WEBSTER'S DICTIONARY AND THESAURUS

WITH COLOR ATLAS

WEBSTER'S DICTIONARY AND THESAURUS

WITH COLOR ATLAS

GEDDES & GROSSET

This edition published 2005 by Geddes & Grosset
David Dale House, New Lanark ML11 9DJ, Scotland

This book is not published by the original publishers of **WEBSTER'S DICTIONARY** or **WEBSTER'S THESAURUS**, or by their successors.

ISBN 1 84205 558 5

Printed and bound in Poland

POLSKABOOK

Contents

Preface

This dictionary has been prepared for the many business and professional people, families, students, office workers, learners of English, word-game enthusiasts and others who need an up-to-date, comprehensive but concise source of reference, but who have no need for the more extensive etymological approach found in larger volumes.

When at first we come across an unfamiliar word, or one which without being totally unknown to us is puzzling, our curiosity may lead us to try to check its correct spelling, its precise meaning, its accepted pronunciation and the appropriateness of its usage in the particular context in which it is found. The crossword solver has of course an additional motive to pick up the dictionary. Even the well-informed reader may occasionally need to check a particular word or phrase – in fact no-one can ever be quite sure that he or she will not find reason to refer to a complete vocabulary of everyday words particularly when communicating with the written word or whenever clarity is essential.

The modern lexicographer's prime role in preparing a dictionary is to reflect the changes taking place in contemporary language. Linguistic change can often be so gradual that we barely notice it, although occasionally there is a sudden realisation that a new word or phrase, previously unknown is in general use, or that a form of usage that was once considered to be 'wrong' has slowly become 'right'.

In presenting a dictionary in a concise manner, the problems faced regarding which words to include and which to leave aside are not easy to resolve. So quickly do additions to the language occur that the choice becomes ever more difficult. A balance must be struck between those words which are so familiar to us, the entries which may seem obsolete and those which merit the status of inclusion.

To compound the editors' difficulties it has to be recognised that language is as quick to absorb foreign importations as it is to develop old words to serve new purposes.

In selecting new words for insertion the editors have been careful to include only those terms which have acquired some stability of form and meaning and show strong signs of surviving within the language at least for a period of time. Words and senses of an archaic and obsolete nature that are frequently found in standard works of literature have been included. A wide range of prefixes, suffixes, and combining forms have been embraced enabling the dictionary user to deduce the meanings of thousands of additional words that are themselves too specialised for entry in their own right in a volume of this scope.

It is appropriate here to draw attention to the arrangement of entries within the text. Words which are derived from a common root have often been grouped together under one head-word. These words can easily be located despite the fact that they are not shown as main entries, as their positions in the dictionary are alphabetically close to the places they would have occupied had they been shown separately.

Derivations given under a head-word are arranged alphabetically. Direct derivatives, i.e. words which are formed by adding a suffix or ending to the root word are given after the head-word is defined. After these follow any one or two word compounds, some of which are hyphenated.

Regarding the order of definitions, where words have more than one definition, the original or oldest meaning of the word is given first, with subsequent definitions illustrating the staged development of the usage of the entry.

Labels relating to grammatical form e.g. *n. v.t. adj.* appear before words or meanings where appropriate. Labels applicable in terms of classification (e.g. *slang obs.*) precede the lists of meanings.

Pronunciation is indicated phonemically, the re-spelling approach being considered simpler than a system of phonetic symbols.

With this arrangement it has been possible to provide good coverage of colloquial and figurative expressions which play such an important part in the language, together with literary vocabulary and listings of technical words and meanings.

What are the advantages of a thesaurus?

To a regular thesaurus-user they become ever more apparent. A thesaurus jogs the memory — it offers help to the person struggling to encapsulate his meaning in a forgotten *mot juste* that might remain tantalizingly on the tip of his tongue. It is indispensable to the student, the journalist, writer and reporter; and to the businessman who wishes to express himself accurately, effectively and concisely. A thesaurus is fun to use, and with the fun comes the opportunity to enhance one's personal command of words and increase one's general knowledge; words that may not be well known to the reader will trigger off investigations in his dictionary and lead him to explore the remoter corners of the language. Finally, a thesaurus is a tool that the word-gamester — compiler, player or solver — cannot do without.

The thing one notices about a thesaurus is that it rarely yields completely interchangeable alternatives for a word — but this is one of its beauties. What it gives is a list of possibles that have more or less of a particular ingredient, are more or less formal, are more or less euphonious, that, in short, have more or less of the precise flavor sought by the user. English has its international origins largely to thank for its richness and subtle variety, and a thesaurus of English words, with their diversity of shape, size, sound and association, will surely yield that ideal, unmistakably usable expression to fit a particular context.

The bias towards abstract terms in the main text has been balanced by the addition of a section that is a virtual newcomer to this type of thesaurus: an appendix of concrete and technical terms, collected alphabetically into categories such as architecture, furniture, vehicles, garments, rhetorical terms, legal terms, anatomical terms. There are also useful lists of collective nouns, names for collectors and enthusiasts, ranks in the armed forces, and wine-bottle sizes. Such words do not fit readily into synonym lists but may be no less sought-after for that.

The editors hope that the reader will get as much enjoyment out of using this thesaurus as they have had in compiling it, and that it will be found to live up to the dictionary definition of **thesaurus** — 'a treasury, a storehouse of knowledge'.

Pronunciation Guide

Accented syllables are marked thus´, e.g. *ban´dit, as-ton´ish-ing*

Vowels and diphthongs in accented syllables

Sound			*Examples*	*Pronunciation*
ā	as in	(1) fate	name, aid, rein	*naām, aād, raān*
		(2) bare	tare, wear, hair, heir	*tār, wār, hār, ār*
ä	as in	(1) father	grass, path	*gräss, päth*
		(2) far	harm, heart, palm	*härm, härt, päm*
a	as in	sat	bad, have	*bad, hav*
ē	as in	(1) me	lean, keel, chief, sieze	*lēn, kēl, chēf, sēz*
		(2) fear	gear, sheer, here, bier	*gēr, shēr, hēr, bēr*
e	as in	pet	red, thread, said, bury	*red, thred, sed, ber´i*
ī	as in	(1) mine	side, shy, dye, height	*sīd, shī, dī, hīt*
		(2) sire	hire, byre	*hīr, bīr*
i	as in	bid	pin, busy, hymn	*pin, biz´i, him*
ō	as in	(1) mote	bone, road, foe, dough	*bōn, rōd, fō, dō*
		(2) more	fore, soar, floor	*fōr, sōr, flōr*
o	as in	got	shot, shone	*shot, shon*
ö	as in	(1) all	haul, lawn, fall, bought	*höl, lön, föl, böt*
		(2) for	swarm, horn	*swörm, hörn*
ōō	as in	(1) moon	fool, sou	*fōōl, sōō*
		(2) poor	boor, tour	*bōōr, tōōr*
oo	as in	foot	good, full, would	*good, fool, wood*
ū	as in	(1) mute	tune, due, newt, view	*tūn, dū, nūt, vū*
		(2) pure	endure	*en-dūr´*
u	as in	bud	run, love	*run, luv*
û	as in	her	heard, bird, world, absurd	*hûrd, bûrd, wûrld, absûrd´*
ow	as in	(1) house	mount, frown	*mownt, frown*
		(2) hour	sour	*sowr*
oi	as in	boy	toy, buoy, soil	*toi, boi, soil*

Certain acceptable variations in pronunciation of vowels
before *r* are not allowed for in the table above. For instance, the *o* in *port* is often pronounced *ö*.

Vowels of Unaccented Syllables

Sound			*Examples*	*Pronunciation*
ȧ	as in	(1) signal	mental, infant, desperate	*men´tȧl, in´fȧnt, des´per-ȧt*
		(2) beggar	altar	*ölt´ȧr*
ė	as in	(1) moment	potent	*pōtėnt*
		(2) silver	never	*nev´ėr*
i	as in	perish	merit, minute, mountain, silly	*mer´it, min´it, mownt´in, sil´i*
ȯ	as in	(1) abbot	faggot, bishop	*fag´ȯt, bish´ȯp*
		(2) doctor	sailor, rigor	*sāl´ȯr, rig´ȯr*
u̇	as in	(1) circus	nimbus, bulbous	*nim´bu̇s, bul´bu̇s*
		(2) figure	treasure	*trez´u̇r*
		(3) tenure	adventure	*ad-ven´tyu̇r* (or *ad-ven´chu̇r* see below)

Consonants

Sound		*Examples*	*Pronunciation*
ch	as in cheap	church, feature, match	*chûrch, fē´chůr* (or *fē´tyůr*), *mach*
f	as in fate	fell, phone, laugh	*fel, fōn, läf*
g	as in good	game, mitigate, guard, ghastly	*gām, mit´i-gāt, gärd, gäst´li*
gw	as in penguin	linguist	*ling´gwist*
gz	as in example	exist	*egz-ist´*
H	as in loch	pibroch, leprechaun	pē´*bro*H, *lep´rė-*Hön
hw	as in where	what	*hwot*
j	as in just	jade, gentle, midge, rigid, region	*jād, jen´tl, mij, rij´id, rē´jȯn*
k	as in keel	kite, cold, chorus	*kīt, kōld, kō´rus* (or *kö´rus*)
ks	as in axe	explain	*eks-plān´*
kw	as in queen	quite, choir, coiffeur	*kwīt, kwīr, kwäf-œr´*
ng	as in sing	rang, rank, longer	*rang, rangk, long´gėr*
s	as in see	sole, cede, scent, mass	*sōl, sēd, sent, mas*
sh	as in shine	shape, machine, sugar, pressure, precious, mention	*shāp, ma-shēn, shoog´ȧr presh´ůr, presh´ůs, men´sh(ȯ)n*
th	as in thin	theme, health	*thēm, helth*
TH	as in then	though, bathe	THO, *bā*TH
y	as in yet	young, super, feature	*yung, s(y)ōō´pėr, fē´tyůr* (or *fē´chůr*)
z	as in zone	zero, maze, muse, xylem, roads	*zē´rō, māz, mūz, zīlem, rōdz*
zh	as in azure	measure, vision, rouge	*mezh´ůr, vizh´(ȯ)n, rōōzh*

Additional sounds in foreign words

Sound		*Examples*	*Pronunciation*
e	as in père	maître	*metr'*
ø	as in deux	douloureux	*dōō-lōō-rø*
œ	as in œuvre	fauteuil, fleur	*fō-tœ-y', flœr*
ü	as in Führer		*fü´rėr*

Nasalised vowels

ã	as in blanc	outrance, mélange	*ōō-trãs, mā-lãzh*
ɛ̃	as in vin	poussin, timbre	*pōōs-ɛ, tɛ̃br'*
ɔ̃	as in mon	accompli, convenance	*a-kɔ̃-plē, kɔ̃´ve-ns*
œ̃	as in lundi	un	*œ̃*

An apostrophe is used to mark such pronunciations as t'h
(where the sound is two separate consonants. It is also used in such words as timbre (*tɛ̃br'*).

Abbreviations used in the Dictionary

abbrev	abbreviation
abl	ablative
acc	accusative
adj(s)	adjective(s)
adv(s)	adverb(s)
aero	aeronautics
alg	algebra
anat	anatomy
anc	ancient(ly)
anthrop	anthropology
aor	aorist
app	apparently
approx	approximately
arch	archaic
archeol	archeology
archit	architecture
arith	arithmetic
astrol	astrology
astron.	astronomy
at no or *at numb*	atomic number
B	Bible (Authorised Version)
biol	biology
book-k	book-keeping
bot	botany
c	(L *circa*) about
cap	capital
cent	century
cf	(L *confer*) compare
chem	chemistry
cog	cognate
coll	colloquial (ly)
comp	comparative
conj	conjunction
conn	connected connection
contr	contracted contraction
cook	cookery
corr	corruption corresponding
dat	dative
demons	demonstrative
der	derived derivation
derog	derogatory derogatorily
dial	dialectal
Dict	Dictionary
dim	diminutive
dub	dubious, doubtful
E	East
econ	economics
eg	(L *exempli gratia*) for example
elect	electricity
erron	erroneous(ly)
esp	especially
ety	etymology
facet	facetiously
fem	feminine
fig	figuratively
foll	followed following
freq	frequently
fut	future
gen	genitive
geog	geography
geol	geology
geom	geometry
gram	grammar
her	heraldry
hist	history
ie	(L *id est*) that is
imit	imitative
imper	imperative
impers	impersonal(ly)
incl	including
indic	indicative
infin	infinitive
inten	intensive
interj	interjection
interrog	interrogative(ly)
intrans	intransitive
lit	literal(ly)
mach	machinery
masc	masculine
math	mathematics

mech	mechanics
med	medicine
mil	military
min	minerology
mod	modern
mus	music
myth	mythology
N	North
n(s)	noun(s)
naut	nautical
neg	negative
neut	neuter
nom	nominative
n pl	noun plural
n sing	noun singular
NT	New Testament (Authorised Version)
obs	obsolete
opp	opposed
orig	original(ly) origin
OT	Old Testament (Authorised Version)
p	participle
p adj	participal adjective
pa p	past participle
part	participle
pass	passive
pa t	past tense
perf	perfect
perh	perhaps
pers	person(al)
pfx	prefix
phil(os)	philosophy
phonet	phonetics
phot	photography
phys	physics
pl	plural
poet	poetical
pop	popular(ly)
poss	possessive possibly
Pr Bk	Book of Common Prayer
pr p	present participle
prep	preposition
pres	present
print	printing
priv	privative
prob	probably
pron(s)	pronoun(s)
pron	pronounced pronunciation
pros	prosody
psych	psychology
qv	(L *quod vide*) which see
RC	Roman Catholic
reflex	reflexive
rel	related, relative
S	South
Shak	Shakespeare
sing	singular
subj	subjunctive
suffx	suffix
superl	superlative
theat	theater
theol	theology
trans	transitive translation
trig	trigonometry
TV	television
ult	ultimately
usu	usually
vb(s)	verbs
v(s)i	verb(s) intransitive
voc	vocative
v(s)t	verb(s) transitive
vulg	vulgar(ly)
W	West
zool	zoology

For abbreviations used in etymologies see next page.

Abbreviations used in Etymologies

A F	Anglo-French
Afrik	Afrikaans
Amer	American
Angl	Anglian
Ar	Arabic
Austr	Australian
Beng	Bengali
Celt	Celtic
Chin	Chinese
Dan	Danish
Du	Dutch
Eng	English
Fr	French
Gael	Gaelic
Ger	German
Gmc	Germanic
Gr	Greek
Heb	Hebrew
Hind	Hindi
Icel	Icelandic (Modern)
Ir	Irish
Ind	Indian
It	Italian
Jap	Japanese
L	Latin
L Ger	Low German
L L	Late Latin
Low L	Low Latin
M E	Middle English
Mex	Mexican
Norm	Norman
Norw	Norwegian
O E	Old English
O Fr	Old French
O H G	Old High German
O N	Old Norse
Pers	Persian
Pol	Polish
Port	Portuguese
Russ	Russian
S Afr	South African
Sans	Sanskrit
Scand	Scandinavian
Scot	Scottish
Sp	Spanish
Sw	Swedish
Turk	Turkish
U S	United States
W	Welsh
W S	West Saxon

DICTIONARY

A

a[1] [a] (when emphatic sometimes *ā*), *adj* the indefinite article, a broken-down form of **an**, used before words beginning with the sound of a consonant; one; any.
a[2] [å], *prep* derived from the prep *on*, still used as a prefix, as in a foot, twice *a* day, *a*-going. [Short for OE *an*, a dialect form of *on*, on, in at.]
A-bomb [ā´bomb] *n* atomic bomb.
aardvark [ärd´värk] *n* an edentate (*Orycteropus afer*) of Africa. [Du *aarde*, earth, *vark* (now *varken*), pig.]
aardwolf [ärd´wŏŏlf] *n* a carnivore (*Proteles crystatus*) of southern and eastern Africa akin to the hyenas. [Du *aarde*, earth, *wolf*, wolf.]
abaca [ä-bä-kä] *n* a plantain (*Musa testilis*) grown in the Philippine Islands; its fiber, called *Manila hemp*. [Native name.]
aback [a-bak´] *adv* (*naut*) (of sails) pressed backward against the mast by the wind—**taken aback**, taken by surprise. [OE *on bǣc*, **on** and **back**.]
abacus [ab´a-kus] *n* a frame with sliding beads for doing arithmatic; (*archit*) a level tablet on the capital of a column:—*pl* **ab´acī** [-sī]. [L,—Gr *abax, -akos*, a board for reckoning on.]
abaft [a-bäft´] *prep* behind. [Pfx *a-* (OE *on*), on, and *bæften*, after, behind; itself made up of pfx *be-*, and *æftan. See* **aft.**]
abalone [ab-a-lōn´ē] *n* a sea mollusk (genus *Haloitis*) with an oval, slightly spiral, shell.
abandon [a-ban´dȯn] *vt* to give up; to desert; to yield (oneself) without restraint (to).—*n* **aban´don**, careless freedom of action.—*adj* **aban´doned**, deserted; very wicked, unrestrained.—*n* **aban´donment**. [OFr *à bandon*, at one's disposal, and *abandoner*, to leave to one's discretion or mercy—*bandon*, ban, control.]
abase [a-bās´] *vt* to humble;—*n* **abase´ment**. [OFr *abaissier*, to bring low—L *ad*, to, and LL *bassus*, low.]
abash [a-bash´] *vt* to disconcert, mortify.—*n* **abash´ment**, confusion from shame. [OFr *esbahir*, to be amazed—L *ex*, out, and Fr interj *bah*, expressive of astonishment.]
abate [a-bāt´] *vti* to make or become less; (*law*) to end.—*n* **abate´ment**, the act of abating; the sum or quantity abated. [OFr *abatre*, to beat down—L *ab*, form, and *batĕre*, popular form of *batuĕre*, to beat; conn with **beat**.]
abatis [a´bat-ēs] *n* a rampart of trees felled and laid side by side, with the branches towards the enemy. [Fr See, **abate**.]
abattoir [ab´a-twär] *n* a slaughter house. [Fr See **abate**.]
abbacy [ab´a-si] *n* the office, tenure, etc.—of an abbot; *adj* **abbatial** [ab-ā´shål]. [App orig a Scottish form for older *abbatie—see* **abbey**.]
abbé [ab´ā] *n* the title of a French priest.
abbess [ab´es] *n* the head of a convent of nuns. [Fr *abesse*—LL *abbātissa*; cf **abbot**.]
abbey [ab´i] *n* a convent or monastery; the church attached to it;—*pl* **abb´eys**. [OFr *abaïe*—LL *abbātia*.]
abbot [ab´ȯt] *n* the head of a monastery. [L *abbās, abbātis*—**Abba**.]
abbreviate [a-brē´vi-āt] *vt* to make shorter, esp to shorten (a word) by omitting letters.—*n* **abbreviā´tion**, an act of shortening; a shortened form. [L *abbreviāre, -ātum—ab*, inten, and *brevis*, short. See **brief**.]
ABC, abcee [ā-bē-sē´] *n* the alphabet; the rudiments of anything.
abdicate [ab´di-kāt] *vti* formally to renounce of give up (office or dignity).—*n* **abdicā´tion**. [L *ab*, from or off, *dicāre, -ātum*, to proclaim.]
abdomen [ab´dȯ-mėn, ab-dō´men] *n* the belly; in mammals, the part between diaphragm and pelvis; in arthropods, the part of the body behind the thorax.—*adj* **abdominal** [-dom´-]. [L.]
abduct [ab-dukt´] *vt* to take away by force.—*ns* **abduc´tion, abduc´tor**. [LL *abdūcĕre-ab*, from, *dūcĕre, ductum*, to draw, lead.]
abeam [a-bēm´] *adv* (*naut*) on a line at right angles to a ship's keel. [Pfx *a-* (OE *on*), on, + **beam**.]
abed [a-bed´] *adv* in bed. [Pfx *a-* (OE *on*), on, + **bed**.]
Aberdeen Angus [ab-ėr-dēn ang-us] *n* a Scottish breed of black hornless cattle.
aberrant [ab-er´ånt] *adj* deviating from what is usual, normal, or right.—*n* **aberrā´tion**, a deviation from truth or rectitude; mental or moral lapse; a distortion, as of an image produced through an imperfect lens. [L *aberrāre, -ātum—ab*, from, *errāre*, to wander.]
abet [a-bet´] *vt* to encourage or aid;—*pr p* **abett´ing**; *pt p* **abbett´ed**.—*n* **abett´er, abett´or**. [OFr *abeter—à* (L *ad*), to, and *beter*, to bait, from root of **bait**.]
abeyance [a-bā´åns] *n* a state of suspension; temporary inactivity. [OFr *abeance—à* (L *ad*), to, and *beer, baer*, to gape.]
abhor [ab-hör´] *vt* to shrink from with horror; to detest, loathe;—*pr p* **abhorr´ing**; *pt p* **abhorred´**.—*n* **abhorr´ence** [-hor´], extreme loathing.—*adj* **abhorr´ent**, detestable. [L *abhorrēre—ab*, from, and *horrēre. See* **horror**.]
abide [a-bīd´] *vt* to endure; to tolerate.—*vi* to remain in a place; (arch) to reside.—*pt* and *pt p* **abode´**.—**abide by**, to live up to (a promise, etc.); to submit to and carry out. [OE *ābīdan*—pfx *ā-*, inten, and *bīdan*, to wait.]
ability [a-bil´i-ti] *n* being able; power to do; talent; skill.—*pl* **abil´ities**. [OFr *ableté* (Fr *habileté*)—L *habilitās—habilis*, apt—*habēre*, to have, hold.]
abject [ab´jekt] *adj* miserable; wretched; degraded.—*n* **abjec´tion**.—*adv* **ab´jectly**. [L *abjectus*, cast away—*ab*, away, *jacĕre*, to throw.]
abjure [ab-jōōr] *vt* to renounce on oath; to renounce.—*n* **abjurā´tion**. [L *ab*, from, *jurāre, -ātum*, to swear.]
ablate [ab-lāt] *vt* to remove, as by surgery; to wear away, burn away, or vaporize.—*vi* to be ablated, as a rocket shield in reentry. [L *ablatus*, carried away.]
ablative [ab´lat-iv] *adj* (*gram*) in or belonging to a case which in Latin, etc. denotes direction from a place, time and source, agent, instrument, etc.—*n* the ablative case. [L *ablātīvus—ab*, from, *ferre, lātum*, to bear.]
ablaze [a-blāz´] *adj* flaming; greatly excited.—*adv* on fire. [Pfx *a-* (OE *on*), on, + **blaze** (1).]
able [ā´bl] *adj* having enough strength, power or means (to do a thing); talented; skilled; (*law*) competent.—*adv* **a´bly**.—*adj* **a´ble-bod´ied**, strong; robust.—**able seaman, able-bodied seaman**, a trained or skilled seaman. [OFr *(h)able*—L *habilis*; see **ability**.]
-able [-å-bl] *suffix* meaning; able to (*durable*); capable of being (*drinkable*); having qualities of (*comfortable*); tending to (*perishable*).
ablution [å-blōō´sh(ȯ)n] *n* the washing of one's body, or part of it. [L *ablūtiō, -ōnis—ab*, away, *luĕre*, to wash.]
Abnaki [ab-näk´i] *n* a confederacy of more than 20 Amerindian tribes of Maine, New Brunswick, and southern Quebec.
abnegate [ab´ni-gāt] *vt* to deny and refuse; to renounce.—*n* **abnegā´tion**. [L *ab*, away, *negāre*, to deny.]
abnormal [ab-nör´mål] *adj* not normal, average, or typical; irregular.—*n* **abnormal´ity**—*adv* **abnor´mally**. [From root of **anomalous**; influenced by **normal**.]
ABO group the classification of human blood into the groups A, B, AB and O according to the reactions to each other.
aboard [a-bōrd´, -börd] *adv, prep* on or in (a ship, a train, etc.); alongside. [Pfx *a-* (OE *on*), on, + **board.**]
abode[1] [a-bōd´] *n* a home, residence. [From **abide**.]
abode[2] [a-bōd´] *pt p, pt p* of **abide**
abolish [ab-ol´ish] *vt* to put an end to; to annul.—*ns* **aboli´tion**, the act of abolishing; **Abolition**, the abolishing of slavery in the US; **aboli´tionist**. [Fr *abolir, abolissant*—L *abolescĕre—abolēre, -itum*.]
abominate [ab-om´in-āt] *vt* to abhor, to detest extremely.—*adj* **abom´inable**, hateful, detestable.—*n* **abom´inableness**.—*adv* **abom´inably**.—*n* **abominā´tion.—abominable snowman**, a hairy manlike creature supposed to live in the snows of Tibet.—Also **yeti**. [L *abōmināri, -ātus*, to turn from as of bad omen. *See* **omen**.]
aborigine [ab-o-rij´in-ē] *n* any of the first known inhabitants of a region.—*adj* **aborig´inal**, existing (in a region) from the beginning; of aborigines.—*n* an aborigine. [L *aborigines—ab origine*, from the beginning. *See* **origin**.]
abort [ab-ört´] *vi* to miscarry in birth; to come to nothing.—*vt* to cause to abort; to terminate prematurely; to stop in the early stages, as because of an equipment failure.—*n* the premature termination of the flight of an aircraft, or any aspect of a rocket or spacecraft launch.—*adj* **abort´ed**.—*n* **abor´tion**, premature expulsion of a fetus, esp if induced on purpose.—*adj* **abort´ive**, unsuccessful, fruitless; arrested in development.—*adv* **abort´ively**.—*n* **abort´iveness**. [L *aborīrī, abortus—ab*, from (reversing meaning), *orīrī*, to rise.]
abound [ab-ownd´] *vi* to overflow, be in great plenty; to teem. [OFr *abunder*—L *abundāre*, to overflow—*ab*, from, *unda*, a wave.]
about [a-bowt´] *prep* on all sides of; near to; with; on the point of; concerning.—*adv* all around; near; nearly; in the opposite direction.—**be about to**, to be on the point of. [OE *on būtan—on*, in, *būtan*, without—*be*, by, and *ūtan*, locative of *ūt*, out.]
above [a-buv´] *prep* over, on top of; better or more than.—*adv* overhead; in a higher position, order, or power; at an earlier point in a writing.—*adj* **above´board**, without deception or concealment; open; done honorably. [OE *ābūfan—on*, on, *bufan*, above—*be*, by, *ufan*, high, upwards, prop the locative of *uf*, up.]
abracadabra [ab-ra-ka-dab´ra] *n* a magical charm or spell; gibberish. [L, origin unknown.]
abrade [a-brād´] *vt* to scrape away, to rub off.—*n* **abrasion** [ab-rā´zh(ȯ)n], the act of rubbing off; an abraded place.—*adj* **abrā´sive** [-ziv, -siv], tending to abrade.—*n* a substance, as sandpaper, used for grinding, polishing, etc. [L *ab*, off, *rādĕre, rāsum*, to scrape.]

abreast [a-brest´] *adv* side by side; informed (of); aware. [Pfx *a-* (OE *on*), on, + **breast**.]

abridge [a-brij´] *vt* to shorten, lessen, curtail; to shorten by using fewer words but keeping the substance.—*n* **abridg´ment, abridge´ment**. [OFr *abregier*—L *abbreviāre*. See **abbreviate**.]

abroad [a-bröd´] *adv* over a wide area; out of doors; in circulation, current; at large; in or to another country.—**from abroad**, from a foreign land; at large; in or to another country. [Pfx *a-* (OE *on*), on, + **broad**.]

abrogate [ab´ro-gāt] *vt* to abolish; to repeal; to annul.—*n* **abrogā´tion**. [L *abrogāre*—*ab*, away, *rogāre, -ātum*, to ask, or to propose a law.]

abrupt [ab-rupt´] *adj* sudden; unexpected; brusque; very steep; disconnected, as some writing.—*adv* **abrupt´ly**.—*n* **abrupt´ness**. [L *abruptus*—*ab*, off, *rumpěre, ruptum*, to break.]

abscess [ab´ses] *n* an inflamed area, containing pus localized in some tissue of the body. [L *absecessus*—*abs*, away, *cēděre, cessum*, to go, to retreat.]

abscission [ab-sizh´(ȯ)n] *n* act of cutting off; state of being cut off; (*bot*) the natural separation of flowers, fruit, and leaves from a plant at a special separation layer.—*n* **abscissa** [ab-sis´a], for rectilineal axes, the distance of a point from the vertical axis (*y*-axis) measured in a direction parallel to the horizontal axis [*x*-axis];—*pl* **absciss´as, absciss´ae** [-ē]. [L *abscinděre, abscissum*—*ab*, from, *scinděre*, to cut.]

abscond [ab-skond´] *vi* to hide, or get out of the way, esp in order to escape a legal process. [L *absconděre*—*abs*, from or away, *conděre*, to hide.]

abseil [ap´zīl, ab-sīl] *vi* to lower oneself down a rock face using a double rope attached to a higher point.—*n* **abseiling**. [Ger *-ab*, down, *seil*, a rope.]

absent [ab´sėnt] *adj* away, not present; not existing; inattentive.—*adv* **ab´sently**, in an inattentive manner.—*vt* **absent´**, to keep (oneself) away.—*ns* **ab´sence**, the state of being away, the time of this; a lack, **absentēē**, one who is absent, as from work. **absentee´ism, absentee ballot**, a ballot marked and sent to a board of elections by a voter (**absentee voter**), who cannot be present to vote in an election.—*adj* **ab´sentmind´ed**, inattentive to surroundings; pre-occupied; habitually forgetful.—**absent without leave**, (*military, naval* absent from duty without official permission. [L *absens, -entis*, pr p of *abesse*—*ab*, away from, *esse*, to be.]

absinthe, absinth [ab´sinth] *n* wormwood; a green liquer flavored with wormwood or a substitute, anise and other aromatics. [Fr,—L *absinthium*—Gr *apsinthion*, wormwood.]

absolute [ab´sȯl-(y)ōōt] *adj* free from limits or conditions; complete; certain, positive; perfect, pure; not relative (*inf*) utter, out-and-out *an absolute shame*.—*adv* **ab´solutely**, independently, unconditionally; positively; completely;—*ns* **ab´soluteness; ab´solutism**, government where the ruler is without restriction, despotism; **absolute alcohol**, waterfree alcohol; **absolute pitch**, the actual pitch of a sound determined by the number of vibrations per second; the ability to recognize or reproduce the pitch of notes in music; **absolute scale**, a temperature scale based on absolute zero; **absolute temperature**, temperature measured on the absolute scale; **absolute value**, the numerical value of a real number without regard to sign; **absolute zero**, a hypothetical temperature marked by the complete absence of heat, approximately equivalent to -273°C or -459°F. [L *absolūtus*, pt p of *absolvěre*. See **absolve**.]

absolution [ab-sol-(y)ōō´sh(ȯ)n] *n* forgiveness; remission of sin or its penalty. [OFr,—L *absolūtiō, -ōnis*—*absolvěre*, See **absolve**.]

absolve [ab-zolv´, or -solv´] *vt* to set free from guilt, a duty, etc.; to give religious absolution to. [L *absolvěre*—*ab*, from, *solvěre*; see **solve**.]

absorb [ab-sôrb´] *vt* to suck up; to take in; to swallow up; to incorporate; to pay for (costs, etc.); to take in (a shock) without recoil; to take up and transform (energy) instead of transmitting or reflecting it; to engage wholly.—*adj* **absorb´able**.—*n* **absorbabil´ity**.—*advs* **absorb´edly; absorb´ingly**.—*adj* **absorb´ent**, able to absorb, as a sponge.—*ns* **absorbent, absorbant, absorb´er**, that which absorbs; **absorp´tion**, the act of absorbing; entire occupation of mind.—*adj* **absorp´tive**, [Fr,—L **absorbēre—ab**, from, *sorbēre, sorptum*, to suck in.]

abstain [ab-stān´] *vi* to keep oneself from some indulgence, esp from drinking alcohol; to refrain from using one's vote.—*ns* **abstain´er**, drinks; **absten´tion**. [Fr *abstenir*—L *abstinēre*—*abs*, from, *tenēre*, to hold.]

abstemious [ab-stēm´i-us] *adj* temperate; sparing in food, drink or enjoyments.—*adv* **abstem´iously**.—*n* **abstem´iousness**. [L *abstēmius*—*abs*, from, *tēmētum*, strong wine.]

abstinent [ab´stin-ėnt] *adj* abstaining from.—*ns* **ab´stinence, ab´stinency**, an abstaining or refraining, esp from food and drink. [Fr,—L *abstinens, -entis*—*abstinēre*. See **abstain**.]

abstract [ab-strakt´] *vt* to remove; to summarize in writing.—*adj* **abstract´ed**, not paying attention.—*adv* **abstract´edly**,—*ns* **abstract´edness; abstraction**, act of abstracting; state of being abstracted; absence of mind; an abstract idea; an example of abstract art.—*adj* **abstract** [ab´strakt], having no material existence; theoretical rather than practical.—*n* a written summary; an example of abstract art.—**abstract art**, art that does not represent things pictorially, but expresses the artist's ideas or emotions; **abstract expressionism**, a form of abstract art in which paint is applied spontaneously.—Also **action painting**.—*adv* **ab´stractly**.—*n* **ab´stractness**.—**in the abstract**, in theory. [L *abstrahěre*—*abs*, away from, *trahěre, tractum*, to draw.]

abstruse [ab-strōōs´] *adj* difficult to understand.—*adv* **abstruse´ly**.—*n* **abstruse´ness**. [L *abstrūsus*, thrust away (from observation)—*abs*, away from, *trūděre, trūsum*, to thrust.]

absurd [ab-sûrd´] *adj* obviously unreasonable, ridiculous.—*ns* **absurd´ness; absurd´ity**,—*adv* **absurd´ly**. [L *absurdus*—*ab*, inten, *surdus*, deaf, dull.]

abundance [ab-und´ȧns] *n* ample sufficiency; great plenty.—*adj* **abund´ant**, plentiful; rich (in).—*adv* **abund´antly**. [*See* **abound**.]

abuse [ab-ūz´] *vt* to use wrongly; to maltreat; to revile; to violate.—*n* **abuse** [ab-ūs´], ill use; misapplication; an unjust or corrupt usage; vituperation.—*adj* **abusive**[-ūs-]—*adv* **abus´ively**.—*n* **abus´iveness**. [L *ab*, away (from what is right), *ūtī, ūsus*, to use.]

abut [a-but´] *vi* to end or lean (on, upon, against); to border (on or upon);—*pr p* **abutt´ing**; *pt p* **abutt´ed**.—*n* **abut´ment** a part supporting a bridge, an arch, etc. [OFr *abouter*, to touch by an end, and OFr *abuter*, to touch at the end (*à*, to, *bout*, end).]

abysm [a-bizm´] *n* (*arch, poet.*) abyss.—*adj* **abys´mal**, bottomless; unfathomable; (of taste) extremely bad—*adv* **abys´mally**. [OFr *abisme*—L *abyssimus*, superl of *abyssus*, bottomless.]

abyss [a-bis´] *n* a bottomless depth; anything too deep to measure (*an abyss of shame*). [Gr *abyssos*, bottomless—*a-*, priv, *byssos*, bottom.]

Abyssinian cat [ab-i-sin´i-in] a breed of small domestic cat, of African origin, grayish or brownish ticked with darker color.

acacia [a-kā´sh(y)a] *n* a genus (*Acacia*) of thorny leguminous plants with pinnate leaves of warm regions. [L—Gr *akakia*—*akē*, a sharp point.]

academic *See* **academy**.

academy [a-kad´em-i] *n* a private secondary school; a school for specialized training, a society of scholars, writers, scientists, etc.—*adj* **academ´ic**, of an academy; scholarly; theoretical as opposed to practical.—*n* member of an institution of learning; an academic person.—*adv* **academ´ically**.—*n* **academician** [ā-kad-ė-mish´n], member of an academy of science, art, or literature.—**academic freedom**, freedom to teach or learn without interference (as by government officials). [Gr *Akadēmia*, name of garden orig outside Athens where Plato taught.]

acanthus [a-kan´thus] *n* a genus (*Acanthus*) of prickly-leaved plants; (*archit*) an ornament resembling their leaves used in the capitals of the Corinthian order. [L,—Gr *akanthos*—*akantha*, thorn, conn with *akē*, point.]

a capella [ä cȧ-pel´ȧ] *adj, adv* choral singing without instrumental accompaniment.

accede [ak-sēd´] *vi* to come into some office or dignity; to agree or assent (*with* **to**). [L *accēděre, accessum*, to go near to—*ad* to, *cēděre*, to go.]

accelerando [ak-sel-ėr-an´dō] *adj, adv* (*mus*) becoming faster. [It]

accelerate [ak-sel´ėr-āt] *vt* to increase the speed of; to hasten the progress or occurrence of.—*vi* to move faster.—*n* **accelerā´tion**, the act of hastening; increase of speed; rate of change of velocity.—*adj* **accel´erative**, tending to cause acceleration; accelerating.—*n* **accel´erator**, one who or that which accelerates, esp a substance that increases the speed of a chemical action, an apparatus for regulating the speed of a machine, or one for imparting high velocities to elementary particles. [L *accelerāre, -ātum*—*ad*, to, *celer*, swift.]

accent [ak´sėnt] *n* stress on a syllable or word; a mark used to direct this stress; any mode of utterance characteristic of a region, a class, or an individual; the emphasis given to something; rhythmic stress in music or verse.—*vt* **ac´cent** or **accent´**, to mark the accent; to emphasize.—*vt* **accent´uate**, to accent; to emphasize.—*n* **accentuā´tion**. [Fr,—L *accentus*, accent—*ad*, to, *cantus*, song.]

accept [ak-sept´] *vt* to receive, esp willingly; to approve; to agree to; to believe in; to agree to pay; to treat as welcome.—*vi* to take something offered (*with* **of**).—*adj* **acceptable** [ak-sept´a-bl, or ak´-], worth accepting; tolerable.—*ns* **accept´ableness, acceptabil´ity**.—*adv* **accept´ably**.—*ns* **accept´ance**, act of accepting or state of being accepted; approval; assent; a promise to pay; **accepta´tion**, a favorable reception; a generally accepted meaning of a word or understanding of an idea;—*adj* **accep´ted**, generally approved or believed in.—*ns* **accept´er; accept´or**, one who accepts; a compound, atom, or subatomic particle that is capable of receiving an entity (as compound atom, etc.) to form a compound. [L *acceptāre*—*accipěre, acceptum*—*ad*, to *capěre*, to take.]

access [ak´ses] *n* approach; or means of approach; the right to enter, use, etc.; an outburst.—*adj* **access´ible**, able to be reached; open (to).—*n* **accessibil´ity**.—*adv* **access´ibly**. [*See* **accede**.]

accessary [ak-ses´ȧr-i] *See* **accessory**.

accession [ak-sesh´(ȯ)n] *n* act of reaching a rank or position; an addition as to a collection. [See **accede**.]

accessory, accessary [ak-ses´ȯr-i] *adj* additional; contributory; aiding; (*law*) participating in a crime; adventitious.—*n* anything additional; an additional item of equipment; one who aids or gives countenance to a crime.—*adj* **accessōr´ial**. [*See* **accede**.]

accidence [ak´si-dėns] *n* (*gram*) the inflectional changes of words to denote changes in number, tense, etc. of the same word; the branch of grammar dealing with these changes. [For *accidents*, or perh directly from *accidentia*, neut pl of pr p of *acciděre*, treated as noun of first declension. See **accident**.]

accident [ak´si-dėnt] *n* an unforeseen or unexpected event; a mishap or disaster; chance.—*adj* **accident´al**,—*n* anything not essential; (*mus*) a sharp, flat, or natural not in the key signature.—*adv* **accident´ally**.—**accident**

insurance, insurance against loss through accidental bodily injury; **accident-prone**, having a greater than average number of accidents; having personality traits that predispose to accidents. [L *accidĕre*, to happen—*ad* to, *cadĕre*, to fall.]

acclaim [a-klām´] *vt* to applaud; to hail.—*vi* to shout applause.—*n* a shout of applause or assent;—*n* **acclamā´tion**, acclaim; shouted assent without recourse to voting.—*adj* **acclam´atory**. [L *acclāmāre*—*ad*, to, *clāmāre*, *-ātum*, to shout.]

acclimatize [a-klīm´a-tīz] *vt* to adapt to a new climate or environment.—*vi* to become acclimatized.—Also **acclim´ate**.—*n* **acclimatizā´tion**.—Also **acclimā´tion, acclimatā´tion**. [Fr *acclimater*, from *à*, to, and *climat*. See **climate**.]

acclivity [a-kliv´i-ti] *n* an upward slope. [L *acclīvitās*—*acclīvis*, uphill—*ad* to, *clīvus*, a slope.]

accolade [ak-ol-ād´, -äd´] *n* a light touch on each shoulder with the flat of a sword conferring knighthood; praise, approval; an award. [Fr,—L *ad* to, *collum*, neck.]

accommodate [a-kom´od-āt] *vt* to adapt; to oblige; to lodge.—*adj* **accommo´dating**, obliging;—*n* **accommodā´tion**, adjustment; willingness to do favors; a help; (*pl*) lodgings; (*pl*) traveling space, as on a train.—*adj* **accomm´odative**, of the nature of an accommodation; **accommodation ladder**, a portable ladder or stairway used for going between a ship and a small boat. [L *accommodāre*, *-ātum*—*ad*, to, *commodus*, fitting. See **commodious**.]

accompany [a-kum´pan-i] *vt* to go with; to supplement (with something); to be present with; an accompaniment to or for.—*ns* **accom´paniment**, that which accompanies; an instrumental part supporting a solo instrument, a voice, or a choir, **accom´panist**, one who performs an accompaniment. [Fr *accompagner*—*à*, to, *compagne*, companion. See **company**.]

accomplice [a-kom´plis, or -kum´-] *n* an associate, esp in crime. [L *complex*, *-icis*, joined; pfx unexplained.]

accomplish [a-kum´plish] *vt* to complete; to effect, fulfill;—*adjs* **accom´plishable**, that may be accomplished; **accom´plished**, done; completed; skilled, expert; polished.—*n* **accom´plishment**, completion, fulfillment; achievement; a social art or skill. [OFr *acomplir*—L *ad*, to, *complēre*, to fill up. See **complete**.]

accord [a-körd´] *vi* to agree; to harmonize (with).—*vt* to make agree; to grant.—*n* agreement; harmony.—*n* **accordance**, agreement; conformity.—*adj* **accordant**, agreeing; harmonious.—*adv* **accord´antly**.—*adj* **accord´ing**, in accordance; agreeing.—*adv* **accord´ingly**, consequently.—**according to**, in accordance with; as asserted by; **with one accord**, all agreeing. [OFr *acorder*—L *ad*, to, *cor*, *cordis*, the heart.]

accordion [a-kör´di-on] *n* a portable musical instrument consisting of folding bellows, keyboard, and free metal reeds.—*adj* hinged or creased or folded with very narrow folds like the bellows of an accordion. [From **accord**.]

accost [a-kost´] *vt* to approach and speak to. [OFr *acoster*—L *ad*, to, *costa*, a side.]

accouchement [a-kōōsh´mä, ment] *n* the time or act of giving birth.—*n*

accoucheur [ä-kōō-shœr´] one who assists at a birth, esp an obstetrician. [Fr,—*accoucher*—*à*, to, *coucher*, bed. See **couch**.]

account [a-kownt´] *vt* to probe into; to think of as, consider.—*vi* to give a financial reckoning (to); to give reasons (for); to kill or otherwise dispose of (*with* **for**).—*n* a counting; (often *pl*) a record of business transactions; a bank account; a charge account; a credit customer; worth, importance; an explanation; a description, report.—*adj* **account´able**, liable; to account, responsible; explicable.—*ns* **account´ableness, accountabil´ity**, liability to give account, responsibility to fulfil obligations.—*adv* **account´ably**.—*ns* **account´ant**, one whose work is accounting, **account´ancy**, the profession or practice of an accountant; **accounting**, the process of keeping and verifying accounts.—**account executive**, a person in business, esp advertising, who is responsible for overseeing a client's account; **on account**, as partial payment; **on account of**, because of; **on no account**, not for any reason or consideration; **take into account**, to consider; **turn to account**, to turn to advantage. [OFr *acconter*—L *ad*, to, *computāre*, to reckon.]

accoutre, accouter [a-kōō´tėr] *vt* to dress or equip;—*pr p* **accoutring** [a-kōō´tėr-ing] *pt p* **accoutred** [a-kōōtėrd].—*n* **accoutrement, accouterment** [a-kōō´tėr-ments], dress; military equipment. [Fr *accoutrer*, earlier *accoustrer*.]

accredit [a-kred´it] *vt* to authorize; to certify; to believe in; to attribute; to furnish with credentials.—*adj* **accred´ited**, certified officially; accepted as valid; certified as being of a prescribed quality.—*n* **accred´itā´tion**. [Fr *accréditer*—*à*, to, *crédit*, credit—L *crēdĕre*, to believe.]

accretion [a-krē´sh(o)n] *n* process of growing or increase by means of gradual additions; accumulated matter; a growing together of parts. [L *accrētiō*, *-ōnis*—*accrescĕre*—*ad*, in addition, *crescĕre*, to grow.]

accrue [a-krōō´] *vi* to grow as a natural result; to accumulate or be added periodically. [OFr *acrewe*, what grows up in a wood to the profit of the owner—*acreistre*—L *accrescĕre*—*ad*, in addition, *crescĕre*, to grow.]

acculturate [a-kul´chůr-āt] *vti* to undergo, or change, by acculturation.—*n* **acculturation´tion**, adaptation to a new culture, esp a different one; the mutual influence of different cultures.

accumulate [a-kūm´ūl-āt] *vti* to pile up, to amass.—*n* **accumulā´tion**,—*adj* **accum´ulative**. [Fr L *accumulātus*, pt p of *accumulāre*—*ad*, to, *cumulus*, a heap.]

accurate [ak´ūr-át] *adj* done with care, exact.—*n* **acc´uracy**, correctness;—*adv* **acc´urately**.—*n* **acc´urateness**. [L *accūrātus*, performed with care—*ad*, to, *cūra*, care.]

accursed [a-kûrs´id, -kûrst] *adj* under a curse; damnable.—Also **accurst´**. [OE pfx *ā*-, inten, and *cursian*, to curse.]

accusative [a-kūz´a-tiv] *adj* (*gram*) or transitive of the case denoting the object of a preposition verb.—*n* the accusative or objective case; a word in this case (as him in 'we saw him'). [Fr *accusatif*—L *accūsātīvus*.]

accuse [a-kūz´] *vt* to bring a charge against; to blame.—*n* **accusā´tion**, the act of accusing; the charge brought against anyone.—*adj* **accus´atory**, containing accusation.—*adj* **accused** [a-kūzd´], charged with a crime;—*n* the person accused.—*n* **accus´er**, one who accuses or brings a charge against another. [OFr *acuser*—L *accūsāre*, *-ātum*—*ad*, to, *causa*, cause.]

accustom [a-kus´tȯm] *vt* to make familiar by habit, use, or custom.—*adj* **accus´tomed**. [OFr *acostumer* (Fr *accoutumer*)—*à*, to, *co(u)stume*. See **custom**.]

ace [ās] *n* the one in dice, cards, dominoes, etc., a point won by a single stroke, as in tennis; an expert, esp in combat flying; (*golf*) a hole in one.—*adj* (*inf*) first-rate.—**ace in the hole**, any advantage held in reserve; **within an ace of**, very near to. [Fr,—L *as*, unity—*as*, a dialectal form of Gr *heis*, one.]

acephalous [a-sef´a-lus] *adj* without a head or having the head reduced; without a governing head or chief. [Gr *a*-, priv, *kephalē*, the head.]

acerbity [a-sûr´bi-ti] *n* sharpness of speech or manner. [Fr,—L *acerbitās*—*acerbus*, bitter—*acer*, sharp.]

acetanilide [as´e-tan´-i-līd] *n* a drug used to lessen pain and fever. [**acetic** + **aniline**.]

acetic [a-sēt´ik, a-set´ik] *adj* of vinegar—*n* **ac´etate**, a salt or ester of acetic acid; a fabric made of an acetate of cellulose; an acetate phonograph recording disk; **acetic acid**, the sour principle in vinegar. [L *acētum*, vinegar—*acēre*, to be sour.]

acetify [a-set´i-fī, a-sēt´i-fi] *vti* to turn into vinegar.—*n* **acetificā´tion**. [L *acētum*, vinegar, *facĕre*, to make.]

acetone [as´é-tōn] *n* a fragrant flammable liquid C_3H_6O used as a solvent and found in abnormal quantities in diabetic urine. [L *acetum*, vinegar.]

acetylene [a-set´i-lēn] *n* a gas formed by the action of water on carbide of calcium which burns with oxygen in a hot flame used for welding, lighting, etc. [**acetic**, + Gr *hylē*, matter.]

acetylsalicylic acid [a-sēt´il-sál´i-sil´ik] *n* aspirin.

Acey Deucy [ā´si dyōō´si, dōōs-] a variation of backgammon.

ache [āk] *n* a dull, continuous pain—*vi* to suffer a dull, continuous mental or physical pain; (*inf*) to yearn.—*pr p* **āch´ing**; *pt p* **āched**.—*adj* **ach´ing**, that aches; causing distress or longing. [The verb was properly *ake*, the noun *ache* (as in *speak* and *speech*)—OE vb *acan* and its derivative n *æce*.]

achene [ā-kēn´é] *n* any small dry fruit with one seed. [Gr *a*-, not, + *chainein*, to gape.]

achieve [a-chēv´] *vt* to perform, accomplish; to gain, win.—*adj* **achiev´able**.—*n* **achieve´ment**, a thing achieved; an exploit. [Fr *achever*, from *à chief* (*venir*)—Low L *ad caput*, to a head. See **chief**.]

Achilles´ heel [a-kil´ēz] *n* vulnerable point.—**Achilles tendon**, the strong tendon connecting the muscles of the calf to the bone of the heel. [from the Gr myth that Achilles was vulnerable only in the heel by which his mother held him when plunging him into the Styx.]

achromatic [a-krōm-at´ik] *adj* refracting light without dispersing it into its constituent colors; not readily colored by the usual staining agents; possessing no hue; (*music*) being without accidentals or modulations.—*n* **achrom´atism**, the state of being achromatic. [Gr *a*-, priv, *chrōma*, gen *chrōmatos*, colour.]

acicular [as-ik´ū-lȧr] *adj* shaped like a needle. [L *acicula*, dim, of *acus*, a needle.]

acid [as´id] *adj* sharp, tart, sour; of an acid; looking or sounding bitter; rich in silica.—*n* a sour substance; (*chem*) any of various compounds that react with a salt to form a base, that reddens litmus, that are hydrogen molecules or ions able to give up a proton to a base or are substances able to accept a pair of unshared electrons from a base; something incisive or sarcastic; (*slang*) LSD—*vti* **acid´ify**, to make or become acid; to convert into an acid.—*vi* to become acid.—*pr p* **acid´ifying**; *pt p* **acid´ified**.—*ns* **acidificā´tion; acid´ity**, being acid; an over-acid condition of the stomach; **acidō´sis**, a condition marked by lower than normal alkali reserves in the body.—*vt* **acid´ulate**, make acid or slightly acid.—*adj* **acid´ulous**, acid in manner.—**acid rain**, rain with a high concentration of acids from the burning of fossil fuels; **acid test**, a crucial, final test. [L *acidus*—*acēre*, to be sour.]

acidophilus milk [a-si-dof´ilus] *n* milk fermented by bacteria used therapeutically to modify intestinal flora.

acknowledge [ak-nol´ij] *vt* to admit that something is true and valid; to report that one has received something; to express thanks for; to show that one has noticed or recognized.—*n* **acknow´ledgment**, [Pfx *a*- (OE *on*), on + **knowledge**.]

acme [ak´mē, -mi] *n* the top or highest point; the culmination or perfection. [Gr *akmē*, a point, the highest point—*akē*, a point.]

acne [ak´nē, -ni] *n* inflammation of sebaceous glands producing pimples. [Perh Gr *akmē*. See **acme**.]

acolyte [ak´o-līt] *n* an altar boy; an attendant or assistant. [Gr *akolouthos*, an attendant.]

aconite [ak´o-nīt] *n* a genus (*Aconitum*) of plants of the buttercup family, including monkshood; a sedative drug made of its roots. [L *aconītum*—Gr *akoniton*.]

acorn [ā´körn] *n* the nut of the oak.—**acorn squash**, a dark green winter squash with yellow flesh, shaped like an acorn. [OE *æcern*, prob.—*æcer*, field, hence meaning 'the fruit of the unenclosed land'; confused with *oak* (OE *āc*) and *corn*.]

acoustic [a-kōōs´tik] *adj* of the sense of hearing; of sounds; of acoustics.—*n pl* **acous´tics**, properties (eg of a room or hall) determining how clearly sounds can be heard in it; (treated as *sing*) the branch of physics dealing with sound. [Fr,—Gr *akoustikos*—*akouein*, to hear.]

acquaint [a-kwānt´] *vt* to make (oneself) familiar (with); to inform.—*ns* **acquaint´ance**, knowledge from personal experience; a person known slightly; **acquaint´anceship**, slight knowledge.—*adj* **acquaint´ed** (*with*), having personal knowledge of. [OFr *acointer*—LL *accognitāre*—L *ad*, to, *cognitus*, known.]

acquiesce [ak-wi-es´] *vi* to rest satisfied with, or make no opposition to (*with* **in**).—*n* **acquiesc´ence**, acceptance; assent.—*adj* **acquiesc´ent**, resting satisfied, submissive. [L *acquiescĕre*—*ad*, *quiēs*, rest.]

acquire [a-kwīr´] *vt* to gain by one's efforts; to get as one's own.—*adj* **acquir´able**, that may be acquired.—*n* **acquisi´tion**, the act of acquiring; that which is acquired; something worth acquiring, a useful gain.—*adj* **acquis´itive**, directed towards, acquiring (possessions); grasping.—*n* **acquis´itiveness. acquired immunodeficiency syndrome**, AIDS. [OFr *aquerre*—L *acquirĕe*. *-quisitum*—*ad*, to, *quaerĕre*, to seek.]

acquit [a-kwit´] *vt* to free from an obligation; to behave or conduct (oneself); to declare innocent;—*pr p* **acquitt´ing**; *pt p* **acquitt´ed**—*ns* **acquitt´al**, a legal discharge from an accusation. [OFr *aquiter*—L *ad*, to, *quiētāre*. See **quit**.]

acre [ā´kėr] *n* a measure of land containing 4840 sq yards.—*n* **acreage** [ā´kėr-ij] the number of acres in a piece of land. [OE *æcer*, cognate with Ger *acker*, L *ager* Gr *agros*, Sans *ajra*.]

acrid [ak´rid] *adj* sharp and bitter to the taste, and smell; sharp in speech, etc.—*ns* **acrid´ity, ac´ridness**. [L *ācer, acris*, sharp.]

Acrilan [ak´ril-àn] *n* trade name for an acrylic fiber.

acrimony [ak´ri-mòn-i] *n* bitterness of feeling or language.—*adj* **acrimō´nious**. [L *acrimōnia*—*ācer*, sharp.]

acrobat [ak´ro-bat] *n* one who performs spectacular gymnastic feats.—*adj* **acrobat´ic**.—*n pl* **acrobat´ics**, an acrobat's tricks; any tricks requiring great skill. [Gr *akrobatos*, walking on tiptoe—*akron*, point, *batos*—*bainein*, to go.]

acronym [ak´rō-nim] *n* a word formed from the initial letters of other words (as *radar*). [Gr *akron*, tip, point, *onoma*, name.]

acrophobia [ak-rō-fō´bi-à] *n* fear of heights. [Gr *akron*, tip, *phobos*, fear.]

Acropolis [a-krop´ol-is] *n* the hill in Athens on which the Parthenon was built; **acropolis**, the upper fortified part of an ancient Greek city. [Gr *akropolis*—*akros*, the highest, *polis*, a city.]

across [a-kros´] *prep* from one side to the other of; on at an angle; on the other side of; into contact by chance.—*adv* crosswise, to or on the opposite side; so as to be understood or accepted.—**across the board**, (of a racing bet) betting in equal amounts to win, place, and show; affecting all classes and groups. [Pfx *a-* (OE *on*), on, and **cross**.]

acrostic [a-kros´tik] *n* a poem or puzzle in which certain letters of each line, spell a word, motto, etc. or a sentence. [Gr *akros*, extreme, and *stichos*, a line.]

acrylic [a-kril´ik] *adj* of a group of synthetic fibers used to make fabrics; of a group of clear, synthetic resins used in making plastic, paints, etc.

act [akt] *vi* to exert force or influence; to produce an effect; to conduct oneself; to perform as on the stage; to function.—*vt* to perform.—*n* something done, a deed; an exploit; the process of doing something; a law; a main division of a play or opera; a short performance, as in a variety show; something done merely for show; **Acts** (*Bible*), 5th book of the New Testament, written by Luke in about 63 AD describing the beginnings of the early Church.—*n* **act´ing**, the art of an actor.—*adj* performing some duty temporarily,—*ns* **act´or**, one who does something; one who acts in plays, movies, etc.; **ac´tress**, a female performer.—**act of God**, a result of forces beyond human control; **act up**, (*inf*) to misbehave; **get one's act together**, (*slang*) get organized; plan or work systematically. [L *agĕre, actum*; Gr *agein*, to put in motion; Sans *aj* to drive.]

actinide series [ak´ti-nīd] *n* series of 15 radioactive elements with increasing atomic numbers from actinium to lawrencium.

actinism [ak´tin-izm] *n* the chemical action of the sun's rays.—*adj* **ac´tinic** [or -tin´-]. [Gr *aktīs, aktīnos*, a ray.]

actinium [ak-tin´i-um] *n* a radioactive element (symbol Ac; at wt 227; at no 89). [Gr *aktīs*, a ray.]

action [ak´sh(ò)n] *n* a state of acting; a deed operation; a gesture; a battle; a lawsuit; the sequence of events in a drama, novel, etc; (*pl*) behavior; the way of working, as of a machine; the moving parts, as of a gun; (*slang*) activity.—adj **ac´tionable**, liable to a lawsuit.—**action painting**, abstract expressionism. [L *actiō, -ōnis*—*agĕre*. See **act**.]

active [akt´iv] *adj* that acts; working; energetic; busy; nimble; effective; (*gram*) of that voice in which the subject of the verb represents the doer of the action.—*adv* **act´ively**.—*ns* **act´iveness; ac´tivism**, a taking direct action to achieve a political or social end; **activist**, a supporter of activism; **activ´ity**, state of being active; a specific action (*student activities*)—**act´ivate**, *vt* to make more active; to make radioactive; to treat (charcoal, etc.) so as to improve adsorptive properties; to put (a military unit) on active status; to aerate (sewage) to hasten decomposition. [L *activus*—*agĕre*. See **act**.]

actual [ak´tū-àl, ak´chŏŏ-àl] *adj* real; existing in fact and now.—*vt* **act´ualize**, to realize in action; to represent realistically.—*n* **actual´ity**.—*adv* **act´ually**, [L *actuālis*—*agĕre*. See **act**.]

actuary [ak´tū-ar-i] *n* one who figures insurance risks, premiums, etc.—*adj* **actuā´rial**. [L *actuārius* (*scriba*), an amanuensis, a clerk.]

actuate [ak´tū-āt] *vt* to put in motion; to incite to action. [L *actus*, action. See **act**.]

acuity [a-kū´i-ti] *n* sharpness of thought or vision. [LL *acuitās*—L *acus*, needle.]

acumen [a-kū´men, a´-] *n* sharpness, of perception, penetration. [L See **acute**.]

acupressure [ak´yoo-presh´ėr] *n* a practice like acupuncture but using hand pressure instead of needles.

acupuncture [ak´yoo-pungk´cher] *n* Chinese treatment involving insertion of needles at various points in the body to treat disease or relieve pain.—Also **needle therapy**.

acute [a-kūt´] *adj* sharp-pointed; keen; sensitive (*acute hearing*); severe, as pain; very serious; less than 90° (*acute angles*); (of a disease) severe but not long-lasting.—*adv* **acute´ly**.—*n* **acute´ness**. [L *acūtus*, pt p of *acuĕre*, to sharpen, from root *ak*, sharp.]

ad [ad] (*inf*) short for advertisement—*n* **ad´man**, a man whose work is advertising.

adage [ad´ij] *n* an old saying, a proverb. [Fr,—L *adagium*—*ad*, to, and root of *āio*, I say.]

adagio [ä-dä´j(y)ō] *adv* (*mus*) slowly.—*n* a slow movement; a slow ballet dance. [It *ad agio*, at ease.]

adamant [ad´a-mànt] *n* a very hard substance.—*adj* inflexible, unyielding. [OFr through L,—Gr *adamas, -antos*—*a-*, priv, and *damaein*, to break, to tame.]

Adam's apple [ad´amz-ap´l] *n* the hard projection in front of the throat, esp of a man.

adapt [a-dapt´] *vt* to make apt or fit; to adjust (oneself) to new circumstances.—*adj* **adapt´able**, that may be adapted; changing readily.—*ns* **adaptabil´ity; adaptā´tion**, the act, process, or result of adapting. [Fr *adapter*—L *adaptāre*—*ad*, to *aptāre*, to fit.]

add [ad] *vt* to join (one thing to another) as an increase or supplement; to put numbers or amounts together to get a total; to say in continuation, to remark further.—*vi* to increase (*with* **to**); to find a sum.—*n* **addi´tion**, an adding of numbers to get a sum; a joining of one thing to another; a part added.—*adj* **addi´tional**, added; more; extra.—**in addition** (**to**), besides. [L *addĕre, additum*—*ad*, to, *dăre*, to put.]

addend [ad´end, à-dend´] *n* a number to be added to another. [See **addendum**.]

addendum [a-den´dum] *n* a thing to be added.—*pl* **adden´da**. [L gerundive of *addĕre*. See **add**.]

adder[1] [ad´ėr] *n* the venomous viper (*Vipera berus*) of Europe; any of several harmless No American snakes, esp puff adder.

adder[2] [ad´ėr] *n* one that adds, esp a device in a computer that performs addition. [OE *nædre*; cf Ger *atter* for *natter*. *An adder* was orig *a nadder*.

addict [a-dikt´] *vt* to give (oneself) up (to a strong habit); to cause (a person) to become dependent upon a drug.—*n* [ad´ikt] one who is addicted (as to a drug).—*adj* **addict´ed**.—*n* **addic´tion**. [L *addīcĕre, addictum*, to consent, devote—*ad*, to, *dicĕre*, to declare.]

Addison's disease [ad´i-sònz] *n* a disease marked by deep bronzing of skin, anemia, and extreme weakness caused by underactivity of the adrenal glands. [Thomas *Addison*, Eng physician (1793–1860).]

additive [ad´i-tiv] *adj* characterized by addition; produced by addition.—*n* something added. [L *additivus*—*addĕre*. See **add**.]

addle [ad´l] *vti* to make, or become rotten; to make or become confused. [ME *adele*—OE *adela*, mud.]

address [a-dres´] *vt* to direct words (to); to speak or write to; to direct in writing; to turn one's skill or energies (to); (*computer*) to indicate or find (the location of a piece of stored information).—*n* a formal communication in writing; a speech; manner, deportment; the place to which a letter is directed [also ad´res] a place of residence.—*adj* **address´able**.—*n* **addressēē´**, the person to whom a letter is addressed. [Fr *adresser*—L *ad*, to, *directum*, straight.]

adduce [a-dūs´] *vt* to offer as example, reason, or proof in discussion or analysis, **adductor**, a muscle that draws one part towards another. [L *adducĕre*—*ad*, to, *ducĕre*, to bring.]

adenine [ad´ėn-ēn] a purine base $C_5H_5N_5$ that codes hereditary information in the genetic code in DNA and RNA. [Gr *adēn*, a gland.]

ad′enoids [ad′en-oidz] *n pl* enlarged masses of tissue in the throat behind the nose. [Gr *adēn*, a gland, *eidos*, form.]
adept [ad-ept′, ad′ept] *adj* highly skilled.—*n* an expert. [L *adeptus* (*artem*), having attained (an art), pt p of *adipisci*—*ad*, to, *apisci*, to reach, obtain.]
adequate [ad′e-kwȧt] *adj* sufficient; equal to requirements.—*adv* **ad′equately**.—*ns* **ad′equateness, adequacy**, [L *adaequātus*, made equal—*ad*, to, and *aequus*, equal.]
adhere [ad-hēr′] *vi* to stick; to remain attached, to give allegiance or support (to).—*n* **adhēr′ence**, state of adhering; steady attachment.—*adj* **adhēr′ent**, sticking (to)—*n* a follower, a partisan. [L *ad*, to, *haerēre*, *haesum*, to stick.]
adhesion′ [ad-hē′zh(ȯ)n] *n, n* the act of adhering or sticking; steady attachment (to); abnormal union of body parts; a band of fibrous tissue joining such parts.—*adj* **adhēs′ive**, sticky; apt to, or intended to, adhere.—*n* an adhesive substance.—*adv* **adhes′ively**.—*n* **adhes′iveness**. [*See* **adhere**.]
ad hoc [ad hok] *adj* (of a committee or other body) constituted for this purpose. [L, to this.]
ad hominem [ad hōm′i-nėm] directed against a person rather than his arguments. [L]
adiabatic [ad-i-a-bat′ik] *adj* occurring without gain or loss of heat. [Gr *adiabatos*, not to be passed—*a*-, not, *dia*, through, *bainein*, to go.]
adieu [a-dū′] *interj, n* goodbye—*pl* **adieus** or **adieux** [a-dūz′] [Fr *à Dieu*, to God.]
ad infinitum [ad in-fin-īt′um, -ēt ŏŏm] to infinity. [L]
ad interim [ad int′ė-rim] for the meantime. [L]
adios [a′dē-ōs] *interj* goodbye. [Sp]
adipose [ad′i-pōs] *adj* of animal fat. [L *adeps, adipis*, soft fat.]
adit [ad′it] *n* a nearly horizontal opening into a mine. [L *adītus*—*ad*, to, *īre*, to go.]
adjacent [a-jās′ėnt] *adj* near (to); adjoining.—*n* **adjac′-ency**.—*adv* **adjac′ently**. [L *ad*, to, jacēre, to lie.]
adjective [aj′ek-tiv] *n* a word added to a noun or other substantive to qualify it or to limit it.—*adj* **adjectīv′al**.—*advs* **adjectīv′ally, ad′jectīvely**, [L *adjectīvum* (*nomen*), an added (word)—*adjicĕre, –jectum*, to throw to, to add—*ad*, to, *jacĕre*, to throw.]
adjoin [a-join′] *vt* to be next to.—*vi* to be in contact.—*adj* **adjoin′ing**, [Through Fr from L *adjungĕre*—*ad*, to, *jungĕre*. See **join**.]
adjourn [a-jûrn′] *vt* to discontinue (a meeting) in order to resume it at another time or place.—*vi* to suspend proceedings for a time; (*inf*) to retire (to another room, etc.)—*n* adjourn′ment, [OFr *ajorner*—LL *adiurnāre*—L *ad*, to, LL *jurnus*—L *diurnus*, daily.]
adjudge [a-juj′] *vt* to decide by law; to declare, order, or award by law. [OFr *ajuger*—L *adjūdicāre*—*ad*, inten, *jūdicāre*.]
adjudicate [a-jōō′di-kāt] *vt* to (*Law*) to hear and decide (a case).—*vi* to serve as a judge (in or on).—*ns* **adjū′dicator; adjudicā′tion**. [L *adjūdicāre, -ātum*—*ad*, inten *jūdicāre*. See **judge**.]
adjunct [a′jungkt] *adj* joined or added; attached in a temporary or subordinate position to the staff of an institution, as a university.—*n* a thing joined or added; (*gram*) any modifying word or clause; an associate or assistant of another.—*adj* **adjunct′ive**,—*adv* **adjunct′ly**, [L See **adjoin**.]
adjure [a-jōōr′] *vt* to charge on oath or solemnly.—*n* **adjurā′tion**, [L *adjūrāre*—*ad*, to, *jūrāre, -ātum*, to swear.]
adjust [a-just′] *vt* to arrange properly; to regulate, to settle rightly; to decide the amount to be paid in settling (an insurance claim).—*vi* to adapt oneself.—*adj* **adjust′able**.—*n* **adjust′ment**. [OFr *ajouster*—LL *adjuxtāre*, to put side by side—L *juxta*, near.]
adjutant [a′jŏŏ-tȧnt] *n* an assistant; a military staff officer who assists the commanding officer.—*ns* **ad′jutancy**, the office or rank of an adjutant. **ad′jutant gen′eral**, the head of a department of the general staff of the army; the executive officer of a major military unit (as a division or corps). [L *adjūtāre*, freq of *adjūvāre*—*ad*, inten, *jūvāre*, to assist.]
ad lib [ad′-lib] *vti* (*inf*) to improvize—*n* (*inf*) an ad-libbed remark.—*adv* (*inf*) as one pleases.—Also **ad lib**. [L *ad libitum*, at pleasure.]
admeasure [ad-mezh′ůr] *vt* to apportion.—*n* **admeas′urement**, determination and apportionment of shares; dimensions; size. [Fr,—L *ad*, to, *mensūra*, measure.]
administer [ad-min′is-tėr] *vt* to manage, direct; to give out as punishment; to apply (medicine, etc.); to tender (an oath, etc.)—*n* **administrā′tion**, management; **Administration**, the executive officials of a government, their policies, and term of office.—*adj* **admin′istrative**, that administers.—*n* **admin′istrātor**, one who manages or directs; (*law*) one appointed to settle an estate. [Through Fr,—L *administrāre*—*ad*, to, *ministrāre*, to minister.]
admiral [ad′mir-ȧl] *n* the commanding officer of a fleet; a naval officer of the highest rank. [Through Fr,—Ar *amīr*, a lord, a chief—*d* introduced through confusion with L *admīrarī*, to wonder at.]
admire [ad-mīr′] *vt* to regard with wonder or surprise; to esteem, often in a somewhat impersonal manner; to regard with enthusiastic approval.—*adj* **admirable** [ad′-mir-ȧ-bl] worthy of being admired.—*adv* **ad′mirably**.—*n* **admirā′tion**,—*n* **admīr′er**,—*adv* **admīr′ingly**. [Fr *admirer*—L *ad*, at, *mīrārī*, to wonder.]
admit [ad-mit′] *vt* to allow to enter or use; to concede; to acknowledge; to be capable of; to leave room for.—*vi* to allow (with of)—*pr p* **admitt′ing**; *pt p* **admitt′ed**.—*adj* **admiss′ible**, that may be admitted or allowed.—*ns* **admissibil′ity; admitt′ance**, the act of admitting; leave to enter; (*elect*) the property of an electric circuit by virtue of which an alternating current flows under the action of an alternating potential difference; **admiss′ion**, an admitting or being admitted; an entrance fee; a conceding, confessing, etc.; a thing conceded, confessed, etc.—*adv* **admitt′edly**. [Through Fr from L *admittĕre, -missum*—*ad*, to, *mittĕre*, to send.]
admixture [ad-miks′chůr] *n* a mixture; a thing added in mixing. [L *ad*, to, and **mix**.]
admonish [ad-mon′ish] *vt* to warn; to reprove mildly. [OFr *amonester*—LL *admonestāre*—*admonēre*—*ad*, inten, *monēre*, to warn.]
admonition [ad-mon-ish′(ȯ)n] *n* gentle or friendly reproof; warning or counsel against fault or oversight.—*adj* **admon′itory**, containing admonition. [L *admonitiō, -ōnis*—*admonēre, -itum*.]
ad nauseam [ad nö′shi-am, now′si] to a sickening degree. [L]
ado [a-dōō] *n* trouble, fuss. [Contr of *at do* = *to do*, a form of the infin borrowed from the Scandinavian.]
adobe [a-dō′bi] *n* a sun-dried brick; clay for making this brick; a house made of such bricks. [Sp *adobar*, to plaster.]
adolescent [ad-o-les′ėnt] *adj* of or in adolescence.—Also *n*—*n* **adolesc′ence**, the period of youth, between childhood and maturity. [Through Fr from L *adolēscēns, -entis*—*adolescĕre*, to grow up.]
adopt [a-dopt′] *vt* to take legally into one's family and raise as one's own child; to take as one's own; to choose or accept and put into effect; to choose (a textbook) for required study in a course.—*n* **adop′tion**, the act of adopting; the state of being adopted.—*adj* **adopt′ive**, that adopts or is adopted. [L *adoptāre*—*ad*, inten, *optāre*, to choose.]
adore [a-dōr′, -dör′] *vt* to worship; to love intensely.—*adj* **ador′able**, worthy of being adored; extremely charming.—*n* **ador′ableness**.—*adv* **ador′ably**.—*ns* **adŏrā′tion**, worship, homage; profound regard; **adōr′er**,—*adv* **ador′ingly**. [L *ad*, to, *ōrāre*.]
adorn [a-dörn′] *vt* to deck or dress; to embellish.—*n* **adorn′ment**, ornament; decoration. [OFr *aörner, adorner*—L *adornāre*—*ad*, to, *ornāre*, to furnish.]
adrenal [ad-rē′nȧl] *adj* near the kidneys.—*ns* **Adren′alin** [-rĕn], trade name for synthesized adrenaline; **adren′aline**, epinephrine.—**adrenal gland**, either of a pair of thumbnailsized glands above the kidneys secreting sex hormones and hormones affecting metabolism. [L *ad*, to *rēnes*, kidneys.]
adrift [a-drift′] *adj, adv* floating without mooring. [Pfx *a*- (OE *on*), on, and **drift**.]
adroit [a-droit′] *adj* skillful and clever.—*adv* **adroit′ly**.—*n* **adroit′ness**. [Fr *à droit*, according to right—L *directus*, straight. See **direct**.]
adscititious [ad-si-tish′ůs] *adj* derived or acquired from something extrinsic. [L *adscīscĕre, -scītum*, to take or assume—*ad*, to, *scīscĕre*, to inquire—*scīre*, to know.]
adsorb [ad-sörb′] *vt* of a solid, to take up a liquid or vapor on its surface.—*n* **adsorption**. [L *ad* to, *sorbēre* to suck in.]
adulation [ad-ū-lā′sh(ȯ)n] *n* fawning; flattery.—*adj* **adulatory** [ad′ū-la-tȯr-i]. [L *adūlārī, adūlātus*, to fawn upon.]
adult [ad′ult, ad-ult′] *adj* grown; mature; euphemism for dealing in pornography, etc.—*n* a mature person, animal, or plant. [L *adultus*—*adolēscĕre*, *adultum*, to grow.]
adulterate [a-dul′tėr-āt] *vt* to make impure, inferior, etc. by adding an improper substance.—*adj* [-ȧt] spurious.—*n* **adul′terant**, a substance used to adulterate—Also *adj*; **adulterā′tion**. [L *adulterāre, -ātum*, to corrupt—*adulterium*. See **adultery**.]
adultery [a-dul′tėr-i] *n* sexual intercourse between a married man and a woman not his wife, or between a married woman and man not her husband.—*ns* **adul′terer**, a man guilty of adultery; **adul′teress**, a woman who commits adultery.—*adj* **adul′terine**, resulting from adultery; spurious; **adul′terous**, guilty of adultery. [OFr *avoutrie*, adultery—L *adulterium*, prob from *ad*, to, *alter*, another. The modern form is due to a later reintroduction of Latin spelling.]
adumbrate [ad-um′brāt, or ad′-] *vt* to foreshadow; to outline vaguely.—*n* **adumbrā′tion**. [L *adumbrāre, adumbrātus*—*ad*, inten, *umbra*, a shadow.]
ad valorem [ad va-lō′rem, -lö′-] *adj* imposed at a percentage of the value. [L]
advance [ad-väns′] *vt* to bring forward; to promote; to raise the rate of; to lend.—*vi* to go forward; to make progress; to rise in rank, price, etc.—*n* progress; improvement; a rise in value; payment beforehand; (*pl*) approaches to get favor;—*adj* in front (*advance guard*); beforehand.—*adj* **advanced′**, in front; old; ahead or higher in progress, price, etc.—*n* **advance′ment**, promotion; improvement—**advance man**, a person hired to travel in advance of a theatrical company, political candidate, etc. to arrange for appearances, etc.; **in advance**, in front; ahead of time. [OFr *avancer*—L *abante*—*ab ante*, from before; the pfx was later refashioned as if it were from L *ad*].
advantage [ad-vänt′ij] *n* superiority over another; gain or benefit; (*lawn tennis*) first point gained after deuce—*vt* to be a benefit to, profit—*adj* **advantā′geous**, of advantage; useful—*adv* **advantā′geously**.—*n* **advanta′geousness**.—**take advantage of**, to use for one's own benefit; to impose upon. [Fr *avantage*—*avant*, before—L *abante*. See **advance**.]
Advent [ad′vent] *n* the period including four Sundays before Christmas; **advent**, a coming. [Through Fr from L *adventus*—*advenīre*—*ad*, to, *venīre*, to come.]

adventitious [ad-ven-tish´ùs] *adj* coming from outside; added by chance; (*bot*) developed out of the usual order or place.—*adv* **adventi´tiously**. [Low L *adventitius*—L *adventicius*—*advenīre*. See **advent**.]

adventure [ad-ven´chùr] *n* a strange or exciting undertaking; an unusual, stirring, often romantic experience.—*vti* to risk; venture.—*n* **adven´turer**, one who engages in hazardous enterprises; one who seeks to better his fortune by bold and discreditable means;—**adven´turess**, a female adventurer, esp a woman who seeks position and livelihood by dubious means.—*adjs* **adven´turous, adven´turesome**, enterprising; ready to incur risk.—*adv* **adven´turously**.—*n* **adven´turousness**. [OFr *aventure*—L *adventūrus*, about to happen, fut part of *advenīre*. See **advent**.]

adverb [ad´vėrb] *n* a word which modifies a verb, adjective, or other adverb—*adj* **adver´bial**,—*adv* **adver´bially**. [L *adverbium*—*ad*, to, *verbum*, a word.]

adversary [ad´vėr-sȧr-i] *n* an opponent; [OFr *a(d)versier*—L *adversārius*—*advertĕre*. See **adverse**.]

adverse [ad´vėrs] *adj* hostile; opposed; unfavorable.—*adv* **ad´versely**.—*ns* **ad´verseness; advers´ity**, adverse circumstances; affliction, misfortune.—*adj* **advers´ative**, denoting opposition or antithesis. [Through Fr from L *adversus*—*advertĕre*—*ad*, to, and *vertĕre, versum*, to turn.]

advert [ad-vûrt´] *vi* to call attention (to) [OFr *avertir, avertissant*—L *advertĕre*—*ad*, to, *vertĕre*, to turn.]

advertise [ad´vėr-tīz, or -tīz´] *vt* to call public attention to, esp in order to sell something, by buying space or time in the media, etc.—*vi* to call public attention to things for sale; to ask (for) by public notice.—*ns* **advert´isement** [-iz, -is-], the act of advertising; a public notice usu. paid for; **adverti´ser**, one who advertises; a paper carrying advertisements; **ad´vertising**, the business of preparing advertisements. [Fr,—L *advertĕre*. See **advert**.]

advice [ad-vīs´] *n* counsel; recommendation with regard to a course of action; (usu. *pl*) information or notice given; an official notice about a business transaction. [OFr *a(d)vis*—L *ad vīsum*, according to what is seen.]

advise [ad-vīz´] *vt* to give advice or counsel to; to recommend; to inform.—*vi* to give advice; to take counsel.—*pr p* **advis´ing**; *pt p* **advīsed** [-vīzd´]—*adj* **advīs´able**, prudent, expedient.—*ns* **advisabil´ity, advis´ableness**.—*adv* **advis´ably**.—*adjs* **advis´ory**, giving advice; **advised´**, thought out (as in *well-advised* and *ill-advised*).—*adv* **advis´edly**, after consideration.—*n* **advis´er, advisor**, one who advises. [OFr *a(d)viser*, from *a(d)vis*. See **advice**.]

advocaat [ad´vō-kä] *n* a liqueur made with egg yolk and brandy.

advocacy [ad´vo-kȧ-si] *n* the function of an advocate; a pleading in support (of). [Fr *advocacie*—L *advocāre*. See **advocate**.]

advocate [ad´vo-kȧt] *n* one who pleads the cause of another, esp in a court of law or before a tribunal; a supporter.—*vt* [-āt] to plead in favor of. [OFr *a(d)vocat*—L *advocātus*—*advocāre, -ātum*, to summon, esp for help—*ad*, to, *vocāre*, to call.]

adz, adze [adz] *n* a carpenter's tool consisting of a thin arched blade with its edge at right angles to the handle. [OE *adesa*.]

aegis [ē´jis] *n* anything that protects; sponsorship.—Also **egis**. [L,—Gr *aigis*.]

Aeolian harp [ē-ō´li-ȧn] *n* a stringed instrument, sounded by currents of air. [L *Aeolus*—Gr *Aiolos*, god of winds.]

aeon *See* **eon**.

aerate [ā´ėr-āt] *vt* to supply (blood) with oxygen by respiration; to supply or impregnate with air; to combine or charge with gas.—*n* **aerā´tion**. [L *āër*, air.]

aerial [ā-ēr´i-ȧl] *adj* belonging to the air; existing in the air; of aircraft or flying.—*n* a radio or TV antenna.—*n aer´ialist*, an acrobat on a high wire, trapeze, etc. [L *āër*, air.]

aerie [ā´ri, also ē´ri, ī´ri] *n* the nest of any bird of prey, esp an eagle.—Also **aery, eyrie, eyry**. [OFr *aire*; origin unknown. The form **eyry**, seems to have been originally due to a confusion with ME *ey*, an egg.]

aerobatics [ā-ėr-ō-bat´iks] *n* stunts done while flying an aircraft [Formed from Gr *āēr*, air, and acro*batics*.]

aerobic [ā-erōb´ik] *adj* living only in the presence of oxygen; of exercise that conditions the heart and lungs by increasing efficient intake of oxygen by the body.—*npl* aerobic exercises (as running, walking, and swimming, etc.) [Gr *āēr*, air, and *bios*, life.]

aerodynamics [ā-ėr-ō-di-nam´iks] *n* the branch of dynamics with forces exerted by air or other gases in motion.—*adj* **aerodynam´ic**. [Gr *āēr*, air, and *dynamis*, power.]

aerolite [ā´ėr-o-līt] *n* a stony meteorite. [Gr *āēr*, air, *lithos*, a stone.]

aeronaut [ā´ėr-o-nöt] *n* one who operates or travels in a balloon or airship.—*n* **aeronaut´ics**, the science dealing with the operation of aircraft; the art or science of flight. [Gr *āēr*, air, *nautēs*, sailor.]

aerophobe [ā´ėr-ō-fōb] a person with an abnormal fear of flying.—*n* **aerophob´ia** (*biol*) movement of organism or part of organism away from air.

aerosol [ā´ėr-ō-sol] *n* a liquid in a container under pressure, with a device for releasing it in a fine spray; the container. [Gr *āēr*, air.]

aerospace [ā´ėr-ō-spās] *n* the earth's atmosphere together with space beyond.—*adj* of missiles, etc. for flight in aerospace. [Gr *āēr*, air + **space**.]

aery [ā´ėr-i] *adj* ethereal. [L *āërius*—*āër*, air.]

Aesculapian [es-kū-lā´pi-ȧn] of the art of healing. [L *Aesculapius*—Gr *Asklēpios*, god of healing.]

aesthetics [es-thet´iks, or ēs-thet´iks] *n* the philosophy of art and beauty—*n* **aesthete** [es´thēt], one who is or pretends to be highly sensitive to art and beauty.—*adj* **aesthet´ic**, of aesthetics; of beauty; appreciative of art and beauty.—*adv* **aesthet´ically**.—*n* **aesthet´icism**, the doctrine that the principles of beauty are basic to other, esp moral principles. Also **esthetics, esthete**, etc. [Gr *aisthētikos*, perceptive—*aisthanesthai*, to feel.]

aestivate [es´ti-vāt] *vi* to pass the summer in a state of torpor; to spend the summer in one place.—*adj* **aes´tival**, of the summer.—*n* **aes´tivātion**.

afar [a-fär] *adv* (*arch, poetic*) at or to a distance. [Pfx *a-* (OE *on* or *of*), on, or from, + **far**.]

affable [af´a-bl] *adj* easy to speak to; approachable;—*ns* **affabil´ity, aff´ableness**.—*adv* **aff´ably**. [Fr,—L *affābilis*—*affārī*, to speak to—*ad*, to, and *fārī*, to speak.]

affair [a-fār´] *n* a thing done or to be done; (*pl*) public or private business; (*inf*) an event; (*inf*) a thing; a temporary romantic or sexual relationship. [OFr *afaire*—*à* (L *ad*) *faire* (L *facĕre*), to do. Cf **ado**.]

affect[1] [a-fekt´] *vt* to act upon; to produce a change in; to move the feelings of.—*n* **affectabil´ity**.—*adjs* **affect´able, affect´ed**, touched with feeling.—*adv* **affect´edly**.—*adj* **affect´ing**, having power to move the feelings.—*adv* **affect´ingly**. [L *afficĕre, affectum*—*ad*, to, *facĕre*, to do.]

affect[2] [a-fekt´] *vt* to make a show or pretence of; to have, show a preference for.—*n* **affectā´tion**, a striving after, or an attempt to assume, what is not natural or real; pretence.—*adj* **affect´ed**, assumed artificially.—*n* **affec´tedness**. [L *affectāre*, freq of *afficĕre*. See **affect** (1).]

affection [a-fek´sh(ȯ)n] *n* fond or tender feeling; liking; a disease or diseased condition.—*adjs* **affec´tionate**, full of affection, loving **affec´tionless**,—*adv* **affec´tionately**. [L *affectiō, -ōnis*—*afficĕre*. See **affect** (1).]

affenpinscher [af´ėn-pinch-ėr] *n* a breed of toy dog with hard wiry black coat, chin tuft, and mustache. [Ger].

afferent [af´ėr-ėnt] *adj* (*anat*) bearing inwards applied to the nerves that convey impulses to the brain or spinal cord.—Also *n* [L *afferens -entis*—*ad*, to, and *ferre*, to carry.]

affiance [a-fī´ȧns] *vt* to betroth. [OFr *afiance, after*—L *ad*, to *fides*, faith.]

affidavit [af-i-dā´vit] *n* a written declaration on oath. [*Affidāvit*, 3rd pers sing perf of a LL *affidāre*, to pledge one's faith.]

affiliate [a-fil´i-āt] *vt* to connect as a subordinate member or branch; to associate (oneself with).—*vi* to join.—*n* an affiliated person club, etc.—*n* **affiliā´tion**, [L *affiliāre, -ātum*, to adopt—*ad*, to, *fil´us*, a son.]

affinity [a-fin´i-ti] *n* relationship by marriage; nearness of kin; structural resemblance; similarity, likeness; attraction, liking; the force that binds atoms together in molecules, enabling elements to form compounds. [Fr *affinité*—L *affinitās*—*affinis*, neighbouring—*ad* at, *finis*, boundary.]

affirm [a-fûrm´] *vt* to assert confidently or positively; (*law*) to make a formal declaration or affirmation, without an oath; to ratify (a judgment).—*adj* **affirm´able**,—*n* **affirmā´tion**, firming; that which is affirmed.—*adj* and *n* **affirm´ative**, that affirms or asserts; the side upholding the proposition in a debate.—*adv* **affirm´atively**.—**affirmative action**, a plan to offset past discrimination in employing or educating women, blacks, etc. [OFr *afermer*—L *affirmāre*—*ad*, to, *firmus*, firm.]

affix [a-fiks´] *vt* to fasten; to add; to attach.—*n* **aff´ix**, a prefix or a suffix. [*affigĕre, -fixum*—*ad*, to, *figĕre*, to fix.]

afflatus [a-flā´tus] *n* inspiration. [L—*afflāre*—*ad*, to, *flāre*, to breathe one.]

afflict [a-flikt´] *vt* to cause pain, distress, or grief to.—*n* **afflic´tion**, pain; suffering; state or cause of distress;—*adj* **afflict´ive**, [L *afflīgĕre, -flictum*—*ad*, to, *flīgĕre*, dash to the ground.]

affluent [af´lōō-ėnt] *adj* abounding; wealthy; rich.—*n* a tributary stream, a rich person.—*n* **aff´luence**, abundance; wealth. [L *affluens, -entis*—*affluĕre*—*ad*, to, *fluĕre*, to flow.]

afford [a-fōrd´, -förd´] *vt* so spare (money, time, etc.) without much inconvenience; to yield, produce. [ME *aforthen*—OE *geforthian* or *forthian*, to further or to cause to come forth.]

afforestation [a-for-estā´shȯn] *n* the planting of trees to form a forest. [LL *afforestāre*—*ad*, to, *forestis*. See **forest**.]

affray [a-frā´] *n* a noisy brawl. [OFr *afrayer, esfreer*—LL *exfrīdiāre*, to break the king's peace—L *ex*, and OHG *fridu* (Ger *friede*), peace.]

affright [a-frīt´] *vt* to frighten.—*n* sudden terror. [OE *āfyrhtan*—*ā-*, inten, and *fyrhtan*. See **fright**.]

affront [a-frunt´] *vt* to insult openly.—*n* an open insult. [OFr *afronter*—LL *affrontāre*—L *ad*, to, *frons, frontis*, forehead.]

affusion [a-fū´zh(ȯ)n] *n* the act of pouring liquid upon, as in baptism. [L *affūsiō, -ōnis*—*affundĕre*—*ad*, to, *fundĕre, fūsum*, to pour.]

Afghan [af´gan] *n* native or inhabitant of Afghanistan; Pashto, **afghan**, a knitted or crocheted blanket or shawl made up of squares or stripes; a large Turkoman carpet with long pile.—**Afghan hound**, a breed of dog with long narrow head and long thick silky coat.

aficionado [ȧ-fish´i-nä´dō] *n* a devotee of some sport, art, etc. [Sp]

afield [a-fēld´] *adv* far away from home; to or at a distance; astray. [Pfx *a-* (OE *on*), on, + **field**.]

afire [a-fīr´] *adj, adv* on fire. [Pfx *a-* (OE *on*), on, + **fire**]

aflame [a-flām´] *adj, adv* in flames, burning. [Pfx *a-* (OE *on*), on + **flame**.]

afloat [a-flōt´] *adv, adj* floating; at sea; flooded. [OE *on flote*. See **float**.]

afoot [a-fōōt´] *adv* on foot; in progress, [Pfx *a-* (OE *on*), on, + **foot**.]

aforementioned [a-fōr´men-shond] *adj* mentioned before.

aforesaid [a-fōr-sed] *adj* spoken of before.
aforethought [a-fōr´thöt] *adj* thought out beforehand; premeditated.
afoul [a-fowl] *adv, adj* in a collision or tangle.—**fall afoul of**, to get into trouble with.
afraid [a-frād´] *adj* frightened (of, that, or to); admit with regret. [Pt p of obs vb *affray*, to startle, frighten. See **affray**.]
afreet *See* **afrit**.
afresh [a-fresh´] *adv* anew; beginning again. [OE pfx *a-* (*of*, off, from), and **fresh**.]
African [af´rik-ȧn] *adj* of Africa, its peoples, or languages.—*n* a native or inhabitant of Africa, esp a dark-skinned person.—*ns* **Africän´a**, materials (as books, documents, or artifacts) relating to African culture and history; **Afr´icanist**, a specialist in African cultures or languages—*African violet*, any of a genus (*Saint paulia*) of tropical African plants often grown as a house plant.
Afrikaans [af-ri-käns´] *n* one of the official languages of South Africa; developed from Dutch. [Du; earlier S African *afrikander*, influenced by Hollander.]
afrit [a-frēt´] *n* an evil demon in Arabian mythology. Also **afreet**. [Ar *'ifrīt*]
aft [äft] *adv* at, near, or toward the stern of a ship or rear of an aircraft. [OE *æftan*.]
Afro [af´rō] *adj* of or denoting a full, bouffant hair style, as worn by some blacks.—Also *n* **Af´ro-**, in composition, Africa; African.—*adj* **Afro-American**, of black Americans, their culture, etc.—*n* an American of African and esp Negroid descent.—**Afro-Asiatic languages**, a family of languages widely distributed over southwestern Asia and northern Africa.
after [äft´ėr] *prep* and *adv* behind in place; later, later than; following in search of; in imitation of; according to; subsequently.—*adj* behind in place; later; nearer the rear.—*ns* **aft´erbirth**, the placenta and membranes which are expelled from the womb after childbirth; **aft´erburner**, a device attached to some engines for burning or utilizing exhaust gases; **af´tercare**, care following a period of treatment; **af´tereffect**, an effect that arises or persists after its cause has gone; **aft´erglow**, the glow often seen in the sky after sunset; **af´terlife**, life after death; **aft´ermath**, a result, esp an unpleasant one; **afternoon** [aft-ėr-nōōn´], the time between noon and evening—Also *adj.*—*ns* **af´tershave**, a lotion for use after shaving; **af´tertaste**, a taste remaining or recurring after eating or drinking something; **af´terthought**, thought or reflection after an action—*adv* **aft´erward, afterwards**, at a later time. [OE *æfter*, comp of *af* or *of*, the primary meaning being 'more off', 'farther away'; *-ter* is the comparative affix seen as *-ther* in **other**.]
Aga Khan [ä-gä´ kän] *n* the spiritual leader of Ismaili Muslims. [Turk *aghā*, Pers *ak, aka*, a lord.]
again [a-gen´] *adv* back into a former condition; once more; besides; on the other hand.—**again and again**, often; **as much again**, twice as much. [OE *ongēan*, again, opposite; Ger *entgegen*.]
against [a-genst´] *prep* in opposition to; in contact or in collision with; in preparation for; as a charge on. [Formed from *again*, with genitive ending *-es*, the *-t* being a later addition.]
agape[1] [ag´a-pē] *n* a love-feast, held by the early Christians in connection with the Lord's Supper. [Gr *agapē*, love.]
agape[2] [a-gāp´] *adj, adv* with the mouth wide open. [Pfx *a-* (OE *on*), on, + **gape**.]
agar [ä´gär] *n* a gelatinous substance obtained from various red seaweeds genera *Gelidium, Gracilaria*, and *Eucheuma*) used as a stabilizing agent in food, a culture medium for bacteria, and as a laxative.—Also **agar-agar**. [Malay.]
agate [ag´ȧt] *n* a chalcedony with striped or clouded coloring used as a gemstone; a playing marble made of or like this. [Gr *achātēs*, said to be so called because first found near the rive *Achates* in Sicily.]
agave [a-gā´vi] *n* a genus (*Agave*) of desert plants with thick fleshy leaves, including some grown for ornament, fiber, and the source of pulque. [L,—Gr *Agauē*, a woman in Greek legend.]
age [āj] *n* the time during which a person or thing has lived or existed; a stage of life; later years of life; a period of time; any great division of geology or history; (*inf*) a long time (often *pl*).—*vti* to grow or make old, ripe, mature, etc.—*pr p* **aging** [aj´ing] *pt p* **aged** [ājd].—*adj* **aged** [āj´id] advanced in age; [ājd] of the age of.—*vti* **age-date**, to determine scientifically the age of archeological or geologic materials.—*n* a specimen's age obtained by scientific dating.—*n* **ageism** [āj´izm], discrimination on grounds of age against the old.—*adjs* **age´ist, age´-ist; age´less**, never growing old; **age´-old**, ancient.—**the ag´ed**, old people [OFr *aage, edage*—L *aetās* = *aevitās*—L *aevum*, age.]
agenda [a-jen´da] *n* a list of things to be done, as items of business to be considered at a meeting. [L neut pl of *agendus*, gerundive of *agĕre*, to do.]
agent [ā´jėnt] *n* a person or thing that acts or exerts power; any natural force acting on matter; one authorized to transact business for another; a representative of a government agency; a spy.—*n* **ag´ency**, action; power; means; a firm, etc. empowered to act for another; an administrative government division.—**Agent Orange**, (*military*) code name for a defoliant containing dioxin. [L *agĕre*, to do. See **act**.]
ageratum [aj´ė-rāt´um] *n* any of a large genus (*Ageratum*) of tropical American herbs grown for their small showy heads of blue or white flowers.
Aggeus [ā-gē´us] *n* (*Bible*) Haggai in the Douay Version of the Old Testament.
agglomerate [a-glom´ėr-āt] *vti* to gather into a mass or a ball.—Also *adj.*—*ns* **agglom´erate** [-āt] something consisting of irregular fragments; **agglomerā´tion**. [L *agglomerāre, -ātum—ad*, to, L *glomus, glomeris*, a ball.]
agglutinate [a-glōōt´in-āt] *vti* to stick together, as with glue.—*n* **agglutinā´tion**, sticking or fusing together.—*adj* **agglut´inative**, tending to, or having power to, cause adhesion; (of languages) in which complex ideas are expressed by words composed of simpler words, the elements retaining their independence and their original form and meaning. [L *agglūtināre, -ātum—ad*, to, *glūten*, glue. See **glue**.]
aggrandize [ag´rand-īz] *vt* to make greater in power, rank, wealth, etc.;—*n* **aggrandizement** [a-gran´diz-ment]. [Fr,—L *ad*, to, *grandis*, large.]
aggravate [ag´ra-vāt] *vt* to make worse. (*inf*) to provoke, irritate.—*adj* **aggr´avated** (*law*), denoting a grave form of a specified offense.—*n* **aggravā´tion**. [L *aggravāre, -ātum—ad*, to, *gravis*, heavy.]
aggregate [ag´re-gāt] *vt* to collect into a mass; to total.—*adj* [-ȧt] formed of parts collected in a mass; taking all units as a whole.—*n* a mass of distinct things gathered into a whole; (*geol*) a mass consisting of rock or mineral fragments; any material mixed with cement to form concrete.—*adv* **agg´regately**.—*n* **aggregā´tion**, act of aggregating; state of being collected together; an aggregate.—**in the aggregate**, considered as a whole. [L *aggregāre, -ātum*, to bring together, as a flock—*ad*, to, *grex, gregis*, a flock.]
aggress [a-gres´] *vi* to act aggressively.—*adj* **aggress´ive**, boldly hostile; quarrelsome; self-assertive, enterprising.—*ns* **aggression** [a-gresh´(ȯ)n], the act of making an unprovoked attack; a hostile action or behavior; **aggress´iveness; aggress´or**, a person or country that attacks first. [L *aggredī, -gressus—ad*, to, *gradī*, to step.]
aggrieve [a-grēv´] *vt* to cause grief or injury to; to offend; to slight; to treat unfairly. [OFr *agrever*—L *ad*, to, *gravis*, heavy.]
aghast [a-gäst´] *adj* stupefied with horror. [Properly *agast*; ME *agasten*, to terrify—OE inten pfx *ā-*, and *gaæstan*, to terrify.]
agile [aj´īl, aj´il] *adj* active, nimble.—*n* **agility** [a-jil´i-ti], quickness of motion, nimbleness. [Fr,—L *agilis*—*agĕre*, to do or act.]
agitate [aj´i-tāt] *vt* to shake, set in motion; to stir violently; to disturb, excite—*vi* to keep up the discussion of, esp with a view to reform.—*ns* **agitā´tion, ag´itator**, one who stirs or keeps up a public agitation; **agitprop** [aj´it-prop], propaganda, esp political and pro-communist. [L *agitāre*, freq of *agĕre*, to put in motion. See **act**.]
aglet [ag´let] *n* the tag or point of a lace or point; any ornamental stud, pin or cord worn in clothing. [Fr *aiguillette*, dim of *aiguille*, a needle—from L *acūcula* = *acicula*, dim of *acus*, a needle.]
aglow [a-glō´] radiant with warmth or excitement. [Pfx *a-* (OE *on*), on + **glow**.]
agnate [ag´nāt] *adj* related on the father's side.—Also *n* [L *agnātus—ad*, to, *((g)nātus*, to be born.]
agnostic [ag-nos´tik] *n* one who holds that we know nothing of God, or of an unseen world beyond material phenomena.—*n* **agnos´ticism**. [Coined by T H Huxley in 1869—Gr *a-*, priv, *gnōstikos*, good at knowing. See **gnostic**.]
Agnus Dei [ag´nus dē´ī] a liturgical prayer addressing Christ as Savior; a figure of a lamb emblematic of Christ. [L 'lamb of God'.]
ago [a-gō] *adv* in the past.—*adj* gone by; past. [Pt p of OE *āgān*, to pass away—inten pfx *ā-*, and *gān*, to go.]
agog [a-gog´] *adj* eager; expectant. [Ety doubtful.]
agony [ag´o-ni] *n* extreme mental or physical suffering; death pangs. *vt* **ag´onize**, to torture.—*vi* to struggle; to be in agony.—*adj* **ag´onizing**.—*adv* **ag´onizingly**.—**agony column**, the part of a newspaper containing advertisements for missing relatives or friends. [Gr *agōnia*—*agōn*, contest.]
agoraphobia [ag´or-ȧfō´bi-a] *n* morbid fear of crossing open places. [Gr *agora*, market-place, *phobos*, fear.]
agouti [ȧ-gōō´ti] *n* a rabbit-sized tropical American rodent (*Dasproctа aguti*). [Fr from Sp *aguti*.]
agrarian [ag-rā´ri-ȧn] *adj* relating to land, or its management.—*n* **agrā´rianism**, a social or political movement advocating land reform and improvement of the economic status of the farmer. [L *agrārius*—*ager*, a field.]
agree [a-grē´] *vi* to get on with one another; to come to an understanding; to consent (to); to assent (to); to concur (with); to be consistent to harmonize (with); to suit a person's health or digestion; (*gram*) to take the same gender, number, case, or person—*vt* to grant. *pr p* **agree´ing**; *pt p* **agreed´**.—*adj* **agree´able**, pleasant; pleasing; willing to consent; conformable.—*n* **agree´ableness**.—*adv* **agree´ably**.—*n* **agree´ment**, concord; conformity; a contract. [OFr *agrer*, to accept kindly—L *ad*, to, *grātus*, pleasing.]
agribusiness [ag´ri-biz-nės] *n* farming together with associated business and industries.
agriculture [ag´ri-kul-chůr] *n* art or practice of producing crops and raising livestock; farming;—*adj* **agricult´ural**—*n* **agricult´urist, agricult´uralist**, one skilled in agriculture. [L *agricultūra*—*ager*, a field, *cultūra*, cultivation. See **culture**.]

aground [a-grownd´] *adj, adv* on or onto the shore, a reef, etc. [Pfx *a-* (OE *on*), on, + **ground**.]

ague [ā´gū] *n* a malarial fever; shivering fits.—*adjs* **aguish** [ā´gū-ish] [OFr *aigue* [Fr *aigu*, sharp)—L *acūta* (*febris*). See **acute**.]

ah [ä, ö] *interj* an exclamation of pain, delight, surprise, etc.

aha [ä-hä´] *interj* an exclamation of satisfaction, triumph, etc.

ahead [a-hed´] *adj, adv* in or to the front; forward; onward; in advance; winning or profiting.—**get ahead**, to advance financially etc. [Pfx *a-* (OE *on*), on, + **head**.]

ahem [a-hem´] *interj* the noise made when cleaning the throat, used to call attention or express doubt.

-aholic [a-höl´ik] *suffix* meaning one addicted to, obsessed with, etc. (*workaholic, bookaholic*).

ahoy [a-hoi´] *interj* a nautical call used in hailing. [Form of interj *hoy*.]

aid [ād] *vti* to help, assist.—*n* help; anything that helps; a helper;—*n* **aid´er**,.—*adj* [OFr *aider*—L *adjūtāre*, to help.]

aide-de-camp [ā´de-kā] *n* a military officer serving as an assistant to a superior etc.;—*pl* **aides´-de-camp**, (pron as *sing*). [Fr, assistant on the field.]

aide-mémoire [ed-, ād-mā-mwär] *n* an aid to the memory; a written summary of the items of a diplomatic document in preparation. [Fr]

AIDS [ādz] *n* a condition, caused by a virus, of deficiency in certain leukocytes leading to cancer, pneumonia, etc. [acquired immune deficiency syndrome.]

aigrette [ā´gret] *n* a spray of feathers for the hair; a plume composed of feathers, or of gems, like a heron's crest. [Fr]

ail [āl] *vi* to be in poor health.—*vt* to cause pain and trouble to.—*n* **ail´ment**, pain; indisposition; disease. [OE *eglan*, to pain.]

ailanthus [ā-lanth´us] *n* a small genus (*Ailanthus*) of Chinese trees, grown widely in American cities because of the ability to survive in pavements, etc.—Also **Tree of Heaven**.

aileron [ā´lėr-on, el´ė-rō] *n* a hinged section at the trailing edge of an airplane wing, used to control its rolling. [Fr, dim of *aile*—L *āla*, a wing.]

aim [ām] *vti* to point or direct towards a mark so as to hit; to direct (one's efforts;) to intend—*n* the action or manner of aiming; the mark aimed at; design, intention.—*adj* **aim´-less**, without purpose or object.—*adv* **aim´lessly**. [OFr *esmer*, to reckon—L *aestimāre*, to estimate.]

ain't [ānt] *inf* contracted form of *are not, am* or *is not*; also *has not, have not*.

Ainu [ī´nōō] *n* member of an indigenous Caucasoid people of Japan. (*pl* **Ainu** or **-s**); their language. [Ainu lit man.]

aioli [ī-ōō´li] *n* garlic mayonnaise. [Fr]

air [ār] *n* the mixture of gases we breathe; the atmosphere; any special condition of atmosphere; a breeze; outward appearance, manner, look; (*mus*) a melody; (*pl*) affectation.—*adj* of aviation.—*vt* to expose to the air; to bring to public notice—*ns* **air bag**, a bag that inflates automatically inside an automobile in a collision, to protect riders from being thrown forward; **air base**, a base for military aircraft; **air bladder**, a sac containing gas and air, esp present in most fishes as an accessory to respiration.—*adj* **air´borne**, carried by or through the air; aloft or flying.—*ns* **air brake**, a brake operated by the action of compressed air on a piston; **air´brush**, an atomizer worked by compressed air and used for spraying on paint, etc.—Also **air brush; air´bus´**, an extremely large passenger aircraft, esp for short trips; **air conditioning**, regulation of air humidity and temperature in buildings, etc.—*vt* **air-condition**.—*n* **air-conditioner**.—*adj* **air-cooled**, cooled by having air passed over, into, or through it.—*ns* **air´craft´**, any machine for traveling through air;—*pl* **air´craft´; aircraft carrier**, a warship with a large flat deck, for carrying aircraft; **air curtain**, a downward-forced air current at an open door to maintain inside temperature; **air-cushion vehicle**, a vehicle supported above surface of ground or water by a cushion of air, used for mowing grass or traveling short distances; **air door**, air curtain; **air´drop**, the parachuting of supplies or troops from an aircraft in flight.—Also *vt*—*ns* **air´field**, a field where aircraft can take off and land; **air´foil**, a wing, rudder, etc. of an aircraft; **air force**, the aviation branch of a country's armed forces; **air gun**, a gun or gunlike device operated by compressed air; **air´head** (*slang*), a stupid or silly person; **air´ing**, exposure to open air for drying or freshening; exercise in open air; exposure to public view; a radio or television broadcast; **air lane**, a route for travel by air; airway; **air´lift**, a system of transporting troops, supplies, etc. by aircraft.—*vt* to transport by airlift.—*n* **air´line**, a system or company for transportation by aircraft.—*adj* of, or on an airline.—*ns* **air´lin´er**, a large passenger aircraft operated by an airline; **air lock**, an airtight compartment, with adjustable air pressure, between places or unequal air pressure; **air´mail´**, mail transported by aircraft.—*vt* to send by airmail.—*ns* **air´man**, an aviator; an enlisted person in the US Air Force ranking above airman basic and below airman first class; **airman basic**, enlisted man of lowest rank in the US Air Force; **airman first class**, enlisted man above airman and below sergeant; **air mass**, a large body of air keeping a uniform temperature as it moves; **air mile**, 6076 feet or 1852 kilometers; **air´plane**, a fixed-wing motor-driven or jet-propelled aircraft kept aloft by the forces of air upon its wings; **air plant**, an epiphyte; **air´play**, the playing of a recording over radio or TV; **air pollution**, waste products in the form of gases and small suspended particles in the atmosphere; **air´port**, a place where aircraft can land and take off, usu. with facilities for repair, etc.; **air power** total capacity of a nation for air war; **air pressure**, the pressure of the atmosphere or of compressed air; **air pump**, machine to extract, compress, or supply air; **air raid**, an attack by aircraft, esp bombers; **air rifle**, a rifle operated by compressed air; **air sac**, air-filled space in the body of birds connected to lungs; air cell of the lungs of mammals; **air shaft**, a well-like ventilating passage; **air´ship**, a self-propelled steerable aircraft that is lighter than air.—*adj* **air´-sick**, nauseated because of air travel.—*ns* **air´space**, the space above a nation over which it maintains jurisdiction; **air´strip**, a temporary airfield.—*adj* **air´tight**, too tight for air or gas to enter or escape; invulnerable (*an airtight alibi*).—*ns* **air trap**, device to prevent the escape of foul gases; **air valve**, air trap; (*npl*) **air´waves**, the medium through which radio signals are transmitted; **air´way´**, air lane; (*pl*) airwaves.—*adj* **air´worthy**, fit for operation in the air.—*n* **air´worthiness**.—*adj* **airy**, of air; open to the air; breezy; light as air, graceful; lighthearted; flippant; (*inf*) putting on airs.—**in the air**, prevalent; **on** (or **off**) **the air**, that is (or not) broadcasting; **up in the air**, not settled; (*slang*) angry, excited, etc. [Fr,—L *āër*—Gr *āēr*, air.]

Airedale [ār´dāl] *n* a breed of large terriers with a hard, wiry black-and-tan coat. [*Airedale*, valley of the Aire river, England.]

aisle [īl] *n* a passageway, as between rows of seats; a side part of a church. [OFr *ele, aisle*—L *axilla, āla*, wing.]

aitchbone [āch´bōn] *n* the bone of the rump; the cut of beef over this bone. [Orig *nache-*, or *nage*-bone—OFr *nache, nage*—L *natis*, buttock; *a nache* became *an aitch*.]

ajar [a-jär´] *adv* partly open, as a door. [Pfx *a-* (OE *on*), on, *cerr*, a turn.]

akimbo [a-kim´bō] *adv, adj* with hands on hip and elbows bent outward.

akin [a-kin´] *adj* related by blood; having similar characteristics. [OE prep *of*, + **kin**.]

à la [a la] *prep* in the manner of. [Fr]

alabaster [al´a-bäs-tėr, or -bäs´-] *n* a semi-transparent gypsum.—Also *adj* [Gr *alabastros*, said to be derived from *Alabastron*, a town in Egypt.]

à la carte [ä lä kärt´] *adj, adv* with a separate price for each item on the menu. [Fr]

alack [a-lak´] *interj* an exclamation denoting sorrow and regret. [Interj *ah* + **lack**.]

alacrity [a-lak´ri-ti] *n* briskness, cheerful readiness. [L *alacritās*—*alacer*, gen *alacris*, brisk.]

à la King [a-lä-king] *adj* in a cream sauce containing mushrooms, pimentos, etc.

à la mode, a la mode [a-lä-mōd´] *adv, adj* according to the fashion. [Fr]

alarm [a-lärm´] *n* notice of danger; sudden surprise with fear; vivid apprehension; a mechanical contrivance to arouse from sleep or to attract attention.—*vt* to give notice of danger; to fill with dread.—*adj* **alarm´ing**, frightening.—*n* **alarm´ist**, one who excites alarm; one given to prophesying danger.—Also *adj* [Fr *alarme*—It *all'arme*, to arms.]

alas [a-läs´] *interj* expressive of grief. [OFr (*h*)*a las* (mod Fr *hélas*); *ha*! ah!*las(se)*, wretched, weary—L *lassus*, wearied.]

Alaskan malamute [ȧl-ask´ăn mal´ă-my] *n* a breed of working dog developed from the Eskimo sled dog.

alate [āl´āt] *adj* having wings or winglike parts.—Also **al´ated**. [L *ālātus*—*āla*, a wing.]

alb [alb] *n* a white robe worn by priests at Mass. [OE *albe*—L *albus*, white.]

albatross [al´ba-tros] *n* any of several large web-footed seabirds (family Diomediadae) of the Pacific Ocean; a heavy burden, as of debt, guilt, etc. [Corr from Sp *alcatraz*, perh with reference to L *albus*, white, from their color.]

albeit [öl-bē´it] *conj* conceding the fact that; even though. [All be it (that) = all though it be that.]

albino [al-bē´no] *n* a person, animal, or plant lacking normal coloration. Human albinos have white skin, whitish hair, and pink eyes.—*pl* **albi´nos**. [Port or Sp *albino*, whitish—L *albus*, white.]

Albion [al´bi-ȯn] *n* Great Britain; England. [L—Celt.]

album [al´bum] *n* a blank book for the insertion of portraits, autographs, etc.; a booklike container for phonograph records; a single long-playing record or tape recording. [L,—*albus*, white.]

albumen [al-bū´men] *n* white of egg; protein in germinating cells; albumin.—*n* **albū´min**, a water-soluble protein found in egg, milk, blood, vegetable tissues, etc.—*adjs* **albū´minous**, [L,—*albus*, white.]

alburnum [al-bûr´num] *n* sapwood. [L,—*albus*, white.]

alchemy [al´ki-mi] *n* the forerunner of modern chemistry, its chief aims being to transmute base metals into gold and to discover the elixir of life.—*n* **al´chemist**. [Ar *al-kīmiā*—*al*, the, *kīmiā* (late Gr *chēmeiā*,) 'transmutation'; confused with Gr *chȳmeiā*, pouring, from *cheein*, to pour, hence the old spellings *alchymy, chymistry*.]

alcohol [al´kō-hol] *n* a liquid generated by the fermentation of sugar or other carbohydrates, and forming the intoxicating element of wine, beer, and spirits; the name for the class of chemical compounds to which common alcohol (ethanol) belongs.—*adj* **alcohol´ic**, of alcohol; suffering from alcoholism.—*n* one addicted to excessive drinking of alcohol.—*n* **al´coholism**, condition of an alcoholic; a resulting diseased condition. [Ar *alkoh'l*—*al*, the, *koh'l*, fine powder of antimony used in the East to stain the eyelids.]

Alcoran [al-ko-rän´] *n* (*arch*) the Koran. [Ar *al*, the, and **Koran**.]

alcove [al´kōv, al-kōv] *n* a recess in a room, as a breakfast nook. [Sp *alcoba*, a place in a room railed off to hold a bed—Ar *al*, the *qobbah*, a vault.]

aldehyde [al´di-hīd] *n* one of the class of chemical compounds with the general formula RCHO, where R is an organic group, the simplest aldehyde being formaldehyde. [From *al dehyd*, a contr for *alcohol dehydrogenatum*, alcohol deprived of hydrogen.]

alder [öl´dėr] *n* genus (*Alnus*) of trees related to the birch, usu. growing in moist ground. [OE *alor*; Ger *erle*; L *alnus*.]

alderman [öl´dėr-man] *n* in some cities, a municipal officer representing a certain district or ward. [OE (Anglian) *aldor* (*ald*, old), senior, chief; *aldorman*, ruler.]

ale [āl] *n* a beverage made from malt by fermentation, similar to beer. [OE (Anglian) *alu*; ON *öl*.]

aleatory [ā´lē-a-tor-ē] *adj* depending on chance or luck; (*mus*) of elements chosen at random.—Also **aleatoric**. [L *aleatorius*, of gambling.]

alee [a-lē´] *adv* on or toward the lee. [Pfx *a-* (OE *on*), on, + **lee**.]

alembic [a-lem´bik] *n* a vessel formerly used in distillation by chemists anything that purifies. [Ar *al*, the, *anbīq*, a still—Gr *ambix*, a cup.]

alert [a-lûrt´] *adj* watchful; brisk.—*n* a danger warning.—*vt* to forewarn, put on the alert.—*adv* **alert´ly**.—*n* **alert´ness.—on the alert**, vigilant. [Fr—It *all' erta*, on the erect—*erto*, erect—L *ērectus*.]

Aleut [al-e-ōōt] *n* member of an Amerindian people inhabiting the Alaskan peninsula and the Aleutian islands; the language of this people.

alewife [āl´wīf] *n* a marine and freshwater fish (*Alosa pseusoharengus*) of N America, used for food and fertilizers.

alexandrine [al-egz-an´drin] *n* a rhyming verse of twelve syllables, six iambic feet, [perh so called from its use in old French poems on *Alexander* the Great.]

alexandrite [al-egz-an´drīt] *n* a variety of chrysoberl, green by daylight and red-violet by artificial light, used as a gemstone. [*Alexander* I, czar of Russia.]

alexia [a-leks´i-a] *n* impaired ability to read.

Alfa [al´fa] communication code word for the letter *a*.

alfalfa [al-fal´fa] *n* a deep-rooted leguminous plant (Medicago sativa) grown widely for hay and forage. [Sp,—Ar *alfaçfaçah*.]

alfresco [al-fres´ko] *adv, adj* in the open air. [It *al fresco*.]

alga [al´ga] *n* any of a group (Algae) of chiefly aquatic lower plants classified according to color; blue-green, green, brown, or red, which may be microscopic unicellular organisms, sometimes colonial, to multicellular seaweed;— *pl* **algae** [-je], **algas**.—*n* **algol´ogist**, a specialist in the study of algae. [L *alga*, seaweed.]

algebra [al´je-bra] *n* the branch of mathematics dealing with the properties and relations of numbers; the generalization and extension of arithmetic.—*adjs* **algebrā´ic, -al**.—*n* **algebrā´ist**. [It and Sp, from Ar *al-jebr*, the resetting of anything broken, hence combination—*jabara*, to unite.]

ALGOL, Algol [al´gäl, -gōl] *n* an algebraic computer programming language designed for mathematical and scientific uses. [*algo*rithmic *l*anguage.]

Algonkin [al-gong´kin] *n* Algonquian; (*geol*) period of Precambrian era, about 6000 000 000 to about 1000 000 000 years ago.

Algonquian [al-gong´kwi-ȧn] *n* Amerindian language group formerly spoken from Labrador south to the Carolinas and westward to the Rockies; people of the Ottawa River Valley; speaker of any of the Algonquian dialects.—Also **Algonquin, Algonkin**.

algorithm [al´go-ridhm] *n* (*math*) any method or procedure for computation.

alias [ā´li-as] *adv* otherwise named.—*n* an assumed name;—*pl* **a´liases**. [L *aliās*, at another time, otherwise—*alius*, other.]

alibi [al´i-bī] *n* (*law*) the plea that a person charged with a crime was elsewhere when it was committed; (*inf*) any excuse.—*vi* (*inf*) to offer an excuse. [L, elsewhere—*alius*, other, *ibi*, there.]

alien [āl´yen, or ā´lē-en] *adj* foreign; strange.—*n* one belonging to another country; one of foreign birth who is not naturalized; a hypothetical being from outer space. [L *aliēnus*—*alius*, other.]

alienate [āl´yėn-āt, ā´li-en-āt] *vt* to transfer (property) to another; to estrange; to divert affection (from).—*adj* **āl´ienable**, capable of being transferred to another.—*ns* **alienabil´ity; alienā´tion**. [L *aliēnāre, -ātum*—*aliēnus*. See **alien**.]

alienist [al´yen-ist, ā´li-en-ist] *n* a psychiatrist, esp one dealing in the legal aspects of psychiatry. [Fr *aliéniste*.]

alight [a-līt] *vi* to come down, as from a horse; to descend after a flight. [OE *ālīhtan*, to come down—*a-*, inten, *līhtan*.]

align [a-līn´] *vt* to arrange in a straight line, to bring (components or working parts) into adjustment; to bring into agreement, etc.—*vi* to line up. [Fr *aligner*—L *ad*, to, *līnea*, a line.]

alike [a-līk´] *adj* like one another.—*adv* equally; similarly. [OE *gelīc, anlīc, onlīc*—*ge*, together, *an, on*, on, *līc*. See like (1).]

aliment [al´i-mėnt] *n* nourishment food.—*adj* **aliment´ary**, pertaining to aliment.—*ns* **alimentā´tion**, the act or state of nourishing or of being nourished; **al´imony**, an allowance for support made to a wife when legally separated from her husband.—**alimentary canal**, the principal part of the digestive apparatus of animals, extending from the mouth to the anus. [L *alimentum*—*alĕre*, to nourish.]

aliphatic [al-i-fat´ik] *adj* (*chem*) of any organic compound having an open chain structure. [Gr *aleiphar*, oil.]

aliquant [al´i-kwant] *adj* (*math*) of a quantity or number that is not an exact divisor of a given quantity or number.

aliquot [al´i-kwot] *adj* (*math*) of a part which is contained in the whole an exact number of times. [L *aliquot*, some, several—*alius*, other, *quot*, how many.]

alive [a-līv´] *adj* in life; alert; in existence, operation, etc.—**alive to**, aware of; **alive with**, teeming with. [OE *on līfe*—*līfe*, dat of *līf*, life.]

aliyah, aliya [a-lē´ya] *n* the immigration of Jews to Israel. [Heb]

alkali [al´ka-li, or -lī] *n* (*chem*) a substance that dissolves in water to form a strongly basic solution, esp the hydroxides of sodium and potasium; **alkalies, alkalis**.—*adj* **alkaline** [al´kalin, or līn].—*n* **alkalinity** [-lin´].—*vt* **al´kalīze**.—*adj* **al´kaloid**.—*n* **alkalōs´is**, condition caused by excess of alkaline substances or shortage of acidic substances in the body fluids.—**alkali metal**, any of the group of elements comprising lithium, sodium, potassium, rubidium, cesium, and francium (so-called because their hydroxides are strongly alkaline). [Ar *alqalīy*, ashes, the term having been originally applied to salts, chiefly potassium carbonate and sodium carbonate, got from plant ashes.]

alkaloid [al´ka-loid] *n* any one of a number of organic bases found in plants and often important in medicine on account of their physiological action. [**alkali**, Gr *eidos*, form.]

all [öl] *adj* the whole of; every one of.—*adv* wholly; completely; entirely.—*n* the whole; everyone; everything.—*adj* **all-American**, comprising wholly American elements; typical of the US; selected as one of the best in the US at the time, esp of an athlete.—*n* an all-American athlete.—**all around**, competent in many fields; having general usefulness or merit; **all fours**, all the limbs of a quadruped; legs and arms of a person when crawling; **all get out** (*inf*), utmost conceivable degree; **all in**, tired; **all in all**, on the whole; **all out**, with enthusiasm; **all over**, over whole extent; everywhere; thoroughly; **all-over**, covering whole surface; **allover**, consisting of repeated pattern; **all right**, adequate; satisfactory; unharmed, safe; very well; satisfactorily; without doubt; **all-round**, all-around; **all there**, mentally alert. [OE *all, eall*; Ger *all*, Gael *uile*, W *oll*.]

Allah [ä´la] *n* the Muslim name of God. [Ar contr of *al-ilāh*, 'the worthy to be adored'.]

allay [a-lā´] *vt* to lighten, relieve; to make quiet or calm. [ME forms, *aleggen, aleyen* (OE *alecgan*—*ā-*, inten, *lecgan*, causal of *licgan*, to lie); identical in form, and accordingly confounded in meaning, with two ME words of Latin origin from which came **alloy** and an obs verb *allege*, to alleviate.]

allege [a-lej´] *vt* to assert or declare, esp without proof; to offer as an excuse.—*n* **allegātion** [al-e-gā´sh(ȯ)n], an assertion, esp without proof.—*adj* **alleged**, declared, but without proof; not actual; so-called. [Through OFr forms from LL *exlītigāre*, to clear at law.]

allegiance [a-lē´j(y)ȧns] *n* the duty of being loyal to one's country, etc.; devotion, as to a cause. [L *ad*, to, + **liege**.]

allegory [al´e-gor-i] *n* a description of one thing under the image of another as in a fable.—*adjs* **allegor´ical**.—*adv* **allegor´ically**.—*vt* **all´egorize**, to put in form of an allegory.—*vi* to use allegory. [Gr *allēgoriā; allos*, other, *agoreuein*, to speak.]

allegro [a-le´grō, or -lā´-] *adv, adj* (*mus*) fast.—*adv, adj* **allegrett´o**, moderately fast. [It,—L *alacer*, brisk.]

alleluia [al-e-lōō´ya] hallelujah.

allergy [al´ėr-ji] *n* an altered or acquired state of sensitivity; abnormal reaction of the body to substances normally harmless; antipathy.—*n* **all´ergen**, a substance inducing an allergic reaction.—*adj* **aller´gic**, (*with* **to**) adversely affected by, supersensitive to (certain substances); feeling distaste, dislike for.—*n* **all´ergist**, a doctor who specializes in treating allergies. [Gr *allos*, other, *ergon*, work.]

alleviate [a-lē´vi-āt] *vt* to lessen or relieve (pain); to mitigate.—*ns* **alleviā´tion; allev´iātor**. [L *alleviāre, -ātum*—*ad* inten, *levis*, light.]

alley [al´i] *n* a narrow street between or behind buildings; a bowling lane;—*pl* **all´eys**.—*n* **all´eyway**, an alley between buildings.—**alley cat**, a homeless mongrel cat. [OFr *alee*, passage—*aller*, to go.]

All Fools' Day [öl fōōlz´ dā] *n* April 1, April Fool's Day.

all hail [öl-hāl´] *interj* used to express greeting, welcome, or acclamation. [**all** + **hail**, interj]

All-hallows [öl-hal´ōz] *n* All Saints' Day. [**all** + **hallow**.]

alliance [a-lī´ȧns] *n* union by marriage or treaty; any union for a common purpose; an agreement for this; the countries, groups, etc. in such an association. [OFr *aliance*—*alier*. See **ally**.]

alligator [al´i-gā-tȯr] *n* a large reptile (genus *Alligator*) of the US similar to the crocodile but having a short, blunt snout.—**alligator clip**, a spring-loaded clip used for making temporary electrical connections; **alligator pear**, an avocado. [Sp *el lagarto*—L *lacerta*, a lizard.]

alliteration [a-lit-ėr-ā´sh(ȯ)n] *n* the recurrence of the same *sound* at the beginning of two or more words in a phrase, etc.—*vi* **allit´erate**, to begin with the same sound.—*vt* to arrange so as to make alliterations.—*adj* **allit´erative**. [Fr,—L *ad*, to, *lītera*, a letter.]

allocate [al´o-kāt] *vt* to distribute or allot; to set apart for a specific purpose.—*n* **allocā´tion**. [L *allocāre*—*ad*, to, and *locāre, -ātum*—*locus*, a place.]

allocution [al-o-kū´sh(ȯ)n] *n* a formal speech, esp a hortatory address. [L *allocūtiō, -ōnis*—*ad*, to, *loquī, locūtus*, to speak.]

allot [a-lot´] *vt* to divide as by lot, to assign as one's share;—*pr p* **allott´ing**; *pt p* **allott´ed**.—*n* **allot´ment**, the act of allotting; part of share allotted. [OFr *aloter; lot* is Gmc, seen in OE *hlot*.]

allotropy [a-lot´ro-pi], **allotropism** [a-lotrōpizm] *n* (*chem*) the property in some elements, of existing in two or more forms (eg carbon in the form of diamond and graphite) each called an **allotrope** [al´o-trōp].—*adj* **allotrŏp´ic**. [Gr *allotropia*, variety—*allos*, another, and *tropos*, turn.]

allow [a-low´] *vt* to permit; to acknowledge, admit, concede; to give, grant (sum of money at regular intervals); to add or deduct in estimating.—*vi* to admit (of).—*adj* **allow´able**, not forbidden; permissible.—*n* **allow´ance**, that which is allowed; a limited portion; a stated quantity; a concession.—**allow for**, take into the reckoning; **make allowance for**, to allow for, esp mitigating circumstances. [OFr *alouer*, to grant, to approve, which combines meanings derived from L *adlocare* (*ad*, to, *locāre*, to place), and L *allaudare* (*ad*, to, *laudāre*, to praise).]

alloy [a-loi´] *vt* to make into an alloy.—*n* [a´loi] a mixture of two or more metals; something that debases another thing when mixed with it. [OFr *aleier* (Fr *aloyer*), to combine—L *alligāre*, to bind.]

all-round [öl-rownd´] *see* **all-around**. [**all**, + **round**.]

All Saints' Day [öl sānts´ dā] *n* November 1, observed in western liturgical churches as a feast to honor all the saints.

All Souls' Day [öl sōlz´ dā] *n* November 2, a day of prayer for the repose of the souls of all the faithful departed.

allspice [öl´spis] *n* the berry of a West Indian tree (*Pimenta dioica*); the tree; an aromatic spice combining the flavor of cinnamon, nutmeg, and clove prepared from allspice berries. [**all**, + **spice**]

all-star [öl´star] *adj* made up entirely of outstanding performers.

all-time [öl tīm] *adj* unsurpassed until now.

allude [a-l(y)ōōd´] *vi* to refer indirectly to.—*n* **allū´sion**, an indirect reference.—*adj* **allus´ive**, containing an allusion; or many allusions.—*adv* **allus´ively**. [L *allūdere*—*ad*, at, *lūdere*, *lūsum*, to play.]

allure [a-l(y)ōōr´] *vt* to draw on as by a lure to entice.—*n* fascination; charm.—*n* **allure´ment**.—*adj* **allur´ing**.—*adv* **allur´ingly**. [OFr *al(e)urer*—*à*, to, *loerre*, a lure.]

alluvium [a-l(y)ōō´vi-um] *n* earth, sand, gravel, etc. deposited by moving water;—*pl* **allū´via**.—*adj* **allū´vial**. [L—*alluĕre*, to wash to or on—*ad*, to, *luĕre*, to wash.]

ally [a-lī´] *vti* to join or unite for a specific purpose; to relate by similarity of structure, etc.—*pt p, adj* **allied´**.—*n* **ally** [a-lī´, or a´lī],—*pl* **all´ies** [-īz] a country or person joined with another for a common purpose. [OFr *alier*—L *alligāre*—*ad*, to, *ligāre*, to bind.]

alma mater [al´ma mā´ter] *n* one's university or school; the song or hymn of a school, college, or university. [L fostering mother.]

almanac [al´, öl´, ma-nak] *n* a calender with astronomical data, weather forecasts, etc. [Most prob the original of the word as in Fr, It, and Sp was a Spanish-Arabic *al-manākh*.]

almighty [öl-mīt´i] *adj* all-powerful.—*adv* **almight´ily**.—*n* **almight´iness**.—**the Almighty**, God. [OE *ælmeahtig*—*eal*, all, *mihtig*, mighty.]

almond [ä´mȯnd] *n* edible kernel of the fruit of a tree (genus *Prunus*) of the rose family; the tree bearing this fruit.—*adj* oval and pointed at one or both ends. [OFr *almande*—L *amygdala*—Gr *amygdalē*.]

almost [öl´mōst] *adv* all but, very nearly. [**all** + **most** (adv).]

alms [ämz] *n* (*sing* and *pl*) relief given out of pity to the poor. [OE ælmysse, through LL, from Gr *eleēmosynē*—*eleos*, compassion.]

aloe [al´ō] *n* a genus (*Aloe*) of plants of the lily family of southern Africa.—*pl* **aloes**, purgative bitter drug, the juice of the leaves of several species of aloe; any of a genus (*Furcraea*) of American plants of the amaryllis family. [OE *aluwan*—L *aloē*—Gr *aloē*.]

aloft [a-loft´] *adv* in the air, flying; at a great height; (*naut*) high above the deck. [ON *ā lopt* (pron *loft*), expressing motion; *ā lopti*, expressing position—ON *ā* = OE *on*, in. *See* **loft**.]

aloha [å-lō´a, ä-lō´hä] *interj* a word used in greeting and farewell. [Hawaiian.]

alone [a-lōn´] *adj* by oneself; solitary; unique.—*adv* singly, by oneself.—**let alone**, to refrain from interfering; not to speak of (*we hadn't a nickel, let alone a dollar*). [**all** (adv), + **one**.]

along [a-long´] *adv* in the direction of the length; together with one; forward.—*prep* by the side of; near.—*prep, adv* **along´side**, beside; side by side;—**all along**, all the time. [OE *andlang*—pfx *and-*, against, and *lang*, **long**.]

aloof [a-lōōf´] *adv* at a distance but in view; apart.—*adj* cool and reserved.—*n* **aloof´ness**. [Pfx *a-* (OE *on*), on + **luff**.]

alopecia [al-o-pēsh´i-å] *n* baldness. [Gr *alōpekia*, fox mange.]

aloud [a-lowd´] *adv* with a normal voice; loudly; [Pfx *a-* (OE *on*), on, and *hlūd*, noise; Ger *laut*.]

alp [alp] *n* a high mountain.—*adj* **al´pine**, of the Alps; of high mountains; denoting ski races that include downhill, slalom, giant slalom, and supergiant slalom.—*n* a mountain plant, esp a small herb.—*ns* **al´pinist**, a mountain climber; **al´penstock**, an iron-shod staff used by climbers; **alpine horn**, primitive wind instrument used by herdsmen in the Alps.—**the Alps**, the high mountain range in south central Europe. [L; of Celtic origin; allied to L *albus*, white (with snow).]

alpaca [al-pak´a] *n* a Peruvian llama, having long silken wool; cloth made of its wool. [Sp *alpaca* or *al-paco*.]

alpha [al´fa] *n* the first letter of the Greek alphabet.—*adj* (*chem*) involving helium nuclei; (*chem*) denoting isomeric or allotropic form of a substance.—**alpha and omega**, the beginning and the end; **alpha particle**, helium nucleus emitted during some radioactive transformations; **alpha rays**, ionizing radiation consisting of a stream of alpha particles. [Gr *alpha*—Heb *aleph*, an ox, the name of the first letter of the Phoenician and Hebrew alphabets.]

alphabet [al´fa-bet] *n* the letters used in writing a language arranged in conventional order.—*adjs* **alphabet´ical**.—*adv* **alphabet´ically**. [Gr *alpha, beta*, the first two Greek letters.]

alphanumeric [al-fa-nōō-mer´ik] *adj* having both alphabetical and numerical symbols.

already [ö-red´i] *adv* previously or before the time specified. [**all** (adv) + **ready**.]

Alsatian [al-sā´sh(y)ån] *adj* of, pertaining to Alsatia or Alsace.—*n* the German Shepherd.

also [öl´sō] *adv* in addition.—*ns* **als´o-ran´**, (*inf*) a defeated contestant in a race, an election, etc; **also-runner**, an also-ran. [**all** (adv), + **so**.]

altar [ölt´år] *n* an elevated place or structure, on which sacrifices are offered; a table, etc. for sacred purposes in a place of worship.—*n* **alt´arpiece**, a work of art placed above and behind an altar. [L *altāre*—*altus*, high.]

alter [öl´tėr] *vti* to make different; to change.—*adj* **al´terable**, that may be altered.—*adv* **al´terably**.—*n* **alterā´tion**, change. *adj* **al´terative**, having power to alter.—*n* a medicine that alters favorably the course of an ailment. [L *alter*, the other—*al* (root of *alius*, other) and the old comp suffix *-ter* = Eng *-ther*.]

altercate [öl´tėr-kāt] *vi* to dispute or wrangle.—*n* **altercā´tion**, an angry or heated quarrel. [L *altercārī, -cātus*, to bandy words from one to the other (*alter*, other).]

alter ego [al´tėr eg´o, öl´tėr ēg´ō] *n* one's other self; a constant companion. [L *alter*, other, *ego*, I.]

alternate [öl´tėr-nāt] *vt* to do or use by turns.—*vi* to act, happen, etc. by turns; to take turns regularly.—*adj* **al´ternȧte** [-nȧt], (of two things) coming or following by turns; (of leaves) placed singly with change of side at each node.—*n* a substitute.—*adv* **alter´nately**.—*n* **alternā´tion**.—*adj* **alter´native**, offering a choice of two things; being or representing an alternative to established institutions, values ideas, etc.—*n* a choice between things; one of the things to be chosen; something left to choose.—*adv* **alter´natively**.—*n* **alt´ernator**, a generator of alternating current.—**alternating current**, an electric current that regularly reverses its direction. [L *alternāre, -ātum*—*alter*. See **alter**.]

although [öl-THō´] *conj* admitting that; notwithstanding that. [**all** (adv), + **though**.]

altimeter [al-tim´e-tėr] *n* an instrument for measuring altitude. [L *altus*, high, + **meter**.]

altitude [al´ti-tūd] *n* height, esp above sea level, a high point or position; angle of elevation above horizon. [L *altitūdō*—*altus*, high.]

alto [ält´o] *n* the range of the lowest female voice; a singer with this range.—*adj* of, for or in the alto. [It,—L *altus*, high.]

altogether [öl-tȯ-geTH´ėr] *adv* in all; on the whole; completely. [**all**, + **together**.]

alto-relievo [al´tō-re-lē´vō] *n* high relief; a sculpture in high relief. [It *altorilievo*. *See* **relief**.]

altruism [al´trōō-izm] *n* the principle of living and acting for the interest of others; animal behavior that seems analogous to human altruism.—*adj* **altruist´ic**. [Fr *altruisme*, formed from It *altrui*—L *alter*, the other.]

alum [al´um] *n* a mineral salt, the double sulphate of aluminum and potassium, used as styptic and astringent. [L *alūmen*.]

alumina [a-l(y)ōō´min-a] *n* the oxide of aluminum.—*adj* **alū´minous**, containing alum or alumina. [L *alūmen, alum*.]

aluminum [a-lōō-min´-um] *n* a silvery metallic element (Symbol Al; at wt 27.0; at no 13) remarkable for its lightness. [**alumina**.]

alumna [al-um´nȧ] *n* a girl (or woman) who has attended or been graduated from a particular school, college or university.

alumnus [al-um´nus] a male alumna.—*pl* **alum´ni**. [L,—*alĕre*, to nourish.]

always [öl´wāz] *adv* at all times; continually; in any case. [**all**, + **way**.]

Alzheimer's disease [älts´hīm-ėrz] *n* a degenerative brain disease. [A *Alzheimer*, 20th century Ger physician.]

am [am] the 1st pers sing pres indic of the verb to be. [OE *eom*; Gr *eimi* (orig *esme*); L *sum* (orig *esum*); Sans *asmi*.]

amalgam [a-mal´gam] *n* a mixture of metals in which one is mercury; a mixture.—*vt* al´gamate, to combine, unite.—*n* **amalgamā´tion**, the blending of different things; consolidation; a close union. [L and Gr *malagma*, an emollient—Gr *malassein*, to soften.]

amanuensis [a-man-ū-en´sis] *n* one who writes to dictation; a copyist; a secretary;—*pl* **amanuen´ses** [-sēz]. [L,—*ab*, from, and *manus*, the hand.]

amaranth [am´år-anth] *n* any of a large genus (*Amaranthus*) of coarse herbs, some cultivated as food crops, others for their large showy flowers; an imaginary flower that never dies; a red azo dye.—*adj* **amaranth´ine**, pertaining to amaranth; undying; of the color amaranth. [Through Fr and L from Gr *amarantos*, unfading—*a-*, priv, + root *mar*, to waste away; allied to L *mori*, to die.]

amass [a-mas´] *vt* to gather in large quantity; to accumulate.—*vi* to come together. [Fr *amasser*—L *ad*, to, and *massa*, a mass.]

amateur [am´a-chûr´, or am-a-tûr´] *n* one who cultivates a particular activity for the love of it, and not for professional gain.—*adj* of or done by amateurs.—*adj* **amateur´ish**, lacking professional skill. [Fr,—L *amātor*, a lover—*amāre*, to love.]

amatory [am´a-tȯr-i] *adj* of or showing sexual love. [L *amātōrius—amāre* to love.]

amaze [a-māz´] *vt* to confound with surprise or wonder, astonish—*n* **amaze´ment**,—*adj* amaz´ing,—*adv* **amaz´ingly**. [OE *āmasian* (preserved in the pt p *āmasod*).]

Amazon [am´a-zȯn] *n* in Greek myth, a race of female warriors; a tall strong masculine woman;—*adj* **Amazō´nian**. [Popular Gr ety from *a-*, priv, *mazos*, a breast—the Amazons' habit of cutting off the right breast that they might draw the bow to its full stretch.]

ambassador [am-bas´a-dȯr] *n* the highest-ranking diplomatic representative from one country to another; an authorized messenger; an unofficial representative.—*adj* **ambassadō´rial**. [Fr *ambassadeur*—L *ambactus*, a vassal.]

amber [am´bėr] *n* a yellowish fossil resin, used for ornaments, etc.—*adj* made of amber; amber-colored. [Fr *ambre*—Ar *anbar*, ambergris.]

ambergris [am´bėr-grēs] *n* a waxy substance found floating in or on the shores of warm seas, believed to originate in the intestines of the sperm whale and used as a fixative for perfume. [Fr *ambre gris*, grey amber.]

ambient [am´bi-ėnt] *adj* surrounding;—*ns* **am´biance, ambience**; surrounding influence, atmosphere. [L *ambiens, -entis*, pr p of *ambīre*—pfx *ambi-*, about, *īre*, to go.]

ambiguous [am-big´ū-us] *adj* admitting of more than one meaning, equivocal; not clear; vague.—**ambigū´ity**, an ambiguous expression.—*adv* **ambig´uously**. [L *ambiguus—ambigĕre*, to go about—pfx *ambi-*, about, *agĕre*, to drive.]

ambit [am´bit] *n* a circuit; space included; scope. [L *ambitus—ambīre*. See **ambient**.]

ambition [am-bish(ȯ)n] *n* desire for power, honor, fame, excellence.—*adj* **ambi´tious**, full of ambition; showing ambition.—*adv* **ambi´tiously**.—*n* **ambi´tiousness**. [Fr,—L *ambitiō, -ōnis*, the canvassing for votes practised by candidates for office in Rome—pfx *ambi-*, about, *īre, itum*, to go.]

ambivalence [am-biv´å-lėns] *n* (*psych*) the coexistence in one person of opposing emotional attitudes (eg love and hate) toward the same object.—*adj* **ambiv´alent**, characterized by ambivalence. [L *ambo*, both, *valens, -entis*, pr p of *valēre*, to be strong.]

amble [am´bl] *vi* (of a horse) to move at an easy gait; to walk in a leisurely way.—*n* a horse's ambling gait; a leisurely walking pace.—*n* **am´bler**. [Fr *ambler*—L *ambulāre*, to walk about.]

ambrosia [am-brō´z(h)i-a] *n* (*Greek and Roman myth*) food of the gods; anything that tastes or smells delicious.—*adj* **ambrō´sial**, fragrant; divine. [L,—Gr *ambrosios=ambrotos*, immortal—*a-*, priv, *brotos*, mortal.]

ambulance [am´būl-åns] *n* a special vehicle for the sick or injured.—Also *adj*—*adjs* **am´bulant**, moving from place to place; **am´bulatory**, having the power of walking.—*n* any part of a building intended for walking in, esp the cloisters of a monastery. [Fr,—L *ambulans, -antis*, pr p of *ambulāre, -ātum*, to walk about.]

ambuscade [am´bus-kād] *vti* ambush. [Fr *embuscade*, OFr *embusche*. See **ambush**.]

ambush [am´bŏŏsh] *n* a concealment of assailants to make a surprise attack; the bushes or other cover in which they are hidden.—*vti* to attack from ambush. [OFr *embusche, embuscher*—LL *emboscāre—in-*, in, *boscus*, a bush.]

ameer [a-mēr´] *n see* **emir**.

ameliorate [a-mēl´yȯr-āt] *vti* to make or become better.—*n* **ameliorā´tion**. [L *ad*, to, *melior*, better.]

amen [ā´men´, or ä´men´] *interj* may it be so! [Gr,—Heb *āmēn*, firm, true.]

amenable [a-mēn´a-bl, a-men´a-bl] *adj* easy to lead, tractable.—*ns* **amenabil´ity, amen´ableness**.—*adv* **amen´ably**. [Fr *amener*, to lead—*à* (L *ad*), *mener*, to lead—LL *mināre*, to lead, to drive (as cattle)—L *minārī*, to threaten.]

amend [a-mend´] *vt* to correct; to improve; to alter in detail.—*vi* to improve one's conduct.—*adj* **amend´able**.—*n* **amend´ment**, correction; improvement; an alteration proposed to a law, bill, etc.—*n pl* **amends´**, as in **make amends**, to make reparation, give compensation, make good a loss. [Fr *amender* for *émender*—L *ēmendāre*, to remove a fault—*ē* (*ex*), out of, *menda*, a fault.]

amenity [a-mēn´i-ti] *n* pleasantness, as regards situation, climate, manners, or convenience; (*pl*) courteous acts.—**amenity horticulture**, the growing of ornamental plants. [Fr *aménité*—L *amoenitās—amoenus*, pleasant, from root of *amāre*, to love.]

amenorrhoea [a-, ā-men-ō-rē´a] *n* abnormal absence of menstruation. [Gr *a-*, priv, *mēn*, month, *rhoiā*, a flowing.]

Amerasian [a-mer-ā´zhyån *or* am-er-ā´shiån] *n* a person of mixed American and Asian lineage.—*also adj*.

amerce [a-mûrs´] *vt* to punish by a fine.—*n* **amerce´ment**. [OFr *amercier*, to impose a fine—L *ad*, to, *mercēs*, reward, punishment.]

American [a-mer´i-kån] *adj* of the American continent or the US.—*n* a native or inhabitant of America.—*npl* **Amer´ican´a**, artifacts typical of American civilization; American culture.—*ns* **Amer´icanism**, a custom, word, phrase or idiom peculiar to Americans; **Ame´ricanist**, an anthropologist specializing in Amerindian languages or cultures; specialist in American culture of history; **Americanīzation**.—*vti* **Amer´icanīze**, to make or become American in character.—*vt* to naturalize as an American.—**American Civil War**, war (1861–65) between the US and 11 Southern states which seceded from the Union and formed the Confederate States of America.—Also **War Between the States; American English**, native language of most US inhabitants, distinguishable from British English in vocabulary and syntax but not sufficiently so as to make it a separate language; **American foxhound**, purebred hound smaller than English foxhound, usu. black, tan, and white; **American Indian**, Amerindian; **American Legion**, organization of veterans of US wars; **American leopard**, jaguar; **American lotus**, a widely-distributed N American water lily (*Nelumbo pentapetala*) of which the entire plant is edible.—Also **water chinquapin, sacred bean**, and **nelumbo; American plan**, hotel plan in which rates cover the costs of meals; **American Revolution**, war (1775–83) for independence waged by the 13 American colonies against Great Britain; **American saddle horse**, 3- or 5- gaited horse of breed developed from thoroughbred and native stock, mainly in Kentucky; **American shorthair**, purebred domestic cat with short plushy coat; **American Standard Version**, an American version of the Bible based on the Revised version published in 1901.—Also **American Revised Version; American water spaniel**, purebred medium-sized sporting dog with curly coat; **American wirehair**, purebred domestic cat with short-haired woolly coat; **America's Cup**, an international yachting trophy first won by the schooner America in 1851; **the Americas**, North and South America considered together. [From *America*, named after *Amerigo* (L *Americus*) Vespucci, in the belief that he was the first explorer to reach the American mainland.]

American Sign Language [a-mer´i-kån sīn´ lang´gwij] a sign language for the deaf that uses hand gestures to convey meaning.—*also* **Ameslan [am'ez'lan]**.

americium [am-ėr-ish´i-um] *n* a transuranic element; (symbol Am at wt 243; at no 95).

Amerindian [a-mer-ind´i-ån] *n* member of any of the aboriginal peoples of the Western Hemisphere.—Also **Amerind´, American Indian**.

amethyst [am´e-thist] *n* a purple or violet quartz or corundum used as a gemstone; purple or violet; a bluish-violet variety of quartz.—*adj* **amethyst´ine**. [Gr *amethystos—a-*, priv, *methyein*, to be drunken—*methy*, wine.]

amiable [ām´i-abl] *adj* lovable; likable.—*ns* **amiabil´ity, am´iableness**, quality, or instance, of being good-natured, obliging.—*adv* **am´iably**. [OFr *amiable*, friendly—L *amīcābilis—amīcus*, a friend; there is confusion in meaning with OFr *amable*, lovable—L *amābilis—amāre*, to love.]

amicable [am´i-ka-bl] *adj* friendly; peaceable.—*ns* **amicabil´ity, am´icableness**.—*adv* **am´icably**. [L *amīcābilis—amīcus*, a friend—*amāre*, to love.]

amice [am´is] *n* a liturgical vestment made of white linen worn about the neck and shoulders. [OFr *amit*—L *amictus—amicĕre*, to wrap about—*ambi-*, about, and *jacĕre*, to throw.]

amid [a-mid´], **amidst** [a-midst´] *prep* in the middle of; among.—*adv* **amid´ships, amid´ship**, in or toward the middle of a ship. [Pfx *a-* (OE *on*), on, and **mid**; for *-st*, see **against**.]

amigo [å-mē´gō] *n* a friend.—*pl* **amigos**. [Sp]

amine [å-men´, or am´ēn] *n* one of the class of basic organic compounds derived from ammonia by replacing one or more hydrogen atoms by hydrocarbon radicals. [**Ammonia**.]

amino acid [a-mē´nō] any of the group of nitrogen-containing organic compounds that form the proteins of plants and animals. [*Ammonia*, *-ine*, and *-o*.]

amir [a-mēr´] *n see* **emir**.

amiss [a-mis´] *adj* wrong; improper; faulty.—*adv* in a faulty manner, astray. [Pfx *a-* (OE *on*), on, + **miss**, failure.]

amity [am´i-ti] *n* friendship; goodwill. [Fr *amitié*—L *amīcitia*, friendship—*amīcus*, a friend—*amāre*, to love.]

ammeter [am´e-tėr] an instrument for measuring electric current in amperes. [*am*pere + **meter**.]

ammonia [a-mō´ni-a] *n* a pungent gas, a compound of nitrogen and hydrogen NH_3 very soluble in water; (loosely) a solution of ammonia in water.—*adj* **ammon´iac**, pertaining to, or having the properties of, ammonia.—*adj* **ammōn´iated**, containing ammonia.—*n* **ammon´ium**, the cation NH_4, which behaves in many ways like the ion of a metal of valency 1. [From **sal ammoniac** traditionally first obtained near the temple of *Ammon*.]

ammonite [am´on-īt] *n* the fossil of an extinct cephalopod.

ammunition [am-ū-nish´(ȯ)n] *n* bullets, gunpowder, bombs, grenades, rockets, etc.; any means of attack or defense; facts and reasoning used to prove a point in an argument. [OFr (*l'*) *amunition*, for (*la*) *munition*—L *munīre*. See **munition**.]

amnesia [am-nē´zh(y)a, or -si-a] *n* partial or total loss of memory. [Gr *amnēsia—a-*, priv, root of *mnaesthai*, to remember.]

amnesty [am´nest-i] *n* a general pardon, esp of political offenders. [Gr *amnēstia—amnēstos*, not remembered.]

amnion [am´ni-ȯn] *n* the innermost membrane enveloping the embryo of reptiles, birds and mammals.—*n* **amniocentesis** [am´-nē-ō-sėn-tē´sis] the insertion of a hollow needle into the uterus of a pregnant woman in order to withdraw a sample of the amniotic fluid to test for foetal abnormalities etc.—*adj* **amniot´ic**, of the amnion.—**amniotic fluid**, the fluid within the amnion in which the embryo is suspended. [Gr]

amoeba [a-mē´ba] *n* any of a genus (*Amoeba*) of one-celled microorganisms found in water, damp soil, and digestive tracts of animals;—*pl* **amoeb´ae**

[-bē].—**amoebic dysentery**, destruction of the intestinal lining by amoeba. [Gr *amoibē*, change, alteration.]

amok [a-mok´] *adv* in a frenzy; to kill.—Also **amuck**. [Malay *amoq*, frenzied.]

among [a-mung´], **amongst** [a-mungst´], prep of the number of; amidst; to or for each or several of (*divide it among the group*); by the joint action of. [OE *on(ge)mang*—*(ge)mengan*, to mingle; for *-st*, see **against**.]

amoral [ā-mor´ál] *adj* neither moral nor immoral; without moral sense. [Gr *a-*, priv, + **moral**.]

amorous [am´or-us] *adj* fond of making love; full of love; of sexual love.—*adv* **am´orously**.—*n* **am´orousness**. [OFr *amorous*—LL *amōrōsus*—L *amor*, love.]

amorphous [a-mör´fus] *adj* without definite shape, shapeless; (*chem*) not crystalline. [Gr *a-*, priv, *morphē*, form.]

amorphous [a-mört´īz] *vt* to put money aside at intervals for gradual payment of (a debt, etc.); to wipe out (as a debt).—*n* **amortizā´tion**. [AFr *amortir*—LL *admortire*—L *ad*, to, *mors, mortis*, death.]

Amos [ā´mōs] *n* (*Bible*) 30th book of the Old Testament written by the prophet Amos, in the 8th century B.C., who pled for social justice.

amount [a-mownt´] *vi* to come in total (to); to be equivalent in substance (to).—*n* the whole sum; the whole value or effect; a quantity. [OFr *amonter*, to ascend—L *ad*, to, *mons, montis*, a mountain.]

amour [am-ōōr´] *n* a usu. illicit love affair.—**amour propre**, self-esteem. [Fr,—L *amor*, love.]

ampere [am´pār, am´pēr] *n* the standard unit by which an electric current is measured equal to one coulomb per second. [*Ampère*, Fr physicist (1775–1836).]

ampersand [am´pėr-sand] *n* a sign (&) meaning 'and'. [A corr of *and per se* and—ie '& standing by itself means *and*'.]

amphetamine [am-fet´â-mēn, -min] *n* a drug used esp as a stimulant, and to suppress appetite. [*a*lpha *m*ethyl *phe*ne*t*hyl + *amine*.]

amphibian [am-fib´i-an] *n* any of a class (Amphibia) of cold-blooded egg-laying vertebrates with soft skin, gills at tadpole stage when aquatic, replaced by lungs as land-living adults (eg frogs, salamanders, toads); vehicle able to travel on land or water; aircraft that can alight on land or water.—*adj* **amphib´ious**. [L,—Gr,—*amphi*, on both sides, *bios*, life.]

amphibrach [am´fi-brak] *n* (*prosody*) a foot of three syllables; a short, a long, and a short. [L,—Gr,—Gr *amphi*, on both sides, *brachys*, short.]

amphitheater [am´fi-thē´a-tėr] *n* an oval or circular edifice having rising rows of seats around an open space. [Gr *amphi*, round about, *theātron*.]

amphora [am´fo-ra] *n* an ancient Greek two-handled jar with a large oval body and a narrow neck. [Gr *amphoreus, amphiphoreus*—*amphi*, on both sides, *pherein*, to bear.]

amphoteric [am-fo-ter´ik] *adj* partly one and partly the other, specifically, capable of reacting chemically either as an acid or as a base. [Gr *amphoteros*, both.]

ample [am´pl] *adj* large in size, scope, etc.; large enough; copious.—*n* **am´pleness**.—*adv* **am´ply**. [Fr,—L *amplus*, large.]

amplify [am´pli-fī] *vt* to express more fully; to strengthen (electrical signals) etc.—*n* **amplificā´tion**.—*adj* **amplificā´tory**.—*n* **am´plifier**, a device that increases electric voltage, current, or power, or the loudness of sound. [L *amplificāre*—*amplus*, large, *facėre*, to make.]

amplitude [am´pli-tūd] *n* largeness; breadth; abundance; range from mean to extreme, as of an alternating current.—**amplitude modulation**, the changing of the amplitude of the transmitting radio wave in accordance with the signal being broadcast. [Fr,—L *amplitūdō*.]

ampoule [am-pōōl´] *n* a small, sealed, glass capsule for one dose of a hypodermic medicine; a vial resembling this.—Also **ampule, ampal**. [Fr,—L *ampulla*, a flask.]

ampulla [am-pul´a] *n* a small two-handled flask used in ancient Rome. [L; *amb-*, on both sides, *olla*, a jar.]

amputate [am´pū-tāt] *vt* to cut off, esp by surgery.—*n* **amputā´tion**. [L *amputāre*—*amb-*, round about, *putāre*, to cut.]

Amtrak [am´trak´] *n* a nationwide system of passenger railroad service. [*Am*erican *t*ravel *track*.]

amuck [a-muk´] *see* **amok**.

amulet [am´ū-let] *n* something worn as a charm against evil. [Fr *amulette*]

amuse [a-mūz´] *vt* to occupy or entertain pleasantly; to divert; to excite mirth in.—*n* **amuse´-ment**.—*adj* **amusing**,—*adv* **amus´ingly**. [Fr *amuser*.]

amylase [am´i-lās or -lāz] *n* an enzyme that hydrolizes starch and glycogen to simple sugar.

an [an] *adj* one; the indefinite article, used before words beginning with the sound of a vowel. [OE *ān*. See **one**.]

-an [en, in, ´n] *suffix* meaning of belonging to (*diocesan*); born in, living in (*Chicagoan*); believing in (*Christian*).

Anabaptist [an-a-bapt´ist] *n* one who holds that baptism ought to be administered only to adults, and therefore that those baptized in infancy ought to be baptized again. [Gr *ana*, again, *baptizein*, to dip in water, to baptise.]

anabolism [an-ab´ol-izm] *n* the constructive part of metabolism in which complex molecules are synthesized from simpler ones in the living organism.—*adj* **anabol´ic**.—**anabolic steroids**, synthetic hormones used to increase the buildup of body tissue, esp muscle,—Also **muscle pull**. [Gr *anabolē*, rising up.]

anachronism [an-a´kron-izm] *n* an error in chronology, whereby a thing is assigned to a period to which it does not belong; the representation of this; a person, custom, or idea regarded as out of date.—*adj* **anachronist´ic**. [Gr *ana*, backwards, *chronos*, time.]

anacoluthon [an-a-ko-lū´thon] *n* want of sequence in the construction of a sentence, when the latter part does not correspond grammatically with the former. [Gr *anakolouthos*—*an-*, priv, and *akolouthos*, following.]

anaconda [an-a-kon´da] *n* a large S American semiaquatic snake (*Eunectus murinus*) that kills its prey by constriction. [Perh a Cingalese name for a different snake.]

anaemia, anae´mic *see* **anemia, anemic**.

anaesthesia, anaesthetic *see* **anesthesia, anesthetic**.

anaglyph [an´a-glif] *n* an ornament carved in low relief, a stereoscopic still or motion picture.—*adj* **anaglypt´ic**. [Gr *anaglyphē*—*ana*, up, *glyphein*, to carve.]

anagram [an´a-gram] *n* a word or sentence formed by rewriting in a different order the letters of another word or sentence; as, 'live' for 'evil', 'Flit on, cheering angel' for 'Florence Nightingale'.—*adjs* **anagrammat´ic, anagrammat´ical**. [Gr *ana*, again, *gramma*, letter—*graphein*, to write.]

anal [ān´ál] *adj* pertaining to or near the anus.

analects [an´a-lekts] *n pl* selected miscellaneous written passages.—Also **analec´ta**. [Gr *analektos*—*ana*, up, *legein*, to gather.]

analgesia [an-al-jē´zi-a] *n* insensibility to pain without loss of consciousness.—*n* **analgē´sic**, a pain-relieving drug.—*adj* that dispels pain. [Gr.—*an-*, priv, *algeein*, to feel pain.]

analogy [an-al´o-ji] *n* an agreement or correspondence in certain respects between things otherwise different; the inference that certain resemblances imply further similarity.—*adj* **analog´ical**.—*adv* **analog´ically**.—*vti* **anal´ogize**, to use, or explain, by analogy.—*adj* **anal´ogous**, similar in certain respects (to).—*n* **an´alogue, an´alog**, a word or thing bearing analogy to, another; an organ that performs the same function as another, though differing from it in structure or origin; a synthetic chemical substance that is similar in function to a natural chemical; a synthetic substance used as a substitute for meat, fish and other foods.—**analog computer**, computer in which voltages, are used to represent numbers of physical quantities. [Gr *ana*, according to, and *logos*, ratio.]

analysis [an-al´i-sis] *n* a resolving or separating a whole into its elements or component parts; a statement of the results of this process; psychoanalysis; (*chem*) separation of compounds and mixtures into their constituents to determine their nature or proportion.—*pl* **anal´yses**. *n* **analysand´**, a person undergoing psychoanalysis.—*vt* **an´alyse** [-īz], to resolve (a whole) into elements; to separate into component parts to psychoanalyze.—*adj* **analyz´able**.—*n* **an´alyst** [-ist], one who analyzes; a psychoanalyst.—*adjs* **analytic** [-it´ik], **-al**, pertaining to analysis;—*adv* **analyt´ically.**—**analytical geometry**, technique of using algebra to deal with geometry; coordinate geometry. [Gr *analysis*—*analyein*, to unloose—*ana*, up, *lyein*, to loose.]

anapest [an´a-pēst, -pest] *n* (*prosody*) a metrical foot consisting of two short syllables before a long,—*adj* **anapaes´tic**, [Gr *anapaistos*, reversed—*ana*, back, *paiein*, to strike.]

anaphylaxis [an-a-fi-laks´sis] *n* instance of severe allergic reaction; anaphylactic shock.—*adj* **anaphylac´tic—anaphylactic shock**, a severe and sometimes fatal systematic reaction produced by exposure to an allergen in a susceptible individual. [Gr *ana*, back, *phylaxis*, protection.]

anarchy [an´ärk-i] *n* the absence of government; political confusion.—*adjs* **anarch´ic**,—*ns* **an´archism**, the theory that all government is unneccessary; **an´archist**, one who strives to create anarchy, esp by violence. [Gr *an-*, priv, *archē*, government.]

anathema [an-ath´em-a] *n* anything greatly detested; any strong curse; a solemn ecclesiastical curse or denunciation; any person or thing anathematized.—*vt* **anath´ematize**, to pronounce accursed. [The classical Gr *anathēma* meant a votive offering set up in a temple—*ana*, up, *tithenai*, to place; the *anathĕma* of the New Testament meant something specially devoted to evil.]

anatomy [an-a´tom-i] *n* the dissection of an organism to study its structure; the science of the structure of plants and animals; the structure of an organism; the analysis of anything;—*adjs* **anatom´ic, -al**, relating to anatomy.—*adv* **anatom´ically**.—*vti* **anat´omize**, to disect; to study structure; to analyze.—*n* **anat´omist**, [Gr *ana*, up, asunder, *temnein*, to cut.]

ancestor [an´ses-tòr] *n* one from whom a person is descended, a forefather.—*adj* **ances´tral**.—*n* **an´cestry**, all one's ancestors; lineage. [OFr *ancestre*—L *antecēssor*—*ante*, before, *cēdĕre, cēssum*, to go.]

anchor [ang´kòr] *n* a hooked implement that sticks into the bed of a sea or river and thus holds a ship in position; anything that gives stability; a newscaster who coordinates the various reports.—*vt* to fix by an anchor; to be the final contestant (on a relay team, etc.); to be the anchor on (a news broadcast.)—*vi* to cast anchor; to be or become fixed.—*ns* **anch´orage**, a place for anchoring.—**an´chorman; anchorwoman**.—**at anchor**, anchored; [OE *ancor*—L *ancora*; cf Gr *ankȳra*—*ankos*, a bend; conn with **angle**.]

anchorite, anchoret, [ang´kòr-īt, ang´kòr-et] *n* one who has withdrawn from the world, usu. for religious reasons.—*n* **anch´oress**, a female anchorite. [Gr *anachōrētēs*—*ana*, apart, *chōreein*, to withdraw.]

anchovy [an´chō-vi, also an´chó´vi] *n* a small Mediterranean fish (*Engraulis* *encrasicholus*) used for pickling, and for making sauce, paste, etc. [Sp and Port *anchova*.]

ancient [ān´shėnt] *adj* very old; belonging to times long past,—*n* an aged person.—*adv* **an´ciently**, in ancient times.—*n* **an´cientness**.—*n pl* **the an´cients**, those who lived in remote times, [Fr *ancien*—LL *antiānus*, former—L *ante*, before.]

ancillary [an´si-lår-ē] *adj* subordinate (to); auxiliary. [L *ancilla*, maid-servant.]

and [and] *conj* signifies addition, repetition, contrast or consequence, and is used to connect words, phrases, clauses, and sentences; informally, as a substitute for *to* (*try and get it*) [OE, and other Gmc languages; prob allied to L *ante*, before, Gr *anti*, against.]

andante [an-dan´tā] *adv, adj, n* (*mus*) moderately slow, [It—pr p of *andare*, to go.]

andiron [and´ī-ėrn] *n* either of a pair of metal supports for logs in a fireplace; a firedog. [OFr *andier*—LL *anderius, andena*; further ety uncertain; early confused with *iron*.]

androecium [an-drē´s(h)i-um] *n* the whole of the stamens in one flower. [Gr *anēr*, gen *andros*, a man, *oikos*, a house.]

androgen [an´drō-jėn] *n* a male sex hormone that can give rise to masculine characteristics. [Gr *andros* + **-gen**].

androgynous an-droj´i-nus] *adj* not distinguishable as to sex in appearance, behaviour, etc.; having roles characteristic of both sexes. [Gr; *anēr*, gen *andros*, a man, *gynē*, woman.]

android [an´droid] *n* in science fiction, an automaton made to look like a man.

andrology [an-drol´ō-jē] *n* branch of medicine dealing with diseases of the male sex, esp disorders of the reproductive system.

anecdote [an´ek-dōt] *n* a brief entertaining account of any curious or interesting incident.—*adj* **an´ecdotal**, [Gr *an-*, priv, *ekdotos*, published—*ek*, out, *didonai*, to give.]

anemia [a-nē´mi-a] *n* a condition in which the blood is low in red cells or in hemoglobin, resulting in paleness, weakness, etc.—*adj* **ane´emic**, [Gr *an*—priv, *haima*, blood.]

anemometer [an-e-mom´it-ėr] *n* an instrument for measuring the force or speed of the wind; wind gauge. [Gr *anemos*, wind, *metron*, measure.]

anemone [a-nem´ȯ-ne] *n* a genus (*Anemone*) of the buttercup family, a sea anemone. [Gr *anemōnē*—*anemos*, wind.]

anent [a-nent´] *prep* concerning, about. [From OE *on efen*, on even, on a level with.]

aneroid barometer [an´ė-roid] *n* a barometer for working by the bending of a thin metal plate instead of by the rise and fall of mercury. [Fr *anéroide*—Gr *a*, priv, *nēros*, wet, *eidos*, form.]

anesthetic [an-es-thet´ik] *n* a drug, gas, etc. used to produce anesthesia, as before surgery.—*adj* of or producing anesthesia.—*ns* **anesthē´sia**, a partial or total loss of the sense of pain, touch, etc.; **anesthēsiológist**, a doctor who specializes in giving anesthetics; **an´esthēsiol´ogy**; **anēs´thetist**, a person trained to give anesthetics.—*vt* **anēs´thetize**, to cause anesthesia in. [Gr *anaisthētos*, without feeling—*an-*, priv, *aisthēsis*, sensation.]

aneurysm, aneurism [an´ūr-izm] *n* the permanent abnormal dilation of an artery. [Gr *aneurysma*—*ana*, up, *eurys*, wide.]

anew [a-nū´] *adv* afresh; again, once more; in a new way or form. [OE perp *of*, and **new**.]

anfractuous [an-frakt´ū-us] *adj* full of windings; tortuous.—*n* **anfractuos´ity**. [*Lanfractuōsus*—*ambi-*, about, *frangĕre, fractum*, to break.]

angel [ān´jėl] *n* a messenger of God; an image of a human figure with wings and a halo; a person of extraordinary beauty or virtue; (*slang*) financial backer as for a play.—*adjs* **angel´ic**, [an-], **angel´ical**.—*adv* **angel´ically**.—**angel dust**, (*slang*) an illicit hallucinogenic drug; **angel food cake**, a light sponge cake made only with egg whites, flour, and sugar. [Gr *angelos*, a messenger.]

Angeleno [an-je-lēn´ō] *n* a native or inhabitant of Los Angeles, California.

angelica [an-jel´i-kȧ] *n* any of a genus (*Angelica*) of herbs of the carrot family used in cookery and medicine.

angelus [an´ji-lus] *n* a short devotional exercise in honor of the Incarnation; the bell rung at morning, noon, and sunset, the times for this exercise. [From its first words. '*Angelus* domini nuntiavit Mariae' (Luke i 28).]

anger [ang´gėr] *n* hot displeasure, often because of opposition, a hurt, etc.—*vti* to make or become angry;—*adj* **ang´ry**, excited with anger; inflamed; of sullen aspect (eg of the sky).—*n* an angry young man.—*adv* **ang´rily**.—*n* **ang´riness**. [ON *angr*; allied to **anguish**.]

angina [an-ji´na] *n* angina pectoris; a spasmodic gripping sensation of pain.—**angina pec´toris**, a disease of the heart marked by paroxysms of intense pain. [L *angina*, conn with L *ang(u)ĕre*, to strangle.]

angiogram [an´ji-ō-gram] *n* an X-ray photograph made by angiography.—*n* **angio´graphy**, process of making X-ray photographs of blood-vessels by injecting the vessels with a substance opaque to the rays. [Gr *angeion*, case, vessel, *gramma*, that which is written.]

angiosperm [an´ji-o-spėrm] *n* any of a class (Angiospermae) of vascular plants (as roses and orchids) in which the seeds are in a closed ovary. [Gr *angeion*, case, *sperma*, seed.]

angle[1] [ang´gl]*n* a corner; the point from which lines or surfaces diverge; (*geom*) the inclination of two straight lines which meet in a point; point of view; (*inf*) a tricky scheme or approach as for personal gain.—*vti* to move or bend at an angle; (*inf*) to present (eg news), not objectively, but in such a way as to serve a particular end.—*adj* **ang´ūlar**, having an angle or angles; forming an angle; measured by an angle; stiff and awkward in manner, bony and lean.—*ns* **angular´ity; angle iron**, an L-shaped iron used to support corners in building, etc.; **an´gleworm**, an earth worm. [Fr,—L *angulus*; cog with Gr *ankylos*; both from root *ank*, to bend, seen also in **anchor, ankle**.]

angle[2] [ang´gl] *vi* to fish with a hook and line; to use tricks to get something.—*ns* **ang´ler; ang´ling**, [OE *angul*, a hook.]

Anglican [ang´glik-ân] *adj* belonging to or of the Church of England;—*n* an Anglican church member.—*n* **Ang´licanism**, attachment to the principles of the English Church.—*adv* **anglice**, [ang´gli-sē], in readily understood English.—*vt* **ang´licize**, [-sīz], to adapt to English standards and practice.—*n* **Ang´licism**, an English idiom or peculiarity. [L *Anglicānus*—*Angli*, English.]

Anglo- [ang´glo] *pfx* English—as in *Anglo*-Saxon, etc.—*n* (and *adj*) **Ang´lo-Catholic**, (member) of a High Church movement in Anglicanism fostering continuity with the RC church by use of RC liturgy, etc.—*n* **Ang´lo-Cathol´icism**.—*n* (and *adj*) **Ang´lo-Nor´man**, the French dialect of the Normans in England, **Ang´lo-French**, the French language used in medieval England.—*adj* **Ang´lo-Sax´on**, of white Protestant culture of the US; *n* Old English; the Germanic settlers of England and southern Scotland and their descendants; an Englishman; plain, blunt English. [L—*Anglus*, English.]

Anglo [ang´glō] *n* (among Hispanics and Amerindians) a person of Caucasian descent; an English-speaking Canadian.

Anglomania [ang´glō-mān´i-a] *n* an absorbing or intense interest in things English. [**Anglo-**, + **mania**.]

anglophil(e) [ang´glō-fil] *n*, and *adj* (one) who admires England and things English. [**Anglo-**, + Gr *phileein*, to love.]

anglophobe [ang´glō-fōb] *n, adj* (one) fearing or disliking England.—*n* **anglophobia**, [ang-glōfō´bi-a;] dislike of England and things English. [Fr *anglophobe*—L *Anglo-* (see **Anglo-**), + Gr *phobos*, fear.]

Angora [ang-gō´, -gö´, ra] *n* a breed of goat with long white silky hair; mohair; a breed cat or a breed rabbit with long silky hair. [*Angora*, now *Ankara*, Asia Minor, famous for its breed of goats.]

angry *see* **anger**.

angst [angst] *n* a feeling of apprehension, fear, or anxiety. [Ger]

angström [ang´strom] *n* one hundred-millionth of a centimeter, a unit used in measuring the length of light waves.—Also **angstrom unit**. [A J Angström (1814–74), Swedish physicist.]

anguish [ang´gwish] *n* excessive pain of body or mind, agony.—*vti* to make or feel anguish. [OFr *angoisse*—L *angustia*, a strait, straitness—*ang(u)ĕre*, to press tightly, to strangle.]

anhydrous [an-hī´drus] *adj* free from water and esp water and crystallization. [Gr *an-*, priv, *hydōr*, water.]

aniline [an´il-in] *n* the amine $C_6H_5NH_2$, a basic, colorless liquid used in the manufacture of dyes. [Port *anil*; Ar *annīl*, for *al-nīl*, the indigo plant.]

anile [an´īl, ān´īl] *adj* of or resembling a senile old woman. [L *ănus, -ūs*, an old woman.]

animadvert [an-im-ad-vůrt´] *vi* (*with* **on** or **upon**) to express criticism of usu. to censure.—*n* **animadver´sion**, criticism, [L, to turn the mind to—*animus*, the mind, *ad*, to, *vertĕre*, to turn.]

animal [an´im-ål] *n* any living organism except a plant or bacterium, typically able to move about; a lower animal as distinguished from man, esp mammals; a brutish or bestial person.—*adj* of or like an animal; bestial; sensual.—*n* **an´i-malism**, sensualism; the doctrine that men are mere animals.—**animal cracker**, a small animal-shaped cookie; **animal husbandry**, the science of breeding and raising farm animals; **animal kingdom**, one of the three basic groups of natural objects that includes all extinct and living animals; **animal magnetism**, quality of being attractive, esp to the opposite sex. [L *animal*—*anima*, air, breath, life.]

animalcule, animalculum [an-im-al´kūl, -um] *n* a small animal; that cannot be seen by the naked eye;—*pl* **animal´cules, animal´cula**. [L *animalculum*, dim of *animal*.]

animate [an´im-āt] *vt* to give life to; to enliven; to actuate.—*adj* [-ȧt] living.—*adj* **an´imated**, lively; full of spirit; endowed with life; moving as if alive.—*n* **animā´tion**, liveliness; vigor.—**animated cartoon**, a film made by photographing a series of drawings, giving the illusion of movement. [L *animāre, -ātum*, to make alive—*anima*, life.]

animism [an´im-izm] *n* the belief that all life is produced by a spiritual force, or that natural objects and phenomena have souls. [L *anima*, life, the soul.]

animosity [an-im-os´i-ti] *n* strong dislike; enmity. [L *animōsitās*—*animōsus*, full of spirit; cf **animus**.]

animus [an´im-us] *n* animosity; feeling of like or dislike; ill-will. [L *animus*, spirit, soul.]

anion [an-ī´ȯn] *n* an ion with a negative charge.

anise [an´is] *n* an umbelliferous plant (*Pimpinella anisum*) whose aromatic seeds are used in flavoring.—Also **an´iseed**. [Gr *anison*.]

ankh [angk] *n* a cross with a loop for its upper vertical arm, an emblem of life.

ankle [angk´l] *n* the joint connecting the foot and leg, the part of the leg between the foot and calf.—*n* **ank´let**, an ornament for the ankle. [OE *anclēow*; cf Ger *enkel*, and **angle**.]

anna [an´ä] *n* a former unit of money in Burma, India, and Pakistan. [Hindustani *ānā*.]

annals [an´älz] *n pl* a written account of events year by year; historical records generally.—*n* **ann´alist**, a writer of annals. [L *annālis*, yearly—*annus*, a year.]

anneal [an-ēl´] *vt* to subject (glass or metals) to heat and gradual cooling to prevent brittleness; to heat in order to fix colors on (eg glass). [OE pfx *an-*, on, *ælan*, to burn.]

annelid [an´el-id] *n* any of the phylum Annel´ida, invertebrate animals with segmented cylindrical bodies, including earthworms, lugworms and leeches. [L *annellus*, *ānellus*, dim of *ānulus*, a ring.]

annex [a-neks´] *vt* to attach esp to something larger; to incorporate into a state the territory of (another state).—*n* [an´eks] something annexed, esp an addition to a building.—*ns* **annexā´tion**; [Fr *annexer*—L *annectĕre*, *annexum*—*ad*, to, *nectĕre*, to tie.]

Annie Oakley [an-ē ōk´lē] *n* a free ticket.

annihilate [a-nī´hil-āt] *vt* to reduce to nothing; to put out of existence.—*ns* **annihilā´tion**. [L *annihilāre*, *-ātum*—*ad*, to, *nihil*, nothing.]

anniversary [an-i-vûrs´ăr-i] *n* the yearly return of the date of some event.—*adj* of an anniversary. [L *anniversārius*—*annus*, a year, *vertĕre*, *versum*, to turn.]

anno Domini [an´ō dom´in-ī, -ē] in the year of our Lord. [L]

annotate [an´ō-tāt] *vti* to provide with explanatory notes.—*ns* **annota´tion; ann´otator**, [L *annotāre*—*ad*, to, *notāre*, *-ātum*, to mark.]

announce [a-nowns´] *vt* to give public notice of; to make known the arrival of; to be an announcer for.—*vi* to serve as an announcer.—*ns* **announce´ment; announc´er**, one who announces, esp who introduces radio or television programs. [OFr *anoncer*—L *annuntiāre*—*ad*, to, *nuntiāre*, to deliver news.]

annoy [a-noi´] *vt* to vex, tease, irritate, as by a repeated action.—*pr p* **annoy´ing**; *pt p* **annoyed´**.—*n* **annoy´ance**, that which annoys; state of being annoyed. [OFr *anoier*; noun, *anoi* (mod *ennui*) perh from L phrase, *in odio*, as in '*est mihi in odio*' 'it is me hateful'.]

annual [an´ū-ăl] *adj* of or measured by a year; yearly; coming every year; living only one year or season.—*n* a plant that lives only one year; a periodical published once a year.—*adv* **ann´ually**. [LL *annuālis*—*annus*, a year.]

annuity [a-nū´i-ti] *n* an investment yielding fixed payments esp yearly; such a payment.—*n* **annū´itant**, one who receives an annuity. [Fr *annuite´*—LL *annuitās*, *-ātis*—L *annus*, year.]

annul [a-nul´] *vt* to do away with; to deprive of legal force, nullify.—*pr p* **annull´ing**; *pt p* **annulled´**.—*n* **annul´ment**, [Fr *annuler*—LL *annullāre*, to make into nothing—L *ad*, to, *nullus*, none.]

annular [an´ūl-ăr] *adj* like or forming a ring.—*adj* **ann´ulate**, formed with rings.—*n* **ann´ulus** (*biol*), a ring-shaped structure.—**annular eclipse**, an eclipse of the sun during which a ring-shaped part of its surface encircles the portion obscured by the moon. [L *annulāris*, or *ānulāris*—*ānulus*, a ring—dim of *a+nus*, a rounding or ring.]

Annunciation [a-nun-si-ā´sh(ò)n] *n* the angel Gabriel's announcement to Mary that she would bear Jesus; the church festival commemorating this; **annunciation**, an announcing. [Fr *annonciation*—L *annuntiātiō*, *-ōnis*—*annuntiāre*. See **announce**.]

anode [an´ōd] *n* the positive electrode by which an electric current enters an electrolytic cell, gas discharge tube, or thermionic valve; the electrode to which electrons flow; the negative electrode in a battery.—*vt* **an´odize**, to give a protective or decorative coat to a metal by using it as an anode in electrolysis. [Gr *anodos*, a way up—*ana*, up,—*hodos*, way.]

anodyne [an´ō-dīn] *n* anything that relieves pain or or soothes. [Gr *anōdўnos*—*an-*, priv, *odynē*, pain.]

anoint [an-oint´] *vt* to consecrate with oil.—*n* **anoint´ment**. [Fr *enoint*, pt p of *enoindre*—L *in*, on, *ung(u)ĕre*, to smear.]

anomaly [a-nom´ă-li] *n* abnormality; anything anomalous.—*adj* **anom´alous**, abnormal; inconsistent or odd. [Gr *anōmalos*—*an-*, priv, *homalos*, even—*homos*, same.]

anon [an-on´] *adv* soon; at another time. [OE *on*, in, *ān*, one (instant).]

anon [a-non´] a contr of **anonymous**.

anonymous [a-non´im-us] *adj* lacking a name; without the name of the author; lacking individuality.—*n* **anonym´ity**, the quality or state of being anonymous.—*adv* **anon´ymously**. [Gr *anōnymos*—*an-*, priv, and *onoma*, name.]

anopheles [ă-nof´i-lēz] *n* a genus (*Anopheles*) of mosquitoes, including all mosquitoes which transmit malaria to man.

anorexia [an-ŏr-ek´si-a] *n* loss of appetite, esp the pathological condition **anorexia nervosa**.—*adj* **anorex´ic**. [Gr *an-*, priv, *orexis*, longing—*oregein*, to reach out.]

another [an-uTH´ĕr] *adj* a different or distinct (thing or person); one more of the same kind; any other.—Also *pron*. [Orig **an other**.]

anserine [an´sĕr-in, or -in] *adj* relating to the goose. [L *anserīnus*—*anser*, goose.]

answer [än´sĕr] *n* a reply or response; retaliation; the solution of a problem.—*vt* to reply or respond; to satisfy (eg one's requirements) or to correspond to (eg a description); to comply with or obey; to defend oneself against (a charge).—*vi* to reply; to act in response (to); to be accountable (for); to conform (to).—*adj* **an´swerable**, capable of being refuted.—**answering machine**, a device that records incoming telephone calls; **answering service**, a commercial service that answers telephone calls for its clients. [OE *andswarn* (n), *andswarian* (vb)—*and-*, against, *swerian*, to swear.]

ant [ant] *n* any of a family (Formicidae) of small, generally wingless insects of many species, all of which form and live in highly organized groups. **ant bear**, a large anteater (*Myrmecophaga jubata*) of S America; **ant cow**, an aphid from which ants obtain honeydew; **ant´eater**, any of several mammals that feed largely or entirely on termites and ants; echidna; aardvark; **ant´hill**, a mound thrown up by ants or termites in digging their nests; **ant lion**, any of various neuropterous insects (as of the genus *Myrmeleon*) that digs a pit in which it lies in wait for ants on which it feeds. [A contr of **emmet**.]

Antabuse [ant´a-bōōs] *n* trade name for disulfiram, used to treat alcoholism.

antacid [ant-as´id] *n* a substance that counteracts acidity. [Gr *anti*, against, + **acid**.]

antagonist [ant-ag´on-ist] *n* an adversary; one who strives against another; an opponent;—*vt* **antag´onize**, to arouse opposition in.—*n* **antag´onism**, opposition; hostility; an opposing force, principle, etc. *adj* **antagonist´ic**.—*adv* **antagonist´ically**. [Gr *anti*, against, *agōn*, a contest.]

antarctic [ant-ärk´tik] *adj* of, near, or relating to, the South Pole or to south polar regions.—*n* **the Antarctic**, land are about the South Pole. [OFr *antartique*—L *antarcticus*—Gr *antarkikos*—*anti*, opposite, and *arktikos*. See **Arctic**.]

ante- [an-ti] *pfx* meaning; in front of (*anteroom*); earlier than (*antediliviam*). [L *ante*; allied to Gr *anti*, against.]

ante [ant´ē] *n* a player's stake in poker.—*vi* to place an ante; **antebellum** [ant-ē-bel´um] *adj* existing before a war, esp the American Civil War.

antecedent [an-ti-sēd´ént] *adj* going before in time; prior (to).—*n* that which precedes in time; (*gram*) the noun or its equivalent to which a relative pronoun refers; (*math*) the first of two terms that compose a ratio; (*pl*) one's ancestry, past life, etc.—*adv* **anteced´ently**. [L *antecēdens*, *-entis*—*ante*, before, *cēdĕre*, *cessum*, to go.]

antechamber [an´ti-chām-bĕr] *n* an anteroom. [Fr *antichambre*—*ante*, before, *camera*, a vault.]

antedate [an´ti-dāt] *vt* to put a date on that is earlier than the actual date; to come before in time. [L *ante*, before, and **date** (1).]

antediluvian [an-ti-di-l(y)ōō´vi-ăn] *adj* existing or happening before the Biblical Flood; antiquated.—Also *n*. [L *ante*, before, and *dīlūvium*, flood.]

antelope [an´ti-lōp] *n* any of an old world family (Bovidae) of swift and graceful ruminant quadrupeds, resembling the deer; pronghorn; leather from an antelope hide. [OFr *antelop*—L *antalopus*—Late Gr *antholops*.]

ante meridian [an-ti-me-ri´di-ăn] *adj* being before noon. [L *antemerīdiānus*—*ante merīdiem*, before noon. See **meridian**.]

antenatal [an-ti-nā´tăl] *adj* prenatal. [L *ante*, before, + **natal**.]

antenna [an-ten´a] *n* either of a pair of feelers on the head of an insect, crab, etc.;—*pl* **antennae** [-nē]; an arrangement of rods and wires, etc. used in sending and receiving the electromagnetic waves in broadcasting;—**antennas**. [L, the yard of a sale.]

antepenult [an-ti-pen-ult´] *n* the third syllable before the end of a word. [L *ante*, before, and **penult**.]

anterior [antē´ri-ŏr] *adj* at or toward the front; earlier, previous. [L *anterior*, comp of *ante*, before.]

anteroom [an´ti-rōōm] *n* a room leading into a larger or main room. [L *ante*, before, + **room**.]

anthelmintic [an-thel-mint´ik] *adj*, *n* (a drug) destroying or expelling worms. [Gr *anti*, against, and *helmins*, *-inthos*, a worm.]

anthem [an´thĕm] *n* a religious choral song; a song of praise or devotion, as to a nation. [OE *antefn*—Gr *antiphōna*—*anti*, in return, *phōnē*, the voice.]

anther [an´thĕr] *n* that part of the stamen in a flower which contains the pollen. [L *anthērea*, a medicine extracted from flowers—Gr *anthēros*, flowery—*anthos*, a flower.]

anthology [an-thol´oj-i] *n* a collection of poetry or prose.—*n* **anthol´ogist**. [Gr *anthos*, a flower, *legein*, to gather.]

anthracite [an´thra-sīt] *n* a hard coal which give much heat and little smoke. [Gr *anthrakītēs*, coal-like—*anthrax*, coal.]

anthrax [an´thraks] *n* a contagious, bacterial disease of cattle and sheep, etc. that can be transmitted to people. [L,—Gr *anthrax*, *-ākos*, coal, a carbuncle.]

anthropo- [an-thrō-po- (or -pō-)] in composition, man. [Gr *anthrōpos*, man.]—eg **anthropography** [an-thrō-pog´ra-fi], *n* the branch of anthropology treating of the geographical distribution of man (*graphein*, to write).

anthropocentric [an-thrō-pō-sent´rik] *adj* regarding man as the center of the universe. [Gr *anthrōpos*, man, and *kentron*, center.]

anthropoid [an´throp-oid, or -thrōp´-] *adj* manlike; applied esp to the great apes, ie chimpanzee, gorilla, orangutan, or gibbon.—*n* an anthropoid ape. [Gr *anthrōpos*, man, *eidos*, form.]

anthropology [an-thrō-pol´oj-i] *n* the scientific study of human beings, their origins, distribution, physical attributes, and culture; the aspect of Christian teaching dealing with the origin, nature, and destiny of human beings.—*adj* **anthropolog´ical**. *n* **anthropol´ogist**. [Gr *anthrōpos*, man, *logos*, discourse.]

anthropomorphism [an-thrōp-o-mörf´izm] *n* the ascription of human characteristics to other beings or to things.—*adj* **anthropomorph´ic**. [Gr *anthrōpos*, man, *morphē*, form.]

anthropophagy [an-thrō-pof´a-ji] *n* cannibalism.—*n* **anthropoph´agi**, cannibals.—*adj* **anthrophoph´agous** [-a-gus]. [Gr *anthrōpos*, man, *phagein*, to eat.]

anti- [ant´i-] *pfx* meaning against, in opposition to; rival; prevents, cures. [Gr *anti*, against, instead of, etc.]

anti [an´tī or -tē] *n* (*inf*) a person opposed to something.—*adj* (*inf*) opposed.

antibiosis [an-ti-bī-ōs´is or an-tī] *n* association between two organisms that is harmful to one of them.

antibiotic [an-ti-bī-ot´ik] *n* any of various chemical, fungal or synthetic substances used against bacterial or fungal infections.—Also *adj*. [Gr *anti*, against, *biōtikos*, pertaining to life—*bios*, life.]

antibody [an´ti-bod-i] *n* a defensive substance produced in an organism in response to the action of a foreign body such as the toxin of a parasite. [Gr *anti*, against, + **body**.]

antic [ant´ik] *adj* grotesque.—*n* a fantastic figure; (*arch*) a buffoon; (usu in *pl*) a fantastic action or trick, a caper.—*vi* to cut capers. [It *antico*, ancient—L *antīquus*; orig used of the fantastic decorations found in the remains of ancient Rome.]

Antichrist [an´ti-krīst] *n* (*Bible*) the antagonist of Christ; an enemy of Christ, or His teachings.—*adj* **antichristian** [-krist´-]. [Gr *anti*, against, and *Christos*.]

anticipate [an-tis´ip-āt] *vt* to be beforehand with (another person or thing), to forestall; to use, spend, deal with, in advance; to foresee; to count upon as certain, to expect.—*vi* to speak, act, before the appropriate time.—*n* **anticipā´tion**.—*adj* **anti-cipātory**. [L *anticipāre, -ātum—ante*, before, *capĕre*, to take.]

anticlerical [an-ti-kler´i-kȧl] *adj* opposed to the clergy or their power in secular matters. [Gr *anti*, against, + **clerical**. *See* **clergy**.]

anticlimax [an-ti-klīmaks] *n* a sudden drop from the important to the trivial; an ineffective or disappointing ending to a story or series of events. [Gr *anti*, against (in this case = the reverse of), + **climax**.]

anticoagulant [an-ti-kō-ag´ū-lȧnt] *n* a substance that hinders clotting of blood.

anticyclone [an-ti-sīklōn] *n* a rotatory outflow of air from an area of high atmospheric pressure. [Gr *anti*, against (in this case = the reverse of), + **cyclone**.]

antidote [an´ti-dōt] *n* that which is given to counteract poison; anything that prevents evil.—*adj* **an´tidotal**. [Gr *antidotos—anti*, against, *didonai*, to give.]

antifreeze. [an´ti-frēz] *n* a substance used, as in an automobile radiator, to prevent freezing up.

antigen [an´ti-jen] a substance that stimulates the production of an antibody. [Gr *anti*, against, *gennoein*, to produce.]

antihero [an´ti-hē´rō] *n* a principal character who lacks noble qualities and whose experiences are without tragic dignity.—*adj* **antiherō´ic**.

antihistamine [an-ti-hist´ȧ-mēn] *n* any of a group of drugs that prevent the action of histamines in allergic conditions.

antilog [an´ti-log], **antilogarithm** [an-ti-log´a-rithm] *n* the number corresponding to a given logarithm, eg 50 is the antilog of 1.69897, which is the logarithm of 50 to the base 10. [Gr *anti*, against (the reverse of), **logarithm**.]

antimacassar [an-ti-ma-kas´ȧr] *n* a small cover on the back or arms of a chair, sofa, etc. to prevent soiling. [Gr *anti*, against, + *Macassar*, an oil once used for the hair.]

antimony [an´ti-mȯn-i] *n* a brittle, bluish-white metallic element (symbol Sb); at wt 121.8; at no 51 used in alloys, drugs, and dyes. [Through Fr from LL *antimonium*.]

antinomy [an-tin´ō-mi] *n* the opposition of one law to another; (*philos*) contradiction between two conclusions correctly derived from two laws both assumed to be correct. [Gr *anti*, against, *nomos*, a law.]

antiparticle [an´tipär´ti-kl] *n* the 'pair' of an elementary particle. (The elementary particles can occur in mutually destructive 'pairs'—particle and antiparticle.)

antipathy [an-tip´ath-i] *n* rooted dislike; aversion; an object of this.—*adjs* **antipathet´ic, -al**. [Gr *anti*, against, *pathos*, feeling.]

antipersonnel [an´ti-pėr-sȯ-el´] *adj* intended to destroy persons rather than objects. [**anti-**, + **personnel**.]

antiphon [an´tif-on] *n* a form of church music sung by two groups, each responding to the other—also **antiph´ony**.—*adj* **antiph´onal**, pertaining to antiphony.—*n* a book of antiphons or of anthems. [Gr,—*anti*, against, in return, and *phōnē*, voice.]

antipodes [an-tip´od-ēz] *n pl* two places on the earth's surface opposite each other.—*adj* **antip´odal**. [Gr *antipŏdĕs—anti*, opposite to, *pous, podos*, a foot.]

antipope [an´ti-pōp] *n* a pope in opposition to one who is held to be canonically chosen. [Gr *anti*, against, + **Pope**.]

antiproton [an-ti-prō´tȯn] *n* the antiparticle of the proton.

antipyretic [an-ti-pī-ret´ik] *adj* counteracting fever.—*n* an agent that reduces fever. [Gr *anti*, against, *pyretos*, fever.]

antiquary [an´ti-kwȧr-i] *n* one who studies or collects monuments and relics of the past.—*adj* **antiquār´ian**, connected with the study of antiquities.—*n* an antiquary.—*n* **antiquār´ianism**, study of, or devotion to the study of, antiquities. [L *antiquārius—antīquus*, old.]

antique [an-tēk´] *adj* ancient; old-fashioned; after the manner of the ancients.—*n* anything very old; a piece of furniture etc. made at an earlier period and according to customs laws at least 100 years old.—*adj* **an´tiquated**, grown old, or out of fashion; obsolete.—*ns* **antiq´uity**, ancient times; ancientness; (*pl*), relics of ancient times. [L *antīquus*, old—*ante*, before; influenced by Fr *antique*.]

antirrhinum [an-ti-rī´num] *n* any of a large genus (*Antirrhinum*) of plants to which snapdragon belongs. [Latinized from Gr *antirrhīnon—anti*, like, mimicking, *rhīs*, gen *rhīnos*, nose.]

antiscorbutic acid [an-ti-skör-būt´ik] *n* Vitamin C.

anti-Semite [an´ti-sem´īt, or -sēm´īt] *n* one who is hostile toward or discriminates against Jews as a religious or racial group. *adj* **anti-Semit´ic**.—*n* **anti-Sem´itism**.

antiseptic [an-ti-sept´ik] *n* a substance that destroys or prevents the growth of disease-producing microorganisms.—Also *adj*—*adv* **antisept´ically**.—*n* **antisep´sis**, antiseptic treatment. [Gr *anti*, against, and *septikos*, rotten.]

antisocial [an-ti-sō´shȧl] *adj* avoiding the company of other people, unsocial; contrary to the interests of society in general. [**anti-** + **social**.]

antithesis [an-tith´i-sis] *n* a contrast or opposition, as of ideas; the exact opposite;—*pl* **antith´esēs** [-sēz]—*adjs* **antithetical** [-thet´-].—*adv* **antithet´ically**. [Gr *anti*, against, *tithenai*, to place.]

antitoxin [an-ti-tok´sin] *n* a substance formed in the body that acts against a specific toxin; a serum containing an antitoxin, injected into a person to prevent disease.—*adj* **antitox´ic**.

antitrades [an´ti-trādz] the prevailing westerly winds of middle latitudes; the westerly winds above the trade winds. [Gr *anti*, against (here = the reverse of), + **trade**.]

antler [ant´lėr] *n* a bony outgrowth from the frontal bone of a deer.—*adj* **ant´lered**. [OFr *antoillier*.]

antonym [ant´ō-nim] *n* either of two words that have opposite meanings, as 'long' and 'short'. [Gr *anti*, against, *onoma*, a name.]

antrum [an´trům] *n* (*anat*) a cavity esp a sinus, in the upper jaw. [L,—Gr *antron*.]

anus [ān´us] the lower orifice of the alimentary canal. [L *ānus*, a ring.]

anvil [an´vil] *n* an iron block on which metal objects are hammered into shape. [OE *anfilte*.]

anxious [angk´shůs] *adj* worried; uneasy; eagerly wishing; causing anxiety.—*n* **anxiety** [ang-zī´i-ti], state of being anxious; state of chronic apprehension as a symptom of mental disorder.—*adv* **an´xiously**.—*n* **an´xiousness**. [L *anxius—ang(u)ĕre*, to press.]

any [en´i] *adj* one out of many (*any book will do*); some (*have you any fresh fruit*?); every (*any child knows that*).—*pron* any person or thing (*keep the cake, I don't want any*); some (*have you any*?).—*adv* at all (*is he any better*?).—*pron* **an´ybody**, any person; an important person.—*advs* **an´yhow**, in any way whatever; in any case; **an´ymore´**, now; nowadays.—*pron* **an´yone**, any person; anybody.—*adv* **an´yplace**, anywhere.—*pron* **an´ything**, any object, event, fact, etc.—*n* a thing, no matter of what kind.—*adv* in any way.—*advs* **an´yway**, in any manner; at any rate; haphazardly; **an´ywhere**, in, at, or to any place; (*inf*) at all.—**any one**, any single (person or thing); **anything but**, not at all; **get anywhere**, (*inf*) to achieve anything. [OE *ǣig—ān*, one.]

Anzac [an´zak] *n* a soldier from Australia or New Zealand. [Coined from initials of Australian-New-Zealand Army Corps.]

A-OK [ā´ō-kā] (*inf*) excellent, fine, in working order, etc. [A(11)OK.]

A one [ā´ wun] (*inf*) superior; first-class. [From Lloyd's classification of risk.]

aorist [ā´ȯr-ist] *n* a tense, expressing past action where time is indefinite or unimportant. [Gr *aoristos*, indefinite—*a-*, priv, *horistos*, limited.]

aorta [ā-ör´ta] *n* the great artery that carries blood from the heart to be distributed by branch through the body.—*adj* **aort´ic**, arteries. [Gr *aortē—aeirein*, to raise up.]

apace [a-pās´] *adv* at a quick pace; swiftly. [Pfx *a-* (OE *on*), on, and **pace**.]

Apache [a-pach´ē] *n* group or member of Amerindian peoples of southwestern US; the Athapascan language of these peoples; **apache** [a-pash´] member of a gang of criminals, esp in Paris. [Fr perh—Amer Indian *apachu*, enemy.]

apart [a-pärt´] *adv* separately; aside; asunder.—**apart from**, leaving out of consideration; **set apart**, to separate, consecrate. [Fr *à part*—L *a parte*, from the part or side.]

apartheid [ȧ-pärt´hāt, -pär´tid] *n* official government policy of racial segregation, esp in South Africa. [Afrikaans.]

apartment [a-pärt´ment] *n* room or rooms, furnished with housekeeping equipment and usu. rented.—**apartment building, apartment house**, building containing separate apartments; **apartment hotel**, hotel containing apartments as well as accommodation for transients. [Fr *appartement*, a suite of rooms forming a complete dwelling—L *ad*, and *partire*, to divide—*pars*, a part.]

apathy [ap´ath-i] *n* lack of feeling; absence of passion; indifference.—*adj* **apathet´ic**.—*adv* **apathet´ically**. [Gr *a-*, priv, *pathos*, feeling.]

ape [āp] *n* a chimpanzee, gorilla, orangutan, or gibbon; any monkey; a mimic; a gross, clumsy man.—*vt* to imitate. [OE *apa*; Ger *affe*.]

apeak [a-pēk´] *adv, adj* being in a vertical position. [Pfx *a-* (OE *on*), on, + **peak**.]

aperient [a-pē´ri-ėnt] *adj* laxative.—Also *n* [L *aperiens, - entis*, pr p of *aperīre*, to open.]

apéritif [ä-pār-i-tēf] *n* an alcoholic drink taken before a meal. [Fr,—L *aperīre*, to open.]

aperture [a´pėr-tyůr, -chůr] *n* an opening; a hole. [L *apertūra—aperīre, apertum*, to open.]

apetalous [a-pet´al-us] *adj* (*bot*) without petals. [Gr *a-*, priv, and *petalon*, a petal.]

apex [ā´peks] *n* the summit; climax; culiminating point; the vertex of a triangle;—*pl* **ā´pexes, apices** [ap´i-sēz, or āp´-]. [L]

aphaeresis, apheresis [a-fēr´i-sis] *n* (*gram*) the taking away of a letter or syllable at the beginning of a word, as in *coon* for *raccoon*. [Gr *aphairesis*, a taking away—*apo*, away, and *haireein*, to take.]

aphasia [a-fā´zi-a] *n* loss of power to use or to understand words. [Gr *a-*, priv, *phasis*, speech.]

aphelion [a-fē´li-on] *n* the point farthest away from the sun in the orbit of a planet, comet, or man-made satellite.—*pl* **aphē´lia**. [Gr *apo*, from, *hēlios*, sun.]

apheresis *see* **aphaeresis**.

aphesis [af´es-is] *n* aphaeresis, in which an unaccented vowel at the beginning of a word is lost, as in *lone* for *alone*.—*adj* **aphet´ic**. [Coined from Gr *apo*, from, *hienai*, to send.]

aphis [af´is, ā´fis] **aphid**, *ns* a plant-louse or greenfly, any of a large number of small insects that suck the juice of plants.—*pl* **aphides** [af´i-dēz, āf´i-dēz]. [Ety unknown.]

aphorism [af´ȯr-izm] *n* a brief, pithy saying, an adage.—*adj* **aphoris´tic**. [Gr *aphorizein*, to mark off by boundaries—*apo*, from, and *horos*, a limit.]

aphrodisiac [af-rō-diz´-i-ȧk] *adj* exciting sexually.—Also *n* [Gr *aphrodīsiakos—Aphroditē*, the goddess of love.]

apiary [āp´i-ȧr-i] *n* a place where bees are kept.—*n* **ap´iarist**, one who keeps bees. [L *apiārium—apis*, a bee.]

apices *pl* of **apex**.

apiculture [ā´pi-cul-tyůr, -chůr] *n* beekeeping. [L *apis*, bee, *cultura*, keeping—*colĕre, cultum*, to keep.]

apiece [a-pēs´] *adv* to or for each one. [**a**, indefinite article, + **piece**.]

apish [āp´ish] *adj* apelike. [**ape**.]

aplomb [a-pl• ´] *n* poise; self-possession. [Fr *aplomb*, perpendicular position—*à plomb*, according to plummet.]

Apocalypse [a-pok´al-ips] *n* (*Bible*) the book of Revelation in the Douay Version of the New Testament; **apocalypse**, prophetic revelation, of Jewish and Christian writing of 200 BC to 150 AD; a cataclysmic event, the end of the world.—**Apocalypse of Baruch**, noncanonical apocalyptic sacred scripture.—adjs **apocalypt´ic, -al**. [Gr, a revelation, an uncovering—*apo*, from, *kalyptein*, to cover.]

apocope [a-pok´o-pe] *n* the loss of the last letter or syllable of a word as *th'* for *the, I* for OE *ic*. [Gr *apo*, off, *koptein*, to cut.]

Apocrypha [a-pok´rif-a] *n* fourteen books of the Septugint rejected in Protestantism and Judaism; eleven are in the Roman Catholic Bible; **apocrypha**, any writings of dubious authenticity.—*ads* **Apocryphal**, of the Apocrypha;—*adj* **apoc´ryphal**, untrue; invented. [Gr, 'things hidden'—*apo*, from, *kryptein*, to hide.]

apodosis [a-pod´o-sis] *n* (*gram*) the main clause of a conditional sentence. [Gr—*apo*, back, *didonai*, to give.]

apogee [ap´o-jē] *n* the greatest distance of the orbit of the moon, or any satellite from the earth, the sun's apogee corresponding to the earth's aphelion, and the moon's being the point of its orbit farthest from the earth. [Gr *apogaion—apo*, from, *gē*, the earth.]

apolitical [ā-pȯl-iti´k-ȧl] *adj* indifferent to political affairs; uninvolved in politics.—*n* **apol´iticism**. [Gr *a-*, priv, + **political**.]

apologetic, -al [a-pol-o-jet´ik, -ȧl] *adj* excusing; penitently acknowledging; said or written in defence.—*adv* **apologet´-ically**.—*n* **apologet´ics**, the defensive argument, esp the defence of Christianity. [See **apology**.]

apologue [ap´o-log] *n* an allegorical tale intended to convey a moral. [Fr,—Gr *apologos*, a fable—*apo*, from, *logos*, speech.]

apology [a-pol´oj-i] *n* a defence or justification; an expression of penitence; a poor substitute (*with* **for**).—*vi* **apol´ogize**, to make excuse; to express regret for a fault.—*n* **apol´ogist**, one who makes an apology; one who defends (a person or cause) by argument. [Gr *apologia—apo*, from, *logos*, speech.]

apoplexy [a´po-pleks-i] *n* sudden loss of sensation and of motion, generally the result of a broken or blocked blood vessel in the brain.—*adjs* **apoplec´tic**, pertaining to or causing apoplexy; suffering from, or having a stroke. [Gr *apoplēzia—apo*, away (with notion of completeness), *plēssein*, to strike.

apostasy [a-pos´ta-si] *n* abandonment, or desertion of one's religion, principles, or political party.—*n* **apost´ate**, one guilty of apostasy;—Also *adj*—*vi* **apost´atize**. [Gr *apostasis*, a revolt or 'standing away'—*apo*, from, *histanai*, to stand.]

a posteriori [ā-pos-te-ri-ō´rī, -ö´rī] *adj* applied to reasoning from effect to cause. [L *a=ab*, from, *posteriori*, abl of *posterior*, comp of *posterus*, after.]

Apostle [a-pos´l] *n* one of the twelve disciples of Christ: **apostle**, the principal champion or supporter of a new system or cause.—*adjs* **apostol´ic** [ap-os-tol´ik, -ȧl].—*n* **apostolic´ity** [-is´i-ti].—**Apostles' Creed**, the oldest form of Christian creed that exists, early ascribed to the apostles; **Apostolic See**, the see of Rome.—**apostolical succession**, transmission of spiritual authority from the time of the apostles to the present day. [Gr, one sent away—*apo*, away, *stellein*, to send.]

apostrophe[1] [a-pos´trof-e], *n* (*rhetoric*) a sudden turning away from the ordinary course of a speech to address some absent person or personified object.—*vt* **apos´trophize**, to address by apostrophe; to make use of apostrophe. [Gr *apostrophē*.]

apostrophe[2] [a-pos´trof-e] *n* a mark (') showing the omission of a letter or letters in a word; also a sign of the possessive case. [Gr *apostrophos*, turned away.]

apothecary [a-poth´ek-ȧr-i] *n* (*arch*) one who dispenses drugs and medicines; (*obs*) a medical practitioner.—**apothecaries' weight**, the system of weights used by pharmacists in which the pound equals 12 ounces. [Through Fr and L, from Gr *apothēkē*, a storehouse—*apo*, away, *tithenai*, to place.]

apothegm [a´pȯ-thėm] *n* a startling or paradoxical aphorism.

apotheosis [a-po-the-ō´sis] *n* the deification of a principle or person. [Gr *apotheōsis—apo*, away from (what he was), *theos*, a god.]

Appaloosa [ap´ȧ-lōōs´ȧ] *n* a rugged saddle horse bred in western N America with small dark blotches on a white coat.

appall, appal [a-pöl´] *vt* to terrify, dismay;—*pr p* **appall´ing**; *pt p* **appalled´**—adj **appall´ing**, *adv* **appall´ingly**. [Perh from OFr *apal(l)ir*, to wax pale, also to make pale.]

appanage [ap´an-ij] *n* the assignation of lands as a provision for younger sons of kings and nobles; any perquisite; an adjunct or attribute. [Fr *apanage*—L *ad*, to, *panis*, bread.]

apparat [ä´pa-rät] an organization, esp a political machine. [Russ, apparatus.]

apparatus [ap-ar-ā´tus, -a´tus] *n* things prepared or provided for a specific use; any complex machine, device, or system. [L *ad*, to, *parātus* (*parāre*), prepared.]

apparel [a-par´ėl] *n* covering for the body, dress.—*vt* to dress; to clothe. [OFr *apareiller*—L *par*, equal, like.]

apparent [a-pār´ent, a-par´ėnt] *adj* that may be seen; evident; seeming.—*adv* **appar´ently**. [Through Fr, from L *appārens, -entis*, pr p of *appārēre*, to appear.]

apparition [a-par-ish´(ȯ)n] *n* an appearance or manifestation; a visionary appearance, a ghost.—*adj* **appari´tional**. [Fr,—L *appāritiō, -ōnis—appārēre*; see **appear**.]

appeal [a-pēl´] *vi* to call, make application, have recourse (*with* **to**); to refer (to a witness or superior authority); to make earnest request; to be pleasing (*with* **to**); to transfer a lawsuit to a higher court.—*vt* to make an appeal of (a law case).—*n* act of appealing; an earnest request for help; transference of a lawsuit for rehearing; attractive power.—*adj* **appeal´able**. [OFr *apeler—L appellāre, -ātum*, to address, call by name; also to appeal to.]

appear [a-pēr´] *vi* to become visible; to come into view; to be published; to present oneself formally; to be manifest; to seem.—*n* **appear´ance**, the act of appearing; that which appears; form, aspect; outward show.—**keep up appearances**, to maintain an outward show of being proper, etc.; **put in an appearance**, to be present for a short time, as at a party. [Through Fr, from L *appārēre—ad*, to, *pārēre, pāritum*, to come forth.]

appease [a-pēz´] *vt* to pacify, esp by granting demands; to propitiate; to allay.—*n* **appease´ment**, the action of appeasing; the state of being appeased. [OFr *apeser*, to bring peace—L *pax, pācis*, peace.]

appellant [a-pel´ȧnt] *n* one who makes an appeal from a lower court to a higher.—*adj* **appell´ate court** [-it], a court that can review appeals and reverse the decision of lower courts. [See **appeal**.]

appellation [ap-el-ā´sh(ȯ)n] *n* that by which anything is called; a name or title.—*n* **appell´ative**, (*obs*) a common noun.—*adj* of the hearer of a language; of the giving of names. [Fr,—L *See* **appeal**.]

append [a-pend´] *vt* to hang (one thing) to another; to add.—*n* **append´age**, something appended; an external organ or part, as a tail.—*ns* **appendect´omy**, surgical removal of vermiform appendix; **appendicī´tis**, inflammation of the vermiform appendix; **append´ix**, something appended or added; supplementary information at the end of a book or document; the vermiform appendix;—*pl* **append´ixes, append´ices**. [L *ad*, to, *pendĕre*, to hang.]

apperception [ap-er-sep´sh(ȯ)n] *n* the mind's perception of itself as a conscious agent. [L *ad*, to, + **perception**.]

appertain [ap-ėr-tān´] *vi* to be the property or attribute of.—*adj* **appertain´ing**, proper, appropriate (to). [Through Fr, from L *ad*, to, *pertinēre*, to belong. See **pertain**.]

appetency [ap´et-ens-i] *n* appetite; desire; a natural affinity.—Also **app´etence**. [L *appetens, -entis*, pr p of *appetĕre*. See **appetite**.]

appetite [ap´et-īt] *n* sensation of physical need and desire; natural desire; desire for food; craving (*with* **for**).—*n* **appetiz´er**; a food that whets the appetite.—*adj* **app´etizing**, stimulating the appetite; savory, delicious. [Through Fr, from L *appetītus—appetēre—ad, to, petēre, petitum*, to seek.]

applaud [a-plöd´] *vt* to praise by clapping the hands; to praise loudly; to extol.—*n* **applause´**, praise loudly expressed, esp by clapping; acclamation. [L *applaudĕre—ad*, to, *plaudĕre, plausum*, to clap.]

apple [ap´l] *n* a round, firm, fleshy, edible fruit; the tree (genus *Malus*) bearing this fruit; (*slang*) derogatory name for Amerindian who is part of or cooperates with the white establishment.—*ns* **apple butter**, jam made from apple-sauce; **app´lejack**, liquor distilled from fermented cider.—*adj* **apple-pie**, having or showing American values and traits.—**apple-pie order**, (*inf*) complete order.—*vi* **apple-polish**, to toady.—*vt* to curry favor with (as by flattery).—*n* **applesauce´**, apples cooked to a pulp and sweetened and strained; (*inf*) nonsense.—**apple of the eye**, someone especially dear. [OE *æppel*; cf Ger *apfel*, ON *epli*, Ir *abhal*, W *afal*.]

Appleton layer [ap´l-tòn lā´ėr] an ionised region in the atmosphere that acts as a reflector of radio waves. [From the physicist Sir Edward *Appleton*.]

appliqué [a-plē´kā] *n* ornamental fabric work applied to another fabric.—*vt* to ornament thus. [Pt p of Fr *appliquer*.]

apply [a-plī´] *vt* to set, place, bring close (to); to bring to bear on; to devote (oneself, to a pursuit).—*vi* to make a request; to be relevant;— *pr p* **apply´ing**; *pt p* **applied** [-plīd´].—*n* **applī´ance**, a device or machine, esp for household use.—*adj* **app´licable**, that may be applied; appropriate, relevant (to).—*adv* **app´licably**.—*ns* **applicability** [ap-li-ka-bil´iti],—*ns* **app´licant**, a person who applies, esp for a job; **applicā´tion**, the act of applying, as the administration of a remedy; diligent effort; attentive study; the process of bringing a general truth to bear on a particular case; the conclusion thus deduced; relevancy; a request, or a form filled out in making one.—*adj* **applied**, used in actual practice. [OFr *aplier*—L *applicāre, -ātum*—*ad*, to, *plicāre, -ātum*, to fold.]

appoggiatura [a-pod-jä-tōō´ra] *n* (*mus*) an embellishing note, usu. written in a smaller size in front of the melodic note. [It *appoggiare*, to lean.]

appoint [a-point´] *vt* to fix; to prescribe; to assign; to select for an office.—*adj* **appoint´ed**, fixed; furnished (as in *well-appointed*).—*n* **appoint´ment**; engagement, rendezvous; a position filled by appointing. (*pl*) furniture. [OFr *apointer*—LL *appunctāre*—L *ad*, to, *punctum*, a point. See **point**.]

apportion [a-pōr´, -pör´, sh(ò)n] *vt* to portion out; to divide in shares.—*n* **appor´tionment**. [L *ad*, to, + **portion**.]

apposite [ap´oz-it] *adj* suitable, appropriate.—*adv* **app´ositely**.—*ns* **app´ositeness; apposi´tion**, state of being placed beside or against; (*gram*) the placing of one noun beside another, in order that the one may explain the other. [L *appositus*, pt p of *appōnĕre*—*ad*, to, *pōnĕre*, to put.]

appraise [a-prāz´] *vt* to set a price on; to value, esp with a view to sale; to estimate the amount and quality of (anything).—*ns* **apprais´al, appraise´ment**, a valuation, estimation of quality; **apprais´er**. [Late in appearing for some time used in the same sense as *praise*.]

appreciate [a-prē´shi-āt] *vt* to esteem highly; to recognize gratefully; to be sensitively aware of.—*vi* to rise in value.—*adj* **apprē´ciable**, capable of being estimated; perceptible.—*adv* **apprē´ciably**.—*n* **appreciā´tion**, appraisement; generous esteem; a sympathetic literary essay; increase in value.—*adj* **apprē´ciative**.—*n* **apprē´ciatory**. [L *appretiātus*, pt p of *appretiāre*—*ad*, to, *pretium*, price.]

apprehend [ap-re-hend´] *vt* to capture or arrest; to perceive by the senses; to grasp by the intellect; to understand; to fear.—*adj* **apprehens´ible**—*n* **apprehen´sion**.—*adj* **apprehens´ive**, uneasy; anxious.—*n* **apprehens´iveness**. [L *apprehendĕre*—*ad*, to, *prehendĕre, -hensum*, to lay hold of.]

apprentice [a-prent´is] *n* one being taught a trade or craft, usu as a member of a labor union; a novice.—*vt* to place or accept as an apprentice.—*n* **apprent´iceship**. [OFr *aprentis-aprendre*, to learn—L *apprehendĕre*. See **apprehend**.]

apprise [a-prīz´] *vt* to give notice to, to inform. [Fr *apprendre*, pt p *appris*—L *apprehendĕre*. See **apprehend**.]

apprize [a-prīz] *vt* to value; to appreciate. [ME *apprisen*.]

approach [a-prōch] *vi* to draw nearer; to make an approach in golf.—*vt* to come near to; to come near in quality, value etc.; to be nearly equal to; to open discussion with, address (a person) with the purpose of getting him to act in a particular way.—*n* a drawing near; a means of access, way leading to; approximation; (*pl*) advances, overtures (to someone); a preliminary step or movement.—*adj* **approach´able**. [OFr *aprochier*—LL *adpropiāre*—L *ad*, to, *prope*, near.]

approbation [ap-rob-ā´sh(ò)n] *n* formal sanction; approval. [Fr,—L *approbātiō, -ōnis*—*approbāre*. See **approve**.]

appropriate [a-prō´pri-āt] *vt* to take as one's own; to set apart for a purpose.—*adj* [-àt] set apart for a particular purpose; peculiar (to); suitable. *adj* **apprō´priately**.—*ns* **apprō´priateness; appropriā´tion**. [L *appropriāre, -ātum*—*ad*, to, *proprius*, one's own.]

approve [a-prōōv´] *vt* to sanction or ratify; to commend.—*vi* to be satisfied with (*with* **of**).—*n* **approv´al**, the act of approving; approbation.—*adj* **approv´ingly**.—**on approval**, (of goods) for the customer to examine and decide whether to buy or return. [Ofr *aprover*—L *approbāre*—*ad*, to, *probāre*, to test or try—*probus*, good.]

approximate [a-proks´im-àt] *adj* nearest or next; approaching correctness.—*vt* to come near to; to be almost the same as.—*vi* to come close.—*adv* **approx´imately**.—*n* **approximā´tion**, a close estimate; a near likeness. [L *approximāre, -ātum*—*ad*, to, *proximus*, nearest, superl of *prope*, near.]

appurtenance [a-pûr´ten-àns] *n* that which appertains (to something else) as an appendage or accessory; (*pl*) apparatus or equipment; (*law*) an additional subordinate right.—*adj, n* **appur´tenant**. [Anglo-Fr *apurtenance*, through LL from L *ad, pertinēre*. See **appertain**.]

après [a-prā] *prefix* meaning after or following some activity (*après-game, après-surgery*) [From après-ski.]

après-ski [a-prā-skē] *n* (evening period of) amusements after skiing.—Also *adj* [Fr]

apricot [ā´, or a´pri-kot] *n* a small, oval orange-pink fruit resembling the plum and peach; the tree (*Prunus armeniaca*) bearing this fruit; the color of an apricot. [Port *albricoque* (Fr *abricot*)—Ar *albirqūq*—*birqūq* is a corr of Late Gr *praikokion*—L *praecoquum* or *praecox*, early ripe; the form is perh due to a fancied connection with L *aprīcus*, sunny.]

April [ā´pril] *n* the fourth month of the year, having 30 days.—*n* **A´pril-fool**, the victim of a hoax on April 1, **All Fools' Day**. [Fr *Avril*—L *Aprīlis*.]

a priori [ä prē-ör´ē, ā prī-ör-ī] *adj* from cause to effect, based on theory instead of experience. [L *a, ab*, from *priōri*, abl of *prior*, preceding.]

apron [ā´pròn] *n* a cloth or piece of leather, etc. worn before one to protect the dress; a short cassock, part of the official dress of a bishop, etc.; applied to a number of things resembling an apron in shape or use, as a paved area where a driveway meets the road.—**apron string**, the string of an apron, a symbol of dominance or complete control. [OFr *naperon*—*nappe*, cloth, tablecloth—L *mappa*, a napkin. *A napron* became *an apron*; cf **adder**.]

apropos [a-pro-pō´] *adv* at the right time; opportunely; appropriately.—*adj* to the purpose, apt. [Fr *à propos*—*à*, to, *propos*, purpose. See **purpose**.]

apse [aps] *n* a domed or vaulted recess, esp at the east end of the choir of a church.—*adj* **ap´sidal**. [From **apsis**.]

apsis [ap´sis] *n* one of the two extreme points in the orbit of a planet or a satellite.—*pl* **apsides** [ap´si-dēz].—*adj* **ap´sidal**. [L *apsis*—Gr *hapsis*, a connection, an arch—*haptein*, to connect.]

apt [apt] *adj* liable, ready, or prone; suitable, appropriate; quick to learn.—*n* **apt´itude**, fitness; readiness; capacity, talent.—*adv* **apt´ly**.—*n* **apt´ness**. [L *aptus*, fit; cog with Gr *haptein*, to connect.]

apterous [ap´tėr-us] *adj* without wings. [Gr *a-*, priv *pteron*, a feather, wing.]

apteryx [ap´tėr-iks] *n* the kiwi. [Gr *a-*, priv *pteryx*, wing.]

aquavit [ak´wà-vēt or äk] *n* a Scandinavian liquor distilled from grain or potatoes and flavored with caraway. [As next entry.]

a´qua vi´tae [a´kwa vītē] *n* a strong alcohol liquor (as brandy). [L *aqua*, water, *fortis*, strong, *vitae*, of life.]

Aqualung [ak´wa-lung] *n* trade name for an apparatus enabling a swimmer to breathe under water. [L *aqua*, water, + **lung**.]

aquamarine [a-kwa-ma-rēn´ (or ā-)] *n* a variety of beryl used as a gemstone.—*adj* bluish-green, sea-colored. [L *aqua*, water, *marīna*—*mare*, the sea.]

aquaplane [ak´wa-plān] *n* a board on which one stands and is towed behind a motorboat.—*vi* to ride on an aquaplane; (of automobile) to be in contact with water on a road, not with the road surface. [L *aqua*, water, + **plane** (1).]

aquarium [a-kwā´ri-um] *n* a tank or series of tanks for keeping aquatic animals or plants; a building in which such tanks are exhibited;—*pl* **aquā´riums, aquā´ria**. [L—*aqua*, water.]

Aquarius [a-kwā´ri-us] *n* the water carrier, 11th sign of the zodiac; in astrology, operative January 20 to February 18. [L—*aqua*, water.]

aquatic [a-kwat´ik] *adj* relating to water; living or growing in water.—*n pl* **aquat´ics**, water sports. [L *aquāticus*—*aqua*, water.]

aquatint [a´kwa-tint or, ā´] *n* a mode of etching in imitation of drawing. [It *acqua tinta*—L *aqua*, water, *tingĕre, tinctum*, to wet, to colour.]

aqueduct [ak´we-dukt] *n* a large pipe or conduit for conveying water; from a distant point; an elevated structure supporting this. [L *aqua*, water, *ducĕre, ductum*, to lead.]

aqueous [ā´kwe-us] *adj* watery; of, like, or formed by water. [L *aqua*, water.]

aquiline [ak´wil-in, or -īn] *adj* relating to or like the eagle; curved or hooked, like an eagle's beak. [L *aquila*, eagle.]

Arab [ar´ab] *n* a native or inhabitant of Arabia; general term for inhabitants of Middle Eastern countries; an Arabian horse, a small breed used for riding.—*adj* of or belonging to Arabia.—*adj* **Arāb´ian**, relating to Arabia.—*n* a native of Arabia.—*adj* **Ar´abic**, relating to Arabia, or to its language.—*n* language of Arabia.—*n* **Ar´abist**, supporter of Arab interests and aspirations.—**Arabic numerals**, the figures 0, 1, 2, 3, 4, 5, 6, 7, 8, 9; **Arab League**, regional organization of sovereign states within the framework of the United Nations. [L *Arabs, Arabis*—Gr *Araps*.]

arabesque [ar´ab-esk] *adj* after the manner of Arabian designs.—*n* a fantastic style of decoration, used by the Spanish Moors, consisting of foliage and other parts of plants curiously intertwined; a posture in classical ballet in which one leg is stretched out backwards parallel with the ground. [Fr,—It *arabesco; -esco* corresponding to Eng *-ish*.]

arable [ar´a-bl] *adj* fit for plowing or planting crops. [L *arābilis*—*arāre*, cog with Gr *aroein*, to plough, OE *erian*, Ir *araim*.]

arachnid [à-rak´nid] *n* any of a class of land-living arthropods with four pairs of legs, as Scorpions, spiders, mites, and ticks. [Gr *arachnē*, spider.]

Aramaic [ar-a-mā´ik] an ancient Semitic language of the Middle East; the language spoken by Christ.—*adj* of, relating to or using this language. [Gr *Aramaios*.]

Aran [ar´an] *adj* (of sweaters, etc.) made with naturally oily, unbleached wool, often with complicated pattern. [*Aran* Islands, Ireland.]

Arapaho, Arapahoe [a-ra´pa-hō] *n* member of an Amerindian people of Algonquian linguistic stock, originally of the Plains, now living in Montana and Wyoming;—*pl* **-ho, hoes,-hoe,-hoes**.

Araucanian [a-row-kan´i-an] *n* American Indian of central Chile and Argentina; language of the Araucanians, which constitutes a language family.

araucaria [ar-ö-kā´ri-a] *n* any of a genus (*Araucaria*) of So American or Australian trees of the pine family. [*Arauco*, a province in S Chile.]

Arawak [ar´a-wäk] *n* member of an American Indian people of Arawakan group now living chiefly along the coast of Guyana; their language.—*n* **Arawak´an**, member of a group of American Indian peoples of S America and the West Indies; their language which constitutes a language family.

arbiter [är´bit-ėr] *n* a judge; an umpire; anyone having absolute power of decision or absolute control.—*n* **arbit´rament**, decision by an arbiter.—*vi* **ar´bitrate**, to act as an arbiter.—*vt* submit to an arbiter; to act as an arbiter upon.—*ns* **arbitrā´tion; ar´bitrātor**, arbiter. [L—*ar=ad*, to, *bitĕre* (cog with Gr *bainein*), to go or come; signifying one who comes to look on, a witness, a judge.]

arbitrary [är´bi-trȧr-i] *adj* not bound by rules; despotic, absolute; capricious, unreasonable.—*adv* **ar´bitrarily**.—*n* **ar´bitrariness**. [L *arbitrārius*, arbiter.]

arboreal [är-bōr´, -bör´i-ȧl] *adj* living in trees; of or like a tree.—*adj* **arboresc´ent**, growing or formed like a tree.—*ns* **arboresc´ence**, tree-like growth; **arborē´tum**, a place in which specimens of trees and shrubs are cultivated;—*pl* **arborē´ta**. [L *arbor*, a tree.]

arbor [är´bȯr] *n* a place shaded by trees, plants, etc.; a bower. [L *herbārium*—*herba*, grass, herb; confused with L *arbor*, tree.]

arborvitae [är-bȯr-vīt´ē] *n* any of various scale-leaved evergreen trees (genus *Thuja*), esp *T. occidentalis*, the white cedar.

arbutus [är´būt-us] *n* a trailing woody vine of the heath family (*Epigaea repens*) of temperate N America. [L *arbŭtus*, akin to *arbor*, tree.]

arc [ärk] *n* a part of the circumference of a circle or other curve; angular measurement (eg 60 *seconds of arc*); (*elect*) a luminous discharge of electricity across a gap between two conductors or terminals.—*vi* to form an electric arc. [OFr,—L *arcus*, a bow.]

arcade [ärk-ād´] *n* a walk arched over; a covered passageway lined with shops. [Fr,—LL *arcāta*, arched—L *arcus*, a bow.]

Arcadian [är-kād´i-ȧn] *adj* pertaining to *Arcadia* (*poet* **Ar´cady**), a rural district in Greece; pastoral; simple, innocent.

arcanum [ärk-ān´um] *n* mysterious knowledge known only to the initiate;—*pl* **arcan´a**.—*adj* **arcane´**, secret or esoteric. [L—*arcānus*—*arca*, a chest.]

arch[1] [ärch] *n* a curved structure so built that the stones or other component parts support each other by mutual pressure and can sustain a load; of the foot, the part from heel to toes.—*vti* to cover with an arch; to curve, raise in an arch.—*n* **arch´way**, an arched or vaulted passage, esp that leading into a castle. [OFr,—L *arca*, chest, and *arcus*, bow.]

arch[2] [ärch] *adj* clever, sly; mischievous, roguish.—*adv* **arch´ly**.—*n* **arch´ness**. [Derived from the prefix *arch-*, in its use in words such as *arch*-rogue, etc.]

arch- [ärch] *prefix* meaning chief, principle (archbishop, archenemy). [OE *arce, ærce*, through L from Gr *archi*, cog with *archein*, to begin, be first, rule.]

-arch [ärk] *suffix* meaning ruler (*matriarch oligarch*).

archaeology, archeology [ärk-e-ol´oj-i] *n* a knowledge of ancient art, customs, etc.; the science that studies the extant relics of ancient times.—*adj* **archaeolog´ical**.—*adv* **archaeolog´ically**.—*n* **archaeol´ogist**. [Gr *archaios*, ancient—*archē*, beginning, *logos*, discourse.]

archaic [ärk-ā´ik] *adj* ancient; old-fashioned, no longer in common use, esp of language.—*n* **arch´āism**, an archaic word or phrase. [Gr *archaikos*—*archaios*, ancient—*archē*, beginning.]

archangel [ärk-ān´jėl] *n* an angel of the highest order.—*adj* **archangel´ic**. [**arch-**, chief, + **angel**.]

archbishop [ärch-bish´ȯp] *n* a bishop of the highest rank.—*n* **archbish´opric**. [**arch-**, chief, + **bishop**.]

archdeacon [ärch-dē´kȯn] *n* the ecclesiastical dignitary next under a bishop.—*ns* **archdeaconate; archdeac´onry**, the jurisdiction, or residence of an archdeacon; **archdeac´onship**, the office of an archdeacon. [**arch-**, chief, + **deacon**.]

archdiocese [ärch-dī´o-sēz] *n* the diocese of an archbishop. [**arch-**, chief, + **diocese**.]

archduke [ärch-dūk´] *n* a sovereign prince; a prince of the imperial house of Austria;—*fem* **archdŭch´ess**.—*adj* **archdū´cal**.—*ns* **archdŭch´y, archdūke´dom**. [**arch-**, chief, + **duke**.]

Archeozoic [är-kē-ȯ-zō´ik] *adj* of the earliest era of geologic history; relating to the system of rocks of this era. [Gr *archaios*, ancient, *zōē*, life.]

archer [ärch´ėr] *n* one who shoots with a bow and arrows.—*n* **arch´ery**, the art of shooting with the bow. [OFr *archier*—L *arcārium*—*arcus*, a bow.]

archetype [ärk´e-tīp] *n* the original pattern or model, a prototype.—*adj* **achetyp´al**. [Gr *archetypon*—*archi-*, first, *typos*, a model.]

archimandrite [är-ki-man´drīt] *n* in the Eastern Catholic Church, the dignitary ranking below a bishop; the superior of a monastery or a group of monasteries. [Late Gr *archimandritēs*—pfx *archi*, first, *mandra*, an enclosure, a monastery.]

Archimedian [ärk-i-mē´di-ȧn] *adj* pertaining to *Archimedes*, a celebrated Greek physical scientist and mathematician of Syracuse (c. 287–212 BC).—**Archimedean solid**, polyhedron whose faces are all regular polygons but not congruent to one another;—**Archimedes´ screw**, device used to raise water.

archipelago [ärk-i-pel´a-gō] *n* a sea abounding in small islands; a group of such islands;—*pl* **archipel´agoes, -s**. [An Italian compound from Gr *archi-*, chief, *pelagos*, sea.]

architect [ärk´i-tekt] *n* one qualified to design buildings and superintend their erection.—*n* **architectonics** [ärk-i-tekton´iks], the science of architecture; structural design, as of a symphony.—*adj* **architectonic**.—*n* **architec´ture** [-tyůr, -chůr], profession or science of building; structure; distinctive style of building (eg *Gothic architecture*); design and construction.—*adj* **architec´tural**. [Gr *architektōn*—*archi*, chief, *tektōn*, a builder.]

architrave [ärk´i-trāv] *n* (*archit.*) the lowest division of the entablature; ornamental band surrounding a door or window. [It from Gr *archi-*, chief, + L *trabs, trabis*, a beam.]

archives [ärk´īvz] *n pl* the place in which public records are kept; public records kept in such a place.—*n* **arch´ivist** [-iv-], a keeper of archives. [Fr,—Gr *archeion*, magisterial residence—*archē*, beginning, power, government.]

archon [ärk´on] *n* a chief magistrate of ancient Athens a presiding officer. [Gr *archōn*—*archein*, to be first, to rule.]

arctic [ärk´tik] *adj* of, near, or relating to the North Pole or to north polar regions; extremely cold.—**Arctic Circle**, an imaginary circle parallel to the equator, 66°33' north of it.—**the Arctic**, the region around the North Pole. [OFr *artique*—L *arcticus*—Gr *arktikos*—*arktos*, a bear.]

ardent [ärd´ėnt] *adj* burning; fiery; passionate.—*adv* **ard´ently**.—*n* **ard´or**, warmth of passion or feeling; eagerness.—*Also* **ard´ency**. [L *ardens, -entis*, pr p of *ardēre*, to burn.]

arduous [ärd´ū-us] *adj* steep; difficult to accomplish; laborious.—*adv* **ard´uously**.—*n* **arduousness**. [L *arduus*, high, cog with Celt *ard*, high.]

are[1] [är] *n* a unit of measure, equals 100 sq meters. [Fr,—L *ārea*.]

are[2] [är] the plural of the present indicative of the verb *to be*. [Old Northumbrian *aron* of Scand origin. This form ousted the older, OE *sind, sindon*. Both are cog with Gr *eisin*, L *sunt*, etc.]

area [ā´rė-a] *n* an expanse of land; a total outside surface, measured in square units; a part of a house, district, etc.; scope or extent; (*geom*) region on a plane enclosed by bounding lines or the measure of the surface of a geometric solid.—**area code**, any of the numbers assigned as a telephone code to the areas into which the US is divided. [L *ārea*.]

arena [a-rē´na] *n* the center of the Roman amphitheater used for the combats of gladiators and wild beasts; a place or sphere of contest or struggle.—*adj* **arenaceous** [a-renā´shůs], sandy.—**arena theater**, a theater with a stage which can have the audience all around it. [L *arēna*, sand.]

argent [ärj´ent] *adj* and *n* silver, or like silver, silvery-white, esp in heraldry. [Fr,—L *argentum*, silver.]

argil [är´jil] *n* clay, esp potter's.—*adj* **argillaceous** [är-jil-ā´shůs]. [L *argilla*—Gr *argilos*, white clay—*argēs*, white.]

argol [är´gol] *n* crude tartar deposits in wine casks during the aging process. [Prob conn with Gr *argos*, white.]

argon [är´gon] *n* an inert gaseous element (symbol A; at wt 39.944; at no 18). [Gr *argon* (neut), inactive—*a-*, priv, *ergon*, work.]

argosy [är´go-si] *n* (*poetic*) a large richly-laden merchant vessel. [Prob from It *Ragusea*, a ship belonging to Ragusa on the Adriatic.]

argot [är´got] *n* the special vocabulary of any set of persons, as of tramps, criminals, etc. [Fr]

argue [ärg´ū] *vt* to prove, or to maintain, by reasoning; to debate, dispute; to persuade (into, out of);—*vi* to offer reasons; to dispute;—*pr p* **arg´ūing**; *pt p* **arg´ūed**.—*adj* **arg´ūable**.—*n* **arg´ument**, a quarrel; a reason put forward in support of an assertion or opinion; discussion, dispute; theme of discourse.—*n* **argumentā´tion**, an arguing or reasoning.—*adj* **argument´ative**, controversial; contentious; characterized by argument; addicted to arguing.—*adv* **argument´atively**.—*n* **argument´ativeness**. [OFr *arguer*—L *argūtāre*, frequentative of *arguĕre*, to prove.]

aria [ä´ri-a] *n* a song, in a cantata, oratorio, or opera, for one voice supported by instruments. [It, from root of **air**.]

arid [ar´id] *adj* dry, parched; uninteresting; dull.—*ns* **arid´ity, ar´idness**. [L *āridus*.]

Aries [ā´ri-ēz] *n* the Ram, the 1st sign of the zodiac; in astrology, operative March 21 to April 21. [L]

aright [a-rīt´] *adv* correctly. [Pfx *a-* (OE *on*), on, and **right**.]

arise [a-rīz´] *vi* to get up, as from bed; to rise, ascend; to come into being, to result (from).—*pt* **arose´**; *pt p* **arisen** [a-riz´n]. [OE *ārīsan*—pfx *ā-*, inten, *rīsan*. See **rise**.]

aristocracy [ar-is-tok´ras-i] *n* government by a privileged minority class; a country with such a government; the nobility, the upper class.—*n* **aristocrat**, [aris´-to-krat or ar´-is-], one who belongs to, or has the characteristics of, or favors, an aristocracy.—*adj* **aristocrat´ic**,—*adv* **aristocrat´ically**. [Gr *aristos*, best, and *kratos*, power.]

Aristotelian [ar-is-to-tē´li-an] *adj* relating to Aristotle, the Greek philosopher, (384–322 BC) master of every field of learning known.—*adj* **Aristotelian, Aristotelean**—**Aristotelean elements** fire, air, earth, and water; **Aristotelian logic**, the logic inventing the syllogism; **Aristote-**

lian theory, the notion that all matter is formed from fire, air, earth, and water.

arithmetic [ar-ith´met-ik] *n* the science of numbers; the art of reckoning by figures.—*adj* **arithmet´ical.**—*adv* **arithmet´ically**.—*n* **arithmetician**, [-ish´ȧn]— **arithmetic mean**, average; an intermediate value between two extremes, **arithmetic progression**, a series of numbers that increase or diminish by a common difference, eg 7, 10, 13, 16 . . . , or 12, 10½, 9, 7½ . . . [Gr *arithmētikē* (*technē*), (art) relating to numbers—*arithmos*, number.]

ark [ärk] *n* (*Bible*) the boat in which Noah and his family and two of every kind of creature survived the flood; an enclosure in a synagogue for the scrolls of the Torah.—**ark of the covenant** (*Bible*) the chest containing the two stone tablets inscribed with the Ten Commandments. [OE *arc*—L *arca*, a chest—*arcēre*, to guard.]

arm[1] [ärm] *n* the limb extending from the shoulder to the hand; anything projecting from the main body, as an inlet of the sea, a rail or support on a chair; a sleeve.—*n* **arm´chair**, a chair with arms.—*adj* (of a critic, etc.) without practical knowledge, doctrinaire.—*ns* **arm´ful**, as much as the arms can hold; **armhole**, the hole in a garment through which the arm is put.—*adj* **arm´less.**—*ns* **arm´let**, an ormental band for the upper arm; **arm´pit** the hollow under the arm at the shoulder; (*slang*) any unpleasant, grimy, or undesirable place.—**with open arms**, with hearty welcome. [OE; cognate with L *armus*. the shoulder-joint, Gr *harmos*, a joint.]

arm[2] [ärm] *n* a weapon; a branch of the military service;—(*pl*) weapons; heraldic bearings.—*vt* to furnish with weapons etc.—*vi* to prepare for war or any struggle; take arms.—*adj* **armed.**—**arms race**, competition among nations in building up armaments.—**under arms**, ready for war; **up in arms**, armed for combat; indignant. [Through Fr, from L *arma*; cog with **arm** (1).]

armada [är-mā´da, är-mä´da] *n* a fleet of warships; a fleet of warplanes. [Sp,—L *armāta*—*armāre*, to arm.]

armadillo [ärm-a-dil´ō] *n* a family (Daspypodidae) of small tropical American quadrupeds, having the body armed with bony plates;—*pl* **armadill´os**. [Sp, dim of *armado*, armed.]

Armageddon [är-ma-ged´ȯn] *n* (*Bible*) the site of the last decisive battle between good and evil; any great, decisive battle. [Heb.—(*H*)*ar* (of doubtful meaning), and *Megiddo*, a famous battlefield (Judges v 19; 2 Kings XXIII 29, 30).]

armament [ärm´a-mėnt] *n* (often *pl*) all the military forces and equipment of a nation; all the military equipment of a warship, etc.; an arming or being armed for war. [L *armāmenta*—*arma*.]

armature [är´ma-tyùr] *n* any protective covering; the iron core wound with wire, in which electromotive force is produced in a generator or motor; the rigid framework used by a sculptor as a foundation for a moldable substance. [L *armātūra*—*armāre*, to arm.]

Armenian [ar-mē´ni-ȧn] *adj* belonging to Armenia in Western Asia.—*n* a native of Armenia; now a republic of in NW Asia; one of Armenian descent; the Indo-European language of Armenians which is the only member of its branch.

armistice [ärm´ist-is] *n* a truce; preliminary to a peace treaty.—**Armistice Day** November 11, anniversary of the signing of armistice that ended World War I; Veteran's Day. [Fr,—L *armistitium* from L *arma*, arms, *sistĕre*, to stop.]

armor [ärm´ȯr] *n* any defensive or protective covering.—*vti* to put armor on.—*adjs* **arm´ored; armō´rial**, of coats of arms; heraldic.—*ns* **armored car**, a vehicle covered with armor plate, as a truck for carrying money to or from a bank; **arm´ory**, an arsenal; an armaments factory; a military drill hall. [OFr *arm(e)ure*—L *armātūra*—*arma*, arms.]

army [ärm´i] *n* a large organized body of soldiers for waging war, esp on land; any large number of persons, animals, etc. [Fr *armée*—L *armāta*, fem *pt p* of *armāre*, to arm.]

aroma [a-rō´ma] *n* a pleasant smell; fragrance.—*adj* **aromat´ic**, fragant; spicy; (*chem*) of the class of cyclic organic compounds derived from or having similar properties to benzene.—*vt* **arom´atize**. [Through Fr and L from Gr *arōma, -atos*, spice.]

arose [a-rōz´] *pt* of **arise**.

around [a-rownd´] *prep* on all sides of; on the border of; in various places in or on; (*inf*) about (*around 1890*);—*adv* in a circle; in every direction; in circumference; to the opposite direction; (*inf*) nearby (*stick around*); **been around** (*inf*), to be experienced, sophisticated. [Pfx *a-* (OE *on*, on, + **round**.]

arouse [a-rowz´] *vt* to wake from sleep; to stir, as to action; to evoke (to arouse pity). [Pfx *ā-*, inten, + **rouse** (1).]

arpeggio [är-pej-(y)ō] *n* (*mus*) a chord whose notes are played in rapid succession. [It *arpeggiare*, to play upon the harp—*arpa*, harp.]

arquebus *see* **harquebus**.

arrack [ar´ak] *n* a coarse spirit distilled from rice, etc. [Ar '*araq*, juice.]

arraign [a-rān] *vt* to call (one) to account; to put (a prisoner) on trial; to accuse publicly.—*n* **arraign´ment**. [OFr *aresnier*—Low L *arrationāre*—L *ad*, to, *ratiō, -ōnis*, reason.]

arrange [a-rānj´] *vt* to set in a rank or row; to put in order; to settle; (*mus*) to adapt (a composition) for performance by instruments or voices other than those for which it was originally written.—*vi* to come to an agreement (with a person); to make preparations.—*n* **arrange´ment**, act of arranging; classification; settlement; (*mus*) an arranging of a composition; the composition as thus arranged. [OFr *arangier*—*à* (L *ad*, to), *rangier, rengier*—*rang*, rank.]

arrant [ar´ȧnt] *adj* downright, notorious (used in a bad sense). [A variant of **errant**, which acquired an abusive sense from its use in phrases like 'arrant thief'.]

arras [ar´as] *n* an elaborate kind of tapestry; a wall hanging, esp of tapestry. [From *Arras* in Northern France, where it was first made.]

array [a-rā´] *n* an orderly grouping, esp of troops; an impressive display; fine clothes.—*vt* to put in order, to arrange; to dress in finery. [OFr *arei*, array, equipage—L *ad*, and a Gmc root found in Eng **ready**.]

arrears [a-rēr´z´] *n pl* overdue debts.—**in arrears**, behind in paying a debt, doing one's work, etc. [OFr *ar(i)ere*—L *ad*, to, *retro*, back, behind.]

arrest [a-rest´] *vt* to stop; to seize; to catch the attention of; to apprehend by legal authority.—*n* an arresting or being arrested.—*adj* **arrest´ing**, attracting attention; interesting.—**under arrest**, in legal custody. [OFr *arester*—L *ad, restāre*, to stand still.]

arrière pensée [ar-yer´ pã´sā´] *n* mental reservation. [Fr]

arrive [a-rīv´] *vi* to reach any place; to come (*the time has arrived*); to achieve success, recognition.—*n* **arrīv´al**, the act of arriving; a person or thing that arrives—**arrive at**, to reach by thinking, etc. [OFr *ariver*—L *ad*, to, *rīpa*, a bank.]

arrivederci [ä rī´ve-der´chē] *interj* goodbye. [It]

arriviste [a-rē-vēst´] *n* a person who is a new and uncertain arrival. [Fr]

arrogate [ar´og-āt] *vt* to claim without right.—*ns* **arr´ogance**, undue assumption of importance.—*adj* **arr´ogant**, haughty; overbearing.—*adv* **arr´ogantly**. [L *arrogāre*—*ad*, to, *rogāre, -ātum*, to ask, to claim.]

arrondissement [a-rō-dēs´mã] *n* the largest division of a French department; an administrative district of some large French cities. [Fr—*arrondir*, to make round.]

arrow [ar´ō] *n* a straight, pointed weapon, made to be shot from a bow; a sign used to indicate direction.(→)—*n* **arr´owhead**, the head or pointed part of an arrow; any triangular shape.—*adj* **arr´owy**, consisting of arrows; swiftly moving. [OE *earh, arwe*]

arrowroot [ar´ō-root] *n* a tropical American plant (genus *Maranta*) with starchy roots; a starch made from its roots. [From its use by South American Indians as an antidote to arrow-poisoning.]

arroyo [ȧ-roi´ō] *n* a dry gully; a rivulet or stream.

arsenal [är´se-nȧl] *n* a magazine or manufactory for weapons and ammunition; a storehouse. [It *arzenale, arsenale* (Sp, Fr *arsenal*)—Ar *dār aççinā'ah*, workshop.]

arsenic [ärs´(e-)nik] *n* a metalloid element (symbol As; at wt 74.9; atomic no 33), highly poisonous.—*adj* **arsen´ical**. [Gr *arsenikon*, yellow orpiment fancifully associated with *arsēn*, male, and the alchemists´ notion that metals have sex.]

arson [ärs´ȯn] *n* the crime of wilfully setting fire to a building. [OFr *arson*—L *ardēre, arsum*, to burn.]

art[1] [ärt] (*arch*) 2d pers sing of the present tense of the verb *to be* used with thou. [OE *eart*.]

art[2] [ärt] *n* human creativity; skill, acquired by study and practice; any craft and its principles; making of things that have form and beauty; any branch of this, as painting, sculpture, etc.; drawings, paintings, statues, etc.; (*pl*) sly trick, wile.—*ns* **art deco** [dek´ō, dā´kō], a decorative style of the late 1920s and the 1930s derived from cubism; **Art Nouveau** [är nōō´vō], style of art and architecture of the 1890s, marked by sinuous outlines and stylized natural forms.—*adj* **art´ful**, cunning; skillful; clever; crafty.—*adv* **art´fully**.—*n* **art´fulness**.—*ns* **art´ist**, one who practices fine art, esp painting; one who does anything very well; **artiste** [-tēst], a professional, usu. musical or theatrical, entertainer.—*adj* **artist´ic**, of art or artists; done skillfully; sensitive to beauty.—*n* **art´istry**, artistic quality, ability, work, etc.—*adj* **art´less**, simple, guileless.—*adv* **art´lessly**.—*n* **art´lessness**.—*adj* **art´y** (*inf*), affectedly artistic.—*n* **art form**, an accepted form of artistic expression.—*adj* **art´sycraft´sy, art´y-craft´y**, arty. [L *ars, artis*.]

artery [är´tėr-i] *n* a tube that conveys blood from the heart; any main channel of communication.—*adj* **artēr´ial**. [L,—Gr *artēria*, orig the windpipe most probably.]

artesian [är-tē´zhȧn, -zi-ȧn] *adj* pertaining to a type of well in which water rises of itself by internal pressure. [in early use at *Artois* (L *Artesium*) in the north of France.]

arthritis [är-thrī´tis] *n* inflammation of a joint.—*adj* **arthritic** [-thrit´ik]. [Gr *arthritikos*—*arthron*, a joint.]

arthropod [är´thropod] *n* any of a member of a phylum (Arthropoda) of invertebrate animals, with bodies consisting of segments bearing jointed appendages—including crustaceans, spiders, insects, etc. [Gr *arthron*, joint, *pous*, gen *podos*, a foot.]

Arthurian [är-thū´ri-ȧn] *adj* relating to King Arthur a legendary 6th-century ruler of the Britons.

artichoke [är´ti-chōk] *n* a thistlelike plant (*Cynara scolymus*) with large scaly heads, parts of which are succulent and edible.—**Jerusalem artichoke**, a perennial American sunflower (*Helianthus tuberosus*) with edible tubers. [Old It *articiocco*—Old Sp *alcarchofa*—Ar *al-kharshōfa, al-kharshūf*.]

article [ärt´i-kl] *n* a section of any document; a literary composition in a newspaper, magazine, encyclopaedia, etc., dealing with a particular subject; a separate item (*an article of luggage*); (*gram*) the name given to the adjectives *the* (definite article) and *a* or *an* (indefinite article).—**Articles of Confederation**, the first compact passed (November 15, 1777) by the congress of the thirteen original States of the United States. [L *articulus*, a little joint—*artus*, a joint.]

articulate [är-tik´ūl-àt] *adj* jointed; capable of speech, or of expressing one's thoughts clearly; distinct, clear, intelligible.—*vt* [-āt] to form into distinct sounds; to put together in a connected way; to express clearly.—*adj* **artic´ular**, of joints or structural components in a joint.—*adv* **artic´ulately**.—*ns* **artic´ulateness; articulā´tion**. [L *articulāre, -ātum*, to furnish with joints, to utter distinctly.]

artifact [är´ti-fakt] *n* any product of human workmanship. [L *ars, artis*, art, *facĕre, factum*, to make.]

artifice [ärt´i-fis] *n* a contrivance; a trick; contrivance; trickery.—*n* **artificer** [ar-tif´is-ėr], a skilled craftsman; an inventor.—*adj* **artificial** [ärt-i-fish´àl], made by art; not natural.—*n* **artificial´ity**.—*adv* **artific´ially**.—*ns* **artificial intelligence**, the means by which computers, robots, etc. perform tasks which normally require human intelligence, such as solving problems, making fine distinctions, etc.; the field of science which studies and develops these means; **artificial respiration**, stimulation of respiration manually or mechanically by forcing air in and out of the lungs. [L *artificium—ars, artis*, art, *facĕre*, to make.]

artillery [är-til´ėr-i] *n* mounted guns, esp cannon; the science of guns; gunnery.—*n* **artill´eryman**, a soldier of the artillery.—**the artillery**, the branch of an army using heavy mounted guns. [OFr *artillerie—artiller*, to arm; through a supposed LL *artillāre*—L *ars, artis*, art.]

artist *see* **art**.

artiste *see* **art.**

Art Nouveau *see* **art**.

Aryan [ā´ri-àn, är´ri-àn] *adj* relating to the Indo European family of languages; non-Jewish and Caucasian, esp Nordic; the language of Iran; the language of India.—*n* member of descendant of prehistoric people who spoke Indo-European; (in Nazi doctrine) non-Jewish Caucasian, esp of Nordic stock. [L *ariānus*, belonging to *Ariana* or *Aria* (Gr *Areia*), the east part of Ancient Persia—Sans *Arya* (cf *Irān*, Persia), often traced to a root *ar*, plough.]

as [az] *adv* equally (*as white as snow*); for instance (*certain colors, as green and blue*); when related in a certain way (*this view as contrasted with that*).—*conj* in the same way that (*run as I do*); to the same amount or degree that (*straight as a die*); while (*she sang as she worked*); because (*as you object, we won't go*); that the consequence is (*so clear as to be obvious*); though (*tall as he is, he can't reach it*).—*prep* in the role or function of (*he poses as a friend*).—*pron* a fact that (*he is tired, as you can see*); that (preceded by **such** or **the same**) (*the same color as yours*).—**as for** (or **to**), concerning; **as is** (or **though**), as it (or one) would if; **as is** (*inf*), just as it is; **as it were**, as if it were so. [A worndown form of *all-so*, OE *all-swā*, wholly so.]

asafetida, asafoetida [as-a-fēt´i-da] *n* an evil-smelling resin formerly used in medicine. [Pers *aza*, mastic, and L *foetida*, stinking.]

asbestos [az-best´os] *n* an incombustible siliceous mineral, of a fine fibrous texture, and capable of being woven. [Gr, unquenchable—*a-*, priv, *sbestos—sbennunai*, to quench; used as noun for various substances including asbestos.]

ascend [a-send´] *vti* to go up; to succeed to (a throne).—*adj* **ascend´ant, -ent.**—*n* the part of the ecliptic rising above the eastern horizon at any moment.—*ns* **ascend´ancy**, controlling influence—also **ascend´ency; ascen´sion**, a rising or going up; **Ascen´sion Day**, the Thursday 40 days after Easter to commemorate Christ's ascension to heaven; **ascent´**, act, or way of ascending; rise; sope or gradient. [L *ascendĕre, ascensum—ad*, to, *scandĕre*, to climb.]

ascertain [as-ėr-tān´] *vt* to obtain certain knowledge of.—*adj* **ascertain´able**.—*n* **ascertain´ment**. [OFr *acertener—à*, to; *see* **certain**.]

ascetic [a-set´ik] *n* one who trains himself to endure severe bodily hardship as a religious discipline; any extremely abstemious person.—*adjs* **ascet´ic**, austere.—*n* **ascet´icism**. [Gr *askētikos—askētēs*, one who trains himself by exercises—*askeein*, to work, take exercise, (*eccles*) to mortify the body.]

ascribe [a-skrīb´] *vt* to attribute; to assign.—*adj* **ascrib´able**.—*n* **ascrip´tion**, act of ascribing; any expression of ascribing, esp arbitrary placement (as at birth) in a particular social class. [L *ascrībĕre, -scriptum—ad*, to, *scrībĕre*, to write.]

asepsis [a-sep´sis] *n* condition of being aseptic.—*adj* **asep´tic**, free from disease-producing germs. [Gr *a-*, priv, *sēpsis—sēpein*, cause to decay.]

asexual [a-seks´ū-àl] *adj* without sex or sexual organs; of reproduction without the union of male and female germ cells. [Gr *a-*, priv, + **sexual**.]

ash[1] [ash] *n* any of a genus (*Fraxinus*) of widely distributed N American tree grown for shade and for its tough, elastic timber. [OE *æsc*; Ger *esche*, ON *askr*.]

ash[2] [ash] *n* powdery remains of anything burnt; fine, volcanic lava; the gray color of wood ash; (*pl*) the substance remaining after a thing has been burned; the remains of the human body when burnt.—*adjs* **ash´en**, like ashes, esp in color; pale.—*n* **Ash Wednesday** [ash-wenz´dā], the first day of Lent (from the putting of ashes on the forehead in penitence). [OE *asce*; ON *aska*.]

ashamed [a-shāmd´] *adj* affected with shame. [Pt p of old verb *ashame*—pfx *a-*, + **shame**.]

Ashkenazi [ash-ke-naz´i] *n* Jew in or from northern Europe;—*pl* **-zim**.—*n* **Ashkenazic** the Yiddish language used by the Ashkenazim or the system of pronunciation, in contrast with Sephardim pronunciation.

ashlar [ash´lår´] *n* hewn stone; a thin facing of squared stones to cover brick or rubble walls. [OFr *aiseler*—L *axillāris—axilla*, dim of *axis, assis*, axle, plank.]

ashore [a-shōr´, shör] *adv, adj* to or on the shore; to or on land. [Pfx *a-* (OE *on*), on, + **shore**.]

ashram [ash´ram] *n* a religious retreat or community where a Hindu holy man lives. [Sanskrit *āsrama*.]

Asiatic [ā-zhi-at´ik, or āsh-i-at´ik] *adj* belonging to *Asia*.—*n* (*offensive*) a native or inhabitant of *Asia*.—Also **Asian** [*āzh´yàn*, or *āsh´i-àn*].

aside [a-sīd´] *adv* on or to one side; in reserve (*put one ticket aside*); notwithstanding (*joking aside*).—*n* words spoken by an actor which the other persons on the stage are supposed not to hear.—**aside from** with the exception of; apart from. [Pfx *a-*, (OE *on*), on, + **side**.]

asinine [as´in-īn] *adj* like an ass; silly; stupid.—*n* **asinity** [-in´i-ti]. [L *asinīnus—asinus*, ass.]

ask [äsk] *vt* to request, beg; inquire; inquire of; invite.—*vi* to make request (for) or inquiry (about).—*n* **ask´er**. [OE *āscian, ācsian*.]

askance [a-skans´], **askant** [a-skant´], *adv* with a sideways glance; with suspicion.

askew [a-skū´] *adv* to one side; awry.—*adj* on one side, awry. [Prob conn with **skew**.]

aslant [a-slänt´] *adv* on a slant.—*prep* slantingly across.—*adj* slanting. [Pfx *a-* (OE *on*), on, + **slant**.]

asleep [a-slēp] *adj* sleeping; inactive; numb; dead.—*adv* into a sleeping condition. [Pfx *a-* (OE *on*), on, + **sleep**.]

aslope [a-slōp´] *adv, adj* being in a sloping or slanting position or direction. [OE *āslopen*, pt p of *āslūpan*, to slip away.]

asocial [ā-sō´shàl] *adj* avoiding contact with others; selfish.

asp [äsp] *n* a small venomous snake of Egypt. [L,—Gr *aspis*.]

asparagus [as-par´a-gus] *n* a genus (*Asparagus*) of plants one species (*A officimalis*) of which is cultivated for its young shoots, esteemed as a table delicacy. [L,—Gr *asparagos*.]

aspect [as´pekt] *n* look; view; appearance of a thing or idea from a specific viewpoint; position in relation to the points of the compass.—**aspect ratio**, (*TV*) ratio of the width to the height of a reproduced image; ratio of the span of an airfoil to its mean chord. [L *aspectus—ad* at, *specĕre*, to look.]

aspen [äsp´en] *n* any of several poplars, esp *Populus tremuloides*, the tree with the widest range in N America, whose small leaves flutter in the slightest breeze.—Also **quaking aspen**. [OE *æspe*, Ger *espe*.]

asperity [as-per´i-ti] *n* roughness; harshness; sharpness of temper. [L *asperitās—asper*, rough.]

asperse [as-pûrs´] *vt* to slander.—*n* **asper´sion**, calumny, slander. [L *aspergĕre, aspersum—ad*, to, *spargĕre*, to sprinkle.]

asphalt [as´fölt] *n* a dark, hard bituminous substance, used for paving and to waterproof cement.—**asphalt jungle**, a big city or a specified part of a big city. [Gr *asphaltos*, from an Eastern word.]

asphyxia [as-fik´si-a] *n* unconsciousness due to deficiency of oxygen or excess of carbon dioxide in the blood.—*vt* **asphyx´iāte**, to cause to suffer asphyxia, to suffocate.—*n* **asphyxiā´tion**. [Gr,—*a*, neg, *sphyxis*, the pulse.]

aspic [as´pik] *n* a jelly used to coat fish, game, hard-boiled eggs, etc. [Fr.]

aspidistra [as-pid-ist´ra] *n* an Asian plant (*Aspidistra lurida*) with large leaves, often grown in pots. [Perh Gr, *aspis, idos*, a shield.]

aspirant [as´pir-ànt, or as-pīr´ànt] *n* one who aspires;—*adj* **aspiring**. [*See* **aspire**.]

aspirate [as´pir-āt] *vt* to pronounce with a full breathing, as *h* in *house*.—*n* [-àt] sound of the letter *h*; a consonant sound consisting of a stop followed by an audible breath; a mark of aspiration (‘); a letter representing an aspirate.—*ns* **aspirā´tion**, pronunciation of a letter with a full breathing; an aspirated sound; the act of drawing a gas or liquid in, out, or through, by suction; **as´pirātor**, a device for drawing a stream of air or liquid through an apparatus by suction. [*See* **aspire**.]

aspire [as-pīr´] *vi* to desire eagerly; to aim at high things.—*n* **aspiration**, [aspir-ā´sh(ó)n], eager desire, ambition.—*adj* **aspīr´ing**.—*adv* **aspīr´ingly**. [Fr,—L *aspīrāre, -ātum—ad*, to, *spīrāre*, to breathe.]

aspirin [as´pir-in] *n* a sedative drug used for relieving pain and fever. [*a*cetyl + *spir*aeic, former.]

ass [as] *n* any of several species of quadrupeds of the same genus (*Equus*) as the horse; a silly, stupid person [OE *assa*, the earlier Gmc form being *esol, esil*—L *asinus*.]. [OE *aers, ears*; Ger *Arsch*; cog. with Gr *orros*.]

assagai *see* **assegai**.

assail [a-sāl´] *vt* to attack suddenly or repeated either physically or with arguments.—*n* **assail´ant**, attacker, esp physical. [OFr *asaillir*—L *assilīre—ad*, upon, and *salīre*, to leap.]

Assamese [as-à-mēz] *n* native or inhabitant of Assam, India;—*pl* **-ese**; the Indic language of the Assamese, one of the languages of the constitution of India.

assassin [as-as´in] *n* one who takes the life of another, esp a politically important person by treacherous violence.—*vt* **assass´inate**.—*n* **assassinā´tion**. [Through Fr or It from Ar *hashshāshin*, 'hashish-eaters', because the assassins drugged themselves with hashish.]

assault [a-sölt´] *n* a violent attack, euphemism for rape; (*law*) an unlawful threat or attempt to harm another physically.—*vti* to make an assault (upon).—**assault and battery**, (*law*) the carrying out of threatened physical harm. [OFr *assaut*—L *ad*, upon, *saltus*, a leap—*salīre*, to leap.]

assay [a-sā´] *vt* to make an assay of; to test.—*vi* to be shown by assay to have a specified proportion of something.—*n* the determination of the quantity of metal in an ore or alloy; a test;—*n* **assay´er**. [OFr *assayer*, n *assai, essai*. See **essay**.]

assegai [as´ė-gī] *n* a spear or javelin used in southern Africa.—*Also* **assagai**. [Ar *azzaghāyah*.]

assemble [a-sem´bl] *vti* to gather together; to collect; to put together the parts of.—*ns* **assem´blage**, a collection of persons or things; (*art*) things assembled in a sculptural collage; **Assembly**, the lower house of some state legislatures; **assem´bly**, the act of assembling; the company so assembled; a gathering of persons for a particular purpose; a fitting together of parts to make a whole; **assembly line**, the machines and workers necessary for the manufacture of an article, arranged in such a way that each worker does a single operation in assembling the work as it is passed along; **assem´blyman**, a member of a legislative assembly. [Fr *assembler*—LL *assimulāre*, to bring together.]

assent [a-sent´] *vt* to agree in thought; to indicate agreement.—*n* consent or agreement. [OFr *asenter*, assent—L *assentīre*—*ad*, to, *sentīre*, to think.]

assert [a-sûrt´] *vt* to maintain or defend (eg rights); to declare, affirm.—*n* **asser´tion**, the act of asserting; affirmation.—*adj* **assert´ive**, persistently positive or confident.—*adv* **assert´ively**.—*n* **assert´iveness**.—**assertiveness training**, method of training submissive individuals to behave with confidence, often by assuming an agressive attitude.—**assert oneself**, to insist on one's rights; to refuse to be ignored. [L *asserĕre* (supine *assertum*) *aliquem manu in libertatem*, to lay a hand on one (a slave) in token of manumission, hence to protect, affirm, declare—*ad*, to, *serĕre*, to join.]

assess [a-ses´] *vt* to fix the amount of, as a tax; to tax or fine; to value, for taxation; to estimate; to judge the worth, importance, etc. of—*adj* **assess´able**.—*ns* **assess´ment; assess´or**. [Fr,—L *assessāre*, freq of *assidēre, assessum*, to sit by, esp of judges in a court—*ad*, to, at, *sedēre*, to sit.]

asset [as´et] *n* anything owned that has value; a desirable thing (*charm is an asset*); (*pl*) all the property, accounts receivable, etc. of a person or business; (*pl*) (*law*) property usable to pay debts. [From the Anglo-Fr law phrase *aver assetz*, to have enough—OFr *asez*, enough—L *ad*, to, *satis*, enough.]

asseverate [a-sev´ėr-āt] *vt* to state positively.—*n* **asseverā´tion**. [L *assevērāre, -ātum*—*ad*, to, *sevērus*, serious.]

assid´uous [as-id´ū-us] *adj*, constant or unwearied in application; diligent.—*adv* **assid´uously**.—*n* **assid´uousness**. [L *assiduitās*—*assiduus*, sitting close at—*ad*, to, at, *sedēre*, to sit.]

assign [a-sīn´] *vt* to designate; to allot; to appoint; to ascribe; (*law*), to transfer (a right, property, etc.).—*n* one to whom any property or right is made over.—*adj* **assign´able**, that may be assigned.—*ns* **assignation** [as-ig-nā´sh(ȯ)n], an appointment to meet, esp one made secretly by lovers; **assignee** [as-in-ē´, or -sīn-], one to whom a right or property is assigned; **assign´ment** [-sīn-], act of assigning; anything assigned; the writing by which a transfer is made; a task allotted. [Fr,—L *assignāre*, to mark out—*ad*, to, *signum*, a mark or sign.]

assimilate [a-sim´il-āt] *vt* to take in as nourishment; to take into the mind and thoroughly absorb; to make similar; to alter by assimilation; to absorb yinto the cultural tradition of a group or population.—*vi* to become assimilated.—*adj* **assim´ilable**.—*ns* **assimilabil´ity; assimila´tion**.—*adj* **assim´ilative**, having the power or tendency to assimilate. [L *assimilāre, -ātum*—*ad*, to, *similis*, like.]

assist [a-sist´] *vti* to help.—*n* **assist´ance**, help; aid.—*adj* **assist´ant**, helping or hending aid.—*n* one who assists; a helper.—**assistant professor**, member of a college or university faculty ranking above instructor and below associate professor. [L *assistĕre*, to stand by—*ad*, to, and *sistĕre*. (Gr *histanai*), to cause to stand.]

assizes [a-siz´-is] *n pl* the sessions or sittings of a court held periodically in English counties; the time or place of these. [OFr *assise*, an assembly of judges, a set rate—*asseoir*—L *asidēre*—*ad*, to, *sedēre*, to sit.]

associate [a-sō´shi-āt] *vt* to join in friendship of partnership, to bring together; to unite in the same body; to connect in thought.—*vi* to keep company (with); to combine or unite.—*adj* [-ȧt], allied or connected; having secondary status or privileges.—*n* one joined or connected with another; a companion, friend, partner, or ally; a degree granted by a junior college at the end of a two-year course.—*n* **associā´tion** [-si-], act of associating; union or combination; a society of persons joined together to promote some object; a connection between ideas, etc.—*adj* **assō´ciative**, tending to association.—**associate professor**, member of college of university faculty ranking above assistant professor and below professor; **association football**, soccer; **associative law** (*math*), of addition, the principle that the sum of several quantities is the same regardless of the way in which the terms are grouped; of multiplication, the principle that the product of several quantities is the same regardless of the way in which the terms are grouped. [L *associāre, -ātum*—*ad*, to, *socius*, a companion.]

assonance [as´on-ȧns] *n* a correspondence in sound; a kind of rhyme, consisting in the coincidence of the vowels of the corresponding syllables, without regard to the consonants as in *mate* and *shape, feel* and *need*.—*adj, n* **ass´onant**, resembling in sound. [Fr,—L *assonāre*—*ad*, to, *sonāre*, to sound.]

assort [a-sört´] *vt* to separate into classes according to kind.—*vi* to agree in kind; to keep company.—*adj* **assort´ed**, arranged in sorts; miscellaneous.—*n* **assort´ment**, act of assorting; that which is assorted; a variety. [Fr *assortir*—L *ad*, to, *sors, sortis*, a lot.]

assuage [a-swāj´] *vt* to soften, mitigate, or allay.—*n* **assuage´ment**, abatement; mitigation.—*adj* **assuā´sive**, soothing, calming. [OFr, formed as if from a L *assuāviāre*—*ad*, to, *suāvis*, mild.]

assume [a-sūm´, or -sōōm´] *vt* to take on; to seize, usurp; to take upon oneself; to take for granted; to pretend to possess.—*adjs* **assumptive** [as-um(p)´tiv], taken as one's own; making undue claims; **assumed´**, appropriated, usurped; pretended; taken as the basis of argument; **assum´ing**, presumptuous, arrogant. [L *assūmĕre*—*ad*, to, *sūmĕre, sumptum*, to take.]

Assumption [a-sum´sh(ȯ)n] *n* (*R C Church*) the ascent of the Virgin Mary into heaven; the festival celebrating this (August 15); act of assuming; that which is taken for granted, supposition. [L *assumptiō, -ōnis*—*assūmĕre*. See **assume**.]

assure [ȧ-shōōr´] *vt* to make sure or certain; to give confidence; to tell positively; to guarantee.—*n* **assur´ance**, feeling of certainty; self-confidence; promise.—*adj* **assured´**, certain; without doubt; self-confident.—*adv* **assur´edly** [-id-li].—*n* **assur´edness**. [OFr *aseürer*—LL *adsēcūrāre*—*ad*, to, *sēcūrus*, safe.]

astatic [ā-stat´ik] *adj* (*Physics*) having no tendency to take a fixed position. [Gr *astatos*, unstable.]

astatine [as´ta-tēn] *n* a highly unstable radioactive element of the halogen group (symbol At; at wt 210; at no 85).

aster [as´tėr] *n* a genus (*Aster*) of composite plants with flowers like little stars, mostly perennial, flowering in the late summer and autumn. [Gr *astēr*, a star.]

asterisk [as´tėr-isk] *n* a star-shaped mark, used in printing to mark footnotes, omission of words, etc., thus*. [Gr *asteriskos*, dim, of *astēr*, a star.]

astern [a-stûrn´] *adv* behind a ship or aircraft; at or toward the rear of a ship, etc.; backward. [Pfx *a-* (OE *on*), on, + **stern** (2).]

asteroid [as´tėr-oid] *n* any of the small planets between Mars and Jupiter.—*adj* **asteroid´al**. [Gr *aster*, a star, *eidos*, form.]

asthma [az´ma] *n* a chronic disorder of the organs of respiration, characterized by paroxysms in which the sufferer gasps painfully for breath.—*adjs* **asthmat´ic**.—*adv* **asthmat´ically**. [Gr *asthma, -atos*—*aazein*, to breathe hard.]

astigmatism [a-stig´ma-tizm] *n* a defective condition of the eye, in which rays proceeding to the eye from one point are not correctly brought to a focus at one point.—*adj* **astigmat´ic**. [Gr *a-*, priv, and *stigma, -atos*, a point.]

astir [a-stûr] *adv* on the move; out of bed. [Pfx *a-* (OE *on*), on, + **stir**.]

astonish [as-ton´ish] *vt* to impress with sudden surprise, to amaze.—*adj* **aston´ishing**.—*adv* **aston´ishingly**.—*n* **aston´ishment**. [From the earlier *astony*—ME *aston(i)en*—OFr *estoner*—L *ex*, out, *tonāre*, to thunder.]

astound [as-townd´] *vt* to astonish greatly.—*pt p* **astound´ed**; *pr p* **astound´ing**.—*adj* **astound´ing**. [ME *aston(i)en*; a doublet of **astonish**.]

astraddle [a-strad´l] *adv* sitting astride. [Pfx *a-* (OE *on*), on, + **straddle**.]

astragal [as´tra-gal] *n* a narrow half-round modelling; a projecting strip on the edge of a folding door. [Gr *astragalos*, one of the vertebrae, a moulding.]

astrakhan [as-tra-kan´] *n* lambskin with a curled wool; a fabric made in imitation of it. [From *Astrakhan* on the Caspian Sea.]

astral [as´trȧl] *adj* belonging to the stars; in theosophy, descriptive of an impalpable essence supposed to pervade all space and enter into all bodies. [L *astrālis*—*astrum*, a star.]

astray [a-strā´] *adv* off the right path; into error. [Pfx *a-* (OE *on*), on, and **stray**.]

astride [a-strīd´] *adv* with a leg on either side.—*prep* with a leg on either side of; extending over and across. [Pfx *a-* (OE *on*), on, + **stride**.]

astringent [as-trin´jėnt] *adj* that contracts body tissues; harsh; biting.—*n* an astringent substance.—*n* **astrin´gency**.—*adv* **astrin´gently**. [L *astringens, -entis*, pr p of *astringĕre*—*ad*, to, *stringĕre*, to bind.]

astro- [as´tro] prefix meaning of a star or stars (*astrophysics*). [Gr *astron*, a star.]

astrolabe [as´trō-lāb] *n* an instrument formerly used for calculating the positions of the sun or stars. [Gr *astron*, a star, and root of *lambanein*, to take.]

astrology [as-trol´o-ji] *n* the study of the positions and motions of the heavenly bodies (out of which grew astronomy) to determine their supposed influence on human affairs.—*n* **astrol´oger**, one versed in astrology.—*adjs* **astrolog´ic, -al**.—*adv* **astrolog´ically**. [Gr *astrologia*—*astron*, star, *logos*, discourse.]

astronaut [as´trō-nöt] *n* one trained to make flights in outer space.—*adj* **astronaut´ical**—*n* **astronaut´ics**, the science of travel in space, navigation in space beyond the earth's atmosphere. [Gr *astron*, a star, *nautēs*, a sailor.]

astronomy [as-tron´ȯm-i] *n* the science of the stars and other heavenly bodies.—*n* **astron´omer**, one versed in astronomy.—*adj* **astronom´ical**,

astronomic, of, or pertaining to, astronomy; (of numbers) very large.—*adv* **astronom´ically**.—**astronomical unit**, the earth's mean distance from the sun, about 92.9 million miles (1.496 x 10^{11}m), used as a measure of distance within the solar system. [Gr *astronomia—astron*, star, *nomos*, a law.]

astrophysics [as-trō-fiz´iks] *n* that branch of astronomy which deals with the physical properties and chemical constitution of the stars. [Gr *astron*, star, + **physics**.]

Astroturf [as´trō-tûrf] *n* trade name of artificial surface for lawns and playing fields, made of a green, grasslike nylon material backed with vinyl.

astute [ast-ūt´] *adj* crafty, cunning; shrewd.—*adv* **astute´ly**.—*n* **astute´ness**. [L *astūtus—astus*, craft.]

asunder [a-sun´dėr] *adv* apart; in direction or position; into pieces. [Pfx *a-* (OE *on*), on, + **sunder**.]

asylum [a-sīl´um] *n* a place of safety, a refuge; an earlier name for an institution for the blind, the mentally ill; orphans, etc. [L,—Gr *asylon—a-*, priv. *sylē*, right of seizure.]

asymmetry [ā-sim´ė-tri] *n* lack of symmetry; (*chem*) condition of not being superimposable on a mirror image.—*adj* **asymmetric, -al**.

asymptote [a´sim-tōt] *n* (*math*) a line that continually approaches nearer to some curve without ever meeting it.—*adjs* **asymptot´ic**. [Gr *asymptōtos*, apt to fall—*piptein*, to fall.]

at [at] *prep* on; in; near; by (*at the office*); to or toward (*look at her*); from (*visible at one mile*); attending (*at a party*); busy with (*at work*); in the state or manner of (*at war, at a trot*); because of (*sad at his death*); with reference to (*good at tennis*); in the amount of, etc. of (*at five cents each*); on or near the age or time of (*at noon*). **-at all**, in any way; to the least extent, under any circumstances; **at bat**, an official time charged to a baseball batter. [OE *æt*; cog with ON *at*, L *ad*, Sans *adhi*, on.]

Atabrine [at´â-brin] *n* a trade name for yellow dye used in the treatment of malaria.

atavism [at´av-izm] *n* appearance of remotely ancestral, characteristics; reversion to a more primitive type.—*adj* **atavis´tic**. [L *atavus*, a great-great-grandfather—*avus*, a grandfather.]

ataxia [a-tak´si-a], **ataxy**, [a-tak´si, at´aks-i] *n* (*med*) inability to coordinate movements of the limbs. [Gr, disorder—*a-*, priv, *taxis*, order.]

ate [et, or āt] *pt p* of **eat**.

atelier [at-ėl-yā´] *n* studio workshop as of an artist or coutourier. [Fr]

Athabaskan [ath-â-bas´kân] *n* an Amerindian people inhabiting central Alaska, closely related to the Navaho, Apache, and Hupas of southwestern US.—Also *adj*.

Athapaskan [ath-â-pas´kân] *n* an Amerindian language family found in the Pacific Northwest, Alaska, and south-western US.

atheism [ā´the-izm] *n* disbelief in the existence of God.—*n* **a´theist**.—*adjs* **atheist´ic, -al**.—*adv* **atheist´ically**. [Fr *athéisme*—Gr *a-*, priv, and *theos*, God.]

athenaeum, atheneum [ath-e-nē´um] *n* a building or room where books, periodicals, and newspapers are kept for use; a literary or scientific association. [Gr *Athēnaion—Athēna* or *Athēnē*.]

atheriosclerosis [ath-ēr-i-ō-skli-rō´sis] *n* degenerative disease of arteries marked by thickening of artery walls caused by deposits of fatty material;—*pl* **-oses** [-ōsēz].

athirst [a-thûrst´] *adj* (*arch*) thirsty; eager (for). [OE *ofthyrst(ed)*, pa p of *ofthyrstan—thyrstan*, to thirst.]

athlete [ath´lēt] *n* a person trained in games or exercises requiring skill, strength, stamina, etc.—*adj* **athlĕt´ic**, relating to athletics; strong, vigorous.—*n pl* **athlet´ics**, athletic sports, games, etc.—**athlete's foot**, ringworm of the feet. [Gr *athlētēs—athlos*, contest.]

athwart [a-thwört´] *prep* across; against.—*adv* crosswise. [Pfx *a-* (OE *on*), on, + **thwart**.]

Atlantic Charter [at-lan´tik] *n* program of peace aims jointly enunciated by Winston Churchill, Prime Minister of Great Britain, and F D Roosevelt, President of the United States, on August 14, 1941. Aims incorporated in the UN declaration of 1942.

atlas [at´las] *n* a book of maps; a bound collection of tables, charts, or plates. [Gr *Atlas*, the Titan condemned to bear the sky on his shoulders, whose figure used to be shown on the title-page of atlases.]

atmosphere [at´mos-fēr] *n* the gaseous envelope that surrounds the earth or any of the heavenly bodies; a unit of pressure equal to 14.69 lb per sq in; any surrounding influence.—*adjs* **atmosphĕr´ic**, of or depending on the atmosphere.—*n pl* **atmospher´ics**, in radio reception, interfering or disturbing signals due to atmospheric conditions.—**atmospheric perspective**, effect of distance in a painting, created by using color. [Gr *atmos*, air, *sphaira*, a sphere.]

atoll [a-tol´, or āt´ol] *n* a coral island formed by a circular belt or coral enclosing a central lagoon. [Dravidian.]

atom [at´ȯm] *n* the smallest particle of an element that can take part in a chemical reaction; anything very small.—*adjs* **atom´ic**, arising from the atom;—*ns* **atomic´ity** [-is-], number of atoms contained in the molecule of an element; the combining power of an atom; **atomizā´tion**, the reduction of liquids to the form of spray.—*vt* **at´omize**, to reduce to a fine spray or minute particles; to destroy by bombing.—*ns* **atomi´zer**, a device for discharging liquids in a fine spray; **at´omy**, a tiny particle; **atom(ic) bomb**, a bomb whose immense power derives from nuclear fission or fusion; **atomic energy**, nuclear energy; **atomic number**, the number of protons in the nucleus of an atom; **atomic pile**, nuclear reactor; **atomic theory**, any theory in which matter is regarded as consisting of atoms; current concept of atom as entity with definite structure; **atomic weight**, the mass of an atom of an element, relative to that of carbon 12; **a´tom smasher**, a particle accelerator. [Gr *atomos*, indivisible—*a-*, priv, *temnein*, to cut.]

atonal [a-tōn´ál] *adj* (*mus*) avoiding traditional tonality; not referred to any scale or tonic.—*n* **atŏnal´ity**—*adj* **atŏn´ic**, uttered without accent or stress. [Gr *a-*, priv, *tonos*, tone. See **tone**.]

atone [at-ōn´] *vi* to give satisfaction or make reparation; to make up (for deficiencies).—*n* **atone´ment**, the act of atoning; expiation; reparation; esp (*theol*) the redemption of man by means of the incarnation and death of Christ. [**at** and **one**, as if to set at one, reconcile.]

atracurium [at-râ-kyōōr´i-u] *n* a drug used as a muscle relaxant during surgery.

atrium [ā´tri-um] *n* the open central court in Greek and Roman dwellings; an auricle of the heart.—*pl* **a´tria**. [L.]

atrocious [a-trō´shùs] *adj* extremely cruel or wicked; abominable; (*inf*) very bad; offensive.—*adv* **atrō´ciously**.—*ns* **atrō´ciousness**, gross cruelty; **atrocity** [a-tros´it-i], atrociousness; an atrocious act; (*inf*) a very displeasing thing. [L *ātrox, ātrocis*, cruel—*āter*, black.]

atrophy [at´rof-i] *n* a wasting away or failure to grow of an organ of the body.—*vt* to cause atrophy in.—*vi* to undergo atrophy. [Gr *a-*, priv, *trophē*, nourishment.]

atropine [at´ro-pin] *n* a poisonous alkaloid obtained from deadly nightshade; used medicinally; main ingredient of belladonna. [Gr *Atropos*, the one of the Fates who cut the thread of life.]

attach [a-tach´] *vt* to bind or fasten (to something); to append, to join (oneself); to associate as an adjunct (eg *to attach a condition*); to attribute (eg importance); to affix (a signature, etc.); to connect by ties of affection, etc.; to seize (property, etc.) by legal process.—*vi* to become attached; to adhere.—*adj* **attach´able**.—*adj* **attached´**, fastened, fixed; joined by taste or affection, devoted (to).—*n* **attach´ment**, act or means of fastening; something attached, esp an extra part attached to a machine to enable it to do special work; a tie of fidelity or affection; (*comput*) a file sent with an e-mail; (*law*) a taking of property, etc. into custody. [OFr *atachier*, from *à* (L *ad*), and perh the root of **tack** (1).]

attaché [a-tash´ā] *n* a technical expert on a diplomatic staff (*commercial attaché*); (*Brit*) a junior member of an ambassador's staff.—*n* **attach´é case**, a briefcase. [Fr, attached.]

attack [a-tak´] *vt* to fall upon violently, to assault; to assail in speech or writing; to begin to affect (of a disease).—*vi* to make an assault.—*n* an assault; onset of illness; severe criticism; a beginning of performance, task, undertaking, etc. [Fr *attaquer*. See **attach**, of which it is a doublet.]

attain [a-tān´] *vt* to reach or gain by effort; to arrive at.—*vi* to come to or arrive at by growth or effort.—*adj* **attain´able**.—*ns* **attain´ableness, attainabil´ity; attain´ment**, act of attaining; the thing attained; accomplishment. [OFr *ataindre*—L *attingĕre—ad*, to, *tangĕre*, to touch.]

attainder [a-tān´dėr] *n* (*law*) loss of civil rights and property, usu. through conviction for high treason.—*vt* **attaint´**, to punish by attainder. [OFr *ataindre*. See **attain**.]

attar [at´ȧr] *n* a fragrant essential oil, esp from rose petals; fragrance. [Pers *atar*.]

attempt [a-tempt´] *vt* to try; to try to do, get, etc.—*n* a try, endeavor, or effort; an attack (eg *an attempt on one's life*). [OFr *atempter*—L *atentāre—ad*, to, *temptāre, tentāre*, to try.]

attend [a-tend´] *vt* to take care of; to accompany; to be present at; to wait for.—*vi* to give heed; to act as an attendant; to wait (on or upon); to apply oneself (to).—*n* **attend´ance**, act of attending; presence; the number of person attending.—*adj* **attend´ant**, giving attendance; accompanying.—*n* one who attends or serves.—**attendance teacher**, an official charged with finding and returning absentee students to school. [OFr *atendre*—L *attendĕre—ad*, to, *tendĕre*, to stretch.]

attention [a-ten´sh(ȯ)n] *n* act or faculty of taking notice or of giving heed; notice, heed; steady application of the mind; care; (usu. *pl*) an act of courtesy; the erect posture of soldiers standing rigidly erect with hands by the sides and heels together.—*adj* **attent´ive**, full of attention; courteous.—*adv* **attent´ively**.—*n* **attent´iveness**. [L *attentiō, -ōnis—attendĕre*. See **attend**.]

attenuate [a-ten´ū-āt] *vt* to make thin; to dilute; to lessen or weaken.—*vi* to become thin or fine.—*adj* **attenuated** [aten´ū-ȧt-id].—*n* **attenuā´tion**. [L *attenuāre, -ātum—ad*, to, *tenuis*, thin.]

attest [a-test´] *vt* to testify, to certify, as by oath; to give proof of, manifest.—*vi* to bear witness (to).—*n* **attestā´tion**.—*adj* **attest´ed**. [L *attestāri—ad*, to, *testis*, a witness.]

attic [at´ik] *n* the room or space just under the roof; a garret. [Gr *Attikos*, Attic, Athenian—*Attikē*, Attica.]

Attila [â-til´â] *n* king of the Huns (died 453 AD) noted for his cruelty and vandalism.

attire [a-tīr] *vt* to clothe; to dress up.—*n* dress, clothing. [OFr *atirer*, put in order—*à tire*, in a row—*à* (L *ad*), to, *tire, tiere*, order.]

attitude [at´i-tūd] *n* posture; position; state of thought or feeling.—*vi* **attitud´inize**, to assume affected attitudes. [Fr or It from LL *aptitūdō, -inis—aptus*, fit.]

attorney [a-tûr´ni] *n* one authorized to act for another, esp a lawyer.—*(pl)* **attor´neys.**—*ns* **attor´ney-gen´eral**, the chief law officer of a government. **attor´neyship**—*(pl)* **attorneys general, attorney generals.**—**attorney at law**, a lawyer. [OFr *atorné*—LL *atornāre*, to commit business to another—*ad*, to, *tornāre*. See **turn**.]

attract [a-trakt´] *vt* to draw (to); to cause to approach; to allure; to get the admiration, attention, etc. of.—*vi* to be attractive.—*adj* **attract´able.**—*ns* **attractabil´ity; attract´ant**, something that attracts; **attrac´tion**, act of attracting; power of attracting, esp charm; *(physics)* the mutual action by which bodies tend to be drawn together.—*adj* **attract´ive.**—*adv* **attract´ively.**—*n* **attract´iveness.** [L *attrahěre, attractum—ad*, to, *trahěre*, to draw.]

attribute [a-trib´ūt] *vt* to consider as belonging (to); to ascribe, impute (to).—*adj* **attrib´utable.**—*ns* **att´ribute**, that which is attributed; a quality or property inseparable from anything; that which can be predicated of anything; **attribū´tion**, act of attributing; that which is attributed.—*adj* **attrib´utive**, expressing an attribute; (of an adjective) standing before the qualified noun (eg a *loud* noise). [L *attribuěre, -tribūtum—ad*, to, *tribuěre*, to give.]

attrition [a-tri´sh(ȯ)n] *n* a wearing away by or as by friction. [L *attrītus—atterěre—ad*, inten, and *terěre, trītum*, to rub.]

attune [a-tūn´] *vt* to put (an instrument) in tune; to harmonize with. [L *ad*, to, **tune**.]

aubade [ō-bäd´] *n* a sunrise song. [Fr *aube*, dawn.]

auburn [ö´bûrn] *adj* reddish brown. [The old meaning was a light yellow, or lightish hue; LL *alburnus*, whitish—L *albus*, white.]

auction [ök´sh(ȯ)n] *n* a public sale of items to the highest bidder.—*vt* to sell by auction.—*n* **auctioneer´**, one who is licensed to sell by auction.—**auc´tion bridge**, a form of bridge in which tricks made are scored toward game.—**acution off**, to sell at auction. L*auctiō, -ōnis*, an increasing—*augēre, auctum*, to increase.]

audacious [ö-dā´shùs] *adj* daring, bold; too bold; insolent; brazen.—*adv* **audā´ciously.**—*ns* **audā´ciousness, audacity** [ö-das´i-ti]. [Fr *audacieux*—L *audax—audēre*, to dare.]

audible [öd´i-bl] *adj* able to be heard.—*ns* **aud´ibleness, audibil´ity.**—*adv* **aud´ibly.**—*n* **aud´ience**, those gathered to hear and see something; all those reached by a broadcast, book, movie, etc.; a hearing, esp a formal interview.—*n* **aud´it**, a formal checking of financial records.—*vti* to check (accounts, energy levels, etc.); to attend (a college class) to listen without credits.—*n* **audi´tion**, a hearing to test a performer—*vti* to try out in an audition.—**aud´itor**, a hearer; one who audits accounts; one who audits classes.—**auditōr´ium**, space allotted to the audience in a building; a building or hall for speeches, concerts, etc. *adj* **aud´itory**, relating to the sense of hearing.—**audit trail**, *(computer)* a record of the passage of data in a computer or data processing machine. [L *audīre, -ītum*, to hear.]

audio [öd´i-ō] *adj* of frequencies corresponding to audible sound waves; of the sound phase of television.—*n* sound; the part of television or motion-picture equipment dealing with sound; the reproduction, transmission or reception of sound.—*ns* **au´diol´ogy**, the science of helping persons with hearing defects; **au´diometer**, an instrument for measuring the sharpness and range of hearing; **au´diophile**, a devotee of high-fidelity sound reproduction.—*adj* **audiovis´ual**, involving both hearing and sight; designed to help learning by making use of both sight and hearing.—*n* **au´diovisuals**, audiovisual teaching aids. [L *audīre*, to hear.]

Audubon Society [ö´du-bȯn] society founded in 1905 for the preservation of wildlife, esp birds. [J J *Audubon* (1785–1851) Amer artist and ornithologist.]

Augean [ö-jē´ȧn] *adj* (of a task, etc.) so repulsively filthy as to demand superhuman effort. [From *Augeas*, a fabled king, whose stalls, containing 3000 oxen, and uncleaned for thirty years, were swept out by Hercules in one day.]

auger [ö´gėr] *n* a carpenter's tool used for boring holes in wood. [ME *nauger* (an *auger* for *a nauger*)—OE *nafugār—nafu*, a nave of a wheel, *gār*, a piercer.]

aught [öt] *n* anything; whatever; a zero.—*adv* in any way; part. [E *ā-wiht*, contr to *aht—ām ō*, ever, *wiht*, creature; cf **ought**.]

augment [ög-ment´] *vti* to increase.—*adj* **augment´ative**, having the quality or power of augmenting.—*ns (gram)* a word formed from another by adding an augmentative suffix; **augmentative suffix**, a suffix added to a word, usu. a noun, to convey the idea of bigness.—*n* **augmentā´tion.**—*adj* **augment´ed**, *(mus)*, of an interval, greater by a semitone than the perfect or the major. [L *augmentum*, increase.]

augur [ö´gūr] *n* a prophet.—*vti* to prophesy; to be an omen (of).—*n* **augury**, [ö´gū-ri] divination from omens; a portent; an omen.—**augur ill**, (or **well**,) to be a bad (or good) omen. [L; prob from *avis*, bird.]

august [ö-gust´] *adj* venerable; imposing; majestic.—*adv* **august´ly.**—*n* **august´ness.** [L *augustus—augēre*, to increase, honour.]

August [ö´gust] *n* the eighth month of the year, having 31 days.—*adj* **Auguš´tan**, pertaining to the Roman Emperor Augustus, or to his reign (31 BC-AD 14); classic, as applied to a period of 18-century English literature.

auk [ök] *n* a family (Alcidae) of black-and-white diving seabirds, found in northern seas, [ON *ālka*.]

auld [öld] *adj (Scot)* old.—**auld lang syne**, [lang sīn], the dear and distant past (*lit* old long since). [Variant of **old**; cf Ger *alt*.]

aunt [änt] *n* a father's or mother's sister; an uncle's wife. [OFr *ante* (Fr *tante*)—L *amita*, a father's sister.]

aura [ör´a] *n* an invisible emanation; a particular quality surrounding a person or thing.—*pl* **aur´ae** [-ē]. [L *aura*, a breeze.]

aural [ör´ȧl] *adj* pertaining to the ear or the sense of hearing.—*adv* **aur´ally.** [L *auris*, ear.]

aureole [ör´i-ōl], **aureola**, [ör-ē´o-la] *n* a halo; a sun's corona.—*adj* **aur´eoled**, encircled with an aureole. [L *aureolus*, dim of *aureus*, golden.]

auric [ör´ik] *adj (chem)* applied to gold when it has a valency of 3. [L *aurum*, gold.]

auricle [ör´i-kl] *n* the external ear; either of the two upper chambers of the heart an earlike part.—*adj* **auric´ular**, pertaining to the ear; known by hearing; told in the ear (ie privately). [L *auricula*, dim of *auris*, the ear.]

auriferous [ör-if´ėr-us] *adj* bearing or yielding gold. [L *aurifer—aurum*, gold, *ferre*, to bear.]

aurochs [ör´oks] *n* the extinct urus of wild ox; (*Bos primogenius*) of the German forests; a nisent. [OHG *ūr-ohso,—ūr* (adopted into L as *ūrus*, into Gr as *ouros*), and *ochs*, ox.]

Aurora [ö-rō´, -rö´, ra] *n* the Roman goddess of dawn; **aurora**, the dawn; *-pl* **-ras -rae**, [rē]; either of the luminous bands seen in the night sky **aurora borealis**, [bō-re-ā´lis] in the northern hemisphere; **aurora australis**, [ös-tra´lis] in the southern hemisphere.—*pl* **auro´ras, -rae** [-rē]. [L *Aurōra*; from a root seen in Sans *ush*, to burn.]

auscultation [ös-kult-ā´sh(ȯ)n] *n* a listening, often with a stethoscope, to sounds in the chest, abdomen, etc. that indicate the patient's condition.—*vti* **aus´cultate.**—*adj* **auscult´atory.** [L *auscultāre, -ātum*, to listen.]

auspice [ö´spis] *n* an omen; good augury; *(pl)* sponsorship; patronage—*adj* **auspi´cious**,—*adv* **auspi´ciously.**—*n* **auspi´ciousness.** [Fr,—L *auspicium*, divination by watching birds, omen—*avis* a bird, *specěre*, to observe.]

Aussie [ös´ē] *n (slang)* an Australian; *(inf)* an Australian terrier.

austere [ös-tēr´] *adj* harsh; stern; strictly upright; severely simple.—*adv* **austere´ly**,—*ns* **austere´ness, austěr´ity**, sternness; *(pl)* an austere practice; a tightened economy. [L *austērus*—Gr *austēros—auein*, to dry.]

austral [ös´trȧl] *adj* southern. [L *austrālis—auster*, the south wind.]

autarchy [öt´är-ki] *n* absolute sovereignty [Gr *autos*, self, *archein*, to rule.]

autarky [öt´är-ki] *n* (of a political unit) policy of economic self-sufficiency. [Gr *autarkeiā—autos*, self, *arkeein*, to suffice.]

authentic [ö-thent´ik] *adj* not spurious or counterfeit; genuine, original; certified by valid evidence; unquestionably true.—*adv* **authent´ically.**—*vt* **authent´icate**, to prove authentic; to make valid; to verify.—*ns* **authenticā´tion**, act of authenticating; confirmation; **authentic´ity**, [-is-], quality of being authentic; state of being in accordance with fact; genuineness. [Fr and L from Gr *authentēs*, one who does anything with his own hand—*autos*, self.]

author [öth´ȯr] *n* one who brings anything into being; the writer of a book, article, etc.—*vt* to be the author of.—*vt* **auth´orize**, to give official approval to; to give authority to; to justify.—*ns* **authorizā´tion; auth´orship**, state of being an author.—**Authorized Version**, the revised English translation of the Bible, published in 1611, authorized by King James I. [Through Fr from L *auctor—augēre, auctum*, produce.]

authority [öth-or´i-ti] *n* legal power of right to command; *(pl)* officials with this power; influence resulting from knowledge, prestige, etc.; a person, writing, etc. cited to support an opinion; an export.—*pl)* **author´ities.**—*adj* **authoritārian**, marked by absolute obedience to authority.—*n* an advocate or enforcer of such obedience.—*Also n*—*adj* **author´itative**, having the sanction or weight of authority based on competent authority; reliable.—*adv* **author´itatively.**—*n* **author´itativeness.** [L *auctoritās, -ātis—auctor*, author, authority.]

autism [öt´izm] *n (psych)* a mental state marked by disregard of external reality—*adj* **autist´ic.** [Gr *autos*, self.]

auto-, aut-, auth- [ötō-, öt-, öth-] in composition pertaining to oneself, for oneself, by oneself, independently. [Gr *autos*, self.]

auto- [ö´tō] *prefix* meaning; self; by oneself or itself. [Gr *autos*, self.]

auto [ö´tō] *n* an automobile. [Contr of **automobile.**]

autobiography [ö-to-bī-og´raf-i] *n* the biography or life of a person written by himself.—*n* **autobiog´rapher.**—*adjs* **autobiograph´ic, -al.** [Gr *autos*, self, *bios*, life, *graphein*, to write.]

autochthon [ö-tok´thon] *n* a person, plant, or animal that is autochthonous.—*adj* **autoch´thonous**, indigenous; formed or originating in the place where found. [Gr *autochthōn—autos*, self, *chthōn*, the soil.]

autocrat [ö´to-krat] *n* an absolute sovereign; any domineering person.—*n* **autoc´racy**, government by one man, with absolute power.—*adj* **autocrat´ic.**—*adv* **autocrat´ically.** [Gr *autokrātes—autos*, self, *kratos*, power.]

auto-da-fé [ö´to-dä-fā] *n* the publication of the judgement passed on heretics by the Inquisition; the infliction of the punishment, esp the public burning of the victims;—*pl* **autos-da-fé.** [Port *auto da fé* (Sp *auto de fe*)—*auto* (L *actum*), act, *da* (L *dē*), of *fé* (L *fidēs*), faith.]

autodyne [ö´tō-dīn] *adj* in radio, of an electrical circuit in which the same elements and valves are used both as oscillator and detector. [Gr *autos*, self, and **(hetero)dyne.**]

autograph [ö´to-gräf] *n* one's own handwriting; a signature;—*vt* to write one's signature in or on.—*adj* **autograph´ic**. [Gr *autos*, self, *graphē*, writing.]

autolysis [ö-tol´is-is] *n* the breakdown of a cell or tissue by self-productive enzymes. [Gr *autos*, self, *lysis*, loosening.]

automaton [ö-tom´a-ton] *n* any automatic device, esp a robot; a human being who acts like a robot.—*pl* **autom´atons, autom´ata**.—*vt* **au´tomate**, to apply automation to.—*adjs* **automat´ic**, acting like an automaton, self-acting; done unthinkingly, as by habit or by reflex; using automatic equipment.—*n* an automatic pistol or rifle.—*adv* **automat´ically**.—*n* **automation** [-mā´sh(ȯ)n], a high degree of mechanization in manufacture in which many or all of the processes are automatically controlled, as by electronic devices.—**automatic pilot**, a gyroscopic instrument that automatically keeps an aircraft, missile, etc. to a predetermined course and altitude. [Gr *automatos*, self-moving.]

automobile [ö-to-mō-bēl´ or ö´-] *n* a self-propelling (usu. by internal-combustion engine) vehicle for passenger transportation on roadways. [Gr *autos*, self; L *mōbilis*, mobile.]

autonomy [ö-ton´om-i] *n* the power or right of self-government.—*adjs* **autonom´ic**, of or controlled by that part of the nervous system that regulates the motor functions of the heart, lungs, etc. and operates independently of the will; **auton´omous**. [Gr *autos*, self, *nomos*, law.]

autopsy [ö´top-si or -top´-] *n* a post-mortem examination to determine the cause of death; a critical analysis. [Gr *autopsia*—*autos*, self, *opsis*, sight.]

autosuggestion [ö´to-su-jes´ch(ȯ)n] *n* a mental process (toward health, etc.) originating in the subject's own mind. [Gr *autos*, self, + **suggestion**.]

autumn [ö´tum] *n* the season between summer and winter; fall.—*adj* **autum´nal**. [L *autumnus*.]

auxiliary [ög-zil´yȧr-i] *adj* helping; subsidiary; supplementary.—*n* a helper; an assistant—**auxiliary verb**, a verb that helps form tenses, moods, voices, etc. of other verbs, as *have, be, may, shall*, etc. [L *auxiliāris*—*auxilium*, help—*augēre*, to increase.]

avail [a-vāl´] *vti* to be of value, use, or service to,—*n* benefit, use or help.—*adj* **avail´able**, that can be obtained or used; accessible.—*ns* **avail´ableness, availabil´ity**,—*adv* **avail´ably**. [Through Fr, from L *ad*, to *valēre*, to be worth.]

avalanche [av´al-änsh -önsh] *n* a mass of snow, ice, and rock sliding down from a mountain; an overwhelming influx; a cumulative process in which photons, etc. produce other photons, etc. through collisions (as with gas molecules). [Fr *avaler*, to slip down—L *ad*, to, *vallis*, valley.]

avant-garde [av-ã-gärd] *n* the leaders in new movements, esp in the arts.—*adj* of such movements. vanguard. [Fr]

avarice [av´ar-is] *n* greed for wealth,—*adj* **avaricious**, [avȧr-i´shùs],—*adv* **avari´ciously**.—*n* **avari´ciousness**. [Fr,—L *avāritia*—*avārus*, greedy—*avēre*, to pant after.]

avast [a-väst´] *interj* (*naut*) hold fast! stop! [Du *houd vast*, hold fast.]

avatar [a-va-tär´] *n* the descent of a Hindu deity in a visible form. [Sans—*ava*, away, down, root *tar*-, pass over.]

avaunt [a-vönt´] *adv* away, hence. [Fr *avant*, forward—L *ab*, from, *ante*, before.]

Ave Maria [ävā Ma-rē´a] (*R C Church*) 'Hail Mary', the first words of a prayer; this prayer (Luke i 28). [Imper of L *avēre*, to be well.]

avenge [a-venj´, -venzh´] *vt* to get revenge for (an injury) to exact due penalty on behalf of (a person).—*n* **aveng´er**. [OFr *avengier*—L *vindicāre*.]

avenue [av´ė-nū] *n* a street; drive, etc. esp when broad; means of access. [Fr,—L *ad*, to, *venīre*, to come.]

aver [a-vûr´] *vt* to declare to be true; to assert;—*pr p* **averr´ing**; *pt p* **averred´**.—*n* **aver´ment**. [Fr *avérer*—L *ad*, and *vērus*, true.]

average [av´ėr-ij] *n* the result of dividing the sum of two or more quantities by number of quantities; the usual kind, amount, etc.—*adj* constituting an average; usual; normal.—*vt* to figure out the average of; to do, take, etc. on an average (*to average six sales a day*).—*vi* to exist as, or form, an average, to have a medial value (*a color averaging a pale green*).—**average out**, to arrive at an average eventually; **on the average**, as an average amount, rate, etc. [The word first appears about 1500 in conn with Mediterranean sea-trade; prob—It *avere* (L *habēre*, to have), goods, the orig sense being a 'charge on property or goods'.]

averse [a-vûrs´] *adj* unwilling; opposed (to).—*ns* **averse´ness; aver´sion**, dislike, hatred;—*vt* **avert´**, to turn from or aside (eg eyes, thoughts); to prevent, ward off.—*adj* **avert´ible**, [L *avertĕre, aversum*—*ab*, from, *vertĕre*, to turn.]

aviary [ā´vi-ȧr-i] *n* a building or large cage for keeping many birds. [L *aviārum*—*avis*, a bird.]

aviation [ā-vi-ā´sh(ȯ)n] *n* the science of flying airplanes; the field of airplane design, construction, etc.—*n* **av´ia´tor**, an airplane pilot. [L *avis*, a bird.]

avidity [a-vid´i-ti] *n* eagerness; greediness.—*adj* **av´id**,—*adv* **av´idly**. [L *aviditās*—*avidus*, greedy—*avēre*, to pant after.]

avionics [ā´vē-än-iks] *npl* electronics as applied in aviation and astronautics. [*avi*(ation) +electr(*onics*).]

avitaminosis [ā-vīt-ȧ-min-ō´sis or -vit-] *n* disease (as scurvy) resulting from a deficiency of vitamins. [Gr *a*-, priv, **vitamin**, + *-osis*, indicating diseased state.]

avocado [av´ȯ-kä´dō or äv-] *n* a tropical tree (genus Persea); its thick-skinned, pear-shaped fruit with yellow buttery flesh.—Also **alligator pear, avocado pear**.

avocation [a-vo-kā´sh(ȯ)n] *n* occupation in addition to one's regular employment; hobby. [Through Fr from L *āvocātiō, -ōnis*, a calling away—*ab*, from *vocāre*, to call.]

Avogadro number [a-vo-gäd´rō] *n* the number of atoms in one gram-atom.—**Avogadro's law**, law stating that gases at the same temperature and pressure have the same number of molecules per unit volume.

avoid [a-void´] *vt* to escape, keep clear of; to shun;—*adj* **avoid´able**.—*n* **avoid´ance**, [Pfx *a* = Fr *es* = L *ex*, out, + **void**.]

avoirdupois [av´ėr-dė-poiz´] *n* a system of weights in which the lb equals 16oz; (*inf*) weight, esp of a person. [OFr *aveier de pes* (*avoir du pois*), to have weight—L *habēre*, to have, *pensum*, that which is weighed.]

avow [a-vow´] *vt* to declare openly; to acknowledge.—*adj* **avowed**, [-vowd´].—*adv* **avow´edly**, [-id-li].—*adj* **avow´able**.—*n* **avow´al**. [OFr *avouer*, orig to swear fealty to—L *ad*, and LL *vōtāre*—*vōtum*, a vow—*vovēre*, to vow.]

avuncular [a-vung´kū-lȧr] *adj* pertaining to an uncle. [L *avunculus*, an uncle.]

await [a-wāt´] *vti* to wait for; to be in store for. [Through Fr from the common Gmc root of Ger *wacht*, Eng **wait**.]

awake [a-wāk´] *vti* to rouse from sleep; to rouse from inaction;—*pt* **awoke´, awaked´**; *pt p* **awaked´**, or **awoke´**.—*adj* not asleep; active; vigilant.—*vti* **awak´en**, to awake; to rouse into interest or attention.—*n* **awak´ening**, ceasing to sleep; an arousing from indifference. [OE *āwæcnan* (pt *āwōc*, pt p *āwacen*) confused with *āwacian* (pt t *āwacode*.) *See* **wake, watch**.]

award [a-wörd] *vt* to give, as by a legal decision; to give (a prize, etc.); to grant.—*n* a decision, as by a judge; a prize. [OFr *ewarder, eswarder*—*es* (L ex, in sense of thoroughly), and *guarder*, watch. *See* **ward, guard**.]

aware [a-wār´] *adj* realizing; informed; conscious.—*n* **aware´ness**. [OE *gewær*—pfx *ge-, wær*, cautious. *See* **wary**.]

awash [a-wosh´] *adj* on a level with the surface of the water; overflowing with water. [Pfx *a-* (OE *on*), on, + **wash**.]

away [a-wā´] *adv* from a place (*run away*); in another place or direction (*away from here*); off, aside (*turn away*); far (*away behind*); from one's possession (*give it away*); at once (*fire away*); continuously (*kept working away*).—*adj* absent; at a distance (*a mile away*).—*interj* be gone!—**away with**, go, come, or take away; **do away with**, get rid of or kill. [OE *aweg*—*on*, on, *weg*, way, *lit* 'on one's way'.]

awe [ö] *n* a mixed feeling of reverential fear, wonder and dread.—*vt* to fill with awe.—*adjs* **awe´some**, full of awe; inspiring awe; **awe´struck**, struck or affected with awe; **aw´ful**, inspiring awe; terrifying; (*inf*) very bad.—*adv* (*inf*) very.—*n* **aw´fulness**. [ON *agi* (OE *ege*), fear; cog with Gael *eaghal*; Gr *achos*, anguish.]

awhile [a-hwīl´] *adv* for a short time. [OE *āne hwīle*, a while.]

awkward [ök´wȧrd] *adj* clumsy; ungraceful; embarrassing; embarrassed; unwieldy; difficult to deal with.—*adv* **awk´wardly**.—*n* **awk´wardness**. [Prob ON *afug*, turned wrong way, and suffx *-ward*, expressing direction.]

awl [öl] *n* a pointed instrument for boring small holes in leather, wood etc. [OE *æl*; cog with ON *alr*, Ger *ahle*.]

awn [ön] *n* the bristles on a head of oats, barley, etc.—*adjs* **awned; awn´less**. [ON *ögn*; Ger *ahne*.]

awning [ön´ing] *n* a structure, as of canvas extended above or in front of a window, door, etc. to afford shelter from the sun or weather. [Ety uncertain.]

awoke [a-wōk´] (*Brit*) *pt, pt p* of **awake**.

AWOL, awol [ā´wöl] *adj* absent without leave. [*a*bsent *w*ith*o*ut *l*eave.]

awry [a-rī´] *adj* twisted to one side; crooked.—*adv* crookedly, obliquely; perversely. [Pfx *a-* (OE *on*), on, **wry**.]

ax, axe [aks] *n* a tool with a long handle and bladed head, for chopping wood, etc.—*pl* **ax´es**.—*vt* to trim, split, etc. with an ax.—**get the ax**, (*inf*) to be discharged from one's job; **have an ax to grind**, (*inf*) to have an object of one's own to gain or promote. [OE *æx*; L *ascia*; Gr *axinē*.]

axil [aks´il] *n* (*bot*) the upper angle between leaf and stem or between branch and trunk. [L *axilla*, the armpit.]

axiom [aks´i-ȯm, aks´yȯm] *n* a self-evident truth; an established principle in an art or science.—*adjs* **axiomat´ic**,—*adv* **axiomat´ically**. [Gr *axiōma*—*axioein*, to think worth, to take for granted—*axios*, worthy.]

axis [aks´is] *n* a real or imaginary straight line about which a body rotates; a central line about which the parts of a figure, body or system are symmetrically arranged; (*math*) a fixed line along which distances are measured or to which positions are referred.—**the Axis**, Germany, Italy, and Japan, in World War II.—*pl* **axes**, [aks´ēz].—*adj* **ax´ial**. [L *axis*; cf Gr *axōn*, Sans *aksa*, OE *eax*.]

axle [aks´l] *n* a rod on or with which a wheel turns; a bar connecting two opposite wheels, as of an automobile; the spindle at each end of such a bar.—*n* **axle-tree**, an axle of a wagon, carriage, etc. [From ON *öxull*.]

axolotl [ak´sȯ-lätl] *n* any of several aquatic salamanders (genus *Ambystoma*) of southwestern No America capable of breeding in the larval state. [Aztec.]

ayatollah [ī´ȧ-tō´lȧ] *n* a Shiite Muslim leader; a title of respect. [Ar, sign of God—*āya*, sign, *ollāh*, God.]

aye,[1] ay [ī] *adv* yes;—*n* **aye**, [ī], a vote in the affirmative; (*pl*) those who vote in the affirmative. [Perh a dial form of *aye*, ever; perh a variant of *yea*.]

aye,[2] ay [ā] *adv* (*poet*) ever; always; for ever. [ON *ei*, ever; conn with OE *ā*, always; also with **age ever**.]

azalea [a-zā´li-a] *n* gardening term for a genus (*Azalea*) of rhododendron. [Gr *azaleos*, dry—reason uncertain.]

azimuth [az´im-uth] *n* the arc of the horizon between the meridian of a place and a vertical circle passing through any celestial body; angular distance of this from meridian.—*adj.* **az´imuthal**. [Ar *as-sumūt—as=al*, the, *sumūt*, pl of *samt*, direction. *See* **zenith**.]

Aztec [az´tek] *adj* of member of Indian race ruling Mexico before the Spanish conquest.—*n* a member of the Aztec people; their extinct language.—**Aztec two-step**, (*i nf*) Montezuma's revenge.

azure [azh´yůr] *adj* sky-blue.—*n* the blue color of the clear sky; the unclouded sky. [OFr *azur*—through LL and Ar from Pers *lājward*, lapis lazuli.]

B

baa [bä] *n* the cry of a sheep.—*vi* to cry or bleat as a sheep. [From the sound.]

Baal [bā´ál] *n* an ancient Semitic fertility god; a false god generally;—*pl* **Bā´alim**. [Heb.]

babble [bab´l] *vi* to speak like a baby; to talk incessantly or incoherently; to murmur, as a brook.—*vt* to prate; to utter.—*ns* **babb´le**, idle senseless talk, prattle; a murmuring sound; **babb´ler**. [Prob imit.]

babe [bāb] *n* a baby; a naive person; (*slang*) a girl or young woman.—**babe in the woods**, a naive person.

Babel [bā´bėl] *n* (*Bible*) city thwarted in building a tower to heaven when God created a confusion of tongues.—*n* **babel**, a confused combination of sounds; a scene of confusion. [Heb **Babel**, explained in Gen XI as confusion.]

baby [bā´bi] *n* an infant or child; one who acts like an infant; a very young animal; the youngest or smallest of a group; (*slang*) a girl or young woman; (*slang*) any person or thing.—Also *adj*.—*vt* to pamper.—*n* **bā´byhood**.—*adj* **bā´byish**.—*ns* **baby beef**, meat from a prime heifer or steer from one to two years old; **baby boomer**, a person born during the birthrate increase (the **baby boom**) after World War II; **baby buggy**, baby carriage; **baby carriage**, a light cotlike carriage for wheeling a baby about; **baby grand**, a small grand piano; **baby's breath**, a hardy perennial (genus *gypsophila*) with small, delicate white or pink flowers; cornflower; **bā´bysitter**, someone who remains in the house with a baby while its mother or usual guardian goes out.—*vi* **bā´by-sit**. [Prob imitative.]

baccalaureate [bak-a-lö´re-át] *n* the university degree of bachelor; a commencement address. [Low L *baccalaureus*.]

baccarat [bak´är-ä] *n* gambling card game in which object is to hold a combination of cards totaling 9, differing from chemin de fer in that players bet against the house. [Fr.]

bacchanal [bak´a-nál] *n* one who indulges in drunken revels.—*adj* relating to drinking or drunken revels—*also* **bacchanā´lian**.—*ns pl* **bacchanā´lia, bacch´anals**, drunken revels. [L *Bacchus*—Gr *Bakchos*, the god of wine.]

bachelor [bach´el-ór] *n* (*hist*) a young knight who followed the banner of another; an unmarried man; one who has completed a four-year course leading to a degree in the humanities (or science, etc.) at a college or a university.—*ns* **bach´elorhood; bach´elor's butt´on**, a plant (*Centaurea cyanus*) with daisylike white, pink, or blue flowers. [OFr *bacheler*—Low L *baccalārius*, a small farmer.]

bacillus [ba-sil´us] *n* any of a genus of a rod-shaped bacteria; (*loosely*) any bacterium;—*pl* **bacill´i**. [Low L *bacillus*, dim of *baculus*, a rod.]

back [bak] *n* the rear surface of the human body from neck to hip; the corresponding part in animals; a part that supports or fits the back; the part or surface of an object that is less used or less important, the part furthest from the front; (*sports*) a player or position behind the front line.—*adj* at the rear (*back teeth*); remote or inferior (*back streets*); of or for the past (*back pay*); backward.—*adv* at or toward the rear; to or toward a former condition, time, etc. (*I'll be back by six*); in return or requittal (*pay him back*); in reserve or concealment.—*vt* to move backward; to support; to bet on; to provide or be a back for.—*vi* to go backward.—*n* **back´ache**, an ache or pain in the back.—*vti* **back´bite´**, to slander (someone absent).—*ns* **backbiter; backboard**, a board at or forming the back of something, esp the board behind the basket in basketball; **backbone**, the spine; a main support; willpower, courage, etc.—*adj* **back´breaking**, very tiring; **back´door´**, indirect, concealed, devious.—*ns* **back´drop´**, a curtain, often scenic, at the back of a stage; background; **back´er**, a patron; one who bets on a contestant; **back´field**, (*football*) the players behind the line, esp the offensive unit; **back´fire´**, the burning out of a small area, as in a forest, to check the spread of a big fire; premature explosion in an internal-combustion engine; reverse explosion in a gun.—*vi* to explode as a backfire; to go wrong, as a plan.—*ns* **back´ground**, the distant part of a scene; surroundings, sounds, data, etc. behind or subordinate to something; one's training and experience; events leading up to something; **back´hand´**, a handwriting that slants to the left; a backhand stroke, blow, catch, etc.—*adj* made with the back of the hand turned outward; written in backhand.—*adv* in a backhand way.—*vt* to hit, catch, swing, etc. backhand.—*adj* **back´hand´ed**, backhand; not direct and open; devious.—*adv* in a backhanded way.—*ns* **back´ing**, something forming a back for support; support given to a person or cause; supporters, backers; **back´lash´**, sharp reaction; recoil; **back´log**, an accumulation or reserve.—*vti* to accumulate as a backlog.—*n* **back order**, an order not yet filled; **back´pack**, a knapsack, often on a light frame, worn by campers or hikers.—*vti* to wear, to carry in, a backpack.—*vi* **back´pedal**, to pedal backward, as in braking a bicycle; to move backward; retreat; withdraw.—*ns* **back´rest**, a support for the back; **back´seat´ driver**, one free of responsibility but full of advice; **back´side´**, the back part; the rump; **back´slapper**, (*inf*) an effusively friendly person.—*vi* **back´slide´**, to slide backward in morals, etc.—*ns* **back´slid´er; back´spin´**, backward spin in a ball, etc. making it bound backward upon hitting the ground.—*adj, adv* behind or off the stage, as in the wings or dressing rooms.—**back´stairs**, involving intrigue or scandal; secret.—*ns* **back´stitch**, a strong hand sewing stitch making a solid line on the right side of the seam; **back´stop´**, a screen, fence, etc. to keep balls from going too far, as behind the catcher in baseball; **back´stretch´**, the straight section of a racetrack opposite the homestretch; **back´stroke´**, a swimming stroke made while lying face upward; **back swimmer**, a water bug (family Notonectidae) that swims on its back; **back talk**, (*inf*) saucy or insolent retorts.—*adj* **back-to-back**, (*inf*) one right after another.—*vi* **back´track´**, to return by the same path; to retreat or recant.—*adj* **back´up, back-up**, standing by as an alternate or auxiliary; supporting.—*n* a backing up, esp an accumulation of support and help.—*adv* **backward, backwards**, toward the back; with the back foremost; in a way opposite the usual; into the past.—*adj* **backward**, turned toward the rear or opposite way; shy; slow or retarded.—*ns* **back´wash**, water or air moved forward by a ship, propeller, etc., a reaction caused by some event; **back´wa´ter**, water moved or held back by a dam, tide, etc.; stagnant water in an inlet, etc.; a backward place or condition.—*n pl* **back´woods´**, heavily wooded, remote areas; any remote, thinly populated area.—*adj* of or like the backwoods.—*n* **backwoods´man.—back and fill**, to maneuver the sails of a boat so as to keep clear of obstructions as it floats down with the current; to take opposite positions alternately; **back and forth**, backward and forward; **back down**, to withdraw from a position or claim; **back off** (*or* **away**, etc.), to move back (or away, etc.); **back out (of)**, to withdraw from an enterprise; to evade keeping a promise, etc.; **back up**, to support; to move backward; to accumulate because of restricted movement; **go back on**, (*inf*) to be disloyal to; to betray; to fail to keep (one's word, etc.); **turn one's back on**, to turn away from, as in contempt; to abandon. [OE *bæc*, Swed *bak*, Dan *bag*.]

backgammon [bak-gam´ón] *n* a game played by two persons on a board with dice and fifteen men or pieces each. [Perh OE *bæc*, back, and ME *gamen*, game.]

bacon [bā´kón] *n* salted and smoked meat from the back or sides of a hog.—**to bring home the bacon**, (*inf*) to achieve an object; provide material support. [OFr *bacon*, of Gmc origin; cf Ger *bache*.]

Baconian [bā-kōn´i-án] *adj* pertaining to Lord Bacon (1561–1626), or to his philosophy, or to the theory that he wrote Shakespeare's plays.

bacteria [bak-tē´ri-a] *n pl* miscroscopic unicellular organisms;—*sing* **bactēr´ium**.—*ns* **bacterēm´ia**, invasion of blood by bacteria without giving rise to symptoms of disease, but resulting in boils or sore throats; **bacter´icide**, an agent that destroys bacteria; **bacteriol´ogy**, the study of bacteria; **bacteriol´ogist; bactē´riophage** [fāj], a virus that infects bacteria; **bacterial endocarditis**, bacterial infection of the lining of the heart, esp the valves. [Gr *baktērion*, dim of *baktron*, a stick.]

bad [bad] *adj* not good; not as it should be; inadequate or unfit; unfavorable; rotten or spoiled; incorrect or faulty; wicked; immoral; mischievous; harmful; severe; ill; sorry, distressed (*he feels bad about it*); offensive;—*comparative* **worse**, *superlaive* **worst**.—*adv* (*inf*) badly.—*ns* anything bad; **badness; bad blood**, mutual emnity; **bad egg**, (*slang*) a mean or dishonest person (*also* **bad actor, bad apple, bad hat**, and **bad lot**.—*vti* **bad´mouth**, (*slang*) to find fault with.—*adj* **bad´temp´ered**, irritable.—**in bad**, (*inf*) in trouble or disfavor; **not bad**, (*inf*) quite good. [ME *badde*.]

bade [bad] *pt* of **bid**.

badge [baj] *n* a distinguishing mark or emblem. [ME *bage*; origin obscure.]

badger [baj´ėr] *na* burrowing hibernating animal (genera *Meles* and *Taxidea*) of the weasel family; the pelt or fur of the badger; **Badger**, nickname for a resident or inhabitant of Wisconsin.—*vt* to pester or annoy persistently.—**badger game**, method of extortion in which the victim is lured into a compromising sexual situation and then threatened with exposure unless money is paid. [Prob from **badge**, and suffix *-ard*, from the white mark like a badge on the badger's forehead.]

badinage [bad´in-äzh] *n* light playful talk, banter. [Fr *badinage*—*badin*, playful.]

badminton [bad´min-ton] *n* a court game for two or four players played with light rackets and a shuttlecock volleyed over a net. [From *Badminton*, a seat of the Duke of Beaufort.]

baffle [baf´l] *vt* to check or make ineffectual; to bewilder.—*n* **baffle plate**, a device for regulating the flow of liquids, gas, etc. [Prob Scottish; but cf Fr *beffler*, from OFr *befe*, mockery.]

bag [bag] *n* a usu. flexible container of paper, plastic, etc. that can be closed at the top; a satchel, suitcase, etc.; a purse; game taken in hunting; a baglike shape or part; (*slang*) an unattractive woman; (*slang*) one's special interest; (*baseball*) a base.—*vt* to make bulge; to capture; to kill in hunting; (*slang*) to get.—*vi* to swell; to hang loosely;—*pr p* **bagg´ing**; *pt p* **bagged**.—*n* **bag´ful**, as much as a bag will hold.—*adj* **bagg´y**, loose like a bag.—*ns* **bag lady**, (*slang*) a homeless poor woman who wanders city streets carrying her belongings in shopping bags; **bag´man**, an agent who collects or distributes illicitly gained money.—**in the bag**, (*slang*) certain; assured. [ME *bagge*.]

bagatelle [bag-a-tel´] *n* a trifle; a game played on a board with nine balls and a cue. [Fr,—It *bagatella*, a conjurer's trick, a trifle.]

bagel [bā´gl] *n* a ring-shaped bread roll, hard and glazed on the outside, soft in the center. [Yiddish.]

baggage [bag´ij] *n* traveler's luggage; a worthless or saucy woman; things that get in the way. [OFr *bagage*—*baguer*, to bind up.]

bagpipe [bag´pīp] *n* (often in *pl*) a wind instrument, consisting of a bag fitted with pipes.—*n* **bag´piper**. [**bag**, + **pipe**.]

Bahaism [bä-hä´izm] *n* a religious movement founded in 1863 stressing unity of all faiths, education, sexual equality, monogamy and the attainment of world peace.—*adj* **Bahai´**.—*n* **Baha´ist**.

bail[1] [bāl] *n* one who procures the release of an accused person by becoming security for his appearing in court; the security given; such a release.—*vt* to set a person free by giving security for him; to help out of financial or other difficulty (*with* **out**).—*adj* **bail´able.**—**bail bond**, a bond deposited as bail for an arrested person as surety that he will appear at his trial; **bails´man**, a person who gives bail for another. [OFr *bail*, jurisdiction—*baillier*, to have in custody; the word became associated with Norm Fr *bailler*, to deliver—L *bājulus*, a carrier.]

bail[2] [bāl] *vti* to dip out (water) from (a boat) (*usu. with* **out**).—*n* a bucket for dipping up water from a boat.—**bail out** to parachute from an aircraft. [Fr *baille*, a bucket, perh from Low L *bacula*, dim of *baca*, a basin.]

Bailey bridge [bā´li-brij] a bridge prefabricated for rapid erection. [Inventor's name.]

bailiff [bāl´if] *n* a minor official in some US courts, usu. a messenger or usher; in England, a district official or a steward of an estate. [OFr *baillif*, acc of *baillis*—Low L *bājulīvus*—*bājulus*, carrier, administrator; cf **bail** (1).]

bait [bāt] *n* food put on a hook to allure fish or make them bite; any allurement.—*vt* to set food as a lure; to set dogs on (a bear, badger, etc.); to worry, persecute, harass, esp by verbal attacks; to lure, to tempt; to entice.—**bait and switch**, a sales tactic in which a customer is attracted by an advertisement for a low-priced item but is then encouraged to buy a more expensive one. [ME *beyten*—Scand *beita*, to cause to bite—*bita*, to bite.]

baize [bāz] *n* a coarse woolen cloth. [Fr *baies*, pl of *bai*—L *badius*, bay-colored.]

bake [bāk] *vt* to dry and harden pottery by the heat of the sun or of fire; to cook food by dry heat, esp in an oven.—*vi* to work as a baker; to become firm through heat;—*pt p* **baked** [bākt]; *pr p* **bāk´ing**.—*ns* **bak´er**, one who bakes bread, etc.; **baker's dozen**, thirteen; **bak´ery**, a bakehouse, a place where bread, etc. is baked or sold; baked goods; **bak´ing**, the process by which bread is baked; **baking powder**, a leavening agent containing baking soda and an acid-forming substance; **baking soda**, sodium bicarbonate. [OE *bacan*; cog with Ger *backen*, to bake, Gr *phōgein*, to roast.]

baksheesh [bak´shēsh] *n* a present of money as a bribe or tip to expedite service. [Pers *bakhshīsh*.]

balalaika [bä-lä-lī´kä] *n* a Russian musical instrument with a triangular body and normally three strings. [Russ.]

balance [bal´ȧns] *n* an instrument for weighing, usu. formed of two dishes or scales hanging from a beam supported in the middle; act of weighing; equality of weight or power (as *the balance of power*); state of mental or emotional equilibrium; harmony among the parts of anything (as in a work of art); equality of debts and credits, or the sum required to make the two sides of an account equal; a remainder.—*vt* to weigh in a balance; to counterpoise; to compare; to bring into, or keep in, equilibrium; to make the debtor and creditor sides of an account agree.—*vi* to have equal weight or power, etc.; to be in equilibrium; to have the credits and debts equal.—*ns* **balance beam**, a narrow wooden beam supported in a horizontal position used for balancing feats in gymnastics; an event in gymnastic competitions; **bal´ance sheet**, a statement showing the financial status of a business; **bal´ance wheel**, a regulating wheel in a watch.—**balance of payments**, difference over a period between a nation's total receipts from foreign countries and its total payments to foreign countries; **in the balance**, not yet settled; **on balance**, all things considered. [Fr,—L *bilanx*, having two scales—*bis*, double, *lanx*, *lancis*, a dish or scale.]

balata [bal´a-ta] *n* the dried juice of a tree (*Manilkara bidentata*) of tropical America, used as a substitute for rubber and gutta-percha; the tree yielding this. [Sp, from South American Indian.]

balcony [balk´on-i] *n* a platform projecting from an upper story and enclosed by a railing; an upper floor of seats in a theater, etc. often projecting over the main floor. [It *balcōne*—*balco*, of Gmc origin; OHG *balcho*, Eng **balk**.]

bald [böld] *adj* lacking a natural or usual covering (as of hair, vegetation, or nap); having little or no tread; plain or blunt; marked with white; bare, unadorned.—*ns* **bald cypress**, a large swamp tree (*Taxodium distichum*) of the southen US yielding hard red wood; **bald eagle**, the common eagle (*Haliaeetus leucocephalus*) of the US, the national bird. **baldpate**, a No American freshwater duck (*Mareca americana*) with a white crown in the male;—*adjs* **bald faced**, brazen, shameless; **bald´ing**, growing bald.—*adv* **bald´ly**.—*n* **bald´ness**. [Orig 'shining', 'white')—Ir and Gael *bal*, 'white' spot.]

balderdash [böl´dėr-dash] *n* nonsense [Origin unknown.]

baldric [böld´rik] *n* a warrior's belt worn over the shoulder to support a sword, etc. [OFr *baldrei*—Low L *baldringus*, perh from L *balteus*, a belt.]

bale[1] [bāl] *n* a large bundle, esp a standardized quantity of goods, as raw cotton compressed and bound.—*vt* to make into bales. [ME *bale*, perh from OFr *bale*—OHG *balla, palla*, ball.]

bale[2] [bāl] *n* great evil; woe.—*adj* **bale´ful**, full of evil; malignant; deadly; ominous.—*adv* **bale´fully**.—*n* **balefulness**. [OE *bealu*; OHG *balo*; ON *böl*.]

baleen [ba-lēn´] *n* whalebone. [OFr *baleine*—L *bālaena*, whale.]

balk [bök] *n* an unploughed ridge of turf; hindrance, obstruction; blunder, error; (*baseball*) an illegal motion by the pitcher entitling base runners to advance one base.—*vt* to obstruct or foil.—*vi* to stop and refuse to move and act; to hesitate or recoil (at). [OE *balca*, ridge; OHG *balcho*, beam.]

ball[1] [böl] *n* anything spherical or nearly so; a globular or egg-shaped object to play with in tennis, football, etc.; any of several such games, esp baseball; a throw or pitch of a ball; a missile for a cannon, rifle, etc.; (*baseball*) a pitched ball that is not a hit and not a strike.—*vti* to form into a ball.—*ns* **ball bearing**, a device for lessening friction by making a revolving part turn on loose steel balls; one of the balls; **ball´boy, ball girl**, a tennis court attendant who retrieves balls for the players; **ball´cock**, a valve in a cistern, shut or opened by the rise or fall of a ball floating in the water; **ball game**, a game played with a ball; (*inf*) a set of circumstances; **ball´park**, a baseball stadium; **ball´point pen, ball´point, ball´-point**, a pen, having a tiny ball rotating against an inking cartridge as its writing tip.—**ball of fire**, a person with unusual drive and energy; **ball up**, (*slang*) to muddle, confuse; **on the ball**, (*slang*) alert, efficient. [ME *bal*, Scand *böllr*.]

ball[2] [böl] *n* a formal social dance; (*slang*) a good time.—*n* **ball´room**. [OFr *bal*—*baller*, to dance—Low L *ballāre*, referred by some to Gr *ballizein*.]

ballad [bal´ȧd] *n* narrative poem or song usu. anonymous, with simple words, short stanzas, and a refrain; a slow, sentimental, 'popular' song. [OFr *balade*, from Low L *ballāre*, to dance.]

ballade [bä-läd´] *n* a medieval form of music or a poem of one or more triplets of stanzas, each of seven or eight lines, including a refrain, usually concluding with an envoy; now frequently used of any poem in stanzas of equal length; the music for each stanza has the form A A B, A providing the music for the first two, and third on fourth lines. [An earlier spelling of **ballad**.]

ballast [bal´ȧst] *n* heavy matter placed in a ship or vehicle to keep it steady when it has no cargo; crushed rock or gravel, etc. used in railroad beds.—*vt* to furnish with ballast. [Prob Old Swed *barlast*—*bar*, bare, and *last*, load.]

ballerina [bal-ler-ēn´ȧ] *n* a female ballet-dancer;—*pl* **ballerin´as, balleri´ne**. [It]

ballet [bal´ā] *n* a theatrical exhibition of dancing and pantomimic action; the troupe that performs it.—*adj* **ballet´ic**.—*ns* **balletomane** [-et´ō-mān] ballet enthusiast; **balletomā´nia**. [Fr; dim of *bal*, a dance.]

ballista [bä-lis´tȧ] *n* a Roman military engine, in the form of a crossbow, which propelled large and heavy missiles.—*adj* **ballistic**, of or pertaining to forcible throwing of missiles; relating to projectiles (**ballistic missile**, a missile guided for only part of its course and falling as an ordinary projectile).—*n* **ballis´tics**, the science of projectiles. [L,—Gr *ballein*, to throw.]

balloon [ba-lōōn´] *n* a large airtight bag, that ascends when filled with a gas lighter than air; an airship with such a bag; a toy of similar form; balloon-shaped drawing enclosing words spoken in a strip cartoon.—*vt* to inflate.—*vi* to swell; to expand. [It *ballone*, augmentative of *balla*, ball.]

ballot [bal´ȯt] *n* a ticket or paper used in voting; act or right of voting, as by ballots; the total number of votes cast.—*vi* to vote;—*pr p* **ball´oting**; *pt p* **ball´oted**.—*n* **ball´ot box**, a box to receive ballots; the action or system of secret voting. [It *ballotta*, dim of *balla*, ball.]

ballyhoo [bal-i-hōō´ (or bal´-)] *n* noisy talk, sensational advertising, etc.—*vti* (*inf*) to promote with ballyhoo.

ballrag [bal´i-rag] *see* **bullyrag**.

balm [bäm] *n* a fragrant and healing ointment; anything that heals or soothes pain.—*adj* **balm´y**, fragrant; soothing; bearing balm.—**balm of Gilead** , balsam poplar. [OFr *basme* (*baume*)—L *balsamum. See* **balsam**.]

balmoral [bal-mor´ȧl] *n* a flat Scottish bonnet; a kind of boot lacing in front. [*Balmoral*, royal castle in Aberdeenshire, built by Queen Victoria.]

balogna [bä-lōn´ē] *n* a large sausage made of pork, veal, pork-suet, etc. sold ready for eating cold. [It.]

baloney [bȧ-lōn´ē] *n* (*inf*) foolish talk; nonsense.

balsa [bäl´sa, böl´sa] *n* a tropical American tree (*Ochroma lagopus*) with very light porous wood; its wood. [Sp, raft.]

balsam [böl´sam] *n* a preparation having a balsamic odor and used esp in medicine;—*ns* **balsam fir**, an American evergreen tree (*Abies balsamea*) grown widely for pulpwood, Christmas trees, and source of Canada balsam; **balsam poplar**, a N American poplar widely cultivated as a shade tree having buds thickly coated with an aromatic resin.—Also **balm of**

Gilead.—*vt* **bal´samize**, to embalm.—*adj* **balsam´ic**, soothing. [L *balsamum*—Gr *balsamon*; prob of Semitic origin.]

Baltic [böl´tik] *adj* denoting the Baltic Sea or the nations bordering it; of the group of Indo-European languages comprising Lithuanian and Latvian.—**Balto-slavic** [böl-to slav´ik] *n* branch of Indo-European languages spoken from eastern Europe to the Pacific comprising the Baltic and Slavic groups.

baluster [bal´us-tėr] *n* any of the small posts of a railing, as on a staircase.—*adj* **bal´ustered**.—*n* **bal´ustrade**, a row of balusters joined by a rail. [Fr *balustre*—Low L *balaustium*—Gr *balaustion*, the pomegranate flower, from the similarity of form.]

bambino [bam-bē´no] *n* a representation of the infant Jesus. [It.]

bamboo [bam-bōō´] *n* any of various often tropical woody grasses (genera *Bambusa, Arundinaria, Dendrocalamus, Phyllostachys, Sasa* and others) ranging in size from a foot to that of a tall tree used for building furniture, or utensils.—**bamboo curtain**, barrier of secrecy in Asian countries; tries; **bamboo shoots**, edible rhizome of certain bamboos. [Malay *bambu*.]

bamboozle [bam-bōō´zl] *vt* to deceive; to confound or mystify. [Origin unknown; first appears about 1700.]

ban [ban] *n* a condemnation by church authorities; a curse; an official prohibition; a strong public condemnation.—*vt* to forbid or prohibit, esp officially. [OE *bannan*, to summon.]

banal [bān´ál, ban´ál, ban-äl´] *adj* commonplace, trivial.—*n* **banality** [ban-al´-i-ti]. [Fr.]

banana [bȧ-nä´nȧ] *n* a herbaceous plant (genus *Musa*) bearing its fruit in compact, hanging bunches.—**banana oil**, a colorless, liquid acetate $C_7H_{14}O_2$ of amyl alcohol having a pleasant fruity odor and used as a solvent and for making artificial fruit essences; **banana republic**, (*inf*) a small country, esp in Central America, that is dominated by foreign interests; **banana seat**, an elongated bicycle saddle; **banana split**, ice cream served on a lengthwise sliced banana and topped with syrup, nuts, and whipped cream.—**go bananas**, (*slang*) go crazy. [Sp or Port from the native name on the Guinea coast.]

band[1] [band] *n* a strip of cloth, etc., to bind round anything; a stripe crossing a surface, distinguished by its color or appearance; (*pl*) the pair of linen strips hanging down in front from the collar, worn as part of clerical, legal, or academic dress; a division of a long-playing phonograph record; (*radio*) a group of wavelengths.—*n* **band´age**, a strip to bind up a wound or fracture, etc.—*vt* to bind with such.—*ns* **Band-Aid**, trade name for a small bandage of gauze and adhesive tape; **band´box**, a thin box for holding millinery, etc.; **band saw**, an endless saw, a toothed steel belt. [ME *bande*—OFr *bande*, of Gmc origin.]

band[2] [band] *n* a number of persons bound together for any common purpose; a troop of conspirators, etc.; a body of musicians, esp brass and percussion players.—*vti* to unite for some purpose.—*ns* **band´lead´er**, the conductor of a band (as a dance band); **band´master**, conductor of a military or concert band; **bands´man**, member of a band of musicians; **band´stand**, a platform, esp outdoors, for accommodating a band of musicians; **band´wagon**, a wagon that carries the band in a parade.—**on the bandwagon**, (*inf*) on the popular or apparently winning side. [Fr *bande*, but with changed sense; cf **band** (1).]

bandanna, bandana [ban-dän´ȧ] *n* a large colored handkerchief. [Hindustani *bāndhnū*, a mode of dyeing.]

bandeau [ban-dō´] *n* a narrow ribbon; a narrow brassiere.—*pl* **bandeaux** [ban-dōz´]. [Fr.].

banderole, banderol [ban´de-rōl] *n* a long, narrow forked flag or streamer; a long scroll bearing an inscription. [Fr.]

bandicoot [ban´di-kōōt] *n* any of several very large rats (*Nesoleia* and related genera) found in India and Ceylon; any of a family (Peramelidae) of small marsupials in Australia, etc. [Dravidian *pandikokku*, pig-rat.]

bandied [ban´did] *pt, pt p* of **bandy** (2).

bandit [ban´dit] *n* an outlaw; a brigand;—*pl* **band´its**. [It *bandito*—Low L *bannīre, bandīre*, to proclaim.]

bandolier, bandoleer [ban-do-lēr´] *n* a belt worn over the chest, esp for holding cartridges. [OFr *bandouillere*—It *bandoliera*—*banda*, a band.]

bandy[1] [ban´di] *n* a game similar to hockey and believed to be its forerunner.

bandy[2] [ban´di] *vt* to bat (as a tennis ball) to and fro; to pass (rumours, etc.) freely; to exchange words, esp angrily);—*pt, pt p* **ban´died**.—*n* **ban´dying**. [Origin obscure.]

bandy[3] [ban´di] *adj* (of legs) bent outward at the knee.—*adj* **ban´dy-legged´**. [Origin obscure.]

bane [bān] *n* destruction, mischief, woe; poison; source or cause of evil.—*adj* **bane´ful**, destructive.—*adv* **bane´fully**.—*n* **bane´fulness**. [OE *bana*, a murderer; ON *bani*, death.]

bang[1] [bang] *n* a heavy blow; a sudden loud noise; (*inf*) a burst of vigor; (*slang*) a thrill.—*vt* to beat; to strike violently; to slam.—*vi* to make a loud noise; to hit noisily or sharply.—*vt* **bang up**, to damage.—*adj* **bang-up**, (*inf*) very good, excellent. [Scan *banga*, to hammer; cf Ger *bengel*, a cudgel.]

bang[2] [bang] *vt* to cut hair short and straight.—*n* (usu. *pl*) banged hair over the forehead. [Origin unknown.]

bangle [bang´gl] *n* a bracelet worn on arms or legs. [Hindustani *bangrī*].

banish [ban´ish] *vt* to condemn to exile; to drive away; to get rid of.—*n* **ban´ishment**, exile. [Fr *bannir*— Low L *bannīre*, to proclaim; of same origin as **ban**.]

banister, bannister [ban´istėr] *n* the railing or supporting balusters in a staircase.

banjo [ban´jō] a stringed musical instrument with a body like a shallow drum, long fretted neck, and usu. six strings that are plucked. [Negro pronunciation of Fr *bandore*, or *pandore*—L *pandūra*—Gr *pandoura*.]

bank[1] [bangk] *n* a mound or ridge; the margin of a river; rising ground in a lake or the sea; the lateral, slanting turn of an aircraft.—*vt* to pile up; to cover (a fire) so as to lessen the rate of combustion; to make (an aircraft) slant laterally on a turn; to make (a billiard ball) recoil from a cushion. [ME *banke*, of Scand origin; cog with **bank** (2 and 3), **bench**.]

bank[2] [bangk] *n* a row of oars; a row or tier, as of keys in a keyboard.—*vt* to arrange in a row or tier. [OFr *banc*, of Gmc origin, cog with **bank** (1).]

bank[3] [bangk] *n* a place where money or other valuable material, eg blood, data (**blood, data bank**) is deposited until required; an institution for the keeping, lending, exchanging etc., of money.—*vti* to deposit in a bank.—*ns* **bank account**, money deposited in a bank and credited to the depositor; **bank´-book**, a book in which record is kept of money deposited in, or withdrawn from, a bank, a passbook; **bank´er**, one who owns or manages a bank; the stakeholder in certain gambling games; a man employed in cod fishery on the Newfoundland banks; a sculptor's or mason's workbench; **bank hol´iday**, a period in which banks are closed, often by government fiat; **bank´ing**, the business of a banker.—*adj* pertaining to a bank.—*ns* **bank´note**, a note issued by a bank, which passes as money, being payable to bearer on demand; **bank´roll´**, a supply of money.—*vt* (*inf*) to supply with money; to finance—**bank on**, to rely or depend on. [Fr *banque*, of Gmc origin, cog with **bank** (1), (2).]

bankrupt [bangk´rupt] *n* a person, etc. legally declared unable to pay his debts; one who becomes insolvent; one lacking a particular thing (*a moral bankrupt*).—*vt* to reduce to bankruptcy.—Also *adj*.—*n* **bank´ruptcy**, the state of being, or act of becoming, bankrupt; utter impoverishment or complete failure. [Fr *banqueroute*, It *banca rotta*—L *ruptus*, broken.]

banner [ban´ėr] *n* a flag or ensign; a headline running across a newspaper page; a strip of cloth bearing a slogan or emblem carried between poles in a parade or stretched between lampposts across a street.—*adj* prominent in support of a political party; excelling (*a banner year*).—*adj* **bann´ered**, furnished with banners. [OFr *banere*—Low L *bandum, bannum*; cog with **band** and **bind**.]

banner ad [ban´ėr ad] *n* (*comput*) an advertisement which appears on websites.

bannerol, banner roll [ban´ėr-ōl] *n* a banderol.

bannock [ban´ȯk] *n* a usu. unleavened biscuit made with oatmeal or barley meal; (*New England*) thin cornbread baked on a griddle. [OE *bannuc*.]

banns [banz] *n pl* a proclamation of intention, esp in church, to marry. [From **ban**.]

banquet [bangk´wėt, -wit] *n* a feast; an elaborate and sometimes ceremonial dinner, in honor of a person or occasion.—*vt* to give a feast to.—*vi* to fare sumptuously.—*ns* **banq´ueter; banq´ueting; banq´uet room**, a large room (as in a hotel or restaurant) suitable for banquets. [Fr,—*banc*, bench, like It *banchetto*, from *banco*.]

banquette [bang-kėt´] *n* a raised gunner's platform behind a parapet; an upholstered bench. [Fr.]

banshee [ban´shē] *n* a female fairy in Irish folklore who wails and shrieks before a death in the family. [Ir *bean sídhe*—Old Ir *ben síde*, woman of the fairies.]

bantam [ban´tȧm] *n* any of several dwarf breeds of domestic fowl; a small, aggressive person.—*adj* like a bantam.—*n* **ban´tamweight**, a professional boxer weighing 112–118 lbs; amateur boxer weighing 112–119 lbs; a wrestler usu. weighing 115–126 lbs. [Prob *Bantam* in Java.]

banter [bant´ėr] *vt* assail with good-humored raillery.—*vi* to exchange banter (with someone).—*n* humorous raillery; jesting.

bantling [bant´ling] *n* a very young child. [Prob Ger *bänkling*, bastard—*bank*, bench.]

Bantu [ban´tōō] *n* member of a group of Negroid peoples in equatorial and southern Africa;—*pl* **-tu,-s**; group of languages of the Niger-Congo group of which Swahili has the largest number of speakers.—Also **Bantic**.—*adj* of the Bantu. [African, meaning 'people'.]

banyan [ban´yȧn] *n* an Indian fig tree (*Ficus benglensis*) with vast rooting branches. [Port *banian*, perh through Ar and Hindustani, from Sans *vanija*, a merchant.]

baobab [bā´o-bab] *n* a broad-trunked tropical tree of Africa and India (*Adonsonia digitata*) marked by angular branches and edible gourdlike fruit. [African.]

baptize [bap-tīz´] *vt* to administer baptism to.—*n* **bap´tism**, immersion in, or sprinkling with, water as a rite of admitting a person to a Christian church; an initiating experience.—*adj* **baptis´mal**.—*adv* **baptis´mally**.—*ns* **Bap´tist**, member of Protestant Christian denomination holding that the true church is of believers only, who are all equal, that the only authority is the Bible, and that adult baptism by immersion is necessary; **bap´tistery**, a place where baptism is administered.—**baptism of fire**, any trying ordeal, as a young soldier's first experience of being under fire; spiritual baptism by a gift of the Holy Spirit. [Gr. *baptizein*—*baptein*, to dip in water.]

bar[1] [bär] *n* a rod of any solid substance; a counter across which alcoholic drinks are served; a place with such a counter; an oblong piece, as of soap; anything that obstructs or hinders; a band or strip; a law court, esp that part where the lawyers sit; lawyers collectively; the legal profession; (*mus*) a vertical line dividing a staff into measures; (*mus*) a measure.—*vt* to fasten or secure, as with a bar; to hinder or exclude; to oppose;—*pr p* **barr´ing**; *pt p* **barred**.—*prep* excluding, excepting (eg *bar none*).—*ns* **bar´bell, bar bell**, a metal bar with weights attached for weight-lifting exercises; **bar´code, bar code**, universal product code; **bar´-graph**, a diagram representing quantities by means of rectangles of different sizes; **bar´keeper**, an owner of a barroom; a bartender; **bar´room**, a room or place whose principal business is the sale of alcoholic drinks; **bar´tend´er**, a man who serves liquor at a bar etc.—*prep* **barr´ing**, excepting, saving.—**cross the bar**, to die. [OFr *barre*—Low L *barra*.]

bar[2] [bar] *n* a unit of pressure equal to one million dynes per square centimeter; the absolute cgs unit equal to one dyne per square centimeter. [Gr *baros*, weight.]

barb[1] [bärb] *n* a beardlike growth; the jag near the point of a fishhook, etc.; a wounding or pointed remark.—*vt* to provide with a barb.—*adj* **barbed**.—*n* **barbed wire, barb´wire´**, wire with barbs at close intervals. [Fr *barbe*—L *barba*, a beard.]

barb[2] [bärb] *n* a swift kind of horse of No Africa, related to Arabians. (See **Barbary ape**.)

barb[3] [bärb] *n* (*slang*) barbiturate.

barbarous [bär´bȧr-us] *adj* uncivilized; primitive; brutal.—*adj* **barbār´ian**.—*n* an uncivilized savage, primitive man; a cruel, brutal man.—*adj* **barbăr´ic**.—*vti* **bar´barize**, to make or become barbarous.—*ns* **bar´barism**, word or expression that is not standard; the state of being primitive or uncivilized; a barbarous act or custom; **barbăr´ity**, cruelty.—*adv* **bar´barously**.—*n* **bar´barousness**. [L,—Gr *barbaros*, foreign, lit stammering, from the unfamiliar sound of foreign tongues.]

Barbary ape [bär´bȧr-i āp] *n* the small tailless ape (*Macaca sylvana*) found in N Africa and Gibraltar. [*Barbary*, the country of the Berbers in N Africa, and **ape**.]

barbecue [bärb´e-kū] *vt* to roast or broil over an open fire (as a pit, a special container, etc.)—*n* a hog, steer, etc. roasted over an open fire; any meat broiled on a spit; a party, picnic, or restaurant featuring this.—**barbecue sauce**, a highly seasoned sauce of vinegar, spices etc. [Sp *barbacoa*—Haitian *barbacòa*, a framework of sticks set upon posts.]

barber [bärb´er] *n* one who shaves faces and cuts hair.—*vti* to cut the hair (of), shave, etc.—*adj* **barbershop**, of a style of unaccompanied group singing, usu. marked by conventionalized close harmony.—*n* a barber's place of business. [OFr *barbeor*—L *barba*, a beard.]

barberry [bär´bėr-i] *n* a genus (*Berberis*) of thorny shrubs with yellow flowers and red berries. [Low L *berberis*; not from *berry*.]

barbican [bär´bi-kan] *n* a tower at the gate of a fortress, esp the outwork defending the drawbridge. [OFr *barbacane*; perh of Ar or Pers origin.]

barbital [bär´bi-tȧl] *n* a white, crystalline, addictive hypnotic.—*n* **barbiturate**, a salt or ester of an organic acid (**barbituric acid**), esp. one used as a sedative, hypnotic or antispasmodic.

barcarole, barcarolle [bär´ka-rōl] *n* a Venetian boatsong; a musical composition in 6/8 or 12/8 meter suggesting the rocking motion of a boat. [It *barcarōla*, boat-song—*barca*, a boat.]

bard [bärd] *n* a poet and singer among the ancient Celts; a poet.—*adj* **bard´ic**. [Gael and Ir *bàrd*.]

bare [bār] *adj* uncovered; naked; open to view; poor, scanty; unadorned; without furnishings; mere or by itself.—*vt* to strip or uncover.—*adj* **bare´back**, on a horse with no saddle.—Also *adv*.—*adj* **bare´faced**, with the face uncovered; shameless.—*adv* **bare´facedly**.—*n* **bare´facedness**.—*adjs* **bare´foot, -ed**, having the feet bare; **bare´hand´ed**, with hands uncovered; without weapons, etc.—Also *adv*.—*adj* **bare´headed; bare´-legged**.—*adv* **bare´ly**, scantily; only just; scarcely.—*n* **bare´ness**. [OE *bær*; Ger *baar, bar*.]

bare [bār] old *pt* of **bear**.

bargain [bär´g(i)n] *n* a contract or agreement; an agreement with regard to its worth (*a bad bargain*); something sold at a price favorable to the buyer.—*n* **bar´gainer**.—*vi* to haggle; to make a bargain.—**into the bargain**, besides; **bargain for** (or **on**), to expect; to count on; **bargain counter**, a store counter where goods at reduced prices are displayed. [OFr *bargaigner*—Low L *barcāniāre*; perh from **barca**, a boat.]

barge [bärj] *n* flat-bottomed freight boat, used on rivers and canals; a large pleasure or state boat.—*vi* to move clumsily; to enter rudely or abruptly (in or into). [OFr *barge*—Low L *barga*.]

barge-board [bärj´-bōrd, börd] *n* a board extending along the edge of the gable of a house to cover the rafters and keep out the rain. [Perh from Low L *bargus*, a gallows.]

barilla [bȧr-il´a] *n* an impure sodium carbonate obtained by burning certain seaside plants (*Salsola kali* and *S soda*) formerly used in making soap, glass, etc. [Sp.]

baritone [bar´i-tōn] *n* a male voice between bass and tenor; a singer with such a voice; a brass or woodwind instrument having a range between tenor and bass. [Through Fr,—Gr *barys*, heavy, deep, and *tonos*, tone.]

barium [bā´ri-ŭm] a metallic element (symbol Ba; at wt 137.3; at no 56).—**barium meal**, a preparation of barium sulfate; **barium sulfate**, a white insoluble fine heavy powder which is opaque to X-rays, swallowed by patient before X-ray of alimentary canal. [From **baryta**.]

bark[1] [bärk] *n* the abrupt cry of a dog, wolf, etc.; any similar sound.—*vi* to yelp like a dog; to speak sharply.— **to bark up the wrong tree**, to direct one's attack, energy, etc. in the wrong direction. [OE *beorcan*.]

bark[2], **barque** [bärk] *n* a three-masted vessel whose mizzenmast is fore-and-aft rigged; any boat propelled by sails or oars. [Fr *barque*—Low L *barca*.]

bark[3] [bärk] *n* the outside covering of a woody stem.—*vt* to strip or peel the bark from; (*inf*) to scrape; to skin (the knees, etc.) [Scand *börkr*; Dan *bark*.]

barley [bär´li] *n* a hardy grain used for food and for making malt liquors and spirits.—*n* **bar´leycorn**, a grain of barley; a former unit of length equal to one-third of an inch. [OE *bærlic* (*adj*), from the same root as *bere*, with suffix *-lic*.]

barm [bärm] *n* the yeast formed on fermenting malt drinks. [OE *beorma*; Dan *bärme*, Ger *bärme*.]

Barmecide [bär´mė-sīd] *adj* providing only the illusion of abundance.—*adj* **Barmecī´dal**. [From an imaginary feast given to a beggar in the *Arabian Nights* by one of the *Barmecide* family.]

bar mitzvah [bär mitz´va] *n* (*Judaism*) the ceremony marking the 13th birthday of a boy, who then assumes full religious obligations; the boy himself.

barn [bän] *n* a farm building in which grain, hay, etc., are stored.—*n* **barn dance**, a social dance featuring several dance forms (as square dancing).—*ns* and *adjs* **barn´-door, barn´-yard**.—*ns* **barn´-owl**, a species (*Tyto alba*) of owl, generally buff-colored above, white below.—*vi* **barn´storm**, to tour rural districts putting on shows or making political speeches.—*vt* to travel across while barn-storming. [OE *bere-ern*, contracted *bern*, from *bere*, barley, *ern*, a house.]

barnacle [bär´na-kl] *n* any of numerous marine shellfish that, in the adult stage, adhere to rocks and ship bottoms; a European goose (*Branta leucopsus*) that breeds in the Arctic, also **bar´nacle goose**. [OFr *bernaque*—Low L *bernaca*.]

barometer [bar-om´et-ėr] *n* an instrument by which the pressure of the atmosphere is measured, and changes of weather indicated; anything that marks change.—*adj* **baromet´ric**.—*adv* **barometrically** [Gr *baros*, weight, *metron*, measure.]

baron [bar´on] *n* a title of rank, the lowest in the British peerage; a powerful businessman; the indeterminate rank of a European nobleman.—*ns* **bar´onage**, the whole body of barons; **bar´oness**, a baron's wife, ex-wife, or widow; a lady holding a baronial title in her own right.—*adj* **barōn´ial**, pertaining to a baron; stately, ample.—*n* **bar´ony**, the territory, rank, or dignity of a baron; a field of activity dominated by an individual or special group; a vast private landholding. [OFr *barun, -on*—Low L *barō, -ōnis*; in the Romance tongues the word meant a man as opposed to a woman, a strong man, a warrior.]

baronet [bar´on-et] *n* the lowest British hereditary title.—*ns* **bar´onetage**, the whole body of baronets; **bar´onetcy**, the rank of baronet. [Dim of **baron**.]

baroque [bar-ōk´] *adj* grotesque, extravagant, whimsical; extravagantly ornamented, esp in architecture and decorative art. [Fr *baroque*; ety uncertain.]

barouche [ba-rōōsh´] *n* a double-seated four-wheeled carriage with a folding top. [Ger *barutsche*—It *baroccio*—L *bis*, twice, *rota*, a wheel.]

barque *see* **bark** (2).

barrack [bar´ȧk] *n* (usu. *pl*) a building for soldiers; a huge bare building. [Fr *baraque* (It *baracca*, Sp *barraca*, a tent).]

barracouta [bar-a-kōō´ta] *n* a large marine food fish (*Thyrsites atun*). [Amer Sp.]

barracuda [bar-a-kōō´dȧ] *n* a fierce, food fish (*Sphyraena barracuda*) of eastern Atlantic waters, a menace to bathers and prized by anglers. [Sp *baracuta*.]

barrage [bar-äzh´] *n* an artificial dam across a river; heavy artillery fire; continuous and heavy delivery (*a barrage of protests*).—*vt* to deliver a barrage against.—**barrage balloon**, a small captive balloon used to support wires or nets to deter low-flying aircraft. [Fr *barrage*—*barre*, bar.]

barratry [bar´ȧ-tri] *n* the fraudulent breach of duty by the master of a ship; the stirring up of law suits.

barrel [bar´ėl] *n* a round wooden vessel made of curved staves bound with hoops; the quantity which such a vessel contains; anything long and hollow, as the barrel of a gun.—*vt* to put in a barrel.—*adj* **barr´elled**, having a barrel or barrels; placed in a barrel.—*n* **barr´el-or´gan**, a mechanical instrument for playing tunes by means of a revolving barrel or cylinder set with pins which operate keys and thus open the valves and admit air to the pipes; also **hurdy-gurdy**. [Fr *baril*—Low L *barile, barillus*, possibly from *barra*, bar.]

barren [bar´ėn] *adj* incapable of bearing offspring; unfruitful; dull, stupid; unprofitable.—*adv* **barr´enly**.—*n* **barr´enness**. [OFr *barain, brahain, brehaing*, perh from *bar*, man, as if 'male-like, not producing offspring'.]

barrette [bar-et´] *n* a bar or clasp for holding a girl's hair in place. [Fr.]

barricade [bar´ik-ād] *n* a temporary fortification raised to block a street; an obstruction.—*vt* to block with a barricade. [Fr *barricade* or Sp *barricada*—perh Fr *barrique* or Sp *barrica*, a cask, the first street barricades being of casks filled with stones, etc.]

barrier [bar´i-ėr] *n* a fence or other structure to bar passage, prevent access, control crowds, etc.—*n* **barr´ier reef**, a coral reef fringing a coast with a navigable channel inside. [OFr *barrière*—Low L *barrāria*—*barra*, bar.]

barrister [bar´is-tėr] *n* one who is qualified to plead at the bar in an English or Irish law-court. [From *barra*, bar, the suffix being unexplained.]

barrow[1] [bar´ō] *n* a small hand-cart used to bear or convey a load. [ME *barewe*, from an assumed OE form *bearwe*—*beran*, to bear.]

barrow[2] [bar´ō] *n* a burial mound. [OE *beorg*; cog with Ger *berg*.]

barter [bär´tėr] *vt* to give (one thing) in exchange (for another); to give (away for some unworthy gain).—*vi* to traffic by exchanging.—*n* traffic by exchange of commodities. [Prob from OFr *barat*, deceit.]

bartizan [bär´ti-zan] *n* a parapet or battlement. [Apparently an adaptation by Sir Walter Scott of Scot *bertisene*, for *bratticing*. *See* **brattice**.]

Baruch [bå-rōōk, bä-] *n* (*Bible*) 30th book of the Old Testament in the Douay Version.

baryon [bar´i-on] *n* elementary particles, as nucleons. [Gr *barys*, heavy.]

baryta [bä-rī´ta] *n* barium oxide, barium hydroxide.—*n* **barytes** [bä-rī´tēz], barium sulfate. [From Gr *barys*, heavy.]

basalt [bas´ölt, bas-ölt´] *n* hard, compact, dark-colored igneous rock.—*adj* **basalt´ic**. [L *basaltes*—an African word.]

base[1] [bās] *n* that on which a thing rests; bottom, foundation, support; the chief or essential ingredient; a place from which operations are conducted; a fixed goal in games such as baseball; the part of a word to which affixes are attached; (*math*) in arithmetic, the number which raised to various powers, forms the main counting unit of a system; in logarithms, the number which when raised to a certain power will produce a certain number; (*chem*) a substance that reacts with an acid to form a salt.—*vt* to found (on);—*pr p* **bās´ing**; *pt p* **based** [bāst].—*adj* **bās´al**.—*n* **basal metabolism**, the quantity of energy used by an organism at rest.—*adj* **base´less**, without a base; unfounded.—*ns* **base´ball**, an outdoor game played with a bat and ball between two teams of nine players on a field with four bases arranged in a diamond in which the object is to score runs; the ball used in this game; **base´line** (*surveying*) measured line through survey area from which triangulations are made; the line at each end of a games court that marks the limit of play; (*baseball*) the line between any two consecutive bases; **baseman** (*baseball*) an infielder stationed at first, second, or third base; **base´ment**, the part of a building that is partly or wholly below ground level; **base pay**, the basic rate of pay, not counting overtime pay, etc.; **base runner** (*baseball*) a batter who has reached, or is trying to reach base.—*adj* **bās´ic**, fundamental; (*chem*) alkaline.—*n* a basic principle, factor, etc.—*n* **basic slag**, a by-product in the manufacture of steel, used as manure.—**Basic English**, term for British American scientific international commercial English devised by C K Ogden consisting of 850 selected English words and simple operating rules. [Fr,—L *basis*—Gr, *ba-*, in *bainein*, to go.]

base[2] [bās] *adj* low in place, value, estimation or principle; mean, vile, worthless; menial.—*adj* **base´born**, illegitimate.—*adv* **base´ly**.—*n* **base´ness**.—**base metal**, any metal other than the precious metals. [Fr *bas*—Low L *bassus*, thick, fat.]

baseball [bās´böl] *see* **base** (1).

bash [bash] *vt* (*inf*) to hit hard.—*n* (*slang*) a party. [Prob Scand.]

bashaw [ba-shö´] *n see* **pasha**.

bashful [bash´fōōl, -fl] *adj* easily embarrassed, shy.—*adv* **bash´fully**.—*n* **bash´fulness**. [Obs *bash* for **abash**.]

BASIC [bās´ik] *n* a simple language for programming and interacting with a computer. [Beginners' All-purpose Symbolic Instruction Code.]

basil [baz´il] *n* a genus (*Ocimum*) of aromatic plants, the leaves of which are used to season food. [OFr *basile*—L *basilisca*—Gr *basilikon*, royal.]

basilica [baz´il´ik-a] *n* a church with a broad nave, side aisles, and an apse; (*RC Church*) a church with special ceremonial rites.—*adj* **basil´ican**. [L *basilica*—Gr *basilikē* (*oikia*), a royal (house), from *basileus*, a king.]

basilisk [baz´il-isk] *n* a fabulous creature with fiery death-dealing eyes; any of several crested tropical American lizards (genus *Basiliscus*) noted for their ability to run on their hind legs. [Gr *basiliskos*, dim of *basileus*, a king.]

basin [bās´n] *n* a wide shallow container for liquid; its contents; a sink; any large hollow, often with water in it; the area drained by a river and its tributaries. [OFr *bacin*—Low L *bachīnus*, perh from *bacca*, a vessel.]

basinet [bas´i-net] *n* a light helmet worn with a visor. [Dim of **basin**.]

basis [bās´is] *n* a base or foundation; a principal constituent; a fundamental principle or theory.—*pl* **bas´es** [bās´ēz]. [L; *see* **base** (1).]

bask [bäsk] *vi* to lie in warmth or sunshine.—Also *fig*. [ON *bathask*, to bathe oneself.]

basket [bäs´kėt] *n* a receptacle made of interwoven cane, wood strips, etc.; (*basketball*) the goal, a round, open hanging net; a scoring toss of the ball through it.—*ns* **bas´ketball**, a team game in which goals are scored by throwing a ball into a basket; this ball; **bas´ketful**, as much as fills a basket; **bas´ket hilt**, a sword hilt with a protective covering like a basket; **Basket Maker**, an ancient culture of the plateau area of the south western US that preceded the Pueblo; **basket weave**, a weave of fabrics where two or more warp or weft threads are interlaced; **bas´ketwork**, work that is woven like a basket.

Basque [bask] *n* one of a people inhabiting the western Pyrenees, in Spain or France, or their language which is a relic of a non-Indo-European language; a continuation of the bodice a little below the waist.—*adj* relating to the Basques or their language or country. [Fr *Basque*—Low L *Vasco*, an inhabitant of *Vasconia*, whence *Gascony*.]

bas-relief [bä´-re-lēf´] *n* sculptures in which the figures do not stand far out from the ground on which they are formed. [Fr *bas-relief. See* **base**, (2), and **relief**.]

bass[1] [bās] *n* the range of the lowest male voice; a singer or instrument with this range; a double-bass; a low, deep sound.—*adj* of, for, or in the range of a bass.—**bass clef**, clef that places the F below middle C on the fourth line of the staff. [From **base** (2).]

bass[2] [bas] *n* any of numerous freshwater food and game fishes of N America (esp families Centrarchidae and Serranidae). [OE *bærs*; cf Ger *bars*, perch.]

basset hound [bas´ėt] *n* a breed like a dachshund, but bigger. [Fr *bas*, low.]

bassinet [bas´i-net] *n* a kind of basket with a hood, used as a cradle. [Fr, dim of *bassin*, a basin.]

basso [bäs´sō] *n* a bass singer, esp one singing opera. [It.]

bassoon [bas-ōōn´] *n* an orchestral woodwind instrument of the oboe family pitched two octaves below the oboe with a tube bent back on account of its great length.—*ns* **bassoon´ist; double bassoon**, sounds an octave lower. [It *bassone*, augmentative of *basso*, low, from root of **base** (2), **bass** (1).]

bass viol [bās-vī´ol] *n* viola da gamba; double bass. See **bass** (1), and **viol**.]

bast [bast] *n* phloem; bast fiber. [OE bæst; Ger *bast*.]

bastard [bas´tärd] *n* a child born of parents not married; something of dubious origin.—*adj* born out of wedlock; not genuine; false.—*vt* **bas´tardize**, to prove or declare to be a bastard; to reduce to a lower state or condition.—*n* **bas´tardy**, the state of being a bastard. [Fr *bâtard*; OFr *fils de bast*, son of the pack-saddle.]

baste[1] [bāst] *vt* to beat severely.—*n* **bast´ing**. [Prob conn with ON *beysta*, Dan *böste*, to beat.]

baste[2] [bāst] *vt* to drop fat over (roasting meat, etc.). [Ety unknown.]

baste[3] [bāst] *vt* to sew with long loose stitches as a temporary seam. [OFr *bastir*, from OHG *bestan*, to sew.]

Bastille [bast-ēl´] *n* an old fortress in Paris long used as a state prison, and demolished (1789) in the French Revolution; **bastille**, a prison. [OFr *bastir*, to build.]

bastinado [bast-in-ād´ō], **bastinade** [bast-in-ād] *vt* to beat repeatedly with a baton or stick. [Sp *bastonada*, Fr *bastonnade*—*baston, bâton. See* **baton**.]

bastion [bast´yȯn] *n* a kind of tower at the angle of a fortification; any strong defense.—*adj* **bast´ioned**. [OFr *bastir*, to build.]

bat[1] [bat] *n* a heavy stick; a club for baseball, etc.; a turn at batting (*at bat*); (*inf*) a blow; a paddle used in various games (as table tennis).—*vt* to hit as with a bat; to advance (a base runner) by batting; to consider or discuss in detail.—*vi* to strike or hit with a bat; to take one's turn at bat; to wander aimlessly;—*pr p* **batt´ing**; *pt p* **batt´ed**.—*ns* **bat´boy**, a boy employed to look after the equipment of a baseball team; **bat´ter**, one who wields the bat at baseball, etc.; layers of raw cotton, wool, etc. for lining clothing, quilts, etc.; a blanket of thermal insulation (as fiberglass); **bat´ting**, management of the bat in games.—**off one's own bat**, through one's own efforts; **off the bat**, immediately. [Perh from OE *bat* (a doubtful form), prob Celt *bat* staff.]

bat[2] [bat] *n* any of an order (Chiroptera) of nocturnal, mouselike, flying mammals with forelimbs modified to form wings.—*adj* **batt´y**, bat-like; bat-infested; (*inf*) crazy. [ME *bakke*, apparently from Scand.]

bat[3] [bat] *vt* to wink.—**not to bat an eyelid**, to show no emotion. [Prob OF *batre*, to beat.]

batch [bach] *n* the quantity of bread etc. baked at one time; one set, group, etc.; an amount of work for processing by a computer in a single run. [ME *bache*—**bake**.]

bath [bäth] *n* water for immersing the body; a bathing; a receptacle or a house for bathing;—*ns* **bath´robe**, a loose-fitting garment of absorbent fabric for wear before and after bathing or as a dressing gown; **bath´room**, a room containing a bathtub and usu. a washbowl and toilet; a toilet; **bath´tub**, a usu. fixed tub for bathing. [OE *bæth*, cog with Ger *bad*.]

bathe [bāTH] *vt* to moisten with any liquid.—*vi* to take a bath; to go swimming; to become immersed.—*ns* **bath´er; bath´ing beauty**, a woman in a bathing suit who is a contestant in a beauty contest; **bath´ing suit**, a swimsuit. [OE *bathian*.]

bathometer [bath-om´et-ėr] *n* an instrument for ascertaining the depth of water. [Gr *bathos*, depth, *metron*, measure.]

bathos [bā´thos] *n* a ludicrous descent from the elevated to the ordinary in writing or speech.—*adj* **bathetic** [bathet´ik]. [Gr, depth.]

bathyscaphe, bathyscaph [bath´i-skāf] *n* a navigable submersible ship having a spherical watertight cabin attached to its underside for deep-sea exploration. [Gr *bathys*, deep, *skaphē*, boat, *skopeein*, to look at.]

bathysphere [bath´i-sfēr] *n* a strongly built steel diving sphere for deep-sea observation. [Gr *bathys*, deep, *sphaira*, sphere.]

batik [bat´ik] *n* a method of producing designs on cloth by covering with wax, for each successive dipping, those parts that are to be protected from the dye. [Malay]

bating [bāt´ing] *prep* excepting. [**abate**.]

batiste [ba-tēst´] *n* a fine sheer fabric of linen and cotton; an imitation made from rayon or wool. [Perh from *Baptiste*, the original maker; perh from its use in wiping the heads of children after baptism.]

batman [bat´, bä´, or bö´man] *n* a British officer's servant. [Fr *bât*, a pack-saddle.]

bat mitzvah [bät mitz´va] *n* a female bar mitzvah; a bar mitzvah ceremony for a girl.

baton [bat´ôn] *n* a staff serving as a symbol of office; a slender stick used by the conductor of an orchestra; a metal rod twirled by a drum major or drum majorette; a policeman's truncheon; a hollow cylinder carried by each member of a relay team in succession. [Fr *bâton*—Low L *basto*, a stick; of unknown origin.]

batrachian [ba-trā´ki-an] *n* any vertebrate amphibian, esp frog or toad.—Also *adj*. [From Gr *batrachos*, a frog.]

battalion [bat-al´yôn] *n* a US Army Unit consisting of four or more companies usu. commanded by a lieutenant colonel; a large group. [Fr, from root of **battle**.]

batten[1] [bat´n] *vti* to fatten, thrive. [ON *batna*, to grow better.]

batten[2] [bat´n] *n* a sawed strip of wood; a strip of wood put over a seam between boards.—*vt* to fasten or supply with battens.

batten[3] [bat´n] *n* in a loom, the frame moved to press the woof threads into place.

batter[1] [bat´ėr] *vt* to beat with successive blows; to wear with beating or by use.—*vi* to strike heavily and repeatedly.—*n* a mixture of flour, egg, and milk or water thin enough to pour or drop from a spoon.—*n* **batt´ering ram**, a large beam with a metal head formerly used in war as an engine for battering down walls.—**battered baby syndrome**, collection of symptoms found in a baby, caused by violence on the part of the parent or other adult. [OFr *batre*—LL *battĕre* (L *batuĕre*), to beat.]

batter[2] [bat´ėr] *n* a receding upward slope of a structure.—*vt* to give a receding upward slope to (as a wall).

battery [bat´ėr-i] *n* a set of heavy guns; the place on which cannon are mounted; the unit of artillery or its personnel; a series of two or more electric cells arranged to produce a current; a similar arrangement of other apparatus; a single cell that furnishes electric current; (*baseball*) the pitcher and catcher; (*law*) an assault by beating or use of force on a person without his consent. [Fr *batterie—battre* (OFr *batre*); *see* **batter**.]

battle [bat´l] *n* a contest between opposing armies; armed fighting; a fight or encounter.—*vti* to fight.—*ns* **batt´le-ax**, a kind of ax once used in battle; (*slang*) a formidable woman; **batt´le cruis´er**, a heavily armed warship that is lighter and more maneuverable than a battleship; **batt´le cry**, a war cry; **battle fatigue**, combat fatigue; **batt´lefield**, the place on which a battle is fought; **battle group**, a military unit normally made up of five companies; **battle royal**, a free-for-all; a heated dispute; **batt´leship**, a heavily armed, heavily armored warship.—**to join, do battle**, to fight. [OFr *bataille—batre*, to beat. *See* **batter**.]

battlement [bat´l-mėnt] *n* a wall or parapet with embrasures, from which to shoot; an indented parapet.—*adj* **batt´lemented**, fortified with battlements. [OFr *batailles*, movable defences on a wall.]

battue [bä-tōō´ or tū´] *n* a method of hunting in which animals are driven into some place for the convenience of the hunters; a hunt in which this method is used. [Fr—*battre*, to beat.]

bauble [bö´bl] *n* a trifling piece of finery; a fool's scepter. [OFr *babel*, prob from the root seen in L *babulus*, a babbler.]

Bauhaus [bow´hows´] *n* the center for teaching and research in architecture, art and design in the 1920s, whose practitioners created the international style in architecture. [Ger *Bauhaus*, lit architecture house.]

bauxite [bök´sīt, -zit, bō´zīt] *n* the most important aluminum ore. [Found at *Les Baux*, near Arles.]

bawbee [bö-bē´] *n* a halfpenny; originally a silver coin worth three pennies Scots. [Prob from a 16th-century Scottish mint-master, the laird of *Sillebawby*; others identify with 'baby'.]

bawd [böd] *n* a woman who keeps a house of prostitution.—*adj* **bawd´y**, obscene, unchaste. [Perh abbrev from *bawd´strot*, a word for a pander, now obsolete.]

bawl [böl] *vti* to shout; to weep loudly.—*n* a loud cry; a noisy weeping.—*ns* **bawl´er, bawl´ing**.—**bawl out**, (*slang*) to reprimand. [Perh Low L *baulāre*, to bark like a dog; but cf ON *baula*, to low like a cow.]

bay[1] [bā] *adj* reddish brown.—*n* a horse of this color. [Fr *bai*—L *badius*, chestnut-colored.]

bay[2] [bā] *n* a wide inlet of a sea or lake, along the shore.—**Bay Stater**, nickname for inhabitant of Massachusetts. [Fr *baie*—Low L *baia*, a harbor.]

bay[3] [bā] *n* a principal compartment in a building; a main division in a structure; any of various sections or compartments used for a special purpose as in an airplane, automobile, filling station, etc.—**bay window**, a window or series of windows projecting outward from the wall and forming a recess in a room; a pot belly. [OFr *baée—baer*, to gape, be open; prob conn with **bay** (2).]

bay[4] [bā] *n* the European laurel (*Laura nobilis*); any of various shrubs (genera *Magnolia, Myrica*, and *Gordonia*) resembling the laurel; (*pl*) honor, fame.—*ns* **bay leaf**, dried leaf of European laurel used as a flavoring agent; **bay rum**, an aromatic liquid used in cosmetics and medicine prepared from leaves of the West Indian bayberry. [OFr *baie*, a berry—L *bāca*.]

bay[5] [bā] *vi* to bark or howl in long, deep tones.—*vt* to bark at; to bring to bay; to utter in deep, long tones.—*n* the position of one forced to turn and fight; the position of one checked; a baying of dogs.—**at bay**, cornered; held off; **bring to bay**, to corner. [A confusion of two distinct words: (1) to hold at bay = OFr *tenir a bay* = It *tenere a bada*—where *bay, bada*, denote suspense indicated by an open mouth; (2) in 'to stand at bay', *bay* is prob OFr *abai* barking—*bayer*, to bark.]

bayberry [bā´beṙ-i] *n* a hardy shrub (*Myrica pensylvanica*) of the east coast of N America with small, waxy berries; the berries; a West Indian tree (*Pementa racemosa*) yielding bay rum.

bayonet [bā´on-et] *n* a stabbing instrument of steel fixed to the muzzle of a musket or rifle.—*vt* to stab with a bayonet. [Fr *baïonnette*, perh from *Bayonne*, in France; or from OFr *bayon*, arrow.]

bayou [bī´ōō] *n* in the Southern US the marshy offshoot of a lake or river. [Perh corrupted from Fr *boyau*, gut.]

bazaar [ba-zär´] *n* an Eastern market-place; a benefit sale for a church, etc. [Pers *bāzār*, a market.]

bazooka [bȧ-zōō´ka] *n* a portable weapon, used chiefly against tanks, consisting of a long tube that launches a projectile with an explosive head. [From the name of a musical instrument used for comic purposes.]

bdellium [del´i-ům] *n* a gum resin resembling myrrh got from various trees (genus *Commiphora*) of the East Indies and Africa. [Gr *bdellion*, used to translate, but prob unconnected with, Heb *b'dōlakh*, Gen ii 12.]

be [bē] *vi* to live; to exist; to have a specified state or quality;—*pr p* **bē´ing**; *pt p* **been**.—**be off**, go away. [OE *bēon*; Ger *bin*; Gael *bi*, to exist; etc.]

beach [bēch] *n* the sandy shore of the sea or of a lake.—*vti* to drive or haul (a boat) up on the beach.—*ns* **beach´head**, a position on a seashore in enemy territory seized by an advance force and held to cover the main landing; **beach´comber**, a long rolling wave; one who lives on what he finds on beaches, etc.; a settler on a Pacific island. [Orig a dial Eng word for shingle.]

beacon [bē´kôn] *n* a light for warning or guiding; a radio transmitter sending guiding signals to aircraft; a source of light or inspiration.—*vt* to furnish with a beacon.—*vi* to shine as a beacon. [OE *bēacn*, a beacon, a sign.]

bead [bēd] *n* a little ball pierced for stringing; (*pl*) a string of beads; (*pl*) a rosary; a bubble or drop of liquid; the small knob of metal forming the front sight of a rifle; a projecting rim, band, or molding.—*vt* to furnish with beads or a beading.—*vi* to form into a bead.—*adjs* **bead´ed**, having beads or a bead; in beadlike form; **bead´y**, small and bright (of eyes); covered with beads or bubbles.—*ns* **bead´ing**, beadwork; an openwork trimming; a beaded molding; **bead´roll**, a list of names; a rosary; **bead´work**, ornamental work in beads for clothing, accessories, etc.; beading in wood for furniture, etc.—**say, tell, count one's beads**, to offer prayers with a rosary. [OE *bed, gebed*, prayer. *See* **bid**.]

beadle [bēd´l] *n* a minor official who keeps order in certain churches. [OE *bydel—bēodan*, to proclaim, to bid; affected by OFr form *bedel*.]

beagle [bē´gl] *n* a breed of small hound with short legs and drooping ears.

beak [bēk] *n* the bill of a bird; anything pointed or projecting; the nose; the projecting mouth parts of various insects, fishes, etc.—*adj* **beaked** [bēkt]. [OFr *bec*—Low L *beccus*, of Celt (Gaulish) origin.]

beaker [bēk´ėr] *n* a large drinking cup, or its contents; a cylindrical vessel with a pouring lip used by chemists and pharmacists. [Scand *bikarr*, prob from Low L *bicārium*, a drinking-bowl.]

beam [bēm] *n* a large and straight piece of timber or metal; the crossbar of a balance; a ship's breadth at its widest point; a slender shaft of light, etc.; a radiant look, smile, etc.; a steady radio or radar signal for guiding aircraft or ships.—*vt* to send forth (light) in a beam; to direct (a radio signal, etc.).—*vi* to shine; to smile radiantly.—*adj* **beam´y**, emitting beams of light; broad in the beam.—**on the beam**, following a guiding beam; proceeding correctly; **on her beam ends**, the position of a ship so much inclined to one side that the beams become nearly vertical. [OE *bēam*, a tree, stock of a tree, a ray of light; Gmc]

bean [bēn] *n* a leguminous plant bearing kidney-shaped seeds; a seed or pod of such a plant; any beanlike seed (*coffee beans*); (*slang*) the head or brain.—*vt* (*slang*) to hit on the head.—*ns* **bean´ery**, (*inf*) a restaurant; **bean´bag**, a small cloth bag filled with dried beans and thrown in games; a pellet-filled cushion used as furniture; **bean´-ball**, a baseball pitched at the batter's head; **bean curd**, soft cheese made from soybean milk.—Also **tofu; bean´-eater**, an inhabitant of Boston, Massachusetts; **bean´o**, bingo; **bean pole**, (*inf*) a tall, skinny person; **bean sprout**, the shoot of bean seeds, esp the mung bean used as a vegetable.—**full of beans**, in high spirits; **spill the beans**, (*inf*) to tell a secret. [OE *bēan*; Ger *bohne*.]

bear[1] [bār] *vt* to carry; to support; to endure; to admit of (eg an interpretation); to behave or conduct (oneself); to bring forth or produce; to need; to give.—*vi* to be patient; to have reference to (*with* **upon**); to be productive; to be situated;—*pr p* **bear´ing**; *pt* **bōre**; *pt p* **borne** [bōrn, börn], **born** [börn]—the latter referring to something brought forth.—*adj* **bear´able**, that may be endured.—*adv* **bear´ably**.—*ns* **bear´er**, one who or that which bears; a plant bearing fruit; one holding a check, draft, or other order for payment, esp if marked payable to bearer; **bear grass**, plants (genera *Yucca, Nolina*, or *Xerophyllum*) of Western and Southwestern US with foliage resembling coarse grass; **bear´ing**, demeanor; a compass direction; relation to, significance in relation to (eg *has no bearing on this question*); a device borne on an escutcheon; the part of a structure that bears the weight; (*pl*) awareness of one's situation; (*pl*) relative direction or position; a machine part on which another part slides, revolves, etc.; **bear´ing rein**, a check rein—**bear down**, to press down by weight; overwhelm; **bear out**, to corroborate; **bear up**, to keep up one's courage. [OE beran; L *ferre*, Gr *pherein*.]

bear[2] [bār] *n* any of a family (Ursidae) of massive mammals with coarse fur, short legs, plantigrade feet and feeding mainly on fruit and insects; any of various other bearlike animals (eg ant bear, Koala bear); **Bear**, either of two constellations in the northern hemisphere, Great Bear (Ursa Major) and Little Bear (Ursa Minor); a rough or ill-bred fellow; one who sells stocks anticipating a fall in price so that he may buy them back at a lower price.—*n* **bear´bait´ing**, the practice of setting dogs on a chained bear.—*adj* **bear´ish**, like a bear; dropping, or causing a drop in price, on the stock exchange.—*ns* **bear´ishness; bear´skin**, the skin of a bear; the high fur cap worn by the Guards in England. [OE *bera*; Ger *bär*; Du *beer*.]

beard [bērd] *n* the hair that grows on the chin and cheeks of a man; any beard-like part; an awn.—*vt* to oppose to the face; to provide with a beard.—*adjs* **beard´ed, beard´less**.—*n* **bearded collie**, a breed of large herding dog with a long rough coat and drooping ears. [OE *beard*, W *barf*, Ger *bart*.]

be´arnaise sauce [bā´ėr-nāz] *n* a sauce of egg yolks, butter, shallots, wine, vinegar, and seasonings usu. served on beef. [Fr.]

beast [bēst] *n* a large four-footed animal; a brutal gross person.—*n* **beast´ie**, a wild or strange beast.—*adj* **beast´ly**, like a beast in actions or behavior; coarse; (*coll*) disagreeable, irksome.—*n* **beast´liness**.—**beast of burden**, any animal used to carry things; **beast of prey**, any animal that hunts and kills for food. [OFr *beste*—L *bestia*.]

beat [bēt] *vt* to strike repeatedly; to thrash; to overcome; to be too difficult for; to mark (time) with a baton, etc.; to mix (eggs, etc.) by hard stirring; to move (esp wings) up and down; to form (a path, way, etc.) by repeated treading or riding; to keep walking on; (*inf*) to puzzle; (*inf*) to cheat; (*slang*) to escape the penalties of.—*vi* to hit, dash, etc. repeatedly; to throb;—*pr p* **beat´ing**; *pt* **beat**; *pt p* **beat´en**.—*n* a recurrent stroke, or its sound, or its moment, as of a watch or the pulse; a habitual route; the unit of musical rhythm; beatnik.—*adj* (*slang*) tired out; of beatniks.—*adj* **beat´en**, made smooth or hard by beating or treading; worn by use; shaped by hammering; exhausted; defeated.—*ns* **beat´er**, an implement for beating (as an eggbeater or the blade of an electric mixer); **beat´ing**, the act of striking; the damage resulting; thrashing; pulsation or throbbing; **beat´nik**, one of the **beat generation**, a group of unconventional poets, etc. who, in the 1950s, refused to accept the aims and standards of contemporary society and led a bohemian existence; a person whose behavior, dress, etc. is unconventional.—*adj* **beat´up**, dilapidated through excessive use.—**beat about the bush, beat around the bush**, to approach a subject in an indirect way; **beat down**, to put or force down; **beat it!** (*slang*) go away!; **beat off**, to drive back; **beat one's brains out**, to make a great mental effort; **beat the bushes**, to search an area meticulously; **beat the drum**, to publicize vigorously; **beat the rap**, (*slang*) to escape the penalties connected with an accusation or charge; **beat up** (**on**), (*slang*) to thrash, knock about severely. [OE *bēatan*, pa t *bēot*.]

beatify [bē-at´i-fī] *vt* to make blissfully happy; (*RC Church*) to declare one who has died to be among the blessed in heaven.—*adj* **beatif´ic**, making blessed; expressing and communicating happiness.—*n* **beatificā´tion**, act of beatifying. [L *beātus*, blessed, and *facĕre*, to make.]

beatitude [bē-at´i-tūd] *n* perfect blessedness or happiness.—**the Beatitudes**, the pronouncements of Jesus in the Sermon on the Mount. [L *beātitūdō*—*beātus*, blessed.]

beau [bō] *n* a woman's suitor or sweetheart.—*pl* **beaux** [bōz].—*ns* **beau geste**, a graceful or magnanimous gesture; an ingratiating reconciling gesture; **beau´idē´al**, a person in whom the highest excellence is embodied; **beau´ monde** [bō´mo•d] the gay or fashionable world. [Fr *beau, bel* (fem *belle*)—L *bellus*, fine, gay, as if for *benulus*, dim of *benus* = *bonus*, good.]

Beaufort scale [bō´fört] *n* system of indicating wind strength (from 0, calm, to 12, hurricane). [Sir Francis *Beaufort*.]

beauty [bū´ti] *n* a pleasing combination of qualities in a person or object; a particular grace or excellence; a beautiful person, esp a woman; good looks.—*adj* **beauteous** [-tiůs, -tyůs] (*poet*) full of beauty, fair.—*adv* **beau´teously**.—*n* **beau´teousness**.—*adj* **beau´tiful**, having beauty.—*adv* **beau´tifully**.—*vti* **beau´tify**, to make or become beautiful.—*ns* **beautician** [bū-tish´an] one who works in a beauty shop; **beautificā´tion; beau´tifier; beautiful people**, persons who are identified with international society; members of the jet set; **beauty contest**, an assemblage of girls or women at which the judges select the most beautiful; **beauty shop, salon**, or **parlor**, a place where women go for hair styling, manicuring, facials, etc.; **beau´ty spot**, a patch placed on the face to heighten beauty; a birthmark resembling such a patch. [OFr *biaute, beaute*—Low L *bellitās, -ātis*—L *bellus. See* **beau**.]

beaver[1] [bēv´ėr] *n* either of two large semiaquatic rodents (genus *Castor*) valuable for their fur and castoreum; the fur of the beaver; a hat with a plush finish; a man's high silk hat; (*slang*) a beard.—*n* **beav´erboard**, trade name for a building board of fiber.—**beaver away**, to work hard. [OE *befer, beofor*; Du *bever*, Ger *biber*, Gael *beabhar*, L *fiber*.]

beaver[2] [bēv´ėr] *n* in medieval armor, the covering for the lower part of the face; a helmet visor. [So called from a fancied likeness to a child's bib. OFr *bavière*, from *bave*, slaver.]

bebop [bē´bop] *n* a style of jazz of the early 1940's characterized by improvised solo performances in dissonant and complex patterns, often by accentuating the second and fourth beats in each 4/4 measure.

becalm [bi-käm´] *vt* to make calm; to make (a ship) motionless from lack of wind.—*adj* **becalmed´**. [Pfx *be*-, inten, + **calm**.]

became [bi-kām´] *pt* of **become**.

because [bi-koz´, bi-köz´] *conj* for the reason that.—**because of**, on account of. [Prep *by*, + **cause**.]

béchamel sauce [bā-shȧ-mel´] *n* a thick, rich white sauce. [Fr.]

bêche-de-mer [bėsh-dė-mā´r] *n* any of several large edible sea cucumbers (esp genera *Actinopyga* and *Holothuria*) used esp in Chinese cooking.—Also **trepang**.

beck [bek] *n* a sign with the finger or head.—**at someone's beck**, subject to someone's slightest whim. [A contraction of **beckon**.]

beckon [bek´ȯn] *vti* to summon by a sign. [OE *bīecnan*—*bēacn*, a sign.]

becloud [bi-klowd´] *vt* to obscure by clouds; to muddle. [Pfx *be*-, around, and **cloud**.]

become [bi-kum´] *vi* to come or grow to be.—*vt* to suit or befit;—*pt* **becāme´**; *pt p* **become´**.—*adj* **becom´ing**, appropriate; seemly; suitable to the wearer.—*adv* **becom´ingly**. [OE *becuman*—pfx *be*-, and *cuman*, to come.]

bed [bed] *n* a piece of furniture for sleeping on; a plot of soil where plants are raised; the bottom of a river, lake, etc.; any flat surface used as a foundation; a stratum.—*vt* to put to bed; to embed; to plant in a bed of earth; to arrange in layers.—*vi* to go to bed, rest, sleep; to stratify.—*ns* **bed´bug**, a wingless bug (*Cimex lectularius*) living in mattresses, cracks in furniture and houses, feeding on human blood by piercing the skin; **bed´clothes**, sheets, blankets, etc. for a bed; **bed´der**, one that makes up beds, a bedding plant; **bedding**, bedclothes; a bottom layer, foundation; material to provide a bed for livestock; stratification.—*adj* **bed´fast**, bedridden.—*ns* **bed´fellow**, one who shares a bed with another; a close associate, an ally; **bed´mate**, one who shares one's bed, esp a sexual partner; **bed´pan**, a shallow vessel used by a person in bed as a toilet.—*adj* **bed´ridd´en**, confined to bed by illness, infirmity, etc.—*n* **bed´rock´**, solid rock underlying soil, etc.; the base or bottom; **bed´roll**, a portable roll of bedding used esp by campers; **bed´room**, a room intended primarily for sleeping.—*adj* suggestive of sexual relations; inhabited by commuters (*bedroom suburbs*).—*n* **bed´side´**, the space beside a bed.—*adj* conducted at the bedside (*bedside diagnosis*); suitable for a bedridden person (*bedside reading*).—*n* **bed´sore**, an ulceration of tissue caused by pressure; **bed´spread**, a decorative cover over the blanket on a bed; **bed´stead**, a framework for the spring and mattress of a bed; **bed´time**, a time for going to bed; **bed´wetting**, enuresis.—**bed of roses**, (*inf*) a situation or position of ease and luxury. [OE *bed(d)*; Ger *bett*, ON *bethr*.]

bedaub [bi-döb´] *vt* to daub over or smear. [Pfx *be*-, and **daub**.]

bedeck [bi-dek´] *vt* to deck or ornament. [Pfx *be*-, and **deck**.]

bedevil [bi-dev´l] *vt* to plague or bewilder.—*n* **bedev´ilment**. [Pfx *be*-, and **devil**, n.]

bedew [bi-dū´] *vt* to moisten gently, as with dew. [Pfx *be*-, and **dew**.]

Bedford cord [bed´fȯrd] *n* a very strong fabric with a prominent rib weave made of cotton, wool, or rayon. [New *Bedford*, Massachusetts.]

bedim [bi-dim´] *vt* make (the eyes or vision) dim;—*pa p* **bedimmed´**. [Pfx *be*-, + **dim**, adj.]

bedizen [bi-dīz´n, bi-diz´n] *vt* to dress gaudily. [Pfx *be*-, + *dizen*.]

bedlam [bed´lȧm] *n* an asylum for lunatics; a place of uproar.—*adj* fit for a madhouse.—*n* **bed´lamite**, a madman. [From the priory of St Mary of *Bethlehem* in London, afterwards a madhouse (*Bethlehem* Royal Hospital).]

Bedlington terrier [bed´ling-tȯn] *n* a breed of woolly-coated terrier with a narrow head and arched back.—Also **Bedlington**. [*Bedlington*, England.]

bedouin, beduin [bed´ōō-in] *n* a nomadic Arab of the north African deserts. [Fr,—Ar *badāwin*, dwellers in the desert.]

bedraggle [bi-drag´l] *vt* to soil by dragging in the wet or dirt. [Pfx *be*-, + **draggle**.]

bee[1] [bē] *n* a social colonial four-winged insect (*Apis melifera*) that is often kept in hives to make honey; any of numerous insects (superfamily Apoidea) that also feed on pollen and nectar and are related to wasps; an eccentric notion.—*ns* **bee´hive**, a container for keeping honeybees; a scene of crowded activity; a woman's hairdo resembling a conical beehive; **bee´keep´er**, one who keeps bees for producing honey; **bee´keep´ing; bee´line**, the most direct course from one point to another; **bees´wax**, the wax secreted by bees and used by them in constructing their cells. [OE *bēo*; Ger *biene*.]

bee[2] [bē] *n* a meeting of people to work together or to compete. [OE *bey*, service.]

beech [bēch] *n* a genus (*Fagus*) of trees with smooth silvery bark and small edible nuts; its wood.—*adj* **beech´en**.—*n* **beech´nut**, the small, three-cornered nut of the beech tree. [OE *bēce* (and related noun *bōc*); Ger *buche*, L *fāgus*, Gr *phēgos* (oak).]

beef [bēf] *n* a full-grown ox, cow, bull, or steer, esp one bred for meat; these animals collectively; their meat; (*inf*) brawn; (*slang*) a complaint;—*pl* **beefs, beeves**.—*vt* to add weight, strength, or power to (*with* **up**).—*vi* (*slang*) to complain.—*ns* **beef´cake´**, (*slang*) photographic display of the muscular development of a nude, or nearly nude man; **beef´eat´er** [bēf´-ēt´ėr] a yeoman of the sovereign's guard, also a warder of the Tower of London; a person who eats beef; (*slang*) an Englishman; **beef´iness; beef´steak**, a thick slice of beef for broiling or frying.—*adj* **beef´y**.—**beef Stroganoff**, thinly-sliced beef cooked in a sour-cream sauce; **beef Wellington**, a fillet of beef covered with paté de foie gras and baked in a pastry case. [OFr *boef*—L *bōs, bovis*.]

Beelzebub [bē-el´ze-bub] *n* a form of Baal worshipped by the Philistines at Ekron; the prince of the evil spirits. [Heb *ba´al z´būb*, fly-lord.]

been [bin] *pt p* of **be**.

beep [bēp] *n* the brief, high pitched sound of a horn or electronic signal.—*vti* to make or cause to make this sound. [Imit.]

beer [bēr] *n* an alcoholic beverage made by slow fermentation, from malted barley and hops; a soft drink made from extracts of roots, etc. (*root beer, birch beer, etc.*).—*adj* **beer'y**, smelling or tasting of beer; of, or affected by, beer.—*n* **beer´iness**. [OE *bēor*; Ger and Du *bier*, ON *bjorr*.]

beestings [bēst´ingz] *n* the first milk drawn from a cow after calving. [OE *bȳsting, bēost*.]

beet [bēt] *n* a genus (*Beta*) of plants with a succulent root used as food and as a source of sugar. [OE *bēte*—L *bēta*.]

beetle[1] [bē´tl] *n* any of an order (Coleoptera) of insects having hard front wings that cover the membraneous back wings when these are folded. [ME *bityl*—OE *bitula, bitela*—*bītan*, to bite.]

beetle[2] [bē´tl] *n* a heavy wooden mallet used for driving wedges, or the like; a wooden pestle. [OE *bīetl*—*bēatan*, to beat.]

beetle[3] [bēt´l] *adj* overhanging.—*vi* to overhang.—**beetle-browed**, having bushy eyebrows; frowning.

beeves [bēvz] plural of **beef**.

befall [bi-föl´] *vti* to happen or occur to;—*pr p* **befall´ing**; *pt* **befell´**; *pt p* **befall´en**. [OE *befeallan*—*be-*, inten, *feallan*, to fall.]

befit [bi-fit´] *vt* to be suitable to; to be right for;—*pr p* **befitt´ing**; *pt p* **befitt´ed**.—*adj* **befitt´ing**.—*adv* **befitt´ingly**. [Pfx *be-*, intensive, + **fit**.]

befog [bi-fog´] *vt* to envelop in fog; to obscure. [Pfx *be-*, + **fog**, n].

before [bi-fōr´, -för´] *prep* in front of; in the presence or sight of; previous to; in preference to.—*adv* in front; earlier; until now.—*conj* previous to the time that; rather than.—*adj, adv* **before´hand**, ahead of time; in anticipation. [OE *beforan*—*be-*, and *foran*, adv. *See* **fore**.]

befoul [bi-fowl´] *vt* to make foul; to soil; to cast aspersions on. [Pfx *be-*, + **foul**, adj].

befriend [bi-frend´] *vt* to act as a friend to, to favor. [Pfx *be-*, + **friend**, n].

beg [beg] *vti* to ask for alms; to ask earnestly; to beseech;—*pr p* **begg´ing**; *pt p* **begged**.—*n* **beggar** [beg´ȧr] one who begs; one who lives by begging; a pauper.—*vt* to impoverish; to make (description, etc.) seem inadequate.—*adj* **begg´arly**, poor; inadequate; worthless.—*ns* **begg´arliness; begg´ary**, extreme poverty; the occupation or practice of begging.—**beg off**, to ask to be released from; **beg the question**, to use circular reasoning; **go begging**, to be available but unwanted. [Ety very obscure; the words *beg* and *beggar* first appear in the 13th century.]

began [bi-gan´] *pt* of **begin**.

beget [bi-get´] *vt* to become the father of; to cause;—*pr p* **begett´ing**; *pt* **begot´** (*arch* **begat´**);—*pt p* **begott´en** (*arch* **begot´**).—*n* **begett´er**, one who begets; a father. [OE *begitan*, to acquire—*be-*, inten, *gitan*, to get.]

begin [bi-gin´] *vti* to start doing, acting, etc.; to originate;—*pr p* **beginn´ing**; *pt* **began´**; *pt p* **begun´**.—*ns* **beginn´er**, one who is beginning to learn or do something; a novice.—**beginn´ing**, origin or commencement; the time or place of starting; the first part of; (*pl*) early stages. [OE *beginnan* (more usually *onginnan*), from *be-* and *ginnan*, to begin.]

begird [bi-gûrd´] *vt* to surround or encompass (with);—*pt* **begirt´, begird´ed**; *pt p* **begirt´**. [OE *begyrdan*. *See* **gird**.]

begone [bi-gon´] *interj* lit be gone! be off! get away!—For **woe´-begone´**, *see* **woe**.

begonia [bi-gōn´ya] *n* a genus (*Begonia*) of tropical plants with showy flowers and remarkable unequal sided and often colored leaves. [Named from Michel *Bégon*, patron of botany, 1638–1710.]

begot [bi-got´] *pt, pt, p*, **begotten** [bi-got´n], *pt p* of **beget**.

begrime [bi-grīm´] *vt* to grime or soil deeply. [Pfx *be-*, + **grime**.]

begrudge [bi-gruj´] *n* to grudge, envy (eg *to begrudge him his success*). [Pfx *be-*, inten, + **grudge**.]

beguile [bi-gīl] *vt* to mislead; to divert attention from.—*ns* **beguile´ment; beguil´er**.—*adv* **beguil´ingly**. [Pfx *be-*, inten, + obs vb *guile*, related to **guile**, n.]

beguine [bė-gēn] *n* a dance of French West Indian origin or its music, resembling the rhumba. [Fr.]

begum [bē´gum] *n* a Muslim princess or lady of rank; a deferential title given to any lady. [Fem of *beg*, or **bey**.]

begun [bi-gun´] *pt p* (sometimes *pt*) of **begin**.

behalf [bi-häf´] *n* support.—**in, on behalf of**, in the interest of; for. [ME *behalve*—OE *be healfe*, by the side. *See* **half**.]

behave [bi-hāv´] *vti* to conduct (oneself) in a specified way; to conduct (oneself) properly;—*pt, pt p* **behaved´**.—*n* **behavior** [bi-hāv´yȯr], way of behaving; conduct or action.—**behavioral science**, a science, eg psychology, sociology, which studies the behavior of human beings; **behavioral scientist; behav´iorism**, a school of psychology that regards observable behavior as the only valid subject for study; **behav´iorist**.—Also *adj*.—*adj* **behavioris´tic**. [Probably formed in 15th century from *be-* and **have**; apparently unconnected with OE *behabban*.]

behead [bi-hed´] *vt* to cut off the head of.—*n* **behead´ing**, the act of cutting off the head of. [OE *behēafdian*—*be-*, privative, *hēafod*, **head**.]

beheld [bi-held´] *pt, pt p* of **behold**.

behemoth [bi-hē´moth] *n* an animal described in the Book of Job; a great beast. [Either pl of Heb *b'hēmāh*, a beast, or a Heb form of Egyptian *p-ehe-mout*, 'water-ox'.]

behest [bi-hest´] *n* a command, charge. [OE *behǣs*, a promise.]

behind [bi-hīnd´] *prep* at the back of; concealed by; later than; supporting.—*adv* in the rear; slow; late.—*adv, adj* **behind´hand**, behind, as in progress, time, etc. [OE *behindan*—*be-, hindan*. *See* **hind** (3).]

behold [bi-hōld´] *vt* to see, observe; to contemplate.—*vi* to look;—*pt, pt p* **beheld´**.—*imper* or *interj* see! lo! observe!—*adj* **behold´en**, bound in gratitude, obliged.—*n* **behold´er**, one who beholds; an onlooker. [OE *behealdan, behaldan*, to hold, observe—pfx *be-*, and *h(e)aldan*, to hold.]

behoof [bi-ōōf´] *n* benefit, convenience. [OE *behōf*.]

behoove, behove [bi-hōōv´] *vt* to be incumbent upon or proper for. [OE *behōfian*, to be fit.]

beige [bāzh] *n* grayish tan wool.—*Also adj*. [Fr.]

being [bē´ing] *n* existence; any person or thing existing; substance, essence.—*adj* **bē´ing**, existing, present.—**being as, being that** (*inf*) since; because; **for the time being**, for now. [From pr p of **be**.]

bel [bel] *n* ten decibels. [From Alexander Graham *Bell* (1847–1922), telephone inventor.]

belabor [bi-lā´bȯr] *vt* to beat soundly; to attack verbally; (*inf*) to labor (a point, etc.). [Pfx *be-*, + **labor**.]

belated [[bi-lāt´ėd] *adj* tardy.—*adv* **belat´edly**. [Pfx *be-*, + **late**, adj.]

belay [bi-lā´] *vti* to secure (a rope) by coiling it round a cleat, etc.; to secure by a rope. [OE *belecgan*—*be-* + *lecgan*. *See* **lay** (2).]

bel canto [bel cän´tō] *n* a style of singing with brilliant vocal display and purity of tone. [It.]

belch [belch, belsh] *vti* to emit gas from the stomach by the mouth; to eject violently.—*n* eructation. [OE *bealcian*; Du *balken*.]

beldam, beldame [bel´dam] *n* an old woman, esp an ugly one. [Formed from *dam*, mother, and *bel-*, used like *grand-*.]

beleaguer [bi-lēg´ėr] *vt* to lay siege to. [Du *belegeren*, to besiege—*leger* a camp.]

belfry [bel´fri] *n* the part of a steeple or tower in which bells are hung. [Orig a watch-tower—OFr *berfroi*; cf Middle High German *berchfrit*—*bergan*, to protect, *frid, frit*, tower.]

Belgian [bel´ji-ȧn, -jȧn] *adj* belonging to *Belgium*, a country of Europe.—*n* a native or citizen of Belgium; any of a breed of usu. roan or chestnut Belgian draft horses.—**Belgian hare**, a breed of slender dark-red domestic rabbit; **Belgian Malinois**, a breed of squarely-built working dog with short straight hair and a dense undercoat; **Belgian sheepdog**, a breed of black dogs developed for sheep herding; **Belgian Tervuren**, a breed of working dog related to the Belgian sheepdog but with long abundant fawn-coloured hair with black tips.

Belial [bēl´yȧl] *n* the devil. [Heb *b'li-ya'al*—*b'li*, without, *ya'al*, usefulness.]

belie [bi-lī] *vt* to give the lie to; fail to justify or act up to (hope, promise); to present in a false character;—*pr p* **bely´ing**; *pt p* **belied´**. [Pfx *be-* + **lie** (1).]

believe [bi-lēv´] *vt* to regard as true; to accept as true what is said by (a person); to think or suppose.—*vi* to have faith in.—*n* **belief´**, persuasion of the truth of anything; religious faith; the opinion or doctrine believed.—*adj* **believ´able**, that may be believed.—*n* **believ´er**.—*adj* **believ´ing**, trustful. [ME *bileven*—*bi-, be-*, + *leven*. The OE form was *gelēfan*; the present compound appears in the 12th century.]

belittle [bi-lit´l] *vt* to make small; to represent as small, to depreciate. [Pfx *be-*, + **little**, adj.]

bell[1] [bel] *n* a hollow vessel of metal which rings when struck; anything bell-shaped; the sound of a bell; (*naut*) a bell rung to mark the periods of the watch.—*vt* to furnish with a bell.—*vi* to become bell-shaped.—*adj* **bell´bottom**, widening towards the ankle, as trousers or slacks.—*ns* **bellboy**, bellhop; **bell´buoy**, a buoy carrying a bell which is rung by the waves; **bell curve** (*statistics*) the symmetrical curve of normal distribution which resembles a bell; **bellhop**, a hotel or club employee who escorts guests to their rooms, and makes himself generally helpful by carrying luggage, running errands, etc.; **bell jar**, a bell-shaped glass used to protect instruments or contain gases, etc. in a laboratory; **bellman**, bellhop; **bell´ met´al**, metal of which bells are made – an alloy of copper and tin; **bell´pull**, a cord or handle used in ringing a bell; **bell´tow´er**, a tower built to contain one or more bells, a campanile; **bell´weth´er**, the leading sheep of a flock, on whose neck a bell is hung; (*fig*) a ringleader; **bellwort**, any of a genus (*Uvularia*) of plants of the lily family with drooping yellow bell-shaped flowers found in eastern No America.—**bell the cat**, to do a daring or risky deed. [OE *belle*; cog with Du *bel*.]

bell[2] [bel] *vi* to bellow, roar; to utter loudly.—*n* bellow. [OE *bellan*, to roar; cf Ger *bellen*.]

belladonna [bel-a-don´a] *n* the deadly nightshade (*Atropa belladonna*), all parts of which are narcotic and poisonous from the presence of atropine; atropine. [It *bella donna*, fair lady; one property of belladonna is to enlarge the pupil, and so add a brilliance to the eyes.]

belle [bel] *n* a pretty woman or girl. [Fr *belle*—L *bella*, fem of *bellus*.]

belles-lettres [bel-let´r] *n pl* nontechnical literature, including poetry, fiction, criticism, etc. [Fr, lit 'fine letters'.]

bellicose [bel´ik-ōs] *adj* contentious, warlike. [L *bellicōsus—bellum*, war.]

belligerent [bel-ij´ėr-ėnt] *adj* at war; of war; warlike; ready to fight or quarrel.—*n* a belligerent person, group, or nation.—*n* **bellig´erency**. [For *belligerant*—L *belligerans, -antis*, pr p of *belligerāre*, to wage war.]

bellow [bel´ō] *vi* to roar like a bull; to make any violent outcry.—*vt* to utter very loudly.—*n* the roar of a bull; any deep sound or cry. [ME *belwen*; OE *bylgian*, to roar; there is an OE *bellan*, to roar—see **bell** (2).]

bellows [bel´ōz] *n pl* (often treated as *sing*) a device for producing and directing a current of air by compression of its collapsible sides; anything collapsible like a bellows. [Same as **belly**; now used only in pl.]

Bell's palsy [belz] *n* paralysis of one side of the face produced by degeneration of the nerve that supplies the muscles of the face. [Sir Charles *Bell*, Scot anatomist.]

belly [bel´i] *n* the part of the body between the chest and the thighs; the abdomen; the stomach; the underside of an animal's body; the deep interior, as of a ship.—*vti* to swell or bulge out;—*pr p* **bell´ying**; *pt p* **bell´ied**.—*n* **bell´yache´**, a pain in the belly; (*slang*) a persistent complaint.—*vi* (*slang*) to complain.—*ns* **bellyache weed**, silverrod; **bell´y-band**, a saddle girth; a band to protect the navel of a newborn baby; **bellybutton, belly button**, (*inf*) the navel; **bell´y dance**, a solo dance with very pronounced movement of abdominal muscles; **bell´y flop**, a dive in which one lands on the snow or in the water on one's stomach; **bell´yful**, a sufficiency; (*slang*) all that one can bear; **bell´y landing**, of an aircraft, a landing without using the landing-wheels; **bell´y laugh**, a deep unrestrained laugh.—*adj* **bell´y-up** (*slang*) done for, esp bankrupt. [ME *bali, bely*—OE *bæl(i)g, bel(i)g*, bag.]

belong [bi-long´] *vi* to have a proper place; to be related (to); to be a member (*with* **to**); to be owned (*with* **to**).—*n pl* **belong´ings**, possessions. [ME *bi-, be-longen*—pfx *be-*, inten, *longen* obs vb to pertain (to).]

beloved [bi-luv´id, bi-luvd´] *adj* dearly loved, much loved, very dear.—*n* one who is much loved. [Pfx *be-*, + **love**.]

below [bi-lō´] *prep* lower than; not worthy of.—*adj, adv* in or to a lower place; beneath; later (in a book, etc.); in or to hell; on earth; under in rank, amount, etc. [Pfx *be-*, + **low**, adj.]

Bel Paese [bel pä-āzi] *n* trade name for a mild soft creamy cheese with a firm rind. [It.]

belt [belt] *n* a band of leather, etc. worn around the waist; any similar encircling thing; a continuous moving strap passing over pulleys and so driving machinery; a distinctive region or strip (*corn belt, a belt of rain*); (*slang*) a hard blow; (*slang*) a gulp of liquor; (*slang*) a thrill.—*vt* to encircle or fasten with a belt; to hit with a belt; (*slang*) to hit hard; (*inf*) to sing loudly (*with* **out**); (*slang*) to gulp (liquor).—*vi* (*inf*) to act in a vigorous or violent manner.—*ns* **belt´ing**, belts, material for belts; **belt highway**, beltway; **belt-tightening**, (*inf*) a reduction in spending; **beltway**, an expressway passing around an urban area.—**below the belt**, unfairly; **under one's belt**, in one's possession. [OE *belt*; ON *belti*, Gael *balt*, L *balteus*.]

belvedere [bel´ve-dēr] *n* a structure (as a cupola) designed to command a view; a shrubby herbaceous perennial (*Kochia trychophylla*) grown for its foliage.—Also **summer cypress**. [It *belvedere—bel*, beautiful, *vedere*, a view.]

bemoan [bi-mōn] *vti* to lament. [OE *bemǣnan*—pfx *be-*, *mǣnan*, to moan.]

bemuse [bi-mūz´] *vt* to muddle; to preoccupy.—*adj* **bemused´**. [Pfx *be-*, inten, + **muse** (1).]

ben [ben] *n* (*Scottish*) a mountain peak [*Gael beann*.]

bench [bench, -sh] *n* a long hard seat for two or more persons; a long worktable (*laboratory bench*); the place where judges sit in a court of law; the status of a judge; judges collectively.—*vt* (*sports*) to take (a player) out of a game.—*ns* **bench mark**, a mark on a permanent object serving as a reference for topographical surveys and tidal observations; **bench´mark**, a point of reference for making measurements; something that serves as a standard; **bench press**, a weight-lifting exercise of pushing a barbell up from the chest while lying on a bench with the feet on the floor; **bench warrant**, an order issued by a judge or court for the arrest of a person; **bench´warmer**, (*sports*) a reserve player or one awaiting return to the field of play. [OE *benc*; cog with Ger and Du *bank*.]

bend [bend] *vt* to curve or make crooked; to subdue; to turn, esp from a straight line; to adapt to one's purpose, distort; (*naut*) to tie.—*vi* to turn, esp from a straight line; to yield from pressure to form a curve; to curve the body (*with* **over** *or* **down**); to give in;—*pt, pt p* **bent**, also **bend´ed** (in *bended knee*).—*n* a bending or being bent; a bent part; any of various knots for tying rope; (*pl*) (*inf*) caisson disease.—*ns* **bend´er**, a spree.—**around the bend**, crazy, mad. *See* **bent**. [OE *bendan*, to bind, to string (a bow).]

beneath [bi´nēth´] *prep* underneath; below; unworthy.—*adj, adv* in a lower place; underneath. [OE *beneothan—be-*, and *neothan*, under.]

benedict [ben´i-dikt] *n* a newly married man, esp one who has long disdained marriage—from *Benedick* in Shakespeare's *Much Ado*.

Benedictine [ben-i-dik´tin] *adj* pertaining to St Benedict or his monastic rule.—*n* a monk or nun of the order founded by St *Benedict* (480–543); devoted, esp to scholarship and liturgical worship; a liqueur once distilled by Benedictine monks.

benediction [ben-i-dik´sh(ó)n] *n* a blessing; a solemn invocation of a blessing esp at the end of a church service.—*adj* **benedict´ory**. [L *benedictiō, -ōnis—bene*, well, and *dīcĕre, dictum*, to say.]

benefaction [ben-i-fak´sh(ō)n] *n* the act of doing good; a good deed done or benefit conferred; the money or help given.—*n* **ben´efactor**, one who confers a benefit. [L *benefactiō, -ōnis—bene*, well, and *facĕre, factum*, to do.]

benefice [ben´i-fis] *n* an endowed church office.—*vt* **ben´efice**. [Through Fr—L *beneficium—bene*, well, *facĕre*, to do.]

beneficence [bi-nef´i-sėns] *n* active goodness, kindness, charity; a gift, benefaction.—*adj* **benef´icent**.—*adv* **benef´icently**. [L *beneficentia*.]

beneficial [ben-i-fish´ál] *adj* useful, advantageous.—*adv* **benefic´ially**.—*n* **benefic´iary**, one receiving or who will be receiving benefit, as from a will, an insurance policy, etc. [L *beneficium. See* **benefice**.]

benefit [ben´i-fit] *n* advantage; anything contributing to improvement; (often *pl*) payments made by an insurance company, public agency, etc. as during sickness or retirement or for death; a public performance, bazaar, etc. the proceeds of which are to help some person or cause.—*vt* to help.—*vi* to receive advantage.—*pr p* **ben´efiting**; *pt, pt p* **ben´efited**.—*n* **ben´efit of clergy**, the privilege of being tried by an ecclesiastical rather than a civil court; the sanction of the church. [ME *benfet*, through Fr from L *benefactum*.]

benevolence [ben-ev´ol-ėns] *n* disposition to do good; an act of kindness; generosity.—*adj* **benev´olent**.—*adv* **benev´olently**. [Through Fr from L *benevolentia*, goodwill—*bene*, well, *volens, -entis* pr p of *velle*, to wish.]

Bengali [ben-gö´lē] *adj* of or belonging to *Bengali*.—*n* a member of a people living chiefly in Bangladesh and West Bengal in India; their language which is Indic.—*ns* **beng´aline**, [-ēn] a cross-wise ribbed fabric made of rayon, silk, wool, or cotton.—**Bengal´light**, a blue light formerly used in signaling and illumination; any of various colored lights or flares.

benighted [bi-nīt´id] *adj* surrounded by darkness; ignorant. [Pt p of obs verb—pfx *be-*, + **night**.]

benign [bin-īn´] *adj* favorable; gracious; kindly; (*med*) of a tumor, not malignant.—*adv* **benign´ly**.—*adj* **benignant** [binig´nánt], kind; gracious.—*n* **benig´nancy**.—*adv* **benig´nantly**.—*n* **benig´nity**, goodness of disposition; kindness and graciousness. [OFr *benigne*—L *benignus*, for *benigenus—bene*, well, and root of *genus*, birth.]

benison [ben´izn] *n* a blessing. [OFr *beneiçun*—L *benedictiō*. See **benediction**.]

benny [ben´ē] *n* (*slang*) an amphetamine pill, esp Benzedrine.

bent [bent] *pt, pt p* of **bend**.—*n* a tendency; natural inclination of the mind.—*adj* curved or crooked; strongly determined (*with* **on**).—*adj* **bent´wood**, of furniture made of pieces of wood permanently bent into various forms by heat, moisture and pressure. [From **bend**.]

bent grass [bent] *n* any of a genus (*Agrostis*) of low-growing perennial grasses which spread by rhizomes and is used widely as a fine lawn grass. [OE *beonnet*, found in placenames; a Gmc word.]

benumb [bi-num´] *vt* to make numb, to deaden the mind, will, etc. of.—*adj* **benumbed´**. [Pfx *be-*, + **numb**.]

Benzedrine [ben´zė-drēn] *n* a trade name for amphetamine in tablet form taken as a stimulant.

benzene [ben´zēn] *n* a colorless, volatile, toxic hydrocarbon; the simplest member of the aromatic series. [From **benzoin**.]

benzine [benzēn, ben-zēn´] *n* a mixture of hydrocarbons from petroleum; gasoline.

benzocaine [ben´zō-kān] *n* a white powder used in ointments as an anesthetic and to protect against sunburn.

benzoin [ben´zō-in, -zoin] *n* the aromatic resin from trees (genus *Styrax*) of southeastern Asia used in medicine, as a perfume fixative and incense.—*adj* **benzo´ic**. [Most prob through It from Ar *lubān jāwi*, frankincense of Jawa (ie Sumatra).]

benzol [ben´zol´] *n* benzene; a mixture of aromatic hydrocarbons.

bequeath [bi-kwēth´] *vt* to leave (property, etc.) by will; to transmit to posterity. [OE *becwethan*—pfx *be-, cwethan*, to say.]

bequest [bi-kwest´] *n* act of bequeathing; that which is bequeathed, a legacy. [ME *biqueste*—OE pfx *bi-, be-, cwethan*, to say.]

Berber [bûr´bėr] *n* a member of various Caucasoid peoples of north Africa; any of the languages of the Afro-Asiatic group of these peoples.—*adj* of these peoples or their languages. [Ar *barbar*; connection with Gr *barbaros*, foreign, is doubtful.]

berceuse [ber-søz´] *n* a lullaby; instrumental pieces of a like character. [Fr].

bereave [bi-rēv´] *vt* to deprive (of); to leave desolate;—*pt, pt p* **bereaved´**—the latter also **bereft´**.—*adj* **bereaved´**, robbed by death.—*n* **bereave´ment**. [OE *berēafian*, to plunder—*be-*, inten, *rēafian*, to rob.]

beret [ber´ā] *n* a flat, round, soft cap. [Fr *béret*.]

berg [bûrg] *n* an iceberg. [Ger, Du, Swed *berg*, hill; cog with **barrow** (2).]

bergamot [bûr´ga-mot] *n* a pear-shaped orange (*Citrus bergamia*) whose aromatic rind yields oil used in perfumery; any of several mints (genus *Monarda*). [Perh from *Bergamo*, a town in Italy.]

beriberi [ber´i-ber´i] *n* a disease, due to lack of vitamin B. [Sinhalese *beri*, weakness.]

berkelium [bûrk´li-ùm] *n* a transuranium element (symbol Bk, at wt 249, at no 97).

berm, berme [bûrm] *n* a ledge or shoulder as along the edge of a paved road.

Bermuda grass [bėr-mū´da] *n* a trailing stoloniferous grass (*Cynodon dactylon*) used for lawns and golf courses in warm parts of the U.S.

Bermuda onion [bėr-mū´da] *n* a large onion with a mild flavour grown in Texas, California, etc.
Bermuda shorts [bė-mū´da] shorts, for men or women, reaching to just above the knees.
berry [ber´i] *n* any small succulent, stoneless fruit; (*bot*) fruit in which seeds are imbedded in pulp (eg tomato, melon, orange, grape); a coffee-bean; the egg of a lobster or crayfish.—*adj* **berr´ied**, bearing berries. [OE *berie*.]
berserk, berserker [bėr-sûrk´(ėr), -zûrk´(ėr)] *n* a Norse warrior filled with a frenzied and resistless fury; one whose actions are recklessly defiant.—*adj, adv* in a violent frenzy. [ON *berserker*, prob bearsark.]
berth [bûrth] *n* a ship's station at anchor or in port; a built-in bed, as in a ship or train; a situation or place of employment.—*vt* to put into or furnish with a berth, to moor a ship at a berth.—*vi* to occupy a berth.—**give a wide berth to**, to keep well away from. [Ety obscure.]
bertha [bûr´tha] *n* a wide round collar covering the shoulders. [From the name *Bertha*.]
beryl [ber´il] *n* a silicate of beryllium and aluminium, a gemstone of which emerald and aquamarine are varieties.—*n* **beryllium**, a metallic element (symbol Be; at wt 9.0; at no 4). [OFr *beryl*—L *bēryllus*—Gr *bēryllos*.]
beseech [bi-sēch´] *vt* to entreat, to implore; to beg, pray earnestly for;—*pt, pt p* **besought´**.—*adv* **beseech´ingly**. [Pfx *be-*, inten + ME *sechen*, to seek.]
beseem [bi-sēm´] *vi* to be seemly or fit for, to suit. [Pfx *be-*, inten + **seem**.]
beset [bi-set´] *vt* to surround or hem in; to attack from all sides; to harass.—*pr p* **besett´ing**; *pt, pt p* **beset´**.—*adj* **besett´ing** constantly harassing one. [OE *besettan*—pfx *be-*, + **set**.]
beside [bi-sīd´] *prep* at, by the side of, near; in comparison with; in addition to; aside from.—**be beside oneself**, to be distraught with anxiety, fear, or anger. [ME *bi siden*—OE *be sīdan*, by the side (dat).]
besides [bi-sīdz´] *prep* other than; in addition to.—*adv* in addition; except for that mentioned; moreover. [**beside** with the *s* of the adverbial gen.]
besiege [bi-sēj´] *vt* to hem in with armed forces; to close in on; to overwhelm, harrass, etc.—*n* **besieg´er**. [ME *besegen*—pfx *be-*, and *segen*, through OFr and LL—L *sedēre*, to sit.]
besmear [bi-smēr´] *vt* to smear over. [OE *bismierwan*—pfx *be-*, inten, *smierwan*, to anoint.]
besmirch [bi-smûrch´] *vt* to soil; to sully. [Pfx *be-* + **smirch**.]
besom [bē´zọm] *n* a bunch of twigs for sweeping, a broom. [OE *besema*; a common Gmc word; Ger *besen*, Du *bezem*.]
besom [bēz´ọm] *n* a reinforcement or decoration around a pocket opening. [Origin unknown.]
besot [bi-sot´] *vt* to make dull, or stupid; esp to muddle with drunkenness or infatuation.—*pr p* **besott´ing**; *pt p* **besott´ed**. [Pfx *be-*, + **sot**, *n*.]
bespatter [bi-spat´ėr] *vt* to spatter with mud; to defame. [Pfx *be-*, + **spatter**.]
bespeak [bi-spēk] *vt* to speak for or engage beforehand;—*pt* **bespoke´**; *pt p* **bespōke´, bespōk´en**. [OE *besprecan*—pfx *be-, sprecan*, to speak.]
bespoke, bespoken [bi-spōk(-n)] *adj* custom-made; dealing in such articles; (*inf*) engaged to be married.
besprinkle [bi-spring´kl] *vt* to sprinkle. [ME *besprengil*—*be-*, intent, *sprenkel*, freq of *sprengen*, to sprinkle.]
Bessemer process [bes´ėm-ėr] *adj* the method of making steel from pig iron by forcing a blast of air through the molten metal in a refractory-lined furnace to remove impurities. [Sir Henry *Bessemer* (1813–1868).]
best [best] *adj* (*superlative* of **good**) most excellent; most suitable, desirable, etc; largest, good in the highest degree, first, highest, most excellent.—*n* one's utmost endeavour; the highest perfection; the best part.—*adv* (*superlative* of **well**) in the highest degree; in the best manner.—*vt* to defeat or outdo.—**best man**, the principal attendant of the bridegroom at a wedding; **best part**, greater part; **best-seller**, a book or other product that has had one of the biggest sales of the season; the writer of such a book.—**all for the best**, ultimately good; under the most favorable conditions; **make the best of**, to do as well as one can with. [OE *betst, betest*. See **better**.]
bestial [best´i-ȧl] *adj* like a beast; brutally sensual.—*n* **bestial´ity**. [L *bestiālis*.]
bestiary [best´i-ȧr-i] *n* a medieval book with fables about real or mythical animals. [LL *bestiārium*, a menagerie.]
bestir [bi-stûr´] *vt* to put into lively action; to rouse (oneself). [OE *bestyrian*—*be-*, inten. *styrian*, to stir.]
bestow [bi-stō´] *vt* to present as a gift.—*n* **bestow´al**, a disposal; act or fact of conferring as a gift. [ME *bistowen*—*be-*, inten *stowen*. See **stow**.]
bestrew [bi-strōō´] *vt* to strew or scatter about.—*pt p* **bestrewed´, bestrown´, bestrewn´** (followed by **with**). [OE *bestrēowian*—*be-, strēowian*. See **strew**.]
bestride [bi-strīd´] *vt* to sit, mount, or stand astride.—*pt* **bestrid´, bestrode´**; *pt p* **bestrid´, bestridd´en**. [OE *bestrīdan*—pfx *be-, strīdan*, to stride.]
bet [bet] *n* a wager, something staked to be lost or won on an uncertain issue; the thing or sum staked; a person or thing likely to bring about a desired result.—*vti* to declare as in a bet; to stake (money, etc.) in a bet (with someone).—*pr p* **bett´ing**; *pt, pt p* **bet** or **bett´ed**.—*ns* **bett´er, bett´or**, one who bets; **bett´ing**, act of betting or proposing a wager. [Possibly from **abet**.]
beta [bēta] *n* the second letter of the Greek alphabet; second in a group or series.—*n* **beta particle**, an electron or positron ejected from the nucleus of an atom during radioactive disintegration; **beta rays**, a stream of beta particles; **beta wave**, an electrical rhythm of the brain associated with normal waking consciousness.
betake [bi-tāk] *vt* (*arch*) to cause (oneself), to go. [Pfx *be-*, + **take**.]
betel [bē´tl] *n* a climbing pepper (*Piper betle*) whose leaves are chewed together with betal nut and lime as a stimulant esp by southeastern Asians;—**betal nut**, the astringent seed of the betal palm; **betel palm**, an Asian palm (*Areca catechu*) that has an orange-colored fruit with a fibrous husk. [Through Port from Dravidian *vetilla*.]
bête noir [bet nwär] pet aversion. [Fr.]
bethel [beth´el] *n* a hallowed spot; a place of worship for Nonconformists or seamen. [Heb *Bēth-ēl*, house of God.]
bethink [bi-thingk´] vt to remember or call to mind;—*pt, pt p* **bethought** [bi-thöt´]. [OE *bithencan*—pfx *be-*, + **think**.]
betide [bi-tīd´] *vti* to befall, to happen to. [ME *betīden*—pfx *be-*, + **tide**.]
betimes [bi-tīmz´] *adv* in good time; early. [Pfx *be-*, + **time**, with adverbial gen *-s*; like *besides* from beside.]
betoken [bi-tō´kn] *vt* to show by a sign, signify; to presage. [ME *bitacnien*—pfx *be-*, + **token**.]
betray [bi-trā´] *vt* to reveal disloyalty to an enemy; to expose treacherously; to fail to uphold; to deceive, esp to seduce and fail to marry; to reveal unknowingly.—*ns* **betray´al, betray´er**. [ME *betraien*—pfx *be-*, OFr *traïr*—L. *tradēre*, to deliver up.]
betroth [bi-trōTH´, -troth´] *vt* to promise in marriage,—*n* **betrōth´al**.—*n, adj* **betrōthed**. [ME *bitreuthien*—pfx *be-*, + **truth** or **troth**.]
better [bet´ėr] *adj* (comparative of **good**) good in a greater degree; preferable; improved; stronger in health; larger.—*adv* (comparative of **well**) in a more excellent manner; in a higher degree; more.—*n* a person superior in position, etc.; a more excellent thing, condition, etc.—*vt* to improve; to surpass.—*n* **bett´erment**, a bettering; an improvement. **be better off**, to be in more desirable circumstances; **get the better of**, to defeat; to outwit. [OE *bet* (adv) *betera* (adj), better; Ger *besser*.]
between [bi-twēn´] *prep* the space time, etc. separating (two things); involving (a struggle between powers); connecting (*a bond between friends*); in the combined possession of; by the joint action of; from one or the other of (*choose between us*).—*adv* in the intermediate space, time, etc.; **between ourselves, between you and me**, in confidence. [OE *betwēonum, betwēonan*—*be, twēgen*, neut *twā*, twain, two.]
betwixt [bi-twikst´] *prep, adv* between.—**betwixt and between**, not altogether one nor altogether the other. [OE *betweox*—*twā*, two, and the suffix, *-ix*, -ish, with added *-t* as in *against*.
bevel [bev´l] *n* an instrument for measuring angles; an angle other than a right angle; angled part or surface.—*adj* having the form of a bevel; slanting.—*vt* to cut to an angle other than a right angle.—*vi* to slope at an angle.—*pr p* **bev´elling**; *pt p* **bev´elled**.—*n* **bev´el gear**, a gearwheel meshing with another at an angle. [Fr *biveau*, an instrument for measuring angles.]
beverage [bev´ėr-ij] *n* any liquid for drinking, esp one other than water. [OFr *bevrage*—*beivre*—L *bibĕre*, to drink.]
bevy [bev´i] *n* a group, esp of girls or women; a flock of birds, esp of quails. [ME *bevey*, prob the same as OFr *bevee, buvee*, drink; the transference of sense being perh from a drink to a drinking-party.]
bewail [bi-wāl´] *vt* to lament; to mourn. [Pfx *be-*, **wail**.]
beware [bi-wār´] *vi* and *vti* to be wary or careful (of). [From the words **be** + **ware** (2), run together. Cf **wary**.]
bewilder [bi-wil´dėr] *vt* to perplex; to confuse hopelessly.—*n* **bewil´derment**. [Pfx *be-*, + obs Eng *wildern*—OE *wilddēoren*, wilderness—*wild*, wild, *deor*, beast.]
bewitch [bi-wich´] *vt* to cast a spell over; to fascinate or charm.—*ns* **bewitch´ery, bewitch´ment**.—*adj* **bewitch´ing**, charming, enchanting.—*adv* **bewitch´ingly**. [ME *biwichen*—*be-*, inten OE *wiccian*—*wicca, wicce*, witch.]
bey [bā] *n* a Turkish governor of a town or province; the native ruler of Tunis. [Turk *bey*, pronounced *bā*, a governor.]
beyond [bi-yond´] *prep* farther on than; past; later than; outside the reach of (*beyond help*); more than.—*adv* farther away.—**the (great) beyond**, whatever follows death. [OE *begeondan*—pfx *be-, geond*, across, beyond.]
bezel [bez´ėl] *n* the oblique side or face of a cut gem; the grooved rim in which a gem or watch crystal is set; the slope at the edge of a chisel or plane. [From OFr (Fr *biseau*); of uncertain origin.]
bezique [be-zēk´] *n* a car game for two players played with a 64-card deck made up of two standard decks with sixes and cards below omitted whose object is to score points by taking tricks and melding; meld of the queen of spades and the jack of diamonds. [Fr *bésigue*, of obscure origin.]
Bhagavad Gita [bä´gȧ-vȧd gē´tȧ] *n* the most popular book of Hindu scripture that conveys the message that there are many ways to salvation. [Sans 'The Song of the Lord'.]
bhang [bang] *n* the leaves and shoots of hemp used as a narcotic and intoxicant. [Hindustani *bhāng*; Pers *bang*.]
bi- [bī] *prefix* meaning: having two; doubly; happening twice during every; using two or both; joining or involving two. [L *bis*, twice, *bīnī*, two by two, for *duis, duīnī*.]
biannual [bī-an´ū-ȧl] *adj* occurring twice a year. [L *bi-*, twice, *annus*, a year.]
bias [bī´as] *n* a slanting or diagonal line, cut or sewn across the grain in cloth; partiality; prejudice.—*vt* to prejudice.—*pt, pt p* **bī´ased** or **bī´assed**.—*adj* slanting; diagonal. [Fr *biais*, slant; of unknown origin.]

biathlon [bī-ath´lon] *n* an athletic event comprising skiing and rifle shooting.
bib [bib] *n* a cloth or plastic cover tied under a child's chin at meals; the upper part of an apron. [ME *bibben*, most prob from L *bibĕre*, to drink.]
Bibb lettuce [bib] *n* a variety of lettuce with a small open head and dark green leaves.
Bible [bī´bl] *n* the sacred writings of the Christian Church, consisting of the Old and New Testaments; the Holy Scriptures of Judaism, the Old Testament; any authoritative book.—*adj* **biblical** [bib´li-kl] of or relating to the Bible; scriptural.—*adv* **bib´lically**.—**Bible belt**, area in the southern US believed to hold uncritically to the literal accuracy of the Bible; an area marked by religious fundamentalism. [Fr—Low L *biblia*, from Gr *ta biblia*, lit 'the books', esp the canonical books, sing *biblion*, a book, dim of *biblos*, papyrus, paper.]
bibliography [bib-li-og´raf-i] n a list of writings on a given subject or by a given author.—*n* **bibliog´rapher**.—*adjs* **bibliograph´ic, bibliograph´ical**. [Gr *biblion*, a book, *graphein*, to write.]
bibliolatry [bib-li-ol´at-ri] *n* an excessive reverence for a book, esp the Bible.—*n* **bibliol´ater**.—*adj* **bibliol´atrous**. [Gr *biblion*, a book, *latreia*, worship.]
bibliomania [bib-li-ō-mān´i-a] *n* a mania for collecting books.—*n* **bibliomān´iac**. [Gr *biblion*, a book, + **mania**.]
bibliophile [bib´li-ō-fil] *n* a lover or collector of books. [Fr,—Gr *biblion*, a book, *philos*, friend.]
bibliopole [bib´li-ō-pōl] *n* a dealer, esp in rare or curious books.—Also **bibliŏp´olist**.—*n* **bibliop´oly**. [Gr *biblion*, a book, *pōleein*, to sell.]
bibulous [bib´ū-lus] *adj* addicted to or fond of alcoholic liquor. [L *bibulus*—*bibĕre*, to drink.]
bicameral [bī-kam´ėr-ål] *adj* having two legislative chambers. [L *bi-*, twice, *camera*, chamber.]
bicarbonate [bī-kär´bon-åt] *n* sodium bicarbonate. [L *bi-*, twice, + **carbonate**.]
bicentenary [bī-sen-ten´å-i, -tēn´-] *adj* pertaining to two hundred years.—*n* the two hundredeth anniversary. [L *bi-*, twice, *centēnārius*, pertaining to a hundred—*centum*, a hundred.]
bicentennial [bī-sen-ten´i-ål] *adj* pertaining to two hundred years.—*n* a two hundredth anniversary or its celebration. [L *bi-*, twice, *centum*, a hundred, *annus*, year.]
biceps [bī´seps] *n* the muscle with two points of origin, esp the large muscle in the front of the upper arm. [L *biceps*, two-headed—*bis*, twice, *caput*, head.]
bicker [bik´ėr] *vi* to squabble, quarrel.—Also *n*. [Perh *bicker* = picker, or *pecker*, to *peck* repeatedly with the beak.]
bicuspid [bī-kus´pid] *adj* having two points.—*n* any of the eight adult teeth with two pointed crowns. [L. *bi-*, twice, + **cusp**.]
bicycle [bī´si-kl] *n* a vehicle consisting of a metal frame on two wheels, and having handlebars and a seat.—*vti* to ride or travel on a bicycle.—*n* **bī´cyclist**. [Formed from L *bi-*, *bis*, twice, + Gr *kyklos*, wheel.]
bid [bid] *vt* to command or ask; to offer (an amount) as the price one will pay or accept; to express (*to bid farewell*); (*cards*) to state (a number of tricks) and declare (trumps).—*vi* to make a bid.—*pr p* **bidd´ing**; *pt* **bade** [bad, sometimes bād], **bid**; *pt p* **bidd´en, bid**,—*n* a bidding; an amount, etc. bid; an attempt or try (for); (*inf*) an invitation.—*adj* **bidd´able**, obedient, docile.—*ns* **bidd´er; bidd´ing**, offer; invitation; command.—**bid fair**, to seem likely. [Partly. OE *bēodan* (Ger *bieten*, to offer; partly OE *biddan* (Ger *bitten*, to pray, ask.]
biddy [bid´ē] *n* a hen; (*slang*) an old woman who is eccentric, gossipy, etc. [Perh *Biddy*, short form of *Bridget*.]
bide [bīd] *vi* (*arch, dial*) to wait; to dwell.—*vt* (*arch, dial*) to endure.—*adj* **bided.—bide one's time**, to wait patiently for an opportunity. [OE *bīdan*; but sometimes for **abide**.]
bidet [bi-dā] *n* a low, bowl-shaped bathroom fixture with running water for bathing the crotch.
biennial [bī-en´i-al] *adj* lasting two years; happening once in two years.—*n* a plant that flowers and fructifies only in its second year, then dies.—*adv* **bienn´ially**. [L *biennālis*—*bi-*, twice, and *annus*, a year.]
bier [bēr] *n* a portable framework on which a coffin is put. [OE *bær*; Ger *bahre*, L *feretrum*—*fĕrre*, to bear. From root of verb **bear**.]
bif [bif] *n* (*slang*) to strike, hit.—Also *vt*. [Imit]
bifocal [bī-fō´kål] *adj* having two foci, used of eyeglasses for near, or for distant, vision.—*n pl* **bi´focals**. [L *bi-*, twice, **focal**. *See* **focus**.]
bifurcate [bī´fůr-kåt or -fûr´-], **bifurcated**, [-id] *adj* divided into two parts or branches.—*n* **bifurcā´tion**. [L *bifurcus*—*bi*, *bis*, twice, *furca*, a fork.]
big [big] *adj* large or great; pregnant; important; pompous (esp *to talk big, to look big*).—*adj* **bigg´ish**, rather big.—*ns* **big´ness**, bulk, size.—*ns* **big business**, an economic group of corporations having great influence on social and political policy; **Big Board**, the New York Stock Exchange; **Big Brother**, person or organization that exercises total dictatorial control; **Big Dipper**, the seven main stars in the constellation Ursa Major; **big game**, large animals or fish sought and taken for sport; an important, usu. risky objective.—*adj* **big´heart´ed**, quick to give or forgive; generous; **bighorn**, a Rocky Mountain wild sheep (*Ovis canadensis*) with a grayish brown coat and long, curved horns; **big league**, the most important leagues in national sport, esp baseball; an enterprise or group at the top of its field; **big mouth** (*slang*), a person who talks too much esp in an opinionated way; **big name**, a person who is well known, esp in entertainment; **big shot** (*inf*), an important person; **big stick** (*inf*), force or the threat of force; **big time**, the top level in any pursuit; **big top**, the main circus tent; **big´wig** (*inf*), a person of importance. [ME *big*, origin very obscure.]
bigamy [big´åm-i] *n* the crime of marrying a second time when one is already legally married.—*n* **big´amist**.—*adj* **big´amous**.—*adv* **big´amously**. [L *bi-*, twice; Gr *gamos*, marriage.]
bight [bīt] *n* a wide bay; a bend or coil of a rope. [OE *byht*; cf Dan and Swed *bugt*, Du *bocht*.]
bigot [big´ȯt] *n* one blindly and obstinately devoted to a particular creed or party.—*adj* **big´oted**.—*n* **big´otry**. [OFr of uncertain origin.]
bijou [bē´zhōō] *n* a trinket; a jewel.—*pl* **bijoux** [bē´zhōō].—*adj* small and elegant.—*n* **bijou´terie**, jewellery. [Fr]
bike [bīk] *n* (*inf*) a bicycle; a motorcycle.
bikini [bi-kē´nē] *n* a very scanty form of two-piece bathing suit for women. [Said to be from *Bikini*, an atoll in the Marshall Islands in the Pacific, partly denuded by atom-bomb experiments.]
bilabiate [bī-lā´bi-åt] *adj* having two lips, as some corollas. [L *bi-*, twice, + **labiate**.]
bilateral [bī-lat´ėr-ål] *adj* having two sides; affecting two parties reciprocally.—*adv* **bilat´erally**. [L *bi-*, twice, + **lateral**.]
bilberry [bil´ber-i] *n* any of several plants (genus *Vaccinium*) that differ from typical blueberries in having their flowers arising singly; its dark blue berry. [Cf Dan *böllebær*.]
bilbo[1], **bilboa** [bil´bō] *n* a rapier or sword. [From *Bilbao*, in Spain.]
bilbo[2] [bil´bō] *n* a long bar of iron used to confine the feet of prisoners, esp on shipboard.
bile [bīl] *n* a gall, a thick bitter fluid secreted by the liver; bad temper.—*adj* **bilious** [bil´-yůs], pertaining to or affected by bile.—*n* **bil´iousness**. [Fr—L *bīlis*.]
bilge [bilj] *n* the bulging part of a cask; the broadest part of a ship's bottom; filth such as collects there; (*slang*) nonsense.—*n* **bilge´ wat´er**, the foul water in a ship's bilge. [Most prob conn with **bulge**.]
bilharzia [bil-här´zi-å] *n* schisto somiasis. [Theodor *Bilharz* (1825–62).]
bilingual [bī-ling´gwål] *adj* expressed in two languages; speaking two languages (eg English and Welsh). [L *bilinguis*—*bi-*, twice, *lingua*, language.]
bilk [bilk] *vt* to cheat, swindle.—*n* **bilk´er**. [Perh a form of **balk**.]
bill[1] [bil] *n* a weapon used formerly, a long staff ending in a hook-shaped blade; a billhook.—*n* **bill´hook**, a cutting or pruning tool with a hooked blade. [OE *bil*; Ger *bille*.]
bill[2] [bil] *n* the beak of a bird; a beaklike mouth part, as of a turtle.—*vi* to touch bills together.—**bill and coo**, to kiss, talk softly, etc. in a loving way. [OE *bile*, most prob the same word as the preceding.]
bill[3] [bil] *n* a statement for goods supplied or services rendered; a list, as a menu or theater program; a poster or handbill; a draft of a proposed law, to be discussed by a legislature; a bill of exchange; a piece of paper money; (*law*) a written declaration of charges and complaints filed.—*vt* to make out a bill of (items); to present a statement of charges to; to advertise by bills; to book (a performer).—*ns* **bill´board´**, a large panel designed to carry outdoor advertising; **bill´fold**, a folding pocketbook for paper money, often with compartments for cards, photographs, loose change, etc.; **bill´ing**, the order in which actors´ names are listed.—**bill of exchange**, a written order to pay a certain sum of money to the person named; **bill of fare**, a menu; a program; **bill of health**, an official certificate of the state of health on board ship before sailing; a usu. favorable report about a condition or situation; **bill of indictment**, an indictment before it is found or ignored by the grand jury; **bill of lading**, a receipt issued to a shipper by a carrier, listing the goods received for shipment; **Bill of Rights**, the first ten amendments to the US Constitution, which guarantees civil rights; **bill of sale**, a written statement transferring ownership by sale.—**fill the bill** (*inf*), to meet the requirements. [Through Low L *billa*, a seal—L *bulla*, a knob. Cf **bull** (2).]
billabong [bil´a-bong] *n* (*Austr*) an effluent from a river; a waterhole, pond, or small lake. [Native words *billa*, river, *bung*, dead.]
billet[1] [bil´ėt] *n* a written order to provide lodging for military personnel; the lodging; a position or job.—*vt* to assign to lodging by billet.—*pr p* **bill´eting**; *pt p* **bill´eted**. [Fr; dim of **bill** (3).]
billet[2] [bil´ėt] *n* a chunky piece of wood (as for firewood); a bar of metal. [Fr *billette*—*bille*, the young stock of a tree; prob of Celt orig.]
billet-doux [bil´e-dōō´] *n* a love letter.—*pl* **billets-doux** [bil´e-dōōz]. [Fr *billet*, a letter, *doux*, sweet.]
billiards [bil´yårdz] *n* a game played with three hard balls driven by a cue on a felt-covered table with raised, cushioned edges.—*adj* **bill´iard**. [Fr *billard*—*bille*, a stick, hence a cue.]
billion [bil´yȯn] *n* a thousand millions, the numeral 1 followed by 9 zeros; in France, Germany and the United Kingdom, a million millions, the numeral 1 followed by 12 zeros. [L *bi-*, twice, + **million**.]
billow [bil´ō] *n* a large wave; any large swelling mass or surge, as of smoke.—*vi* to surge or swell in a billow.—*adjs* **bill´owed, bill´owy**. [Scand ON *bylgja*.]
billy [bil´i] *n* a club, esp a policeman's heavy stick.—*pl* **bill´ies**. [OFr *bille*, a tree trunk.]

billy goat [bil´i] *n* (*inf*) a male goat.

biltong [bil´tong] *n* (*S Africa*) jerked meat. [Du *bil*, buttock, *tong*, tongue.]

bimbo [bim´bō] *n* a generalized disparaging term for a man or a woman; a prostitute.

bimetallism [bī-met´ȧl-izm] *n* the use of two metals, esp gold and silver, as the monetary standard, with fixed values in relation to each other.—*adj* **bimetall´ic.**—*n* **bimet´allist**. [L *bi-*, twice + **metal**.]

bimonthly [bī-munth´li] *adj* once in two months; loosely twice a month. [L *bi-*, twice + **month**.]

bin [bin] *n* a box or crib etc. for storing grain, coal, etc. [OE *binn*, a manger.]

binary [bī´nȧr-i] *adj* made up of two parts; double; denoting or of a number system in which the base is two, each number being expressed by using only two digits, specifically 0 and 1.—**binary operation**, a rule which assigns to each pair of elements in a set a uniquely defined third element which is also uniquely the consequence of the given operation in the given pair; **binary star**, a double star system containing two associated stars revolving around a common center of gravity. [L *bīnārius*—*bīnī*, two by two—*bis*.]

bind [bīnd] *vt* to tie together, as with rope; to hold or restrain; to encircle with a belt, etc.; to bandage (*often with* **up**); to constipate; to reinforce or ornament the edges of by a band, as of tape; to fasten together the pages of (a book) and protect with a cover; to obligate by duty, love, etc.; to compel, as by oath or legal restraint.—*vi* to become tight or stiff; to stick together; to be obligatory.—*n* anything that binds; (*inf*) a difficult situation.—*pt, pt p* **bound**.—*n* **bind´er**, one who binds, as books; a cover for holding sheets of paper together; a binding substance, as tar.—*adj* **bind´ing**, restraining; obligatory.—*n* the act of binding; anything that binds; the covering of a book.—*ns* **bind´weed**, any of a genus *Convolvulus* of plants that entwine the stems of other plants; **bine**, the slender stem of a climbing plant. [OE *bindan*.]

bingo [bing´gō] *n* a game of chance played by covering on a card each number called.

binnacle [bin´ȧ-kl] *n* (*naut*) the box in which a ship's compass is kept. [Formerly *bittacle*—Port *bitácola*—L *habitāculum*, a dwelling-place—*habitāre*, to dwell.]

binocular [bīn-ok´ūl-ȧr] *adj* having two eyes; suitable for two eyes.—*n* (*pl*) a field glass having two tubes, one for each eye. [L *bīnī*, two by two, *oculus*, an eye.]

binomial [bī-nōm´i-ȧl] *adj, n* (denoting) a mathematical expression consisting of two terms connected by a plus sign or a minus sign.—**binomial nomenclature**, a system for naming plants and animals giving every species an official scientific name accepted internationally; **binomial theorem**, a general formula that expresses any power of a binomial. [L *bi-*, *bis*, twice, *nōmen*, a name.]

bio- [bī-ō] in composition, life; of living things. [Gr *bios*, life.]

bioavailability [bī-ō-a-vāl-a-bil´it-i] *n* the rate at which a drug, etc. enters the bloodstream and circulates, as to organs.

biochemistry [bīō-kem´is-tri] *n* a science concerned with the chemistry of plants and animals.—*adj* **biochem´ical**.—*n* **biochem´ist**. [Gr *bios*, life and **chemistry**.]

biocide [bī´ō-sīd] *n* a chemical agent that can kill living organisms.

bioclean [bī´ō-klīn] *adj* as free as possible from microorganisms; aseptic.

biodegradable [bī-ō-dė-grā´di-bl] readily decomposed by bacterial action.

biofeedback [bī-ō-fēd´bak] *n* the mechanical monitoring of bodily functions for the purpose of gaining control of the functions monitored.

biogenesis [bī-ō-jen´es-is] *n* the theory that life can come only from living things; biosynthesis. [Gr *bios*, life and **genesis**.]

biography [bī-og´raf-i] *n* an account of a person's life written by another; biographical writings in general; account of the chronology of something (as an animal, a coin, a building).—*n* **biog´rapher**.—*adjs* **biograph´ic, -al**.—*adv* **biograph´ically**. [Gr *bios*, life, *graphein*, to write.]

biology [bī-ol´oj-i] *n* the science that treats of living organisms.—*adj* **biolog´ical**.—*adv* **biolog´ically**.—*n* **biol´ogist**.—**biological clock**, means by which living organisms can time their rhythmic periods without external cues; **biological control**, control of destructive organisms by nonchemical means; **biological warfare**, the use of living organisms or their toxic products as weapons of war. [Gr *bios*, life, *logos*, a discourse.]

biomass [bi´ō-mas] *n* the amount of living material (animals, plants, etc.) in a unit of area; fuel from plant materials and animal waste. [Gr *bios* life + **mass**.]

bionics [bī-on´iks] *n* the science of designing instruments or systems modeled after living organisms.—*adj* **bion´ic**, of bionics; having an artificial body part of parts, as in science fiction, so as to enhance strength, abilities, etc. [Gr *bios*, life.]

biophysics [bī-o-fiz´iks] *n* the application of physics to the study of living things. [Gr bios, life + **physics**.]

biopsy [bī´op-si] *n* the removal of bits of living tissue for diagnosis of disease; such examination. [Gr *bios*, life, *opsis*, appearance.]

biorhythm [bī´ō-riTH´m] *n* an inherent rhythm that seems to control or initiate biological processes.

biosynthesis [bī-ō-sin´thė-sis] *n* the formation of chemical compounds by living organisms.

biotin [bī´ō-tin] *n* a factor of the Vitamin B group.

bipartisan [bī-pär´ti-zn] *adj* of, representing, or supported by two political parties.

bipartite [bī-pärt´īt] *adj* having two parts, involving two. [L *bi-*, *bis*, twice, *partītus*, divided—*partīre*, or *-īrī*, to divide.]

biped [bī´ped] *n* an animal with two feet.—*adj*. [L *bipēs*—*bi-*, *bis*, twice, *pēs*, *pedis*, foot.]

biplane [bī´plān] *n* an airplane with two sets of wings, one above the other. [L *bi-*, twice + **plane**.]

birch [bûrch] *n* a genus (*Betula*) of trees having many forms and sizes; a rod for punishment, consisting of a birch twig or twigs.—*vt* to flog.—*adjs* **birch, birch´en**. [OE *berc, bierce*; ON *björk*, Sans *bhūrja*.]

bird [bûrd] *n* any of a class (Aves) of warm-blood egg-laying vertebrates with a feathered body, scaly legs, and forelimbs modified to form wings; a game bird; a shuttlecock; (*inf*) a fellow, esp a peculiar person; anything resembling a bird esp by flying or being aloft.—*vi* to observe or identify birds in their wild environment.—*ns* **bird´call**, a device for imitating the sound of a bird; the note or cry of a bird; a sound imitating it; **bird dog**, a gundog trained to hunt or retrieve fowl; one (as a canvasser) who seeks out something for someone else; one who steals another's date.—*vi* **bird-dog**, to follow closely.—*vt* to watch closely.—*ns* **bird´ie** (*golf*), a hole in one stroke less than par; **bird´lime**, a sticky substance for catching birds; **bird´seed**, a mixture of seeds for feeding caged and wild birds; **bird's eye**, a speedwell (*Veronica chamaedrys*); an allover pattern for fabrics consisting of a diamond with a dot in the center; a small spot in wood surrounded by irregular elipses—*adj* marked with spots resembling birds' eyes; seen from above as if by a flying bird; cursory; of wood (as maple) containing bird's-eyes.—**bird of paradise**, any of various brilliantly plumed birds (family Paradiseidae) of the New Guinea area; a house plant (*Strelitzia reginae)* having an orange and purple resembling a bird's head; **bird of passage**, a person leading a wandering life; a migratory bird; **bird of prey**, a carnivorous bird (as a hawk, falcon, or vulture) that lives on meat taken by hunting or on carrion; **bird's-foot trefoil**, a plant (Lotus corniculatus) closely related to true clovers and used widely for fodder. **for the birds** (*slang*) not to be taken seriously, of little value; **get the bird** (*slang*), be rejected. [OE *brid*, the young of a bird, a bird.]

bireme [bī´rēm] *n* an ancient vessel with two tiers of oars. [Fr,—L *birēmis*—*bi*, twice, and *rēmus*, an oar.]

biretta [bir-et´a] *n* a square cap with three projections worn by Roman Catholic clergy. [It *berretta*—Low L *birretum*, a cap.]

birth [bûrth] *n* the act of bearing or bringing forth; coming into the world; the offspring born; lineage; dignity of family; beginning or origin.—*ns* **birth´control**, the control of reproduction by contraceptives; **birth´day**, the day on which one is born, or the anniversary of that day.—*adj* relating to the day of one's birth.—*ns* **birth´mark**, a peculiar mark on one's body at birth; **birth´place**, the place of one's birth; **birth´rate**, the number of births per thousand of population per year; **birth´right**, the right to which one is entitled by birth; **birth´stone**, a gem symbolizing the month of one's birth.—**give birth to**, to bring forth (offspring); to create; **in one's birthday suit**, (*inf*), naked. [Prob ON *byrth*.]

bis [bis] *adv* twice; (*mus*) a direction for repetition. [L.]

biscuit [bis´kit] *n* a quick bread baked in small pieces; pottery that has undergone the first firing before being glazed.—*adj* pale brown in color. [OFr *bescoit*—L *bis*, twice, *coquĕre, coctum*, to cook or bake.]

bisect [bī-sekt´] *vt* to cut into two equal parts; (*geom*) to divide into two equal parts.—*ns* **bisec´tion; bisec´tor**, a line that bisects. [L *bi-*, twice, and *secāre*, *sectum*, to cut.]

bisexual [bī-seks´ū-ȧl] *adj* attracted sexually to both sexes.—Also *n*. [L *bi-*, twice, + **sexual**.]

bishop [bish´ȯp] *n* a high-ranking Christian clergyman governing a diocese or church district; a chessman that can move in a diagonal direction.—*n* **bish´opric**, the office and jurisdiction of a bishop; a diocese. [OE *biscop*—L *episcopus*—Gr *episkopos*, an overseer—*epi*, upon, *skopeein*, to look at.]

bismuth [biz´muth, or bis´-] *n* a metallic element (symbol Bi; at wt 209.0; no 83). [Ger *bismuth, wissmuth* (now *wismut*).]

bison [bī´son] *n* a large wild ox (genus *Bison*), wisent; the buffalo. [From L *bisōn*, prob of Gmc origin.]

bisque[1] [bisk] *n* unglazed white porcelain. [Corr of **biscuit**.]

bisque[2] [bisk] *n* a handicap whereby the recipient chooses the time at which to claim the concession allowed. [Fr.]

bisque[3] [bisk] *n* a thick cream soup made of shellfish, game, or pureed vegetables; an ice cream containing ground nuts or powdered macaroons.

bister, bistre [bis´tėr] *n* a warm brown pigment used in art. [Fr *bistre*.]

bit[1] [bit] *n* a bite, a morsel (of food); a small piece; (*inf*) a coin in former use (12½ cents); the smallest degree; a brief space of time; a small part in a theatrical performance; the aggregation of identifying characteristics of a situation, condition, activity, etc.—*adj* **bitt´y**, small, tiny; made up of scraps of something.—**a bit**, rather, somewhat; **a bit much**, a little more than one is willing to tolerate; **bit by bit**, gradually; **do one's bit**, to do one's share. [From **bite**.]

bit[2] [bit] *n* a metal mouthpiece in a bridle, used as a control; a drilling or boring tool for use in a brace, drill press, etc.; something bit and held between the teeth, as the stem of a pipe or cigar holder.—*vt* to put the bit in the mouth; to curb or restrain; **take the bit between one's teeth**, to be beyond restraint. [From **bite**.]

bit[3] [bit] *n* a unit of information in computers equivalent to on, off or yes, no; the physical representation of this (as in a computer tape or memory). [Contracted *b*inary dig*it*.]

bit[4] *ptp* of **bite**.

bitch [bich] *n* the female of the dog, wolf and other carnivorous animals; (*slang*) a spiteful woman. [OE *bicce*.]

bite [bīt] *vti* to seize or tear with the teeth; to puncture with the mouth parts, as an insect; to eat into chemically; to cause to smart; to wound by a sharp weapon;—*vi* to press or snap the teeth (into, at, etc.); to cause a biting sensation; to grip; to seize a bait; to be caught, as by a trick.—*pt* **bit**; *pt p* **bit** or **bitt´en.**—*n* a grasp by the teeth; a puncture by an insect; something bitten off; a mouthful; a snack; (*inf*) a sum deducted, as by tax.—*n* **bit´er.**—*adj* **bit´ing,—bite the bullet**, to confront a painful situation bravely. [OE *bītan*.]

bitt [bit] *n* a post on a ship's deck for fastening cables (usu. in *pl*).—*vt* to fasten round the bitts. [Perh ON *biti*, a cross beam.]

bitter [bit´ėr] *adj* biting or acrid to the taste; sharp; sorrowful, painful; acrimonious; harsh; resentful; cynical.—*adj* **bitt´erly.**—*n* **bitt´erness.**—*n pl* **bitt´ers**, a liquor containing bitter herbs etc. used in some cocktails.—*ns* **bitt´ernut**, a tall N American tree (*Carva cordiformis*) found throughout the central and eastern US; **bitt´erroot**, a perennial herb (*Lewisia rediviva*) of the Rocky mountains with pink or white flowers; **bitt´ersweet**, something that is pleasurable but alloyed with pain; a sprawling poisonous nightshade (*Solanum dulcamara*) with reddish-orange oval berries; a N American climbing, twining vine (*Celastrus scandens*); pipsissewa.—*adj* being at once bitter and sweet; of chocolate containing little sugar.—**bitter end**, (*naut*) the inboard end, as of a cable or rope; the last extremity, however painful. [OE *biter—bītan*, to bite.]

bittern [bit´ėrn] *n* any of various American herons, esp the American bittern (*Botaurus lentiginosus*) marked by their booming cry. [ME *bittour, botor*—OFr *butor*.]

bitumen [bi-tū´men, or bit´-] *n* any of several substances obtained as residue in the distillation of coal tar, petroleum, etc. or occurring naturally as asphalt.—**bituminous coal**, coal that yields pitch or tar when it is burned; soft coal.—*adj* **bitūminous.**

bivalent [bī-vā´lėnt, or biv´a-lėnt] *adj* (*chem*) having a valency of two; pertaining to one of a pair of homologuous chromosomes (also *n*).—*ns* **bivalence, bivalency**. [L *bī*-, twice, and **valent**.]

bivalve [bī´valv] *n* any mollusk having two valves or shells hinged together, as a clam. [L *bi*-, twice, *valva*, a leaf of a door.]

bivouac [biv´ōō-ak] *n* a temporary camp, esp one without tents or other cover.—*vi* to pass the night in a bivouac.—*pr p* **biv´ouacking**; *pt p* **biv´ouacked**. [Fr,—Ger *bei*, by, *wachen*, to watch.]

biweekly [bī´wēk´li] *adj* occurring once in two weeks, or twice a week.—*n* a periodical issued twice a week. [L *bi*-, twice, and **weekly**.]

bizarre [bi-zär´] *adj* odd, fantastic, extravagent. [Fr,—Sp *bizarro*, gallant.]

blab [blab] *vti* to reveal (a secret); to gossip.—*pr p* **blabb´ing**; *pt p* **blabbed**—*n* gossip.—*n* **blabb´er**. [ME *blabbe*, a chatterer, also *blabber*, to babble.]

black [blak] *adj* of the darkest color, like coal or soot; having dark-colored skin and hair, esp Negro; without light; dirty; evil, wicked; sad, dismal; sullen.—*n* black color; or pigment, absence of color; a Negro; black clothes, esp when worn in mourning.—*vti* to make or become black;—*n* **black´amoor**, a dark-skinned person, esp a Negro.—*adj* **black´-and-tan**, having black hair on the back, and tan or yellowish-brown elsewhere, esp of a terrier.—*n* an auxilliary policeman in Ireland about 1920 (from his khaki uniform with black cap and armlet).—*adj* **black´-a-vised** [blak´ä-vist], swarthy in complexion.—*vt* **black´ball**, to vote against; to ostracize; to reject in voting by putting a black ball into a ballot-box.—*ns* **black´ball; black bear**, the common American bear (*Euarctos americanus*) having a brown, black, or white coat; **black belt**, a black belt awarded to an expert of the highest skill in judo or karate; **black´berry**, the fruit of the bramble (genus *Rubus*); a plant bearing the fruit; **black´bird**, any of various birds (family Icteridae) the male of which is almost all black; **black´board**, a board painted black for writing in chalk; **black´cap**, chickadee;—*vt* **black´en**, to make black; to defame.—*ns* **Black English**, a nonstandard dialect of English held to be spoken by Afro-Americans; **black´flag**, the flag of a pirate; **Black´foot**, a confederacy of Amerindians of Montana, Alberta, and Saskatchewan; a member of the Blackfoot;—*pl* **Blackfoot, Blackfeet**; the Algonquian language of the Blackfoot; **blackguard** [blag´ärd], a scoundrel, villain; one who uses foul or abusive language.—*adj* low; scurrilous.—*vt* to vituperate, abuse.—**black gum**, a woodland tree (*Nyssa sylvatica*) of eastern N America of the dogwood family;—*ns* **black´head**, a dark plug or dried fatty matter in a pore of the skin; **black´ing**, a substance used for blacking leather, etc.—*adj* **black´ish.**—*n* **black´jack**, a small leather-covered bludgen with a flexible handle; the card game twenty-one.—*vt* to hit with a blackjack.—*n* **black´lead**, graphite; **black´letter**, a heavy, angular condensed typeface; this style of handwriting; **black´list**, a list of those censured, refused employment, etc. Also *vt*—*n* **black´mail**, money extorted by threat of revealing something discreditable in the victim's life—*vt* to coerce (into doing something) by threats.—*ns* **blackmail´er; Black´Maria**, a patrol wagon. **black mark**, mark indicating something unfavorable on one's record; **black mar´ket**, illicit buying and selling.—Also *adj*—*ns*; **black mass**, a travesty of the Christian Mass performed by practicioners of black magic; **Black Muslim**, a member of an Islamic sect of American blacks; **black´ness; black´out**, the darkness produced by total extinction or concealment of lights; temporary loss of consciousness; **black power**, political and economic power sought by American blacks in the struggle for civil rights.—Also *adj*—*ns* **black´sheep**, a disreputable member of a family or group; **Black´shirt**, a member of a Fascist organization, esp the Italian Fascist party; **black´smith**, a smith who works in iron; **black tie**, a black bow tie worn with a tuxedo.—*adj* **black-tie**, donoting an occasion when a tuxedo should be worn.—*ns* **black´top**, a bituminous mixture, usu. asphalt, used as a surface for roads, etc. *vt* to cover with black top; **black widow**, a venomous New World spider (*Latrodectus mactans*), the female of which is black and has an hourglass-shaped mark on the underside of the abdomen.—**black and blue**, with the livid color of a bruise; **black art**, magic used for evil purposes; **black´body**, an ideal body or surface that absorbs all radiant energy falling upon it with no reflection; **black book**, a book containing a blacklist; (*inf*), an address book, esp one owned by a man; **black box**, a flight recorder; something with mysterious internal functions or mechanisms; **the Black Death**, the name given to the bubonic plague which was pandemic in 14th century Europe; **black eye**, a discoloration around the eye; a bad reputation; **-black-eyed Susan**, either of two N American cone-flowers (*Rudbeckiea hirta* and *R serotina*) having flower heads with orange or yellow rays and a dark centre; **black hole**, a hypothetical invisible region in space held to be caused by the collapse of a massive star.—**in black and white**, in writing or in print; in no colors but black and white, and shades of gray. [OE *blæc*, black.]

bladder [blad´ėr] *n* a sac that fills with fluid, esp one that holds urine flowing from the kidneys; a thing resembling this (a football bladder).—*ns* **bladd´ernut**, a shrub or small tree (*Staphylea trifolia*) of temperate N America grown as an ornamental; **bladd´erwort**, a genus (*Utricularia*) of aquatic insectivorous plants with bladders to catch their prey; **bladd´erwrack**, a common brown seaweed (*Fucus visiculosus*) which is covered with bladders filled with gelatin. [OE *blædre*.]

blade [blād] *n* the flat part of a leaf or petal, esp a leaf of grass; the cutting part of a knife, sword, etc; the flat part of an oar or paddle; the free outer part of the tongue; a sword or swordsman; the runner of an ice skate; a dashing fellow.—*adj* **blad´ed**. [OE *blæd*; ON *blath*; Ger *blatt*.]

blain [blān] *n* an inflamed swelling or sore. [OE *blegen*.]

blame [blām] *vt* to censure; to attribute the responsibility to.—*n* imputation of a fault; censure.—*adjs* **blam´able, blame´ful**, deserving of blame or censure;—*adv* **blame´fully.**—*adj* **blame´less**, without blame; innocent.—*adv* **blame´lessly.**—*n* **blame´lessness.**—*adj* **blame´worthy**, worthy of blame.—*n* **blame´worthiness**. [Fr *blâmer*—OFr *blasmer*—Gr *blasphēmeein*, to speak ill. See **blaspheme**.]

blanch [blänch or -sh] *vt* to whiten or bleach; to make pale; to scald (vegetables, almonds, etc.);—*vi* to turn pale. [Fr *blanchir—blanc*, white.]

blancmange [blämän(g)zh´] *n* a dessert made from gelatinous or starchy ingredients (as cornstarch) and milk. [Fr *blancmanger—blanc*, white, *manger*, food.]

bland [bland] *adj* smooth; gentle; mild; insipid.*adv* **bland´ly.**—*n* **bland´ness.** [L *blandus*.]

blandish [bland´ish] *vti* to flatter and coax; to cajole.—*n* **bland´ishment**. [Fr *blandir*, pr p *blandissant*—L *blandīrī*.]

blank [blangk] *adj* of paper, without writing or marks; empty, vacant; empty of thought (*a blank mind*); utter, complete. (*a blank denial*).—*n* an empty space; esp one to be filled out on a printed form; such a printed form; an empty place or time; a powder-filled cartridge without a bullet.—*vt* to hold (an opponent) scoreless.—*adv* **blank´ly.**—*n* **blank´ness, blank verse**, unrhymed verse, usually written in iambic pentameter. [Fr *blanc*, from root of Ger *blinken*, to glitter.]

blanket [blang´ket] *n* a large, soft piece of cloth used for warmth, esp as a bed cover; a covering generally.—*adj* applying generally or covering all cases.—*vt* to cover.—**blanket stitch**, a reinforcing hand stitch used on blankets on other thick fabrics to prevent wear. [OFr *blankete*, dim of *blanc*, white.]

blare [blār] *vti* to sound loudly.—*n* a loud, harsh sound. [ME *blaren*.]

blarney [blär´ni] *n* flattery.—*vti* to flatter or coax. [*Blarney* Castle, near Cork, where a stone, difficult to reach, confers the gift on those who kiss it.]

blasé [blä-zā] *adj* satiated and bored. [Fr, pt p of *blaser*, to cloy.]

blaspheme [blas-fēm´] *vt* to speak impiously of, (God).—*vi* to utter blasphemy.—*n* **blasphem´er.**—*adj* **blasphemous** [blas´femus], profane; impious.—*adv* **blas´phemously.**—*n* **blas´phemy**, profane speaking; contempt or indignity offered to God. [Gr *blasphēmia—blasphēmeein*. See **blame**.]

blast [bläst] *n* a blowing or gust of wind; a forcible stream of air; the sound of a horn; an explosion or detonation; an outburst of criticism.—*vt* to blight; to blow up, explode; to criticize sharply.—*vi* to make a loud, harsh sound; to set off explosives, etc.—*adj* **blast´ed**, blighted.—*ns* **blast´fur´nace**, a smelting furnace in which a blast of air produces the intense heat; **blast-off; blast´off**, the launching of a rocket, space vehicle, etc. [OE *blæst*; cf ON *blāsa*; Ger *blasen*.]

blatant [blāt´ánt] *adj* noisy, obtrusive, glaring; boldly conspicuous.—*adv* **blat´antly**. [Prob a coinage of Spenser.]

blather [blaTH´er] *vi* to chatter foolishly.—*n* foolish chatter.—**blath´erskite**, a loquacious fool. [ME *blather*—ON *blathra*, to talk foolishly, *blathr*, nonsense. *Blether* is the Scots form.]

blaze[1] [blāz] *n* a rush of light or flame; an active display, outburst; intense light.—*vi* to burn with a strong flame; to throw out a brilliant light; to be excited, as with anger.—*n* **blaz´er**, a light sports jacket of bright color. [OE *blæse*, a torch.]

blaze[2] [blāz] a white mark on a beast's face; a mark made on a tree by chipping the bark.—*vt* to mark a tree with a blaze; to indicate a forest track by trees so marked. [Perh Du *bles* or ON *blesi*; or **blaze** (1).]

blaze[3] [blāz] *vt* to proclaim. [Connected with ON *blāsa*, to blow; confused with **blazon**.]

blazon [blā´zn] *vt* to make public; to adorn; to describe (heraldic or armorial bearings) in technical terms.—*n* the science or rules of coats of arms; a heraldic shield; a coat of arms; a showy display.—*n* **blaz´onry**, the art of drawing coats of arms, heraldry; brilliant display. [Fr *blason*, shield, confused with ME *blasen*, infin, **blaze** (3).]

bleach [blēch] *vti* to make or become white or colorless.—*n* a substance for bleaching. [OE *blǣcan*, from root of **bleak**.]

bleachers [blēch´ers] *n pl* outdoor uncovered plank seats for spectators at sporting events.

bleak [blēk] *adj* cold, unsheltered, bare; harsh; gloomy; not hopeful.—*adv* **bleak´ly**.—*n* **bleak´ness**. [Apparently ON *bleikr*, answering to OE *blǣc*, *blāc*, pale, shining, black.]

blear [blēr] *adj* dim with water or tears; obscure to the view of imagination.—Also *vt*—*adj* **blears**. [Cf Low Ger *bleeroged*, 'blear-eyed'.]

bleat [blēt] *vi* to cry as sheep, goat, or calf.—*n* a bleating cry or sound. [OE *blǣtan*; L *balāre*, Gr *blēchē*, a bleating; root *bla*-; imit]

bled [bled] *pt*, *pt p* of **bleed**.

bleed [blēd] *vi* to lose blood; to ooze sap; to be filled with grief or sympathy.—*vt* to draw blood or sap from; (*inf*) to extort money from;—*pt*, *pt p* **bled**.—*ns* **bleed´er**, one who is liable to bleed, esp hemophiliac; **bleed´ing**, a discharge of blood; the operation of letting blood. [OE *blēdan*.]

bleep [blēp] *vi* to give out a high sound or radio signal, beep. [Imit]

blemish [blem´ish] *n* a flaw or defect, as a spot.—*vt* to mar; to spoil. [OFr *blesmir*, *blemir*, pr p *blemissant*, to stain.]

blench[1] [blench] *vti* to bleach (something); to blanch.

blench[2] [blench] *vi* to shrink back, to flinch. [OE *blencan*.]

blend [blend] *vt* to mix or mingle (varieties of tea, etc.); to mix so that the elements cannot be distinguished.—*vi* to mix, merge; to shade gradually into each other, as colors; to harmonize;—*pt p* **blend´ed**.—*n* a mixture.—*ns* **blend´er**, one that blends; an electrical appliance that can chop, whip, mix, or liquefy foods; **blend´ing**. [ME *blenden*; cf OE *blandan*, ON *blanda*.]

blende [blend] *n* a zinc ore; any of several sulfide ones. [Ger *blende*—*blenden*, deceive, from its resemblance to lead sulphide.]

Blenheim [blen´em] *n* a variety of English toy spaniel with rich chestnut markings on a pearly whitecoat. [*Blenheim*, Duke of Marlborough's seat.]

bless [bles] *vt* to consecrate; to praise; to invoke divine favor upon; to make happy; to make the sign of the cross over;—*pt p* **blessed** [blest], or **blest**.—*adj* **bless´ed** [-id], holy, sacred; fortunate; blissful; beatified.—*adv* **bless´edly**.—*ns* **bless´edness; bless´ing**, a wish or prayer for happiness or success; any cause of happiness; good wishes or approval; a grace said before or after eating. [OE *blēdsian*, *blētsian*, to bless, prob from *blōd*, blood. The word was used as equivalent to *benedīcĕre*.]

blest [blest] *pt p* of **bless**.

blew [bloo̅] *pt p* of **blow**.

blight [blīt] *n* any insect, disease, etc. that destroys plants; anything that injures or destroys.—*vt* to affect with blight; to blast; to frustrate. [First appears in literature in the 17th century; prob of Scand origin.]

blimp [blimp] *n* (*inf*) a non rigid airship; Colonel Blimp.

blind [blīnd] *adj* without sight; ignorant or undiscerning; not directed, or affording no possibility of being directed, by sight or by reason concealed; closed at one end; (*aeronautics*) by the use of instruments.—*n* something to mislead; a window-screen, a shade.—*vt* to make sightless; to deprive of insight; to dazzle; to deceive;—*pt*, *pt p* **blīnd´ed**.—*n* anything that obscures sight or keeps out light, as a shade for the window or eyes; a place of concealment; a decoy.—*adj* **blind´ing**, tending to make blind.—*pr p* making blind.—*adv* **blind´ly**.—*n* **blind´ness**, want of sight; failure or inability to perceive and understand.—*adj* **blind´fold**, having the eyes bandaged, so as not to see; thoughtless, reckless.—*vt* to cover the eyes of.—*n* a cloth used to cover the eyes.—ns **blind´side**, the side on which a blind person fails to see; the side away from which one is looking; **blind´worm**, a slowworm.—**blind alley**, a fruitless course of action; **blind date** (*inf*), a date with a stranger, arranged by a third person; either person involved; **blind gut**, the caecum; **blind spot**, the point on the retina that is insensitive to light and on which no images are formed; any sphere within which perception or understanding fails; a portion of a field that cannot be seen or inspected with available equipment; a locality with markedly poor radio reception; **blind tiger**, a place that sells alcoholic liquors illegally; **blind trust**, an arrangement by which a person, usu. in high government service, gives up management of his financial affairs to an agent for a specified period.—**blind man's buff**, a game in which one of the party is blindfolded and tries to catch the others; **blind to**, unaware of, unable to appreciate. [OE *blind*; ON *blindr*.]

blink [blingk] *vi* to twinkle, or wink; flash on and off; to ignore (*with* **at**).—*vt* to shut out of sight, to avoid or evade.—*n* a glimpse, glance; a momentary gleam.—*n pl* **blink´er**, a flashing warning light; a cloth hood with projecting sidepieces at the eye openings used in skittish racecourses.—**on the blink** (*slang*), out of order. [ME a variant of *blenk*, prob the same as **blench**.]

blip [blip] *n* a luminous image on an oscilloscope.

bliss [blis] *n* the highest happiness; spiritual joy.—*adj* **bliss´ful**.—*adv* **bliss´fully**.—*n* **bliss´fulness**. [OE *blītho*—*blīthe*, joyful.]

blister [blis´tėr] *n* a raised patch on the skin, containing watery matter, as caused as by burning or rubbing; a similar raised spot on any other surface.—*vt* to raise a blister; to lash with words.—*vi* to form blisters.—*adj* **blis´tering**, (of criticism) savage, cruel.—*n* **blister beetle**, various beetles (family Meloidae) used for blistering. [ME; most prob OFr *blestre*, conn with ON *blāstr*, *blāsa*, to blow.]

blithe [blīTH] *adj* happy, gay, sprightly.—*adv* **blithe´ly**.—*n* **blithe´ness**.—*adj* **blithe´some**, joyous.—*adv* **blithe´somely**.—*n* **blithe´someness**. [OFr *blīthe*, joyful.]

blitz [blits] *n* any sudden destructive attack.—*vt* to subject to a blitz. [Ger *blitzkrieg*, lightning war.]

blizzard [bliz´ȧrd] *n* a blinding storm of wind and snow. [Most prob onomatopoeic, on the analogy of *blow*, *blast*, etc.]

bloat [blōt] *vti* to swell as with water or air; puff up, as with pride.—*adj* **bloat´ed**.—*n* **bloat´er**, a common cisco (*Coregonus hoyi*) of the Great Lakes; a lightly salted and briefly smoked herring or mackeral. [Scand, as in Swed *blöt*, soft.]

blob [blob] *n* a drop of liquid; a round spot; zero.—*vti* to splash with blobs. [Imit]

bloc [blok] *n* a combination of parties, nations, etc. to achieve a common purpose. [Fr]

block [blok] *n* a solid piece of wood or stone, etc.; a piece of wood; an auctioneer's platform, used as a support (for chopping, etc.), or as a mold (for hats), or for printing (illustrations), or as a toy (for building); a city square; a group or row of buildings; a number of things as a unit; a pulley with its framework; an obstruction.—*vt* to enclose or shut up; to obstruct; to shape; to sketch roughly (*often with* **out**).—*vi* to block an opponent in sports.—*ns* **blockade´**, the isolation of a place by blocking every approach by land or sea (*vt* to isolate by blockade); any strategic barrier; **block´age**, act or instance of obstructing or state of being obstructed.—*ns* **blockade-runn´er**, a person or ship that passes through a blockade; **block busting** (*inf*), the inducing of owners to sell their houses out of fear that a minority group may move into their neighborhood; **block grant**, a grant of Federal funds to a State or local government to fund a block of programs; **block´head**, a stupid fellow; **block´house**, formerly a small temporary fort; a reinforced structure for observers, as of missile launchings; **block´sys´tem**, a system of signalling by which no train can enter a block or section of the railway till the previous train has left it.—**block and tackle**, pulley blocks and ropes, used for lifting heavy objects. [Fr *bloc*, prob Gmc in origin.]

blond, blonde [blond] *adj* having light-colored hair and skin; light-colored.—*n* a blond(e) person. [Fr]

blood [blud] *n* the red fluid in the arteries and veins of animals; the sap of a plant; the essence of life; life; kinship; descent; temper, anger; bloodshed; (among blacks) an Afro-American.—*adjs* **blood´ed**, having a specific kind of blood (*hot-blooded*); of fine breed; **blood´y**, stained with blood; blood thirsty; (*Brit slang*) murderous, cruel.—*vt* to make bloody.—*adv* **blood´ily**.—*ns* **blood´bath**, a massacre; **blood cell**, a cell normally present in the blood.—*adj* **blood´curd´ling**, exciting horror.—*ns* **blood´feud**, a feud between different clans or families; **blood´group**, any one of the four kinds (designated O, A, B, AB) into which human blood is classified for transfusion; **blood´guilt, blood´guilt´iness**, the guilt of shedding blood.—*adj* **blood´-guil´ty**.—*ns* **blood´heat**, the temperature of the human blood (about 98° F); **blood´hound**, a large keen-scented tracking dog.—*adj* **blood´less**, without blood, anaemic; without spirit; without the shedding of blood.—*ns* **blood´lessness; blood´lett´ing**, the act of letting blood, or bleeding by opening a vein; **blood´ mon´ey**, a reward for cooperation in action by which the life of another is endangered; money paid to next of kin as reparation for manslaughter; **blood´ pois´oning**, septicemia; **blood pudding**, blood sausage; **bloodroot**, a plant (*Sanguinaria canadensis*) of the poppy family having a red root and sap and a white flower in early spring; **blood sausage**, a very dark sausage containing a large proportion of blood; **blood serum**, blood from which the fibrin and suspended material (as cells) have been removed; **blood´shed**, the shedding of blood; slaughter.—*adjs* **blood´shot** (of the eye), red or inflamed with blood; **blood´-stained**, stained with blood; guilty of murder.—*ns* **blood´stain; blood´stone**, a green chalcedony with bloodlike spots; **bloodstream**, the flow of blood through the blood vessels in the living body; **blood´suck´er**, an animal that sucks blood, esp a leech; a person who sponges or preys on another; **blood sugar**, the glucose in the blood; its concentration (as in milligrams per 100 milliliters); **blood test**, a test of the blood, esp a test for syphilis; **blood´thirst´iness**, thirst or desire for shedding blood.—*adj* **blood´thirst´y**.—*ns* **blood-typing**, the process of determining the blood group of someone; **blood´ vess´el**, any vessel in which blood flows.—

blood bank, a supply of blood; the place or institution where it is kept; **blood count**, the number of red or white corpuscles in the blood; **blood pressure**, the pressure of the blood on the walls of the blood vessels.—**bad blood**, anger, hatred; **in cold blood**, with cruelty; deliberately. [OE *blōd.*]

bloom [blōōm] *n* a blossom or flower; the state of being in flower; a period of most health, vigor, etc.; a youthful, healthy glow; the powdery coating on some fruit and leaves.—*vi* to blossom; to be at one's prime; to glow with health, etc.—*adj* **bloom´ing**. [ON *blōm*; cf Ger *blume*.]

bloomers [blōōm´ėrz] *n pl* a woman's underpants gathered above the knee. [Amelia *Bloomer*, US feminist.]

blooper [blōōp-ėr] *n* (*slang*) a stupid mistake; (*baseball*) a fly that falls just beyond the infield for a hit. [Imit.]

blossom [blos´ȯm] *n* a flower, esp one that precedes edible fruit; a state or time of flowering.—*vi* to put forth blossoms or flowers; to begin to flourish. [OE *blōstm, blōstma*, from the same root as *blōstm, blōstma*; see **bloom**.]

blot [blot] *n* a spot or stain, esp of ink; a stain in reputation.—*vt* to spot or stain; to obliterate; to disgrace; to dry with blotting paper.—*pr p* **blott´ing**; *pt p* **blott´ed**.—*ns* **blott´er**, a piece of blotting paper; a book for recording events as they occur; **blott´ing pāper**, absorbent paper, used to dry freshly-written ink.

blotch [bloch] *n* an irregular discoloration on the skin; any large blot or stain.—*vt* to mark or cover with blotches.—*adjs* **blotched, blotch´y**.

blouse [blowz] *n* a shirtlike garment worn by women and children; a uniform coat worn by soldiers, etc.—*vti* to gather in and drape at the waistline. [Fr.]

blow[1] [blō] *n* a hard hit, as with the fist; a sudden attack, a sudden misfortune or calamity.—**come to blows**, to fight. [Prob from vb **blow** (3)—OE *blāwan*.]

blow[2] [blō] *vi* to bloom or blossom.—*pr p* **blō´ing**; *pt* **blew** [blōō]; *pt p* **blown** [blōn]. [OE *blōwan*; Ger *blühen*.]

blow[3] [blō] *vi* to produce a current of air; to drive air; to move, as air or the wind; to burst suddenly (*often with* **out**); to breathe hard or with difficulty; to spout, as whales; to emit a sound produced by a current of air; (*inf*) to brag; (*slang*) to leave.—*vt* to drive by a current of air; to sound by blowing; to drive air into; to burst by an explosion (*often with* **up**); to melt (a fuse, etc.); (*inf*) to spend (money) freely; (*slang*) to leave; (*slang*) to bungle.—*pt* **blew** [blōō]; *pt p* **blown** [blōn].—*n* **blow´er**, one that blows; a braggart; a device for producing a stream of gas or air.—*vt* **blow´dry´**, to arrange (hair) by simultaneously brushing and drying by a hand-held hair drier.—*n* **blow-dry´er**;—*ns* **blow´fly**, any of various two-winged flies (family Calliphoridae) that lay their eggs on meat, etc.; a widely distributed bluebottle (Calliphora vicina); **blow´hole**, a hole of gas in metal captured during the solidifying process; a nostril in the top of the head of a whale, etc.; a hole in the ice to which aquatic mammals come to breathe.—*adj* **blown**, swollen or bloated; having fly excrement deposited; being out of breath.—*n* **blowout** (*inf*), a festive social event; a bursting of a container (as a tire) by pressure on a weak spot; an uncontrolled eruption of a gas or oil well.—*vi* **blow out**, to become extinguished by a gust of air; (of a gas or oil well) to erupt out of control.—*vt* to extinguish by a gust; (of a storm) to dissipate (itself) by blowing.—*ns* **blow´pipe**, a pipe through which air is blown on a flame, to increase its heat; a long straight tube from which an arrow is blown by the breath; **blow´torch**, a small gasoline torch that shoots out in a hot flame; **blow´up**, an explosion; an enlarged photograph; (*slang*) an angry outburst.—*adj* **blow´y**, windy.—**blow off** (*inf*), to release emotions, as by shouting; **blow over**, to pass over or pass by; **blow up** (*inf*), to lose one's temper. [OE *blāwan*; Ger *blähen, blasen*; L *flāre*.]

blubber [blub´ėr] *n* the fat of whales and other large sea animals; excessive fat on the body; the action of blubbering.—*adj* puffed out; thick.—*vi* to weep effusively. [ME *blober, bluber*; most likely onomatopoeic.]

blucher [blōōch´ėr or blōōk´-] *n* a kind of shoe in which the vamp and tongue are made in one piece. [Prussian Field-Marshal *Blücher* (1742–1819).]

bludgeon [bluj´ȯn] *n* a short stick with a heavy end for striking.—*vti* to strike with a bludgeon; to bully or coerce.

blue [blōō] *adj* of the color of the clear sky; (of the skin) livid; dismal; depressed; (of a story) indecent; puritanical (*blue laws*).—*n* the color of the spectrum lying between green and violet; any blue pigment; (*pl*) (*inf*) a depressed feeling (*with* **the**); (*pl*) a style of vocal and instrumental jazz having usu. slower tempo than ragtime in a 12-measure pattern; clothing, esp of a police force.—*ns* **bluebell**, any of various plants bearing blue bell-shaped spring flowers as a European squill (*Scilla nonscripta*) or the wild hyacinth; (*pl*) a herb of eastern N America (*Mertensia virginica*).—Also **Virginia bluebells; blue´berry**, the edible blue or blackish berry of any of several plants (genus *Vaccinium*) of the heath family; a shrub, such as the huckleberry, producing these berries; **bluebird**, any of several small No American songbirds (genus *Sialia*) related to the robin but more or less blue on top; **blue book**, a volume of specialized information, esp that published by the Federal government; a directory of socially prominent persons; a booklet in which students answer examination questions; the examination itself; **blue´bott´le**, a large fly with metallic blue abdomen; a bachelor's button; **blue catfish**, a large bluish catfish (*Ictalurus furcatus*) of the Mississippi valley that may exceed 100 pounds in weight; **blue cheese**, any cheese having veins of bluish mold; **blue chip**, a stock issue of reliable investment quality; a successful and profitable enterprise that has endured; an outstandingly valuable property or asset; **blue coat**, a Union soldier during the Civil War; a police officer.—*adj* **blue´-coll´ar**, pertaining to those engaged in manual work.—*ns* **blue crab**, an edible crab (*Callinectus sapidus*) of the Atlantic and Gulf coasts; **Blue Cross Plans**, US nonprofit organizations providing hospital care to subscribers; **bluefin tuna, bluefin**, a very large tuna (*Thunnus thynnus*); **blue flag**, a common blue- flowered iris (*Iris versicolor*) of the eastern US; **blue flu**, a sick-out staged by police officers; **blue gill**, a common sunfish (*Lepomis macrochirus*) of the eastern and central US prized for food and sport; **bluegrass**, any of several grasses (genus *Poa*) having bluish green blades, esp in Kentucky; country music played on unamplified instruments, marked by free improvisation and close harmony; **blue´-jacket**, a seaman in the US navy; **blue jeans**, blue denim pants; **blue law**, a statute regulating work, commerce, and amusements on Sundays; **blue-mold**, a genus of fungi (*Penicillium*) that produces blue or blue-green surface growths; **blueness; blue nose** (*inf*), a puritanical person.—*vt* **blue-pen´cil**, to edit esp by shortening or deletion.—*n* **blue´print**, a white photographic print, on blue sensitised paper, made from a photographic negative or from a drawing on transparent paper; a preliminary sketch of proposed reforms; a plan of work to be done or a guide or model provided by agreed principles.—*adj* **blue-ribbon**, selected for quality, reputation, or authority.—*ns* **blue ribbon**, a blue ribbon awarded as an honor (as to the first-place winner in a competition); **blue-sky law**, a law providing for the regulation of the sale of securities (as stock).—*adj* **blū´ish**, slightly blue.—**blue baby**, a baby suffering from congenital cyanosis; **blue blood**, aristocratic blood; **blue peter**, a blue flag with white rectangle hoisted on a ship ready to sail.—*adj* **blue plate**, denoting a main course with accompanying vegetable offered at a restaurant at a discount price.—*n* **bluepoint**, a small edible oyster from the south shore of Long Island, New York.—*adj* (of a domestic cat) having a bluish cream body with dark gray points.—*ns* **Blue Shield Plans**, US nonprofit organizations providing medical and surgical care to subscribers; **blue streak**, something that moves very fast; a constant stream of words; **blue whale**, the largest animal that ever lived, a whale (*Sibbaldus musculus*) attaining 100 feet in length and weighing up to 100 tons.—**(out of) the blue**, without warning, as a thunderbolt from a clear sky; **once in a blue moon**, exceedingly seldom; **the blue**, the sky; the sea. [ME *blew*—OFr *bleu*, of Gmc origin.]

bluff[1] [bluf] *adj* rough and hearty in manner; outspoken; ascending steeply with a flat front.—*n* a high steep bank or cliff.—*n* **bluff´ness**. [Prob Du.]

bluff[2] [bluf] *vti* to mislead or frighten by a false, bold front.—*n* a bluffing; one who bluffs.—*n* **bluff´er**.—**call someone's bluff**, to expose or challenge someone's bluff. [Perh Du.]

blunder [blun´dėr] *vi* to make a foolish mistake; to flounder about.—*n* a foolish mistake. [ME *blondren*; prob conn with obs *bland*, to mix; perh from ON *blunda*, to doze.]

blunderbuss [blun´dėr-bus] *n* a muzzle-loading short gun with a wide bore; a blundering person. [Corr of Du *donderbus*—*donder*, thunder, *bus*, a box, barrel of a gun.]

blunt [blunt] *adj* having a dull edge or point; rough, outspoken.—*vti* to make or become dull.—*adv* **blunt´ly**.—*n* **blunt´ness**. [Orig sleepy, dull; prob conn with ON *blunda*, to doze.]

blur [blûr] *n* a smudge, smear; a confused impression.—*vti* to blot; to make or become indistinct in shape, etc.; to dim.—*n* **blurr´iness**.—*adj* **blurr´y**.—*pr p* **blurr´ing**; *pt p* **blurred**. [**blear**.]

blurb [blûrb] *n* (*inf*) a publisher's descriptive notice of a book; an exaggerated advertisement. [Attributed to an American writer and illustrator, Gelet Burgess.]

blurt [blûrt] *vt* to utter impulsively (*with* **out**). [From sound.]

blush [blush] *n* a red glow on the skin caused by embarrassment; any rosy color.—*vi* to show shame, confusion, joy, etc., by blushing (*with* **for** *or* **at**); to become rosy.—*n* **blush´er**, a cosmetic that gives color to the face; a person who blushes readily.—*adv* **blush´ingly**.—**at the first blush**, at the first glance or appearance; off-hand. [ME *blusche, blysche*.]

bluster [blus´tėr] *vi* to make a noise like a blast of wind; to bully or swagger.—*n* a blast or roaring as of the wind; bullying or boastful language.—*adv* **blus´teringly**. [Prob conn with **blast**.]

boa [bō´ä] *n* a large snake (as the anaconda, boa constrictor or python) that kills by constriction; a woman's long, flexible scarf of fur, feathers, etc.—**boa-constric´tor**, a tropical American boa (*Constrictor constrictor*) having a mottled or barred brown body and reaching to 10 feet or more in length. [L *bŏa*, a kind of snake.]

boar [bōr, bör] *n* an uncastrated male pig, the wild hog (*sus scrofa*) of Europe from which most domestic swine derive. [OE *bār*; Du *beer*.]

board [bōrd, börd] *n* a table to put food on; meals, esp when provided regularly for pay; a long, flat piece of sawed wood; a flat piece of wood, etc. for some special use; pasteboard; a council; a body of persons who direct or supervise; the side of a ship (*overboard*)—*vt* to supply with board and fixed terms; come onto the deck of (a ship); to get on (a train, bus, etc.).—*vi* to receive meals or room and meals, regularly for pay.—*ns* **board´er**, one who received board; **board´inghouse**, a house where residents pay for their board; **board´ing school**, a school in which board is given; **board foot**, a unit of quantity for lumber equal to the volume of a board 12 x 12 x 1 inches; **board game**, a game of strategy (as chess, checkers, backgammon, etc.) played by moving pieces on a board; **board measure**, a measurement in board feet; **boardroom**, a room designated for meetings of a board; **boardwalk**, a walk make of thick boards, esp one along a beach.—**board up**, to cover with boards; **on board**, on a ship, aircraft, etc.; **the boards**, the stage (of a theater). [OE *bord*, a board, the side of a ship; ON *borth*.]

boast [bōst] *vi* to talk vaingloriously; to brag.—*vt* to brag of, speak proudly of; to possess with pride.—*n* a bragging; a subject of pride, a cause of boasting.—*n* **boast´er**.—*adj* **boast´ful**.—*adv* **boast´fully**.—*n* **boast´fulness**. [ME *bost*.]

boat [bot] *n* a small open craft; a ship; a dish shaped like a boat.—*vt* to place in or bring into a boat.—*vi* to go about in a boat.—*ns* **boat´er**, a flat straw hat with a brim; **boat´hook**, an iron hook fixed to a pole used for pulling or pushing a boat into position; **boat´ing**, rowing, sailing, etc.; **boat´man**, a man who works on, deals in, or operates boats; **boat people**, refugees fleeing by boat.—**in the same boat**, in the same plight. [OE *bāt*; Du *boot*; Fr *bateau*.]

boatswain [bō´sn] *n* a ship's officer in charge of hull maintenance and related work; a petty officer on a merchant ship; a naval warrant officer in the US Navy. [**boat**, + **swain**.]

bob [bob] *vi* to move quickly up and down; to curtsey; to fish with a bob.—*vt* to move in short jerks; to cut (hair, etc.) short;—*pr p* **bobb´ing**; *pt p* **bobbed**.—*n* a short jerking motion; the weight on a pendulum, plumbline, etc.; a woman or girl's short haircut.—*n* **bob´sled**, a long racing sled.—*vi* to ride or race on a bobsled. [Perh Celt, Gael *baban, babag*.]

bobbin [bob´in] *n* a reel or spool for winding yarn, wire, etc. [Fr *bobine*, prob Celt; cf Gael *baban*, a tassel.]

bobby pin [bob´ē] *n* a small metal hairpin with the prongs pressing close together. [From the use with bobbed hair.]

bobby socks, bobby sox [bob´ē] *n* (*inf*) girls' ankle-length socks.—**bobby-soxer**, an adolescent girl.

bobcat [bob´kat] *n* a medium-sized feline (*Lynx rufus*) of eastern N America with a black-spotted reddish-brown coat.—Also **wildcat**. [From the stubby tail.]

bobeche [bō-besh´, -bāsh´] *n* a usu. glass collar on a candlestick to catch drippings. [Fr]

bobolink [bob´ō-lingk] *n* a N American songbird (*Dolichonyx oryzivorus*). [At first *Bob Lincoln*, from the song of the bird.]

bobstay [bob´stā] *n pl* (*naut*) stay for holding the bowsprit down. [*bob* (meaning uncertain), + **stay**.]

bobtail [bob´tāl] *n* a short or cut tail; a horse, dog, or cat with a very short tail; something abbreviated. [**bob**, + **tail**.]

bobwhite [bob´hwit] *n* any of a genus (*Colinus*) of quail, esp the favorite game bird (*C. virgianus*) of the eastern and central US. [Imit]

boccie, bocci, or bocce [bach´ē] *n* a grass court game played by two players or two teams of two to four players in which the object is to bowl eight wooden balls close to the jack ball. [It *bocce*, (wooden) balls.]

bock beer [bok] *n* a strong, dark, sweet beer brewed in winter for use in spring. [*Einbeck*, Germany, where first brewed.]

bode [bōd] *vt* to portend; to prophesy.—*vt* to be an omen of.—**bode ill** (or **well**) to be a bad (or good) omen. [OE *bodian*, to announce—*(ge)bod*, a message; allied to **bid**.]

bodega [bo-dē´ga] *n* a wineshop; a store specializing in Hispanic groceries. [Sp]

bodice [bod´is] *n* the upper part of a dress. [A form of *bodies*, pl of **body**.]

bodkin [bod´kin] *n* a small dagger; a small instrument for pricking holes in cloth; a large blunt needle. [Perh conn with W *bidog*, a dagger.]

body [bod´i] *n* the whole physical substance of a man, animal, or plant; the trunk of a man or animal; a corpse; the main part of anything; a distinct mass (*a body of water*); substance or consistency, as of liquid; a richness of flavor; a person; a distinct group;—*pl* **bod´ies**.—*vt* to give form to; to embody;—*pr p* **bod´ying**; *pt p* **bod´ied**.—*adjs* **bod´iless; bod´ily**, physical; relating to the body.—*adv* in the flesh; as a whole; altogether.—*ns* **bod´ybuild´er**, person who excercises and diets in preparation for competitive exhibition of physique; **bodybuilding; bod´yguard**, person or persons assigned to guard someone; **body language**, gestures, unconscious bodily movements, etc. which function as a means of communication; **bod´ysnatch´er**, one who secretly removes dead bodies from their graves; **body stocking**, a tightfitting garment that covers the torso and sometimes the legs; **body types**, categories of human physique based on major anatomical characteristics developed by theories relating body type and personality—**bod´y pol´itic**, the people as a political unit. [OE *bodig*.]

Boer [bōōr] *n* a South African of Dutch or Huguenot descent.—Also *adj*. [Du, a farmer. See **boor**.]

bog [bog] *n* soft spongy ground, a small marsh.—*vti* sink in as in a bog.—*adj* **bogg´y**.—*n* **bog asphodel**, a herb (*Narthecium americanum*) of the lily family. [Ir and Gael *bogach*; bog, soft.]

bogey [bō´gi] *n* (*golf*) one stroke more than par on a hole.—Also **bogie**. [Perh **bogy**.]

boggle [bog´l] *vi* to start back in fear or agitation; to hesitate (at).—*vt* to confuse (the imagination, mind, etc.). [From **bogle**.]

bogie, bogey [bō´gi] *n* a low strongly built cart; a small supporting or aligning wheel. [Ety unknown.]

bogus [bō´gus] *adj* counterfeit, spurious. [An American cant word, of doubtful origin.]

bogy, bogie [bō´gi] *n* a goblin; a bugbear or special object of dread.—*n* **bo´gyman**. [Ety uncertain.]

bohea [bō-hē´] *n* a black tea. [Chinese.]

Bohemian [bō-hē´mi-ȧn] *n* a Czech; a gipsy; one who defies social conventions.—Also *adj*. [Fr *bohémien*, a gipsy, from the belief that these wanderers came from *Bohemia*.]

boil[1] [boil] *vi* to pass rapidly from the liquid state into vapor; to seethe like boiling liquid; to cook in boiling liquid; to be excited, esp with anger.—*vt* to heat to a boiling state; to cook by boiling.—*ns* **boil´er**, a container in which to boil things; a tank in which water is heated and stored, or steam is generated; **boil´ersuit**, a coverall; **boil´ing point**, the temperature at which a liquid boils; the point at which a person loses his temper; the point of crisis.—**boil down**, to reduce by boiling; to condense; **boil over**, to bubble over the sides of the containing vessel; to burst into passion. [OFr *boillir*—L *bullīre*—*bulla*, a bubble.]

boil[2] [boil] *n* an inflamed, pus-filled, painful swelling on the skin. [OE *bȳl*]

boisterous [bois´tėr-us] *adj* wild, noisy, turbulent; loud and exuberant.—*adv* **bois´terously**.—*n* **bois´terousness**. [ME *boistous*.]

bok choy [bäk choi] *n* a cabbage (*Brassica Chinensis*) forming an open head with long white stalks and dark green leaves. [Chin]

bola, bolas [bō´la, bō´las] a weapon used for hunting consisting of weights joined by cords or things;—*pl* **bo´las**. [Amer Sp]

bold [bōld] *adj* daring or courageous; forward, impudent, presumptuous; executed with spirit; striking to the sight.—*adj* **bold´faced**, impudent.—*adv* **bold´ly**.—*n* **bold´ness.—make bold**, to take the liberty (to). [OE *bald*; OHG *bald*.]

bole [bōl] *n* a tree trunk. [Scand *bolr*; Ger *bohle*, a plank.]

bolero [bo-lā´ro, or bo-lē´ro] *n* a Spanish dance; the music to which it is danced; a short open vest. [Sp]

boll [bōl] *n* the pod of a plant, esp of cotton or flax.—*ns* **boll´wee´vil**, a weevil (*Anthonomus grandis*) that feeds on cotton bolls as a larvae and as an adult; **boll´worm**, the corn earworm; any of several moth caterpillars that destroys cotton bolls. [A form of **bowl**; OE *bolla*.]

bollard [bol´ȧrd] *n* a short post on a wharf or ship round which ropes are secured; one of a line of short posts barring the passage of motor vehicles. [Prob **bole**.]

bologna [ba-lōn´ē] *n* a baloney sausage. [*Bologna*, in Italy.]

Bolshevik [bol´shė-vik, böl-] *n* (*pl* **bol´sheviks, bolshev´iki**), a member of the majority faction that came into power in Russia in 1917; a Communist, esp of the Soviet Union.—*vt* **bol´shevize**, to make Bolshevist.—*ns* **Bol´shevism; Bol´shevist**, a Bolshevik; a revolutionary communist (of any country). [Russ *bolshe*, greater.]

bolster [bōl´stėr] *n* a long narrow pillow; any bolsterlike object or support.—*vt* to support as with a bolster, (*often with* **up**). [OE *bolster*; from root of **bowl**.]

bolt[1] [bōlt] *n* a bar used to fasten a door, etc.; an arrow, esp for a crossbow; a flash of lightening; a threaded metal rod used with a nut to hold parts together; a roll (of cloth, paper, etc.); a sudden dash.—*vt* to fasten with a bolt; to swallow hastily; to say suddenly; blurt (out); to abandon (a party, group, etc.).—*vi* to rush away (like a bolt from a bow); to withdraw support from one's party, etc.—*adv* erectly upright. [OE *bolt*; OHG *bolz*.]

bolt[2] [bōlt] *vt* to sift (as flour) usu. through a fine-meshed cloth.—*n* **bolt´er**, a machine for bolting flour; the operator of such a machine. [OFr *bulter*, or *buleter=bureter*, from *bure*—LL *burra*, a coarse reddish-brown cloth—Gr *pyrrhos*, reddish.]

bolus [bō´lus] *n* a small, round lump; a large pill. [L *bōlus*—Gr *bōlos*, a lump.]

bomb [bom] *n* a hollow case containing explosives, incendiary, or chemicals thrown, dropped, or otherwise reaching its target; a small container with compressed gas in it; (*slang*) a complete failure.—*vt* to attack with bombs.—*vi* (*slang*) to be unsuccessful, to flop.—*vt* **bombard´**, to attack with artillery or bombs; to assail (as with questions); (*phys*) to subject, as the atom, to a stream of particles at high speed.—*ns* **bombardier** [-bȧr-dēr], one who releases the bombs in a bomber; **bombard´ment; bomber** [bom´er], one who bombs; an airplane designed for bombing.—*adjs* **bomb´-happ´y**, shocked into insouciance by shell or bomb explosions; **bomb´proof**, secure against the force of bombs.—*n* **bomb´shell**, a bomb; startling news. [Fr *bombe*—L *bombus*—Gr *bombos*, a humming sound.]

bombazine [bom´ba-zēn´] *n* a twilled or corded fabric of silk and worsted, or of cotton and worsted. [Fr *bombasin*, through Low L—Gr *bombyx*, silk.]

bombast [bom´-bast] *n* pompous language.—*adj* **bombas´tic**.—*adv* **bombas´tically**. [Low L *bombax*, cotton—Gr *bombyx*, silk.]

bombe [b•b] a dessert, usu. ice cream, frozen in a round mould. [Fr]

bon mot [b´ōn mō] a witty saying;—*pl* **bons mots** [b• mō]; **bon ton** [bän tän], good style, the fashionable world; **bon vivant** [bän vē-vänt], one who lives well or luxuriously. [Fr].

bona fide [bō´na fīd, bän´á, bō´nė fī´dē, -fid´e] *adj* in good faith; genuine. [L.]

bonanza [bon-an´zä] *n* a rich vein of ore; any source of wealth. [Sp good weather.]

bonbon [bän bän] *n* a small piece of candy. [Fr 'very good'—*bon*, good.]

bond[1] [bond] *n* anything that binds, fastens, or unites; (*pl*) shackles; an obligation imposed by a contract, promise, etc.; the status of goods in a warehouse until taxes are paid; an interest-bearing certificate issued by the government or business, redeemable on a specified date; surety against theft, absconding, etc.; an amount paid as surety or bail; a systematic lapping of bricks in a wall.—*vt* to join, bind, or otherwise unite; to provide a bond for; to place or hold (goods) in bond.—*vi* to hold together by means of a bond.—*ns* **bond´hold´er**, one who holds a government or corporation bond; **bond´man**, a slave or serf; **bonds´man**; one who assumes the responsibility of a bond; **bond paper**, a durable paper orig intended for bonds. [A variant of *band*—OE *bindan*, to bind.]

bond[2] [bond] *adj* (*arch*) in a state of servitude.—*n* **bond´age**, captivity, slavery; subjugation to a person or force. [OE *bonda*, a peasant, a householder—ON *bōndi*; meaning affected by association with **bond** (1).]

bone [bōn] *n* a hard substance forming the skeleton of higher animals; a piece of the skeleton; a bonelike substance or thing; (*slang*) dice.—*vt* to take the bones out of, as meat.—*vi* (*slang*) to study hard (usu. with up).—*adjs* **boned**, having the bones removed; **bon´y**, full of, or consisting of, or like, bones; having large bones or little flesh.—*ns* **bone´ash**, the remains when bones are burnt in an open furnace; **bone´black**, the remains when bones are heated in a close vessel.—*adj* **bone´-dry´**, absolutely dry.—*ns* **bone china**, translucent china made with bone ash as a constituent;—*adj* **bone´less**.—*ns* **bone meal**, fertilizer or feed made of crushed or ground bone; **boner** (*slang*), a blunder; **bone´-sett´er**, one who treats broken or displaced bones without being a licensed physician. [OE bān.]

bonfire [bon´fīr] *n* an outdoor fire. [**bone, fire**.]

bongo, bongo drum [bong´ō] *n* either of a pair of small drums of different pitch struck with the fingers. [Amer Sp.]

bonhomie [bon´o-mē] *n* easy good natured. [Fr—*bon homme*, a good fellow.]

bonito [bȯ-nēt´ō] *n* any of various medium-sized tunas (esp genera *Sarda* and *Euthynnus*) important as food fishes. [Sp.]

bonne [bon] *n* a French maidservant, nursemaid. [Fr; fem of *bon*, good.]

bonnet [bon´ėt] *n* a hat with a chin ribbon, worn by women and children. [OFr,—Low L *bonnetum*, orig the name of a stuff.]

bonus [bōn´us] *n* a voluntary addition to the sum due as interest, dividend, or wages. [L *bonus*, good.]

bonze [bonz] *n* a Buddhist monk. [Jap *bonzô* or *bonzi*, a priest.]

boo [bōō] *interj* expressive of disapprobation or contempt.—*vti* to utter 'boo!', to hoot.—*vt* **boo´-hoo´**, to weep noisily. [Imit.]

boob [bōōb] *n* a stupid awkward person; a boor; a Philistine; (*slang*) a woman's breast.—**boob tube**, television or a TV set. [**booby**.]

booby [bōō´bi] *n* a simpleton; any of several small gannets (genus *Sula*) of tropical seas.—*ns* **boo´by prize**, a prize for the lowest score; **boo´by trap**, a device for playing a practical joke on a guileless victim; an apparently harmless mechanical contrivance which, if touched, automatically injures the finder. [Perh Sp *bobo*.]

boogie-woogie [bōōg´i-wōōg´i] *n* a style of fast jazz for the piano, with a persistent rhythm in the bass.

book [bŏŏk] *n* a collection of sheets of paper bound together, either printed, written on, or blank; a literary composition; a division of such; a libretto; a record of bets; six tricks gained by a side at bridge; any source of information; (*pl*) formal records of financial transactions.—*vt* to note in a book; to engage in advance; of police, to take the name of, for an alleged offence.—*vi* to make a reservation.—*ns* **book´binding**, the art or practice of putting the covers on books; **book´binder; book´case**, a case with shelves for books; **book´club**, a society (esp mail order) that produces books for its members; **book´end**, a prop for the end of a row of books; **book´ie** (*slang*), a bookmaker;—*adj* **book´-ish**, fond of books; acquainted only with books.—*ns* **book´ishness; book´keep´er; book´keep´ing**, the art of keeping accounts in a regular and systematic manner; **book´let**, a small book; a pamphlet; **book´-mak´er**, a printer, binder, or designer of books; one who makes money by inducing others to bet with him on the terms he offers; **book´man**, a scholar, student; one involved in writing, publishing or selling of books. **book´mark, book´marker**, something placed in a book to mark a particular page; **book´plate**, a label, usually pasted inside the cover of a book, bearing the owner's name, **book´stall**, a stall or stand where books are sold; **book´worm**, a grub that eats holes in books; one who reads assiduously.—**in one's book**, in one's own opinion; **in one's good books**, in favor with one; **one for the book**, an act or occurrence worth noting; **on the books**, on the records. [OE *bōc*, book, the beech; Ger *buche*, the beech, *buch*, a book, because the Germanic peoples first wrote on beechen boards.]

Boolean algebra [bōō´lē-an al´ji-bra] the science of symbols denoting logical propositions and their combination according to certain rules which correspond to the laws of logic. [Named after George **Boole** (1815–64).]

boom[1] [bōōm] *n* a pole by which a sail is stretched; a chain or bar stretched across a harbor. [Du *boom*, beam, tree.]

boom[2] [bōōm] *vi* to make a hollow sound or roar.—*n* a hollow sound, as of the sea; the cry of the bittern. [From a Low Ger root found in OE *byme*, a trumpet, Du *bommen*, to drum.]

boom[3] [bōōm] *vi* to become suddenly active or prosperous.—*vt* to push into sudden prominence.—*n* a sudden increase of activity in business, or the like; a sudden rise in price or value.—**boom town**, a town that booms and enjoys abnormal economic prosperity. [Prob from **boom** (2).]

boomerang [bōōm´e-rang] *n* a curved hardwood missile used by the natives of Australia, so balanced that, when thrown to a distance, it returns towards the thrower; an act that recoils on the agent. [Australian.]

boon[1] [bōōn] *n* a petition; a gift, favor. [ON *bōn*, prayer; OE *bēn*.]

boon[2] [bōōn] *adj* (*arch*) gay, merry, congenial (of a companion); kind (eg *boon nature*). [Fr *bon*—L *bonus*, good.]

boondoggle [bōōn´dog-l] *n* an article of simple handcraft; work of little or no practical value. [Scout coinage.]

boor [bōōr] *n* a peasant; a coarse or awkward person.—*adj* **boor´ish**.—*adv* **boor´ishly**.—*n* **boor´ishness**. [Du *boer*; Ger *bauer*; OE *gebūr*, a farmer.]

boost [bōōst] *vt* to help forward; to raise; to advertize fervently; to supplement voltage of; to increase supply of air to, or pressure.—*n* a push.—*n* **boost´er**, any device which increases the effect of another mechanism; an auxiliary motor in a rocket, usu. breaking away after delivery of its impulse; a substance that increases the effectiveness of medication; (*slang*) a shop lifter. [Orig US.]

boot[1] [bōōt] *n* a covering for the foot and lower part of the leg, generally made of leather; an instrument for torturing the leg; (*slang*) unceremonious dismissal, (*with* **the**); a navy or marine corp recruit undergoing basic training.—*vt* to put boots on; to kick; to bring a computer program from a disc into computer memory.—*ns* **boot´black**, one who shines shoes; **boot camp**, a Navy or Marine Corp camp for basic training; **boot´jack**, an instrument for taking off boots; **boot´leg**, the leg of a high boot; something bootlegged, esp moonshine; a football play where the quarterback hides the ball and rolls out; **boot´legger**, one who deals illicitly in alcoholic liquor; (*slang*—also *vti* and *adj* **boot´leg**); [OFr *bote*—Low L *botta, bota*.]

boot[2] [bōō] (*arch, poetic*) *vt* to profit or advantage.—*n* advantage, profit.—*adj* **boot´less** (of an action) useless.—*adv* **boot´lessly**.—*n* **boot´lessness.—to boot**, in addition. [OE *bōt*, compensation, amends, whence *bētan*, to amend to make **better**.]

bootee, bootie [bōōt-ē´] *n* an ankle-length boot, slipper or sock, esp a knitted or crocheted one for an infant. [Dim of **boot**.]

booth [bōōTH, or -th] *n* a stall for selling goods; a small enclosure for voting at elections; a small structure to house a public telephone, etc; a restaurant seating arrangement consisting of a table between two high-backed benches. [ON *būth*; Ger *bude*.]

booty [bōōt´i] *n* spoil, plunder; a prize. [ON *bȳti*, share—*bȳta*, to divide.]

booze [bōōz] *vi* to drink deeply or excessively.—*n* intoxicating liquor esp hard liquor. [Apparently Middle Du *bûsen*, to drink deeply.]

bop [bop] *n* a style of jazz in the 1950s, the earliest form of 'cool' jazz, a development of *bebop*.

boracic acid [bō-ras´ik] *n* a weak acid composed or boron, oxygen and hydrogen.—Also **boric acid**, formerly in wide use as an antiseptic before the discovery of its poisonous properties.—**bo´rax**, the mineral composed of the sodium salt of boracic acid chiefly from the dried beds of certain lakes; (*slang*) shoddy merchandise. [Through Fr and Low L *borax, boracis*, from Ar *bûraq*.]

Bordeaux [bör-dō´] *n* any of several red, white, or rosé wines produced around Bordeaux in southwest France.

border [bōrd´ėr] *n* the edge or margin of anything; a dividing line between two countries; a narrow strip along an edge; (*slang*) the US—Mexican border.—*vi* to come near, to adjoin (*with* **on, upon**).—*vt* to adorn with a border; to adjoin; to be a border to.—*ns* **bord´erland**, land near a border; a vague condition; **bord´erline**, a boundary.—*adj* on a boundary; indefinite. [OFr *bordure*; from root of **board**.]

bore[1] [bōr, bör] *vt* to pierce so as to form a hole; to weary, to fail to interest.—*n* a hole made by boring; the size of the cavity of a gun; a tiresome person or thing.—*n* **bore´dom**, tedium. [OE *borian*, to bore; cf Ger *bohren*; allied to L *forāre*, to bore, Gr *pharynx*, the gullet.]

bore[2] [bōr, bör] *pt* of **bear**.

bore[3] [bōr, bör] *n* a tidal flood which rushes violently up the estuaries of certain rivers. [ON *bāra*, a wave or swell.]

boreas [bō´re-as] *n* the north wind personified. [L and Gr]

boric *see* **boracic acid**.

born [börn] *pt p* of **bear**, to bring forth—**born-again**, of a person having undergone a revival of a personal faith or conviction or of a former activity; **not born yesterday**, difficult to deceive.

borne [bȯrn, bōrn] *pt p* of **bear**, to carry.

boron [bō´ron] *n* metalloid element (symbol B; at wt 10.8; at no 5), found in borax, etc. [See **borax**.]

borough [bur´ȯ] *n* a self-governing, incorporated town; any of the five administrative units of New York City. [OE *burg, burh*, a city, akin to *beorgan*, to protect.]

borrow [bor´ō] *vt* to obtain or loan or trust; to adopt (an idea, etc.) as one's own.—*n* **borr´ower**. [OE *borgian*—*borg, borh*, a pledge, security.]

borscht, borsch [börsh(t)] *n* Russian soup made with beetroot, etc. Also **bortsch—borscht belt, borscht circuit**, the theaters and nightclubs in the Jewish summer resorts in the Catskills in New York State. [Russ *borshch*.]

borzoi [bör´zoi] *n* breed of tall hound with long, silky coat and narrow head; the Russian wolfhound. [Russ *borzoy*, swift.]

boscage [bosk´ij] *n* a thicket; woodland. [Fr *boscage, bocage*—Low L *boscus*]

bosh [bosh] *n* (*inf*) nonsense.—Also *interj*. [Turk *bosh*, worthless.]

bosky [bosk´i] *adj* woody or bushy; [Prob ME *bosk*, a bush; cf **boscage**.]
bosom [bŏŏz´-, bōōz´ȯm] *n* the breast of a human being, or the part of the dress that covers it; the seat of the passions and feelings, the heart; the interior.—*adj* confidential; intimate. [OE *bōsm*; Ger *busen*.]
boson [bō´son] *n* any of a class of subatomic particles whose spin is zero or an integral number. [SN *Bose*, physicist.]
boss[1] [bos] *n* a knob or stud; a raised ornament.—*vt* to ornament with bosses. [OFr *boce*, from Old Ger *bōzan*, to beat.]
boss[2] [bos] *n* the master, manager, or foreman; the person who pulls the wires in political intrigue.—*vt* to manage; (*inf*) to keep in subjection.—*adj* (*slang*) excellent. [New York Dutch *baas*, master.]
Boston [bö´stȯn] *n* a variation of whist played with a double deck of cards; a dance resembling the waltz.—**Boston cream pie**, a round yellow layer cake filled with custard or creme patisserie and iced on the top only with a chocolate frosting; **Boston fern**, a fern (*Nephrolepis exaltata bostoniensis*) with many much-divided fronds; **Boston ivy**, a woody vine (*Parthenocissus tricuspidata*) of the grape family with 3-lobed leaves; **Boston terrier, Boston bull**, an American breed of non-sporting dog developed from the bulldog and bullterrier with a brindle and white smooth coat. [*Boston*, Massachusetts.]
bot, bott [bott] *n* the maggot of the bot´fly, esp one infesting the horse.
botany[1] [bot´ȧn-i] *n* the science of plants.—*adjs* **botan´ic, -ical**.—*n* **botan´ical**, a vegetable drug, esp in the crude state.—*adv* **botan´ically**.—*vi* **bot´anize**, to study plants, esp on a field trip.—*n* **bot´anist**, one skilled in botany.—**botanical garden**, a park stocked with indigenous and exotic plants, frequented by students of botany and by the public. [Gr *botanē*, grass; cf boskein, to feed, L *vescī*, to feed.]
botany[2] [bot´ȧn-i] *adj* a fine grade of wool from the merino sheep. [Originally shipped from *Botany Bay*, Australia.]
botch [boch] *n* a swelling on the skin; a clumsy patch; ill-finished work.—*vt* to patch or mend clumsily; to put together unsuitably or unskillfully. [Per from root of **boss** (1).]
botfly [bot´flī] *n* any of various stout two-winged flies (group Oestroidea) with larvae parasite in tissues of various mammals including man.—Also **gadfly**.
both [bōth] *adj* and *pron* the two; the one and the other.—*conj* (or *adv*) as well, equally. *Both . . . and* is nearly equivalent to *not only . . . but also* (eg *both the cat and the dog, both wise and learned*). [ON *bāthar*; OE *bā*; Ger *beide*; cf L *ambo*, Gr *amphō*.]
bother [boTH´ėr] *vt* to perplex or tease.—*ns* **both´er, botherā´tion**.—*adj* **both´ersome**. [Poss Anglo-Irish for **pother**.]
bo tree [bō´-trē] *n* the sacred fig tree (*Ficus religiosa*) planted close to Buddhist temples in Ceylon. [Sinhalese *bo*.]
botryoidal [botrioid´al] *adj* resembling a bunch of grapes. [Gr *botrys*, a bunch of grapes, *eidos*, form.]
Botticelli [bot-i-chel´i] *n* a parlor game in which players attempt to discover the identity selected by the person who is 'it'.
bottle [bot´l] *n* a hollow narrow-necked vessel for holding liquids; the contents of such a vessel.—*vt* to enclose in bottles; to confine as if in a bottle.—*adj* **bott´led**, enclosed in bottles; shapped like a bottle; kept in restraint.—*ns* **bott´led gas**, gas under pressure in portable cylinders; **bott´le green**, a dark green, **bott´le-nosed dolphin, bottlenose dolphin**, a moderately large toothed whale (genus *Tursiops*) with a prominent beak; **bott´leneck**, a narrow section of a road where traffic is apt to be congested; any stage of a process at which facilities for progress are inadequate.—**bottle up**, to confine repress; **hit the bottle** (*slang*), to drink much alcoholic liquor. [OFr *bouteille*, dim of *botte*, a vessel for liquids—Low L *butis*.]
bottom [bot´ȯm] *n* the lowest part of anything; that on which anything rests or is founded; the sitting part of the body; the seat of a chair; the hull of a ship lying below the water; the bed of the sea, etc.; the basis of anything.—*vt* to found or rest upon, to bring to the bottom, to get to the bottom of.—*vi* to become based; to reach the bottom.—*adj* **bott´omless**.—*ns* **bott´omland**, low-lying land along a watercourse; **bottom line**, the crux; the line at the bottom of a financial report that shows the net profit or loss; the final result.—Also *adj adj* **bott´ommost**, lowest, deepest; most basic.—*n* **bottom round**, meat (as steak) from the outer part of a round of beef.—**at bottom**, fundamentally. [OE *botm*.]
botulism [bot´yŏŏl-izm] *n* food poisoning caused by contamination by anerobic soil bacillus. [L *botulus*, sausage.]
bouclé [bōō´klā] *n* a yarn having the threads looped to give a bulky effect; a textile fabric of bouclé yarn. [Fr]
boudoir [bōōd´wär] *n* a lady's private room. [Fr—*bouder*, to pout, to be sulky.]
bouffant [bōōf´ã] *adj* puffed out. [Fr]
bougainvillea [bōōg-ān-vil´-ēä] *n* a genus (*Bougainvillaea*) of woody vines of tropical America, conspicuous for the beauty of their rosy or purple bracts. [French explorer de *Bougainville* (1729–1811).]
bough [bow] *n* a branch of a tree. [OE *bög, bōh*, an arm, the shoulder; *būgan*, to bend.]
bought [böt] *pt, pt p* of **buy**.
bouillon [bool-yän´] *n* a strong broth, a clear seasoned soup made from lean beef.—**bouillon cube**, a cube of evaporated seasoned meat extract. [Fr, from same root as **boil**.]
boulder [bōld´ėr] *n* a large stone or mass of rock rounded by the action of water, weathering, etc.—*adj* containing boulders. [Prob from Swed *bullrà*, Dan *buldre*, to roar like thunder.]
boulevard [bool´e-vär] *n* a broad road, often lined by trees. [Fr,—Ger *bollwerk*; same root as **bulwark**.]
bounce [bowns] *vi* to jump or spring suddenly; to rebound like a ball; (*slang*) (of a worthless check) to be returned; to boast, to exaggerate.—*vt* to cause a ball to bounce; (*slang*) to put (a person) out by force; (*slang*) to fire from a job.—*n* a thud; a leap or spring; capacity for bouncing; (*inf*) energy, dash, etc.—*n* **bounc´er**, (*slang*) a man hired to remove disorderly people from nightclubs, etc.—*adj* **bounc´ing**, big, healthy, etc. [Du *bonzen*, strike, *bons*, a blow.]
bound[1] [bownd] *pt, pt p* of **bind**.—In composition, restricted to or by, as *housebound, stormbound*.—**bound to**, obliged to; sure to.
bound[2] [bownd] *n* the limit of a definite area; (*pl*) the area so defined; (*pl*) the limits (of what is reasonable or what is permitted).—*vt* to set bounds to; to limit, restrain, or surround; to name the boundaries of.—*n* **bound´ary**, the line by which an area is defined.—*adj* **bound´less**, having no limit; vast.—**out of bounds**, beyond the boundaries; forbidden. [OFr *bonne*—Low L *bodina*.]
bound[3] [bownd] *vi* to spring or leap.—*n* a spring or leap. [Fr *bondir*, to spring, in OFr to resound—L *bombitāre*.]
bound[4] [bownd] predicative *adj* ready to go to, on the way to (eg *bound for the North, outward bound*). [ON *būinn*, pt p of *būa*, to prepare.]
bounden [bownd´n] *adj* obligatory (*bounden duty*). [Archaic pt p of **bind**.]
bounty [bown´ti] *n* liberality in bestowing gifts; the gifts bestowed; a reward or premium.—*adjs* **bounteous**, [-tiùs], **boun´tiful**, liberal in giving; generous.—*advs* **boun´teously, boun´tifully**.—**bounty hunter**, one that hunts predatory animals for the reward offered; one that tracks down outlaws and captures them when a reward is offered. [OFr *bontet*, goodness—L *bonitās, -ātis*—*bonus*, good.]
bouquet [bōōk´-ā, or -ā´] *n* a bunch of flowers, a nosegay; the perfume exhaled by wine.—**bouquet garni**, [gär´nē], a bunch of herbs used in cooking, removed before serving. [Fr *bosquet*, dim of *bois*, a wood; cf It *bosco*.]
bourbon [bûr´bȯn, bōōr-] *n* a whiskey distilled from corn mash. [*Bourbon County*, Kentucky.]
bourgeois [bōōrzh´wä] *n* one of the **bourgeoisie** [bōōrzh´wäzē or -zē´], the social class between the very wealthy and the middle class.—*adj* smug, respectable, conventional; humdrum. [Fr *bourgeois*, citizen.]
bourgeon *See* **burgeon**.
bourn[1], **bourne** [bōrn, bōōrn] *n* (*arch*) a boundary, a limit, a goal. [Fr *borne*, a limit.]
bourn[2], **bourne** [bōōrn] *n* a stream, a brook.
bourse [bōōrs] *n* a European stock exchange. [Fr *bourse* See **purse**.]
bout [bowt] *n* a turn, spell a period spent in some activity; a contest or struggle. [Doublet of **bight**; from root of **bow** (1).]
boutique [bōō-tēk´] *n* a small shop, or department in a shop, selling one type of goods, esp clothing. [Fr]
bovine [bō´vīn] *adj* pertaining to cattle; dull, unemotional. *n* an ox, cow, etc. [L *bōs, bovis*, an ox or cow.]
bow[1] [bow] *vi* to bend the neck, body, in saluting a person, etc.; to submit.—*vt* to bend, incline downwards; to weigh down, crush; to usher with a bow; to express by a bow.—*n* a bending of the neck or body in salutation.—**take a bow**, to acknowledge applause, etc. [On *būgan*, to bend; akin to L *fugĕre*, to flee, to yield.]
bow[2] [bō] *n* anything in the shape of an arch, as the rainbow; a tough, flexible curved rod by which arrows are shot from a string; the instrument by which the strings of a violin or the like are sounded; a looped knot of ribbon, etc.—*vti* to bend, curve; to play (a violin, etc.) with a bow.—*n* **bow´leg**, a leg bowed outward at or below the knee.—*adj* **bow´legged**.—*ns* **bow´man**, an archer; a boatman, oarsman, or paddler stationed at the front of the boat; **bow´string**, the string by which a bow is drawn; **bowstring hemp**, the soft tough leaf fiber of sanseveria used esp in cordage; **bow´ window**, a window projecting in a curve. [OE *boga*; cog with Ger *bogen*.]
bow[3] [bow] *n* the forward part of a ship.—*ns* **bow´er**, an anchor carried at the bow of a ship. [From a Low Ger, Du, or Scand word for shoulder Fr *bough*.]
bowdlerize [bowd´lėr-īz] *vt* to expurgate (a book) by altering or omitting indelicate expressions, esp to do so unnecessarily. [From Dr T *Bowdler*, who thus edited Shak in 1818.]
bowel [bow´ėl] *n* an interior part of the body; (in *pl*) the entrails, the intestines; (*pl*) the deep and remote part of anything; (*pl arch*) the heart, pity, tenderness.—**move one's bowels**, to defecate. [OFr *boel*—L *botellus*, a sausage, also an intestine.]
bower [bow´ėr] an arbor; a lady's private apartment in a medieval castle; a shelter (as in a garden made with entwined vines and tree boughs.)—*ns* **bow´erbird**, an Australian bird (family Paradisaeidae) in which the male makes a bower ornamented with gay feathers, shells, etc. **bow´ery**, a colonial Dutch plantation or form; a city district notorious for homeless usu. alcoholic derelicts. [OE *būr*, a chamber.]
bowie knife [bō´i-nīf] *n* a stout hunting knife with a sharp curved, concave back edge sharpened at the point. [designed by Colonel *Bowie* in 1827.]
bowl[1] [bōl] *n* a wooden ball used for rolling along the ground; (*pl*) a game

played on a smooth lawn with bowls having a bias.—*vti* to play at bowls; to speed smoothly (along) like a bowl.—*ns* **bowl´er**, one who bowls; **bowling**, a game in which a heavy ball is bowled along a bowling alley at ten wooden pins; **bowl´ing all´ey**, a long narrow wooden lane, usu. one of several in a building designed for them; **bowl´ing green**, a smooth grassy plot for bowls.—**bowl over**, to knock over; (*inf*) to astonish. [Fr *boule*—L *bulla*.]

bowl[2] [bōl] *n* a deep, rounded dish; a large drinking cup; an amphitheater, stadium; the contents of a bowl. [OE *bolla*.]

bowler [bō´ler] *n* a derby hat.

bowline [bō´lin] *n* a rope to keep a sail close to the wind; a knot used to tie a bowline so that it will not slip or jam. [ME; of doubtful origin.]

bowsprit [bow´sprit] *n* a strong spar projecting over the bows of a sailing ship. [Apparently Du *boegspriet*.]

box[1] [books] *n* a genus (*Buxus*) of evergreen shrubs and small trees with very compact habit of growth and hard, strong, heavy wood; a case or receptacle for holding anything; the contents of a box; a boxlike thing or space; in a theater, a group of enclosed seats; the driver's seat on a carriage; a television set; (*slang*) a guitar; (*baseball*) any of six areas on a baseball diamond designated for the batter, pitcher, catcher, etc.—*vt* to put into a box; to enclose.—*ns* **box´-board**, paperboard used for making boxes and cartons; **box car**, a fully enclosed railroad freight car; **box´er**, one that makes boxes or packs things in boxes; **box elder**, a N American maple (*Acer negundo*); **boxing**, an act of enclosing in a box; a boxlike enclosure; material used for boxes and casing; **box kite**, a tailless kite made up of two or more connected open boxes; **box lunch**, a packed lunch; **box office**, in a theater, etc., the office at which tickets are sold.—*adj* (*inf*) ability to draw an audience.—*ns* **box pleat**, a double pleat made by forming two facing folded edges; **box score**, the printed score of a baseball or basketball game recording the names of the players, their positions, and activity for each phase of the game; **box social**, a fund-raising event at which box lunches are auctioned; **box spring**, a bedspring consisting of spiral springs enclosed in a cloth-covered frame; **box stall**, an enclosure in a barn or stable for an individual horse, cow, etc.; **box turtle, box tortoise**, any of several No American land turtles (genus *Terrapene*) capable of closing its shell by hinged joints in the lower half; **boxwood**, the close-grained tough hard wood of the box (*Buxus*); a wood with similar properties; a plant producing boxwood.—*adj* **box´y**, resembling a box.—**box the compass**, to name the 32 points in their order; to make a complete reversal. [OE *box*—L *buxus*—Gr *pyxos*, a box-tree.]

box[2] [boks] *n* a blow on the head or ear with the hand.—*vt* to strike with the hand or fist.—*vi* to fight with the fists.—*ns* **box´er**, one who boxes; **Boxer**, a member of a Chinese secret society that in 1900 attempted to drive foreigners out of China and to eradicate foreign influence, esp Christianity; **boxer**, a breed of medium-sized working dog with a short-haired brindled or pale brown coat; one that engages in the sport of boxing; **boxer shorts**, a man's underpants resembling the brief pants worn by a boxer; **box´ing**, the skill or sport of fighting with the fists; **box´ing glove**, a padded mitten worn in boxing. [Possibly connected with Gr *pyx* (adv) 'with the fist'.]

boy [boi] *n* a male child; a lad; a servant.—*n* **boy´hood**, time, or state, of being a boy.—*adj* **boy´ish**.—*adv* **boy´ishly**.—*n* **boy´ishness**.—*ns* **boy´friend**, a male friend with whom a person is romantically or sexually involved; **Boy Scout**, a member of the scouting program of the Boy Scouts of America, for boys aged 11 to 17; one who follows an uncomplicated mode of morals and behavior; **boy wonder**, a young man whose achievements arouse admiration.—**the boys**, (*slang*) men, esp drinking and poker companions of the speaker; (*slang*) a gang of organized criminals. [ME *boi boy*;, Ger *bube*.]

boycott [boi´kot] *vt* to shut out from all social and commercial intercourse in order to punish or coerce. [From Captain *Boycott*, who was so treated by his Irish neighbors in 1880.]

boysenberry [boi´zen-ber-i] *n* a type of bramble, the cross of various blackberries and raspberries; the raspberry-flavored fruit. [Rudolph *Boyes*, American horticulturist.]

bra [brä] *n* short for **brassière**.

brace [brās] *n* anything that draws together and holds tightly; a rod or bar connecting two parts of a structure for stiffening purposes; an instrument for turning a bit; in printing, a mark connecting two or more words or items to be considered together ({); a pair, couple; (*pl*) (*Brit*) straps for supporting the trousers; ropes for turning the yards of a ship; a dental appliance for straightening the teeth.—*vt* to tighten or to strengthen.—*adj* **brac´ing**, invigorating. [OFr *brace*, the arm, power—L *brachium*—Gr *brachīōn*, the arm, that which holds.]

bracelet [brās´lėt] *n* an ornament for the wrist. [Fr—L *brachiāle*—*brachium*, the arm.]

bracero [brä-sėr´-ō] *n* a Mexican laborer admitted to the US esp for seasonal contract work in agriculture. [Sp.]

brachial [brāk´-, or brak´i-ȧl] *adj* belonging to the arm. [L *brachiālis*—*brachium*, arm.]

brachiopod [brak´i-ō-pod] *n* any of a phylum (Brachiopoda) of marine invertebrates with bivalve shells which feed by generating currents of water with ciliated arms. [L *brachium*, arm = Gr *pod*, foot.]

brachycephalic [brak-i-sef-al´ik, also -sef´-], **brachycephalous** [brak-i-sef´al-us].—*adj* short-headed, applied to skulls of which the breadth is at least four-fifths of the length. [Gr *brachys*, short, *kephalē*, head.]

bracken [brak´ėn] *n* a large, coarse fern, esp the brake (*Pteridium aquilinum latiuscalum*) whose young shoots are edible, found in eastern and central N America; a growth of brakes. [Ety obscure.]

bracket [brak´ėt] *n* a support for a shelf, etc., projecting from a wall; people classified according to income (eg *in the lower, middle, upper income bracket*); (*pl*) in printing and writing, the marks [] used to enclose one or more words.—*vt* to support by brackets; to enclose by brackets; to classify together. [Fr *braguette*—L *brācae*, breeches.]

brackish [brak´ish] *adj* somewhat salty; nauseating.—*n* **brack´ishness**. [Du *brak* + suffx *-ish*.]

bract [brakt] *n* a modified leaf growing at the base of a flower.—*adj* **brac´teal** [-ti-ȧl]. [L *bractea*, gold-leaf.]

brad [brad] *vt* a small nail having a slight projection at the top on one side instead of a head; a thin wire nail having a barrel-shaped head.—*vt* to fasten with brads.—*n* **brad´-awl**, an awl to pierce holes. [ON *broddr*, a pointed piece of iron.]

brag [brag] *vti* to boast.—*pr p* **bragg´ing**; *pt p* **bragged**.—*n* a boast or boasting. [Most prob Celt.]

braggadocio [brag-a-dō´shi-ō] *n* a braggart or boaster; empty boasting.—Also *adj*. [From *Braggadochio*, a boastful character in Spencer's *Faerie Queene*.]

braggart [brag´ȧrt] *adj* boastful.—*n* a loud, arrogant boaster. [Fr *bragard*, vain, bragging.]

Brahman [brä´man] *n* a person of the highest or priestly caste among the Hindus; a breed of domestic cattle related to the zebu of India.—*n* **Brah´manism**, the worship of **Brah´ma** [brā´mȧ, brä´m-e, or bram-], an impersonal supreme spirit, and also the supreme deity and creator; **Brah´min**, a person of high social standing, and cultivated intellect and taste, esp one from Boston.

braid [brād] *vt* to interweave three or more strands (of hair, straw, etc.); to make by such interweaving.—*n* a narrow band made by such interweaving used to bind or decorate clothing; a strip, as of hair, formed by braiding. [OE *bregdan*; ON *bregtha*, to weave.]

braille [brāl] *n* printing for the blind, using a system of dots in relief.—Also *adj*. [From Louis *Braille*, the inventor (1809–52).]

brain [brān] *n* the part of the central nervous system which is contained within the skull of vertebrates; the intellect; a person of exceptional intelligence; (often *pl*), the chief planner of an organization or enterprise.—*vt* to dash out the brains of; to hit on the head.—*ns* **brain´child** (*inf*), an original thought or work; **brain death**, irreversible cessation of activity in the central nervous system esp as indicated by a flat electroencephalogram for a specified length of time.—*adj* **brain´less**, foolish or stupid.—*ns* **brain´pan**, the skull; **brain´picking**, the act of getting information from another person; **brain´power**, intellectual ability; people with developed intellectual ability; **brain´storm** (*inf*), sudden inspiration; **brain´storming**, the unrestrained offering of ideas by all members of a group to seek solutions to problems; **brain trust**, unofficial and sometimes unacknowledged panel of experts and advisers, esp to the President of the US; **brain´wash´ing**, a systematic attempt to change what a person thinks and believes by methods, not necessarily violent, which applied persistently, usu. over a long period, shake his faith in his accepted views (*vt* **brain´wash**).—**brain drain** (*inf*), continuing loss of persons of high intelligence and creativity through emigration; **brain wave**, the rhythmic fluctuations of voltage between parts of the brain resulting in the production of an electric current; a current produced by brain waves; (*inf*) a brainstorm.—*adj* **brain´y** (*inf*), having a good mind; intelligent. [OE *brægen*; Du *brein*.]

braise [brāz] *vt* to stew in a closed vessel. [Fr *braiser*.]

brake[1] [brāk] obsolete *pt* of **break** (1).

brake[2] [brāk] *n* a fern, esp any of the genus *Pteridium*; bracken. [Perh **bracken**.]

brake[3] [brāk] *n* rough or marshy land overgrown usu. with one kind of plant.—*adj* **brak´y**. [Ety uncertain.]

brake[4] [brāk] *n* an instrument to break flax or hemp; a harrow; a contrivance for retarding the motion of a wheel by friction; a kind of vehicle.—*vt* to retard or stop by a brake.—*vi* to apply the brake on a vehicle; to become checked by a brake.—See **break** (1).—*ns* **brake´man**, the person on a freight or passenger train who inspects the train and assists the conductor; the end man on a bobsled team who operates the brake. [From root of **break**.]

bramble [bram´bl] *n* any rough prickly shrub or vine of the genus *Rubus*, esp raspberries and blackberries. [OE *brēmel*; Du *braam*; Ger *brom-beere*.]

bran [bran] *n* the husks of cereal grain sifted from the flour. [OFr *bran*, bran; perh Celt.]

branch [bränch or -sh] *n* an armlike extension of a tree; any offshoot from a parent stem; a separately located department of a business or enterprise; the tributary of a river; a subdivision, section of a subject.—*vi* to spread out as a branch, or in branches to come out (from the main part) as a branch.—*vt* to ornament with designs of branches; to divide up.—**branch off**, to separate into branches; to diverge; **branch out**, to extend one's interests, activities, etc. [Fr *branche*—Low L *branca*, paw.]

brand [brand] *n* a piece of wood burning or partly burned; a mark stamped with a hot iron; such a mark inflicted on the person as a sign of guilt or disgrace, now used to identify cattle; particular make (of goods); a trademark.—*vt* to mark with a hot iron; to fix a mark of infamy upon.—*ns* **brand´er; brand name**, the name by which a certain make of commodity is known.—Also *adj*.—*adj* **brand´new**, entirely new and unused. [OE *brand, brond*, from root of **burn** (2).]

brandish [brand´ish] *vt* to wave or flourish as a brand or weapon.—*n* a waving or flourish. [Fr *brandissant—brandir*, from root of **brand**.]

brandy [brand´i] *n* an alcoholic liquor distilled from wine or from fermented fruit juice. [Formerly *brandwine*—Du *brandewijn—branden*, to burn, to distil, and *wijn*, wine.]

brant [brant] *n* any of several wild geese (genus *Branta*) esp the American brant (*B bernicla*) which has a black head, neck, and breast and is prized for its flesh.—(*pl*) **brant, brants**.

brash [brash] *adj* impetuous; bumptious; bold.

brass [bräs] *n* an alloy of copper and zinc; (*inf*) effrontery; (often *pl*) the brass instruments of an orchestra or band; (*slang*) officers or officials of high rank.—*ns* **brass´hat**, a high-ranking military officer; a person in a high position in civilian life; **brass´y** (or **brassie**), a wooden golf club with sole of brass or other metal.—*adj* of or like brass; impudent; pitiless; harsh in tone.—**brass band**, a band consisting of percussion and brass instruments; **brass tacks**, (*inf*) basic facts. [OE *bræs*.]

brassard [bras´ärd] *n* a cloth worn around the upper arm usu. with an identifying symbol. [Fr—*bras*, arm.]

brassière [bras´i-er] *n* a woman's undergarment supporting the breasts. [Fr.]

brat [brat] *n* an ill-mannered, annoying child.—*n* **bratt´iness**. [OE *bratt*; of Celt origin.]

brattice [brat´is] *n* a wooden partition or lining, esp to control ventilation in a mine.—*vt* to furnish with a brattice. [OFr *breteshe*—Low L *bretachia*; prob Gmc.]

bratwurst [brat´wûrst] *n* a highly spiced fresh pork sausage for cooking. [Ger.]

braunschweiger [brown´shwī-gėr] *n* smoked liver sausage. [Ger.]

bravado [brav-ä´dō, brav-ā´dō] *n* pretended bravery; a boastful threat.—*pl* **brava´do(e)s**. [Sp *bravada—bravo*, brave.]

brave [brāv] *adj* courageous; noble; finely dressed, handsome.—*vt* to meet boldly; to defy; to face (it out).—*n* any brave man; a N American Indian warrior.—*adv* **brave´ly**.—*n* **brav´ery**, heroism; finery.—**brave new world**, a future society characterized by totalitarianism and technological advance. [Fr *brave*; It and Sp *bravo*; perh from Celt.]

Bravo communication word for the letter *B*.

bravo[1] [bräv´ō] *n* a daring villain; a hired assassin.—*pl* **bravo(e)s** [bräv´ōz]. [It, Sp.]

bravo[2] [bräv´ō] *interj* well done! excellent! [It.]

bravura [bräv-ōōr´a] *n* bold daring; dash; (*mus*) bold and spirited execution; a passage requiring such execution. [It.]

brawl [bröl] *n* a noisy quarrel.—*vi* to quarrel noisily. [ME *bralle*; perh conn with Du *brallen*, Ger *prahlen*, to boast.]

brawn [brön] *n* strong, well-developed muscles; muscular strength.—*adj* **brawn´y**, muscular. [OFr *braon*, flesh (for roasting); of Gmc origin.]

bray[1] [brā] *vt* to break, pound, or grind small. [OFr *breier*.]

bray[2] [brā] *n* the cry of the donkey; any harsh sound.—*vi* to utter such sounds. [OFr *brai, brait—braire*—Low L *bragire*; perh of Celt origin.]

brayer [brā´ėr] *n* a printer's hand inking roller.

braze [brāz] *vt* (*arch*) to harden.—*adjs* **brā´zen**, of or belonging to brass; impudent; **brazen-faced**, marked by bold disrespect.—*vt* to face (a situation) with impudence (as in *to brazen it out*).—*n* **brazier** [brāzh´(y)ėr], a worker in brass. [OE *bræsian—bræs*, brass.]

braze [brāz] *vt* to solder with a metal having a high melting point.—*n* **brazier**, [brāz´yėr, brāzh´(y)ėr] a pan for hot coals. [Fr *braser*, to burn; perh influenced by **brass**.]

Brazil´ian [bra-zil´yȧn] *n* a native of Brazil, in South America.—*adj* belonging to Brazil.—*ns* **Brazil´ nut**, a tall S American tree (*Bertholletia excelsa*) that bears an edible, three-sided seed; its nut; **brazil´wood**, the heavy wood of various tropical leguminous trees (esp genus *Caesalpina* used as dyewood and in cabinet work. [OFr *bresil*; Sp, Port, *brasil*—Low L *brasilium*, a red dyewood brought from the East. When a similar wood was discovered in South America the country became known as *terre de brasil*, whence *Brasil*, Brazil.]

breach [brēch] *n* an act of breaking; a break or gap, as in the walls of a fortress; a breaking of law, contract, covenant, promise, etc.; a break in friendship.—*vt* to make a breach or opening in.—**breach of promise**, breach of a promise of a marriage. [OE *bryce, brice*; related to **break**.]

bread [bred] *n* food made of flour or meal baked; livelihood (also **bread-and-butt´er**,); food; (*slang*) money; being as basic as earning a living; that can be depended on; sent or given as thanks for hospitality.—*ns* **bread and butter**, a means of livelihood; **bread´basket**, (*slang*) stomach; an important cereal-producing region; **bread´board**, a board on which bread is cut; a board on which components are mounted for breadboarding.—*vt* to make an experimental arrangement of (as an electronic circuit or a mechanical system) to test feasibility.—*ns* **bread´fruit**, a tall tropical tree (*Arctocarpus altilis*) whose fruit, when roasted, forms a good substitute for bread; **bread´winner**, one who earns a living for a family; **breadline**, a line of people waiting to receive free food (as from a welfare agency or charity.) [OE *bread*, prob from a Gmc root meaning of fragment, like the Scot and North country use of 'a *piece*', for a bit of bread. The usual OE word was *hlāf*.]

breadth [bredth] *n* extent from side to side, width; liberality (eg of mind); in art, subordination of details to the harmony of the whole. [OE *brǣdu*; Ger *briete*; same root as **broad**.]

break [brāk] *vt* to sever forcibly; to divide; to shatter; to crush; to tame; to violate; to fail to fulfil; to check, as a fall; to interrupt (eg silence); to discontinue; to cure (of a habit); to make poor, ill, bankrupt etc.; to impart (news); to surpass; to decipher or solve.—*vi* to fall asunder; to pass suddenly (into a condition or action); to force a passage; to dawn or come into view; to become bankrupt; to crack (as the voice); to sever a connection; to stop activity temporarily; to suffer a collapse, as of spirit; (of news, etc.) suddenly and sensationally to become public;—*pt* **brōke**, (*arch*) **brāke**; *pt p* **brok´en**,—*n* state of being broken; an opening; a pause or interruption; a sudden change; an escape; (*slang*) a stroke of luck.—*adj* **break´able**.—Also *n* in *pl*—*ns* **break´age**, the action of breaking, or its consequences; the sum allowed for such loss. **break´away**, revolt, secession; **breakbone fever**, dengue; **break dancing**, dancing which involves acrobatic moves; **break´down**, failure of health; a stoppage; an anyalysis; **break´er**, a wave that breaks into foam.—*adj* **break-even**, having equal cost and income.—*vi* **break in**, to enter premises by force; to interrupt a conversation, to intrude; to begin a new enterprise or activity.—*vt* to accustom to a new activity; to overcome the stiffness or newness of.—*ns* **break´ing**, (*phonetics*) change of a vowel to a diphthong by the influence of following sounds; **breaking point**, the point at which a person give way under stress; the point at which a situation becomes critical.—*adj* **break´neck**, reckless.—*n* **breakout**, a military attack to break from encirclement.—*vi* **break out**, to emerge suddenly and forcefully; to become affected with a skin eruption; to emerge from a restraining condition.—*vt* to make ready for action; to produce for consumption; to separate from a mass of data.—*ns* **break´through**, action of breaking through an obstruction; a very important advance or discovery; **break-up**, a dispersion; a disintegration; a collapse; **break´water**, a barrier to break the force of the waves as before a harbour, **break down**, to crush; to collapse; to fail completely; to separate into component parts; to analyze; **break the heart**, to cause or feel, crushing sorrow; **break the ice**, to make a beginning; to overcome initial difficulties, esp reserve or restraint; **break up**, to break open; to break in pieces; (*inf*) to go to pieces; to decay; to disperse; **break wind**, expel gas from anus, **break with**, to quarrel with; to cease adherence to (tradition, a habit, etc.). [OE *brecan*; Ger *brechen*.]

breakfast [brek´fȧst] *n* a break or breaking of a fast—the first meal of the day.—*vi* to take breakfast.

bream [brēm] *n* a small freshwater fish (*Lepomus gibbosus*) common in streams and ponds with sand and mud bottoms throughout eastern and central US.—Also **sunfish, pumpkin seed**; any of various European or Australian marine food fishes. [OFr *bresme*, from OHG; Ger *brassen*.]

breast [brest] *n* the forepart of the human body between the neck and the belly; one of the two mammary glands; the corresponding part of any vertebrate; conscience, disposition, affections.—*vt* to bear the breast against; to oppose; to mount.—*ns* **breast´bone**, sternum; **breast´plate**, a piece of armor for the breast; **breast´stroke**, a swimming stroke in which both arms are brought out sideways from the chest; **breast´work**, a hastily constructed low earthwork. [OE *brēost*; Ger *brust*; Du *borst*.]

breath [breth] *n* the air drawn into and then expelled from the lungs; power of breathing; life; a single act of breathing; a very slight breeze; an exhalation.—*adjs* **breath´less**, out of breath; panting; gasping; unable to breathe easily because of emotion; **breath´taking**, very exciting.—*n* **breath´lessness.—catch the breath**, to stop breathing for an instant; to pause or rest; **take one's breath away**, to thrill. [OE *brǣth*; Ger *brodem*, steam, breath.]

breathe [breTH] *vi* to draw in and expel breath or air from the lungs; to take breath, to rest or pause; to live; to speak or sing softly; to whisper.—*vt* to draw in or expel from the lungs, as air; to infuse (into); to give out as breath; to whisper; to exercise; to let (a horse) recover breath.—*ns* **breath´er** a spell of exercise; (*inf*) a rest to recover breath; **breathing**, the act of breathing; respite; one or other of two signs used in Greek to signify presence or absence of the aspirate; **breath´ing space, breathing spell, breathing room**, time in which to recover, get organized or get going.—**breathe again**, to have a feeling of relief. [ME *brethen*, from OE *brǣth*, breath.]

breccia [brech´yä] *n* a rock composed of angular fragments. [It]

bred [bred] *pt, pt p* of **breed**.]

breech [brēch] *n* the lower part of the body behind; the hinder part of a gun; the bottom part of a pulley block.—*n pl* **breeches** [brich´ez], a garment for the lower limbs of the body coming just below the knee.—*ns* **breeching** [brēch´-, brich´-], part of a horse's harness that comes round the breech; **breech´es buoy**, a canvas seat in the form of breeches hung from a life buoy used to haul persons from one ship to another; **breech´load´er**, a firearm loaded by introducing the charge at the breech. [OE *brēc*; found in all Gmc languages; cf Ger *bruch*, Du *brock*.]

breed [brēd] *vt* to generate or bring forth; to train or bring up; to propagate, raise (eg *he breeds horses*); to cause or occasion.—*vi* to be with young; to produce offspring; to be produced (eg *trouble breeds there*).—*pt, pt p* **bred**.—*n* progeny or offspring; race or type.—*ns* **breed´er; breed´ing**, act of producing; education and training; good manners resulting from good training.—**breeder reactor**, a nuclear reactor capable of creating more fissile material than it consumes in maintaining the chain reaction. [OE *brēdan*, to cherish, keep warm; Ger *brüten*, to hatch.]

breeze[1] [brēz] *n* a light gentle wind; a wind from 4 to 31 miles an hour; (*inf*) a thing easy to do.—*adj* **breez´y**, fanned with or subject to breezes; airy; nonchalant; bright, lively.—*n* **breezeway**, a covered passageway, as between a house and garage. [Old Sp *briza*, It *brezza*.]

breeze[2] [brēz] *n* furnace refuse from coal or coke. [Perh OFr *brese*.]

brethren [breTH´ren] *pl* of **brother**.

Breton [bret´ȯn] *n* a native of Brittany (*Bretagne*), France; the Celtic tongue of Brittany.—*adj* pertaining to Britanny.

breve [brēv] *n* an obsolescent note, ‖ twice as long as a whole note; the curved mark (˘) placed over a vowel to indicate pronunciation. [It *breve*—L *brevis*, short.]

breviary [brēv´i-ȧr-i also brev´-] *n* book containing the daily service of the RC Church. [L *breviārium*—*brevis*, short.]

brevity [brev´it-i] *n* shortness; conciseness. [L *brevitās*—*brevis*, short.]

brew [brōō] *vt* to make (beer, ale, etc.) from malt and hops by boiling and fermenting; to steep (tea, etc.); to plot, scheme.—*vi* to perform, or undergo, the operation of brewing; to be in preparation.—*n* something brewed.—*ns* **brew´er**, one who brews; **brew´ery**, a place for brewing beer, etc.—**brewer's yeast**, the dried, pulverized cells of a yeast (*Saccharomyces cerevisiae*) used in brewing and also as a source of B-complex vitamins. [OE *brēowan*, cf Ger *brauen*.]

briar See **brier** (1).

briar [brī´ėr] *n* a tobacco pipe made from the root of a brier.

bribe [brīb] *n* something offered to influence the judgment unduly or corrupt the conduct, esp to do something illegally.—*vt* to offer or give a bribe to.—*n* **brib´ery**, the act of giving or taking bribes. [OFr *bribe*, a lump of bread; origin uncertain.]

bric-a-brac [brik´a-brak] *n* curios, treasured odds and ends. [Fr]

brick [brik] *n* a block of baked clay for building; a similar block of other material.—*vt* to lay or pave with brick.—*ns* **brick´bat**, a piece of brick, esp as a missile; an unfavorable remark; **brick´layer**, one who lays bricks; **brick´work**, work of bricks or a structure formed of bricks; **brick´yard**, a place where bricks are made.—**drop a brick**, to make a blunder. [Fr *brique*, from root of **break**.]

bridal [brīd´ȧl] *n* a wedding.—*adj* belonging to a bride or a wedding, nuptial. [**bride** + **ale**, a feast.]

bride [brīd] *n* a woman about to be married or newly married.—*ns* **bride´groom**, a man about to be married; a man newly married; **bride-price**, a payment (as of money, cattle, etc.) given by a prospective husband to the bride's family in many cultures; **bridesmaid**, a young woman attending the bride during a wedding. [OE *brȳd*; ON *brūthr*, Ger *braut*, a bride.]

bridewell [brīd´wel] *n* a prison. [From such a place, once a palace, near St *Bride's Well* in London.]

bridge[1] [brij] *n* a structure by which traffic is conveyed over a river or intervening space; the narrow raised platform whence the captain of a ship gives directions; the bony part of the nose; an arch to raise the strings of a violin, etc.; a mounting for false teeth; anything that connects across a gap.—*vt* to be, or to build, a bridge over.—*n* **bridge´head**, a fortification covering the end of a bridge nearest to the enemy's position; any advanced position seized in enemy territory; **bridge´work**, dental bridges.—**burn one's bridges**, to follow a course from which there is no retreat. [OE *brycg*; Ger *brücke*.]

bridge[2] [brij] *n* any of various card games for four players in two partnerships that bid for the right to name a trump suit, score points for tricks above six, and played with the declarer's hand exposed, esp contract bridge. [Ety uncertain.]

bridle [brī´dl] *n* the headgear to which a horse's reins are attached; any restraint.—*vt* to put a bridle on; to manage by a bridle; to restrain.—*vi* to draw one's head back as an expression of anger, scorn, etc.—*ns* **brī´dle path**, a trail suitable for horseback riding. [OE *brīdel*; OHG *brittel*.]

Brie [brē] *n* a flat, round cheese with an edible crust made from fermented, mold-inoculated whole milk. [Fr]

brief [brēf] *n* a short account of a client's case for the instruction of counsel in a trial at law; an outline of an argument, esp that setting out the main contentions; (*pl*) snug, legless underpants.—*vt* to furnish with precise, final instructions.—*adj* short; concise.—*adv* **brief´ly**.—*n* **brief´ness**.—*adj* **brief´less**, having no legal clients.—*n* **brief´case**, a flat, flexible case for carrying papers, books, etc.—**in brief**, in a few words. [Fr *bref*—L *brevis*, short.]

brier[1] [brī´ėr] *n* a plant (as of the genera *Rosa, Rubus* and *Smilax*) with a thorny or prickly woody stem; a mass of these. [OE (Anglian) *brēr*.]

brier[2] [brī´ėr] *n* a heath (*Erica arborea*) of southern Europe from whose root tobacco-pipes are made.—*n* **brier´root**, the root of the brier. [Fr *bruyère*, heath.]

brig [brig] *n* a two-masted, square-rigged vessel. [Shortened from **brigantine**.]

brigade [brig´ād´] *n* a US army unit consisting of three or more battalions and usu. commanded by a colonel; a group of people organized to function as a unit in some work.—*n* **brigadier´ gen´eral**, a commissioned officer in the army, air force, or marine corps ranking above a colonel and below a major general whose insignia is one star. [Fr *brigade*—It *brigata*—Low L *briga*, strife.]

brigand [brig´ȧnd] *n* a bandit, usu. one of a roving gang.—*n* **brig´andage**, plundering. [Fr—It *brigante*—*briga*, strife.]

brigantine [brig´ȧn-tēn] *n* a brig without a square mainsail. [Fr *brigantin*—It *brigantino*, a pirate ship.]

bright [brīt] *adj* shining; clear; (*arch*) beautiful; cheerful; brilliant in color or sound; favorable or hopeful; clever; illustrious.—*adv* brightly; clearly.—*vti* **bright´en**, to make or become bright or brighter.—*adv* **bright´ly**.—*n* **bright´ness**. [OE *byrht, beorht*; cog with L *flagrāre*, to flame.]

Bright's-disease [brīts´-diz-ēz´] *n* a group of diseases of the kidney marked by albumin in the urine. [From Dr Richard *Bright* (1789–1858).]

brilliant [bril´yȧnt] *adj* sparkling; splendid; talented.—*n* a gem (as a diamond) cut in a particular form with from 80 to 88 facets giving it a special brilliance.—*adv* **brill´iantly**.—*ns* **brill´iance, brill´iancy**, brightness; splendor; great cleverness; **brilliantine** [bril´yȧn-tēn], a dressing to make the hair glossy; a light lustrous fabric resembling alpaca and with a cotton warp and worsted weft. [Fr *brillant*, pr p of *briller*, to shine—Low L *beryllus*, a beryl.]

brim [brim] *n* the upper edge of a hollow vessel; the rim of a hat.—*vti* to fill or be full to the brim.—*pr p* **brimm´ing**; *pt p* **brimmed**.—*adj* **brim´ful**, full to the brim; completely full.—**brim over**, to overflow. [ME *brymme*.]

brimstone [brim´stōn] *n* sulfur. [Lit burning stone; from the OE *brȳne*, a burning—*byrnan*, to burn + **stone**.]

brindled, brindle [brin´dld, brin´dl] *adj* brownish or gray, marked with darker spots or streaks. [Prob connected with **brand**.]

brine [brīn] *n* water saturated with common salt; a strong saline solution (as of calcium chloride); the water of a sea or salt lake.—*vt* to treat (as by steeping) with brine.—*adj* **brīn´y**, pertaining to brine or to the sea; salt. [OE *brȳne*, a burning; applied to salt liquor, from its burning, biting quality.]

bring [bring] *vt* to fetch, to lead or carry 'here' or to the place where the speaker will be; to cause to come (eg rain, relief), to result in; to lead to an action or belief; to sell for.—*pt, pt p* **brought** [brawt].—*n* **bringer**.—**bring about**, to bring to pass, to effect; **bring around**, to restore to consciousness; **bring down**, to cause to fall by or as if by shooting; to carry (a total) forward; **bring down the house**, to cause tumultuous applause; **bring forth**, to give birth to, produce; **bring home**, to make unmistakably clear; **bring in**, to introduce; to yield as profit; (*baseball*) to enable (a man on third base) to reach home plate by a hit; to cause (as an oil well) to be productive; to earn; **bring off**, to rescue; to achieve; **bring on**, to cause to happen; **bring out**, to make clear; to develop (a quality) effectively; to put before the public; to introduce formally into society; **bring to**, to restore to consciousness; **bring to account**, to reprimand; **bring to bear**, to put to use; to apply, exert; **bring to book**, to compel to give an account; **bring to light**, to disclose, reveal; **bring to mind**, to cause to be recalled; **bring to terms**, to compel to agree, assent, or submit; **bring up**, to rear or educate; to introduce as into discussion; to cough or vomit up; **bring up the rear**, to come last or behind. [OE *bringan*, to carry, to bring; allied perh to **bear**.]

brink [bringk] *n* the edge or border of a steep place or of a river; the point of onset; the threshhold of danger.—*n* **brink´manship**, the action of going to the very edge of, but not into, war or other disaster, in pursuit of a policy. [Prob Dan *brink*, declivity.]

brioche [brē-osh´] *n* a light, rich roll made with eggs, flour, yeast, etc. [Fr]

briquette, briquet [bri-ket´] *n* a brick-shaped block of usu. fine compressed material. [Fr *briquette*, dim of *brique*, a **brick**.]

brisk [brisk] *adj* full of life and spirit; active, energetic; pleasingly tangy; sharp in tone.—*adv* **brisk´ly**.—*n* **brisk´ness**. [Perh Celtic; perh Fr *brusque*.]

brisket [brisk´ėt] *n* meat from the breast of an animal. [Perh Fr *brechet, brichet*.]

brisling, bristling [bris´ling] *n* a small herring (*Clupea sprattus*) resembling, and processed like, a sardine. [Norw, sprat.]

bristle [bris´l] *n* a short, stiff hair.—*vi* to stand erect, as bristles; to have the bristles erect; to show anger or desire to resist; to be thickly covered (with).—*pr p* **brist´ling**; *pt p* **brist´led**.—*adj* **brist´ly**, set with bristles; rough.—**bristle with**, to be full of, beset with. [Conn with OE *byrst*, a bristle.]

bristol board [bris´tȯl bōrd, -bȯrd] *n* a smooth pasteboard, paperboard, esp for artwork.—Also called **bristol**. [From the town *Bristol*, England.]

Britannia [brit-an´i-a] *n* Britain; female figure personifying it.—*adj* **Britann´ic**.—**Britannia metal**, an alloy of tin with antimony and a little copper or zinc resembling pewter. [L *Britannia*.]

British [brit´ish] *adj* pertaining to Great Britain or the British Commonwealth; relating to the English language as spoken in Britain.—*n* natives or inhabitants of Britain; the Celtic language of the ancient Britons, Welsh.—**British thermal unit**, amount of heat required to raise the temperature of one pound of water through on degree Fahrenheit. [OE *Brettisc*—*Bret*, a Briton, Welshman.]

Briton [brit´ȯn] *n* one of the Brythonic inhabitants of Britain, or one of their descendants; a native or citizen of Great Britain. [L *Britto*, from root of **Brython**.]

brittle [brit´l] *adj* easily broken; frail.—*n* **britt´leness**. [OE *brēotan*, to break.]

broad [bröd] *adj* of large extent from side to side; wide; large, free or open; obvious; coarse, indelicate; strongly marked in pronunciation or dialect; tolerant; giving prominence to main elements, or harmony of the whole, without insisting on detail.—*n* (*slang*) a woman.—*advs* **broad, broad´ly**.—*ns* **broad´ arr´ow**, an arrow with a flat barbed head; **broad bean**, the large flat edible seed of a vetch (*Vicia faba*); this plant widely grown for its seed and fodder.—*adj* **broad´cast**, scattered or sown by hand; widespread.—*adv* in all directions.—*n* sowing by broadcasting general dissemination; transmission by radio or television for public reception; the matter so transmitted.—*vt* to scatter broadcast; to make widely known; to transmit by radio or television.—*pt, pt p* **broad´cast**.—*ns* **broad´caster; broad´cloth**, a woolen or worsted densely textured fabric with a smooth lustrous finish; a soft, semiglossy durable fabric of cotton, silk, or rayon.—*vti* **broad´en**, to make or grow broad or broader.—*ns* **broad´ gauge**, a railroad gauge wider than standard gauge; **broad´ness; broad´side**, the side of a ship; all the guns on one side of a ship of war, or their simultaneous discharge; a large sheet of paper with matter (often popular) printed on one side only (also **broadsheet**).—*adj* **broad´-spectrum**, effective against various insects and microorganisms.—*n* **broad´sword**, a cutting sword with a broad blade; **broad´tail**, the fur or skin of a very young or unborn karakul lamb; **Broad´way**, the commercial theater and amusement world of New York City.—**broad jump**, long jump. [OE *brād*.]

Brobdingnagian [brob-ding-nag´i-ȧn] *n* an inhabitant of the fabulous region of **Brobdingnag** (in *Gulliver's Travels*), where everything was gigantic; hence, a giant.—*adj* gigantic.

brocade [brok-ād´] *n* a fabric characterized by woven, raised designs.—*adj* **brocad´ed**. [It *broccato*, Fr *brocart* from It *broccare*, Fr *brocher*, to prick, stitch.]

Broca's area [brō´käz] *n* a brain center associated with the motor control of speech. [Paul P *Broca*, Fr surgeon.]

broccoli [brok´o-li] *n* a kind of cauliflower (*Brassica oleracea*) with loose heads of tiny green buds. [It; pl of *broccolo*, a sprout, dim of *brocco*, a skewer, a shoot.]

brochette [brō-shet´] *n* a skewer for broiling chunks of meat, etc.; food broiled on a brochette. [Fr]

brochure [bro-shōōr´] *n* a pamphlet. [Fr lit a small book, stitched—*brocher*, to stitch.]

brock [brok] *n* a badger. [OE *brocc*, from Celt.]

brogan [brō´gn] *n* a heavy work shoe, fitting high on the ankle. [Ir.]

brogue [brōg] *n* a stout shoe; a manner of pronunciation, esp that of English by the Irish (perh a different word). [Ir *bróg*, Gael *bròg*, a shoe.]

broider [broid´ėr], **broidery** [broid´ėr-i] *See* **embroider, embroidery**

broil[1] [broil] *n* a noisy quarrel; a confused disturbance.—Also *vti*. [Fr *brouiller*, to entangle, disorder.]

broil[2] [broil] *vti* to cook by exposure to direct heat.—*n* **broil´er**, a pan, grill, etc. for broiling; a bird fit for broiling esp a young chicken of up to 2½ pounds dressed weight. [Ety dub]

broke [brōk] *pt*, old *pt p* of **break**, surviving as *pt p* chiefly in the informal sense of hard up.

broken [brō´kn] *pt p* of **break**.—*adj* splintered, fractured; violated; ruined; tamed; incomplete, interrupted, intermittent; irregular; imperfect (eg *he speaks broken English*).—*adv* **brok´enly**.—*adjs* **brok´en-down**, extremely infirm; worn out; **brok´en-field**, achieved (as by a ball carrier in football) against widely scattered opposition; **brok´enheart´ed**, crushed with grief; **brok´en-wind´ed**, having short breath or disordered respiration, as a horse.

broker [brōk´ėr] *n* an agent who arranges marriages; an agent who negotiates contracts of purchase and sale (as of real estate, commodities, or securities); a power broker.—*n* **brok´erage**, the business of a broker; the commission charged by a broker. [ME *brocour*—Anglo-Fr *brocour*.]

bromeliad [brō-mel´i-ȧd] *n* any of various plants of the pineapple family (Bromeliaceae) chiefly tropical American and grown widely as house plants for their decorative flowers and leaves. [Olaf *Bromelius*, Swed botanist.]

bromine [brō´mēn] *n* a nonmetallic element (symbol Br; at wt 79.9; at no 35), named from its pungent fumes.—*n* **brō´mīde**, a compound of bromine and another element or radical, esp those used as medicinal sedatives; (*slang*) an old joke; a trite saying; a dull person.—**bromide paper**, in photography, paper with a highly sensitive surface containing bromide of silver, used in printing from a negative. [Gr *brōmos*, a stink.]

bronchus [brongk´us] *n* either of the main forks of the windpipe.—*pl* **bronch´ī**.—*adjs* **bronch´ial; bronchit´ic**, pertaining to bronchitis.—*n* one suffering from bronchitis.—*n* **bronchitis** [brongk-ī´tis] inflammation of the lining of the bronchial tubes. [Gr *bronchos*, windpipe.]

bronco [brong´ko] *n* a wild or half-tamed horse or pony of the western US.—*n* **bron´co buster** (*inf*), a tamer of broncos. [Sp *bronco*, rough, sturdy.]

brontosaurus [bron-to-sö´rus] *n* a genus (*Apatosaurus*) of dinosaurs, found fossil in the US. [Gr *brontē*, thunder, *sauros*, lizard.]

bronze [bronz] *n* an alloy of copper and tin and sometimes other elements; a copper alloy without tin; anything cast in bronze; a reddish-brown color.—*adj* made of, or like, bronze.—*n* **bronzing**, a bronze coloring or discoloration (as of leaves).—**Bronze Age**, the prehistoric period that began between 4000 and 3000 BC in which tools and weapons were made from bronze. [Fr—It *bronzo* L *Brundusium*, Brindisi.]

brooch [brōch] *n* an ornament held by a pin or a clasp and usu. worn near the neck. [Fr *broche*, a spit. Cf **broach**.]

brood [brōōd] *vi* to sit as a hen on eggs; to hang or hover (over); to meditate silently (on, over); to think anxiously for some time.—*n* a group having a common nature or origin, esp the children in a family; the number hatched at once.—*adj* kept for breeding, as in *brood* mare, etc.—*n* **brood´er**, one that broods; a heated shelter for raising fowl.—*adj* **brood´y**, inclined to sit or incubate; contemplative, moody. [OE *brōd*; Du *broed*; from the same root as **breed**.]

brook[1] [brŏŏk] *n* a small stream.—*ns* **brook´let**, a little brook; **brook trout**, a mottled stream trout (*Salvelinus fontinalis*) of N America. [OE *brōc*, water breaking forth; Du *broek*, Ger *bruch*.]

brook[2] [brŏŏk] *vt* to bear or endure. [OE *brūcan*, to use, enjoy; Ger *brauchen*, L *frui, fructus*.] *brauchen*, L *frui, fructus*.]

broom [brōōm] *n* any of various evergreen shrubs (genera *Cytisus, Genista*) of the pea family with yellow flowers; a bundle of fibers or twigs attached to a long handle used for sweeping.—*n* **broom´stick**, the handle of a broom [OE *brōm*.]

broth [broth] *n* a thin soup made by boiling meat, etc. in water; a fluid culture medium. [OE *broth*—*brēowan*, to brew.]

brothel [broth´-, broTH´ėl] *n* a house of prostitution. [ME *brothel*, a worthless person—OE *brothen*, ruined—*brēothen*, to go to ruin.]

brother [bruTH´ėr] *n* the name applied to a male child by the other children of his parents; a friend who is like a brother; a fellow member of any group or association; a lay member of a men's religious order;—*pl* **broth´ers; breth´ren**, used chiefly in formal address or in referring to the members of a society or sect.—*ns* **broth´erhood**, the state of being a brother; an association of men for any purpose; **broth´er-in-law**, the brother of a husband or wife; a sister's husband;—*pl* **brothers-in-law**.—*adj* **broth´erly**, like a brother; kind; affectionate.—*n* **broth´erliness**. [OE *brōthor*; cog with Ger *bruder*, Gael, *brathair*, L *frater*, etc.]

brougham [brōō´ȧm, brōōm] *n* a closed carriage (or automobile) with the driver's seat outside. [After Lord *Brougham* (1778–1868)]

brought [bröt] *pt, pt p* of **bring**.

brouhaha [brōō´hä-hä] *n* fuss, clamor. [Fr; perh from Heb].

brow [brow] *n* the eyebrow, the ridge over the eyes; the forehead; the edge of a cliff.—*vt* **brow´beat**, to cow by stern looks or speech, to bully. [OE *brū*; ON *brūn*.]

brown [brown] *adj* having the color of chocolate, a mixture of red, black, and yellow; tanned.—*n* a brown color.—*vti* to make or become brown.—*ns* **brown bagging**, the practice of bringing lunch from home to work, school, etc.; the practice of taking a bottle of liquor into a club or restaurant where setups are available; **brown bear**, any of several bears largely brown in color often lumped in a single species (*Ursus arctos*), including the grizzly bear that formerly inhabited the whole of western N America; **brown Betty**, a baked dessert of apples, bread crumbs, and spices; **brown bread**, bread made of wholewheat flour; a dark brown steamed bread usu. or cornmeal, flour, molasses, etc.; **brown´coal**, lignite; **brown fat**, a mammalian heat-producing tissue; **Brownie**, a member of the Girl Scouts of the USA from 6 through 8 years of age; **brownie**, a flat, nutty chocolate cake, served in squares; in Scottish folklore, a friendly domestic goblin; **brownie point**, a credit earned esp by cultivating a superior.—*adj* **brown´ish; brown´y**.—*n*—**brown study**, a reverie, orig a gloomy one; **brown sugar**, refined or partially refined sugar. [OE *brūn*; Du *bruin*, Ger *braun*.]

browse [browz] *vti* to feed on the rough shoots or leaves of plants; to read desultorily. [OFr *brouster*—*broust*, a sprout.]

browser [brow´zeer] *n* someone who browses; a computer software package that allows the user to locate and read hypertext files.

brucellosis [brōō-sėl-ō´sis] *n* a bacterial disease occurring in goats, cattle, hogs, and man.—Also **undulant fever**. [Sir David *Bruce*, bacteriologist.]

bruin [brōō´in] *n* a bear. [Du *bruin*, **brown**.]

bruise [brōōz] *vt* to injure and discolor (body tissue) without breaking the skin; to dent the surface (of wood); to break down (as leaves and berries) by pounding; to inflict psychological pain on.—*vi* to inflict a bruise; to undergo bruising.—*n* discoloration of the skin; a similar injury to plant tissue; an abrasion, scratch on furniture; an injury, esp to the feelings.—*n* **bruis´er**, a strong, pugnacious man. [OE *brӯsan*, to crush.]

bruit [brōōt] *vt* to noise abroad. [Fr *bruit*—Fr *bruire*; cf Low L *brugītus*; prob imit].

brummagem [brum´a-jem] *adj* showy but worthless. [Another form of *Birmingham*.]

brunch [brunch] *n* breakfast and lunch combined.

brunette [brŏŏn´et´] *n* a woman with black or dark-brown hair, often with dark eyes and complexion.—Also *adj*. [Fr dim of *brun*, brown.]

brunt [brunt] *n* the shock of an onset, the force of a blow; the chief shock or strain of anything (*bear the brunt of*); the hardest part. [Origin obscure.]

brush [brush] *n* an instrument set with bristles or the like for cleansing or for applying friction or a coating of some material; a painter's hair pencil; a bushy tail; a grazing contact.—*vt* to pass a brush over; to remove by a sweeping motion.—*vi* to pass with light contact.—*ns* **brush´off**, a curt dismissal; **brush´wood**, loppings and broken branches; underbrush;—**to brush up**, to revive in the memory. [OFr *brosse*, brushwood.]

brusque, brusk [brusk] *adj* blunt and abrupt in manner.—*adv* **brusque´ly**.—*ns* **brusque´ness, brusquerie** [brŏŏs´kerē]. [Fr]

Brussels carpet [brus´lz] *n* a kind of carpet having a woolen surface on a foundation of linen.—*ns* **Brussels griffon**, a breed of short-faced rough- or smooth-coated toy dog; **Brussels lace**, a fine needlepoint or bobbin lace with floral designs; a machine-made net of hexagonal mesh; **bruss´els sprout**, a plant (*Brassica oleracea gemmifera*) with small edible green heads on its stem. [Named from *Brussels* in Belgium.]

brut [brōōt] *adj* (of champagne) the driest made by the producer. [Fr]

brute [brōōt] *adj* belonging to, or as if belonging to, the lower animals; soulless; irrational; stupid; cruel; material, without consciousness.—*n* one of the lower animals; a brutal man.—*adj* **brut´al**, like a brute; unfeeling; inhuman.—*vt* **brut´alize**, to make like a brute, to degrade.—*n* **brutal´ity**.—*adv* **brut´ally**.—*adj* **brut´ish**, brutal; stupid.—*adv* **brut´ishly**.—*n* **brut´ishness.—brute force**, sheer strength. [Fr *brut*—L *brūtus*, dull, irrational.]

bryony [brī´o-ni] *n* any of a genus (*Bryonia*) of climbing vines of the gourd family with large leaves and red or black fruit. [Through L—Gr *bryōnia*.]

bryophyllum [brī-o-fil´um] *n* a succulent kalanchoe (*Kalanchoe pinnata*) grown as a foliage plant. [Gk *bryon*, a moss, liverwort, *pyllon*, a leaf.]

bryophyte [brī´o-fīt] *n* a plant phyllum comprising mosses and liverworts. [Gk *bryon*, a moss, liverwort, *phyton*, a plant.]

Brython [brith´on] *n* a Celt of the group to which Welsh, Cornish and Bretons belong.—*adj* **Brython´ic**. [W *Brython*, Briton.]

bubble [bub´l] *n* a film of liquid forming a ball around air or gas; a tiny ball of gas or air in a liquid or a solid; a transparent dome; an unsound or fraudulent scheme; to boil; to make a gurgling sound;—*pr p* **bubb´ling**; *pt p* **bubb´led**.—*adj* **bubb´ly**.—*n* **bubb´le chamber**, device for showing the path of a charged particle by the string of bubbles left in its track. [Cf Swed *bubbla*, Du *bobbel*.]

bubo [bū´bo] *n* an inflammatory swelling of the glands in the groin or armpit.—*adj* **bubon´ic**, accompanied by buboes—**bubonic plague**, an epidemic caused by a bacterium (*Yevsinia pestis*) and marked by buboes and fever, transmitted from rats to man through fleas. [L,—Gr *boubōn*, the groin, a bubo.]

buccaneer [buk´ȧn-ēr´] *n* one of the freebooters in the West Indies during the seventeenth century; a pirate; an unscrupulous adventurer, esp in politics or business.—*vi* to act as a buccaneer. [Fr *boucaner*, to smoke meat—Carib *boucan*, a wooden grid-iron. The French settlers in the West Indies cooked their meat on a *boucan* in native fashion, and were hence called *boucaniers*.]

buck [buk] *n* the male of the antelope deer, goat, hare, rabbit, and rat; a dashing fellow; (*slang*) a dollar.—*vi* (of a horse) to rear upward quickly; (*inf*) to resist.—*vt* (*football*) to charge against; to throw by bucking; (*inf*) to resist stubbornly.—*adj* of the lowest grade within a military rank.—*ns* **buck´passer** (*inf*), one who regularly shifts blame or responsibility to someone else; **buck´shot**, a large kind of shot, used in shooting deer; **buck´skin**, a soft leather made of deerskin or sheepskin; (*pl*) breeches or suit of buckskin.—*adj* made of or like the skin of a buck.—*n* **buck´tooth**, a projecting front tooth.—**buck for** (*slang*), to work eagerly for (a promotion, raise, etc.); **buck up** (*inf*) to cheer up. [OE *buc, bucca*; Du *bok*, Ger *bock*, he-goat.]

buckboard [buk´bōrd, -börd] *n* a four-wheeled wagon with a springy platform. [OE *būc*, body, + **board**.]

bucket [buk´ėt] *n* a container with a handle for drawing or holding liquid or substances in small pieces; the amount held by a bucket; etc.; one of the compartments on the circumference of a water-wheel, or one of the scoops of a steam shovel.—*n* **buck´etshop**, a dishonest brokerage firm; formerly, a saloon selling liquor in open containers or a gambling parlor using market fluctuations as a basis for betting; **buck seat**, a single, contoured seat with a movable back in an automobile.—**kick the bucket**, to die. [Prob conn with OE *būc*, a pitcher; or OFr *buket*, a pail.]

buckeye [buk´ī] *n* a horsechestnut (genus *Aesculus*), esp the tall trees (*A hippocastanum* and *A glabra*) grown for ornament and shade throughout temperate. No America; the large burs enclosing shiny brown seeds; **Buckeye**, nickname for a resident or native of Ohio.

buckle [buk´l] *n* a fastening for a strap or band; a bend or bulge.—*vti* to connect with a buckle; to bend or crumple under pressure, etc.—*n* **buck´ler**, a small shield used for parrying; **buckle down**, to apply oneself. [Fr *boucle*, the boss of a shield, a ring—Low L *buccula*.]

buckram [buk´rȧm] *n* a coarse fabric of jute, cotton, or linen, stiffened with size.—*adj* made of buckram; stiff; precise. [OFr *boquerant*.]

buckthorn [buk´thorn] *n* a tall thorny shrub (*Rhamnus cathartica*) widely used as a hedge plant in N America.

buckwheat [buk´hwēt] *n* any of a genus (Fagopyrum) esp two plants (*F esculentum* and *F tartaricum*) cultivated for their edible seeds; the seed used as cereal grain. [Prob Du *boekweit*, or Ger *buchweizen*, beech-wheat.]

bucolic [bū-kol´ik] *adj* pertaining to the tending of sheep; pastoral; rustic.—*n* **bucol´ic**, a pastoral poem. [L,—Gr *boukolikos—boukolos*, a herdsman.]

bud [bud] *n* an embryo shoot, flower, or flower cluster of a plant; an early stage of development.—*vi* to put forth buds; to begin to grow.—*vt* to produce or develop from buds; to cause (as a plant) to bud; to graft by inserting a bud under the bark of another tree;—*pr p* **budd´ing**; *pt p* **budd´ed**.—*n* **budd´ing**, being in an early stage of development.—**in the bud**, in a budding condition; in an early stage. [ME *budde*; perh related to Du *bot*, a bud.]

Buddah [bŏŏd´ä] *n* the state of perfect enlightenment; an image of Siddharta Gautama (about 563–483 BC), founder of Buddhism.—*ns* **Buddhism**, a system of ethics and philosophy based on the belief that the purpose of life is to attain enlightenment, manifested in many forms such as Lamaism, Zen, etc.; **Buddhist**, a believer in Buddhism. [Sans *buddha*, wise, from *budh*, to know.]

buddy [bud´ē] *n* (*inf*) a friend; a term of informal address.—**buddy system**, an arrangement on which two persons are paired, usu. for mutual safety.

budge [buj] *vti* to move or stir. [Fr *bouger*—It *bulicare*, to boil—L *bullire*.]

budgerigar [buj-er-i-gär´] *n* a small Australian parrot (*Melopsittacus undulatus*) usu. light green in the wild, but bred in many colors.—Also (*coll*) **budgie**. [Austr native *budgeri*, good, *gar*, cockatoo.]

budget [buj-ėt] *n* a collection stock; any plan of expenditure.—*vi* to prepare a budget or plan of revenue and expenditure; to allow (for) in a budget.—*vt* to put on a budget; to plan (*budget your time*). [Fr *bougette*, dim of *bouge*, a pouch—L *bulga*.]

buff [buf] *n* a heavy, soft, brownish-yellow leather; a military coat made from this; a dull brownish yellow; (*inf*)a devotee, fan.—*adj* made of buff; of a buff color.—*vt* to clean or shine with leather or a leather-covered wheel.—*n* **buffer**.—**in the buff**, naked. [Fr *buffle*, a buffalo.]

buffalo [buf´a-lō] *n* any of various wild oxen, any of a genus (*Bison*), esp the large shaggy-maned N American wild Ox (*B bison*); a freshwater fish (*Ictiobus cyprinellus*) related to the carp;—*pl* **buff´alo, buff´aloes**.—*ns* **buffalow bug**, carpet beetle; **buff´alo robe**, the hide of an American buffalo lined with fabric and used as a coverlet. [It *buffalo*, through L from Gr *boubalos*.]

buffer [buf´ėr] *n* anything that lessens shock, as of collision; something that serves as a protective barrier; a temporary storage area in a computer.—*vt* to treat or supply with a buffer.—*ns* **buff´er state**, a neutral country lying between two rival states; **buffer zone**, an area designed to separate. [Prob from obs *buff*, to strike.]

buffet[1] [buf´ėt] *n* a blow with the fist, a slap.—*vt* to strike with the hand or fist; to contend against.—*vi* to make one's way esp under difficult conditions.—*n* **buffet´ing**, repeated blows. [OFr *buffet—buffe*, a blow, esp on the cheek.]

buffet[2] [bůfā´] *n* a sideboard or table at which guests serve themselves food; a meal served thus. [Fr *buffet*.]

buffoon [buf-ōōn´] *n* one who amuses by jests, grimaces, etc.; a clown; a fool.—*n* **buffoon´ery**, ludicrous or vulgar jesting. [Fr *booffon*—It *buffone; buffare*, to jest.]

bug[1] [bug] *n* an object of terror.—*ns* **bug´aboo**, a bogy; **bug´bear**, an object of terror (generally imaginary) or of abhorrence; a continuing source of irritation. [ME *bugge*.]

bug[2] [bug] *n* an insect with sucking mouth parts; any insect; (*inf*) a germ or virus; (*slang*) a defect, as in a machine; (*slang*) a hidden microphone.—*vt* (*slang*) to plant a concealed listening device in; (*slang*) to annoy, anger, etc.—*adj* **bug´eyed** (*slang*), with bulging eyes.

buggy [bug´i] *n* a light four-wheeled, one-horse carriage with one seat; a small carriage for a baby. [Ety unknown.]

bugle[1] [bū´gl] *n* valveless brass instrument like a small trumpet used esp for military calls.—*vti* to signal by blowing a bugle.—*n* **bū´gler**. [OFr *bugle*—L *būculus*, dim of *bōs*, an ox.]

bugle[2] [bū´gl] *n* any of a genus (*Ajuga*) of low-growing plants with spikes of blue flowers with basal rosettes.

bugle[3] [bū´gl] *n* a small cylindrical bead used for trimming, esp on women's clothing.

build [bild] *vt* to erect; to form or construct, to establish, base; to create or develop (*often with* **up**).—*vi* to put up buildings; to grow or intensify (*often with* **up**).—*pt p* **built** (*arch* **build´ed**).—*n* the way a thing is built or shaped.—*ns* **build´er; build´ing**, the art of erecting houses etc.; anything built; **build´up**, a building up, strengthening; favorable publicity; preliminaries leading up to a climax in a story, etc.—*adjs* **built´-in**, formed as part of a main structure, present as part of one's genetic inheritance (as *built-in aptitude*); firmly fixed; **built´-up**, made higher, stronger, etc. with added parts; having many buildings on it, **build up**, to develop gradually by increments; to promote the reputation, health, etc. of; to accumulate or develop appreciably. [OE *gebyld*, pt p of an assumed *byldan*, to build—*bold*, a dwelling.]

bulb [bulb] *n* a subterranean bud with swollen leaf bases in which reserve materials are stored, as in onions, narcissi, etc.; any similar protuberance; the globe of an electric light.—*adjs* **bulbed, bul´bous**. [L *bulbus*—Gr *bolbos*, an onion.]

bulbul [bŏŏl´bŏŏl] *n* the 'Persian nightingale'; any of several birds (family Pycnonotidae) of Asia and Africa. [Ar.]

bulge [bulj] *n* a swelling; a rounded projecting part;—*vti* to swell or bend outward.—*adj* **bul´gy**. [OFr *boulge*, prob L *bulga, knapsack*; cf **bilge**.]

bulgur [bul´gur] *n* parched cracked wheat. [Turk.]

bulk [bulk] *n* magnitude or size; great size; large quantity; the greater part;—

vi to have, or increase in size or importance.—*adj* total, aggregate; not packaged.—*adj* **bulk´y**, having bulk; unwieldy.—*adj* **bulk´iness**. [ON *bulki*, a heap.]

bulkhead [bulk´hed] *n* a watertight, fireproof, etc. partition separating one part of a ship's interior from another; a retaining wall, a boxlike structure over an opening.

bull[1] [bŏŏl] *n* the male of bovine and certain other animals, as the whale, walrus, elephant, moose; one who seeks to raise the price of stocks and speculates on a rise; a bull's-eye; (*slang*) nonsense;—*adj* male; rising in price.—*ns* **bull´bait´ing**, the sport of baiting or exciting bulls with dogs; **bull´dog**, a breed of compact, muscular, short-haired dog with widely separated forelegs and an undershot lower jaw.—*vt* to throw (a steer) by holding its horns and twisting its neck—*adj* stubborn, like a bulldog. **bull´fight**, a popular Hispanic spectacle in which a bull is goaded to fury and finally despatched by a matador; **bull´frog**, a large N American frog (*Rana catesbeiana*) with a deep, loud croak;—**bull´-head´ed**, impetuous and obstinate.—*ns* **bull´horn**, a portable electronic voice amplifier; **bull´ock**, a castrated bull; young bull; **bull´pen**, a temporary detention room in a jail; (*baseball*) a practice area for relief pitchers; **bull´ring**, the enclosure in which a bullfight takes place; **bull´s-eye**, the center of a target, of a different color from the rest, and usually round; a direct hit; **bull´terr´ier**, a crossbreed between the bulldog and the terrier. [ME *bole*, prob Scand *bole, boli*.]

bull[2] [bŏŏl] *n* an edict of the pope which has his seal affixed. [L *bulla*, a knob, a leaden seal.]

bull[3] [bŏŏl] *n* a ludicrous blunder in speech. [Prob OFr *boul*, cheat.]

bulldoze [bŏŏl´dōz] *vt* (*inf*) to intimidate; to clear by bulldozer.—*n* **bull´dozer**, tractor with horizontal ram for clearing and leveling.

bullet [bŏŏl´ėt] *n* the ball fired from any kind of small-arm.—*adj* **bull´etproof**, proof against bullets. [Fr *boulette*, dim of *boule*, a ball—L *bulla*.]

bulletin [bŏŏl´e-tin] *n* an official report of public news, or of a patient's progress. [Fr,—It *bullettino*.]

bullion [bŏŏl´yȯn] *n* gold and silver in the mass and uncoined; dress trimming of gold and silver threads.

bullock *See* **bull** (1)

bully[1] [bŏŏl´i] *n* a cruel and boastful oppressor of the weak.—*adj* blustering; brisk; (*inf*) excellent.—*vt* to treat with persistent petty cruelty; to domineer over; to coerce (into).—*pr p* **bull´ying**; *pt p* **bull´ied**.—*vt* **bull´y-rag** (*inf*), to overawe by threats and taunts. [Per Du *boel*, a lover; cf Ger *buhle*.]

bully[2] [bŏŏl´i] *ns* canned or pickled beef. [Prob Fr *bouilli*, boiled beef, influenced by **bull** (1).]

bulrush, bullrush [bŏŏl´rush] *n* any of a genus (*Scirpus*) of annual or perennial sedges with a bristly spikelet of flowers. [Perh **bull** (1), in sense of great, + **rush** (2).]

bulwark [bŏŏl´wȧrk] *n* a fortification or rampart; the side of a ship projecting above the deck; any means of defence or security.—*vt* to defend; to fortify. [Cf Ger *bollwerk*.]

bum [bum] *n* (inf) a tramp; a devotee, as of skiing or tennis.

bumble [bum´(b)l] *vi* to utter indistinctly; to bungle.—*n* **bum´blebee**, a large wild loud-humming bee (genus *Bombus*). [Freq of **bum**.]

bumboat [bum´bōt] *n* a boat bringing provisions for sale to ships. [Origin doubtful.]

bump [bump] *vi* to knock dully; to jolt.—*vt* to strike against or on; to jolt.—*n* a dull, heavy blow, a thump; a lump or swelling; one of the protuberances on the surface of the skull supposed to indicate certain mental characteristics.—*n* **bump´er**, a bar on a motorcar to lessen the shock of collision; a cup or glass filled to the brim; anything large or generous in measure.—Also *adj*—**bump off** (*slang*), to murder. [Onomatopoeic.]

bumpkin [bump´kin] *n* an awkward clumsy rustic; a clown. [Prob Du *boomken*, a log.]

bumptious [bump´shus] *adj* offensively self-assertive.—*adv* **bump´tiously**.—*n* **bump´tiousness**. [Prob formed from **bump**.]

bun [bun] *n* a kind of sweet cake; a rounded mass of hair. [Prob from OFr *bugne*, a swelling.]

Buna [bōō´na] *n* one form of synthetic rubber. [From parts of the names of its chemical constituents; orig trademark.]

bunch [bunch or -sh] *n* a lump (*rare*); a number of things fastened together; a cluster; something in the form of a tuft or knot; (*inf*) a group of people.—*vi* to cluster.—*vt* to make a bunch of, to concentrate.

bundle [bun´dl] *n* a number of things bound together; a loose package; (*biol*) a strand of conducting vessels, fibers, etc.—*vt* to make into bundles; to put, push hastily or unceremoniously.—*vi* to go hurriedly or in confusion (away, off, out).—**bundle up**, to dress warmly. [Conn with **bind** and **bond**.]

bung [bung] *n* the stopper of the hole in a barrel; a large cork.—*vt* to stop up with a bung.—*n* **bung´hole**, a hole for a bung.

bungalow [bung´ga-lō] *n* a lightly built house of one story occupied by Europeans in India; any similar house of one story. [Hindi *baṅglā*, (house) in the style of Bengal house.]

bungle [bung´gl] *n* anything clumsily done; a gross blunder.—*vi* to act in a clumsy awkward manner.—*vt* to make or mend clumsily; to manage awkwardly.—*n* **bung´ler**. [Ety obscure; prob onomatopoeic.]

bunion [bun´yȯn] *n* a lump or inflamed swelling on the first joint of the great toe.

bunk [bungk] *n* a box or recess in a ship's cabin; a sleeping berth anywhere.—*n* **bunk´er**, a large bin or chest, esp for stowing coal on a ship; an obstacle on a golf course.—*vti* to fuel.—*adj* **bunk´ered**.—*n* **bunk´ering**, loading fuel into a ship. [Prob of Scand origin; cf ON *bunki*, Dan *bunke*, a heap.]

bunkum, buncombe [bung´kum] *n* (*inf*) shallow pretentious oratory, humbug; pretentious nonsense—also **bunk**. [From *Buncombe*, USA, whose member in Congress confessed that he was talking simply to please Buncombe.]

bunny [bun´i] *n* child's word for a rabbit.

Bunsen burner [bun´sen] *n* a gas burner in which air mingles with the gas and produces a smokeless flame of great heating power. [R. W. *Bunsen* (1811–1899).]

bunt[1] [bunt] *vti* (*baseball*) to bat (a pitch) lightly so that it does not go beyond the infield.—*n* a bunted ball.

bunt[2] [bunt] *n* a disease of wheat or the fungus that causes it. [Ety unknown.]

bunting[1] [bunt´ing] *n* a thin worsted stuff for ships' colors; flags, cloth decorations.

bunting[2] [bunt´ing] *n* a genus (*Emberiza*) of finches nearly allied to the crossbills. [Ety uncertain.]

bunting[3] [bunt´ing] an infant's hooded sleeping bag made from thickly napped fabric.

buntline [bunt´līn] *n* a rope passing from the foot of a square sail, led up to the masthead and thence on deck, to help in hauling up the sail. [*bunt*, part of a sail, and **line** (2).]

buoy [boi] *n* a floating secured mark, serving as a guide or as a warning for navigation, or as a mooring point.—*vt* to fix buoys or marks to; to keep afloat, or sustain; to raise the spirits of—in last two meanings usu. with **up**.—*n* **buoy´ancy**, capacity for floating lightly on water or in the air; cheerfulness, elasticity of spirit.—*adj* **buoy´ant**, tending to float; cheerful. [Du **boei**, buoy, fetter, through Romance forms, from Low L *boia*, a collar of leather.]

bur *See* **burr** (1).

burble [bûrb´l] *vi* to talk incoherently, esp from excitement; to gurgle.—*n* **burb´ling**, the breaking up of a streamline flow of air about a body (as an airplane). [Prob onomatopoeic.]

burbot [bûr´bot] *n* a fish (*Lota lota*) having a longish beard on its lower jaw, the only freshwater species of the cod family. [Fr *barbote*.—L *barba*, a beard.]

burden[1] *n* a load; cargo; tonnage (of a ship); that which is oppressive or difficult to bear; responsibility.—*vt* to load; to oppress; to encumber.—*adj* **bur´densome**, heavy, oppressive. [OE *byrthen—beran*, to bear.]

burden[2] [bûrd´n] *n* part of a song repeated at the end of every stanza, a refrain; the leading idea (of anything). [Fr *bourdon*, a humming tone in music—Low L *burdo*, a drone bee.]

bureau [bū´rō, bū´rō] *n* a chest of drawers; a branch of a newspaper, magazine, or wire service in an important news center; a government department.—*pl* **bureaus, bureaux** [-ōz]. [Fr *bureau*—OFr *burel*, russet cloth—L *burrus*, red.]

bureaucracy [bū-rok´ra-si or -rōk´-] *n* a system of government by officials, responsible only to their chiefs.—*n* **bur´eaucrat**, one who practises or favors bureaucracy.—*adj* **bureaucrat´ic**. [**bureau**, + Gr *krateein*, to govern.]

burette, buret [bū-ret´] *n* graduated glass tube, usu. with a tap, for measuring the volume of liquids. [Fr.]

burgeon [bûr´jȯn] *n, vi* to put forth buds, etc.; to grow or develop rapidly.—Also **bourgeon**.

burgess [bûr´jės] *n* a freeman or citizen of a borough. [OFr *burgeis*.]

burgh [bur´ȯ] *n* another spelling of **borough**, used for Scottish burghs.—*ns* **burg** (same as **borough**); **burgher** [bûrg´ėr], an inhabitant of a borough; a citizen or freeman.

burglar [bûrg´lȧr] *n* one who enters a building to commit a felony, eg to steal.—*adj* **burglār´ious**.—*adv* **burglār´iously**.—*vt* **burg´le** (a back-formation).—*n* **burg´lary**. [Ety uncertain.]

burgomaster [bûr´gȯ-mäs-tėr] *n* the chief magistrate of a Dutch, Flemish, or German town. [Du *burgemeester*; Ger *Bürgermeister*.]

burgundy [bûr´gun-di] *n* a French wine, so called from *Burgundy*, the district where it is made; a blended red wine produced elsewhere (as California).

burial [ber´i-ȧl] *n* the act of burying. [OE *byrgels*, a tomb—*byrgan*, to bury.]

burin [būr´in] *n* a chisel used in copper engraving. [Fr; from root of **bore** (1).]

burke [bûrk] *vt* to stifle, to suppress. [From *Burke* (hanged 1829), who committed this crime in order to sell the bodies of his victims for dissection.]

burlesque [bûr-lesk´] *n* a ludicrous and exaggerated imitation.—*adj* of the nature of burlesque.—*vt* to mock by burlesque. [It *burlesco*; prob from Low L *burra*, a flock of wool, a trifle.]

burly [bûr´li] *adj* big and sturdy.—*n* **bur´liness**. [ME *borlich*.]

Burmese [bur´mēz, -mēz´] *adj* relating to *Burma* or its Sino-Tibetan language.—*n* a native of Burma, or the language of Burma.

burn [bûrn] *vt* to consume or injure by fire; to expose to great heat.—*vi* to be on fire; to consume through fire; to feel excess of heat; to be inflamed with passion.—*pt, pt p* **burned, burnt**.—*n* a hurt or mark caused by fire.—*n* **burn´ing**, conflagration.—Also *adj*—*ns* **burn´er**, in a lamp or stove, the part from which the flame arises.—**burning bush**, the emblem of the

Presbyterian churches of Scotland, adopted from Ex iii 2; any of several plants esp summer cypress; **burn one's boats**, to destroy all means of retreat, to stake everything on success; **burn someone's ears**, to rebuke strongly; **burn the candle at both ends**, to strain one's energies or resources; **burn the midnight oil**, to study far into the night. [OE weak trans verb *bærnan*, confused with strong intrans *beornan*.]

burnish [bûrn´ish] *vt* to make bright by rubbing.—*n* polish; luster. [Fr *burnir, burnissant*, to burnish—*brun*, brown.]

burnous [bûr-nōōs´] *n* a mantle with a hood much worn by the Arabs. [Fr,—Ar *burnus*.]

burnt *pt, pt p* of **burn**.

burp [bûrp] *vi* (*slang*) to belch.—*vt* to pat a baby's back to cause it to belch.—Also *n*.

burr, bur[1] [bûr] *n* the prickly adhesive seed-case or head of certain plants; rough edge to a line on a dry-point plate.—*n* **bur´dock**, a plant (genus *Arctium*) with a bur or prickly head and docklike leaves. [Cog with Dan *borre*, a bur.]

burr[2] [bûr] the rough sound of *r* pronounced in the throat, as in Northumberland, England. [Prob preceding, but perh from the sound.]

burrito [bù-rē´tō] *n* a tortilla baked with a savory filling.

burro [bûr´ō] *n* a donkey. [Sp.]

burrow [bûr´ō] *n* a hole excavated by certain animals for shelter.—*vi* to make, live in, holes underground, as rabbits; to dwell in a concealed place.—*vti* to tunnel. [Prob a variant of **borough**—OE *beorgan*, to protect.]

bursa [bûr´sȧ] *n* a sac or cavity with a lubricating fluid, as between a tendon and a bone.—*n* **bursīt´is**, inflammation of a bursa.

bursar [bûrs´ȧr] *n* a treasurer. [Low L *bursa*, a purse—Gr *byrsa*, skin or leather.]

burst [bûrst] *vt* to break into pieces; to break open suddenly or by violence.—*vi* to fly open or break in pieces; to break forth or away; to force one's way (into); to break (into—some sudden expression of feeling, condition, or activity).—*pt, pt p* burst.—*n* a sudden outbreak; a spurt; a volley of shots. [OE *berstan*; Ger *bersten*.]

bury [ber´i] *vt* to hide in the ground; to cover; to consign to the grave, the sea, etc., as a dead body; to hide or blot out of remembrance.—*pr p* **bur´ying**; *pt p* **bur´ied**.—**bury the hatchet**, to renounce enmity. [OE *byrgan*, to bury; Ger *bergen*, to hide.]

bus [bus] *n* an omnibus; (*slang*) a car.—*pl* **buses, busses**.—*vt* to transport by bus.—*vi* to go by bus; to do the work of a busboy.—*ns* **bus´boy**, a waiter's assistant who cleans tables, brings water, etc.; **bus´ing, buss´ing**, the transporting by bus of children from one district to school in another, esp to achieve a more even racial balance.—**busman's holiday**, a holiday spent in activities similar to one's work; **miss the bus**, to lose an opportunity. [Short for **omnibus**.]

busby [buz´bi] *n* a tall, fur hat, esp one worn by a guardsman. [Prob Hungarian.]

bush[1] [bŏŏsh] *n* a shrub thick with branches; anything of bushy tuft-like shape; forest; wild uncultivated country.—*vi* to grow thickly.—*adj* **bush´y**, full of bushes; thick and spreading.—*ns* **bush´iness; bush´man**, one who lives in the Australian bush; one of an almost extinct aboriginal race in southern Africa; a Khoisian language of the Bushmen; **bush´rang´er** [-rānj´-], in Australia, one who leads a lawless life in the bush.—**bush league** (*slang*) (*baseball*), a small or second-rate minor league; **bush´master**, to tropical American viper (*Lachesis mutis*) that is the largest New World venomous snake; **bush shirt, jacket**, a garment, often of cotton, with four patch pockets and a belt; **bush telegraph**, the obscure and rapid transmission of news through a country or population.—**beat about the bush**, to talk without coming to the point. [ME *busk, busch*; from a Gmc root found in Ger *busch*, Low L *boscus*, Fr *bois*.]

bush[2] [bŏŏsh] *n* the metal box or lining of any cylinder in which an axle works. [Du *bus*—L *buxus*, the box-tree.]

bushel [bŏŏsh´l] *n* a dry measure equal to 4 pecks or 32 quarts. [OFr *boissiel*, from the root of **box**.]

Bushido [bōō´shi-dō] *n* a Japanese code of chivalry valuing honor above life. [Jap.]

business [biz´nis] *n* trade, profession, or occupation; one's concern or affair; one's duty; a matter or affair; (*theat*) the details of action, as distinguished from dialogue, that make up a part.—*adj* **bus´inesslike**, methodical, systematic, practical.—*n* **business college, business school**, a school of typing, bookkeeping, etc.—**mean business**, to be in earnest; **mind one's own business**, to avoid meddling with the affairs of others; **no business**, no right; **send about one's business**, to dismiss abruptly. [**busy**.]

buskin [busk´in] *n* a half-boot, esp one with thick soles worn in ancient times by actors of tragedy—hence, the tragic drama as distinguished from comedy.—*adj* **busk´ined**, tragic; dignified. [Ety uncertain.]

buss [bus] *n* a kiss.—Also *vti*. [ME *bass*; cf Old Ger *bussen*, to kiss, Fr *baiser*.]

bust[1] *n* a sculpture representing the head and breast of a person; the upper front part of the human body, esp a woman's. [Fr *buste*; It and Sp *busto*.]

bust[2] [bust] *vti* (*slang*) to burst or break; to make or become bankrupt or demoted; to hit; to arrest.—*n* (*slang*) a failure; financial collapse; a punch; a spree; an arrest.—*n* and *v*.

bustard [bus´tȧrd] *n* a family (Otididae) of large heavy birds of Australia and the Old World related to cranes. [Fr *bistard*, corr of L *avid tarda*, slow bird (a misnomer).]

bustle[1] [bus´l] *vi* to busy oneself noisily or fussily.—*n* hurried activity, stir, tumult. [ME *bustelen*.]

bustle[2] [bus´l] a frame or pad for causing a skirt to hang back from the hips.

busy [biz´i] *adj* fully employed; active; diligent; meddling; of a design or picture, having too much detail; (of a telephone in use).—*vt* to make busy; to occupy (esp oneself).—*pr p* **busying** [biz´i-ing]; *pt p* **busied** [biz´id].—*adv* **bus´ily**.—*ns* **bus´yness**, state of being busy; **bus´ybody**, a meddling person. [OE *bysig*.]

but [but] *prep* only; except.—*conj* on the other hand; in contrast; nevertheless; except that (merging in *prep*.—eg *they had all left but he, him*); that not (developing into negative rel pron.—eg *there is none of them but thinks*).—*adv* only; merely; just.—*pron* who . . . not; which . . . not.—**but for**, if it were not for. [OE *be-ūtan, būtan*, without—*be*, by and *ūtan*, out, ie near and yet outside.]

butane [bū´tān] *n* a hydrocarbon used as a fuel, in organic synthesis, etc.

butch [bŏŏch] *n* (*slang*) a very short haircut; (*slang*) the 'male' parter in a lesbian relationship. [Amer boy's nickname.]

butcher [bŏŏch´ėr] *n* one whose business is to kill cattle for food, or who deals in their flesh; one who delights in slaughter.—*vt* to kill for food; to put to a bloody death, to kill cruelly; to spoil by bad acting, reading, etc.—*ns* **butch´-er-bird**, any of various strikes; **butch´ery**, the preparation of meat for sale; a butching; great or cruel slaughter. [OF *bochier, bouchier*, one who kills he-goats—*boc*, a he-goat.]

butler [but´lėr] *n* a manservant, usu. the head servant of a household, etc. [Norm Fr *butuiller*—Low L *buticulārius*—*butis*. See **bottle**.]

butt[1] [but] *vti* to strike with the head, as a goat, etc.—*n* a push with the head.—**butt in**, to intervene; to intrude. [OFr *boter*, to push, strike.]

butt[2] [but] *n* a large cask for wine and beer. [Cf Fr *botte*, Sp *bota*, Low L *butta*.]

butt[3] [but] *n* a mound behind targets; a victim of ridicule; (*pl*) a shooting range. [Fr *but*, goal.]

butt[4] [but] *n* the thick and heavy end; the stump; (*slang*) a cigarette.—*vti* to join end to end. [Ety uncertain.]

butte [byōōt] *n* a steep hill standing alone on a plain. [Fr.]

butter [but´ėr] *n* an oily substance obtained from cream by churning.—*vt* to spread over with butter; (*inf*) to flatter (*with* **up**).—*ns* **butter bean**, lima bean; wax bean; **butt´ercup**, a genus of plants (*Ranunculus*), with a cup like flower of a golden yellow; **butt´erfing´ers**, one who lets a ball, etc., he ought to catch slip through his fingers; **butt´erfly**, an insect (order Lepidoptera) with a slender body and four usu. brightly colored wings; a gay flighty person; a swimming stroke executed in a prone position by moving both arms simultaneously in a circular motion while kicking the legs simultaneously.—*pl* **butt´erflies**.—Also *adj*.—*ns* **butt´ermilk**, the milk that remains after the butter has been separated from the cream by churning; **butt´ernut**, the edible oily nut of a tree (*Juglans cinerea*) of the walnut family; the tree; **butt´erscotch**, a kind of toffee containing a large admixture of butter; a syrup with this flavor; **butt´erwort**, a genus (*Pinguicula*) of insectivorous plants with glistening leaves.—*adj* **butt´ery**, like, containing, or with, butter; offensively flattering. [OE *butere*; Ger *butter*; both from L *būtyrum*—Gr *boutyron*—*bous*, ox, *tyros*, cheese.]

buttery [but´ėr-i] *n* a storeroom for liquors. [Fr *bouteillerie*, lit 'place for bottles'.]

buttock [but´ȯk] *n* either half of the rump or protuberant part of the body behind. [Dim of **butt**, end.]

button [but´n] *n* a knob or disk of metal, bone, etc., used as a fastening, ornament, or badge; any similar knob or disk.—*vti* to fasten by a button or buttons.—*n* **butt´onhole**, the hole or slit into which a button is passed; a flower of flowers therein.—*vt* to work with a stitch (*buttonhole stitch*) suitable for defence of edges; to detain in talk.—*n* **butt´onhook**, a hook for pulling the buttons of gloves and shoes through the buttonholes. [Fr *bouton*, any small projection, from *bouter*, to push.]

buttress [but´res] *n* a projecting support built on to the outside of a wall; any support or prop.—*vt* to prop or support. [Apparently from OFr *bouterez* (*bouteret*)—*bouter*, to push, bear against.]

Butyl[1] [bū´tīl] *n* trade name for any of various synthetic rubbers.

butyl[2] [bū´tīl] *n* an alcohol radical C_4H_9.

buxom [buks´ȯm] *adj* yielding, elastic; plump and comely. [ME *buhsum*, pliable, obedient—OE *būgan*, to yield, and *-some*.]

buy [bī] *vt* to purchase (for money); to bribe; to obtain in exchange for something not necessarily concrete; (*inf*) to accept, believe.—*pr p* **buy´ing**, *pt, pt p* **bought** [bawt].—Also *n*—*n* **buy´er**.—**buyer's market**, one in which, because the supply exceeds the demand, the buyers control the price. [OE *bycgan*, pt *bohte, boht*.]

buzz [buz] *vi* to make a noise like that of an insects' wings; to murmur; to hover (about).—*vt* to whisper or spread secretly; (*aero*) to fly very low over or very close to; to interfere with in flight by flying very close to.—*n* the noise of bees and flies; a whispered report.—*n* **buzz´er**, an electrical or other apparatus producing a buzzing sound.—**buzz word**, a hackneyed, almost meaningless word used as part of the jargon of a particular subject. [Imit.]

buzzard [buz´ȧrd] *n* any of various large birds of prey, as the turkey buzzard; a contemptible or rapacious person. [Fr *busard*; prob conn with L *buteo*, a kind of hawk.]

by [bī] *prep* at the side of; near to; along a route passing through, via; past; through denoting the agent, cause, means, etc.; to the extent of (eg *short by three inches*); measured in terms of (eg *by the yard, by this standard*); of time, at or before; during, or under specified conditions (*by day, by candlelight*).—*adv* near; in reserve; past; aside.—*adv* **by´-and-by**, at some future time.—*ns* **by´(e)elec´tion**, an election held between regular elections in order to fill a vacancy.—*adj* **by´gone**, past.—*ns* **by´name**, a nickname; **by´pass**, a side track to avoid an obstruction or a congested area; a channel carrying a fluid around a part and back to the main stream; shunt.—*vt* to avoid by means of a bypass.—*ns* **by´path**, a secluded or indirect path; **by´play**, action apart from the main action; dumbshow aside on the stage; **by´-pro´duct**, a product formed in the process of making something else; **by´road**, byway; **by´stander**, a chance spectator; **by´way**, a private and obscure way; **by´word**, a common saying; a proverb; an object of common reproach.—**by and large**, on the whole; **by the way**, incidentally; **let bygones be bygones**, let the past be forgotten. [OE *bi, big*; Ger *bei*, L *ambi-*.]

bye [bī] *n* the state of one who has not drawn an opponent and passes without contest to the next round; in golf, the holes played after the match is won.—*adj* and *prefix* subsidiary. [**by**.]

bylaw, byelaw [bī´lö] *n* a law adopted by an organization or assembly for its own meetings or affairs. [From ON *byjarlög*, Dan *by-lov*, townlaw; from ON *būa*, to dwell.]

Byronic [bī-ron´ik] *adj* possessing the characteristics, or alleged characteristics, of Lord *Byron* (1788–1824), or of his poetry, esp overstrained in sentiment, cynical and libertine.

byte [bīt] *n* in computers, a set of usually six or eight bits treated as a unit. [From **bit**[3] and **bite** or *binary digit eight*.]

Byzantine [biz-an´tīn, biz´-] *adj* relating to *Byzantium* or Constantinople (now Istanbul).—**Byzantine Empire**, the Eastern or Greek Empire in southeast Europe and southwest Asia from AD 395 to 1453.

C

cab [kab] *n* a carriage for public hire; a taxicab; the place where the driver sits in a truck, crane, etc.—*ns* **cabb´ie, cabb´y** (*inf*) one who drives a cab for hire; **cab´driver**.—*n* **cabstand**, a place where cabs stand for hire. [Shortened from **cabriolet**.]
cabal [ka-bal´] *n* a small party united for some secret design; a conspiracy. [Fr *cabale*; from Heb; see **cabbala**.]
cabala, cabbala, caballah [käb´ä-la] *n* a secret system of the Jewish rabbis for the interpretation of the hidden sense of Scripture.—*n* **cab´alist**, one versed in the cabbala.—*adj* **cabalist´ic**, relating to the cabbala; having a hidden meaning. [Heb *qabbālāh*, tradition—*qibbēl*, to receive.]
caballero [kab-à-ler´ō, -ä-yer´ō] *n* a Spanish gentleman; (*southwest US*) a horseman or a lady's escort.
cabaret [kab´a-rā] *n* a restaurant with musical entertainment; an entertainment of the type given in such a restaurant. [Fr tavern; prob for *cabanaret*—*cabane*, a hut.]
cabbage [kab´ij] *n* a garden plant (*Brassica oleracea capitata*) with thick leaves formed usu into a round compact head, used as a vegetable. [Fr *caboche*, head; from L *caput*, the head.]
caber [kāb´ėr, käb´ėr] *n* a long, heavy pole tossed by Scottish Highland athletes. [Gael *cabar*.]
cabin [kab´in] *n* a hut or cottage; a small room, esp in a ship; a compartment for passengers in an aircraft.—*vt* to shut up in a cabin.—*n* **cab´in boy**, a boy who serves the occupants of a ship; **cab´in cruis´er**, a power-driven boat with full provision for living on board. [Fr *cabane*—Low L *capanna*.]
cabinet [kab´in-et] *n* a case with drawers or shelves; a case holding a TV, radio, etc.; a body of official advisers to a chief executive.—*n* **cab´inetmak´er**, a maker of cabinets and other fine furniture. [Dim of **cabin**.]
cable [kā´bl] *n* a strong rope often of wire strands for hauling or tying anything; a wire for carrying electric current; a cablegram—*vt* and *vi* to telegraph by cable.—*ns* **cable car**, a car drawn by a moving cable, as up a steep incline; **cā´blegram**, a telegram sent by undersea cable; **cā´ble stitch**, (a series of knitting stitches producing) a pattern resembling twisted cables; **cable television**, the transmission of TV programmes by cable to individual subscribers. [Fr,—Low L *caplum*, a halter—*capĕre*, to hold.]
caboose [ka-bōōs´] *n* the trainman's car at the rear of a freight train. [Du *kombuis*]
cabriolet [kab-ri-ō-lā´] *n* a light carriage with two wheels; a former style of convertible coupé; a cab. [Fr.]
cacao [ka-kä´o, or ka-kā´o] *n* the tropical American tree (*Theobroma cacao*) from whose seeds cocoa and chocolate are made. [Mexican *cacauatl*.]
cachalot [kash´a-lot, -lö] *n* sperm whale. [Fr]
cache [kash] *n* a hiding-place for treasure stores, etc.; treasure, stores, etc., hidden.—*n* **cachepot, cache pot**, a decorated jar for holding potted plants. [Fr *cacher*, to hide.]
cachet [kash´ā] *n* a seal; any distinctive stamp, esp something showing or conferring prestige; a design, advertisement, etc. stamped or printed on mail.
cachinnate [kak´in-āt] *vi* to laugh loudly.—*n* **cachinnā´tion**. [L *cachinnāre*, to laugh loudly.]
cachou [kash´ōō] *n* a pill or pastille used to perfume the breath. [Fr]
cacique [ka-sēk´] *n* a native Indian chief in areas dominated by Spanish culture. [Sp—native word in Haiti.]
cackle [kak´l] *n* the sound made by a hen; talk or laughter of similar sound.—*vti* to make such a sound.—**cut the cackle**, to stop the useless talk. [ME *cakelen*.]
cacophony [ka-kof´o-ni] *n* a disagreeable sound; discord of sounds.—*adj* **cacoph´onous**. [Gr *kakos*, bad, *phōnē*, sound.]
cactus [kak´tus] *n* any one of a family (Cactaceae) of prickly plants whose stems store water and do the work of leaves;—*pl* **cac´ti** or **cac´tuses**. [L,—Gr *kaktos*, a prickly plant in Sicily.]
cad [kad] *n* one who lacks the instincts of a gentleman.—*adj* **cadd´ish**. [Short for **cadet**.]
cadaverous [ka-dav´ėr-us] *adj* gaunt, haggard; pallid, livid.—*n* **cadav´er**, a dead body intended for dissection. [L *cadāver*, a dead body—*cadĕre*, to fall dead.]
caddie, caddy [kad´i] *n* one who carries clubs for a golfer.—Also *vt* [Scot, from **cadet**.]
caddisfly, caddicefly [kad´is] *n* any of an order (Trichoptera) of four-winged insects with vestigial mouthparts and aquatic larvae.—*n* **caddis worm**, larva of the caddisfly, which lives in water in a silken sheath. [Ety uncertain.]
caddy [kad´i] *n* a small box for holding tea. [Malay *kati*, the weight of a small packet of tea.]
cadence [kā´dens] *n* the fall of the voice; rhythm; measured movements as on marching.—*n* **caden´za** [kä-den´zä] an elaborate passage for the solo instrument in a concerto. [Fr,—L *cadĕre*, to fall.]
cadet [ka-det´] *n* a student at an armed forces academy; any trainee, as a practice teacher.—*n* **cadet´ship**. [Fr *cadet*, formerly *capdet*—dim of L *caput*, the head.]
cadge [kaj] *vti* to beg or get by begging.—*n* **cadg´er**. [Prob conn with **catch**.]
cadmium [kad´mi-ùm] *n* a metallic element (symbol Cd; at wt 112.4; at no 48). [Gr *kadmeia*, calamine.]
cadre [kad´r] *n* a nucleus, framework, esp the officers of a political or military unit. [Fr]
caducous [ka-dū´kus] *adj* falling early, as leaves. [L *cadūcus*—*cadĕre*, to fall.]
caecum [sē´kum] *n See* **cecum**.
Caesar [sē´zàr] *n* the title assumed by the Roman Emperors as heirs of Julius *Caesar*; an absolute monarch.
caesium [sēz´i-ùm] *See* **cesium**.
caesura [sē-zū´rä] *n* (*pros*) division of a foot between two words; a pause in a line of verse (generally near the middle).—*adj* **caesū´ral**. [L *caedĕre, caesum*, to cut off.]
café, cafe [kaf´ā] *n* a small restaurant, a barroom, a nightclub, etc.—**café au lait, café noir**, (the color of) white, black, coffee. [Fr]
cafeteria [ka-fe-tēr´i-a] *n* a self-service restaurant. [Cuban Spanish *cafetería*, a tent in which coffee is sold.]
caffeine [kaf´-ēn] *n* an alkaloid present in coffee, tea and kola [Fr *caféine*—ultimately from Turkish *qahveh*. See **coffee**.]
caftan [kaf´tan] *n* a long-sleeved Persian or Turkish garment. [Turk *qaftān*.]
cage [kāj] *n* a box made of wire and wood for holding captive birds or animals; any similar structure.—*vt* to imprison in a cage.—*n* **cager** (*slang*), a basketball player. [Fr,—L *cavea*, a hollow.]
cagey, cagy [kāj´i] *adj* (*coll*) wary, not frank.
caiman, cayman [kā´màn] *n* any of several tropical American crocodiles related to the alligator. [Sp.]
Cain [kān] *n* a murderer, from *Cain*, who killed his brother Abel (Gen iv).—**to raise Cain**, to make a violent disturbance.
caique [kä-ēk´] *n* a light skiff used on the Bosporus. [Fr,—Turk, *kaik*, a boat.]
cairn [kārn] *n* (*Scottish*) a heap of stones; a small breed of Scottish terrier.—*n* **cairngorm´**, brown or yellow quartz found in Cairngorm Mts in Scotland. [Celt *carn*.]
caisson [kās´ón] *n* an ammunition chest or wagon; a strong case for keeping out the water while the foundations of a bridge are being built; an apparatus for lifting a vessel out of the water for repairs or inspection.—**caisson disease**, pain in the joints, paralysis, etc., caused by a too sudden change from a higher to a lower pressure; bends. [Fr, from *caisse*, a case or chest.]
caitiff [kā´tif] *n* a mean despicable fellow.—*adj* mean, base. [OFr *caitif* (Fr *chétif*)—L *captīvus*, a captive—*capĕre*, to take.]
cajole [ka-jōl´] *vti* to coax by flattery. [Fr *cajoler*, to chatter; ety uncertain.]
Cajun, Cajan [kā´jùn] *n* inhabitant of Louisiana descended from 18th-century French-Canadian immigrants; the dialect spoken by Cajuns; **Cajan**, a person of mixed white, black, and Amerindian ancestry living in southwest Alabama and southeast Mississippi.
cake [kāk] *n* a mass of fried dough, batter, hashed food etc.; a mixture of flour, eggs, sugar, etc. baked in small flat shapes or a loaf; a small block of compacked or congealed matter.—*vti* to form into a cake or hard mass.—**take the cake** (*slang*) to win the prize. [ON *kaka*.]
calabash [kal´a-bash] *n* a tree (*Crescentiae cujete*) of tropical America bearing a large gourdlike fruit, the shell of which, called a calabash, is dried and used for holding liquids, etc. [Fr *calebasse*—Sp *calabaza*—Pers *kharbuz*, melon.]
calamary [kal´à-màr-i] *n* squid.
calamine [kal´a-mīn, -min] *n* a zinc oxide powder used in skin lotions, etc. [Fr.—Low L *calamīna*.]
calamity [kal-am´i-ti] *n* a great misfortune; affliction.—*adj* **calam´itous**, disastrous.—*adv* **calam´itously**. [Fr *calamité*—L *calamitās, -ātis*.]
calamus [kal´a-mus] *n* the traditional name of the sweet flag, an aromatic plant; the reed pen used by the ancients;—*pl* **calamī**. [L—Gr *kalamos*, reed, cane.]
calash [ka-lash´] *n* a light low-wheeled carriage with a folding top; a hood formerly worn by ladies. [Fr *calèche*; of Slavonic origin.]
calcareous [kal-kā´re-us] *adj* like or containing limestone, chalk or lime. [L *calcārius*, from *calx*, lime.]
calcium [kal´si-ùm] *n* the metal (symbol Ca; at wt 40.1; at no 20) present in chalk and lime.—*adj* **calcif´erous**, containing lime.—*vti* **cal´cify**, to change into a hard, stony substance by the deposit of lime or calcium salts.—*vti* **cal´cine** [kal´sīn, -sin] to change into an ashy powder by heat.—**calcium**

carbonate, white crystalline compound found in bones, shells, limestone, chalk, etc. [Formed from L *calx*, a stone, lime.]
calculate [kal´kū-lāt] *vt* to count or reckon; to think out, esp mathematically; to plan, think, purpose, suppose.—*vi* to make a calculation; to rely, base one's plans or forecasts (on).—*adj* **cal´culable**.—*adjs* **cal´culated**, fitted (to), likely (to); deliberate; **cal´culating**, given to forethought; selfish and scheming.—*n* **calculā´tion**, the art or process of calculating; estimate; forecast.—*n* **cal´culātor**, a machine for doing arithmetic rapidly; one who calculates. [L *calculāre, -ātum*, to reckon by help of little stones—*calculus* (dim of *calx*), a little stone.]
calculus [kal´kū-lus] *n* an abnormal stony mass in the body (*pl* **cal´culi**); (*math*) the study of the changes of a continuously varying function (*pl* **cal´culuses**). [L]
caldron, cauldron [köl´drȯn] *n* a large kettle or boiler; a state of violent agitation. [OFr *caudron*—L *caldārium-calidus*, hot.]
Caledonian [kal-e-dō´ni-ȧn] *adj* pertaining to ancient *Caledonia*, the Highlands, or Scotland generally.—*n* a Scot. [L *Călēdŏnia*.]
calefactory [kal-e-fak´tȯr-i] *n* a room in which monks warmed themselves. [L *calēre*, to grow hot, *facĕre*, to make.]
calendar [kal´en-dȧr] *n* a system of determining the length and divisions of a year; an almanac or table of months, days, and seasons; a schedule, as of pending court cases. [OFr *calendier*—L *calendārium*, an account-book—*kalendae*, calends.]
calender [kal´en-dėr] *n* a press with rollers for finishing the surface of cloth, paper, etc.—*vt* to press in a calender. [Fr *calandre*—L *cylindrus*—Gr *kylindros*, roller.]
calends [kal´endz] *n* among the Romans, the first day of each month from which days were counted backward to the ides. [L *kalendae*—*calāre*, to call (because the beginning of the month was proclaimed).]
calenture [kal´en-tyůr] *n* tropical fever caused by exposure to heat. [Fr and Sp,—L *calens, -entis*, pr p of *calēre*, to be hot.]
calf[1] [käf] *n* the young of the cow, elephant, whale, and certain other mammals; calfskin leather;—*pl* **calves** [kävz].—*ns* **calf´ love**, immature affection of a boy for a girl; **calf's-foot jelly**, jelly made from gelatin obtained by boiling calves' feet. [OE *cealf*; Ger *kalb*.]
calf[2] [käf] *n* the fleshy back part of the leg below the knee.—*pl* **calves** [kävz]. [ON *kālfi*; perh the same word as the preceding.]
caliber, calibre [kal´i-bėr] *n* the size of the bore of a tube; diameter; (*fig*—of a person) degree of excellence or importance.—*vt* **cal´ibrāte**, to determine the caliber of; to mark or correct the scale on a measuring instrument. [Fr *calibre*, the bore of a gun.]
calico [kal´i-kō] *n* a cotton cloth first brought from *Calicut* in India.
calif *See* **caliph**.
californium [kal-i-för´-ni-ům] a transuranic element (symbol cf; at wt 251; at no 98)
caliper, calliper [kal´i-pėrz] *n* measuring instrument with legs suitable for measuring the inside or outside diameter of bodies. [Corr of **caliber**.]
caliph, calif [kal´if, or kā´lif] *n* the name assumed by the successors of Mohammed.—*n* **cal´iphate**, the office, rank, or government of a caliph. [Fr *calife*—Ar *khalīfah*, a successor.]
calisthenics [kal-is-then´iks] *n pl* exercises for promoting gracefulness and strength of body.—*adj* **calisthen´ic**. [Gr *kallos*, beauty, *sthenos*, strength.]
calk *See* **caulk**.
calk [kök] *n* a spike in a horseshoe to prevent slipping; a similar device worn on the sole of a shoe.—*vt* to provide or wound with a calk. [L *calx, calcis*, a heel.]
call [köl] *vi* to cry aloud; to make a short visit; to telephone.—*vt* to name; to summon; to appoint or proclaim; to describe as specified; to awaken; to give orders for; to stop (a game); to demand payment of; (*poker*) to require a player to show his hand by equaling his bet.—*n* a summons or invitation; a sense of vocation; a demand; a short visit; a telephone connection or conversation or a request for one; a cry, esp of an animal or a bird; need, or demand, as for a product.—*ns* **call´boy**, a bellhop; a page; **call´er**, one who pays a short visit; **call girl**, a prostitute who is called by telephone to assignations; **call´ing**, vocation, trade, profession; **call letters**, the letters that identify a radio station.—**call out**, to summon into action; to instruct (members of a trade union) to come out on strike; **call up**, to summon from beneath or from another world; to summon for active military duty; to bring into the memory; **on call**, ready to answer summons; subject to demand for immediate payment; **within call**, subject to summons. [OE *ceallian*; ON *kalla*, Du *kallen*.]
calligraphy [kal-ig´ra-fi] *n* handwriting, esp fine penmanship. [Gr *kallos*, beauty, *graphein*, to write.]
callous [kal´us] *adj* hardened; unfeeling.—*ns* **callos´ity**, a hard thickening of the skin; **call´us**, a hardened, thickened place on the skin.—*adv* **call´ously**.—*n* **call´ousness**. [L *callōsus*—*callus*, hard skin.]
callow [kal´ō] *adj* inexperienced, immature. [OE *calu*; Ger *kahl*, L *calvus*, bald.]
calm [käm] *adj* still or quiet, serene, tranquil.—*n* absence of wind; repose; serenity.—*vti* to become or make calm; to quiet.—*adv* **calm´ly**.—*n* **calm´ness**. [Fr *calme*, from Low L *cauma*—Gr *kauma*, noonday heat.]
calomel [kal´ō-mel] *n* a white tasteless powder $Hg_2 Cl_2$ used in medicine, esp as a purgative and fungicide. [Fr]
calorie, calory [kal´or-i] *n* the amount of heat needed to raise the temperature of a gram of water from 15°C to 16°C, equal to 4.186 joules, a heat unit 1000 times as great as this (also kilogram calorie or large calorie), used in measuring the energy-producing value of food.—*adjs* **calor´ic**, of heat; of calories; **calorif´ic**, causing heat;—*ns* **calorificā´tion; calorim´eter**, an instrument for measuring quantities of absorbed or evolved heat; **calorim´etry**, the art or process of measuring heat. [L *calor*, heat.]
caltrop, calthrop [kal´trop, köl´trop, kal´throp, köl´] *n* an instrument armed with four spikes so arranged that one always stands upright, used to obstruct the progress of an enemy. [OE *coltetræppe, calcatrippe*—L *calx, calcis*, heel.]
calumet [kal´ū-met] *n* a long-stemmed ceremonial pipe smoked by N American Indians as a symbol of peace. [Fr,—L *calamus*, a reed.]
calumny [kal´um-ni] *n* false accusation; slander.—*vt* **calum´niāte**, to accuse falsely; to slander.—*vi* to spread evil reports.—*ns* **calum´niātion; calum´niātor**.—*adj* **calum´nious**, of the nature of calumny, slanderous.—*adv* **calum´niously**. [L *calumnia*.]
calvary [kal´va-ri] *n* an open-air representation of Christ's crucifixion; an experience of intense mental suffering. [L *calvāria*, a skull.]
calve [käv] *vt* and *vi* to bring forth (a *calf*).
calves *See* **calf**. (2)
Calvinism [kal´vin-izm] *n* the doctrines of the great Genevan religious reformer, John *Calvin* (1509–64). The distinguishing doctrine of his system is predestination, coupled with the irresistibility of God's grace.—*n* **Cal´vinist**.—*adjs* **Calvinist´ic, -al**.
calx [kalks] *n* the substance of a metal or mineral that remains after strong heating (an oxide or oxides);—*pl* **calxes** [kalk´sēz] or **calces** [kal´sēz]. [L *calx*, a stone, lime.]
calypso [kȧ-lip´sō] *n* folk song, usu a commentary on a current happening, made up as the singer goes along, originally from Trinidad.
calyx [kal´iks, or kā´liks] *n* the outer green covering or cup of a flower, consisting of sepals.—*pl* **calyces**, or **calyxes**. [Gr *kalyx*, a covering—*kalyptein*, to cover.]
cam [kam] *n* a device to change rotary to reciprocating motion.—*n* **cam´shaft**, the rotating shaft to which cams are fitted to lift valves in motors. [Du.]
camaraderie [kam-a-räd´ėr-ē] *n* the spirit of comradeship. [Fr.]
camarilla [kam-ar-il´ä] *n* a body of secret unofficial advisers; a cabal. [Sp dim of *cámara*, a chamber.]
camber [kam´bėr] *n* a slight convexity upon an upper surface, as of a road surface.—*vti* to arch slightly. [Fr *cambrer*—L *camerāre*, to vault.]
cambium [kam´bi-ům] *n* the layer of cells between the wood and the bark of a stem from which new wood and bark grow. [L *cambīre*, to change.]
Cambrian [kam´bri-ȧn] *adj* Welsh.—*n* the period of the earliest geological era of the Paleozoic era or the rocks formed during this period. [Formed from *Cymry*, Welshmen, or *Cymru*, Wales.]
cambric [kām´brik] *n* a fine white linen or cotton cloth, orig manufactured at *Cambrai* (then Flanders, now France).
came [kām] *pt* of **come**.
camel [kam´ėl] *n* an animal (genus *Camelus*) of Asia and Africa with one or two humps on its back, used as a beast of burden and for riding.—**camel('s) hair**, the hair of the camel; the hair of the squirrel's tail used for paintbrushes; the soft, durable cloth made from this hair, usu tan in color. [L *camēlus*—Gr *kamēlos*—Heb *gāmāl*.]
camellia [ka-mēl´ya, -mel´] *n* a genus (*Camellia*) of evergreen shrubs of the tea family, natives of eastern Asia, grown for the singular beauty of their flowers. [Named from *Camellus*, a Jesuit botanist.]
camelopard [kam-el´ō-pärd] *n* early name for the giraffe. [Gr *kamēlopardălis*—*kamēlos*, camel, *pardălis*, panther.]
Camembert [kam-ā-ber´] *n* a soft rich cheese made near *Camembert*, in Normandy.
cameo [kam´ē-ō] *n* an engraved gem in which the figure or subject is carved in relief; an outstanding bit role, esp in a motion picture; a bit of fine writing.—*pl* **cam´eos** [It *camméo* (Fr *camée*)—Low L *cammaeus*.]
camera [kam´er-a] *n* a vaulted room; a judge's private chamber (**in camera**, of a case, tried in secret); the apparatus in which a photographer exposes a sensitive plate or film; (*TV*) the apparatus that forms the image of the scene and converts it into electrical impulses for transmission.—**cam´era obscū´ra**, an instrument for throwing the images of external objects on a white surface placed within a dark chamber or box. [L]
camisole [kam´is-ōl] *n* a woman's loose underbodice without sleeves. [Sp *camisa*—L *camisia*.]
camomile *See* **chamomile**.
camouflage [ka´mōō-fläzh] *n* any device (esp deceptive coloring) for deceiving an adversary.—*vti* to disguise in order to conceal. [Fr *camouflet*, a whiff of smoke blown in the face, etc.]
camp[1] [kamp] *n* the ground on which tents are pitched; a recreational place in the country for vacationers, esp children; the supporters of a particular cause.—*vi* to encamp or pitch tents.—*ns* **camp´er**, one who camps; a specially equipped trailer or automotive vehicle for casual travel and camping; **camp´fire**, an outdoor fire at a camp; a social gathering around such a fire; **camp´foll´ower**, a non-combatant who follows in the rear of an army, a prostitute; a politician who joins a movement solely for personal gain; **camp´ meet´ing**, an evangelical religious gathering held in the open air.—

break camp, to dismantle a camp and leave. [Fr *camp*, a camp—L *campus*, a plain.]
camp[2] [kamp] *adj* (*slang*) theatrical, affected, exaggerated. Also *n*.—*adj* **cam´py**.
campaign [cam-pān´] *n* a series of military operations with a particular objective; organized action in support of a cause as for electing a candidate.—*vi* to serve in a campaign.—*n* **campaign´er**. [Fr *campagne*—L *campania*—*campus*, a field.]
campanile [kam-pan-ē´lā] *n* a bell tower, esp one detached from the church; (*pl*) **campaniles** [ē´lez], **campanili** [-ē´lē]. [It, from *campana*, a bell.]
campanology [kam-pan-ol´o-ji] *n* the art of bell ringing. [It *campana*, a bell, and Gr *logos*, a discourse.]
campanula [kam-pan´ū-la] *n* a genus (*Campanula*) of flowers, commonly known as bellflowers.—*adj* **campan´ulate**. [It *campana*, a bell.]
campestral [kam-pes´tràl] *adj* growing in, or pertaining, to, fields or open country; rural. [L *campestris*, from *campus*, a field.]
camphor [kam´fòr] *n* a solid essential oil, obtainable from the camphor tree (*Cinnamomum camphora*) of the laurel family, having a peculiar aromatic taste and smell used to repel insects, as a stimulant in medicine, etc.—*adj* **cam´phorated**, impregnated with camphor. [Fr *camphre*—Low L *camphora*—Malay, *kāpūr*, chalk.]
campus [kam´pùs] *n* the grounds, and sometimes buildings of a school, college, or university.—Also *adj*. [L, a field.]
can[1] [kan] *vt* to be able, to have sufficient power.—*pt* **could**. [OE *cunnan*, to know (how to do), to be able; pres indic (orig past) *can*].
can[2] [kan] *n* a container, usu metal, with a separate cover; a vessel of tinplate in which meat, fruit, etc., are hermetically sealed; a jar for packing and preserving fruits and vegetables; (*slang*) a jail; (*slang*) a toilet; (*slang*) an ounce of marijuana.—*vt* to put up for preservation in cans.—*adj* **canned**, prepared or recorded in advance for wide distribution; lacking originality as if mass produced; (*slang*) drunk.—*n* **cann´ery**, a factory where goods are canned.—**in the can** (of a film or a videotape), completed and ready for release. [OE *canne*.]
Canadian [ka-nā´di-àn] *adj* and *n* pertaining to *Canada*; a native of Canada.—*ns* **Canadian bacon**, bacon cut from the loin; **Canadian French**, the language of the French Canadians; **Canadianism**, a custom or belief of Canada; a word or idiom originating in Canadian English.
canal [kan-al´] *n* an artificial watercourse for navigation or irrigation; a duct in the body for conveying fluids.—*vt* to construct a canal through or across.—*vt* **can´alize**, to provide with a canal or channel.—*vi* to flow in or into a channel; to establish new channels. [L *canālis*, a waterpipe.]
canard [ka-när(d)´] *n* a false rumor. [Fr, *lit* 'duck'.]
canary [ka-nā´ri] *n* a small finch (*Serinus canarius*) found in the Canary islands that is usu greenish to yellow and kept as a cage bird and singer; (*slang*) an informer.—*adj* canary-coloured.
cancan [kan-kan] *n* a high-kicking dance of French origin. [Ety obscure.]
cancel [kan´sel] *vt* to strike out by crossing with lines or marking a postage stamp, check, etc. as used; to annul or suppress; to countermand; to counterbalance or compensate for; to remove like quantities from opposite sides of an equation or like factors from numerator and denominator of a fraction.—*n* a printed page, etc., canceled, or substituted for one canceled.—*n* **cancellā´tion**. [Fr *canceller*—L *cancellāre*, from *cancelli*, railings, lattice-work.]
Cancer [kan´sėr] *n* the crab, the 4th sign of the zodiac; in astrology, operative June 21 to July 21; **cancer**, the abnormal and uncontrollable growth of the cells of living organisms, esp a malignant tumor that expands by metasisis; any spreading evil.—**tropic of cancer**, parallel of latitude 23½° north of the equator.—*adj* **canc´erous**, of or like a cancer. [L *cancer*; cog with Gr *karkinos*, a crab.]
candela [kan-del´a] *n* unit of luminous intensity such that the luminous intensity of a black body radiator at the temperature of solidification of platinum is 60 candela per sq cm [**candle**.]
candelabrum [kan-de-lā´brum] *n* a branched and ornamented candlestick or lampstand;—*pl* **candelā´bra**—also used as *sing* with *pl* **candelā´bras**. [L.]
candid [kan´did] *adj* frank, ingenuous; free from prejudice, impartial.—*adv* **can´didly**.—*n* **can´didness**. [Fr *candide*—L *candidus*, white.]
candidate [kan´di-dàt] *n* one who has nomination for an office or qualification for membership or award; a student taking examinations for a degree.—**can´didacy**. [L *candidātus*—*candidus*, white.]
candied *See* **candy**.
candle [kan´dl] *n* a cylinder of wax, tallow, or like substance surrounding a wick; a light.—*ns* **can´dlepow´er**, illuminating power in terms of a 7/8 inch sperm candle burning at the rate of 120 grains per hour; candelas; **can´dlestick**, portable stand for holding a candle.—**not fit to hold a candle to**, utterly inferior to; **the game is not worth the candle**, the thing is not worth the cost. [OE *candel*—L *candēla*, from *candēre*, to shine, to glow.]
Candlemas [kan´dl-mas] *n* the RC festival of the purification of the Virgin Mary and of the presentation of Christ in the temple, February 2, when candles are blessed. [**candle** + **mass**.]
candor [kan´dòr] *n* freedom from prejudice; sincerity, frankness. [L *candor*, whiteness, from *candēre*, to shine.]
candy [kan´di] *n* a solid confection of sugar or syrup with flavoring, fruit, nuts, etc.—*vt* to cook in sugar, esp to preserve; to crystallize into sugar.—*vi* to become crystallized into sugar—*pr p* **can´dying**; *pt, pt p* **can´died**.—**candy striper**, a teenage volunteer working at a hospital. [Fr *candi*, from Ar *qandah*, candy.]
candytuft [kan´di-tuft] *n* a genus (*Iberis*) of plants with white, pink or purple flowers in tufts. [*Candia* (Crete) + **tuft**.]
cane [kān] *n* the slender, jointed stem of certain plants, as bamboo; a plant with such a stem, as sugar cane; a walking stick.—*vt* to beat with a cane.—*n* **cane´brake**, a dense growth of cane plants. [Fr *canne*—L *canna*—Gr *kannē*, a reed.]
canine [kan´īn, kān´īn, kan-īn´] *adj* like or pertaining to a dog; of the family of animals that includes wolves, dogs, and foxes.—**canine teeth**, in man, four sharp pointed teeth between the incisors and premolars. [L *canīnus*—*canis*, a dog.]
canister [kan´ist-ėr] *n* a small box or can for holding tea, coffee, flour, etc. [L *canistrum*, a wicker basket—Gr *kanastron*—*kannē*, a reed.]
canker [kang´kėr] *n* an erosive or spreading sore; an area of necrosis in a plant; a plant disease marked by cankers; anything that corrupts or consumes.—*vt* to eat into, corrupt, or destroy; to infect or pollute.—*vi* to grow corrupt; to decay.—*adj* **cank´erous**, corroding like a canker.—*ns* **canker sore**, a small painful ulcer, esp of the mouth; **cank´erworm**, either of two moths (*Alsophila pometaria* and *Paleacrita vernata*) and esp their larvae which are serious pests of trees. [L *cancer*, a crab, gangrene.]
cannabis [kan´àbis] *n* a narcotic drug variously known as hashish, bhang, marijuana, etc.; (*cap*) the hemp genus. [Gr *kannabis*].
cannel coal [kan´ėl] *n* a bituminous coal that burns with a bright flame. [Prob **candle**.]
cannibal [kan´i-bàl] *n* an eater of the flesh of his own species.—*adj* relating to, or indulging in, cannibalism.—*vti* **cann´ibalize**, to strip (old equipment) of parts for use in other units.—*n* **cann´ibalism**, the practice of eating one's own kind. [Sp, a corr of *Caníbal, Caríbal* (Eng *Carib*), a people who formerly ate human flesh.]
cannikin [kan´i-kin] *n* a small can or drinking vessel. [Dim of **can**.]
cannon [kan´òn] *n* a large mounted piece of artillery; an automatic gun on an aircraft.—*vi* to discharge cannon.—*vt* cannonade.—*n* **cannonade´**, an attack with cannon.—*vt* to attack with cannon.—*ns* **cann´onball**, a ball to be shot from a cannon; **cannon fodder**, soldiers at risk from artillery fire. [Fr *canon*—L *canna*, a reed.]
cannot [kan´ot] am, is, or are, unable to. **cannot but**, have no choice but to. [Neg form of pres indic of **can**.]
canoe [ka-nōō´] *n* a narrow, light boat propelled by paddles.—Also *vi*.—*n* **canoe´ist**. [Sp *canoa*—Haitian.]
canon [kan´òn] *n* a law or rule, esp in ecclesiastical matters; a standard; the books of the Bible accepted by the Christian Church; the recognized genuine works of any author; a clerical dignitary belonging to a cathedral; (*mus*) a round.—*adj* **canon´ical**, according to, or included in, a canon; authoritative; ecclesiastical.—*adv* **canon´ically**.—*vt* **can´onize**, to declare (a dead person) a saint, to glorify.—*ns* **canonizā´tion; can´on law**, codified ecclesiastical law; **can´onry**, the office or endowment of a canon. [OE *canon*—L *canon*—Gr *kanōn*, a straight rod.]
canopy [kan´o-pi] *n* a covering hung over a throne, bed or person; a rooflike projection.—*vt* to cover as with a canopy;—*pr p* **can´opying**; *pt p* **can´opied**. [Fr *canapé*—Low L *canopeum*—Gr *kōnōpeion*, a couch with a mosquito net—*kōnōps*, a mosquito.]
cant[1] [kant] *vi* to talk in an affectedly solemn or hypocritical way.—*n* a hypocritical or affected style of speech; the language peculiar to a class (eg to thieves); conventional talk of any kind. [L *cantāre*, freq of *canĕre*, to sing.]
cant[2] [kant] *n* an inclination from the level; a sloping or tilted position.—*vti* to slant; to tilt. [Prob conn with Du *kant*; Ger *kante*, corner.]
can't [kant, känt] contraction for **cannot**.
Cantab [kan´tab] for **Cantabrigian**, *adj* of or pertaining to Cambridge, Massachusetts or Cambridge University, England. [L *Cantabrigia*, Cambridge.]
cantabile [kän-täb´ē-lā, -lē] *adj* (*mus*) in a singing manner. [It.]
canteloupe, cantaloup [kan´ta-lōōp] *n* a small muskmelon (*Cucumus melo reticulatus*) with a rough, netted rind and juicy orange flesh. [Fr,—It *Cantalupo*, a town near Rome, where it was first grown in Europe.]
cantankerous [kan-tang´kėr-us] *adj* perverse in temper, quarrelsome.—*adv* **cantan´kerously**.—*n* **cantan´kerousness**. [ME *contek*, strife.]
cantata [kan-tä´tä] *n* a choral composition for a story, intended for concert performance only.—*n* **cantatrice** [kän-tä-trē´chā] a female singer. [It,—L *cantāre*, freq of *canĕre*, to sing.]
canteen [kan-tēn´] *n* a recreation center for servicemen, teenagers, etc.; a flask for carrying water. [Fr *cantine*—It *cantina*, a cellar.]
canter [kan´tėr] *n* a horse's 3-beat gait resembling a slow, smooth gallop.—*vi* to move at a canter.—*vt* to make to canter. [Orig *Canterbury-gallop*, from the easy pace at which the pilgrims rode to Canterbury.]
Canterbury bell [kan´tėr-ber-i bel] *n* any of several bell-flowers as (*Campanula medium*) grown for their showy flowers. [Supposed to resemble the bells on the horses of pilgrims to Canterbury.]
cantharides [kan-thar´i-dēz] *n pl* a preparation used in medicine made from dried blister beetles, esp those known as Spanish flies. [L,—Gr *kantharis*, a blister beetle, pl *kantharidĕs*.]
canticle [kan´ti-kl] *n* a song, particularly one of several liturgical songs (as

the Magnificat) taken from the Bible; **Canticle of Canticles** (*Bible*), the Song of Solomon in the Douay Version of the Bible. [L *canticulum*, dim of *canticum—cantus*, a song.]

cantilever [kan´ti-lēv-ėr] *n* a bracket or block projecting as a support, esp a projecting structure anchored at one end only.—*vt* to support by means of cantilevers.—**cantilever bridge**, one composed of self-supporting projecting arms built inwards from the piers and meeting in the middle of the span, where they are connected together. [**cant**, angle, + **lever**.]

cantle [kan´tl] *n* a corner, edge, or slice of anything; the upward, projecting rear part of a saddle. [**cant** (2).]

canto [kan´tō] *n* a division of certain long poems.—*pl* **can´tos**. [It,—L *cantus—canĕre*, to sing.]

canton [kan´tȯn, kan-ton´] a division of a country; one of the Swiss federal states.—*vt* to divide into cantons; [mil pron kan-tōōn´] to allot quarters to troops.—*n* **canton´ment**, the temporary quarters of troops; in India, a permanent military town. [OFr *canton*; It *cantone*, corner, district—*canto*, a corner; cf **cant** (2).]

Cantonese [kan-ton-ēz] *adj* of Canton (now Kwangchow), China, its people or language.—*n* the dialect of Chinese spoken in Kwangchow.

cantor [kan´tȯr] a singer of liturgical solos in a synogogue; the leader of singing in a church choir. [L, singer—*canĕre*, to sing.]

Canuck, Kanuck [kan-uk´] *n* a Canadian-American; a French Canadian.

canvas [kan´vȧs] *n* a coarse cloth made of hemp or other material, used for sails, tents, etc., and for painting on; the sails of a ship; a tent; an oil painting on canvas.—*n* **can´vasback**, a N American wild duck. (*Athya valiserinia*) with a grayish back and an elongated head profile.—[OFr *canevas*—L *cannabis*—Gr *kannabis*, hemp.]

canvass [kan´vȧs] *vti* to go through (places) or among (people) asking for votes, opinions, orders, etc.—*n* a canvassing.—*n* **can´vasser**. [From **canvas**.]

canyon [kan´yon] *n* a long, narrow valley between high cliffs. [Sp *cañon*, tube.]

caoutchouc [kow´chŏŏk] *n* raw rubber, gum-elastic, the latex or juice of rubber trees. [Fr,—Carib *cahuchu*.]

cap [kap] *n* any closefitting head covering, visored or brimless; a caplike thing; a cover; a top.—*vt* to cover with a cap; to cover (the end of); to equal or excel.—*pr p* **capp´ing**; *pt p* **capped**.—*n* **capp´ing**, a covering; **cap in hand**, humbly, respectfully, or sometimes fearfully. [OE *cæppe*—Low L *cappa*, a cape or cope.]

capable [kāp´a-bl] *adj* having ability or skill to do (*often with* **of**); competent; susceptible (of); suitable for, adapted to.—*n* **capabil´ity**, quality or state of being capable; (usu in *pl*) feature capable of being used or developed.—*adv* **cap´ably**. [Fr,—Low L *capābilis*—L *capĕre*, to hold, take.]

capacity [kap-as´i-ti] *n* power of holding; containing, absorbing, or grasping; volume; ability; power of mind; character (eg *in his capacity as leader*); legal competence; maximum possible content, or output.—*adj* **capā´cious**, roomy, wide.—*adv* **capā´ciously**.—*n* **capā´ciousness**.—*n* **capăc´itance**, property that allows a system or body to store an electric charge; the value of this expressed in farads.—*vt* **capăc´itate**, to make capable, to qualify.—*n* **capăc´itor**, an electric device having capacitance. [Fr,—L *capācitās—capĕre*, to take, hold.]

cap-à-pie [kap-a-pē´] *adv* from head to foot (eg *armed cap-à-pie*—of a knight). [OFr *cap a pie*—L *caput*, head, *pēs*, foot.]

caparison [ka-par´is-ȯn] *n* the covering of a horse; a rich cloth laid over a warhorse.—*vt* to cover with a cloth, as a horse. [Fr *caparaçon*—Sp *caparazón—capa*, a cape, cover—Low L *cappa*.]

cape[1] [kāp] *n* a sleeveless garment fastened at the neck and hanging over the back and shoulders. [OFr *cape*—Low L *cappa*.]

cape[2] [kāp] *n* a head or point of land running into the water. [Fr *cap*—L *caput*, the head.]

caper[1] [kā´pėt] *n* any of a genus (*Capparis*) of a low prickly Mediterranean shrub, esp one (*C spinosa*) which is cultivated for its green flower bud, pickled and used as seasoning. [L, *capparis*—Gr *kapparis*.]

caper[2] [kā´pėr] *vi* to leap or skip like a goat; to dance in a frolicsome manner.—*n* a leap; a prank.—**to cut a caper**, to frisk. [Shortened form of **capriole**.]

capercaillie, capercailzie [kā-pėr-kāl´yi] *n* the largest Old World grouse (Tetroa urogallus). [Gael *capull coille*, 'horse of the wood'.]

capillary [ka-pil´ȧr-i, kap´il-ȧr-i] *adj* as fine or minute as a hair; having a very small bore, as a tube.—*n* a tube with a fine bore; (*pl*) the minute vessels that unite the veins and arteries in animals.—*n* **capillar´ity**, a phenomenon depending on surface tension and angle of contact, of which the rise of liquids in capillary tubes and the action of blotting paper and wicks are examples. [L *capillāris—capillus*, hair, akin to *caput*.]

capital [kap´it-ȧl] *adj* relating to the head; involving the loss of life; chief, principal; of, or being the seat of government; of capital or wealth; excellent.—*n* a city that is the seat of government; a large letter; capitalists collectively; the stock or money for carrying on any business; a city preeminent in some special activity.—*vt* **cap´italize**, to convert into capital or money; to furnish with capital; to turn to advantage; to begin a word with capital letters.—*ns* **capitalizā´tion; cap´italism**, the economic system in which the means of production and distribution are privately owned and operated for profit.—**cap´italist**, an owner of wealth used in business; an upholder of capitalism; a wealthy person.—*adv* **cap´itally**, excellently.—**capital gain**, the increase in value of an asset between the time it is bought and the time it is sold; **capital goods**, producers' goods; **capital letter**, the form of a letter used to begin a sentence or a proper name, as A, B, C. etc.; **capital punishment**, penalty of death for a crime; **capital stock**, the capital of a corporation, divided into shares. [OFr *capitel*—L *capitālis—caput*, the head.]

capital [kap´it-ȧl] *n* the head or top part of a column, etc. [L *capitellum—caput*, head.]

capitation [kap-it-ā´sh(ȯ)n] *n* a direct uniform tax imposed on each head or person, a poll tax; a uniform per capita fee. [L *capitātus*, headed, *capitātiō*, poll tax—*caput*, head.]

Capitol Hill [kap´it-ol] *n* the legislative branch of the US government. [L *Capitōlium—caput*, the head.]

capitulate [kap-it´ūl-āt] *vi* to yield or surrender on certain conditions; to stop resisting.—*n* **capitulā´tion**. [Low L *capitulātus*, pa p of *capitulāre*, to arrange under heads—*capitulum*, a chapter.]

capon [kā´pȯn] *n* a castrated cock fattened for eating. [OE *capun*; L *capō, -ōnis*—Gr *kapōn—koptein*, to cut.]

capote [ka-pōt´] *n* a long hooded cloak or mantle. [Fr dim of *cape*, a cloak.]

caprice [ka-prēs´] *n* a change of humor or opinion without reason, disposition or mood inclining to such changes; a fanciful and sprightly work in music.—*adj* **capri´cious** [-ri´-shu̇s] full of caprice; changeable.—*adv* **capri´ciously**.—*n* **capri´ciousness**. [Fr *caprice* and It *capriccio*; perh from L *caper*, a goat.]

Capricorn [kap´ri-körn] *n* the goat, the 10th sign of the zodiac; in astrology, operative December 21 to January 19. [L *capricornus—caper*, a goat, *cornu*, a horn.]

caprine [kap´rin] *adj* of, relating to, or being a goat. [L *caprīnus—caper*, a goat.]

capriole [kap´ri-ōl] *n* a playful leap; (of a trained horse), a leap without advancing.—*vi* to leap; to caper. [OFr *capriole*—It *capriola*—L *caper, capra*, a goat.]

capsicum [kap´si-ku̇m] *n* a genus (*Capsicum*) of tropical herbs and shrubs widely cultivated for their many-seeded fleshy-walled berries, also called peppers. [Perh L *capsa*, a case—*capĕre*, to take, hold.]

capsize [kap-sīz´] *vt* to upset.—*vi* to be upset.

capstan [kap´stan] *n* an upright drum, around which cables are wound to haul them in. [Fr *cabestan, capestan*—L *capĕre*, to take.]

capsule [kap´sūl] *n* a dry, dehiscent seedpod consisting of two or more carpels; a fibrous or membraneous covering; a gelatin case for holding a dose of medicine; a metal or other container; a self-contained spacecraft or a part of one, manned or unmanned, recoverable or non-recoverable. [Fr,—L *capsula*, dim of *capsa*, a case.]

captain [kap´tin] *n* a chief, leader; (*US Military*) an officer ranking just above lieutenant; a navy officer ranking just above commander, the master of a ship; the leader of a team, as in sports.—*vt* to be captain of.—*n* **cap´taincy**, the rank or commission of a captain. [OFr *capitaine*—Low L *capitāneus*, chief—L *caput*, head.]

caption [kap´sh(ȯ)n] *n* a newspaper heading, or a note accompanying an illustration; (*motion pictures*) a subtitle.—*vt* to give a caption (heading, etc.) to.—*adj* **cap´tious**, ready to catch at faults or to take offence, carping, made for the sake of argument, as a remark.—*adv* **cap´tiously**.—*n* **cap´tiousness**. [L *captiō, -ōnis—capĕre*, to take.]

captivate [kap´tiv-āt] *vt* to charm; to engage the affections of. [L *captīvāre, -ātum*, to take captive.]

captive [kap´tiv] *n* a prisoner; one kept in confinement.—*adj* confined; kept in bondage; restrained by a rope (as a balloon); charmed, captivated by (*with* **to**).—*ns* **captiv´ity; cap´tor**, one who takes a captive or a prize; **cap´ture**, the act of taking; the thing taken; an arrest.—*vt* to take as a prize; to take by force; to take possession of (the attention, imagination). [L *captīvus—capĕre, captum*, to take.]

Capuchin [kap´ū-chin or kap-ōō-shēn´] *n* a friar of a branch of the Franciscan order, so called from the hood he wears; **capuchin**, any of a genus (*Cebus*) of So American monkeys, esp one (*C capucinus*) with hair resembling a monk's cowl. [Fr *capuchin*, It *cappucino*, a cowl—Low L *cappa*.]

capybara [kap-i-bär´a] *n* the largest living rodent (*Hydrochoerus capybara*), a native of S America, allied to the guineapig. [Brazilian.]

car [kär] *n* a vehicle moved on wheels, as an automobile, etc.; a vehicle moved on rails; an elevator cage.—*ns* **carpool**, a plan by a group to use their cars in rotation, to and from work, etc.; **car´port**, a covered parking space, esp a space under a roof projecting from a building. [Norm Fr *carre*—Low L *carra*, itself a Celt word.]

caracal [kar´a-kȧl] *n* a long-legged reddish-brown nocturnal cat (*Felis caracal*) of savannas in Africa having long pointed ears with tufts of black hair. [Fr, prob from Turk *qaraqulaq*, black ear.]

caracole [kar´a-kōl] *n* a half turn made by a horseman. [Fr *caracole*—It *caracollo*—Sp *caracol*, a spiral snail-shell.]

carafe [ka-räf] *n* a bottle holding water or wine. [Fr *carafe*, prob from Ar *gharafa*, to draw water.]

caramel [kar´a-mėl] *n* a dark-brown substance produced by heating sugar above its melting-point, used for coloring or flavoring; a chewy candy made with sugar, butter, etc.—*adj* made of or containing caramel.—*vti* **car´amelize**, to burn sugar. [Fr,—Sp *caramelo*.]

carat [kar´ȧt] *n* a measure of weight for precious stones equal to 200 milligrams. [Fr,—Ar *qirāt*, perh from Gr *keration*, a carob seed used as a weight.]

caravan [kar´a-van] *n* a company traveling together for security, esp in crossing the desert; a train of pack animals; a van.—*n* **caravansary** [kar-a-van´ser-ē], **caravanserai** [kar-a-van´ser-ī], a kind of unfurnished inn or extensive enclosed court where caravans stop in eastern countries; a hotel, inn. [Pers *kārwānsarāi—kārwān*, caravan, *sarāi*, inn.]

caravel [kar´av-el] *n* a kind of light sailing-vessel of the 15th and 16th centuries. [Fr,—It *caravella*; cf Low L *carabus*, Gr *karabos*, a bark.]

caraway [kar´a-wā] *n* a biennial plant (*Carum carvi*) with aromatic seeds, used as a tonic and flavoring. [Prob Sp *alcaravea* (*carvi*)—Ar *karwiyā*.]

carbide [kär´bīd] *n* a compound of carbon with another element; calcium carbide, used to generate acetylene. [**carbon**.]

carbine [kär´bīn] *n* a short-barreled rifle; a light, semiautomatic or automatic .30-caliber rifle. [Fr *carabine*.]

carbohydrate [kär-bō-hī´drāt] *n* a compound of carbon, hydrogen, and oxygen, the last two being in the same proportion as in water, esp in sugars and starches as components of food. [See **carbon, hydrate**.]

carbolic acid [kar-bol´ik as´id] *n* phenol. [L *carbō*, coal, *oleum*, oil.]

carbon [kär´bon] *n* a nonmetallic element (symbol C; at wt 12.0; at no 6) a constituent of all organic matter, occurring as pure charcoal, diamond and graphite; a carbon copy.—*adj* **carbonā´ceous**, pertaining to, or composed of, carbon.—*n* **car´bonate**, a salt of carbonic acid.—*adj* **carbonif´erous**, producing carbon or coal.—*n* **Carboniferous**, the period of the Paleozoic geological era between the Devonian and the Permian; the rocks (containing great coal-measures) formed during this period.—*vt* **car´bonize**, to convert into carbon or a carbon residue; to impregnate with, or combine with, carbon.—*n* **carbonizā´tion**.—**carbon 14**, a radioactive isotope of carbon used as a tracer element in biochemical studies; **carbon black**, a fine carbon used in the manufacture of pigments and inks; **carbon copy**, a duplicate of writing made by means of **carbon paper**, a paper coated with a black, waxy pigment; etc.; **carbon dating**, estimating the date of death of prehistoric organic material from the amount of carbon-14 still present in it; **carbon bisulfide, carbon disulphide**, a poisonous, flammable liquid used as a solvent for rubber, etc.; **carbonic acid**, a weak acid formed by the solution in water of **carbon dioxide**, a gas evolved by respiration and combustion; **carbon monoxide**, a colorless, odorless, highly poisonous gas; **carbon tetrachloride**, a nonflammable mixture used in cleaning fluids, etc. [Fr *carbone*—L *carbō, -ōnis*, coal.]

Carborundum [kä-bȯr-un´dum] *n* a trade name for various abrasives.

carboy [kär´boi] *n* an often cushioned container of glass, plastic, or metal holding between 5 and 15 gallons. [Pers *qarābah*.]

carbuncle [ka´bung-kl] *n* a fiery red gemstone (a garnet); an inflamed ulcer.—*adj* **carbun´cular**. [L *carbunculus*, dim of *carbō*, coal.]

carburetor [kär´bū-ret-ȯr] *n* part of an internal-combustion engine in which air is mixed with gasoline spray to make an explosive mixture. [Fr *carbure*—L *carbō*, coal.]

carcass [kär´kȧs] *n* the dead body of an animal; a framework or shell. [OFr *carquois*.]

carcinoma [kär-si-nō´ma] *n* any of several kinds of epithelial cancer.—*n* **carcin´ogen**, a substance that produces cancer.—*adj* **carcinogen´ic**. [Gr *karkinōma—karkinos*, crab.]

card[1] [kärd] *n* a small piece of pasteboard; one with figures for playing a game, with a person's name and address, with a greeting, invitation, message, etc.; an attraction; (*inf*) a witty or clowning person. (*pl*) any game played with a deck of cards; a sports program.—*n* **card´board**, a stiff, finely finished pasteboard.—*adj* **card´-carr´ying**, openly expressing membership of, or support for, a party or group, esp the Communist party.—*n* **card´sharp´er, card shark** (*inf*), a professional cardplayer who habitually cheats at cards.—**in** or, **on the cards**, inevitable. [Fr *carte*—L *c(h)arta*—Gr *chartēs*, a leaf of papyrus.]

card[2] [kärd] *n* an instrument for combing fibers of cotton, wool and flax.—*vt* to comb (wool, etc.). [Fr *carde*—L *carduus*, a thistle.]

cardiac [kär´di-ak] *adj* belonging to the heart.—*ns* **car´diograph**, an instrument for recording movements of the heart; **car´diogram**, a tracing obtained from a cardiograph; **cardiol´ogy**, the branch of medicine concerned with diseases of the heart.—*adj* **cardiovas´cular**, of the heart and the blood vessels as a unified system. [Gr *kardia*, the heart.]

cardigan [kär´di-gan] *n* a knitted woolen sweater that opens down the front. [Lord *Cardigan* (1797–1868).]

cardinal [kär´din-ȧl] *adj* denoting that on which a thing hinges or depends, fundamental.—*n* an official appointed by the Pope to his council; bright red; a crested finch (*Richmondena cardinalis*) of the eastern US, southwestern US and Mexico with a black face and completely red in the male.—*ns* **car´dinalate, car´dinalship**, the office or dignity of a cardinal.—**cardinal flower**, a N American lobelia (*Lobelia cardinalis*) that bears a brilliant red spike; **cardinal numbers**, numbers expressing how many (1,2,3, etc.); **cardinal points**, the four chief points of the compass—north, south, east, and west; **cardinal virtues**, justice, prudence, temperance, fortitude. [Fr,—L *cardinālis—cardō, cardinis*, a hinge.]

care [kär] *n* affliction; anxiety; heedfulness; charge, keeping; the cause or object of anxiety.—*vi* to be anxious (for, about); to be disposed, willing (to); to have a liking or fondness (for); to provide (for).—*adjs* **care´free´**, light-hearted; **care´ful**, full of care; heedful.—*adv* **care´fully**.—*n* **care´fulness**.—*adj* **care´less**, without care; heedless, unconcerned.—*adv* **care´lessly**.—*ns* **care´lessness; care´tak´er**, one put in charge of anything; one exercising temporary control or supervision.—*adj* **care´worn**, worn or vexed with care.—**care of**, at the address of; **take care**, to be cautious; **take care of**, to look after with care; to provide for. [OE *caru*; ON *kœra*, to lament.]

careen [ka-rēn´] *vti* to lean or cause to lean sideways; tip; tilt; lurch. [Fr *carène*—L *carīna*, the bottom of a ship, the keel.]

career [ka-rēr´] *n* a race; a rush; progress through life, esp advancement in calling or profession.—*adj* having a professional career; dedicated to a career.—*vi* to move or run rapidly. [Fr *carrière*, a racecourse.]

caress [kä-res´] *vt* to touch endearingly, to fondle.—*n* an endearing touch. [Fr *caresser*—It *carezza*, an endearment; Low L *cāritia—cārus*, dear.]

caret [kar´ėt] *n* a mark, △, to show where to insert something omitted. [L, 'there is wanting'.]

cargo [kär´gō] *n* the load carried by a ship, truck, aircraft, etc.; freight.—*pl* **car´goes, cargos**. [Sp from root of **car**.]

Carib [kar´ib] *n* member of a group of American Indian peoples of northeast S America and the Lesser Antilles;—*pl* **Caribs, Carib**; the family of languages spoken by these peoples.—*adj* **Caribbē´an**. [From Sp; cf **cannibal**.]

caribou [kar´i-bōō´] *n* a large deer (*Rangifer caribou*) of northern N America with palmate antlers in both sexes and grouped with reindeer in one species. [Canadian Fr]

caricature [kar´i-kä-chůr] *n* a likeness or imitation so exaggerated or distorted as to appear ridiculous.—*vt* to make ridiculous by an absurd likeness or imitation.—*n* **caricatur´ist**. [It *caricatura—caricare*, to load, from root of **car**.]

caries [kā´ri-ēz] *n* decay of bones or esp of teeth.—*adj* **cā´rious**. [L]

carillon [kar´il-on] *n* a set of bells usu hung from a tower and played by means of a keyboard or other mechanism; the orchestral glockenspiel.—*n* **carillonneur´**. [Fr,—Low L *quadriliō, -ōnis*, a quaternary, because carillons were formerly rung on four bells.]

carking [kärk´ing] *adj* burdensome, annoying. [Norm Fr *kark(e)*—Low L *carcāre—carricāre*, to load.]

carl, carle [kärl] *n* a man; a fellow. [ON *karl*, a man, a male. Cr **churl**.]

Carmelite [kär´mel-īt] *n* a medicant friar of the order of Our Lady of Mount *Carmel*, in Syria, founded about 1156; a nun of a corresponding order.

carminative [kär-min´ä-tiv] *n* a medicine to relieve flatulence.—Also *adj*. [L *carmināre*, to card or cleanse (wool).]

carmine [kär´mīn, -min] *n* the red coloring prepared from cochineal. [Fr *carmin*, through Sp from Ar; cf **crimson**.]

carnage [kär´nij] *n* slaughter. [Fr,—It *carnaggio*, carnage—L *carō, carnis*, flesh.]

carnal [kär´nȧl] *adj* fleshy; sensual; worldly.—*n* **carnal´ity**, state of being carnal.—*adv* **car´nally**.—**carnal knowledge** (*law*), sexual intercourse. [L *carnālis—car(ō), carnis*, flesh.]

carnation [kär-nā´sh(ȯ)n] *n* the color of human flesh; a garden flower developed in many forms from the Old World pink (*Dianthus caryophyllus*). [L *carnātiō*, fleshiness.]

carnival [kär´ni-vȧl] *n* a feast observed by Roman Catholics just before the fast of Lent; any revelry or indulgence; an entertainment with sideshows, rides, etc. [It *carnevale*—Low L *carnelevārium*, apparently from L *carnem levāre*, to put away flesh.]

carnivora [kär-niv´ō-ra] *n pl* carnivorous mammals.—*adj* **carniv´erous**, flesh-eating.—*adv* **carniv´orously**.—*ns* **carniv´orousness; car´nivore**, any of an order (Carnivora) of flesh-eating animals; an insectivorous plant. [L *carō, carnis*, flesh, *vorāre*, to devour.]

carob [kar´ob] *n* a leguminous Mediterranean tree, (Ceratonia siliqua); the long blackish sugary pod of this tree, used for fodder and human food. [Through Fr from Ar *kharrūbah*; cf **carat**.]

carol [kar´ol] *n* a song of joy or praise.—*vi* to sing a carol; to sing or warble.—*vt* to praise or celebrate in song;—*pr p* **car´olling**; *pt p* **car´olled**. [OFr *carole*; It *carola*, orig a ring-dance.]

carotid [ka-rot´id] *adj* relating to the two great arteries of the neck. [Gr *karōtidēs* (pl)—*karos*, sleep, the ancients supposing that deep sleep was caused by compression of them.]

carouse [kar-owz´] *n* a noisy drinking party.—*vi* to engage in a noisy drinking party; freely and noisily.—*n* **carous´al**, a carouse [OFr *carous*, Fr *carrousse*—Ger *gar aus*, quite out!—that is, empty the glass.]

carousel *See* **carrousel**.

carp[1] [kärp] *vi* to catch at small faults or errors (with *at*).—*n* **car´per**. [Most prob Scand, ON *karpa*, to boast, modified in meaning through likeness to L *carpěre*, to pluck, deride.]

carp[2] [kärp] *n* a freshwater fish (*Cyprinus carpio*) often raised for food. [OFr *carpe*—Low L *carpa*; perh Gmc]

carpal [kär´pȧl] *adj* pertaining to the wrist.—*n* a carpal bone. [Gr *karpos*, wrist.]

carpel [kär´pėl] *n* a modified leaf forming the whole or part of the pistil of a flower. [Gr *karpos*, fruit.]

carpenter [kär´pent-ėr] *n* a worker in timber as used in building houses, etc.—*vi* to do the work of a carpenter.—*n* **car´pentry**, the trade or work of a carpenter. [OFr *carpentier*—Low L *carpentārius*—*carpentum*, a wagon, car, from root of **car**.]

carpet [kär´pėt] *n* the woven or felted covering of floors, stairs, etc.; anything that covers like a carpet.—*vt* to cover with, or as with, a carpet.—*pr p* **car´peting**; *pt p* **car´peted**.—*ns* **car´petbag**, a traveling-bag made of carpeting; **car´petbagg´er**, a Northerner who went South after the Civil War to profit from unsettled conditions; an outsider, esp a nonresident who meddles in politics; **carpetbag steak**, a thick piece of steak in which a pocket is cut and stuffed with oysters; **car´peting**, material of which carpets are made.—**on the carpet**, up before someone in authority for reprimand. [OFr *carpite*—Low L *carpeta*, a coarse fabric made from rags pulled to pieces—L *carpĕre*, to pluck.]

carrack [kar´ak] *n* a beamy merchant vessel of the 14th and 15th centuries.—Also **car´ack**. [OFr *carraque*.]

carrageen [kar-a-gēn´] *n* an edible red seaweed; also known as Irish moss; carrageenan—*n* **carragee´nan, carragee´nin**, a colloid extracted from carrageen and used as a suspending agent in foods, a clarifying agent in beverages, and in controlling crystal growth in frozen confections. [Prob Ir *carraigín*, little rock.]

carriage [kar´ij] *n* act, or cost, of carrying; a vehicle for carrying; behavior, bearing; a baby buggy; a moving part, as on a typewriter, that supports and shifts something.—*n* **carriage trade**, trade from well-to-do or upper-class people; rich people. [From **carry**.]

carrier *See* **carry**.

carrion [kar´i-ȯn] *n* the dead and putrid flesh of any animal; flesh unfit for food.—*adj* relating to, or feeding on, putrid flesh. [Fr *carogne*—L *carō, carnis*, flesh.]

carrot [kar´ȯt] *n* a biennial herb (*Daucus carota*) grown for its edible, fleshy, orange root; the root; an inducement, often illusory.—**carrot-and-stick**, marked by the use of alternate reward and punishment.—*adj* **carr´oty**, carrot-colored (applied to the hair). [Fr *carotte*—L *carōta*.]

carrousel, carousel [kar-ōō-sel´, -zel] *n* a tournament; a merry-go-round; a rotating conveyor, eg for luggage at an airport. [Fr *carrousel*.]

carry [kar´i] *vt* to convey or transport; to bear; to support, sustain; to bear (oneself); to extend; to take by force; to gain; to gain by a majority of votes; to keep in stock; to keep on one's account books, etc.—*vi* to act as a bearer, conductor, etc.; (of a voice, a gun, etc.) to reach, indicating its range.—*pr p* **carr´ying**; *pt p* **carr´ied**—*n* the distance over which anything is carried.—*ns* **carr´ier**, one who carries, esp for hire; one in the business of transporting; a receptacle or other device for carrying; one who transmits an infectious disease without himself suffering from it; an individual having a specified gene that is not expressed in the phenotype; (*radio, etc.*) a steady current by modulations of which signals are transmitted; non-active material mixed with, and chemically identical to, a radioactive compound; **carr´ier pig´eon**, a pigeon with homing instinct, used for carrying messages; **carrying charge**, interest paid on the balance owed in installment buying.—*adj* **carr´y-on**, small enough to fit under an airplane seat.—*n* a piece of carryon luggage.—*adj* **carr´y-out**, denoting prepared food or beverages sold as by a restaurant to be consumed elsewhere.—*n* **carr´y-over**, something carried over, as a remainder of crops or goods.—**carry the torch**, to crusade; to be in love, esp without reciprocation; **carry the ball**, to bear the major responsibility; **carry the day**, to win, to prevail. [OFr *carier*—Low L *carricāre*, to cart—L *carrus*, a car.]

cart [kärt] *n* a small wagon.—*vti* to carry in a cart, truck, etc.; to transport.—*ns* **cart´age**, the act, or cost, of carting; **car´ter**, one who drives a cart; **cart´wheel**, a large coin (as a silver dollar); a lateral handspring with arms and legs extended.—**put the cart before the horse**, to reverse the natural order of things. [Ety uncertain; OE *cræt*, or ON *kartr*.]

carte blanche [kärt blãsh] *n* a blank paper, duly signed, to be filled up at the recipient's pleasure; freedom of action. [Fr.]

cart´el [kär-tel´] *n* a written agreement between belligerent nations; an association of business in an international monopoly. [Fr,—L *c(h)arta*. *See* **card** (1).]

Cartesian [kar-tē´zi-ȧn, -zhyȧn] *adj* relating to the French philosopher *Descartes* (1596–1650), or to his philosophy or mathematical methods.

Carthusian [kär-thū´zi-ȧn] *n* a monk of an order founded in 1086, noted for its strictness.—*adj* of or pertaining to the order. [L *Cartusiānus*; from a village (now *La Grande Chartreuse*) near Grenoble near which their first monastery was founded.]

cartilage [kär´ti-lij] *n* in vertebrate animals, a firm elastic substance, lacking blood vessels and nerves; gristle.—*adj* **cartilaginous** [-laj´-]. [Fr,—L *cartilāgō*; cf *crātis*. (See **crate**).]

cartography [kär-tog´ra-fi] *n* map-making.—*ns* **cartog´rapher**. [L *c(h)arta*—Gr *chartēs*, a leaf of papyrus, and Gr *graphein*, to write.]

carton [kär´tȯn] *n* a cardboard box or container. [Fr. See **cartoon**.]

cartoon [kär-tōōn] *n* a preparatory drawing on strong paper to be transferred to frescoes, tapestry, etc., any large sketch or design on paper; a comic or satirical drawing; a comic strip; an animated cartoon. [Fr *carton* (It *cartone*)—*carte*; see **carte** (2).]

cartouche [kär-tōōsh´] *n* a case for holding cartridges; (*archit*) an ornament resembling a scroll of paper with the ends rolled up; an oval figure on ancient Egyptian monuments or papyri enclosing characters expressing royal names.—Also **cartouch´**. [Fr,—It *cartoccio*—L *c(h)arta*. See **card** (1).]

cartridge [kär´trij] *n* a case containing the charge for a gun. [A corr of **cartouche**.]

carve [kärv] *vt* to cut into forms, devices, etc., to make or shape by cutting; to cut up (meat) into slices or pieces.—*vi* to carve statues or designs; to carve meat.—*adj* **carv´en**, carved.—*ns* **carv´er**, one who carves; a sculptor; a carving-knife; **carving**, the act or art of carving; the device or figure carved.—**carve out**, to hew out; to gain by one's exertions; **carve up**, to subdivide, apportion. [OE *ceorfan*, to cut; Du *kerven*; Ger, *kerben*, to notch.]

carvel [kär´vel] *n* caravel.—*adj* **car´vel-built**, built with planks meeting flush at the seams. [Older form of **caravel**.]

caryatid [ka-i-at´id] *n* a column carved in the shape of a draped female figure used to support an entablature;—*pl* **caryat´ides** [-id-ēz]. [Gr *Karyātis*.]

Casanova [kas-ȧ-nō´va] *n* (*inf*) a person conspicuous for his amorous adventures, as was Giovanni Jacopo *Casanova* de Seingalt (1725–1798), whose Memoirs, written in French, tell a tale of adventure, roguery, intrigue, scandal, of many kinds.

cascade [kas-kād´] *n* a small, steep waterfall; a shower, as of sparks, etc.—*vti* to fall in cascades. [Fr,—It—L *cadĕre*, to fall.]

cascara [kȧs-kä´ra] *n* cascara buckthorn; cascara sagrada.—*ns* **cascara buckthorn**, a tree (*Rhamnus purshiana*) of the U.S. Pacific coast yielding cascara sagrada; **cascara sagrada**, the dried bark of cascara buckthorn used as a laxative. [Sp *cáscara*, bark.]

case[1] [kās] *n* a covering, box, or sheath; the boards and back of a book; the tray in which a compositor has his types before him.—*vt* to enclose in a case.—*vt* **case´ hard´en**, to harden on the surface; to make callous or insensible.—*adj* **case-hardened**.—*ns* **case´ knife**, a sheath knife; a table knife; **case´ment**, a window that opens on hinges at the side; **cas´ing**, the skin of a sausage; the outer covering of a pneumatic tire; a frame, as for a door; space formed between two layers of fabric for enclosing a cord, etc. [O North Fr *casse*—L *capsa*—*capĕre*, to take.]

case[2] [käs] *n* that which falls or happens, event; state or condition; subject of question or inquiry; a person under medical treatment; a legal statement of facts; (*gram*) the grammatical relation of a noun, pronoun, or adjective to other words in a sentence, etc.; convincing arguments; a lawsuit.—*vt* (*slang*) to look over carefully.—*ns* **case´ law**, law as decided in previous cases; **case´load**, the number of cases handled by a court, caseworker, etc.; **case´work**, social work in which guidance is given in cases of personal and family maladjustment; **case´worker.**—**in case**, in the event that; lest; **in no case**, by no means. [OFr *cas*—L *cāsus*, from *cădĕre*, to fall.]

casein [kāsē-in] *n* a protein, the principal albuminous constituent of milk or cheese.—*adj* **cā´sēous**, pertaining to cheese. [Fr,—L *caseus*, cheese.]

casemate [kās´māt] *n* a heavily protected chamber or compartment on a warship, esp one in which a gun is mounted.—*adj* **case´mated**. [Fr; ety uncertain.]

cash [kash] *n* coin or money; ready money; money, a check, etc. paid at the time of purchase.—*vt* to exchange for money.—*ns* **cash flow**, the measure of liquidity of a business usu. consisting of net income after taxes plus noncash charges (as depreciation) against income; **cashier´**, one who has charge of the receiving and paying of money; **cash´reg´ister**, a device, usu. with a money drawer, that automatically and visibly records the amount put in.—**cash in**, to turn into cash. [OFr *casse*, a box.]

cashier [kash-ēr´] *vt* to dismiss from a post in disgrace; to discard or put away. [Du. *casseren*, to cashier—L *cassāre*—*cassus*, void.]

cashmere [kash´mēr] *n* a fine, carded wool from goats of northern India, Tibet, and China; the yarn spun from this wool.

casino [ka-sē´no] *n* a room or building for gambling, dancing, etc. [It, from L *casa*, a cottage.]

cask [käsk] *n* a barrel of any size, esp one for liquids; its contents. [Fr *casque*—Sp *casco*, skull, helmet, cask.]

casket [käsk´et] *n* a small box or chest for holding jewels, etc.; a coffin. [Ety uncertain; hardly a dim of **cask**.]

casque [käsk] *n* a cover for the head; a helmet. [A doublet of **cask**.]

cassava [ka-sä´vä] *n* a tropical plant (genus *Manihot*) with starchy roots; the starch from the root, used in tapioca.

casserole [kas´e-rōl] *n* a vessel in which food is both cooked and served; the food itself. [Fr.]

cassette [kas-et´] *n* a case with magnetic tape or film in it, for loading in a tape recorder or camera. [Fr dim of *casse*, case.]

cassia [kas(h)´ya] *n* a coarse cinnamon bark (as from *Cinnamonum cassia*); any of a genus (*Cassia*) of leguminous herbs, shrubs, and trees of warm regions. [L *casia*—Gr *kasia*—Heb.]

cassimere [kas´i-mēr] *n* a twilled cloth of the finest wools. [Corr of **cashmere**.]

cassock [kas´ȯk] *n* a long black robe worn by Roman Catholic and Anglican clergy and by laymen assisting in services. [Fr *casaque*—It *casacca*.]

cassowary [kas´ō-wȧr-i] *n* a genus (*Casuarius*) of running birds, found esp in Australia, New Guinea etc. nearly related to the emus. [Malay *kasuārī* or *kasavārī*.]

cast [käst] *vt* to throw or fling; to shed, drop; to reckon; to direct; to mold or shape.—*vi* to throw, hurl.—*pt, pt p* **cast**.—*n* act of casting; a throw; the thing thrown; the distance thrown; a motion, turn, or squint, as of the eye; matter ejected by an earthworm; a plaster form for immobilizing a limb; a mold; the form received from a mold; type or quality; a tinge; the assignment of the various parts of a play to the several actors; the company of actors playing roles.—*n* **cast´away**, a person or thing cast off; one ship-wrecked in a desolate place; an outcast.—*adj* **cast´ down**, dejected.—*ns* **cast´ing**, act of casting or molding; that which is cast; a mold; **cast´ing-vote**, the vote by which the chairman of a meeting decides the issue when the other votes are equally divided; **cast´ i´ron**, an iron alloy that is cast in a mold.—*adj* rigid; unyielding, inflexible.—*adj* **cast´-off**, laid aside or rejected.—*n* a person or thing cast off.—**cast about**, to look round enquiringly, to search; **cast off**, to throw off; to set aside as useless; to unmoor; to remove a stitch or stitches from a piece of knitting in such a way that it does not unravel; to disown; **cast on**, to make stitches on a knitting needle to begin a piece of knitting; **cast lots**, to draw lots to determine something by chance. [ON *kasta*, to throw.]

castanets [kas´ta-nets] *n pl* two hollow shells of ivory or hard wood, joined by a band passing round the thumb, and struck by the fingers to produce an accompaniment to dances and guitars; orchestral castanets with springs and handles. [Sp *castañeta*—L *castanea*, a chestnut.]

caste [kast] *n* a hereditary Hindu social class in India; any exclusive social class.—**lose caste**, to descend in social rank. [Port *casta*, breed, race—L *castus*, pure, unmixed.]

castellan, castellated *See* **castle**.

caster [kast´ėr] *n* a small wheel on the legs of furniture; a small vessel with perforated top for pepper, sugar, etc.—Also **cas´ter**. [**cast**.]

castigate [kas´tig-āt] *vt* to chastise; to criticise severely.—*ns* **castigā´tion; cas´tigātor**. [L *castigāre, -ātum*, from *castus*, pure.]

castle [käs´l] *n* a fortified house or fortress; anything built in the likeness of such; a piece in chess (also called *rook*).—*vt* to move (the chess king) in castling.—*vi* to move a chess king in a specified way.—*n* **castellan** [kas´tel-an] governor or captain of a castle.—*adj* **cas´tellated**, having turrets and battlements like a castle.—**castles in the air**, or **in Spain**, visionary projects. [OE *castel*—L *castellum*, dim of *castrum*, a fortified place.]

castor [käs´tȯr] *n* the beaver; a hat made of its fur. [L,—Gr *kastōr*.]

castor oil [käs´tȯr-oil] *n* a medicinal and lubricating oil obtained from a tropical plant (*Ricinus communis*).

castrate [kas´trāt] *vt* to deprive of the power of generation by removing the testicles, to geld; to deprive of the ovaries, to spay; to deprive of vitality by psychological means.—*n* **castrā´tion**. [L *castrāre, -ātum*.]

casual [kaz(h)´ū-ȧl] *adj* accidental; unforeseen; occasional; careless; unceremonious.—*n* a casual or migratory worker; a member of the armed forces awaiting assignment or transportation to his unit.—*adv* **cas´ually**.—*n* **cas´ualty**, that which falls out; an accident, esp a fatal one; (*mil*) a loss by wounds, death, desertion, etc.; a person injured or killed in an accident. [L *cāsuālis*—*cāsus*. See **case** (2).]

casuarina [kas-ū-a-rī´na] *n* a genus (*Casuarina*) of trees, mainly Australian, some of which yield hard heavy wood. [Named from their resemblance to *cassowary* plumage.]

casuistry [kas´ū-is-tri] (or kazh´-) *n* a method of solving conflicts of obligation by applying general principles of ethics and moral theology to particular case of human conduct; subtle but false reasoning, esp about moral issues.—*n* **cas´uist**, one who practises casuistry.—*adjs* **casuist´ic, -al**, relating to casuistry; subtle; specious. [Fr *casuiste*—L *cāsus*. See **case** (2).]

cat [kat] *n* a wild or domesticated animal of genus *Felis*; a spiteful woman; short for the **cat-o'-nine-tails**, a whip with nine lashes; (*slang*) a man, a fellow; **catamaran**, a strong tackle used to hoist an anchor.—*ns* **cat´amount**, a wild cat, esp a cougar or lynx; **cat-a-mountain**, any of various wild cats;—*adj* **cat and mouse**, quarrelsome.—*ns* **cat´bird**, a N American songbird (*Dumetalla carolinses*) with a mewing, catlike call; **cat´call**, raucous cry made to express disapproval (as at a sports event); **cat´gut**, a kind of cord made from the intestines of sheep; **cat´kin**, a spike or tuft of small flowers, as in the willow, hazel, etc.—*adj* **cat´-like**, noiseless, stealthy.—*ns* **cat's´ cra´dle**, a pastime in which a string looped about the fingers and passed from player to player is transformed from one pattern to another; intricacy; **cat's´-eye**, a variety of quartz showing opalescent reflections; a playing marble with eyelike concentric circles; **cat's´-paw** (*naut*), a light breeze; a dupe or tool; a hitch in the bight of a rope made to form two eyes; **catt´ery**, a place where cats are bred or cared for.—*adj* **catt´y**, like a cat; spiteful.—*n* **cat´walk**, a narrow footway, as on a bridge; the platform used in fashion shows. (see **bell**). [OE *cat*; found in many languages; Low L *cattus*, prob Celt.]

catabolism [kat-ab´ol-izm] *n* the breaking down of complex molecules in the living organism to release energy; destructive metabolism. [Gr *katabolē*—*katabollein*, to throw down—*kata*, down, *ballein*, to throw.]

cataclysm [kat´a-klizm] *n* a flood of water; any sudden violent change.—*adj* **cataclys´mic**. [Gr *kataklysmos*—*kata*, downward, *klyzein*, to wash.]

catacomb [kat´a-kōm] *n* a subterranean burial-place, esp the famous Catacombs near Rome, where many of the early Christian victims of persecution were buried; any underground passage or groups of passages; a complicated set of interrelated things. [It *catacomba*—through Late L, prob from Gr *kata*, downward, and *kymbē*, a hollow.]

catafalque [kat´a-falk] *n* a temporary structure representing a tomb placed over the coffin during a lying in state; the stand on which the coffin rests; a pall-covered coffin-shaped structure used at requiem masses after burial. [Fr,—*It catafalco*.]

catalectic [kat-a-lek´tik] *adj* incomplete—applied to a verse wanting one syllable at the end. [Gr *katalēktikos*, incomplete—*katalēgein*, to stop.]

catalepsy [kat´a-lep-si] *n* a state of temporary insensibility with bodily rigidity, as in epilepsy.—*adj* **catalep´tic**. [Gr *kata*, down, *lēpsis*, seizure.]

catalog, catalogue [kat´a-log] *n* a classified list of names, books, etc.—*vti* to put in a catalog; to make a catalog of;—*pr p* **cat´aloguing**; *pt p* **cat´alogued**. [Fr through LL—Gr *katalogos*—*kata*, down, *legein*, to choose.]

catalysis [ka-tal´i-sis] *n* the acceleration or retardation of a chemical reaction by a substance which itself undergoes no permanent chemical change.—*n* **cat´alўst** (or **catalyt´ic agent**), a substance acting as the agent in catalysis.—*vt* **cat´alyze**. [Gr *katalysis*—*kata*, down, *lyein*, to loosen.]

catamaran [kat-a-mär-an´] *n* a raft of logs lashed together, propelled by sails or paddles; a boat with two hulls. [From Tamil, 'tied wood'.]

catamount *See* **cat**.

catapult [kat´a-pult] *n* anciently an engine of war for throwing stones, arrows, etc.; any similar device, as for launching an airplane, rocket missile, etc. from a deck or ramp. [L *catapulta*—Gr *katapeltēs*.]

cataract [kat´a-rakt] *n* a waterfall; an opaque condition of the lens of the eye causing blindness or partial blindness; the opaque area. [L *cataracta*—Gr *kataraktēs*, a waterfall (*kata*, down).]

catarrh [kat-är´] *n* (*old fashioned*) a discharge of fluid due to the inflammation of a mucous membrane, esp of the nose; a cold.—*adj* **catarrh´al**. [L *catarrhus*—Gr *katarrhous*—*kata*, down, *rheein*, to flow.]

catastrophe [kat-as´trō-fe] *n* a sudden, violent change in a feature of the earth; utter failure; a calamity.—*adj* **catastroph´ic**. [Gr *kata*, down, *strophē*, a turn.]

catcall *See* **cat**.

catch [kach] *vt* to take hold of, esp a thing in motion; to seize after pursuit; to trap or ensnare; to be in time for; to surprise, detect; to become infected with (a disease); (*inf*) to see, hear, etc.; to grasp (eg a meaning).—*vi* to be contagious; to be entangled or fastened;—*pt, pt p* **caught** [köt].—*n* seizure; anything that seizes or holds; that which is caught; anything worth catching; a snare; a song in which the parts are successively caught up by different voices; (*inf*) a tricky qualification.—*adj* **catch´-as-catch´-can´**, using any available means or methods.—*n* **catch´er**, (*baseball*) the player behind home plate, who catches pitched balls.—*adj* **catch´ing**, infectious; captivating, attractive.—*ns* **catch´ment a´rea**, a geographical area served by an institution; **catch´penny**, any worthless thing, esp a publication, intended merely to gain money (also *adj*); **catch´phrase**, a phrase that becomes popular and is much repeated; a slogan; **catch´word**, a guide word; a word or expression representative of a party, school, or point of view through constant repetition.—*adj* **catch´y**, attractive; deceptive; readily caught up, as a tune, etc.—**catch fire**, to become ignited; to become inspired by passion or zeal; to increase greatly in scope etc. **catch it**, to get a scolding or the like; **catch on**, to comprehend; to catch the popular fancy; **catch out**, to detect in error.—*n* **catch 22**, an absurd situation in which one can never win, being constantly balked by a clause, rule, etc. which itself can change to block any change in one's course of action.—**catch up**, to overtake; to bring about arrest for illicit activities; to acquire belated information. [From OFr *cachier*—Late L *captiāre* for *captāre*, inten of *capĕre*, to take.]

catchpole, catchpoll [kach´pōl] *n* a sheriff's deputy esp one who arrests debtors. [Through OFr from Low L *cachepolus, chassipullus*, one who chases fowls.]

catchup, catsup *See* **ketchup**.

catechize [kat´e-kīz] *vt* to instruct by question and answer; to question, examine searchingly.—*adjs* **catechis´mal, catechis´tic**, relating to a catechism or to oral instruction.—*adv* **catechet´ically**.—*ns* **cat´echīzer; cat´echism**, oral instruction; a manual, esp a summary of instruction in the form of question and answer; **cat´echist**, one who catechizes; a native teacher in a mission church. [L *catēchismus*, formed from Gr *katēchizein, katēcheein*, to din into the ears, teach—*kata*, down, *ēchē*, a sound.]

catechumen [kat-e-kū´men] *n* one who is being taught the rudiments of Christianity. [Gr *katēchoumenos*, being taught, pr p pass of *katēcheein*, to teach.]

category [kat´e-gor-i] *n* a class or division in a scheme of classification.—*adj* **categor´ical**, (of a statement) positive; absolute, without exception; of, as, or in a category.—*adv* **categor´ically**.—**categorical imperative**, the absolute unconditional command of the moral law which is universally binding. [Gr *katēgoria; katēgoros*, an accuser.]

cater [kā´tėr] *vi* to provide food and service, as for parties (*with* **for**); to seek to gratify another's desires (*with* **to**).—*n* **cā´terer**. [Lit to act as a *cater*, the word being orig a noun (spelled *catour*)—OFr *acateor, achetour*—LL *acceptāre*, to acquire.]

caterpillar [kat´ėr-pil-ȧr] *n* the wormlike larvae of a butterfly or moth; extended to other larvae; a tractor made for use on rough or soft ground running on endless articulated tracks (from **Caterpillar**, trademark). [Prob OFr *chatepelose*, 'hairy cat'.]

caterwaul [kat´ėr-wöl] *n* the shriek or cry of the cat.—*vi* to make such a noise. [The second part is prob imit.]

catgut *See* **cat**.

cathartic [kath-ärt´ik] *adj* having the power of cleansing; purgative, esp of the bowels.—*ns* **cathar´sis**, a relieving of the emotions, as through the arts or psychotherapy; **cathar´tic**, a purgative medicine. [Gr *kathartikos*, for cleansing—*katharos*, clean.]

Cathay [ka-thā] (*obs*) name for China.

cathedral [kath-ēd´rȧl] *n* the principal church of a diocese, in which is the see of a bishop; any large, imposing church.—*adj* belonging to a cathedral. [L *cathĕdra*—Gr *kathĕdra*, a seat.]

catherine wheel [kath´ė-rin-hwēl] *n* a wheel with spikes protruding from the rim; an acrobatic cartwheel; a kind of firework which in burning rotates like a wheel. [St *Catherine* of Alexandria (4th cent), who escaped torture on a wheel.]

catheter [kath´e-tėr] *n* a tube for admitting gases or liquids through the channels of the body, or for removing them, esp for removing urine from the bladder.—*vt* **cath´eterize**. [Through L—Gr *kathetēr*—*kathienai*, to send down.]

cathode [kath´ōd] *n* the negative terminal of an electrolytic cell at which positively charged ions are discharged into the exterior electric circuit; in valves and tubes, the source of electrons; the positive terminal in a battery.—*adjs* **cath´odal; cathod´ic**.—**cathode rays**, streams of negatively charged particles (electrons) emitted normally from the surface of the cathode during an electrical discharge in a rarefied gas, producing X-rays when they strike solids. **cathode-ray tube**, a device in which a narrow beam of electrons strikes against a fluorescent screen and produces a luminous spot. [Gr *kata*, down *hodos*, a way.]

catholic [kath´ol-ik] *adj* universal; general, embracing the whole body of Christians; liberal, the opposite of exclusive; relating to the Roman Catholic Church or church claiming historical continuity from the early church, esp Anglicans.—*n* **Catholic**, an adherent of the RC Church.—*ns* **Cathol´icism**, the tenets of the RC Church; (without *cap*) catholicity (*rare*); **catholic´ity** [-is´-], universality; liberality or breadth of view; Catholicism (*rare*).—**Catholic Epistles**, the five New Testament letters including James, Peter I and II, John I, and Jude addressed to the early Christian churches at large. [Gr *katholikos*, universal—*kata*, throughout, *holos*, the whole.]

catkin *See* **cat**.

CAT scan *c*omputer-*a*ssisted *t*omography. See **compute**.

cattle [kat´l] *n pl* oxen, bulls, and cows, held as property or raised for use; human beings, esp en masse etc. [OFr *catel, chatel*—Low L *captāle*, orig capital, property in general, then esp animals—L *capitālis*, chief—*caput*, the head.]

Caucasian [kö-kā´z(h)i-ȧn] *adj* pertaining to the Caucasus; Caucasoid.—*n* a native of the Caucasus; a Caucasoid—*adj* **Caucasoid**, denoting or of one of the major groups of mankind, loosely called the white race.—*n* a member of the Caucasoid group.

caucus [kö´kus] *n* private meeting of leaders of a political party or faction, usu to plan strategy.

caudal [kö´dȧl] *adj* pertaining to the tail.—*adj* **cau´dāte**, tailed. [L *cauda*, a tail.]

caudle [kö´dl] *n* a warm drink, usu of wine or ale mixed with egg, spices, etc., given to the sick. [OFr *chaudel*—L *calidus*, hot.]

caught [köt] *pt, pt p* of **catch**.

caul [köl] *n* the membrane covering the head of some infants at their birth. [OFr *cale*, a little cap.]

cauldron *See* **caldron**.

cauliflower [kol´i-flow(ė)r] *n* a variety of cabbage (*Brassica oleracea botrytis*) whose inflorescence is eaten. [Earlier *cole-florye, colie-florie*—Low L *cauli flora*—L *caulis*, cabbage.]

caulk [kök] *vt* to render (a boat) watertight by pressing oakum, etc., into the seams; to stop up (cracks) with a filler.—*n* **caulk´er**. [OFr *cauquer*, to press—L *calcāre*, to tread—*calx*, heel.]

cause [köz] *n* that which produces an effect; ground, motive, justification; a legal action; the aim proposed, or the opinions advocated, by an individual or party.—*vt* to produce; to bring about; to induce.—*adj* **caus´al**, relating to a cause or causes.—*ns* **causal´ity**, the relation of cause and effect; **causā´tion**, the operation of cause and effect.—*adj* **caus´ative**, producing an effect, causing.—*adv* **caus´atively**.—*adj* **cause´less**, without cause; without just cause.—*adv* **cause´lessly**.—*n* **cause´lessness**. [Fr,—L *causa*.]

cause célèbre [kōz sā-leb-r´] a legal case that excites much public interest; a notorious incident. [Fr.]

causerie [kōz´ėr-ē] *n* a talk or gossip; a short and informal essay. [Fr.]

causeway [köz´wā] *n* a pathway raised and paved with stone as across wet ground or water.—*vt* to pave. [ME *causee*—OFr *caucie*—Low L (*via*) *calciata*—L *calx*, heel and **way**.]

caustic [kös´-, kos´tik] *adj* burning tissue by chemical action; corrosive; sarcastic, cutting.—*n* a substance that burns or wastes away the skin and flesh.—*adv* **caus´tically**.—*n* **caustic´ity**, quality of being caustic.—**caustic potash, soda**, potassium, sodium hydroxide. [L,—Gr *kaustikos*—*kaiein, kausein*, to burn.]

cauterize [kö´tėr-īz] *vt* to burn with caustic or a hot iron so as to destroy dead tissue, etc.; to deaden.—*ns* **cau´tery**, a burning with caustics or a hot iron; an iron or caustic used for burning tissue; **cauterizā´tion**. [Fr *cautériser*—Low L *cautērizāre*—Gr *kautēr*, a hot iron—*kaiein*, to burn.]

caution [kö´sh(ȯ)n] *n* heedfulness; warning.—*vt* to warn.—*adj* **cau´tionary**, containing caution; **cau´tious**, possessing or using caution; watchful; prudent.—*adv* **cau´tiously**.—*n* **cau´tiousness**. [Fr,—L *cautiō, -ōnis*—*cavēre*, to beware.]

cavalcade [kav-ȧl-kād´] *n* a procession of persons on horseback; a dramatic sequence or procession. [Fr, through It and Low L—L *caballus*, a horse.]

cavalier [kav-ȧl-ēr´] *n* a knight; a swaggering fellow; a gallant gentleman, esp a lady's escort.—*adj* like a cavalier; gay; haughty, offhand, disdainful.—*adv* **cavalier´ly**. [Fr,—It *cavallo*—L *caballus*, a horse.]

cavalry [kav´ȧl-ri] *n* combat troops originally mounted on horseback but now on motorized armored vehicles; horsemen. [Fr *cavallerie*—It *cavalleria*—L *caballārius*, horseman.]

cave [kāv] *n* a hollow place inside the earth open to the surface.—*vti* to collapse or make collapse (*with* **in**).—*n* **cave´man**, one, esp of the Stone age, who lived in a cave; (*inf*) one who acts with primitive violence. [Fr,—L *cavus*, hollow.]

caveat [kā´ve-at] *n* a notice or warning; a notice to stay proceedings in a court of law.—**caveat emptor**, let the buyer beware. [L, 'let him take care'—*cavēre*, to take care.]

cavern [kav´ėrn] *n* a cave, esp a large cave.—*adj* **cav´ernous**, full of caverns; (of animal tissue) composed of vascular sinuses and capable of dilating with blood. [Fr,—L *caverna*—*cavus*, hollow.]

caviar, caviare [kav´i-är] *n* salted roe of the sturgeon, etc. [Prob the 16th-cent It *caviale*.]

cavil [kav´il] *vi* to make empty, trifling objections.—*pr p* **cav´illing**; *pt p* **cav´illed**.—*n* a frivolous objection.—*n* **cav´iller**. [OFr *caviller*—L *cavillārī*, to practise jesting—*cavilla*, jesting.]

cavity [kav´it-i] *n* a hollow; a hollow place. [L *cavitās, -ātis*—*cavus*, hollow.]

cavort [kav-ört´] *vi* to curvet, frolic, bound. [Explained as a corr of **curvet**.]

cavy [kāv´i] *n* any of several short-tailed S American rodents (family Caviidae), esp the guinea pig. [*cabiai*, the native name in French Guiana.]

caw [kö] *vi* to cry as a crow.—*n* the cry of a crow. [From the sound.]

cayenne [kā-en´] *n* a very pungent red pepper (*Capsicum frutescens*).—**cayenne pepper**, the powder of the dried pods and seeds of this capsicum. [Usually referred to *Cayenne* in French Guiana; but prob the word is Brazilian.]

cayman *See* **caiman**

CD ROM [abbrev] compact disc read-only memory. A CD used for distributing text and images in electronic publishing, for computer software, and for permanent storage of computer data.

CDV [abbrev] CD-video; compact video disc.

cease [sēs] *vt* and *vi* to give over, to stop.—*vi* to be at an end.—*adj* **cease´less**, without ceasing; incessant.—*adv* **cease´lessly**. [Fr *cesser*—L *cessāre*, to give over—*cēdĕre*, to yield, give up.]

cecum, caecum [sē´kum] *n* a sac or bag, having only one opening, connected with the intestine of an animal.—*pl* **ce´ca**. [L—*caecus*, blind.]

cedar [sē´dȧr] *n* any of a genus (*Cedrus*) of large coniferous evergreen trees remarkable for the durability and fragrance of their wood.—*adj* made of cedar.—Also (*poet*) **cē´darn**. [L *cedrus*—Gr *kedros*.]

cede [sēd] *vt* to yield or give up to another, esp by treaty; to assign or transfer the title of. [L *cēdĕre, cessum*, to yield, give up.]

cedilla [se-dil´a] *n* a mark placed under the letter *c* (thus *ç*) to show that it is to have the sound of *s*. [Sp (Fr *cédille*, It *zediglia*), all from *zēta*, the Greek name of *z*.]

ceil [sēl] *vt* to furnish (as a wooden ship) with a lining; to provide with a ceiling.—*n* **ceil´ing**, the inner roof of a room; the upper limit of visibility; an upper limit usu. prescribed. [Prob conn with Fr *ciel*, It *cielo*, Low L *caelum*, a canopy.]

celandine [sel´an-dīn] *n* a variety of poppy (*Chelidonium majus*) with yellow flowers; an European buttercup (*Ranunculus ficaria*) that has been introduced locally into the US.—Also **lesser celandine**. [OFr *celidoine*—Gr *chelīdonion*—*chelīdōn*, a swallow.]

celebrate [sel´e-brāt] *vt* to make famous; to honor with solemn ceremonies; to perform with proper rites and ceremonies.—*vi* (*inf*) to have a good time.—*n* **cel´ebrant**, one who performs a rite.—*adj* **cel´ebrated**, distinguished, famous.—*ns* **celebrā´tion**, act of celebrating; **celeb´rity**, the condition of being celebrated, fame; a notable person. [L *celebrāre, -ātum*—*celeber*, much visited, renowned.]

celerity [sel-er´it-i] *n* quickness, rapidity of motion. [L *celeritās*—*celer*, quick.]

celery [sel´ėr-i] *n* a kitchen vegetable with long succulent stalks. [Fr *célerie*—Gr *selīnon*, parsley.]

celestial [sel-est´yȧl] *adj* heavenly; dwelling in heaven; in the visible heavens.—*n* an inhabitant of heaven. [Through Fr from L *caelestis*—*caelum*, heaven.]

celibacy [sel´i-bas-i] *n* the unmarried state; complete sexual abstinence.—*adj* **cel´ibate**, of or in a state of celibacy.—*n* one unmarried, or bound by vow not to marry. [L *caelebs*, single.]

cell [sel] *n* a small room in a prison, etc.; a small cavity, as in a honeycomb; a small unit of protoplasm; a unit within a larger organization; the unit of an electrical battery, in which chemical action takes place between an anode and a cathode both separately in contact with an electrolyte; a part of the atmosphere that behaves as a unit.—*n* **cell´ule**, a little cell.—*adj* **cell´ūlar**, consisting of, or containing, cells; containing cavities; having a porous texture.—*ns* **celluloid**, a motion-picture film; **Cell´uloid**, a trade name for a flammable plastic substance made from nitrocellulose and camphor; **cell´ulose**, the chief component of cell membrane of plants, used in making paper, textiles, etc. [OFr *celle*—L *cella*, conn with *celāre*, to cover.]

cellar [sel´ár] *n* a basement; a covered excavation; the lowest grade or rank, esp in the standings (as of an athletic league); a stock of wines.—*ns* **cell´arage**, cellar space, esp for storage; **cell´arer**, the caretaker of provisions in a monastery; **cell´aret**, a case for holding bottles of wine or liquor. [OFr *celier*—L *cellārium*—*cella*; see **cell**.]

cello [chel´ō] *n* an instrument of the violin family, between the viola and double bass in pitch.—*n* **cellist**. [Short for **violin cello**.]

cellophane [sel´ō-fān] *n* a tough transparent wrapping material made from cellulose. [Orig trademark—**cell(ul)o(se)**, and Gr *phainein*, to show.]

cellular phone [sel´ū-lar fōn] *n* a portable mobile telephone operated by microwave radio. Also **cellphone** [sel´fōn].

Celsius *See* **centigrade**.

celt [selt] *n* a prehistoric stone or metal implement shaped like a chisel or ax head. [Ety uncertain.]

Celt [kelt, selt] *n* a Gaul; extended to include members of other Celtic-speaking peoples.—*adj* **Celt´ic**, pertaining to the Celts.—*n* a branch of the Indo-European family of languages, including Breton, Welsh, Cornish, Irish, Gaelic, Manx. [L *Celtae*; Gr *Keltoi* or *Keltai*.]

cement [se-ment´] *n* a powdered substance of lime and clay, mixed with water, etc. to make mortar or concrete, which hardens upon drying; any adhesive substance.—*vt* to unite with cement; to cover with cement.—*vi* to be cemented.—*n* **cementā´tion**, the act of cementing; the process of surrounding a solid with a powder and heating the whole so that the solid is changed by chemical combination with the powder. [OFr *ciment*—L *caementum*, chip of stone used to fill up in building a wall.]

cemetery [sem´e-tėr-i (or -tri)] *n* a place for the burial of the dead. [Low L *coemētērium*—Gr *koimētērion*.]

cenotaph [sen´ō-täf] *n* a sepulchral monument to one who is buried elsewhere. [Fr,—L—Gr *kenotaphion*—*kenos*, empty, and *taphos*, a tomb.]

Cenozoic [sē-no-zō´ik] *adj* denoting the geologic era that included the present marked by the evolution of mammals and the higher flowering plants; the system of rocks formed in this era.

censer [sens´ėr] *n* a pan in which incense is burned. [OFr *censier, encensier*—Low L *incensorium*—L *incendĕre, incensum*, to burn.]

censor [sen´sȯr] *n* an official with the power to examine literature, mail, etc. and remove or prohibit anything considered obscene, objectionable, etc.; a hypothetical inhibitive mechanism in the mind that prevents what is painful from emerging into consciousness.—*vt* to delete, suppress as a censor might.—*adjs* **censo´rial**, belonging to a censor, or to the correction of public morals; **censō´rious**, expressing censure; fault-finding.—*adv* **censō´riously**.—*ns* **censō´riousness; cen´sorship**, office or action of a censor. [L; cf **censure**.]

censure [sen´shụr] *n* an unfavorable judgment, blame, reproof.—*vt* to blame; to condemn as wrong.—*adj* **cen´surable**. [L *censūra*—*censēre*, to estimate or judge.]

census [sen´sus] *n* an official enumeration of inhabitants and recording of age, sex, etc. [L *census*, a register.]

cent [sent] *n* a coin = the hundredth part of a dollar; a penny. [L *centum*, a hundred.]

centaur [sen´tör] *n* a fabulous monster, half man, half horse. [L *Centaurus*—Gr *Kentauros*.]

centavo [sen-tä´vō] *n* a unit of money in Mexico, the Phillipines, and some countries of S America. [Sp.]

centenary [sen-ten´ár-i or sen´tin-] *n* a century or hundred years; a hundredth anniversary.—*adj* pertaining to a hundred.—*n* **centenā´rian**, one at least a hundred years old. [L *centenī*, a hundred each—*centum*.]

centennial [sen-ten´i-ȧl] *adj* happening once in a hundred years.—*n* a hundredth anniversary or its celebration. [Coined from L *centum*, and *annus*, a year.]

center [sen´tėr] *n* the middle point of a circle or sphere; the approximate middle point or part of anything, a pivot; a political party of moderate political opinions; (*sports*) a player at the center of a line, floor, etc.—*vt* to place in, or collect to, the center.—*vi* to be centered.—*pr p* **cen´tering**; *pt p* **cen´tered**.—*adj* **central**, belonging to the center, principal, dominant.—*n* **centralizā´tion**, the tendency to administer affairs by a central rather than a local authority.—*vt* **cen´tralize**, to draw to a center.—*adv* **cen´trally**.—*ns* **cen´terpiece**, an ornament for the middle of a table; **central nervous system**, the brain and spinal cord; **center of gravity**, the point at which the weight of a body may be supposed to act, and at which the body may be supported in equilibrium; **central processing unit**, part of a computer that performs logical and arithmetical operations on data; **Central Standard Time**, time reckoned from the 90th to 105th meridians west of Greenwich. [Fr,—L *centrum*—Gr *kentron*, a sharp point.]

centesimal [sen-tes´i-mȧl] *adj* hundredth. [L *centēsimus*—*centum*.]

centi- [sen-ti-] in composition 1/100 of the unit named. [L *centum*, a hundred.]

centigrade [sen´ti-grād] *adj* divided into a hundred degrees, as the *centigrade thermometer* (first constructed by Celsius, 1701–44), in which freezing point (of water) is zero and boiling point (of water) is 100°. *Celsius* is now the preferred term. [L *centum, gradus*, a step.]

centigram [sen´ti-gram] *n* a unit of weight, the hundredth part of a gram. [Fr,—L *centum*, a hundred + **gram(me)**.]

centiliter [sen´ti-lē-tėr] *n* a unit of volume, the hundredth part of a liter, 10 cubic centimeters. [Fr,—L *centum*, a hundred + **liter**.]

centimeter [sen´ti-mē-tėr] *n* a unit of measure, the hundredth part of a meter.—**centimeter-gram-second system**, a system of measurement based on the centimeter as the unit of length, the gram as the unit of mass, and the solar second as the unit of time. [Fr,—L *centum*, a hundred and **meter**.]

centipede [sen´ti-pēd] *n* any of a class (Chilopoda) of long flattened arthropods with a pair of legs for each body segment. [L *centum*, and *pēs, pedis*, a foot.]

cento [sen´to] *n* a literary composition made up of scraps from various sources.—*pl* usually **cen´tos**. [L *cento*, Gr *kentrōn*, patchwork.]

centrifugal [sen-trif´ū-gȧl] *adj* tending away from the center of rotation, as in *centrifugal force*.—*n* **centrifuge** [sen´trifūj] an apparatus that separates liquids, etc. of different density by rotating them at very high speed. [L *centrum*, center, *fugĕre*, to flee from.]

centripetal [sen-trip´et-ȧl] *adj* tending towards the center of rotation by centripetal force. [L *centrum*, center, *petĕre*, to seek.]

century [sen´tū-ri] *n* a period of a hundred years, esp of the Christian era or of the preceding period of human history; a race over a hundred units (as yards).—*n* **centū´rion**, the commander of a hundred Roman soldiers. [L *centuria*—*centum*, hundred.]

cephalic [se-fal´ik] *adj* belonging to the head.—*adj* **ceph´alous**, having a head.—**cephalic index**, the ratio of the breadth to the length of the skull expressed as a percentage. [Gr *kephalē*, head.]

cephalopod [sef´-al-opod] *n* any of a class (Cephalopoda) of marine mollusks characterized by a well-developed head and eyes and a ring of sucker-bearing tentacles which include the squids, octopuses, and cuttlefishes. [Gr *kephalē*, head, *pous*, gen *podos*, foot.]

Cepheid [sē´fē-id] *n* any of a class of stars whose characteristic is that over a short period (in most cases less than three weeks) they dim and brighten again; they are used in the estimation of distances in outer space. [Gr.]

ceraceous. *See* **cere**.

ceramic [se-ram´ik] *adj* of earthenware, porcelain, or brick, or any product manufactured by the firing at a high temperature of a nonmetalic mineral (as clay).—*n* (in *pl*; treated as *sing*) the art or process of making ceramic articles; articles made of ceramic. [Gr *keramos*, potter's earth.]

cere [sēr] *vt* (*obs*) to cover with wax; to wrap in or as if in a cerecloth.—*adj* **cērā´ceous** [-shus], of or like wax.—*ns* **cere´cloth**, a cloth dipped in melted wax in which to wrap a dead body; **cere´ment**, a cere´cloth; a shroud; **cerumen**, the yellow waxy secretion from the glands of the outer ear, earwax. [L *cēra*, wax.]

cereal See **Ceres**.

cerebrum [ser´e-brum] *n* the front and larger part of the brain of vertebrates; the dominant part of the brain in man, associated with intellectual function; the brain as a whole.—*n* **cerebell´um**, the section of the brain behind and below the cerebrum whose function is coordination of voluntary movements.—*adj* **cer´ebral**, pertaining to the cerebrum.—*n* **cerebrā´tion**, thinking.—*adjs* **cer´ebrospīn´al**, of the brain and the spinal cord; **cer´ebrovas´cular**, relating to the brain and its blood vessels. [L *cerebrum*, the brain]

ceremony [ser´e-mo-ni] *n* a sacred rite; behavior that follows rigid etiquette; pomp or state.—*adj* **ceremō´nial**, relating to ceremony.—*n* outward form; a system of ceremonies.—*adv* **ceremō´nially**.—*adj* **ceremō´nious**, full of ceremony; precise.—*adv* **ceremō´niously**.—**stand on ceremony**, to insist on formality. [Fr,—L *caerimōnia*, sanctity.]

Ceres [sē-rēz] *n* the Roman goddess of tillage and corn.—*adj* **cē´real**, relating to corn or edible grain.—*n* (usu. *pl*) a grain used as food, as wheat, barley, etc.; a food prepared from this. [L prob from *creāre*, create.]

cerise [ser-ēz, also -ēs´] *n, adj* a light and clear red. [Fr, 'cherry'.]

cerium [sē´ri-ụm] *n* a rare metallic element (symbol Ce; at wt 140.1 at no 58). [Named from planet *Ceres* discovered about the same time.]

certain [sûr´tin, -tn] *adj* sure, convinced; unerring; sure to happen; regular, inevitable; sure (to do); indisputable; some; one.—*adv* **cer´tainly**.—*ns* **cer´tainty**, that which is undoubted; that which is inevitable; assurance of a truth or of a fact; **cer´titude**, freedom from doubt.—**for certain**, without doubt. [OFr,—L *certus*—*cernĕre*, to decide.]

certificate [sėr-tif´i-kȧt] *n* a written declaration of some fact; a testimonial of character.—*vt* to give a certificate to.—*n* **certificā´tion**.—*vt* **cer´tify**, to declare formally or in writing, and usu. with authority; to inform;—*pr p* **cer´tifying**; *pt p* **cer´tified**.—**certified public accountant**, a public accountant certified as passing a State examination. [Fr *certificat*—L *certificāre*—*certus*, certain, *facĕre*, to make.]

cerulean [si-rōō´li-ȧn] *adj* sky blue. [L *caeruleus*.]

ceruse [sē´roos, or si-roos´] *n* white lead used as a pigment. [Fr,—L *cērussa*, conn with *cēra*, wax.]

cervical [sûr´vi-kȧl, sėr-vī´kȧl] *adj* belonging to the neck; belonging to the neck of the womb. [Fr,—L *cervix, cervicis*, the neck.]

cervine [sûr´vīn] *adj* relating to deer; like deer. [L *cervīnus*—*cervus*, a stag.]

cesarean, cesarian section [sē-zar´i-an] *n* the delivery of a child by cutting through the walls of the abdomen, as is (improbably) said to have been the case with Julius Caesar or one of his ancestors.

cesium, caesium [sēz´i-ụm] *n* a metallic element (symbol Cs; at wt 132.9, at no 55); used in form of compounds or alloys in photoelectric cells. [L *caesius*, bluish grey.]

cessation [ses-ā´sh(o̐)n] *n* a ceasing or stopping; a pause. [Fr,—L *cessātiō, -ōnis—cessāre*. See **cease**.]
cession [sesh´(o̐)n] *n* a yielding up, a surrender. [Fr,—L *cessiō, -ōnis—cedere*. See **cede**.]
cesspool [ses´pōōl] *n* a pool or pit for collecting filthy water. [Origin obscure.]
cestus [ses´tus] *n* a girdle, esp one worn by a bride. [L,—Gr *kestos*.]
cesura *See* **caesura**.
cetacean [se-tā´shi-an] *adj* of an order (Cetacea) of aquatic mammals, mostly marine, including the whales, dolphins, porpoises, etc. with fishlike bodies and paddle-shaped forelimbs.—*n* **cetā´cean**.—*adj* **cetā´ceous**. [L,—Gr *kētos*, any sea-monster.]
cetane [sē´tān] *n* a paraffin hydrocarbon found in petroleum.—**cetane number**, a measure of the ignition quality of diesel engine fuel.
cha-cha(-cha) [chä-chä (-chä)] *n* a Latin American ballroom dance.
chafe [chāf] *vt* to make hot by rubbing; to fret or wear by rubbing; to cause to fret or rage.—*vt* to fret or rage.—*n* heat; anger.—*n* **chaf´ing dish**, a dish or vessel in which anything is heated by hot coals, etc.; a dish for cooking on the table. [Fr *chauffer*—L *calefacĕre—calēre*, to be hot, *facĕre*, to make.]
chafer [chāf´ėr] *n* any of various large beetles, esp of family Scarabaeidae. [OE *cefer*.]
chaff [chäf] *n* the husks of grain as threshed or winnowed; cut hay and straw; worthless matter; light banter.—*vt* to banter. [OE *ceaf*.]
chaffer [chaf´ėr] *vi* to bargain; to haggle about the price.—*n* **chaff´erer**. [ME *chapfare*, a bargain, from OE *cēap*, price, barter, *faru*, way.]
chaffinch [chaf´inch, -sh] *n* a European songbird (*Fringilla coelebs*) of the finch family. [Said to delight in *chaff*.]
Chagas' disease [shäg´as] *n* tropical American disease caused by a parasite (*Trypanosoma cruzi*). [Carlos *Chagas*, Brazilian physician.]
chagrin [shä-grin´] *n* that which wears or gnaws the mind; vexation; annoyance.—*vt* to vex or annoy. [Fr *chagrin*, shagreen, rough skin, ill-humor.]
chain [chān] *n* a series of links or rings passing through one another; any continuous series; anything that binds; a measure of 100 links used in surveying; a unit of length equal to 66 feet; (*pl*) fetters, bonds, confinement; a series of related things or events; a group of stores, etc. owned by a company.—*vt* to fasten; to fetter.—*ns* **chain gang**, a gang of convicts chained together, as when working; **chain´mail**, armor made of iron links; **chain reaction**, chemical, atomic, or other process in which each reaction is in turn the stimulus of a similar reaction, eg ordinary combustion, or nuclear fission; **chain´-smoker**, a nonstop smoker; **chain´ stitch**, an ornamental stitch resembling the links of a chain. [Fr *chaîne*—L *catēna*.]
chair [chār] *n* a moveable seat for one, with a back to it; the seat or office of one in authority; a chairman.—*vt* to install in office; to preside as chairman of.—*ns* **chair´ lift**, a set of seats suspended from overhead wires for taking sightseers or skiers up a hill; **chair´man, -woman, -person**, one who takes the chair, or presides at a meeting; **chair´manship**. [Fr *chaire*—L—Gr *kathedra*.]
chaise [shāz] *n* a light open carriage for one or more persons.—**chaise longue, chaise lounge**, a couchlike chair with a long seat. [Fr, from *chaire*. See **chair**.]
chalcedony [kal-sed´ō-ni, or kal´-] *n* a kind of quartz with the luster of wax, generally pale blue or gray in color. [Gr *chalkēdōn*, possibly from *Chalcedon*, in Asia Minor.]
chalet [shal´ā] *n* a summer hut used by Swiss herdsmen in the Alps; any similar building. [Fr.]
chalice [chal´is] *n* a cup or bowl; a communion cup; the cup-shaped interior of a flower. [Fr *calice*—L *calix, calisis*; cf Gr *kylix*, a cup.]
chalk [chök] *n* a soft limestone, composed of calcium carbonate; a substitute for this used for writing on a blackboard.—*vt* to rub or mark with chalk.—*adj* **chalk´y**.—*n* **chalk´iness.—chalk up**, to score, get, achieve; to charge or credit. [OE *cealc*—L *calx*, limestone.]
challenge [chal´enj] *vt* to summon to a combat or contest; to defy; to accuse (*of—with* **with**); to object to; to claim (as due).—*n* a demand for identification; a summons to a contest of any kind; a calling of anyone or anything in question; a difficulty which stimulates interest or effort.—*n* **chall´enger**. [OFr *chalenge*, a dispute, a claim—L *calumnia*, a false accusation.]
chalybeate [ka-lib´e-āt] *adj* containing iron.—*n* a water or medicine containing iron. [Gr *chalyps*, gen *chalybos*, steel, so called from the *Chalybes*, a nation famous for steel.]
cham [kam] *n See* **khan**.
chamber [chām´bėr] *n* a room, esp a bedroom; the place where an assembly meets; a legislative or deliberative assembly; a compartment; the back end of the bore of a gun; (*pl*) a judge's office.—*vi* to be wanton.—*adj* **cham´bered**.—*ns* **cham´bermaid**, a female servant in charge of bedrooms; **cham´ber mu´sic**, music for performance by a small group, as a string quartet.—**chamber of commerce**, an association formed in a town or district to promote the interests of local commerce. [Fr *chambre*—L *camera*—Gr *kamara*, a vault.]
chamberlain [chām´bėr-lin] *n* an officer in charge of the private apartments of a king or nobleman; (*Brit*) the treasurer of a corporation. [OFr *chambrelenc*; OHG *chamerling*—L *camera*, a chamber, and affix *-ling* or *-lenc*.]
chameleon [ka-mēl´yȯn, or ē-ȯn] *n* any of various American lizards (genus *Anolis*) capable of changing their color; an inconstant person. [L *chamaeleon*—Gr *chamaileōn—chamai* (=L *humi*), on the ground (ie dwarf), and *leōn*, a lion.]
chamfer [cham´fėr, or sham´] *n* a bevel or slope; a groove, channel, or furrow.—*vt* to groove or bevel. [Fr *chanfrein*—OFr *chanfraindre*.]
chamois [sham´wä] *n* a small Alpine antelope (*Rupicapra rupicapra*) of Europe and the Caucasus; **chamm´y, shamm´y** [sham´i] a soft pliable leather made from its skin; any material resembling this. [Fr, perh from Romansh.]
chamomile, camomile [kam´o-mīl] *n* any of a genus (*Anthemis*) of plants, or their dried flowers, used in medicine, affording a bitter stomachic and tonic. [Fr,—L—Gr *chamaimēlon*, lit earthapple, from the apple-like smell of the blossoms—*chamai*, on the ground, *mēlon*, an apple.]
champ[1] [champ] *vti* to make a snapping noise with the jaws in chewing. [Older form *cham*, most prob from Scand]
champ[2] [champ] *n* (*slang*) a champion.
champagne [sham´pān´] *n* a white sparkling wine from *Champagne* in France.
champaign [sham-pān´] *n* open, level country. [A doublet of **campaign**, from OFr *champaigne*—L *campānia*, a plain.]
champion [cham´pi-ȯn] *n* one who fights in single combat for himself or for another; one who defends a cause; in games, a competitor who has excelled all others.—*adj* firstclass.—*vt* to defend, to support.—*n* **cham´pionship**. [Fr,—Low L *campiō, -ōnis*—L *campus*, a plain, a place for games.]
chance [chäns] *n* that which falls out or happens without assignable cause; an unexpected event; risk; opportunity; possibility; probability; a ticket in a lottery.—*vt* to risk.—*vi* to happen.—*adj* happening accidentally, without assignable cause, without design.—*adj* **chanc´y**, lucky; risky, uncertain.—**by chance**, accidentally; **chance on** (or **upon**), to find or meet by chance; (**the**) **chances are**, the likelihood is. [OFr *cheance*—Low L *cadentia*—L *cadĕre*, to fall.]
chancel [chän´sl] *n* the part of the church around the altar, for the clergy and the choir. [OFr,—L *cancelli*, lattice.]
chancellery, chancellory [chän´sė-lė-ri] *n* office attached to embassy; the office or staff of an embassy or consulate;—*pl* **-ies**. [Same as next.]
chancellor [chän´sel-ȯr] *n* a high government official, as, in certain countries, a prime minister; in some universities, the president or other executive officer; a chief judge of a court of chancery or equity in some States; any of several church officials.—*n* **chan´cellorship**. [Fr *chancelier*—Low L *cancellārius*, orig an officer who had charge of records, and stood near the *cancelli* (L), the crossbars that surrounded the judgement-seat.]
chance-medley [chäns´-med-li] *n* unintentional homicide in which the killer is not entirely without blame; action with an element of chance. [OFr *chance medlée*, mingled chance.]
chancery [chän´sėr-i] *n* a court of equity; an office of public archives; a chancellery. [Fr *chanellerie*.]
chandelier [shan-dė-lēr´] *n* a frame with branches for holding lights.—*n* **chandler** [chand´lėr] a candle maker; a dealer in candles; a dealer retailing supplies of a specified kind (*a yacht chandler*). [Fr,—Low L *candelāria*, a candlestick.—L *candēla*, a candle.]
change [chānj] *vt* to alter or make different; to make to pass from one state (into another); to put, give, take, put on, in place of another or others; to exchange; to give or get smaller coin for.—*vi* to suffer alteration, become different; to put on different clothes; to leave one station, train, etc., and take one's place in another.—*n* a substitution; the act of changing; alteration or variation of any kind; variety; small coins, esp those given to adjust a payment; an exchange.—*adj* **change´able**, subject or prone to change; fickle; inconstant.—*adv* **change´ably**.—*ns* **changeabili´ity, change´ableness**, fickleness; power of being changed.—*adj* **change´ful**—*adv* **change´fully**.—*n* **change´fulness**.—*adj* **change´less**, unchanging; constant.—*n* **change´ling**, a child secretly left in place of another.—**change of life**, menopause; **change off**, to take turns. [Fr *changer*—Late L *cambiāre*—L *cambīre*, to barter.]
channel [chan´l] *n* the bed or the deeper part of a river, harbor, etc.; a body of water joining two larger ones; a navigable passage; (*pl*) an official means of communication; a path for information in a computer; a narrow range or group of frequencies, part of a frequency band, assigned to a particular station so that it may transmit radio or television programmes without interference from other transmissions.—*vt* to make a channel; to furrow; to direct (into a particular course); to send through a channel. [OFr *chanel, canel*—L *canālis*, a canal.]
chant [chänt] *vti* to sing; to celebrate in song; to recite in a singing manner.—*n* song; a kind of sacred music in which a number of syllables are recited to one tone; a manner of singing or speaking in a musical monotone.—*ns* **chànt´er**, a singer; a precentor; the tenor or treble pipe of a bagpipe, on which the melody is played; **chant´ry**, an endowment, or chapel, for the chanting of masses. [Fr *chanter*—L *cantāre—canĕre*, to sing.]
chanticleer [chant´i-klēr] *n* a rooster. [From the name of the cock in the old beast epic of Reynard the Fox. O Fr *chanter*, to sing, *cler*, clear.]
Chanuka, Channuka or Hanuka [hä´nu-kȧ] *n* (*Judaism*) the Feast of Lights, an eight-day holiday in December memorializing the successful rebellion against Greco-Syrian despots and the rededication of the Temple. [Heb.]
chaos [kā´os] *n* disorder; the state of matter before it was reduced to order by the Creator.—*adj* **chaot´ic**, confused.—*adv* **chaot´ically**. [L,—Gr, the first unformed state of the universe.]

chap[1] [chap] *vti* to crack open, split, roughen, the skin in cold weather.—*n* a chapped place in the skin. [ME *chappen*; cog with Du and Ger *kappen*.]
chap[2] [chap] *n* (*inf*) a fellow [from **chapman**.]
chap[3] [chap] *n* (*pl*) the mouth and lower cheeks.—*adj* **chap´fall´en**, having the lower jaw hanging loosely; depressed. [Northern Eng and Scot *chaft*; ON *kjaptr*, the jaw.]
chapbook [chap´book] *n* a small book containing poems, stories, tales, etc. [*Chap*man + **book**.]
chapel [chap´ėl] *n* a building for Christian worship, not so large as a church; a subordinate or private place of worship; a division of a church with its own altar; a room for services in a funeral home; an association of printers in a printing office. [OFr *capele*—Low L *cappella*, dim of *cappa*, a cloak or cope.]
chaperon, chaperone [shap´e-rōn] *n* a lady under whose care a girl appears in society; one delegated to ensure proper behavior.—*vt* to act as chaperon to. [Fr, a large hood—*chappe*, a hooded cloak—Low L *cappa*, a cloak.]
chapiter [chap´i-tėr] *n* the capital of a column. [Fr *chapitre*—L *caput*, the head.]
chaplain [chap´lin] *n* a clergyman attached to a chapel; a clergyman serving in a religious capacity with the armed forces, or in a prison, hospital, etc.—*n* **chap´laincy**. [OFr *chapelain*—Low L *cappellānus*—*cappella*. See **chapel**.]
chaplet [chap´let] *n* a garland or wreath for the head; a string of beads used in counting prayers; a small molding carved with small ornaments. [OFr *chapelet*—*chape*, a head-dress.]
chapman [chap´man] *n* (*arch*) one who buys or sells;—*pl* **chapmen**. [OE *cēap-mann*—*cēap*, price, barter, *mann*, man. See **cheap**.]
chaps [chaps] *npl* leather trousers without a seat, worn over ordinary trousers by cowboys to protect their legs. [Mex Sp.]
chapter [chap´tėr] *n* a main division of a book; a subject or category generally; an assembly of the canons of a cathedral or the members of a religious or military order; an organized branch of some society or fraternity.—*n* **chap´ter house**, a house or room where a chapter meets; the residence of a local chapter of a fraternity or sorority. [O Fr *chapitre*—L *capitum*, dim of *caput*, the head.]
char[1] [chär] *n* any of a genus (*Salvelinus*) of small trouts. [Prob Celt; cf Gael *ceara*, red, blood-colored.]
char[2] [chär] *vt* to reduce to charcoal or carbon by burning.—*vti* to scorch;—*pr p* **charr´ing**; *pt p* **charred**. [Origin obscure.]
charabanc [shar´-a-bang] *n* a sightseeing bus. [Fr *char à bancs*, carriage with benches.]
character [kar´ak-tėr] *n* a letter or distinctive mark; writing generally, handwriting; a secret cipher; any essential feature or peculiarity; the aggregate of peculiar qualities which constitutes personal or national individuality; a formal statement of such qualities; a person of remarkable individuality; a personality as created in a play or novel; (*inf*) an eccentric person.—*vt* **char´acterize**, to describe by (its or his) peculiar qualities; to describe (as); to distinguish, be characteristic of.—*ns* **characteriza´tion; characteris´tic**, that which marks or constitutes the character; the integral part of a logarithm.—*adj* **characteris´tic**, marking or constituting the peculiar nature.—*adv* **characteris´tically**.—*n* **character witness**, one that gives evidence concerning the reputation and conduct of a party to a legal action.—*adv* **in character**, in keeping with the person's usual conduct or attitudes; **out of character**, unlike what one would expect from the person concerned. [Fr *caractère*—L *character*—Gr *charaktēr, charassein*, to engrave.]
charade [shar-äd´] *n* an acted riddle in which the syllables of the word proposed and the whole word are represented in successive scenes. [Fr.]
charcoal [chär´kōl] *n* the carbonaceous residue from the partial combustion of wood or animal matter; a pencil of fine charcoal used in drawing; a charcoal drawing. [**char** (2) + **coal**.]
charge [chärj] *vt* to load, to fill (with); to burden; to lay a task, trust upon (one); to exhort; to accuse; to ask as the price; to attack at a rush.—*vi* to make an onset.—*n* that which is laid on; cost or price; the load of powder, etc., for a gun; care, custody; the object of care; an accumulation of electricity; command; exhortation; accusation; attack or onset; (*pl*) expenses.—*adj* **charge´able**, liable to be charged; blamable.—*n* **charg´er**, a large flat dish or platter; a war-horse; an instrument or device for charging.—**charge account**, an account in which goods obtained are entered to be paid for later. [Fr *charger*—Low L *carricāre*, to load—L *carrus*, a wagon.]
chargé d'affaires [shär´zhā-dä-fer´] *n* a minor diplomat; an ambassador's deputy. [Fr]
chariness *See* **chary**.
chariot [char´i-ȯt] *n* a pleasure or state carriage; a car used in ancient warfare or racing.—*n* **charioteer´**, one who drives a chariot. [Fr, dim of *char*, a car.]
charisma [kar-is´mȧ] *n* a spiritual power given by God; personal quality that enables an individual to influence his fellows; a similar quality felt to reside in an office or position.—*adj* **charismat´ic**. [Gr *charis, -itos*, grace.]
charity [char´i-ti] *n* (*NT*) universal love; benevolence; the disposition to think favorably of others, and do them good; almsgiving; a benevolent fund or institution.—*adj* **char´itable**, of or relating to charity; lenient, kindly; liberal to the poor.—*n* **char´itableness**.—*adv* **char´itably**. [Fr *charité*—L *cāritās*—*cārus*, dear.]
charlatan [shär´la-tȧn] *n* a mere talking pretender; a quack.—*n* **char´latanry**. [Fr,—It *ciarlatano*—*ciarlare*, to chatter.]
Charlie [chär´lē] *n* word used in communication for the letter *c*.
charlock [chär´lok] *n* wild mustard (*Brassica kaber*), a common weed with yellow flowers. [OE *cerlic*.]
charlotte [shär´lot] *n* a molded dessert consisting of fruit, whipped cream or custard enclosed by strips of bread, ladyfingers, or biscuits. [From the name *Charlotte*.]
charm [chärm] *n* a spell; something thought to possess occult power, as words in metrical form or an amulet or trinket; attractiveness; personal attractions; (*phys*) the quantum number used to account for the unusual behavior of certain elementary particles.—*vt* to influence by a charm; to enchant; to delight.—*adj* **charmed**, protected, as by a spell; delighted.—*n* **charm´er**.—*adv* **charm´ingly**. [Fr *charme*—L *carmen*, a song.]
charnel [chär´nėl] *n* a place where the bones thrown up by gravediggers are put.—Also **charnel house**. [OFr *charnel*—L *carnālis*—*carō, carnis*, flesh.]
chart [chärt] *n* a map, esp for use in navigation; an information sheet with tables, graphs, etc.; a table, graph, etc.—*vt* to make a chart of; to plan (a course of action). [OFr *charte*—L *c(h)arta*; see **card** (1).]
charter [chärt´ėr] *n* any formal writing conferring or confirming titles, rights, or privileges, or the like, esp one granted by the sovereign or government; a deed or conveyance; privilege.—*vt* to establish by charter; to let or hire, as a ship, on contract.—*adj* hired, as *charter plane*; made in a hired airplane, as *charter flight*. [O Fr *chartre*—L *c(h)artula*, dim of *c(h)arta*; see **card** (1).]
Chartism [chärt´izm] *n* a movement in 19th century England in support of the reforms demanded by the People's *Charter* of 1838.—*n* **Chart´ist**.
chartreuse [shär-trœz´] *n* a yellowish green liqueur first manufactured by the monks of the monastery of La Grande *Chartreuse*. [See **Carthusian**.]
chary [chār´i] *adj* sparing (of, in); unwilling to risk (*with* **of**); cautious.—*adv* **char´ily**.—*n* **char´iness**. [OE *cearig*—*cearu*, care.]
chase[1] [chās] *vt* to pursue; to hunt; to drive away.—*n* pursuit; a hunting; that which is hunted; an unenclosed game preserve.—*n* **chas´er.—wild-goose chase**, futile pursuit of the unattainable. [OFr *chacier, chasser*—L *captāre*, freq of *capĕre*, to take.]
chase[2] [chās] *vt* to decorate (metal) with engraving.—*n* **chas´er**. [Short for **enchase**.]
chase[3] [chās] *n* a frame for holding printing types. [Fr *châsse*, a shrine, a setting—L *capsa*, a chest. See **case** (1).]
chasm [kazm] *n* a yawning or gaping hollow; a gap or opening; a void space. [Gr *chasma*, from *chainein* (pr indic *chaskō*), to gape.]
chassé [shas´ā] *n* a gliding step in dancing. [Fr]
chassis [chas´ē, shas´ē] *n* the frame of an automobile or airplane; the working parts of a radio; the recoiling parts of a cannon; the roof, walls, floors, and facing of a building; a frame, as for the parts of a TV set; the assembled frame and parts;—*pl* **chassis** [shas´ez]. [Fr *châssis*, frame.]
chaste [chāst] *adj* modest; virtuous; virgin; pure in taste and style.—*adv* **chaste´ly**.—*ns* **chaste´ness; chăs´tity**, abstention from unlawful sexual activity; sexual purity; virginity; refinement of style. [OFr *chaste*—L *castus*, pure.]
chasten [chās´n] *vt* to free from faults by punishing—hence, to punish or correct. [**chaste**, + suffix *-en*.]
chastise [chas´tīz´] *vt* to punish for the purpose of correction; to reduce to order or to obedience.—*n* **chas´tisement**. [Related to *chasten*; exact history of word unknown.]
chasuble [chaz´- or chas´ū-bl] *n* a sleeveless vestment worn by the priest celebrating Mass. [Fr,—Low L *casubula*—L *casula*, dim of *casa*, a hut.]
chat [chat] *vi* to talk easily or familiarly;—*pr p* **chatt´ing**; *pt p* **chatt´ed**.—*n* familiar, easy talk.—*adj* **chatt´y**, inclined to talk much and in familiar style. [Short for **chatter**.]
château [shä´tō] *n* a castle, a great country-seat; a vineyard estate around a castle, esp in Bordeaux, France (common in names of wines);—*pl* **châ´teaux** [-tōz].—*ns* **chatelain** [shat´e-lā], a castellan; **chat´elaine** [-len], a female castellan; an ornamental clasp or chain. [OFr *chastel* (Fr *château*)—L *castellum*, dim of *castrum*, a fort.]
chattel [chat´ėl] *n* any kind of property that is not freehold. [OFr *chatel*—Low L *captāle*—L *capitāle*, etc., property, goods.]
chatter [chat´ėr] *vi* to talk idly or rapidly; (of birds) to utter a succession of rapid short notes; to sound as the teeth when one shivers.—*n* idle talk.—*ns* **chatt´erbox**, one who chatters or talks incessantly; **chatt´erer**. [From the sound.]
Chaucerian [chö-sē´ri-ȧn] *adj* pertaining to, or like, *Chaucer* (1345–1400).
chauffeur [shō´fėr, shō-fœr´] *n* one employed to drive a private automobile for someone else. [Fr]
chauvinism [shō´vin-izm] *n* excessive national pride and contempt for other countries; excessive attachment to any group, cause, etc.—*n* **chau´vinist**.—*adj* **chauvinist´ic**.—See also **male chauvinist pig**. [From Nicolas *Chauvin*, ardent Napoleonic veteran.]
chaw [chö] *vt* (*dial*) to chew, as tobacco. [By-form of **chew**.]
cheap [chēp] *adj* low in price; charging low prices; of small value; paltry; inferior.—*vti* **cheap´en**, to make or become cheaper.—*adv* **cheap´ly**.—*ns* **cheap´ness; cheap´skate** (*slang*) a stingy person.—**cheap shot** (*slang*) an uncalled-for, rough or mean act or remark. [Originally *good cheap*, ie a good bargain; OE *cēap*, price, barter; OE *cēapian*, ON *kaupa*, Ger *kaufen*, to buy—all from L *caupo*, a huckster.]
cheat [chēt] *vt* to deceive; to defraud.—*vi* to practice deceit.—*n* a fraud; one who cheats.—*n* **cheat´er**. [ME *cheten*, a form of *escheten*, to escheat.]

check[1] [chek] *vt* to bring to a stand; to restrain or hinder; to rebuke; to scrutinize; to verify; to mark with a pattern of squares.—*n* in chess, a threat to the king; anything that checks; a sudden stop or repulse; a mark put against items in a list; a token or counter; a pattern of small squares.—*ns* **check´er**, one that checks; an employee who checks out purchases in a self-service store; **check´mate**, in chess, a position from which the king cannot escape; disaster that cannot be retrieved.—*vt* in chess, to make a move that causes checkmate; to frustrate.—*ns* **check off**, the deduction of union dues from an employee's paycheck by the employer; **check´out**, the desk at a self-service store, etc., where one pays for goods.—**hold in check**, to restrain, keep back. [OFr *eschec, eschac*, through Low L and Ar from Pers *shāh*, king—**checkmate** being OFr *eschec mat*—Ar *shāh māt(a), 'king is dead'*.]

check[2] [chek] *n* a money order to a bank.—*vt* to mark in squares of different colors; to diversify.—*n* **checkbook**, a book containing blank checks to be drawn on a bank.—*adj* **check´ered**, variegated, like a chessboard; varying in character; eventful, with alternations of good and bad fortune. [A variant of **check**.]

checker [chek´er] (*arch*) chessboard.

checkers [chek´ėrz] *n pl* a board game for two played with 12 thick disks called checkers or men.—*n* **checkerboard**, a board with 64 squares of alternating color for playing checkers.

cheddar [ched´ȧr] *n* a kind of cheese first made at *Cheddar* in Somersetshire, England.

cheek [chēk] *n* the side of the face below the eye; (*inf*) effrontery, impudence.—*adj* **cheek´y**, insolent, saucy.—**cheek by jowl**, side by side. [OE *cēce*, jaw.]

cheep [chēp] *vi* to chirp, as a young bird.—*n* any chirping sound. [From the sound.]

cheer [chēr] *n* disposition, frame of mind; joy; a shout of approval or welcome; entertainment; fare, food.—*vt* to comfort; to encourage; to applaud.—*adjs* **cheer´ful**, in good spirits; lively; ungrudging; **cheer´y**, cheerful, lively, merry.—*advs* **cheer´fully; cheer´ily**.—*ns* **cheer´fulness; cheer´iness**.—*adj* **cheer´less**, without comfort, gloomy.—*n* **cheer´lessness**. [OFr *chiere*, the face—Low L *cara*, the face.]

cheese [chēz] *n* the curd of milk coagulated and often pressed into a hard mass.—*ns* **cheese´cake**, a pastry shell filled with a mixture of cheese, sugar, eggs, etc.; a cake made with cottage or cream cheese; (*slang*) photographic display of a figure, esp the legs of a pretty girl; **cheese´par´ing**, miserly economy.—*adj* miserly, niggardly.—*adj* **chees´y**, having the consistency or odor of cheese; containing cheese; (*slang*) shabby, cheap. [OE *cēse, cȳse*, curdled milk—L *cāseus*.]

cheetah [chē´tä] *n* a large spotted cat (*Acinonyx jubatus*) of Africa, like the leopard, used in hunting. [Hindustani *chītā*.]

chef [shef] *n* a master cook (**chef de cuisine** [dė kwē-zēn´].—*n* **chef d'œuvre** [shā dœvr], masterpiece, esp in art and literature;—*pl* **chefs d'œuvre** (pron as *sing*). [Fr See **chief**.]

chemise [she-mēz´] *n* a woman's short, one-piece undergarment; a loose-fitting dress hanging straight from the shoulders. [Fr *chemise*—Low L *camisia*, a nightgown, surplice.]

chemistry [kem´is-tri] *n* the science that treats of the properties of substances both elementary and compound, and of the laws of their combination and action one upon another.—*adjs* **chem´ical** (**chem´ico-, chem´o-**, in compound words).—*adv* **chem´ically**. *n pl* **chem´icals**, substances used in chemical processes.—*n* **chem´ist**, one skilled in chemistry;—**chemical engineering**, design, construction, and operation of chemical plant and works, esp in industrial chemistry; **chemical warfare**, warfare involving the use of irritating or asphyxiating gases, oil, flames, etc. [From **alchemy**.]

chemotherapy [kem-ō-ther´ȧ-pi] *n* treatment or control of a mental illness or a disease by means of a chemical compound. [**chemo-** (see **chemistry**), + **therapy**.]

chemurgy [kem´ûr-ji] *n* the application of chemistry to agriculture, esp the use of farm products to provide raw organic materials for industrial applications.—*adj* **chemur´gic**. [Coined in USA in 1934.]

chenille [she-nēl´] *n* a wool, cotton, silk, or rayon yarn with a protruding pile; a fabric knitted or woven with this yarn. [Fr, a caterpillar.]

cheongsam [chöng´säm´] *n* a tight dress with a mandarin collar and slits at each side of the skirt. [Chin]

cherish [cher´ish] *vt* to protect and treat with affection; to entertain in the mind, hold in the heart, to nurse. [Fr *chérir, chérissant*—*cher*, dear—L *cārus*.]

Cherokee [cher´ō-kē] *n* a member of an Amerindian people originally of Tennessee and N Carolina; the Iroquoian language of this people.

cheroot [she-rōōt´] *n* a cigar cut square at each end. [Fr *cheroute*—Tamil (qv) *shuruttu*, roll.]

cherry [cher´i] *n* any of several species of trees of the same genus (*Prunus*) as the plum; the small fruit, often bright red, which they bear; a variable color, averaging a moderate red. [OE *ciris*—L *cerasus*—Gr *kerasos*, a cherry-tree.]

chert [chûrt] *n* any impure flintlike rock usu. dark in color, occurring in nodules in chalcedony. [Ety doubtful.]

cherub [cher´ŭb] *n* a winged creature with human face; a celestial spirit; a beautiful child;—*pl* **cher´ubs, cher´ubim** [(-y)ōō-bim], **cher´ubims**.—*adjs* **cheru´bic** [-ōō´bik], **-al.** [Heb *k'rūb*, pl *k'rūbīm*.]

chess [ches] *n* a game played by two persons with figures or 'men', which are moved on a checkerboard;—*n pl* **chess´men**, pieces used in chess. [Fr *échecs*; It *scacchi*; Ger *schach*. Orig from Pers *shāh*, a king.]

chest [chest] *n* a large strong box; a treasury; the part of the body between the neck and the abdomen, the thorax.—**chest of drawers**, a set of drawers fitted in a single piece of furniture. [OE *cyst*; Scot *kist*—L *cista*.]

chesterfield [chest´ėr-fēld] *n* a long overcoat; a heavily padded sofa. [A 19th century Lord *Chesterfield*.]

chestnut [ches´nut] *n* any of a genus (*Castanea*) of trees or shrubs of the beech family, esp an American tree (*C. dentata*); the edible nut of a chestnut; a horse chestnut; a chestnut-colored horse which is a shade of pure or reddish brown; (*slang*) a stale joke.—*adj* of chestnut color, grayish to reddish brown.—**pull the chestnuts out of the fire**, to take control and rescue someone from a difficult situation. [OFr *chastaigne*—L *castanea*.]

cheval-de-frise [she-val´-de-frēz] *n* a spiky defensive structure, used esp to stop cavalry (often in *pl* form);—*pl* **chevaux-de-frise** [she-vō´-]. [Fr,—*cheval*, horse, *de*, of, *Frise*, Friesland.]

cheval glass [shė-val´ gläs] *n* a large glass or mirror supported on a frame. [Fr *cheval*, horse, stand.]

chevalier [shev-a-lēr´] *n* a cavalier; a knight; a gallant. [Fr,—*cheval*—L *caballus*, a horse.]

cheviot [shev´ē-ot] *n* a breed of hardy sheep that are a source of quality mutton; a cloth made from their wool. [*Cheviot* hills, England, Scotland.]

chevron [shev´ròn] *n* a rafter; the V-shaped bar on the sleeve of a uniform, showing rank. [Fr *chevron*, a rafter—L *capreolus*, dim of *caper*, a goat.]

chew [choo] *vt* to bruise and grind with the teeth, to masticate.—*n* action of chewing; a quid of tobacco.—*n* **chew´ing gum**, a preparation made from chicle, sweetened and flavored.—**chew out** (*slang*) to reprimand; **chew over** (*inf*) to meditate on. [OE *cēowan*; Ger *kauen*.]

Cheyenne [shī-an´] *n* a member of an Amerindian people of the western plains;—*pl*—**enne,-s**; the Algonquian language of this people.

chez [shā] *prep* at the home of. [Fr]

chi [kī] *n* 22d letter of the Greek alphabet.

Chianti [kē-an´ti] *n* a wine (usu. red) of Tuscany. [Named from the *Chianti Mts*]

chiaroscuro [kyär-o-skōō´rō] *n* management of light and shade in a picture. [It,—L *clārus*, clear, *obscurus*, dark.]

chic [shēk] *n* style, fashion.—*adj* stylish. [Fr]

chicane [shi-kān´] *vi* to use shifts and tricks.—*vt* to deceive.—*n* (also **chicā´nery**), trickery or artifice, esp in legal proceedings. [Fr *chicane*, sharp practice at law.]

Chicano [chi-kän´ō] *n* a US citizen or inhabitant of Mexican descent;—*pl*—**nos**. [Amer Sp]

chichi [shē-shē] *adj* pretentious; fussy; affected; stylish, self-consciously fashionable.—*n* something that is, or the quality of being, chichi; red tape; fuss. [Fr]

chick [chik] *n* the young of a fowl, esp of the hen; a child, as a term of endearment; (*slang*) a girl or a young woman.—*ns* **chick´en**, a chick; flesh of a fowl; a child; a coward; **chick´en feed** (*slang*) a paltry sum (as in profit or wages).—*adj* **chick´enheart´ed**, timid, cowardly.—*ns* **chick´enpox**, a contagious febrile disease, chiefly of children; **chick´weed**, a low-growing plant (*Stellaria media*) often found as a lawn weed. [OE *cicen*; cf Du *kieken*, Ger *küchlein*.]

chickahominy [chik-ȧ-hom´in-i] *n* member of an Amerindian people of Virginia;—*pl* **-ny, -nies**.

chicle [chik´l, chick´li] *n* the gum of the sapodilla tree. [Sp,—Mexican.]

chicory, chickory [chik´o-ri] *n* a plant (*Cichorium intybus*) with blue flowers, grown for its root and as a salad plant; its dried, ground, roasted root used to adulterate and flavor coffee. [Fr *chicorée*—L *cichorium*—Gr *kichōrion*.]

chide [chīd] *vt* to scold, rebuke, reprove by words;—*pr p* **chīd´ing**; *pt*, **chĭd**, sometimes **chīd´ed**; *pt p* **chĭd, chidd´en**. [OE *cidan*.]

chief [chēf] *adj* head; principal, most important.—*n* the head of a clan or tribe; a leader; the head of a department or business.—*adv* **chief´ly**, in the first place, principally; for the most part.—*ns* **chief´tain**, [-tin], the head of a clan; a leader; **chief´taincy, chief´tainship**.—**chief executive**, a principal executive officer, esp the president of a republic or the governor of a State; **chief justice**, the presiding or principal judge of a court of justice.—**chief of naval operations**, the commanding officer of the US Navy and a member of the Joint Chiefs of Staff; **chief of staff**, the ranking officer of a staff in the armed forces serving as principal adviser to a commander; the commanding officer of the US Army or US Air Force and a member of the Joint Chiefs of Staff; **chief of state**, the formal head of a national state as distinguished from the head of the government. [Fr *chef*—L *caput*, the head.]

chiffon [shē´f•, shif´on] *n* a thin gauzy material—*adj* of chiffon; made fluffy with beaten egg whites (as of a cake).—*n* **chiffonier**, [shif-on-ēr], *n* a high bureau or chest of drawers, often with a mirror. [Fr rag, adornment—*chiffe*, rag.]

chignon [shē´ny•] *n* a fold or roll of hair worn on the back of the head and neck. [Fr]

chigoe [chig´ō] *n* a tropical flea (*Tunga penetrans*) of which the fertile female causes discomfort by burrowing under the skin.—*Also* **chigger**, [chig´ėr]. [Fr *chique*.]

chihuahua [chi-wä´-wä] *n* a very small dog with pointed ears. [*Chihuahua* in Mexico.]

chilblain [chil´blān] *n* a painful red swelling, esp on hands and feet, in cold weather. [**chill** + **blain**.]

child [chīld] *n* a very young person; a son or daughter; one connected with a person, place, or state by resemblance or origin (eg *a child of the devil, of the East, of shame*); a youth of gentle birth, esp in ballads, etc. (*arch.*) **childe**;—*pl* **chil´dren**, offspring; descendants; inhabitants.—*ns* **child´bear´ing**, the act of bringing forth children; **child´bed**, the state of a woman brought to bed with child; **child´birth**, parturition; **child´hood**, state of being a child.—*adj* **child´ish**, of or like a child—silly, trifling.—*adv* **child´ishly**.—*n* **child´ishness**.—*adjs* **child´less**, without children; **child´like**, like a child; innocent; trusting—**child's play**, an easy task; **second childhood**, childishness sometimes characterizing old age; **with child**, pregnant. [OE *cild*, pl *cild*, later *cildru, -ra*.]

chiliad [kil´i-ad] *n* a group of 1000; millenium. [Gr *chilioi*, 1000.]

chill [chil] *n* coldness; a cold that causes shivering; anything that damps or disheartens.—*adj* shivering with cold; slightly cold.—*vti* to make or become cold;—*adj* **chill´y**, chill.—*ns* **chill´ness, chill´iness. chill factor**, the combined effect of low temperatures and high winds on exposed skin. [OE *cele, ciele*, cold.]

chili, chille, chilli [chil´i] *n* the pod of some of the capsicums, pungent and stimulant; a thick sauce of meat and chilies.—**chili con carne**, a spiced stew of beef, chilies or chili powder, beans, and often tomatoes. [Mexican.]

chime [chīm] a set of bells or metal tubes, etc. tuned in a scale; the ringing of such bells; a single bell, as in a clock; a definite sequence of bell-like notes; the harmonious sound of bells, etc.; accord; harmony.—*vi* to sound in harmony; to accord or agree.—*vt* to strike, or cause to sound in harmony.—**chime in**, to break into a conversation or discussion esp to express an opinion. [ME *chimbe*, prob OFr *cymbale*—L *cymbalum*, a cymbal.]

chimera, chimaera [kī-mir-à or ki-] *n* in Greek mythology, a fire-breathing she-monster made up of the parts of various animals; **chimera, chimaera**, an impossible fancy; a living organism in which two separate kinds of tissue exist; **chimaera**, any of a family (Chimaeridae) of marine fishes with a tapering tail.—*adjs* **chimer´ic**, of a genetic chimera; **chimer´ical**, fantastically visionary or improbable; given to fantastic schemes. [L,—Gr *chimaira*, a she-goat.]

chimney [chim´ni] *n* a passage for the escape of fumes, smoke, or heated air from a fireplace or furnace; anything of a like shape.—*ns* **chim´ney pot**, a cylindrical pipe at the top of a chimney; **chim´ney piece**, an ornamental shelf over and around the fireplace; **chim´ney sweep, chim´ney sweep´er**, one who sweeps or cleans chimneys. **chimney swift, chimney swallow**, a small sooty-grey bird (*Chaetura pelagica*) that often nests inside an unused chimney. [Fr *cheminée*—L *camīnus*; Gr *kaminos*, a furnace.]

chimpanzee [chim-pan´zē also shim-] *n* an anthropoid ape (*Pan troglodytes*) of equatorial Africa that is smaller, weaker, and more arboreal than the gorilla. (Kongo dial *chimpenzi*.]

chin [chin] *n* the face below the mouth.—*vt* to pull (oneself) up, while hanging by the hands from a bar, until the chin is just above the bar.—*n* and *vi* **chin´wag**, (*slang*) talk. [OE *cin*; Ger *kinn*, Gr *genys*.]

china [chīn´ä] *n* porcelain originally made in China; vitrified ceramic ware; any earthenware, esp dishes used at the table.—*ns* **chin´a-clay**, kaolin; **Chin´aman**, (*offensive*) Chinese; **chin´aware**, tableware made of china; **Chinese´**, a native of China; a person of Chinese descent; (*pl* **Chinese´**); a group of languages of the Sino-Tibetan family that share a single system of writing but may be mutually unintelligible when spoken; mandarin.—*Also adj*—**Chinese lantern**, a paper lantern.

chinchilla [chin-chil´a] *n* a small rodent (*Chincilla laniger*) of S America valued for its soft gray fur; the fur itself. [Sp]

chine [chīn] *n* the spine or backbone; a piece of the backbone and adjoining parts for cooking; a ridge, crest.—*vt* to cut through the backbone of (as in butchery). [OFr *eschine*, prob from OHG *scina*, a pin.]

chink[1] [chingk] *n* a cleft, a narrow opening; a narrow beam of light showing through a chink.—*vt* to close up the chinks in. [ME *chine*, a crack.]

chink[2] [chingk] *n* the clink, as of coins.—*vti* to give forth a clink. [From the sound.]

Chinook [chin-ook´] *n* member of an Amerindian people of Oregon; *-pl* **-nook, -s; chinook**, a warm moist wind that blows down the eastern side of the Rocky Mountains.—*ns* **Chinook´an**, language of the Chinook; **chinook salmon**, a large commercially important salmon (*Oncorhynchus tshawytscha*) of the North Pacific. [*Chinook*, an Amer Indian tribe.]

chintz [chints] *n* glazed cotton printed in several colors.—*adj* **chintzy** (*inf*) cheap, stingy, etc. [Orig pl—Hindustani *chint*, spotted cotton-cloth.]

chip [chip] *vt* to strike small pieces from the surface of;—*pr p* **chipp´ing**; *pt p* **chipped**.—*n* a small piece chipped off; a place where a small piece has been chipped off; a thin slice of food; a games counter; a minute piece of semi-conducting material on which microcircuits can be printed.—*n* **chip´board**, a paperboard made from wastepaper.—**chip in**, to pay part of the cost of something.—**a chip off the old block**, one with the characteristics of his father; **have a chip on one's shoulder**, to be defiant and aggressive; to be ready to take offence; **in the chips**, (*slang*) wealthy. [ME *chippen*, to cut in pieces. Conn with **chop**.]

chipmunk [chip´mungk] *n* any of various small striped semi-terrestial American squirrels (genera *Tamias* and *Eutamias*) [Algonquian.]

Chippendale [chip´ėn-dāl] *adj* applied to a style of furniture made in England in the 18th century, characterized by the use of Chinese and Gothic motifs. [Thomas *Chippendale*.]

Chippewa [chip´ė-wö, or wä] See **Ojibwa**.

chiromancy [kī´rō-man-si] *n* palmistry. [Gr *chier*, the hand, *manteia*, prophecy.]

chiropodist [kī-rop´o-dist] *n* one who practices chiropody; a podiatrist.—*n* **chirop´ody**, the care and treatment of minor ailments of the feet. [Gr *cheir*, hand, and *pous*, gen *podos*, foot.]

chiropractic [kī´rō-prak-tik] *n* method or practice of curing diseases by manipulating joints, esp of the spine;—*n* **chi´ropractor**, one who carries out such treatment. [Gr *cheir*, the hand, *prāktikos*, fit for action.]

chiropteran [kī-rop´tėr-an] *n pl* the order (Chiroptera) of mammals consisting of the bats. [Gr *chier*, the hand, *pteron*, a wing.]

chirp [chûrp] *n* the sharp, thin sound of certain birds and insects.—*vi* to make such a sound; to talk in a lively strain.—*adj* **chirp´y**, lively; merry. [From the sound.]

chisel [chiz´ėl] *n* tool with the end beveled to a cutting edge.—*vt* to cut, carve, etc., with a chisel; (*inf*) to swindle or get by swindling.—*pr p* **chisel(l)ing**, *pt p* **chisel(l)ed**.—*adj* **chis´eled**, cut with a chisel; (*fig*) sharply defined. [OFr *cisel*—L *caedĕre*, to cut.]

chit[1] [chit] *n* a voucher or a sum owed for drink, food, etc.; a brief note; an order or pass.—*Also* **chitt´y**. [Hindustani *chitthī*.]

chit[2] [chit] *n* a child (*slightingly*) a girl. [A contraction of **kitten**.]

chitin [kī´tin] *n* the substance that forms most of the hard parts of crustaceans, insects, and spiders.—*adj* **chi´tinous**. [Fr *chitine*—Gr *chiton*, a tunic.]

chivalry [shiv´ȧl-ri] *n* the usages and qualifications of chevaliers or feudal knights; bravery and courtesy.—*adjs* **chival´ric, chiv´alrous**, pertaining to chivalry; showing the qualities of an ideal knight, generous, courteous, etc.—*adv* **chiv´alrously**. [Fr *chevalerie*—*cheval*—L *caballus*, a horse.]

chive [chīv] *n* a perennial herb (*Allium schoeneprasum*) related to the onion. [Fr *cive*—L *coepa*, an onion.]

chivy, chivvy [chiv´i] *vt* to annoy or tease persistently; to obtain by small maneuvers.

chlorine [klō´rēn, -rin, rīn] *n* a nonmetallic element (symbol Cl; at wt 35.5; at no 17), a yellow green gas used in bleaching, disinfecting, and in industry.—*ns* **chlōr´al**, strongly narcotic substance obtained by the action of chlorine on alcohol; chloral hydrate; **chloral hydrate**, a bitter cystalline drug used as a sedative or in knockout drops; **chlō´rate**, a salt containing the group $C10_3$.—*n* **chlō´ride**, a compound of chlorine with another element or radical.—*vt* **chlō´rinate**, to treat or cause to combine with chlorine or a chlorine compound.—*ns* **chloroform**, [klor´ō-förm[2] or [1]klō´rō-förm], a colorless, volatile liquid used to induce insensibility (also *vt*); **chlō´rophyll**, the ordinary green photosynthetic coloring matter of vegetation; **chlorō´sis**, an iron-deficiency anemia of young girls marked by a greenish color of the skin; a diseased condition of plants marked by yellowing or blanching. [Gr *chlōros*, pale-green.]

chock [chok] *vt* to fasten as with a wedge.—*n* a wedge to keep a cask from rolling; a log.—*adjs* **chock-a-block´, chock´-full, choke´-full**, quite full. [Ety obscure.]

chocolate [chok´ō-lȧt] *n* a paste made of the roasted pounded cacao bean with sugar and flour or similar material; a beverage made by dissolving this paste in boiling water; a small candy with a center (as fondant, etc.) and chocolate coating.—*adj* **chocolate-colored**, dark reddish brown; made of or flavored with chocolate.—*adj* **choc´-olate-box**, pretty-pretty or oversentimental. [Sp *chocolate*; from Mexican *chocólatl*.]

Choctaw [chok´tö] *n* member of an Amerindian people of Mississippi, Alabama, and Louisiana;—*pl* **-taw, -s**; the Muskogean language of the Choctaw people.

choice [chois] *n* act or power of choosing; the thing chosen; alternative; preference; the best (part.—*adj* worthy of being chosen; select. [Fr *choix*—*choisir*; from same Gmc root as **choose**.]

choir [kwīr] *n* a chorus or band of singers, esp those belonging to a church; the part of a church appropriated to the singers; a division of angels.—*n* **choir loft**, a gallery occupied by a church choir. [Fr *chœur*—L *chorus*. See **chorus**.]

choke [chōk] *vt* to interfere with the breathing of; to throttle; to suffocate; to stop or obstruct; to cut off some air from the carburetor of (a gasoline engine) so as to make a richer gasoline mixture.—*vi* to be choked.—*n* the action of choking; the sound of choking; the valve that chokes a carburetor.—*adj* **chok´y**, tending to cause choking; inclined to choke, as with emotion.—*n* **choke´berry**, a shrub (genus *Aronia*) bearing chokeberries; a small berry-like astringent fruit; **chokecherry**, any of several American wild cherries (esp *Prunus virginiana*); **chok´er**, one who chokes; a high collar; a high tight necklace.—**choke back**, to repress; **choke down**, to swallow with difficulty; **choke off**, to bring to an end. [Ety obscure.]

choler [kol´ėr] *n* the bile; anger; irascibility.—*adj* **chol´eric**, irascible, prone to anger; angry. [Fr,—L,—Gr *cholera*—*cholē*, bile.]

cholera [kol´ėr-a] *n* any of several severe, infectious intestinal diseases of man and domestic animals. [Gr *cholera*—*cholē*, bile.]

cholesterol [kȯ-les´tė-rȯl] *n* a crystalline alcohol found esp in animal fats, blood, and bile. [Gr *cholē*, bile, and *stereos*, solid.]

choose [chōōz] *vt* to take (one thing) in preference to another; to select.—*vi* to will or determine, to think, fit;—*pt* **chose**; *ptp* **chos´en**.—*adj* **choos´(e)y**, (*inf*) difficult to please, fastidious.—**I cannot choose but**, I must. [OE *cēosan*, Du *kiesen*.]

chop[1] [chop] *vt* to cut with a sudden blow; to cut into small pieces.—*n* a cut of meat and bone from the rib, loin, or shoulder; a sharp downward blow.—*ns* **chop´-house**, an eating house where chops and steaks are served; **chopp´er**, one that **chops**; (*pl*) (*slang*), teeth; (*inf*) a helicopter.—*adj* **chopp´y**, running in irregular waves, making abrupt starts and stops. [A form of **chap** (1).]

chop[2] [chop] *vi* to change direction; to veer with or as of with the wind.—*pr p* **chopp´ing**; *pt p* **chopped**—**chop logic**, to argue contentiously. [Connection with **chop** (1) is not clear.]

chop[3] [chop] *n* the chap or jaw, generally used in *pl.*—*adj* **chop´-fall´en**, cast down; dejected. [See **chap** (3).]

chopsticks [chop´-stiks] *n* two small sticks held together and used in many Asian countries in eating. [Pidgin Eng *chop-chop*, quick, and **stick**.]

chop suey [chop sōō´ē] *n* a Chinese American dish of stir-fried vegetables and meat or shellfish served with rice. [Chin.]

choral, chorale *See* **chorus**.

chord[1] [körd] *n* (*mus*) three or more notes played together. See also **common**. [From **accord**.]

chord[2] [körd] *n* (*poet*) a string of a musical instrument; (*geom*) a straight line joining any two points on a curve; (*aero*) the straight line joining the leading and the trailing edges of an airfoil. [L *chorda*—Gr *chordē*, a gut string.]

chore [chōr, chör] *n* a household task; an unenjoyable task. [Form of **char** (3).]

chorea [ko-rē´ä] *n* a nervous disorder (as of man or dogs) causing involuntary movements of limbs or face. [L,—Gr *choreia*, dancing.]

choreography [kor-i-og´ra-fi] *n* dancing; the art of arranging dances, esp ballets; the arrangement of a ballet.—*adj* **choreograph´ic**.—*n* **choreog´rapher**. [Gr *choreia*, dancing, *graphē*, description—*graphein*, to write. Cf **chorus**.]

choreology [[kor-ė-ol´ō-jē] *n* the notation of ballet dancing.

chortle [chört´l] *vi* to utter a low deep laugh.—Also *n* [Coined by Lewis Carroll in 1872, perh from *chuckle* and *snort*.]

chorus [kō´rus, kö´] *n* a band of singers and dancers performing together; in Greek plays, a number of persons who commented on the action; that which is sung by a chorus; a refrain; a combined utterance.—*vt* to sing or say together.—*adj* **chōr´al**, pertaining to a chorus or choir.—*n* **chōrale´**, **chōrral´**, a psalm or hymn tune sung to a traditional or composed melody; a choir, chorus.—*adv* **chōr´ally**, in the manner of a chorus.—*adj* **cho´ric**, in the manner of a chorus, esp a Greek chorus.—*n* **chŏr´ister**, a member of a choir. [L,—Gr *choros*, dance.]

chose, chosen *See* **choose**.

chow [chow] *n* (*inf*), food [perhaps Chin.]

chow chow [chow chow] *n* a breed of thick-coated dog with a black tongue and curled tail, originally from China where it was formerly bred for food.—Also **chow**.

chrism [krizm] *n* consecrated or holy oil, used in Greek and Latin churches, esp for baptism, confirmation, and ordination. [OFr *chresme*—Gr *chrisma*, from *chriein*, to anoint.]

Christ [krīst] *n* the Anointed, the Messiah.—*vt* **christen** [kris´n], to baptize in the name of Christ; to give a name to.—*ns* **Christendom** [kris´n-], the part of the world in which Christianity prevails; the whole body of Christians; **Chris´tian** [chȧn], a follower of Christ.—*adj* relating to Christ or His religion.—*vt* **chris´tianize**, to make Christian; to convert to Christianity.—*n* **Christian´ity**, the religion of Christ; the spirit of this religion.—**Christian era**, the era counted from the birth of Christ; **Christian name**, a given name at baptism; loosely, a forname; **Christian Science**, a religion which includes the belief that healing, mental and physical, can be achieved without medicine by means of the patient's Christian faith—founded in 1866 by Mary Baker Eddy. [OE *Crist*—Gr *Christos*—and *chriein*, to anoint.]

Christmas [kris´mas] *n* an annual festival, originally a mass, in memory of the birth of Christ, held on December 25, which is a US national holiday. *n* **Christ´mas cactus** a S American cactus (*Zygocactus truncatus*) with flat stems, short joints, and showy red flowers.—*adj* **Christ´massy, Christmasy**, appropriate to Christmas.—*ns* **Christ´mastide**, the festival season from Christmas Eve till after New Year's Day; **Christmas time**, the season around Christmas; **Christ´mas tree**, a tree, usu. an evergreen, decorated at Christmas; an oil-well control device placed at the top of the well. [**Christ, + mass**.]

Christology [kris-tol´o-ji] *n* that branch of theology which treats of the nature and person of Christ. [Gr *Christos*, Christ, *logos*, a discourse.]

chromatic [krō-mat´ik] *adj* relating to color or colors; (*mus*) proceeding by half tones;—*ns* **chromatic´ity**, the color quality of light depending on hue and saturation (ie excluding brightness), one method of defining it being by its purity and dominant wavelength; **chrōmat´ics**, the science of colors; **chromatog´raphy**, methods of separating substances in a mixture which depend on the fact that different absorbents will take up different constituents of the mixture, that certain solvents will not mix but will be in layers one over the other, etc.—methods which finally present the substances as a **chromat´ogram**, such as a series of visible bands in a verticle tube; **chrōme**, chromium; a chromium pigment; something plated with an alloy of chromium.—*vt* to treat with a chromium compound (as in dying). **chrō´mium**, metallic element (symbol Cr; at wt 52.0; at no 24).—*adj* **chrōm´ic**, relating to or derived from chromium esp with a valence of three.—*ns* **chrō´minance** (TV), difference between any color and a reference color (usu. a white of specified chromaticity) of equal luminance; **chrō´mosome**, any of the microscopic rod-shaped bodies bearing genes. **chrō´mosphere**, the lower part of the atmosphere of the sun which is thousands of miles thick, consisting chiefly of hydrogen gas; a similar part of the atmosphere of any star. [Gr *chrōmatikos-chrōma*, colour.]

chronic [kron´ik, -ȧl] *adj* lasting a long time; of a disease, deep seated or long continued, as opposed to *acute*. [Gr *chronikos—chronos*, time.]

chronicle [kron´i-kl] *n* a record of events in order of time; a history.—*vt* to record.—*n* **chron´icler**, a writer of a chronicle.—*n* **Chronicles** (*Bible*) 13th and 14th books of the Old Testament, which record the geneologies of Adam, Saul's life and David's victory over the Philistines, the reign of Solomon, the Kings of Judea. [OFr *chronique*, through L—Gr *chronika*, annals—*chronos*, time.]

chronobiology [krō´no-bī-ol´ō-ji] *n* branch of biology concerned with recurring rhythms in living organisms.

chronograph [kron´o-gräf] *n* an instrument for taking exact measurements of time, eg a *stop watch*. [Gr *chronos*, time, *graphein*, to write.]

chronology [kron-ol´o-ji] *n* the science of computing time and of dating events; a scheme of time; order in time.—*ns* **chronol´oger, chronol´ogist**.—*adjs* **chronolog´ic, -al**.—*adv* **chronolog´ically**. [Gr *chronos*, time, *logos*, a discourse.]

chronometer [kron-om´ė-tėr] *n* a very accurate form of timekeeper. [Gr *chronos*, time, *metron*, a measure.]

chrysalis [kris´a-lis], **chrysalid** [kris´a-lid], *n* the pupa of a butterfly, enclosed in a cocoon; the cocoon.—*adj* **chrys´alid**. [Gr *chrȳsallis—chrȳsos*, gold.]

chrysanthemum [kris-an´thė-mum] *n* a genus (*Chrysanthemum*) of composite plants including weeds, garden ornamentals, and others grown as sources of medicines and insecticides; the flower head of a garden form. [Gr *chrȳsos*, gold, *anthemon*, flower.]

chrysolite [kris´ō-līt] *n* olivine; a form of asbestos. [Gr *chrȳsos*, gold, *lithos*, stone.]

chrysoprase [kris´o-prāz] *n* a green chalcedony, valued as a gem. [Gr *chrȳsos*, gold, *prason*, a leek.]

chub [chub] *n* a small freshwater fish (*semotilus atromaculatus*) common in small streams from Maine to Wyoming, south to Alabama and New Mexico.—*adj* **chubb´y**, short and thick, plump.—*n* **chubb´iness**. [Origin unknown.]

chuck[1] [chuk] *vi* to call, as a hen. [A variety of **cluck**.]

chuck[2] [chuk] *n* a word of endearment.

chuck[3] [chuk] *n* a gentle blow (under the chin).—*vt* to pat gently (under the chin); to toss; to pitch.—**chuck it**, to quit, yield; **chuck up**, (*inf*) to vomit. [Fr *choquer*, to jolt; allied to **shock**.]

chuck[4] [chuk] *n* a device on a machine tool for gripping revolving work or a drill; a cut of beef from part of the neck, the shoulder blade, or the first three ribs. [Ety uncertain.]

chuckle [chuk´l] *n* a quiet laugh; the cry of a hen.—*vi* to laugh quietly; to call as a hen does her chickens. [Akin to **chuck** (1).]

chum [chum] *n* (*inf*) a close companion.—*vi* (*inf*) to be a chum.—*adj* **chumm´y**, sociable. [Perh a mutilation of **chamber-fellow**.]

chump [chump] *n* (*inf*) a stupid person; a fool. [Per related to **chunk**.]

chunk [chungk] *n* a short, thick piece of anything, as wood, bread, etc.—*adj* **chunk´y**. [Perh related to **chuck** (3).]

Church [chûrch] *n* all Christians; a particular Christian denomination; **church**, a building for public worship, esp Christian worship; the clerical profession; a religious service.—*vt* to bring to a church service on a special occasion.—*adj* **church´less**, not belonging to a church.—*ns* **church´man**, a clergyman or ecclesiastic; a member of a church; **church´war´den**, a lay officer who looks after certain secular interests of a church; a long-stemmed clay pipe; **church´yard**, the yard around a church often used as a burial ground. [OE *circe*—Gr *kȳriakon*, belonging to the Lord—*Kȳrios*, the Lord.]

churl [chûrl] *n* a rustic; an ill-bred, surly fellow—*adj* **churl´ish**.—*adv* **churl´ishly**.—*n* **churl´ishness**. [OE *ceorl*, a countryman; ON *karl*.]

churn [chûrn] *n* a container for the production of butter from cream or milk.—*vt* to agitate so as to obtain butter; to shake or beat violently, as milk in a churn; to turn over persistently (ideas in the mind).—*vi* to perform the act of churning.—**churn out**, to produce copiously. [OE *cyrin*; ON *kirna*, a churn.]

chute [shōōt] *n* a waterfall, rapid; an inclined trough or a passage for sending down water, logs, rubbish etc. [Fr *chute*, a fall.]

chutney [chut´ni] *n* a relish of fruits, spices, and herbs. [Hindustani *chatni*.]

chutzpa, chutzpah [hŏŏts´pȧ] *n* shameless audacity, presumption, or gall. [Yiddish.]

chyle [kīl] *n* a white fluid drawn from the food while in the intestines.—*adj* **chyl´ous**. [Fr,—Gr *chȳlos*, juice—*cheein*, to pour.]

chyme [kīm] *n* the pulp to which the food is reduced in the stomach. [Gr *chȳmos*.]

cicada [si-kā´da], **cicala** [si-kä´la] *ns* any of a family (Cicadidae) of large flylike insects with transparent wings, the male producing a loud, shrill sound. [L *cicāda*; It *cicala*.]

cicatrix [sik´a-triks] *n* a scar over a wound that is healed;—*pl* **cicatrices** [si-kat´ri-sēz].—*vt* **cic´atrize**, to help the formation of a cicatrix on. [L *cicatrix, -icis*, a scar.]

cicerone [chich-er-ō´nā] *n* one who shows strangers the curiosities of a place; a guide;—*pl* **cicero´ni** [-nē]. [It,—L *Cicero*, the Roman orator.]

Ciceronian [sis-er-ō´ni-ȧn] *adj* relating to or like *Cicero* (BC 106–43), Roman orator and essayist.

cider [sī´dėr] *n* a drink made from apples. [Fr *cidre*, through LL—Gr *sikera*, strong drink—Heb *shēkar*.]

ci-devant [sē-de-vã] *adj* former (eg *the ci-devant ruler*). [Fr formerly.]

cigar [si´gär] *n* a compact roll of tobacco leaves for smoking.—*ns* **cigarette´**, finely cut tobacco rolled in thin paper. **cigarill´o**, a small, thin cigar. [Sp *cigarro*.]

cilium [sil´i-ùm] *n* a hairlike process of a cell;—*pl* **cil´ia**, the eyelashes.—*adjs* **cil´iary; cil´iāted**, having cilia. [L *cilium*, pl *cilia*, eyelids, eyelashes.]

cinch [sinch] *n* saddle or pack girth; (*coll*) something easy to do.—*vt* to tighten a girth on; (*slang*) to make sure of. [Sp *cincha*—L *cingula*.]

cinchona [sing-kō´na] *n* a genus (*Conchona*) of S American trees and shrubs, yielding the bark from which quinine is obtained—also called *Peruvian bark*. [Said to be so named from the Countess of *Chinchon*, who was cured of a fever by it in 1638.]

cincture [singk´tyùr] *n* a girdle or belt.—*vt* to gird, encompass. [L *cinctūra*—*cingĕre, cinctum*, to gird.]

cinder [sin´dėr] *n* a tiny piece of partly burned wood, etc.; (*pl*) ashes from wood or coal.—*adj* **cin´dery**. [OE *sinder*, slag.]

cine- [sin´i-] in composition, motion picture as **cinecamera**, a camera for taking motion pictures; **cinefilm**, film for a **cinecamera; cine-X Ray**, an X ray of a process in motion.

cinematography [sin-i-mat-o´gräf-i] *n* the art or science of motion-picture photography.—*n* **cinematog´rapher**, a motion-picture cameraman; a motion-picture projectionist. [Fr *cinématographie*—Gr *kinēma, -atos*, motion, *graphein*, to write.]

cinema verité [sin´ė-mȧ ve´-ri-tā] *n* the art of filming a motion picture so as to represent realism. [Fr]

cingulum [sing´gū-lum] *n* (*anat*) a band or encircling ridge. [L]

cinnabar [sin´a-bȧr] *n* sulphide of mercury, called vermilion when used as a pigment. [L,—Gr *kinnabari*, a dye, from Persian.]

cinnamon [sin´a-mȯn] *n* the spicy bark of any of several trees (genus *Cinnamomum*) of the laurel family; the tree, a light yellowish-brown.—Also *adj*. [L *cinnamomum*—Heb *kinnamon*.]

cipher [sī´fėr] *n* (*arith*) the symbol O; any of the Arabic numerals; anything of little value; a nonentity; an interweaving of the initials of a name; a secret mode of writing.—*vi* to use figures on a mathematical process.—*vt* to convert (a message) into cipher; to compute arithmetically. [OFr *cifre* (Fr *chiffre*)—Ar *cifr*, empty.]

circa [sûr´ka] *prep, adv* about. [L]

circadian [sûr-kȧ-dē´ȧn] *adj* pertaining to any biological cycle which is repeated, usu. approx every 24 hours. [From L *circa*, about, *di*(*em*), day, and suffix *-an*.]

Circassian [sėr-kash´yȧn] *n* a member of a group of peoples of the Caucasus of Caucasian race but not of Indo-European speech; the language of the Circassian peoples.

Circean [sėr-sē´ȧn] *adj* like, pertaining to, *Circe*, a sorceress who changed the companions of Ulysses into swine.

circle [sûr´kl] *n* a plane figure bounded by one line every point of which is equally distant from a certain point called the center; the line which bounds the figure; a ring; a series ending where it began; a company or group (of people); extent, scope, as of influence.—*vt* to move round; to encompass.—*vi* to move in a circle.—*n* **cir´clet**, a little circle, esp a circular ornament, (as a ring). [OE *circul*—L *circulus*, dim of *circus*.]

circuit [sûr´kit] *n* the way or path round; the path of an electric current; area, extent; a round made in the exercise of a calling; a chain or association, as of theaters or resorts.—*adj* **circū´itous**, roundabout, not direct.—*adv* **circū´itously**.—*n* **circuitry**, detailed plan of a circuit, as in radio or television, or its components.—*n* **cir´cuit break´er**, a switch or other device for interrupting an electric circuit. [Fr,—L *circuitus*—*circuīre*—*circum*, round, *īre*, to go.]

circular [sûr´kū-lȧr] *adj* round; ending in itself; circuitous.—*n* an advertisement, etc. sent to a number of persons.—*n* **circular´ity**.—*vt* **cir´cularize**, to canvass; to make circular; to send circulars to.—**circular function**, any of the trigonometrical functions with argument in radians; **circular saw**, a steel disk with teeth on its periphery, used for sawing wood, metal, etc., and generally power driven. [OFr *circulier*—L *circulāris*.]

circulate [sûr´ku-lāt] *vt* to make or go round as in a circle; to spread.—*vi* to move around; to be spread about.—*n* **circulā´tion**, the act of moving in a circle or in a closed path (as the blood); the sale of a periodical.—*adj* **cir´culatory**, circulating. [L *circulāre, -ātum*.]

circumambient [sûr-kum-am´bi-ėnt] *adj* surrounding. [L *circum*, about, *ambīre*, to go round.]

circumambulate [sûr-kum-am´bū-lāt] *vi* to circle on foot, esp as part of a rite.—*n* **circumambulā´tion**. [L *circum*, about, *ambulāre, -ātum*, to walk.]

circumcise [sûr´kum-sīz] *vt* to cut off the foreskin of (a male) or the clitoris of (a female).—*n* **circumci´sion**. [L *circumcīdĕre, circumcīsum*—*circum*, about, *caedĕre*, to cut.]

circumference [sûr-kum´fėr-ėns] *n* the boundary line of a circle, a ball, etc.; the length of this line.—*adj* **circumferen´tial**. [L *circum*, about, *ferre*, to carry.]

circumflex [sûr´kum-fleks] *n* an accent (ˆ) originally denoting a rising and falling of the voice on a vowel or syllable.—Also *adj* [L *circum*, about, *flectĕre, flexum*, to bend.]

circumfluence [sûr-kum´flōō-ėns] *n* a flowing around; (*zool*) circumvallation.—*adj* **circum´fluent**. [L *circum*, about, *fluĕre*, to flow.]

circumfuse [sûr-kum-fūz´] *vt* to surround; to envelop.—*n* **circumfū´sion**. [L *circum*, about, *fundĕre, fūsum*, to pour.]

circumjacent [sûr-kum-jā´sėnt] *adj* bordering on every side. [L *circum*, about, *jacens*, lying—*jacēre*, to lie.]

circumlocution [sûr-kum-lō-kū´sh(ȯ)n] *n* roundabout and evasive speech; a roundabout phrase.—*adj* **circumloc´utory**. [L *circum*, about, *loquī, locūtus*, to speak.]

circumnavigate [sûr-kum-nav´i-gāt] *vt* to sail or fly around (the earth, etc.)—*ns* **circumnavigā´tion; circumnav´igator**. [L *circum*, about, and **navigate**.]

circumscribe [sûr-kum-skrīb´] *vt* to draw a line round; to draw (one plane figure) so as to enclose another, the outer touching the inner at as many points as possible; (of a plane figure) to enclose (another) thus; to confine within limits, restrict.—*n* **circumscrip´tion** [L *circum*, about, *scrībĕre*, to write.]

circumspect [sûr´kum-spekt] *adj* looking round on all sides watchfully, cautious, prudent.—*n* **circumspec´tion**.—*adv* **cir´cumspectly**.—*n* **cir´cumspectness**. [L *circum*, about, *spicĕre, spectum*, to look.]

circumstance [sûr´kum-stȧns] *n* a fact or event, esp in relation to others; a detail; ceremony (*pl*) time, place, and occasion, etc., of an act; the state of one's affairs.—*vt* to place in particular circumstances.—*adj* **circumstantial**, [-stan´shȧl] consisting of details; minute.—*adv* **circumstan´tially**.—*vt* **circumstan´tiate**, [-shi-] to prove by circumstances; to describe exactly.—**circumstantial evidence**, evidence inferred from circumstances proved by direct evidence. [L *circum*, about, *stans, stantis*, standing—*stāre*.]

circumvallate´ [sûr-kumval´āt] *vt* to surround with a defensive rampart.—*adj* of the pappilae near the back of the tongue supplied with taste buds responsive to bitter flavors.—*n* **circumvallā´tion**, a surrounding with a wall; an encircling rampart. [L *circum*, about, *vallum*, rampart.]

circumvent [sûr-kum-vent´] *vt* to surround so as to intercept or capture; to outwit (a person).—*n* **circumven´tion**. [L *circum*, about, *venīre, ventum*, to come.]

circumvolution [sûr-kum-vȯ-lū´shȯn] *n* act or instance of turning around an axis. [L *circum*, about, *volvĕre, volūtum*, to roll.]

circus [sûr´kus] *n* a large arena enclosed by tiers of seats on three or four sides for the exhibition of games, feats of horsemanship etc.; a traveling show consisting of exhibitions of horsemanship, acrobatics, performances by animals, etc.; (usu. with *adj*) a group of people giving a display, esp in a number of places, as *tennis circus, flying circus*; a noisy entertainment or scene; (*inf*) a source of much fun. [L *circus*; cog with Gr *kirkos*.]

cirrhosis [si-rō´sis] *n* a hardening of tissues of various organs, esp a disease of the liver characterized by an increase of fibrous tissue and destruction of liver cells. [Gr *kirros*, orange-tawny.]

cirrus [sir´us] *n* thin, wispy, feathery clouds formed of ice crystals;—*pl* **cirri**, [sir´ī].—*adjs* **cirr´ous**. [L a curl.]

cis- [sis-] a prefix signifying on this side, as in **cisalpine**, on this side—ie on the Roman (south) side—of the Alps. [L *cis*, on this side.]

Cistercian [sis-tûr´shȧn] *n* one of the order of monks established in 1098 in the forest of Cîteaux (*Cistercium*), in France.

cistern [sis´tėrn] *n* an artificial reservoir or tank for storing water, esp an underground tank for the storage of rainwater; a fluid-containing sac or cavity in an organism. [L *cisterna*, from *cista*, a chest.]

citadel [sit´a-dėl] *n* a fortress in or near a city; a stronghold. [It *cittadella*, dim of *città*, a city—L *cīvitās*.]

cite [sīt] *vt* to call or summon; to summon to appear in court; to quote; to adduce.—*n* **citā´tion**, an official summons to appear; the document containing it; the act of quoting; that which is quoted; official recognition of achievement. [L *citāre, -ātum*, to call.]

cithara [sith´a-ra] *n* an ancient Greek musical instrument differing from the lyre in its flat, shallow sound box.—*ns* **citt´ern; cith´ern**, a metal-stringed musical instrument of the 15th and 16th centuries like a guitar with a flat pear-shaped body. [L,—Gr *kitharā*; cf **guitar, zither**.]

citizen [sit´i-zėn] *n* a member of a state or nation who owes allegiance to it by birth or naturalization and is entitled to full civil rights.—*n* **cit´izenship**, rights and duties of a citizen; membership in a community (as a college).—**citizen's band**, a system of two-way radio, limited in range and restricted to certain wavelengths, which in the US is allocated officially for private communication. [ME *citisein*—OFr *citeain*—*cité*.]

citron [sit´ròn] *n* a fruit resembling a lemon; the tree (*Citrus medica*) bearing this fruit; the preserved rind of the citron used esp in cakes and puddings; a small hard-fleshed melon used esp in pickles and preserves.—*n* **cit´rate**, a salt or ester of citric acid.—*n* **cit´rus**, a genus (*Citrus*) including the citron, lemon, lime, orange, etc.—**citric acid**, the acid to which lemons and certain other fruits owe their sourness. [Fr,—L *citrus*, a citron.]

cittern *See* **cithern** (under **cithara**).

city [sit´i] *n* a large town; in the US an incorporated municipality with boundaries, powers, etc. defined by State charter; the people of a city.—*n* **city hall**, a building housing a municipal government.—**Eternal City**, Rome. [Fr *cité*, a city—L *civitās*, the state.]

civet [siv´et] *n* a civet cat; the musky secretion of the civet cat used in perfume.—*n* **civ´et cat**, any of several carnivorous mammals, esp a long-bodied, short-legged African animal (*Civettitis civetta*) that produces the civet of commerce; a small spotted skunk (genus *Spilogale*) of western N America. [Fr *civette*—Ar *zabād*.]

civic [siv´ik] *adj* pertaining to a city or citizen.—*n* **civics**, the science of citizenship. [L *cīvicus*—*cīvis*, citizen.]

civil [siv´il] *adj* pertaining to the community or to a citizen; having the refinement of city-bred people; polite; pertaining to ordinary, as opposed to military or ecclesiastical, life; (*law*) relating to actions or suits concerned not with crime but with private rights and the remedy of injuries other than criminal; denoting the law established by a nation or state for its own jurisdiction.—*ns* **civil´ian**, one engaged in civil as distinguished from military and other pursuits; **civil´ity**, good breeding; politeness.—*adv* **civ´illy.**—**civil disobedience**, refusal to obey laws and regulations, pay taxes, etc.—a nonviolent means of forcing concessions from government; **civil engineer**, an engineer concerned with the design and construction of public works (as roads, harbors, sewage systems, etc.) and of various private works; **civil rights**, those rights guaranteed to the individual, esp by the 13th, 14th, 15th, and 19th amendments to the US Constitution; **civil service**, those employed in government service, esp through public competitive examination; **civil war**, a war between citizens of the same state; **the Civil War**, the war between the North and the South in the US (1861–65). [L *cīvīlis*—*cīvis*, a citizen.]

civilize [siv´il-īz] *vt* to reclaim from barbarism; to instruct in arts and refinements.—*n* **civilizā´tion**, state of being civilized; a making civilized; civilized peoples; culture.—*adj* **civ´ilized**, beyond barbarism; refined; sophisticated. [**civil**.]

civvies, civies [siv´ēz] *npl* (*inf*) civilian clothes.

clack [klak] *vi* to make a noise as by striking wood with wood; to talk noisily.—*n* a clacking sound; the clatter of voices. [Imit.]

clad [klad] *pt, pt p* of **clothe**.—*adj* clothed or covered.—*vt* to cover one material with another, eg one metal with another (as in nuclear reactor), or brick or stonework with a different material (in building).—*n* **cladd´ing**.

claim [klām] *vt* to call for; to demand as a right; to maintain or assert.—*n* a demand for something supposed due; right or ground for demanding; the thing claimed, esp a piece of land appropriated by a miner or other.—*adj* **claim´able**.—*n* **claim´ant**, one who makes a claim. [OFr *claimer*—L *clamāre*, to call out.]

clairvoyance [klār-voi´àns] *n* the alleged power of seeing things not present to the senses.—*n* and *adj* **clairvoy´ant**. [Fr *clair* (L *clārus*), clear, *voir* (L *vidēre*), to see.]

clam [klam] *n* an edible marine bivalve molusk; a freshwater mussel; (*inf*) a close mouthed person; a clamshell.—*n* **clam´bake**, a picnic at which steamed clams are served; (*inf*) any large noisy party, esp a political rally.—**clam up** (*coll*), to be silent. [OE *clam*, fetter.]

clammy [klam´ē] *adj* moist and sticky; moist and cold.—*n* **clamm´iness**. [OE *clæman*, to anoint.]

clamant [klam´ànt, klām´ànt] *adj* calling loudly, insistently. [L *clāmans*, -*antis*—*clāmāre*, to cry out.]

clamber [klam´bėr] *vi* to climb with difficulty, grasping with the hands and feet.—*n* **clamb´erer**. [From root of **climb**.]

clamor [klam´òr] *n* a loud continuous outcry; uproar.—*vi* to cry out aloud in demand; to make a loud continuous outcry.—*adj* **clam´orous**, noisy, boisterous.—*adv* **clam´orously**.—*n* **clam´orousness**. [L *clāmor*.]

clamp [klamp] *n* a piece of timber, iron, etc. used to fasten things together or to strengthen any framework.—*vt* to bind with a clamp.—**clamp down on**, to suppress, or suppress the activities of, firmly. [From a root seen in OE *clam*, fetter; Du *klamp*, a clamp; akin to *clip* (2), **climb**.]

clan [klan] *n* a tribe or collection of families subject to a single chieftain, commonly bearing the same surname, and supposed to have a common ancestor; a clique, sect or group.—*adj* **clann´ish**, closely united and holding aloof from others.—*adv* **clann´ishly**.—*ns* **clann´ishness; clans´man**, a member of a clan. [Gael *clann*, offspring, tribe—L *planta*, a shoot.]

clandestine [klan-des´-tin] *adj* concealed or hidden, private, sly.—*adv* **clandes´tinely**. [L *clandestīnus*—*clam*, secretly.]

clang [klang] *vi* to produce a loud, deep ringing sound.—*vt* to cause to do so.—*n* a ringing sound, like that made by metallic substances struck together:—*n* **clang´or**, a clang; a loud ringing noise.—*adj* **clang´orous**.—*adv* **clang´orously**. [L *clangĕre*, to sound.]

clank [klangk] *n* a sound, less prolonged than a clang, such as is made by a chain.—*vt* to make or cause a clank. [Prob formed under the influence of **clink** and **clang**.]

clap[1] [klap] *n* a sudden blow or stroke; the noise made by the sudden striking together of two things, as the hands; a burst of sound.—*vt* to strike together so as to make a noise; to thrust or drive together suddenly; to applaud with the hands; to put suddenly (eg *to clap one in prison; to clap eyes on*).—*vi* to strike together with noise; to applaud;—*pr p* **clapp´ing**; *pt p* **clapped**.—*ns* **clapp´er**, one who claps; that which claps, as the tongue of a bell; **clap-trap**, flashy display; empty words. [ON *klappa*, to pat; Du and Ger *klappen*.]

clap[2] [klap] *n* gonorrhea (*often with* **the**). [MF *claprir*, bubo.]

claret [klar´et] *n* a dry dark red wine of Bordeaux; a similar wine produced elsewhere; a dark purplish red. [Fr *clairet*—*clair*—L *clārus*, clear.]

clarify [klar´i-fī] *vt* to make clear or pure.—*vi* to become clear;—*pr p* **clar´ifying**; *pt p* **clar´ified**.—*ns* **clarificā´tion; clar´ifier**. [L *clārus*, clear, and *facĕre*, to make.]

clarinet [klar-in-et´] *n* an orchestral woodwind instrument, formed like a pipe with holes closed by keys ending in a bell, with a single reed fixed to the mouthpiece, available in many sizes and types. [Fr,—L *clārus*, clear.]

clarion [klar´i-òn] *n* a kind of trumpet whose note is clear and shrill; a thrilling note. [Fr *clairon*—*clair*—L *clārus*, clear.]

clarity [klar´i-ti] *n* clearness. [ME *clarte*—L *clāritās*.]

clash [klash] *n* a loud noise, such as is caused by the striking together of weapons; opposition; contradiction.—*vi* to dash noisily (against, into); to meet in opposition; to disagree.—*vt* to strike noisily together. [Formed from the sound, like Ger and Swed *klatsch*.]

clasp [kläsp] *n* a hinged fastening; an embrace.—*vt* to fasten with a clasp; to grasp in the hand; to hold in the arms, embrace.—*n* **clasp´knife**, a pocket knife, esp a large knife whose blade can be held open by a catch. [ME *claspe, clapse*; ety uncertain.]

class [kläs] *n* a rank or order of persons or things; high rank or social standing; a number of students or scholars who are taught together; a group of things alike in some respect; in biological classification, a division above an order and below a phylum or division.—*vt* to form into a class or classes; to place in a class.—*adj* **class´-con´scious**, acutely conscious of membership of a social class; believing in and actively aware of class struggle.—*ns* **class´mate**, a member of the same class in a school or college; **class´ic**, any standard writer or work; a student of the ancient classics; (*pl*) Greek and Latin studies.—*adjs* **class´ic, -al**, of the highest class or rank, esp in literature; of the best Greek and Roman writers; of music conforming to certain standards of form, complexity, etc. traditional; authoritative; standard, stock (as in *classic example*; of clothes, made in a style that does not soon go out of fashion.—*adv* **class´ically**.—*ns* **class´icism** [-is-izm], a classical idiom; principle, character, tendency such as is seen in Greek and Roman literature; **class´icist**, one versed in the classics; one supporting their use in education.—*adj* **class´less**, having no class distinctions; not belonging obviously to any social class.—*adj* **class´y** (*inf*), first-class, esp in style; elegant.—**class action** (**suit**) a legal action brought by one or more persons on behalf of themselves and a much larger group. [L *classis*, a division of the Roman people.]

classify [klas´i-fī] *vt* to arrange in classes; to make secret for security reasons;—*pr p* **class´ifying**; *pt p* **class´ified**—*n* **classificātion**.—*adj* **class´ified**, arranged in classes; on the secret list; of advertisements in a newspaper, grouped according to goods or services offered. [L *classis*, a division of the Roman people, *facĕre*, to make.]

clatter [klat´ėr] *n* a repeated rattling noise; a repetition of abrupt sharp sounds; noisy talk.—*vti* to make or cause to make rattling sounds; to chatter noisily. [OE *clatrung*, clattering (verbal noun).]

clause [klöz] *n* a sentence; part of a sentence with subject and predicate; an article or part of a contract, will, etc. [Fr *clause*—L *clausus*—*claudĕre*, to shut.]

claustral [klö´stràl] *adj* cloistral.

claustrophobia [klö-strō-fō´bi-a] *n* a morbid dread of confined places. [L *claustrum*, a barrier, Gr *phobos*, fear.]

clave [klāv] *pt p* of **cleave** (2).

clavichord [klav´i-körd] *n* a stringed musical instrument with a keyboard, predecessor of the piano. [L *clāvis*, a key, *chorda*, a string.]

clavicle [klav´i-kl] *n* the collarbone, connecting the shoulder blade and breastbone.—*adj* **clavic´ular**. [Fr *clavicule*—L *clāvicula*, dim of *clāvis*, a key.]

clavier [kla-vēr´] *n* the keyboard of an organ, piano, etc.; any stringed keyboard instrument. [Fr,—L *clāvis*, a key.]

claw [klö] *n* the hooked nail of an animal or bird; the leg of a crab, insect, etc. or its pointed end or pincer; anything like a claw.—*vti* to scratch or tear as with the claws or nails.—*n* **claw hammer**, a hammer fitted with a claw for drawing nails. [OE *clawu*; a kin to **cleave**, to stick.]

clay [klā] *n* a tenacious ductile earthy material, hydrated aluminium silicates more or less impure; earth in general; the human body.—*adj* **clay´ey**, made of clay; covered with clay.—**feet of clay**, faults and weaknesses of character not at first suspected. [OE *clǣg*.]

claymore [klā-mōr´, -mör´] *n* a large sword formerly used by the Scottish Highlanders. [Gael *claidheamh-mór*—Gael and Ir *claidheamh*, sword, *mór*, great.]

clean [klēn] *adj* free from dirt or defilement; sportsmanlike; pure; guiltless; neat; complete; free of radioactive fallout.—*adv* quite; entirely; smoothly, neatly.—*vti* to make or to be clean or free from dirt.—*ns* **clean´er**, one who, or that which, cleans, esp one who dry-cleans; **cleanness** [klēn´ne+s].—*adj* **cleanly** [klen´li], clean in habits or person; pure; neat.—*adv* [klēn´li].—*n* **cleanliness** [klen´lines], habitual cleanness or purity.—*adj* **clean´-limbed**, well-proportioned.—**clean room**, a room, as in a computer center, designed to be nearly 100% free of dust, pollen etc., **clean up**, to make clean; to free from vice, corruption, etc.; (*slang*), to make (large profits); **have clean hands**, to be free from guilt; **clean up one's act**, to behave in a more acceptable manner. [OE *clǣne*; Ger *klein*, small.]

cleanse [klenz] *vt* to make clean or pure.—*n* **cleans´er**, one who, or that which, cleanses. [OE *clǣsian*.]

clear [klēr] *adj* pure, bright, undimmed; transparent; free from obstruction or difficulty; plain, distinct, obvious; without blemish, defect, drawback, or diminution.—*adv* in a clear manner; plainly; wholly; apart from (eg *stand clear of the gates*).—*vt* to make clear; to empty; to free from obscurity or obstruction; to free from suspicion, acquit or vindicate; to declare free from security restrictions; to decode; to leap, or pass by or over; to make a profit of; to set free for sailing.—*vi* to become clear; to go away; to sail after satisfying demands and obtaining permission.—*adv* **clear´ly**, in a clear manner; distinctly.—*ns* **clear´ness, clear´ance**, act of clearing; the adjustment of accounts in a clearing house; a certificate that a ship has satisfied all demands of the customhouse and procured permission to sail; the distance between two objects, or between a moving and a stationary part of a machine.—*adj* **clear´-cut**, sharp in outline; distinct, definite.—*ns* **clear´ing**, the act of making clear; a tract of land cleared of wood, etc., for cultivation; **clear´inghouse**, an office in which banks adjust their mutual claims; a central agency for the collection, classification, and distribution of information; **clearstory**, clerestory.—**clear away** (or **off**), to remove so as to leave a cleared space; to depart.—**clear out** (*inf*), to go away; **clear up**, to make or become clear. [Fr *clair*—L *clārus*, clear.]

cleat [klēt] *n* a wedge; a piece of wood nailed across a structure to keep it firm; a projection to which ropes are made fast. [From a supposed OE *clēat*; cf Du *kloot*; Dan *klode*; Ger *kloss*.]

cleave[1] [klēv] *vti* to divide by a blow; split; sever.—*pr p* **cleav´ing**; *pt* **clōve** or **cleft**; *pt p* **cleaved** or **clov´en** or **cleft**.—*ns* **cleav´age**, a split; tendency to split; **cleav´er**, one who or that which cleaves, esp. a butcher's heavy, broad knife. [OE *clēofan*.]

cleave[2] [klēv] *vi* to stick or adhere; to be united closely (to), remain faithful (to);—*prp* **cleaving** *pt* **cleaved** or **clove** or **clave**; *pt p* **cleaved**. [OE *clifian*; cog, with Ger *kleben*.]

clef [klef] *n* a sign placed on a musical staff by which the pitch of notes is fixed. [Fr, from L *clāvis*; Gr *kleis*, a key.]

cleft[1] [kleft] *pt, ptp* of **cleave** (1).

cleft[2] [kleft] *n* an opening made by cleaving or splitting; a crack, fissure, or chink.—**cleft palate**, congenital fissure of the roof of the mouth. [Cf Ger *kluft*, Dan *klyft*, a hole.]

clematis [klem´a-tis] *n* a vine or herb (genera *Clematis, Atragene*, or *Viorma*) of the buttercup family having three leaflets on each leaf and showy flowers. [L—Gr *klēmatis*, a plant, probably periwinkle—*klēma*, a twig.]

clement [klem´ėnt] *adj* (of weather) mild; kind, merciful.—*n* **clem´ency**.—*adv* **clem´ently**. [Fr—L *clēmens*.]

clench [klench] *vt* to close (the teeth or fist) tightly; to grasp; to clinch.—*n* a firm grip. [See **clinch**.]

clepsydra [klep´si-dra] *n* an instrument for measuring time by the trickling of water; a water clock. [L—Gr *klepsydra*—*klepstein*, to steal, *hydōr*, water.]

clerestory [klēr-stō´ri] *n* an outside wall with windows that rises above a roofed section of a building.—Also **clearstory**. [**clear** + **story**.]

clergy [klûr´ji] *n* ministers, priests, rabbis, etc. collectively; the ministers of the Christian religion, as holders of an allotted office, in contradistinction to the laity.—*n* **cler´gyman**, one of the clergy; a regularly ordained minister.—*adjs* **cler´ic, -al** [kler´ik, -ȧl] belonging to the clergy; pertaining to a clerk.—*ns* **cler´ic**, a clergyman; **cler´icalism**, political power of the clergy. [Fr *clergé*—Late L *clēricus*—Gr *klērikos*, from *klēros*, a lot, a heritage, then the clergy.]

clerihew [kler´i-hū] *n* a jingle in two short couplets purporting to give the quintessence of the life and character of some notable person. [First used by E. *Clerihew* (Bentley) in his *Biography for Beginners* (1905).]

clerk [klûrk] *n* a layman with minor duties in a church; an office worker who types, files, etc.; a public official who keeps the records of a court, town, etc.; a salesclerk.—*vi* to work as a salesclerk.—*adj* **cler´ical**, pertaining to a clerk. [OE *clerc*, a priest—Late L *clēricus*.]

clever [klev´ėr] *adj* able or dexterous; ingenious; intelligent; skilful.—*n* **clev´erness**.—*adv* **clev´erly**. [Ety uncertain.]

clew, clue [klōō] *n* a ball of thread, or the thread in it; a thread that guides through a labyrinth; anything that points to the solution of a mystery (usu. **clue**); the corner of a sail; a metal loop in the corner of a sail. [OE *cliwen*.]

cliché [klē-shā] *n* a hackneyed phrase; something (as a menu item) that has become commonplace. [Fr *clicher*, to stereotype.]

click [klik] *n* a short, sharp ticking sound; anything that makes such a sound, as a small piece of iron falling into a notched wheel.—*vi* to make a light, sharp sound. [Dim of **clack**.]

client [klī´ėnt] *n* one who employs a lawyer, accountant, or consultant; one using the services of a social agency; a customer.—*ns* **clientele** [klī´en-tēl], **clientèle** [klē-ā-tel´] a group of clients; **clientage**.—**client state**, a country that is economically, politically, or militarily dependent on another country. [L *cliens, -entis*, for *cluens*, one who listens (to advice)—*cluēre*, to hear.]

cliff [klif] *n* a high steep rock; the steep side of a mountain.—*n* **cliff´hanger**, a tense, exciting adventure or contest; an ending line that leaves one in suspense. [OE *clif*; Du *clif*; ON *klif*.]

clift *See* **cleft** (2).

climacteric [klī-mak´tėr-ik or klī-mak-ter´ik] *n* menopause; a critical period in human life, in which some great bodily change takes place.—*adj* critical.—*adj* **climacter´ical**. [Gr *klīmaktēr*—*klīmax*, a ladder.]

climate [klī´mȧt] *n* the average weather conditions of a region (temperature, moisture, etc.); a region with reference to its prevailing weather; the prevailing influence characterizing a group or period.—*adjs* **climat´ic, -al**.—*n* **climatol´ogy**, the science of the causes on which climate depends. [OFr *climat*—Gr *klima*, gen *klimatos*, slope—*klinein*, to slope.]

climax [klī´maks] *n* the arrangement of a series of ideas, or of words or phrases, in ascending order of emphasis; the last term of the arrangement, a culmination.—*vti* to reach, or bring to a climax. [Gr *klīmax*, a ladder—from *klinein*, to slope.]

climb [klīm] *vti* to ascend or mount by clutching with the hands and feet; to ascend with effort; of plants, to ascend by clinging to other objects.—*pt* **climbed** (*arch* **clomb**).—*n* an ascent.—*ns* **climb´er**, one who or that which climbs; one who attempts to gain a superior position in society; **climbing iron**, a steel framework with spikes for attaching to one's boots for climbing. [OE *climban*, conn with **clamber** and **cleave**, to stick.]

clime [klīm] *n* climate. [A variant of **climate**.]

clinch [klinch] *vt* to fasten a nail by bending down the point; to settle or confirm (an argument, a bargain).—*vi* (*boxing*) to grip the opponent with the arms to hinder his punching; (*slang*) to embrace.—*n* the act of clinching.—*n* **clinch´er**, one that clinches; a decisive point in an argument.—*adj* **clinch´er-built** (same as **clinker-built**). [Same as **clench**; causal form of **clink**.]

cline [klīn] *n* (*biol*) a gradation of differences of form, etc., seen eg within one species over a specified area of the world. [Gr *klīnein*, to lean.]

cling [kling] *vi* to adhere or stick close; to adhere in interest or affection.—*pr p* **clinging**; *p t, pt p* **clung**. [OE *clingan*.]

clinic [klin´ik] *n* the teaching of medicine by treating patients in the presence of students; a place where medical specialists practice as a group; an outpatient department, as of a hospital.—*adj* **clin´ical**, based on observation; strictly objective.—*adv* **clin´ically**.—**clinician** [kli-nish´ȧn] one who practices clinical medicine, psychology, etc. [Gr *klīnikos*—*klīnē*, a bed.]

clink[1] [klingk] *n* a ringing sound made by striking metal, glass, etc.—*vti* to make or cause to make a ringing sound.—*n* **clink´er**, (*arch*) hard brick; the incombustible cinder or slag formed in furnaces; (*slang*) a mistake.—*adj* **clink´erbuilt**, made of planks overlapping those below. [A form of **click** and **clank**.]

clink[2] [klingk] *n* (*slang*) a prison cell; (*slang*) prison. [Name of a former prison in Southwark, London.]

clinometer [klin-, klīn-om´i-tėr] *n* any of various instruments for measuring angles of elevation or inclination. [Gr *klīnein*, to lean.]

clip[1] [klip] *vt* to cut with shears; to trim; to pare down; to shorten (utterance); (*inf*) to hit sharply; (*slang*) to swindle.—*vi* to move rapidly.—*pr p* **clipp´ing**; *pt p* **clipped**.—*n* the thing clipped off, as wool shorn off sheep; (*inf*) a smart blow; a single instance or occasion.—*ns* **clip´ joint**, a store or place of entertainment, eg a night club, where customers are overcharged; **clipped form, clipped word**, a shortened form of a word, as pike for turnpike; **clipp´er**, one that clips; a sailing vessel with very sharp lines and great spread of canvas; **clipp´ing**, an item cut out from a publication. [ON *klippa*, cut.]

clip[2] [klip] *vt* to hold firmly; to fasten with a clip.—*n* any device that grips, clasps, or hooks; a piece of jewelry held in place by a spring clip. [OE *clyppan*, to embrace; ON *klўpa*, to pinch.]

clique [klēk] *n* an exclusive group of persons in union for a purpose; a faction.—*adj* **cliqu´ish**. [Fr.]

clitoris [klit´ȯr-is] *n* a small sensitive organ of the vulva. [Gr *kleitoris*.]

cloaca [klō-ā´kä] *n* (*zool*) the common chamber in birds, reptiles, amphibians and many fishes into which the urinary, intestinal, and generative canals discharge; a comparable chamber in some invertebrates.—*pl* **cloacae** [klō-ā´sē]. [L.]

cloak [klōk] *n* a loose outer garment; a covering; that which conceals, a disguise, pretext.—*vt* to put a cloak on; to cover; to conceal.—*adj* **cloak´-and-dagg´er**, concerned with plot and intrigue.—*n* **cloak´room**, a room for keeping coats and hats; a room or cubicle where luggage, etc. may be checked for temporary safekeeping; an anteroom of a legislative chamber for the private use of its members. [OFr *cloke*—Low L *cloca*, bell.]

clobber [klob´ėr] *vt* (*slang*) to strike very hard; to defeat overwhelmingly. [Origin unknown.]

clock[1] [klok] *n* a device for measuring and indicating time, usu. by means of pointers moving over a dial.—*vt* to time by a stopwatch or by an electronic timing device; to register on a mechanical recording device.—*adv* **clock´wise**, in the direction of the hands of a clock.—*n* **clock´work**, the mechanism of a clock or any similar mechanism with springs and gears.—

adj as steady and regular as that of a clock.—**like clock´work**, very regularly. [ME *clokke*.]

clock[2] [klok] *n* an ornament on a sock or stocking.

clod [klod] *n* a thick round mass or lump that sticks together, esp of earth or turf; the ground; a stupid fellow.—*n* **clod´hopper**, a countryman, a peasant; a dolt; a coarse, heavy shoe.—*adj* **clodhopp´ing**, boorish. [A later form of **clot**.]

clog [klog] *n* a block of wood; an impediment; a shoe with a wooden sole.—*vt* to accumulate in a mass and cause stoppage in; to obstruct; to encumber.—*n* **clog´ dance**, a dance performed in clogs. [Ety uncertain.]

cloisonné [kloi-són-ā´] *adj* denoting enamel work in which the surface decoration is set in hollows formed by thin strips of wire. [Fr.]

cloister [klois´tėr] *n* a covered arcade forming part of a monastery; a place of religious retirement, a monastery or nunnery; an enclosed place.—*vt* to confine in a cloister; to confine within walls.—*adjs* **clois´tral, claus´tral** [klös´trål] pertaining to, or confined to, a cloister; secluded; **clois´tered**, dwelling in cloisters; solitary. [OFr *cloistre* (OE *clauster*)—L *claustrum*-*claudĕre, clausum*, to shut.]

clone [klōn] *n* an individual grown from a single somatic cell of its parent and genetically identical to it; the whole stock of individuals derived asexually.—*vt* to propagate a clone from; to make a copy of.—*vi* to produce a clone. [Gr *klōn*, shoot.]

close[1] [klōs] *adj* shut up; with no opening; hot and airless, stifling; narrow, confined; stingy; near, in time or place; intimate; compact, dense (eg of texture); hidden; reserved, secretive; strict, careful; nearly alike; nearly even or equal; (of a vowel) pronounced with slight opening or with the tongue tense.—*adv* in a close manner; nearly; densely.—*n* an enclosed place.—*adv* **close´ly**.—*ns* **close´ness; close´ corporā´tion**, a corporation whose stock is not publicly traded.—*adjs* **close´fist´ed**, stingy; **close´-grained**, having a compacted smooth texture, esp having small annual rings; **close´-hauled**, with sails trimmed for sailing as near as possible to the wind.—*ns* **close-up**, a photograph taken near at hand and thus detailed and big in scale; a close scrutiny.—**close call, close shave**, (*inf*) a narrow escape. [Fr *clos*, shut—L *claudĕre, clausum*, to shut.]

close[2] [klōz] *vt* to make close; to stop up (an opening); to draw together and unite; to shut, to end; to complete, conclude (eg a bargain).—*vi* to come together; to grapple (with); to agree (with); to come to an end.—*n* the manner or time of closing; a pause or stop; the end.—*n* **clos´ure**, the act of closing; the condition of being closed; something that closes; cloture.—**close down**, to cease operations; **closed circuit** (*TV*) a system in which the signal is transmitted by cable only to receivers connected in the circuit; **closed shop**, an establishment in which the employer by agreement hires only union members in good standing. [ME *closen*—L *claudĕre, clausum*.]

closet [kloz´ėt] *n* a small room or cupboard for clothes, supplies, etc.; a small private room; a toilet or toilet bowl.—*vt* to shut up in a private room for a confidential talk.—*pr p* **clos´eting**; *pt p* **clos´eted**. [OFr *closet*, dim of *clos*. See **close** *adj*.]

clot [klot] *n* a thickened mass or soft lump, as blood.—*vti* to form into clots, to coagulate.—*pr p*, **clott´ing**; *pt p* **clott´ed**. [OE *clott*, clod.]

cloth [kloth] *n* woven, knitted, or pressed material from which garments, coverings, etc. are made; a piece of such material; a tablecloth, washcloth, dustcloth, etc.—*pl* **cloths** [kloths].—*vt* **clothe** [klōTH] to cover with a garment; to provide with clothes; to cover; *pr p* **clōth´ing** [TH]; *pt pt p* **clōthed** [TH], clad.—*n pl* **clothes** [klōz, klōTHz] garments or articles of dress.—*ns* **clothes´horse**, frame for hanging clothes on; a conspicuously dressy person; **clothes´pin**, forked piece of wood or plastic or a small spring clamp to secure clothes on a line; **clothier** [klōTH´i-ėr] one who makes or sells clothes; **clothing** [klōTH´ing] clothes, garments; a covering.—**the cloth**, the clergy. [OE *clāth*, cloth; Ger *kleid*, a garment.]

cloture [klō´chûr] *n* the ending of legislative debate by having the bill put to immediate vote.—Also **closure**.

cloud [klowd] *n* a mass of fog, consisting of minute particles of water, often in a frozen state, floating in the atmosphere; a great number or multitude; a great volume (of dust or smoke); anything that obscures as a cloud; anything gloomy or ominous.—*vt* to darken or obscure as with clouds; to sully.—*vi* to become clouded or darkened.—*adj* **cloud´ed**, hidden by clouds; darkened; indistinct.—*adj* **cloud´y**, darkened with, or consisting of, clouds; obscure; gloomy.—*adv* **cloud´ily**.—*n* **cloud´iness**.—*adj* **cloud´less**.—*ns* **cloud´berry**, a creeping herbaceous raspberry (*Rubus chamaemorus*) of north temperate regions; its pale amber-colored edible fruit; **cloud´burst**, a sudden flood of rain; **cloud chamber**, an apparatus in which the path of charged particles is made visible by means of droplets condensed on gas ions.—**in the clouds**, impractical; in a daydream; **under a cloud**, under suspicion. [OE *clūd*, a hill, then a cloud, the root idea being a mass or ball; **clod** and **clot** are from the same root.]

clout [klowt] *n* a blow; (*inf*) influence.—*vt* (*inf*) to strike, as with the hand; (*slang*) to hit (a ball) a far distance. [OE *clūt*; cf ON *klūtr*, a kerchief.]

clove[1] [klōv] *pt* of **cleave**.—*n* **clove´hitch**, a kind of temporary knot that holds firmly round an object.

clove[2] [klōv] *n* the dried flower bud of a tropical tree (*Eugenia aromatica*), as a spice, and yielding an essential oil.—*n* **clove´ pink**, a variety of pink smelling of cloves. [Fr *clou*, a nail—L *clāvus*.]

clove[3] [klōv] *n* a segment of a bulb, as of garlic. [OE *clufu*.]

cloven [klōv´ėn] *adj* split; divided.—*adjs* **clov´en-foot´ed, clov´en-hoofed**, having the hoof divided, as the ox or sheep.—**the cloven hoof**, a symbol of devilish agency or of evil character. [*Pt p* of **cleave**, to divide.]

clover [klōv´ėr] *n* a genus (*Trifolium*) of three-leaved plants, growing among grass and affording rich pasturage.—*n* **clov´erleaf**, a traffic arrangement in which one road passes over the top of another and the roads connecting the two are in the pattern of a four-leaved clover.—**live in clover**, to live luxuriously. [OE *clāfre*; Du *klaver*; Dan *klöver*; Ger *klee*.]

clown [klown] *n* a clumsy or boorish person; one who entertains, as in a circus, by antics, jokes, etc.—*vi* to act the clown.—*adj* **clown´ish**.—*adv* **clown´ishly**.—*n* **clown´ishness**. [Prob conn with **clod**.]

cloy [kloi] *vt* to sate by too much that is rich, sweet, etc.—*pr p* **cloy´ing**; *pt p* **cloyed**.—Also *vi*. [For *accloy*—OFr *encloyer*, to drive a nail into, to spike or stop, as a gun.—L *in*, in, *clāvus*, a nail.]

club [klub] *n* a heavy tapering stick, knobby or massy at one end, used to strike with, a cudgel; an implement for striking a ball as in golf; an association of persons for social, political, athletic, or other ends; the premises occupied by a club; any of one of the four suits of cards marked by a black trefoil; (*pl*) this suit.—*vt* to beat with a club.—*vi* to combine (for a common end).—*adj* **club(b)´able**, sociable.—*n* **club´foot**, a deformed foot twisted out of position from birth; this deformity.—*adj* **club´-foot´ed**.—*ns* **club´house**, a house occupied by a club or used for club activities; locker rooms used by an athletic team; **club´ moss**, a moss (order Lycopodiales) with scaly leaves and clublike stems; **club sandwich**, a sandwich of three slices of bread with two layers of meat, lettuce, tomato and mayonnaise. [ON and Swed *klubba*; same root as **clump**.]

cluck [kluk] *n* the call of a hen to her chickens; any similar sound.—*vi* to make such a sound. [From the sound, like Du *klokken*, Ger *glucken*, Dan *klukke*.]

clue [klōō] *See* **clew**

clump [klump] *n* a thick, short, shapeless piece of anything; a cluster (eg of trees or shrubs); the sound of heavy footsteps.—*vi* to walk heavily; to form clumps. [Prob Scand; Dan *klump*, a lump.]

clumsy [klum´zi] *adj* shapeless; ill-made; unwieldy; awkward in movement; without adroitness or tact.—*adj* **clum´sily**.—*n* **clum´siness**. [ME *clumsen*, to be stiff.]

clung [klung] *p t, pt p* of **cling**.

cluster [klus´tėr] *n* a number of things of the same kind growing or joined together; a bunch; a group or crowd.—*vti* to grow or gather into clusters. [OE *clyster*; prob conn with **clot**.]

clutch[1] [kluch] *vt* to seize or grasp; to hold tightly in the hand.—*n* (usu *pl*) power; control; a grasp; a device by which two shafts or rotating members of a machine may be connected or disconnected. [OE *clyccan*, to clench.]

clutch[2] [kluch] *n* a nest of eggs; a brood of chicks; a cluster. [From *cleck* (now chiefly Scot), to hatch.—ON.]

clutter [klut´ėr] *n* confusion; stir; noise; irregular interference on radar screen from echoes, rain, buildings, etc.—*vi* (*dial*) to go about in disorder.—*vt* to jumble, put into disorder (*often with* **up**). [A variant of **clatter**.]

Clydesdale [klīdz´dāl] *n* a heavy, feather-legged draft horse of the breed originating in *Clydesdale*, Scotland.

co- [kō-] a prefix signifying jointness, accompaniment, connection. [L *cum*, with.]

coach [kōch] *n* a large, closed, four-wheeled carriage; a railroad passenger car; a bus; the lowest-price class of airline accommodations; an instructor or trainer, as of athletes, actors, singers, etc.—*vti*, to instruct and train (students, etc.).—*n* **coach´dog**, a Dalmatian; **coach´man**, the driver of a coach. [Fr *coche*—Hungarian *kocsi*, from *Kocs*, a village in Hungary.]

coadjutor [kō-aj´ū-tor or kō´â-jōō´ter] *n* a helper or assistant, esp to a bishop. [L *co-*, with, *adjūtor*, a helper—*ad*, to, *juvāre*, to help.]

coagulate [kō-ag´ū-lāt] *vt* to clot; to make to curdle or congeal.—*vi* to curdle or congeal.—*adj* **coag´ulable**.—*ns* **coag´ūlant**, a substance that causes curdling, as rennet; **coagulā´tion**.—*adj* **coag´ulātive**.—*n* **coag´ulum**, what is coagulated; a clot. [L *coāgulāre, -ātum*—*co-*, together, *agĕre*, to drive.]

coal [kōl] *n* a solid, black, combustible mineral, derived from vegetable matter, used for fuel; a piece of coal; an ember.—*vi* to take in coal.—*vt* to supply with coal.—*ns* **coal´field**, a district containing coal; **coal´ gas**, the mixture of gases produced by the distillation of coal, used for lighting and heating.—*n pl* **coal´ meas´ures**, the group of carboniferous strata in which coal is found.—*ns* **coal oil**, kerosene; **coal seam**, a bed of coal, usu. thick enough to be mined for profit; **coal´ tar**, a thick, black, opaque liquid formed when coal is distilled.—**coaling station**, a port at which steamships take in coal.—**haul** (or **call**) **over the coals**, to reprimand sharply. [OE *col*; cog with ON *kol*, Ger *kohle*.]

coalesce [kō-al-es´] *vi* to grow together or unite into one body; to combine in an association.—*n* **coales´cence**, growing into each other; fusion.—*adj* **coales´cent**.—*ns* **coali´tion**, a usu. temporary combination or alliance, esp of states or political parties; **coali´tionist**. [L *coalescĕre*—*co-*, together, *alescĕre*, to grow up.]

coarse [kōrs, körs] *adj* common, base, or inferior; rough; rude; gross; consisting of rather large particles.—*adv* **coarse´ly**.—*n* **coarse´ness**.—*vti* **coars´en**, to make or become coarse.—*adj* **coarse´-grained**, large in grain, as wood; lacking in fine feelings. [From phrase 'in course', hence *ordinary*.]

coast [kōst] *n* border of land next to the sea; the seashore; a slide down an incline, as on a sled.—*vi* to sail along or near a coast; to travel downhill in a vehicle without mechanical propulsion.—*vt* to sail along the shore of.—*adj* **coast´al**, pertaining to the coast.—*ns* **coast´er**, a person or thing that coasts; a small mat to protect the surface of a table, etc. from the imprint of glasses; **coast´ guard**, a branch of the US armed forces whose duties include defending the nation's coast, aiding vessels in distress, etc.—**coaster brake**, a brake on a bicycle operated by reverse pressure on the pedals; **coaster wagon**, a child's toy wagon often used for coasting. [OFr *coste* (Fr *côte*)—L *costa*, a rib, side.]

coat [kōt] *n* a kind of front-opening outer garment with sleeves; the natural covering of a plant or animal; a membrane or layer, as of paint, etc.—*vt* to cover with a coat or layer.—*ns* **coat´dress**, a tailored dress with fastening from neckline to hem; **coat´ing**, a surface coat or layer cloth for coats.—**coat of arms**, the heraldic bearings or family insignia embroidered on the surcoat worn over the coat of mail; the coat itself; such bearings wherever displayed; **coat of mail**, a piece of armor for the upper part of the body, made of metal scales or rings linked one with another; **coatt´ail**, either half of the divided lower half of a coat. [OFr *cote* (Fr *cotte*)—Low L *cottus, cotta*, a tunic.]

coati [kō-ä´ti or kō´ä-ti] *n* an American plantigrade carnivorous mammal (genus *Nasua*) allied to the raccoons.—Also **coatimundi** [kō-wät´i-mon´dē or kwät-, mūn]. [South American Indian.]

coax [kōks] *vt* to persuade by fondling or flattery; to humor or soothe.—*adv* **coax´ingly**. [ME *cokes*, a simpleton.]

coaxial [kō-ak´si-àl] *adj* having the same axis; denoting a double-conductor, high-frequency transmission line, as for television.

cob [kob] *n* a corncob; a short-legged strong riding horse; a male swan.—*n* **cob´nut**, the fruit of a European hazel (*Corylus arellana grandis*); the tree.

cobalt [kō´bölt] *n* metallic element (symbol Co; at wt 58.9; at no 27); blue pigment prepared from it.—**cō´balt blue**.—*adj* of this greenish blue color.—**cobalt 60**, a radioactive isotope of cobalt used in the gammaray treatment of cancer. [Ger *kobalt*, from *kobold*, a demon, so called by the German miners, who supposed it to be mischievous and hurtful.]

cobble[1], **cobblestone** [kob´l-stōn] *ns* a rounded stone used in paving.—*vt* to pave with such. [Ety uncertain.]

cobble[2] [kob´l] *vt* to repair, to make (shoes); to put together roughly or hastily.—*n* **cobbler**, one who cobbles or mends shoes. [Ety unknown.]

cobelligerent [kō-be-lij´e-rènt] *adj* cooperating in warfare.—Also *n*. [**co-** + **belligerent**.]

COBOL, cobol [kō-bòl] *n* a standardized business language for programming a computer. [*co*mmon *b*usiness *o*riented *l*anguage.]

cobra [kō´bra] *n* a poisonous snake (genus *Naja*) found in India and Africa, which dilates its neck so as to resemble a hood. [Port 'snake of the hood'.]

cobweb [kob´web] *n* the spider's web; anything flimsy, gauzy, or ensnaring like this. [Prob OE *attercop—web—ātor*, poison, *coppa*, a head, tuft. See also **web**.]

coca [kō´ka] *n* any of several S American shrubs (genus *Erythroxylon*) esp one (*E coca*) with leaves resembling tea; dried leaves of this coca.—*n* **cocaine** [kō-kān] an alkaloid obtained from coca leaves, used as a local anesthetic and as an intoxicant. [Sp—Peruvian.]

coccus [kok´us] *n* a spherical bacterium.—*pl* **cocci** [kok´sī]. [L—Gr *kokkos*, a grain.]

coccyx [kok´siks] *n* the small triangular bone at the end of the spinal column. [Gr *kokkyx*, cuckoo, as resembling its bill.]

cochineal [koch´i-nēl] *n* a red dye consisting of the dried bodies of female cochineal insects.—*n* **cochineal insect**, a small bright-red cactus-feeding insect (*Dactylopius coccus*). [Sp *cochinilla*.]

cochlea [kok´le-a] *n* anything spiral shaped, esp a snail shell; (*anat*) the spiral cavity of the ear. [L—Gr *kochlias*, a snail.]

cock[1] [kok] *n* the adult male of the domestic fowl (*Gallus gallus*); male of other birds; a faucet or valve; the hammer in the lock of a gun; its position, as **at half cock**, drawn back half-way.—*vt* to set erect or upright; to set up, as the brim of the hat; to draw back the cock of a gun; to tilt up.—*vi* to strut, to swagger.—*adj* **cockahoop´**, exultant; *ns* **cock´chafer**, a large European beetle (*Melolontha melolontha*) destructive to vegetation; any of various related beetles; **cock´crow**, early morning; **cock´er**, a keeper or handler of fighting cocks; **cock´erel**, a young cock; **cocker spaniel**, a breed of small spaniel with long ears, square muzzle, and silky coats; **cock´eye**, a squinting eye.—*adj* **cock´eyed**.—*ns* **cock´fight, cockfighting**, a contest between gamecocks; **cock´horse**, a child's rocking horse; **cock´pit**, a pit or enclosed space where gamecocks fought; a frequent battleground; part of a ship-of-war used for the wounded in action; a compartment in the fuselage of an aircraft for pilot or passenger; the driver's seat in a racing car; **cocks´comb**, the comb or crest on a cock's head; a coxcomb; a garden plant (genus *Celosia*); **cock´shy**, a throw at a thing, as for amusement; an object or a person taken as a butt (as of criticism).—*adj* **cock´sure**, very sure; over-confident.—*n* **cock´tail**, a mixture of spirituous or other liquors; an appetizer served as the first course of a meal.—*adj* **cock´y**, impudent.—*ns* **cock-and-bull story**, an incredible story told as true; **cock-a-leekie**, soup made of a fowl boiled with leeks; **cocked hat**, an old-fashioned three-cornered hat; **cock of the walk**, chief of a set; **cock´sfoot**, a tall hay and pasture grass (*Dactylis glomerata*) whose flowers branch from the stem like the talons of a cock.—**knock into a cocked hat**, to overwhelm and utterly discomfit. [OE *coc*; ON *kokkr*.]

cock[2] [kok] *n* a small pile of hay. [Swed *koka*, a lump of earth; Ger *kugel*, a ball.]

cockade [kok-ād´] *n* a rosette worn on the hat as a badge. [Fr *cocarde—coq*, cock.]

Cockaigne [kok-ān´] *n* an imaginary country of luxury and delight. [Ety uncertain; Fr *cocagne*, acc to some from L *coquěre*, to cook.]

cockatoo [kok-a-tōō´] *n* any of numerous large, noisy and usu. crested parrots (genus *Kakatoe*) of Australasia. [Malay, *kakatúa*.]

cockatrice [kok´a-trīs, -tris] *n* a fabulous monster supposedly able to kill by a look. [OFr *cocatris*.]

cockboat [kok´bōt] *n* a small boat, esp one that is used as a tender. [ME *cogge*, ship, + **boat**.]

cocker [kok´ėr] *vt* to pamper, fondle, indulge. [Ety uncetain; cf Du *kokelen*, OFr *coqueliner*, to dandle.]

cockle[1] [kok´l] *n* a cornfield weed. [OE *coccel*.]

cockle[2] [kok´l] *n* a bivalve mollusk (family Cardiidae) with a heart-shaped shell.—*n* **cock´leshell**, the shell of a cockle; a shell suggesting a cockleshell; a frail boat.—**warm the cockles of the heart**, to cheer up or gladden. [Fr *coquille—*Gr *konchylion—konchē*, a cockle.]

cockney [kok´ni] *n* (often **Cockney**) one born in London, strictly, within hearing of Bow Bells—*ns* **cock´neydom**, the domain of Cockneys; **cock´neyism**, dialect or manners of a Cockney.

cockroach [kok´rōch] *n* any of an order (Blattaria) of chiefly nocturnal insects, including the common household pest. [Sp *cucaracha*.]

coco [kō´kō] *n* the coconut palm.—*ns* **co´conut**, the fruit of the coconut palm whose outer husk yields coir and whose nut contains thick edible meat and coconut milk; **coconut milk**, the fluid inside a fresh coconut; the creamy liquid extracted from the grated flesh or from dried, shredded coconut used for cooking; **coconut oil**, a colorless fatty oil or white semisolid fat extracted from fresh coconuts and used in making soap and food products; **coconut palm**, a tall tropical palm (*Cocos nucifera*) probably of American origin. [Port and Sp *coco*.]

cocoa [kō´kō] *n* a powder made from roasted cacao seeds; a drink made from the powder—*n* **cocoa butter**, a pale yellow fat made from cacao seeds, the basis of chocolate. [A corr of **cacao**.]

cocoon [ko-kōōn´] *n* the silken sheath spun by many insect larvae in passing into the pupa stage, and by spiders for their eggs. [Fr *cocon*, from *coque*, a shell—L *concha*, a shell.]

cod [kod] *ns* a food fish (*Gadus morrhua*) of northern seas; a fish of the cod family (Gadidae), esp a Pacific fish (*G macrocephalus*). Also **cod´fish**.—*n* **cod´ling**, a small cod.—**cod-liver oil**, an oil obtained from the liver of the cod and related fishes used as a source of Vitamins A and D.

coda [kō´da] *n* (*mus*) a passage forming the conclusion of a piece. [It,—L *cauda*, a tail.]

coddle [kod´l] *vt* to pamper, treat as an invalid; to cook (as eggs) in water not quite boiling.

code [kōd] *n* a collection or digest of laws, rules, or regulations; a standard of behavior; a system of words, letters, or symbols, to ensure economy or secrecy in transmission of messages.—*vt* to codify.—*vt* **cod´ify**, [kod´-, kōd´-] to put into the form of a code; to digest, to systematize;—*pr p* **cod´ifying**; *pt p* **cod´ified**.—*n* **codificā´tion**. [Fr *code*—L *cōdex*, book.]

codex [kō´deks] *n* a manuscript volume esp of the Scriptures or classical texts;—*pl* **codices**, [kōd´isēz]. [L *cōdex* or *caudex*, a book.]

codfish [kod´fish] *n* cod.

codicil [kod´i-sil] *n* an addition to a will. [L *cōdicillus*, dim of *cōdex*, book.]

codling [kod´ling] *n* an immature apple; any of several elongated greenish English cooking apples. [Ety uncertain.]

codon [kō´dòn] *n* a triplet of bases in the DNA of the chromosomes which is part of the genetic code. [**code**.]

coeducation [kō-ed-ū-kā´sh(ò)n] *n* education of pupils or students of each sex in the same school or college. [**co-**, + **education**.]

coefficient [kō-ef-ish´ėnt] *n* that which acts together with another thing to produce an effect; (*math*) the numerical or literal factor prefixed to an unknown quantity in any algebraic term; (*phys*)— a numerical *constant* used as a multiplier of a *variable* quantity in calculating the magnitude of a particular physical property (eg expansion when heated) of a particular substance. [**co-**, + **efficient**.]

coenzyme [kō-en´zīm] *n* a substance necessary for the activity of an enzyme.

coerce [kō-ûrs´] *vt* to restrain by force; to compel (a person) to (*with* **into**); to enforce.—*adj* **coer´cible**.—*n* **coer´cion**, [-sh(ó)n]], restraint.—*adj* **coer´cive**, having power to coerce; compelling.—*adv* **coer´cively**. [L *coercēre—co-*, together, *arcēre*, to shut in.]

coeval [kō-ē´vàl] *adj* of the same age.—*n* one of the same age, a contemporary. [L *coaevus—co-*, together, and *aevum*, age.]

coexist [kō-egz-ist´] *vi* to exist at the same time.—*n* **coexis´tence**.—*adj* **co-exist´ent**.— [L *co-* together, + **exist**.]

coextensive [kō-eks-ten´siv] *adj* extending equally in time or space. [L *co-*, together + **extensive**.]

coffee [kof´i] *n* a drink made from the roasted, ground beanlike seeds of the coffee tree; the seeds; whole or ground, or the shrub.—*ns* **coffee cake**, a sweet rich quickbread made with nuts, fruit etc. **coff´ee table**, a small low table.—*adj* of a book, large and expensively illustrated.—**coffee tree**, a large shrub or small tree (*Coffea arabica*) native to Africa, but now cultivated in warm regions for its seeds. [Turk *qahwah*, orig meaning wine.]

coffer [kof´ėr] *n* a chest for holding money or treasure.—*n* **coff´erdam**, a watertight structure used for building the foundations of bridges, etc., under water. [OFr *cofre*, a chest—L *cophinus*, a basket—Gr *kophinos*, a basket.]

coffin [kof´in] a coffer or chest for a dead body.—*vt* to place within a coffin. [OFr *cofin*—L *cophinus*—Gr *kophinos*, a basket.]

cog [kog] *n* a catch or tooth on a wheel.—*vt* to fix teeth in the rim of a wheel;—*pr p* **cogg´ing**; *pt p* **cogged**.—*n* **cog´wheel**, a toothed wheel.

cogent [kō´jėnt] *adj* powerful, convincing.—*n* **cō´gency**, convincing power.—*adv* **cō´gently**. [L *cogĕre*—*co-*, together, *agĕre*, to drive.]

cogitate [koj´i-tāt] *vi* to turn a thing over in one's mind, meditate, ponder.—*n* **cogitā´tion**, meditation.—*adj* **cog´itātive**, meditative, reflective. [L *cōgitāre, -ātum*, to think deeply—*co-*, together and *agitāre*. See **agitate**.]

cognac [kon´yak] *n* a French brandy, so called because much of it is made near the town of *Cognac*.

cognate [kog´nāt] *adj* related, esp on the mother's side; allied to (*with* **with**); of the same kind, nature, or origin; (of words) developed from the same original word but having undergone a different series of sound changes in separate languages (eg Eng *father*, L *pater*, etc.).—*n* one related by blood, a kinsman (often, any kinsman other than an agnate).—**cognate object**, a word akin in origin or meaning to a normally intransitive verb and used as its object (eg *to live a life*). [L *cognātus*—*co-*, together, *(g)nasci, (g)nātus*, to be born.]

cognition [kog-nish´(ȯ)n] *n* knowledge; the mental processes (sensation, perception, etc.) by which knowledge is apprehended.—*adj* **cog´nizable**, that may be judicially investigated.—*n* **cog´nizance**, knowledge or notice, judicial or private; observation; jurisdiction; a badge.—*adj* **cog´nizant**, having cognisance or knowledge (of).—*adj* **cog´nitive**, capable of, or pertaining to, cognition. [L, from *cognoscĕre, cognitum*—*co-*, together, and *(g)noscĕre*, to know.]

cognomen [kog-nō´men] *n* a surname; a nickname; a name; the last of the three names usu. borne by a Roman, as Marcus Tullius *Cicero*. [L,—*co-*, together, *(g)nomen*, a name—*(g)noscĕre*, to know.]

cohabit [kō-hab´it] *vi* to dwell together as, or as if, husband or wife.—*n* **cohabitā´tion**. [L *cohabitāre*—*co-*, together, *habitāre*, to dwell.]

cohere [kō-hēr´] *vi* to stick together; to be consistent.—*ns* **cohēr´ence**, a sticking together; a consistent connection between several parts; **coher´ency**, the quality of being coherent.—*adj* **coher´ent**, sticking together; connected; consistent.—*adv* **coher´ently**.—*n* **cohē´sion**, the act of sticking together; a form of attraction by which particles of bodies stick together.—*adv* **cohē´sive**, tending to unite into a mass.—*adv* **cohē´sively**.—*n* **cohē´siveness**. [L *cohaerēre, cohaesum*—*co-*, together, *haerēre*, to stick.]

cohort [kō´hört] *n* a tenth part of a Roman legion; any band of warriors; a group of individuals having a statistical factor (as age, income, educational attainment) in common in a demographic study; an associate; a companion [Fr,—L *cohors, -tis*, an enclosed place, a multitude enclosed, a company of soldiers.]

coif [koif] *n* a covering for the head, esp a hoodlike cap worn under a veil by nuns; a close-fitting cap of lawn or silk formerly worn by lawyers; a woman's headdress.—*ns* **coiff´eur**, [kwäf-œr´] a hairdressing; a head-dress. [Fr *coiffe*—LL *cofia*, a cap.]

coign of vantage [koin] *n* a commanding position.

coil [koil] *vt* to wind (flexible material) in concentric rings.—*vi* to wind in rings.—*n* a length (of flexible material) coiled in rings; one of these rings; an arrangement of one or more turns of bare or insulated wire in an electrical circuit; a roll of postage stamps; a stamp from such a roll. [OFr *coillir*—L *colligĕre*—*col-*, together, *legĕre*, to gather.]

coil [koil] *n* tumult; fuss; the turmoil and vexation of everyday life.

coin [koin] *n* a piece of metal legally stamped and current as money.—*vt* to convert a piece of metal into money; to stamp; to invent (a word, phrase).—*ns* **coin´age**, the act of coining money; the currency; the pieces of metal coined; invention, fabrication; what is invented; **coin´er**, one who coins money; a maker of counterfeit coins; an inventor. [Fr *coin*, a wedge, also the die to stamp money—L *cuneus*, a wedge.]

coincide [kō-in-sīd´] *vi* to occupy the same space or time; to be identical; to agree, correspond (*often with* **with**).—*n* **coin´cidence**, act or condition of coinciding; the occurrence of one event at the same time as, or following, another without any causal connection.—*adj* **coin´cident**.—*adv* **coin´cidently**. [L *co-*, together, *incidĕre*—*in*, in, *cadĕre*, to fall.]

Cointreau [kwɛ-trō] *n* an orange-flavored liqueur. [Trademark.]

coir [koir] *n* the strong fiber from the outer husk of the coconut. [Dravidian *kāyar*, cord—*kāyaru*, to be twisted.]

coitus [kō´it-ůs] *n* sexual intercourse.—Also **coition** [kōish´ȯn]. [L *coitiō, -ōnis*,—*co-*, together, *īre, ītum*, to go.]

coke [kōk] *n* a fuel obtained by distilling coal, driving off its more volatile constituents; residue when any substance (eg petroleum) is carbonized.

col [kol] *n* a depression or pass in a mountain range. [Fr,—L *collum*, a neck.]

cola [kō´la] *n* a carbonated soft drink of sugar, caffeine, phosphoric acid or citric acid and flavored with extracts usu. from the Kola nut and coca leaves. [From *Coca-cola*, a trademark.]

colander [kul´end-ėr, or kol´-] *n* a vessel having small holes in the bottom, used as a strainer. [L *cōlāre*, to strain—*cōlum*, a strainer.]

cold [kōld] *adj* the opposite of hot; chilly, without passion or zeal; indifferent; unfriendly; reserved; without application of heat; (of a hunting scent) not fresh or off the track; (*inf*) unprepared; (*slang*) perfectly memorized; (*slang*) unconscious.—*n* lack of heat; the feeling or sensation caused by the absence of heat; cold weather; a virus infection of the respiratory tract, causing sneezing, coughing, etc.—*adv* **cold´ly**.—*n* **cold´ness**.—*adj* **cold´blood´ed**, having a body temperature that varies with the surrounding air or water, as fish and reptiles; unfeeling, cruel; frigid, unemotional.—*n* **cold´cream**, a creamy preparation for cleansing and softening the skin;—**cold feet**, lack of courage; **cold front**, the forward edge of a cold air mass advancing into a warmer mass; **cold storage**, storage and preservation of goods in refrigerating chambers; abeyance; **cold turkey**, (*slang*) abrupt and total withdrawal of narcotics; (slang) without preparation; **cold shoulder**, (*inf*) indifference, a rebuff.—**have** (or **get**) **cold feet**, (*inf*) to be (or become) timid; **in the cold**, neglected. [OE *cald, ceald*; Ger *kalt*; cog also with Eng **cool**.]

cole [kōl] *n* any of a genus (*Brassica*) of herbaceous plants (as bok choy, broccoli, cabbage, kohlrabi, and rape).—*ns* **cole´slaw, cole slaw** a salad of shredded cabbage; **cole´wort**, cole, esp one that forms no head (as kale). [OE *cāwel*; Ger *kohl*, Scot *kail*; L *colis, caulis*, a stem, esp of cabbage.]

coleopeteran [kol-e-op´ter-an] an order (coleoptera) of insects having two pairs of wings, the outer pair being hard or horny; the beetles. [Gr *koleos*, a sheath, and *pteron*, a wing.]

colic [kol´ik] *n* severe pain in the abdomen. [Fr, through L—Gr *kolikos*—*kolon*, the large intestine.]

coliseum [käl´i-sē´-um] *n* a large stadium. [Cf **Colosseum**.]

colitis *See* **colon** (2).

collaborate [kol-ab´ȯr-āt] *vi* to work in association; to work with, help, an enemy of one's country, etc.—*ns* **collaborā´tion; collab´orator**. [L *collaborāre, -atum*—*col-*, with, *laborāre*, to work.]

collage [kol-äzh] *n* an art form made up from scraps of paper and other odds and ends pasted down; any work made from assembled fragments. [Fr, pasting.]

collapse [kol-aps´] *n* a falling away or breaking down; any sudden or complete breakdown or prostration.—*vi* to fall or break down; to go to ruin.—*adj* **collaps´ible**, capable of collapsing or being reduced to a more compact form. [L *collapsus*—*col-*, together, *lābi, lapsus*, to slide or fall.]

collar [kol´ȧr] *n* something worn round the neck; the part of a garment at the neck; a band for an animal's neck.—*vt* to seize by the collar; to put a collar on; to seize.—*n* **coll´arbone**, the clavicle. [OFr *colier*—L *collāre*—*collum*, neck.]

collate [kol-āt´] *vt* to examine and compare, as books, and esp old manuscripts; to place in, appoint to, a benefice; to place in order, as the sheets of a book for binding.—*ns* **collā´tion**, act of collating; a bringing together for examination and comparison; presentation to a benefice; a repast between meals; **collā´tor**, one who collates or compares; one who bestows or presents. [L *collātum*, used as supine of *conferre*—*col-*, together, and *lātum* (*ferre*, to bring).]

collateral [kol-at´ȧr-ȧl] *adj* side by side; running parallel or together; descended from the same ancestor, but not in direct line; related (to a subject etc.) but not forming an essential part.—*n* a collateral kinsman; a collateral security.—*adv* **collat´erally**. [L *col-*, together, and *latus, lateris*, a side.]

colleague [kol´ēg] *n* one associated with another in a profession or occupation. [Fr *collègue*—L *collēga*—*col-*, together, and *legĕre*, to choose.]

collect [kol-ekt´] *vt* to assemble or bring together; to call for and remove; to gather (payments or contributions); to infer; to put (one's thoughts) in order; to regain control of (oneself).—*vi* to accumulate.—*n* **coll´ect**, a short prayer, consisting of one sentence, conveying one main petition.—*adj* **collect´ed**, composed, cool.—*adv* **collect´edly**.—*ns* **collect´edness**, self-possession, coolness; **collec´tion**, act of collecting; gathering of contributions, esp money; the money collected; an assemblage; a book of selections; range of new fashion clothes by a couturier.—*adj* **collect´ive**, pertaining to a group of individuals, common (eg interests, action, responsibility); derived from a number of flowers, as the fruit of the mulberry; (*gram*) expressing a number of individuals as a single group (*with sing verb*).—*n* a collective enterprise, esp a collective farm; the people who work together in it; a collective noun.—*adv* **collect´ively**.—*ns* **collect´ivism**, the political or economic theory advocating collective control, esp over production and distribution; a system marked by such control; **collect´ivist**.—Also *adj*—*n* **collect´or**, one who collects, as tickets, money specimens, etc.; **collective bargaining**, negotiation on conditions of service between an organized body of workers on one side and an employer or association of employers on the other; **collective farm**, state-controlled farm consisting of a number of small holdings operated on a cooperative basis. [L *colligĕre, -lectum*—*col-*, together, *legĕre*, to gather.]

colleen [kol´ēn] *n* an Irish girl. [Irish *cailín*.]

college [kol´ij] *n* a group of individuals with certain powers and duties (*the* *electoral college*); an institution of higher learning that grants degrees; any of the schools of a university; a school offering specialized instruction.—*adj* **collē´gial**, pertaining to a college.—*ns* **College Boards**, sets of examinations taken by aspirants to certain colleges; **collegial´ity**, the participation of bishops in the government of the Roman Catholic Church in collaboration with the Pope; **collē´gian**, a college student.—*adj* **collē´giate**, pertaining to or resembling a college.—**college try**, (*inf*) an all-out effort. [Fr *collège*—L *collegium*, from *col-*, together, and *legĕre*, to gather.]

collet [kol´ėt] *n* a collar holding the balance spring in a timepiece; the part of a ring that contains the stone. [Fr,—L *collum*; cf **collar**.]

collide [kol-īd´] *vi* to dash together; to clash.—*adjs* **collid´ed, collid´ing**.—*n* **colli´sion**, state of being struck together; a violent impact, a crash; conflict, opposition. [L *collīdĕre, collīsum*—*co-*, together, *laedĕre*, to strike.]

collie [kol´i] *n* a breed of sheepdog originating in Scotland. [Ety uncertain.]

collier [kol´yėr] *n* one that produces charcoal; one who works in a coal mine; a ship that carries coal.—*n* **coll´iery**, a coal mine and its connected buildings. [**coal**.]

collinear [ko-lin´e-ȧr] *adj* in the same straight line. [L *col-*, together, *līnea*, a line.]

collocate [kol´ō-kāt] *vt* to place together; to arrange.—*n* **collocā´tion**. [L *collocāre, -ātum*—*col-*, together, *locāre*, to place.]

collodion [kol-ō´di-on] *n* a gluey solution of cellulose nitrates in alcohol and ether, used in surgery and photography. [Gr *kollōdēs*—*kolla*, glue, *eidos*, form, appearance.]

collogue [ko-lōg´] *vi* to converse confidentially. [Prob—L *colloquī*, to speak together.]

colloid [kol´oid] *n* a substance in a state in which it can be suspended in a liquid, but (unlike a substance in true solution) is not able to pass through a semipermeable membrane.—*adj* **colloid´al**. [Gr *kolla*, glue, *eidos*, form.]

collop [kol´op] *n* a small piece or slice of meat. [Ety dub]

colloquy [kol´o-kwi] *n* a speaking together, mutual discourse, conversation.—*adj* **collō´quial**, pertaining to, or used in, common conversation.—*ns* **collō´quialism**, a form of expression used in familiar talk; **collo´quium**, an organised conference or seminar or some subject.—*adv* **collō´quially**. [L *colloquium*—*col-*, together, *loquī*, to speak.]

collotype [kol´o-tīp] *n* a printing process using gelatin, used esp for high quality work; a print made by collotype. [Gr *kolla*, glue + **type**.]

collude [kol-(y)ōōd´] *vi* to act in concert, esp in a fraud.—*n* **collu´sion**, act of colluding; a secret agreement to deceive.—*adj* **collu´sive**, fraudulently concerted; acting in collusion.—*adv* **collu´sively**. [L *collūdĕre, collūsum*, from *col-*, together, *ludĕre*, to play.]

colon[1] [kō´lon] *n* a punctuation mark (:) used esp to indicate a distinct member or clause of a sentence. [Gr *kōlon*, a limb.]

colon[2] [kō´lon] *n* the greater portion of the large intestine extending from the caecum to the rectum.—*ns* **colī´tis**, inflammation of the colon; **colic**, acute abdominal pain; **colos´tomy**, making of an artificial anus by surgical means. [L,—Gr *kolon*, the large intestine.]

colonel [kûr´nėl] *n* (*US mil*) a commissioned officer ranking just above a lieutenant colonel and below a brigadier general; an honorific title used for a minor titular official of a State, esp in southern or midland US.—*ns* **Colonel Blimp**, a pompous person with ultraconservative views; **col´onelcy**, office or rank, of a colonel. [Fr and Sp *coronel*; a corr of It *colonello*, the leader of a *colonna*, or column—L *columna*.]

colonnade [kol-ėn-ād´] *n* a range of columns placed at regular intervals; a similar row, as of trees. [Fr,—L *columna*.]

colony [kol´ŏn-i] *n* a body of persons under the laws of their native land who form a fixed settlement in another country; the settlement so formed (*zool*) a collection of organisms in close association; a community of the same nationality or pursuits, as within a city; a group of persons institutionalized away from others.—*adj* **Colon´ial**, of or in the thirteen British colonies that became the US; **colon´ial**, of, in, or having a colony.—*n* an inhabitant of a colony,—*ns* **colon´ialism**, a trait of colonial life or speech; the theory that colonies should be exploited for the benefit of the mother country; the practice of treating them this way; **colon´ialist**.—*vt* **col´onize**, to plant or establish a colony in; to form into a colony.—*ns* **colonizā´tion; col´onist**, an inhabitant of a colony. [L *colōnia*—*colĕre*, to till.]

colophon [kol´o-fon] *n* an inscription at the end of a book or literary composition with name, date, etc.; a publisher's imprint or device. [L *colophōn*—Gr *kolophōn*, end.]

colophony [kol-of´o-ni or kol´-] *n* rosin. [Gr from *Colophon*, in Asia Minor.]

color [kul´ȯr] *n* a sensation induced in the eye by light of certain wavelengths—particular color being determined by the wavelength; a property whereby bodies present different appearances to the eye through their differing ability to absorb or reflect light of different wavelengths; color of the face or skin; any coloring matter; pigment; dye; paint; (*pl*) a colored badge, etc. to identify the wearer; outward appearance; vivid quality; (*pl*) a flag.—*vt* to put color on, to stain, to paint; to set in a fair light; to exaggerate; to misrepresent; to give a certain quality to (eg *fear of loss colored his attitude to the problem*).—*vi* to show color; to blush.—*adj* **colorif´ic** [kol-], producing colors.—*ns* **colorā´tion; col´or bar´**, social discrimination between white and other races.—*adj* **col´or blind**, unable to distinguish certain colors; free from racial prejudice.—*n* **col´or blind´ness**.—*adjs* **col´ored**, having color; belonging to a dark-complexioned race; **col´orfast**, with color not subject to fading or running; **col´orful**, full of color; vivid.—*ns* **col´oring**, any substance used to give color; manner of applying colors; specious appearance; **col´orist**, one who colors or deals with color.—*adj* **col´orless**, without color; without distinctive quality, not vivid; dull, uninteresting.—**show one's colors**, reveal one's true self; **primary colors** (See **primary**). [OFr *color*—L *color*; akin to *celāre*, to cover.]

Colorado potato beetle [kol-ȯr-ä´dō] a black-and-yellow striped bettle (*Leptinotarsa decimlineata*) that feeds on the leaves of potatoes.—Also **potato beetle, potato bug**. [*Colorado*, state of US.]

coloratura [kol-or-ä-tōō´rä] *n* (*mus*) florid ornaments, or florid passages, in vocal music; a high and flexible soprano voice, capable of singing coloratura passages; a singer with such a voice. [It lit colouring.]

Colossians [kȯ-los´i-ȧnz] *n* (*Bible*) 12th book of the New Testament, an epistle written by St Paul to Christians of Colossal and Laodicea.

colossus [kol-os´us] *n* a gigantic statue, esp that of Apollo which stood at (but not astride of) the entrance to the harbor of Rhodes.—*adj* **coloss´al**, like a colossus; gigantic.—*n* **Colossē´um**, Vespasian's amphitheater at Rome, which was the largest in the world; **Colosseum**, a coliseum. [L,—Gr *kolossos*.]

colporteur [kol´pōr-tûr, -pör, or kol-pōrt-ėr´] *n* a peddler, esp one selling tracts and religious books.—*n* **col´portāge** [or kol´pōr´täzh], the distribution of books by colporteurs. [Fr *colporteur*, from *col* (L *collum*), the neck, and *porter* (L *portāre*), to carry.]

colt [kōlt] *n* a young male horse, esp one that has not reached an arbitrarily denoted age; horse; an inexperienced youth.—*adj* **colt´ish**, like a colt; frisky; wanton.—*n* **colts´foot**, any of various plants having leaves resembling a colt's foot, esp a perennial (*Tussilago farfara*) with yellow flowers appearing before the leaves. [OE *colt*; Swed *kult*, a young boar, a stout boy.]

columbine [kol´um-bīn] *n* any of a genus (*Aquilegia*) of plants with showy spurred flowers as the red-flowered plant (*A. canadensis*) of eastern N America and the blue-flowered herb (*A. coerulea*) of the Rocky Mountains.—*n* **columbā´rium**, a niche for a sepulchral urn. [L *columba*, a dove.]

Columbia [kȯ-lum´bi-ȧ] *n* the United States.—*adj* **Colum´bian**, of or relating to the US or Christopher Columbus.—*n* **columb´ium**, former name for niobium.—**Columbus Day**, October 12, formerly observed as a legal holiday in many States of the US; the second Monday in October observed as a legal holiday in many states of the US. [Christopher *Columbus*, who landed in the Bahamas in 1492.]

column [kol´um] *n* a long, round body, used to support or adorn a building; any upright body or mass suggestive of a column; a body of troops with narrow front; a perpendicular row of figures etc.; a perpendicular section of a page of print, etc.; a feature article appearing regularly in a newspaper, etc.—*adj* **column´nar**, like a column; formed in columns. [L *columen, columna*, akin to *celsus*, high; Gr *kolōnē*, a hill.]

colza [kol´za] *n* cole seed, yielding oil. [Du *koolzaad*, cabbage-seed.]

coma [kō´ma] *n* deep prolonged unconsciousness.—*adj* **com´atose**. [Gr *kōma*.]

Comanche [kȯ-man´chė] *n* member of an Amerindian people ranging from Wyoming and Nebraska into New Mexico and Texas;—*pl* **-che, -s**; the Uto-Aztecan language of the Comanche.

comb [kōm] *n* a toothed instrument for separating and cleaning hair, wool, flax, etc.; the fleshy crest of some birds; the top or crest of a wave, of a roof, or of a hill; an aggregation of cells for honey.—*vt* to separate, arrange, or clean by means of a comb; to search thoroughly.—*n* **comb´er**, one who, or that which, combs wool, etc.; a long foaming wave of the sea.—*n pl* **comb´ings**, hairs combed off. [OE *camb*.]

combat [kumbat´, or kom´bat] *vi* to contend or struggle.—*vt* to contend against, oppose.—*n* [kom´bat´] a struggle; a fight.—*adj* **com´batant**, fighting.—*n* one who is fighting.—*adj* **com´bative**, contentious.—*n* **com´bativeness**.—**combat fatigue**, mental disturbance in a fighting soldier. [Fr *combattre*, to fight—L *com-*, together, *bātuĕre*, to strike.]

combine [kom´bīn´] *vt* to join together in one whole; to unite closely; to possess together (diverse qualities); to follow (various pursuits), hold (various offices).—*vi* to come into close union; to cooperate toward (an end or result—*with* **to**); (*chem*) to unite and form a compound.—*n* [kom´bīn], an association formed for commercial or political, often unethical, purposes; a machine for harvesting and threshing grain.—*n* **combinā´tion**, the act of combining; union; persons united for a purpose; (*math*) a possible set of a given number of things selected from a given number, irrespective of arrangement within the set; the series of letters or numbers that must be dialled to move the mechanism of a combination lock and so open it; any of various one-piece undergarments.—*adj* **com´binative**.—**combining form**, a word form occurring only in compounds and derivatives. [L *combināre*, to join—*com-*, together, and *bīnī*, two and two.]

combustible [kom-bust´ibl] *adj* liable to take fire and burn; excitable.—*n* anything that will take fire and burn.—*ns* **combustibil´ity; combustion** [kombus´ch(ȯ)n], burning; oxidation or analogous process with evolution of heat. [L *combūrĕre, combustum*, to consume—*com-*, inten, *ūrĕre*, to burn.]

come [kum] *vi* to move towards this place; to draw near; to extend (to); to issue; to arrive at (a certain state or condition—*with* **to**); to amount (to); to become (eg *to come loose*); to chance, to happen; to occur in a certain order; to be derived or descended; to be caused; to result; to be available;—*pr p* **com´ing**; *pt* **came**; *pt p* **come**.—*interj* (or *imper*) as in **come,**

come or **come now**, implying remonstrance or encouragement.—(With sense of *prep*) by, on, or before, as in 'come Monday' = 'let Monday come', ie 'when (or before) Monday comes'.—*n* **com´er**, one who comes (usu. qualified, as *new-comer, late-comer, all comers*).—**come about**, to happen; (*naut*) to turn about; **come across**, to meet or find by chance; **come along**, to appear or arrive; to proceed or succeed; **comeback** (*inf*) a return to a previous position, as of power; (*inf*) a witty answer; a retort; **come by**, to make a visit; **come down**, to descend; to be reduced (*n* **come´down**, a descent; loss of prestige); **come in**, to enter a room, etc.; to reply to a radio signal or call; to find a place; to become fashionable; to place among those finishing in a race or contest; to assume power or office; **come in for**, to become subject to; **come into**, to enter into; to inherit; **come off**, to acquit oneself; to appear, seem; to happen; **come out**, to become known; to enter society; to end up; **come out for**, to announce endorsement of; **come out with**, to utter; **come around**, to recover; to yield; **come to**, to recover consciousness; to be a question of; **come to pass**, to happen; **come true**, to be fulfilled; **come up**, to arise, as a point in a discussion; **comeup´pance** (*inf*) deserved punishment; **how come**? (*inf*) why; **to come** (*predicative adj*) future. [OE *cuman*; Ger *kommen*.]

comedy [kom´e-di] *n* a play with a pleasant or humorous character; an amusing event.—*n* **comē´dian**, one who writes comedies; an actor of comic parts. [Through Fr and L,—Gr *kōmōidia*—*kōmos*, revel, *ōidē*, song.]

comely [kum´li] *adj* pleasing, graceful, handsome.—*n* **come´liness**. [OE *cȳmlic*—*cȳme*, suitable, *lic*, like.]

comestible [kom-est´ibl] *adj* edible.—Also *n* (usu. *pl*) food. [Fr,—*comedĕre*, to eat up.]

comet [kom´ėt] *n* a heavenly body which moves around the sun with a very eccentric orbit, having a definite nucleus and commonly a luminous tail.—*adj* **com´etary**. [Gr *komētēs*, long-haired—*komē*, the hair.]

comfit [kum´fit] *n* a candy that has a center of a piece of fruit, a nut, etc. coated and preserved with sugar. [Fr *confit*.]

comfort [kum´fört] *vt* to relieve from pain or distress; to cheer, revive.—*n* relief; encouragement; ease; quiet enjoyment; freedom from annoyance; any source of ease, enjoyment, etc.—*adj* **com´fortable**, imparting, or enjoying, comfort.—*adv* **com´fortably**.—*n* **com´forter**, one who comforts; a quilted bed covering; a long narrow, usu. knitted scarf; **Comforter**, the Holy Spirit.—*adj* **com´fortless**, without comfort.—**comfort station**, a public toilet or restroom. [OFr *conforter*—L *con-*, inten, *fortis*, strong.]

comic [kom´ik] *adj* pertaining to comedy; raising mirth; droll.—*n* (*inf*) an amusing person; an actor of droll parts, a comedian; a comic book; a comic strip; (*pl*) a section of comic strips.—*adj* **com´ical**, funny.—*n* **comical´ity**.—*adv* **com´ically**.—*ns* **comic book**, a magazine containing comic stories told in pictures like those of a comic strip; **comic opera**, a light opera, with a comic or farcical plot and much spoken dialogue; **comic relief**, comic scene in a tragedy affording, or supposed to afford, relief to the harrowed feelings; **comic strip**, a strip of small pictures showing consecutive stages in an adventure normally one of a series of adventures befalling a stock character or stock characters. [L *cōmicus*—Gr *kōmikos*.]

Comintern [kom´in-tûrn] *n* the *Com*munist *Intern*ational (1919–43) or Third International. [See **international**.]

comity [kom´i-ti] *n* courtesy, civility. [L *cōmitās*—*cōmis*, courteous.]

comma [kom´a] *n* in punctuation, the point (,) which marks a slight separation in a sentence; any of several butterflies (genus *Polygonia*) with a silvery comma-shaped mark on the hind wings.—**comma fault**, the use of a comma in a misleading way. [L,—Gr *komma*, a section of a sentence, from *koptein*, to cut off.]

command [kom´änd´] *vt* to order; to bid; to exercise supreme authority over; to have within sight, influence, or control; to deserve and get.—*vi* to have authority, to govern.—*n* an order; authority; control; the thing commanded; in a remote-control guidance system, a signal activating a mechanism or setting in motion a sequence of operations by instruments; a unit of the US Air Force higher than an air force; a military or naval force, or district, under a specified authority.—*n* **commandant´**, an officer who has the command of a place or of a body of troops.—*vt* **commandeer´**, to seize for military use.—*ns* **command´er**, one who commands; an officer in the navy or coast guard above a lieutenant commander and next in rank under a captain; **command´er in chief**, the officer in supreme command of an army, or of the entire forces of the state; **command´ership**.—*adj* **command´ing**, fitted to impress, or to control; dominating.—*adv* **command´ingly**.—*ns* **command´ment**, a command; a precept; one of the ten Biblical laws; **command´o**, member of a small force trained to raid enemy territory.—**command post**, the field headquarters of a military unit, from which operations are directed. [Fr *commander*—L *commendāre*—*com-*, inten, *mandāre*, to entrust.]

commemorate [ko-mem´o-rāt] *vt* to call to remembrance, esp by a solemn or public act; to celebrate; to serve as a memorial of.—*n* **commemorā´tion**, preserving the memory (of some person or thing) by a solemn ceremony, etc.—*adj* **commem´orative**. [L *commemorāre, -ātum*, to remember—*com-*, inten, and *memor*, mindful.]

commence [kom-ens´] *vi* and *vt* to begin; to originate.—*n* **commence´ment**, act, instance, or time of commencing; the day or ceremonies for conferring diplomas or degrees; the activities during this time. [OFr *com(m)encer*—L *com-*, inten, *initiāre*, to begin.]

commend [kom-end´] *vt* to commit as a charge (to); to recommend as worthy; to praise.—*adj* **commend´able**, praiseworthy.—*n* **commend´ableness**.—*adv* **commend´ably**.—*n* **commendā´tion**, the act of commending; praise; declaration of esteem.—*adj* **commend´atory**, commending, containing praise or commendation.—**commend me to**, give me for preference. [L *commendāre*—*com-*, inten, *mandāre*, to trust.]

commensalism [ko-men´sál-izm] *n* the association of two kinds of organisms in which one obtains food or other benefits from the other without damaging it or benefitting it.—*adj, n* **commen´sal**. [L *com-*, together, *mensa*, a table.]

commensurable [ko-men´sū-ra-bl] *adj* having a common standard of measurement.—*adv* **commen´surably**.—*adj* **commen´surate** [-át], equal in measure or extent; in due proportion (with, to).—*adv* **commen´surātely**. [L *com-*, with, *mensūra*, a measure—*mētīrī, mensus*, to measure.]

comment [kom´ent] *n* a note conveying an illustration or explanation; a remark, observation, criticism; talk, gossip.—*vi* to make critical or explanatory notes.—*ns* **comm´entary**, a series of explanatory notes or remarks; **comm´entator**, one who reports and analyzes events, trends, etc. as on television. [Fr,—L *commentārī*—*com-*, and *mens*, the mind.]

commerce [kom´érs] *n* interchange of merchandise on a large scale between nations or individuals; social intercourse; sexual intercourse.—*adj* **commer´cial**, pertaining to commerce, mercantile.—*n* an advertisement broadcast on television or radio.—*n* **commer´cialism**, the commercial spirit, institutions, or methods; excessive emphasis on profit.—*adv* **commer´cially**.—*vt* **commer´cialize**, to put on a business basis, esp so as to make a profit.—**commercial traveler**, a traveling salesman. [Fr,—L *commercium*—*com-*, with, *merx, mercis*, merchandise.]

commination [kom´in-ā-shȯn] *n* denunciation.—*adj* **comm´inatory**, threatening punishment. [L *comminārī, -ātum*—*com-*, inten, *minārī*, to threaten.]

commingle [ko-ming´gl] *vti* to mingle together. [L *com-*, together, + **mingle**.]

comminute [kom´in-ūt] *vt* to break in minute pieces, to pulverize.—*n* **comminū´tion**. [L *comminuĕre, -ūtum*—*com-*, *minus*, less.]

commiserate [kom-iz´ė-āt] *vt* to feel or express compassion for, to pity.—*vi* to condole (with).—*n* **commiserā´tion**. [L *com-*, with, *miserārī*, to deplore—*miser*, wretched.]

commissary [kom´is-ár-i] *n* formerly, an army officer in charge of supplies; a store, as in an army camp, where food and supplies are sold; a restaurant in a movie or TV studio.—*ns* **commissar** [-är], formerly, in USSR the head of a government department; **commissā´riat**, the department charged with the furnishing of provisions, as for an army; the supply of provisions; a government department in the former USSR until 1946. [Low L *commissārius*—L *committĕre, commissum*, to entrust.]

commission [kom-ish´(ȯ)n] *n* act of committing; that which is committed; a document conferring authority, or the authority itself; something to be done by one person on behalf of another; (*mil*) an official certificate conferring rank; (*mil*) the rank conferred; an order for a work of art, etc.; the fee paid to an agent for transacting business; a body of persons appointed to perform certain duties.—*vt* to give a commission to or for; to empower; (*naut*) to put (a vessel) into service.—*ns* **commiss´ioner**, one who holds a commission to perform some business, as to exercise authority on behalf of a government department; a member of a commission; a man appointed to regulate and control a professional sport. **commiss´ionership.—commissioned officer**, an officer in the armed forces holding a commission.—**in** (or **out of**) **commission** in (or not in) working order. [From **commit**.]

commit [kom-it´] *vt* to give in charge or trust; to consign; to become guilty of, perpetrate; to compromise, involve; to pledge (oneself);—*pr p* **committ´ing**; *pt p* **committ´ed**.—*ns* **commit´ment**, act of committing; an order for sending to prison, or mental institution; an obligation, promise, engagement; declared attachment to a doctrine or a cause; **committ´al**, commitment; a pledge, actual or implied.—*adj* **committ´ed**, having entered into a commitment; (of literature) written from, (of author) writing from, a fixed standpoint or with a fixed purpose, religious, political, or other.—*n* **committ´ee**, a number of persons, selected from a more numerous body, to whom some special business is committed. [L *committĕre*—*com-* with, *mittĕre, missum*, to send.]

commix [kom-iks´] *vt* to mix together.—*vi* to mix.—*n* **commix´ture**, act of mixing together; the state of being mixed; the compound so formed. [L *com-*, with, + **mix**.]

commodious [kom-ō´di-ùs] *adj* convenient; spacious; comfortable.—*n* **commode´**, a chest of drawers; a movable washstand; a toilet.—*adv* **commō´diously**.—*ns* **commō´diousness; commŏdity**, convenience; an article of traffic; (*pl*) goods, produce. [L *commodus*—*com-*, with, *modus*, measure.]

commodore [kom´o-dōr] *n* a naval officer intermediate between a rear admiral and a captain; the senior captain in a fleet of merchantmen; the chief officer of a yacht club or boating association. [Perh from Du *kommandeur*.]

common [kom´ȯn] *adj* belonging equally to more than one; public; general; widespread; familiar; usual; frequent; easy to be had; of little value; vulgar; denoting a noun (as a book) that refers to any of a group.—*n* a tract of open land, used in common by the inhabitants of a town, etc.—*ns* **comm´onalty**, the general body of the people; **comm´oner**, one who is not a noble.—*adv* **comm´only**.—*ns* **common carrier**, a person or company in the business of transporting people or goods for a fee; **common denominator**, a common multiple of the denominators of two or more fractions; a characteristic in common; **comm´onness; comm´onplace**, a common topic; a platitude;—*adj* lacking distinction; hackneyed.—*ns* **comm´onplace book**, a book of memorabilia; **comm´on room**, a lounge available to all members of a residential community; a room in a college for the use of the faculty.—*n pl* **comm´ons**, the common people; **Commons** (*Brit*) the lower House of Parliament or House of Commons.—*ns* **common chord**, a tone with its third and fifth; **common gender**, a noun having only one form to denote male or female (eg L *bōs*, bull, cow, or Eng *teacher, pupil*); **common law**, law based on custom, usage, and judicial decisions; **common market**, an association of countries as a single economic unit with internal free trade and common external tariffs; **common noun**, a name that can be applied to all the members of a class and is not the name of any specific member of a group; **comm´on sense**, good sense or practical sagacity; **common time**, (*mus*) four beats to the bar with the quarter note receiving a single beat.—**in common**, shared; equally (with others). [Fr *commun*—L *commūnis*, prob from *com-*, together, and *mūnis*, serving, obliging.]

commonwealth [kom´ón-welth] *n* the people of a nation or state; a democracy or republic; a federation of states; a state of the US, used officially of Kentucky, Massachusetts, Pennsylvania, and Virginia; **Commonwealth**, a federal union of constituent states, used officially of Australia; a political unit voluntary allied to the US, used officially of Puerto Rico and of the Northern Mariana islands; the English state from the death of Charles I to the Restoration in 1660; a loose association of self-governing autonomous states declaring a common allegiance (as to the British crown).—*n* **comm´onweal** [-wēl], (*arch*) commonwealth; the common good.

commotion [kom-ō´sh(ó)n] *n* a violent motion or moving; excited or tumultuous action, physical or mental; agitation; tumult. [L *com-*, inten, and *movēre, mōtum*, to move.]

commune[1] [kom´ūn] *n* in France, etc., a small territorial division; a group of people living together and sharing possessions.—*adj* **commū´nal** [or kom´-], pertaining to a commune or a community; owned in common. [Fr *commune*—L *commūnis*. See **common**.]

commune[2] [kom-ūn´] *vi* to converse together spiritually or confidentially. [OFr *comuner*, to share.]

communicate [kom-ū´ni-kāt] *vt* to make known; to give.—*vi* to have mutual access; to exchange information by letter, etc.; to partake of Holy Communion; to succeed in conveying one's meaning to others.—*adj* **commū´nicable**, that may be communicated, as an idea, or transmitted, as a disease.—*ns* **commū´nicant**, one who receives the Holy Communion; **communicā´tion**, act, or means, of communicating; information given; a letter, message; (in *pl*) routes and means of transport; (in *pl*) means of giving information, as the press, radio, and television.—*adj* **commū´nicative**, inclined to give information, unreserved.—*n* **commū´nicativeness**.—*adj* **commū´nicatory**, imparting knowledge.—*n* **communiqué** [kom-ū´ni-kā], official announcement. [L *commūnicāre, -ātum*—*commūnis*, common.]

communion [kom-ūn´yón] *n* act of communing; spiritual intercourse; fellowship; common possession; union in religious service; the body of the people who so unite.—**Communion Sunday**, a Sunday (as the first Sunday of the month) on which a Protestant church regularly holds a Communion service. [L *commūniō, -ōnis*—*commūnis*, common.]

communism [kom´ū-nizm] *n* a social order under which private property is abolished, and all things held in common; (loosely) the form of socialism developed in the former USSR; socialism as formulated by Marx, Lenin, etc.—*n* **comm´unist**, one who believes in or supports communism.—*adj* **communist´ic**. [Fr *communisme*—L *commūnis*; cf **common**.]

community [kom-ūn´i-ti] *n* common possession or enjoyment; agreement; a society of people having common rights, etc.; the public in general; any group having work, interests, etc. in common.—**community antenna television**, a system by which telecasts are received by a single high antenna and sent to local subscribers by direct cable; **community center**, a place where members of a community may meet for social, recreational, educational, and other activities; **community college**, a junior college serving a certain community; **community property** (*law*), in the States formerly under Spanish dominion, the union of assets upon marriage. [OFr,—L *commūnitās*—*commūnis*, common.]

commute [kom-ūt´] *vt* to exchange; to exchange (a punishment) for one less severe.—*vi* to travel regularly between two places, esp between surburban home and place of work in a city.—*adj* **commut´able**, that may be commuted or exchanged.—*ns* **commutabil´ity; commuta´tion**.—*adj* **commu´tative** (*math*), such that x*y = y*x—where * denotes a binary operation.—*ns* **comm´utātor**, an apparatus for reversing electric currents; **commut´er**, one who commutes.—*adj* **commut´ual**, mutual. [L *commūtāre*—*com-*, with, *mūtāre*, to change.]

compact[1] [kom-pakt´] *adj* closely placed or fitted together; firm; brief.—*vt* to press closely together; to consolidate.—*n* [kom´pakt] a small cosmetic case, usu. containing face powder and a mirror; a smaller model of automobile.—*n* **compac´tor**, a device that compresses trash into small bundles.—**compact disc**, a small plastic optical disc usu. containing recorded music.—*adv* **compact´ly**.—*n* **compact´ness**. [Fr,—L *compactus, pt p* of *compingĕre*—*com-*, together, *pangĕre*, to fix.]

compact[2] [kom´pakt] *n* a mutual bargain or agreement; a league, treaty, or union. [L *compactum*—*compacīscī*, from *com-*, together, and *pacīscī*, to make a bargain.]

companion[1] [kom-pan´yón] *n* one who keeps company or frequently associates with another, including one who is paid for doing so; an associate or partner; one of a pair or set.—*adj* of the nature of a companion; accompanying.—*adj* **compan´ionable**, fit to be a companion; agreeable.—*adv* **compan´ionably**.—*adj* **compan´ionless**.—*n* **compan´ionship**. [Fr *compagnon*, from Low L *compānium*, a messmate—L *com-*, with, and *pānis*, bread.]

companion[2] [kom-pan´yón], *n* a hood covering at the top of a companionway; a companionway;—*n* **compan´ionway**, the ladder or stair from an upper to a lower deck. [Du *kompanje*, store-room.]

company [kum´pa-ni] *n* any assembly of persons; a number of persons associated together for trade, etc.; a society; a military unit (as of infantry) consisting of usu. a headquarters and two or more platoons; the crew of a ship; fellowship; society; those members of a partnership firm whose names do not appear in the firm name.—**keep company**, to associate (with); to go together as a couple intending to marry; **part company**, to stop associating (with). [Fr *compagnie*.]

compare [kom-pār] *vt* to set (things) together to ascertain how far they agree or disagree; to set (one thing) beside another for such a purpose (*with* **with**); to liken or represent as similar (**to**); (*gram*) to give the degrees of comparison of.—*vt* to stand in comparison; to reflect or modify (an adjective or adverb) according to the degree of comparison.—*vi* to bear being compared; to make comparisons; to be equal or alike.—*adj* **com´părable**, that may be compared (**with**); worthy to be compared (**to**).—*n* **com´parableness**.—*adv* **com´parably**.—*adj* **compăr´ative**, pertaining to comparison; estimated by comparing with something else; not positive or absolute; (*gram*) expressing more.—*adv* **compar´atively**.—*n* **compăr´ison**, the act of comparing; comparative estimate; a simile or figure by which two things are compared; (*gram*) the inflection of an adjective or adverb to express different relative degrees of its quality.—**beyond compare, past compare, without compare**, without equal; **in comparison with**, compared with. [Fr,—L *comparāre*, to match, from *com-*, together, *parāre*, to make or esteem equal.]

compartment [kom-pärt´mėnt] *n* a separate part or division of any enclosed space; a separate section or category.—**compartment´alize**, to divide into categories or into units. [Fr, from *compartir*—L *com-*, with, *partire*, to part.]

compass [kum´pås] *n* a circuit or circle; space; limit, bounds; range of pitch of a voice or instrument; an instrument consisting of a magnetized needle, used to find directions; (often *pl*) an instrument consisting of two movable legs, for describing circles, etc.—*vt* to pass or go around; to surround or enclose; to besiege; to bring about or obtain; to contrive or plot. [Fr *compas*, a circle, prob from Low L *compassus*—L *com-*, together, *passus*, a step.]

compassion [kom-pash´(ó)n] *n* fellow feeling, or sorrow for the sufferings of another; pity.—*adj* **compassionate** [-sh(ó)n-åt] inclined to pity or mercy.—*adv* **compass´ionately**.—*n* **compass´ionateness**. [Fr—L *compassiō*—*com-*, with, *patī, passus*, to suffer.]

compatible [kom-pat´ibl] *adj* consistent; consistent (with); able to coexist.—*n* **compatibil´ity**, ability to coexist; ability of a television set not made for color to receive color signals in black and white.—*adv* **compat´ibly**. [Fr—L *com-*, with, *patī*, to suffer.]

compatriot [kom-pā´tri-ót or -pat´-] *n* a fellow countryman.—Also *adj*. [Fr—L *com-*, with, and **patriot**.]

compeer [kom-pēr] *n* one who is equal (to another—eg in age, rank); a companion. [L *compar*—*com-*, with, *par*, equal.]

compel [kom-pel´] *vt* to drive or urge on forcibly; to oblige (eg *to compel to go*); to force (eg obedience).—*pr p* **compell´ing**; *pt p* **compelled´**.—*adjs* **compell´able; compell´ing**, forcing attention. [L *com-*, inten, *pellĕre, pulsum*, to drive.]

compendium [kom-pen´di-ům] *n* a shortening or abridgment; a summary; a collection.—*pl* **compendiums, -dia**.—*adj* **compen´dious**, short; comprehensive.—*adv* **compen´diously**.—*n* **compen´diousness**. [L *compendium*, what is weighed together, hung up together, stored, or saved—*com-*, together, *pendĕre*, to weigh.]

compensate [kom´pen-sāt] *vt* to recompense (make up for loss, or remunerate for trouble); to counterbalance.—*vi* to make up (for).—*n* **compensā´tion**, act of compensating; that which counterbalances; reward for service; amends for loss sustained; process of compensating for sense of failure or inadequacy by concentrating on some other achievement or superiority, real or fancied.—*adj* **compen´satory**, giving compensation. [L *com-*, inten, and *pensāre*, freq of *pendĕre*, to weigh.]

compete [kom-pēt] *vi* to seek or strive for something in opposition to others; to contend (for a prize).—*n* **competition** [-pet-i´-] act of competing; rivalry; a contest; a match.—*adj* **compet´itive**, pertaining to, or characterized by, competition; (of eg price) such as to give a chance of successful result in conditions of rivalry.—*n* **compet´itor**, one who competes; a rival or opponent. [L *competĕre*—*com-*, together, *petĕre*, to seek.]

competent [kom´pe-tėnt] *adj* suitable; sufficient; capable; legally qualified; permissible (eg *it is competent to you to do so*).—*ns* **com´petence, com´petency**, fitness; sufficiency; enough to live on with comfort; capacity; legal power or capacity.—*adv* **com´petently**. [Fr—L *competěre*—*com-*, with, *petěre*, to seek, to strive after.]

compile [kom-pīl´] *vt* to write or compose by collecting the materials from other books; to draw up or collect.—*ns* **compilā´tion**, the act of compiling; the thing compiled, a literary work made by gathering the material from various authors; **compīl´er**. [Fr *compiler*, prob from L *compilāre*—*com-*, together, *pilāre*, to plunder.]

complacent [kom-plā´sėnt] *adj* showing satisfaction; self-satisfied.—*ns* **complā´cence, complā´cency**, contentment; self satisfaction.—*adv* **complā´cently**. [L *complacēre*—*com-* inten, *placēre*, to please.]

complain [kom-plān´] *vi* to express grief, pain, sense of injury (*absol or with* **of** *or* **about**); to state a grievance or make a charge (against someone—*with* **of** *and* **to**); to find fault.—*ns* **complain´ant** (*law*) a plaintiff; **complain´er**, a murmurer; complainant; **complaint´**, a complaining; an expression of grief, distress, or dissatisfaction; the thing complained of; (*law*) a formal charge; an ailment. [Fr *complaindre*—Low L *complangěre*—L *com-*, inten, *plangěre*, bewail.]

complaisant [kom-plā´zȧnt] *adj* desirous of pleasing, obliging; lenient.—*n* **complai´sance** [or kom-plāz´-ȧns] care or desire to please; an obliging civility.—*adv* **complai´sāntly**. [Fr—*complaire*—L *complacēre*.]

complement [kom´pli-mėnt] *n* that which completes or fills up; full number or quantity; that by which an angle or arc falls short of a right angle or quadrant; (*math*) all members of a set not included in a given subset.—*vt* to make complete.—*adjs* **complement´al**, of the nature of a complement; **complement´ary**, supplying a mutual deficiency; together making up a whole, or a right angle; constituting one of a pair of contrasting colors that produce a neutral color when combined in suitable proportions. [L *complēmentum*—*com-*, inten, *plēre*, to fill.]

complete [kom-plēt´] *adj* free from deficiency; perfect; entire; finished.—*vt* to finish; to make perfect or entire.—*adv* **complete´ly**.—*ns* **complete´ness**, the state of being complete; **complē´tion**, the act of completing; the state of being complete; fulfilment. [L *complēre*, *-ētum*, to fill up; *com-*, inten.]

complex [kom´pleks] *adj* composed of more than one, or of many, parts; not simple, intricate, difficult.—*n* a complex whole; a collection of interrelated buildings or units.—*n* (*psychoanalysis*) a group of mostly unconscious impulses, etc. strongly influencing behavior; (loosely) an obsession.—*n* **complex´ity**, state of being complex; complication.—*adv* **com´plexly**.—**complex number**, a number of the form $a + b\sqrt{-1}$ where *a* and *b* are real numbers; **complex sentence**, a sentence containing one or more subordinate clauses. [L *complex*—*com-*, *plicāre*; see **complicate**.]

complexion [kom-plek´sh(ȯ)n] *n* color or look of the skin, esp of the face; nature, character, temperament.—*adj* **complex´ioned**, having a specified complexion. [Fr—L *complexiō*, *-ōnis*, a combination, physical structure of body—*com-*, and *plectěre*, to plait.]

compliance [kom-plī´ȧns] *n* action in obedience to another's wish, request, etc.—the act of complying.—*adj* **complī´ant**, yielding, submissive.—*adv* **complī´antly**. [**comply** + suffx *-ance*.]

complicate [kom´pli-kāt] *vt* to entangle; to render complex, intricate, difficult.—*adj* **com´plicated**, intricately involved; hard to solve, analyze, etc.—*ns* **com´plicacy**, the quality or state of being complicated; **complicā´tion**, an intricate blending or entanglement; an involved state of affairs; an additional circumstance making (eg situation) more difficult; a condition or additional disease making recovery from the primary disease more difficult; **complicity** [komplis´i-ti] partnership in wrongdoing. [L *com-*, together, and *plicāre*, *-ātum*, to fold.]

compliment [kom´pli-mėnt] *n* an expression of regard or praise, or of respect or civility; (*pl*) respects.—*vt* **compliment´**, to pay a compliment to; to congratulate (on).—*adj* **compliment´ary**, conveying, or expressive of, civility or praise; using compliments; given free as a courtesy. [Fr *compliment*—L *complēmentum*.]

compline [kom´plin] *n* the seventh and last of the canonical hours. [OFr *complie*—L *complēta* (*hora*).]

comply [kom-plī´] *vi* to act in accordance (with the wishes or command of another, or with conditions laid down, etc.).—*pr p* **comply´ing**; *pt, pt p* **complied´**. [It *complire*, to fulfil, to suit, to offer courtesies—L *complēre*, to fill full, to fulfil.]

compo [kom´po] *n* any composite material. [Abbrev of **composition**.]

component [kom-pō´nėnt] *adj* making up; forming one of the elements of a compound whole.—*n* one of the elements of a compound; one of the parts of which anything is made up. [L *compōněre*, to make up.]

comport [kom´pōrt´] *vi* to agree, suit (with).—*vt* to bear, behave (oneself). [L *comportāre*—*com-*, together, *portāre*, to carry.]

compose [kom-pōz´] *vt* to form by putting together or being together; to set in order or at rest; to settle (eg dispute); to set up for printing; to create (esp in literature or music).—*vi* to create musical works, etc.—*adj* **composed´**, self-possessed; settled, quiet, calm.—*adv* **compos´edly**.—*ns* **compos´edness; compos´er**, a writer, an author, esp of a piece of music.—*adj* **com´posite**, made up of two or more distinct parts; **Composite** (*architecture*) a blending of the Ionic and the Corinthian orders; (*bot*) belonging to the family Compositae, a very large group of plants having small flowers or florets arranged in heads resembling single flowers (eg the daisy).—*n* a composite thing; a composite plant.—*adv* **com´positely**.—*ns* **com´positeness; composi´tion**, the act or process of composing, esp the arrangement of elements into proper proportion or relation into artistic form; the arrangement of type for printing; general makeup; the makeup of a chemical compound; a work in literature, music, or painting; a coming together or agreement, an arrangement or compromise; **compos´itor**, one who puts together, or sets up, type for printing; **com´post**, a mixture of decomposed organic matter for fertilizing soil.—*vt* to convert (plant debris) into compost.—*n* **compō´sure**, calmness, self-possession, tranquility. [Fr *composer*, from L *com-*, together, *pōnere*, to place, influenced in some meanings by confusion with *pausāre*, to cease, to rest.]

compos mentis [kom´pos ment´is] of sound mind, sane. [L.]

compote [kom´pōt] *n* fruit stewed in syrup. [Fr *compote*.]

compound[1] [kom-pownd´] *vt* to mix or combine; to make by combining parts; to compute (compound interest); to intensify by adding new elements; to settle or adjust by agreement; to agree for a consideration not to prosecute (a felony).—*vi* to become joined in a compound; to come to terms of agreement.—*adj* **com´pound**, mixed or composed of a number of parts; not simple.—*n* [kom´pownd] a mass made up of a number of parts; a word made up of two or more words; (*chem*) a distinct substance formed from two or more elements in definite proportions.—*ns* **compound´er**.—**compound fracture**, a fracture in which the bone pierces the skin; **compound interest**, interest paid on the principal and the accumulated unpaid interest; **compound sentence**, a sentence containing more than one principal clause. [OFr from L *compōněre*—*com-*, together, *pōněre*, to place.]

compound[2] [kom´pownd] *n* an enclosure around a building or buildings. [Malay *kampong*, enclosure.]

comprehend [kom-prė-hend´] *vt* to seize or take up with the mind, to understand; to comprise or include.—*adj* **comprehen´sible**, capable of being understood.—*adv* **comprehen´sibly**.—*ns* **comprehensibil´ity, comprehen´sibleness**.—*n* **comprehen´sion**, power of the mind to understand; act of understanding, or of including; comprehensiveness.—*adj* **comprehen´sive**, having the quality or power of comprehending much; inclusive; including much.—*adv* **comprehen´sively**.—*n* **comprehen´siveness**, fullness, completeness. [L *comprehenděre*—*com-*, together, *prehenděre*, *-hensum*, to seize.]

compress [kom-pres´] *vt* to press together; to force into a narrower space; to condense.—*n* **com´press**, a pad used in surgery to apply pressure to any part; a folded cloth applied to the skin.—*adj* **compress´ible**, that may be compressed.—*ns* **compress´ibleness**, the property of being reduced in volume by pressure; **compressibil´ity**, compressibleness; **compress´ion**, act of compressing; state of being compressed; the stroke that compresses the gases in an internal-combustion engine.—*adj* **compress´ive**, able to compress.—*n* **compress´or**, anything that compresses, thereby raising pressure, as a device that compresses air or gas. [L *compressāre*—*com-*, together, *pressāre*, to press—*preměre*, *pressum*, to press.]

comprise [kom-prīz´] *vt* to contain, include; to consist of. [Fr *compris*, *pt p* of *comprehendre*—L *comprehenděre*.]

compromise [kom´prō-mīz] *n* a settlement of differences by mutual concession; partial waiving of one's theories or principles for the sake of settlement; anything of intermediate or mixed kind.—*vti* to adjust by compromise; to lay open to suspicion, disrepute, etc.—*adj* **com´promised**, exposed to discredit. [Fr *compromis*—L *comprōmittěre*, *-missum*—*com-*, together, *prōmittěre*, to promise.]

compulsion [kom-pul´sh(ȯ)n] *n* the act of compelling; force, constraint, coercion.—*adj* **compul´sive**, coercive; with power to compel.—*adv* **compul´sively**.—*adj* **compul´sory**, obligatory; enforced; compelling.—*adv* **compul´sorily**. [Fr—LL *compulsiō*, *-ōnis*—L *compellěre*. See **compel**.]

compunction [kom-pungk´sh(ȯ)n] *n* uneasiness of conscience; remorse tinged with guilt.—*adj* **compunc´tious**, repentant; remorseful.—*adv* **compunc´tiously**. [OFr—L *compunctiō*, *-ōnis*—*com-*, inten, and *pungěre*, *punctum*, to prick.]

compurgation [kom-pûr-gā´sh(ȯ)n] *n* the clearing of the accused by **compurgators**, witnesses testifying to his innocence or veracity; evidence in favor of the accused; vindication. [L *compurgāre*, to purify wholly—*com-*, inten. See **purge**.]

compute [kom-pūt´] *vt* to determine, esp by mathematical means; to calculate by means of a computer.—*vi* to reckon; to use a computer.—*adj* **comput´able**, calculable.—*ns* **computā´tion**, act of computing; reckoning; **comput´er**, a calculator; a mechanical, electric or electronic device that stores numerical or other information and provides logical answers at high speed to questions bearing on that information.—*vt* **comput´erize**, to store in a computer; to put in a form that a computer can use; to equip with computers; to bring computer(s) into use to control (an operation); to process (data) by computer.—**computer-assisted tomography**, the production of X-ray pictures of sections of the body with the assistance of a computer.—Also **CAT scan**. [L *computāre*—*com-*, together, *putāre*, to reckon.]

comrade [kom´rȧd] *n* a close companion, intimate associate; in some socialist and communist circles used as a term of address or prefixed to a name.—*n* **com´radeship**. [Sp *camarada*, a roomful, a room-mate—L *camera*, a room.]

con[1] [kon] a contraction of L *contrā*, against, as in **pro and con**, for and against.

con[2] [kon] *vt* to study carefully; to commit to memory.—*pr p* **conn´ing**; *pa p* **conned**. [OE *cunnian*, to try to know—*cunnan*, to know.]

con[3] [kon] *adj* abbrev for **confidence** as in (*slang*) **con game**, a swindle; **con man** (*slang*) a swindler, esp one with a persuasive way of talking.—*vt* (*slang*) to swindle, trick.

con[4] [kon] *n* (*slang*) a convict.

concatenate [kon-kat´e-nāt] *vt* to link together, to connect in a series.—*n* **concatenā´tion**, act of concatenating; state of being linked or mutually dependent; a series of things (eg events) linked to each other. [L *con-*, together, and *catēna*, a chain.]

concave [kon´kāv] *adj* curved inward like the inside of a bowl.—*n* a concave line or surface.—*n* **concăv´ity**, the quality of being concave; the inner surface of a concave or hollow body. [L *concavus*, from *con-*, inten, *cavus*, hollow. See **cave**.]

conceal [kon´sēl] *vt* to hide; to keep secret.—*n* **conceal´ment**, act of concealing; secrecy. [OFr *conceler*—L *concēlāre*—*con-*, inten, and *cēlāre*, to hide.]

concede [kon-sēd´] *vt* to admit as true, valid, etc. (eg a claim, a point in argument); to grant (eg a right).—*vi* to admit or grant (that); to yield. [L *concēdĕre, -cessum*—*con-*, wholly, *cēdĕre*, yield.]

conceit [kon-sēt´] *n* overweening self-esteem; vanity; a witty thought, esp far-fetched, affected, or over-ingenious.—*adj* **conceit´ed**, having a high opinion of oneself; egotistical.—*adv* **conceit´edly**.—*n* **conceit´edness**. [From **conceive**, on the analogy of *deceive, deceit*.]

conceive [kon-sēv´] *vt* to become pregnant with; to form in the mind; to imagine or think; to understand.—*vi* to become pregnant; to form an idea of.—*adj* **conceiv´able**.—*adv* **conceiv´ably**.—*ns* **conceivabil´ity, conceiv´ableness**. [OFr *concever*—L *concipĕre, conceptum* from *con-*, and *capĕre*, to take.]

concentrate [kon´sen-trāt] *vt* to bring towards a common center; to focus; to direct with a single purpose or intention; to condense, to render more intense the properties of.—*vi* to draw towards a common center; to direct one's energies to a single aim.—*n* a product of concentration, esp a food reduced in bulk by eliminating fluid; foodstuff relatively high in nutrients.—*n* **concentrā´tion**, act or process of concentration; direction of attention to a single object.—*adj* **concen´trative**, tending to concentrate.—**concentration camp**, a camp where persons (as prisoners of war, political prisoners, and refugees) are detained or confined. [A lengthened form of *concentre*, to bring, or come, together to a focus or center.]

concentric [kon-sent´rik] *adj* having a common center, as circles. [Fr *concentrique*—L *con-*, with, *centrum*—Gr *kentron*, a point.]

concept [kon´sept] *n* a thing conceived, a general notion.—*n* **concep´tion**, the act of conceiving or being conceived in the womb; the thing conceived; the formation in the mind of an image or idea; a concept; an original idea or design.—*adj* **concep´tual**, pertaining to conception or to concepts.—*n* **concep´tualism**, a theory in philosophy standing between normalism and realism holding that universals exist in the mind as concepts of discourse which may exist in reality. [L *concipĕre, -ceptum*, to conceive.]

concern [kon-sûrn´] *vt* to relate or belong to; to affect or interest; to make uneasy; to interest, trouble (oneself—*with* **with, in, about**).—*n* that which concerns or belongs to one; interest in or regard for a person or thing; anxiety; a business, or those connected with it.—*adj* **concerned´**, having connection with; interested; anxious.—*adv* **concern´edly**.—*prep* **concern´ing**, regarding; pertaining to.—*n* **concern´ment**, something in which one is concerned; importance; anxiety.—**as concerns**, in regard to; **concern oneself**, to busy oneself; to be worried. [Fr—L *concernĕre*—*con-*, together, *cernĕre*, to distinguish, perceive.]

concert [kon´sėrt] *n* union or agreement in any undertaking; harmony; musical harmony; a musical entertainment.—*vt* **concert´**, to frame or devise together; to arrange, plan.—*vi* to act in harmony or conjunction.—*ns* **concertina** [konsėr-tē´na] a musical instrument the sounds of which are produced by free vibrating reeds of metal, as in the accordion; coiled barbed wire for use as an obstacle; **concerto** [kon-chėr´to] a composition for solo instrument(s), with orchestral accompaniment.—*pl* **concer´tos, concer´ti**.—*n* **con´certmas´ter**, the leader of the first violin section in a symphony orchestra.—**concert pitch**, the (higher) pitch at which instruments are tuned; international pitch, at which A over middle C is at 440 vibrations per second; (*inf*) a state of extreme readiness. [It *concertare*, to sing in concert.]

concession [kon-sesh´(ȯ)n] *n* the act of conceding; the thing conceded; a privilege granted by a government, company, etc. as the right to sell food at a park.—*n* **concessionaire´**, one who has obtained a concession to sell, etc.—*adj* **concess´ive**, implying concession; expressing concession. [**concede**.]

conch [kongk] *n* a marine gastropod mollusk (genera *Strombus* and *Cassis*) with a large spiral shell; the outer ear or its cavity.—*adj* **conchoid´al**, having the form of a conch; (*minerology*) having elevations and depressions shaped like the inside of a conch, esp of a surface produced by a fracture.—*ns* **conchol´ogy**, that branch of natural history which deals with the shells of mollusks; **conchol´ogist**. [L *concha*—Gr *konchē*, a cockle.]

concierge [k•-si-erzh´] *n* a resident doorkeeper, janitor, landlord's representative, esp in France; a hotel staff member in a European hotel who helps guests with luggage, arranges tours, etc. [Fr; ety unknown.]

conciliate [kon-sil´i-āt] *vt* to gain or win over; to appease.—*ns* **conciliā´tion**, act of conciliating; **concil´iator**.—*adj* **concil´iatory**. [L *conciliāre, -ātum*—*concilium*, council.]

concise [kon-sīs´] *adj* cut short; brief, using, or expressed in, few words.—*adv* **concise´ly**.—*ns* **concise´ness; concision** [-sizh´-] conciseness. [Fr—L *concīdĕre, concīsum*, from *con-*, and *caedĕre*, to cut.]

conclave [kon´klāv] *n* a private meeting, esp of Roman Catholic cardinals secluded continuously while choosing a pope; a gathering of an association. [L *conclāve*, from *con-*, together, *clāvis*, a key.]

conclude [kon-klōōd´] *vt* (*arch*) to enclose, shut up; to end; to decide; to infer; to arrange (a treaty, etc.).—*vi* to end; to form a final judgment.—*n* **conclusion** [-clōō´zh(ȯ)n] act of concluding; the end, close, or last part; inference; judgment.—*adj* **conclusive** [clōō´siv] final; convincing.—*adv* **conclus´ively**.—*n* **conclus´iveness**. [L *conclūdĕre, conclūsum*—*con-*, together, *claudĕre*, to shut.]

concoct [kon-kokt´] *vt* to make by combining ingredients; to devise, to plan; to fabricate (as a dish in cookery); to fabricate (eg a story).—*n* **concoc´tion**, act of concocting; preparation of a mixture; the mixture so prepared. [L *concoquĕre, concoctum*—*con-*, together, and *coquĕre*, to cook, to boil.]

concomitant [kon-kom´i-tȧnt] *adj* connected with some thing, action, or state, and accompanying it (eg *concomitant pleasures, circumstances*).—Also *n*.—*ns* **concom´itance, concom´itancy**, coexistence. [L *con-*, with, *comitans*, pr p of *comitārī*, to accompany—*comes*, a companion.]

concord [kon´körd or kong´-] *n* state of being of the same heart or mind; agreement; a treaty; a combination of sounds satisfying to the ear; grammatical agreement.—*n* **concord´ance**, agreement; an alphabetical list of the words in a book, with references to the passages where they occur; a similar list for the works of an author.—*adj* **concord´ant**, harmonious; in harmony (with).—*n* **concord´at**, an agreement, esp a treaty between the pope and a secular government for the regulation of church matters. [Fr *concorde*—L *concordia*—*concors*, of the same heart, from *con-*, together, *cor, cordis*, the heart.]

concourse [kon´-, kong´-körs] *n* a moving or flowing together of persons; a meeting resulting from a voluntary or spontaneous coming together; an open space for crowds as in a park; an open space or hall (as in a railroad terminal) where crowds gather. [Fr—L *concursus*—*con-*, together, *currĕre*, to run.]

concrescence [kon-kres´ėns] *n* a growing together. [L *concrescentia*—*con-*, together, *crescĕre*, to grow.]

concrete [kon-krēt´] *adj* having a material existence; denoting a thing, not a quality or state; particular, not general; made of concrete.—*n* [kon´krēt] anything concrete; a mixture of lime, sand, pebbles, etc., bonded together with cement, used in building.—*vti* **concrēte´**, to form into a solid mass; to cover with concrete.—*adv* **concrēte´ly**.—*ns* **concrēte´ness; concrē´tion**, a mass concreted; a solidified mass.—**concrete poetry**, an art form which makes use of visual effects such as the arrangement of letters on the printed page. [L *concretus*—*con-*, together, *crescĕre, crētum*, to grow.]

concubine [kong´kū-bīn] *n* a woman living in a socially recognized state of concubinage; a mistress.—*n* **concū´binage**, state of living together as man and wife without being married; state of being a secondary wife. [Fr—L *concubīna*—*con-*, together, *cubāre*, to lie down.]

concupiscence [kon-kū´pis-ėns] *n* violent desire; sexual appetite, lust.—*adj* **concū´piscent**. [Fr—L *concupiscentia*—*concupiscĕre*—*con-*, inten, *cupĕre*, to desire.]

concur [kon-kûr´] *vi* (*obs*) to run together; to meet in one point; to coincide; to act together; to agree in opinion (with).—*pr p* **concurr´ing**; *pt p* **concurred´**.—*n* **concurr´ence**, the meeting of lines in one point; coincidence; joint action; assent.—*adj* **concurr´ent**, meeting in the same point; coming, acting, or existing together; coinciding; accompanying.—*adv* **concurr´ently**. [L *concurrĕre*—*con-*, together, *currĕre*, to run.]

concuss [kon-kus´] *vt* to affect with concussion.—*n* **concussion** [-kush´-], a violent shock caused by sudden impact; impaired functioning produced by a heavy blow, esp on the head.—*adj* **concuss´ive**, having the power or quality of concussion. [L *concussus*, pa p of *concutĕre*—*con-*, together, *quatĕre*, to shake.]

condemn [kon-dem´] *vt* to pronounce guilty; to censure or blame; to sentence to punishment or to an unpleasant fate; to pronounce unfit for use; to appropriate (property) for public use.—*adj* **condem´nable** [-dem´nȧ-bl].—*n* **condemnation**, state of being condemned; blame; cause of being condemned.—*adj* **condem´natory**, expressing or implying condemnation. [L *condemnāre*, from *con-*, inten, *damnāre*, to condemn.]

condense [kon-dens´] *vt* to render more dense or compact; to express in fewer words; to change to a denser form, as from gas to liquid; to reduce to smaller compass.—*vi* to become condensed.—*adj* **condens´able**.—*ns* **condensabil´ity; condensā´tion**, act, or process, of condensing; what is produced by condensing; **condens´er**, a lens or mirror used to concentrate light on an object; an apparatus in which gas or vapor is condensed; a capacitor; **condensed milk**, milk reduced by evaporation, and sugared. [L *condensāre*—*con-*, inten, and *densus*, dense.]

condescend [kon´di-send´] *vi* to act graciously or patronizingly to inferiors; to deign; to stoop (to what is unworthy).—*adj* **condescend´ing**, gracious to inferiors; patronizing.—*adv* **condescend´ingly**.—*n* **condescen´sion**. [L *con-*, inten, *descendĕre*, to descend.]

condign [kon-dīn´] *adj* well merited; adequate (of punishment).—*adv* **condign´ly**.—*n* **condign´ness**. [L *condignus—con-*, wholly, *dignus*, worthy.]

condiment [kon´di-mėnt] *n* a seasoning or relish used to give flavor to food. [L *condīmentum—condīre*, to preserve, to pickle.]

condition [kon-dish´(ȯ)n] *n* anything required for the performance, completion, or existence of something else; (*inf*) an illness; a healthy state; (*pl*) attendant circumstances; an unsatisfactory academic grade that may be raised by further work; a particular state of being (eg *in a liquid condition*); rank, standing; a prerequisite (eg *air to breathe is a condition of survival*).—*vt* to agree upon; to limit, determine, control; to put into the required state, eg to clean, warm, and render humid (the air admitted to a building); to prepare, train (person, animal) for a certain activity or for certain conditions of living; to make accustomed (to).—*adj* **condi´tional**, expressing condition; depending on conditions; not absolute.—*adv* **condi´tionally**.—*adj* **condi´tioned**, having a (specified) condition, state, or quality; circumstanced; subject to condition.—*ns* **condi´tioner**, a person, substance, or apparatus that brings into good or required condition; **condi´tioning**, a bringing into a state of fitness for an objective.—**on condition that**, provided that. [L *condīciō, -ōnis*, a compact (later false spelling *conditio*)—*condīcĕre—con-*, together, *dīcĕre*, to say.]

condole [kon-dōl´] *vi* to grieve (with another); to express sympathy in sorrow.—*n* **condol´ence**, expression of sympathy with another's sorrow. [L *con-*, with, *dolēre*, to grieve.]

condom [kön´-dȯm, kän´-] *n* a sheath, usu. of rubber, for the penis, used as a prophylactic or contraceptive. [Origin unknown.]

condominium [kon-dō-min´i-um] *n* an apartment in an apartment building owned by an individual; joint sovereignty; a government administered by two or more powers; a region under such a government. [L *con-*, together, *dominium*, lordship.]

condone [kon-dōn´] *vt* to pass over without blame, to excuse.—*n* **condonā´tion**, an overlooking of an offense. [L *con-*, inten, *donāre*, to give. See **donation**.]

condor [kon´dȯr] *n* a large vulture (*Vulture gryphus*) found in the high Andes of S America. [Sp,—Peruvian *cuntur*.]

condottiere [kon-dot-tyā´rā] *n* a leader of a band of mercenary soldiers in 14th and 15th centuries; a mercenary soldier;—*pl* **condottieri** [-rē]. [It,—*conditto* way—L *con-, ducĕre*, to lead.]

conduce [kon-dūs´] *vi* to tend, to contribute (to some end).—*adj* **conduc´ive**, leading or tending (to), having power to promote.—*n* **conduc´iveness**. [L *condūcĕre—con-*, together, *dūcĕre*, to lead.]

conduct [kon-dukt´] *vti* to lead or guide; to convey (water, etc.); to direct (eg an orchestra); to manage (eg a business); to behave (oneself); (*elect, heat*) to transmit.—*ns* **con´duct**, act or method of leading or managing; guidance; management; behavior; **conduct´ance**, power of conducting electricity.—*adj* **conduct´ible**, capable of conducting heat, etc.; capable of being conducted or transmitted.—*ns* **conductibil´ity; conduc´tion**, act or property of conducting or transmitting; transmission (eg of heat) by a conductor; transmission of excitation through nervous tissue.—*adj* **conduct´ive**, having the quality or power of conducting or transmitting.—*ns* **conductiv´ity**, a power that bodies have of transmitting heat and electricity; **conduct´or**, a director of an orchestra or choir; one in charge of passengers on a train, etc.; that which has the property of transmitting electricity, heat, etc. [L *conductus—condūcĕre*. See **conduce**.]

conduit [kun´dit, or kon´-] *n* a channel or pipe to convey water, etc.; a tube for electric wires. [Fr *conduit*—L *conductus—condūcĕre*, to lead.]

cone [kōn] *n* a solid figure with a circular or elliptical base tapering to a point; any cone-shaped object; the scaly fruit, more or less conical, as that of the pine, fir, etc.; any of numerous conical gastropod mollusks (family Conidae).—*ns* **cone´flower**, any of several composite plants having cone-shaped flower disks, esp rudbeckia; **cŏ´nic**, a conic section.—*adj* **conical**, resembling a cone, esp in shape.—**conic section**, a curve formed by the intersection of a plane with a right circular cone, a parabola or ellipse. [Gr *kōnos*.]

Conestoga [kon-ė-stōg´ȧ] *n* a broad, covered wagon used by settlers of America traveling across the prairies. [*Conestoga*, Pa]

coney, cony [kō´nē] *n* a rabbit or its fur; any of various small short-eared mammals (family Ochotonidae) of the rocky parts of high mountains related to rabbits. [Prob through OFr *connil*, from L *cunīculus*, a rabbit.]

confabulate [kon-fab´ū-lāt] *vi* to chat.—*n* **confabulā´tion; con´fab** (*inf*) an informal talk, chat. [L *con-*, together, *fābulārī*, to talk.]

confection [kon-fek´sh(ȯ)n] *n* a candy, ice cream, preserve, etc.; a medicine prepared with sugar, syrup, or honey; a piece of fine craftsmanship.—*ns* **confec´tionary**, a confectioner's shop; **confec´tioner**, one who makes or sells sweets; **confec´tionery**, the art; sweet foods (as candy or pastry); a confectioner's shop.—**confectioners' sugar**, a finely powdered sugar. [L *conficĕre, confectum*, to make up together—*con-*, together, *facĕre*, to make.]

confederate [kon-fed´ėr-ȧt] *adj* leagued together, allied; **Confederate**, of the Confederacy.—*n* one united in a league, an ally, accomplice; **confederate**, a southern supporter of the confederacy.—*vti* [-āt] to league together or join in a league.—*ns* **confed´eracy**, a league, alliance; **the Confederacy**, the eleven Southern States that seceded from the US in 1860 and 1861; **confederā´tion**, an alliance; **the Confederation**, the United States from 1781 to 1789. [L *confoederāre, -ātum—con-*, together, *foedus, foedĕris*, a league.]

confer [kon-fûr´] *vt* to give or bestow; to compare views or take counsel; to consult;—*pr p* **conferr´ing**; *pt p* **conferred´**.—*n* **con´ference**, the act of conferring; an appointed meeting for consultation or discussion; an association of schools, churches, etc. [Fr—L *conferre—con-*, together, *ferre*, to bring.]

confess [kon-fes´] *vt* to acknowledge fully, esp something wrong; to own or admit; to make known, as sins to a priest; to hear confession from, as a priest.—*vi* to make confession; to hear a confession.—*ns* **confess´ion**, acknowledgement of a crime or fault; a thing confessed; a statement of religious belief; acknowledgement of sin to a priest; a sect; a denomination; **confess´ional**, an enclosure in a church where a priest hears confessions.—*adj* pertaining to confession or to a creed.—*n* **confess´or**, a priest who hears confessions and grants absolution; one who confesses.—*adj* **confessed´**, admitted, avowed.—*adv* **confessedly** [kon-fes´id-li] admittedly. [Fr *confesser*—L *confitērī, confessus—con-*, signifying completeness, *fatērī*, to confess.]

confetti [kon-fet´tē] *n pl* bits of colored paper thrown about at celebrations, esp weddings. [It (sing *confetto*); cf **comfit, confection**.]

confide [kon-fīd´] *vi* to trust wholly or have faith (*with* **in**); to impart secrets with trust.—*vt* to entrust (to one's care); to impart with reliance upon secrecy.—*ns* **confidant´**, one to whom secrets are confided; a bosom friend; **con´fidence**, firm trust, belief, or expectation; admission to knowledge of private affairs, etc.; a confidential communication; belief in one's own abilities.—*adj* **con´fident**, trusting firmly; positive; bold.—*adv* **con´fidently**.—*adj* **confiden´tial**, confided (eg information); entrusted with secrets (eg *confidential secretary*).—*adv* **confiden´tially**.—**confidence game**, a swindle effected by one (**confidence man**) who first gains the confidence of his victim. [L *confīdĕre—con-*, inten, *fīdĕre*, to trust.]

configuration [kon-fig-ū-rā´sh(ȯ)n] *n* external figure or shape, outline; relative position or aspect, as of planets; the spatial arrangement of atoms in a molecule. [L *configūrātiō—con-*, together, and *figurāre*, to form—*figūra*, shape. Cf **figure**.]

confine [kon´fīn] *n* border, boundary, or limit—generally in *pl*—*vt* [kon-fīn´] to restrict, to keep within limits; to keep shut up, as in prison, a sickbed, etc. limit; to imprison.—*adj* **confīn´able**.—*n* **confine´ment**, state of being shut up; restraint from going out esp of women in childbirth. [Fr *confiner*—L *confinis*, bordering—*con-*, together, *finis*, the end.]

confirm [kon-fûrm´] *vt* to strengthen, to establish more firmly; to make (a person) more firm (eg in belief, habit); to ratify; to corroborate; to verify; to admit to full church membership.—*n* **confirmā´tion**, a making firm or sure; convincing proof; the rite by which persons are admitted to full church membership.—*adjs* **confirm´ative**, tending to confirm; **confirm´atory**, giving further proof, confirmative, corroborative; **confirmed´**, settled, inveterate, habitual. [OFr *confermer*—L *confirmāre—con-*, inten, *firmāre—firmus*, firm.]

confiscate [kon´fis-kāt] *vt* to seize (private property) for the public treasury; to seize by authority.—*adj* forfeited to the state.—*adjs* **confis´cable**, liable to confiscation; **confis´catory** [or kon´-], effecting, of the nature of, characterized by, confiscation.—*ns* **confiscā´tion**, act of confiscating; state of being confiscated; **con´fiscator**. [L *confiscāre, -ātum—con-*, together, *fiscus*, the state treasury.]

conflagration [kon-fla-grāsh´(ȯ)n] *n* a great destructive burning or fire. [L *conflagrāre—con-*, inten, and *flagrāre*, to burn.]

conflict [kon´flikt] *n* violent collision; a struggle or contest; emotional disturbance.—*vi* [kon-flikt´] to fight, contend; to be in opposition; to clash.—*adj* **conflict´ing**, clashing; contradictory.—**conflict of interest**, a conflict between the obligation to the public and the self-interest of a public officeholder, etc. [L *conflīgĕre—con-*, together, *flīgĕre*, to strike.]

confluence [kon´flŏŏ-ėns] *n* a flowing together; the place of meeting, as of rivers; a concourse.—*adj* **con´fluent**, flowing together; uniting.—*n* a stream uniting and flowing with another; a tributary.—*adv* **con´fluently**.—*n* **con´flux**, a flowing together. [L *confluĕre, confluxum*, from *con-*, together, *fluĕre*, to flow.]

conform [kon-förm´] *vi* to be or become of the same form; to comply with (*with* **to**); to act in accordance with rules, customs, etc.—*vt* to make (something) like (to); to adapt.—*adj* **conform´able**, corresponding in form; suitable; compliant.—*adv* **conform´ably**.—*ns* **conformā´tion**, particular form, shape, or structure; a symmetrical arrangement of the parts of a thing; **conform´er, conform´ist**, one who conforms, esp with the worship of the established church; **conform´ity**, correspondence; agreement; conventional behavior; compliance; consistency. [L *conformāre—con-*, with, *formāre—forma*, form.]

confound [kon-fownd´] *vt* to confuse, fail to distinguish between; to throw into disorder; to discomfit; to perplex;—*adj* **confound´ed**, confused; astonished; (*inf*) abominable, horrible.—*adv* **confound´edly.—confound you**, a mild execration. [OFr *confondre*—L *confundĕre, -fūsum—con-*, together, *fundĕre*, to pour.]

confraternity [kon-fra-tûr´ni-ti] *n* a brotherhood; a religious society, usu. of laymen. [L *con-*, intensive, + **fraternity**.]

confrère [k•-frer] *n* a colleague; an associate. [Fr,—L *con-*, together, *frāter*, a brother.]

confront [kon-frunt´] *vt* to face in a hostile manner; to oppose; to bring face to face (with); to encounter.—*n* **confrontā´tion**. [Fr *confronter*, through Low L—L *con-*, together, *frons, frontis*, forehead.]

confucianism [con-fū´shyȧn-izm] *n* ethical system of Confucius, the Chinese philosopher (551–479 BC) emphasizing devotion to family, peace, and justice.—*adj* **confu´cian**.

confuse [kon-fūz´] *vt* to throw into disorder; to perplex; to fail to distinguish.—*adj* **confused´**, perplexed; abashed; disordered.—*adv* **confus´edly**.—*n* **confū´sion**, disorder; a mixing up in thought or in statement; overthrow; perplexity; embarrassment. [A doublet of **confound**.]

confute [kon-fūt´] *vt* to prove to be false (eg an argument), to refute.—*adj* **confūt´able**.—*n* **confutā´tion**. [L *confutāre*.]

conga [kong´ga] *n* a dance of Cuban origin in which dancers follow a leader, usu. in single file; music for it; a tall drum of Afro-Cuban origin that is played with the hands. [Amer Sp, Congo.]

congé [k•´zhā], **congee** [kon´ji] *n* a bow; dismissal; leave to depart; an architectural molding with a concave profile. [Fr *congé*—L *commeātus*, leave of absence—*com-*, together, *meāre*, to go.]

congeal [kon-jēl´] *vti* to freeze; to change from fluid to solid by cold, to jell; to solidify, as by cold.—*adj* **congeal´able**.—*ns* **congeal´ment, congelā´tion**, act or process of congealing. [L *congelāre*, from *con-*, and *gelu*, frost.]

congener [kon´je-nėr] *n* a plant or animal of the same taxonomic genus as another; a person or thing of the same kind or nature. [L, —*con-*, with, and *genus, generis*, kind.]

congenial [kon-jē´niȧl] *adj* of the same nature or tastes, kindred, sympathetic; in accordance with one's tastes; agreeable (to).—*n* **congēnial´ity**.—*adv* **congē´nially**. [L *con-*, with, *geniālis*, genial. See **genial**.]

congenital [kon-jen´i-tȧl] *adj* begotten or born with a person, said of diseases or deformities dating from birth.—*adv* **congen´itally**. [L *congenitus*, from *con-*, together, *gignĕre, genitum*, to beget.]

conger eel [kong´gėr] *n* a strictly marine eel (*Conger oceanus*) important as a food fish; (*loosely*) any related eel (family Congridae). [L,—Gr *gongros*.]

congeries [kon-jûr´i-ēz] *n* an aggregation of things in a heap or pile. [L,—*con-*, together, *gerĕre, gestum*, to bring.]

congest [kon-jest´] *vt* to pack closely; to cause congestion in.—*vi* to accumulate excessively.—*adj* **congest´ed**, affected with an unnatural accumulation of blood; overcrowded.—*n* **congest´ion**, an accumulation of blood in any part of the body; an overcrowded condition; an accumulation causing obstruction.—**congestive heart failure**, heart failure in which the heart is unable to maintain adequate blood circulation or to pump out the venous blood returned by the veins. [L *congerĕre, congestum*—*con-*, together, and *gerĕre, gestum*, to bring.]

conglob´ate [kon-glōb´āt] *vt* to form into a round compact mass.—Also *adj*.—*n* **conglobā´tion**.—*vt* **conglobe´**, to conglobate. [L *con-*, together, *globāre, -ātum*—*globus*, a ball.]

conglomerate [kon-glom´ėr-ȧt] *adj* gathered into a rounded mass.—*vt* to gather into a ball.—*n* (*geol*) gravel cemented into a compact and coherent mass; a large corporation made up of companies which often have diverse and unrelated interests.—*n* **conglomerā´tion**, state of being conglomerated; collection (of things of mixed kind or origin). [L *conglomerāre, -ātum*—*con-*, together, and *glomus, glomeris*, a ball of yarn.]

conglutinate [kon-glōō´tin-āt] *vt* to stick together with glue or with a glutinous substance.—*vi* to become conglutinated, as blood platelets.—*n* **conglutinā´tion**. [L *conglūtināre, -ātum*—*con-*, together, and *glūten*, glue.]

Congoese [kong´gō-ēz], **Congolese** [kong´gō-lēz] *ns* (*sing* and *pl*) a native, or natives of the Congo.

congratulate [kon-grat´ū-lāt] *vt* to express pleasure in sympathy with, to felicitate; to deem happy (esp *reflex*).—*n* **congratulā´tion**, act of congratulating; an expression of joyful sympathy.—*adj* **congrat´ulatory**, expressing congratulations. [L *congrātulārī, -ātus*—*con-*, inten, *grātulāre*—*grātus*, pleasing.]

congregate [kong´grė-gāt] *vt* to gather together, to assemble.—*vi* to flock together.—*n* **congregā´tion**, an assemblage of persons or things; a body of people united to worship in a particular church.—*adj* **congregā´tional**, pertaining to a congregation.—*ns* **Congregā´tionalism**, a form of church government in which each congregation is independent in the management of its own affairs; **Congregā´tionalist**, an adherent of Congregationalism. [L *congregāre, -ātum*—*con-*, together, and *grex, gregis*, a flock.]

congress [kong´gres] *n* the supreme legislative body of a nation, esp a republic; an association or society; an assembly or conference, esp for discussion and usu. action on some question; a single meeting or session of a group; coitus; **Congress**, the legislature of the US, comprising the Senate and the House of Representatives.—*adj* **congressional** [kon-gresh´ȯn-ȧl].—*n* **con´gressman, congresswoman**, a member of the US Congress, esp of the House of Representatives.—**Congressional Medal**, Medal of Honor. [L *con-*, together, *gradī, gressus*; to step, to go.]

congruence [kong´grōō-ėns] *n* quality or state of agreeing, coinciding or being congruent; a statement that two numbers or geometric figures are congruent.—*adj* **cong´ruent**, agreeing; harmonious; (*math*) the relationship between two numbers with respect to another number, if their difference is a multiple of that number; (*geom*) the relationship between figures identical in shape whose corresponding parts are equal.—*n* **congru´ity**, agreement, harmony, consistency; fitness.—*adj* **cong´ruous**, suitable; consistent (with).—*adv* **cong´ruously**.—*n* **cong´ruousness**. [L *congruĕre*, to run together.]

conic, conical *See* **cone**.

conifer [kon´i-fėr] *n* any of an order (Coniferales) of mainly evergreen trees and shrubs including forms with true cones (as pines) and others (as yews).—*adj* **conif´erous**. [**cone**, + L *ferre*, to bear.]

conjecture [kon-jek´tyůr] *n* an opinion formed on slight or defective evidence; the act of forming such; a guess.—*vt* to infer on slight evidence; to guess.—*adj* **conjec´tural**.—*adv* **conjec´turally**. [L *conjicĕre, conjectum*, to throw together—*con-*, together, *jacĕre*, to throw.]

conjoin [kon-join´] *vti* to join together for a common purpose.—*adj* **conjoint´**, united (eg *conjoint efforts*).—*adv* **conjoint´ly**. [Fr *conjoindre*—L *conjungĕre*—*con-*, together, and *jungĕre, junctum*, to join.]

conjugal [kon´jŏŏ-gȧl] *adj* pertaining to marriage.—*adv* **con´jugally**.—**conjugal rights**, the right of sexual intercourse between husband and wife. [L *conjugālis*—*conju(n)x*, a spouse—*con-, jugum*, a yoke.]

conjugate [kon´jŏŏ-gāt] *vt* (*gram*) to give the various inflections or parts of a verb; to couple, unite.—*adj* [-ȧt] joined, connected.—*n* a word agreeing in derivation with another word.—*n* **conjugā´tion**, the act of joining; union; (*gram*) the inflection of the verb; a class of verbs inflected in the same manner. [L *conjugāre, -ātum*—*con-*, together, *jugāre*—*jubum*, a yoke.]

conjunct [kon-junkt´] *adj* conjoined; (*mus*) of melodic progression by intervals of no more than a major second.—*ns* **conjunc´tion**, connection, union; (*gram*) a word that connects sentences, clauses, and words; one of the aspects of the sun, moon, or planets when two of these bodies have the same celestial longitude; **conjuncti´va**, the modified epidermis of the front of the eyeball; **conjunctivītis**, inflammation of the conjunctiva.—*adj* **conjunc´tive**, serving to unite; (*gram*) introduced by, or of the nature of, a conjunction.—*adv* **conjunc´tively**.—*n* **conjunc´ture**, combination of circumstances, usu. producing a crisis. [L *conjunctus*—*conjungĕre*. See **conjoin**.]

conjure [kon´jė] *vi* to practice magical arts.—*vt* [kȯn-jōōr´] to invoke by a sacred name or in a solemn manner; to compel (a spirit) by incantation; to implore earnestly; to call before the imagination; to effect by magic or jugglery;—*pr p* **con´juring**; *pt p* **con´jured**.—*ns* **conjurā´tion**, act of summoning by a sacred name or solemnly; enchantment; **con´jurer, -or**, one who practices magic; a juggler. [Fr,—L *con-*, together, and *jurāre*, to swear.]

conn [kon] *vt* to control or direct the steering of (as a ship).—*n* one that conns.—*n* **conning tower**, an armored pilothouse (as on a battleship); a raised cylindrical structure on an early submarine. [Apparently—Fr *conduire*—L *condūcĕre*; see **conduct**.]

connate [kon´āt] *adj* inborn, innate. [L *con-*, with, *nascī, nātus*, to be born.]

connect [kon-ekt´] *vt* to tie or fasten together; to establish a relation between; to associate in the mind.—*vi* to join.—*adj* **connect´ed**, linked; related; coherent.—*adv* **connect´edly**, in a connected manner.—*n* **connec´tion**, act of connecting; that which connects; (*pl*) opportunity of change of trains, buses, etc.; context; a relative, esp by marriage; (usu. *pl*) an associate; a source of contraband (as illegal drugs).—*adj* **connect´ive**, binding together.—*n* a word that connects sentences and words.—**connecting rod**, a rod that transmits motion from one rotating part of a machine to another in a reciprocating motion; **connective tissue** (*anat*) fibrous tissue connecting and supporting organs. [L *con-*, and *nectĕre, nexum*, to tie.]

conning tower *See* **conn**.

connive [kon-īv´] *vi* to wink (at a fault); to give tacit consent; to be an accomplice.—*n* **conniv´ance**. [Fr,—L *connīvēre*, to wink.]

connoisseur [kon´-es-ûr´] *n* one who has knowledge, an expert critic of art, music, etc.—*n* **connoisseur´ship**, the skill of a connoisseur. [Fr (now *connaisseur*)—*connoître* (*connaître*)—L *cognoscĕre*, to know.]

connote [kon-ōt´] *vt* to signify secondarily; to imply as inherent attributes; to include.—*vt* **conn´otāte**, to connote.—*n* **connotā´tion**, the sum of attributes implied by a term; what is implied in a word or suggested by it beyond its recognized simple meaning.—*adj* **conn´otātive** [or -nōt´a-tiv]. [L *con-*, with, *notāre*, to mark.]

connubial [kon-ū´bi-ȧl] *adv* pertaining to marriage.—*adv* **connū´bially**. [L *con-*, with, *nubĕre*, to marry.]

conoid [kōn´oid] *n* anything like a cone in form.—*adjs* **con´oid, conoid´al**. [Gr *kōnos*, a cone, *eidos*, form.]

conquer [kong´kėr] *vt* to gain by force; to overcome or vanquish.—*vi* to be victor.—*adj* **con´querable**, that may be conquered.—*ns* **con´queror**, a victor; **conquest** [kong´-kwest], the act of conquering; that which is conquered or acquired by physical or moral force. [OFr *conquerre*—L *conquīrĕre*—*con-*, inten *quaerĕre*, to seek.]

conquistador [kon-kwis´tȧ-dör] *n* a leader in the Spanish conquest of America, esp of Mexico and Peru in the 16th century.—*pl* **-dors, -dores** [-dor´es]. [Sp,—L *conquīrĕre*; see **conquer**.]

consanguine [kon-sang´gwin] *adj* related by blood, of the same family or descent—also **consanguin´eous**.—*n* **consanguin´ity**, relationship by blood. [L *consanguineus*—*con-*, with, *sanguis*, blood.]

conscience [kon´shėns] *n* the knowledge, or the consciousness, of our own acts and feelings as right or wrong with a compulsion to do right; (*psychoanalysis*) the part of the superego that transmits commands and admonitions to the ego.—*adj* **conscientious** [-shi-ensh´-], regulated by a regard to conscience; scrupulous.—*adv* **conscien´tiously**.—*ns* **conscien´tiousness; conscience money**, money given to relieve the conscience, by discharging a claim previously evaded; **conscientious objector**, one who objects on grounds moral or religious to bearing arms or to military service.—**in all conscience**, or **in conscience**, in all fairness. [Fr,—L *conscientia*, knowledge—*conscīre*, to know well.]

conscious [kon´shůs] *adj* having awareness or knowledge (of); aware (that); unduly aware; awake mentally; deliberate, intentional.—*adv* **con´sciously**.—*n* **con´sciousness**, the totality of mental states and processes (perceptions, feelings, thoughts), mind in its widest sense; awareness; the waking state of the mind. [L *conscius*—*conscīre*, to know well, be conscious of (wrong).]

conscript [kon´skript] *adj* enrolled into service by compulsion; drafted; made up of conscripted persons.—*n* a conscripted person (as a military recruit.)—*vt* [kon-script´] to enlist compulsorily.—*n* **conscrip´tion**, a compulsory enrollment, esp for military service. [L *conscrībĕre, conscriptum*, to enrol.]

consecrate [kon´se-krāt] *vt* to set apart for a holy use; to devote; to render holy or venerable.—*n* **consecrā´tion**. [L *consecrāre, -ātum*.]

consecution [kon-se-kū´sh(ȯ)n] *n* a series of things that follow one another.—*adj* **consec´utive**, following in regular order;—*adv* **consec´utively**.—*n* **consec´utiveness**. [L *consequī*—*con-, sequī, secūtus*, to follow.]

consensus [kon-sen´sus] *n* an opinion held by all or most; general agreement, esp in opinion. [L *consentīre*]

consent [kon-sent´] *vi* (*arch*) to be of the same mind; to agree; to give assent (to).—*n* agreement, permission; concurrence; voluntary agreement by a people to organize a civil society and give authority to the government.—*adjs* **consentā´neous**, agreeable (to), unanimous. [L *consentire*—*con-*, with, *sentīre*, to feel, to think.]

consequence [kon´si-kwėns] *n* that which follows or comes after as a result, or as an inference; importance; social standing.—*adj* **consequent**, following, esp as a natural effect or deduction.—*n* the natural effect of a cause; the conclusion of a conditional sentence; the second number in a ratio.—*adv* **con´sequently**.—*adj* **consequen´tial** [-shǎl], following as a result; self-important.—*adv* **consequen´tially**.—**take the consequences**, to accept the results of one's actions. [Fr,—L *consequī*—*con-*, together, *sequī*, to follow.]

conserve [kon-sûrv´] *vt* to keep entire; to keep from damage or loss; to preserve in sugar; to maintain (a quantity) constant during a process of chemical, physical or evolutionary change.—*n* [usu. kon´sûrv] (often *pl*) a jam of two or more fruits.—*adj* **conser´vable**.—*ns* **conser´vancy**, conservation; an area or organization designated to conserve and protect natural resources; **conservā´tion**, planned management in conserving (flora and fauna, environment); **conservā´tionist**, one interested in conservation; **conser´vatism**, a disposition in politics to preserve what is established.—*adj* **conser´vative**, tending or having power to conserve; (loosely) moderately estimated, understated.—*n* one of the political party that desires to preserve the institutions of the country against innovation; one who adheres to traditional methods or views; a cautious or discreet person.—*ns* **conser´vativeness; conservatoire** [kon-sėr-vä-twär´] a school specializing in one of the fine arts, esp music; **conser´vator**, one who preserves from injury, an official custodian; **conser´vatory**, a greenhouse in which exotic plants are kept; a conservatoire; **conser´ver.—conservation of energy**, the law that in any isolated system the total amount of energy is constant. **conservation of mass, conservation of matter**, a principle in classical physics that the total mass of any material system is neither increased nor diminished by reaction between the parts. [L *con-*, together, *servāre*, keep.]

consider [kon-sid´ėr] *vt* to look at carefully; to think or deliberate on; to weigh advantages and disadvantages, with a view to action (eg *to consider going abroad*); to take into account; to show regard or consideration for; to believe, think.—*vi* to think seriously or carefully, to deliberate.—*adj* **consid´erable**, worthy of being considered; important; more than a little.—*adv* **consid´erably**.—*adj* **consid´erāte**, serious; prudent; mindful of the feelings or claims of others.—*adv* **consid´erately**.—*ns* **consid´erateness**, thoughtfulness for others; **considerā´tion**, deliberation; motive, reason, inducement, argument for or against; a taking into account; importance; compensation or reward; considerateness.—*prep* **consid´ering**, in view of.—*conj* seeing that.—**in consideration of**, as payment for. [Fr,—L *considerāre*, supposed to have been orig a term of augury—*con-, sīdus, sīderis*, a star.]

consign [kon-sīn´] *vt* (*obs*) to sign or seal; to entrust; to commit (to); to transmit; send or deliver goods.—*ns* **consignee´**, one to whom anything is consigned or sent; **consign´er; consign´ment**, the act of consigning; the thing consigned; a shipment of goods sent to an agent for sale.—**on consignment**, with payment due after sale of the consignment. [Fr,—L *consignāre*, to attest.]

consist [kon-sist´] *vi* (*arch*) to exist; to be composed (of); to be comprised (in), or to be essentially; to agree, be consistent (with).—*ns* **consist´ence, consist´ency**, degree of density; agreement.—*adj* **consist´ent**, (*obs*) fixed; not fluid; agreeing together, compatible; true to one's principles; (*statistics*) close to the true value of an estimated parameter as the sample becomes large.—*adv* **consist´ently**, uniformly, invariably; in accordance (with).—*n* **con´sistory** [or kon-sist´-], an assembly or council; a solemn meeting of Roman Catholic cardinals convoked and presided over by the pope.—*adj* **consistō´rial**. [L *consistĕre*—*con-*, together, *sistĕre*, to stand.]

consociate [kon-sō´shi-āt] *vti* to associate together.—*n* **consociation** [kon-sō-shi-ā´sh(ȯ)n]. [L *consociāre, -ātum*—*con-*, with, *sociāre*. See **sociable**.]

console [kon-sōl´] *vt* to give solace or comfort to.—*adj* **consol´able**, that may be comforted.—*ns* **consolā´tion**, solace; alleviation of misery; **consolā´tion prize**, a prize given to the runner-up or a loser in a contest.—*adj* **consol´atory**, offering, or giving, consolation.—*n* **consol´er**. [L *con-*, inten, and *sōlārī*, to comfort.]

console [kon´sōl] *n* a bracket to support cornices; the desk-like frame containing the keys, stops, etc. of an organ; a large radio or television set standing on the floor; a panel or cabinet with dials, switches, etc.; control unit of an electrical, electronic, or mechanical system; a storage cabinet between bucket seats in an automobile.—*n* **con´solette´**, a small cabinet containing a radio, television, or record player. [Fr *console*.]

consolidate [kon-sol´i-dāt] *vt* to make solid; to strengthen; to merge, combine.—*vi* to grow solid or firm; to unite.—*n* **consolidā´tion**, act of consolidating; strengthening. [L *consolidāre, -ātum*—*con-*, inten, and *solidus*, solid.]

consommé [k•-som-ā´] *n* a kind of clear soup made from well-seasoned stock. [Fr,—L *consummāre*, to consummate.]

consonant [kon´son-ånt] *adj* consistent (with, to); harmonious.—*n* an articulation that can be sounded only with a vowel; a letter of the alphabet representing such a sound.—*ns* **con´sonance**, a state of agreement; agreement or unison of sounds; **con´sonancy**, harmony.—*adj* **consonant´al**, pertaining to a consonant.—*adv* **con´sonantly**, consistently, harmoniously.—**consonant shift**, a set of regular changes in consonant articulation in the history of a language or dialect. [L *consonans, -antis, pr p of consonāre*, to harmonise—*con-*, with, *sonāre*, to sound.]

consort[1] [kon´sört] *n* a partner, companion; a wife or husband, esp of a reigning queen or king; an accompanying ship.—*vti* **consort´**, to associate.—*n* **consortium** [kon-sör´tium, or -shi-um], an international banking or financial combination—*pl* **consor´tia**. [L *consors, consortis*, from *con-*, with, *sors*, a lot.]

consort[2] [kon´sört] *n* group; assembly; a group of instrumentalists or singers performing together; a set of musical instruments of the same family.—**in consort**, in company, in harmony. [MF *consorte*, Fr *consort*.]

conspectus [kon-spek´tus] *n* a comprehensive survey; a synopsis. [L *conspectus*—*conspicĕre*, to look at.]

conspicuous [kon-spik´ū-us] *adj* catching the eye, noticeable.—*n* **conspic´uousness**.—*adv* **conspic´uously**. [L *conspicuus*—*conspicĕre*—*con-*, inten, *specĕre*, to look.]

conspire [kon-spīr´] *vi* to plot or scheme together; to cooperate (towards one end).—*vt* to plot.—*ns* **conspĭr´acy**, a secret union for an evil purpose; a plot; joint action, concurrence; **conspĭrator**, one who conspires.—*adj* **conspĭratō´rial**, like a conspirator. [L *conspīrāre*—*con-*, together, *spīrāre*, to breathe.]

constable [kon´sta-bl] *n* a public officer usu. of a town or township responsible for keeping the peace and minor judicial duties; (*Brit*); a policeman.—*n* **constab´ūlary**, an organized body of constables of a particular district; an armed police force organized on military lines, but distinct from the regular army.—*adj* of or pertaining to constables. [OFr *conestable*—L *comes stabulī*, count of the stable.]

constant [kon´stånt] *adj* fixed; unchangeable; faithful; continual.—*n* (*math*) a symbol which is assigned a fixed value for all specific instances in a statement.—*n* **con´stancy**, fixedness; unchangeableness; faithfulness.—*adv* **con´stantly**, firmly; continually. [L *constans, -antis*, from *constāre*, to stand firm —*con-*, inten, *stāre*, to stand.]

constellation [kon-stel-ā´sh(ȯ)n] *n* any of 88 groups of fixed stars; an assemblage of brilliant persons. [L *constellātus*, studded with stars—*con-*, with, *stellāre*—*stella*, a star.]

consternation [kon-stėr-nā´sh(ȯ)n] *n* fear; shock; dismay; panic. [L *consternāre, -ātum*, from *con-*, wholly, *sternĕre*, to strew.]

constipate [kon´stip-āt] *vt* to cause constipation in.—*n* **constipā´tion**, infrequent and difficult movement of the bowels. [L *con-*, together, *stīpāre, -ātum*, to pack.]

constitute [kon´stit-ūt] *vt* to establish (a law, government, etc.); to set up (an assembly, etc.) in a legal form; to appoint; to form, to make up, be equivalent to.—*n* **constit´uency**, the voters in a district.—*adj* **constit´uent**, constituting or forming; essential, elemental, electing; authorized to make or revise a constitution.—*n* an essential part; a voter in a district.—*n* **constitū´tion**, the natural condition of body or mind; disposition; structure; the system of basic laws and principles of a government, society, etc.; a document stating these specifically; the Constitution of the US; (*chem*) molecular structure, taking into account not only the kind and numbers of atoms but the way in which they are linked.—*adj* **constitū´tional**, inherent in the natural frame, natural; agreeable to the constitution or frame of government, legal.—*n* a walk for the sake of one's health.—*ns* **constitū´tionalism**, adherence to government according to constitutional principles; a constitutional system of government; **constitū´tionalist**, a supporter of constitutional government.—*adv* **constitū´tionally**.—*adj*

con´stitutive, that constitutes or establishes; constituent; essential component. [L *constituĕre, constitūtum*, from *con-*, together, *statuĕre*, to make to stand, to place.]

constrain [kon-strān´] *vt* to force, compel; to confine, imprison.—*adj* **constrained´**, forced, not natural, embarrassed.—*n* **constraint´**, compulsion; confinement; a reserved or embarrassed manner. [OFr *constraindre*—L *constringĕre*—*con-*, together, *stringĕre*, to press.]

constrict [kon-strikt´] *vt* to press together, to cramp; to cause to contract.—*n* **constric´tion**, a pressing together; tightness.—*adj* **constric´tive**.—*n* **constrict´or**, that which constricts or draws together; the boa-constrictor. [L *constringĕre, constrictum*.]

constringe [kon-strinj´] *vt* to draw together; to cause to contract.—*adj* **constrin´gent**, having the quality of contracting. [L *constringĕre*.]

construct [kon-strukt´] *vt* to build up; to put together the parts of; (*fig*) to compose; to draw.—*ns* **construct´or; construc´tion**, the act of constructing; anything piled together, building; manner of forming; (*gram*) the syntactic relations of words in a sentence; meaning, interpretation as of a statement.—*adj* **construc´tional**, pertaining to construction.—*n* **construc´tionist**, a person who interprets a law, document, etc. in a specified way.—*adj* **construc´tive**, declared such by judicial interpretation; promoting improvement or development relating to construction or creation; capable of, or tending towards, constructing; not direct or expressed, but inferred (eg *constructive permission*).—*adv* **construct´ively**.—*n* **construct´iveness**, the faculty of constructing; **construct´ivism**, a non-objective 20th century art movement originating in Russia concerned with the creation of three-dimensional abstracts using wire, iron, or wood. [L *construĕre, -structum*—*con-*, *struĕre*, to build.]

construe -[kon-strōō´] *vti* to elucidate grammatically; to translate literally; to interpret. [L *construĕre, constructum*, to build.]

consubstantial [kon-sub-stan´shȧl] *adj* of the same substance, nature, or essence,—*n* **consubstantiā´tion** (*theol*) the Lutheran doctrine of the actual, substantial presence of the body and blood of Christ in eucharistic bread and wine. [L *con-*, with, + **substantial**.]

consuetude [kon´swe-tūd] *n* custom; social usage.—*adj* **consuetū´dinary**, customary.—*adj* a ritual of customary devotions. [L *consuētūdō*, custom.]

consul [kon´sul] *n* one of the two chief magistrates in the Roman republic; a government official appointed to live in a foreign city to attend to the interests of his country's citizens and business there.—*adj* **con´sūlar**, pertaining to a consul.—*ns* **con´sulate**, the office or residence of a consul; **con´sulship**. [L.]

consult [kon-sult´] *vt* to ask advice or information of; to act in accordance with (eg wishes).—*vi* to consider in company; to take counsel; to give professional advice.—*ns* **consult´ant**, one who consults another; one who gives technical or professional advice; **consultā´tion**, a deliberation between physicians on a case or its treatment.—*adj* **consult´ative**, of or pertaining to consultation; advisory; **consult´ing**, providing expert or professional advice. [L *consultāre*, inten of *consulĕre*, to consult.]

consume [kon´sūm´] *vt* to destroy by wasting, fire, etc.; to devour; to waste or spend.—*vi* to waste away; to utilize economic goods.—*adj* **consum´able**.—*ns* **consum´er**, one who uses goods and services for his own needs rather than to produce other goods; **consum´erism**, the protection of the interests of buyers of goods and services; a preoccupation with and an inclination toward the buying of consumer goods.—**consumer price index**, an index measuring the change in cost of specified goods and services expressed as a percentage of the cost of the same goods and services in some base period. [L *consūmĕre*, to destroy—*con-*, signifying completeness, *sūmĕre, sumptum*, to take.]

consummate [kon´sum-āt] *vt* to complete or finish, esp to complete (a marriage) by sexual intercourse.—*adj* **consumm´ate** [-āt] complete, supreme, perfect.—*adv* **consumm´ately**.—*n* **consummā´tion**, act of completing; perfection; the final issue or result. [L *consummāre*, to perfect—*con-*, with, and *summa*, the sum.]

consumption [kon-sum´sh(ȯ)n] *n* the act or process of consuming; the amount consumed; tuberculosis of the lungs.—*adj* **consump´tive**, wasting away; inclined to tubercular disease.—*n* one affected by consumption.—*adv* **consump´tively**.—*n* **consump´tiveness**, a tendency to consumption. [See **consume**.]

contact [kon´takt] *n* touch; meeting; association; close proximity allowing passage of electric current or communication of disease; a place where electric current may be allowed to pass; a person who has been exposed to contagion; a person through whom one can get in touch (esp secretly) with an individual or group, esp with disreputable or criminal person(s); an influential acquaintance.—*vti* to bring or come into touch, connection, with.—*adj* **contact´ual**, pertaining to contact.—**contact flying**, navigation of an aircraft by observation of land or sea over which it is flying; **contact lens**, a tiny, thin correctional lens placed in the fluid over the cornea of the eye; **contact print**, a photographic print made by placing the negative in direct contact with a sensitized surface. [L *contingĕre, contactum*, to touch—*con-*, wholly, *tangĕre*, to touch.]

contagion [kon-tā´jȯn] *n* (transmission of a disease by) direct contact with an infected person or object; a contagious disease; the spreading of an emotion, idea, etc.—*adj* **contā´gious**, communicable by contact.—*adv* **contā´giously**.—*n* **contā´giousness**. [L *contagiō, -ōnis*—*con-*, together, *tangĕre*, to touch.]

contain [kon-tān´] *vt* to have within, enclose; to comprise, include; to restrain; to hold back or restrain within fixed limits.—*adj* **contain´able**.—*n* **contain´er**, a receptacle.—*vt* **contain´erize**, to put (cargo) into huge standardized containers for shipment.—*n* **contain´ment**, the policy of preventing the expansion of a hostile power or ideology. [Through Fr from L *continēre, contentum*—*con-*, together, *tenēre*, to hold.]

contaminate [kon-tam´i-nāt] *vt* to defile by touching or mixing (with); to pollute, corrupt, infect.—*ns* **contaminā´tion**, pollution; **contam´inent**, a contaminating substance. [L *contāmināre, -ātum*—*contāmen* (for *contagmen*), pollution—root of *tangĕre*. See **contact**.]

conte [k•t] *n* a short story. [Fr.]

contemn [kon-tem´] *vt* to express contempt.—*n* **contem´ner**. [Fr—L *contemnĕre, -temptum*, to value little—*con-*, inten, *temnĕre*, to slight.]

contemplate [kon´tem-plāt] *vt* to consider or look at attentively; to meditate on or study; to intend.—*vi* to muse.—*n* **contemplā´tion**, attentive study or observation.—*adj* **con´templātive** [or -tem´-plȧ-] given to, concerned with, marked by, contemplation.—*adv* **con´templatively**. [L *contemplārī, -ātus*, to mark out a *templum* or place for auguries.]

contemporaneous [kon-tem-po-rā´ne-us] *adj* living, happening, or being at the same time.—*adv* **contemporā´neously**.—*n* **contemporā´neousness**.—*adj* **contem´porary**, contemporaneous; of about the same age; present day.—*n* one who lives at the same time. [L *con-*, together, *temporāneus*—*tempus*, time.]

contempt [kon-tempt´] *n* the feeling one has toward someone or something considered low, worthless, etc.; the condition of being despised; (*law*) disregard of the dignity (of a court).—*adj* **contempt´ible**, deserving contempt or scorn; despicable.—*adv* **contempt´ibly**.—*adv* **contempt´uous**, haughty, scornful.—*adv* **contempt´uously**.—*n* **contempt´uousness**. [L *contemptus*—*contemnĕre*.]

contend [kon-tend´] *vi* to strive; to struggle in emulation or in position; to dispute or debate.—*vt* to assert.—*ns* **contend´er; conten´tion** [-sh(ȯ)n] a struggle to attain an object; strife; debate; an opinion maintained in debate.—*adj* **conten´tious** [-shùs] quarrelsome; involving dispute.—*adv* **conten´tiously**.—*n* **conten´tiousness**. [L *contendĕre, -tentum*—*con-*, with, *tendĕre*, to stretch.]

content[1] [kon´tent] *n* (usu. *pl*) what is in a container; (usu *pl*) what is in a book; what is dealt with in a talk; substance or meaning; amount contained; the matter dealt with in a field of study. [OFr—L *contentus*, pt p of *continēre*. See **contain**.]

content[2] [kon-tent´] *adj* satisfied; willing; assenting.—*n* satisfaction—often 'heart's content'.—*vt* to make content; to satisfy.—*adj* **content´ed**, content.—*adv* **content´edly**.—*ns* **content´edness, content´ment**. [Fr—L *contentus*, contained, hence satisfied—*con-*, *tenēre*, hold.]

conterminous [kon-tėr´min-us] *adj* having a common boundary; coextensive (with). [L *conterminus*, neighboring—*con-*, together, *terminus*, boundary.]

contest [kon-test´] *vt* to call in question or make the subject of dispute; to contend for.—*n* **con´test**, a struggle for superiority; strife; debate.—*adj* **contest´able**.—*n* **contest´ant**, a competitor in a game, etc.; one who contests. [Fr—L *contestārī*, to call to witness—*con-*, and *testārī*, to be a witness.]

context [kon´tekst] *n* the parts of a discourse or treatise that precede and follow a passage under consideration and may fix its meaning; associated surroundings, setting.—*n* **contex´ture**, the interweaving of parts into a whole; the structure or system so made. [L *contextus*—*con-*, together, *texĕre, textum*, to weave.]

contiguous [kon-tig´ū-us] *adj* touching, adjoining; near.—*ns* **contigū´ity, contig´uousness**.—*adv* **contig´uously**. [L *contiguus*—*contingĕre*, to touch on all sides.]

continent [kon´ti-nėnt] *n* a large extent of land not broken up by seas; one of the six or seven great divisions of the land surface of the globe.—*adj* restraining the indulgence of pleasure, esp sexual.—*n* **con´tinence**, the restraint imposed by a person upon his desires, esp total abstinence; the ability to retain a bodily discharge voluntarily.—*adj* **continent´al**, characteristic of a continent; often **Continental**, of or relating to the colonies later forming the US.—Also *n* an American soldier of the Revolution in the Continental army.—**continental drift**, a hypothetical slow movement of the continents; **continental shelf**, a gently sloping zone, under relatively shallow seas, offshore from a continent ending in a steep slope to the oceanic abyss.—**the Continent**, the mainland of Europe. [L *continens, -entis*—*continēre*, to contain.]

contingent [kon-tin´jėnt] *adj* dependent (on something else); liable but not certain to happen; accidental.—*n* a quota or group, esp of soldiers.—*ns* **contin´gence, contin´gency**, quality of being contingent; an uncertain event.—*adv* **contin´gently**. [L *contingens, -entis*—*con-*, *tangĕre*, to touch.]

continue [kon-tin´ū] *vt* to draw out or prolong; to extend; to go on with; to resume.—*vi* to remain in the same place or state; to last or endure; to preserve.—*adj* **contin´ual**, unceasing; very frequent.—*adv* **contin´ually**.—*ns* **contin´uance**, duration; uninterrupted succession; (*law*) postponement or adjournment; **continuā´tion**, going on; constant succession; extension; resumption; a further installment.—*adj* **contin´uātive**, continuing.—*n* **contin´uātor**, one who continues.—*adj* **contin´ued**, uninterrupted; unceasing; resumed; in installments; extended.—*ns* **continū´ity**, state of being continuous; uninterrupted connection; a script or scenario in the performing arts.—*adj* **contin´uous**, joined together without interruption.—*adv* **contin´uously**.—*n* **contin´ūum**, a continuous whole, quantity, or series; a compact set which cannot be separated into two sets neither of which contains a limit of the other.—**continuing education**, formal courses of study for parttime students, esp adults. [Fr—L *continuāre—continuus*, joined, connected, from *continēre*.]

continuo [kon-tin´ū-ō] *n* (*mus*) a bass part consisting of a succession of bass notes with figures that indicate the required chords. [It.]

contort [kon-tört´] *vti* to twist or turn violently, distort.—*ns* **contor´tion**, a violent twisting; **contor´tionist**, one who can twist his body into unnatural positions. [L *con*, inten, *torquēre, tortum*, to twist.]

contour [kon´tōōr or kon-tōōr´] *n* the outline of a figure, land, etc.; the line representing this outline; the general form of something.—**contour feather**, one of the mediumsized feathers that form the general covering of a bird and determine the general contour; **contour line**, a line drawn on a map through all points at the same height above sea level; **contour map**, a map in which the configuration of land is shown by contour lines. [Fr *con*, and *tour*, a turning—L *tornus*, a lathe.]

contra[1] [kon´tra] *prep* against.—*n* an argument against, used in the phrase **pro and contra**. [L *contrā*.]

contra[2] [kon´tra] *n* one of a rebel group trying to overthrow the Nicaraguan government established in 1979. [Amer Sp.]

contraband [kon´tra-band] *adj* illegal to import or export.—*n* smuggled goods. [Sp *contrabanda*—It *contrabbando*—L *contrā*, against, LL *bandum*, ban.]

contrabass [kon´tra-bās] *n* the double bass.

contraception [kon-tra-sep´sh(ȯ)n] *n* the deliberate prevention of conception.—*n* **contracep´tive**, a means of contraception.—Also *adj*. [L *contrā*, against + (**con**)**ception**.]

contract [kon-trakt´] *vt* to draw together; to lessen; to undertake by agreement; to incur (eg a debt); to shorten (a word or phrase).—*vi* to shrink, to become less; to make a contract.—*n* **con´tract**, an agreement, esp a written one enforceable by law, between two or more people.—*adjs* **contract´ed**, drawn together; **contract´ible**, capable of being contracted; **contract´īle** [or -īl] tending or having power to contract.—*ns* **contractĭl´ity; contrac´tion**, act of contracting; a shortening or thickening of a functioning fiber; a reduction in business activity; a word shortened in speech or spelling;—*n* **contract´or**, one of the parties to a bargain or agreement; one who engages to execute work or furnish supplies on a large scale; one that contracts to erect buildings; something (as a muscle) that contracts and shortens.—**contract bridge**, a bridge game distinguished by the fact that overtricks do not count toward game or slam bonuses. [L *contractus—con*, together, *trahĕre, tractum*, to draw.]

contradict [kon-tra-dikt´] *vt* to assert the contrary of, to deny; to accuse (a person) of a misstatement; to be contrary to.—*n* **contradic´tion**, act of contradicting; denial; logical incongruity; inconsistency.—*adjs* **contradic´tive, contradict´ory**, involving, causing, or constituting a contradiction.—*n* a proposition so related to another that if either of the two is true the other must be false and if either is false the other must be true.—*n* **contradict´oriness**.—*adj* **contradic´tious** [shùs] prone to contradict. [L contrādīcĕre, -dictum.]

contradistinction [kon-tra-dis-tingk´sh(ȯ)n] *n* distinction by contrast.—*adj* **contradistinct´ive**.—*vt* **contradistin´guish**, to contrast and mark the difference by opposite qualities. [L *contrā*, against + **distinction**.]

contrail [kon´trāl] *n* a trail of condensed vapor created in the air by an airplane or rocket at high altitudes. [**con(densation)** and **trail**.]

contralto [kon-tral´tō] *n* a singing voice having a range between tenor and mezzo-soprano; a person having this voice; the part sung by a contralto. [It *contra*, against, *alto*, alto.]

contraption [kon-trap´sh(ȯ)n] *n* (*inf*) a contrivance. [Perh arbitrarily from **contrive**.]

contrapuntal *See* **counterpoint**

contrary [kon´tra-ri] *adj* opposed; opposite in nature; [kon-trā´ri] perverse.—*n* a thing that has opposite qualities.—*n* **contrarī´ety**, opposition; inconsistency.—*adv* **contrarily** [kon´- or -trā´-].—*n* **contrariness** [kon´- or -trā´-].—*adv* **con´trariwise**, on the other hand; vice versa; in the opposite way.—**contrary to**, in conflict with; despite; **on the contrary**, just the opposite; **to the contrary**, notwithstanding. [L *contrārius—contrā*, against.]

contrast [kon-träst´] *vi* to show marked difference from.—*vt* to compare so as to point out the differences.—*n* [kon´träst] opposition or unlikeness in things compared; exhibition of differences; thing showing marked unlikeness (to another). [Fr *contraster*—L *contrā*, opposite to, *stāre*, to stand.]

contravene [kon-tra-vēn´] *vt* to go against; to oppose in argument; to infringe (a law).—*n* **contraven´tion**. [L *contrā*, against, *venīre*, to come.]

contretemps [kän-trė-tän´] *n* a confusing, embarrassing or awkward occurrence. [Fr *contre* (L *contrā*), against, and *temps* (L *tempus*), time.]

contribute [kon-trib´ūt] *vti* to give, along with others, for a common purpose; to write (an article, etc.) as for a magazine; to furnish ideas, etc.—*n* **contribū´tion**, the act of contributing; anything contributed.—*adjs* **contrib´utive, contrib´utory**, giving a share; helping towards a result.—*n* **contrib´utor**.—**contribute to**, to share in bringing about. [L *con-*, with, *tribuĕre, -ūtum*, to give, pay.]

contrite [kon´trīt] *adj* brokenhearted for sin; showing penitence.—*adv* **con´tritely**.—*ns* **con´triteness, contrĭ´tion**, state of being contrite; remorse. [L *contrītus—conterĕre—con-*, wholly, *terĕre*, to rub, bruise.]

contrive [kon-trīv´] *vt* to plan; to invent; to manage; to effect (sometimes with difficulty or by artifice).—*n* **contriv´ance**, act of contriving; the thing contrived; invention; artifice.—*adj* **contrived**, having been contrived; artificial, overelaborated.—*n* **contriv´er**. [OFr *controver—con-*, and *trover*, to find.]

control [kon-trōl´] *n* restraint; authority, command; a means of controlling or testing; an experiment performed to afford a standard of comparison for other experiments.—Also **control experiment**, one (as an organism, culture, or group) that is part of the experiment; an apparatus to regulate a mechanism.—*vt* to verify (an experiment) by comparison; to restrain; to govern.—*pr p* **controll´ing**; *pt p* **contrōlled´**.—*adj* **controll´able**.—*n* **controll´er**, a person in charge of finances, as in a business. [Fr *contrôle*, from *contre-rôle*, a duplicate register—L *contrā*, against, *rotulus*, a roll.]

controvert [kon´tro-vûrt] *vt* to dispute or oppose by reasoning.—*vi* to engage in controversy.—*adj* **controvert´ible**, disputable.—*adv* **controvert´ibly**.—*n* **con´troversy**, a discussion of opposing views; contention; strife.—*adj* **controver´sial** [-shȧl] relating to controversy; open to dispute (eg a statement).—*n* **controver´sialist**, one given to controversy.—*adv* **controver´sially**. [L *contrā*, against, *vertĕre*, to turn.]

contumacious [kon-tū-mā´shùs] *adj* obstinately disobedient; rebellious.—*adv* **contumā´ciously**.—*ns* **contumā´ciousness, con´tumacy**, willful contempt of court. [L *contumax -ācis*, insolent—*con-*, *tumēre*, to swell, or *temnĕre*, to despise.]

contumely [kon´tūm´li, kėn-, kon´tū-mē-lē] *n* humiliating treatment or scornful insult; an instance of such language or treatment.—*adj* **contumē´lious**, haughtily reproachful; insolent.—*adv* **contumē´liously**.—*n* **contumē´liousness**. [L *contumēlia*, prob from the same source as *contumax*; see **contumacious**.]

contuse [kon-tūz´] *vt* to bruise.—*n* **contū´sion**, a bruise. [L *contundĕre, contūsum—con-*, *tundĕre*, to bruise.]

conundrum [kon-un´drum] *n* a riddle turning on a play on words; any puzzling question.

conurbation [kon-ûr-bā´sh(ȯ)n] *n* a vast urban area around and including a large city. [L *con-*, together, *urbs*, a city.]

convalesce [kon-val-es´] *vi* to regain health and strength; to get better.—*adj* **convales´cent**, gradually recovering health.—*n* one recovering health.—*n* **convales´cence**. [L *con-*, *valescĕre—valēre*, to be strong.]

convection [kon-vek´sh(ȯ)n] *n* transmission, esp that of heat through fluid by means of currents due to the greater density of the colder parts.—**convection oven**, an oven having a fan that circulates hot air continuously and uniformly around food. [L *convectiō, -ōnis*, a bringing together—*con-*, *vehĕre*, to carry.]

convene [kon-vēn´] *vti* to assemble for a meeting.—*n* **conven´er, conven´or**, one who convenes a meeting. [Fr *convenir*—L *convenīre*, from *con-*, together, *venīre*, to come.]

convenient [kon-vēn´yėnt] *adj* suitable; handy; commodious; occasioning little or no trouble (as, *it is convenient for me to go today*).—*n* **conven´ience**, suitableness; an advantage; material advantage (as, *marriage of convenience*); any means or device for promoting ease or comfort.—*adv* **conven´iently**.—**convenience store**, a small often franchised market that is open long hours.—**at one's convenience**, at a time or place suitable to one. [L *conveniens, -entis—convenīre*, to come together, to fit.]

convent [kon´vent] *n* a house of a religious order or congregation, esp an establishment of nuns. [Through Fr from L *conventus—convenīre, conventum*, to come together.]

conventicle [kon-vent´i-kl] *n* an illegal gathering; an assembly for religious worship, esp a secret meeting against the law; a meetinghouse. [L *conventiculum*, a secret meeting of monks, dim of *conventus*, see **convent**.]

convention [kon-ven´sh(ȯ)n] *n* the act of convening; an assembly, often periodical, of representatives for some common object; agreement, as between nations; established usage.—*adj* **conven´tional**, formed by convention; customary; bound or influenced by convention or tradition; not natural, spontaneous, or original.—*n* **conventional´ity**, state of being conventional; that which is established by use or custom; adherence to convention.—*adv* **conven´tionally**.—*n* **conventioneer´**, a person attending a convention. [Fr—L *conventiō, -ōnis—convenīre*. See **convene**.]

converge [kon-vûrj] *vti* to come or bring together at one point.—*ns* **conver´gence, conver´gency**.—*adj* **conver´gent**. [L *con-*, together, *vergĕre*, to bend, incline.]

conversazione [kon-vėr-sat-se-ō´ne] *n* a meeting for conversation, particularly on literary subjects;—*pl* **conversaziō´nes**, or **conversaziō´ni** [-nē]. [It.]

converse [kon-vûrs´] *vi* to talk familiarly.—*n* **con´verse**, familiar intercourse; conversation.—*adjs* **convers´able**, disposed to converse; sociable; **con´versant**, acquainted by study, familiar (with a subject, etc.).—*n* **conversā´tion**, intercourse; talk, familiar discourse.—*adj* **conversā´tional**.—*n* **conversā´tionalist**, one who excels in conversation.—**conversation piece**, a painting of a number of persons in their customary surroundings; something (as a novel or unusual object) that stimulates conversation. [Fr—L *conversārī*, to live with.]

convert [kon-vûrt´] *vt* to change or turn from one thing, condition, or religion to another; to alter (into); to apply (to a particular purpose); to exchange for an equivalent, as paper money for specie; to misappropriate.—*n* **con´vert**, a converted person, esp one whose religious convictions have been changed.—*adj* **con´verse**, reversed in order of relation.—*n* that which is the opposite of another; a theorem formed by interchanging the hypothesis and conclusion of a given theorem; a proposition in which the subject and predicate have changed places.—*adv* **converse´ly**.—*ns* **conver´sion** [-sh(ò)n] change from one state, opinion, or religion to another; something converted from one use to another; **convert´er**, one that converts, esp the furnace used in the Bessemer process; **convertor**; an apparatus for making a change in an electrical energy; a radio device for converting one frequency to another; a device that accepts data in one form and converts it to another; a device for adapting a television or radio receiver to receive channels for which it was not originally designed.—*adj* **convert´ible**, that may be converted; exchangeable at a fixed price for gold or other currency.—*n* anything convertible, esp a car with a folding top.—*adv* **convert´ibly**.—*n* **convertibil´ity**. [L *convertĕre, conversum—con-, vertĕre*, to turn.]

convex [kon´veks, kon-veks´] *adj* curving outward like the surface of a sphere.—*n* **convex´ity**, roundness of form on the outside.—*adv* **con´vexly** [or -veks´]. [L *convexus—convehĕre*, to carry together.]

convey [kon-vā´] *vt* to carry; to transmit; to impart, communicate; to make over in law.—*ns* **convey´er, -or** (also *adj*); **convey´ance**, act of conveying; a vehicle of any kind; (*law*) the act of transferring property; the writing which transfers it; **convey´ancer**, one who effects transference of property; **convey´ancing**. [OFr *conveier* (Fr *convoyer*)—L *con-*, and *via*, a way.]

convict [kon-vikt´] *vt* to prove guilty; to pronounce guilty.—*n* [kon´vikt] a convicted person serving a prison sentence.—*n* **convic´tion**, act of convincing or convicting; strong belief; consciousness (of sin). [Same root as **convince**.]

convince [kon-vins´] *vt* to persuade by argument or evidence; to satisfy (as to truth or error).—*adj* **convinc´ible**.—*adv* **convinc´ingly**.—*n* **conviction**, a being convinced. [L *convincĕre—con-*, signifying completeness, *vincĕre, victum*, to conquer.]

convivial [kon-viv´i-ål] *adj* pertaining to a feast; social, jovial.—*n* **convivial´ity**.—*adv* **conviv´ially**. [From L—*convivium*, a living together, a feast—*con-*, together, *vīvĕre*, to live.]

convoke [kon-vōk´] *vt* to call together, to assemble.—*n* **convocā´tion**, act of convoking; the ceremonial assembly of members of a college or university. [L *convocāre—con-*, together, *vocāre, -ātum*, to call.]

convolve [kon-volv´] *vt* to roll together, or one part on another.—*adj* **con´voluted**, convolved.—*n* **convolū´tion**, a twisting; a fold. [L *convolvĕre—con-*, together, *volvĕre, volūtum*, to roll.]

convolvulus [kon-vol´vū-lus] *n* any of a genus (*Convolvolus*) of twining, trailing or erect herbs and shrubs of the morning-glory family. [L—*convolvĕre. See* **convolve**.]

convoy [kon-voi´] *vt* to accompany for protection.—*n* [kon´voi] the act of convoying; protection; that which convoys or is convoyed. [Fr *convoyer. See* **convey**.]

convulse [kon-vuls´] *vt* to agitate violently; to shake with irregular spasms.—*n* **convul´sion**, any involuntary contraction of the muscles by which the body is thrown into violent spasms; any violent disturbance.—*adj* **convuls´ive**, attended with convulsions;—*adv* **convuls´ively**.—*n* **convuls´iveness**. [L *con-*, inten, and *vellĕre, vulsum*, to pluck, to pull.]

cony *See* **coney**.

coo [kōō] *vi* to make a sound as a dove or pigeon; to talk caressingly;—*pr p* **cōō´ing**; *pt p* **cōōed**.—*n* the sound emitted by doves. [Imit]

cook [kŏŏk] *vt* to prepare (food) by boiling, baking, frying, etc.; (*inf*) to manipulate for any purpose, or falsify, as accounts, etc.; to subject to the action of heat or fire.—*vi* to be a cook; to undergo cooking; (*slang*) to perform or proceed well.—*n* one who cooks; one whose business is to cook.—*ns* **cook´ book**, a book of recipes and other information for preparing food; **cook´out**, a meal cooked and eaten outdoors.—**to cook one's goose**, (*slang*), to ruin one's plan (*inf*) irretrievably; **to cook up**, to devise; to invent. [OE *cōc*, a cook—L *coquus*.]

cookie[1], **cooky** [kŏŏk´i] *n* a small, sweet flat cake. [Du *koekje*, a cake.]

cookie[2] *n* (*comput*) a small file created by a Web server which is transmitted to, and stored on, the hard disk of the computer.

cool [kōōl] *adj* slightly cold; tending to reduce the effects of heat; free from excitement, calm; not zealous, ardent, or cordial; indifferent; impudent; (*inf*) without exaggeration; (*slang*) very good.—*vti* to make or become cool;—*n* that which is cool; coolness; (*slang*) self-possession.—*ns* **cool´ant**, a fluid or other substance for cooling engines, etc.; **cool´er**, a place for keeping things cool; (*slang*) jail.—*adjs* **cool´head´ed**, not easily excited, capable of acting with composure; **cooling-off**, designed to permit negotiations between parties after time has passed; **coolish**.—*adv* **cool´ly**, in a cool manner; indifferently; impudently.—*n* **cool´ness**, moderate cold; indifference; want of zeal; lack of agitation; self-possession.—**cool it**, (*inf*) to calm down; **cool off**, to become less angry and more amenable to reason; **cool one's heels**, (*inf*) to be kept waiting for a long time, esp from discourtesy or disdain. [OE *cōl*; Ger *kühl* Cog with **cold**, and **chill**.]

coolie [kōōl´i] *n* formerly, an Indian or Chinese hired laborer. [Prob *Kulī*, a tribe of Bombay; or orig Tamil cf *kūli*, hire.]

coon [kōōn] *n* the raccoon.—*n* **coonskin**, the skin of a raccoon used as a fur. [Abbreviated form of **raccoon**.]

coop [kōōp] *n* a small pen for poultry; a small building for housing poultry; (*slang*) jail.—*vt* to confine as in a coop.—Also **coop up**. [ME *cupe, coupe*, basket.]

cooper [kōōp´ėr] *n* one who makes and repairs barrels, etc.—*n* **coop´erage**, the work or workshop of a cooper. [App Low German—LL *cūpārius—cūpa*, cask.]

cooperate [kō-op´ėr-āt] *vi* to work together (toward some end).—*ns* **co´-op**, a cooperative; **cooperā´tion, coop´erative**, an organization or enterprise owned by and operated for the benefit of those using its services; a cooperative store.—*n* **coop´erātor**. [**co-**, + **operate**.]

co-opt [kō-opt´] *vt* to elect or chose as a member; to appoint as assistant or colleague; to take into a group, to assimilate.—*ns* **co-optā´tion, co-op´tion**.—*adj* **co-op´tative**. [L *cooptāre, -ātum—co-*, together, *optāre*, to choose.]

coordinate [kō-ör´di-nåt] *adj* holding the same order or rank *n* (eg *coordinate clauses in a sentence*).—*vt* [-āt] to make coordinate; to adjust the relations or movements of, to harmonize.—*n* an equal thing or person; any of a series of numbers which, in a given frame of reference, locate a point in space; one of two or more measures that determine the position of a point, etc. with reference to a fixed system of axes, etc.; (*pl*) clothing designed to be used together, attaining their effect through pleasing contrast (of color, texture, etc.).—*adv* **coor´dinately**.—*n* **coordinā´tion**, state of being coordinate; act of co-ordinating; harmonious functioning of parts or agents toward the production of a normal or a desired result.—**coordinate geometry**, analytical geometry. [L *co-*, and *ordināre, -ātum. See* **ordain**.]

coot [koot] *n* a genus (*Fulica*) of birds of the rail family resembling ducks; any of several N American scoters; (*inf*) a harmless simple person. [ME *cote*; Du *koet*.]

cootie [kōō´tē] (*slang*) a louse.

cop [kop] *vt* (*slang*) to catch.—*n* (*slang*) policeman.—**cop out**, (*slang*) to confess to police; to renege; to give up, quit. [Ety uncertain.]

copacetic, copesetic, copasetic [kō-på-set´ik] *adj* sound; excellent (*slang*).—*interj* all clear. [unknown.]

copal [kō´pal] *n* a hard resin got from many tropical trees, and also fossil. [Sp,—Mexican *copalli*, resin.]

cope[1] [kōp] *n* an ecclesiastical vestment consisting of a long semicircular cloak, a covering like this, esp one that envelops or conceals; a coping.—*vt* to cover with a cope, or with coping.—*ns* **cope´stone**, the stone that tops a wall; a finishing touch; **cop´ing**, the covering course of a wall, usu. with a sloping top. [From root of **cap**.]

cope[2] [kōp] *vi* to contend (with) esp on equal terms or successfully; to deal with successfully. [Fr *couper*—L *colaphus*—Gr *kolaphos*, a buffet.]

Copernican [ko-pûr´ni-kån] *adj* relating to *Copernicus*, the Polish astronomer (1473–1543), or to his discovery that the earth revolves about the sun; of major importance or degree.

coping *See* **cope** (1).

copious [kō´pi-us] *adj* plentiful, overflowing.—*adv* **cō´piously**.—*n* **cō´piousness**. [L *cōpiōsus—cōpia*, plenty.]

copper [kop´ėr] *n* a reddish metallic element (symbol Cu; at wt 63.5; at no 29); money made of copper; any of various small butterflies (family Lycaenidae) with usu. copper-colored wings.—*adj* made of copper; copper-colored.—*vt* to cover with copper.—*ns* **copp´erhead**, a common poisonous snake (*Agkistrodon contortrix*) of the eastern and central US with a copper-colored head and reddish-brown marking on the body; **copp´erplate**, a plate of polished copper on which something has been engraved; an impression taken from the plate; faultless handwriting; **copp´ersmith**, a smith who works in copper.—*adj* **copp´ery**, like copper. [Low L *cuper*—L *cuprum*, a contr of *cyprium aes*, 'Cyprian brass', because found in *Cyprus*.]

copperas [kop´ėr-as] *n* sulphate or iron, used in making ink and pigments. [Fr *couperose*.]

coppice [kop´is], **copse** [kops] *n* a thicket of small trees and shrubs. [OFr *copeiz*, wood—Low L *colpāre*, to cut.]

copra [kop´ra] *n* the dried coconut meat yielding coconut oil. [Port, from Malay.]

coprolite [kop´ro-līt] *n* fossil excrement. [Gr *kopros*, dung, *lithos*, a stone.]

copse *See* **coppice**.

Copt [kopt] *n* a member of the Coptic Church; an Egyptian descended from ancient Egyptians.—*adj* **Cop´tic**.—*n* an Afro-Asiatic language, written in the Greek alphabet but descended from ancient Egyptian.—*adj* of this language; of Copts.—**coptic art**, Christian art in Egypt from the 3d to 9th centuries; **Coptic Church**, an independent sect of the Eastern Church. [A corr of Gr *Aigyptios*, Egyptian.]

copula [kop´ū-la] *n* that which joins together, a bond or tie.—*vi* **cop´ulāte**, to unite in sexual intercourse.—*n* **copulā´tion**.—*adj* **cop´ulative**, uniting.—*n* (*gram*) a verb form that links a subject with a predicate. [L]

copy [kop´i] *n* an imitation; a reproduction; a transcript; an individual specimen of a book; a model for imitation; matter for printing; material for a newspaper writer; text for an advertisement.—*vt* to write, paint, etc., after an original; to imitate; to transcribe; to reproduce or duplicate mechanically.—*pt p* **cop´ied**.—*ns* **cop´ybook**, a writing or drawing book with models for imitation; **cop´yholder**, a device for holding copy, esp for a typesetter; one who reads copy for a proofreader; **copy´right**, the exclusive legal right to the publication and sale of a literary, dramatic, musical, or artistic work in any form.—*adj* protected by copyright.—*n* **copywriter**, a writer of advertising or publicity copy. [Fr *copie*—Low L *cōpia*, a transcript—L *cōpia*, plenty.]

coquet, coquette [ko-ket´] *vi* to play the coquette; to deal with something playfully rather than seriously.—*ns* **cō´quetry**, act of coquetting; attempt to attract admiration without genuine affection; fickleness in love; **cŏquette´**, a woman addicted to coquetry.—*adj* **cŏquett´ish**. [Fr *coqueter—coquet*, dim of *coq*, a cock.]

coracle [kör´a-kl] *n* a small oval rowboat used in Wales made of skins or oilcloth stretched on wickerwork. [W *corwgl*.]

coral [kör´ȧl] *n* the hard skeleton secreted by certain marine polyps; a polyp or polyp colony together with its membranes and skeletons; the ovary of a lobster or scallop, coral red when cooked; a color averaging deep pink.—*adj* made of or like coral.—*ns* **cor´albells**, a perennial (*Heuchera sanguinea*) widely cultivated for its spikes of tiny coral flowers; **cor´alline**, a family (*Carollinaceae*) of calcareous red algae.—*adj* of, or resembling coral or coralline.—*n* **cor´al reef**, a reef formed by the growth and deposit of coral. [OFr,—L *coralium*—Gr *korallion*.]

corban [kör´ban] *n* among the ancient Hebrews, an offering to god. [Heb *qorbān*.]

corbel [kör´bel] *n* (*archit*) a projection from the face of a wall, supporting a cornice, arch, etc. [OFr *corbel*—Low L *corvellus*, dim of *corvus*, a raven.]

cord [körd] *n* a small rope or thick string; (*anat*) something resembling a cord; anything that binds or restrains; a measure of cut wood (128 cubic feet); a rib on the surface of a fabric; a ribbed fabric; a slender electric cable.—*vt* to bind with a cord.—*ns* **cord´age**, cords and ropes; **cord´ite**, a smokeless explosive made of nitroglycerin, guncotton, etc.—*adj* **cordless**, operated by batteries, as an electric shaver. [Fr *corde*—L *chorda*. See **chord**.]

cordial [kör´di-ȧl] *adj* hearty, sincere; affectionate; reviving the heart of spirits.—*n* an invigorating medicine or drink.—*n* **cor-dial´ity**.—*adv* **cor´dially**. [Low L *cordiālis*—L *cor, cordis*, the heart.]

cordillera [kör-dil-yā´rä or -dil´ėr-ȧ] *n* a system or chain of mountains. [Sp,—Old Sp *cordilla*—L *chorda*, cord.]

cordon [kör´don, -dȯn] *n* a cord or ribbon bestowed as an award; a line of sentries or policemen to prevent access to an area.—*vt* to enclose with a cordon. [Fr]

corduroy [kör-dụ̇-roi´] *n* a thick cotton fabric, corded or ribbed; (*pl*) trousers made of corduroy; a road laid transversely with logs. [Perh Fr *corde du roi*, king's cord.]

cordwain [kïrd´wān] *n* (*arch*) fine leather, originally from *Cordova* in Spain.—*n* **cord´wainer**, a shoemaker.

core [kōr, kör] *n* the heart; the inner part of anything, esp of fruit; the most important part.—*vt* to take out the core of. [Perh conn with L *cor*, heart.]

correspondent [kö-rė-spond´ėnt] (*law*) a person named as having committed adultery with the husband or wife from whom a divorce is sought.

corgi [kör´gē] *n* a Welsh corgi. [Welsh *corr*, dwarf, *ci*, dog.]

coriaceous [kōr-i-ā´shụs] *adj* leathery, of or like leather. [L *corium*, skin, leather.]

coriander [kor-i-an´dėr] *n* an umbelliferous plant (*Coriandrum sativum*) whose seeds are used as spice, etc. [Fr,—L *coriandrum*—Gr *koriannon*.]

Corinthian [kor-inth´i-ȧn] *adj* of *Corinth*, Greece, or an ornate style of Greek architecture; profligate.—*n* man of fashion. *n* **Corinthians**, (*Bible*) 7th and 8th books of the New Testament, epistles written to Christians at Corinth by St Paul, probably in 55 and 56 AD.

cork [kork] *n* the light, thick elastic outer bark of the cork oak used esp for stoppers and insulation; a stopper made of cork; any stopper.—*adj* made of cork.—*vt* to stop with a cork; to plug.—*ns* **cork oak**, an oak (*Quercus suber*) of southern Europe and northern Africa that produces the cork of commerce; **cork´screw**, a screw for drawing corks from bottles.—*adj* like a corkscrew in shape. [Sp *corcho*—L *cortex*, bark, rind.]

corm [körm] *n* the storage organ of a plant, a compact thickened underground stem like a bulb, but without the separate scales. [Gr *kormos*, the lopped trunk of a tree.]

cormorant [kör´mȯ-rȧnt] *n* any of various web-footed seabirds (family Phalocrocoracidae) of great voracity and used in eastern Asia for catching fish; a glutton. [Fr *cormoran*, from L *corvus marīnus*, sea crow.]

corn[1] [körn] *n* a small hard seed, esp of a cereal plant; the plants themselves; (in N America) maize, a cereal grass with kernals growing in rows along a corncob; (in England) wheat, (in Scotland and Ireland) oats; (*slang*) something old-fashioned or hackneyed.—*vt* to pickle (meat, etc.) in brine.—*ns* **corn´ball**, an unsophisticated person; **corn´cob**, the elongated woody center of the ear of maize; **corn cockle**, an annual weed (*Agrostemma githago*), with purplish red flowers found in cornfields; **corn earworm**, a moth (*Heliothis zea*) whose yellow-headed larva is destructive to maize, tomatoes, and cotton bolls; **corn´flower**, corn cockle; batchelor's button; **Corn´ Law**, one of a series of laws in Great Britain before 1846 prohibiting or discouraging the importation of grain; **corn´meal**, meal ground from corn; **corn oil**, a yellow oil got from the germ of maize kernels and used in salad oil, soft soap, and margarine; **corn snow**, coarse granules of snow formed by partial melting then freezing; **corn starch**, starch made from maize used in cooking and a wide range of industrial processes. [OE *corn*; akin to L *grānum*.]

corn[2] [körn] *n* a small hard growth chiefly on the foot.—**tread on one's corns**, to injure one's feelings. [L *cornū*, a horn.]

cornea [kör´ne-a] *n* the transparent membrane that forms the front covering of the eyeball—*adj* **cor´neal**. [L *cornea* (*tela*), horny (tissue).]

cornel [kör´nėl] *n* any of various shrubs or trees (genus *Cornus*) with perfect flowers, esp the dwarf cornel (*C canadensis*) found throughout N America, and related dogwoods. [Low L *cornolium*—L *cornus*, cornel.]

cornelian [kör-nē´li-ȧn] *n* a fine chalcedony generally translucent and red.—Also **carnē´lian**. [Fr *cornaline*—L *cornū*, a horn; or *cornum* (*cornus*), see previous word.]

corner [kör´nėr] *n* the point where two lines meet; a secret or confined place; an awkward position, difficulty; in association football, a free kick from the corner flag; an operation by which a few speculators gain control of the whole available supply of a commodity.—*vt* to put in a corner; to drive into an embarrassing position from which escape is difficult; to gain control of the supplies of (a commodity).—*vi* to turn a corner; to meet at a corner or angle.—*n* **cor´nerstone**, the stone that unites the two walls of a building at a corner; the principal stone, esp the corner of the foundation of a building—hence (*fig*) something of great importance.—**cor´nerback** (*football*) either of two defensive backs stationed between the line of scrimmage and the safety man.—**around the corner**, at hand; imminent; **cut corners**, to do a piece of work skimpily or with the minimum of effort; **turn the corner**, to go round the corner; to get past a difficulty or danger. [OFr *corniere*—L *cornū*, a horn.]

cornet [kör-net´] *n* a valved musical instrument of brass, more tapering than the trumpet; any cone-shaped object. [Fr *cornet*, dim of *corne*, a horn, trumpet—L *cornū*, a horn.]

cornice [kör´nis] *n* (*classical archit*) the highest molded projection of a wall or column; plaster molding round a ceiling; a decorative band used to conceal curtain fixtures. [Fr,—It perh Gr *korōnis*, a curved line; cf L *corōna*.]

Cornish [körn´ish] *adj* pertaining to *Cornwall*.—*n* the people or Celtic dialect of Cornwall; a breed of domestic fowls.

cornucopia [kör-nū-kō´pi-a] *n* a horn-shaped container overflowing with fruits, flowers, etc. emblematic of abundance, an inexhaustible store. [L *cornū*, horn, and *cōpia*, plenty.]

corny[1] [kör´ni] *adj* (*inf*) old-fashioned, out-of-date, uninteresting from frequent use, dull, foolish.

corny[2] [kör´ni] *adj* having corns on the feet.

corolla [kor-ol´a] *n* the inner covering of a flower composed of one or more leaves called petals. [L *corolla*, dim of *corōna*, a crown.]

corollary [kor´ol-ȧ-ri] *n* an obvious inference; a consequence or result. [L *corollārium*, a garland—*corolla*; see above.]

corona [ko-rō´na] *n* a colored ring round the sun or moon; the halo seen around the sun during a total eclipse; the upper portion of a bodily part (as of a tooth or skull); a long cigar.—*n* **cor´onal; cor´onary**, pertaining to a crown.—**coronary arteries**, arteries that supply blood to the heart muscle; **coronary thrombosis**, the formation of a clot in one of these arteries.—*n* **coronā´tion**, the act of crowning a sovereign. [L *corōna*, a crown.]

coroner [kor´o-nėr] *n* a public officer who holds inquests into the causes of accidental or suspicious deaths. [OFr—L *corōna*.]

coronet [kor´o-net] *n* a small crown worn by the nobility; a band of jewels, flowers, etc. for the head.—*adj* **cor´oneted**. [OFr, dim of *corone*, crown—L *corōna*, a crown.]

corporal[1] [kör´po-rȧl] *n* the lowest rank of non-commissioned officer, just below a sergeant;—*n* **cor´poralship**. [Fr *caporal*—It *caporale*—*capo*, the head—L *caput*, the head.]

corporal[2] [kör´po-rȧl] *adj* belonging or relating to the body; having a body; not spiritual.—*n* the cloth used for covering the elements of the Eucharist.—*adv* **cor´porally**.—*adj* **cor´porate**, legally united into a body so as to act as an individual; belonging to a corporation; united.—*adv* **cor´porately**.—*ns* **corpora´tion**, a group of people organized as to operate a business, under a charter granting them as a body some of the legal rights, etc. of an individual; (*inf*) a potbelly; **cor´poratism**, the organization of a society into industrial and professional corporations serving as organs of political representation and exercising control over persons within their jurisdiction.—*adj* **corpō´real**, having a body or substance, material. [L *corporālis*—*corpus, corpŏris*, the body.]

corps [kōr] *n* an organized subdivision of the military establishment; a tactical unit usu. consisting of two divisions or more and auxiliary arms and services; a body of persons with a common activity or occupation; a corps de ballet.—*pl* **corps** [kōrz]. [Fr from L *corpus*, the body.]

corps de ballet [kör dė ba-le´] the ensemble of a ballet company. [Fr]

corpse [körps, or körs] *n* a dead body esp of a human being. [ME *corps*, earlier *cors*—OFr *cors*, the body—L *corpus*.]

corpus [kör´pus] *n* a corpse; a body of laws, etc.—*pl* **cor´pora**.—*ns* **cor´pūlence, cor´pulency**, fleshiness of body, excessive fatness.—*adj* **cor´pūlent**, fleshy or fat.—*adv* **cor´pulently**.—*n* **cor´puscle** [or -pus´l], a minute particle; a cell not in continuous contact with others (eg lying in a fluid such as the blood plasma)—also **corpus´cule** [-kūl].—*adj*

corpus´cular [-kū-].—**Corpus Christi**, the Roman Catholic festival in honor of the Eucharist held on the Thursday after Trinity Sunday; **corpus delicti** [dėlik´tī], the facts constituting a crime; (*loosely*) the body of a murder victim. [L *corpus*, the body.]

corral [kor-al´] *n* an enclosure for cattle, etc.; a defensive enclosure in an encampment, made by placing wagons in a circle.—*vt* to form, or put in, a corral. [Sp.]

correct [kor-ekt´] *vt* to remove faults from; to mark faults in; to set right (a person); to punish; to counteract, neutralize (eg a tendency).—*adj* free from faults; true; in accordance with the accepted standard (of conduct, taste, etc.)—*adv* **correct´ly**.—*n* **correc´tion**, amendment; punishment.—*adjs* **correc´tional, correct´ive**, tending, or having the power, to correct.—*ns* **correct´ive**, that which corrects; **correct´ness, corrector**.—**corrected time**, in yacht racing, a boat's elapsed time less her time allowance. [L *corrigĕre, correctum*—*con-*, inten, *regĕre*, to rule.]

correlate [kor´e-lāt] *vt* to be related to one another esp by close or necessary connection.—*vt* to bring into relation with each other, to connect systematically.—*n* **correlā´tion**.—*adj* **correl´ative**, mutually or reciprocally related; corresponding and used together (eg the words *either—or*).—Also *n*. —*adv* **correl´atively**. [Coined from L *con-*, with, + **relate**.]

correspond [kor-e-spond´] *vi* to suit, to agree (*with* **to, with**); to be analogous (to) in function, position or other respect; to hold intercourse, esp by letter.—*n* **correspond´ence**, harmony, relation of agreement part to part (also) **correspond´ency**; communication by letters; letters sent or received.—*adj* **correspond´ent**, answering; analogous.—*n* one with whom intercourse is kept up by letters; a journalist supplying news from a place away from home office; person or firm that regularly does business with another.—*adv* **correspond´ingly**. [Coined from L *con-*, with, and *respondēre*, to promise, answer.]

corridor [kor´i-dör] *n* a passageway into which compartments or rooms open; a usu. narrow passageway or route, as land held in foreign territory or a restricted lane for air traffic; a densely populated strip of land including two or more major cities. [Fr,—It *corridore*—It *correre*, to run—L *currĕre*.]

corrie [kor´i] *n* a semicircular recess in a mountain. [Gael *coire*, a cauldron.]

corrigendum [kor-i-jen´dum] *n* an error in a printed work discovered after printing and shown with its correction on a separate sheet;—*pl* **corrigen´da**, [L, gerundive of *corrigĕre*, to correct.]

corrigible [kor´ij-ibl] *adj* that may be corrected; open to correction.—*n* **corrigibil´ity**. [Fr,—L *corrigĕre. See* **correct**.]

corroborate [kor-ob´o-rāt] *vt* to confirm, esp by evidence.—*adj* **corrob´orative**, tending to confirm.—*n* that which corroborates.—*n* **corroborā´tion**, confirmation. [L *cor-*, intensive, *rōborāre, -ātum*, to make strong—*rōbur*, oak, strength.]

corroboree [ko-rob´ō-rē] *n* festive or warlike dance of Australian Aborigines; a song for such a dance; a noisy gathering. [Native word.]

corrode [kor-ōd´] *vti* to eat into or wear away by degrees as by rust, chemicals, etc.—*n* **corrō´sion**, act or process of wasting away; a product of corroding.—*adj* **corros´ive**, having the quality of eating away.—*n* that which has the power of corroding.—*adv* **corros´ively**.—*n* **corros´iveness**.—**corrosive sublimate**, a highly poisonous compound of mercury and chlorine. [L *cor-*, inten, *rōdĕre, rōsum*, to gnaw.]

corrugate [kor´(y)ōō-gāt] *vt* to form into parallel ridges and grooves.—*n* **corrugā´tion**.—**corrugated iron**, sheet iron shaped into a wavy surface for the sake of strength. [L *cor-*, inten, *rūgāre, -ātum*, to wrinkle—*rūga*, a wrinkle.]

corrupt [kor-upt´] *vti* to make or become corrupt.—*adj* putrid; depraved; defiled; not genuine; full of errors; venal; taking bribes; dishonest.—*adv* **corrupt´ly**.—*ns* **corrupt´ness; corrupt´er; corrup´tion**, decomposition; impurity; bribery; perversion (eg of language).—*adjs* **corrupt´ive**, having the quality of corrupting; **corrupt´ible**, liable to corruption; capable of being bribed.—*n* **corruptibil´ity**. [L *cor-*, inten, and *rumpĕre, ruptum*, to break.]

corsage [kör´sij, kör-säzh´] *n* the bodice or waist of a woman's dress; a bouquet to be worn. [OFr, —*cors*—L *corpus*, the body.]

corsair [kör´sār] *n* a pirate ship or pirate, esp of the Barbary coast (North Africa); any pirate. [Fr *corsaire*, one who courses or ranges—L *cursus*, a running—*currĕre*, to run.]

corselet *See* **corslet**.

corset [körs´et] *n* a closefitting undergarment worn, chiefly by women, to support the torso. [Dim of OFr *cors*—L *corpus*, the body.]

corslet, corselet [körs´let] *n* (*hist*) a defensive covering for the body, chiefly of leather; a form of corset. [Fr *corselet*, dim of OFr *cors*—L *corpus*, the body.]

cortege, cortège [kör-tezh´] *n* a train of courtiers; a procession, esp a funeral procession. [Fr—It *corte*, court.]

cortex [kör´teks] *n* the outer layer of plant tissue surrounding xylem; (*zool*) the outer layer of an organ, esp the brain;—*pl* **cortices** [kör´tisēz].—*n* **cortisone** [kör´ti-sōn] a substance present in the adrenal cortex; the hormone used esp in the treatment of rheumatoid arthritis. [L *cortex, corticis*, bark.]

corundum [ko-run´dum] *n* a mineral consisting of alumina, second in hardness only to the diamond, that can be synthesized, and is used as an abrasive; forms include sapphire, ruby. [Tamil *kurundam*, ruby.]

coruscate [kor´us-kāt] *vi* to sparkle, throw off flashes of light.—*adj* **corus´cant**, flashing.—*n* **coruscā´tion**, a glittering; sudden flashes of light. [L *coruscāre, -ātum*, to vibrate, glitter.]

corvée [kör-vā´] *n* the obligation to perform unpaid labor for the sovereign or feudal lord; labor extracted in lieu of taxes by public authorities, esp for highway construction and repair. [Fr—Low L *corrogāta*—L *corrogāre*—*cor-*, together, *rogāre*, to ask.]

corvette [kör-vet´] *n* (*Brit*) formerly a vessel with flushdeck and one tier of guns; now an escort vessel, specially designed for protecting convoys against submarine attack. [Fr—Sp *corbeta*—L *corbīta*, a slow-sailing ship, from *corbis*, a basket.]

corvine [kör´vīn] *adj* pertaining to the crow; resembling a crow. [L *corvinus*—*corvus*, a crow.]

Corybant [kor´i-bant] *n* a priest of the goddess Cybele, whose rites included frantic music and dances;—*pl* **Cor´ybants; Corybantes** [kor-i-ban´tēz].—*adj* **coryban´tic**, wildly excited. [Gr *Korybās*, gen *Korybantos*.]

coryphaeus [kor-i-fē´us] *n* the chief or leader, esp the leader of a chorus;—*pl* **coryphaei** [-fē´ī]. [L—Gr *koryphaios*—*koryphē*, the head, top.]

cos lettuce [kos] *n* romaine. [Introduced from the Aegean island of *Cos*, Gr *Kōs*.]

cosecant [kō-sē´kȧnt, -sek´-] *n* one of the six trigonometrical functions of an angle, the reciprocal of the sine, identical with the secant of the complementary angle.

cosignatory [kō-sig´na-to-ri] *adj* uniting with others in signing.—Also *n* **cosign´er**, one who does so. [**co-** + **signatory**.]

cosine [kō´sīn] *n* one of the six trigonometrical functions of an angle, the ratio of the base to the hypotenuse—identical with sine of complementary angle.

cosmetic [koz-met´ik] *adj* beautifying or correcting faults in the face, hair, etc.; done or made to enhance the appearance of anything.—*n* a preparation to enhance beauty.—*adv* **cosmet´ically**. [Gr *kosmētikos*—*kosmeein*—*kosmos*, order.]

cosmic *see* **cosmos** (1).

cosmogony [koz-mog´o-ni] *n* the creation or origin of the world or universe; a theory, or a myth, of the origin of the universe.—*n* **cosmog´onist**. [Gr *kosmogonia*—*kosmos*, order, and root of *gignesthai*, to be born.]

cosmography [koz-mog´rȧ-fi] *n* a description of the world; the science of the constitution of the universe.—*n* **cosmog´rapher**.—*adjs* **cosmograph´ic, -al**. [Gr *kosmographia*—*kosmos*, order, the universe, *graphein*, to write.]

cosmology [koz-mol´o-ji] *n* a branch of philosophy that deals with the nature of the universe; a branch of astronomy dealing with the origin, structure, and space-time relations of the universe; a theory about these.—*adj* **cosmolog´ical**.—*n* **cosmol´ogist**, one versed in cosmology. [Gr *kosmos*, order, the universe, *logos*, discourse.]

cosmonaut [koz´mō-nöt] *n* a Russian who has traveled round the world in space; an astronaut. [From Russian—Gr *kosmos*, the universe, *nautes*, sailor.]

cosmopolitan [koz-mo-pol´i-tȧn], **cosmopolite** [koz-mop´ōlīt] *n* a citizen of the world; one free from local or national prejudices.—*adj* belonging to all parts of the world; having international tastes; unprejudiced.—*n* **cosmopol´itanism**. [Gr *kosmopolītēs*—*kosmos*, the world, *polītēs*, a citizen—*polis*, a city.]

cosmos[1] [koz´mos] *n* the universe as an orderly or systematic whole; any orderly system.—*adjs* **cos´mic**, of, or relating to, the cosmos; vast in extent, intensity, or comprehensiveness; **cos´mical**, cosmic.—*adv* **cos´mically**.—**cosmic rays**, streams of highly penetrating charged particles bombarding the earth from outer space. [Gr.]

cosmos[2] [koz´mos] *n* any of a genus (*Cosmos*) of tropical American composite herbs, esp a tall fall-blooming annual (*C. bipinnatus*) with red or yellow disks.

cossack [kos´ak] *n* one of a people in southeastern Russia, famous as horsemen. [Turk.]

cosset [kos´et] *n* a pet lamb.—*vt* to pamper. [Ety uncertain.]

cost [kost] *vt* to bring, or be valued at (a specified price); to require, involve (in suffering, or loss); to estimate the cost of production of;—*pt, pt p* **cost**.—*n* what is paid or suffered to obtain anything; (*pl*) expenses of a lawsuit.—*adj* **cost´ly**, of great cost; valuable.—*n* **cost´liness**.—**at all costs**, by any means required; **cost of living**, the total cost of goods ordinarily required in order to live up to one's usual standard; **cost-of-living index**, consumer price index. [OFr *couster* (Fr *coûter*)—L *constāre*, to stand at.]

costive [kos´tiv] *adj* constipating; constipated.—*adv* **cos´tively**.—*n* **cos´tiveness**. [OFr *costivé*—L *constīpātus*—*constīpāre. See* **constipate**.]

costume [kos´tūm, kos-tūm´] *n* a manner of dressing; dress; a woman's outer dress.—*adj* **costumed´**.—*ns* **costum´er**, one who makes or deals in costumes.—**costume jewelry**, jewelry worn as an adornment only, without pretense of value. [Fr—L *consuētūdō*, custom.]

cosy *see* **cozy**.

cot[1] [kot] *n* a small dwelling, a cottage; a sheath, as for a hurt finger. [OE *cot(e)*; cf ON and Du *kot*; Low L *cota* is from Gmc.]

cot[2] [kot] *n* a narrow collapsible bed as one made of canvas on a folding frame. [Anglo-Ind—Hindustani *khāt*.]

cotangent [kō-tan´jėnt] *n* one of the six trigonometrical functions of an angle, the reciprocal of the tangent, identical with the tangent of the complementary angle.

cote [kōt] *n* a cot; a small shelter for fowl, sheep, etc. [OE *cote; see* **cot** (1).]
coterie [kō´te-rē] *n* a social, literary, or other exclusive circle. [Fr; orig a number of peasants obtaining a joint tenure of land from a lord—Low L *cota*, a hut—Gmc.]
cothurnus [kō-thûr´nus], **cothurn** [kō´thûrn] *n* a high thick-soled laced boot worn by actors in Greek or Roman tragic drama; a style of ancient tragedy;—*pl* **cothur´nī**. [L *cothurnus*—Gr *kothornos*.]
cotillion [ko-til´yon], **cotillon** [ko-tē´y•] *n* an intricate, formal group dance; a formal ball. [Fr, petticoat—*cotte*, a coat—Low L *cotta*, a tunic; cf **coat**.]
cottage [kot´ij] *n* a small house; a house used for vacations.—*n* **cott´ager**, one who lives in a cottage.—**cottage cheese**, a soft white cheese made from sour milk curds. [LL *cottagium*—OE *cot; see* **cot** (1).]
cotter[1], **cottar** [kot´ėr] *n* a peasant or farm laborer occupying a cottage for which he has to give service in lieu of rent. [From root of **cot** (1), partly through Low L.]
cotter[2] [kot´ėr] *n* a tapered piece used to fasten together parts of a structure; a cotter pin.—*n* **cotter pin**, a split pin fastened in place by spreading apart its ends after insertion.
cotton [kot´n] *n* a soft fibrous substance; the hairs covering the seeds of a tropical plant (genus *Gossypium*) of the mallow family; such a plant, esp one grown to produce cotton; thread; yarn or cloth made of cotton.—*adj* made of cotton.—*vi* to agree (with); to become attached (to).—*ns* **cotton candy**, a candy made of spun sugar; **cotton gin**, a machine which separates the seeds, hulls, and foreign material from cotton; **cotton grass**, any of a genus (*Eriophorum*) of sedges with tufted spikes; **cottonmouth, cottonmouth moccasin**, water moccasin.—*adj* **cotton-picking**, damned, used as an expression of disapproval; damned, used as an intensive.—*ns* **cottontail**, any of several small N American rabbits (genus *Silvalagus*) with a sandy brown coat and a white underside to the tail; **cottonwood**, a poplar (*Populus deltoides*) of the eastern and central US with a tuft of cottony hairs on the seed.—*adj* **cotton´y**.—**cotton on** (*inf*) to take a liking to; to become aware of (a situation). [Fr *coton*—Ar *qutun*.]
cotyledon [kot-i-lē´don] *n* (*bot*) the first leaf or first pair of leaves developed by the embryo of a seed plant or of some lower plants (as ferns).—*adj* **cotylē´donary**. [L—Gr *kotylēdōn*—*kotylē*, a cup.]
couch [kowch] *vt* to lay down on a bed, etc.; to express (in words); to embroider (a design) by fastening the main threads with small stitches at regular intervals.—*vi* to lie down for the purpose of sleep, concealment, etc.—*n* any place for rest or sleep; a bed.—*adj* **couch´ant**, lying down with the head raised. [Fr *coucher*, to lay down—L *collacāre*. *See* **collocate**.]
couchgrass [kowch´, kōōch´ (-gräs)] *n* quack grass; any of several grasses resembling quack grass in spreading by creeping rhizomes. [A variant of *quitch*—OE *cwice*, prob akin to *cwic*, living.]
cougar [kōō´gär] *n* a large tawny cat (*Felis concolor*] formerly found throughout the Americas.—Also **catamount, mountain lion, painter, puma**. [Fr *cougar*, adapted from a South American name.]
cough [kof] *vi* to expel air with a sudden opening of the glottis and a harsh sound.—*n* the act or sound of coughing.—*vt* **cough up**, (*slang*) to hand over, deliver, or produce. [ME *coughen*; cf Du *kuchen*, Ger *keuchen, keichen*, to gasp.]
could [kŏd] *pt* of **can**. [ME *coude, couth*—OE *cūthe* for *cunthe*, was able; *l* is inserted from the influence of *would* and *should*.]
coulee [kōō-lā´, kōō´li] *n* a small stream; a gully; a sheet or stream of lava. [Fr,—*couler*, to flow.]
coulisse [kōō-lēs´] *n* a side scene of a theater stage; the space between the side scenes; the backstage area; a grooved piece of timber on which something slides. [Fr,—*couler*, to glide, to flow—L *cōlāre*, to strain, purify.]
coulomb [kŏŏ-lom´] *n* a unit of electric charge equal to 6.25 x 10^{18} electrons passing a point in one second. [From the French physicist, C A de *Coulomb*.]
coulter [kōl´tėr] *n* the cutting tool attached to the beam of a plow. [OE *culter*—L *culter*, knife.]
council [kown´sil] *n* an elected or appointed legislative or advisory body; a central body uniting a group of organizations; an executive body whose members are equal in power and authority.—*ns* **coun´cilman, coun´cilor, coun´cilwoman**, a member of a council. [Fr *concile*—L *concilium*.]
counsel [kown´sel] *n* consultation, deliberation; advice; plan, purpose; one who gives counsel, a lawyer or a group of lawyers; a consultant.—*vt* to advise; to recommend.—*vi* to give or take advice.—*pr p* **coun´seling**; *pt p* **coun´seled**.—*ns* **coun´selee´**, one receiving counsel; **coun´seling**, professional guidance for an individual or a couple from a qualified person (as a psychologist, priest, rabbi, minister, etc.); **coun´selor**, one who counsels; a lawyer, esp one managing a client's case in court; a supervisor in a summer camp; **counselor-at-law**, lawyer managing a client's case; **coun´selorship**. [Fr *conseil*—L *consilium*, advice—*consulĕre*, to consult.]
count[1] [kownt] *n* a European noble equal in rank to a British earl; **count´ess**, a woman of this rank; the wife, ex-wife, or widow of a count or earl.—*n* **coun´ty**, the domain of a count; the largest territorial division for local government in a state of the US; a territorial division of Great Britain and Ireland, now abolished in Scotland.—Also *adj*. [OFr *conte*—L *comes, comitis*, a companion.]
count[2] [kownt] *vt* to number, sum up; to ascribe; to esteem, consider; to call aloud (beats or time units); to include or exclude by counting.—*vi* to name numbers or add up items in order; to have a (specified) value; to be of account; to be reckoned; to depend (*with* **on**).—*n* act of numbering; the number counted; a particular charge in an indictment.—*ns* **count´down**, the schedule of operations just before firing a rocket, etc.; the descending count to zero which marks the moment of action, as eg the moment of firing a rocket; **count´er**, he who, or that which, counts; that which indicates a number; a token used in reckoning; a table on which money is counted or goods laid; **coun´terman**, a man who serves customers at the counter of a lunchroom or cafeteria; **count´inghouse**, the premises in which a merchant keeps his accounts and transacts business.—*adj* **count´less**, innumerable.—**count heads** or **count noses**, count the number present; **over the counter**, through a broker's office rather than through the stock exchange; (of drugs) without a prescription; **under the counter**, in an illicit and private manner. [OFr *cunter* (Fr *compter*)—L *computāre*.]
countenance [kown´ten-àns] *n* the face; the expression of the face; appearance; goodwill, support.—*vt* to favor or approve. [OFr *contenance*—L *continentia*, restraint, demeanor—L *continēre*, to contain.]
counter[1] *see* **count** (2).
counter[2] [kown´tėr] *adv* in the opposite direction; in opposition.—*adj* contrary; opposite.—*n* that which is counter or opposite; the part of a horse's breast between the shoulders and under the neck; (*naut*) the curved part of a ship's hull over the sternpost and rudder.—*vt* to contradict, combat; to meet or answer by a stroke or move.—*vi* to meet attacks or arguments with defensive or retaliatory measures.—*vt* **counteract´**, to act in opposition to, to hinder or defeat; to neutralize.—*n* **counterac´tion**.—*adj* **counterac´tive**, tending to counteract.—*n* **coun´terattack**, an attack in reply to an attack.—*vt* **counterbal´ance**, to balance by weight on the opposite side; to act against with equal weight, power, or influence.—*ns* **coun´terbalance**, an equal weight, power, or agency working in opposition; **coun´terclaim**, an opposing claim, esp in law.—*adv* **coun´terclock´wise**, in a direction contrary to that of the hands of a clock.—*ns* **coun´tercul´ture**, the culture of those people whose life style is opposed to the prevailing culture; **coun´tercurr´ent**, a current flowing in the opposite direction; **coun´teresp´ionage**, spying directed against an enemy's spy system; **coun´terfoil**, a coupon detached from a ticket or check, etc., and kept as a receipt or record; **coun´terinsur´gency**, measures taken by a state against rebels or terriorists; **coun´terintell´igence**, activities aimed at preventing an enemy from obtaining correct information to prevent sabotage, and to gather military and political information; **coun´terirr´itant**, an irritant used to relieve another irritation.—*vi* **coun´termarch**, to march back or in a contrary direction.—*n* a marching back by which a body of troops change front, and still retain the same men in the front rank; a march (as of political demonstrators) intended to counter the effect of another march.—*n* **coun´termine´**, (*mil*) a tunnel for intercepting an enemy mine; any means of counteraction.—*vt* **countermine´**, to make a mine in opposition to; to frustrate by secret measures.—*ns* **coun´terpart**, (*law*) one of two corresponding parts of a legal instrument; part that answers to another part; that which fits into or completes another; a duplicate, double; **coun´terplot**, plot or stratagem intended to frustrate another plot.—*vts* to intrigue against; to foil with a plot; **coun´terpoise**, to poise or weigh against or on the opposite side; to act in opposition to with equal effect.—*n* counterbalance.—*ns* **Count´er-Reformation**, (*hist*) a reform movement within the Roman Catholic Church, following the Reformation; **coun´terrevolū´tion**, a revolution undoing a previous revolution.—*vt* **countersign´**, to sign in addition to another, to attest the authenticity of a document.—*ns* **coun´tersign**, a military private sign or word, which must be given in order to pass a sentry; (also **coun´tersig´nature**) a name countersigned to a writing.—*vt* **countervail´**, to be of avail against; to compensate for.—*vi* to exert force against an opposing usu. bad force or influence. [Fr,—L *contrā*, against.]
counterfeit [kown´tėr-fit] *vt* to imitate; to copy without authority, to forge.—*n* something false or copied that pretends to be genuine.—Also *adj*. [OFr *contrefet*, from *contrefaire*, to imitate—L *contrā*, against, *facĕre*, to do.]
countermand [kown-tėr-mänd´] *vt* to recall or to stop by a command in opposition to one already given (eg reinforcements); to revoke, cancel (a command, an order).—*n* a revocation of a former order.—*adj* **countermand´able**. [OFr *contremander*—L *contrā*, against, and *mandāre*, to order.]
counterpane [kown´tėr-pān] *n* a bedspread. [OFr *contrepointe*, a corr of *coultepointe*—L *culcita puncta*, stitched pillow or cover; cf **quilt**.]
counterpoint [kown´tėr-point] *n* (*mus*) the art of combining melodies; a melody added as accompaniment to another.—*adj* **contrapunt´al**, according to the rules of counterpoint. [Fr,—*contre*, against, *point*, a point, from the pricks, points, or notes placed against those of the original melody.]
countertenor [kown´tėr-ten´ȯr] *n* an adult male voice singing in the alto range. [Fr *contre-teneur*.]
country [kun´tri] *n* a rural, as distinct from an urban, region; the land in which one was born, or in which one resides; the territory of a nation; a nation.—*adj* belonging to the country; of farm supplies and procedures; relating to country music.—*adj* **coun´trified, coun´tryfied**, rustic, unsophisticated; performed in the manner of country music.—*ns* **coun´try-dance**, dance in which partners are arranged in opposite lines.—*ns* **country house, country seat**, a mansion or estate in the country; **coun´tryman**,

one who lives in the country; a farmer; one born in the same country with another; **country music**, rural folk music, esp of the Southern US; **country and western**, country music including Western cowboy style; **coun´trywoman; coun´tryside**, a district or part of the country. [OFr *contrée*—L *contrā*, opposite.]

county *see* **count** (1).

coup [kōō] *n* a blow, stroke; a successful stroke or stratagem.—**coup de grâce** [dė gräs], a finishing blow; **coup d'état** [dā-tä], a sudden and violent change in government; **coup d'oeil** [dėi´], a glance, a brief survey; **coup de théâtre** [dė tā-ä-tr'], a sudden and dramatic happening or action. [Fr, through L—Gr *kolaphos*, a blow.]

coupé [kōō-pā], **coupe** [kōōp] *n* a closed, two-door automobile. [Fr *couper*, to cut.]

couple [kup´l] *n* that which joins two things together; two of a kind joined together, or connected; two; a pair.—*vt* to join together.—*ns* **coup´let**, two consecutive lines of verse that rhyme with each other; **coup´ling**, a joining together, esp in sexual union; a mechanical device for joining parts or things together; means of joining two electric circuits by having a common part to both. [OFr *cople*—L *copula*.]

coupon [kōō´pon(g)] *n* a detachable certificate on a bond, presented for payment of interest; a certificate entitling one to a discount, gift, etc., or for use in ordering goods; a voucher that payment will be made, goods sold, etc.; a piece cut from an advertisement entitling one to some privilege.—*n* **coup´oning**, the distribution or redemption of coupons. [Fr,—*couper*, to cut off.]

courage [kur´ij] *n* the quality that enables people to meet dangers without giving way to fear, bravery; spirit.—*adj* **courā´geous**, full of courage, brave.—*adv* **courā´geously**.—*n* **courā´geousness**. [OFr *corage* (Fr *courage*)—L *cor*, heart.]

courier [kōō´ri-ėr] *n* a messenger, esp a member of the diplomatic service bearing messages, a spy transferring secret information, or a runner of contraband; a member of the armed services responsible for carrying mail, information, or supplies; a person hired to take care of hotel accommodation, etc. for a traveler. [Fr,—L *currĕre*, to run.]

course [kōrs, körs] *n* act of running; path in which anything moves; a channel for water; the direction pursued; the ground over which a race is run, golf is played, etc.; a race; regular progress; method of procedure; conduct; a prescribed series of studies; any of the studies; each of the successive divisions of a meal; a range of bricks or stones on the same level in building.—*vt* to run, chase, or hunt after.—*vi* to move with speed along an indicated path.—*ns* **cours´er**, a runner; a swift horse; one who courses or hunts; **cours´ing**, hunting with hounds.—**in due course**, in the usual sequence (of events); **in the course of**, during; **of course**, naturally, needless to say. [Fr *cours*—L *cursus*, from *currĕre, cursum*, to run.]

court [kōrt, kört] *n* an uncovered space surrounded by buildings or walls; a short street; a playing space, as for tennis, etc.; the palace of a sovereign; the body of persons who form his suite or council; attention designed to procure favor, affection, etc., as 'to pay court'; (*law*) the hall of justice; the judges and officials who preside there; any body of persons assembled to decide causes.—*vt* to pay attention to; to woo; to solicit, to seek.—*vi* to carry on a courtship.—*ns* **court´house**, a building housing law courts; a building housing offices of a county government; **court´ier**, one in attendance at a royal court; one who courts or flatters.—*adj* **court´ly**, having stately manners like those of a court.—*ns* **court´liness; court´-mar´tial** [-shål], a court held by officers of the armed forces to try offences against service discipline;—*pl* **courts´-mar´tial; court´ plas´ter**, a glycerin coated adhesive plaster made of silk, originally applied as patches on the face of ladies at court; **court´ship**, the act of wooing; **courtside´**, an area at the edge of a court (as for tennis or basketball); **court´yard**, a court or enclosed ground adjoining or in a large building. [OFr *cort*—Low L *cortis*, a courtyard—L *cors, cohors*, an enclosure.]

courtesan [kōrt´i-zan] *n* a prostitute with a courtly, upperclass clientele. [Fr *courtisane*—It *cortigiana*.]

courteous [kûr´tē-us] *adj* polite, considerate and respectful in manner and action.—*adv* **court´eously**.—*ns* **court´eousness; courtesy** [kûrt´e-si], courteous behavior; an act of civility or respect.—*n* **court´esy tī´tle**, a title allowed, by courtesy of society and not by legal right, to near relations of peers and to some others, as 'Professor' for any teacher. [OFr *corteis, cortois*—*cort, see* **court**.]

cousin [kuz´n] *n* a kinsman generally, esp one descended from a remote ancestor in a different line; the son or daughter of an uncle or aunt; a term used by a sovereign in addressing another, or to one of his own noblemen; a person of a race or culture ethnically related.—*n* **cous´inger´man**, a first cousin, esp one with four common grand-parents;—*pl* **cousins-german**. [Fr,—L *consōbrīnus*—*con-*, signifying connection, *sōbrīnus*, applied to the children of sisters—from the root of *soror*, a sister.]

couture [kōō-tür] *n* the business of designing, making, and selling custom-made men's and women's clothing; the garments created by couture.—*ns* **couturier** [kōō-tür-yā] a firm engaged in couture; the owner or designer in such a firm; **couturière** [-yer], a woman couturier. [Fr.]

cove [kōv] *n* a small bay or inlet in a body of water; a cavern, rocky recess or small valley in the side of a mountain. [OE *cofa*, a room; ON *kofi*, Ger *koben*.]

covenant [kuv´ė-nånt] *n* a mutual agreement, esp for the performance of some action; the writing containing the agreement; the common-law action to recover damages for breach of a covenant.—*vt* to promise by a covenant.—*vi* to enter into an agreement.—*adj* **cov´enanted**, agreed to by covenant; bound by covenant.—*ns* **Cov´enanter**, [usu. in Scot kuv-ėn-ant´ėr], one who signed or adhered to the *Scottish National Covenant* of 1638; **cov´enanter**, one that makes a convenant. [OFr,—L *con-*, together, *venīre*, to come.]

Coventry [kov´-, kuv´ėnt-ri] *n* in **to send to Coventry**, to exclude from social intercourse.

cover [kuv´ėr] *vt* to put or spread something on, over, or about; to overspread; to clothe, be a covering to; to hide; to screen, protect; to extend over; to comprise; to be sufficient for; to traverse; to command with a weapon; to report (an occurrence) for a newspaper.—*vi* to spread over, as a liquid does; to provide an excuse (for).—*n* that which covers or protects; undergrowth; thicket, concealing game, etc; a tablecloth and setting; something used to hide one's real actions, etc.—*ns* **cov´erage**, the amount, extent, etc. covered by something; **cov´erall**, (usu.*pl*) a one-piece protective garment often worn over regular clothing; **cov´ering**, anything that covers or conceals.—*adj* **cov´ert**, covered; secret, concealed.—*n* a place that covers or affords protection.—*adv* **cov´ertly**.—*n* **cov´erture**, covering; shelter; (*law*) the condition of a married woman under common law.—*ns* **cover charge**, a fixed charge additional to the price of food and service, made by some restaurants; **cover crop**, a crop planted to prevent soil erosion and to provide humus; **covered bridge**, a bridge that has its roadway protected by a roof and enclosing sides; **cover story**, a story accompanying a magazine-cover illustration; **cover-up**, something used to hide one's real activities, etc.; a concerted effort to keep an illegal or unethical act or situation from being made public; a loose outer garment.—**cover one's tracks**, to conceal traces in order to elude pursuers; **cover ground**, to deal with a subject in a particular manner; **take cover**, to seek shelter; **under cover**, in secrecy. [Fr *couvrir*—L *co-operire*.]

coverlet [kuv´ėr-let] *n* a bedspread. [Fr *couvrir*, to cover, *lit*, a bed—L *lectum*.]

covet [kuv´et] *vt* to desire or wish for eagerly; to wish for (what belongs to another);—*pr p* **cov´eting**; *pt p* **cov´eted**.—*adjs* **cov´etable; cov´etous**, inordinately desirous; avaricious.—*adv* **cov´etously**.—*n* **cov´etousness**. [OFr *coveiter*—L *cupiditās, -ātis*—*cupĕre*, to desire.]

covey [kuv´i] *n* a mature bird or pair of birds with a brood of young; a small flock of birds, esp partridge or quail. [OFr *covée*—L *cubāre*, to lie down.]

cow[1] [kow] *n* the mature female of domestic cattle (genus *Bos*), valued for its milk; the mature female of certain other animals, as the elk, elephant, whale, etc.—*ns* **cow´boy**, one who tends cattle or horses, esp a usu. mounted ranch hand; **cow´catch´er**, an apparatus on the front of a locomotive to throw off obstacles; **cow´hand**, cowboy; **cow´hide**, the hide of a cow made into leather; a whip made of cowhide; **cow´parsnip**, a tall perennial N American plant (*Heracleum lanatum*) of the carrot family with large leaves and broad umbrels of white or purple flowers; a related plant (*H sphoridylium*) naturalized in the US from the Old World; **cow´pox**, a mild disease of the cow that protects against smallpox when transmitted to man. [OE *cū*, pl *cȳ*; Ger *kuh*; Sans *go*.]

cow[2] [kow] *vt* to subdue, intimidate. [Perh from ON *kūga*; Dan *kue*, to subdue.]

coward [kow´ård] *n* one who turns tail, one without courage; one who is shamefully afraid.—*adjs* **cow´ard, cow´ardly**, afraid of danger, timid; befitting a coward.—*ns* **cow´ardice, cow´ardliness**, want of courage, timidity. [OFr *couard*—L *cauda*, a tail.]

cower [kow´ėr] *vi* to sink down through fear, etc.; to crouch timidly. [Cf ON *kūra*, Dan *kure*, to lie quiet.]

cowl [kowl] *n* a cap or hood; a monk's hood; a cover for a chimney, etc.; a draped neckline on a woman's garment; the part of an automobile body supporting the windshield and instrument board; a cowling.—*adj* **cowled**, wearing a cowl.—*n* **cowl´ing**, the casing of an airplane engine. [OE *cugele*; ON *kofl*; L *cucullus*, hood.]

cowrie, cowry [kow´ri] *n* a marine gastropod (family Cypraeidae) widely distributed in warm seas and having glossy often brightly-coloured shells. [Hindi *kaurī*.]

cowslip [kow´slip] *n* a common British primrose (*Primula veris*) with fragrant yellow flowers; marsh marigold. [OE *cū*, cow, *slyppe*, slime.]

coxcomb [koks´kōm] *n* a strip of red cloth notched like a cock's comb, which professional fools used to wear; a fool; a fop. [**cockscomb**.]

Coxsackie virus [kok-sak´i] *n* any of several viruses related to that of poliomyelitis, usu. affecting children in late summer and fall. [*Coxsackie*, NY]

coxswain [kok´sn, or kok´swān] *n* one who steers a boat or racing shell.—Often contr **cox.** [**cock** (cf **cock-boat**) and **swain**.]

coy [koy] *adj* modest; coquettishly bashful.—*adv* **coy´ly**.—*n* **coy´ness**. [Fr *coi*—L *quiētus*, quiet.]

coyote [kī´ōt, or kī-ōt´ē] *n* a small wolf (*Canis latrans*) native to western N America. [Mex Sp *coyotl*.]

coypu [koi´poo] *n* nutria. [Amer Sp *coipú*—Araucanian *coypu*.]

coz [kuz] *n* cousin. [clipped form.]

cozen [kuz´n] *vt* to cheat.—*ns* **coz´enage**, deceit; **coz´ener**. [Perh Fr *cousiner*, to claim kindred.]

cozy, cosy [kō´zi] *adj* warm and comfortable, snug.—*n* a padded cover for a teapot, to keep the tea warm.

crab[1] [krab] *n* any of numerous chiefly marine broadly built crustaceans; **Crab**, the constellation Cancer.—*vi* (*inf*) to complain.—**catch a crab**, in rowing, to fail to raise the oar. [OE *crabba*; Ger *krebs*.]
crab[2] [krab] *n* a sour-tempered person.
crab´apple [krab] *n* a small, wild sour apple, esp any native species of genus *Malus*, as *M ioensis, M coronaria*; a cultivated variety of apple having usu. highly colored, acid fruit; a tree that produces crab apples. [Ety doubtful.]
crabbed [krab´id] *adj* ill-natured, morose; (of writings) intricate, difficult to understand; (of handwriting) ill-formed, cramped.—*adv* **crabb´edly**.—*n* **crabb´edness**. [**crab** (1), intermixed in meaning with **crab** (2).]
crab grass [krab] *n* a grass (esp *Digitaria sanguinalis*) that has creeping stems which root freely and is a pest in lawns and turf.
crack [krak] *vt* to make, or cause to make, a sharp sudden sound; to break into chinks; to split; to break partially or suddenly and sharply; in distilling petroleum, to break down hydrocarbons into simpler ones; to break up (chemical compounds) into simpler compounds by means of heat; (*slang*) to make (a joke); (*inf*) to break open (as a safe); to solve the mystery of (a code).—*vi* to make a sharp explosive sound; to break or split, usu. without separation; (*inf*) to lose control under pressure (*usu. with* **up**); to shift erratically in vocal tone; to break down into simpler chemical compounds usu. as a result of heating.—*n* a sudden sharp splitting sound; a chink; a flaw; (*inf*) a blow; (*slang*) a biting comment.—*adj* (*inf*) excellent.—*n* **crack´brain**, a crazy person.—*adjs* **crack´brained; cracked**, damaged by crack or cracks; (*inf*) crazy.—*ns* **crack´er**, one who or that which cracks; a thin crisp biscuit; a firecracker; **Crack´er**, a nick-name for a resident of Georgia or Florida; **cracks´man**, a burglar; a safecracker; **crack´erjack**, (*slang*) a first-rate person or thing.—Also *adj*.—*ns* **Cracker Jack**, trade name for a candied popcorn confection.—**crack down** (**on**), to become strict with; **cracked up to be**, (*inf*) believed to be; **crack up**, to crash; (*inf*) to break down mentally or physically; **get cracking**, to start moving fast. [OE *cracian*, to crack; cf. Du *kraken*, Gael *crac*.]
crackle [krak´l] *vi* to give out slight but frequent cracks.—*n* the sound of such cracks; a finely cracked surface, as on some pottery.—*n* **crack´ling**, (usu. *pl*) the rind of roast pork.—*adj* **crack´ly**, brittle.—*n* **crack´nel**, a light, brittle biscuit. [Freq of **crack**.]
cradle [krā´dl] *n* a small bed, usu. on rockers, in which a child is rocked; infancy; a place where anything is nurtured in the earliest period of its existence; a supporting framework, a frame in which anything is enclosed or partly enclosed; a frame to keep bedclothes from pressing on a patient.—*vt* to lay or rock in a cradle; to nurture. [OE *cradol*; ety obscure.]
craft [kräft] *n* cunning; dexterity; an art, skilled trade; the members of a skilled trade; (*pl* **craft**) a boat, ship, or aircraft.—*ns* **crafts´man**, one engaged in a craft; **crafts´manship**, skill in a craft.—*adj* **craf´ty**, having skill; cunning, wily.—*adv* **craft´ily**.—*n* **craft´iness**. [OE *cræft*; Ger *kraft*, power.]
crag [krag] *n* a rough steep cliff.—*adjs* **cragg´ed, cragg´y**, full of crags or broken rocks; rough, rugged.—*ns* **cragg´i-ness; crags´man**, one skilled in climbing rocks. [W *craig*, a rock; Gael *creag, carraig*.]
cram [kram] *vt* to press close; to stuff, to fill to superfluity; (*inf*) to stuff the memory with (information required for an examination).—*vi* to eat greedily; to learn by cramming;—*pr p* **cramm´ing**; *pt p* **crammed**.—*n* a crush.—*n* **cramm´er**, one who crams a pupil, or a subject, for an examination. [OE *crammian*; ON *kremja*, to squeeze.]
crambo [kram´bo] *n* a game in which one gives a word to which another finds a rhyme. [Prob from L *crambē repetīta*, cabbage served up again.]
cramp [kramp] *n* a spasmodic contraction of the muscles; (*pl*) abdominal spasms and pain; a clamp.—*vt* to affect with spasms; to confine narrowly; to restrict, restrain unduly (eg efforts).—*vi* to suffer from cramps.—*ns* **cramp´on**, an iron plate with spikes, for the foot, for hill climbing, walking on ice, etc. [OFr *crampe*; cf Du *kramp*, Ger *krampf*.]
cranberry [kran´bėr-i] *n* the red acid berry of a genus (*Vaccinium*) of small evergreen shrubs growing in marshy ground; any of the shrubs themselves.—*n* **cranberry bush**, a shrubby viburnum (*Viburnum trilobum*) of N America with red fruit resembling the cranberry. [For *craneberry*; origin obscure; cf Ger *kranbeere, kranich-beere*, crane berry.]
crane [krān] *n* any of a family (Gruidae) of large wading birds, with long legs, neck, and bill; a machine for raising, shifting, and lowering heavy weights using a movable projecting arm.—*vt* to raise with a crane.—*vti* to stretch out (the neck).—*ns* **crane´ fly**, any of numerous flies (family Tipulidae) which resemble large mosquitoes but do not bite; **cranes´bill**, any wild geranium. [OE *cran*; Ger *kranich*, W *garan*.]
cranium [krā´ni-um] *n* the skull; the bones enclosing the brain;—*pl* **crā´niums, crā´nia**.—*adj* **crā´nial**, pertaining to the cranium.—*ns* **craniol´ogy**, the study of skulls; **craniot´omy**, surgical opening of the skull.—*adj* **craniolog´ical**.—*n* **craniol´ogist**, one skilled in craniology. [Low L *crānium*—Gr *kṛānion*.]
crank[1] [krangk] *n* a conceit in speech; a whim; (*inf*) an eccentric person; a handle bent at right angles; (*mach*) an arm on a shaft for communicating motion to or from the shaft.—*vt* to move or seek to move by turning a crank (also **crank up**).—*adj* **crank´y**, crooked; in bad condition, shaky; full of whims; cross.—*n* **crank´iness**.—*ns* **crank´case**, a casing for the crankshaft and connecting rods of some types of reciprocating engine; **crank´shaft**, a shaft with one or more cranks for transmitting motion.—*adj* **crank´y**, peevish; eccentric.—**crank out**, to produce, esp in a mechanical manner. [OE *cranc*; cf Ger *krank*.]
crank[2] [krangk] *adj* (of a boat) liable to be upset by an external force.—*n* **crank´ness**.
cranny [kran´i] *n* a fissure, chink; a secret place.—*adj* **crann´ied**, having crannies or fissures. [Fr *cran*, a notch.]
crape [krāp] *n* crêpe; a band of crêpe worn as a sign of mourning (on a hat or sleeve). [OFr *crespe* (Fr *crêpe*)—L *crispus*, crisp.]
crap´ulous [krap´yů-lės] *adj* characterized by intemperance esp in drinking and eating; sick from drinking excessively. [Fr *crapule*—L *crāpula*, intoxication.]
crash[1] [krash] *n* a noise as of things breaking or being crushed by falling; a collision; a sudden failure, as of a business; a collapse, as of the financial market.—*adj* involving suddenness or speed or great effort; planned to deal with an emergency speedily; intended to lessen effects of a crash.—*vi* to fall to pieces with a loud noise; to be violently impelled (against, into); to land in such a way as to be seriously damaged, or destroyed.—Also *vt*.—*ns* **crash´dive´**, a sudden dive of a submarine; **crash´ hel´met**, a cushioned safety headdress worn by racing-motorists, motor cyclists, etc.—*vti* **crash´-land**, to land (an aircraft) in an emergency without lowering the undercarriage.—*ns* **crash´ land´ing; crash pad**, (*slang*) temporary sleeping place or quarters. [From the sound.]
crash[2] [krash] *n* a coarse strong linen cloth. [Perh from Russ.]
crasis [krā´sis] *n* (*gram*) the mingling or contraction of two vowels into one long vowel, or into a diphthong;—*pl* **crā´sēs**. [Gr *krāsis*—*kerannȳnai*, to mix.]
crass [kras] *adj* thick; coarse; stupid.—*ns* **crass´itude; crass´ness**. [OFr *cras*—L *crassus*.]
cratch [krach] *n* a crib or rack to hold hay for cattle. [Fr *crèche*, a manger; from a Gmc root, whence also **crib**.]
crate [krāt] *n* an open box of wood slats, for shipping; (*slang*) a dilapidated automobile.—*vt* to pack in a crate. [L *crātis*, a hurdle.]
crater [krāt´ėr] *n* a bowl-shaped mouth of a volcano; a hole made in the ground by the explosion of a shell, mine, bomb, etc. [L *crātēr*—Gr *krātēr*, a large bowl for mixing wine, from *kerannȳnai*, to mix.]
cravat [kra-vat´] *n* a kind of necktie worn chiefly by men. [Fr *cravate*—introduced in 17th cent from the *Cravates* or Croatians.]
crave [krāv] *vt* to beg earnestly, to beseech; to long for; to require.—*n* **crav´ing**, desire, longing. [OE *crafian*; ON *krefja*.]
craven [krāv´n] *n* a coward, a spiritless fellow.—*adj* cowardly, spiritless.—*adv* **crav´enly**.—*n* **crav´enness**. [Origin obscure.]
craw [krö] *n* the crop of a bird or insect; the stomach of lower animals. [ME *crawe*; cf Du *kraag*, neck.]
crawfish [krö´fish´] *n* a crayfish; the spiny lobster.
crawl [kröl] *vi* to move as a worm; to behave abjectly; to move slowly or stealthily; to be covered with crawling things.—*n* the act of crawling; a slow pace; an alternate overhand swimming stroke.—*n* **crawl´er**. [Scand,—Ger *krabbeln*, to creep.]
crayfish [krā´fish] *n* any of numerous freshwater crustaceans, one genus (*Cambarus*) in eastern N America, and another genus (*Astacus*) found in the Pacific states; the spiny lobster. [ME *crevice*—OFr *crevice*—Old High Ger *krebiz*, a crab.]
crayon [krā´on] *n* a stick made of wax or chalk, variously colored, used for drawing; a drawing in crayons. [Fr *crayon*—*craie*, chalk, from L *crēta*, chalk.]
craze [krāz] *vt* to weaken; to derange (of the intellect).—*n* a foolish enthusiasm, fashion, hobby.—*adj* **craz´y**, frail; demented; fantastically composed of irregular pieces (as a quilt).—*n* **craz´iness**. [Scand; Swed *krasa*, Dan *krase*, to crackle; whence also Fr *écraser*, to crush.]
creak [krēk] *vi* to make a sharp, grating sound, as of a hinge, etc.—*n* a noise of this kind.—*adj* **creak´y**. [From sound, cf *crake, croak*.]
cream [krēm] *n* the oily part of milk; the best part of anything; any creamlike preparation or refreshment; a yellowish white.—*vt* to add cream to; to beat into a soft, smooth consistency.—*vi* to gather or form cream; to break into a creamy froth.—*n* **cream´ery**, an establishment where butter and cheese are made or where milk and cream are processed and sold.—*adjs* **cream´y**, full of or like cream; gathering like cream.—*n* **cream´iness.—cream of tartar**, a white crystalline salt, an ingredient in baking powder. [OFr *cresme, creme*—L *chrisma*.]
crease [krēs] *n* a mark made by folding or doubling anything; a specially marked area in various sports, esp that in front of or surrounding the goal, as in hockey or lacrosse.—*vt* to make creases in anything.—*vi* to become creased.
create [krē-āt´] *vt* to bring into being; to invest with (a new form, character, rank, or office); to produce, as any work of imagination; to act for the first time (a character in a new play); to make (eg an impression).—*vi* to make something new.—*n* **creā´tion**, the act of creating, esp the universe; that which is created; the universe.—*adj* **creā´tive**, having power to create; that creates; showing imagination or originality.—*adv* **creā´tively**.—*ns* **creā´tiveness; creativ´ity; creā´tor**, one who creates; a maker; **creature** [krē´ -chůr], what has been created, esp an animated being, an animal, a person; a dependent or puppet.—**the Creator**, God; **creature comfort**, something that gives bodily comfort. [L *creāre, -ātum*.]

creatine [krē´a-tin] *n* a nitrogenous substance $C_4H_9N_3O_2$ found esp in the striped muscle of vertebrates. [Gr *kreas*, gen *kreatos*, flesh.]
creature *See* **create**.
crèche [kresh] *n* a display of the stable scene of Jesus' birth. [Fr.]
credence [krē´dėns] *n* belief esp in the reports or testimony of another; small table beside the altar on which the bread and wine are placed before being consecrated.—*adj* **crĕden´tial**, giving a title to belief or credit.—*n* that which entitles to credit or confidence; (*pl*) written evidence of trustworthiness or authority.—*adj* **credible** [kred´-] that may be believed.—*ns* **credibil´ity**.—*adv* **cred´ibly**.—*n* **cred´it**, belief; honor; reputation; influence derived from good reputation; a source of honor; sale on trust; time allowed for payment; the side of an account on which payments received are entered; a sum placed at a person's disposal in a bank; (*pl*) a list of acknowledgments of work done as on a motion picture; a completed unit of study in a school.—*vt* to believe; to enter on the credit side of an account; to attribute to.—*adj* **cred´itable**, trustworthy; bringing credit or honor.—*n* **cred´itableness**.—*adv* **cred´itably**.—*n* **cred´itor**, one to whom a debt is due.—*adj* **cred´ulous**, apt to believe without sufficient evidence; unsuspecting.—*adv* **cred´ulously**.—*ns* **cred´ulousness, credū´lity**. disposition to believe on insufficient evidence.—**credibility gap**, gap between what is claimed and what seems likely; inability to have one's truthfulness or honesty accepted; **credit card**, a card issued by a credit card company which enables the holder to have purchases debited to an account kept by the company; **credit hour**, the unit of measuring educational credit based on a given number of classroom periods over a defined period; **credit line**, a note acknowledging the source of an item (as a news dispatch or television program; **credit union**, a cooperative association for pooling savings of members and making low-interest loans to them.—**do credit to**, to bring honor to; **on credit**, agreeing to pay later. [L *crēdere*, to believe.]
Cree [krē] *n* member of an Amerindian people of Manitoba and Saskatchewan;—*pl* **Cree, -s**; the Algonquian language of this people.
creed [krēd] *n* a summary of articles of religious belief. [OE *crēda*—L *credo*, I believe.]
creek [krēk] *n* a natural stream of water smaller than a river; **Creek**, confederacy of Amerindian people of Alabama, Georgia, and Florida; member of any of these peoples; the Muskogean language of the Creek nation.—**up the creek**, (*slang*) in trouble. [Prob Scand, ON *kriki*, a nook; cf Du *kreek*, a bay.]
creel [krēl] *n* an angler's fishing basket. [Prob Celt; cf Old Ir *criol*, a chest.]
creep [krēp] *vi* to move on or near the ground; to move slowly or stealthily; to grow along the ground or on supports, as a vine; to fawn or cringe; to shudder;—*pt, pt p* **crept**.—*n* a crawl; a narrow passage; (*slang*) an annoying or disgusting person.—*n* **creep´er**, a creeping plant; a bird (as of the family Certhiidae) that creeps about on trees or bushes seeking insects.—*adj* **creep´y**, creeping; causing creeps, weird.—**the creeps**, a feeling of fear, repugnance, etc. [OE *crēopan*; Du *kruipen*.]
creese *see* **kris**.
cremation [krem-ā´sh(ȯ)n] *n* act of burning, esp of the dead.—*vt* **cremate´**.—*n* **crematōr´ium**, a place where cremation is done. [L *crematiō, -ōnis*—*cremāre*, to burn.]
crême (properly **crème**) [krem] *n* French for cream, applied to various creamy substances.—**crème de la crème** [dė la krem], the very best; **crême** (**crème**) **de menthe** [dė mãt], a peppermint flavored liqueur.
crenate, -d [krēn´āt, -id] *adjs* (*bot*) having rounded teeth between sharp notches.—*n* **crenā´tion**, a formation of this type. [Low L *crēna*, a notch.]
crenellated [kre´nel-āt-id] *adj* furnished with battlements; indented. [Fr,—Low L *crēna*, a notch.]
Creole [krē´ōl] *n* a person descended from the original French settlers of Louisiana; a person of mixed Creole and Negro descent; **creole**, a language based on two or more languages that serves as the native language of its speakers.—*adj* prepared with sautéed tomatoes, green peppers, onions, etc. [Fr *créole*—Sp *criollo*—*criadillo*, a nursling.]
creosote [krē´ō-sōt] *n* an oily liquid obtained by the destructive distillation of wood tar or coal tar.—*vt* to treat with creosote as a preservative. [Gr *kreas*, flesh, *sōtēr*, savior—*sōzein*, to save.]
crêpe [krāp] *n* a thin, crinkled cloth of silk, rayon, wool, etc.; thin paper like crêpe; rubber rolled in thin crinkly sheets; a thin pancake.—*vt* to frizz, as hair.—*n* **crêpe-de-chine** [dė shēn], a soft, fine, sheer clothing crêpe, esp of silk. [Fr, *see* **crape**.]
crepitate [krep´i-tāt] *vi* to crackle, snap.—*n* **crepitā´tion**, the sound detected in the lungs by auscultation in certain diseases. [L *crepitāre, -ātum*, freq of *crepāre*, to crack, rattle.]
crept [krept] *pt, pt p* of **creep**.
crepuscular [kre-pus´kū-lȧr] *adj* of or pertaining to twilight. [L *crepusculum*—*creper*, dusky, obscure.]
crescendo [kresh-en´dō] *adv* (*mus*) gradually increasing in force or loudness.—*n* a passage so marked; increasing loudness or intensity.—Often *cres, cresc*, or <1. [It.]
crescent [kres´ėnt] *adj* increasing; shaped like the new or old moon.—*n* the moon as it increases towards half-moon; the Turkish standard or emblem.—*adjs* **crescent´ic**. [L *crescens, -entis*, pr p of *crescĕre*, to grow.]
cress [kres] *n* any of numerous crucifers (esp genera *Lepidium* and *Nasturtium*) with moderately pungent leaves used in salad and garnishes. [OE *cresse, cerse*; cf Du *kers*, Ger *kresse*.]
cresset [kres´et] *n* an iron basket, or the like, for combustibles, placed on a beacon, lighthouse, wharf, etc. [OFr *cresset, crasset*—Old Du *kruysel*, a hanging lamp.]
crest [krest] *n* the comb or tuft on the head of a cock or other bird; the summit of anything; a plume of feathers or other ornament on the top of a helmet; a badge or emblem.—*vt* to furnish with, or serve for, a crest; to surmount.—*vi* to rise to a crest.—*adjs* **crest´fallen**, dejected, dispirited. [OFr *creste*—L *crista*.]
cretaceous [krė-tā´shùs] *adj* composed of or like chalk; **Cretaceous**, of, relating to, or being the last period of the Mesozoic era; the corresponding system of rocks. [L *crētāceus*—*crēta*, chalk.]
cretin [krē´tin (or kre´-)] *n* one affected with cretinism.—*n* **crē´tinism** [or kre´-], a state of mental defect, associated with bodily deformity or arrested growth, as a result of congenital thyroid deficiency.—*adj* **cre´tinous**. [Fr *crétin*—Swiss *crestin*—L *christianus*—cf the frequent use of *innocent* for *idiot*.]
cretonne [kret-on´, or kret´on] *n* a strong printed linen or cotton fabric used for curtains or for covering furniture. [Fr; *Creton* in Normandy.]
crevasse [krėv-as´] *n* a crack or split, esp applied to a cleft in a glacier.—*n* **crevice** [krev´is], a crack, fissure; a narrow opening. [OFr *crevace*—L *crepāre*, to creak.]
crew [krōō] *n* a group of people working together.—*vi* to act as a member of the crew of a ship, etc.—**crew cut**, a short, cropped hair style. [OFr *creue*, increase—*croistre*, to grow.]
crewel [krōō´ėl] *n* a loosely twisted worsted yarn used for embroidery and tapestry. [Orig a monosyllable, *crule, crewle*; ety uncertain.]
crib [krib] *n* a manger or fodder receptacle; a child's bed with high sides; an enclosure for storing grain; an underwater structure serving as a pier, water undertake, etc.; (*inf*) a translation or other aid used dishonestly in doing schoolwork.—*vt* to put in a crib, confine; to furnish with a crib; (*inf*) to plagiarize;—*pr p* **cribb´ing**; *pt p* **cribbed**.—*n* **cribbage** [krib´ij], a card game in which each player discards a certain number of cards for the *crib*, and scores by holding certain combinations, etc. [OE *crib*; Ger *krippe*.]
crick [krik] *n* a spasm or cramp of the muscles, esp of the neck or back. [Prob onomatopoeic.]
cricket[1] [krik´et] *n* a leaping orthopteran insect (family Gryllidae) noted for the chirping noise produced by the male by rubbing together the forewings; a low wooden footstool; a metal signaling device that makes a click when pressed, often used as a toy. [OFr *criquet*; cf Du *krekel*, Ger *kreckel*.]
cricket[2] [krik´et] *n* an outdoor game played with bats, a ball, and wickets, between two sides of eleven each.—*n* **crick´eter**. [Fr *criquet*; ety uncertain.]
cried [krīd] *pt, pt p* of **cry**.—*n* **crī´er**, one who cries or proclaims, esp one who makes public announcements.
crime [krīm] *n* an act punishable by law; such acts collectively; an offense, sin.—*adj* **criminal** [krim´-], relating to crime; guilty of crime; of the nature of crime.—*n* one guilty of crime.—*n* **criminal´ity**, guiltiness.—*adv* **crim´inally**.—*vt* **crim´ināte**, to accuse.—*ns* **criminā´tion; criminol´ogy**, the scientific study of crime and criminals. **criminol´ogist**. [Fr,—L *crīmen, -inis*.]
crimp [krimp] *adj* made crisp or brittle.—*vt* to press into folds or pleats; to give a corrugated appearance to; to curl (hair).—*n* a pleat. [OE *gecrympan*, to curl; same root as **cramp**.]
crimson [krim´zn] *n* a deep-red color, tinged with blue.—*adj* deep-red.—*vti* to make or become crimson. [ME *crimosin*—OFr *cramoisin*—Ar word—*qirmiz*, kermes, the insect from which the dye was first made.]
cringe [krinj] *vi* to bend or crouch with servility or fear; to behave obsequiously.—*n* **cringe´ling**, one who cringes. [Related to OE *crincan, cringan*, to shrink.]
cringle [kring´gl] *n* an eyelet of rope or metal in the edges of a sail. [Gmc; cf Ger *kringel*.]
crinkle [kring´kl] *vt* to twist, wrinkle, crimp.—*vi* to wrinkle up, curl.—*n* a wrinkle.—*adj* **crink´ly**, wrinkly. [Frequentative of OE *crincan*; same root as **cringe**.]
crinoline [krin´o-lin] *n* a stiff fabric of horsehair and flax, employed to distend a woman's attire; a petticoat or skirt distended by hoops. [Fr, *crin* (L *crīnis*), hair, and *lin* (L *līnum*), flax.]
cripple [krip´l] *n* a lame or otherwise disabled person.—*adj* lame.—*vt* to lame; to disable, deprive of power. [OE *crypel*; conn with **creep**.]
crisis [krī´sis] *n* point or time for deciding anything; the decisive moment or turning point;—*pl* **crises** [krī´sēz]. [Gr *krisis*, from *krinein*, to decide.]
crisp [krisp] *adj* curling closely; having a wavy surface; dry and brittle; fresh and bracing; firm, decided (eg style).—*vt* to curl or twist; to make crisp or wavy.—*adv* **crisp´ly**.—*n* **crisp´ness**.—*adj* **crisp´y**. [OE,—L *crispus*.]
crisscross [kris´kros] *n* a mark formed by two lines in the form of a cross; (*hist*) the cross at the beginning of the alphabet on a hornbook (also *Christ-cross*); a network of crossing lines.—*adj* and *adv* crosswise.—*vti* to cross repeatedly. [**Christ('s) cross**.]
criterion [krī-tē´ri-on] *n* a means or standard of judging;—*pl* **critē´ria**. [Gr *kritērion*—*kritēs*, a judge.]
critic [krit´ik] *n* one who appraises literary or artistic work; a faultfinder.—

adj **crit´ical**, relating to criticism; discriminating; captious; at or relating to a turning point, transition, or crisis; decisive.—*adv* **crit´ically**.—*n* **crit´icalness**.—*vt* **crit´icize**, to pass judgment on; to censure.—*ns* **crit´icism**, the art of judging, esp in literature or the fine arts; a critical judgment or observation; **critique** [kri-tēk´], a critical examination of any production, a review. [Gr *kritikos*—*krīnein*, to judge.]

croak [krōk] *vi* to utter a low hoarse sound, as a frog; to grumble; to forebode evil; (*slang*) to die.—*n* the sound of a frog.—*n* **croak´er**.—*adj* **croak´y**. [From the sound. Cf **crow**.]

crochet [krō´shā] *n* needlework done by means of a small hook.—*vti* to do, or to make in, such work. [Fr *crochet*—*croche, croc*, a hook.]

crock[1] [krok] *n* a pot or jar.—*n* **crock´ery**, earthenware, vessels of baked clay. [OE *croc*; Ger *krug*; perh of Celt origin.]

crock[2] [krok] *n* a decrepit person. [Cf Norw and Swed *krake*, a poor beast.]

crocodile [krok´o-dīl] *n* a genus (*Crocodylus*) of large amphibious reptiles found in the warm rivers of Asia, Africa, America, and Australia.—*n* **crocodilian**, any of an order (Loricata) of reptiles including the crocodiles, alligators, caimans, and gavials.—Also *adj*.—**crocodile tears**, affected tears, hypocritical grief. [OFr *cocodrille*—L *crocodīlus*—Gr *krokodeilos*, a lizard.]

crocus [krō´kus] *n* a bulbous plant (genus *Crocus*) with brilliant yellow, purple, or white flowers, growing in early spring. [L *crocus*—Gr *krokos*; prob of Eastern origin.]

Crohn's disease [krōnz] *n* an inflammatory disease of the small intestine giving rise to a wide range of symptoms.

cromlech [krom´lek] *n* a stone circle; formerly applied to a dolmen. [W *cromlech*—*crom*, curved, circular, and *llech*, a stone.]

crone [krōn] *n* an ugly, withered old woman. [Per OFr *carogne*, a crabbed woman; or Celt.]

crony [krōn´i] *n* a close companion.

crook [kro͝ok] *n* a bend; anything bent; a staff bent at the end, as a shepherd's or bishop's; a trick; a swindler.—*vt* to bend or form into a hook.—*vi* to bend or be bent.—*adj* **crook´ed** [-id], not straight; dishonest; [*in this sense* krookt] bent like a crook.—*adv* **crook´edly**.—*n* **crook´edness**. [Prob Scand; cf ON *krōkr*, Dan *krog*.]

croon [kro͞on] *vti* to sing or hum in an undertone; to sing quietly in an extravagantly sentimental manner.—Also *n*.—*n* **croon´er**. [Cf Du *kreunen*, to groan.]

crop [krop] *n* a hunting whip; mode of cutting or wearing short hair; the total quantity of any agricultural product cut or harvested; total growth of produce; the craw of a bird.—*vt* to cut off the top or ends; to cut short; to raise crops on; to cut the hair of;—*pr p* **cropp´ing**; *pt p* **cropped**.—*adj* **crop´-eared**, having ears cropped, or hair cropped to show the ears.—**crop up**, to come up unexpectedly. [OE *crop*, the top shoot of a plant, the crop of a bird.]

cropper [krop´ėr] *n* a fall; a failure.—**come a cropper**, (*inf*) to have a fall, to fail.

croquet [krō´kā] *n* a game in which wooden balls are driven by long-handled mallets through a series of arches set in the ground. [Fr *croquet*, a dial form of *crochet*, dim of *croc, croche*, a crook.]

croquette [krok´et´] *n* a deep-fried ball or cake of minced meat or fish. [Fr *croquer*, to crunch.]

crosier, crozier [krō´zhyėr] *n* the pastoral staff or crook of a bishop or abbot. [ME *crose* or *croce*—Late L *crocia*, a crook.]

cross [kros] *n* a gibbet on which the Romans exposed malefactors, consisting of two beams, one placed transversely to the other; the gibbet on which Christ suffered; (the symbol of) the Christian religion; the sufferings of Christ; anything that crosses or thwarts; adversity or affliction in general; a hybrid; a monument, often in the form of a cross, where proclamations are made, etc.; a cross-shaped decoration.—*vti* to mark with a cross, or to make the sign of the cross over; to set something across; to draw a line across; to place crosswise; to pass, or cause to pass, from one side to the other of; to thwart; to interbreed.—*adj* lying across, transverse; oblique; adverse; ill-tempered; reciprocal; hybrid.—*adv* **cross´ly**, peevishly.—*n* **cross´bill**, a genus (*Loxia*) of finches with the mandibles of the bill crossing each other near the points.—*n pl* **cross´bones**, two arm or leg bones laid across each other—forming, with the skull, a conventional emblem of death or piracy.—*ns* **cross´bow**, a weapon for shooting arrows formed by a bow placed crosswise on a stock or wooden bar; **cross´breed**, a breed produced by the crossing or intermixing of different races.—*adj* **cross´bred**.—*vt* **cross´-check´**, to test the accuracy of a statement, etc. by consulting various sources of information.—Also *vi* and *n*.—*adjs* **cross´-country**, denoting cross-country racing or skiing; **cross´cut**, cut transversely; made or used for cutting transversely.—*vt* **cross´-exam´ine**, to test the evidence of a witness by subjecting him to an examination by the opposite party; to question searchingly (often impertinently).—*n* **cross´-examinā´tion**.—*adj* **cross´-eyed**, having a squint.—*ns* **cross´-fertilization**, the fertilization of a plant by pollen from another; **cross´fire**, (*mil*) the crossing of lines of fire from two or more points.—*adj* **cross´-grained**, having the grain or fibers crossed or intertwined; perverse, contrary, intractable.—*ns* **cross´ing**, act of going across; the place where a road etc., may be crossed; thwarting; crossbreeding.—*adj* **cross´-legged**, having the legs crossed.—*ns* **cross´over**, a road passing over the top of another; **cross´patch**, an ill-natured person; **cross´-pur´pose**, a contrary purpose (eg *at cross-purposes*).—*vt* **cross´-question**, to question minutely, to cross-examine.—*ns* **cross´-reference**, a reference in a book to another title or passage; **cross´road**, a road crossing the principal road; (*pl*) the place of crossing of two roads; (*fig*) a point where a critical choice of action has to be made; **cross´ section**, a transverse section; a comprehensive representation (eg of the people of a locality, of their opinions); effective target area of a nucleus for a particular reaction under specified conditions.—*n pl* **cross´trees**, pieces of timber placed across the upper end of the lower masts and topmasts of a ship.—*n* **cross´wind´**, a wind blowing across the path of, eg an airplane.—*adv* **cross´wise**, in the form of a cross; across.—*ns* **cross´word**, a puzzle in which a square with blank spaces is to be filled with letters which, read across or down, will make words corresponding to given clues.—**cross swords**, to engage in a dispute. [OE *cros*—ON *kross*—L *crux, crucis*.]

cross-platform [kros-plat´förm] *adj* (*comput*) applies to the compatibility of files on computers with different operating systems.

crotchet [kroch´ėt] *n* a perverse whim or stubborn notion.—*adj* **crotch´ety**, having crotchets or peculiarities, whimsical. [Fr *crochet*, dim of *croche*, a hook.]

croton [krō´ton] *n* a genus (*Croton*) of tropical plants, one (*C tiglium*) of East India producing a brownish-yellow oil; another (*C eluteria*) of the Bahamas, a violent purgative. [Gr *krotōn*, a tick or mite, which the seed of the plant resembles.]

croton bug [krō´ton] *n* a winged cockroach (*Blatella germanica*) common in US urban buildings. [*Croton* river, NY, a source of water for New York City.]

crouch [krowch] *vi* to squat or lie close to the ground; to cringe, to fawn. [ME *cruchen, crouchen*; possibly connected with **crook**.]

croup[1] [kro͞op] *n* inflammation of the larynx and trachea associated with labored breathing and hoarse coughing. [Imitative.]

croup[2] [kro͞op] *n* the rump of a horse; the place behind the saddle. [Fr *croupe*, protuberance.]

croupier [kro͞o´pi-ėr] *n* an employee of a gambling casino who watches the cards and collects the money at the gambling tables. [Fr 'one who rides on the *croup*'; *see* **croup** (2).]

crow [krō] *n* any of various usu. large entirely glossy black birds (genus *Corvus*); uttering a cawing cry, the cry of a cock; a child's inarticulate cry of joy; **Crow**, member of an Amerindian people of Montana; the Siouan language of this people.—*vi* to croak; to cry as a cock; to boast, swagger;—*pt* **crew** [kro͞o] or **crowed**; *pt p* **crowed**.—*ns* **crow´bar**, a large iron lever bent at the end like the beak of a crow; **crowfoot**, any of a genus (*Ranunculus*) of plants of the buttercup family that are usu. yellow-flowered herbs; **crow's´-foot**, one of the wrinkles produced by age, spreading out from the corners of the eyes; **crow's nest**, a lookout platform high on a ship's mast.—**as the crow flies**, in a straight line. [OE *crāwe*. a crow, *crāwan*, to cry like a cock; imit.]

crowd [krowd] *n* a number of persons or things closely pressed together, without order; the rabble, multitude; (*inf*) a set; a clique.—*vt* to fill by pressing or driving together; to fill excessively full; to compress (*with* **into**).—*vi* to press on; to press together in numbers, to swarm.—*adj* **crowd´ed**.—**crowd sail**, to hoist every available sail. [OE *crūdan*, to press.]

crown [krown] *n* a wreath worn on the head, esp as a mark of honor; reward; completion or consummation; the head covering of a monarch; kingship; the sovereign; governing power in a monarchy; the top of anything, as a head, hat, tree, hill; a British coin stamped with a crown, esp a silver five shilling piece; the part of a tooth projecting above the gum line.—*vt* to cover or invest with a crown; to invest with royal dignity; to adorn; to dignify; to complete happily; (*slang*) to hit on the head.—*n* **crown´glass**, a kind of window glass formed in circular plates or discs.—*n pl* **crown´ jew´els**, jewels (as crown and scepter) pertaining to the crown or sovereign.—*n* **crown´ prince**, the prince who is heir apparent to the crown. [OFr *corone*—L *corōna*; cf Gr *korōnos*, curved.]

crozier *See* **crosier**.

crucial [kro͞o´shål] *adj* testing or decisive; severe; critical. [Fr *crucial*, from L *crux, crucis*, a cross.]

crucible [kro͞o´si-bl] *n* a heat-resistant container for melting ores, metals, etc.; severe trial. [Low L *crucibulum*.]

crucifer [kro͞o´sif´ėr] *n* any of a family (Cruciferae) of plants with a corolla of four petals arranged in the form of a cross (eg cabbage, mustard, wallflower).—*adj* **crucif´erous**. [L *crux, crucis*, a cross, *ferre*, to bear.]

cruciform [kro͞o´si-förm] *adj* in the form of a cross. [L *crux, crucis*, a cross, + **form**.]

crucify [kro͞o´si-fī] *vt* to put to death on a cross; to subject to comparable torment; to subdue completely, to mortify (eg the flesh);—*pt p* **cru´cified**.—*ns* **cru´cifix**, a figure or picture of Christ fixed to the cross; **Crucifix´ion**, death on the cross, of Christ; **crucifixion**, extreme and painful punishment, suffering, or affliction. [OFr *crucifier*—L *crucifigĕre, crucifixum*—*crus*, cross, *figĕre*, to fix.]

crude [kro͞od] *adj* raw, unprepared; not reduced to order or form, unfinished, undigested; immature; unrefined.—*adv* **crude´ly**.—*ns* **crude´ness; crud´ity**, rawness; unripeness; that which is crude. [L *crūdus*, raw.]

cruel [kro͞o´el] *adj* disposed to inflict pain, or pleased at suffering; void of pity, merciless, savage.—*adv* **cru´elly**.—*n* **cru´elty**. [Fr *cruel*—L *crūdēlis*.]

cruet [krōō´et] *n* a small glass bottle for vinegar and oil, etc. for the table. [Anglo-Fr, dim of OFr *cruye*, a jar.]

cruise [krōōz] *vi* to sail, fly, drive, or wander to and fro; to move at the most efficient speed for sustained travel.—*vt* to cruise over or about.—*n* a voyage from place to place for pleasure or on a naval commission.—*ns* **cruis´er**, one who cruises; anything that cruises, as a police car; a fast warship smaller than a battleship.—**cruise missile**, a guided missile with a terrain-seeking radar system that flies at low altitude. [Du *kruisen*, to cross.]

crumb [krum] *n* a small bit or morsel of bread; any small particle; the soft part of bread.—*vt* (*cooking*) to cover with crumbs.—*n* **crumb structure**, a soil condition suitable for growing crops in which the soil is aggregated into crumbs.—*adj* **crumb´y**, in crumbs; soft. [OE *cruma*; Du *kruim*; Ger *krume*.]

crumble [krum´bl] *vt* to break into crumbs.—*vi* to fall into small pieces; to decay.—*adj* **crum´bly**, apt to crumble, brittle. [Orig dim of **crumb**.]

crumpet [krump´et] *n* a batter cake baked on a griddle. [ME *crompid*, cake.]

crumple [krump´l] *vti* to twist or crush into wrinkles; to crease; to collapse.—*n* a wrinkle or crease made by crumpling.—*adj* **crump´ly**. [Formed from *crump* (obs), to curve, curl up.]

crunch [krunch] *vt* to crush with the teeth or underfoot; to chew (anything) hard, and so make a noise.—*n* the act or sound of crunching; (*slang*) (*with* **the**) crucial, testing moment. [From the sound; cf Fr *grincer*.]

crupper [krup´ėr] *n* a strap of leather fastened to the saddle and passing under the horse's tail to keep the saddle in its place; the hind part of a horse. [OFr *cropiere—crope*, the croup.]

crural [krōō´ràl] *adj* relating to the thigh or leg, specifically femoral. [L *crūrālis*, from *crūs, crūris*, the leg.]

crusade [krōō-sād´] *n* any of the Christian military expeditions (11th to 13th centuries) to recover the Holy Land from the Muslims; any daring or romantic undertaking; concerted action to further a cause.—*vi* to go on a crusade.—*n* **crusad´er**. [Fr *croisade*—L *crux*, a cross.]

cruse [krōōz] *n* a small pot or jar for holding liquid. [Cf ON *krūs*; Dan *kruus*; Ger *krause*.]

crush [krush] *vt* to break, bruise, or crumple; to squeeze together; to beat down or overwhelm, to subdue.—*vi* to become crushed.—*n* a violent squeezing; a throng; (*slang*) an infatuation. [OFr *croissir*.]

crust [krust] *n* the hard rind or outside coating of anything; the outer part of bread; the pastry shell of a pie; any hard surface layer, as of snow; (*slang*) insolence; the solid exterior of the earth.—*vti* to cover or become covered with a crust.—*adj* **crust´y**, of the nature of or having a crust; having a hard or harsh exterior; surly.—*adv* **crust´ily**.—*n* **crust´iness**. [L *crusta*, rind.]

crustacean [krus-tā´s(h)i-an] *n* any of a large class (Crustacea) of mostly aquatic arthropods including crabs, lobsters, shrimps, wood lice, water fleas, and barnacles.—Also *adj*.—*adj* **crustā´ceous**, of, having, or forming a crust or shell. [**crust**, + suffx *-acea*, neut pl of *-aceous*.]

crutch [kruch] *n* a staff with a cross-piece at the head to place under the arm of a lame person; any prop or support. [OE *crycc*.]

crux [kruks] *n* a difficult problem; the essential or deciding point;—*pl* **crux´es, cruces** [krōō´sez]; cf **crucial**. [L *crux*, cross.]

cry [krī] *vi* to utter a shrill loud sound, esp one of pain or grief; to shed tears, weep.—*vt* to utter loudly, to exclaim; to proclaim or make public; to offer for sale by crying;—*pt, pt p* **cried**.—*n* any loud sound, esp of grief or pain; a call or shout; a watchword or slogan; a prayer; a fit of weeping; lamentation; particular sound uttered by an animal;—*pl* **cries**.—*adj* **cry´ing**, calling loudly; claiming notice, notorious.—**cry down**, to disparage, decry; **cry off**, to cancel, as an agreement; **cry havoc**, to sound an alarm; **cry over spilt milk**, to express regrets for what cannot be undone; **cry up**, to praise; **cry wolf**, to give unnecessary alarm. [Fr *crier*—L *quiritāre*, to scream—*quěri*, to lament.]

cryogen [krī´ō-jen] *n* a substance used to obtain low temperatures.—*adj* **cryogen´ic**, pertaining to the science of cryogenics or to work done, apparatus used, or substances kept, at low temperatures.—*n* **cryogen´ics**, the branch of physics concerned with phenomena at very low temperatures. [Gr *kryos*, frost, and root of *gignesthai*, to become.]

cryolite [krī´o-līt] *n* a sodium-aluminum fluoride found in Greenland, usu. in white cleavable masses of waxy luster. [Gr *kryos*, frost, *lithos*, a stone.]

cryosurgery [krī´ō-sûr´jėr-i] *n* surgery at very low temperatures. [Gr *kryos*, frost, + **surgery**.]

crypt [kript] *n* an underground vault, esp one under a church, used for burial.—*adj* **cryp´tic**, hidden, secret; enigmatic (eg *a cryptic saying*). [L *crypta*—Gr *kryptē—kryptein*, to conceal.]

crypt-, crypto- [krip´t(o)-] in composition, hidden.—*n* **crypto** [krip´to], a secret member of a party, sect, organization, etc.—*ns* **crypto-Christian; crypto-communist**. [Gr *kryptos*, hidden.]

cryptogram [krip´tō-gram] *n* a message in code or cipher; a representation having a hidden significance.—*ns* **cryp´tograph**, a cryptogram; a device for enciphering and deciphering; **cryptog´raphy**, secret writing; the enciphering and deciphering of messages in secret code or cipher. [Gr *kryptos*, secret, and *graphein*, to write.]

crystal [krist´l] *n* rock crystal; a body, generally solid, whose atoms are arranged in a definite pattern, expressed outwardly by geometrical form with plane faces; anything clear, as a covering over a watch face; very clear, brilliant glass; articles of such glass, as goblets.—*adjs* **crys´tal, crys´talline**, made of crystals; like crystal in clearness, structure, etc.—*vti* **crys´tallīze**, to become or cause to become crystalline; to make or become definite or concrete.—*ns* **crystal ball**, a sphere of quartz crystal traditionally used by fortune tellers; a means of predicting future events; **crystallizā´tion; crystallog´raphy**, the branch of chemistry dealing with the system of forms among crystals, their structure, and forms of aggregation. [OFr *cristol*—L *crystallum*—Gr *krystallos*, ice—*kryos*, frost.]

cub [kub] *n* a young carnivorous mammal (as a bear, lion, fox, etc.); a young shark; a young person; an inexperienced newspaper reporter.—*n* **Cub Scout**, a member of the scouting program of the Boy Scouts of America for boys of the age range 8 to 10. [Ety dub.]

cube [kūb] *n* a solid body having six equal square faces, a solid square; the third power of a quantity.—*vt* to raise to the third power; to cut into cubes.—*adjs* **cū´bic**, of the third power or degree; being the volume of a cube whose edge is a specified unit; isometric; three-dimensional; cubical; **cū´bical**, shaped like a cube; relating to volume.—*adv* **cū´bically**.—*ns* **cū´bism**, a movement in painting which seeks to represent several aspects of an object seen simultaneously, fragmenting their forms, and reorganizing the elements in new combinations; **cū´boid**, a rectangular parallelepiped, esp one whose faces are not all equal.—*adjs* **cū´boid, cuboid´al**, somewhat resembling a cube in shape.—**cube root**, the number or quantity that produces a given cube by being raised to the third power—thus 2 is the cube root of 8; **cubic foot**, the volume of a cube one foot in length, width, and breadth. [Fr—L *cubus*—Gr *kybos*, a die.]

cubicle [kū-bi-kl] *n* a small place (esp for sleeping) partitioned off from a larger room. [L *cubiculum—cubāre*, to lie down.]

cubit [kū´bit] *n* a measure employed by the ancients, equal to the length of the arm from the elbow to the tip of the middle finger, from 18 to 22 inches. [L *cubitum*, the elbow; cf L *cubāre*, to lie down.]

cucking stool [kuk´ing-stōōl] *n* a chair formerly used for punishing offenders (as dishonest tradesmen) by public exposure or ducking in water.

cuckold [kuk´old] *n* a man whose wife has proved unfaithful.—*vt* to wrong (a husband) by unchastity. [OFr *cucuault—cucu*, cuckoo.]

cuckoo [kŏŏ´kōō] *n* a grayish brown European bird (*Cuculus canorus*) remarkable for depositing its eggs in the nests of other birds; any of a large family (Cuculidae) to which this bird belongs.—*ns* **cuck´oo clock**, a clock in which the hours are told by a cuckoo call; **cuck´ooflow´er**, a bitter cress (*Cardamine pratensis*) of Europe and America; ragged robin; **cuck´oopint** [-pint], a European arum (*Arum maculatum*); **cuck´oospit**, a froth secreted on plants by the nymphs of spittle insects; a spittle insect. [Imitative.]

cucumber [kūkum-bėr] *n* a creeping plant (*Cucumis sativus*) with large elongated fruit used as a vegetable. [L *cucumis, -eris*.]

cud [kud] *n* the food brought from the first stomach of a ruminating animal back into the mouth and chewed again.—*n* **cud´weed**, any of several composite plants (as of the genus *Gnaphalium*) with silky or woolly foliage.—**chew the cud**, to meditate. [OE *cwidu*.]

cuddle [kud´l] *vt* to hug, to embrace, to fondle.—*vi* to lie close and snug together.—*n* a close embrace. [Origin unknown.]

cuddy [kud´i] *n* a small cabin formerly under the poopdeck; the galley of a small ship; a small room or cupboard.

cudgel [kuj´l] *n* a heavy staff; a short thick club.—*vt* to beat with a cudgel;—*pr p* **cudg´elling**; *pt p* **cudg´elled.—cudgel one's brains**, to think hard. [OE *cycgel*.]

cue[1] [kū] *n* the last word of an actor's speech serving as a hint to the next speaker; any signal to do something; a hint.—*vt* to give a cue to. [According to some from Fr *queue* (see next word); in 17th century written Q, and derived from L *quando*, 'when', ie when to begin.]

cue[2] [kū] *n* a rod used in playing billiards and pool to strike the cue ball.—*n* **cue ball**, the ball the player strikes in order to hit other balls in billiards or pool. [Fr *queue*—L *cauda*, a tail.]

cuff[1] [kuf] *n* a stroke with the open hand.—*vt* to strike with the open hand. [Origin obscure; cf Swed *kuffa*, to knock.]

cuff[2] [kuf] *n* the end of the sleeve near the wrist; a covering for the wrist; a turned-up fold at the bottom of a trouser leg.—**off the cuff**, (*slang*) unofficially and extempore; **on the cuff**, (*slang*) on credit. [Prob cog with **coif**.]

cuirass [kwi-ras´ or kū-] *n* a defensive covering for the breast and back, esp one of leather or iron fastened with straps and buckles.—*n* **cuirassier**, [-ēr´] a mounted soldier so armed. [Fr *cuirasse—cuir*, leather—L *corium*, skin, leather.]

cuisine [kwi-zēn´] *n* a style of cooking or preparing food; the food prepared. [Fr (It *cucina*)—L *coquīna—coquěre*, to cook.]

cul-de-sac [kŭ(l)-dė-sak] *n* a blind pouch; a blind alley. [Fr *cul*, bottom, *de*, of, *sac*, sack.]

culinary [kū´lin-år-i] *adj* of or relating to cooking. [L *culīnārius—culīna*, a kitchen.]

cull [kul] *vt* to select; to pick out, gather.—*n* something picked out for rejection as not being up to standard. [Fr *cueillir*, to gather.—L *colligěre—col-*, together, *legěre*, to gather. Doublet of **collect**.]

culm[1] [kulm] *n* refuse coal screenings; a Mississippian formation in which marine fossil-bearing beds alternate with those of plant remains.

culm[2] [kulm] *n* a monocotyledonous stem.—*adj* **culmif´erous**, bearing a culm. [L *culmus*, a stalk.]

culminate [kul´min-āt] *vi* (*astron*) to be at, or come to, the meridian and thus the highest point of altitude; to reach the highest point (*with* **in**).—*vt* to bring to a head or the highest point.—*n* **culminā´tion**, act of culminating; the highest point; (*astron*) transit of a body across the meridian. [Low L *culmināre, -ātum*—L *culmen*, properly *columen*, a summit.]

culpable [kul´pa-bl] *adj* deserving of blame.—*ns* **culpabil´ity, cul´pableness**, liability to blame.—*adv* **cul´pably**. [OFr *coupable*—L *culpābilis*—*culpa*, a fault.]

culprit [kul´prit] *n* a person accused, or found guilty, of a crime. [From the fusion in legal phraseology of *cul* (Anglo-Fr *culpable*, or L *culpābilis*) and *prit, prist* (OFr *prest*), ready.]

cult [kult] *n* a system of religious belief; devoted attachment to a person, principle, etc., esp regarded as a literary or intellectual fad; a religion regarded as unorthodox or spurious; its body of adherents.—Also **cult´us**. [L *cultus*—*colĕre*, to worship.]

cultivate [kul´ti-vāt] *vt* to till or prepare for crops; to produce by tillage; to loosen the soil and kill weeds around (plants); to devote attention to; to civilize or refine.—*ns* **cultivā´tion**, the art or practice of cultivating; cultivated state; refinement or culture; **cul´tivator**, an agricultural implement for breaking up the surface of the ground among crops. [Low L *cultivāre, -ātum*—L *colĕre*, to till, to worship.]

culture [kul´chůr] *n* cultivation of the soil; a growth of bacteria, etc. in a prepared substance; improvement of the mind, manners, etc.; the skills, arts, etc. of a given people in a given period; the customary beliefs, social forms, and material traits of a religious, social, or racial group.—*vt* to cultivate; to improve.—*adj* **cul´tural**.—*adj* **cul´tured**, cultivated; well educated, refined.—**culture shock**, a sense of disorientation experienced when exposed to an alien culture. [L *cultūra*—*colĕre*.]

cultus *See* **cult**.

culverin [kul´vėr-in] *n* an early form of cannon of great length. [Fr *coulevrine*, from *couleuvre*, a snake—L *coluber*, a snake.]

culvert [kul´vėrt] *n* a drain or conduit under a road, etc. [Perh from Fr *couler*, to flow—L *colāre*.]

cumber [kum´bėr] *vt* to impede, to get in the way of; to burden uselessly.—*adjs* **cum´bersome**, unwieldy; burdensome; **cum´brous**, hindering, obstructing; heavy.—*adv* **cum´brously**.—*n* **cum´brousness**. [OFr *combrer*, to hinder—Low L *cumbrus*, a heap; corr of L *cumulus*, a heap.]

cummerbund [kum´ėr-bund] *n* a sash worn as a waistband, esp with a man's tuxedo. [Anglo-Ind—Pers *kamarband*, a loin-band.]

cumin [kum´in] *n* a low plant (*Cuminum cyminum*) of the carrot family, cultivated for its seeds which are used as a spice. [L *cuminum*—Gr *kyminon*.]

cum laude [kumlowd´ē] *adj, adv* with distinction. [L.]

cumulate [kūm´ū-lāt] *vt* to heap together; to combine into one; to build up by adding new material.—*adj* **cum´ulative**, becoming greater by successive additions (eg force, effect, evidence, sentence).—*adv* **cum´ulatively**. [L *cumulāre, -ātum*—*cumulus*, a heap.]

cumulus [kū´mū-lus] *n* a heap; a cloud form having a flat base and rounded outlines resembling a cauliflower;—*pl* **cumulī**. [L.]

cuneate [kū´ni-āt, or āt] *adj* of the form of a wedge.—*adj* **cuneiform**, [kū-nē´i-förm, kū´n(ē)i-förm] wedge-shaped; written in wedge-shaped characters.—*n* the wedge-shaped syllabary written by being impressed in wet clay, used for Assyro-Babylonian, Sumerian, Hittite, and Old Persian from about 4000 BC to 1000 BC. [L *cuneus*, a wedge.]

cunning [kun´ing] *adj* (*arch*) knowing; sly; crafty; pretty; cute.—*n* slyness, craftiness.—*adv* **cunn´ingly**. [OE *cunnan*, to know.]

cup [kup] *n* a small, bowl-shaped container for liquids, usu. with a handle; a cupful; the liquid contained in a cup; an ornamental vessel used as a prize; anything shaped like a cup; a half pint or eight fluid ounces; the symbol ∪ indicating the union of two sets.—*vt* to take or place as in a cup; to curve into the shape of a cup; to treat by cupping;—*pr p* **cupp´ing**; *pt p* **cupped**.—*ns* **cup´bear´er**, an attendant at a feast to pour out and hand the wine; **cupboard**, [kub´örd] a closet or cabinet with shelves for cups, plates, utensils, food, etc. **cup´ful**, as much as fills a cup;—*pl* **cup´fuls; cupp´ing**, an operation of drawing blood to the surface of the body by using a glass vessel evacuated by heat.—**cup of tea**, something one likes or excels in; a thing to be reckoned with; **in his cups**, drunk. [OE *cuppe*—L *cūpa*, a tub.]

Cupid [kū´pid] *n* the Roman god of love, son of Venus, represented by a mischievous boy with a bow and arrows.—*n* **cūpid´ity**, covetousness. [L *Cupīdō, -inis*—*cupĕre*, to desire.]

cupola [kū´po-la] *n* a spherical vault on the top of a building; a dome, esp a small one. [It—L *cūpola*, dim of *cūpa*, a cask.]

cupri-, cupro- [kū´pri, -ō] (in composition) of or containing copper [L *cuprum*, copper];—eg **cupri´ferous**, of rocks, yielding copper; **cup´ronick´el**, an alloy of copper and nickel). *Adjs* **cupric, cuprous** are used for compounds in which copper has respectively its higher and its lower combining power (the former a valency of 2, the latter a valency of 1);—eg **cupric oxide** (CuO), black copper oxide; **cuprous oxide** (Cu_2O), red copper oxide.

cur [kûr] *n* a worthless dog, of low breed; a churlish fellow.—*adj* **curr´ish**.—*adv* **curr´ishly**.—*n* **curr´ishness**. [ME *curre*; cf ON *kurra*, to grumble.]

curaçao, curaçoa [kū´ra-sō, kū-ra-sow, sä-o] *n* a liqueur flavored with the dried peel of the sour orange, named from the island of *Curaçoa* in the West Indies, where it was first made.

curare [kū-rä´ri] *n* a dried aqueous extract of a vine (*Strychnos toxifera* or *Chondodendron tomentosum*) used in arrow poisons by S American Indians and in medicine to produce muscle relaxation.—*n* **curarine**, [kū-rä´rēn] any of several alkaloids from curare. [Port, from South American Indian.]

curate [kūr´ āt] *n* a clergyman in charge of a parish; a clergyman assisting a rector or vicar.—*ns* **cur´acy, cur´ateship**. [LL *cūrātus*—L *cūra*, care.]

curator [kūr-ā´tör] *n* a superintendent, esp. of a museum, zoo, or other place of exhibit.—*n* **curā´torship**, the office of a curator. [L *cūrātor*.]

curb [kûrb] *n* a chain or strap attached to the bit for restraining a horse; a check or restraint; a stone or concrete edging along a street; a market dealing in stocks and bonds not listed on the exchange.—*vt* to restrain or control.—*n* **curb´stone**, the stone or stones making up a curb. [Fr *courbe*—L *curvus*, bent.]

curd [kûrd] *n* the coagulated part of soured milk from which cheese is made; any similar substance.—*vti* **curd´le**, to turn into curd; to coagulate. [Prob Celt; Gael *gruth*, Ir *cruth*.]

cure [kūr] *n* act of healing; that which heals; a method of medical treatment.—*vt* to heal; to rid (one) of (eg a bad habit); to preserve, as by drying, salting, etc.; to process (tobacco, leather, etc.) as by drying or aging;—*pr p* **cur´ing**; *pt p* **cured**.—*adj* **cūr´able**, that may be cured.—*n* **cūrabil´ity**.—*adjs* **cur´ative**, tending to cure; **cure´less**, that cannot be cured. [OFr *cure*—L *cūra*, care; not the same as **care**.]

curé [kū´rā] *n* a parish priest in France. [Fr,—LL *cūrātus; see* **curate**.]

curfew [kûr´fū] *n* in feudal times the ringing of a bell as a signal to put out all fires and lights; a prohibition against being abroad in the streets after a specified hour. [OFr *covrefeu* (Fr *couvre-feu*—*couvrir*, to cover, *feu*, fire).]

Curia [kū´ri-a] *n* the official body governing the Roman Catholic Church under the authority of the Pope. [L.]

curio [kū´ri-o] *n* any rare and unusual article;—*pl* **cu´rios**. [For **curiosity**.]

curious [kū´ri-ůs] *adj* anxious to learn; inquisitive; singular, rare; odd.—*n* **curios´ity**, state or quality of being curious; inquisitiveness; anything rare or unusual.—*adv* **cū´riously**.—*ns* **cū´riousness; curio´sa**, unusual or erotic books. [Fr *curieux*—L *cūriōsus*—*cūra*.]

curium [kū´ri-ům] *n* a transuranic element (symbol Cm; at wt 248; at no 96) named after Marie and Pierre Curie, discoverers of radium.

curl [kûrl] *vt* to twist into ringlets, to coil; to furnish with curls.—*vi* to grow into coils; to move in curves; to play at the game of curling.—*n* a ringlet of hair, or anything like it; a wave, bending, or twist.—*ns* **curl´er**, one who, or that which, curls; a player at the game of curling; **curl´ing**, a game in which two teams of four persons each slide curling stones over a stretch of ice toward a target circle.—*ns* **curl´ing i´ron**, a heated, rod-shaped implement for forming curls by winding a lock around the rod; **curl´ing stone**, a heavy stone with a handle, used in the game of curling.—*adj* **curl´y**, having curls; full of curls.—*n* **curl´iness**. [ME *crull*; Du *krullen*, Dan *krolle*, to curl.]

curlew [kûr´l(y)ōō] *n* any of a number of largely brownish migratory birds (esp genus *Numenius*) related to the woodcocks, but having long curved bill and long legs, and a plaintive cry. [OFr *corlieu*; prob from its cry.]

curmudgeon [kûr-muj´ön] *n* a churlish, ill-natured fellow; a miser.—*adj* **curmudge´only**. [Origin unknown.]

currant [kur´ånt] *n* a small kind of black raisin or dried seedless grape; the fruit of several garden shrubs (genus *Ribes*); a plant bearing currants. [From *Corinth*.]

current [kur´ėnt] *adj* running or flowing; generally received; now passing; present.—*n* a running stream; a body of water or air moving in a certain direction; a flow of electricity; course (eg of events).—*n* **curr´ency**, circulation; that which circulates, as the money of a country; prevalence; general acceptance.—*adv* **curr´ently**. [L *currens, -entis*—*currĕre*, to run.]

curricle [kur´i-kl] *n* a two-wheeled open carriage, drawn by two horses abreast.—*n* **curric´ulum**, a course of study at a school or university.—**curriculum vitae**, [ků-rik´ū-lum vē´tī] (biographical sketch of) the course of one's life. [L *curriculum*, from *currĕre*, to run, *vita*, life.]

curry[1] [kur´i] *n* a food or dish seasoned with curry powder; curry powder.—*vt* to cook with curry powder or a curry sauce.—*n* **curry powder**, a blend of several pungent ground spices usu. including cayenne pepper, turmeric, cardamom, cumin, ginger, and coriander. [Tamil *kari*, sauce.]

curry[2] [kur´i] *vt* to dress (leather); to rub down and dress (a horse); to drub;—*pr p* **curr´ying**; *pt p* **curr´ied**.—*ns* **curr´ier**, one who curries or dresses tanned leather; **curr´ycomb**, a metal comb used for grooming horses.—**curry favor**, to seek to gain favor by flattery or attention. [OFr *correier*—*conrei*, outfit.]

curse [kûrs] *vt* to invoke or wish evil upon; to consign to perdition; to vex or torment.—*vi* to utter imprecations; to swear.—*n* invocation or wishing of evil or harm; evil invoked on another; any great evil.—*adj* **curs´ed** [also kûrst], under, blasted by, a curse; hateful.—*adv* **curs´edly**.—*n* **curs´er**. [OE *cursian*—*curs*, a curse; ety doubtful; not conn with **cross**.]

cursive [kûr´siv] *adj* (of handwriting) written with a running hand flowing.—*adv* **cur´sively**. [Low L *cursīvus*—L *currĕre*, to run.]

cursory [kûr´sör-i] *adj* running quickly over, hasty, superficial.—*adv* **cur´sorily**. [L *currĕre, cursum*, to run.]

curt [kûrt] *adj* short; concise; discourteously brief.—*adv* **curt´ly**.—*n* **curt´ness**. [L *curtus*, shortened.]

curtail [kûr-tāl´] *vt* to cut short; to deprive of a part (of); to abridge;—*pr p*

curtail´ing; *pt p* **curtailed´**.—*n* **curtail´ment**. [Old spelling *curtal*—OFr *courtault*—L *curtus*.]

curtain [kûr´t(i)n] *n* the hanging drapery at a window, around a bed, etc.; the part of a rampart between two bastions; the movable screen separating the stage from the auditorium; (*pl*) (*inf*) the end, esp death.—*vt* to enclose, or to furnish, with curtains.—*ns* **cur´tain rais´er**, a short play preceding the main performance in a theater; **curtain wall**, a nonbearing exterior wall between columns or piers. [OFr *cortine*—Low L *cortina*; prob L *cors, cortis*, a court.]

curtsy, curtsey [kûrt´si] *n* an obeisance, made by bending the knees, proper to women and children.—*vi* to make a curtsy. [A variant of **courtesy**.]

curule [kū´rōōl] *adj* applied to the official chair of the higher Roman magistrates. [L *curūlis*—*currus*, a chariot.]

curve [kûrv] *n* a bend in a direction continuously deviating from a straight line; anything so bent; a line (including a straight line) answering to an equation.—*vti* to bend, or to be bent, in a curve; to move in a curve.—*adj* **curvaceous, curvacious** [kûrvā´shus], (*inf*) of a woman, having shapely curves.—*ns* **cur´vature**, a curving or bending; the continual bending or the amount of bending from a straight line; **curve ball**, a baseball pitch thrown so that it swerves from its expected course. [L *curvus*, crooked.]

curvet [kûr´vet, kûr-vet´] *n* a light leap of a horse in which he curves his body; a leap, frolic.—*vi* to leap in curvets; to frisk;—*pr p* **cur´vetting, curvett´ing**; *pt p* **cur´veted, curvett´ed**. [It *corvetta*, dim of *corvo*—L *curvus*, crooked.]

curvilinear [kûr-vi-lin´i-ȧr] *adj* bounded by curved lines; represented by a curved line; marked by flowing tracery. [L *curvus*, and *lineāris*—*līnea*, a line.]

Cushing's disease [kŏŏsh´ingz] *n* a tumor of the pituitary gland.—*n* **Cushing's syndrome**, disease of the adrenal gland marked by excessive secretions from the gland. [Harvey *Cushing*, Amer surgeon.]

cushion [kŏŏsh´ȯn] *n* a case filled with some soft, elastic stuff, for resting on; a pillow; any elastic pad or lining; anything that serves to deaden a blow.—*vt* to seat on, or furnish with, a cushion; to serve as a cushion for or against. [OFr *coissin*—L *coxīnum*—*coxa*, hip.]

cushy [kŏŏsh´i] *adj* easy and comfortable. [Perh Hindustani *khushī*, pleasure.]

cusp [kusp] *n* an apex; a prominence on a tooth; the point or horn of the moon, etc.—*adjs* **cus´pidāte**, having a cusp; terminating in a rigid point. [L *cuspis, -idis*, a point.]

cuspidor [kus´-pi-dör, dōr] *n* a spittoon. [Port—L *conspuĕre*, to spit upon.]

cuss [kus] *n* (*inf*) a curse; a fellow.—*adj* **cuss´ed**, cursed; obstinate; perverse.—*n* **cuss´edness**. [Obviously **curse**; in the personal sense, prob with a supposed reference to **customer**.]

custard [kus´tȧrd] *n* a boiled or baked mixture of milk, eggs, etc., sweetened and flavored.—*n* **cus´tard app´le**, any of several chiefly tropical American soft-fleshed edible fruits; any of a genus (*Annona*) of shrubs or trees bearing this fruit, esp a small West Indian tree (*A. reticulata*). [Earlier *custade*, a corr of *crustade*, a pie with **crust**.]

custody [kus´to-di] *n* a watching or guarding; care; imprisonment.—*adj* **custō´dial**.—*n* **custō´dian**, a keeper; a guardian; a caretaker. [L *custōdia*, from *custōs, -ōdis*, a keeper.]

custom [kus´tȯm] *n* what one is wont to do; usage; frequent repetition of the same act; regular trade or business; a tax on goods; (*pl*) taxes or duties imposed on imports.—*adj* **cus´tomary**, usual; habitual; holding, or held, by custom.—*adv* **cus´tomarily**.—*adjs* **cus´tom-built, cus´tom-made**, built or made to a customer's order.—*ns* **cus´tomer**, one who buys from one, esp one who buys regularly; (*slang*) a person having a specified distinctive trait; **cus´tomhouse**, the place where customs or duties are paid. [OFr *custume, costume*—L *consuētūdō, -inis*—*consuescĕre*, to accustom.]

cut [kut] *vt* to make an incision in; to cleave or pass through; to sever a piece, pieces of, from a larger portion; to fell, hew, mow, trim; to carve, hew, or fashion by cutting; to strike sharply; to have (a new tooth) grow through the gum; to reduce or curtail; to divide (a pack of cards) into two portions, or to draw (a card) from the pack; (*inf*) to refuse ostentatiously to recognize (an acquaintance); to intersect (a line); (*inf*) to absent oneself from (a school, class, etc.); to execute (as *to cut a caper*); to strike (a ball) obliquely to the off side by a sharp movement; to impart spin to (a ball); (*slang*) to stop.—*vi* to make an incision; to intersect; to change direction suddenly; to swing a bat, etc. (at a ball); to take cutting; (in motion pictures) to cease photographing;—*pr p* **cutt´ing**; *pt, pt p* **cut**.—*n* a cleaving or dividing; a stroke or blow; a passage or channel cut out; an incision or wound; a piece cut off, as of meat; a length of cloth varying from 40 to 100 yards; an engraved block, or the picture from it; manner of cutting, or fashion; type, kind; a degree, grade; a stroke that cuts a ball; spin imparted by such a stroke; (*inf*) an unauthorized absence from school, etc.; (*slang*) a share, as of profits.—*ns* **cut´back**, a going back in a plot to earlier happenings; a reduction; **cut´glass**, glass decorated with designs cut into its surface by an engraving tool or abrasive wheel; **cut´off**, the point at which something ceases to operate or apply; (*pl*) shorts made from jeans with the legs cut off at the knees or higher; **cut´purse**, a pickpocket; **cutt´er**, the person or thing that cuts; a small swift vessel with one mast and sharp prow, fore-and-aft rigged; a light sleigh; **cut´throat**, an assassin; **cutt´ing**, a dividing or lopping off; an incision; a piece cut out or off; a piece of plant cut off for propagation; editing of film or recording; a recording.—*adj* **cut-and-dry**, or **cut-and-dried**, done according to a plan or formula, routine; **cut-rate**, selling or on sale at a *reduced price*.—*adjs* **cut down**, to reduce, curtail; **cut in**, to interpose; to intrude; to mix with cutting motions; to interrupt a dance couple and take one as a partner; to give a share; **cut off**, to destroy; intercept; stop; **cut out**, to shape; prepare; to eliminate; to form by erosion; to supplant; to disconnect from the source of power; (*vi* of an engine) to fail, stop; (*adj*) innately suited; **cut up**, to carve; to criticize severely; (to be) distressed. **cut mustard**, to achieve the standard necessary for success.

cutaneous *see* **cutis**.

cute [kūt] *adj* (*inf*) acute, shrewd; pretty or attractive, esp in a dainty way. [**acute**.]

cutis [kū´tis] *n* the vascular layer of the skin.—*adj* **cūtā´eous**, belonging to the skin.—*n* **cū´ticle**, the outermost layer of the skin. [L.]

cutlass [kut´las] *n* a short, broad sword, with one cutting edge, formerly used in the navy. [Fr *coutelas*—L *cultellus*, dim of *culter*, a knife.]

cutler [kut´lėr] *n* one who makes or sells knives.—*n* **cut´lery**, the business of a cutler; edged or cutting instruments in general, often implements for eating food. [Fr *coutelier*—L *culter*, knife.]

cutlet [kut´let] *n* a small slice of meat cut off from the ribs or leg; a small flat croquette of chopped meat or fish. [Fr *côtelette*, dim of *côte*, from L *costa*, a rib.]

cuttlebone [kut´l-bōn] *n* the shell of cuttlefishes used for polishing powder or as a source of lime and salts for caged birds.—*n* **cuttlefish**, any of a family (Sepiidae) of 10-armed marine mollusks having a calcified internal shell. [OE *cudele*.]

cyanide [sī´ȧn-īd] *n* a chemical compound containing the group CN, as in hydrogen cyanide (prussic acid), HCN, and metal cyanides.—*adj* **cyan´ic**, of or belonging to cyanogen.—*ns* **cy´an**, one of the primary colors in color printing and photography; a greenish blue color; **cy´anide**, a direct compound of cyanogen with a metal; **cy´aniding**, extraction of gold or silver from ore by means of potassium cyanide; **cy´anin**, a plant pigment; **cy´anine**, any of a group of dyes used in photography; **cyanogen**, the poisonous gas $(CN)_2$; **cyanō´sis**, morbid blueness of the skin. [Gr *kyanos*, blue.]

cyber café [sī´bėr kaf´ā] *n* a café which has facilities that enable customers to browse the Internet.

cybernetics [sī-bėr-net´iks] *n* (*pl* treated as *sing*) the comparative study of automatic communication and control in functions of living bodies and in mechanical and electric systems (such as in computers). [Gr *kybernētēs*, a steersman.]

cyberspace [sī´bėr-spās] *n* all of the data stored on a large computer network.

cyclamate [sik´la-māt, -mȧt] *n* a salt of calcium or sodium used esp formerly as a sweetener but now discontinued because of harmful metabolic effects.

cyclamen [sik´la-men] *n* a genus (*Cyclamen*) of the same family as the primrose, with nodding flowers and petals bent back. [Gr *kyklaminos*.]

cycle [sī´kl] *n* a period of time in which events happen in a certain order, and which constantly repeats itself; an age; a recurring series of changes; a series of poems, prose romances, etc.; centering around a figure or event; a series of narratives dealing with the exploits of a legendary hero; a bicycle, motorcycle, or tricycle; a series of a single, double, triple, and home run hit in any order by one player during one baseball game.—*vi* to move in cycles; to recur in cycles; to ride a bicycle or tricycle.—*vt* to cause to pass through a cycle of operations or events.—*adjs* **cy´clic, -al**, pertaining to or containing a cycle; recurring in cycles; arranged in a ring or rings; contained in a circle.—*ns* **cy´clist**, one who rides a bicycle; **cy´cloid**, a curve made by a point in a circle, when the circle is rolled along a straight line.—*adjs* smooth with concentric lines of growth; of a personality marked by alternating high and low moods; **cycloid´al**. [Gr *kyklos*, a circle.]

cyclone [sī´klōn] *n* a storm blowing spirally inwards toward a center of low pressure; (in the midwest US) a tornado.—*adj* **cyclon´ic**. [Gr *kyklōn*, pr p of *kykloein*, to whirl round—*kyklos*, a circle.]

cyclopedia [sī-klō-pē´di-a] *See* **encyclopedia**.

cyclopentadiene [sī´klȯ-pent´ȧ-dī-ēn] *n* a chemical compound consisting of a ring of five carbon atoms with six attached hydrogen atoms.

cyclorama [sī-klō-rä´mȧ] *n* a circular panorama; a curved background in stage and cinematograph sets, used to give impression of sky distance, and for lighting effects. [Gr *kyklos*, circle, *horāma*, view.]

cyclostyle [sī´klō-stīl] *n* an apparatus for replicating copies of a writing. [Gr *kyklos*, circle, and **style**.]

cyclotron [sī´klō-trȯn] *n* an apparatus for giving high energy to particles, as protons, etc., used in atomic research.

cygnet [sig´net] *n* a young swan. [Dim of L *cygnus*, a swan, directly or through Fr *cygne*.]

cylinder [sil´in-dėr] *n* a figure generated by a straight line remaining parallel to a fixed axis and moving round a closed curve (ordinarily a circle perpendicular to the axis); a roller-shaped object; applied to many parts of machinery of cylindrical shape, esp the turning part of a revolver and the piston chamber of an engine.—*adjs* **cylin´drical, cylin´dric**, having the form or properties of a cylinder.—**cylinder seal**, a cylinder (as of stone) engraved in intaglio and used esp in ancient Mesopotamia to roll an impression on wet clay. [Gr *kylindros*—*kylindein*, to roll.]

cymbal [sim´bȧl] *n* (*mus*) one of a pair of two brass plates struck together to produce a ringing or clashing sound in a symphony orchestra. [L *cymbalum*—Gr *kymbalon*—*kymbē*, the hollow of a vessel.]

cyme [sīm] *n* an inflorescence the main shoot of which ends in a flower, subsequent flowers growing on lateral branches.—*adj* **cym´ose**. [L *cȳma, cīma*, a sprout—Gr *kȳma*.]

Cymric [kim´rik] *adj* Welsh. [W *Cymru*, Wales.]

cynic, -al [sin´ik- -ȧl] *adj* sneering; disinclined to recognize goodness or selflessness as a motive for behavior.—*ns* **cyn´ic**, one who takes a low view of human character and conduct; **Cyn´ic**, adherent of an ancient Greek school of philosophy which held that virtue is the only good in that its essence lies in independence and self-control; **Cyn´icism**, the doctrine of the cynics; **cynicism** [sin´-i-sizm], contempt for human nature; a saying characterized by such contempt.—*adv* **cyn´ically**. [Gr *kynikos*, dog-like—*kyōn*, gen *kynos*, a dog; cf L *canis*.]

cynosure [sīn´ō-shōōr, or si´-] *n* a center of attraction or admiration; **Cynosure**, the constellation Ursa Minor; the North Star. [Gr *kyōn*, gen *kynos*, a dog, *oura*, a tail.]

cypress [sī´pres] *n* a genus (*Cupressus*) of mostly evergreen trees with overlapping leaves resembling scales; any of several other coniferous trees; the wood of a cypress; a symbol of mourning. [OFr *ciprès*—L *cupressus*—Gr *kyparissos*.]

Cyrillic [si-ril´ik] *adj* denoting the alphabet used in Russia, Bulgaria, Serbia, and the Ukraine, mainly based on the Greek alphabet. [St *Cyril*, 9th cent AD, reputed inventor.]

cyst [sist] *n* a closed sac with a distinct membrane developing abnormally in the structure of plants or animals.—*adj* **cyst´ic**. [Gr *kystis*, a bladder.]

cytology [sī-tol´ō-ji] *n* the branch of biology that deals with cells. [Gr *kytos*, vessel.]

cytoplasm [sīt´ō-plazm] *n* the protoplasm of a cell apart from that of the nucleus. [Gr *kytos*, vessel, *plasma*, form, body.]

cytosine [sī´to-sēn] *n* one of the four bases in deoxyribonucleic acids, in close association with guanine. [Gr *kytos*, vessel.]

czar [zär] *n* the title of any of the former emperors of Russia; an autocrat.—*ns* **czar´evitch**, an heir apparent of a czar; **czarina** [zär-ēnȧ] the wife of a czar.—Also **tsar, tsarina**. [Russ,—L *Caesar*.]

Czech [chek] *adj* of, or pertaining to, the Czech Republic.—*n* a native or inhabitant of the Czech Republic, esp. an inhabitant of Bohemia or Moravia; the Slavic language of the Czechs.—*adjs* **Czecholslovak**, **Czecholslovakian** of the former Czechoslovakia, its peoples or languages.—n (loosely) either of the two languages of the former Czechoslovakia, Czech or Slovak. [Polish.]

D

D-day [dē´dā] (D for unnamed *day*), the opening day (6th June 1944) of the Allied invasion of Europe in World War II; any critical day of action.
D layer lowest region of the ionosphere from about 25 to 50 miles above the surface of the earth in which occurs the absorption of radio waves.
dab[1] [dab] *vt* to strike gently with something soft or moist; to peck;—*pr p* **dabb´ing**; *pt p* **dabbed**.—*n* a gentle blow; a small lump of anything soft or moist; (*usu. in pl; slang*) fingerprint.—*n* **dab´chick** the pied-billed grebe of America; the little grebe of Europe. [First appears about 1300; cf Ger *tappe*, a pat. Confused with **daub** and **tap**.]
dab[2] a species of flounder of light-brown color.
dab[3] [dab] *n* (*inf*) an expert person—*also* **dab-hand**. [Prob a corr of **adept**.]
dabble [dab´l] *vi* to do anything in a superficial or dilettante way.—*n* **dabb´ler**. [Freq of **dab**.]
da capo [dä kä´pō] a term in music, indicating 'return to the beginning'—*usu. written* **DC**. [It, 'from the beginning'—L *da*, from, *caput*, head.]
dace [dās] *n* any small fresh-water fish of the carp family. [ME *darce*—Low L *dardus*, a dart or javelin. So called from its quickness.]
dachshund [däks´hŏŏnt] *n* a breed of short-legged, long-bodied hound. [Ger *dachs*, a badger, *hund*, dog.]
dacoit [da-koit´] *n* in India and Burma, one of a gang of robbers or brigands.—*n* **dacoit´y**, brigandage. Also **dakoit**. [Hindustani.]
Dacron [dak´ron] *n* trade name for polyester fiber.
dactyl [dak´til] *n* in poetry, a word or word-group consisting of one heavily-stressed syllable followed by two lightly-stressed syllables.—*adj* **dactyl´ic**.—**dactylol´ogy**, the art of communicating with the fingers, esp the manual alphabet. [Gr *daktylos*, a finger.]
dad [dad], **daddy** [dad´i] *n* (*inf*) father.—*n* **dadd´y-long-legs** (*inf*) any of various spiders or insects with long slender legs. [Ety uncertain.]
Dada *or* **Dadaism** [dä´dä] *n, adj* (of) artistic movement from about 1915 to 1922 intended to outrage and scandalize by its anti-art and anti-sense artefacts.
dado [dādo] *n* the lower part of the walls of a room when paneled or painted separately; the part of the pedestal in a classical column below the surbase and above the base. [It]
daffodil [daf´o-dil] *n* a yellow-flowered narcissus. Also **lentlily**. [ME *affodille*—Gr *asphodelos*; the *d* is unexplained.]
daft [däft] *adj* silly; insane.—*adv* **daftly**.—*n* **daft´ness**. [From same root as **deft**.]
dagger [dag´er] *n* a short sword for stabbing; a mark of reference (†).—**at daggers drawn**, in a state of hostility. [ME.]
dago [dāgo] *n* a man of Italian origin. [Prob Sp *Diego*—L *Jacobus*, James.]
daguerreotype [dä-ger´-ō-tīp] *n* an early method of photography on a copper plate; a photograph so taken. [Fr, from Louis *Daguerre*.]
dahlia [däl´yä] *n* a genus (*Dahlia*) of half-hardy tuberous perennials of the aster family grown for its range of colors and flower forms. [From *Dahl*, a Swedish botanist.]
Dail [doil] *n* the lower house of the legislature of Eire. [Irish, assembly.]
daily [dā´li] *adj, adv* every day.—*n* a daily paper. [day.]
daimyo [dī´myō] *n* a Japanese noble under the old feudal system (1600–1867). [Jap from Chin.]
dainty [dān´ti] *adj* delicate; tasteful; fastidious.—*n* a delicacy.—*adv* **dain´tily**.—*n* **dain´tiness**. [ME *deintee*—L *dignitās, -ātis*—*dignus*, worthy.]
daiquiri [dīkiri, däk] *n* a cocktail made of rum, lemon or lime juice, and sugar. [From *Daiquiri*, Cuba.]
dairy [dā´ri] *n* the place where milk is kept, and butter and cheese made; an establishment for the supply of milk.—**dai´ry farm; dai´rymaid; dai´ryman**.—**dairy cattle**, cows raised mainly for production of milk; **dairy products**, milk, butter, cheese, yogurt, etc. [OE *dǣge*, a dairymaid.]
dais [dā´is, dās] *n* a raised floor at the end of a hall; a raised floor with a seat and canopy. [OFr *deis*—Gr *diskos*, a disk.]
daisy [dā´zi] *n* any of various composite plants having heads with white or pink rays and a yellow disk, esp English daisy; **dai´sy-chain**, a row of daisies linked together; **daisy stitch**, embroidery stitch made with small loop and securing stitch; **daisy-wheel**, flat wheel-shaped printing device with characters at the ends of spokes; **push up daisies**, (*inf*) to be dead. [OE *dæges ēage*, day's eye.]
dakoit *see* **dacoit**.
Dalai Lama [däl-ī läm´a] *n* the head of Tibetan Buddhism. [Mongolian *dalai*, ocean, Tibetan *lama* a high priest.]
dale [dāl] *n* the low ground between hills; the valley through which a river flows. [OE *dæl*.]
dally [dal´i] *vi* to lose time by idleness or trifling; to play (with); to exchange caresses;—*pr p* **dally´ing**; *pt p* **dall´ied**.—*n* **dall´iance**, trifling; interchange of embraces; delay. [OFr *dalier*, to chat.]
Dalmation [dal-mā´sh(à)n] *n* a large short-haired dog with black markings on a white body. [Conn, prob erroneously, with *Dalmatia*, on the NE Adriatic.]
dalmatic [dal-mat´ik] *n* a loose-fitting, wide-sleeved ecclesiastical vestment. [Low L *dalmatica*, a robe on the pattern of a dress worn in *Dalmatia*.]
Daltonism [döl´ton-izm] *n* congenital, usu. red-green color blindness.
Dalton's Law [döl´tonz] the physical law that the total pressure exerted by a mixture of gases is equal to the sum of the partial pressures of the gases of the mixture. [From John *Dalton* (1766–1844).]
Dalton System [döl´tonz] a method of progressive education whereby a pupil contracts to undertake a year's work at his or her pace. [From *Dalton*, Massachusetts, where it was first used in 1920.]
dam[1] [dam] *n* a barrier to restrain water; the water thus confined.—*vt* to keep back by a bank or similar obstruction (*also fig*);—*pr p* **damm´ing**; *pt p* **dammed**;—*n* **damsite**, the place to be dammed. [ME, of Germanic origin.]
dam[2] [dam] *n* a mother of a four-footed animal. [A form of *dame*.]
damage [dam´ij] *n* injury; loss; the value of what is lost; (*inf*) cost; (*pl*) payment due for loss or injury sustained by one person through the fault of another.—*vt* to harm.—*adj* **damageable**, fragile. [O Fr *damage*—L *damnum*, loss.]
damask [dam´ask] *n* reversible, figured, woven fabric esp linen; Damascus steel or its surface pattern.—*adj* of a red color, like that of a damask rose.—*n* **damascene** [dam´asēn], (*cap*) a native of Damascus; a Damascus sword; inlay of metal on steel.—*vt* to decorate metal (esp steel) by inlaying; to ornament with the wavy appearance of Damascus steel; **dam´ask-rose**, a hardy, large, fragrant, pink rose (*Rosa damascena*). [From *Damascus*, in Syria, where damask was orig made.]
dame [dām] *n* title of a woman having the same rank as a knight; (*slang*) a woman. [Fr *dame*—L. *domina*, a mistress.]
damn [dam] *vt* to censure or condemn; to sentence to eternal punishment.—*n* an oath, a curse.—*adj* **dam´nable**, deserving damnation; hateful, pernicious; (*inf*) very annoying.—*adv* **dam´nably**.—*n* **damnā´tion**, condemnation; eternal punishment.—*adj* **dam´natory**, consigning to damnation.—*adj* **damned**, sentenced to everlasting punishment; hateful, deserving of condemnation, used as a mild oath (in this sense often **damn**). **damnedest** (*inf*) most remarkable.—*adv* very, exceedingly (often **damn**).—*adj* **damning** exposing (a person) to conviction of fault or crime, or to condemnation. [Fr *damner*—L *damnāre*, to condemn—*damnum*, loss.]
Damocles, Sword of [dam´-ō-klēs] *n* a symbol of insecurity.—*adj* **Damoclean** (*dam-ō-clē´an*). [Damocles, a sycophant of Dionysius, was invited to sample the life he envied. At a banquet, he suddenly looked up and saw a sword suspended by a single horsehair above his head.]
damp [damp] *n* humidity; in mines, any gas other than air.—*vt* to moisten; to discourage.—*adj* moist, *vti* **damp´en**, to make or become damp or moist.—*n* **damper**; a depressive influence; a metal plate in a flue for controlling combustion; (*mus*) device for stopping vibration of stringed instruments; unleavened bread made with flour and water—(*Australia*) *n* **damp´ness**. [ME *dampen*; akin to Ger *dampf*, vapor.]
damsel [dam´zėl] *n* a young unmarried woman; a girl. [OFr *dameisele*—Low L *domicella*, dim of L *domina*, lady.]
damson [dam´z(ò)n, -sòn] *n* a small dark-purple oval-fruited variety of plum; the tree producing this fruit. [Shortened from *Damascene*—*Damascus*.]
dan [dan] *n* a degree of proficiency in martial arts; person attaining this. [Jap]
dance [däns] *vi* to move with the rhythm of sound, esp to music; to move lightly and gaily; (*fig*) to seem to move in such a way (eg of eyes).—*vt* to make to dance or to move up and down; to perform (a dance).—*n* a dance performance of an artistic nature; a social function at which dancing is the chief entertainment; a tune to which dancing is performed.—**dan´cer**, one who dances, esp as a profession; **Dance of Death**, Death, sometimes represented as a skeleton, leading all men to the grave. Also **Dance Macabre**. [OFr *danser*.]
dandelion [dan´di-līòn] *n* a common composite (*Taraxacum officinale*) with jagged-tooth leaves, (edible) yellow flower and fluffy seed head. [Fr *dent de lion*, lion tooth.]
dander [dan´dėr] *n* (*inf*) anger, passion. [A form of **dandruff**.]
Dandie Dinmont [dan´di din´mònt] *n* a short-legged terrier with pendulous ears and a long wiry pepper and mustard coat. [Called after *Dandie Dinmont* in Scott's *Guy Mannering*, who owned such dogs.]
dandle [dan´dl] *vt* to fondle or toss in the arms, as a baby. [Origin unknown.]
dandruff [dand´rùf] *n* a scaly scurf on the scalp. [Origin unknown.]
dandy [dan´di] *n* a man who pays too much attention to dress.—*adj* (*inf*) excellent, fine—*vt* **dan´dify**, to dress up.—*n* **dandification**. [Origin unknown.]

Dane [dān] *n* a native of *Denmark*; **a Great Dane**, a large, short-haired breed of dog.—*adj* **Dan´ish**, belonging to Denmark.—*n* the language of the Danes; (*inf*) Danish pastry.—*n* **Danish pastry**, a sweet yeast roll filled or topped with fruit and nuts. [Dan. *Daner* (pl); OE *Dene*.]

danger [dān´jėr] *n* a state or circumstances involving injury or risk; a source of harm or risk.—*adj* **dan´gerous**, very unsafe; (of persons) not to be trusted.—*adv* **dan´gerously**.—**dan´gerousness; danger line, danger point**. [OFr *dangier* absolute power, hence power to hurt—L *dominus*, a lord.]

dangle [dang´gl] *vi* to hang loosely; to follow (after someone), to hang (about, around someone);—*vt* to make to dangle.—*n* **dangler**, (*gram*) in a sentence, a modifier lacking its intended substantive, esp **dangling participle**. [Scand; cf ON *dingla*, to swing.]

Daniel [dan´yel] *n* the 27th book of the Old Testament written by the prophet Daniel describing Jerusalem under Gentile control.

dank [dangk] *adj* unpleasantly moist.

danseur [dã-sæ´] *n* a male ballet dancer. [Fr]

danseuse [dã-soez´] *n* a female ballet dancer. [Fr]

dap [dap] *vi* to drop (bait) gently into the water.

dapper [dap´ėr] *adj* quick; little and active; spruce. [Du *dapper*, brave.]

dapple [dap´l] *adj* marked with spots.—*vt* to variegate with spots.—*adj* **dapple-gray**, mottled with darker gray. [Origin unknown.]

DAR [abbrev] Daughters of the American Revolution, a society open to women descended from patriots who fought in the Revolution.

dare [dār] *vti* to be bold enough; to venture;—*3rd pers sing* **dare(s)**;—*vt* to challenge; to defy.—*n* a challenge.—*n* **daredev´il**, a rash, venturesome person; **daredeviltry**, reckless boldness.—*adj* reckless.—*adj* **dar´ing**, bold; courageous.—*n* boldness.—*adv* **dar´ing-ly**. [OE *dearr*, present sing (orig preterite) of *durran*.]

dark [därk] *adj* having little or no light; of a shade of color closer to black than white; (of a person) having brown or black skin or hair; gloomy; (*inf*) secret, unknown; mysterious.—*n* absence of light; obscurity; a state of ignorance.—*vt* **dark´en**, to make dark or darker (*lit and fig*); to sully.—*vi* to grow dark or darker.—*adj* **dark´ish**, somewhat dark; dusky.—*adv, adj* **dark´ling**, in the dark; dark.—*adv* **dark´ly**.—*n* **dark´ness**.—**Dark Ages**, the period of intellectual darkness in Europe, from the 5th to the 10th century; **Dark Continent**, Africa before exploration; **a dark horse**, in racing, a horse whose capabilities are not known; a person whose character is not easily read; **darkroom**, a room protected from actinic light for processing film.—**be in the dark about**, be ignorant of; **darken someone's door**, pay unwelcome visit, **keep dark**, be silent or secret about, conceal; **Prince of Darkness**, Satan. [OE *deorc*.]

darling [där´ling] *n* one dearly loved; a favourite. [OE *dēorling*—adj *dēore*, dear.]

darn[1] [därn] *vt* to replace or reinforce broken or worn threads in a fabric.—*n* the place darned.—*n* **darn´ing-need´le**. A long needle with a long narrow eye; (*inf*) a dragonfly.

darn[2] [därn] *vti n, adj; interj* form of **damn** as a mild oath.

dart [därt] *n* a small pointed missile; anything that pierces; a tapering fold sewn on fabric; (*in pl*) a game in which darts are thrown at a board.—*vti* to move rapidly.—**dart´board**, the target in the game of darts; **dar´ter**, any of several small fresh-water fishes allied to the perch. [OFr *dart*.]

Darwinism [där´win-izm] *n* the theory that new species of plants and animals originate from those descendents of parent forms which are naturally selected through survival of the fittest, propounded by Charles *Darwin* (1809–82).—*adj* and *n* **Darwin´ian**.

dash [dash] *vt* to throw, thrust, or drive violently; to bespatter; to frustrate (hopes); to depress, confound (eg one's spirits); to write quickly.—*vi* to rush violently.—*n* a short race; a violent striking; a rush; a small amount of something added to food; a blow; a punctuation mark (—); verve; display.—*n* **dashboard**, a panel in an automobile or airplane to carry instruments; a board or screen in front of a driver in a horse-vehicle to keep off splashes of mud.—*adj* **dash´ing**, spirited; showy. [ME *daschen, dassen* to rush.]

dashiki [däshē´kē] *n* a brightly-colored loose-fitting shirt, [WAfr].

dastard [das´tard] *n* a mean, sneaky coward—*adj, adv* **das´tardly**.—*n* **das´tardliness**. [From a Scand stem *dast*=Eng *dazed*, and Fr suffx—*ard*]

data [dā´ta] *n pl* (now often with sing verb) facts, statistics, or information either historical or derived by calculation or experimentation.—*sing* **dātum**.—**dat´a bank, dat´abase**, a large body of information stored in a computer for analysis or use.—**data processing**, analysis of information stored on a computer by using strictly defined systems of procedure. [L, pt p neut pl of *dăre*, to give.]

date[1] [dāt] *n* day of month; a statement of time of writing, sending, executing, as on a letter, book, document; the time of an event; period to which something belongs; an appointment or engagement; a social engagement; the person with whom a social engagement is made.—*vt* to affix a date to; to ascertain or suggest the date of; (*inf*) to make a date with; (*inf*) to go out regularly esp with a member of the opposite sex.—*vi* to reckon from a point in time; to show signs of belonging to a particular period.—*adj* **dāt´able**.—*adj* **dāte´less**, undated; endless; having unknown beginning; of permanent interest; immemorial.—*n* **dāteline**, the 180th meridian, east of which is one day earlier than west of it (*Also* **International Dateline**); a line giving the date in periodical.—**out-of-date** *see* **out; up-to-date** *see* **up**. [L *datum* as in *datum Romae*=given at Rome.]

date[2] [dāt] *n* the sweet, oblong fruit of a palm; the tall tree (*Phoenix dactylfera*) of the palm family yielding this fruit. [Fr *datte*—Gr *daktylos*, a finger.]

dative [dāt´iv] *adj* (*gram*) expressing an indirect object.—*n* the dative case; a word in the dative. [L *datīvus*—*dăre*, to give.]

datum [dā´tum] *n* singular of **data**; (*engineering and surveying*) **datums**; *pl* **data**, [L *dătum*, given—*dăre*, to give.]

datura [datū´ra] *n* a genus of half-hardy annuals and shrubby tender perennial garden plants of the nightshade family. [Hindi *dhortūra*, Jimson weed]

daub [döb] *vt* to smear; to paint coarsely.—*n* a coarse painting.—*n* **daub´er**. [OFr *dauber*, to plaster—L *dē*, down, and *albus*, white.]

daughter [dö´tėr] *n* a female child; a female descendant; a female personification (*the US is the daughter of the original British colonies*).—*n* **daugh´ter-in-law**, a son's wife;—*pl* **daughters-in-law; Daughters of the American Revolution** *see* **DAR**. [OE *dohtor*.]

daunt [dönt] or *dänt, vt* to frighten; to discourage.—*adj* **daunt´less**, not to be daunted.—*adv* **daunt´lessly**.—*n* **daunt´-lessness**. [OFr *danter*—L *domitāre*—domāre, to tame.]

dauphin [dö´fin] *n* the eldest son of a king of France.—*n* **dau´phine**, his wife. [OFr *daulphin*. From *Delphinus*, family name of lords of part of south-east France (province of Dauphiné) ceded to the king in 1349.]

davenport [dav´ėn-pōrt, -port *n* a large, upholstered couch or settee often convertible to a bed; a small desk with drawers and lift-up top. [From the maker.]

davit [dav´it] *n* one of a pair of pieces of timber or iron to raise a boat over a ship's side or stern. [Cf Fr *davier*, a forceps.]

Davy Jones [dā´vi jōnz] *n* personification of the bottom of the sea. **Davy Jones's locker**, the bottom of the ocean.

daw [döw] *n* a jackdaw. [ME *dawe*.]

dawdle [dö´dl] *vi* to waste time by acting or moving slowly.—*n* **daw´dler**. [Perh connected with (dial.) *daddle*, to totter.]

dawn [dön] *vi* to become day; to begin to grow light; to begin to appear.—*n* daybreak; beginning.—Also **dawn´ing**.—**dawn (up)on**, to become suddenly clear to. [OE *dagian*, to dawn, *dæg*, day.]

day [dā] *n* twenty-four hours, the time the earth takes to make a revolution on her axis; the time of light, from sunrise to sunset; a day set apart for a purpose; a successful period of vogue, or influence;—**day´book**, a diary; book-keeper's daily ledger; **day´break**, dawn; **daycare center**, place where young children of working parent(s) stay; **day-dream**, a dreaming or musing while awake (also *vi*); **day´light**, light of day; clear space.—*adj* **day´long**, during the whole day.—*n* **daylight saving time**, the creation of day-light by advancing the clock during summer months; **day boy, day girl, day student**, a pupil who attends a boarding-school during the school-hours, but boards at home; **day lily**, hemerocallis; **Day of Atonement**, Yom Kippur; **day´star**, the morning star; **day´time**.—**day by day**, daily; **day in day out**, for an indefinite succession of days; **day off**, a break from scheduled activity; **the time of day** *see* **time**. [OE *dæg*.]

Dayak [dī´ak] *or* **Dyak** *n* a member of the Indonesian peoples of Borneo; their language.

Day-Glo [da´glo] *n* trade name for luminous printing ink.

daze [dāz] *vt* to stun, to stupefy.—*n* bewilderment.—*adj* **dazed** (*dāzd*).—*adv* **dazedly** (*dāz´id-li*). [ON *dasask*, to be breathless.]

dazzle [daz´l] *vt* to daze or overpower with a strong light; to confound by brilliancy, beauty, or cleverness.—*n* the act of dazzling; that which dazzles.—*n* **dazz´ler**. [Freq of *daze*.]

DDT [dichloro-diphenyl-trichloroethane] *abbrev* of a chemical insecticide.

de- [dē- di-] down; away from; completely. [L *dē*, from, down from, away from];—eg **depose, derail, denude** (see these words). Also used (as a living prefix) to form words reversing or undoing, in action;—eg **decentralize, denazification**.

deacon [dē´kön] *n* in certain churches, a member of the clergy under priests; an elected or appointed church officer; the lowest grade in the Mormon priesthood;—*fem* **dea´coness**, in some Protestant churches a woman officer who helps the minister;—**dea´conry, dea´conship**. [L *diāconus*—Gr *diākonos*, a servant.]

dead [ded] *adj* without life; death-like; without vegetation; extinguished (*eg of fire*); numb (*eg of a limb*); spiritually or emotionally insensitive; dull (*of color, sound, etc.*); without motion; out of play (*of a ball*); obsolete; unsaleable; complete; absolutely accurate; unerring;—*adv* in a dead manner; absolutely; utterly.—*n* one who is dead; the time of greatest stillness, as 'the dead of night'; **the dead**, those who are dead; **dead´-beat´**, (*inf*) quite overcome, exhausted;—*vt* **dead´en**, to make dead; to deprive partly of vigor or sensibility; to lessen (*a sensation, as pain*); to deprive of force or brightness (*eg a sound*).—**dead-end**, a pipe, passage, etc. closed at one end; (*lit and fig*) a cul-de-sac; **dead´-eye** (*naut*) a round, flattish wooden block with a rope or iron band passing round it, and pierced with three holes for a lanyard; **dead´head**, (*inf*) a useless person; **dead heat**, a race in which two or more competitors are equal at the end; **dead language**, one no longer spoken; **dead´-lett´er**, a law or rule which has been made but is not enforced; a letter undelivered and unclaimed at the post-office; **dead´line**, the date by which something must be done; a line drawn in a military prison, by going beyond which a prisoner makes himself liable to be shot instantly; **dead´lock**, a complete standstill, also *vt*; **dead loss**, a loss without any compensation; **dead man's handle** *or* **dead man's pedal**, switch on machinery that allows operation only when depressed by operator;—*adj* **dead´ly**, causing death; fatal; death-like; implacable (eg *deadly hatred*); bringing damnation (eg *deadly sin*); intense (eg *deadly earnestness*);—**dead´liness; dead´ly-night´shade**, belladonna; **dead´march**, a solemn march played at funerals;—**dead´ness; deadpan** an expressionless face; one having such;—*adj* (*of manner*) expressionless, emotionless, esp when the situation implies feeling of some kind, eg amusement.—**dead reck´oning**, an estimation of a ship's place by the logbook and compass; **dead set**, a determined and prolonged attempt; **dead´weight**, unrelieved weight; a heavy or oppressive burden; **dead´wood**, useless material, pieces of timber laid on the upper side of the keel at either end; **dead to the world**, (*slang*) very soundly asleep; unconscious from drinking. [OE *dēad*.]

deaf [def] *adj* dull of hearing; unable to hear; not willing to hear;—*vt* **deaf´en**, to make deaf; to stun; to render impervious to sound.—**deaf´ening**, *adj* making deaf; very loud.—**deaf´-mute**, one who is both deaf and dumb; **deaf´ness**. [OE *dēaf*.]

deal[1] [dēl] *n* a portion, amount (**a great, good, deal**); (*inf*) a large amount; the act of dividing playing cards; a business transaction, esp a favorable one.—*vt* to divide, to distribute; to deliver (*eg a blow*).—*vi* to transact business (with); to trade (in); (*with* **with**) to act towards; to distribute cards;—*pt, p p* **dealt** [delt].—**deal´er**, a trader; in cards, one whose turn it is to deal or who has dealt the hand in play; **dealership**, a sales agency for a specific brand of goods; **deal´ing**, manner of acting towards others (**double dealing** *see* **double**); intercourse of trade, etc. (*usu. pl*).—**deal with**, to tackle and dispose of (any problem or task). [OE *dǣlan*—*dǣl*, a part; Ger *teilen*—*teil*, a part or division. A doublet of **dole**.]

deal[2] [dēl] *n* fir or pine wood.—*adj* of deal. [Middle Low Ger *dele*; cf OE *thille*.]

dean [dēn] *n* a dignitary in cathedral and collegiate churches who presides over the canons; the head of a faculty in a university or college; high school administrator in charge of discipline; **dean´ery**, group of parishes presided over by a dean; a dean's house; **dean´ship**, the office of a dean. [OFr *deien*—Low L *decānus*, a chief of ten—L *decem*, ten.]

dear [dēr] *adj* high in price, costly; highly valued; beloved; a conventional form of address used in letter-writing.—*n* one who is beloved.—*adv* at a high price.—*interj* indicating surprise, pity, or other emotion, as in 'Oh dear!' 'Dear me!'—*adv* **dear´ly**.—**dear´ness; dearth** [*dûrth*], high price; scarcity; famine. [OE *dēore*.]

death [deth] *n* the end of life; manner or cause of dying; state of being dead; the destruction of something.—**death´ag´ony**, the struggle often preceding death; **death´bed**, the bed on which one dies; the last illness; **death´blow**, a blow that causes death; a mortal blow; **death cap**, a destroying angel (*Amanita phalloides*);—*adj* **death´less**, never dying; everlasting.—*n* **death´lessness**.—*adj* **deathly**, deadly; deathlike.—**death march**, a forced trek on which many will die of exhaustion; **death´mask**, a plaster-cast taken from the face after death; **death´rate** the proportion of deaths to the population; **death´ratt´le**, a rattling in the throat which sometimes precedes death; **death's´-head**, a human skull, emblematic of death; **deathtrap**, an unsafe structure or place; **deathwatch**, a vigil with a dying person; **death´watch beetle** (family **Anobiidae**) name for several insects that produce a ticking noise; **death´-wish**, conscious or unconscious wish for death for oneself or for another; [OE *dēath*.]

debacle [dā-bäk´l, di-bak´l] *n* a breaking up of ice on a river; a complete break-up or collapse. [Fr *débâcle; dé*-(—*des*-), and *bâcler*, to bar—L *baculus*, a stick.]

debar [di-bär´] *vt* to bar out (from); to exclude;—*pr p* **debarr´ing**; *pp* **debarred´**.—*n* **debar´ment**. [Fr *débarrer*—LL *dēbarrāre*, which meant 'to unbar'.]

debark [di-bärk´] *vt* to disembark.—*n* **dēbarkā´tion**, (Fr *débarquer*—*des*- (L *dis*-), away, and *barque*, a ship.]

debase [di-bās´] *vt* to lower; to make mean or of less value, to degrade; to adulterate, as the coinage.—*adj* **debased´**, degraded.—*n* **de-base´ment**. [**de-** + obs *base*—**abase**.]

debate [di-bāt´] *n* a contention in words; a formal argument; a (parliamentary) discussion.—*vt* to argue about.—*vi* to deliberate; to join in debate.—*adj* **debāt´able**, liable to be disputed.—*n* **debāt´er**. [OFr *debatre*—L *dē* and *bātuěre*, to beat.]

debauch [di-bŏch´] *vt* to corrupt; to seduce; to lead away from duty or allegiance.—*vi* to over-indulge.—*n* a fit of intemperance or debauchery.—*p adj* **debauched´**, corrupt; profligate.—*n* **debauch´ery**, indulgence in harmful or immoral sensual behavior. [OFr *desbaucher*, to corrupt; origin uncertain.]

debenture [di-ben´tyůr, -chůr] *n* a written acknowledgment of a debt; a security issued by a company for borrowed money [L *dēbentur*, there are due, 3rd pers pl pass of *dēbēre*, to owe—the first word of the receipt.]

debilitate [di-bil´i-tāt] *vt* to make weak, to impair the strength of.—**debilitā´tion; debil´ity**, bodily weakness and languor. [L *dēbilitāre*, -*ātum*—*dēbilis*, weak.]

debit [deb´it] *n* an entry in a ledger of a debt.—*vt* to charge (a person, with a debt); to enter on the debit side of an account. [L *dēbitum*, what is due, from *dēbēre*, to owe.]

debonair [deb-o-nār´] *adj* having a carefree manner; courteous, gracious, charming. [OFr *de*, of, *bon*, good, *aire*, manner.]

debouch [di-bowch´, di-bōōsh´] *vi* to come out from a narrow pass or confined place.—*n* **debouchure´**, the mouth of a river or strait. [Fr *déboucher*—*de*, from, *bouche*, the mouth.]

debrief [dē-brēf´] *vt* to gather information from (a soldier, astronaut, etc.) on his return from a mission. [**de-**, + **brief**.]

debris [deb´rē] *n* remains of wreckage, (*geol*) a mass of rocky fragments. [Fr, from *briser*, to break; akin to **bruise**.]

debt [det] *n* something one person owes to another; liability to pay or to do something; a state of obligation or of indebtedness.—*n* **debt´or**, one who owes money to another.—**debt of honor**, a debt not recognized in law, but binding in honor;—**bad debt**, a debt of which there is no prospect of payment; **in a person's debt**, under an obligation to a person. [OFr *dette*—L *dēbitum, dēbēre*, to owe.]

debug [dē-bug´] *vt* to remove concealed listening devices from; to find faults or errors in and remove them from. [**de-**, + **bug´**]

debunk [de-bungk´] *vt* to show up (a claim or theory as false. [**de-** + **bunk**.]

début [dā-bü´] *n* a beginning or first attempt; a first appearance before the public or in society.—**debutant**, person making a first professional appearance; **debutante** [*deb´ūtant*], a girl making her first appearance in society usu. at a designated event (dim **deb**). [Fr *début*, a first stroke—*débuter*—*de*, from, *but*, aim, mark.]

deca-, deka- [dek´a] to indicate quantities or magnitudes in multiples of ten. [Gr *deka*, ten.]

decade [dek´ad, -ad´, dek´ad] *n* a group of ten, esp a series of ten years (*eg the 80s*), [Fr *décade*—Gr *dekas, -ados*—*deka*, ten.]

decadence [dek´a-dėns] or *de-kā´-*, **dec´adency** (or *de-kā´-*), *n* state of decay; deterioration in standard,—*adj* **dec´adent** (or *de-kā´-*), decaying; lacking in moral and physical vigor—*n* one who is degenerate; one of a group of late 19th-century writers in France and in England characterized by *over-refinement* of style [Fr,—L *de*, down, *caděre*, to fall.]

decaffeinated [dēkaf´ināted] *adj* (of coffee or tea) with caffeine reduced or removed. [**de-** + **caffeine**.]

decagon [dek´a-gon] *n* a plane figure of ten angles and sides, a ten-sided polygon—*adj* **decag´onal**. [Gr *deka*, ten, and *gōnia*, an angle.]

decahedron [dek-a-hē´dron] *n* a solid figure having ten faces.—*adj* **decahē´dral**. [Gr *deka*, ten, and *hedra*, a seat.]

decal [dē´-kal] *n* a process of transferring a picture or design from specially-prepared paper to another surface; the paper bearing the design. Also **décalmania**, [Fr *calguer* and mania.]

Decalogue [dek´a-log] *n* the ten commandments of the Bible. [Gr *deka*, ten, *logos*, a discourse.]

decameter *see* **dekameter**.

decamp [di-kamp´] *vi* to leave suddenly or secretly.—*n* **decamp´ment**. [Fr *décamper*.]

decant [di-kant´] *vt* to pour off, leaving sediment; to pour from one vessel to another.—**decantā´tion; decant´er**, an ornamental bottle for holding decanted liquid. [Fr *décanter*—L *dē*, from, *canthus*, beak of a vessel—Gr *kanthos*, corner of the eye.]

decapitate [di-kap´i-tāt] *vt* to behead.—*n* **decapitā´tion**. [L *dē*, from, *caput, capitis*, head.]

Decapoda [di-kap´o-da] *n pl* an order of Crustaceans with five pairs of walking limbs; cephalopods with eight short tentacles and two longer ones—*n* **dec´apod**, a member of either of these orders.—Also *adj*. [Gr *deka*, ten, *pous*, gen *podos*, a foot.]

decarbonate [dē-kär´bon-āt] *vt* to remove carbon dioxide or carbonic acid from. [**de-** + **carbonate**.]

decarbonize [dē-kär´bon-īz] *vt* to remove carbon from. Also **decarburize**.—*n* **decarbonizā´ation**. [pfx **de-**, and **carbonize**.]

decasyllable [dek-a-sil´a-bl] *n* a verse line, or a word, with ten syllables.—*adj* **decasyllab´ic**. [Gr *deka*, ten, *syllabē*, a syllable.]

decathlon [dek-ath´lon] *n* a track-and-field contest consisting of ten events. [Gr *deka*, ten, *athlon*, a contest.]

decay [di-kā´] *vi* to fall away from a state of health or excellence; to waste away; to rot.—*vt* to cause to decompose or rot.—*n* a falling into a worse state; a wearing away; (*chem, phys*) disintegration of a radioactive substance.—*p adj* **decayed´**, (*fig*) reduced in circumstances.—*n* **decayed´ness**. [L *dē*, from, *caděre*, to fall.]

decease [di-sēs´] *n* death.—*vi* to die.—*adj* **deceased´**, dead.—*n* the dead person previously referred to. [L *dē*, away, *cēděre, cessum*, to go.]

decedent [dē-sēd´-ent] *n* a deceased person.—*n* **decedent estate**, the estate left by a decedent. [L *dēcēdens* – departing].

deceit [di-sēt´] *n* act of deceiving; anything intended to mislead; fraud; falseness.—*adj* **deceit´ful**, disposed or tending to deceive; insincere.—*adv* **deceit´fully**.—*n* **deceit´fulness**.—*vt* **deceive** (di-sēv´), to mislead; to cheat; to disappoint.—*n* **deceiv´er**. [L *dēcipěre, dēceptum*—*dē*, from, *capěre*, to take.]

decelerate [dē-sel´ėr-āt] *vti* to slow down. [L *dē*, down, *celer*, swift.]

December [di-sem´bėr] *n* the twelfth and last month of the year with 31 days. [L *decem*, ten.]

decennial [de-sen´yȧl] *adj* of period of ten years.

decent [dē´sėnt] *adj* respectable, proper; moderate; not obscene; (*inf*) quite good; kind, generous—*n* **dē´cency**, seemliness, propriety, modesty; (*inf*) considerateness, sense of what may be expected of one.—*adv* **dē´cently**. [L *decens, -entis*, pr p of *decēre*, to be becoming.]

decentralize [dē-sen´trȧl-īz] *vt* to transfer functions from central government, organization or head to local centers.—*n* **decentraliza´tion**. [**de-** + **centralize**.]

deception [di-sep´sh(ȯ)n] *n* act of deceiving; state of being deceived; means of deceiving or misleading; trick; illusion.—*adj* **decep´tive**, tending to deceive; misleading.—*adv* **decep´tively**.—*n* **decep´tiveness**. [Low L *dēceptiō, -ōnis*—*dēcipĕre*, to deceive.]

deci- [des´i] to indicate a quantity or magnitude of one-tenth unit. [L *decimus*, tenth—*decem*, ten.]

decibel [des´i-bel] *n* a unit for measuring sound level. [**deci-** + **bel**.]

decide [di-sīd´] *vt* to determine, to end, to settle; to resolve.—*vi* to make up one's mind.—*adj* **decid´ed**, determined, settled; clear, unmistakable; resolute.—*adv* **decid´edly**. [OFr *decider*—L *dēcīdĕre*—*dē*, away, *caedĕre*, to cut.]

deciduous [di-sid´ū-us] *adj* liable to be shed at a certain period; shedding (teeth, leaves, antlers, etc.). [L *dēciduus*—*dēcidĕre*—*dē*, from, and *cadĕre*, to fall.]

decigram [des´i-gram] *n* a tenth of a gram. [**deci-** + **gram**.]

deciliter [desi´-lēter] *n* a tenth of a liter. [**deci-** + **liter**.]

decimal *adj* of tenths, of numbers written to the base 10.—**decimalize**, to express as a decimal or to convert to a decimal system.—*adv* **dec´imally.**—**decimal currency**, currency in which units can be divided by ten; **decimal fraction**, fraction whose denominator is ten or a power of ten; **decimal number system**, the ordinary number system which denotes real numbers according to place values for multiples of ten; **decimal point**, a dot written before the numerator in a decimal fraction, thus 0.5 = ½. [Low L *decimālis*—*decem*, ten.]

decimate [des´i-māt] *vt* to reduce greatly in number, as by slaughter or disease; to punish by killing every tenth man.—*n* **decimā´tion**. [L *decimāre, -ātum*—*decem*, ten.]

decimeter [des´i-mēter] *n* a tenth of a meter. [**deci-** + **meter**.]

decipher [di-sī´fėr] *vt* to read or transliterate from secret writing; to make out what is unknown or difficult.—*adj* **decī´pherable**. [**de-**, + **cipher**.]

decision [di-sizh´(ȯ)n] *n* the act of deciding; a settlement; a judgment; firmness (eg *to act with decision*); the quality of being decided in character.—*adj* **decī´sive**, having the power of deciding; showing decision; final; positive.—*adv* **decī´sively**.—*n* **decī´siveness**. [L *dēcisiō, -ōnis*—*dēcidĕre*. See **decide**.]

deck [dek] *vt* to cover; to adorn.—*n* the floor on a ship, airplane, bus, or bridge; an extension to a dwelling made of planks; a pack of playing cards; the turntable of a phonograph; the playing mechanism of a tape recorder; (*slang*) the ground, the floor; a portion of narcotics.—**deck´chair**; folding chair made of canvas suspended in a frame. Also **steamer chair.**—**deck´hand**, (*inf*) a stagehand; **decking**, any treated flexible material used as waterproof covering for a roof or deck; any self-supporting flooring or roofing units laid between joists or rafters; **hit the deck**, (*slang*) to fall to the ground; to get up out of bed. [Du *dekken*, to cover.]

deckle [dek´l] *n* in paper-making a frame for fixing the width of a sheet.—*n* **deck´le-edge**, the rough edge of hand-made paper, or imitation of it. [Ger *deckel*, lid.]

declaim [di-klām´] *vti* to make a rhetorical speech; to recite.—*n* **declamation**, [de-kla-māsh´(ȯ)n], act of declaiming; a set speech.—*adj* **declăm´ătory**, appealing to the passions; noisy and rhetorical merely. [L *dēclāmāre*—*dē*, inten, *clāmāre*, to cry out.]

declare [di-klār´] *vt* to make known; to assert; to make a full statement of, as of goods at a custom-house.—*vi* (*law*) to make a statement; (*with* **for, against**) to announce one's decision or sympathies;—*adj* **declār´able** capable of being declared, or proved.—**declaration**, [dek-la-rā´sh(ȯ)n], act of declaring; that which is declared; a written affirmation.—*adj* **declared´**, avowed.—**declar´er** (*bridge*) the person playing the hand. **Declaration of Independence**, the public act on July 4, 1776 by which the American colonies were declared to be free and independent of England; the document affirming this. [Fr *déclarer*, from L *dēclārāre, -ātum*—pfx, *dē-*, *clārus*, clear.]

déclassé [dā-klä-sā] *adj* having lost caste or social standing. [Fr *déclasser*.]

declassify [dē-klas´i-fī] *vt* to take off the secret list. [*de-* + **classify**.]

declension [di-klen´sh(ȯ)n] *n* (*gram*) inflection of a noun and its modifiers to show case and number; the whole set of such reflected forms; a decline. [From L *dēclīnātiō, ōnis*, a bending aside—*dēclīnāre*; perh through Fr *déclinaison*. See **decline**.]

decline [di-klīn´] *vi* to deviate; to move down; to deteriorate; to fail; to draw to an end; to refuse.—*vt* to turn away from, to refuse; (*gram*) to give the various cases of a declension.—*n* a falling off; a down-slope; decay; a gradual sinking of the bodily faculties.—*n* **declinā´tion** act of declining; a sloping downward; (*astron*) angular distance from the celestial equator. [Fr *décliner*—L *dēclīnāre*—*dē*, down, away from, *clīnāre*, to bend.]

declivity [di-kliv´i-ti] *n* a place that slopes downward; a gradual descent.—*adj* **decliv´itous**. [Fr,—L *dēclīvitās*—*dē*, downward, *clīvus*, sloping, akin to *clīnāre*, to bend.]

decoct [di-kokt´] *vt* to prepare or extract by boiling.—*n* **decoc´tion**, an extract of anything got by boiling. [L *dēcoquĕre, dēcoctum*—*dē*, down, *coquĕre*, to cook.]

decode [dē-kōd´] *vt* to translate from a code. [**de-** + **code**.]

décolleté [dā-kol-tā] *adj* cut low at the neckline.

décolletage [dā-kol-tāj] *n* a low-cut dress or neckline. [Fr; ultimately from L *collum*, neck.]

decolorize [dē-kul´ȯr-īz] *vt* to deprive of color. [Fr *décolorer*—L *dē*, from, *color*, color.]

decompose [dē-kom-pōz´] *vt* to separate the component parts of; to resolve into elements.—*vi* to decay.—*adj* **decompos´able**.—*n* **decomposi´tion** act or state of decomposing; decay.—*vt* **decompound´**, to decompose. [Fr *décomposer*—pfx *dé*, apart, and *composer*. See **compose**.]

decompress [dē-kom-pres´] *vt* to decrease the pressure on, esp gradually.—*n* **decompression** (*presh´(ō)n*. [Pfx *de-*, and **compress**.]

decontaminate [dē-kon-tam´in-āt] *vt* to free from contamination.—*n* **decontaminā´tion**.—**decontamination squad**, a party equipped to cleanse from poison gas. [L pfx *dē*, and **contaminate**.]

decontrol [dē-kon-trōl´] *vt* to remove (esp) official control.—*n* removal of control. [Pfx **de-**, and **control**.]

décor [dā-kör] *n* scenery and stage embellishments; disposition of ornament; general decorative effect, eg of a room. [Fr].

decorate [dek´o-rāt] *vt* to ornament; to honour with a badge or medal.—*adj* **dec´orated**,—*n* **decorā´tion**, ornamènt; badge of an order.—*adj* **dec´orātive**, ornamental.—*n* **dec´orātor**, one who decorates, esp houses.—**decorated style** (*archit*), a style of Gothic architecture elaborated and richly decorated. [L *decorāre, -ātum*—*decus*, what is becoming—*decēre*, to be becoming.]

decorous [dek´o-rus] or [de-kō´rus] *adj* becoming, proper, decent; showing propriety and dignity.—*adv* **decō´rously** [or dek´o-rus-li].—*ns* **decō´rousness** [or dek´o-]; **decō´rum**, what is becoming in outward appearance, propriety of conduct, decency. [L *decōrus*, becoming.]

decorticate [dē-kör´ti-kāt] *vt* to deprive of the bark, husk, or peel.—*n* **decorticā´tion**. [L *decorticāre, -ātum*—*de*, from, and *cortex*, bark.]

decoy [di-koy´] *vt* to lure into a trap.—*n* anything intended to allure into a snare; a trap for wild ducks. [Perh Du *kooi*—L *cavea*, a cage.]

decrease [di-krēs´] *vi* to become less.—*vt* to make less.—*n* (*dē´krēs*) a growing less; the amount of diminution.—*adj* **decreas´ingly**, [L *dēcrescĕre*—*dē*, from, *crescĕre*, to grow.]

decree [di-krē´] *n* an order, edict or law; a judicial decision; a predetermined purpose (of God).—*vt* to decide by sentence in law; to appoint.—*vi* to make a decree;—*pr p* decree´ing; *pt p* decreed´.—*adj* **decrē´tive**, having the force of a decree.—**decree nisi** [nī´sī]—L *nisi*, unless), a decree that becomes absolute unless cause be shown to the contrary—granted esp in divorce cases. [L *dēcrētum*—*dēcernĕre*, to decide.]

decrement [dek´re-mėnt] *n* the act or state of decreasing; the quantity lost by decrease. [L *dēcrēmentum*.]

decrepit [di-krep´it] *adj* worn out by the infirmities of old age; in the last stage of decay.—*ns* **decrep´itness, decrep´itude**. [L *dēcrepitus*, noiseless, very old—*crepitus*, a noise.]

decrepitate [di-krep´i-tāt] *vi* to crackle, as salts when heated.—*n* **decrepitā´tion**. [L *dē-*, inten, *crepitāre*, to rattle much.]

decrescent [di-kres´ėnt] *adj* becoming gradually less.—*n* (*mus*) **decresen´do** (*dā-kre-shen´-dō*), diminuendo (qv). [L pfx *dē-*, and *crescĕre*, to increase.]

decretal [di-kre+´tal] *n* a decree, esp of the Pope; a book containing decrees. [L *dēcrētālis*—*dēcrētum*; see **decree**.]

decry [di-krī´] *vt* to cry down, to censure as worthless;—*pt p* decried´.—ns **decrī´al, decrī´er**. [Fr *dé-*, *des-* (L *dis*), and *crier*, to cry. See **cry**.]

decuman [dek´ū-man] *n* a great wave, as every tenth wave was supposed to be. [L *decumānus*—*decem*, ten.]

decumbent [di-kum´bėnt] *adj* reclining on the ground. [L *dēcumbens*—*dē*, down, *cumbĕre* for *cubāre*, to lie.]

decussate [di-kus´āt] *vt* to divide in the form of an X.—*vi* to cross in such a form. Also *adj* [From L *decussis*, a Roman coin of ten asses (*decem asses*) marked with X, ie 10.]

dedicate [ded´i-kāt] *vt* to consecrate (to some sacred purpose); to devote wholly or chiefly; to inscribe (to someone).—*ns* **dedicā´tion**, the act of dedicating; an address to a patron; or a similar inscription, prefixed to a book; **ded´icātor**.—*adj* **ded´icātory**. [L *dēdicāre, -atum*—*dē*, down, *dicāre*, to declare.]

deduce [di-dūs´] *vt* to derive; to infer from what precedes or from premises.—*adj* **deduc´ible** [-dūs´-].—*vt* **deduct´**, to take (from); to subtract.—*adj* **deduct´ible**.—*n* **deduc´tion**, (1) the act of deducing; that which is deduced; the drawing of a particular truth from a general, as distinguished from *induction*, rising from particular truths to a general; (2) the act of deducting; that which is deducted, abatement.—*adj* **deduct´ive**, concerned with deduction from premises.—*adv* **deduct´ively**. [L *dēdūcĕre, dēductum*—*dē*, from, *dūcĕre*, to lead.]

deed [dēd] *n* an act; an exploit; a legal document recording a transaction.—*n* **deed´-pōll** (*see* **poll**, head). [OE *dǣd*—*dōn*, to do.]

deem [dēm] *vt* or *vi* to judge; to think, to believe.—*ns* **deem´ster, demp´ster**, a judge, esp in the Isle of Man. [OE *dēman*, to form a judgment—*dōm*, judgment.]

deep [dēp] *adj* extending or placed far down or far from the outside; far involved (in eg difficulties); engrossed (in, eg study); profound, intense (eg learning, sleep, distress, sin), heartfelt (eg thankfulness), penetrating (eg understanding); difficult to understand; secret; cunning; sunk low; low in pitch; (of a color) of high saturation and low brilliance; (*cricket*) in the outfield, not close to the wicket.—*adv* in a deep manner; far in, into (eg *deep in the forest, in the night*).—*n* that which is deep; the sea.—*adj* **deep´-eyed**, thorough-going, extreme—in a bad sense.—*vt* **deep´en**, to make deeper in any sense; to increase.—*vi* to become deeper.—*n* **deep´-freeze´**, storage of foodstuffs, or other perishable substances, at very low temperature; the container in which the material is stored—Also *vt*—*adv* **deep´ly**.—*n* **deep´ness**.—*adj* **deep´seat´ed** (*fig*, firmly rooted.—**deep litter**, a method of keeping hens with a peat material on the floor of the hen-house; **Deep South**, the region of the South-east United States, esp with reference to its clinging to the ways of the past; **in deep water**, in difficulties; **go off the deep end**, to express strong feelings freely; **two deep, three deep**, etc. in two, three layers or rows. [OE *dēop*.]

deer [dēr] *n* any animal of the *Cervidae*, a family characterised by the possession of antlers, by the males at least, including stag, reindeer, etc.;—*pl* **deer**.—*ns* **deer´-for´est**, wild tract (not necessarily woodland) reserved for deer; **deer´-stalk´er**, one who stalks deer; a sportsman's cap peaked at back and front. [OE *dēor*.]

de-escalate [de-es´ka-lāt] *vt* to reverse or slow down escalation—*n* **de-escalation**.

deface [di-fās´,] *vt* to disfigure; to obliterate.—*n* **deface´ment**. [OFr *desfacer*—L *dis-*, away, *faciēs*, face.]

de facto [dē fak´tō] *adv* and *adj* in fact (eg the *ruler de facto of the country*); actual, real (eg *the de facto ruler*). See **de jure**. [L]

defaecate *see* **defecate**.

defalcate [dē´-] or [de´fal-kāt] or [di-fal´kāt] *vi* to embezzle.—*ns* **defalcā´tion, def´alcātor**. [Low L *dēfalcāre, -ātum*, to cut away—L *dis-*, away, *falx, falcis*, a sickle.]

defame [di-fām´] *vt* to destroy the good reputation of; to speak evil of.—*n* **defamā´tion**, slander.—*adv* **defam´atorily**.—*adj* **defam´atory**, injurious to reputation. [OFr,—L *diffāmāre*—*dis*, away, *fāma*, report.]

default [di-fölt´] *n* a fault or failure; neglect to do what duty or law requires; failure to fulfil a financial obligation.—*vi* to fail in one's duty (as honoring a financial obligation, or appearing in court).—*n* **default´er**, one who defaults.—**in default of**, in the absence of; for lack of; **judgment by default**, judgment given against a person because he fails to plead. [OFr,—L *pfx dē-*, and *fallěre*. See **fault**.]

defeasible [di-fēz´ibl] *adj* that may be defeated or annulled. [From OFr *defaire*, to undo.]

defeat [di-fēt´] *vt* to frustrate; to win a victory over.—*n* a frustration of plans; overthrow, as of an army in battle; loss of a game, race, etc.—*ns* **defeat´ism**, disposition to accept defeat; **defeat´ist**—also *adj* [OFr *defeit, de(s)-fait, pa p of desfaire*, to undo—L *dis-*, neg *facěre*, to do.]

defecate [def´e-kāt, dēf´-] *vt* to clear from impurities or extraneous matter (also *fig*).—*vi* to void excrement.—*n* **defecā´tion**. [L *dēfaecāre, -ātum*, to cleanse—*dē*, from, *faex, faecis*, dregs.]

defect [di-fekt, dē´fekt] *n* a deficiency; a blemish, fault.—*vi* (*di-fekt´*), to desert one's country or a cause, transferring one's allegiance (to another).—*ns* **defec´tion**, failure; a falling away from duty or allegiance; **defec´tionist**.—*adj* **defec´tive**, having a defect; faulty; incomplete; (*gram*) not having all the inflections.—*n* a person defective in physical or mental powers.—*adv* **defect´ively**.—*ns* **defect´iveness; defect´or**.—**the defects of one's qualities**, virtues carried to excess, the faults apt to accompany or flow from good qualities, [L *dēficěre, dēfectum*, to fail—*dē*, down, and *facěre*, to do.]

defence [di-fens´] *n* a defending; capability or means of resisting an attack; protection; vindication; (*law*) a defendant's plea; the defending party in legal proceedings.—*pa p* **defenc´ed** (*B*), fortified.—*adj* **defence´less**.—*adv* **defence´lessly**.—*n* **defence´lessness**. [**OFr** *defense*(*e*)—L *dēfenděre*. See **defend**.]

defend [di-fend´] *vt* (*arch*) to prohibit; to guard or protect; to maintain against attack (*law*) to resist, as a claim; to contest (a suit).—*adj* **defend´able**, that may be defended.—*ns* **defend´ant**, a defender; (*law*) a person accused or sued; **defnd´er; defense**, American spelling of **defence**.—*adj* **defens´ible**, that may be defended.—*n* **defnsibil´ity**.—*adj* **defens´ive**, serving to defend; in a state or posture of defence.—*n* that which defends; posture of defence.—*adv* **defens´ively**.—**Defender of the Faith**, a title borne by the sovereigns of England since Henry VIII, on whom it was conferred by the Pope. [L *dēfenděre, dēfensum*, to ward off—*dē*, off, and *fenděre*, to strike (found in compounds).]

defer [di-fûr] I*vt* to put off to another time; to delay;—*pr p* deferr´ing; *pa p* deferred´.—*n* **defer´ment**.—**deferred annuity**, an annuity, payment of which does not begin till after a certain number of years; **deferred payment**, payment by instalments; **deferred shares**, shares not entitling the holder to a full share of profits, and sometimes to none at all, until the expiration of a specified time or the occurrence of some event. [L *differre*—*dis-*, asunder, *ferre*, to bear, carry.]

defer [di-fûrl] *vi* to yield (to wishes or opinions of another, or to authority);—*pr p* deferr´ing; *pa p* deferred´.—*n* **deference** (def´-ėr-ėns), a deferring or yielding in judgment or opinion; respectful or courteous willingness to defer.—*adj* **deferen´tial**, expressing deference or respect.—*adv* **deferen´tially**. [L *dēferre*—*dē*, down, and *ferre*, to bear.]

defiance [di-fi´ȧns] *n* the act of defying; a challenge to combat; contempt of opposition.—*adj* **defi´ant**, full of defiance, insolently bold.—*adv* **def´antly**. [OFr,—*defier; see* **defy**.]

deficient [di-fish´ėnt] *adj* wanting, lacking.—*ns* **defic´iency**, defect; lack; **def´icit**, deficiency, esp of revenue, as compared with expenditure.—**deficiency disease**, one due to the lack of an essential element (as a vitamin or vitamins) in the diet—eg rickets, scurvy. [L *dēficěre*; see **defect**.]

defile [di-fīl´] *vi* to march off in file or line, or file by file.—*n* (*dē´fīl*), *di-fīl´* a long narrow pass or way, in which troops can march only in file or with a narrow front.—*n* **defile´ment**. [Fr *défiler*—L *dis-*, and *filum*, a thread.]

defile [di-fīl´] *vt* (*lit* and *fig*) to pollute or corrupt; (*arch*) to ravish.—*ns* **defile´ment**, act of defiling; foulness; **defil´er**. [L *dē*, and OE *fȳlan*—*fūl*, foul; confused with OFr *defouler*, to trample, violate.]

define [di-fīn´] *vt* to fix the bounds or limits of; to mark the limits or outline of clearly; to describe accurately; to fix the meaning of.—*adjs* **defin´able**, that may be defined; **def´inite**, defined; having distinct limits; fixed; exact; clear—*adv* **def´initely**.—*ns* **def´initeness; defini´tion**, a defining; a description of a thing by its properties; an explanation of the exact meaning of a word, term, or phrase; sharpness of outline.—*adj* **defin´itive**, defining or limiting; decisive, final—*n* (*gram*) an adjective used to limit the signification of a noun.—*adv* **defin´itively**. [Fr,—L *dēfinīre, -ītum*, to set bounds to—*dē*, and *finis*, a limit.]

deflagrate [def´la-grāt, or dē´-] *vt* to burn suddenly, generally with flame and crackling noise.—*n* **deflagrā´tion**. [L *dēflagrāre*—*dē*, down, *flagrāre*, to burn.]

deflate [dē-flāt´] *vt* to undo or reverse the process of inflation.—*n* **deflā´tion**. [L *dē*, down, *flāre, flātum*, to blow.]

deflect [di-flekt´] *vti* to turn aside; to swerve or deviate from a right line or proper course.—**deflec´tion**, deviation; **deflec´tor**, a device for deflecting a flame, electric arc, etc. [L *dē*, from, and *flectěre, flexum*, to bend, turn.]

deflower [di-flow´(ė)r] *vt* to deprive of virginity.—*n* **defloration**. [OFr *deflorer*—Low L *dēflōrāre*, to strip flowers off—L *dē*, from, *flōs, flōris*, a flower.]

defoliation [di-fo-li-ā´sh(ȯ)n] *n* the falling off of leaves; the time of shedding leaves. [Low L *dēfoliāre, -ātum*—*dē*, off, *folium*, a leaf.]

deforce [di-fōrs´, -förs´] *vt* to keep out of possession by force.—*n* **deforce´ment**. (Anglo-Fr *deforcer*—*de-* (L *dis-*). [See **force**.]

deforest [dē-for´est] *vt* to clear of forests.—*n* **deforestā´tion**. [OFr *desforester*—*des-* (L *dis-*). See **forest**.]

deform [di-förm´] *vt* to spoil the natural form of; to put out of shape.—**deformā´tion**, the result of deforming; the act of deforming; **deform´ity**, a deformed part of the body, depravity. [L *dēformis*, ugly—*dē*, from, *forma*, beauty.]

defraud [di-fröd´] *vt* to deprive by cheating or deceiving. [L *dēfraudāre*—*dē*, from, *fraus, fraudis*, fraud.]

defray [di-frā´] *vt* to pay (the expenses of),—*pr p* **defray´ing**; *pt p* **defrayed´; defrayment, defray´al**. [OFr *desfrayer*—*des-* (L *dis-*), *frais*, expenses.]

defrost [dē-frost´] *vt* to thaw out; to remove frost or ice from;—also *vi*. [**de-** +**frost**.]

deft [deft] *adj* adroit, skilful, quick and neat in action.—*adv* **deft´ly**.—*n* **deft´ness**. (ME *defte, dafte*, simple, meek; OE *gedæfte*, meek—*dæftan, gedæftan*, prepare, make fit.]

defunct [di-fungkt´] *adj* no longer being in existence or functioning or in use. [L *dēfungī, dēfunctus*, to finish—*dē, fungī*, to perform.]

defuse [de´fūz´] *vt* to remove the fuse from (a bomb or mine); to intervene in a tense situation. [**de-** + **fuse**.]

defy [di-fī´] *vt* to challenge; to brave, to flout, or to resist (eg convention, order, person);—*pr p* **defy´ing**; *pt p* **defied´**. [OFr *defier*—Low L *diffidāre*, renounce allegiance.]

degauss [dē-gows´] *vt* to demagnetize. [**de-** + **gauss**, unit of intensity of magnetic field—KF *Gauss*, physicist.]

degenerate [di-jen´ėr-ȧt] *adj* having declined in physical or moral qualities; sexually deviant.—Also *n*—*vi* become or grow worse; (*biol*) to return to a simpler state.—**degen´eracy, degenerā´tion**, the act or process of becoming degenerate; the state of being degenerate.—*adv* **degen´erately**.—*n* **degen´erateness**.—*adj* **degen´erative**, tending or causing to degenerate. [L *dēgenerāre, -ātum*, to depart from its kind—*dē*, from *genus, generis*, kind.]

degrade [di-grād´] *vt* to lower in grade or rank; to deprive of office or dignity; to debase; to disgrace.—*n* **degradation** [deg-ra-dā´sh(ȯ)n], disgrace; abasement; degeneration. [Fr *dégrader*—L *dē*, down, and *gradus*, a step.]

degree [di-grē´] *n* a step in an ascending or descending series; a stage in intensity; the relative quantity in intensity; a unit of measurement in a scale; an academic title awarded as of right or as an honor; the classification of a crime; a point on the earth's surface as measured by degrees latitude or longitude; (*algebra*) an equation defined by the sum of its exponents; (*geom*) the 360th part of the circumference of a circle; (*mus*) a step of the diatonic scale; (*gram*) one of three grades in the comparison of adjectives or adverbs.—**by degrees**, gradually;—**degree Celsius** *see* **Celsius**;—**third degree** *see* **third**. [Fr *degré*—L *dē*, down, *gradus*, a step.]

dehisce [dē-his´] *vi* to gape, to burst open as the fruits of some plants.—*n* **dehis´cence**.—*adj* **dehis´cent**. [L *dehiscēns* pr p of *dehiscĕre*—*dē*, inten, *hiscĕre*, to gape.]

dehumanize [dē-hū´man-īz] *vt* to deprive of human qualities, to brutalize. [**de-** + **humanize**.]

dehumidify [dē-hūmid´ifī] *vt* to remove moisture from air—*n* **dehumid´ifier**, an electrical appliance for removing moisture from the air. [**de** + **humidify**.]

dehydrate [dē-hī-drāt´] *vt* to deprive of water chemically; to dry (foodstuffs); (*fig*) to deprive of strength, interest, etc.—*n* **dehydrā´tion**, loss of moisture; (*med*) excessive loss of water from the tissues of the body. [L *dē*, from, Gr *hydōr*, water.]

dē-ice [de-īs] *vt* to prevent the formation of or to remove ice from a surface. [**de-** + **ice**]

deicide [dē´i-sīd] *n* the killing of a god; the putting to death of Jesus Christ. [From a supposed Low L form *deicidium*—*deus*, a god, and *caedĕre*, to kill.]

deify [dē´i-fī] *vt* to exalt to the rank of a god; to worship as a deity;—*pr p* **dē´ifying**; *pt p* **dē´ified**.—*n* **deificā´tion**, the act of deifying. [Fr *déifier*—L *deificāre*—*deus*, a god, and *facĕre*, to make.]

deign [dān] *vi* to condescend.—*vt* to condescend to give. [Fr *daigner*—L *dignārī*, to think worthy—*dignus*, worthy.]

deist [dē´ist] *n* one who believes in the existence of God, but not in revealed religion.—*n* **dē´ism**, the creed of a deist.—*adjs* **deist´ic, -al**. [Fr *déiste*, *déisme*—L *deus*, a god.]

deity [dē´i-ti] *n* divinity; godhead; a god or goddess; **Deity**, the Supreme Being. [Fr,—Low L *deitās*—L *deus*, god.]

déjà vu [dā-zhä vü] *n* an illusion of having experienced something that is really being experienced for the first time. [Fr, already seen.]

deject [di-jekt´] *vt* to cast down the spirits of.—*adj* **deject´ed**, cast down, disheartened.—*adv* **deject´edly**.—**deject´edness; dejec´tion**, lowness of spirits. [L *dējicĕre*, *-jectum*—*dē*, down, *jacĕre*, to cast.]

de jure [dē jōō´rē] *adv, adj* by right and by a lawful title; rightful, lawful. [L]

deka- *see* **deca-**.

Delaware [del´-awār] *n* a member of an Indian tribe originally of the Delaware valley; the Algonquian language of this tribe; a dry white table wine; the grape used to make this wine. [the place-name.]

delay [di-lā´] *vt* to put off to another time, to postpone; to hinder, retard.—*vi* to pause, linger, or put off time;—*pr p* **delay´ing**; *pt p* **delayed´**.—*n* the act of delaying; an instance of being delayed. [OFr *delaier*.]

delectable [di-lekt´a-bl] *adj* delightful, pleasing.—*n*. **delect´ableness**.—*adv*. **delect´ably**.—*n* **delectā´tion**, delight. [Fr,—L *dēlectābilis*—*dēlectāre*, to delight.]

delegate [del´e-gāt] *vt* to send as a representative; to entrust power, task or responsibility to (an agent or assembly).—*n* [-gȧt] a deputy or an elected representative.—*adj*. delegated, deputed.—*n* **delegā´tion**, a delegating; a body of delegates. [L. *dē*, away, and *lēgāre*, *-ātum*, to send as ambassador.]

delete [di-lēt´] *vt* to blot out, to erase.—*n* **delē´tion**. [L *dēlēre*, *dēlētum*, to blot out.]

deleterious [del-e-tē´ri-us] *adj* hurtful or destructive.—*adv* **deletē´riously**.—*n* **deletē´riousness**. [Gr *dēlētērios*, hurtful—*dēleesthai*, to hurt.]

delft [delf(t)] *n*, a kind of tin-glazed earthenware originally made at *Delft*, Holland.

deliberate [di-lib´ėr-āt] *vt* to weigh in the mind.—*vi* to discuss or debate thoroughly; to consider.—*adj* [-ȧt] well considered; intentional; considering carefully; cautious; quiet, unflurried.—*adv* **delib´erately**.—**delib´erateness; deliberā´tion**, the act of deliberating; mature reflection; calmness, coolness.—*adj* **delib´erative**, proceeding or acting by deliberation. [L *dēlīberāre*, *-ātum*—*dē-*, inten, *lībrāre*, to weigh—*lībra*, a balance.]

delicate [del´i-kȧt] *adj* fine in texture; fragile, not robust; requiring tactful handling; of exquisite workmanship; requiring skill in techniques.—*n* **del´icacy**, a luxurious food; sensibility or behaviour.—*adv* **del´icately**, in a delicate manner;—*n* **del´icateness**. [L *dēlicātus*—*dēliciae*, allurements, luxury—*dēlicĕre*—*dē-*, inten, and earlier *lacĕre*, to entice.]

delicatessen [del-i-kȧ-tes´n] *n* a store selling prepared foods, esp meat. Also **deli**. [Ger pl of Fr *délicatesse*, delicacy.]

delicious [di-lish´us] *adj* highly pleasing to the senses, esp taste; giving exquisite pleasure.—*adv* **deli´ciously**, delightfully;—*n* **deli´ciousness**. [L *dēliciōsus*—*dēliciae*. *See* **delicate**.]

delight [di-līt´] *vt* to please highly.—*vi* to have or take great pleasure.—*n* a high degree of pleasure; that which gives great pleasure.—*adjs* **delight´ful, delight´some**, affording delight.—*adv* **delight´fully**.—*n* **delight´fulness**. [OFr *deliter*—L *dēlectāre*, inten of *dēlicĕre*; spelling influenced by confusion with *light*.]

delimit [di-lim´it] *vt* to fix or mark the limit of.—*n* **delimitā´tion**. [L *dēlīmitāre*—*dē-*, inten, and *līmitāre*. *See* **limit**.]

delineate [di-lin´e-āt] *vt* to describe accurately in pictures or words.—*ns* **delineā´tion**, the act of delineating; a sketch, representation, or description; **delin´eator**. [L *dēlīneāre*, *-ātum*—*dē*, down, and *līnea*, a line.]

delinquent [di-ling´kwėnt] *adj* failing in duty; guilty of an offense; (of a bill) overdue.—*n* a person guilty of misdeed, esp young person who breaks the law.—*n* **delin´quency**, failure in or omission of duty; a fault; a crime.—*adv* **delin´quently**. [L *dēlinquens*, *-entis*, pr p of *dēlinquĕre*—*dē-*, inten, *linquĕre*, to leave.]

delirious [di-lir´i-us] *adj* wandering in mind, light-headed; wildly excited.—*adv* **delir´iously**.—*ns* **delir´iousness; delir´ium**, state of being delirious; strong excitement; wild enthusiasm.—**delirium trēmens**, a disorder of the brain produced by excessive drinking. *Also* **DTs**. [L *dēlīrus*, crazy—*dēlīrāre*, lit to turn aside—*dē*, from *līra*, a furrow; *tremens*, the pr p of *tremĕre*, to tremble.]

deliver [de-liv´ėr] *vt* to transport (goods) to their destination; to distribute regularly; to liberate, to rescue; to give birth; to assist at a birth; to launch (a blow); to pitch (a baseball); to utter (a speech).—*adj* **deliv´erable**.—**deliv´erance**, act of delivering or freeing; **deliv´erer; deliv´ery**, the act of delivering; anything delivered or communicated; a giving up; the manner of delivering anything; the act of giving birth. [Fr *déliver*—L *dē*, from, *liberāre*, to set free—*līber*, free.]

dell [del] *n* a little hollow, usu. with trees. [Same root as **dale**.]

Delphic utterance [del´fik] a statement open to more than one interpretation. [From the oracle at the shrine of Apollo in Delphi, Greece.]

delphinium [del-fin´i-um] *n* any of a genus (*Delphinium*) of hardy annual or perennial flowering plants of the Crowfoot family. Also **larkspur**. [*Gr delphinion*, larkspur.]

delta [del´ta] *n* the fourth letter of the Greek alphabet, the capital form of which is Δ a tract of land of like shape formed at the mouth of a river; word used in communication for the letter *d*.—*adj* **del´toid**, of the form of the Greek Δ, triangular. **deltoid** or **deltoid muscle**, triangular muscle covering front, side and rear portions of shoulder joint.—**del´ta-wing** (**airplane**), a jet airplane with triangular wings. [Gr,—Heb *daleth*, a tent-door.]

delude [di-l(y)ōōd´] *vt* to deceive. [L *dēlūdĕre*, to play false—*dē*, down, *lūdĕre*, *lūsum*, to play.]

deluge [del´ūj] *n* a flood, esp that in the days of Noah; (*fig*) anything happening in a heavy rush.—*vt* to inundate (*lit, fig*). [Fr,—L *dīluvium*—*dīluĕre*—*dis-*, away, *luĕre*, to wash.]

delusion [di-l(y)ōō´zh(ȯ)n] *n* a false belief; a persistent false belief that is a symptom of mental illness.—*adjs* **delu´sive, delu´sory**, apt or tending to delude, deceptive.—*adv* **delu´sively**.—*n* **delu´siveness**. [L. *dēlūsiō*, *-ōnis*—*dēlūdĕre; see* **delude**.]

de luxe [dė lüks´, di lōōks´, luks´] adj sumptuous, luxurious. [Fr]

delve [delv] *vti* to search deeply; (*literary*) to dig.—*n* **delv´er**. [OE *delfan*, to dig.]

demagnetize [dē-mag´net-īz] *vt* to remove magnetic power from.—*n* **demagnetizā´tion**. [Pfx de-, and **magnetize**.]

demagogue [dem´a-gog] *n* a political orator who appeals to the passions and prejudices of the people.—*adjs* **demagogic, -al** [-gog´- or -goj´-].—*n* **demagogy** [-goj´-]. [Fr,—Gr *dēmagōgos*—*dēmos*, people, *agōgos*, leading—*agein*, to lead.]

demand [di-mänd´] *vt* to ask for in an imperious manner.—*n* the asking for what is due; an asking for with authority; an urgent claim; desire shown by consumers.—*n* **demand´ant**; a plaintiff—**in demand**, sought after; **demand deposit**, bank deposit that may be withdrawn without notice; **demand note**, a note payable upon presentation; **supply and demand** *see* **supply**. [Fr *demander*—Low L *dēmandāre*—L *dē-*, inten, and *mandāre*, to put into one's charge.]

demarcation [dē-märk-ā´sh(ȯ)n] *n* the act of marking off or setting bounds to;—*vt* **dē´marcate**, to mark off or limit. [Sp *demarcación*—*de*, from, *marcar*, to mark.]

demean[1] [di-mēn´] *vt* to behave.—*n* **demeanor**, conduct; bearing. [OFr *demener*—*de-* inten, *mener*, to lead—Low L *mināre*, to drive cattle—L *minārī*, to threaten.]

demean[2] [di-mēn´] *vt* to lower in dignity. [Prob on the analogy of *debase*, from **de-**, + **mean**[1].]

dement [di-ment´] *vt* to deprive of reason.— *adj* **dement´ed**, out of one's mind; insane.—*n* **dementia** [de-men´shi-a], the failure or loss of mental powers.—*n* **dementia praecox** [pre´kaks] schizophrenia. [L *dēmēns*, *dēmentis*, out of one's mind—*dē*, from, and *mēns*, the mind.]

demerara [dem-ė-rā´ra] *n* (*Brit*) brown sugar in large crystals. [*Demerara* (-rä´-) in Guyana.]

demerit [dē-mer´it] *n* a defect, a fault. [L *dēmerērī*, *dēmeritum*, to deserve fully, later understood as 'to deserve ill'—*dē-*, fully, *merērī*, to deserve.]

Demerol [dem´erol] *n* trade name for meperidine.

demesne [di-mān´, -mēn´] *n* a mansion, with lands adjacent to it not let out to tenants; any estate in land. [form of **domain**.]

demi- [dem´i] half. [Fr; *see* **demy**.]

demigod [dem´i-god] *n* the offspring of a god and a mortal; a person who seems to possess godlike powers. [Fr *demi*, half + **god**.]

demi-john [dem´i-jon] *n* a glass bottle with a full body and narrow neck holding from one to ten gallons. [Fr *damejeanne*, Dame Jane.]

demilitarize [dē-mil´itārīz] *vt* to remove armed forces, installations, etc. from; to replace military with civilian government.—*n* **demilitariza´tion**.—**demilitarized zone**, an area required by treaty to have no military installations or forces in it.

demimonde [dem´i-mond] *n* a class of women of dubious reputation.—*n* **demimondaine** [-ān] a woman of the demimonde; a courtesan. [Fr *demi*, half, *monde*, world.]

demise [di-mīz´] *n* death, esp of a distinguished person.—*vt* to bequeath to a successor. [OFr *demise*, pt p of *desmettre*, to lay down—L *dis-*, aside, *mittĕre, missum*, to send.]

demission [di-mish´(ȯ)n] *n* relinquishment (of). [Same root as **demise**.]

demobilize [dē- or di-mōb´il-īz, or -mob´-] *vt* to take out of mobilization, to disband; (*inf*) to discharge from the armed forces.—*n* **demobilizā´tion**. [**de-** + **mobilize**.]

democracy [di-mok´ra-si] *n* a form of government in which the supreme power is retained by the people collectively and exercised directly or indirectly through their representatives; a state or society characterized by recognition of equality of rights and privileges; political, social or legal equality;—*n* **dem´ocrat**, one free from snobbery; one who adheres to or promotes democracy as a principle; a member of the Democratic party.—*adjs* **democrat´ic**, relating to democracy;—*adv* **democrat´ically**.—*vt* **democratize´**, to render democratic. [Fr *démocratie*—Gr *dēmokratiā*—*dēmos*, the people, and *krateein*, to rule—*kratos*, strength.]

demoded [dē-mōd´id] *adj* no longer in fashion. [**de-** + **mode**.]

demography [di-mog´ra-fi] *n* the study of population statistics concerning birth, marriage, death and disease. [From Gr *dēmos*, people, *graphein*, to write.]

demolish [di-mol´ish] *vt* to pull down or knock down (a building); to destroy (an argument); (*inf*) to eat up.—*n* **demoli´tion** [dem-]. [Fr *démolir*—L *dēmōlīrī*, to throw down—*dē*, down, and *mōlīrī*, to build—*mōles*, a heap.]

demon [dē´mon] *n* an evil spirit, a devil; an energetic and skillful person.—*adjs* **demoniac** [di-mōn´i-ak], **demoniacal** [dē-mo-nī´a-kl], of or like demons or evil spirits; influenced by demons.—*n* **demon´iac**, one possessed by a demon or evil spirit.—*adv* **demonī´acally**.—**demonology**, the study of demons; belief in demons; a catalog of enemies. [L *daemon*—Gr *daimōn*, a spirit, genius; in NT and Late Greek, a devil.]

demonetize [dē-mon´i-tīz] *vt* to remove the money value from (coins etc.). [Fr *démonétiser*—L. *monēta*. See **money**.]

demonstrate [de´mon-strāt or di-mon´strāt] *vt* to show or point out clearly; to prove with certainty.—*vi* to exhibit one's feelings.—*adj* **demon´strable** [or dem´-], which may be demonstrated.—*n* **demon´strability**.—*adv* **demon´strably** (or *dem´-*).—*n* **demonstrā´tion**, a pointing out; proof by evidence; a practical display or exhibition; a display of emotion; a public manifestation of opinion, as by a rally or parade etc. (*Also* **demo**); a display of armed force.—*adj* **demon´strative**, showing one's feelings; making evident; proving with certainty; of the nature of proof; (*gram*) indicating the thing referred to.—*adv* **demon´stratively**.—**demon´strativeness; dem´onstrator**, one who demonstrates products, equipment, etc., esp to potential buyers; one who takes part in a public manifestation of opinion. [L *dēmonstrāre, -ātum*—*dē*, inten, *monstrāre*, to show.]

demoralize [dē-mor´al-īz] *vt* to corrupt in morals; to lower the *morale* of—that is, to deprive of spirit and confidence or to throw into confusion.—*n* **demoralizā´tion**. [Fr *démoraliser*—*dé-* (L *dis-*), *un-*, *moraliser*.]

demotic [dē-mät´ik] *adj* of ordinary people; of a simplified form of Egyptian hieroglyphics—*n* **demotic** demotic language. [Gr. *demos*, people.]

demote [dē-mōt´] *vt* to reduce in rank. [on the analogy of **promote**—L *dē*, down.]

demulcent [di-mul´sėnt] *adj* soothing. [L *dē-mulcēns, -entis*—*dē*, down, *mulcēre*, to stroke, to soothe.]

demur [di-mûr´] *vi* to raise objections—*pr p* **demurr´ing**; *pt p* **demurred´**.—*n* a hesitation; an objection.—**demurr´age**, the charge for undue delay in unloading a ship, truck, or freight car; **demurr´er**, one who demurs. [Fr *demeurer*—L *dēmorārī*, to loiter, linger—*dē-*, inten, and *morārī*, to delay—*mora*, delay.]

demure [di-mūr´] *adj* sober, staid, modest; affectedly modest; making a show of gravity.—*adv* **demure´ly**.—*n* **demure´ness**. [OFr *meur* (Fr *mûr*)—L *maturus*, ripe; prefix unexplained.]

demy [di-mī´] *n* a size of paper 16 by 21 in; a holder of certain scholarships in Magdalen College, Oxford;—*pl* **demies´**.—*n* **demy´ship**. [Fr *demi*—L *dimidium*, half—*di-*, apart, *medius*, the middle.]

den [den] *n* a cave or lair of a wild beast; a place where people gather for illegal activities, esp gambling or smoking opium; a room in a house for relaxation or study; a group of Boy Scout cubs forming a unit.—**den dad, den mother**, the adult serving as leader of a cub scout den. [OE *denn*, a cave, akin to *denu*, a valley.]

denationalize [dē-nash´on-ȧl-īz] *vt* to transfer from government to private ownership. [**de-** + **nationalize**.]

denaturalize [dē-nat´ūr-ȧl-īz] *vt* to make unnatural; to deprive of citizenship. [**de-** + **naturalize**.]

denature [dē-nā´tyůr, -chůr] *vt* to render (alcohol, etc.) unfit for consumption.—*n* **denā´turant**, a substance used for this purpose. [**de-** + **nature**.]

denazify [dē-not´sifī] *vt* to obliterate Nazi influence from. [**dē** + **Nazi**]

dendroid [den´droid] *adj* having the form of a tree. [Gr. *dendron*, a tree, and *eidos*, form.]

dendrology [den-drol´o-ji] *n* the natural history of trees. [Gr *dendron*, a tree, and *logos*, a discourse.]

dengue [deng´gē, -gā] *n* disease of tropical and subtropical regions transmitted by the mosquito. Also **breakbone fever**.

denial [di-nī´al] *n* act of denying or saying no; contradiction; refusal (of request, claim, etc.); disavowal, rejection.—*adj* **denī´able**, that may be denied. [**deny**.]

denier [den´i-ėr] a gauge of yarn for hosiery and panty hose. [Fr—L *dēnārius*, a Roman silver coin.]

denigrate [den´i-grāt] *vt* to sully the character of; to belittle.—*n* **denigrā´tion**. [L *dē-*, inten, *nigrāre*, to blacken—*niger*, black.]

denim [den´im] *n* a durable twilled cotton cloth; used for jeans, overalls, etc. [Fr *de*, of, *Nîmes*, a town in France.]

denizen [den´i-zn] *n* an inhabitant, esp any animal or plant indigenous to a different region. [OFr *deinzein*—*deinz, dens* (Fr *dans*), within—L *dē intus*, from within.]

denominate [di-nom´in-āt] *vt* to name; to designate.—*n* **denominā´tion**, the act of naming; a name or title; a religious group comprising many local churches, larger than a sect; one of a series of related units, esp monetary.—*adj* **denomina´tional**, belonging to a denomination.—*n* **denominā´tionalism**, devotion to the interests of a denomination; a policy governed by such devotion.—*adj* **denom´inative**, giving or having a name.—*adv* **denom´inatively**.—*n* **denom´inator**, (*arith*) the part of a fractional expression written below the fraction line. [L *dē-*, inten, *nōmināre*, to name—*nōmen*, a name.]

denote [di-nōt´] *vt* to note, mark; to indicate, be the sign of; to mean; (*logic*) to name.—*n* **denotā´-tion**. [Fr,—L *dēnotāre, -ātum*—*dē-*, inten, and *notāre*, to mark—*nota*, a mark or sign.]

dénouement [dā-nōō´mā] *n* the unraveling of a plot or story; the issue, event, or outcome. [Fr *dénouement* or *dénoûment; dénouer*, to untie—L *dis-*, apart, *nodāre*, to tie—*nodus*, a knot.]

denounce [di-nowns´] *vt* to inform against publicly; to give information against; to notify formally the ending of (treaties, etc.).—*n* **denounce´ment** (same as **denunciation**). [Fr *dénoncer*—L *dēnuntiāre*—*dē-*, inten, *nuntiāre*, to announce.]

dense [dens] *adj* difficult to see through; massed closely together; dull-witted.—*adv* **dense´ly.**—**dense´ness; dens´ity**, the quality of being dense; the ratio of mass to volume.—*n* **densitometer** [-tom´eter] instrument for measuring density. [L *densus*, thick.]

dent [dent] *n* a small hollow made by the pressure or blow of a harder body on a softer.—*vt* to make a mark by means of a blow. [A variant of **dint**.]

dental [den´tȧl] *adj* of, or for, the teeth; produced by the aid of the teeth.—*n* a sound produced by applying the tongue to the teeth.—**dental floss**, waxed thread for cleaning between teeth. [L *dens, dentis*, a tooth. See **tooth**.]

dentate, -d [den´tāt, id] *adj* toothed; notched; set as with teeth. [L *dentātus*, toothed—*dens*, a tooth.]

denticle [den´ti-kl] *n* a small tooth or toothlike part.—*adjs* **dentic´ulāte, -d**, having notches.—*n* **denticulā´tion**. [L *denticulus*, dim of *dens*, a tooth.]

dentiform [den´ti-förm] *adj* having the form of a tooth; of teeth. [L *dens, dentis*, tooth, *forma*, form.]

dentifrice [den´ti-fris] *n* a substance used in cleaning the teeth. [Fr,—L *dentifricium*—*dens*, a tooth, *fricāre*, to rub.]

dentine, dentin [den´tin] *n* the hard bonelike part of teeth. [L *dens, dentis*, a tooth.]

dentist [den´tist] *n* licensed practitioner who treats diseases of the teeth and gums or inserts artificial teeth.—*n* **den´tistry**, the profession of a dentist. [Fr *dentiste*—L *dens, dentis*, a tooth.]

dentition [den-tish´(ȯ)n] *n* the cutting or growing of teeth; the conformation, number, and arrangement of the teeth; a set of teeth (eg *the milk dentition*). [L *dentītiō, -ōnis*—*dentīre*—*dens, dentis*, a tooth.]

denture [den´tyůr, -chůr] *n* a set of artificial teeth. [L *dens, dentis*, a tooth.]

denude [di-nūd´] *vt* to make naked; to deprive, strip.—*n* **dēnudā´tion**, a making bare; (*geol*) laying bare by erosion. [L *dēnūdāre*—*dē-*, inten, *nūdāre, -ātum*, to make naked—*nūdus*, naked.]

denunciate [di-nun´s(h)i-āt] *vt* same as **denounce**.—*n* **denunciation** (*-shi-ā´-*, or *-si-ā´-*), act of denouncing; an arraignment (of);—*adj* **denun´ciatory**, containing, or of the nature of, a denunciation. [L *dēnuntiātus*, pt p of *dēnuntiāre*. See **denounce**.]

deny [di-nī´] *vt* to declare not to be true; to reject; to refuse; to disown;—*pr p* **deny´ing**; *pt p* **denied´**.—**deny oneself**, to restrict one's pleasure, esp in food and drink. [Fr *dénier*—L *dēnegāre*—*dē-*, inten, *negāre*, to say no. See **negation**.]

deodar [dē-o-där´] *n* a Himalayan cedar (*Cedrus deodara*). [Sans. *deva-dāru*, divine tree.]

deodorize [dē-ō´dor-īz] *vt* to take the odor or smell from.—**deō´dorant, deō´dorizer**, a substance that destroys or conceals unpleasant smells. [L *dē*, from, *odor*, smell.]

Deo volente (abbrev **DV**) [dā´ō vo-len´tā] God willing. [L] **deoxidate** [dē-oks´i-dāt] *vt* to take oxygen from; to reduce from the state of an oxide—also **deox´idize**.—*n* **deoxidā´tion**. [L *dē*, from, + **oxide**.]

deoxygenate [dē-oks´-i-jenāt] *vt* to remove oxygen from.—*n* **deoxygenātion**. [L *dē*, from + **oxygenate**.]

deoxyribonucleic acid [dē-oks-i-rī´bō-nū-klē´ik as´id] any of a class of nucleic acids in the chromosomes storing genetic information.—abbrev **DNA**.

depart [di-pärt´] *vi* to go away; to leave, start; to deviate, diverge (from).—**departed**, the dead; **depart´ure**, act of departing; a going away from a place; deviation.—**a new departure**, a change of purpose or procedure. [Fr *départir*—L *dis-*, apart, and *partīrī*, to part, to divide.]

department [di-pärt´mėnt] *n* a unit of specialized functions into which an organization or business is divided; a province.—*n* **department store**, a large store in which departments sell separate types of goods.—*adj* **departmental** [dēpärt-ment´ål].—*adv* **department´ally**. [Fr *départementdépartir*. See **depart**.]

depend [di-pend´] *vi* to hang down; to be based on or connected with anything; to be contingent (on); to rely (on).—*adj* **depend´able**, that may be relied on.—*n* **depend´ent** (also **-ant**), one who depends on, or is supported by, another.—*adj* **depend´ent** (also **-ant**), depending, relying on, contingent; (*gram*) subordinate.—**depend´ence** (**-ance**), state of being dependent; reliance, trust; that on which one depends; **depend´ency**, a territory dependent on a distant country. [Fr *dépendre*—L *dēpendēre*—*dē* from, and *pendēre*, to hang.]

depict [di-pikt´] *vt* to draw a likeness of: to describe minutely. [L *dēpingĕre, dēpictum*—*dē-*, inten, *pingĕre*, to paint.]

depilatory [di-pil´a-tòr-i] *adj* taking hair off.—*n* a substance for removing superfluous hair. [L *dēpilāre, -ātum*—*dē*, from, *pilus*, hair.]

deplete [di-plēt´] *vt* to use up a large quantity of.—*n* **deplē´tion**, the act of emptying or exhausting;—**depletion allowance**, a tax concession for industries that deplete unrenewable resources, esp oil, in the course of production. [L *dēplēre, dēplētum*, to empty—*dē-*, neg, *plēre*, to fill.]

deplore [di-plōr´, -plör´] *vt* to regret deeply; to complain of; to deprecate.—*adj* **deplor´able**, lamentable, sad; hopelessly bad.—*n* **deplor´ableness**.—*adv* **deplor´ably**. [Fr,—L *dēplōrāre*—*dē-*, inten, *pilōrāre*, to weep.]

deploy [di-ploi´] *vt* to spread out and place strategically (any forces).—*vi* to open; to extend from column into line, as a body of troops.—*n* **deploy´ment**. [Fr *déployer*—L *dis-*, apart, *plicāre*, to fold. Doublet of **display**.]

deplume [di-plōōm´] *vt* to take the feathers from; to deprive of honors.—*n* **deplumā´tion**. [Fr *déplumer*—L *dē*, from, *plūma*, a feather.]

depolarize [dē-pō´lår-īz] *vt* to deprive of polarity.—*n* **depōlarizā´tion**. [**de-** + **polarize**.]

depone [di-pōn´] *vt* to testify upon oath.—*adj* **depōn´ent**.—*n* one who makes a deposition under oath. [L *dēpōnĕre*; pr p *dēpōnēns, -entis*—*dē*, down, *pōnĕre*, to place.]

depopulate [di-pop´ū-lāt (or dē-)] *vt* to reduce the population of.—*vi* to become depopulated.—**depopulā´tion**, act of depopulating; **de-pop´ulator**. [L *dēpopulārī, -ātus*—*dē-*, inten, *populārī*, to spread over a country, said of a hostile people (L *populus*)—hence to ravage, to destroy.]

deport [di-, dē-pōrt´, -pört´,] *vt* to expel from a country.—*n* **deportā´tion**. [Fr *déporter*—L *dēportāre*—*dē-*, away, and *portāre, -ātum*, to carry.]

deport [di-pōrt´, -pört´] *vt* to behave (*reflexive*).—*n* **deport´ment**, bearing, manners; behavior. [OFr *deporter*—L *dē-*, inten, *portāre*, to carry.]

depose [di-pōz´], *vt* to remove from power; to attest.—*adj* **depos´able**.—*n* **depos´al**. [Fr *déposer*—L *dē*, from, *pausāre*, to pause, to place.]

deposit [di-poz´it] *vt* to put or set down; to entrust for safekeeping; to let fall, leave.—*n* that which is deposited; something entrusted to another's care, esp money put in a bank; money given in part payment or security; matter let fall or left in a layer.—**depos´itary**, the one receiving a deposit; a depositary; **depos´itor; depos´itory**, a place where anything is deposited. [L *dēpŏsitum*, placed—*dēpōnĕre*—*dē*, down, *pōnĕre*, to place.]

deposition [dep-o-zish´(ò)n] *n* act of deposing; removal from office; sworn testimony, esp in writing; an act or process of depositing; sediment. [**deposit**; blended with root of **depose**.]

depot [dep´ō, dē´pō] *n* a storehouse; a bus station, a railroad station. [Fr *dépôt*—L *dēpōnĕre, -pŏsitum*.]

deprave [di-prāv´] *vt* to make bad or worse; to corrupt.—*n*. **deprăvā´tion**, act of depraving; state of being depraved, depravity.—**deprave´ment**.—*adj* **deprāved´**, corrupt.—*adv* **deprāv´edly**.—*ns* **deprāv´edness; depraver; deprăv´ity**, a vitiated or corrupt state of moral character; extreme wickedness; corruption. [L *dēprāvāre*—*dē-*, inten, *prāvus*, bad.]

deprecate [dep´ri-kāt] *vt* to express disapproval of; to seek to avert, esp by prayer.—*n* **deprecā´tion**, act of deprecating; earnest prayer, esp in litanies, a petition against a particular evil.—*adv* **dep´recatingly**.—*adjs* **dep´recative, dep´recatory**, apologetic, trying to avert evil by prayer. [L *dēprecārī, -ātus – dē*, away, and *precārī*, to pray.]

depreciate [di-prē´shi-āt] *vt* to lower the worth of; to disparage.—*vi* to fall in value.—*n* **depreciā´tion**, the falling of value; disparagement.—*adjs* **deprē´ciative, deprē´ciatory**, tending to depreciate; disparaging. [L *dēpretiāre, -ātum*—*dē*, down, and *pretium*, price.]

depredate [dep´ri-dāt] *vt* to lay waste; to plunder or ravage;—**depredā´tion**, act of plundering; state of being depredated; **dep´redator**. [L *dēpraedārī, -ātus*—*dē-*, inten, *praedārī*—*praeda*, plunder.]

depress [di-pres´] *vt* to press down; to lower; to make less active; to make sad;—*adj* **depressed´**, pressed down; dejected, dispirited.—*adj* **depress´ing**, able or tending to depress.—*adv* **depress´ingly**.—*n* **depress´ion**, a falling in or sinking; an area of law; atmospheric pressure; a hollow; (*med*) an abnormal state of inactivity; a phase of the business cycle characterized by stagnation, widespread unemployment, etc.—**The Depression** or **The Great Depression**—business beginning in 1929 and ending upon the outbreak of World War II. [L *dēprimĕre, -pressum*—*dē*, down, *premĕre*, to press.]

deprive [di-prīv´] *vt* to take a thing away from; to prevent from using or enjoying.—**deprived child**, child who has been prevented from having a normal life.—*n* **deprĭvā´tion**, act of depriving; state of being deprived; loss.—*adj* **deprived**, underprivileged; suffering from hardship. [Low L *dēprīvāre*, to degrade—L *dē*, from, *prīvāre*, to deprive—*prīvus*, one's own.]

depth [depth] *n* deepness; the degree of deepness down or inwards; an abyss; the intensity of color; the intensity of emotion or feeling; the profundity of thought; the midtime of night or of winter; the lowness of sound or pitch; the quality of being deep.—*n* **depth´-charge**, a bomb that explodes under water.—**beyond** or **out of one's depth**, beyond one's capability or knowledge;—**in depth**, intensively and extensively (investigated). [Not in OE; possibly ON *dýpth*, or formed from *deep* on the analogy of *length*.]

depute [di-pūt´] *vt* to appoint as a substitute; to delegate.—*n* **depūtā´tion**, act of deputing; the person or persons deputed or appointed to transact business for another.—*vi* **dep´utize**, to act as deputy.—*n* **dep´ūty**, a delegate or representative, or substitute.—**deputy sheriff**, an acting sheriff. [Fr,—L *dēputāre*, to prune (late) to select.]

derail [dē-rāl´] *vt* to cause to leave the rails.—*vi* (of a streetcar, subway train, etc.) to leave the rails.—*n* **derail´ment**. [**de-** + **rail**.]

derange [di-rānj´] *vt* to throw into confusion; to make insane.—*adj* **deranged´**, disordered; insane.—*n* **derange´ment**, disorder; insanity. [Fr *déranger*—*dé-* (L *dis-*), asunder, and *ranger*, to rank.]

Derby [dër´bi] *n* an annual horse race held at Churchill Downs, Kentucky and at Epsom, England; **der´by**, contest of any kind open to all; stiff felt hat with dome-like crown.

derelict [der´e-likt] *adj* abandoned; falling in ruins.—*n* a person abandoned by society; a wrecked vehicle.—*n* **derelic´tion**, neglect (of duty), remissness; state of being abandoned. [L *dērelinquĕre, -lictum*—*dē-*, inten, *re-*, behind, *linquĕre*, to leave.]

derestrict [dē´rēstrikt] *vt* to free from restriction. [**de-** + **restrict**.]

deride [di-rīd´] *vt* to laugh at, to mock.—*n* **derid´er**.—*adj* **derid´ingly**. [L *dērīdēre, -rīsum*—*dē-*, inten, *rīdēre*, to laugh.]

derision [di-rizh´(ò)n] *n* act of ridiculing; mockery; a laughing-stock.—*adjs* **derī´sive, derīs´ory**, mocking. [L *dērīsiō*—*dērīdēre*. See **deride**.]

derive [di-rīv´] *vt* to take from a source or origin; to infer, deduce (from); to trace (a word) to its root.—*vi* to descend or issue (from).—*adj* **derīv´able**.—*n* **derivation** [dėr-ivā´sh(ò)n], act of deriving; the tracing of a word to its root; that which is derived; source; descent.—*adj* **deriv´ative**, derived or taken from something else; not radical or original.—*n* that which is derived; a word formed from another word.—*adv* **deriv´atively**. [OFr *deriver*—L *dērīvāre*—*dē*, down, from, *rīvus*, a river.]

-derm [dûrm] suffix denoting the skin.—**der´mis** [dûr´mis] the fine skin below the epidermis containing blood vessels.—*adj* **der´mal**, pertaining to the skin; consisting of skin.—*n* **dermatol´ogy**, the science of skin.—**dermatologist**, physician specializing in skin disorders and disease. [Gr *derma, -atos*, the skin—*derein*, to flay.]

dernier cri [der-ne-ā krē] the last word; the latest fashion. [Fr (*lit* the last cry).]

derogate [der´o-gāt] *vi* (*with* **from**) to detract.—*n* **derogā´tion**, a taking from, detraction, depreciation.—*adj* **derog´atory**, contemptuous; disparaging, deprecating.—*adv* **derog´atorily**.—*n* **derog´atoriness**. [L *dērogāre, -ātum*, to repeal part of a law—*dē*, down, from, and *rogāre*, to propose a law.]

derrick [der´ik] *n* any apparatus using a tackle at the end of a beam; a tower-like structure over a drilled hole, esp an oil well. [From *Derrick*, the name of a hangman in the 17th century.]

derring-do [der´ing-dōō] *n* (*false archaic*) daring action. [Spenser mistook for a noun *derrynge do*, misprinted in Lydgate (*c* 1370 – *c* 1450) in place of *dorrying do*, ie daring (to) do.]

derringer [der´in-jer] *n* a pocket pistol with a large bore. [From Henry *Deringer*, American gunsmith.]

derris [der´is] *n* any of a genus (*Derris*) of the pea family, esp *D elliptica*, the roots of which yield an insecticide. [Formed from Gr *derris*, a leather covering.]

dervish [dûr´vish] *n* a member of any Muslim religious order vowing chastity and poverty, noted for frenzied, whirling dancing. [Pers *darvīsh*, a poor man.]

desalinate [dēsal´ināt] or **desalinize** [-īze] *vt* to remove salt from (esp sea water).—*pr p* **desalinating, desalinizing**; *pt p* desalinated, **desalinized** (also—**sā**.)

descant [des´kant] *n* an accompaniment higher than and harmonizing with the main melody. [OFr *descant*—L *dis-*, apart, *cantus*, a song.]

descend [di-send´] *vi* to climb down; to pass from a higher to a lower place or condition; to incline downward; to invade (*with* **on, upon**); to be derived.—*vt* to go down.—*n* **descendant**, one who descends, as offspring from an ancestor.—*adjs* **descend´ent**, going down; proceeding from an ancestor; **descend´ible**, that may descend or be descended; heritable.—*n* **descent´**, act of descending; motion or progress downward; slope; a raid or invasion; transmission by succession; derivation from an ancestor. [Fr *descendre*—L *dēscendĕre*—*dē*, down, *scandĕre*, to climb.]

describe [di-skrīb´] *vt* to give an account of; to trace out or delineate;—*adj* **describ´able**. [L *dēscrībĕre*—*dē*, down, *scrībĕre, scriptum*, to write.]

description [di-skrip´sh(ò)n] *n* act of describing; an account of anything in words; sort, class, or kind.—*adj* **descrip´tive**, serving to describe; containing description.—*adv* **descrip´tively**.—*n* **descrip´tiveness**. [OFr,—L *descriptiō, -ōnis*—*describere*. See **describe**.]

descry [di-skrī´] *vt* to catch sight of;—*pr p* **descry´ing**; *pt p* **descried´**.

[Apparently two words: (1) OFr *descrire* for *descrivre*—L *dēscrībĕre*; a doublet of **describe**; (2) O Fr *descrier*, announce—*des-*, *de-*, *crier*, to cry; a doublet of **decry**.]

desecrate [des´i-krāt] *vt* to profane; to divert from a sacred purpose;—*n* **desecration**, profanation; act of desecrating. [Coined on the analogy of **consecrate**—L *dē*, from; L *dēsecrāre* meant 'consecrate'.]

desegregate [dēseg´ri-gāt] *vt* to abolish racial segregation in.—*n* **desegregā´tion**. [**de-** + **segregate**.]

desert[1] [di-zûrt´] *n* that which is deserved; claim to reward; merit. [OFr pt p of *deservir*. See **deserve**.]

desert[2] [di-zûrt´] *vt* to leave; to forsake.—*vi* to run away; to leave the armed forces without permission.—**desert´er; deser´tion**, act of deserting; state of being deserted. [L *dēserĕre, dēsertum*—*dē-*, neg, *serĕre*, to join together.]

desert[3] [dez´ėrt] *n* a barren place; a waste; a solitude.—*adj* desolate; uninhabited; uncultivated; barren.—**desert boot**, a laced, suede shoe that extends above the ankle.—**desert rat**, any of various mouse-like rodents found in arid regions; (*inf*) a soldier, esp British, fighting in N African desert in World War II. [OFr *desert*—L *dēsertum*—*dēserĕre*, to desert, disjoin.]

deserve [di-zûrv´] *vt* to earn by service; to merit.—*vi* to be worthy of reward.—*adj* **deserv´ing**, worthy.—*advs* **deserv´ingly, deserv´edly** [-id], according to desert, justly. [OFr *deservir*—L *dēservīre*—*dē-*, inten, *servīre*, to serve.]

desiccate [des´i-kāt] *vt* to dry up; to preserve by drying;—*vi* to grow dry.—*adjs* **des´iccant, desicc´ative**, drying; having the power of drying.—*n* a drying agent.—**desiccā´tion; des´iccātor**, substance or apparatus for drying. [L *dēsiccāre, -ātum*, to dry up—*dē*, *siccus*, dry.]

desiderate [di-sid´er-āt] *vt* to wish for or want.—*adj* **desid´erative**, implying desire.—*n* **desiderā´tum**, something desired or much wanted;—*pl* **desiderā´ta**. [L *dēsiderāre, -ātum*, to long for. A doublet of **desire**.]

design [di-zīn´] *vt* to make working drawings for; to contrive; to intend—*n* a working drawing; a plan or scheme formed in the mind; intention; relation of parts to the whole, disposition of forms and colors; pattern.—*adj* **design´able**.—*adv* **design´edly** [-id-li], intentionally.—*n* **design´er**, one who furnishes designs or patterns; a plotter.—*adj* **design´ing**, artful, scheming.—*n* the art of making designs or patterns.—*vt* **des´ignate** [-ig-nāt], to mark out, specify, make known; to name; to be a name for; to appoint or nominate.—*adj* [-āt] appointed to office but not yet installed (*placed after noun*).—*n* **designà´tion**, a pointing out; name; title. [Fr,—L *dēsignāre, -ātum*—*dē*, off, *signum*, a mark.]

desire [di-zīr´] *vt* to long for, wish for; request, ask.—*n* an earnest longing or wish; a prayer or request; the object desired; lust.—*adj* **desir´able**, worthy of desire; pleasing, agreeable.—**desir´ableness, desirabil´ity**.—*adv* **desir´ably**.—*adj* **desir´ous**, full of desire; wishful; (*obs*) desirable. [Fr *désirer*—L *dēsiderāre*. See **desiderate**.]

desist [di-zist´, -sist´] *vi* to stop [L *dēsistĕre*—*dē-*, away, and *sistĕre*, to cause to stand.]

desk [desk] *n* a table for writing or reading; a counter; the specialized section of an organization such as a newspaper or the Department of State; position in an orchestra.—**deskbound**, doing sedentary work. [ME *deske*—L *discus*—Gr *diskos*.]

desktop publishing [desk´top pub´lish-ing] *n* the use of a computer with page-layout programs and a laser printer to produce professional-looking printed matter.

desolate [des´o-lāt] *vt* to make joyless, wretched; to deprive of inhabitants; to lay waste.—*adj* [des´o-lȧt] solitary; joyless; destitute of inhabitants; laid waste.—*adv* **des´olately**.—**des´olateness; desolā´tion**, waste, destruction; a place desolated; sorrow without hope. [L *dēsōlāre, -ātum*—*dē-*, inten, *sōlāre*, to make alone—*sōlus*, alone.]

desorption [dē-sörp´shȯn] *n* release from an absorbed or adsorbed state.—*vt* **desorb´**. [**de-**.]

despair [di-spār´] *vi* to be without hope; to despond.—*n* hopelessness; that which causes despair.—*adv* **despair´ingly**. [OFr *desperer*—L *dēspērāre, -ātum*—*dē-*, neg, *spērāre*, to hope.]

despatch *see* **dispatch**.

desperado [des-pėr-ä´dō, -ā´dō] *n* a reckless criminal;—*pl* **despera´do(e)s**. [OSp (mod *desesperado*)—L *dēspērātus*.]

desperate [des´pėr-ȧt] *adj* in a state of despair; hopeless; despairingly reckless; frantic; (of a remedy) extreme.—*adv* **des´perately**.—**des´perateness, desperā´tion**, state of despair; disregard of danger, recklessness. [L *dēsperāre*.]

despicable [des´pi-ka-bl, -pik´] *adj* deserving to be despised, contemptible, worthless.—*n* **des´picableness**.—*adv* **des´picably**. [L *dēspicĕre*. See **despise**.]

despise [di-spīz´] *vt* to look down upon with contempt; to scorn. [OFr *despire*—L *dēspicĕre*—*dē*, down, *specĕre*, to look.]

despite [di-spīt´] *n* a looking down upon with contempt; violent malice or hatred.—*prep* in spite of, notwithstanding.—*adj* **despite´ful**.—*adv* **despite´fully**.—*n* **despite´fulness**. [OFr *despit*—L *dēspectus*—*dēspicĕre*. See **despise**.]

despoil [di-spoil´] *vt* to spoil or strip completely (eg of possessions); to rob.—**despoil´er; despōliā´tion**. [OFr *despoiller* (mod *dépouiller*)—L *dēspoliāre*—*dē*, inten, *spolium*, spoil.]

despond [di-spond´] *vi* to be wanting in hope, to be dejected.—**despond´ence, despond´-ency**, dejection.—*adj* **despond´ent**, desponding.—*advs* **despond´ently; despond´ingly**. [L *dēspondēre*—*dē*, away, *spondēre*, to promise.]

despot [des´pot] *n* one invested with absolute power; a tyrant.—*adjs* **despot´ic, -al**, of or like a despot; having absolute power; tyrannical.—*adv* **despot´ically**.—*n* **des´potism**, absolute power; a state governed by a despot. [OFr *despot*—Gr *despotēs*, a master.]

desquamate [des´kwa-māt] *vi* to scale off.—*n* **desquamā´tion**, a scaling off; the separation of the cuticle or skin in scales. [L *dēsquāmāre, -ātum*—*dē*, off, and *squāma*, a scale.]

dessert [diz-ûrt´] *n* the sweet course at the end of a meal.—*n* **dessert´spoon**, (*Brit*) a spoon used for eating dessert. [OFr *dessert*—*desservir*, to clear the table—*des-* (L *dis-*), away, and *servir* (L *servīre*), to serve.]

destine [des´tin] *vt* to predetermine; (*in passive*) to be fated; to doom (to good or evil).—**destinā´tion**, the place to which one, anything, is going; **des´tiny**, the purpose or end to which any person or thing is appointed; unavoidable fate. [Fr,—L *dēstināre*—*dē-*, inten, root *sta-*, in *stāre*, to stand.]

destitute [des´ti-tūt] *adj* in utter want; (*with* **of**) entirely lacking in.—*n* **destitū´tion**, the state of being destitute; poverty. [L *dēstituĕre, -ūtum*—*dē*, away, *statuĕre*, to place.]

destroy [di-stroi´] *vi* to pull down, demolish; to ruin, to put an end to; to do away with, to kill;—*pr p* **destroy´ing**; *pt p* **destroyed´**.—*n* **destroy´er**, a person or thing that destroys; a fast small warship. [OFr *destruire*—L *dēstruĕre, dēstructum*—*dē*, down, and *struĕre*, to build.]

destruction [di-struk´sh(ȯ)n] *n* act, or means, of destroying; ruin.—*vt* **destruct´**, (*inf*) to destroy (a rocket or missile) in flight.—*adj* **destruc´tible**, able, or liable, to be destroyed.—*n* **destructibil´ity**.—*adj* **destruc´tive**, causing destruction; mischievous; (*with* **of** *or* **to**) ruinous, deadly; (opp to *constructive*) merely negative (eg *destructive criticism*).—*adv* **destruc´tively**.—**destruc´tiveness; destruc´tor**, a destroyer; a furnace for burning up refuse. [L *dēstructiō, -ōnis*—*dēstruĕre*. See **destroy**.]

desuetude [des´wi-tūd] *n* passing into disuse. [L *dēsuētūdō*—*dē-*, neg, *suescĕre*, to become used.]

desultory [des´ùl-tȯr-i] *adj* going aimlessly from one thing to another, unmethodical.—*adv* **des´ultorily**.—*n* **des´ultoriness**. [L *dēsultōrius*—*dēsultor*, a vaulter—*dēsilīre, -sultum*, to leap—*dē*, from, *salīre*, to jump.]

detach [di-tach´] *vt* to release; to separate, disengage; (*mil*) to send off on special service.—*vi* to separate.—*adj* **detach´able**.—*p adj* **detached´**, unconnected; separate; aloof; free from emotion.—*n* **detach´ment**, state of being detached; that which is detached, as a body of troops. [Fr *détacher*—OFr *des-* (L *dis-*), apart, neg, and root of **attach**.]

detail [di-tāl´] *vt* to relate minutely; to enumerate; (*mil*) to set apart for a particular duty.—*n* (*dē´tāl*, or *di-tāl´*) a small part; an item; an account that goes into particulars; intricate decoration.—*adj* **detailed´**, giving full particulars; exhaustive. [Fr *détailler*—*dē-*, inten, *tailler*, to cut; cf **tailor**.]

detain [di-tān´] *vt* to delay, stop; to keep in custody.—**detainee** (*di-tān´ē*), one who is held in custody; **detain´er**, one who detains; **detain´ment**. [OFr *detenir*—L *dētinēre*—*dē*, from, *tenēre*, to hold.]

detect [di-tekt´] *vt* to discover; to find out; to discern.—*adj* **detect´able, detect´ible**.—*n* **detec´tion**, discovery (of something hidden); state of being found out.—*adj* **detect´ive**, of detection or detectives.—*n* a person, usually a police-officer employed to find evidence of crimes.—*n* **detec´tor**, one who detects; a device for detecting the presence of something.—**lie detector** *see* **lie**. [L *dētegĕre, -tectum*—*dē-*, neg, *tegĕre*, to cover.]

détente [dā-tāt] *n* relaxation of strained relations between countries. [Fr]

detention [di-ten´sh(ȯ)n] *n* act of detaining; state of being detained; confinement;—**detention center**, place where offenders are held while awaiting trial. [L *dētentiō; -ōnis*—*dētinēre*. See **detain**.]

deter [di-tûr´] *vt* to frighten, hinder, or prevent (from);—*pt p* **deterr´ing**; *pt p* **deterred´**.—*adj* **deterrent** [di-ter´ėnt], serving to deter.—*n* anything that deters; specifically a nuclear weapon. [L *dēterrēre*—*dē*, from, *terrēre*, to frighten.]

detergent [dē-tûr´jent] *n* a cleaning agent. Also *adj*. [L *dētergēre, dētersum*—*dē*, off, and *tergēre*, to wipe.]

deteriorate [di-tē´ri-ō-rāt] *vt* to make worse.—*vi* to grow worse.—*n* **dēteriorā´tion**. [L *dēteriōrāre, -ātum*, to make worse—*dēterior*, worse—*dē*, down.]

determine [di-tûr´min] *vt* to limit; to fix or settle; to find out; to put an end to; to regulate; to impel.—*vi* to come to a decision; to come to an end.—*adj* **deter´minable**, capable of being determined, decided, or finished.—*adj* **deter´minant**, serving to determine.—*n* that which serves to determine; (*math*) an algebraic term expressing the sum of certain products of numbers represented by arranging the terms in a square or matrix.—*adj* **deter´mināte**, determined or limited; fixed; decisive.—*adv* **deter´minātely**.—*n* **determinā´tion**, that which is determined or resolved on; direction to a certain end; resolution; fixed purpose; decision of character.—*adjs* **deter´minātive**, that determines, limits, or defines; **deter´mined**, firm in purpose, resolute; fixed.—*adv* **deter´minedly**.—*n* **deter´minism**, the doctrine that all things, including the will, are determined by causes. [Fr,—L *dēterminăre, -ātum*—*dē-*, inten, *terminus*, a boundary.]

detest [di-test´] *vt* to dislike intensely.—*adj* **detest´able**, worthy of being detested, extremely hateful, abominable.—*n* **detest´ableness**.—*adv* **detest´ably**.—*n* **dētestā´tion**, extreme hatred. [Fr *détester*—L *dētestārī*—*dē-*, inten, *testārī*, to call to witness, execrate—*testis*, a witness.]

dethrone [di-thrōn´] *vt* to remove from a throne; depose.—*n* **dethrone´ment**. [**de-**+ **throne**.]

detonate [det´o-nāt, dē´to-nāt] *vi* to explode rapidly and violently.—*vt* to cause so to explode.—**detonā´tion**, the act of detonating; **det´onātor**, a device that initiates an explosion. [L *dētonāre, -ātum—dē*, down, *tonāre*, to thunder.]

detour [dē´tōōr, di-tōōr´] *n* a deviation from an intended course, esp one temporarily replacing a more direct route.—**make a detour**, to go by a roundabout way. [Fr *dé-* (L *dis-*), asunder, *tour*, turning.]

detoxify [de-tox´ifi] *vt* to remove a poison or toxin or the effect of from.—*n* **detoxification**.

detract [di-trakt´] *vt* to take away.—*vi* to take away (from), lessen, esp reputation or worth.—**detrac´ter, detrac´tor; detrac´tion**, depreciation, slander. [L *dē*, from, *trahěre, tractum*, to draw.]

detrain [dē-trān´] *vt* to set down from a railroad car.—*vi* to come out of a train. [**de-** + **train** (n).]

detriment [det´ri-mėnt] *n* damage, injury.—*adj, n* **detriment´al**. [L *dētrīmentum—dē*, off, *terěre, trītum*, to rub.]

detritus [di-trī´tus] *n* fragments formed by the rubbing away from a larger mass, any waste, esp of rock.—*n* **detrĭ´tion**, a wearing away. [L,—*dē*, off, *terěre, tritum*, to rub.]

de trop [di trō] *adj* (of a person; used predicatively) in the way, unwelcome. [Fr]

detrude [de-trood] *vt* to thrust (something) down.—*n* **detrusion**. [L *detruder*]

detumescence [dē-tū-mes´ėns] *n* diminution of swelling. [L *dētumescěre—de-*, neg, *tumescěre*, to swell.]

deuce[1] [dūs] *n* a card or die with two spots; a two-dollar bill; the sum of two dollars; (*lawn tennis*); the score of forty all in a game or five all in a set. [Fr *deux*, two—L *duos*, acc of *duo*, two.]

deuce[2] [dūs] *n* the devil—in exclamatory phrases. [Prob from *deuce*—see **deuce** (1)—the lowest throw at dice.]

deus ex machina [dē´ùs eks mak´in-a] *n* any person, thing, event, that solves a difficulty in an unpredictable or an unnatural manner. [L **deus**, god, **ex** from, **machina**, a machine]

deuterium [dū-tēr´i-ùm] *n* heavy hydrogen.—*n* **deuteron** (*dū´tėr-on*), the nucleus of a heavy hydrogen atom, consisting of one proton and one neutron. Also **deuton**. [Gr *deuteros*, second.]

deuterogamy [dū-tėr-og´a-mi] *n* second marriage. [Gr *deuteros*, second, *gamos*, marriage.]

Deuteronomy [dū-tėr-on´o-mi] or [dū-ter-on-o-mi] *n* the fifth book of the Pentateuch, containing a repetition of the decalogue and laws given in Exodus. [Gr *deuteros*, second, *nomos*, law.]

deutsche mark [doich´ė mark] *n* the unit of money in West Germany. Abbrev **DM**.

deutzia [doit´sē-å] *n* any of a genus (*Deutzia*) of ornamental shrubs of the hydrangea family. [From Deutz, a Dutch naturalist.]

devalue [dē-val´ū] *vt* to reduce the value of.—*vt* **deval´uate**.—*n* **devaluā´tion** [**de-** + **value**.]

devastate [dev´as-tāt] *vt* to lay waste; to plunder—*vi* to be overwhelmed.—*adj* **dev´astating**, overwhelming.—*adv* **dev´astatingly**.—*n* **devastā´tion**, act of devastating; state of being devastated; havoc. [L *dēvastāre, -ātum—dē*, inten, *vastāre*, to lay waste.]

develop -e [di-vel´op] *vt* to lay open by degrees; to evolve; to bring to maturity; to show, reveal the symptoms of (eg a habit, a disease); to elaborate (eg a plan); (*chess*) to bring into a position of usefulness in attack; (*math*) to express in expanded form; to treat photographic film or plate to reveal image; to improve the value of, or to change the use of (land).—*vi* to grow (into); to open out; to evolve; to become apparent;—*pr p* **de-vel´oping**; *pt p* **devel´oped**.—**devel´oper**, one who or that which develops; a reagent for developing photographs; an apparatus for developing muscles; **devel´opment**, a gradual unfolding or growth, evolution; the act of developing; (*math*) the expression of a function in the form of a series; a new situation that emerges. (*mus*) the elaboration of a theme.—**developing country**, poor country seeking to industrialize. [Fr *développer*, opposite of *envelopper*; of obscure origin.]

deviate [dē´vi-āt] *vi* to turn aside (from a course, topic, principle, etc.); to diverge, differ, from a standard, norm, etc.; to vary from type.—**dē´viant**, that which deviates from an accepted norm.—also *adj*; **deviā´tion** [*naut*] error of a magnetic compass.—**deviated septum**, abnormal displacement of the partition in the nasal cavity. [L *dēviāre, -ātum—dē*, from, *via*, the way.]

device [di-vīs´] *n* a contrivance; an invention; a scheme, a plot; a heraldic or emblamatic figure or design. (*pl*) desire, will. [OFr *devise*.]

devil [dev´l] *n* (**Devil**) supreme spirit of evil, Satan; any evil spirit; a very wicked person; (*inf*) a reckless, lively person; (*inf*) someone or something difficult to deal with; an expletive; an apprentice; a highly seasoned dish.—*vt* to season highly.—*vi* to drudge for another;—*pr p* **dev´illing**; *pt p* **dev´illed**.—*adj* **dev´ilish**, fiendish, malignant.—*adv* (*inf*) very, exceedingly.—*adv* **devilishly**.—*adj* **dev´il-may-care**, reckless, audacious.—*n* **dev´ilry** or **dev´iltry**, conduct worthy of the devil; **devil's advocate**, one who advocates opposing cause, esp for the sake of argument; in RC Church, an official appointed to present arguments against beatification or canonization.—**devil's food cake**, a rich chocolate cake;—**between the devil and the deep blue sea**, between equally bad alternatives; **Tasmanian devil**, the black bear-like carnivorous marsupial (*Sarcophilus harrisi*) of Tasmania. [OE *dēofol, dēoful*—L *diabolus*—Gr *diabolos*, from *diaballein*, to slander, from *dia*, across, *ballein*, to throw.]

devious [dē´vi-us] *adj* indirect; not straightforward; underhand.—*adv* **dē´viously**.—*n* **dē´viousness**. [L *dēvius*. See **deviate**.]

devise [di-vīz´] *vt* to invent, contrive; to plan; to leave real estate by will.—*n* act of leaving property by will; a will; property bequeathed by will.—*ns* **devīs´er**, one who contrives; **devīs´or**, one who bequeaths. [OFr *deviser, devise*—Low L *dīvīsa*, a division of goods, a mark.]

devitalize [dē-vī´ta-līz] *vt* to deprive of life or vitality.—*n* **devitalizā´tion**. [**de-** + **vitalize**.]

devitrification [de-vitri-fica´shun] *n* loss of glassy or vitreous condition.—*vt* **devitrify**, deprive of the character of glass. [dē + L *vitrum*, glass.]

devoid [di-void´] *adj* (*with* **of**) lacking; free from. [OFr *desvoidier—des-* (L *dis-*), away, *voidier*—L *viduāre—viduus*, deprived.]

devolution [dev-] or [dēv-ol-ū´sh(ò)n] *n* a transference from one person to another; (*biol*) degeneration. [Low L *dēvolūtiō*—L *dēvolvěre*. See **devolve**.]

devolve [di-volv´] *vt* to hand on to a successor or deputy; to deliver over. [L *dēvolvěre, -volūtum—dē*, down, *volvěre, -ūtum*, to roll.]

Devonian [di-vō´ni-ån] *adj* of the period of the Paleozoic era between the Silurian and the Mississippian or the corresponding system of rocks. [Devonshire, England]

devote [di-vōt´] *vt* to set apart; to dedicate by solemn act; to give or use for a particular activity or purpose.—*adj* **devōt´ed**, given up, as by a vow; zealous; strongly attached;—*adv* **devōt´edly**.—*ns* **devotee** [-tē´ or dev´-], one wholly or superstitiously devoted (*with* **of** *or* **to**); a fanatic; **devō´tion**, consecration; given to the worship of God; piety; strong affection, or attachment (to); ardor; (*pl*) prayers.—*adj* **devō´tional**.—*adv* **devō´tionally**. [L *dēvovēre, dēvōtum—dē-*, away, *vovēre*, to vow.]

devour [di-vowr´] *vt* to swallow greedily; to eat up; to consume or waste; to take in eagerly by the senses or mind.—*n* **devour´er**. [OFr *devorer*—L *dēvorāre—dē-*, inten, *vorāre*, to swallow.]

devout [di-vowt´] *adj* given up to religious thoughts and exercises, pious; solemn, earnest.—*adv* **devout´ly**.—*n devout´ness*. [OFr *devot*—L *dēvōtus—dēvovēre*. See **devote**.]

dew [dū] *n* air moisture, deposited on a cool surface, esp at night; any beaded moisture.—*vt* to wet with dew; to moisten.—*ns* **dew´drop; dew´point**, the temperature at which dew begins to form; the temperature at which a vapor begins to condense.—*adj* **dew´y**. [OE **dēaw**; cf ON *dögg*, Ger *thau*, dew.]

Dewey Decimal System [doo´ē de´-simal sis´tem] system of library book classification with ten main subject classes. [Melvin Dewey, American librarian.]

dewlap [dū´lap] *n* the pendulous skin under the throat etc.—*adj* **dew´lapped**. [Prob **dew** and OE *læppa*, a loose hanging piece.]

DEW line [doo´lin] Distant Early Warning line, network of sensors located in Arctic regions in N America.

Dexedrine [deks´edrin] *n* trade name for amphetamine.

dexter [deks´ter] *adj* (of a heraldic shield) on the right-hand side; right.—*n* **dexter´ity** right-handedness; readiness and skill, adroitness.—*adjs* **dex´terous, dex´trous**, right-handed; adroit, clever.—*adv* **dex´terously**.—*n* **dex´terousness**.—*adj* **dex´tral**, right, as opposed to left. [L *dexter*; Gr *dexios*, Sans *daksina*, on the right, on the south.]

dextran [dek´stran] *n* gummy polysaccharide produced by certain bacteria from sucrose used as partial substitute for blood plasma.

dextrin, dextrine [deks´trin] *n* a *soluble* gummy mixture got from starch.

dex´trose [deks´trōs] *n* glucose. [Fr]

dhow [dow] *n* a lateen-sailed Arab vessel of the Indian Ocean. [Origin unknown.]

di- [dī] two, twice, double. [Gr *dis* twice.]

dia- [dī´a] through. [Gr]

diabetes [dī-a-bē´tēz] *n* a disorder marked by the persistent and excessive discharge of urine.—*n, adj* **diabet´ic**, (of) a person who suffers from diabetes.—**diabetis insipidus**, a condition whereby large quantities of dilute urine are discharged.—**diabetes mellitus** [melī´tes], a disorder marked by inability of the body to use carbohydrates due to the failure of the pancreas to secrete insulin. [Gr *diabetes* a siphon—*dia*, through, *bainein*, to go.]

diablerie [dē-äb´lė-rē] *n* black magic, sorcery. [Fr,—*diable*—L *diabolus*. See **devil**.]

diabolic, -al [dī-ä-bol´ik, -al] *adjs* devilish.—*adv* **diabol´ically**, [L—Gr *diabolikos—diabolos* the devil. *See* **devil**.]

diaconate [dī-ak´o-nåt] *n* the office of a deacon; an official body of deacons.—*adj* **diac´onal**, a deacon or deaconess [LL *diaconātus*—L *diāconus*. See **deacon**.]

diacritical, diacritic [dī-a-krit´ik-al] *adjs* distinguishing between—used of marks or points attached to letters to indicate differences of sound. [Gr *diakritikos, diakrinein—dia* between, *krinein*, to distinguish.]

diadem [dī´a-dem] *n* a band or fillet worn round the head as a badge of royalty; a crown; royalty. [OFr *diademe*—L *diadēma*—Gr *diadēma—dia* round, *deein*, to bind.]

diagnosis [dī-ag-nō´sis] *n* the identification of a disease by means of its symptoms; the analysis of the nature or cause of a problem; the classification of natural objects on a scientific basis.—*pl* **diagnō´ses**.—*vt* **diagnose** [-nōz´, -nōs´], to ascertain, or to recognize, from symptoms.—*adj* diagnŏs´tic; of or for diagnosis.—*n* that by which anything is known; a symptom. [Gr, *dia* between, *gnōsis—gnōnai* to know.]

diagonal [dī-ag´o-nál] *adj* stretching from one corner to an opposite corner of a figure with four or more sides; slantwise.—*n* a straight line so drawn.—*adv* **diag´onally**. [Fr,—L *diagōnālis*, from Gr *diagōnios—dia* through, *gōnia*, a corner.]

diagram [dī´a-gram] *n* a figure or plan drawn in outline to illustrate any statement.—*adj* **diagramma´tic**. [Through L—Gr *diagramma—dia*, round, *graphein*, to write.]

dial [dī´ál] *n* an instrument for showing the time of day by the sun's shadow; the face of a watch or clock; a circular plate with a moveable index used for various purposes.—*vt* to measure or indicate by dial; to make a telephone connection by using a dial.—**dial tone**, a sound given over the telephone that the line is available. [ME *dial*—Low L *diālis*, daily—L *diēs*, a day.]

dialect [dī´a-lekt] *n* a variety or form of language peculiar to a district or class. [Through Fr and L from Gr *dialektos*, speech, peculiarity of speech—*dia* between, *legein*, to speak.]

dialec´tic [dī-alek´tik] *n* branch of logic which teaches the art of arriving at the truth by logical discussion, esp in matters of opinion;—*adv* **dialec´tically**.—*n* **dialecti´cian** [-shán], one skilled in dialectic, a logician.—**dialectical materialism**, theory of Marx and Engels interpreting history as a series of contradictions produced by the struggle between the ruling and working classes. [Gr *dialektikos—dialegesthai*, to argue.]

dialogue, dialog [dī´a-log] *n* conversation between two or more persons, esp in a play or novel; an exchange of views in the hope of ultimately reaching agreement. [Fr,—L *dialogus*—Gr *dialogos*, a conversation—*dialegesthai*, to discourse.]

dialysis [dī-al´i-sis] *n* (*med*) the filtering of blood through a membrane to remove waste productions; (*chem*) the separation of a colloid from a true solution by diffusing it through a membrane; dissolution;—*pl* **dial´yses** [-sēz].—*vt* **dialyze** [dī´á-līz], to separate by dialysis.—*n* **dialyzer**.—*adj* **dialy´tic**. [Gr *dialysis—dia*, asunder, *lyein*, to loose.]

diamagnetic [dī-a-mag-net´ik] *adj* (*phys*) of the magnetic properties of bodies of substances whose permeability is less than that of a vacuum. [Gr *dia*, through + **magnetic**.]

diameter [dī-am´ė-tėr] *n* a straight line passing through the center of a circle; the length of this line.—*adjs* **diamet´ric, -al**, in the direction of a diameter; pertaining to the diameter; like the opposite ends of the diameter (as in *diametrical opposition*).—*adv* **diamet´rically**. [Through Fr and L from Gr *diametros—dia*, through, *metron*, a measure.]

diamond [dī´a-mónd] *n* a valuable gem, a crystallized form of pure carbon, and the hardest of all minerals; (*baseball*) the playing field, esp the infield; a suit of playing cards denoted by a red lozenge; 1½ point printing type.—*adj* resembling diamonds; made of diamonds; marked with diamonds; lozenge-shaped.—**dī´amond-wed´ding**, a sixtieth anniversary of marriage. [ME *adamaunt*—OFr *adamant*. See **adamant**.]

dianetics [dī-anet´iks] *n sing* theory and method of treating personality disorders held to be caused by prenatal experiences. [Gr *dia*, through, *nous*, mind.]

dianthus [dī-anthės] *n* a **pink**[2].

diapason [dī-a-pā´zón] *n* (*mus*) an interval of an octave; a full volume of various sounds in concord; the compass of a voice or instrument; a tuning fork; one of two organ stops (**open** and **stopped diapason**). [Gr *dia*, through, and *pasōn*, gen pl fem of *pas*, all—part of the Gr phrase, *dia pasōn chordōn symphōnia*, concord through all the notes.]

diaper [dīa-pėr] *n* absorbent material worn by an infant to retain bodily waste; woven fabric or design in diamond pattern. [OFr *diaspre, diapre*—Gr *dia*, through, *aspros*, white.]

diaphanous [dī-af´a-nus] *adj* allowing to shine or appear through, transparent, clear; light, delicate.—*adv* **diaph´anously**. [Gr *diaphanēs—dia*, through, *phainein*, to show, shine.]

diaphoretic [dī-a-for-ret´ik] *adj* promoting perspiration.—*n* a medicine that increases perspiration. [Gr *diaphoreein*, to carry off sweat.—*dia*, through, *pherein*, to bear.]

diaphragm [dī´a-fram] *n* a thin partition or dividing membrane; the midriff, a structure separating the chest from the abdomen; device for regulating aperture of a camera lens; contraceptive cap covering cervix.—*adj* **diaphragmat´ic** [-frag-mat´ik]. [Gr *diaphragma—dia*, across, *phragma*, a fence.]

diarchy [dīär-ki] *n* a form of government in which two persons, states, or bodies are jointly vested with supreme power. [Formed from Gr *di-*, twice, *archein*, to rule.]

diarrhea, diarrhoea [dī-a-rē´a] *n* excessive looseness of the bowels.—*adjs* **diarrheic, diarrhoet´ic**. [Gr *diarroia—dia*, through, *rheein*, to flow.]

diary [dī´á-ri] *n* a daily record.—*n* **dī´arist**, one who keeps a diary. [L *diārium—diēs*, a day.]

Diaspora [dīas´por-ė] *n* the dispersion of the Jews from Palestine after the Babylonian captivity.—**diaspora**, Jewish communities living outside Palestine or modern Israel; the dispersion of peoples from their native place. [Gr *diasporā—dia*, through, *speirein*, to scatter.]

diastase [dī´as-tās] *n* any enzyme having the power of converting starch into sugar. [Gr *diastasis*, division—*dia*, apart, *stasis*, setting.]

diastole [dī-as´tol] *n* the dilation of the chambers of the heart during which they fill with blood. [Gr *diastolē—dia*, asunder, *stellein*, to place.]

diathermy [dī-a-thûr´mi] *n* the generation of heat in body tissues by the passage of an electric current through them for medical or surgical purposes. [Gr *dia*, through, *thermē*, heat.]

diatom [dī´a-tom] *n* any of a group of unicellular algae inhabiting fresh and salt water, and the soil.—*n* **dī-a´tomite**, loose material derived chiefly from diatom remains used esp as a filter. Also **kieselguhr**, [Gr *diatomos—diatemnein*, to cut in two.]

diatonic [dī-a-ton´ik] *adj* of major and minor scales as opposed to chromatic scale; of melodies and harmonies excluding chromatic tones.—*adv* **diaton´ically**. [Gr *dia*, through, *tonos*, tone.]

diatribe [dī´a-trīb] *n* an abusive harangue. [Gr *diatrībē*, a spending of time—*dia*, through, *trībein*, to rub, wear away.]

dibble [dib´l] *n* a pointed tool used for making holes to put seeds or plants in—also **dibb´er**.—vt **dibb´le**, to plant with a dibble.—*vi* to make holes; to dip, as in angling. [Prob conn with **dab**.]

dice [dīs] Plural of **die**.

dicentra [dī-sen´trė] *n* any of a genus (*Dicentra*) of herbs of the fumitory family with dissected leaves and irregular flowers.

dicephalous [dī-sef´a-lus] *adj* two-headed. [Gr *dikephalos—di-*, double, *kephalē*, a head.]

dichlor(o)- [dī-klȯr(-ō)-, -klör-] having two atoms of chlorine.

dichotomy [dī-kot´o-mi] *n* a division into two parts; strongly contrasted groups or classes.—*adj* **dichot´omous**. [Gr *dicha*, in two, and *temnein*, to cut.]

dick [dik] *n* (*slang*) man; (*slang*) detective. [*Dick* for Richard.]

dickens [dik´ėnz] *n* the deuce, the devil. [App from *Dickon* = Richard, used as a substitute for *devil*.]

Dickensian [dik-en´ziėn] *adj* of Charles Dickens, English novelist (1812–70); denoting squalor and exploitation as depicted in his novels. *n* an admirer or student of Dickens.

dicker [dik´ėr] *n* haggling, bargaining; petty trade by barter, etc.—*vi* to haggle. [Prob obs *dicker*, the number ten, esp of hides or skins.]

dickey, dicky [dik´i] *n* a false shirt front; an apron; a seat at the back of an automobile. [Perh from *dick*, a dial Eng word for a leather apron; prob Du *dek*, a cover.]

dicotyledon [dī-kot-i-lē´dȯn] *n* a flowering plant having two embryonic seed leaves—*adj* **dicotylē´donous**. [Gr *di-*, twice + **cotyledon**.]

Dictaphone [dik´ta-fōn] *n* trade name for an apparatus that records and plays back dictation. [L *dictāre*, to dictate, Gr *phōnē*, sound.]

dictate [dik-tāt´] *vt* to say or read for another to write; to lay down with authority; to command, require.—*vi* to give orders (to).—*n* [dik´tāt] an order, rule, direction, impulse.—**dictā´tion**, act of dictating; overbearing command; something dictated; **dictā´tor**, one invested with absolute authority.—*adj* **dictătō´rial**, like a dictator; absolute; overbearing.—*adv* **dictătō´rially**.—*n* **dictā´torship**. [L *dictāre, -ātum—dīcĕre*, to say.]

diction [dik´sh(ȯ)n] *n* manner of speaking, enunciation; choice of words, style. [Fr, or L *dictiō, -ōnis—dīcĕre, dictum*, to say.]

dictionary [dik´sh(ȯ)n-á-ri] *n* a book containing the words of a language alphabetically arranged, with their meanings, etc., a lexicon; a work containing information on any department of knowledge, alphabetically arranged. [Low L *dictiōnārium—dīcĕre*.]

Dictograph [dik´to-gräf] *n* trade name for a telephone for transmitting speech from room to room, with or without the speaker's knowledge. [L *dictum*, thing said, and Gr *graphein*, to write.]

dictum [dik´tum] *n* an authoritative saying;—*pl* **dic´ta**. [L]

dicumarol [dī-kōōm´ärol] *n* a drug used to prevent the formation of blood clots in arteries and veins, an anticoagulant.

did [did] [**didst**] *pa t* of **do**.

didactic, -al [di-dak´tik, -á (or dī-)] *adjs* fitted, or intended, to teach; instructive.—*adv* **didac´tically**. [Gr *didaktikos—didaskein*, to teach; akin to L *docēre, discĕre*.]

diddle [did´l] *vi* (*slang*) to make any nervous gesture; to handle an object idly. [Origin uncertain.]

die[1] [dī] *vi* to cease existence; to become extinct;—*pr p* **dy´ing**; *pt, and pt p* **died** (*dīd*).—*n* **diehard**, one who prolongs vain resistance; usu. an extreme conservative.—**die away**, to fade from sight or hearing; **die off**, to die one by one; **die out**, to pass out of existence. [Prob from a lost OE *dēgan*; but commonly referred to a Scand root seen in ON *deyja*. The OE word is *steorfan*, whence our *starve*.]

die[2] [dī] *n* a small cube with one to six spots on each face; a stamp for impressing coin, etc.;—*pl* (playing games and the like) **dice** (*dīs*); (stamping) **dies** (*dīz*).—*vi* **dice**, to play with dice (*inf*) to take a risk; *vt* to cut into small cubes.—*pr p* **dic´ing**; *pt p* **diced** (*dīst*).—*n* **die-sinking**, the engraving of dies.—**no dice**, no success; **the die is cast**, an irrevocable step has been taken. [OFr *de*, pl *dez*, from Low L *dadus*—L *datus*, given or cast (*talus*, a piece of bone used in play, being understood).]

dieldrin [dēl´drin] *n* a chemical insecticide.

dielectric [dī-e-lek´trik] *adj* of non-conducting material;—*n* any substance which insulates against electricity. [Gr *dia*, through + **electric**.]

diesel [dēz´l] *n* a vehicle driven by a diesel engine.—**diesel engine**, an oil-burning engine in which ignition is produced by the heat of highly-compressed air,—**diesel fuel**, the oil for this. [Rudolf *Diesel* (1858–1913), the inventor.]

diet[1] [dī´et] *n* mode of living, with special reference to food; food selected to adjust weight, to control illness, etc.—*vt* to put on a diet.—*vi* to take food according to rule.—**dī´etary laws**, (*Judaism*) rules governing the prohibition of certain foods and the fitness of certain foods for eating.—*n* course of diet; allowance of food, esp in large institutions.—*adjs* **dīetĕt´ic**, pertaining to diet.—**dīetet´ics**, application of the principles of nutrition; **dietitian** (*-ish´ȧn*), a person trained to plan meals in hospitals, schools etc. [Fr *diète*—LL *diaeta*—Gr *diaita*, mode of living, diet.]

diet[2] [dī´et] *n* a formal assembly; the English name for various legislative bodies. [OFr *diete*—Low L *diēta*—Gr *diaita*, way of life; or from L *diēs*, a (set) day.]

differ [dif´ėr] *vi* to be unlike (*used by itself, or followed by* **from**); to disagree with (*with* **with, from**); to quarrel, be at variance (with);—pr p **diff´ering**; pt p **diff´ered**.—*n* **diff´erence**, that which distinguishes one thing from another; the amount or manner of being different.—*adj* **diff´erent**, distinct, separate; unlike, not the same (*with* **than**); novel.—*n* **differen´tia** (-*shi-ä*; L), that which distinguishes a thing from others, esp of species within a genera.—*pl* **differen´tiae** [shi-ē].—*adj* **differen´tial**, of, or showing a difference.—*vt* **differen´tiāte**, to make different; to become specialized; to note differences.—*n* **differentiātion**.—*adv* **diff´erently**.—**differential calculus**, (*math*) a system of mathematical analysis dealing with the rate of change of a variable function; **differential equation** (*math*) an equation containing differentials or derivatives; **differential gear**, a gear permitting relative rotation of two shafts driven by a third. [L. *differre*—*dif-* (=*dis-*), apart, *ferre*, to bear.]

difficult, [dif´i-kult] *adj* hard to understand; hard to make, do, or carry out; hard to please.—*n* **difficulty**, thing that is hard to understand; obstacle; hard work; trouble. [The adj was formed from *difficulty*, Fr *difficulté*—L *difficultās*—*difficilis*—*dif-* (=*dis-*), neg, *facilis*, easy.]

diffident [dif´i-dėnt] *adj* shy, lacking self-confidence, not assertive.—*n* **diff´idence**.—*adv* **diff´idently**. [L *diffidens, -entis*, pr p of *diffīdĕre*, to distrust—*dif-* (=*dis-*), neg, *fīdĕre*, to trust.]

diffraction [di-frak´sh(ȯ)n] *n* the breaking up of a ray of light into colored bands of the spectrum or into a series of light and dark bands. [L *diffringĕre, diffractum*—*dis-*, asunder, *frangĕre*, to break.]

diffuse [di-fūz´] *vt* to spread in all directions.—*vi* to spread.—*vti* (*of gases, fluids or small particles*) to intermingle.—*adj* **diffūsed´**, spread widely, not concentrated.—*adj* **diffuse** (*di-fus*), diffused, widely spread; wordy, not concise.—*adv* **diffuse´ly**.—*n* **diffuse´ness**.—*adj* **diffūs´ible**, that may be diffused.—**diffūsibil´ity, diffū´sion**.—*adj* **diffus´ive**, extending; spreading widely.—*adv* **diffus´ively**.—*n* **diffus´iveness**. [L *diffundĕre, diffūsum*—*dif-* (=*dis-*), asunder, *fundĕre*, to pour out.]

dig [dig] *vt* to use a tool or hands, claws etc. in making a hole in the ground; to unearth by digging; to excavate; to thrust; to nudge; (*slang*) to understand, approve.—*pr p* **digg´ing**; *pt, pt p* **dug**.—*n* (*slang*) a thrust, a poke (—*fig often with* **at**); an archaeological excavation.—*n* **digger**, one who or that which digs; **Digger**, a N American Indian (as a Paiute) who digs roots for food.—*n pl* **digg´ings**, places where mining is carried on, esp for gold; (*Brit*) lodgings. Also **digs.**—**dig in**, to cover by digging; (*lit or fig*) to entrench; **dig up**, (*slang*) to find or meet someone or something, usu. someone disagreeable or eccentric or something old-fashioned. [Prob O Fr *diguer*, to dig.]

digest [di-jest´] *vt* to convert (food) into assimilable form; to reduce (facts, laws etc.) to convenient form by classifying or summarizing; to form clear view of (a situation) by reflection.—*vi* to undergo digestion.—*adj* **digest´ible**, that may be digested (*lit or fig*).—**digestibil´ity; digestion** [dijes´ch(ȯ)n], the ability to digest; the act or process of digesting. [L *dīgerĕre, dīgestum*, to carry asunder or dissolve—*dī* (=*dis-*), asunder, *gerĕre*, to bear.]

digest [dī´jest] *n* an orderly summary of any written matter; a periodical synopsis of published or broadcasted material. [L *dīgesta*, neut pl of *dīgestus, pt p* of *dīgerĕre*, to carry apart, to arrange.]

digit [dij´it] *n* any of the basic counting units of a number system, including zero; a human finger or toe; a beast's toe.—*adj* **dig´ital**, of or using digits; (*of clock or watch*) showing hours and minutes in figures; (*of computer*) operating on data in the form of digits—*n* **digitā´lis**, a genus of plants including the foxglove; a powerful heart stimulant obtained from the foxglove.—*adjs* **dig´itate**, (*bot*) having finger-like sections.—*n* **digitā´tion**.—*adj* **dig´itigrade**, walking on the toes.—*n* an animal that walks on its toes, not touching the ground with heel.—*vt* **dig´itize**, to put (data) into digital form for use in a digital computer. [L *digitus*, a finger or a toe.]

dignify [dig´ni-fī] *vt* to invest with honor; to exalt;—*pr p* **dig´nifying**; *pt p* **dig´nified**.—*adj* **dig´nified**, marked with dignity; stately; noble; serious in manner. [Low L *dignificāre*—*dignus*, worthy, *facĕre*, to make.]

dignity [dig´ni-ti] *n* the state of being dignified; the claim(s) to respect, worthiness.—*n* **dig´nitary**, one in a high position or rank, esp in the church.—**beneath someone's dignity**, not worthy enough for someone to do;—**stand on one's dignity**, to insist on being treated with respect. [Fr *dignité*—L *dignitās*—*dignus*, worthy.]

digraph [dī´gräf] *n* two letters expressing one sound, as *ea* in bread, *ng* in sing, *th* in that. [Gr *di-*, twice, *graphē*, a mark, a character—*graphein*, to write.]

digress [di-gres´, dī-gres´] *vi* to turn aside from the main subject in speaking or writing.—*n* **digress´ion**.—*adjs* **digress´ional, digress´ive**, of the nature of a digression.—*adv* **digress´ively**. [L *dīgredī, dīgressus*—*di-* (*dis-*), aside, *gradī*, to step.]

dihedral [dī-hē´drȧl] *adj* formed by two half-planes meeting along a common line. [Gr *di-*, twice, *hedra*, seat.]

dike [dīk] *n* a ditch; a causeway; (*geol*) a wall-like mass of igneous rock. Also **dyke**. [OE *dic*; Du *dijk*, Ger *teich*, a pond.]

delapidate [di-lap´i-dāt] *vt* to bring (a building) to ruin.—Also *vi*—*adj* **dilap´idated**, in structural disrepair.—**dilapidā´tion**, state of damage or disrepair; **dilap´idator**. [L *dīlapidāre*—*dī*, asunder, *lapis, lapidis*, a stone.]

dilate [di-lāt´, dī-lāt´] *vt* to enlarge;—*vi* to widen; to be enlarged, esp pupil of eye.—*adj* **dilāt´able**, that may be dilated or expanded.—**dilātabil´ity, dilātā´tion, dilā´tion**, expansion; **dilāt´or**. [L *dīlātus* (used as pt p of *differre*) from *dī-* (=*dis-*), apart, *lātus*, wide.]

dilatory [dil´a-tȯr-i] *adj* tardy; causing or intending to delay.—*adv* **dil´atorily**.—*n* **dil´atoriness**. [L *dīlātōrius*, extending or putting off (time)—*dīlatus*. See **dilate**.]

dilemma [di-lem´a] *n* a situation where each of two alternative courses (or of all the feasible courses) is eminently undesirable. [L,—Gr *dilēmma*—*di-*, twice, double, *lēmma*, an assumption—*lambanein*, to take.]

dilettante [dil-et-an´ti] *n* a person who dabbles in a subject for amusement.—*pl* **dilettan´ti** [-tē].—*n* **dilettan´tism**. [It pr p of *dilettare*, to take delight in—L *dēlectāre*, to delight.]

diligent [dil´i-jėnt] *adj* industrious.—*n* **dil´igence**, hard work, industry; a public stagecoach [also pronounced dēlē-zhōs].—*adv* **dil´igently**. [Fr,—*dīligēns, -entis, pr p of L dīligĕre*, to choose.]

dill [dil] *n* an edible hardy annual herb (*Anethium graveolens*) of the carrot family.—**dill pickle**, a cucumber pickled in dill water. [OE *dile*; Ger and Swed *dill*.]

dillydally [dil´i-dal´i] *vi* to loiter, trifle.—*pr p* **dillydallying**; *pt* **dillydallied**. [A kind of reduplication of **dally**.]

dilute [di-l(y)ōōt´, dī-l(y)ōōt´] *vt* to diminish the strength etc., of, by mixing, esp with water.—*adj* [also dī´l(y)ōōt], diminished in strength by mixing.—*adj* **dil´uent**, diluting.—*n* that which dilutes.—*n* **dilu´tion**. [L *diluĕre, dīlūtum*—*dī*, away, *luĕre*, to wash.]

dilū´vial, dilū´vian [dil-(y)ōō´vi-al, -en] *adj* of a flood. [L *dīluvium*—*dīluĕre*.]

dim [dim] *adj* faintly lit, not seeing, hearing, understanding, etc. clearly.—*vt* to make dark;—*vi* to become dim;—pr p **dimm´ing**; pt p **dimmed**.—*adv* **dim´ly**.—*n* **dimm´er**, a device for regulating the supply of light; **dim´ness; dimout**, reduction of public night lighting; **dimwit**, a slow-thinking person.—*adj* **dimwitted**. [OE *dimm*; akin to ON *dimmr*, dark, and Ger *dämmerung*, twilight.]

dime [dīm] *n* the tenth part of a US or Canadian dollar, 10 cents. [Fr orig *disme*, from L *decima* (*pars*), a tenth (part).]

dimenhydrinate [dī-men-hī´drenāt] *n* an antihistamine used to prevent and to treat motion sickness. Also **Dramamine**.

dimension [di-, dīmen´sh(ȯ)n *n* any linear measurement of width, length, or thickness; extent; size.—*adj* **dimen´sional**, concerning dimension. [Fr,—L *dimensiō*—*dīmetīrī, dīmensus*—*dī-* (=*dis-*), apart, mētīrī, to measure.]

dimeter [dim´e-tėr] *n* in verse, a line with two major stresses. [L,—Gr *dimetros*—*di-*, twice, *metron*, a measure.]

diminish [di-min´ish] *vti* to make or become smaller in size, amount, or importance.—*p adj* **dimin´ished** (*mus*), of an interval, less by a semitone than the perfect or the minor of the same name.—*adj* **dimin´ishable**.—*adv* **dimin´ishingly**. [Coined from **minish** in imitation of L *dīminuĕre*—*dī-* (*dis-*), apart, *minuĕre*, to make less.]

diminuendo [di-min-ū-en´dō] *adv* (*mus*) gradually becoming quieter.—*n* (phrase or passage) diminishing in sound.—*pl* **-s.** [It,—L *dēminuĕre*, to lessen.]

diminution [dim-in-ū´sh(ȯ)n] *n* act or process of being made smaller.—*adj* **dimin´utive**, very small; expressing diminution (eg of a suffix).—*n* a word formed by a suffix (as -ette, -kin, -ling), by clippings (Nan for Nancy), or by altering (Jack for John) to express small size, familiarity, etc.—*adv* **dimin´utively**.—*n* **dimin´utiveness**. [L. *dīminūtiō, -ōnis*—*dīminuĕre, dīminūtum*, to lessen.]

dimity [dim´i-ti] *n* a fine, thin, corded cotton fabric. [Gr *dimitos*—*di-*, twice, *mitos*, a thread.]

dimorphism [dī-mör´fizm] *n* (*biol*) occurrence of two forms in the same species; (*chem*) crystallization in two forms of the same compound.—*adj* **dimor´phic, dimor´phous**. [Gr *di-*, twice, *morphē*, form.]

dimple [dim´pl] *n* a small hollow, usu on the cheek or chin. [Apparently cog with Ger *tümpel*, pool.]

din [din] *n* a loud continued noise.—*vt* to repeat loudly and persistently;—*pr p* **dinn″ing**; *pt p* **dinned**. [OE *dynn, dyne*; cf ON *dynr*, Dan *dön*, noise.]

dinar [din-är´] *n* the unit of money of Iraq, Jordan, Libya, and Yugoslavia.

dine [dīn] *vi* to eat dinner.—*vt* to give a dinner.—**din´er**, one who dines.—**dinette´**, an alcove used for meals; **dining car**, a restaurant car on a railroad train; **dining hall**, a large room where meals are served to members of a group, esp at a school, college etc.; **din´ing room**, a room used for meals.—**dine out**, to dine elsewhere than at home—**dinerout´, diners-out**. [Perh OFr *disner* (Fr *dîner*)—*Low L disjūnāre*, for *disjējūnāre*, to break one's fast.]

ding dong [ding dong´] *n* the sound made by bells. [Imit]
dinghy [ding´gi] *n* a small open boat propelled by oars or sails. [Hindi *dīngī*, a small boat.]
dingle [ding´gl] *n* a dell. [Origin unknown.]
dingo [ding´gō] *n* the wild dog of mainland Australia;—*pl* **ding´oes** (*-ōz*) [Native name.]
dingy [din´ji] *adj* dirty-looking, shabby.—*n* **din´giness**. [Origin obscure.]
dinner [din´ėr] *n* the main meal of the day; a formal meal in honor of a person or occasion.—**dinner jacket**, a tuxedo; **dinnerware**, the china and glasses used at a dinner table. [OFr *disner*, properly breakfast.]
dinosaur [dī´no-sör] *n* any of an order of extinct (Mesozoic) reptiles. [Gr *deinos*, terrible, and *sauros*, lizard.]
dint [dint] *n* the mark of a blow; force (as in *by dint of*).—*vt* to make a dint in. [OE *dynt*, a blow; Scot *dunt*, a blow with a dull sound, ON *dyntr*.]
diocese [di´o-sēs, -sis] *n* the district over which a bishop has authority.—*adj* **diocesan** (*dī-os´esn,-ezn*), of a diocese.—*n* a bishop having jurisdiction. [Through Fr and L from Gr *dioikēsis*—*dioikeein*, to keep house—*oikos*, a house.]
diode [dī´ōd] *n* a two-electron tube with a cathode and an anode; a rectifier analogous in use to a diode. [Gr *di-*, twice, *hodos*, way.]
dioecious [dī-ē´shùs] *adj* having male and female flowers on different plants. [Gr *di-*, twice, *oikos*, a house.]
diopter [dī-op´ter] *n* a unit for measuring the reflective power of light.—*n pl* (*with sing v*) **diop´tics**, the science of the refraction of light.
diorama [dī-o-rä´ma] *n* a miniature three-dimensional scene, esp a museum exhibit; device for producing changing effects by manipulating light on a partly translucent picture.—*adj* **dioram´ic**. [Gr *dia*, through, *horama*, a sight.]
dioxide [dī-oks´īd] *n* an oxide with two molecules of oxygen to one molecule of the other constituents.
dioxin [dī-oks´in] *n* any of various byproducts resulting from the manufacture of certain herbicides and insecticides.
dip [dip] *vt* to put (something) under the surface (as of a liquid) and lift quickly out again; to immerse (as a hog) in an antiseptic solution; to lower and raise again.—*vi* to go into water and come out quickly; to suddenly drop down or sink out of sight; to read superficially; to incline downward from the plane of the horizon.—*pr p* **dipping**; *pt p* **dipped**.—*n* a dipping of any kind; a sudden drop; a mixture in which to dip something.—*n* **dipstick**, a rod with graduated markings to measure the depth (as of oil in an engine). [OE *dyppan*, causal of *dȳpan*, to plunge in—*dēop*, deep.]
dipetalous [dī-pet´a-lus] *adj* having two petals. [Gr *di-*, twice, and *petalon*, a leaf.]
diphtheria [dif-thē´ri-a] *n* an infectious throat disease.—*adjs* **diphther´ial, diphtherit´ic**. [Gr *diphthera*, leather.]
diphthong [dif´thong] *n* two vowel-sounds (represented by one letter or by two) pronounced as one syllable, as in *my* [ma´i], roam [*rō´ùm*] and other so-called 'long vowels'. [Gr *diphthongos*, with two sounds—*di-*, twice, *phthongos*, sound.]
diploma [di-plōma] *n* a certificate given by a school, college or university to its graduating students.—*n* **diploma mill**, an institution of higher learning operating without accreditation; a college or university with minimal academic demands. [L,—Gr *diplōma*, a letter folded double—*diploos*, double.]
diplomacy [di-plō´ma-si] *n* the management of relations between nations; skill in handling affairs without arousing hostility.—*adj* **diplomat´ic**, of diplomacy; employing tact and conciliation.—*adv* **diplomat´ically**.—**diplō´matist, dip´lomat**, one employed or skilled in diplomacy. [From **diploma**.]
diplopia [dip-lap´ēa] *n* double vision.—*adj* **diplop´ic**. [NL]
dipole [dī´pōl] *n* two equal and opposite electric charges or magnetic poles of opposite sign a small distance apart; a body or system having such; a type of radio antenna.—*adj* **dipol´ar**, having two poles. [**di-** + **pole**.]
dipper [dip´ėr] *n* something used for dipping articles; any of several birds (as a water ouzel) skilled in diving; the seven principal stars in the constellation Ursa Major called **Big Dipper**; the seven principal stars in Ursa Minor, with the handle pointing to the North Star, called **Little Dipper**.—*n* **dipperful** [**dip**].
dipsomania [dip-sō-mā´ni-a] *n* the abnormal craving for alcoholic beverages.—*n* **dipsoma´niac**. [**Gr** *dipsa*, thirst, and *mania*, madness.]
Diptera [dip´tėr-a] *n pl* order of insects with single pair of wings and sucking or piercing mouth parts.—*adjs* **dip´terous; dip´teran** (*bot*) having two winglike parts. [Gr *dipteros*, two-winged—*di-*, twice, *pteron*, a wing.]
diptych [dip´tik] *n* a pair of paintings or carvings on two panels hinged together. [Gr *diptychos*—*di-*, twice, *ptyssein*, to fold.]
dire [dīr] *adj* dreadful; desperately urgent.-*adv* **dire´ly**.—*n* **dire´ness**. [L *dīrus*; cf Gr *deinos*, frightful.]
direct [di-rekt´, dī´rekt] *adj* straight; in an unbroken line; frank; truthful.—*vt* to manage, to control; to tell or show the way; to point to, to aim at; to address (a letter or package); to carry out the organizing and supervising of; to train and lead performances.—*vi* to determine a course; to act as director.—*n*. **direc´tion**, management, control; order, command; knowing or telling what to do, where to go, etc.; a name and address on a letter or package; onward movement; tendency; any way in which one may face or point.—*adjs* **direc´tional**, relating to direction in space; **direc´tive**, directing—*n* an order as to procedure.—*adv* **direct´ly**, in a direct manner, immediately; in a little while.—*n* **direct´ness; direct´or**, a person who directs, esp the production of a show for stage or screen; one of the persons directing the affairs of a company or an institution; **direct´orate**, a group of directors; **directorship**, the office of director.—*adjs* **directo´rial**, of a director; of theatrical directions; **direct´ory**, advising, guiding.—*n* a book or collection of rules, ordinances, etc.; an alphabetical or classified list (as of names and telephone numbers etc. in an organization); a body of directors.—**direct current**, an electric current flowing in one direction only (abbrev **DC**); **direct discourse**, speech reported in the words used by the speaker; **direct object**, (*gram*) the person or thing directly affected by the action expressed in the sentence; **direct primary**, a primary election in which nominations for candidates are made by a direct vote; **direct tax**, one levied directly on the person who bears the burden of it; **direction find´er**, a radio receiving device that determines the direction of incoming radio waves. [L *dīrigĕre, dīrectum*—*di-*, apart, and *rĕgere*, to rule, to make straight.]
dirge [dûrj] *n* a funeral song or hymn; a slow, mournful piece of music. [ME *dirige*, from L.]
dirigible [dir´i-ji-bl] *adj* that can be steered.—*n* an airship. [From root of **direct**.]
dirk [dûrk] *n* a dagger.—*vt* to stab with a dirk. [Ety unknown.]
dirndl [dûrn´dėl] *n* a full, gathered skirt.
dirt [dûrt] *n* matter in the wrong place, esp filth; loose earth; obscenity; spiteful gossip.—**dirt farmer**, a farmer who earns his own living by farming his own land, esp one without hired labor; **dirt road**, an unpaved road;—*adj* **dirt´y**, foul, filthy, unclean, despicable; mean.—*vt* to soil with dirt.—*pr p* **dirt´ying**; *pt p* **dirt´ied**.—*adv* **dirt´ily**.—*n* **dirt´iness**.—**dirty linen**, private matters whose public exposure brings distress; **dirty old man**, a lecherous man; **dirty pool**, unsportsmanlike conduct; **dirty work**, treacherous mean act. [ME *drit*, prob.—ON *drit*, excrement.]
dis- [dis-] opposite of (**discontent**); reverse of (**disentangle**); exclude or expel (**disbar**); negative (disagreeable). [L *dis-, di-*]
disable [dis-ā´bl] *vt* to make useless; to cripple.—*ns* **disablement, disability**, state of being disabled.
disabuse [dis-a-būz´] *vt* to undeceive or set right. [L *dis-* + **abuse**.]
disadvantage [dis-ad-vänt´ij] *n* unfavorable circumstance or condition; loss, detriment.—*adjs* **disadvant´aged**, deprived of the civil rights and resources (housing, medical and educational facilities) enjoyed by the majority of people; **disadvantā´geous**, attended with disadvantage; unfavorable—*adv* **disadvantā´geously**. [L *dis-* + **advantage**.]
disaffect [dis-a-fekt´] *vt* to make discontented or unfriendly.—*adj* **disaffect´ed**, ill-disposed, disloyal.—*n* **disaffec´tion**, state of being disaffected. [L *dis-* + **affect**.]
disaffirm [dis-a-fûrm´] *vt* to deny (what has been affirmed). [L *dis-* + **affirm**.]
disagree [dis-a-grē´] *vi* to differ; to dissent; to quarrel; to have a bad effect.—*adj* **disagree´able**, unpleasant, bad-tempered.—*n* **disagree´ableness**.—*adv* **disagree´ably**.—*n* **disagree´ment**, failure to agree; incongruity; a dispute. [L *dis-* + **agree**.]
disallow [dis-a-low´] *vt* to refuse to sanction; to deny the truth or value of; to reject. [OFr *desalouer*—*des-* (L *dis-*), *alouer*. See **allow**.]
disappear [dis-a-pēr´] *vi* to vanish from sight; to fade out of existence.—*n* **disappear´ance**. [L *dis-* + **appear**.]
disappoint [dis-a-point´] *vt* to frustrate, fall short of, the hopes of (a person); to defeat the fulfilment of (eg hopes).—*adjs* **disappointed; disappointing**.—*adv* **disappointingly**.—*n* **disappoint´ment**, the defeat of one's hopes; frustration; vexation due to failure. [OFr *desapointer*—*des-* (L *dis-*), away, and *apointer*, to appoint. See **appoint**.]
disapprobation [dis-ap-ro-bā´sh(ò)n] *n* disapproval. [L *dis-* + **approbation**.]
disapprove [dis-a-prōōv´] *vti* to give or have an unfavorable opinion (*vi with* **of**).—*n* **disapprov´al**.—*adv* **disapprov´ingly**. [L *dis-* + **approve**.]
disarm [dis-ärm´] *vt* to deprive of weapons; to render defenseless or harmless; (*fig*) to conciliate.—*vi* to reduce national armaments.—*n* **disarm´ament**—*adj* **disarm´ing**, (*fig*) conciliating, instantly gaining good will or favor. [L *dis-*, + *arm*.]
disarrange [dis-a-rānj´] *vt* to undo the arrangement of, to disorder, to derange.—*n* **disarrange´ment**. [L *dis-* + **arrange**.]
disarray [dis-a-rā´] *vt* to throw into disorder; to strip of array or dress.—*n* want of array or order; undress. [L *dis-* + **array**.]
disassemble [dis-asėm´bel] *vti* to take or to come apart.—*adj* **disassemblable**.—*n* **disassembly**. [*dis* + **assemble**.]
disassociate [dis-a-sō´shi-āt] *vt* to disconnect; to dissociate. [L *dis-* + **associate**.]
disaster [diz-äs´tėr] *n* an adverse or unfortunate event; great and sudden misfortune, calamity.—*adj* **disas´trous**, calamitous, ruinous; gloomy, foreboding disaster.—*adv* **disas´trously**. [OFr *desastre*—*des-* (L *dis-*), with evil sense, *astre*, a star, destiny—L *astrum*, Gr *astron*, star.]
disavow [dis-a-vow´] *vt* to disclaim, to disown, to deny.—*n* **disavow´al**. [OFr *desavouer*—*des-* (L *dis-*), away, *avouer*, to avow.]
disband [dis-band´] *vt* to disperse, break up (esp an army).—*vi* to break up.—*n* **disband´ment**. [OFr *desbander*, to unbind—*des-* (L *dis-*), *bander*.]

disbar [dis-bär´] *vt* to deprive (a lawyer) of status or privileges;—*pr p* **disbarring**; *pt p* **disbarred**.—*n* **disbarment**. [L *dis-* + **bar**].

disbelieve [*dis-bi-lēv´*] *vt* to believe to be false; to refuse belief or credit to.—*vi* to have no faith (in).—**disbelief´, disbeliev´er**. [L *dis-* + **believe**.]

disbud [dis-bud´] *vt* to remove buds from (plants) or horn buds from (cattle).

disburden [dis-bûr´dn] *vt* to rid of a burden, unload (eg a ship);—*n* **disbur´denment**. [L *dis-* + **burden**.]

disburse [dis-bûrs´] *vt* to pay out.—*n* **disburse´ment**. [OFr *desbourser—des-* (L *dis-*), apart, + *bourse*, a purse.]

disc *see* **disk**; abbrev of discount.

discard [dis-kärd´] *vti* to throw away (a card) as useless; to cast off, get rid of.—*n* that which is thrown aside. [L *dis-*, away, + **card**.]

discern [di-sûrn´, di-zûrn´] *vt* to perceive; to seeclearly.—*n* **discern´er**.—*adj* **discern´ible, discernable**.—*adv* **discern´ibly**.—*adj* **discern´ing**, discriminating, acute; having insight and understanding.—*n* **discern´ment**, power or faculty of discriminating; acuteness, insight. [L, *discernĕre—dis-*, thoroughly, *cernĕre*, to perceive.]

discharge [dis-chärj´] *vt* to unload, as a cargo; to set free; to acquit; to dismiss; to fire, as a gun; to let out, emit; to perform, as duties; to pay, as a debt.—*vi* to unload; to be released from a charged state.—*n* act or process of discharging; that which is discharged; release; dismissal; acquittal; payment.—*n* **discharg´er**.—**discharge tube**, a tube in which an electric discharge takes place in a vacuum or in a gas at low pressure. [OFr *descharger—des-*, apart + *charger*. See **charge**.]

disciple [dis-ī´pl] *n* one who follows or believes in the doctrine of another; one of the twelve apostles of Christ.—*n* **disci´pleship**. [Fr,—L *discipulus—discĕre*, to learn.]

discipline [dis´i-plin] *n* instruction; a branch of learning; branch of sport; training, or mode of life in accordance with rules; subjection to control; order maintained by control; penance.—*vt* to subject to discipline; to train; to bring under control; to chastise.—*adj* **dis´ciplinable**.—*n* **disciplinā´rian**, one who enforces strict discipline.—*adj* **dis´ciplinary**, of the nature of discipline. [L *disciplīna*, from *discipulus*. See **disciple**.]

disclaim [dis-klām´] *vi* to deny connection with; to renounce all legal claim to.—*n* **disclaim´er**, a denial of legal claim; a writing embodying this. [OFr *disclaimer—*L *dis-*, apart, *clāmāre*, to cry out.]

disclose [dis-klōz´] *vt* to lay open, bring to light, to reveal.—*n* **disclō´sure**, act of disclosing; a revelation; that which is disclosed. [OFr *desclos—*L *dis-*, apart, *claudĕre, clausum*, to shut.]

discobolus [dis-kob´o-lus] *n* a discus thrower. [L,—Gr *diskos*, a quoit, *ballein*, to throw.]

discoid, -al [dis´koid, -âl] *adj* having the form of a disk. [Gr *diskos*, a quoit, *eidos*, form.]

discolor [dis-kul´òr] *vt* to change or to spoil the color of; to stain.—Also *vi*—*n* **discolorā´tion**, act of discoloring; state of being discolored; stain. [OFr *descolorer—*L *dis-*, apart, *colōrāre—color*, color.]

discombobulate [dis-kumbob´èlāt] *vt* to disconcert, upset, confuse.—*n* **discombobulation**. [prob alteration of **discompose**.]

discomfit [dis-kum´fit] *vt* to defeat the plans or hopes of; to frustrate;—*pr p* **discom´fiting**; *pt p* **discom´fited**.—*n* **discom´fiture**. [OFr *desconfit*, pt p of *desconfire—*L *dis-, conficĕre*, to prepare—*con-, facĕre*, to make.]

discomfort [dis-kum´fòrt] *n* uneasiness.—*vt* to deprive of comfort, to make uneasy. [OFr *desconforter—des-*, apart, *conforter*, to comfort. See **comfort**.]

discommode [dis-kom-ōd´] *vt* to inconvenience. [L *dis-* + obs *commode—*L *comodāre—commodus*. See **commodious**.]

discompose [dis-kom-pōz´] *vt* to disturb the self-possession of; to disarrange, disorder.—*n* **discompō´sure**. [L *dis-* + **compose**.]

disconcert [dis-kon-sûrt´] *vt* to confuse; to upset. [OFr *disconcerter—des-* (L *dis-*), apart, *concerter*, to concert.]

disconnect [dis-kon-ekt´] *vt* to separate or disjoin.—*adj* **disconnect´ed**, separated; incoherent.—*n* **disconnec´tion**. [L *dis-* + **connect**.]

disconsolate [dis-kon´so-lát] *adj* forlorn; dejected.—*adv* **discon´solately**. [L *dis-, consōlārī, consōlātus*, to console.]

discontent [dis-kon-tent´] *adj* not content.—*n* want of contentment; dissatisfaction; ill-humor.—*vt* to deprive of content.—*p adj* **discontent´ed**, dissatisfied; fretful.—*adv* **discontent´edly**.—**discontent´edness; discontent´ment**, discontent. [L *dis-* + **content**.]

discontinue [dis-kon-tin´ū] *vt* to stop; to give up.—*vi* to cease.—**discontin´uance, discontinuā´tion**, a breaking off or ceasing; **discontinu´ity**, want of continuity or of coherence.—*adj* **discontin´uous**, not continuous, interrupted, intermittent. [OFr *discontinuer—*L *dis-, continuāre*, to continue.]

discord [dis´körd] *n* disagreement, strife; (*mus*) a lack of harmony; harsh clashing sounds.—**discord´ance**—*adj* **discord´ant**, without concord or agreement; harsh, jarring; inconsistent, contradictory.—*adv* **discord´antly**. [OFr *descord—*L *discordia—dis-, cor, cordis*, the heart.]

discotheque [dis´kô-tek] *n* a nightclub for dancing to live or recorded music. [Fr]

discount [dis´kownt] *n* a deduction from the amount or cost; the percentage charged for doing this.—*vt* **discount´**, to deduct from the amount a cost; to allow for exaggeration; to disregard; to make less effective by anticipation.—*vi* to make and give discounts.—*adj* **discount´able**.—**discount´er, discount house, discount store**, a store where merchandise is sold at below the suggested retail price; **discount rate**, the annual interest rate deducted in advance on a loan; the charge levied by a central bank for advances and rediscounts. [OFr *descompter—des-* (L *dis-*), away, *compter*, to count.]

discountenance [dis-kown´tèn-àns] *vt* to refuse support to; to discourage. [OFr *descontenancer—des-, contenance*, countenance.]

discourage [dis-kur´ij] *vt* to take away the courage of; to try to prevent; to hinder.—**discour´ager, discour´agement**, act of discouraging; that which discourages;—*adj* **discourageable**. [OFr *descourager* (—*descoragier*)—L *dis-*. See **courage**.]

discourse [dis-kōrs´, -körs´, or dis´-] *n* a formal speech or writing; conversation.—*vi* to talk. [Fr *discours—*L *discursus—dis-*, away, *currĕre*, to run.]

discourteous [dis-kûrt´yus] *adj* lacking in courtesy, rude.—*adv* **discourt´eously**.—**discourt´eousness, discourt´esy**. [L *dis-* + **courtesy**.]

discover [dis-kuv´ėr] *vt* to see, find or learn of for the first time.—*adj* **discov´erable**.—**discov´erer; discov´ery**, the act of discovering; the thing discovered. [OFr *descouvrir—des-* (L *dis-*), away, *couvrir*, to cover.]

discredit [dis-kred´it] *n* doubt; disgrace.—*vt* to cast doubt on; to refuse belief in;—*adj* **discred´itable**, not creditable, disgraceful.—*adv* **discred´itably**. [L *dis-* + **credit**.]

discreet [dis-krēt´] *adj* wisely cautious, prudent.—*adv* **discreet´ly**.—*n* **discreet´ness**. [OFr *discret—*L *discrētus—discernĕre*, to separate, to perceive.]

discrepancy [dis-krep´án-si, or dis´-] *n* difference; disagreement.—*adj* **discrep´ant**, contrary, disagreeing.—*adv* **discrepantly**. [Fr,—L *discrepāns, -antis*, different—*dis-*, asunder, *crepāns*, pr p of *crepāre*, to sound.]

discrete [dis´krēt, dis-krēt´] *adj* separate; consisting of distinct parts; not mathematically continuous.—*adv* **discrete´ly**.—*n* **discrete´ness**. [A doublet of **discreet**.]

discretion [dis-kresh´(ò)n] *n* the freedom to judge or to choose; good judgment.—*adj* **discre´tionary**, left to discretion; unrestricted. [OFr *discrecion—*L discrētiō, -ōnis—discernĕre, -crētum. See **discern**.]

discriminate [dis-krim´i-nāt] *vi* to make a difference or distinction; (*with* **in favor of, against**) to treat favorably or unfavorably in comparison with others.—*adj* **discrim´inating**, making a distinction; gifted with judgment and penetration.—*n* **discriminā´tion**, act or quality of discriminating; discernment,—judgment.—*adj* **discrim´inative**, making distinctions.—*adv* **discrim´inatively**.—*adj* **discrim´inatory**, discriminative. [L *discrīmināre, -ātum—discrīmen*, that which separates—root of *discernĕre*. See **discern**.]

discursive [dis-kûr´siv] *adj* wandering from one subject to another; rambling.—*adv* **discur´sively**.—*n* **discur´siveness**. [L *dīs-, currĕre*, run.]

discus [dis´kus] *n* a heavy, circular plate of stone or metal used for throwing by atheletes;—*pl* **discuses**. [L,—Gr *diskos*.]

discuss [dis-kus´] *vt* to talk over; to investigate by reasoning or argument.—**discuss´ant**, one who takes part in a formal discussion; **discuss´ion**, debate. [L *discutĕre, discussum—dis-*, asunder, *quatĕre*, to shake.]

disdain [dis-dān´] *vt* to scorn, reject.—*n* scornful aversion; haughtiness.—*adj* **disdain´ful**.—*adv* **disdain´fully**.—*n* **disdain´fulness**. [OFr *desdaigner* with substitution of *des-* (L *dis-*) for L *dē* in L *dēdignārī—dignus*, worthy.]

disease [diz-ēz´] *n* sickness; illness, ailment; any particular illness.—*adj* **diseased´**, affected with disease. [OFr *desaise—des-* (L *dis-*), *aise*, ease.]

disembark [dis-em-bärk´] *vt* to set ashore.—*vi* to leave a ship, to land.—*n* **disembarkā´tion**. [OFr *desembarquer—des-* (L *dis-*), *embarquer*. See **embark**.]

disembarrass [dis-èm-bar´as] *vt* to free from something that holds back; to relieve.—*n* **disembarr´assment**. [L *dis-* + **embarrass**.]

disembody [dis-èm-bod´i] *vt* to separate (a soul, spirit etc.) from the body. [L *dis-* + **embody**.]

disembogue [dis-èm-bōg´] *vti* to discharge at the mouth, as a stream.—*n* **disembogue´ment**. [Sp *desembocar—des-* (L *dis-*), asunder, *embocar*, to enter the mouth—*em* (L *in*) into, *boca* (L *bucca*), cheek, mouth.]

disembowel [dis-èm-bow´el] *vt* to remove the entrails of; to remove the substance of. [L dis- + **embowel**.]

disenchant [dis-èn-chänt´] *vt* to free from a magic spell or illusion.—*n* **disenchant´ment**. [L *dis-* + **enchant**.]

disencumber [dis-èn-kum´ber] *vt* to free from a burden.—*n* **disencum´brance**. [L dis- + **encumber**.]

disendow [dis-ên-dow´] *vt* to take away the endowments of (esp of a school or church).—*n* **disendow´ment**. [L *dis-* + **endow**.]

disenfranchise [dis-en-fran´chīz] *vt* take the rights of citizenship away from.—*n* **disenfranchisement**. Also **disfranchise, disfranchisement**. [L *dis-* + **franchise**.]

disengage [dis-èn-gāj´] *vt* to separate or free from being engaged; to separate; to release.—*n* **disengage´ment**, a separating, releasing; a mutual withdrawal of potential combatants from a position.—*adj* **disengaged´**, at leisure. [OFr *desengager—des-* (L *dis-*), *engager*, to engage.]

disentangle [dis-èn-tang´gl] *vt* to free from complications.—*n* **disentang´lement**. [L *dis-* + **entangle**.]

disenthrall, disenthral [dis-èn-thröl´] *vt* to release from enchantment. [L *dis-* + **enthral**.]

disentomb [dis-èn-tōōm´] *vt* to remove from a tomb. [L *dis-* + **entomb**.]

disequilibrium [dis-ē-kwil-i´brium] loss or lack of equilibrium.

disestablish [dis-es-tab´lish] *vt* to deprive of an established position.—*n* **disestab´lishment**. [L *dis-* + **establish**.]

diseur [dē-soe´] *n* a professional entertainer who talks, recites, etc. [Fr *diseur*, one who recites.]

diseuse [dē-zœz] *n* a female diseur.

disfavor [dis-fāvȯr] *n* dislike; condition of being out of favor.—*vt* to withhold favor from, to disapprove. [L *dis-* + **favor**.]

disfigure [dis-fig´ūr] *vt* to spoil the beauty or excellence of, to deface.—**disfig´urement**. [OFr *desfigurer*—L *dis-*, *figūrāre*, to figure.]

disfranchise *see* **disenfranchise**.

disfrock [dis-frok´] *vt* to unfrock. [L *dis-* + **frock**.]

disgorge [dis-görj´] *vt* to discharge from the throat, to vomit; to give up (what one has wrongfully seized). [OFr *desgorger*—*des-* (L *dis-*) away, *gorge*, throat. See **gorge**.]

disgrace [dis-grās´] *n* loss of trust, favor, or honor; something that disgraces.—*vt* to put out of favor; to bring disgrace or shame upon.—*adj* **disgrace´ful**, causing shame; dishonorable.—*adv* **disgrace´fully**.—*n* **disgrace´fulness**. [Fr *disgrâce*—L *dis-*, neg, *gratia*, favor, grace.]

disgruntle [dis-grun´tl] *vt* to make ill-humored and dissatisfied.—*adjs* **disgruntling, disgruntled**.—*n* **disgruntlement**. [L *dis-* + *gruntle*, freq of **grunt**.]

disguise [dis-gīz´] *vt* to hide what one is by appearing as something else; to hide what (a thing) really is.—*n* the use of a changed appearance to conceal the identity of the wearer; a false appearance. [Fr *desguiser*—*des-* (L dis-), neg, *guise*, manner. See **guise**.]

disgust [dis-gust´] *n* sickening dislike.—*vt* to excite disgust in.—*adjs* **disgust´ed; disgust´ing**.—*adv* **disgust´ingly**. [OFr *desgouster*—*des-* (L *dis-*), gouster (L *gustāre*), *to taste*.]

dish [dish] *n* anything to serve food in; the amount of food served in a dish; the food served; any of various shallow concave vessels; a directional microwave antenna having a concave reflector; the state of being concave; an attractive woman.—*vt* to put (as food) into a dish; to present food (*with* **up**); to make concave like a dish.—*adj* **dished**, concave; (of a pair of wheels) closer together at the bottom than at the top.—**dishcloth**, a cloth for washing dishes; **dishcloth gourd**, the fruit of any of several gourds (genus *Luffa*) having a fibrous interior that is dried and used like a sponge; **dishpan**, a large flat-bottomed vessel for washing dishes; **dishpan hands** (*n pl* but *sing* or *pl* in construction) condition of dryness and redness of the hands resulting from reaction to household chemicals, esp detergents; **dishrag**, a dishcloth; **dish towel**, a cloth for drying dishes; **dishwasher**, a person hired to wash dishes; a machine for washing dishes; **dishwater**, water in which dishes have been or are to be washed. [OE *disc*, a plate, a dish, a table—L *discus*—Gr *diskos*.]

dishabille [dis-a-bēl´] *n* state of careless or casual dress. [Fr *déshabillé*, *pt p of déshabiller*, to undress—*des-* (L *dis-*), apart, *habiller*, to dress.]

disharmony [dis-här´mo-ni] *n* lack of harmony; discord; incongruity. [L *dis-* + **harmony**.]

dishearten [dis-härt´n] *vt* to discourage. [L *dis-* + **hearten**.]

dishevel [di-shev´el] *vt* to throw into disorder;—pr p **dishev´eling**; pt p *adj* **dishev´eled**, rumpled. [OFr *discheveler*—Low L *discapillāre*, to tear out or disorder the hair—L *dis-*, in different directions, *capillus*, the hair.]

dishonest [dis-on´ėst] *adj* not honest.—*adv* **dishon´estly**.—*n* **dishon´esty**. [OFr *deshoneste*—*des-* (L *dis-*), *honeste* (L *honestus*), honest.]

dishonor [dis-on´ȯr] *n* disgrace; shame.—*vt* to deprive of honor; to bring shame on, to disgrace; to refuse the payment of, as a check.—*adj* **dishon´orable**, having no sense of honor; disgraceful.—*n* **dishonorableness**.—*adv* **dishon´orably**. [OFr *deshonneur*—*des-* (L *dis-*), *honneur* (L *honor*), honor.]

disillusion [dis-i-l(y)ōō´zh(ȯ)n] *n* act of setting free from illusion; state of being freed from illusion.—*vt* to set free from illusion; to undeceive.—*adj* **disillusioned**, freed from illusions.—*n* **disillu´sionment**. [L. *dis-* + **illusion**.]

disincentive [dis-in-sen´tiv] *n* a discouragement to effort.—Also *adj*. [L *dis*,- + **incentive**.]

disinclination [dis-in-kli-nā´sh(ȯ)n] *n* unwillingness.—*vt* **disincline´**, to make unwilling (to, for).—*adj* **disinclined´**, not inclined; averse (to). [L *dis-* + **incline**.]

disinfect [dis-in-fekt´] *vt* to destroy germs.—*n* **disinfect´ant**, any chemical agent that inhibits the growth of or destroys germs.—Also *adj*—*n* **disinfec´tion**. [L *dis-* + **infect**.]

disinformation [dis-informa´shun] *n* false information given out by intelligence agencies to mislead foreign spies. [**dis-** + **information**.]

disingenuous [dis-in-jen´ū-us] *adj* insincere.—*adv* **disingen´uously**.—*n* **disingen´uousness**. [L *dis-* + **ingenuous**.]

disinherit [dis-in-her´it] *vt* to deprive of an inheritance.—*n* **disinher´itance**. [L *dis-* + **inherit**.]

disintegrate [dis-in´ti-grāt] *vti* to separate into parts; to crumble.—*ns* **disintegrā´tion; disin´tegrator**—*adj* **disintegrative**. [L *dis-* + **integrate**.]

disinter [dis-in-tûr´] *vt* to take out of a grave; to bring to light.—*n* **disinter´ment**. [L *dis-* + **inter**.]

disinterested [dis-in´tėr-est-ed] *adj* impartial; uninterested.—*adv* **disin´terestedly**.—*n* **disin´terestedness**. [L *dis-* + **interested**.]

disjoin [dis-join´] *vt* to separate what has been joined.—*vti* **disjoint´**, to take or come apart at the joints.—*adj* **disjoint´ed**, incoherent, esp of speech or writing.—*adv* **disjoint´edly**.—*n* **disjoint´edness**. [OFr *desjoindre*—L *disjungĕre*—*dis-*, apart, *jungĕre*, to join.]

disjunct [dis-jungkt´] *adj* disjoined.—*n* **disjunc´tion**, the act of disjoining; disunion; separation.—*adj* **disjunct´ive**, disjoining; separating; (gram) uniting sentences but marking a contrast in sense (eg of conjunctions such as *either, or*).—*n* a word which disjoins.—*adv* **disjunct´ively**. [OFr *desjoinct*—*desjoindre*. See **disjoin**.]

disk, disc [disk] *n* any flat thin circular body; the circular figure presented by a spherical body, as the sun; a cylindrical elastic pad made of fibrocartilage between vertebrae; a phonograph record; a storage device in a computer; see **floppy disk** (under **flop**) and **hard disk** (under **hard**).—**diskectomy**, the surgical removal of a portion of an intervertebral disk.—**disk´ jockey** one who provides a commentary on a program of recorded music.—**floppy disk** *see* **floppy**. [Gr *diskos*.]

dislike [dis-līk´] *vt* to be displeased with.—*n* aversion, distaste. [L *dis-* + **like**]

dislocate [dis´lo-kāt] *vt* to put out of joint; to disturb—*n* **dislocā´tion**, a dislocated joint; displacement; [Low L *dislocāre*, *-ātum*—L *dis-*, apart, *locāre*, to place.]

dislodge [dis-loj´] *vt* to drive from a place of rest, or of hiding, or of defense; to force, or to knock accidentally, out from its place.—*n* **dislodg´ment**. [OFr *desloger, des-* (L *dis-*), apart, *loger*, to lodge.]

disloyal [dis-loi´ȧl] *adj* not *loyal*—*adv* **disloy´ally**.—*n* **disloy´alty**. [OFr *desloyal*—*des-* (L *dis-*), loyal, leial—L *lēgālis*, legal.]

dismal [diz´mȧl] *adj* gloomy, dreary, cheerless.—*adv* **dis´mally**. [OFr *dismal*—L *dies malī*, evil, unlucky days.]

dismantle [dis-man´tl] *vt* to strip of guns, covering, etc.; to pull down; to take apart. [OFr *desmanteller*—*des-* (L *dis-*), away, *manteler*—*mantel*, a mantle.]

dismast [dis-mäst´] *vt* to take the mast from; to break down the mast of. [L *dis-*, + **mast**.]

dismay [dis-mā´] *vt* to make afraid.—*n* loss of courage through fear. [Apparently through OFr—L *dis-*, and OHG *magan* (OE *magan*), to have might or power. See **may**.]

dismember [dis-mem´ber] *vt* to cut or tear the limbs from.—*n* **dismem´berment**. [O Fr *desmembrer*—*des-* (L *dis-*), *membre* (L *membrum*), a member.]

dismiss [dis-mis´] *vt* to send away; to remove from office or employment; to stop thinking about; (*law*) to put out of court.—**dismiss´al, dismiss´ion**. [L *dis-*, away, *mittĕre, missum*, to send.]

dismount [dis-mownt´] *vt* to get off a horse, bicycle, etc.; to throw from a horse; to take (a thing) from its setting or support. [OFr *desmonter*—*des-* (L *dis-*), *monter*, to mount.]

Disneyesque [diz-ne-esk´] *adj* whimsical, resembling anthropomorphic cartoon characters created by Walt Disney.

disobedient [dis-o-bēd´yėnt] *adj* neglecting or refusing to obey.—*n* **disobē´dience**.—*adv* **disobē´diently**. [L *dis-* + **obedient**.]

disobey [dis-o-bā´] *vt* to neglect, to refuse, to obey or do what is commanded. [OFr *desobeir*—*des-* (L *dis-*) + *obeir*, to obey.]

disoblige [dis-o-blīj´] *vt* to neglect or refuse to oblige.—*adj* **disoblig´ing**.—*adj* **disoblig´ingly**. [L *dis-* + **oblige**.]

disorder [dis-ör´der] *n* confusion; riot; an illness in which symptoms are produced without the intervention of germs.—*vt* to disarrange; to upset the health of.—*adj* **disor´dered**, confused, deranged.—*adj* **disor´derly**, out of order, in confusion;—*n* **disor´derliness**—**disorderly conduct**, (*law*) a petty offense against public order and decency. [OFr *desordre*—*des-* (L *dis-*), neg, *ordre*.]

disorganize [dis-ör´gan-īz] *vt* to destroy the structure of; to throw into disorder.—*n* **disorganizā´tion**. [L *dis-* + organize.]

disown [dis-ōn´] *vt* to refuse to acknowledge as one's own. [L *dis-* + **own**.]

disorient [dis-orē´ent] *vt* to cause the loss of sense of time, place, or identity; to confuse.—*n* **dis-orientation**. Also **disorientate** [-āt]. [Fr *désorienter*.]

disparage [dis-par´ij] *vt* to belittle.—**dispar´agement, dispar´ager**.—*adv* **dispar´agingly**. [OFr *desparager*—*des-* (L *dis*). *parage*, equality of birth.—L. *par*, equal.]

disparate [dis´pȧr-ȧt] *adj* unequal, incapable of being compared. [L *disparātus*—*dis-*, *parāre*, make ready; influenced by *dispar*. unequal.]

disparity [dis-par´i-ti] *n* essential difference; the quality of being unlike. [L *dispar*, unequal—*dis-*, *par*, equal.]

dispassion [dis-pash´(ȯ)n,] *n* freedom from passion; calm state of mind.—*adj* **dispass´ionate** (*-ȧt*), cool; impartial.—*adv* **dispass´ionately**. [L *dis-* + **passion**.]

dispatch [dis-pach´] *vt* to send off to some place; to perform speedily; to kill.—*n* a sending off (of a letter, a messenger etc); rapid performance; haste; a written message, esp of news. Also **despatch**.—**dispatcher** [dis-pach´er] a person in a transportation company overseeing the departure of taxis, trains, planes, buses; a person at police headquarters directing the destination of police cars. [It *dispacciare*, or Sp *despachar*—L *dis-*, apart, and root of *pangĕre, pactum*, to fasten; not conn with Fr *dépêcher*.]

dispel [dis-pel´] *vt* to drive away and scatter;—pr p **dispell´ing**; pt p **dispelled´**. [L *dispellĕre*—*dis*, away, *pellĕre*, to drive.]

dispensable [dis-pens´ȧ-bl] *adj* which can be done without. [Low L *dispensābilis*—L *dispensāre*.]

dispensary [dis-pens´ȧr-i] *n* a place where medicines are made up and dispensed. [Root of **dispensation**.]

dispensation [dis-pen-sā´sh(ȯ)n] *n* the act of distributing or dealing out; licence or permission to neglect a rule.—*adjs* **dispens´ātional, dispens´atory**, granting permission.—*vt* **dispense**, to deal out in portions; to distribute; to administer.—*n* **dispens´er**, one who dispenses; a container that gives out a product in prearranged quantities.—**dispense with**, to do without. [OFr,—L *dispensatiō, -ōnis—dispensāre—dis-*, asunder, *pensāre*, inten of *pendĕre*, to weigh.]

disperse [dis-pûrs´] *vt* to scatter; to send in different directions; to cause to evaporate or vanish.—*vi* to separate; to spread; to vanish.—**dispers´al**, the act or result of dispersion; **dispers´er**.—*adj* **dispers´ive**, of dispersion; tending to disperse. [L *dīspergĕre, dīspersum—dī* (*dis-*), asunder, apart, *spargĕre*, to scatter.]

dispersion [dis-pûr´sh(ȯ)n] *n* a scattering, or state of being scattered; the separation of light into colors by diffraction or refraction. [**disperse**.]

dispirit [dis-pir´it] *vt* to depress.—*adj* **dispir´ited**, dejected.—*adv* **dispir´itedly**. [L *dis-* + **spirit**.]

displace [dis-plās´] *vt* to take the place of; to remove from a position of authority; to put out of place.—*adj* **displace´able**.—*n* **displace´ment**, a putting or being out of place; the quantity of water displaced by a floating object.—**displaced person**, a refugee [OFr *desplacer—des-* (L *dis-*), + *place*, place.]

display [dis-plā´] *vt* to show; to exhibit; to set out ostentatiously.—*n* a displaying; exhibition; ostentatious show;—*n* **display´er**. [OFr *despleier—des-* (L *dis-*), + *plier, ploier* (L *plicāre*), to fold; doublet of **deploy**. *See* **ply**.]

displease [dis-plēz] *vt* to offend; to annoy.—*vi* to raise aversion.—*adj* **displeased´**, vexed, annoyed.—*n* **displeasure** (*dis-plezh´ůr*), the feeling of one who is offended; discomfort. [OFr *desplaisir—des-* (L *dis-*), *plaisir*, to please.]

disport [dis-pōrt, -pört´] *vt* to divert, amuse; (*reflexive*) to amuse oneself. [OFr *desporter* (with *se*), to carry (oneself) away from one's work, to amuse (oneself)—*des-* (L *dis-*), and *porter* (L *portāre*), to carry. See **sport**.]

dispose [dis-pōz´] *vt* to arrange; to influence—*vi* to settle a matter finally.—*adj* **dispos´able**, intended to be thrown away or destroyed after use.—*n* **dispos´al**, order, arrangement; selling; settling; the getting rid (of);—*adj* **disposed´**, inclined;—*n* **dispos´er**.—**dispose of**, to settle what is to be done with; to sell. [Fr *disposer—dis-* (L *dis-*), asunder, *poser*, to place—L *pausāre*.]

disposition [dis-po-zish´(ȯ)n] *n* natural way of behaving toward others; tendency; arrangement. [Fr,—L from *dis-*, apart, *pōnĕre*, to place.]

dispossess [dis-poz-es´] *vt* to force to give up ownership of a house, land, etc.—*adj* **dispossessed´**, deprived of possessions and security etc.—*n* **dispossess´or**. [L *dis-* + **possess**.]

dispraise [dis-prāz´] *n* expression of disapproval; blame, reproach.—*vt* to censure. [OFr *despreisier—des-* (L dis-), *preisier*, to praise.]

disproof [dis-prōōf´] *n* a disproving; refutation. [L *dis-* + **proof**.]

disproportion [dis-pro-pōr´sh(ȯ)n] *n* lack of symmetry.—*vt* to make out of proportion.—*adj* **dispropor´tional**.—*adv* **dispropor´tionally**.—*adj* **dispropor´tionate**, ill-proportioned; too large or too small in relation to something else.—*adv* **dispropor´tionately**.—*n* **dispropor´tionateness**. [L *dis-* **proportion**.]

disprove [dis-prōōv´] *vt* to prove to be false [OFr *desprover—des-* (L *dis-*) *prover*. See **prove**.]

dispute [dis-pūt´] *vt* to make a subject of argument; to oppose by argument; to call in question; to resist; to contend for.—*vi* to argue; to debate.—*n* an argument; a quarrel.—*adj* **disput´able** [also dis-], that may be disputed; of doubtful certainty.—*adv* **dis´putably**.—*ns* **dis´putant, disputā´tion**, a contest in argument; an exercise in debate.—*adjs* **disputātious**. inclined to dispute, cavil, or controvert.—*adv* **disputā´tiously**.—*n* **dispū´tatiousness**. [OFr *desputer*—L *disputāre—dis-*, apart, + *putāre*, to think.]

disqualify [dis-kwol´i-fi] *vt* to deprive of qualification; to declare unqualified; to make unfit, to disable.—*n* **disqualificā´tion**, state of being disqualified; anything that disqualifies or incapacitates. [L *dis-* + **qualify**.]

disquiet, *dis-kwī´et, n.* uneasiness, restlessness: anxiety.—*v.t.* to make uneasy.—**disquīetude**, state of disquiet. [L. *dis-* + **quiet**.]

disquisition [dis-kwi-zish´(ȯ)n] *n* a careful inquiry into any matter by speech or writing.—*adj* **disquisi´tional**. [L *disquīsītiō, -onis—disquīrĕre—dis-, quaerĕre, quaesītum*, to seek.]

disregard [dis-ri-gärd´] *vt* to pay no attention to.—*n* neglect (of—*also with* **for**). [L *dis-*, + **regard**.]

disrelish [dis-rel´ish] *vt* to dislike the taste of.—*n* distaste, dislike. [L *dis-*, + **relish**.]

disrepair [dis-ri-pār´] *n* state of being out of repair. [L *dis-*, + **repair**.]

disrepute [dis-ri-pūt´] *n* disgrace.—Also **disreputability, disreputableness**.—*adj* **disrep´utable**, not respectable.—*adv* **disrep´utably**. [L *dis-*, + **repute**.]

disrespect [dis-ri-spekt] *n* lack of respect. Also **disrespectfulness**.—*adj* **disrespect´ful**, showing disrespect; irreverent;—*adv* **disrespect´fully**. [L *dis-*, neg, + **respect**.]

disrobe [dis-rōb´] *vt* to undress. [L *dis-*, + **robe**.]

disrupt [dis-rupt´] *vti* to break up.—*n* **disrup´tion**, the act of breaking up.—*adj* **disrup´tive**, causing, or accompanied by, disruption. [L *disruptus, dīruptus—dīrumpĕre—dis-*, asunder, *rumpĕre*, to break.]

dissatisfy [dis-sat´is-fī] *vt* to fail to satisfy; to make discontented.—**dissatisfac´tion**, state of being dissatisfied. [L *dis-*, + **satisfy**.]

dissect [di-sekt´] *vt* to cut apart (a plant, an animal, etc.) in order to determine the structure of; to analyze and interpret minutely.—*adj* **dissect´ed**. (*bot*) cut deeply into fine lobes; divided by hills and ridges.—**dissec´tion**, the act or process of dissecting, a specimen prepared by dissecting. [L *dissecāre, dissectum—dis-*, asunder, *secāre*, to cut.]

dissemble [di-sem´bl] *vt* to pretend.—*vi* to assume a false appearance; to play the hypocrite.—*n* **dissem´bler**. [L *dissimulāre—dissimilis*, unlike—*dis-, similis*, like.]

disseminate [di-sem´i-nāt] *vt* to sow or scatter (*usually fig*), to spread (knowledge etc.).—*n* **disseminā´tion**.—*n* **dissem´inator**. [L *dissēminare, -ātum—dis-*, asunder, *sēmināre*, to sow—*sēmen, sēminis*, seed.]

dissent [di-sent´] *vi* to disagree; to withhold assent.—*n* difference of opinion; religious nonconformity; a justice's non-concurrence with a majority decision.—**dissen´sion, dissention**, disagreement; **dissent´er**, one who dissents; **Dissenter**, an English Nonconformist.—*adj* **dissen´tient** [-shėnt], declaring dissent;—*n* one who disagrees. [Fr,—L *dissentīre, dissensum—dis-*, apart, *sentīre*, to think.]

dissertate [dis´ėr-tāt] *vi* to discourse.—*n* **dissertā´tion**, a treatise.—*adj* **dissertā´tional**.—*n* **diss´ertātor**. [L *dissertāre*, intensive of *disserĕre*, to discuss—*dis-, serĕre*, to put together.]

disserve [dis-sûrv´] *vt* to do an ill turn to.—*n* **disserv´ice**, injury, an ill turn.—*adj* **disserv´iceable**. [OFr *desservir*—L *dis-, servīre*, to serve.]

dissever [di-sev´ėr] *vt* to sever; to separate, disunite.—*vi* to come apart.—*n* **dissev´erance**. [OFr *dessevrer*—L *dis-*, apart, *sēparāre*, to separate.]

dissident [dis´i-dėnt] *adj* dissenting, disagreeing, esp with the views of a government.—*n* a dissenter.—*n* **diss´idence**, disagreement. [L *dissidens, -entis*, pr p of *dissidēre—dis-*, apart, *sedēre*, to sit.]

dissimilar [di-sim´i-lȧr] *adj* unlike—**dissimilar´ity, dissimil´itude**. [L *dissimilis—dis-, similis*, like.]

dissimulate [di-sim´u-lāt] *vt* to conceal or disguise, dissemble.—*vi* to practise dissimulation.—*n* **dissimulā´tion**, the act of dissembling; hypocrisy. [L *dissimulāre, -ātum*, to dissimulate—*dis-, similis*, like.]

dissipate [dis´i-pāt] *vt* to scatter; to cause to spread thinly; to dissolve; to lose (heat or electricity) irrecoverably; to squander.—*vi* to separate and disappear; to be extravagant in the pursuit of pleasure.—*adjs* **diss´ipated**, dissolute, esp addicted to drinking, **dissipative**; of dissipation, esp of heat.—*n* **dissipā´tion**, dispersion; state of being dispersed; wasteful expenditure (eg of energy, funds); intemperate living; frivolous amusement. [L *dissipāre, -ātum—dis-*, asunder, archaic *supāre*, to throw.]

dissociate [di-sō´shi-āt] *vt* to think of apart (from), separate in thought; (*reflexive*) to repudiate connection with; to separate (*also vi*).—*n* **dissociā´tion** (*-sō-si*). [L *dissociāre, -ātum—dis-*, asunder, *sociāre*, to associate.]

dissolve [di-zolv´] *vt* to cause to pass into solution; to disperse (as an assembly); to break up (as a partnership or marriage) legally.—*vi* to become liquid; to be overcome by emotion.—*n* the gradual disappearance of an image in a motion-picture or television shot.—*adj* **dissol´vent**, having power to dissolve.—*n* that which can dissolve.—*adj* **dissoluble** [dis´ol-(y)ōō-bl, or disol´ū-bl], capable of being dissolved.—*n* **dissolubil´ity**.—*adj* **diss´olūte**, loose, esp in morals, lewd, licentious.—*adv* **diss´olūtely**.—**diss´olūteness; dissolū´tion**, death; undoing; breaking up of an assembly; change from a solid to a liquid state; decomposition. [L *dissolvĕre, -solūtum—dis-*, asunder, *solvĕre, solūtum*, to loose.]

dissonant [dis´-o-nȧnt] *adj* not agreeing or harmonizing in sound, etc.; discordant.—*n* **diss´onance**, a clashing musical interval; discord, disagreement. [Fr,—L *dissonans, -antis—dis-*, apart, *sonāre*, to sound.]

dissuade [di-swād´] *vt* to prevent or deter by advice or persuasion.—*n* **dissuā´sion**.—*adj* **dissuā´sive**, tending to dissuade.—*n* that which tends to dissuade.—*adv* **dissuā´sively**. [L *dissuādēre—dis*, apart, *suādēre, suāsum*, to advise.]

distaff [dis´täf] *n* the stick that holds the bunch of flax, tow, or wool in spinning.—**distaff side**, the female part of a family. [OE *distæf* from Low Ger *diesse*, the bunch of flax on the staff, and *stæf*, staff.]

distal [dis´tal] *adj* farthest from the point of attachment; of or situated at the outer end. [Formed from **distance**.]

distance [dis´tȧns] *n* a space or interval (between); a distant place or point (eg *in the distance*); remoteness; reserve of manner.—*vt* to place at a distance; to leave at a distance behind.—**keep one's distance** (*lit and fig*), to keep aloof. [OFr *distance*—L *dīstantia—dīstans*. See **distant**.]

distant [dis´tȧnt] *adj* far away in time, place, or connection; at a great distance; far apart in time, likeness, etc.; not friendly.—*adv* **dis´tantly**. [Fr,—L *dīstans, -antis—dis-*, apart, *stans, stantis*, pr p of *stāre*, to stand.]

distaste [dis-tāst´] *n* disrelish, dislike.—*adj* **distaste´ful**, unpleasant to the taste; disagreeable.—*adv* **distaste´fully**.—*n* **distastefulness**. [L *dis-* + **taste**.]

distemper[1] [dis-tem´pėr] *n* a paint made by mixing the color with eggs or glue instead of oil; a painting made with distemper. [L *dis-*, *temperāre*, to regulate, mix in proportion. See next word.]

distemper[2] [dis-tem´pėr] *n* an infectious often fatal disease of dogs and other animals; sickness of the mind or body. [OFr *destemprer*, to derange.—L *dis-*, apart, *temperāre*, to govern, regulate.]

distend [dis-tend´] *vt* to stretch; to swell, esp from internal pressure.—*vi* to swell.—*adjs* **disten´sible**, that may be stretched;—*n* **distension, disten´tion**, act of distending or stretching. [L *distendĕre—dis-*, asunder, *tendĕre, tensum* or *tentum*, to stretch.]

distich [dis´tik] *n* a couple of lines or verses making complete sense, a couplet. [Gr *distichos—dis*, twice, *stichos*, a line.]

distill, distil [dis-til´] *vi* to fall in drops; to use a still.—*vt* to let or cause to fall in drops; to convert a liquid into vapor by heat, and then to condense it again; to extract the spirit or essential oil from anything by evaporation and condensation;—*pr p* **distill´ing**; *pt p* **distilled´**.—**distilla´tion**, the act of distilling; **dis´tillate**, the product of distillation; something distilled; **distill´er**, one who or that which distills; **distill´ery**, a place where distilling esp of alcoholic liquor is carried on. [OFr *distiller*, with change of prefix—L *dēstillāre, -ātum—dē*, down, *stillāre*, to drop—*stilla*, a drop.]

distinct [dis-tingkt´] *adj* separate; different; well-defined; clear.—*adj* **distinct´ive**, marking or expressing difference; characteristic.—*adv* **distinct´ly**.—*n* **distinct´ness**. [OFr,—L *distinctus*. See **distinguish**.]

distinction [dis-tingksh(ò)n] *n* separation or division; difference; that which distinguishes; discrimination; excellence, superiority; a mark of honor. [Fr,—L *dīstinctiō, -ōnis—dīstinguĕre*. See **distinguish**.]

distingué [dis-tang´gā, dē̆s-tɛ-gā] *adj* (with appearance or manner) suggesting birth and breeding; **distingueé**, when referring to a woman. [Fr]

distinguish [dis-ting´gwish] *vt* to tell apart; to see or hear clearly; to confer distinction on; to make eminent or known.—*vi* to perceive a difference.—*adj* **disting´uishable**, capable of being distinguished.—*adv* **disting´uishably**.—*adjs* **disting´uished**, illustrious; distingué; **disting´uishing**, characteristic.—**Distinguished Flying Cross**, US military decoration awarded for heroism, esp in aerial combat; **Distinguished Service Cross**, US Army decoration awarded for heroism in battle; **Distinguished Service Medal**, US military decoration awarded for meritorious government service in wartime. [L *dīstinguĕre, dīstinctum—dī-*, asunder, *stinguĕre*, orig to prick.]

distort [dis-tört´] *vt* to twist out of shape; to misrepresent.—*n* **distor´tion**, a twisting out of regular shape; crookedness; any departure from the initial wave-form during transmission of radio or video signals. [L *dis-*, asunder, *torquĕre, tortum*, to twist.]

distract [dis-trakt´] *vt* to draw away, esp of the mind or attention; to confuse.—*adjs* **distract´ed, distractible**.—*adv* **distract´edly**.—*n* **distrac´tion**, state of being distracted; perplexity; agitation; that which distracts or diverts attention. [L *distrahĕre, -tractum—dis-*, apart, *trahĕre*, to draw.]

distrait [dis-trā´] *adj* absent-minded; inattentive because worried or harassed. [Fr]

distraught [dis-tröt´] *adj* distracted, wildly perplexed; crazed, [**distract**, modified by association with words like **caught, taught**.]

distress [dis-tres´] *n* suffering; that which causes suffering; calamity; condition of being in danger and requiring help.—*vt* to afflict with pain or suffering; to harass; to grieve.—*adj* **distress´ful**.—*adv* **distress´fully**.—*adj* **distress´ing**.—*adv* **distressingly**.—**distress call**, pre-arranged code sign indicating that the sender needs help, eg Mayday, SOS; **distressed finish**, treatment applied to furniture to minimize wear. [OFr *destresse*—L *dīstringĕre*; see **distrain**.]

distribute [dis-trib´ūt] *vt* to divide and share out; to spread; to divide into parts; to arrange; to transport goods to retail outlets.—*adj* **distrib´utable**, that may be allotted.—*n* **distrib´utary**, a river branch flowing away from the main stream.—**distrib´utor**, an agent who sells goods, esp wholesale; a device for distributing current to the spark plugs in an engine.—**distribū´tion**, allotment; dispersal; the manner of allotment or dispersal; the manner in which the products of industry are shared among the people; classification.—**Distrib´utive Education** a vocational program in which a student receives both school instruction and on-the-job training; **distributive law** (*math*) stating that multiplication is distributive with respect to addition, ie the effects of a multiplier are distributed impartially over the terms of a sum.—*adv* **distrib´utively**. [L *distribuĕre—dis-*, asunder, *tribuĕre, tribūtum*, to allot.]

district [dis´trikt] *n* a portion of territory defined for political, judicial, educational, or other purposes; a region or area with a distinguishing character.—*vt* to divide into districts.—*adj* **districtwide**.—**district attorney**, law officer acting for the people or government in a specified district. [Fr,—LL *dīstrictus—dīstringĕre*, to draw tight.]

distrust [dis-trust´] *n* lack of trust.—*vt* to have no trust in.—*adj* **distrust´ful**, suspicious.—*adv* **distrust´fully**.—*n* **distrust´fulness**. [L *dis-* + **trust**.]

disturb [dis-tûrb´] *vt* to interrupt; to throw into confusion; to disquiet.—*adj* **disturbed**, showing symptoms of emotional illness.—*ns* **disturb´ance**, tumult; interruption or confusion (of procedure, arrangement, etc.); **disturb´er**. [OFr *destourber*—L *disturbāre—dis-*, asunder, *turbāre*, to agitate—*turba*, a crowd.]

disunion [dis-ūn´y(ò)n] *n* breaking up of union; separation. [L *dis-* + **union**.]

disunite [dis-ū-nīt´] *vt* to divide, to separate.—*n* **disū´nity**. [L *dis-*, priv, + **unite**.]

disuse [dis-ūs´, or dis´ūs] *n* cessation of use or practice; state of not being used.—*vt* (*dis-ūz´*) to stop using or practicing. [L *dis-* + **use**.]

ditch [dich] *n* any long narrow depression dug in the ground.—*vt* to dig a ditch in or around; to drive (a car) into a ditch; to make a forced landing of (an airplane) on water; to get rid of.—**ditchdigger**, one who digs ditches; person employed in hard manual labor; **ditch reed**, a tall N American reed (*Phragmites communis*) with broad flat leaves. [OE *dīc*, whence also **dike**.]

ditheism [dī´thē-izm] *n* the doctrine of the existence of two supreme gods. [Gr *di-*, twice, *theos*, a god.]

dither [dith´er] *vi* to tremble, quake; to waver.—*n* a trembling; agitation; perturbation. [Prob imit.]

dithyramb [dith´i-ram(b)] *n* (*derog*) any extravagantly emotional passage of prose or verse.—*adj* **dithyram´bic**, of or like a dithyramb; wildly enthusiastic. [L,—Gr *dithyrambos*.]

dittany [dit´à-ni] *n* gas plant; any of various plants of the mint family. [OFr *dictame*—L *dictamnus*—Gr *diktamnos*; prob from Mt *Diktē* in Crete.]

ditto [dit´ō] *n* that which has been said; the same thing represented by two turned commas. **ditto marks**, in lists or tables to avoid repetition.—*adv* as before. [It *ditto*—L *dictum*, said, *pt p* of *dīcĕre*, to say.]

ditty [dit´i] *n* a song; a little poem to be sung. [OFr *ditie*—L *dictātum*, neut of *dictātus*, perf part of *dictāre*, to dictate.]

ditty-bag [dit´i-bag] *n* a sailor's bag for needles, thread, etc.—Also **ditty-box**.

diuretic [dī-ū-ret´ik] *adj* promoting the discharge of urine.—*n* a substance causing this discharge. [Fr,—Gr *diourētikos—dia*, through, *ouron*, urine.]

diurnal [dī-ûr´nàl] *adj* daily; of the daytime; having a daily cycle.—*adv* **diur´nally**. [L *diurnālis—dies*, a day.]

diva [dē-va] *n* a great woman singer. [It,—L *dīva*, fem of *dīvus*, divine.]

divagate [dī´va-gāt] *vi* to wander about; to digress.—*n* **dīvagā´tion**. [L *dīvagārī*.]

divalent [div´àl-ènt, or dī-vā´lènt] *adj* (*chem*) having a valence of two; associated in pairs in synapsis.—*n* a pair of synaptic chromosomes. [Gr *di-*, twice, + L *valens, -entis, pr p* of *valēre*, to have power.]

divan [di-van´] *n* a large couch without back or sides often used as a bed; an Oriental council of state; a court of justice; a council chamber with cushioned seats; an Eastern couch; a smoking room. [Ar and Pers *dīwān*, a long seat.]

divaricate [dī-var´i-kāt] *vt* to spread apart; to branch off; to diverge.—*adj* widely divergent, spreading apart.—*n* **divaricā´tion**, a divergence of opinion. [L *dīvaricāre, -ātum—dī-*, asunder, *varicāre*, to spread the legs—*vārus*, bent apart.]

dive [dīv] *vi* to plunge headfirst into water or down through the air; to plunge (the body, hand, or mind) suddenly into anything.—*pr p* **diving**; *pt p* **dove, dived**.—*n* a plunge; a swoop; (*slang*) a disreputable public place, a speakeasy; in prizefighting, a pre-arranged feigned knockout.—*n* **dive´bomb´er**, an airplane that discharges a bomb while in a steep dive.—**div´er**, one who dives; one who works from a diving bell or in a diving suit; a loon or any bird skillful at diving.—**diving bell**, a hollow vessel supplied with air for respiration, in which one may work under water; **diving board**, a springboard; **diving suit**, a weighted, sealed costume supplied with air, worn underwater. [OE *dȳfan, dūfan*; ON *dȳfa*.]

diverge [di- or dī-vûrj´] *vi* to branch off; to differ, deviate (from a standard).—**diverg´ence, diverg´ency**.—*adj* **diverg´ent**. [L *dis-*, asunder, *vergĕre*, to incline.]

diverz [dīv´ėrs] *adj* sundry, several, more than one. [*See* **divert**.]

diverse [dīvėrs, or dī-vûrs´] *adj* different, unlike; multiform, various.—*adv* **dī´versely** (or *dīverse´ly*).—*n* **diver´sity**, state of being diverse; difference, unlikeness; variety.

diversify [di-vûr´si-fī] *vt* to make (investments) in securities of different types so as to lessen risk of loss; to engage in production of a variety of (manufactures, crops).—Also *vi*—*pr p* **diver´sifying**; *pt p* **diver´sified**.—*n* **diversificā´tion**. [Fr,—Low L *dīversificāre—dīversus*, diverse, *facĕre*, to make.]

diversion [di-vûr´sh(ò)n] *n* amusement, recreation; act of diverting or turning aside; that which diverts; a tactical move to take an enemy's attention off a more important operation.—*adj* **diver´sionary**, of the nature of a diversion. [See **divert**.]

divert [di-vûrt´] *vt* to turn aside; to amuse.—*adj* **divert´ing**.—*adv* **divert´ingly**. [Fr,—L *dīvertĕre, dīversum—dī-*, aside, *vertĕre*, to turn.]

divertimento [di-vėr-ti-men´tō] *n* (*mus*) a divertissement. [It]

divertissement [dē-ver-tēs´mō] *n* a diversion, amusement; a short ballet, primarily for presentation between longer ballets; a short light-hearted piece of music; a musical pot-pourri. [Fr]

divest [di- or dī-vest´] *vt* to strip or deprive (of anything). [OFr *desvestir*, with change of prefix (*dis-* for *dē-*) from L. *dēvestīre—dē*, away from, *vestīre*, to clothe—*vestis*, a garment.]

divide [di-vīd´] *vt* to break up, or mark off, into parts, actually or in imagination; to separate into equal parts; to keep apart; (*math*) to ascertain how many times one quantity contains another.—*vi* to separate; to fall apart.—*n* a watershed.—*adv* **divid´edly**.—*n* **divid´er**, furniture, plants, etc. used to separate functions in a room; one who or that which divides.—*adj* **divid´ing**, separating. [L *dīvidĕre, dīvīsum—dis-*, asunder, root *vid*, to separate.]

dividend [div´i-dend] *n* a number or quantity which is to be divided by another number or quantity; the money earned by a company and divided by the owners of the company. [L *dīvidendum—dīvidĕre*. See **divide**.]

divine [di-vīn´] *adj* of, from, or like God or a god; excellent in the highest degree.—*n* a minister of the gospel; a theologian.—*vt* to discover intuitively; to dowse.—*vi* to profess or practise divination; to prophecy.—*ns* **divinā´tion**, the act or practice of foretelling the future or of finding a hidden thing by supernatural means; intuitive perception; **divin´er**, one who divines or professes divination.—*adv* **divine´ly**.—*n* **divin´ingrod**, a forked rod, used by those professing to discover water or metals underground. [OFr *devin*, soothsayer—L *dīvīnus*, from *dīvus, deus*, a god.]

divinity [di-vin´i-ti] *n* any god; theology; the quality of being God or a god.—**divinity drops, divinity fudge**, a confection made of eggwhites, chopped nuts, sugar; etc. [OFr *devinite*—L *dīvinitās, -ātis. See* **divine**.]

division [di-vizh´(ò)n] *n* act of dividing; state of being divided; that which divides, a partition, a barrier; a portion or section; a military unit; separation; difference in opinion, etc.; disunion; *(math)* the process of dividing one number by another.—*adj* **divis´ible**, capable of being divided or separated;—*n* **divisibil´ity**.—*adv* **divis´ibly**.—*adjs* **divi´sional** (*-vizh´-*), pertaining to or marking a division or separation; **divīs´ive**, creating discord.—*n* **divī´sor** *(math)*, the number that divides the dividend. [OFr—L *divīsiō, -ōnis—dividěre*.]

divorce [di-vōrs´, -vörs´] *n* the legal dissolution of marriage; separation.—*vt* to dissolve the marriage of; to become divorced from; to separate.—*ns* **divorcee**, a divorced person; **divorce´ment**. [Fr,—L *dīvortium—dīvortěre*, another form of *dīvertěre*. See **divert**.]

divot [div´òt] *n* a piece of turf dug from a golf course while making a shot.

divulge [di-vulj´] *vt* to tell; ro reveal. [Fr—L *dīvulgāre—dī-*, abroad, *vulgāre*, to publish—*vulgus*, the common people.]

divvy [div´ē] *vt (inf)* divide and share.

dixie [dik´sē] *n (inf)* cooking utensil or mess tin.—**Dixie**, southern states of the US.—**Dixieland**, New Orleans and Chicago jazz.

DIY [or **diy**] Abbrev for **do-it-yourself**.

dizzy [diz´i] *adj* not steady; confused; causing dizziness; *(slang)* silly; foolish.—*vt* to make dizzy; to confuse.—*adv* **dizz´ily**.—*n* **dizz´iness**, giddiness. [OE *dysig*, foolish; cf Dan *dösig*, drowsy.]

djellaba, djellabah [je-la´bà] *n* a loose cloak with a hood and full sleeves.

DNA [dē-en-ā] *n* deoxyribo-nucleic acid.

do[1] [dōō] *vt* to perform; to work; to end, to complete; to make.—*vi* to act or behave; to be satisfactory.—*2nd sing* **do´est, dost** [dust], *3rd* **does** [duz], *also* **do´eth, doth** [duth]; *pt* **did**; *pr p* **do´ing**; *pt p* **done** [dun]. **Do** has special uses where it has no definite meaning, as in asking questions (*Do you like milk?*), emphasizing a verb (*I do want to go*), and standing for a verb already used (*My dog goes where I do*).—*adj* **do´ing**, active.—**doings**, things done; actions.—**do´-good´er**, a well-meaning but unrealistic social reformer, usu. one who is naive and ineffectual.—*adj* **do-it-yourself**, for use by an amateur.—Also *n*—**do away with**, to abolish; **do in**, *(inf)* to get the better of; *(slang)* to exhaust; to murder.—*adj* **do"nothing**, marked by inactivity.—*n* a shiftless person; **do someone proud**, to treat someone lavishly; to make someone feel flattered; **do time** *(slang)*, to serve a prison sentence; **do up**, to wrap; to repair; to renovate; **do without**, to forgo.—**do one's stuff** *(slang)*, to do what is one's business to do; **do out of** *(slang)*, to cheat; **dos and don'ts**, customs; **do someone dirt** *(slang)*, to cause another trouble, esp by informing. [OE *dōn, dyde, gedōn*; Du *doen*, Ger *tun*; conn with Gr *tithenai*, to put.]

do[2] [dō] *n (mus)* the first tone or keynote of a diatonic scale; the tone C in the fixed system of solemization.

Doberman pinscher [dō-berman pin´sher] *n* a breed of working dog with a glossy black-and-tan coat. [L Dobermann, a 19th-century German dog breeder + *pinscher*, a Ger breed of hunting dog.]

dobbin [dob´in] *n* a workhorse. [An altered dim of *Robert*.]

docile [dō´sil or dos´il] *adj* teachable; easily managed.—*n* **docīl´ity**. [Fr,—L *docilis—docēre*, to teach.]

dock[1] [dok] *n (Rumex)* of the polyonaceae with long leaves and a strong deep root some of which are eaten or used as medicine, but generally a pernicious weed. [OE *doice*.]

dock[2] [dok] *vt* to cut short; to curtail; to clip.—*n* the part of a tail left after clipping. [ME *dok*, prob—ON *dokkr*, a stumpy tail.]

dock[3] [dok] *n* a wharf; an artificial basin for the reception of ships.—*vt* to join (spacecraft) together in space.—Also to enter a dock.—*ns* **dock´age**, accommodation in docks for ships; charge for using a dock; **dock´er**, one who works at the docks; **dock´yard**, an establishment with storage, and facilities for repairing and refitting ships.—**dry´-dock** *see* **dry**. [Old Du *dokke*.]

docket [dok´et] *n* a list of lawsuits to be tried by a court.—*vt* to enter on a docket.—*pr p* **dock´eting**; *pt p* **dock´eted**. [Perh a dim of **dock** (2).]

doctor [dok´tor] *n* person qualified to treat diseases or physical disorders; the highest academic degree; the holder of such a degree. Also **doc**.—*vt* to treat medically; to patch up (machinery, etc.); to tamper with, falsify; *(inf)* to castrate. or spay.—*n* **doc´torate**, the degree of doctor given by a university.—*adj* **doctoral**. [L, a teacher—*docēre*, to teach.]

doctrinaire [dok-tri-nār´] *n* one whose opinions are formed by theory rather than by experience.—*adj* applying theory without regard for practical consequences. [Fr—Late L *doctrīnārius*.]

doctrine [dok´trin] *n* a thing taught; a principle of belief.—*adj* **doc´trinal** (or *-trīnàl*), relating to, or containing, doctrine; relating to the act of teaching.—*adv* **doc´trinally**. [Fr—L *doctrīna—docěre*, to teach.]

document [dok´ū-mėnt] *n* a paper containing information, or proof or evidence of anything.—*vt* [dok´ū-mėnt, or -ment´] to furnish with documents; to support or prove by documents.—*adj* **document´ary**, relating to, or found in, documents; aiming at presentation of reality.—*ns* **documentary**, a motion picture portraying a particular human activity without fictional coloring and without professional actors; **documentā´tion**. [Fr—L *documentum—docēre*, to teach.]

dodder[1] [dod´ėr] *n* any of a genus (*Cuscata*) of leafless, twining, pale-colored parasitic plants. [ME *doder*; cf Ger *dotter*.]

dodder[2] [dod´er] *vi* to tremble or shake as a result of old age or weakness; to progress unsteadily. [Poss conn with Norw *dudra*, to tremble.]

dodeca- [dō-deka-] having twelve (Gr *dōdeka*, twelve).—**dodec´agon**, a plane figure having twelve angles and sides (Gr *gonia*, an angle); **dodecahe´dron**, a solid figure having twelve plane faces.—**dodecasyll´able**, etc.

dodge [doj] *vi* evade an obligation by trickery; to move quickly in an irregular course.—*vt* to avoid by a sudden movement or shift of place; to trick.—*n* a trick.—*n* **dodg´er**.—**dodge ball**, an informal team game where players forming a circle try to hit their opponents inside the circle with a large inflated ball. [Origin obscure.]

dodo [dō´dō] *n* a large clumsy bird, now completely extinct; a stupid person.—*pl* **do´does**. [Port *doudo*, **silly**.]

doe [dō] *n* a female deer, rabbit, or hare.—*n* **doe´skin**, the skin of a deer, lamb, or sheep; the very supple leather made from this; a heavy smooth woven cloth. [OE *dā*; Dan *daa*, a deer.]

doer [dōōer] *n* one who does, or habitually does, anything; an agent. [**do**.]

does [duz] 3rd pers sing pres indic of **do**.

doff [dof] *vt* to take off, remove (esp one's hat). [**do, off**.]

dog [dog] *n* a domestic carnivorous mammal closely related to the wolf with great differences in form; the male of wolf, fox, etc.; a worthless person; any of various usu. simple mechanical devices for holding, gripping or fastening by a spike, rod or bar; andiron; **Dog**, either of the constellations Canis Major or Canis Minor; *(pl)* feet; anything inferior of its kind; *(pl)* ruin (*go to the dogs*); an investment not worth its price; slow-moving merchandise; an unattractive woman or girl; a theatrical flop.—*adj* **dog-like**.—*vt* to hunt, to track like a hound; to worry as if by dogs;—*pr p* **dogging**; *pt p* **dogged**.—*adv* extremely, utterly.—*adj* canine; spurious, unlike that used by native speakers.—**dogbane**, any of a genus (*Apocynum* of Apocynaceae, the dogbane family) comprising often poisonous chiefly tropical plants; **dog-berry**, any of several plants bearing unpalatable fruit; **dog biscuit**, a hard dry biscuit for dogs; hardtack; **dogcart**, a cart drawn by a dog; a two-wheeled carriage with crosswise seats set back to back; **dogcatcher**, a community official who catches and disposes of stray dogs; **dog collar**, a collar for a dog; *(slang)* a clerical collar; a wide, snug-fitting necklace; **dog days**, hot sultry weather between early July and early September in the northern hemisphere; a period of inactivity or stagnation; **dog-ear**, the turned down corner of a page, esp of a book.—*adj* **dog-eared**, having dog-ears; shabby, worn; **dogged**, tenacious.—*adv* **doggedly**.—*n* **doggedness**.—*adj* **doggish**, canine; stylish in a showy way.—*adv* **doggishly**.—*n* **doggishness. dogface**, a soldier, esp an infantryman; **dogfight**, a fight between dogs; *(loosely)* a fiercely disputed contest; a fight between two fighter planes esp at close quarters; **dogfish**, a bowfin; any of various small sharks; **doghouse**, a shelter for a dog; **dogleg**, something having a sharp angle or a sharp bend.—*adj* crooked like a dog's hind leg.—*vi* to go along a dogleg course.—*vt* **dognap**, to steal (a dog).—*pr p* **dognapping** or **dognaping**; *pt p* **dognapped** or **dognaped**;—*n* **dognapper** or **dognaper**.—**dog paddle**, an elementary form of swimming in which the arms paddle in the water.—*vi* **dogpaddle**.—**dogsled**, a sled drawn by a dog; **Dog Star**, Sirius; Procyon; **dog tag**, a disk or plate on a dog collar bearing a license registration number; a military identification worn around the neck; **dogtooth**, canine, eyetooth; an architectural ornament consisting of four leaves radiating from a raised point in the center; **dogtooth violet** [dog´tōōth vī´ōlet] *n* any of a genus (*Erythronium*) of small spring-flowering bulbous herbs of the lily family; **dogtrot**, a quick easy gait like that of a dog.—*vi* to move at a dogtrot; **dogwatch**, either of two half watches on shipboard between 4–6 pm or 6–8 pm; any of various night shifts, esp the last shift; **dogwood** [dog´wŏŏd] *n* any of a genus (*cornus*) of trees, shrubs, and subshrubs (family Cornaceae, the dogwood family).—**dog-eat-dog**, marked by ruthless self-interest; **doggie-bag**, a bag of leftover food from a meal eaten at a restaurant; **dog in the manger**, a person who refuses to give up something that is useless to him; **in the doghouse**, in disfavor. [Late OE *docga*; cf Du *dog*, a mastiff; Ger *dogge*.]

doge [dōj or dō´jā] *n* the chief magistrate in republican Venice and Genoa. [It (Venetian dial), for *duce* (= Eng *duke*—L *dux*, a leader.]

dogey [dō´gē] *n* a young calf.

doggerel [dog´ėr-ėl] *n* worthless verse [Origin unknown.]

dogma [dog´ma] *n* a belief taught or held as true, esp by a church; a doctrine; a belief.—*adjs* **dogmăt´ic, -al**, pertaining to a dogma; asserting a thing as if it were a dogma; asserting positively; overbearing.—*adv* **dogmat´ically**.—*n* **dogmat´ics**, branch of theology that tries to interpret the dogmas of religious faith.—*vi* **dog´matize**, to state one's opinion dogmatically or arrogantly.—**dog´matizer; dog´matism**, dogmatic or positive assertion of opinion; **dog´matist**, one who makes positive assertions. [Gr, an opinion, from *dokeein*, to think, seem.]

doily [doi´li] *n* a small ornamented mat, often laid on or under dishes. [From *Doily* or *Doyley*, a famous haberdasher.]
doings [dōō´ingz] *n pl.* See **do** (*vb*).
doit [doit] *n* a thing of little or no value. [Du *duit.*]
dojo [dō´jō] *n* a school for training in the arts of self-defence. [Jap.]
dol [dol] *n* a unit for measuring pain.
Dolby [dol´bē] *n* trade name for a system which reduces the noise level on tape-recorded sound.
dolce [dol´chā] *adj* (*mus*) sweet.—*n* a soft-toned organ-stop. [It.]
doldrums [dol´drumz] *n pl* those parts of the ocean about the equator where calms and light baffling winds prevail; low spirits. [Prob conn with obs *dold*, stupid, or *dol*, dull.]
dole[1] [dōl] *n* something given in charity; a small portion.—*vt* to deal (out) in small portions. [OE *dāl*; cf **deal**.]
dole[2] [dōl] *n* (*arch*) grief; heaviness at heart.—*adj* **dole´ful**, full of dole or grief, melancholy.—*adv* **dole"fully**.—*n* **dole´fulness**. [OFr *doel* (Fr *deuil*), grief—L *dolēre*, to feel pain.]
dolicho- [dol-i-kō-] long.—*adj* **dolichocephalic** [dol-i-kosef-al´ik], long-headed, applied to skulls whose breadth is less than four-fifths of their length (opp to *brachycephalic*)—also **dolichoceph´alous**. [Gr *dolichos*, long, *kephalē*, the head.]
doll [dol] *n* a toy in human form; a pretty woman without personality; a woman.—*n* **doll´y**, a child's name for a doll; a low platform on wheels for moving heavy objects.—*n* **doll´house**, a small-scale toy house; a dwelling so small that it suggests this. [Prob from *Dolly*, familiar dim of *Dorothy*.]
dollar [dol´ȧr] *n* the unit of money in the US, Canada, Australia and many other countries.—**dollar-a-year**, of a person earning a token salary in public service; **dollar diplomacy**, using money to influence political transactions. [Ger *t(h)aler* (Low Ger *daler*), short for *Joachimsthaler*, because first coined at the silver-mines in Joachimsthal (Joachim's dale) in Bohemia.]
dolly See **doll**.
dolman [dol´mȧn] *adj* of a sleeve on a woman's garment that is wide at the armhole and tapers to fit the wrist.—*n* a woman's coat with cape-like flaps instead of sleeves. [Fr—Turk *dōlāmān*.]
dolmen [dol´mėn] *n* a prehistoric structure of two or more erect unhewn stones, supporting a large flattish stone, found esp in Britain and France. [Fr *dolmen*; usually explained as Breton *dolmen—dol, taol*, table, *men*, a stone. But *tolmēn* in Cornish meant 'hole of stone'.]
dolomite [dol´o-mīt] *n* a limestone consisting of calcium magnesium carbonate. [Named in honor of the French geologist *Dolomieu* (1750–1801).]
dolor [dol´ȯr, dōl´ȯr] *n* pain, grief, anguish.—*adj* **dol´orous**, full of pain or grief; doleful.—*adv* dol´orously.—*n* **dol´orousness**. [OFr,—L *dolēre*, to grieve.]
dolphin [dol´fin] *n* any of various whales (family *Delphinidae*) with a beak-like snout; either of two large food fishes (genus *Coryphaena*) of tropical and temperate seas.—**dolphinarium**, a pool or aquarium where dolphins are displayed. [OFr *daulphin*—L *delphīnus*—Gr *delphis, -phīnos*.]
dolt [dōlt] *n* a dull or stupid fellow.—*adj* **dolt´ish**, dull, stupid.—*adv* **dolt´ishly**.—*n* **doltishness**. [Dolt=*dulled* (see **dull**) or blunted.]
Dom [dom] *n* a title given to certain RC dignitaries, [Port *Dom*—L *dominus*, lord.]
domain [do-mān´] *n* territory under the control of one ruler or government; field of thought, action, etc. (*math.*) the set on which a function is defined. [Fr,—L *dominium—dominus*, a master.]
dome [dōm] *n* a large, rounded roof; something high and rounded.—*adj* **domed**, having a dome. [L *domus*, a house; Fr *dôme*, It *duomo*, Ger *dom*.]
domestic [do-mes´tik] *adj* belonging to the house; fond of home; private; tame; not foreign.—*n* a servant in the house.—*adv* **domes´tically**.—*vt* **domes´ticāte**, to make domestic; to tame;—**domesticā´tion; domestic´ity** (*-tis´-*), domestic or domesticated state; home life. [L *domesticus—domus*, a house.]
domicile [dom´i-sil, -sīl] *n* a house, home; a person's legal place of residence.—*vt* to establish in a fixed residence.—*adj* **domicil´iary**, pertaining to the domicile. [Fr—L *domicilium—domus*, a house.]
dominant [dom´in-ȧnt] *adj* prevailing, predominant; overtopping others.—*n* (*mus*) the fifth note above the tonic.—*n* **dom´inance**, ascendancy.—*adv* **dom´inantly**. [L *dominans, -antis*, pr p of *dominārī*, to be master.]
dominate [dom´in-āt] *vt* to control or rule by strength; to hold a commanding position over.—*n* **dominā´tion**, control; rule. [L *dominārī, -ātus*, to be master—*dominus*, master—*domāre* (from the same Indo—Gmc root as Eng *tame*).]
domineer [dom-in-ēr´] *vi* to exercise arrogant mastery; *vt* to tyrannize over. [Prob through Du—OFr *dominer*—L *dominārī*, see above.]
dominical [do-min´ik-ȧl] *adj* belonging to the Lord, as the Lord's Prayer, the Lord's Day. [Low L *dominicālis*—L *dominicus—dominus*, lord, master.]
Dominican [do-min´i-kan] *adj* belonging to St *Dominic* or to the monastic order founded by him in 1215.—*n* a friar or monk of that order.
dominie [dom´i-ni] *n* a teacher; a clergyman. [L *domine*, voc of *dominus*, master.]
dominion [do-min´yȯn] *n* a domain or territory with one ruler, owner, or government; control; (*in pl*) one of the orders of angels.—**Dominion Day**, a Canadian festival on the anniversary of the union of the provinces, July 1, 1867. [Low L *dominiō, -ōnis—dominus*, master.]
domino [dom´i-nō] *n* one of the oblong pieces, with two compartments each blank or marked with from one to six spots, with which the game of **dom´inoes** [-nōz] is played; a half-mask worn with a masquerade costume. [Sp *domino*—L *dominus*.]
don [don] *n* **Don**, a Spanish title, corresponding to English Sir, Mr; (*inf*) a fellow or tutor at Oxford University or Cambridge University. [Sp,—L *dominus*.]
don [don] *vt* to put on (clothing, etc.).—*pr p* **donn´ing**; *pt p* **donned**. [A contr of **do, on**.]
Doña [don´ya] *n* a Spanish title, corresponding to Mrs or Madam; a Spanish lady.
donation [do-nā´sh(o)n] *n* a contributing; a contribution.—*vt* **donāte´**, to give as a gift; to contribute, esp to a charity; to give off or transfer (as electrons).—**dōnee´**, the person to whom a gift is made; **dō´nor**, a giver; one used as a source of blood, semen, tissue, or organs. [Fr,—L *dōnāre, -ātum—dōnum*, a gift—*dăre*, to give.]
done [dun] *pt p* of **do**.
dong [dong] *n* the unit of money in Vietnam.
donjon [dun´jȯn] *n* a strong central tower in ancient castles. [A doublet of **dungeon**.]
Don Juan [don jōōȧn] a legendary Spaniard famous for his seduction of women; any libertine. [**don** (1), Sp *Fuan*, John.]
donkey [dong´ki] *n* a small animal resembling a horse, an ass; a stupid person.—**don´key-en´gine**, a portable auxiliary engine; a small locomotive used for switching; **donkey's years**, a very long time; **don´keywork**, drudgery. [Perh.= *dun-ik-ie*, a double dim of *dun*, from its color; or from *Duncan*.]
Donna [don´a] *n* honorific form of address to an Italian woman.
donnée [do´nā] *n* the set of assumptions upon which a work of fiction or drama proceeds. [Fr]
don't [dōnt] for **do not**.—*n*, don't know respondent to an opinion poll who does not reveal his position on an issue.
donut *see* **doughnut**.
doodle [dōōd´l] *vi* to scrawl, scribble meaninglessly.
doohickey [dōō´hikē] *n* a small article whose name is unknown or forgotten.
doom [dōōm] *n* destiny; ruin; final judgment.—*vt* to pronounce judgment on; to condemn, destine (often in *pass*, eg *it was doomed to failure*);—*pr p* **dōōm´ing**; *pt p* **dōōmed**.—**dooms´day** the day of God's final judgment of mankind; **doomsayer, doomster** a person who predicts calamity. [OE *dōm*, judgment.]
door [dōr, dör] *n* a movable barrier to close an opening in a wall; a similar part of a piece of furniture; a doorway.—**doorjamb** [*-jam*] an upright pieceforming the side of a door opening; **doorkeeper**, person who attends a door; **doorknob** [*-nob*] a knob that releases a door latch when turned; **doorman**, one who tends the door of a public building and assists people (as in calling taxis); **doormat**, a mat placed in front of or inside a doorway for wiping dirt from shoes; a person who submits without protest to indignities or abuse; **doorpost**, a doorjamb; **door prize**, a prize awarded to the holder of a winning ticket given out at the entrance to a function; **doorstop**, a device (as a wedge or weight) for holding a door open; a projection attached to a wall or floor for preventing damaging contact between an opened door and the wall; **doorway**, the opening in a wall that a door closes; a means of gaining access, as knowledge is the doorway to success.—**at one's door**, as a charge against one's being responsible; **door-to-door**, being or making a usu. unsolicited call at every residence in an area; providing delivery at a specified address; **revolving door** *see* **revolving**. [OE *duru*; Ger *tor, tür*; Gr *thyra*, L *fores* (pl), a door.]
dopa [dō´pa] *n* an amino acid used in the treatment of Parkinson's disease.
dope [dōp] *n* a thick pasty material; lubricating grease; airplane varnish; opium; a drug, narcotic or stimulative; anything calculated to dull mental and moral energy; a stupid person; information.—*vt* to drug (*lit* and *fig*).—*n* **dop´ing** (*electronics*), addition of known impurities to a semiconductor to achieve the desired properties in diodes and transistors. [Du *doop*, a dipping, sauce; *doopen*, to dip.]
Doppelganger [dop´elgang-er] *n* ghostly duplicate of a living person.
Doppler effect [dop´ler] *n* change in apparent frequency of sound of light waves as a result of the relative motion between the observer and source.
Doric [dor´ik] *adj* denoting the simplest of the Greek orders of architecture.—*n* a dialect of ancient Greek spoken esp in the Peloponnesus, Crete, Sicily, and southern Italy. [Fr *dorique*—L *Dōricus*—Gr *Dōrikos—Dōris*.]
dormant [dor´mant] *adj* sleeping; quiet, as if asleep; inactive; (*heraldic*) in a sleeping posture.—*n* **dor´mancy**. [Fr *dormir*—L *dormīre*, to sleep.]
dormer [dör´mer] *n* an upright window that projects from a sloping roof. [L *dormītorium—dormīre*, to sleep.]
dormitory [dör´mi-tȯr-i] *n* a building with many sleeping rooms; a large sleeping room with many beds. [L *dormītōrium—dormīre*, to sleep.]
dormouse [dör´mows] *n* any of several Old World rodents (family *Gliridae*) that resembles a squirrel;—*pl* **dor´mice**. [Perh conn with L *dormīre*, to sleep (from their hibernation), and prob **mouse**.]
dormy, dormie [dör´mi] *adj* (*golf*) said of a player when he is as many holes 'up' or ahead as there are holes still to play. [Poss conn with L *dormīre*, to sleep.]
dorsal [dör´sȧl] *adj* of, on, or near the back. [Fr,—L *dorsum*, the back.]
dory [dōr´ē] *n* a small rowing boat with a flat bottom. [Miskito *dóri*, a dugout.]

dose [dōs] *n* the quantity of medicine, X-rays, etc. administered at one time; a part of an experience; a gonorrheal infection.—*vt* to divide (as a medicine) into doses; to give medicine in doses to; to treat with an agent.—*ns* **dōs´age**, a method or rate of dosing; **dosim´eter**, an instrument for measuring radiation. [Fr,—Gr *dosis*, a giving—*didonai*, to give.]

do-si-do [dō-si-dō] *n* a square dance figure in which the dancers pass and circle each other back to back.

dossier [dos´i-ėr, do-syā] *n* a collection of documents about some subject or person. [Fr]

dost [dust] 2nd pers sing pres indic of **do**.

dot[1] [dot] *n* a small spot, a point; a centered point used as a multiplication sign; (*mus*) a point indicating augmentation of a note or rest or one that is to be played staccato; a precise point in time; the short element in the Morse code.—**dotted swiss**, a sheer light muslin ornamented with evenly spaced raised dots. [Du *dot* knot, tuft.]

dot[2] [dot] *n* a marriage portion.—*adj* **dō´tal**, pertaining to dowry. [Fr—L *dōs, dōtis—dōtare*, to endow.]

dote [dōt] *vi* to be weak-minded because of old age; to show weak or excessive affection (*with* **on** *or* **upon**).—**dōt´age**, childishness of old age; **dōt´ard**, one showing the weakness of old age. [Cf Old Du *doten*, to be silly and Fr *radoter*, to rave.]

doth [duth] 3rd pers sing pres indic of **do**.

dotterel [dot´ėr-el] *n* an old world plover (*Chardrius morinellus*). [**dote**]

dottle [dot´l] *n* plug of tobacco left in pipe after smoking.

Douay Version [doo-ā´] *n* an English translation of the Bible used by Roman Catholics. Also **Douay Bible**. [*Douay*, France.]

double [dub´l] *adj* twice as large, as strong, etc.; for two; made of two like parts; having two meanings, characters, etc.; (*bot*) flowers with more than the normal number of petals.—*adv* twice.—*n* number or amount that is twice as much; person or thing just like another; in motion-pictures, a person who acts in the place of a leading character; a sharp turn.—*vt* to make twice as much or as many; to fold, to bend; to bend sharply backward; to go around.—*vi* become twice as much or as many.—*ns* **double agent**, a spy secretly acting for two governments at the same time; **double-barrel**, a double-barreled gun; **double bass**, the largest instrument in the violin family; **double bassoon**, the contrabassoon; **double bind**, a psychological dilemma in which a dependent person usu. a child receives conflicting messages from a single source or faces disparagement no matter how he responds to a situation.—*adj* **doubleblind**, of an experimental procedure in which neither the subjects nor the experimenters know the makeup of the test and control groups during the course of the experiment; **double boiler**, a cooking utensil consisting of two saucepans fitting into each other so that the contents of the upper can be cooked by boiling in the lower; **double bond** (*chem*) a chemical bond consisting of two covalent bonds between two atoms in a molecule.—*adj* **double-breasted** (of a garment) having one half of the front lapped over the other and usu. a double row of buttons; **double cross**, an act of winning a fight or match after agreeing to lose it; the betrayal of an associate; a cross between first-generation hybrids of four separate inbred lines; **double header**, a train pulled by two locomotives; two games, contests or events held consecutively on the same program; **double jeopardy**, two adjudications for one offense;—*adj* **doublejointed**, having a joint with an exceptional degree of freedom of movement between the parts joined; **double standard**, bi-metallism; a code of morals that applies different and more severe standards to one group than another, esp that of sexual behavior; **doublethink**, a simultaneous belief in two contradictory ideas.—*vi* **doub´le-tongue**.—**double star**.—**at the double**, running. [OFr *doble*—L *duplus*, double—*duo*, two.]

double entendre [dōō-blā-tā-dr´] *n* a word or phrase with two meanings, one usually risqué. [Fr of 17th century, superseded now by (*mot*) *à double entente*.]

doublet [dub´lėt] *n* (formerly) a man's close-fitting jacket; one of a pair, eg *balm, balsam*. [OFr, dim of *double*.]

doubloon [dub-lōōn´] *n* an old gold coin of Spain and Spanish America. [Sp *doblón*.]

doubt [dowt] *vi* to be undecided.—*vt* to hold in doubt; to distrust; to suspect.—*n* uncertainty of mind; suspicion; fear.—*n* **doubt´er**.—*adj* **doubt´ful**, full of doubt; not confident; suspicious; undetermined, uncertain; not clear.—*adv* **doubt´fully**.—*n* **doubt´fulness**.—*advs*. **doubt´less**, without doubt, certainly; **doubt´lessly**.—**no doubt** certainly; **doubting Thomas**, a habitually doubting person. [OFr *douter*—L *dubitāre*, akin to *dubius*, doubtful.]

douche [dōōsh] *n* a jet of water directed on or into the body. [Fr,—It *doccia*, a water-pipe—L *dūcĕre*, to lead.]

dough [dō] *n* a mixture of flour and other ingredients stiff enough to knead or roll; something resembling dough, esp in consistency.—*n* **dough´nut**, a small usu. ring-shaped cake fried in fat; something that resembles a doughnut in shape, esp a torus.—*adj* **dough´y**, like dough; soft; pallid, pasty. [OE *dāh*; Ger *teig* ON *deig*.]

doughty [dow´ti] *adj* able, strong; brave.—*adv* **dough´tily**. [OE *dyhtig*, valiant—*dugan*, to be strong.]

dour [dōōr] *adj* obstinate; sullen; grim. [Apparently L *dūrus*, hard.]

douse [dows] *vt* to plunge into water; to strike or lower, as a sail; to put out, quench. [Cf Old Du *dossen*, to beat.]

dove [duv] *n* a small bird of the same family (*Columbidae*) as the pigeon; an advocate of peace or a peaceful policy, emblem of innocence, gentleness; **dove´cote**, a box or building in which pigeons breed; **dove´tail**, a mode of fastening boards together by fitting pieces shaped like a wedge or a dove's tail spread out (*tenons*) into like cavities (*mortises*).—*vt* to fit (one thing exactly into another).—Also *vi*. [OE *dūfe*, as in *dūfedoppe*, diving bird.]

dowager [dow´á-jėr] *n* a widow with a dower or jointure; a dignified elderly woman. [OFr *douagere*—Low L *dōtārium*—L *dōtāre*, to endow.]

dowdy [dow´di] *adj* poorly dressed, not stylish.

dowel [dow´el] *n* a pin of wood or iron inserted in the edges of two adjacent boards for the purpose of fastening them together. [Prob related to Ger *döbel*, a plug.]

dower *n* [dow´ėr] a widow's life share in her husband's estate. [OFr *douaire*—Low L *dōtārium*—L *dōtāre*, to endow.]

Dow-Jones average [dow-jōnz´] *n* financial index compiled from the relative daily movement of prices of selected common stocks. [Charles H. Dow and Edward D. Jones, American financial statisticians.]

down[1] [down] *n* soft feathers; a covering of fluffy hairs.—*adj* **down´y**, covered with, or made of, down or the like; soft. [ON *dūnn*.]

down[2] [down] *adv* toward or in a lower physical position; to a lying or sitting position; toward or to the ground, floor, or bottom; in cash (*pay $5 down*); on paper (*write down what is said*); to a source or hiding place (*tracked them down*); in a direction opposite of up; toward or in the center of a city; to or in a lower status or worse condition; from a past time; to or in a state of less activity; from a thinner to a thicker consistency.—*adj* occupying a low position, esp lying on the ground; directed or going downward; being at a lower level (*sales were down*); depressed, dejected; sick (*down with measles*); having a low opinion or dislike (*down on the boy*); being part of a price (*a down payment*).—*prep* in a descending direction in, on, along, or through; to or toward the lower end or bottom of.—*n* a low period (as in activity, emotional life, or fortunes); one of a series of attempts to advance a football.—*vti* to go or cause to go or come down; to defeat.—*ns* **downbeat**, (*mus*) the downward stroke of a conductor indicating the accented note; the first beat of a measure; a decline in prosperity; **downer**, a depressant drug esp barbiturate; a depressing experience or situation; **downfall**, a sudden fall (as from high rank or power); a sudden or heavy fall of rain or snow; something that causes a downfall; **downhill**, a descending gradient; a skiing race against time down a trail; **downstage**, the part of the stage nearest the audience or camera; **downstate**, the chief southerly sections of a state of the US as distinguished from the northern part; **downtown**, the main business district of a town or city; **downturn**, a downward turn esp in business activity.—*adv* **down under**, into or in Australia or New Zealand.—**down the line**, all the way, **down-to-earth**, practical, realistic; **down to the ground**, perfectly, completely. [ME *a-down, adun*—OE *of dūne*, from the hill.]

download [down´lōd] *n* to copy a file from an on-line information service or from another computer to your computer.

Down's syndrome [downz sin´drom] *n* chromosomal abnormality resulting in a flat face, a fold of skin at the inner eye, and some mental retardation.—Also **mongolism**. [From JHL Downs, English physician.]

dowry [dow´ri] *n* the property which a woman brings to her husband at marriage. [Same root as **dower**.]

dowse [dowz] *vi* to use a divining-rod.—*vt* to find by dowsing.—*n* **dowser**, a rod used for dowsing; a person who uses such. [Orig uncertain.]

doxology [doks-ol´o-ji] *n* a hymn or statement praising God. [Gr *doxologia*—*doxa*, praise, and *legein*, to speak.]

doyen [doi´ėn, dwä-yā] *n* a senior member of a group; an expert in a field; the oldest example of a category. [Fr,—L *decānus*.]

doze [dōz] *vi* to sleep lightly; to be half-asleep or in a stupefied state.—*vt* to spend in drowsiness (*with away*).—*n* a short light sleep. [Cf ON *dūsa*, Dan *döse*, to dose.]

dozen [duz´n] *n* a set of twelve.—**baker's dozen**, thirteen; **dozens**, an indefinitely large number; **daily dozen**, *see* **daily**. [OFr *dozeine*—L *duodecim*—*duo*, two, and *decem*, ten.]

drab [drab] *adj* dull, monotonous, uninteresting.—*n* **drab´ness**. [Fr *drap*, cloth—Low L *drappus*.]

dracaena [dra-sē´na] *n* any of two genera (*Dracaena* or *Cordyline*) of the lily family, small evergreen shrubs with sword-shaped leaves.

drachm [dram] *n* a drachma; a dram.—*n* **drachma** [drak´ma] the unit, money in Greece. [Gr *drachmē*—*drassesthai*, to grasp.]

draconian [dra-ko´nyȧn] *adj* (of laws, etc.) severe, harsh.—Also **dracŏn´ic**. [After *Draco*, author of a severe code of laws at Athens (621 BC).]

draft [dräft] *n* anything drawn; a smaller body (of men, animals, things) selected from a larger; conscription; an order for the payment of money; a demand (on resources, credulity, etc.); a plan; a preliminary sketch.—*vt* to draw an outline of; to draw up in preliminary form; to draw off (for a special purpose).—*n* **drafts´-man**, one who draws up documents, plans, designs, etc. [Same word as **draught**.]

drag [drag] *vt* to draw by force; to draw slowly; to pull roughly and violently; to explore (a river-bed) with a dragnet or hook.—*vi* to hang so as to trail on the ground; to move slowly and heavily;—*pr p* **dragg´ing**; *pt p* **dragged**.—*n* a net (**dragnet**) or hook for dragging along to catch things under water; a heavy harrow; a long open carriage, with transverse or side seats; a contrivance for retarding a wheel; any obstacle to progress; (*aero*) the component of the aerodynamic force on an aircraft which lies along the longitudinal axis of the machine; (*slang*) something boring or tedious; influence; (*slang*) women's clothing worn by a man.—**drag one's feet**, to hang back deliberately in doing something. [OE *dragan* or ON *draga*; Ger *tragen*; cf **draw**.]

drag´ee [drä-zhā] a sugar-coated nut; a silver-coated candy for cake decoration; a sugar-coated pill. [Fr]

draggle [drag´l] *vt* to make or become wet and dirty as by dragging along the ground.—*n* **dragg´le-tail** a slattern. [Freq of **drag** and a doublet of **drawl**.]

dragoman [drag´o-màn] *n* an interpreter or guide in the Middle East.—*pl* **drag´omans**. [Fr from Ar *tarjumān—tarjama* to interpret.]

dragon [drag´ȯn] *n* a fabulous winged reptile; the constellation Draco; a fierce person; a genus of lizards of the E Indies.—*ns* **drag´onet**, a little dragon; a fish of the goby family; **drag´onfly**, any of a suborder [Anisoptera] of large harmless four-winged insects. Also **darning needle.—drag´ons-blood**, the red resinous exudation of several kinds of trees, used for coloring varnishes, etc. [Fr—L *drakō, -ōnis*—Gr *drakōn, -ontos*.]

dragoon [dra-gōōn´] *n* a soldier who fights on horseback—*vt* to harass or compel by bullying commands. [Fr *dragon*, dragon, dragoon.]

drain [drān] *vt* to draw (off or away) by degrees; to clear of water by drains; to make dry; to exhaust.—*vi* to flow off gradually; to lose moisture by its flowing or trickling away.—*n* watercourse; ditch; sewer; exhausting expenditure.—**drain´age**, act, process, method, or means of draining, a system of drains; **drain´er**, a utensil on which articles are placed to drain; **drain´pipe**, a pipe to carry away waste water or rainwater; (*in pl, (inf)*) very narrow trousers.—**down the drain**. (*slang*) gone for good, wasted. [OE *drēahnian*.]

drake [drāk] *n* the male of the duck [Ety obscure; cf dial Ger *draak*.]

Dralon [dra´lon] *n* a trade name for acrylic fiber with velvety nap.

dram [dram] *n* a unit of capacity (1/8 fluid ounce); a unit of weight (avoirdupois 27.243 grains or 0.00265 ounce; apothecaries', 3 scruples or 60 grains); a small portion of something to drink; a small amount. [Fr and L, from Gr *drachmē. See* **drachma**.]

drama [dräm´à] *n* a story of life and action for representation by actors; a composition intended to be represented on the stage; dramatic literature; a dramatic situation or a series of deeply interesting events—*adjs* **dramatic** [dràmat´ik], **-al**, belonging to, or in the form of, a drama; vivid, striking, often with an element of unexpectedness.—*adv* **dramat´ically**.—*n* **dramat´ics** (*pl* treated as *sing*), the acting, production, study of plays; (*inf*) show of excessive, exaggerated emotion.—*vt* **dram´atize**. to compose in, or turn into, the form of a drama or play; to exaggerate the importance or emotional nature of.—*n* **dram´atist**. a writer of plays.—**dramat´ic ūn´ities** (*see* **unity**); **dram´atis persōnae** [ē]) the characters of a drama or play [L,—Gr *drāma, -atos—drāein*, to do.]

Dramamine [dram´-a-min] *n* trade name for dimenhydrinate.

dramaturgy [dram´a-tûr-ji] *n* the principles of dramatic composition; theatrical art [Gr *drāmatourgia—drāma* and *ergon*, work.]

drambuie [dram-boo´e] *n* Scottish liqueur made from whisky, heather honey, etc.

drank [drangk] *pa t* of **drink**.

drape [drāp] *vt* to cover with cloth; to hang cloth in folds about; (*refl*) to assume a casual, graceful pose.—*n* a hanging or curtain.—*ns* **drāp´ery**, hangings; [O Fr *draper*, to weave, drape—*drap*, cloth, prob of Gmc origin.]

drastic [dras´tik] *adj* acting with force and violence. [Gr. *drastikos—drāein*, to act, to do.]

drat [drat] *vt* a mild oath. [Shortened from **God rot**]

Dravidian [dra-vid´i-àn] *n* an individual of a non-Aryan race of Southern India.—**Dravidian languages**, a family of languages spoken by the Dravidian peoples. [Sans *Drāvida*, an ancient province of S India.]

draw [drö] *vti* to haul, to drag; to cause to go in a certain direction (*drew her aside*); to pull out (as a hand from a pocket); to attract; to delineate, to sketch; to extract the essence (as of tea); to require (a specified depth) to float in; to accumulate; to gain; to receive (as a salary); to bend (a bow) by pulling back the string; to leave (a contest) undecided; to write up, to draft (a will); to elongate (metal) by pulling through dies; to produce or allow a current of air.—*pa t* **drew** [drōō], *pt p* **drawn**.—*n* the act, process, or result of drawing; a lot or chance drawn at random; a tie; an attraction, a spectator event.—**drawback**, a hindrance, handicap; **drawbridge**, a bridge made to be drawn up, down, or aside; **drawer**, one that draws; a sliding boxlike compartment (as in a table, chest, or desk); *pl* an undergarment for the lower part of the body; **drawing**, an act or instance of drawing esp when something is decided by drawing lots; the act or art of making a figure, plan, or sketch by using lines; a representation made by drawing.—**draw a bead on**, take aim at; **draw a blank**, to fail to gain desired information; **draw on** or **draw upon**, to use as a source of supply; **draw straws**, to decide something by lottery in which straws of unequal length are used; **draw a line** or **draw the line**, to fix a boundary between things that tend to intermingle (as between painting and photography); to fix a boundary excluding what one will not tolerate; **draw in** to retract; to become shorter.

drawl [dröl] *vt* to speak or utter in a slow, lengthened tone.—*n* a slow, lengthened utterance. [Connected with **draw**.]

dray [drā] *n* a low strong cart for heavy goods. [Cf OE *dræge*, drag-net—*dragan*, to draw.]

dread [dred] *n* great fear; awe; an object of fear or awe.—*adj* dreaded, inspiring great fear or awe.—*vt* to fear greatly; to reverence.—*adj* **dreadful** (*orig*) full of dread; producing great fear or awe; terrible; (*inf*) very bad, annoying, boring, etc.—*adv* **dread´fully**.—*n* **dread´fulness**.—*n* **dread´nought** a type of warship, both swift and heavily armoured, esp of the early 20th century. [ME *dreden*—OE *ondrædan* to fear.]

dream [drēm] *n* a sequence of thoughts and fancies, or a vision during sleep; a state of abstraction, a reverie; an unrealised ambition; something only imaginary.—*vi* to fancy things during sleep; to think idly.—*vt* to see in, or as in, a dream;—*pa t* and *pt p* **dreamed** or **dreamt** [dremt].—*n* **dream´er**.—*adj* **dreamy**, full of dreams, languid; addicted to dreaming, abstracted, unpractical; (*inf*) lovely.—*adv* **dream´ily**.—*n* **dream´iness.—dream´land**, the land of dreams, reverie, or imagination; **dream´world**, a world of illusions.—**dream up**, to plan in the mind, often unrealistically. [ME *dream, drēm*; not recorded in OE; cf OHG *troum*, ON *draumr*.]

dreary [drēr´i] *adj* gloomy; cheerless.—*adv* **drear´ily**.—*n* **drear´iness**. [OE *drēorig*, mournful, bloody—*drēor*, gore.]

dredge[1] [drej] *n* a bag-net for dragging along the ocean or river bottom to take specimens of plants and animals, mud, etc.; apparatus for deepening a harbor or channel by removing mud from the bottom, or for raising alluvial deposits containing minerals.—*vt* to gather with a dredge; to deepen.—*n* **dredg´er**, a vessel fitted with dredging apparatus. [Conn with **drag, draw**.]

dredge[2] [drej] *vt* to coat (food) by sprinkling.—*n* **dred´ger**, container with perforated lid for sprinkling. [OFr *dragie*, sugar-plum—Gr *tragēmata*, dessert.]

dregs [dregz] *n pl* impurities in liquid that fall to the bottom; the most worthless part of anything. [Prob ON *dreggjar*.]

drench [drench or -sh] *vt* to wet thoroughly, to soak; to saturate.—*n* a dose of medicine forced down the throat of an animal.—*n* **drench´ing**, a soaking, as by rain. [OE *drencan*, to cause to drink, from *drincan*, to drink.]

Dresden [dres´den] *adj* (of) delicate and decorative porcelain ware made near Dresden, Germany.

dress [dres] *vt* to straighten; to set in order; to prepare; to draw (fowl); to trim; to treat, bandage; to tend; to clothe; to adorn.—*vi* to come into line; to put on clothes;—*pt* and *pt p* **dressed**.—*n* the covering or ornament of the body; a lady's gown; manner of clothing.—*adj* **dress´y**, showy; too fond of dress or adornment.—**dress´ cir´cle; dress´er**, one who dresses; a person who assists an actor to dress; a kind of kitchen sideboard; **dress´ing**, dress or clothes; any application used in a preparation process (as manure applied to land, sauce or stuffing added to food); the bandage, etc. applied to a wound; **dress´ing gown**, a loose garment used in dressing, or in deshabille; **dress´ing sta´tion**, a place where wounded are collected and tended by members of a field ambulance.—**dress down**, to scold severely; **dress up**, to dress elaborately; to dress for a part or in masquerade; to treat so as to make appear better, more interesting etc., than it really is; **dress rehearsal**. [OFr *dresser*, to prepare, through Low L—L *dīrigēre* to direct.]

dressage [*dres-äzh*] *n* training of a horse in deportment and response to controls. [Fr]

drew [drōō] *pt* of **draw**.

dribble [drib´l] *vi* to fall in small drips; to allow saliva to trickle from the mouth.—*vt* to spend in small amounts; (*football*) to kick (the ball) along little by little.—*n* **drib´let** a drop, trickle, small quantity. [Freq of obs vb *drib*, akin to **drip**.]

dried [drīd] *pt* and *pt p* of **dry**.

drift [drift] *n* a heap of matter driven together, as snow; the direction in which a thing is driven; natural course, tendency; the general sense or intention (of what is said); (*geol*) one of the superficial, as distinct from the solid, formations of the earth's crust.—*vt* to carry by drift.—*vi* to be floated or blown along; to be driven into heaps; to wander around without any definite aim.—*ns* **drifter**, a person who or thing which drifts; a fisherman or a fishing-boat that uses a drift-net; **drift´wood**, wood drifted by water. [**drive**.]

drill[1] [dril] *n* a West African baboon (*Mandrillus leucophaeus*) closely related to the mandrill. [Obs Fr *drill*, a man.]

drill[2] [dril] *vt* to bore, pierce, as with a drill; to exercise (soldiers, pupils, etc.).—*n* an implement that bores; the exercising of soldiers, etc.; exercise, practice; correct procedure or routine; a furrow with seed or growing plants in it.—*ns* **drillmaster**, an instructor in military drill; an instructor who maintains severe discipline and often stresses the trivial; **drill press**, an upright drilling machine in which the drill is pressed to the work by hand or by a lever; **drill team**, an exhibition marching team. [Prob borrowed from Du *drillen*, to bore; *dril, drille*, a borer; cf. **thrill**.]

drill[3] [dril] *n* a kind of strong twilled cloth. [Ger *drillich*, ticking—L *trilīx*, three-threaded—*trēs, tria*, three, *līcium*, thread.]

drily *see* **dry**.

drink [dringk] *vt* to swallow, as a liquid; to take in through the senses.—*vi* to swallow a liquid; to take intoxicating liquors to excess;—*pr p* **drinking**; *pt* **drank**; *pt p* **drunk**.—*n* something to be drunk; intoxicating liquor.—*n* **drink´er**, a tippler.—**drink in**, to absorb; to take in, understand, with appreciation; **drink to** (**a person's health**), to drink wine or other beverage with good wishes for a person's health.—**strong drink**, alcoholic liquor. [OE *drincan*; Ger *trinken*.]

drip [drip] *vi* to fall in drops; to let fall drops;—*pr p* **dripping**; *pt p* **dripped**.—

n a falling in drops; that which falls in drops; the edge of a roof; a device for passing a fluid slowly and continuously, esp into a vein of the body; the material so passed; (*slang*) a forceless person.—*adj* **drip´dry´**, of a material or garment, requiring little or no ironing when allowed to dry by dripping.—Also *vi, vt*—*ns* **dripp´ing**, that which falls in drops, as fat from meat in roasting; **drip´stone**, a projecting molding over doorways, etc., serving to throw off the rain. [OE *dryppan—drēopan*.]

drive [drīv] *vt* to urge, push or force onward; to direct the movement or course of; to convey in a vehicle; to set or keep in motion or operation; to carry through strongly (*drive a hard bargain*); impress forcefully (*drove the lesson home*); to propel an object of play (as a ball or shuttlecock) by a hard blow.—*vi* to be forced along; to be conveyed in a vehicle; to work, to strive (at).—*pr p* **driving**, *pt* **drove**, *pt p* **driven**.—*n* a trip in an automobile; a driving together of animals (as for capture or slaughter); the guiding of logs downstream to a mill; the act of driving a ball; a driveway; a military attack; an intensive campaign (as *a membership drive*); dynamic quality; the apparatus by which motion is imparted to a machine.—**drive at**, to have as an ultimate meaning or conclusion.—**drive-in**, place of business (as a theater, restaurant, or bank) so laid out that patrons can be accommodated in their automobiles.—Also *adj* **driveway**, a short private road leading from the street to a house, garage, or parking lot. [OE *drīfan*, to drive; Ger *trieben*, to push.]

drivel [driv´l] *vi* to slaver; to speak like an idiot;—*pr p* **driv´eling**; *pt p* **driv´eled**.—*n* slaver; nonsense. [ME *drevelen, dravelen*—OE *dreflian*.]

drizzle [driz´l] *vi* to rain in small drops.—*n* a small, light rain.—*adj* **drizz´ly**. [Freq of ME *dresen*—OE *drēosan*, to fall.]

drogue [drog] *n* a sea anchor; a small parachute for slowing down or stabilizing something (as an astronaut's capsule); a funnel-shaped device enabling an airplane to be refueled from a tanker airplane while in flight.

droll [drōl] *adj* odd; amusing.—*n* a jester.—*n* **droll´ery**. [Fr *drôle*, prob from Du *drollig*, odd—*trold*, a hobgoblin.]

dromedary [drom´i-dár-i, or drum´-] *n* a swift camel; a one-humped Arabian camel. [Fr,—Low L *dromedārius*—Gr *dromas, -ados*, running—*dromos*, a course, run.]

drone [drōn] *n* the male of the honey-bee; one who lives on the labor of others, like the drone-bee—a lazy, idle fellow; a deep humming sound; a bass-pipe of a bagpipe; a monotonous tiresome speaker or speech; an aircraft piloted by remote control.—*vi* to emit a monotonous humming sound. [OE *drān*, bee.]

drool [drōōl] *vi* to slaver—a form of **drivel**.

droop [drōōp] *vi* to sink or hang down; to grow weak or faint; to decline. [ON *drūpa*, to droop; from the same root as **drop**.]

drop [drop] *n* a small amount of liquid in a roundish shape; a sudden fall; the distance down.—*vi* to fall in drops; to fall suddenly; to go lower, to sink; to stop, to end; to come (in); to let go; to dismiss; to leave out, to omit.—*vt* to let fall, to cause to fall; to lower or cause to descend; to set down from a ship or vehicle; to cause (the voice) to be less loud; to bring down; to give up (as an idea); to leave incomplete; to lose; to kill.—*pr p* **dropping**; *pt p* **dropped**—*ns* **dropkick**, a kick made by dropping a football to the ground and kicking it at moment it starts to rebound; **droplet**, a tiny drop (as of liquid); **drop-off**, a very steep descent; a marked decline; **dropout**, one who drops out of school; one who drops out of conventional society; a spot on a magnetic tape from which data has disappeared. **drop seat**, a hinged seat (as in a taxi) that may be dropped down; a seat (in an undergarment) that falls down when unbuttoned.—**drop back**, to move toward the rear of an advancing line; **drop behind**, to fail to keep up; **drop by**, to pay a brief casual visit; **drop in**, to pay an unexpected visit. [OE *dropa*, drop—*dropian, droppian*, to drop; Du *drop*, Ger *tropfe*.]

dropsy [drop´si] *n* edema.—*adj* **drop´sical**. [Through Fr from L *hydrōpisis*—Gr *hydrōps, -ōpos*—*hydōr*, water.]

droshky [drosh´ki], **drosky** [dros´ki] *n* a low four-wheeled open carriage used in Russia. [Russ *drozhki*.]

dross [dros] *n* the scum of melting metals; waste matter; refuse. [OE *drōs*.]

drought [drowt], **drouth** [drowth] *n* dryness; want of rain or of water.—*adjs* **drought´y, drouth´y**. [OE drūgath, dryness—*drūgian*, to dry.]

drove [drōv] *pt* of **drive**.—*n* a number of cattle, or sheep, driven.—*n* **drov´er**, one whose occupation is to drive cattle. [OE *drāf*—*drīfan*, to drive.]

drown [drown] *vi* to die of suffocation in liquid.—*vt* to kill by suffocation in liquid; to submerge; to flood; to overwhelm. [ME *drounen*; origin obscure.]

drowse [drowz] *vi* to be heavy with sleep.—*vt* to make heavy with sleep; to stupefy.—*adj* **drows´y**, sleepy.—*adv* **drows´ily**.—*n* **drows´iness**. [Apparently OE *drūsian*, to be sluggish.]

drub [drub] *vt* to beat or thrash;—*pr p* **drubb´ing**; *pt p* **drubbed**.—*n* **drubbing**, a beating. [Possibly Ar *daraba*, to beat.]

drudge [druj] *vi* to do dull, laborious, or very menial work.—*n* one who does such work—a hack, or a menial servant.—*n* **drudg´ery**, the work of a drudge, hard, dull or humble labor. (Ety unknown; perh from root of OE *drēogan*, to perform, undergo.]

drug [drug] *n* any substance used in the composition of medicine; a substance used to stupefy or poison or self-indulgence; an article that cannot be sold, generally owing to overproduction.—*vt* to mix or season with drugs; to dose to excess, poison, or stupefy, with, or as with, drugs.—*vi* (*inf*) to be addicted to taking drugs;—*pr p* **drugg´ing**; *pt p* **drugged**.—**drug´ add´ict, drug´ fiend**, a habitual taker of drugs; **drugg´ist**, a pharmacist.—**drugstore**, a retail store selling medicines and other miscellaneous articles such as cosmetics, film, etc.—**drugstore cowboy**, one who wears cowboy clothes but has no experience of being a cowboy; one who loafs on street corners and in drugstores. [OFr *drogue*, of uncertain origin.]

druid [drōō´id] *n* (also **Druid**) a priest among the ancient Celts of Britain, Gaul, and Germany; an Eisteddfod official.—*adjs* **druid´ic, -al**.—*n* **dru´idism**, the doctrines and ceremonies of the druids. [L pl *druidae*, from a Celtic stem *druid-*, whence Gael *draoi*, magician.]

drum [drum] *n* an instrument of percussion, stretched on a frame (usu. cylindrical or hemispherical in shape); anything shaped like a drum, as a container for liquids; the tympanum of the ear; (*archit*) the upright part of a cupola.—*vi* to beat a drum; to beat or tap rhythmically; to thump continuously.—*vt* to expel with beat of drum (*with* **out, down**); to summon as by drum (*with* **up**); to impress by continued repetition (with *into*);—*pr p* **drumm´ing**; *pt p* **drummed**.—**drumhead**, the material stretched over each end of a drum; the top of a capstan that is pierced with sockets for the use of levers turning it; **drumhead court-martial**, a summary court-martial that tries offenses on the battlefield; **drum major**, the marching leader of a band; **drum majorette**, a female drum major; a baton twirler who accompanies a marching band; **drummer**, one who plays a drum; a traveling salesman; **drum printer**, a line printer in which the printing element is a revolving drum; **drum up**, to bring about by persistent effort; to invent or originate. [From a Gmc root; cf Ger *trommel*, drum; prob imit]

drunk [drungk] *pt p of* **drink**.—*adj* intoxicated.—*n* a drunk person.—*n* **drunk´**, one who frequently drinks to excess.—*adj* **drunk´en**, giving to excessive drinking; resulting from, showing the effects of (or as if of), intoxication.—*n* **drunk´enness**, intoxication; habitual intoxication.

drupe [drōōp] *n* a fleshy fruit containing a stone, as the plum, etc.—*adj* **drupā´ceous**. [L *drūpa*—Gr *dryppā*, an over-ripe olive.]

dry [drī] *adj* free or freed from water or liquid; (of land) not being in or under water; thirsty; characterized by the absence of alcoholic beverages; not giving milk; (of a cough) lacking natural lubrication; austere; marked by a matter-of-fact, ironic, or terse manner of expression; uninteresting, wearisome; (of wine) not sweet. *comparative* **drier**; *superlative* **driest**.—*vt* to free from water or moisture.—*vi* to become dry; *pr p* **drying**; *pt p* **dried**.—*ns* **drier**, something that extracts or absorbs moisture; a substance that accelerates drying (as of oils, paints, and printing inks); **dryness; dryer**, an appliance for drying (as of clothes or hair).—*adv* **dryly.—dry cell**, a battery whose contents are not spillable.—*vt* **dryclean**, to clean with solvents other than water.—**dry dock**, a dock that can be kept dry during ship construction and repair; **dry farming**, farming without irrigation in areas of limited rainfall; **dry goods**, textiles, ready-to-wear clothing and notions; **dry ice**, solidified carbon dioxide used chiefly as a refrigerant; **dry measure**, units of capacity for dry commodities (as bushel, peck, quart, or pint); **drypoint**, an engraving made with a steel or jeweled point without the use of acid; a print made from such an engraving; **dry rot**, the decay of wood caused by fungi; **dry run**, practice of firing without ammunition; a practice exercise; a rehearsal; **dry well**, a hole filled with gravel and rubble to receive water (as drainage from a roof) and allow it to drain away.—*vi* **dry out** (*inf*) to recover from alcohol abuse; **dry up**, to disappear by evaporation, draining, or cutting off, a source of supply; to wither or die through gradual loss of vitality; to stop talking. [OE *drȳge*; cf Du *droog*, Ger *trocken*.]

dryad [drī´ad] *n* a wood nymph;—*pls* **dry´ads, -adēs**. [Gr *dryas, -ados*, from *drys*, oak tree.]

dual [dū´ál] *adj* twofold; consisting of two.—*n* **dū´alism** (*philos*) any of various theories which admit of two independent and mutually irreducible substances in any given domain; **dual citizenship**, the status of a person who is a citizen of two or more nations; **dū´alist**, a believer in dualism; **dual´ity**, doubleness, state of being double.—*adj* **du´al-pur´pose**, serving or intended to serve two purposes; **dual-purpose fund**, an investment company with two classes of stockholders, one entitled to dividends and the other to gains from capital appreciation. [L *duālis*—*duo*, two.]

dub [dub] *vt* to confer knighthood upon, by touching each shoulder with a sword; to confer any dignity upon; to nickname, style;—*pr p* **dubb´ing**; *pt p* **dubbed**.—*n* **dubb´ing**, the accolade; (or **dubb´in**) a preparation of grease for softening leather. [OE *dubbian*.]

dub [dub] *vt* to give (a film) a new sound-track, eg one in a different language; to add sound effects or music to (a film, etc.); to transfer (recorded music, etc.) to a new disk or tape; to combine so as to make one record (music, etc., from more than one source, eg a live performance and a recording).—*n* **dubb´ing**. [Abbrev of **double**.]

dubious [dū´bi-us] *adj* doubtful (about, of); uncertain as to the result (eg *a dubious contest*); equivocal (eg *dubious reply*); of questionable nature (eg *dubious dealings; a dubious compliment*).—*adv* **dūbiously**.—*ns* **dūbiousness, dūbī´ety**. [L *dubius*.]

ducal [du´kal] *adj* of a duke.

duchy [duch´i] *n* the territory of a duke, a dukedom.—**duch´ess** [duch´es] the wife or widow of a duke; a woman of the same rank as a duke in her own right; **duchess potatoes**, mashed potatoes formed into cakes or as a border around a dish. [OFr duché—Low L *ducātus*.]

duck[1] [duk] *n* coarse cloth for small sails, sacking, etc.; (*pl*) garments made of duck. [Du *doeck*, linen cloth; Ger *tuch*.]
duck[2] [duk] *vt* to dip for a moment in water; (*coll*) to avoid.—*vi* to dip or dive; to lower the head suddenly.—*n* a quick lowering of the head or body.—*n* **duck´ing-stool**, a stool or chair in which scolds, etc. were formerly tied and ducked in the water. [ME *douken*.]
duck[3] [duk] *n* any of a family (Anatinae) of water birds related to geese and swans; the female of this bird.—*ns* **duckbill**, platypus; **duckboard**, slatted flooring laid on a wet, muddy, or cold surface; **duckpin**, a small bowling pin shorter and wider in the middle than a tenpin; **duck soup**, something easy to do.—*adv* **duckfooted**, with feet pointed outward; **make ducks and drakes of, play ducks and drakes with**, to squander, waste. [OE *duce*, a duck; from the same root as **duck**(2).]
duck[4] [duk] *n* an amphibious truck. [From manufacturers' code initials, DUKW.]
duct [dukt] *n* a tube or pipe for fluids, electric cable, etc.—**ductless gland**, an endocrine gland. [L *ductus—dūcěre*, to lead.]
ductile [duk´-til]—*adj.* easily led; yielding; capable of being drawn out into threads.—*n.* **ductil´ity**. [Fr,—L *ductilis—dūcěre, to lead.*]
dud [dud] *n* anything worthless.—Also *adj* [Origin unknown.]
dude [dūd] *n* fop, dandy. [Origin unknown.]
dude ranch a vacation resort offering activities (such as horseback riding) typical of western ranches.
dudgeon [duj´ȯn] *n* resentment; angry feeling.
duds [dudz] *n pl* poor or ragged clothes; (*coll*) clothes. [Perh ME *dudde*, cloak.]
due [dū] *adj* owed; that ought to be paid or done to another; proper; expected to arrive, be ready, be paid, etc.—*adv* directly (eg *due east*).—*n* what is owed; what one has a right to; perquisite; fee or tribute.—**due to**, because of. [OFr *deü*, *pt p* of *devoir*—L *dēbēre*, to owe.]
duel [dū´ėl] *n* combat, under fixed conditions, between two persons over a matter of honor, etc; (*fig*) single combat of any kind (eg *a verbal duel*).—*vi* to fight in a duel.—*pr p* du´elling; *pt p* **du´eled.—dū´eler, dū´elist**. [It *duello*—L *duellum*, the original form of *bellum*, war—*duo*, two.]
duenna [dū-en´a] *n* an elderly lady who acts as guardian to a younger. [Sp *dueña*, a form of *doña*, mistress—L *domina*, fem of *dominus*, lord.]
duet [dū-et´] *n* a composition in music for two performers; the performance of such.—*n* **duett´ist**. [It *duetto—duo*, two—L *duo*, two.]
duffel [duf´l] *n* a thick, coarse woolen cloth with a thick nap. Also **duffle.—duffelbag**, a large cylindrical bag for personal belongings. [Du, from *Duffel*, a town near Antwerp.]
duffer [duf´ėr] *n* an ineffectual or clumsy man. [Origin unknown.]
duffle *see* **duffel**.
dug[1] [dug] *n* a nipple or udder of a cow or other beast. [Cf Sw *dægga*, Dan *dægge*, to suckle.]
dug[2] [dug] *pt* and *pt p* of **dig**.—*n* **dug´out**, a boat made by hollowing out the trunk of a tree; a rough dwelling or shelter, *dug out* of a slope or bank or in a trench; either of the two shelters near a baseball diamond that contain the players' benches.
dugong [doo´gong] *n* a genus (*Dugong*) of large herbivorous mammals of tropical seas related to the manatee. Also **sea cow**. [Malayan *dūyong*.]
duiker [dī´kėr, di´ker] *n* any of several small African antelopes (*Cephalophus*) or related species. [Du]
duke [dūk] *n* the highest order of British nobility; a title of European nobility.—*n* **duke´dom**, the title, rank, or territories of a duke. [OFr *duc*—L *dux, ducis*, a leader—*dūcěre*, to lead.]
Dukhobor *see* **Doukhobor**.
dulcet [duls´et] *adj* sweet to the taste, or to the ear; melodious, harmonious. [L *dulcis*, sweet.]
dulcimer [dul´si-mėr] *n* a musical instrument played by striking the strings with two hammers. [Sp *dulcemele*—L *dulce melos*, a sweet song—*dulcis*, sweet, *melos* (Gr *melos*), a song.]
dull [dul] *adj* not sharp or pointed; not bright or clear; stupid; boring; not active.—*vti* to make or to become dull.—*adv* **dul´ly—dull´ness, dul´ness; dull´ard**, a dull and stupid person. [Related to OE *dol*, foolish, and *dwellan*, to err; Ger *toll*, mad.]
dulse [duls] *n* an edible red seaweed (*Rhodymenia palmata*). [Gael *duileasg*, perh *duille*, leaf, *uisge*, water.]
duly [dū´li] *adv* properly; fitly; at the proper time. [See *due*.]
duma [dōō´ma] *n* a representative council in Russia. [Russ.]
dumb[1] [dum] *adj* not able to speak; silent; stupid.—*n* **dumb´ness.—dumb´bell**, a short bar with heavy disks or round ends used to exercise the muscles; a very stupid person; **dumb´show´**, gesture without words; pantomime; **dumb´wait´er**, a portable serving table; a small elevator for moving food from one floor to another.—*vti* **dum(b)-found´, -er**, to confound briefly, usu. with astonishment. [OE *dumb*; Ger *dumm*, stupid.]
dumdum [dum´dum] *n* a soft-nosed expanding bullet. [First made at *Dum Dum* near Calcutta.]
dummy [dum´ē] figure of a person used to display clothes; a stupid person; an imitation; (*bridge*) the exposed cards of the declarer's partner; the declarer's partner—*adj* imitating; existing in name only, fictitious (as of a corporation or bank account)—*vt* to make a dummy of (a book).—*vi* (*slang*) to refuse to talk (*with* **up**).
dump [dump] *vt* to unload; to discard, as on a rubbish heap; to sell goods abroad at a price lower than the market price abroad.—*n* a place for refuse or other unwanted material; a dirty, dilapidated place.—**dump truck** a vehicle for transporting and unloading loose materials. [Cf Dan *dumpe*, Norw *dumpa*, to fall plump.]
dumpling [dump´ling] *n* a rounded piece of dough cooked by boiling or steaming; a short, fat person. [Origin obscure.]
dumpy [dump´i] *adj* short and thick.—**dump´iness; dump´y lev´el**, a spirit level used in surveying, having a short telescope rigidly connected to the vertical spindle.
dumps [dump] *n* gloominess, low spirits [Cf Ger *dumpf*, gloomy.]
dun [dun] *adj* greyish-brown in color.—*n* a dun horse. [OE *dun*, prob Celt].—
dun [dun] *vt* to importune for payment;—*pr p* **dunn´ing**; *pt p* **dunned**. [Perh allied to **din**.]
dunce [duns] *n* one slow at learning; a stupid person. [*Duns* Scotus.]
dunderhead [dun´dėr-hed] *n* a stupid person.—[Origin unknown.]
dune [dūn] *n* a hill of sand piled up by the wind.—**dune buggy**, a beach buggy, **duneland**, an area having many dunes. [Fr—ODu *dūna*; cf **down**.]
dung [dung] *n* excrement; manure.—*vt* to manure with dung.—*ns* **dung beetle**, a beetle (as a dorbeetle or tumblebug) that rolls balls of dung in which to lay eggs; **dung´hill**, a heap of dung; a situation that is repulsive. [OE].
dungaree [dung-gȧ-rē´ or dung´-] *n* a kind of coarse cotton cloth, trousers, often bibbed, made from this. (*pl*) [Hindustani *dungrī*.]
dungeon [dun´jȯn] *n* a close, dark prison, esp a cell underground. [OFr *donjon*—Low L *domniō,-ōnis*—L *dominus*, a lord.]
dunk [dungk] *vti* to dip cake, etc., that one is eating in one's coffee or other beverage. [Ger *tunken* to dip.]
dunlin [dun´lin] *n* the red-backed sandpiper (*Pelidna alpina*). [Dim of **dun**.]
duo [dū´ō] *n* a duet; two persons associated in some way. [It—L *duo*, two.]
duodecennial [dū-ō-di-sen´yȧl] *adj* occurring every twelve years. [L *duodecim*, twelve, *annus*, year.]
duodecimo [dū-ō-des´i-mō] *n* size of book in which each sheet is folded into 12 leaves; a book of this size—*adj* of this size.
duodecimal [dū-ō-des´i-ml] *adj* computed by twelves; twelfth.—**duodecimal system**, a numeration system whose base is 12, the numbers 10 and 11 being denoted by special symbols and regarded as digits. [L *duodecim*, twelve—*duo*, two, and *decem*, ten.]
duodenum [dū-o-dēnum] *n* the first part of the small intestine.—*adj* **duodē´nal**. [Formed from L *duodēni*, twelve each.]
duologue [dū´ō-log] *n* a piece spoken between two. [Irregularly formed from L *duo* (or Gr *dyo*), two, Gr *logos*, discourse.]
dupe [dūp] *n* one who is cheated.—*vt* to deceive; to trick.—*n* **dū´pery**, the art of deceiving others. [Fr *dupe*; of uncertain origin.]
duple [dū´pl] *adj* double, twofold; (*mus*) having two beats to the bar. [L *duplus*; cf **double**.]
duplex [dū´pleks] *adj* twofold, double.—*n* an apartment on two floors; a two-family house.—**duplicity** (dū-plis´i-ti), contradictory, doubleness, esp in conduct and intention; treachery. [L *duplex, -icis*.]
duplicate [dū´pli-kāt] *adj* double; twofold; exactly like.—*n* another thing of the same kind; a copy or transcript.—*vt* [dū´pli-kāt] to double; to make an exact copy or copies of; to repeat.—**duplicā´tion; dū´plicātor**, a copying apparatus.—**in duplicate**, in two copies. [L *duplicāre, -ātum—duo*, two, *plicāre*, to fold.]
durable [dūr´a-bl] *adj* able to last or endure; resisting wear, etc.—**dur´ableness, durabil´ity.—dur´ance** imprisonment; **duration**, continuing in time; the time in which an event persists. [L dūrāre, to harden, endure, last.]
duralumin [dūr-al´-ūm-in] *n* an aluminum-based alloy. [L dūrus, hard, + **aluminum**.]
durbar [dûr´bar] *n* a reception or levee, esp of Indian princes. [Pers *dar-bār*, a prince's court, lit, a 'door of admittance'.]
duress [dūr´es or dūr-es´] *n* unlawful constraint; imprisonment. [OFr *duresse*—L *dūritia—dūrus*, hard.]
durian [dōōr´ian] *n* a large, oval, tasty but foul-smelling fruit with a prickly rind; the tree of SE Asia bearing this fruit.
during [dū´ring] *prep* throughout the time of; in the course of. [Orig pr p of obs *dure*, to last.]
durra [dōō´ra] *n* any of several grain sorghums grown widely in warm dry regions.—Also **dura**. [Ar *dhurah*.]
durst [dûrst] *pt* of **dare**, to venture. [OE *dorste*, pa t of *durran*, to dare.]
dusk [dusk] *adj* dark brown.—*n* twilight; partial darkness.—*adj* **dusk´y**, having dark skin.—*n* **dusk´iness**. [Connected with OE *dox*, dark.]
dust [dust] *n* fine particles of solid matter; earth; the grave.—*vt* to free from dust; to sprinkle with flour, sugar, or the like.—*adj* **dust´y**, covered with, containing, or characterized by dust.—**dust bowl**, a drought area subject to duststorms; **dustcloth**, a cloth for removing dust; **dustcover**, a cover for protecting furniture from dust; **dust devil**, a small whirlwind containing sand or dust; **duster**, a cloth for removing dust; a woman's lightweight coat; a device for dusting crops with insecticides or fungicides; **dustheap**, a mound of dry refuse; **dustjacket**, a paper cover for a book; **dustpan**, a shovel-shaped pan for sweepings; **duststorm**, strong winds bearing clouds of dust; **dusty miller**, any of several plants having leaves covered with ashy-gray or white matted hairs.—**bite the dust** *see* **bite**. [OE dust.]

Dutch [duch] *adj* pertaining to Holland, its people, or language; (*obs*) German.—*ns* **Dutch cheese** cottage cheese; **Dutch Colonial architecture**, a style characterized by a gambrel roof and overhanging eaves; **Dutch courage**, courage due to intoxicants; **Dutch door**, a door divided horizontally so that each part can be opened or shut separately; **Dutch elm disease**, a fungus disease of elms marked by yellowing foliage, defoliation and death; **Dutch hoe**, a scuffle hoe; **Dutchman's breeches**, a spring-flowering herb (*Dicentra cucullaria*) of the fumitory family with finely divided leaves and cream-white double-spurred flowers; **Dutchman's pipe**, a vine (*Aristolochia durior*) with large leaves and early summer flowers resembling a pipe; **Dutch oven**, a metal shield for roasting before an open fire; a brick oven in which cooking is done by residual heat; a castiron kettle or pot with a tight cover for baking in an open fire; **Dutch treat**, a meal or entertainment for which each person pays his or her own way; **Dutch uncle**, one who admonishes sternly and bluntly; **Pennsylvania Dutch** [pen-sil-vān´-yȯ duch] *n* a dialect of German mixed with English words spoken in parts of Pennsylvania; the descendents of 17th and 18th century immigrants to Pennsylvania from Germany and Switzerland. [Ger *deutsch, (lit)* belonging to the people—OHG *diutis*, of which *-is* = the Eng suffx *-ish*, and *diut* = OE *thēod*, a nation.]

duty [dūti] *n* that which one is bound by any obligation to do; one's business, occupation, functions, etc. (eg *on duty, the duties of this post*); service; respect; tax on goods, etc.—*adjs* **dū´teous**, devoted to duty; obedient; **dū´tiable**, liable to be taxed; **dū´tiful**, attentive to duty; respectful; **dū´ty-free**, free from tax or duty. [Anglo-Fr *dueté; cf* **due**.]

duumvirate [dū-um´vi-rāt] *n* the union of two men (**dūum´virs**) in the same office—a form of government in ancient Rome. [L—*duo*, two, and *vir*, a man.]

DVD [abbrev] digital video disc.

dwarf [dwörf] *n* an animal or plant much below normal size; a star (as the sun) of ordinary or low luminosity and relatively small mass and size.—*vt* to hinder from growing; to make to appear small.—*adj* **dwarf´ish**, like a dwarf; very small. [OE *dweorg*; Ger *zwerg*.]

dwell [dwel] *vi* to abide (in a place); to remain, to continue long; (*with* **on**) to rest the attention on, to talk at length about;—*pr p* **dwell´ing**; *pt* and *pt p* **dwelt** or **dwelled**.—*ns* **dwell´er; dwell´ing**, the place where one dwells, habitation. [OE *dwellan*, to cause to wander, lead astray, delay.]

dwindle [dwin´dl] *vi* to grow less; to grow feeble; to become degenerate. [Dim of *dwine* (Scot), to waste away—OE *dwīnan*, to fade.]

Dyak *see* **Dayak**.

dybbuk [dib´ek] *n* a wandering soul believed in Jewish folklore to enter the body of a person and control his actions until exorcised by a religious rite.—*pl* **dybbukim**. [Heb *dibbiq*.]

dye [dī] *vt* to stain; to give a new color to;—*pr p* **dye´ing**; *pt p* **dyed**.—*n* color; tinge; a coloring material, esp in solution.—*ns* **dy´er**, one whose trade is to dye cloth, etc.; **dye´stuff**, material used in dyeing; **dye´wood**, any wood from which coloring matter is obtained for dyeing.—**dyed-in-the-wool**, dyed in the raw state; of firmly fixed convictions. [OE *dēagian*, to dye, from *dēag* or *dēah*, color.]

dying [dī´ing] *pr p of* **die**.—*adj* occurring immediately before death, as *dying words*; pertaining to death; declining, becoming extinct.—*n* death.

dyke *see* **dike**.

dynam-, dynamo- [din´am(-ō) or dī´] [Gr *dynamis*, power—*dynasthai*, to be able.]—*adjs* **dynam´ic, -al**, relating to force; causal; forceful, very energetic.—*adv* **dynam´ically**.—*ns* **dynam´ic**, a moving or driving force; **dynamics** (*pl* as sing), the science which treats of matter and motion, or mechanics, sometimes restricted to kinetics; **dyn´amite**, a powerful explosive agent (nitroglycerine and kieselguhr); **dyn´amītard, dyn´amīter**, user of dynamite, esp for political purposes; **dynamo**, contr for **dynamo-electric machine**, a machine which generates electric currents by means of the relative movement of conductors and magnets;—*pl* **dyn´amos; dynamom´eter**, an instrument for measuring force or power (Gr *metron*, a measure).

dynast [din´ast or dīn´-] *n* a ruler.—*n* **dyn´asty**, a succession of hereditary rulers or of members of any powerful family or connected group.—*adj* **dynas´tic**. [Gr *dynastēs*, a lord.]

dyne [dīn] *n* the unit of force in the centimeter-gram-second system—that which, acting on a mass of 1 g imparts to it an acceleration of 1 cm per s per s.—Equals 10^{-5} newtons. [Fr, formed from Gr *dynamis*, power.]

dys- [dis-] ill, bad, abnormal. [Gr.]

dysentery [dis´en-tri] *n* painful inflammation of the large intestine with associated diarrhea.—*adj* **dysenter´ic**. [Gr *dysenteria*—*dys-*, ill, *enteron*, intestine.]

dysfunction [dis-fung(k)´sh(ȯ)n] *n* imperfect functioning of an organ of the body. [**dys-** + **function**.]

dyslexia [dis-leks´i-ȧ] *n* impaired ability in learning to read or spell.—*adjs* **dyslec´tic, dyselx´ic**. [**dys-** + Gr *lexis*, word.]

dysmenorrhea [dis-men-ō-rē´ȧ] *n* painful menstruation. [**dys-** + Gr *mēn*, month, *rhoiā*, flow.]

dyspepsia [dis-pep´si-a] *n* indigestion—also **dyspep´sy**.—*n* **dyspep´tic**, a person afflicted with dyspepsia.—*adjs* **dyspep´tic, -al** pertaining to, or suffering from, dyspepsia; (*fig*) gloomy, bad-tempered.—*adv* **dyspep´tically**. [Gr **dys-**, ill, *pessein, peptein*, to digest.]

dysprosium [dis-prō´si-ùm] *n* a metallic element (symbol Dy; at wt 162.5. no 66) of the rare-earth group. [Gr *dysprositos*, hard to get at.]

dystrophy [dis´trȯ-fi] *n* imperfect nutrition; any of several disorders in which there is wasting of muscle tissue, etc. [**dys-** + Gr, *trophē*, nourishment.]

E

E layer a layer of the ionosphere occurring at about 60 miles above the earth's atmosphere and capable of reflecting radio waves.—**E region**, the part of the ionosphere 40 to 90 miles above the surface of the earth, containing the daytime E layer and the sporadic E layer.

each [ēch] *adj* every one, separately considered, in any number. [OE *ǣlc—ā*, ever, *gelīc*, alike.]

eager [ē´gėr] *adj* excited by desire (to do, or for); earnest, keen, enthusiastic.—*adv* **ea´gerly**.—*n* **ea´gerness.**—**eager beaver**, an enthusiast; a zealous person. [OFr *aigre*—L *ācer*, sharp.]

eagle [ē´gl] *n* any of various large, brownish diurnal birds of prey (family Accipitridae) with feathered legs, keen eyes, and powerful wings; a gold coin of the United States, worth ten dollars; (golf) score of two strokes under par.—*adj* **ea´gle-eyed.**—*n* **ea´glet**, a young eagle. [OFr *aigle*—L *aquila*.]

eagre [ē´gėr] *n* a tidal bore. [Ety uncertain.]

ear [ēr] *n* a spike, as of corn.—*vi* to put forth ears. [OE *ēar*; Ger *ähre*.]

ear [ēr] *n* the organ of hearing, or the external part merely; the sense of hearing; the faculty of distinguishing sounds, esp of different pitch; attention; anything shaped like an ear.—*ns* **ear´ache**, a pain in the ear; **ear´drum**, the tympanic membrane; **ear´mark**, an owner's mark set on the ears of sheep; a distinctive mark.—*vt* to put an earmark on; to set aside (for a particular purpose).—*adj* **ear´splitting**, shrill, screaming.—*ns* **earmuff**, one of a pair of ear coverings connected by a flexible band and worn as protection against cold or noise; **earphone**, a device that converts electrical energy into sound and is worn over or in the ear; **earplug**, a protective device for insertion into the outer opening of the ear; **earring**, an ornament for the earlobe or rim of the ear; **earshot**, within range of hearing; **earwax**, cerumen; **earwig**, any of numerous insects (order Dermaptera) with slender many-jointed antennae and appendages like forceps at the end of the body.—*vt* to annoy or attempt to influence by talk. (OE *ēarwicga—ēare*, ear, *wicga*, insect, beetle). [OE *ēare*; cf Ger *ohr*, L *auris*.]

earl [ûrl] *n* a British nobleman ranking between a marquis and a viscount; courtesy title given to the eldest son of a marquis etc.—*fem* **count"ess.**—*n* **earl´dom**, the dominion or dignity of an earl. [OE *eorl*, a warrior, hero; cf ON *jarl*.]

early [ûr´li] *adj* belonging to or happening in the first part (of a time, period, series); happening in the remote past or near future.—*adv* near the beginning; soon; in good time; before the appointed time.—*n* **ear´liness.**—**Early American**, a style of furniture, architecture, or fabric characteristic of colonial America.—**early bird**, an early riser; one who gains by acting more promptly than his competitors; **early on**, at or during an early point or stage. [OE *ǣlīce—ǣr*, before.]

earn [ûrn] *vt* to gain by work or service; to acquire; to deserve.—*n pl* **earn´ings**, something earned; the balance of revenue after deducting costs. [OE *earnian*, to earn; cf OHG *aran*, harvest; Ger *ernte*.]

earnest [ûr´nest] *adj* intent; sincere; serious.—*n* seriousness.—*adv* **ear´nestly**.—*n* **ear´nestness.**—**in earnest**, serious, not jesting; intent on one's purpose, not trifling; seriously; purposefully. [OE *eornost*, seriousness; Ger *ernst*.]

earnest [ûr´nest] *n* money given in token of a bargain made; a pledge. [Ety obscure.]

earth [ûrth] *n* the third planet in order from the sun; the world; the inhabitants of the world; the matter on the surface of the globe; soil; dry land, as opposed to sea; dirt; dead matter; the human body; a burrow.—*vt* to hide or cause to hide in the earth or in a hole.—*adj* **earth´en**, made of earth.—*ns* **earth´enware**, ceramic ware made of coarse clay fired at low heat.—*adj* **earth´ly**, belonging to the earth; passed on earth; worldly, not spiritual.—*n* **earth´liness.**—**earth´quake**, a shaking of the earth's crust caused by changes far beneath the surface.—**earth science**, any of the sciences (as geology, meteorology, or oceanology) that deal with the earth or one of its parts.—*adj* **earthshaking**, of fundamental importance—*n* **earthshaker; earth´work**, a fortification of earth; **earth´worm**, any of a family (Lumbricidae) of annelid terrestial hermaphroditic worms that live in the soil.—*adj* **earth´y**, consisting of, relating to, or resembling earth or soil; gross; crude.—*n* **earth´iness**. [OE *eorthe*; cf Du *aarde*, Ger *erde*.]

ease [ēz] *n* freedom from pain or disturbance; rest from work; quiet; freedom from difficulty; naturalness.—*vt* to free from pain, trouble, or anxiety; to relieve (the mind); to relax, slacken, release (pressure, tension); to moderate; to facilitate; to move slowly and carefully.—*vi* to become less intense (also **ease off**); to become less in demand.—*n* **ease´ment**, the right held by one person in land owned by another.—*adj* **eas´y**, at ease; free from pain, trouble, anxiety, difficulty; unconstrained (eg of manner); not tight; not strict; equally pleased with either alternative.—*adv* **eas´ily**.—*n* **eas´iness.**—*interj* **easy**! a command to go gently.—*adjs* **eas´ygō´ing** indolent; placid.—**at ease** free from pain or discomfort; free from formality; standing silently (in a military formation) with feet apart.—**easy as pie** (*slang*) very easy; **easy mark**, one easily imposed upon or duped; **easy street**, a situation of no financial worries. [OFr *aise*; cog with It *agio*; Provençal *ais*, Port *azo*.]

easel [ēz´l] *n* the frame on which painters support their pictures while painting. [Du *ezel*, or Ger *esel*, an ass.]

east [ēst] *n* the direction of the sunrise; the direction toward the right of one facing north; the compass point opposite west; **East**, regions lying to the east of a point of orientation as East Asia, East Germany, East Indies; a person (such as a bridge or mah-jongg player) occupying this position during a game.—*adj* **eastbound**, traveling or heading east.—*adj, adv* **eastward**; *adv* **eastwards**; *adj, adv* **easterly**, situated toward or belonging to the east, coming from the east.—*n* a wind from the east; *pl* **easterlies. easternize**, imbue with qualities of residents of the eastern US; orientalize.—*n* **easting**, difference in longitude to the east from the last preceding point of reckoning;—*adj, adv* **easterly**, situated toward or belonging to the east; coming from the east.—*adjs* **Eastern**, of a region designated East; of the Christian Churches originating in the church of the Eastern Roman Empire; Eastern Orthodox; **eastern, easternmost**, lying toward the east; coming from the east.—**Eastern Orthodox**, of the Eastern Catholic churches that accord primacy to the patriarch of Constantinople and adhere to the Byzantine rite.—**eastern hemisphere**, the half of the earth to the east of the Atlantic Ocean including Europe, Asia, and Africa.—**east by north**, compass point one point north of due east (N 78° 45´E); **east by south** compass point one point south of due east (S78° 45´E); **Eastern time**, 5th time zone west of Greenwich that includes the eastern US. [OE *ēast*; Ger *ost*; akin to Gr *ēōs*, the dawn.]

Easter [ēstėr] *n* a church feast observed on a Sunday in March or April in commemoration of the resurrection of Christ.—*ns* **Easter bonnet**, a woman or girl's hat bought to wear at Easter; **Easter bunny**, a rabbit said to bring presents for children at Easter; **Easter egg**, an egg dyed in bright colors that is associated with Easter celebrations; **Easter lily**, any of several white cultivated lilies (esp *Lilium longiflorum*) that bloom in early spring; **Easter parade**, a promenade on Easter Sunday to show off new clothes. [OE *ēastre*; Ger *ostern*. Perh from *Eostre*, a goddess whose festival was held at the spring equinox.]

eat [ēt] *vt* to chew and swallow, or to swallow; to consume; (*also with* **into**) to waste away, to corrode.—*vi* to take food;—*pr p* **eat´ing**; *pt* **ate** (*āt*); *pt p* **eaten** (*ētn*).—*adj* **eat´able**, fit to be eaten.—*n* anything used as food; *pl* food.—*n* **eatery**, a place where meals are sold, a restaurant.—**eat crow**, to accept what one has fought against; **eat humble pie**, to apologize under pressure; **eat one's heart out**, to grieve bitterly; **eat one's words**, to take back what one has said; **eat out of someone's hand**, to accept the domination of another. [OE *etan*; cf Ger *essen*; L *edĕre*, Gr *edein*.]

eau de Cologne [ō dė kō-lōn´] *n* cologne.

eau de vie [ō dė vē] brandy. [Fr *eau*, water, *de*, of, *vie*, life.]

eaves [ēvz] *n pl* the projecting edge of a roof.—*vi* **eaves´drop**, to listen secretly to private conversation.—*n* **eaves´dropper**. [OE *efes*, the clipped edge of thatch.]

ebb [eb] *n* the fall of the tide; a decline.—*vi* to flow back; to sink, to decline.—*n* **ebb´tide**, the ebbing tide. [OE *ebba*.]

ebony [eb´ȯn-i] *n* a hard heavy wood yielded by Old World tropical trees (genus *Diospyrus*).—Also *adj*—*vt* **eb´onize**, to stain black in imitation of ebony.—*pr p* **eb´onizing**; pt p **ebonized**.—*adj* **eb´on**, made of ebony; black as ebony.—*n* **eb´onite**, vulcanized rubber. [L *(h)ebenus*—Gr *ebenos*; cf Heb *hobnīm*, pl of *hobni, obni—eben*, a stone.]

ebullīent [e-bul´yėnt] *adj* exuberant, enthusiastic; boiling up or over.—*n* **ebulli´tion**, outburst (of feeling, etc.); act of boiling (also **ebull´ience**); an outbreak. [L *ēbulliēns, -entis—ē*, out, *bullire*, boil.]

eccentric [ek-sen´trik] *adj* deviating from a usual or accepted pattern; deviating from a circular path; set-up axis or off-center; support; being off-center.—*n* **eccen´tric** an eccentric person.—*adv* **eccen´trically**.—*n* **eccentric´ity** [-tris´-], condition of being eccentric; singularity of conduct; oddness. [Gr *ek*, out of, *kentron*, centre.]

ecclēsias´tic [e-klēzi-as´tik] *n* a priest, a clergyman.—*adjs* **ecclēsias´tic, -al**, of, belonging to, the church.—*ns* **ecclesiol´ogy**, the study of building and decorating churches; theological doctrine relating to churches; **ecclesiol´ogist**. [Gr *ekklēsia*, assembly summoned by crier; (later) the Church—*ek*, out of, *kalein*, to call.]

Ecclesiastes [e-klēzi-as´tēz] *n* (*Bible*) 21st book of the Old Testament traditionally ascribed to Solomon, the theme of which is the excellence of wisdom.

Ecclesiasticus [e-klēzi-as´tik-us] *n* a didactic book in the RC canon of the Old Testament and the Protestant Apocrypha.

ECG Abbrev of **electrocardiogram**.

echelon [esh´e-lon, āsh´e-l•] *n* a stepwise arrangement of troops, ships, or airplanes, each line being a little to the right or left of that in front of it; a level (of authority) in a hierarchy. [Fr *échelon*, from *échelle*, a ladder or stair—L *scala*.]

echidna [ek-id´nä] *n* a genus of Australian toothless, spiny, egg-laying, burrowing nocturnal mammals. [Gr, viper.]

echo [ek´ō] *n* the repetition of a sound caused by a sound-wave being reflected; imitation; the reflection of a radar signal by an object; word used in communications for the letter *e*.—*pl* **echoes** [ek´ōz].—*vi* to reflect sound; to be sounded back.—*vt* to send back the sound of; to repeat; to imitate.—*pr p* **ech´oing**; *pt p* **ech´oed**.—*ns* **ech´olocā´tion**, determining the position of unseen objects by means of sound echoes (as a bat or submarine); **ech´osound´er**, an instrument for locating an object underwater or for determining the depth of a body of water by using sound waves. [L—Gr *ēchō*, a sound.]

éclair [ā-klār´] *n* a usu. chocolate-frosted small oblong shell of choux pastry with cream or custard filling. [Fr, lightning.]

eclampsia [e-klamp´sē-a] *n* a convulsive state, esp an attack during pregnancy or childbirth. [Gr *eklampsis*, to flash forth.]

éclat [ā-klä´] *n* a striking effect; fame; striking success; applause. [Fr from OFr *esclater*, to break, to shine.]

eclectic [ek-lek´tik] *adj* selecting or borrowing; choosing the best out of everything.—*n* one who selects opinions from different systems. [Gr *eklektikos*—*ek*, from, *legein*, to choose.]

eclipse [e-klips´] *n* the total or partial disappearance of a heavenly body by the interposition of another between it and the spectator, or by its passing into the shadow of another; temporary failure; loss of brilliancy; darkness.—*vt* to hide wholly or in part; to darken; to throw into the shade, surpass.—*n* **eclip´tic**, the line in which eclipses take place, ie a great circle (*celestial ecliptic*), the apparent path of the sun's annual motion among the fixed stars; a great circle on the globe corresponding to the celestial ecliptic.—*adj* pertaining to an eclipse or the ecliptic. [OFr,—L *eclīpsis*—Gr *ekleipsis*—*ek*, out of, *leipein*, to leave.]

eclogue [ek´log] *n* a short pastoral poem. [L *ecloga*—Gr *eklogē*, a selection esp of poems—*ek*, out of, *legein*, to choose.]

eco- [ek´ō] concerned with habitat and environment in relation to living organisms; **ec´ocide** destruction of an environment; **ec´osphere**, the habitable parts of the universe; **ec´osystem**, the complex of a community and its environment as a functioning unit in nature. [Gr *oikos*, a house.]

ecology [ē-kol´o-ji] *n* the study of organisms in relation to environment; human ecology. [Gr *oikos*, house, *logos*, discourse.]

e-commerce [ē´kom-ėrs] *n* (*comput*) electronic commerce; undertaking business transactions online.

economy [ek- or ēk-on´o-mi] *n* the thrifty and judicious use of money or goods; an instance of this; the economic system of a country.—*adjs* **econom´ic, -al**, pertaining to economy; (usu. **economic**) considered from the point of view of supplying man's needs; capable of yielding a profit; (usu. **economical**) thrifty.—*adv* **econom´ically**.—*n* **econom´ics**, a social science concerned with the production, consumption, and distribution of goods and services.—*vti* **econ´omize**, to spend money carefully; to save; to use prudently.—*n* **econ´omist**, one who studies economics;—**economic system**, the structure of economic life in a country, area, or period. [L *oeconomia*—Gr *oikonomia*—*oikos*, a house, *nomos*, a law.]

ecru [ā´krōō] *adj* beige. [Fr]

ecstasy [ek´stȧ-si] *n* excessive joy; poetic frenzy; any exalted feeling.—*adj* **ecstat´ic**, causing ecstasy; rapturous.—*adv* **ecstat´ically**. [Gr *ekstasis*—*ek*, from, *histanai*, to make to stand.]

ecto- [ek-to-] outside [Gr *ektos*, outside.], eg:—*adj* **ectop´ic**, occurring in an unusual position, form or manner esp an **ectopic pregnancy**, when gestation takes place in the peritoneal cavity.—*ns* **ec´tomorph**, an individual of slender build; **ectopar´asite**, an external parasite; **ectoplasm**, the outer layer of the cytoplasm of a cell; an emanation of bodily appearance believed by some spiritualists to come from a medium.

ecumenical [ek-ū-men´ik -al] *adj* of the whole Christian world; worldwide; universal; of relations between religions. [L *oecumenicus*—Gr *oikoumenē* (*gē*), inhabited (world).]

eczema [ek´si-ma] *n* inflammation of the skin with itching and the formation of patches of red scales. [Gr *ek*, out of, *zeein*, to boil.]

edacious [e-dā´shus] *adj* of eating; gluttonous.—*n* **edac´ity**. [L *edax*, *edācis*—*edĕre*, to eat.]

Edam [ē´dȧm] *n* a firm cheese of mild flavor made from cow's milk, molded into a ball and covered with red wax. [Edam, Netherlands.]

Edda [ed´a] *n* the name of two Scandinavian books, the one a collection of ancient mythological and heroic songs, the other a prose composition of the same kind. [ON, apparently akin to *ōdr*, mad, *ōthr*, spirit, mind, poetry.]

eddy [ed´i] *n* a whirlpool or whirlwind.—*vi* to move round and round;—*pr p* **edd´ying**; *pt p* **edd´ied**. [Prob conn with OE pfx *ed-*, back.]

edelweiss [ā´dėl-vīs] *n* a small white-flowered alpine perennial herb (*Leontopodium alpinum*). [Ger *edel*, noble, *weiss*, white.]

edema [i-dēm´a] *n* swelling caused by an abnormal accumulation of watery fluid in the tissues of the (plant or animal) body. Also **dropsy**, [Gr *oidēma*, swelling.]

Eden [ē´dn] *n* the garden where Adam and Eve lived; a paradise. [Heb *ēden*, delight, pleasure.]

edentate [e-den´tāt] *adj* toothless.—*n* **Edentā´ta**, an order of mammals, having few or no teeth, including sloths, armadillos, New World anteaters and formerly pangolins and aardvarks. [L *ēdentātus*, toothless—*ē*, out of, *dens*, *dentis*, a tooth.]

Edgar [ed´gȧr] *n* statuette awarded annually by a professional society for notable achievement in mystery-novel writing. [From Edgar Allan Poe, regarded as the father of the detective story.]

edge [ej] *n* the border of anything; the brink; the cutting side of an instrument; something that wounds or cuts; sharpness (eg of mind, appetite), keenness.—*vt* to put an edge on; to border; to move by little and little; to insinuate.—*vi* to move sideways.—*adjs* **edged; edge´less**.—*advs* **edge´ways, edge´wise**, in the direction of the edge; sideways.—*adj* **edg´y**, with edges, sharp, hard in outline; irritable.—*ns* **edg´iness**, angularity; irritability; **edg´ing**, any border or fringe round a garment, etc.; a border of box, etc. round a flowerbed.—**on edge**, nervous, anxious. [OE *ecg*; cf Ger *ecke*, L *acies*.]

edible [ed´i-bl] *adj* fit or safe to eat.—*n* something for food.—*ns* **edibil´ity, ed´ibleness**. [L *edibilis*—*edĕre*, to eat.]

edict [ē´dikt] *n* a decree. [L *ēdictum*—*ē*, out of, *dīcĕre*, *dictum*, to say.]

edifice [ed´i-fis] *n* a large building or house. [Fr *édifice*—L *aedificium*—*aedificāre; see* **edify**.]

edify [ed´i-fī] *vt* to build up the faith of; to comfort; to improve the mind of;—*pr p* **ed´ifying**; *pt p* **ed´ified**.—*n* **edificā´-tion**, instruction; progress in knowledge or in goodness.—*adjs* **ed´ificātory; ed´ifying**, instructive; improving. [Fr *édifier*—L *aedificāre*—*aedes*, a house, *facĕre*, to make.]

edit [ed´it] *vt* to prepare for publication, broadcasting, etc; to superintend the publication of; to make up the final version of a motion picture by selection, rearrangement, etc; of material photographed previously.—*ns* **edi´tion**, number of copies of a book, etc., printed at a time; form in which a book is issued (eg the annual edition of the yearbook, a limited edition); **ed´itor**, one who edits books, etc.; one who conducts a newspaper, periodical, etc.—*adj* **editō´rial**, of or belonging to an editor.—*n* an article in a newspaper or periodical expressing the opinions of the publishers or editors.—**ed´itorship; editor in chief**. [L *ēdĕre*, *ēditum*—*ē*, from, *dăre*, to give.]

educate [ed´ū-kāt] *vt* to provide schooling according to an accepted standard.—*adj* **ed´ucable.—educabil´ity; educā´tion**, the bringing up or training, as of a child; the development (of one or all of a person's powers of body and mind); instruction as given in schools or universities; a course or type of instruction (eg *a college, a classical education*); the principles and practice of teaching.—*adj* **educā´tional**.—*adv* **educā´tionally**.—*n* **educā´tionist**, an educational theorist; **ed´ucator**, a teacher or school administrator.—*adj* **ed´ucative**, tending to teach.—**educational television**, public television; television that provides instruction, esp for students and sometimes by closed circuit. [L *ēducāre*, *-ātum*, to rear.]

educe [e-dūs´] *vt* to draw out; to infer.—*adj* **educ´ible**. [L *ēdūcĕre*—*ē*, from, and *dūcĕre*, to lead.]

Edwardian [ed-wörd´i-ȧn] *adj* of the time of Edward VII of England (1901–10), characterized by opulence and material security; (of clothing) the hourglass silhouette for women and narrow fitted suits for men.

EEC Abbrev for **European Economic Community**.

EEG Abbrev for **electroencephalogram**.

eel [ēl] *n* a snakelike fish (*Anguilla rostrata*) with a smooth slimy skin. [OE *ǣl*; Ger, Du *aal*]

e'en [ēn] (*poetic*) a contraction of **even**.

e'er [ār] (*poetic*) a contraction of **ever**.

eerie [ē´ri] *adj* exciting fear, weird; affected with fear, timorous.—*adv* **ee´rily**.—*n* **ee´riness**. [ME *arh, eri*—OE *ærg* (*earg*), timid.]

efface [e-fās´] *vt* to destroy the surface of a thing; to rub out; (*fig*) to obliterate, wear away; to eclipse; to treat (oneself) as insignificant, to shun notice.—adj **efface´able**, that can be rubbed out.—*n* **efface´ment**. [Fr *effacer*—L *ex*, out, *faciēs*, face.]

effect [e-fekt´] *n* the result, consequence, outcome; impression produced; purport (*what he said was to this effect*); reality (*in effect*); efficacy; (*pl*) goods, property; (*pl*) in the theatre, cinema, sound and lighting devices contributing to the illusion of the place and circumstances in which the action is carried on.—*vt* to produce; to accomplish.—*n.* **effec´tor**, a bodily organ (as a gland or muscle) that becomes active in response to stimulation; a substance that induces protein synthesis in the body.—*adjs* **effec´tive**, having power to produce a specified effect; powerful; serviceable (eg fighting force); not merely nominal; striking (eg illustration, speech).—*n* one capable of service.—*adv* **effec´tively**.—*n* **effec´tiveness**.—*adjs* **effec´tual**, successful in producing the desired effect (eg of measures).—*n* **effectual´ity**.—*adv* **effec´tually.—in effect**, in truth, really; substantially; **take effect**, to come into force; **to the effect**, with the meaning. [OFr—L *effectus*—*ex*, out, *facĕre*, to make.]

effeminate [e-fem´in-ȧt] *adj* womanish; unmanly; weak, soft; voluptuous.—*n* an effeminate person.—*n* **effem´inacy**. [L *effēmināre*, *-atum*, to make womanish—*ex*, out, and *fēmina*, a woman.]

effendi [e-fen´di] *n* a man of property, authority, or education in an eastern Mediterranean country. [Turk; from Gr *authentēs*, an absolute master.]

efferent [ef´ė-rėnt] *adj* conveying outward or away, as **efferent nerve**, one carrying impulses away from the central nervous system. [L *ē*, from, *ferens*, *-entis*, pr p of *ferre*, to carry.]

effervesce [ef-ėr-ves´] *vi* to emit bubbles of gas; to be exhilarated.—*n* **efferves´cence**.—*adj* **efferves´cent**. [L *effervescĕre*—*ex*, inten, and *fervēre*, to boil.]

effete [e-fēt´] *adj* decadent; effeminate. [L *effētus*, weakened by having brought forth young—*ex*, out, *fētus*, a bringing forth, young.]

efficacious [ef-i-kā´shus] *adj* producing the result intended (of an impersonal agent, e.g. a medicine).—*adv* **efficā´ciously**.—*n* **eff´icacy**. [L *efficax, -ācis*—*efficĕre*; see **efficient**.]

efficient [e-fish´ėnt] *adj* capable of doing what may be required (of a person or other agent or of an action).—*n* **efficiency** [e-fish´n-si], power to produce the result intended; the ratio of the energy output of a machine, etc., to the energy input; capability, competence.—*adv* **effi´ciently**. [Fr,—L *efficiens, -entis*, pr p of *efficĕre*—*ex*, out, *facĕre*, to make.]

effigy [ef´i-ji] *n* a crude figure of a hated person; the head on a coin. [Fr,—L *effigiēs*—*effingĕre*—*ex*, inten, *fingĕre*, to form.]

effloresce [ef-lo-res´] *vi* to blossom forth; (*chem*) to change to a powder as the result of the loss of water.—*n* **efflores´cense**.—*adj* **efflores´cent**. [L *efflōrescĕre*—*ex*, out, *flōrescĕre*, to blossom—*flōs, flōris*, a flower.]

effluent [eflŏŏ-ėnt] *adj* flowing out.—*n* a stream that flows out of another stream or a lake; that which flows out (eg smoke, liquid industrial waste, sewage).—**eff´luence**, a flowing out. [L *effluens, -entis*, pr p of *effluĕre*—*ex*, out, *fluĕre*, to flow.]

effluvium [e-flōō´vi-um] *n* disagreeable vapors, esp rising from decaying matter;—*pl* **efflu´via**.—*adj* **efflu´vial**. [Low L,—L *effluĕre*.]

effort [ef´ŏrt] *n* exertion; attempt; struggle.—*adj* **eff´ortless**, without effort, or apparently so. [Fr,—L *ex*, out, *fortis*, strong.]

effrontery [e-frunt´ėr-i] *n* impudence; insolence. [Fr *effronterie*—L *effrōns, effrontis*—*ex*, out, *frons, frontis*, the forehead.]

effulgence [e-fulj´ėns] *n* radiant splendor; brilliance.—*adj* **effulg´ent** shining forth; extremely bright; splendid. [L *effulgēre*, to shine out, pr p *effulgens, -entis*—*ex*, out, *fulgēre*, to shine.]

effuse [e-fūz´] *vt* to pour out; to pour forth (as words).—*n* **effū´sion**, act of pouring out; that which is poured out or forth; a wordy expression of feeling in speech or writing.—*adj* **effū´sive**, gushing, expressing one's emotions freely.—*adv* **effūsively**.—*n* **effū´siveness**. [L *effundĕre, effūsum*—*ex*, out, *fundĕre*, to pour.]

eft [eft] *n* a newt. [OE *efeta*. Origin obscure. See **newt**.]

egalitarian [ē-gal-i-tā´ri-ȧn] *adj, n* equalitarian.—*n* **egalitā´rianism**. [OFr *egal*—L *aequālis*—*aequus*, equal.]

egg[1] [eg] *n* a round or oval body laid by birds, reptiles, and fishes from which the young is hatched; an ovum: anything resembling an egg; a fellow, a guy.—*ns* **egg beater**, hand operated utensil for stirring or mixing eggs; helicopter; **egg cell**, ovum; **egg cup**, cup composed of two small bowls joined at the bottoms, one for holding upright a soft-boiled egg, the other larger bowl for holding a soft-boiled egg emptied into it; **egg foo yong**, Chinese type of omelet filled with chicken, shellfish, or meat, and vegetable mixture; **egghead**, an intellectual; **eggnog**, a drink made of eggs, milk, sugar, spices, brandy or rum, etc.; **eggplant**, a widely-cultivated perennial herb (*Solanum melongena*) of the nightshade family; the smooth dark purple egg-shaped fruit of this plant; **egg roll**, Chinese dish made of a thin egg-dough casing filled with chopped meat or shellfish and vegetables and deep-fried; **egg´shell**, the hard outer covering of an egg.—*Also adj* thin and fragile; slightly glossy; **egg timer**, a small sandglass running about three minutes for timing the boiling of eggs; **egg tooth**, a hard sharp prominence on the beak of an unhatched bird or the nose of an unhatched reptile that is used to break through the shell. [ON *egg*; cf OE *æg*, Ger *ei*, perh L *ōvum*, Gr *ōon*.]

egg[2] [eg] *vt* (*followed by* **on**) to incite (a person to do something). [ON *eggja*—*egg*, an edge; cog with OE *ecg*, edge.]

egis [ē´jis] *see* **aegis**.

eglantine [eg´lan-tīn] *n* the sweetbrier. [Fr,—OFr *aiglent*, as if from a L *aculentus*, prickly—*acus*, a needle, and suffx *-lentus*.]

ego [e´gō, ē´gō] *n* the 'I', or self—that which is conscious and thinks.—*adj* **egocen´tric**, self-centered.—*ns* **e´gōism**, (*phil*) the doctrine that we have proof of nothing but our own existence; the theory that self-interest is the basis of morality; egotism; **e´gōist**, one who holds the doctrine of egoism; one who thinks and speaks too much of himself.—*adjs* **egōist´ic, -al**.—*n* **e´gotism**, a frequent use of the pronoun I, speaking much of oneself, self-exaltation.—*n* **e´gotist**.—*adjs.* **egotist´ic, -al**. [L *ego*, I.]

egrēgious [e-grē´jyus] *adj* glaringly bad; outrageous; notorious.—*adv* **egrē´giously**.—*n* **egrē"giousness**. [L *ēgregius*, chosen out of the flock—*ē*, out of, *grex, gregis*, a flock.]

egress [ē´gres] *n* act of going out; the power or right to depart; the way out.—*n* **egress´ion** [-gresh´(ȯ)n]. [L *ēgredī, ēgressus*—*ē*, out of, *gradī*, to go.]

egret [ē´gret] any of various herons bearing long plumes during the breeding season.

Egyptian [ē-jip´sh(ȧ)n] *adj* of, relating, to a native or inhabitant of Egypt.—*n* the Hamitic language used from earliest times to about the 3d century AD; a type-face having little contrast between thick and thin strokes and slab serifs; **Egyptology**, the study of Egyptian antiquities; **Egyptologist; Egyptian cotton**, a fine long-staple cotton grown chiefly in Egypt.

eh [eh] *interjection* an explanation expressing doubt, surprise, or failure to hear exactly; exclamation suggesting yes for an answer,

eider [īdėr] *n* the *eider-duck*, any of several northern sea ducks (*Somateria* or related genera).—*n* **ei´derdown**, the soft down of the eider; a comforter stuffed with eiderdown. [Prob from ON *æthr*, an eider-duck.]

eidetic [ī-det´ik] *adj* marked by or having exceptionally accurate and vivid recall, esp of visual images. [Gr *eidētikos*, of a form.]

eight [āt] *adj n* one more than seven; the symbol for this (8, VIII, viii); the eighth in a series or set; something having eight units as members. Also *n*—*adj* **eightfold**, having eight units as members; being eight times as great or as many.—*n* **eighth**, (*mus*) an octave; the last of eight.—Also *adj, adv*.—*ns* **eight ball**, a black pool ball numbered eight; a person who is a misfit; **eighth note**, (*mus*) a note with the time value of 1/8 of a whole note; **eighth rest**, (*mus*) a rest corresponding to an eighth note. [OE *eahta, ahta*; Ger *acht*, L *octō*, Gt *oktō*.]

eighteen [āt-ēn] *adj* one more than seventeen; the symbol for this (18, XVIII, xviii). Also *n*—*adj* **eighteenth**, the last of eighteen.—Also *n*. [OE *eahtatēne*.]

eighty [ā´te] *adj, n* eight times ten; symbol for this (80, LXXX, lxxx).—*pl* **eighties** (80s); the numbers from 80 to 89; the same numbers in a life or a century.—*adj* **eightieth**, the last of eighty. Also *n*. [OE *eahtatig*—*eahta*, eight, *tig*, ten (related to *tien, tēn*).]

einsteinium [īn-stīn´i-ùm] *n* a transuranic element (Symbol E, at wt 254, at no 99). [named after Albert *Einstein* (1879–1955).]

eisteddfod [ī-steTH´vod] *n* a Welsh competitive festival of the arts, esp singing. [W *eistedd*, to sit.]

either [ī´THėr, or ē´THėr] *adj, pron* the one or the other; one of two; each of two.—*conj* correlative to *or*. [OE *ǣgther*, a contr of *ǣghwæther=ā*, aye, the pfx *ge-*, and *hwæther*, mod Eng *whether*.]

ejaculate [e-jak´u-lāt] *vt* to eject a fluid (as semen); to exclaim. Also *vi*—*n* **ejaculā´tion**.—*adj* **ejac´ulatory**. [L *ē*, from, and *jaculāri, -ātus*—*jacĕre*, to throw.]

eject [e-jekt´] *vt* to cast out; to emit; to turn out, to expel.—*vi* to cause oneself to be ejected from an aircraft or space-craft.—*ns pl* **eject´a**, matter thrown out, esp by volcanoes.—*n* **ejec´tion**, act of ejecting; that which is ejected.—*adj* **ejec´tive**.—*ns* **eject´ment**, expulsion; (*law*) an action for recovery of the possession of land, etc.; **eject´or**, one who ejects; any mechanical apparatus for ejecting.—*n* **eject´ion seat**, seat that can be shot clear with its occupant in an emergency. [L *ējectāre*, freq of *ējicĕre, ējectum*—*ē*, from, *jacĕre*, to throw.]

eke[1] [ēk] *vt* to add to, to lengthen.—**eke out**, to supplement (with); to use sparingly so as to make suffice; to manage to make (a scanty living), or to support (existence). [OE ēcan—L *augēre*, to increase.]

eke[2] [ēk] *adv* in addition to; likewise. [OE *ēac*; Ger *auch*; perh from root of **eke**[1].]

ekistics [e-kist´iks] *n* the study of human settlements, drawing on the knowledge and experience of architects, city planners, engineers, and sociologists. [NGr *oikistikē*, relating to settlement.]

elaborate [e-lab´ȯr-āt] *vt* to work out in detail; to improve by successive operations; to fashion, develop (usu. a natural product) from elements.—Also *vi* (*often with* **on, upon**).—*adj* [-ȧt] worked out with fullness and exactness; highly detailed.—*adv* **elab´orately**.—*ns* **elab´orateness; elaborā´tion**, act of elaborating; refinement; the process by which substances are built up in the bodies of animals or plants.—*adj* **elab´orative**.—*n* **elab´orator**. [L *ēlabōrāre, -ātum*—*ē*, from, *labōrāre*—*labor*, labor.]

élan [ā-lā´] *n* verve, spirit characterized by poise. [Fr]

eland [ē´land] *n* either of two large African antelopes (*Taurotragus oryx* and *T derbianus*) with short spirally-twisted horns. [Du—Ger *elend*, elk.]

elapse [e-laps´] *vi* to slip or glide away; to pass silently, as time.—*n* passing. [L *ē* from, *lābī, lapsus*, to slide.]

elastic [e-las´tik] *adj* having the ability to recover the original form, when forces that changed that form are removed; springy; able to recover quickly a former state or condition after a shock.—*n* fabric, tape, etc., woven partly of elastic thread.—*adv* **elas´tically**.—*adj* **elast´icized**, made with elastic threads or inserts.—**elasticity**, [tis´-], tendency of a body to return to its original size or shape, after having been stretched, compressed, or deformed; springiness; power to recover from depression; **elas´tin**, a protein, chief constituent of elastic tissue.—**elastic clause**, a clause in the US Constitution that provides the constitutional basis of the implied or potential powers of Congress; **elastic collision**, a collision in which the total kinetic energy of the colliding particles remains unchanged; **elastic scattering**, a scattering of particles as a result of elastic collision. [Late Gr *elastikos*—*elaunein*, to drive.]

elate [e-lāt´] *vt* to make exultant or proud.—*adv* **elat´edly**.—*n* **ela´tion**, pride resulting from success; elevation of spirits. [L *ēlātus*, used as pt p of *efferre*—*ē* from, *lātus*, carried.]

elbow [el´bō] *n* the joint of the arm; any sharp turn or bend.—*vt* to push with the elbow; to jostle.—*ns* **el´bow grease**, hard work; **el´bow room**, room to extend the elbows; space enough for moving or acting; free scope.—**at one's elbow**, close at hand; **out at elbows**, shabbily dressed; short of funds. [OE *elnboga*. See **ell; bow**, *n vt*.]

elder[1] [eld´ėr] *n* any of a genus (*Sambucus*) of trees or shrubs of the honeysuckle family with flat clusters of white or pink flowers.—**el´derberry**, the edible black or red berry borne by the elder. [OE *ellærn*.]

elder[2] [eld´ėr] *adj* older.—*n* one who is older; an ancestor; one of a class of office-bearers in Presbyterian churches; a Mormon ordained to the Melchizadek priesthood.—*adj* **eld´erly**, somewhat old; bordering on old age.—*n* **eld´ership**, the office of an elder.—*adj*. **eld´est**, oldest. [OE *eldra*, comp, of *eald*, old.]

El Dorado [el dō-rä´dō] the golden land of imagination of the Spanish conquerors of America; any place where wealth is easily to be made. [Sp *el*, the, *dorado*, gilded.]

elect [e-lekt´] *vt* to choose by voting; to make a selection of (subjects in a course); to decide on (a course of action).—*vi* to make a selection.—*adj* chosen; chosen for an office but not yet in it (as *the president-elect*); chosen by God for salvation.—*n* the chosen of God; any group of persons set apart by excellence.—*pl* **elect**.—*n* **elec´tion**, the act of electing; the public choice of a person for office; predestination to eternal life.—*vi* **electioneer´**, to work to secure the election of a candidate.—*adj* **elec´tive**, pertaining to, dependent on, or exerting the power of, choice.—*n* an elective course or subject.—*n* **elect´or**, one who has a vote at an election; a member of the US electoral college.—*adj* **elect´oral**, pertaining to elections or to electors.—*n* **elect´orate**, the body of electors.—**Election Day**, a day legally established for the election of public officials, esp the first Tuesday after the first Monday in November in an even year; **electoral college**, a body of electors who elect the president and vice-president of the US. [L *ēligĕre, ēlectum*—*ē*, from, *legĕre*, to choose.]

electrical, -al [e-lek´trik -ȧl] *adj* of electricity; charged with electricity; producing electricity; run by electricity; exciting, thrilling.—*adv* **elec´trically**.—*ns* **electrician** [e-lek-trish´ȧn], person whose work is installing or repairing electric wires, motors, lights etc.; **electricity** [tris´-], a form of energy that can produce light, heat, magnetism, and chemical changes; an electric current; a feeling of excitement.—*vt* **elec´trify**, to charge with electricity, to equip for the use of electric power; to excite suddenly; to astonish;—*pt p* **elec´trified**.—*n* **electrificātion**.—**electric chair**, a chair used in electrocuting condemned criminals; **electric eye**, a photo-electric cell; **electric guitar**, guitar with a solid body which must be electrically amplified; **electric motor**, any device for converting electrical energy into mechanical energy; **electric organ**, a specialized tract of tissue (as in the electric ray and the electric eel) in which electricity is generated. [L *ēlectrum—Gr ēlektron*, amber, in which electricity was first observed.]

electro- [e-lek´trō-] of, associated with, accomplished by, electricity.—**elec´trocar´diogram**, the tracing made by an electrocardiograph; **elec´trocar´diograph**, an instrument for recording the changes of electrical potential occurring during the heartbeat; **electrochemistry**, the branch of chemistry that deals with chemical changes produced by electricity and the production of electricity by chemical changes.—*vt* **elec´trocute**, to kill by electricity.—*ns* **electrocū´tion; elec´troenceph´alogram** [-sef´], the tracing made by an electro encephalograph. **elec´troenceph´alograph**, an instrument for detecting and recording the electrical activity of the brain.—*vt* **elec´trolyze**, [-īz], to subject to electrolysis.—*ns* **electrol´ysis** [-isis], the decomposition of a chemical compound by electricity; the destruction of hair roots with an electric current.—**elec´trolyte** [-līt], a solution that will conduct a current.—*adj* **electrolytic** [-lit´ik], pertaining to, associated with or made by electrolysis.—*n* **electrolytic cell**, a vessel in which electrolysis is carried out.—*ns* **elec´tromagnet**, a piece of iron rendered magnetic by a current of electricity passing through a coil of wire wound round it; **elec´tromag´netism**, a branch of science which treats of the relation of electricity to magnetism: magnetism developed by a current of electricity.—*adj* **elec´tromagneti´c**, pertaining to, or produced by, electromagnetism.—**electromagnetic waves**, waves propagated in space by variations of electric and magnetic field intensity, of which light, radio, X-rays, gamma rays are examples.—*ns* **electrom´eter**, an instrument for measuring difference of electric potential; **electromo´tive force** (*abbrev* **EMF**), the force which tends to cause a movement of electricity round an electric circuit; **electromo´tor**, an apparatus for applying electricity as a motive-power.—*vt* **elec´troplate**, to plate or cover with metal by electrolysis.—*n* articles covered with silver in this way.—*ns* **elec´troplating; elec´trotype**, a printing plate made by electrolytically coating a mould with copper.

electrode [el-ek´trōd] *n* a conductor through which a current of electricity enters or leaves an electrolytic cell, gas discharge tube, or thermionic valve. [**electro-**, and Gr *hodos*, way.]

electron [el-ek´tron] *n* a negatively charged elementary particle that forms the part of the atom outside the nucleus.—*adj* **electronic**.—*n* **electronics**, the physics of electrons and their use.—*ns* **electron microscope**, an instrument in which a focused beam of electrons produces an enlarged image of a minute object on a fluorescent screen or photographic plate; **electron pair**, two electrons of opposite spin in the same orbital; **electronic music**, music made by recording musical ideas generated by electronic and conventional instruments on tape and then reproduced by electroacoustical means, the performance being the playback; **electronic organ**, an organ in which electric signals created by electronic oscillators are amplified and converted into sound by a loudspeaker; **electron shell**, one of several groups of electrons arranged concentrically round the nucleus of an atom; **electron tube**, an electronic device in which the electron conduction is in a vacuum or gas inside a gas-tight enclosure—including thermionic valve; **electronvolt**, unit of energy associated with an electron which has freely changed its potential by one volt (*abbrev* **´eV**). [Gr]

electrum [e-lek´trum] *n* a natural pale yellow alloy of gold and silver.

electuary [e-lek´tū-ȧr-i] *n* a medicine mixed with honey, sugar, or syrup. [Low L *ēlectuārium*—perhaps Gr *ekleikton—ekleichein*, to lick up.]

eleemosynary [el-i-ē-moz´i-nar-i or -mos´-] *adj* of a nonprofit organization; given in charity. [Gr *eleēmosynē*, alms—*eleos*, pity.]

elegant [el´e-gȧnt] *adj* expensive and in good taste (eg of clothes); graceful (eg of manner); refined (eg of literary style).—*n* **el´e-gance**.—*adv* **el´egantly**. [Fr,—L *ēlegāns*, -antis—*ē*, from, and root of *legĕre*, to choose.]

elegy [el´e-ji] *n* a slow plaintive song; a poem praising and mourning a specific dead person.—*adj* **elegī´ac, -al** belonging to elegy.—*n* **-elegiac stanza**, a quatrain in iambic pentameter with a rhyme scheme of *abab* **el´egist**, a writer of elegies.—*vi* **el´egize**, to write an elegy. [Through Fr and L—Gr *elegos*, a lament.]

element [el´e-mėnt] *n* the natural environment (*she was in her element*); a constituent part; the simplest principles (as of an art or science), rudiments; the basic member of a mathematical set; a substance not separable by ordinary chemical means into substances different from itself; any of the four substances (earth, air, fire, water) in ancient and medieval thought believed to constitute the universe.—*pl* weather conditions, esp severe weather.—*adjs* **element´al**, pertaining to elements, or produced by elements; **element´ary**, primary; pertaining to the elements; treating of first principles.—*ns* **elementary particle**, (*physics*) one of several subatomic particles not known to be composed of simpler particles; **elementary school**, a school usu. consisting of the first six or first eight grades. [L *elementum*, pl *elementa*, first principles.]

elephant [el´e-fȧnt] *n* any of a family (*Elefantidae*) of huge heavy mammals with a long trunk, thick skin, and ivory tusks.—*n* **elephantī´asis**, a disease caused by threadworms in which the limbs or the scrotum become greatly enlarged.—*adj* **elephant´ine**, very large and clumsy.—*n* **elephant seal**, a nearly extinct large seal (*Mirounga angustirostrïs*) with a long inflatable proboscis inhabiting California coasts; a related seal (*M leonina*) of the southern hemisphere.—**white elephant** *see* **white**. [Fr—L *elephās, -antis*—Gr *elephas*; or possibly from OE *olfend*, camel.]

elevate [el´e-vāt] *vt* to lift up; to raise in rank, to improve in mind or morals; to elate. **elevā´tion**, a raised place; the height above the earth's surface or above sea level; the act of elevating or raising; the state of being raised; a drawing that shows how the front, rear, or side of something looks from the outside; exaltation.—**el´evator**, a cage or platform for moving something from one level to another; a building for storing grain; a movable surface on an airplane to produce motion up or down. [L *ēlevāre, -ȧtum—ė*, from, *levāre*, to raise—*levis*, light.]

eleven [e-lev´n] *adj, n* one more than ten.—*ns* the symbol for this (11, XI, xi); a team of eleven (football).—*adj* **elev´enth**, the last of eleven; being one of eleven equal parts.—Also *n*—**at the eleventh hour**, at the last moment. [OE *en(d)le(o)fan*; perh (ten and) *one* left.]

elevon [el´ė-vȯn] *n* a wing flap on delta-wing or tailless aircraft acting both as *elev*ator and as an ailer*on*.

elf [elf] *n* a mischievous fairy.—*pl* **elves**.—*adjs* **elf´in**, of, like, or relating to elves; **elf´ish, elv´ish**, elf-like; mischievous, tricky.—*adv* **elfishly**. [OE *ælf*; cf ON *ālfr*, Swed *elf*.]

elicit [e-lis´it] *vt* to draw forth, esp *fig* (eg a truth, information, an admission).—*n* **elicitā´tion**. [L *ēlicĕre, ēlicitum*.]

elide [e-līd´] *vt* to omit or slur over in pronunciation, as a vowel or syllable.—*n* **elī´sion** the suppression of a vowel or syllable; an omission. [L. *ēlīdĕre, ēlīsum—ē*, from, *laedĕre*, to strike.]

eligible [el´i-ji-bl] *adj* fit or worthy to be chosen; legally qualified; desirable.—**el´igibleness, eligibil´ity**. [Fr,—L *ēligĕre. See* **elect**.]

eliminate [e-lim´in-āt] *vt* to thrust out, expel; to remove, to exclude (eg errors); to ignore, leave out of consideration; to get rid of (eg an unknown from an equation).—*adj* **elim´inative**.—*n* **eliminā´tion**. [L *ēlimināre, -ātum—ē*, from, *līmen, -inis*, a threshold.]

elision *see* **elide**.

elite [ā-lēt´] *n* the choice part; a superior group; a typewriter type providing 12 characters to the inch.—*n* **elit´ism**, leadership or rule by an elite; advocacy of such rule. [Fr *élite*—L *electa* (*pars*), a chosen (part).]

elixir [e-liks´ėr] n a substance supposed to have the power of indefinitely prolonging life; a panacea; a sweetened alcoholic medicine. [Low L,—Ar *al-iksīr* the philosopher's stone.]

Elizabethan [e-liz-a-bēth´an] *adj* of Queen Elizabeth of England or her time (reigned 1558–1603)—also of Elizabeth II; used of dress, manners, literature, etc.—*n* a poet, dramatist, or other person of that age.

elk [elk] *n* the largest existing deer (*Alces alces*) of Europe and Asia resembling but not so large as the moose; the wapiti; soft tan rugged leather.—*n* **Elk**, a member of the Benevolent and Protective Order of Elks, a major benevolent and fraternal order. [ON *elgr*, Swed *elg*, L *alcēs*, Gr *alkē*.]

ell[1] [el] *n* an old measure of length. [OE *eln*; Du *el*, Ger *elle*. L *ulna* Gr *ōlenē*, elbow.]

ell[2] [el] *n* an extension at right angles to a building.

ellipse [el-ips´] *n* (geom) an oval; having both ends alike.—*n* **ellip´sis**, the omission of a word or words needed to complete the grammatical construction of a sentence; the marks (. . .) used to show an omission in writing or printing.—*pl* **ellip´sēs**.—*n* **ellip´soid** (*math*), a surface of which every plane section is an ellipse or a circle.—*adjs* **ellipsoi´dal; ellip´tic,**

-al pertaining to an ellipse or ellipsis; oval; of extreme economy of speech or writing.—*adv* **ellip´tically**. [L,—Gr *elleipsis—el-leipein*, to fall short—*en*, in, *leipein*, to leave.]

elm [elm] *n* a genus (*Ulmus*) of the elm family; a tall deciduous shade tree with spreading branches and broad top; its hard heavy wood. [OE *elm*; Ger *ulme*, L *ulmus*.]

elocution [el-o-kū´sh(o)n] *n* the art of public speaking.—*adj* **elocū´tionary**.—*n* **elocu´-tionist**. [Fr,—L *ēlocūtiō, -ōnis—ēloquī, ēlocutus—ē*, from, *loquī*, to speak.]

Elohim [e-lo-him´] *n* a Hebrew name for God. [Heb *pl* of *Eleoh*, a plural of intensity.]

elongate [ē´long-gāt] *vt* to make longer, to extend.—*adj* **e´longāted**, long and usu. narrow.—*n* **elongā´tion**, act of lengthening out; the part thus added to the length; the angular distance of a planet from the sun. [Low L *ēlongāre, -ātum—ē*, from, *longus*, long.]

elope [e-lōp´] *vi* to run away esp with a lover; **elope´ment; elop´er**. [Cf Old Du *ontlōpen*, Ger *entlaufen*, to run away.]

eloquence [el´o-kwėns] *n* flow of speech that has grace and force; the power to persuade by speaking.—*adj* **el´oquent**, having eloquence; persuasive.—*adv* **el´oquently**. [L *ēloquens, -entis*, pr p of *ēloquī*.]

else [els] *adv* otherwise; besides, except that mentioned.—*adv* **else´where** in or to another place. [OE *elles*, otherwise—orig gen of *el*, other; cf OHG *alles* or *elles*.]

elucidate [e-l(y)ōō´si-dāt] *vt* to make clear; to explain.—*n* **elucidā´tion**—*adjs* **elu´cidative, elu´cidatory**.—*n* **elu´cidator**. [Low L *ēlūcidāre, -ātum—ē*, inten, *lūcidus*, clear.]

elude [e-l(y)ōōd´] *vt* to slip away from; to baffle (eg the memory, understanding).—*adj* **elu´sive**.—*adv* **elu´sively**.—*n* **elu´siveness**. [L *ēlūdere, ēlūsum—ē* from, *lūdere*, to play.]

elves, elvish *see* **elf**.

elver [el´vėr] *n* a young eel. [Variant of *eelfare*, the passage of young eels up a river (OE *fær*, a journey), hence a brood of eels.]

Elysium [e-liz(h)´i-um] *n* the abode of the blessed after death; any delightful place.—*n* **elys´ian fields** Elysium; exceedingly delightful. [L,—Gr *ēlysion (pedion)*, the Elysian (plain).]

em [em] *n* (*printing*) the unit for measuring the area of composition; the square of the body of any type.—*Also* **em quad**.

em- [em-] *pfx See* **en-**.

emaciate [e-mā´sh-āt, ´si-āt] *vt* to make unnaturally thin.—*vi* to become lean, to waste away.—*adjs* **emā´ciate** (*-ȧt*), **-d.**—*n* **emaci-ā´tion**. [L *ēmaciāre, -ātum—maciēs*, leanness.]

email, e-mail [ē´māl] *n* (*comput*) electronic mail; mail sent via the Internet.

emanate [em´a-nāt] *vi* to come forth from a source.—*n* **emanā´tion**, that which issues or proceeds (from some source); something that emanates or is produced by emanation; a heavy gaseous element produced by radioactive disintegration. [L *ē*, out from, *mānāre*, to flow.]

emancipate [e-man´si-pāt] *vt* to set free, esp from bondage or slavery.—*ns* **emancipā´tion; emancipā´tionist**, an advocate of the emancipation of slaves; **eman´cipātor.—Emancipation Proclamation**, the proclamation issued by President Abraham Lincoln giving freedom to slaves in states still in conflict with the Union, effective January 1, 1863. [L *ē*, away from, *mancipāre, -ātum*, to transfer property—*manus*, the hand, *capere*, to take.]

emasculate [e-mas´kū-lāt] *vt* to castrate; to deprive of strength.—*adj* [-lat], deprived of vigor or strength; **emasculā´tion**.—*adj* **emas´culātor**. [Low L *ēmasculāre, -ātum—ē*, from, *masculus*, dim, of *mas*, a male.]

embalm [em-bäm´] *vt* to preserve (a dead body) with drugs, chemicals, etc.; to perfume; to preserve with care and affection.—*ns* **embalm´er; embalm´ing; embalm´ment**. [Fr *embaumer*, from *em-*, in, and *baume; see* **balm**.]

embank [em-bangk´] *vt* to enclose or confine with a bank or dike.—*n* **embank´ment**, the act of embanking; a bank, mound, or ridge, made to hold back water or to carry a roadway. [Pfx *em-*, in, + **bank**.]

embargo [em-bär´gō] *n* an order of a government forbidding ships to enter or leave its ports; any restriction put on commerce by law; a prohibition, ban;—*pl* **embar´goes**.—*vt* to place an embargo on;—*pr p* **embar´gōing**; *pt p* **embar´gōed**. [Sp,—*embargar*, to impede, to restrain—Sp pfx *em-*, in, Low L (and Sp) *barra*, a bar.]

embark [em-bärk´] *vt* to put on board a ship or airplane.—*vi* to board a boat or airplane for transportation; to make a start in an activity or enterprise.—*n* **embarkā´tion**. [Fr *embarquer*, from *em-*, in, *barque*, ship.]

embarrass [em-bar´as] *vt* to impede; to involve in difficulty, esp in money matters; to perplex; to put out of countenance, disconcert.—*a adj* **embarr´assed**.—*n* **embarr´assment**, perplexity; money difficulties; a perplexing amount (as of choice, riches). [Fr *embarrasser—em-*, in *barre*, bar.]

embassy [em´bas-i] *n* a person or group officially sent as ambassadors; an ambassador's official residence. [OFr *ambassée*; from same root as **ambassador**.]

embattle [em-bat´l] *vt* to arrange in order of battle; prepare for battle.—*adj* **embatt´led**.—*n* **embatt´lement**, battlement. [*em-* + OFr *bataillier*, to embattle. See **battlement**.]

embay [em-bā´] *vt* to lay or force (a ship) within a bay.—*n* **embay´ment**, a bay. [*em-*, in, + **bay**.]

embed [em-bed´] *vt* to fix in a mass of matter; to lay, as in a bed.—Also **imbed**. [Pfx *em-* + **bed**.]

embellish [em-bel´ish] *vt* to decorate, to adorn.—**embell´isher; embell´ishment**. [Fr *embellir, embellissant—em-*, in, *bel* (*beau*), beautiful.]

ember [em´bėr] *n* a piece of live coal or wood; (*pl*) smouldering remains of a fire (*lit* and *fig*). [OE *ǣmerge*; ON *eimyrja*.]

emberday [em´bėr-dā] *n* any of appointed days of fasting and prayer in each of four seasons in certain Western churches. [OE *ymbryne*, a circuit—*ymb*, round, and *ryne*, a running, from *rinnan*, to run.]

embezzle [em-bez´l] *vt* to steal (money, securities, etc. entrusted to one's care).—*ns* **embezz´lement**, fraudulent appropriation of property entrusted; **embezz´ler**. [Anglo-Fr *enbesiler*, to make away with.]

embitter [em-bit´ėr] *vt* to make bitter; to arouse bitter feelings in.—*adj* **embitt´ered**, soured.—Also **imbitter**. [*em-* + **bitter**.]

emblazon [em-blā´zȯn] *vt* to adorn with heraldic devices, etc.; to make bright with color; to celebrate, extol.—*ns* **emblā´zoner; emblā´zonment; emblā´zonry**, the art of emblazoning or adorning; devices on shields. [*em-* + **blazon**.]

emblem [em´blem] *n* an object or a picture suggesting another object or an idea; a symbol; a figure adopted and used as an identifying mark; a heraldic device, a badge.—*adjs* **emblemat´ic, -al**, pertaining to or containing emblems; symbolical.—*adv* **emblemat´ically**. [Through L—Gr *emblēma*—Gr *en*, in, *ballein*, to throw.]

embody [em-bod´i] *vt* to put (as a spirit) into visible form; to express in definite form; to bring together and include in a single book, law, system, etc.—*adj* **embod´ied**.—*n* **embod´iment**, act of embodying; state of being embodied; the representation (of a quality) in living form. [*em-*, in, + **body**.]

embolden [em-bōld´n] *vt* to inspire with courage. [*em-*, **bold**, + suffx *-en*.]

embolism [em´bo-lizm] *n* the obstruction of a blood vessel by a foreign or abnormal particle (as an air bubble or blood clot) during life.—*adj* **embolic**.—*ns* **embolus**, an abnormal particle circulating in the blood; **embolization**, the process or state in which a blood vessel or organ is obstructed by the lodgment of a mass. [Late Gr *embolismos—emballein*, to throw in.]

embonpoint [ã-b•-pwɛ̃] *n* plumpness of person; stoutness. [Fr,—*en bon point*, in good form.]

embosom [em-bŏŏz´ȯm] *vt* to shelter closely.—Also **imbosom**. [*em-* + **bosom**.]

emboss [em-bos´] *vt* to raise bosses on, to ornament with raised-work; to mould or carve in relief.—*adjs* **embossable; embossed´**.—*ns* **embosser; emboss´ment**, raised-work. [*em-* + **boss**.]

embouchure [ã-bōō-shür´] *n* the position of the lips on the mouthpiece of a wind instrument. [Fr,—*emboucher*, to put to the mouth—*en*, in, *bouche*, a mouth.]

embowel [em-bow´ėl] *vt* to disembowel.—*pr p* **embow´eling**; *pt p* **embow´eled**.—*n* **embow´elment**. [*em-*, in, + **bowel**.]

embower [em-bow´ėr] *vt* to place in a bower. [*em-* + **bower**.]

embrace [em-brās´] *vt* to take in the arms; to press to the bosom with affection; to take eagerly (eg an opportunity); to adopt or receive (eg Christianity); to comprise.—*vi* to join in an embrace.—Also *n*. [OFr *embracer* (Fr *embrasser*)—L *in*, in, into, *brā(c)chium*, an arm.]

embrasure [em-brā´zhůr] *n* a recess of a door or window; an opening in a wall for cannon. [Fr,—OFr *embraser*, to slope the sides of a window—*em-* (L *in*), *braser*, to skew.]

embrocate [em´brō-kāt] *vt* to moisten and rub, as with a lotion.—*n* **embrocā´tion**, act of embrocating; the lotion used. [Low L *embrocāre, -ātum*, from Gr *embrochē*, a lotion.]

embroider [em-broid´ėr] *vt* to ornament with stitches; to elaborate in florid detail.—*ns* **embroid´erer; embroid´ery**, the art of producing ornamental designs in needlework on textile fabrics, etc.; ornamental needlework; embellishment; exaggerated or invented detail. [ME *embrouderie*—OFr *embroder*.]

embroil [em-broil´] *vt* to involve (a person) in a quarrel; to bring (persons) into a state of discord; to throw into confusion.—*n* **embroil´ment**. [Fr *embrouiller*—pfx *em-*, and *brouiller*; see **broil** (1).]

embryo [em´bri-ō] *n* an animal during the period of its growth from the fertilized egg to the eighth week of life; (*bot*) a rudimentary plant contained in the seed; a thing in a rudimentary state.—*pl* **em´bryos**.—*ns* **embryol´ogy**, the study of the embryo; **embryol´ogist**.—*adj* **embryon´ic**, immature, undeveloped. [Low L,—Gr *embryon—en*, in, *bryein*, to swell.]

emcee [em´sē] *n* master of ceremonies.—Also **MC**.

emend [ē-mend´, e-mend´] *vt* to correct errors in a text.—Also **em´endate**.—*ns* **emendā´tion**, the act of emending; an alteration designed to correct or improve; **e´mendātor**.—*adj* **emendable; emen´datory**. [L *ēmendāre, -ātum—ē*, from, *menda*, a fault.]

emerald [em´ėr-ȧld] *n* a rich green variety of beryl prized as a gemstone; any of various gemstones resembling this.—*ns* **emerald green**, brightly or richly green; **the Emerald Isle**, Ireland. [OFr *esmeralde*—L *smaragdus*—Gr *smaragdos*.]

emerge [e-mûrj´] *vi* to rise out of (orig a liquid—*with* **from**); to come forth, come into view; (*fig*) to come out as a result of enquiry; to crop up (eg a difficulty).—*ns* **emer´gence**, act of emerging or coming out (*lit* and *fig*); **emer´gency**, an unexpected occurrence or situation demanding immediate action; a substitute in reserve.—*adj* **emer´gent**, emerging; coming into being in the course of evolution; urgent.—*n* **emer´sion**, act of emerging. [L *ēmergĕre, ēmersum—ē*, out of, *mergĕre*, to plunge.]

emeritus [e-mer´i-tus] *adj* and *n* retired from active service, but still holding one's rank and title. [L *ēmeritus*, having served one's time.]

emery [em´ėr-i] *n* a hard granular mineral consisting of corundum and used for grinding and polishing; a hard abrasive powder.—*ns* **emery board**, a nail file made of cardboard and covered with crushed emery; **emery paper**, a stiff paper coated with finely powdered emery. [OFr *esmeril, emeril*—Low L *smericulum*—Gr *smēris, smȳris*.]

emetic [e-met´ik] *adj* causing vomiting.—*n* a medicine that causes vomiting.—*n* **emē´sis**, an act or instance of vomiting.—*pl* **emeses**. [Gr *emetikos—emeein*, to vomit.]

emigrate [em´i-grāt] to leave one's country in order to settle in another.—*adj* **em´igrant**, emigrating or having emigrated.—Also *n*—*ns* **emigrā´tion; émigré** [ā-mē-grā´], or **emigré** [ė-] an emigrant; a refugee, esp from the French or Russian revolution. [L *ēmigrāre, -ātum—ē*, from, *migrāre*, to remove.]

eminent [em´i-nėnt] *adj* rising above others; conspicuous; distinguished; exalted in rank or office.—*adv* **em´inently**, in a distinguished manner; in a conspicuous degree.—*ns* **em´inence, em´inency**, a rising ground, hill; (*lit* and *fig*) height; distinction; a title of honor.—**eminent domain**, the right of a government to take private property for public use.—*n* **eminence**, high rank or position; a person of high rank or attainments; a high place; **Eminence**, the title for a cardinal of the RC church; **eminence grise**, [ā-mē-nās grēz´] a confidential agent, esp one exercising unsuspected or unofficial power; *pl* **eminences grises**—*adj* **eminent**, rising above others; conspicuous. [L *ēminens, -entis*, pr p of *ēminēre—ē*, from, *minēre*, to project.]

emir [ām-ēr´, or ē´mir] *n* a native ruler in parts of Africa and Asia.—*n* **emir´ate**, the office, jurisdiction, or state of an emir.—Also **ameer**. [Ar *amīr*, ruler.]

emit [e-mit´] *vt* to give out (eg light, heat, sound, water); to put (as money) into circulation; to express, to utter.—*pr p* **emitt´ing**; *pt p* **emitt´ed**.—*ns* **em´issary**, one sent out on a secret mission (often used rather contemptuously); **emiss´ion**, the act of emitting; that which is issued at one time.—*adj* **emiss´ive**. [L *ēmittĕre, ēmissum—ē*, out of, *mittĕre*, to send.]

Emmenthal [em´en-tal], **Emmenthaler** [-er] *n* a hard cheese, pale yellow in color with large, shiny holes and a nutty sweet flavor.—Also **Swiss cheese**. [From *Emmenthal*, Switzerland.]

emmet [em´et] *n* (*dial*) the ant. [OE *ǣmete*.]

Emmy [em´ē] *n* a statuette awarded annually by a professional organization for notable achievement in television.—*pl* **Emmys**. [from alteration of *Immy*, nickname for image orthicon (a camera tube used in television).]

emollient [e-mol´yėnt] *adj* softening; making supple; soothing, esp to the skin or mucous membrane.—*n* something that softens and soothes. [L *ēmollīre, ēmollītum—ē-*, inten, *mollīre*, to soften—*mollis*, soft.]

emolument [e-mol´ū-mėnt] *n* the product (as salary or fees) of an employment. [L *ēmolimentum*—prob from *ēmŏlĕre*, to grind out.]

emoticon [e-mō´ti-kon] *n* an icon representing emotion made up of standard keyboard characters. A few examples are— :) smiling face; :-) smile; :-D big smile. Also known as **smilies**.

emotion [e-mō´sh(ȯ)n] *n* a strong feeling of any kind.—*vi* **emote´**, to show or express exaggerated emotion.—*adj* **emō´tional**, of the emotions; liable to emotion.—*adv* **emō´tionally**.—*adj* **emō´tive**, tending to arouse emotion. [L *ēmōtiō, -ōnis—ēmovēre, -mōtum*, to stir up—*ē*, and *movēre*, to move.]

emp- for words not found under this, *see* **imp-**.

empanel *see* **impanel**.

empathy [em´pa-thi] *n* capacity for participating in the feelings or ideas of another.—*vi* **em´pathize**. [Gr *en*, in, *pathos*, feeling.]

empennage [em-pen´aj] *n* the tail assembly of an airplane. [Fr *empannage*, feather of an arrow.]

emperor [em´pėr-ȯr] *n* the sovereign ruler of an empire.—*fem* **em´press**. [OFr *emperere*—L *imperātor* (fem *imperātrix*)—*imperāre*, to command.]

emphasis [em´fa-sis] *n* particular stress or prominence given (as to a phrase in speaking or to a phase of action).—*pl* **em´phases** [-sēz].—*vt* **em´phasize**, to lay stress on.—*adjs* **emphat´ic, -al**, expressed, or expressing, with emphasis; forcible (of an action).—*adv* **emphat´ically**. [Gr *emphasis*, image, significance—*en*, in, *phainein*, to show.]

emphysema [em-fiz-ēm´a] *n* a disorder marked by distension of the air sacs of the lungs. [NL from Gr *emphysema*, bodily inflation.]

empire [em´pīr] *n* a large state or group of states under a single sovereign, usu. an emperor; nations dominated by the same sovereign state; a country ruled by an emperor. [Fr—L *imperium*.]

empiric, empirical [em-pir´ik, -ȧl] *adj* resting on trial or experiment; known by experience only.—*n* **empir´ic**, one who makes trials or experiments; one whose knowledge is got from experience only.—*adv* **empir´ically**.—*ns* **empir´icism** (*phil*), the system which regards experience as the only source of knowledge; **empir´icist.—empirical formula** (*chem*), a formula expressing the simplest numerical relationship between the atoms of the elements present in a compound—eg the empirical formula of benzene is CH, though its molecular formula is C_6H_6. [Fr,—L *empīricus*—Gr *empeirikos—en*, in, *peira*, a trial.]

emplacement [em-plās´mėnt] *n* the act of placing; (*mil*) a gun platform. [Fr]

emplane [em-plān´] *see* **enplane**.

employ [em-ploi´] *vt* to give work and pay to; to make use of.—*n* **employment**.—*adj* **employ´able**.—*p adj* **employed´**, having employment.—*ns* **employ´ēē**, a person employed; **employ´er; employ´ment**, act of employing; state of being employed; occupation, esp regular trade, business, or profession. [Fr *employer*—L *implicāre*, to enfold.—*in*, in, *plicāre*, to fold.]

emporium [em-pō´ri-um, -pö´] *n* a large store carrying many different things.—*pl* **emporiums, empō´ria**. [L,—Gr *empŏrion—empŏros*, a trader, *en*, in, *poros*, a way.]

empower [em-pow´ėr] *vt* to authorize. [*em-* + **power**.]

emprise [em-prīz´] *n* an undertaking, esp an adventurous, daring or chivalric enterprise. [OFr *emprise*.]

empty [emp´ti] *adj* containing nothing; not occupied; null (*an empty set*); lacking reality, substance, or value; hungry; marked by the lack of human life, activity, or comfort.—*vt* to make empty; to transfer by emptying.—*vi* to become empty; to discharge its contents.—*pt p* **emp´tied**.—*n* an empty vessel, box, sack, etc.—*pl* **emp´ties**.—*n* **emp´tiness**, state of being empty.—*adjs* **empty-handed**, having or bringing nothing; having acquired or gained nothing; **empty-headed**, scatterbrained.—*ns* **empty calorie**, one that has no nutritive value; **empty nester**, (*inf*) middle-aged couple whose grown children have left the family home. [OE *æmetig—æmetta*, leisure, rest. The *p* is excrescent.]

empyema [em-pī-ē´ma] *n* the presence of pus in a bodily cavity.—*pl* **empye´mata, empye´mas**. [Gr—*en*, in, *pyon*, pus.]

empyreal [em-pir-ē´ȧl´, em-pir´i-ȧl] *adj* formed of pure fire or light; pertaining to the highest and purest region of heaven; sublime.—*adj* **empyrē´an** [or -pir´-], empyreal.—*n* the highest heaven; the region of pure light. [Gr *empyros*, fiery—*en*, in, and *pyr*, fire.]

emu [ē´mū] *n* a fast-running Australian bird (*Dromaius novae-hollandiae*), related to the ostrich, with rudimentary wings and drooping feathers. [Port *ema*, an ostrich.]

emulate [em´ū-lāt] *vt* to strive to equal or excel; to rival; (*loosely*) to imitate.—*n* **emulā´tion**, act of emulating or attempting to equal or excel; rivalry, competition.—*adj* **em´ulative**, inclined to emulation, rivalry, or competition.—*n* **em´ulator**.—*adj* **em´ulatory**.—*adj* **em´ulous**, eager to emulate; engaged in competition or rivalry.—*adv* **em´ulously**. [L *aemulārī, aemulātus—aemulus*, emulous.]

emulsion [e-mul´sh(ȯ)n] *n* a mixture of mutually insoluble liquids in which one is dispersed in droplets throughout the other; a light-sensitive coating on photographic paper or film.—*vt* **emul´sify**.—*adjs* **emulsible, emul´sive**. [Fr,—L *ēmulgēre, ēmulsum*, to milk out—*ē*, from, *mulgēre*, to milk.]

en- [en-] used to form verbs, meaning: (1) to put into, eg **encage**; (2) to bring into the condition of, eg **enslave**; (3) to make, eg **endear**. Before *b, p*, and sometimes *m, en-* becomes *em-*, eg **embed, emplane, emmesh** for **enmesh**. [Fr—L *in*.]

enable [en-ā´bl] *vt* to make able, by supplying the means; to give legal power or authority to. [*en-* + **able**.]

enact [en-akt´] *vt* to establish by law; to act the part of.—*adjs* **enact´ing, enact´ive**, that enacts.—*n* **enact´ment**, the passing of a bill into law; that which is enacted; a law. [*en-* + **act**.]

enamel [en-am´el] *n* a glasslike substance used to coat the surface of metal or pottery; the hard outer layer of a tooth; a usu. glossy paint that forms a hard coat.—*vt* to coat with or paint in enamel; to form a glossy surface upon, like enamel.—*pr p* **enameling, enam´elling**; *pt p* **enameled, enam´elled.—enamelware**, metal utensils coated with enamel. [OFr *enameler—en*, in, *esmail*, enamel.]

enamor [en-am´ȯr] *vt* to inflame with love. [OFr *enamourer*—pfx *en-*, *amour*.—L *amor*, love.]

en bloc [ā blok] *adj, adv* as a whole, in a mass. [Fr]

encage [en-kāj´] *vt* to shut up as in a cage. [*en-* + **cage**.]

encamp [en-kamp´] *vt* to settle in a camp.—*vi* to make a stay in a camp.—*n* **encamp´ment**, the act of encamping; a camp. [*en-* + **camp**.]

encase [en-kās´] *vt* to enclose as in a case.—*n* **encase´ment**.—Also **incase**. [*en-* + **case**(1).]

encaustic [en-kös´tik] *n* a paint made from pigment mixed with melted beeswax and resin and fixed by heat after application; the method of using encaustic.—*adj* prepared by heat; burnt in. [Gr *enkaustikos—en*, in, *kaiein*, to burn.]

enceinte[1] [ã-s•t´] *n* (*fort*) an enclosure, generally the whole area of a fortified place. [Fr,—*enceindre*, to surround—L *in*, in, *cingĕre, cinctum*, to gird.]

enceinte[2] [ã-s•t´] *adj* pregnant, being with child. [Fr prob through LL—L *in*, *cingĕre, cinctum*, to gird.]

encephal(o)-[en-sef´al(-ȯ)-, -kef´] of the brain.—*ns* **encephalī´tis**, inflammation of the brain; **encephalomyelitis**, concurrent inflammation of the brain and spinal cord; **encephalon** [en-sef´a-lon], the vertebrate brain. [Gr *enkephalos*, the brain—*en*, in, *kephate*, head.]

enchain [en-chān´] *vt* to put in chains; to fetter.—*n* **enchain´ment**. [Fr *enchaîner—en*, and *chaîne*, a chain—L *catēna*.]

enchant [en-chänt´] *vt* to bewitch, to charm.—*adj* **enchant´ed**, under the power of enchantment; delighted.—*n* **enchant´er**:—*fem* **enchant´ress**.—*adv* **enchant´ingly**.—*n* **enchant´ment**, act of enchanting; enchanted state. [Fr *enchanter*—L *incantāre*, to sing a magic formula over—*in*, on, *cantāre*, to sing.]

enchase [en-chās´] *vt* to engrave; to set with jewels; to ornament with engraved designs. [Fr *enchâsser—en*, in, *châsse*, a shrine, setting—L *capsa*, a case.]

enchilada [en-chil-ad´a] *n* a tortilla rolled with meat filling and served with chili sauce.—**the whole enchilada** (*slang*) the entire affair, the whole matter. [American Spanish.]

encipher [en-sī´fer] *vt* to convert a message into cipher.—*n* **encipherment**. [See **cipher**.]

encircle [en-sûrk´l] *vt* to surround (with); to go or pass round. [*en-* + **circle**.]

enclave [en´klāv], also en-kläv´, or ā-kläv´] *n* a piece of territory entirely enclosed within foreign territory. [Fr,—Late L *inclāvāre*—L *in*, and *clāvis*, a key.]

enclitic [en-klit´ik] *n* (*gram*) a word or particle without accent which always follows another word and usually modifies the accentuation of the word it follows (eg Gr *te*, L *-que*, *-ne*).—Also *adj*. [Gr *enklitikos*—*en*, in, *klīnein*, to lean.]

enclose [en-klōz´] *vt* to shut up or in; to surround.—*n* **enclos´ure**, the act of enclosing; state of being enclosed; that which is enclosed; that which encloses.—Also **inclose**. [Fr,—L *inclūdĕre*, *in-clūsum*—*in*, in, *claudĕre*, to shut.]

encomium [en-kō´mi-um], also **encōm´ion**, *n* high commendation; a formal expression of praise.—*pl* **encōm´iums, encō´mia**.—*adjs* **encomias´tic**. [L,—Gr *enkōmion*, a song of praise—*en*, in, *kōmos*, festivity.]

encompass [en-kum´pȧs] *vt* to surround or enclose.—*n* **encom´passment**. [*en-* + **compass**.]

encore [ong-kōr´] *interj* again!—*n* [also ong´-] a call for the repetition of a performance; repetition (or a further performance) in response to a call.—*vt* to call for a repetition of (a performance), or a further performance by (a person). [Fr (It *ancora*)—perh from L (in) *hanc horam*, till this hour, hence=still.]

encounter [en-kown´tėr] *vt* to meet, esp hostilely or unexpectedly.—*n* a meeting; a fight, passage of arms (*lit* and *fig*).—**encounter group**, a usu. leaderless group that seeks to develop a person's capacity to express his feelings and to form close emotional ties by encouraging unrestrained physical contact and uninhibited speech. [OFr *encontrer*—L *in*, in, *contra*, against.]

encourage [en-kur´ij] *vt* to put courage in; to inspire with spirit or hope; to incite.—*n* **encour´agement**, act of encouraging; that which encourages.—*adj*. **encour´aging**.—*adv* **encour´agingly**. [OFr *encoragier* (Fr *encourager*)—*en-*, *corage*, courage.]

encroach [en-krōch´] *vi* to extend into (territory, sphere, etc. of others—*with* **on**), to seize on the rights of others.—*n* **encroach´er**.—*n* **encroach´ment**, act of encroaching; that which is taken by encroaching. [OFr *encrochier*, to seize—*en-*, *croc*, a hook.]

encrust [en-krust´] *vt* to cover with a crust or hard coating eg of precious materials; to form a crust on the surface of.—*vi* to form a crust.—Also **incrust** [in-].—*n* **incrusta´tion, encrustā´tion**, act of encrusting; a crust or layer of anything; an inlaying of marble, mosaic, etc. [Fr,—L *incrustāre*, *-ātum*—*in*, on, *crusta*, crust.]

encumber [en-kum´bėr] *vt* to weigh down; to hinder the function or activity of.—Also **incumber**.—*n* **encum´brance**, that which encumbers or hinders; a legal claim on an estate. [OFr *encombrer*, from *en-*, *combrer*. See **cumber**.]

encyclical [en-sīk´lik-ȧl, or -sik´-] *adj* sent round to many persons or places.—*n* a letter addressed by the pope to all his bishops. [Gr *enkyklios*—*en*, in, *kyklos*, a circle.]

encyclopedia, -paedia [en-sī-klo-pē´di-a] *n* a work containing information on all branches of knowledge or treating comprehensively a particular branch of knowledge usu. in alphabetical order.—*adj* **encyclope´dic, encyclopae´dic**, of the nature of an encyclopedia; comprehensive.—*ns* **encyclope´dist**, the compiler, or one who assists in the compilation, of an encyclopedia.—**Encyclopedist** one of the writers of a French encyclopedia (1751–80) who were identified with the Enlightenment. [Gr *enkyklios*, circular, *paideia*, instruction.]

end [end] *n* the last part; the place where a thing stops; purpose; result, outcome.—*vt* to bring to an end; to destroy.—*vi* to come to an end; to result (in).—*adj* final; ultimate.—*adj* **end´ed**, brought to an end.—*n* **end´ing**, the thing that constitutes an end; (*gram*) one or more letters or syllables added to a word base to denote inflection.—*adj* **end´less**, without end; returning upon itself; extremely numerous.—*adv* **end´lessly**.—*n* **end´lessness**.—*advs*—*adj* **endmost** situated at the very end. **end´ways, end´wise** on end; with the end forward (toward the observer).—**end game**, the last stage in various games, esp bridge, checkers, and chess; **end line**, a line marking a boundary, esp of a playing area; **endpaper**, either of two once-folded sheets of paper pasted against the covers of a book and attached to the first and last pages; **end product**, the final result of a process, etc.; **end run**, a play in football in which the ball carrier tries to run wide of the opponents to reach the goal line.—**end it all**, (*inf*) to commit suicide; **in the end**, after all; **no end**, exceedingly; **on end**, with the end down; upright; without a stop or letup. [OE *ende*; cf Ger and Dan *ende*; Sans *anta*.]

endanger [en-dān´jėr] *vt* to place in danger. [Pfx *en-*, and **danger**.]

endear [en-dēr´] *vt* to make dear or more dear.—*adv* **endear´ingly**.—*n* **endear´ment**, act of endearing; a caress or utterance of love. [**en-** + **dear**.]

endeavor [en-dev´ȯr] *vi* to strive or attempt (to).—Also (*arch*) *vt*—*n* a strenuous attempt. [From Fr *se mettre en devoir*, to make it one's duty, to do what one can; Fr *en*, in, *devoir*, duty.]

endemic [en-dem´ik] locally prevalent (*an endemic disease, endemic plants*).—*adv* **endem´ically**. [Gr *endēmios*—*en*, in, and *dēmos*, a people, a district.]

endive [en´dīv´] *n* an annual or biennial herb (*chicorium endiva*) widely cultivated as a salad plant.—Also **escarole**; the blanched shoot of chicory. [Fr,—L *intibus*.]

endo- within [Gr *endon*, within], eg:—**end´omorph**, person having a heavy rounded build, with a tendency to become fat; **endopar´asite**, an internal parasite; **end´oplasm**, the inner portion of the cytoplasm of a cell; **endoskel´eton**, the internal skeleton or framework of the body; **en´doscope** (Gr *skopeein*, to view), an instrument for viewing the inside of hollow organs of the body. See **ento-**.

endocardium [en-dōkär´di-um] *n* the lining membrane of the heart.—*n* **endocardī´tis**, disease of this membrane. [Gr *endon*, within, *kardia*, heart.]

endocrine [en´do-krin] *adj* secreting internally, specifically producing secretions that are distributed in the body by the bloodstream.—*ns* **endocrine gland**, a gland (as the thyroid or pituitary) that produces an endocrine secretion.—Also **ductless gland**.—*ns* **endocrinologist**, person specializing in study or treatment of endocrine diseases; **endocrinology**, the science dealing with endocrine glands. [Gr *endon*, within, *krinein*, to separate.]

endogamy [en-dag´am-ē] *n* marriage within a specific group as required by custom or law. [**endo** + Gr *gamos*, marriage.]

endogenous [en-daj´en-is], **endogenic** [-ik] *adj* growing from or on the inside; originating within the body. [**endo** + **gene**.]

endorse [en-dörs´] *vt* to write one's name, comment, etc. on the back of (a check or other document); to approve; to support.—*ns* **endors´ee**, the person to whom a bill, etc., is assigned by endorsement; **endorse´ment**, act of endorsing; **endors´er**.—Also **indorse**. [Changed from ME *endosse* under the influence of Low L *indorsāre*—*in*, on, *dorsum*, the back.]

endorphin [en-dorf´in] *n* chemical occurring in the brain which has a similar effect to morphine. [**endo** + **morphine**.]

endosperm [en´dō-spûrm] *n* (*bot*) the nutritive material enclosed with the embryo in a seed. [**endo-** + **sperm**.]

endothermic [en-do-thurm´ik], **endothermal** [-al] *adj* characterized or formed with absorption of heat; warm-blooded.—*n* **endotherm**, a warm-blooded animal. [**endo** + **therm**].

endow [en-dow´] *vt* to give money or property to provide an income for; to enrich (with any gift or faculty).—*n* **endow´ment**, act of endowing; that which is settled on any person or institution; a quality or faculty bestowed on anyone by nature. [Fr *en* (= L *in*) *douer*, to endow—L *dōtāre*—*dōs*, *dōtis*, a dowry.]

endrin [en-drin] *n* a chemical insecticide.

endue [en-dū´] *vt* to provide with a quality or power. [OFr *enduire*—L *indūcĕre*—*in*, into, *dūcĕre*, to lead, with meaning influenced by *induĕre*, to put on.]

endure [en-dūr´] *vt* to bear with patience; to undergo; to tolerate.—*vi* to remain firm; to last.—*adj* **endur´able**, that can be endured or borne.—*adv* **endur´ably**.—*n* **endur´ance**, state, or the power, of enduring or bearing; continuance. [OFr *endurer*—L *indūrāre*—*in*, in, *dūras*, hard.]

enduro [en-door´ō] *n* a long race (as for automobiles or motorcycles) stressing endurance rather than speed. [See **endure**.]

enema [en´e-ma, or e-nē´ma] *n* liquid injected into the rectum; the material injected. [Gr—*enienai*, to send in—*en*, in, and *hienai*, to send.]

enemy [en´e-mi] *n* one who hates or dislikes and wishes to injure another, a foe, esp a military opponent; something harmful or deadly. [OFr *enemi*—L *inimīcus*—*in-*, neg, *amīcus*, a friend.]

energy [en´ėr-ji] *n* capacity of acting or being active; vigorous activity; capacity to do work; vigor; forcefulness;—*pl* **energies**.—*adjs* **energet´ic**, strenuously active; operating with force, vigor and effect.—*adv* **energet´ically**.—*vt* **en´ergize**, to give strength or active force to; to stimulate to activity.—*vi* to act with force. [Gr *energeia*—*en*, in, *ergon*, work.]

enervate [en´ėr-vāt] *vt* to lessen the strength or vigor of; to weaken in mind and body.—*adj* **enervated** [-vȧt] weakened; spiritless.—*adj* **en´ervating**. [L *ēnervāre*, *-ātum*—*ē*, out of, *nervus*, a nerve.]

enfant terrible [ã-fã te-rē-bl´] *n* a person whose behavior is embarrassing, indiscreet, or irresponsible. [Fr]

enfeeble [en-fē´bl] *vt* to make feeble; to weaken.—*n* **enfee´blement**, weakening; weakness. [OFr *enfe(i)blir*—*en-* (L *in*), *feible*, *foible*. See **feeble**.]

enfilade [en-fi-lād´] *n* gunfire that rakes a line of troops, or a position, from end to end.—*vt* to rake with shot through the whole length of a line. [Fr,—*enfiler*—*en* (= L *in*), *fil*, a thread. Cf **file**, a line or wire.]

enfold [en-fōld´] *vt* to wrap up (in, with); to embrace.—Also **infold**. [**en** + **fold** (1).]

enforce [en-fōrs´, -förs´] *vt* to compel obedience by threat (of penalty); to execute (the law) with vigor.—*n* **enforce´ment**, act of enforcing. [OFr *enforcer*—*en* (= L *in*), *force*. See **force**.]

enfranchise [en-fran´chīz] *vt* to set free (as from slavery); to admit to citizenship; to grant the vote to.—*n* **enfran´chisement**, act of enfranchising. [OFr *enfranchir*—*en*, *franc*, free.]

engage [en-gāj´] *vt* to pledge as security; to promise to marry; to keep busy; to hire; to attract and hold, esp attention or sympathy; to cause to participate; to bring or enter into conflict; to begin or take part in a venture; to connect or interlock, to mesh.—*adj* **engaged´**.—*n* **engage´ment**, act of engaging; state of being engaged; betrothal; promise; appointment; employment; a fight or battle; commitment.—*adj* **engag´ing**, winning, attractive (eg of manner).—*adv* **engag´ingly**. [Fr *engager—en gage*, in pledge—OFr *guage*.]

engender [en-jen´dėr] *vt* to bring into being, to produce; to cause to develop (eg hatred, strife, heat). [Fr *engendrer*—L *ingenerāre—in*, and *generāre*, to generate.]

engine [en´jin] *n* a machine by which physical power is applied to produce a physical effect; a locomotive; a mechanical device, esp a machine used in war.—*ns* **engineer**, a member of a military group devoted to engineering work; a designer or builder of engines; one trained in engineering; one that operates an engine; etc.—*vt* to arrange, contrive.—*n* **engineer´ing**, the art or profession of an engineer. [OFr *engin*—L *ingenium*, skill.]

English [ing´glish] *adj* of, relating to, or characteristic of England, the English people, or the English language.—*n* the language of the English people, the US and many areas now or formerly under British control; English language and literature as a subject of study; (*pl in construction*) the people of England; the spin given to a ball (as in pool or bowling).—*ns* **English Channel**, the body of water dividing Great Britain from continental Europe; **English cocker spaniel**, a breed of sporting dog with a square muzzle and distinctive arched and slightly flattened skull; **English foxhound**, a breed of hound characterized by a large heavily boned form, short ears, and slightly fringed tail; **English horn**, an alto oboe; **English muffin**, a bread dough rolled and cut into rounds, baked on a griddle, and split and toasted just before eating; **English saddle**, a shallow-seated saddle without a pommel; **English setter**, a breed of sporting dog with a moderately long silky coat of white or white with color and feathering on the tail and legs; **English sonnet**, a sonnet consisting of three quatrains and a couplet with a rhyme scheme of abab cdcd efef gg.—Also **Shakespearean sonnet; English sparrow**, a sparrow (*Passer domesticus*) native to Europe and parts of Asia that has been widely introduced everywhere; **English springer spaniel**, a breed of sporting dog with a deep-bodied muscular build and a black and white moderately long straight or slightly wavy silky coat; **English toy spaniel**, a breed of diminutive spaniel presenting in different varieties; **English toy terrier**, the Manchester terrier; **English walnut**, a Eurasian tree (*Juglans regia*) valued for its large edible nut and hard richly figured wood. [OE *Englisc, Engle*, Angles.]

engorge [en-gorj´] *vi* congest with blood; eat (food) greedily; gorge (oneself).—*n* **engorgement** [**en** + **gorge**.]

engram [en´gram] *n* a hypothetical change in neural tissue postulated in order to account for the persistence of memory. [Gr **en-**, *ingramma*, that which is written.]

engraft en-gräft´] *vt* to graft; to insert, incorporate (into); to join on to something already existing (with *upon*); to implant in the mind. [**en** + **graft** (1).]

engrain [en-grān] *see* **ingrain**.

engrave [en-grāv´] *vt* to produce (as letters or lines) by incising a surface; to incise (as stone or metal) to produce a representation (as of letters or designs) that may be printed from; to impress deeply (upon, eg the memory).—*ns* **engrav´er; engrav´ing**, act or art of cutting designs on metal, etc.; an impression taken from an engraved plate, a print. [**en-** + **grave**, vb.]

engross [en-grōs´] *vt* to occupy fully; to copy in a large hand; to prepare the final text of (an official document).—*adv* **engrossingly**.—**engross´er; engross´ment**, act of engrossing; that which has been engrossed; a fair copy. [From Fr *en gros*, in large. See **gross**.]

engulf [en-gulf´] *vt* to swallow up; to flow over and enclose.—*n* **engulf´ment**. [**en-** + **gulf**.]

enhance [en-häns´] *vt* to heighten or intensify; to raise in value or in importance; to add to, increase.—*n* **enhance´ment**. [Prob from OFr *enhaucer*—L *in*, and *altus*, high.]

enharmonic [en-här-mon´ik] *adj* (mus) of intervals that differ only in name, eg a and b; of chords identical in sound, but written differently. [LL *enharmonicus*—Gr *enarmonikos—en*, in, *harmonia*, harmony.]

enigma [en-ig´ma] *n* a statement with a hidden meaning to be guessed, a riddle; a puzzling person or thing.—*adjs* **enigmat´ic, -al**.—*adv* **enigmat´ically**. [L *aenigma*—Gr *ainigma—ainissesthai*, to speak in riddles—*ainos*, a fable.]

enjambment, enjambement [en-jamb´mėnt, ā-zhāb´mā] *n* the continuation of the sense without a pause beyond the end of a line of verse. [Fr *enjambement—enjamber*, to stride, encroach—*en*, in, *jambe*, leg.]

enjoin [en-join´] *vt* to order or direct with authority; to forbid, to prohibit. [Fr *enjoindre*—L *injungĕre—in, jungĕre*, to join.]

enjoy [en-joi´] *vt* to take pleasure or satisfaction in; to possess or use (with satisfaction); to experience.—*adj* **enjoy´able.—enjoy´ableness; enjoy´ment**. [OFr *enjoier*, to give joy to—*en* (= L *in*), and *joie*, joy; or OFr *enjoir*, to enjoy—*en*, and *joir*—L *gaudēre*, to rejoice.]

enlarge [en-lärg´] *vti* to make or grow larger; to expand or increase the capacity of (eg ideas, heart, mind); to exaggerate; to be diffuse in speaking or writing; to expatiate (upon).—*adj* **enlarged´**.—*ns* **enlarge´ment**, an act, instance, or state of enlarging; a photograph or other thing that has been made larger, an addition.—**enlar´ger**. [OFr *enlarger—en* (= L *in*), *large*, broad.]

enlighten [en-līt´n] *vt* to instruct; to inform, esp to free from prejudice and ignorance.—*p ad* **enlight´ened**, free from prejudice or superstition; informed.—*n* **enlight´enment**, act of enlightening; information; state of being enlightened; **Enlightenment**, the spirit of the French philosophers of the 18th century. [OE *inlīhtan—in*, in, and *līhtan*, to light.]

enlist [en-list´] *vt* to engage for service in the armed forces; to secure the aid or support of.—*vi* to register for services; to enter heartily into a cause.—*n* **enlistment; enlisted man**, a man or woman in the armed forces ranking below a commissioned or warrant officer. [**en** + **list** (2).]

enliven [en-līv´n] *vt* to excite or make active; to make sprightly or cheerful. [*en-*, **life** + suffx *-en*.]

en masse [ā mas] *adv* in a body, as a whole. [Fr]

enmesh [en-mesh´] *vt* to catch, entangle, as in a mesh or net.—Also **immesh´**.—*n* **enmesh´ment**. [**en-** + **mesh**.]

enmity [en´mi-ti] *n* ill-will, esp mutual hatred. [OFr *enemistié*—L *inimīcus*. See **enemy**.]

ennoble [e-nō´bl], *vt* to dignify; to exalt, to raise to the nobility.—*n* **ennō´blement**. [Fr *ennoblir*—Fr *en* (= L *in*), and **noble**.]

ennui [on-wē´] *n* boredom.—*adj* **ennuyé** [-yā]. [Fr,—OFr *anoi*. See **annoy**.]

enormous [e-nör´mus] *adj* very large.—*n* **enor´mity**, a great crime; great wickedness; huge size.—*adv* **enor´mously**. [L *ēnormis—ē*, out of, *norma*, rule.]

enough [e-nuf´] *adj* sufficient.—*adv* sufficiently; (foll another *adv*) rather (eg *funnily enough*).—*n* a sufficient number, quantity or amount.—**have enough of**, to be tired of; **well, good, enough**, quite well, quite good. [OE *genōh, genōg*; Ger *genug*; ON *gnōgr*.]

enow [e-now´] *adj adv* (*arch*) = **enough**.

en passant [ā pâs ānt] *adv* in passing, used in chess of the capture of a pawn. [Fr]

enplane [en-plān] *vi* to board an airplane.—Also **emplane**. [**en-** + **plane**.]

en prise [ā prēz] *adj* (of a man in chess or checkers) exposed to capture. [Fr]

en quad [en kwad] *n* a quad whose set dimension is one half of that of an em quad. (From its use for the letter *n*.]

enquire *See* **inquire**.

enrage [en-rāj´] *vt* to make angry.—*adj* **enraged´**. [OFr *enrager—en* (= L *in*), and *rage*, rage.]

enrapture [en-rap´tyůr, -chůr] *vt* to transport with pleasure or delight. [**en-** + **rapture**.]

enrich [en-rich´] *vt* to make rich or richer; to adorn (with costly ornaments); to increase the proportion of some valuable substance to; to expand a school curriculum by increasing the range of subjects and the depth of treatment.—*n* **enrich´ment**. [Fr *enrichir—en-* (L *in*), *riche*, rich.]

enroll, enrol [en-rōl´] *vti* to enter or register on a roll or list.—*pr p* **enrōll´ing**; *pt p* **enrōlled**.—*ns* **enrollee; enrollment**. [O Fr *enroller—en*, and *rolle*, roll.]

en route [ā rōōt] *adj, adv* along or on the way. [Fr]

ensample [en-säm´pl] *n* example, instance.

ensconce [en-skons´] *vt* to establish in a safe, secure, or comfortable place. [Fr *en* (= L *in*) and Eng **sconce** (1).]

ensemble [āsābl´] *n* all the parts of a thing taken together; the general effect; the performance of the full number of musicians, dancers, etc.; a complete harmonious costume. [Fr *ensemble*, together—L *in*, in, *simul*, at the same time.]

enshrine [en-shrīn´] *vt* to enclose in or as if in a shrine; to cherish as sacred. [Fr *en* (= L *in*), Eng **shrine**.]

enshroud [en-shrowd´] *vt* to cover; to hide; to veil. [**en-** + **shroud**.]

ensiform [en´si-förm] *adj* sword-shaped, as a leaf. [L *ensis*, sword, suffx *-form*.]

ensign [en´sīn, en'sin] *n* a flag; a mark or badge; a commissioned officer in the navy ranking below a lieutenant junior grade. [OFr *enseigne*—L *insignia*, pl of *insigne*, a distinctive mark—*in*, and *signum*, a mark.]

ensilage [en´sil-ij] *n* silage.—*vt* **ensile**, to prepare and store (fodder) for silage. [Fr,—Sp *en*, in, *silo*—L *sirus*—Gr *siros*, etc., pit for corn.]

enslave [en-slāv´] *vt* to reduce to slavery; to subject to a dominating influence.—**enslave´ment; enslav´er**. [**en-** + **slave**.]

ensnare [en-snār´] *vt* to snare; to trap. [**en-** + **snare**.]

ensue [en-sū´] *vi* to follow as a consequence or in time.—*pr p* **ensū´ing**; *pt p* **ensūed´**. [OFr *ensuir*—L *in*, after, *sequī*, to follow.]

en suite [ā swēt] *adj, adv* in a succession, series, or set. [Fr].

ensure [en-shōōr´] *vt* to make sure, certain, or safe. See **insure**.

entablature [en-tab´la-tyůr] *n* the part of a building resting on the top of columns. [It *intavolatura—in*, in, *tavola*, a table—L *tabula*.]

entail [en-tāl´] *vt* to settle on a series of heirs, so that the immediate possessor may not dispose of the estate; to bring on as an inevitable consequence; to necessitate.—*n* an estate entailed; the rule of descent of an estate. [**en-** + **tail** (2).]

entangle [en-tang´gl] *vt* to twist into a tangle; to involve in complications or difficulties; to ensnare.—*n* **entang´lement**, act of entangling; state of being entangled; a tangled obstacle or snare; conditions causing perplexity, embarrassment, or anxiety. [**en-** + **tangle**.]

entente [ā-tāt] *n* an understanding; a friendly agreement or relationship between states. [Fr]

enter [en´tėr] *vi* to go or come in or into; to become a member of; to put down one's name (*with* **for**).—*vt* to come or go into; to penetrate; to join or engage in; to begin; to put into; to enroll or record.—**enter into**, to become a party to; to participate actively or heartily in; to understand sympathetically (another's feelings); to take up the discussion of; to be part of. [Fr *entrer*—L *intrāre*, to go into, related to *inter*, between.]

enter- [en´tėr-] between, among. [Fr *entre*—L *inter*.]

enteric, enteral [en-ter´ik, en´-ter-al] *adj* intestinal.—*n* **enterī´tis**, inflammation of the intestines. [Gr *enteron*, intestine.]

enterprise [en´tėr-prīz] *n* a bold or dangerous undertaking; a business project; willingness to engage in undertakings of risk.—*adj* **en´terprising**, forward in undertaking projects; adventurous. [OFr *entreprise*, pt p of *entreprendre*—*entre*, between (L *inter*), *prendre* (L *prehendĕre*), to seize.]

entertain [en-tėr-tān´] *vt* to receive and treat as a guest; to hold in mind; to amuse; to consider.—*n* **entertain´er**.—*p adj* **entertain´ing**.—*adv* **entertain´ingly**.—*n* **entertain´ment**, act of entertaining; that which entertains; performance or show intended to give pleasure; amusement. [Fr *entretenir*—L *inter*, among, *tenēre*, to hold.]

enthrall [en-thröl´] *vt* to enslave; to hold spellbound;—*pr p* **enthrall´ing**, *pt p* **enthralled´**.—*n* **enthral´ment**, act of enthralling; slavery. [**en-** + **thrall**.]

enthrone [en-thrōn´] *vt* to place on a throne; to install as a king or bishop.—*n* **enthrōne´ment**. [**en-** + **throne**; cf Fr *enthroner*, from *en*, and *trône*—Gr *thronos*, a throne.]

enthusiasm [en-thū´zi-azm] *n* intense interest; passionate zeal.—*n* **enthūsiast**, one filled with enthusiasm.—*adjs* **enthūsias´tic**, zealous; ardent.—*adv* **enthūsias´tically**.—*vti* **enthūse´**, to make, be, become, or appear enthusiastic. [Gr *enthousiasmos*, a god-inspired zeal—*enthousiazein*, to be inspired by a god—*en*, in, *theos*, a god.]

entice [en-tīs´] *vt* to attract by offering some pleasure or reward; to lead astray.—*n* **entice´ment**, act of enticing; that which entices or tempts; allurement.—*adj* **entic´ing**. [OFr *enticier*, provoke; prob related to L *titiō*, a firebrand.]

entire [en-tīr´] *adj* whole; complete; unimpaired, unbroken, unmingled.—*adv* **entire´ly**.—*ns* **entire´ness, entire´ty**, completeness; the whole. [OFr *entier*—L *integer*, whole, from *in-*, not, and root of *tangĕre*, to touch.]

entitle [en-tī´tl] *vt* to give the title of, to style; to give a claim (to). [OFr *entiteler*—Low L *intitulāre*—*in*, in, *titulus*, title.]

entity [en´ti-ti] *n* a real substance; a thing that exists. [Low L *entitās, -ātis*—*ens, entis*, being—*esse*, to be.]

ento- in, inside [Gr *entos*, within]. It often interchanges with **endo-**;—eg **entopar´asite, endopar´asite**.

entomb [en-tōōm´] *vt* to place in a tomb; to bury.—*n* **entomb´ment**, burial. [OFr *entoumber*—*en*, in, *tombe*, a tomb.]

entomology [en-to-mol´o-ji] *n* the branch of zoology that deals with insects.—*adj* **entomolog´ical**.—*n* **entomol´ogist**, one learned in entomology. [Fr *entomologie*—Gr *entoma*, insects, *logos*, discourse.]

entourage [ā-tōō-räzh´] *n* retinue, group of attendants. [Fr—*entourer*, to surround—*en*, in, *tour*, a circuit.]

entozoan [en-tō-zō´an] *n* an animal living parasitically within the body of its host.—*(pl)* **entozō´a**. [Gr *entos*, within, *zōon*, an animal.]

entr'acte [ã-trakt´] *n* the interval between acts in a play; a piece of music or other performance between acts. [Fr *entre*, between, *acte*, an act.]

entrails [en´trālz] *n pl* the internal parts of an animal's body, the bowels. [OFr *entraille*—Low L *intrālia*—*inter*, within.]

entrain[1] [en-trān´] *vti* to put (troops) into or to go into a railroad car. [**en-** + **train**.]

entrain[2] [in-trān´] *vt* to suspend bubbles or particles in a moving fluid; to incorporate (air bubbles) into concrete; to modify the phase or period of (as a circadian rhythm).—*n* **entrain´ment**. [Fr]

entrance[1] [en´trans] *n* act of entering; power or right to enter; a place of entering; a door.—*n* **en´trant**, one who, or that which, enters (esp a competition, a profession, etc.). [Fr *entrer*—L *intrāre*, to enter.]

entrance[2] [en-träns´] *vt* to put into a trance; to fill with rapturous delight.—*n* **entrance´ment**. [**en-** + **trance**.]

entrap [en-trap´] *vt* to catch, as in a trap; to ensnare; to entangle.—*n* **entrap´ment**. [OFr *entraper*—*en*, in, *trappe*, a trap.]

entreat [en-trēt´] *vt* to ask earnestly; to beg for.—*Also* **intreat**.—*n* **entreat´y**, act of entreating; earnest prayer. [OFr *entraiter*—*en*, *traiter*, to treat.]

entrechat [ã-trė-shä] *n* in ballet dancing, a leap during which the calves are struck together. [Fr]

entrée, entree [ā´trā] *n* the right or privilege of admission; the principal dish of the meal in the US. [Fr]

entremets [ā-trė-mā] *n* dishes served between the chief courses of a meal. [Fr]

entrench [en-trench´, -sh] *vt* to dig a trench around; to establish in a strong position.—*vi* to encroach (upon).—*n* **entrench´ment**, defensive earthwork of trenches and parapets; an encroachment.—Also **intrench´**. [**en-** + **trench**.]

entrepôt [ā´trė-pō] *n* an intermediate center of trade and transshipment. [Fr]

entrepreneur [ā-trė-prė-nœr´] *n* one who undertakes a business enterprise, esp one involving risk.—*adj* **entrepreneur´ial**, [Fr]

entresol [en´trė-sol] *n* mezzanine. [Fr,—*entre*; between, *sol*, the ground.]

entropy [en´trò-pi] *n* a measure of the unavailable energy of a system; an ultimate state of inert uniformity.—*pl* **entropies**. [Gr *en*, in, *tropē*, turning, intended to represent 'transformation content'.]

entrust [en-trust´] *vt* to commit as a trust (to); to commit to another with confidence.—Also **intrust**. [**en-** + **trust**.]

entry [en´tri] *n* act of entering (in any sense); entrance; act of committing to writing in a record; the thing so written; the person or thing that takes part in a contest; the right or privilege of entering. [Fr *entrée*. See **enter**.]

entwine [en-twīn´] *vt* to twine together or around. [**en-** + **twine**.]

entwist [en-twist´] *vt* to entwine. [**en-** + **twist**.]

enumerate [e-nū´mer-āt] *vt* to count the number of; to list.—*n* **enumerā´tion**, act of numbering; a detailed list. [L *ē*, from, *numerāre, -ātum*, to number.]

enunciate [e-nun´s(h)i-āt] *vt* to state definitely; to pronounce distinctly.—*n* **enunciation** [e-nun-s(h)i-ā´sh(ò)n], act of enunciating; manner of uttering or pronouncing; a distinct statement or declaration.—*n* **enun´ciator**. [L *ēnuntiāre, -ātum*—*ē*, from, *nuntiāre*, to tell—*nuntius*, a messenger.]

enure [en-ūr´] *see* **inure**.

enuresis [en-u-rē´sis] *n* the involuntary discharge of urine; bed-wetting. [Gr *en-*, in, *ourisēs*, urination.]

envelop [en-vel´op] *vt* to enclose completely with or as if with a covering.—*ns* **envelope** [en´vėl-ōp, on´-], that which envelops, wraps, or covers; a paper container for a letter; the bag containing the gas in a balloon or airship; **envel´opment**, a wrapping or covering on all sides. [OFr *enveloper*; origin obscure.]

envenom [en-ven´òm] *vt* to make poisonous; to embitter.—*n* **envenomization**, poisoning caused by a bite or a sting. [OFr *envenimer*—*en, venim*, venom.]

environ [en-vī´ròn] *vt* to surround, to encircle.—*n* **envī´ronment**, surroundings.—*n pl* **environs** [en-vī´rònz or en´vi], the outskirts of a place; neighborhood.—*adj* **environmen´tal**.—*n* **environmentalist**, a person concerned about the quality of the human environment. [Fr *environner*—*environ*, around—*virer*, to turn round; cf **veer**.]

envisage [en-viz´ij] *vt* to have a mental picture of. [Fr *envisager*—*en, visage*, the face.]

envoi, envoy [en´voi] *n* the concluding part of an essay, a poem or a book. [OFr *envoye*—*envoiier*, to send—*en voie*, on the way.]

envoy [en´voi] *n* a diplomatic agent; a representative.—*n* **en´voyship**. [For Fr *envoyé*—pt p of *envoyer*, to send.]

envy [en´vi] *n* ill-will or discontent at another's well-being or success; an object of envy.—*vt* to feel envy towards; to feel envy on account of, to grudge.—*pr p* **en´vying**; *pt p* **en´vied**.—*adjs* **en´viable**, that is to be envied; **en´vious**, feeling envy; directed by envy.—*adv* **en´viously**.—*n* **en´viousness**. [Fr *envie*—L *invidia*—*in*, on, *vidēre*, to look.]

enwrap [en-rap´] *vt* to cover by wrapping; to wrap (in); to engross. [**en-** + **wrap**.]

enzyme [en´zīm] *n* a complex substance produced by living cells, which induces or speeds chemical reactions in plants and animals without itself undergoing any alteration. Cf *catalyst*. [Gr *en*, in, *zȳmē*, leaven.]

Eocene [ē´ō-sēn] *adj* (*geol*) belonging to the oldest period of the Tertiary era. [Gr *ēōs*, daybreak, *kainos*, new.]

eolian [ē-ōlien] *adj* borne, deposited, produced or eroded by the wind. [L *Aeolus*, god of the winds.]

eolith [ē´ō-lith] *n* a very crudely-chipped flint. *n*—*adj* **Eolith´ic**, of a very early stage of human culture. [Gr *ēōs*, dawn, *lithos*, stone.]

epact [ē´pakt] *n* a period added to harmonize the solar calendar with the lunar calendar. [Fr *épacte*—Gr *epaktos*, brought on—*epi*, on, *agein*, to bring.]

epaulet [ep´òl-et] *n* a shoulder ornament, esp on a uniform. [Fr *épaulette*—*épaule*, the shoulder.]

epergne [e-pûrn´] *n* a branched ornamental centerpiece for the dinner table. [Perh from Fr *épargne*, saving—*épargner*, to save.]

ephedrine [e-fed´rin] *n* a drug used to treat asthma, hay fever and other allergic disorders. [Gr *ephedrā*, horsetail.]

ephemeral [ef-em´ėrėl] *adj* existing only for a day; shortlived.—**efem´erid**, mayfly. [Gr *ephēmeros*, living a day—*epi*, for, during, *hēmera*, a day.]

Ephesians [e-fēs´ians] the tenth book of the New Testament, an epistle written by St Paul to the Christians of Ephesus from his captivity at Rome at about 60 AD.

epi- above, outside [Gr *epi*, upon], eg:—*n* **ep´iblast**, the outer germinal layer of an embryo.—*adj* **epicer´ebral**, above or upon the brain.

epic [ep´ik] *n* a long poem in elevated language narrating the deeds of a hero.—**epic drama**, 20th century narrative drama that seeks to provoke critical thought, esp about social conditions, by appealing to the viewer's reason rather than emotion; **epic theater**, theater employing epic drama. [Gr *epikos*—*epos*, a word.]

epicene [ep´i-sēn] *adj* common to both sexes; having characteristics of both sexes. [Gr *epi*, upon, *koinos*, common.]

epicenter [ep´i-sen-tėr] *n* the earth's surface directly above the focus of an earthquake. [Gr *epi*, upon, *kentron*, a point.]

epicure [ep´i-kŷr] *n* a person of refined and fastidious taste, esp in food and wine.—*adj* **Epicurē´an**; given to luxury.—*n* a follower of Epicurus; one given to the luxuries of the table.—*ns* **epicurē´anism**, the doctrines of Epicurus; attachment to these doctrines; **ep´icurism**, pursuit of pleasure; fastidiousness in luxury. [Through L—Gr *Epikouros*.]

epicycle [ep'i´-sīkl] *n* a circle having its center on the circumference of a greater circle on which it moves. [Gr *epi*, upon, *kyklos*, a circle.]

epidemic [ep-i-dem´ik, -âl] *adj* affecting many persons at one time.—*n* **epidem´ic**, an epidemic outbreak, esp of disease.—**epidemiol´ogy**, branch of medicine dealing with the incidence, distribution, and control of disease in a population; **epidemiol´ogist**. [Gr *epi*, among, *dēmos*, the people.]

epidermis [ep-i-dûr´mis] *n* an outer layer, esp of skin; a thin surface layer of tissue in higher plants.—*adjs* **epider´mal, epider´mic**. [Gr *epidermis—epi*, upon, *derma*, the skin.]

epidiascope [ep-i-dī´a-skōp] *n* a projector for images of objects whether opaque or transparent. [Gr *epi*, upon, *dia*, through, *skopeein*, to look at.]

epidural [ep-i-door´al] *n* spinal anesthetic used for relief of pain during childbirth.—Also *adj*. [Gr *epi-*, upon, *dura (mater)*.]

epiglottis [ep-i-glot´is] *n* a cartilaginous flap over the glottis. [Gr *epi*, over, *glōttis*, glòttis.]

epigram [ep´i-gram] *n* a short witty poem or saying.—*adjs* **epigrammat´ic, -al**, relating to or dealing in epigrams; like an epigram; concise and pointed.—*adv* **epigrammat´ically**.—*vt* **epigramm´atize**, to make an epigram on.—*n* **epigramm´atist**. [Through Fr and L from Gr *epigramma—epi*, upon, *gramma*, a writing—*graphein*, to write.]

epigraph [ep´i-gräf] *n* an inscription, esp on a building; a citation or motto at the beginning of a book or of one of its parts. [Gr *epigraphē—epi*, upon, *graphein*, to write.]

epilepsy [ep´i-lep-si] *n* a nervous disorder marked typically by convulsive attacks and loss of consciousness.—*adj, n* **epilep´tic**. [Gr *epilēpsia—epi*, upon, and root of *lambanein*, to seize.]

epilogue [ep´i-log] *n* a speech or short poem at the end of a play; the concluding section of a book, etc. [Fr, through L—Gr *epilogos*, conclusion—*epi*, upon, *legein*, to speak.]

Epiphany [e-pif´ȧn-i] *n* a church festival celebrated on January 6, in commemoration of the coming of the Magi to Jesus at Bethlehem. [Gr *epiphaneia*, appearance—*epi*, to, *phainein*, to show.]

epiphyte [ep´i-fīt] *n* a plant which derives its moisture and nutrients from the air and rain and grows usu. on another plant. [Gr *epi-*, upon, *phyton*, a plant.]

episcopacy [e-pis´ko-pȧs-i] *n* the government of the church by bishops; the office of bishop; a bishop's period of office; the bishops, as a class.—*adj* **epis´copal**, governed by bishops; belonging to or vested in bishops; **Episcopal**, of or relating to the Protestant Episcopal Church.—*adj* **episcopā´lian**, pertaining to bishops, or to government by bishops.—*n* one who belongs to an episcopal church; **Episcopalian**, a member of the Protestant Episcopal Church.—*ns* **episcopā´lianism**, episcopalian government and doctrine; **epis´copate**, a bishopric; the office of a bishop; a body of bishops. [L *episcopātus*—Gr *episkopos*, an overseer.]

episcope [ep´i-skōp] *n* a projector for images of opaque objects. [Gr *epi*, on, over, *skopeein*, to look.]

episode [ep´i-sōd] *n* a unit of action in a dramatic or literary work; an incident in a sequence of events.—*adj* **episŏd´ic(al)**, pertaining to or contained in an episode; brought in as a digression; consisting largely of episodes. [Gr *epeisodion—epi*, upon, *eisodos*, a coming in—*eis*, into, *hodos*, a way.]

epistemology [ep-is-te-mol´oj-i] *n* the theory of knowledge. [Gr *epistēmē*, knowledge, *logos*, discourse.]

epistle [e-pis´l] *n* a letter; **Epistle**, a letter written by one of Christ's Apostles to various churches and individuals.—*adj* **epis´tolary**. [OFr,—L *epistola*—Gr *epistolē—epi*, on the occasion of, *stellein*, to send.]

epitaph [ep´i-täf] *n* an inscription in memory of a dead person, usu. on a tombstone. [Gr *epitaphion—epi*, upon, *taphos*, a tomb.]

epithalamium [ep-i-tha-lā´mi-um] *n* a song or poem in celebration of a marriage. [Gr *epithalamion—epi*, upon, *thalamos*, a bride-chamber.]

epithelium [ep-i-thē´li-um] *n* the cellular membrane that covers the outer surface and lines the closed cavities of the body. [Mod L—Gr *epi*, upon, *thēlē*, nipple.]

epithet [ep´i-thet] *n* a characterizing and often abusive word or phrase.—*adj* **epithet´ic(al)**. [Gr *epitheton*, neut of *epithetos*, added—*epi*, on, *tithenai*, to place.]

epitome [e-pit´o-mē] *n* a condensed account; something that represents or typifies another on a small scale.—*vt* **epit´omize**, to condense; to represent on a small scale. [Gr,—*epi*, *tomē*, a cut.]

epizoon [ep-i-zō´ȯn] *n* an animal that lives on the surface of another animal; *pl* **epizō´a**. [Gr *epi*, upon, *zōion*, an animal.]

epoch [ēp´ok, ep´ok] *n* a point of time fixed or made remarkable by some great event from which dates are reckoned; an age in history; *(geol)* a division of time constituting part of a period *(see this entry)*.—*adj* **ep´ochal**. [Gr *epochē—epechein*, to stop—*epi*, upon, *echein*, to hold.]

epode [ep´ōd] *n* a lyric poem in which a long line is followed by a shorter one; the last part of a lyric ode, sung after the strophe and antistrophe. [Gr *epōidos—epi*, on, *ōidē*, an ode.]

eponym [ep´o-nim] *n* one who gives his name to something; a hero invented to account for the name of a place or people.—*adj* **epon´ymous**. [Gr *epōnymos—epi*, upon, to, *onoma*, a name.]

epoxy [e-pok´sē] *adj* containing oxygen bound to two other atoms, often carbon, which are already attached in some way.—*n* epoxy resin; **expox´y resin**, a synthetic resin used in coatings and adhesives.

epsilon [ep´si-lon] *n* fifth letter of the Greek alphabet. [Gr *epsilon*, bare or mere *e*.]

Epsom salts [ep´sum saltz] *npl* a bitter magnesium salt with cathartic properties. [*Epsom*, England.]

Epstein-Barr virus [ep´stīn bar vī´res] *n* a virus which causes glandular fever and is marked persistent weakness. [From M A *Epstein* and Y M *Barr*, British virologists.]

equable [ek´wȧ-bl or ēk´-] *adj* uniform; free from extremes (eg of climate); of even temper, not easily annoyed or agitated.—*n* **equabil´ity**.—*adv* **e´quably**. [L *aequābilis—aequāre—aequus*, equal.]

equal [ē´kwal] *adj* the same in amount, size, number, or value; *(with* **to***)* strong enough for; impartial, regarding or affecting all objects in the same way; tranquil of mind; capable of meeting a task or situation.—*n* one that is equal.—*vt* to be equal to, esp to be identical in value; to make or do something equal to;—*pr p* **equaling** or **equalling**; *pt p* **equaled** or **equalled**.—*vt* **equalize** to make equal; to compensate for; to adjust or correct the frequency (of an electric signal).—*n* **equalization**.—*adj* **equalitarian** egalitarian.—*ns* **equalitarianism; equality**, sameness in size, number, value, rank, etc.—*adv* **equally**.—*vt* **equate**, to make, treat, or regard as comparable;—*vi* to correspond as equal.—*n* **equation**, an act of equaling; the state of being equal; a usu. formal statement of equivalence (as in logical and mathematical expressions) with the relations denoted by the sign =; an expression representing a chemical reaction by means of chemical symbols.—**Equal Rights Amendment**, a proposed amendment to the US Constitution providing for equal rights of both sexes. [L *aequālis—aequāre*, to make equal—*aequus*, equal.]

equanimity [ē-kwa-nim´i-ti, e-] *n* composure. [L *aequanimitās—aequus*, equal, *animus*, the mind.]

equator [e-kwā´tȯr] *n (geog)* an imaginary circle passing round the globe, equidistant from N and S poles and dividing the earth's surface into the northern and southern hemispheres.—*adj* **equatō´rial**. [LL *aequator*—L *aequus*, equal.]

equerry [ek´swė-ri] *n* an officer in charge of the horses of a prince or nobleman; a personal attendant of a male member of the British royal family. [Fr *écurie*—Low L *scūria*, a stable.]

equestrian [e-kwes´tri-ȧn] *adj* pertaining to horsemanship; on horseback.—*n* one who rides on horseback;—*fem* (sham Fr) **equestrienne´**. [L *equester, equestris—eques*, a horseman—*equus*, a horse.]

equi- [ē´kwi-] equal [L *aequus*, equal], eg:—*adjs* **equian´gular**, having equal angles; **equidis´tant**, equally distant (from); **equilat´eral**, having all sides equal.

equilibrium [ēk-wi-lib´ri-um] *n* balance; a state of even balance; a state in which opposing forces or tendencies neutralize each other.—*pl* **-riums** or **-ria**.—**equil´ibrist** [or -lib´-, or -līb´-], one who does balancing tricks. [L *aequilibrium—aequus*, equal, *lībra*, balance.]

equine, equinal [e´kwīn, e-kwīn´ȧl] *adj* of a horse. [L *equīnus-equus*, a horse.]

equinox [ek´wi-noks, ēk´wi-noks] *n* the time when the sun crosses the equator, making the night equal in length to the day, about March 21 and September 23.—*adj* **equinoc´tial** [-shȧl], pertaining to the equinoxes, to the time of these, or to the regions about the equator.—*n* the equator or equinoctial line; an equinoctial storm. [L *aequus*, equal, *nox, noctis*, night.]

equip [e-kwip´] *vt* to supply with everything needed;—*pr p* **equipp´ing**; *pt p* **equipped´**.—*ns* **e´quipāge**, a horse-drawn carriage and attendants; **equip´ment**, the act of equipping; the state of being equipped; things used in equipping. [Fr *équiper*, prob—ON *skipa*, to set in order—*skip*, a ship.]

equipoise [ek´wi-poiz] *n* a state of balance; a counterpoise.—Also *vt*. [L *aequus*, equal, and **poise**.]

equipollent [ē-kwi-pol´ėnt] *adj* having equal power or force; equivalent.—*n* **equipoll´ence**. [L *aequus*, equal, *pollens, pollentis, pr p* of *pollēre*, to be able.]

equiponderate [ē-kwi-pon´dėr-āt] *vi* to be equal in weight; to balance.—*n* **equipon´derance**.—*adjs* **equipon´derant**. [L *aequus*, equal, *pondus, ponderis*, weight.]

equitation [ek-wi-tā´sh(ȯ)n] *n* the art of riding on horseback. [L *equitāre*, to ride—*equus*, a horse.]

equity [ek´wi-ti] *n* fairness; a legal system developed into a body of rules supplementing the common law; the value of a property or of an interest in it in excess of the claims against it.—*adj* **e´quitable**, fair; pertaining to equity in the legal sense.—*n* **eq´uitable-ness**.—*adv* **eq´uitably**. [OFr *equité*—L *aequitās, -ātis—aequus*, equal.]

equivalent [e-kwiv´ȧ-lėnt] *adj* equal in value, power, meaning, etc.; virtually identical, esp in effect or function.—*n* a thing equivalent.—*n* **equiv´alence**.—*adv* **equiv´alently**.—**equivalent weight**, *(chem)* the weight of a substance in grams which combines with one mole of a monovalent atom or group, eg with one gram of hydrogen. [Fr,—L *aequus*, equal, *valens, valentis*, pr p of *valēre*, to be worth.]

equivocal [e-kwiv´o-kȧl] *adj* ambiguous; uncertain; suspicious; questionable.—*adv* **equiv´ocally**.—*n* **equiv´ocalness**.—*vi* **equiv´ocāte**, to use equivocal words in order to mislead.—**equivocā´tion; equiv´ocātor**. [L *aequus*, equal, *vox, vōcis*, the voice, a word.]

era [ē´ra] *n* a period typified by some special feature; a chronological order or system of notation reckoned from a given date as basis; a main division of geological time, subdivided into **periods** *(see this entry)*. [Late L *aera*, a number, orig counters, pieces of copper used in counting, pl of *aes*, copper.]

ERA abbrev for Equal Rights Amendment.

eradicate [e-rad´i-kāt, or ē] *vt* to pull up by the roots; to extirpate.—*adjs* **erad´icable, eradicative**, that can be eradicated.—*ns* **erad´icā´tion**, the act of eradicating; state of being eradicated; **eradicator**. [L *ērādicāre, -ātum*, to root out—*ē*, from *rādix, -īcis*, a root.]

erase [e-rāz´, e-rās´] *vt* to rub or scratch out (as written words).—**erā´ser**, that which erases; **erā´sure** [-zhùr, -zhūr], a rubbing out. [L *ērādere*—*ē* from, *rādĕre, rāsum*, to scrape.]
erbium [ûr´bi-ùm] *n* a metallic element (symbol Er; at wt 167.3, at no 68), of the rare-earth group. [Name formed from Ytt*erby* in Sweden.]
ere [ār] *prep* and *conj*, before. [OE *ǣr*; cf Du *eer*.]
erect [e-rekt´] *adj* upright; not leaning or lying down.—*vt* to build; to set upright.—*n* **erec´tion**, construction; the turgid state of a previously flaccid body when it becomes engorged with blood.—*adv* **erect´ly**.—*n* **erect´ness**. [L *ērectus, ērigĕre*, to set upright—*ē*, from, *regĕre*, to direct.]
eremite [er´e-mit] *n* a hermit, esp a religious recluse. *adj* **eremitic (-al)**.—*n* **erimitism**. [LL *erēmīta*—Gr *erēmītēs*—*erēmos*, desert.]
erg [ûrg] *n* the unit for measuring work in the centimeter-gram-second system. See **joule**. [Gr *ergon*, work.]
ergo [ûr´gō] *adv* therefore. [L *ergō*.]
ergonomics [ėr-go-nom´iks] *n* biotechnology.
ergosterol [ēr-gäs´te-rėl] *n* a steroid alcohol ($C_{28}H_{44}O$), that occurs esp on yeasts, molds, and ergot and that is converted to Vitamin D by ultraviolet radiation. [International Scientific Vocabulary.]
ergot [ûr´got] *n* a disease of rye and other cereals caused by a fungus; this fungus; a medicine derived from an ergot fungus.—*n* **er´gotism**, toxic condition caused by eating food contaminated by ergot fungus or chronic excessive use of an ergot drug. [Fr]
erica [er-ik´al] *n* any of a large genus (*Erica*) of the heath family of low much-branched evergreen shrubs.—*adjs* **ericaceous**, of, relating, or being of the heath family; **ericoid**, resembling heath. [L—Gr *ereikē*, heath.]
Erie [ēr´ē] *n* a member of an Amerindian people of the Lake Erie region; the language of the Erie people.
ermine [ûr´min] *n* the weasel (genus *Mustela*) in its winter coat; the white fur of the winter coat; a rank or office whose official robe is edged with ermine.—*adj* **er´mined**, adorned with ermine. [OFr *ermine*, perh from L (*mus*) *Armēnius*, lit mouse of Armenia, whence it was brought to Rome.]
erne [ûrn] *n* the eagle, esp the white-tailed sea eagle (*Haliätus albicilla*). [OE *earn*; cf ON *örn*.]
erode [e-rōd´] *vt* to eat or wear away gradually.—*n* **erō´sion** [e-rō´zh(ó)n], the action or process of eroding.—*adj* **erō´sive**. [L *ē*, from, *rōdĕre, rōsum*, to gnaw.]
erotic [e-rot´ik] *adj* of sexual love.—*n* **erotica**, literary or artistic works with an erotic quality or theme.—*vt* **erot´icize**, to make erotic. [Gr *Erōs, -rōtos*, Greek god corresponding to Cupid.]
err [ûr] *vi* to be or do wrong.—*adjs* **errat´ic, -al**, capricious; irregular; eccentric, odd.—*adv* **errat´ically**.—*ns* **errat´ic**, a stone or boulder transported by ice and deposited far from its original source; **errā´tum**, an error in writing or printing; —*pl* **errā´ta**, a page bearing list of corrigenda. —*adj* **errō´neous**, wrong; mistaken.—*adv* **errō´neously**.—*ns* **errō´neousness; err´or**, (*arch*) wandering; a blunder or mistake; wrong-doing. [Fr *errer*—L *errāre*, to stray; cog with Ger *irren*, and *irre*, astray.]
errand [er´ànd] *n* a short journey on which one is sent to say or do something on behalf of another; the object of this journey.—**a fool's errand** *see* **fool**. [OE *ǣrende*; ON *eyrindi*.]
errant [er´ànt] *adj* wandering; going astray, esp doing wrong; moving aimlessly.—*n* **err´antry**, a wandering state, esp in search of chivalrous adventure. [Fr,—L *errans, errantis*, pr p of *errāre*.]
ersatz [er-zäts´] *adj* substitute; synthetic. [From a Ger noun meaning compensation, replacement.]
Erse [ers, ûrs] *n* Scottish Gaelic; Irish Gaelic.
erst [ûrst] *adv* at first; formerly.—*adv* **erst´while**, formerly.—*adj* former. [OE *ǣrest*, superl of *ǣr*. See **ere**.]
erubescent [er-(y)ōō-bes´ėnt] *adj* growing red; blushing.—*n* **erubes´cence**. [L *ērubescĕre*, to grow red—*ē*-, intent, and *rubescĕre*—*rubēre*, to be red.]
eruct [e-rukt´, -āt] *vt* to belch.—*n* **eructā´tion** (*ē*-). [L *ēructāre, -ātum*—*ē*, from, *ructāre*, to belch forth.]
erudite [er´(y)ŏŏ-dīt] *adj* learned.—*adv* **er´uditely**.—*n* **erudĭ´tion**, state of being learned; knowledge gained by study. [L *ērudīre, ērudītum*, to free from roughness—*ē*, from *rudis*, unformed.]
erupt [e-rupt´] *vi* to burst forth; to break out into a rash.—*n* **erup´tion**, a breaking or bursting forth (eg of lava from a volcano, of strong feeling); that which bursts forth; a breaking out of spots on the skin.—*adj* **erupt´ive**, breaking forth; attended by or producing eruption; produced by eruption.—*adv* **eruptible**. [L *ērumpĕre, ēruptum*—*ē*, from, *rumpĕre*, to break.]
erysipelas [er-i-sip´e-làs] *n* an acute bacterial (streptoccal) disease, marked by a fever and severe skin inflammation, esp around the nose and lips. [Gr; prob from the root of *erythros*, red, *pella*, skin.]
erythema [er-i-thē´mà] *n* abnormal redness of the skin due to capillary congestion (as in inflammation).—*adjs* **erythematic, erythem´atous**. [Gr *erythēma*—*enythainein*, to redden—*erythros*, red.]
erythrocyte [e-rith´ō-sīt] *n* a red blood cell of vertebrates that transports oxygen and carbon dioxide.
escalade [es-ka-lād´] *n* the scaling of the walls of a fortress by means of ladders.—*vt* to scale; to mount and enter by means of ladders.—**escalator clause**, a clause in an agreement providing for upward or downward adjustment (as of prices or wages).—**es´calate**, to ascend, descend on an escalator; to increase rapidly in scale or intensity.—Also *vt*.—**escalā´tion; es´calātor**, a power-driven set of stairs arranged to ascend or descend continuously. [Fr—Sp *escalada*—*escala*, a ladder—L *scāla*.]
escallop [es-kal´óp] *n see* **scallop**.
escape [es-kāp´] *vt* to get clear away from (eg custody); to evade (eg punishment); to go unnoticed (by eye or ear, etc.); to elude the memory; of words or sounds, to issue inadvertently from (a person, lips).—*vi* to emerge into or gain freedom; to flee; to leak (eg of gas).—*n* act of escaping; a means of escaping; flight; a leakage; flight from reality.—*adj* **escāp´able**, that can be avoided, evaded.—*ns* **escapāde´**, a mischievous adventure; **escāpe´ment**, a device in a timepiece by which the motions of the wheels and of the pendulum wheel are accommodated to each other; the mechanism that controls the movement of a typewriter carriage; **escāp´ism**, desire or tendency to escape from reality into fantasy; **escāp´ist**, one who seeks escape, esp from reality (also *adj*).—**escape artist**, one (as a showman or criminal) unusually adept at escaping from confinement **escape clause**, clause in a contract which renders the contract void under specified conditions; **escapee**, one that escaped, esp an escaped prisoner; **escape hatch**, an opening through which one can escape (as from a space vehicle); **escape mechanism**, a mode of behavior or thinking adopted to evade unpleasant facts or responsibilities; **escape velocity**, the minimum velocity that a moving body (as a rocket) must have to escape from the gravitational field of the earth and move outward into space.—*ns* **escapology**, the art of escaping for entertainment; **escapologist**. [OFr *escaper* (Fr *échapper*)—L *cappā* (lit) 'out of one's cape or cloak.']
escargot [es-kar-gō´] *n* a snail prepared for food. [Fr—MF—escargol.]
escarole [es´kar-ol] *n* endive.
escarp [es-kärp´] *n* a steep slope or scarp; (*fort*) the side of the ditch next the rampart.—*vt* to make into an escarp.—*n* **escarp´ment**, the precipitous side of a hill or rock, an escarp. [Fr *escarper*, to cut down steep.]
eschatology [es-ka-tol´o-ji] *n* the doctrine of the last or final things, as death, judgement, the state after death. [Gr *eschatos*, last, *logos*, a discourse.]
escheat [es-chēt´] *n* property that falls to the state for want of an heir, or by forfeiture.—*vi* to fall to the state. [OFr *eschete*—*escheoir* (Fr *échoir*)—L *ex*, from, *cadĕre*, to fall.]
eschew [es-chōō´] *vt* to shun on moral grounds. [OFr *eschever*; cog with Ger *scheuen*, to shun.]
eschscholzia, eschscholtzia [e-sholt´zē-a] *n* a genus of hardy annual and perennial herbs of the poppy family with bright showy flowers; the California poppy.
escort [es´kört] *n* a person or persons, ship or ships, etc. accompanying for protection, guidance, custody, or merely courtesy.—*vt* **escort´**, to attend as escort. [Fr *escorte*—It *scorta*—*scorgere*, to guide—L *ex*, out, *corrigĕre*, to set right.]
escritoire [es-kri-twär´] *n* a writing-desk. [Fr *escritoire*—Low L *scrīptōrium*—L *scrībĕre, scrīptum*, to write.]
escrow [es´krō] *n* a deed, bond, or other written agreement put in charge of a third person until certain conditions are fulfilled. [MF *escroue*, scroll.]
escudo [es-kōōdō] *n* unit of money in Chile and in Portugal. [Sp and Port from L *scutum*, a shield.]
esculent [es´kū-lėnt] *adj* fit to be used for food by man.—*n* something that is eatable. [L *esculentus*, eatable—*esca*, food—*edĕre*, to eat.]
escutcheon [es´kuch´ón] *n* a shield on which a coat of arms is represented; a family shield; the part of a vessel's stern bearing her name; a plate round an opening, eg a key-hole plate. [OFr *escuchon*—L *scūtum*, a shield.]
Esdras [ez´dres] *n* (Bible) Ezra and Nehemiah in the Douay Version of the Old Testament.
Eskimo [es´ki-mō] *n* a group of peoples of northern Canada, Greenland, Alaska, and eastern Siberia; a member of this group; their language.—Also *adj*.—*pl* **Eskimo** or **Eskimos**.—Also **Esquimau**.—*n* **Eskimo dog**, a breed of broad-chested dog with a long shaggy outer coat and soft dense woolly inner coat; a sled dog of American origin. [Algonquian].
esophagus [e-sof´a-gus] *n* a muscular tube connecting the mouth and stomach.
esoteric [es-o-ter´ik] *adj* understood by a select few; secret; private. [Gr *esōterikos*—*esōterō*, comp of *esō, eisō*, within.]
ESP *See* **extra-sensory**.
espadrille [es´pa-dril] *n* a flat shoe usu. having a fabric upper and rope soles. [Fr]
espalier [es-pal´yėr] *n* a plant (as a fruit tree) trained to grow flat against a support. [Fr,—It *spalliera*, a support for the shoulders—*spalla*, a shoulder.]
esparto [es-pär´tō] *n* either of two Spanish and Algerian grasses (*Stipa tenacissima* and *Lygeum spartum*) used esp to make cordage, shoes, and paper. [Sp,—L *spartum*—Gr *sparton*, a kind of rope.]
especial [es-pesh´(à)l] *adj* particular; special.—*adv* **espec´ially**. [OFr,—L *speciālis*—*speciēs*, species.]
Esperanto [es-pėr-an´tō] *n* an auxiliary international language. [From the pseudonym of L L Zamenhof, the inventor.]
espionage [es´pyon-äzh, es´pi-ó-nij, es-pī´ó-nij] *n* spying; use of spies. [Fr *espionnage*—*espionner*—*espion*, a spy.]
esplanade [es-pla-nād´] *n* any level space for walking or driving, esp along a shore. [Fr,—Sp *esplanada*—L *explānāre*—*ex*, out, *plānus*, flat.]
espouse [es-powz´] *vt* to give or take in marriage; to support or embrace, as a

cause.—*n* **espous´al**, the act of espousing, adoption, support (of a cause); (*pl*) a contract or mutual promise of marriage. [OFr *espouser* (Fr *épouser*)—L *sponsāre—spondēre, sponsum*, to vow.]

espresso [es-pres´ō] *n* coffee brewed by forcing steam through finely-ground darkly roasted coffee beans. [It, pressed.]

esprit [es-prē] *n* wit; liveliness.—**esprit de corps**, the common spirit existing in the members of a group. [Fr *esprit*, spirit, *corps*, body.]

espy [es-pī´] *vt* to catch sight of. [OFr *espier*.]

Esquimau [es´ki-mō] (*pl* **Esquimaux**, *es´ki-mōz*). *See* **Eskimo**.

esquire [es-kwīr´, sometimes es´-] *n* a title of dignity next below a knight; a general title of respect in addressing letters. Abbrev **Esq.** [OFr *esquier*—L *scūtārius—scūtum*, a shield.]

essay [es´ā] *n* a trial; an attempt; a written composition usu. dealing with a subject from a limited or personal point of view.—*vt* **essay´**, to try, to attempt;—*pr p* **essay´ing**; *pt p* **essayed´**.—*n* **ess´ayist**, a writer of essays.—**essay question**, an examination question that requires an answer in a sentence, paragraph, or short composition; **essay test** a test made up of essay questions. [OFr *essai*—LL *exagium*, a weighing.]

essence [es´ėns] *n* that which makes a thing what it is; a substance distilled or extracted from another substance (as a plant or drug) and having the special qualities of the original substance; a perfume.—*adj* **essen´tial** [-shȧl], relating to, constituting, or containing the essence; indispensable, important in the highest degree.—*n* an absolutely necessary element or quality.—**essential´ity**, the quality of being essential; an essential quality or element. —**essential amino acid**, an amino acid (as lysine) that is required for normal health and growth, is manufactured in the body in insufficient quantities if at all and is usu. supplied by dietary protein.—*n* **essentialness**.—*adv* **essen´tiālly**, in essence, characteristically. [Fr,—L *essentia—essens, -entis*, assumed pr p of *esse*, to be.]

Essene [is-sēn, es-sēn´] *n* a member of a monastic brotherhood of Jews in Palestine from the 2d century BC to the 2d century AD.—*adjs* **Essenian; Essenic**.—*n* **Essenism**.

establish [es-tab´lish] *vt* to set up (as a system, business, etc.) permanently; to settle (a person in office); get generally accepted; place beyond dispute as of a custom, belief; place beyond dispute as of a custom, belief; to prove as a fact.—*n* **establishment**, act of establishing; a fixed state; that which is established.—*ns* **the Establishment**, social group exercising power by virtue of traditional superiority and in the interest of maintaining the status quo; **established church**, a church recognized by law as the official church of the nation and supported by civil authority. [OFr *establir*, pr p *establissant*—L *stabilīre—stabilis*, firm—*stāre*, to stand.]

estate [es-tāt´] *n* condition or rank; total possessions; property, esp landed property; a social or political class (eg the three estates of nobility, clergy and commons).—**estate tax**, an excise in the form of a percentage of the net estate that is levied on the privilege of an owner of property in transmitting his property to others after his death.—**fourth estate** *see* **fourth; real estate** *see* **real**. [OFr *estat* (Fr *état*)—L *status*. See **status**.]

esteem [es-tēm´] *vt* to set a high value on; to consider or think.—*n* high estimation, favorable opinion.—*adj* **es´timable**, that can be estimated, valued; deserving a good opinion.—*adv* **es´timably**.—*vt* **es´timate**, to judge the worth of; to calculate.—*n* judgement or opinion of the worth or size of (anything); a preliminary calculation of cost.—*n* **estimā´tion**, a reckoning; judgment; esteem, honor. [Fr *estimer*—L *aestimāre*.]

ester [es´ter] *n* (*chem*) a compound which can be hydrolyzed to an acid and an alcohol or phenol, eg fats and major constituents of fruit essences. [Ger *essig*, vinegar, and *äther*, ether.]

Esther [es´ter] *n* (*Bible*) 17th book of the Old Testament telling the story of Esther, who became queen to Xerxes and saved the Jews from massacre, which is commemorated annually in the feast of Purim.

esthetic *see* **aesthetic**.

estimate. See **esteem, estival, estivate, estivation** *see* **aestival, aestivate, aestivation**.

Estonian [e-stōn´ē-en] *n* a member of a Finno-Ugric, speaking people of Estonia; the Finno-Ugric language of the Estonian people.—Also *adj*.

estrange [es-trānj´] *vt* to alienate the affections or confidence of.—*adj* **estranged´**.—*n* **estrange´ment**. [OFr *estranger*—L *extrāneus*.]

estrogen [es´trė-jen] *n* a substance (as a hormone) that stimulates the development of female characteristics and promotes estrus.—*adjs* **estrogen´ic**, promoting estrus; of relating to, or caused by estrogen.—*n* **es´trus** or **es´trum**, a regularly occurring state of sexual excitability during which the female of most mammals is capable of conceiving and will accept the male.—*adj* **estrous, estrual**.—**estrous cycle**, the phenomenon of the correlated endocrine and generative systems of a female mammal from the onset of one period of estrus to the next. [L *oestrus*.]

estuary [es´tū-ȧr-i] *n* an arm of the sea at the mouth of a river.—*adjs* **estuarial, es´tūarine**. [L *aestuārium—aestus*, burning, commotion, tide.]

étagere, etagere [a-ta-jer´] *n* an elaborate whatnot often with a mirrored back. [Fr]

et cetera [et set´ėr-a] and so forth; usually written **etc.** or **&c.** [L *et*. and, *cētera*, the rest.]

etch [ech] *vti* to make lines on (as metal or glass) usu. by the action of acid; to produce (as a design) by etching; to delineate clearly.—*n* **etch´ing**, the act, art or process of etching; the design produced on or print made from an etched plate. [Ger *ätzen*, to corrode by acid; from same root as Ger *essen*, to eat.]

eternal [e- or ē-tûr´nȧl] *adj* without beginning or end; everlasting; unchangeable; seemingly endless.—*vt* **eter´nize** [or ē´tėr-nīz], to make eternal; to immortalize; to prolong indefinitely.—*adv* **eter´nally**.—*n* **eter´nity**, eternal duration; the state or time after death.—**the Eternal**, God. [Fr *éternel*—L *aeternus—aevum*, a period of time, an age.]

ethane [ē-thān] *n* a colorless odorless gaseous hydrocarbon found in natural gas and used esp as fuel. [See **ether**.]

ethonal [eth´a-nl] *n* alcohol.—Also **ethyl alcohol**.

ether [ēthėr] *n* (*chem*) a light flammable liquid used as an anesthetic or solvent; the upper regions of space; the invisible elastic substance supposed to be distributed evenly through all space.—*vt* **etherize**, to treat or anesthetize with ether; to make numb as if by anesthetizing.—*adj* **ethē´real**, consisting of ether; heavenly; airy; spirit-like.—*vt* **ethē´realize**, to convert into ether, or the fluid ether; to render spirit-like. [L,—Gr *aithēr—aithein*, to burn, light up.]

ethics [eth´iks] *n sing or pl* study of standards of right and wrong; system of conduct or behavior, moral principles.—*adj* **eth´ical**.—*adv* **eth´ically**. [Gr *ēthikos—ēthos*, custom, character.]

Ethiopian [ē-thi-ō´pi-ȧn] *adj* of *Ethiopia*.—*n* a native or inhabitant of Ethiopia.—*adj* **Ethiopic**, of the Christian liturgical language of Ethiopia.—Also *n* of Ethiopia. [Gr *Aithiops—aithein*, to burn, *ōps*, face.]

ethnic, -al [eth´nik, -ȧl] *adj* of races or large groups of people classed according to common traits and customs.—*ns* **ethnobiology**, a branch of biology dealing with the relation between usu. primitive human societies and the plants and animals of their environment.—*adj* **ethnocentric**, having race as a central interest; characterized by the attitude that one's group is superior.—*n* **ethnography**, ethnology, esp descriptive anthropology.—*adj* **ethnograph´ic(al)**.—*ns* **ethnographer; ethnol´ogy**, the science that deals with races of people, their origin, distribution, characteristics, customs, and culture; anthropology dealing with comparison and analysis of cultures.—*adj* **ethnolog´ical**.—*adv* **ethnolog´ically**.—*n* **ethnol´ogist**.—*ns* **ethnomusicology**, a study of the music of non-European cultures; **ethnoscience**, the nature lore (as folk taxonomy of plants and animals) of primitive peoples. [Gr *ethnos*, a nation, *graphē*, writing, *logos*, discourse.]

ethology [eth-ol´ōjē´] *n* a branch of knowledge dealing with human ethos and its formation and evolution; the scientific and objective study of animal behavior.—*n* **ethos**, the distinguishing character, sentiment, moral nature, or guiding beliefs of a person, group, or institution. [Gr *ethos*, custom, character.]

ethyl [eth´il] *n* the radical (C_2H_5) from which common alcohol (C_2H_5OH) and ether are derived; the abbreviation for tetraethyllead, a gasoline additive.—**ethyl alcohol**, alcohol. [**ether** + Gr *hȳlē*, matter.]

ethylene [eth´il-ēn] *n* a colorless flammable gaseous unsaturated hydrogen C_2H_4 found in coal gas or obtained by pyrolysis of petroleum hydrocarbons. [International Scientific Vocabulary, ethyl.]

etiolate [ē´-ti-o-lāt] *vt* to cause (as a plant) to grow pale from want of light; to make pale and sickly; to take away the natural vigor (as by pampering).—*vi* to become pale.—*n* **etiolā´tion**. [Fr *étoiler*, to become pale, to grow into stubble—*éteule*, stubble—L *stipula*, a stalk.]

etiology [ē-ti-ol´o-ji] *n* the study of causes.

etiquette [et´i-ket, or -ket´] *n* the forms of conduct or behavior prescribed by custom or authority to be observed in social, official or professional life. [Fr *étiquette*. See **ticket**.]

Etruscan [e-trus´kȧn] of or pertaining to Etruria, a region of ancient Italy west of the Tiber and the Apennines, or to its people or their language or civilization. [L *Etruscus*.]

et seq and the following one. [L *et sequentia*.]

étude [ā-tüd´] *n* (*mus*) a composition intended either to train or to test the player's technical skill. [Fr, study.]

etui [ā-twē´] *n* a small ornamental case. [Fr]

etymology [et-i-mol´oj-i] *n* the science or investigation of the derivation and original meaning of words; the source and history (of a word).—*adj* **etymolog´ical** [-loj´-].—*adv* **etymolog´ically**.—*n* **etymol´ogist** [-jist]. [Through OFr and L from Gr *etymologia—etymos*, true, *logos*, a discourse.]

eucalyptus [ū-kȧ-lip´tus] *n* any of a genus (*Eucalyptus*) of mostly Australian evergreen trees wholly grown for useful products.—Also *gum tree*.—*n* **eucalyptus oil**, oil distilled from leaves of eucalyptus and used medicinally and industrially.—*pl* **eucalyp´tī, eucalyp´tuses**, Latinised from Gr *eu*, well, *kalyptos*, covered.]

Eucharist [u´kä-rist] *n* the sacrament of communion; (*Christian Science*) communion with God.—*adj* **eucharist´ic**, [Gr *eucharistia*, thanksgiving—*eu*, well, and *charizesthai*, to show favor—*charis*, grace, thanks.]

euchre [ū´kėr] *n* a card game in which the side naming the trump must take three tricks out of five to win.

Euclidean geometry [yōō-kli´dē-an] the study of points, lines, and planes (which are not defined, but are assumed to be intuitively given) and their relations as defined by axioms. [*Euclid*, a geometrician of Alexandria c. 300 B.C.]

eugenics [ū-jen´iks] *npl* science of improving the human race by selective breeding. [Gr *eugenēs*, of good stock.]

Euler circles [oy´ler ser-klz] *npl* concentric or enclosing circles to show relations between sets and subsets. [Leonhard D. Euler, Swiss mathematician (1707–83).]

eulogy [ū´lo-ji] *n* a speech or writing in warm praise of (someone, occasionally something—*with* **on**).—*vt* **eu´logize**, to praise.—*n* **eu´logist**, one who praises or extols another.—*adj* **eulogist´ic**, full of praise.—*adv* **eulogist´ically**. [Late L *eulogium*—Gr *eulogion* (classical *eulogia*)—*eu*, well, *logos*, a speaking.]

eunuch [ū´nuk] *n* a castrated man, esp one in charge of a harem. [Gr *eunouchos*—*eunē*, a bed, *echein*, to have (charge of).]

euphemism [ū´fem-izm] *n* a mild or inoffensive term employed to express what is disagreeable; the use of such a term.—*adj* **euphemist´ic**. [Gr *euphēmismos*—*euphēmizein*, to speak words of good omen—*eu*, well, *phanai*, to speak.]

euphony [ū´fo-ni] *n* agreeableness of sound; pleasing to the ear.—*adjs* **euphon´ic, -al, euphō´nious**.—*adv* **euphō´niously**. [Gr *euphōnia*—*eu*, well, *phonē*, sound.]

euphonium [u-fōn´ē-um] *n* a brass musical instrument larger than the cornet with its oval bell pointed backwards, used in brass bands.

euphorbia [ū-for´bē-a] *n* any of a large genus (*Euphorbia*) of plants that have a milky juice and flowers lacking a calyx; a spurge.

euphoria [ū-fō´ri-å, -fö´] *n* a feeling of well-being.—*adj* **euphoric** [-for´]. [Gr *euphŏriā*.]

euphuism [u´fū-izm] *n* any affected elegant style of writing; flowery, artificial language.—*n* **eu´phuist**.—*adj* **euphuist´ic**. [Gr *euphyēs*, graceful.]

Eurasian [ūr-ā-zh(y)ån, -shån] *adj* of Mongolian and Caucasian parents; of Europe and Asia (Eurasia) taken as one continent.—*Also n.*

eureka [ū-rēk´a] *interjection* used to express triumph on a discovery. [Gr *heurēka*, I have found it.]

eurhyth´mics [ūr-rith´miks] *npl* the art of representing musical harmony by physical gestures. [Gr *eu*, well, *rhythmos*, rhythm.]

European [ū-ro-pē´an] *adj* belonging to *Europe*.—*n* a native or inhabitant of Europe; a person of European descent; a white person.—*ns* **European chafer**, an Old World beetle (*Amphimallon majalis*) now established in eastern N America where its larva destroys the roots of turf grasses; **European Common Market**, popular name for the European Economic Community whose members aim to eliminate all obstacles to the free movement of goods, services, capital and labor between the member countries and to set up a common external commercial policy, agricultural policy, and transport policy; **European plan**, a hotel plan where the daily rates cover only the cost of the room.—**European Economic Community** (EEC) European Common Market.

europium [ūrō´pi-ům] *n* a metallic element (symbol Eu; at wt 152.0 at no 63), a member of the rare-earth group. [*Europe*.]

eustachian tube [u-sta´shē-en toob] *n* a tube connecting the inner cavity of the ear with the throat and equalizing pressure on both sides of the eardrum. [Bartolommeo *Eustachio*, Italian physician, died 1574.]

euthanasia [ū-than-ā´zi-a] *n* the act or practice of putting to death painlessly, esp in order to release from incurable suffering. [Gr *euthanasia*—*eu*, well, *thanatos*, death.]

euthenics [u-then´iks] *n* a science dealing with the improvement of human qualities by changes in the environment.

evacuate [e-vak´ū-āt] *vti* to make empty; to discharge wastes from the body; to leave empty, to vacate.—**evacuā´tion**, act of evacuating; that which is discharged; **evac´uātor; evac´uēē**, a person removed in an evacuation. [L *ē*, from, *vacuāre*, *-ātum*, to empty—*vacuus*, empty.]

evade [e-vād, ē-vād´] *vt* to manage to avoid, esp by dexterity or slyness. [Fr *évader*—L *ēvādĕre*—*ē*, from *vādĕre*, to go.]

evaluate [ē, or e-val´ū-āt] *vt* to fix the value of.—*n* **evaluā´tion**. [Fr *évaluer*.]

evanescent [ev-ån-es´ėnt] *adj* fleeting; vanishing.—*n* **evanes´cence**.—*adv* **evanes´cently**. [L *ēvānescens, -entis*—*ē*, from, *vānescĕre*, to vanish—*vānus*, empty.]

evangel [e-van´jėl] *n* gospel; evangelist.—*adjs* **evangelical, evangel'ic** [e-, ē-van-jel´ik-ål], of, according to, being in agreement with the Christian gospel esp as presented in the four Gospels; Protestant; emphasizing salvation by faith through personal conversion, the authority of Scripture, and the importance of preaching as contrasted with ritual; low church.—*adv* **evangel´ically**.—*n* **evangel´icalism**, evangelical principles.—*vt* **evan´gelize**, to make acquainted with the gospel.—*vi* to preach the gospel from place to place.—*n* **evan´gelist**, one who evangelizes; one of the writers of the four gospels.—*adj* **evangelis´tic**. [LL *ēvangelium*—Gr *euangelion*—*eu*, well, *angellein*, to bring news.]

evaporate [e-vap´ȯr-āt] *vti* to change into a vapor; to remove water from; to give off moisture; to vanish; to disappear.—*adj* **evap´orable**.—*n* **evaporā´tion**. [L *ē*, from *vapōrāre*, *-ātum*—*vapor*, vapor.]

evasion [e-vā´zh(ȯ)n] *n* act of eluding; a means of evading, esp an equivocal statement used in evading.—*adj* **evā´sive**, that evades or seeks to evade; not straightforward.—*adv* **evā´sively**.—*n* **evā´siveness**. [Fr *évasion*—LL *ēvāsiō, -ōnis*—L *ēvādĕre*. See **evade**.]

eve see **even**².

even¹ [ēv´n] *adj* level, flat; smooth; regular, equal; balanced; fully revenged; exact; divisible by 2.—*vt* to make or become even.—*adv* exactly; precisely; fully, quite; at the very time; used as an intensive to emphasize the identity of something (*he looked content, even happy*), to indicate something unexpected (*she refused even to look at him*), or to stress the comparative degree (*she did even better*).—*adv* **ev´enly**.—*adjs* **ev´enhand´ed**, fair, impartial;—*n* **ev´enness**. [OE *efen*; Du, *even*, Ger *eben*.]

even² [ēv´n] *n* (poet.) evening; (*obs* or *dial.*) eve.—*Also* **e´en** [ēn].—*ns* **eve** [ēv], the night, or the whole day, before a festival; the time just preceding an event; (*poet.*) evening; **evening** [ēv´ning], the close of the day and early part of the night.—*ns* **evening primrose** [prim´rōz], any of several plants of the genus *Oenethera*, esp one with yellow flowers opening in the evening; **evening star**, a bright planet (as Venus) seen in the western sky at sunset; a planet that rises before midnight; **e´vensong** vespers; evening prayers; **ev´entide** the time of evening. [OE *æfen, æfnung*.]

event [e-vent´] *n* something that happens; a social occasion; contingency; any occurrence; a contest in a program of sports.—*adjs* **event´ful**, full of events; momentous; **event´ūal**, happening as a consequence; final.—*n* **event´ūal´ity**, a contingency.—*adv* **event´ūally**, finally, at length.—*vi* **event´ūāte**, to turn out. [L *ēventus*—*ēvenīre*—*ē*, from *venīre*, to come.]

ever [ev´ėr] *adv* always; at any time; in any case.—*adj* **ev´ergreen**, having foliage that remains green.—*n*.—*adj* **everlast´ing**, enduring forever; eternal.—*n* eternity; a plant whose flowers may be dried without loss of form or color.—*adv* **everlast´ingly**.—*n* **everlast´ingness**.—*adv* **evermore´**, forever. [OE æfre, always.]

every [ev´ėr-i, ev´ri] *adj* being one of the total.—*prons* **ev´erybody, ev´eryone**, every person.—*adj* **ev´eryday**, daily; common, usual; pertaining to weekdays, not Sunday.—*pron* **ev´erything**, all things; all.—*n* **Ev´eryman**, the hero of an old morality play, representing mankind.—*adv* **ev´erywhere**, in every place.—**every now and then, every now and again**, or **every so often**, at intervals; occasionally. [OE *æfre*, ever, and *ælc*, each.]

evict [ē-, or e-vikt´] *vt* to expel (a tenant) from land or from a building by lawful methods; to expel.—*n* **evic´tion**, [L ēvictus, pt p of *ēvincĕre* to overcome.]

evident [ev´i-dėnt] *adj* easy to see or understand.—*adv* **ev´idently**.—*n* **ev´idence**, an outward sign; proof, testimony, esp matter submitted in court to determine the truth of alleged facts.—*vt* to indicate; to prove.—*adj* **eviden´tial** [-shål], furnishing evidence; tending to prove. [L *ēvidens, -entis*—*ē*, from *vidēre*, to see.]

evil [ē´vl, ē´vil] *adj* wicked; causing or threatening distress or harm.—*adv* **ē´villy**, in an evil manner.—*n* sin; a source of sorrow or distress; calamity.—**e´vildo´er**, one who does evil; **e´vil eye**, a supposed power to cause harm by a look.—*adj* **e´vil-mind´ed**, inclined to evil thoughts; malicious. [OE *yfel*; Du *euvel*; Ger *übel*; **ill** is a doublet.]

evince [e-vins´] *vt* to show (eg a quality).—*adj* **evinc´ible**.—*adv* **evinc´ibly**.—*adj* **evinc´ive**, showing, tending to show. [L *ēvincĕre*—*ē*-, inten, *vincĕre*, to overcome.]

eviscerate [ē-, or e-vis´ėr-āt] *vt* to tear out the entrails of; to deprive of vital content or force.—*n* **eviscerā´tion**. [L *ē*, from, *viscera*, the bowels.]

evocative *see* **evoke**.

evoke [e-vōk] *vt* to call forth or up.—*adj* **evoc´ative** [-vok´], having power to evoke; serving to awaken (eg feelings, memories). [L *ēvocāre*—*ē*, from, and *vocāre*, to call.]

evolution [ev-, ēv-ol-(y)ōō´sh(ȯ)n] *n* a process of change in a particular direction; one of a series of prescribed movements (as in a dance or military exercise); the process by which something (as an organism) attains its distinctive characteristics; a theory that existent types of plants and animals have developed from previously existing kinds.—adj **evolu´tionary**, of or pertaining to evolution.—*n* **evolu´tionist**, one who believes in evolution as a principle in science.—*vi* **evolve** [ē-volv´] to develop by or as if by evolution.—[L *ēvolvērea*—*ē*, from, *volvĕre, volūtum*, to roll.]

ewe [ū] *n* a female sheep.—*n* **ewe´-neck**, a thin neck with a faulty arch occurring as a defect on dogs and horses. [OE *ēowu*; cf L *ovis*, Gr *oïs*, Sans *avi*, a sheep.]

ewer [ū´ėr] *n* a large water jug with a wide spout. [Through Fr from L *aquārium*—*aqua*, water, whence also Fr *eau*.]

ex- [eks-] indicating that the following term is no longer applicable [L *ex*, out of, from], eg:—**ex-pres´ident**, a former president; **ex-wife**, a former wife.

exacerbate [eks-, or egz-as´ėr-bāt] *vt* to make more violent, bitter, or severe.—*n* **exacerbā´tion**. [L *exacerbāre, -ātum*—*ex*, inten., *acerbāre*, from *acerbus*, bitter.]

exact [egz-akt´] *vt* to compel to furnish; to extort, to require as indispensable.—*adj* without any error; absolutely correct.—*adj* **exacting**, greatly demanding; requiring close attention and precision.—*ns* **exac´tion**, act of demanding strictly; an oppressive demand; that which is exacted; **exact´itūde**, exactness; correctness.—*adv* **exact´ly**.—*n* **exact´ness**. [L *exigĕre, exactum*, to drive out, to exact—*ex*, from, *agĕre*, to drive.]

exaggerate [egz-aj´er-āt] *vt* to enlarge (as a statement) beyond bounds.—*ns* **exaggerā´tion**, extravagant representation; a statement in excess of the truth; **exagg´erātor**.—*adjs* **exagg´erative, exagg´eratory**. [L *exaggerāre, -ātum*—*ex-*, *aggerāre*, to heap up—*agger*, a heap.]

exalt [egz-ölt´] *vt* to raise up, esp in rank, power, or dignity.—*n* **exaltā´tion**, elevation in rank or dignity; high estate; elation.—*adj* **exalt´ed**, elevated; lofty; dignified. [L *exaltāre*.—*ex*, inten, *altus*, high.]

examine [egz-am´in] *vt* to look at closely and carefully, to investigate; to test, esp by questioning.—*ns* **examinā´tion**, close inspection; test of knowl-

edge. Also **exam.**—**examinee**, person who is examined; **examiner**. [Fr,—L *exāmināre—exāmen*, the tongue of a balance.]
example [egz-am´pl] *n* a representative sample; a model to be followed or avoided; a problem to be solved in order to show the application of some rule; a warning to others.—**for example**, as an example. [OFr,—L *exemplum—eximĕre*, to take out—*ex*, out of, *emĕre, emptum*, to take, buy.]
exasperate [egz-as´pėr-āt] *vt* to irritate in a high degree; to make worse.—*n* **exasperā´tion**. [L *ex-*, inten, *asperāre*, to make rough—*asper*, rough.]
ex cathedra [eks ka-thē´drȧ] *adj, adv* with authority from the seat of authority. [L]
excavate [eks´ka-vāt] *vt* to hollow out; to form by hollowing out; to dig out and remove (as earth); to reveal to view by digging away a covering.—*ns* **excavā´tion**, act of excavating; a hollow or cavity made by excavating; **ex´cavātor**, one that excavates, esp a power-driven shovel. [L *excavāre—ex*, out, *cavus*, hollow.]
exceed [ek-sēd´] *vt* to go beyond (the limit set or required); to be greater than; to surpass or excel.—*vi* to go beyond a given or proper limit.—*p adj* **exceed´ing**, surpassing; excessive.—*adv* **exceed´ingly**. [L *ex-*, beyond, *cēdĕre, cessum*, to go.]
excel [ek-sel´] *vt* to outdo, to surpass.—*vi* to do better than others (*with* **in, at**);—*pr p* **excell´ing**; *pt p* **excelled´**.—**exc´ellence, exc´ellency**, great merit; any excellent quality; (usually **Excellency**) a title of honor given to persons high in rank or office.—*adj* **exc´ellent**, surpassing others, in some good quality; of great virtue, worth, etc.—*adv* **exc´ellently**. [L *excellĕre—ex-*, out, up, *celsus*, high.]
except [ek-sept´] *vt* to leave out, to take out.—*vi* to object.—*prep* (also **except´ing**) not including; other than.—*n* **excep´tion**, the act of excepting; something excepted; an objection.—*adjs* **exceptionable**, liable to objection **excep´tional**, unusual, esp superior; **except´ive**, including, making, or being an exception.—**except for** but for. [L *excipĕre, exceptum—ex*, from, *capĕre*, to take.]
excerpt [ek´sûrpt, or ek-sûrpt´] *n* a passage selected from a book, opera, etc.; an extract. [L *excerptum, pt p* of *excerpĕre—ex*, from, *carpĕre*, to pick.]
excess [ek-ses´] *n* a part that is too much, surplus; intemperance; that which exceeds; the degree or amount by which one thing exceeds another.—*adj* **excess´ive**, beyond what is right and proper, immoderate.—*adv* **excessively**.—**in excess of** over; to an amount or degree beyond. [L *excessus—ex-cēdĕre, excessum*, to go beyond.]
exchange [eks-chānj´] *vt* to give and take (one thing in return for another); to give and take mutually.—*n* the giving and taking of one thing for another; the thing exchanged; the interchange of valuables and esp of bills of exchange or money of different countries; a place where things and services are exchanged, esp a marketplace for securities; a central office where telephone lines are connected for communication.—*adj* **exchange´able**.—*n* **exchangeabil´ity**. [OFr *eschangier* (Fr *échanger*)—Low L *excambiāre*—L *ex*, from, *cambīre*, to barter.]
Exchequer [eks-chek´ėr] *n* the British governmental department in charge of finances. [OFr *exchequier*, a chessboard. See **check**.]
excise[1] [*ek-sīz´*] *n* a tax on the manufacture, sale, or use of certain articles within a country.—*adj* **excīs´able**, liable to excise duty. [Old Du *excijs*—OFr *acceis*, tax—Low L *accēnsāre* to tax—*ad*, to, *cēnsus*, tax.]
excise[2] [ek-sīz´] *vt* to remove by cutting out.—*n* **excision** [ek-sizh´(ȯ)n]. [L *excīdĕre*, to cut out—*ex*, from, *caedĕre*, to cut.]
excite [ek-sīt´] *vt* to arouse strong emotion in, to agitate; to rouse to activity; to stimulate.—*adj* **excīt´able**, capable of being excited; easily excited.—*ns* **excītabil´ity; excitant** [ek´si-tȧnt, or ek-sītȧnt], that which excites or rouses the vital activity of the body, a stimulant; **excitā´tion**, act of exciting.—*adjs* **excīt´ative, excīt´atory**, tending to excite.—*adj* **excīt´ed**, agitated; roused emotionally; in a state of great activity; **excited state**. state of physical system (as an atomic nucleus, atom, or molecule) that is higher energy than the ground state.—**excīte´ment**, agitation; stimulation; that which excites. [Fr,—L *excitāre, -ātum—exciēre—ex-*, out, *ciēre*, to set in motion.]
exclaim [eks-klām´] *vi* to cry out.—*vt* to utter or speak vehemently.—*n* **exclămā´tion**, vehement protest, etc., an uttered expression of surprise, and the like.—**exclamation point** the mark expressing this (!).—*adj* **exclamatory**, containing or expressing exclamation. [Fr *exclamer*—L *exclāmāre, -ātum—ex-*, out, *clāmāre*, to shout.]
exclude [eks-klōōd´] *vt* to shut out.—*n* to drive out; to keep out.—**exclu´sion**, a shutting or putting out; exception.—*adj* **exclus´ive**, reserved for particular persons; snobbishly aloof; sole, undivided (as of rights).—*adv* **exclu´sively**.—*n* **exclu´siveness**. [L *exclūdĕre—ex-*, out, *claudĕre*, to shut.]
excogitate [eks-koj´i-tāt] *vt* to think out; to devise.—*n* **excogitā´tion**. [L *excōgitāre, -ātum—ex-*, out, *cōgitāre*, to think.]
excommunicate [eks-kom-ū´i-kāt] *vt* to expel from communion with the church; to exclude from fellowship.—*n* **excommunicā´tion**. [From Late L *excommūnicāre*—L *ex*, from, *commūnis*, common.]
excrement [eks´krė-mėnt] *n* waste matter discharged from the bowels.—*adj* **excrement´al**. [L *excrēmentum—excernĕre—ex-*, out, *cernĕre*, to sift.]
excrescence [eks-kres´ėns] *n* an outgrowth or projection, esp abnormal, grotesque, or offensive; an outbreak.—*adj* **excres´cent**, growing out; superfluous. [Fr,—L,—*excrēscĕre—ex-*, out, *crēscĕre*, to grow.]
excrete [eks-krēt´] *vt* to separate and discharge wastes from the body, esp in urine.—*n pl* **excrē´ta**, matter eliminated from an organism.—*n* **excrē´tion**, the excreting of matter from an organism; that which is excreted.—**excrē´tory**, having the quality of excreting. [L *ex*, from, *cernĕre, crētum*, to separate.]
excruciate [eks-krōōshi-āt] *vt* to torture.—*adj* **excru´ciāting**, intensely painful or distressful, agonizing.—*adv* **excru´ciātingly**.—*n* **excructiā´tion**. [L *ex-*, out, *cruciāre, -ātum*, to crucify—*crux, crucis*, a cross.]
exculpate [eks´kul-pāt, or -kul´-] *vt* to clear from alleged fault or guilt.—*n* **exculpā´tion**.—*adj* **excul´patory**, tending or serving to exculpate. [L *ex*, from, *culpa*, a fault.]
excursion [eks-kûr´sh(ȯ)n] *n* a pleasure trip; a digression; an outward movement or a cycle of movement (as of a pendulum).—*n* **excur´sionist**, one who goes on a pleasure trip.—*adj* **excur´sive**, rambling;—*adv* **excur´sively**.—**excur´siveness; excur´sus**, an appendix or a digression containing further exposition on a point or topic.—*pl* **excursuses, excursus**. [L *ex-*, out, *currĕre, cursum*, to run.]
excuse [eks-kūz´] *vt* to pardon; to forgive; to give a reason or apology for; to be a reason or explanation of; to let off.—*n* [eks-kūs´] the reason given.—*adj* **excusable** [eks-kūz´ȧbl]).—*adv* **excus´ably**.—*adj* **excūs´atory**, making or containing excuse. [L *excūsāre—ex*, from, *causa*, a cause, accusation.]
execrate [eks´e-krāt] *vt* to curse; to detest utterly.—*adj* **ex´ecrable**, deserving to be execrated, abominable.—*adv* **ex´ecrably**.—*n* **execrātion**, act of execrating; a curse pronounced. [L *exsecrārī, -ātus*, to curse—*ex*, from, *sacer*, sacred.]
execute [ekse´e-kūt] *vt* to perform; to carry into effect; to put to death by law.—*adj* **executable** [eg-zek´ūt-ȧ-bl, or ek-sek´-] that can be performed.—*ns* **exec´ūtant**, one who executes or performs; **ex´ecūter; execū´tion**, act of executing or performing; carrying into effect the sentence of a court of law; the warrant for so doing; **execū´tioner**, one who executes, esp one who inflicts capital punishment.—*adj* **exec´ūtive**, designed or fitted to execute; concerned with performance, administration, or management; qualifying for or pertaining to the execution of the law.—*n* the power or authority in government that carries the laws into effect; the persons who administer the government or an organization; one concerned with administration or management.—*adv* **exec´ūtively**.—*n* **exec´ūtor**, one who executes or performs; the person appointed to see a will carried into effect;—*fem* **exec´utrix**.—*n* **exec´utorship**.—*adj* **exec´ūtory**, executing official duties; designed to be carried into effect. [Fr *exécuter*—L *exsequi, exsecūtus—ex*, out, *sequī*, to follow.]
exegesis [eks-e-jē´sis] *n* interpretation, esp Biblical.—*adjs* **exegĕt´ic, -al**, pertaining to exegesis, explanatory.—*adv* **exegĕt´ically**.—*npl* **exegĕt´ics**, the science of exegesis. [Gr *exēgēsis—exēgeesthai*, to explain—*ex-*, out, *hēgeesthai*, to guide.]
exemplar [eg-zem´plȧr, -plär] *n* an ideal model; a typical instance or example.—*adj* **exemplary** [eg-zem´plȧr-i, or ig], worthy of imitation; serving as a warning.—*adv* **exem´plarily**. [L *exemplar*, a copy; also OFr *exemplaire*—Low L *exemplārium—exemplum*, example.]
exemplify [egz-em´pli-fī] *vt* to illustrate by example; to be an example of; to make an attested copy of; to prove by an attested copy;—*pr p* **exem´plifying**; *pt p* **exem´plified**.—*n* **exemplificā´tion**, act of exemplifying; that which exemplifies; a copy or transcript. [L *exemplum*, example, *facĕre*, to make.]
exempt [egz-emt´] *vt* to free, or grant immunity (*with* **from**).—*adj* not liable.—*n* **exemp´tion**, act of exempting; freedom from any service, duty, burden, etc. [Fr,—L *eximĕre, exemptum—ex*, from *emĕre*, to buy.]
exercise [eks´ėr-sīz] *n* a putting in practice; exertion of the body for health or amusement or acquisition of skill; a similar exertion of the mind; a lesson or task; a written school task; military mock battle.—*vt* to train by use; to give exercise to; to trouble, worry (eg *he was exercised about the matter*); to put in practice, to use (eg discretion, authority). [OFr *exercice*—L *exercitium*—L *exercēre, -citum—ex-*, inten, *arcēre*, to shut up, restrain.]
exert [egz-ûrt´] *vt* to bring into active operation (eg strength, influence).—*n* **exer´tion**, a bringing into active operation; striving; activity. [L *exserĕre, exsertum*, to put, thrust, forth or out—*ex*, from, *serĕre*, to put together.]
exfoliate [eks-fōli-āt] *vti* to cast off or to come off in scales, laminae, or splinters.—*n* **exfoliā´tion**. [L *exfoliāre, -ātum—ex*, from, *folium*, a leaf.]
exhale [eks-hāl´, egz-āl´] *vt* to breathe out; send out as vapor.—*vi* to emit breath; to rise as vapor.—*n* **exhalation** [eks-, egz-a-lā´sh(ȯ)n, or eks´ha-], act or process of exhaling; that which is exhaled. [Fr *exhaler*—L *exhālāre—ex*, from, *hālāre, -ātum*, to breathe.]
exhaust [egz-öst´] *vt* to draw out completely; to empty; to use the whole strength of; to wear or tire out; to treat of or develop completely (a subject).—*n* the escape of used gas or steam from an engine; the matter that escapes.—*adj* **exhaust´ed**, emptied; consumed; tired out.—*adj* **exhaust´ible**.—*n* **exhaust´ion**, act of exhausting or consuming; state of being exhausted; extreme fatigue.—*adj* **exhaust´ive**, tending to exhaust; comprehensive, thorough.—*adv* **exhaust´ively**, very thoroughly. [L *exhaurīre, exhaustum—ex*, from, *haurīre*, to draw.]
exhibit [egz-ib´it] *vt* to display, esp in public; to present to a court in legal form.—*n* an act or instance of exhibiting, something exhibited; something produced and identified in court for use as evidence.—*n* **exhib´itor**.—*adj* **exhib´itory**, exhibiting.—*ns* **exhibi´tion**, a showing, a display (*exhibition of bad manners*); a public show (of works of art or products of commerce);

exhibi´tionism, tendency to show what should not be shown; excessive tendency to show off one's abilities; **exhibi´tionist**. [L *exhibēre, -itum—ex*, out, *habēre, -itum*, to have.]

exhilarate [egz-il´a-rāt] *vt* to make hilarious or merry; to enliven.—*adj* **exhil´arant**, exhilarating.—*n* **exhilarā´tion**, state of being exhilarated; joyousness. [L *exhilarāre, -ātum—ex-*, inten, *hilaris*, cheerful.]

exhort [eg-zört´] *vt* to urge strongly and earnestly (a course of action, a person to do); to warn.—*n* **exhortā´tion**, act of exhorting; language intended to incite or encourage.—*adjs* **exhort´ative, exhort´atory**, tending to exhort or advise. [L *exhortārī, -ātus—ex-*, inten, *hortārī*, to urge.]

exhume [eks-hūm´] *vt* to take (a dead person) out of the ground; to bring (a subject) back from neglect or obscurity.—*n* **exhumā´tion**. [L *ex*, out of, *humus*, the ground.]

exigent [eks´i-jėnt] *adj* pressing, urgent; exacting.—*ns* **ex´igence, ex´igency**, pressing necessity; emergency. [L *exigens, -entis, pr p* of *exigĕre—ex*, from, *agĕre*, to drive.]

exiguous [egz-, eks-ig´ū-ůs] *adj* scanty in amount. [L *exiguus—exigĕre*. See **exact**.]

exile [eks´īl, or egz´īl] *n* a person driven from his native place; banishment.—*vt* to expel from one's country, often as punishment; to banish. [OFr *exil*—L *exsilium*, banishment—*ex*, out of, and root of *salīre*, to leap; affected by L *exsul*, an exile.]

exist [egz-ist´] *vi* to have an actual being.—*n* **exist´ence**, state of existing or being; livelihood; life; anything that exists.—*adj* **exist´ent**, having being; at present existing.—*n* **existen´tialism**, a doctrine, popularly understood to be that life is purposeless and man petty and miserable. [L *existĕre, exsistĕre*, to stand forth—*ex*, out, *sistĕre*, to stand.]

exit [eks´it, egz´-] *n* a way out of an enclosed space; a going out or away; death; a departure from a stage.—*pl* **ex´its**.—*vi* to make an exit. [L *exit*, he goes out, *exīre*, to go out—*ex*, out, and *īre, itum*, to go.]

exo- outside [Gr *exō*, without], eg:—**exoskel´eton**, a hard supporting or protective structure on the outside of the body, eg a shell; applied also to scales, hoofs, etc.

ex libra [eks lib´ra] from the library of. [L]

exodus [eks´o-dus] *n* the departure of many people; **Exodus**, the departure of the Israelites from Egypt led by Moses; (*Bible*) 2d book of the Old Testament, the account of the founding of the nation of Israel and the building of the tabernacle. [L,—Gr *exodus—ex*, out, *hodus*, a way.]

ex officio [eks o-fish´i-ō] *adj, adv* by virtue of or because of an office. [L]

exogamy [eks-og´a-mi] *n* the practice of marrying only outside of one's own group, esp as required by custom or law. [Gr *exō*, out, *gamos*, marriage.]

exonerate [egz-on´ėr-āt] *vt* to free from blame; to acquit.—*n* **exonerā´tion**.—*adj* **exon´erative**, freeing from blame. [L *exonerāre, -ātum—ex*, from, *onus, oneris*, burden.]

exorbitant [egz-ör´bi-tånt] *adj* going beyond the usual limits; excessive.—*n* **exor´bitance**.—*adv* **exor´bitantly**. [L *exorbitans, -antis*, pr p of *exorbitāre—ex*, out of, *orbita*, a track—*orbis*, a circle.]

exorcise [eks´ȯr-sīz] *vt* to expel an evil spirit.—*ns* **ex´orcism**, act of exorcising; **ex´orcist** (also **exorcis´er**). [Late L, from Gr *exorkizein—ex*, out, *horkos*, an oath.]

exoteric [eks-o-ter´ik] *adj* suitable for communication to the public or multitude; not included among the initiated. [Gr *exōterikos—exōterō*, comp of *exō*, outside.]

exotic [egz-ot´ik] *adj* foreign; strange; excitingly different or unusual; of or relating to striptease.—*n* a rare plant; stripteaser.—*ns* **exotica**, literary or artistic items having an exotic theme; **exoticism**, quality or state of being exotic. [L,—Gr *exōtikos—exō*, outside.]

expand [eks-pand´] *vt* to spread out; to enlarge in bulk or surface; to develop in fuller detail, to express at length.—*vi* to become opened; to increase in size; (*fig*) to become communicative.—*n* **expanse´**, a wide extent; amount of spread or stretch.—*adj* **expans´ible**, capable of being expanded.—*ns* **expansibil´ity, expan´sion**, act of expanding; state of being expanded; enlargement; extension.—*adj* **expans´ive**, widely extended; having a capacity to expand; causing expansion; worked by expansion; comprehensive; talkative, communicative.—*adv* **expans´ively**.—*n* **expans´iveness**.—**expanded metal**, sheet metal cut and expanded into a lattice and used esp as lath; **expanded plastic**, light-weight cellular plastic used esp as insulation and protective packing meterial.—Also **foamed plastic, plastic foam**. [L *expandĕre—ex*, out, *pandĕre, pansum*, to spread.]

ex parte [eks pär´tē] *adj, adv* from a one-sided point of view (eg *an ex parte statement*). [L]

expatiate [eks-pā´shi-āt] *vi* to talk or write at length.—*n* **expatiā´tion**.—*adj* **expā´tiātory**, expansive. [L *exspatiārī, -ātus—ex*, out of, *spatārī*, to roam—*spatium*, space.]

expatriate [eks-pā´tri-āt] *vti* to banish or exile (oneself, another).—Also *n, adj* (person) expatriated, exiled by self or other(s).—*n* **expatriā´tion**, act of expatriating; exile, voluntary or compulsory. [Low L *expatriāre, -ātum—ex*, out of, *patria*, fatherland.]

expect [eks-pekt´] *vt* to look forward to as likely to come or happen, or as due; to suppose.—*ns* **expect´ance, expect´ancy**, act or state of expecting; that which is expected; hope.—*adj* **expect´ant**, looking or waiting for something.—Also *n*—*adv* **expect´antly**.—*n* **expectā´tion**, act or state of expecting; that which is, or may fairly be, expected; (*pl*) prospect of fortune or profit by a will.—**expected value**, (*math*) the mean value of a random variable. [L *exspectāre, -ātum—ex*, out, *spectāre*, to look, freq of *specĕre*, to see.]

expectorate [eks-pek´to-rāt] *vti* to expel (mucus) from the respiratory tract by coughing; to spit.—*ns* **expectorā´tion**, act of expectorating; that which is expectorated; **expec´torant**, a medicine that promotes expectoration.—Also *adj*. [L *expectorāre, -ātum—ex*, out of, from, *pectus, pectoris*, the breast.]

expedient [eks-pē´di-ėnt] *adj* suitable or desirable under the circumstances.—*n* means suitable to an end; means devised or used for want of something better.—*ns* **expē´dience, expē´diency**, fitness, prudence, advisability; that which is opportune or politic; self-interest.—*adv* **expē´diently**. [L *expediens, -entis, pr p* of *expedīre*. See **expedite**.]

expedite [eks´pe-dīt] *vt* to carry out promptly; to facilitate.—*n* **expedi´tion**, speek, promptness; an organized journey to attain some object, as exploration, etc.; the party undertaking such a journey.—*adj* **expedi´tionary**, belonging to an expedition; **expedi´tious**, speedy, characterized by speed and efficiency. [L *expedīre, -ītum—ex*, from, *pēs, pedis*, foot.]

expel [eks-pel´] *vt* to drive out, to eject; to banish;—*pr p* **expell´ing**; *pt p* **expelled´**. [L *expellĕre, expulsum—ex*, from, *pellĕre*, to drive.]

expend [eks-pend´] *vt* to spend (*often with* **on, upon**); to employ or consume in any way.—*adj* **expend´able**, that may be sacrificed to achieve some end.—*ns* **expend´iture** [-tyůr, -chůr], act of expending; that which is expended; money spent; **expense´**, outlay; cost; cause of expenditure.—*adj* **expens´ive**, causing or requiring much expense, costly.—*n* **expens´iveness**.—**expense account**, account of expenses reimbursable to an employee. [L *expendĕre—ex*, out, *pendĕre, pensum*, to weigh.]

experience [eks-pēri-ėns] *n* observation or practice resulting in or tending toward knowledge; knowledge gained by seeing and doing; a state of being affected from without (as by events); an affecting event (*a startling experience*).—*vt* to meet with, undergo; to prove or know by use.—*adj* **expē´rienced**, taught by experience—skillful, wise.—*adj* **expērien´tial** [-shål], pertaining to or derived from experience. [Fr,—L *experientia*, from *experīrī—ex-*, inten, and old verb *perīrī*, to try.]

experiment [eks-per´i-mėnt] *n* any test or trial to find out something; a controlled procedure carried out to discover, test, or demonstrate something.—*vi* to carry out experiments.—*adj* **experiment´al**, of, based on, or proceeding by experiment; based on experience; tentative.—*ns* **experiment´alist, experiment´er**, one who makes experiments. [L *experīmentum—experīrī*; see **experience**.]

expert [eks-pûrt´] *adj* thoroughly skilled; knowledgeable through training and experience.—*vti* to examine and give judgement on.—*ns* **ex´pert**, one who is specially skilled in any art or science; a scientific or professional witness; **expert´ness**, skill, adroitness. [Fr—L *expertus-experīrī*; see **experience**.]

expertise [eks-pûrt-ēz´] *n* expert knowledge; expertness, skill; expert appraisal, valuation. [Fr]

expiate [eks´pi-āt] *vt* to pay the penalty for; to make amends for.—*adj* **ex´piable**, capable of being expiated.—*ns* **expiā´tion**, act of expiating; the means by which atonement is made; **ex´piātor**, one who expiates.—*adj* **ex´piātory**. [L *expiāre, -ātum—ex-*, inten, *piāre*, to appease, atone for.]

expire [eks-pīr´] *vti* to breathe out; to die; to come to an end; to lapse or become void.—*n* **expirā´tion**, the act of breathing out; end, termination.—*adj* **expī´ratory**, pertaining to emission of the breath.—*adjs* **expīred´**, lapsed, invalid; **expī´ring**, dying; (of words) uttered at the time of, dying.—*n* **expī´ry**, exhalation of breath; termination, esp by lapse of time; death. [Fr *expirer*—L *ex*, from, *spīrāre, -ātum*, to breathe.]

explain [eks-plān´] *vt* to make plain or intelligible; to expound; to account for.—*adj* **explain´able**.—*n* **explănā´tion**, act of explaining or clearing from obscurity; that which explains or clears up; the meaning or sense given; a mutual clearing up of misunderstanding.—*adj* **explan´atory**, serving to explain or clear up.—**explain away**, to modify, lessen the force of, by explanation (eg *he tried to explain away his previous statement*).—**explain oneself**, to make one's meaning, or the reason of one's actions, clear. [OFr *explaner*—L *explānāre—ex*, out, *plānāre—plānus*, plain.]

expletive [eks´ple-tiv, eks-plē´tiv] *adj* filling out; added merely to fill up.—*n* a word inserted to fill up a gap; a meaningless oath.—**expletive deleted**, indicating the omission from print of an obscene word or phrase. [L *explētīvus—ex*, out, *plēre*, to fill.]

explicate [eks´pli-kāt] *vt* to develop the implications of, to explain.—*adj* **explic´able**, capable of being explained.—*n* **explicā´tion**, act of explicating or explaining; explanation.—*adjs* **ex´plicātive, ex´plicatory**, serving to explicate or explain. [L *explicāre, explicātum* or *explicitum—ex*, out, *plicāre*, to fold.]

explicit [eks-plis´it] *adj* not implied merely, but distinctly stated; plain in language; outspoken.—*adv* **explic´itly**.—*n* **explic´itness**. [*See* **explicate**.]

explode [eks-plōd´] *vt* to bring into disrepute, and reject; to cause to blow up.—*vi* to burst with a loud report; to burst out (eg into laughter).—*adj* **explō´ded**, blown up; rejected, discarded.—*n* **explō´sion** [-zh(ȯ)n], act of exploding; a sudden violent burst with a loud report; an outburst of feelings, etc.; a great and rapid increase or expansion, as *population explosion*.—*adj* **explōs´ive** [-siv, -ziv], worked by an explosion; liable to or causing explosion; bursting out with violence and noise.—*n* something that will explode; (*linguistics*) the sudden opening of the oral air passage, resulting in a sudden rush of air to produce the consonants *p* and *b.*—*n* **explodent.**—**exploded diagram**, a drawing showing the parts (of something) separated but in correct relation to each other. [L *explōdĕre, explōsum—ex*, from, *plaudĕre*, to clap hands.]

exploit [eks-ploit´, or eks´ploit] *n* a deed or achievement, esp a heroic one.—*vt* [eks-ploit´] to work, make available (eg natural resources); to make gain out of, or at the expense of (eg a person).—*n* **exploitā´tion**, the act of successfully applying industry to any object, as the working of mines, etc.; the act of using for selfish purposes; the operations involved in obtaining ore from a mine. [OFr *exploit*—L *explicitum*, unfolded.]

explore [eks-plōr´, -plör´] *vti* to search or travel through for the purpose of discovery; to examine thoroughly.—*n* **explorā´tion**, act of searching thoroughly; travel for the sake of discovery.—*adjs* **explor´ative, explor´atory**, serving, or intended, to explore or investigate (eg an *exploratory operation*); for exploration (eg *exploratory zeal*).—*n* **explor´er**. [Fr *explorer*—L *explōrāre, -ātum*, to search out—prob from *ex*, from, *plōrāre*, to call out.]

exponent [eks-pō´nėnt] *n* a symbol, usu. a number written above and to the right of a mathematical expression to indicate the operation of raising to a power; one who interprets, esp in the performance of music; one who champions, advocates, or exemplifies.—*adj* **exponen´tial** [ekspōn-en´-shȧl], having to do with algebraic exponents; involving unknown or variable quantities as exponents.—**exponential growth**, increasingly rapid growth. [L *expōnens—ex*, out, *pōnĕre*, to place.]

export [eks-pōrt´, -pört´] *vt* to send out (goods) of one country for sale in another.—*n* **ex´port**, act of exporting; the article exported.—*adj* **export´able**.—*ns* **exportā´tion; export´er**. [L *exportāre, -ātum—ex*, out of, *portāre*, to carry.]

expose [eks-pōz´] *vt* to display; to lay bare; to deprive of protection or shelter; to subject to an influence (as light, weather).—*adj* **exposed**, open to view; not shielded or protected.—*ns* **exposé** [eks-pō-zā], a showing up of crime, dishonesty, etc.; **expō´sure** [-zhůr], an exposing or state of being exposed; time during which light reaches and acts on a photographic film, paper, plate or segment of a roll of film.—**exposure meter**, a device for indicating correct photographic exposure under varying light conditions.—**expose oneself**, to expose one's body indecently. [Fr *exposer*—L *ex*, out, and Fr *poser*, to place, from LL *pausāre*, to rest, not from L *pōnĕre, positum*, to place.]

exposition [eks-po-zish´(ȯ)n] *n* a public show or exhibition; a detailed explanation; a speech or writing explaining a process, thing, or idea.—*ns* **ex´po**, a large public exhibition, esp one with international participation; **expos´itor**, one who expounds.—*adj* **expos´itory**, serving to explain, explanatory. [L *expositiō, -ōnis*, exposition—*expōnĕre, expositum*, to expose, set forth; see **exponent**.]

ex post facto [eks pōst fak´tō] *adj, adv* done, made, or formulated after the fact. [L]

expostulate [eks-post´ū-lāt] *vi* to remonstrate.—*n* **expostūlā´tion**.—*adj* **expost´ūlatory**, containing expostulation. [L *expostulāre, -ātum—ex-*, inten, *postulāre*, to demand.]

expound [eks-pownd´] *vt* to present in detail (eg a doctrine); to explain, interpret (eg the Scriptures). [OFr *espondre*—L *expōnĕre—ex-*, out, *pōnĕre*, to place.]

express [eks-pres´] *vt* to represent or make known by a likeness, signs, symbols, etc.; to put into words; (*reflex*) to put one's thought, feeling into words; to reveal (eg an emotion, a quality).—*adj* exact (eg *his express image*); directly stated, explicit; expeditious (eg method); traveling at high speed with few or no stops along the way.—*adv* by express.—*n* a system or company for sending articles, money, etc. at rates higher than standard freight charges.—*adv* **express´ly**, definitely, explicitly; of set purpose.—*adjs* **express´ible; express´ive**, serving to express (*with* **of**); conveying vividly or forcibly meaning or feeling, full of expression.—*adv* **express´ively**.—*ns* **express´iveness; expression**, act of representing or giving utterance; representation or relevation by language, art, the features, etc.; look; intonation; due indication of feeling in performance of music; word, phrase; **express´ionism**, a theory or practice that art seeks to depict the subjective emotions aroused in the artist by objects and events, not objective reality.—*adj* **express´ionless**.—**expressman**, a person employed in the express business; **expressway**, a high-speed divided highway with controlled access points. [OFr *expresser*—L *ex*, from, *pressāre*, frequentative of *premĕre, pressum*, to press.]

expropriate [eks-prō´pri-āt] *vt* to take (property) from its owner.—*n* **expropriā´tion**. [L *expropriāre, -ātum—ex*. from, *proprium*, property.]

expulsion [eks-pul´sh(ȯ)n] *n* the act of expelling or being expelled.—adj **expul´sive**, able or serving to expel. [L *expulsāre*, frequentative of *expellĕre*. See **expel**.]

expunge [eks-punj´] *vt* to obliterate, to erase. [L *ex*, out, *pungĕre*, to prick.]

expurgate [eks´pûr-gāt] *vt* to purify (esp a book) from anything supposed to be noxious or erroneous.—*ns* **expurgā´tion; expurgator** [eks´pûr-gā-tȯr, or eks-pûr´gȧ-tȯr].—*adj* **expur´gătory**, tending to expurgate or purify. [L *expurgāre, -ātum—ex*, out, *purgāre*, to purge.]

exquisite [eks'kwi-zit, also -kwiz´] *adj* of consummate excellence (eg of workmanship); very beautiful; showing delicate perception or close discrimination; fastidious; extreme, as pain or pleasure.—*n* one extremely fastidious in dress, a fop.—*adv* **ex´quisitely**.—*n* **ex´quisiteness**. [L *exquīsītus—ex*, out, *quaerĕre, quaesītum*, to seek.]

exscind [ek-sind´] *vt* to cut off or out. [L *ex*, from, *scindĕre*, to cut.]

exsiccate [ek´si-kāt] *vt* to dry up.—*n* **exsiccā´tion**. [L *exsiccāre—ex, siccus*, dry.]

extant [eks´tánt´] *adj* still existing. [L *ex(s)tans, -antis—ex*, out, *stāre*, to stand.]

extempore [eks-tem´po-re] *adv* on the spur of the moment; without preparation.—*adj* composed and delivered or performed impromptu—also **extemporān´eous, extem´porary**.—*vi* **extem´porize**, to do something extemporaneously.—*n* **extemporizā´tion**. [L *ex*, out of, and *tempore*, ablative of *tempus, temporis*, time.]

extend [eks-tend´] *vt* to stretch out; to prolong in any direction; to enlarge (eg power, meaning); to hold out (eg the hand); to offer, accord (eg sympathy).—*vt* to stretch, reach.—*adjs* **extens´ible, extens´ile** [or-il], that may be extended.—*ns* **extensibil´ity; exten´sion**, act of extending; condition of being extended; an added part; the property of occupying space; an additional telephone using the same line as the main one.—*adj* **extens´ive**, large; comprehensive.—*adv* **extens´ively**.—*ns* **extens´iveness; extent´**, the space or degree to which a thing is extended; scope; degree or amount (as, *to some extent*); **exten´sor**, a muscle which straightens a limb.—**extended play**, a 45-rpm phonograph record with a playing time of 6 to 8 minutes. [L *extendĕre, extentum*, or *extensum—ex*, out, *tendĕre* to stretch.]

extenuate [eks-ten´ū-āt] *vt* to make (guilt, a fault; or offense) seem less.—*adj* **exten´ūāting**.—*n* **extenūā´tion**, act of representing anything as less wrong or criminal than it is, mitigation.—*adj* **exten´ūātory**, tending to extenuate. [L *extenuāre, -ātum*, to make thin, weaken—*ex*, inten, *tenuis*, thin.]

exterior [eks-tē´ri-ȯr] *adj* outer; external; suitable for use on the outside, as paint.—*n* the outside, outer surface; outward manner or appearance; representation of an outdoor scene. [L *exterior*, comp of *exter*, outward—*ex*, from.]

exterminate [eks-tûr´mi-nāt] *vt* to destroy utterly.—*n* **exterminā´tion**, complete destruction or extirpation.—*adj* **exter´minatory**, serving or tending to exterminate.—*n* **exter´minātor**. [L *extermināre, -ātum—ex*, out of, *terminus*, boundary.]

external [eks-tûr´nȧl] *adj* outwardly perceivable; of, relating to, or located on the outside or outer part; arising or acting from without.—*n* an external feature.—*adv* **exter´nally**.—*vt* **exter´nalize**, to give external expression to; to ascribe to causes outside oneself. [L *externus*, outward—*exter*, outside.]

extinct [eks-tingkt´] *adj* put out, extinguished (as fire, life); (of a volcano) no longer erupting; no longer existing.—*n* **extinc´tion**, extinguishing, quenching, or wiping out; becoming extinct. [See **extinguish**.]

extinguish [eks-ting´gwish] *vt* to quench; to destroy; to obscure by superior splendour.—*adj* **exting´uishable**.—*n* **exting´uisher**, a device for putting out fire. [L *ex(s)tinguĕre, ex(s)tinctum—ex*, out, *stinguĕre*, to quench.]

extirpate [eks´tėr-pāt] *vt* to root out; to destroy totally.—*ns* **extirpā´tion**, extermination, total destruction; **ex´tirpātor**. [L *ex(s)tirpāre, -ātum—ex*, out, and *stirps*, a root.]

extol, extoll [eks-tol´] *vt* to praise highly;—*pr p* **extoll´ing**; *pt p* **extolled´**. [L *extollĕre—ex*, up, *tollĕre*, to lift or raise.]

extort [eks-tört´] *vt* to obtain (money, promises, etc.) by force or improper pressure.—*n* **extor´tion**, the act of extorting; that which is extorted.—*adjs* **extor´tionary**, pertaining to or implying extortion; **extor´tionāte**, exorbitant.—*n* **extor´tioner**. [L *extorquēre, extortum—ex*, out, *torquēre*, to twist.]

extra [eks´tra] *adj* additional.—*adv* unusually.—*n* what is extra or additional, esp a charge; a special edition of a newspaper; an additional worker or a performer (as in a crowd scene in a motion picture). [L *extrā*, outside.]

extra- [eks´tra-] used to form adjectives, meaning beyond, beyond the scope of, eg:—*adjs* **ex´tracurric´ular**, of a subject or activity, outside, and additional to, the regular academic course; **ex´tragalac´tic**, outside, beyond our galaxy; **ex´trajudi´cial**, not made in court, beyond the usual course of legal proceeding; **ex´tramar´ital**, of relations, etc., outside marriage, though properly confined to marriage; **ex´tramun´dāne**, beyond the material world; **ex´tramū´ral**, beyond the walls; **ex´trasens´ory**, beyond the powers of ordinary senses (**extrasensory perception**, an awareness of objects or of facts which seems to have been given by means other than through the senses, as in telepathy and clairvoyance—abbrev **ESP**), **ex´traterres´trial**, outside, or from outside, the earth. [L]

extract [eks-trakt´] *vt* to draw out by force (eg a tooth, money, a confession); to withdraw (as a juice or constituent) by chemical or physical means; to select, quote (passages from a book, etc.); (*math*) to find (the root of a number).—*n* **ex´tract**, anything drawn from a substance; a passage taken from a book or writing.—*adj* **extract´able, extract´ible**.—*n* **extrac´tion**, act of extracting; lineage; that which is extracted.—*adj* **extract´ive**, tending or serving to extract.—*n* an extract.—*n* **extract´or**. [L *extrahĕre, extractum—ex*, from, *trahĕre*, to draw.]

extradition [eks-tra-dish´(ȯ)n] *n* a surrendering of an alleged criminal to a different jurisdiction for trial.—*vt* **ex´tradīte**. [L *ex*, from, *trāditiō—trādĕre, trāditum*, to deliver up.]

extraneous [eks-trān´yůs] *adj* coming from without; foreign (eg to other substances with which it is found, as *extraneous matter*); not belonging (to eg the subject under consideration); not essential.—*adv* **extrān´eously**. [L *extrāneus*, external—*extrā*, outside.]

extraordinary [eks-trör´di-nàr-i, or eks-tra-ör´-] *adj* beyond ordinary, not usual or regular; wonderful, surprising; additional (eg *envoy extraordinary*).—*adv* **extraor´dinarily**. [L *extrā*, outside, *ordō, -inis*, order.]

extrapolate [eks-trap´ō-lāt] *vti* to infer (unknown data) from known data.—*n* **extrapolā´tion**. [L *extrā*, outside, and **interpolate**.]

extraterritorial [eks-trà-ter-i-tō´ri-àl, -tö´-] *adj* outside the territorial limits of a jurisdiction.—*n* **extraterritoriality**, exemption for the application or jurisdiction of local laws or tribunals.—**extraterritorial rights**, extraterritoriality. [L *extrā*, outside, and *territōriālis* (*—territōrium*, territory).]

extravagant [eks-trav´a-gànt] *adj* (*obs*) wandering beyond bounds; unrestrained, excessive (eg grief, praise); lavish in spending; wasteful; exorbitant (price).—*n* **extrav´agance**, excess; lavish expenditure. [L *extrā*, beyond, *vagans, -antis*, pr p of *vagāri*, to wander.]

extravaganza [eks-trav-a-gan´za] *n* an extravagant or eccentric musical, dramatic, or literary production. [It (*e*)*stravaganza*.]

extravasate [eks-trav´a-sāt] *vt* to force out of vessels or arteries, as blood; to pour out from a vent in the earth, as lava or water.—*vi* to escape from its proper vessels. [L *extrā*, out of, *vas*, a vessel.]

extravert *see* **extrovert**.

extreme [eks-trēm´] *adj* outermost; most remote; last; highest in degree, greatest (eg *extreme penalty*); very violent (eg pain); stringent (eg measures); (of opinions) thoroughgoing, marked by excess—opp to *moderate*.—*n* the utmost point or verge, the end; utmost or highest limit or degree.—*adv* **extrēme´ly**.—*ns* **extrē´mist**, one ready to use extreme measures; **extremity** [-trem´i-ti], the utmost limit; the highest degree; greatest necessity or distress; (*pl*) extreme measures; (*pl*) hands or feet.—**extreme unction**, in RC and Orthodox Church, the sacrament of anointing a dying person by a priest.—**in the extreme**, to the greatest possible extent. [OFr *extreme*—L *extrēmus*, superl of *exter*, outside.]

extricate [eks´tri-kāt] *vt* to free (from difficulties or perplexities); to set free, to disentangle.—*adj* **ex´tricable**.—*n* **extricā´tion**, disentanglement; act of setting free. [L *extrīcāre, -ātum*—*ex*, from, *trīcae*, hindrances.]

extrinsic [eks-trin´sik] *adj* not contained in or belonging to a body; operating from without; not essential. [Fr,—L *extrinsecus*—*exter*, outside, suffx *-in*, *secus*, beside.]

extrovert [eks´tro-vert] *n* one whose interests are in matters and objects outside of himself.—Also **extravert**. [L *extrā*, outside, *vertĕre*, to turn; *extro-*, by analogy with *intro-*.]

extrude [eks-trōōd´] *vt* to force or thrust out.—*vi* to protrude.—*n* **extrusion** [-trōōzh(ò)n], act of extruding, thrusting, or throwing out.—*adj* **extru´sive**, forcing out; (of rocks) consolidated on the surface of the ground. [L *extrūdĕre, extrūsum*—*ex*, out, *trūdĕre*, to thrust.]

exuberant [egz-, eks-(y)ōō´bėr-ànt] *adj* luxuriant; lavish; effusive; in high spirits.—*ns* **exū´berance**, luxuriance; copiousness; superabundance; high spirits.—*adv* **exū´berantly**. [L *exūberans*, pr p of *exūberāre*—*ex-*, inten, *ūber*, rich.]

exude [egz-, eks-ūd´] *vt* to discharge by sweating; to discharge through pores or incisions.—*vi* to ooze out of a body as through pores.—*n* **exudā´tion** [eks-], act of exuding or discharging through pores; that which is exuded. [L *ex*, from, *sūdāre*, to sweat.]

exult [egz-ult´] *vi* to rejoice exceedingly (at); to triumph (over).—*adj* **exult´ant**, exulting; triumphant.—*n* **exultā´tion**, triumphant delight.—*adv* **exult´ingly**. [L *ex(s)ultāre, -ātum*, from *ex(s)ilire*—*ex*, out or up, *salīre*, to leap.]

exuviae [egz-, eks-(y)ōō´vi-ē] *n pl* cast-off skins, shells, or other coverings of animals; (*geol*) fossil remains of animals.—*vti* **exū´viāte**, to shed (an old covering). [L from *exuĕre*, to draw off.]

eyas [ī´as] *n* an unfledged hawk. [*eyas*, a corr of *nyas*—Fr *niais*—L *nīdus*, nest.]

eye [ī] *n* the one of two organs of sight; the power of seeing; sight; regard; keenness of perception; anything resembling an eye, as the hole of a needle, loop or ring for a hook, etc.; an undeveloped bud (as of a potato); the center of a flower, esp of a composite; a device (as a photoelectric cell) that functions analogously to the human eye; (*slang*) a detective, esp a private one.—*vt* to look on; to observe narrowly;—*pr p* **eye´ing** or **ey´ing**; *pt p* **eyed** [īd].—*ns* **eye´ball**, the globe of the eye; **eye´bright**, any of the several herbs (genus *Euphrasia*) of the figwort family with opposite cut leaves; **eye´brow**, the hairy arch above the eye.—*adj* **eye´cat´ching**, striking.—*n* **eye´lash**, hair, line of hairs that edges the eyelid.—*adj* **eyeless**, without eyes; **eyelet**, [ī´let], a small eye or hole to receive a lace or cord, as in garments, sails, etc.; **eye´lid**, the lid of skin and muscle covering the eye; **eye´ō-pener**, something astonishing or startling; **eye´piece**, the lens or combination of lenses at the eye-end of an optical instrument; **eye´ shadow**, a cosmetic applied to the eyelids; **eye´shot**, the range of sight; **eye´sight**, power of seeing; **eye´sore**, anything that is offensive to look at; **eye´tooth**, a canine tooth in the upper jaw; **eye´wash**, a lotion for the eye; humbug, deception; **eye´wit´ness**, one who sees a thing done; **eyeball-to-eyeball**, face-to-face; **eye rhyme**, a pair of words that rhyme in spelling but not in pronunciation (seat, great); **eyes-only**, (of confidential information) intended to be read only by the recipient, top secret; **make eyes at**, to look at in an amorous way, to ogle; **my eye**, used to express mild astonishment or surprise; **with an eye to**, with a view to. [OE *ēage*; Ger *auge*, Du *oog*, ON *auga*.]

eyrie *see* **aerie**.

Ezechiel [i-zēk´iel] *n* (*Bible*) Ezekiel in the Douay Version of the Old Testament.

Ezekiel [i-zēk´iel] *n* (*Bible*) 26th book of the Old Testament written by the prophet Ezekiel concerning the fate of the nation of Israel after the Babylonian captivity.

Ezra [ez´ra] *n* (*Bible*) 15th book of the Old Testament, a postexilic book relating the experiences of the Jews as they reunited.

F

f-stop [ef´stop] *n* a camera lens aperture indicated by an f-number.

fa [fa] *n* (Music) the fourth note of the diatonic scale.

Fabian [fā´bi-ȧn] *adj* delaying, avoiding battle, cautious; favoring the gradual introduction and spread of socialism.—*n* (*Brit*) a supporter of the Fabian Society. [From Q, *Fabius* Maximus, who baffled Hannibal by evading conflict.]

fable [fā´bl] *n* a short story, often with animal characters, intended to teach the moral lesson; any tale in literary form intended to instruct or amuse; a falsehood.—*vti* to invent (fables), tell (stories without basis in fact).—*adj* **fā´bled.**—*n* **fab´ulist** [fab´-], one who invents fables.—*adj* **fab´ūlous**, feigned, related in fable; incredible, astonishing; wonderful, marvelous. [Fr *fable*—L *fābula*—*fārī*, to speak.]

fabric [fab´rik] *n* framework, structure; manufactured cloth; pattern produced by crystal grains on a rock. [Fr *fabrique*—L *fabrica*—*faber*, a worker in hard materials.]

fabricate [fab´ri-kāt] *vt* to manufacture; to devise falsely (eg a lie).—*ns* **fabricā´tion**, construction; manufacture; that which is fabricated or invented; a story; a falsehood; **fab´ricator**. [L *fabricārī*—*fabrica*, fabric].

fabulist, fabulous *see* **fable**.

facade [fa-säd´] *n* the exterior front or face of a building; an imposing appearance concealing something inferior. [Fr,—*face*, after It *facciata*, the front of a building—*faccia*, the face.]

face [fās] *n* the front of the head; the main or front surface of anything; outward show or appearance; cast of features; dignity, self respect; boldness, effrontery; a mine, drift, or excavation which is being worked.—*vt* to meet in the face or in front; to stand opposite to; to confront; to cover with a new surface.—*vi* to turn the face; to take or have a direction.—*ns* **face card**, a king, queen or jack in a deck of cards; **face´cloth**, a cloth for washing the face.—*adj* **face´less**, anonymous.—*ns* **face´lift**, an operation to smooth and firm the face; a renovating process, esp one applied to the outside of a building; **fac´er**, one that faces, esp a cutter for facing surfaces; a stunning defeat.—*n, adj* **face´-saving**, avoiding the appearance of climbing down or humiliation.—*n* **fac´ing**, a lining at the edge of a garment; a covering in front for ornament or protection; a material for facing.—**face the music**, to meet an unpleasant situation, esp as a consequence of one's actions; **face-to-face**, confronting one another; very close (*with* **with**); **face up to**, to meet boldly; **face value**, the value as stated on the face of a coin, etc.; nominal worth; apparent worth; **in the face of**, in the presence of; in spite of; **lose face**, to suffer open loss of dignity or prestige; **make a face**, to grimace; **to one's face**, in one's presence. [Fr *face*—L *faciēs*, form, face; perh from *facĕre*, to make.]

facet [fas´et] *n* a small plane surface (as on a cut gem); any of a number of sides or aspects, as of a personality.—*adj* **fac´eted**. [Fr *facette*, dim of *face*, face.]

facetious [fa-sē´shus] *adj* joking, esp in an inappropriate manner.—*n pl* **facetiae** [fasē´shi-ē], witty or humorous sayings or writings.—*adv* **facē´tiously.**—*n* **facē´tiousness**. [Fr. from L *facētia*—*facētus*, merry, witty.]

facial [fā´shȧl] *adj* of or relating to the face.—*n* beauty treatment to the face.—**facial index**, ratio of the breadth of the face to its length multiplied by 100; **facial tissue** a sheet of soft tissue paper used as a handkerchief, etc.—*adv* **fā´cially**. [Fr—L *faciēs*, face.]

facile [fas´il, or -il] *adj* not hard to do; fluent; superficial.—*vt* **facil´itāte**, to make easy.—*n* **facil´ity**, ease; dexterity; easiness to be persuaded, pliancy; a building, etc. that facilitates some activity.—*pl* **facil´ities**, means that render anything easily done. [Fr,—L *facilis*, easy—*facĕre*, to do.]

facsimile [fak-sim´i-le] *n* an exact copy.—*n* **fax** [fax] facsimile transmission device which transmits graphic matter by telephone.—Also *vt*. [L *fac*, imper of *facĕre*, to make, *simile*, neut of *similis*, like.]

fact [fakt] *n* a deed, esp a criminal deed; anything known to have happened or to be true; anything alleged to be true and used as a basis of argument; reality.—*adj* **fact´ual**, of, or containing, facts; actual.—*adj* **fact´-finding**, appointed to ascertain, directed towards ascertaining, all the facts of a situation.—Also *n*. **in fact, as a matter of fact**, really.—**fact of life**, something that exists and must be taken in consideration; (*pl*) the fundamental processes concerning sex and reproduction. [L *factum*—*facĕre*, to make.]

faction[1] [fak´sh(ȯ)n] *n* a group of persons in an organization working together in a common cause against the main body; dissension.—*vt* **fac´tionalize**, to divide into opposing groups; to make factional.—*adj* **fac´tious**, turbulent; disloyal.—*adv* **fac´tiously**.—*n* **fac´tiousness**. [L *factiō, -ōnis*—*facĕre*, to do.]

faction[2] [fak´sh(ȯ)n] *n* a book based on facts but written in the form of a novel and published as fiction. [**fact** + **fiction**.]

factitious [fak-tish´us] *adj* produced or induced artificially.—*adv* **facti´tiously**. [L *factitius*—*facĕre*, to make.]

factor [fak´tȯr] *n* a transactor of business for another; any circumstance that influences the course of events; (*math*) one of two or more quantities, which, when multiplied together, produce a given quantity.—*n* **fac´torage**, the fees of a factor.—*adj* **fac´tōrial**, of or pertaining to a factor.—*n* the product of all whole numbers from a given number down to 1.—*vt* **fac´torize**, to resolve into factors.—*n* **fac´tory**, a building or buildings where things are manufactured. [L,—*facĕre*.]

factotum [fak-tō´tum] *n* a person employed to do all kinds of work. [Low L,—L *fac*, imper of *facĕre*, to do, *tōtum*, all.]

faculty [fak´ul-ti] *n* any natural power of a living organism; special aptitude; all the teachers of a school or of one of its departments. [Fr,—L *facultās, -ātis*—*facilis*, easy.]

fad [fad] *n* a whim, craze.—*adjs* **fadd´ish, fadd´y.**—*ns* **fadd´ishness; fadd´ism; fadd´ist**. [Ety uncertain.]

fade [fād] *vi* to lose freshness or color gradually; to grow faint, to die away.—*vt* to cause (an image or a sound) to become gradually less distinct or loud.—*adj* **fade´less**, not liable to fade. [OFr *fader*—*fade*—L *vapidum*.]

faeces, faecal [fē´sēs, fē´kel] *see* **feces**.

fag [fag] *vti* to become or be tired by hard work.—*pr p* **fagg´ing**; *pt p* **fagged**.—*n* drudgery; a cigarette.—*n* **fag´ end**, the end of a web of cloth that hangs loose; the untwisted end of a rope; the extreme end of a thing. [Ety uncertain; perh a corr of **flag**, to droop.]

fagot, faggot [fag´ȯt] *n* a bundle of sticks for fuel; a bundle of iron or steel rods. [Fr *fagot*, a bundle of sticks, perh from L *fax*, a torch.]

Fahrenheit [fä´ren-hīt or far´en-īt] *adj* (of a thermometer or thermometer scale) having the freezing-point of water marked at 32 degrees, and the boiling point at 212 degrees. [Named from the inventor, Gabriel D. *Fahrenheit* (1686–1736).]

fail [fāl] *vi* to fall short; to be insufficient; to weaken, to die away; to stop operating; to be negligent on duty, expectation, etc.; to be unsuccessful; (*education*) to get a grade of failure; to become bankrupt.—*vt* to disappoint (a person); to leave, to abandon; to neglect (to fail to go); (*education*) to give a grade of failure.—*pr p* **fail´ing**; *pt p* **failed.**—*ns* **fail**, the failure of a broker or brokerage firm to deliver securities by a given time; **failing**, a fault, weakness; a foible.—*prep* in default of.—*n* **fail´ure**, lack of success; cessation; omission; decay; bankruptcy; an unsuccessful person.—*adj* **fail´-safe**, pertaining to a mechanism incorporated in a system to ensure that there will be no accident if the system does not operate properly.—**without fail**, assuredly. [OFr *faillir*—L *fallĕre*, to deceive; cf Du *feilen*, Ger *fehlen*.]

faille [fīl] *n* a ribbed, soft fabric of silk, rayon, or cotton. [Fr]

fain [fān] *adj* (*arch*) glad or joyful; content for want of better (to); compelled (to).—*adv* gladly. [OE *fægen*, joyful.]

fainéant [fen´ā-ā] *n* an irresponsible idler.—Also *adj*. [Fr as if from *faire*, to do, *néant*, nothing; really—OFr *faignant*, pr p of *faindre*, to skulk.]

faint [fānt] *adj* lacking strength; dim; lacking distinctness; weak in spirit; done in a feeble way.—*vi* to lose strength, color, etc.; to swoon; to lose courage or spirit.—*n* syncope.—*adv* **faint´ly.**—*adjs* **faint´heart´ed**, lacking courage and resolution, timid; **faint´ish.**—*n* **faint´ness**. [OFr *feint* (Fr *feindre*), feigned—L *fingĕre*, to feign.]

fair[1] [fār] *adj* pleasing to the eye; clean, unblemished; blond; clear and sunny; easy to read (*a fair hand*); just and honest; according to the rules; moderately large; average (*in fair condition*); that may be hunted (*fair game*); (*baseball*) that is not foul.—*adv* in a fair manner; squarely.—*adv* **fair´ly.**—*n* **fair´ness.**—*ns* **fair´ copy**, a clean copy after correction; **fair-haired boy**, a favorite who can do no wrong **fair´ing**, adjustment or testing of curves in ship-building; means of reducing head-resistance in an airplane; **fair´ play**, honest dealing; justice.—*adj* **fair-spok´en**, courteous and pleasant in speech.—*n* **fair´-way**, the channel by which vessels enter or leave a harbor; any open path or space; the mowed part of a golf course between the tee and the green.—*adj* **fair´-weath´er**, suitable only in favorable conditions; (of a friend) loyal only in prosperous times.—**not fair** something not according to the rules. [OE *fæger*.]

fair[2] [fār] *n* a regular gathering for barter and sale of goods; a carnival or bazaar, esp for charity; a competitive exhibition of farm, household, and manufactured goods, with amusements and educational displays. [OF *feire*—L *fēria*, holiday.]

fairy [fār´i] *n* an imaginary being, of diminutive and graceful human form with magic powers.—*adj* like a fairy, fanciful, delicate.—*ns* **fairy godmother**, a generous friend or benefactor; **fair´yland**, the country of the fairies; a lovely, enchanting place; **fair´y ring**, a ring of mushrooms, esp *Marasmius oreades*.—*n* **fair´y tale**, a story about fairies; an incredible tale.—*adj* beautiful, fortunate, as in a fairy tale. [OF *faerie*, enchantment—*fae* (Fr *fée*). *See* **fay**.]

fait accompli [fet a-k•-plē] *n* a thing already done and presumably irrevocable.—*pl* **faits accomplis**. [Fr]

faith [fāth] *n* trust or confidence; belief in the statement of another; a belief in the truth of revealed religion; confidence and trust in God; that which is believed; any system of religious belief; fidelity to promises; honesty of intention; word or honor pledged.—*adj* **faith´ful**, full of faith, believing; firm in adherence to promises, duty, allegiance, etc.; loyal; true, true to an original, accurate.—*adv* **faith´fully**.—*ns* **faith´fulness; faith´ healing**, a method of treating disease by prayer and exercise of faith in God.—*adj* **faith´less**, treacherous, disloyal; untrustworthy.—*adv* **faith´lessly**.—*n* **faith´lessness**.—**bad faith** treachery; **in good faith**, with sincerity; **the Faithful**, the body of adherents of the Muslim religion. [ME *feith, feyth*—OFr *feid*—L *fidēs*—*fīdĕre*, to trust.]

fake [fāk] *vt* to falsify or counterfeit.—*n* a swindle, dodge, sham; a faked article.—*n* **fak´er**, a counterfeiter. [Cf Ger *fegen*, to furbish up.]

fakir [fa-kēr´ or fā´kir] *n* a (esp Muslim) religious mendicant in India, etc. [Ar *faqīr*, a poor man, *fakr, fagr*, poverty.]

falcate, -d [fal´kāt, -id] *adj* hooked or curved like a sickle. [L *falx, falcis*, a sickle.]

falcon [föl´kȯn or fö´kn] *n* any of various hawks trained for use in falconry, esp the peregrine; any of various hawks (family Falconidae) characterized by long wings and a notch and tooth on the edge of the upper mandible.—*ns* **fal´coner**, one who hunts with, or who breeds and trains hawks for hunting.—**fal´conry**, the art of training or hunting with falcons. [OFr *faucon*—Low L *falcō, -ōnis*.]

falderol *see* **fol´derol**.

faldstool [föld´stōōl] *n* a kind of stool for the sovereign of Great Britain at his coronation; a bishop's armless seat; a small desk at which the litany is read in Anglican churches. [Low L *faldistolium*—OHG *faldan* (Ger *falten*), to fold, *stuol* (Ger *stuhl*), stool.]

fall[1] [föl] *vi* to descend by force of gravity; to drop prostrate; to collapse; to be wounded or killed in battle; to take a downward direction; to become lower, weaker, less; to lose power, status, etc., to do wrong, to sin; to take on a sad look (*his face fell*); to pass into a specified condition (*he fell ill*); to take place; to be directed by chance; to come by inheritance; to be divided (**into**).—*pr p* **fall´ing**; *pt* **fell**; *pt p* **fallen** [fö´l(ė)n].—*n* the act of falling, in any of its senses; that which falls; as much as comes down at one time (*a fall of snow*); overthrow; descent from a better to a worse position; slope or declivity; (*pl*) a descent of water; length of a fall; decrease in value; a sinking; the time when the leaves fall, autumn; a long tress of hair added to a woman's hairdo.—*adj* of, relating to, or suitable for autumn.—*adj* **fall´en**, killed in war; in a degraded state, ruined.—*ns* **fall´ing-off**, decline; **fall´ing star**, a meteor; **fall´-out**, a deposit of radioactive dust from a nuclear explosion or plant; by-product, side benefit.—**fall away**, to withdraw support; to renounce one's faith; to drift off a course; **fall back**, to retreat, give way; **fall back upon**, to have recourse to (an expedient or resource in reserve); **fall flat**, to be unsuccessful; **fall for** (*inf*), to fall in love with; to be tricked by; **fall from grace**, backslide; **fall in**, to line up in formation; **fall off**, a decline, esp in quality or quantity; **fall on**, to meet, find; **fall on one's feet**, to succeed where failure was to be feared; to land fortunately, be lucky; **fall out**, to quarrel; to leave one's place in a formation; **fall over oneself, fall over backward**, to display excessive eagerness; **fall short of**, to fail to reach; **fall through**, to fail; **fall to**, to begin; to start eating. [OE *fallan* (WS *feallan*); Ger *fallen*; prob conn with L *fallĕre*, to deceive.]

fall[2] [föl] *n* a trap.—*n* **fall´guy**, a dupe, easy victim; a scape-goat. [OE *fealle*—*feallan*, to fall.]

fallacy [fal´à-si] *n* a false idea; a mistake in reasoning.—*adj* **fallacious** [fa-lā´shủs], misleading; not logical.—*adv* **fallā´ciously**.—*n* **fallā´ciousness**. [OFr *fallace*, deceit—L *fallācia*—*fallax*, deceptive—*fallĕre*, to deceive.]

fallal [fal-al´] *n* a trifling ornament, esp in dress.—*adj* foppish. [Ety uncertain.]

fallible [fal´i-bl] *adj* liable to error or mistake.—*n* **fallibil´ity**, liability to err.—*adv* **fall´ibly**. [Fr,—Low L *fallibilis*, from *fallĕrė*, to deceive.]

Fallopian tube [fål-lō´pi-ån] *n* either of two tubes through which the ova pass from the ovary to the uterus. [*G Fallopius*, 16th c Italian anatomist.]

fallow [fal´ō] *adj* (of land) plowed and left unseeded for a season or more.—Also *n*—*vt* to plow land without seeding it.—*n* **fall´owness**. [OE *fealgian*, to fallow; *fealh*, fallow land.]

fallow deer [fal´ō dēr] *n* a yellowish-brown deer (*Dama dama*) with broad antlers and a pale yellow coat of Europe and Asia Minor. [OE *falu*; cf ON *folr*, Ger *fahl*.]

false [föls] *adj* wrong, incorrect, untrue; untruthful; unfaithful; misleading; artificial—*adv* **false´ly**.—*ns* **false´hood**, falsity; a lie; **false´ness; fals´ity**, quality of being false; a false assertion; **false title**, occupation used as a title for a person (eg entrepreneur Geddes). [OFr *fals* (Fr *faux*)—L *falsus*, pt p of *fallĕre*, to deceive.]

falsetto [föl-set´ō] *n* an artificial way of singing in which the voice is higher-pitched than normal.—*pl* **falsettos**.—Also *adj*. [It *falsetto*, dim of *falso*, false.]

falsify [föls´i-fī] *vt* to misrepresent; to alter (a document, etc.) fraudulently.—*pr p* **fals´ifying**; *pt p* **fals´ified**.—*ns* **falsificā´tion, fals´ifier**. [Fr,—Low L *falsificāre*—L *falsus*, false, *facĕre*, to make.]

falter [föl´tėr] *vi* to stumble; to fall or stammer in speech; to flinch; to waver, hesitate in action.—*adv* **fal´teringly**, in a faltering or hesitating manner. [Prob a freq of ME *falden*, to fold.]

fame [fām] *n* reputation, esp for good; state of being well known.—*adj* **famed**. [Fr,—L *fāma*, from *fārī*, to speak.]

familiar [fa-mil´yår] *adj* well acquainted or intimate; showing the manner of an intimate, having a thorough knowledge of (*with* **with**); well known; common.—*n* one well or long acquainted; a spirit or demon supposed to attend a person at call.—*vt* **famil´iarize**, to make thoroughly acquainted; to accustom; to make easy by practice or study.—*n* **familiar´ity**, intimate acquaintanceship; freedom from constraint; undue freedom in speech or behavior.—*adv* **famil´iarly**. [OFr *familier*—L *familiāris*, from *familia*, a family.]

family [fam´i-li] *n* a household; parents and their children; the descendants of one common progenitor; a group of related plants or animals forming a category ranking above a genus and below an order; (*math*) a set of curves or surfaces whose equations differ only in parameters; a unit of a crime syndicate (as the Mafia) operating within a given geographical area.—**family circle**, a gallery in a theater or opera house above or behind more expensive seats; **family planning**, regulating size and spacing of family by using effective methods of birth control; **family tree**, a genealogical diagram. [L *familia*—*famulus*, a servant.]

famine [fam´in] *n* an acute general scarcity of food; extreme scarcity of anything. [Fr,—L *famēs*, hunger.]

famish [fam´ish] *vti* to make or be very hungry. [Obs *fame*, to starve—L *famēs*, hunger.]

famous [fā´mus] *adj* renowned, noted; (*inf*) excellent.—*adv* **fā´mously**. [OFr,—L *fāmōsus*—*fāma*. *See* **fame**.]

fan[1] [fan] *n* any device used to set up a current of air, esp a hand-waved triangular piece or a mechanism with blades; folding object of paper, feathers, etc. used for cooling the face.—*vt* to cool, as with a fan; to ventilate; to stir up, to excite.—*pr p* **fann´ing**; *pt p* **fanned**.—*ns* **fan-jet**, a jet engine having a fan that draws in extra air whose compression and expansion provides extra thrust; an airplane powered by such an engine; **fan´light**, a semicircular window with radiating bars like the ribs of a fan; **fann´er, fan´tail**, a fan-shaped tail or end; a domestic pigeon having a broad rounded tail with 30 or 40 feathers. [OE *fann*, from L *vannus*, a fan.]

fan[2] [fan] *n* an enthusiastic follower of some sport, or hobby, or public favorite.—**fan club**, group united by devotion to a celebrity.—**fandom**, fans collectively (of a sport). [From **fanatic**.]

fanatic [fa-nat´ik] *adj* extravagantly or unreasonably zealous, excessively enthusiastic.—Also *n*—*adj* **fanat´ical**, fanatic.—*adv* **fanat´ically**.—*n* **fanat´icism**, wild and excessive enthusiasm. [Fr,—L *fānāticus*, belonging to a temple, inspired by a god, *fānum*, a temple.]

fancy [fan´si] *n* imagination when playful, light, etc.; a mental image; caprice, a whim; fondness.—*adj* pleasing to, or guided by, fancy or caprice; elegant or ornamental.—*vt* to portray in the mind; to imagine; to have a fancy or liking for; to be pleased with;—*pr p* **fan´cying**; *pt p* **fan´cied**.—*n* **fan´cier**, a person with a special interest in something, esp plant or animal breeding.—*adj* **fan´ciful**, guided or created by fancy; imaginative; whimsical.—*adv* **fan´cifully**.—*n* **fan´cifulness**.—*ns* **fan´cy dress ball**, a ball at which fancy dresses are worn; **fancy dress**, dress chosen according to the wearer's fancy.—*adj* **fan´cy-free**, not married, engaged, etc; carefree; **fancywork**, embroidery, crocheting, and other ornamental needlework. [Contracted from **fantasy**.]

fandango [fan-dang´go] *n* Spanish dance, performed in triple time by a man and a woman to a guitar and castanet accompaniment; music for this dance; tomfoolery. [Sp].

fane [fān] *n* temple; a church. [L *fānum*.]

fanfare [fan´fār, f•´fār] *n* a flourish of trumpets or bugles.—*n* **fanfaronāde´**, vain boasting; bluster. [Fr, perh from the sound.]

fang [fang] *n* a long sharp tooth as one by which an animal's prey is seized or the long hollow tooth through which venomous snakes inject venom.—*adj* **fanged**. [OE *fang*, from the same root as *fōn*, to seize.]

fantasia [fan-tā´zi-a] *n* a musical or prose composition not governed by the ordinary rules of form. [It—Gr *phantasiā*. See **fantasy**.]

fantasy [fan´tȧ-si] *n* fancy; imagination; mental image; an imaginative poem, play or novel.—*adjs* **fantas´tic, -al**.—*adv* **fantas´tically**. [OFr, through Low L from Gr *phantasiā*—*phantazein*, to make visible. **fancy** is a doublet.]

fantoccini [fant´o-chē-nē] *npl* a puppet show using puppets operated by strings or mechanical devices; such puppets. [Ital]

far [fär] *adj* distant in space or time.—*adv* very distant in space, time, or degree; to or from a distance in time or position, very much.—*adjs* **far´away´**, distant; dreamy, **farfetched´**, brought from a remote time or place; **far´-off´**, remote; **far´sight´ed**, able to see to a great distance; having hyperopia; foreseeing what is likely to happen and preparing for it; **by far, far and away**, by a great deal; **Far East**, East Asia (China, Japan, etc.); **far and wide**, in every direction. [OE *feor(r)*; Du *ver*; ON *fiarre*.]

farad [far´ad] *n* SI derived unit of electrical capacitance, the capacitance of a capacitor between the plates of which appears a difference of potential of one volt when it is charged by one coulomb of electricity (symbol F); **faraday**, the quantity of electricity transferred in electrolysis per equivalent weight of an ion equal to about 96,500 coulombs. [From Michael *Faraday* (1791–1867).]

farce [färs] *n* a style of comedy, marked by broad humor and extravagant wit; ridiculous or empty show; a savory stuffing; mockery.—*adj* **far´cical**, ludicrous.—*adv* **far´cically**. [Fr *farce*, stuffing, from L *farcīre*, to stuff, apparently applied orig to a gag introduced into a religious play.]

fardel [fär´dėl] *n* a bundle; a burden. [OFr *fardel*, dim, of *farde*, a burden—possibly Ar *fardah*, a package.]

fare [fār] *vi* to happen; to be in a specified condition (*to fare well*); to eat.—*n* money paid for transportation; a passenger in a public conveyance; food.—*interj* **farewell´**, goodbye.—*n* good wishes at parting.—*adj* parting; final (*a farewell gesture, farewell address*). [OE *faran*; Ger *fahren*.]

farina [fa-rē´na] *n* flour or meal made from cereal grains, eaten as a cooked cereal.—*adj* **farinā´ceous**, mealy. [L,—*far*, grain.]

farm [färm] *n* a piece of land (with house, barns, etc.) on which crops and animals are raised; a minor-league baseball team associated with a major-league team which trains recruits for the major-league team.—*vt* to cultivate, as land.—*ns* **farm´er**, a person who manages or operates a farm; yokel; **farmhouse**, a house on a farm, **farm´ing**, the business of operating a farm; agriculture; **farm´stead**, a farm with the buildings belonging to it; **farm´-yard**, the yard or enclosure surrounded by the farm buildings.—**farm out**, to board out for fixed payment; to give, eg work for which one has made oneself responsible, to others to carry out. [OE *feorm*, goods, entertainment, from Low L *firma*, a fixed payment—L *firmus*, firm.]

faro [fār´o] *n* a gambling game in which players bet on cards drawn from a box. [Perh from *Pharaoh*; reason unknown.]

farrago [fa-rä´gō, or -rā´] *n* a confused mixture, [L *farrāgō*, mixed fodder—*far*, grain.]

farrier [far´i-ėr] *n* one who shoes horses [OFr *ferrier*—L *ferrum*, iron.]

farrow [far´ō] *n* a litter of pigs.—*vti* to bring forth (pigs). [OE *fearh*, a pig.]

farther [färTHėr] *adj* at or to a greater distance—*Also adv* to a greater degree.—*adj* **far´thermost, far´thest**. [A variant (ME *ferther*) of **further** that came to be thought a comp of **far**.]

farthing [fär´THing] *n* a former British monetary unit; a coin representing this unit; something of small value. [OE *fēorthing*, a fourth part—*fēortha*, fourth, and *-ing*.]

farthingale [fär´THing-gāl] *n* a support (as of hoops) worn, esp in the 16th century, beneath a skirt to expand it at the hipline. [OFr *verdugale*—Sp *verdugado*, hooped.]

fasces [fas´ēz] *npl* a bundle of rods, with the projecting blade of an axe, borne before ancient Roman magistrates as a badge of authority. [L pl of *fascis*, a bundle.]

fascicle [fas´i-kl] *n* (*bot*) a bunch, a bundle; a part of a book issued in parts.—*Also* **fascicule** [fas´i-kūl].—*adjs* **fascic´ular** [fas-ik´-], **fascic´ulate, -d**, united as in a bundle. [L *fasciculus*, dim of *fascis*, a bundle.]

fascinate [fas´i-nāt] *vt* to hold spellbound; to charm, attract irresistibly.—*adj* **fas´cinating**.—*n* **fascinā´tion**. [L *fascināre, -ātum*, perh allied to Gr *baskainein*, to bewitch.]

fascism [fash´izm] *n* a system of government characterized by dictatorship, belligerent nationalism, racism, and militarism.—*n* and *adj* **fasc´ist**. [It *fascismo*—*fascio*, a political group, a bundle—L *fascis*. Cf **fasces**.]

fashion [fash´(ȯ)n] *n* the form or shape of a thing; manner; the current style of dress, conduct, speech, etc.—*vt* to make; to suit or adapt.—*n* **fash´ioner**.—*adj* **fash´ionable**, according to prevailing fashion; prevailing or in use at any period; observant of the fashion in dress or living.—*n* **fash´ionableness**.—*adv* **fash´ionably**.—*ns* **fash´ionmonger**, one who studies, imitates, or sets the fashion; **fash´ion plate**, a pictorial representation of the latest style of dress; a very smartly dressed person.—**after a fashion**, in an approximate or rough way. [OFr *fachon*—L *factiō, -ōnis*—*facěre*, to make.]

fast[1] [fäst] *adj* firm; fixed; loyal, devoted; non-fading; swift, quick; ahead of time (as a timepiece); wild, promiscuous; (*inf*) glib.—*adv* firmly, thoroughly, sound (*fast asleep*); rapidly.—*ns* **fast and loose**, in a craftily deceitful way; in a reckless and irresponsible manner; **fast´-food**, a business, as a hamburger stand, that offers food prepared and served quickly; **fastness**, fixedness; swiftness; colorfast quality; a stronghold. [OE *fæst*; Ger *fest*.]

fast[2] [fäst] *vi* to abstain from all or certain foods.—*n* abstinence from food, a period of fasting.—*n* **fast´ing**. [OE *fæstan*, to fast; Ger *fasten*, to keep.]

fasten [fäs´n] *vti* to fix securely; to attach.—*ns* **fast´ener** [fäsn´ėr], a clip, catch, or other means of fastening; **fas´tening**, that which fastens.—**fasten (up) on**, to direct (eg one's eyes) on; to seize on (eg a fact, a statement); to fix (something disagreeable—eg blame) on. [OE *fæstnian*.]

fastidious [fas-tid´i-us] *adj* difficult to please; daintily refined; oversensitive.—*adv* **fastid´iously**.—*n* **fastid´iousness**. [L *fastīdiōsus*—*fastīdium*, loathing.]

fat [fat] *adj* plump; corpulent; fruitful, profitable.—*n* an oily or greasy material found in animal tissue and plant seeds; the richest part of anything; superfluous part.—*vt* to make fat.—*ns* **fat cat** (*slang*), a wealthy influential donor esp. to a political campaign; **fat´ness**, quality or state of being fat; fullness of flesh; richness; fertility.—*vt* **fatt´en**, to make fat or fleshy; to make fertile.—*n* fatt´ening, the process of making fat; state of growing fat.—*adj* **fatt´y**, containing fat or having the qualities of fat.—*n* one that is fat, esp an overweight person.—*pl* **fatties**.—*n* **fatt´iness**.—**fatty acid**, any of a series of organic acids which includes those organic acids obtained by hydrolysis of fats. [OE *fǣtt*, fatted.]

fata morgana [fä´ta mor-gä´na] a mirage, [the fairy (*fata*) Morgana of Arthurian romance.]

fate [fāt] *n* inevitable destiny, appointed lot; ill-fortune; doom; ultimate lot; **the Fates**, the three goddesses who determined the birth, life and death of man.—*adj* **fāt´al**, belonging to, or appointed by, fate; causing ruin or death; mortal; disastrous (to); ill-advised.—*ns* **fāt´alism**, belief that all events happen by fate and are hence inevitable; acceptance of this doctrine; **fāt´alist**, one who believes in fatalism.—*adj* **fāt´alistic**, belonging to or partaking of fatalism.—*n* **fatal´ity**, an occurrence resulting in death; a death caused by a disaster or accident.—*adv* **fat´ally**.—*adjs* **fāt´ed**, doomed; destined (to); **fate´ful**, charged with fate. [L *fātum*, a prediction—*fātus*, spoken—*fārī*, to speak.]

father [fä´THėr] *n* a male parent; **Father**, God; an ancestor or forefather; a fatherly protector; a founder or originator; a title of respect applied to Christian monks, priests, etc.—*vt* to be the father of.—*ns* **fa´ther fig´ure**, a senior person of experience and authority looked on as a trusted leader; **fa´therhood**, state of being a father; **father-in-law**, the father of one's husband or wife; **fa´therland**, one's native land; the land of one's fathers.—*adjs* **fa´therless**, destitute of a living father; **fa´therly**, like a father in affection and care.—*n* **fa´therliness**.—**the Holy Father**, the Pope. [OE *fæder*; Ger *vater*; L *pater*, Gr *patēr*, Sans *pitr*.]

fathom [faTH´ȯm] *n* a nautical measure = 6 feet.—*vt* to measure the depth of; to comprehend.—*adjs* **fath´omable; fath´omless**.—*n* **Fathom´eter**, trade name for sonic depth finder. [OE *fæthem*; Du *vadem*, Ger *faden*.]

fatigue [fa-tēg´] *n* weariness from labor of body or of mind; menial or manual work performed by military personnel; (*pl*) the clothing worn on fatigue or in the field; tendency of a material to break under repeated stress (as metal fatigue); (of muscle or nerve ending) temporary loss of power to respond after repeated stimulation.—*vt* to reduce to weariness.—*vi* to tire;—*pr p* **fatigu´ing**; *pt p* **fatigued´**. [Fr *fatigue*—L *fatigāre*, to weary.]

fatuous [fat´ū-us] *adj* silly, idiotic.—*ns* **fat´ūousness; fatū´ity**, silliness, inanity, an instance of this. [L *fatuus*.]

fauces [fö´sēz] *n pl* the upper part of the throat, from the root of the tongue to the entrance of the gullet. [L]

faucet [fö´set] *n* a fixture for draining off liquid (as from a pipe or cask). [Fr *fausset*.]

faugh [fō, fö] *interj* an exclamation of contempt or disgust. [Prob from the sound.]

fault [fölt] *n* failing; blemish; a minor offence; an error in a racket game (as tennis); (*geol*) a fracture in the earth's crust causing displacement of strata.—*vt* to find fault with; to find flaw(s) in; (*geol*) to cause a fault in.—*adj* **fault´y**, imperfect.—*adv* **fault´ily**.—*n* **fault´iness**.—*adj* **fault´less**, without fault or defect.—*adv* **fault´lessly**.—*n* **fault´lessness**.—**to a fault**, to an excessive degree; **find fault (with)**, to censure.—*ns* **fault´finder, fault´finding**. [OFr *faute, falte*—L *fallěre*, to deceive.]

fauna [fön´a] *n* the animals or animal life of a region or a period;—*pl* **faun´as, faun´ae** [-ē].—*n* **faun**, a figure of Roman mythology similar to the satyr. [L *Fauna, Faunus*, tutelary deities of shepherds—*favēre, fautum*, to favor.]

faute de mieux [fōt dė my_] for want of something better. [Fr]

faux pas [fō´ pä´] *n* a false step; a social blunder;—*pl* **faux pas** [usu. päz]. [Fr, lit false step.]

favor [fā´vȯr] *n* goodwill; approval; a kind deed; partiality; a small gift given out at a party; (*usu. pl*) a privilege granted or conceded, esp sexual.—*vt* to regard with goodwill; to be on the side of; to treat indulgently; to afford advantage to; to oblige (with).—*adj* **fā´vorable**; friendly; propitious; conducive (to); expressing approval.—*n* **fā´vorableness**.—*adv* **fa´vorably**.—*adj* **fā´vored**, preferred; enjoying advantages.—*ns* **fā´vorite**, a person or thing regarded with favor or preference; one unduly preferred; one expected to win.—*adj* esteemed, preferred; **fā´voritism**, the showing of undue favor; **favorite son**, one favored by the delegates of his state as presidential candidate at a national political convention; **in one's favor**, in one's good graces; to one's advantage; **out of favor**, unpopular, disliked. [OFr,—L *favor*—*favēre*, to favor, befriend.]

fawn[1] [fön] *n* a young deer, esp one still unweaned or retaining a distinctive baby coat; a young goat, or any young animal related to the goat; a light grayish brown color.—*adj* **fawny**, of a color close to fawn.—*n* **fawn lily** *see* **dogtooth violet** in **dog**. [OFr *faon*, through LL from L *fētus*, offspring.]

fawn[2] [fön] *vi* to make demonstrations of affection as a dog does; to flatter in a servile way (*with* **(up) on**).—*n* **fawn´er**.—*adv* **fawn´ingly**. [A variant of obs *fain*, to rejoice—OE *fægen*, glad.]

fax *see* **facsimile**.

fay [fā] *n* a fairy. [OFr *fae*—LL *fāta* (sing)—L *fāta* (pl), the Fates. See **fate**.]

faze [fāz] *vt* (*inf*) to disturb. [OE *fēsian*, to drive away.]

fealty [fē´ȧl-ti or fēl´ti] *n* the vassal's obligation of fidelity to his feudal lord; intense and compelling loyalty. [OFr *fealte*—L *fidēlitās, -ātis*—*fidēlis*, faithful—*fiděre*, to trust.]

fear [fēr] *n* a painful emotion excited by danger, alarm; apprehension of danger or pain; the object of fear; risk; deep reverence, piety towards God.—*vt* to regard with fear; to expect with alarm; to be regretfully inclined to think; (*B*) to stand in awe of, to venerate.—*vi* to be afraid or apprehensive.—*adj* **fear´ful**, timorous; apprehensive (of); exciting intense fear, terrible; very bad, excessive.—*adv* **fear´fully**.—*n* **fear´fulness**.—*adj* **fear´less**, without fear; daring, brave.—*adv* **fear´lessly**.—*n* **fear´lessness**.—*adj* **fear´some**, causing fear, frightful. [OE *fǣr*, fear, *fǣran*, to terrify.]

feasible [fēz´i-bl] *adj* practicable, possible.—*ns* **feas´ibleness, feasibil´ity**.—*adv* **feas´ibly**. [Fr *faisable*, that can be done—*faire, faisant*—L *facĕre*, to do.]

feast [fēst] *n* an elaborate meal prepared for some special occasion; something that gives abundant pleasure; a periodic religious celebration.—*vi* to take part in a feast.—*vt* to entertain sumptuously; to delight.—*ns* **feast´er; Feast of Tabernacles**, Sukkoth. [OFr *feste* (Fr *fête*)—L *festum*, a holiday, *festus*, solemn, festal.]

feat [fēt] *n* a deed manifesting extraordinary strength, skill, or courage. [Fr *fait*—L factum—L *facĕre*, to do.]

feather [feTH´ėr] *n* one of the growths that form the covering of a bird; plumage;—(*pl*) plumage; attire; class, kind (*birds of a feather*).—*vt* to furnish or adorn with feathers; to turn (an oar or propeller blade) so that the edge is foremost.—*ns* **feath´erbed**, a feather mattress; a bed with a feather mattress; **featherbedding**, the employment of extra, standby workers; **feath´erhead, feath´erbrain**, a foolish person; **feath´erstitch**, an embroidery stitch consisting of diagonal blanket stitches worked alternatively to the left and right; **feath´erweight**, a boxer weighing from 119 to 126 lbs; a wrestler weighing from 124 to 134 lbs.—*adj* **feath´ery**, pertaining to, resembling, or covered with, feathers.—**feather one's nest**, to accumulate wealth for oneself while serving others in a position of trust.—**a feather in one's cap**, mark of distinction. [OE *fether*; Ger *feder*; L *penna*, Gr *pteron*.]

feature [fē´tyůr, -chůr] *n* (*pl*) facial form or appearance; any of the parts of the face; a characteristic trait of something; a special attraction, sale item, newspaper article, etc.; a full-length motion picture.—*vti.* to make or be a feature of (something).—*adj* **fea´tureless**, lacking distinct features. [OFr *faiture*—L *factūra*—*facĕre*, to make.]

febrifuge [feb´ri-fūj] *n* a medicine for reducing fever. [L *febris*, fever, *fugāre*, to put to flight.]

febrile [fēb´ril, or feb´ril] *adj* pertaining to fever; feverish.—*n* **febril´ity**. [Fr,—L *febris*, fever.]

February [feb´rŏŏ-ȧr-i] *n* the second month of the year, having 28 days (or 29 days in leap years). [L *Februārius* (*mensis*), the month of expiation, *februa*, the feast of expiation.]

feces [fē´sēz] *n pl* excrement.—*adj* **fec´al**. [L, pl of *faex, faecis*, dregs.]

feckless [fek´les] *adj* shiftless, worthless, inefficient. [Scot *feck*, perh from **effect**, and suffx *-less*.]

feculent [fek´ū-lent] *adj* foul with impurities.—*n* **fec´ulence**. [L *faecula*, dim of *faex*, dregs.]

fecund [fek´und] *adj* fruitful, fertile, prolific.—*vt* **fec´undāte** [or fek-und´āt], to make fruitful; to impregnate.—*ns* **fecundā´tion**, the act of impregnating; the state of being impregnated; **fecund´ity**, fruitfulness, prolificness. [Fr,—L *fēcundus*, fruitful.]

fed *pt* and *pt p* of **feed**.

fedayeen [fed-ä´yēn] *n pl* Arab guerillas. [Arabic, the sacrificers.]

federal [fed´ėr-ȧl] *adj* designating or of a union of states, etc., in which each member surrenders some of its power to a central authority; of a central government of this type, esp the government of the US; **Federal**, of or supporting a former US political party which favored a strong centralized government; of or supporting the Union in the Civil War.—*ns* **fed´eralism**, the principles or cause maintained by federalists; **fed´eralist**, a supporter of a federal constitution or union.—*vt* **fed´eralize**, to unite (states, etc.) in a federal union; to put under federal authority.—*vti* **fed´erate**, to unite in a federation.—*ns* **federa´tion**, a union of states, groups, etc., in which each subordinates its power to a central authority; a federated organization; **Federal Bureau of Investigation**, a division of the US Department of Justice which gathers facts on federal offences; **fed´eral court**, a court established by authority of a federal government, esp one established under the laws and Constitution of the US; **Federal Reserve Bank**, one of 12 reserve banks set up to hold reserves and discount commercial paper for affiliated banks in their areas; **fed´erated church**, a local church uniting two or more congregations with differing denominational ties.—*n* a supporter of federation.—*vt* **fed´eralize**.—*ns* **fed´eralism**, the principles or cause maintained by federalists; **fed´eralist**, a supporter of a federal constitution or union. [L *foedus, -eris*, a league.]

fedora [fe-dor´a] *n* a low soft felt hat with the crown creased lengthwise, usu. worn by men. [Fr]

fee [fē] *n* price paid for professional services, licenses, etc.; (*law*) an inheritance in land. [OE *feoh*, cattle, property; a special kind of property, property in land; Ger *vieh*, ON *fē*; allied to L *pecus*, cattle, *pecūnia*, money.]

feeble [fē´bl] *adj* weak, infirm; lacking force or effectiveness.—*adj* **fee´blemind´ed** mentally retarded.—*n* **fee´bleness**.—*adv* **fee´bly**. [OFr *feble, foible*, for *floible*—L *flēbilis*, lamentable, from *flēre*, to weep.]

feed [fēd] *vt* to give food to; to furnish with necessary material; to gratify.—*vi* to take food.—*pr p* **feed´ing**; *pt, pt p* **fed**.—*n* food for animals; material fed into a machine; the part of a machine supplying this material.—*n* **feed´er**, one who feeds, or that which supplies.—*adj* secondary, subsidiary, tributary.—*ns* **feed´back**, return of part of the output of a system to the input as of electricity or of information; **feed´lot**, a plot of land on which livestock are fattened for market; **feed´stock**, raw material supplied to a machine or processing plant.—**fed up**, sated, wearied or disgusted beyond endurance. [OE *fēdan*, to feed.]

feel [fēl] *vt* to perceive by the touch, to try by touch; to grope (one's way); to be conscious of; to have an inward persuasion of; to experience.—*vi* to know by the touch, to have the emotions excited; to produce a certain sensation when touched (*to feel hard* or *hot*);—*pr p* **feel´ing**; *pt, pt p* **felt**.—*n* the sense of touch; a quality as revealed to the touch (*it has a soapy feel*); a quality of atmosphere of which one is conscious (*an eerie feel*).—*ns* **feel´er**, a remark or an action intended to sound the opinions of others; a tactile process (as a tentacle or antenna) of an animal; **feel´ing**, the sense of touch; perception of objects, by touch; consciousness of pleasure or pain; tenderness; emotion; emotional responsiveness; belief as resulting from emotion; (*pl*) the affections or passions; (*pl*) sensibilities.—*adj* expressive of great sensibility or tenderness; easily affected.—*adv* **feel´ingly**.—**feel (a person) out**, to find out the opinions of (a person) cautiously; **feel like**, (*inf*) to have a desire for; **feel one's way**, to advance cautiously; **feel up to**, (*inf*) to feel capable of. [OE *fēlan*, to feel; Ger *fühlen*; prob akin to L *palpāre*, to stroke.]

feet [fēt] *pl* of **food**.—**feet of clay**, a flaw of character that is usu. not readily apparent.

feign [fān] *vt* to invent; to dissemble.—*adj* **feigned**, pretended. [Fr *feindre*, pr p *feignant*, to feign—L *fingĕre, fictum*, to form.]

feint [fānt] *n* a pretended attack, intended to take the opponent off his guard, as in boxing.—*vi* to make a feint. [Fr *feinte*—*feindre*. See **feign**.]

feldspar [fel(d)´spär] *n* any member of the most important group of rock-forming minerals, compounds of aluminum and silicon, containing also potassium, calcium or sodium.—*adj* **feldspathic**, pertaining to or consisting of feldspar. [Swed *feldetspat*—*feld*, field, *spat*, spar.]

felicity [fe-lis´i-ti] *n* happiness; a happy event; apt and pleasing expression in writing, etc.—*vt* **felic´itāte**, to express joy or pleasure to; to congratulate.—*n* **felicitā´tion**, the act of congratulating.—*adj* **felic´itous**—*adv* **felic´itously**. [Fr,—L *fēlicitās, -ātis*—*fēlix, -icis*, happy.]

feline [fē´līn] *adj* pertaining to the cat or the cat family; like a cat; sly.—Also *n* [L *fēlīnus*, a cat.]

fell[1] [fel] *pt t* of **fall**.

fell[2] [fel] *vt* to cut, beat, or knock down; to kill, to sew (a seam) by folding one raw edge under the other.—*n* **fell´er**. [**OE** *fellan*, causal form of *fallan*, to fall.]

fell[3] [fel] *n* a skin, hide, pelt; a thin tough membrane covering a carcass directly under the hide. [OE *fel*; cf L *pellis*, Gr *pella*, Ger *fell*.]

fell[4] [fel] *adj* cruel, fierce, bloody, deadly. [OFr *fel*, cruel—Low L *fellō, -ōnis*. See **felon**.]

fellah [fel´ä] *n* a peasant, esp in Egypt;—*pl* **fell´aheen, fell´ahîn**. [Ar *fellāh*, tiller of the soil.]

fellow [fel´ō] *n* an associate; a comrade; one of a pair, a mate; one holding a fellowship in a college; (*inf*) a man or boy; a member of a learned society.—*adj* belonging to the same group or class, as **fell´ow cit´izen, fell´ow worker**, etc.—*ns* **fell´ow feel´ing**, feeling between fellows or equals, sympathy; **fell´owship**, companionship; a mutual sharing; a group of people with the same interests; an endowment for the support of a student or scholar doing advanced work; **fellow traveller**, a nonmember who supports the cause of a party. [ME *felawe*—ON *fēlagi*, a partner in goods, from *fē* (Ger *vieh*), cattle, property, and root *lag-*, a laying together, a law.]

felo-de-se [fel´ō di sē´] *n* one who kills himself; self-murder. [Anglo-L, a felon towards himself.]

felon [fel´ȯn] *n* one guilty of felony; a convict; a whitlow.—*adj* **felō´nious**, of, relating to, or having the nature of a felony.—*adv* **felō´niously**.—*n* **fel´ony**, a grave crime declared to be a felony by the nature of the punishment; crime for which the penalty may be death or more than one year of punishment under federal law. [OFr,—Low L *fellō, -ōnis*, a traitor.]

felt[1] [felt] *pt, pt p* of **feel**.

felt[2] [felt] *n* a fabric of wool, often mixed with fur or hair, worked together by pressure.—*vi* to become like felt.—*vt* to make into felt.—*n* **felt´ing**, the art or process of making felt; the felt itself. [OE *felt*; cf Du *vilt*, Ger *filz*.]

female [fē´māl] *adj* of the sex that produces young; pertaining to females; (*bot*) having a pistil or fruit-bearing organ; having a hollow part (as a pipe fitting) for receiving an inserted part.—*n* a female person, animal, or plant. [Fr *femelle*—L *femella*, dim of *fēmina*, a woman.]

feminine [fem´i-nin] *adj* pertaining to women; womanly; womanish; (*gram*) of that gender to which words denoting females belong.—*adv* **fem´ininely**.—*ns* **fem´inism**, the movement to win political, economic and social equality for women; **fem´inist**, supporter of feminism; **femininity**, the quality of being feminine. [L *fēmina*, woman.]

femme fatale [fam fä-täl] a woman of irresistible charm. [Fr, fatal woman.]

femur [fē´můr] *n* the thighbone.—*adj* **fĕm´oral**. [L *fĕmur, -ŏris*, thigh.]

fen [fen] *n* an area of low marshy land; swamp; bog.—*adj* **fenn´y**. [OE *fenn*; ON *fen*.]

fence [fens] *n* a barrier for enclosing, bounding, or protecting land; a receiver of stolen goods.—*vt* to enclose with a fence; to keep (out) as by a fence.—

vi to practise the art of fencing; to make evasive answers; to be a receiver of stolen goods.—*ns* **fenc´er**, a maker of fences; one who practises fencing with a sword; **fencing**, the art of fighting with a foil or other sword; material for making fences; a system of fences. [Abbrev of **defence**.]

fend [fend] *vi* to resist; **fend for oneself**, to manage by oneself; **fend off**, ward off. [Abbrev of **defend**.]

fender [fend´ėr] *n* anything that protects or fends off something else, as the part of an automobile body over the wheel. [**fend**.]

fenestra [fe-nes´tra] *n* a window.—*adj* **fenes´tral**, belonging to, or like, a window; perforated—also **fenes´trāte(d)**.—*n* **fenestrā´tion**, the arrangement of windows in a building. [L]

Fenian [fē´ni-ȧn] *n* a member of an association of Irishmen founded in 1857 for the overthrow of the English government in Ireland.—*n* **Fē´nianism**. [Old Ir *Féne*, one of the names of the ancient population of Ireland.]

fennel [fen´ėl] *n* a European herb (*Foeniculum officinale*) of the carrot family grown for its foliage and aromatic seeds; a herb (*F vulgare*) grown for its edible bulbous stem tasting of licorice. [OE *finul*—L *fēniculum*, fennel—*fēnum*, hay.]

feral [fē´rȧl] *adj* wild; untamed; pertaining to or like a wild beast.—Also **fēr´ine** [-rīn, -rin]. [L *fera*, a wild beast.]

feria[1] [fē´ri-ȧ] *n* an Hispanic market festival often in observance of a religious holiday. [Sp]

feria[2] [fē´ri-ȧ] *n* a weekday of a church calendar of which no feast falls.—*adj* **fer´ial**. [Fr,—L *fēria*, a holiday.]

ferment [fûr´mėnt] *n* a substance causing fermentation, as yeast; excitement, agitation.—*vt* **ferment´**, to cause fermentation in; to excite, to agitate.—*vi* to be in the process of fermentation; to be stirred with anger.—*adj* **ferment´able**, capable of fermentation.—*ns* **fermentā´tion**, the breakdown of complex molecules in organic components caused by the influence of a ferment; restless action of the mind or feelings.—*adjs* **ferment´ative**, causing, or consisting in, fermentation; **fermenter**, an organism that causes fermentation; **fermentor**, an apparatus for carrying out fermentation. [Fr,—L *fermentum*, for *fervi mentum*—*fervēre*, to boil.]

fermi [fûr´mi] *n* a unit of length = 10^{15} m.—*ns* **fer´mion**, one of a group of subatomic particles; **fer´mium**, a transuranic element (symbol Fm; at wt 253; at no 100). [Italian physicist Enrico *Fermi* (1901–54).]

fern [fûrn] *n* any of a large class (Filicinae) of nonflowering plants having roots, stems, and fronds, and reproducing by spores.—*adj* **fern´y**. [OE *fearn*; Ger *farn*.]

ferocious [fe-rō´shȯs] *adj* savage, fierce; cruel.—*adv* **ferō´ciously**.—*ns* **ferō´ciousness; feroc´ity**, savage cruelty of disposition; untamed fierceness; an act showing this. [L *ferōx*, *ferōcis*, wild—*ferus*, wild.]

ferret [fer´et] *n* a half-tamed albino variety of the polecat (*Mustela furo*), employed in unearthing rabbits.—*vt* to drive out of a hiding-place; to search (out) cunningly and persistently;—*pr p* **ferr´eting**; *pt p* **ferr´eted**. [OFr *furet*, a ferret—Low L *fūrō, -ōnis*, ferret—L *fūr*, a thief.]

ferri-, ferro-, (ferr-) of, containing iron [L *ferrum*, iron].—*n* **ferr´ite**, any of a type of magnetic material, mixed oxides of iron, manganese, aluminum, etc., which are also electric insulators.—*adjs* **ferrug´inous** [-ōōj- or -ūj-; L *ferrūgō, -inis*, iron rust], of, containing, or related to iron, resembling iron rust in color; **ferri´ferous** [*-ferous* from L *ferre*, to bear], of rocks, iron-yielding; **ferr´ocon´crete** reinforced concrete; **ferr´otype** a photograph made on a thin iron plate.—**ferri-, ferro-**, and similarly the *adjs* **ferric** and **ferrous** are used for compounds in which iron has respectively its higher (3) and its lower (2) combining power.—*adj* **ferromagnet´ic**, having high magnetic permeability.

Ferris wheel [fer´us] *n* an amusement ride comprising a large upright wheel revolving on a fixed axis and having suspended seats. [G. *Ferris*, 1859–96, US engineer.]

ferrocene [fer´ō-sēn] *n* (*chem*) $G_{10}H_{10}Fe$, stable compound in which iron is linked to two rings each of five carbon atoms. [**ferro + cyclopentadiene**.]

ferrule [fer´ȯl, fer´(y)ōōl] *n* a metal ring or cap on a cane, umbrella, etc., to keep it from splitting. [OFr *virole*—L *viriola*, a bracelet.]

ferry [fer´i] *vt* to carry or convey over water (or land), esp along a regular route, in a boat, ship, or aircraft; to deliver (an aircraft coming from a factory) under its own power;—*pr p* **ferr´ying**; *pt p* **ferr´ied**.—*n* a place or route of carriage across water; the right of ferrying; a ferryboat. [OE *ferian*, to convey, *faran*, to go; Ger *fähre*, a ferry—*fahren*, to go, to carry.]

fertile [fûr´tīl, -til] *adj* able to bear or produce (abundantly); rich in resources; inventive.—*adv* **fer´tilely**.—*vt* **fer´tilize**, to make fertile or fruitful; to enrich; to impregnate; to pollinate.—*ns* **fertilizā´tion; fer´tilizer; fertil´ity**, fruitfulness, richness; abundance. [Fr,—L *fertilis*—*ferre*, to bear.]

ferule [fer´(y)ŏŏl] *n* a rod used for punishment. [L *ferula*, a cane—*ferīre*, to strike.]

fervent [fûr´vėnt] *adj* hot; ardent, zealous, warm in feeling.—*n* **fer´vency**, eagerness; emotional warmth.—*adv* **fer´vently**.—*adj* **fer´vid** very hot; having burning desire or emotion; zealous.—*adv* **fer´vidly**.—*ns* **fer´vidness; fer´vor**, heat; heat of mind, zeal. [Fr,—L *fervēre*, to boil.]

fess, fesse [fes] *n* (*her*) a band drawn horizontally across the middle of an escutcheon. [Fr *fasce*—L *fascia*, a band.]

festal [fes´tȧl] *adj* pertaining to a feast or holiday; joyous; gay.—*adv* **fes´tally**. [Fr,—OFr *fest*. See **feast**.]

fester [fes´tėr] *vi* to become corrupt; to suppurate; to rankle.—*vt* to cause to fester or rankle.—*n* a wound discharging pus. [OFr *festre*—L *fistula*, an ulcer.]

festive [fes´tiv] *adj* merry, joyous.—*n* **fes´tival**, a joyful celebration; a feast; a season of performances of music, plays, or the like.—*adv* **fes´tively**.—*n* **festiv´ity**, social mirth; a festive celebration; gaiety. [L *fēstīvus*—*fēstus*.]

festoon [fes-tōōn´] *n* a garland suspended between two points; (*archit*) an ornament like a wreath of flowers, etc.—*vt* to adorn as with festoons. [Fr *feston*, app conn with L *fēstum*. See **feast**.]

feta [fet´a] *n* a white soft Greek cheese made from sheep or goat's milk and cured in brine. [modern Greek.]

fetal *see* **fetus**.

fetch [fech] *vt* to go and bring back; to cause to come; to sell for.—*n* range, sweep (eg of imagination); a stratagem, trick.—*adj* **fetch´ing**, fascinating.—**fetch up**, to recover; to stop suddenly. [OE *feccan*, app an altered form of *fetian*, to fetch; cf Ger *fassen*, to seize.]

fetch[2] [fech] *n* the apparition of a living person.—[Ety unknown.]

fête [fet, fāt] *n* a festival; a holiday.—*vt* to entertain at a feast; to honor with festivities. [Fr]

fetich *see* **fetish**.

feticide *see* **fetus**.

fetid [fē´tid or fet´id] *adj* stinking, having a strong offensive smell. [L *foetidus*—*foetēre*, to stink.]

fetish [fet´ish] *n* an object believed to procure for its owner the services of a spirit lodged within it; something regarded with irrational reverence.—*n* **fet´ishism, fet´ichism**, the worship of a fetish; a belief in charms.—Also **fetich**, [Fr *fétiche*—Port *feitico*, magic; a name given by the Portuguese to the gods of West Africa—Port *feitiço*, artificial—L *factītius*—*facĕre*, to make.]

fetlock [fet´lok] *n* a tuft of hair that grows above a horse's hoof; the part where this hair grows; the joint of the limb at the fetlock. [History obscure; compounded of *foot* and *lock* (of hair); cf Ger *fissloch*.]

fetter [fet´ėr] *n* (used chiefly in *pl*) a chain or shackle for the feet; anything that restrains.—*vt* to put fetters on; to restrain.—*adj* **fett´ered**. [OE *feter*—*fōt*, foot.]

fettle [fet´l] *n* condition, as *in fine fettle*. [ME *fetlen*, make ready.]

fetus [fēt´us] *n* the unborn young of an animal, esp in its later stages; in man, the offspring in the womb from the fourth month until birth.—*adj* **fet´al**.—*ns* **fē´ticide** [-sīd], the act of causing the death of a fetus; **fētos´copy** [kopē] examination of the pregnant uterus by means of a fiberoptic tube. [L *fētus*, offspring.]

feud[1] [fūd] *n* a deadly quarrel, esp between families or clans.—*vi* to carry on a feud. [OFr *faide*, *feide*—Low L *faida*—OHG *fēhida*. Akin to **foe**.]

feud[2] [fūd] *n* a fief or land held on condition of service.—*adj* **feud´al**, pertaining to feuds or fiefs; belonging to feudalism.—*n* **feud´alism**, the economic and social system in medieval Europe, in which land, worked by serfs, was held by vassels in exchange for military and other services to overlords.—*adj* **feud´atory**, holding lands or power by feudal tenure.—Also *n*. [Low L *feudum*—Gmc; connected with **fee** (2).]

fever [fē´vėr] *n* an abnormally increased body temperature; any disease marked by a high fever; a restless excitement.—*vt* to put into a fever.—*vi* to become fevered.—*adj* **fē´vered**, affected with fever; excited.—*ns* **fē´verfew**, a perennial European composite herb (*Chrysanthemum parthenium*).—*adj* **fē´verish**, slightly fevered; indicating fever; restlessly excited.—*adv* **fē´verishly**.—*n* **fē´verishness**. [OE *fēfor*—L *febris*.]

few [fū] *adj* small in number, not many.—*n* **few´ness**.—**a few**, a small number (of)—used as a noun, or virtually a compound adjective.—**quite a few**, (*inf*) a large number; **the few**, the minority. [OE *fēa*, pl *fēawe*; Fr *peu*; L *paucus*, small.]

fey [fā] *adj* fated; strange and unusual. [ME *fay*, *fey*—OE *fǣge*, doomed; cf Du *veeg*, about to die.]

Feynman diagram [fīn´man] a graphic representation of various interactions of elementary particles such as electrons, positrons, and photons.

fez [fez] *n* a red tapering cap usu. with black tassel worn esp by men in eastern Mediterranean countries.—*pl* **fezz´es**. [From *Fez* in Morocco.]

fiancé *fem* **fiancée** [fē-ã´sā] *n* a person engaged to be married (with possessive case of noun or pronoun—eg *her fiancé was there*). [Fr]

fiasco [fi-as´kō] *n* an utter failure of any kind.—*pl* **fiascoes**. [It *fiasco*, bottle, perh—L *vasculum*. *See* **flask**.]

fiat [fi´at] *n* a formal or solemn command; a decree. [L 'let it be done', 3rd pers sing pres subj of *fiěrī*, passive of *facĕre*, to do.]

fib [fib] *n* a lie about something unimportant.—*vi* to tell a fib or lie;—*pr p* fibb´ing; *pt p* fibbed. [Perh **fable**.]

fiber [fī´bėr] *n* any fine thread-like object of animal, vegetable or mineral origin, natural or synthetic; a structure of material composed of fibers; texture; short for dietary fiber.—*n* **fiber´board** stiff sheet made by compressing fibers (as of wood).—*adj* **fibered**, having fibers.—*ns* **fiber´glass**, glass in fibrous form used in making various products (as glass wool, yarns, textiles, and structures); **fiber optics**, thin transparent fibers of glass or plastic inclosed by material of lower index of refraction and that transmit light throughout their length by internal reflections; a bundle of such fibers used in an instrument as for viewing body cavities; (*sing*) the technique of using fiber optics; **fī´bril**, a small filament or fiber; one of the fine threads composing muscle fiber, etc. **fī´brin**, a threadlike elastic protein formed in blood clots; **fi´brinogen**, a protein in the blood from which fibrin is formed; **fibrōsīt´is**, inflammation of fibrous tissues.—*adj* **fi´brous**, composed of fibers.—*n* **fi´brousness**. [Fr,—L *fibra*, a thread.]

Fibonacci series [fē-bo-nach´ē] *n* the series of numbers 0, 1, 1, 2, 3, 5, 8, 13, 21, . . ., in which each term is the sum of the two preceding terms. [L *Fibonacci*, 1170–1250, Ital mathematician.]

fibula [fib´u-la] *n* the outer of the two bones from the knee to the ankle.—*pl* **fibulae**. [L]

fichu [fē´shü] *n* a woman's three-cornered cape of lace or muslin for the neck and shoulders. [Fr]

fickle [fik´l] *adj* inconstant; changeable.—*n* **fick´leness**. [OE *ficol; gefic*, fraud.]

fictile [fik´tīl -til], *adj* of pottery. [L *fictilis—fingĕre*, to fashion.]

fiction [fik´sh(ò)n] *n* an invented story; any literary work with imaginary characters and events as a novel, play, etc.; such works collectively.—*adjs* **fic´tional**, imaginative, not restricted to fact; pertaining to fiction; **ficti´tious** [-tish´ùs], imaginary, not real, feigned.—*adv* **ficti´tiously**. [Fr,—L *fictiō, -ōnis—fictus*, pt p of *fingĕre*.]

fiddle [fid´l] *n* (among musicians) a violin; a device to keep dishes from sliding off a table aboard ship; a swindle.—*vt* to play on a violin.—*vt* to swindle; to falsify.—*vi* to be busy over trifles.—*interjs* **fiddle-faddle, fidd´lesticks**, nonsense!—*ns* **fiddle-head**, an ornament on a ship's bow resembling the scroll at the head of a violin; a young unfurling frond of some ferns often eaten as greens; **fidd´ler**, one who fiddles; **fiddler crab**, a burrowing crab (genus *Uca*) having one claw much enlarged in the male.—**play second fiddle**, to take a subordinate part in anything. [OE *fithele*; Ger *fiedel*. From same root as **viol, violin**.]

fidelity [fi-del´i-ti] *n* faithful performance of duty; loyalty; faithfulness to a husband or wife; exactness in reproducing sound or picture, esp by electronic devices such as a record player, radio, or television. [L *fidēlitās, -ātis—fidēlis*, faithful—*fidĕre*, to trust.]

fidget [fij´et] *vi* to be unable to rest; to move uneasily;—*pr p* **fidg´eting**; *pt p* **fidg´eted**.—*n* one who fidgets; restlessness; (*pl*) general nervous restlessness.—*adj* **fidg´ety**, restless; uneasy.—*n* **fidg´etiness**. [Perh related ON *fikja*.]

fiducial [fi-dū´shi-àl] *adj* showing confidence or reliance; of the nature of trust.—*adj* **fidū´ciary**, of the nature of a trust; held in trust.—*n* trustee,—*pl* **fiduciaries**. [L *fidūcia*, confidence, from *fidĕre*, to trust.]

fief [fēf] *n* in feudalism, heritable land held by a vassal. [OFr *see* **fee** (2).]

field [fēld] *n* area of land free from trees and buildings; a piece of ground cleared for tillage, pasture, or sport; the locality of a battle; the battle itself; an unbroken wide expanse (eg *icefield*); a tract yielding a natural product (eg gold, coal); an area affected in a particular way (eg *magnetic field*); the area visible through an optical lens; sphere of activity, knowledge, etc.; (*her*) the surface of a shield; the background on which figures are drawn; all entrants in a contest; (*math*) a set of elements upon which binary operations of addition, subtraction, multiplication, and division can be performed except that division by 0 is excluded; (*physics*) a space within which magnetic or electrical lines of force are active.—*vt* at baseball, to catch or stop and return to the fixed place; to put (eg a team) into the field to play.—*vi* to stand ready to stop the ball in baseball.—*ns* **field´ day**, a day when troops are drawn out for instruction in field exercises; a day of sports and athletic competition; any day of unusual bustle or success; **field´er**, one who fields; **field´ event**, an athletic event other than a race; **field´fare**, a medium-sized Eurasian thrush (*Turdus pilaris*) with ash-colored head and chestnut wings; **field´glass(es)**, a small, portable binocular telescope for use outdoors; **field´ goal**, (in basketball) a goal made while the ball is in play; (in football) a goal made by drop-kicking or place-kicking from the field; **field´ house**, a building providing facilities for athletic events, seats for spectators, and storage of equipment; **field´ marshal**, an officer of the highest rank in some armies; **field´ mouse**, any of various mice, esp a vole; **field´ officer**, a major, lieutenant colonel, or colonel in the US Army, Air Force or Marine Corps; **field´stone**, a stone (as in building) usu. in unaltered form used in construction; **field´ trial**, a trial of sporting dogs in actual practice; a test in practice, as distinct from one under laboratory conditions; **field´work**, a temporary fortification thrown up by troops in the field; work (as by students) done in the field through firsthand observation; the gathering of anthropological and sociological data through observation and interviews.—**play the field**, to expand one's activities. [OE *feld*; cf Du *veld*, the open country, Ger *feld*.]

fiend [fēnd] *n* an evil spirit; an inhumanly wicked person; an enthusiast; an addict.—*adj* **fiend´ish**, like a fiend; devilishly cruel.—*n* **fiend´ishness**. [OE *fēond*, enemy; Ger *feind*, Du *vijand*.]

fierce [fērs] *adj* ferocious, angry; violent.—*adv* **fierce´ly**.—*n* **fierce´ness**. [OFr *fers* (Fr *fier*)—L *ferus*, wild, savage.]

fiery [fīr´i] *adj* like, or consisting of, fire; ardent, impetuous; irritable.—*adv* **fier´ily**.—*ns* **fier´iness** [**fire**.]

fiesta [fē-es´ta] *n* a saint's day; holiday; festivity. [Sp]

fife [fīf] *n* a small keyless variety of the flute. [Ger *pfeife*, pipe, or Fr *fifre*, fife, fifer; both from L *pīpāre*, to cheep.]

fifteen [fif´tēn] (when used absolutely, [fif-tēn´] adj, n one more than fourteen; the symbol for this (15, XV, xv,); the first point scored by a side in a game of tennis.—*adj* **fifteenth**, the last of fifteen; being one of fifteen equal parts.—*Also n*. [OE *fiftēne*.]

fifth [fifth] *adj* last of five; being one of five equal parts.—*Also n* (*music*) the interval embracing five diatonic degrees; a unit of measurement for liquor equal to one fifth of a US gallon.—**Fifth**, the Fifth Amendment of the US constitution.—*n* **Fifth Amendment**, amendment guaranteeing certain legal safeguards, esp that no person in a criminal case is compelled to testify against himself; **fifth column**, traitors among the population who give help to an enemy attacking from outside; **fifth wheel**, one that is unnecessary. [OE *fifta*; affected in ME by the *-th* in *fourth*.]

fifty [fif´ti] *adj n* five times ten; symbol for this (50, L, 1.—*pl* **fifties** (50s), the numbers from 50 to 59; the same numbers in a life or century.—*adj* **fif´tieth**, the last of fifty; being one of fifty equal parts.—*Also n* **fif´ty-fif´ty**, half-and-half; (of chances) equal. [OE *fiftig—fif*, five, *tig*, ten, related to *tiēn, tēn*.]

fig [fig] *n* any of a very large genus (*Ficus*) of trees of the mulberry family, yielding a pear-shaped fruit; the edible fruit of *F carica*; a thing of little consequence.—*n* **fig´ leaf**, symbol of affected modesty; something intended to conceal the reality of actions or motives. [Fr *figue*—L *ficus*, a fig-tree.]

fight [fīt] *vi* to strive (for); to contend in war or in single combat.—*vt* to engage in conflict with; to win (one's way) by conflict;—*pr p* **fight´ing**; *pt* and *pt p* **fought** (*föt*).—*n* a struggle; a combat; a battle or engagement; strong disagreement; the will, or strength, to contend.—*n* **fight´er**, one who fights; one who does not give in easily; an airplane designed to destroy enemy aircraft.—*adj* **fight´ing**, engaged in, or fit for, combat.—*n* the act of fighting or contending.—**fighting chair**, a chair from which a salt-water angler plays a hooked fish; **fighting chance**, a chance to success given supreme effort. [OE *fehtan*; Ger *fechten*.]

figment [fig´mėnt] *n* a fabrication or invention. [L. *figmentum—fingĕre*, to form.]

figure [fig´ūr] *n* the form of anything in outline; a geometrical form; a representation in drawing, etc.; a design; a statue; appearance; a personage; a character denoting a number; a number; value or price; a deviation from the ordinary mode of expression, in which words are changed from their literal signification or usage; (*geom*) a surface or space bounded by lines or planes; a set of steps in a dance or a series of movements in skating; a type or emblem; (*pl*) arithmetic.—*vt* to make an image of; to mark with figures or designs; (*inf*) to believe, to consider; to calculate with figures.—*vi* to play a part (in), be conspicuous (in); to do arithmetic.—*adj* **figurative**, representing by means of a figure or symbol; not in its usual or exact sense, metaphorical; using figures of speech.—*adv* **figuratively**.—*adj* **figured**, adorned with figures, marked with figures.—*ns* **figure eight**, something resembling the Arabic numeral 8 in form or shape; **figurehead**, a carved figure on the bow of a ship; a nominal head or leader; **figure skating**, skating in which the skater outlines prescribed figures; **figurine**, a small carved or molded figure.—**figure of speech**, an expression, as a metaphor or simile, using words in a nonliteral or unusual sense; **figure on**, to rely on; **figure out**, to solve, to understand; **figure up**, to add, to total. [Fr,—L *figūra*, cognate with *fingĕre*, to form.]

filament [fil´a-mėnt] *n* a slender thread or threadlike part; a fiber; the fine wire in a light bulb or electron tube; (*bot*) the stalk of a stamen; a chain of cells.—*adj* **filament´ous**, thread-like. [L *filum*, a thread.]

filbert [fil´bėrt] *n* the nut of the cultivated hazel. [Prob from *St Philibert*, whose day fell in the nutting season.]

filch [filch] *vt* to steal, to pilfer.—*n* **filch´er**, thief. [Ety. unknown.]

file [fīl] *n* an container for keeping papers, etc., in order; an orderly arrangement of papers; a line of persons or things.—*vt* to dispatch or register (a news story, an application, etc.); to put on public record.—*vi* to move in a line; to apply (for divorce, for candidacy, esp in a primary election). **-on file** available for ready reference; **(in) single file, Indian file**, (moving forward) singly, one behind another. [L *filum*, a thread.]

file[2] [fīl] *n* a steel instrument with sharp-edged furrows for smoothing or grinding.—*vt* to cut or smooth with, or as with, a file; to polish, improve.—*n* **fil´ing**, a particle rubbed off with a file. [OE *fȳl*; Ger *feile*; Du *vijl*.]

filial [fil´yàl] *adj* pertaining to, or becoming in, a son or daughter; bearing the relation of a child.—*adv* **fil´ially**. [Fr,—Low L *filiālis*—L *filius*, a son.]

filiation [fil-e-a´shun] *n* filial relationship, esp of a son to his father; the adjudication of paternity; descent or derivation, esp from a culture or language; the process of determining such relationship.

filibuster [fil´i-bus-tėr] *n* a member of a legislature who obstructs a bill by making long speeches.—*vti* to obstruct (a bill) by such methods. [Sp *filibustero*, through Fr from Du *vrijbueter, vrijbuiter*. See **freebooter**.]

filiform [fil´i-förm] *adj* having the form of a filament; long and slender. [L *filum*, thread, *forma*, form.]

filigree [fil´i-grē] *n* a kind of ornamental work in which threads of precious metal are interlaced; anything delicate and fragile like such metalwork.—Also *adj*. [Fr *filigrane*—It *filigrana*—L *filum*, thread, *granum*, a grain.]

Filipino [fil-i-pē´no] *n* a native of the Philippine Islands, specif a member of a Christianized Philippine people; a citizen of the Republic of Philippines.

fill [fil] *vt* to put as much as possible into; to occupy wholly; to put a person into (a position or job, etc.); to supply the things called for (in an order, etc.); to close or plug (holes, etc.).—*vi* to become full.—*n* enough to make full or to satisfy; anything that fills.—*ns* **filler; fill´ing**, anything that fills a hole, etc.; **filling station**, service station.—**fill in**, to complete by supplying something; to supply for completion; to be a substitute; **fill out**, to make or become larger; to complete (a document, etc.) with data; **fill up**, to make or become completely full. [OE *fyllan—full*, full.]

fillet [fil´et] *n* a thin strip or band; a thin boneless strip of meat or fish; (*archit*) a small space or band used along with mouldings.—*vt* to bone and slice (fish or meat);—*pr p* **fill´eting**; *pt p* **fill´eted**. [Fr *filet*, dim of *fil*, from L *filum*, a thread.]

fillip [fil´ip] *vt* to strike with the nail of the finger, forced from the thumb with a sudden jerk;—*pr p* **fill´iping**; *pt p* **fill´iped**.—*n* a snap of the finger from the thumb; a stimulus. [A form of **flip**.]

filly [fil´i] *n* a young female horse. [Dim of *foal*.]

film [film] *n* a fine, thin skin, coating, etc.; a flexible cellulose material covered with a light-sensitive substance used in photography; haze or blur; a motion picture.—*vti* to cover or be covered as with a film; to photograph or make a motion picture (of).—*adj* **filmy**, gauzy, sheer; blurred, hazy.—*n* **filminess**.—*ns* **filmcard**, microfiche; **film´strip**, a strip of film bearing photographs, diagrams, or graphics for still projection. [OE *filmen*, conn with *fell*, a skin.]

Filofax [fil´o-fax] *n* trade name for a loose-leaf pocket filing system.

filter [fil´ter] *n* a device or substance straining out solid particles, impurities, etc., from a liquid or gas; a device or substance for screening out electric oscillations, light waves, etc., of certain frequencies; a screen for absorbing light of certain colors.—*vti* to pass through or as through a filter; to remove with a filter.—*ns* **filterable virus**, any of the infectious agents that remain virulent after a fluid containing them passes through a filter of diatomite or unglazed porcelain; **filter bed**, a bed of sand, gravel, etc., used for filtering water or sewage; **filter paper**, porous paper for use in filtering. [OFr *filtre*—Low L *filtrum*, felt.]

filth [filth] *n* foul matter; obscenity.—*adj* **filth´y**, foul, unclean; obscene.—*n* **filth´iness**.—*adv* **filth´ily**. [OE *fȳlth—fūl*, foul.]

filtrate [fil´trāt] *vt* to filter.—*n* a liquid that has been filtered.—*n* **filtrā´tion**, act or process of filtering. [**filter**.]

fimbriate, -d [fim´bri-āt, -ed] *adj* fringed. [L *fimbriātus—fimbriae*, fibers.]

fin [fin] *n* an organ by which an aquatic animal balances itself and swims; anything like this in shape and use.—*adjs* **fin´like; finned**, furnished with fins. [OE *finn*; L *pinna*.]

final [fī´nål] *adj* of or coming at the end, last; decisive, conclusive.—*n* (*pl*) the last of a series of contests; a final examination.—*vt* **fī´nalize**, to make complete.—*ns* **fin´alist**, a contestant in the final, deciding contest of a series; **final´ity**, state of being final; completeness or conclusiveness.—*adv* **fī´nally**.—**final cause** (see **cause**). [Fr,—L *fīnālis—finis*, an end.]

finale [fi-nä´lā] *n* the end; the last movement in a musical composition; the concluding piece in a concert. [It *finale*, final—L *fīnālis*.]

finance [fi-nans´, fī] *n* the art of managing money; (*pl*) money resources.—*vt* to supply or get money for.—*adj* **finan´cial** [-shål], pertaining to finance.—*adv* **finan´cially**.—*n* **finan´cier**, one skilled in finance. [Fr,—Low L *financia*—Low L *fināre*, to pay a fine—*finis*. See **fine** (2).]

finch [finch, -sh] *n* any of numerous songbirds of the family Fringillidae having a short stout conical bill adapted for crushing seeds. [OE *finc*; Ger *fink*.]

find [fīnd] *vt* to discover by chance; to get by searching; to perceive; to recover (something lost); to reach, attain; to decide and declare to be.—*vi* to reach a decision (as by a jury).—*pr p* **finding**; *pt p* **found**.—*n* a finding; something found.—*ns* **finder**, one that finds; a camera device for sighting the field of view; **finding**, a discovery; something found; the verdict of a judge, scholar, etc.—**find fault**, to criticize unfavorably; **find out**, to learn by study, observation, or search. [OE *findan*; Ger *finden*.]

fin de siècle [fẽ de sye-kl´] the end of the (19th) century or of an era; characteristic of the ideas, etc., of that time; decadent. [Fr]

fine [fīn] *adj* very good; with no impurities, refined; clear and bright (*fine weather*); not heavy or coarse (*fine sand*); very thin or small (*fine print*); sharp (*a fine edge*); subtle (*a fine distinction*); elegant.—*adv* in a fine manner; (*inf*) very well.—*adv* **finely**.—*ns* **fineness, fin´ery** elaborate clothes, jewelry, etc.—*adj* **fine´spun**, finely spun out; artfully contrived.—**fine art(s)**, as painting, sculpture, music, those chiefly concerned with the beautiful. [Fr,—L *fīnītus*, finished, from *fīnire*, to finish, *finis*, an end.]

fine [fīn] *n* a sum of money imposed as a punishment.—*vt* to impose a fine on.—**in fine**, in short. [Low L *finis*, a fine—L *finis*, an end.]

finesse [fi-nes´] *n* subtlety of contrivance; a cunning strategy; (*bridge*) an attempt to take a trick with a card lower than a higher card held by an opponent.—*vi* to use artifice. [Fr]

finger [fing´gėr] *n* one of the five terminal parts of the hand, or of the four other than the thumb; anything shaped like a finger; the breadth of a finger.—*vt* to touch with the fingers; (*mus*) to use the fingers in a certain way when playing.—*ns* **fing´erboard**, the part of stringed musical instrument against which the strings are pressed to produce the desired tones; **fing´er bowl**, a small water bowl for rinsing the fingers at the table.—*adj* **fing´ered**, having fingers, or anything like fingers.—*ns* **fing´ering**, act or manner of touching; the choice of fingers as in playing a musical instrument; the indication of this; **fing´erpost**, a post with a finger pointing the way; **fing´erprint**, the impression of a fingertip on any surface, esp an ink impression taken for purposes of identification.—*vt* to take the fingerprints of.—**have** (or **keep**) **one's fingers crossed**, to hope for something; **put one's finger on**, to ascertain exactly; **put one's finger on**, (*fig*) to identify, diagnose, define exactly. [OE *finger*.]

finial [fin´i-ål] *n* the decorative terminal part at the top of a spire, lamp, curtain rod, etc. [From L *finis*, end.]

finicky [fin´i-kē] *adj* too particular, fussy.—Also **fin´ical, fin´icking**. [Prob conn with **fine** (1).]

finis [fī´nis] *n* the end, conclusion. [L]

finish [fin´ish] *vt* to bring to an end, to come to the end of; to consume all of; to perfect; to give a desired surface effect to.—*vi* to come to an end.—*n* the last part, the end; anything used to finish a surface; the finished effect; means or manner of completing or perfecting; polished manners, speech, etc.—*adj* **fin´ished**, incapable of further effort; debarred from further success; polished, excellent.—*n* **fin´isher**, one who completes or perfects.—**finish off**, to end; to kill or ruin; **finish with**, to bring to an end. [Fr *finir, finissant*—L *fīnīre—finis*, an end.]

finite [fī´nīt] *adj* having definable limits; (*gram*) of a part of a verb, limited by number and person, forming a predicate (eg *he speaks*)—not an infinitive, participle, or gerund (eg *to speak, speaking*).—*adv* **fī´nītely**.—*n* **fī´nīteness**. [L *fīnītus*, pt p of *fīnīre*.]

fink [fink] *n* a despicable person; an informer; a strike-breaker. [Origin unknown.]

Finn [fin] *n* an inhabitant or native of Finland. [OE *Finnas*, Finns.]

finnan-haddie [fin´ån-had´ē] *n* a kind of smoked haddock, originally prepared at Findon, Kincardineshire, Scotland.

fiord *see* **fjord**.

fir [fûr] *n* a genus (*Abies*) of cone-bearing, evergreen trees; its timber. [OE *fyrh*; cf Ger *föhre*.]

fire [fīr] *n* the flame, heat, and light of combustion; something burning; a destructive burning (*a forest fire*); a strong feeling; a discharge of firearms.—*vti* to ignite; to supply with fuel; to bake (bricks, etc.) in a kiln; to excite or become excited; to shoot (a gun, etc.); to hurl or direct with force; to dismiss from a position.—*ns* **fire´arm**, a hand weapon discharged by an explosion; **fire´ball**, a ball of fire; a meteor; the cloud created by a nuclear explosion; **firebox**, a chamber (as of a furnace or steam boiler) that contains a fire; a box containing a device that transmits an alarm to a fire station; **fire´brand**, a brand or piece of wood on fire; one who foments strife; **fire´break**, a strip of land cleared to stop the spread of a fire; **fire´brick**, a brick so made as to resist the action of fire; **fire´ brigade´**, a brigade or company of men for extinguishing fires or conflagrations; **fire´clay**, a kind of clay, capable of resisting fire, used in making firebricks; **fire´damp**, a combustible mine gas; **fire´-dog**, andiron, **fire´-eater**, a juggler who pretends to eat fire; one given to needless quarrelling; **fire´ escape´**, an iron stairway or other special means of exit from a building for use in case of fire; **fire´fly**, a winged nocturnal beetle (esp family Lampyridae) whose abdomen glows with a soft intermittent light; **fireguard**, who who watches for the outbreak of fire; one whose duty is to extinguish fires; a metal screen placed in front of a fireplace; **fire´man**, a man whose business it is to assist in extinguishing fires; a man who tends a fire in a furnace, etc.; **fire´place**, a place for a fire, esp an open place built in a wall; **fire´plug**, a street hydrant supplying water for fighting fires.—*adj* **fire´proof**, not easily destroyed by fire.—*vt* to make fireproof.—*ns* **fire´side**, the side of the fireplace; home.—*adj* homely, intimate.—*ns* **fire´stone**, pyrite formerly used for striking fire; **fire´tower**, a tower used as a lookout for forest fires; **fire´trap**, a building easily set afire or hard to get out of if on fire; **fire´water**, strong alcoholic beverage; **fire´wood**, wood used as fuel; **fireworks**, firecrackers, rockets, etc., for noisy effects or brilliant displays; such a display; a display of temper or intense conflict; **fir´ing**, application of fire or heat to; discharge of guns; fuel; **firing squad**, a detachment detailed to fire volleys over the grave of one buried with military honors; a detachment detailed to shoot a condemned prisoner.—**catch fire**, to begin to burn; **on fire**, burning; greatly excited; **under fire**, under attack. [OE *fȳr*; Ger *feuer*; Gr *pyr*.]

firkin [fûr´kin] *n* a small wooden vessel or cask; a British measure equal to the fourth part of a barrel. [With dim suffx *-kin*, from Old Du *vierde*, fourth.]

firm[1] [fûrm] *adj* fixed; compact; strong; not easily moved or disturbed; unshaken; resolute; definite.—*adv* **firm´ly**.—*n* **firm´ness**. [OFr *ferme*—L *firmus*.]

firm[2] [fûrm] *n* a business company. [It *firma* from L *firmus*. See **farm**.]

firmament [fûr´må-mėnt] *n* the sky, viewed poetically as a solid arch or vault.—*adj* **firmament´al**, celestial. [Fr,—L *firmāmentum—firmus*, firm.]

first [fûrst] *adj* before all others in a series; 1st; earliest; foremost, as in rank, quality, etc.—*adv* before anyone or anything else; for the first time; sooner.—*n* any person or thing that is first; the beginning; the winning place, as in a race; low gear.—*n* **first aid**, emergency treatment for an injury, etc., before regular medical aid is available.—*adj* **firstborn**, born first in a family; eldest.—Also *n*.—*adj* **firstclass**, of the highest quality.—*n* **first degree burn**, a mild burn marked by pain, heat, reddening of the skin but without blistering; **first´fruits**, the fruits first gathered in a season; the first profits or effects of anything.—*adj* **first´hand**, obtained directly.—Also *adv*.—**First Lady**, the wife of the US president; *n* **first´ling**, the first produce or offspring.—*adv* **first´ly**, in the first place.—**first person**, that form of a pronoun or verb which refers to the speaker.—*adj* **first´-rate**, of the highest class, excellence; very well.—*adj* **first-string**, that is the first choice for regular play (as on a sports team).—**first wa´ter**, (of gems) the purest lustre; **First World**, the chief industrialized nations within the political power blocs of the world comprising the US, Japan, the Soviet Union, and many western European countries; **at first**, at the beginning. [OE *fyrst*, superl of *fore*, before.]

first-generation [fûrst jen-ēr-ā´shùn] *adj* denoting a native-born citizen of a country whose parents were foreign; denoting a foreign-born, naturalized citizen or inhabitant of a country.

firth [fûrth] *n* an arm of the sea, esp a rivermouth.—Also **frith**. [ON *fiörthr*; Norw *fjord*.]

fisc [fisk] *n* a state or royal treasury.—*adj* **fisc´al** of or relating to the public treasury and revenues; financial.—*n* revenue stamp; fiscal year.—**fiscal year** an accounting period of twelve months. [OFr—L *fiscus*, a purse.]

fish[1] [fish] *n* any of a large group of coldblooded animals living in water having backbones, gills for breathing, and fins; the flesh of fish used as food;—*pl* **fish**, or **fish´es** when referring to different species.—*vi* to catch or try to catch fish; to seek to obtain by artifice (*with* **for**).—*vt* to grope for, find, and bring to view (*often with* **out**).—*ns* **fish´bowl**, a bowl for keeping live fish; a place or condition that affords no privacy; **fisher**, a large dark brown N American arboreal carnivorous mammal (*Martes pennantes*) related to the weasel; its fur; **fish´erman**, a person who fishes for sport or for a living; a ship used in fishing; **fish farm**, a commercial facility for raising aquatic animals for human food; **fishing expedition**, a legal interrogation to discover information for a later proceeding; an investigation that does not stick to its stated objective and hopes to uncover incriminating evidence; **fish´net**, netting fitted with floats and weights for catching fish; a coarse open-mesh fabric.—*adj* **fish-net**.—*n* **fish story**, an incredible and extravagant story.—*vi* **fishtail**, to swing the tail of an airplace from side to side to reduce speed, esp while landing; to have the rear end of a vehicle move from side to side out of control while moving forward.—*n* **fish´wife**, a coarse, scolding woman.—*adj* **fishy**, like a fish in odor, taste, etc.; creating doubt or suspicion.—**fish-and-chips**, fried fish in batter and french fried potatoes; **fish or cut bait**, to make a choice between alternatives; **fish out of water**, a person out of his sphere or element; **neither fish nor fowl**, one not belonging to a particular class or category. [OE *fisc*; Ger *fisch*; ON *fiskr*; L *piscis*; Gael *iasg*.]

fish[2] [fish] *n* (*naut*) a piece of wood placed alongside another to strengthen it.—*n* **fish´plate**, an iron plate, one of a pair used to join railway rails. [Prob Fr *fiche*, peg.]

fissile [fis´il, -īl] *adj* that may be cleft or split in the direction of the grain; fissionable.—*n* **fission** [fish´ȯn], a split or cleavage.—*adj* **fiss´ionable**.—**fission bomb**, atom bomb. [L *fissilis*, from *findĕre*, *fissum*, to cleave.]

fissiparous [fi-sip´a-rus] *adj* propagated by fission or self-division. [L *fissus* pt p of *findĕre*, to cleave, *parĕre*, to bring forth.]

fissure [fish´ùr] *n* a narrow opening or chasm. [Fr,—L *fissūra*, from *findĕre*, *fissum*, to cleave.]

fist [fist] *n* the closed or clenched hand.—*vt* to strike or grip with the fist.—*n pl* **fist´icuffs**, a fight with the fists. [OE *fȳst*; Ger *faust*.]

fistula [fist´ū-la] *n* an abnormal passage as from an abscess to the skin.—*adjs* **fist´ular**, hollow like a pipe; **fist´ulous**. [L *fistula*, a pipe.]

fit[1] [fit] *adj* suited to some purpose, function, etc.; proper, right; healthy; (*slang*) inclined, ready.—*n* the manner of fitting.—*vt* to be suitable to; to be the proper size, shape, etc., for; to adjust so as to fit; to equip, to outfit.—*vi* to be suitable or proper; to have the proper size or shape.—*pr p* **fitt´ing**; *pt p* **fitt´ed**.—*adv* **fit´ly**.—*ns* **fitt´er; fit´ness**.—*adj* **fitting**, appropriate.—*n* an act of one that fits, esp a trying on of altered clothes; a small often standardized electrical part.—*adv* **fittingly**.—**fit to be tied**, extremely angry; **fit to kill**, to a striking degree. [Origin unknown.]

fit[2] [fit] *n* any sudden, uncontrollable attack, as of coughing; an outburst, as of anger; a seizure involving convulsions or loss of consciousness.—*adj* **fit´ful**, marked by intermittent activity; spasmodic.—*adv* **fitfully**.—*n* **fitfulness**.—**by fits (and starts)**, in an irregular way; **have** *or* **throw a fit** (*inf*) to become very angry or upset. [OE *fitt*, a struggle.]

fit[3] [fit] *n* (*arch*) a division of a poem or song. [OE *fitt*, a song.]

fitch [fich] *n* a polecat; the fur of the polecat. [OFr *fissel*, from root of Du *visse*, nasty.]

five [fiv] *adj, n* one more than four; the symbol for this (5, V, v).—*adjs* **fifth**, see separate entry; **fivefold**, having five units or members; being five times as great or as many.—*ns* **five-and-ten**, a store that sells a wide variety of inexpensive merchandise.—Also **five-and-dime; fiver**, a 5-dollar bill.—*adj* **five-star**, of first class or quality.—**five of a kind**, (*poker*) four cards of the same kind plus another in one hand; **take five**, (*slang*) to take a rest; relax. [OE *fīf*.]

fix [fiks] *vt* to fasten firmly; to set firmly in the mind; to direct (one's eyes) steadily at something; to make rigid; to make permanent; to establish (a date, etc.) definitely; to set in order; to repair; to prepare (food or meals); (*inf*) to influence the result or action of (a race, jury, etc.) by bribery; (*inf*) to punish.—*vi* to become fixed; (*inf*) to prepare or intend.—*n* the position of a ship, etc., determined from the bearings of two known positions; (*inf*) a predicament; (*inf*) a situation that has been fixed; (*inf*) something whose supply becomes continually necessary or greatly desired as a drug, entertainment, activity, etc.—*ns* **fixation**, a fixing or being fixed; an obsession; a remaining at an early stage of psychosexual development; **fixative**, a substance used to make permanent by preventing fading, evaporation, or protecting from the elements.—*adj* **fixed**, settled; not apt to evaporate; steadily directed; fast, lasting.—*adv* **fix´edly** [-id-li].—*ns* **fix´edness, fix´ity; fix´er; fix´ture**, what is fixed to anything, as to land or to a house; a fixed article of furniture; a fixed or appointed time or event.—**fixed star**, a star so distant that its motion can be measured only by observations over long periods. [L *fixus, figĕre*, to fix, prob through Low L *fixāre*.]

fizz [fiz] *vi* to make a hissing or spluttering sound.—*n* any effervescent drink.—*adj* **fizz´y**, effervescent.—*vi* **fizz´le**, to hiss or sputter;—*n* an abortive effort; failure. [Formed from the sound.]

fjord [fyörd] *n* a narrow inlet of the sea between cliffs or steep slopes.—Also **fiord**. [Norw.]

flabbergast [flab´ėr-gäst] *vt* to stun, confound. [Prob conn with **flabby** and **aghast**.]

flabby [flab´i] *adj* soft, yielding; weak and ineffective.—*n* **flabb´iness**. [From **flap**.]

flaccid [flak´sid] *adj* not firm or stiff; lacking vigor and force; (*bot*) deficient in turgor.—*adv* **flac´cidly**.—*n* **flaccid´ity**. [Fr,—L *flaccidus—flaccus*, flabby.]

flag[1] [flag] *vi* to grow languid or spiritless.—*pr p* **flagg´ing**; *pt p* **flagged**. [Perh OFr *flac*—L *flaccus*; prob influenced by imit forms as *flap*.]

flag[2] [flag] *n* a plant with sword-shaped leaves—an iris, or a reed. [Ety obscure; cf Du *flag*.]

flag[3] [flag] *n* a piece of bunting, usu. with a design, used to show nationality, party, a particular branch of the armed forces, etc., or to mark a position, or to convey information.—*vt* to decorate with flags; to inform by flag-signals.—*ns* **Flag´ Day**, June 14, observed in various states in commemoration of the adoption in 1777 of the official US flag; **flag day**, a day on which charitable donations are solicited in exchange for small flags; **flag´ship**, the chief or leading item of a group or collection; **flag´staff**, a staff or pole on which a flag is displayed; **flag-waving**, a passionate appeal to patriotic sentiment. [Origin unknown; cf Dan *flag*; Du *vlag*, Ger *flagge*.]

flag[4] [flag] *n* a stone that separates in flakes or layers; a flat stone used for paving.—Also **flagstone**. [ON *flaga*, a slab.]

flagellate [flaj´ėl-āt] *vt* to whip.—*ns* **flagellā´tion; flagell´ant** [also flaj´-], one who scourges himself in religious discipline. [L *flagellāre, -ātum—flagellum*, dim of *flagrum*, a whip.]

flagellum [flȧ-jel´um] *n* (*zool.*) any of various elongated threadlike appendages of plants and animals, esp one that is the primary organ of motion of many microorganisms. [L. see **flagellate**.]

flageolet [flaj-o-let´ or flaj´-] *n* a small flute resembling the treble recorder. [Fr dim of OFr *flageol, flajol*, a pipe.]

flagitious [fla-jish´ùs] *adj* grossly wicked, guilty of enormous crimes.—*adv* **flagi´tiously**.—*n* **flagi´tiousness**. [L *flāgitiōsus—flāgitium*, a disgraceful act—*flagrāre*, to burn.]

flagon [flag´ȯn] *n* a pottery or metal container for liquids with handle and spout and often a lid; a large bulging short-necked bottle; the contents of a flagon. [Fr *flacon* for *flascon*—Low L *flascō, -ōnis*. See **flask**.]

flagrant [flā´grȧnt] *adj* glaring, notorious.—*n* **flā´grancy**.—*adv* **flā´grantly**. [L *flagrāns, -antis*, pr p of *flagrāre*, to burn.]

flail [flāl] *n* a hand threshing implement.—Also *vt.* [OE *fligel*, prob from L *flagellum*, a scourge.]

flair [flār] *n* intuitive discernment; aptitude, bent. [Fr 'scent'.]

flak [flak] *n pl* anti-aircraft guns; the missiles of such a gun; criticism, opposition. [Ger, abbrev of *flieger-abwehr-kanone*, anti-aircraft gun.]

flake [flāk] *n* a small layer or film; a very small loose mass, as of snow or wool; (*slang*) cocaine.—*vt* to form into flakes.—*adjs* **flak´y, flak´ey**, (*slang*) very unconventional; eccentric; crazy.—**flake out** (*coll*), to collapse from weariness or illness. [Prob Scand; ON *floke*, flock of wool; OHG *floccho*.]

flambé [flam-bā´] *adj* served with a brandy or rum sauce set afire to flame.—*n* a dessert so served. [Fr]

flambeau [flam´bō] *n* a flaming torch;—*pl* **flam´beaux** [-bōz]. [Fr, *flambe*—L *flamma*.]

flamboyant [flam-boi´ȧnt] *adj* flamelike or brilliant; ornate; strikingly elaborate. [Fr *flamboyer*, to blaze.]

flame [flām] *n* the burning gas of a fire, appearing as a tongue of light; the state of burning with a blaze; a thing like a flame; an intense emotion; (*inf*) a sweetheart.—*vi* to burst into flame, to grown red or hot; to become excited.—*n* a strong reddish orange color.—*adj* **flammable**, easily set on fire; that will burn readily.—*n* **flammability**.—*ns* **flame´out**, a failure of combustion in a jet engine during flight; **flame´thrower**, a weapon that shoots flaming gasoline, oil, etc. [OFr *flambe*—L *flamma—flagrāre*, to burn.]

flamenco [fla-men´kō] *n* vigorous rhythmic dance style or music of Spanish gypsies. [Sp]

flamingo [fla-ming´gō] *n* any of several aquatic birds (family Phoenicopteridae) with rosy-white plumage, long legs and neck;—*pl* **flaming´o(e)s**. [Sp *flamenco*—L *flamma*, a flame.]

flan [flan] *n* (Brit) an open case of pastry or sponge cake with custard, or fruit, or other filling. [Fr]

flâneur [flä-nœr´] *n* a loafer. [Fr,—*flâner*, to stroll, idle.]

flange [flanj] *n* a projecting or raised edge, as of a wheel or of a rail.—*adj* **flanged**. [Prob related to **flank**.]

flank [flangk] *n* the side of an animal from the ribs to the hip; the side or wing of anything.—*vt* to attack the side of; to pass round the side of; to be situated at the side of. [Fr *flanc*.]

flannel [flan´ėl] *n* a cotton or woolen cloth of loose texture; (*pl*) trousers of such cloth.—*n* **flannelette**, a soft, fleecy cotton fabric.—*adj* **flann´elly**. [Perh OFr *flaine*, blanket, or Welsh *gwlan*, wool.]

flap [flap] *n* the blow, or motion, of a broad loose object; anything broad and flexible hanging loose, as material covering an opening; (*inf*) fluster, panic.—*vt* to beat or move with a flap; (*inf*) to fluster.—*vi* to move, as wings; to hang like a flap; (*inf*) to get into a panic or fluster.—*pr p* **flapp´ing**; *pt p* **flapped**.—*ns* **flap´doodle** nonsense; **flap´jack**, a pancake; **flapp´er** one that flaps; a fly swatter. [Prob imit.]

flare [flār] *vi* to burn with a glaring, unsteady light, to flash suddenly; to blaze (**up**—*lit* or *fig*); to widen out bell-wise.—*n* an unsteady glare; a flash; a bright light used as a signal or illumination; a widening, or a part that widens like a bell.—*n* **flare-up**, a sudden outburst of flame or of anger, trouble, etc. [Perh conn with Norw *flara*, to blaze.]

flash [flash] *n* a sudden, brief light; a brief moment; a sudden brief display; a brief news item sent by radio, etc.; a gaudy display.—*vi* to send out a sudden, brief light; to sparkle; to come or pass suddenly.—*vt* to cause to flash; to send (news, etc.) swiftly.—*adj* **flashy**.—*n* **flash´back**, an interruption in the continuity of a story, etc., by telling or showing an earlier episode; **flash´bulb**, a bulb giving a brief, dazzling light, for taking photographs; **flasher**, a man who exposes himself indecently; **flash point**, the lowest temperature at which vapor, as of an oil, will ignite with a flash; a point at which something or someone bursts into action or being. [Prob imit; cf Swed prov *flash*, to blaze.]

flask [fläsk] *n* a narrow-necked vessel for holding liquids; a bottle; a vessel for holding gunpowder. [OE *flasce*; Ger *flasche*; prob from Low L *flascō*—L *vasculum*, a small vessel—*vas*, a vessel.]

flat [flat] *adj* having a smooth level surface; lying spread out; broad, even, and thin; absolute (*a flat denial*); not fluctuating (*a flat rate*); emptied of air (*a flat tire*); without gloss (*flat paint*); (*mus*) below true pitch.—*adv* in a flat manner or position; exactly; (*mus*) below true pitch.—*n* anything flat, esp a surface, part, or expanse; a deflated tire; (*mus*) a note one half step below another; the symbol for this.—*adv* **flatly**.—*ns* **flatfish**, any of an order (Heterosomata) of marine fishes (as halibuts, flounders, turbots, and soles) that as adults have both eyes on one side; **flat´foot**, condition of the foot in which the instep arch is flattened; (*slang*) a policeman; **flat silver**, eating or serving utensils (as forks, knives, and spoons) made of or plated with silver; **flat´top**, an aircraft carrier; a modified crew cut; **flat´worm**, platyhelminth.—**flat out**, in a blunt and direct manner; at top speed or peak performance. [ON *flatr*, flat.]

flatter [flat´ėr] *vt* to treat with insincere praise and servile attentions; to represent over-favorably; to please (with false hopes).—*n* **flatt´erer**.—*adj* **flatt´ering**, uttering false praise; pleasing to pride or vanity.—*adv* **flatt´eringly**.—*n* **flatt´ery**, false praise. [OFr *flater* (Fr *flatter*)—Gmc.]

flatulent [flat´ū-lėnt] *adj* affected with air in the stomach; apt to generate such; pretentious, vain.—*ns* **flat´ūlence, flat´ūlency**, air generated in the stomach; windiness, emptiness.—*adv* **flat´ūlently**.—*n* **flatus** [flā´tus], a puff of wind; air generated in the stomach or intestines. [Fr,—Low L *flātulentus*—L *flāre, flātum*, to blow.]

flaunt [flönt] *vi* to wave in the wind; to move or behave ostentatiously.—*vt* to display.—Also *n*. [Prob Scand.]

flautist [flöt´ist] *n* a flute player. [It *flautista*.]

flavor [flā´vȯr] *n* that quality of anything which affects the smell or the taste; a relish; (*fig*) savor; characteristic quality.—*vt* to impart flavor to.—*adj* **flā´vorous**.—*n* **flā´voring**, any substance used to give a flavor.—*adj* **flā´vorless**. [OFr *flaur*; prob influenced by **savor**.]

flaw[1] [flö] *n* a gust of wind. [Cf Du *vlaag*, Swed *flaga*.]

flaw[2] [flö] *n* a break, a crack; a defect; a fault in a legal paper that may nullify it.—*vt* to crack or break.—*adj* **flaw´less**. [ON *flaga*, a slab.]

flax [flaks] *n* any of a genus (*Linus*) of herbs, esp a blue-flowered annual cultivated for its fiber and seed; the fiber of this plant.—*adj* **flax´en**, made of or resembling flax; light yellow.—*n* **flax seed**, the seed of the flax, a source of linseed oil. [OE *flæx*; Ger *flachs*.]

flay [flā] *vt* to strip off the skin;—*pr p* **flay´ing**; *pt p* **flayed**.—*n* **flay´er**. [OE *flēan*; ON *flā*, to skin.]

flea [flē] *n* an order of parasitic insects of great agility.—*ns* **flea´bag**, an inferior hotel or rooming house; **flea´-bane**, a genus of plants whose smell is said to drive away fleas; **flea´-bite**, the bite of a flea; (*fig*) a trifle; **flea market**, a usu. open-air market for second-hand goods.—**a flea in one's ear**, a stinging rebuff. [OE *flēah*, cf *floh*, Du *vloo*.]

flèche [flesh] *n* a slender spire above the nave and transepts of a church. [Fr, arrow.]

fleck [flek] *n* a spot or speckle; a little bit of a thing.—*vs t* **fleck, fleck´er**, to spot; to streak. [ON *flekkr*, a spot; Ger *fleck*, Du *vlek*.]

flection *see* **flexion**.

fled [fled] *pa t* and *pt p* of **flee**.

fledge [flej] *vt* to bring up a bird until it is ready to fly; to furnish with feathers, as an arrow.—*vi* to acquire feathers for flying.—*n* **fledgling**, a little bird just fledged; an immature or inexperienced person; one that is new. [ME *fligge, flegge*—OE *flycge*, fledged—*flēogan*, to fly (Ger *fliëgen*).]

flee [flē] *vi* to run away, as from danger; to disappear.—*vt* to keep at a distance from;—*pr p* **flee´ing**; *pt p* **fled**. [OE *flēon* (Ger *fliehen*). Not akin to *fly*, but influenced by it.]

fleece [flēs] *n* a sheep's coat of wool.—*vt* to clip wool from; to plunder; to cover, as with wool.—*adjs* **fleeced**, having a fleece; **fleece´less; fleec´y**, woolly. [OE *flēos*; Du *vlies*, Ger *fliess*.]

fleet[1] [flēt] *n* a number of warships under one command; any group of ships, trucks, etc., under one control. [OE *flēot*, a ship—*flēotan*, to float.]

fleet[2] [flēt] *adj* swift; nimble; transient.—*adv* **fleet´ly**.—*n* **fleet´ness**, [Prob. ON *fliōtr*, swift; but ult cog with succeeding word.]

fleet[3] [flēt] *vi* to move, pass swiftly, hasten.—*vt* to while away;—*pr p* **fleet´ing**; *pt p* **fleet´ed**. [OE *flēotan*, to float.]

Flemish [flem´ish] *adj* of or belonging to the *Flemings* or people of Flanders, or their language. [Du *Vlaamsch*.]

flense [flenz, -sh] *vt* to cut out the blubber of, as a whale. [Dan *flense*.]

flesh [flesh] *n* the soft substance of the body, esp the muscular tissue; the pulpy part of fruits and vegetables; meat; the body as distinct from the soul; all mankind; yellowish pink.—*vt* to initiate or habituate by giving a foretaste; to give substance to (*usu. with* **out**); to free from flesh.—*vi* to become fleshy (*with* **up** *or* **out**).—*adj* **fleshed** [flesht], having flesh, esp of a specified kind (*pink-fleshed*).—*adjs* **fleshly**, corporeal; sensual; **fleshy**.—*ns* **fleshiness**, state of being fleshy; corpulence; **fleshpots**, luxury; place of lascivious entertainment; **flesh wound**, an injury involving penetration of the body without damaging bone or internal organs.—**in the flesh**, alive; in person; **one's (own) flesh and blood**, one's close relatives. [OE *flæsc*; cog forms in all Gmc languages.]

fleur-de-lis [flœr´-de-lē´ or -lēs´] *n* the flower of the lily; an ornament and heraldic bearing borne by the kings of France;—*pl* **fleurs´-de-lis´**. [Fr *lis*—L *lilium*, a lily.]

flew [flōō] *p t* of **fly**.

flex [fleks] *vti* to bend (arm, etc); to contract (a muscle).—*n* a bending.—*adjs* **flexible** [fleks´i-bl], **flexile** [fleks´īl], easily bent, pliant; docile.—*n* **flexibil´ity**, pliancy; easiness to be persuaded.—*adv* **flex´ibly**.—*ns* **flex´ion**, a bend; a fold; **flex´or**, a muscle that bends a limb.—*adjs* **flex´ūous**, full of windings and turnings; lacking rigidity.—*n* **flex´ūre**, a bend or turning. [L *flectĕre, flexum*, to bend.]

flextime [fleks´tim] *n* the staggering of working hours to enable each employee to work the full quota of time but at periods most convenient for the individual.—*Also* **flexitime, flexible time, gliding time**. [**flexible** + **time**.]

flick [flik] *vt* to strike lightly.—*n* a flip. [Imit.]

flicker [flik´ėr] *vi* to flutter and move the wings, as a bird; to burn unsteadily, as a flame. [OE *flicorian*; imit.]

flier [flī´ėr] *n* one who flies, a pilot; a reckless or speculative venture; an advertising circular; a step in a straight flight of stairs. [**fly**.]

flight[1] [flīt] *n* the act, manner, or power of flying; distance flown; a group of things flying together; an airplane scheduled to fly a certain trip; a trip by airplane; a soaring above the ordinary (*a flight of fancy*); a set of stairs, as between landings; a unit of the US Air Force below a squadron.—*adjs* **flight´less**, without power of flight; **flight´y**, fanciful; changeable; giddy.—*adv* **flight´ily**.—*ns* **flight´iness; flight attendant** a person who attends passengers in an airplane; **flight deck**, the uppermost deck of an aircraft carrier; the forward compartment in some airplanes; **flight´-recorder**, a device which records information about the functioning of an aircraft and its systems.—**flightstrip**, an emergency landing field beside a highway. [OE *flyht*—*flēogan*, to fly.]

flight[2] [flīt] *n* an act of fleeing. [Assumed OE *flyht*—*flēon*, to flee.]

flimsy [flim´zi] *adj* thin; without solidity, strength, or reason; weak.—*adv* **flim´sily**.—*n* **flim´siness**. [First in 18th century. Prob suggested by **film**.]

flinch [flinch, -sh] *vi* to shrink back; to wince.—*n* **flinch´er**.—*adv* **flinch´ingly**. [Prob conn with ME *fleechen*, OFr *flechir*, L *flectĕre*, to bend.]

fling [fling] *vt* to cast, toss, throw; to dart; to scatter.—*vi* to kick out; to dash or rush; to throw oneself impetuously;—*pr p* **fling´ing**; *pt p* **flung**.—*n* a cast or throw; a taunt; a season of freedom to indulge impulses; a bout of pleasure; a lively dance. [ON *flengja*; Swed *flänga*.]

flint [flint] *n* a very hard siliceous rock, usu. gray, that produces sparks when struck with steel; a material used for producing a spark used in lighters.—*adj* made of flint, hard.—*ns* **flint´ glass**, a heavy brilliant glass containing lead oxides used for optical structures; **flint´lock**, a gun having a flint fixed in the hammer for striking a spark to ignite the charge.—*adj* **flint´y**, consisting of or like flint; hard, cruel.—*n* **flint´iness**. [OE *flint*; Dan *flint*; Gr *plinthos*, a brick.]

flip[1] [flip] *n* a hot drink of beer (or egg and milk) and spirits sweetened. [Prob—**flip** (2).]

flip[2] [flip] *vt* to toss with a quick jerk; to snap (a coin) in the air with the thumb; to turn or turn over.—*vi* to move jerkily; (*slang*) to lose self control.—*ns* **flip chart**, a chart to display information in sequences, consisting of large sheets attached at the top that can be turned over one after the other; **flip´-flop**, the sound or motion of something flapping loosely; a somersault, esp when performed in the air; a usu. electronic device or circuit (as in a computer) capable of assuming either of two stable states; **flip´-flops**, flat sandals made of composition rubber, held on the foot by a thong between the big toe and smaller toes; **flipp´er**, a limb adapted for swimming; a rubber shoe expanded into a paddle, used in skin diving; **flip´-side**, the side of a phonograph record carrying the song, etc., of lesser importance. [Cf **fillip, flap.**]

flippant [flip´ȧnt] *adj* quick and pert of speech; frivolous.—*ns* **flipp´ancy, flipp´antness**, pert fluency of speech; levity.—*adv* **flipp´antly**. [Cf **flip** (2) and ON *fleipa*, to prattle.]

flirt [flûrt] *vi* to trifle with love; to trifle or toy (to flirt with an idea).—*vt* to move (a light article) jerkily.—*n* a sudden jerk; a trifler with the opposite sex.—*n* **flirta´tion**, the act of flirting—*adj* **flirta´tious**, given to flirting. [Onomatopoeic.]

flit [flit] *vi* to move lightly and rapidly.—*n* **flitt´ing**. [ON *flytja*; Swed *flytta.*]

flitch [flich] *n* the side of a hog salted and cured. [OE *flicce*; ON *flikki.*]

flitter [flit´ėr] *vi* to flutter. [**flit.**]

float [flōt] *vi* to be supported or suspended in a liquid; to be buoyed up; to move lightly; to drift about aimlessly.—*vt* to cause to float; to put into circulation (*to float a bond issue*); to arrange for (a loan).—*n* anything that floats; a low flat vehicle decorated for exhibit in a parade; a tool for smoothing.—*adj* **float´able**.—*ns* **float´age**, charge for shipping railroad cars on a barge; **floatā´tion**, *see* **flotā´tion**; **float´er**.—*adj* **float´ing**, that floats, in any sense; not fixed; circulating.—*ns* **float´ing dock**, a dock that can be partly submerged to permit entry of a ship and raised to keep the ship high and dry; **floating rib**, rib not attached to the sternum. [OE *flotian*, to float; ON *flota.*]

flock[1] [flok] *n* a group of certain animals as birds, sheep, etc., living and feeding together; a group of people or things.—*vi* to assemble or travel in a flock or crowd. [OE *flocc*, a flock, a company; ON *flokkr.*]

flock[2] [flok] *n* tuft of wool or cottom fiber; woolen or cotton refuse used for stuffing furniture.—*n* **flocking**, tiny fibers applied to a fabric, wallpaper, etc. as a velvety surface. [OFr *floc*—L *floccus*, a lock of wool.]

floe [flō] *n* a field of floating ice. [Prob Norw *flo*, layer.]

flog [flog] *vt* to beat with a rod or stick. [Prob an abbrev of **flagellate.**]

flood [flud] *n* an overflowing of water on an area normally dry; the rising of the tide; a great outpouring, as of words.—*vt* to cover or fill, as with a flood; to put too much water, fuel, etc. on or in.—*vi* to gush out in a flood; to become flooded.—*ns* **flood´gate**, a gate for allowing or stopping the flow of water, a sluice; **flood´-light, flood´-lighting**, strong illumination from many points to eliminate shadows.—*vt* **flood¸light**—*n* **flood´tide**, the rising tide; an overwhelming quantity; a high point.—**the Flood**, Noah's deluge. [OE *flōd* Du *vloed*, Ger *flut*; cog with **flow**.]

floor [flor] *n* the inside bottom surface of a room; the bottom surface of anything (*the ocean floor*); a story in a building; the right to speak in an assembly; the lower limit, the base.—*vt* to furnish with a floor; to knock down; (*inf*) to defeat; (*inf*) to shock, to confuse.—*ns* **floor´board**, a board in a floor; the floor of an automobile; **floor exercise**, any gymnastic exercise done without apparatus; **flooring**, a floor or floors; material for making a floor; **floor show**, a show presenting singers, dancers, etc., in a nightclub. [OE *flōr*; Du *vloer*, a flat surface, Ger *flur*, flat land.]

flop [flop] *vi* to swing or bounce loosely; to move in a heavy, clumsy or relaxed manner.—*n* a fall plump on the ground; a collapse; a complete failure; (*slang*) a place to sleep.—*adj* **floppy**.—*n* **floppy disk´** a small flexible magnetic disk on which to store data for a computer. [A form of **flap.**]

flora [flō´ra, flö´] *n* the plants (collectively) of a region or of a period; a list of these;—*pl* **flōras, flōrae** [-ē].—*adj* **flō´ral**, pertaining to the goddess Flora or to flowers; (*bot*) containing the flower.—*n* **flōres´cence**, a bursting into flower; (*bot*) the time when plants flower.—*adj* **flōres´cent**.—*n* **flō´ret** (*bot*), one of the small flowers forming the head of a composite plant.—*adj* **flō´riated**, decorated with floral ornaments; having a floral form;—*n* **flō´riculture**, the culture of flowers—*adj* **floricul´tural**.—*n* **flōricul´turist**, a florist.—*adj* **flŏr´id**, flowery; flushed with red; fully developed, esp of a disease.—*adv* **flor´idly**.—*n* **flor´idness**.—*adjs* **flōrif´erous**, blooming freely.—*n* **flŏr´ist**, one who sells or grows flowers and ornamental plants for sale. [L *Flōra*, goddess of flowers—*flōs, flōris*, a flower.]

Florentine [flor´ėn-tīn] *adj* pertaining to the Italian city of *Florence*; of dishes made with spinach.

floruit [flō´rŏŏ-it] *n* a period of flourishing, as of a person or movement. Abbrev **fl.** [L 3rd pers sing perf of *flōrēre*, to flourish.]

floss [flos] *n* the rough outside of the silkworm's cocoon and other waste of silk manufacture; fine silk used in embroidery; any loose downy plant substance; dental floss.—*vti* to use dental floss.—*adj* **floss´y**, slick, stylish. [Prob OFr *flosche*, down; or from some Gmc word cog with *fleece*; cf ON *flos*, nap.]

flotage [flō´taj] *n* flotation, material that floats.

flōtation [flo-tā´sh(ȯ)n] *n* the act of floating; the science of floating bodies; act of starting a business, esp by issuing stock. [See **float.**]

flotilla [flō-til´a] *n* a fleet of ships, esp two or more squadrons of small warships; a large force of moving things. [Sp dim of *flota*, a fleet.]

flotsam [flot´sȧm] *n* floating debris. [Anglo-Fr *floteson* (Fr *flottaison*)—OF *floter*, to float.]

flounce[1] [flowns] *vi* to move abruptly or impatiently.—*n* an impatient fling, flop, or movement. [Prob cog with Norw *flunsa*, to hurry, Swed dial *flunsa*, to plunge.]

flounce[2] [flowns] *n* a hanging strip sewed to the skirt of a dress.—*vt* to furnish with flounces.—*n* **floun´cing**, material for flounces. [Earlier form *frounce*—OFr *froncir*, to wrinkle.]

flounder[1] [flown´dėr] *vi* to struggle with violent and awkward motion; to stumble helplessly in thinking or speaking. [Prob an onomatopoeic blending of the sound and sense of earlier words like *founder, blunder.*]

flounder[2] [flown´dėr] *n* any of various flatfish, esp of two families (Pleuronectidae and Bothidae) that include important marine food fishes. [Anglo-Fr *floundre*—OFr; most prob of Scand origin.]

flour [flowr] *n* the finely ground meal of wheat or other grain; the fine soft powder of any substance.—*vt* to sprinkle with flour.—*adjs* **flour´less flour´y**. [Same word as **flower.**]

flourish [flur´ish] *vi* to grow luxuriantly; to thrive, be prosperous; to live and work (in, at, about, a specified time); to use copious and flowery language; to make ornamental strokes with the pen; to show off.—*vt* to adorn with flourishes or ornaments; to brandish in show or triumph.—*n* decoration; showy splendor; a figure made by a bold stroke of the pen; the waving of a weapon or other thing; a musical fanfare.—*adj* **flour´ishing**, thriving; prosperous; making a show. [OFr *florir*—L *flōs, flōris*, flower.]

flout [flowt] *vt* to jeer at, to mock; to treat with contempt.—Also vi—n a scornful act or remark. [Prob a specialised use of *floute*, ME form of *flute*, to play on the flute.]

flow [flō] *vi* to run, as water; to rise, as the tide; to move in a stream; to glide smoothly; to circulate, as the blood; to be plentiful; to hang loose and billowing.—*n* a flowing; the rate of flow; anything that flows; the rising of the tide.—*adj* **flow´ing**.—*adv* **flow´ingly**.—**flowchart**, a diagram showing the progress of work in a series of operations. [OE *flōwan.*]

flower [flow´ėr] *n* the seed-producing structure of a flowering plant, blossom; a plant cultivated for its blossoms; the best or finest part.—*pl* a finely divided powder produced esp by condensation or sublimation (*flowers of sulfur*).—*vt* to cause to bear flowers; to decorate with floral designs.—*vi* to produce blossoms; to reach the best stage.—*n* **flow´eret**, a floret.—*adj* **flow´ery**, full of or adorned with flowers; full of ornate expressions and fine words.—*n* **flow´eriness**. [OFr *flour* (Fr *fleur*)—L *flōs, flōris*, a flower.]

flown [flōn] *pt p* of **fly**.

flu [flōō] *n* short for influenza; popularly, a respiratory or intestinal infection caused by a virus.

fluctuate [fluk´tū-āt] *vi* to be continually varying in an irregular way.—*n* **fluctuā´tion**. [L *fluctuāre, -ātum—fluctus*, a wave—*fluěre*, to flow.]

flue [flōō] *n* a shaft for the passage of smoke, hot air, etc., as in a chimney.—*adj* **flue-cured**, cured with heat transmitted through a flue without exposure to smoke or fumes.—*n* **flue pipe**, (*mus*) an organ pipe in which the sound is produced by air impinging on an edge (cf **reed pipe**). [Origin doubtful.]

fluent [flōō´ėnt] *adj* flowing smoothly; ready in the use of words.—*n* **flu´ency**.—*adv* **flu´ently**. [L *fluēns, fluentis*, pr p of *fluěre*, to flow.]

fluff [fluf] *n* soft, light down; a loose, soft mass, as of hair.—*vt* to shake or pat until loose or fluffy; to bungle (one's lines) as in acting.—*adj* **fluffy**, like fluff; feathery. [Origin doubtful.]

fluid [flōō´id] *adj* that can flow as a liquid or gas does; that can change rapidly or easily; available for investment as cash.—*n* a liquid or gas.—*ns* **fluid´ics**, the technology of using a flow of liquid or gas for certain operations; **fluid´ity, flu´idness**, state or quality of being fluid; physical property of a substance enabling it to flow.—**fluid drive**, a system of transmitting power smoothly through the medium of the change in momentum of a fluid, usu. oil; **fluidounce**, a US unit of measure equal to 1/16 pint. [Fr,—L *fluidus*, fluid—*fluěre*, to flow.]

fluke[1] [flōōk] *n* a flatfish; a flattened trematode worm. [OE *flōc*, a plaice; cf ON *flōke.*]

fluke[2] [flōōk] *n* the part of an anchor which fastens in the ground; a barbed head as of a harpoon; a lobe of a whale's tail. [Prob a transferred use of **fluke** (1).]

fluke[3] [flōōk] *n* a stroke of luck.

flume [flōōm] *n* an inclined chute for carrying water, as to transport logs, furnish power, etc.; a gorge with a stream running through it. [OFr *flum*—L *flūmen*, a river—*fluěre*, to flow.]

flummery [flum´ėr-i] *n* a soft jelly made from flour or meal; any of several sweet desserts; mumbo-jumbo. [W *llymru—llymrig*, harsh, raw—*llym*, sharp, severe.]

flung [flung] *pa t* and *pt p* of **fling**.

flunk [flunk] *vti* to fail, as in schoolwork.—Also *n.*

flunky [flung´ki] *n* a liveried manservant; a toady; a person with menial tasks. [Perh orig *flanker*, one who runs alongside.]

fluorite [flōō´rīt] *n* a mineral (CaF_2) of different colors used as a flux and for making opalescent and opaque glass.—Also **flu´or, flu´orspar**.—*n* **fluores´cence**, the property of producing light when acted upon by radiant energy; light so produced.—*adj* **fluores´cent**.—*n* **flu´oride**, any of various compounds of fluorine.—*vt* **flu´oridate**, to treat (drinking water) with a fluoride to reduce tooth decay.—*n* **fluoridā´tion**—*vt* **flu´orinate** to treat with flourine.—*n* **flu´orine**, an element (symbol F; at wt 190; no 9); a pale greenish-yellow gas.—**fluorescent lamp**, a glass tube coated on the inside with a fluorescent substance that gives off (fluorescent) light when mercury vapor in the tube is acted upon by a stream of electrons. [L *fluor*, flow, from its use as a flux.]

flurry [flur´i] *n* a sudden gust of wind, rain, or snow; a sudden commotion; a brief advance or decline in prices (on the stock exchange).—*vti* to cause or become agitated and confused. [Prob onomatopoeic, suggested by **flaw** (1), **hurry**, etc.]

flush[1] [flush] *n* a rapid flow, as of water; sudden, vigorous growth; a sudden excitement; a blush; a sudden feeling of heat, as in a fever.—*vi* to flow rapidly; to blush or glow; to be washed out by a sudden flow of water.—*vt* to wash out with a sudden flow of water; to cause to blush; to excite.—*adj* abundant, well supplied, esp with money. [Prob onomatopoeic, but meaning influenced by **flash, blush**.]

flush[2] [flush] *adj* having the surface in one plane with the adjacent surface. [Prob related to **flush** (1).]

flush[3] [flush] *vi* (of birds) to start up suddenly and fly away.—*vt* to rouse (game birds) suddenly.—*n* a number of birds roused at the same time. [ME *fluschen*. Perh imitative.]

flush[4] [flush] *n* a run of cards all of the same suit. [OFr *flux*. See **flux**.]

fluster [flus´tėr] *vti* to make or become confused.—*n* being flustered. [ON *flaustr*, hurry.]

flute [flōōt] *n* an orchestral woodwind instrument in the form of a straight pipe (with finger holes and keys) held horizontally and played through a hole located near one end; a groove in the shaft of a column; a grooved pleat.—*vi* to play a flute.—*n* **flutist**, one who plays a flute. [OFr *fleüte*.]

flutter [flut´ėr] *vi* to flap the wings; to move about with bustle; to be in agitation or in uncertainty.—*vt* to throw into disorder.—*n* quick, irregular motion; agitation; confusion. [OE *flotorian*, to float about, from *flot*, the sea, stem of *flēotan*, to float.]

fluvial [flōō´vi-ȧl] *adj* of or belonging to streams and rivers. [L *fluviālis*—*fluvius*, a river, *fluěre*, to flow.]

flux [fluks] *n* a flowing; a continual change; any abnormal discharge from the body; a substance used to help metals fuse together, as in soldering.—*vt* to melt.—*vi* to flow.—*n* **fluxion** [fluk´sh(ȯ)n], a flowing or discharge.

fly [flī] *vi* to move through the air, esp on wings or in aircraft; to move swiftly; to flee.—*vt* to avoid, flee from; to cause to fly, as a kite; to cross by flying;—*pr p* **fly´ing**; *pt p* **flew** [flōō]; *pt p* **flown** [flōn].—*n* a stout-bodied, two-winged insect; a fish-hook dressed with silk, etc., in imitation of a fly; a flap that conceals a fastening on a garment; a flap over the entrance to a tent; *(mech)* a fly-wheel; *(pl)* in a theatre, the space above the stage; a baseball hit high in the air.—*adj* **fly´blown**, tainted; covered with flyspecks.—*ns* **fly-by-night**, one that seeks to evade responsibilities by flight; **fly´-catch´er**, a bird (order Passeriformes) that catches flies on the wing; **fly-drive**, travel in which a tour provides air transportation and car rental; **fly´er**, a crack train; a handbill; **fly´ing bomb**, a robot bomb; **fly´ing butt´ress**, a buttress connected to a wall by an arch, serving to resist outward pressure.—*n pl* **fly´ing-colors**, triumphant success.—*ns* **Fly´ing-Dutch´man**, a Dutch black spectral ship, whose captain is condemned to sweep the seas around the Cape of Storms for ever; **fly´ing fish**, any of numerous fishes (family Exocoetidae) of warm seas with winglike fins used in gliding through the air; **fly´ing-fox**, any of a suborder (Megachiroptera) of large Old World fruit-eating bats of warm regions; **fly´ing machine**, an apparatus for navigating the air; **flying saucer**, a disklike flying object in the sky repeatedly reported to have been seen; **fly´ing squirrel**, either of two N American squirrels (*Glaucomys volans* and *G sabrinus*) with folds of skin connecting the forelegs and hind legs enabling it to make long gliding leaps; any similar squirrel; **fly´ing-start**, in a race, a start in which the signal is given after the competitors are in motion; **fly´leaf**, a blank leaf at the beginning or end of a book; **fly´man**, one who works the ropes in theater flies; **fly´over**, a processional flight of aircraft; **fly´pā´per**, a sticky or poisonous paper for destroying flies; **fly´speck**, a speck made by fly excrement; something small and insignificant; **fly´weight**, a boxer weighing not more than 112 pounds; **fly´wheel**, a wheel, usu. relatively massive, which stores energy by inertia, used eg to equalize effect of driving effort.—**fly blind**, to fly an airplane solely by instruments; **fly high**, to be elated; **fly in the face** or **teeth of**, to stand brazenly in defiance of; **fly in the ointment**, a detracting factor; **fly into**, have a violent outburst of; **let fly (at)** to hurl (at); to direct a verbal attack (at); **on the fly**, *(inf)* while in a hurry; (baseball) while still in the air. [OE *flēogan*, to fly, *flēoge*, fly; Ger *fliegen*.]

foal [fōl] *n* the young of the horse family.—*vti* to bring forth (a foal). [OE *fola*; Ger *fohlen*, Gr *pōlos*; L *pullus*.]

foam [fōm] *n* froth on the surface of liquid; something like foam, as frothy saliva; a rigid or springy cellular mass made from liquid rubber, plastic, etc.—*vi* to froth out.—*adjs* **foam´less, foam´y**, frothy; **foamed plastic**, expanded plastic; **foam rubber**, spongy rubber of fine texture made by foaming (as by whipping before vulcanization). [OE *fām*; Ger *feim*, prob akin to L *spuma*.]

fob [fob] *n* a small pocket for a watch; the watch chain or ribbon hanging from such a pocket. [Perh conn with Low Ger *fobke*, High Ger dial *fuppe*, pocket.]

fo'c'sle *see* **forecastle**.

focus [fō´kus] *n* a point where rays of light, heat, etc. meet after being bent by a lens, curved mirror, etc.; distance of a focus from the surface of a lens or concave mirror, focal length; correct adjustment of the eye, lens, etc. to form a clear image; the central point.—*pl* **foci** [fō´sī], **fō´cuses**.—*vt* to bring to a focus; to concentrate.—*pt p* **fō´cused**.—**in focus**, clear; **out of focus**, blurred. [L *focus*, a hearth.]

fodder [fod´ėr] *n* food for cattle.—*vt* to supply with fodder. [OE *fōdor*; alied to **food, feed**.]

foe [fō] *n* an enemy, an adversary; something injurious. [ME *foo*—OE *fāh, fā* (adj) and *gefā* (noun).]

foehn, föhn [fœn] *n* a hot dry wind blowing down a mountain valley. [Ger—L *Favōnius*, the west wind.]

foetid *see* **fetid**.

foetus *see* **fetus**.

fog [fog] *n* a large mass of water vapor condensed to fine particles just above the earth's surface; a state of mental confusion.—*vti* to make or become foggy.—*adjs* **fog´bound**, surrounded by fog; unable to move because of fog; **fog´less**, free of fog; **fogg´y**, misty; clouded in mind; confused, indistinct.—*ns* **fogg´iness; foghorn**, a horn sounded as a warning signal in foggy weather; a large hoarse voice; **Foggy Bottom**, the US Department of State. [Perh conn with Dan *fog*, as in *snee-fog*, thick falling snow.]

fogy, fogey [fō´gi] *n* a dull old fellow; a person with antiquated notions. [Prob from **foggy** in sense of 'mossgrown'.]

foible [foi´bl] *n* a weakness; a failing; a penchant. [OFr *foible*, weak; cf **feeble**.]

foil[1] [foil] *vt* to defeat; to baffle; to frustrate.—*pr p* **foil´ing**; *pt p* **foiled**.—*n* a light, blunted fencing sword with a circular guard.—*pl* sport of fencing with the foil. [OFr *fuler*, to stamp or crush.—L *fullō*, a fuller of cloth.]

foil[2] [foil] *n* a very thin sheet of metal; anything that sets off or enhances another by contrast. [OFr *foil* (Fr *feuille*)—L *folium*, a leaf.]

foist [foist] *vt* to bring in by stealth; to palm off (upon); to pass off as genuine. [Prob Du prov *vuisten*, to take in the hand; *vuist*, fist.]

fold[1] [fōld] *n* a doubling of anything upon itself; a crease; a part laid over on another; *(geol.)* a bend produced in layers of rock.—*vt* to lay in folds; to wrap up, envelop; to interlace (one's arms); clasp (one's hands); to embrace, to incorporate (an ingredient) into a food mixture by gentle overturnings.—*vi* to become folded; to fail completely; to collapse, esp to go out of business.—*n* **fold´er**, a person or thing that folds; a folded cover or large envelope for holding or filing papers.—*adjs* **fold´away**, designed to fold out of the way and out of sight; **fold´ing**, that folds or that can be folded.—*ns* **foldboat**, a small collapsible canoe; **fold-boating**, sport of shooting rapids and cruising on swift waters in a foldboat; **folding money**, paper money; **foldout**, a folded leaf in a publication (as a book) that is larger than the page. [OE *fealdan*, to fold; Ger *falten*.]

fold[2] [fōld] *n* a pen for sheep; a flock of sheep; a group of people or institutions having a common belief, activity, etc.—*vt* to confine in a fold. [OE *falod, fald*, a fold, stall.]

folderol [fol´de-rol] *n* a useless ornament; nonsense. [*fol-de-rol*, a refrain in some old songs.]

foliaceous [fō-li-ā´shus] *adj* pertaining to or consisting of leaves or laminae. [L *foliăceus*—*folium*, a leaf.]

foliage [fō´li-ij] *n* leaves, as of a plant or tree; a representation of leaves, flowers, and branches in architectural ornamentation.—*adj* **fō´liaged; fō´liāted**, decorated with leaf ornaments; consisting of layers or laminae.—*n* **fō´liātion**, the process of forming into a leaf; the state of being in leaf; the numbering of the leaves of a manuscript; the act of beating a metal into a thin plate. [Fr *feuillage*—L *folium*, a leaf.]

folio [fō´li-ō] *n* a large sheet of paper folded once; a book of such sheets; the number of a page in a book.—*vt* to put a serial number on each leaf or page of. [Ablative of L *folium*, a leaf, a sheet of paper.]

foliole [fō´li-ōl] *n* *(bot)* a leaflet of a compound leaf. [Fr, dim of L *folium*, a leaf.]

folivore [fou´lī-vor] *n* an animal, esp a primate, that feeds on leaves.—*adj* **foliv´orous**. [L *folium*, leaf + **vore**.]

folk [fōk] *n* a people, a nation; the common people of a nation.—*pl* **folk, folks**. *(pl)* people, persons.—*adj* of or originating among the common people.—*ns* **folklore**, the traditional beliefs, legends, etc. of a people; **folk mass**, (RC) a mass using folk music, often with the congregation joining in the singing; **folk medicine**, traditional medicine as practised nonprofessionally, esp the use of vegetable remedies on an empirical basis; **folk song**, a traditional or composed song marked by simplicity of melody, stanzaic form, and refrain;—*adj* **folksy**, friendly, informal in manner.—*adv* **folksily**.—*n* **folksiness**.—*n* **folktale**, an anonymous, timeless, and placeless tale circulated orally among a people; **folkway**, a traditional social custom. [OE *folc*; ON *folk*; Ger *volk*.]

follicle [fol´i-kl] *n* any small sac, cavity, or gland. [Fr—L *folliculus*, dim of *follis*, a windbag.]

follow [fol´ō] *vt* to go or come after or behind; to pursue; to proceed along (a road); to practise (a profession); to imitate; to obey; to adopt, as an opinion; to keep the eye or mind fixed on; to grasp or understand the whole course of; to come after in time; to result from.—*vi* to come after another; to result.—*ns* **foll´ower**, one who comes after; a disciple or adherent; **foll´owing**, the whole body of supporters.—*adj* coming next after; to be next after; to be next mentioned.—**follow out**, to follow to the end; to carry out (an order); **follow through**, to continue a stroke or motion to the end of its arc; to press on in an activity to a conclusion; **follow up**, to pursue a question, inquiry, etc., that has been started (*n* **foll´ow-up**). [OE *folgian, fylgan*; Ger *folgen*.]

folly [fol´i] *n* a lack of sense; a foolish thing; an extravagant and fanciful building; esp one in a garden. [OFr *folie—fol*, foolish.]

foment [fo-ment´] *vt* to stir up (trouble); to apply a warm lotion to.—*ns* **fomenta´tion**, the application of hot moist substances to ease pain; instigation; **foment´er**. [Fr *fomenter*—L *fōmentāre—fōmentum* for *fovimentum—fovēre*, to warm.]

fond [fond] *adj* tender and loving; weakly indulgent; prizing highly (*with* **of**).—*vt* **fond´le**, to treat with fondness; to caress.—*adv* **fond´ly**.—*n* **fond´ness**. [For *fonned*, pt p of ME *fonnen*, to act foolishly—*fon*, a fool.]

fondant [fon´dȧnt] *n* a soft sugar mixture for candies and icings; a candy made from this. [Fr *fondre*, to melt—L *fundĕre*.]

fondue, fondu [fon-dōō] *n* melted cheese usu. Emmental and Gruyère flavored with white wine, used for dipping cubes of bread; small pieces of meat cooked at the table in hot oil; a chafing dish in which fondue is made. [Fr *fondre*, to melt.]

font[1] [font] *n* a receptacle for baptismal water; a receptacle for holy water; a source (*font of knowledge*). [OE *font*—L *fons, fontis*, a fountain.]

font[2] [font] *n* (*printing*) set of type all of one size and style. [Fr *fonte—fondre*—L *fundere*, to cast.]

food [fōōd] *n* any substance, esp a solid, taken in by a plant or animal to enable it to live and grow; anything that nourishes.—*ns* **food chain**, a sequence (as fox, rabbit, and grass) of organisms in a community in which each feeds on the member below it; **food cycle**, all the individual food chains in an ecological community; **food poisoning**, sickness caused by contaminants, as bacteria, in food; **food processor**, an electrical appliance with a set of interchangeable blades revolving inside a container for blending, chopping, slicing, etc., food; **food stamp**, any of the Federal stamps sold at less than face value to persons with low incomes for buying food; **foodstuff**, any material made into or used as food. [OE *fōdal*; Swed *föda*.]

fool [fōōl] *n* a person showing lack of wisdom, or of common sense; a person of weak mind; a jester.—*vt* to deceive; to treat as a fool.—*vi* to play the fool; to joke.—*n* **fool´ery**.—*adj* **fool´hardy**, foolishly bold; rash, incautious.—*n* **fool´hard´iness**.—*adj* **fool´ish**, unwise; ridiculous.—*adv* **fool´ishly**.—*n* **fool´ishness**.—*adj* **fool´proof**, not liable to sustain or inflict injury as a result of wrong usage (that even a fool could not misunderstand).—*ns* **fool's´ err´and**, a useless mission; **fool's paradise**, a state of delusory happiness; **fool's parsley**, a poisonous weed (*Aethusa cynapium*) of the carrot family resembling parsley.—**fool around**, to engage in casual sexual activity. [OFr *fol* (Fr *fou*), It *folle*—L *follis*, a wind-bag.]

foolscap [fōōlz´kap] *n* a size of writing paper 13 by 16 inches, in the US, originally bearing the watermark of a fool's cap and bells.

foot [fŏŏt] *n* the end part of the leg, on which one stands; the lower part or base; a measure of length equal to 12 inches (symbol: ´); a group of syllables serving as a unit of meter in verse.—*pl* **feet** (**foot** in *a ten-foot pole*).—*vi* to dance; to walk; (of a sailboat) to make speed.—*vt* to put new feet to; to add up (a column of figures); to pay (a bill).—*pr p* **foot´ing**; *pt p* **foot´ed**.—*ns* **foot´age**, measurement in feet; **foot´ball**, a field game played with an inflated leather ball by two teams; the ball used; **foot´bridge**, a narrow bridge for pedestrians.—*adj* **foot´ed**, provided with a foot or feet, esp of a specified kind (eg *light-footed*).—*ns* **foot´fall**, the sound of a footstep; **footgear**, shoes and boots; **foot´hill**, a hill at the foot of higher hills.—*pl* a hilly region at the base of a mountain range; **foot´hold**, space on which to plant the feet; a position usable as a base for further advance; **foot´ing**, place for the foot to rest on; placing of the feet; foundation; position, status, conditions (eg *on a friendly footing, on this footing*); settlement; **foot´lights**, a row of lights in front of a stage floor; the stage as a profession; **foot´man**, a servant or attendant in livery.—*pl* **foot´men; foot´mark, foot´print**, the mark or print of a foot; **foot´note**, a note of reference or comment, esp at foot of page; **foot´path**, a narrow path for pedestrians; **foot´pound**, the energy needed to raise a mass of one pound the height of one foot.—*adj* **foot-pound-second**, of a system of measurement based upon the foot as the unit of length, the pound as the unit of weight, and the second as the unit of time.—Abbrev. *fps*; **foot´race**, a race by humans on foot.—*vi* **foot´slog**, to march or tramp through mud.—*n* **foot´sol´dier**, infantryman.—*adj* **foot´sore**, having sore feet, as by much walking.—*ns* **foot´step**, the step or impression, or the sound, of the foot; trace of a course pursued.—*pl* a way of life; **foot´stool**, a stool to support the feet; **foot´wear**, boots and shoes.—**foot-and-mouth-disease**, an acute contagious febrile virus disease, esp of cloven-footed animals.—**at one's feet**, under one's influence; **foot in the door**, the first step toward a goal; **off one's feet**, in a sitting or lying position; **on foot**, by walking or running; **on one's feet**, standing; in a recovered condition (as from illness); in an extemporaneous manner; **to one's feet**, to a standing position; **under foot** in the way. [OE *fōt*, pl *fēt*; Ger *fuss*, L *pēs, pedis*, Gr *pous, podos*, Sans *pād*.]

footle [fōōt´l] *vi* to trifle, potter.—*adj* **foot´ling**, trivial, ineffectual, purposeless. [Ety obscure.]

foozle [fōōz´l] *n* a tedious fellow; a bungled stroke at golf, etc.—*vi* to fool away one's time.—*vti* to bungle. [Cf Ger dial *fuseln*, to work badly.]

fop [fop] *n* an affected dandy.—*n* **fopp´ery**, vanity in dress or manners; affectation.—*adj* **fop´pish**.—*adv* **fopp´ishly**.—*n* **fopp´ishness**. [Cf Ger *foppen*, to hoax.]

for [för, fȯr] *prep* generally used in phrases indicating a relation of cause or purpose:—because of, in consequence of (eg *he wept for shame*); in payment of, or recompense of; in order to be, to serve as, with the object of (eg *enlisted for a soldier, use this for a plate, a case for holding books*); appropriate to, or adapted to; in quest of; in the direction of; on behalf of; in place of; in favor of; with respect to; notwithstanding, in spite of; to the extent of; through the space of; during.—*conj* because. [OE *for*.]

forage [for´ij] *n* food for domestic animals, esp when taken by browsing or grazing; a search for provisions.—*vi* to search for food.—*vt* to get or take food from; to raid. [Fr *fourrage*, OFr *feurre*, fodder, of Gmc origin.]

foramen [fo-rā´mėn] *n* a small opening;—*pl* **forăm´ina, fora´mens**.—*adj* **foram´inous**, pierced with small holes. [L—*forāre*, to pierce.]

forasmuch as [for-az-much´ az] *conj* because, since.

foray [for´ā] *n* a raid.—*vti* to plunder. [Ety obscure, but ult identical with **forage**.]

forbade [fȯr-bad´] *pt t* of **forbid**.

forbear [fȯrbār´] *vi* to endure, to avoid.—*vt* to hold oneself back from.—*pt* **forbore´**; *pt p* **forborne´**.—*n* **forbear´ance**, exercise of patience, command of temper; clemency.—*adj* **forbear´ing**, long-suffering, patient. [OE *forberan*, pt *forbær*, pt p *forboren*. Pfx *for-*, signifying abstention, and **bear**.]

forbid [fȯr-bid´] *vt* to prohibit; to prevent;—*pt* **forbade** [forbad´], *pt p* **forbidd´en**.—*adjs* **forbidd´en**, prohibited; unlawful; **forbidd´ing**, looking dangerous or disagreeable; repellent.—*adv* **forbidd´ingly**, [OE *forbēodan*, pt *forbēad*, pt p *forboden*. Pfx *for-*, signifying prohibition, and **bid**; cf Ger *verbieten*.]

force [fōrs, fȯrs] *n* strength, power, energy; efficacy; validity (of an argument); significance; influence; vehemence; violence; coercion or compulsion; a body of people prepared for action (eg *police force, armed forces*); (*mech*) any cause which changes the direction or speed of the motion of a portion of matter.—*vt* to draw, push, by exertion of strength; to thrust; to compel, to constrain; to ravish; to take by violence; to achieve by force; to produce with effort; to cause (a plant) to grow by artificial means.—*adj* **forced**, accomplished by great effort (eg *a forced march*); strained,; caused to grow or develop unnaturally fast.—*adj* **force´ful**, effective.—*adv* **force´fully**.—*n* **force´ pump**, a pump with a solid piston for drawing and forcing through valves a liquid (as water) to a great height above the pump.—*adj* **forc´ible**, having force; done by force.—*n* **forc´ibleness**.—*adv* **forc´ibly**.—*n* **forc´ing**.—**in force**, in full strength; in effect, valid; **force one's hand**, to cause one to act prematurely; to force one to reveal his purpose or intention. [Fr,—Low L *fortia*—L *fortis*, strong.]

forcemeat [fōrs-mēt] *n* meat chopped fine and highly seasoned, used as a stuffing or alone. [For **farce**—Fr *farcir*, to stuff.]

forceps [fȯr´seps] *n* an instrument for grasping and holding firmly, or exerting traction upon objects, esp by jewelers and surgeons.—*pl* **for´ceps**. [L, from *formus*, hot, and *capĕre*, to hold.]

ford [fōrd, fȯrd] *n* a place where water may be crossed on foot.—*vt* to cross water on foot.—*adj* **ford´able**. [OE *ford—faran*, to go; Ger *furt—fahren*, to go on foot.]

fore [fōr, fȯr] *adj* front.—*n* the front.—*adv* at or towards the front (of a ship).—*interj* (*golf*) a warning cry to anybody in the way of the ball.—*adj* **fore-and-aft**, from the bow to the stern; set lengthwise, as a rig.—**at the fore**, displayed on the foremast (of a flag); **to the fore**, prominent. [OE *fore*, radically the same as **for**, prep.]

forearm[1] [fō´rärm] *n* the part of the arm between the elbow and the wrist; the corresponding part in other vertebrates. [Pfx *fore-*, front part of + **arm** (1).]

forearm[2] [fōr-ärm´] *vt* to arm in advance. [Pfx *fore-*, before + **arm** (2).]

forebear [fōr´bār] *n* an ancestor. [Pfx *fore-*, before, **be** + suffix *-ar, -er*.]

forebode [fōr-bōd´] *vt* to portend; to have a premonition (esp of evil).—*n* **forebod´ing**. [Pfx *fore-*, before + OE *bodian*, to announce—*bod*, a message.]

forecast [fōr´käst] *vt* to reckon beforehand; to predict; to foreshadow.—*vi* to estimate beforehand;—*pt* and *pt p* **fore´cast, forecast´ed**.—*n* **fore´cast**, a prediction. [Pfx *fore-*, before + **cast**, to reckon.]

forecastle, fo'c'sle [fōk´sl, sometimes fōr´käs-l] *n* a short raised deck at the forward part of a ship; the forepart of the ship under the maindeck, the quarters of the crew. [**fore** + **castle**.]

foreclose [fōr-klōz´] *vt* to preclude; to prevent; to take away the right of redeeming (a mortgage).—*n* **foreclos´ure**, a foreclosing; (*law*) the process by which a mortgager failing to repay the loan is deprived of his right to redeem the property. [OFr *forclos*, pt p of *forclore*, to exclude—L *forīs*, outside, *claudĕre, clausum*, to shut.]

foredeck [fōr´dek] *n* the forepart of a ship's main deck. [**fore** + **deck**.]

foredoom [fōr-dōōm´] *vt* to doom beforehand. [Pfx *fore-*, before + **doom**.]

forefather [fōr´fä-THėr] *n* an ancestor. [Pfx *fore-*, before + **father**.]

forefinger [fōr´fing-gėr] *n* the finger next to the thumb. [**fore** + **finger**.]

forefoot [fōr´fŏŏt] *n* one of the anterior feet of a quadruped. [**fore** + **foot**.]

forefront [fōr´frunt] *n* the very front or foremost part. [**fore** + **front**.]

forego [fōr-gō´] *vt* to go before, precede; chiefly used in *pr p* **foregoing** and *pt p* **foregone´**.—**foregone conclusion**, a conclusion come to before examination of the evidence; an inevitable result. [Pfx *fore-*, before + **go**.]

foreground [fōr´grownd] *n* the part of a picture or field of view nearest the observer's eye. [**fore** + **ground** (2).]

forehand [fōr´hand] *n* a stroke in a racket game made with the palm of the hand turned in the direction in which the hand is moving; the part of a horse that is in front of its rider.—*adj* **fore´handed**, with the palm in front. [**fore** + **hand**.]

forehead [for´id, -ed, or -hed] *n* the part of the face above the eyes. [Pfx *fore*, front part of + **head**.]

foreign [for´in] *adj* belonging to another country; from abroad; alien (to), not belonging (to), not appropriate; introduced from outside (as *foreign body*); dealing with, or intended for dealing with, countries other than one's own.—*n* **for´eigner**, a native of another country. [OFr *forain*—Low L *forāneus*—L *forās, foris*, out of doors.]

forejudge [fōr-juj´] *vt* to expel, oust, or put out by judgement of a court; to judge before hearing the facts and proof. [Pfx *fore-*, before + **judge**.]

foreknow [fōr-nō´] *vt* to know beforehand; to foresee.—*n* **foreknowl´edge**. [Pfx *fore-*, before + **know**.]

foreland [fōr´lȧnd] *n* a promontory, a headland. [**fore** + **land**.]

foreleg [fōr´leg] *n* a front leg. [**fore** + **leg**.]

forelock [fōr´lok] *n* the lock of hair on the forehead. [**fore** + **lock** (2).]

foreman [fōr´mȧn] *n* the first or chief man; an overseer;—*pl* **fore´men**. [**fore** + **man**.]

foremast [fōr´mäst, -mȧst] *n* the mast nearest the bow of a ship. [**fore** + **mast**.]

foremost [fōr´mōst] *adj* first in place; most advanced; first in rank or dignity. [OE *forma*, first, superl of *fore*, and superl suffx *-st*; it is therefore a double superl. The OE form *formest* was wrongly divided *for-mest* instead of *formest*, and *-mest* mistaken for *-most*.]

forenoon [fōr´nōōn, fōr-nōōn´] *n* the part of the day before noon; morning. [Pfx *fore-*, before + **noon**.]

forensic [fo-ren´sik] *adj* belonging to courts of law; used in law pleading.—**forensic medicine**, a science dealing with the relation and application of medical facts to legal problems. [L *forēnsis*—*forum*, market-place.]

foreordain [fōr-or-dān´] *vt* to arrange beforehand; to predestine.—*n* **foreordinā´tion**. [Pfx *fore-*, before + **ordain**.]

forepart [fōr´pärt] *n* the front; the early part. [**fore** + **part**.]

foreplay [fōr´plā] *n* erotic stimulation before sexual intercourse. [*fore-*, before + **play**.]

forequarter [fōr´kwater] *n* the front half of a lateral half of the carcass of a quadruped. [*fore-*, before + **quarter**.]

foreran [fōr-ran´] *pt t* of **forerun**.

forerun [fōr-run´] *vt* to run before; to precede.—*n* **forerunn´er**, a runner or messenger sent before, a skier who runs the course before the start of a race; a predecessor, a forebear. [Pfx *fore-*, in front of + **run**.]

foresail [fōr´s(ā)l] *n* the lowest square sail on the foremast; a triangular sail on the forestay. [**fore** + **sail**.]

foresee [fōr-sē´] *vt* to see or know beforehand; *pt* **foresaw´**; *pt p* **foreseen´**. [Pfx *fore-*, before + **see** (2).]

foreshadow [fōr-shad´ō] *vt* to represent or indicate beforehand.—*n* **foreshad´owing**. [Pfx *fore-*, before + **shadow**.]

foreshore [fōr´shōr] *n* a strip of land margining a body of water; the space between the high and low water marks. [Pfx *fore-*, the front part of + **shore** (2).]

foreshorten [for-shört´n] *vt* in drawing, etc. to shorten some lines of (an object) to give the illusion of proper relative size.—*n* **foreshort´ening**. [**fore** + **shorten**.]

foresight [fōr´sīt] *n* act of foreseeing; the power to foresee; prudent provision for the future. [Pfx *fore-*, before + **sight**.]

foreskin [fōr´skin] *n* the skin that covers the glans penis. [**fore** + **skin**.]

forest [for´est] *n* a thick growth of trees, etc. covering a large tract of land; something resembling a forest.—*ns* **for´ester**, a person trained in forestry; an inhabitant of a forest; **for´estry**, the science of developing forests; the management of growing timber. [OFr *forest* (Fr *forêt*)—Low L *forestis* (*silva*), the outside wood, as opposed to the *parcus* (park) or walled-in wood—L *foris*, out of doors.]

forestall [fōr-stöl´] *vt* to prevent by doing something ahead of time; to anticipate.—*n* **forestall´er**. [OE *foresteall*, an ambush—*fore-*, before, *steall*, stall.]

forestay [fōr´stā] *n* a stay from the foremost head to the deck of a ship. [**fore** + **stay** (2).]

foretaste [fōr-tāst] *vt* to taste beforehand; to anticipate.—*n* **fore´taste**, a warning, a taste beforehand. [Pfx *fore-*, before + **taste**.]

foretell [fōr-tel´] *vt* to tell beforehand, to predict. [Pfx *fore*,- before + **tell**.]

forethought [fōr´thöt] *n* thought or care for the future, provident care. [Pfx *fore-*, before + **thought**.]

foretoken [fōr´tō-kn] *n* a token or sign beforehand.—*vt* **foretō´ken**, to portend. [Pfx *fore-*, before + **token**.]

foretop [fōr´top] *n* (*naut*) the platform at the head of the foremast.—*n* **fore´-topmast**, a mast next above the foremast. [**fore** + **top** (1).]

forever [for-ev´ėr] *adv* for all time to come; continually.—*adv* **forev´ermore´**, forever.

forewarn [fōr-wörn´] *vt* to warn beforehand—*n* **forewarn´ing**. [Pfx *fore-*, before + **warn**.]

forewing [fōr´wing] *n* one of a 4-winged insect's front pair of wings. [**fore** + **wing**.]

forewoman [fōr´wŏŏm-ȧn] *n* a female overseer;—*pl* **fore´women** [fōr´wim-ėn]. [**fore** + **woman**.]

foreword [fōr´wûrd] *n* a preface. [**fore** + **word**—a 19th century coinage, on analogy of Ger *vorwort*.]

forfeit [för´fit] *vt* to lose the right to by some fault or crime; to penalise by forfeiture; (*loosely*) to give up voluntarily (a right).—*n* a penalty for a fault; something deposited and redeemable.—*adj* **for´feitable**.—*n* **for´feiture**, act of forfeiting; state of being forfeited; the thing forfeited. [OFr *forfait*—Low L *forisfactum*—*forisfacĕre*, to transgress.]

forfend [fȯr-fend´] *vt* to protect, to preserve. [Pfx *for-*, signifying prohibition + **fend**.]

forgather [fōr-gaTH´ėr] *vi* to assemble. [Pfx *for-*, inten + **gather**.]

forgave [fȯr-gāv] *pt* of **forgive**.

forge[1] [förj, fōrj] *n* a furnace, esp one in which iron is heated; a smithy.—*vt* to shape (metal) by heating and hammering; to form; to counterfeit (eg a signature).—*vt* to commit forgery.—*ns* **forg´er**, one who forges or makes; one guilty of forgery; **forg´ery**, fraudulently making or altering any writing; that which is forged or counterfeited. [OFr *forge*—L *fabrica*—*faber*, a workman.]

forge[2] [förj, fōrj] *vt* to move steadily on (usu. with **ahead**). [Origin obscure.]

forget [fȯr-get´] *vti* to be unable to remember; to overlook or neglect.—*pr p* **forgett´ing**; *pt* **forgot´**; *pt p* **forgot´, forgott´en**.—*adj* **forget´ful**, apt to forget, inattentive.—*adv* **forget´fully**.—*ns* **forget´fulness; forget´-me-not**, any of a genus (Myosotis) of small herbs of the borage family having bright-blue or white flowers.—**forget oneself**, act in an improper manner. [OE *forgietan*—pfx *for-*, away, *gietan*, to get.]

forgive [fȯr-giv] *vt* to pardon, or cease to feel resentment against (a person); to pardon, overlook (a debt or trespass).—*vi* to be merciful or forgiving;—*pt* **forgave´**; *pt p* **forgiv´en**.—*n* **forgive´ness**, pardon, remission; disposition to pardon.—*adj* **forgiv´ing**, ready to pardon, merciful. [OE *forgiefan*—pfx *for-*, away, *giefan*, to give; cf Ger *vergeben*.]

forgo [fȯr-gō´, fōr-gō´] *vt* to give up; to forbear the use of. [Pfx *for-*, signifying abstention, and **go**.]

forgot, forgotten *see* **forget**.

fork [förk] *n* a pronged instrument; anything that divides into prongs or branches; the space or angle between two branches; one of the branches into which a road or river divides; the point of separation.—*vi* to divide into branches.—*vt* to form as a fork; to move with a fork.—*adjs* **forked, fork´y**, shaped like a fork.—**forklift**, a power-driven truck for hoisting and transporting heavy objects by means of steel fingers inserted under the load.—**fork out, over** or **up** (*inf*) to pay out; to hand over. [OE *forca*—L *furca*.]

forlorn [fȯr-lörn] *adj* (*obs*) quite lost; forsaken; wretched.—*adv* **forlorn´ly**. [OE *forloren*, pt p of *forlēosan*, to lose—pfx *for-*, away, *leōsan*, to lose.]

forlorn hope [fȯr-lörn´-hōp] *n* a body of men selected for some service of uncommon danger; a desperate enterprise. [From the Du *verloren hoop*, the lost troop.]

form [förm] *n* general structure; the figure of a person or animal; a mold; a particular mode, kind, type, etc. (*ice is a form of water, the forms of poetry*); arrangement; a way of doing something requiring skill; a conventional procedure; a printed document with blanks to be filled in; condition of mind or body; a chart giving information about racehorses; changed appearance of a word to show inflection; type locked in a frame for printing.—*vt* to shape; to train; to develop (habits); to constitute.—*vi* to be formed.—*adj* **form´al**, according to form or established mode; ceremonial; punctilious; stiff.—*n* a formal dance; a women's evening dress.—*ns* **form´alism**, strict observance of form or conventional usage; **form´alist**, one having exaggerated regard to rules or established usages; **formal´ity**, the precise observance of forms or ceremonies; a conventional method of procedure; stiffness; conventionality.—*adv* **form´ally**.—*n* **formā´tion**, form of making or producing; that which is formed; structure; regular array or prearranged order helping development; (*geol*) any igneous, sedimentary, or metamorphic rock represented as a unit.—*adj* **form´ative**.—*Also n* element in a word serving to give it form and not part of the base; the minimal element in a transformational grammar.—*adj* **formless**, shapeless. [OFr *forme*—L *forma*, shape.]

formaldehyde [för-mal´de-hīd] *n* a colorless pungent gas (CH_2O) used in solution as a disinfectant and preservative.

formalin [förm´alin] *n* an aqueous solution of formaldehyde used as an antiseptic, germicide or preservative.

format [för´mat] *n* of books, etc., the size, form, shape in which they are issued; general plan and arrangement (as of a television show). [Fr]

former [förm´ėr] *adj* before in time; past; first mentioned (of two).—*adv* **form´erly**, in former times, heretofore. [Formed late on analogy of ME *formest*, foremost, by adding comp suffx *-er* to base of OE *forma*, first, itself superlative.]

formic [för´mik] *adj* of formic acid.—*n* **formic acid**, a colorless pungent liquid (CH_2O_2) found esp in ants and many plants, used chiefly in textile manufacture.—*n* **for´micary**, an ant nest. [L *formica*, an ant.]

formidable [för´mi-dȧ-bl] *adj* causing fear; redoubtable; difficult to deal with.—*n* **for´midableness**.—*adv* **for´midably**. [Fr,—L *formīdābilis*—*formīdō*, fear.]

formula [förm´ū-la] *n* a prescribed form; a formal statement of doctrines; a list of ingredients, as for a prescription or recipe; (*math*) a general expression for solving problems; (*chem*) a set of symbols expressing the composition of a substance; a fixed method according to which something is to be done; technical specification governing cars entered for certain motor-racing events;—*pl* **form´ūlas, formulae** [form´ū-lē]—*ns* **formularizā´tion, formūlā´tion; form´ūlary**, a formula; a book of formulae or precedents.—*adj* prescribed; ritual.—*vst* **form´ūlāte**, to reduce to or express in a formula; to state or express in a clear or definite form. [L, dim of *forma*.]

fornicate [för´ni-kāt] *vi* to commit fornication—*ns* **fornicā´tion**, sexual intercourse outside marriage; **for´nicātor**. [L *fornicārī, -ātus—fornix*, a brothel.]

forsake [fȯr-sāk´] *vt* to desert; to give up;—*pr p* forsāking; *pt* **forsook´**; *pt p* **forsāk´en**. [OE *forsacan—for-*, away, *sacan*, to strive.]

forsooth [fȯr-sōōth´] *adv* in truth, certainly, used ironically. [**for** + **sooth**.]

forswear [fȯr-swār´] *vt* to renounce under oath.—*vi* to swear falsely;—*pt* **forswore´**; *pt p* **forswōrn´**. [Pfx *for*, signifying abstention, and **swear**.]

forsythia [for-siTH´ē-a] *n* any of a genus (*Forsythia*) of shrubs with yellow, bell-shaped flowers in early spring. [W. Forsyth, 18th century British botanist.]

fort [fōrt, fört] *n* a fortified place for military defense; a permanent army post. [Fr,—L *fortis*, strong.]

forte[1] [fōrt] *n* that in which one excels. [Fr *fort*, strong.]

forte[2] [för´te] *adj, adv* (*mus*) loud;—*superl* **fortis´simo**, very loud. [It]

forth [fōrth, förth,] *adv* forward; onward; out; into the open; progressively.—*adj* **forth´coming**, about to appear; approaching; ready to be produced; readily available.—*adv* **forth´right**, straightforward.—*adj* straightforward; honest; downright.—*adv* **forthwith´**, immediately. [OE *forth—fore*, before.]

fortify [för´ti-fī] *vt* to strengthen physically, emotionally, etc.; to strengthen against attack, as with forts; to support; to add alcohol to (wine, etc.); to add vitamins, etc. to (milk, etc.);—*pt p* **for´ti-fied**.—*ns* **fortificā´tion**, act or process of fortifying; that which fortifies; **for´tifier**. [Fr *fortifier*—Low L *fortificāre—fortis*, strong, *facĕre*, to make.]

fortissimo *see* **forte**.

fortitude [för´ti-tūd] *n* courage in endurance. [L *fortitūdō—fortis*, strong.]

fortnight [fört´nīt] *n* (*Brit*) two weeks or fourteen days.—*adj, adv* **fort´nightly**, once a fortnight. [Contr of OE *fēowertēne niht*, fourteen nights.]

fortress [för´tres] *n* a fortified place. [OFr *forteresse*, another form of *fortelesce. See* **fortalice**.]

fortuitous [fȯr-tū´i-tus] *adj* happening by chance.—*adv* **fortū´itously**.—*ns* **fortū´itousness, fortū´ity**. [L *fortuitus—forte*, by chance.]

fortune [för´tūn, -chùn] *n* whatever comes by chance or luck; the arbitrary ordering of events; prosperity, success; riches; wealth.—*adj* **for´tunāte**, having good luck.—*adv* **for´tunātely**.—*ns* **for´tune cook´ie**, a thin folded cookie containing a slip of paper on which is printed a fortune, a proverb, or joke; **for´tune hunt´er**, one seeking wealth, esp by marriage.—*adj* **for´tuneless**, without fortune; luckless.—*ns* **for´tunetell´er**, one who professes to foretell someone's fortune; **for´tunetell´ing**. [Fr,—L *fortūna*.]

forty [för´ti] *adj n* four times ten, symbol for this (40, XL, xl);—*pl* **forties** (40s), the numbers from 40 to 49; the same numbers in a life or a century.—*adj* **for´tieth** [för´ti-ėth], the last of forty; being one of forty equal parts.—Also *n* **for´ty-five**, a .45 caliber handgun, usu. written .45; a microgroove phonograph record played at a speed of 45 revolutions per minute, usu. written 45; **forty-niner**, one taking part in the rush to California for gold in 1849; **forty winks**, a short nap. [OE *fēowertig—fēower*, four, *tig*, ten, related to *tien, tēn*.]

forum [fō´-, fö´rum] *n* the marketplace in Rome, where public business was transacted and justice dispensed; an assembly, program or meeting to discuss topics of public concern. [L *fŏrum*, akin to *forīs*, out of doors.]

forward [för´wȧrd] *adj* at, toward, or of the front; advanced; onward; prompt; bold; presumptuous; of or for the future.—*vt* to promote; to send on.—*adv* toward the front; ahead.—*n* a player in any of several games who plays at the front of the team's formation.—*adv* **for´wardly**.—*n* **for´wardness**. [OE *foreweard—fore*, and *-weard*, signifying direction. *Forwards* (ME *forwardes*) was orig the gen form (cf Ger *vorwärts*).]

fosse [fos] *n* (*fort*) a ditch or moat in front of a fortified place.—Also **foss**. [Fr *fosse*—L *fossa—fodĕre, fossum*, to dig.]

fossil [fos´il] *n* the petrified remains of an animal or vegetable found embedded in the strata of the earth's crust; a person with outmoded ideas or ways.—*adj* of or like a fossil; dug from the earth (*coal is a fossil fuel*); antiquated.—*adj* **fossilif´erous**, containing fossils.—*vti* **foss´ilize**, to convert into or become changed to a fossil.—*ns* **fossilizā´tion**, a changing into a fossil. [Fr *fossile*—L *fossilis—fodĕre*, to dig.]

foster [fos´tėr] *vt* to bring up; to encourage.—*adj* having a specified standing in a family but not by birth (*a foster brother*). [OE *fōstrain*, to nourish, *fōstor*, food.]

fought [föt] *pt, pt p* of **fight**.

foul [fowl] *adj* stinking, loathsome; extremely dirty; indecent; wicked; stormy (*foul weather*); tangled (*a foul rope*); outside the limits set; denoting lines setting limits on a playing area; treacherous (*a foul deed*); (*inf*) unpleasant, disagreeable; encrusted or clogged with a foreign substance (*the chimney was foul*).—Also *adv*.—*vt* to make filthy; to dishonor; to obstruct (*grease fouls drains*); to entangle (a rope, etc.); to make a foul against, as in a game; (*baseball*) to bat (the ball) foul.—*vi* to be or become fouled.—*n* (*sports*) a hit, blow, move, etc. that is foul.—*ns* **foulness; foulbrood**, a bacterial disease of honeybee larvae; **foul line**, (*baseball*) either of two lines extending from the corners of home plate to the corners of first and third base; (*bowling*) the line over which the player must not step when delivering the ball; (*basketball*) either of two lines on a basketball court parallel to the backboard from which a player delivers a free throw.—*adj* **foul-mouthed**, given to the use of obscene, profane, or abusive language.—*ns* **foul play**, violence esp murder; **foul-up**, state of confusion caused by ineptitude, carelessness, or mismanagement; a mechanical difficulty. [OE *fūl*; Ger *faul*.]

foulard [fool´ard] *n* a lightweight silk, usu. decorated with a printed pattern; an imitation of this fabric; an article, esp a necktie, made from this.

found[1] *pt, pt p* of **find**.—*n* **found´ling**, a little child found deserted.

found[2] [fownd] *vt* to set on something solid; to bring into being; to establish (as an institution) often with provision for future maintenance.—*ns* **foundation**, a founding or being founded; an endowment for an institution; such an institution; the base of a house, wall, etc.; a woman's supporting undergarment; **foundation stone**, a stone in the foundation of a building, esp one laid with public ceremony; **founder**, one that founds or establishes; **founding father**, an originator of an institution or movement; **Founding Father**, a member of the American Constitutional Convention of 1787. [Fr *fonder*—L *fundāre, -ātum*, to found—*fundus*, the bottom.]

found[3] [fownd] *vt* to melt and pour (metal) into a mold.—*ns* **found´er**, one who founds metal, esp a typefounder; **found´ry**, the art of founding or casting; the place where founding is carried on. [Fr *fondre*—L *fundĕre, fūsum*, to pour.]

founder [fownd´ėr] *vi* to subside, to collapse; (of a ship) to fill with water and sink; to go lame.—*vt* to cause to founder. [OFr *fondrer*, to fall in—*fond*, bottom—L *fundus*, bottom.]

fount [fownt] *n* a spring of water; a source. [L *fons, fontis*.]

fountain [fownt´in, -ėn] *n* a natural spring of water; a source; an artificial jet or flow of water; the basin where this flows; a reservoir, as for ink.—*ns* **fount´ainhead; fount´ain pen**, a pen having a reservoir for holding ink. [Fr *fontaine*—Low L *fontāna*—L *fons, fontis*, a spring.]

four [fōr, för] *adj, n* one more than three; the symbol for this (4, IV, iv); the fourth in a series or set; something having four units as members (as *a four-oared boat, a four-cylinder engine*).—*adj* **fourfold**, having four units or members; being four times as great or as many.—*n* **four-bagger**, a home run.—*adj* **four-channel**, of or relating to quadriphony.—*ns* **four-color conjecture**, the hypothesis that only four colors are needed to color any map on a plane surface so that no adjacent region will be the same color; **four flush**, four cards of the same suit in a 5-card poker hand.—*vi* **four-flush**, to bluff in poker holding a four flush; (*loosely*) to make a false claim.—*ns* **Four Freedoms**, freedom of speech and expression, freedom of worship, freedom from want, and freedom from fear; **4-H Club**, club(s) sponsored by the US Department of Agriculture to instruct young people in agriculture and citizenship (improving head, heart, hands, and health).—*adj* **four-handed**, (of a piano work) designed for two players; of card game engaged in by four players.—*n* **four-in-hand**, a necktie with long overlapping ends; a team of horses driven by one person; a vehicle drawn by such a team; **four-letter word**, any of a group of vulgar or obscene words made up of four letters; **four o'clock**, any of a genus (*Mirabilis*) of chiefly American annual or perennial herbs, esp a garden form (*M jalapa*) with fragrant flowers opening late in the afternoon; **fourplex**, a house or building containing four separate apartments; a four-family condominium; **fourscore**, four times twenty; eighty.—*adj* **four-star**, of a superior degree of excellence. [OE *fēower*; Ger *vier*.]

fourteen [för´tēn] (when used absolutely, fōrtēn´) *adj, n* four and ten.—*adj* **fourteenth**, the last of fourteen; being one of fourteen equal parts.—Also *n*. [OE *fēowertēne*.]

fourth [fōrth] *adj* last of four; being one of four equal parts.—Also *adv, n*. **Fourth**, Independence Day.—*adv* **fourth´ly**, in the fourth place.—**fourth dimension**, a dimension in addition to length, breadth, and depth, interpreted as the time coordinate in a space-time continuum; something outside the range of ordinary experience; **fourth estate**, the public press; the **Fourth of July**, Independence Day. [OE *fēowertha, fēortha*.]

fowl [fowl] *n* a bird; any of the domestic birds used as food, as the chicken, duck, etc.; the flesh of these birds.—*pl* **fowl, fowls**.—*vi* to kill, or try to kill, wildfowl.—*ns* **fowl´er**, one who takes wildfowl; **fowl´ing-piece**, a light gun for small-shot, used in fowling. [OE *fugol*; Ger *vogel*.]

fox [foks] *n* any of various small, alert mammals (esp genus *Vulpes*) of the dog family; the fur of the fox; a sly, crafty person; **Fox**, a member of an Amerindian people formerly living in Wisconsin.—*vt* to trick by cunning; to repair (a shoe) by renewing the upper.—*adj* **foxed**, discolored with yellowish brown stains.—*ns* **fox´fire**, a luminous fungus (as *Armillaris mellea*) that causes decaying wood to glow; **fox´glove**, any of a genus (*Digitalis*) of erect herbs of the figwort family, esp *D purpurea*, cultivated for its tubular flowers and as a source of digitalis; **fox´hole**, a pit dug in the ground as a protection against enemy fire; **fox´hound**, any of various large swift powerful hounds of great endurance used in hunting foxes; **fox´terr´ier**, any of a breed of small lively terriers formerly used to dig out foxes; **Fox´trot**, a communication code word for the letter f; **fox-´trot**, a short broken slow gait in which the hind foot of a horse hits the ground before the diagonal forefoot; a dance for couples in 4/4 time; the music for this dance.—*vi* to dance the fox-trot.—*adj* **foxy**, resembling or suggestive of a fox; warily guileful; of a warm reddish brown color; having a sharp brisk flavor; physically attractive. [OE *fox*; Ger *fuchs*.]

foyer [foy´er, fwä´yā] *n* an anteroom; an entrance hallway, as in a hotel or theater. [Fr,—L *focus*, hearth.]

fracas [frak´ä, frä-kä´] *n* uproar; a noisy quarrel. [Fr,—It *fracasso—fracassare*, to make an uproar.]

fraction [frak´sh(ȯ)n] *n* a small part, amount, etc.; (*math*) a quantity less than a whole, expressed as a decimal or with a numerator and denominator.—*adj* **frac´tional**, belonging to, or containing, a fraction or fractions.—*vt* **frac´tionalize**, to break up into parts. [OFr *fraccion*—L *fractiō, -ōnis—frangĕre, fractum*, to break.]

fractious [frak´shu̇s] *adj* ready to quarrel; peevish—*adv* **frac´tiously**.—*n* **frac´tiousness**. [From *fraction* in obs sense of quarrelling, dissension.]

fracture [frak´tyu̇r, -chu̇r] *n* the breaking of any hard body; the breach or part broken; the breaking of a bone.—*vt* to break. [L *fractūra—frangĕre, fractum*, to break.]

fragile [fraj´īl, fraj´il] *adj* easily broken; frail; delicate.—*n* **fragil´ity**, the state of being fragile. [Fr,—L *fragilis—frangĕre*, to break.]

fragment [frag´ment] *n* a piece broken off; an unfinished portion; an extant portion of something of which the rest has been destroyed or lost.—*adjs* **fragment´al** (also frag´-; *geol*), composed of fragments of older rocks; **frag´mentary**, consisting of fragments or pieces; existing or operating in separate parts; **fragmentā´tion**, division into fragments. [Fr,—L *fragmentum—frangĕre*, to break.]

fragrant [frāg´rȧnt] *adj* sweet-scented.—*ns* **frā´grance, frā´grancy**, pleasantness of smell.—*adv* **frā´grantly**. [Fr,—L *frāgrans, -antis*, pr p of *frāgrāre*, to smell.]

frail [frāl] *adj* very easily shattered; of weak health or physique; morally weak.—*ns* **frail´ness, frail´ty**, weakness; infirmity. [OFr *fraile*—L *fragilis*, fragile.]

fraise [frāz] *n* (*fort*) a horizontal or nearly horizontal palisade of pointed stakes. [Fr]

frame [frām] *vt* to form according to a pattern; to construct; to put into words (*to frame an excuse*); to enclose (a picture) in a border; to falsify evidence against (an innocent person) so that a verdict of guilty is obtained; to prearrange (a contest) so that the desired outcome is assured.—*n* something composed of parts fitted together and united; physical makeup of an animal, esp a human body; the framework of a house; the structural case enclosing a window, door, etc.; an ornamental border, as around a picture; temper (*good frame of mind*); one exposure in a filmstrip, motion picture, etc.; (*bowling*) a division of a game.—*adj* having a wood frame.—**frame of reference**, an arbitrary system of axes for describing the position or motion of something or from which physical laws are derived; a set or system (as of facts and ideas) serving to orient; a viewpoint, a theory; **frame-up**, an act in which someone is framed; an action that is framed; **framework**, a structural frame; a basic structure (as of ideas); frame of reference; the larger branches of a tree that determine its shape. [OE *framian*, to be helpful, *fram*, forward.]

franc [frangk] *n* a unit of money in France, Belgium, and Switzerland. [OFr *franc*, from the words *Francorum rex* (King of the Franks) on the first coins.]

franchise [fran´chīz, -shīz, -chiz] *n* a privilege or right granted; the right of voting. [OFr,—*franc*, free.]

Franciscan [fran-sis´kȧn] *n* a member of the Order of Friars Minor founded by St Francis of Assisi in 1209 and dedicated to preaching, missions, and charities. [L *Franciscus*, Francis.]

Franco- [frangk´ō] French, in combinations as *Franco-German, Franco-Russian, etc.*—*ns* **Franc´ophil(e)** [-fīl], a lover of things French [Gr *philos*, dear]; **Franc´ophobe** [-fōb], a hater of things French, [Gr *phobos*, fear.]

francolin [fran´ko-lin] *n* any of numerous partridges (*Francolinus* and related genera) of southern Asia and Africa.

franc-tireur [frã-tē-rœr] *n* a civilian fighter or sniper. [Fr *franc*, free, *tireur*, a shooter.]

frangible [fran´ji-bl] *adj* easily broken.—*n* **frangibil´ity**. [OFr; same root as **fraction**.]

frangipani, frangipanni [fran´ji-pan-ē] *n* a perfume derived from or resembling the odor of the red jasmine; any of several shrubs (genus *Plumeria*) of the dogbane family (as red jasmine) native to the American tropics.

frank [frangk] *adj* free in expressing oneself; clinically evident (*frank pus*).—*vt* to send (mail) free of postage.—*n* the right to send mail free; a mark indicating this right.—*n* **frank´ness**. [OFr *franc*—Low L *francus*—OHG *Franko*, Frank, hence a free man.]

Frankenstein [frangk´en-stīn] *n* the title character in a novel (1818) by Mary W. Shelley, creator of a monster that destroys him; a work that ruins its originator; a monster in the shape of a man.

Frankfurter [frangk´fōōr-tėr] *n* a small cured cooked sausage. [Ger]

frankincense [frangk´in-sens] *n* a fragrant gum resin from chiefly East African or Arabian trees (genus *Boswellia*) that is an important incense resin. [OFr *franc encens*, pure incense.]

frantic [fran´tik] *adj* mad; furious, wild.—*advs* **fran´tically, fran´ticly**. [OFr *frenetique*—L *phrenēticus*,—Gr *phrenētikos*, mad—*phrēn*, the mind. Cf **frenzy**.]

frappé, frappe [fra´pā, frap] *n* a partly frozen drink (as of fruit juice); a liqueur served over shaved ice; a thick milk shake.—Also *adj*. [Fr]

fraternal [fra-tûr´nȧl] *adj* belonging to a brother or brethren; brotherly.—*adv* **frater´nally**.—*vi* **frat´ernize**, to associate as brothers; to seek brotherly fellowship.—*ns* **fraternizā´tion, frat´ernizer; frater´nity**, the state of being brethren; a society formed on a principle of brotherhood. [L *frāter*, a brother, Gr *phrātēr*, a clansman.]

fratricide [frat´ri-sīd] *n* one who kills his brother; the murder of a brother.—*adj* **frat´-ricīdal**. [Fr,—L *frāter, frātis*, brother, *caedĕre*, to kill.]

fraud [frōd] *n* deceit; (*law*) intentional deception; imposter.—*adj* **fraud´ulent**.—*adv* fraud´ulently.—*n* **fraud´ulence**. [OFr,—L *fraus, fraudis*, fraud.]

fraught [frōt] *adj* filled or loaded (with). [Prob Old Du *vracht*. Cf **freight**.]

fraxinella [frȧks-en-el´ȧ] *n* a Eurasian perennial herb (*Dictamnus albus*) of the rue family with flowers that exhale a flammable vapor in hot weather.—Also **gas plant**. [Dim of L *fraximus*, ash tree.]

fray [frā] *n* a conflict; a brawl. [Abbrev of **affray**.]

fray [frā] *vt* to wear off by rubbing; to ravel out the edge of.—*vi* to become frayed. [Fr *frayer*—L *fricāre*, to rub.]

freak[1] [frēk] *n* a whim; an unusual happening; any abnormal animal, person, or plant; (*slang*) a sexual deviate; (*slang*) a user of an illicit drug; an ardent enthusiast (*a chess freak*).—*adj* abnormal.—*adj* **freak´ish**.—*adv* **freak´ishly**.—*n* **freak´ishness**.—**freak-out**, withdrawal from reality, esp by using drugs; a drug-induced state of mind, a bad trip; an irrational act; one who freaks out. [A late word; cf OE *frīcian*, to dance.]

freak[2] [frēk] *vt* to streak with color. [Perh same as **freak** (1).]

freckle [frek´l] *vti* to make or become spotted with freckles.—*n* a small, brownish spot on the skin. —*adjs* **freck´ly, freck´led**, full of freckles. [ON *freknur* (pl), Dan *fregne*.]

free [fre] *adj* not under the control or power of another; having liberty; independent; able to move in any direction; not burdened by obligations; not confined to the usual rules (*free verse*); not exact (*a free translation*); generous (*a free spender*); frank; with no cost or charge; exempt from taxes, duties, etc.; clear of obstruction (*a free road*); not fastened (*a rope's free end*).—*adv* without cost; in a free manner.—*vt* to release from bondage or arbitrary power; to clear of obstruction, etc.—*pr p* **free´ing**; *pt p* **freed**.—*adv* **free´ly**.—*ns* **free agent**, a professional athlete (as a footballer) who is free to negotiate a contract with any team; **free´board**, the distance between the waterline and the freeboard deck of a ship or between the water and the upper edge of the side of a small boat; the height above the recorded high-water mark of a structure (as of a dam); the space between the ground and the undercarriage of an automobile; **freebie, freebee** [frē´bē], something (as a theater ticket) given or received without charge; **free´board deck**, the deck below which all bulkheads are watertight.—*adj* **free´born** not born in slavery.—*n* **freed´man**, a man freed from slavery; **free´dom**, being free, esp independence, civil or political liberty, exemption from obligation, being able to act, use, etc., freely, ease of movement; frankness; a right or privilege; **free ent´erprise**, the conduct of business without interference from the state; **freefall´**, unchecked fall, as of a parachutist before the parachute opens; **free flight´**, the flight of a rocket after the fuel supply has been used up or shut off; **free-for-all´**, a competition, dispute, or fight open to all comers and usu. without rules; a brawl.—*adj* **free´hand**, done without mechanical aids or devices (*a freehand drawing*).—Also *adv*.—*ns* **free hand´**, freedom of action or decision; **free kick´**, a kick (as in football or soccer) with which an opponent may not interfere; **free´lance**, a soldier available for hire; one who acts independently without regard to party lines; one who pursues a profession without long-term commitment to any employer.—*vi* **freeload´**, to impose upon another's hospitality.—*ns* **free lunch´**, something given entirely free of charge or obligation; **free mark´et**, an economic market operating by free competition; **free´martin**, a sexually imperfect usu. sterile female calf twinborn with a male; **Free´mason**, a member of an international secret society based on brotherhood and mutual aid; **free´masonry**, natural or instinctive fellowship or sympathy; the institutions, principles, or practices of Freemasons; **free´ port**, a port where goods are received and shipped free of customs duty; **free rad´ical**, (*chem*) an esp reactive atom or group of atoms that has one or more unpaired electrons; **free´stone**, a peach etc in which the pit does not cling to the pulp; **freethink´er**, one who rejects authority in religion; a rationalist; **free trade´**, trade based on the unrestricted international exchange of goods with tariffs used only as a source of revenue; **free univers´ity**, an unaccredited autonomous free institution established within a university by students to present and discuss subjects not usu. dealt with in the academic curriculum; a loosely organized forum for studying subjects not normally offered at universities; **free´way**, an expressway with fully controlled access; a toll-free highway; **freewheel´**, a power-transmission system in a motor vehicle with a device that allows the propellor shaft to run freely when its speed is greater than that of the engine shaft; a clutch fitted in the rear hub of a bicycle that permits the rear wheel to run on free when the pedals are stopped; **free will´**, voluntary choice or decision; freedom of human beings to make choices that are not determined by prior causes or by divine intervention; **free world´**, the part of the world where democracy and capitalism or moderate socialism rather than totalitarian systems prevail.—**free from** (*or* **of**), without; **free on board**, without charge for delivery to the train, ship, etc.; **make free with**, to use freely. [OE *frēo*; Ger *frei*, ON frī.]

freebooter [frē´bōōt-ėr] *n* a pirate; a plunderer. [Du *vrijbuiter—vrij*, free, *buit*, booty.]

freesia [fre´zhȧ] *n* any of a genus (*Freesia*) of the iris family of sweet-scented African herbs with red, white, or yellow flowers. [F.H.T. *Freese*, Ger. physician.]

freeze [frēz] *vi* to be formed into, or become covered by ice; to become very cold; to be damaged or killed by cold; to become motionless; to be made speechless by strong emotion; to become formal and unfriendly.—*vt* to harden into ice; to convert from a liquid to a solid with cold; to make extremely cold; to act toward in a stiff and formal way; to act on usu. destructively by frost; to anesthetize by cold; to fix (prices, etc.) at a given level by authority; to make (funds, etc.) unavailable to the owners by authority.—*pr p* **freez´ing**; *pt* **froze**; *pt p* **frozen**.—*n* a state of weather marked by low temperature, esp below freezing point; an act or instance of freezing.—*ns* **freeze´-dry´ing**, process of drying (food) in a frozen state under high vacuum, esp for preservation; **freeze´-frame´**, a frame of a motion-picture or television film that is repeated to give the illusion of a static picture; **freezer**, something that freezes or keeps cool, esp a compartment, room, or device for freezing food or keeping it frozen; **freez´ing point**, the temperature at which a liquid solidifies (*the freezing point of water is 0° Celsius or 32° Fahrenheit*).—**freeze out**, to die out through freezing, as plants; (*inf*) to keep out by competition, a cold manner, etc.; **freeze over**, to become covered by ice. [OE *frēosan*, pa p *froren; vriezen*, Ger *frieren*, to freeze.]

freight [frāt] *n* the transportation of goods by water, land, or air; the cost for this; the goods transported.—*vt* to load with freight; to send by freight.—*ns* **freight´age; freight´er**, one that loads or charters and loads a ship; shipper; a ship or airplane used chiefly to carry freight; **freight ton**, 100 cubic feet; **freight train**, a railroad train for transporting goods. [Prob Old Du *vrecht*, a form of *vracht*. See **fraught**.]

French [french] *adj* of France, its people, culture, etc.—*n* the Romance language that developed from Vulgar Latin and became the official and literary language of France.—*ns* **French bull´dog**, any of a breed of small compact heavy-boned dogs having erect ears; **French Canad´ian**, one of the descendants of French settlers in Lower Canada; **French chalk´**, a soft white variety of steatite used esp for drawing lines on cloth and for removing grease in dry cleaning; **French cuff´**, a shirtsleeve cuff turned back and fastened with a link; **french curve´**, a template used for drawing curved lines; **French dress´ing**, a salad dressing made of vinegar, oil, and seasonings; a creamy, tomato-flavored commercial salad dressing; **french fries**, strips of potato fried in deep fat; **French horn**, orchestral brass instrument with a narrow conical tube wound twice in a circle, funnel-shaped mouthpiece, and a flaring bell.—*vt* **french´ify, French´ify**, to make French in qualities, traits, or typical practices; **French kiss´**, an open-mouth kiss usu. involving tongue contact; **French leav´e**, an informal, hasty, or secret departure; **French´man**, a native or inhabitant of France; **French provin´cial**, a style of furniture, architecture, or fabric characteristic of the French provinces in the 17th and 18th centuries; **French wind´ow**, a pair of casement windows that reaches the floor, opens in the middle, and is placed on an outside wall; **French´woman**, a woman who is a native or inhabitant of France.

frenetic [fren-e´tik] *adj* frantic, frenzied.

frenzy [fren´zi] *n* a violent excitement; paroxysm of madness.—*adj* **fren´zied**. [OFr *frenesie*—Gr *phrenītis*, inflammation of the brain—*phrēn*, the mind.]

frequent [frē´kwėnt] *adj* coming or occurring often.—*vi* [frė-kwent´] to visit often; to resort to.—*ns* **frē´quency**, repeated occurrence; commonness of occurrence; the number per second of vibrations, cycles, or other recurrences; **frē´quentā´tion**, the act of visiting often.—*adj* **frequent´ative** (*gram*), denoting the frequent repetition of an action.—*n* (*gram*) a verb expressing such repetition.—*n* **frequent´er**.—*adv* **frē´quently**.—*ns* **frē´quentness; frequency distribution**, an arrangement of statistical data that shows the frequency of occurrence of a variable; **frequency modulation**, the modulation of the frequency of the carrier wave in accordance with speech or signal data; a broadcasting system using such modulation. [L *frequēns, frequentis*; conn with *farcīre*, to stuff.]

fresco [fres´kō] *n* a painting executed on walls covered with damp freshly-laid plaster.—*vt* to paint in fresco. [It *fresco*, fresh.]

fresh [fresh] *adj* recently made, grown, etc. (*fresh coffee*); not salted, pickled, etc.; not spoiled; lively, not tired; not worn, soiled, faded, etc.; new, recent; inexperienced; cool and refreshing; (of wind) brisk; (of water) not salt.—Also *adv*—*n* an increased flow or rush (as of water); a stream of fresh water running into fresh water.—*vi* **freshen**, to make or become fresh.—*adv* **freshly**.—*ns* **fresh breeze**, a wind from 19 to 24 miles per hour (5 on the Beaufort scale); **freshet**, a rise or overflowing of a stream caused by heavy rains or melting snow; **freshman**, a person in the first year of high school, college, university, or Congress; **freshness**.—*adj* **freshwater**, of, relating to, or living in fresh water.—**freshen up**, to bathe, to put on fresh clothes; to refill (a glass holding a drink). [OE *fersc*; cf Du *versh*, Ger *frisch*.]

fret[1] [fret] *vti* to eat into; to wear away or roughen by rubbing; to ripple (water); to irritate or be irritated.—*pr p* **frett´ing**; *pt p* **frett´ed**;—*n* irriration.—*adj* **fret´ful**, peevish.—*adv* **fret´fully**.—*n* **fret´fulness**. [OE *fretan*, to gnaw—pfx *for-*, inten, and *etan*, to eat; Ger *fressen*.]

fret[2] [fret] *n* a running design of interlacing small bars.—*vt* to furnish with frets.—*n* **fret´saw**, a saw with a narrow blade and fine teeth held under tension in a frame.—*adj* **frett´ed**, ornamented with frets.—*n* **fret´work**, ornamental carving or fancywork consisting of a combination of frets. [OFr *frete*, trellis-work.]

fret[3] [fret] *n* a wooden or metal ridge on the fingerboard of a guitar, banjo etc. [Prob same as **fret** (2).]

Freudian [froid´i-ȧn] *adj* pertaining to Sigmund *Freud* (1856–1939) and his psychology of the unconscious.—**Freudian slip**, an error in speech motivated by and revealing some unconscious state of the mind.

friable [frī´ȧ-bl] *adj* easily crumbled.—*n* **friabil´ity**. [Fr,—L *friābilis—friāre, friātum*, to crumble.]

friar [frī´ȧr] *n* a member of a mendicant order.—*n* **frī´ary**, a monastery of friars; **friar's lantern**, the will o' the wisp. [OFr *frere*—L *frāter*, a brother.]

fribble [frib´l] *vi* to trifle.—*n* a trifler. [Onomatopoeic; prob influenced by **frivol**.]

fricassee [frik-a-sē´] *n* a dish made of fowl, rabbit, etc. cut into pieces and cooked in sauce.—*vt* to cook as a fricassee;—*pr p* **fricassee´ing**; *pt p* **fricasseed´**. [Fr *fricassée*.]

fricative *see* **friction**.

friction [frik´sh(ȯ)n] *n* a rubbing of one object against another; conflict, as because of differing opinions; the resistance to motion of things that touch.—*adj* **frict´ional**.—*n* **fric´ative**, a consonant produced by the breath being forced through a narrow opening (as *f, th*), an open consonant, a spirant.—Also *adj*. [L *fricāre, frictum*, to rub.]

Friday [frī´dā] *n* the sixth day of the week. [OE *Frīgedæg*, day of (the goddess) *Frigg*.]

fried [frīd] *pt, pt p* of **fry**.

friend [frend] *n* a person whom one knows well and is fond of; an ally, supporter, or sympathizer; **Friend**, a member of the Society of Friends, a Quaker.—*adj* **friend´less**, without friends—**friend´lessness**.—*adj* **friend´ly**, like a friend; having the disposition of a friend; favourable.—*ns* **friend´liness; friend´ship**, attachment from mutual esteem; friendly assistance.—**friend of the court**, amicus curiae; **Friends of the Earth**, an organization of conservationists and environmentalists. [OE *frēond*, orig a pr p; cf *frēon*, to love; Ger *freund*.]

frieze [frēz] *n* the part of the entablature between the architrave and cornice; a decorative band along the top of the wall of a room. [OFr *frize*; It *fregio*; perh L *Phrygium*, Phrygian.]

frigate [frig´ȧt] *n* a fast, three-masted sailing warship of the 18th and early 19th century; a warship smaller than a destroyer used for escort, antisubmarine, and patrol duties.—*n* **frig´ate bird**, any of several strong-winged seabirds (family Fregatidae) noted for their rapacious habits. [OFr *fregate*—It *fregata*; ety uncertain.]

fright [frīt] *n* sudden fear; alarm; something unsightly.—*vs* **fright, fright´en**, to make afraid; to alarm.—*adj* **fright´ful**, terrible, shocking; extreme.—*adv* **fright´fully**.—*n* **fright´fulness**. [OE *fyrhto*; cf Ger *furcht*, fear.]

frigid [frij´id] *adj* extremely cold; not warm or friendly; sexually unresponsive.—*n* **frigid´ity**.—*adv* **frig´idly**.—*n* **frig´idness**.—*adj* **frigorif´ic** [frig-], causing cold.—**Frigid Zone** either of two zones of the earth's surface within the polar circles. [L *frīgidus—frīgēre*, to be cold—*frīgus*, cold.]

frill [fril] *vt* to furnish with a frill or frills.—*n* any superfluous ornament; a ruffle.

fringe [frinj] *n* a border of loose threads; an outer edge; marginal or minor part.—*vt* to be or make a fringe for.—*adj* at the outer edge; additional; minor.—*vt* to adorn with fringe; to border.—**fringe benefit**, payment other than wages.—*adj* **fringe´less**. [OFr *frenge*—L *fimbriae*, threads, fibres, akin to *fibra*, a fibre.]

frippery [frip´ėr-i] *n* cheap, gaudy clothes. [OFr *freperie, frepe*, a rag.]

Frisbee [friz´bē] *n* trade name for a plastic saucer-shaped disk tossed back and forth in a game. ["Mother Frisbie's" cookie jar lids.]

Frisian [frizh´ȧn, friz´i-ȧn] *n* a member of a people inhabiting the Netherlands province of Friesland and the Frisian Islands along the coast of West Germany and Denmark; the Germanic language of this people.—Also *adj*.

frisk [frisk] *vi* to gambol; to leap playfully.—*vt* (*slang*) to search the pockets, etc., of (a person) for concealed weapons.—Also *n*.—*adj* **frisk´y**.—*adv* **frisk´ily**.—*n* **frisk´iness**. [OFr *frisque*.]

frisson [frē-s•] *n* shiver; shudder; thrill.

frit [frit] *n* the mixed materials for making glass, pottery, etc. [L *frīgēre, frīctum*, to roast.]

frith [frith] *see* **firth**.

fritter[1] [frit´ėr] *n* a piece of fruit or meat fried in batter. [OFr *friture*—L *frīgēre*, to fry.]

fritter[2] [frit´ėr] *vt* to squander piecemeal (*with* **away**); to break into fragments. [Obs n pl *fitters*, rags, fragments.]

frivolous [friv´ō-lůs] *adj* trifling; silly.—*vti* **friv´ol**, to trifle.—*n* **frivol´ity**, trifling habit or nature; levity; an act, or a thing, that is frivolous.—*adv* **friv´olously**.—*n* **friv´olousness**. [L *frīvolus*, perh—*fricāre*, to rub.]

frizz [friz] *vti* to form into, or to be or become, small short crisp curls.—*n* hair that is frizzed. [OFr *friser*, to curl; perh conn with *frieze*, cloth.]
frizzle[1] [friz´l] *vti* to frizz. [Related to **frizz**.]
frizzle[2] [friz´l] *vti* to sizzle, as in frying. [Perh onomatopoeic adaptation of **fry**.]
fro [frō] *adv* away; back; used in the phrase *to and fro*. [ON *frā*.]
frock [frok] *n* a robe worn by friars, monks, etc.; a dress.—*n* **frock´ coat**, a double-breasted full-skirted coat for men.—*adj* **frocked**, clothed in a frock. [OFr *froc*, a monk's frock—Low L *frocus*—L *floccus*, a flock of wool; or from Low L *hrocus*—OHG *hroch*, a coat.]
frog[1] [frog] *n* any of numerous tailless web-footed amphibians (as of the suborder Diplasiocoela); a fancy loop used to fasten clothing; the nut of a violin bow; a small holder for fixing flowers in a vase.—*ns* **frog´man**, one trained and equipped for underwater demolition, exploration, etc.; **frog spit**, cuckoo spit; an alga that forms slimy masses on quiet water.—**frog in the throat**, hoarseness. [OE *frogga*; also *frox*; cog with ON *froskr*; Ger *frosch*.]
frog[2] [frog] *n* a V-shaped band of horn on the underside of a horse's hoof. [Perh **frog**, (1).]
frog[3] [frog] *n* on a railway or a tramway, a structure in the rails allowing passage across, or to, another line. [Perh **frog** (1).]
frolic [frol´ik] *n* a lively party or game; merriment, fun.—*vi* to play wild pranks or merry tricks; to gambol;—*pr p* **frol´icking**; *pt p* **frol´icked**.—*adj* **frol´icsome**, gay; sportive.—*n* **frol´icsomeness**. [Du *vrolijk*, merry; cf Ger *fröhlich*, joyful, gay.]
from [from] *prep* beginning at, starting with (*from noon to midnight*); out of (*from her purse*); originating with (*a letter from me*); out of the possibility or use of (*kept from going*); as not being like (*to know good from evil*); because of (*to tremble from fear*). [OE *fram, from*; akin to ON *frā*.]
frond [frond] *n* (*bot*) a large leaf with many divisions, esp of a palm or fern.—*adj* **frond´ed**, having fronds. [L *frons, frondis*, a leaf.]
front [frunt] *n* outward behavior; (*inf*) an appearance of social standing, etc.; the part facing forward; the first part; a forward or leading position; the land bordering a lake, street, etc.; the advanced battle area in warfare; an area of activity (*the home front*); a person or group used to hide another's activity; (*meteorology*) the boundary between two air masses.—*adj* at, to, in, on, or of the front.—*vti* to face; to serve as a front (for).—*n* **frontage**, the front part of a building; the front boundary line of a lot or the length of this line; land bordering a street, etc.—*adj* **front´al**, of or belonging to the forehead or a front—*n* something worn on the forehead or face; a covering for the front of an altar; a facade.—*n* **front´let**, a band worn on the forehead.—*adjs* **front´-line**, of or having to do with a country that is close to or borders on a hostile nation or area of potential conflict; **front´-page**, of special interest or importance.—**front man**, a figurehead; the lead performer in a musical group; **front office**, the management, as of a company.—**in front of**, before. [OFr,—L *frōns, frontis*, the forehead.]
frontier [frunt´-ēr´] *n* the border between two countries; the part of a country which borders on unexplored region; any new field of learning, etc.—*adj* of or on the frontier.—*n* **front´iersman**. [OFr *frontier*—L *frōns, frontis*.]
frontispiece [frunt´i-spēs] a picture in front of a book before the textual matter. [Fr,—Low L *frontispicium*—*frōns, frontis*, forehead, *specĕre*, to see; not conn with **piece**.]
frost [frost] *n* the process of freezing; temperature at or below freezing point; frozen dew; coldness of manner.—*vt* to cover as if with frost, esp to put icing on (a cake); to give a frostlike opaque surface to (glass).—*ns* **Frostbelt**, snowbelt; **frost´bite**, injury to a part of the body by exposure to cold.—*adjs* **frost´-bitt´en; frost´ed**, quick-frozen (as vegetables); having undergone frosting (*frosted hair*).—*n* **frost´ing**, material or treatment to give appearance of frost.—*adj* **frost´y**, producing or containing frost; briskly cold; marked by coolness or extreme reserve in manner.—*adv* **frost´ily**.—*n* **frost´iness**. [OE *frost, forst*—*frēosan*; cf Ger *frost*.]
froth [froth] *n* foam; foaming saliva; frivolity; chatter.—*vi* to foam.—*adj* **froth´y**.—*adv* **froth´ily**.—*n* **froth´iness**. [ON *frotha*, Dan *fraade*.]
froward [frō´wȧrd] *adj* perverse.—*adv* **frō´wardly**.—*n* **frō´wardness**. [**fro** + suffx *-ward*.]
frown [frown] *vi* to wrinkle the brow as in anger or concentration; to regard with displeasure or disapproval (*with* **upon**).—*vt* to force by a frown.—*n* a wrinkling or contraction of the brow in displeasure, etc.; a stern look.—*adj* **frown´ing**, gloomy. [From OFr *froignier* (mod *refrogner*), to knit the brow; origin unknown.]
frowzy [frow´zi] *adj* dirty and untidy; unkempt. [Origin unknown.]
frozen [frōz´n] *ptp* of **freeze**.
fructify [fruk´ti-fī] *vti* to bear or cause to bear fruit.—*ns* **fructificā´tion**, the forming or producing of fruit; (*bot*) a structure that contains spores; **fruc´tōse**, a sugar, found in sweet fruit and honey. [L *frūctus*, fruit.]
frugal [frōō´gȧl] *adj* economical in the use of resources; inexpensive, meager.—*n* **frugality**.—*adv* **fru´gally**. [L *frūgālis*—*frux, frūgis*, fruit.]
frugiv´orous [frōō-jiv´ȯr-us] *adj* feeding on fruit.—*n* **frug´ivore**, an animal esp a primate that feeds on fruit. [L *frux, frūgis*—*ferre*, to bear, *vorāre*, to eat.]
fruit [frōōt] *n* a product of plant growth (as grain, vegetables, cotton, etc.); an edible plant structure containing the seeds inside a juicy pulp; (*bot*) the seed-bearing part of any plant; the result or product of any action.—*vt* to cause to bear fruit.—*vi* to bear fruit.—*ns* **fruit´age**, condition or process of bearing fruit; fruit; product or result of an action; **fruit´cake** a rich cake containing nuts, preserved fruit, and spices; **fruit fly**, any of various small two-winged insects (as drosophila) whose larvae feed on fruit; **fruiting body**, a plant organ specialized for producing spores.—*adj* **fruit´ful**, producing fruit abundantly; productive.—*adv* **fruit´fully**.—*n* **fruit´fulness**.—*adj* **fruit´less**, barren; without profit; useless.—*adv* **fruit´lessly**.—*n* **fruit´lessness**.—*adj* **frui´ty**, like or tasting like, fruit; (*slang*) crazy.—*n* **fruitiness**. [OFr *fruit, fruict*—L *frūctus*—*fruī, frūctus*, to enjoy.]
fruition [frōō-ish´(ȯ)n] *n* the bearing of fruit; a coming to fulfillment, realization. [OFr *fruition*—L *fruī*, to enjoy.]
frumenty [frōō´men-ti] *n* food made of hulled wheat boiled in milk. [OFr *frumentee*—*frument*—L *frumentum*.]
frump [frump] *n* a plain and dowdy woman.
frustrate [frus-trāt´] *vt* to cause to have no effect; to prevent from achieving a goal or gratifying a desire.—*adj* **frustrate´; frustrat´ed**, having sense of discouragement and dissatisfaction.—*n* **frustrā´tion**, act of frustrating; state or instance of being frustrated; a deep chronic sense of dissatisfaction; something that frustrates. [L *frustrāre*—*frustrā*, in vain.]
frustum [frus´tum] *n* a slice of a solid body; the part of a cone or pyramid between the base and a plane parallel to it, or between two planes. [L *frustum*, a bit.]
fry[1] [frī] *vti* to cook over direct heat usu. in hot fat.—*n* a social gathering at which food is fried and eaten.—*n pl* **fries**, fried potatoes.—*n* **fryer**, a utensil for deep frying; a chicken for frying.—**out of the frying pan into the fire**, clear of one difficulty only to fall into a greater one.—*pr p* **fry´ing**; *pt p* **fried**. [Fr *frire*—L *frīgĕre*; cf Gr *phrygein*.]
fry[2] [frī] *n* recently hatched fishes; the young of other animals; very small adult fishes.—**small fry**, children; persons of little importance. [ON *friō*, Dan and Swed *frö*.]
fuchsia [fū´shi-a] *n* any of a genus (*Fuchsia*) of decorative shrubs with long pendulous flowers; a vivid reddish purple. [Leonard *Fuchs*, a German botanist, 1501–66.]
fuddle [fud´l] *vt* to make drunk; to make confused.—*vi* to take part in a drinking bout.—*n* a fuddled state. [Cf Du *vod*, soft, Ger dial *fuddeln*, to swindle.]
fuddy-duddy [fud´i-dud´i] *n* an old fogy, stick-in-the-mud.—*adj* stuffy; prim; censorious.
fudge [fuj] *n* a soft candy made of butter, milk, sugar, flavoring, etc.—*vi* to refuse to commit oneself; to cheat.—*vt* to fake; to fail to come to grips with.—*interj* nonsense!
fuel [fū´ėl] *n* anything burned to supply heat and power; material from which atomic energy may be obtained; anything that intensifies strong feeling.—*vti* to supply with or get fuel. [OFr *fowaille*—Low L *focāle*—L *focus*, a fire-place.]
fug [fug] *n* a hot, stuffy atmosphere.
fugacious [fū-gā´shůs] *adj* fugitive; fleeting.—*ns* **fugā´ciousness, fugac´ity** [-gas´i-ti]. [L *fugax, fugācis*, from *fugĕre*, to flee.]
fugitive [fūj´i-tiv] *adj* fleeing, as from danger or justice; apt to flee away; fleeting.—*n* one who flees or has fled; a refugee. [L *fugitīvus*—*fugĕre*, to flee.]
fugue [fūg] *n* polyphonic musical composition with theme taken up successively by different voices; (*psych*) flight from one's own identity, esp involving travel. [Fr,—It *fuga*—L *fuga*, flight.]
fulcrum [ful´krum] *n* (*mech*) the fixed point on which a lever moves.—*pl* **ful´crums, ful´cra**. [L *fulcrum*, a prop—*fulcīre*, to prop.]
fulfill, fulfil [fōōl-fil´] *vt* to carry out (a promise, etc.); to do (a duty, etc.); to satisfy (a condition); to bring to an end, complete.—*pr p* **fulfill´ing**; *pt p* **fulfilled´**.—*n* **fulfill´ment, fulfilment**. [OE *fullfyllan*—*full*, full, *fyllan*, to fill.]
fulgent [ful´jėnt] *adj* shining; bright.—*n* **ful´gency**.—*adv* **ful´gently**. [L *fulgēns, -entis*, pr p of *fulgēre*, to shine.]
fulgurant [ful´gū-rant] *adj* flashing like lightning. [L *fulgur*, lightning.]
fuliginous [fū-lij´i-nůs] *adj* sooty; dusky. [L, *fūlīgō, -inis*, soot.]
full[1] [fōōl] *adj* having all that can be contained; having eaten all one wants; having a great number (of); complete (*a full dozen*); having reached to greatest size, extent, etc.; plump, round; with wide folds (*a full skirt*).—*n* the greatest amount, extent, etc.—*adv* completely, directly, exactly.—*adv* **full´y**, thoroughly; at least.—*n* **full back**, (*football*) a member of the offensive backfield; a defensive player stationed nearest the defended goal (as in soccer, field hockey).—*adjs* **full´-blooded**, of unmixed ancestry; vigorous; **full´-blown**, in full bloom; matured.—*n* **full´ dress´**, the style of dress worn at ceremonial and formal social occasions.—*adjs* **full-fash´ioned**, (of knitted garments) made so as to fit the curves of the body exactly; **full´-length**, showing the whole length of the human figure.—*ns* full moon, the moon with its whole disk illuminated; **full´-ness, ful´ness**, the state of being full.—*adjs* **full´-out**, at full power; total; **full´-scale**, of the same size as the original; involving full power or maximum effort; **full-time**, of or engaged in work, study, etc. that takes the standard amount of time for working; **full stop**, a point marking the end of a sentence. [OE *full*; ON *fullr*, Ger *voll*.]

full[2] [fŏŏl] *vt* to shrink and thicken (wool cloth).—*ns* **full´er**, one that fulls cloth; **fuller's earth**, a soft earth or clay, capable of absorbing grease, used in fulling cloth, refining oils, etc. [OFr *fuler*—Low L *fullāre*—L *fullō*, a cloth-fuller.]

fulmar [fŏŏl´mär, -mȧr] *n* an arctic seabird (*Fulmarus glacialus*) closely related to the petrels; any of several related birds of the southern seas. [Perh ON *fūll*, foul, *mār*, gull.]

fulminate [ful´min-āt] *vi* to thunder or make a loud noise; to issue decrees with violence or threats; to inveigh (against).—*vt* to cause to explode; to send forth, as a denunciation.—*n* a salt of fulminic acid (often dangerously detonating).—*n* **fulminā´tion**, an act of fulminating or detonating; a denunciation.—*adj* **fulmin´ic**, pertaining to an acid used in preparing explosive compounds. [L *fulmināre, -ātum*—*fulmen*, lightning—*fulgēre*, to shine.]

fulsome [fŏŏl´sum, ful´sum] *adj* gross; offensive to smell or other sense; disgustingly fawning; very flattering or complimentary; profuse in praise, full, rounded, complete.—*adv* **ful´somely**.—*n* **ful´someness**. [**full** (1) + suffx *-some*.]

fulvous [ful´vus] *adj* deep or dull yellow, tawny. [L *fulvus*, tawny.]

fumble [fum´bl] *vi* to grope about awkwardly; to use the hands awkwardly.—*vt* to handle or manage awkwardly.—*n* **fum´bler**. [Du *fommelen*, to fumble.]

fume [fūm] *n* smoke or vapor, esp if offensive or suffocating.—*vi* to give off fumes; to show anger.—*adj* **fum´y**.—**fumed oak**, darkened oak. [OFr *fum*—L *fūmus*, smoke.]

fumigate [fūm´i-gāt] *vt* to expose to fumes, esp to destroy pests.—*ns* **fūmigā´tion; fūm´igātor**, a fumigating apparatus. [L *fūmigāre, -ātum*.]

fun [fun] *n* what provides amusement and enjoyment.—**fun and games**, light amusement; diversion; **make fun of**, to ridicule. [Prob a form of obs *fon*, to befool; cf Ir *fonn*, delight.]

funambulate [fū-nam´bū-lāt] *vi* to walk on a rope.—*ns* **funambulā´tion; funam´bulist**, a rope-walker. [L *fūnis*, a rope, *ambulāre*, to walk.]

function [fungk´sh(ȯ)n] *n* activity proper to anything; duty peculiar to any office; a ceremony or formal entertainment; a thing so connected with another that any change in the one produces a corresponding change in the other.—*vi* to perform a function; to act, operate.—*adj* **func´tional**, pertaining to, or performed by, functions; designed with special, or exclusive, regard to the purpose which it is to serve (as a building).—*n* **func´tionalism**, the theory or practice of adapting method, form, materials, etc., primarily with regard to the purpose in hand.—*adv* **func´tionally**.—*ns* **func´tionary**, one who discharges a duty or holds an office; **functional shift**, (*gram*) changes in the function of a word from noun to verb or adjective, noun use of adjectives, etc. [OFr,—L *functiō, -ōnis*—*fungī, functus*, to perform.]

fund [fund] *n* a supply that can be drawn upon; a sum of money set aside for a purpose; (*pl*) ready money.—*vt* to provide funds for; to put or convert into a long-term debt that bears interest.—**fund-raiser**, a person employed to raise funds; a social event (as a party) held for the purpose of raising funds. [Fr *fond*—L *fundus*, the bottom.]

fundamental [fun-dȧ-ment´ȧl] *adj* basic; essential, primary.—*n* that which serves as a groundwork; an essential.—*ns* **funda´ment**, an underlying theory or principle; buttocks, anus; land surface unaltered by human activity; **fundament´alism**, belief in the literal truth of the Bible; **fundament´alist**, one who holds this belief.—*adv* **fundament´ally**.—**fundamental particle**, elementary particle. [Fr,—L *fundāmentum*—*fundāre*, to found.]

funeral [fū´nėr-ȧl] *n* the ceremony connected with burial or cremation.—*adj* pertaining to or used at a funeral.—*adj* **fūnēr´eal** [-ė-ȧl], pertaining to or suiting a funeral; dismal, mournful.—**funeral director**, the manager of an establishment (**funeral home** or **funeral parlor**) where funeral services can be held. [OFr,—Low L *fūnerālis*—L *fūnus, fūněris*, a funeral procession.]

fungus [fung´gus] *n* any of a major group (Fungi) of lower plants, as molds, mildews, mushrooms, yeasts, etc. that lack chlorophyll, and reproduce by spores.—*pl* **fungi** [fun´jī], or **funguses** [fung´gus-ez].—*n* **fungicide** [fun´jisīd], any substance that kills fungi.—*adjs* **fung´al, fungici´dal**, pertaining to a fungicide; **fung´oid**, fungus-like; **fung´ous**. [L *fungus*, a mushroom—Gr *sphongos, spongos*, a sponge.]

funicular [fun-ik´yulȧr] *n* a cable railway ascending a mountain. [L *fūniculus*, dim of *fūnis*, a rope.]

funk [fungk] *n* panic; one who funks.—*vti* to shrink through fear; to shirk.—*n* **funk hole**, a dug-out; any place to which one flees for safety. [Ety uncertain.]

funky [fung´kē] *adj* having an offensive odor; having an earthy style derived from the early blues; odd or quaint in appearance. [*funk*, offensive odor.]

funnel [fun´l] *n* a passage for the escape of smoke, etc.; a vessel, usually a cone ending in a tube, for pouring fluids into bottles, etc.—*adj* **funn´elled**, provided with a funnel. [Prob through Fr from L *infundibulum*—*funděre*, to pour.]

funny [fun´i] *adj* causing laughter; perplexing, odd.—*adv* **funn´ily**.—**funny bone**, name for a place on the ulnar nerve because of the tingling sensation produced by a blow on the elbow; **funny paper**, the comic strip section of a newspaper. [**fun**.]

fur [fûr] *n* the thick, soft, fine hair of certain animals; their skins with the hair attached; a garment of fur; a fur-like coating on the tongue; the thick pile of a fabric (as chenille).—*vt* to line with fur; to coat.—*vi* to become coated;—*pr p* **furr´ing**; *pt p* **furred**.—*ns* **furr´ier**, a dealer in furs; a dresser of furs; **furr´iery**, the fur business; fur craftmanship.—*adj* **furr´y**, consisting of, like, covered with, or dressed in, fur. [OFr *forre, fuerre*, sheath.]

furbelow [fûr´bė-lō] *n* a plaited border or flounce; a superfluous ornament. [Fr, It, and Sp *falbala*; of unknown origin.]

furbish [fûr´bish] *vt* to polish, to burnish, to renovate. [OFr *fourbir, fourbissant*, from OHG *furban*, to purify.]

furcation [fûr-kā´shȯn] *n* something that is branched, a fork; the act or process of branching. [L *furca*, fork.]

furious [fū´ri-ȯs] *adj* full of fury; violent.—*adv* **fū´riously**.—*n* **fū´riousness**. [OFr *furieus*—L *furiōsius*—*furia*, rage.]

furl [fûrl] *vt* to roll up (a sail, flag, etc.) tightly and make secure. [Perh conn with **fardel**.]

furlong [fûr´long] *n* 220 yards, one-eighth of a mile. [OE *furlang*—*furh*, furrow, *lang*, long.]

furlough [fûr´lō] *n* leave of absence, esp for military personnel.—*vt* to grant furlough to. [Du *verlof*.]

furnace [fûr´nis] *n* an enclosed structure in which heat is produced, as by burning fuel. [OFr *fornais*—L *fornāx, -ācis*—*fornus*, an oven.]

furnish [fûr´nish] *vt* to fit up or supply completely, or with what is necessary; to supply (a person with); to provide (eg food, reasons).—*n* **fur´nisher**.—*n pl* **fur´nishings**, fittings of any kind, esp articles of furniture, etc., within a house; things to wear (*men's furnishings*). [OFr *furnir, furnissant*—OHG *frummen*, to accomplish.]

furniture [fûr´ni-tyůr, -chůr] *n* the things in a room, etc. which equip it for living, as chairs, beds, etc.; necessary equipment. [Fr *fourniture*.]

furor [fū´rör] *n* fury, frenzy; widespread enthusiasm, a craze. [L]

furrow [fur´ō] *n* the trench made by a plow; a groove; a wrinkle.—*vti* to form furrows in; to wrinkle. [OE *furh*; cf Ger *furche*, L *porca*, a ridge.]

further[1] [fûr´THėr] *adv* at or to a greater distance or degree; in addition.—*adj* more distant; additional.—*adv* **fur´thermore**, in addition to what has been said, moreover, besides.—*adj* **fur´thermost**, most remote.—*adv* **fur´thest**, at or to the greatest distance.—*adj* most distant. [OE *furthor* (adv) *furthra* (adj)—*fore* or *forth* with comp suffx.]

further[2] [fûr´THėr] *vt* to help forward, promote.—*n* **fur´therance**, a helping forward. [OE *fythran*.]

furtive [fûr´tiv] *adj* stealthy; secret.—*adv* **fur´tively**.—*n* **fur´tiveness**. [Fr *furtif, -ive*—L *furtīvus*—*fūr*, a thief.]

fury [fū´ri] *n* rage; violent passion; madness; **Fury**, one of the three goddesses of vengeance; hence, a passionate, violent woman. [Fr *furie*—L *furia*—*furěre*, to be angry.]

furze [fûrz] *n* gorse.—*adj* **furz´y**, overgrown with furze. [OE *fyrs*.]

fuscous [fus´kůs] *adj* of any color averaging brownish gray. [L *fuscus*, akin to *furvus*.]

fuse [fūz] *vti* to melt or be melted; to join as if by melting together.—*n* a tube or wick filled with combustible material for setting off an explosive charge; a bit of fusible metal inserted as a safeguard in an electric circuit.—*adj* **fū´sible**, that may be fused or melted.—*ns* **fūsibil´ity; fū´sion**, act of melting; the state of fluidity from heat; a close union of things; a political partnership. [L *funděre, fūsum*, to melt.]

fusee [fū-zē´] *n* the spindle in a watch or clock on which the chain is wound; a match with long, oval head for outdoor use; a red signal flare used esp for protecting stalled trains and trucks. [OFr *fusée*, a spindleful—L *fūsus*, a spindle.]

fuselage [fūz´ėl-ij or -äzh] *n* the body of an airplane. [Fr,—L *fūsus*, a spindle.]

fusel oil [fū´zl-oil] *n* any oily liquid occurring in insufficiently distilled liquors used esp as a source of alcohol and as a solvent. [Ger *fusel*, bad spirits.]

fusil [fū´zil] *n* a flint-lock musket.—*ns* **fusilier´, fusileer´**, formerly a British soldier armed with a fusil; **fusillade** [-ād´], simultaneous or continuous discharge of firearms.—*vt* to shoot down by a simultaneous discharge of firearms. [OFr *fuisil*, a flint-musket, same as It *focile*—Low L *focile*, steel (to strike fire with), dim of L *focus*, a fireplace.]

fuss [fus] *n* excited activity, bustle; a nervous state; (*inf*) a quarrel; (*inf*) a showy display of approval.—*vi* to worry over trifles; to whine, as a baby.—*adj* **fuss´y**, worrying over details, hard to please, whining; full of needless, showy details.—*n* **fuss´iness**.—*adv* **fuss´ily**.—*ns* **fuss´budget, fuss´pot**, (*inf*) a fussy person.

fustian [fust´yȧn] *n* kinds of twilled cotton fabric having a pile face; a pompous and unnatural style of writing or speaking, bombast.—*adj* made of fustian; bombastic. [OFr *fustaigne*—It—Low L—prob from *El-Fustat* (Old Cairo) where it may have been made.]

fustic [fus´tik] *n* the wood of a tropical American tree, yielding a yellow dye (*old fustic*). [Fr *fustoc*, yellow—L *fustis*.]

fustigate [fus´ti-gāt] *vt* to cudgel; to criticize severely.—*n* **fustigā´tion**. [L *fustīgāre, -ātum*—*fustis*, a stick.]

futile [fū´tīl, fū´til] *adj* useless; frivolous.—*adv* **fū´tilely**.—*n* **fūtil´ity**, uselessness. [Fr,—L *fūtilis*—*funděre*, to pour.]

futon [fōō´ton] *n* a thick cotton mattress. [Japanese.]

future [fūt´yůr, -chůr] *adj* about to be; that is to come; (*gram*) expressive of time to come.—*n* time to come.—*ns* **fūt´ūrism**, a movement in art, music, and literature begun in Italy about 1909 marked by an effort to give formal expression to the energy of mechanical processes; a point of view that finds meaning or fulfillment in the future; **fūt´ūrist**; a believer or practitioner of futurology; **futur´ity**, time to come; the state of being yet to come; an event yet to come; **fut´urology**, study dealing with future possibilities based on current trends. [Fr,—L *futūrus*, used as fut p of *esse*, to be.]

fuzz [fuz] *n* fine light particles of fiber (as of down or fluff); a blurred effect; fluff; (*slang*) police.—*vi* to fly off in minute particles; to become blurred.—*vt* to make fuzzy; to blur.—*adj* **fuzz´y**, fluffy; blurred.—**fuzzbuster**, (*slang*) an electronic device for detecting radar; **fuzzbuzz**, (*slang*) fuss or inconvenience, commotion; **fuzzy set**, (*math*) a set whose elements converge or overlap with other sets.

G

G-man [jē´man] (G for government) a special agent of the US Federal Bureau of Investigation; **G-string** [jē´string] (origin obscure), a string or strip worn round the waist and between the legs; **G suit** [jē-sūt] (gravity suit), a suit designed to counteract the physiological effects of acceleration on an aviator or astronaut.

gab [gab] *n* idle talk.—*vi* to talk in a rapid or thoughtless manner, chatter. [Prob short for **gabble**.]

gabble [gab´l] *vti* to talk or utter rapidly or incoherently; to utter inarticulate or animal sounds.—*n* such talk or sounds. [Prob imit.]

gabardine [gab´er-dēn] *n* a firm cloth with a fine diagonal weave on the right side of wool, rayon, or cotton. [Variant of **gaberdine**.]

gaberdine [gab´er-dēn] *n* a loose coat worn by Jews in medieval times; a garment, esp a raincoat, of gabardine. [OFr *gaverdine*.]

gable [gā´bl] *n* the triangular wall enclosed by the sloping ends of a ridged roof. [Prob through OFr *gable*, from ON *gafl*.]

gad [gad] *vi* to rove restlessly or idly (*often with* **about**);—*pr p* **gadd´ing**; *pt p* **gadd´ed**.—*n* **gad´about**, one who rushes from place to place. [Prob conn with *gad* in **gadfly**; or obsolete *gadling*, vagabond.]

gadfly [gad´flī] *n* any of various flies (as a horsefly, botfly, or warble fly) that bite or annoy livestock; a mischievous gadabout. [ME *gad* (ON *gaddr*), a spike, or OE *gād* (*See* **goad**) + **fly**.]

gadget [gaj´ėt] *n* any small ingenious device. [Ety uncertain.]

gadolinium [gad-ō-lin´i-ům] *n* a metallic element (symbol Gd; at wt 157.3; at no 64), a member of the rare-earth group. [Named from *Gadolin*, a Finnish chemist.]

Gael [gāl] *n* one whose language is Gadhelic, esp a Scottish Highlander.—*adj* **Gaelic** [gāl´ik, also gal´ik], pertaining to the Gaels.—*n* the language of Ireland and (now *esp*) that of the Scottish Highlands. [Gael *Gaidheal*.]

gaff [gaf] *n* a spear or spearhead for taking fish or turtles; a butcher's hook; the spar to which the head of a fore-and-aft sail is bent; a hoax; rough treatment; gaffe.—**stand the gaff**, bear up under punishment, ridicule, etc. [Fr *gaffe*.]

gaffe [gaf] *n* a social blunder. [Fr.]

gag [gag] *vt* to cause to retch; to keep from speaking, as by stopping the mouth of.—*vi* to retch.—*n* something put over or into the mouth to prevent talking; any restraint of free speech; a joke.—*ns* **gag´man**, a gag writer; a comedian who uses gags; **gag order**, a court order prohibiting members of the news media from reporting on an issue that is before a court of law; **gag´ster**, a gagman; one who plays practical jokes. [ME *gaggen*, to strangle.]

gaga [gag´a] *adj* fatuous; doddering; marked by wild enthusiasm. [Fr.]

gage [gāj] *n* a pledge; something thrown down as a challenge, as a glove.—*vt* to bind by pledge or security; offer as a guarantee; to stake, wager. [OFr *guage, gage*, from Gmc; vb from Fr *gager*. See **wage**.]

gage [gāj] *n* an instrument for or a means of testing and measuring. [OFr *gauge*.]

gaggle [gag´l] *n* a flock of geese when not in flight. [Prob imit.]

gaiety, gaily *see* **gay**.

gain [gān] *vt* to earn; to win; to attract; to get as an addition (esp profit or advantage); to make an increase in; to reach.—*vi* to make progress; to increase in weight.—*n* an increase esp in profit or advantage; an acquisition.—*n* **gainer**.—*adj* **gainful**, productive of gain; profitable.—*adv* **gainfully**.—*n* **gainfulness**.—**gain ground**, to make progress; **gain on**, to draw nearer to (an opponent in a race, etc.). [OFr *gain, gaain, gaigner, gaaignier*, from Gmc.]

gainsay [gān-sā´ gān´sā´] *vt* to contradict; to deny;—*pt* and *pt p* **gainsaid** [-sād´, -sed´].—*n* **gain´sayer** (*B.*), an opposer. [OE *gegn*, against, and **say**.]

gait [gāt] *n* way or manner of walking or running; any of the various foot movements of a horse (as a trot, pace, canter, etc.). [ON *gata*, a way.]

gaiter [gāt´ėr] *n* a covering for the lower leg fitting down upon the shoe. [Fr *guêtre, guietre*.]

gal[1] [gal] *n* a girl or woman. [Alteration of **girl**.]

gal[2] [gal] *n* a unit of acceleration equivalent to one centimeter per second per second, used especially for values of gravity. Abbrev g. [*Gal*ileo Galilei.]

gala [gā´la, gäla] *n* a celebration. [Fr *gala*, show—It *gala*, finery.]

galabia [gal-a´bē-a] *n* a long loose cotton gown worn in Arab countries.—*Also* **gala´bieh, gala´biya**. [Ar.]

galantine [gal´ȧn-tēn, -tin] *n* a cold dish of poultry, veal, etc., covered in aspic. [Fr,—Low L *galatina* for *gelatina*, jelly. See **gelatine**.]

galaxy [gal´ak-si] *n* (usu. **Galaxy**) the Milky Way, a luminous band of stars stretching across the heavens; any similar system of stars; any splendid assemblage.—*adj* **galactic**, of a galaxy or galaxies; huge. [Through Fr and L, from Gr *galaxias*—*gala, -aktos*, milk.]

gale [gāl] *n* a wind from 32 to 63 miles per hour (7 to 8 on the Beaufort scale). [Origin obscure.]

galena [ga-lē´na] *n* native lead sulphide; a lead-gray mineral with metallic luster. [L *galēna*, lead-ore.]

Galilean [gal-i-lē´ȧn] *adj* of or pertaining to *Galileo*, a great Italian mathematician (1564–1642).

gall[1] [göl] *n* bile; something bitter or distasteful; bitter feeling; brazen boldness marked by impudence and insolence.—*ns* **gall´ bladder**, a membranous sac attached to the liver in which bile is stored; **gall´-stone**, a small solid mass in the gall bladder or bile ducts. [OE *galla, gealla*, gall; cf Ger *galle*, Gr *cholē*, L *fel*.]

gall[2] [göl] *n* an abnormal growth on plant tissue produced by fungi, insect parasites, etc.—*n* **gall´nut**, a nutlike gall. [Fr *galle*—L *galla*, oak-apple (one type of oak-gall).]

gall[3] [göl] *n* a sore due to chafing.—*vt* to hurt by rubbing: to irritate. [OE *galla, gealla*, a sore place.]

gallant [gal´ȧnt] *adj* stately, imposing; brave; noble; polite and attentive to women.—*Also n* [gal-ȧnt´].—*adv* **gall´antly**.—*n* **gall´antry**, heroic courage; the behavior of a gallant; a courteous act or remark. [Fr *galant*—OFr *gale*, a merrymaking; prob Gmc; cf **gala**.]

galleon [gal´i-ȯn] *n* a large Spanish ship of the 15th and 16th centuries. [Sp *galeón*—Low L *galea*. Cf **galley**.]

gallery [gal´ėr-i] *n* a covered walk or porch open at one side; a long narrow outside balcony; an upper floor of seats, esp (in a theater) the highest and cheapest; the occupants of the gallery; a body of spectators; a room or building for the exhibition of works of art. [OFr *galerie* (It *galleria*).]

galley [gal´i] *n* a long, low-built ship of ancient times with one deck, propelled by oars; the kitchen of a ship or airplane; (*printing*) a shallow tray for holding composed type; proof printed from such type.—*n* **gall´ey proof**, a galley. [OFr *galie*—Low L *galea*.]

galliard [gal´yȧrd] *n* a spirited dance popular in the 16th century. [OFr *gaillard*.]

Gallic [gal´ik] *adj* of ancient Gaul or its people; French.—*n* **gall´icism** [-is-izm], the use in another language of a French expression or idiom or a French trait.—**Gallo-** [gal´o-], in composition, French:—as, **Gall´ophil, Gall´ophile**, one who is friendly to the French; **Gall´ophobe**, one who dislikes or fears the French or what is French; Francophil, -phile, -phobe.) [L *Gallus*, a Gaul; *Gallicus*, Gaulish.]

gallinaceous [gal-in-ā´shůs] *adj* of or relating to an order (*Galliformes*) of heavy-bodied largely terrestial birds including pheasants, turkey, grouse, and the common domestic fowl. [L *gallīna*, a hen—*gallus*, a cock.]

gallipot [gal´i-pot] *n* a small glazed pot, esp for medicine. [Prob a pot brought in a *galley*.]

gallium [gal´i-ům] *n* a metallic element (symbol Ga; at wt 69.7; at no 31), that is hard and brittle at low temperatures, melts at room temperature, and expands upon freezing. [Name formed from *Gallia*, Gaul, France.]

gallivant [gal-i-vant´] *vi* to go about in search of amusement. [Perh **gallant**.]

gallon [gal´ȯn] *n* a unit of liquid measure comprising four quarts or 231 cubic inches. [O Norm Fr *galun, galon* (OFr *jalon*).]

gallop [gal´ȯp] *vti* to go or cause to go at a gallop—*n* the fastest gait of a horse, etc.; a succession of leaping strides.—*pr p, adj* **gall´oping**. [OFr *galoper, galop*; prob Gmc.]

gallows [gal´ōz] *n* a wooden frame on which criminals are hanged.—*ns* **gall´ows bird**, one who deserves hanging; **gall´ows humor**, humor that makes fun of a very serious or terrifying situation. [ME *galwes* (pl)—OE *galga*; Ger *galgen*.]

galop [ga-lop´, gal´ȯp] *n* a lively dance; music for such a dance. [Fr; cf **gallop**.]

galore [ga-lōr´, -lör´] *adv* in abundance (*bargains galore*). [Ir *go*, a particle used in forming advs, *leór*, sufficient.]

galosh [gȧ-losh´] *n* a high overshoe worn esp in snow and slush. [Fr *galoche*—Gr *kālopodion*, dim of *kālopous*, a shoemaker's last—*kālon*, wood, *pous*, foot.]

galumph [ga-lumf´] *vi* to prance along boundingly and exultingly. [A coinage of Lewis Carroll (C L Dodgson; 1832–1898)—prob *gallop* and *triumph*.]

galvanism [gal´vȧn-izm] *n* electricity produced by chemical action.—*adj* **galvanic** [-van´-].—*vt* **gal´vanīze**, to apply an electric current to; to startle; to excite; to plate (metal) with zinc.—*ns* **galvanom´eter**, an instrument for measuring electric current. [From *Galvani*, of Bologna, the discoverer (1737–98).]

gambit [gam´bit] *n* (*chess*) an opening in which a sacrifice is offered for the sake of an advantage; an action intended to gain an advantage. [It *gambetto*, a tripping up—*gamba*, leg.]

gamble [gam´bl] *vi* to play games of chance for money; to take a risk for some advantage.—*vt* to risk in gambling, to bet.—*n* an undertaking involving risk.—*n* **gam´bler**. [For *gamm-le* or *gam-le*, a freq which has ousted ME *gamenen*—OE *gamenian*, to play at games—*gamen*, a game.]

gambol [gam´bl, -bol] *vi* to jump and skip about in play; to frisk.—*pr p* **gam´bolling**; *pt p* **gam´bolled**.—Also *n*. [Formerly *gambold*—OFr *gambade*—It *gambata*, a kick—Low L *gamba*, a leg.]

game[1] [gām] *n* any form of play, amusement; activity or sport involving competition under rules; a single contest in such a competition; the number of points required for winning; a scheme, a plan; wild birds or animals hunted for sport or food, the flesh of such animals; (*inf*) a business or job, esp one involving risk.—*adj* having a resolute spirit (*game to the end*); of or relating to game (*game laws*).—*vi* to play for a stake.—*ns* **game´cock**, a specially bred rooster trained for cockfighting; a male game fowl; **game´keeper**, a person who takes care of game birds and animals, as on an estate; **game park**, a large tract of land, esp in Africa, set aside as a game reserve; **game plan**, a strategy for achieving an objective; **game point**, the situation when the next point scored will win the game; the winning point; **gamesmanship**, the art or practice of winning games by questionable expedients without actually cheating; the use of dubious methods to gain an objective; **gamester**, a gambler; **game theory**, a mathematical method of selecting the best strategy for a game, war, competition, etc. so as to minimize one's maximum losses.—*adj* **gam´y, gam´ey**, having the strong flavor of cooked game; slightly tainted; plucky; risqué.—**the game is up**, failure is certain. [ME *gamen*, a game; ON *gaman*, Dan *gammen*.]

game[2] [gām] *adj* lame. [Most prob not the Celt *cam*, crooked.]

gamete [gam´ēt, gam-ēt´] *n* a reproductive cell that unites with another to form the cell that develops into a new individual. [Gr *gametēs*, husband, *gametē*, wife—*gameein*, to marry.]

gamin [gam´in] *n* a street Arab; **gamine** [-mēn], a girl of a pert, impish appearance and disposition.—Also *adj*. [Fr.]

gamma [gam´a] *n* third letter of the Greek alphabet.—**gamm´a glob´ulin**, fraction of blood serum which contains most antibodies; **gamma rays**, strong electromagnetic radiation from a radioactive substance. [Gr.]

gamut [gam´ut] *n* the whole compass of a voice or instrument; the full extent of anything. [From *gamma*, the Greek letter G, and *ut*, the syllable later superseded by *doh*.]

gander [gan´dėr] *n* an adult goose; a look. [OE *ganra, gandra*; Du and Low Ger *gander*.]

gang [gang] *n* a number of persons associating together.—*n* **gang´ster**, a member of a gang of criminals.—**gang up on**, to attack as a group. [OE *gang* (Dan *gang*, Ger *gang*), *gangan*, to go.]

gangling [gang´gling] *adj* loosely and awkwardly built; lanky.—Also **gangly** [gang´gli]. [Orig Scot and Eng dialect.]

ganglion [gang´gli-on] *n* a mass of nerve cells from which nerve impulses are transmitted.—*pl* **gang´lia**. [Gr.]

gangplank [gang´plank] *n* a movable ramp by which to board or leave a ship.

gangrene [gang´grēn] *n* death of soft body tissue when the blood supply is obstructed; a pervasive moral evil.—*vti* to make or become gangrenous.—*adj* **gang´rěnous**. [L *gangraena*—Gr *gangraina, grainein*, to gnaw.]

gangway [gang´wā] *n* a passageway, esp an opening in a ship's side for loading, etc.; a gangplank.—*interj* clear the way! [OE *gangweg*; cf **gang** + **way**.]

gannet [gan´et] *n* any of several large fish-eating seabirds (family Sulidae) that breed in large colonies chiefly on off-shore islands. [OE *ganot*, a sea-fowl; Du *gent*.]

ganoid [gan´oid] *adj* of or relating to a subclass (Ganoedi) of fishes having hard glistening scales, as the sturgeon.—Also *n*. [Gr *ganos*, brightness, *eidos*, appearance.]

gantlet [gant´let] *n* former punishment in which the offender ran between two rows of men who struck him; a series of troubles.—Also **gaunt´let**; a stretch of railroad track where two lines overlap with one rail within the rails of the other to avoid switching.

gantry [gan´tri] *n* a framework, often on wheels, for a traveling crane; a wheeled framework with a crane, platforms, etc. for readying a rocket to be launched; a stand for barrels; a working platform for a traveling crane, etc.; a structure to which are attached railroad signals for a number of tracks. [Perh OFr *gantier*—L *cantērius*, a beast of burden.]

gaol, gaoler British, esp English, spellings of **jail, jailer**.

gap [gap] *n* an opening or breach; a passage; a mountain pass; any breach of continuity.—*adj* **gappy**. [ON *gap*.]

gape [gāp] *vi* to open the mouth wide; to yawn; to stare with the mouth open.—*n* act of gaping; a wide opening.—(*pl*) a disease of young birds in which gapeworms invade and irritate the trachea; a fit of yawning.—*n* **gape´worm**, a nematode (*Syngamus trachea*) that causes gapes. [ON *gapa*, to open the mouth; Ger *gaffen*, to stare.]

gar [gar] *n* any of several predaceous N American freshwater ganoid fishes (family Lepisosteidae) with rank tough flesh; any of various fishes having an elongated body and a beaklike snout. [OE *gar*, a spear.]

garage [ga-räzh´] *n* an enclosed shelter for automotive vehicles; a business place where such vehicles are repaired, serviced, etc.—*vt* to put or keep in a garage.—*n* **garage sale**, a sale of unwanted household goods, held in a garage or other part of the house. [Fr *garer*, to secure—Gmc; related to **wary**.]

garb [gärb] *n* clothing, style of dress; external appearance.—*vt* to clothe. [It *garbo*, grace; of Gmc origin.]

garbage [gär´bij] *n* food waste; unwanted or useless material; trash; (*computer*) inaccurate or useless data. [Of doubtful origin.]

garble [gär´bl] *vt* to distort (a message, story, etc.) so as to mislead; to introduce textual error into (a message). [It *garbellare*—Ar *ghirbál*, a sieve.]

garçon [gär-s•] *n* a waiter in a restaurant. [Fr.]

garden [gär´dn] *n* a piece of ground for growing herbs, fruits, flowers, or vegetables; a fertile, well-cultivated region; a public parklike place, usu. ornamented with plants and trees.—*vi* to make, or work in, a garden.—*ns* **garden apartment**, a multiple-unit low-rise dwelling having considerable lawn or garden space; **garden city**, a planned residential community with park and planted areas.—*adj* **garden-variety**, of a cultivar; ordinary, commonplace. [OFr *gardin* (Fr *jardin*); from Gmc; allied to **yard**.]

gardenia [gär-dē´ni-a] *n* any of a genus (*Gardenia*) of tropical shrubs, with beautiful fragrant white or yellow flowers. [Named from the American botanist, Dr. Alex *Garden* (died 1791).]

garfish [gär´fish] *n* gar.

gargantuan [gär-gan´tū-ȧn] *adj* like, or worthy of, *Gargantua*, Rabelais's hero, a giant of vast appetite; enormous, prodigious.

gargle [gär´gl] *vti* to wash (the throat), preventing the liquid from going down by expelling air against it.—*n* a liquid for washing the throat. [OFr *gargouiller*—*gargouille*, the throat.]

gargoyle [gär´goil] *n* a projecting spout, usually grotesquely carved, from a roof gutter; a grotesquely carved figure; a person with an ugly face. [OFr *gargouille*—L *gurgulio*, throat.]

garish [gār´ish] *adj* showy, gaudy; glaring (eg of light).—*adv* **gar´ishly**.—*n* **gar´ishness**. [Earlier *gaurish, gawrish*—*gaure*, to stare.]

garland [gär´lȧnd] *n* a wreath of flowers or leaves; a book of selections in prose or poetry.—*vt* to deck with a garland. [OFr *garlande*.]

garlic [gär´lik] *n* a bulbous herb (*Allium sativum*) of the lily family widely cultivated for its compound bulbs used in cookery; its bulb.—*adjs* **garlicked, garlicky.—garlic salt**, a seasoning of ground dried garlic and salt. [OE *gārlēac*—*gār*, a spear, *lēac*, a leek.]

garment [gär´mėnt] *n* any article of clothing. [OFr *garniment*—*garnir*, to furnish.]

garner [gär´nėr] *n* a granary; a store of anything.—*vt* to store; to acquire by effort; to collect. [OFr *gernier* (Fr *grenier*)—L *grānārium* (usu. in pl), a granary.]

garnet [gär´net] *n* a hard glasslike mineral used as a semiprecious stone; a variable color averaging a dark red. [OFr *grenat*—Low L *grānātum*, pomegranate; or Low L *grānum*, grain, kermes, red dye.]

garnish [gär´nish] *vt* to decorate; to decorate (food) with something that adds color or flavor; to equip with accessories; to garnishee.—*n* a decoration, something used to garnish food.—*ns* **garnishee**, one who is served with a garnishment; **garnishment**, garnish; a legal summons or warning concerning the attachment of property to satisfy a debt; a stoppage of a specified sum from wages to satisfy a creditor; **garniture**, an embellishment; a decoration. [OFr *garnir, garnissant*, to furnish, from a Gmc root seen in OE *warnian*, to warn.]

garret [gar´et] *n* a room just under the roof of a house. [OFr *garite*, a place of safety, *guarir, warir*, to defend. (Fr *guérir*)—from the Gmc root seen in **wary**.]

garrison [gar´i-s(o)n] *n* troops stationed at a fort; a fortified place with troops.—*vt* to station (troops) in (a fortified place) for its defense.—**garrison cap**, a visorless folding cap worn as part of a military uniform; **garrison state**, a state organized primarily on a military basis. [OFr *garisongarir, guarir*, to defend, furnish; Gmc, see **garret**.]

garrotte, garotte [ga-rot´] *n* a method of execution by strangling with an iron collar; the iron collar used; strangulation with a cord, thong, etc., esp with robbery as the motive.—*vt* to execute or attack by such strangling.—*n* **garroter**. [Sp *garrote*, cf Fr *garrot*, a stick.]

garrulous [gar´ū-lus, -oo-lus] *adj* talkative.—*ns* **garrulity** [gar-(y)ōō´li-ti]; **garr´ulousness**, pointless or annoying talkativeness. [L *garrulus*—*garrire*, to chatter.]

garter [gär´tėr] *n* a band used to support a stocking; **Garter**, badge of the highest order of knighthood in Great Britain.—*vt* to fasten with a garter.—*n* **garter belt**, a woman's undergarment with suspended fastenings to hold up stockings; **garter snake**, a small, harmless snake (genus *Thamnopis*) with longitudinal stripes on the back. [OFr *gartier*—*garet* (Fr *jarret*), the ham of the leg, prob Celt.]

gas [gas] *n* airlike substance with the capacity to expand indefinitely and not liquify or solidify at ordinary temperatures; any mixture of flammable gases used for lighting or heating; any gas used as an anesthetic; any poisonous substance dispersed in the air, as in war; gasoline; (*inf*) the accelerator pedal in a motor vehicle; empty talk; (*slang*) something that is very appealing or enjoyable (*the party was a gas*).—*pl* **gases**.—*vt* to supply with gas esp gasoline; to treat chemically with gas; to poison or affect adversely with gas.—*vi* to give off gas; to talk idly; to fill the tank (as of an automobile) with gasoline.—*pr p* **gass´ing**; *pt p* **gassed**.—*vti* to convert into gas or to become gaseous.—*ns* **gasification, gasifier**.—*adj* **gaseous**, having the form of or being gas; of or being related to gases; lacking substance or solidity.—*n* **gaseousness**.—*ns* **gas´bag**, a bag for holding gas; an idle talker; **gas chamber**, a room in which prisoners are executed by poison gas; **gas chromatograph**, an instrument used to separate a sample into components in gas chromotography; **gas gangrene**, progressive gangrene marked by impregnation of the dead and dying tissue with gas and caused by certain toxins; **gasohol**, a fuel consisting of 10 percent ethyl alcohol and 90 percent gasoline; **gasoline, gasolene**, a volatile, flammable liquid distilled from petroleum and used chiefly as a fuel in internal-combustion engines; **gas plant**, fraxinella; **gas turbine**, an internal-combustion engine in which expanding gases from the combustion chamber drive the blades of a turbine; **gasworks**, a plant for manufacturing gas. [Based on Gr *chaos*, space; chaos.]

gash [gash] *vt* to cut deeply into.—*n* a deep, open cut. [Formerly *garse*—OFr *garser*, to scarify—Low L *garsa*, scarification, possibly—Gr *charassein*, to scratch.]

gasket [gas´kit] *n* a piece or ring of rubber, metal, etc. used to make a piston or joint leakproof; sealing material over a crack; material between opening surfaces to prevent air leaking (as on a refrigerator); a cord to secure a furled sail. [Fr *garcette*, a small cord.]

gasogene [gas´-e-jēn] a portable apparatus for carbonating liquids; an apparatus carried by a vehicle to produce gas for fuel by partial burning of charcoal or wood. [Fr *gazogène*.]

gasp [gäsp] *vi* to catch the breath with effort.—*vt* to utter with gasps.—*n* the act of gasping. [ON *geispa*, to yawn; cf *geip*, idle talk.]

gastric [gas´trik] *adj* of, in, or near the stomach—also **gas´tral**.—*ns* **gastrec´tomy**, surgical removal of the stomach, or part of it; **gastrī´tis**, inflammation of the stomach; **gas´troenterī´tis**, inflammation of the mucous membrane of the stomach and the intestines; **gas´troenterol´ogy**, the study of the diseases and pathology of the stomach and intestines. [Gr *gastēr*, the belly.]

gastronomy [gas-tron´o-mi] *n* the art or science of good eating.—*n* **gas´tronome**, an epicure. [Gr *gastēr*, belly, *nomos*, law.]

gastropod [gas´trōpod] *n* any of a large class (Gastropoda) of mollusks (as snails) with a univalve shell or none and usu. with a distinct head bearing sense organs. [Gr *gastēr*, belly, *podos*, a foot.]

gat [gat] *n* (*slang*) a handgun. [**Gatling gun**.]

gate [gāt] *n* a movable structure controlling passage through an opening in a fence or wall; a gateway; a movable barrier; a structure controlling the flow of water, as in a canal; a device (as in a computer) that outputs a signal when specified input conditions are met; the total amount or number of paid admissions to a performance.—*vt* to supply with a gate.—*ns* **gate´-crasher**, one who attends an affair without being invited or a performance without paying; **gate´fold**, an oversize page in a magazine or book, bound so that it can be folded out; **gateleg table**, a table with drop leaves supported by movable paired legs; **gateway**, an opening for a gate; means of entrance or exit.—**give** (**someone**) **the gate**, (*slang*) to get rid of. [OE *geat*, a way; Du *gat*, ON *gat*.]

gate [gāt] combining form added to nouns and meaning any scandal involving charges of corruption and usu. of coverup. [From *Watergate*.]

gather [gaTH´er] *vt* to bring together in one place or group; to get gradually; to collect (as taxes); to harvest; to draw close to something (*gathering her skirts*); to pucker fabric by pulling a thread or stitching; to infer.—*vi* to come together in a body; to cluster around a focus of attention; to swell and fill with pus.—*n* a puckering in cloth made by gathering; an act´or instance of gathering.—*ns* **gatherer; gathering**, an assembly; a meeting; an abscess; the collecting of food and raw materials from the wild; a collection; a gather in cloth. [OE *gaderian, gæderian*; same root as **together**.]

Gatling gun [gat´ling gun] *n* an early machine gun invented by R. J. *Gatling* about 1861.

gauche [gōsh] *adj* clumsy; tactless; not planar (*gauche conformation of molecules*).—*n* **gaucherie** [gōshė-rē´], a tactless or awkward act. [Fr,—*gauche*, left.]

gaucho [gow´chō] *n* a cowboy of the pampas of South America. [Sp.]

gaud [göd] *n* an ornament, a piece of finery.—*n* **gaud´y**, an English college or other festival.—*adj* **gaud´y**, showy; vulgarly bright.—*adv* **gaud´ily**.—*n* **gaud´iness**, showiness. [In part app—OFr *gaudir*—L *gaudēre*, to be glad, *gaudium*, joy; in part directly from L.]

gauge [gāj] *n* measurement according to some standard or system; any device for measuring; the distance between rails of a railway; the size of the bore of a shotgun; the thickness of sheet metal, wire, etc.—*vt* to measure the size, amount, etc. of; to judge. [OFr *gauge* (Fr *jauge*).]

Gaul [göl] *n* ancient division of the Roman Empire in what is now France; an inhabitant of Gaul. [Fr *Gaule*—L *Gallia, Gallus*; perh conn with OE *wealh*, foreign.]

gaunt [gönt] *adj* excessively thin as from hunger or age; looking grim or forbidding. [Per allied to Norw *gand*, pointed stick, and Swed dial *gank*, a lean horse.]

gauntlet[1] [gönt´let] *n* a knight's armored glove; a long glove, often with a flaring cuff.—**throw down the gauntlet**, to challenge, as to combat. [Fr *gantelet*, dim of *gant*, glove, of Gmc origin.]

gauntlet[2] [gönt´let] *see* **gantlet**.

gauze [göz] *n* any very thin, loosely woven fabric, as of cotton or silk; a firm woven material of metal or plastic filaments.—*adj* **gauz´y**. [Fr *gaze*; origin uncertain.]

gave [gāv] *pt* of **give**.

gavel [gav´l] *n* a mallet used as a chairman's hammer.

gavotte [ga-vot´] *n* a lively dance of French peasant origin marked by rising of the feet; the music for such a dance. [Fr.]

gawk [gök] *vi* to stare at stupidly.—*adj* **gawk´y**, awkward, ungainly.—Also *n*. [Ety obscure; most prob not related to Fr *gauche*, left.]

gay [gā] *adj* joyous and lively; brilliant (*gay colors*).—*n* **gai´ety**.—*adv* **gai´ly**. [OFr *gai*—perh OHG *wâhi*, pretty.]

gaze [gāz] *vi* to look steadily.—*n* a steady look. [Prob cog with obs *gaw*, to stare, ON *gā*, to heed.]

gazebo [gȧ-zē´bō] *n* a belvedere. [Ety dub.]

gazelle [ga-zel´] *n* any of numerous small swift antelopes (*Gazella* and related genera of Africa and Asia) noted for their large, lustrous eyes. [Fr,—Ar *ghazāl*, a wild-goat.]

gazette [ga-zet´] *n* a newspaper, now mainly in newspaper titles; (*Brit*) an official publication listing government appointments; legal notices, etc.—*n* **gazatteer´** [gaz-], a geographical dictionary. [Fr,—It *gazzetta*, a small coin; or from It *gazzetta*, dim of *gazza*, magpie.]

gazogene *see* **gasogene** in **gas**. [Fr *gaz-ogène*—*gaz*, gas. Gr suffx *-genēs*—root of *gignesthai*, to become.]

gazpacho [gäz-päch´o] *n* a spicy, thick vegetable soup usu. served cold. [Sp.]

gear [gēr] *n* clothing; equipment, esp for some task or activity; a toothed wheel designed to mesh with another; (*often pl*) a system of such gears meshed together to pass motion along; a specific adjustment of such a system (*high gear*); a part of a mechanism with a specific function.—*vt* to connect by or furnish with gears; to adapt (one thing) to conform with another (*to gear supply to demand*).—*ns* **gear´shift**, a device for connecting or disconnecting transmission gears; **gear´wheel**, a cogwheel.—**in gear**, connected to the motor; in proper working order; **out of gear**, not connected to the motor; not in proper working order. [ME *gere*.]

gecko [gek´ō] *n* any of a family (Gekkonidae) of small harmless insectivorous lizards. [Malay *gēkoq*.]

gee [jē] *interj* (*slang*) an exclamation of surprise. [Euphemism for *Jesus*.]

geese *pl* of **goose**.

gefilte fish [ge-fil´te] *n* chopped, seasoned fish, boiled and served in balls or cakes. [Yiddish.]

Geiger (-Müller) counter [gī´gėr (mül´ėr) kown´tėr] an instrument for detecting and counting ionizing particles, as from radioactive sources. [H. *Geiger* (1882–1945), Ger physicist.]

geisha [gā´sha] *n* a Japanese girl trained as an entertainer to serve as a hired companion to men. [Jap].

gel [jel] *n* a jelly-like substance.

gelatin, gelatine [jel´a-tin] *n* a tasteless, odorless substance extracted by boiling bones, hoofs, etc., or a similar vegetable substance; when dissolved and cooled forms a jellylike material used in foods, photographic film, etc.—*vt* **gelat´inize**, to make into gelatin.—*n* **gelat´inization**.—*adj* **gelat´inous**. [Fr,—It *gelatina, gelata*, jelly—L *gelāre*, to freeze.]

gelation[1] [jel-a´shůn] *n* the action or process of freezing. [L *gelare*, to freeze.]

gelation[2] [jel-a´shůn] *n* the formation of a gel from a solid. [**gel** + -tion.]

geld [geld] *vt* to castrate, esp a horse.—*n* **geld´ing**, a castrated horse. [ON *gelda*; Dan *gilde*.]

gelid [jel´id] *adj* icy cold;—*adv* **gel´idly**.—*n* **gelid´ity**. [L *gelidus*—*gelū*, frost.]

gelignite [jel´ig-nīt] *n* a powerful explosive consisting of dynamite in gelatin form. [Perh from **gelatine** and L *ignis*, fire.]

gem [jem] *n* any precious stone, esp when cut for use as a jewel; anything extremely precious or valuable.—*n* **gem´stone**, any mineral that can be used as a gem when cut and polished. [OE *gim*; OHG *gimma*—L *gemma*, a bud.]

geminate [jem´in-āt] *adj* (*bot*) in pairs.—*n* **geminā´tion**. [L *gemināre, -ātum*—*geminus*, twin.]

Gemini [jem´in-ē] *npl* the 3d sign of the zodiac in astrology operative May 21 to June 20; the 3d zodiacal constellation represented pictorially as the twins Castor and Pollux. [L *geminus*, twin.]

gemma [jemm´a] *n* an asexual reproductive structure that becomes detached from the parent and develops into a new individual; (*loosely*) a bud.—*pl* **gemm´ae** [-ī].—*n* **gemma´tion**, reproduction by gemmae. [L *gemma*, a bud.]

gendarme [zhā-därm´] *n* an armed policeman in France and other places.—*n* **gendar´merie** [-ė-rē], an armed police force. [Fr *gendarme*, sing from pl *gens d'armes*, men-atarms—*gens*, people, *de*, of, *armes*, arms.]

gender [jen´dėr] *n* (*gram*) the classification by which words are grouped as feminine, masculine, or neuter. [Fr *genre*—L *genus, generis*, a kind, kin.]

gender *see* **engender**.

gene [jēn] *n* any of the complex chemical units in the chromosomes by which hereditary characteristics are transmitted.—*ns* **gene´bank**, a place in which specific genetic materials are stored alive for study and research; **gene´therapy**, the elimination of genetic defects by genetic engineering; **gen´ome**, the whole set of chromosomes of an individual; all of the genes in such a set. [Gr *genos*, race.]

genealogy [jēn-i-al´o-ji, or jen-] *n* a recorded history of one's ancestry; the study of family descent; lineage.—*adj* **genealog´ical**.—*n* **geneal´ogist**, one who studies or traces genealogies or descents. [Gr *geneālogia—genea*, race, *logos*, discourse.]

genera *pl* of **genus**.

general [jen´er-ȧl] *adj* not local, special, or specialized; of or for a whole genus, relating to or covering all instances or individuals of a class or group; widespread, common to many; not specific or precise (*in general terms*); holding superior rank (*attorney general*).—*n* something that involves or is applicable to the whole; a commissioned officer ranking next below a general of the army or a general of the air force, a commissioned officer of the highest rank in the marine corps.—*ns* **general assembly**, a legislative assembly, esp a US state legislature; **General Assembly**, the supreme deliberative body of the United Nations; **general delivery**, delivery of mail at the post office to addressees who call for it; **generaliss´imo**, in some countries, the commander-in-chief of the armed forces; **general´ity**, the quality or state of being general; a vague or inadequate statement;—*vti* **gen´eralize**, to formulate or state in terms of a general law; to talk (about something) in general terms.—*adv* **gen´erally**, widely; popularly; usually; not specifically.—*ns* **general staff**, a group of officers who assist a high-level commander in planning, coordinating, and supervising operations; **general practitioner**, a physician or veterinarian who does not limit his practice to a speciality.—**in general**, for the most part. [OFr,—L *generālis—genus*, birth, kind.]

generate [jen´er-āt] *vt* to bring into existence; to produce, esp to originate (as electricity) by a vital or chemical process.—*n* **generation**, a body of living beings constituting a single step in a line of descent from an ancestor; the average period between generations; production as of electric current.—*adj* **gen´erative**, having the power to generate.—**gen´erator**, one that generates, esp a machine which changes mechanical energy to electrical energy. [L *generāre, -ātum—genus*, a kind.]

generic, -al, generically *see* **genus**.

generous [jen´ėr-us] *adj* magnanimous; of a noble nature; willing to give or share; large, ample.—*adv* **gen´erously**.—*ns* **gen´erousness, generos´ity**. [Fr *généreux*—L *generōsus*, of noble birth—*genus*, birth.]

genesis [jen´es-is] *n* the beginning, origin; **Genesis**, (*Bible*) 1st book of the Old Testament, an account of the creation of the world, the fall of man, and the promise of redemption. [Gr.]

genet [jen´et] *n* a genus (*Genetta*), mostly African, of carnivorous animals allied to the civet; their fur. [Fr *genette*—Sp *gineta*—Ar *jarnait*.]

genetic, -al [jen-et´ik, -ȧl] *adjs* of or relating to the origin, development or causes of something; of or relating to genetics.—*ns* **genetic code**, the biochemical basis of the heredity of an organism consisting of the order in which chemical constituents are arranged in DNA and RNA; **genetic marker**, a gene or genetic characteristic that can be identified and followed from generation to generation; **gene´tics**, the branch of biology dealing with heredity and variation in plants and animals.—*adv* **gene´tically**.—*n* **genet´icist**. [Gr *genos*, race.]

Genevan [je-nē´vȧn] *adj* pertaining to *Geneva*.—**Geneva Convention**, an international agreement of 1865 providing for the neutrality of hospitals in war, and for the security of those whose business it was to tend the wounded and of chaplains; **Geneva Cross**, Red Cross.

genial [jē´ni-ȧl] *adj* cheering; kindly, sympathetic; healthful.—*ns* **gēnial´ity, gē´nialness**.—*adv* **gē´nially**. [L *geniālis—genius*, a guardian spirit. See **genius**.]

geniculate, -d [je-nik´ū-lȧt, -id] *adjs* bent abruptly at an angle like a bent knee.—*n* **geniculā´tion**. [L *geniculātus—geniculum*, a little knee—*genū*, the knee.]

genital [jen´i-tȧl] *adj* of reproduction or the sexual organs.—*n* **genital´ia**, the external organs of the reproductive system.—*npl* **genitals**, genitalia. [L *genitālis—gignĕre, genitum*, to beget.]

genitive [jen´i-tiv] *adj* (*gram*) of or belonging to the case expressing origin, possession, or similar relation; having to do with its forms and constructions, eg the use of the preposition *of* in English to denote possession or origin.—*n* the genitive case. [L *genitīvus* (*gignĕre, genitum*, to beget), for Gr *genikos—genos*, a class.]

genius [jēn´yus] *n* the particular spirit of a nation, place, age, etc.; natural ability, strong inclination (*with* **for**); great mental capacity and inventive ability; one having extraordinary intellectual power.—*pl* **geniuses, genii**. [L *genius—gignĕre, genitum*, to beget.]

genocide [jen´ō-sīd] *n* the systematic killing of a whole people or nation.—*adj* **genocīd´al**. [Gr *genos*, race, L *caedĕre*, to kill.]

genre [zhän´rė] *n* a distinctive type of category, esp of literary composition; a style of painting in which everyday objects are treated realistically. [Fr,—L *genus*.]

gent [jent] *n* (*inf*) a gentleman, used as a humorous or vulgar term.

genteel [jen-tēl´] *adj* polite or well-bred; now esp affectedly refined.—*n* **genteel´ism**, a word believed by its user to be genteel (as *stomach* for *belly*).—*adv* **genteel´ly**.—*n* **genteel´ness**. [Due to a second borrowing of Fr *gentil*, later than that which gave **gentle**.]

gentian [jen´shȧn] *n* any of two genera (*Gentiana* and *Dasystephana*) of plants of alpine regions, usu. with blue flowers; the roots and rhizome of the yellow gentian (*G. lutea*) used in medicine.—**gentian violet**, a mixture of dyes used as a bactericide, fungicide, and anthelmintic. [L *gentiāna*, according to Pliny from *Gentius*, king of Illyria, who introduced it in medicine (2nd cent BC).]

gentile [jen´tīl] *n* anyone not a Jew; a heathen; (among Mormons) anyone not a Mormon.—Also *adj*. [L *gentīlis—gens*, a nation.]

gentle [jen´tl] *adj* belonging to a family of high social station; refined, courteous; generous; kind; tame (*a gentle dog*); kindly; patient; not harsh or rough; gradual (*a gentle slope*).—*ns* **gentle breeze**, wind having a speed of 8 to 12 miles an hour (3 on the Beaufort scale); **gentil´ity**, the gentry or their status; good manners; the quality of being genteel. [Fr *gentil*—L *gentīlis*, belonging to the same *gens* or clan, later, well-bred. *See* **genteel**.]

gentleman [jen´tl-mȧn] *n* a man of good family and social standing; a courteous, gracious, and honorable man; (*pl*) polite term of address.—*ns* **gentleman farm´er**, a man who farms for pleasure rather than profit; **gentleman's agree´ment**, an agreement secured only by the honor of the participants; **gent´lewoman**, a woman of noble or gentle birth; a lady. [**gentle + man**.]

gentry [jen´tri] *n* people of high social standing; formerly, landed proprietors not belonging to the nobility; people of a particular class or group (*the academic gentry*).—*vt* **gen´trify** [fī], to convert (a poor or working-class property) to one that is more expensive, esp in order to raise property values.—*n* **gentrifica´tion**. [OFr *genterise, gentelise*, formed from adj *gentil*, gentle.]

genuflect [jen-ū-flekt´] *vi* to bend the knee in worship or respect.—*n* **genūflex´ion** (also **genūflec´tion**). [L *genū*, the knee, *flectĕre, flexum*, to bend.]

genuine [jen´ū-in] *adj* not fake or artificial, real; sincere.—*adv* **gen´uinely**.—*n* **gen´uineness**. [L *genuīnus—gignĕre*, to beget.]

genus [jē´nus] *n* (*biol*) a taxonomic division of plants and animals below a family and above a species; the first word of a name in binomial nomenclature (eg *homo sapiens*); a class of objects divided into several subordinate species.—*pl* **genera** [jen´ėr-a].—*adjs* **generic** [jener´ik], of a whole class, kind, or group; that is not a trade name; of a genus.—*n* a product without a brand name.—*adv* **gener´ically**. [L *gĕnus, generis*, birth; cog with Gr *genos*.]

geo- [jē´ō] earth, world, forming words such as: *ns* **geochem´istry**, study of the chemical changes of the solid matter of the earth or a celestial body (as the moon); **geochronol´ogy**, the chronology of the past as indicated by geologic strata; its study; **geomag´netism**, study of magnetic forces at the surface of the earth at different places and times; **geomorphol´ogy**, study of present-day landscapes and explanations of the changes by which their features (hills, valleys, etc.) have been formed; **geophys´ics**, the physics of the earth including the fields of meteorology, hydrology, oceanography, seismology, volcanology, magnetism, radioactivity, and geodesy. [Gr *gē*, the earth.]

geocentric [jē-ō-sen´trik] *adj* viewed as from the center of the earth; having the earth as a center.—*adv* **geocen´trically**. [Gr *gē*, the earth, *kentron*, the center.]

geode [jē´ōd] *n* a nodule of stone having a cavity lined with crystals; the cavity in a geode. [Fr,—Gr *geōdēs*, earthy—*gē*, earth, *eidos*, form.]

geodesy [jē-od´e-si] *n* a branch of applied mathematics that determines the exact positions of points and the figures and areas of large portions of the earth's surface, the shape and size of the earth, and the variations of terrestrial gravity and magnetism.—*n* **geodes´ic**, the shortest line between two points on a given surface.—*adj* of or concerned with the measurement of the earth and its surface; designating the shortest line between two points on a curved surface; of the geometry of such lines; having a surface formed of straight bars in a grid of polygons (*geodesic dome*).—*adj* **geodetic**, concerning the measurement of the earth and its surface; designating the shortest line between two points on a curved surface. [Fr *géodésie*—Gr *geōdaisia—gē*, the earth, *daiein*, to divide.]

geoduck [gōō´-e-duk] *n* a large edible clam (*Panope generosa*) of the Pacific coast. [Chinook.]

geography [jē-og´ra-fi] *n* the science that describes the earth and its life; the physical features of a region.—*n* **geog´rapher**.—*adjs* **geograph´ic** [-graf´-], **-al**.—*adv* **geograph´ically**. [Fr,—L,—Gr *geōgraphia—gē*, earth, *graphē*, a description—*graphein*, to write.]

geology [jē-ol´o-ji] *n* the science relating to the history and development of the earth's crust, its rocks and fossils.—*n* **geol´ogist**.—*adjs* **geolog´ic, -al**.—*adv* **geolog´ically**.—*vi* **geol´ogize**, to study geology.—**geologic time**, the period of time occupied by the earth's geologic history. [Fr *géologie*—Gr *gē*, earth, *logos*, a discourse.]

geometry [jē-om´e-tri] *n* the branch of mathematics dealing with the properties, measurement, and relationships of points, lines, planes, and solids; any of a number of mathematical systems in which a family of theorems is derived from a set of axioms or postulates, neither of which are derived from everyday life.—*ns* **geom´eter, geometri´cian** [-shȧn] a specialist in geometry.—*adjs* **geomet´ric, -al**.—*adv* **geomet´rically**.—**geometrical progression**, a series of numbers such that the ratio of successive terms is constant, eg 2, 4, 8, 16. [Fr *géométrie*—L, Gr *geōmetria—gē*, earth, *metron*, a measure.]

geophagy [[jē-of´ȧ-ji] *n* the practice of eating earth. [Gr *gē*, earth, *phagein*, to eat.]

geopolitics [jē-o-pol´i-tiks] *n* a study of the influence of such factors as geography, economics, and demography on the politics and esp the foreign policy of a state.—*adj* **geopolit´ical**. [Gr *gē*, earth, and **politics**.]

georgette [jör-jet´] *n* a thin strong fabric woven from hardtwisted yarns to produce a dull pebbly surface. [From *Georgette*, a trade name.]

Georgian [jörj´i-ȧn] *adj* relating to or contemporary with any of the various *Georges*, kings of Great Britain; belonging to *Georgia* in the Caucasus; of the US state of *Georgia*.

georgic [jörj´ik] *n* a poem dealing with agriculture.—*adj* of or relating to agriculture. [The *Georgics*, poems by Vergil.]

geothermal, geothermic [jē-ō-therm´al, -ik] *adj* of, relating to, or using the heat of the earth's interior; produced or permeated by such heat. [**geo-** + **thermal**.]

geotropism [jē-ot´ro-pizm] *n* (*bot*) tendency to growth downward under the influence of gravity.—*adj* **geotrop´ic**. [Gr *gē*, the earth, *tropos*, a turning.]

geranium [je-rān´i-um] *n* a genus (*Geranium*) of plants with seed-vessels similar in shape to a crane's bill; popular name for a pelargonium. [L,—Gr *geranion—geranos*, a crane.]

gerbil, gerbille [jûr´bil] *n* any of numerous Old World burrowing rodents (*Gerbillus* and related genera) with long hind legs adapted for leaping. [Fr *gerbille*.]

gerfalcon *see* **gyrfalcon**.

geriatric [jer-ē-ȧ´trik] *n* (*pl*) a branch of medicine dealing with diseases and disorders of aging and old age; an aged person.—Also *adj*.—*ns* **geriatrici´an, geria´trist**. [Gr *gēras*, old age.]

germ [jûrm] *n* a bit of living matter capable of growth and development into an organism; any microscopic, diseasecausing organism; an origin (*the germ of an idea*).—*n* **germ´icide**, any antiseptic, etc. used to destroy germs.—*adj* **germ´inal**, of or relating to a germ cell; embryonic.—*vti*, **germ´inate**, to start developing; to sprout, as from a seed.—*n* **germina´tion**.—**germ cell**, an ovum or sperm; **germ plasm**, germ cells; genes. [Partly through Fr *germe*, from L *germen, -inis*, a sprout, bud, germ—*germināre, -ātum*, to sprout.]

german [jûr´mȧn], **germane** [-mān] *adj* having the same parents or same grandparents (*brother-german, cousin-german*). [OFr *germain*—L *germānus*.]

German [jûr´man] *n* a native or inhabitant of Germany; the language of Germany, Austria, etc.—Also *adj*.—*n* **German´ic**, a branch of the Indo-European family of languages including English, Dutch, German, etc.; the unrecorded language from which these languages developed.—*adj* of this group of languages; of Germany or its inhabitants.—**German measles**, rubella; **German Shepherd**, a wolflike breed of working dog often used in police work and as a guide dog for the blind; **German silver**, nickel silver. [L *Germāni*, Germans; origin unknown.]

germanium [jėr-mā´ni-ům] *n* a rare metallic element (symbol Ge; at wt 72.6; at no 32), used in transistors. [Formed from *Germany*.]

gerontology [jer-ont-ol´o-ji] *n* the scientific study of the processes of growing old. [Gr *gerōn, -ontos*, an old man, *logos*, a discourse.]

gerrymander [ger-, jer-i-man´dėr] *vt* to rearrange (voting districts) in the interests of a particular party or candidate.—Also *n*. [Formed from the name of Governor Elbridge *Gerry* (1744–1814) and sala*mander*, from the likeness to that animal of the gerrymandered map of Massachusetts in 1811.]

gerund [jer´und] *n* an English verbal noun ending in *-ing*; a Latin verbal noun expressing generalized or uncompleted action. [L *gerundium—gerěre*, to bear.]

gest, geste [jest] *n* an exploit; a tale of adventure, a romance. [OFr *geste*—L *gesta*; see **jest**.]

gestalt [gė-shtält] *n* form, structure, pattern; an organised whole (eg a living organism, a picture, a melody, the solar system) in which each individual part affects every other, the whole being more than the sum of its parts.—**gestalt psychology**, the psychology of a school which demonstrated the tendency of the mind to perceive situations as a whole, rather than as a number of isolated elements or sensations. [Ger.]

gestapo [ge-stä´pō] *n* the secret police in Germany under the Nazis. [From Ger *ge*heime *sta*ats *polizei*, secret state police.]

gestate [jes-tāt´] *vt* to carry in the womb during the period from conception to birth; to conceive and develop slowly in the mind.—*vi* to be in the process of gestation.—*n* **gesta´tion**. [Fr,—L *gestātiō, -ōnis—gestāre, -ātum*, to carry—*gerěre*, to bear.]

gesticulate [jes-tik´ū-lāt] *vi* to make vigorous gestures, esp when speaking.—*n* **gesticulā´tion**, act of making gestures in speaking; a gesture.—*adj* **gestic´ulātory**. [L *gesticulāri, -ātus—gesticulus*, dim of *gestus*, gesture—*gerěre*, to carry.]

gesture [jes´tyůr, -chůr] *n* movement of part of the body to express or emphasize ideas, emotions, etc.; any remark or act conveying a state of mind, intention, etc., often made merely for effect. [Low L *gestūra*—L *gestus*, from L *gerěre*, to carry.]

get [get] *vt* to come into the state of having; to receive; to obtain; to acquire; to arrive at (*get home early*); to go and bring (*get your books*); to catch; to persuade (*get him to go*); to cause to be (*get the jar open*); to prepare (*get dinner*); (*inf*) (*with* **have** *or* **has**) to be obliged to (*he's got to go*); to possess (*she's got green eyes*); (*inf*) to strike, kill, baffle, defeat, etc.; (*inf*) to understand; (*slang*) to cause an emotional response in (*her singing gets me*).—*vi* to come; to go; to arrive; to come to be (*to get caught*); to manage or contrive (*to get to do something*).—*pr p* **gett´ing**; *pt p* **got, gott´en**.—as an auxiliary verb for emphasis in passive construction (*to get praised*).—**get around**, to move from place to place; to circumvent; to influence as by flattery; **get away**, to go away, to escape.—*n* **get´away**, the act of starting as in a race; the act of escaping.—**get away with**, (*slang*) to do something without being discovered; **get by**, (*inf*) to survive; to manage; **get it**, (*inf*) to understand; to be punished; **get off**, to come off, down, or out of; to leave or start; to escape or help to escape; **get on**, to go on or into; to put on; to proceed; to grow older; to succeed; **get out**, to go out or away; to take out; to be disclosed; to publish; **get over**, to recover from; to forget; **get through**, to finish; to manage to survive; **get together**, to assemble; (*inf*) to reach an agreement.—*n* **get´-together**, an informal social gathering or meeting.—**get up**, to rise (from sleep, etc.); to organize.—*n* **get´-up**, (*inf*) dress, costume.

geum [jē´um] *n* a genus (*Geum*) of the rose family; the Latin name for arens. [L, herb-bennet.]

gewgaw [gū´gö] *n* a showy trifle; a bauble. [Origin unknown.]

geyser [gī´zėr] *n* a spring from which columns of boiling water and steam gush into the air at intervals. [*Geysir*, a geyser in Iceland—ON *geysa*, to gush.]

ghastly [gäst´li] *adj* terrifying, horrible; intensely disagreeable; ghostlike; (*inf*) very great (*a ghastly mistake*); (*inf*) very bad or unpleasant—*n* **ghast´liness**. [ME *gastlich*, terrible—OE *gǣstan*. See **aghast**.]

ghat [göt] *n* in India, a flight of steps at a river landing. [Hindustani *ghāt*, descent.]

ghee [gē] *n* clarified butter. [Hindustani *ghī*.]

gherkin [gûr´kin] *n* a small cucumber (*Cucumis anguria*) used for pickling; the immature fruit of the cucumber. [From an earlier form of Du *aūgurkje*, a gherkin; app from Slavonic.]

ghetto [get´ō] *n* a section of some European cities to which Jews were restricted; any section of a city in which members of a minority group live, esp because of social, legal or economic pressure.—*vt* **ghett´oize**, to isolate in or as if in a ghetto.—*n* **ghettoiza´tion**.—**ghetto blaster**, a large portable radio or tape player that is often played loudly in public places. [It.]

ghost [gōst] *n* the supposed disembodied spirit of a dead person, appearing as a shadowy apparition; a faint trace or suggestion (*a ghost of a smile*); a false image in a photographic negative or on a television screen; an absentee who is counted as present at school or work.—*adj* **ghostly**, of or related to apparitions.—*ns* **ghost story**, a story about ghosts; a tale based on imagination rather than fact; **ghost town**, a wholly or nearly deserted once-flourishing town; **ghost word**, a word never in established usage, esp one arising from a typographical error or a mistaken pronunciation; **ghost´writer**, one who writes speeches, articles, books, etc. for another who professes to be the author.—*vti* **ghost´write**.—**give up the ghost**, to die. [OE *gāst*, Ger *geist*.]

ghoul [gōōl] *n* in oriental folklore, an evil spirit that robs graves and feeds on the dead; one suggestive of a ghoul; an Eastern demon that preys on the dead; a human being whose tastes or pursuits are equally grim or revolting.—*adj* **ghoul´ish**. [Ar *ghūl*.]

GI [jē-ī´] *adj* provided by an official US military supply department; (*inf*) of or characteristic of the US armed forces.—*n* (*inf*) a member or former member of the US armed forces, esp an enlisted man.—*pl* **GI's, GIs**. [Abbreviation of *government issue*.]

giant [jī´ȧnt] *n* a huge legendary manlike being of great strength; a person or thing of great size, strength, intellect, etc.—Also *adj*.—*n* **gi´antess**, a female giant; **giant panda** *see* **panda; giant slalom**, a race for skiers on a longer and steeper course than that used for the regular slalom; **giant star**, a star of great luminosity and of large mass. [OFr *geant* (Fr *géant*), through L from Gr *gigās*, gen *gigantos*.]

gibber [jib´ėr] *vi* to utter senseless or inarticulate sounds.—*n* **gibberish** [gib´ėr-ish], unintelligible chatter. [Imit.]

gibberelin [jib-e-rel´in] *n* any of several plant-growth regulators that promote shoot growth. [From *Gibberella fujikoroi*, fungus from which it was first isolated.]

gibbet [jib´et] *n* a gallows; a structure from which bodies of executed criminals were hung and exposed to public scorn.—*vt* to hang on a gibbet. [OFr *gibet*, a stick; origin unknown.]

gibbon [gib´ȯn] *n* any of several small tailless apes (genera *Hylobates* and *Symphalangus*) of southeastern Asia and the East Indies.

gibbous [gib´us] *adj* of the shape of the moon or a planet when between half full and full. [L *gibbōsus—gibbus*, a hump.]

giblets [jib´lets] *n pl* the edible viscera of a fowl. [OFr *gibelet*.]

Gibralter [gibral´ter] *n* an impregnable stronghold. [*Gibralter*, fortress in the British colony of Gibralter.]

Gibson [gib´son] *n* a drink made from gin and vermouth and garnished with a cocktail onion.

giddy [gid´i] *adj* dizzy; that causes giddiness; whirling; light-headed; flighty.—*adv* **gidd´ily**.—*n* **gidd´iness**. [OE *gidig* (for *gydig*), possessed by a god, insane.]

gift [gift] *n* something given; the act of giving; a natural ability.—*vt* to present with or as a gift.—*adj* **gift´ed**, having great natural ability.—**gift certificate**, a document entitling the recipient to select merchandise in the establishment of the issuer.—**gift of gab**, the ability to talk glibly and persuasively; **gift of tongues**, the charismatic gift of ecstatic speech. [Root of **give**.]

gig [gig] *n* a light two-wheeled carriage; a long, light boat. [ME *gigge*, a whirling thing (cf **whirligig**); origin obscure.]
giga- [jī-gȧ-] billion (eg *giga*volt).
gigantic [jī-gan´tik] *adj* exceeding the usual or expected (as in size, force or prominence).—*adv* **gigan´tically**.—*n* **gigan´tism**, state of being gigantic; development to abnormally large size; excessive vegetative growth. [L *gigās, gigantis*, Gr *gigās, -antos*, a giant.]
giggle [gig´l] *vi* to laugh with short catches of the breath, or in a silly manner.—*n* a laugh of this kind.—*ns* **gigg´ler; gigg´ling**. [Imit.]
GIGO [**gī´gō**] (*computing*) garbage in, garbage out.
gigolo [jib´ō-lō] *n* a man paid to be a woman's escort. [Fr.]
Gila monster [he´la] *n* a poisonous black-and-orange lizard (*Heloderma suspectum*) of the southwestern US. [*Gila River*, Arizona.]
gild [gild] *vt* to coat with gold leaf; to give money to; to give a deceptively attractive appearance to.—*ns* **gild´er**, one who coats articles with gold; **gild´ing**, act or trade of a gilder; gold laid on any surface for ornament.—**gild the lily**, to embellish to an unnecessary extent. [OE *gyldan—gold*. See **gold**.]
gill[1] [gil] *n* an organ for breathing in water; the flap below the beak of a fowl; one of the radiating plates under the surface of a mushroom. [Cf Dan *giælle*; Swed *gäl*.]
gill[2] [jil] *n* a liquid measure equal to ¼ pint. [OFr *gelle*.]
gillyflower [jil´i-flow-(ė)r] *n* a name for various flowers that smell like cloves, esp a carnation. [OFr *girofle*—Gr *karyophyllon*, the clove-tree—*karyon*, a nut, *phyllon*, a leaf.]
gilt [gilt] *pt, pt p* of **gild**—*n* gilding.—*adjs* **gilt-edge, gilt´edged**, having the edges of gilt; of the highest quality (*gilt-edge securities*).
gimbals [jim´bȧlz] *n pl* a pair of rings so pivoted that one swings freely within the other, used to keep a ship's compass level. Also called a **gim´bal ring**. [L *gemelli*, twins.]
gimcrack [jim´krak] *adj* showy but cheap and useless.—*n* a gimcrack thing.—*n* **gimcrackery**. [Origin obscure.]
gimlet [gim´let] *n* a small tool for boring holes, with a screw point and a wooden crosspiece as handle.—*vt* to pierce as with a gimlet.—*adj* **gim´let-eyed**, sharp-sighted. [OFr *guimbelet*, from Gmc.]
gimmick [gim´ik] *n* (*inf*) a tricky device; (*slang*) an attention-getting feature or device, as for promoting a product, etc.—**gimmi´ckry**, gimmicks in quantity; use of gimmicks.—*adj* **gimm´icky**. [Orig unknown.]
gimp [gimp] *n* an ornamental flat braid or round cord used as trimming. [Fr *guimpe*, app from OHG *wimpal*, a light robe; Eng **wimple**.]
gin[1] [jin] *n* an alcoholic liquor distilled from grain and flavored with juniper berries.—*n* **gin mill**, a bar, a saloon; **gin rummy**, form of rummy for two players in which 'gin' is called by the first player melding all ten cards. [Du *genever, jenever*, OFr *genevre*—L *jūniperus*, the juniper; confused with the town of Geneva.]
gin[2] [jin] *n* a snare or trap; a machine, esp one for hoisting; a cotton gin. [Abbreviated form of OFr *engin*. See **engine**.]
ginger [jin´jėr] *n* a tropical plant (genus *Zingiber*) with fleshy rhizomes used as a flavoring and in medicine; the spice prepared by drying and grinding; (*inf*) vigor; a strong brown.—*adv* **gin´gerly**, very carefully.—*ns* **ginger ale**, a carbonated soft drink flavored with ginger; **gin´gerbread**, a cake flavored with ginger; showy ornamentation; **gin´gersnap**, a crisp cookie flavored with ginger and molasses. [ME *gingivere*—OFr *gengibre*—L *zingiber*—Gr *zingiberis*.]
gingerly [jin´jėr-li] *adv* with care or caution. Also *adj*.—*n* **gin´gerliness**. [Perh OFr *gensor*, comp of *gent*—L *gentīlis*, gentle.]
gingham [ging´ȧm] *n* a kind of cotton cloth, woven from colored yarns with stripes or checks. [Fr *guingan*, orig from Malay *ging-gang*, striped.]
gingivitis [jin-ji-vīt´is] *n* inflammation of the gums. [L *gingiva*, the gum.]
ginkgo [ging´ko] *n* a tree (*Ginkgo biloba*) of eastern China with fan-shaped leaves often grown as a shade tree.—Also **gingko**.—*pl* **ginkgoes, ginkgos**. [Chin.]
ginseng [jin´seng] *n* the root of ginseng; a perennial herb (*Panax schinseng*) having an aromatic root valued as medicine; any of several related plants, esp a N American herb (*P. quinque folius*); its root, said to be a remedy for exhaustion of body or mind. [Chin *jên-shên*.]
gipsy *see* **gypsy**.
giraffe [ji-räf´] *n* a large cud-chewing mammal (*Giraffa camelopardus*) of Africa, the tallest living quadruped, with very long legs and neck. [Fr,—Sp *girafa*—Ar *zarāfah*.]
gird[1] [gûrd] *vti* to gibe, jeer (*with* **at**). [From obs *gird*, to strike; same as **gird**(2).]
gird[2] [gûrd] *vt* to encircle or fasten with a belt; to surround; to prepare (oneself) for action.—*pt, pt p* **gird´ed** or **girt**.—*n* **gird´er**, a large wooden or steel beam for supporting joists, the framework of a building, etc. [OE *gyrdan*; cf Ger *gürten*.]
girdle [gûrd´l] *n* a belt for the waist; anything that encircles; a woman's elasticized garment supporting the waist and hips.—Also *vt*. [OE *gyrdel*—*gyrdan*, to gird.]
girl [gûrl] *n* a female child; a young woman.—*n* **girl´hood**, the state or time of being a girl.—*adj* **girlish**, of or like a girl.—*adv* **girl´ishly**.—*n* **girl´ishness**.—**girl Friday**, a female assistant (as in an office) entrusted with wide variety of tasks; **Girl Scout**, a member of any of the programs of the Girl Scouts of the USA for girls ages 6 through 17. [Origin obscure.]
girt [gûrt] *pt p* of **gird**.—*vt* to fasten with a girth. [**gird**.]
girth [gûrth] *n* a band put around the belly of a horse, etc. to hold a saddle or pack; the circumference, as of a tree trunk. [ON *gjörth*.]
gist [jist] *n* the ground of a legal action; the main point or pith of a matter. [OFr *gist* (Fr *gît*)—OFr *gesir* (Fr *gésir*), to lie—L *jacēre*.]
give [giv] *vt* to hand over as a present; to hand over (*to give a porter a bag*); to hand over in or for payment; to pass (regards etc.) along; to cause to have (*to give pleasure*); to act as host or sponsor of; to supply (*cows give milk*); to yield; to offer (*give advice*); to perform (*to give a concert*); to inflict (punishment, etc.); to sacrifice.—*vi* to bend, move, etc. from force or pressure; *pr p* **giv´ing**; *pt p* **gave**.—*n* capacity or tendency to yield to force or strain; the quality or state of being springy.—*ns* **give´away**, an unintentional revelation; something given free or sold cheap; a radio or television program giving prizes.—**giver**, one who gives.—*vt* **give away**, to make a gift of; to give (the bride) to the bridegroom; (*inf*) to reveal or betray.—*n* **give´back**, a workers' benefit relinquished to management, usu. in exchange for some concession.—*adj* **given**, accustomed (to) by habit, etc.; specified; assumed, granted.—**give forth**, to emit; **give in**, to yield; **give it to**, (*inf*) to beat or scold; **give off**, to emit; **give or take**, plus or minus; **give out**, to make public; to distribute; to become worn out, etc.; **give up**, to hand over; to cease; to stop trying; to despair of; to devote wholly. [OE gefan (WS *giefan*); Ger *geben*.]
gizzard [giz´ȧrd] *n* the muscular second stomach of a bird. [ME *giser*—OFr *guiser*.]
glacé [glä´sā] *adj* glossy, as silk; candied, as fruit. [Fr]
glacial [glā´shi-ȧl] *adj* extremely cold; of or relating to glaciers or a glacial epoch.—*vt* **glac´iate**, to subject to glacial action; to produce glacial effects in or on.—*n* **glacia´tion**.—**glacial epoch**, any period when much of the earth was covered by glaciers. [L *glaciālis*, icy, *glaciāre, -ātum*, to freeze—*glaciēs*, ice.]
glacier [glas´i-ėr, -yėr (also glāsh´-)] *n* a large mass of snow and ice moving slowly down a mountain. [Fr,—*glace*, ice—L *glaciēs*, ice.]
glacis [glās´is] *n* a gentle slope; a buffer state. [Fr,—OFr *glacier*, to slip.]
glad [glad] *adj* happy; causing joy; very willing; bright.—*vti* **gladd´en**, to make or become glad.—*adv* **glad´ly**.—*n* **glad´ness**.—*adj* **glad´some**.—**glad hand**, (*slang*) a warm welcome often prompted by ulterior motives. [OE *glæd*; Ger *glatt*, smooth, ON *glathr*, bright, Dan *glad*.]
glade [glād] *n* an open space in a wood. [Origin obscure; poss conn with **glad**.]
gladiator [glad´i-ā-tȯr] *n* in ancient Rome, a professional combatant with men or beasts in the arena.—*adjs* **gladiătō´rial, glad´iatory**. [L *glădiātor*—*glădius*, a sword.]
gladiolus [glad-i-ō´lus] *n* any of a genus (*Gladiolus*) of the iris family with swordlike leaves and tall spikes of funnel-shaped flowers.—*pl* **gladiol´uses, gladiol´i**. [L *glădiŏlus*, dim of *glădius*, a sword.]
gladstone-bag [glad´stȯn-bag] *n* a traveling bag hinged to open flat. [After Brit statesman, W E Gladstone (1809–98).]
glair(-e) [glār] *n* egg white used as varnish; any viscous, transparent substance.—*vt* to varnish with white of eggs.—*adj* **glair´y**. [Fr *glaire*—Low L *clāra* (*ōvī*), white (of egg)—L *clārus*, clear.]
glamour, glamor [glam´ȯr] *n* seemingly mysterious allure; bewitching charm.—*adj* **glam´orous**. [Scot]
glance [gläns] *vi* to strike obliquely and go off at an angle; to flash; to look quickly.—*n* a glancing off; a flash; a quick look.—**at first glance**, on first consideration.
gland [gland] *n* any organ for secreting substances to be used in, or eliminated from, the body.—*adj* **gland´ūlar**.—**glandular fever** *see* **infectious mononucleosis** at **infect**. [L *glans, glandis*, an acorn.]
glanders [gland´ėrz] *n* a contagious bacterial disease esp of horses, often fatal.—*adj* **gland´ered**. [OFr *glandre*, a gland.]
glare [glār] *n* a harsh uncomfortably bright light, esp painfully bright sunlight; an angry or fierce stare; a bright, glassy surface, as of ice.—*vi* to shine with a steady, dazzling light; to stare fiercely.—*vt* to express with a glare.—*adj* **glar´ing**.—*adv* **glar´ingly**. [ME *glāren*, to shine; akin to **glass**, OE *glær*, amber, L Ger *glaren*, to glow.]
glass [glas] *n* a hard brittle substance, usu. transparent, made by fusing silicates with soda, lime, etc.; glassware; a glass article, as a drinking container; (*pl*) eyeglasses or binoculars; the amount held by a drinking glass.—*adj* of or made of glass.—*vt* to equip with glass panes.—*adj* **glass´y**.—*ns* **glass arm**, (*baseball*) an injured or sore arm resulting from tendons weakened by or damaged by training or pitching; **glass´blowing**, the art of shaping a mass of glass that has been softened by heat by blowing air into it through a tube; **glass harmonica**, a musical instrument consisting of a series of graded glass disks which produces sound by rubbing the fingers against the wetted rims; **glass snake**, a limbless lizard (*Ophisauris ventralis*) of the southern US with a tail that breaks readily into pieces; **glassware**, articles made of glass; **glass wool**, glass fibres in a mass used for thermal insulation and filtering air. [OE *glaes*.]
glaucoma [glow-kō´mȧ] *n* a disease of the eye marked by increased pressure within the eyeball. [Gr *glaukōma*.]
glaucous [glö´kus] *adj* pale yellow-green; light bluish gray or bluish white;

having a powdery or waxy coating giving a frosted appearance that tends to rub off. [L *glaucus*—Gr *glaukos*, bluish-green or grey (orig gleaming).]

glaze [glāz] *vt* to provide (windows, etc.); to give a hard, glossy finish to (pottery, etc.); to cover (foods) with a coating of sugar syrup, etc.—*vi* to become glassy or glossy.—*n* a glassy finish or coating.—*ns* **glā´zier** [-zyėr], one who sets glass.—**glāz´ing**, the act or art of setting glass; the art of covering with a vitreous substance. [ME *glasen*—*glas*, glass.]

gleam [glēm] *vi* to glow or shine, transiently or not very brightly.—*n* a faint or moderate glow (of light); a transient show of some emotion, esp hope.—*n* **gleam´ing**. [OE *glǣm*, gleam, brightness.]

glean [glēn] *vti* to collect (grain left by reapers); to collect (facts, etc.) gradually.—*n* **gleanings**, things acquired by gleaning. [OFr *glener* (Fr *glaner*).]

glee [glē] *n* mirth and gaiety; delight; (*mus*) a song in parts.—*adj* **glee´ful**, merry.—**glee club**, a group singing part songs. [OE *glēo, glīw*, mirth; ON *glȳ*.]

gleet [glēt] *n* a chronic inflammation of a bodily orifice usu. accompanied by a discharge; the discharge. [OFr *glette, glecte*, a flux.]

glen [glen] *n* a narrow secluded valley.—**glen plaid**, a plaid pattern with thin crossbarred stripes. [Gael *gleann*; cf W *glyn*.]

glengarry [glen-gar´i] *n* a woolen cap, generally rising to a point in front, with ribbons hanging down behind. [*Glengarry*, in Scotland.]

glib [glib] *adj* speaking or spoken smoothly, to the point of insincerity; lacking depth and substance.—*adv* **glib´ly**.—*n* **glib´ness**. [Cf Du *glibberig*, slippery.]

glide [glīd] *vi* to slide smoothly and easily; (*aeronautics*) to descend with little or no engine power.—*n* a gliding; a disk or ball, as of nylon, under a furniture leg to provide a smooth surface.—*n* **glider**, one that glides; an engineless aircraft carried along by air currents; a porch swing suspended in a frame. [OE *glīdan*, to slip; Ger *gleiten*.]

glimmer [glim´ėr] *vi* to give a faint, flickering light; to appear faintly.—Also *n*.—*n* **glimmering**, a faint manifestation. [ME *glemern*, freq from root of **gleam**.]

glimpse [glimps] *n* a brief, quick view; appearance; a momentary view.—*vi* to look quickly.—*vt* to get a glimpse of. [ME *glymsen*, to glimpse.]

glint [glint] *vi* to shine, gleam, sparkle.—*vt* to reflect.—*n* a gleam. [Earlier *glent*; prob Scand.]

glissade [glēs-äd´] *vi* to slide down a snow-covered slope without the aid of skis; to perform a sliding step in ballet.—Also *n*. [Fr from *glisser*, to slip.]

glisten [glis´n] *vi* to shine as light reflected from a wet or oily surface. [ME *glistnen*—OE *glisnian*, to shine.]

glister [glis´tėr] *vi* to glitter. [ME *glistren*; cf **glisten**, and Du *glisteren*.]

glitter [glit´ėr] *vi* to sparkle with light; to be splendid; to be showy.—*n* sparkle; showiness; bits of glittering material.—*adj* **glitt´ering**. [ME *gliteren*; cf ON *glitra*, Ger *glitzern*.]

gloaming [glōm´ing] *n* twilight, dusk. [OE *glōmung*—*glōm*, twilight.]

gloat [glōt] *vi* to gaze exultingly, esp with a wicked or a malicious joy. [Perh ON *glotta*, to grin.]

globe [glōb] *n* anything spherical or almost spherical; the earth, or a model of the earth.—*adjs* **glōb´al**, worldwide; **glob´ose** [-ōs], spherical; **globular** [glob´ū-lȧr], spherical; made up of globules.—*ns* **glōb´alism**, a policy, outlook, etc. that is worldwide in scope; **globe artichoke**, the edible head of a tall perennial plant (*Cynara scolymus*); the plant itself; **globe flower**, any of a genus (*Trollius*) of plants of the buttercup family with globose yellow flowers; **globe trotter**, one who travels widely about the world; **globule**, a tiny ball; a very small drop. [L *globus*.]

globulin [glob´yŏŏl-in] *n* any of a class of simple proteins (as myosin) that are insoluble in pure water but are soluble in dilute salt and that occur widely in plant and animal tissue.

glockenspiel [glok´en-spēl] *n* an orchestral percussion instrument with tuned metal bars, played with hammers. [Ger *glocke*, bell, and *spiel*, play.]

gloom [glōōm] *n* partial darkness; deep sadness.—*vi* to be or look sullen or dejected; to be cloudy or obscure.—*adj* **gloom´y**, dim or obscure; depressed in spirits; depressing, disheartening.—*adv* **gloom´ily**.—*n* **gloom´iness**. [ME *gloumbe*. See **glum**.]

glorify [glō´-, glö´ri-fī] *vt* to make glorious, invest with glory; to advance the glory of (God); to extol, to honor; to transform (an ordinary thing) into something more splendid—to regard it, or to speak of it, in such a way;—*pt p* **glo´rified**.—*n* **glorificā´tion**. [L *gloria*, glory, *facĕre*, to make.]

glory [glō´-, glö´ri] *n* great honor or fame, or its source; adoration; great splendor; heavenly bliss.—*vi* to exult (*with* **in**);—*pr p* **glor´ying**; *pt p* **glō´ried**.—*adj* **glō´rious**, noble, splendid; conferring renown.—*adv* **glō´riously**.—*n* **glō´riousness**.—**Old Glory**, the US flag. [OFr *glorie* and L *glōria*.]

gloss[1] [glos] *n* the shine of a polished surface; external show.—*vt* to give a shiny surface to; to hide (an error, etc.) or make seem right or inconsequential.—*n* **glosser**, any shiny or glossy cosmetic, esp one for the lips.—*adj* **gloss´y**, smooth and shining; highly polished.—*adv* **gloss´ily**.—*n* **gloss´iness**. [Cf ON *glossi*, blaze, *glōa*, to glow; akin to **glass**.]

gloss[2] [glos] *n* a marginal or interlinear explanation of an unusual word; an explanation; a collection of explanations of words.—*vt* to comment or make explanatory remarks; to read a different sense into.—*n* **gloss´ary**, a collection of glosses.—*adj* **glossā´rial**, relating to a glossary: containing explanation.—*n* **gloss´arist**, a writer of a glossary. [Gr *glōssa, glōtta*, tongue, a word requiring explanation.]

glottis [glot´is] *n* the opening between the vocal cords in the larynx; the structures surrounding this space.—*adj* **glott´al**.—**glottal stop**, the interruption of the breath stream during speech by closure of the glottis. [Gr *glōttis*—*glōtta*, the tongue.]

glove [gluv] *n* a covering for the hand, esp with a sheath for each finger; a baseball player's mitt; a boxing glove.—*vt* to cover with, or as with, a glove.—*ns* **glove compartment**, a small storage cabinet in the dashboard of an automobile; **glov´er**, one who makes or sells gloves. [OE *glōf*.]

glow [glō] *vi* to shine with an intense heat; to burn without flame; to emit a steady light; to flush; to tingle with bodily warmth or with emotion; to be ardent.—*n* shining due to heat; steady, even light; warmth of feeling.—*n* **glow´worm**, a larva or wingless female of a firefly (family Lampyridae) that emits light from the abdomen. [OE *glōwan*, to glow; Ger *glühen*, ON *glōa*, to glow.]

glower [glow´ėr] *vi* to stare frowningly; to scowl.—*n* a fierce or threatening stare.

glucose [glōō´kōs] *n* a crystalline sugar ($C_6H_{12}O_6$) occurring naturally in fruits, honey, etc.; a light-colored syrup made from cornstarch. [Gr *glykys*, sweet.]

glue [glōō´] *n* a sticky, viscous liquid made from animal gelatin, used as an adhesive; any similar substance.—*vt* to join as with glue;—*pr p* **glu´ing**; *pt p* **glued**.—*adj* **glu´ey**, sticky, viscous. [Fr *glu*—Low L *glus, glūtis*.]

glum [glum] *adj* sullen; gloomy.—*adv* **glum´ly**. [ME *glombe, glome*, to frown.]

glume [glōōm] *n* a chaff-like bract which encloses the spikelet in grasses. [L *glūma*, husk—*glūbĕre*, to peel.]

glut [glut] *vt* to gorge; to overstock (the market);—*pr p* **glutt´ing**; *pt p* **glutt´ed**.—*n* a surfeit; an oversupply. [L *gluttīre*, to swallow.]

gluten [glōō´tėn] *n* a tenacious elastic protein substance, esp of wheat flour that gives cohesiveness to dough.—*adj* **glu´tinous**. [L *glūten, -inis*, glue; akin to **glue**.]

glutton [glut´(ò)n] *n* one who eats and drinks to excess; one who has a great appetite (eg for work); a wolverine.—*adj*, **glutt´onous**, given to, or consisting in gluttony.—*n* **glutt´ony**, excess in eating or drinking. [Fr *glouton*—L *glūtō, -ōnis*—*glūtīre, gluttīre*, to devour.]

glycerin, glycerine [glis´ėr-in, ēn] *n* the popular and commercial name for glycerol.

glycerol [glis´er-ōl] *n* a colorless, syrupy liquid made from fats and oils, used in making skin lotions, explosives, etc. [Gr *glykeros*, sweet—*glykys*, sweet.]

glycogen [glik´ō-jėn, or glīk´-] *n* a substance in animal tissues that is changed into a simple sugar as the body needs it. [Gr *glykys*, sweet, and the root of *gennaein*, to produce.]

glyph [glif] *n* an ornamental vertical groove, esp in a Doric frieze; a symbol (as a curved arrow on a road sign) that conveys information nonverbally. [Gr *glyphē*—*glyphein*, to carve.]

glyptic [glip´tik] *n* the cut or process of carving or engraving, esp on gems. [Gr *glyptos*, carved.]

gnar [när] *vi* to snarl or growl.—Also **gnarl**. [Onomatopoeic; cf Ger *knurren*, Dan *knurre*, to growl.]

gnarl [närl] *vt* to twist into a state of deformity.—*adj* **gnarled**, (of tree trunks) full of knots; crabby in disposition. [Cf ON *gnerr*, Ger *knurren*, Dan *knort*, a knot, gnarl.]

gnash [nash] *vti* to grind (the teeth) in rage or pain; (of teeth) to strike together. [ME *gnasten*; prob from ON, ultimately onomatopoeic.]

gnat [nat] *n* any of various small, two-winged insects that bite or sting. [OE *gnæt*.]

gnaw [nö] *vti* to bite away bit by bit; to torment, as by constant pain. [OE *gnagan*: cf Du *knagen*, mod Icel *naga*.]

gneiss [nīs] *n* a granitelike rock formed by layers of quartz, mica, etc.—*adj* **gneiss´oid**, like gneiss. [Ger *gneis*.]

gnome [nōm] *n* in folklore, a dwarf who dwells in the earth and guards its treasure.—**the gnomes of Zürich, Europe**, etc., the big bankers. [*gnomus*, Medieval Latin word used by Paracelsus (see **sylph**).]

gnomon [nō´mon] *n* an object that by the position or length of its shadow serves as an indicator, esp of the hour of the day; (*geom*) that which remains of a parallelogram when a similar parallelogram within one of its angles is taken away. [Gr *gnōmōn*, a gnomon, a carpenter's square—*gnōnai* (aorist), to know.]

Gnostic [nos´tik] *n* (*theology*) one of a sect, esp in early Christian times, who maintained that knowledge, not faith, was the way of salvation, claiming themselves to have superior knowledge of spiritual things.—*adj* having knowledge; pertaining to the Gnostics.—*n* **gnos´ticism** [-tisizm], the doctrines of the Gnostics. [Gr *gnōstikos*, good at knowing—*gignōskein*, to know.]

gnu [nōō, nū] *n* either of two large African antelopes (*Connochaetes gnou* and *C. taurinas*) with an oxlike head and a horselike tail. [From Hottentot.]

go [gō] *vi* to move on a course; to proceed; to work properly (*the motor won't go*); to act, sounds, as specified (*the balloon went 'pop'*); to result (*the game went badly*); to become (*to go mad*); to be expressed, sung (*as the saying goes*); to harmonize (*blue goes with gold*); to be accepted, valid; to leave, to depart; to die; to fail (*his eyesight is going*); to be allotted or sold; to be able to pass (through); to fit (into); to be capable of being divided (into) (*five goes into ten twice*); to belong (*socks go into this drawer*).—*vt* to travel along; (*inf*) to put up with; (*inf*) to provide (bail) for an arrested person.—*n* a success; (*inf*) a try; (*inf*) energy.—*pl* **goes**.—*n* **go-´ahead**, permission or a signal to proceed (*usu. with* **the**).—**go back on**, (*inf*) to betray or break a promise, etc.; **go for**, to try to get; (*inf*) to attack; (*inf*) to be attracted by; **go in for**, (*inf*) to engage or indulge in; **go off**, to be extinguished, become outdated, etc.; to attend social functions, performances, etc.; **go over**, to examine thoroughly; to do again; (*inf*) to be successful; **go places**, (*inf*) to be on the way to success; **go through**, to endure; to look through; **go through with**, to pursue to the end; **go to bat for**, (*inf*) to champion, to defend; **go together**, to harmonize; (*inf*) to be sweethearts; **go under**, to fail, as in business; **let go**, to allow to escape; **let oneself go**, to be unrestrained; **on the go**, (*inf*) in constant motion; **to go**, to be taken out, as of food from a restaurant; still to be done, etc. [OE *gan*, to go; cf Ger *gehen*, Du *gaan*.]

goad [gōd] *n* a sharp-pointed stick, often shod with iron, for driving oxen; a stimulus.—*vt* to drive with a goad; to urge forward; to irritate, annoy excessively. [OE *gād*, a goad.]

goal [gōl] *n* the place at which a race, trip, etc. is ended; an end that one strives to attain; in some games, the place over or into which the ball or puck must go to score; the score made.—*ns* **goal´ie** [-ē], **goal´keeper**, a player who defends the goal (as in soccer or hockey). [ME *gol*, boundary.]

goat [gōt] *n* a cud-chewing mammal (genus *Capra*) related to the sheep that has backward curving horns, short tail, and usu. straight hair; a lecherous man; (*inf*) a scapegoat.—*n* **goat´ee** [-ē], a small, pointed beard on a man's chin.—**get one's goat**, to irritate one. [OE *gāt*; Ger *geiss*, Du *geit*.]

gobbet [gob´et] *n* a mouthful; a lump to be swallowed. [OFr *gobet*, dim of *gobe*, mouthful, lump; cf Gael *gob*, mouth.]

gobble [gob´l] *vt* to eat greedily; to take eagerly (*often with* **up**); to read rapidly (*often with* **up**).—*vi* to make a noise in the throat, as a turkey. [OFr *gober*, to devour.]

Gobelin [gob´ė-lin, -lē̃] *adj* of, relating to, or characteristic of tapestry produced at the Gobelin works in Paris. [From the *Gobelin*, French dyers settled in Paris in the 15th century.]

goblet [gob´let] *n* a large drinking cup without a handle. [OFr *gobelet*, dim of *gobel*.]

goblin [gob´lin] *n* in folklore, an evil or mischievous sprite. [OFr *gobelin*—Low L *gobelinus*, perh—*cobālus*—Gr *kobālos*, a mischievous spirit.]

goby [gō´bi] *n* any of a family (Gobiidae) of small sea fishes, with ventral fins forming a sucker. [L *gōbius*—Gr *kōbios*.]

god [god] *n* any of various beings conceived of as supernatural and immortal, esp a male deity; an idol; a person or thing deified; **God**, in monotheistic religions, the creator and ruler of the universe.—*ns* **god´child**, the person a godparent sponsors; **goddess**, a female god; a woman of great beauty, charm, etc.; **godfather**, male godparent; man having analogous relationship to an enterprise, field of activity, etc.; (*slang*) the head of a Mafia family or other group involved in organized crime; **godhead**, the state of being a god; **Godhead**, God (*usu. with* **the**); **godhood**, the state of being a god.—*adjs* **godless**, irreligious; wicked; **god´ly**, devout; devoted to God; **god´parent**, a person who sponsors a child, as at baptism or confirmation, taking responsibility for its faith; **god´send**, anything that comes unexpectedly and when needed or desired, as if sent by God.—**God's acre**, a churchyard. [OE *god*; Ger *gott*; from a Gmc root *guth-*, god, and quite distinct from **good**.]

go-down [gō-down´] *n* a warehouse in an oriental country. [Malay *godong*.]

godwit [god´wit] *n* any of a genus (*Limosa*) of wading birds with a long bill, related to the snipes but resembling curlews. [Origin obscure.]

gofer [gō´fėr] *n* an employee whose duties include running errands.—Also **gopher**. [**go** + **for**.]

goffer [gof´ėr] *vt* to plait or crimp with a heated iron.—Also *n*. [OFr *gauffrer*—*goffre*, a wafer.]

goggle [gog´l] *vi* to stare with bulging eyes.—*npl* large spectacles, sometimes fitting snugly against the face, to protect the eyes.—*adj* **gogg´le-eyed**, having bulging or rolling eyes. [Possibly related to Ir and Gael *gog*, to nod.]

going [gō´ing] *n* a departure; condition of the ground for, eg walking, racing; advance toward an objective.—*adj* that goes (*easygoing*); commonly accepted (*going price*); existing (*the best novelist going*); conducting business with the expectation of indefinite continuance.—**be going to**, will or shall; **going-over**, (*inf*) a severe scolding; a thorough inspection; **goings-on**, events or actions, esp when disapproved of. [**go**.]

goiter [goi´tėr] *n* an enlargement of the thyroid gland visible as a swelling in the front of the neck.—*adj* **goi´trous**. [Fr *goître*—L *guttur*, the throat.]

gold [gōld] *n* a malleable yellow metallic element (symbol Au, at wt 197.0; at no 79) used esp for coins and jewelry; a precious metal; money, wealth; a yellow color.—*adj* of, or like gold.—*ns* **gold´brick**, (*inf*) anything worthless passed off as valuable; (*military slang*) one who avoids work; **gold´digger**, (*inf*) a woman who uses feminine charms to extract money or gifts from men.—*adj* **golden**, made of or relating to gold; bright yellow; very valuable; flourishing.—*ns* **gold´en-ager**, (*inf*) an elderly and often retired person usu. engaging in club activities; **golden eagle**, a large eagle (*Aquila chryaetos*) of the northern hemisphere with brownish yellow tips on the head and neck feathers; **gol´deneye**, either of two diving ducks (genus *Bucephala*); **golden mean**, the medium between two extremes; **golden plover**, either of two gregarious plovers (genus *Pluvialis*), esp one (*P. dominica*) that breeds in arctic America and winters in Hawaii and the southern hemisphere; **gol´denrod**, any of several N American plants (genus *Solidago*) with long branching stalks bearing clusters of small, yellow flowers; **golden rule**, a guiding principle; the precept that one should act toward others as he would want them to act toward him; **golden section**, a proportion in which the ratio of the whole to the larger part is the same as the ratio of the larger part to the small.—*adj* **gold-filled**, made of a base metal overlaid with gold;—*n* **goldfinch**, a small American finch (genus *Spinus*), the male of which has a yellow body; **gold leaf**, gold beaten into very thin sheets, used for gilding; **gold standard**, a monetary standard in which the basic currency unit equals a specified quantity of gold. [OE *gold*; ON *gull*, Ger *gold*.]

golem [gō´lem, goi´lem, gā´lem] *n* in Hebrew folklore, an artificial human being endowed with life; something resembling a golem, as a blockhead. [Yiddish.]

golf [golf, galf] *n* an outdoor game in which the player attempts to propel a small resilient ball with clubs around a turfed course with widely spaced holes in regular progression with the smallest number of strokes; **Golf**, word used in communication, for the letter g.—*vi* to play this game.—*ns* **gol´fer; golf ball**, a hard dimpled ball used in golf; the spherical printing element of an electric typewriter; **golf club**, a long-shafted club with wooden or metal head used to strike a golf ball; the premises of an association of golfers, usu. having its own course and facilities; **golf course**, a tract of land for playing golf; **golf widow**, a woman whose husband spends much time playing golf. [Origin obscure; perh Du *kolf*, a club.]

Goliath [gō-lī´ath] *n* a Philistine champion who in I Samuel 17 is killed by David; a giant.

golliwog, golliwogg [gol´i-wog] *n* a grotesque black doll with staring eyes and bristling hair. [*Golliwogg*, an animated doll in children's fiction by Bertha Upton, died 1912, American writer.]

gonad [gon´ad] *n* (*biol*) an animal organ that produces reproductive cells; ovary or testis.—*n* **gonadotrop(h)´in**, a substance which stimulates the gonads and which is used as a drug to promote fertility. [Gr *gonē*, generation.]

gondola [gon´do-la] *n* a long, narrow, black boat used on the canals of Venice; a railroad freight car with low sides and no top; a cabin suspended under an airship or balloon; an enclosed car suspended from a cable used to transport persons esp skiers up a mountain.—*n* **gondolier** [-lēr´], on who propels a gondola. [It.]

gone [gon] *pt p* of **go**, lost, passed beyond help; departed; dead; insane, or acting so; (*slang*) in an exalted state; (*slang*) enamored of (*with* **on**).

gonfalon [gon´fa-lon] *n* an ensign of princes or states, as in medieval Italy; a flag that hangs from a crosspiece or frame. [It *gonfalone* and OFr *gonfanon*—OHG *gundfano*—*gund*, battle, *fano*, a flag.]

gong [gong] *n* a disk-shaped percussion instrument struck with a usu. padded hammer; a saucer-shaped bell (as in a fire alarm) struck with a mechanical hammer. [Malay.]

gonif [gän´if] *n* (*slang*) a thief; a rascal. [Yiddish.]

gonorrhea [gon-o-rē´a] *n* a contagious infection of the mucous membrane of the genital tract. [Gr *gonorroia*—*gonos*, seed, *rheein*, to flow, from a mistaken notion of its nature.]

goo [gōō] *n* (*slang*) sticky substance; sentimentality.—*adj* **goo´ey**. [Origin unknown.]

good [gŏŏd] *adj* having the proper qualities; beneficial; valid; healthy or sound (*good eyesight*); honorable (*one's good name*); enjoyable, pleasant, etc.; skilled; considerable (*a good many*).—*comparative* **better**; *superlative* **best**.—*n* something good; benefit; something that has economic utility; good persons (*with* **the**);—*pl* personal property; cloth; wares, commodities.—*adv* (*inf*) well; fully.—*n, interj*.—**good-bye, good-by**, a concluding remark at parting; farewell.—*n* **Good Friday**, the Friday before Easter, commemorating the Crucifixion of Christ.—*adjs* **good-looking**, handsome; **goodly**, of pleasing appearance; ample.—*ns* **good Samaritan**, anyone who helps others unselfishly; **good turn**, a friendly, helpful act; **goodwill**, benevolence; willingness; the value of a business in patronage, reputation, etc., beyond its tangible assets.—**as good as**, nearly; **for good (and all)**, permanently; **good and**, (*inf*) very and altogether; **good for**, able to endure or be used for (a period of time); worth; able to pay or give; **good-for-nothing**, an idle worthless person; **make good**, make up for; carry out, fulfill; succeed; **to the good**, in a position of net gain.—**get the goods on**, (*inf*) to discover something incriminating about. [OE *gōd*; Du *goed*, Ger *gut*, ON *gōthr*.]

goof [gōōf] *n* (*slang*) a stupid person; a mistake; a blunder.—*vi* (*slang*) to err; to waste time, shirk duties (*with* **off** *or* **around**).

googol [gōō´gȯl] *n* (*math*) the figure 1 followed by 100 zeroes (10^{100}).

googolplex [gōō´gȯl-plex] *n* (*math*) the figure 1 followed by a googol of zeroes (10^{googol} or $10^{10^{100}}$).

gook [gook, gōōk] *n* (*slang*) any sticky or slimy substance.

goon [gōōn] (*slang*) a ruffian or thug; a stupid person.

goop [gōōp] *n* (*slang*) any sticky, semiliquid substance.

goose [gōōs] *n* a large, long-necked, web-footed bird (family Anatidae) related to the swans and ducks; its flesh as food; a female goose as distinguished from a gander; a foolish person.—*pl* **geese**.—*pl* **gooses**, a tailor's smoothing iron.—*ns* **goose bumps**, gooseflesh; **goose egg**, zero, esp as a score in a game or contest; **gooseflesh**, a roughening of the skin caused usu. by cold or fear; **goose grass**, cleavers; yard grass; **gooseneck**, something (as the flexible tubing of a lamp) that can assume the shape of a goose's neck; **goose pimples**, gooseflesh; **goose step**, a stiff-legged marching step used by some armies when passing in review.—*vi* **goose-step**, to march in goose step; to practice blind allegiance to a policy.—**cook one's goose**, to spoil one's chances. [OE *gōs* (pl *gēs*); ON *gās*, Ger *gans*, L *anser* (for *hanser*), Gr *chēn*.]

gooseberry [gōōs´ber-i] *n* the acid berry of a shrub (genus *Ribes*) related to the currant and used esp in jams and pies. [Perh **goose** and **berry**; or *goose* may be from MHG *krus*, crisp, curled; cf OFr *groisele, grosele*, gooseberry, Scot *grossart*.]

gopher[1] [gō´fėr] *n* a burrowing edible land tortoise (*Gopherus polyphemus*) of the southern US; any of several burrowing rodents (family Geomyidae) with wide cheek pouches; any striped ground squirrel (genus *Citellus*); a gopher ball.—*ns* **gopher ball**, a pitched baseball hit for a home run; **gopher snake**, indigo snake; bull snake. [Perh Fr *gaufre*, honeycomb.]

gopher[2] [gō´fėr] *see* **gofer**

Gordian knot [görd´yan] *n* an intricate problem, esp one unsolvable in its own terms. [Alexander, unable to untie the knot tied by *Gordius*, king of Phrygia, cut it through with his sword.]

gore[1] [gōr, gör] *n* blood from a wound, esp clotted blood.—*adj* **gōr´y**. [OE *gor*, filth, dung; ON *gor*, cud, slime.]

gore[2] [gōr, gör] *n* a tapering piece let into a garment to widen it.—*vt* to shape with gores; to pierce as with a spear or horns. [OE *gāra*, a pointed triangular piece of land; cf *gār*, a spear.]

Gore-tex [gör-teks] *n* trade name for a waterproof, breathable laminated fabric. [Name of inventor.]

gorge [görj] *n* the throat; a ravine.—*vt* to swallow greedily; to glut.—*vi* to feed gluttonously.—*n* **gorg´et**, a piece of armor for the throat; an ornamental collar; a part of a wimple covering the throat and shoulders. [OFr.]

gorgeous [gör´jus] *adj* brilliantly colored; magnificent.—*n* **gor´geousness**. [OFr *gorgias*, gaudy.]

gorgon [gör´gȯn] *n* one of three fabled female monsters of horrible and petrifying aspect; any ugly or formidable woman.—*adjs* **gor´gon, gorgō´nian**. [Gr *Gorgō*, pl. *-ŏnės—gorgos*, grim.]

gorgonzola [gör-gȯn-zō´la] *n* a semihard blue-veined cheese made from cow's milk, with a rich piquant flavor, originally from Italy. [From *Gorgonzola*, near Milan.]

gorilla [gor-il´a] *n* an anthropoid ape (*Gorilla gorilla*) of western equatorial Africa related to the chimpanzee but much larger; (*slang*) an ugly or brutal man. [Gr *gorillai* (pl), reported by Hanno the Carthaginian as a tribe of hairy women; supposed to be an African word.]

gormandise [gör´mȧnd-iz] *vti* to eat like a glutton. [*See* **gourmand**.]

gorp [görp] *n* a mix of raisins, nuts, etc. eaten for energy. [Unknown.]

gorse [görs] *n* a spiny yellow-flowered European shrub (*Ulex europaeus*); (*loosely*) any of several related plants (genera *Ulex* and *Genista*). [OE *gorst*.]

goshawk [gos´hawk] *n* any of several long-tailed hawks with short rounded wings, esp a hawk (*Accipiter gentilis*) of the northern hemisphere. [OE *gōshafoc—gōs*, goose, *hafoc*, hawk.]

gosling [goz´ling] *n* a young goose. [OE *gōs*, goose, and double dim *-l-ing*.]

gospel [gos´pėl] *n* the message concerning Christ, the Kingdom of God, and salvation; **Gospel**, any of the first four books of the New Testament; anything proclaimed or accepted as the absolute truth. [OE *godspel—gōd*, good (with shortened vowel being understood as *god*, God), and *spell*, story; a translation of LL *evangelium*.]

gossamer [gos´ȧ-mėr] *n* very fine spider-threads which float in the air or form webs on bushes in fine weather; any very thin material. [ME *gossomer*; perh goose-summer, a St Martin's summer, when geese are in season and gossamer abounds.]

gossip [gos´ip] *n* one who chatters idly about others; such talk.—*vi* to be a gossip.—*adj* **goss´ipy**. [OE *godsibb*, god-father, one who is *sib* (i.e. related) in God, spiritually related.]

got, gotten *see under* **get**.

Goth [goth] *n* any member of a Germanic people that conquered most of the Roman Empire in the 3d, 4th, and 5th century, AD.—*adj* **Goth´ic**, of the Goths or their language; of a style of architecture with pointed arches, steep roofs, elaborate stonework, etc.; barbarous; of style of fiction marked by gloom, the grotesque, and violent incidents.—*n* German black letter type; a bold type style without serifs. [The native names *Gutans* (sing *Guta*) and *Gutôs* (sing *Guts*), *Gutthiuda*, 'people of the Goths'; Latinised as *Gothī, Gotthi*.]

gouache [gwash, gōō-ash´] *n* a method of painting with opaque watercolors; a picture painted by gouache; the pigment used in gouache. [Fr, through It, from L *aquātiō*, a watering-place, pool.]

Gouda [gōōd´ė] *n* a firm cheese of mild flavor made from cow's milk, shaped like a flattened ball and covered with red wax. [*Gouda*, Holland.]

gouge [gowj, also gōōj] *n* a chisel with a hollow blade, for cutting grooves, or holes.—*vt* to scoop out, as with a gouge; to force out, as the eye with the thumb. [OFr, Low L *gubia*, a kind of chisel.]

goulash [gōō´lash] *n* a beef or veal stew seasoned with paprika. [Hung *gulyás* (*hús*), herdsman, (meat).]

gourd [görd or gōōrd] *n* any trailing or climbing plant of a family (Cucurbitaceae) that includes the squash, melon, pumpkin, etc.; the fruit of one species or its dried, hollowed out shell, used as a cup, vessel, etc. or ornament. [OFr *gourde*, contr from *cougourde*—L *cucurbita*, a gourd.]

gourmand [gōōr´mȧnd, -mã] *n* one who likes good food and drink, often to excess. [Fr; cf **gormand**.]

gourmet [gōōr-mā] *n* one who likes and is an excellent judge of fine foods and drinks. [Fr, a wine-merchant's assistant.]

gout [gowt] *n* an acute inflammation of the joints, esp in the great toe.—*adj* **gout´y**. [OFr *goutte*—L *gutta*, a drop.]

govern [guv´ėrn] *vti* to exercise authority over; to rule, to control; to influence the action of; to determine; (*grammar*) to require (a word) to be in a certain case.—*adj* **governable**.—*ns* **governance**, the action, function, or power of government; **governess**, a woman employed in a private home to teach and train the children; **government**, the exercise of authority over a state, organization, etc.; a system of ruling, political administration, etc.; those who direct the affairs of a state, etc.; **Government**, the executive branch of the US federal government.—*adj* **government´al**, of government.—*ns* **governor**, the elected head of any State of the US; one appointed to govern a province, etc.; a mechanical device for automatically controlling the speed of an engine; **governor-general**, a governor of high rank, esp the representative of the British monarch in certain countries of the Commonwealth. [OFr *governer*—L *gubernāre*—Gr *ky bernaein*, to steer.]

gown [gown] *n* a loose outer garment, specifically a woman's formal dress, a nightgown, a long, flowing robe worn by clergymen, judges, scholars, etc.; a coverall worn in the operating room; the body of students and faculty of a college or university (*rivalry between town and gown*).—Also *vt*.—*n* **gownsman**, a professional or academic person. [OFr *goune*—Low L *gunna*.]

goy [goi] *n* a non-Jew, Gentile;—*pl* **goy´im**. [Heb, nation.]

grab [grab] *vt* to seize or grasp suddenly; to appropriate unscrupulously; *pr p* **grabb´ing**; *pt p* **grabbed**.—*n* a sudden grasp or clutch. [Cf Swed *grabba*, to rasp.]

grabble [grab´l] *vi* to grope; to sprawl. [Freq of **grab**.]

grace [grās] *n* beauty or charm of form, movement, or expression; good will; favor; a delay granted for payment of an obligation; a short prayer of thanks for a meal; **Grace**, a title of an archbishop, duke, or duchess.—the love and favor of God toward man; **Graces**, in Greek mythology, three sister goddesses who are the givers of charm and beauty.—*vt* to decorate; to dignify.—*adj* **grace´ful**, having beauty of form, movement, or expression.—*n* **grace´fulness**.—*adj* **grace´less**, lacking sense of what is proper; clumsy.—*n* **grace note**, a musical note added as an ornament; a small embellishment.—*adj* **gracious** [gra´shus] having or showing kindness, courtesy, etc.; compassionate; polite to supposed inferiors; marked by luxury, ease, etc. (*gracious living*).—*adv* **graciously**.—*n* **graciousness**.—**in the good graces of**, in favor with; **in the bad graces of**, in disfavor with.—[Fr *grâce*—L *grātia*, favor—*grātus*, agreeable.]

grade [grād] *n* a stage or step in a progression; a degree in a scale of quality, rank, etc.; a group of people of the same rank, merit, etc.; the degree of slope; a sloping part; any of the divisions of a school course, by years; a mark or rating in an examination, etc.—*vt* to arrange in grades; to give a grade to; to make level or evenly sloping.—*ns* **graduation**, an arranging in grades, or stages; a gradual change in stages; a step in a graded series; **grade crossing**, the place where a railroad intersects another railroad or a roadway on the same level; **grade school**, elementary school; **grade separation**, a crossing with an overpass or underpass; **grad´ient**, a slope, as of a road; the degree of slope.—*adj* **grad´ual**, taking place by degrees.—**make the grade**, to succeed. [L *gradus*, a step—*gradī*, to step, walk, go.]

graduate [grad´yū-āt] *n* one who has completed a course of study at a school, college, or university; a receptacle marked with figures for measuring contents.—*adj* holding an academic degree or diploma; of or relating to studies beyond the first or bachelor's degree.—*vt* to grant a degree or diploma upon completion of a course of study; to mark with degrees for measuring; to sort according to size, quality, etc.—*vi* to become a graduate.—*n* **graduat´ion**, a mark that graduates something; an act or process of graduating; commencement. [See **grade**.]

graffiti [gräf-fē´tē] *n pl* scribblings or drawings, often indecent, on a wall or other public surface. [It,—Gr *graphein*, to write.]

graft [graft] *n* a shoot or bud of one plant inserted into another, where it grows permanently; the transplanting of skin, bone, etc.; the getting of money or advantage dishonestly; the money or advantage so gained.—*vti* to insert (a graft); to obtain (money, etc.) by graft.—*n* **graft´er**. [OFr *graffe*—L *graphium*—Gr *graphion, grapheion*, a stylus.]

graham [grā´ėm] *adj* designating or made of finely-ground wholewheat flour. [Sylvester *Graham*, died 1851, American dietary reformer.]

grail [grāl] *n* in medieval legend the cup used by Jesus at the Last Supper. [OFr *graal* or *grael*, a flat dish—Low L *gradālis*, ultimately from Gr *krātēr*, a bowl.]

grain [grān] *n* the seed of any cereal plant, as wheat, corn, etc.; cereal plants; a tiny, solid particle, as of salt or sand; a unit of weight, 0.002083 ounce, in avoirdupois, troy, or apothecaries' system; the arrangement of fibers, layers, etc. of wood, leather, etc.; the markings or texture due to this; natural disposition.—*vt* to form into grains; to paint in imitation of the grain of wood, etc.—*vi* to become granular.—**grain of salt**, a skeptical view. [L *grānum*, seed, akin to **corn**.]

gram, gramme [gram] *n* the basic unit of weight in the metric system, equal to about 1/28 of an ounce. [Fr,—L,—Gr *gramma*, a letter, a small weight.]

-gram [-gram] something written (*telegram*); a specified number of grams (*kilogram*). [Gr *gramma*, a letter.]

Gramineae [gra-min´e-ē or grā-] *n pl* the grass family.—*adjs* **graminā´ceous, gramin´eous**, like or pertaining to grass; grassy; **graminiv´orous**, grass-eating. [L *grāmen, grāminis*, grass.]

grammar [gram´ȧr] *n* language study dealing with the forms of words and with their arrangement in sentences; a system of rules for speaking and writing a language; one's manner of speaking and writing as judged by such rules; a grammar textbook; the principles or rules of an art, science, or technique.—*ns* **grammarian**, one skilled in grammar; **grammar school**, elementary school; a secondary school emphasizing Latin and Greek in preparation for college.—*adj* **grammatical**, of, or relating to, grammar; conforming to the rules of grammar.—*adv* **grammatically**. [OFr *gramaire*; from Low L *gramma*, a letter (with the termination *-ārius*)—Gr *gramma*, a letter—*graphein*, to write.]

gram-negative [gram neg´a-tiv] *adj* (of bacteria) not holding the purple dye when stained by Gram's dye. [Hans C. J. *Gram*, Danish physician.]

gram-positive [gram pos´i-tiv] *adj* (of bacteria) holding the purple dye when stained by Gram's dye. [See **gram-negative**.]

grampus [gram´pus] *n* a marine mammal (*Grampus griseus*), as the blackfish or killer whale; the giant whip scorpion (*Mastigoproctus giganteus*) of the southern US. [16th century *graundepose*—L *crassus*, fat, *piscis*, fish, confused with Fr *grand*, big.]

granary [gran´ȧr-i] *n* a building for storing grain. [L *grānārium*—*grānum*, seed.]

grand [grand] *adj* higher in rank than others (*a grand duke*); most important; imposing in size, beauty, extent, etc.; distinguished; illustrious; overall (the grand total); (*inf*) very good; delightful.—*n* (*slang*) a thousand dollars. A combining form meaning the generation older or younger than (eg **grand´mother**, the mother of one's father or mother; **grand´child**, the child of one's son or daughter).—*ns* **grandee´**, a high-ranking Spanish or Portuguese nobleman; **grand´eur**, splendor; magnificence; nobility; dignity; **grand´father clock**, a large clock with a pendulum in a tall, upright case; **grandiflor´a**, a tall bush rose marked by the production of both single blooms and clusters of blooms on the same plant.—*adj* **grandil´oquent**, using pompous words.—*n* **grand mal**, severe epilepsy.—*adj* **grandiōse´**, having grandeur; pompous and showy.—*ns* **grand jury**, a jury that investigates accusations and indicts persons for trial if there is sufficient evidence; **grand master**, an expert player (as of chess) who has scored consistently well in international competition; **grand opera**, opera in which the whole text is set to music; **grand piano**, a large piano with a horizontal, harp-shaped case; **grand prix**, one of a series of long-distance auto races; **grand slam**, (*baseball*) a home run hit when there is a runner on each base; (*bridge*) bidding for and winning all the tricks in a deal; (*tennis*) winning of Australian, French, US and Wimbledon championships within a calendar year; the winning of all the specified tournaments on a tour; **grandstand**, the main structure for seating spectators at a sporting event. [Fr *grand*—L *grandis* great.]

grange [grānj] *n* a farm, esp a farmhouse with outbuildings attached; **Grange**, an association of farmers or a local lodge of this. [OFr *grange*, barn—Low L *grānea*—L *grānum*, grain.]

granite [gran´it] *n* a hard, igneous rock consisting chiefly of feldspar and quartz; unyielding firmness of endurance.—*adj* **granit´ic**.—**gran´olith**, an artificial stone of crushed granite and cement. [It *granito*, granite, lit grained—L *grānum*, grain.]

granivorous [gran-iv´ȯr-us] *adj* feeding on seeds or grain. [L *grānum*, grain, *vorāre*, to devour.]

granny, grannie [gran´e] *n* (*inf*) a grandmother; (*inf*) an old woman; (*inf*) any fussy person.—*pl* **grann´ies**.—*adj* of an old-fashioned style.—*ns* **granny dress**, a long loose-fitting dress usu. with high neck and long sleeves; **granny glasses**, eyeglasses with round lenses and thin wire frames; **granny knot**, a square knot wrongly tied and thus insecure. [By shortening and alteration of *grandmother*.]

granola [gran-ō´lė] *n* a breakfast cereal of rolled oats, wheat germ, sesame seeds, brown sugar or honey, nuts or dried fruit. [Trademark.]

grant [grant] *vt* to consent to; to give or transfer by legal procedure; to admit as true.—*n* the act of granting; something granted, esp a gift for a particular purpose; a transfer of property by deed; the instrument by which such transfer is made.—*ns* **grant-in-aid**, a grant of funds, as by a foundation to a scientist, artist, etc. to support a specific project; **grants´manship**, the skill of getting grants-in-aid.—**take for granted**, to consider as true, already settled, etc. [OFr *graanter, craanter, creanter*, to promise—L *crēdĕre*, to believe.]

granule [gran´ūl] *n* a small grain or particle.—*adjs* **gran´ūlar**, consisting of granules; having a grainy texture; **gran´ūlōse**, having the surface roughened with granules.—*vt* **gran´ūlāte**, to form or crystallize into grains or granules.—*vi* to collect into grains or granules; to form granulations.—*n* **granūlā´tion**, act or process or condition of granulating; one of the minute red granules of new capillaries formed on the surface of a healing wound. [L *grānulum*, dim of *grānum*, grain.]

grape [grāp] *n* a small, round, juicy berry, growing in clusters on a vine; a grapevine; a dark purplish red.—*ns* **grape´fruit**, a large, round, sour citrus fruit with a yellow rind; a small, roundheaded tree (*Citrus paradisi*) yielding this fruit; **grape hy´acinth**, a small bulbous spring-flowering herb (genus *Muscari*) with usu. blue flowers; **grape sugar**, dextrose; **grape´vine**, woody vine (genus *Vitis*) that usu. climbs by tendrils and produces grapes; an informal means of circulating information or gossip; a secret source of information.—*adj* **grāpey, grap´y**, of a wine, having the taste or aroma of fresh grapes.—**sour grapes** *see* **sour**. [OFr *grape, grappe*, a cluster of grapes—*grape*, a hook; orig Gmc.]

graph [graf] *n* a diagram representing the successive changes in the value of a variable quantity or quantities.—*adj* **graphic**, described in realistic detail; represented by a graph.—*ns* **graphite**, a soft, black form of carbon used in pencils, for lubricants, etc.; **graphology**, the study of handwriting, esp as a clue to character; **graph paper**, paper ruled for drawing graphs.—**graphic arts**, those arts that include any form of visual artistic representation, writing and printing on flat surfaces. [Gr *graphē*, a writing—*graphein*, to write.]

grapnel [grap´nėl] *n* a small anchor with several claws or arms; a grappling iron. [Dim of OFr *grapin*—*grape*, a hook; of Gmc origin.]

grapple [grap´l] *n* an instrument for hooking or holding.—*vt* to seize; to lay fast hold of; to grip.—*vi* to contend in close fight; to try to deal (with, eg a problem).—*n* **grapp´ling ī´ron**, an iron bar with hooks at one end for anchoring a boat, grappling ships to each other, or recovering sunken objects. [Cf OFr *grappil*—*grape*, a hook.]

grasp [gräsp] *vt* to grip, as with the hand; to seize; to comprehend.—*vi* try to seize; (*with* **at**) to accept eagerly.—*n* grip; power of seizing; mental power of comprehension—*adj* **grasp´ing**, seizing; avaricious. [ME *graspen, grapsen*, from the root of *grāpian*, to grope.]

grass [gras] *n* any of a large family (Gramineae) of plants with jointed stems and long narrow leaves including cereals, bamboo, etc.; such plants grown as lawn; pasture; (*slang*) marijuana.—*vt* to feed (livestock) on grass; to cover with grass, esp to seed to grass.—*vi* to produce grass.—*ns* **grass´hopper**, any of a group of plant-eating, winged insects (suborder Saltatoria) with powerful hind legs for jumping; **grass roots**, (*inf*) the common people; (*inf*) the basic source or support, as of a movement; **grass widow**, (*inf*) a wife whose husband is absent. [OE *gærs, græs*; ON, Ger, Du, *gras*; prob allied to **green** and **grow**.]

grate[1] [grāt] *n* a framework of bars set in a window, door, etc.; a frame of metal bars for holding fuel in a fireplace; a fireplace.—*vt* to furnish with a grate.—*n* **grating**, a framework of bars. [Low L *grāta*, a grate—L *crātis*, a hurdle; cf **crate**.]

grate[2] [grāt] *vt* to grind into particles by scraping; to rub against (an object) or grind (the teeth) together with a harsh sound; to irritate.—*vi* to rub or rasp noisily; to cause irritation. [OFr *grater*, through Low L, from OHG *chrazzōn* (Ger *kratzen*), to scratch, akin to Swed *kratta*.]

grateful [grāt´fŏŏl, -fl] *adj* appreciative; welcome.—*adv* **grate´fully**.—*n* **grate´fulness**.—*vt* **grăt´ify**, to please; to indulge;—*pt p* **grat´ified**.—*adj* **grat´ifying**.—*n* **gratificā´tion**, a pleasing or indulging; that which gratifies; delight. [OFr *grat*—L *grātus*, pleasing, thankful, and suffx *-ful*]

gratis [grā´tis, grä´-] *adj, adv* free of charge. [L *grātis*, contr of *grātīs*, abl pl of *grātia*, favor—*grātusa*, pleasing.]

gratitude [grat´i-tūd] *n* thankful appreciation for favors received. [Fr,—Low L *grātitūdō*—L *grātus*, pleasing.]

gratuity [gra-tū´i-ti] *n* a gift as of money, esp for a service, a tip.—*adj* **gratū´itous**, given free of charge; uncalled-for.—*adv* **gratū´itously**. [Fr,—Low L *grātuitās, -ātis*—L *grātus*, pleasing.]

gravamen [grav-ā´men] *n* the essence or most important part of a complaint or accusation. [L *gravāmen*—*gravis*, heavy.]

grave[1] [grāv] *vt* (*obs*) to dig; (*obs*) to carve, sculpture; to engrave.—*vi* to engrave;—*pt p* **graved** or **grav´en**.—*n* a pit or hole dug out, esp one to bury the dead in; any place of burial; (*fig*) death, destruction.—*ns* **grav´er**, an engraver's tool, eg a burin; **grave´-stone**, a stone placed as a memorial at a grave; **grave´yard**, a burial-ground.—**with one foot in the grave**, on the brink of death. [OE *grafan*, to dig, *græf*, a cave, grave, trench; Du *graven*, Ger *graben*.]

grave[2] [grāv] *vt* to clean (by burning, etc.) and smear with tar (a wooden ship's bottom).—*n* **graving dock**, a dry-dock. [Perh OFr *grave*, beach.]

grave[3] *adj* of importance, weighty; threatening, serious; not gay or showy, sober, solemn; low in pitch.—*adv* **grave´ly**.—*n* **grave´ness**. [Fr,—L *gravis*.]

gravel [grav´l] *n* an assemblage of small rounded stones; small collections of gravelly matter in the kidneys or bladder.—*vt* to cover with gravel; to puzzle, nonplus;—*pr p* **grav´elling**; *pt p* **grav´elled**.—*adj* **grav´elly**. [OFr *gravele*; prob Celt.]

gravity [grav´i-ti] *n* importance, esp seriousness; weight; the attraction of bodies toward the center of the earth, the moon, or a planet; specific gravity.—*vi* **grav´itate**, to move or tend to move under the force of gravitation; to move toward something.—*ns* **gravim´eter**, a device for determing specific gravity; a device for measuring variations in a gravitational field; **gravita´tion**, a natural force of attraction that tends to draw bodies together. [L *gravitās, -ātis*—*gravis*, heavy.]

gravy [grāv´i] *n* the juice given off by meat in cooking; the sauce made from this juice; (*slang*) money easily obtained.—*n* **gravy train**, (*inf*) a much exploited source of easy money. [Perh *gravé*, a copyist's mistake for OFr *grané*—*grain*, a cookery ingredient.]

gray [grā] *n* any of a series of neutral colors ranging between black and white; something (as an animal, garment, cloth, or spot) of a gray color; a soldier in the Confederate army during the American Civil War; (*slang*) a member of the Caucasian race.—*adj* of this color; having hair this color; darkish; dreary; designating a vague, intermediate area; (*slang*) of or relating to the Caucasian race.—*vti* to make or become gray.—*ns* **gray´beard**, an old man; **gray eminence**, a person who exercises power behind the scenes; **gray´ling**, any of several freshwater salmoid fishes (genus *Thymallus*) valued as food and sport fishes; **gray matter**, the brownish grey neural tissue of the brain and spinal cord; (*inf*) intelligence. [OE *graeg*; cf Ger *grau*.]

graze[1] [grāz] *vt* to eat or feed on (growing grass or pasture); to put to feed on growing grass; (of land) to supply food for (animals).—*vi* to eat grass; to supply grass.—*ns* **grazier** [grā´-zi-ėr, -zyėr, zhyėr], one who grazes or pastures cattle and rears them for the market; **graz´ing**, the act of feeding on grass; the feeding or raising of cattle; pasture. [OE *grasian*—*græs*, grass.]

graze[2] [grāz] *vt* to pass lightly along the surface of; to scrape.—*n* a passing touch; scratch, abrasion. [Ety uncertain.]

grease [grēs] *n* melted animal fat; any thick, oily substance or lubricant.—*vt* to smear with grease, to lubricate.—*adj* **greas´y**, soiled with grease; oily.—*ns* **greas´iness; grease-paint**, a tallowy composition used by actors in making up; theater makeup; **greasy spoon**, a small cheap usu. insanitary restaurant. [OFr *gresse*, fatness, *gras*, fat—L *crassus*.]

great [grāt] *adj* of much more than ordinary size, extent, etc.; much above the average; intense (*great pain*); eminent (*a great writer*); most important; more distant in a family relationship by one generation (*great-grandparent*); (*inf*) skillful (*often with* **at**); (*inf*) excellent; fine.—*n* a distinguished person.—*ns* **great circle**, a circle on the surface of the earth of which an arc connecting two points on it gives the shortest path on the earth's surface; **Great Dane**, any of a breed of tall massive powerful smooth-coated dogs; **great divide**, a watershed between major drainage systems, a significant point of division, esp death; **great horned owl**, a large N American owl (*Bubo virginianus*) with conspicuous ear tufts; **Great Power**, a nation that figures decisively in international affairs. [OE *grēat*; Du *groot*, Ger *gross*.]

greave [grēv] *n* armor for the leg below the knee. [OFr *grève*, shin, greave.]

grebe [grēb] *n* any of a family (Podicipitidae or Podicipedidae) of swimming and diving birds closely allied to the loon. [Fr *grèbe*.]

Grecian [grēsh´(y)ȧn] Greek.—*n* a Greek; one well versed in the Greek language and literature. [L *Graecia*, Greece—Gr *Graikos*, Greek.]

greedy [grēd´i] *adj* wanting more than one needs or deserves; having too strong a desire for food and drink.—*n* **greed**, excessive desire, esp for wealth.—*adv* **greed´ily**—*n* **greed´iness**. [OE *grǣdig*; Du *gretig*.]

Greek [grēk] *adj* of Greece, its people, or its language.—*n* a native or citizen of Greece; the language of Greece which constitutes a branch of Indo-European; something unintelligible (*chemical formulas are greek to me*); a member of a Greek-letter fraternity or sorority.—*ns* **Greek Catholic**, a member of an Eastern church; a member of an Eastern rite of the RC Church; **Greek cross**, a cross having arms of equal length; **Greek Orthodox Church**, the national church of Greece, recognizing the Patriarch of Constantinople as its head. [OE *Grēcas, Crēcas*, Greeks, or L *Graecus*—Gr *Graikos*, Greek.]

green [grēn] *adj* of the color green; covered with plants or foliage; having a sickly appearance; unripe; inexperienced, naive; not fully processed or treated (*green liquor, green hides*); (*inf*) jealous.—*n* a color between blue and yellow in the spectrum; the color of growing grass; something of a green color; (*pl*) green leafy vegetables, as spinach, etc.; a grassy plot, esp the end of a golf fairway.—*adj* **green´ish**.—*ns* **green´ness; green´back**, US paper money; **green bean**, the edible, immature green pod of the kidney bean; **green´belt**, a belt of parkways or farms surrounding a community designed to prevent urban sprawl; **green´ery**, green vegetation; **green´horn**, an inexperienced person; a person easily duped; **green´house**, a heated building, mainly of glass, for growing plants; **green manure**, a crop, as of clover, plowed under to fertilize the soil; **green pepper**, the immature fruit of the sweet red pepper; **green power**, money, as the source of power; **green thumb**, a knack for growing plants. [OE *grēne*; Ger *grün*, Du *groen*, green, ON *grœnn*.]

greengage [grēn´gāj´] *n* a greenish yellow, very sweet variety of plum. [Said to be named from Sir W *Gage*, Eng botanist, died 1820.]

Greenwich time [grin´ij, gren´ich] the time of the meridian of Greenwich used as the basis of worldwide standard time. [*Greenwich*, England.]

greet [grēt] *vt* to address with friendliness; to meet (a person, event, etc.) in a specified way; to present itself to.—*pr p* **greet´ing**; *pt p* **greet´ed**.—*n* **greet´ing**, a salutation at meeting; an expression of good wishes; (*pl*) a message of regards. [OE *grētan*, to greet, to meet; Du *groeten*, Ger *grüssen*, to salute.]

gregarious [gre-gā´ri-us] *adj* associating in flocks and herds; fond of company.—*adv* **gregā´riously**.—*n* **gregā´riousness**. [L *gregārius*—*grex*, *gregis*, a flock.]

Gregorian calendar [gre-gō´, -gö´, ri-an] the calendar as reformed by Pope Gregory XIII (1582); adopted in England and in the American colonies in 1752 in place of the Julian calendar.

gremlin [grem´lin] *n* an imaginary creature blamed for disruption of any procedure or of malfunction of equipment esp in an aircraft.

grenade [gre-nād´] *n* a small missile thrown by the hand or projected (as by a rifle or special launcher). [Fr,—Sp *granada*, pomegranate—L *grānātus*, full of seeds (*grāna*).]

grew [grōō] *pt* of **grow**.

greyhound [grā´hownd] *n* any of a breed of tall and slender dogs with great speed and keen sight. [OE *grīghund*; cf ON *greyhundr*—ON *grey*, a dog, *hundr*, a hound.]

grid [grid] *n* a gridiron, a grating; a metallic plate in a storage battery; an electrode (as of wire mesh) for controlling the flow of electrons in an electron tube.

griddle [grid´l] *n* a flat iron plate for cooking pancakes. [Anglo-Fr *gridil*, from a dim of L *crātis*, a hurdle.]

gridiron [grid´ī-ėrn] *n* a frame of iron bars for broiling; anything resembling this, as a football field. [ME *gredire*, a griddle. From the same source as **griddle**; but the term *-ire* became confused with ME *ire*, iron.]

grief [grēf] *n* deep sorrow caused as by a loss; distress.—*adj* **grief´-strick´en**, bowed down with sorrow.—**come to grief**, meet with reverse, mishap, disaster. [OFr,—L *gravis*, heavy.]

grieve [grēv] *vti* to feel or cause to feel grief.—*n* **griev´ance**, a circumstance thought to be unjust and ground for complaint; a complaint against a real or imagined wrong, ground of complaint.—*adj* **griev´ous**, causing grief; full of grief; deplorable; severe.—*adv* **griev´ously**.—**griev´ousness**. [OFr *grever*—L *gravāre*—*gravis*, heavy.]

griffin, griffon, gryphon [grif´in, -ȯn] *n* mythical animal, with lion's body and eagle's beak and wings. [Fr—*griffon*—L *grȳphus*—Gr *gryps*, a bird, probably the great bearded vulture—*grȳpos*, hook-nosed.]

griffon [grif´ȯn] *vt* either of two breeds of dog; the Brussels griffon or the wirehaired pointing griffon. [Prob from **griffin**.]

grill [gril] *n* to broil; to question relentlessly.—*n* a gridiron; grilled food; a restaurant specializing in grilled food. [Fr *griller*—*gril*, a gridiron—from a dim of L *crātis*, a hurdle.]

grille [gril] *n* an open grating forming a screen. [Fr. same root as **grill**.]

grilse [grils] *n* a young salmon on its first return from the sea. [Origin unknown.]

grim [grim] *adj* hard and unyielding, stern; appearing harsh, forbidding; repellent, ghastly in character.—*adv* **grim´ly**.—*n* **grim´ness**. [OE *grim(m)*; Ger *grimmig*—*grimm*, fury, Du *grimmig*, ON *grimmr*.]

grimace [gri-mās´] *n* a distortion of the face, in jest etc.; a smirk.—Also *vi*. [Fr.]

grimalkin [gri-mal´kin or -mawl´kin] *n* an old female cat. [**grey** + *malkin*, a dim of Maud, Matilda.]

grime [grīm] *n* sooty; dirt, rubbed into a surface, as of the skin.—*vt* to soil deeply.—*adj* **grim´y**, foul, dirty. [Cf Flem *grijm*.]

Grimm's law the law formulated by Jacob Grimm in 1822, stating the regularity of consonantal sound shifts in languages of the Teutonic family.

grin [grin] *vi* to smile broadly as in amusement; to show the teeth in pain, scorn, etc.—*pr p* **grinn´ing**; *pt* and *pt p* **grinned**.—*n* act of grinning. [OE *grennian*; ON *grenja*, Ger *greinen*, Du *grijnen*, to grumble, Scot *girn*.]

grind [grīnd] *vt* to reduce to powder by crushing; to wear down, sharpen, smooth, or roughen by friction; to rub (the teeth) together gratingly; to oppress; to work by a crank.—*vi* to be moved or rubbed together; to jar or grate; to drudge at any tedious task; to study hard; to rotate the hips in an erotic manner.—*pr p* **grīnd´ing**; *pt, pt p* **ground** [grownd].—*n* the act or sound of grinding; long, difficult work or study; (*inf*) a student who studies hard.—*ns* **grind´er**, he who, or that which, grinds; (*pl*) (*inf*) the teeth; a hero sandwich; **grind´stone**, a circular revolving stone for grinding or sharpening tools. [OE *grindan*.]

gringo [gring´ō] *n* (*offensive*) among Hispanics, a foreigner, esp N Americans.—*pl* **gring´os**. [Sp.]

grip [grip] *n* a secure grasp; the manner of holding a bat, club, racket, etc.; the power of grasping firmly; mental grasp; mastery; a handle; a small traveling bag.—*vt* to take firmly and hold fast; to get and hold the attention of.—**come to grips**, to struggle (*with* **with**). [OE *gripe*, grasp, *gripa*, handful, *grippan*, to seize.]

gripe [grīp] *vt* to cause sharp pain in the bowels of; (*slang*) to annoy.—*vi* (*slang*) to complain.—*n* (*pl*) sharp pains in the bowels; (*slang*) a complaint.—*n* **griper**. [OE *gripan* (*grāp*, *gripen*); ON *grīpa*, Ger *greifen*, Du *grijpen*.]

grippe [grēp] *n* earlier term for influenza. [Fr,—*gripper*, to seize.]

grisly [griz´li] *adj* terrifying; ghastly; arousing horror, [OE *grislic*.]

grist [grist] *n* grain that is to be or has been ground; matter forming the basis of a story or analysis.—**grist for one's mill**, something turned to advantage. [OE *grist*; same root as **grind**.]

gristle [gris´l] *n* cartilage.—*adj* **grist´ly**.—*n* **grist´liness**. [OE *gristle*.]

grit [grit] *n* rough particles, as of sand; a coarse sandstone; firmness of character; stubborn courage.—*adj* **gritt´y**.—*n* **gritt´iness**. [OE *grēot*; Ger *griess*, gravel.]

grizzle [griz´l] *n* a gray or roan animal.—*adjs* **grizz´led**, gray or streaked with gray; having gray hair; **grizz'ly**, grayish; grizzled.—*n* **grizzly** (**bear**), a very large powerful brown bear (*Ursus horribilis*) of western N America. [ME *grisel*—Fr *gris*, grey.]

groan [grōn] *vi* to utter a deep sound as in distress or disapprobation; to make a harsh sound (as of creaking) under sudden or prolonged strain.—Also *n*.—*vt* to utter or express with groaning. [OE *grānian*.]

groat[1] [grōt] *n* an old English silver coin. [Old Low Ger *grote*, or Du *groot*, lit great, ie thick.]

groat[2] [grōt] *n* hulled grain broken into fragments larger than grits; the grain of oats deprived of the husks. [OE *grotan* (pl).]

grocer [grōs´ėr] *n* a dealer in food and household supplies.—*n* **groc´ery** (gen *pl* **groc´eries**), articles sold by grocers. [Earlier *grosser*, wholesale dealer; OFr *grossier*—Low L *grossārius*—*grossus*. *See* **gross**.]

grog [grog] *n* originally, rum diluted with water, liquor (as rum) cut with water, often spiced and served hot.—*adj* **grogg´y**, partially intoxicated; dizzy; dazed. [From 'Old Grog', the nickname (apparently from his grogram cloak) of Admiral Vernon, who in 1740 ordered that rum (until 1970 officially issued to sailors) should be mixed with water.]

grogram [grog´ràm] *n* a kind of coarse cloth of silk and mohair. [OFr *gros grain*, coarse grain.]

groin [groin] *n* the fold between the belly and the thigh; (*archit.* the angular curve formed by the crossing of two vaults.—*n* **groin´ing**. [Early forms *grind, grine*, perh—OE *grynde*, abyss.]

groom [grŏŏm, grōōm] *n* one who has the charge of horses; a bridegroom.—*vt* to tend, esp a horse; to make tidy and neat; to train (a person) for a particular purpose. [Origin obscure; influenced by OE *guma* (as in bride-*groom*), a man.]

groove [grōōv] *n* a long, narrow furrow, cut with a tool; any channel or rut; a settled routine.—*vt* to make a groove in.—*vi* to react with empathy.—*adj* **groov´y**, (*slang*) very pleasing or attractive. [Prob Du *groef, groeve*, a furrow; cog with ON *grōf*, Eng **grave**.]

grope [grōp] *vi* to search (for something) as if blind or in the dark.—*vt* to search by feeling (*to grope one's way*).—*adv* **grop´ingly**. [OE *grāpian*; allied to **grab, gripe**.]

grosbeak [grōs´bēk] *n* any finchlike bird of Europe or America with a large stout conical bill. [Fr *grosbec*—*gros*, thick, *bec*, beak.]

grosgrain [grō´grān] *n* a heavy ribbed silk or rayon fabric.—*n* **grosgrain ribbon**, a sturdy ribbon used to trim or reinforce clothing, etc. [Fr.]

gross [grōs] *adj* fat and coarse-looking; flagrant, dense, thick; lacking in refinement; earthy; obscene; total, with no deductions; (*slang*) of anything objectionable.—*n* an overall total; twelve dozen.—*pl* **gross**.—**gross national product**, the total value of a nation's annual output of goods and services; **in gross**, in bulk, wholesale. [Fr *gros*—L *grossus*, thick.]

grotesque [grō-tesk´] *adj* distorted or fantastic in appearance, shape, etc.; ridiculous; absurdly incongruous.—Also *n*.—*adv* **grotesque´ly**.—*n* **grotesque´ness**. [Fr *grotesque*—It *grottesca*—*grotta*, a grotto.]

grotto [grot´ō] *n* a cave; an imitation cave, usu. fantastic.—*pl* **grott´oes**. [It *grotta* (Fr *grotte*)—L *crypta*—Gr *kryptē*, a crypt, vault.]

grouch [growch] *vi* to grumble or complain sullenly.—*n* one who grouches; a sulky mood. [ME *grucchen*.]

ground [grownd] *pt, pt p* of **grind**.

ground [grownd] *n* the solid surface of the earth; soil; a basis for belief, action, or argument; the background, as in a design; the connection of an electrical conductor with the earth; (*pl*) the area about and relating to a building; a tract of land; sediment.—*vt* to set on the ground; to cause to run aground; to base, found, or establish; to instruct in the first principles of; to keep (an aircraft or pilot) from flying; to connect (a conductor of electricity) with the ground.—*vi* to run ashore; (*baseball*) to be put out on a grounder.—*ns* **ground cover**, low, dense-growing plants used for covering bare ground; **ground crew**, a group of workers who repair and maintain aircraft; **grounder**, (*baseball*) a batted ball that travels along the ground; **ground floor**, the floor of a building more or less level with the ground, the first floor; **groundhog**, a woodchuck; **grounding**, basic general knowledge of a subject; **ground ivy**, a trailing mint (*Nepeta hederacea*) with rounded leaves and blue-purple flowers.—*adj* **groundless**, without reason.—*ns* **ground rule**, (*baseball*) a rule adapted to playing conditions in a specific ballpark; any basic rule; **groundswell**, a large rolling wave; a wave of popular feeling; **groundwork**, foundation, basis.—**gain ground**, to gain in achievement, etc.; **give ground**, to yield; **hold one's ground**, to remain firm; **in on the ground floor**, in at the start of (of a business, etc.); **lose ground**, lose in popularity, etc.; **run into the ground**, (*slang*) to overdo. [OE *grund*; cog with Ger *grund*, ON *grunnr*.]

groundsel [grown(d)´sėl] *n* any of a large genus (*Senecio*) of composite plants with usu. yellow flower heads. [OE *gundæswelgiæ*, appar from *gund*, pus, *swelgan*, to swallow, from its use in poultices, influenced by *grund*, ground.]

group [grōōp] *n* a number of persons or things considered as a collective unit; a small musical band of players or singers; two or more figures forming one artistic design.—*vti* to form into a group or groups.—*n* **group therapy**, a form of treatment for a group of patients with similar emotional problems, as by mutual criticism. [Fr *groupe*—It *groppo*, a bunch, knot; from Gmc.]

grouse[1] [grows] *n* any of numerous birds (family Tetraonidae) that have a plump body, strong feathered legs and that include many important game birds, esp the ruffed grouse, spruce grouse, and sharp-tailed grouse.—*pl* **grouse, grouses**. [Origin unknown.]

grouse[2] [grows] *vi* (*inf*) to complain. [OFr *groucher, grocher, gruchier*, to grumble.]

grout [growt] *n* a thin mortar used as between tiles.—*vt* to fill in with grout. [OE *grūt*, coarse meal; or perh in part Fr *grouter*, to finish with grout.]

grove [grōv] *n* a small wood, generally without undergrowth. [OE *grāf*.]

grovel [gruv´el] *vi* to lie and crawl in a prostrate position, esp in token of subservience; to behave abjectly.—*n* **groveler**. [ME *groveling, grofling*, prone—ON *grūfa*.]

grow [grō] *vi* to come into being; to be produced naturally; to develop, as a living thing; to increase in size, quantity, etc.; to become (*to grow weary*).—*vt* to cause or let grow; to raise, to cultivate.—*pt* **grew** [grōō]; *pt p* **grown** [grōn].—*ns* **grow´er; growth**, a growing; gradual increase; development; that which has grown; a **grown-up**, adult—Also *adj*.;—**grow on**, to have an increasing affection; **grow up**, to mature. [OE *grōwan*; ON *grōa*.]

growl [growl] *vi* to utter a rumbling, menacing sound such as an angry dog makes.—*vt* to express by growling.—Also *n*.—*n* **growl´er**, one that growls; a can or pitcher for beer bought by the measure; a small iceberg; an electromagnetic device used for magnetizing, demagnetizing, and finding short-circuited coils. [Cf Du *grollen*, to grumble; allied to Gr *gryllizein*, to grunt.]

groyne [groin] *n* a breakwater, to check erosion and sand-drifting. [Prob **groin**.]

grub [grub] *vi* to dig in the ground; to work hard.—*vt* to clear (ground) of roots; to uproot.—*pr p* **grubb´ing**; *pt p* **grubbed**.—*n* the wormlike larva of a beetle; a drudge; (*slang*) food.—*adj* **grubb´y**, dirty.—*ns* **grubb´er; grubb´iness**. [ME *grobe*.]

grudge [gruj] *vt* to give or allow unwillingly; to be unwilling (to).—*n* a feeling of resentment (*with* **against**) due to some specific cause.—*adj* **grudg´ing**, unwilling, reluctant.—*adv* **grudg´ingly**. [OFr *groucher, grocher, gruchier*, to grumble.]

gruel [grōō´ėl] *n* a thin broth of meal cooked in water or milk.—*adj* **gru´eling, grue´lling**, exhausting. [OFr *gruel*, groats.—Low L *grūtellum*, of Gmc origin.]

gruesome [grōō´sùm] *adj* causing horror or loathing. [Cf Du *gruwzaam*, Ger *grausam*.]

gruff [gruf] *adj* rough or surly; hoarse.—*adv* **gruff´ly**.—*n* **gruff´ness**. [Du *grof*; cog with Swed *grof*, Ger *grob*, coarse.]

grumble [grum´bl] *vi* to growl; to murmur with discontent; to rumble.—*n* the act of or an instance of grumbling.—*n* **grum´bler**.—*adj* **grum´bly**, inclined to grumble. [Cf Du *grommelen*, freq of *grommen*, to mutter; Ger *grummeln*.]

grumpy [grum´pi] *adj* surly.—*adv* **grum´pily**.—*n* **grum´piness**. [Obs *grump*, a snub, sulkiness.]

grunt [grunt] *vi* to make a sound like a hog.—Also *n*.—*n* **grunt´er**. [OE *grunnettan*, freq of *grunian*.]

Gruyère [grōō-yâr] *n* a cooked, hard, pale yellow cheese, honeycombed with holes, made from whole cow's milk. [Gruyère, Switzerland.]

guanaco [gwä-nä´ko] *n* a S American mammal (*Lama guanico*) related to the camel but lacking a hump. [American Sp.]

guano [gwä´no] *n* manure of sea birds used as fertilizer; a similar substance (as bat excrement and cannery waste) used as fertilizer. [Sp *guano*, or *huano*, from Peruvian *huanu*, dung.]

guarantee [gar-àn-tē´] *n* a pledge or security for another's debt or obligation; a pledge to replace something if it is not as represented; assurance that something will be done as specified; a guarantor.—*vt* to give a guarantee for; to promise.—*ns* **guar´antor**, one who gives a guaranty or guarantee; **guar´anty**, an undertaking to answer for another's failure to pay a debt or perform a duty; an agreement that secures the existence or maintenance of something; guarantor. [Anglo-Fr *garantie*—*garant*, warrant. Cf **warrant**.]

guard [gärd] *vt* to watch over and protect; to defend; to keep from escape or trouble.—*vi* to keep watch (against); to act as a guard.—*n* defense; protection; a posture of readiness for defense; any device to protect against injury or loss; a person or group that guards; a defensive basketball player or offensive football lineman.—*adj* **guard´ed**, kept safe; cautious.—*ns* **guard´house**, (*military*) a building used by a guard when not walking a post; a jail for temporary confinement; **guard´ian**, custodian; a person legally in charge of a minor or someone incapable of taking care of his own affairs. —*adj* protecting.—*n* **guard´rail**, a protective railing, as along a highway.—**on one's guard**, vigilant. [OFr *garder*—OHG *warten*; OE *weardian*; compare **ward**.]

guava [gwä´vä] *n* a tropical American shrubby tree (*Psidium guajava*) widely cultivated for its sweet acid yellow fruit; its fruit. [Sp *guayaba*, guava fruit; of S America origin.]

gubernatorial [gū-bėr-nǎ-tō´ri-àl] *adj* of a governor or the office of a governor. [L *gubernātor*, steersman, governor.]

guelder rose [gel´dėr rōz] *n* a cultivated variety of the cranberry bush with large globose heads of sterile flowers. [From *Geldern* (Prussia) or from *Gelderland* (Holland).]

guerdon [gûr´dòn] *n* a reward or recompense. [OFr *guerdon, gueredon*—Low L *widerdonum*.]

guernsey [gûrn´zi] *n* any of a breed of dairy cattle usu. fawn-coloured with white markings. [From *Guernsey* in the Channel Islands.]

guerrilla, guerilla [gėr-il´a] *n* a member of a small force of irregular soldiers, making surprise raids.—Also *adj*. [Sp *guerrilla*, dim of *guerra*, war—OHG *werra*, cf **war**; Fr *guerre*.]

guess [ges] *vt* to judge upon inadequate knowledge or none at all; to judge correctly by doing this; to think or suppose.—Also *vi, n*.—*n* **guess´work**, process or result of guessing. [ME *gessen*; cog with mod Icel *giska, gizka*, for *gitska*—*geta*, to get, think.]

guest [gest] *n* a person entertained at the home, club, etc. of another; any paying customer of a hotel, restaurant, etc.—*adj* for guests; performing by special invitation (*guest artist*).—*vt* to receive as a guest.—*vi* to appear as a guest. [OE (Anglian) *gest* (WS *giest*); allied to L *hostis*, stranger, enemy.]
guff [guf] *n* empty talk, humbug. [Perh imit.]
guffaw [guf-ö´] *vi* to laugh loudly.—*n* a loud laugh. [From the sound.]
guide [gīd] *vt* to point out the way for; to lead; to direct the course of; to control.—*n* one who leads or directs another in his way or course; one who exhibits and explains points of interest; something that provides a person with guiding information; a device for controlling the motion of something; a book of basic instruction.—*ns* **guid´ance**, leadership; advice or counsel; **guide´book**, a book containing directions and information for tourists; **guided missile**, a military missile whose course is controlled by radar, etc.; **guide´line**, an indication or outline of policy or conduct; **guide word**, either of the terms at the head of a page of an alphabetical reference work that indicate the first and last words on that page. [OFr *guider*; prob from a Gmc root, as in OE *witan*, to know, etc.]
guild [gild] *n* an association for mutual aid and the promotion of common interests. [OE *gield*, influenced by ON *gildi*.]
guilder [gild´ėr] *n* a unit of money in the Netherlands. [Du *gulden*.]
guile [gīl] *n* cunning, deceit.—*adj* **guile´ful**, crafty, deceitful.—*n* **guile´fulness**.—*adj* **guile´less**, without deceit; artless.—*adv* **guile´lessly**.—*n* **guile´lessness**. [Norm Fr *guile*, deceit, prob Gmc; cf **wile**.]
guillemot [gil´i-mot] *n* any of several narrow-billed auks of northern seas constituting two genera (*Uria* and *Cepphus*.) [Fr, dim of *Guillaume*, William, perh suggested by Breton *gwelan*, gull.]
guillotine [gil´o-tēn, -tēn´] *n* an instrument for beheading by descent of a heavy oblique blade; a machine for cutting paper; a rule for limiting time for discussion in a legislature. Also *vt*. [From *Guilloton* (1738–1814), French physician.]
guilt [gilt] *n* the fact of having done a wrong or committed an offense; a feeling of self-reproach from believing one has done a wrong.—*adj* **guilt´y**, having guilt; legally judged an offender; of or showing guilt.—*adv* **guilt´ily**.—*n* **guilt´iness**.—*adj* **guilt´less**, innocent.—*adv* **guilt´lessly**.—*n* **guilt´lessness**. [Orig a payment or fine for an offence; OE *gylt*.]
guinea [gin´i] *n* a former English gold coin equal to 21 shillings.—*ns* **guin´ea fowl**, an African bird (*Numida meleagris*) of the pheasant family, dark grey with white spots; **guin´ea pig**, a small S American rodent (*Cavia cobaya*) often kept as a pet and widely used in biological research; any subject used in an experiment.
guise [gīz] *n* external appearance; assumed appearance (*in the guise of*). [OFr *guise*; cf OHG *wisa*, a way, guise, OE *wise*, way.]
guitar [gi-tär´] *n* a musical instrument with usu. six strings, a long, fretted neck, and a flat body. [Fr *guitare*—L *cithara*. See **cithara**.]
gulag, Gulag [gōō´läg] *n* a forced labor camp esp for political prisoners. [From Russian acronym GULag.]
gulch [gulch, gulsh] *n* a deep, narrow ravine. [Origin doubtful.]
gulf [gulf] *n* a large area of ocean reaching into land; a wide, deep chasm; a vast separation.—**Gulf Stream**, a warm ocean current flowing from the Gulf of Mexico northward toward Europe; **gulfweed**, sargasso. [OFr *golfe*—Gr *kolpos*, bosom.]
gull [gul] *n* any of numerous long-winged web-footed aquatic birds (family Laridae). [Perh W *gwylan*, to weep, wail.]
gull [gul] *n* a dupe; an easily tricked person.—*vt* to cheat, trick.—*adj* **gull´ible**, easily deceived.—*n* **gullibil´ity**. [Origin uncertain.]
gullet [gul´et] *n* the esophagus; the throat. [OFr *goulet*, dim of *goule*—L *gula*, the throat.]
gully [gul´i] *n* a channel worn by running water after rain.—*vt* to wear a gully or channel in.—*vi* to undergo erosion. [Prob **gullet**.]
gulp [gulp] *vt* to swallow hastily or greedily; to choke back as if swallowing.—*n* a gulping or swallowing. [Cf Du *gulpen, gulp*.]
gum[1] [gum] *n* the firm flesh that surrounds the teeth.—*n* **gum´boil**, an abscess on the gum. [OE *gōma*, palate; ON *gōmr*.]
gum[2] [gum] *n* a sticky substance found in certain trees and plants; an adhesive; chewing gum.—*vt* to coat or unite with gum.—*vi* to become sticky or clogged.—*adj* **gum´my**.—*ns* **gum arabic**, a gum from certain acacia trees, used in medicine, candy, etc.; **gum´drop**, a small, firm candy made of sweetened gelatin, etc.; **gum´shoe**, a detective.—*vi* to engage in detective work.—*n* **gum tree**, a tree (as a sour gum or sapodilla) that yields gum; the eucalyptus. [OFr *gomme*—L *gummi*—Gr *kommi*; prob of Egyptian origin.]
gumbo [gum´bō] *n* a rich soup thickened with okra. [American French *gombo*, of Bantu origin.]
gumption [gum(p)´sh(ȯ)n] *n* shrewd practical commonsense; initiative. [Perh conn with ON *gaumr*, heed.]
gun [gun] *n* a weapon with a metal tube from which a projectile is discharged by the force of an explosive; any similar device not discharged by an explosive (*an air gun*); the shooting of a gun as a signal or salute; anything like a gun; a throttle.—*vi* to shoot or hunt with a gun.—*vt* (*inf*) to shoot (a person); (*slang*) to advance the throttle of an engine.—*ns* **gun´boat**, a small armed ship; **gun´fight**, a fight between persons using pistols or revolvers; **gun´man**, an armed gangster; a hired killer; **gun´metal**, bronze with a dark tarnish; its dark-gray color; **gunn´er**, a soldier, etc. who helps fire artillery; a naval warrant officer in charge of a ship's guns; **gun´powder**, an explosive powder used in guns, for blasting, etc.; **gun´shy**, afraid of a loud noise; markedly distrustful.—**-gun for**, (*slang*) to try to get; **jump the gun**, (*slang*) to begin before the proper time; **stick to one's guns**, to stand fast; **under the gun**, (*inf*) in a tense situation, often involving a deadline. [ME *gonne*, poss from the woman's name *Gunhild*.]
gung-ho [gung-hō´] *adj* enthusiastic.—Also *n*. [Chin.]
gunny [gun´i] *n* a strong coarse fabric of jute or hemp esp for bagging. [Hindustani *gōn, gōnī*, sacking.]
Gunter's chain [gun´tėr] *n* a chain 66 feet long, that is the unit of length for surveys of US public lands. [Edmund *Gunter*, astronomer (1581–1626).]
gunwale [gun´l] *n* the upper edge of a ship's or boat's side. Also **gunnel**.
gurgle [gûr´gl] *vi* to make a bubbling sound. [Cf It *gorgogliare*.]
gurnard [gûr´nȧrd] a sea robin. [OFr *gornard*, related to Fr *grogner*, to grunt—L *grunnīre*, to grunt; from the sound they emit when taken.]
guru [gōō´rōō] *n* a spiritual teacher; a venerable person. [Hind *gurū*—Sans *guru*, venerable.]
gush [gush] *vi* to flow out plentifully; to have a sudden flow; to talk or write effusively.—*vt* to cause to gush.—*n* a gushing.—*n* **gush´er**, one who gushes; an oil well from which oil spouts forth.—*adj* **gush´ing**. [ME *gosche, gusche*.]
gusset [gus´et] *n* a triangular piece inserted in a garment to strengthen or enlarge some part of it. [OFr *gousset*—*gousse*, a pod, husk.]
gust[1] [gust] *n* a sudden brief rush of wind; a sudden outburst.—*vi* to blow in gusts. [ON *gustr*, blast.]
gust[2] [gust] *n* inclination; keen delight.—*n* **gustā´tion**, the act of tasting; the sense of taste.—*adj* **gust´ătory**, of or pertaining to the sense of taste.—*n* **gust´o**, taste; zest—*pl* **gustoes** [L *gustus*, taste; cf Gr *geuein*, to cause to taste.]
gut [gut] *n* (*pl*) the bowels or the stomach; the intestine; tough cord made from animal intestines; (*pl*) (*slang*) daring; courage.—*vt* to remove the intestines from; to destroy the interior of; *pr p* **gutting**; *pt* **gutted**.—*adj* (*slang*) basic, not difficult.—*adjs* **gut´less**, (*slang*) lacking courage; **guts´y**, (*slang*) courageous, forceful, etc.—**gutty** (*inf*) marked by courage or fortitude; having a vigorous challenging quality. [OE *guttas* (*pl*); cf *gēotan*, to pour.]
gutta-percha [gut´a-pûr´cha or -ka] *n* solidified juice of various Malayan trees (genera *Payena* and *Pala*-guium). [Malay *getah*, gum, *percha*, a tree producing it.]
gutter[1] [gut´ėr] *n* a channel for conveying away water, esp at a roadside or at the eaves of a roof; a channel or groove to direct something (as of a bowling alley); the lowest condition of human life.—*adj* marked by extreme vulgarity or indecency.—*vt* to provide with a gutter.—*vi* to flow in rivulets; (of a candle) to melt away or to incline downward in a draft. [OFr *goutiere*—*goute*—L *gutta*, a drop.]
gutter[2] *see* **gut**.
guttural [gut´ùr-ȧl] *adj* pertaining to the throat; formed in the throat.—*n* velar.—*adv* **gutt´urally**. [Fr,—L *guttur*, the throat.]
guy[1] [gī] *n* a rope, rod, etc., to steady anything.—*vt* to keep in position by a guy. [OFr *guis, guie*; Sp *guia*, a guide.]
guy[2] [gī] *n* (*slang*) a man or boy.—*vt* to tease. [*Guy Fawkes*, Eng conspirator.]
guzzle [guz´l] *vti* to swallow greedily.—*n* **guzz´ler**. [Perh conn with Fr *gosier*, throat.]
gymkhana [jim-kä´na] *n* a meeting featuring sports contests or athletic skills. [Hindustani *gend-khāna* ('ball-house'), racket-court, remodelled on *gymnastics*.]
gymnasium [jim-nā´zi-um] *n* a room or building equipped for physical training and sports.—*pl* **gymna´siums, -ia**.—*ns* **gym; gym´nast** [-nast], one skilled in gymnastics; **gymnas´tic**, a system of training by exercise; (*usu. in pl* **gymnas´tics**, *used as sing*.) exercises devised to strengthen the body; feats or tricks of agility.—*adjs* **gymnas´tic, -al**. [Latinised from Gr *gymnasion*—*gymnos*, naked.]
gymn(o)- [gim´n(o)-, jim´n(ō)-, gimn(o)´-, jimn(o)´-] naked.—*ns* **gymnos´ophist** (Gr *sophos*, wise), one of a sect of ascetics in ancient India who went naked and practiced meditation; **gymn´osperm** (Gr *sperma*, seed), any of the lower or primitive group of seed plants (as conifers) whose seeds are not enclosed in an ovary. [Gr *gymnos*, naked.]
gynecocracy [gīn, jin-ē-kok´ra-si] *n* political supremacy of women.—*pl* **gynecoc´racies**, [Gr *gynē, -aikos*, a woman, *krateein*, to rule.]
gynecology [gīn-, jin-ē-kol´o-ji] *n* that branch of medicine which treats of the diseases and hygiene of women.—*adj* **gynecolog´ical**.—*n* **gynecol´ogist**. [Gr *gynē*, a woman, *logos*, discourse.]
gynoecium [jin-, jīn-ē´si-um] *n* (*bot*) the aggregate of carpels on a flower; pistil. [Mod L,—Gr *gynē*, woman, *oikos*, house.]
gyp [jip] *n* (*inf*) a swindle; a swindler. [Perh—obs Fr *jupeau*.]
gypsum [jip´sum] *n* hydrous calcium sulphate (hydrated sulphate of lime). [L—Gr *gypsos*, chalk.]
Gypsy [jip´si] *n* a member of a wandering Caucasoid people of Indian origin; a Romany; **gypsy**, who looks or lives like a Gypsy.—*pl* **gypsies**.—*n* **gypsy moth**, a moth (*Porthetria dispar*) which is a destructive defoliator of many trees. [**Egyptian**, because once thought to have come from Egypt.]

gyre [jīr] *n* a circular or spiral motion.—*vi* **gyr´āte** [or -āt´], to spin, whirl.—*n* **gyra´tion**, whirling motion.—*adjs* **gy´ral, gyr´ătory**, spinning round; **gyromagnet´ic**, pertaining to magnetic properties of rotating electric charges.—*ns* **gyr´oscōpe**, a wheel mounted in a ring so that its axis is free to turn in any direction; when the wheel is spun rapidly, it will keep its original plane of rotation.—*adj* **gyroscop´ic**.—*ns* **gyrostab´ilizer, gyr´ostat**, a gyroscopic device for countering the roll of a ship, etc. [L *gȳrus*—Gr *gȳros*, a ring.]

gyrfalcon [jer´falkon] *n* an arctic falcon (*Falco rusticolus*) that occurs in several forms and is the largest of all falcons. *Also* **gerfalcon**. [OFr *gerfaucon*—Low L *gyrfalcō*, most prob OHG *gîr*, a vulture (Ger *geier*). *See* **falcon**.]

gyrus [jīr´ŭs] *n* a convoluted ridge between two grooves; a convolution of the brain. [*See* **gyre**.]

gyve [jīv] *vt* to fetter.—*n* shackle, fetter. [ME *gives, gyves*.]

H

H´-bomb [āch´bom] hydrogen bomb.
ha [ha, hȧ] *interj* used to express surprise.
Habacuc [häb´ȧ-kuk] *n* (*Bible*) Habakkuk in the Douay Version of the Old Testament.
Habakkuk [häb´ȧ-kuk] *n* (*Bible*) the 35th book of the Old Testament, written by the prophet Habakkuk, a group of psalms on the triumph of justice and divine mercy over evil.
habanera [(h)ä-bä-nā´rä] *n* a Cuban dance or dance-tune in 2–4 time. [*Habana* or Havana, in Cuba.]
habeas corpus [hā´be-as-kör´pus] *n* a writ requiring that a prisoner be brought before a court to decide the legality of his detention. [L, lit 'have the body', from L *habēre*, to have, and *corpus*, the body.]
haberdasher [hab´ėr-dash-ėr] *n* a dealer in men's hats, shirts, neckties, etc.—*n* **habe´erdashery**. [OFr *hapertas*; ety uncertain.]
habiliment [ha-bil´i-mėnt] *n* clothing, attire (esp in *pl*). [Fr *habillement*—*habiller*, to dress—L *habilis*, fit, ready—*habēre*.]
habit [hab´it] *n* a distinctive costume, as of a nun, etc.; a thing done often and hence, easily; a usual way of doing things; an addiction, esp to narcotics.—*vt* to clothe.—*adjs* **habit-forming**, leading to the formation of a habit or addiction; **habit´ual**, having the nature of a habit; inherent in an individual.—*vt* **habit´uate**, to accustom.—*ns* **habituation; hab´itūde**, characteristic condition; custom; **habitué** [habit´ū-ā], a habitual frequenter (of any place). [Fr.—L *habitus*, state, dress—*habēre*, to have.]
habitable [hab´it-a-bl] *adj* capable of being lived in.—*ns* **habitability, hab´itableness**.—*adv* **hab´itably**.—*ns* **hab´itat**, the normal locality of an animal or plant; a controlled environment in which people can live in hostile physical conditions (as under the sea); **habitat group**, a museum exhibit showing plants and animals in their natural surroundings; **habitā´tion**, act of inhabiting; a dwelling or residence. [Fr.—L *habitābilis*—*habitāre, -ātum*, to inhabit, frequentative of *habēre*, to have.]
habitant [ab-ē-tā] *n* a native of Canada or of Louisiana of French descent. [Fr, inhabitant.]
hacienda [(h)as-i-en´da] *n* (*Sp Amer*) an estate or ranch. [Sp.—L *facienda*, things to be done.]
hack[1] [hak] *vt* to cut with rough blows; to chop or mangle.—*n* a tool for hacking; a gash or notch; a harsh, dry cough.—*adj* **hack´ly**, rough and broken, as if hacked or chopped.—*n* **hack´saw**, a fine-toothed saw for cutting metal. [Assumed OE *haccian*, found in composition *tō-haccian*; cf Du *hakken*, Ger *hacken*.]
hack[2] [hak] *n* a horse for hire; an old worn-out horse; a literary drudge; a coach for hire; (*inf*) a taxicab.—*adj* hired; hackneyed.—*vti* to use, let out, or act, as a hack.—*n* **hack´work**, professional, literary, or artistic work usu. done according to a formula to satisfy commercial standards. [Contr of **hackney**.]
hackle [hak´l] *n* a comb for hemp or flax; the neck features of a rooster, pigeon, etc. collectively; (*pl*) the hairs on a dog's neck; an angler's artificial fly made from a cock's hackle.—*vt* to comb out with a hackle, as flax. [Allied to **hook**.]
hackney [hak´ni] *n* a horse for driving or riding; any of an English breed of high-stepping horses; a carriage or automobile for hire.—*adj* kept for public hire; hackneyed.—*adj* **hackneyed**, made trite by overuse. [OFr *haquenée*, an ambling nag.]
had *pa t* and *pt p* of **have**.
haddock [had´ȯk] *n* an important Atlantic food fish (*Melanogrammus aeglefinus*) related to the cod. [ME *haddok*.]
Hades [hā-dēz] *n* the home of the dead; (*inf*) hell. [Gr *Aides, Haides*.]
haemo *see* **hemo**.
hafnium [haf´ni-ụm] *n* a metallic element (symbol HF; at wt 178.5, at no 72). [L *Hafnia*, Copenhagen.]
haft [häft] *n* the handle of a weapon or tool. [OE *hæft*, Ger *heft*.]
hag [hag] *n* an ugly old woman; a witch.—*adj* **hag´ridd´en**, obsessed, tormented. [OE *hægtesse*, a witch; Ger *hexe*.]
Haggadah [hä-gȧ´dȧ] *n* (*Judaism*) the reading at a Passover Seder recounting Israel's bondage and flight from Egypt. [Heb.]
Haggai [hag´ē-ī, hag´ī] *n* (*Bible*) 37th book of the Old Testament written by the prophet Haggai about 520 BC urging the renewal of work on restoring the temple after the Babylonian captivity.
haggard [hag´ärd] *n* (*falconry*) an adult hawk caught wild.—*adj* (*of a hawk*) untamed; having a wild, wasted, worn look.—*adv* **hagg´ardly**. [OFr *hagard*.]
haggis [hag´is] *n* a Scottish dish made of the heart, lungs and liver of a sheep, calf, etc., chopped up with suet, onions, oatmeal, etc., seasoned and boiled in the animal's stomach.
haggle [hag´l] *vt* to cut unskilfully.—*vi* to bargain contentiously; to stick at trifles, to cavil.—*n* **hagg´ler**. [A variant of **hackle**.]
Hagiographa [hag-i-og´ra-fa or hāj-] *n pl* the third part of the Jewish scriptures.—*ns* **hagiog´rapher**, a writer of hagiography; **hagiog´raphy**, a biography of saints or venerated persons; an idealizing or idolizing biography. [Gr *hagiographa* (*biblia*)—*hagios*, holy, *graphein*, to write.]
hagiology [hag-i-ol´o-ji or hāj-] *n* history and legends of saints; a list of venerated persons. [Gr *hagios*, holy, *logos*, discourse.]
hagioscope [hag´i-ō-skōp or hāj´-] *n* an opening through an interior wall of a church to allow people in the transepts to see the altar. [Gr *hagios*, holy, *skopeein*, to look at.]
ha-ha [hä´-hä] *n* a sunk fence. [Fr *haha*.]
haiku [hī´kōō] *n* a Japanese verse form of three lines of 5, 7 and 3 syllables. [Jap.]
hail[1] [hāl] *n* a calling to attract attention; a greeting; hearing distance.—*vt* to call to, from a distance; to greet, welcome (as).—*interj* an exclamation of tribute, greeting, etc.—*adj* **hail´-fell´ow-well-met´**, readily friendly and familiar.—also *n* and *adv*.—**hail from**, to come from, belong to (a place). [ON *heill*, health.]
hail[2] [hāl] *n* frozen raindrops.—*vti* to pour down in rapid succession.—*n* **hail´stone**, a pellet of hail. [OE *hægl* (*hagol*); Ger *hagel*.]
hair [hār] *n* a filament growing from the skin of an animal; a mass of hairs, esp that covering the human head; a thread-like growth on a plant; a fiber; anything very small and fine.—*ns* **hair´ball**, a ball of hair often found in the stomach of a cat, cow, or another animal that licks its coat; **hair´breadth, hairs´breadth**, a very small space or amount; **hair´do**, the style in which hair is arranged; **hair´line**, a very thin line; the outline of the hair on the head.—*adj* **hair-´raising**, (*inf*) terrifying or shocking; **hair´splitting**, making petty distinctions; quibbling.—Also *n*.—*n* **hair´spring**, a slender, hairlike coil spring, as in a watch.—*adj* **hair´trigger**, immediately responsive.—*n* **hairworm**, any of a genus (*Capillaria*) of nematode worms that include serious parasites of fowls and of man; any of a group (*Gordiacea*) of slender elongated worms that are parasitic in arthropods.—*adj* **hair´y**, covered with hair; (of plants) having a downy fuzz; (*inf*) tending to cause tension as from danger.—**get in one's hair**, to annoy. [OE *hǣr*; Ger, Du and Dan *haar*.]
Haitian [hā´ti-ȧn] *adj* of, or pertaining to, *Haiti*, in the W Indies.—*n* a native or citizen of Haiti; **Haitian Crē´ole**, the language of most Haitians that is based on French and various West African languages.
hajj [häj] *n* the pilgrimage to Mecca that every Muslim is required to make.—*n* **hajj´i** [(-ē)], one who has made the pilgrimage. [Ar, 'a pilgrimage'.]
hake [hāk] *n* a marine food fish (genera *Merliccius* and *Urophycis*) allied to the cod.—*pl* **hake, hakes**. [Prob Scand; cf Norw *hake-fisk*, lit 'hook-fish'.]
hakim[1] [hä-kēm´] *n* a Muslim physician. [Ar.]
hakim[2] [hä´kim] *n* a Muslim ruler, governor, or judge. [Ar.]
Halakah [hä-läk´a] *n* the body of Jewish law supplementing the scriptural law and forming the legal part of the Talmud.
halberd [hal´bėrd] *n* a weapon combining a spear and a battleax.—*n* **halberdier´** [-dēr´], one armed with a halberd. [OFr *halebard*—Mid High Ger *helmbarde*—*halm*, handle, or *helm*, helmet; OHG *barta*, an axe.]
halcyon [hal´si-ȯn] *adj* calm, peaceful, happy. [L *alcyōn*—Gr *alkyōn*; as if *hals*, sea, *kyōn*, conceiving.]
hale[1] [hāl] *adj* healthy, robust. [North form, from OE *hāl*; the S and Midl development gives **whole**; parallel form **hail** (1)—ON.]
hale[2] [hāl] *vt* to force (a person) to go. [OFr *haler*.]
half [haf, häf] *n* either of two equal parts of something; either of the two equal periods of some games.—*pl* **halves** [havz, hävz].—*adj* being a half; incomplete; partial.—*adv* to the extent of a half; (*inf*) partly (*half done*); (*inf*) at all (*with* **not**).—*ns* **half-and-half**, something half one thing and half another, as a mixture of milk and cream.—*adj* partly one thing and partly another.—*adv* in two equal parts.—*ns* **halfback**, (*football*) either of two backs, in addition to the fullback and the quarterback; **half-´breed**, one whose parents are of different races; **half brother**, a brother through one parent only; **half-caste**, half-breed; **half dollar**, a coin of the US and Canada, worth 50 cents; *adjs* **half-hardy**, (of plants) being able to stand low but not freezing temperatures; **half´hearted**, with little interest, enthusiasm, etc.—*ns* **half hitch**, a knot made by passing the end of a piece of rope around an object, across the main part of the rope, and through the resulting loop; **half-life**, the time taken for half the atoms in radioactive material to decay; **half-mast**, (of flag) the position to which a flag is lowered as a sign of mourning; **half-moon**, the moon when its disk is half illuminated; **half note**, (*music*) a note having one half the duration of a whole note; **half sister**, a sister through one parent only; **half-size**, clothing size for the full-figured woman; **half sole**, a sole (of a shoe or boot) from the arch to the toe; **halftone**, an illustration printed from a relief plate, showing light and shadow by means of minute dots; **halftrack´**, an

army truck, armored vehicle, etc. with a continuous tread instead of rear wheels.—*adj* **half´way´**, midway between two points, etc.; partial (*half-way measures*).—*adv* to the midway point; partially.—**half´way house**, a place for helping people adjust to society after being imprisoned, hospitalized, etc.; **half-wit**, a stupid, silly, or imbecilic person.—**meet halfway**, be willing to compromise with. [OE *half, healf*, side, half; cf Ger *halb*, Dan *halv*.]

halibut [hal´i-but] *n* a marine food fish that is found in northern seas (*Hippoglossus hippoglossus* in the Atlantic and *H. stenolepis* in the Pacific), the largest of the flat-fishes. [ME *hali*, holy, and *butte*, a flounder, plaice, the fish being much eaten on holy days; cf Du *heilbot*, Ger *heilbutt*.]

halidom [hal´i-dòm] *n* something held sacred. [OE *hāligdōm—hālig*, holy.]

halitosis [hal-i-tō´sis] *n* bad-smelling breath. [L *hālitus*, breath.]

hall [höl] *n* the main dwelling on an estate; a public building with offices, etc.; a large room for exhibits, gatherings, etc.; a college building; a vestibule at the entrance of a building; a hallway.—*ns* **hall´mark**, a mark or symbol of high quality; **hall´way**, a passageway in a building.—**Hall of Fame**, a building containing memorials to outstanding Americans; a place set aside to honor illustrious persons in any profession, esp sport. [OE *hall* (*heall*); Du *hal*, ON *höll*, etc.]

hallelujah [hal-ė-lōō´ya] *interj* and *n* the exclamation 'Praise Jehovah'; a song of praise to God. [Heb *hallelū*, praise ye, and *Jáh*, Jehovah.]

hallo *see* **hollo**.

hallow [hal´ō] *vt* to make or regard as holy.—*ns* **Hall´oween**, the evening of October 31; observed esp by children in playing tricks; **Hall´owmas**, the Feast of All Saints, November 1. [OE *hālgian*, to hallow—*hālig*, holy.]

hallucination [hal-ōō-sin-ā´sh(ò)n] *n* the apparent perception of sights, sounds, etc. that are not actually present.—*vti* **hallu´cinate**, to have or cause to have hallucinations.—*adjs* **hallū´cinative, hallū´cinatory**.—*n* **hallū´cinogen**, a drug producing hallucinations.—*adj* **hallūcinogen´ic**. [L *(h)a(l)lūcinārī, -ātus*, to wander in mind.]

hallux vulgus [häl´uks vûl´gus] *n* a bunion. [L.]

halm *see* **haulm**.

halo [hā´lō] *n* a ring of light, as around the sun; a symbolic ring of light around the head of a saint in pictures; the aura of glory surrounding an idealized person or thing.—*pl* **halo(e)s** [hā´lōz]. [L *halōs*—Gr *halōs*, a round threshingfloor.]

halogen [hal´ō-jėn] *n* a group of elements comprising fluorine, chlorine, bromine, iodine, astatine (in ascending atomic number order). [Gr *hals*, salt, *gennaein*, to produce.]

halothane [hal´ō-THān] *n* a nonexplosive inhaled anesthetic.

halt[1] [hölt] *vti* to stop.—Also *n*. [Ger *halt*, stoppage.]

halt[2] [hölt] *vi* to hesitate.—**the halt**, those who are lame. [OE *halt* (*healt*); Dan *halt*.]

halter [hölt´ėr] *n* a rope or strap for tying or leading an animal; a hangman's noose; a woman's upper garment held up by a loop around the neck.—*vt* to catch with or as if with a halter. [OE *hælftre*; Ger *halfter*.]

halvah, halva [häl´vė] *n* a sweet, sticky confection from the Middle East and India made of honey and sesame seeds or semolina and fruit. [Turkish.]

halve [häv] *vt* to divide into halves; in golf, to play one hole in the same number of strokes as one's opponent. [**half**.]

halyard [hal´yȧrd] *n* (*naut*) a rope or tackle for hoisting or lowering a sail, yard, or flag. [From *halier, hallyer*—**hale** (2); altered through association with **sail-yard**.]

ham [ham] *n* the back of the thigh; the upper part of a hog's hind leg, salted, smoked, etc.; (*inf*) an amateur radio operator; (*slang*) an actor who overacts.—*n* **ham´string**, any of three muscles at the back of the thigh that flex and rotate the leg.—*vi* to overact.—*adjs* **ham´-fist´ed, ham´-hand´ed**, clumsy. [OE *hamm*; cf dial Ger *hamme*.]

hamadryad [ha-ma-drī´ad] *n* (*myth*) a wood-nymph who lived and died with the tree in which she dwelt; a king cobra.—*pl* **hamadry´ads, hamadry´ades** [-ēz]. [Gr *hamadryas—hama*, together, *drys*, a tree.]

hamadryas baboon [ha-ma-drī´es] *n* a baboon (*Pipio hamadryus*) with a reddish pink muzzle and calloused buttocks that was venerated by the ancient Egyptians.—Also **sacred baboon**. [**hamadryad**.]

hamburger [ham´bûrg-ėr] *n* ground beef; a cooked patty of such meat, often in a sandwich.—Also **ham´burg**. [*Hamburg*, Germany.]

hame [hām] *n* either of two curved bars to which the traces are attached in the harness of a draft horse. [Cf Du *haam*, Low Ger *ham*.]

Hamitic [ham-it´ik] *n* a group of N African languages related to Semitic.—*adj* of this group of languages; of, relating to, or characteristic of the Hamites.—*n* **Ham´ite**, a member of a group of N African peoples that are mostly Muslim and mainly Caucasoid although widely variable in appearance.

hamlet [ham´let] *n* a very small village. [OFr *hamelet*, dim of *hamel*—from Gmc; OE *hām*.]

hammer [ham´ėr] *n* a tool for pounding, having a heavy head and a handle; a thing like this in shape or use, as the part of the gun that strikes the firing pin; a bone of the middle ear.—*vti* to strike repeatedly, as with a hammer; to drive, force, or shape, as with hammer blows.—*ns* **hammerhead**, the head of a hammer; a blockhead; a shark with a mallet-shaped head having an eye at each end; **hamm´ertoe**, a deformed toe, with its first joint bent downward.—**hammer and sickle**, an emblem on the flag of the former USSR symbolizing communism; **hammer and tongs**, with great force; **hammer away at**, to keep emphasizing. [OE *hamor*; Ger *hammer*; ON *hamarr*.]

hammock [ham´òck] *n* a piece of strong cloth or netting suspended by the ends, and used as a bed or couch. [Sp *hamaca*, of Carib (qv) origin.]

Hammond organ [ham´ànd] *n* musical instrument shaped like a small upright piano with two keyboards which generates tone electronically. [L. *Hammond*, inventor.]

hamper[1] [ham´pėr] *vt* to hinder; to impede; to encumber. [Cf ON and Mod Icel *hemja*, to restrain; Ger *hemmen*.]

hamper[2] [ham´pėr] *n* a large basket, usu. with a lid. [Obs *hanaper*—OFr *hanapier*, a case for a *hanap* or drinking-cup.]

hamster [ham´stėr] *n* a small short-tailed Old World rodent (*Cricetus* or a related genus) with cheek pouches. [Ger.]

hamstring *see* **ham**.

Han [hän] *n* a Chinese dynasty (202 B.C.–220 A.D.) marked by the introduction of a uniform written language and the adoption of Buddhism; the dominant ethnic group of China, the Chinese people.

hand [hand] *n* the part of the arm below the wrist, used for grasping; a side or direction (*at my right hand*); possession or care (*in safe hands*); control (*to strengthen one's hand*); an active part; a promise to marry; skill; one having a special skill; handwriting; applause; help; a hired worker; a source (*news at first hand*); anything like a hand, as a pointer on a clock; the breadth of a hand, 4 inches when measuring the height of a horse; the cards held by a player at one time; a round of card play.—*adj* of, for, or controlled by the hand.—*vt* to give as with the hand; to help or conduct with the hand.—*ns* **hand´ball**, a game in which players bat a ball against a wall or walls with the hand; **hand´bill**, a small printed notice to be passed out by hand; **hand´cart**, a small cart pulled or pushed by hand; **hand´cuff**, either of a pair of connected rings for shackling the wrists of a prisoner (*usu. pl*).—*vt* to manacle.—*adj* **hand´ed**, having or involving (a specified kind or number of) hands.—*ns* **hand´ful**, as much as will fill the hand; a few; (*inf*) someone or something hard to manage; **hand´-me-down**, (*inf*) a used garment, etc. passed on to one; **hand´out**, a gift of food, etc. as to a beggar; a leaflet handed out; an official news release.—*vt* **hand´pick´**, to pick by hand; to choose carefully for a purpose.—*ns* **hand´rail**, a narrow rail for grasping as a support; **hand´set**, a telephone mouthpiece and receiver in a single unit.—*adjs* **hands-off**, of a policy of not interfering; **hands-on**, involving active participation and operating experience.—*ns* **handspring**, a gymnastic feat in which a person leaps forward or backward into a handstand and then onto his feet; **handstand**, an act of supporting the body in an upside-down position by the hands alone.—*adjs* **hand-to-hand**, at close quarters, esp fighting; **hand-to-mouth**, having barely enough food and money to satisfy immediate needs.—*n* **handwriting**, writing done by hand; a style of such writing.—**at hand**, near.—**hand in hand**, together; **hand it to**, (*slang*) to give credit to; **hand over fist**, (*inf*) easily and in large amounts; **hands down**, easily; **on hand**, near; available; present; **on the one hand**, from one point of view; **on the other hand**, from the opposite point of view. [OE *hand*.]

handicap [hand´ikap] *n* a competition in which difficulties are imposed on, or advantages given to, the various contestants to equalize their chances; such a difficulty or advantage; any hindrance.—*vt* to give a handicap to; to hinder.—*ns* **hand´icapper**, a person, as a sports writer, who tries to predict the winners in horse races.—**the handicapped**, those who are physically disabled or mentally retarded. [Prob *hand i´ cap*, from the drawing from a cap in an old lottery game.]

handicraft [hand´i-kräft] *n* skill with the hands, or work calling for it. [OE *handcræft—hand* and *cræft*, craft, assimilated to **handiwork**.]

handiwork [hand´i-wûrk] *n* handmade work; work done by a person himself. [OE *handgewerc—hand*, and *gewerc*, work.]

handkerchief [hang´kėr-chif] *n* a small cloth for wiping the nose, etc. [**hand** and **kerchief**.]

handle [hand´l] *vt* to touch, hold, or feel with the hand; to wield, use; to manage (a person, affair); to deal with; to deal in (goods).—*n* that part of anything held in the hand.—*ns* **hand´ler**, one who handles; one who controls or shows off an animal at a show, etc.; **hand´ling**.—**fly off the handle**, to lose one's temper. [OE *handlian—hand*, a hand.]

handsome [han´sòm] *adj* good-looking; dignified; generous; ample.—*adv* **hand´somely**.—*n* **hand´someness**. [**hand** + suffx *-some*; cf Du *handzaam*.]

handy [han´di] *adj* dexterous; ready to the hand, near; convenient.—*n* **hand´yman**, a man who does odd jobs. [**hand**.]

hang [hang] *vt* to support from above against gravity, to suspend; to decorate with pictures, etc., as a wall; to put to death by suspending by the neck; to exhibit (works of art); to prevent (a jury) from coming to a decision.—*vi* to be suspended, so as to allow of free lateral motion; to droop; to hover or impend; to be in suspense.—*pt t, pt p* **hanged** (by the neck) or **hung**.—*n* action of hanging; manner in which anything hangs or is disposed.—*adj* **hang´dog**, abject or ashamed.—*ns* **hanger**, one who hangs things; that on which something is hung; **hang glider**, a glider like a kite from which the harnessed pilot hangs; **hang gliding**, the sport of gliding through the air in a hang glider; **hanging**, an execution by hanging; something hung as a tapestry, etc.—*adj* that hangs.—*ns* **hang´man**, a public executioner; **hang´nail**, a bit of torn skin next to a fingernail; **hang´out**, a favorite place to meet; **hang´over**, a survival; disagreeable effects of too much alcoholic liquor; **hang´up**, (*slang*) an unresolved personal problem.—**get the hang of**, to learn the knack of; to understand the meaning of; **hang around**, (*inf*) to loiter; **hang back**, to be reluctant as from shyness; **hang on**, to persevere; to depend on; to listen attentively to; **hang out**, (*slang*) to spend much time; **hang up**, to put on a hook, etc.; to end a telephone call by replacing the receiver; to delay. [OE *hangian* and ON *hanga* and *hengja*; Du, Ger *hangen*.]

hangar [hang´ȧr, hang´gär] *n* a repair shed or shelter for aircraft. [Fr.]

hank [hangk] *n* a coiled or looped bundle, usu. containing specified yardage. [ON *hanki*, a hasp.]

hanker [hangk´ėr] *vi* to yearn (*with* **after, for**). [Perh conn with **hang**; cf Du *hunkeren*.]

Hannukkah *see* **Chanukah**.

Hansen's disease [han´senz] *n* leprosy. [A. *Hansen*, Norwegian physician, died 1921.]

hansom [han´sȯm] *n* a light two-wheeled covered carriage, pulled by one horse, with driver's seat raised behind. [Invented by Joseph A. *Hansom*, 1803–82.]

hap [hap] *n* luck.—*adj* **hap´less**, unlucky.—*adv* **hap´lessly**.—*n* **hap´lessness**.—*adv* **hap´ly**, by hap, chance, or accident; perhaps, it may be. [ON *happ*, good luck.]

haphazard [hap-haz´ȧrd] *n* chance.—*adj* not planned; random.—*adv* by chance. [**hap, hazard**.]

happen [hap´ėn] *vi* to take place; to be, occur, or come by chance; to have the luck or occasion (*I happened to see it*).—*n* **happ´ening**, an occurrence; an event that is especially interesting, entertaining, or important. [**hap**.]

happy [hap´i] *adj* lucky; possessing or enjoying pleasure or good; pleased; furnishing or expressing enjoyment; apt, felicitous (eg a phrase).—*adv* **happ´ily**.—*n* **happ´iness**.—*adj* **happ´y-go-luck´y**, easygoing; irresponsible.—**happy medium**, a prudent or sensible middle course. [**hap**.]

hara-kiri [hä´ra-kē´rē] *n* ritual suicide by disembowelment. [Jap *hara*, belly, *kiri*, cut.]

harangue [ha-rang´] *n* a tirade; a pompous, wordy address.—*vti* to deliver a harangue.—*pr p* **haranguing** [*-rang´ing*]; *pt p* **harangued** [-rangd´].—*n* **harang´uer**. [OFr *arenge, harangue*, from OHG *hring*, a ring of auditors.]

harass [har´as] *vt* to annoy, to pester, to trouble by constant raid and attacks.—*pr p* **har´assing**, *pt, pt p* **har´assed**.—*ns* **har´asser; har´assment**. [OFr *harasser*; prob from *harer*, to incite a dog.]

harbinger [här´bin-jėr] *n* a forerunner; a herald. [ME *herbergeour*, allied to **harbor**.]

harbor [här´bȯr] *n* any refuge or shelter; a protected inlet for anchoring ships; a port.—*vt* to shelter or house; to hold in the mind (*to harbor envy*).—*vi* to take shelter.—*n* **har´borage**, place of shelter.—*adj* **har´borless**.—*n* **har´bormas´ter**, the public officer who has charge of a harbor; **harbor seal**, a small seal (*Phoca vitulina*) of oceanic coasts of the northern hemisphere that often ascends rivers. [ME *herberwe*—an assumed OE *herebeorg*—*here*, army, *beorg*, protection.]

hard [härd] *adj* not easily penetrated, firm, solid; stiff; difficult to understand; difficult to do; difficult to bear, painful; severe, strenuous, rigorous; unfeeling; ungenerous; intractable; (of sound) harsh; (of color) brilliant and glaring; (of drug) habit-forming and seriously detrimental to health; (of news) definite, substantiated; (of drink) very alcoholic; (of water) that prevents lathering with soap.—*adv* with urgency, vigor, etc.; earnestly, forcibly, with difficulty, as in **hard-earned**, etc.; close, near, as in **hard by**.—*adv* **hard-a-lee**, close to the lee-side, etc.—*adj* **hard´-and-fast´**, strict.—*ns* **hard´back**, a hard-cover book; **hard´ball**, baseball.—*adj* **hard´bitten**, tough, seasoned.—*ns* **hardboard**, a composition board made from wood chips.—*adj* **hard-boiled**, (of eggs) boiled until solid; (*inf*) unfeeling.—*n* **hard candy**, a candy made of boiled sugar and usu. fruit-flavored; **hardcopy**, output (as from microfilm or computer storage) that can be read by eye.—*adjs* **hard´-core**, extremely resistant to change; **hard-cover**, of any book bound in a stiff cover.—*vti* **harden**, to make or become hard.—*ns* **hard goods**, durable consumer goods; **hard hat**, a protective helmet; a construction worker.—*adjs* **hard´head´ed**, shrewd and unsentimental; stubborn; **hard´heart´ed**, unfeeling; cruel; **hard-hitting**, forcefully effective; **hard´-line**, aggressive; unyielding; **hard-nosed**, (*slang*) tough and stubborn or shrewd.—*ns* **hard palate**, the bony arch forming the roof of the mouth; **hard rock**, music with a heavy beat and extreme amplification; **hard sauce**, butter creamed with sugar and flavorings, esp brandy; **hard sell**, high-pressure salesmanship; **hard-shell clam**, a quahog; **hardship**, something that causes suffering or privation; **hard´stand**, a paved area for parking aircraft or other vehicles; **hard´tack**, unleavened bread made in large wafers; **hard´top**, an automobile resembling a convertible but having a fixed metal top; **hardware**, articles made of metal as tools, nails, etc.; the mechanical, magnetic, and electronic devices of a computer; necessary (parts of) machinery; **hard´wood**, any timber with a tough compact texture; the wood of deciduous trees with broad, flat leaves, as maple, oak, etc.; **hard of hearing**, partially deaf; **hard up**, (*inf*) in need of money. [OE *heard*, Du *hard*, Ger *hart*; allied to Gr *kratys*, strong.]

hardy [härd´i] *adj* brave; resolute; audacious; robust; vigorous; able to bear cold, exposure or fatigue.—*ns* **hard´ihood, hard´iness**.—*adv* **hard´ily**. [OFr *hardi*—OHG *hartjan*, to make hard.]

hare [hār] *n* any of various timid and swift mammals, esp genus *Lepis* related to and resembling the rabbit.—*ns* **hare and hounds**, a game where some of the players scatter a paper trail and the others try to follow and find them; **hare´bell**, a plant (*Campanula rotundifolia*) with blue bell-shaped flowers.—*adj* **hare´brained**, flighty; foolish.—*n* **hare´lip**, a congenital deformity in the upper human lip, being split like that of a hare.—*adj* **hare´lipped**. [OE *hara*; Du *haas*, Dan, *hare*, Ger *hase*.]

harem [hā´rem, hä-rēm´] *n* the usu. secluded part of a Muslim's house where the women live; the women in a harem. [Ar *harīm, haram*, anything forbidden—*harama*, to forbid.]

haricot [har´i-kō, -kot] *n* the ripe seed or the unripe pod of any of several beans, esp *Phaseolus vulgaris*. [Fr *haricot*.]

hark [härk] *vi* to listen carefully (*usu with* **to**); **hark back**, to revert to a previous topic or circumstance. [Same root as **hearken**.]

harken *see* **hearken**.

Harlequin [hár´lė-kwin, or -kin] *n* a comic character in pantomime who wears a mask and colorful tights.—*n* **harlequin**, a clown, a buffoon.—*adj* (of textiles) having a bold multi-colored pattern; (of an animal's coat) having patches of different colors on a solid ground.—*n* **harlequināde´**, the portion of a pantomime in which the harlequin plays a chief part. [Fr *harlequin, arlequin*, prob the same as OFr *Hellequin*, a devil in mediaeval legend.]

harlot [här´lot] *n* a prostitute.—Also *adj*.—*n* **har´lotry**, prostitution; unchastity. [OFr *herlot, arlot*, a base fellow; origin unknown.]

harm [härm] *n* hurt; damage; injury.—*vt* to injure.—*adj* **harm´ful**, hurtful.—*adv* **harm´fully**.—*n* **harm´fulness**.—*adj* **harm´less**, not injurious; (*arch*) innocent; unharmed.—*adv* **harm´lessly**.—*n* **harm´lessness**. [OE *hearm*; Ger *harm*.]

harmattan [här-mä-tan´, här-mät´an] *n* a dust-laden wind on the Atlantic coast of Africa. [African word.]

harmonic [här-mon´ik] *adj* (*music*) of or in harmony.—*n* an overtone; (*pl*) the science of musical sounds.—*adv* **harmonically**.—*ns* **harmonica**, a small wind instrument that produces tones when air is blown or sucked across a series of metal reeds; a mouth organ; **harmonium**, a keyboard musical instrument whose tones are produced by thin metal reeds set in motion by foot-operated bellows; a reed organ.—*adj* **harmō´nious**, having parts arranged in an orderly or pleasing way; having similar ideas, interests, etc.; having musical tones combined to give a pleasing effect.—*vi* **har´monize**, to be in harmony; to sing in harmony.—*vt* to make harmonious.—*ns* **harmonization; harmony**, pleasing agreement of parts in color, size, etc.; agreement in action, ideas, etc.; friendly relations; the pleasing combination of tones in a chord; **harmonic minor scale**, a minor scale which has the semitones between the 2d and 3d and 5th and 6th, with an interval of three semitones between the 6th and 7th; **harmonic progression**, a series of numbers whose reciprocals form an arithmetic progression; **harmonic motion**, a type of vibration which may be represented by projecting on to a diameter the uniform motion of a point round a circle—the motion of a pendulum bob is approximately this. [Gr *harmonia*, music—*harmos*, a joint, fitting.]

harness [här´nes] *n* the leather straps and metal pieces by which a draft animal is fastened to a vehicle, plow, etc.; something resembling a harness; prefabricated wiring ready to be attached; the part of the loom controlling the heddles.—*vt* to put a harness on; to control so as to use the power of.—**in harness**, at work; able to work closely with others. [OFr *harneis*, armour.]

harp [härp] *n* a musical instrument with strings stretched across a triangular frame played by plucking.—*vi* to play on the harp; to persist in talking or writing tediously (on anything).—*n* **harp´ist**. [OE *hearpe*; Ger *harfe*.]

harpoon [här-pōōn´] *n* a barbed spear with an attached line, for spearing whales, etc.—*vt* to strike with the harpoon.—*n* **harpoon´er**. [Fr *harpon*—*harpe*, a clamp, perh—L *harpa*, Gr *harpē*, sickle.]

harpsichord [härp´si-körd] *n* a musical instrument resembling a grand piano whose strings are plucked rather than struck. [OFr *harpechord*—Low L *harpa*, of Gmc origin. See **harp, chord** (2).]

harpy [här´pi] *n* (*myth.*) a malign monster, part woman and part bird; a predatory person; a shrewish woman. [L *harpȳia*—Gr, pl *harpyiai*, lit snatchers, symbols of the stormwind—*harpazein*, to seize.]

harquebus [här´kui-bus] *see* **arquebus**.

harridan [har´i-dȧn] *n* a disreputable, shrewish old woman. [Prob OFr *haridelle*, a lean horse, a jade.]

harrier [har´i-ėr] *n* a small dog with a keen smell, for hunting hares; a cross-country runner. [**hare** or **harry**.]

harrier *see* **harry**.

Harris tweed [har´is] *n* trade name for tweed spun, dyed and woven on the Scottish island of Lewis and Harris.

harrow [har´ō] *n* a heavy frame with spikes, spring teeth, or disks for breaking up and leveling plowed ground.—*vt* to draw a harrow over (land); to cause mental distress to.—*adj* **harr´owing**, acutely distressing to the mind. [ME *harwe*.]

harry [har´i] *vt* to raid and ravage or rob; to torment or worry.—*pr p* **harr´ying**; *pt p* **harr´ied**.—*n* **harr´ier**, one that harries; any of a genus (*Circus*) of small hawks feeding chiefly on small mammals, reptiles, and insects; a hunting dog resembling a foxhound used esp for hunting rabbits; a runner on a cross-country team. [OE *hergian*—*here*, an army; Ger *heer*.]

harsh [härsh] *adj* unpleasantly rough; jarring on the senses or feelings; rigorous; cruel.—*adv* **harsh´ly**.—*n* **harsh´ness**. [ME *harsk*, a northern word; cf Swed *härsk* and Dan *harsk*, rancid, Ger *harsch*, hard.]

harts´horn [härtz´horn] *n* a preparation of ammonia used as smelling salts.

hartebeest [här´tė-bēst] *n* either of two large African antelopes (*Alcelaphus buselaphus* or *A. lichtensteini*); a South African antelope. [S Afr Du, 'hartbeast'.]

harum-scarum [hā´rum-skā´rum] *n* a giddy, rash person.—Also *adj*. [Prob from obs *hare*, to harass, and **scare**.]

Havarti [hȧ-vär´tē] *n* a semisoft Danish cheese having a porous texture and usu. mild flavor. [*Havarti*, Denmark.]

harvest [här´vest] *n* the time of gathering in the ripened crops; a season's crop; the crops gathered in; fruits; the product of any labor or action.—*vti* to gather in (a crop).—*vt* to win by achievement.—*ns* **harvest fly**, cicada; **harvest home**, the time of harvest; a feast at the close of harvest; **harvest´man**, an arachnid (order Phalangida) resembling a spider with a small rounded body and very long slender legs, also called **daddy-long-legs; harvest mite**, a mite larva (family Trombiculidae) that sucks the blood of vertebrates and causes intense irritation; **harvest moon**, the full moon nearest the time of the September equinox; **har´vest time**, the time during which an annual crop (as wheat) is harvested. [OE *hærfest*; Ger *herbst*, Du *herfst*.]

has [haz] 3d pers sing pres ind of **have**.

has-been [haz-bin] *n* a person or thing whose popularity is past.

hash [hash] *vt* to chop up (meat or vegetables) for cooking.—*n* a chopped mixture of cooked meat and vegetables, usu. baked or fried; a mixture; a muddle or mess; (*slang*) hashish.—**hash out**, (*inf*) to settle by long discussion; **hash over**, (*inf*) to discuss at length. [Fr *hacher—hache*, hatchet.]

Hasid [ha-sid´] *n* a sect of Jews holding fundamental, mystical views, identified by dress and customs.—*pl* **Hasid´im**. [Hebrew.]

hashish [hash´ish, -ēsh] *n* the leaves, shoots, or resin of Indian hemp, smoked or swallowed in various forms as an intoxicant. [Ar.]

hasp [häsp] *n* a hinged fastening for a door, etc., esp a metal piece fitted over a staple and fastened as by a bolt or padlock. [OE *hæpse*; Dan and Ger *haspe*.]

hassock [has´ȯk] *n* a firm cushion used as a footstool or seat. [OE *hassuc*.]

hast [hast] 2d pers sing pres indic of **have**.

hastate, -d [hast´āt, -id] *adjs* (*bot*) spear-shaped. [L *hastātus—hasta*, spear.]

haste [hāst] *n* quickness of motion.—*vt* **hasten** [hās´n], to accelerate; to hurry on.—*vi* to move with speed; to do without delay (eg *he hastened to add*).—*pr p* **hast´ening** [hās´ning]; *pt p* **hastened** [hās´nd].—*adj* **hast´y**, speedy; hurried; rash.—*adv* **hast´ily**.—*ns* **hast´iness; hast´y pudd´ing**, cornmeal mush; Indian pudding.—**make haste**, to hurry. [OFr *haste* (Fr *hâte*), from Gmc; cf OE *hǣst*, Du *haast*, Ger *hast*.]

hat [hat] *n* a covering for the head, generally with crown and brim.—*vti* to provide with a hat.—*ns* **hatt´er**, one who makes or sells hats; **hat´trick**, the scoring of three goals in one game (as of hockey) by the same player.—**pass the hat**, to take up a collection; **talk through one's hat**, to talk nonsense; **throw one's hat into the ring**, to enter a contest, esp for political office; **under one's hat**, (*inf*) confidential. [OE *hæt*; Dan *hat*.]

hatch[1] [hach] *n* a small door or opening (as on an aircraft or spaceship); an opening in the deck of a ship or in the floor or roof of a building; a lid for such an opening; a hatchway.—*ns* **hatchback**, an automobile with a rear that swings up giving wide entry to a storage area; **hatchway**, an opening in a ship's deck or in a floor or roof; a passage giving access to an enclosed space (as a cellar). [OE *hæcc*, *hæc*, a grating; Du *hek*, a gate.]

hatch[2] [hach] *vt* to produce from the egg; to develop or concoct (eg a plot).—*vi* to produce young from the egg; to come from the egg.—*n* **hatch´ery**, a place for hatching eggs, esp of poultry or fish. [Early ME *hacchen*, from an assumed OE *hæccean*.]

hatch[3] [hach] *vt* to shade by fine lines, incisions, etc., in drawing and engraving.—*n* **hatch´ing**, the mode of so shading. [OFr *hacher*, to chop.]

hatchet [hach´et] *n* a small ax with a short handle.—*adj* **hatch´et-faced**, having a narrow, sharp-featured face.—*ns* **hatchet job**, (*inf*) a biased, malicious attack on another's character; **hatchet man**, one hired for murder, coercion, or attack; a writer specializing in invective; person hired to perform hatchet jobs.—**bury the hatchet**, to make peace. [Fr *hachette—hacher*, to chop.]

hate [hāt] *vt* to dislike intensely; to wish to avoid.—*vi* to feel hatred.—*n* a strong feeling of dislike or ill will; the person or thing hated.—*adj* **hate´ful**, deserving hate.—*adv* **hate´fully**.—*ns* **hate´fulness; hat´er; hat´red**, hate.—**hate someone's guts**, to hate someone with great intensity. [OE *hete*, hate, *hatian*, to hate; Ger *hasz*.]

hath [hath] (*arch*), 3d pers sing pres indic of **have**.

hauberk [hö´bėrk] *n* a long coat of chain mail. [OFr *hauberc*—OHG *halsberg—hals*, neck, *bergan*, to protect.]

haughty [hö´ti] *adj* proud, arrogant.—*adv* **haught´ily**.—*n* **haught´iness**. [Ofr *halt, haut*, high—L *altus*, high.]

haul [höl] *vti* to move by pulling; to transport by wagon, truck, etc.—*n* the act of hauling; the amount gained, caught, etc. at one time; the distance over which something is transported.—*ns* **haul´age**, act of hauling; charge for hauling; **haul´er**, one that hauls, esp a business; a commercial vehicle for hauling.—**haul off**, (*inf*) to draw the arm back before hitting; **in, over the long haul**, over a long period of time. [A variant of **hale** (2).]

haulm [höm] *n* the stalk of beans, peas, etc., esp after the crop has been gathered. [OE *healm*; Du, Ger *halm*.]

haunch [hönch, -sh] *n* the part of the body around the hips; leg and loin of a deer, sheep, etc. used for food.—**on one's haunches**, in a squatting position. [OFr *hanche*; prob of Gmc origin.]

haunt [hönt] *vt* to visit often or continually; to recur repeatedly to (*haunted by memories*).—*vi* to linger; to appear habitually as a ghost.—*n* a place often visited.—*adj* **haunt´ed**, supposedly frequented by ghosts. [OFr *hanter*; perh a corr of L *habitāre*.]

hausfrau [hows´frow] *n* a housewife. [Ger.]

haute, haut [ōt] *adj* fashionable; high-class.—**haute couture** [kōōtür], clothing designers or houses that create exclusive fashions; the fashions created; **haute cuisine** [kwē-zēn´], elaborate cuisine, esp traditional French; **haute école** [ākol´], a highly stylized form of horsemanship; **haut(e) monde** [m´Þd], high society. [Fr.]

hauteur [ō-tûr´, hō-tœr´] *n* haughtiness. [Fr.]

Havana [ha-vän´a] *n* a cigar made from Cuban tobacco; a tobacco originally grown in Cuba. [*Havana*, Cuba.]

have [hav] *vt* to hold; to keep; to possess; to own; to entertain in the mind; to enjoy; to experience; to give birth to; to allow, or to cause to be (eg *I will not have it; you should have the picture framed*); to be obliged; (*inf*) to hold at a disadvantage; (*inf*) to deceive; as an auxiliary, used with the pt p to form the perfect tenses (eg *they have gone*).—*pr p* **hav´ing**; *pt t, pt p* **had**.—*n* **have-not´**, a person or nation with little or no wealth.—**have coming**, to deserve; **have done**, finish, stop; **have done with**, have no further concern with; (*inf*) **have had it**, to be unable or unwilling to tolerate more; (*inf*) **have it in for**, to intend to do harm to; **have it out**, to settle a problem by frank discussion; **have on**, to be wearing; **have over**, to invite someone to visit; **have to**, must; **have to do with**, to be connected with. [OE *habban*, pt *hæfde*, pt p *gehæfd*, Ger *haben*, Dan *have*.]

haven [hā´vn] *n* an inlet of the sea, or mouth of a river, where ships can get good and safe anchorage; any place of safety, an asylum. [OE *hæfen*, Du *haven*, Ger *hafen*.]

haversack [hav´ėr-sak] *n* a bag similar to a knapsack but worn over one shoulder. [Fr *havresac*—Ger *habersack*, oatsack—*haber, hafer*, oats.]

havoc [hav´ȯk] *n* great destruction and devastation.—**play havoc with**, to devastate. [OFr *havot*, plunder.]

haw[1] [hö] *n* the berry of the hawthorn; the hawthorn.—*n* **haw´thorn**, any of a genus (*Crataegus*) of spring-flowering spiny shrubs or trees. [OE *haga*, a yard or enclosure; Du *haag*, a hedge, Ger *hag*, a hedge, ON *hagi*, a field.]

haw[2] [hö] *vi* to grope for words; to equivocate. [Imit.]

Hawaiian [hȧ-wī´yȧn] *n* a native or resident of Hawaii, esp one of Polynesian ancestry; the Polynesian language of the Hawaiians.—*ns* **Hawaiian goose**, nene; **Hawaiian guitar**, an acoustic guitar with a long neck and six to eight steel strings.—Also *n*.

hawk[1] [hök] *n* any of numerous diurnal birds of prey (suborder Falcones) with short, rounded wings, a long tail, and a hooked beak and claws; an advocate of war.—*vi* to hunt birds by using a trained hawk.—*vt* to hunt on the wing like a hawk.—*n* **Hawk´eye**. a nickname for a native or resident of Iowa.—*adj* **hawk-eyed**, keen-sighted.—*ns* **hawkmoth**, any of numerous stout-bodied moths (family Sphingidae) with a long proboscis which is kept coiled at rest. Also called **sphinx**.—**hawksbill**, a carnivorous sea turtle (*Eretmochelys imbricata*) whose shell yields tortoiseshell. [OE *hafoc*, Du *havik*, Ger *habicht*, ON *haukr*.]

hawk[2] [hök] *vti* to clear the throat (of) audibly. [Imit.]

hawker [hök´ėr] *n* one who goes about offering goods for sale.—*vt* **hawk**, to convey about for sale; to cry for sale. [Cf Low Ger and Ger *höker*, Du *heuker*.]

hawse [höz] *n* part of a vessel's bow in which the hawseholes are cut.—*n pl* **hawse´holes**, holes through which a ship's cables pass. [ON *hāls*, the neck.]

hawser [hö´zėr] *n* a large rope for towing, etc.—**hawser bend**, a method of joining two heavy ropes together by seizing. [OFr *haucier, haulser*, to raise—Low L *altiāre*—L *altus*, high.]

hawthorn *see* **haw** (1).

Hawthorne effect [haw´THȯrn] *n* the change in output or results in a situation purely as an effect of applying different stimuli. [*Hawthorne* works in Illinois where its existence was established in 1926.]

hay [hā] *n* grass, clover, etc. cut down and dried for fodder.—*ns* **hay´cock**, a conical pile of hay in the field; **hay´fē´ver**, irritation of the nose, throat, and eyes, caused by an allergic reaction to pollen; **hay´loft**, a loft in which hay is kept; **hay´mak´er**, a powerful blow; **hay´mow**, a mass of hay stored in a barn; hayloft; **hay´rick, hay´stack**, a pile of stacked hay.—*adj, adv* **hay´wire**, (*slang*) out of order; disorganized; crazy.—**to go haywire**, to become crazy. [OE *hīeg, hīg, hēg*, Ger *heu*, Du *hooi*, ON *hey*.]

hazard [haz´ȧrd] *n* risk; danger; an obstacle on a golf course.—*vt* to risk.—*adj* **haz´ardous**, dangerous; risky. [OFr *hasard*; prob through the Sp from Arab *al zār*, the die; perh from *Hasart*, a castle in Syria, where a game of chance was invented during the Crusades.]

haze[1] [hāz] *n* a thin vapor of fog, smoke, etc. in the air; slight vagueness of mind.—*vti* to make or become hazy (*often with* **over**).—*adj* **haz´y**.—*adv* **haz´ily**.—*n* **haz´iness**.

haze[2] [hāz] *vt* to force to do ridiculous or painful things, as an initiation.

hazel [hā´zl] *n* a genus (*Corylus*) of small trees yielding an edible nut enclosed in a leafy cup.—*adj* pertaining to the hazel; of a light-brown color.—*n* **hā´zelnut**, the nut of a hazel. [OE *hæsel*, Ger *hasel*, ON *hasl*, L *corylus*.]

he [hē] *nom masc pron of 3d pers* the male (or thing spoken of as male) named before; used in a generic sense or when the sex of the person is unspecified.—*adj* male, eg **hē´goat**.—**hē´-man**, a man of extreme virility. [OE *hē, he*.]

head [hed] *n* the part of the animal body containing the brain, eyes, ears, nose and mouth; the top part of anything; the foremost part; the chief person; (*pl*) a unit of counting (*ten head of cattle*); the striking part of a tool; mind; understanding; the topic of a chapter, etc.; crisis, conclusion; pressure of water, steam, etc.; source of a river, etc.; froth, as on beer.—*adj* at the head, top, or front; coming from in front; chief, leading.—*vt* to command; to lead; to cause to go in a specified direction.—*vt* to set out; to travel (*head eastward*).—*adj* **head´less**.—*ns* **head´ache**, a continuous pain in the head; (*inf*) a cause of worry or trouble; **head´board**, a board that forms the head of a bed, etc.; **head cold**, a common cold with congestion of the nasal passages; **head´dress**, a decorative covering for the head; a hairdo.—*adj* **head´first´**, with the head in front; recklessly.—*ns* **head´gear´**, a hat, cap, etc; **head´hunter**, one who preserves the heads of enemies as trophies; one who recruits executive personnel; **heading**, something forming the head, top, or front; the title, topic, etc. of a chapter, etc.; the direction in which a vehicle is moving; **head´land**, a promontory; **head´light´**, a light at the front of a vehicle; **head´line´**, printed lines at the top of a newspaper article giving the topic.—*vt* to give featured billing or publicity to.—*adj, adv* **head´long´**, with the head first; with uncontrolled speed or force; rash(ly); **head louse**, the common louse (*Pediculus humanus capitis*) that lives on the scalp of man; **head´master, head´mis´tress**, the principal of a private school.—*adj, adv* **head´-on´**, with the head or front foremost.—*ns* **head´phone**, a radio receiver held to the head by a band; **head´quarters**, the center of operations of one in command, as in an army; the main office in any organization; **head´rest**, a support for the head; **head´room**, space overhead, as in a doorway or tunnel; **head´shrinker**, a headhunter who shrinks the heads of his victims; (*inf*) a psychotherapist, esp a psychoanalyst; **head´start´**, an early start or any other competitive advantage; **head´stone**, a marker placed at the head of a grave.—*adj* **head´strong´**, determined to do as one pleases.—*ns* **head´waiter**, the head of the dining-room staff in a restaurant; **head´wa´ters**, the small streams that are the source of a river; **head´way**, forward motion; progress; **head´word**, term placed at the beginning (as of an entry in a dictionary).—**come to a head**, to be about to suppurate, as a boil; to reach a crisis; **go to one's head**, to intoxicate one; to make one vain; **head and shoulders**, beyond comparison; **head off**, to get ahead of and intercept; **head over heels**, deeply; completely; **head-to-head**, in direct confrontation; **heads up**! (*inf*) look out! **keep** or **lose one's head**, to keep or lose one's poise; **on** or **upon one's head**, as one's responsibility; **out of one's head**, delirious; **over one's head**, too difficult to understand; to a higher authority; **turn one's head**, to make one vain. [OE *hēafod*, Du *hoofd*, Ger *haupt*.]

heal [hēl] *vt* to make whole and healthy; to cure; to remedy, repair.—*vi* to grow sound.—*pr p* **heal´ing**; *pt p* **healed**.—*ns* **heal´er, heal´ing**, the act or process by which anything is healed or cured; the power to heal.—*adj* tending to cure or heal. [OE *hǣlan*—*hāl*, whole; cf Ger *heil*, Du *heel*, ON *heill*, cf **hail** (1), **hale**, (1), **whole**.]

health [helth] *n* physical and mental well-being; freedom of disease, etc.; condition of body or mind (*poor health*); a wish for one's health and happiness, as in a toast; soundness, as of a society.—*adjs* **healthful**, helping to produce or maintain health; wholesome; **healthy**, having good health; showing or resulting from good health.—*ns* **healthiness; health food**, food thought to be very healthful, as food grown with natural fertilizers and free of additives; **health insurance**, insurance against loss through illness of the insured, esp that providing compensation for medical expenses; **health maintenance organization**, an organization providing comprehensive medical care within a specified geographical area financed by its users through fixed periodical payments in advance. Also called **HMO**. [OE *hælth*—*hāl*, whole.]

heap [hēp] *n* a mass or pile of jumbled things; (*inf*) a large amount.—*vt* to throw in a heap; to pile high; to fill (a plate, etc.) full or to overflowing.—*pr p* **heap´ing**; *pt p* **heaped**. [OE *hēap*; ON *hōpr*, Ger *haufe*, Du *hoop*.]

hear [hēr] *vt* to perceive by the ear; to listen to; to conduct a hearing of (a law case, etc.); to be informed of; to learn.—*vi* to be able to hear sounds; to be told (*with* **of** *or* **about**).—*pr p* **hear´ing**; *pt* and *pt p* **heard** [hûrd].—*ns* **hear´er; hear´ing**, act of perceiving by the ear; the sense of perceiving sound; opportunity to be heard; earshot; **hear´say**, rumor, gossip.—**hear from**, to get a letter, etc. from; **not hear of**, to refuse to consider. [OE *hȳran*, Du *hooren*, ON *heyra*, Ger *hören*.]

hearken [härk´n] *vi* to listen carefully; to pay heed. [OE *he(o)rcnian*; cf **hark, hear**; Ger *horchen*.]

hearse [hûrs] *n* a vehicle in which a corpse is conveyed to the grave. [OFr *herse* (It *erpice*)—L *hirpex*, a harrow.]

heart [hart] *n* the hollow, muscular organ that circulates the blood; the central, vital, or main part; the human heart as the center of emotions, esp sympathy, spirit, etc.; a conventionalized design of a heart; a suit of playing cards marked with such a symbol in red; (*pl*) a card game played with a standard 52-card deck in which the object is to avoid taking tricks or certain cards.—*ns* **heart´ache**, sorrow or grief; **heart attack**, any sudden instance of heart failure, esp a coronary thrombosis; **heart´beat**, one full contraction and dilation of the heart; **heart´break**, overwhelming sorrow or grief.—*adj* **heart´broken**.—*n* **heart´burn**, a burning sensation beneath the breastbone.—*vt* **heart´en**, to encourage.—*n* **heart failure**, inability of the heart to supply enough blood to the body.—*adj* **heart´felt**, sincere.—*n* **heart´land**, a central and vital area considered by geopoliticians to be of vital strategic importance in political dominance of the world.—*adj* **heart´less**, unfeeling.—*n* **heart-lung machine**, a mechanical pump that takes over the functions of the heart and lungs during heart surgery.—*adjs* **heart´-rending**, causing much mental anguish; **heart´sick**, extremely unhappy or despondent.—*n* **hearts´ease**, tranquility; any of various violas, esp johnny-jump-up.—*npl* **heart´strings**, deepest feelings.—*adjs* **heart´-to-heart´**, intimate; candid; **heart´warming**, such as to cause genial feelings.—*n* **heart´wood**, the non-living central portion of wood.—*adj* **heart´y**, warm and friendly; unrestrained, as laughter; strong and healthy; nourishing and plentiful.—**after one's own heart**, that pleases one perfectly; **at heart**, in one's innermost nature; **by heart**, by memory; **set one's heart on**, to have a fixed desire for; **take to heart**, to consider seriously; to be troubled by. [OE *heorte*; Du *hart*, Ger *herz*.]

hearth [härth] *n* the part of the floor on which the fire is made; the fireside; the house itself. [OE *heorth*; Du *haard*, Ger *herd*.]

heat [hēt] *n* the quality of being hot; the perception of hotness; hot weather or climate; strong feeling, esp ardor, anger, etc.; a single bout, round, or trial in sports; the period of sexual excitement in female animals; (*slang*) coercion.—*vti* to make or become warm or hot; to make or become excited. [OE *hǣto*, heat; *hāt*, hot; Ger *hitze*.]

heath [hēth] *n* any of a family (Evicaceae, the health family) of shrubby evergreen plants that thrive on open barren usu acid soil; a tract of open wasteland, esp in the British Isles. [OE *hæth*.]

heathen [hē´THn] *n* anyone not a Christian, Jew, or Muslim; a person regarded as irreligious, uncivilized, etc.—*pl* **heathens, heathen**.—*adj* strange; uncivilized.—*adj* **hea´thenish**, relating to the heathen; barbarous. [OE *hæthen*; Du *heiden*.]

heather [heTH´ėr] *n* a common heath (*Calluna vulgaris*) of northern and alpine regions with small sessile leaves and tiny usu purplish pink flowers.—*adjs* **heather, heathery**, of, relating to, resembling, heather; having flecks of various soft colors. [Older Scots *hadder*.]

heave [hēv] *vt* to lift, esp with great effort; to lift in this way and throw; to utter (a sigh, etc.) with effort; (*naut*) to raise, haul, etc. by pulling as with a rope.—*vi* to swell up; to rise and fall rhythmically; to vomit; to pant; to gasp; (*naut*) to haul.—*pr p* **heav´ing**; *pt p* **heaved** or **hove**.—*n* the act or effort of heaving.—**heave-ho**, (*inf*) dismissal, as from a job.—**heave to**, (*naut*) to stop. [OE *hebban*, pt *hōf*, pt p *hafen*; Ger *heben*.]

heaven [hev´n] *n* (usu. *pl*) the visible sky; **Heaven**, the dwelling place of God and his angels where the blessed go after death; God; any place or state of great happiness.—*adj* **heavenly**, of or relating to heaven or heavens; beatific; delightful.—*adj, adv* **heavenward, heavenwards**, toward heaven. [OE *heofon*.]

heavy [hev´i] *adj* hard to lift or carry; of more than the usual, expected, or defined weight; to an unusual extent (*a heavy vote, a heavy drinker*); hard to do; hard to digest; clinging, penetrating (*a heavy odor*); cloudy (*a heavy sky*); using massive machinery to produce basic materials, as chemicals and steel; (*theatre*) a villain.—*adjs* **heav´y-duty**, made to withstand great strain, bad weather, etc.; **heav´y-handed**, clumsy; tactless; tyrannical; **heav´y-hearted**, sad; unhappy.—*n* **heavy hydrogen**, deuterium.—*adj* **heav´y-set**, having a stout or stocky build.—*ns* **heavy water**, deuterium oxide, water in which the normal hydrogen content has been replaced by deuterium; **heav´yweight**, a boxer or wrestler who weighs over 175 pounds. [OE *hefig*—*hebban*, to heave; OHG *hebig*.]

hebdomadal [heb-dom´a-dål] *adj* weekly. [L *hebdomadālis*—Gr *hebdomas*, a period of seven days—*hepta*, seven.]

Hebrew [hē´brōō] *n* a member of an ancient Semitic people; an Israelite; a Jew; the ancient Semitic language of the Israelites; its modern form, the language of Israel.—*Also adj*.—*vt* **hebra-ize´**, to make Hebraic in form or character. [OFr *Ebreu*—L *Hebraeus*—Gr *Hebraios*—Heb '*ibrī*, lit 'one from the other side (of the river)'.]

Hebrews [hē´brōōz] (*Bible*) 19th book of the New Testament, epistle of disputed authorship espousing the perfection of Christ.

hecatomb [hek´a-tom] *n* a great public sacrifice; any large number of victims. [Gr *hekatombē*—*hekaton*, a hundred, *bous*, an ox.]

heck [hek] *interj, n* (*inf*) a euphemism for *hell*.

heckle [hek´l] *vt* to harass (a speaker) with questions or taunts.—*n* **heck´ler**. [ME *hekelen*.]

hectare [hek´tar] *n* a metric measure of area, 10,000 square meters; 100 ares—2.47 acres.

hectic, -al [hek´tik, -ål] *adj* pertaining to the constitution or habit of body; affected with hectic fever; intense, feverish, rushed. [Fr.—Gr *hektikos*, habitual—*hexis*, habit.]

hecto- [hek´to-] **hect-**, 100 times, as in **hectogram**, 100 grams; **hectoliter**, 100 liters; **hectometer**, 100 meters.

hectograph [hek´to-gräf] *n* a gelatine pad for printing copies of a writing or drawing. [Gr *hakaton*, hundred, *graphein*, to write.]

hector [hek´tȯr] *n* a bully, a braggart.—*vt* to treat insolently; to annoy.—*vi* to play the bully. [Gr *Hector*, the Trojan hero.]

heddle [hed´l] *n* an arrangement on a loom for moving the threads of the warp so as to allow the shuttle to pass bearing the weft.

hedge [hej] *n* a close row of bushes or small trees serving as a fence; a barrier.—*vt* to enclose with a hedge; to surround; to hem in; to guard; to place secondary bets as a precaution.—*vi* to avoid committing oneself, as in argument.—*ns* **hedge´hog**, a small insectivorous Old World mammal (genus *Erinaceous*) with sharp spines on the back; a porcupine; **hedge´pig**, a hedgehog; **hedge´row**, a line of shrubs or trees separating or enclosing fields. [OE *hecg, hegg*; Du *hegge*, Ger *hecke*.]

hedonism [hē´dȯn-izm] *n* the doctrine that pleasure is the highest good.—*n* **hē´donist**. [Gr *hēdonē*, pleasure.]

heed [hēd] *vt* to pay close attention (to).—*n* careful attention.—*adj* **heed´ful**.—*adv* **heed´fully**.—*n* **heed´fulness**.—*adj* **heed´less**, inattentive; careless.—*adv* **heed´lessly**.—*n* **heed´lessness**. [OE *hēdan*; Du *hoeden*.]

heehaw [hē´hö] *vi* to bray. [Imit.]

heel [hēl] *n* the back part of the foot, under the ankle; the part covering or supporting the heel in stockings, etc. or shoes; one of the crusty ends of a loaf of bread; a solid attachment forming the back of the sole of a shoe; a rear, low, or bottom part; anything like a heel in shape, crushing power, etc.; (*inf*) a despicable person.—*vt* to furnish with a heel; to follow closely; (*inf*) to provide with money, etc.—*vi* to follow along at the heels of someone.—**down at the heel(s)**, shabby; seedy; **kick up one's heels**, to have fun; **on** or **upon the heels of**, close behind; **under heel**, under subjection. [OE *hēla*; Du *hiel*.]

heel [hēl] *vi* to incline; to lean to one side, as a ship.—*vt* to tilt. [Earlier *heeld, hield*—OE *hieldan*, to slope; cf Du *hellen*.]

heft [heft] *vt* to lift; to estimate a weight by lifting. [Same root as **heave**.]

hefty [heft´i] *adj* (*inf*) heavy; large and strong; big. [Same root as **heave**.]

hegemony [hē-, he-gem´ȯn-i, or -jem´-, or hē´-, he´-] *n* leadership; preponderant influence, esp of one nation over others. [Gr *hēgemonia*—*hēgemōn*, leader.]

hegira, hejira [hej´i-ra] *n* the flight of Mohammed from Mecca in 622 AD. [Ar *hijrah*, flight, *hajara*, to leave.]

heifer [hef´ėr] *n* a young cow that has not calved. [OE *hēahfore, hēahfru, -fre*; prob 'high-goer'—*hēah*, high, *faran*, to go.]

heigh-ho [hā´-, or hī´-hō] *interj* an exclamation of weariness; a cry of encouragement. [Imit.]

height [hīt] *n* the topmost point; the highest limit; the distance from the bottom to the top; altitude; a relatively great distance above a given level; an eminence; a hill.—*vti* **heighten**, to make or come to a higher position; to make or become larger, greater, etc. [For *highth*—OE *hīehtho, hēahthu*—*hēah*, high.]

Heimlich maneuver [hīm´lik] *n* applying manual pressure to the lower chest to dislodge a foreign object from the windpipe. [H.J. *Heimlich*, b. 1920, Amer surgeon.]

heinous [hā´nùs] *adj* outrageously evil.—*adv* **hei´nously**.—*n* **hei´nousness**. [OFr *haïnos*—*haïr*, to hate.]

heir [ār] *n* one who inherits or is entitled to inherit another's property, title, etc.—*ns* **heir apparent**, the heir whose right to inherit cannot be denied if he outlives the ancestor; **heir at law**, an heir entitled by law to an intestate's real property; **heir´ess**, a woman or girl who is an heir, esp to great wealth; **heir´loom**, any possession handed down from generation to generation; **heir presumptive**, an heir whose legal right to inheritance may be defeated, esp by the birth of a brother in the case of a girl. [OFr *heir*—L *hērēs*, an heir.]

hejira *see* **hegira**.

Helanca [hė-langk´ė] *n* a trade name for nylon stretch yarn.

held *pt* and *pt p* of **hold**.

helical *see* **helix**.

helicopter [hel´i-kop-tėr] *n* a kind of aircraft lifted and moved, or kept hovering, by large rotary blades mounted horizontally. [Gr *helix*, screw, *pteron*, wing.]

helio- or heli- [hē-li(-ō-] sun [Gr *hēlios*, sun].—eg **heliocentric** [hē-li-ō-sen´trik], *adj* referred to the sun as center.

heliograph [hē´li-ō-gräf] *n* an apparatus for signalling by using the sun's rays reflected by a mirror.—*vt* to signal to by heliograph. [Gr *hēlios*, sun, *graphē*, a drawing—*graphein*, to write.]

heliolatry [hē-li-ol´a-tri] *n* sun worship. [Gr *hēlios*, sun, *latreia*, worship.]

heliometer [hē-li-om´e-tėr] *n* an instrument for measuring the angular distance between two celestial objects or between points on the moon. [Gr *hēlios*, sun, *metron*, a measure.]

heliport [hel´i-port] *n* a landing and takeoff place for a helicopter. Also **helipad**.

heliostat [hē´li-ō-stat] *n* an instrument by means of which a beam of sunlight is reflected in an invariable direction. [Gr *hēlios*, sun, *statos*, fixed—*histanai*, to stand.]

heliotrope [hē´li-ō-trōp] *n* any of a genus (*Heliotropium*) of plants with fragrant clusters of small white or reddish-purple flowers; reddish purple; a bloodstone.—*n* **heliot´ropism**, the tendency of a plant to bend toward the light. [Gr *hēliotropion*—*hēlios*, the sun, *tropos*, a turn.]

helium [hēl´i-um] *n* a gaseous element (symbol He; at wt 4.003; at no 2), in the sun's atmosphere. [Gr *hēlios*, sun.]

helix [hē´liks] *n* a spiral; the rim of the ear.—*pl* **helices** [hel´i-sēz] or **hel´ixes**.—*adj* **helical** [hel´i-kȧl]. [L *helix, -icis*—Gr *helix*, a spiral—*helissein*, to turn round.]

hell [hel] *n* in Christian belief, the place or state of punishment of the wicked after death; the abode of evil spirits; any place of vice or misery; (a state of) supreme misery or discomfort; severe censure or chastisement.—*ns* **hell´-er**, an obstreperous person; **hell´hound**, a hound of hell; an agent of hell; **hellion** [hel´yȯn], one given to diabolical conduct.—*adj* **hell´ish**, pertaining to or like hell; very wicked.—*adv* **hell´ishly**.—*n* **hell´ishness**. [OE *hel*; ON *hel*, Ger *hölle*.]

hellebore [hel´ė-bōr, -bör] *n* any of a genus (*Helle borus*) of plants of the buttercup family, esp the Christmas rose (*H. iniger*). [Gr *helleboros*.]

Hellenic [hel-en´ik] *adj* Greek; of the history, language, or culture of the ancient Greeks.—*n* **Hellenist**, a person living in ancient Greece who adopted the language and way of life but was of foreign ancestry, esp a hellenized Jew; a specialist in ancient Greek.—*adjs* **Hellenist´ic**, pertaining to the Hellenists; pertaining to Greek language and culture affected by foreign influences after the time of Alexander the Great (356–323 BC). [Gr *Hellēn*, a Greek.]

hello [hul-ō, he´-lō] *interj*; a form of greeting.—*n* a call of hello.—*vi* to call hello. [Imit.]

helm[1] [helm] *n* the apparatus by which a ship is steered.—*n* **helms´man**, one who steers. [OE *helma*; ON *hjālm*, a rudder, Ger *helm*, a handle.]

helm[2] [helm], **helmet** [hel´met] *n* a covering of armor for the head; the hood-shaped petals of certain flowers.—*adj* **hel´meted**, [OE *helm*; Ger *helm*.]

helminth [hel´minth] *n* a worm, esp an intestinal one.—*adj* **helmin´thic**.—*ns* **helminthol´ogy**, the study of worms; **helminthol´ogist**. [Gr *helmins, -inthos*, a worm.]

helot [hel´ot] *n* a serf or slave.—*n* **hel´ot-ism**, a symbiotic relationship in which one member functions as the slave of the other. [Gr *Heilōtēs*, also *Heilōs*.]

help [help] *vt* to make things better or easier for; to aid; to assist; to remedy (*to help a cough*); to keep from (*can't help crying*); to serve or wait on (a customer, etc.).—*vi* to give aid; to be useful; *pt p* **helped**.—*n* a helping; aid; assistance; a remedy; one that helps, esp a hired person.—*n* **helper**.—*adj* **helpful**, giving help; useful.—*adv* **help´fully**.—*ns* **help´fulness; help´ing**, a portion served to one person.—*adj* **help´less**, unable to help oneself.—*adv* **help´lessly**.—*ns* **help´lessness; help´mate, help´meet**, a helpful companion, esp a wife or husband.—**help oneself to**, to take without asking; **help out**, to help in getting or doing something. [OE *helpen*, pt *healp*, pt p *holpen*; ON *hjālpa*, Ger *helfen*.]

helter-skelter [hel´tėr-skel´tėr] *adv* in haste and confusion.—*adj* disorderly. [Imit.]

helve [helv] *n* the handle of an axe or similar tool.—*vt* to furnish with a helve. [OE *helfe*, a handle.]

hem [hem] *n* the border of a garment etc.—*vt* to form a hem on by preventing the fabric from fraying, usu. by folding and sewing down the edge; to edge; to sew with a stitch used in making a hem.—*pr p* **hemm´ing**; *pt p* **hemmed**.—*n* **hem´-stitch**, an ornamental finish on fabric made by pulling out several adjoining threads.—*vt* to decorate with hemstitch.—**hem in**, to surround, confine. [OE *hemm*, a border.]

hem [hem, hm] *n, interj* a sort of half-cough to draw attention. [Imit.]

he-man [hē´man] (*inf*) a strong, virile man.

hematite [hē´mȧ-tīt] *n* native ferric oxide, an important iron ore.

hematology [hē-ȧ-tol´ōjī] *n* the study of blood and its diseases. [Gr *haima*, blood, *logos*, discourse.]

hematoma [hēm-ȧ-tōm´a] *n* a tumorlike swelling containing blood. [Gr *haimat- (haima)* blood.]

heme [hēm] *n* the iron-containing pigment in hemoglobin. [Gr *haima*, blood.]

hemi- [hem´i-] half. [Gr **hēmi-**, half.]

hemiplegia [hem-i-plēj´ē-ȧ] *n* paralysis of one side of the body.

Hemiptera [hem-ip´tėr-a] *n pl* an order of insects with piercing and sucking mouthparts, usu. two pairs of wings, including many important pests. [Gr *hēmi-*, half, *pteron*, a wing.]

hemisphere [hem´i-sfēr] *n* half of a sphere or globe; any of the halves (northern, southern, eastern, or western) of the earth; the left or the right half of the cerebrum.—*adjs* **hemispher´ic, -al**. [Gr *hēmisphairion*—*hēmi-*, half, *sphaira*, a sphere.]

hemistich [hem´i-stik] *n* half a line, an incomplete line of poetry.—*adj* **hem´istichal** [or *-is´-*]. [L *hēmistichium*—Gr *hēmistichion*—*hēmi-*, half, *stichos*, a line.]

hemlock [hem´lok] *n* a poisonous plant (*Conium maculatum*) of the parsley family; a poison made from this plant; an evergreen tree (*Tsuga canadensis*) of the pine family; its wood. [OE *hymlīce*.]

hemoglobin [hēm´ō-glō-bin] *n* the red coloring matter of the red blood corpuscles.

hemophilia [hēm-ō-fil´ē-a] *n* a hereditary condition in which the blood fails to clot normally.—*adj, n* **he´mophiliac**. [Gr *haima*, blood, *philia*, love.]

hemorrhage [hem´er-ij, hem´rij] *n* the escape of blood from a blood vessel; heavy bleeding. [Gr *haimorrhagia*—*haima*, blood, *rhēgnynai*, to burst.]

hemorrhoid [hem´e-roid, hem´roid] *n* a painful swelling of a vein near the anus, often with bleeding.—Also **piles**. [Gr *haima*, blood, *rheein*, to flow.]

hemp [hemp] *n* a widely cultivated Asian herb (*Cannabis sativa*) of the mulberry family; its fiber, used to make rope, sailcloth, etc.; a substance, as hashish, made from its leaves and flowers.—*adj* **hemp´en**, made of hemp. [OE *henep, hænep*; cf Gr *kannabis*.]

hen [hen] *n* the female of many birds, esp the chicken.—*ns* **henn´ery**, a poultry farm; an enclosure for poultry; **hen´party**, a party for women only.—*vt* **henpeck**, to nag and domineer over (one's husband); **hen´track, hen´scratch**, illegible handwriting. [OE *henn*, fem of *hana*, a cock; Ger *henne* (*hahn*, cock).]

hence [hens] *adv* from this place; from this time; from this cause or reason.—*interj* away! begone!—*advs* **hence´forth, hencefor´ward**, from this time forth or forward. [ME *hennes*, formed with genitive ending from *henne*—OE *heonan*, from base of **he**.]

henchman [hench´man, -sh´-] *n* a trusted helper or follower. [OE *hengest*, a horse + **man**.]

hendecasyllable [hen´dek-à-sil´à-bl] *n* a metrical line of eleven syllables.—*adj* **hendecasyllab´ic**. [Gr *hendeka*, eleven, *syllabē*, a syllable.]

hendiadys [hen-dī´a-dis] *n* the expression of an idea (such as that normally contained in a noun and an adjective) by using two words connected by 'and', as 'with might and main', meaning 'by main strength'. [Gr *hen dia dyoin*, lit 'one by two'.]

henequen [hen´ē-ken] *n* a tropical American agave (*Agave fourcroydes*); its leaf-fiber used for binder twine. Cf **sisal**. [Sp *jeniquén*.]

henna [hen´a] *n* an Old World tropical shrub (*Lawsonia inermis*); a dye extracted from its leaves used to tint the hair or skin; reddish brown.—*adj* reddish-brown.—*vt* to dye with henna. [Ar *hennā´*.]

henry [hen´ri] *n* (*elect*) the unit of inductance such that an electromotive force of one volt is induced in a circuit by rate of change of current of one ampere per second; symbol H. [Joseph *Henry*, American physicist (1797–1878).]

hep [hep] *n see* **hip**³.

hepatic [hep-at´ik] *adj* belonging to the liver.—**heparin** [hep-ar´in], a substance produced by the liver that inhibits clotting of the blood.—*n* **hepatī´tis**, inflammation of the liver. [Gr *hēpar, hēpătos*, the liver.]

hept(a)- seven [Gr *hepta*, seven]—eg **heptangular** [heptang´gū-lår], *adj* having seven angles.

heptad [hep´tad] *n* a group of seven. [Gr *heptas, -ados—hepta*, seven.]

heptagon [hep´ta-gon] *n* a polygon of seven angles and seven sides.—*adj* **heptag´onal**. [Gr *heptagōnos*, seven-cornered—*hepta*, seven, *gōnia*, an angle.]

her [hûr] *pron* the objective case (*dat* or *acc*) of the *pron* **she**; also the possessive case (*gen*)—in this use described also as *possessive adjective*. [ME *here*—OE *hire*, gen and dat sing of *hēo*, she.]

herald [her´åld] *n* in former times, an official who made public proclamations and arranged ceremonies; a British official who records coats-of-arms, etc.; a proclaimer; a forerunner.—*vt* to usher in; to proclaim.—*adj* **heral´dic**, of or relating to heralds or heraldry.—*adv.* **heral´dically**.—*n* **her´aldry**, the science of dealing with genealogies and coats of arms; ceremony; pomp. [OFr *herault*; of Gmc origin.]

herb [ûrb, hûrb] *n* any seed plant whose stem withers away annually; any plant used as a medicine, seasoning, etc.—*adj* **herbā´ceous**, of the nature of, or containing, herbs.—*n* **herb´age**, pasturage; the succulent parts of herbs.—*adj* **herb´al**, pertaining to herbs.—*n* a book containing descriptions of plants with medicinal properties.—*ns* **herb´alist**, one who practices healing by using herbs; one who grows or deals in herbs; **herbä´rium**, a classified collection of dried plants.—*pl* **herbä´ria; herb´icide** [-i-sīd], a substance for killing plants; **herb´ivore** [-vōr, -vör], a plant-eating animal.—*adj* **herbiv´orous**, living on plants.—*n* **herb´Rob´ert**, a sticky low geranium (*Geranium robertianum*) with small reddish purple flowers. [Fr *herbe*—L *herba*.]

Herculean [hûr-kū-lē´ån] *adj* extremely difficult or dangerous; of extraordinary strength and size.—*n* **Her´cules**, a very strong man. [*Hercules*, son of Zeus, noted for the twelve difficult tasks imposed on him.]

herd [hûrd] *n* a number of animals of one kind, esp large animals, that habitually keep together.—*vi* to go in herds.—*vt* to tend, as a herdsman.—*n* **herds´man**, one who manages, breeds, or tends a herd. [OE *hæord, hirde, hierde*; Ger *heerde, hirte*.]

here [hēr] *adv* at or in this place; used as an intensive (*John here is an actor*); to or into this place; now; on earth.—*n* this place.—*advs* **here´about**, also **-abouts**, near this place; **hereaf´ter**, after this, in some future time or state.—*n* the state after death.—*advs* **hereby´**, by this means; **herein´**, in here; in this writing, container, etc.; **hereof´**, of this; **hereon´**, on this; **hereto´**, for this object; **heretofore´**, up to now, **hereunto´** [also -un´-], to this; **hereupon´**, on this, immediately after this; **herewith´**, with this.—**neither here nor there**, irrelevant. [OE *hēr*, from base of *hē*, he; Du and Ger *hier*, Swed *här*.]

heredity [he-red´i-ti] *n* the transmission of physical characteristics from ancestors to their descendants.—*adj* **hered´itable**, that may be inherited.—*n* **heredit´ament**, any property that may pass to an heir.—*adj* **hered´itary**, descending by inheritance; transmitted to offspring. [L *hērēditā, -ātis*—*hērēs, -ēdis*, an heir.]

heresy [her´i-si] *n* an opinion or belief (esp in theology) adopted in opposition to that accepted or usual in the community to which one belongs.—**her´etic**, a dissenter from an established belief or doctrine.—*adj* **heret´ical**.—*adv* **heret´ically**. [OFr *heresie*—L *haeresis*—Gr *hairesis*—*haireein*, to take.]

heritable [her´i-ta-bl] *adj* that may be inherited.—*n* **her´itor**, one that inherits. [Fr *héritable, héréditable*—Low L *hērēditābilis—hērēs*, heir.]

heritage [her´it-ij] *n* that which is inherited; tradition, etc. handed down from one's ancestors or the past. [OFr *heritage, heriter*—Late L *hērēditāre*, to inherit.]

hermaphrodite [hûr-maf´rod-īt] *n* an animal or a plant with the organs of both sexes.—*adjs* **hermaphrodīt´ic**. [Gr *Hermaphrodītos*, the son of *Hermēs* and *Aphrodītē*, who grew together with the nymph Salmacis into one person.]

hermeneutical hermeneutic [hûr-mė-nū´tik, (-ål,)] *adj* interpreting, explanatory.—*adv* **hermeneu´tically**.—*n sing* **hermeneu´tics**, the science of interpretation, esp of the Scriptures. [Gr *hermēneutikos—hermēneus*, an interpreter, from *Hermēs*, the herald of the gods.]

hermetic [hûr-met´ik] *adj* airtight.—*adv* **hermet´ically**. [From *Hermēs Trismegistos*, Hermes 'the thrice-greatest', the Greek name for the Egyptian Thoth, god of science, esp alchemy.]

hermit [hûr´mit] *n* a recluse.—*n* **her´mitage** [-ij]), the dwelling of a hermit. [ME *eremite*, through Fr and L from Gr *erēmītēs—erēmos*, solitary.]

hernia [hûr´ni-a] *n* the protrusion of an organ, esp part of the intestine, through an opening in the wall of the surrounding structure; a rupture.—*adj* **her´nial**. [L.]

hero [hē´rō] *n* a man of distinguished bravery; one admired for his exploits; the central male character in a novel, play, etc..—*pl* **hēroes**.—**heroine** [her´ō-in], a woman with the attributes of a hero.—*adj* **heroic** [hė-rō´ik], of or like a hero; of or about heroes and their deeds; daring and risky.—*n pl* **herō´ics**, extravagant talk or action.—*adv* **hero´ically**.—*ns* **heroism** [her´ō-izm], the qualities of a hero; high courage; **hero sandwich**, a sandwich made of a long roll sliced lengthwise and well filled with meat, cheese, onions, lettuce, etc.; **hē´ro wor´ship**, the worship of heroes; excessive admiration.—**hero´ic coup´let**, a pair of rhyming lines in iambic pentameter. [Through OFr and L from Gr *hērōs*; akin to L *vir*, OE *wer*, a man, Sans *vīra*, a hero.]

heroin [her´ō-in, her-ō´in] *n* a habit-forming derivative of morphine. [*Heroin*, a trademark.]

heron [her´ȯn] *n* wading bird (family Ardeidae), esp the New World species including the Black-crowned night heron and bitterns.—*n* **her´onry**, a heron rookery. [OFr *hairon*—OHG *heigir*.]

herpes [hûr´pēz] *n* any of several virus diseases marked by small blisters on the skin or mucous membranes. [Gr *herpēs—herpein*, to creep.]

Herr [her] a German title equivalent to English Mr. [Ger.]

herring [her´ing] *n* a small food fish (family Clupeidae) abundant in the N Atlantic and N Pacific, canned and sold as sardines on the young state.—*adj* **herr´ingbone**, like the spine of a herring with the ribs extending in rows of parallel, slanting lines; having such a pattern.—**red herring** *see* **red**. [OE *hǣring, hēring*; cf Ger *häring, heer*.]

hers [hėrz] *pron* the possessive (*gen*) case of **she**. *See* **theirs**.

herself [hėr-self´] *pron* the emphatic form of **she** (nominative), **her** (objective—accusative or dative); in her real character; the reflexive form of **her** (objective).

hertz [hûrts] *n* SI unit of frequency, equal to one cycle per second.—**Hertzian waves**, electromagnetic radiation resulting from the oscillations of electricity in a conductor; symbol Hz. [Heinrich *Hertz* (1857–94), German physicist.]

hesitate [hez´i-tāt] *vi* to pause irresolutely; to be in doubt; to be reluctant (to); *ns* **hes´itancy, hesitā´tion**, wavering; doubt.—*adj* **hes´itant**, hesitating.—*adv* **hes´itātingly**. [L *haesitāre, -ātum*, freq of *haerēre, haesum*, to stick.]

Hespē´rian [he-spir´ē-ån] *adj* in the west. [Gr *hesperos*, evening.]

Hessian [hes´i-ån] sometimes [hesh´-] *adj* of or pertaining to *Hesse*.—*n* a native of Hesse; **hessian**, a German mercenary serving in the British army during the American Revolution; burlap; (*pl*) short for **Hessian boots**, a kind of long boots first worn by Hessian troops.—**Hessian fly**, a two-winged fly (*Mayetiola destructor*) destructive to wheat crops in America. [From *Hesse*, Ger *Hessen*, in Germany.]

hetaera, hetaira [hi-tir´ė, hi-tīr-e] *n* a highly-educated courtesan in Ancient Greece; a demimondaine.—*pl* **hetaerae, hetaeras, hetairas, hetairai**. [Gr *hetaira*, companion.]

hetero- [het´ėr-o-, -ō´-] **heter**, different, other [Gr *heteros*].—eg **heterochromatic** [het-ėr-ō-krōm-å-tik], having different colors; made up of different wavelengths or frequencies; **heterosexual** [het-ėr-ō-seks´ū-ål], having sexual attraction towards the opposite sex.

heteroclite [het´ėr-ō-klīt] *adj* (*gram*) irregularly inflected.—Also *n.* [Gr *heteroklitos—heteros*, other, *klitos*, inflected—*klinein*, to inflect.]

heterodox [het´ėr-ō-doks] *adj* holding an opinion other than, different from, the one generally received, esp in theology; heretical.—*n* **het´erodoxy**, heresy. [Gr *heterodoxos—heteros*, other, *doxa*, an opinion—*dokeein*, to think.]

heterodyne [het´ėr-ȯ-dīn] in (radio) communication, applied to a method of imposing on a carrier wave another of different frequency to produce audible beats. [Gr *heteros*, other, *dynamis*, strength.]

heterogeneous [het-ėr-ō-jē´ni-ůs] *adj* dissimilar; composed of parts or elements of different kinds.—*ns* **heterogenē´ity, heterogēn´eousness**.—*adv* **heterogēn´eously**. [Gr *heterogenēs—heteros*, other, *genos*, a kind.]
heuristic [hū-ris´tik] *adj* helping to learn, as by a method of self-teaching.—Also *n*. [Gr *heuriskein*, to find.]
hew [hū] *vt* to cut with blows; to shape; to cut (a path; eg *to hew one's way*).—*vi* to conform (to a rule, principle, etc..—*pt p* **hewed**, or **hewn**.—*n* **hew´er**, one who hews. [OE *hēawan*; Ger *hauen*.]
hexa-, hex-, six [Gr *hex*].—eg **hexad** [hek´sad], *n* a group of six (Gr *hexas*, *-ados*); **hexose**, a sugar (as glucose) with six carbon atoms to the molecule.
hexachord [hek´sa-körd] *n* a series of six notes having a semitone between the third and fourth tones. [**hexa-** + Gr *chordē*, a string.]
hexagon [heks´a-gon] *n* a figure with six sides and six angles.—*adj* **hexag´onal**.—*adv* **hexag´onally**. [Gr *hexagōnon—hex*, six, *gōnia*, an angle.]
hexahedron [heks-a-hē´dron] *n* a solid with six faces, esp a cube.—*adj* **hexahē´dral**. [Gr *hex*, six, *hĕdra*, a base.]
hexameter [hek-sam´et-ėr] *n* a line of verse of six metrical feet. [L.—Gr *hex*, six, *metron*, a measure.]
hexapod [heks´a-pod] *n* an insect. [Gr *hexapous*, *-podos—hex*, six, *pous*, a foot.]
hey [hā] *interj* expressive of joy or interrogation or calling attention.—*n* **hey´day**, a period of fullest vigor. [Imit.]
hi [hī] *interj* an exclamation of greeting.
hiatus [hī-ā´tus] *n* a break in continuity; (*gram*) a slight pause between two vowels coming together in successive words or syllables.—*pl* **hīā´tuses**. [L.—*hiāre, hiātum*, to gape.]
hibachi [hi-bäch´ē] *n* a portable barbecue. [Jap.]
hibernate [hī´bėr-nāt] *vi* to winter; to pass the winter in torpor; to remain in a state of inactivity.—*n* **hibernā´tion**. [L *hībernāre, -ātum—hībernus*, wintry—*hiems*, winter.]
Hibernian [hī-bür´ni-ȧn] *adj* relating to *Hibernia* or Ireland.—*n* a native or inhabitant of Ireland. [L *Hibernia*, Ireland.]
Hibiscus [hib-is´kůs] *n* a genus (*Hibiscus*) of plants of the mallow family, esp Rose of Sharon (*H. syriacus*), a temperate zone tree or shrub. [L.—Gr *ibiskos*, marshmallow.]
hiccup [hik´up] *n* a sudden spasm of the diaphragm followed immediately by closure of the glottis; the sound caused by this.—*vi* to be affected with hiccup.—*pr p* **hicc´uping**; *pt p* **hicc´uped**.—Also **hiccough** [hik´up]. [Imit; cf Du *hik*, Dan *hik*, Breton *hik*.]
hick [hik] *n* (*inf*) an unsophisticated person, esp from a rural area. [A familiar form of *Richard*.]
hickory [hik´ȯr-i] *n* a genus (*Carya*) of N American trees of the walnut family; its hard, tough wood; its smooth-shelled edible nut.—Also **hickory nut**. [Earlier *pohickery*; of Amer Indian origin.]
hid, hidden *see* **hide**.
hidalgo [hi-dal´gō] *n* a Spanish nobleman of the lowest class.—*pl* **hidalgōs**. [Sp *hijo de algo*, 'the son of something'.]
hide[1] [hīd] *vt* to conceal; to put out of sight; to keep secret; to screen.—*vi* to go into, or stay in, concealment.—*pt* **hid**; *pt p* **hidd´en, hid**.—*adj* **hidd´en**, concealed; unknown.—*ns* **hide´away** (*inf*) a place where one can hide; **hide´out**, (*inf*) a hiding place, as for gangsters. [OE *hȳdan*, to hide.]
hide[2] [hīd] *n* the skin of an animal either raw or tanned.—*adj* **hide´bound** (of an animal), having the hide clinging too closely to the body; obstinately conservative and narrow-minded.—*n* **hid´ing**, a thrashing. [OE *hȳd*; Ger *haut*, L *cutis*.]
hideous [hid´i-ůs] *adj* frightful, horrible, ghastly; extremely ugly.—*n* **hid´eousness**.—*adv* **hid´eously**. [OFr *hideus, hisdos—hide, hisde*, dread; perh from L *hispidus*, rough, rude.]
hie [hī] *vti* to hasten.—*pr p* **hie´ing**; *pt p* **hied**. [OE *hīgian*.]
hiemal [hē´māl, hī´e-mȧl] *adj* belonging to winter. [L *hiems*, winter.]
hierarch [hī´ėr-ärk] *n* a religious leader, esp of high authority.—*adjs* **hī´erarchal**, of a hierarch; **hierarch´ical**, of, or relating to a hierarchy.—**hī´erarchy**.—*n* church government by clergy in graded ranks; the highest officials in such a system; a group of persons or things arranged in order of rank, grade, etc. [Gr *hierarchēs—hieros*, sacred, *archein*, to rule.]
hieratic [hī-ėr-at´ik] *adj* priestly; applying to a kind of ancient Egyptian writing consisting of simplified forms of hieroglyphics. [L *hierāticus*—Gr *hierātikos—hieros*, sacred.]
hieroglyph [hī´ėr-ō-glif] *n* a character used in a system of hieroglyphic writing.—*n* **hieroglyph´ic**, a picture or symbol representing a word, sound, etc. in a system used by ancient Egyptians and others; a symbol hard to understand; a hieroglyph; any written character difficult to read.—*adjs* **hieroglyph´ic, -al**.—*adv* **hieroglyph´ically**. [Gr *hieroglyphikon—hieros*, sacred, *glyphein*, to carve.]
hi-fi [hī-fī] *n* high fidelity; equipment for reproduction of sound with high fidelity.
higgle [hig´l] *vi* to haggle.—*n* **higg´ler**. [Prob a form of **haggle**.]
higgledy-piggledy [hig´l-di-pig´l-di] *adv* and *adj* haphazard; in confusion.
high [hī] *adj* lofty, tall; extending upward a (specified) distance; situated at or done from a height; above others in rank, position, etc.; greater in size, amount, cost, etc. than usual; raised or acute in pitch; (of meat) slightly tainted; (*slang*) drunk; (*slang*) under the influence of a drug.—*adv* in or to a high degree, rank, etc.—*n* a high level, place, etc.; that gear of a motor vehicle, etc. producing the greatest speed; (*slang*) euphoric condition induced as by drugs.—*n* **high´ball**, whiskey or brandy mixed with soda water, etc.—*adj* **high´born**, of noble birth.—*ns* **high´boy**, a high chest of drawers mounted on legs; **high´brow**, (*inf*) an intellectual; **high-energy physics**, a branch of physics dealing with elementary particles esp as in experiments using particle accelerators; **higher-up** (*inf*) a person of higher rank, etc.—*adj* **high´falut´in, hi´falut´in**, (*inf*) pretentious; pompous.—*n* **high fidelity**, nearly exact reproduction of a wide range of sound waves in recording, broadcast transmission, etc.—*adj* **high´-flown**, extravagantly ambitious; bombastic.—*ns* **high frequency**, any radio frequency between 3 and 30 megahertz; **High German**, German as spoken by native speakers in central and southern Germany.—*adjs* **high´hand´ed**, overbearing; **high-hat**, (*slang*) snobbish.—*vt* (*slang*) to snub.—*ns* **High Holiday**, either Rosh Hashanah or Yom Kippur; **highland**, a region with many hills or mountains; **the Highlands**, the mountainous region occupying most of northern Scotland; **high jump**, a jump for height in a track-and-field event.—*adj* **high-level**, of or by persons of high office; in a high office.—*n* **high-level language**, (*computing*) language suitable for problem-solving where a single instruction can correspond to several instructions; **high´light, high light**, the part on which light is brightest; the most important or interesting scene, part, etc.—*vt* to give highlights to; to give prominence to.—*adv* **highly**, very much; favorably; at a high level, wage, rank, etc.—*adj* **high-mind´ed**, having high ideals, etc.—*n* **highness**, height; **Highness**, a title used in speaking to or of royalty.—*adjs* **high-octane** (of gasoline) having a high octane number and thus good antiknock properties; **high-pressure**, having or withstanding high pressure; using insistent methods.—*vt* (*inf*) to urge with such methods.—*ns* **high relief**, a sculptural relief in which at least half of the sculptured form projects beyond the background; **high-rise**, an apartment house, office building, etc. of many stories; **high school**, a secondary school for students in grades 10, 11 and 12, and sometimes grade 9; **high seas**, open ocean waters outside the territorial limits of any nation; **high sign**, (*inf*) a secret warning signal.—*adj* **high´-spirited**, courageous; lively; **high´-strung**, nervous and tense; excitable; **high-tech**, of specialized complex technology; of furniture, fashions, etc. utilitarian in design.—*n* **high technology**.—*adj* **high tension**, having or carrying a high voltage.—**high tide**, the highest level to which the tide rises; **high time**, time before the proper time but before it is too late; **high treason**, an act of treason directly affecting the security of a nation; **high´way**, a public road; a main thoroughfare; **high´wayman**, one who robs travelers on a highway.—**high and low**, everywhere; **on high**, in heaven. [OE *hēah*; ON *hār*, Ger *hoch*.]
hijacker, highjacker [hī´jak-ėr] *n* one who hijacks.—*vt* **hi´jack, high´jack**, to steal (goods in transit) by force; to force (an aircraft) to make an unscheduled flight. [Origin obscure.]
hike [hīk] *vi* to take a long walk.—*vt* (*inf*) to pull up; (*inf*) to raise (prices, etc.).—*n* a long walk; a tramp; (*inf*) a rise.—*n* **hiker**. [Perh **hitch**.]
hilarious [hi-lā´ri-ůs] *adj* gay, very merry.—*adv* **hilā´riously**.—*n* **hilarity** [hi-lar´-], gaity. [L *hilaris*—Gr *hilaros*, cheerful.]
hill [hil] *n* a high mass of land, less than a mountain; a mound; an incline on a road.—*n* **hill´ock**, a small hill.—*adj* **hill´y**, full of hills. [OE *hyll*; allied to L *collis*, a hill, *celsus*, high.]
hilt [hilt] *n* the handle of a sword, dagger, tool, etc. [OE *hilt*; MDu *hilte*, OHG *helza*; not conn with **hold**.]
hilum [hī´lum] *n* the scar on a seed where it joined its stalk.—*pl* **hī´la**. [L *hīlum*, a trifle, 'that which adheres to a bean'.]
him [him] *pron* the objective case (*dat* or *acc*) of the *pron* **he**. [OE *him*, dat sing of *hē*, *he*, he, *hit*, it.]
himself [him-self´] *pron* the emphatic form of **he, him**; in his real character; having command of his faculties; sane; in good form; the reflexive form of **him** (objective).
hind [hīnd] *adj* placed in the rear; of the part behind; back.—Also **hind´er**.—*adj* **hind´most**, farthest behind.—*n pl* **hind´quarters**, the rear parts of a quadruped.—*n* **hind´-sight**, wisdom after the event. [OE *hinder*, backwards; Ger *hinter*, behind; cf OE *hindan* (adv), back.]
hinder [hin´dėr] *vt* to keep back, or prevent progress of.—*vi* to be an obstacle.—*n* **hin´drance**, act of hindering; that which hinders, an obstacle. [OE *hindrian*; Ger *hindern*.]
Hindi [hin´dē] *n* the federal language of India; the literary language of northern India.—Also *adj*. [From *Hind*, India.]
Hindu, Hindoo [hin´-dōō] *n* any of several peoples of India; a follower of Hinduism.—*n* **Hin´duism, Hin´dooism**, the dominant religion of India emphasizing the duty of the individual to observe custom and religious law; the religion and customs of the Hindus. [Pers *Hindu—Hind*, India.]
Hindustani, Hindostani [hin-dōō-stä´nē] *n* a dialect of Hindi; all spoken forms of Hindu and Urdu considered together.—Also *adj*.
hinge [hinj] *n* a movable joint on a door or lid; a natural joint, as of a clam.—*vti* to attach or hang by a hinge.—*pr p* **hing´ing**; *pt p* **hinged**.—*n* **hinge´ joint** (*anat*), a joint (as the elbow) that allows movement in one plane only. [Related to **hang**.]
hinny [hin´i] *n* the offspring of a stallion and a female donkey. [L *hinnus*—Gr *ginnos*, later *hinnos*, a mule.]
hint [hint] *n* a distant or indirect indication or allusion; slight mention; a

helpful suggestion.—*vt* to intimate or indicate indirectly.—*vi* to give hints. [OE *hentan*, to seize.]

hinterland [hint´ėr-land] *n* the land behind that bordering a coast or river; a remote area. [Ger.]

hip[1] [hip] *n* either side of the body below the waist and above the thigh.—*ns* **hipbone**, a large flaring bone forming half of the pelvis in mammals; **hipline**, the line formed by measuring the hip at its widest part. [OE *hype*; Ger *hüfte*.]

hip[2] [hip], **hep** [hep] *n* the fruit of the dog-rose or other rose. [OE *hēope*.]

hip[3] [hip] *adj* (*slang*) sophisticated; aware; fashionable; of hippies.—*n* **hippie**, (*slang*) a person usu. young who has turned to mysticism, psychedelic drugs, communal living in his alienation from conventional society.—Also **hippy**.—**get** or **be hip** (*slang*) to become or be informed about.

Hippeastrum [hip-ē-äst´rûm] *n* a genus (*Hippeastrum*) of subtropical and tropical bulbs of the lily family related to and often sold as amaryllis, with showy funnel-shaped flowers. [Gr *hippos*, a horse, *astron*, a star.]

hippocampus [hip-ō-kam´pus] *n* a genus (*Hippocampus*) of small fishes with horselike head and neck, the sea-horse; (*anat*) elongated ridges on the floor of each lateral ventricle of the brain. [Gr *hippokampos—hippos*, a horse, *kampos*, a sea-monster.]

Hippocratic oath an oath taken by a doctor binding him to observe the code of medical ethics contained in it. [Hippocrates, Greek physician, 4th century, BC.]

hippodrome [hip´o-drōm] *n* a stadium for horses and chariots in ancient Greece; an arena for equestrian performances. [Fr—Gr *hippodromos—hippos*, a horse, *dromos*, a course.]

hippogriff [hip´-ō-grif] *n* a fabulous animal, a winged horse with the head of a griffin. [Fr *hippogriffe*—Gr *hippos*, a horse, *gryps*, a griffin.]

hippopotamus [hip-ō-pot´a-mus] *n* any of several large African quadrupeds (genus *Hippopotamus*) of aquatic habits, with very thick skin, short legs, and a large head and muzzle.—*pl* **-muses, -mi**. [L—Gr *hippopotamos—hippos*, a horse, *potamos*, a river.]

hire [hīr] *n* wages for service; the price paid for the use of anything.—*vt* to pay for the services of (a person) or the use of (a thing).—Also *adj*.—*ns* **hire´ling**, one who will follow anyone's order for pay; **hir´er**, one who hires.—**hire out**, to work for pay. [OE *hȳr*, wages, *hȳrian*, to hire.]

hirsute [hėr-sūt´] *adj* hairy; rough, shaggy; (*bot*) having long, stiffish hairs. [L *hirsūtus—hirsus, hirtus*, shaggy.]

his [hiz] *pron* possessive (*gen*) form of **he**—described also as a *possessive adjective*. [OE *his*, gen of *hē, he*, he, and of *hit*, it.]

Hispanic [his-pan´ik] *adj* of, or derived from Spain or the Spanish.—*ns* **Hispan´ist**, one specializing in Spanish language, literature, or civilization; **Hispan´ō**, a native or resident of southwestern US descended from Spanish settlers before annexation. [*Hispania*, Iberian peninsula.]

hispid [his´pid] *adj* (*bot*) rough with, or having, spines, stiff hairs or bristles. [L *hispidus*.]

hiss [his] *vi* to make a sound like that of a prolonged *s*; to show disapproval by hissing.—*vt* to say or indicate by hissing.—*n* the act or sound of hissing.—*n* **hissing**. [Imit.]

hist [hist] *interj* be quiet! [Imit.]

hist(o) [hist(ō)-, -o´-] *n* tissue, as in *ns* **histamine** [hist´àmēn], a substance released by the tissues in allergic reactions; **histology** [his-tol´o-ji], the study of the minute structure of the tissues of organisms. [Gr *histos*, web, and *logos*, discourse.]

history [hist´ȯr-i] *n* an account of the origin and progress of a nation, institution, etc.; all recorded past events; the branch of knowledge that deals with the recording, analysis, etc. of past events; a known past (*my coat has a history*.)—*pl* **-ies**.—*n* **historian**, [hist´-ōr´i-ȧn] a writer of history; one who is learned in history.—*adjs* **histŏr´ical**, pertaining to history; containing history; derived from history; famous in history; **histŏr´ic**, famous in history, memorable.—*adv* **histor´ically**.—*ns* **historic´ity** [-is´-], historical truth, actuality; **historiog´rapher**, historian; **historiog´raphy**, the principles of historical writing, esp that based on the use of primary sources and techniques of research.—**historic present**, the present tense used in relating past events. [L *historia*—Gr *historia—histōr*, knowing.]

histrionic [his-tri-on´ik, -ȧl] *adj* relating to the stage or actors; melodramatic.—*adv* **histrion´ically**.—*n pl* **histrionics**, dramatics; an artificial manner or outburst. [L *histriōnicus—histrio*, an actor.]

hit [hit] *vti* to come against (something) with force; to give a blow (to), to strike; to strike with a missile; to affect strongly; to come (upon) by accident or after a search; to arrive at; (baseball) to get (a hit).—*n* a blow that strikes its mark; a collision; a successful and popular song, book, etc.; (*slang*) a murder; (*slang*) a dose of a drug, a drink of liquor, etc.; (*baseball*) a ball struck by which a batter gets on base.—*n* **hitter.—hit-and-miss**, random; **hit-and-run** (*baseball*) play in which the base runner moves off as soon as the pitcher delivers the ball and the batter swings; an automobile accident usu. involving a pedestrian in which the driver leaves the scene without stopping; **hit it off**, to get along well; **hit the books**, (*inf*) to study; **hit the fan**, (*inf*) to have a stunningly undesirable impact; **hit the jackpot**, to become unexpectedly successful; **hit´list**, (*inf*) a list of persons or programs to be opposed or eliminated; **hit´man**, (*slang*) a hired murderer; **hit the nail on the head**, to be exactly right; **hit the spot**, (*inf*) that gives special satisfaction, usu. of food or drink. [OE *hyttan*, app ON *hitta*, to light on, to find.]

hitch [hich] *vi* to move jerkily; to become fastened or caught.—*vt* to move, pull, etc. with jerks; to fasten with a hook, knot, etc.; (*slang*) to get (a ride) in hitchhiking.—*n* a tug; a limp; a hindrance; a catching; a kind of knot; (*slang*) a period of time served.—*vi* **hitch´hike**, to travel by asking for rides from motorists along the way.—*n* **hitchhiker**. [ME *hicchen*.]

hither [hiTH´ėr] *adv* to this place.—*adj* toward the speaker; nearer.—*adj* **hith´ermost**, nearest on this side.—*advs* **hith´erto**, up to this time; **hith´erward(s)**, towards this place.—**hither and thither**, in various directions. [OE *hider*; ON *hethra*.]

Hitlerism [hit´lėr-izm] *n* the nationalistic and totalitarian principles and policies associated with Hitler.—*adj, n* **Hit´lerite**. [From Adolf *Hitler*, German Nazi dictator 1933–1945.]

hive [hīv] *n* a shelter for a colony of bees; a beehive; the bees of a hive; a crowd of busy people; a place of great activity.—*vt* to gather (bees) into a hive.—*vi* to enter a hive.—**hive off** (*inf*) to separate from a group. [OE *hȳf*.]

hives [hīvs] *n pl* urticaria. [Origin unknown.]

hoar [hōr, hör] *n* a covering of minute ice crystals; ice crystals formed from gas.—*adj* **hoar´y**, white or grey with age; (*bot*) covered with short, dense, whitish hairs.—*n* **hoar´frost**, hoar. [OE *hār*, hoary, gray; ON *hārr*.]

hoard[1] [hōrd, hörd] *n* a store; a hidden stock.—*vti* to amass and deposit in secret.—*n* **hoard´er**. [OE *hord*; ON *hodd*, Ger *hort*.]

hoard[2] [hōrd, hörd], **hoarding** [hōrd´ing, hörd-] *n* a screen of boards, esp for enclosing a place where construction is taking place. [OFr *hurdis—hurt, hourt, hourd*, a palisade.]

hoarse [hōrs, hörs] *adj* having a rough, husky voice, as from a cold; harsh; discordant.—*adv* **hoarse´ly**.—*n* **hoarse´ness**. [ME *hōrs, hoors*—OE recorded from *hās*, inferred *hārs*.]

hoax [hōks] *n* a deceptive trick; a practical joke.—*vt* to deceive by a hoax.—*n* **hoax´er**. [Prob **hocus**.]

hob [hob] *n* a surface beside a fireplace, on which anything may be laid to keep hot.—*n* **hob´nail**, a nail with a thick, strong head, used on the soles of heavy shoes to prevent wear.—*adj* **hob´nailed**. [Ety uncertain.]

hobble [hob´l] *vi* to walk with short unsteady steps; to limp.—*vt* to fasten the legs of (horses, etc.) loosely together.—*n* a limp; a rope etc. used to hobble a horse. [Cf Du *hobbelen, hobben*, to toss.]

hobbledehoy [hob´l-di-hoi´] *n* an awkward youth. [Origin obscure.]

hobby [hob´i] *n* a hobbyhorse; a spare-time activity.—*n* **hobb´yist**, a person pursuing a hobby.—*n* **hobb´yhorse**, a child's toy comprising a stick with a horse's head; a rocking horse. [ME *hobyn, hoby*, prob *Hob*, a by-form of *Rob*.]

hobgoblin [hob´gob-lin] *n* a mischievous goblin; a bugbear. [ME *Hobbe*, a form of Robert.]

hobnail *see* **hob** (1)

hobnob [hob´nob] *vi* to associate familiarly. [Prob *hab, nab*, have, have not (*ne-have*).]

hobo [hō´bō] *n* a vagrant workman; a tramp.—*pl* **-s, -oes**. [Origin unknown.]

Hobson's choice [hob´sȯnz chois] a choice of one or none. [*Hobson*, a Cambridge horse hirer, gave his customers no choice but to take the horse nearest the door.]

hock[1] [hok] *n, vt* (*slang*) to give something in security for a loan.

hock[2] [hok] *n* the joint bending backward on the hind leg of a horse, etc. [OE *hoh*, heel.]

hockey [hok´i] *n* a team game played on ice skates, with curved sticks and a rubber disk, called a puck; a similar game played on foot in a field with a ball. [Prob OFr *hoquet*, a crook.]

hocus-pocus [hō´kus-pō´kus] *n* meaningless words used by a conjurer; sleight of hand; deception.—*vt* **hō´cus**, to cheat; to drug. [Sham Latin.]

hod [hod] *n* a tray or V-shaped stemmed trough for carrying bricks or mortar on the shoulder.—*n* **hod carrier**. [Cf dial *hot, hott*, Ger *hotte*, obs Du *hodde*, Fr *hotte*, a basket.]

hodgepodge [hoj´poj] *n* a jumbled mixture. [Fr *hochepot—hocher*, to shake, and *pot*, a pot.]

Hodgkin's disease [hoj´kinz] *n* a neoplastic disease marked by enlargement of the lymph glands, etc. [T. *Hodgkin*, Eng physician.]

hoe [hō] *n* an instrument for scraping or digging up weeds and loosening the earth.—*vti* to cultivate with a hoe.—*pr p* **hoe´ing**; *pt p* **hoed**. [OFr *houe*—OHG *houwâ*, a hoe.]

hog [hog] *n* a full-grown pig raised for its meat; (*inf*) a selfish, greedy, or filthy person; (*inf*) one that uses something to excess.—*n* **hogback**, a hill ridge, esp one with steeply sloping sides.—*vt* **hog´tie**, to tie the hands or four feet of; (*inf*) to make incapable of effective action; **hog´wash**, the refuse given to pigs; insincere talk, writing, etc.—**go the whole hog**, (*inf*) to go the whole way; **high on** or **off the hog**, (*inf*) in a luxurious way. [OE *hogg*.]

hogshead [hogz´hed] *n* a large cask or barrel holding from 63 to 140 gallons; a liquid measure equal to 63 US gallons. [Apparently **hog's + head**.]

Hohokum [hō-hōkûm] *n* an Amerindian culture of Arizona of 800 A.D.

hoi polloi [hoi po-loi´] the common people; the masses. [Gr, pl of definite article and *adj*.]

hoist [hoist] *vt* to raise aloft, esp with a pulley, crane, etc.—*n* a hoisting; an apparatus for lifting. [Perh Old Du *hijssen*, Du *hijschen*, to hoist.]

hoity-toity [hoi´ti-toi´ti] *adj* giddy; huffy; haughty. [From obs *hoit*, to romp.]

hokum [hō´kum] *n* (*slang*) mawkish sentiment in a play, story, etc.; nonsense; humbug. [Conn with **hocus-pocus**.]

hold[1] [hōld] *vt* to keep fast; to grasp; to maintain in position; to restrain or control; to retain; to contain; to own, to occupy; to remain firm; to carry on, as a meeting; to regard.—*vi* to go on being firm, loyal, etc.; to remain unbroken or unyielding; to be true or valid; to continue; *pr p* **holding**; *pt p* **held**.—*n* a grasping or seizing; a grip; a thing for holding something; a dominating force; a prison.—*ns* **hold´all**, a container for miscellaneous articles; **holder**, one that holds, esp a title deed, lease, etc.; **holdfast**, the part of a plant clinging to a flat surface; the means of attachment of a parasite to its host; something that will hold something else securely; **holding** (often *pl*) property, esp land, stocks and bonds; **holdup**, a delay; an armed robbery; **holding company**, a company formed to hold the stock of other companies, which it then controls; **holding pattern**, the oval course taken by aircraft while waiting for clearance to land.—**hold out on**, (*inf*) to withhold vital information; **on hold**, in a brief state (as of an interrupted telephone call) or indefinite period of suspension. [OE *haldan* (WS *healdan*); OHG *haltan*.]

hold[2] [hōld] *n* the interior of a ship or of an aircraft used for cargo. [**hole**.]

hole [hōl] *n* a hollow place; a cavity; a pit; an animal's burrow; an aperture; a perforation; a small, squalid, dingy place; (*golf*) a small cavity into which the ball is to be hit; the tee, fairway, etc. leading to this.—*vti* to make a hold in (something); to drive into a hole.—*adjs* **hole´-and-cor´ner**, secret, underhand; **hol´ey**, having holes; **hole up**, (*inf*) to hibernate, as in a hole; **in the hole**, (*inf*) financially embarrassed. [OE *hol*, a hole, cavern; Du *hol*, Dan *hul*, Ger *hohl*, hollow.]

holiday [hol´i-dā] *n* a religious festival; a day of freedom from work, etc., esp one set aside by law. [**holy** + **day**.]

holland [hol´ȧnd] *n* a usu. heavily sized, plain-woven cotton or linen fabric used for window shades and bookbinding.—*n* **Holl´ands**, gin made in Holland.

hollo [hol´ō], **holloa** [hol-ō´] *n, interj* a shout of encouragement or to call attention.—*vt* to shout. [Cf **holla, hello**.]

hollow [hol´ō] *n* a hole; a cavity; a depression; a groove, channel.—*adj* having an empty space within or below; sunken; empty or worthless (*hollow praise*).—*vti* to make or become hollow; **holl´owware; holl´oware**, vessels used in the home (as cups, vases, etc.) that have a significant depth. [OE *holh*, a hollow place—*hol*. See **hole**.]

holly [hol´i] *n* a genus (*Ilex*) of evergreen shrubs having prickly leaves and scarlet or yellow berries. [OE *hole(g)n*; cf W *celyn*, Ir *cuileann*.]

hollyhock [hol´i-hok] *n* a tall, widely cultivated perennial herb (*Althaea rosea*) of the mallow family, with spikes of large flowers. [ME *holihoc—holi*, holy, + OE *hoc*, mallow.]

holmium [hōl´mi-ùm] *n* metallic element (symbol Ho; at wt 164.9; at no 67), of the rare-earth group. [*Holmia*, Latinised form of Stockholm.]

holm oak [hōm´ōk´] *n* the evergreen oak (*Quercus ilex*). [ME *holin*—OE *hole(g)n*, holly.]

holo- [hol´ō-], **hol-** [hol-] whole; wholly. [Gr *holos*, hole.]

holocaust [hol´ō-köst] *n* a great destruction of life, esp by fire; **Holocaust**, the murder of Jews by the Nazis. [Gr *holokauston—holos*, whole, *kaustos*, burnt.]

hologram [hol´ō-gram] *n* a photograph made without use of a lens by means of interference between two parts of a laser beam, the result appearing as a meaningless pattern until suitably illuminated, when it shows as a 3-D image (a number of pictures can be 'stored' on the same plate or film).

holograph [hol´ō-gräf] *n* a document wholly in the handwriting of the signer.—Also *adj*.—*adj* **holographic** [-graf´ik].—*n* **holography**, [hol-o´grafi] (the technique of) making or using holograms. [Gr *holos*, whole, *graphein*, to write.]

holster [hōl´stėr] *n* a pistol case attached to a belt.—*adj* **hol´stered**. [Perh Du *holster*, pistol case; cf OE *heolster*, hiding-place.]

holus-bolus [hōl´us-bōl´us] *adv* all at once. [Sham L; perh—Eng *whole bolus* or Gr *holos* and *bōlos*, lump, bolus.]

holy [hō´li] *adj* dedicated to religious use; without sin; deserving reverence.—*ns* **hol´iness**, sanctity; **Holiness**, a title of the Pope (*with* **His** *or* **Your**); **holy city**, a city that is the center of religious traditions; **Holy Communion**, a Christian rite in which bread and wine or substitutes are received as symbols of the body and the blood of Jesus; **Holy Ghost**, the third person of the Trinity; the Holy Spirit; **Holy Grail**, the grail; **Holy Land**, Palestine; **holy of holies**, the most sacred chamber of the Jewish tabernacle and temple; **Holy Roman Empire**, an empire of west central Europe existing from 962 A.D. until 1806; **Holy Spirit**, Holy Ghost; **holystone**, a soft sandstone used for scrubbing a ship's deck; **holy war**, a war waged by religious believers to defend their faith or to preempt invasion; **Holy Week**, the week before Easter. [OE *hālig*, lit whole, perfect, healthy—*hāl*, sound, whole; conn with **hail, heal, whole**.]

homage [hom´ij] *n* anything done or given to show honor, reverence, etc. [OFr *homage*—Low L *homināticum*—L *homō*, a man.]

homburg [hom´bûrg] a man's hat, of felt, with narrow brim, and crown dinted in at the top. [First worn at *Homburg*, Germany.]

home [hōm] *n* the place where one lives; the city, etc. where one was born or reared; a place thought of as home; a household and its affairs; an institution for the aged, orphans, etc.; home plate.—*adj* of one's home or country; domestic; central (*home office*).—*adv* at, to, or in the direction of home; to the point aimed at.—*ns* **home economics**, the art and science of homemaking, nutrition, etc.; **home front**, civilian concerns during a war.—*adj* **home´grown´**, grown or produced at home or nearby; characteristic of a particular locale; **home´like**, cozy; cheerful; wholesome; **homely**, everyday; crude; not good-looking; **home´made**, made, or as if made, at home.—*ns* **home´maker**, a housewife or one who manages a home; **home plate**, (*baseball*) the slab that the batter stands beside which is the last base touched in scoring a run; **home run**, (*baseball*) a hit that allows the batter to touch all bases and score a run.—Also **hom´er** (*inf*).—*adj* **home´sick´**, longing for home.—*n* **home´sick´ness**.—*adj* **home´spun**, cloth spun at home; made of homespun; plain.—*n* cloth made of yard spun at home; coarse cloth like this.—*ns* **home´stead**, a place for a family's home, including the land and buildings; a 160-acre tract of US public land, granted as a farm.—*n* **homesteader**.—*n* **home´stretch´**, the part of a race track between the last turn and the finish line; the final part.—*adj, adv* **homeward**, toward home.—*adv* **homewards**.—*n* **home´work´**, work, esp piecework, done at home; school-work to be done outside the classroom; preliminary study for a project.—*adj* **homey**, cozy, familiar, etc.—**at home**, in one's home, esp to welcome visitors; at ease; **bring home to**, to impress upon; **home free**, (*inf*) out of peril. [OE *hām*; Du and Ger *heim*.]

homeopathy [hōm-i-o´pathi] *n* the system of treating disease by small quantities of drugs that cause symptoms similar to those of the disease.—*ns* **hom´eopath; homeo´pathist**, one who believes in or practices homeopathy.—*adj* **homeopath´ic**.—*adv* **homeopath´ically**. [Gr *homolos*, similar, *pathos*, feeling.]

homer [hō´mėr] *n* a pigeon trained to fly home from a distance.—*vi* to hit a home run. [**home**.]

Homeric [hō-mer´ik] *adj* pertaining to *Homer*, the great Greek epic poet of the 8th century B.C.; worthy of Homer; heroic. [Gr *hŏmērikos—Hŏmēros*, Homer.]

homicide [hom´i-sīd] *n* the killing of a person by another; one who kills another.—*adj* **homicī´dal**, [Fr.—L *homicidium—homō*, a man, *caedĕre*, to kill.]

homily [hom´i-li] *n* a sermon; a solemn talk or writing.—*adjs* **homilet´ic, -al**.—*n* **homilet´ics**, the art of preaching. [Gr *homīlia*, an assembly, a sermon—*homos*, the same, *īlē*, a crowd.]

hominid, hominoid *see* **Homo sapiens**.

hominy [hom´i-ni] *n* hulled and coarsely ground dry corn.—**hominy grits**, dish of boiled hominy. [Amerindian.]

Ho´mo sapiens man.—*adj* **ho´minid**, of, or relating to man and his ancestors.—Also *n*.—*adj* **ho´minoid**, manlike; of or belonging to primates.—*n* a hominoid animal. [L *hŏmō*, man, *sapiens*, wise, (here) intelligent, able to reason.]

homo- [hom´ō-, hō´mo-], **hom-** [hom-], same [Gr *homos*].—eg **homograph** [hom´o-gräf] *n* a word of the same spelling as another but of different meaning and origin (Gr *graphein*, to write).

homogeneous [hom-ō-jēn´i-ùs] *adj* of the same kind or nature; having all the constituent parts or elements similar.—*ns* **homogene´ity**, homogeneousness; (*math*) the state of having identical values or distribution functions; **homogē´neousness**, uniformity of nature or kind.—*vt* **homog´enize**, to make homogenous; to process (milk) so that the cream does not separate. [Gr *homogenēs—homos*, one, same, *genos*, kind.]

homologate [hom-ol´o-gāt] *vt* to confirm or approve officially.—*n* **homologā´tion**. [Low L *homologāre, -ātum*—Gr *homologeein*, to agree—*homos*, same, *logos*, speech.]

homologous [hom-ol´o-gùs] *adj* corresponding in relative position, general structure and descent.—*ns* **hom´ologue, homolog** [-log], something (as a chromosome or chemical compound) that exhibits homology; **homology**, a similarity often attributed to a common origin; (*chem*) the relation of elements in the same group of the periodic table.—*adj* **homological** [-loj´-]. [Gr *homologos*; cf **homologate**.]

homonym [hom´o-nim] *n* a word having the same sound as another, but a different meaning and origin and usu. spelling.—*adj* **homon´ymous**, [Gr *homōnymos—homos*, the same, *onyma, onoma*, name.]

homophobia [hō´mȧ-fōb-ē-ȧ] *n* hatred or fear of homosexuals. [**homo** + **phobia**.]

homophone [hom´o-fōn] *n* a word pronounced exactly as another but differing from it in meaning.—*adj* **homophonous** [-of´-].—*n* **homoph´ony**, (*mus*) the sound of a chord. [Gr *homos*, the same, *phōnē*, sound.]

homosexual [hom-ō-seks´ū-ȧl] *adj* having sexual desire directed toward one of the same sex.—Also *n*.—*n* **homosexual´ity**. [**homo-** + **sexual**.]

hone [hōn] *n* a hard stone used to sharpen cutting tools.—*vt* to sharpen as on a hone. [OE *hān*; ON *hein*; allied to Gr *kōnos*, a cone.]

honest [on´ėst] *adj* truthful; trustworthy; sincere or genuine; gained by fair means; frank, open.—*adv* **hon´estly**.—*n* **hon´esty**, the state of being honest; a perennial garden plant (*Lunaria annua*) grown for its flowers and dead tops with their flat, transparent seedpods. [Fr.—L *honestus—honor*.]

honey [hun´i] *n* a sweet thick substance that bees make as food from the nectar of flowers; sweetness; a darling.—*adj* of, resembling honey; much loved.—*ns* **hon´eybee**, a honey-producing bee (*Apis mellifica*) kept for its honey and wax; **hon´eycomb**, the structure of six-sided wax cells made by bees to hold their honey, eggs, etc; anything like this.—*vt* to fill with holes like a honeycomb.—*adj* of or like a honeycomb.—*ns* **hon´eydew**, a sugary deposit on leaves secreted by aphids, scale insects, or a fungus; **hon´eydew melon**, a variety of melon with a smooth whitish rind and sweet, green flesh; **hon´ey locust**, a tall, N American tree (*Gleditsia triacanthos*) yielding a hard, durable wood and edible fruits; **hon´eymoon**, the vacation spent together by a newly-married couple.—Also *vi.*—*n* **hon´eysuckle**, any of a genus (*Lonicera*) of shrubs with small, fragrant flowers. [OE *hunig*; Ger *honig*, ON *hunang*.]

honk [hongk] *n* the cry of the wild goose; the noise of an automobile horn.—Also *vti.* [Imit.]

honorarium [hon-or-ā´ri-um, on-] *n* a voluntary fee paid, esp to a professional man for his services. [L *honōrārium* (*dōnum*), honorary (gift).]

honorary [on´ȯr-ȧr-i] *adj* given as an honor; holding a title or office without performing services, or without reward. [L *honōrārius*.]

honorific [on-ȯr-if´ik] *see* **honor**.—Also *n.* [L *honōrificus—honor*, honor, and suffx *-ficus—facĕre*, to make.]

honor [on´or] *n* high regard or respect; glory; fame; good reputation; integrity; chastity; high rank; distinction; **Honor**, a title of certain officials, as judges (*with* **Her, His**, *or* **Your**); something done or given as a token of respect; a source of respect and fame; the ace, king, queen, jack or ten in a deck of cards.—*vt* to respect greatly; to do or give something in honor of; to accept and pay.—*adjs* **hon´orable**, worthy of being honored; honest; upright; bringing honor; **hon´orary**, given as an honor; designating or in an office held as an honor, without service or pay; **honorific** [on-or-if´ik], conferring honor.—Also *n.*—*ns* **hon´or roll**, a list of persons, esp students deserving honor; public display of the names of local citizens who have served in the armed forces; **hon´or society**, organization for the recognition of academic achievement; **hon´or system**, system whereby members of institutions are trusted to abide by rules without supervision.—**debt of honor** *see* **debt; do the honors**, to act as host; **point of honor** *see* **point**. [Anglo-Fr *(h)onour*—L *honor, honōs, -ōris*.]

hooch [hōōch] *n* (*slang*) alcoholic liquor, esp when illicitly distilled or obtained. [*Hootchino*, an Amerindian tribe.]

hood [hŏŏd] *n* a flexible covering for the head and back of the neck; the metal cover over an automobile engine; any hoodlike thing as the (adjustable) top of an automobile, baby carriage, canopy over stove, etc; the ornamental scarf worn with an academic gown.—*vt* to cover with a hood.—*adj* **hood´ed**. [OE *hōd*.]

-hood [-hŏŏd] *n suffx* indicating state, nature, as *hardihood, manhood*.—Also **-head** [-hed], as *Godhead*. [OE *hād*, Ger *-heit*, state.]

hoodlum [hōōdl´ŭm] *n* a member of a lawless gang.

hoodoo [hōō´dōō] *n* voodoo; a person or thing that brings bad luck; bad luck. [App **voodoo**.]

hoodwink [hŏŏd´wingk] *vt* to mislead by trickery. [**hood + wink**.]

hooey [hōō´i] *n* (*slang*) nonsense.

hoof [hōōf] *n* horny substance on the feet of certain animals, as horses, etc., or the entire foot.—*vti* (*inf*) to walk.—*pl* **hoofs, hooves**.—*adj* **hoofed**. [OE *hōf*; Ger *huf*, ON *hōfr*.]

hook [hŏŏk] *n* an object of bent metal, such as would catch or hold anything; a fishhook; something shaped like a hook; a strike, blow, etc., in which a curving motion is involved.—*vt* to catch, fasten, hold, as with a hook.—*vi* to be curved.—*adj* **hooked** [hŏŏkt], addicted to some activity or substance (*with* **on, by**).—*n* **hook´er**, (*slang*) a prostitute.—*ns* **hook´up**, the establishment of a connection; an alliance; **hookworm**, a parasitic intestinal worm with hooks in the mouth; the disease it causes.—**by hook or by crook**, one way if not another; **off the hook**. (*inf*) out of trouble. [OE *hōc*; Du *hoek*.]

hookah [hŏŏk´a] *n* an Oriental tobacco-pipe of Arabs, Turks, etc., in which the smoke is passed through water. [Ar *huqqah*, bowl, casket.]

hooligan [hōōl´i-gȧn] *n* a hoodlum.—*n* **hoo´liganism**. [Said to be the name of a leader of a gang.]

hoop [hōōp] *n* a circular band for holding together the staves of casks, etc.; anything like this, as a ring in a hoop skirt.—*vt* to bind with hoops; to encircle. [OE *hōp*; Du *hoep*.]

Hoosier [hōō´zhėr] *n* a native or resident of Indiana.—Also *adj.* [Origin obscure.]

hoot [hōōt] *n* the sound that an owl makes; a shout of scorn.—*vi* to utter a hoot.—*vt* to express (scorn) of (someone) by hooting.—*n* **hoot´er**. [Imit prob immediately Scand.]

hootenanny [hōōt´n-an-ē] *n* a gathering or performance of folk singers. [Origin unknown.]

hop[1] [hop] *vi* to leap on one leg; to leap with all feet at once, as a frog, etc.; (*inf*) to go briskly.—*pr p* **hopp´ing**; *pt, pt p* **hopped**.—*n* a hopping; (*inf*) a dance; (*inf*) a short flight in an airplane.—*ns* **hopp´er**, one who hops; a hopping insect; a container from which the contents can be emptied slowly and evenly; **hop´scotch**, a game in which children hop over lines drawn on the ground. [OE *hoppian*, to dance; Ger *hopfen, hüpfen*.]

hop[2] [hop] *n* a twining vine (*Humulus lupulus*) with small cone-shaped flowers; (*pl*) the dried ripe cones, used for flavoring beer, etc.—**hop up**, (*slang*) to stimulate, as by a drug; (*slang*) to supercharge (an automobile engine, etc.). [Du *hop*; Ger *hopfen*.]

hope [hōp] *n* a feeling that what is wanted will happen; the object of this; a person or thing on which one may base some hope.—*vt* to want and expect.—*vi* to have hope (for).—*adj* **hope´ful**, full of hope; having qualities that promise good or success.—*n* a person aspiring to a job, etc.—*adv* **hope´fully**, in a hopeful manner; it is hoped.—*n* **hope´fulness**.—*adj* **hope´less**, without hope; giving no ground to expect good or success; incurable.—*adv* **hope´lessly**.—*n* **hope´lessness. hope´chest**, a young woman's accumulation of household goods in anticipation of marriage; a chest for such a collection; **hope against hope**, to cherish hope in spite of every discouragement. [OE *hopian—hopa*, hope; Du *hopen*; Ger *hoffen*.]

Hopi [hō´pē] *n* a member of an Amerindian people of north-eastern Arizona.—*pl* **Hopi, -s**.—Also *adj*; the Uto-Aztecan language of the Hopi. [Hopi *hopi*, good, peaceful.]

horary [hōr´ȧr-ē, hȯr-, här-] *adj* pertaining to an hour; hourly. [L *hōra*, an hour.]

Horatian [hor-ā´shȧn] *adj* pertaining to Horace (Quintus *Horatius* Flaccus; 65 BC-8 BC), the Latin poet, or to his manner or verse.]

horde [hōrd, hörd] *n* a crowd or throng; a swarm. [Fr—Turk *ordū*, camp.]

horehound [hōr´-, hör´hownd] *n* a bitter mint (*Marrubium vulgare*); a medicine or candy made from its juice. [OE *hār*, hoar, *hūne*, horehound.]

horizon [hor-ī´zȯn] *n* the circle in which earth and sky seem to meet; the boundary or limit of one's experience, interests, etc.—*adj* **horizontal** [hor-i-zont´ȧl], not vertical; flat and even; level; parallel to the plane of the horizon.—*adv* horizon´tally. [Fr from Gr *horizōn* (*kyklos*), bounding (circle), *pr p* of *horizein*, to bound—*horos*, a limit.]

hormone [hör´mōn] *n* a product of living cells formed in one part of the organism and carried to another part, where it takes effect; a synthetic substance that has the same effect.—*adjs* **hormonal, hormonelike**. [Gr *hormōn*, pr p of *hormaein*, to set in motion.]

horn [hörn] *n* a hard outgrowth on the head of an animal; the material of which this is made; any projection resembling a horn; a crescent tip; something made of, or curved like, a horn; a wind instrument, esp the French horn or trumpet; one of the equally unacceptable alternatives in a dilemma; a device to sound a warning; (*slang*) a telephone.—*vt* to furnish with horns; to remove horns from.—*adj* **horn´y**, like horn; hard; callous; (*slang*) lustful.—*ns* **hornbeam**, any of a genus (*Carpinus*) of the birch family with a smooth grey bark and hard white wood; **horn´book**, formerly, a child's primer consisting of a page bearing an alphabet or religious text, held in a frame with a thin pane of horn; **horned lizard**, horned toad; **horned toad**, a small harmless lizard (genus *Phrynosoma*) having hornlike spines of the western US; **horn´fly**, a small black fly (*Haematobia irritans*) that is a bloodsucking pest of cattle; **horn´ist**, a French horn player; **horn of plenty**, a cornucopia; **horn´pipe**, a lively dance formerly popular with sailors; the music for such a dance; **horn rims**, eyeglasses with genuine or imitation horn rims.—**horn in** (*inf*) to intrude. [OE *horn*, Scand and Ger *horn*, Gael and W *corn*, L *cornu*, Gr *keras*.]

hornblende [hörn´blend] *n* a mineral consisting of silica, with magnesia, lime or iron, found in igneous or metamorphic rock. [Ger *horn*, horn, and -*blende—blenden*, to dazzle.]

hornet [hörn´et] *n* a large wasp with a severe sting. [OE *hyrnet*.]

hornpipe *see* **horn**.

horologe [hor´o-loj] *n* a device for keeping time.—*ns* **horol´oger, horol´ogist**, a maker of clocks, etc.—*adjs* **horolog´ic, -al**.—*n* **horol´ogy**, the science of measuring time; the art of making timekeepers. [OFr *orloge*—L *hōrologium*—Gr *hōrologion—hōra*, an hour, *legein*, to tell.]

horoscope [hor´o-skōp] *n* a chart of the zodiacal signs and positions of planets, etc. by which astrologers profess to predict future events, esp in the life of an individual; the telling of a person's fortune by this method. [Gr *hōroskopos—hōra*, an hour, *skopeein*, to observe.]

horrible [hor´i-bl] *adj* exciting horror; dreadful; (*inf*) very bad; ugly, unpleasant, etc.—*adv* **horr´ibly**. [L *horribilis—horrēre*, to shudder, bristle.]

horrid [hor´id] *adj* terrible; horrible.—*adv* **horr´idly**.—*n* **horr´idness**. [L *horridus—horrēre*, to bristle.]

horrify [hor´i-fī] *vt* to strike with horror.—*pr p* **horr´ifying**; *pt p* **horr´ified**.—*adj* **horrif´ic**, exciting horror; frightful. [L *horrificus*—root of *horrēre* and *facĕre*, to make.]

horror [hor´ȯr] *n* the strong feeling caused by something frightful or shocking; strong dislike; a source of such feeling; a disagreeable person or thing.—*adj* inspiring feelings of horror; bloodcurdling. [L *horror, horrēre*, to bristle, shudder.]

hors de combat [ör dė k p-ba] disabled. [Fr.]

hors-d'œuvre [ör-dœ-vr´] *n* an appetizer served before a meal. [Fr.]

horse [hörs] *n* four-legged, solid-hoofed herbivorous mammal (*Equus caballus*) with flowing mane and tail, ranging in size from 24 to 68 inches at the shoulders, domesticated for drawing loads, carrying riders, etc.; (*pl*) cavalry; a vaulting horse; a frame with legs to support something.—*vt* to supply with a horse or horses; to put on horseback.—*vi* to engage in horseplay.—*ns* **horse´back**, the back of a horse; **horse chestnut**, a large tree (*Aesculus hippocastanum*) with large palmate leaves and erect clusters of flowers; its large glossy brown seed.—*interj* **horse feathers** (*slang*) nonsense.—*ns* **horse´fly**, a two-winged usu. large blood-sucking fly (family Tabanidae); gadfly; **horse´hair**, hair from the mane or the tail of a horse; stiff fabric woven from this hair or a synthetic resembling it;

horse´hide, the hide of a horse; leather made from this; **horse latitude**, either of two oceanic regions between 30° north and 30° south latitude marked by calms; **horse´laugh**, a boisterous, usu. derisive laugh; **horse´less carriage**, an automobile; **horse´man**, a person skilled in the riding or care of horses; **horse´manship**, the art of being a horseman; **horse opera**, (*slang*) a cowboy movie; **horse´play**, rough, boisterous fun; **horse´power**, a unit for measuring the power of engines, etc. equal to 746 watts or 33,000 foot-pounds per minute; **horse´radish**, a tall herb (*Armoracia lapathifolia*) of the mustard family; a relish made up from its pungent root; **horse's ass**, (*slang*) a blockhead; **horse´sense**, (*inf*) common sense; **horse´shoe**, a flat, U-shaped, protective metal plate nailed to a horse's hoof; anything shaped like this; (*pl*) a game in which the players toss horseshoes at a stake; **horse´shoe crab**, any of several related marine arthropods (order Xiphosura) with a fused head and thorax shaped like a broad crescent.—Also **king crab.—horse´trade**, a negotiation marked by shrewd bargaining and mutual concessions; **horse´whip**, a whip for driving horses.—*vt* to lash with a horsewhip.—*adj* **hor´sy, hors´ey**, of, like, or suggesting a horse; of or like people who like horses, fox hunting, or horse racing.—**from the horse's mouth**, from the original source; **hold one's horses**, (*slang*) to curb one's impatience; **horse around**, (*slang*) to engage in horseplay. [OE *hors*; ON *hross*; OHG *hross, hros*.]

hortative [hört´a-tiv] *adj* inciting; encouraging; giving advice.—Also **hort´atory**. [L *hortārī, -ātus*, to incite.]

horticulture [hör´ti-kul-tyůr, -chůr] *n* the art or science of growing flowers, fruits, and vegetables.—*adj* **horticul´tural**.—*n* **horticul´turist**. [L *hortus*, a garden, *cultūra*—*colĕre*, to cultivate.]

hosanna, hosannah [hō-zan´a] *n* an exclamation of praise to God. [Gr *hōsanna*—Heb *hōshīʿāhnnā*—*hōshīāʿ*, save, *nā*, pray.]

hose [hōz] *n* stockings; socks; a flexible tube used to convey fluids.—*pl* **hoses, hose.**—*n* **hos´iery** [hō´zhėr-ē], stockings; socks. [OE *hosa*, pl *hosan*, Du *hoos*, Ger *hose*.]

Hosea [hō-za-ė, -zē-å] *n* (*Bible*) the 28th book of the Old Testament, written by the prophet Hosea in which he uses his domestic life as an analogy for the relationship between God and Man.

hospice [hos´pis, -pēs] *n* a guesthouse for travelers; a homelike facility for the care of the dying. [Fr—L *hospitium*—*hospes*, a stranger treated as a guest.]

hospitable [hos´pit-å-bl] *adj* kind to strangers; giving a generous welcome to guests.—*n* **hos´pitableness**.—*adv* **hos´pitably**.—*n* **hos´pital´ity**, the act, practice, or quality of being hospitable. [L *hospes, -itis*, stranger, guest.]

hospital [hos´pit-ål] *n* an institution for the treatment of the sick or injured; a building for any of these purposes.—*vt* **hos´pitalize**, to send to hopsital. [OFr *hospital*—LowL *hospitāle*—*hospes*, a guest.]

host[1] [hōst] *n* one who lodges or entertains a stranger or guest at his house; an innkeeper; an animal or plant on or in which another lives; a radio or television emcee.—*vti* to act as host (to).—*n* **hostess**, a female host. [OFr *hoste*—L *hospes, hospitis*, a guest, also host.]

host[2] [hōst] *n* an army, a large multitude.—**Lord of hosts**, a favorite Hebrew term for Jehovah. [OFr *host*—L *hostis*, an enemy.]

host[3] [hōst] *n* the wafer or bread used in the Eucharist or Holy Communion. [L *hostia*, a victim.]

hosta [hōst´a, host´a] *n* plantain lily. [Nicholas *Host*, Austrian botanist.]

hostage [hos´tij] *n* a person given or kept as a pledge until certain conditions are met. [OFr *hostage*—L *obses, obsidis*, a hostage.]

hostel [hos´tėl] *n* a lodging place.—Also **hos´telry**. [OFr *hostel, hostellerie*—L *hospitāle*; cf **hospital**.]

hostile [hos´til], -til] *adj* belonging to an enemy; showing enmity; warlike; adverse; resistant (to; esp to new ideas, change).—*n* **hostil´ity**, enmity.—*pl* **hostil´ities**, acts of warfare. [L *hostīlis*—*hostis*, enemy.]

hostler [hos´lėr or os´-] *n* one who takes care of horses and mules; one who services a vehicle (as a locomotive) or machine (as a crane). [**hostel**.]

hot [hot] *adj* of high temperature; very warm; giving or feeling heat; full of intense feeling; following closely; electrically charged; (*inf*) recent, new; (*slang*) stolen; (*slang*) excellent.—*adv* **hot´ly**.—*ns* **hot air´**, (*slang*) empty talk; **hot´bed**, a bed of heated earth enclosed by low walls and covered by glass for forcing plants; anything that fosters rapid growth or extensive activity.—*adj* **hot´blooded**, easily excited.—*ns* **hot´box´**, an overheated bearing on an axle or shaft; **hot´cake**, a pancake; **hot corn´er**, (*baseball*) the position of the third baseman; **hot´dog**, (*inf*) a wiener, esp one served in a long soft roll.—*interj* used to express pleasure.—*vi* **hot´dog**, to perform ostentatious stunts (as while skiing or surfing).—*adv* **hot´foot´**, in haste.—*ns* **hot´house**, a heated structure for growing plants; **hot´line**, a telephone line for immediate communication, as between heads of state in a crisis; **hot money**, investment money moved about quickly to profit from short-term interest rates; **hot´plate**, a small cooking stove; **hot potato**, (*inf*) a problem that no one wants to handle; **hot´rod**, (*slang*) an automobile, usu. old, with a supercharged engine; **hot seat**, (*slang*) an electric chair; (*inf*) a difficult situation; **hot´shot**, (*slang*) an aggressive expert in any field; **hot spring**, a thermal spring, esp one at a health resort.—*adj* **hot´tempered**, having a fiery temper.—*n* **hot tub**, a large tub in which several people can soak in hot water; **hot water**, (*inf*) a distressing difficulty.—**make it hot for**, (*inf*) to make things uncomfortable for; **sell like hot cakes**, (*inf*) sell rapidly and in large quantities. [OE *hāt*, Ger *heiss*, Swed *het*.]

hotel [hō-tel´] *n* a commercial establishment providing lodging and meals for travelers, etc.; **Hotel**, communication code word for the letter *h*.—*n* **hotel keeper; hotel´ier**, one who owns or manages a hotel. [ME *hostel*—OFr *hostel* (Fr *hôtel*)—L *hospitālia*, guestchambers—*hospes*, guest.]

Hottentot [hot´n-tot] *n* a member of a people of southwest Africa related to the Bushmen.—*pl* **-tot, -s**; the 'click' language of the Khoisan family spoken by the Hottentot. [Du imit; from their staccato manner of speech.]

hound [hownd] *n* any of a class of purebred dogs defined by the American Kennel Club, typically with large drooping ears, which hunt by scent, and are used in the chase; any dog.—*vt* to hunt or chase as with hounds; to urge on by harassment.—*adj* **hounds´tooth check** or **hound's tooth check**, of a pattern or fabric with a broken-check design. [OE *hund*; Gr *kyōn*, gen *kynos*, L *canis*.]

hour [owr] *n* 60 min or the 24th part of a day; the time for a particular activity (*lunch hour*); the time of day (*the hour is 2:30*); (*education*) a credit, equal to each hour spent in class per week.—*pl* the prescribed times for doing business.—*ns* **hour´-glass**, an instrument for measuring the hours by the running of sand from one part to another through a narrow neck; **hour´ hand**, the short hand on the face of a watch or clock that marks the hour.—*adj* **hour´ly**, happening every hour; frequent.—*adv* at every hour; frequently done during an hour.—**after hours**, after the regular hours for business, school, etc.; **hour after hour**, every hour. [OFr *hore*—L *hōra*—Gr *hōra*.]

houri [hōō´ri, how´ri] *n* a beautiful woman of the Muslim paradise; (*inf*) a voluptuous young woman. [Pers *huri*—Ar *hūriya*, a black-eyed girl.]

house [hows] *n* a building to live in esp by one person or family; a household; a family as including relatives, ancestors, and descendants; the audience in a theater; a business firm; a legislative assembly.—*pl* **houses** [howz´iz].—*vt* **house** [howz], to shelter; to store; to provide houses for.—*vi* to take shelter.—*ns* **house´ arrest´**, confinement to one's house, instead of imprisonment; **house´ boat**, a barge furnished and used as a dwelling place or for cruising; a dwelling on the water supported by floats; **house´break´er**, one who breaks open and enters a house for a felonious purpose; **house´break´ing**.—*adj* **house´broken** (of dogs, cats) trained to void in a special place; (*inf*) (of persons) well-mannered; **house´coat**, a woman's garment with a long skirt, for wearing in the house; **house´hold**, those living together in the same house.—*adj* pertaining to the house and family.—*ns* **house´hold word**, a familiar saying or name; **house´keeper**, a woman who runs a home, esp one hired to do so; **house´keeping**, the management of a house or of domestic affairs.—*adj* domestic.—*ns* **house´maid**, a female servant employed to do housework; **house´man**, a person who performs general work around a house or hotel; **house physician**, a physician who is employed by and lives in a hotel.—*adj* **house´-proud**, taking pride in the condition of one's house.—*ns* **house´-warming**, a party given after moving into a new house; **housewife** [hows´wīf], the mistress of a house; a pocket sewing outfit.—*adj* **house´wifely**.—*ns* **housewifery** [huz´if-ri, hows´wīf-ri]; **house´work**, the work of housekeeping; **housing** [howz´ing], the providing of shelter or lodging; shelter or lodging; houses collectively; an enclosing frame, box, etc.—Also *adj*.—**housing project**, a publicly-supported planned development for housing usu. low-income families; **housemaid's knee**, a swelling over the knee caused by enlargement of the bursa in front of the kneecap; **house of representatives**, the lower house of a legislative assembly (as the US Congress).—**keep house**, to maintain or manage an establishment. [OE *hūs*; Ger *haus*.]

housing [howz´ing] *n* an ornamental covering for a horse. [OFr *houce*, a mantle.]

hove *pt, pt p* of **heave**.

hovel [hov´ėl, huv´ėl] *n* any small wretched dwelling; a shed.

hover [huv´ėr, hov´ėr] *vi* to remain aloft flapping the wings; to remain suspended; to linger.—*n* **Hov´ercraft**, trade name for an air-cushion vehicle used to cross water.

how [how] *adv* in what manner; to what extent; by what means; in what condition. [OE *hū*, prob an adverbial form from *hwā*, who.]

howdah [how´da] *n* a pavilion or seat fixed on the back of an elephant or camel. [Ar *houdaj*.]

however [how-ev´ėr] *adv* in whatever manner or degree; nevertheless. [**how, ever**.]

howitzer [how´its-ėr] *n* a short cannon used for shelling at a steep angle. [Ger *haubitze*—Czech *houfnice*, a sling.]

howl [howl] *vi* to utter the long, wailing cry of wolves, dogs, etc.; to utter a similar cry of anger, pain, etc.; to shout or laugh in mirth, etc.—*vt* to utter with a howl; to drive by howling.—*n* the wailing cry of a wolf, dog, etc.; any similar sound; (*inf*) a joke.—*n* **howler**, one who howls; (*inf*) a ludicrous blunder. [OFr *huller*—L *ululāre*, to shriek or howl—*ulula*, an owl.]

howsoever [how-so-ev´ėr] *adv* to whatever extent or degree; by whatever means. [**how, so, ever**.]

hoy [hoi] *n* a large one-decked boat, commonly rigged as a sloop; a barge for bulky cargo. [Du *heu*, Flem *hui*.]

hoyden [hoi´dėn] *n* a bold, boisterous girl. [Perh Du *heyden*, a heathen, a gipsy—*heyde*, heath.]

HTML [abbrev] (*comput*) hypertext markup language, the basic language in which pages on the Web are written.

HTTP [abbrev] (*comput*) hypertext transport protocol. The structure used to connect the many servers on the Web.

huarache [wŭ-rach´ē, hă-] *n* a low-heeled sandal with upper made of interwoven leather thongs. [Mexican Spanish.]
hub [hub] *n* the center part of a wheel; a center of activity. [Prob a form of **hob** (1).]
hubble-bubble [hub´l-bub´l] *n* a hookah; a bubbling sound; confusion. [**bubble**.]
hubbub [hub´ub] *n* a confused sound of many voices, riot, uproar. [App of Irish origin.]
hubris [hū´bris], **hybris** [hī´bris] *n* arrogant pride.—*adj* **hūbris´tic**. [Gr, wanton violence arising from passion or pride.]
huckaback [huk´a-bak] *n* an absorbent linen or cotton fabric with raised surface used for towels, etc.
huckleberry [huk´l-bėr-i] *n* a genus (*Gaylussacia*) of N American shrubs with dark-blue to black berries; the edible berry; the blueberry. [App for *hurtleberry*. See derivation of **whortleberry**.]
huckster [huk´stėr] *n* a person using aggressive or questionable methods of selling; (*inf*) an advertising copywriter.
huddle [hud´l] *vti* to crowd close together; to draw (oneself) up.—*n* a confused crowd or heap; (*slang*) a private conference; (*football*) a grouping of a team to get signals before a play. [Poss conn with **hide**.]
hue[1] [hū] *n* color; a particular shade or tint of a color. [OE *hiow, heow*; Swed *hy*, complexion.]
hue[2] [hū] *n* a shouting; now only in **hue and cry**. [Fr *huer*, imit.]
huff [huf] *n* state of smoldering resentment.—*vi* to blow; to puff.—*adj* **huff´y**.—*adv* **huff´ily**.—*n* **huff´iness**. [Imit.]
hug [hug] *vt* to clasp close with the arms; to cling to (a belief, etc.); to keep close to (a shore, etc.).—*vi* to embrace one another.—*pr p* **hugg´ing**; *pt p* **hugged**.—*n* a close embrace.
huge [hūj] *adj* enormous; gigantic; very large.—*adv* **huge´ly**.—*n* **huge´ness**. [OFr *ahuge*.]
hugger-mugger [hug´ėr-mug´ėr] *n* secrecy; confusion. [Origin obscure.]
Huguenot [hū´gė-not or -nō] *n* a French Protestant of the 16th and 17th centuries. [Fr—earlier *eiguenot*—Ger *eidgenoss*, confederate, assimilated to the name *Hugues*, Hugh.]
hulk [hulk] *n* the body of a ship, esp if old and dismantled; a large, clumsy person or thing.—*adjs* **hulk´ing, hulk´y**, clumsy. [OE *hulc*, perh—Gr *holkas—helkein*, to draw.]
hula, hula-hula [hōō´la, hōō´la-hōō´la] *n* a native Hawaiian dance.—*n* **Hula-Hoop**, trade name for large ring of plastic swung around body by wriggling hips. [Hawaiian.]
hull [hul] *n* the outer covering of a fruit or seed; the frame or body of a ship.—*vt* to remove the hulls of; to pierce the hull of. [OE *hulu*, a husk, as of corn—*helan*, to cover; Ger *hülle*, a covering—*hehlen*, to cover.]
hullabaloo [hul´a-ba-lōō] *n* an uproar. [Perh from **hullo** (**hello**).]
hum [hum] *vi* to make a sound like bees; to sing with closed lips; to pause in speaking and utter an inarticulate sound; to be busily active.—*vt* to render music by **humming**.—*pr p* **humm´ing**; *pt p* **hummed**.—*n* the noise of bees; a murmur.—*ns* **humming**, a low murmuring sound; **humm´ing bird**, a tiny brightly colored American bird (family Trochilidae) with wings that vibrate rapidly, making a humming sound.—**make things hum**, to cause brisk activity. [Imit; cf Ger *hummen, humsen*.]
human [hū´mȧn] *adj* belonging or pertaining to man or mankind; having the qualities of a man.—*n* **hū´mankind**, people, mankind.—*adv* **hū´manly**, according to, in keeping with, human standards, qualities, or abilities.—**human nature**, the nature of man; the qualities of character common to all men. [Fr *humain*—L *hūmānus—homō*, a human being.]
humane [hū-mān´] *adj* having the feelings proper to man; kind, tender, merciful; benevolent.—*adv* **humane´ly**. [**human**.]
humanize [hū´man-īz] *vti* to make or become human or humane.
humanist [hū´mȧn-ist] *n* advocate of humanism.—*adj* **humanist´ic**.—*n* **hu´manism**, any system which puts human interests and the mind of man paramount, rejecting religion. [L (*līterae, literae*) *hūmāniōres*, polite literature.]
humanitarian [hū-man-i-tā´ri-ȧn] *n* a philanthropist.—*adj* of or belonging to humanity, benevolent.—*n* **humanitā´rianism**. [**humanity**.]
humanity [hū-man´it-i] *n* the nature peculiar to a human being; the kind feelings of man, benevolence; mankind collectively.—*pl* **human´ities**. [Fr—L *hūmānitās—hūmānus—homō*, a man.]
humble [hum´bl] *adj* lowly; unpretentious, modest.—*vt* to bring down in condition or rank; to abase (oneself).—*n* **hum´bleness**.—*adv* **hum´bly**. [Fr—L *humilis*, low—*humus*, the ground.]
humble-bee [hum´bl-bē] *n* the bumble-bee. [Perh from *humble*, freq of **hum**.]
humble pie [hum´bl pī] *n* apology, usu. under pressure.—**eat humble pie**, to undergo humiliation. [OFr *nombles*, for *lomble—le omble—le*, the, *omble*, navel—L *umbilīcus*.]
humbug [hum´bug] *n* fraud, sham, hoax.—*vt* to deceive; to hoax.—*pr p* **hum´bugging**; *pt p* **hum´bugged**.
humdinger [hum-ding´ėr] *n* (*inf*) an exceptionally excellent person or thing. [Prob **hum** + **ding** (1).]
humdrum [hum´drum] *adj* dull, monotonous.—Also *n*. [**hum** and perh **drum**.]
humerus [hū´mėr-us] *n* the bone of the upper arm.—*pl* **hūm´erī**.—*adj* **hū´meral**, of the region of the humerus or shoulder. [L *(h)umerus*, the shoulder.]
humid [hū´mid] *adj* moist, damp, rather wet.—*adv* **hū´midly**.—*vt* **humid´ify**, to make humid.—*ns* **humid´ifier**, a device for increasing or maintaining humidity; **hūmid´ity**, moisture, degree of moistness.—**relative humidity**, see **relative**. [L *hūmidus—hūmēre*, to be moist.]
humiliate [hū-mil´i-āt] *vt* to humble; to wound the selfrespect of, or mortify.—*n* **humiliā´tion**. [L *humiliāre, -ātum—humilis*, low.]
humility [hū-mil´i-ti] *n* the state of being humble. [OFr *humilite*—L *humilitās—humilis*, low.]
humming *see* **hum**.
hummock [hum´ȯk] *n* a small hillock; a ridge of ice. [Origin unknown.]
humor [hū´mȯr] *n* (*arch*) a fluid of the body, esp one of the four that were formerly believed to determine temperament; temperament, disposition; state of mind (eg *good humor, ill humor*); inclination; caprice; the ability to appreciate or express what is funny, amusing, etc.; the expression of this.—*vt* to indulge; to gratify by compliance.—*adj* **hū´moral**, of or proceeding from a bodily humor (as a hormone).—*ns* **humoresque´**, a musical caprice; **hū´morist**, one whose behavior is regulated by a price; one who portrays the ludicrous in human life and character; a maker of jokes.—*adj* **hū´morous**, (*arch*) capricious; having a sense of the ludicrous and incongruous; funny, exciting laughter.—*adv* **hū´morously**.—*n* **hū´morousness**.—**comedy of humors**, see **comedy; out of humor**, out of sorts. [OFr *humor*—L *(h)ūmor—(h)ūmēre*, to be moist.]
hump [hump] *n* a lump on the back of an animal (as a camel or whale).—*vt* to hunch; to arch.—*n* **hump´back**, a humped or crooked back; a hunchback.—*adj* **hump´backed**, having a humpback; having a convex curve (as a bridge).—**over the hump**, past the crisis or difficulty.
humus [hūm´us] *n* decomposed organic matter in the soil. [L *humus*; cf Gr *chamai*, on the ground.]
Hun [hun] *n* one of a savage nomad race of Asia, which overran Europe in 5th century AD; a ruthless savage; (*offensive*) a German. [OE (pl) *Hūne, Hūnas*; L *Hunni*.]
hunch [hunch, -sh] *n* a hump; (*inf*) a premonition.—*vt* to arch into a hump.—*vi* to move forward jerkily.—*n* **hunch´back**, a person with a humpback. [Origin obscure.]
hundred [hun´dred] *adj, n* ten times ten.—*n* the symbol for this (100, c, C); the hundredth in a series or set; something having a hundred units as members; a hundred dollar bill; a subdivision of some American counties.—*pl* the numbers 100 to 999.—*adj* **hun´dredfold**, having a hundred units or members; being a hundred times as great or as many.—*adj* **hun´dredth**, the last of a hundred.—*n* one of a hundred equal parts.—*n* **hun´dred weight**, a unit of weight, equal to 100 pounds in the US and 112 pounds in Britain.—**hundreds place**, the 3rd number to the left of the decimal point in a number in Arabic notation. [OE *hundred*—old form *hund*, a hundred, with the suffx *-red*, a reckoning.]
hung *pt, pt p* of **hang**.
Hungarian [hung-ār´ēȧn] *adj* of Hungary, its people, etc.—*n* a native or inhabitant of Hungary; the language of the Hungarians.
hunger [hung´gėr] *n* craving for food; need, or lack, of food; any strong desire.—*vi* to crave food; to long (for).—*adj* **hung´ry**, having, showing, eager desire, esp for food; greedy; lean, barren, poor.—*adv* **hung´rily**.—*n* **hung´er-strike**, prolonged refusal of all food by a prisoner until certain demands are granted as a form of protest. [OE *hungor* (n), *hyngran* (vb); cf Ger *hunger*, Du *honger*.]
hunk [hungk] *n* (*inf*) a large piece, lump, etc.; (*inf*) an attractive, well-built man.—**hunker** [hungk´ėr] *vi* to squat.—*n pl*, haunches or buttocks. [Perhaps Scand.]
hunt [hunt] *vti* to seek out to kill or capture (game) for food or sport; to search (for); to chase.—*n* a chase; a search; a party organized for hunting.—*ns* **hunter**, one who hunts; a horse or dog bred for hunting; **hunts´man**, a person who manages a hunt and looks after the hounds; **hunt´ress**, a woman who hunts game. [OE *huntian*; prob conn with *hentan*, to seize.]
hurdle [hûr´dle] *n* a portable frame of bars for temporary fences or for jumping over by horses or runners; an obstacle.—*pl* race over hurdles.—*vi* to race over hurdles.—*vt* to jump over; to overcome (an obstacle).—*n* **hurd´ler**, [OE *hyrdel*; Ger *hürde*.]
hurdy-gurdy [hûr´di-gûr´di] *n* a barrel organ. [Imit.]
hurl [hûrl] *vt* to fling with violence; to cast down; to utter vehemently.—*vi* (*inf*) (*baseball*) to pitch.—*n* **hurl´er**. [Cf Low Ger *hurreln*, to hurl; influenced by **hurtle** and **whirl**.]
hurly-burly [hûr´li-bûr´li] *n* tumult; confusion. [Perh from **hurl**.]
Huron [h(y)ŏŏr´ėn] *n* confederacy of Amerindian peoples of the St Lawrence valley; a member of any of these peoples.
hurrah [hur-ä´, hŏŏr-ä´] *interj* an exclamation of enthusiasm or joy.—*Also* **huzzah**. [Cf Scand *hurra*, Ger *hurrah*, Du *hoera*.]
hurricane [hur´i-kin, -kȧn] *n* a violent tropical cyclone with winds of at least 74 miles per hour (12, the highest, on the Beaufort scale).—*ns* **hurr´icane lamp**, a candlestick or oil lamp with a glass chimney to protect the flame; an electric lamp like this. [Sp *huracán*, from Carib.]
hurry [hur´i] *vt* to urge forward; to hasten.—*vi* to move or act with haste.—*pt p* **hurr´ied**.—*n* rush; urgency; eagerness to do, go, etc.—*adv* **hurr´iedly**.—*n* **hurr´y-skurr´y**, confusion and bustle.—*adv* confusedly. [Prob imit. Cf Old Swed *hurra*, to whirl round.]
hurt [hûrt] *vt* to cause bodily pain to; to damage; to offend.—*vi* to give pain; to have pain.—*pt, pt p* **hurt**.—*n* a pain; injury.—*adj* **hurt´ful**, causing hurt or loss; injurious.—*adv* **hurt´fully**.—*n* **hurt´fulness**.—*adj* **hurt´less**, harmless; without hurt or injury. [OFr *hurter*, to knock, to run against.]

hurtle [hûrt´l] *vti* to move or throw with great speed and much force. [Freq of **hurt** in its original sense (see ety).]
husband [huz´bȧnd] *n* a man to whom a woman is married.—*vt* to conserve; to manage thriftily.—*ns* **hus´bandman**, (*arch*) a farmer; **hus´bandry**, economical management; farming. [OE *hūsbonda*, ON *hūsbōndi*—*hūs*, a house, *būandi*, inhabiting, *pr p* of ON *būa*, to dwell.]
hush [hush] *interj* or *imper* silence! be still!—*vti* to quieten.—*n* a silence.—*adj* **hush´-hush´**, (*inf*) secret.—**hush up**, (*inf*) to keep secret.—[Imit. Cf **hist** and **whist**.]
husk [husk] *n* the dry, thin covering of certain fruits and seeds; any dry, rough, or useless covering.—*vt* to remove the husk from.—*adj*. [ME *huske*, perh connected with **house**.]
husky[1] [husk´i] *adj* (of the voice) hoarse; rough in sound; sturdy, strong.—*adv* **husk´ily**.—*n* **husk´iness**. [From **husk**, a dry covering.]
husky[2] [hus´ki] *n* a New World arctic sled dog; a Siberian husky. [App—*Eskimo*.]
hussar [hŏŏ-zär´] *n* a European soldier of a light cavalry regiment usu. with a brilliant dress uniform. [Hungarian *huszar*, through Old Serbian—It *corsaro*, a freebooter.]
hussy [hus´i, huz´i] *n* a woman of low morals; a brazen young woman or girl. [Abreviation of **housewife**.]
hustings [hus´tingz] *n sing* the process of, or a place for, political campaigning. [OE *hūsting*, a council—ON *hūsthing*—*hūs*, a house, *thing*, an assembly.]
hustle [hus´l] *vt* to shake or push together; to push roughly or unceremoniously; to jostle.—*vi* to move hurriedly; (*inf*) to work energetically; (*slang*) to obtain money illegally.—*n* a hustling; (*inf*) energetic action.—*n* **hus´tler**, an energetic person. [Du *hutsen, hutselen*, to shake to and fro.]
hut [hut] *n* a very plain or crude little house or cabin. [Fr *hutte*—OHG *hutta*.]
hutch [huch] *n* a chest or cupboard; a pen or coop for small animals; a hut. [Fr *huche*, a chest—Low L *hūtica*, a box; prob Gmc.]
hutzah, hutzpa *see* **chutzpah**.
huzzah, huzza [huz-ä´] *interj, n* hurrah. [Perh Ger *hussa*.]
hyacinth [hī´a-sinth] *n* a bulbous genus (*Hyacinthus*) of the lily family with spikes of bell-shaped flowers; a blue stone of the ancients; the orange gemstone jacinth; a light violet to moderate purple.—*adj* **hyacin´thine**. [Through L from Gr *Hyakinthos*.]
hyaline [hȳ´a-lin] *adj* glassy; of or like glass. [Gr *hyalos*, glass, prob Egyptian.]
hybrid [hī´brid] *n* the offspring of two plants or animals of different species; a mongrel.—*adj* crossbred.—*vti* (to cause) to produce hybrids; to crossbreed.—*adjs* **hy´brid, hyb´ridous**. [Fr.—L *hibrida*, a mongrel.]
hybris *see* **hubris**.
hydra [hī´dra] *n* a legendary many-headed water serpent; any persistent problem; any of numerous freshwater polyps (genus *Hydra*) having a mouth surrounded by tentacles.—*adj* **hy´dra-head´ed**, difficult to root out. [Fr *hydra*—*hydōr*, water.]
hydrangea [hī-drān´j(y)a] *n* a genus (*Hydrangea*) of shrubby plants with large heads of showy flowers, natives of China and Japan. [Gr *hydōr*, water, *angeion*, vessel.]
hydrant [hī´drȧnt] *n* a large pipe with a valve for drawing water from a water main. [Gr *hydōr*, water.]
hydrate [hī´drāt] *n* a chemical compound of water and some other substance.—*vt* to combine with water.—*vi* to become a hydrate.—*ns* **hydrā´tion, hydrator**. [Gr *hydōr*, water.]
hydraulic [hī-dröl´ik] *adj* relating to hydraulics: conveying water; worked by water or other liquid.—*adv* **hydraul´ically**.—*n pl* **hydraul´ics**, used as *sing*; the science dealing with the mechanical properties of liquids, as water, and their application in engineering; **hydraulic ram**, a pump that forces running water to a higher level by using the kinetic energy of flow. [From Gr *hydōr*, water, *aulos*, a pipe.]
hydro-, hydr- water. [Gr *hydōr*.]
hydrocarbon [hī-drō-kär´bȯn] *n* a chemical compound containing only hydrogen and carbon.
hydrocephalus [hī-drō-sef´a-lus] *n* the accumulation of cerebrospinal fluid in the ventricles of the brain.—*adjs* **hydrocephal´ic, hydroceph´alous**. [Gr *hydōr*, water, *kephalē*, the head.]
hydrochloric acid [hī-drō-klor´ik] a strong, highly corrosive acid that is a solution of the gas hydrogen chloride in water.
hydrodynamics [hī-drō-di-nam´iks or -dī-] *n pl* used as *sing*, the science that treats of the motions and equilibrium of a material system partly or wholly fluid.—*adjs* **hydrodynam´ic, -al**. [Gr *hydōr*, water, and *dynamics*.]
hydroelectricity [hī-drō-el-ek-tris´i-ti] *n* electricity produced by water power.—*adj* **hydroelec´tric**. [Gr *hydōr*, water, and **electricity**.]
hydrogen [hī´drō-jėn, -jen] *n* a flammable, colorless, odorless, gaseous chemical element (symbol H; at wt 1.0; at no 1), the lightest known substance.—*vt* **hy´drogenate** [-droj´], to combine with or treat with hydrogen.—*ns* **hydrogenā´tion; hydrogen bomb**, an extremely destructive atom bomb in which atoms of hydrogen are fused by explosion of a nuclear-fission unit in the bomb; **hydrogen peroxide**, a colorless liquid used as a bleach or disinfectant.—*adj* **hydrog´enous**.—**heavy hydrogen** *see* **heavy**. [From Gr *hydōr*, water, and *gennaein*, to produce.]
hydrography [hī-drog´ra-fi] *n* the study of bodies of water (as seas, lakes, and rivers) including the measurement of flow and charting, etc.—*n* **hydrog´rapher**.—*adjs* **hydrographic** [-graf´ik]. [Gr *hydōr*, water, *graphein*, to write.]
hydrokinetic [hī-drō-ki-net´ik] of the motion of fluids and forces affecting this motion.
hydrology [hī-drol´o-ji] *n* the science of water, esp its distribution on the earth and in the atmosphere. [Gr *hydōr*, water, *logos*, discourse.]
hydrolysis [hī-drol´i-sis] *n* the decomposition of organic compounds by interaction with water.—*adj* **hydrolyt´ic**. [Gr *hydōr*, water, *lysis*, loosing—*lyein*, to loose.]
hydrometer [hī-drom´ėt-ėr] *n* a device for measuring specific gravities of liquids, esp alcoholic beverages.—*adjs* **hydrometric** [-met´-], **-al.**—*n* **hydrom´etry**. [Gr *hydōr*, water, *metron*, a measure.]
hydropathy [hī-drop´a-thi] *n* the treatment of disease by water.—*adjs* **hydropathic** [hī-drō-path´ik]. [Gr *hydōr*, water, *pathos*, suffering—*pathein*, to suffer.]
hydrophobia [hī-drō-fō´bi-a] *n* a morbid fear of water; rabies.—*adj* **hydrophobic** [-fob´ik]. [Gr *hydōr*, water, *phobos*, fear.]
hydroplane [hī´drō-plān] *n* a light, flat-bottomed speedboat with airfoils. [Gr *hydōr*, water, L *planus*, plane.]
hydroponics [hī-drō-pon´iks] *n* the art or practice of growing plants in a chemical solution without soil. [Gr *hydōr*, water, *ponos*, toil.]
hydrosphere [hī´drō-sfēr] *n* the water envelope of the earth including aqueous vapor and bodies of water. [Gr *hydōr*, water, *sphaira*, sphere.]
hydrostatics [hī-drō-stat´iks] *n pl* used as *sing*, a branch of physics dealing with fluids at rest; esp with the pressures they exert or transmit.—*adj* **hydrostat´ic**. [Gr *hydōr*, water, *statikē* (*epistēme*), statics.]
hydrotropism [hī-drot´rop-izm] *n* the directional growth of plants toward water. [Gr *hydōr*, water, *tropos*, turn.]
hydrous [hī´drůs] *adj* (*chem, min*) containing water. [Gr *hydōr*, water.]
hydroxide [hī-droks´īd] *n* a chemical compound containing an OH group (eg NaOh, sodium hydroxide). [**hydrogen, oxygen**.]
hydrozoan [hī-drō-zō´an] *n* any coelenterate of the class Hydrozoa, which includes hydra and the Portuguese man-of-war.—Also *adj*.
hyena, hyaena [hī-ē´na] *n* a nocturnal, carnivorous, scavenging mammal, family Hyaenidae, of Asia and Africa with a howl like wild laughter. [L—Gr *hyaina*—*hȳs*, a pig.]
hygiene [hī´ji-ēn, also -jen] *n* the principles and practice of health and cleanliness.—*adj* **hygienic** [hī-jēn´-ik].—*adv* **hygien´ically**.—*n pl* (as *sing*) **hygien´ics**, hygiene. [Fr *hygiène*—Gr *hygieinē* (*technē*), hygienic (art)—*hygieia*, health, *hygiēs*, healthy.]
hygrometer [hī-grom´ėt-ėr] *n* an instrument for measuring the relative humidity of air.—*adjs* **hygrometric** [-met´rik], **-al.**—*n* **hygrom´etry**. [Gr *hygros*, wet, *metron*, a measure.]
hygroscope [hī´grō-skōp] *n* an instrument that shows changes in the humidity of the atmosphere.—*adj* **hygroscopic** [-skop´ik], readily absorbing moisture from the atmosphere. [Gr *hygros*, wet, *skopeein*, to view.]
Hymen [hī´men] *n* (*myth*) the Greek god of marriage.—*adjs* **hymenē´al, hymenē´an**. [Gr wedding-cry, perh also a god.]
hymen [hī´men] *n* a thin membrane partially closing the vaginal orifice.—*n pl* **hymenop´tera**, a large order of insects which have two pairs of membraneous wings, complete metamorphosis, often associate in large colonies, and include ants, bees, wasps, etc.—*adjs* **hymeopteran, hymenopterous**. [Gr *hy̆men*, a membrane.]
hymn [him] *n* a song of praise.—*vt* to celebrate in song; to worship in hymns.—*vi* to sing in adoration.—*ns* **hym´nal, hym´nary**, hymn book.—*ns* **hymnol´ogy**, the study or composition of hymns. [Gr *hymnos*.]
hyoscine [hī´ō-sēn] *n* a poisonous alkaloid occurring in belladonna and related plants and used like atropine. [Gr *hyoskyanos*, henbane.]
hype [hīp] *n* (*slang*) hypodermic; (*slang*) a drug addict; (*slang*) deception, esp exaggerated promotion.—*vt* to stimulate, excite, as by a drug injection; (*inf*) to promote (something) in a sensational way.
hyper- [hī´pėr-] beyond; over, in excess [Gr *hyper*].—eg **hyperphys´ical**, beyond physical laws, supernatural; **hypersen´sitive**, over-sensitive; **hypersen´sitiveness**.
hyperbaric [hī-pėr-bar´ik] *adj* pertaining to conditions of high atmospheric pressure with a greater concentration of oxygen than normal. [Gr *hyper*, beyond, *barys*, heavy.]
hyperbola [hī-pûr´bo-la] *n* (*geom*) a curve, one of the conic sections, being the intersection of a double cone and a plane making a greater angle with the base than the side of the cone makes.—*adjs*. **hyperbol´ic, -al.** [L.—Gr *hyperbolē*, overshooting—*hyperballein*—*hyper*, beyond, *ballein*, to throw.]
hyperbole [hī-pûr´bo-lē] *n* a figure of speech that produces a vivid impression by obvious exaggeration.—*adjs* **hyperbol´ic, al.**—*adv* **hyperbol´ically**.—*vti* **hyper´bolize**, to indulge in exaggeration.—*n* **hyper´bolism**. [A doublet of the above.]
hyperborean [hī-pėr-bō´ri-ȧn] *adj* belonging to the extreme north.—*n* an inhabitant of the extreme north. [Gr *hyperboreos*—*hyper*, beyond, *Boreas*, the north wind.]
hypercritic [hī-pėr-krit´ik] *n* one who is excessively critical.—*adjs* **hypercrit´ical**.—*adv* **hypercrit´ically**.—*n* **hypercrit´icism**. [Gr *hyper*, over, and **critic**.]

hyperglycemia [hī-pėr-glī-sēm´i-ȧ] *n* abnormal rise in the sugar content of the blood. [Gr *hyper*, beyond, *glykys*, sweet.]

hypermetrical [hī-pėr-met´rik-ȧl] *adj* beyond or exceeding the ordinary meter of a line; having an additional syllable. [Gr *hyper*, beyond, and **metrical**.]

hypermetropia [hī-pėr-me-trō´pi-a] *n* long-sightedness. [Gr *hyper*, beyond, *metron*, measure, *ōps*, eye.]

hyperon [hī´pėr-ȯn] *n* an unstable heavy elementary particle. [Gr *hyper*, beyond, exceeding.]

hypersonic [hī-pėr-son´ik] *adj* of speeds, above Mach 5, or 5 times the speed of sound. [Gr *hyper*, beyond, and **sonic**.]

hypertension [hī-pėr-ten´sh(ȯ)n] *n* blood pressure higher than normal. [Gr *hyper*, beyond, and **tension**.]

hypertext [hī´pėr-tekst] *n* (*comput*) text which provides a link from one document to another area of that document or another.

hypertrophy [hī-pûr´tro-fi] *n* abnormal enlargement of an organ or part.—*vi* to increase in size beyond the normal.—*adj* **hyper´trophied**. [Gr *hyper*, over, *trophē*, nourishment.]

hyperventilation [hī-pûr-vėnt´il-ā-shûn] *n* an increase in the rate of breathing, often resulting in dizziness. [G *hyper*, beyond + **ventilation**.]

hypha [hī-fa] *n* one of the threadlike elements of the mycelium of a fungus.—*pl* **hyph´ae** [-ē]. [Gr *hyphē*, web.]

hyphen [hī´fėn] *n* a short stroke (–) joining two syllables or words.—*vt* to join by a hyphen.—*vt* **hy´phenate**, to hyphen.—*p adj* hy´phenated, hyphened. [Gr.—*hypo*, under, *hen*, one.]

hypnosis [hip-nō´sis] *n* a sleeplike state in which the mind responds to external suggestion.—*n* **hypnother´apy**, treatment of illness by hypnosis.—*adj* **hypnot´ic**, of or relating to hypnosis.—*n* any agent causing sleep.—*vt* **hyp´notize**, to put in a state of hypnosis; to fascinate.—*n* **hyp´notism**,- the art or practice of inducing hypnosis. [Gr *hypnos*, sleep.]

hypo- [hī´pō], **hyp-**, under, below [Gr *hypo*].—eg **hypoglycem´ia**, abnormal reduction of sugar content of the blood; **hypoten´sion**, blood pressure lower than normal.

hypochondria [hip-, hīp-ō-kon´dri-a] *n* morbid anxiety about health, often with imaginary illnesses.—*adj* **hypochon´driac**, relating to or affected with hypochondria.—Also *n*. [Gr *hypochondria* (neut pl)—*hypo*, under, *chondros*, a cartilage.]

hypocrisy [hi-pok´ri-si] *n* pretending to be what one is not, as good or virtuous; simulating feeling one does not experience.—*n* **hyp´ocrite**, one who practises hypocrisy.—*adj* **hypocrit´ical**.—*adv* **hypocrit´ically**. [Gr *hypokrisis*—*hypokrinesthai*, to play on the stage, from *hypo*, under, *krinesthai*, to dispute.]

hypodermic [hip-, or hīp-ō-dûr´mik] *adj* injected under the skin.—*n* a hypodermic needle, syringe or injection.—*ns* **hypodermic needle**, a hollow needle attached to a hypodermic syringe; **hypodermic syringe**, a syringe used for the injection of material beneath the skin. [Gr *hypo*, under, *derma*, skin.]

hypoglycemia [hī-pō-glī-sēm´i-ȧ] *n* abnormal drop in the sugar content of the blood. [Gr *hypo*, under, *glykys*, sugar.]

hypostasis [hip-, or hīp-os´ta-sis] *n* (*med*) sediment; (*med*) excessive blood in a part of the body; essential substance; the essence or real personal substance of each of the three divisions of the Trinity.—*adjs* **hypostatic** [-stat´ik].—*adv* **hypostat´ically**. [Gr *hypostatis*—*hypo*, under, *stasis*, setting.]

hypotenuse [hīp-, or hip-ot´ėn-ūs, or -ūz] *n* the side of a right-angled triangle opposite to the right angle; the length of a hypotenuse. [Fr.—Gr *hypoteinousa* (*grammē*), (a line) subtending or stretching under—*hypo*, under, *teinein*, to stretch.]

hypoth´ecāte [hip-oth´ė-kāt] *vt* to pledge without delivery of title or possession (of a property).—*n* **hypothecā´tion**. [L *hypothēca*—Gr *hypothēkē*, a pledge.]

hypothermia [hī-pō-thûr´mi-ȧ] *n* subnormal body temperature. [Gr *hypo*, under, *thermē*, heat.]

hypothesis [hī-poth´e-sis] *n* an unproved theory, etc. tentatively accepted to explain certain facts.—*pl* **hypoth´eses** [-sēz].—*adjs* **hypothet´ical**, assumed.—*adv* **hypothet´ically**. [Gr *hypothesis*—*hypo*, under, *thesis*, placing.]

hyson [hī´son] *n* a Chinese green tea made from twisted, thinly-rolled leaves. [From Chinese.]

hyssop [his´ȯp] *n* an aromatic plant (*Hyssopus officinalis*) of the mint family with blue flowers. [L *hyssōpum*—Gr *hyssōpos*, or *-on*; cf Heb *´ēzōb*.]

hysterectomy [his-tėr-ek´tȯm-i] *n* surgical removal of the womb. [Gr *hystera*, the womb, *ectomē*, a cutting out.]

hysteria [his-tē´ri-a] *n* a mental disorder marked by excitability, anxiety, imaginary organic disorders, etc.; any outbreak of wild uncontrolled feeling.—*n pl* **hyster´ics**, fits of hysteria.—*adjs* **hysteric** [-ter´-ik], **-al**.—*adv* **hyster´ically**. [Gr *hystera*, the womb, with which hysteria was formerly thought to be connected.]

hysteron-proteron [his´tėr-on-prot´ėr-on] *n* a figure of speech consisting of an inversion of the natural or rational order (eg line, hook, and sinker). [Gr, lit latter-former.]

I

I [ī] *pron* the nominative case singular of the first personal pronoun; the word used by a speaker or writer in mentioning himself. [ME *ich*—OE *ic*; Ger *ich*, ON *ek*, L *ego*, Gr *egō*.]

iambus [ī-am´bus] *n* a metrical foot of two syllables, the first short and the second long, as in L *fidēs*; or the first unaccented and the second accented, as in *deduce*.—Also **i´amb**.—*adj* **iam´bic**, consisting of iambuses. [L *iambus*—Gr *iambos*, from *iaptein*, to assail, this metre being first used by writers of satire.]

iatrogenic [ī-à-trė-jėn´ik] *adj* of a disease or disorder inadvertently induced by a physician. [Gr *iatros* physician + *genic* produced by.]

Iberian [ī-bē´ri-àn] *adj* of Spain and Portugal; of ancient Iberia (now Georgia) in the Caucasus. [L and Gr *Ibēria*, Spain and Portugal, Georgia.]

ibex [ī´beks] *n* any of several large-horned mountain wild goats. [L *ibex*.]

ibid [ib-id] in (of a book, page, etc. cited) in the same place. [L *ibidem*.]

ibis [ī´bis] *n* a genus of wading birds with curved bill, akin to the spoonbills, one species worshipped by the ancient Egyptians. [L and Gr *ībis*, prob an Egyptian word.]

ice [īs] *n* water frozen solid by cold; a frozen dessert of fruit juice, sugar, etc.; (*slang*) diamonds.—*vt* to freeze; to cool with ice; to cover with icing.—*vi* to freeze (*often with* **up** *or* **over**).—*ns* **ice age**, glacial epoch; **ice´berg**, a great mass of ice broken off a glacier and floating in the sea; **iceberg lettuce**, a crisp light-green head lettuce; **ice´boat**, a frame on runners propelled by sails on ice; an icebreaker; **ice´box**, a refrigerator, esp one in which ice is used; **ice´breaker**, a sturdy boat for breaking a channel through ice; **ice´cap**, a mass of slowly spreading glacial ice; **ice cream´**, a sweet, frozen food made from flavored cream or milk; **ice´field**, an extensive field of ice in the sea; **ice´floe**, a sheet of floating sea ice; *ice´hockey*, an indoor or outdoor hockey game played by six players; **ice´man**, one who sells or delivers ice; **ice´milk**, a dessert like ice cream, but with less butterfat; **ice´skate**, a boot with a steel blade fixed to the sole; **ic´ing**, a semisolid flavored sweet mixture used to coat cakes and cookies.—*adj* **icy** [ī´sē], full of or covered with ice; of ice; slippery or very cold; cold in manner.—*adv* **ic´ily**.—*n* **ic´iness**.—**break the ice**, to make a start, as in getting acquainted; **cut no ice**, (*inf*) have no influence; **on thin ice** (*inf*) in danger. [OE *īs*; ON *īss*; Ger *eis*, Dan *is*.]

Icelandic [īs-land´ik] *adj* of Iceland.—*n* the Germanic language of the Icelanders.

Iceland moss [īs´lànd-mos] *n* a lichen (*Cetraria islandica*) of northern regions, used as a medicine and for food.

Iceland poppy [īs´lànd-pop´i] *n* a perennial poppy (genus *Papaver*) with grey-green pinnate leaves and flowers varying from white to orange-scarlet.

Iceland spar [īs´lànd-spär] *n* a transparent calcite with double refraction.

ichneumon [ik-nū´mòn] *n* a mongoose; an ichneumon fly.—*n* **ichneumon fly**, any of a large superfamily (Ichneumonoidea) of insects whose larvae are parasitic in or on other insects. [Gr *ichneumōn*, lit tracker—*ichneuein*, to hunt after—*ichnos*, a track.]

ichthyology [ik-thi-ol´o-ji] *n* the branch of zoology dealing with fishes.—*adj* **ichthyolog´ical**.—*n* **ichthyol´ogist**. [Gr *ichthȳs*, a fish, *logos*, discourse.]

ichthyophagous [ik-thi-of´a-gus] *adj* subsisting on fish. [Gr *ichthȳs*, a fish, *phagein*, to eat.]

ichthyosaurus [ik´thi-ō-sör-us] *n* any of an order (Ichthyosaurus) of extinct marine reptiles shaped like a fish with an elongated snout. [Gr *ichthȳs*, a fish, *sauros*, a lizard.]

icicle [īs´i-kl] *n* a hanging piece of ice formed by the freezing of dripping water. [OE *īsesgicel; īses* being the gen of *īs*, ice, and *gicel*, an icicle.]

icon [ī´kon] *n* an image; in the Eastern Church, a sacred image usu on a wooden panel; an object of uncritical reverence; (*comput*) a symbol on a screen that represents something or some process or function in the computer. [L *īcōn*—Gr *eikōn*, an image.]

iconoclast [ī-kon´ō-klast] *n* one who attacks old cherished errors and superstitions.—*adj* **iconoclast´ic**.—*n* **icon´oclasm**, act of breaking images (*lit, fig*). [Gr *eikōn*, an image, *klaein*, to break.]

iconoscope [ī-kon´ō-skōp] *n* a form of electron camera. [*Iconoscope* a trademark.]

ictus [ik´tus] *n* a rhythmical accentuation. [L, a blow.]

id [id] *n* in psychoanalytic theory, that part of the psyche which is the source of psychic energy. [L *id*, it.]

ID card [ī-dē´] *n* a card bearing data (as a photograph and description) about the person whose name appears on it.—Also **identification card, identity card**.

idea [ī-dē´a] *n* an image of an external object formed by the mind; a notion, thought, any product of intellectual action; an opinion or belief; a scheme; meaning or significance.—*adj* **idē´al**, existing in idea; existing in imagination only; highest and best conceivable; perfect.—*n* the highest conception of anything; a perfect model; a goal or principle.—*vti* **idē´alize**, to regard as, or to represent as, ideal.—*ns* **idealiza´tion; idē´alism**, behavior or thought based on a conception of things as one thinks they ought to be; a striving to achieve one's ideals; **idē´alist**.—*adj* **idealist´ic**, of idealists or to idealism.—*n* **ideal´ity**, ideal state; ability and disposition to form ideals of beauty and perfection; something idealized or imagined.—*adv* **idē´ally**. [L *idĕa*—Gr *idĕā*; cf *idein* (aor), to see.]

idée fixe [ē-dā fēks] a fixed idea; an obsession. [Fr.]

identify [ī-den´ti-fī] *vt* to ascertain or prove to be the same; to ascertain the identity of; to regard or wish to regard (oneself) as sharing interests, experiences, attitudes, behavior, etc. with a person or group.—*pt p* **iden´tified**.—*ns* **identificā´tion; identification card**, ID card. [LL *identificāre*—*idem*, the same, *facĕre*, to make.]

identity [ī-den´ti-ti] *n* state of being the same; sameness; individuality; personality; who or what a person is; (*math*) an equation true for all values of the symbols involved.—*adj* **iden´tical**, the very same; having the same origin.—*adv* **iden´tically**.—*ns* **iden´ticalness; identity card**, ID card; **identity crisis**, the state of being uncertain about oneself, one's goals, etc., esp in adolescence. [Fr *identité*—Low L *identitās, -ātis*—L *idem*, the same.]

ideogram [id´i-ō-gram, or īd´-] **ideograph** [-gräf] *ns* a symbol that stands not for a word or sound but for the thing itself; a logogram.—*adjs* **ideograph´ic**. [Gr *idea*, idea, *gramma*, a drawing—*graphein*, to write.]

ideology [id-, or īd-i-ol´o-ji] *n* the doctrines, beliefs, opinions, etc. of an individual, class, political party, etc.—*adjs* **ideolog´ic, -al**. [Gr *idea*, idea, *logos*, discourse.]

ides [īdz] *n pl* in ancient Rome, the 15th day of March, May, July, October, and the 13th of the other months. [Fr *ides*—L *īdūs* (pl).]

idiocy *See idiot*.

idiom [id´i-òm] *n* the dialect of a people, region, etc.; the usual way in which the words of a language are used to express thought; an accepted phrase or expression with a different meaning from the literal; a characteristic style, as in art or music.—*adjs* **idiomat´ic, -al**.—*adv* **idiomat´ically**. [Gr *idiōma*, peculiarity—*idios*, one's own.]

idiosyncrasy [id-i-ō-sing´kra-si] *n* peculiarity of temperament or mental constitution; any characteristic of a person.—*adj* **idiosyncratic** [-krat´ik]. [Gr *idios*, own, *synkrāsis*, a mixing together—*syn*, together, *krāsis*, a mixing.]

idiot [id´i-òt, id´yòt] *n* an adult mentally inferior to a child of three; a foolish or unwise person.—*n* **id´iocy** [-si], state of being an idiot; imbecility; folly.—*adjs* **idiotic** [-ot´ik].—*adv* **idiot´ically**.—*ns* **id´iotism**, the state of being an idiot; **idiot box** (*slang*) a television. [Fr,—L *idiōta*—Gr *idiōtēs*, a private person, one who holds no public office or has no professional knowledge—*idios*, own, private.]

idle [ī´dl] *adj* unemployed; averse to labor; not occupied or in use; useless, vain; baseless.—*vt* to spend in idleness.—*vi* to move slowly or aimlessly; to be unemployed or inactive; to operate without transmitting power (*the motor idled*)—*vt* to waste; to cause (a motor) to idle.—*ns* **i´dleness; idler pulley**, a tightening pulley or guide for a chain or belt; **idler wheel**, a wheel, gear, or roller used to transfer motion or to support or guide something; an idler pulley.—*adv* **i´dly**. [OE *īdel*; Du *ijdel*, Ger *eitel*.]

idol [ī´dòl] *n* an image of some object of worship; a person or thing too much loved, admired, or honored.—*vt* **i´dolīze**, to make an idol of, for worship; to love to excess. [OFr *idole*—L *īdōlum*—Gr *eidōlon*—*eidos*, what is seen—*idein* (aor) to see.]

idolater [ī-dol´à-tėr] *n* a worshipper of idols; a great admirer;—*fem* **idol´atress**.—*vt* **idol´atrīse**.—*adj* **idol´atrous**.—*adv* **idol´atrously**.—*n* **idol´atry**, the worship of idols; excessive love. [Fr *idolâtre*—Gr *eidōlolatrēs*—*eidōlon*, idol, *latreiā*, worship.]

idyll [id´il, īd´il] *n* a short pictorial poem, chiefly on pastoral subjects; a story, episode, or scene of happy innocence or rusticity; a work of art of like character, in music, etc.—*adj* **idyll´ic**. [L *īdyllium*—Gr *eidyllion*, dim of *eidos*, image.]

if [if] *conj* on condition that; in case that; supposing that; whether. [OE *gif*, cf Du *of*, ON *ef*.]

igloo [ig´lōō] *n* an Eskimo house built of soil, wood, or stone or of snow and ice. [Eskimo.]

igneous [ig´nė-us] *adj* of fire; (*geol*) produced by volcanic action or intense heat. [L *ignis*, fire.]

ignis fatuus [ig´nis-fat´ū-us] *n* the light of combusion of marsh gas, any delusive ideal.—*pl* **ignes-fatui** [ig´nēz-fat´ū-ī]. [L *ignis*, fire, *fatuus*, foolish.]

ignite [ig-nīt´] *vt* to set on fire; to heat to the point at which combustion occurs; to render luminous by heat.—*vi* to take fire.—*adj* **ignīt´able, ignīt´ible**.—*n* **ignī´tion**, act of igniting; the firing of an explosive mixture of gases, vapors, or other substances, eg by an electric spark; the means of igniting; state of being ignited. [L *ignīre, ignītum*, to set on fire, make red hot—*ignis*, fire.]

ignoble [ig-nō´bl] *adj* of low birth; mean or worthless; dishonorable.—*n* **ignō´bleness**.—*adv* **ignō´bly**. [Fr,—L *ignōbilis—in-*, not, *gnōbilis* (*nōbilis*), noble.]

ignominy [ig´nō-min-i] *n* the loss of one's good name, disgrace; infamy.—*adj* **ignomin´ious**, dishonorable; humiliating, degrading; contemptible, mean.—*adv* **ignomin´iously**.—*n* **ignomin´iousness**. [Fr,—L *ignōminia—in-*, not, *(g)nōmen, -inis*, name.]

ignoramus [ig-nō-ra-´mus] *n* an ignorant person, esp one making a pretence to knowledge.—*pl* **ignorā´muses**. [L *ignōrāmus*, we are ignorant, 1st pers pl pres indic of *ignōrāre*.]

ignorant [ig´nȯr-ȧnt] *adj* without knowledge; uninformed; resulting from want of knowledge.—*n* **ig´norance**.—*adv* **ig´norantly**. [Fr,—L *ignōrans, -antis*, pr p of *ignōrāre*. See **ignore**.]

ignore [ig-nōr´, -nör´] *vt* to disregard. [L *ignōrāre*, not to know—*in-*, not, and the root of *(g)nōscĕre*, to know.]

iguana [i-gwä´na] *n* any of a family (iguanidae) of large herbivorous arboreal lizards of tropical America. [Sp from Carib.]

ikebana [ē´ke-bä´nȧ] *n* Japanese art of flower arrangement.

il [il-] a form of **in-** used before *l*.

ilex [ī´leks] *n* the holm oak; the holly genus. [L *īlex*, holm-oak.]

Iliad [il´i-ad] *n* a Greek epic, ascribed to Homer, about the Trojan War. [Gr *Ilias, -ados—Ilios* or *Ilion*, Ilium, Troy.]

ilk [ilk] *adj* same. only in—**of that ilk**, of the estate of the same name as the family. [OE *ilca*, prob—*līk*, like.]

ill [il] *adj* (comparative **worse**; superlative **worst**) not in good health; bad; evil; faulty; unfavorable..—*adv* badly, not well; with difficulty.—*n* mild disorder or disease; evil; misfortune.—*adjs* **ill´-advised´**, imprudent.—**ill at ease**, uncomfortable; embarrassed.—*ns*—*adj* ill´-bred, uncivil.—*n* **ill´-breed´ing**.—*adjs* **ill´-fāt´ed**, unlucky; **ill´-fāvored**, ugly; unpleasant; **ill´-gott´en**, obtained by evil or dishonest means; **ill´-hum´ored**, bad-tempered; **ill´-mann´ered**, rude; **ill´-nā´tured**, malevolent; spiteful;—*adv* **ill´-nā´turedly**.—*n* **ill´ness**, sickness; disease.—*adjs* **ill´-starred´**, unlucky; **ill-suit´ed**, not appropriate; quarrelsome.—*vt* **ill-treat**, to treat unkindly, unfairly, etc.—*n* **ill-treatment, ill´-used´**, badly used or treated.—*vt* **ill´-use**, to abuse.—*n* **ill´-will´**, enmity. [ON *illr*; not connected with OE *yfel*, evil, but formerly confused with it.]

illation [il-ā´sh(ȯ)n] *n* act of inferring; conclusion inferred.—*adj* **illative**, inferential.—*n* a word (as *thus*) or phrase (as *as a result*) introducing an inference. [L *illātiō, -ōnis—illātus*, used as pt p of *inferre*, to infer—*il-(in-)*, in, *lātus*, carried.]

illegal [il-ē-gȧl] *adj* contrary to law.—*n* an illegal immigrant.—*vt* **illē´galīze**, to unlawful.—*n* **illegal´ity**, the quality or condition of being illegal, or an instance of it.—*adv* **illē´gally**. [L *il- (in-)*, not, and **legal**.]

illegible [il-ej´i-bl] *adj* impossible to read because badly written or printed.—*ns* **illeg´ibleness, illegibil´ity**.—*adv* **illeg´ibly**. [L *il- (in-)*, not, and **legible**.]

illegitimate [il-ė-jit´i-mȧt] *adj* born of parents not married to each other; contrary to law, rules, or logic.—*n* **illegit´imacy**.—*adv* **illegit´imātely**. [L *il- (in-)*, not, + **legitimate**.]

illiberal [il-ib´ėr-ȧl] *adj* narrow-minded; not generous.—*n* **illiberal´ity**. [Fr *illibéral*—L *illiberālis—il- (in-)*, not, *liberālis*, liberal.]

illicit [il-is´it] *adj* improper; unlawful.—*adv* **illic´itly**.—*n* **illic´itness**. [L *illicitus—il- (in-)*, not, *licitus*, pt p of *licēre*, to be allowed.]

illimitable [il-im´it-ȧ-bl] *adj* immeasurable; infinite.—*n* **illim´itableness**.—*adv* **illim´itably**. [L *il- (in-)*, not, + **limitable**.]

illiterate [il-it´ėr-ȧt] *adj* uneducated, esp not knowing how to read or write.—Also *n*.—*ns* **illit´erateness, illit´eracy** [-si]. [L *illīterātus* (or *-litt-*)—*il- (in-)*, not, *līterātus* (or *litt-*), learned.]

illogical [il-oj´i-kȧl] *adj* not logical or reasonable.—*adv* **illog´ically**.—*n* **illog´icalness**. [L *il- (in-)*, not, + **logical**.]

illume *See* **illuminate**.

illuminate [il-(y)ōō´min-āt] *vt* to give light to; to light up; to make clear; to inform; to decorate as with gold or lights.—*ns* **illuminant**, a substance or device that illuminates; **illumination**, an illuminating; the intensity of light.—*adj* **illu´minative**, tending to give light; illustrative or explanatory.—*n* **illu´minator**.—*vs t* **illu´mine, illume´**, illuminate. [L *illūmināre, -ātum—in*, in, upon, *lūmināre*, to cast light.]

illusion [il-(y)ōō´zh(ȯ)n] *n* a false idea or conception; an unreal or misleading image or appearance.—*n* **illu´sionist**, a magician or sleight-of-hand performer.—*adjs* **illu´sive, illu´sory**, deceiving by false appearances.—*adv* **illu´sively**.—*n* **illu´siveness**. [Fr,—L *llūsiō, -ōnis,—illūdĕre—in*, on, *lūdĕre*, to play.]

illustrate [il´us-trāt, il-us´trāt] *vt* to make clear as by examples; to furnish (books, etc.) with explanatory pictures, charts, etc.—*n* **illustrā´tion**, act of making clear, explaining; an example; a picture or diagram accompanying a text.—*adjs* **ill´ustrated** [or -us´-], having illustrations; **illustrative** [il´us-trā-tiv or il-us´tra-tiv], **illus´tratory**, having the quality of making clear or explaining.—*n* **ill´ustrātor**.—*adj* **illus´trious**, highly distinguished; noble.—*adv* **illus´triously**.—*n* **illus´triousness**. [L *illūstris—illūstrāre, —ātum—lūstrāre*, to light up, prob—*lūx*, light.]

im- [im-] a form of **in-** used before *b, m* and *p*.

image [im´ij *n* a representation of a person or thing; the visual impression of something in a lens, mirror, etc.; a copy; a likeness; a mental picture; the concept of a person, product, etc. held by the public at large; a metaphor or simile.—*vt* to make a representation of; to reflect; to imagine.—*ns* **imagery** [*im´ij-ri* or *im´ij-ėr-i*], the work of the imagination; mental pictures; figures of speech; images in general or collectively; **im´agist**, one of a 20th-century school of poetry aiming at concentration, exact and simple language, and freedom of form and subject; **im´agism**, the theory or practice of this school. [OFr,—L *imāgō*, image; cf *imitārī*, to imitate.]

imagine [im-aj´in] *vt* to form an image of in the mind; to conceive; to think vainly or falsely; to suppose, conjecture;—*vi* to form mental images.—*adj* **imag´inable**.—*n* **imag´inableness**.—*adv* **imag´inably**.—*adj* **imag´inary**, existing only in the imagination.—*n* **imaginātion**, act of imagining; the faculty of forming images in the mind; the artist's creative power; that which is imagined.—*adj* **imag´inātive**, full of imagination.—*ns* **imag´inātiveness; imag´iner; imag´ining**, that which is imagined. [OFr *imaginer*—L *imāginārī—imāgō*, an image.]

imago [i-mā´gō] *n* the last, adult, state of insect life; an idealized mental image of oneself or another.—*pl* **imagines** [i-mā´jin-ēz], **imā´gōs**. [L.]

imam [i-mäm´] *n* the one who leads the devotions in a mosque; a title among Muslims. [Ar *imām*, chief.]

imbalance [im-bal´ȧns] *n* lack of balance as in proportion or force. [L *in-*, not, + **balance**.]

imbecile [im´be-sil, -sēl] *adj* stupid or foolish.—*n* an adult with a mental age of a three- to eight-year-old child; a stupid or foolish person.—*n* **imbecil´ity**. [Fr *imbécille* (now *imbécile*)—L *imbēcillus*; origin unknown.]

imbed [im-bed´] *vt See* **embed**.

imbibe [im-bīb´] *vti* to drink esp alcoholic liquor; to receive into the mind.—*n* **imbib´er**. [L *imbibĕre—in*, in, into, *bibĕre*, to drink.]

imbitter, imbosom, embitter *See* **emboson**.

imbricate [im´bri-kāt] *vt* (*bot, zool*) to lay one over another, as tiles on a roof.—*vi* to be so placed.—*adj*(*-ȧt*) overlapping like roof-tiles.—Also **im´bricāted**.—*n* **imbricā´tion**. [L *imbricāre, -ātum*, to tile—*imbrex*, a tile—*imber*, a shower.]

imbroglio [im-brōl´yō] *n* a complicated, confusing situation; a confused misunderstanding. [It confusion—*imbrogliare*, to confuse, embroil.]

imbrue [im-brōō´] *vt* to stain. [OFr *embreuver—bevrer* (Fr *boire*)—L *bibĕre*, to drink.]

imbue [im´bū´] *vt* to dye; to permeate (with ideas, feelings, etc.). [OFr *imbuer*—L *imbuĕre—in*, and root of *bibĕre*, to drink.]

imitate [im´i-tāt] *vt* to strive to produce something like, or to be like; to mimic.—*adj* **im´itable**, that may be imitated or copied.—*ns* **imitabil´ity; imitā´tion**, act of imitating; that which is produced as a copy or counterfeit; a performance in mimicry.—*adj* sham, counterfeit.—*adj* **im´itātive**, inclined to imitate; formed after a model; mimicking.—*ns* **im´itātiveness; am´itātor**. [L *imitārī, imitātus*.]

immaculate [im-ak´ū-lȧt] *adj* spotless; unstained; pure.—*adv* **immac´ulately**.—*n* **immac´ulateness**.—**immaculate conception**, the RC dogma that the Virgin Mary was conceived without original sin. [L *immaculātus—in-*, not, *maculāre*, to spot.]

immanent [im´a-nėnt] *adj* inherent; pervading.—*n* **imm´anence**, the pervasion of the universe by an intelligent and creative principle. [L *in*, in, *manēre*, to remain.]

immaterial [im-a-tē´ri-ȧl] *adj* spiritual; unimportant.—*vt* **immatē´rialize**, to separate from matter.—*ns* **immatē´rialism**, the doctrine that there is no material substance; **immatē´rialist**, one who believes in this; **immaterial´ity**, the quality of being immaterial or of not consisting of matter. [Low L *immāteriālis—im- (in-)*, not, *māteriālis. See* **material**].

immature [im-ȧ-tūr´] *adjs* not ripe; not perfect; not come to full development.—*n* **immatur´ity**. [L *immātūrus—im- (in-)*, not, *mātūrus*. See **mature**.]

immeasurable [im-ezh´ůr-ȧ-bl] *adj* that cannot be measured; boundless; vast.—*n* **immeas´urableness**.—*adv* **immeas´urably**. [L *im- (in-)*, not, and **measurable**.]

immediate [im-ē´di-ȧt] *adj* with nothing between; not acting by second causes, direct; next, nearest; without delay.—*adv* **immē´diately**.—*ns* **immē´diacy** [*-si*], state of being immediate; **immē´diateness**. [Low L *immediātus—im- (in-)*, not, *mediātus—mediāre*. See **mediate**.]

immemorial [im-e-mōr´, mör´, i-ȧl] *adj* beyond the reach of memory; very old. [Low L *immemoriālis*—L *im- (in-)*, not, *memoriālis—memor*, memory.]

immense [i-mens´] *adj* vast in extent; very large.—*adv* **immense´ly**.—*ns* **immense´ness; immens´ity**. [Fr,—L *immensus—in-*, not, *mensus*, pa p of *metīrī*, to measure.]

immerge [im-(m)ûrj´] *vti* to plunge in. [L *in*, into, *mergĕre, mersum*, to plunge.]

immerse [im-(m)ûrs´] *vt* to dip under the surface of a liquid; to baptize by dipping the whole body; to engage or involve deeply (eg of thought, of difficulties).—*adj* **immers´ible**, capable of being immersed, or of working under water.—*n* **immer´sion**, act of immersing; state of being immersed; deep absorption or involvement; baptism by immersing.—*n* **immersion heater**, an electric coil or rod immersed in water to heat the water. [Same root as **immerge**.]

immesh *same as* **enmesh**.

immigrate [im´i-grāt] *vi* to come into a new country, esp to settle there.—*ns*

imm´igrant, one who immigrates; **immigrā´tion**. [L *immigrāre—in*, into, *migrāre, -ātum*, to remove.]

imminent [im´i-nėnt] *adj* near at hand; impending; threatening.—*ns* **imm´inence, imm´inency**.—*adv* **imm´inently**. [L *imminens, -entis—in*, upon, *minēre*, to project.]

immiscible [im-is´i-bl] *adj* not capable of being mixed. [L *im- (in-)*, not, and **miscible**.]

immitigable [im-it´i-gȧ-bl] *adj* incapable of being made less severe, painful, etc.—*adv* **immit´igably**. [L *immītigābilis—im- (in-)*, not, *mītigābilis—mītigāre*, to soften.]

immobile [im-(m)ō´bil, -bīl, bēl] *adj* immovable; not readily moved; motionless; stationary.—*n* **immobilīzā´tion**.—*vt* **immob´ilize**, to render immobile; to keep out of action or circulation.—*n* **immobil´ity**. [Fr,—L *immōbilis—im- (in-)*, not, *mōbilis*. See **mobile**.]

immoderate [im-od´ėr-ȧt] *adj* exceeding due bounds, excessive, unrestrained.—*n* **immoderā´tion**, want of moderation, excess. [L *immoderātus—im- (in-)*, not, *moderātus*. See **moderate**.]

immodest [im-od´est] *adj* lacking restraint; exceedingly self-assertive; indecent.—*adv* **immod´estly**.—*n* **immod´esty**. [L *immodestus—im- (in-)*, not, *modestus*. See **modest**.]

immolate [im´ō-lāt] *vt* to kill as a sacrifice.—*ns* **immolā´tion**, sacrifice; that which is offered in sacrifice; **imm´olātor**. [L *immolāre, -ātum*, to sprinkle meal (on a victim), hence to sacrifice—*in*, upon, *mola*, meal.]

immoral [im-(m)or´ȧl] *adj* inconsistent with what is right; wicked; lewd.—*n* **immorality** [im-or-al´i-ti], quality of being immoral, esp unchaste; an immoral act or practice. [L *im- (in-)*, not, + **moral**.]

immortal [im-ör´tȧl] *adj* exempt from death; enduring; having lasting fame.—*n* an immortal being.—*vt* **immortalize** [im-ör´tȧl-iz], to make immortal as in fame.—*n* **immortality**. [L *immortālis—im- (in-)*, not, *mortālis*. See **mortal**.]

immortelle [im-ör-tel´] *n* an everlasting flower. [Fr *(fleur) immortelle*, immortal (flower).]

immovable [im-ōōv´ȧ-bl] *adj* firmly fixed; steadfast, unyielding.—*ns* **immov´ableness, immovabil´ity**.—*adv* **immov´ably**. [L *im- (in-)*, not, and **movable**.]

immune [im-ūn´] *adj* exempt from or protected against something disagreeable or harmful; not susceptible to a specified disease.—*vt* **imm´unize**, to render immune, esp to a disease.—*ns* **immunīzā´tion; immun´ity**, state of being immune; **immunol´ogy**, the branch of medicine dealing with immunity to disease or with allergic reactions. [L *immūnis—in-*, not, *mūnus*, service.]

immure [i-mūr´] *vt* to shut (oneself) up; to imprison; to entomb in a wall. [L *in*, in *mūrus*, a wall.]

immutable [im-ūt´ȧ-bl] *adj* unchangeable; invariable.—*ns* **immūtabil´ity, immūt´ableness**.—*adv* **immūt´ably**. [L *immūtābilis—im- (in-)*, not, *mūtābilis*. See **mutable**.]

imp [imp] *n* a teasing or mischievous child; a little devil or wicked spirit.—*adj* **imp´ish**. [OE *impa*—Low L *impotus*, a graft—Gr *emphytos*, engrafted.]

impact [im-pakt´] *vt* to force tightly together; *(inf)* to have an effect on.—*vi* to hit with force; *(inf)* to have an effect (on).—*n* **im´pact**, violent contact; a shocking effect.—*n* **im´pact**, the blow of a body in motion impinging on another body; collision; *(fig)* effect, influence.—*adj* **impact´ed** (of a tooth) abnormally lodged in the jaw. [L *impactus*, pt p of *impingěre*. See **impinge**.]

impair [im-pār´] *vt* to make worse, less, etc. [OFr *empeirer—Fr empirer*, from L *im- (in-)*, intensive, *pējōrāre*, to make worse.]

impale [im-pāl´] *vt* to fix on, or pierce through, with something pointed.—*n* **impale´ment**. [Fr *empaler*—L *in*, in, *pālus*, a stake.]

impalpable [im-pal´pȧ-bl] *adj* not perceivable by touch; eluding apprehension.—*n* **impalpabil´ity**. [Low L *impalpābilis—im- (in-)*, not, *palpābilis*. See **palpable**.]

impart [im-pärt´] *vt* to give a share of; to make known. [OFr *empartir*—L *impartīre*—in, on, *pars, partis*, a part.]

impartial [im-pär´sh(ȧ)l] *adj* not favoring one more than another; just.—*n* **impartiality** [-shi-al´i-ti], quality of being impartial, freedom from bias.—*adv* **impar´tially**. [L *im- (in-)*, not, + **partial**.]

impartible [im-pärt´i-bl] *adj* not subject to partition.—*n* **impartibil´ity**. [LL *impartibilis—im- in-)*, not, *partibilis*. See **partible**.]

impassable [im-päs´ȧ-bl] *adj* not capable of being passed or traversed.—*ns* **impassabil´ity, impass´ableness**.—*adj* **impass´ably**.—*n* **impasse** [ē-päs´, im-päs´], a place from which there is no outlet; a deadlock. [L *im- (in-)*, not, + **passable**.]

impassioned [im-pash´ōnd] *adj* passionate; ardent; fiery. [It *impassionāre*—L *in*, in, *passiō, -ōnis*, passion.]

impassive [im-pas´iv] *adj* not feeling or showing emotion; imperturbable.—*adv* **impass´ively**.—*ns* **impass´iveness, impassiv´ity**. [L *im- (in-)*, not, + **passive**.]

impasto [im-pas´tō] *n* paint applied thickly to a canvas; this method of applying color. [It.]

impatient [im-pā´shėnt] *adj* lacking patience; annoyed because of delay; restlessly eager (for, to do).—*n* **impā´tience**.—*adv* **impā´tiently**. [L *im- (in-)*, not, and **patient**.]

impeach [im-pēch´] *vt* to discredit (a person's honor); to try (a public official) on a charge of wrongdoing.—*adj* **impeach´able**, liable to impeachment; chargeable with a crime.—*ns* **impeach´ėr**, one who impeaches; **impeach´ment**. [OFr *empescher*, to hinder—L *impedicāre*, to fetter.]

impeccable [im-pek´ȧ-bl] *adj* without defect or error; faultless.—*n* **impeccabil´ity**. [L *im- (in-)*, not, *peccāre*, to sin.]

impecunious [im-pi-kū´ni-us] *adj* habitually without money, poor.—*n* **impecunios´ity**. [L *im- (in-)*, not, *pecūnia*, money.]

impedance [im-pēd´ȧns] *n* the total resistance in an electric circuit to the flow of an alternating current of a single frequency. [**impede**, suffx *-ance*.]

impede [im-pēd´] *vt* to hinder to obstruct.—*n* **impĕd´iment**, that which impedes; hindrance; a defect preventing fluency (in speech).—*n pl* **impediment´a**, military baggage, baggage generally.—*adj* **imped´itive**, causing hindrance. [L *impedīre—in*, in, *pēs, pedis*, a foot.]

impel [im-pel´] *vt* to urge forward, to propel; to excite to action;—*pr p* **impell´ing**; *pt p* **impelled´**.—*n* **impell´er**. [L *impellěre, impulsum—in*, on, *pellěre*, to drive.]

impend [im-pend´] *vi* to hang over; to threaten; to be about to happen.—*adj* **impend´ent**, ready to act or happen. [L *impendēre—in*, on, *pendēre*, to hang.]

impenetrable [im-pen´e-trȧ-bl] *adj* incapable of being pierced or penetrated; inaccessible to reason or to an emotional appeal; inscrutable.—*n* **impenetrabil´ity**, the inability of two parts of matter to occupy the same space at the same time; the state of being impenetrable.—*adv* **impen´etrably**. [Fr *impénétrable*—L *impěnětrābilis—im- (in-)*, not, *penetrābilis—penetrāre*. See **penetrate**.]

impenitent [im-pen´i-tėnt] *adj* not repenting of sin or transgression.—*adv* **impen´itently**. [L *im- (in-)*, not, and **penitent**.]

imperative [im-per´ȧ-tiv] *adj* expressive of command; authoritative; obligatory; urgently necessary; designating or of the mood of a verb that expresses a command, etc.—*adv* **imper´atively**. [L *imperātīvus—imperāre*, to command—*in*, in, *parāre*, to prepare.]

imperceptible [im-pėr-sep´ti-bl] *adj* not discernible, insensible; minute; gradual.—*adv* **impercep´tibly**. [L *im- (in-)*, not, + **perceptible**.]

imperfect [im-pûr´fekt] *adj* falling short of perfection; incomplete; defective; *(gram)* designating a verb tense that indicates a past action or state as incomplete or continuous.—*n* an imperfect tense, the verb form expressing it.—*adv* **imper´fectly**.—*ns* **imper´fectness, imperfec´tion**. [L *im- (in-*), not, + **perfect**.]

imperforate [im-pûr´fo-rāt] *adjs* not pierced through; having no opening esp lacking the normal opening; (of postage (stamps) lacking perforations). [L *im- (in-)*, not, + **perforate**.]

imperial [im-pē´ri-ȧl] *adj* of the nature of an empire, emperor, or empress; majestic; august; or great size or superior quality; of the British system of weights and measures.—*n* a small pointed chin beard.—*adv* **impē´rially**.—*ns* **impē´rialism**, imperial state or authority; the policy of forming and maintaining an empire, as by subjugating territories, establishing colonies, etc.; the policy of seeking to dominate weaker countries; **imperialist**, an advocate or supporter of imperialism.—Also *adj*.—*adj* **imperialistic**.—**imperial gallon**, the standard British gallon, equal to 1/5 US gallons.—**imperial moth**, a large American moth (*Eacles imperialis*) with yellow and purplish brown marks. [Fr,—L *impěriālis—impěrium*, sovereignty.]

imperil [im-per´il] *vt* to put in peril, to endanger. [L *in*, in, and **peril**.]

imperious [im-pē´ri-us] *adj* haughty, tyrannical; arrogant; imperative.—*adv* **impē´riously**.—*n* **impē´riousness**. [L *imperiōsus—imperium*, command, rule.]

imperishable [im-per´ish-ȧ-bl] *adj* indestructible; everlasting.—*ns* **imper´ishableness, imperishabil´ity**.—*adv* **imper´ishably**. [L *im- (in-)*, *not*, + **perishable**.]

impermanent [im-pûr´mȧn-ent] *adj* not permanent, not lusting.—*n* **impeŕmanence**. [L *im-(in-)*, not + **permanent**.

imper´meable [im-pûr´mė-ȧ-bl] *adj* not permitting passage, esp to fluids; impervious.—*ns* **impermeabil´ity, imper´meableness**.—*adv* **imper´meably**. [L *im- (in-)*, not + **permeable**.]

impersonal [im-pûr´sȯn-ȧl] *adj* without reference to any particular person; not existing as a person; *(gram.)* denoting or of a verb occurring only on the third person singular, usu with 'it' as subject.—*n* **impersonal´ity**.—*adv* **imper´sonally**. [L *im- (in-)*, not + **personal**.

impersonate [im-pûr´sȯn-āt] *vt* to assume the role of another person for purposes of entertainment or fraud.—*ns* **impersonā´tion; imper´sonātor**. [L *in*, in, + **personate**.

impertinent [im-pûr´ti-nėnt] *adj* not pertinent; impudent; insolent.—*n* **imper´tinence**.—*adv* **imper´tinently**. [L *im- (in-)*, not, + **pertinent**.

imperturbable [im-pėr-tûr´bȧ-bl] *adj* that cannot be disturbed; calm; impassive.—*n* **imperturbabil´ity**.—*adv* **impertur´bably**. [L *imperturbābilis—in-*, not, *perturbāre*, to disturb.]

impervious [impėr´vi-ùs] *adj* incapable of being penetrated, as by water; not easily influenced by ideas, arguments, etc.—*n* **imper´viousness**.—*adv* **imper´viously**. [L *impervius*; cf **pervious**.]

impetigo [im-pe-tīgo] *n* a contagious bacterial skin disease characterized by thickly set clusters of pustules. [L—*impetěre*, to rush upon, attack.]

impetuous [im-pet´ū-us] *adj* acting or done suddenly with headlong energy; impulsive.—*adv* **impet´uously**.—*ns* **impet´uousness, impetuos´ity**. [L *impetus*, an attack; cf **impetus**.]

impetus [im´pė-tus] *n* the force with which a body moves against resistance; driving force or motive. [L—*in*, into, on, *petěre*, to seek.]

impiety [im-pī´ėti] *n* lack of reverence for God; disrespect [L *impietās, -ātis*; cf. **piety**.]

impinge [im-pinj´] *vi* (*with* **on, upon**) to strike or fall, to encroach. [L *impingĕre—in*, against, *pangĕre*, to fix, drive in.]

impious [im´pi-us] *adj* lack of reverence for God, profane.—*adj* **im´piously**. [L *impius*; cf **piety**.]

implacable [im-plak´á-bl, or -plāk´-] *adj* not to be appeased, inexorable.—*n* **implăcabil´ity**.—*adv* **implac´ably**. [L *implācābilis; cf.* **placable**.]

implant [im-plänt´] *vt* to plant firmly; to fix firmly in the mind.—*n* something implanted in tissue, as a graft or a pellet.—*n* **implantā´tion**, the act of infixing. [L *in*, in, + **plant**.]

implausible [im-plö´zė-bl] *adj* not plausible.—*adv* **implau´sibly**.

implead [im-plēd´] *vt* to prosecute a suit at law.—*n* **implead´er**. [L *in*, in, + **plead**]

implement [im-´ple-ment´] *n* something used in a given activity.—*vt* [im-ple-ment´] to fulfil or perform. [Low L *implementum*—L *implēre*, to fill.]

implicate [im´pli-kāt] *vt* to show to have a part or to be connected.—*n* **implicātion**, the act of implicating; entanglement; that which is implied.—*adjs* **im´plicative**, tending to implicate; **implic´it** [plis´it], implied; unquestioning (eg trust).—*adv* **implic´itly**.—*n* **implic´itness**. [L *implicāre, -ātum—in*, in, *plicāre*, to fold.]

implore [im-plōr´, -plör´] *vt* to ask earnestly (for); to beg (a person) to do something.—*adv* **implor´ingly**, beseechingly. [Fr,—L *implōrāre—in*, in, *plōrāre*, to weep.]

imply [im-plī´] *vt* to have as a necessary condition, part, etc.; to express indirectly; to hint, suggest.—*pr p* **imply´ing**; *pt p* **implied**. [OFr *emplier*—L *implicāre*. See **implicate**.]

impolite [im-po-līt´] *adj* having bad manners; uncivil.—*adv* **impolite´ly**.—*n* **impolite´ness**. [L *impŏlītus*; cf **polite**.]

impolitic [im-pol´i-tik] *adj* not politic; unwise. [L *im-(in)*, not, + **politic**.]

imponderable [im-pon´dėr-à-bl] *adj* that cannot be weighed or measured.—*ns* **imponderabil´ity; impon´derable**. [L *im-(in-)*, not, + **ponderable**.]

import [im-pōrt´, -pört´] *vt* to bring (goods) in from a foreign country for sale or use; to mean; to signify.—*vi* to be of importance, to matter.—*n* [im´pōrt] something imported; meaning; importance.—*adj* **import´able**, that may be brought into a country.—*adj* **import´ant** of great weight, significance, or consequence; having, or acting if having, power, authority etc.—*n* **import´ance**.—*adv* **import´antly**.—*ns* **importā´tion**, the act of importing; the goods imported; **import´er**, one who brings in goods from a foreign country. [Fr,—L *importāre,-ātum—in*, in, *portāre*, to carry.]

importune [im-pȯr-tūn´] *vt* to ask urgently and repeatedly.—*n* **importa´unāteness**.—*adj* **import´unāte**, persistent in asking or demanding.—*adv* **import´unātely**.—*ns* **importun´er; importun´ity**, urgency in demand. [Fr,—L *importūnus*, inconvenient—*im- (in-)*, not, *portus*, a harbour; cf **opportune**.]

impose [im-pōz´] *vt* to put (a burden, tax, punishment) on or upon; to force (oneself) on others.—*vi* (*with* **on** *or* **upon**) to take advantage of; to cheat or defraud. *adj* **impos´ing**, impressive because of size, appearance, dignity, etc.—*adv* **impos´ingly**.—*n* **imposition**. [L *impositiō, -ōnis—in*, on, *pōnĕre, pŏsitum*, to place.]

impossible [im-pos´i-bl] *adj* not capable of existing, being done, or happening; not capable of being endured, used, etc. because disagreeable or unsuitable.—*n* **impossibil´ity**. [L *im- (in-)*, not + **possible**.]

impost [im´pōst] *n* a tax. [OFr *impost*—L *impōnĕre, impŏsitum*, to lay on]

impost [im´pōst] *n* (*archit*) the upper part of a pillar supporting a vault or arch. [Fr *imposte—It imposta*—L *impōnĕre, impōsitum*.]

impostor, imposter [im-pos´tȯr] *n* one who assumes a false character or impersonates another.—*n* **impos´tūre**, a fraud. [LL—*impōnĕre, impŏsitum*, to impose.]

impotent [im´po-tėnt] *adj* powerless; helpless; (of a man) unable to engage in sexual intercourse.—*n* **im´potence**.—*adv* **im´potently**. [L *impŏtens, -entis*; cf **potent**.]

impound [im-pownd´] *vt* to confine (an animal) in a pound; to take legal possession of; to collect and enclose (water) as for irrigation. [**in** + **pound**, enclosure.]

impoverish [im-pov´ėr-ish] *vt* to make poor; to deprive of strength, resources, etc.—*n* **impov´erishment**. [From OFr *empovrir*—L *in*, in, *pauper*, poor.]

impracticable [im-prak´tik-à-bl] *adj* not able to be done or used; unmanageable.—*ns* **impracticabil´ity**,—*adv* **imprac´ticably**. [L*im- (in-)*, not, + **practicable**.]

impractical [im-prak´tik-àl] *adj* not practical.

imprecate [im´pre-kāt] *vt* to invoke evil on; to curse.—*vi* to utter curses.—*n* **imprecā´tion**,—*adj* **im´precatory**. [L *imprecārī—in*, upon, *precari-ātus*, to pray.]

impregnable [im-preg´nȧ-bl] *adj* that cannot be taken by force, unyielding.—*n* **impregnabil´ity**.—*adv* **impreg´nably**. [Fr *imprenable*—L *in-*, not, *prendĕre, prehendĕre*, to take; *g*, a freak spelling, has come to be pronounced.]

impregnate [im-preg´nāt] *vt* to make pregnant; to saturate (with); to imbue (with—eg feelings, principles).—*n* **impregnā´tion**, the act of impregnating; that with which anything is impregnated. [Low L *impraegnāre, -ātum—in*, in, *praegnans*, pregnant.]

impresario [im-pre-zä´ri-ō, or -sä´-] *n* the manager of an opera, a concert series, etc. [It—*impresa*, enterprise.]

impress [im-pres´] *vt* to stamp; to imprint; to affect strongly the mind or emotions of; to fix in the memory.—*n* [im´pres] an impressing; an imprint.—*adj* **impress´ible**, susceptible.—*n* **impression** [-presh´(ȯ)n], act or result of impressing; a single printing of a book; the idea or emotion left in the mind by any experience; a vague, uncertain memory.—*adj* **impress´ionable**, easily impressed.—*ns* **impressionabil´ity; impress´ionism**, a 19th-century French movement in painting based on the principles of conveying an impression of nature as though seen for the first time and using only the spectrum range of colors, to depict light. **impress´ionist**.—*adj* **impress´ive** tending to impress the mind or emotions; eliciting wonder or admiration.—*adv* **impressively**.—*n* **impress´iveness**. [L *imprimĕre, impressum—im- (in-)*, in *premĕre*. See **press** (1).]

impress [im-pres´] *vt* to force into military service; to seize for public use; to enlist by forcible persuasion.—*n* **impress´ment**, the act of seizing for public use or of impressing into public service. [L *im- (in-)*, in, and *prest*. See **press** (2).]

imprimatur [im-pri-mā´tůr] *n* permission or licence, esp to publish. [Lit 'let it be printed'; from L *imprimĕre—in*, on, *premĕre*, to press.]

imprimis [im-prī´mis] *adv* in the first place. [L—*in prīmis* (abl pl).]

imprint [im-print´] *vt* to print; to stamp; to impress.—*n* **imprint** [im´print] a mark made by imprinting; a lasting effect; a note in a book giving the facts of publication.—*n* **imprinting** the learning process in a young animal in which it identifies with the species of the mother substitute. [L *im- (in-)*, on, + **print**.]

imprison [im-priz´n] *vt* to put in or as prison.—*n* **impris´onment**. [L *im- (in-)*, into + **prison**.]

improbable [im-prob´á-bl] *adj* unlikely.—*n* **improbabil´ity**.—*adv* **improb´ably**. [L *im- (in-)*, not, + **probable**.]

impromptu [im-promp´tū] *adj* unprepared.—Also *adv*.—*n* an extempore speech; a musical composition with the character of an extemporization. [L *in promptū* (abl)—*promptus*, readiness.]

improper [im-prop´ėr], *adj* not suitable, unfit; incorrect, wrong; not in good taste.—**improper fraction**, a fraction in which the numerator is greater than the denominator, as 4/3.—*adv* **improp´erly**.—*n* **impropri´ety**. [L *im- (in-)*, not, *proprius*, own.]

improve [im-prōōv´] *vt* to use (time) well; to make better; to make (land or structures) by cultivation, construction etc.—*vi* to become better.—*adj* **improv´able**.—*n* **improvabil´ity**.—*adv* **improv´ably**.—*ns* **improve´ment**, the act of improving; progress; a change for the better; **improv´er**. [Anglo-Fr *emprower*—OFr *en preu*, into profit.

improvident [im-prov´i-dėnt] *adj* not provident or thrifty; lacking foresight.—*n* **improv´idence**.—*adv* **improv´idently**. [L *imprōvidus*, improvident; cf; **provide**.]

improvise [im-pro-vīz´] *vti* to compose and perform without preparation; to make or do with whatever is at hand.—*ns* **improvisā´tion**, the act of improvising; that which is improvised; **improvisā´tor, improvīs´er**. [Fr *improviser*—L *in-*, not, *prōvīsus*, foreseen—*prōvidēre*.]

imprudent [im-prōōdėnt] *adj* lacking foresight or discretion; rash—*n* **impru´dence**.—*adv* **impru´dently**. [L *imprūdens,—entis*, rash.]

impudent [im´pūdėnt] *adj* shamelessly bold; insolent.—*n* **impudence**.—*adv* **im´pudently**. [L *im-, (in-)*, not, *pudens, -entis—pudēre*, to be ashamed.]

impugn [im-pūn´] *vt* to oppose or challenge as false.—*adj* **impugn´able**.—*n* **impugn´er**. [L *impugnāre—in*, against, *pugnāre*, to fight.]

impulse [im´puls] *n* the act of impelling; effect of an impelling force; force suddenly and momentarily communicated; a stimulus traveling along a nerve or a muscle; incitement to action by a stimulus; a sudden inclination to act.—*n* **impul´sion**, impelling force; strong desire to perform an irrational act.—*adj* **impuls´ive**, having the power of impelling; acting or actuated by impulse.—*adv* **impuls´ively**.—*n* **impuls´iveness**. [L *impulsus*, pressure—*impellĕre*. See **impel**.]

impunity [im-pūn´i-ti] *n* freedom from punishment. [L *impūnitās, -ātis—in-*, not, *poena*, punishment.]

impure [im-pūr´] *adj* unclean; immoral; mixed with foreign matter.—*adv* **impure´ly**.—*ns* **impur´ity, impure´ness**. [L *impūrus—in-*, not, *pūrus*, clean.]

impute [im-pūt´] *vt* to attribute (esp a fault or misbehaviour) to another.—*adj* **imput´able**, capable of being imputed or charged, attributable.—*n* **imputabil´ity**.—*adv* **imput´ably**.—*n* **imputā´tion**, act of imputing; something imputed. [Fr *imputer*—L *imputāre—ātum—in*, in, *putāre*, to reckon.]

in [in] *prep* expressing the relation of a thing to that which surrounds, encloses, or includes it, as contained by (*in a room*), wearing (*in formal dress*), during (*done in a day*), at the end of (*due in a day*), not beyond (*in sight*), affected by (*in trouble*); being a member of (*serving in the army, works in the business*); using (*speak in English*); because of (*he cried in pain*); into (*come in the house*).—*adv* to or at a certain place; so as to be contained by a certain space, condition, etc.—*adj* that is in power; inner; inside; gathered, counted, etc.; (*inf*) currently smart, fashionable, etc.—*n* (*pl*) the political party in office; (*inf*) special influence or favor.—**have it in for** (*inf*) to hold a grudge against; **ins and outs** all the details and complications; **in that** since, because; **in with** associated with. [OE *in*; Du, Ger, *in*, ON, ī, W *yn*, L *in*, Gr *en*.]

in- [in-] *prefix* not [L];—eg **insincere, insincerity**. It appears also as **i-, il-, im-, ir-**; eg **ignoble, illegal, immortal, irregular** (see these words). It is

allied to OE *un-* and is sometimes interchangeable with it;—eg *inexpressive, unexpressive*.
in- [in-] *prefix* in, into [L];—eg **include, infuse, ingredient** (see these words). It appears also as **il-, im-, ir-**;—eg **illuminate, immerse, irrigate** (see these words). There is also an Old English prefix of the same form and meaning seen in words of Gmc origin;—eg **income, inland, insight**.
-in [-in] *suffix* (*Chem*) forming names of neutral substances (*gelatin, protein*) and of antibiotics (*penicillin*); forming terms to denote organized public protest (*teach-in, love-in, be-in*) a or public group activity (*sing-in*).
inability [in-å-bil´i-ti] *n* lack of ability. [L *in-*, not, + **ability**.]
in absentia [in ab-sen´ti-ä, ab-sensh´yå] although not present. [L]
inaccessible [in-ak-ses´i-bl] *adj* not accessible. *ns* **inaccess´ibility, inaccess´ibleness.**—*adv* **inaccess´ibly**. [L *inaccessibilis*, unapproachable—*in-*, not, *accessibilis*; cf **accede**.]
inaccurate [in-ak´ūr-åt] *adj* not exact or correct.—*n* **inacc´uracy**, want of exactness; a mistake.—*adv* **inacc´urately**. [L *in-*, not, + **accurate**.]
inactive [in-akt´iv] *adj* not active.—*n* **inac´tion**, idleness; rest.—*adv* **inact´ively**.—*n* **inactiv´ity**, idleness; lack of action. [L *in-*, not, + **active**.]
inadequate [in-ad´e-kwåt] *adj* not adequate—*ns* **inad´equacy, inad´equateness.**—*adv* **inad´equately**. [L *in-*, not, + **adequate**.]
inadmissible [in-ad-mis´i-bl] *adj* not admissable.—*n* **inadmissibil´ity**.—*adv* **inadmiss´ibly**. [L *in-*, not, + **admissible**.]
inadvertent [in-ad-vûrt´ėnt] *adj* not attentive or observant; due to oversight.—*ns* **inadvert´ence, inadvert´ency**.—*adv* **inadvert´ently**. [L *in-*, not, and *advertens, -entis*—*advertĕre*. See **advert**.]
inadvisable [in-ad-vīz´å-bl] *adj* not advisable.—*n* **inadvisabil´ity**. [L *in-*, not, + **advisable**.]
inalienable [in-āl´yen-å-bl] *adj* not capable of being taken away or transferred.—*n* **inal´ienableness**. [L *in-*, not, + **alienable**.]
inamorata [in-am-o-rä´ta] *n* a woman beloved. [It *innamorata, -to*—Low L *inamorāre*, to cause to love—L *in*, in, *amor*, love.]
inane [in-ān] *adj* empty, lacking sense, silly.—*ns* **inanition** [in-a-nish´(ȯ)n], exhaustion from lack of food; **inan´ity**, senselessness. [L *inānis*.]
inanimate, -d [in-an´im-åt, -id] *adj* not animate; spiritless; dull.—*n* **inanimā´tion**. [L *inanimātus*, lifeless; cf **animate**.]
inapplicable [in-ap´lik-å-bl] *adj* not applicable.—*n* **inapplicabil´ity**. [L *in-*, not, + **applicable**.]
inapposite [in-ap´oz-it] *adj* not apposite—*adv* **inapp´ositely**. [L *in-*, not, + **apposite**.]
inappreciable [in-a-prē´sh(y)å-bl] *adj* too small to be perceived. [L *in-*, not, + **appreciable**.]
inappropriate [in-a-prō´pri-åt] *adj* not suitable.—*adv* **inapprō´priately**.—*n* **inapprō´priateness**. [L *in-*, not, + **appropriate**.]
inapt [in-apt´] *adj* not apt; not suitable; unskilful.—*n* **inapt´itude, inapt´ness**, lack of aptitude.—*adv* **inapt´ly**. [L *in-*, not, + **apt**.]
inarticulate[1] [in-är-tik´ūl-āt] *adj* indistinctly uttered; incapable of clear and fluent expression.—*adv* **inartic´ulately**.—*ns* **inartic´ulacy, inartic´ulateness, inarticulā´tion**, indistinctness of sounds in speaking. [L *inarticŭlātus*; cf **articulate**.]
inarticulate[2] [in-är-tik´ūl-āt] *n* any of a class (Inarticulata) of brachiopods without a hinge between the shell valves.
inartistic [in-är-tis´tik] *adj* not artistic; not appreciative of art.—*adv* **inartis´tically**. [L *in-*, not, + **artistic**.]
inasmuch as [in-az-much´] since; because; to the extent that.
inattentive [in-a-tent´iv] *adj* not attentive.—*ns* **inattention** [-ten´sh(ȯ)n], **inattent´iveness**.—*adv* **inattent´ively**. [L *in-*, not, + **attentive**.]
inaudible [in-öd´i-bl] *adj* not able to be heard.—*ns* **inaudibil´ity, inaud´ibleness**.—*adv* **inaud´ibly**. [L *inaudībilis*; cf **audible**.]
inaugurate [in-ö´gūr-āt] *vt* to induct formally into an office; to cause to begin; to open formally to the public.—*n* **inaugurā´tion**.—*adj* **inau´gural**, of an inauguration; first in a series.—*n* a speech made at an inauguration; an inauguration.—*n* **inau´gurātor**.—*adj* **inau´guratory**.—**Inauguration Day** January 20 following a presidential election when the new president is inaugurated. [L *inaugurāre, -ātum*, to inaugurate with taking of the auspices—*in*, in, *augurāre*—*augur*. See **augur**.]
inauspicious [in-ö-spish´us] *adj* not auspicious.—*adv* **inauspic´iously**.—*n* **inauspic´iousness**. [L *inauspicātus*, without auspices, ill-omened—*in-*, not, *auspicātus*—*auspicāre*.]
inborn [in´börn] *adj* born in or with one; hereditary, inherited. [L *in*, in, + **born**.]
inbound [in-bownd] *adj* traveling or going inward.
inbreathe [in-brēTH´, in´brēTH] *vt* to breathe (something) in [L *in*, in, + **breathe**.]
inbreed [in´brēd, in-brēd´] *vti* to breed by continual mating of individuals of the same or closely related stocks; to make or become too effete, refined, etc.—*adj* **inbred´** innate; produced by inbreeding.—*n* **inbreed´ing**. [L *in*, in, + **breed**.]
inc Abbrev of **incorporated**.
Inca [ing´ka] *n* a member of the Quecha peoples of Peru that dominated ancient Peru until the Spanish conquest. [Sp—South American Indian, prince.]
incalculable [in-kal´kū-lå-bl] *adj* not calculable or able to be reckoned; too many to be counted; unpredictable.—*adv* **incal´culably**. [L *in-*, not, + **calculable**.]
in camera [in-kam´ėr-å] *adv* secretly; in private.
incandescent [in-kan-des´ėnt] *adj* glowing or white with heat.—*n* **incandescence** [-es´ens], white heat.—**incandescent lamp**, a lamp with a filament in a vacuum heated to incandescence by an electric current. [L *in*, in, *candēscĕre*—*candēre*, to glow.]
incantation [in-kan-tā´sh(ȯ)n] *n* words chanted in magic spells or rites. [L *incantātiō, -ōnis*—*incantāre*, to sing a magical formula over.]
incapable [in-kāp´å-bl] *adj* not capable.—*n* **incapabil´ity**.—*adv* **incap´ably**. [L *in-*, not, + **capable**.]
incapacitate [in-kap-as´it-āt] *vt* to make unable or unfit; (*law*) to disqualify.—*n* **incapac´ity**. [L *incapax, -ācis*.]
incarcerate [in-kär´sėr-āt] *vt* to imprison, to confine.—*n* **incarcerā´tion**, imprisonment. [L *in*, in, *carcer*, a prison.]
incarnadine [in-kär´na-din, -dīn] *vt* to make red.—*adj* flesh-colored; bloodred. [Fr *incarnadin(e)*—Low L *incarnātus*—*incarnāre*. See **incarnate**.]
incarnate [in-kär´nåt] *adj* endowed with a human body; personified.—*vt* [-nāt] to give bodily form to; to be the type or embodiment of.—*n* **incarnā´tion**. [Low L *incarnāre, -ātum*—L *in*, in, *carō, carnis*, flesh.]
incase *See* **encase**.
incautious [in-kö´shus] *adj* not cautious.—*n* **incau´tiously**. [L *incautus*—*in-*, not, *cautus*—*cautiō*. See **cautious**.]
incendiary [in-sen´di-år-i] *n* one that sets fire to a building, etc., maliciously; an incendiary agent (as a bomb); one who promotes strife.—*adj* relating to incendiarism; used for setting buildings, etc., on fire; tending to excite or inflame.—*n* **incen´diarism**, the act or practice of setting on fire maliciously or of stirring up strife. [L *incendiārius*—*incendium*—*incendĕre, incensum*, to kindle.]
incense[1] [in-sens´] *vt* to inflame with anger. [OFr *incenser*—L *incendĕre, incensum*, to set on fire.]
incense[2] [in-sėns] *n* any material burned to give fragrant fumes, the fumes so obtained; any pleasant smell. [OFr *encens*—L *incensum*—*incendĕre*, to set on fire.]
incentive [in-sent´iv] *n* a stimulus; a motive. [L *incentīvus*, striking up a tune—*incinĕre*—*in*, in *canĕre*, to sing.]
inception [in-sep´sh(ȯ)n] *n* a beginning.—*adj* **incep´tive**, beginning, or marking the beginning. [L *inceptiō, -ōnis*—*incipĕre, inceptum*, to begin—*in*, on, *capĕre*, to take.]
incertitude [in-sûr´ti-tūd] *n* doubt; insecurity. [Fr,—Low L *incertitūdō*—L *incertus*, uncertain.]
incessant [in-ses´ånt] *adj* never ceasing; continual, constant.—*adv* **incess´antly**. [L *incessans, -antis*—*in-*, not, *cessāre*, to cease.]
incest [in´sest] *n* sexual intercourse between persons too closely related to marry legally.—*adj* **incest´ūous**, guilty of incest.—*adv* **incest´uously**. [L *incestum*—*in-*, not, *castus*, chaste.]
inch [inch] *n* a measure of length equal to 1/12 foot; symbol ´´.—*vti* to move very slowly, or by degrees.—**by inches**, gradually; **every inch**, in all respects; to the utmost degree; **inch by inch**, gradually; **within an inch of**, very close to. [OE *ynce*, an inch—L *uncia*, the twelfth part of anything; cf **ounce**.]
inchoate [in´kō-āt, in-kō´āt] *adj* only begun; rudimentary.—*adv* **inchoately** [in´-, or -ko´-].—*adj* **inchō´ative**, incipient; (*gram*) denoting the beginning of an action. [L *inchoāre* (for *incohāre*), *-ātum*, to begin.]
incident [in´si-dėnt] *adj* likely to happen as a result; falling upon or affecting.—*n* something that happens; an event, esp a minor one; a minor conflict.—*n* **in´cidence**, the degree or range of occurrence or effect.—*adj* **incident´al**, happening in connection with something more important—Also *n* (*pl*) miscellaneous items.—**incidental music**, background music to enhance the mood or action (as for a love scene, a storm) on the stage.—*adv* **incident´ally**, in passing, as an aside. [L *incidens, -entis*—*in*, on, *cadĕre*, to fall.]
incinerate [in-sin´ėr-āt] *vt* to reduce to ashes.—*ns* **incinerā´tion; incin´erātor**, a furnace for burning trash. [L *incinerāre, -ātum*—*in*, in, *cinis, cineris*, ashes.]
incipient [in-sip´i-ėnt] *adj* beginning; nascent.—*ns* **incip´ience, incip´iency**.—*adv* **incip´iently**. [L *incipiens, -entis*, pr p of *incipĕre*, to begin.]
incise [in-sīz´] *vt* to cut into with a sharp tool; to engrave.—*n* **incision** [in-sizh´(ȯ)n], the act of cutting into a substance; a cut, a gash.—*adj* **incisive** [-sīs´-], having the quality of cutting in; acute in mind; sharp; penetrating.—*adv* **incisively**.—*ns* **incisiveness; incisor** [-sīz´ȯr], any of the front cutting teeth between the canines. [Fr *inciser*—L *incīdĕre, incīsum*—*in*, into, *caedĕre*, to cut.]
incite [in-sīt´] *vt* to urge to action; to rouse.—*ns* **incitant** [in-sīt´ånt], **incitā´tion** [-sit-, sīt-], an act of inciting or rousing; an incentive; **incite´ment; incit´er**.—*adv* **incit´ingly**. [Fr,—L *incitāre*—*in*, in, *citāre*, to rouse—*ciēre*, to put in motion.]
incivility [in-si-vil´i-ti] *n* lack of civility, impoliteness; an act of discourtesy (*pl*) **incivil´ities**. [Fr,—L *incīvīlis*—*in*, not; cf **civil**.]
inclement [in-klem´ėnt] *adj* rough; stormy; lacking mercy; harsh.—*n* **inclem´ency**.—*adv* **inclem´ently**. [L *inclēmens*, unmerciful—*in*, not; cf **clement**.]
incline [in-klīn´] *vi* to lean; to slope; to be disposed; to have a preference or liking.—*vt* to cause to bend downwards; to cause to deviate; to dispose.—*n* [in´klīn, in-klīn´] a slope.—*adj* **inclīn´able**, capable of being tilted or

sloped; somewhat disposed.—*n* **inclīnā´tion**, a bend or bow; a slope or tilt; angle with the horizon or with any plane or line; tendency; disposition of mind, natural aptness; favourable disposition, affection.—*adj* **inclīned´**, bent; sloping; disposed.—**inclined plane**, a plane surface forming an oblique angle with the plane of the horizon. [Fr,—L *inclīnāre*, to bend towards—*in*, into, *clīnāre*, to lean.]

inclose, inclosure *See* **enclose, enclosure**.

include [in-klōōd´] *vt* to enclose; to comprise as a part; to take in.—*n* **inclusion** [-klōō´zh(ȯ)n], act of including; that which is included.—*adj* **inclu´sive**, including everything; including the terms or limits mentioned (the first to the tenth inclusive).—*adv* **inclu´sively**. [L *inclūdĕre, inclūsum*—*in*, in, *claudĕre*, to shut.]

incognito [in-kog´ni-tō] *adj, adv* disguised under an assumed name.—*n* one appearing or living incognito.—*adj, adv, n* **incog´nita** (of a woman) living or appearing incognito. [It,—L *incognitus*—*in-*, not, *cognitus*, known—*cognoscĕre*, to know.]

incoherent [in-kō-hēr´ėnt] *adj* not coherent; loose, rambling.—*n* **incoher´ence**.—*adv* **incoher´ently**. [L *in-*, not, + **coherent**.]

incombustible [in-kom-bust´i-bl] *adj* incapable of combustion.—*n* **incombustibil´ity**.—*adv* **incombust´ibly**. [L *in-*, not, + **combustible**.]

income [in´-kŭm] *n* the money etc. received for labor or services, or from property, investments, etc.—*n* **in´come tax**, a tax levied on the net income of a person or a business.—*adj* **in´coming**, coming in; taking a new position esp as part of a succession (*the incoming president*); just beginning (*the incoming period*). [**in, come**.]

incommensurable [in-kom-en´sū-rȧ-bl] *adj* having no basis of comparison.—*ns* **incommensurabil´ity, incommen´surableness**.—*adv* **incommen´surably**.—*adj* **incommen´surāte**, disproportionate; not adequate; incommensurable.—*adv* **incommen´surātely**. [L *in-*, not, + **commensurable**.]

incommode [in-kom-ōd´] *vt* to cause trouble or inconvenience to.—*adj* **incommō´dious**, inconvenient, uncomfortable.—*adv* **incommō´diously**.—*n* **incommō´diousness**. [Fr,—L *incommodāre*—*in-*, not, *commodus*, commodious.]

incommunicable [in-kom-ūn´i-kȧ-bl] *adj* that can not be communicated or imparted.—*n* **incommunicabil´ity**.—*adv* **incommun´icably**.—*adj* **incommun´icative**, uncommunicative. [L *in-*, not, + **communicable**.]

incommunicado [in-kȯm-ūn-i-kä´dō] *adj, adv* without means of communication. [Sp *incommunicado*.]

incomparable [in-kom´pȧr-ȧ-bl] *adj* not admitting comparison (with); matchless.—*n* **incom´parableness**.—*adv* **incom´parably**. [Fr,—L *incompărābilis*; cf **comparable**.]

incompatible [in-kom-pat´i-bl] *adj* incapable of existing together in harmony, or at all; (of propositions) not both true.—*n* **incompatibil´ity**.—*adv* **incompat´ibly**. [Low L *incompatābilis*; cf **compatible**.]

incompetent [in-kom´pė-tėnt] *adj* without adequate ability, knowledge, fitness, etc.—*n* an incompetent person.—*ns* **incom´petence, incom´petency**.—*adv* **incom´petently**. [Fr *incompétent*—Low L; cf **competent**.]

incomplete [in-kom-plēt´] *adj* lacking a part or parts; imperfect; unfinished.—*adv* **incomplete´ly**.—*n* **incomplete´ness**. [Low L *incomplētus*; cf **complete**.]

incompliant [in-kom-plī´ánt] *adj* not pliable or compliant. [L *in-*, not, + **compliance**.]

incomprehensible [in-kom-pre-hen´si-bl] *adj* not capable of being understood.—*ns* **incomprehensibil´ity, incomprehen´sibleness, incomprehen´sion**, failure or inability to understand.—*adv* **incomprehen´sibly**.—*adj* **incomprehen´sive**. [L *incomprehensībilis*; cf **comprehensible**.]

incompressible [in-kom-pres´i-bl] *adj* that cannot be compressed.—*n* **incompressibil´ity**. [L *in-*, not + **compressible**.]

inconceivable [in-kon-sēv´ȧ-bl] *adj* impossible to comprehend; unbelievable.—*n* **inconceiv´ableness**.—*adv* **inconceiv´ably**. [L *in-*, not, + **conceivable**.]

inconclusive [in-kon-klōōs´iv] *adj* leading to no definite result.—*adv* **inconclus´ively**.—*n* **inconclus´iveness**. [L *in-*, not + **conclusive**.]

incongruous [in-kong´grŏŏ-us] *adj* lacking harmony or agreement of parts; unsuitable; inappropriate.—*n* **incongru´ity** [-grōō´-].—*adv* **incong´ruously**. [L *incongrūus*; cf **congruous**.]

inconsequent [in-kon´si-kwėnt] *adj* lacking reasonable sequence; inconsequential; irrelevant.—*n* **incon´sequence**.—*adj* **inconsequential** [-kwen´shȧl], of no consequence.—*advs* **inconsequen´tially, incon´sequently**. [L *inconsĕquens, -entis*; cf **consequent**.]

inconsiderable [in-kon-sid´ėr-ȧ-bl] *adj* not worthy of notice; trivial.—*adv* **inconsid´erably**. [Fr *inconsidérable*; cf **considerable**.]

inconsiderate [in-kon-sid´ėr-ȧt] *adj* not mindful of the claims of others; thoughtless.—*adv* **inconsid´erately**.—*n* **inconsid´erateness**. [L *inconsīdĕrātus*; cf **considerate**.]

inconsistent [in-kon-sist´ėnt] *adj* not compatible with other facts; containing incompatible elements; changeable; not having the same set of variables for unknowns.—*ns* **inconsist´ence, inconsist´ency**.—*adv* **inconsist´ently**. [L *in-*, not, + **consistent**.]

inconsolable [in-kon-sōl´ȧ-bl] *adj* not to be comforted.—*adv* **inconsol´ably**. [L *inconsōlābilis*; cf **consolable**.]

inconsonant [in-kon´sȯn-ȧnt] *adj* not harmonizing with. [L *in-*, not + **consonant**.]

inconspicuous [in-kon-spik´ū-us] *adj* not conspicuous.—*adv* **inconspic´uously**.—*n* **inconspic´uousness**. [L *inconspĭcŭus*; cf **conspicuous**.]

inconstant [in-kon´stȧnt] *adj* subject to change; fickle.—*n* **incon´stancy**.—*adv* **incon´stantly**. [L *inconstans, -antis*; cf **constant**.]

incontestable [in-kon-test´ȧ-bl] *adj* too clear to be called in question, indisputable.—*adv* **incontest´ably**. [Fr; cf **contestable**.]

incontinent[1] [in-kon´ti-nėnt] *adj* not restraining the passions or appetites; unable to restrain the natural discharges from the body.—*ns* **incon´tinence, incon´tinency**.—*adv* **incon´tinently**. [L *incontinens, -entis*—*in-*, not, *continens*. See **continent**.]

incontinent[2] [in-kon´ti-nėnt] *adv* immediately.—Also **incon´tinently**. [Fr—LL *in continenti* (*tempore*), in unbroken time.]

incontrovertible [in-kon-tro-vûrt´i-bl] *adj* too clear to be called in question.—*n* **incontrovertibil´ity**.—*adv* **incontrovert´ibly**. [L *in-*, not, + **controvertible**.]

inconvenient [in-kon-vēn´yėnt] *adj* causing trouble or difficulty.—*vt* **inconven´ience**, to put to trouble.—*ns* **inconven´ience, inconven´iency**.—*adv* **inconven´iently**. [Fr *inconvénient*; cf **convenient**.]

inconvertible [in-kon-vûrt´i-bl] *adj* not convertible, (of paper money) not exchangeable for coins, (of a currency) not exchangeable for foreign money.—*n* **inconvertibil´ity**. [Low L *inconvertībilis*; cf **convertible**.]

inconvincible [in-kon-vin´si-bl] *adj* not capable of being convinced. [L *in-*, not, + **convincible**.]

incorporate [in-kör´pȯ-rāt] *vt* to combine; to include; to embody; to merge; to form into a corporation.—*vi* to unite into one group or substance; to form a corporation.—Also *adj*. **incor´porated**, united in one mass; formed into a legal corporation.—*n* **incorporā´tion**. [L *incorporāre, -ātum*—*in*, in, into, *corpus, -oris*, body.]

incorporeal [in-kör-pōr-ē-ȧl] *adj* not having a body; of, or relating a right based on property (as bonds or patents) without intrinsic value. [-pō´, -pö´ri-ȧl].—*adv* **incorpō´really**. [L *incorporātus, incorporālis*, bodiless—*in-*, not, *corpus, -oris*, body.]

incorrect [in-kor-ekt´] *adj* faults; not accurate; wrong; not proper.—*adv* **incorrect´ly**.—*n* **incorrect´ness**. [L *incorrectus*; cf **correct**.]

incorrigible [in-kor´i-ji-bl] *adj* beyond correction or reform esp of bad habits.—Also *n*—*ns* **incorr´igibleness, incorrigibil´ity**.—*adv* **incorr´igibly**. [Fr; see **correct**.]

incorrupt [in-kor-upt´] *adj* free from corruption; free of error.—*adj* **incorrupt´ible**, not capable of decay; that cannot be bribed or morally corrupted.—*ns* **incorrupt´ibleness, incorruptibil´ity**.—*adv* **incorrupt´ibly**.—*ns* **incorrup´tion, incorrupt´ness**.—*adv* **incorrupt´ly**. [L *incorruptus*; cf **corrupt**.]

increase [in-krēs´] *vi* to become greater in size, numbers, amount, etc.—*vt* to make greater in size, numbers, etc.—*n* [in´krēs] an increasing or becoming increased; the result or amount of an increasing.—*adv* **increas´ingly**. [ME *encressen*—Anglo-Fr *encresser*—L *increscĕre*—*in*, in, *crescĕre*, to grow.]

incredible [in-kred´i-bl] *adj* surpassing belief; seeming too unusual to be possible.—ns **incredibil´ity, incred´ibleness**.—*adv* **incred´ibly**. [L *incrēdibilis*; cf **credible**.]

incredulous [in-kred´ū-lus] *adj* unbelieving; showing disbelief.—*ns* **incredū´lity, incred´ūlousness**.—*adv* **incred´ūlously**. [L *incrēdulus*; cf **credulous**.]

increment [ing´- or in´kri-mėnt] *n* an increase; the amount of increase; an amount or thing added. [L *incrēmentum*—*increscĕre*, to increase.]

incriminate [in-krim´in-āt] *vt* to accuse of a crime; to implicate; to involve in a crime.—*adj* **incrim´inatory** [or -ā-]. [Low L *incrīmināre, incrīminātum*; cf **criminate** (see **crime**).]

incrust [in-krust´] *vt* to cover as with a crust.—*vi* to form a crust.—*n* **incrusta´tion**.—Also **encrust, encrustation**. [Fr,—L *incrustāre, -ātum*—*in*, on, *crusta*, crust.]

incubate [in´kū-bāt, or ing´-] *vti* to sit on and hatch (eggs); to keep (eggs, embryos, etc.) in a favorable environment for hatching or developing; to develop, as by planning.—*n* **incubā´tion**, the act or process of incubating; the period between infection and appearance of symptoms; **in´cubātor**, an apparatus for hatching eggs by artificial heat, for rearing prematurely born children, or for cultivating microorganisms. [L *incubāre, -ātum* (usu -*ĭtum*)—*in*, on, *cubāre*, to lie, recline.]

incubus [in´kū-bus] *n* a nightmare; any oppressive burden;—*pl* **in´cubuses, incubi** [in´kū-bī]. [L *incŭbus*, nightmare—*in*, on, *cubāre*, to lie.]

inculcate [in´kul-kāt (or -kūl´-] *vt* to teach by frequent admonitions or repetitions.—*ns* **inculcā´tion; in´culcātor**. [L *inculcāre, -ātum*—*in*, into, *calcāre*, to tread—*calx*, the heel.]

inculpate [in´kul-pāt (or -kūl´-] *vt* to incriminate.—*n* **inculpā´tion**.—*adj* **incul´patory**. [Low L *inculpāre, -ātum*—L *in*, in, *culpa*, a fault.]

incumbent [in-kum´bėnt] *adj* resting (on or upon) one as a duty or obligation; currently in office.—*n* the holder of an office, etc.—*n* **incum´bency**, a duty or obligation; a term of office. [L *incumbens, -entis*, pr p of *incumbĕre*, to lie upon.]

incunabula [in-kū-nab´ū-la] *n pl* books printed before the year 1500; the origin, early stages of anything, (*sing*) **incunab´ula**. [L *incūnābŭla*, swaddling-clothes, infancy, earliest stage—*in*, in, *cūnābula*, dim of *cūnae*, a cradle.]

incur [in-kûr´] *vt* to bring upon oneself; *pt* (something undesirable); **incurr´ing**; *pt p* **incurred´**. [L *incurrĕre, incursum*—*in*, into, *currĕre*, to run.]

incurable [in-kūr´á-bl] *adj* not curable; (*loosely*) not likely to be changed.—Also *n*.—*adv* **incur´ably**. [OFr,—L *incūrābilis*—*in*-, not, *cūrābilis*, curable.]

incurious [in-kū´ri-us] *adj* not curious; uninterested. [L *incūriōsus*—*in*-, not, *cūriōsus*, attentive, inquisitive.]

incursion [in-kûr´sh(ȯ)n] *n* an invasion or raid; an entering into as an activity. [L *incursiō, -ōnis*—*incurrĕre*.]

incurve [in-kûrv´] *vti* to bend so as to curve inward.—*vt* **incur´vāte** [or in´-], to cause to bend inward.—*adj* curved inward.—*n* **incurvā´tion, incur´vature**. [L *incurvāre*, to bend in—*incurvus*, bent.]

indebted [in-det´id] *adj* in debt; obliged; owing gratitude.—*n* **indebt´edness**. [OFr *endetté*, pa p of *endetter*—*en*, in, *dette*, debt.]

indecent [in-dē´sėnt] *adj* offensive to common modesty or propriety.—*n* **indē´cency**.—*adv* **indē´cently**. [L *indĕcens*; cf **decent**.]

indecipherable [in-di-si´fėr-á-bl] *adj* incapable of being deciphered. [L *in*-, not, + **decipherable**. *See* **decipher**.]

indecision [in-di-sizh´(ȯ)n] *n* want of decision or resolution; hesitation.—*adj* **indecisive** [-sīz´iv], inconclusive; irresolute.—*adv* **indecī´sively**.—*n* **indecī´siveness**. [L *in*-, not, + **decisive**.]

indeclinable [in-di-klīn´á-bl] *adj* (*gram*) not varied by inflection.—*adv* **indeclin´ably**. [Fr *indéclinable*—L *indēclīnābilis*.]

indecorous [in-dek´ō-rus, -di-kō´-, or -kö´-] *adj* unseemly; violating good manners.—*adv* **indec´ōrously**.—*n* **indecō´rum**, want of propriety of conduct. [L *indĕcōrus*.]

indeed [in-dēd´] *adv* in fact; in truth; in reality.—*interj* expresses surprise, disbelief, sarcasm, etc. [**in, deed**.]

indefatigable [in-di-fat´i-gá-bl] *adj* tireless, unremitting in effort.—*n* **indefat´igableness**.—*adv* **indefat´igably**. [Fr,—L *indēfatīgābilis*—*in*, not, *dē*, from, *fatīgāre*, to tire.]

indefeasible [in-di-fēz´i-bl] *adj* not capable of being annulled.—*n* **indefeasibil´ity**.—*adv* **indefeas´ibly**. [L *in*-, not, + **defeasible**.]

indefensible [in-di-fens´i-bl] *adj* that cannot be defended, maintained, or justified.—*adv* **indefens´ibly**. [L *in*-, not, + **defensible**. See **defend**.]

indefinable [in-di-fīn´á-bl] *adj* that cannot be defined.—*adv* **indefin´ably**. [L *in*-, not, + **definable**. See **define**.]

indefinite [in-def´i-nit] *adj* without clearly marked outlines or limits; not precise in meaning; vague; (*gram*) not limiting or specifying, such as *a* and *an*, which are indefinite articles; (*gram*) not referring to a particular person or thing.—*adv* **indef´initely**.—*n* **indef´initeness**. [L *indēfīnītus*; cf **definite** (see **define**).]

indehiscent [in-dē-his´ėnt] *adj* (*bot*) not opening naturally when ripe. [L *-in*, not, + **dehiscent**.]

indelible [in-del´i-bl] *adj* that cannot be blotted out or effaced; making a mark that cannot easily be removed.—*n* **indelibil´ity**.—*adv* **indel´ibly**. [L *indēlēbilis*—*in*-, not, *dēlēre*, to destroy.]

indelicate [in-del´i-kȧt] *adj* improper; lacking in fineness of feeling or tact; coarse.—*n* **indel´icacy** [-kȧ-si].—*adv* **indel´icately**. [L *-in*, not + **delicate**.]

indemnify [in-dem´ni-fī] *vt* to insure against loss, damage, etc.; to repay (for loss, damage, etc.)—*pt p* **indem´nified**.—*n* **indemnification** [-fi-kā´sh(ȯ)n]. [*indemnis*, unhurt (*in*-, not, *damnum*, loss), and suffx *-fy*.]

indemnity [in-dem´ni-ti] *n* insurance against damage or loss, compensation for loss or injury. [Fr *indemnité*—L *indemnis*, unharmed—*damnum*, loss.]

indemonstrable [in-dem´ȯn-strȧ-bl, or in-di-mon´-] *adj* that cannot be demonstrated or proved. [L *-in*, not, + **demonstrable**. See **demonstrate**.]

indent [in-dent´] *vt* to notch; to begin farther in from the margin than the rest of a text.—*vi* to form an indentation.—*n* [in´dent, also in-dent´] a dent or notch.—*ns* **indentā´tion**, being indented; a notch, cut, inlet, etc.; a dent; a spacing in from the margin, usu **inden´tion** in this sense; **inden´ture**, a written agreement, a contract binding one person to work for another.—*vt* to bind by indentures; to indent. [Two different words fused together; (1)—Low L *indentāre*—L *-in*, in, *dens, dentis*, a tooth; (2)—English **in** and **dint, dent**.]

independent [in-di-pend´ėnt] *adj* freedom from the influence or control of others; self-governing; self-determined; not adhering to any political party; not connected with others (*an independent grocer*); not depending on another for financial support.—*n* one who is independent in thinking, action etc.—*ns* **independ´ence; independ´ency**, a self-governing political unit.—*adv* **independ´ently**.—**Independence Day**, the anniversary of the adoption of the American Declaration of Independence on July 4, 1776; **independent clause**, main clause. [L *-in*, not, + **dependent**. See **depend**.]

indescribable [in-di-skrī´á-bl] *adj* that cannot be described; vague, difficult to define; possessing its characteristic quality in a high degree. [L *-in*, not + **describable**.]

indestructible [in-di-struk´ti-bl] *adj* that cannot be destroyed.—*n* **indestructibil´ity**.—*adv* **indestruc´tibly**. [L *in*-, not + **destructible**. *See* **destruction**.]

indeterminable [in-di-tûr´min-á-bl] *adj* not to be ascertained or fixed.—*adv* **indeter´minably**.—*adj* **indeter´minate** [-ȧt], not determinate; uncertain; having no defined or fixed value.—*adv* **indeter´minately**.—*n* **indeterminā´tion**, want of determination; want of fixed direction.—*adj* **indeter´mined**, not determined; unsettled. [L *indēterminābilis*; cf **determinable**.]

index [in´deks] *n* the forefinger (also **in´dex fing´er**); a pointer or hand on a dial or scale, etc.; anything that gives an indication; an alphabetical list of subjects dealt with, usu at the end of a book; a figure showing ratio or relative change; **Index** (RC Church) formerly, a list of books forbidden to be read; (*math*) the number denoting a power; (*math*) the root to be extracted from an expression written as a radical, as 3 in $\sqrt[3]{27}$.—*pl* **in´dexes** (*math*) **indices** [in´disez].—*vt* to make an index of or for. [L *index, indicis*—*indicāre*, to show.]

Indian [in´di-ȧn] *n* a member of any of the aboriginal peoples of the Americas; a native of India or the East Indies.—Also *adj*—*ns* **Indian club**, a bottle-shaped club, used by jugglers, gymnasts, etc.; **Indian corn**, maize; **Indian file**, single file; **Indian giver**, a person who gives something and then takes it back; **Indian ink**, black drawing ink; **Indian pipe**, a white leafless saprophytic plant (*Monotropa uniflora*) of the US and Asia; **Indian pudding**, a baked dessert made of cornmeal, milk, and molasses; **Indian red**, a moderate-to-strong brownish red; **Indian summer**, a period of unusually warm weather in the fall; **Indian wrestling**, contest in which opponents attempt to make the other lose balance; arm wrestling; **Indian paper**, extremely thin, opaque printing paper used esp for Bibles. [L *India*—*Indus* (Gr *Indos*), the Indus (Pers *Hind*)—Sans *sindhu*, a river.]

indicate [in´di-kāt] *vt* to point out; to show; to give some notion of; (*med*) suggest or point to (as suitable treatment); also (*pass*) used loosely of any desirable course of action.—*n* **indicā´tion**, act of indicating; mark; token; symptom.—*adj* **indic´ative**, showing the existence, presence, or nature (of), giving intimation (of); (*gram*) applied to the mood of the verb that affirms or denies.—*adv* **indic´atively**.—*n* **ind´icātor**, one who, or that which, indicates; a measuring contrivance with a pointer or the like; any device for exhibiting condition for the time being.—*adj* **in´dicatory** [or -dik´-]. [L *indicāre, -ātum*—*in*, in, *dicāre*, to proclaim.]

indict [in-dīt´] *vt* to charge with a fault or offense; to accuse; to charge with a crime through the due process of law as by a grand jury.—*adj* **indict´able**, subject to being indicted; making one liable to indictment.—*n* **indict´ment**, the legal process of indictment; a formal written statement framed by a prosecuting authority charging a person of a crime. [With Latinised spelling (but not pronunciation) from Anglo-Fr *enditer*, to indict—L *in*, in, *dictāre*, to declare.]

indifferent [in-dif´ėr-ėnt] *adj* neutral; without importance (to); unconcerned; fair; average.—*ns* **indiff´erence, indiff´erentism**, the belief that religious differences are of equal value.—*adv* **indiff´erently**, in an indifferent manner. [L *indiffĕrens, -entis*; cf **different**.]

indigenous [in-dij´ėn-us] *adj* existing naturally in a country region, or particular environment; native.—*n* **in´digēne, in´digėn**. [L *indigena*, a native—*indu*, old form of *in*, in, and *gen*-, root of *gignĕre*, to produce.]

indigent [in´di-jėnt] *adj* poor, needy.—Also *n*. [Fr,—L *indigens, -entis*, pr p of *indigēre*—from the old word *indu*, in, *egēre*, to need.]

indigested [in-di-jest´id] *adj* not thought out; not arranged.—*n* **indigestion** [in-di-jes´ch(ȯ)n], difficulty in digesting food.—*adj* **indigest´ible**, not easily digested.—*n* **indigestibil´ity**.—*adv* **indigest´ībly**. [L *indīgestus*, unarranged—*in*-, not, *dīgerĕre*, to arrange, digest.]

indignant [in-dig´nȧnt] *adj* expressing anger, esp at mean or unjust action.—*adv* **indig´nantly**.—*ns* **indignā´tion**, righteous anger; **indig´nity**. [L *indignus*, unworthy—*in*-, not, *dignus*, worthy.]

indigo [in´di-gō] *n* a violet-blue dye obtained from the leaves of plants of the indigo (genus *Indigofera*), or synthetically. [Sp *índico, índigo*—L *indicum*—Gr *Indikon*, Indian (neut adj).]

indirect [in-di-rekt´, or -dī-] *adj* not straight; not straight to the point; dishonest *indirect dealing*); secondary (*an indirect result*).—*adv* **indirect´ly**.—*n* **indirect´ness**.—**indirect evidence**, circumstantial or inferential evidence; **indirect object** (*gram*), a noun or pronoun denoting the person or object *to, toward* or *for* whom or which the action expressed by the sentence takes place (eg *her* in 'I gave her the book'.). [L *indīrectus*; cf **direct**.]

indiscernible [in-di-sûrn´i-bl or -zûrn´-] *adj* not discernible. *adv* **indiscern´ibly**. [L *in*-, not, + **discernible**. *See* **discern**.]

indiscreet [in-dis-krēt´] *adj* not discreet, imprudent, injudicious.—*adv* **indiscreet´ly**.—*ns* **indiscreet´ness, indiscretion** [-kresh´(ȯ)n], want of discretion; rashness; an indiscreet act. [L *in*-, not, and **discreet**.]

indiscrete [in-dis-krēt] *adj* not separated; undivided. [L *indiscretus*.]

indiscriminate [in-dis-krim´i-nȧt] *adj* confused; random; making no distinctions; not distinguishing relative merits.—Also **indiscrim´inating**.—*n* **indiscrimina´tion**.—*adv* **indiscrim´inately**. [L *in*-, not + **discriminate**.]

indispensable [in-dis-pens´á-bl] *adj* absolutely necessary.—*ns* **indispensabil´ity, indispens´ableness**.—*adv* **indispens´ably**. [Low L *indispensābilis*.]

indispose [in-dis-pōz´] *vt* to make indisposed.—*pt p, adj* **indisposed´**, slightly ill; unwilling; disinclined.—*ns* **indispos´edness, indisposition** [-poz-ish´(ȯ)n], state of being indisposed; disinclination; slight illness. [L *in*-, not, + **dispose**.]

indisputable [in-dis-pū´tȧ-bl also -dis´] *adj* unquestionable; certain.—*n* **indisputableness**.—*adv* **indisputably**. [Low L *indisputābilis*; cf **disputable**.]

indissoluble [in-dis´ol-(y)ōō-bl or -di-sol´-] *adj* that cannot be broken or violated; inseparable; lasting.—*ns* **indiss´olubleness, indissolubil´ity** [-ū-bil´-].—*adv* **indiss´olubly**. [L *indissŏlūbilis*; cf **dissoluble**.]

indistinct [in-dis-tingkt´] *adj* not clearly marked; dim; not clearly recognizable.—*adv* **indistinct´ly**.—*n* **indistinct´ness**.—*adj* **indistinctive**, not distinctive. [L *indistinctus*; cf **distinct**.]

indistinguishable [in-dis-ting´gwish-å-bl] *adj* that cannot be distinguished, lacking identifying characteristics.—*adv* **indisting´uishably**. [L *in-*, not + **distinguishable**.]

indite [in-dīt´] *vt* to compose or write.—*n* **indit´er**. [OFr *enditer*, to make known; cf **indict**.]

indium [in´di-ům] *n* a metallic element (symbol In; at wt 114.8; at no 49). [L *ind*icum, indigo (from two indigo-colored lines in the spectrum), and -*ium*.]

individual [in-di-vid´ū-ål] *adj* existing as a separate thing or being; of, by, for, or relating to a single person or thing.—*n* a single thing or being; a person.—*vt* **individ´ualīze** to make individual; to treat as an individual.—*n* **individualīzā´tion**.—*ns* **individ´ualism**, individuality; the doctrine that the state exists for the individual; the leading of one's life in one's own way; **individ´ualist**, one who thinks and acts with great independence; one who advocates individualism; **individual´ity** [-al´i-ti], the sum of the characteristics that set one person or thing apart; existence as an individual.—*adv* **individ´ually**.—*vt* **individ´uāte**, to individualize; to give individuality to.—*n* **individuā´tion**. [L *indīviduus*—*in-*, not, *dīviduus*, divisible—*dīvidĕre*, to divide.]

indivisible [in-di-viz´i-bl] *adj* not divisible.—*ns* **indivisibil´ity, indivis´ibleness**.—*adv* **indivis´ibly**. [L *indīvisibilis*; cf **divisible** (*see* **division**).]

indocile [in-dō´sīl or in-dos´il] *adj* not docile; not disposed to be instructed.—*n* **indocil´ity**. [L *indŏcilis*; cf **docile**.]

indoctrinate [in-dok´trin-āt] *vt* to instruct in doctrines, theories, beliefs, etc.—*n* **indoctrinā´tion**. [Low L *in*, in, *doctrināre*, to teach; cf **doctrine**.]

Indo-European [in´dō-ū-rō-pē´ån] *adj* denoting the most geographically widespread and numerically important family of languages which includes English, a member of the Germanic branch.—Also *n*. [Indo=Indian—L *Indus*—Gr *Indos*.]

indolent [in´dȯl-ėnt] *adj* idle; lazy.—*n* **in´dolence**.—*adv* **in´dolently**. [L *in-*, not, *dolens, -entis*, pr p of *dolēre*, to suffer pain.]

indomitable [in-dom´it-å-bl] *adj* not easily discouraged or defeated.—*adv* **indom´itably**. [Low L *indŏmitābilis*—*dŏmitāre*, to tame.]

indoor [in´dōr, -dör] *adj* practised, used, or being, within a building.—*adv* **indoors´**, in or into a building. [**in, door**.]

indorse *See* **endorse**.

indubitable [in-dū´bit-å-bl] *adj* that cannot be doubted.—*n* **indū´bitableness**.—*adv* **indū´bitably**. [L *indŭbitābilis*—*in*, not, *dŭbitāre*, to doubt.]

induce [in-dūs´] *vt* to persuade; to bring on; to draw (a conclusion) from particular facts; to bring about (an electric or magnetic effect) in a body by placing it within a field of force.—*n* **induce´ment**, that which induces; an incentive; a motive. [L *indūcĕre, inductum*—*in*, into, *dūcĕre*, to lead.]

induct [in-dukt´] *vt* to place formally in an office, a society, etc.; to enroll (esp a draftee) in the armed forces.—*ns* **inductance**, the property of inducing an electromotive force by variation of current in a circuit; **induc´tion**, installation in office, etc.; reasoning from particular cases to general conclusions; the inducing of an electric or magnetic effect by a field of force.—*adj* **induc´tive**.—*adv* **induc´tively**.—*n* **induc´tor**. [Same root as **induce**.]

indue *See* **endue**.

indulge [in-dulj´] *vt* to satisfy (a desire); to gratify the wishes of; to humor.—*vi* to give way to one's desire.—*n* **indul´gence**, the act or practice of indulging; a thing indulged in; a favor or privilege; (*R C Church*) a remission of punishment still due for a sin after the guilt has been forgiven.—*adj* **indul´gent**, ready to gratify the wishes of others; compliant; lenient, often to excess.—*adv* **indul´gently**. [L *indulgēre*, to be kind to, indulge—*in*, in, and prob L *dulcis*, sweet.]

indurate [in´dū-rāt] *vti* to make or become hard either physically or emotionally.—*n* **indurā´tion**. [L *indūrāre, -ātum*—*in*, in, *dūrāre*, to harden.]

industry [in´dus-tri] *n* quality of being diligent; steady application to labor; any branch of productive, manufacturing enterprise or all of these collectively; any large-scale business activity; the owners and managers of industry.—*adj* **indus´trial**, relating to or consisting in industry.—*vt* **indus´trialīze**, to make industrial.—*vi* to become industrial.—*ns* **indus´trialism**, social and economic organization characterized by large industries, machine production, urban workers, etc.; **indus´trialist**, one who owns or manages an industrial enterprise.—*adj* **indus´trious**, hard-working; diligent.—*adv* **indus´triously**.—**industrial arts**, the mechanical and technical skills used in industry; a subject taught in elementary and secondary schools that aims at developing these skills; **industrial park**, an area zoned for industrial and business use, usu on the outskirts of a city; **industrial relations**, relations between workers, management, government agencies, labor and management in the same field, and the general public; **industrial school**, a school in which some industrial art is taught, esp one for juvenile delinquents. [L *industria*, perh from the old word *indu*, in, within, and *struĕre*, to build up.]

indwelling [in´dwel-ling] *adj* left within a bodily organ esp to facilitate drainage (as a catheter). [**in, dwell**.]

inebriate [in-ē´bri-āte] *vt* to make drunk.—Also *n*.—*ns* **inebriā´tion, inebriety** [in-ē-brī-´iti]. [L *inēbriāre, -ātum*—*in-*, inten *ēbriāre*, to make drunk—*ēbrius*, drunk.]

inedible [in-ed´i-bl] *adj* unfit to be eaten. [L *in-*, not + **edible**.]

ineducable [in-ed´ū-kå-bl] *adj* thought to be incapable of being educated.—*n* **ineducabil´ity**. [L *in-*, not, + **educable**. See **educate**.]

ineffable [in-ef´å-bl] *adj* inexpressible; too sacred to be spoken.—*n* **ineff´ableness**.—*adv* **ineff´ably**. [L *ineffābilis*—*in-*, not, *effābilis*, that can be uttered—*fārī*, to speak.]

ineffaceable [in-e-fās´å-bl] *adj* ineradicable.—*adv* **inefface´ably**. [L *in-*, not, + **effaceable**. *See* **efface**.]

ineffective [in-e-fek´tiv] *adj* not effective.—*adv* **ineffec´tively**.—*adj* **ineffec´tual** [in-e-fek-chūål], not effectual; futile.—*n* **ineffec´tualness**.—*adv* **ineffec´tually**.—*adj* **inefficā´cious** [in-ef-i-kā´shs]—*adj* **inefficacious** not having power to produce an effect.—*adv* **inefficā´ciously**.—*n* **ineff´icacy** [-kå-si], want of efficacy.—*adj* **inefficient** [ine(fish´ėnt)] not efficient.—*n* **ineffic´iency**.—*adv* **ineffici´ently**. [L *in-*, not. See **effective** and **effectual** (under **effect**), **efficacious, efficient**.]

inelastic [in-ē-las´tik], *adj* not elastic; unyielding—**inelastic collision** a collision of particles in which part of the kinetic energy generated by the colliding particles changes into another form of energy. [L *in-*, not, + **elastic**.]

inelegance [in-el´i-gåns] *n* lack of elegance.—*adj* **inel´egant**.—*adv* **inel´egantly**. [Fr *inélégance*; cf **elegance** (*see* **elegant**).]

ineligible [in-el´i-ji-bl] *adj* not qualified for election; not suitable for choice; (*football*) not permitted under the rules to catch a forward pass.—*n* **ineligibil´ity**.—*adv* **inel´igibly**. [L *in-*, not + **eligible**.]

ineluctable [in-e-luk´tå-bl] *adj* not to be escaped from. [L *inēluctābilis*—*in-*, not, *ē*, from, *luctārī*, to struggle.]

inept [in-ept´] *adj* unsuitable; unfit; foolish; awkward; clumsy.—*n* **inept´itūde**.—*adv* **inept´ly**. [L *ineptus*—*in-*, not, *aptus*, apt.]

inequality [in-e-kwol´i-ti] *n* lack of equality; unevenness; (*math*) a statement indicating that value of one quantity or expression is not equal to another. [OFr *inequalité*—Low L; cf **equality**. *See* **equal**]

inequitable [in-ek´wi-tå-bl] *adj* unfair, unjust.—*adv* **ineq´uitably**.—*n* **inequity**. [L *in-*, not + **equitable**.]

ineradicable [in-e-rad´i-kå-bl] *adj* not able to be eradicated or rooted out.—*adv* **inerad´icably**. [L *in-*, not, + **eradicable**.]

inert [in-ûrt´] *adj* without power to move or to resist; inactive; dull; slow; with few or no active properties.—Also *n*. *ns* **inert´ness; inertia** [in-ûr´-shi-a], (physics) the tendency of matter to remain at rest (or continue in a fixed direction) unless acted on by an outside force; disinclination to act.—*adj* **iner´tial**, of, or pertaining to, inertia.—*adv* **inert´ly**.—**inert gas**, noble gas. [L *iners, inertis*, unskilled, idle—*in-*, not, *ars, artis*, art.]

inescapable [in-es-kā´på-bl] *adj* not to be escaped. [L *in-*, not, + **escapable**.]

inessential [in-es-en´sh(å)l] *adj* not necessary. [L *in-*, not + **essential**.]

inestimable [in-es´tim-å-bl] *adj* too great to be properly estimated.—*adv* **ines´timably**. [OFr,—L *inaestimābilis*; cf **estimable**. See **esteem**.]

inevitable [in-ev´it-å-bl] *adj* that must happen—*ns* **inev´itableness, inevitabil´ity**.—*adv* **inev´itably**. [L *inēvītābilis*—*in-*, not, *ē*, from, *vītāre*, to avoid.]

inexact [in-egz-akt´] *adj* not precisely correct or true; inaccurate; not careful and rigorous.—*ns* **inexact´itude, inexact´ness**. [L *in-*, not, and **exact**.]

inexcusable [in-eks-kūz´å-bl] *adj* not justifiable; unpardonable.—*n* **inexcus´ableness**.—*adv* **inexcus´ably**. [L *inexcūsābilis*; cf **excusable**. See **excuse**.]

inexhaustible [in-egs-ös´tibl] *adj* incapable of being used up; incapable of being worn out.—*n* **inexhaustibil´ity**.—*adv* **inexhaust´ibly**. [L *in-*, not, and **exhaustible**.]

inexorable [in-eks´ȯr-å-bl] *adj* not to be moved by entreaty, unrelenting.—*ns* **inex´orableness, inexorabil´ity**.—*adv* **inex´orably**. [L *inexōrābilis*—*in-*, not, *exōrāre*—*ex*, out of, *ōrāre*, to entreat.]

inexpedient [in-eks-pē´di-ėnt] *adj* contrary to expediency; unadvisable.—*ns* **inexpē´dience, inexpē´diency**.—*adv* **inexpē´diently**. [L *in-*, not, + **expedient**.]

inexpensive [in-eks-pens´iv] *adj* not costly. [L *in-*, not, + **expensive**.]

inexperience [in-eks-pē´ri-ėns] *n* lack of experience or of the knowledge or skill resulting from experience.—*adj* **inexpē´rienced**. [Fr *inexpérience*; cf **experience**.]

inexpert [in-eks´pûrt or in-eks-pûrt´] *adj* unskillful.—*n* **inexpert´ness**. [OFr,—L *inexpertus*; cf **expert**.]

inexpiable [in-eks´pi-å-bl] *adj* not able to be expiated or atoned for.—*n* **inex´piableness**.—*adv* **inex´piably**. [L *inexpiābilis*; cf **expiable**. See **expiate**.]

inexplicable [in-eks´pli-kå-bl] *adj* that cannot be explained.—*ns* **inexplicabil´ity, inex´plicableness**.—*adv* **inex´plicably**. [L *inexplicābilis*; cf **explicable**. *See* **explicate**.]

inexpressible [in-eks-pres´i-bl] *adj* that cannot be expressed.—*adv* **inexpress´ibly**.—*adj* **inexpress´ive**, lacking expression.—*n* **inexpress´iveness**. [L *in-*, not + **expressible**.]

inextinguishable [in-eks-ting´gwish-å-bl] *adj* that cannot be extinguished or quenched.—*adv* **inexting´uishably**. [L *in-*, not + **extinguishable**.]

inextricable [in-eks´tri-kȧ-bl] *adj* that one cannot extricate himself from; that cannot be disentangled; insolvable.—*adv* **inex´tricably**. [L *inextrīcābilis*; cf **extricable**. *See* **extricate**.]
infallible [in-fal´i-bl] *adj* incapable of error; dependable; reliable.—*n* **infallibil´ity**.—*adv* **infall´ibly**. [Low L *infallibilis*; cf **fallible**.]
infamous [in´fa-mus] *adj* having a bad reputation; notorious; causing a bad reputation; scandalous.—*adv* **in´famously**.—*n* **in´famy**, very bad reputation; disgrace; great wickedness; an infamous act.—*pl* **infamies**. [LL *infāmōsus*—*in-*, not, *fāma*, fame.]
infant [in´fȧnt] *n* a very young child; a baby.—*adj* of or for infants; in a very early stage.—*n* **in´fancy**, the state or time of being an infant; the beginning of anything.—*adjs* **infantile** [in´fȧnt-īl, also -til] of infants; like an infant, babyish.—Also **infantine** [-īn].—**infantile paralysis**, poliomyelitis. [L *infāns, -antis*—*in-*, not, *fāns*, pr p of *fārī*, to speak.]
infanticide [in-fant´i-sīd] *n* child murder; the murderer of an infant.—*adj* **infant´icidal**. [LL *infanticīdium*, child-killing, *infanticīda*, child-killer—*infāns*, an infant, *caedĕre*, to kill.]
infantry [in´fȧnt-ri] *n* that branch of an army consisting of soldiers trained to fight on foot. [Fr *infanterie*—It *infanteria*—*infante*, youth, servant, foot-soldier—L *infāns, -antis*.]
infarct [in-färkt´] *n* a portion of body tissue that is dying because blood supply to it has been cut off.—*n* **infarct´ion**. [Mediaeval L *īnfarctus*—*in*, in, *far(c)tus*—*farcīre*, to cram, stuff.]
infatuate [in´fat´ū-āt] *vt* to inspire with foolish passion.—*adj* **infat´uated**.—*n* **infatuā´tion**. [L *infatuāre, -ātum*—*in*, in, *fatuus*, foolish.]
infect [in-fekt´] *vt* to contaminate with microorganisms that cause disease; to imbue with one's feelings or beliefs, esp so as to harm.—*n* **infection** [in-fek´sh(ȯ)n], act of infecting; an infectious disease.—*adjs* **infec´tious**, having the quality of infecting; denoting a disease caused in the body by the presence of germs; tending to spread to others; **infec´tive**, capable of producing infection; affecting others.—*adv* **infec´tiously**.—*n* **infec´tiousness**. [L *inficĕre*—*in*, into, *facĕre*, to make.]
infelicitous [in-fe-lis´i-tus] *adj* not happy or fortunate; inappropriate, inapt.—*n* **infelic´ity**. [L *in-*, not + **felicitous**.]
infer [in-fûr´] *vt* to deduce; to conclude; to imply.—*pr p* **inferr´ing**.—*pt p* **inferred´**.—*adjs* **in´ferable**, that may be inferred or deduced.—*n* **in´ference**, that which is inferred or deduced, conclusion; the act of drawing a conclusion from premises.—*adj* **inferential** [-en´sh(ȧ)l], based on or relating to inference.—*adv* **inferen´tially**. [L *inferre*—*in*, into, *ferre*, to bring.]
inferior [in-fē´ri-ȯr] *adj* lower in space; subordinate; poor or poorer in quality.—*n* one lower in rank or station.—*n* **inferior´ity**.—**inferior´ity complex** (*psych*), an acute sense of inferiority expressed by a lack of confidence or in exaggerated aggression. [L *inferior*, comp of *inferus*, low.]
infernal [in-fûr´nȧl] *adj* of hell or Hades; hellish; fiendish.—*adv* **infer´nally**.—**infernal machine**, a contrivance made to resemble some ordinary harmless object, but charged with a dangerous explosive. [L *infernus*—*inferus*, low.]
inferno [in-fûr´nō] *n* hell; intense heat; a conflagration. [It.]
infertile [in-fûr´til, tīl] *adj* not productive; barren.—*n* **infertility** [-til´-]. [Low L *infertilis*; cf **fertile**.]
infest [in-fest´] *vt* to overrun in large numbers, usu so as to be harmful; to be parasitic in or on. [L *infestāre*, from *infestus*, hostile.]
infidel [in´fi-del] *n* one who does not believe in a certain religion; one who has no religion.—*n* **infidel´ity**, unfaithfulness, esp in marriage. [OFr *infidèle*—L *infidēlis*—*in-*, not, *fidēlis*, faithful—*fidēs*, faith.]
infield [in´fēld] *n* the area of a baseball field enclosed by the baselines; the players whose field positions are there.—*n* **infielder**. [**in**, + **field**.]
infiltrate [in´fil-trāt] *vti* to filter or pass gradually through or into; to penetrate (enemy lines, a region, etc.) gradually or stealthily, so as to attack or seize control from within.—*ns* **infiltrā´tion; infiltrator**. [L *in*, into, + **filtrate**.]
infinite [in´fin-it] *adj* without end or limit; very great; vast.—*n* something infinite (in extent, number, or duration.—*adv* **in´finitely**.—*ns* **infin´itūde, infin´ity**, immensity; a countless number; an infinite quantity.—*adj* **infinites´imal**, immeasurably small.—Also *n*.—*adv* **infinites´imally**.—**infinite set** (*math*), a set which can be put in a one-to-one correspondence with part of itself. [L *infinītus*; cf **finite**.]
infinitive [in-fin´it-iv] *n* (*gram*) the form of a verb without reference to person, number or tense (*usu with* **to**, as in "I want to go."). [L *infinītīvus*—*in-*, not, *fīnīre*, to limit.]
infirm [in-fûrm´] *adj* feeble; weak; not firm; unstable; frail; shaky.—*ns* **infirm´ity; infirmary** [in-fûrm´ȧr-i], a hospital or place for the treatment of the sick. [L *infirmus*—*in-*, not, *firmus*, strong.]
infix[1] [in-fiks´] *vt* to fix in; to set in by piercing; to inculcate. [L *infixus*—*in*, in, *fīgĕre, fixum*, to fix.]
infix[2] [in´fiks] an inflectional form appearing in the body of a word.
inflame [in-flām´] *vti* to arouse, excite, etc. or to become aroused, excited, etc.; to undergo or cause to undergo inflammation. [OFr *enflammer*—L *inflammāre*—*in*, into; *flamma*, a flame.]
inflammable [in-flam´ȧ-bl] *adj* flammable; easily excited.—*ns* **inflammabil´ity, inflamm´ableness**.—*adv* **inflamm´ably**.—*n* **inflammā´tion**, an inflaming or being inflamed; redness, pain, heat, and swelling in the body, due to injury or disease.—*adj* **inflamm´atory**, rousing excitement, anger, etc.; of or caused by inflammation. [L *inflammāre*—*in*, into, *flamma*, a flame.]
inflate [in-flāt´] *vt* to blow full with air or gas; to puff up with pride; to increase beyond what is normal, esp the supply of money and credit.—*adj* **inflat´ed**.—*n* inflation [in-flāsh(ȯ)n], the condition of being inflated; an increase in the currency in circulation or a marked expansion of credit, resulting in a fall in currency value, and a sharp rise in prices.—*adj* **inflationary**, pertaining to inflation. [L *inflāre, -ātum*—*in*, into, *flāre*, to blow.]
inflect [in-flekt´] *vt* to turn from a direct line or course; to change the form (of a word) by inflection; to vary the tone of (the voice).—*n* **inflec´tion**, a bend; the change in the form of a word to indicate number, case, tense, etc.; a change in the tone of the voice.—*adjs* **inflec´table, inflective**. [L *inflectere*—*in*, in, *flectĕre, flexum*, to bend, *flexiō, -ōnis*, a bend.]
inflexible [in-flek´si-bl] *adj* not flexible; stiff, rigid; fixed; unyielding.—*ns* **inflexibil´ity, inflex´ibleness**.—*adv* **inflex´ibly**. [L *in-*, not, + **flexible**.]
inflict [in-flikt´] *vt* to cause (wounds, pain, etc.); to impose (as punishment) (*with* **on** *or* **upon**).—*n* **inflic´tion**, act of inflicting or imposing; that which is inflicted.—*adj* **inflictive**, tending or able to inflict. [L *inflīgĕre, inflictum*—*in*, against, *flīgĕre*, to strike.]
inflorescence [in-flor-es´ȩns] *n* the producing of blossoms; the arrangement of flowers on a stem; a flower cluster; flowers collectively. [L *inflōrēscĕre*, to begin to blossom.]
influence [in´flŏŏ-ȩns] *n* the power to affect others; the power to produce effects by having wealth, position, ability, etc.; one with influence.—*vt* to have influence on.—*adj* **influential** [-en´shȧl], having much influence; effectively active (in).—*adv* **influen´tially**. [OFr—Low L *influentia*—L *in*, into, *fluĕre*, to flow.]
influenza [in-flŏŏ-en´zȧ] *n* a contagious feverish virus disease marked by muscular pain and inflammation of the respiratory system. [It Allied to **influence**.]
influx [in´fluks] *n* a flowing in. [L *influxus*—*influĕre*.]
info [in´fō] *n* (*inf*) information.
infold [en-fōld] *vt* to envelope. *vi* to fold inward.—Also **enfold**.
inform [in-förm´] *vt* to give knowledge of something to.—*vi* to give information, esp in accusing another.—*ns* **inform´ant**, a person who gives information; **informā´tion**, something told or facts learned; news; knowledge; data stored in or retrieved from a computer.—*adjs* **inform´ative**, instructive; **inform´atory**, instructive.—*n* **inform´er**, one who gives information; one who informs against another.—**information retrieval**, the techniques of recovering stored data esp by means of a computerized system; **information science**, technology concerned with devising means for providing more efficient access to documents and improving the dissemination of information. [OFr *enformer*—L *informāre*—*in*, into, *formāre*, to form.]
informal [in-förm´ȧl] *adj* not formal; not according to fixed rules, customs, etc.; casual; not requiring formal dress; colloquial.—*n* **informal´ity**.—*adv* **inform´ally**. [L *in-*, not, *forma*, form; *informis*, formless, misshapen.]
infraction [in-frak´sh(ȯ)n] *n* a violation of a law, pact, etc. [L *in*, in, *frangĕre, fractum*, to break.]
infra dig [in´frȧ dig] *adj* beneath one's dignity. [L *infra dignitatem*.]
infrangible [in-fran´ji-bl] *adj* that cannot be broken; not to be violated.—*ns* **infrangibil´ity, infran´gibleness**. [L *in-*, not, *frangĕre*, to break.]
infrared [in´fra-red´] *adj* denoting, of those invisible rays just beyond the red end of the visible spectrum (which have a penetrating heating effect). [L *infra*, below, + **red**.]
infrastructure [in´frȧ-struk-chủr] *n* basic installations and facilities, as sewers, roads, power plants, transportation and communication systems of a community or nation; the permanent installations required for military services. [L *infra*, below, + **structure**.]
infrequent [in-frē´kwȩnt] *adj* seldom occurring.—*n* **infrē´quency**.—*adv* **infrē´quently**. [L *infrĕquens, -entis*; cf **frequent**.]
infringe [in-frinj´] *vt* to violate, esp a pact or a law.—*n* **infringe´ment**. [L *infringĕre*—*in*, in, *frangĕre*, to break.]
infuriate [in-fū´ri-āt] *vt* to enrage; to madden. [L *in*, in, *furiāre, -ātum*, to madden—*furĕre*, to rave.]
infuse [in-fūz´] *vt* to instill or impart (qualities, etc.); to inspire; to steep (tea leaves, etc.) to extract the essence.—*n* **infusion** [in-fū´zh(ȯ)n], something obtained by infusing. [L *infundĕre, infūsum*—*in*, into, *fundĕre, fūsum*, to pour.]
infusible [in-fūz´i-bl] *adj* that cannot be fused. [L *in-*, not, + **fusible**.]
infusorian [in-fūzō´ri-an] *n* any of a group of minute organisms found in semiliquid organic decomposition, esp a cililiated protozoan.—*n* **infusorial earth**, kieselguhr. [Neut pl of modern L *infūsōrius*—*infundĕre*. See **infuse**.]
ingather [in´gaTH-ėr] *vt* to gather in.—*vi* to assemble.—*n* **ingathering**. [**in**, + **gathering**.]
ingenious [in-jē´ni-ůs] *adj* clever, resourceful, etc.; made or done in an original or clever way; skilfully contrived.—*adv* **ingē´niously**.—*n* **ingē´niousness**. [L *ingenium*, natural ability, skill—root, of *gignĕre*, to beget, produce.]
ingenuity [in-jen-ū´i-ti] *n* cleverness; ingenious quality. [L *ingenuitās, -ātis*—*ingenuus*; see below.]

ingenuous [in-jen´u-us] *adj* frank, artless; simple; naive.—*adv* **ingen´uously**.—*ns* **ingen´uousness; ingénue** [ẽ-zhänü] (*theatre*), the role of a naive young woman, or an actress in this role. [L *ingenuus*, free-born, ingenuous.]

ingle [ing´gl] *n* a fire, a fireplace.—*n* **ing´lenook**, a recess by a large open fireplace; a bench or settee in this recess; a fireside corner. [Possibly Gael *aingeal*; or L *igniculus*, dim of *ignis*, fire.]

inglorious [in-glō´ri-us, -glö´-] *adj* disgraceful; shameful.—*adv* **inglō´riously**.—*n* **inglō´riousness**. [L *in-*, not, and *glōriōsus*—*gloria*, glory.]

ingot [ing´got] *n* a mass of metal, esp gold or silver, cast into a bar. [Perh OE *in*, in, and the root *got*, as in *goten*, pt p of *gēotan*, to pour; Ger *giessen*.]

ingraft *See* **engraft**.

ingrain [in-grān´] *vt* to fix firmly into a natural texture or into a person's behavior pattern.—*adj* **ingrained** firmly established, as habits; inveterate.—Also **engrain**. [**in**, + **grain**.]

ingrate [in-grāt´, in´grāt] *n* one who is ungrateful. [L *ingrātus*—*in-*, not, *grātus*, pleasing, grateful.]

ingratiate [in-grā´shi-āt] *vt* to bring (oneself) into another's favor. [L *in*, into, *grātia*, favor.]

ingratitude [in-grat´i-tūd] *n* lack of gratitude; ungratefulness. [Low L *ingrātitūdō*—*L ingrātus*, unthankful.]

ingredient [in-grē´di-ent] *n* that which enters into a mixture; a component. [L *ingrediens, -entis*, pr p of *ingredī*—*in*, into, *gradī*, to walk.]

ingress [in´gres] *n* entrance: [L *ingressus*—*ingredī*—*in*, into, *gradī*, to walk.]

ingrowing [in´grō-ing] *adj* growing inward; growing into the flesh—*adj* **in´grown**. [**in, growing**.]

inguinal [ing´gwin-ȧl] *adj* relating to the groin. [L *inguinālis*—*inguen, inguinis*, the groin.]

ingurgitate [in-gûr´ji-tât] *vt* to swallow up greedily. [L *ingurgitāre, -ātum*—*in*, into, *gurges, -itis*, a whirlpool.]

inhabit [in-hab´it] *vt* to live in.—*adj* **inhab´itable**, that may be inhabited.—*ns* **inhab´itant**, a person or animal inhabiting a specified place. **inhabitā´tion**, the act of inhabiting; the state of being inhabited. [L *inhabitāre*—*in*, in *habitāre*, to dwell.]

inhale [in-hāl´] *vti* to breathe in.—*ns* **inhā´lant**, a medicine, etc. to be inhaled; **inhalātion** [in-hä-lā´sh(ȯ)n], the act of drawing into the lungs; something to be inhaled. **in´halator** an apparatus used in inhaling medicinal vapors; an apparatus to maintain breathing. [L *in*, in *hālāre*, to breathe.]

inharmonious [in-här-mō´ni-us] *adj* discordant; characterized by dissension.—*adv* **inharmō´niously**.—*n* **inharmō´niousness**. [L *in-*, not,+ **harmonious**.]

inhere [in-hēr´] *vi* to be inherent.—*adj* **inher´ent**, existing in and inseparable from something else; innate.—*n* **inher´ence**—*adv* **inher´ently**. [L *inhaerēre, inhaesum in*, in, *haerēre*, to stick.]

inherit [in-her´it] *vt* to get as heir; to possess by transmission from past generations.—Also vi—adj **inher´itable** heritable.—*ns* **inher´itance** the action of inheriting; something inherited; **inher´itor** [OFr *enhériter*, to put in possession as heir—Low L *inhērēditāre*, to inherit—L *in*, in, *hērēs, hērēdis*, an heir.]

inhibit [in-hib´it] *vt* to hold in or back; to check;—*n* **inhibi´tion**, an inhibiting or being inhibited; a mental process that restrains an action, emotion, or thought—*adj* **inhib´ited**.—*n* **inhib´itor**, that which inhibits esp a substance that interferes with a chemical process. [L *inhibēre, -hibitum*—*in*, in, *habēre*, to have.]

inhospitable [in-hos´pit-ȧ-bl] *adj* not showing hospitality; lacking shelter or sustenance.—*ns* **inhos´pitableness, inhospital´ity**.—adv **inhos´pitably**. [OFr,—Low L *inhospitābilis*; cf **hospitable**.]

inhuman [in-hūmȧn] *adj* barbarous, cruel, unfeeling.—*n* **inhumanity** [in-hū-man´i-ti] *adv* **inhū´manly**. [L *inhūmānus*; cf **human**.]

inhumane [in-hū-mān´] *adj* not humane; inhuman. [L *in-*, not, + **humane**.]

inhume [in-hūm´] *vt* to inter—*n* **inhumā´tion**, burial. [L *inhumāre*—*in*, in, *humus*, the ground.]

inimical [in-im´i-kȧl] *adj* unfriendly, hostile; unfavorable (to); opposed (to).—*adv* **inim´ically**. [L *inimīcālis*—*inimīcus*, enemy—*in-*, not, *amīcus*, friend.]

inimitable [in-im´it-ȧ-bl] *adj* that cannot be imitated; matchless.—*adv* **inim´itably**. [L *inimitābilis*; cf **imitable**.]

iniquity [in-ik´wi-ti] *n* wickedness; gross injustice.—*adj* **iniq´uitous**, marked by iniquity.—*adv* **iniq´uitously**. [Fr,—L *iniquitās, -ātis*—*iniquus*, unequal—*in-*, not, *aequus*, equal.]

initial [in-ish´ȧl] *adj* of or at the beginning.—*n* the first letter of each word in a name; a large letter at the beginning of a chapter, etc.—*vt* to put the initials of one's name to;—*pr p* **ini´tialling**; *pt p* **ini´tialled**.—*adv* **ini´tially**.—*vt* **ini´tiate**, to bring (something) into practice or use; to teach the fundamentals of a subject to; to admit as a member into a club, etc. esp with a secret ceremony.—*n* one who is initiated.—*adj* begun; initiated.—*ns* **initiā´tion**, act or process of initiating; act of admitting to a society; **ini´tiative** the action of taking the first step; ability of originate new ideas or methods; the introduction of proposed legislation by voters' petitions.—*adj* **ini´tiatory**, introductory. [L *initium*, beginning.]

inject [in-jekt´] *vt* to force (a fluid) into a vein, tissue, etc. with a syringe or the like; to introduce (a remark, quality, etc.); to throw, drive, force into something.—*n* **injec´tion**, act of injecting [L *injicēre, injectum*—*in*, into, *jacēre*, to throw.]

injudicious [in-jōō-dish´us] *adj* lacking in judgment; indiscreet; unwise; ill-judged.—*adv* **injudic´iously**.—*n* **injudic´iousness**. [L *in-*, not + **judicious**.]

injunction [in-jung(k)´sh(ȯ)n] *n* a command; an order; a court order prohibiting or ordering a given action. [Low L *injunctiō, -ōnis*—*in*, in, *jungēre, junctum*, to join.]

injure [in´jùr] *vt* to wrong; to harm, damage, hurt.—*adj* **injurious** [in-jōō´ri-us].—*adv* **inju´riously**.—*ns* **inju´riousness; injury** [in´jùr-i], that which injures; wrong; damage. [L *injūria*, injury—*in-*, not, *jūs, jūris*, law.]

injustice [in-jus´tis] *n* violation of, or withholding of, another's rights; a wrong; an unjust act. [Fr,—L *injūstitia*—*in-*, not. See **justice**.]

ink [ingk] *n* a colored liquid used for writing, printing, etc.; the dark protective secretion of a cephalopod.—*vt* to cover, mark, or color with ink.—*adj* **ink´y**, like very dark ink in color; black; covered with ink.—*ns* **ink´iness; ink´blot**, any of the patterns that are used in the Rorschuch test; **ink´stand**, inkwell; a small tray with fittings for holding ink and pens; **ink´well**, a container for ink; **ink´y cap, ink cap**, a mushroom (genus *Coprinus*) whose fruiting body melts into an inky fluid after the spores have matured. [OFr *enque* (Fr *encre*)—Low L *encaustum*, purple-red ink used by later Roman emperors.]

inkling [ingk´ling] *n* a hint; a vague notion. [ME *inclen*, to hint.]

inlaid [in-lād´, or in´-] *adj* inserted by inlaying; having a pattern set into the surface. [Pt p of **inlay**.]

inland [in´land, in´lȧnd] *adj* of or in the interior of a country.—*n* [inland´] an inland region.—*adv* [inland´] into or toward this region.—*n* **in´lander**, one who lives inland. [OE *inland*, a domain—**in**, + **land**.]

in-law [in-lö´] *n* a relative by marriage.—*pl* **in-laws´**.

inlay [in-lā´] *vt* to insert; to ornament by inserting pieces of metal, ivory, etc.—*pt p* inlaid.—*n* [in´-] inlaying; inlaid work; material inlaid.—*ns* **inlayer** [in´lā-ėr, in-lā´ėr]; **inlay´ing**. [Adv **in**, + **lay** (2).]

inlet [in´let] *n* a narrow strip of water extending into a body of land. [Adv **in**, + **let** (1).]

in loco parentis [in lō´kō pȧ-ren´tis] in place of a parent. [L.]

inly [in´li] *adv* inwardly; in the heart; thoroughly, entirely. [OE *inlīc*—*in, līc*, like.]

inmate [in´māt] *n* a person confined with others in a prison or institution. [**in** or **inn**, + **mate**.]

inmost [in´mōst] *adj* farthest within; most secret.

inn [in] *n* a small hotel; a restaurant or tavern.—*n* **inn´keeper**, one who keeps an inn. [OE *inn*, an inn, house—*in, inn*, within (adv), from the prep *in*, in.]

innards [in´ȧrdz] *n pl* (*inf*) inner organs or parts. [**inwards**.]

innate [in-āt´, or in´āt] *adj* inborn; inherent.—*adv* **inn´ātely**.—*n* **inn´āteness**. [L *innātus*—*in*, in, *nāsci, nātus*, to be born.]

inner [in´ėr] *adj* farther within; most secret.—*adj* **in´nermost**, inmost.—**inner circle**, the small, exclusive, most influential part of a group; **inner city**, the blighted central sections of a large city; **inner space**, space near the earth's surface, esp under the sea; one's inner self; **in´nerspring mattress**, a mattress with built-in coil springs. [OE *in*, comp *innera*, superl *innemest=inne-m-est*—thus a double superlative.]

inning [in´ing] *n* (*baseball*) a team's turn at bat; a numbered round of play in which both teams have a turn at bat. [**in or inn**.]

innocent [in´o-sėnt] *adj* harmless; inoffensive; blameless; guileless; ignorant of evil; simple, not guilty of a specific crime.—*n* an innocent person, as a child.—*ns* **inn´ocence, inn´ocency**, the quality of being innocent.—*adv* **inn´ocently**. [OFr,—L *innocens, -entis*—*in-*, not, *nocēre*, to hurt.]

innocuous [in-ok´ū-us] *adj* harmless.—*adv* **innoc´uously**.—*n* **innoc´uousness**. [L *innocuus*—*in-*, not, *nocuus*, hurtful—*nocēre*, to hurt.]

innominate [i-nom´i-nāt] *adj* having no name.—**innominate artery**, the first branch given off from the arch of the aorta; **innominate bone**, the large flaring bone forming half of the pelvis in mammals.—Also **hopbone**. [L *in-*, not, *nōmināre, -ātum*, to name.]

innovate [in´o-vāt] *vi* to introduce new methods, devices, etc.; to make changes.—*ns* **innovā´tion; inn´ovātor**. [L *innovāre, -ātum,*—*in*, in, *novus*, new.]

innuendo [in-ū-en´dō] *n* a hint or sly remark usu derogatory; an insinuation.—*pl* **innuen´do(e)s**. [L *innuendō*, by nodding at, ablative gerund of *innuĕre*, to nod to, indicate—*in*, to *nuĕre*, to nod.]

innumerable [in-(n)ū´mėr-ȧ-bl] *adj* too numerous to be counted.—*ns* **innūmerabil´ity, innū´merableness**.—*adv* **innū´merably**. [L *innumerābilis*—L *in-*, not, *numerābilis*, that can be counted.]

inobservant [in-ob-zėr´vȧnt] *adj* lacking attention.—*n* **inobser´vance**. [LL *inobservans* (L *inobservantia*, carelessness)—*in-*, not, *observans*—*observāre*. See **observe**.]

inoculate [in-ok´ū-lāt] *vt* to inject a serum or a vaccine into, esp in order to create immunity; to protect as if by inoculation.—*n* **inoculā´tion**, the process or instance of inoculating; substance used for inoculating, esp an antigen or pathogen to stimulate the production of antibodies. [L *inoculāre, -ātum*—*in*, into, *oculus*, an eye, a bud.]

inoffensive [in-o-fen´siv] *adj* giving no offence; harmless.—*adv* **inoffen´sively**.—*n* **inoffen´siveness**. [L *in-*, not, + **offensive**.]

inoperable [in-op´er-ȧ-bl] *adj* not suitable for surgery. [L *in-*, not, **operate**, suffx *-able*.]

inoperative [in-op´ėr-a-tiv] *adj* not working or functioning. [L *in-*, not, + **operative**. See **operate**.]

inopportune [in-op'ör-tūn, -tūn'] *adj* unseasonable; inconvenient.—*adv* **inopp'ortunely** [or -tūn'-]. [L *inopportūnus*—*in-*, not, *opportūnus*, suitable.]

inordinate [in-ör'di-nȧt] *adj* excessive, immoderate.—*n* **inor'dinateness**.—*adv* **inor'dinately**. [L *inordinātus*—*in-*, not, *ordināre, -ātum*, to arrange, regulate.]

inorganic [in-ör-gan'ik] *adj* not having the structure or characteristics of living organisms.—*adv* **inorgan'ically**.—**inorganic chemistry**, the branch of chemistry dealing with substances not usu classed as organic. [L *in-*, not, + **organic**. See **organ**.]

inosculate [in-os'kū-lāt] *vti* to unite closely.—*n* **inosculā'tion**. [L *in*, in, and *ōsculārī, -ātus*, to kiss.]

inpatient [in'pā-shent] *n* a patient being treated in a hospital while living there.

input [in'po͝ot] *n* what is put in, as power into a machine, data in a computer, etc.—*vt* to enter into a computer. [**in** + **put**.]

inquest [in'kwest] *n* judicial inquiry before a jury esp any case of violent or sudden death. [OFr *enqueste*—LL *inquesta*—L *inquīsīta (rēs)*—*in-quīrēre*, to inquire.]

inquietude [in-kwī'et-ūde] *n* restlessness; uneasiness. [Fr *inquiétude*—LL *inquietūdō*—L *inquiētus*, restless—*in-*, not. See **quiet**.]

inquire [in-kwīr'] *vi* to ask a question or questions; to investigate (*usu with* **into**).—*vt* to seek information about.—*n* **inquir'er**.—*adv* **inquir'ingly**.—*n* **inquir'y**, act of inquiring; investigation; a question.—**inquire after**, to ask about the health of. [Fr,—L *inquīrēre*—*in*, in, *quaerĕre, quaesītum*, to seek.]

inquisition [in-kwi-zish'(ȯ)n] *n* a searching examination; investigation; **Inquisition** (*RC Church*) formerly, the tribunal for suppressing heresy; any relentless questioning or harsh suppression.—*adjs* **inquisit'ional**, relating to inquisition or the Inquisition; **inquis'itive**, inclined to ask many questions; unnecessarily curious; prying.—*adv* **inquis'itively**.—*ns* **inquis'itiveness; inquis'itor**, one who inquires, esp with undue hostility; a member of the Inquisition tribunal.—*adj* **inquisitō'rial**.—*adv* **inquisitō'rially**. [L *inquīsītiō, -ōnis*—*inquīrēre*. See **inquire**.]

in re [in rē, rā] in the matter (of). [L].

in-residence [in rez-id-ėns] *adj* having specific duties, often as a teacher, but given time to work at one's profession.

inroad [in'rōd] *n* an incursion into an enemy's country, a raid; (*fig*) encroachment. [**in** + **road**; cf **raid**.]

insalubrious [in-sa-l(y)o͞o'bri-us] *adj* unhealthy.—*n* **insalū'brity**. [L *insalūbris*—*in-*, not, *salūbris*. See **salubrious**.]

insane [in-sān'] *adj* not sane, mentally ill; of or for insane people; very foolish.—*adv* **insane'ly**.—*n* **insanity** [in-san'iti], lack of sanity; mental disorder. [L *in-*, not, + **sane**.]

insanitary [in-san'i-tȧr-i] *adj* dirty enough to endanger health; contaminated. [L *in-*, not, + **sanitary**.]

insatiable [in-sā'sh(y)ȧ-bl] *adj* that cannot be satisfied.—*ns* **insā'tiableness, insātiabil'ity**.—*adv* **insā'tiably**.—*adj* **insā'tiate**, insatiable. [Fr,—L *insatiābilis*—*in-*, not. See **satiate**.]

inscribe [in-skrīb'] *vt* to mark or engrave (words, etc.) on (a surface); to add (a person's name) to a list; to dedicate (a book) to someone; to autograph; to fix in the mind.—*ns* **inscrīber; inscription** [in-skrip'sh(ȯ)n], something inscribed.—*adj* **inscript'ive**. [L *inscrībĕre, inscriptum*—*in*, upon, *scrībĕre*, to write.]

inscrutable [in-skro͞ot'ȧ-bl] *adj* that cannot be understood; inexplicable; enigmatic.—*ns* **inscrutabil'ity, inscrut'ableness**.—*adv* **inscrut'ably**. [L *inscrūtābilis*—*in-*, not, *scrūtārī*, to search into.]

inseam [in'sēm] *n* the seam from the crotch to the bottom of a trouser leg.

insect [in'sekt] *n* any of a class (Insecta) of small arthropods with three pairs of legs, head, thorax, and abdomen and two or four wings.—*adj* like an insect.—*n* **insec'ticide**, a substance for killing insects. [L *insectum*, pa p of *insecāre*—*in*, into, *secāre*, to cut.]

insectivore [in-sek-tiv'ōr] *n* an order (Insectivora) of mammals, mostly terrestrial, insect-eating, nocturnal in habit, and small in size (as moles and hedgehogs); an insectivorous plant or animal.—*adj* **insectiv'orous**, living on insects. [Modern L *insectum*, an insect, *vorāre*, to devour.]

insecure [in-se-kūr'] *adj* not safe; feeling anxiety; not firm or dependable.—*adv* **insecure'ly**.—*n* **insecur'ity**. [L *in-*, not, + **secure**.]

inseminate [in-sem-'in-āt] *vt* to fertilize; to impregnate; to imbue (with ideas, etc.)—*n* **insemina'tion**. [L *insēmināre*—*in-*, in, *sēmen, -inis*, seed.]

insensate [in-sen'sȧt] *adj* not feeling sensation; stupid; without regard or feeling; cold. [L *insensātus*—*in*, not, *sensātus*, intelligent—*sensus*, feeling.]

insensible [in-sen'si-bl] *adj* unable to perceive with the senses; unconscious; unaware; indifferent; virtually imperceptible.—*n* **insensibil'ity**.—*adv* **insen'sibly**. [L *in-*, not, + **sensible**.]

insensitive [in-sen'si-tiv] *adj* not sensitive; not responsive. [L *in-*, not, and **sensitive**.]

insentient [in-sen'sh(y)ėnt] *adj* not having perception; without life or consciousness. [L *in-*, not, + **sentient**.]

inseparable [in-sep'ȧr-ȧ-bl] *adj* that cannot be separated.—*n* an inseparable companion.—*ns* **insep'arableness, inseparabil'ity**.—*adv* **insep'arably**. [L *in-*, not, + **separable**.]

insert [in-sûrt'] *vt* to put or fit (something) into something else.—*n* [in'sėrt] something inserted.—*n* **inser'tion**. [L *inserĕre, insertum*—*in*, in, *serĕre*, to join.]

inset [in'set] *n* something set in; an insertion or insert.—*vt* [in-set'] to set in, to insert.) [**in** + **set**.]

inshore [in'shōr'] *adj, adv* near or in toward the shore. [**in** + **shore**.]

inside [in'sīd] *n* the inner side, surface, or part; (*pl*) (*inf*) the viscera.—*adj* internal; known only to insiders; secret.—*adv* [in-sīd'] on or in the inside; within; indoors.—*prep* [insīd'] in or within.—*n* **insī'der**, a person inside a given place or group; one having secret or confidential information.—**inside of**, within the time or space of; **inside out**, reversed; (*inf*) thoroughly; **inside track**, an advantageous position. [**in** + **side**.]

insidious [in-sid'i-us] *adj* marked by slyness or treachery; more dangerous than seems evident.—*adv* **insid'iously**.—*n* **insid'iousness**. [L *insidiōsus*—*insidiae*, an ambush—*insidēre*—*in*, in, *sedēre*, to sit.]

insight [in'sīt] *n* the ability to see and understand clearly the inner nature of things esp by intuition; an instance of such understanding. [**in** + **sight**.]

insignia [in-sig'ni-a] *n pl* marks by which anything is known. [L neut pl of *insignis*, remarkable, distinguished—*in*, in, *signum*, a mark.]

insignificant [in-sig-nif'i-kȧnt] *adj* inconsequential; unimportant; petty.—*ns* **insignif'icance, insignif'icancy**.—*adv* **insignif'icantly**. [L *in-*, not, + **significant**.]

insincere [in-sin-sēr'] *adj* not sincere; dissembling; not frank.—*adv* **insincere'ly**.—*n* **insincerity** [-ser'i-ti]. [L *insincērus*—*in*, not. See **sincere**.]

insinuate [in-sin'ū-āt] *vt* to introduce or work in slowly, indirectly, etc.; to hint.—*adj* **insin'uating**, gradually winning confidence and favor; causing doubt by subtle hints.—*adv* **insin'uatingly**.—*n* **insinuā'tion**.—*adj* **insin'uative**.—*n* **insin'uātor**. [L *insinuāre, -ātum*—*in*, in, *sinus*, a curve.]

insipid [in-sip'id] *adj* tasteless; without flavor; dull.—*adv* **insip'idly**.—*ns* **insip'idness, insipid'ity**. [LL *insipidus*—L *in-*, not, *sapidus*, well-tasted—*sapĕre*, to taste.]

insist [in-sist'] *vi* to take and maintain a stand (*often with* **on** *or* **upon**).—*vt* to demand strongly; to declare firmly.—*adj* **insist'ent**, insisting or demanding.—*n* **insist'ence**. [L *insistĕre*—*in*, upon, *sistĕre*, to stand.]

in situ [in sī'tū] in its original place or position. [L *in*, in, *sitū*, abl of *situs*, position, site.]

insobriety [in-so-brī'ė-ti] *n* lack of sobriety. [L *in-*, not, + **sobriety**. *See* **sober**.]

insofar [in-sō-fär'] *adv* to such a degree or extent.

insolate [in'so-lāt] *vt* to expose to the sun's rays.—*n* **insolā'tion** [L *insōlāre, -ātum*—*in*, in, *sōl*, the sun.]

insolent [in'sol-ėnt] *adj* boldly disrespectful; insulting; rude.—*n* **in'solence**.—*adv* **in'solently**. [L *insolens, -entis*—*in-*, not, *solens*, pt p of *solēre*, to be wont.]

insoluble [in-sol'ū-bl] *adj* not capable of being dissolved; not capable of being solved or explained.—*ns* **insolubil'ity, insol'ubleness**. [L *insolūbilis*—*in-*, not, + **soluble**.]

insolvent [in-solv'ėnt] *adj* not able to pay one's debts; bankrupt; pertaining to insolvent persons.—*n* one unable to pay his debts.—*n* **insolv'ency**. [L *in-*, not, + **solvent**. *See* **solve**.]

insomnia [in-som'ni-a] *n* abnormal inability to sleep.—*n* **insom'niac**. [L *insomnis*, sleepless.]

insomuch [in-sō-much'] *adv* to such a degree (that, as); inasmuch (as). [**in, so, much**.]

insouciant [in-so͞o'si-ȧnt] *adj* calm and unbothered, carefree.—*n* **insouciance** [in-so͞o'si-ȧns, ẽ-so͞o-sē-ãs]. [Fr—*in-*, not, *souciant*, pr p of *soucier*—L *sollicitāre*, to disturb.]

inspect [in-spekt'] *vt* to look at carefully; to examine or review officially.—*ns* **inspec'tion, inspec'tor**, one who inspects; an examining officer; a police officer ranking below a superintendent; an examining officer at a polling place; **inspec'torāte**, a body of inspectors. [L *inspectāre*, freq of *inspicĕre, inspectum*—*in*, into, *specĕre*, to look.]

inspire [in-spīr'] *vt* to inhale; to impel, as to some creative effort; to motivate by divine influence; to arouse (a thought or feeling) in (someone); to cause.—*vt* to inhale; to give inspiration.—*n* **inspirā'tion** [in-spir-], an inhaling; a mental or emotional inspiring; any stimulus to creative thought; an inspired idea, action, etc.—*adjs* **inspiratory** [in-spir'atȯr-i, in'spir-], belonging to or aiding inspiration; **inspīred'**, moved or directed as if by divine influence.—*n* **inspīr'er**. [L *inspīrāre*—*in*, in, into, *spīrāre*, to breathe.]

inspirit [in-spir'it] *vt* to fill with spirit. [**in** + **spirit**.]

inspissate [in-spis'āt or in'-] *vti* to thicken.—*n* **inspissā'tion**. [L *in*, in, *spissāre*—*spissus*, thick.]

instability [in-sta-bil'i-ti] *n* lack of firmness, determination. [Fr *instabilité*—L *instabilitās*—*in-*, not. See **stable** (1).]

install, instal [in-stöl'] *vt* to formally place in an office, rank, etc.; to establish in a place; to fix in position for use.—*ns* **installā'tion; instal(l)'ment**, to place in an office by seating in an official seat; **install'ment**, an installing or being installed; a sum of money to be paid at regular specified times; any of several parts, as of a serial.—**install'ment plan**, a system by which debts, as by purchased articles, are paid in installments. [LL *in, stallum*, stall—OHG *stal*.]

instance [in'stȧns] *n* an example; a step in proceeding; an occasion (in the first instance).—*vt* to give as an example.—**at the instance of**, at the suggestion of. [OFr,—L *instantia—instans*. See **instant**.]

instant [in´stànt] *adj* pressing, urgent; (*old fashioned*) as the current month; imminent; immediate; concentrated or precooked for quick preparation, as a food or beverage.—*n* a moment; a particular moment.—*adj* **instantān´eous**, occurring very quickly.—*advs* **instantān´eously; instanter** [in-stan´tėr] L, immediately; **in´stantly**, immediately. **the instant**, as soon as. [L *instans, -antis*, pr p of *instāre*, to be near, press upon, urge—*in*, upon, *stāre*, to stand.]

instead [in-sted´] *adv* in place of the one mentioned. [Prep **in**, + **stead**.]

instep [in´step] *n* the upper part of the arch of the foot, between the ankle and the toes. [Origin obscure.]

instigate [in´sti-gāt] *vt* to urge on, incite; to foment rebellion.—*ns* **instigā´tion**, the act of inciting, esp to evil; **in´stigātor**, an inciter, generally in a bad sense. [L *instigāre, -ātum*.]

instill, instil [in-stil´] *vt* to drop in; to infuse slowly; to put in drop by drop; to put (an idea, etc.) in or into gradually (into the mind).—*pr p* **instill´ing**; *pt p* **instilled´**.—*ns* **instillā´tion; instill´er; instil´ment**. [L *instillāre—in*, in, *stillāre*, to drop.]

instinct [in´stingkt] *n* (an) inborn tendency to behave in a way characteristic of a species; a natural or acquired tendency; a knack.—*adj* [in-stingkt´] infused; imbued.—*adj* **instinc´tive**.—*adv* **instinctively**. [L *instinctus—instinguěre*, to instigate.]

institute [in´sti-tūt] *vt* to set up, establish; to start, initiate.—*n* an organization for the promotion of science, art, etc.; a school, college, or department of a university specializing in some field.—*n* **institū´tion**, an established law, custom, etc.; an organization having a social, educational, or religious purpose; the building housing it; (*inf*) a long-established person or thing.—*adjs* **institut´ional, institut´ionalized**, of a person unable to live independently of the structures of an institution.—*n* **in´stituter; in´stitutor**. [L *instituěre, -ūtum—in*, in, *statuěre*, to cause to stand—*stāre*, to stand.]

instruct [in-strukt´] *vt* to inform; to teach; to educate; to inform; to order or direct.—*n* **instruc´tion**.—*adjs* **instruc´tional; instruc´tive**.—*adv* **instruc´tively**.—*ns* **instruc´tiveness; instruc´tor**, a teacher, a college teacher of the lowest rank. [L *instruěre, instructum—in*, in, *struěre*, to pile up.]

instrument [in´strōō-mėnt] *n* a thing by means of which something is done; a tool or implement; any of various devices for indicating, measuring, controlling, etc.; any of various devices producing musical sound; (*law*) a formal document.—*vt* [-ment´], to address a legal document; to score for musical performance; to equip with indicating, measuring, or controlling devices.—*adj* **instrumental** [-ment´àl], serving as a means; helpful; of, performed on, or written for a musical instrument or instruments.—*ns* **instrument´alist**, one who plays on a musical instrument; **instrumentality** [-mėnt-al´i-ti], agency—*adv* **instrument´ally**.—*n* **instrumentā´tion**, use or provision of instruments; (*mus*) the arrangement of a composition for performance by different instruments; a science concerned with developing and manufacturing instruments for particular purposes.—**instrument flying**, the flying of an aircraft by instruments only; **instrument landing**, a landing made by an aircraft in poor visibility by means of instruments and radio directive and ground devices; **instrument panel**, a panel on which instruments are mounted; a dashboard. [L *instrūmentum—instruěre*, to instruct.

insubordinate [in-sub-ör´din-àt] *adj* not submitting to authority; rebellious.—*n* **insubordinā´tion**. [L *in-*, not, + **subordinate**.]

insubstantial [in-sub-stan´shėl] *adj* unreal; imaginary; weak or flimsy. [L *in-*, not + **substantial**.]

insufferable [in-suf´ėr-à-bl] *adj* intolerable; unbearable.—*adv* **insuff´erably**. [L *in-*, not, + **sufferable**.]

insufficient [in-suf-ish´ėnt] *adj* not enough; not of sufficient power or ability; inadequate.—*n* **insuffic´iency**.—*adv* **insuffic´iently**. [OFr—LL *insufficiens—in-*, not, *sufficěre*. See **suffice**.]

insular [in´sū-làr] *adj* of or like an island or islanders; narrow-minded; illiberal.—*n* **insularity** [-ar´i-ti].—*adv* **in´sularly**.—*vt* **in´sulate**, to set apart; to isolate; to cover with a nonconducting material in order to prevent the escape of electricity, heat, sound, etc.—*ns* **insulā´tion; in´sulator**, one that insulates. [L *insulāris—insula*, an island.]

insulin [in´sė-lin] *n* a hormone vital to carbohydrate metabolism, secreted by islets of tissue in the pancreas; an extract from the pancreas of animals used in the treatment of diabetes. [L *insula*, an island.]

insult [in-sult´] *vt* to treat with indignity or contempt; to affront.—*n* [in´sult] affront, a remark or act hurtful to the feelings or pride.—*adj* **insult´ing**.—*adv* **insult´ingly**. [L *insultāre—insilīre*, to spring at—*in*, upon, *salīre*, to leap.]

insuperable [in-sū´pėr-à-bl] *adj* that cannot be overcome.—*n* **insuperabil´ity**.—*adv* **insu´perably**. [L *insuperābilis—in-*, not, *superābilis—superāre*, to pass over—*super*, above.]

insupportable [in-sup-ōrt´à-bl, ört´] *adj* unbearable, insufferable; that cannot be justified.—*n* **insupport´ableness**.—*adv* **insupport´ably**. [Fr—LL *insupportābilis—in-*, not. See **support**.]

insure [in-shōōr´] *vt* to take out or issue insurance on; to ensure.—*vi* to contract to give or take insurance.—*adj* **insur´able**, that may be insured.—*ns* **insur´ance**, the act or system of insuring; a contract (or **insurance policy**) purchased to guarantee compensation for a specified loss by fire, death, etc.; the amount for which something is insured; the business of insuring against loss; **insur´ed**, a person whose property, life, etc. is insured against loss; **insur´er**, a person or company that insures others against loss. [OFr *enseurer—en*, and *seur*, sure. See **sure**.]

insurgent [in-sûr´jėnt] *adj* rising in revolt.—*n* one who rises in opposition to established authority, a rebel.—*ns* **insur´gence, insur´gency**. [L *insurgens, -entis—in*, upon, *surgěre*, to rise.]

insurmountable [in-sûr-mownt´à-bl] *adj* not surmountable; that cannot be overcome.—*adv* **insurmount´ably**. [L *in-*, not, + **surmountable**.]

insurrection [in-sur-ek´sh(ò)n] *n* a rising or revolt.—*adjs* **insurrec´tional, insurrec´tionary**.—*n* **insurrec´tionist**. [L *insurrectiō, -ōnis—insurgěre*. See **insurgent**.]

insusceptible [in-sus-ep´ti-bl] *adj* not susceptible.—*n* **insusceptibil´ity**. [L *in-*, not, + **susceptible**.]

intact [in-takt´] *adj* unimpaired; whole. [L *intactus—in-*, not, *tangěre*, to touch.]

intaglio [in-tāl´yō] *n* a design carved or engraved below the surface; a printing process in which the ink-carrying areas of the printing surface are hollows below the surface. [It—*in*, into, *tagliare*, to cut—L *tālea*, a cutting, layer.]

intake [in´tāk] *n* that which is taken in; amount taken in; the place in a pipe, etc. where a fluid is taken in. [Adv **in** + **take**.]

intangible [in-tan´ji-bl] *adj* that cannot be touched, incorporeal; representing value but without material being, as good will; that cannot be easily defined.—*n* something intangible.—*ns* **intan´gibleness, intangibil´ity**.—*adv* **intan´gibly**. [Low L *intangibilis*; cf **tangible**.]

integer [in´tė-jėr] *n* any member of the set consisting of the positive and negative whole numbers and zero. Examples: -5, 0, 5.—*adj* **in´tegral** [-gràl], necessary for completeness; whole or complete; made up of parts forming a whole.—*n* the result of a mathematical integration.—*adv* **in´tegrally**.—*vti* **in´tegrāte** to make whole or become complete; to bring (parts) together into a whole; to remove barriers imposing segregation upon (racial groups); to abolish segregation.—*ns* **integrā´tion, integrity** [in-teg´ri-ti], completeness, wholeness; unimpaired condition; honesty, sincerity, etc.—**integral calculus**, a branch of mathematics concerned with finding the limit of a sum of terms; **integrated circuit**, a tiny electronic circuit, usu on a silicon chip. [L *integer—in-*, not, root of *tangěre*, to touch.]

integument [in-teg´ū-mėnt] a natural covering as skin, a rind, a husk, etc.—*adj* **integumentary** [-ment´ār-i]. [L *integumentum—in*, upon, *tegěre*, to cover.]

intellect [int´ė-lekt] *n* the ability to reason or understand; high intelligence; a very intelligent person.—*n* **intellec´tion**, reasoning; thought.—*adjs* **intellect´ive**, of, or related to the intellect; **intellectual** [-ek´tū-àl], of, involving, or appealing to the intellect; requiring intelligence; showing high intelligence.—*n* one with intellectual tastes and interests.—*ns* **intellect´ualism**, adherence to intellectual pursuits or to the exercise of intellect; **intellect´ualist; intellectuality** [-al´i-ti].—*adv* **intellect´ually**. [L *intellectus—intelligěre, intellectum*, to understand—*inter*, between, *legěre*, to choose.]

intelligent [in-tel´i-jėnt] *adj* having or showing intelligence; clever, wise, etc.—*n* **intell´igence**, the ability to learn or understand; the ability to cope with a new situation; news or information; those engaged in gathering secret, esp military, information.—*adj* **intelligential** [-jen´shàl].—*adv* **intell´igently**.—*adj* **intell´igible**, that may be understood; clear.—*ns* **intell´igibleness, intelligibil´ity**.—*adv* **intell´igibly; intelligence quotient**, ratio, commonly expressed as a percentage, or a person's mental age to his actual age; **intelligence test**, a test to determine a person's relative mental capacity. [L *intelligens, -entis*, pr p of *intelligěre*.]

intelligentsia [in-tel-i-jent´si-a] *n* intellectuals collectively. [Russ—L *intelligentia*.]

intemperance [in-tem´pėr-àns] *n* excess of any kind; habitual over-indulgence in intoxicating liquor.—*adj* **intem´perate**, indulging to excess any appetite, esp intoxicating liquors.—*adv* **intem´perately**.—*n* **intem´perateness**. [Fr *intempérance*—L *intemperantia—in-*, not. See **temperance**.]

intend [in-tend´] *vt* to design, to purpose; to mean something to be or be used (for); to mean, to signify.—*adj* **intend´ed**, expected to be in the future.—*n* one's future wife or husband. [OFr *entendre*—L *intenděre, intentum* and *intensum—in*, towards, *tenděre*, to stretch.]

intense [in-tens´] *adj* very strong, concentrated; strained to the utmost, strenuous; marked by much action, strong emotions, etc.—*adv* **intense´ly**.—*ns* **intense´ness, inten´sity**.—*vti* **inten´sify**, to make or become more intense.—*pr p* **intens´ifying**; *pt p* **intens´ified**.—*ns* **intensificā´tion; inten´sion**, intensity; (*logic*) the sum of the qualities implied by a general name.—*adj* **inten´sive**, of or characterized by intensity; thorough; denoting careful attention given to patients right after surgery, etc. (*gram*) giving force or emphasis.—*n* an intensive word.—*adv* **inten´sively**.—*n* **inten´siveness**. [*See* **intend**.]

intent [in-tent´] *adj* firmly directed; having one's attention or purpose firmly fixed.—*n* an intending; something intended; purpose or meaning.—*n* **intention** [in-ten´sh(ò)n], a determination to act in a specified way; anything intended.—*adjs* **inten´tional**, done purposely.—*advs* **inten´tionally, intent´ly**.—*n* **intent´ness**.—**to all intents and purposes**, in every important respect. [See **intend**.]

inter [in-tûr´] *vt* to bury.—*pr p* **interr´ing**; *pt p* **interred´**.—*n* **inter´ment**. [Fr *enterrer*—Low L *interrāre*—L *in*, into, *terra*, the earth.]

inter- [in´tėr] *prefix* [L] meaning: between, among, or involving the individual elements named in the base adjective or singular noun, as *intercultural, interdepartmental, interfaith, intergroup, interracial*; with or on each other.

interact [in-tėr-akt´] *vi* to act upon one another.—*n* **interaction** —*adj* **interactive** [in-tėr-ak´tiv] interacting; allowing two-way communication between a device such as a computer or a compact video disc, and its user. [in-tėr-ak´sh(ȯ)n], mutual action. [L *inter* between, + **act.**]

inter alia [in-tėr a´li-a, ā´] among other things. [L.]

interallied [in-tėr-al´īd or -īd´] *adj* between or among allies. [L *inter*, between, + **allied**. *See* **ally**.]

intercalate [in-tėr´kál-āt] *vt* to insert between others, as a day in a calendar; to interpolate.—*adj* **inter´calary**, inserted between others.—*n* **intercalā´tion**. [L *intercalāre, -ātum*—*inter*, between, *calāre*, to proclaim. See **calends**.]

intercede [in-tėr-sēd´] *vi* to plead on behalf of another; to mediate.—*n* **interced´er**. [L *intercēdĕre, -cessum*—*inter*, between, *cēdĕre*, to go.]

intercept [in-tėr-sept´] *vt* to stop or seize in its course; (*math*) to mark off between two points, lines, etc.—*n* [in´tėr-sept], a point of intersection of two geometric figures; interception by an interceptor.—*ns* **intercep´tor, intercep´ter**, one who or that which intercepts; a light, swift airplane for pursuit or missile designed for defense. **intercep´tion**. [L *intercipĕre, -ceptum*—*inter*, between, *capĕre*, to seize.]

intercession [in-tėr-sesh´(ȯ)n] *n* act of interceding or pleading for another.—*adj* **intercess´ional**.—*n* **intercessor** [-ses´ȯr], one who intercedes; a bishop who acts during a vacancy in a see.—*adjs* **intercessō´rial, intercess´ory**, interceding. [Fr *intercession*—L *intercessiō, -ōnis*—*intercēdĕre*. See **intercede**.]

interchange [in-tėr-chānj´] *vt* to give and take mutually; to exchange, put (each of two things) in the other's place; to alternate.—*n* **in´terchange**, an interchanging; a place on a freeway where traffic can enter or depart.—*adj* **interchange´able**, that may be interchanged.—*ns* **interchange´ableness, interchangeabil´ity**.—*adv* **interchange´ably**. [L *inter*, between, + **change**.]

intercollegiate [in-tėr-ko-lē´ji-ȧt] *adj* between or among colleges and universities. [L *inter*, between, + **collegiate**.]

intercom [in-tėr-kom´] *n* a radio or telephone intercommunication system, as between rooms. [*Inter*nal *com*munication.]

intercommunicate [in-tėr-kom-ūn´ikāt] *vti* to communicate with or to each other or one another.—*n* **intercommunicā´tion**.—**intercommunication system**, a local system for two-way communication using a microphone and loudspeaker at each station.

intercommunion [in-ter-kom-ūn-yûn] *n* interdenominational communion. [L *inter*, between, and **commune**, vb.]

intercostal [in-tėr-kost´ȧl] *adj* (*anat*) between the ribs. [L *inter*, between, *costa*, a rib.]

intercourse [in´tėr-kōrs, -körs] *n* a connection by dealings; sexual union. [OFr *entrecours*—L *intercursus*, a running between—*inter*, between, *currĕre, cursum*, to run.]

interdenominational [in-ter-dė-nom´ina´shunl] *adj* between or among religious denominations. [L *inter*, between, + **denomination**.]

interdict [in-tėr-dikt´] *vt* to prohibit (an action); to restrain from doing or using something.—*n* an official prohibition.—*n* **interdic´tion**.—*adjs* **interdic´tive, interdic´tory**, containing interdiction; prohibitory. [L *interdīcĕre, -dictum*—*inter*, between, *dīcĕre*, to say.]

interest [int´(ė-)rest, -rist] *n* a share in, or a right to, something; anything in which one has a share; (often *pl*) benefit; (usu *pl* those having a common concern or power in a cause, industry, etc.; a feeling of curiosity about something; the power of causing this feeling; money paid for the use of money; the rate of such payment.—*vt* to excite the attention of; to cause to have a share in; to regard as a personal concern.—*adj* **in´terested**, having an interest or concern; affected or biased by personal considerations, etc.—*adv* **in´terestedly**.—*adj* **in´teresting**, engaging or apt to engage the attention or regard; exciting emotion or passion.—*adv* **in´terestingly**.—**compound interest**, interest added to the principal at the end of each period (usually a year) to form a new principal for next period; **in the interest(s) of**, for the sake of, with a view to furthering or to helping. [From obs *interess*, influenced by OFr *interest*—L *interest*, it concerns, 3rd pers sing pres ind of *interesse*—*inter*, between, among, *esse*, to be.]

interface [in´-ter-fās] *n* a surface that forms the common boundary between two parts of matter or space. [L *inter*, between, + **face**.]

interfere [in-tėr-fēr´] *vi* to clash; to come between; to intervene; to meddle; (*sport*) to hinder an opponent in any of various illegal ways.—*ns* **interfēr´ence**, the act of interfering; (radio and television) the interruption of reception by atmospherics or by unwanted signals; **interfēr´er**. [OFr *enterférir*—L *inter*, between, *ferīre*, to strike.]

interferon [in-tėr-fer´on] *n* a protein produced naturally in the body usu by cells in response to a virus. [**interfere**.]

interfuse [in-tėr-fūz´] *vt* to blend; to infuse.—*n* **interfusion** [-fū´zh(ȯ)n]. [L *interfūsus*—*inter*, between, *fundĕre, fūsum*, to pour.]

intergalactic [in-tėr-gal-ak´tic] *adj* between or among galaxies. [L *inter*, between, + **galactic**.]

interglacial [in-tėr-glā´shi-ȧl] *adj* (*geol*) occurring between two glacial epochs. [L *inter*, between, + **glacial**.]

interim [in´tėr-im] *n* the period of time between; meantime.—*adj* temporary.—*adv* meanwhile. [L.]

interior [in-tē´ri-ȯr] *adj* situated within; inner; inland; private.—*n* the interior part, as of a room, country, etc.; the internal or domestic affairs of a country.—*adv* **inte´riorly**.—**interior decoration**, the art or business of decorating and furnishing interiors of homes, offices, etc.—*n* **interior decorator**. [L, comp of assumed *interus*, inward.]

interject [in-tėr-jekt´] *vt* to throw in between; to interrupt with.—*n* **interjec´tion**, (*gram*) an exclamation.—*adj* **interjec´tional**, parenthetical. [L *inter(j)icere, interjectus*—*inter*, between, *jacĕre*, to throw.]

interlace [in-tėr-lās´] *vti* to lace or weave together.—*n* **interlace´ment**. [OFr *entrelacier*—*entre*, between. See **lace**.]

interlard [in-tėr-lärd´] *vt* to intersperse; to diversify. [Fr *entrelarder*—*entre*, between. See **lard**.]

interleave [in-tėr-lēv´] *vt* to arrange (sheets of something) in alternate layers. [L *inter*, between. See **leaf**.]

interline [in-tėr-līn´] *vt* to insert between lines; to write between the lines of.—*adj* **interlinear** [-lin´i-ȧr], written between lines.—*ns* **interlineā´tion**. [L *inter*, between, and **line**—or perh from Low L *interlineāre*.]

interlink [in-tėr-lingk´] *vti* to link together. [L *inter*, between, + **link** (1).]

interlock [in-tėr-lok´] *vt* to lock together; to join with one another.—*vi* to be locked together. [L *inter*, between, + **lock** (1).]

interlocution [in-tėr-lo-kū´sh(ȯ)n] *n* conference.—*n* **interloc´utor**, one who speaks in dialogue.—*adj* **interloc´utory**. [L *interlocūtiō, -ōnis*—*inter*, between, *loquī, locūtus*, to speak.]

interloper [in´tėr-lōp-ėr] *n* one who meddles.—*vi* **interlope´**, to encroach on the rights of others; to intrude. [Prob L *inter*, between, + **lope**.]

interlude [in´tėr-l(y)ōōd] *n* anything that fills time between two events, as music between acts of a play. [L *inter*, between, *lūdus*, play.]

interlunar [in-tėr-l(y)ōō´nȧr] *adj* belonging to the moon's monthly period of invisibility.—Also **interlu´nary**. [L *inter*, between, *lūna*, the moon.]

intermarry [in-tėr-mar´i] *vi* to marry, esp of different races or groups, or of close relatives.—*n* **intermarr´iage**. [L *inter*, between, + **marry**.]

intermeddle [in-tėr-med´l] *vi* to meddle, to interfere officiously.—*n* **intermedd´ler**. [OFr *entremedler, entremesler*—*entre*, between. See **meddle**.]

intermediate [in-tėr-mē´di-ȧt] *adj* in the middle; in between.—*n* (*chem*) a compound formed as a step between the starting material and the final product.—*adj* **intermē´diary**, acting between others; intermediate.—*n* an intermediate agent.—*adv* **intermē´diately**. [Low L *intermediātus*—L *intermedius*—*inter*, between, *medius*, middle.]

interment [in-tėr´mėnt] *n* burial. [**inter**.]

intermezzo [in-tėr-med´zo´ or -met´sō] *n* a short dramatic or musical entertainment between parts of a play, etc.; a movement in a larger instrumental work; a similar independent work. [It,—L *intermedius*.]

interminable [in-tûr´min-ȧ-bl] *adj* lasting, or seeming to last forever; endless.—*n* **inter´minableness**.—*adv* **inter´minably**. [LL *interminābilis*—*in-*, not, *terminus*, a boundary.]

intermingle [in-tėr-ming´gl] *vti* to mingle or mix together. [L *inter*, among, + **mingle**.]

intermit [in-tėr-mit´] *vti* to stop for a time.—*n* **intermission** [-mish´ȯn], act of intermitting; interval of time between parts of a performance.—*adj* **intermitt´ent**, stopping and starting again at intervals; periodic.—*n* **intermitt´ence**. *adv* **intermitt´ently**. [L *intermittĕre, -missum*—*inter*, between, *mittĕre*, to cause to go.]

intermix [in-tėr-miks´] *vt* to mix or to become mixed together.—*n* **intermix´ture**. [L *intermiscēre, -mixtum*—*inter*, among, *miscēre*, to mix.]

intern [in-tûrn´] *vt* to detain and confine within an area.—*n* [in´tûrn], a doctor serving in a hospital, usu just after graduation from medical school; an apprentice journalist, teacher, etc.—Also **interne**.—*ns* **internēē´**, one confined within fixed bounds; **intern´ment**, confinement of this kind. [Fr, *interne*—L *internus*, inward.]

internal [in-tûr´nȧl] *adj* of or on the inside; to be taken inside the body (*internal remedies*); intrinsic; domestic.—*adv* **inter´nally**.—**inter´nal-combust´ion en´gine**, an engine as the automobile, powered by the explosion of a fuel-and-air mixture within the cylinders.—**internal medicine**, the branch of medicine dealing with the treatment of diseases, esp of adults, not requiring surgery; **Internal Revenue Service**, the division of the US Department of the Treasury that collects income and excise taxes and enforces revenue laws. [L *internus*—*inter*, within.]

international [in-tėr-nash´ȯn-ȧl] *adj* between or among nations; concerned with the relations between nations; for the use of all nations; of or for people in various nations.—*ns* **internat´ionalism**, an attitude, belief or policy favoring the practice of cooperation and understanding between nations.—**internat´ionalist**.—*adv* **internat´ionally**.—**international date line**, date line; **international law**, the body of rules accepted by nations as governing their relations to one another; **international air mile, international nautical mile**, a unit of distance in air and sea navigation equal to 6067.1033 feet or 1.852 kilometers; **International Phonetic Alphabet**, a set of signs and letters used to represent human speech sounds; **international pitch** (*mus*), the tuning standard of 440 vibrations per second for A above middle C; **international relations**, a branch of political science dealing with relations, esp foreign policies, between nations; **international unit**, a quantity of a substance, esp a vitamin, that produces a particular biological effect agreed upon as an international standard. [L *inter*, between, + **national**.]

internecine [in-tėr-nē´sīn] *adj* extremely destructive to both sides. [L *internecīnus, -īvus—internecare—inter*, between (used intensively), *necāre*, to kill, *nex, necis*, murder.]

Internet [in´tėr-net] *n* the worldwide system of linked computer networks.

internuncio [in-tėr-nun´shi-ō] *n* a messenger between two parties; a papal legate ranking below a nuncio.—*adj* **internun´cial**, concerning an internuncio; linking sensory and motor neurons. [It *internunzio*, Sp *internuncio*, and L *internuntius—inter*, between, *nuntius*, a messenger.]

interpellation [in-tėr-pel-ā´sh(ō)n] *n* formal questioning of (a foreign minister) concerning an official policy or personal conduct.—*vt* **interpell´ate**. [Fr,—L *interpellāre, -ātum*, to disturb by speaking—*inter*, between, *pellĕre*, to drive.]

interpenetrate [in-tėr-pen´e-trāt] *vt* to penetrate thoroughly;—*n* **interpenetrā´tion**. [L *inter*, between, + **penetrate**.]

interplanetary [in-tėr-plan´ėt-ȧr-i] *adj* between planets. [L *inter*, between, + **planetary**.]

interplay [in´ter-plā] *n* interchange of action and reaction. [L *inter*, between, + **play**.]

Interpol [in´tėr-pol] *n* the *Inter*national Criminal *Pol*ice Commission, directed to international co-operation in the suppression of crime.

interpolate [in-tėr´po-lāt] *vt* to change (a text) by inserting new material; to insert between or among others; (*math*) to estimate a value between two known values.—*ns* **interpolā´tion; inter´polātor**. [L *interpolāre, -ātum—inter*, between, *polīre*, to polish.]

interpose [in-tėr-pōz´] *vti* to place or come between; to intervene (with); to interrupt (with).—*ns* **interpos´er; interposition** [in-tėr-poz-ish´(ō)n], act of interposing; the action of a state when it places its sovereignity between its citizens and the federal government. [Fr *interposer*—L *inter*, between, Fr *poser*, to place. See **pose**].

interpret [in-tûr´pret] *vt* to explain; to translate; to construe; to give one's own conception of, as in a play or musical composition.—*vi* to translate between speakers of different languages.—*adj* **inter´pretable**, capable of being explained.—*n* **interpretā´tion**, act or result of interpreting; an instance of interpretation.—*adj* **inter´pretātive**, containing interpretation.—*adv* **inter´pretatively**.—*n* **inter´preter**, one who translates orally for persons speaking in different languages; a computer program that translates an instruction into machine language. [L *interpretārī, -ātus—interpres, -etis*.]

interregnum [in-tėr-reg´num] *n* the time between two reigns; the time between the cessation of one and the establishment of another government; a pause in a continuous series. [L *inter*, between, *regnum*, rule.]

interrelation [in-tėr-ri-lā´sh(ō)n] *n* reciprocal relation.—*vti* **interrelate´**, to make or be mutually related.—*n* **interrelā´tionship**. [L *inter*, between, + **relation**.]

interrogate [in-ter´ō-gāt] *vti* to question esp formally.—*n* **interrogā´tion**.—*adj* **interrogative** [in-tėr-og´ȧ-tiv], asking a question.—*n* a word (as *who, what, which*) used in asking a question.—*adv* **interrog´atively**.—*ns* **inter´rogātor**, one that interrogates; a radio transmitter and receiver with facilities for displaying the reply; **interrog´atory**, a written question requiring to be answered at the direction of the court.—*adj* **interrogative**.—**interrogation point**, question mark. [L *interrogāre—inter*, between, *rogāre*, to ask.]

interrupt [in-tėr-upt´] *vt* to break into (a discussion, etc.) or break in upon (a speaker, worker, etc.); to make a break in the continuity of.—*vi* to interrupt an action, talk, etc.—*adj* **interrupt´ed**, broken in continuity.—*adv* **interrup´tedly**.—*ns* **interrup´ter, interrup´tion**, act of interrupting.—*adj* **interrup´tive**, tending to interrupt. [L *interrumpĕre, -ruptum—inter*, between, *rumpĕre*, to break.]

intersect [in-tėr-sekt] *vti* to cut across; to cut or cross mutually; to divide by cutting or crossing.—*n* **intersec´tion**, an intersecting; the place where two lines, roads, etc. meet or cross. [L *inter*, between, *secāre, sectum*, to cut.]

interservice [in-tėr-sûr´vis] *adj* between or among branches of the armed forces. [L *inter*, between + **service**.]

intersperse [in-tėr-spûrs´] *vt* to scatter or set here and there; to diversify with things scattered here and there.—*n* **interspersion** [-spėr´sh(ō)n]. [L *interspergĕre, -spersum—inter*, among, *spargĕre*, to scatter.]

interstate [in´tėr-stāt] *adj* between and among states of a federal government. [L *inter*, between, + **state**.]

interstellar [in-tėr-stel´ȧr] *adj* taking place or located among the stars. [L *inter*, between, *stella*, a star.]

interstice [in-tûr´stis] *n* a crack; a crevice; a minute space.—*adj* **interstitial** [-stish´ȧl], occurring in interstices.—[L *interstitium—inter*, between, *sistĕre, stătum*, to stand, set.]

intertidal [in-tėr-tī´dȧl] *adj* (living) between low-water and high-water mark. [L *inter*, between. See **tide**.]

intertwine [in-tėr-twīn´] *vti* to twine together. [L *inter*, together, + **twine**.]

interval [in´tėr-vȧl] *n* a space between things; the time between events; (*mus*) the difference of pitch between two tones. [L *intervallum—inter*, between, *vallum*, a rampart.]

intervene [in-tėr-vēn´] *vi* to come or be between; to occur between two events, etc.; to come in to modify, settle, or hinder some action, etc.—*n* **intervention** [-ven´sh(ō)n], intervening; interference. [L *inter*, between, *venīre*, to come.]

interview [in´tėr-vū] *n* a personal meeting for conference; a meeting in which a person is asked about his views, etc. as by a reporter; a published account of this.—*vt* to have an interview with.—*ns* **interviewee´; interviewer**. [OFr *entrevue—entre*, between, *voir*, to see.]

interweave [in-tėr-wēv´] *vti* to weave together; to connect closely. [L *inter*, together, + **weave**.]

intestate [in-tes´tȧt] *adj* having made no will.—*n* one who dies intestate.—*n* **intes´tacy** [-tȧ-si], the state of being or dying intestate. [L *intestātus—in-*, not, *testārī, -ātus*, to make a will.]

intestine [in-tes´tin] *n* (usu *pl*) lower part of the alimentary canal between the stomach and the anus.—*adj* **intes´tinal**. [L *intestīnus—intus*, within.]

intimate [in´ti-mȧt] *adj* most private or personal; very close or familiar; deep and thorough.—*n* an intimate friend.—*vt* [-māt], to hint or imply.—*n* **in´timacy** [-mȧ-si], state of being intimate.—*adv* **in´timately**.—*ns* **intimā´tion**, indication, hint. [L *intimāre, -ātum—intimus*, innermost—*intus*, within.]

intimidate [in-tim´i-dāt] *vt* to strike fear into esp by threats.—*n* **intimidā´tion**. [L *in*, into, *timidus*, fearful.]

into [in´tŏŏ, in´tōō] *prep* noting passage inwards (*lit, fig*); noting the passage of a thing from one state to another; noting parts made by dividing (eg *folded into four, broken into fragments*. 6 *into* 42 *gives* 7); by (*multiplied into*); (*inf*) interested in. [**in, to**.]

intolerable [in-tol´ėr-ȧ-bl] *adj* that cannot be endured.—*n* **intol´erableness**.—*adv* **intol´erably**.—*adj* **intol´erant**, unwilling to tolerate others' beliefs, etc.—*n* **intol´erance**.—*adv* **intol´erantly**. [L *intolerābilis—in-*, not. See **tolerable**.]

intonate [in´ton-āt] *vti* to intone, to utter.—*n* **intonā´tion**, an intoning; the manner of producing tones with regard to accurate pitch; variations in pitch within an utterance. *vti* **intone** [in-tōn´], to speak or recite in a singing tone; to chant.—*n* **intōn´er**. [Low L *intonāre, -ātum*—L *in tonum*, according to tone.]

in toto [in tō´tō] entirely. [L.]

intoxicate [in-toks´i-kāt] *vt* to poison; to excite greatly.—*ns* **intox´icant**, something that intoxicates esp a drug or an alcoholic drink; an intoxicating agent; **intoxic´ātion**, state of being poisoned; condition of being drunk; excitement to excess. [Low L *intoxicāre, -ātum—toxicum*—Gr *toxikon*, arrow-poison—*toxon*, a bow.]

intra- [in´tra-] *prefix* within, as in **intramus´cūlar**, within a muscle; **in´traur´ban**, within a city; **intravē´nous**, within, or introduced into, a vein. [L *intrā*, within.]

intractable [in-trakt´ȧ-bl] *adj* unmanageable; obstinate.—*ns* **intractabil´ity, intract´ableness**.—*adv* **intract´ably**. [L *intractābilis—in-*, not, and **tractable**.]

intramural [in-trȧ-mūr-el] *adj* within an institution or organization; competitive within the student body; (*med*) occurring within the walls of an organ.

intranet [in´trȧ-net] *n* a system that works in a similar way to the Internet, but which has limited access and may work, for example, in an office.

intransigent [in-tran´si-jėnt or -zi-] *adj* refusing to compromise, irreconcilable.—*n* **intran´sigence**. [Fr *intransigeant*—Sp *intransigente*—L *in-*, not, *transigens, -entis*, pr p of *transigĕre*, to transact. See **transact**.]

intransitive [in-tran´si-tiv] *adj* (*gram*) not transitive; denoting a verb that does not take a direct object.—*adv* **intran´sitively**. [LL *intransitīvus—in-*, not. See **transitive**.]

intreat *See* **entreat**.

intrench *See* **entrench**.

intrepid [in-trep´id] *adj* bold; fearless; brave.—*n* **intrepid´ity**.—*adv* **intrep´idly**. [L *intrepidus—in-*, not, *trepidus*, alarmed.]

intricate [in´tri-kȧt] *adj* involved; complicated.—*ns* **in´tricacy** [-ȧ-si], **in´tricateness**.—*adv* **in´tricately**. [L *intrīcātus—in*, in, *trīcāre*, to make difficulties—*trīcae*, hindrances.]

intrigue [in-trēg´] *n* a secret or underhanded plotting; a secret or underhanded plot or scheme; a secret love affair.—*vi* to engage in intrigue.—*vt* to excite the interest or curiosity of.—*n* **intriguer** [-trēg´ėr].—*adj* **intrigu´ing**.—*adv* **intrigu´ingly**. [Fr,—L *intrīcāre*. See **intricate**.]

intrinsic [in-trin´sik] *adj* belonging to the real nature of a thing; inherent.—*adv* **intrin´sically**. [Fr *intrinsèque*—Low L *intrinsecus—intra*, within, suffx *-in*, *secus*, following.]

intro- [in´trō-, in-trō´-] *prefix* within, into. [L *intrō, inwards*.]

intro [in´tro] *n* (*inf*) introduction. Contraction of **introduction**.

introduce [in-trō-dūs´] *vt* to lead to bring in; to put (into a place); formally to make known or acquainted; to make acquainted with (*with* **to**); to bring into notice, or into practice; to preface.—*n* **introduction** [-duk´sh(ō)n] act of introducing, or of being introduced; first acquaintance with (*with* **to**); preliminary matter to a book.—*adj* **introduc´tory**, serving to introduce; preliminary; prefatory. [L *intrōdūcĕre, -ductum—intrō*, inwards, *dūcĕre*, to lead.]

introit [in-trō´it] *n* (*often cap*) the first part of the Mass (*often* **Introit**); a piece of music at the beginning of a christian worship service. [L *introitus—introīre—intrō*, inwards, *īre, itum*, to go.]

intromit [in-trō-mit´] *vt* to send or put in; to insert.—*pr p* intromitt´ing; *pt p* intromitt´ed.—*n* **intromission** [-mish´(ō)n]. [L *intrō*, inward, *mittĕre, missum*, to send.]

introspect [in-tro-spekt´] *vti* to (engage in) an inspection of one's own mind and feelings, etc.—*n* **introspection** [-spek´sh(ò)n].—*adj* **introspec´tive**. [L *intrō*, within, *specĕre*, to see.]
introvert [in´-trō-vûrt] one who is more interested in his own thoughts, feelings, etc. than in external objects or events.—*vt* to turn inward.—*n* **introver´sion**. [L *intrō*, inwards, *vertĕre, versum*, to turn.]
intrude [in-trōōd´] *vti* to force (oneself) upon others unasked. *ns* **intruder; intrusion** [-trōōzh(ȯn], act of intruding; the forcible entry of rock in a molten state among and through existing rocks.—*adj* **intrusive**, tending or apt to intrude; inserted without justification in spelling or word origin.—*adv* **intrusively**.—*n* **intrusiveness**. [L *in*, in *trūdĕre, trūsum*, to thrust.]
intrust *See* **entrust**.
intuition [in-tū-ish´(ȯ)n] *n* the capacity of the mind by which it immediately perceives the truth of things without reasoning or analysis; a truth so perceived.—*vt* **intu´it**, to apprehend by intuition.—*adj* **intūit´ional**.—*n* **intūit´ionism**, a doctrine that the perception of truth is by intuition; a doctrine that moral principles can be intuited.—*adj* **intū´itive**.—*adj* **intu´itively**. [L *in*, into or upon, *tuērī, tuitus*, to look.]
intumescent [in-tū-mes´ent] *adj* marked by intumescence; (of paint) swelling when exposed to high heat.—*n* **intumes´cence**, a swelling or bubbling up; something swollen or enlarged. [L *in*, in, *tumēscĕre*, to swell.]
Inuit [in-yōō´it] *n* an Eskimo of N America or Greenland; the language of the Inuit people. [Aleut *inuit*, pl of *inuk*, person.]
Inuktitut [i-nook´-ti-toot] *n* the language of the Inuit.
inundate [in´un-dāt] *vt* to cover as with a flood; to deluge.—*n* **inundā´tion**. [L *inundāre, -ātum—in*, in, *undāre*, to rise in waves—*unda*, a wave.]
inure [in-ūr´] *vt* to accustom to pain, hardship, etc.; to habituate.—Also **enure´**.—*n* **inure´ment**. [Prefix *in- en-*, in, and obsolete word *ure*, practice, operation.]
in vacuo [in vak´ū-ō, -ŏŏ-ō, wak´-] in a vacuum. [L.]
invade [in-vād´] *vt* to enter as an enemy; to encroach upon, to violate.—*ns* **invad´er; invasion** [vā´zh(ȯ)n].—*adj* **invasive** [-vā´ziv], marked by military aggression; (of cancer cells) tending to spread; tending to infringe; (*med*) diagnostic methods involving entry into living tissue. [L *invādĕre, invāsum—in*, in, *vādĕre*, to go.]
invalid [in-val´id] *adj* not valid—*adj* **invalid**, [in´val-id], sick, weak and sickly; of or for invalids.—*n* one who is ill or disabled.—*vt* **inval´idāte**, to render invalid; to deprive of legal force.—*ns* **invalidā´tion; invalid´ity**, want of cogency or force; state of illness or disability. [Fr *invalide*—L *invalidus—in-*, not, *validus*, strong—*valēre*, to be strong.]
invaluable [in-val´ū-à-bl] *adj* too valuable to be measured in money.—*adv* **inval´uably**. [L *in-*, not, + **valuable**.]
Invar [in´vär, in-vär´] *n* an alloy of iron and nickel that expands little on heating. [Trademark.]
invariable [in-vā´ri-à-bl] *adj* without variation or change; unalterable; constantly in the same state.—*n* **inva´riableness**.—*adv* **invā´riably**.—*n* **invā´riant**, that which does not alter. [L *in-*, not, and **variable**.]
invasion, invasive *See* **invade**.
invective [in-vek´tiv] *n* a violent abusive attack in speech or writing; abusive or insulting language.—Also *adj*. [Fr,—LL *invectiva* (*ōrātiō*) abusive (speech)—*invehĕre, invectum*. See **inveigh**.]
inveigh [in-vā´] *vi* to make an attack with words, to rail (against). [L *invehĕre, invectum—in*, in, *vehĕre*, to carry.]
inveigle [in-vē´gl also in-vā´gl] *vt* to entice or trick into doing something.—*n* **invei´glement**. [Prob altered from Anglo-Fr *enveogler* (Fr *aveugler*), to blind to—L *ab*, from, oculus, the eye.]
invent [in-vent´] *vt* to think up; to think out or produce (a new device, process, etc.) to originate.—*n* **inven´tion**, that which is invented; the power of inventing.—*adj* **inven´tive**, of invention; skilled in inventing.—*adv* **inven´tively**.—*ns* **inven´tiveness; inven´tor**. [L *invenīre, inventum—in*, upon, *venīre*, to come.]
inventory [in´ven-tȯr-i] *n* an itemized list of goods, property, etc. as of a business; the store of such goods for such listing; a list of the property of an individual or an estate.—*vt* to make an inventory of. [LL *inventōrium*, for L *inventārium*, a list of things found—*invenīre*, to find.]
inverse [in´vėrs, in-vûrs´] *adj* inverted; directly opposite.—*n* any inverse thing.—*adv* **inverse´ly**.—*n* **inver´sion**, the act of inverting; the state of being inverted; a change of order or position; homosexuality; conversion of direct current into alternating current. [L *inversus*, pr p of *invertĕre*. See **invert**.]
invert [in-vûrt´] *vt* to turn upside down; to reverse the customary order or position of.—*adj* **inver´ted**, turned upside down; reversed.—**invert sugar**, dextrose obtained from starch. [L *invertĕre, inversum—in*, in, *vertĕre*, to turn.]
invertebrate [in-vûrt´e-brāt] *n* an animal without a backbone.—Also *adj*. [L *in-*, not, + **vertebrate**.]
invest [in-vest´] *vt* to clothe; to install in office with ceremony; to furnish with power, authority, etc.; to put (money) into business, bonds, etc. for profit.—*vi* to invest money.—*ns* **inves´titure**, ceremony of investing; **invest´ment**, the act of investing; money invested; that in which money is invested; **inves´tor**, one who invests money.—**investment company**, a company whose primary function is holding securities of other companies purely for investment purposes. [L *investīre, -ītum—in*, on, *vestīre*, to clothe.]
investigate [in-vest´i-gāt] *vti* to search (into); to inquire.—*n* **investigā´tion**.—*adjs* **invest´igātive, invest´igātory**.—*n* **invest´igātor**. [L *investīgāre, -ātum—in*, in, *vestīgāre*, to track.]
inveterate [in-vet´ėr-àt] *adj* firmly established; habitual.—*adv* **invet´erately**.—*ns* **invet´erateness, invet´eracy** [-à-si] state of being obstinate. [L *inveterātus*, stored up, long continued—*in*, in, *vetus, veteris*, old.]
invidious [in-vid´i-us] *adj* likely to provoke ill-will; offensively discriminating (eg *an invidious distinction*).—*adv* **invid´iously**.—*n* **invid´iousness**. [L *invidiōsus—invidia*, envy.]
invigorate [in-vig´ȯr-āt] *vt* to give vigor to; to fill with energy.—*n* **invigorā´tion**. [L *in*, in, *vigor*. See **vigor**.]
invincible [in-vin´si-bl] *adj* that cannot be overcome; unconquerable.—*ns* **invin´cibleness, invincibil´ity**.—*adv* **invin´cibly**. [Fr,—L *invincibilis—in-*, not, *vincĕre*, to overcome.]
inviolable [in-vī´ōl-à-bl] *adj* not to be violated; not to be profaned or injured; sacred; indestructible.—*ns* **inviolabil´ity, invī´olableness**, the quality of being inviolable.—*adv* **invī´olably**.—*adjs* **invī´olāte, -d**, not violated; unprofaned; not broken. [Fr,—L *inviolābilis—in-*, not, *violābilis—violāre*, to injure, profane.]
invisible [in-viz´i-bl] *adj* incapable of being seen; unseen; out of sight; imperceptible.—*ns* **invisibil´ity, invis´ibleness**.—*adv* **invis´ibly**. [Fr,—L *invīsibilis—in-*, not. See **visible**.]
invite [in-vīt´] *vt* to ask to come somewhere or do something; to ask for; to give occasion for (*his conduct invites gossip*); to tempt; to entice.—*n* (*inf*) an invitation.—*ns* **invitation** [in-vi-tā´sh(ȯ)n], the act of inviting; a message used in inviting; **invitēe**, an invited person; **invīt´er**.—*adj* **invīt´ing**, alluring, attractive.—*adv* **invit´ingly**, in an inviting manner. [L *invītāre, -ātum*.]
in vitro [in vēt´ro] *adj, n* outside the living body. [L.]
in vivo [in vē´vō] in the living organism. [L.]
invocation [in-vō-kā´sh(ȯ)n] *n* an invoking of God, the Muses, etc.—*adj* **invocatory** [in-vok´a-tȯr-i]. [OFr,—L *invocātiō, -ōnis—invocāre*. See **invoke**.]
invoice [in´vois] *n* a letter of advice of the dispatch of goods, with particulars of their price and quantity.—*vt* to present an invoice for or to. [Prob pl of Fr *envoi*.]
invoke [in-vōk´] *vt* to call on (God, the Muses, etc.) for help, blessing, etc.; to resort to (a law, etc.) as pertinent; to conjure; to beg for; to implore. [Fr *invoquer*—L *invocāre, -ātum—in*, on, *vocāre*, to call.]
involucre [in´vol-(y)ōō-kėr] *n* (*bot*) a whorl of bracts close to a flower, a flower cluster or fruit. [L *involūcrum—involvĕre*, to involve.]
involuntary [in-vol´un-tàr-i] *adj* not done by choice; not consciously controlled.—*adv* **invol´untarily**.—*n* **invol´untariness**. [LL *involuntārius—in-*, not. See **voluntary**.]
involute [in´vol-(y)ōōt] *adj* curled spirally; curled or curved inward; involved; intricate; rolled inward at the margins; turned inward.—*n* that which is involved or rolled inward; a curve traced by the end of a string unwinding itself from another curve.—*n* **involu´tion**, the action of involving; state of being entangled; a complication (*math*) raising to a power. [L *involūtus—involvĕre*. See **involve**.]
involve [in-volv´] *vt* to complicate; to implicate; to affect or include; to require; to occupy, to make busy.—*n* **involve´ment**. [L *involvĕre—in*, in, *volvĕre, volūtum*, to roll.]
invulnerable [in-vul´nėr-àbl] *adj* that cannot **invulnerabil´ity, invul´nerableness**.—*adv* **invul´nerably**. [L *invulnerābilis—in-*, not. See **vulnerable**.]
inward [in´wȧrd] *adj* placed or being within, internal; mental or spiritual; directed toward the inside.—*adv* toward the inside; into the mind or soul.—*advs* **in´wardly**, within; in the mind or spirit; toward the inside or center; **in´wards**, inward. [OE *inneweard* (adv).]
in-wrought [in-röt´] *adj* worked in, esp as embroidered decoration. [Adv **in**, + **wrought**.]
iodine [īo-dēn, -dīn, -din] *n* a nonmetallic element (symbol I; at wt 126.9. no 53); tincture of iodine.—*vt* **i´odize**, to treat with iodine.—*n* **iōd´oform**, a compound of iodine used as an antiseptic. [Gr *ioeidēs, iōdēs*, violet-coloured—*ion*, a violet, *eidos*, form.]
ion [ī´ȯn] *n* an electrically charged atom or group of atoms formed through the gain or loss of one or more electrons.—*vti* **i´onize**, to dissociate into ions, as a salt dissolved in water, or become electrically charged, as a gas under radiation.—*n* **ion´osphere**, the region of the earth's atmosphere about 30 to 300 miles above the earth.—**ion exchange**, transfer of ions from a solution to a solid or another liquid used in water-softening and many industrial processes. [Gr *iȯn*, neut pr p of *ienai*, to go.]
Ionic [ī-on´ik] *adj* denoting a Greek style of architecture distinguished by the ornamental scrolls on the capitals. [Gr *Iōnikos, Iōnios*.]
iota [ī-ō´ta] *n* the ninth letter of the Greek alphabet; a very small quantity; a jot. [Gr *iōta*, the smallest letter in the alphabet, I, *i*; Heb *yōd*.]
IOU [īōū] standing for *I owe you*; a signed note bearing these letters, acknowledging a specified debt.
ipecac [ip´e-kak] *n* an emetic made from the dried roots of a S American plant; any of several roots used in the same way. [Port from Amer Indian.]
ipse dixit [ip´sē dik´sit] an unproved assertion. [L.]

ipso facto [ip´sō fak´tō] by the fact (or act) itself. [L.]

IQ, I.Q a number indicating a person's level of intelligence based on a test. [*i*ntelligence *q*uotient.]

ir- [ir-] *pfx* a form of **in-** used before *r*.

Iranian [ī-rān´i-ȧn] *adj, n* (native or inhabitant) of Iran.—*n* branch of the Indo-European languages to which Persian, the official language of Iran, belongs. [Pers *Irān*, Persia.]

Iraqi [i-rä´kē] *n* a native of Iraq; the form of Arabic spoken in Iraq.—Also *adj* [Ar *'Irāqi*.]

irascible [ir-as´i-bl] *adj* easily angered; hot-tempered.—*n* **irascibil´ity**.—*adv* **iras´cibly**. [Fr,—L *īrāscibilis—īrāscī*, to be angry—*īra*, anger.]

ire [īr] *n* anger; wrath.—*adjs* **irate** [ī-rāt´ or īr´āt], enraged, angry; **ire´ful**, full of wrath; resentful.—*adv* **ire´fully**. [L *īra*, anger.]

iris [ī´ris] *n* the round, pigmented membrane surrounding the pupil of the eye; any of a large genus (*Iris*) of perennial herbaceous plants with sword-shaped leaves and a showy flower; the rainbow; an appearance resembling the rainbow.—*pl* **i´rises**.—*n* **iridescence** [ir-i-des´ėns], play of rainbow colors, as on bubbles, mother-of-pearl.—*adjs* **irides´cent**.—*ns* **irid´ium**, noble metallic element (symbol Ir; at wt 192.2; at no 77); **iridosmine** [ir-id-oz´min, or īr-, or -os´-], a native alloy of iridium and osmium. **irī´tis**, inflammation of the iris of the eye. [Gr *Iris, -idos*, the messenger of the gods, the rainbow.]

Irish [ī-rish] *adj* of Ireland, its people, etc.—*n* the Celtic language of Ireland; the English dialect of Ireland.—the **Irish**, the natives or inhabitants of Ireland.—**Irish coffee**, brewed coffee with Irish whiskey, topped with whipped cream; **Irish setter**, a breed of bird dog with a mahogany red coat; **Irish whiskey**, whiskey made in Ireland chiefly of barley; **Irish wolf´hound**, a breed of tall sturdy hound with a rough wiry coat.

irk [ûrk] *vt* to annoy, irritate, tire out, etc.—*adj* **irk´some**, tedious; burdensome.—*adv* **irk´somely**.—*n* **irk´someness**. [ME *irken*.]

iron [ī´ėrn] *n* a metallic element (symbol Fe; at wt 55.9; at no 26), the most common of all metals; tool, etc. of this metal, esp one with a heated flat underface for pressing cloth; (*pl*) shackles of iron; firm strength; power; any of certain golf clubs with angled metal heads.—*adj* of iron; like iron, strong and firm.—*vti* to press with a hot iron.—**i´ronclad**, clad in iron; difficult to change or break (*an ironclad lease*)—*ns* **i´ron gray´**, a slightly greenish dark gray; **i´ron hand**, strict and rigorous control.—*adj* **i´ron-heart´ed**, unfeeling; cruel.—*ns* **i´ronside**, a man of great strength or bravery; **i´ronstone**, any rock consisting of mainly iron-bearing ore; tough durable earthenware; **i´ronware**, things made of iron; **i´ronwood**, the hop hornbeam (*Ostrya virginiana*), a deciduous tree of eastern N America; the tough wood of this tree; **i´ronwork**, work, esp decorative, done in iron (*pl*) building in which iron is smelted, cast, or wrought.—**Iron Age**, the era of iron implements beginning in central Europe from about the 7th century BC until the Christian era; **iron curtain**, any barrier that separates communities or ideologies. **iron lung**, a large respirator that encloses all of the body but the head; **i´ron maiden**, a medieval instrument of torture, consisting of an enclosed space lined with spikes; **iron ration**, an emergency ration. [OE *īren*, (*īsern, īsen*); Ger *eisen*.]

irony [ī´rȯni or ī-ėr-nī] *n* expression in which the intended meaning of the words is the opposite of their usual sense; an event or result that is the opposite of what is expected.—*adjs* **ironic** [ī-ron´ik], **iron´ical**.—*adv* **iron´ically**. [L *irōnia*—Gr *eirōneiā*, dissimulation—*eirōn*, a dissembler, perh *eirein*, to talk.]

Iroquois [ir´ekwoi,-kwä] *n* Amerindian confederacy of New York comprising Cayuga, Mohawk, Oneida, Onandaga, Seneca, and later Tuscaroro tribes; any member of these peoples.—*pl* **-ois**.—*n* **Iroquoi´an**, Amerindian language family spoken in upper New York state, Oklahoma, and North Carolina. [Algonquin.]

irradiate [ir-ā´di-āt] *vt* to shine upon; to light up; to enlighten; to radiate; to expose to X-rays or other radiant energy.—*vi* to emit rays; to shine.—*n* **irrā´diance**.—*adj* **irrā´diant**.—*n* **irradiā´tion**, emission of radiant energy; exposure to radiation (as X-rays). [L *irradiāre, -ātum—in*, on; cf **radiate**.]

irrational [ir-ash´ȯn-ȧl] *adj* lacking the power to reason; senseless; unreasonable; absurb.—**irrational number**, a real number which cannot be expressed as a ratio of two integers, as the square root of minus two.—*n* **irrational´ity**.—*adv* **irra´tionally**. [L *irratiōnālis—in-*, not. See **rational**.]

irreclaimable [ir-i-klām´ȧ-bl] *adj* that cannot be reclaimed.—*adv* **irreclaim´ably**. [L *in-*, not, and **reclaimable**.]

irreconcilable [ir-ek-ȯn-sīl´ȧ-bl] *adj* that cannot be brought into agreement; incompatible.—*n* **irreconcil´ableness**.—*adv* **irreconcil´ably**. [L *in-*, not, + **reconcilable**.]

irrecoverable [ir-i-kuv´ėr-ȧ-bl] *adj* irretrievable, beyond recovery.—*adv* **irrecov´erably**. [L *in-*, not, + **recoverable**.]

irredeemable [ir-i-dēm´ȧ-bl] *adj* that cannot be brought back; that cannot be converted into coin, as certain paper money; that cannot be changed or reformed.—*adv* **irredeem´ably**. [L *in-*, not, + **redeemable**.]

irreducible [ir-i-dūs´i-bl] *adj* that cannot be reduced or brought from one degree, form, or state to another; not to be lessened.—*adv* **irreduc´ibly**. [L *in-*, not, + **reducible**.]

irrefragable [ir-ef´rȧ-gȧ-bl] *adj* that cannot be refuted; that cannot be changed.—*n* **irrefragability**.—adv irref´ragably. [L *irrefrāgābilis—in-*, not, *re-*, backwards, *frangěre*, to break.]

irrefutable [ir-ef´ūt-ȧ-bl or -ūt´-] *adj* indisputable.—*adv* **irref´ūtably** [also -ūt´-]. [LL *irrefūtābilis—in-*, not. See **refutable**.]

irregular [ir-eg´ū-lȧr] *adj* not regular; not conforming to rule; not straight, even, or uniform; (*gram*) not inflected in the usual way.—*n* **irregularity** [-lar´i-ti].—*adv* **irreg´ularly**. [OFr *irregular*—Low L *irrēgulāris—in-*, not. See **regular**.]

irrelevant [ir-el´ė-vȧnt] *adj* not pertinent; not to the point.—*ns* **irrel´evance, irrel´evancy**.—*adv* **irrel´evantly**. [L *in-*, not, + **relevant**.]

irreligious [ir-i-lij´us] *adj* impious.—*adv* **irrelig´iously**.—*n* **irrelig´ion**, state of being irreligious. [L *irreligiōsus—in-*, not. See **religious**.]

irremediable [ir-i-mē´di-ȧ-bl] *adj* beyond remedy or correction.—*n* **irremē´diableness**.—*adv* **irremē´diably**. [L irremediābilis—in-, not. See **remediable**.]

irremovable [ir-i-mōōv´ȧ-bl] *adj* not removable.—*n* **irremovabil´ity**.—*adv* **irremov´ably**. [L *in-*, not, + **removable**.]

irreparable [ir-ep´ȧr-ȧ-bl] *adj* irretrievable.—*n* **irrep´arableness**.—*adv* **irrep´arably**. [Fr *irréparable*.—L *irreparābilis—in-*, not. See **reparable**.]

irreplaceable [ir-i-plās´ȧ-bl] *adj* that cannot be replaced. [L *in-*, not, + **replaceable**.]

irrepressible [ir-i-pres´i-bl] *adj* that cannot be repressed.—*adv* **irrepress´ibly**. [L *in-*, not, + **repressible**.]

irreproachable [ir-i-prōch´ȧ-bl] *adj* free from blame; faultless.—*adv* **irreproach´ably**. [L *in-*, not, + **reproachable**.]

irresistible [ir-i-zist´ibl] *adj* that cannot be resisted; too strong, fascinating, etc. to be withstood with success; overmastering; extremely charming.—*ns* **irresist´ibleness**.—*adv* **irresist´ibly**. [L *in-*, not, + **resistible**.]

irresolute [ir-ez´ȯl-(y)ōōt] *adj* not firm in purpose; hesitating.—*adv* **irres´olutely**.—*ns* **irres´oluteness, irresolūtion** [-ōō´sh(o)n, -ū´sh(ȯ)n], want of resolution. [L *irresolūtus—in-*, not, + **resolute**.]

irrespective [ir-i-spek´tiv] *adj* regardless (*with* **of**).—*adv* **irrespec´tively**. [L *in-*, not, + **respective**.]

irresponsible [ir-i-spons´i-bl] *adj* not responsible for actions; lacking a sense of responsibility.—*n* **irresponsibil´ity**.—*adv* **irrespons´ibly, irresponsive** [ir-i-spons´iv] *adj* not responding; not inclined to respond.—*n* **irrespons´iveness**. [L *in-*, not, + **responsible**.]

irretrievable [ir-i-trēv´ȧ-bl] *adj* not to be retrieved.—*n* **irretriev´ableness**.—*adv* **irretriev´ably**. [L *in-*, not, + **retrievable**.]

irreverent [ir-ev´ėr-ėnt] *adj* not reverent; showing disrespect.—*n* **irrev´erence**.—*adv* **irrev´erently**. [L *irreverens—in-*, not. See **reverent**.]

irreversible [ir-i-vûrs´i-bl] *adj* not reversible; that cannot be recalled or annulled.—*ns* **irreversibil´ity, irrevers´ibleness**.—*adv* **irrevers´ibly**. [L *in-*, not, + **reversible**.]

irrevocable [ir-ev´ok-ȧ-bl] *adj* that cannot be undone or revoked.—*n* **irrev´ocableness**.—*adv* **irrev´ocably**. [Fr *irrévocable*—L *irrevocābilis—in-*, not, **revocable**. See **revoke**.]

irrigate [ir´i-gāt] *vt* to supply (land) with water as by means of artificial ditches, pipes, etc.; (*med*) to wash out (a cavity, wound, etc.).—*ns* **irrigā´tion, irrigāt´or**. [L irrigāre, -ātum, to water—*in*, upon, *rigāre*, to wet.]

irritate [ir´i-tāt] *vt* to provoke to anger; to annoy; to make inflamed or sore.—*adj* **irr´itable**, easily annoyed, irritated, or provoked; (*med*) excessively sensitive to a stimulus.—*ns* **irr´itableness, irritabil´ity**, the quality of being easily irritated; the susceptibility to stimuli possessed by living matter.—*adv* **irr´itably**.—*adj* **irr´itant**, irritating.—*n* that which causes irritation.—*n* **irritā´tion**, act of irritating or exciting; excitement; anger, annoyance; (*med*) a condition of irritability, soreness, inflammation of a part of the body.—*adj* **irr´itātive**, tending to irritate or excite; accompanied with or caused by irritation. [L *irrītāre, -ātum*.]

irruption [ir-up´sh(ȯ)n] *n* a breaking or bursting in; (*ecology*) an abrupt increase in size of population; a sudden invasion or incursion.—*adj* **irrup´tive**, rushing suddenly in.—*adv* **irrup´tively**. [L *irrumpěre, irruptum—in*, in, *rumpěre*, to break.]

IRS, I.R.S. Internal Revenue Service.

is [iz] third pers sing pres indic of **be**. [OE *is*; Ger *ist*, L *est*, Gr *esti*, Sans *asti*.]

Isaiah [ī-zā´e] *n* (*Bible*) 23d book of the Old Testament, written by Isaiah, a prophet, about the deliverance of man.

Isais [i-zā´es] *n Bible* Isaiah in the Douay Version of the Bible.

isch emia [is-kē´mi-ȧ] *n* a deficiency of arterial blood in a part of the body. [Gr *ischein*, to restrain, *haima*, blood.]

ISDN [abbrev] integrated services digital network. A means of transmitting data, voice and video digitally over a telecommunications line.

-ish *adj suffix* meaning: of a specified people [Span*ish*], like (boy*ish*), somewhat (tall*ish*), and (*inf*) approximately (thirty*ish*). [OE *-isc*].]

isinglass [ī´zing-glās] *n* a gelatin prepared from fish bladders; mica, esp in thin sheets. [App from obs Du *huizenblas—huizen*, a kind of sturgeon, *blas*, a bladder.]

Islam [is´läm or iz´-, or is-läm´] *n* the Muslim religion, a montheistic religion founded by Mohammed; Muslims collectively or the lands in which they predominate.—*adj* **Islam´ic**.—*n* **Is´lamism**, the faith or cause of Islam.—*vt* **Is´lamize**, to convert to Islam.—**Islamic Calendar**, a lunar calendar organized in 30-year cycles and reckoned from the Hegira in 622 AD; **Islamic era**, the era for numbering Islamic calendar years from 622 AD. [Ar *islām*, surrender (to God).]

island [ī´land] *n* a land mass smaller than a continent and surrounded by water; anything like this in position or isolation.—**islander** [ī´land-ėr], a native or inhabitant of an island. [ME *iland*—OE *īegland, īgland, ēgland*—*īeg, īg, ēg*, island (from a root which appears in Angles*ea*, Alder*ney*, etc., OE *ēa*, L *aqua*, water), and *land*. The *s* is due to confusion with *isle*.]

isle [īl] *n* an island, esp a small one. **islet** [ī´let], a little isle. [ME *ile, yle*—OFr *isle*—L *insula*.]

-ism, -asm or [(with **-ic**) **-icism**], *suffx* forming abstract nouns signifying condition, system, as ego*ism*, Calvin*ism*, Angl*icism*. [L *-ismus, -asmus*—Gr *-ismos, -asmos*.]

ism [izm] *n* any distinctive doctrine, theory or practice. [From the suffx *-ism*.]

iso- [ī-sō-] in composition, equal. [Gr *isos, equal*];—eg **isochromatic** [ī-sō-krō-mat´ik].—*adj* having the same colour (Gr *chrōma, -ātos*, colour); **isochronal** [ī-sok´ron-ȧl], **isoch´ronous** [-us].—*adjs* of equal time; performed in equal times. [Gr *chronos*, time.]

isobar [ī´sō-bär] *n* a line on a map passing through places of equal barometric pressure. [Gr *isos*, equal, *baros*, weight.]

isohyet [ī-sō-hī´et] *n* a line on a map connecting areas of equal rainfall. [Gr *isos*, equal, *hȳetos*, rain—*hȳein*, to rain.]

isolate [ī´sō-lāt] *vt* to set apart from others; to place alone.—*n* a person or thing that is isolated.—*ns* **isolā´tion; isolā´tionism**, the policy of avoiding political entanglements with other countries; **isolātionist**. [It *isolare*—*isola*—L *insula*, an island.]

isomer [ī´sō-mer] any of two or more chemical compounds whose molecules contain the same atoms but in different arrangements.—*adj* **isomer´ic**.—*n* **isom´erism**. [Gr *isos*, equal, *meros*, part.]

isometric [ī-sō-met´rik] *adj* equal in measure; of isometrics.—*ns* **isometr´ics**, system of strengthening the muscles by opposing one muscle to another or to a resistant object; **isom´etry**, mapping of a metric space.—**isometric drawing**, representation of an object in isometric drawing but with parallel lines drawn in true length; **isometric projection**, an isometric drawing in which all the edges are equally foreshortened. [Gr *isos*, equal, *metron*, measure.]

isomorphic [ī-sō-mörf´ik] *adj* having identical or similar form or shape or structure.—*n* **isomorph´ism**. [Gr *isos*, equal, *morphē*, form.]

isopod [ī´sō-pod] *n* any of an order (Isopoda) of crustaceans with no shell, unstalked eyes, and seven pairs of nearly equal legs.—Also *adj*. [Gr *isos*, equal, *pous, podos*, a foot.]

isosceles [ī-sos´e-lēz] *adj* denoting a triangle with two equal sides. [Gr *isoskelēs*—*isos*, equal, *skelos*, a leg.]

isotherm [ī´so-thėrm] *n* a line on a map connecting points of the same temperature.—*adv* **isotherm´ally**. [Gr *isos*, equal, *thermē*, heat—*thermos*, hot.]

isotope [ī´sō-tōp] *n* any of two or more forms of an element having the same atomic number but different atomic weights.—*adj* **isotopic** [-top´ik].—*n* **i´sotopy** [-tō-pē, ī-sät´ė-pē]. [Gr *isos*, equal, *topos*, place.]

Israelite [iz´ri-ėl-īt] *n* any of the people of ancient Israel.—*adj* **Israeli** [iz-rā´li] of modern Israel or its people.—*n* a native or inhabitant of modern Israel (*pl*)—**lis, -li**. [Gr *Israēlītēs*—*Israēl*, Heb *Yisrāēl*, perh contender with God—*sara*, to fight, *El*, God.]

issue [ish´(y)ōō, is´ū] *n* an outgoing; an outlet; a result; offspring; a point under dispute; a sending or giving out; all that is put forth at one time (an issue of bonds, a periodical, etc.); (*med*) a discharge of blood, etc.—*vi* to go or flow out; to result (from) or end (in); to be published.—*vt* to let out; to discharge; to give or deal out, as supplies; to publish—**at issue**, in dispute; **take issue**, to disagree. [OFr *issue*—*issir*, to go or flow out—L *exire*—*ex*, out, *ire*, to go.]

-ist [-ist] a suffix meaning: one who does, makes, or practices (satir*ist*), one skilled or occupied with (violin*ist*, drugg*ist*), an adherent (anarch*ist*). [L *-ista*—Gr *istēs*.]

isthmus [is(th)´mus] *n* a narrow strip of land having water at each side and connecting two larger bodies of land. [L,—Gr *isthmos*, from root of *ienai*, to go.]

it [it] *pron* the thing spoken of; the subject of an impersonal verb (*it is raining*); a subject or object of indefinite sense in various constructions (*it's all right, he lords it over us*).—*n* the player, as in tag, who must catch another.—**with it**, (*slang*) alert, informed, or hip. [OE *hit*, neut of *he*; Du *het*; akin to Ger *es*, L *id*, Sans *i*, pronominal root = here. The *t* is an old neuter suffix, as in *that, what*, and cognate with *d* in L *illud, istud, quod*.]

Italian [i-tal´yȧn] *adj* of or relating to Italy or its people. *n* a native or citizen of Italy; the language of Italy, which is a Romance language.—*vt* **Ital´ianīse**, to make Italian.—*adjs* **Italianate, Italianes´que** [-ešk], Italian in style or character. [L *Italiānus* and Gr *Italikos*—*Italia*, Italy.]

italic [i-tal´ik] *adj* denoting a type in which the letters slant upward to the right (*this is italic type*).—*n* (usu *pl*) italic type or handwriting. **Italic**, the branch of the Indo-European language family including all of the modern Romance languages. [its early use in Italy.]

itch [ich] *n* an uneasy irritating sensation in the skin; an eruptive disease in the skin, caused by a parasitic mite; a constant teasing desire.—*vi* to have an uneasy irritating sensation in the skin; to have a constant, teasing desire.—*adj* **itch´y**, pertaining to or affected with itch.—*n* **itch´iness**. [OE *giccan*, to itch; Ger *jucken*, to itch.]

item [ī´tem] *n* an article; a unit; a separate thing; a bit of news or information.—*vt* **i´temize**, to specify the items of; to set down by items.—*n* **itemiza´tion**. [L *item*, likewise.]

iterate [it´ėr-āt] *vt* to do again; to say again, repeat. *n* **iterā´tion**.—*adj* **it´erātive**. [L *iterāre, -ātum*—*iterum*, again.]

itinerant [īt-in´ėr-ȧnt] *adj* traveling from place to place.—*n* a traveler.—*ns* **itin´eracy, itin´erancy**.—*n* **itin´erary**, a route; a record of a journey; a detailed plan of a journey.—*vi* **itin´erāte**, to travel, esp for the purpose of judging or preaching. [L *iter, itineris*, a journey.]

-itis [-ītis] *n suffix* meaning inflammation of (a specified part or organ) (neur*itis*).

its [its] *poss pron* the possessive of **it**. [The old form was *his, its* not being older than the end of the 16th century. *Its* does not occur in the English Bible of 1611, or in Spenser, occurs rarely in Shakespeare, and is not common until the time of Dryden.]

itself [it-self´] *pron* the intensive and reflexive form of **it**; its true self.—**by itself**, alone, apart; **in itself**, by its own nature.

ivory [ī´vȯ-ri] *n* the hard, white substance composing the tusks of elephants, walruses, etc., any substance like ivory; creamy white; (*slang*) piano keys; (*slang*) dice.—*adj* of, or like ivory; creamy-white.—*ns* **i´vory black**, a black pigment made from burnt ivory; **i´vory nut**, the nut of a species of palm (*Phytelephas macrocarpa*) of So America used for carving and turning; **ivory tower**, a retreat away from reality or action. [OFr *ivurie*—L *ebur, eboris*, ivory; Sans *ibhas*, an elephant.]

ivy [ī´vi] *n* a climbing or creeping vine (*Hedera helix*) with a woody stem and evergreen leaves widely cultivated in many species as an ornamental; poison ivy.—**Ivy League**, an association of colleges in the northeastern US widely regarded as high in scholastic and social prestige. [OE *īfig*, OHG *ebah*.]

-ize [īz] *suffix*: meaning; to cause to be (steril*ize*), to become (like) (crystal*lize*), to combine with (oxid*ize*), to engage in (soliloqu*ize*).

J

jab [jab] *vti* to poke as with a sharp instrument; to punch with short, straight blows.—*n* a sudden thrust or stab. [App imitative.]
jabber [jab´ėr] *vti* to talk rapidly, incoherently, or foolishly.—*n* **chatter**.—*n* **jabb´erer**. [Imit.]
jabot [zha´bō] *n* a frill of lace, etc., worn in front of a blouse or shirt. [Fr.]
jacinth [jas´inth] *n* a reddish-orange variety of zircon. [OFr *iacinte*—L *hyacinthus*. See **hyacinth**.]
jack [jak] *n* a man or boy; any of various machines used to lift something heavy; a playing card with a page boy's picture on it, ranking below the queen; a small flag flown on a ship's bow as a signal or to show nationality; any of the small 6-pronged metal pieces tossed and picked up in the game of jacks; a plug-in receptacle used to make electric contact; the target ball in lawn bowling; (*inf*) money.—*vt* to raise by means of a jack.—*ns* **Jack Frost**, frost or cold weather personified; **jack´-in-the-box**, a toy consisting of a box from which a figure on a spring jumps up when the lid is lifted; **jack´-in-the-pulpit**, a plant (*Arisaema triphyllum*) with a flower spike partly arched over by a hoodlike covering; **jack´knife**, a large pocketknife; a dive in which the diver touches his feet with knees straight and then straightens out; **jack-of-all-trades´**, one who can do many kinds of work acceptably; **jack-o´-lantern**, a hollow pumpkin cut to resemble a face and used as a lantern; a luminescant wood-destroying fungus (*Clitodyes illudens*); **jack´pot**, cumulative stakes, as in poker; **jack rabbit**, a large hare (*Lepus californicus*) of western N America, with strong hind legs; **jack´screw**, a screw-operated jack for lifting. **jack up**, (*inf*) to raise prices, wages, etc. [ME *jacke*, from *Jacke*, nickname for *Johan*, John.]
jackal [jak´öl] *n* any of several wild dogs esp (*Canis aureus*) of Asia and No Africa; a person who does another's dirty work. [Pers *shaghāl*.]
jackanapes [jak´a-nāps] *n* an impudent fellow; a coxcomb; a forward child.
jackass [jak´as] *n* a male donkey; a fool. [**jack, ass**.]
jackdaw [jak´dö] *n* an Old World black bird (*Corvus monedula*) like the crow, but smaller. [**jack, daw**.]
jacket [jak´et] *n* a short coat; an outer covering, as the removable paper cover of a book, the cardboard holder of a phonograph record, the skin of a potato, etc. [OFr *jaquet*, dim of *jaque*. See **jack**.]
Jacobean [jak-o-bē´an] *adj* of, or characteristic of, the period of James I of England (1603–1625). [L *Jacōbus*, James.]
Jacob´s ladder [jā´kobz-lad´ėr] *n* any of a genus (*Polemonium*) of herbs with flat-topped blue or white flowers and leaves resembling a ladder; (naut) a ladder of ropes with wooden steps. [From the *ladder Jacob* saw in his dream, Gen XXVIII 12.]
jacquard [jak´ärd] *n* a brocade or damask fabric with an intricately woven pattern.—**jacquard loom**, a loom head for producing such a fabric. [J M *Jacquard*, who invented it, 1801.]
Jacussi [je-kōōz´ē] *n* trade name for a device which swirls water in a bath; a bath containing such a device. [*Jacuzzi*, Amer developers.]
jade[1] [jād] *n* a worthless nag; a disreputable woman.—*vt* to tire; to satiate. [Origin unknown; cf ON *jalda*, a mare; Scot *yaud*.]
jade[2] [jād] *n* a hard, ornamental semiprecious stone; its light green color.—**jade plant**, any of several succulents (genus *Crassula*) cultivated as foliage plants. [Fr.—Sp *ijada*, the flank—L *ilia*.]
jag[1] [jag] *n* a sharp, toothlike projection.—*adj* **jagged**, having sharp projecting points; notched or ragged.
jag[2] [jag] *n* a small load; (slang) intoxication from drugs or alcohol; a bout of drinking, crying, etc. a notch; a sharp or rugged point of rock, etc.; (*bot*) a cleft or division; (*Scot*) a prick; an inoculation, injection; a thrill; a bout of indulgence, eg in liquor or narcotics.—*vt* to cut into notches; to prick.—*pr p* **jagg´ing**; *pt p* **jagged**.—*adj* **jagged** [jag´id] notched, rough-edged.—*adv* **jaggedly** [jag´id-li].—*n* **jaggedness** [jag´id-nes]. [Origin unknown.]
jaguar [jag´wär or jag´ū-ar] *n* a medium-sized, black-marked feline (*Felis onca*) of tropical America. [South American Indian *jaguāra*.]
jai alai [hī´lī´ hī´ė-lī] *n* a court game in which the ball is caught in a wicker racket and hurled against the walls of an enclosed arena. [Basque.]
jail [jāl] *n* a prison—*vt* to send to or confine in prison—*ns* **jail´-bird**, one who is or has been in jail; **jail´er**, one who has charge of a jail. [Norm Fr *gaiole*—Low L *gabiola*, a cage—L *cavea*, a cage—*cavus*, hollow.]
jalap [jal´ap] *n* the purgative root of a plant (*Exogonium purga*) [*Jalapa* or Xalapa, in Mexico.]
jalopy [jȧ-lop´i] *n* (*inf*) a decrepit old automobile.
jalousie [zhal-ŏŏ-zē´ or zhal´-] *n* a shutter constructed with angled slats to allow ventilation and prevent entry of rain; window made of angled slats of glass. [Fr *jalousie*, jealousy.]
jam[1] [jam] *n* fruit boiled with sugar until thickened.—*adj* **jamm´y**. [Perh from **jam** (2).]
jam[2] [jam] *vt* to squeeze into a confined space; tight; to crowd full; to block by crowding; to wedge; to bring (machinery) to a standstill by wedging; to interfere with a radio signal by sending out other signals on the same wavelength.—*vi* to become stuck.—*pr p* **jamm´ing**; *pt p* **jammed**.—*n* a crush; a block; a difficulty; (*inf*) a difficult or embarrassing situation. [Perh allied to **champ**.]
jamb [jam] *n* the sidepost of a door, fireplace, etc. [Fr *jambe*, perh Celt *cam*, bent.]
jamboree [jam-bō-rē´] *n* (*slang*) a boisterous frolic, a spree; a large assembly of Boy Scouts from many places.
James [jāmz] *n* (*Bible*) 20th book of the New Testament epistle addressed to converted Jews living around the Mediterranean, written by a half-brother of Jesus.
jangle [jang´gl] *vi* to sound harshly or discordantly, as bells.—*vt* to cause to jangle; to irritate.—*n* dissonant clanging.—*ns* **jang´ler; jang´ling**. [OFr *jangler*.]
janitor [jan´i-tȯr] *n* one who takes care of a building, doing routine maintenance, etc.—*adj* **janitor´ial**. [L *jānitor*—*jānua*, a door.]
January [jan´ū-ȧr-i] *n* the first month of the year, having 31 days. [L *Jānuārius*.]
japan [ja-pan´] *n* a hard, glossy varnish.—*vt* to lacquer with japan.
Japanese´ [ja-pan-ēz´] *adj* of Japan, of its people, or of its language which is the only member of its family—**Japanese beetle**, a shiny, green and brown beetle (*Popillia japonica*) orig from Japan, severely damaging to plants.—Also *n*.
jar[1] [jär] *vi* to make a harsh sound; to have an irritating effect (on one); to vibrate from an impact; to clash.—*vt* to jolt.—*n* a grating sound; a vibration due to impact; a jolt.—*adv* **jarr´ingly**. [Imit.]
jar[2] [jär] *n* an earthen or glass bottle with a wide mouth; the amount this will contain. [Fr *jarre*, or Sp *jarra*—Ar *jarrah*.]
jargon [jär´gȯn] *n* confused talk, gibberish; the special or technical vocabulary of a science, art, profession, etc. [Fr *jargon*.]
jasmine [jaz´min] *n* any of a genus (*Jasminum*) of climbing shrubs of warm regions with fragrant white or yellow flowers; a light yellow.—Also **jessamine**. [Fr *jasmin, jasemin*—Ar *yāsmīn, yāsamin*—Pers *yāsmīn*.]
jasper [jas´pėr] *n* a red, yellow, dark green or brown quartz used as a gemstone. [OFr *jaspe, jaspre*—L *iaspis, -idis*—and Gr *iaspis, -idos*; of Eastern origin.]
jaundice [jön´dis] *n* a disease, symptom characterized by a yellowing of the eyes, skin, etc., by bile; bitterness; ill-humor; prejudice.—*vt* to cause to have jaundice; to make prejudiced through envy, etc.—*adj* **jaun´diced**, affected with jaundice; (of person, judgment) biassed by envy, disillusionment, etc. [Fr *jaunisse*—*jaune*, yellow—L *galbīnus*, yellowish, *galbus*, yellow.]
jaunt [jönt] *vi* to go from place to place; to make an excursion.—*n* an excursion; a ramble.—*adj* **jaunt´ing**.
jaunty [jönt´i or jänt´i] *adj* having an airy or sprightly manner.—*adv* **jaunt´ily**.—*n* **jaunt´iness**. [Fr *gentil*.]
javelin [jav´(ė-)lin] *n* a light spear esp one thrown for distance in a contest. [Fr *javeline*; prob Celt.]
jaw [jö] *n* one of the bones in which teeth are set; either of two movable parts that grasp or crush something, as in a vise; the narrow opening of a gorge; (*slang*) a friendly chat.—*vi* (*slang*) to talk at length.—*ns* **jaw´bone**, a bone of a jaw, esp of the lower jaw.—*vti* to try to persuade by using the influence of one's office; **jaw´breaker**, a machine for crushing rocks, etc.; a hard usu round candy; (*slang*) a word hard to pronounce. [Perh *chaw* (a chew), modified by Fr *joue*, cheek.]
jay [jā] *n* any of several Old World birds of the crow family with raucous voices, roving habits, and destructive behaviour to other birds.—*vi* **jay´walk**, to walk across a street carelessly without obeying traffic rules or signals.—*n* **jay´walker**. [OFr *jay*.]
jazz [jaz] *n* a general term for American popular music embracing ragtime, blues, swing, jive, and bebop; (*slang*) talk, acts, etc. regarded disparagingly.—*vt* to play as jazz; (*slang*) to enliven or embellish, (*with* **up**).—*adj* **jazz´y**, of or like jazz; (*slang*) lively, flashy, etc. [Origin unknown.]
jealous [jel´us] *adj* suspicious of or incensed at rivalry: envious (of); anxiously heedful.—*adv* **jeal´ously**.—*n* **jeal´ousy**. [OFr *jalous*—L *zēlus*—Gr *zēlos*, emulation.]
jean [jēn, jān] *n* a twilled cotton cloth; (*pl*) trousers or overalls or jean; (*pl*) casual trousers of jean or denim. [OFr *Janne*—L *Genua*, Genoa.]
jeep [jēp] *n* a light military vehicle with heavy duty tyres and good ground clearance for use on rough terrain; **Jeep**, trade name for a civilian automotive vehicle resembling a jeep. [GP = general purpose.]
jeer [jēr] *vt* to treat with derision.—*vi* to scoff (at).—*n* a railing remark.—*adv* **jeer´ingly**.

Jehovah [ji-hō´vä] *n* God.—**Jehovah's Witness**, a member of a Christian sect that witnesses by distributing literature, practices personal evangelism, and believes the end of the world is near. [Hebrew.]

jejune [ji-jōōn´] *adj* lacking interest; naïve, immature.—*adv* **jejune´ly**—*n* **jejune´ness**. [L *jējūnus*, fasting, empty.]

jejunum [ji-jōōn´ėm] *n* the middle part of the small intestine. [L, neuter of *jējūnus*, fasting, empty.]

jelly [jel´i] *n* a soft, gelatinous food made from cooked fruit syrup or meat juice; any substance like this.—*vti* to jell.—*vti* **jell**, to become, or make into jelly; to crystallize, as a plan.—*adj* **jell´ied**.—*ns* **jelly bean**, a small, bean-shaped candy with a gelatinous center; **jellyfish**, a coelenterate with a nearly transparent body and long tentacles; (*inf*) a weak-willed person; **jelly roll**, a thin sheet of sponge cake spread with jelly and rolled up. [Fr *gelée*, from *geler*—L *gelāre*, to freeze.]

jennet [jen´et] *n* a small Spanish horse; a female donkey; a hinny. [OFr *genet*—Sp *jinete*, a light horseman; perh of Arab origin.]

jenny [jen´i] *n* a female bird; a female donkey, a spinning jenny. [From the name *Jenny*.]

jeopardy [jep´ȧrd-i] *n* great danger or risk.—*vt* **jeop´ardize**, to put in jeopardy. [Fr *jeu parti*, a divided or even game—Low L *jocus partītus*—L *jocus*, a game, *partītus*, divided—*partīrī*, to divide.]

jerboa [jėr-bō´ä] *n* any of several Old World desert rodents (family Dipodidae) with long hind legs and a long tail. [Ar *yarbū´*.]

jeremiad [jer-e-mī´ad] *n* a lamentation; a doleful story. [From *Jeremiah*, reputed author of the Book of Lamentations.]

Jeremiah [jer-ė-mī´ė] *n* (*Bible*) 24th book of the Old Testament written by a major prophet who lived at the time of the fall of Jerusalem.

Jeremias [jer-ė-mī´ės] *n* (*Bible*) Jeremiah in the Douay version of the Old Testament.

jerk[1] [jûrk] *n* a sudden sharp pull or twist; a sudden muscular contraction or reflex; (*slang*) a person regarded as stupid, foolish, etc.—*vti* to move with a jerk; to pull sharply; to twitch.—*adj* **jerk´y**.—*n* **jerki´ness**. [An imitative word.]

jerk[2] [jûrk] *vt* to preserve (meat) by cutting it into long strips and drying it in the sun.—*n* **jerk´y**. [Amer Sp, *charqui*—Amer Indian.]

jerkin [jûr´kin] *n* a close-fitting jacket, often sleeveless. [Origin unknown.]

jerry-builder [jer´i-bild´ėr] *n* one who builds flimsy houses cheaply and hastily.—*adj* **jerr´y-built**. [Prob the personal name.]

jersey [jûr´zi] *n* any plain machine-knitted fabric of natural or man-made fibers; a circular-knitted sweater; **Jersey**, a breed of small short-horned dairy cattle known for their rich milk. [From the island *Jersey*.]

jerusalem artichoke [jer-ōōs´ȧ-lem är´ti-chōk] *n* a perennial American sunflower (*Helianthus tuberosus*) with edible tubers. [It *girasole*.]

jess [jes] *n* a short strap round the leg of a hawk for attaching a leash.—*adj* **jessed**, having jesses on. [OFr *ges*—L *jactus*, a cast—*jacĕre*, to throw.]

jessamine [jes´a-min] *see* **jasmine**.

jest [jest] *n* a mocking remark; a joke; a thing to be laughed at.—*vi* to jeer; to joke; **jest´er**, one who jests; esp one kept in a king's or nobleman's household. [Orig 'a deed, a story', ME *geste*—OFr *geste*—L *gesta*, things done, doings—*gerĕre*, to do.]

Jesuit [jez´ū-it] *n* one of the Society of Jesus, founded in 1534 by Ignatius Loyola; an intriguer.—*adjs* **jesuit´ic, -al**.—*adv* **jesuit´ically**.—*n* **jes´uitism**, the principles and practices of the Jesuits.

Jesus [jē´zus] *n* the founder of the Christian religion.—Also **Jesus Christ**. [Gr *Iēsous*—Heb *Yēshūa´*, contr of *Yehōshūa´*, Joshua.]

jet[1] [jet] *n* a black, very hard and compact coal that takes a high polish and is used in jewelry; a lustrous black. —Also *adj* used for ornaments. [OFr *jaiet*—L and Gr *gagātēs*—*Gagas* or Gangai, a town and river in Lycia, in Asia Minor, where it was obtained.]

jet[2] [jet] *n* a stream of liquid or gas suddenly emitted; a spout for emitting a jet; a jet-propelled airplane (in full **jet (air) plane**).—*vti* to gush out in a stream; to travel or convey by jet airplane.—**jet´lag**, disruption of the daily body rhythyms associated with crossing time zones at high speed; **jet propulsion**, propulsion of aircraft, boats, etc. by the discharge of gases from a rear vent.—*adj* **jet-prop´elled**.—**the jet set**, moneyed social set who travel widely for pleasure.—*n* **jet´setter**. [OFr *jetter*—L *jactāre*, to fling, freq of *jacĕre*, to throw.]

jetsam [jet´sȧm] *n* goods thrown overboard and washed up on the shore.—*vt* **jett´ison**, to abandon, to throw overboard. [Af *jetteson*—L *jactātiō, -ōnis*, a casting—*jactāre*, freq of *jacĕre*, to cast.]

jetty [jet´i] *n* a wharf; a small pier. [OFr *jettee*, thrown out—*jetter*. See **jet** (2).]

jeu d´esprit [zh_ des-prē´] a witticism; a witty literary trifle.—*pl* **jeux** [zh_] **d´esprit**. [Fr.]

Jew [jōō] *n* a person descended, or regarded as descended, from the ancient Hebrews; a person whose religion is Judaism.—*adj* **Jew´ish**.—*ns* **Jew´ishness; Jew´ry**, the Jewish people; **Jew's harp, Jews' harp**, a small metal musical instrument held between the lips and plucked to produce a twanging tone. [OFr *Jueu*—L *Jūdaeus*—Gr *Ioudaios*—Heb *Yehūdāh*, Judah.]

jewel [jōō´ėl] *n* a precious stone; a gem; anything or anyone highly valued; a small gem used as a bearing in a watch.—*ns* **jeweler, jew´eller**, one who makes or deals in jewels; **jew´elry**, jewels in general. [OFr *jouel* (Fr *joyau*); either a dim of Fr *joie*, joy, from L *gaudium*, or derived through Low L *jocāle*, from L *jocārī*, to jest.]

Jezebel [jez´ė-b(ė)l] *n* a bold, vicious woman. [1 Kings, xvi 31; 2 Kings, ix 30–37.]

jib [jib] *n* a triangular sail in front of the foremast in a ship.—*vi* (of a sail) to gybe or swing from one side to the other.—*vt* to cause to gybe.—*n* **jib´boom**, a boom or an extension to the bow-sprit.

jibe *See* **gibe**.

jig [jig] *n* a lively dance usually in 6–8 time; the music for this; a device used to guide a tool.—*vt* to dance (a jig).—*n* **jigg´er**, anything that jigs, or operates a jig; any of several salls; an apparatus that works with a jerky, reciprocating motion; a measure for drinks, about 1½ ounces.—*ns* **jig´saw**, a saw consisting of a narrow blade set in a frame used for cutting irregular lines; **jigsaw puzzle**, a picture cut up into irregular pieces, to be fitted together.

jihad [ji-häd´] *n* a holy war waged by Muslims against unbelievers or heretics; a war for a doctrine or principle. [Ar *jihād*.]

jilt [jilt] *n* one who encourages and then rejects a lover.—*vt* to discard a lover after encouragement. [Possibly *jillet* or *gillet*, dim of the name Jill.]

jim crow [jim krō] *n* the policy or practice of discrimination by legal sanction against Afro-Americans.

jimsonweed [jim´son-wēd] *n* a poisonous annual weed (*Datura stramonium* of the nightshade family. [*Jamestown*, Va.]

jingle [jing´gl] *n* a sound like that of small bells or of coins shaken together; a catchy verse or song with easy rhythm, simple rhymes, etc.—*vti* (to cause) to jingle like small bells. [Imit.]

jingoism [jing´gō-ism] *n* advocacy of an agressive foreign policy.—*n* **jing´oist**.—*adj* **jingoist´ic**. [From the mild oath "By Jingo" in a chauvinistic British music-hall song.]

jinricksha [jin-rik´shä, -shö] *n* a rickshaw.

jinx [jingks] *n* (*inf*) a bringer of bad luck.

jitter [jit´ėr] *vi* to be nervous, to show nervousness.—*adj* **jitt´ery**.—*ns* **jitt´ers** (*inf*), an uneasy nervous feeling; fidgets (*with* **the**); **jitt´erbug**, a fast acrobatic dance for couples, esp in the 1940s.

jive [jīv] *n* (*slang*) foolish, exaggerated, or insincere talk; formerly, improvised jazz usu played at a fast tempo.—Also *vti*.

job [job] *n* a piece of work done for pay; a task; a duty; the thing or material being worked on; work; employment; a criminal enterprise.—*adj* hired or done by the job.—*vti* to deal in (goods) as a jobber; to sublet (work, etc.).—*ns* **jobb´er**, one who buys goods in quantity and sells them to dealers; one who does piecework.—**job action**, a refusal by a group of employees to perform their duties in order to win certain demands, esp when forbidden by law to strike; **job lot**, an assortment of goods for sale as one quantity.

Job [jōb] *n* (Bible) 18th book of the Old Testament, a poetical book of the Bible written by the man whose name has become synonymous with patience.—**Job's comforter**, a person who adds to distress while purporting to give sympathy.

jockey [jok´i] *n* one whose job is riding horses in races—*vti* to cheat; to swindle; to maneuver for position or advantage; to ride a horse as a jockey. [Dim of *Jock*, northern Eng for **Jack**.]

jockstrap [jok´strap] *n* a genital support worn by men participating in athletics, (*slang*) an athlete.—Also **jock**.

jocose [jo-kōs´] *adj* full of jokes; facetious.—*adv* **jocose´ly**.—*n* **jocose´ness**. [L *jocōsus*—*jocus*, a joke.]

jocular [jok´ū-lȧr] *adj* joking; full of jokes.—*n* **jocularity** [-ar´i-ti].—*adv* **joc´ularly**. [L *joculāris*—*jocus*, joke.]

jocund [jōk´ünd, jok´ünd] *adj* genial, cheerful, pleasant.—*n* **jocundity** [-kund´i-ti].—*adv* **joc´undly**. [Fr.—LL *jocundus* for L *jūcundus*, pleasant, modified by association with *jocus*.]

jodhpurs [jod´pûrz] *n pl* riding breeches fitting tightly from knee to ankle. [*Jodhpur* in India.]

Joel [jō´el] *n* (*Bible*) 29th book of the Old Testament, a prophetic book built around the plague of locusts present at the time of its writing.

jog [jog] *vt* to shake with a push or a jerk; to stir up, as the memory.—*vi* to move up and down with a jerking motion; to move up and down with unsteady motion.—*n* a slight shake; a push; a slow walk or trot.—*ns* **jogg´ing**, exercising by running in a slow bouncing manner; **jog´-trot**, a slow jogging trot.

joggle [jog´l] *vti* to jog or shake slightly.—*n* a slight jolt. [App dim or freq of **jog**.]

John [jon] *n* (*Bible*) the 4th book of the New Testament, the Gospel of John; the 23d, 24th, and 25th books of the New Testament epistles written by John; the apostle, writer of the Gospel, the epistles, and Revelation; (*slang*) a prostitute's client; **john** (*slang*), a toilet.

John Bull [jon bōōl] *n* England, or an Englishman, personified. [From Arbuthnott's *History of John Bull*, 1712.]

John Doe [jon dō] *n* a fictitious name used in legal documents for an unknown person.

John Hancock [jon han´kök] *n* an autograph signature. [From the prominence of his signature on the Declaration of Independence.]

johnnycake [jon´ē-kāk] *n* a bread made with cornmeal.

Johnny-jump-up [jon-ē-jump´up] *n* any of various small-flowered pansies developed from the European viola (*Viola tricolor*); any of various American violets.

Johnsonese [jon-son-ēz´] *n* a literary style, full of antitheses, balanced sets of clauses, and words of Latin origin. [Dr Samuel *Johnson*, man of letters and lexicographer (1709–84).]

joie de vivre [zhwa dė vē-vr´] joy in living; high spirits, zest. [Fr.]

join [join] *vti* to bring and come together (with); connect; unite; to become a part or member of (a club, etc.); to participate (in a conversation, etc.).—*n* a joining; a place of joining.—*ns* **join´er**, a carpenter who finishes interior woodwork; (*inf*) one who joins many organizations; **join´ery**, the trade of a joiner; the work done by a joiner.—*n* **joint**, a place where, or way in which, two things are joined; any of the parts of a jointed whole; in an animal, the parts where two bones move on one another; (*slang*) a cheap bar, restaurant, etc. or any house, building, etc.; (*slang*) a marijuana cigarette.—*adj* common to two or more (*joint property*); sharing with another (a *joint owner*).—*vt* to connect by a joint or joints.—*adv* **joint´ly**, in common.—**Joint Chiefs of Staff**, a US advisory group comprising the chief of the army and air force, the chief of naval operations, and sometimes the commandant of the marine corps; **joint resolution**, a resolution passed by the US Congress that has the force of law when signed by or passed over the veto of the President.—**out of joint**, dislocated; disordered. [OFr *joindre*—L *jungĕre, junctum*, to join.]

joist [joist] *n* a beam supporting the boards of a floor or the laths of a ceiling. [OFr *giste*—*gesir*—L *jacēre*, to lie.]

jojoba [hō-hō´ba] *n* a broadleaf evergreen shrub (*Simmondsia californica*) of southwestern No America with edible seeds yielding a valuable oil. [Mexican Sp].

joke [jōk] *n* anything said or done to excite a laugh; a thing done or said merely in fun; a person or thing to be laughed at.—*vi* to make jokes.—*n* **jok´er**, one who jokes; a hidden provision, as in a legal document, etc. to make it different from what it seems to be; an extra playing card.—*adv* **jok´ingly**. [L *jocus*.]

jolly [jol´i] *adj* merry; full of fun; delightful; (*inf*) enjoyable.—*vti* (*inf*) to try to make (a person) feel good; to make fun of (someone).—*n* **jollificā´tion**, noisy festivity and merriment.—*ns* **joll´iness, joll´ity**.—**Jolly Roger**, a pirate's flag with a white skull and crossbones on a black field. [OFr *jolif, joli*.]

jolt [jōlt] *vi* to shake; to proceed with sudden jerks.—*vt* to shake with a sudden shock.—*n* a sudden jerk. [Etymology obscure.]

Jonah [jō´na] *n* (*Bible*) 32d book of the Old Testament written by the prophet who was swallowed by a great fish; a person believed to bring bad luck to those around him.

Jonas [jō´nas] *n* (*Bible*) Jonah in the Douay Version of the Old Testament.

Jonathan [jon-a-thȧn] *n* a New Englander; a variety of red eating apple. [Perh from the sagacious Governor *Jonathan* Trumbull, 1710–85.]

jongleur [zh•-glœr´] *n* a wandering minstrel. [Fr.—OFr *jogleor*—L *joculātor*. Same root as **juggler**.]

jonquil [jon´kwil] *n* a species (*Narcissus jonquilla*) of narcissus with small yellow flowers. [Fr *jonquille*—L *juncus*, a rush.]

Jordan almond [jor´dȧn] *n* a large Spanish almond when coated with salt or colored, candied sugar. [*Jordan*, the Middle Eastern country.]

jorum [jōr, jōr´ům] *n* a large drinking vessel; its contents. [Ety unknown; perh from *Joram* in 2 Sam viii 10.]

Joshua [josh´e-wė, -shwė] *n* (*Bible*) 6th book of the Old Testament in which the successor to Moses describes the return to Palestine.

joss [jos] *n* a Chinese idol; fortune.—*n* **joss stick**, a stick of Chinese incense. [Port *deos*, god—L *deus*.]

jostle [jos´l] *vti* to shake or jar by collision; to elbow.—Also *n*. [Freq of **joust, just**.]

Josue [josh´e-wi, -shwi] *n* (*Bible*) Joshua in the Douay Version of the Old Testament.

jot [jot] *n* a very small amount.—*vt* to set (down) briefly.—*pr p* **jott´ing**; *pt p* **jott´ed**.—*ns* **jott´er**, one who jots; **jott´ing**, a brief note. [L *iōta* (read as *jōta*)—Gr *iōta*, the smallest letter in the alphabet equivalent to *i*; Heb *yōd*.]

joule [jōōl, jowl] *n* a unit of energy equal to work done when a force of one newton acts over a distance of one meter. [J. P. *Joule*, physicist.]

journal [jûr´n(ȧ)l] *n* a daily record of happenings, as a diary; a newspaper or periodical; (*bookkeeping*), a book of original entry for recording transactions; that part of a shaft or axle that turns in a bearing.—*ns* **journalese´**, a facile style of writing found in many magazines, newspapers, etc.; **journalism**, the work of gathering news for, or producing a newspaper or magazine; **journ´alist**, a writer for a newspaper or magazine.—*adj* **journalist´ic**. [Fr.—L *diurnālis*. See **diurnal**.]

journey [jûr´ni] *n* any travel; a tour.—*vi* to travel.—*pr p* **jour´neying**; *pt p* **jour´neyed** [-nid].—*n* **jour´neyman**, one whose apprenticeship is completed; an average or mediocre performer. [Fr *journée*—*jour*, a day—L *diurnus*.]

joust [jowst, just] *n* the encounter of two knights on horseback at a tournament.—*vi* to tilt. [OFr *juste, jouste, joste*—L *juxtā*, near.]

Jove [jōv] *see* **Jupiter**.

jovial [jō´vi-ȧl] *adj* full of playful good humor.—*ns* **joviality** [-al´i-ti].—*adv* **jo´vially**. [L *joviālis*—*Jovis*, the god Jove or Jupiter, or the planet Jupiter, an auspicious star.]

jowl [jōl, jowl] *n* the lower jaw; the cheek esp of a hog. [Probably several different words. ME forms are *chaul, chol*, OE *ceafl*, jaw.]

joy [joi] *n* intense gladness; a cause of this.—*vi* to rejoice.—*adj* **joy´ful**, feeling, expressing, or giving joy.—*adv* **joy´fully**.—*n* **joy´fulness**.—*adj* **joy´less**, without joy; not giving joy.—*adv* **joy´lessly**.—*n* **joy´lessness**.—*adj* **joy´ous**, joyful.—*adv* **joy´ously**.—*n* **joy´ousness**.—**joy ride** (*inf*), an automobile ride, often at reckless speed, just for pleasure; action like a joy ride, esp ignoring cost of consequences; **joy´stick** (*inf*), the control lever of an airplane; a manual device for positioning a lighted indicator, as on a video screen. [Fr *joie* (cf It *gioja*)—L *gaudium*.]

jubilant [jōō´bi-lȧnt] *adj* joyful and triumphant; elated; rejoicing.—*ns* **ju´bilance**.—*vi* **ju´bilate**, to exult, rejoice.—*ns* **Jubilate** [jōō-bi-lā´t], the 100th Psalm. [L *jūbilāre*, to shout for joy.]

jubilee [jōō´bi-lē] *n* a 50th or 25th anniversary; a time of rejoicing; jubilation. [Fr *jubilé*—L *jūbilaeus*—Heb *yōbēl*, a ram, ram's horn (trumpet).]

Judaic, -al [jōō-dā´ik, -ȧl] *adj* of the Jews or Judaism.—*vt* **Judaize** [jōō´dā-īz], to make Jewish; to conform or bring into conformity with Judaism.—*ns* **Juda´ica**, historical and literary material relating to Jews or Judaism; **Judaism** [jōō´dā-izm], the religion of the Jews; the religious and cultural traditions of the Jews; the Jews collectively. [L *Jūdaicus*—*Jūda*, Judah, a son of Israel.]

Judas [jōō´das] *n* the apostle in the Gospel accounts who betrayed Jesus; a person who betrays a friend; a traitor; **judas**, a peephole.

Jude [jōōd] *n* (*Bible*) 26th book of the New Testament, an epistle exhorting believers to guard against apostasy.

judge [juj] *n* a public official with authority to hear and decide cases in a court of law; a person chosen to settle a dispute or decide who wins; a person qualified to decide on the relative worth of anything.—*vti* to hear and pass judgment (on) in a court of law; to determine the winner of (a contest) or settle (a dispute); to form an opinion about; to criticize or censure; to suppose, think.—*ns* **Judges** (*Bible*) 7th book of the Old Testament, describing a period of 400 years during which the people of Israel suffered repeated judgments by God for their sins; **judge´ship**, the office of a judge; **judg´ment**, a judging; deciding; a legal decision; an opinion; the ability to come to an opinion; **Judgment Day** (*Christianity*), the time of God's final judgment of all people. [Anglo-Fr *juger*—L *jūdicāre*—*jūs*, law, *dīcĕre*, to declare.]

judicature [jōō´di-ka-tyůr] *n* the administering of justice; jurisdiction; judges or courts collectively. [L *jūdicāre, -ātum*, to judge.]

judicial [jōō-dish´ȧl] *adj* of judges, courts, or their functions; allowed, enforced, etc. by a court; befitting a judge; fair; impartial.—*adv* **judic´ially**.—**judicial review**, the power granted by the US Constitution that gives the court system the right or duty to annul legislation or executive orders which the judges deem to be unconstitutional. [L *jūdiciālis*—*jūdicium*.]

judiciary [jōō-dish´(y)ar-i] *adj* of judges or courts.—*n* the part of government that administers justice; judges collectively. [L *jūdiciārius*.]

judicious [jōō-dish´ůs] *adj* according to sound judgment; possessing sound judgment; discreet.—*adv* **judic´iously**.—*n* **judic´iousness**. [Fr *judicieux*—L *jūdicium*.]

Judith [jōō´dith] *n* (*Bible*) the 18th book in the Douay Version of the Old Testament.

judo [jōō´dō] *n* ju-jitsu. [Jap.]

juggernaut [jug´ėr-nöt] *n* a terrible, irresistible force. [Sans *Jagannātha*, lord of the world.]

juggle [jug´l] *vi* to toss up balls, etc. and keep them in the air.—*vt* to manipulate so as to deceive.—*n* a juggling.—*ns* **jugg´ler; jugg´lery**. [OFr *jogler*—L *joculārī*, to jest—*jocus*, a jest.]

jugular [jug´ū-lȧr] *adj* of the neck or throat.—*n* either of the large veins on each side of the neck carrying blood from the head.—Also **jugular vein**. [L *jugulum*, the collar-bone—*jungĕre*, to join.]

juice [jōōs] *n* the liquid part of fruit, vegetables, or of animal tissue; (*inf*) vitality; (*slang*) electricity.—*vt* to extract juice from.—*adj* **juice´less**.—*n* **juic´er**, a device for extracting juice from fruit.—*adj* **juic´y**, full of juice; (*inf*) very interesting; (*inf*) highly profitable.—*n* **juic´iness**. [Fr *jus*—L *jūs* broth, lit mixture.]

jujitsu [jōō-jit´sŏŏ] *n* a Japanese system of wrestling in which the strength and weight of the opponent are used against him. [Jap *jū-jutsu*.]

ju-ju [jōō´jōō] *n* an object of superstitious worship in West Africa; a fetish or charm. [App Fr *joujou*, a toy.]

jujube [jōō´jōōb] *n* a gelatinous, fruit-flavored candy; the fruit of any of several small trees (genus *Ziziphus*) of the buckthorn family; the trees themselves. [Fr *jujube*, or Low L *jujuba*—Gr *zizyphon*.]

juke box [jōōk boks] coin-operated electric phonograph. [Gullah *juke*, disorderly.]

julep [jōō´lep] *n* a sweet drink of syrup, flavoring and water; tall drink of bourbon or brandy and sugar over crushed ice, garnished with mint.—Also **mint julep**. [Fr.—Sp *julepe*—Ar *julāb*—Pers *gulāb*—*gul*, rose, *āb*, water.]

Julian calendar [jōōl´yȧn] *n* calendar introduced in 46 BC by Julius Caesar in which the year was made to consist of 365 days, 6 hours instead of 365 days by introducing a leap year. [C *Julius* Caesar (100–44 BC.]

julienne [zhü-li-en´] *adj* (of vegetables and meat) cut into thin strips.—*n* a clear meat soup containing julienne vegetables. [French name.]

Juliett [jōō-lē-ėt] communication code word for the letter *j*.

July [jōō-lī] *n* the seventh month of the year having 31 days. [L *Jūlius* from Caius (or Gaius) Julius Caesar, who was born in it.]

jumble [jum´bl] *vt* (*often with* **up**); to throw together without order.—*vi* to become mixed together confusedly.—*n* a hodge podge.

jumbo [jum´bō] *n* anything very big of its kind.—Also *adj*.—**jumbo jet** (*inf*), large jet-propelled airplane. [Amer Negro, *jamba*, elephant.]

jump [jump] *vi* to spring or leap from the ground, a height, etc.; to jerk; to act swiftly and eagerly (*often with* **at**); to pass suddenly, as to a new topic; to rise suddenly, as prices; (*slang*) to be lively.—*vt* to leap or pass over (something); to leap upon; to cause (prices, etc.) to rise; (*inf*) to attack suddenly; (*inf*) to react to prematurely; (*slang*) to leave suddenly.—*n* a jumping; a distance jumped; sudden transition; a nervous start.—*adj* **jump´y**, moving in jumps, etc.; easily startled.—*ns* **jump´er**, one that jumps; wire used to close an electric circuit; **jumping bean**, a seed of several Mexican shrubs (genus *Sebastiana* and *Sapium*) that tumbles about because of the movement of a moth larva inside it; **jumping mouse**, a small hibernating No American rodent (family Zapodidae) with long hind legs and tail; **jumping-off place**, a remote or isolated place; a place from which a project is launched; **jump seat**, a folding seat behind the front seat of a passenger automobile; **jump suit**, a coverall worn by paratroops, etc.; any one-piece garment like this.—**get** or **have the jump on** (*slang*), to get or have an advantage over; **jump bail**, to forfeit bail by running away; **jump the gun** (ie the starting-gun in a race), to get off one's mark too soon, start before time, act prematurely, take an unfair advantage; **jump the queue**, to take a position in a queue to which one is not entitled; to get ahead of one's turn; **jump to conclusions**, to arrive at a conclusion. [Prob onomatopoeic.]

jumper [jump´er] *n* a loose jacket; a sleeveless dress for wearing over a blouse, etc.; rompers.

junco [junk´ō] *n* any of a genus (*Junco*) of widely distributed American finches.

junction [jungk´sh(ȯ)n] *n* a joining, a union or combination; place or point of joining, esp of roads or railroad lines. [L *junctiō, -onis—jungĕre*. See **join**.]

juncture [jungk´tyủr, -chủr] *n* a junction; a point of time; a crisis. [L *junctūra—jungĕre*. See **join**.]

June [jōōn] *n* the sixth month having 30 days. [L *Jūnius*.]

jungle [jung´gl] *n* a dense tropical growth of thickets, brushwood, etc.; any wild tangled mass; (*slang*) a place or situation where there is ruthless competition, or struggle for survival.—*ns* **jung´lefowl**, a bird (*Gallus gallus*) of south-eastern Asia from which domestic fowls have evolved; **jungle gym**, a structure of vertical and horizontal bars used in children's playgrounds, etc. [Sans *jāngala*, desert.]

junior [jōon´yȯr] *adj* the younger, written 'Jr.' after the son's name if it is the same as his father's; of more recent or lower status; of juniors.—*n* one who is younger, of lower rank, etc.; a student in the next-to-last year, as of a high school or college.—**junior college**, a school offering courses two years beyond high school; **junior high school**, a school usu including 7th, 8th, and 9th grades; **Junior League**, an organization of women under the age of 40 for voluntary civic and social service; **junior varsity**, athletic team for those not eligible for the varsity. [L *jūnior*, compar of *jŭvenis*, young.]

juniper [jōō´ni-pėr] *n* a genus (*Juniperus*) of evergreen shrubs, one species of which yields berries used to flavour gin. [L *jūniperus*.]

junk[1] [jungk] *n* a Chinese sailing vessel, with high forecastle and poop, sometimes large and three-masted. [Port *junco*, app—Javanese *djong*.]

junk[2] [jungk] *n* discarded useless objects; (*inf*) trash; (*slang*) heroin.—*vt* (*inf*) to scrap.—*ns* **junk´er**, (*slang*) an old, rundown truck or car; **junk´ie, junk´y**, (*slang*) a narcotics addict.—**junk food**, snack food with little nutritional value.

junket [jung´ket] *n* curdled milk, sweetened and flavored; a picnic; an excursion, esp one by an official at public expense.—*vi* to go on a junket. [Anglo-Fr *jonquette*, rush-basket—L *juncus*, a rush.]

junta [jun´ta] *n* a government, esp military, formed by a group following a coup d´état. [Sp—L *jungĕre, junctum*, to join.]

Jupiter [jōō´pi-tėr] *n* the chief god among the Romans—also **Jove**; the largest planet of the solar system. [L *Jūpiter, Juppiter*.]

Jurassic [jōō-ras´ik] *adj* the second period of the Mesozoic era—*n* Jurassic period or rock system. [*Jura* Mountains, France and Switzerland.]

juridical [jōō-rid´ik-ȧl] *adj* of judicial proceedings or law.—*adv* **jurid´ically**. [L *jūridicus—jūs, jūris*, law, *dīcere*, to declare.]

jurisconsult [jōō-ris-kon-sult´] *n* a specialist in international and public law; a jurist. [L *jūs, jūris*, law, *consulĕre, consultum*, to consult.]

jurisdiction [jōō-ris-dik´sh(ȯ)n] *n* the distribution of justice; legal authority; extent of power; district over which any authority extends.—*adj* **jurisdic´tional**. [L *jūrisdictiō, -ōnis*.]

jurisprudence [jōō-ris-prōō´dėns] *n* the science or philosophy of law; a division of law. [L *jūrisprūdentia—jūs, jūris*, law, *prūdentia*, knowledge.

jurist [jōō´rist] *n* an expert on law or a writer on law.—*adjs* **jurist´ic**.—*adv* **jurist´ically**. [Fr *juriste*.]

jury [jōō´ri] *n* a body of persons sworn to give a verdict on evidence before them; a committee that decides winners in a contest.—*n* **ju´ror**, one who serves on a jury. [Ango-Fr *juree-jurer*—L *jūrāre*, to swear.]

jussive [jus´iv] *adj* (*gram*) expressing command. [L *jubēre*, perf *jussī*, to command.]

just [just] *adj* fair, (*impartial*) righteous, deserved, due; in accordance with facts; exact.—*adv* exactly; nearly; only; barely; a very short time ago; immediately; (*inf*) really.—*adv* **just´ly**, equitably; by right; **just the same**, nevertheless. [Fr *juste*, or L *jūstus—jūs*, law.]

justice [jus´tis] *n* quality of being just; integrity; impartiality; the use of authority to uphold what is just; the administration of law; the awarding of what is due; a judge.—**justice of the peace**, a local magistrate who decides minor cases, performs marriages, etc.—**do justice to**, to treat fairly. [Fr.—L *justitia*.]

justify [jus´ti-fī] *vt* to prove or show to be just or right, to vindicate; (of circumstances) to furnish adequate grounds for; to corroborate; (*theology*) to absolve.—*pr p* **jus´tifying**; *pt p* **jus´tified**.—*adj* **just´ifiable** [or fī´-], that may be justified or defended.—*adv* **justifī´ably**.—*n* **justificā´tion**, vindication; sufficient grounds or reason (for); absolution.—*adjs* **jus´tificātive, jus´tificā´tory**, having power to justify.—*n* **jus´tifier**, one who defends, or vindicates; he who pardons and absolves from guilt and punishment. [Fr *justifier* and L *jūstificāre—jūstus*, just, *facĕre*, to make.]

jut [jut] *vti* to stick out; to project.—*n* a part that juts. [A form of **jet** (2).]

jute [jōōt] *n* the fiber of two Indian plants (*Corchorus olitorius* and *C capsularis*) of the linden family, used for making coarse bags, mats, etc.; a plant producing jute. [Bengali *jhuto*—Sans, *jūta*, matted hair.]

juvenile [jōō´vė-nīl] *adj* young; immature; of or for young persons.—*n* a young person; an actor who plays youthful roles; a book for children.—*n pl* **juvenilia** [-il´ya], writings or works of one's childhood or youth, artistic or literary works intended for children.—*ns* **juvenility** [-il´i-ti]; **juvenile delinquency**, antisocial or illegal behavior by minors, usu 18 years or younger; **juvenile delinquent; juvenile officer**, a police officer responsible for dealing with juvenile delinquents. [L *juvenīlis—juvenis*, young.]

juxtaposition [juks-tȧ-poz-ish´(ȯ)n] *n* a placing or being placed side by side.—*vt* **juxtapose´**. [L *juxtā*, near, + **position**.]

K

Kaaba [kä'bä] *n* the holy building at Mecca which contains a sacred black stone, is the goal of Islamic pilgrimage, and the point toward which Muslims turn when praying. [Ar *ka'bah—ka'b*, cube.]
Kabuki [ka-book-i] *n* traditional Japanese popular drama performed in a highly conventional manner.
kachina [ka-chēn'a] *n* in Pueblo culture, a doll symbolizing powers and manifestations of ancestors.
Kaddish [käd'ish] *n* (*Judaism*) a hymn in praise of God, recited at the daily service or as a mourner's prayer; (*inf*) a son. [Aramaic *qaddish*, holy.]
kaffeeklatsch [kä'fē-kläch] *n* an informal gathering to drink coffee and chat. [Ger *kaffee*, coffee + *klatsch*, gossip.]
kaiser [kī'zėr] *n* an emperor, esp a German Emperor.—*n* **kai'sership**. [Ger,—L *Caesar*.]
kale [kāl] *n* a cabbage (*Brassica olevacea acephala*) with open curled leaves; (*slang*) money. [Scots form of **cole**.]
kaleidoscope [ka-lī'dō-skōp] *n* a small tube containing bits of colored glass reflected by mirrors to form symmetrical patterns as the tube is rotated; anything that constantly changes.—*adj* **kaleidoscop'ic** [-skop'ik]. [Gr *kalos*, beautiful, *eidos*, form, *skopeein*, to look at.]
kamikaze [kä-mi-kä'zē] *n* (A Japanese airman, or plane, esp during World War II, making) a suicidal attack. [Jap, divine wind.]
kangaroo [kang-går-ōō'] *n* a leaping, herbivorous marsupial mammal (family Macropodidae) of Australia and nearby islands, with short forelegs and strong, large hind legs.—**kangaroo court**, a court operated by any improperly constituted body; a tribunal before which a fair trial is impossible; **kangaroo justice**, the kind of justice dispensed by a kangaroo court; **kangaroo rat**, a burrowing nocturnal rodent (genus *Dipodymus*) of desert areas of southwestern US. [Supposed to be a native name.]
Kantian [kant'i-ån] *adj* pertaining to the great German philosopher, Immanuel *Kant* (1724–1804), or his philosophy.
kaolin [kā'ō-lin] *n* a white clay used in porcelain, etc. [From the mountain *Kao-ling* ('high ridge') in China.]
kappa [kä'pä] *n* 10th letter of the Greek alphabet.
kapok [kāp'ok] *n* the silky fibers around the seeds of the ceiba tree, used for stuffing cushions, etc. and as insulation. [Malay *kāpoq*.]
kaput, kaputt [kȧ-pŏŏt'] *adj* (*slang*) ruined; broken. [Ger.]
karakul [kār'ȧ-cûl] *n* a breed of hardy, fat-tailed sheep of central Asia; the curly lustrous black coat from the fleece of its young lambs, usu spelled caracul.
karat [kār'ėt] *n* a measure of fineness for gold equal to 1/24 part of pure gold in any alloy.
karate [ka-rä'tā] *n* a Japanese system of self-defense by sharp, quick blows with the hands and feet.
karma [kär'mä] *n* (*Buddhism and Hinduism*) the totality of one's acts in each state of one's existence; (*loosely*) fate. [Sans *karma*, act.]
kart [kärt] *n* a small, flat motorized vehicle used in racing. [From **cart**.]
katydid [kā'ti-did] *n* any of a number of American grasshoppers (family Tettigoniidoe); tree katydid (*Pterophylla*) lives in trees. [Imit of its note.]
kayak [kī'ak] *n* an Eskimo canoe made of skins on a wooden frame. [Eskimo.]
kebab [kė-bab'] *n* small cubes of meat cooked with vegetables, seasoning and usu served on skewers.
kedge [kej] *n* a small anchor for kedging a ship.—*vt* to move (a ship) by dropping a kedge at the destination required. [Origin doubtful.]
kedgeree [kej'ė-rē] *n* a dish made with fish, rice, etc. [Hindustani *khichrī*.]
keel [kēl] *n* the lowest part of a ship extending along the bottom from stem to stern, and supporting the whole frame.—*vti* (to cause) to turn over.—*vt* **keel'haul**, to torture or punish by hauling under the keel of a ship; to rebuke severely.—**keel over**, (*inf*) to capsize; to fall over suddenly.—**on an even keel**, in an upright, level position. [ON *kjölr*.]
keen[1] [kēn] *adj* having a sharp point or a fine edge; affecting one as if by cutting; piercing; shrewd; perceptive; intense.—*adv* **keen'ly**.—*n* **keen'ness**. [OE *cēne*, bold, fierce, keen; Ger *kühn*, bold; ON *kœnn*, expert.]
keen[2] [kēn] *n* a lament for the dead.—*vi* to wail over the dead.—*n* **keen'er**, a professional mourner. [Ir *caoine*.]
keep [kēp] *vt* to celebrate, observe; to fulfill; to protect, guard; to take care of; to preserve; to provide for; to make regular entries in; to maintain in a specified state; to hold for the future; to hold and not let go; to stay in or on (a place, course, etc.).—*vi* to stay in a specified condition; to continue, go on; to refrain or restrain oneself; to stay fresh, not spoil.—*pr p* **keep'ing**; *p t, pt p* **kept**.—*n* food and shelter; care and custody; the inner stronghold of a castle.—*ns* **keep'er**, one who guards, watches, or takes care of persons or things; any device for keeping things in position; **keeping**, care, charge; observance; agreement; **keep'sake**, something kept in memory of the giver.—**for keeps** (*inf*) permanently; **in keeping with**, in conformity with; **keep at**, to persist in doing; **keep one's hand in**, to keep in practice; **keep to**, to stay in; to limit oneself to; to abide by; **keep to oneself**, to keep secret; to remain solitary; **keep up**, to maintain in good condition; to continue, to maintain the pace; to remain informed (*with* **with**). [OE *cēpan*.]
keg [keg] *n* a small barrel; a unit of weight for nails, equal to 100lb. [Earlier *cag*—ON *kaggi*.]
kelp [kelp] *n* any large brown seaweed (orders Laminariales and Fucales); the ashes used as a source of iodine. [ME *culp*.]
kelpie [kel'pi] *n* (*Scot*) a water-sprite in the form of a horse. [Origin uncertain.]
kelvin [kel'vin] *n* unit of temperature.—**Kelvin temperature**, temperature on a scale where absolute zero (-273.15° Celsius) is taken as zero degrees. (abbrev K). [Lord *Kelvin* (1824–1907), physicist.]
ken [ken] *n* understanding; view; sight.
kennel [ken'ėl] *n* a doghouse; (often *pl*) a place where dogs are bred or kept.—*vt* to keep in a kennel. [Norm Fr *kenil* (Fr *chenil*)—L *canile—canis*, a dog.]
kepi [kāp'ē] *n* a military cap with circular top and visor. [Fr *képi*.]
kept *p t, pt p* of **keep**.]
keratin [ker'ȧ-tin] *n* a tough, fibrous protein, the substance of hair, nails, feathers, etc.
kerchief [kûr'chif] *n* a square head cloth; a scarf; [OFr *cuevrechief* (Fr *couvrechef*)—*couvrir*, to cover, *chief*, the head.]
kernel [kûr'nėl] *n* a seed within a hard shell; the edible part of a nut; the important part of anything. [OE *cyrnel—corn*, grain, and dim suffix *-el*; Ger *kern*, a grain.]
kerosene [ker'o-sēn] *n* a thin oil obtained by distillation of petroleum.—Also **ker'osine**. [Gr *kēros*, wax.]
kestrel [kes'trėl] *n* a small European falcon (Falco tinnunnculus). [OFr *quercerelle*.]
ketch [kech] *n* a fore-and-aft rigged sailing vessel. [Earlier *catch*, perh from the verb **catch**.]
ketchup [kech'ûp] *n* a sauce for meat, fish, etc.; esp a thick sauce (**tomato ketchup**) of tomatoes, onions, spices, etc.—Also **catch'up, cat'sup**. [Malay *kēchap*.]
ketone [kē'tōn] *n* one of a class of chemical compounds with the general formula R'COR, the simplest ketone being acetone.—*adj* **keton'ic**.—*n* **ketos'is**, disturbance of body chemistry produced by the use of fat as a source of energy.
kettle [ket'l] *n* a metal container for boiling or cooking things; a teakettle.—*n* **kett'ledrum**, a musical instrument consisting of a hollow metal hemisphere with a parchment head, tuned by screws.—**a fine kettle of fish**, an awkward state of affairs. [OE *cetel*; Ger *kessel*; perh from L *catillus*, dim of *catinus*, a deep cooking-vessel.]
key[1] [kē] *n* a device for locking and unlocking something; a thing that explains or solves, as the legend of a map, a code, etc.; a controlling position, person, or thing; one of a set of parts pressed in a keyboard; (*mus*) a system of related tones based on a keynote and forming a given scale; style or mood of expression.—*vt* to furnish with a key; (*mus*) to regulate the pitch or tone of; to bring into harmony.—*adj* controlling; important.—*n* **key'board**, a set of keys in a piano, organ, typewriter, etc.—Also *adj*.—*n* **key club**, a private nightclub, etc. to which each member has a key.—*adj* **keyed**, having keys; set or pitched in a particular key; fastened or strengthened with a key; constructed with a keystone.—*ns* **key'hole**, an opening (in a lock) into which a key is inserted; **key'note**, the basic note of a musical scale; the basic idea or ruling principle.—*vt* to give the keynote of; to give the keynote speech at.—*n* **keynote speech**, a speech as at a convention setting forth the policy of a party; **key'pad**, a small usu hand-held keyboard of numbered buttons used to tap in a telephone number, to operate a television receiver, or to enter data in a computer; **key'punch**, a keyboard machine for recording data by punching holes in cards for use in data processing; **key signature**, sharps or flats placed after the clef at the beginning of a staff of music to indicate the key; **key'stone**, the middle stone at the top of an arch, holding the stones or other pieces in place; **key word**, a significant word used to facilitate the filing, etc. of documents.—**key up**, to make nervous; to raise the courage of. [OE *cæg*.]
key[2] [kē] *n* a low island or reef. [Sp *cayo*.]
Keynesianism [kān'zi-en-ism] *n* group of theories and programs of J. M. Keynes (1883–1946) and his followers, esp advocacy of government intervention to maintain high employment.—*adj, n* (denoting) one who supports the economic ideas propounded by Keynes.
khaki [kä'ki] *adj* dull yellowish-brown.—*n* strong, twilled cloth of this color; (often *pl*) a khaki uniform or trousers. [Hindustani and Pers *khākī*, dusty.]

khan [kän] *n* formerly, (title borne by) medieval Chinese emperors and Mongol and Turkic rulers; title of various dignatories in India, Iran, etc.—Also **cham**. [Turki, and thence Pers, *khān*, lord or prince.]

Khmer [kmer] *n* a member of a people of Cambodia; the Mon-Khmer language of the Khmer people that is the official language of Cambodia.

kibbutz [kē-bōōts´] *n* an Israeli collective settlement, esp a collective farm.—*pl* **kibbutzim** [kē-bōōts-ēm]. [Modern Heb.]

kibitzer [kib´it-zer] *n* (*inf*) one who watches a game of cards, esp bridge, without comment; a person giving unsolicited advice. [Yiddish.]

kibosh [kī´bosh] *n* (*slang*) end.—**put the kibosh on**, to silence, get rid of, check, etc.

kick [kik] *vt* to strike with the foot; to drive, force, etc. as by kicking; to score (a goal, etc.) by kicking; (*slang*) to get rid of (a habit).—*vi* to strike out with the foot; to recoil, as a gun; (*inf*) to complain; (*football*) to kick the ball.—*n* an act or method of kicking; a sudden recoil; (*inf*) a complaint; (*inf*) an intoxicating effect; (*inf*) (often *pl*) pleasure.—*ns* **kick´back**, (*slang*) a giving back of part of money received in payment; the money returned; **kick´off**, (*football*) a kick that puts the ball into play; a beginning, as part of a campaign; **kick pleat**, a short inverted pleat at the hem of a narrow skirt; **kick´stand**, a short metal bar which when kicked into position holds a bicycle, etc. upright; **kick turn**, a skiing turn in a stationary position used to change position.—*adj* **kick´y**, (*slang*) fashionable; (*slang*) exciting.—**kick in**, (*slang*) to pay (one's share); **kick over**, to start working, as an automobile engine; **kick (someone) upstairs**, to promote (someone) to an apparently better position. [ME *kiken*; origin unknown. W *cicio*, to kick, comes from Eng.]

kickshaw [kik´shö] *n* a delicacy; a trinket. [Fr *quelque chose*, something.]

kid [kid] *n* a young goat; anything of kidskin; (*inf*) a child.—*vti* (*inf*) to tease or fool playfully.—*vi* (of a goat or antelope) to bring forth young.—*n* **kid glove**, a glove made of kid leather.—**with kid gloves**, with great tact or caution. [ON *kith*; cf Dan *kid*.]

kidnap [kid´-nap] *vt* to seize and hold to ransom, as of a person; **kid´napping**; *pt p* **kid´napped**.—*n* **kid´napper**. [*kid*, a child, *nap*, to seize, steal.]

kidney [kid´ni] *n* either of a pair of glandular organs excreting waste products from the blood as urine; an animal's kidney used as food; disposition; class; kind (*of the same kidney*).—**kidney bean**, any of various cultivated beans (*Phaseolus vulgaris*), esp a large dark red bean seed; **kidney stone**, a hard mineral deposit in the kidney. [ME *kidenei* (pl *kideneiren*), the second element perh being *ei* (pl *eiren*), egg, confused sometimes with *nere*, kidney.]

kieselguhr, kieselgur [kē´z(ė)l-gŏŏr] *n* loose or porous diatonite. [Ger—*kiesel*, flint, *guhr*, fermentation.]

kilim [kē´-lēm] *n* a type of pileless rug woven in the Near East with identical patterns on both sides. [Turkish, fr Persian *kilim*.]

kill [kil] *vt* to cause the death of, to slay; to destroy; to defeat or veto (legislation); to neutralize (a color); to spend (time) on trivial matters; to turn off (an engine, etc.); to stop publication of.—*n* the act of killing; an animal or animals killed.—*n* **kill´er**, a person, animal or thing that kills.—*adj* **killing**, causing death, deadly; exhausting; fatiguing.—*n* slaughter; murder; (*inf*) a sudden great profit.—**kill´joy**, a person who spoils other people's enjoyment. [ME *killen*, or *cullen*.]

kiln [kil, kiln] *n* a furnace or oven for drying, burning bricks, pottery, etc. [OE *cyln, cylen*—L *culīna*, a kitchen.]

kilo [kē´lō, kil´ō] *n* kilogram; kilometer; **Kilo**, a communications code word for the letter *k*. [Shortened form.]

kilo- *prefix* a thousand. [Gr *chīlioi*]

kilobit [ki´lō- or kil´ō-bit] *n* 1000 bits; 1024 bits.

kilobyte [ki´lō-bīt] *n* 1024 bytes.

kilocycle [kil´ō-sī-kl] *n* former term for kilohertz.

kilogram [kil´ō-gram] *n* a unit of weight and mass, equal to 1000 grams or 2.2046 pounds.

kilohertz [kil´ō-hurts] *n* one thousand cycles per second, 1000 hertz.

kilometer [kil´ė-mētėr] *n* a unit of length equal to 1000 meters or 3,2808.8 feet.

kiloton [kil´ė-tun] *n* 1000 tons; explosive force equal to power of 1000 tons of TNT.

kilowatt [kil´ė-wät] *n* a unit of electrical power, equal to 1000 watts.—**kilowatt-hour**, a unit of energy equal to work done by one kilowatt in one hour.

kilt [kilt] *n* a kind of short pleated skirt, forming part of the Scottish Highland dress; a similar skirt worn by women.—*vt* to tuck up (skirts); to pleat vertically. [Scand; cf Dan *kilte*, to tuck up; ON *kilting*, a skirt.]

kimono [ki-mō´nō] *n* a loose Japanese robe with wide sleeves, fastening with a sash; a western garment resembling this. [Jap]

kin [kin] *n* relatives; family.—*adj* related as by blood.—*n* **kin´ship**, blood-relationship; close connection. [OE *cynn*; ON *kyn*, family, race; cog with L *genus*, Gr *genos*.]

-kin *noun suffix* denoting a diminutive as in lamb*kin*. [Prob Du or LG]

kind [kīnd] *n* sort; variety; class; a natural group or division; essential character.—*adj* sympathetic; friendly; gentle; benevolent.—*adjs* **kind´heart´ed; kind´ly**, kind; gracious; agreeable; pleasant.—*adv* in a kind gracious manner; favorably; please (*kindly shut the door*).—*ns* **kind´liness´; kind´ness**.—**in kind**, in the same way; **kind of** (*inf*), somewhat; rather; **of a kind**, alike. [OE (*ge*)*cynde*—*cynn*, kin.]

kindergarten [kin´dėr-gär-t(ė)n] *n* a class or school for children, usu four to six years old that teaches basic skills and social behavior. [Ger—*kinder*, children, *garten*, garden.]

kindle [kin´dl] *vt* to set on fire; to excite (feelings, interest, etc.).—*vi* to catch fire; to become aroused or excited.—*n* **kind´ling**, material, such as bits of dry wood, for starting a fire. [Cf ON *kyndill*, a torch—L *candēla*, candle.]

kindred [kin´dred] *n* a person's family or relatives; family relationship; resemblance.—*adj* related; like, similar. [ME *kinrede*—OE *cynn*, kin, and the suffix *-rǣden*, expressing mode or state.]

kine [kīn] *n pl* (*arch*) cows; cattle. [ME *kyen*, a doubled plural of OE *cū*, a cow, the plural of which is *cȳ*; cf Scots *kye*, cows.]

kinematics [kin-ė-mat´iks, or kīn-] *n* the branch of physics that deals with the characteristics of different kinds of pure motion, without reference to mass or the causes of the motion;—*adjs* **kinemat´ic, -al**. [Gr *kīnēma*, motion—*kīneein*, to move.]

kinesis [ki-nē´sis, kī] *n* a movement that depends on the force of the stimulus. [Gr *kīnēsis*, movement.]

kinetics [ki-net´iks, or kī-] *n* the science of the action of force in producing or changing motion.—*adjs* **kinet´ic; kinetic art, sculpture**, art, sculpture, in which movement (produced by air currents, electricity, etc.) plays an essential part; **kinetic energy**, energy derived from motion. [Gr *kīnētikos*—*kīneein*, to move.]

king [king] *n* the man who rules a country and its people; a man with the title of ruler, but with limited power to rule; man supreme in a certain sphere; something best in its class; the chief piece in chess; a playing card with a picture of a king on it; ranking above a queen; a checker that has been crowned.—*ns* **king´bird**, any of various American flycatchers (genus *Tyrannus*); **king cobra**, hamadryad; **king crab**, a hermit crab; any of several large crabs; **king´cup**, any of several yellow-flowered plants, esp buttercup; **king´dom**, a country headed by a king or queen; a realm, domain (*the kingdom of poetry*); any of the three divisions of the natural world; the animal kingdom, the vegetable kingdom, the mineral kingdom; **king´fisher**, a short-tailed diving bird (family Alcedinae) that feeds chiefly on fish; **king´let**, a small songbird (genus *Regulus*) found throughout the American continent; **king´nut**, tall American tree (*Carya laciniosa*) planted for its timber and nuts; **Kings** (*Bible*) 11th and 12th books of the Old Testament, which record the reign of Solomon.—*adj* **king´-size; king´-sized**, larger than standard size.—*n* **king snake**, a brightly-marked snake (genus *Lampropeltis*) of the central and southern US which feeds on rodents.—**King Charles Spaniel**, a toy breed of spaniel with very long ears; **King James Version**, Authorized Version of the Bible. [OE *cyning*—*cynn*, a tribe, with suffix *-ing*; cog with **kin**.]

kink [kingk] *n* a twisted loop in a string, rope, hair, etc.; a painful cramp in the neck, back, etc.; a mental twist; a whim.—*vti* to form or cause to form a kink or kinks.—*adj* **kink´y**. [Prob Du *kink*; but cf Ger, Swed, and Norw, *kink*.]

kinsfolk [kinz´fōk] *n* relatives.—*ns* **kins´man**, a male relative; **kins´woman**, a female relative. [**kin**, + **folk**.]

kiosk [ki-osk´] *n* a small open structure used as a newsstand. [Turk *kiöshk*—Pers *kūshk*.]

Kiowa [ki´ewö, or -wä] *n* a member of the Amerindian people of Colorado, Kansas, New Mexico, Oklahoma, and Texas.—*pl* **wa, -s**; the Uto-Aztecan language of this people.

kipper [kip´ėr] *vt* to cure (herring, salmon etc.) by salting and drying or smoking.—*n* a kippered herring, etc. [Perh OE *cypera*, a spawning salmon.]

kirsch [kiērsh] *n* a brandy made from cherries.

kismet [kis´met] *n* fate, destiny. [Turk *qismet*.]

kiss [kis] *vti* to caress or salute with the lips; to touch gently or lightly.—*n* an act of kissing; a light, gentle touch; any of various candies.—*n* **kisser**, one that kisses; (*slang*) mouth; (*slang*) face.—**kiss of death**, a disastrous act or association; **kiss of peace**, a ceremonial embrace or handshake in Christian liturgy. [OE *cyssan*, to kiss—*coss*, a kiss; Ger *küssen*.]

kit [kit] *n* an outfit; equipment; a container and/or the tools, instructions, etc. assembled in it for some specific purpose.—*n* **kitbag**, a strong bag for holding one's kit or outfit.—**the whole kit and caboodle** (*inf*), the whole lot. [Prob Middle Du *kitte*, a hooped beer can.]

kitchen [kich´ėn] *n* a place where food is prepared and cooked.—*ns* **kitchenette´**; a compact kitchen; **kitchen gar´den**, a garden where vegetables are cultivated for the kitchen; **kitch´en midden**, a prehistoric refuse heap.—**kitchenware**, kitchen utensils. [OE *cycene*—L *coquīna*—*coquěre*, to cook.]

kite [kīt] *n* any of several long-winged birds of the hawk family (Accipitridae); a light frame covered with paper or cloth for flying in the wind at the end of a string; a person who preys on others.—*vt* to cause to soar; (*inf*) to use (a check) knowing that there are insufficient funds to cover it.—*vi* to rise rapidly. [OE *cȳta*.]

kith [kith] friends and relatives, now only in **kith and kin**. [OE *cȳth*—*cunnan*, to know.]

kithara [kith´er-ė] *n* the foremost stringed instrument of the ancient Greeks, with a U-shaped frame, a crossbar between the arms and at least five strings.

kitsch [kich] *n* work in any of the arts that is pretentious and inferior or in bad taste. [Ger]

kitten [kit´n] *n* a young cat; the young of other small mammals.—*vt* and *vi* (of a cat) to bring forth.—*adj* **kitt´enish**, coyly playful. [ME *kitoun*, dim of **cat**.]
kittiwake [kit´i-wāk] *n* any of several gulls (genus *Rissa*) with long wings and rudimentary hind toe. [Imit]
kitty[1] [kit´i] *n* a kitten; a pet name for a cat.
kitty[2] [kit´i] *n* the stakes in a poker game; money pooled for some purpose.
kitty-corner, kitty cornered. *See* **catercornered**.
kiwi [kē´wi] *n* a flightless bird (genus *Apteryx*) of New Zealand; **Kiwi** (*inf*), a native or inhabitant of New Zealand; the fruit of a Chinese gooseberry.—*n* **kiwifruit**. [Maori, from its cry.]
kleptomania [klep-to-mā´ni-a] *n* an uncontrollable impulse to steal.—*n* **kleptomā´niac**. [Gr *kleptein*, to steal, *maniā*, madness.]
klutz [kluts] *n* (*slang*) a clumsy or stupid person.
knack [nak] *n* ability to do something easily; a trick; a habit. [Orig imit; cf Du *knak*, a crack.]
knackwurst [nak´wûrst] *n* a thick, highly seasoned sausage. [Ger]
knapsack [nap´sak] *n* a bag for carrying equipment or supplies on the back. [Du *knappen*, to crack, eat.]
knave [nāv] *n* a tricky or dishonest man; (*Brit*) a playing card: the jack.—*n* **knav´ery**, dishonesty.—*adj* **knav´ish**; rascally.—*adv* **knav´ishly**. [OE *cnafa, cnapa*, a boy, a youth; Ger *knabe, knappe*.]
knead [nēd] *vt* to squeeze and press together into a mass, as flour into dough; to massage. [OE *cnedan*; Ger *kneten*.]
knee [nē] *n* the joint between the thigh and the lower leg; anything shaped like a bent knee.—*vt* to hit or touch with the knee.—*n pl* **knee´breech´es**, breeches reaching to or just below the knee.—*ns* **knee´cap**, the kneepan or patella; **knee´hole**, an open space (as under a desk) for the knees; **knee jerk**, an involuntary kick when the tendon below the patella is tapped.—*adj* denoting an automatic response.—*n* **knee´pan**, the knee-cap. [OE *cnēow, cnēo*; Ger *knie*, L *genu*, Gr *gony*.]
kneel [nēl] *vi* to go down on one's knee or knees; to remain in this position.—*pt* and *pt p* **kneeled, knelt**. [OE *cnēowlian*.]
knell [nel] *n* the sound of a bell at a death or funeral; a warning of death, failure, etc.—*vi* to sound slowly as a bell; to toll; to sound ominously.—*vt* to call or announce as by a knell. [OE *cnyllan*, to beat noisily; Du and Ger *knallen*.]
knew [nū] *pt* of **know**.
knickerbockers [nik´ėr-bok-ėrz] *n pl* loose breeches gathered in at the knee.—Also **knick´ers**. [From the widebreeched Dutchmen in 'Knickerbocker's' (Washington Irving's) humoros *History of New York* (1809).]
knickknack [nik´-nak] *n* a small ornamental article. [A double of **knack**.]
knife [nīf] *n* a flat piece of steel, silver, etc., with a sharp edge, set in a handle so that it can be used to cut; a sharp blade forming a part of a tool or machine.—*pl* **knives** [nīvz].—*vt* to cut or stab with a knife; (*inf*) to injure or defeat by treachery.—**under the knife**, undergoing surgery. [ME *knif*.—OE *cnīf*.]
knight [nīt] *n* in the Middle Ages, a man raised to an honorable military rank and pledged to do good deeds; in modern times in Britain, a man who for some achievement is given honorary rank entitling him to use 'Sir' before his given name; a chessman shaped like a horse's head.—*vt* to make (a man) a knight. **knight´err´ant**, a knight who travelled in search of adventures; a man of chivalrous or quixotic spirit; **knight´err´antry; knight´hood**, the rank, title, or status of knight; the order or fraternity of knights.—*adj, adv* **knight´ly**.—**Knight of Columbus**, a member of a benevolent and fraternal society of Roman Catholic men; **Knight Templar**, a member of an order of Freemasonry. [OE *cniht*, youth, servant, warrior; Ger and Du *knecht*, servant.]
knit [nit] *vt* to form (material, or a garment) by interlooping yarn by means of knitting needles; to cause to grow together (eg broken bones); (of common interests, etc.) to draw (persons) close together; to contract, wrinkle (the brows).—*vi* to make material from yarn by means of needles; to grow together;—*pr p* **knitt´ing**; *pt, pt p* **knitt´ed** or **knit**.—*ns* **knitt´er; knitt´ing**, the work of a knitter; union, junction; the material formed by knitting; **knitt´ing need´le**, a thin rod of steel, bone or other substance used in knitting; **knit´wear**, knitted clothing. [OE *cnyttan—cnotta*, a knot.]
knives *pl* of **knife**.
knob [nob] *n* a rounded lump or protruberance; a handle, usu round, of a door, drawer, etc. **knobbed**, containing or set with knobs; **knobb´y**, full of knobs; like a knob.—*ns* **knobb´iness**. [Cf Low Ger *knobbe*.]
knock [nok] *vi* to strike a blow; to rap on a door; to bump, collide; (of an engine) to make a thumping noise.—*vt* to strike; to hit so as to cause to fall (*with* **down** *or* **off**); to make by hitting (*knock a hole in the wall*); (*inf*) to find fault with; *n* a knocking, a hit, a rap.—*n* **knock´er**, one that knocks, a device suspended to a door for making a knock.—*adj* **knock´kneed**, having knees that *bend inward at the knee*.—**knock about**, or **around** (*inf*) to wander about; **knock down**, to take apart; to indicate the sale of (an article) at an auction; **knock off** (*inf*), to stop working; (*inf*) to deduct; (*slang*) to kill, overcome, etc.; **knock out**, to make unconscious or exhausted; **knock together** (*inf*), to make or compose hastily; **knock up**, (slang) to make pregnant. [OE *cnocian*; perh imit.]
knoll [nōl] *n* a round hillock. [OE *cnol*; Ger *knollen*, a knob, lump.]
knot [not] *n* a lump in a thread, etc. formed by a tightened loop or tangling; a fastening made by tying lengths of rope, etc.; an ornamental bow; a small group, cluster; a hard mass of wood where a branch grows out from a tree, which shows as a roundish, cross-grained piece in a board; a unit of speed of one nautical mile (6,076.12 feet) per hour; something that ties closely, esp the bond of marriage.—*vti* to make or form a knot (in); to entangle or become entangled.—*ns* **knot´grass**, a cosmopolitan weed (*Polygonum aviculare*) of the buckwheat family with jointed stems; any of several grasses with jointed stems; **knot´hole**, a hole where a knot has fallen out; **knot´weed**, any of several herbs of the genus *Polygonum*.—*adj* **knott´y**, full of knots; hard to solve; puzzling.—*n* **knott´iness**. [OE *cnotta*; Ger *knoten*, Dan *knude*, L *nōdus*.]
know [nō] *vt* to be well-informed about; to be aware of; to be acquainted with; to recognize or distinguish.—*pr p* **knowing**; *pt* **knew** [nū]; *pt p* **known** [nōn].—*adj* **know´ing**, having knowledge; shrewd; clever; implying a secret understanding.—*adv* **know´ingly**, in a knowing way; to one's own knowledge.—*ns* **know-how** (*inf*), technical skill; **know´-all, know-it-all** (*inf*), one who acts as if he knows much about everything.—**in the know** (*inf*), having confidential information. [OE *cnāwan*; ON *knā*, L *noscĕre*, for *gnoscere*, Gr *gignōskein*.]
knowledge [nol´ij] *n* what one knows; the body of facts, etc. accumulated by mankind; fact of knowing (eg *the knowledge of success*); range of information or understanding; the act of knowing.—*adj* **knowl´edgeable**, having knowledge or intelligence. [ME *knowleche*, where *-leche* is unexplained; see **know**.]
knuckle [nuk´l] *n* a joint of the finger, esp at the roots of the fingers; the knee of an animal used as food.—*ns* **knuck´leduster**, a metal covering for the knuckles used as a weapon; **knuck´lehead** (*inf*), a stupid person.—**knuckle down**, to work hard; **knuckle under**, to yield; to give in. [ME *knokel*.]
knurl [nûrl] *n* a small knob or ridge; one of a series of knurls on a metal surface to prevent slippage.—*adj* **knurl´ed**. [OE *knur*.]
koala [kō-ä´la] *n* an Australian tree-dwelling marsupial (*Phascolarctos cinereus*) with thick, gray fur. The model for the teddy bear. [Australian native name *kūlā*.]
kohl [kōl] *n* a black powder used in Middle Eastern countries for staining the eyelids. [Ar *koh´l*.]
kohlrabi [kōl´rä-bi] *n* a cabbage with a turnip-shaped stem. [Ger,—It *cavalo rapa*, cole-turnip.]
koine [koi´na, kē´ne] *n* a lingua franca; **Koine**, the Greek language consisting of an amalgamation of dialects spoken during the time of the Roman Empire (from about 31 BC to 476 AD).
kokanee [kō´kä-ni] *n* a small, freshwater salmon of N America.
kola tree [kō´lä] *n* either of two tropical trees (genus *Cola*) whose seeds (called **ko´la-nuts**) have stimulant properties. [West African name.]
Kol Nidre [kōl nidrȧ, or köl´nidre] *n* (*Judaism*) the prayer chanted just before sunset on Yom Kippur eve.
kolinsky [ko-lin´ski] *n* any of several Asian minks (esp *Mustela siberica*); its fur. [Russ *kolinski—Kola*, a peninsula in the north-west of European Russia.]
Komsomol [kom´sō-mol] *n* a youth organization of the former USSR.
kook [ko͝ok] *n* (*slang*) a person regarded as silly, eccentric, etc.
kookaburra [ko͝ok´ȧ-bur-a] *n* an Australian kingfisher (*Dacelo novaguineae*) with a harsh cry like loud laughter. [Austr native name.]
kookie, kooky [ko͝ok´i] *adj* eccentric, crazy; (of clothes) smart and eccentric.
kopeck, kopek [kō-pek´] *n* a unit of money in Russia, the hundredth part of a rouble. [Russ *kopeika*.]
Koran [kō-rän´, kȯ-rȧn´] *n* the sacred book of the Muslims. [Ar *qurān*, reading.]
kosher [kō´shėr] *adj* (*Judaism*) clean or fit to eat according to dietary laws; (*slang*) proper, legitimate. [Heb *kāshēr*, right.]
kowtow [kow´tow´] *vi* to show great respect (to) by bowing. [Chinese *k'o*, knock, *t'ou*, head.]
koumiss [ko͞omis] *n* fermented mare's milk.—Also **kumiss**. [Russ *kumis*.]
kraal [kräl] *n* a S African native village; a corral; also, a native hut with bush stockade round it. [Du *kraal*—Port *curral*—L *currĕre*.]
kraut [krowt] *n* sauerkraut.
Krebs cycle [krebz] *n* a series of chemical reactions occurring in the tissues of mammals by which food is made available for energy.—Also **citric acid cycle, tricarboxylic acid cycle**. [H A *Krebs*, Brit biochemist.]
Kremlin [krem´lin] *n* the citadel of Moscow, formerly housing many Soviet government offices; the Soviet government.—*ns* **krem´linol´ogy**, the study of the policies, etc. of the Soviet Union; **Kremlinologist**. [Russ *kreml´*.]
krill [kril] *n* small shrimplike plankton (order Euphausiacea) that is the principal food of many whales.
kris [krēs] *n* a Malay dagger with wavy blade. [Malay.]
Krishna [krish´na] *n* a Hindu god, an incarnation of Vishnu.
krone [krōn´ė] *n* a monetary unit of Denmark or Norway.—*pl* **kron´er. krona** [krōn´ė] *n* unit of money in Iceland or Sweden.—*pl* **kron´or**.
krypton [krip´ton] *n* a noble gaseous element (symbol Kr; at wt 83.80; atomic no 36). [Gr *kryptein*, to hide.]
kudos [kū´dos] *n* (*inf*) fame, renown. [Gr *kȳdos*.]
kudzu [ko͝od´zo͞o] *n* a prostrate vine (*Pueraria thunbergiana*) of the pea family used widely for erosion control and for forage. [Jap *kuzu*.]
Ku Klux Klan [kū´kluks klan] a US secret society that is anti-Negro,

anti-Semitic, anti-Catholic, etc. whose membership is confined to American-born white Christians.—*n* **Ku Kluxer**. [Gr *kyklos*, a circle, and **clan**.]

kulak [kōō-lak´] *n* a rich peasant in 19th century Russia. [Russ, fist.]

kumiss *See* **koumiss**.

kümmel [kim´él] *n* a German liqueur flavored with caraway seeds and cumin. [Ger.]

kumquat [kum´kwot] *n* a small, orange-colored, oval citrus fruit with a sour pulp and a sweet rind; the tree (genus *Fortunella*) that bears it. [From Chinese; lit 'golden orange'.]

kung fu [kung foo] a Chinese system of self-defense, like Karate but with flowing movements.

Kuomintang [kwo´min-däng´] *n* the nationalist people's party in China, exiled to Taiwan in 1949. [Chinese.]

kurchatovium [kûr-chá-tō´vi-ùm] *n* element 104 named by Russians, who claimed its discovery in 1966, after a Russian physicist.—Also **rutherfordium**.

Kurd [kōōrd, kûrd] *n* one of the pastoral and agricultural people inhabiting a region in Turkey, Iran, Iraq, Syria, and the Armenian and Azerbaidzhan republics.—*n* **Kurd´ish**, the Iranian language of the Kurds.

kwashiorkor [kwä-shi-ör´kör] *n* a severe nutritional disease of children due to deficiency of protein. [Ghanaian name.]

kyphosis [ki-fō´sis] *n* curvature of the spine in which the back is rounded. [Gr *kyphos*, humpbacked.]

kymograph [kī´mō-graf] *n* a device for graphically recording motion or pressure (as of blood).—*n* **kym´ogram**, record produced by a kymograph. [Gr *kyma*, wave + **graph**.]

Kyrie [kēr´i-e] *n* a short, liturgical prayer that begins with the words "Lord, have mercy".—Also **kyrie eleison** [el-ā´i-son]. [LL from Gr *kȳrie, eleēson*, Lord, have mercy.]

L

laager [lä´gėr] *n* in South Africa, a camp made by a ring of ox-wagons set close together for defence; an encampment. [Cape Du *lager*—Ger *lager*, a camp.]

label [lā´b(ė)l] *n* a small slip attached to anything to denote its nature, contents, ownership, etc.; term of generalized classification.—*vt* to affix a label to; to designate (as);—*prp* **lā´belling**; *pt, ptp* **lā´belled**.—[OFr *label* (Fr *lambeau*); perh—OHG *lappa* (Ger *lappen*).]

labial [lā´bi-ȧl] *adj* of the lips;—*n* a sound as *b, m*, and *p* formed by the lips.—*adv* **lā´bially**.—*adj* **lā´biate**, lipped; having a lipped corolla.—*adj, n* **lābiodent´al**, of a sound pronounced by lips and teeth as *f* and *v* [L *labium*, a lip.]

laboratory [lab´ȯ-rȧ-tȯ-ri] *n* a place where scientific work and research is carried out. [L *labōrāre*—*labor*, work.]

labor [lā´bȯr] *n* work, physical or mental exertion; a specific task; all wage-earning workers; labor unions collectively; the process of childbirth.—*vi* to work; to work hard; to move with difficulty; to suffer (delusions, etc.); to be in childbirth.—*vt* to develop in unnecessary detail.—*adj* **laborious** requiring much work; industrious; labored.—*adv* **laboriously**.—*n* **laboriousness**.—*adj* **labored**, done with effort; strained.—*ns* **labor camp**, a penal colony where forced labor takes place; a camp for migrant workers; **laborer**, one who labors, esp one whose work requires strength rather than skill; **labor union**, an association of workers to promote and protect the welfare, rights, etc. of its members.—**Labor Day**, the first Monday in September in the US and Canada, a legal holiday honoring labor; May 1 in many countries; **Labour Party**, a British political party, generally supporting the interests of organized labor. [OFr *labour, labeur*—L *labor*.]

Labrador retriever [lab´rȧ-dör ri-trēv´ėr] *n* a breed of large, smooth-coated sporting dog. [*Labrador*.]

laburnum [la-bûr´num] *n* a small genus (*Laburnum*) of poisonous trees or shrubs of the pea family with hanging yellow flowers. [L]

labyrinth [lab´i-rinth] *n* a structure containing winding passages through which it is hard to find one's way; a maze.—*adjs* **labyrinth´ian, labyrinth´ine**. [Gr *labyrinthos*, perh conn with *labrys*, the double axe.]

lac[1] *See* **lakh**.

lac[2] [lak] *n* a resinous substance secreted on certain Asiatic trees by a scale insect which is the source of shellac. [Hindustani, *lākh*—Sans *lākṣā*, 100 000, hence the (teeming) lac insect.]

lace [lās] *n* a string, etc. used to draw together and fasten parts of a shoe, a corset, etc.; an ornamental fabric of delicately woven fine thread—*vt* to fasten with a lace; to interwine, weave; to thrash, whip.—*n* **lac´ing**, the act of fastening with a lace or cord through eyelet-holes; a cord used in fastening. [OFr *las*, a noose—L *laqueus*, a noose.]

lacerate [las´ėr-āt] *vt* to tear jaggedly.—*n* **lacerā´tion**.—*adj* **lac´erative**, tearing; having power to cause mental distress. [L *lacerāre, -ātum*, to tear—*lacer*, torn.]

lachrymal, lacrimal [lak´ri-mȧl] *adj* of tears.—*adj* **lach´rymose**, shedding tears; given to weeping.—*adv* **lach´rymosely**. [*lachryma*, mediaeval spelling of L *lacrima*, a tear; Gr *dakry*, Eng **tear**.]

lack [lak] *n* the fact or state of not having any or not having enough; the thing that is needed.—*vti* to be deficient in or entirely without.—*adj* **lack´luster**, dull; lacking brightness. [ME *lak*, defect; cf Middle Low Ger and Du *lak*, blemish.]

lackadaisical [lak-a-dā´zi-kȧl] *adj* showing lack of spirit or interest; listless. [From archaic interj *lackadaisy*!]

lackey [lak´i] *n* a male servant of low rank; a servile, obsequious person; a toady. [OFr *laquay* (Fr *laquais*)—Sp *lacayo*, a lackey; perh Ar *luka*', servile.]

laconic [la-kon´ik] *adj* using few words; concise.—*adv* **lacon´ically**. [Gr *Lakōnikos*.]

lacquer [lak´ėr] *n* a varnish made of lac and alcohol.—*vt* to cover with lacquer, to make glossy.—*n* **lac´querer**. [Fr *lacre*—Port *lacre, laca*—Hindustani. *See* **lac** (2).]

lacrosse [la-kros´] *n* a game played by two teams of twelve, the ball being driven through the opponents' goal by a crosse. [Fr]

lacteal [lak´ti-ȧl] *adj* of or like milk; milky.—*n* any of the lymphatic vessels of the intestines which convey the chyle to the thoracic duct.—*n* **lactā´tion**, the secretion of milk.—*adjs* **lac´tic** of or relating to milk; obtained from sour milk or whey; involving the production of lactic acid; **lactif´erous**, conveying or producing milk or milky juice.—*n* **lac´tose**, a sugar present in milk yielding glucose upon hydrolysis and lactic acid upon fermentation.—**lactic acid**, a hygroscopic organic acid $C_3H_6O_3$ normally present in animal tissue, produced by bacterial fermentation of carbohydrate matter and used widely in food, medicine, and industry. [L *lacteus*, milky—*lac*, gen *lactis*, milk; Gr *gala*, gen *galaktos*, milk.]

lacuna [la-kū´na] *n* a gap esp a missing portion in a text;—*pl* **lacū´nae** [-nē]. [L *lacūna*, hollow, gap.]

lad [lad] *n* a boy; a youth; [ME *ladde*, youth, servant.]

ladder [lad´ėr] *n* a contrivance, often portable, with rungs between two supports, for going up and down; something that resembles a ladder in form or use, esp in ascending. [OE *hlǣder*; Ger *leiter*.]

lade [lād] *vt* to load; to throw in or out, as a fluid, with a ladle or dipper.—*adj* **lad´en**, laded or loaded; burdened.—*n* **lad´ing**, the act of loading; that which is loaded; cargo; freight. [OE *hladan*, pt *hlōd*, to load, to draw out water.]

Ladino [lȧ´dēnō] *n* a dialect of Spanish and Portuguese, the vernacular of Sephardic Jews; **ladino**, a Spanish-speaking Latin-American. [Spanish.]

ladle [lād´l] *n* a long-handled, cuplike spoon; a device like a ladle in shape or use. [OE *hlædel*—*hladan*, to lade.]

lady [lā´dē] *n* a woman of high social position; a woman who is polite, refined, etc.; **Lady**, a British title given to women of certain ranks;—*pl* **la´dies** term used to address a group of women.—*ns* **la´dy beetle**, ladybug; **la´dybird**, ladybug; **la´dybug**, a small, roundish often brightly-colored beetle (family Coccinellidae) with a spotted back; **Lady Chapel**, a chapel dedicated to the Virgin Mary; **lady fern** either of two ferns (genus *Athyrium*), Northern Ladyfern (*A filixfoemina*) is evergreen; Southern Lady fern (*A filix-foemina asplenioides*) is not; **la´dyfinger** a small finger-shaped sponge cake; **lady-in-waiting** a woman waiting upon a queen or princess.—*adj* **la´dylike** like or suitable for a lady.—*ns* **la´dylove** a sweetheart; **la´dyship** the rank or position of a lady; a title used in speaking to or of a titled Lady (*with* **your** *or* **her**); **lady-slipper** a N American temperate-zone orchid (genus *Cypripedium*) with flowers somewhat like slippers; **la´dy-killer** a man who is extremely attractive to women. [OE *hlǣfdige*, lit app the bread-kneader—*hlāf*, loaf, and a lost word from the root of **dough**.]

lag[1] [lag] *n* a falling behind; the amount of this.—*vi* to move or walk slowly; to loiter; to become less intense; to roll a cue ball in billiards or a marble in a game of marbles to decide the order of play.—*vt* to lag behind; to shoot (as a marble) at a mark. *prp* **lagg´ing**; *ptp* **lagged**.—*adj* **lagg´ard**, lagging; slow;—*ns* **lagg´ard, lagg´er**, one who lags behind; a loiterer. [Origin unknown.]

lag[2] [lag] *n* a barrel stave; a slat or strip forming part of a lid for a cylindrical object.—*vt* to cover or provide with lags. [Prob ON *lögg*, barrel-rim; cf Swed *lagg*, stave.]

lager [lä´ger] *n* a beer that has been aged for several months. [Ger *lagerbier*—*lager*, a store-house, *bier*, beer.]

lagoon [la-gōōn´] *n* a shallow lake or pond esp one connected with a larger body of water; the water enclosed by a circular coral reef; shallow water separated from the sea by sand dunes. [It *laguna*—L *lacūna*.]

laid [lād] *pt, ptp* of **lay** (2)—*adj* **laid-back** (*slang*) relaxed, easy-going, etc.; not hurried.

lain *ptp* of **lie** (2).

lair [lār] *n* the den or retreat of a wild animal. [OE *leger*, a couch—*liegan*, to lie down; Du *leger*, Ger *lager*.]

laissez-faire [les´ā-fer´] *n* noninterference with the free action of the individual, esp the absence of governmental control over industry and business.—Also **laiss´er-faire´**. [Fr *laisser* (imper *laissez*) to allow (L *laxāre*, to relax), *faire* (L *facĕre*), to do.]

laity *See* **lay** (4).

lake[1] [lāk] *n* a purplish-red pigment prepared from lac or cochineal; carmine. [Fr *laque*—Hindustani. *See* **lac** (2).]

lake[2] [lāk] *n* a large inland body of usu. fresh water.—*ns* **lake´dwell´ing**, a dwelling, esp prehistoric, built on piles in a lake; **lake´front** an area fronting a lake; **lake herring** a cisco (*Coregonus artedii*) which is an important food fish; **Lakeland terrier** a breed of small, straight-legged, harsh-coated terrier; **lak´er** one associated with a lake, esp a fish; **lake trout** any of various freshwater salmon and trout, esp a N American char (*Salvelinus namaycush*). [ME *lac*—L *lacus*.]

lakh [lak] *n* one hundred thousand; a great number.—Also **lac**. [Hindustani *lākh*—Sans *lākṣā*, 100 000.]

lam[1] [lam] *n* (*slang*) headlong flight.—*vi* (*slang*) to flee; escape.—**on the lam** (*slang*) in flight, esp from the police.

lam[2] [lam] *vt* to beat. [Cf OE *lemian*, to subdue, to lame.]

lama [lä´mä] *n* a monk or priest in lamaism.—*ns* **Lamaism** [lä´mä-izm] a form of Buddhism in Tibet and Mongolia; **la´masery** [lä-mä´sėr-i] a Tibetan monastery. [Tibetan *blama*, the *b* silent.]

lamaze [lė-mäz] *n* a training program in natural childbirth, involving the help of the father.

lamb [lam] *n* a young sheep; its flesh as food; a simple, innocent, or gentle person.—*vi* to bring forth (a lamb); to tend (ewes) at lambing time.—*n* **lamb´skin**, a lamb's skin dressed with the wool on and made into winter garments; leather from such a skin. [OE *lamb*; Ger *lamm*, Du *lam*.]

Lambda [lam´dȧ] *n* the 11th letter of the Greek alphabet.

lambent [lam´bėnt] *adj* licking; moving about as if touching lightly; gliding over; flickering. [L *lambĕre*, to lick.]

lame [lām] *adj* crippled, esp in the use of a leg; stiff and painful; poor; ineffectual.—*vt* to make lame;—*adv* **lame´ly**.—*n* **lame´ness**.—**lame duck**, an elected official continuing to hold office during the interim between the end of his term and the inauguration of a successor. [OE *lama*, lame; Du *lam*, Ger *lahm*.]

lamé [la-mā] *n* a fabric interwoven with flat metallic threads. [Fr.]

lamella [la-mel´ȧ] *n* a thin plate, scale, or layer, esp one of the thin plates in the gills of a bivalve mollusk or the gill of a mushroom.—*pl* **lamell´ae** [-mel´ē] **lamell´as**.—*adj* **lamell´ar, lam´ellate**. [L, dim of *lamina*, a thin plate.]

lament [la-ment´] *vti* to feel or express deep sorrow (for); mourn.—*n* a lamenting; an elegy, dirge, etc. mourning some loss or death.—*adj* **lamentable** [lam´ėntȧbl or lėmėn´tȧbl].—*ns* **lamenta´tion; Lamenta´tions** (*Bible*) 25th book of the Old Testament, written by Jeremiah, describing the capture and destruction of Jerusalem by the Babylonians. [Fr *lamenter*—L *lāmentārī*.]

lamina [lam´i-na] *n* a thin plate or layer; the expanded part of a foliage leaf;—*pl* **lam´inae** [-nē, nī], **lamin´as**—*adj* **lam´inar**, consisting of, arranged in, or like laminae.—*n* **laminaria**, any of a genus (*Laminaria*) of large kelps.—*vt* **lam´inate**, to cover with one or more thin layers; to make by building up in layers.—*vi* to divide into laminae.—*n* a product made by laminating.—*adj* built in thin sheets or layers.—*n* **laminā´tion**.—**laminar flow**, a streamline flow in a fluid near a boundary. [L *lāmina*, a thin plate.]

lamp [lamp] *n* a container with a wick for burning oil, etc. to produce light or heat; any device for producing light or therapeutic rays; a holder or base for such a device.—*ns* **lamp´black**, a fine soot used as a pigment; **lamp´post**, a post supporting a street lamp. [Fr *lampe* and Gr *lampas, -ados*—*lampein*, to shine.]

lampoon [lam-pōōn´] *n* a satirical writing attacking someone.—*vt* to ridicule maliciously in a lampoon.—*ns* **lampoon´er, lampoon´ery**. [OFr *lampon*, orig a drinking-song, with the refrain *lampons* = let us drink—*lamper*, to drink (*lapper*, to lap).]

lamprey [lam´pri] *n* any of an order (*Hyperoartia*) of aquatic vertebrates resembling an eel but having a jawless, round sucking mouth. [OFr *lamproie*—Low L *lamprēda, lampetra*—explained as from L *lambĕre*, to lick, *petra*, rock.]

lance [läns] *n* a long wooden spear with a sharp iron or steel head; a soldier armed with a lance; a surgeon's lancet;—*vt* to pierce, as with a lance; to open with a lancet.—*n* **lanc´er**, a cavalry soldier armed with a lance, (*pl*) a set of five quadrilles each in a different meter; the music for such dances. [Fr,—L *lancea*; Gr *lonchē*, a lance.]

lanceolate, -d [län´si-ō-lāt, -id] *adjs* shaped like a lance head; (*bot*) tapering towards both ends. [L *lanceolātus*—*lanceola*, dim of *lancea*, a lance.]

lancet [län´set] *n* a small, usu. two-edged, pointed surgical knife; a lancet window; a lancet arch.—**lancet arch**, an acutely pointed arch; **lancet window**, a high narrow window terminating in an acutely pointed arch without tracery. [OFr *lancette*, dim of *lance*. *See* **lance**.]

land [land] *n* the solid portion of the earth's surface; ground, soil; a country and its people; real estate.—*vt* to set (an aircraft) down on land or water; to put on shore from a ship; to bring to a particular place; to catch (a fish); (*inf*) to get or secure (a job); (*inf*) to deliver (a blow).—*vi* to go ashore from a ship; (of a ship) to come to port; to arrive at a specified place; to come to rest.—*adj* **land´ed** owning land;—*ns* **land´fall**, a sighting of land from a ship at sea; the land sighted; **land´fill**, disposal of garbage or trash by burying it in the ground; **land´holder**, an owner of land.—*adj, n* **land´holding**.—*n* **landing**, the act of coming to shore or to the ground; the place where persons or goods are loaded or unloaded from a ship; a platform at the end of a flight of stairs.—*adj* **land´locked**, surrounded by land, as a bay; cut off from the sea and confined to fresh water.—*ns* **land´lord**, a man who leases land, houses, etc. to others; a man who keeps a rooming house, inn, etc.; **land´lubber**, one who has had little experience on boats; **land´mark**, something that marks the boundary of a piece of land; any prominent feature of the landscape distinguishing a locality; an important event or turning point; **land´mass**, a very large piece of land, esp a continent; **land mine**, an explosive charge placed in the ground, usu. detonated by stepping or driving on it.—*adj* **land-poor**, needing money while owning land.—*ns* **landslide**, the sliding of a mass of soil or rocks down a slope; the mass sliding down; an overwhelming victory, esp in an election; **lands´man**, a fellow countryman; a landlubber. *adj, adv* **landward**, toward the land.—*adv* **land´wards**.—**land contract**, a contract in which the seller of real estate transfers his interest to the buyer only after the purchase price has been fully paid in regular payments over a specified period; **land grant**, a grant of land made by the government, esp for railroads, roads, or colleges; **land-grant college**, college or university in the US entitled to federal government support under certain laws; **landing gear**, the undercarriage of an aircraft, including wheels, etc.; **land office**, a government office that handles the sales of public lands; **land-office business** (*inf*) a booming business. [OE *land*; Du, Ger *land*.]

landau [lan´dö] *n* a four-wheeled carriage with a top that may be opened centrally and thrown back.—*n* **landaulet´**, a closed automobile, the back portion of which can be uncovered by lowering part of the roof and sides; a small landau. [*Landau* in Germany, where it is said to have been first made.]

landscape [land´skāp] *n* a picture of natural, inland scenery; an expanse of natural scenery seen in one view.—*vt* to make (a plot of ground) more attractive as by adding lawns, bushes, trees, etc.—*n* **land´scaper**.—**landscape architect**, one whose profession is the arrangement of land for human use, esp the placing of structures, pathways, and plantings; **landscape gardener**, one skilled in the decorative planting of gardens and grounds; **landscape painter**, one who depicts landscapes in paintings, watercolors, etc. [Du *landschap*, from *land* and *-schap*, a suffix equivalent to Eng *-ship*.]

lane [lān] *n* a narrow road, path, etc.; a path or strip designated, for safety reasons, for ships, aircraft, automobiles, etc. [OE *lane, lone*.]

language [lang´gwij] *n* human speech or the written symbols for speech; any means of communicating; a special set of symbols used in a computer; the speech of a particular nation, etc.; the particular style of verbal expression characteristic of a person, group, profession, etc.—**language arts**, the subjects (as reading and writing) that aim at developing the student's understanding of and the ability of use both oral and written language. [Fr *langage*—*langue*—L *lingua*, the tongue.]

languid [lang´gwid] *adj* feeble, flagging, exhausted, sluggish, spiritless.—*adv* **lang´uidly**.—*n* **lang´uidness**. [L *languidus*—*languēre*, to be weak.]

languish [lang´gwish] *vi* to become languid; to lose strength and animation; to pine.—*adj* **lang´uishing** expressive of languor, or merely of sentimental emotion.—*adv* **lang´uishingly**.—*n* **lang´uishment**. [Fr *languiss-* (serving as pr p stem of *languir*)—L *languescĕre*—*languēre*, to be faint.]

languor [lang´g(w)ȯr] *n* state of being languid, faint; dullness, listlessness.—*adj* **lang´uorous**. [L *languor, -ōris*.]

lank [langk] *adj* tall and lean; straight and limp.—*adv* **lank´ly**.—*n* **lank´ness**.—*adj* **lank´y**, lean, tall, and ungainly.—*n* **lank´iness**. [OE *hlanc*.]

lanolin [lan´ō-lin] *n* a fat extracted from wool, used in cosmetics, ointments, etc. [L *lāna*, wool, *oleum*, oil.]

lantern [lant´ėrn] *n* a transparent case for holding or carrying a light; an ornamental structure surmounting a building to give light and air.—*adj* **lant´ern-jawed**, having long thin jaws, and sunken cheeks. [Fr *lanterne*—L *lanterna*—Gr *lamptēr*—*lampein*, to give light.]

lanthanum [lan´thȧn-ŭm] *n* a metallic element (symbol La; at wt 138.9; at no 57).—**lan´thanide series** class of 15 chemically related elements (lanthanides) with atomic numbers from 57 (lanthanum) to 71 (lutetium). [From Gr *lanthanein*, to be unseen.]

lanyard [lan´yȧrd] *n* a short rope used on board ship for fastening or stretching; a cord for hanging a knife, whistle, or the like about the neck. [Fr *lanière*, perh from L *lānārius*, made of wool—*lāna*, wool.]

lap[1] [lap] *vti* to lick up with the tongue; (of waves) to wash or flow against. [OE *lapian*; Low Ger *lappen*; L *lambĕre*; Gr *laptein*.]

lap[2] [lap] *n* the part from waist to knees of a person sitting; the part of the clothing covering this; that in which a person or thing is cared for; an overlapping; a part that overlaps; one complete circuit of a race track.—*vt* to fold (over or on); to wrap; to enfold; to overlap; to get a lap ahead of (an opponent) in a race.—*vi* to overlap; to extend over something in space or time (*with* **over**).—*ns* **lap´belt**, a seat belt that fastens across the lap; **lap´board**, a board placed on the lap for use as a table or desk; **lap dog**, any pet dog small enough to be held in the lap; **lap of honor**, a round of the field run by a person or a team that has just had a victory. [OE *læppa*, a loosely hanging part; Ger *lappen*, a rag.]

lapel [la-pel´] *n* part of a garment folded back, continuing the collar.—*adj* **lapelled´**. [Dim of **lap**[2]]

lapidary [lap´i-dȧr-i] *n* a cutter of gemstones.—*adj* pertaining to stones and the cutting of stones; inscribed on stone. [L *lapidārius*—*lapis, -idis*, a stone.]

lapillus [lȧ-pil´ŭs] *n* a glassy fragment of lava thrown out in a volcanic eruption.—*pl* **lapilli** [la-pil´ī].

lapin [lap´in] *n* a castrated male rabbit; rabbit fur, often dyed and sheared to resemble other fur. [Fr.]

lapis lazuli [lap´is laz´ūlī] *n* an azure, opaque, semiprecious stone. [L *lapis*, a stone, Med L *lazulus*, azure.]

Lapp *n* a member of a nomadic people inhabiting northern Scandinavia, Finland and the Kola peninsula of northern Russia; the Finno-Ugric languages of the Lapps.

lapse [laps] *vi* to fall away by cessation or relaxation of effort or cause; to fall from the faith; to fail in duty; to pass into disuse; to become void.—*n* a small error; a failure (in virtue, memory, etc.).—*adj* **lapsed**, having fallen into disuse or become void; fallen into sin or from the faith. [L *lapsāre*, to slip, *lapsus*, a slip—*lābī, lapsus*, to slip.]

lapwing [lap´wing] *n* a crested Old World plover (*Vanellus vanellus*). [ME *lappewinke*—OE *læpewince, hlēpewince, hlēawince*; modified by confusion with **wing**.]

larceny [lär´sėn-i] *n* the unlawful taking of another's property; theft. [OFr *larrecin* (Fr *larcin*)—L *latrōcinium*—*latrō*, a robber.]

larch [lärch] *n* a genus (*Larix*) of cone-bearing trees of the pine family that sheds its leaves annually. [Gr *larix*.]

lard [lärd] *n* the melted and clarified fat of the hog.—*vt* to insert strips of bacon or fat pork (in meat) before cooking; to embellish. [OFr—L *lāridum, lārdum*; cf Gr *lārinos*, fat, *lāros*, pleasant to taste.]

larder [lärd´ėr] *n* a place where food supplies are kept; food supplies. [OFR *lardier*, a bacon-tub—*lard*. See **lard**.]

lares and penates [ler´ēz and pi-nāt´ēz] *n pl* the household gods of the ancient Romans. [L (sing *lar*).]

large [lärj] *adj* great in size, amount, or number; bulky; big; spacious; bigger than others of its kind; operating on a big scale.—*adj* **large´-heart´ed**, sympathetic, kindly, generous.—*adv* **large´ly**, much, in great amounts; mainly, for the most part.—*n* **large´ness**.—**at large**, at liberty; fully; in detail; (of a congressman) representing no particular district. [Fr—L *largus*, copious.]

largess, largesse [lärj´es] *n* a present or donation; money liberally bestowed. [Fr *largesse* and L *largitiō, -ōnis—largus*, copious.]

largo [lär´gō] *adj* (*mus*) slow and dignified.—*n* a movement to be so performed. [It—L *largus*, copious.]

lariat [lar´i-at] *n* a rope for tethering grazing horses; a lasso. [Sp *la*, the, *reata*, a rope for tying animals together.]

lark[1] [lärk] *n* any of a family of Old World songbirds (family *Alaudidae*), esp the skylark. [ME *laverock*—OE *læwerce, lāwerce*, Ger *lerche*.]

lark[2] [lärk] *n* a frolic; a piece of mischief.—*vi* to frolic.—*adj* **lark´y**. [Perh from the preceding; some connect it with OE *lāc*, play.]

larkspur [lärk´spûr] *n* an annual delphinium.

larva [lär´va] *n* an animal in an immature but active state markedly different from the adult, eg a caterpillar.—*pl* **larvae** [lär´vē].—*adj* **lar´val**. [L *lārva, lārua*, a spectre, a mask.]

larynx [lar´ingks] *n* the structure at the upper end of the windpipe, containing the vocal cords.—*pl* **lar´ynes, larynges** [lė-rin´jėz].—*adj* **laryngeal** [*lar-in´ji-ál*].—*n* **laryngitis** [-jī´tis] inflammation of the larynx.—*n* **laryng´oscope** [-ing´gō], a mirror for examining the larynx. [L—Gr *larynx, -yngos*.]

lasagna [la-sän´yė] *n* pasta formed in wide, flat strips; a dish of lasagna baked in layers with cheese, tomato sauce, and ground meat.—Also **lasagne**. [Ital, the noodle.]

lascivious [la-siv´i-ùs] *adj* lustful; tending to produce lustful emotions.—*adv* **lasciv´iously**.—*n* **lasciv´iousness**. [LL *lasciviōsus—lascīvus*, playful.]

laser [lāz´ėr] *n* a device which amplifies an input of light, producing an extremely narrow and intense monochromatic beam.—*vi* **lase**, to emit coherent light.—**laser disc**, a video disc for recording audio and video data to be read by a laser beam. [*L*ight *a*mplification by *s*timulated *e*mission of *r*adiation.]

lash [lash] *n* the flexible part of a whip; an eyelash; a stroke as with a whip; a stroke of satire.—*vt* to strike with or as if with a lash; to switch back and forth; to fasten or secure with a rope or cord; to scourge with censure or satire.—*vi* to make strokes as with a whip.—*n* **lash´ing**, act of whipping; a rope for making things fast.—*vt* **lash out**, to strike out violently; to speak angrily. [Origin obscure; perh several different words, with possible connections with **latch** and **lace**.]

lass [las] *n* a young woman. [Origin obscure.]

Lassa fever [la´sȧ fē´vėr] An infectious tropical virus disease, often fatal. [*Lassa*, Nigeria.]

lassitude [las´i-tūd] *n* faintness, weakness, weariness, languor. [L *lassitūdō—lassus*, faint.]

lasso [las´ō, also la-sōō] *n* a long rope with a running noose for catching wild horses, etc.—*pl* **lassos, lassoes**.—*vt* to catch with the lasso.—*pr p* **lass´ōing** [or -ōō´-]; *pt p* **lass´oed** [las´ōd or -ōōd]. [S Amer pronunciation of Sp *lazo*—L *laqueus*, a noose.]

last[1] [läst] *n* a shoemaker's model of the foot on which boots and shoes are made or repaired.—*vt* to shape with a last. [OE *lāst*, footprint.]

last[2] [last] *vi* to remain in existence, use, etc.; to endure.—*vt* to continue during; to be enough for.—*adj* **lasting**, that lasts a long time.

last[3] [last] alternative superlative of **late**.—*adj* being or coming after all the others in time or place; only remaining; the most recent; least likely; conclusive.—*adv* after all the others; most recently; finally.—*n* the one coming last.—*adjs* **last-ditch´**, being a final effort to avoid disaster; **last-in first-out**, of a method of inventory valuing all stock in hand at the cost of the lot last received; (*inf*) of the practice of firing the newest employees when the work force is reduced.—*n* **last hurrah**, a final attempt or appearance, as in politics.—*ns* **Last Judgment** (*Christianity*), the final judgment at the end of the world; **last name**, surname; **last straw**, a final trouble that results in defeat, loss of patience, etc.; **Last Supper**, the meal eaten by Jesus and His disciples on the eve of His betrayal; **last word**, the final remark in a dispute; a definitive statement; the latest fashion.—**at last, at long last**, finally; **on its last legs, on one's last legs**, near the end of usefulness. [OE *latost*, superl of *læt*, slow, late.]

Lastex [last´eks] *n* trade name for an elastic yarn made of silk, rayon, or cotton wound around a rubber core.

latakia [lat-a-kē´a] *n* a highly aromatic smoking tobacco. [*Latakia*, in Syria.]

latch [lach] *n* a fastening for a door, gate, or window, esp a bar, etc. that fits into a notch.—*vti* to fasten with a latch.—*ns* **latch´key**, the key of an outer door; **latchkey child**, a young child who regularly returns home to an empty house; **latch´string**, a string fastened to a latch and left hanging outside the door for use in raising the latch.—**latch onto**, (*inf*) to get or obtain; to take in as an idea. [OE *læccan*, to catch.]

late [lāt] *superlative*: **lāt´est** or **last**.—*adj* slow, tardy; behindhand; coming after the expected time; long delayed; far advanced towards the close; last in any place or character; deceased; departed; out of office; not long past.—*advs* **late; late´ly**, recently.—*n* **late´ness**. [OE *læt*, slow; Du *laat*; ON *latr*; Ger *lass*, weary; L *lassus*, tired.]

lateen [la-tēn´] *adj* of a triangular sail rigged to the low mast used esp on the coast of northern Africa.—*n* a lateen-rigged ship; a lateen sail. [Fr (*voile*) *latine*—L *Latīnus*, Latin.]

latent [lā´tėnt] *adj* hidden; not visible or apparent; dormant; undeveloped, but capable of development.—*n* **lā´tency**.—*adv* **lā´tently**.—**latent heat**. [L *latens, -entis*, pr p of *latēre*, to lie hid, Gr *lanthanein*, to be unseen.]

lateral [lat´ėr-ál] *adj* of, at, from, toward the side.—*adv* **lat´erally**. [L *laterālis—latus, latĕris*, a side.]

latex [lā´teks] *n* the milky juice of plants. [L.]

lath [läth] *n* a thin slip of wood used in slating, plastering, etc.; any framework for plaster.—*pl* **laths** [läTHZ].—*vt* to cover or line with laths. [OE *lætt*.]

lathe [lāTH] *n* a machine for turning and shaping articles of wood, metal, etc.

lather [läTH´ėr] *n* a foam made with water and soap; froth from sweat; (*inf*) an excited state.—*vti* to cover with or form lather. [OE *lēathor*.]

Latin [lat´in] *adj* of ancient Rome, its people, their language, etc.; denoting or of the languages derived from Latin, the peoples who speak them, their countries, etc.—*n* a native or inhabitant of ancient Rome; the language of ancient Rome; a person, as a Spaniard or Italian, whose language is derived from Latin.—*vt* **lat´inīze**, to give Latin forms to; to render into Latin.—*ns* **Lat´inism**, a Latin idiom.—*n* **Lat´inist**, one skilled in Latin; **Latin alphabet**, an alphabet used for writing Latin that has been modified for writing many modern languages including English; **Latin America**, that part of the Western Hemisphere south of the US where a language derived from Latin (Spanish, Portuguese, French) is the official language. [L *Latīnus*, belonging to *Latium*, the district round Rome.]

latitude [lat´i-tūd] *n* extent; scope; freedom from restrictions on actions of opinions; distance north or south of the equator, measured in degrees; a region with reference to this distance; the angular distance of a celestial body from its ecliptic.—*adjs* **latitūd´inal; latitu+dinar´ian** broad and liberal in standards of religious belief and conduct.—*n* a person who regards the details of particular creeds and forms of worship as unimportant.—*n* **latitūdina´rianism**. [Fr—L *lātitūdō, -inis—lātus*, broad.]

latrine [la-trēn´] *n* a toilet for the use of many people, as in an army camp. [L *lātrīna—lavātrīnā—lavāre*, to wash.]

latter [lat´ėr] *adj* later; more recent; nearer the end; being the last mentioned of two.—*adv* **latt´erly**, of late.—**Latter-day Saint**, a Mormon. [OE *lætra*, comp of *læt*, slow, late.]

lattice [lat´is] *n* a network of crossed laths or bars.—*n* **latt´icework**, a lattice, lattices collectively. [Fr *lattis—latte*, a lath.]

laud [löd] *vt* to praise; to extol.—*adj* **laud´able**, praise-worthy.—*n* **laud´ableness**.—*adv* **laud´ably**.—*adj* **laud´atory**, containing praise; expressing praise. [L *laudāre—laus, laudis*, praise.]

laudanum [löd´(a)-num] *n* formerly, any of various opium preparations; a solution of opium in alcohol. [L *laudanum*, a dark resin.]

laugh [läf] *vi* to emit explosive inarticulate sounds of the voice under the influence of amusement, joy, scorn, or other emotion.—*vt* to render, put, or drive with laughter.—*n* an act of laughing; a sound of laughing.—*adj* **laugh´able**, ludicrous.—*n* **laugh´ableness**.—*adv* **laugh´ably**.—*ns* **laugh´ing gas**, nitrous oxide; **laugh´ing jack´ass**, a kookaburra.—*adv* **laugh´ingly**.—*ns* **laugh´ingstock**, an object of ridicule; **laugh´ter**, the act or sound of laughing.—**laugh at**, to be amused by; to make fun of. [OE (Anglian) *hlæhhan* (WS *hliehhan*); Ger *lachen*.]

launch[1] [lönch] *vt* to throw or hurl; to send forth; to start on a course; to cause to slide into the water or to take off from land.—*vi* to throw oneself into some activity.—*n* the act or occasion of launching; **launch pad, launch´ing pad**, a platform from which a rocket, guided missile, etc. is launched; **launch window**, a favorable time period for launching a spacecraft. [OFr *lanchier, lancier* (Fr *lancer*)—*lance*. See **lance**.]

launch[2] [lönch] *n* an open, or partly enclosed, motor boat. [Sp *lancha* perh from Malay *lanchār*, swift.]

launder [lön´dėr] *vti* to wash and iron, as clothes.—*vt* to legitimize (money) obtained from criminal activity.—*ns* **laun´derette**, a place equipped with laundry equipment that customers may use for a fee; **Laun´dromat**, a trade name for a self-service laundry; **laun´dry**, a place where clothes are washed; clothes sent to be washed. [ME *lavander*—OFr *lavandier*—L *lavandāria*, neut pl from gerundive of *lavāre*, to wash.]

laureate [lö´ri-ąt] *adj* crowned with laurel (as a mark of honor).—*n* the recipient of an honor for high achievement in science or art, as a Nobel Laureate.—*n* **pō´et lau´reate**, official poet attached to the British royal household, who writes odes, etc., for court and national occasions. [L *laureātus*, laurelled—*laurus*, laurel.]

laurel [lö´rėl] *n* evergreen shrub (genuis *Laurus*) of southern Europe, with large, glossy leaves; the leaves of *L nobilis* used by the ancient Greeks to crown victors in games; (*pl*) fame; honor; any of various trees and shrubs resembling the true laurel. [Fr *laurier*—L *laurus.*]

lava [lä´va] *n* molten rock discharged in a molten stream from a volcano; such rock when solidified by cooling. [It—L *lavāre*, to wash.]

lavaliere, lavalliere [lav´e-lir´] *n* an ornament on a fine chain, worn around the neck. [Fr.]

lave [lāv] *vti* (*poetic*) to wash; to bathe.—*ns* **lavä´bō**, a washbasin and water tank hung on the wall; a wall planter resembling this; **làv´atory**, a washbowl with faucets and drain; a room with a washbowl and toilet; **lā´ver**, (*Judaism*) a large vessel for washing, esp ritual washing. [L *lavāre, -ātum*; Gr *louein*, to wash.]

lavender [lav´ėn-dėr] *n* a Mediterranean mint (*Lavendula officinalis*) dried and used in sachets; pale purple. [Anglo-Fr *lavendre* (Fr *lavande*), perh conn with *līvidus*, livid.]

lavish [lav´ish] *vt* to give or spend freely or too freely.—*adj* bestowing profusely, prodigal; extravagant, unrestrained.—*adv* **lav´ishly**.—*n* **lav´ishness**. [Per OFr *lavasse, lavache*, deluge of rain—*laver*—L *lavāre*, to wash.]

law [lö] *n* all the rules of conduct established by the authority of a nation or smaller political authority; any one of such rules; obedience to such rules; the study of such rules, jurisprudence; the seeking of justice in courts under such rules; the profession of lawyers, judges, etc.; a sequence of events occurring with unvarying uniformity under the same conditions; the stating of such a sequence; any rule expected to be observed.—*adj* **law´-abiding**, obeying the law.—*n* **law´breaker**, one who violates the law.—*adj, n* **law´breaking**.—*adj* **law´ful**, in conformity with the law; recognized by law.—*n* **law´giver**, a lawmaker; a legislator.—*adj* **law´less**, not regulated by law; not in conformity with law, illegal; not obeying the law, unruly.—*ns* **law´maker**, one who makes or helps to make laws, esp a legislator; **law´suit**, a suit between private parties in a law court; **law´yer**, one whose profession is advising others in matters of law or representing them in a court of law.—**the Law**, the Mosaic law, or part of the Bible containing it; **the law**, (*inf*) a policeman or the police. [ME *lawe*—late OE, of ON origin, from the same root as **lie, lay**.]

lawn[1] [lön] *n* a fine sheer cloth of linen or cotton.—*adj* made of lawn. [Prob from *Laon*, near Rheims.]

lawn[2] [lön] *n* land covered with closely-cut grass, esp around a house.—*ns* **lawn bowling**, a bowling game played on a green with balls which are rolled at a jack; **lawn mower**, a hand-propelled or power-driven machine to cut lawn grass; **lawn tennis**, tennis (see **tennis**). [Earlier *laund*—OFr *launde, lande*; prob Celt.]

lawrencium [lö-ren´si-ům] *n* transuranic element (symbol Lr; at wt 257; at no 103). [E O *Lawrence*, US physicist (1901–58).]

lax [laks] *adj* slack, loose; not tight; not strict or exact.—*adj* **lax´ative**, having the power of loosening the bowels and relieving constipation.—*n* any laxative medicine.—*ns* **lax´ity, lax´ness**, state or quality of being lax.—*adv* **lax´ly**. [L *laxus*, loose.]

lay[1] [lā] *pt* of **lie** (2).

lay[2] [lā] *vt* to beat or knock down; to put down; to allay or suppress; to place in a resting position; to place or set; to place in a correct position; to put down as a bet, wager; to produce (an egg); to devise; to present or assert:-*pt, pt p* **Paid**.—*n* way or position in which a thing is situated.—*n* **lay´er**, one that lays; a single thickness, fold, etc.—*vt* to propagate (a plant) by layering.—*vi* to separate into layers; to form by superimposing layers; (of a plant) to form roots when a stem is fixed to the earth.—*ns* **lay´off**, a putting out of work temporarily; the period of this; **lay´out**, the manner in which anything is laid out, esp the makeup of a newspaper, advertisement, etc.; the thing laid out.—*vt* **lay out**, to plan in detail; to arrange for display; (*inf*) to knock unconscious; to prepare (a corpse) for viewing.—*n* **lay´over**, a stop in a journey.—**layaway plan**, a method of buying by making a deposit on something which is delivered only after full payment; **laying on of hands**, the act of laying hands on a person's head to confer a blessing (as in ordination of a minister or a bishop, confirmation, faith healing, etc.). [OE *lecgan*, to lay, causative of *licgan*, to lie; cf ON *leggja*, Ger *legen*.]

lay[3] [lā] *n* a short narrative poem; a lyric. [OFr *lai*; origin obscure.]

lay[4] [lā] *adj* of a layman; not belonging to a profession.—*ns* **lā´ity**, laymen collectively; **lay analyst**, a psychoanalyst who is not a medical doctor; **lay´man**, a person not belonging to a given profession, esp the clergy; **lay reader**, an Anglican or Roman Catholic layman authorized to conduct part of the church service. [OFr *lai*—L *lāicus*—Gr *lāikos*—*lāos*, the people.]

layette [lā-yet´] *n* a complete outfit for a newborn child. [Fr.]

lay figure [lā´-fig´ůr] *n* a jointed figure used by painters in imitation of the human body, as a support for drapery; a person resembling a puppet or lay figure. [Earlier *layman*—Du *leeman*—*led* (now *lid*), joint, *man*, man.]

lazy [lā´zi] *adj* disinclined to exertion, averse to labor; sluggish.—*vti* **laze**, to idle or loaf.—*adv* **lā´zily**.—*n* **lā´ziness.—la´zybones** (*inf*) a lazy person; **Lazy Susan**, a revolving tray for food, etc. [Origin unknown.]

LCD [el-sē-dē] *n* a device for alphanumeric displays, as on digital watches, using a crystalline liquid. [*l*iquid *c*rystal *d*isplay.]

L-dopa [el-dō´pä] *n* a substance found naturally esp in broad beans and synthesized for use in treating Parkinson's disease.

lea [lē] *n* (*poetic*) meadow. [OE *lēah*.]

leach [lēch] *vt* to wash (wood ashes, etc.) with a filtering liquid; to extract (a soluble substance) from some material.—*vi* to lose soluble matter through a filtering liquid. [OE *leccan*, to moisten.]

lead[1] [lēd] *vt* to show the way by going first; to precede; to guide; to direct by influence; to be head of (an expedition, orchestra, etc.); to be at the head of (one's class, etc.); to be ahead of in a contest; to live, spend (*lead a full life*).—*vi* to show the way, as by going first; to tend in a certain direction (*with* **to**); to be or go first; *pt, pt p* **led**.—*n* the role of a leader; first place; the amount or distance ahead; anything that leads, as a clue; the leading role in a play; etc.; the right of playing first in cards or the card played.—*ns* **lead´er**, one who leads or goes first; a member of a political party chosen to manage party activities in a legislative assembly; the principal officer of a political party in a parliamentary system; **lead´ership**, office of leader or conductor; the quality of a leader, ability to lead; **leading edge**, the front edge of a propeller blade or an airfoil; the forward part of a moving object; **lead time**, the period of time needed from the decision to make a product to the start of production.—**lead off**, to begin; **lead on**, to lure; **lead up to**, to prepare the way for. [OE *lǣdan*, to lead, *lād*, a way; Ger *leiten*, to lead.]

lead[2] [led] *n* a heavy, soft, bluish-gray, metallic element (symbol Pb; at wt 207.2; at no 82); a weight for sounding depths at sea, etc.; bullets; a stick of graphite, used in pencils.—*adj* of or containing lead.—*vt* to cover or fit with lead.—*adj* **lead´en**, made of lead; heavy; dull; gloomy; gray.—*n* **lead´ poi´soning**, poisoning by the absorption of lead into the system. [OE *lēad*; Ger *lot*.]

leaf [lēf] *n* any of the flat, thin parts, usu. green growing from the stem of a plant; a sheet of paper; a very thin sheet of metal; a hinged or removable part of a table top.—*pl* **leaves** [lēvz].—*vi* to bear leaves; to turn the pages of (*with* **through**).—*adj* **leaf´less**.—*n* leaf´let, a small or young leaf; a separate sheet of printed matter, often folded; **leaf mold**, decayed leaves used as compost; a mold or mildew affecting foliage.—*adj* **leaf´y**, having many or broad leaves.—*n* **leafy spurge**, a tall perennial plant (*Euphorbia esula*) that is a troublesome weed in northern N America. [OE *lēaf*; Ger *laub*, Du *loof*, a leaf.]

league[1] [lēg] *n* a varying measure of distance, averaging about 3½ miles. [LL *leuga, leuca*, a Gallic mile of 1500 Roman paces.]

league[2] [lēg] *n* an association of nations, groups, etc. for promoting common interests; (*sports*) groups of teams formed to play one another.—*vti* to form into a league.—**League of Nations**, an association of nations (1920–46) succeeded by UN. [Fr *ligue*—Low L *liga*—L *ligāre*, to bind.]

leak [lēk] *n* a crack or hole in a vessel through which liquid may pass; passage through such an opening; confidential information made public, deliberately or accidentally.—*vi* to have a leak; to pass through a leak; to give out information surreptitiously.—*n* **leak´age**, a leaking; that which enters or escapes by leaking.—*adjs* **leak´proof; leak´y**. [OE *hlec*, leaky; or perh re-introduced from Du or Low Ger *lek*, leak; or ON *leka*, to leak.]

lean [lēn] *vi* to bend or slant from an upright position; to rest (against); to bend (over); to rely (on).—*vt* to cause to lean.—*pt, pt p* **leaned**, or **leant** [lent].—*ns* **leaning**, inclination; **lean´-to**, a structure whose sloping roof abuts a wall, etc. [OE *hleonian, hlinian*, and causative *hlǣne*; Du *leunen*.]

lean [lēn] *adj* thin, with little flesh or fat; spare; meager.—*n* meat with little or no fat.—*adv* **lean´ly**.—*n* **lean´ness**. [OE *hlǣne*; Low Ger *leen*.]

leap [lēp] *vi* to jump; to accept something offered eagerly (*with* **at**).—*vt* to pass over by a jump; to cause to leap.—*pr p* **leaping**; *pt, pt p* **leaped**, or **leapt** [lept or lēpt].—*n* act of leaping; bound; space passed by leaping; an abrupt transition.—*ns* **leap´-frog**, a sport in which one places his hands on the back of another stooping in front of him, and vaults over his head; **leap´ year**, every fourth year (excluding centesimal years not exactly divisible by 400), consisting of 366 days, adding one day in February. [OE *hlēapan*; Ger *laufen*, to run.]

learn [lûrn] *vti* to be informed, to get to know; to gain knowledge, skill, or ability in; to commit to memory.—*pt, pt p* **learned** [lėrnd].—*adj* **learned** [lėrn´id], having learning; erudite; [lėrnd] acquired by study, experience, etc.—*adv* **learn´edly**.—*ns* **learn´edness; learn´er; learning**, the acquiring of knowledge or skill; acquired knowledge or skill. [OE *leornian*; Ger *lernen*; cf *lǣran* (Ger *lehren*), to teach.]

lease [lēs] *n* a contract letting a house, farm, etc., for a term; the period of time for which the contract is made.—*vt* to grant or take under lease.—*pr p* **leas´ing**; *pt, pt p* **leased**.—*n* **lease´hold**, the act of holding by lease; land, buildings, etc. held by lease.—*n* **lease´holder**. [Fr *laisser*, to leave—L *laxāre*, to loose, *laxus*, loose.]

leash [lēsh] *n* a cord, strap, etc. by which a dog or animal is held in check.—*vt* to control and check as by a leash. [OFr *lesse* (Fr *laisse*), a thong to hold a dog by—L *laxus*, loose.]

least [lēst] *adj* alternative superlative of **little**. *adj* smallest in size, degree, etc.; slightest.—*adv* in the smallest degree.—*n* the smallest in amount, importance, etc.—**at (the) least** at the lowest; at any rate; **not in the least** not at all. [OE *lǣst* (adj and adv); comp *lǣssa* (adj), *lǣs* (adv); no positive.]

leather [leTH´ėr] *n* the skin of an animal prepared for use by removing the hair and tanning.—*ns* **leath´erback**, the largest existing sea turtle (*Dermochylys coriacea*) having a flexible carapace; **leath´erbark**, leatherwood; **leath´erneck**, (*slang*) a US Marine; **leath´erwood**, a small shrub (*Dircus palustris*) of woodland in eastern No America whose bark was used by Indians and pioneers as emergency fiber for thongs, etc.—*adj* **leath´ery**, like leather; tough and flexible. [OE *lether*, leather; Du and Ger *leder*.]

leave[1] [lēv] *n* permission; permission to be absent; period covered by this; formal parting; farewell.—**take leave of**, to bid farewell to. [OE *lēaf*, permission, cog. with *lēof*, dear. See **lief**.]

leave[2] [lēv] *vt* to allow to remain; (*slang*) to let (*leave us go*); to depart from; to have remaining at death, to bequeath; to refer for decision (to); to allow (a person to do) without supervision; to abandon.—*vi* to depart.—*pr p* **leav´ing**; *pt, pt p* **left**.—*n pl* **leav´ings**, leftovers; remnants; refuse.—**leave off** to stop; **leave out** to omit. [OE *lǣfan*.]

leaven [lev´n] *n* a substance to make dough rise, esp yeast; anything that makes a general change.—*vt* to raise with leaven; to spread through, causing gradual change. [Fr *levain*—L *levāmen*—*levāre*, to raise—*levis*, light.]

leaves [lēvz] *pl* of **leaf**.

lecher [lech´ėr] *n* a man addicted to lewdness.—*adj* **lech´erous**, lustful; provoking lust.—*adv* **lech´erously**.—*ns* **lech´erousness, lech´ery**. [OFr *lecheor*—*lechier*, to lick; OHG *leccōn*, Ger *lecken*, Eng **lick**.]

lecithin [lės´ė-thin] *n* a nitrogenous, fatty compound found in animal and plant cells used in medicine, foods, etc. [Gr. *lekithos*, egg yolk.]

lectern [lek´tėrn] *n* a reading stand. [Low L *lectrīnum*—*lectrum*, a pulpit—Gr *lektron*, a couch.]

lection [lek´sh(ȯ)n] *n* a liturgical lesson for a specified day; a variant reading of a text.—*n* **lec´tionary**, a book of lections for the church year. [L *lectiō, -ōnis*—*legĕre, lectum*, to read.]

lecture [lek´chur] *n* an informative talk to a class, etc.; a lengthy scolding.—*vti* to give a lecture (to); to scold.—*n* **lecturer**. [L *lectura*—*legĕre, lectum*, to read.]

led [led] *pt, pt p* of **lead**, to show the way.

LED [el´ē-dē] *n* a semiconductor that emits light when voltage is applied and used in an electronic display (as for a digital watch). [*l*ight-*e*mitting *d*iode.]

ledge [lej] *n* a shelf; a ridge of rocks. [ME *legge*, prob from the root of **lay** (2).]

ledger [lej´ėr] *n* a book of final entry, in which a record of debits, credits, etc. is kept.—*n* **ledger line** a short line added above or below a musical staff to extend its range. [App from OE *licgan*, to lie, *lecgan*, to lay.]

lee [lē] *n* shelter; (*naut*) the side or part away from the wind.—*adj* of or on the lee; the quarter toward which the wind blows.—*adj* sheltered; on or toward the sheltered side.—*ns* **lee´ shore**, a shore on the leeward of a ship.—*adj* **lee´ward** [*naut* lōō´ȧrd] away from the wind.—*n* the lee side.—*adv* toward the lee.—*n* **lee´way**, the distance a ship, aircraft, etc., is driven to leeward of its course; (*inf*) a margin of time, money, etc.; (*inf*) room for freedom of action. [OE *hlēo(w)*, shelter.]

leech [lēch] *n* any of a class (*Hirudinea*) of blood-sucking worms; one who clings to another to get what he can from him.—*vi* to cling (on to) thus. [OE *lǣce*.]

leek [lēk] *n* a vegetable (*Allium porrum*) that resembles a greatly enlarged green onion. [OE *lēac*, a leek plant.]

leer [lēr] *n* a sly, sidelong, or lecherous look.—*vi* to look with a leer.—*adv* **leer´ingly**.—*adj* **leer´y**, suspicious; wary (*with* **of**). [OE *hlēor*, face, cheek.]

lees [lēz] *n pl* dregs of liquor. [Fr *lie*.]

left[1] [left] *pt, pt p* of **leave**.—*n* **left´over**, something, esp food, left over.

left[2] [left] *adj* of or on the side that is toward the west when one faces north; on, for, or belonging to the side which is less skilful in most people.—*n* the left side; **left**, in politics, a radical or liberal position, party, etc. (often with **the**).—*adjs* **left-hand; left´-handed**, having the left hand stronger than the right; done with or made for use with the left hand; ambiguous or backhanded.—*adv* with the left hand. [ME *lift, left*—OE *left* for *lyft*, weak.]

leg [leg] *n* one of the limbs on which men and animals support themselves and walk; the part of a garment covering the leg; anything shaped or used like a leg; a stage, as of a trip.—*vi* (*inf*) to walk or run (*usu. with* **it**).—**legged** [leg´id or legd] having (a specified number or kind of) legs.—*n* **legg´ing**, a covering for the leg (usu. *pl*).—*adjs* **legg´y**, having disproportionately long legs; having attractive legs; (of a plant) spindly.—**leg´less**, without legs. [ON *leggr*, a leg; Dan *læg*, Swed *lägg*.]

legacy [leg´a-si] *n* that which is left to one by will; anything handed down by an ancestor.—**legatee´**, one to whom a legacy is bequeathed. [L *lēgāre, -ātum*, to leave by will.]

legal [lē´gȧl] *adj* of or based on law; permitted by law; of or for lawyers.—*vt* **lē´galize**, to make lawful.—*n* **lēgal´ity**.—*adv* **lē´gally**.—*ns* **legal holiday**, one established by legal authority and marked by restrictions on work and official business; **legal tender**, money that must be accepted in payment of an obligation. [L *lēgālis*—*lex, lēgis*, law.]

legate [leg´ȧt] *n* an envoy, esp from the Pope; an official emissary.—*n* **leg´ateship**.—*adj* **leg´atine** [ēn, īn] of or relating to a legate.—*n* **legā´tion**, a diplomatic minister and his staff and headquarters. [From L *lēgātus*—*lēgāre*, to send with a commission.]

legato [lā-gä´tō] *adj, adv* (*mus*) smooth, smoothly, the notes running into each other without a break. [It tied—L *ligāre*, tie.]

legend [lej´ėnd] *n* a traditional story; a myth; a notable person or the stories of his exploits; an inscription on a coin, etc.; words accompanying an illustration or map.—*adj* **leg´endary**, of, based on, or presented in legends. [Fr *légende*—Low L *legenda*, to be read, a book or chronicles of the saints read at matins—*legĕre*, to read.]

legerdemain [lej-ėr-dē-mān´] *n* sleight-of-hand; trickery. [Lit light of hand—Fr *léger*, light, *de*, of, *main*, hand.]

leghorn [leg´hörn, leg-örn´] *n* fine straw plait made in Tuscany; a hat made of it; a breed of domestic fowl. [*Leghorn*, in Italy.]

legible [lej´i-bl] *adj* clear enough to be read.—*ns* **leg´ibleness, legibil´ity**.—*adv* **leg´ibly**. [L *legibilis*—*legĕre*, to read.]

legion [lē´jȯn] *n* a large body of soldiers; a large number, a multitude.—*ns* **lē´gionary, legionnaire** [lē-jȯn-ār´] a member of a legion.—**Legionnaires´ disease**, (*med*) a severe bacterial disease affecting the lungs, occurring sporadically. [L *legiō, -ōnis*—*legĕre*, to levy.]

legislate [lej´is-lāt] *vi* to make or pass laws—*vt* to cause to be, go, etc. by making laws.—*n* **legislā´tion**.—*adj* **leg´islative**, of legislation or a legislature.—*ns* **leg´islātor**, a member of a legislative body; **leg´islāture**, the body of those in a state who have the power of making laws. [L *lex, lēgis*, law, *lātum*, serving as supine to *ferre*, to bear.]

legitimate [le-jit´i-mȧt] *adj* born of parents married to each other; lawful; reasonable, justifiable; conforming to accepted rules, standards, etc.; (of stage plays) as distinguished from burlesque, etc.—Also *vt* **legit´imize; legit´imatize**, to make or declare legitimate.—*n* **legit´imacy**, state of being legitimate.—*adv* **legit´imately**.—*ns* **legitimā´tion**, act of rendering legitimate; **legit´imist**, one who believes in the right of royal succession according to the principle of heredity and primogeniture. [Low L *lēgitimāre, -ātum*—L *lēgitimus*, lawful—*lex*, law.]

legume [leg´ūm] *n* any of a large family (Leguminosae) of plants having seeds growing in pods, including peas, beans, etc.; the pod or seed of such a plant used as food.—*adj* **legū´minous**. [Fr *légume*, a vegetable—L *legūmen*, pulse, prob —*legĕre*, to gather.]

lei [lā´ē] *n* a garland of flowers. [Hawaiian.]

leisure [lēzh´ůr, lezh´ůr] *n* time free from employment and at one's own disposal; freedom from occupation.—*adj* free and unoccupied.—*adj* **lei´sured**, having leisure.—*adj* **lei´surely**, without haste; slow.—*adv* in an unhurried manner. [OFr *leisir*—L *licēre*, to be permitted.]

leitmotiv, leitmotif [līt´mō-tēf] *n* a dominant theme. [Ger,—*leiten*, to lead, and *motiv*, a motif.]

lemma [lem´a] *n* a preliminary proposition used in the main argument or proof; argument or subject of literary composition, etc., prefixed as heading; a glossed word or phrase.—*pl* **lemm´as, lemm´ata**. [Gr *lēmma*, from the root of *lambanein*, to take.]

lemming [lem´ing] *n* any of several small arctic rodents (genus *Lemmus*). [Norw *lemming*.]

lemon [lem´ȯn] *n* a small oval fruit (genus *Citrus*) with an acid pulp; the tree that bears it; (*slang*) something defective.—*ns* **lemonade´**, a drink made with lemon juice, sugar and water.—*adj* **lemon yellow** a pale greenish yellow. [Fr *limon* (now the lime); cf Pers *līmūn*; cf **lime** (2).]

lemur [lē´můr] *n* a superfamily (Lemuroidea) of arboreal, usu. nocturnal primates chiefly in Madagascar, related to monkeys.—*pl* **lē´murs**. [L *lěmŭrēs*, ghosts.]

lend [lend] *vt* to give the use of for a time; to let out (money) at interest; to give, impart.—*vi* to make loans.—*pr p* **lending**; *pt, pt p* **lent**.—*ns* **lend´er; lend-lease**, in World War II, material aid granted countries whose defense the US deemed vital.—**lend itself to** to be useful for or open to. [OE *lǣnan*—*lǣn, lān*, a loan.]

length [length] *n* extent from end to end; the longest measure of anything; long continuance; a piece of a certain length.—*vti* **length´en**, to increase in length.—*advs* **length´ways, length´wise**, in the direction of the length.—*adj* **length´y**, long, esp too long.—*adv* **length´ily**.—*n* **length´iness**.—**at length**, finally; in full. [OE *lengthu*—*lang*, long.]

lenient [lē´ni-ėnt, lē´nyėnt] *adj* not harsh or severe; merciful.—*ns* **lē´nience, lē´niency**.—*adv* **lē´niently**.—*adj* **lenitive** [len´-], soothing; mitigating.—*n* (*med*) an application for easing pain.—*n* **lenity** [len´-], mildness; clemency. [L *lēniens, -entis*, pr p of *lēnīre*, to soften—*lēnis*, soft.]

lens [lenz] *n* a curved piece of transparent glass, plastic, etc. for bringing together or passing rays of light through it, used in optical instruments to form an image; any device used to focus electromagnetic rays, sound waves, etc.; a similar transparent part of the eye which focuses light rays on the retina.—*pl* **lens´es**.—*adj* **lentik´ūlar** shaped like a double-convex lens; of or relating to a lens; using lenticules.—*n* **lent´icule**, a minute lens on the base side of stereoscopic film; the grooves in the surface of a projection screen. [L *lens, lentis*, lentil.]

Lent [lent] *n* an annual fast of forty weekdays in commemoration of Christ's fast in the wilderness from Ash Wednesday to Easter.—*adj* **lent´en**, relating to, or used in, Lent; sparing. [OE *lencten*, the spring; Du *lente*, Ger *lenz*.]

lentil [len´til] *n* any of several leguminous plants (*Lens culinaris*) with flattened seeds and leafy stalks used as fodder; their seed used for food. [OFr *lentille*—L *lens, lentis*, the lentil.]

lento [len´tō] *adj* (*mus*) slow.—*adv* slowly.—*n* a slow passage or movement. [It—L *lentus*.]

Leo [lē´ō] *n* the 5th sign of the zodiac, in astrology operative July 22 to August 21; the 5th zodiacal constellation represented as the lion; the Lion, a constellation.—*adj* **lē´onine** of or like a lion. [L *leō, -ōnis*, lion.]

leopard [lep´ärd] *n* a large tawny feline (*Felis pardus*) with black spots of southern Asia and Africa.—Also **panther**. [OFr—L *leopardus*—Gr *leopardos* (for *leontopardos*)—*leōn*, lion, *pardos*, pard.]
leotard [lē´ō-tärd] *n* a skintight garment worn by dancers and acrobats. [Julius *Leotard*, 19th-cent Fr trapeze artist.]
leper [le´pėr] *n* one affected with leprosy. [OFr *lepre*—L and Gr *lepra*—Gr *lepros*, scaly—*lepos* or *lepis*, a scale.]
lepidopteran [lep-i-dop´tėr-an] *adj* any of a large order (Lepidoptera) of insects comprising butterflies, moths, and skippers that as adults have four wings covered with fine, often colorful scales and that as larvae are caterpillars.—*adjs* **lepidop´teral, lepidop´terous**. [Gr *lepis, -idos*, a scale, *pteron*, a wing.]
leprechaun [lep-rė-hön´] *n* in Irish folklore, a fairy who, if caught, can reveal hidden treasure. [Perh Old Irish *luchorpan*—*lu* small, *corp(an)*, a body.]
leprosy [lep´ro-si] *n* a chronic infectious bacterial disease of the skin, Hansen's disease.—*adj* **lep´rous**, affected with leprosy; scaly, scurfy. [Through OFr—LL *leprōsus*—*lepra*. See **leper**.]
lepton [lep´ton] *n* any of a group of subatomic particles with weak interactions as electrons, muons and neutrinos. [Gr *leptos*, small, light.]
leptospirosis [lep-tō-spī-rōs´is] *n* a disease caused by a bacterium (genus *Leptospira*) that is parasitic in rodents and man and is usu. transmitted through water contaminated by a rodent's urine.
lesbian [lez´bi-ȧn] *n* a homosexual woman.—*n* **les´bianism**.
lese-majesty [lēz´-maj´es-ti] *n* an offence against the sovereign; any lack of proper respect toward one in authority. [Fr *lèse majesté*—L *laesa mājestās*, injured majesty—*laedĕre*, to hurt.]
lesion [lē´zh(o̊)n] *n* an injury of tissue or an organ resulting in impairment of function. [Fr *lésion*—L *laesiō, -ōnis*—*laedĕre, laesum*, to hurt.]
less [les] an alternative comparative of **little**. *adj* not so much, not so great, etc.; fewer; smaller.—*adv* to a smaller extent.—*n* a smaller amount.—*prep* minus.—**less and less**, decreasingly. [OE *-lǣssa*, less, *lǣs* (adv); not conn with **little**.]
-less [-les] *suffix* meaning without (value*less*); that does not (tire*less*); that cannot be (daunt*less*). [OE *-lēas*, Ger *-los*, Goth *-laus*.]
lessee [les-ē´] *n* one to whom a lease is granted. [OFr *lessé*; root of **lease**.]
lessen [les´n] *vti* to make or become less. [**less**.]
lesser [les´ėr] *adj* less; smaller; less important. [Double comp formed from **less**.]
lesson [les´(o̊)n] *n* something to be learned or studied; something that has been learned or studied; a unit of learning or teaching; (*pl*) a course of instruction; a selection from the Bible, read as a part of a church service. [Fr *leçon*—L *lectiō, -ōnis*—*legĕre*, to read.]
lessor [les´ör] *n* one who grants a lease. [Anglo-Fr; root of **lease**.]
lest [lest] *conj* that not; for fear that. [From OE *thȳ lǣs the*, for the reason less that, which became in ME *les te*.]
let [let] *vt* to allow, permit; to rent; to assign (a contract); to cause to run out, as blood; as an auxiliary in giving suggestions or commands (eg *let us go*).—*vi* to be rented. *pr p* **lett´ing**, *pt, pt p* **let**.—**let alone** leave alone; **let be** leave be; **let down** to lower; to slow up; to disappoint; **let it all hang out**, (*inf*) to reveal one's true feelings; **let know**, tell; **let off** to give forth; to deal leniently with; **let on** (*inf*) to pretend; (*inf*) to indicate one's awareness; **let out**, to release; to rent out; to make a garment larger; **let up** to relax; to cease. [OE *lǣten*, to permit, pa t *lēt*, pa p *lǣten*; Ger *lassen*.]
let [let] *n* an obstacle in **without let or hindrance**. [OE *lettan*, to hinder—*lǣt*, slow.]
-let [-let] *suffix* meaning small (leaf*let*)
lethal [lē´thȧl] *adj* deadly.—*n* a fatal genetic abnormality. [L *lēt(h)ālis*—*lēt(h)um*, death.]
lethargy [leth´ȧr-ji] *n* an abnormal drowsiness; sluggishness; apathy.—*adj* **lethar´gic**, [-är´-]—*adv* **lethar´gically**. [L and Gr *lēthargia*, drowsy forgetfulness—*lēthē*, forgetfulness.]
Lett [let] *n* one of a people closely related to the Lithuanians and mainly inhabiting Latvia. [Ger *Lette*—Lettish *Latvi*.]
letter [let´ėr] *n* any character of the alphabet; a written or printed message; (*pl*) literature; learning; knowledge; literal meaning; a single piece of printing type; a style of type; the initial of a school awarded for achievement in athletics.—*vt* to mark with letters.—*vi* to win an athletic letter.—*ns* **letter bomb**, small explosive device mailed in an envelope; **letter carrier**, a postman, mailman;—*adj* **lett´ered**, literate; highly educated; marked with letters.—*ns* **lett´erhead**, the name, address, etc. as a heading on stationery; **lett´ering**, the act of making or inscribing letters, or such letters.—*adj* **letter perfect**, correct to the last detail, esp verbatim.—*ns* **letters patent**, a document granting a patent. [Fr *lettre*—L *lītera, littera*.]
lettuce [let´is] *n* a plant (*Lactuca sativa*) with succulent leaves; its leaves used in salads. [Fr *laitue*—L *lactūca*—*lac*, milk.]
leukocyte [lū´kō-sīt] *n* a white corpuscle in the blood which destroys disease-causing organisms. [Gr *leukos*, white, *kytos*, hollow.]
leukemia [lū-kē´mi-ȧ] *n* a disease in which there is an abnormal increase in the number of leukocytes. [Gr *leukos*, white, *haima*, blood.]
Levant [le-vant´] *n* the Eastern Mediterranean and its shores.—*n* **levant´er**, a strong easterly wind in the Levant.—*adj* **levant´ine**, belonging to the Levant. [Fr *levant*, rising—L *levāre*, to raise.]
levee[1] [lev´ē, le-vē´, lev´ā] *n* a morning assembly of visitors; an assembly received by a sovereign or other great personage; a reception usu. in honor of a particular person. [Fr *levée*—*lever*—L *levāre*, to raise.]
levee[2] [lev´e, le-vē´] *n* an embankment to prevent a river from flooding bordering land. [Fr *levée*, raised.]
level [lev´l] *n* an instrument for determining the horizontal; a horizontal line or plane (*sea level*); a horizontal area; normal position with reference to height; position in a scale of values.—*vti* to make or become level; to demolish; to raise and aim (a gun etc.); *pr p* **lev´eling** or **-lling**; *pt, pt p* **lev´eled** or **-lled**.—*adj* **lev´el-head´ed**, having an even temper and sound judgment.—*ns* **lev´eler; lev´eller**, one who levels; one who would remove all social or political inequalities; **lev´elness**, state of being level; **level with** (*slang*) to be honest with; **level off**, to reach and maintain equilibrium; **on the level** (*inf*) honest, bona fide. [OFr *livel, liveau*—L *lībella*, a plummet, dim of *lībra*, a balance.]
lever [le´vėr or lē´vėr] *n* a bar used as a pry; a means to an end; a device consisting of a bar turning about a fixed point, using force at a second point to lift a weight at a third.—*vt* to move, as with a lever—*n* **lē´verage**, the mechanical power gained by the use of a lever; power, that can be used to achieve a purpose. [Fr *levier*—*lever*—L *levāre*, to raise.]
leveret [lev´ėr-et] *n* a hare in its first year. [OFr *levrette*—L *lepus, lepŏris*, a hare.]
leviable [lev´i-ȧ-bl] *adj* able to be levied or levied upon. [From **levy**.]
leviathan [le-vī´a-thȧn] *n* (*Bible*) a sea monster; anything huge. [Heb *livyāthān*.]
Levis [lē´vīz] *n* trade name for blue denim jeans. [*Levi* Strauss, US manufacturer.]
levitation [lev-i-tā´sh(o̊)n] *n* the illusion of raising a body in the air without support.—*vt* **lev´itate**. [L *levis*, light.]
Levite [lē´vīt] *n* a member of the priestly Hebrew tribe of Levi.—*n* **Levit´icus** (*Bible*) 3d book of the Old Testament, containing the laws relating to the priests.
levity [lev´iti] *n* frivolity; improper gaiety. [L *levitās, -ātis*—*levis*, light.]
levulose [lev´ū-lōs] *n* fructose. [L *laevus*, left.]
levy [lev´i] *vt* to raise, collect, esp by authority, as an army or a tax; to make (war);—*pr p* **lev´ying**; *pt, pt p* **lev´ied**.—*n* the act of collecting by authority; the troops or money so collected. [L *levāre*, to raise.]
lewd [l(y)ōōd] *adj* indecent; lustful; obscene.—*adv* **lewd´ly**.—*n* **lewd´ness**. [OE *lǣwede*, ignorant, belonging to the laity.]
lexicon [leks´i-kon] *n* a dictionary; a special vocabulary; the total stock of morphemes in a language.—*adj* **lex´ical**, belonging to a lexicon.—*ns* **lexicog´raphy**, the editing or making of a dictionary; the principles and practices of dictionary making; **lexicog´rapher**, one skilled in lexicography.—*adjs* **lexicograph´ic, -al**.—*n* **lexicol´ogy**, branch of linguistics which treats of the proper signification and use of words. [Gr *lexicon*, a dictionary—*lexis*, a word, *legein*, to speak.]
Leyden jar [lī´dėn jär] *n* an electrical condenser consisting of a glass jar coated inside and outside with tinfoil or other conducting material. [*Leyden* in Holland, where it was invented.]
Lhasa apso [lä´sà äp´sō] *n* a small dog of Tibetan breed with a long dense coat and a well-feathered tail curled over the back. [*Lhasa* in Tibet.]
liable [lī-ȧ-bl] *adj* legally bound or responsible; subject to; likely (to).—*n* **liabil´ity**, state of being liable; that for which one is liable; (*pl* **-ies**) the debts of a person or business; something that works to one's disadvantage. [Fr *lier*—L *ligāre*, to bind.]
liaison [lē-āz•, li-āz´(o̊)n] *n* intercommunication as between units of a military force; an illicit love affair; (*cookery*) a thickening of flour and fat, egg yolk, etc. used in sauces, soups, etc.—*vi* **liaise** [lē-āz´] to form a link; to be or get in touch. [Fr,—L *ligātiō, -ōnis*—*ligāre*, to bind.]
liana [li-än´a] *n* a general name for climbing plants in tropical forests. [Fr *liane*—*lier*—L *ligāre*, to bind.]
liar [lī-ȧr] *n* one who utters lies. [From **lie** (1).]
Lias [lī´as] *n* (*geol*) the lowest division of the Jurassic system in Europe—of argillaceous limestone, etc.—*adj* **Liass´ic**, pertaining to the lias formation. [A Somerset quarryman's word, app—OFr *liois*.]
libation [lī-bā´sh(o̊)n] *n* the pouring forth of wine or other liquid in honor of a deity; the liquid poured; an alcoholic drink. [L *lībātiō, -ōnis*—*lībāre, -ātum*—Gr *leibein*, to pour.]
libel [lī-bėl] *n* any written or printed matter tending to injure a person's reputation unjustly; the act or crime of publishing such a thing.—*vt* to defame by a libel.—*n* **lī´beller**.—*adj* **libellous**.—*adv* **lī´bellously**. [L *libellus*, dim. of *liber*, a book.]
liberal [lib´ėr-ȧl] *adj* ample, abundant; not literal or strict; tolerant; favoring reform or progress.—*n* one who favors reform or progress.—*vti* **lib´eralize**, to make or become liberal.—*ns* **lib´eralism**, the principles of a liberal; **liberal´ity**, the quality of being generous and broadminded; an instance of this.—*adv* **lib´erally**.—**liberal arts**, literature, languages, history, etc. as courses of study. [Fr—L *līberālis*, befitting a freeman—*līber*, free.]
liberate [lib´ėr-āt] *vt* to release from slavery, enemy occupation, etc.; to secure equal rights for (women, etc.); (*inf*) to steal.—*ns* **liberā´tion; lib´erator**. [L *līberāre, -ātum*—*līber*, free.]
liberty [lib´ėr-ti] *n* freedom from slavery, captivity, etc.; a particular right, freedom, etc.; an impertinent attitude; leave given a sailor to go ashore.—*n* **Liberty Bell**, the bell of Independence Hall, Philadelphia, rung July 4,

1776, to proclaim US independence.—**take liberties**, to be impertinent or too familiar; to deal inaccurately (with facts, data, etc.) *n* **libertinage** [lib´ėr-tin-aj] debauchery.—*n* **lib´ertine**, formerly one who professed free opinions, esp in religion; one who leads a licentious life; a rake or debauchee.—*adj* belonging to a freedman; unrestrained; licentious.—*n* **lib´ertinism**, licentiousness of opinion or practice; lewdness or debauchery. [Fr *liberté*—L *lībertās, -ātis*—L *lībertīnus*, a freedman—*līber*, free.]

libido [li-bē´dō] *n* the sexual urge; in psychoanalytic theory, psychic energy comprising goal-directed biological urges.—*adj* **libid´inous**, lustful, lascivious.—*n* **libid´inousness**.—*adv* **libid´inously**. [L *libīdō, -inis*, desire.]

Libra [lī´bra, lē´-] *n* the 7th sign of the zodiac; in astrology operative September 24 to October 23; the 7th zodiacal constellation represented as a pair of scales. [L]

library [lī´brår-i] *n* a collection of books, etc.; a room or building for, or an institution in charge of, such a collection.—*ns* **librari´an**, one in charge of a library or trained in library science; **librar´ianship; library paste**, a thick white adhesive made from starch; **library science**, the practice, principles, or study of library care and administration. [L *librārium*—*liber*, a book.]

libretto [li-bret´ō] *n* the words of an opera, oratorio, etc.—*pl* **librett´os; librett´i**. [It, dim of *libro*—L *liber* a book.]

lice [līs] *pl* of **louse**.

license [lī´sėns] *n* a formal or legal permission to do something specified; a document granting such permission; freedom to deviate from rule, practice, etc. (*poetic license*); excessive freedom, an abuse of liberty.—*vt* to permit formally.—*ns* **licensee´**, a person to whom a license is granted; **licentiate**, a person having a professional license.—*adj* **licen´tious**, morally unrestrained; lascivious.—*adv* **licen´tiously**.—*n* **licen´tiousness**. [Fr *licence*—L *licentia*—*licēre*, to be allowed.]

lichee *See* **litchi**.

lichen [lī´kėn] *n* any of a large group of plants consisting of an alga and a fungus in close association, growing on stones, trees, etc.; any of several skin diseases marked by eruptions on the skin. [L *līchēn*—Gr *leichēn*—*leichein*, to lick.]

lich-gate [lich´-gāt] *See* **lych-gate**.

licit [lis´it] *adj* lawful. [L *licitus*.]

lick [lik] *vt* to pass the tongue over; to lap; (*inf*) to whip; (*inf*) to vanquish.—*n* a licking with the tongue; a small quantity; a salt lick; (*inf*) a sharp blow; (*inf*) a short, rapid burst of activity.—*a lick and a promise*, a short burst of activity. [OE *liccian*; Ger *lecken*, L *lingĕre*, Gr *leichein*.]

licorice [lik´or-is] *n* a black flavoring extract made from the root of a European plant (*Glycyrrhiza glabra*); candy flavored with this extract. [Low L *liquiritia*, a corr of Gr *glykyrriza*—*glykys*, sweet, *rhīza*, root.]

lid [lid] *n* a removable cover as for a box, etc.; an eyelid; (*inf*) a restraint. [OE *hlid* (Du *lid*)—hlīdan, to cover.]

lie[1] [lī] *n* a false statement made to deceive, an intentional violation of truth; anything that misleads.—*vi* to utter falsehood with an intention to deceive.—*pr p* **ly´ing**; *pt, pt p* **lied**.—**lie detector**, a polygraph. [OE *lēogan* (*lyge*, a falsehood); Du *liegen*, Ger *lügen*, to lie.]

lie[2] [lī] *vi* to be or put oneself in a reclining or horizontal position; to rest on a support in a horizontal position; to be in a specified condition; to be situated; to exist.—*n* the way in which something is situated; lay.—*pr p* **ly´ing**; *pt* **lay**; *pt p* **lain; lie low**, to lie prostrate, defeated, or disgraced; to keep quiet or hidden; to bide one's time; **lie to**, (of a ship) to lie almost with head to windward; **lie up**, to rest in bed; (of a ship) to be in dock or beached for the winter. [OE *licgan*; Ger *liegen*.]

lied [lēt] *n* a German art song, esp of the 19th century.—*pl* **lieder** [lē´der]. [Ger]

Liederkranz [lē´der-krants] *n* trade name for a creamy cheese with edible russet crust which develops a robust odor as it changes from white to cream.

liege [lēj] *adj* loyal, faithful.—*n* in feudalism, a lord or sovereign; a subject or vassal. [OFr *lige*, prob from OHG *ledic*, free, *līdan*, to depart.]

lien [lē´ėn, lēn] *n* (*law*) a right to retain possession of another's property until the owner pays a debt due to the holder. [Fr—L *ligāmen*, tie, band.]

lieu [l(y)ōō] *n* place.—**in lieu of**, in place of, instead of. [Fr—L *locus*, place.]

lieutenant [lōōten´ånt] *n* one acting for a superior in the US Air Force, Army and Marine Corps, a commissioned officer ranking below a captain; in the US Navy an officer ranking above a lieutenant junior grade.—*ns* **lieutenant colonel** (*US Military*) an officer ranking above a major; **lieutenant commander** (*US Navy*) an officer ranking above a lieutenant; **lieutenant general** (*US Military*) an officer ranking above a major general; **lieutenant governor** an elected official of a state who ranks below and substitutes for the governor. [Fr—*lieu*, place, *tenant*, prp of *tenir* to hold.]

life [līf] *n* that property of plants and animals (ending at death) that enables them to use food, grow, reproduce, etc.; the state of having this property; a human being; living things collectively; the time a person or thing exists; one's manner of living; the people and activities of a specified time, place, etc.; one's animate existence; a biography; the source of liveliness (*the life of the party*); vigor, liveliness;—*pl* **lives**.—*adj* of animate being; lifelong; using a living model; of or relating to or provided by life insurance.—*ns* **life belt**, a life preserver in belt form; a safety belt; **life´blood´**, the blood necessary to life; a vital element; **life´boat´**, a small rescue boat carried by a ship; **life buoy**, a ring-shaped life preserver; **life cycle**, a sequence of stages through which a living being passes during its lifetime; **life´guard´**, an expert swimmer employed (as at a beach or pool) to prevent drownings; **life history**, the history of an individual's development in his social environment; **life insurance**, insurance in which a stipulated sum is paid at the death of the insured; **life jacket**, a life preserver like a sleeveless jacket or vest.—*adjs* **life´less**, inanimate; dead; dull; **life´like**, resembling real life or a real person or thing.—*ns* **life´line´**, the rope for raising or lowering a diver; a very important commercial route; **life list**, a record kept by a birder of all birds sighted and identified.—*adj* **life´long´**, lasting nor changing during one's whole life.—*ns* **life net**, a strong net used by firemen to catch people jumping from a burning building; **life peer**, a British peer whose title is not hereditary; **life preserver**, a buoyant device for keeping a person from drowning by keeping him afloat; **lifer** (*slang*), a person sentenced to prison for life; **life raft**, an inflatable raft or boat for emergency use by people forced into the water; **life´sav´er**, a lifeguard; (*inf*) a help in time of need.—*adj* **life´saving**, something (as drugs) designed to save lives.—*n* the skill or practice of saving lives, esp from drowning.—*n* **life science**, a branch of science dealing with living organisms and life processes.—*adj* **life´-size**, of the size of the original.—*ns* **life span**, the duration of existence of an individual; **life style**, particular attitudes, habits, etc. of a person or group; **life´time´**, the length of time that one lives or that a thing lasts.—Also *adj.*—*n* **life´work´**, the work to which a person devotes his life.—**life-and-death, life-or-death**, vitally important; **life of Riley**, a carefree comfortable life; **life-support system**, an artificial system providing the items (as oxygen, food, water, etc.) necessary for maintaining life. [OE *līf*; ON *līf*, Swed *līf*; Ger *leib* body.]

lift [lift] *vt* to bring to a higher position, raise; to raise in rank, condition, etc.; to pay off (a mortgage, debt, etc.) to end (a blockade, etc.); (*slang*) to steal.—*vi* to exert oneself in raising something; to rise; to go up.—*n* act or fact of lifting; distance through which a thing is lifted; lifting power or influence; elevation of mood, etc.; elevated position or carriage; a ride in the direction in which one is going; help of any kind; (*British*) an elevator.—*ns* **lift´off´**, the vertical thrust of a spacecraft, missile, etc. at launching; the time of this; **lift truck**, a small truck for lifting and transporting loads. [ON *lypta*—*lopt*, the air.]

ligament [lig´a-mėnt] *n* a band of tissue connecting bones or holding organs in place; a unifying bond.—*adj* **ligament´ous**.—*n* **lig´ature** [lig´å-chur] a tying or binding together; a tie, bond, etc.; two or more letters united, as æ ffi; (*surgery*) a thread used to suture a blood vessel, etc.—*n* **liga´tion**, an act of ligating; something that binds.—*vt* **ligate** [lī´gāt, lī-gāt´], to tie with a ligature. [L *ligāre*, to bind.]

light[1] [līt] *n* the radiant energy by which the eye sees; ultraviolet or infrared radiation; brightness, illumination; a source of light, as the sun, a lamp, etc.; daylight; thing used to ignite something; a window or windowpane; knowledge, enlightenment; public view (*bring things to light*); aspect (*viewed in another light*); an outstanding person.—*adj* having light; bright; pale in color.—*adv* palely.—*vt* to ignite; to cause to give off light; to furnish with light; to brighten, animate; *prp* **light´ing**; *pt* and *ptp* **light´ed** or **lit**.—*vti* **light´en**, to make or become light or lighter; to shine, flash.—*ns* **light´er**, a person or thing that starts something burning; **light´house**, a tower with a bright light to guide ships at night; **light´ing**, the process of giving light; **light meter**, a device for measuring illumination used esp in photography; **light´ness**, the amount of light; brightness; paleness in color; **light´ning**, discharge or flash of electricity in the sky; **lightning bug**, firefly; **lightning rod**, a metal rod placed high on a building and grounded to divert lightning from the structure; **light pen**, a pen-shaped device for direct interaction with a computer; **light´ship**, a ship with a bright light moored at a place dangerous to navigation; **light´year**, the distance that light travels in one year, about 6 trillion miles.—**in the light of**, considering; **see the light of day**, to come into being; to come into public view; to understand. [ME *liht*—OF *leht*, lēoht; Ger licht.]

light[2] [līt] *adj* having little weight; not heavy, esp for its size; less than usual in weight, amount, force, etc.; of little importance; easy to bear; easy to do; gay, happy; dizzy, giddy; not serious; moderate; moving with ease; producing small products.—*adv* lightly.—*vi* to come to rest after traveling through the air; to come or happen on or upon; to strike suddenly, as a blow.—*prp* **light´ing**; *pt*, and *pt p* **light´ed**, or **lit**.—*vti* **light´en**, to make or become lighter in weight; to make or become more cheerful.—*n* **light-emitting diode**, LED.—*adj* **light´-fingered**, thievish;—*n* **light flyweight**, amateur boxer weighing not more than 106lbs.—*adjs* **light´-footed**, stepping lightly and gracefully; **light-´head´ed**, dizzy; delirious; frivolous; **light-´heart´ed**, carefree.—*n* **light heavyweight**, a professional boxer or wrestler weighing 161 to 175lbs; amateur boxer weighing 165 to 179lbs.—*adv* **light´ly**, with little weight or pressure, gently; to a small degree or amount; nimbly, deftly; cheerfully; with indifference.—*n* **light middleweight**, amateur boxer weighing 148–157lbs.—*adj* **light´-minded**, silly.—*ns* **light muscat**, a dry or semisweet white table wine; **lightness**, not being heavy; being gay or cheerful; lack of proper seriousness; **light opera**, operetta; **light´weight**, a boxer or wrestler weighing 127 to 135lbs.—*adj* light in weight.—*n* **light welterweight**, amateur boxer weighing 132 to 140 lbs.—**lighter-than-air**, of less weight than the air displaced; **light out**(*inf*), to depart suddenly; **make light of**, to treat as unimportant. [OE *līht, lēoht*.]

light[3] [līt] *vi* to dismount, to alight; to arrive by chance (upon);—*prp* **light´ing**; *pt, pt p* **light´ed** or **lit**.—**light into** to attack forcefully. [OR līhtan, to dismount.]

lighter [līt´er] *n* a large barge used in loading or unloading larger ships lying offshore.—*n* **light´erage** act or instance of using a lighter; price paid for the service; lighters collectively. [ME from MDu *lichter*, from *lichten*, to unload.]

lignin [lig´nin] *n* an amorphous substance related to cellulose, with which it forms the woody cell walls of plants and the material between them. [L *lignum*, wood.]

lignite [lig´nīt] *n* a soft, brownish-black coal with the texture of the original wood. [L *lignum*, wood.]

lignum vitae [lig´num vit´ē] *n* the very heavy hard wood of several tropical American trees (genus *Guaiacum*); a tree yielding lignum vitae. [L *lignum*, wood.]

ligule [lig´ūl] *n* a scalelike projection esp on a plant. [L *ligula* dim of *lingua*, a tongue.]

like[1] [līk] *adj* having the same characteristics; similar; equal.—*adv* (*inf*) likely.—*prep* similar to; similarly to; characteristic of; in the mood for; indicative of; as for example.—*conjunction* (*inf*) as; as if.—*n* an equal; counterpart.—*n* **like´lihood**, probability.—*adj* **like´ly**, credible; reasonably to be expected; suitable.—*adv* probably.—*n* **like´mind´ed**, having the same tastes, ideas, etc.—*vt* **lik´en**, to compare.—*n* **like´ness**, a being like; something that is like, as a copy, portrait, etc.; appearance, semblance.—*adv* **like´wise**, the same; also; moreover.—**and the like**, and others of the same kind; **as like as not**, probably; **the likes of**, (*inf*) any person or thing like. [OE *līc*, seen in *gelīc*; ON *líkr*, Du *gelijk*.]

like[2] [līk] *vt* to be pleased with; to wish.—*vi* to be so inclined.—*npl* preferences, tastes.—*adj* **lik´able, like´able**, attractive, pleasant, genial, etc.—*n* **lik´ing**, fondness; affection; preference. [Orig impersonal—OE *līcian*—*līc*, like.]

lilac [lī´làc] *n* a European shrub (*Syringa vulgaris*) now widely naturalized in temperate zones, with large clusters of tiny, fragrant flowers.—*n, adj* a pale purple. [Sp—Pers *lilak*, bluish.]

Lilliputian [lil-i-pū´sh(y)àn] *adj* tiny; petty.—*n* [A tiny inhabitant of *Lilliput*, an island described by Swift in his *Gulliver's Travels*.]

lilt [lilt] *vi* to sing or play merrily.—*vt* to sing easily or gaily.—*n* a cheerful song or air; springy movement. [ME *lulte*.]

lily [lil´i] *n* a bulbous plant (genus *Lilium*) having typically trumpet-shaped flowers; its flower; any similar plant.—*adj* resembling a lily as in whiteness, purity.—*adjs* **lil´ied**, adorned with lilies; **lil´y-liv´ered**, cowardly; timid.—**lily of the valley**, a small perennial plant (*Convallaria majalis*) of the lily family with a raceme of fragrant white bell-shaped flowers. [OE *lilie*—L *lilium*—Gr *leirion*, lily.]

limb[1] [lim] *n* an arm, leg, or wing; a large branch of a tree.—*vt* to dismember; to cut off the limbs of (a felled tree).—**out on a limb**, (*inf*) in a precarious position. [OE *lim*; ON *limr*.]

limb[2] [lim] *n* an edge or border, as of the sun, etc.; the edge of a sextant, etc. [Fr *limbe*—L *limbus*, a border.]

limber [lim´bėr] *adj* flexible, able to bend the body easily.—*vti* to make or become limber.

limbo [lim´bō] *n* in some Christian theologies, the abode after death assigned to the unbaptized; a place of oblivion. [From the Latin phrase *in limbo*—*in*, in, and abl of *limbus*, border.]

Limburger [lim´bėrg-ėr] *n* a semisoft, fermented cow's-milk cheese with a full flavor and strong odor. [*Limburg*, Belgian province.]

lime[1] [līm] *n* any slimy or gluey material; bird-lime; quick-lime; the white caustic substance (calcium oxide when pure) obtained by calcining limestone, etc., used for cement.—*vt* to cover with lime; to cement; to manure with lime; to ensnare.—*ns* **lime´kiln**, a kiln or furnace in which limestone is burned to lime; **lime´light**, light produced by a blowpipe-flame directed against a block of quicklime; the glare of publicity; **lime´stone**, a sedimentary rock composed essentially of calcium carbonate; **lime´twig**, a twig smeared with bird-lime; a snare.—*adjs* **lim´ous**, gluey; slimy; muddy; **lim´y**, glutinous; sticky; containing, resembling, or having the qualities of lime. [OE *līm*; Ger *leim*, glue, L *līmus*, slime.]

lime[2] [līm] *n* a small globose yellowish-green fruit (genus *Citrus*) with a juicy, sour pulp; the tree that bears it.—*ns* **limeade´**, a drink made with sweetened lime juice mixed with plain or carbonated water; **lime-juicer**, (*slang*) a British ship or sailor.—**lim´ey**, (*slang*) an Englishman. [Arabic, *līm*.]

lime[3] [līm] *n* the linden tree. [Variant of obs *lind*, **linden**.]

limerick [lim´er-ik] *n* a form of humorous verse in a five-line jingle. [*Limerick*, Ireland.]

limit [lim´it] *n* boundary; (*pl*) bounds; the greatest amount allowed.—*vt* to set a limit to; to restrict.—*adjs* **lim´itable; lim´itary**, limiting; enclosing.—*n* **lim´itā´tion**.—*adjs* **lim´itless**, having no limits; **limited**, confined within bounds; (of a train, bus, etc.) making a restricted number of stops; lacking breadth and originality. [L *līmes, -itis*, boundary.]

limn [lim] *vt* to draw or paint; to outline in clear sharp detail; to describe.—*n* **lim´ner**. [OFr *enluminer*—L *illumināre*.]

limousine [lim´ōō-zēn] *n* a large luxury automobile, esp one driven by a chauffeur. [Fr.]

limp [limp] *vi* to walk with or as with a lame leg.—*n* a halt or lameness in walking.—*adj* lacking firmness; wilted, flexible, etc.—*adv* **limp´ly**.—*n* **limp´ness**. [OE *lemp-healt*, halting.]

limpet [lim´pet] *n* any of a number of marine gastropod mollusks (esp families Acmeidae and Patellidae) with a low conical shell that cling to rocks; one that clings tenaciously to someone or something; an explosive designed to cling to the hull of a ship. [OE *lempedu*, lamprey.]

limpid [lim´pid] *adj* perfectly clear; transparent.—*ns* **limpid´ity, lim´pidness**.—*adv* **lim´pidly**. [L *limpidus*, liquid.]

linchpin [linch´pin] *n* a pin used to keep a wheel on its axle. [OE *lynis*, axle, and **pin**.]

linden [lin´den] *n* any tree of the genus *Tilia*, having deciduous, heart-shaped, serrated leaves. [OE *lind*; cf ON *lind*, Ger *linde*.]

line[1] [līn] *vt* to put, or serve as, a lining in.—*n* **lin´ing**, the material covering an inner surface. [OE *līn*, flax.]

line[2] [līn] *n* a length of cord, rope, or wire; a cord for measuring, making level; system of conducting fluid, electricity, etc.; a thin threadlike mark; anything like such a mark, as a wrinkle; edge, limit, boundary; border, outline, contour; row of persons or things, as printed letters across a page; a succession of persons, lineage; a connected series of things; the course a moving thing takes; a course of conduct, actions, etc.; whole system of transportation; a person's trade or occupation; field of experience or interest; (*inf*) glib, persuasive talk; a verse; the forward combat position in warfare; line, trenches or other defenses used in war; a stock of goods; a piece of information; a short letter, note; (*pl*) all the speeches of a character in a play; (*football*) the players in the front row; (*math*) the path of a moving point.—*vt* to mark with lines; to form a line along; to cover with lines; to arrange in a line; to hit (as a baseball or a tennis ball) hard in a straight line.—*vi* to hit a line drive in baseball; to align.—*ns* **līn´age**, the number of written or printed lines as on a page; **lineage** [lin´ē-ij] direct descent from an ancestor; ancestry, family.—*adj* **lineal** [lin´i-àl] hereditary; linear; descended in a direct line from an ancestor.—*adv* **lin´eally**.—*n* **lin´eament**, (*usu pl*) feature; distinguishing mark in the form, esp of the face.—*adj* **lin´ear**, of, made of, or using a line or lines; narrow and long; in relation to length only.—*n* **linēar´ity**.—*adv* **lin´early**.—**linear equation**, an equation of the first degree, that is, one whose graph is a straight line; **linear function**, a mathematical function in which first-degree variables are multiplied by constants and are combined only by addition and subtraction; **linear measure**, a measure or a system of measures of length; **linear park**, a hiking, biking, jogging trail converted from an old train route; **linear programming**, a mathematical method of solving practical problems by means of linear functions where the variables are subject to limitations; **lineat´ion**, a marking with lines; arrangement of lines; **line´backer**, (*football*) a defensive player directly behind the line; **line drawing**, a drawing made in solid lines; **line drive**, a ball (as in tennis or baseball) hit in a straight line parallel to the ground; **line engraving**, an engraving cut by hand directly in a metal plate; **line judge**, (*football*) a linesman whose duties include being official timekeeper; **line´man**, a man who sets up and repairs telephone or electric power lines; (*football*) a player in the line; **line printer**, a high-speed printing device (as for a computer) that prints each line as a unit; **lin´er**, a steamship, airplane, etc. in regular service for some line; a cosmetic applied in a fine line; **line score**, (*baseball*) a score giving the runs, hits, and errors by each team; **lines´man**, (*football*) an official who marks the gains or losses in ground; (*tennis*) an official who determines if the balls land outside the foul lines; **line´up**, an arrangement of persons or things in a line.—**line of credit**, the maximum credit allowed a borrower or buyer; **line of duty**, all that is associated with some field of responsibility; **line of force**, a line in a magnetic or electric field whose tangent gives the direction of the field at that point.—**bring** or **come into line**, to bring or come into conformity; **draw the line**, to set a limit; **hold the line**, to stand firm; **in line for**, being considered for. [Partly from OE *līne*, cord (from or cognate with L *līnum*, flax); partly through Fr *ligne*, and partly directly, from L *līnea*, thread.]

linen [lin´ėn] *n* thread or cloth made of flax; (often *pl*) sheets, cloths, etc. made of linen, or of cotton, etc.; paper made from linen fibers or with a linen finish.—*adj* made of flax; resembling linen cloth. [OE *līnen* (adj)—*līn*, flax.]

ling [ling] *n* heather. [ON *lyng*.]

-ling [-ling] *n suffix* denoting a diminutive, as duck*ling*.

linger [ling´gėr] *vi* to remain long; to loiter; to delay.—*n* **ling´erer**.—*adj* **ling´ering**, remaining long, protracted. [OE *lengan*, to protract—*lang*, long.]

lingerie [lẽzh-(ė)rē] *n* women's underwear. [Fr—*linge*, linen—L *līnum*.]

lingo [ling´gō] *n* a dialect, jargon, etc. that one is not familiar with. [L *lingua*, language.]

lingua franca [ling´gwa frangk´a] *n* a hybrid language used for communication by speakers of different languages. [Ital, Frankish language.]

lingual [ling´gwàl] *adj* of, or pronounced with, the tongue.—*adv* **ling´ually**.—*n* **ling´uist**, a specialist in linguistics; a polyglot.—*adjs* **linguist´ic, -al**.—*adv* **linguist´ically**.—*n pl* **linguist´ics**, the science of language; the study of a particular language. [L *lingua*, the tongue.]

liniment [lin´i-mėnt] *n* a soothing medicated liquid to be rubbed on the skin; a thin ointment; an embrocation. [L *linīmentum*—*linĕre*, to besmear.]

link[1] [lingk] *n* a loop or ring of a chain; anything connecting a single part of a series.—*vti* to connect; to join.—*ns* **link´age** [-ij], a linking; a series or system of links; **link´up**, a linking together. [OE *hlence*; ON *hlekkr*; Ger *gelenk*, a joint.]

link[2] [lingk] *n* (*formerly*) a torch made of pitch and tow.—*ns* **link´boy, link´man**, an attendant carrying a link in dark streets.

links [lingks] *n pl* a golf course. [OE *hlinc*, a ridge of land, a bank.]

Linnaean, Linnean [lin-ē´ȧn] *adj* of, or relating to, or following the methods of Carl Linné, the Swedish botanist (1707–78), who established the system of binominal nomenclature.

linnet [lin´et] *n* a common small finch (*Carduelis cannabina*) of Europe, Africa, and Asia. [OFr *linot*—*lin*, flax—L *līnum*.]

linoleum [lin-ō´li-um] *n* a floor covering of burlap with a smooth, hard decorative coating made of powdered cork, linseed oil, etc. [L *līnum*, flax, *oleum*, oil.]

linocut [li´nō-kut] *n* a linoleum block cut in relief, or a print from it. [*lino*leum and **cut**.]

Linotype [līn´ō-tīp] *n* a keyboard-operated typesetting machine for producing castings of complete lines of words, etc. [**line o' type**. Trademark.]

linseed [lin´sēd] *n* flax seed.—*n* **lin´seed oil**, yellow drying oil from flax seed. [OE *līn*, flax, *sǣd*, seed.]

linsey-woolsey [lin´zi, -wōōl´zi] *ns* a sturdy coarse fabric of linen or cotton and wool mixed. [**line** (1) + **wool**.]

lint [lint] *n* scraped and softened linen; bits of fluff, thread, etc. from cloth or yarn. [ME *lynt*, perh—L *linteus*, of linen—*līnum*, flax.]

lintel [lint´(ė)l] *n* the horizontal crosspiece over a doorway or window. [OFr *lintel*, dim of L *līmes, -itis*, border.]

lion [lī´ȯn] *n* a large, tawny social feline (*Felis Leo*) of Africa and southern Asia, with a shaggy mane in the adult male; a person of great courage or strength; a celebrity; **Lion**, a member of the Lion's Club, a major national and international service club.—**li´oness**, a female lion.—*adj* **lī´on-heart´ed**, very brave.—*vt* **lī´onize**, to treat as a celebrity.—**lion's share**, the largest share. [Anglo-Fr *liun*—L *leō, -ōnis*—Gr *leōn*.]

lip [lip] *n* either of the muscular flaps in front of the teeth by which things are taken into the mouth; anything like a lip, as the rim of a pitcher; (*slang*) insolent talk.—*adj* spoken, but insincere (*lip service*).—*vt* to touch the edge of.—*pr p* **lipp´ing**; *pt p* **lipped**.—*adjs* **lipped**, having (a specified number or kind of) lips; **lipp´y**, (*slang*) impudent; insolent.—*n* **lip reading**, recognition of a speaker's words, as by the deaf, by watching lip movement.—*vti* **lip´-read**.—*n* **lip´stick**, a small stick of cosmetic for coloring the lips.—*vti* **lip´-sync´, lip´-synch´** [-singk], to move the lips silently in synchronization to recorded song or speech. [OE *lippa*; Du *lip*; Ger *lippe*, L *labium*.]

lip-, lipo- [lip-, lip-(ō-)] in composition, fat; fatty tissue; fatty, as in **lip´ase**, an enzyme that breaks up fats.—**lipoma** [lī-pō´mȧ], a slow-growing tumor of fatty tissue. [Gr *lipos*, fat.]

liquate [lik´wāt] *vt* to cause to separate by applying heat (to mixed metals that solidify or fuse at different temperatures).—*n* **liquā´tion**. [L *liquāre, -ātum*, to liquefy.]

liquefy [lik´we-fī] *vti* to change to a liquid.—*pt, pt p* **liq´uefīed**.—*n* **liquefac´tion**.—*adj* **liq´uefiable**.—*n* **liq´uefier**.—*adj* **liques´cent**, melting. [L *liquefacĕre*—*liquēre*, to be liquid, *facĕre*, to make.]

liqueur [li-kûr´] *n* a sweet, syrupy-flavored alcoholic liquor. [Fr—L *liquor*.]

liquid [lik´wid] *adj* flowing; fluid; clear; limpid; flowing smoothly and musically, as verse; readily convertible into cash.—*n* a substance that, unlike a gas, does not expand indefinitely and unlike a solid, flows readily.—*n* a liquid substance; a flowing consonant sound, as *l, r*.—*ns* **liquid´ity, liq´uidness**.—*vt* **liq´uidate**, to settle the accounts of (a business); to pay (a debt); to convert into cash; to get rid of, as by killing.—*ns* **liquidā´tion; liquidāt´or**.—*vt* **liq´uidize´**, to make liquid.—*ns* **liquid measure**, a unit for measuring liquid capacity.—**liquid crystal display** LCD. [L *liquidus*, liquid, clear—*liquēre*, to be clear.]

liquor [lik´ȯr] *n* any liquid; an alcoholic drink, esp one distilled, as whiskey or rum. [OFr *licur, licour*—L *liquor, -ōris*.]

lira [lē´ra] *n* a unit of money in Italy or Turkey.—*pl* **lire** [lē´rā], **lir´as**. [It—L *lībra*, a pound.]

lisle [līl] *n* a fine hard-twisted cotton thread. [*Lille*, France.]

lisp [lisp] *vi* to substitute the sounds *th* for *s* or TH for *z*; to utter imperfectly.—*vt* to utter with a lisp.—*n* the act or habit of lisping. [OE *wlisp*, stammering.]

lissome, lissom [lis´ȯm] *adj* lithe; supple; agile, etc. [Form of **lithesome** (see **lithe**).]

list[1] [list] *n* a series of names, numbers, words, etc. usu. set forth in order.—*vt* to make a list of; to enter in a directory, etc.—*n* **list price**, the retail price as given in a list or catalog. [OFr *liste* of Gmc origin, ultimately same word as above.]

list[2] [list] *vti* to tilt to one side, as a ship.—*n* such a tilting.—*adj* **list´less**, having no desire or wish because of illness, dejection, etc.; languid.—*adv* **list´lessly**.—*n* **list´lessness**. [OE *lystan*, impers please—*lust*, pleasure.]

listen [lis´n] *vi* to try to hear; to follow advice.—*n* **list´ener**.—*vi* **list´en in**, to tune in to a radio broadcast; to listen to others talking on a telephone; to eavesdrop. [OE *hlysnan*.]

listeriosis [lis-tėr-ē-ō´sis] *n* a serious, commonly fatal bacterial (*Listeria monocytogenes*) disease of many animals including man, usu. transmitted through food. [Joseph *Lister*, English surgeon.]

lists [lists] *n* a fenced area in which knights jousted.—**enter the lists**, to engage in contest. [OE *liste; lelste*, border.]

lit *pt, pt p* of **light** (*vb* **1 and 3**).—**lit up** (*inf*) drunk.

litany [lit´ȧ-ni] *n* a prayer with responses, in public worship. [OFr—Low L *litanīa*—Gr *litaneia*—*litesthai*, to pray.]

litchi [lē´chē] *n* the raisinlike fruit, when dried enclosed in a papery brown shell, of a Chinese tree (*Litchi chinensis*); a tree bearing litchis.—Also **lī´chee**. [Chinese.]

literal [lit´ėr-ȧl] *adj* following the exact words of the original (*a literal translation*); in a basic or strict sense (*the literal meaning*); prosaic, matter-of-fact (*a literal mind*); real (*the literal truth*).—*adv* **lit´erally**.—*n* **lit´eralness**. [L *līterālis*—*lītera*, a letter.]

literary [lit´er-ar-i] *adj* of or dealing with literature; knowing much about literature.—*n* **lit´eracy**, ability to read and write.—*adj* **lit´erate** [-ȧt] able to read and write; educated.—Also *n*.—*n pl* **literä´ti**, scholarly people.—*adj, adv* **litera´tim** [-rā or -rä] letter for letter.—*n* **lit´erature** [-chůr], writings of a period or of a country, esp those kept alive by their excellence of form, permanent value, etc.; all the books and articles on a subject; (*inf*) any printed matter. [L *līterātūra, litterātūra*—*lītera, littera*, a letter.]

lithe [līTH] *adj* flexible, pliant.—*adv* **lithe´ly**.—*n* **lithe´ness**.—*adj* **lithe´some**.—*n* **lithe´someness**. [OE *līthe*, soft, mild.]

lithium [lith´i-um] *n* the lightest metallic element (symbol Li; at wt 6.9; at no 3).—*n* **lithium carbonate**, a white powdery salt used in making glass, dyes, etc. and in treating manic-depressive disorders. [Gr *lithos*, stone.]

lithograph [lith´ō-gräf] *n* a print made by lithography.—*vti* to make (prints or copies) by this method.—*n* **lithog´raphy**, printing from a flat stone or metal plate, parts of which have been treated to repel ink.—*n* **lithog´rapher**.—*adj* **lithograph´ic**.—*adv* **lithograph´ically**.—*n* **lithog´raphy**. [Gr *lithos*, a stone, *graphein*, to write.]

lithology [lith-ol´o-ji] *n* the study of rocks; the character of a rock formation.—*adjs* **litholog´ic, litholog´ical**. [Gr *lithos*, a stone, *logos*, discourse.]

lithophyte [lith´ō-fīt] *n* a plant that grows on rocks. [Gr *lithos*, stone, *phyton*, plant.]

lithosphere [lith´ō-sfēr] *n* the rocky crust of the earth. [Gr *lithos*, stone, *sphaira*, sphere.]

lithotomy [lith-ot´o-mi] *n* surgical removal of a stone in the urinary bladder. [Gr *lithos*, stone, *tomē*, a cutting—*temnein*, to cut.]

litigate [lit´i-gāt] *vti* to dispute by a lawsuit.—*adjs* **lit´igable**, that may be contested in law; **lit´igant**, contending at law, engaged in a lawsuit.—*n* person engaged in a lawsuit.—*n* **litigā´tion**.—*adj* **litigious** [li-tij´-us] inclined to engage in lawsuits; contentious.—*n* **litig´iousness**.—*adv* **litig´iously**. [L *lītigāre, -ātum*—*lis, lītis*, a dispute, lawsuit, *agĕre*, to do.]

litmus [lit´mus] *n* a substance obtained from certain lichens, turned red by acids, blue by bases. [ON *litr*, color, *mosi*, moss.]

litotes [līt´- or lit´ō-tēz] *n* a kind of understatement denying the opposite of what is meant (eg Mount Everest is not exactly a foothill). [Gr *lītotēs*, simplicity—*lītos*, plain.]

liter [lēt´ėr] *n* the basic unit of capacity in the metric system, equal to 0.908 dry quarts and 1.057 liquid quarts. [Fr.]

litter [lit´ėr] *n* things scattered about or left in disorder; young animals produced at one time; straw, hay, etc. used as bedding for animals; a stretcher for carrying a sick or wounded person; a framework with a couch usu. enclosed by curtains, on which a person can be carried.—*vt* to make untidy; to scatter about carelessly.—*n* **litt´erbug**, one who litters public places with refuse, etc. [OFr *litiere*—Low L *lectāria*—L *lectus*, a bed.]

little [lit´l] *adj* (comparative **less** or **lesser**; superlative **least** or **littl´est**) not great or big, small in size, amount, degree, etc.; short in duration; small in importance or power; narrow-minded.—*n* small amount, degree, etc.—*adv* **less, least**, slightly; not much; not in the least.—*ns* **Little Bear**, Ursa Minor; **Little Dipper**, the seven principal stars in Ursa Minor; **Little League**, a commercially sponsored baseball league for boys and girls from 8 to 12 years old; **Little Leaguer; little magazine**, a literary magazine, usu. subsidized, featuring little-known writers; **littleneck**, quahog; **little people**, tiny imaginary beings (as fairies, brownies, elves, etc.) of folklore; **little slam**, (*bridge*) the bidding of and winning of all but one trick in a deal.—**little by little**, gradually; **make little of, think little of**, consider as not very important. [OE *lȳtel*.]

littoral [lit´ȯr-ȧl] *adj* of or along the seashore.—*n* the shore zone between high and low watermarks. [L—*lītus, littus, lītoris, littoris*, shore.]

liturgy [lit´ûr-ji] *n* the prescribed ritual of a church.—*adjs* **litur´gic, -al**.—*adv* **litur´gically**. [Gr *leitourgiā*.]

live [liv] *vi* to have life; to remain alive; to endure; to pass life in a specified manner; to enjoy a full life; to feed (*to live on fruit*); to reside.—*vt* to carry out in one's life; to spend; pass (*to live a useful life*).—*adjs* **livable; live** [līv], having life; of the living state or living beings; of present interest; still burning; unexploded (*a live shell*); carrying electric current; (*of a broadcast*) broadcast during the actual performance; (*sports*) in play (*a live ball*).—*n* **līve´stock**, domestic animals esp cows, horses, sheep, pigs, etc. raised for use or sale—**live down**, to live as to wipe out the shame of (a misdeed); **live up to**, to act in accordance with one's ideals. [OE *lifian*.]

livelihood [līv´li-hood] *n* means of living or of supporting life. [OE *līflād*—*līf*, life, *lād*, course; confused with *livelihood*, liveliness.]

livelong [liv´long] *adj* long in passing; whole; entire. [**lief**, used intensively + **long**.]

lively [līv´li] *adj* full of life; spirited; exciting; gay, cheerful; vivid; keen; bounding back with great resilience.—*adv* in a lively manner.—*n* **līve´liness**. [OE *līflic*—*līf*, life.]

liver [liv´ėr] *n* the largest glandular organ in vertebrate animals which secretes bile, etc. and is important in metabolism; the liver of an animal used as food.—*ns* **liver fluke**, any of various parasitic flatworms that invade the mammalian liver; **liver spot**, light brown spot on the skin of usu. middle-aged or older persons; **liv´erwort**, a bryophyte of the same class (Hepatica) as mosses but lacking the radial symmetry of mosses; **liv´erwurst**, a sausage containing ground pork liver. —*adjs* **liv´erish, liv´ery**, suffering from disordered liver; irritable. [OE *lifer*; Ger *leber*, ON *lifr*.]

livery [liv´ėr-i] *n* an identifying uniform as of a servant; the care and feeding of horses for a fee; the keeping of horses or vehicles for hire.—*adj* **liv´eried**. [Fr *liverée*—*livrer*, to deliver—L *līberāre*, to free.]

lives [līvz] *pl* of **life**.

livid [liv´id] *adj* discolored; black and blue; of a lead color; pale with emotion.—*n* **liv´idness**. [L *līvidus*—*līvēre*, to be of a lead color.]

living [liv´ing] *adj* having life; full of life, strong (*a living faith*); still in use; true to life, vivid; of life, for living in.—*n* a being alive; livelihood; manner of existence.—*ns* **living death**, life emptied of satisfaction; **living fossil**, an organism that has remained unchanged from earlier geologic times (as a horseshoe crab or a gingko tree); **living wage**, a wage sufficient to maintain a reasonable standard of comfort; **living will**, a document directing that the signer's life not be artificially supported during a terminal illness.—**the living**, those alive. [**live**, vb.]

lizard [liz´ȧrd] *n* any of a suborder (*Lacertilia*) of reptiles with a slender body, four legs, and a tapering tail. [Fr *lézard*—L *lacerta*.]

llama [lä´mä] *n* a wild or domesticated ruminant (genus *Lama*), related to the camel, of So America used as a beast of burden and a source of wool. [Sp from native name.]

llano [lyä´no or lä´no] *n* an open grassy plain in the southwestern US or Spanish America.—*pl* **lla´nos**. [Sp—L *plānus*, plain.]

Lloyd's [loidz] *n* an association of underwriting firms specializing in marine insurance and known for insuring against losses of almost every conceivable kind. [From *Lloyd's* coffee-house in London, 17th-century meeting-place of merchants, to exchange shipping news, etc.]

load [lōd] *n* an amount carried at one time; something borne with difficulty; burden; (often *pl*) (*inf*) a great amount.—*vt* to put (a load) into or upon (a carrier); to burden; to oppress; to supply in large quantities; to alter, as by adding a weight to dice or an adulterant to alcoholic drink; to put film into (a camera); (*baseball*) to put runners on first, second, and third base; to add to an insurance premium or to a price; to put a charge of ammunition into (a firearm).—*vi* to take on a load.—*adj* **loaded** (*slang*) having a large amount of money.—*ns* **load factor**, a proportion of seats paid for and occupied in a commercial aircraft; **load line**, the line on a ship indicating its depth in the water when properly loaded; **load´star**, lodestar; **load´stone**, lodestone. [OE *lād*, course, journey, conveyance; meaning affected by the unrelated **lade**.]

loaf[1] [lōf] *n* a regularly shaped mass of bread; food shaped like a load of bread.—*pl* **loaves** [lōvz]. [OE *hlāf*, bread.]

loaf[2] [lōf] *vi* to loiter, pass time idly.—*n* **loaf´er**.

Loafer [lōf´ėr] *n* trade name for a shoe resembling a mocassin.

loam [lōm] *n* a fertile soil, of clay, sand, and animal and vegetable matter.—*adj* **loam´y**. [OE *lām*; Ger *lehm*; allied to **lime** (1).]

loan [lōn] *n* the act of lending; something lent, esp money at interest.—*vti* to lend.—*ns* **loan shark**, one who lends money at an exorbitant rate of interest; **loanword**, a word of one language taken and used in another. [ON *lān*; related to OE *lǣnan*; cf **lend**.]

loath, loathe [lōth] *adj* reluctant, unwilling (to).—[OE *lāth*, hateful.]

loathe [lōTH] *vt* to dislike greatly, to feel disgust at.—*n* **loath´ing**, extreme hate or disgust, abhorrence.—*adjs* **loath´some** exciting loathing or abhorrence, detestable.—*adv* **loath´somely**.—*n* **loath´someness**. [OE *lāthian*—*lāth*. *See* **loath**.]

loaves *See* **loaf** (1).

lob [lob] *vti* to toss or hit (a ball) in a high curve.—*n* a high-arching throw or kick. [Allied to Du *lob*.]

lobby [lob´i] *n* an entrance hall of a public building; a person or group that tries to influence legislators.—*vti* to act as a lobbyist.—*n* **lobby´ist** one who tries to get legislators to support certain measures. [Low L *lobia*—Middle High Ger *loube*, portico, arbour—*laub*, leaf.]

lobe [lōb] *n* a rounded projection, as the lower end of the ear; any of the divisions of the lungs or brains.—*adjs* **lob´ar, lob´āte, lobed**, of or relating to a lobe.—*n* **lob´ule** a small lobe; a subdivision of a lobe.—*adj* **lob´ūlar**, shaped like a lobule. [Gr *lobs*, lobe.]

lobelia [lob-ē´li-a] *n* a large genus (*Lobelia*) of garden plants, usually with blue flowers. [*Lobel*, a Flemish botanist.]

lobotomy [lob-ot´ō-mi] *n* cutting off of certain fibers of the brain in order to relieve certain mental disorders. [Gr *lobos*, lobe, *tomē*, cut.]

lobster [lob´stėr] *n* any of a family (Homaridae, esp genus *Homarus*) of edible sea crustaceans with four pairs of legs and a pair of large pincers.—*ns* **lobster pot**, a trap for catching lobsters, usu. an oblong cage with slat sides and a funnel-shaped net; **lobster tail**, the edible tail of various crayfish; **lobster thermidor**, cooked lobster meat in a rich wine sauce stuffed into a lobster shell. [OE *loppestre*—L *locusta*, a lobster.]

local [lō´kȧl] *adj* of or belonging to a place, confined to a spot or district; of or for a particular part of the body; making all stops along its run.—*n* a local train, bus, etc.; a branch, as of a labor union.—*n* **locale** [-käl´], the scene of some event.—*vt* **lōc´alize**, to limit, confine, or trace to a particular place;—*n* **localizā´tion**.—*n* **local´ity**, existence in a place; position; a district.—*adv* **lō´cally**.—*vt* **locāte´**, to place, to set in a particular position; to find the place of, to show the position of.—*vi* (*inf*) to settle.—*n* **locā´tion**, act of locating; position; place; (*movies*) away from the studio.—**local anesthetic**, anesthetic which produces insensitivity in one part of the body; **local color**, details of dress, etc. characteristic of a certain region or time introduced into a novel, video, etc. to supply realism. [L *locālis*—*locus*, a place.]

lock [lok] *n* a device to fasten doors, etc. as with a key or combination; part of a canal, dock, etc. in which the level of the water can be changed by the operation of gates; the part of a gun by which the charge is fired; a controlling hold.—*vt* to fasten with a lock; to shut (up, in, or out); to fit, link; to jam together so as to make immovable.—*vi* to become locked; to interlock.—*ns* **lock´age**, toll paid for passage through a lock; a system of locks; (of a ship) a passing through a lock. **lock´er**, a closet, chest, etc. that can be locked; a large compartment for freezing and storing food; **locker room**, a room for changing clothes and storing clothes and equipment, esp one used by athletes.—*adj* **locker-room**, of an earthy or sexual nature.—*n* **lock´et**, a little hinged ornamental case, usu. containing a picture, and hung from the neck; **lock´jaw**, an early symptom of tetanus, marked by the inability to open the jaws; tetanus; **lock´keeper**, one who attends the locks of a canal; **lock´out**, the closing of a business establishment by the owners or managers in order to gain concessions from the employees; **lock´smith**, one whose work is making and repairing locks and keys; **lock´stitch**, a stitch formed by the locking of two threads together; **lock´up**, a jail.—**lock horns**, to come into conflict; **lock, stock, and barrel**, completely. [OE *loc*.]

lock [lok] *n* a curl of hair; a tuft of wool, etc. [OE *locc*; ON *lokkr*, Ger *locke*, a lock.]

loco[1] [lō´-kō] *adj, adv* (*mus*) at the pitch level as written. [L *loco*, in the place.]

loco[2] [lō´-kō] *adj* (*slang*) mentally disordered.—*vt* to poison with locoweed; to make crazy.—*ns* **lo´coism**, a disease of grazing animals caused by chronic locoweed poisoning; **lo´coweed´**, any of various leguminous plants (genera *Astragalus* and *Oxytropis*) of the southwestern US causing locoism. [Mexican Sp]

locomotive [lō-ko-mōt´iv] *adj* of locomotion.—*n* an electric, steam, or diesel engine on wheels, designed to move a railroad train.—*n* **locomō´tion**, motion, or the power of moving, from one place to another. [L *locus*, a place, *movēre*, *mōtum*, to move.]

locomotor ataxia [lō-kō-mōt´ėr ä-tak´si-a] tabes dorsalis.

locum tenens [lō´kum (tēn´enz)] *n* a substitute, esp for a doctor or clergyman. [L *locus*, a place, *tenēre*, to hold.]

locus [lō´kus] *n* a place; (*math*) the path of a point or a curve, moving according to some specific rule; the aggregate of all possible positions of a moving or generating element.—*pl* **loci** [lō´sī]—**locus classicus** [klas´i-kus], a passage regarded as most authoritative in establishing the meaning of a word or the facts of a subject. [L *locus*, place.]

locust [lō´kust] *n* any of various large grasshoppers often traveling in swarms and destroying crops; cicada; any of various hard-wooded leguminous trees, esp honey locust (*Gleditsia triacanthos*) and black locust (*Robinia pseudoacacia*).—*n* **lō´cust-bean**, the sweet pod of the carob tree. [L *locusta*, lobster, locust.]

locution [lō-kū´sh(ȯ)n] *n* act or mode of speaking esp a word or expression characteristic of a region, group, or cultural level. [L *locūtiō*, *-ōnis*—*loquī*, *locūtus*, to speak.]

lode [lōd] *n* an ore deposit;—*ns* **lode´star**, the star that guides esp the North Star; **lode´stone**, a strongly magnetic iron ore.—Also **loadstar, loadstone**. [OE *lād*, a course.]

lodge [loj] *n* a small house for some special use; a resort hotel or motel; the local chapter or hall of a fraternal society.—*vt* to house temporarily; to shoot, thrust, etc. firmly (in); to bring (a complaint, etc.) before legal authorities; to confer (powers) upon (*with* **in**.)—*vi* to live in a place for a time; to live as a paying guest; to come to rest and stick firmly (in).—*ns* **lod´ger**, one who lives in a rented room in another's home; **lodg´ing**, temporary habitation; *pl* a room or rooms rented in the house of another; **lodg´ment, lodge´ment**, act of lodging, or state of being lodged. [OFr *loge*—OHG *lauba*, shelter.]

loess [lœs, lō´es] *n* a loamy deposit found in N America, Europe, and Asia. [Ger *löss*.]

loft [loft] *n* a room or space immediately under a roof; a gallery in a hall or church; height given to a ball hit or thrown.—*vt* to send (a ball) into a high curve.—*adj* **loft´y**, very high, elevated; noble; haughty.—*adv* **loft´ily**.—*n* **loft´iness**. [Late OE *loft*—ON *lopt*, the sky, an upper room; OE *lyft*, Ger *luft*, the air.]

log[1] [log] *n* a section of the trunk or of a large limb of a felled tree; a device for ascertaining the speed of a ship; a record of speed, progress, etc. esp one kept on a ship's voyage or aircraft's flight.—*vt* to saw (trees) into logs; to record in a log; to sail or fly (a specified distance).—*vi* to cut down trees and remove the logs.—*ns* **log´book**, an official record of a ship's or aircraft's progress and proceedings on board; **logg´er**, one engaged in logging; **logg´erhead**, a blockhead; any of various marine turtles, esp a carnivorous turtle (*Caretta caretta*) of the warm waters of the western Atlantic; **log´jam**, a jumble of logs jammed together in a watercourse; (*inf*) a deadlock, an impasse; a blockage; **log´roll´ing**, mutual exchange of favors, esp among legislators; the sport of balancing oneself while revolving a floating log with one's feet; **log´wood**, a central American leguminous tree (*Haemotoxylon campechianum*); its very hard heartwood; the brown or brownish-red dye from its heartwood.—**at loggerheads**, in sharp disagreement.

log[2] [log] abbrev for **logarithm**.

loganberry [lō´gàn-ber-i] *n* a hybrid developed from the blackberry and the red raspberry; its purplish red fruit. [J H *Logan*, US lawyer.]

logarithm [log´a-riTHm] *n* the exponent of the power to which a fixed number is to be raised to produce a given number. The fixed number is called the base, which can be any positive number except 1.—*adjs* **logarith´mic,—a.**—*adv* **logarith´mically**. [Gr *logos*, ratio, *arithmos*, number.]

loggia [lōj´a, lōj´ya] *n* a roofed open gallery or balcony. [It]

logic [loj´ik] *n* correct reasoning, or the science of this; way of reasoning; what is expected by the working of cause and effect.—*adj* **log´ical** according to the rules of logic; skilled in logic.—*adv* **log´ically**.—*n* **logic´ian** one skilled in logic. [Gr *logikē* (*technē*), logical (art)—*logos*, word, reason.]

logistic, -al [loj-is´tik, -àl] *adj* of or relating to symbolic logic; of or relating to logistics. [Gr *logistikos—logizesthai*, to compute.]

logistics [loj-is´tiks] *n* the branch of military art concerned with transport, housing, and supply of troops; the organizing of a large operation. [Fr *logistique—loger*, to quarter.]

logogram [log´o-gram] *n* a single sign for a word. [Gr *logos*, word, *gramma*, letter.]

logogriph [log´ogrif] *n* a word puzzle (as an anagram). [Gr *logos*, word, *graphein*, to write.]

logomachy [lo-gom´a-ki] *n* contention about words; a wordy controversy. [Gr *logomachia—logos*, word, *machē*, fight.]

logotype [log´ė-tip] *n* a symbol representing a company, etc.—Also **logo**. [Gr *logos*, a word.]

-logy [-lo-ji] *suffix* meaning: a (specified kind of) speaking; science, doctrine, or theory of. [Gr *logos*, word, reason.]

loin [loin] *n* (usu. *pl*) the lower part of the back between the hipbones and the ribs; the front part of the hindquarters of an animal used for food; (*pl*) the hips and the lower abdomen regarded as the region of strength, etc.—*n* **loin´cloth**, a piece of cloth worn round the loins, esp in India. [OFr *loigne*—L *lumbus*, loin.]

loiter [loi´tėr] *vi* to proceed slowly; to dawdle.—*n* **loi´terer**. [Du *leuteren*, to dawdle; Ger dial *lottern*, to waver.]

loll [lol] *vi* to lie lazily about, to lounge; to hang loosely (now mainly of the tongue).—*vt* let hang loosely. [Perh imit]

lollipop [löl´i-pop] *n* a piece of candy at the end of a stick. [Perh N English dial *lolly*, tongue.]

lolygag [läl´ē-gag´] *vi* (*inf*) to waste time in aimless activity.

London broil [lun´don] *n* a grilled, boneless cut usu. flank of beef served sliced diagonally across the grain.

lone [lōn] *adj* by oneself; isolated; solitary.—*n* **loner**, (*inf*) one who avoids the company, counsel of others.—*adj* **lone´some**, having or causing a lonely feeling.—*adv* **lone´somely**.—*n* **lone´someness**.—**lone wolf**, one who prefers to act, live, or work alone. [**alone**.]

lonely [lōn´li] *adj* isolated; unhappy at being alone. [**alone**.]

long [long] *adj* measuring much in space or time; in length (*five feet long*); having a greater than usual length, quantity, etc.; tedious, slow; far-reaching; well-supplied.—*adv* for a long time; from start to finish; at a remote time.—*vi* to desire earnestly esp for something not likely to be attained.—*n* a long time; one taking a long position (as in securities or commodities); (*pl*) long trousers; a clothing size for tall men.—*ns* **long´bow**, a hand-drawn bow that is usu. 5½ to 6 feet long; **long distance**, a telephone exchange for calls between distance places.—*adj, adv* **long distance**, of or relating to a telephone communication or place far away.—*n* **longevity** [-jev´-] long life.—*adj* **long´-faced**, glum.—*n* **long green**, (*slang*) paper money.—*adj* **long´hair´**, (*inf*) of intellectuals or intellectual tastes.—*ns* **long´hand´**, ordinary handwriting as distinguished from shorthand; **long´horn´**, long-horned cattle of Spanish origin formerly common in southwestern US; a firm-textured cheese ranging from white to orange in color and from mild to sharp in flavor; **long hundredweight**, 112 lbs; **long johns**, long underwear; **long jump**, a jump for distance in track-and-field athletics.—*adj* **long-lived´**, having or tending to have a long life span.—*n* **long play**, a long-playing record.—*adj* **long´-range´**, reaching over a long distance or period of time.—*ns* **long´shore´man**, one who loads and unloads ships at a port; **long shot**, (*inf*) in betting, a choice that is not favored and thus carries great odds.—*adjs* **long´stand´ing**, having continued for a long time; **long´-suff´ering**, enduring trouble, pain, etc. patiently; **long suit**, a holding of more than the average number of cards; something at which a person excels; **long´-term´**, for or extending over a long time.—**long ton**, 2,240 lbs; **long view**, an approach to a situation that emphasizes long-range factors.—*adj* **long´-winded**, speaking or writing at great length; tiresomely long; **as long as**, during the time that; since; provided that; **before long**, soon; **in the long run**, a relatively long period of time; **the long and the short**, gist; **long in the tooth**, old; **not long for**, having little time left to do or enjoy something; **so long**, good-bye. [OE *lang*; Ger *lang*, ON *langr*.]

longitude [lon´ji-tūd] *n* distance east or west of the prime meridian, expressed in degrees or time.—*adj* **longitud´inal**, of or in length; running or placed lengthwise; of longitude.—*adv* **longitud´inally**. [L *longitūdō, -inis*, length—*longus*, long.]

loofah [lōō´fà] *n* any of a genus (*Luffa*) of gourds with white flowers and large fruits; its fruit; the fibrous skeleton of the fruit used as a washcloth.

look [lŏŏk] *vi* to try to see; to see; to search; to appear, seem; to be facing in a specified direction.—*vt* to direct one's eyes on; to have an appearance befitting (*to look the part*).—*n* a looking, glance; appearance; aspect; (*inf*) (*pl*) personal appearance.—*interj* see! pay attention!—*ns* **lookalike**, one that looks like another; **look´er**, one that looks; (of a woman or girl) beauty; **look´er-on´**, a spectator; **looking glass**, a (glass) mirror; **look´out´**, a careful watching; a place for keeping watch; a person assigned to watch; (*inf*) concern; **look´-see´** (*slang*) a quick look.—**look after**, to take care of; **look down on, or upon**, to view with contempt; **look down one's nose**, to regard with disdain or disapproval; **look for**, to expect; **look forward to**, to anticipate; **look in on**, to pay a brief visit; **look into**, to investigate; **look out**, to be careful; **look over**, to examine; **look to**, to take care of; to rely on; **look up**, to search for as in a reference book; (*inf*) to call on; **look up to**, to admire. [ON *lōcian*, to look.]

loom[1] [lōō] *n* a machine in which yarn or thread is woven into a fabric.—*vt* to weave on a loom. [OE *gelōma*, a tool.]

loom[2] [lōō] *vi* to appear indistinctly or as in a mirage, often with a suggestion of exaggerated size or of menacing quality; to take shape, as an impending event.—*n* a looming shadow or reflection.

loon[1] [lōōn] *n* any of several large fish-eating diving birds (genus *Gavia*) of N America, best known for its haunting cry. [ON *lomr*]

loon[2] [lōōn] *n* a clumsy, stupid person; a crazy person.—*adj* **loon´y**, (*slang*) crazy, demented. [ME *loun*.]

loop [lōōp] *n* a figure made by a curved line crossing itself; a similar rounded shape in cord, rope, etc. crossed on itself; anything forming this figure; an intrauterine contraceptive device; a segment of a movie film or magnetic tape.—*vt* to make a loop of; to fasten with a loop.—*vi* to form a loop or loops.—*npl* **loop´ers**, the caterpillars of certain moths (families Geometridae and Noctuidae) which move by drawing up the hindpart of their body to the head.—*n* **loophole** [lōōp´hōl] a slit in a wall for looking or shooting through; a means of evading an obligation, etc.—*vt* to make loopholes in; **loop´line**, a branch of a railroad that returns to the main line.—*adj* **loop´y**, crazy. [Perh Middle Du *lûpen*, to peer.]

loose [lōōs] *adj* not confined; free; not firmly fastened; not tight or compact; not precise; inexact; (of a woman) sexually immoral; (*inf*) relaxed.—*vt* to unfasten; to untie; to release; to relax.—*vi* to become loose.—*adv* **loose´ly**.—*vti* **loos´en**, to make or become loose or looser.—*ns* **loose´ness; loose end**, something left hanging loose; (*pl*) unsettled details.—*adj* **loose´-leaf´**, having leaves or sheets that can be easily replaced or removed.—**at loose end** unsettled, idle, etc; **on the loose**, unconfined; free. [ON *lauss*; OE *lēas*.]

loot [lōōt] *n* plunder; (*slang*) money.—*vti* to plunder, ransack. [Hindi *lūt*.]

lop[1] [lop] *vi* to hang down loosely.—*adjs* **lop´-eared**, having drooping ears; **lop´-sīd´ed**, ill-balanced. [Perh conn with **lob**.]

lop[2] [lop] *vt* to cut off the top or ends of, esp of a tree; to curtail by cutting away superfluous parts;—*prp* **lopp´ing**; *pt, ptp* **lopped**—*n* twigs of trees cut off. [OE *loppian*.]

lope [lōp] *vi* to run with a long stride. [ON *hlaupa*; allied to **leap**.]

loquacious [lo-kwā´shùs] *adj* very talkative.—*adv* **loquā´ciously**.—*ns* **loquā´ciousness, loquac´ity** [-kwas´-] [L *loquax, -ācis—loquī*, to speak.]

loran [lō´-, lö´ran] *n* long range aid to navigation (a form of radar). [From the initial letters.]

lord [lörd] *n* an owner, ruler, or master; **Lord** title used in speaking to of a British nobleman of certain rank; (*pl*) the upper house of the British parliament.—*adj* **lord´ly**, noble; magnificent; haughty.—*adv* in the manner of a lord.—*ns* **Lord's day**, Sunday; **lord´ship´**, the rank or authority of a lord; rule, dominion; a title used in speaking of or to a lord (*with* **his** *or* **your**); **Lord's prayer**, the prayer beginning Our Father; Matthew 6:9–13.—**the Lord**, God; Jesus Christ; **lord it over**, to be overbearing toward. [ME *loverd, laverd*—OE *hlāford—hlāf*, bread, *weard*, guardian.]

lordosis [lör-dōs´is] *n* the exaggeration of the normal forward curve of the lower spine; a hollow back.

lore[1] [lōr, lör] *n* knowledge; learning, esp of a traditional nature; a particular body of tradition. [OE *lār*.]

lore[2] [lōr] *n* the space between the eye and the bill on a bird; the corresponding space in a reptile or fish. [L *lōrum*, a thong.]

lorgnette [lörn-yet´] *n* eye or opera glasses with a handle. [Fr *lorgner*, to look sidelong at, to ogle.]

lorn [lörn] *adj* (*arch*) lost; forsaken. [OE *loren*, pap of *lēosan*, to lose.]

lory [lōri] *n* any of a number of parrots (genera *Domicella, Trichoglossus, Chalsopsitta*) native to Australia, New Guinea, and adjacent islands etc. [Malay *luri*.]

lose [lōōz] *vt* to have taken from one by death, accident, removal, etc.; to be unable to find; to fail to keep, as one's temper; to fail to see, hear, or understand; to fail to have, get, etc.; to fail to win; to cause the loss of; to wander from (one's way, etc.); to squander.—*vi* to suffer (a) loss; *prp* **los´ing**; *pt, ptp* **lost**.—*adj* **los´able**.—*n* **los´er**.—*adj* **los´ing**.—*n* **loss**, a losing or being lost; the damage, trouble caused by losing; the person, thing, or amount lost.—*adj* **lost**, no longer possessed; missing; not won; destroyed or ruined; having wandered astray; wasted.—**at a loss**, uncertain; **lose ground**, to suffer loss; to fail to advance or improve; **lose oneself**, to become absorbed; **lose one's heart**, to fall in love. [OE *losian*, usually impersonal, to be a loss.]

lot [lot] *n* an object drawn from among a number to reach a decision by chance; the decision thus arrived at; one's share by lot; fortune; a plot of ground; a group of persons or things; (often *pl*) (*inf*) a great amount; (*inf*) sort (*a bad lot*).—*n* **lottery**, a scheme for distributing prizes by lot or chance.—*vt* to allot; to separate into lots.—*pr p* **lott´ing**; *pt p* **lott´ed**. [OE *hlot*, a lot—*hlēotan*, to cast lots.]

lothario [lō-thā´ri-ō] *n* a seducer of women. [From *Lothario*, in Rowe's play, *The Fair Penitent* (1703).]

lotion [lō´sh(ó)n] *n* a liquid preparation for cosmetic or external medical use. [L *lōtiō, -ōnis—lavāre, lōtum*, to wash.]

lotus [lō´tus] *n* the American lotus; bird's-foot trefoil; in Greek legend, a plant whose fruit induced contented forgetfulness.—*ns* **lotus tree**, the native N American persimmon (*Diospyros virginiana*); **lotus position**, an erect sitting position in yoga with the legs crossed close to the body. [L,—Gr *lōtos*.]

louche [lōōsh] *adj* not reputable; shady. [Fr.]

loud [lowd] *adj* making a great sound; noisy; emphatic; (*inf*) showy or flashy.—*advs* **loud, loud´ly**.—*n* **loud´ness**.—*adj* **loud´mouthed´** [moutht or mouTHt], talking in a loud, irritating voice; given to offensive talk.—*n* **loud´speak´er** a device for converting electrical energy into sound. [OE *hlūd*; Ger *laut*; L *inclytus*, renowned, Gr *klytos*, heard.]

lounge [lownj] *vi* to move, sit, lie, etc. in a relaxed way; to spend time idly.—*n* a room with comfortable furniture for lounging; a couch or sofa.—*ns* **lounge lizard**, a ladies' man; a social parasite; **lounge´wear**, casual clothing for wearing at home.

lour, louring [lowr, low´ring] *see* **lower, lowering**

louse [lows] *n* any of various (orders Anoplura and Mallophaga) wingless insects parasitic on men and animals; any similar small parasites on plants; (*slang*) a mean, contemptible person.—*pl* **lice** [līs].—*adj* **lousy** [low´zi], swarming with lice; (*slang*) disgusting, of poor quality, or inferior; (*slang*) well supplied (with).—**louse up**, (*slang*) to spoil; to ruin. —*n* **lous´iness**. [OE *lūs*, pl *lȳs*; Ger *laus*.]

lout [lowt] *n* a clumsy, stupid fellow.—*adj* **lout´ish**.—*adv* **lout´ishly**.—*n* **lout´ishness**. [OE *lūtan*, to stoop.]

louver, louvre [lōō´vėr] *n* one of a set of slats set parallel and slanted to admit air but not rain.—Also *adj*.—*n* a ventilatory structure of these. [OFr *lover, lovier*.]

love [luv] *n* a strong liking for someone or something; a passionate affection for another person; the object of such affection; (*tennis*), a score of zero.—*vti* to feel love (for).—*adj* **lov´able, lov´eable**.—*ns* **love affair**, a romantic attachment or episode; a lively enthusiasm; **love apple**, a tomato; **love´bird**, any of various small parrots (as of the genera *Agapornis* of Africa, *Loriculus* of Asia, and *Psittacula* of So America) that show great affection for their mates; **love feast**, a communal meal eaten by a Christian congregation in token of brotherly love; **love-in**, a gathering of people to show their mutual love; **love-in-a-mist**, a garden plant (*Nigella damascena*) of the buttercup family; **love knot**, a stylized knot used as a token of love.—*adjs* **love´less**, without love; **love´lorn**, pining from love; **love´ly**, beautiful; (*inf*) highly enjoyable.—*n* **loveliness; love´making**, courtship; sexual activity, esp copulation; **lov´er**, a sweetheart; a paramour; (*pl*) a couple in love with each other; a devotee, as of music.—*adj* **lover´ly**, resembling or fit for a lover.—*n* **love seat**, a small sofa for two people;—*adjs* **love´sick**, languishing with love; **lov´ing** affectionate.—*n* **loving cup**, a large drinking cup with two handles, often given as a prize; **loving-kindness**, benevolent affection.—**in love**, feeling love; **make love**, to woo, embrace, etc.; to have sexual intercourse. [OE *lufu*, love; Ger *liebe*.]

low[1] [lō] *vi* to moo.—*n* the sound a cow makes, mooing. [OE *hlōwan*; Du *loeien*.]

low[2] [lō] *adj* not high or tall; near the ground, floor, base; below the normal level; less in size, degree, amount, etc. than usual; deep in pitch; depressed in spirits; humble, of low rank; vulgar, coarse; not loud.—*adv* in or to a low degree, level, etc.—*n* a low level, degree, etc.; an arrangement of gears giving the lowest speed and greatest power.—*adj* **low´born´**, of humble birth.—*ns* **lowboy´**, a chest of drawers mounted on short legs; **low´brow´**, (*inf*) one considered to lack cultivated tastes.—Also *adj*.—*ns* **lowcomedy**, comedy approaching farce and employing burlesque or the representation of low life; **Low Countries**, the Netherlands, Belgium, and Luxembourg; **low´down**, (*slang*) the true, pertinent facts (*with* **the**)—*adj* **lowdown´**, (*inf*) mean, contemptible.—*adj* **low´er**, (comparative of **low**) below in place, rank, etc.; less in amount, degree, etc.—*vt* to let or put down; to reduce in height, amount, etc.; to bring down in respect, etc.—*vi* to become lower.—*n* **lowercase**, small-letter type used in printing, as distinguished from capital letters; **lower class**, a social class below the middle class and having the lowest status in society; **low frequency**, any radio frequency between 30 and 300 kilohertz; **Low German**, the vernacular dialects of north Germany; the branch of Germanic languages including English, Dutch, etc.—*adjs* **low-´grade**, of low quality, degree, etc.; **low´key´**, of low intensity, subdued.—*n* **low´land**, land below the level of the surrounding land.—**the Lowlands**, the lowlands of central Scotland.—*adjs* **low´ly**, of low position; humble; **low-´minded**, showing a coarse, vulgar mind.—*ns* **low profile**, a barely noticeable presence; **Low Sunday**, the Sunday following Easter; **low tide**, the lowest level of the tide.—**lay low**, to overcome or kill; **lie low**, to keep oneself hidden; **lowest common denominator**, something acceptable to the greatest number of people. [ON *lāgr*, Du *laag*, low.]

lower[1] [low´er, lō´ėr] *vi* to look sullen; to become dark, gloomy, threatening.—*adj* **low´ery**, gloomy, lowering.—*Also* **lour** [low´ėr]. [ME *louren*, cf Du *loeren*.] *See* **lour**.

lower[2] [lō´ėr] *see* **low** (2).

loyal [loi´ál] *adj* faithful; showing firm allegiance.—*n* **loy´alist** one who supports the government during a revolt.—*adv* **loy´ally**.—*n* **loy´alty**. [Fr,—L *lēgālis*—lex, *lēgis*, law.]

lox[1] [loks] *n* a kind of smoked salmon. [Ger *lachs*, a salmon.]

lox[2] [loks] *n* liquid oxygen, used in a fuel mixture for rockets.

lozenge [loz´enj] *n* a diamond-shaped figure; a cough drop, candy, etc. orig diamond-shaped; (*heraldry*) the diamond-shaped figure in which the arms of maids, widows, and deceased persons are borne. [Fr *losange*; of unknown origin.]

LSD [ėl-ės-dē] *n* a chemical compound used in the study of mental disorders and as a psychedelic drug. [*ly*sergic acid *d*iethylamide.]

luau [lōō-ow] *n* a Hawaiian feast.

lubber [lub´ėr] *n* an awkward, sturdy, clumsy fellow; an inexperienced, clumsy sailor.—*adj, adv* **lubb´erly**. [Origin doubtful.]

lubricate [l(y)ōō´bri-kāt] *vt* to make smooth or slippery; to oil.—*ns* **lūbricant; lubricā´tion; lubricity** [lū-bris´i-ti] slipperiness; smoothness; lewdness. [L *lūbricāre, -ātum—lūbricus*, slippery.]

lucent [l(y)ōō´sėnt] *adj* shining; clear.—*n* **lū´cency**, brightness. [L *lūcens, -entis*, pr p of *lūcēre*, to shine—*lux, lūcis*, light.]

lucid [l(y)ōō´sid] *adj* shining; transparent; sane; easily understood;—*ns* **lucid´ity, lu´cidness**.—*adv* **lu´cidly**.—[L *lūcidus—lux, lūcis*, light.]

Lucifer [l(y)ōō´si-fėr] *n* Satan; a match of wood tipped with a combustible substance ignited by friction. [L *lūcifer*, light-bringer—*lux, lūcis*, light, *ferre*, to bring.]

luck [luk] *n* that which seems to happen or come to one by chance; chance; good fortune.—*adj* **luck´less**, unfortunate.—*adv* **luck´lessly**.—*n* **luck´lessness**.—*adj* **luck´y**, having or bringing good luck;—*adv* **luck´ily**.—*n* **luck´iness**.—**luck out** (*inf*) to be lucky. [Ger or Du *luk*; cf Ger *glück*, prosperity.]

lucre [l(y)ōō´kėr] *n* (*derogatory*) riches, money.—*adj* **lu´crative**, producing wealth or profit; profitable.—*adv* **lu´cratively**. [L *lucrum*, gain.]

ludricrous [l(y)ōō´dik-rùs] *adj* absurd, laughable.—*adv* **lu´dricrously**.—*n* **lu´dicrousness**.—*adj* **lud´ic** of or with playful behavior. [L *lūdicrus—lūdĕre*, to play.]

luff [luf] *n* the windward side of a ship.—*vt* to turn a ship towards the wind. [Origin obscure.]

lug[1] [lug] *vt* to pull along, to drag with effort;—*pr p* **lugg´ing**; *pt, pt p* **lugged**.—*n* **lugg´age**, the trunks and other baggage of a traveller. [Swed *lugga*, to pull by the hair—*lugg*, the forelock.]

lug[2] [lug], **lugsail** [lug´sāl, lug´sl] *ns* a square sail bent upon a yard that hangs obliquely to the mast.—*n* **lugg´er**, a small vessel with lugsails.

lug[3] [lug] *n* the ear; an earlike projection by which a thing is held or supported; a heavy nut for securing a wheel to an axle.

luge [lōōj] *n* a small sled that is ridden lying on the back and used esp in competition. [Fr]

lugubrious [l(y)ōō-gu´bri-us] *adj* mournful, dismal, esp in an exaggerated way.—*adv* **lugū´briously**. [L *lūgubris—lūgēre*, to mourn.]

lugworm [lug´wûrm] *n* any of a genus (*Arenicola*) of worms found in the sand on the seashore, used for bait by fishermen.

Luke [lōōk] *n* (*Bible*) 3d book of the New Testament, synoptic gospel presenting Jesus as a man among men, written by the author of Acts.

lukewarm [lōōk´wörm] *adj* barely warm, tepid; lacking enthusiasm.—*adv* **luke´warmly**. [ME *leuk, luke*; cf Du *leuk*.]

lull [lul] *vt* to soothe, to quiet.—*vi* to become calm.—*n* a short period of calm.—*n* **lull´aby** [-bī] a song to lull children to sleep. [Swed *lulla*]

lumbago [lum-bā´gō] *n* pain in the lower back.—*adj* **lum´bar**, of or near the loins. [L*lumbus*, loin.]

lumber[1] [lum´bėr] *n* timber, logs, beams, boards, etc., roughly cut and prepared for use; household articles no longer in use.—*vi* to cut down timber and saw it into lumber.—*vt* to clutter with lumber; to heap in disorder.—*ns* **lum´berjack´**, a man whose work is cutting down trees and preparing it for the sawmill; **lum´berman**, lumberjack; one who deals in lumber. [Perh from **lumber** (2).]

lumber[2] [lum´bėr] *vi* to move heavily and noisily. [ME *lomeren*; cf dial Swed *lomra*, to resound.]

lumen [l(y)ōō´mėn] *n* unit of luminous flux, one candela per steradian. [L *lumen, -inis*, light.]

luminary [l(y)ōō´min-ȧr-i] *n* a body that gives off light, such as the sun; a famous or notable person.—*n* **lumines´cence** [-es´ėns], the emission of light without heat, as in fluorescence or phosphorescence.—*adj* **lumines´cent**.—*adjs* **luminif´erous**, transmitting or producing light; **lū´minous**, giving light; shining; clear, lucid.—*adv* **lū´minously**.—*ns* **lū´minousness, luminos´ity**. [L *lūmen, -inis*, light—*lūcēre*, to shine.]

lummox [lum´oks] *n* (*inf*) a clumsy, stupid person. [Origin unknown.]

lump[1] [lump] *n* a small shapeless mass of something; a swelling; (*pl*) (*inf*) hard blows, criticism, etc.—*adj* in a lump or lumps.—*vt* to put together in a lump or lumps; to treat or deal with in a mass.—*vi* to become lumpy.—*ns* **lump´er**, a laborer employed in handling cargo.—*adj* **lump´ish**, like a lump; heavy; gross; dull.—*adv* **lump´ishly**.—*ns* **lump´ishness**.—*adj* **lump´y**, full of lumps. [Origin doubtful; found in various Gmc languages.]

lump[2] [lump] *vt* (*inf*) to have to put up with (something disagreeable).

lunar [lōō´nȧr] *adj* of or like the moon.—*adj* **lu´nāte** crescent-shaped.—*n* **lunā´tion**, the period between one new moon and the next; a lunar month averaging 29 days and 12 hours.—*ns* **lunar caustic**, fused and molded crystals of silver nitrate; **lunar eclipse**, an eclipse which takes place when the moon enters the shadow of the earth; **lunar excursion, module**, used to carry astronauts from the spacecraft to the surface of the moon and back. [L *lūnāris*—*lūna*, the moon—*lūcēre*, to shine.]

lunatic [lōō´nȧ-tik] *adj* insane or for the insane; utterly foolish.—*n* an insane person.—*n* **lu´nacy**, insanity; utter folly.—**lunatic fringe**, fanatical or visionary minority of a political party or social movement; strip of false color in an optical image. [From the belief that lunacy fluctuated with phases of the moon.]

lunch [lunch] *n* a light meal, esp between breakfast and dinner.—*vi* to eat lunch.—*ns* **lunch´eon** [lunch´ȯn] lunch, esp a formal lunch; **lunch´eonette´**, a small restaurant serving light lunches; **luncheon meat** meat processed in loaves, etc. and ready to eat. [Perh altered from **lump**; or from Sp *lonja*, a slice of ham.]

lune [lōōn] *n* the part of a plane surface bounded by two intersecting arcs or a sphere bounded by two great circles.—*n* **lunette´** something shaped like a crescent or half-moon.—*n* **lunette´**. [Fr *lune*—L *lūna*.]

lung [lung] *n* either of the two spongelike breathing organs in the chest of vertebrates. [OE *lungen*.]

lunge [lunj] *n* a sudden thrust, as with a sword; a sudden plunge forward.—*vti* to move, or cause to move, with a lunge. [Fr *allonger*, to lengthen—L *ad* to, *longus*, long.]

lupine, lupin [lōō´pin] *n* a genus (*Lupinus*) of plants of the pea family some of which are cultivated for their flowers, others for green manure, fodder, and edible seed. [L *lupinus*.]

lupine [lū´pīn] *adj* wolfish. [L *lupinus*—*lupus*, a wolf.]

lupus [lōō´pus] *n* any of several diseases marked by lesions of the skin.—*ns* **lupus erythematosus** [er-ith-ē-mȧ-tōs´ės], inflammatory disease of the connective or supporting tissues of the body; **lupus vulgaris** [vul-gär´is], tuberculosis of the skin. [L *lupus*, a wolf.]

lurch[1] [lûrch] *n* a difficult situation, only in **leave in the lurch**. [OFr *lourche*.]

lurch[2] [lûrch] *vi* to roll or pitch suddenly to one side.—*n* a sudden roll or pitch.

lurcher [lûr´chėr] *n* a crossbred dog trained to hunt silently. [From *lurch*, obs variant of **lurk**.]

lure [l(y)ōōr] *n* any enticement; fishing bait.—*vt* to entice, attract, or tempt. [OFr *loerre*—Middle High Ger *luoder*, bait.]

Lurex [lŏŏr´eks] *n* trade name for metallic thread made from plastic-coated aluminum.

lurid [lōō´rid] *adj* lighted up with red or fiery glare; shocking; sensational.—*adv* **lū´ridly**. [L *lūridus*.]

lurk [lûrk] *vi* to lie in wait; to skulk. [Perh freq from **lour**.]

luscious [lush´ùs] *adj* delicious, richly sweet; delighting any of the senses.—*n* **lusc´iousness**.

lush[1] [lush] *adj* tender and juicy; of or showing abundant growth. [Obs *lash*—ME *lasche*, slack.]

lush[2] [lush] *n* (*slang*) an alcoholic.

lust [lust] *n* longing desire (for), eagerness to possess; sensual appetite.—*vi* to feel an intense desire.—*adj* **lust´ful**.—*adv* **lust´fully**.—*n* **lust´fulness**.—*adj* **lust´y**, vigorous; healthy; stout.—*n* **lust´iness**.—*adv* **lust´ily**. [OE *lust*, pleasure.]

luster [lus´tėr] *n* gloss; sheen; brightness; radiance; brilliant beauty or fame; glory.—*adj* **lus´trous**. [Fr,—L *lustrāre*, to shine.]

lusty *see* **lust**.

lute [lōōt, lūt] *n* an old stringed instrument shaped like half a pear.—*ns* **lut´anist** a player on a lute. [OFr *lut*; like Ger *laute*, from Ar *al*, the *´lūd*, wood, lute.]

lutetium [lū-tē´shi-ùm] *n* a metallic element (symbol Lu; at wt 175.0; at no 71), a member of the rare-earth group. [L *Lutetium*, Paris.]

Lutheran [lōō´thėr-ȧn] *n* a member of a Protestant Christian denomination believing that salvation is by faith alone through grace.—*adj* of the Lutheran Church.—*n* **Luth´eranism**. [Martin *Luther* (1483–1546), Ger religious reformer.]

lux [luks] *n* unit of illumination, one lumen per square meter.

luxury [luk´shù-ri, lug´zhù-ri] *n* free indulgence in costly pleasures; something beyond what is essential or what one is accustomed to—*adj* relating to or providing luxury.—*adj* **luxū´riant**, [lug-zhōō´ri-ȧnt, luk-] exuberant in growth; overabundant.—*ns* **luxū´riance, luxūriancy**.—*adv* **luxūriantly**.—*vi* **luxū´riate**, to live luxuriously; to revel (in).—*adj* **luxū´rious**, fond of or indulging in luxury; constituting luxury; rich, comfortable, etc.—*adv* **luxūriously**.—*n* **luxū´riousness**. [OFr *luxurie*—L *luxuria*, luxury—*luxus*, excess.]

Lyceum [lī-sē´um] *n* a lecture hall; an organization providing lectures, debates, etc. [L *lȳceūm*—Gr *Lykeion*—*Lykeios*, an epithet of Apollo.]

lychgate [lich-gāt] *n* a roofed churchyard gate under which the bier rest before interment. [ME from *lich*, a corpse, *gate*, a gate.]

lyddite [lid´īt] *n* a powerful explosive chiefly of picric acid. [Tested at *Lydd* in Kent, England.]

lye [lī] *n* a strong alkaline solution obtained by leaching wood ashes used in cleaning and in making soap. [OE *lēah, lēag*; Ger *lauge*; allied to L *lavāre*, to wash.]

lying [lī´ing] *adj* not truthful.—*n* the telling of a lie or lies. [From **lie** (1).]

lymph [limf] *n* a clear, yellowish body fluid resembling blood plasma, found in intercellular spaces and the lymphatic vessels.—*adj* **lymphat´ic**, of or containing lymph; sluggish.—*n* a vessel which conveys the lymph.—*adj* **lymph´oid**, of or like lymph, or the tissue of lymph glands.—*n* **lymph node**, any of the compact structures lying along the course of the lymphatic vessels. [L *lympha*, water.]

lynch [linch, -sh] *vt* to murder (an accused person) by mob action, without lawful trial, as by hanging.—*n* **lynch´law**. [Captain William *Lynch* of Virginia, vigilante in 1780.]

lynx [lingks] *n* a wildcat (*Lynx lynx*) found throughout the northern hemisphere with a short tail, tufted ears, and relatively long legs; bobcat; a N American lynx (*L canadensis*) is larger and has a wholly black tail tip.—*adj* **lynx´eyed**, sharpsighted. [L,—Ger *lynx*.]

lyonnaise [lī´ō-nāz] *adj* prepared with sliced, fried onions. [Fr]

lyre [līr] *n* an ancient stringed musical instrument like the harp.—*adj* **ly´rate**, lyre-shaped.—*n* **lyre´ bird**, either of two Australian passerine birds (genus *Menura*), the male of which displays a tail shaped like a lyre.—*adj* **lyr´ic**, denoting or of poetry, expressing the writer's emotion; of, or having a high voice with a light, flexible quality.—*n* a lyric poem; (*pl*) the words of a song.—*adj* **lyr´ical** lyric; expressing rapture or enthusiasm.—*n* **lyr´icist** a writer of lyrics, esp for popular songs. [Fr,—L *lyra*—Gr]

lysis [lī´sis] *n* the gradual abatement of a disease; breaking down as of a cell.—*n* **ly´sin**, a substance that causes lysis.—**lysergic acid** [lī-sûr´jik], LSD. [Gr *lysis*, dissolution, *lyein*, to loose.]

lysogeny [lī-soj´e-nē] *n* coexistence between a virus and bacterium.

M

Mab [mab] *n* the queen of the fairies in English literature.

macabre [mȧ-käb´rė, mȧ-käb´] *adj* gruesome; grim; horrible. [Fr.]

macadam [mȧ-kad´ȧm] *n* small, broken stones, rolled until solid, often with tar and asphalt, to make roads. [J L *McAdam* (1756–1838) Scottish engineer.]

macaroni [mak-a-rō´ni] *n* pasta in the form of tubes; in the 18th century, a dandy.—*adj* **macaronic** [-on´ik], mixing vernacular words with Latin words or adding Latin endings to non-Latin words; characterized by a mixture of two languages. [It *maccaroni* (now *maccheroni*), pl of *maccarone*, prob—*maccare*, to crush.]

macaroon [mak-a-rōōn´] *n* a small, sweet cookie made of crushed almonds or coconut. [Fr *macaron*—It *maccarone*.]

macaw [ma-kö´] *n* any of numerous large long-tailed (genus *Ara*), showy tropical American parrots. [Port *macao*.]

Maccabees [mak´ȧ-bēz] *n* (*Bible*) 45th and 46th books in the Douay Version of the Old Testament.

mace[1] [mās] *n* a heavy, spiked war club used in the Middle Ages; a staff used as a symbol of authority by certain institutions; one who carries a mace. [OFr *mace* (Fr *masse*)—hypothetical L *mat(t)ea*, whence L dim *mat(t)eola*, a kind of tool.]

mace[2] [mās] *n* an aromatic spice made from the husk of the nutmeg. [OFr *macis*, possibly—L *maccis, -idis*, a word supposed to have been invented by Plautus, Roman comic poet (250–184 BC), for an imaginary spice.]

macerate [mas´ėr-āt] *vt* to soften or separate the parts of by soaking in liquid; to tear, chop, etc. into bits or to a pulp.—*ns* **macerā´tion; mac´erator**. [L *mācerāre, -ātum*, to steep.]

Machabees [mak´ȧ-bēz] *n* (*Bible*) the last two books of the Apocrypha in the Protestant canon, named for the family of Jewish patriots who led a successful revolt against Syria (175–164 BC) and established a line of priest-kings which lasted until the reign of Herod in 37 BC.

machete [mȧ-shet´ē, -chet´ē] *n* a large knife used for cutting sugar cane, underbrush, etc. [Sp.]

Machiavellian [mak-i-a-vel´yȧn] *adj* crafty; deceitful.—*n* **Machiavell´ianism**, the political doctrine that any means may be used by a ruler to establish and maintain a strong central government. [From *Niccolò Machiavelli*, a statesman and political writer of Florence (1469–1527).]

machinate [mak´i-nāt] *vi* to plot or scheme, esp for doing harm.—*vt* to plan or contrive to bring about.—*ns* **machinā´tion; mach´inator**. [L *māchinārī, -ātus*—*māchina*—Gr *mēchanē*, contrivance.]

machine [ma-shēn´] *n* a structure of fixed and moving parts, for doing some kind of work; an organization functioning like a machine; the controlling group in a political party; a device, as the lever, etc. that transmits, or changes the application of energy.—*vt* to shape or finish by machine-operated tools.—*adj* of machines; done by machinery.—*ns* **machine gun**, an automatic gun, firing a rapid stream of bullets; **machine language**, the system of signs, symbols, etc. used by a computer.—*adj* **machine-readable**, directly usable by a computer.—*ns* **machinery**, machines collectively; the working parts of a machine; the means for keeping something going; **machin´ist**, one who makes, repairs, or operates machinery; **machine shop**, a workshop where work is machined to size and assembled; **machine tool**, a machine for shaping solid work. [Fr,—L *māchina*—Gr *mēchanē*.]

machismo [mä-chēz´mō] *n* strong or assertive masculinity; virility.—*adj* **ma´chō**. [Sp.]

Mach number [mäk] *n* the number indicating the ratio of an object's speed to the speed of sound. [E *Mach*, Austrian physicist (1838–1916).]

macho *see* **machismo**.

mackerel [mak´ėr-ėl] *n* an important food fish (*Scomber scombrus*) of the N Atlantic, dark blue above and plain silvery below with about 30 dark wavy stripes across the back; related species of the Pacific coast.—*ns* **mackeral shark**, any of a family (*Lamnidae*) of large fierce sharks of the open sea; **mackerel sky**, a sky full of cirrocumulus clouds, which resemble the stripes on a mackerel's back. [OFr *makerel* (Fr *maquereau*).]

mackinaw [ma´ki-nö] *n* a short heavy plaid coat.—*n* **Mackinaw trout**, a N American lake trout (*Salvelinus namaycush*). [*Mackinaw City*, Michigan, formerly an Indian trading post.]

mackintosh, macintosh [mak´in-tŏsh] *n* a thin waterproof fabric, formerly of rubberized cotton. [C *Macintosh*, Scottish chemist and inventor.]

macramé [mak-rȧ-mā´] *n* coarse string or lace knotted in designs. [Fr.]

macro- [mak-rō-] in composition, large, long. [Gr *makros*, large].—eg **macrocosm** [mak´rōkozm] the universe; any large, complex entity. [Gr *kosmos*, world.]

macrobiotic [mak-rō-bī-ö´tik] *adj* of the art of prolonging life as by eating an extremely restricted range of foods.—*n* **macrobiot´ics**. [**macro-** + Gr *biōtikos*, of life.]

macron [mā´kron, ma´kron] *n* a mark (-) placed over a vowel to indicate that it has a long sound.

macroscopic [mak-rō-skop´ik] *adj* visible to the naked eye; considered in terms of large units. [Gr *makros*, large, *skopeein*, to look at.]

macula [mak´ū-la] *n* a spot or blotch, as on the skin.—*pl* **maculae** [-lē].—*vt* **mac´ulāte**, to mark with spots.—*n* **maculā´tion**, a blemish on the skin, as an acne scar; the arrangement of markings on an animal or plant. [L *macula*, a spot.]

mad [mad] *adj* insane; frantic; foolish and rash; infatuated; wildly gay; having rabies; angry.—*n* an angry mood.—*n* **mad´cap**, a reckless, impulsive person.—*adj* reckless and impulsive.—*vti* **madd´en**, to make or become insane, angry, or wildly excited.—*adv* **mad´ly**.—*ns* **mad´house**, an insane asylum; a place where there is noise and confusion; **mad´man**, an insane person; a lunatic; **mad´ness**.—**like mad** (*inf*), to a great degree; (*inf*) at a high rate; **mad as a hatter**, harmlessly crazy. [OE *gemæd(e)d*; Old Saxon *gimēd*, foolish.]

madam [mad´ȧm] *n* a courteous form of address to a woman; a woman in charge of a brothel.—*pl* **mad´ams**, or (in letters) **mesdames** [mā-dam´].—*n* **madame´**, a married woman; title equivalent to Mrs.—*pl* **mesdames**. [Fr *madame*, ie *ma*, my, *dame*, lady.—L *mea domina*.]

madder [mad´ėr] *n* any of various plants of the genus *Rubia*, esp a vine with yellow flowers and a red root; a red dye made from the root; a moderate to strong red. [OE *mæd(d)re*; ON *mathra*.]

made [mād] *pt, pt p* of **make**.—*adjs* **made-to-order**, produced to a customer's specifications; being ideally suited for a particular purpose; **made-up**, put together; invented; false; with cosmetics applied.

Madeira [ma-dē´ra] *n* an amber-colored fortified dessert wine. [*Madeira* islands, Portugal.]

madeleine [mad´ė-lėn] *n* a small rich cake shaped like a shell. [Fr.]

mademoiselle [mad-mwä-zel´, mad-ė-mō-zel´] *n* a form of address to a young lady; Miss.—*pl* **mesdemoiselles** [mēd-mwä-zel]. [Fr *ma*, my, *demoiselle*, young lady. See **damsel**.]

Madonna [ma-don´a] *n* the Virgin Mary, esp as seen in works of art.—*n* **Madonna lily**, a white lily (*Lilium candidum*) with large funnel-shaped flowers. [It lit 'my lady'—L *mea domina*]

madras [mad´ras, mė-dras´] *n* a firm cotton cloth of varying weights, usu. in stripes or plaids. [*Madras*, India.]

madrepore [mad´re-pör] *n* any coral (order Madreporaria) of the common reef-building type. [It *madrepora*—*madre*, mother—L *māter*, and Gr *pōros*, a soft stone, stalactite, etc., or L *porus*, a pore.]

madrigal [mad´ri-gȧl] *n* (*mus*) an unaccompanied song in several parts. [It *madrigale*, perh from *mandr(i)a*, a cattleshed—L *mandra*—Gr *mandrā*.]

madrilene [mad´-ri-len´, -lān´] *n* a tomato-flavored consommé. [Fr.]

madrona, madrone, madrono [ma-drō´nȧ] *n* an evergreen tree (*Arbutus menziesii*) of the Pacific coast of N America with large leaves, reddish-brown bark, of considerable commercial importance; related species grown as an ornamental. [Sp *madrona*.]

maelstrom [māl´strom] *n* a large and violent whirlpool; an agitated state of affairs, mind, etc. [Du (now *maalstroom*), a whirlpool.]

maestro [mä-es´trō, mī´strō] *n* a master, esp an eminent musical composer or conductor. [It.]

Mafia [mä´fē-ä] *n* a secret society composed chiefly of criminal elements; **mafia**, a group of people with similar backgrounds, interests, or aims; a clique. [Sicilian Italian.]

magazine [mag-ȧ-zēn´ also mag´-] *n* a place for military stores; a space where explosives are stored, as in a fort; a supply chamber as in a camera, a rifle, etc.; a periodical publication containing articles, stories, etc. [Fr *magasin*—It *magazzino*—Ar *makhāzin*, pl of *makhzan*, a storehouse.]

magdalen, magdalene [mag´dȧ-lėn] *n* a repentant prostitute. [From Mary *Magdalene* (ie of *Magdala*—Luke viii 2); see **maudlin**.]

magenta [ma-jen´ta] *n* a purplish-red dye; purplish red.—Also *adj*. [*Magenta*, Italy.]

maggot [mag´ȯt] *n* a wormlike larva, as of the housefly; a fantastic idea, a whim.—*adj* **magg´oty**, full of maggots. [Perh modification of ME *maddok, mathek*, dim; same root as **mawkish**.]

magi *pl* of **magus**.

magic [maj´ik] *n* the use of charms, spells, etc. in seeking or pretending to control events; any mysterious power; the art of producing illusions by sleight of hand, etc.—*adjs* of, produced by or using magic; producing astonishing results, as if by magic.—**mag´ical**.—*adv* **mag´ically**.—*ns* **magician** [mȧ-jish´ȧn], one skilled in magic; **mag´ic lan´tern**, an early form of optical projector of still pictures; **magic square**, an arrangement of numbers in the form of a square characterized by the fact that every row, column, or diagonal has the same sum. [Gr *magikē (technē)*, magic (art)—Pers. See **magus**.]

magisterial [maj-is-tē´ri-al] *adj* of, or suitable for a magistrate; authoritative.—*adv* **magistē´rially**.—*ns* **mag´istrate**, a civil officer empowered to administer the law; a minor official, as a justice of the peace. [L *magister*.]

magma [mag´ma] *n* the molten material existing within the earth from which igneous rocks are the results by cooling. [Gr.]

Magna Charta, Magna Carta [mag´na kär´ta] *n* the Great Charter obtained from King John of England at Runnymede, 1215; any charter of liberty. [L.]

magna cum laude [mag´nȧ kōōm low´dė] with great distinction. [L.]

magnanimity [mag-na-nim´i-ti] *n* that quality of mind which raises a person above all that is mean or unjust; generosity of spirit.—*adj* **magnan´imous**.—*adv* **magnan´imously**. [L *magnanimitās—magnus*, great, *animus*, the mind.]

magnate [mag´nāt] *n* a very influential person. [L *magnās, -ātis—magnus*, great.]

magnesium [mag-nē´zi-um, -z(h)yum, -shium, -shyum] *n* metallic element (symbol Mg; at wt 24.3; at no 12) of a bright, silver-white color.—*n* **magnē´sia**, a white powder, oxide of magnesia, used as a laxative. [Prob *Magnēsia*. See **magnet**.]

magnet [mag´net] *n* any piece of iron, steel, or lodestone that has the property of attracting iron or steel; anything that attracts.—*adj* **magnet´ic**, having the properties of a magnet; of, producing, or caused by magnetism; that can be magnetized; powerfully attractive.—*adv* **magnet´ically**.—*vt* **mag´netize**, to give magnetic properties to (steel, iron, etc.); to charm (a person).—*ns* **mag´netizer; mag´netism**, the property, quality, or condition of being magnetic; the force to which this is due; personal charm; **mag´netite**, a black iron oxide, an important iron ore; **magneto** [magnē´tō], a small generator in which one or more permanent magnets produce the magnetic field; **magnetic field**, any space in which there is an an appreciable magnetic force; **magnetom´eter**, an instrument for measuring magnetic forces of which one form is used to check airline passengers for concealed weapons; **magnetic needle**, a light slender bar of magnetized steel which constitutes the essential part of a compass when mounted so that it can turn freely in any direction; **magnetic north**, direction indicated by the magnetic needle; **magnetic storm**, a disturbance in the magnetic field of the earth; **magnetic tape**, a thin plastic ribbon with a magnetized coating for recording sound, digital computer data, etc. **magnet school**, a public school offering new and special courses to attract students from a wide urban area so as to promote desegregation. [Through OFr or L from Gr *magnētis (lithos)*, magnesian (stone), from *Magnēsia* in Lydia or *Magnēsia*, eastern part of Thessaly.]

magnetron [mag´nė-tron] *n* a diode vacuum tube which generates power at microwave frequencies.

Magnificat [mag-nif´i-kat] *n* the song of the Virgin Mary, Luke i 46–55, beginning in the Vulgate with this word. [L '(my soul) doth magnify', 3rd pers sing pres ind of *magnificāre*.]

magnificence [mag-nif´i-sėns] *n* the quality of being magnificent.—*adj* **magnif´icent**, splendid, stately, sumptuous, as in form; (of ideas) exalted; (*inf*) excellent.—*adv* **magnif´icently**. [L *magnificens, -entis*.]

magnify [mag´ni-fī] *vt* to exaggerate; to increase the apparent size of (an object) as (with) a lens—*pt p* **mag´nified**.—*ns*, **magnificā´tion**, act of magnifying; state of being magnified; the apparent enlargement of an object by a lens or lenses; **mag´nifier**, a lens or combination of lenses that makes an object appear larger. [L *magnificāre—magnus*, great, *facĕre*, to make.]

magniloquent [mag-nil´o-kwėnt] *adj* speaking in a grand or pompous style.—*n* **magnil´oquence**.—*adv* **magnil´oquently**. [L *magnus*, great, *loquens, -entis*, pr p of *loquī*, to speak.]

magnitude [mag´ni-tūd] *n* greatness of size, extent, etc.; importance; the degree of brightness of a fixed star. [L *magnitūdō—magnus*, great.]

magnolia [mag-nōl´i-a or -ya] *n* an American and Asiatic genus (*Magnolia*) of shrubs and trees with evergreen or deciduous leaves and usu. showy flowers appearing in early spring. [Pierre *Magnol* (1638–1715), a botanist.]

magnum [mag´nùm] *n* a wine bottle holding about 2/5 of a gallon. [L *magnum* (neut), big.]

magnum opus [mag´nùm ō´pùs] a great work, esp a writer or artist's greatest achievement; a masterpiece. [L.]

magpie [mag´pī] *n* any of a large number of black and white chattering birds of the crow family esp *Pica pica*, found throughout the US; a chattering person.—*adj* collected indiscriminately; acquisitive. [*Mag*, for *Margaret* + **pie** (1).]

magus [mā´gus] *n* a priest of the ancient Persians and Medes; **Magus**, one of the wise men from the East paying homage to the infant Jesus; a sorcerer, a magician.—*pl* **Magi** [-jī].—*adj* **Ma´gian**, pertaining to the magi or (without *cap*) to a sorcerer. [L—Gv *magos*—O Pers *magus*. See **magic**.]

Magyar [mag´yär or mod´yor] *n* a member of the main ethnic group in Hungary; the Hungarian language. [Hungarian.]

Maharajah, Maharaja [mä-hä-rä´jä] *n* in India, a prince; formerly, the ruler of a native state.—*n* **Maharani, Maharanee** [-rä´nē], the wife of a maharajah; a Hindu princess ranking above a rani. [Hindustani—Sans *mahāt*, great, *rājan*, king, *rānī*, queen.]

mahatma [ma-hat´ma] *n* (*Buddhism, Hinduism*) any of a class of wise and holy persons held in high regard. [Sans *mahātman*, 'high-souled'.]

mah-jongg [mä-jong´] *n* a game for four players played with 144 tiles comprising 108 suit tiles, 28 honors and 8 flowers or seasons, the object of which is to obtain sets of tiles. [Chinese.]

mahlstick *see* **maulstick**.

mahogany [ma-hog´ȧ-ni] *n* a tropical American tree (family Meliaceae); its wood; reddish-brown. [Origin unknown.]

mahout [mä-howt´] *n* in India, the keeper and driver of an elephant. [Hindustani *mahāut, mahāwat*.]

maid [mād] *n* a maiden; a girl or woman servant. [Shortened from **maiden**.]

maiden [mād´n] *n* a girl or young unmarried woman.—*adj* of or for a maiden; unmarried or virgin; untried; first (*a maiden voyage*).—*ns* **maid´enhair**, a fern (genus *Adiantum*) with fine hairlike stalks; **maid´enhead**, virginity; **maid´enhood**, the state or time of being a maiden.—*adj* **maid´enly**, of, or becoming to, a maiden.—*ns* **maid´enliness**.—**maiden name**, surname of a married woman before her marriage; **maid of honor**, an unmarried woman acting as chief attendant to a bride; **maid´servant**, a female servant. [OE *mægden*.]

mail[1] [māl] *n* a body armor made of small metal rings or links; a hard enclosing cover of an animal (as a tortoise).—*vt* to arm with mail.—**mailed fist**, a threat of armed force. [Fr *maille*—L *macula*, a spot or a mesh.]

mail[2] [māl] *n* letters, packages, etc. transported and delivered by the post office; a postal system.—*adj* of mail.—*vt* to send by mail.—*ns* **mail´box, mail box**, a box into which mail is delivered or a box for depositing outgoing mail; **mail drop**, an address used in transmitting secret communications; a slot or receptacle for depositing mail; **mail´gram**, trade name for a letter transmitted electronically between post offices for regular mail delivery; **mail´ing**, the mail dispatched at one time by a sender; **mail´man**, a man who carries and delivers mail; **mail order**, an order for goods to be sent by mail; **mail-order house**, a retail establishment whose business is conducted by mail. [OFr *male*, a trunk, a mail—OHG *malha, malaha*, a sack.]

maillot [mī-ō´, mä-yō´] *n* a woman's one-piece bathing suit. [Fr.]

maim [mām] *vt* to cripple; to mutilate; to render defective. [OFr *mahaing*.]

main [mān] *n* a principal pipe in a distribution system for water, gas, etc.; (*poetic*) the ocean; the essential point.—*adj* chief in size, importance, etc.; principal.—*ns* **main clause** (*gram*), a clause that can function as a complete sentence; **main drag** (*slang*), the principal street of a city or town; **main´frame´**, a large computer that can handle multiple tasks concurrently; **main´land**, the principal land mass of a continent, as distinguished from nearby islands; **main´line**, the principal road, course, etc.—*vt* (*slang*) to inject (a narcotic drug) directly into a large vein.—*adv* **main´ly**, chiefly, principally.—*ns* **main´mast** [-mėst, -mast´], the principal mast of a sailing vessel; **main´sail** [-sl, sāl´], the principal sail of a vessel, set from the mainmast; **main´spring**, the principal spring in a clock, watch, etc.; the chief incentive, motive, etc.; **main´stay**, the supporting line extending forward from the mainmast; a chief support; **main´stream´**, a major trend, line of thought, etc.—*vt* to cause to undergo mainstreaming.—*ns* **main´stream´ing**, the placement of disabled persons into regular school classes, work places, etc.; **Main Street**, the principal street of a small town; an environment marked by materialistic provincial complacency.—**by main force** or **strength**, by sheer force or strength; **in the main**, mostly; **with might and main**, with all one's strength. [Partly OE *mægen*, strength, partly ON *meginn*, strong; influence of OFr *maine, magne* (L *magnus*), great, is questioned.]

Maine coon [mān kōōn] *n* a breed of large long-haired domestic cats with a very full tapered tail.—Also **coon cat, Maine cat**.

maintain [mān-tān´, mėn-, men-] *vt* to keep in a particular condition; to preserve, continue in; to keep up; to support, to bear the expenses of; to give support to; to give support by supplying what is needed; to affirm.—*adj* **maintain´able**.—*n* **maintenance** [mān´tėn-ȧns], the act of maintaining; the means of support; the upkeep as of property. [Fr *maintenir*—L *manū* (abl) *tenēre*, to hold in the hand.]

maître d'hôtel [me´tr dö-tėl] *n* a headwaiter or steward.—*n* **maître d'** [-dē] (*inf*), the head of a dining-room staff (as of a restaurant). [Fr.]

maize [māz] *n* corn; light yellow. [Sp *maiz*—Haitian.]

majesty [maj´es-ti] *n* grandeur; **Majesty**, a title used in speaking to or of a sovereign (*with* **Your, His**, or **Her**).—*adjs* **majes´tic**, having majesty; stately. [Fr *majesté*—L *mājestās, -ātis—mājor, mājus*, comp of *magnus*, great.]

majolica [ma-jol´i-ka or -yol´-] *n* glazed earthenware esp an Italian decorated ware. [Perh from *Majorca*.]

major [mā´jȯr] *adj* greater in size, importance, amount, etc.; (*mus*) higher than the corresponding minor by half a tone.—*vi* (*education*) to specialize (in a field of study).—*n* (*US Military*) an officer ranking just above a captain; (*education*) a principal field of study.—*ns* **major-dōmō**, a head steward; a butler; **major general** (*US Military*), an officer ranking just above a brigadier general; **majority**, the greater number; the excess of the larger number of votes cast for a candidate in an election; full legal age; the military rank of a major; **majority leader**, leader of the majority party in a legislative assembly; **majority rule**, a political principal that a decision made by an organized group constituting fifty-one percent of the members will be binding on the whole group; **major league**, a league of the highest classification in US professional sport, esp baseball and football; the top rank of an enterprise or activity.—*adj* **major-medical**, of a form of medical insurance designed to pay at least most of the costs of medical treatment for a major illness.—*ns* **major premise**, the premise of a syllogism containing the major term; **major scale** (*mus*), a scale with half steps between the third and fourth and the seventh and eighth tones; **major suit**, either spades or hearts in bridge as they have superior scoring values; **major term**, the term in a syllogism that appears as a predicate of the conclusion. [L *mājor*, comp of *magnus*.]

make [māk] *vt* to cause to exist, occur, or appear; to build, create, produce, etc.; to prepare for use (*make the bed*); to amount to (*two pints make a quart*); to have the qualities of (*to make a fine leader*); to acquire, earn; to cause the success of (*that book made him*); to understand (*what did she make of that*); to do, execute; to cause or force; to arrive at, reach; (*inf*) to get on or in (*make the team*).—*n* **make´er**.—*n* **make´-believe´**, pretense; a feigning.—*adj* imagined; pretended; **make´fast´**, something to which a boat can be fastened, as a post or buoy; **make´shift**, a temporary substitute.—*adj* that will do as a temporary substitute.—*ns* **make´up´, make´-up´**, the way something is put together, composition; nature, disposition; the cosmetics, etc. used by an actor; cosmetics generally. **make´weight**, something that is thrown into a scale to make up the weight; something of little value added to supply a deficiency.—*adj* **make´-work´**, that serves no other purpose than to give an idle person something to do.—**make a face**, grimace; **make a mountain out of a molehill**, to exaggerate the importance of a trifling matter; **make away with**, to steal; to kill; **make book**, to accept bets at calculated odds on all entrants in a contest; **make eyes**, ogle, **make fun of**, to mock, ridicule; **make good**, to make valid or complete; to succeed; **make it**, (*inf*) to achieve a certain thing; (*inf*) to have sexual intercourse; **make light of**, to treat of as little account; **make much of**, to treat with fondness; to treat as if of importance; **make public**, disclose; **make the grade**, to be successful; **make off with**, to steal; **make out**, to see with difficulty to understand; to fill out (a blank form, etc.) to (try to) show or prove to be; to succeed; to get along; (*slang* to make love; **make over**, to change, renovate; to transfer the ownership of; **make time**, to travel fast; to gain time; to progress toward winning favour; **make up**, to put together; to form, to constitute; to invent; to provide (what is lacking); to compensate for; to become friends again after a quarrel; to decide (one's mind); **make up to**, to try to win over, as by flattery; **make waves**, to disturb the status quo; **make way**, to give room for passings, etc.; to make progress. [OE *macian*.]

mal- [mal-] *prefix* meaning bad or badly, wrong, ill. [Fr—L *male*, badly.]

malabsorption syndrome [mal-åb-sörp´shȯn] *n* a disease in which the digestive tract is unable to absorb certain nutrients.

malacca [mal-ak´a] *n* a brown walking-cane made from the stem of one of the rattan palms. [*Malacca*, in the Malay Peninsula.]

Malachi [mal´å-kī] *n* (*Bible*) 39th book of the Old Testament, written by the prophet Malachi, stating the final message from God to a rebellious people.

Malachias [Mal-å-kī´ės] *n* (*Bible*) Malachi in the Douay Version of the Old Testament.

malachite [mal´a-kīt] *n* a mineral that is a green basic carbonate of copper used as an ore and for making ornamental objects. [Gr *malachē*, mallow, as of the color of a mallow leaf.]

maladjusted [mal-å-just´ėd] *adj* poorly adjusted, esp to the environment—*n* **maladjust´ment**. [Fr *mal*, ill, + **adjusted**.]

maladministration [mal-ad-min-is-trā´sh(ȯ)n] *n* corrupt or incompetent management of public affairs; incorrect dosage (as of drugs). [Fr *mal*, ill, + **administration**.]

maladroit [mal´a-droit (or -droit´)] *adj* inept, clumsy, bungling [Fr.]

malady [mal´a-di] *n* an illness, disease, either of the body or of the mind. [Fr *maladie—malade*, sick—L male habitus, in ill condition—*male*, badly, *habitus*, ptp of *habēre*, have, hold.]

malaise [mal´āz, mälez´] *n* a feeling of discomfort or of uneasiness. [Fr *malaise*.]

malapropism [mal´a-prop-izm] *n* a ludicrous misuse of words. [Mrs *Malaprop* in Sheridan's play, *The Rivals*.]

malapropos [mal-a-prō-pō] *adj* out of place.—Also *adv*. [Fr *mal*, ill, + **apropos**.]

malaria [ma-lā´ri-a] *n* an infectious disease caused by parasites (genus *Plasmodium*) in the red blood cells, transmitted by the anopheles mosquito characterized by intermittent chills and fever.—*adjs* **malā´rious, malā´rial**. [It *mal´aria*—L *malus*, bad, *āēr, āĕris*, air.]

malcontent [mal´kon-tent] *adj* dissatisfied, rebellious.—Also *n*.—*adj* **malcontent´ed**. [OFr *malcontent*.]

maldistribution [mal-dis-tri-bū´shȯn] *n* uneven, unfair, or inefficient distribution. [Fr *mal*, ill, + **distribution**.]

male [māl] *adj* denoting or of the sex that fertilizes the ovum; of, like, or suitable for men and boys; masculine. (*mechanics*) having a part shaped to fit into a corresponding hollow part.—*n* a male person, animal, or plant.—**male bonding**, fellowship or cameraderie among males; **male chauvinist pig** (*derogatory*), a man who thinks that women are inferior to men. [OFr *male*—L *masculus*, male—*mās*, a male.]

malediction [mal-ė-dik´sh(ȯ)n] *n* a curse; reviling.—*adj* **maledict´ory**. [L *maledīcĕre, -dictum*—male, ill, *dīcĕre*, to speak.]

malefactor [mal´ė-fak-tor] *n* an evildoer; a criminal. [L *male*, ill, *facĕre*, to do.]

malevolent [mal-ev´o-lėnt] *adjs* wishing evil to others; malicious.—*n* **malev´olence**.—*adv* **malev´olently**. [L *male*, ill, *volens, -entis*, prp of *velle*, to wish.]

malformation [mal-för-mā´sh(ȯ)n] *n* faulty or abnormal formation of a body or part. [Fr *mal*, ill, + **formation**.]

malice [mal´is] *n* active ill will, intention to harm another; (*law*) evil intent.—*adj* **malicious** [må-lish´ùs].—*adv* **malic´iously**.—*n* **malic´iousness**. [Fr,—L *malitia—malus*, bad.]

malign [ma-līn´] *adj* injurious; malignant.—*vt* to speak evil of; to slander.—*adv* **malign´ly**. [Fr *malin, fem maligne*—L *malignus* for *maligenus*, of evil disposition—*malus* band, and *gen-*, root of *genus*, race.]

malignant [ma-lig´nånt] *adj* having an evil influence; wishing evil; very harmful; causing or likely to cause death.—*ns* **malig´nance; malig´nancy**, state of being malignant; aggressively malicious; a malignant tumor.—*adv* **malig´nantly**. [L *malignans, -antis*, prp of *malignāre*, to act maliciously.]

malinger [ma-ling´gėr] *vi* to feign sickness in order to avoid duty.—*n* **maling´erer**. [Fr *malingre*, sickly.]

mall [möl] *n* a level shaded walk; a public walk; a shoplined street for pedestrians only; an enclosed shopping center. [Same root as **maul**; see **pall-mall**.]

mallard [mal´ård] *n* the common wild duck (*Anias platyrhynchos*), often raised in captivity for food or for sport. [OFr *mallart, malart*.]

malleable [mal´ė-abl] *adj* capable of being beaten, rolled, etc., into a new shape; adaptable.—*ns* **mal´eableness, malleabil´ity**; hammering; a hammer mark. [L *malleus*, a hammer.]

mallet [mal´et] *n* a small short-handled wooden hammer; a long-handled hammer for playing croquet or polo; a small hammer for playing a xylophone, etc. [Fr *maillet*, dim of *mail*, a mall.]

mallow [mal´ō] *n* a genus (*Malva*) of plants including the hollyhock, cotton, and okra with palm-shaped leaves, usu showy flowers. [OE *m(e)alwe*—L *malva*; Gr *malachē—malassein*, to soften.]

malmsey [mäm´zi] *n* the sweetest variety of Madiera wine. [LL *malmasia*.]

malnutrition [mal-nū-trish´(ȯ)n] *n* imperfect or faulty nutrition. [Fr *mal*, ill, + **nutrition**.]

malodorous [mal-ō´dȯr-us] *adj* having a bad odour, stinking. [Fr *mal*, ill, + **odour**.]

malpractice [mal-prak´tis] *n* professional misconduct, esp by a medical practitioner. [Fr *mal*, ill, + **practice**.]

malt [mölt] *n* barley or other grain soaked in water, allowed to sprout, and dried in a kiln.—*vt* to make into malt; to treat or combine with malt.—*vi* to become malt; to make grain into malt.—*ns* **malted milk**, powdered malt and dried milk used in drink with milk, etc.; **malt liquor**, a fermented liquor (as beer) made with malt; **mal´tōse**, a fermented sugar $C_{12}H_{22}O_{11}$ formed from starch; **malt´ster**, one who makes malt; **malt sugar**, maltose.—*adj* **malt´y**.—*n* **malt whisky**, unblended whisky distilled from fermented malt. [OE *m(e)alt*; cf Ger *malz*.]

Malthusian [mal-thū+z´i-ån] *adj* of Malthus or his theory that as population increases faster than food production and unless checked by contraception, war, famine, disease, or other disaster, universal poverty is the inevitable result. [Rev T R *Malthus* (1766–1834).]

maltreat [mal-trēt´] *vt* to use roughly or brutally.—*n* **maltreat´ment** [Fr *maltraiter*—L male, ill, *tractāre*, to treat.]

mama, mamma [mä´mä] *n* mother, (*slang*) wife, woman. [Repetition of *ma*, one of the first syllables a child naturally utters.]

mamba [mam´ba] *n* any of several tropical and southern African snakes (genus *Dendraspis*) allied to the cobras, esp a large deadly, black or green snake (*D angusticeps*) of southern Africa, very quick in movement. [Kaffir *im mamba*, large snake.]

mambo [mam´bō] *n* a ballroom dance, like the rumba and cha-cha, originating in Cuba.

mamillary [mam´il-år-i] *adj* pertaining to the breast; studded with breast-shaped protruberances. [L *mam(m)illa*, dim of *mamma*.]

mamma [mam´å] *n* a mammary gland and its accessory parts.—*pl* **mammae** [-ē,-ī].—*adj* **mamm´ary**, of the nature of, relating to the mammae.—*ns* **mamm´ogram**, an x-ray photograph of the breasts; **mammog´raphy**, radiological examination of the breast. [L *mamma*.]

mammal [mam´ål] *n* any member of a class (Mammalia) of warm-blooded vertebrates comprising man and all other animals that suckle their young with milk.—*adj* **mammā´lian**. [L *mammālis*, of the breast—*mamma*, the breast

mammon [mam´ȯn] *n* riches regarded as an object of worship and greedy pursuit.—*ns* **mamm´onist**, a person devoted to riches. [Low L *mam(m)ōna*—Gr *mam(m)onās*—Aramaic *māmōn*, riches.]

mammoth [mam´ȯth] *n* any of several extinct elephants.—*adj* resembling a mammoth in size; very large. [Former Russ *mammot*, (now *mamont*).]

man [man] *n* a human being (*Homo sapiens*) esp an adult male; the human race; one having in high degree the qualities considered distinctive of manhood; a husband; an adult male servant or employee; one of the pieces used in chess, checkers. etc.; (*slang*) (*often* **Man**) white society or people.—*vt* to furnish with men for work, defense, etc.; to brace (oneself for an ordeal).—*ns* **man-about-town**, a worldly and and socially active man; **man ape**, a chimpanzee, gorilla, or orangutan; any of various fossil primates between these and recent man; **man-day**, the labor of one man in a normal working day; a unit consisting of a hypothetical average man-day; **man´-eater**, an animal that eats human flesh; **man Friday**, an efficient and devoted employee.—*adj* **man´ful**, showing courage and resolution.—*vt* **man´han´dle**, to handle roughly; to move by human force.—*ns* **man´hole**, a hole through which one can enter a sewer, conduit, etc.; **man´hood´**, the state or time of being a man; virility, courage, etc.; men collectively; **man´hour**, the time unit equal to one hour of work done by one person; **man´hunt´**, a hunt for a fugitive; **man jack**, individual man (*every man jack*); **man´kind´**, the human race; men as distinguished from women.—*adjs* **man´ly**, appropriate in character to a man; strong; virile; **man´made´**, manufactured or created by man, esp. synthetic fibers; **manned**, performed by a man, as a space flight; **mann´ish**, like a man or man's.—*ns* **man-of-war´**, a combatant warship of a recognized navy; **man-o´-war bird**, a frigate bird; **man´power**, power furnished by human strength; the collective availability for work of people in a given area, nation, etc., **man´slaughter**, the killing of a human being by another, esp. when unlawful but without malice.—*adj* **man´tailored**, made with the severity associated with men's suits and coats.—*n* **man´trap´**, a trap or snare for catching men; **man-year**, the work of one man in a year comprising a standard number of working days; **-as a man**, as one man in unison; **man in the street**, an average or ordinary man; **man of letters**, a writer, scholar, etc., esp in the field of literature; **man of straw**, a straw man; **man-to-man**, frank and honest; **one's own man**, independent; **to a man**, with no exception. [OE *mann*; Ger *mann* Du *man*.]

manacle [man´á-kl] *n* a handcuff (usu. *pl*)—*vt* to handcuff; to restrain. [OFr *manicle*—L *manicula*, dim of *manica*, sleeve, glove, handcuff—*manus*, hand.]

manage [man´ij] *vt* to control the movement or behavior of; to have charge of; to direct; to succeed in accomplishing.—*vi* to carry on business; to contrive to get along.—*adj* **man´ageable**, that can be managed; submitting to control.—*n* **man´ageableness**.—*ns* **man´agement**, art or act of managing; manner of directing or of using anything; a body of managers; **man´ager**.—*adjs* **managerial**, of, pertaining to, management, a manager; **man´aging**, controlling; administering; domineering. [It *maneggio*—L *manus*, the hand.]

manana [man-yän´à] *n* tomorrow or an indefinite future time.—*adv* at an indefinite time in the future. [Sp.]

manatee [man-a-tē´] *n* a genus (*Trichechus*) of large, plant-eating aquatic mammals of tropical waters. [Sp *manaté*—Carib *mantoui*.]

Manchu [man-chōō´] *n* a member of a Mongolian people of Manchuria who ruled China from 1644 to 1912; their language;—*pl*—**chus**,—**chu´**.—Also *adj*.

mandamus [man-dā´mus] *n* a writ issued by a superior court commanding the performance of an official act or duty. [L, 'we command'.]

mandarin [man´da-rin] *n* formerly, a high-ranking bureaucrat of the Chinese empire; any high-ranking government official, esp one given to pedantic sometimes obscure public pronouncements; **Mandarin**, Beijing, formerly Peking, dialect which is the official pronunciation of the Chinese language; the fruit of a small, spiny Chinese tree (*Citrus reticulata*) which has been developed in cultivation.—Also **tangerine**.—**mandarin collar**, a narrow, stand-up collar, open in front. [Port *mandarim*—Malayan *mantrī*, counsellor—Sans *mantra*, counsel.]

mandate [man´dāt] *n* an order or command; formerly, a League of Nations' commission to a country to administer some region; this region; the will of constituents expressed to their representatives in legislatures.—*n* **man´datory**, the holder of a mandate.—containing a command; obligatory because of a command. [L *mandātum, mandāre*—*manus*, hand, *dåre*, give.]

mandible [man´di-bl] *n* the lower jaw of a vertebrate; either jaw of a beaked animal; one of the first pair of mouth appendages in insects or crustaceans.—*adj* **mandib´ular**, relating to the jaw. [L *mandibula*—*mandĕre*, to chew.]

mandolin, mandoline [man´do-lin] *n* a round backed instrument like a guitar with four or five pairs of strings. [It *mandola, mandora*, a lute, dim *mandolino*.]

mandragora *same as* **mandrake**.

mandrake [man´drāk] *n* a poisonous plant (*Mandagora officinarum*) of the nightshade family, with a thick, forked root suggesting the human form; may apple.—Also **mandrag´ora**. [L *mandragora*—Gr *mandragorās*.]

mandrel, mandril [man´drėl] *n* blunted steel cone fitted to a lathe center by which articles are secured while they are being turned. [Fr *mandrin*.]

mandrill [man´dril] *n* a large fierce gregarious west African baboon (*Mandrillus sphinx*). [Prob **man**, + **drill** (baboon).]

mane [mān] *n* long hair on the back of the neck of the horse, lion etc. [OE *manu*; ON *mön*; Ger *mähne*.]

maneuver [ma-nōō´vėr] *n* a planned and controlled movement of troops, warships, etc.; a skillful or shrewd move; a strategem.—*vti* to perform or cause to perform maneuvers; to manage or plan skillfully; to move, get, make, etc. by some scheme.—*adj* **maneu´vrable**.—*n* **maneuvrabil´ity**. [Fr,—Low L *manuopera*—L *manū*, by hand, *opera*, work. Cf **manure**.]

manganese [mang´ga-nēz, or -nēz´] *n* a hard brittle greyish-white metallic element (symbol Mn; at wt 54.9; at no 25).—*adj* **manganē´sian**. [Fr *manganese*—It *manganese*—L *magnesia*.]

mange *see* **mangy**.

mangel [mang´gl] *n* mangel-wurzel. [Abbrev]

mangel-wurzel [mang´gl-wûr´zl] *n* a variety of beet cultivated as cattle food. [Ger *mangold*, beet, *wurzel*, root.]

manger [mānj´ėr] *n* a trough in which hay, etc. is laid for horses and cattle.—**dog in the manger**, one who will neither enjoy something himself nor let others do so—also used adjectivally. [OFr *mangeoire*—L *mandūcāre*, to chew, eat.]

mangle[1] [mang´gl] *vt* to mutilate by roughly cutting, tearing, crushing, etc.; to spoil, botch, mar. [Anglo-Fr *ma(ha)ngler*, prob a freq of OFr *mahaigner*, to maim—*mahaing*, a hurt.]

mangle[2] [mang´gl] *n* a machine for ironing sheets, etc. between rollers.—*vt* to smooth with a mangle.—*n* **mang´ler**. [Du *mangel*—Gr *manganon*.]

mango [mang´gō] *n* the yellow-red fleshy fruit with a firm central stone; the evergreen tropical tree (*Mangifera indica*) bearing this fruit.—*pl* **mang´oes**. [Port *manga*—Malay *manggā*—Tamil *mān-kāy*, mango-fruit.]

mangrove [mang´grōv] *n* a genus (*Rhizophora*) of trees that throw out root-forming branches, growing in tropical swamps and forming dense masses important in land building; a tree (genus *Avicennia*) resembling the true mangrove.

mangy [mānj´i] *adj* affected with mange; shabby, seedy.—*ns* **mange** [mānj], a skin disease of mammals, causing itching, hair loss, etc. transmitted by a minute parasite mite; **mang´iness**. [Fr *mangé*, eaten, pt p of *manger*—L *mandūcāre*, to chew.]

mania [mā´ni-a] *n* violent madness; excessive or unreasonable desire, excitement, or enthusiasm.—*adj* **ma´nic**.—*n* **mā´niac**, a person affected with mania; a madman.—*adj* **maniacal** [má-nī´á-kl].—*adj* **man´ic-depress´ive**, of a mental illness characterized by periods of elation and periods of depression. [L,—Gr *maniā*.]

manicure [man´i-kūr] *n* trimming, polishing, etc. of fingernails and removing dead cuticle.—*vt* to do manicure work; to trim closely and evenly, as a lawn.—*n* **man´icurist**. [L *manus*, hand, *cūra*, care.]

manifest [man´i-fest] *adj* that may be easily seen by the eye or perceived by the mind.—*vt* to show plainly; to reveal.—*n* an itemized list of a ships cargo; a list of passengers on an aircraft.—*n* **manifestā´tion**, act of disclosing; display; revelation.—*adv* **man´ifestly**. [L *manifestus*, prob—*manus*, the hand, *festus*, pt p of obs *fendĕre*, to dash against (as in *offendĕre*).]

manifesto [man-i-fest´ō] *n* a public written declaration of intentions by an important person or group. [It,—L See **manifest**.]

manifold [man´i-fōld] *adj* having many forms, parts, etc.; of many sorts; being such in many ways; operating several parts of one kind.—*n* a pipe with many outlets, as for conducting cylinder exhaust from an engine.—*vti* to make copies of, as with carbon paper.—*adv* many times; a great deal. [**many**, and suffx *-fold*.]

manikin, mannikin [man´i-kin] *n* a mannequin. [Du *manneken*, double dim of *man*; Eng **man**.]

Manila [ma-nil´a] *adj* made from Manila hemp; **manil´a**, made of manilla paper.—*ns* **Manila hemp**, abaca; **manila paper**, a strong, buff-colored paper originally made from Manila hemp. [*Manila*, Phillipines.]

manioc [man´i-ok] *n* cassava. [S Amer Indian *mandioca*.]

manipulate [ma-nip´ū-lāt] *vt* to work or handle skillfully; to manage shrewdly or artfully, often in an unfair way; to alter (figures, etc.) for one's own purposes.—*n* **manipulā´tion**.—*adjs* **manip´ulative, manip´ulatory**.—*n* **manip´ulator**. [Low L *manipulāre, -ātum*—L *manipulus*.]

manitou, manitu, manito [man´i-tō] *n* the Algonguian concept denoting the supernatural force of the natural world. [Algonguian.]

manna [man´a] *n* the food of the Israelites in the wilderness; any help that comes unexpectedly. [Heb *mān hū*, what is it? or from *man*, a gift.]

mannequin [man´i-kin] *n* a dummy figure; a person usu. a woman, employed to wear and display clothes. [Fr—Du; see **manikin**.]

manner [man´er] *n* the way in which anything is done; personal style of acting or deportment; distinguished deportment; style of writing, painting, thought, etc.; habit; (*pl*) morals, social customs; (*pl*) breeding, social conduct esp good.—*adj* **mann´ered**, having manners of a specified kind, artificial, stylized, etc.—*n* **mann´erism**, a peculiarity of style or manner in art, literature, etc., carried to excess; a peculiarity of manner in speech, behavior, etc.—*adj* **mann´erly**, showing good manners.—*n* **mann´erliness**. [Fr *manière*—*main*—L *manus*, the hand.]

manor [man´ȯr] *n* in England, a landed estate; the main house on such an estate.—*adj* **manorial** [ma-nō´ri-ăl]. [OFr *manoir*—L *manēre, mansum*, to stay.]

manqué [mā-kā] *adj* (placed after the noun) unfulfilled; would-be (eg *he is a poet manqué*). [Fr]

mansard [man´särd] *n* a roof having the lower part steeper than the upper.—*adj* **mansard´ed**. [Designed by François *Mansart* (1598–1666).]

mansion [man´sh(ȯ)n] *n* a large, imposing house. [OFr,—L *mansiō, -onis*—*manēre, mansum*, to remain.]

mantel [man´tl] *n* the facing about a fireplace, including a projecting shelf; the ornamental shelf over a fireplace.—Also **man´telpiece, man´telshelf**. [Same word as **mantle**.]

mantilla [man-til´a] *n* a woman's scarf, as of lace covering the head and shoulders. [Sp; dim of *manta*.]

mantis [man´tis] *n* a genus (*Mantis*) of orthopterous insects somewhat like locusts, carrying their large spinous forelegs in the attitude of prayer. [Gr *mantis*.]

mantissa [man-tis´a] *n* the decimal part of a logarithm. [L, make-weight.]

mantle [man´tl] *n* a cloak or loose outer garment; anything that envelops or conceals; a small hood which when placed over a flame becomes white-hot and gives off light.—*vt* to cover as with a mantle.—*vi* to be or become covered; to blush or flush. [Partly through OE *mentel*, partly through OFr *mantel* (Fr *manteau*)—L *mantellum*.]

mantra [man´trȧ] *n* a chant of Vedic hymn, text, etc. [Sans]

manual [man´ū-ȧl] *adj* of the hand; done, worked, or used by the hand; involving skill or hard work with the hands.—*n* a handy book for use as a guide, reference, etc.; prescribed drill in the handling of a weapon; a keyboard for the hands esp of an organ or harpsichord having several keyboards.—*adv* **man´ually**.—**manual alphabet**, the signs for letters made by the deaf and dumb; **manual training**, training in practical arts and crafts, as woodworking; **manual worker**, one who works with his hands. [L *manuālis*—*manus*, the hand.]

manufacture [man-ū-fak-chůr] *vt* to make, esp by machinery and on a large scale; to fabricate, concoct.—*n* the process of manufacturing; anything manufactured.—*n* **manufact´ory**, a place where goods are manufactured.—*n* **manufact´urer**, one who manufactures, esp one who employs workers in manufacturing. [Fr,—L *manū* (abl) by hand, *factūra*, a making, from *facĕre, factum*, to make.]

manumit [man-ū-mit´] *vt* to release from slavery; to set free;—*pr p* **manūmitt´ing**; *pt, pt p* **manūmitt´ed**.—*n* **manumission** [-mish´(ȯ)n]. [L *manūmittĕre*—*manū*, from the hand, *mittĕre, missum*, to send, release.]

manure [man-ūr´] *vt* to enrich with any fertilizing substance.—*n* any substance applied to land to make it more fruitful.—*n* **manūr´er**. [Anglo-Fr *maynoverer* (Fr *manœuvrer*). See **manoeuvre**.]

manuscript [man´ū-skript] *adj* written by hand or type written; written with printlike letters.—*n* book, etc. as submitted to a publisher; writing or typewriting as opposed to print. [L *manū* (abl), by hand, *scrībĕre, scrīptum*, to write.]

Manx [mangks] *n* the language of the Isle of Man, a Celtic language of the same group as Gaelic.—*adj* pertaining to the Isle of Man or to its inhabitants.—**Manx cat**, a breed of cat with only a rudimentary tail.

many [men´i] *adj* (comparative **more**, superlative **most**) numerous.—*n* a large number of persons or things.—*adj* **man´y-sid´ed**, having many qualities or aspects; having wide interests or varied abilities.—*n* **man´y-sid´edness**.—**as many**, the same in number. [OE *manig*.]

Maoism [mow-izm] *n* form of Marxism developed in China chiefly by Mao Tse-tung (in Pinyin, Mao Zedong).

Maori [mow´ri] *n* any of the Polynesians native to New Zealand; their language.—Also *adj*.

mao-tai, mao tai [mow tī] *n* a potent Chinese liquor distilled from millet. [Chinese.]

map [map] *n* a representation of all or part of the earth's surface, showing either natural features as continents and seas, etc. or manmade features as roads, railroad stations, parks, buildings, etc.; a similar plan of the stars in the sky; a representation or scheme of the disposition or state of anything.—*vt* to make a map of; (*math*) to place (the elements of a set) in one-to-one correspondence with the elements of another set;—*pr p* **mapp´ing**; *pt, pt p* **mapped**. [L *mappa*, a napkin, a painted cloth, orig Punic (qv).]

maple [mā´pl] *n* any of a genus (*Acer*) of trees with two-winged fruits, grown for shade, wood, or sap; its hard light-colored wood; the flavor of the syrup or sugar made from the sap of the sugar maple (*A. saccharum*) [OE *mapul*, maple.]

maquis [mä´kē] *n* a thicket formation of shrubs, esp along the Mediterranean coast; members of the French underground guerilla movement in World War II. [Fr,—It *macchia*—L *macula*, mesh.]

mar [mär] *vt* to spoil, to impair, to injure, to damage, to disfigure;—*pr p* **marring**; *pt, pt p* **marred**. [OE *merran*.]

marabou, marabout [mar´a-bōō] *n* a large African stork (*Leptoptilos crumeniferus*), the feathers of which are used in trimming, women's clothes or hats. [Fr—prob from the following.]

maraca [ma-räk´ȧ] *n* a percussion instrument made of a dried gourd or a gourd-shaped rattle with pebbles in it. [Brazilian native name.]

maraschino [mar-as-kē´nō, -shē-] *n* a liqueur distilled from the black wild cherry.—**maraschino cherries**, cherries in a syrup flavored with marachino. [It—*marasca, amarasca*, a sour cherry—L *amārus*, bitter.]

marathon [mar´a-thon] *n* a foot race of 26 miles, 385 yards; any endurance contest. [*Marathon*, town and plain 22 miles from Athens. A soldier ran this distance without stopping, bringing news of a Greek victory over the Persians, 490 BC.]

maraud [ma-röd´] *vi* to rove in quest of plunder.—*n* **maraud´er**. [Fr *maraud*, rogue.]

marble [mär´bl] *n* any limestone taking a high polish; a slab, work of art, or other object made of marble; anything like marble in hardness, coldness, etc.; a little ball of stone, glass, etc; (*pl*) a children's game played with such balls; (*pl*) (*slang*) brains, good sense.—*adj* of or like marble.—*vt* to stain or vein like marble.—*vt* **mar´bleīze**, to make look like marble.—*n* **mar´bler**.—*adjs* **mar´bling; mar´bly**, like marble.—**marble cake**, a cake made with light and dark batter combined to give a streaked appearance. [OFr *marbre*—L *marmor*; cf Gr *marmaros*—*marmairein*, to sparkle.]

marc [märc] *n* remains of grapes etc. that have been pressed for wine-making; brandy distilled from these. [Fr].

marcel [mär-sel´] *n* a deep soft wave in the hair made by using a heated curling iron. Also *vt*. [*Marcel*, a French hairdresser, the inventor (1872).]

March[1] [märch] *n* the third month of the year having 31 days.—**March hare**, a hare at breeding time, a proverbial example of madness. [L *Martius* (*mēnsis*), (the month) of Mars.]

march[2] [märch] *n* a boundary; border; a frontier, esp a district set up to defend a boundary. **march´es**.—*vi* to have a common frontier (with). [Fr *marche*; cf **mark** (1).]

march[3] [märch] *vi* to walk with regular steps, as in military formation; to advance steadily.—*vt* to cause to march.—*n* a marching; a steady advance; progress; a regular, steady step; the distance covered in marching; a piece of music for marching.—**on the march**, advancing, moving steadily; **steal a march on**, to get a secret advantage over. [Fr *marcher*, to walk.]

marchioness [mär´shȯn-es] *n* the wife or widow of a marquess; a lady of the rank of a marquess. [LL *marchionissa*, fem of *marchiō, -ōnis*, a lord of the marches.]

Mardi Gras [mär´dē grä] *n* the last day before Lent; a day of carnival in New Orleans, etc. [Fr fat Tuesday.]

mare[1] [mār] *n* a mature female horse, mule, donkey, etc.—*ns* **mare's nest**, a hoax; a jumble, a mess.—**mare´tails**, cirrus clouds blown into strands. [OE *mere*, fem of *mearh*, a horse; cog with Ger *mähre*, ON *merr*, W *march*, a horse.]

mare[2] [mā´rē] *n* one of several large dark areas on the moon or Mars.—*pl* **maria** [mā´ri-a]. [L sea.]

mare[3] [mār] *n* (*obs*) an evil supernatural being causing nightmares.

margarine [mär´jȧr-ēn] *n* a butter substitute made from vegetable oils and fats, etc. [Gr *margarītēs*, a pearl.]

margin [mär´jin] *n* a border, edge; the blank border of a printed or written page; an amount beyond what is needed; provision for increase, error, etc.; the difference between the cost and selling of goods.—*adj* **mar´ginal**, pertaining to a margin; placed in the margin; close to the limit; barely sufficient.—*n* **marginā´lia**, notes written on the margin.—*adv* **mar´ginally**. *adjs* **mar´ginate, -d**, having a margin.—**marginal utility**, the amount of additional utility provided by increasing the quantity of the goods consumed by one unit. [L *margō, -inis*; cf **mark, march** (2).]

margarita [mär-gȧ-rēt-ȧ] *n* a cocktail consisting of a tequila, lime or lemon juice, and an orange flavored liqueur. [Mexican Sp]

margay [mär´gā, mär-gā´] *n* a small American spotted cat (*Felis tigrina*) ranging from Texas to Brazil.

mariachi [mar-ē-ä´chē] *n* one of a strolling band of musicians in Mexico; such a band; its music. [Mexican Sp]

marigold [mar´i-gōld] *n* a yellow-flowered composite (genus *Tagetes*) or its flower. [From the Virgin Mary + **gold**.]

marijuana, marihuana [mä-ri-wä´nȧ] *n* dried flowers and leaves of hemp smoked for their intoxicating effect. [Amer Sp]

marimba [ma-rim´bȧ] *n* a kind of xylophone with a resonant tube beneath each bar. [Native African name.]

marina [mȧ-rēn´ȧ] *n* a small harbor with docks, services, etc. for pleasure craft. [Formed from marine.]

marinade [mar´i-nād] *n* a savory usu acidic solution in which meat, fish, etc. is soaked to enhance flavor or to tenderize it before cooking.—*vt* to marinate.—*vt* **marinate**, to steep (fish, meat, etc.) in a marinade.—*vi* to become marinated. [Prob from It *marinato*.]

marine [ma-ren] *adj* of, in, near, or belonging to the sea; maritime; nautical; naval.—*n* a soldier trained for service at sea; a member of the Marine Corps; naval or merchant ships.—*ns* **Marine Corps**, a branch of the US armed forces trained for land, sea, and aerial combat; **mariner**, a sailor. [Fr,—L *marinus*—*mare*, sea.]

Mariolatry [mā-ri-ol´a-tri] *n* excessive veneration of the Virgin *Mary*. [Gr *Maria*, Mary, *latreiā*, worship.]

marionette [mar-i-o-net´] *n* a little jointed doll moved by strings or wires. [Fr, dim of the name *Marion*.]

mariposa lily [mar-i-pōs´ȧ] *n* a bulbous plant (*Calochortus venustus*) of western No America with a white tulip-like flower, whose underground stem has been used as food.—Also **mariposa tulip**. [Amer Sp]

marital [mar´i-tȧl] *adj* of marriage, matrimonal. [L *maritālis*—*maritus*, a husband.]

maritime [mar´i-tīm] *adj* on, near, or living near the sea; of navigation, shipping, etc. [L *maritimus*—*mare*, sea.]

marjoram [mär´jo-rȧm] *n* any of various fragrant mints (genera *Origanum* and *Majorama*) used in cooking. [OFr *marjorane*.]

mark[1] [märk] *n* a spot, scratch, etc. on a surface; a printed or written symbol, as a punctuation mark; a brand or label on an article showing the maker, etc.; an indication of some quality, character, etc.; a grade (*a mark of A in*

Latin); a standard of quality; impression, influence, etc.; an object of known position serving as a guide; a line, dot, etc. indicating position as on a graduated scale; a target, goal.—*vt* to make a mark or marks on; to identify as by a mark; to show plainly (*her smile marked her joy*); to set off, characterize; to heed (*mark my words'.*); to grade, rate.—*n* **mark'down'**, a selling at a reduced price; the amount of reduction.—*adj* **marked** [märkt], having a mark or marks; noticeable; obvious.—*adv* **mark'edly**.—*ns* **mark'er**, one that marks; something used for marking; **mark'ing**, a mark or marks; the characteristic arrangement of marks, as on fur or feathers; **marks'man**, one who shoots, esp one who shoots well; **marks'manship'**; **mark'up**, a selling at an increased price; the amount of increase; the process of putting legislative bill into its final form.—**make one's mark**, to achieve fame; **mark time**, to keep time while at a halt by lifting the feet as if marching; to suspend progress for a time. [OE (Mercian) *merc* (WS *mearc*), a boundary.]

mark[2] [märk] *n* a unit of money in Germany, the deutshe mark in Federal Republic of Germany, the ostmark in the German Democratic Republic.

Mark[3] [märk] *n* (*Bible*) 2d book of the New Testament, a synoptic gospel presenting Jesus in the role of servant, written by a disciple.

market [mär'ket] *n* a meeting of people for buying and selling; the people at such a meeting; space or building in which provisions, cattle, etc. are shown for sale; store for the sale of food; the chance to sell or buy; demand for (goods, etc.); region where goods can be sold.—*vt* to offer for sale; to sell.—*vi* to buy provisions.—*adj* **marketable**, fit to be offered for sale; wanted by purchasers or employers; of or relating to buying and selling.—*ns* **marketabil'ity; marketing**, act of buying or selling in a market; all of the processes involved in moving goods from the producer to the consumer; **marketing research**, research conducted to determine the extent of demand for specified goods or services or to analyze comparative costs of alternative processes; **market order**, an order to buy or sell securities immediately at the best price obtainable; **marketplace**, a market in a public square; the world of trade and economic activity; a sphere in which intangibles compete for acceptance (*the marketplace of ideas*); **market price**, an actual price in current market dealings; **market research**, the gathering of factual information from consumers concerning their preferences for goods and services; **market value**, the price at which both buyer and seller is willing to do business. [Late OE *market*—Norman-Fr *market*—L *mercātus*, trade, a market—*merx*, merchandise.]

marl [märl] *n* a limy clay often used as a soil conditioner esp on limy soil; manure.—*vt* to dress (land) with marl.—*adj* **mar'ly**, like marl; abounding in marl. [OFr *marle* (Fr *marne*)—Low L *margila*, a dim of L *marga*.]

marline, marlin [mär'lin] *n* a small rope for winding round a larger one to keep it from wearing.—*n* **mar'linespike**, a spike for separating the strands of a rope. [Du *marling*—*marren*, to bind, and *lijn*, rope.]

marmalade [mär'mȧ-lād] *n* a jamlike preserve generally made of the pulp and rind of oranges. [Fr *marmelade*, through Port and L—Gr *melimēlon*, a sweet apple—*meli*, honey, *mēlon*, an apple.]

marmoreal [mär-mōr'e-ȧl, -mȯr'-] *adj* of, or like, marble or a marble statue. [L *marmor*, marble.]

marmoset [mär'mō-set, -zėt] *n* any of numerous small monkeys (family Callithricidae) of South and Central America. [Fr *marmouset*, grotesque figure.]

marmot [mär'mot] *n* a genus (*Marmota*) of stout burrowing rodents esp hoary marmot (*M caligata*); the woodchuck; the prairie dog. [It *marmotto*—L *mūs, mūris*, mouse, *mons, montis*, mountain.]

maroon[1] [ma-rōōn'] *n* a dark brownish red. [Fr *marron*, a chestnut.]

maroon[2] [ma-rōōn'] *n* a marooned person; **Maroon**, a fugitive Negro slave of the West Indies and Guiana in the 17th and 18th centuries; a descendant of such a slave.—*vt* to put on shore on a desolate island; to leave helpless and alone. [Fr *marron*—Sp *cimarrón*, wild.]

marquee [mär-kē'] *n* a rooflike projection over an entrance, as to a theater; a large tent. [From **marquise**, as if that word were pl.]

marquetry, marqueterie [märk'et-ri] *n* decorative inlaid work, as in furniture. [Fr *marqueterie*—*marqueter*, to inlay—*marque*, a mark.]

marquess, marquis [mär'kwis] *n* a British title of nobility next below that of a duke; in some European countries, a nobleman ranking above a count.—*n* **marquise** [mär-kēzl], in various countries, a marchioness; a gemstone cut in the shape of a pointed oval. [From OFr *marchis* (but assimilated later to Fr *marquis*)—Low L *marchensis*, a prefect of the marches.]

Marrano [mȧ-rän'ō] *n* Spanish or Portuguese Jew forcibly converted to Christianity in the 15th century. [Sp.]

marriage [mar'ij] *n* the ceremony, act, or contract by which a man and woman become husband and wife; a wedding; a close union.—*adj* **marr'iageable**, suitable, or at a proper age, for marriage.—**marriage of convenience**, a marriage entered into because of the ensuing political, economic, etc. advantages instead of mutual affection. [OFr *mariage*—*marier*. See **marry**.]

marron glacé [mar-ō gla-sā] *n* a sweet chestnut preserved in syrup. [Fr.]

marrow [mar'ō] *n* the soft tissue in the hollow parts of the bones; the essence or best part of anything.—*n* **marr'owbone**, a bone (as a shinbone) rich in marrow; (*pl*) knees; **marrowfat**, any of several wrinkle-seeded garden peas.—*adj* **marr'owy**, full of marrow; pithy. [OE (Anglian) *merg, mærh* (WS *mearg*), Ger *mark*.]

marry [mar'i] *vt* to join as husband and wife; to take for husband or wife; to give in marriage; to unite.—*vi* to get married.—*pr p* **marr'ying**; *pt, pt p* **marr'ied**.—**marry into**, to become a member of by marriage, **marry off**, to give in marriage. [Fr *marier*—L *maritare*, to marry, *maritus*, a husband—*mās, maris*, a male.]

Mars [märz] *n* the Roman god of war; the planet consipicuous for the redness of its light. [L *Mārs, Mārtis*.]

Marsala [mär-sä'lä] *n* a fortified Sicilian wine varying from dry to sweet. [*Marsala*, Sicily.]

marsh [märsh] *n* a tract of soft wet land.—*ns* **marsh' gas**, methane; **marsh hawk, marsh harrier**, a widely distributed No American hawk (*Circus cyaneus*) with a conspicuous white rump; **marshmall'ow**, a pink flowered perennial (*Althea officinalis*) which has a mucilaginous root used in confectionery and in medicine; a soft, spongy confection of sugar, gelatin, etc.; **marsh marigold**, a swamp herb (*Caltha palustris*) of the buttercup family.—*adj* **marsh'y**, resembling a marsh; relating to or occurring in marshes.—*n* **marsh'iness**. [OE *mersc, merisc*, orig adj—*mere*. See **mere** (1).]

marshal, marshall [mär'shȧl] *n* an official in charge of ceremonies, parades, etc.; in some foreign armies, a general officer of the highest rank; a Federal officer appointed to a judicial duties with duties like those of a sheriff; the head of some police or fire departments.—*vt* to arrange (ideas, troops, etc.) in order; to guide.—*pr p* **mar'shalling**; *pt, pt p* **mar'shalled**.—*n* **mar'shalship**. [OFr *mareschal* (Fr *maréchal*); from OHG *marah*, a horse, *schalh* (Ger *schalk*), a servant.]

marsupial [mär-sū'pi-ȧl] *adj* of an order (Marsupialia) of mammals that carry their incompletely developed young in an abdominal pouch on the mother.—*n* an animal of this kind, as an opossum. [L *marsūpium*—Gr *marsipion, marsypion*, a pouch.]

mart [märt] *n* a market. [Du *markt, mart*; cf **market**.]

marten [mär'tėn] *n* any of several carnivorous mammals (genus *Martes*) allied to the weasel, valued for their fur. [Fr *martre*, from the Gmc root seen in Ger *marder*, and OE *mearth*, marten.]

martial [mär'shȧl] *adj* of or belonging to war; warlike; bold; military;—*adv* **mar'tially**.—**martial arts**, systems of self-defense, usu from the Orient, as Karate or Kung fu; **martial law**, rule by military authorities over civilians, as during a war. [Fr *martial*—L *mārtiālis*—*Mārs*.]

martian [mär'shȧn] *adj* of Mars.—*n* an imagined inhabitant of Mars. [L *Mārtius*—*Mārs*.]

martin [mär'tin] *n* a small European swallow (*Delichon urbica*) with a forked tail, black head and back, and white rump and underparts; any of various other swallows and flycatchers. [The name *Martin*; cf **robin**, etc.]

martinet [mär-ti-net' or mär'-] *n* a strict disciplinarian. [From *Martinet*, a very strict officer in the army of Louis XIV of France.]

martingale [mär'tin-gāl, -gal] *n* a strap fastened to a horse's girth, passing between his forelegs, and attached to the bit or reins, so as to keep his head down; a short spar under the bowsprit. [Fr perh from a kind of breeches worn at *Martigues* in Provence.]

martyr [mär'tėr] *n* one who by his death bears witness to his belief; one who suffers for his belief; a chronic sufferer from a disease (*with* **to**).—*vt* to put to death for his belief; to inflict suffering on.—*ns* **mar'tyrdom**, the sufferings or death of a martyr; **martyrol'ogy**, a history of martyrs; a discourse on martyrdom; **martyrol'ogist**. [OE—L—Gr a witness.]

marvel [mär'vėl] *n* anything astonishing or wonderful.—*vti* to become full of wonder.—*adj* **mar'velous**, astonishing; beyond belief, improbable; (*inf*) very good, splendid.—*adv* **mar'velously**.—*n* **mar'velousness**. [Fr *merveille*—L *mīrābilis*, wonderful—*mīrārī*, to wonder.]

Marxism [märks'izm] *n* the system of thought developed by Karl Marx and Friedrich Engels advocating public ownership of the means of production and the dictatorship of the proletariat until the establishment of a classless society.—*adj* **Marxist**. [Karl *Marx* (1818–83).]

marzipan [mär-zi-pan'] *n* a pastry confection of ground almonds, sugar, and egg white. [Through Low L from Ar; older form *marchpane*; marzipan is Ger form.]

Masai [mä'sī] *n* an African people of the highlands of Kenya and Tanzania; a Nilotic language of the Masai people.—Also *adj*.

mascara [mas-kä'rä] *n* a cosmetic for coloring the eyelashes. [Sp *máscara*. See **mask**.]

mascon [mas'kon] *n* dense material lying beneath the moon's surface. [*mass concentration*.]

mascot [mas'kot] *n* a person, creature, or thing supposed to bring good luck. [Fr *mascotte*.]

masculine [mas'kū-lin] *adj* characteristic of, peculiar to, or appropriate to, a man or the male sex; mannish; (*gram*) of that gender to which belongs words denoting males.—*adv* **mas'culinely**.—*n* **masculin'ity**. [Fr—L *masculīnus*—*masculus*, male—*mās*, a male.]

maser [māz'er] *n* a device that stimulates atoms, as in a gas, to emit radiation in a narrow beam. [*M*icrowave *a*mplification by *s*timulated *e*mission of *r*adiation.]

mash [mash] *n* in brewing, a mixture of crushed malt and hot water; a mixture, as of bran with meal beaten and stirred as a food for animals; any soft mass.—*vt* to make into a mash; to crush or injure. [OE *masc*(*-wyrt*), mash(-wort).]

mask [mäsk] *n* a covering to conceal or protect the face; anything that conceals or disguises; a masquerade; a molded likeness of the face; a grotesque representation of the face worn to amuse or frighten; a masque—*vt* to cover or conceal as with a mask.—*vi* to take part in a masquerade; to disguise one's intentions or character.—*adj* **masked**. [Fr *masque*—Sp *máscara* or It *maschera*, of doubtful origin.]

maskanonge [mas´kȧ-nónj], **maskelonge** [-lónj], **maskinonge**. *See* **muskellunge**.

masochism [maz´o-kizm] *n* (*psych*) abnormal pleasure obtained from the suffering of physical or mental pain, esp as inflicted by a member of the other sex. [From the novelist Sacher-*Masoch* who described it.]

mason [mā´sn] *n* one who cuts, prepares, and lays stones, a builder in stone; a Freemason.—*adj* **Masonic** [ma-son´ik], relating to Freemasonry.—*n* **mā´sonry**, work executed by a mason, stonework; the art of building in stone. [OFr *masson* (Fr *maçon*)—Low L *maciō, -ōnis*, prob Gmc.]

masque [mäsk] *n* a masked ball; in the 16th and 17th centuries, a dramatic entertainment with a mythical or allegorical theme.—Also **mask**.

masquerade [mäsk-ėr-ād] *n* a ball or party at which fancy dress and masks are worn; acting or living under false pretences.—*vi* to join in a masquerade; to assume a false appearance.—*n* **masquerad´er**. [Fr *mascarade*, from Sp cf **mask**.]

mass [mas] *n* a quantity of matter of indefinite shape and size; a large quantity or number (*a mass of bruises*); bulk; size; the main part; (*physics*) the quantity of matter in a body as measured in its relation to inertia.—*adj* of or for the masses or for a large number.—*vti* to gather or form into a mass.—*ns* **mass´cult´**, (*inf*) a commercialized culture popularized through the mass media; **mass defect**, the difference between the mass of an isotope and its mass number;—*adj* **mass´ive** [-iv], forming or consisting of a large mass; big and solid; large and imposing.—*adv* **mass´ively**.—*ns* **mass´iveness; mass media**, newspapers, magazines, radio and television as the means of reaching the mass of people; **mass noun**, a noun (as water or bread) denoting a concept, property, or thing which ordinarily cannot be separated into distinct component parts and that in English is preceded by 'some' rather than 'a' or 'an' in indefinite singular constructions; **mass number**, the number of neutrons and protons in the nucleus of an atom; **mass production**, quantity production of goods, esp by machinery and division of labor; **mass spectrometer**, an instrument for identifying the constituents of a chemical compound by separating gaseous ions according to their differing mass and charge; **mass spectrometry**, the method of using a mass spectrometer; **mass spectrum**, the spectrum of a stream of gaseous ions separated according to their mass and charge.—**the masses**, the common people, esp the lower social classes. [Fr *masse*—L *massa*, a lump, prob.—Gr *māza*, a barley cake—*massein*, to knead.]

Mass [mass] *n* the celebration of the Eucharist in RC churches;—**mass card**, a card notifying the recipient (as a bereaved family) that a mass is to be offered for the repose of the soul of the mourned. [OE *mæsse*—Low L *missa*—L *mittěre*, to send away, perh from the phrase at the close of the service, *Ite, missa est* (*ecclesia*), 'Go, (the congregation) is dismissed'.]

massacre [mas´ak-ėr] *n* the indiscriminate cruel killing of many people or animals.—*vt* to kill in large numbers. [Fr]

massage [ma-säzh] *n* a kneading and rubbing of the muscles to stimulate the circulation of the blood and make them work better.—*vt* to give a massage to.—*ns* **masseur** [-œr´], a man whose work is giving massages; **masseuse** [-œz´], a woman masseur. [Fr, from Gr *massein* to knead.]

massif [ma-sēf´, mas´if] *n* a principal mountain mass. [Fr]

mast[1] [mäst] *n* a tall vertical spar used to support the sails, yards, etc. on a ship; a vertical pole.—*vt* to furnish with a mast.—*n* **mast´head**, the top part of a ship's mast; a newspaper or magazine listing of owner, address, etc. [OE *mæst*; Ger *mast*.]

mast[2] [mäst] *n* nuts (as acorns and beechnuts) accumulated on the forest floor. [OE *mæst*; Ger *mast*.]

mastectomy [mas-tek´tȯ-mi] *n* surgical removal of a breast. [Gr *mastos*, breast, *ektomē*, cutting out.]

master [mäs´tėr] *n* a man who rules others or has control over something, esp the head of a household; an employer; an owner of an animal or slave; the captain of a merchant ship; a male teacher in a private school; an expert craftsman; a writer or painter regarded as great; an original from which a copy can be made, esp a phonograph record or magnetic tape; **Master**, a title for a boy too young to be addressed as Mr; one holding an advanced academic degree.—*adj* being a master; chief; main; controlling.—*vt* to be or become master of; to become an expert (in art, etc.).—*ns* **master-at-arms**, a naval petty officer whose duty is to maintain discipline aboard ship; **master bedroom**, a large or principal bedroom in a house; **master chief petty officer**, a petty officer of the highest rank in the navy; **master class**, a seminar for advanced music students conducted by a master musician.—*adj* **mas´terful**, acting the part of a master; domineering; expert; skillful.—*ns* **master gunnery sergeant**, a non-commissioned officer in the marine corps ranking above a master sergeant; **master key**, a key that will open up every one of a set of locks.—*adj* **mas´terly**, expert; skillful.—*adv* in a masterly manner.—*n* **mas´termind´**, a very clever person, esp one who plans or directs a project.—*vt* to be the mastermind of.—*ns* **master of arts**, the recipient of a degree in the humanities of social sciences that is awarded after two years research to the holder of a bachelor's degree; the degree itself; **master of ceremonies**, a person who acts as host at a formal event or a program of entertainment;—Also **emcee; master of science**, the recipient of a degree in the sciences that is awarded usu after two years research to the holder of a bachelor's degree; the degree itself; **mas´terpiece´**, a work done with extraordinary skill; the greatest work of a person or group; **master plan**, an overall plan; **master race**, a people held to be racially preeminent and thus entitled to rule and enslave other peoples; **master sergeant**, a noncommissioned officer in the US Army ranking next below a sergeant major; a noncommissioned office in the US Air Force ranking next below a senior master sergeant; a noncommissioned officer in the US Marine Corps ranking next below a master gunnery sergeant; **mas´tership´**, dominion; superiority; the status, office, or function of a master; mastery; **master stroke**, a masterly action, move or achievement; **mas´terwork**, a masterpiece; **mastery**, control as by a master; ascendancy or victory; expert skill or knowledge. [Partly OE *mægester*, partly OFr *maistre* (Fr *maître*), both from L *magister*, from root of *magnus*, great.]

mastic [mas´tik] *n* an aromatic resin from mastic trees used chiefly in varnishes; any pasty material used as cements and protective coatings.—*n* **mastic tree**, a small European tree (*Pistacia lentiscus*) yielding mastic. [Fr *mastic*—LL *mastichum*—Gr *mastichē*.]

masticate [mas´ti-kāt] *vt* to chew; to reduce to a pulp by kneading or crushing—*n* **masticā´tion**.—*adj* **mas´ticatory**, used for chewing; adapted for chewing.—*n* a substance chewed to increase the saliva. [L *masticāre, -ātum*; cf Gr *mastax*, jaw.]

mastiff [mas´tif] *n* a thick-set and powerful breed of dog, formerly used in hunting now used chiefly as watchdogs. [OFr *mastin*, app L *mansuētus*, tame; perh confused with OFr *mestif*, mongrel.]

mastodon [mas´to-don] *n* a genus (*Mammut*) of extinct elephants differing from mammoths and elephants in the form of the molar teeth. [Gr *mastos*, breast, *odous, -ontos*, a tooth.]

mastoid [mas´toid] *n* the bony prominence behind the ear.—*n* **mastoidī´tis**, inflammation of the air cells of the mastoid. [Gr *mastos*, a breast, *eidos*, form.]

masturbation [mas-tûr-bā´shȯn] *n* manipulation of the genitals for sexual gratification.—*vi* **mas´turbate**. [L *masturbārī*.]

mat[1] [mat] *n* a piece of fabric of woven rushes, straw, coarse fiber, etc.; variously used for protection, as under a vase, etc. or on the floor; a thickly padded floor covering used for wrestling, etc.; anything interwoven or tangled into a thick mass.—*vti* to cover as with a mat; to interweave or tangle into a thick mass.—**go to the mat**, (*inf*) to engage in a struggle or dispute.—*n* **matt´ing**, process of becoming matted; material used as mats. [OE *matt(e), meatte*—L *matta*, a mat.]

mat[2] matt, matte [mat] *adj* having a dull surface. [Fr *mat*; Ger *matt*, dull.]

matador [mat´a-dör] *n* the bullfighter who kills the bull with a sword. [Sp *matador*—*matar*, to kill—L *mactāre*, to kill, to honor by sacrifice.]

match[1] [mach] *n* a short stick of wood or other material tipped with an easily ignited material.—*ns* **matchbook´**, a small cardboard folder containing rows of paper matches; **match´lock**, (*hist*) the lock of a musket containing a match for firing it; a musket so fired; **match´wood**, wood suitable for matches; splinters. [OFr *mesche* (Fr *mèche*).]

match[2] [mach] *n* any person or thing equal or similar to another; two persons or things that go well together; a contest or game; a mating or marriage.—*vt* to join in marriage; to put in opposition (with, against); to be equal or similar to; to get a counterpart to; to suit (one thing) to another.—*vi* to be equal, similar, suitable, etc.—*adj* **match´less**, having no equal.—*adv* **match´lessly**.—*ns* **match´lessness; match´mak´er**, one who arranges marriages for others. [OE *gemæcca*.]

mate[1] [māt] *n* a companion; a fellow worker; one of a matched pair; a husband or wife; the male or female of paired animals; an officer of a merchant ship, ranking below the captain.—*vti* to join as a pair; to couple in marriage or sexual union. [Prob Middle Low Ger *mate*, or Du *maet* (now *maat*); cf OE *gemetta*, a messmate, and **meat**.]

mate[2] [māt] *vt* to checkmate;—*n* and interj checkmate. [OFr *mat*, checkmated. *See* **checkmate**.]

maté, mate [mätā] *n* a South American holly (*Ilex paraguayensis*) an infusion of its leaves and green shoots. [Sp *mate*, orig the vessel in which it was infused for drinking.]

material [ma-tē´ri-ȧl] *adj* of matter; physical; of the body or bodily needs, comfort, etc.; not spiritual; important, essential, etc.—*n* what a thing is, or may be made of; elements or parts; cloth; fabric; (*pl*) tools, etc. needed to make or do something.—*vt* **matē´rialize**, to give material form to.—*vi* to assume bodily form; to make an unexpected appearance.—*ns* **materializa´tion; mate´rialism**, the doctrine that everything in the world, including thought, can be explained only in terms of matter; the tendency to be more concerned with spiritual or intellectual values; **mate´rialist**. *Also adj*. -*adj* **materialist´ic**.—*adv* **mate´rially**, physically; to a great extent; substantially. [L *māteriālis*—*māteria*, matter.]

materia medica [mȧ-tē´ri-a med´i-ka] (the science of) the substances used as remedies in medicine; a treatise on materia medica. [Mediaeval L.]

materiel, matériel [ma-tė´rē-ėl] *n* equipment, apparatus, and supplies used by an organization, esp armed forces. [Fr]

maternal [ma-tûr´nȧl] *adj* of, like, or from a mother; related through the mother's side of the family—*adv* **mater´nally**.—*n* **mater´nity**, the state, character, or relation of a mother.—*adj* intended for pregnant women; for the care of mothers and their newborn babies. [Fr *maternel* (It *maternale*) and *maternité*.—L *māternus*—*māter*, mother.]

mathematical, mathematic [math-ė-mat´ik, -ål] *adj* of, like or concerned with mathematics; very accurate and precise.—*adv* **mathemat´ically**.—*ns* **mathematician** [-ish´ån], one versed in mathematics; **mathemat´ics** (treated as *sing.*), the science dealing with quantities, forms, etc. and their relationships by the use of numbers and symbols.—*Also* **math**. [Gr *mathēmatikē* (*epistēmē*), mathematical (knowledge, science)—*mathēma*—*manthanein*, to learn.]

matin [mat´in] *n* (*pl*) the daily morning service of the Anglican Church; (*pl*) one of the seven canonical hours of the R C Church usually sung between midnight and daybreak;—*adjs* **matin; mat´inal**.—*n* **matinee, matinée** [mat´i-nā], an afternoon performance of a play, etc. [Fr *matines* (fem pl)—L *mātūtīnus*, belonging to the morning.]

matriarchy [mā´tri-är-ki] *n* form of social organization in which the mother is the ruler of the family or tribe and in which descent is traced through the mother.—*n* **mā´triarch**, a woman who is head and ruler of her family and descendants; an elderly woman who dominates her family or associates; an old woman of great dignity.—*adj* **matria´rchal**. [From L *māter*, mother, on analogy of **patriarch(y)**.]

matricide [mat´ri-sīd] *n* one who murders his (her) own mother; the murder of one's own mother.—*adj* **matrici´dal**. [L *mātricīda, mātricīdium*—*māter*, mother, *caedĕre*, to kill.]

matriculate [ma-trik´ū-lāt] *vti* to enroll, esp as a student.—*n* **matriculā´tion**, [Late L *mātrīcula*, a register, dim of *mātrīx; See* **matrix**.]

matrimony [mat´ri-mȯn-i] *n* the act or rite of marriage; the married state.—*adj* **matrimonial** [-mō´ni-al].—*adv* **matrimō´nially**—*ns* **matrimony plant**, honesty; **matrimony vine**, a climbing shrub (genus *Lycium*) with bright berries. [OFr *matrimoine*—L *mātrimōnium*—*māter, mātris*, mother.]

matrix [mā´triks, or mat´riks] *n* (*anat*) the womb; the cavity in which anything is formed; that in which anything is embedded; a mould; (*math*) a rectangular array of quantities or symbols;—*pl* **matrices** [māt-, or mat´-ris-ēz] or **matrixes**. [L *mātrīx, -īcis*, a breeding animal, later, the womb—*māter*, mother.]

matron [mā´trȯn] *n* a wife or widow, esp one of mature appearance and manner; a woman in charge of nursing and domestic arrangements in a hospital, school, or other institution.—*adj* **mā´tronly**, sedate.—*n* **matron of honor**, a married woman acting as chief attendant to a bride. [Fr *matrone*—L *mātrōna*—*māter*, mother.]

matt *see* **mat** (2).

matter [mat´ėr] *n* what a thing is made of; material; whatever occupies space and is perceptible to the senses; any specified substance; content of thought or expression; a quantity; a thing or affair; cause or occasion; significance; trouble, difficulty; pus; mail.—*vi* to be of importance; to form pus. **-as a matter of fact**, in fact; really; **for that matter**, as far as that is concerned; **no matter**, it is not important; in spite of; **the matter**, wrong (*nothing's the matter*). [OFr *matiere*—L *māteria*, matter.]

Matthew [math´yōō] *n* (*Bible*) 1st book of the New Testament, synoptic gospel presenting Jesus as the Redeemer and King of Israel, written by a disciple.

mattock [mat´ȯk] *n* a kind of pickax for loosening the soil, digging out roots, etc. [OE *mattuc*.]

mattress [mat´res] *n* a casing of strong cloth filled with cotton, foam rubber, coiled springs, etc., used on a bed; an inflatable airtight sack for use as a mattress. [OFr *materas* (Fr *matelas*)—Ar *matrah*, a place where anything is thrown.]

mature [ma-tūr´] *adj* fully developed, ripe; completely worked out (of a plan); due (of a bill).—*vt* to bring ripeness, full development or perfection; to bring to a head.—*vi* to become ripe; to become due (of a loan).—*adj*.—*adv* **matūre´ly**.—*ns* **matūre´ness; matūr´ity**, ripeness; full development; the time when a loan becomes due.—*vti* **mat´ūrate**, to mature.—*n* **matūrā´tion**. [L *mātūrus*, ripe.]

matutinal [ma-tūt´i-nål] *adj* of, relating to, or occurring in the morning; early. [L *mātūtīnālis, mātūtīnus*. See **matin**.]

matzo [mät´zō] *n* flat, unleavened bread resembling a soda cracker. [Yiddish.]

maudlin [möd´lin] *adj* foolishly sentimental. [ME *Maudelein*, through OFr and L from G *Magdalēnē*, (woman) of Magdala, from the assumption that Mary Magdalene was the penitent woman of Luke vii 37 ff; see **Magdalen**.]

maul [möl] *n* a heavy hammer for driving stakes.—*vt* to bruise or lacerate; to handle roughly. [OFr *mail*—L *malleus*.]

maulstick [möl´stik] *n* a long stick used by painters etc., as a support for the wrist.—Also **mahl´stick**. [Du *maalstok*—*malen*, to paint, *stok*, stick, assimilated to **stick**.]

maunder [mön´dėr] *vt* to talk or move in a confused or aimless way.

Maundy Thursday [mön´di thûrz´dā] the day before Good Friday. [Fr *mandé*—L *mandātum*, command (John xiii 34).]

mausoleum [mö-sō-lē´um] *n* a magnificent tomb.—*pl*—**eums**. [L *mausōlēum*—Gr *Mausōleion*, the magnificent tomb of a certain *Mausōlus* (d 353 BC).]

mauve [mōv, möv] *n* any of several shades of pale purple.—*adj* of this color. [Fr,—L *malva*, mallow.]

maven, mavin [mā´vėn] *n* (*inf*) an expert; a connoisseur. [Yiddish.]

maw [mö] *n* the throat, gullet, jaws or oral cavity of a voracious animal; something like a gaping maw. [OE *maga*; Ger *magen*.]

mawkish [mök´ish] *adj* insipid; sickly sentimental, maudlin.—*adv* **mawk´ishly**.—*n* **mawk´ishness**. [ON *mathkr*, maggot.]

maxi [maks´i] *n* a long skirt, dress or coat.

maxilla [maks-il´a] *n* the upper jawbone in vertebrates; in anthropods, the first or second part of mouthparts behind the mandibles.—*adj* **maxillary** [maks-il´ár-i, or maks´-]. [L *maxilla*, jawbone.]

maxim [maks´im] *n* a concise rule of conduct; a precept. [Fr *maxime*—L *maxima* (*sententia*, or some other word), greatest (opinion, etc.), fem superl of *magnus*, great.]

maximum [maks´i-mum] *n* the greatest quantity, number, etc. possible; the highest point or degree reached.—*adj* highest; greatest possible reached.—*pl* **max´ima**.—*adj* **maximal**. [L, superl neut of *magnus*, great.]

maxwell [maks´wėl] *n* the centimeter-gram-second electromagnetic unit of magnetic flux equal to 10^{-8} *weber*. [James Clerk-*Maxwell* (1831–79), Scottish physicist.]

may [mā] *verbal auxiliary expressing*: possibility (*it may snow*); permission (*you may go*); contingency (*come what may*); wish or hope (*may she live*).—pt **might** [mīt].—*adv* **may´be**, perhaps. [OE *mæg*, pr t (old pt) of *magan*, to be able, pt *mihte*; cog with Ger *mögen*.]

May [mā] *n* the fifth month of the year, having 31 days; early or gay part of life; **may**, the hawthorn or its blossom; spring-blooming spirea; any other spring-blooming plant esp genera *Arabis, Syringus, Ulmus* and *Viburnum*.—*vi* to take part in the festivities of May or May Day; to gather flowers in May; *pr p* **may´ing**.—*ns* **may´apple**, a N American herb (*Podophyllum peltatum*) with a poisonous root that is used medicinally, and a single, white saucer-shaped flower.—Also **man´drake**.—*ns* **May Day**, May 1, celebrated as a traditional spring festival; observed in many countries as a labor holiday; **may´flower**, an early spring flower, esp the trailing arbutus and windflower; **May´flower**, the ship on which the Pilgrims came to America in 1620; **may´fly´**, any of an order (Ephemeroptera) of short-lived insects; ephemerid; **may´ing**, the celebration of May Day; **may´pole´**, a flower-crowned pole forming the center of activities on May Day; **may´pop**, the insipid yellow applelike fruit of a passionflower (*Passiflora incarnata*) of the southern US; the plant itself or its blossom; **May´time**, the month of May. [OFr *Mai*—L *Māius* (*mēnsis*, month), sacred to *Māia*, mother of Mercury.]

Maya [mī´å] *n* a member of an Amerindian people of Yucatán, Belize and northern Guatemala; a language of the ancient Mayans recorded in inscriptions; the language of the Mayan people. [Sp.]

maybe *See* **may**.

Mayday [mā´dā] *n* the international radio-telephonic distress signal for ships and aircraft. [Fr *m'aidez*, help me.]

mayo [mā´yō] *n* (*inf*) mayonnaise. [Clipped form of **mayonnaise**.]

mayonnaise [mā´ȯn-āz´] *n* a salad dressing composed of the yolk of eggs, olive-oil, and vinegar or lemon-juice, seasoned. [Fr.]

mayor [mā´ȯr, mār] *n* the chief administrative officer of a municipality.—*ns* **may´oralty**, the office or term of office of a mayor. [Fr *maire*—L *mājor*, comp of *māgnus*, great.]

maze [māz] *n* a confusing, intricate network of pathways; a confused state.—*vt* to bewilder; to confuse.—*adj* **maz´y**, resembling a maze. [Prob from lost OE word; compound *āmasod*, amazed, occurs.]

mazel [mäz´ėl] *n* (*inf*) luck.—**mazel tov** [töf], congratulations!, good luck! [Heb.]

mazurka [ma-zōōr´ka, or -zûr´-] *n* a lively Polish dance; a piece of music for it in triple time. [Pol Masurian woman—ie a woman of the province of Mazovia.]

me [mē] *personal pron* the objective case of **I.** [OE *mē*.]

mea culpa [mē´a kul´pa, mā´a kōōl´pa] through my fault. [L.]

mead[1] [mēd] *n* an alcoholic liquor made from fermented honey. [OE *meodu*; Ger *met*, W *medd*.]

mead[2] [mēd] *n* (*poetic*) meadow.

meadow [med´ō] *n* a piece of land where grass is grown for hay; low, level, moist grassland.—*vt* to make a meadow of.—*ns* **meadow boots**, marsh marigold; **meadow lark**, a N American songbird (*Sturnella magna*) with a chunky light brown body, a black bib on a yellow breast and throat; any of related species found throughout continental US, all of which are important predators of harmful insects; **meadow rue**, any of a genus (*Thalictrum*) of plants of the buttercup family with thin, pale green, lobed compound leaves; **meadow saffron**, colchicum; **meadowsweet**, a N American spirea (*Spirea latifolia*), a tall shrub with purplish-red nearly smooth stems and flowers in dense, wand-shaped clusters.

meager, meagre [mē´gėr] *adj* lean; poor in quality; scanty, deficient in quantity.—*adv* **mea´gerly**.—*n* **mea´gerness**. [Fr *maigre*—L *macer*, lean; cf Ger *mager*.]

meal[1] [mēl] *n* any of the times for eating, as lunch, dinner, etc.; the food served at such a time.—*ns* **meal pack**, a frozen meal prepackaged in a tray and heated before serving; **meal ticket**, someone that is the source of one's income. [OE *mæl*, time, portion of time; Du *maal*, Ger. *mahl*.]

meal[2] [mēl] *n* any edible grain coarsely ground; any substance similarly ground.—*adj* **meal´y**, resembling meal; covered with meal.—*n* **meal´iness.**—*adj* **meal´y-mouthed´**, not outspoken and blunt; euphemistic; devious in speech. [OE *melu, melo*; Ger *mehl*, Du *meel*, meal.]

mean[1] [mēn] *adj* low in quality or value; inferior; shabby; ignoble; contemptibly selfish, bad-tempered, etc.; stingy; (*slang*) difficult; (*slang*) expert.—*n* **mean´ie, mean´y** (*inf*), one who is mean, selfish, etc.—*adv* **mean´ly.**—*n* **mean´ness.** [OE *gemǣne*; Ger *gemein*, L *commūnis*, common.]

mean[2] [mēn] *adj* halfway between extremes; average.—*n* what is between extremes; (*math*) a number between the smallest and largest values of a set of quantities, esp an average.—*n pl* **means**, that by which something is done or obtained; agency; resources; wealth.—*advs* **mean´time, mean´while**, in or during the intervening time; at the same time.—*n* the intervening time.—**mean sun**, a fictitious sun used for time keeping that moves at a constant rate uniformly along the celestial equator; **mean time, mean solar time**, time as given by the position of the mean sun.—**by all means**, without fail; certainly; **by means of**, by using; **by no means**, not at all. [OFr *meien* (Fr *moyen*)—L *mediānus*—*medius*, middle.]

mean[3] [mēn] *vt* to have in mind; to intend; to intend to express; to signify, denote (*'aye' means 'yes'*).—*vi* to have a (specified) degree of importance, effect, etc (*honors mean little to her*).—*pr p* **meaning**; *pt, pt p* **meant** [ment].—*n* **mean´ing**, signification; the sense intended; import.—*adj* significant.—**mean well**, to have good intentions. [OE *mǣnan*; Ger *meinen*, to think.]

meander [mē-an´dėr] *n* a winding path esp a labyrinth; a winding of a stream or river.—*vi* (of a stream) to take a winding course; to wander idly.—*adjs* **mean´dering, mean´drous** [drôs]. [L *Maeander*—Gr *Maiandros*, a winding river in Asia Minor.]

meanie, meany *See* **mean** (1).

meant [ment] *pt, pt p* of **mean** (3).

measles [mē´zlz] *n* an acute, contagious virus disease, usu. of children, characterized by small red spots on the skin, high fever, etc.—Also **rubeola**, a similar but milder disease, German measles or rubella; a disease affecting pigs and cattle due to infection by larval tapeworms (genus *Taenia*).—*adjs* **mea´sled**, infected with measles; spotty; **mea´sly**, measled; (of meat) infected with tapeworm larvae; (*inf*) contemptibly slight or worthless. [ME *maseles*; cf Du *mazelen*, Ger *masern*.]

measure [mezh´ůr] *n* the extent, dimension, capacity, etc. of anything; a determining of this, measurement; a unit of measurement; any standard of valuation; a system of measurement; an instrument for measuring; a definite quantity measured out; a course of action; a statute, law; a rhythmical unit, esp the notes and rests between bars on a musical staff.—*vt* to find out the extent, dimensions, etc. of, esp by a standard; to mark off by measuring; to be a measure of.—*vi* to take measurements; to be of specified measurements.—*adj* **meas´urable.**—*adv* **meas´urably.**—*adjs* **meas´ureless; meas´ured**, set or marked off by a standard; regular or steady (*measured steps*); planned with care (*measured words*).—*n* **meas´urement**, a measuring or being measured; extent or quantity determined by measuring; a system of measuring or of measures.—**beyond measure**, exceedingly; **for good measure**, as something extra; **in a measure**, to some extent; **measure up to**, to prove to be competent. [OFr *mesure*—L *mensūra*, a measure—*mētīrī, mensus*, to measure.]

meat [mēt] *n* anything eaten as food; the flesh of animals used as food; the edible part (*a nut meat*); the substance or essence.—*ns* **meat´-ax**, a cleaver; a heavy-handed method of changing something; **meat´ball**, a small ball of ground meat usu. mixed with bread crumbs and spices; **meat loaf**, a dish of ground meat, etc. baked in the form of a loaf; **meat´packing**, the industry of preparing the flesh of animals for market.—*adj* **meat´y**, full of meat; substantial.—**meat and drink**, food; **meat and potatoes**, a main object of interest; **meat-and-potatoes**, basic, practical; everyday.—*adj* **meat´y**, full of meat; (*fig*) full of substance. [OE *mete*.]

Mecca [mek´a] *n* the birthplace of Mohammed and goal of Muslim pilgrimage; **mecca**, any place that one yearns to go to.

mechanic [me-kan´ik] *adj* of or relating to manual work or skill; of the nature of or resembling a machine (as in automatic performance).—*n* a manual worker; a machinist, esp one who maintains machinery.—*adj*—*adj* **mechan´ical**, having to do with machinery or tools; produced or operated by machinery; of the science of mechanics; machinelike; spiritless.—*adv* **mechan´ically.**—*ns* **mechanician** [mek-ån-ish´ån], **mechanic, machinist; mechan´ics**, the science of motion and the action of forces on bodies; knowledge of machinery; the technical aspect (*the mechanics of poetry*).—*vt* **mech´anize**, to make mechanical; to equip (an industry) with machinery or (an army, etc.) with motor vehicles, tanks, etc.—*n* **mech´aniza´tion.**—*ns* **mech´anism**, the working parts of a machine; any system of interrelated parts; any physical or mental process by which a result is produced; a doctrine that holds natural processes (as life) to be mechanically determined and can be completely explained by the laws of physics and chemistry; **mech´anist**, a believer in mechanism; **mech´another´apy**, the treatment of disease by mechanical means, as massage. [Gr *mēchanikos*—*mēchanē*, a contrivance.]

Mechlin [mek´lin] *n* a delicate bobbin lace used for trimming clothing. [*Mechlin*, Belgium.]

medal [med´ål] *n* a small, flat piece of inscribed metal, commemorating some event or awarded for some distinction; a disk bearing a religious symbol.—*adj* **medallic** [mēdal´ik], of or shown on a medal.—*ns* **medallion** [mėdal´yȯn], a large medal; a design, portrait, etc. shaped like a medal; a small round or oval serving (as of meat); **med´alist**, one awarded a medal; **Medal for Merit**, a US civilian decoration for outstanding services; **Medal of Freedom**, a US civilian decoration for meritorious achievement; **Medal of Honor**, a US military decoration awarded in the name of Congress for conspicuous bravery in battle; **medal play**, golf competition scored by total number of strokes. [Fr *médaille*—It *medaglia*; through a Low L form from L *metallum*, metal.]

meddle [med´l] *vi* to interfere in another's affairs.—*n* **medd´ler.**—*adj* **medd´lesome**, to meddling. [OFr *medler*, a variant of *mesler* (Fr *mêler*)—Low L *misculāre*—L *miscēre*, to mix.]

media [mē´di-a] *pl* of **medium**.

mediaeval *See* **medieval**.

medial [mē´di-ål] *adj* middle; ordinary.—*adj* **mē´dian**, middle; intermediate; denoting the middle number in a series.—*n* a medium number, point, line, etc.—*n* **median strip**, a planted or paved strip dividing a highway into lanes. [LL *mediālis*, L *mediānus*, LL *medians, -antis*—L *medius*, middle.]

mediate [mē´di-åt] *adj* occupying a middle position; acting through an intervening agency; showing indirect causation or relation.—*vi* [-āt´] to be in an intermediate position; to be an intermediary.—*vt* to settle (differences) between persons, nations, etc. by intervention.—*adv* **mē´diately.**—*ns* **mē´diateness; mēdiā´tion**, the act of mediating.—*n* **mē´diator**, one that mediates; a mediating agent in a biological or chemical process. [Low L *mědiāre*, to be in the middle—L *mědius*.]

medical [med´i-kål] *adj* of or connected with the practice or study of medicine; requiring medical treatment.—*ns* **med´ic**, (*inf*) a physician or surgeon; (*inf*) a member of a military medical corps; **Med´icaid**, a State and Federal health program for paying certain medical expenses of persons having a low income; **medical examiner**, a public officer who makes postmortem examinations of bodies to find the cause of death; **Med´icare´**, a federal health program for paying certain medical expenses of the aged.—*vt* **med´icate**, to treat with medicine.—*adv* **med´ically.** [Low L *medicālis*—L **medicus**, pertaining to healing, a physician—*medēri*, to heal.]

medicament [med-ik´å-ment] *n* any substance used in curative treatment. [L *medicāmentum*—*medicāre*.]

medicate [med´i-kāt] *vt* to treat with medicine.—*adj* **med´icable**, that may be cured.—*adj* **med´icated**, treated with medicine.—*n* **medicā´tion.**—*adj* **med´icative**, healing. [L *medicāre, -ātum*, to heal.]

medicine [med´sin, -sn] *n* any substance used for the treatment or prevention of disease; the science or art of preventing, alleviating, or curing disease, esp the branch dealt with by the physicians as opposed to surgery.—*adj* **medicinal** [med-is´in-ål], used in medicine; curative; relating to medicine.—*adv* **medic´inally.**—*ns* **medicine ball**, a heavy leather ball used for exercise; **medicine dropper**, a short glass tube with a rubber bulb used to administer medicine drop by drop; **med´icine man**, among N American Indians, a man supposed to have supernatural powers to heal the sick. [OFr *medecine*—L *medicina*.]

medieval, mediaevel [med-i-ē´val] *adj* of the Middle Ages.—*ns* **medie´valist, mediae´valist**, a specialist in medieval history and culture; a connoisseur of medieval arts and culture; **Medieval Latin**, the Latin used from the 7th to 15th centuries inclusive, esp for liturgical and literary purposes. [L *medius*, middle, *aevum*, age.]

medio [mē´di-ō-] in composition, middle. [L *medius*, middle.]

mediocre [mē´di-ō´kėr] *adj* of middling goodness, ability, etc.; inferior.—*n* **mediocrity** [-ok´-], a middling degree of merit; a mediocre person. [Fr *médiocre*—L *mediocris*—*medius*, middle.]

meditate [med´i-tāt] *vi* to consider thoughtfully (*with* **on, upon**); to engage in contemplation, esp religious.—*vt* to consider deeply; to intend.—*adj* **med´itated.**—*n* **meditā´tion**, deep thought; serious continuous contemplation esp on a religious or spiritual theme; a meditative treatment of a literary or a musical theme.—*adj* **med´itative**, marked by deep or serious contemplation.—*adv* **med´itatively.**—*n* **med´itativeness.** [L *meditārī*, prob cog with L *medērī*, to heal.]

Mediterranean [med-i-tėr-ā´nė-ån] *adj* of the Mediterranean Sea; denoting furniture made to imitate heavy, ornately carved Renaissance furniture; **mediterranean**, enclosed or nearly enclosed with land; of a physical type of the Caucasian race characterized by medium or short stature, a relatively long head, and dark complexion. [L *mediterrānus*—*medius*, middle, *terra*, earth.]

medium [mē´di-um] *n* the middle condition or degree; any intervening means, instrument, or agency; a substance through which any effect is transmitted; a channel (as newspapers, radio, television) through which information is transmitted; in spiritualism, the person through whom spirits are said to communicate with the material world.—*pl* **mē´dia**, or **mē´diums.**—*adj* **mē´dium**, intermediate in amount, quality, position, etc. [L *mědium*.]

medlar [med´lår] *n* a small (*Mespilus Germanica*) tree akin to the apple; its fruit. [OFr *medler, mesler*—L *mespilum*—Gr *mespilon*.]

medley [med´li] *n* a miscellany; a musical piece made up of various tunes or passages. [OFr *medler, mesler*, to mix.]

medullary [me-dul´ăr-i] *adj* consisting of, or resembling, marrow or pith. [L *medulla*, marrow.]

medusa [me-dū´za] *n* a small hydrozoan jellyfish, from the likeness of its tentacles to the snakes of Medusa's head.—*pl* **medū´sae** [-zē, -sē]. [L *Medūsa*—Gr *Medousa*.]
meek [mēk] *adj* mild and gentle of temper, submissive.—*adv* **meek´ly**.—*n* **meek´ness**. [ON *mjūkr*; early modern Du *muik*.]
meerschaum [mēr´sham] *n* a fine light whitish clay; a tobacco pipe made of it. [Ger,—*meer*, sea, *schaum*, foam.]
meet[1] [mēt] *adj* precisely suitable; proper.—*adv* **meet´ly**. [Prob from an OE (Anglian) form answering to WS *gemǣte*—*metan*, to measure.]
meet[2] [mēt] *vt* to come face to face with; to come into contact with; to be present at the arrival of; to contend with, deal with; to experience; to be perceived by (the eye, etc.); to satisfy (a demand, etc.); to pay (a bill, etc.).—*vi* to come together; to assemble; to be introduced; to have an encounter.—*pt, pt p* **met**.—*n* a meeting, as of huntsmen.—*ns* **meet´ing**, a coming together; an assembly; a junction; **meet´inghouse**, a house or building where people, esp Protestants meet for public worship.—**meet halfway**, to compromise with; **meet with**, to be subjected to; to encounter. [OE *mētan*, to meet—*mōt, gemōt*, a meeting.]
mega- [meg´a-], **meg-**, [meg´-], in composition, great, powerful, or (metric system) a million of.—*ns* **meg´abyte** [bīt], a unit of computer information approximately equal to one million bytes; **meg´adeath**, death of a million people, unit used in estimating casualties in nuclear war; **megadōse**, a large dose (as of vitamin)—*vt* to provide with a megadose.—*n* **meg´ahertz**, a unit of frequency equal to one million hertz; **meg´awatt**, one million watts; **meg´ohm**, one million ohms; **megaton**, an explosive force equivalent to one million tons of TNT (trinitrotoluene). [Gr *megas*, great.]
megalith [meg´a-lith] *n* a huge stone.—*adj* **megalith´ic**. [Gr *megas*, great, *lithos*, a stone.]
megalomania [meg-a-lō-mā´ni-a] *n* the delusion that one is great or powerful. [Gr *megas*, great, *mania*, madness.]
megaphone [meg´a-fōn] *n* a funnel-shaped device for causing sounds to be heard better and at a greater distance. [Gr *megas*, great, *phōnē*, voice.]
megrim [mē´grim] *n* a migraine; vertigo; a whim or fancy; (*pl*) low spirits. [Fr *migraine*—Gr *hēmikrānia*—*hēmi*, half, *krānion*, skull.]
meiosis [mī-ō´sis] *n* understatement, as a figure of speech; the process in cell division that results in the number of chromosomes in gamete-producing cells being reduced to one half.—*adj* **meiot´ic**.—Cf **mitosis**. [Gr *meiōsis*, diminution.]
melamine [mel´à-mēn] *n* a white crystalline organic base $C_3H_6N_6$ used in making synthetic resins.—*n* **melamine resin**, a thermosetting resin used for adhesives, coatings, and laminated products.
melancholy [mel´àn-kol-i, -kȯl-i] *n* depression of spirits, dejection; sadness, pensiveness.—*adj* depressed; depressing.—*n* **melanchō´lia**, a mental state characterized by dejection and often with delusions.—*adj* **melancholic** [-kol´ik]. [OFr *melancholic*—L *melancholia*—Gr *melancholiā*—*melās, -ănos*, black, *cholē*, bile.]
Melanesian [mel-àn-ēz´i-àn] *adj* of Melanesia, its people or their languages.—*n* a language group consisting of the Austronesian languages of Melanesia; a member of the dominant native group in Melanesia. [Gr *melās, -ănos*, black, *nēsos*, island.]
mélange [mā-lãzh´] *n* a mixture; a medley. [Fr.]
melanin [mel´à-nin] *n* a dark brown pigment found in animals and plants.—*ns* **mel´anism**, an increased amount of melanin (as of skin, hair, feathers); **melanom´a**, a usu. malignant skin tumour containing melanin; **melanos´is**, excessive deposit of melanin in the tissues. [Gr *melās, -ănos*, black.]
Melba toast [mel´bà] *n* very thin crisp toast. [Nellie *Melba*, singer.]
meld [meld] *vti* in card games, to expose and declare (certain cards) for a score.—*n* the cards melded.
melee, mêlée [mel´ā] *n* a confused conflict between opposing parties. [Fr—*mêler*, to mix.]
meliorate [mē´li-ȯ-rāt] *vt* to make better.—*vi* to grow better.—*n* **meliorā´tion**.—*adj* **mē´liorātive**, tending towards improvement. [L *melior*, better.]
mellifluous [mel-if´lōō-us] *adj* honey-producing; sweet as honey (eg of voice, words).—*advs* **mellif´luently, mellif´luously**. [L *mel*, honey.]
mellophone [mel´ō-fōn] *n* a brass band instrument resembling the French horn. [**mellow + phone**.]
mellow [mel´ō] *adj* soft and ripe (of fruit); well matured (of wine); soft, not harsh (of sound, color, light); softened by age or experience (of character).—*vt* to soften by ripeness or by age; to mature.—*vi* to become soft; to be matured; to become gentler and more tolerant.—*n* **mell´owness**.—*adj* **mell´owy**, soft. [Prob OE *melu*, meal, influenced by *mearu*, soft, tender.]
melodrama [mel´ō-drä-ma] *n* a kind of sensational drama.—*adj* **melodramatic** [-at´ik], of the nature of melodrama; overstrained; sensational.—*n* **melodramatist** [-dram´a-tist], a write of melodramas. [Gr *melos*, a song, *drāma*, action.]
melody [mel´o-di] *n* an air of tune; sweet music; tunefulness; the tune in harmonised music.—*n* **melō´deon**, a small reed organ; a kind of accordion.—*adjs* **melŏd´ic**, of the nature of, or pertaining to, melody; **melō´dious**, full of melody; agreeable to the ear.—*adv* **melō´diously**.—*ns* **melō´diousness; mel´odist**.—**melodic minor scale**, a minor scale with the semitones between the 2d and 3d and the 7th and 8th notes ascending, and between the 5th and 6th and 2d and 3d descending. [Fr—Late L—Gr *medōidiā*—*melos*, a song, *ōidē*, a lay.]
melon [mel´ȯn] *n* the large, juicy many-seeded fruit of trailing plants (family Cucurbitacee), as the watermelon, cantaloupe, etc; (*inf*) protruding abdomen; (*inf*) a financial windfall. [Fr,—L *mēlō, -ōnis*—Gr *mēlon*, an apple.]
melt [melt] *vti* to become liquid; to dissolve; to dwindle or cause to dwindle away; to soften or to be softened emotionally.—*n* a material in the molten state; the condition of being melted; **melt´ing**.—*adv* **melt´ingly**.—*ns* **melt´down´**, the melting of the fuel core of a nuclear reactor; the drastic collapse of almost anything; **melting point**, the temperature at which a solid melts; **melting pot**, a vessel for melting something in; a place where people of various nationalities, races, etc. are assimilated; **melt´water**, water derived from the melting of snow or ice.—*adj* **mōlt´en**, melted; made of melted metal. [OE *meltan* (intr strong vb), and *mæltan, meltan* (causative weak vb; WS *mieltan*).]
melton [mel´tȯn] *n* a heavy smooth woolen fabric with a short nap. [*Melton* Mowbray, England.]
member [mem´bėr] *n* a limb of an animal; one of a society; a representative in a legislative body; any essential part of a structure.—*adj* membered, having limbs.—*n* **mem´bership**, the state of being a member or one of a society; the members of a body regarded as a whole. [Fr *membre*—*membrum*.]
membrane [mem´brān, -brin] *n* a thin flexible solid sheet or film, esp of animal or vegetable origin; a skin of parchment.—*adjs* **mem´branous**, like, or of the nature of, a membrane. [Fr,—L *membrāna*—*membrum*.]
memcon [mem´kän] *n* (*inf*) a memorandum of a conversation.
memento [me-men´tō] *n* a reminder esp a souvenir.—*pl* **memen´tos** or **-toes**. [L, imper of *meminisse*, to remember.]
memo [mem´ō] *n* note sent between employees about company business. [**memorandum**.]
memoir [mem´wär, -wör] *n* (*pl*) record of events set down from personal knowledge and intended as material for history or biography; a biographical sketch. [Fr *mémoire*—L *memoria*, memory—*memor*, mindful.]
memorable, memorial *See* **memory**.
memorandum [mem-ȯr-an´dum] *n* a note to assist the memory; an informal written communication, as within an office.—*pl* **memoran´dums, memoran´da**. [L a thing to be remembered, neut gerundive of *memorāre*, to remember.]
memory [mem´ȯ-ri] *n* the power of retaining and reproducing mental or sensory impressions; an impression so reproduced; a having or keeping in the mind; time within which past things can be remembered; commemoration; remembrance; of computers, a store.—*adj* **mem´orable**, deserving to be remembered; remarkable.—*adv* **mem´orably**.—*adj* **memō´rial**, serving, or intended, to preserve the memory of anything; pertaining to memory.—*n* that which serves to keep in remembrance; a monument.—*vt* **memō´rialize**, to present a memorial to; to petition by a memorial.—*n* **memō´rialist**, one who writes, signs, or presents a memorial.—*vt* **mem´orize**, to commit to memory.—**Memorial Day**, a legal holiday in the US (the last Monday in May in most states) in memory of dead servicemen of all wars. [L *memoria*, memory.]
men *pl* of **man**.
menace [men´ás] *n* a threat; a threatening danger.—*vt* to threaten.—*adj* **men´acing**.—*adv* **man´acingly**. [Fr,—L *minăciae*, threats—*minae*, overhanging parts, threats.]
ménage [mā-näzh´] *n* a household; the management of a house.—**ménage à trois** [a trwa], a household composed of a husband and wife and the lover of one of them. [Fr through Late L,—L *mānsiō, -ōnis*, a dwelling.]
menagerie [men-aj´ėr-i] *n* a place for keeping wild animals for exhibition; a collection of such animals, esp traveling. [Fr *ménagerie*—*ménage*; see above.]
mend [mend] *vt* to repair; to correct, improve (one's ways, manners).—*vi* to grow better.—*ns* **mend´er; mend´ing**, the act of repairing; things requiring to be mended.—**on the mend**, improving, recovering. [Shortened form of **amend**.]
mendacious [men-dā´shùs] *adj* lying, untruthful.—*adv* **mendā´ciously**.—*n* **mendacity** [-das´i-ti], lying, untruthfulness. [L *mendāx, -ācis*, conn with *mentīrī*, to lie.]
mendelevium [men-del-lē´(-lā´-)vi-um] *n* a transuranic element (symbol MV; at wt 256; at no 101). [Named after the Russian scientist *Mendeleev* (1834–1907) who developed the periodic table.]
Mendel's law [mend´ėlz] *n* a principle of genetics that hereditary units occur in pairs which separate in meiosis so that every zygote but one member of a pair of genes from each parent.—*adj* **Mendēl´ian**.—*ns* **Mendelian factor**, a gene; **Mend´elism**, the principles or operation of Mendel's law. [Gregor *Mendel* (1834–1907) Austrian botanist.]
mendicant [men´di-kànt] *adj* begging.—*n* a beggar.—*ns* **men´dicancy, mendicity** [-dis´i-ti], the condition of a beggar; begging. [L *mendīcans, -antis*, pr p of *mendīcāre*, to beg—*mendīcus*, a beggar.]
menial [mē´ni-àl] *adj* servile, humiliating.—*n* a domestic servant; one performing servile work; a person of servile disposition. [Anglo-Fr *menial*, cf OFr *mesnie*—L *mansiō, -ōnis*, a dwelling.]
Ménière's disease [men´yerz, men-yerz´] a progressive disorder of the inner ear marked by severe vertigo, tinnitus, and deafness. [Prosper *Ménière*, Fr physician.]
meningitis [men-in-jī´tis] *n* inflammation of the membranes enveloping the brain or spinal cord. [Gr *mēninx, -ingos*, a membrane.]

meniscus [men-is´kus] *n* a crescent-shaped figure; a lens convex on the one side and concave on the other; the curved upper surface of a liquid column that is concaved when wetted by the liquid and concave when not. [Gr *mēniskos*, dim of *mēnē*, the moon (*iskos*, small).]

Mennonite [men´ō-nīt] *n* a member of an evangelical Christian sect living and dressing plainly and rejecting military service, oaths, etc. [*Menno* Simons, 16th century Dutch reformer.]

menopause [men-ō-pöz] *n* permanent end of menstruation. [Gr *mēn*, month, *pausis*, end.]

menorah [mė-nör´å] *n* (*Judaism*) a candelabrum with seven (or nine) branches.

mensch [mensh] *n* (*inf*) a person of integrity and honor. [Yiddish.]

menses [men´sēz] *n pl* the monthly discharge from the uterus. [L. *mēnsēs*, pl of *mēnsis*. month.]

menstruum [men´strŏŏ-um] *n* a solvent.—*pl* **menstru´ums, men´strua**.—*adj* **men´strual**, monthly; pertaining to the menses.—*vi* **men´struāte**, to discharge the menses.—*n* **menstruā´tion**.—*adj* **men´struous**. [L neit of *mēnstruus*, monthly.]

mensurable [men´sh(y)ůr-å-bl, or -sūr-, -shūr-] *adj* measurable.—*n* **mensurabil´ity**.—*adj* **mens´ural**, pertaining to measure.—*n* **mensurā´tion**, the act or art of finding by measurement and calculation the length, area, volume, etc., of bodies. [L *mēnsūrāre*, to measure.]

mental [men´tål] *adj* of, or relating to the kind; of, relating to, or affected with a disorder of the mind.—*n* **mentality** [-tal´-i-ti], **mental capacity or power**.—*adv* **men´tally**.—**mental age**, a measure used in psychological testing that expresses mental attainment in terms of the number of years it takes the average child to reach the same level; **mental deficiency**, retarded development of learning ability; **mental reservation**, qualification of (a statement) that one makes to oneself but does not express; **mental retardation**, congenital lowness of intelligence. [Fr,—L *mēns, mentis*, the mind.]

menthol [men´thol] *n* an alcohol obtained from oil of peppermint by cooling, which gives relief in colds, etc. [L *mentha*, mint.]

mention [men´sh(ȯ)n] *n* a brief notice; a casual introduction into speech or writing.—*vt* to notice briefly; to remark; to name.—adj **men´tionable**, fit to be mentioned. [L *mentiō*.]

mentor [men´tȯr] *n* a wise counsellor.—*n* **men´torship**. [Gr *Mentōr*, the tutor by whom Telemachus was guided.]

menu [men´ū, mė´nü] *n* the bill of fare; a list on a computer display from which the user can select the operation the computer is to perform. [Fr,—L *minūtus*, small.]

meow [mē-ow´] *n* the cry of a cat; a spiteful remark.—Also *vi*.—Also **mew, miaow**. [Imit.]

meperidine [mė-per´i-dēn] *n* a synthetic pain-relieving drug with sedative and antispasmodic properties; a morphine substitute.—Also **Demeral**.

Mephistopheles [mef-is-tof´i-lēz] *n* a medieval devil found in Marlowe's *Dr Faustus* and Goethe's *Faust*.—*adj* **Mephistophē´lian, Mephistophelē´an**, cynical, scoffing, fiendish. [Ety unknown; prob influenced by Gr *mē*, not, *phōs*, gen *phōtos*, light, *philos*, loving.]

mephitis [me-fī´tis] *n* a poisonous exhalation; a foul stink.—*adjs* **mephitic** [-fit´-], **-al**. [L *mephītis*.]

mercantile [mûr´kån-tīl] *adj* of merchants or trade.—*n* **mer´cantilism**, the growth of international trade at the end of the medieval era, marked by strict governmental regulation of the entire national economy. [Fr,—It *mercantile*—L *mercāri*, to trade.]

Mercator projection [mėr-kā´tȯr pro-jėk´sh(ȯ)n] a representation of the surface of the globe in which the meridians are parallel straight lines, and the parallels of latitude at right angles to these, the distance between the parallels of latitude increasing towards the poles. [*Mercator* (merchant), a Latin translation of the name of the cartographer Gerhard Kremer (lit shopkeeper); 1512–94.]

mercenary [mûr´sėn-år-i] *adj* working or done for money only.—*n* a soldier hired into foreign service. [L *mercēnārius*—*mercēs*, hire.]

mercerize [mûr´sėr-īz] *vt* to treat cotton so as to give it a gloss and to strengthen it. [From John *Mercer* (1791–1866), the inventor of the process.]

merchant [mûr´chånt] *n* a trader; a shopkeeper.—*adj* commercial.—*ns* **mer´chandise, merchandize** [-dīz], goods bought and sold for gain; **mer´chantman**, a trading-ship.—*pl* **mer´chantmen**. [OFr *march(e)ant*—L *mercārī*, to trade.]

Merchurochrome [mer-kyŏŏ-o-krōm] *n* trade name for a red solution of a compound of mercury, used as an antiseptic.

Mercury [mûr´kū-ri] *n* a Roman god who was the messenger of the gods; the smallest planet in the solar system and nearest the sun; **mercury**, a silvery, liquid metallic element (symbol Hg, at wt 200.8; at no 80); quicksilver.—*adj* **mercū´rial**, having the qualities of quicksilver, active, volatile in temperament; etc.—*adjs* **mercu´ric, mercu´rous**, used respectively of compounds in which mercury has a valency of 2 and a valency of 1, eg *mercuric chloride* ($HgCl_2$), corrosive sublimate, *mercurous chloride* (HgCl), calomel. [Fr,—L *Mercūrius*, prob *merx, mercis*, merchandise.]

mercy [mûr´si] *n* forbearance towards one who is in one's power; a forgiving disposition; clemency; compassion for the unfortunate.—*adj* **mer´ciful**, full of, or exercising, mercy.—*adv* **mer´cifully**.—*n* **mer´cifulness**.—*adj* **mer´ciless**, without mercy; unfeeling; cruel—*adv* **mer´cilessly**.—*ns* **mer´cilessness;—mercy killing**, killing to prevent incurable suffering.—**at the mercy of**, wholly in the power of. [Fr *merci*, grace—L *mercēs*, -*ēdis*, pay, later favour.]

mere[1] [mēr] *n* a pool or lake. [OE *mere*, sea, lake, pool; Ger *meer*, L *mare*, the sea.]

mere[2] [mēr] *adj* only what the noun indicates and nothing else.—*adj* **mere´ly**, simply; solely. [L *merus*, unmixed.]

mere[3] [mēr] *n* a boundary.—*n* **mere´stone**, a boundary stone. [OE *gemǣre*.]

meretricious [mer-ė-trish´ůs] *adj* flashy; gaudy or showily attractive (of dress, literary style, etc.).—*adv* **meretric´iously**.—*n* **meretric´iousness**. [L *meretrix, -īcis*, a harlot—*merēre*, to earn.]

merganser [mer-gan´sėr] *n* a large, fish-eating diving duck (subfamily Merginae) of N America. [L *mergus*, a diving bird, *ānser*, a goose.]

merge [mûrj] *vti* to cause to lose identity by being absorbed; to unite.—*n* **mer´ger** [L *mergêre, mersum*.]

meridian [me-rid´i-ån] *n* an imaginary circle on the earth's surface passing through the poles and any given place; (*astron*) an imaginary circle, passing through the poles of the heavens, and the zenith of the spectator, the highest point of power, etc.—*adj* **merid´ional**, pertaining to the meridian; southern—*adv* **merid´ionally**. [L *merīdiānus, merīdiōnālis*—*merīdiēs* (for *medīdiēs*), midday—*medius*, middle, *diēs*, day.]

meringue [mė-rang´] *n* a dessert topping made of a mixture of sugar and white of eggs. [Fr; origin unknown.]

merino [mė-rē´nō] *n* a breed of sheep with fine silky wool; the wool; yarn or cloth made from it. [Sp a merino sheep, also a governor.—L *mājōrīnus*, greater, also (LL) *mājōrīnus*, a headman—L *mājor*, greater.]

merit [mer´it] *n* excellence that deserves honor or reward; that which one deserves; worth value; (*pl*) rights and wrongs (of a case).—*vt* to deserve as reward or punishment.—*ns* **meritoc´racy**, a system (as an educational system) whereby intellectual achievement is rewarded by rapid advancement; leadership selected on intellectual criteria; **merit system**, a system by which appointments and promotion in the civil service are based on competence rather than political favoritism.—*adj* **meritō´rious**, deserving (in a moderate degree) of reward, honor, or praise.—*adv* **meritō´riously**.—*n* **meritō´riousness**.—[OFr *merite*—L *meritum*—*merēre, -ītum*, to obtain as a lot, to deserve.]

merle, merl [mûrl] *n* the blackbird. [Fr,—L *merula*.]

merlin [mûr´lin] *n* a species of small falcon *Falco colum barius*). [Anglo-Fr *merilun*—OFr *esmerillon*.]

merlot [mûr-lō] *n* a dry red wine made from a grape widely grown in California. [Fr].

mermaid [mûr´mād] *n* in legend, a woman with a fish's tail. [OE *mere*, lake, sea, *mægden*, maid.]

merman [mûr´man] *n* in fable, a creature with the head and torso of a man and a fish's tail.

merry [mer´i] *adj* pleasant; cheerful, noisily gay; causing laughter; lively.—*adv* **merrily**.—*ns* **merr´iment**, gaiety with laughter and noise, mirth, hilarity; **merr´iness; merr´y-an´drew**, a buffoon; one who clowns publicly; **merr´y-go-round**, a revolving ring of hobbyhorses, etc.; **merr´ymaking**, a merry entertainment; a festival. [OE *myr(i)ge*.]

mesa [mā´så] *n* a high plateau with steep sides. [Sp]

mescal [mė-skal] *n* a small cactus (*Lophophora williamsii*) that is the source of a stimulant used esp by Mexican Indians; a liquor distilled from the leaves of an agare.—*n* **mesc´aline** [-len, -lēn], a hallucinatory alkaloid from the mescal cactus.

mesdames *pl* of **madam**.

mesembryanthemum [me-zem-bri-an´-the-mum] *n* genus (*Mesebryanthemum*) of succulent plants, mostly of southern African. [Gr *mesēmbriā*, midday (*mesos*, middle, *hēmerā*, day), *anthemon*, a flower.]

mesentery [mes´ėn-tėr-i or mez´-] *n* a membrane in the cavity of the abdomen, attached to the back bone, and serving to keep the intestines in place.—*adj* **mesenteric** [-ter´ik] [Gr *mesos*, middle, *enteron*, intestine.]

mesh [mesh] *n* an opening between the threads of a net, wires of a screen, etc.; (*pl*) the threads and knots bounding the opening; trap; engagement (eg of geared wheels)—*vt* to catch in a net, ensnare.—*vt* to become engaged or interlocked, as the teeth on geared wheels. [Perh Middle Du *maesche*; cf OE *max*, net; Ger *masche*.]

meshugge [mė-shŏŏg´ė] *adj* (*inf*) crazy; obsessed; phobic; bizarre.—*ns* **meshugg´ene**, a meshugge man; **meshugg´ener**, a meshugge woman. [Yiddish.]

mesmerize [mez´mėr-īz] *vt* to hypnotize; (*loosely*) to fascinate, dominate the will or fix the attention of.—*adjs* **mesmeric** [-mer´ik] **-al**.—*ns* **mes´merizer, mes´merist; mes´merism**, hypnotism. [From Friedrich Anton or Franz *Mesmer*, a German physician (1734–1815)]

meson [mes´on, mēz´on, mēs´-, mes´-] *n* an elementary atomic particle of small mass and very short life. [From Gr *mesos*, neut *meson*, middle.]

Mesozoic [mes-o-zō´ik] *adj* of the Secondary geological era, or second of the three main divisions of geological time.—Also *n*. [Gr *mesos*, middle, *zōē*, life.]

mesquite [mes-kēt´] *n* a leguminous tree or shrub (*Prosapis fuliflora*) that forms extensive thickets in the south western US, bears pods rich in sugar, and is an important foliage food. [Sp]

mess [mes] *n* a serving, as of porridge; a number of persons who take their meals together regularly; a dish of soft, pulpy or liquid stuff; a mixture disagreeable to the sight or taste; disorder, confusion.—*vt* to supply with a mess; to make a mess of; to muddle.—*vi* to belong to a mess (with), eat one's meals (with); to potter (about).—*n* **mess hall**, a room or building where soldier's etc. regularly have meals; **mess kit**, a compact kit of nested cooking and eating utensils.—*adj* **mess´y**, involving or causing dirt or mess; confused, disordered. [OFr *mes* (Fr *mets*), a dish—L *mittěre, missum*, to send, in Low L to place.]

message [mes´ij] *n* any communication, oral or written, from one person to another; the chief idea that the writer, artist, etc. seeks to communicate in a work—*ns* **message unit**, a unit used by a telephone company to charge for calls that are timed, such as long-distance calls; **messenger**, one who carries messages or a message; a forerunner; **get the message**, (*inf*) to understand a hint. [Fr,—Low L *missāticum*—L *mittěre, missum*, to send.]

Messiah [mė-sī´a] *n* the anointed one, the Christ—also **Messī´as**.—*adj* **Messianic** [mes-i-an´ik] [Heb *māshīah*, anointed—*māshah*, to anoint.]

messieurs [mes-y_] *pl* of **Monsieur**

Messrs [mes´ėrz] *pl* of Mr.

mestiza [mes-tē´zȧ] *n* a woman who is a mestizo.

mestizo [mes-tē´zō] *n* a person of mixed European and Amerindian ancestry. [Sp *mestizo*—L *mixticius*—*miscēre*, to mix.]

met *pt, pt p* of **meet** (2).

met(a)- [met(-ȧ)-] in composition, among with; after, later; often implies change; beyond.

metabolism [met-ab´ol-izm] *n* the process in organisms by which protoplasm is formed by food and broken down into waste matter, with release of energy.—*adj* **metabol´ic**, relating to changes in metabolism. [Gr *metabolē*, change.]

metacarpal [met-a-kär´pȧl] *adj* pertaining to the part of the hand between the wrist and the fingers. [Gr *meta*, after, *karpos*, wrist.]

metacenter [met´a-sen-tėr] *n* the point of intersection of the vertical line through the center of buoyancy (also through the center of gravity) of a body floating in equilibrium and that through the center of buoyancy when equilibrium is disturbed.—*adj* **metacen´tric**. [Gr *meta, kentron*, point.]

metal [met´l] *n* any of a class of chemical elements having a peculiar luster and possessing fusibility, conductivity for heat and electricity, etc., such as gold, iron, copper, etc.; any alloy of such elements as brass, bronze et.; anything consisting of metal.—*adjs* **met´alled; metallic** [mė-tal´ik], consisting of metal; like a metal (eg in appearance, hardness, sound); **metallif´erous**, producing or yielding metal.—*vt* **met´allize**, to coat, treat, or combine with metal.—*ns* **metallizā´tion; met´alloid**, a nonmetal that can combine with a metal to form an alloy.—Also *adj* (OFr,—L *metallum*—Gr *metallon*, a mine.]

metallurgy [met´ȧ´l-ûr-ji] *n* the science of separating metals from their ores and preparing them for use by smelting, refining, etc.—*adj* **metallur´gical**,—*n* **met´allurgist**. [Gr *metallourgeein*, to mine—*metallon*, a mine, *ergon*, work.]

metamorphosis [met-a-mör´fos-is] *n* transformation; change of form, structure, substance, appearance, character, etc., by natural development; change of condition (eg of affairs); the marked change that some living beings undergo in the course of their growth, as caterpillar to butterfly, tadpole to frog, etc.;—*pl* **metamor´phoses** [-sēz].—*adj* **metamor´phic**, showing or relating to, change of form; (*geol*) formed by alteration of existing rocks by heat, pressure, etc.,—*n* **metamor´phism**, processes of transformation of rocks in the earth's crust.—*vt* **metamor´phose** [-fōz], to transform. [Gr *metamorphōsis*—*meta*, expressing change, *morphē*, form.]

metaphor [met´a-fȯr] *n* a figure of speech by which a thing is spoken of as being that which it resembles, not fundamentally, but only in a certain marked characteristic, or marked characteristics (eg *he is a tiger when roused*, when roused, he shows ferocity suggestive of that of a tiger; cf *simile*).—*adjs* **metaphor´ic, -al**.—*adv* **metaphor´ically**.—**mixed metaphor**, an expression in which two or more metaphors are confused (eg *to take arms against a sea of troubles*). [Gr *metaphorā*—*meta*, over, *pherein*, to carry.]

metaphysics [met-a-fiz´iks] *n* the branch of philosophy that seeks to explain the nature of being and reality; speculative philosophy in general.—*adj* **metaphys´ical**, pertaining to metaphysics;—*n* **metaphysician** [-ish´-ȧn], one versed in metaphysics. [From certain works of Aristotle to be studied after his physics—Gr *meta*, after, *physika*, physics—*physis*, nature.]

metastable [met´a-stā-bl] *adj* having only a slight margin of stability. [Gr *meta*, beside, and **stable** (1).]

metastasis [mė-tas´tȧ-sis] *n* the transfer, as of malignant cells, from one part of the body to another through the bloodstream.

metatarsal [met-a-tär´sȧl] *adj* belonging to the front part of the foot,—*n* **metatar´sus**, the part of the foot between the ankle and the toes. [Gr *meta*, beyond, *tarsos*, the flat of the foot.]

metathesis [met-ath´ė-sis] *n* transposition or exchange of places, esp between the sounds or letters of a word (eg OE *brid, thridda*, ME *drit*, give modern Eng *bird, third, dirt.*) [Gr,—*metatithenai*, to transpose—*meta*, in exchange, *tithenai*, to place.]

metazoan [met-a-zō´an] *n* any of a group (Metazoa) that comprises all animals having a body of cells differentiated into tissues and organs.—*adjs* **metazō´an** (also *n* **metazō´ic**.—*n sing* **met´azōon**. [Gr *meta*, after, *zōion*, animal.]

mete [mēt] *vt* to allot; to portion (out) (punishment, reward). [OE *metan*; Gr *messen*.]

metempsychosis [met-emp-si-kō´sis] *n* transmigration of the soul. [Gr,—*meta*, expressing change, *empsȳchōsis*, an animating—*en*, in, *psȳchē*, soul.]

meteor [mētyȯr] *n* a small particle of matter traveling through space, revealed to observation when it enters the earth's atmosphere, friction causing it to glow; the streak of light produced by the passage of a meteor.—*adj* **meteoric** [mē-tė-or´ik], of or relating to a meteor; transiently brilliant.—*n* **mē´teorite**, a meteor, that has reached the ground without being completely vaporized.—*n* **mēteorol´ogy**, a study of weather and climate.—*adjs* **mēteorolog´ical**.—*n* **mēteorol´ogist**. [Gr *ta meteōra*, things on high—*meta*, beyond, and the root of aeirein, to lift.]

-mēter *suffix meaning*: device for measuring (**speedometer**); meter(s) in length (**kilometer**)

meter[1] [mē´ter] *n* rhythmic pattern in verse, the measured arrangement of syllables according to stress; rhythmic pattern in music.—*adj* **met´ric, met´rical** of, relating to, or composed in meter. [OE *meter*, OFr *metre*, both from L *metrum*, Gr *metron* measurement.]

meter[2] [mē´ter] *n* the basic unit of length in the metric system, equal to 39.37 inches.—*adj* **meter-kilogram-second**, being a system of units based on the meter as the unit of length, the kilogram as the unit of mass, and the mean solar second as the unit of time; **met´ric, met´rical**, based on the meter as a standard of measurement; of, relating to, or using the metric system.—*n* **met´ricātion**, conversion of an existent system of units into the metric system.—*vt* **met´ricīze**, to express in the metric system.—*n* **metric system**, a decimal system of weights and measures based on the meter and the kilogram.

meter[3] [mē´tėr] *n* an apparatus for measuring and recording the quantity of gas, water, etc. passing through it; parking meter.—*n* **meter maid**, a woman employed by a police department to issue summons for illegal parking, jaywalking, etc. [**mete**.]

methane [mēth´ān] *n* a colorless, odorless flammable gas formed by the decomposition of vegetable matter, as in marshes.

method [meth´ȯd] *n* the mode or rule of accomplishing an end; orderly procedure; orderly arrangement; system; classification.—*adjs* **methodic** [mė-thod´ik], **-al**, arranged with method; acting with method or order.—*adv* **method´ically**.—*vt* **meth´odize**, to reduce to method; to arrange in an orderly manner.—*ns* **Meth´odism**, the principles and practice of the Methodists; **Meth´odist**, one of a sect of Christians founded Protestant by John Wesley (1703–91), noted for the strictness of its discipline.—*adjs* **methodist´ic**. [Gr *methodos-meta*, after, *hodos*, a way.]

meticulous [me-tik´ū-lus] *adj* over-careful, scrupulously careful about small details.—*adv* **metic´ulously**. [L *meticulōsus*, frightened—*metus*, fear.]

métier [mā-tyā] *n* one's calling or business; that in which one is specially skilled. [Fr,—L *ministěrium*.]

métis [mā-tē(s)] *n* one of mixed blood.

metonymy [met-on´i-mi] *n* a figure of speech in which the name of one thing is put for that of another related to it as 'the bottle' for 'drink', etc.—*adjs* **metonym´ic, -al**.—*adv* **metonym´ically**. [L,—Gr *metōnymiā*—*meta*, expressing change, *onoma*, a name.]

metric [met´rik] *See* **meter** (1,2). [Gr *metron*, measure.]

metronome [met´ro-nōm] *n* an instrument that sets a musical tempo.—*adj* **metronom´ic**. [Gr *metron*, measure, *nomos*, law.]

metropolis [me-trop´o-lis] *n* the main city, often a capital of a country, state, etc.; capital of a country; any large and important city.—*pl* **metrop´olises**.—*adj* **metropol´itan**,—*n* the primate of an ecclesiastical province. [Gr *mētropolis*—*mētēr*, mother, *polis*, a city.]

mettle [met´l] *n* ardor spirit, courage.—*adjs* **mett´led, mett´lesome**, high-spirited, ardent.—**on one's mettle**, prepared to do one's best. [From the **metal** of a blade.]

mew[1] [mū] *n* the common European gull (*Larus canus*). [OE *mǣw*; Du *meeuw*, ON *mār*, Ger *möwe*; all imit]

mew[2] [mū] *See* **meow**.

mew[3] [mū] *vt* to shut up; to confine (*often with* **up**).—*n* (*pl*) an enclosure for trained hawks; a place for hiding. [OFr *muer*—L *mutāre*, to change.]

mezzo forte [met´sō-, med´zō-för´tā] *adj, adv* rather loud. [It]

mezzo-soprano [met´sō-, med´zō-si-prä´nō] *n* a range of voice between soprano and alto; a woman having a mezzo-soprano voice. [It]

mezzotint [met´sō-tint or med´zō-tint] *n* a method of copperplate engraving, producing an even gradation of tones; an engraving produced by mezzotint. [It,—*mezzo*, middle, half, *tinto, tint*.]

mi [mē] *n* (*mus*) 3d tone of the diatonic scale.

miasma [mī-az´ma, mi-] *n* an unwholesome exhalation;—*pl* **mias´mata, mias´mas**.—*adjs* **mias´mal, miasmat´ic**. [Gr *miasma, -atos*, pollution—*miainein*, to stain.]

miaow [mē-ow´] *See* **meow**.

mica [mīka] *n* a mineral that crystallizes in thin, flexible layers, resistant to heat.—*adj* **micā´ceous** [-shůs]. [L *mīca*, a crumb.]

Micah [mī´ka] *n* (*Bible*) 33d book of the Old Testament written by the prophet Micah, displaying the character and acts of Jehovah in relation to the nations of Israel.

mice [mīs] *pl* of **mouse**.

Micheas [mī´ki-as] *n* (*Bible*) Micah in the Douay Version of the Old Testament.
Mickey Finn [mik´i fin] a drink of liquor doctored with a narcotic or purgative.
Mickey Mouse [mik´i mows] *adj* insignificant; annoyingly petty.
Micmac [mik´mak] *n* a member of an Indian people of Canada; the Algonquian language of the Micmac people. [Micmac *Migmac*, lit allies.]
micro- [mīkrō] in composition, small;—eg **microcephalic** [mī-krō-sefål-ik] *adj*, small headed (Gr *kephalē*, head); **microampere**, a millionth part of an ampere. [Gr *mīkros*, small.]
microbe [mī´krōb] *n* an organism which can be seen by the aid of a microscope, esp a disease-causing bacterium. [Fr,—Gr *mīkros*, small, *bios*, life.]
microbiological [mī-krō-bī-ō-log´i-kål] *adj* of or pertaining to microscopic living things; used in the study of such living things. [Gr *mikros*, small, and **biological**.]
Microcard [mī´kro-kard] trade name for a card having microcopies of printed data.
microchip [mīkro-chip] *n* a small wafer of silicon, etc. containing electronic circuits.—Also **chip**.
microcircuit [mīkro-sir-kit] *n* a miniature electronic circuit, esp an integrated circuit.—*n* micro-circū´itry.
micrococcus [mī-krō-kok´us] *n* a spherical bacillus. [Gr *mīkros*, small, *kokkos*, a grain.]
microcomputer [mī´kro-kom-pyōōt´er] *n* a computer in which the central processing unit is contained in one or more silicon chips.
microcopy [mī´krō-cop-ē] *n* a reduce photographic copy of graphic matter.
microcosm [mīkrō-kozm] *n* a little universe or world.—*adjs* **microcos´mic**. [Gr *mīkros*, little, *kosmos*, world.]
microdot [mī´kro-dot] *n* a microcopy reduced to the size of a dot.
microelectronics [mī´kro-el-ek-tron´iks] *npl* a branch of electronics concerned with microcircuits.
microfauna [mī´krō-fön-å] *n* minute animals, esp those invisible to the naked eye; the fauna of a strictly localized environment.
microfiche [mī´krō-fesh] *n* a sheet of microfilm containing pages of printed manner.—Also **film card**.
microfilm [mī´krō-film] *n* a roll of film on which documents are photographed in a reduced size for convenience.—*vti* to photograph on microfilm. [Gr *mīkros*, small **film**.]
micrograph [mi´krō-graf] a pictorial reproduction of an object as seen through the microscope. [Gr *mīkros*, little, *graphein*, to write.]
microgroove [mī´kro-grōōv] *n* the fine groove of a long-playing phonograph record. [Gr *mīkros*, small, and **groove**.]
micrometer[1] [mī-krom´ė-tėr] *n* an instrument for measuring minute distances or angles.—*adjs* **micromet´ric, -al**. [Gr *mīkros*, little, *metron*, measure.]
micrometer[2] *See* **micron**.
micromicron [mī´kro-mī´krōn] in a millionth of a millionth part. [Gr *mīkros*, small.]
microminiaturisation [mī-krō-min´i-(å)chůr-iz-ā-shỏn] *n* reduction to extremely small size. [Gr *mīkros*, small, and **miniature**.]
micron [mī´kron] *n* unit of length, 10^{-6} metres.—Also **micrometer** (%3m). [Gr *mīkros*, small.]
microorganism [mīkrō-ör´gan-izm] *n* a very small living animal or plant esp any of the bacteria, protozoans, viruses, etc. [Gr *mikros*, small, *organon*, instrument.]
microphone [mī´kro-fōn] *n* an instrument for transforming sound waves into electric signals.—Also (*inf*) **mike**. [Gr *mīkros*, small, *phōnē*, voice.]
microprint [mī´krō-print] *n* a greatly reduced photocopy of print, readable by a magnifying device.
microprocessor [mīk-rō-prō´ses-ỏr] *n* a computer processor contained on an integrated-circuit chip. [Gr *mīkros*, small, **processor**.]
micropyle [mī´krō-pīl] *n* (*bot*) a tiny opening in the integument at the apex of an ovule, through which the pollen tube usually enters; an area on the surface of an egg through which a sperm enters. [Gr *mīkros*, small, *pylē*, a gate.]
microscope [mīkrō-skōp] *n* an optical instrument for making magnified images of minute objects by means of a lens or lenses.—*adjs* **microscop´ic, -al**, pertaining to a microscope; visible only by the aid of a microscope;—*adv* **microscop´ically**.—*n* **mi´croscopy**, use of the microscope. [Gr *mikros*, little, *skopeein*, to look at.]
microsurgery [mī´krō-sur´jer-e] *n* minute surgical dissection or manipulation of individual cells under a microscope.
microwave [mī´krō-wāv] *n* a radio wave between 1 and 100 centimeters in length.—*n* **microwave oven**, an oven in which food is cooked by the heat produced as a result of microwave penetration of the food. [Gr *mīkros*, small, and **wave**.]
micturate [mik´cher-rāt, mik´te-] *vi* to urinate.—*n* **mic´turi´tion**.
mid [mid] *adj* middle;—*prep* amid.—*n* **mid´day**, the middle of the day,—*adj* **mid´land**, inland.—*n* the interior of a country.—*n* **mid´night**, twelve o'clock at night.—*adj* being at midnight; very dark.—*n* **mid´shipman**, a student naval officer.—*adv* **mid´ships**.—*ns* **mid´summer**, the middle of summer; the summer solstice about June 21; **mid´way**, that part of a fair where sideshows, etc. are located.—*adj* being in the middle of the way or distance.—*adv* halfway.—*n* **mid´winter**, the middle of winter; the winter solstice (December 21 or 22). [OE **midd**; cf Ger *mitte*, L *medius* Gr *mesos*.]
midden [mid´ėn] *n* a refuse heap. [Scand, as Dan *mödding*—*mög*, dung.]
middle [mid´l] *adj* halfway between two given points, times, etc.; intermediate; intervening.—*n* the middle point or part; something intermediate, waist.—*adj* **midd´ling**, of middle rate, state, size, or quality; second-rate; moderate.—*adv* moderately.—**middle age**, the time between youth and old age; **Middle Ages**, the period of European history between about 500 to 1500 AD; **Middle America**, the midwestern section of the US; the traditional and conservative element of the middle class; **midd´lebrow**, a moderately intellectual person.—Also *adj*,—*ns* **middle C**, (*mus*) the note written on the first ledger line below the treble staff and the first above the bass staff; **middle class**, the social class comprising business and professional people, bureaucrats, and some farmers and skilled workers sharing common aspirations and values; a social class between the very rich and the poorer working class; **Middle East**, the area from Afghanistan to Egypt, including the Arabian Peninsula and eastern Turkey; the Near East, excluding the Balkans; **middle ear**, the sound-conducting part of the ear which is separated from the outer ear by the eardrum; **Middle English**, the English language from about 100 to about 1500 AD; **midd´leman**, a dealer who intervenes between producer and consumer; an agent; **middle school**, in some school systems, a school with usu. grades 5 to 8; **middle term**, (*logic*) the term of a syllogism which appears in both premises but not in the conclusion; **middleweight**, weighing 154–160 lbs; an amateur boxer weighing 157–165 lbs; a wrestler weighing usu. 172–192 lbs.; **Middle West**, region of north central US between the Rocky Mountains and the eastern border of Ohio.—**middle-of-the-road**, avoiding extremes, esp political extremes. [OE *middel*—*mid*; Du *middel*, Ger *mittel*.]
midge [mij] *n* any small gnat or fly.—*n* **midg´et**, a very small person; something very small of its kind. [OE *mycg(e)*; Ger *mücke*.]
midi [mid´i] *adj* of a skirt or dress, having the hemline about mid-calf. Cf **maxi, mini**.
midriff [mid´rif] *n* the middle part of the torso between the abdomen and the chest. [OE *mid*, middle, *hrif*, the belly.]
midst [midst] *n* middle.—*prep* amidst. [ME *middes*, with excrescent *t*.]
midwife [mid´wīf] *n* a woman who assists women in childbirth;—*pl* **midwives** [mid´wīvz].—*n* **mid´wifery** [-wif-ė-ri, -if-ri, -wīf-ri], art or practice of a midwife. [OE *mid*, with (Ger *mit*, Gr *meta*), *wīf*, woman.]
mien [mēn] *n* the air or look, expression of face, manner, bearing. [Perh from obs *n demean*—**demean** (2); influenced by Fr *mine*.]
might[1] [mīt] *ptp* of **may** (1).
might[2] [mīt] *n* power, strength; vigor—*adj* **might´y**, having great power; very large; (*Bible*) wonderful, miraculous.—*adj* (*inf*) very.—*adv* **might´ily**.—*n* **might´iness**, power; greatness. [OE *miht, mecht*; Ger *macht*; cf **may** (1).]
mignonette [min-yo-net´] *n* a sweet-scented garden plant (genus *Reseda*) with spikes of greenish-yellow flowers. [Fr, fem dim of *mignon*, daintily small.]
migraine [mē-grān´] *n* an intense, periodic headache, usu. limited to one side of the head.
migrate [mī´grāt] *vi* to settle in another country or region; to move to another region with the change in season, as many birds.—*adj* **mī´gratory**, migrating or accustomed to migrate; wandering.—*n* **migrā´tion**. [L *migrāre*, *-ātum*.]
mikado [mi-kä´dō] *n* (*obs*) an emperor of Japan. [Jap 'exalted gate'.]
Mike [mīk] *n* communication code word for the letter *m*.
mike [mīk] *n*(*inf*) microphone. [Abbrev of **microphone**.]
mil [mil] *n* a unit of length, .001 of an inch. [L *mīlle*, 1000.]
milch [milk, milch, milks] *adj* kept for milking (*milch cows*). [OE *milce*; cf **milk**.]
mild [mīld] *adj* gentle in temper and disposition; not sharp or bitter; acting gently; gently and pleasantly affecting the senses, temperate, soft—*adv* **mild´ly**.—*n* **mild´ness**. [OE *milde*, mild; cf Ger *mild*, ON *mildr*, gracious.]
mildew [mil´dū] *n* a fungus that attacks some plants or appears on damp cloth, etc. as a whitish coating.—*vti* to affect or be affected with mildew. [OE *meledēaw, mildēaw*, from a lost word for honey, and *dēaw*, dew.]
mile [mīl] *n* a unit of linear measure equal to 5,280 feet; the nautical mile is 6,076.12 feet.—*ns* **mile´age**, an allowance per mile for traveling expenses; total miles traveled; the average number of miles that can be traveled, as per gallon of fuel. **mile´stone**, a stone set up to mark the distance of a mile; a significant event. [OE *mīl*—L *mīlia*, thousands.]
miliary [mil´yȧr-i] *adj* made up of many small projections or lesions. [L *milium*, millet.]
milieu [mēl-y_] *n* environment, esp social setting. [Fr, middle.]
militant [mil´i-tȧnt] *adj* fighting; ready to fight, esp for some cause; combative;—Also *n* **mil´itancy**.—*adv* **mil´itantly**.—*vt* **mil´itarize**, to equip and prepare for war.—*ns* **militarizā´tion; mil´itarism**, military spirit; a policy of aggressive military preparedness.—*adj* **mil´itary**, pertaining to soldiers or to warfare; warlike.—*n* soldiery; the army.—*vi* **mil´itate**, to contend; **military police**, soldiers assigned to carry on police duties for the army. [L *mīles, -itis*, a soldier, *mīlitāris*, military, *mīlitāre*, to serve as a soldier.]
militia [milish´a] *n* an army composed of civilians called out in time of emergency.—*n* **milit´iaman**. [L *mīlitia*, military service or force.]
milk [milk] *vt* to squeeze or draw milk from: to extract juice, poison, money,

etc., from; to exploit.—*n* a white liquid secreted by female mammals for the nourishment of their young; a milk-like juice or preparation.—*ns* **milk´er**, one who milks; a machine for milking cows; a cow that gives milk; **milk´ fē´ver**, a fever of cows, sheep, or goats accompanying the secretion of milk shortly after parturition.—*adj* **milk´y**, made of, full of, like or yielding milk;—*ns* **milk´iness; milk´ing**, the act of drawing milk from cows, etc.; **milk glass**, a nearly opaque whitish glass; **milk´maid**, a girl or woman who milks cows or works in a dairy; **milk´man**, a man who sells or delivers milk for a dairy; **milk of magnesia**, a milky white suspension of magnesium hydroxide in water, used as a laxative and antacid; **milk punch**, a beverage made of milk and rum or whisky; **milk shake**, a drink of milk, flavoring, and ice cream, shaken until frothy; **milk´sop**, an unmanly man; **milk´tooth**, one of the first, temporary teeth of a mammal;—**milk-and-water**, weak; insipid; **Milk´y Way**, (*astron*), the Galaxy. [OE *milc, meolc*, milk; Ger *milch*, milk; L *mulgēre*, to milk.]

milium [mil´i-um] *n* a whitish lump in the skin due to a blocked duct in an oil gland.

Milium [mil´i-um] *n* a trade name for metal-insulated fabric used for lining outer clothing and curtains.

mill [mil] *n* a machine for grinding by crushing between hard, rough surfaces; a building where grain is ground; one where manufacture of some kind is carried on.—*vt* to grind; to press or stamp in a mill; to put ridges and furrows on the rim of, as coin.—*vi* (of cattle or a crowd) to move around confusedly.—*ns* **mill´dam, mill´pond**, a dam or pond to hold water for driving a mill; **mill´er**, one who owns or works a mill; **mill´ing**, ridges and furrows on the rim of a coin; **mill´race**, the current of water that turns a mill-wheel, or the channel in which it runs; **mill´stone**, one of the two stones used in a mill for grinding corn; an oppressive burden; **mill´stream**, water flowing in a millrace; **mill´wheel**, the waterwheel used for driving a mill; **mill´wright**, a worker who builds and repairs mills. [OE *myln*—L *mola*, a mill—*molĕre*, to grind.]

millennium [mil-en´i-um] *n* a thousand years; the thousand years mentioned in *Revelation* XX between the second coming of Christ, when the righteous are raised from the dead, and the time when the wicked are raised; a coming golden age;—*pl* **millenn´ia**.—*adj* **millenā´rian**, pertaining to the millennium.—*n* one believing in the millennium.—*adj* **mill´enary**, consisting of a thousand.—*n* a thousand years; a thousandth anniversary.—*adj* **millenn´ial**, of or relating to a millennium. [L *mīlle*, 1000, *annus*, a year.]

millesimal [mil-es´im-ȧl] *adj* thousandth; consisting of thousandth parts.—Also *n*.—*adv* **milles´imally**. [L *millēsimus*—*mille*, a thousand.]

millet [mil´et] *n* a food-grain. [Fr *millet*—L *milium*.]

milliard [mil´yȧrd, mil´i-ärd] *n* in England, France and Germany, the term for one billion, the number one followed by nine zeros; 1,000,000,000. [Fr—L *mille*, a thousand.]

milli- [mil´i-] in composition, in names of units a thousandth part, as *ns* **milligram, millimeter**, etc., a thousandth part of a gram, meter etc. [L *mille*, a thousand.]

millimicro- [mil´i-mī´kro] in composition, a billionth, as **millimicrosecond**, a billionth of a second. [**milli-, micro-**.]

milliner [mil´in-ėr] *n* one who makes or sells women's headgear, trimmings, etc.—*n* **mill´inery**, the articles made or sold by milliners; the work or business of a milliner. [Prob orig *Milaner*, a trader in Milan wares, esp silks and ribbons.]

million [mill´yȯn] *n* a thousand thousands (1,000,000); a very great number.—*n* **mill´ionaire** [-ār], a man worth a million of money or more or enormously rich.—*adj* **mill´ionary**, pertaining to, or consisting of, millions.—*adj, n* **mill´ionth**, the ten hundred thousandth.—**the million**, the great body of the people generally. [Fr,—Low L *mīlliō, -ōnis*—L *mille*, 1000.]

millipede [mil´i-pēd] *n* a myriapod. [*mīllepeda—mīlle*, a thousand, *pēs, pedis*, a foot.]

mime [mīm] *n* any dramatic representation consisting of action without words; a mimic or pantomimist.—*adjs* **mimet´ic**, apt to imitate; characterized by imitation.—*n* **mimic** [mim´ik], one who imitates, esp an actor skilled in mimicry.—*adj* imitative; mock or sham.—*vt* to imitate, esp in ridicule; to ape;—*prp* **mim´icking**;; *ptp* **mim´icked**.—*n* **mim´icry** [-kri], practice, art, or way of mimicking. [Gr *mīmos*.]

mimosa [mim-ō´za] *n* a genus (*mimosa*) of leguminous trees or shrubs growing in warm regions having fragrant spikes of yellow flowers. [Gr *mīmos*, a mimic.]

minaret [mi´-när-et´] *n* a high, slender tower on a mosque, from which the call to prayer is sounded. [Ar *manār, manārat*, lighthouse—*nār*, fire.]

minatory [min´a-tȯr-i] *adj* menacing. [L *minārī, -ātus*, to threaten.]

mince [mins] *vt* to cut up (meat etc.) into small pieces, to diminish or suppress a part of (one's meaning) in speaking;—*vi* to speak or act with affected daintiness.—*prp* **minc´ing**; *ptp* **minced** [minst].—*ns*. **mince´meat**, a mixture of chopped apples, raisins etc. used as a filling for pie.—*adj* **minc´ing**, speaking or walking with affected nicety.—*adv* **minc´ingly**. [OFr *mincier, minchier*—L *minūtus*; cf **minute**.]

mind [mīnd] *n* the faculty by which we think, etc.; the understanding; the whole spiritual nature; memory; intellect; reason; opinion; sanity.—*vt* to pay attention to; to obey; to take care of; to be careful about; to care about; object to.—*vi* to pay attention; to be obedient; to be careful, object.—*adjs* **mind-blowing**, psychedelic; causing a similar mental state; overwhelming; **mind-expanding**, causing an exposure of normally repressed psychic elements; psychedelic.—*adjs* **mind´ed**, having a mind (esp in compounds—eg *small-, narrow-minded*); disposed; **mind´ful**, bearing in mind (*with* **of**); attentive; observant.—*adv* **mind´less**, without mind; stupid.—**blow one's mind** (*slang*), to undergo hallucinations, etc. as from psychedic drugs; **make up one's mind**, to decide; **never mind**, do not concern yourself; **of one mind**, agreed; **of, in two minds**, uncertain (what to think or do); **on one's mind**, filling one's thoughts; worrying one; **out of one's mind**, frantic; **to one's mind**, in exact accordance with one's wishes. [OE *gemynd—munan*, to think; L *mens*, the mind.]

mine[1] [mīn] *pron* the possessive (*gen*) case of I (eg *the watch is mine*).—Also *possessive adj* (now used without noun—eg *this is John's watch, that is mine*). [OE *mīn*.]

mine[2] [mīn] *n* a place from which metals, etc., are dug; an excavation dug under a fortification to blow it up; an explosive charge for this purpose; a submerged or floating charge of explosives to destroy ships; a rich source.—*vt* to excavate, make passages in or under; to obtain by excavation; to beset with, or destroy by, mines.—*vi* to dig or work a mine.—*ns* **mī´ner**, one who works in a mine; **mine´layer**, vessel for laying mines; **mine´sweeper**, a vessel for removing mines. [Fr *mine*.]

mineral [min´ėr-ȧl] *n* an inorganic substance, found naturally in the earth; any substance neither vegetable nor animal.—*adj* of or containing minerals.—*adj* relating to, or having the nature of, minerals.—*vt* **min´eralize**, to impregnate with mineral matter.—*ns* **mineralizā´tion; mineral´ogy**, the science of minerals.—*adj* **mineralog´ical**.—*adv* **mineralog´ically**.—*n* **mineral´ogist**, one versed in mineralogy.—*ns* **mineral jelly**, petrolatum; **mineral kingdom**, one of the three great groups of natural objects that includes inorganic objects; **mineral oil**, an oil of mineral origin, esp refined petroleum oil; **mineral water**, water impregnated with mineral salts or gases; **mineral wool**, a lightweight vitreous fibrous material used in heat and sound insulation. [Fr,—*miner*, to mine; cf **mine** (2).]

minestrone [min-i-strōn´ē] *n* a thick vegetable soup with pieces of pasta, etc. [It]

Ming [ming] *adj* of, pertaining to, produced during, the *Ming* dynasty in Chinese history (1368–1643), famous for works of art.

mingle [ming´gl] *vti* to mix; to join in mutual intercourse.—*ns* **ming´ler, ming´ling**, mixture; a mixing or blending together. [OE *mengan*; Ger *mengen*.]

mini- [min´i-] in composition, small (abbrev of **miniature**) as in eg the following; **minicar**, a subcompact; **miniskirt**, a skirt whose hemline is well above the knees.

miniature [min´ē-a-chûr, min´i-chûr] *n* a painting on a very small scale; a small or reduced copy of anything.—*adj* on a small scale, minute.—*vt* **min´iaturize**, much to reduce the size of (electronic equipment).—*n* **miniaturiz´ation**. [It *miniatura*—L *minium*, red lead; meaning affected by association with L *minor*, less, smaller, etc.]

minim [min´im] *n* (*mus*) a half note; (apothecaries' measure) one-sixtieth of a fluid dram.—*adj* **min´imal**, of least, or of least possible, size, amount, or degree.—*vt* **min´imize**, to reduce to or estimate at a minimum.—*n* **min´imum**, the least number, quantity, or degree possible; the lowest degree or print reached.—*pl* **min´ima**.—*adj* **min´imum; minimum wage**, the lowest wage permitted by law. [L *minimus*, the smallest.]

minion [min´yȯn] *n* a favorite, esp term of contempt for a servile dependent; a subordinate official. [Fr *mignon*, a darling.]

minister [min´is-tėr] *n* a clergyman serving a church; pastor; the responsible head of a department of government; the representative of a government at a foreign country.—*vi* to serve as a minister in a church; to give help (to).—*adj* **ministē´rial**, pertaining to a ministry or minister.—*adv* **ministē´rially**.—*adj* **min´istrant**, administering; attendant.—*n* **ministrā´tion**, the act or process of ministering.—*n* **min´istry**, act of ministering; office or duties of a pastor; the clergy; the department under a ministry of government. [L,—*minor*, less.]

miniver [min´i-vėr] *n* white fur worn by medieval nobles. [OFr—*menu*, small (L *minūtus*), *vair*, fur.]

mink [mingk] *n* any of several carnivorous weasel like mammals (genus *Mustela*) living on land and in water, valued for its durable, soft fur. [Perh from Swed *mänk*.]

minnow [min´ō] *n* a very small freshwater fish commonly used as bait. [OE *myne*.]

minor [mī´nȯr] *adj* lesser in size, importance, degree, bulk, etc.; (*mus*) lower than the corresponding major by a semitone.—*n* a person under full legal age; (*education*) a secondary field of study.—*vi* (*education*) to have a secondary field of study (in).—*ns* **minor´ity**, the state of being under age; the smaller number; a racial, religious, or political group that differs from the larger, controlling group; **minor league**, a league of professional clubs in a sport (as baseball or football) other than the recognized major leagues; **minor premise**, (*logic*) the premise of a syllogism that introduces the minor term; **minor suit**, either of two bridge suits of inferior scoring value; **minor term**, (*logic*) the term in syllogism that forms the subject of the conclusion. [L *minor*, less.]

minotaur [min´ō-tör] *n* a fabulous bull-headed monster, to whom human sacrifices were made in a labyrinth built for Minos, King of Crete. [Gr *Mīnōtauros—Mīnōs* and *tauros*, a bull.]
minstrel [min´strėl] *n* a traveling singer of the Middle Ages; a member of a comic variety show in which the performers blacken their faces.—*ns* **minstrel show**, a troupe of performers; **min´strelsy**, the art or occupation of a minstrel; music; a company of minstrels; a collection of songs. [OFr *menestrel*—L *ministeriālis—minister*, attendant.]
mint[1] [mint] *n* the place where money is coined by government; a place where anything is invented or made; a vast sum (of money).—*vt* to coin; to invent.—*ns* **mint´age**, coining; coinage; duty for coining; **mint´er**, one who mints or coins; an inventor. [OE *mynet*, money—L *monēta*. See **money**.]
mint[2] [mint] *n* any of a large genus of aromatic plants producing highly odoriferous oil. [OFr *minte*—L *mentha*—Gr *minthē*.]
minuend [min´ū-end] *n* the number from which another is to be subtracted. [L *minuendum—minuĕre*, to lessen.]
minuet [min-ū-et´] *n* a slow, graceful dance with short steps; the music for such a dance. [Fr *menuet—menu*, small—L *minūtus*, small.]
minus [mī´nus] *prep* less (*four minus two*); (*inf*) without (*minus a toe*).—*adj* involving subtraction; negative; less than (*a grade of A minus*).—*n* a sign (-), indicating subtraction or negative quantity.—Also **minus sign**.—*n* **minuscule** [-us´kūl], a cursive script originated by the monks in the 7th–9th centuries; any lowercase letter. [L, *neuter* or *minor*, less.]
minute[1] [mīn-ūt´] *adj* extremely small; attentive to small things; exact.—*adv* **minute´ly**.—*n* **minute´ness**. [L *minūtus*, pt p of *minuĕre*, to lessen.]
minute[2] [min´it] *n* the sixtieth part of an hour; the sixtieth part of a degree; an indefinitely small space of time; (*pl*) an official record of a meeting.—*vt* to make a brief jotting or note of anything.—*ns* **minute hand**, the hand that indicates the minutes on a clock or watch; **min´uteman´**, a member of the American citizen army at the time of the Revolution; **minute steak**, a small, thin steak that can be cooked quickly.—**the minute that**, just as soon as. [Same word as above.]
minutiae [mi-nū´shi-ē] *n pl* small or unimportant details. [L, pl of *minūtia*, smallness.]
minx [mingks] *n* a pert young girl.
minyan [min´yȧn] *n* (*Judaism*) the ten male Jews required for a religious service.—*pl* **minyan´in** [min-yän´in]. [Heb]
Miocene [mī´o-sēn] *adj* of the period of the Tertiary geological era preceding the Pliocene. [Gr *meiōn*, less, *kainos*, recent.]
miracle [mir´ȧ-kl] *n* a wonder; supernatural event.—*adj* **mirac´ulous** [-ak´ū-lus], of the nature of a miracle; able to perform miracles.—*adv* **mirac´ulously**.—*n* **mirac´ulousness**.—*ns* **miracle drug**, a drug that causes a dramatic improvement in a patient's condition; **miracle play**, a medieval drama based on episodes from the life of a saint or martyr; mystery play. [Fr,—L *mīrāculum—mīrārī, -ātus*, to wonder at.]
mirage [mi-räzh´] *n* an optical illusion in which a distant object seems to be nearby. [Fr—*mirer*, to look at—L *mīrārī*, to wonder at.]
Miranda [mir-and´ȧ] *adj* of, relating to, or upholding the legal rights of a person suspected of a crime to remain silent and to be represented by a lawyer, esp during questioning by the police.—*vt* **mirand´ize**, (*slang*) to read a suspect his rights. [from a Supreme Court ruling in the case of Ernesto *Miranda* in 1967.]
mire [mīr] *n* an area of wet, soggy ground; deep mud.—*vt* to plunge and fix in mire; to soil with mud.—*vi* to sink in mud.—*adj* **mī´ry**. [ON *mȳrr*, bog.]
mirror [mir´ȯr] *n* a smooth reflecting surface; a faithful representation; an example, good or bad.—*vt* to reflect as in a mirror;—*pr p* **mirr´oring**; *pt p* **mirr´ored**. [OFr *mireor, mirour*—L *mīrārī, -ātus*, to wonder at.]
mirth [mûrth] *n* gaiety esp with laughter.—*adj* **mirth´ful**, full of mirth, merry, jovial.—*adv* **mirth´fully**.—*n* **mirth´fulness**.—*adj* **mirth´less**, joyless, cheerless. [OE *myrgth—myrige*, merry.]
mis- prefix meaning; wrong(ly); bad(ly); no, not. [OE *mis-*, of Gmc origin; OFr *mes-* (L *minus*, neut of *minor*, less).]
misadventure [mis-ad-vent´-chu̇r] *n* bad luck; mishap. [**mis-** + **adventure**.]
misadvise [mis-ad-vīz´] *vt* to give bad advice to.—*adj* **misadvised´**, ill-advised. [**mis** + **advise**.]
misalliance [mis-a-lī´ȧns] *n* an unsuitable alliance, esp marriage. [After Fre *mésalliance*.]
misanthrope [mis´ȧn-thrōp] *n* a hater of mankind.—*adjs* **misanthrop´ic**, hating or distrusting mankind.—*adv* **misanthrop´ically**.—*n* **misan´thropy**. [Gr *mīsanthrōpos—mīseein*, to hate, *anthrōpos*, a man.]
misapply [mis-a-plī´] *vt* to use for a wrong purpose.—*n* **misapplication**. [**mis-** + **apply**.]
misapprehend [mis-ap-rė-hend´] *vt* to misunderstand.—*n* **misapprehen´sion**. [**mis-** + **apprehend**.]
misappropriate [mis-a-prō´pri-āt] *vt* to use (another's money or goods) wrongly or dishonestly.—*n* **misappropriā´tion**. [**mis-** + **appropriate**.]
misbecome [mis-bi-kum´] *vt* to be unbecoming or unsuitable to. [**mis-** + **become**.]
misbegotten [mis-bi-got´n] *adj* illegitimate. [**mis** + pt p of **beget**.]
misbehave [mis-bi-hāv´] *vi* to behave wrongly or improperly.—*n* **misbehav´iour**. [**mis-** + **behave**.]
misbelieve [mis-bi-lēv´] *vt* to believe wrongly or falsely.—*ns* **misbelief´**, belief in false doctrine; **misbeliev´er**. [**mis-** + **believe**.]
miscalculate [mis-kal´kū-lāt] *vti* to calculate wrongly.—*n* **miscalculā´tion**. [**mis** + **calculate**.]
miscall [mis-köl´] *vt* to call by a wrong name; to misname. [**mis-** + **call**.]
miscarriage [mis-kar´ij] *n* an act of miscarrying; the act of expelling a foetus prematurely and accidentally.—*vi* **miscarr´y**, to be unsuccessful; to fail of the intended effect; to bring forth prematurely. [**mis-** + **carriage, carry**.]
miscegenation [mis-ė-jėn-ā´sh(ȯ)n] *n* marriage or sexual relations between a man and woman of different races. [L *miscēre*, to mix, *genus*, race.]
miscellaneous [mis-ėl-ān´i-us] *adj* consisting of several kinds of qualities.—*adv* **miscellān´eously**,—*ns* **miscellān´eousness; miscell´any**, a mixture of various kinds; a collection of writings on different subjects or by different authors; **miscell´anist**, a writer of miscellanies. [L *miscellāneus—miscēre*, to mix.]
mischance [mis-chäns´] *n* bad luck; mishap. [OFr *mescheance*.]
mischief [mis´chif] *n* damage; source of harm of annoyance; action or conduct that causes trivial annoyance.—*adj* **mischievous** [mis´chi-vus], harmful, prankish.—*adv* **mis´-chievously**.—*ns* **mis´chievousness**. [OFr *meschef*, from **mis-** + *chef*—L *caput*, the head.]
misch metal [mish´met-l] *n* an alloy of cerium with rare earth metals used esp in tracer bullets etc. [Ger *mischen*, to mix + **metal**.]
miscible [mis´i-bl] *adj* that may be mixed.—*n* **miscibil´ity**. [Fr,—L *miscēre*, to mix.]
misconceive [mis-kon-sēv´] *vti* to misunderstand.—*n* **misconcep´tion**, an erroneous idea. [**mis-** + **conceive**.]
misconduct [mis-kon´dukt] *n* dishonest management; improper behaviour.—*vt* **misconduct´**. [**mis-** + **conduct**.]
misconstrue [mis-kon-strōō´ or -koṅ] *vt* to misinterpret.—*n* **misconstruc´tion**. [**mis-** + **construe**.]
miscount [mis-kownt´] *vti* to count incorrectly.—*n* an incorrect count. [**mis-** + **count** (2).]
miscreant [mis´kri-ȧnt] *adj* villainous; evil.—*n* a villain. [OFr *mescreant*—**mis-** + L *crēdens, -entis*, pr p of *crēdĕre*, to believe.]
misdate [mis-dāt´] *vt* to date wrongly.—*n* a wrong date. [**mis-** + **date** (1).]
misdeal [mis-dēl´] *n* a wrong deal.—*vti* to deal (playing cards) wrongly. [**mis** + **deal**.]
misdeed [mis-dēd´] *n* a wrong or wicked act; crime; sin, etc. [OE *misdǣd*—**mis-** + **deed**.]
misdemean´our [mis-di-mēn-´er] *n* (law) any minor offense bringing a lesser punishment than a felony. [**mis-** + **demean** (1).]
misdirect [mis-di-rekt´, -dī-] *vt* to direct wrongly.—*n* **misdirec´tion**. [**mis-** + **direct**.]
misdoubt [mis-dowt´] *vt* to doubt the reality or truth of; to suspect; to fear (that). [**mis-** + **doubt**.]
misemploy [mis-em-ploi´] *vt* to misuse. [**mis-** + **employ**.]
mise-en-scène [mēz ā sān] scenery and properties, stage setting; the setting, circumstances of an event. [Fr]
miser [mī´zėr] *n* a greedy, stingy person who hoards money for its own sake.—*adj* **mī´serly**, avaricious. [L *miser*, wretched.]
miserable [miz´ėr-ȧ-bl] *adj* wretched; causing misery; bad, inadequate; pitiable.—*n* **mis´erableness**.—*adv* **mis´erably**. [Fr,—L *miserābilis—miser*.]
miserere [miz-e-rā´re] *n* Psalm 51, from its first words, 'Miserere mei, Domine'; a musical composition adapted to this psalm. [L, 2nd pers sing imper of *miserērī*, to have mercy, to pity—*miser*, wretched.]
misery [mis´ėr-i] *n* wretchedness; extreme pain or sorrow; a cause of such suffering. [OFr,—L *miseria—miser*, wretched.]
misfeasance [mis-fēz´ȧns] *n* (*law*) trespass, esp the doing of a lawful act in a wrongful manner. [OFr *mesfaisance—mes-*, wrong, and *faisance* (L *facĕre*, to do).]
misfire [mis-fīr´] *vi* to fail to explode or ignite; to produce no effect, achieve no success.—*n* such a failure. [**mis-** + **fire**.]
misfit [mis´fit] *n* a thing that fits badly; a maladjusted person.—Also *vti*. [**mis-** + **fit** (1).]
misfortune [mis-för´tūn, -chu̇n] *n* ill fortune; trouble; a calamity. [**mis-** + **fortune**.]
misgive [mis-giv´] *vti* to give or cause fear or doubt.—*n* **misgiv´ing**, a feeling of apprehension and mistrust. [**mis-** + **give**.]
misgovern [mis-guv´ėrn] *vt* to govern badly.—*n* **misgov´ernment**. [**mis-** + **govern**.]
misguide [mis-gīd´] *vt* to lead astray.—*n* **misguid´ance**. [**mis-** + **guide**.]
mishandle [mis-han´dl] *vt* to handle unskilfully to abuse. [**mis-** + **handle**.]
mishap [mis´hap] *n* an unlucky accident. [**mis-** + **hap**.]
mishear [mis-hēr´] *vt* to hear incorrectly. [**mis-** + **hear**.]
misinform [mis-in-förm´] *vt* to supply with wrong information.—*ns* **misinformā´tion**. [**mis** + **inform**.]
misinterpret [mis-in-tėr´pret] *vt* to understand, explain wrongly.—*ns* **misinterpretā´tion**. [**mis-** + **interpret**.]
misjudge [mis-juj´] *vti* to judge wrongly.—*n* **misjudg´ment**. [**mis-** + **judge**.]
mislay [mis-lā´] *vt* to lay in a place not remembered; to put down or install improperly.—*pt p* **mislaid´**. [**mis-** + **lay** (2).]
mislead [mis-lēd´] *vt* to lead astray; to deceive; to lead into wrongdoing.—*pt, pt p* **misled´**.—*adj* **mislead´ing**, deceptive. [**mis-** + **lead**, vb.]

mismanage [mis-man´ij] *vt* manage badly or dishonestly —*n* **misman´agement**. [**mis-** + **manage**.]
misname [mis-nām´] *vt* to give an appropriate name to. [**mis-** + **name**.]
misnomer [mis-nō´mėr] *n* a wrong or unsuitable name. [OFr, from **mis-** + *nommer*—L *nōmināre*, to name.]
miso [mē´sō] *n* a high-protein food paste based on soybeans ranging in taste from very salty to very sweet. [Jap.]
misogynist [mis-oj´i-nist] *n* a woman hater.—*n* **misog´yny**. [Gr *mīseein*, to hate, *gynē*, a woman.]
misplace [mis-plās´] *vt* to put in a wrong place; to set (eg trust, affection) on an unworthy object.—*n* **misplace´ment**. [**mis-** + **place**.]
misplay [mis-plā´] *vti* to play wrongly or badly, as in games or sports.—*n* a bad or wrong play. [**mis-** + **play**.]
misprint [mis-print´] *vt* to print wrongly.—*n* a mistake in printing. [**mis-** + **print**.]
misprision [mis-prizh´(ȯ)n] *n* misconduct or neglect of duty by a public official. [OFr **mis** + Low L *prēnsiō, -ōnis*—L *praehendĕre*, to take.]
misprize [mis-prīz´] *vt* to hold in contempt; to undervalue. [OFr, **mis** + Low L *prēnsiō, -ōnis*—*praehendĕre*, to take.]
mispronounce [mis-pro-nowns´] *vt* to pronounce wrongly.—*n* **mispronunciā´tion** [-nun-]. [**mis-** + **pronounce**.]
misquote [mis-kwōt´] *vt* to quote wrongly.—*n* **misquotā´tion**, an incorrect quotation. [**mis-** + **quotation**.]
misread [mis-rēd´] *vt* to read wrongly esp so as to misinterpret.—*n* **misreading**. [**mis-** + **read**.]
misrepresent [mis-rep-rė-zent´] *vt* to represent falsely; to give an untrue idea of.—*n* **misrepresentā´tion**.—*adj* **misrepresent´ative**, not representative (of), tending to misrepresent. [**mis-** + **represent**.]
misrule [mis-rōōl´] *n* misgovernment.—*vt* to rule badly. [**mis-** + **rule**.]
miss[1] [mis] *n* **Miss**, a title used before the name of an unmarried woman or girl; a young woman or girl.—*pl* **misses**. [Shortened form of **mistress**.]
miss[2] *vt* to fail to hit, reach, attain, find, observe, hear; to fail to take advantage of (an opportunity); to omit, fail to have; to discover the absence of; to feel the want of.—*vi* to fail to hit; to fail to be successful; to misfire, as an engine.—*n* a failure to hit, obtain, etc.—**miss out on**, to lose a good opportunity for; **miss the boat**, to lose one's opportunity. [OE *missan*; Du *missen*, to miss.]
missal [mis´ȧl] *n* (*RC Church*) the book that contains the prayers used in celebrating Mass throughout the year. [Low L *missāle*, from *missa*, mass.]
misshape [mis-shāp´] *vt* to shape badly; to deform.—*adj* **misshap´en**. [**mis-** + **shape**.]
missile [mis´il, -īl] *n* an object, as a rock, spear, rocket, etc. to be thrown, fired, or launched at a target. [L *mittĕre, missum*, to throw.]
missing [mis´ing] *adj* absent from the place where expected to be found. [**miss** (2).]
mission [mish´(ȯ)n] *n* a sending of an agent, delegate, or messenger; a flight with a specific purpose, as a task assigned to an astronaut; the purpose for which one is sent; a vocation; persons sent on a mission; an embassy; the sending out of persons to spread a religion; a station or establishment of missionaries.—*n* **miss´ionary**, one sent on a mission, esp religious.—*adj* pertaining to missions.—*n* **mission control**, a command center that controls space flights from the ground. [L *missiō, -ōnis*—*mittĕre*, to send.]
missive [mis´iv] *n* a letter or written message. [Low L *missivus*—L *mittĕre, missum*, to send.]
misspell [mis-spel´] *vt* to spell wrongly.—*pt p* **misspelt´, misspelled´**.—*n* **misspell´ing**. [**mis-** + **spell** (2).]
misspend [mis-spend´] *vt* to spend improperly or wastefully.—*pt, pt p* **misspent´**. [**mis-** + **spend**.]
misstate [mis-stāt´] *vt* to state wrongly or falsely.—*n* **misstate´ment**. [**mis-** + **state**.]
mist [mist] *n* a large mass of water vapor, less dense than a fog; anything that dims or obscures.—*vti* to obscure, or become obscured.—*adj* **mist´y**.—*adv* **mist´ily**.—*n* **mist´iness**. [OE *mist*, darkness; Du *mist*.]
mistake [mis-tāk´] *vt* to understand to perceive wrongly.—*vi* to make a mistake.—*pt* **mistook´**; *pt p* **mistak´en**.—*n* an idea, answer, act, etc. that is wrong; an error or blunder.—*adjs* **mistak´able; mistak´en**, understood wrongly; erroneous; guilty of a mistake.—*adv* **mistak´enly**. [ME *mistaken*—ON *mistaka*, to take wrongly—*mis-*, wrongly, *taka*, to take.]
mister [mis´tėr] *n* a title of address to a man, written **Mr**; (*inf*) sir. [**master**.]
mistime [mis-tīm´] *vt* to do or say at an inappropriate time. [**mis-** + **time**.]
mistletoe [miz´l-tō, or mis´-] *n* a parasitic evergreen plant, with white berries. [OE *misteltān*—*mistel, mistil*, mistletoe, *tān*, twig.]
mistral [mis´träl] *n* a violent, cold, dry, north-west wind in the south of France. [Fr *mistral*—L *magistrālis*, masterful—*magister*.]
mistranslate [mis-trans-lāt´ or -tranz-] *vt* to translate incorrectly.—*n* **mistranslā´tion**. [**mis-** + **translate**.]
mistreat [mis-trēt] *vt* to treat wrongly or badly.—*n* **mistreat´ment**. [**mis-** + **treat**.]
mistress [mis´tres] *n* a woman who is head of a household; a country or state having supremacy; a woman with whom a man is having a prolonged affair; a form of address once applied to any woman, now given to a married woman, usu. written **Mrs** [mis´iz]. [OF *maistress*—L *magister*, master.]
mistrial [mis-trī´ȧl] *n* (*law*) a trial void because of an error in the proceedings or the inability of the jury to reach a verdict. [**mis-** + **trial**.]
mistrust [mis-trust´] *n* lack of trust.—*vti* to suspect; to doubt.—*adj* **mistrust´ful**.—*adv* **mistrust´fully**.—*n* **mistrust´fulness**. [**mis-** + **trust**.]
misunderstand [mis-un-dėr-stand´] *vt* to misinterpret.—*n* **misunderstand´ing**, a mistake as to meaning; a quarrel or disagreement.—*adj* **misunderstood´**. [**mis-** + **understand**.]
misuse [mis-yōōs´] *n* incorrect or improper use; application to a bad purpose.—*vt* **misuse** [mis-yōōz´], to use wrongly; to treat badly, abuse. [**mis-** + **use**.]
mite [mīt] *n* any of a large number of very small parasitic on other insects or vertebrates or plants, or infesting food such as cheese (the name *Acarus* is applied to a genus including some of the mites, and also, loosely, to any mite). [OE *mīte*.]
miter, mitre [mī´tėr] *n* a headdress worn by archbishops, bishops, and abbots; a joint between two pieces of wood to form a corner.—*adj* **mī´tral**, of or like a miter. [Fr—Gr *mitrā*, a fillet.]
mitigate [mit´i-gāt] *vt* to alleviate (eg pain); to appease (eg anger); to lessen the severity of (punishment); to temper (eg severity); to lessen the gravity of, partially excuse, an offence (eg *mitigating circumstances*).—*adj* **mit´igable**.—*n* **mitigā´tion**.—*adj* **mit´igātive**, mitigating, tending to mitigate; soothing.—*n* **mit´igātor**. [L *mītigāre, -ātum*—*mītis*, mild.]
mitosis [mi-, or mī-tō´sis] *n* division of a cell by which each daughter cell has the same set of chromosomes as the parent.—*adj* **mitotic** [-tot´ik]. [Gr *mitos*, fiber.]
mitre *See* **miter**.
mitt [mitt] *n* a glove covering the hand and forearm, but only the base of the fingers; (*slang*) a hand; (*baseball*) a padded glove worn for protection; a boxing glove [contracted form of **mitten**.]
mitten [mit´n] *n* a glove with a thumb but no separate fingers. [OFr *mitaine*.]
mittimus [mit´i-mus] *n*(*law*) a warrant of commitment to prison. [L, 'we send'—*mittĕre*, to send.]
mix [miks] *vt* to blend together in a single mass; to make by blending ingredients, as a cake; to combine.—*vi* to be mixed or blended; to get along together.—*n* a mixture; a beverage for mixing with alcoholic liquor.—*adj* **mixed**, blended; made up of different parts, classes, races, etc.; confused.—*ns* **mix´er**, one who, or a machine or contrivance which, mixes; (with *good* or *bad*) one who gets on well, with miscellaneous casual acquaintances; **mix´ture** [-chůr], act of mixing or state of being mixed; a blend formed by mixing.—**mix up**, to implicate or involve; to confuse.—**mixed marriage**, one between persons of different religions, races, etc.; **mixed number**, a number made up of a whole number and a fraction, as 8 2/3. [OE *miscian*; Ger *mischen*; L *miscēre, mixtum*, to mix.]
mizzen, mizen [miz´n] *n* a fore-and-aft sail on the mizzenmast.—*adj* belonging to the mizzen.—*n* **mizz´enmast**, the mast nearest the mainmast in a sloop. [Fr *misaine*—It *mezzana*—Low L *mediānus*—L *medius*, the middle.]
mizzle [miz´l] *vi* to rain in very fine drops. [Cf L Ger *miseln*.]
mnemonic [nē-mon´ik] *adj* assisting the memory.—Also *n*—*n* **mnemon´ics**, a technique of improving the memory. [Gr *mnēmonikos*—*mnēmōn*, mindful—*mnēmē*, memory.]
moa [mō´a] *n* any of numerous extinct gigantic, flightless birds (family Dinornithidae) in New Zealand. [Maori.]
moan [mon] *n* a low mournful sound as of sorrow or pain.—*vti* to utter a moan; to complain. [OE *mǣnan*, to moan.]
moat [mōt] *n* a deep trench round a castle or fortified place, sometimes filled with water.—*vt* to surround with a moat.—*adj* **moat´ed**. [OFr *mote*, mound.]
mob [mob] *n* a disorderly crowd; a large herd or flock; contemptuous term for the masses; (*slang*) a gang of criminals.—*vt* to attack in a disorderly crowd; to crowd around.—*pr p* **mobb´ing**; *pt p* **mobbed, moboc´racy**, rule or ascendancy exercised by the mob. [L *mōbile* (*vulgus*), the fickle (multitude)—*movēre*, to move.]
mobcap [mob´kȧp] *n* a woman's indoor morning cap. [Old Du *mop*.]
mobile [mō´bil, -bēl] *adj* able to move; easily moved; changing rapidly; characterized by ease in change of social status.—*n* an artistic structure composed of dangling forms which move with any movement of the air.—*vt* **mō´bilize**, to put in readiness for service; to call into active service, as troops.—*ns* **mobilizā´tion; mobil´ity**, quality of being mobile.—**mobile home**, a large trailer outfitted as a home. [Fr, L *mōbilis*—*movēre*, to move.]
Möbius Strip [mō´bi-us] *n* a surface with only one side and one edge made by putting a single twist in a long rectangular strip of paper and pasting the ends together. [A F *Möbius*, Ger mathematician.]
moccasin [mok´a-sin] *n* a flat shoe based on Amerindian footwear; any soft, flexible shoe resembling this; water mocassin. [Native word.]
mocha [mō´ka] *n* a superior Arabian coffee; a flavoring combining coffee and chocolate.—Also *adj*. [*Mocha* on the Red Sea.]
mock [mok] *vt* to laugh at, to deride; to mimic in ridicule; to disappoint (hopes); to deceive; to defy.—*n* ridicule; an object of scorn.—*adj* sham, false.—*ns* **mock´er; mock´ery, mock´ing**, derision, ridicule; subject of ridicule; vain imitation; false show.—*adj* **mock´-herō´ic**, burlesquing the heroic style, or the actions or characters of heroes.—*n* **mock´ingbird**, a common bird (*Mimus polyglottos*), esp in southern US noted for its

exact imitations of other birds.—*adv* **mock´ingly**.—**mock orange**, any of several ornamental shrubs resembling the orange, esp philadelphus; **mock turtle soup**, an imitation of turtle soup, made of calf's head or veal. [OFr *mocquer*.]

mode [mōd] *n* manner of acting, doing, or existing; fashion; form; a manifestation or state of being of a thing; (*mus*) any of the scales used in a composition; in terms such as major mode, minor mode, and pentatonic mode; the item in a series of statistical items that occurs most frequently; (*gram*) mood.—*adj* **mō´dal**, relating to mode or form; (*mus*) written in one of the medieval modes.—*n* **modal´ity**. [Fr,—L *modus*.]

model [mod´l] *n* something to be copied; something worthy to be imitated; an imitation, esp on a smaller scale; one who poses for an artist or photographer; one who displays clothes by wearing them.—*adj* serving as a model; representative of others of the same style, etc. (*a model home*).—*vt* to form after a model (*with* **after, on**); to make a model; to display clothes by wearing.—*vi* to serve as a model for an artist, etc.; practise modelling.—*ns* **mod´eler; mod´eling**, the act or art of making a model. [OFr *modelle*—It *modello*, dim of *modo*—L *modus*, a measure.]

modem [mō´dem] *n* an electronic device used to convert signals from one form to a form compatible with another kind of equipment. [*mo*dulator *dem*odulator.]

moderate [mod´ėr-āt] *vti* to make or become moderate; to preside over (a meeting, etc.)—*adj* [-ȧt] kept within reasonable limits; avoiding extremes; mild, calm; of medium quality, amount, etc.—*n* one whose views are not extreme.—*adv* **mod´erately**.—*ns* **moderate breeze**, wind having speed of 13 to 18 miles per hour, 4 on the Beaufort scale; **moderate gale**, wind having speed of 32 to 38 miles per hour, 7 on the Beaufort scale; **mod´erateness; moderā´tion**, state of being moderate.—*adv* **moderato** [-ä´to] (*mus*), with moderate quickness.—*ns* **mod´erātor**, one who, or that which, moderates or restrains; a president or chairman, in a Presbyterian governing body; the material in which neutrons are slowed down in an atomic pile; **mod´eratorship**. [L *moderārī, -ātus*—*modus*, a measure.]

modern [mod´ėrn] adj of the present or recent times; up-to-date; **Modern**, denoting the most recent form of a language.—*n* one living in modern times, whose views or tastes are modern.—*vti* **mod´ernize**, to make or become modern.—*ns* **Modern English**, the English language since about the mid-15th century; **modernizā´tion; mod´ernizer; mod´ernism**, modern practice or views; **mod´ernist**, an advocate of modern ideas or habits.—*adv* **mod´ernly**.—*ns* **modern´ity, mod´ernness**. [L *modernus*—*modo*, just now.]

modest [mod´est] *adj* restrained by a sense of propriety; decent; having a moderate estimate of one's own merits, not vain, boastful, or pushing; unobtrusive; moderate.—*adv* **mod´estly**.—*n* **mod´esty**, the fact or quality of being modest. [L *modestus*—*modus*, a measure.]

modicum [mod´i-kum] *n* a small quantity. [L *modicus*, moderate—*modus*, a measure.]

modify [mod´i-fī] *vt* to change the form or quality of; to alter slightly, (*gram*) to limit in meaning, qualify.—*adj* modifiable.—*ns* **modificā´tion**, act of modifying; **mod´ifier**. [Fr *modifier*—L *modificāre, -ātum*—*modus*, a measure, *facĕre*, to make.]

modish [mō´dish] *adj* fashionable, stylish.—*adv* **mō´dishly**.—*ns* **mō´dishness; modiste** [mod-ēst´], a fashionable dressmaker or milliner. [L *modus*, a measure.]

modulate [mod´ū-lāt] *vt* to regulate, to adjust; to vary the pitch, intensity, etc. of the voice; to vary the frequency of (radio waves, etc.).—*vi* to pass from one state to another; (*mus*) to pass from one key into another.—*ns* **modulā´tion**, the act of modulating; **mod´ulātor**, one who, or that which, modulates; **mod´ule**, a unit of size used in standardized plannings of buildings and design of components; a self-contained unit forming part of a spacecraft.—*adj* **mod´ular**, of modules.—*n* **mod´ulus** (*math*), a constant multiplier or coefficient; a quantity used as a divisor to produce classes of quantities, each class distinguished by its members yielding the same remainders.—*pl* **moduli** [mod´ū-lī]. [L *modulārī, -ātus*, to regulate—*modulus*, dim of *modus*, a measure.]

Mogen David [mō´gėn dō´vid] *n* double triangle forming the six-pointed star of David; a symbol of Jewry and of the state of Israel. [Heb]

Mogul[1], **Moghul** [mō-gul] *n* an Indian Muslim descended from Mongol, Turkish, or Persian conquerors of India; **Mogul**, an important person, magnate. [Pers, properly 'a *Mongol*'.]

mogul[2] [mō´gul] *n* a bump in a ski run.

mohair [mō´hār] *n* the long, white, fine silken hair of the Angora goat; cloth made of it. [Ar *mukhayyar*, influenced by **hair**.]

Mohammedan [mō-ham´ė-dȧn] *See* **Muhammadan**.

Mohawk [mō-hök] *n* an Amerindian people of Mohawk River Valley, New York; Iroquoian language of this people. [Algonquian.] [Native word.]

Mohave [mō-häv´e] *n* Amerindian of a Yuman tribe of the Colorado River in Arizona, California, and Nevada.

Mohican [mō-hē´kȧn] *n* a confederacy of Amerindian peoples of the upper Hudson River Valley, New York.

Mohs´ scale [mōz, mōs, mō´sėz] *n* a scale of hardness for minerals and gemstones ranging from 1 for the softest to 10 for the hardest. [F *Mohs*, Ger minerologist.]

moiety [moi´e-ti] *n* a half; an infinite part. [OFr *moite*—L *medietās*—*medius*, middle.]

moire [mwär, mör], **moiré** [mwär´ā, moi´ri] *n* a fabric, esp silk, etc. having a wavy pattern. [Fr, from English **mohair**.]

moist [moist] *adj* damp; slightly wet.—*vti* **moisten** [mois´n], to make or become moist.—*ns* **moist´ness; moist´ure**. [OFr *moiste*, perh—L—*mustum*, juice of grapes, new wine.]

molar[1] [mō´lȧr] *adj* used for grinding.—*n* a back tooth. [L *molāris*—*mola*, a millstone—*molĕre*, to grind.]

molar[2] [mō´lȧr] *adj* of a mass of matter as distinguished from the properties or motions of atoms or molecules. [L *moles*, mass.]

molasses [mo-las´ėz] *n* the thick brown sugar that is produced during the refining of sugar. [Port *melaco* (Fr *mélasse*)—Low L *mellāceum*, honey-like—*mel, mellis*, honey.

mold[1] [mōld] *n* a fungus producing a furry growth on the surface of organic matter; this growth.—*vi* to become moldy.—*adj* **mold´y**.—*n* **mold´iness**. [ME *mowle*; cf ON *mygla*.]

mold[2] [mōld] *n* a hollow form in which anything is cast; a pattern; the form received from a mold; a thing formed in a mold; distinctive character.—*vt* to make in or on a mold; to form, shape.—*ns* **mold´er; mold´ing**, the act of one that molds; anything formed by or in a mold; a shaped strip of wood, as around the upper walls of a room.

mold[3] [mōld] *n* soft, loose soil rich in decayed vegetable matter. [Fr *moule*—*modulus*, a measure.]

mole[1] [mōl] *n* a small spot on the skin usu dark-colored and raised. [OE *māl*.]

mole[2] *n* any of numerous small burrowing insectivores (esp family Talpidae) with very small eyes, concealed ears and soft fur; a machine for tunneling; one who works in the dark; a spy who establishes a cover long before his services are called upon; a spy within an organization.—*ns* **mole´-hill**, a little heap of earth cast up by a mole; **mole´-skin**, the skin of a mole used as fur; a durable, napped cotton fabric. [ME *molle, mulle*; cf Du *mol*, L Ger *mol, mul*; according to some a shortened form of **mouldwarp**.]

mole[3] [mōl] *n* a massive breakwater; the harbor formed by a mole. [Fr,—L *mōlēs*, mass.]

mole[4] [mōl] the amount of substance that contains as many elementary entities as there are atoms in 12 grams of carbon-12. [Ger,—*molekül*, molecule.]

mole[5] [mō-lā] *n* a spicy sauce of chilis, onions, etc., unsweetened chocolate, thickened with tortillas. [Mexican Sp]

molecule [mol´ė-kūl] *n* the smallest particle of any substance that retains the properties of that substance; a small particle.—*adj* **molec´ular**.—*ns* **molecular´ity; molecular biology**, branch of biology dealing with the molecular basis of hereditary and of protein synethesis; **molecular weight**, the weight of a molecule of a substance referred to that of an atom of carbon-12 taken as 12. [Fr *molécule*, dim—L *mōlēs*, a mass.]

molest [mō-lest´,mȯ-lest´] *vt* to annoy; to make improper sexual advances.—*ns* **molestа´tion; molest´er**. [Fr *molester*—L *molestāre*—*molestus*, troublesome.]

mollify [mol´i-fī] *vt* to soften, to assuage; to make less severe or violent.—*pt p* **moll´ified**.—*ns* **mollificā´tion; moll´ifier**. [Fr,—L *mollificāre*—*mollis*, soft, *facĕre*, to make.]

mollusk, mollusc [mol´usk] *n* any of a large phylum (Mollusca) of invertebrate animals, characterized by a soft body often enclosed in a shell, as oysters, snails, squid.—*adj* **mollus´can, molluskan**. [L *molluscus*, softish—*mollis*, soft.]

molly, mollie [mol´i] *n* a brightly-colored live-bearer (genus *Poecilia*) highly valued as an aquarium fish.

mollycoddle [mol´i-kädl] *n* a pampered man or boy.—*vt* to pamper. [Dim of Mary.]

Molotov cocktail [mol´ȯ-tof] a crude hand grenade consisting of a bottle with inflammable liquid, and a wick to be ignited just before the missile is thrown. [VM *Molotov*, Russian statesman.]

molt, moult [mōlt] *vi* to shed hair, skin, horns, etc. prior to replacement of new growth as birds, snakes, etc. [L *mūtāre*, to change.]

molten [mōlt´n] *adj* melted by heat; made of melted metal. [Old pt p of **melt**.]

molybdenum [mol-ib-dē´num, -ib-den-um] *n* a silvery-white metallic element (symbol Mo; at wt 95.9; no 42). [L,—Gr,—*molybdos*, lead.]

mom and pop [mom and pop] *adj* (*inf*) of or relating to a small, family-run retail business.

moment [mō´mėnt] *n* an indefinitely brief period of time; a definite point in time; a brief time of importance; importance.—*adv* **mo´mentar´ily**, for a short time; in an instant; at any moment.—*adjs* **mo´mentary**, lasting only for a moment; **momen´tous**, of great moment, very important.—*n* **momen´tum**, the impetus of a moving object, equal to the product of its mass and its velocity.—*pl* **-tums, ta** [tȧ].—**moment of force**, effective tendency of a force to rotate a body to which it is applied; **moment of truth** (*inf*), moment when a person or thing is put to the test. [L *mōmentum*—*movēre*, to move.]

monad [mon´ad] *n* the number one; a unit; unit of being, material and psychical; a hypothetical primitive organism.—*adjs* **monad´ic, -al**. [Gr *monas, -ados*, a unit—*monos*, alone.]

monadelphous [mon-a-delf´us] *adj* (*bot*) of stamens, united by the filaments in one bundle. [Gr *monos*, single, *adelphos*, brother.]

monarch [mon´ärk] *n* a hereditary sovereign, one that holds preeminent power.—*adjs* **monarch´al; monarch´ical; monarch´ic**, vested in a single ruler.—*ns* **mon´archy**, government by a monarch; **mon´archism**, the principles of a monarchy; **mon´archist**, an advocate of monarch. [Gr *monarchēs*—*monos*, alone, *archein*, to rule.]

monastery [mon´às-tėr-i, -tri] *n* the residence of a group of monks, or nuns.—*adj* **monas´tic**.—*n* **monas´tic**, a monk.—*adv* **monas´tically**.—*n* **monas´ticism** [-sizm], the corporate monastic life. [Gr *monastērion, monastikos*—*monastēs*, monk—*monos*, alone.]

monaural [mon-ö´ràl] *adj* of sound reproduction using a single channel to carry and reproduce sound.—Also **monophonic**. [Gr *monos*, single, L *auris*, the ear.]

Monday [mun´di, -dā] *n* the second day of the week. [OE *mōnandæg*, — *mōnan*, gen of *mōna*, moon, *dæg*, day.]

monetary [mon´-, or mun´e-tar-i] *adj* of the coinage or currency of a country; of or relating to money.—*n* **mon´etarist**, one who advocates an economic policy based on the control of a country's money supply. [L *monēta*. See **money**.]

money [mun´i] *n* pieces of stamped metal, or any paper notes authorized by a government as a medium of exchange; property; wealth—*pl* **mon´eys, monies**.—*vt* **monetize** [mon´e-tīz], to make into or recognize as money.—*n* **mon´eybag´**, a bag for money; (*pl*) (*inf*), a rich person.—*adj* **mon´eyed**, rich.—*n* **mon´eymaker**, one good at acquiring money; something profitable; **money market**, any short-term system for providing loanable funds, usu. for 6 to 30 months; **money order**, an order for payment of a specified sum of money, issued for a fee at one post office, bank, etc. and payable at another.—**in the money**, (*slang*), among the winners in a race, etc.; (*slang*) wealthy; **make money**, to gain profits; **money of account**, a monetary denomination not issued as currency or a coin but used in keeping accounts; **on the money** (*slang*), on target; precisely to the point; **put money into**, to invest money in. [OFr *moneie*—L *monēta*, a mint, *Monēta*, being a surname or Juno, in whose temple at Rome money was coined.]

monger [mung´gėr] *n* a trader; a dealer; one who tries to stir up or spread something usu. discreditable. (chiefly in composition as *gossipmonger, warmonger*). [OE *mangere*—L *mangō*, a dealer who polishes up his wares, a slave-dealer.]

Mongolian [mon-gōl´i-àn, mong-go-lē´an] *n* a native or inhabitant of Mongolia; a person of Mongoloid racial stock; the Mongolic language of the Mongol people; **mongolian**, one affected with Down's syndrome.—Also *adj*.—*n* **Mongol**, Mongolian.—Also *adj*.—*n* **mongol´ianism**, Down's syndrome.—*adj* **Mongoloid**, of or denoting most of the peoples of Asia, Eskimos, and Amerindians, one of the major groups of mankind.

mongoose [mong´gōōs] *n* a common ichneumon of India, noted as a slayer of snakes.—*pl* **mong´ooses**. [Marathi, *mangūs*.]

mongrel [mung´grėl] *n* an animal or plant, esp a dog, of mixed breed.—Also *adj*. [Perh from root of OE *mengan*, to mix.]

monition [mon-ish´(ò)n] *n* an admonishing; a warning.—*n* **mon´itor**, a student chosen to help the teacher; any device for regulating the performance of a machine, aircraft, etc.; (*radio, TV*) a receiver for checking the quality of transmission.—*vti* to watch or check on (a person or thing).—*adj* **mon´itory**, giving admonition or warning.—*n* a letter containing an admonition or warning.—*pl* **-ies**. [L,—*monēre*, *-itum*, to remind.]

monk [mungk] *n* one of a religious community living in a monastery.—*adj* **monk´ish**.—*ns* **monk´s cloth**, a heavy cloth with a basket weave; **monks´hood**, a woodland plant (genus *Aconitum*), found throughout the US with a poisonous root and a blue flower like a monk's hood. [OE *munuc*—L *monachus*—Gr *monachos*—*monos*, alone.]

monkey [mungk´i] *n* any of the primates except man and the lemurs, esp the smaller, long-tailed primates.—*pl* **monk´eys**.—*vi* (*inf*) to play, trifle, or meddle.—*ns* **monkey bars**, a three-dimensional structure of horizontal and vertical bars from which children can swing and hang; **monkey business** (*inf*), foolishness, mischief, or deceit; **mon´key shines**, playful pranks; **monkey wrench**, a wrench with an adjustable jaw.—**throw a monkey wrench into** (*inf*), to disrupt the orderly functioning of. [Origin doubtful.]

mono-, mon- *prefix* one, single [Gr *monos*, alone, single], eg **monotint** [mon´ōtint], *n* a drawing or painting in a single tint.

mono [mōn´ō] *n* abbrev of mononucleosis.

monochromatic [mon-ō-krō-mat´ik] *adj* consisting of one color; consisting of radiation (as light) of a single wavelength.—*n* **mon´ochrome**, a painting, drawing, picture, print, in a single color; the art or process of making such pictures or prints. [Gr *monos*, single, chrōma, -atos, colour.]

monocle [mon´o-kl] *n* a single eyeglass. [Fr *monocle*—Gr *monos*, single, L *oculus*, eye.]

monocotyledon [mon-ō-kot-i-lē´don] *n* a plant with only one cotyledon.—*adj* **monocotylē´donous**. [**mono-**, and **cotyledon**.]

monocular [mon-ok´ū-làr] *adj* with or for one eye only. [Gr *monos*, single, L *oculus*, an eye.]

monody [mon´o-di] *n* dirge, elegy; a song for one voice.—*adjs* **monod´ic, -al**.—*n* **mon´odist**. [Gr *monōidiā*—*monos*, single, *ōidē*, song.]

monoecious [mon-ē´shùs] *adj* (*bot*) having separate staminate and pistillate flowers on the same plant; (*zool*) hermaphroditic. [Gr *monos*, single, *oikos*, house.]

monogamy [mon-og´a-mi] *n* marriage to one wife or husband only.—*adjs* **monogam´ic, monog´amous**.—*n* **monog´amist**. [Gr *monis*, one, single, *gamos*, marriage.]

monogram [mon´ō-gram] *n* a figure consisting of several letters interwoven or written into one. [Gr *monos*, single, *gramma*, a letter.]

monograph [mon´ō-gräf] *n* a treatise written on one particular subject or any branch of it.—Also *vt*.—*adjs* **monograph´ic**. [Gr *monos*, single, *graphein*, to write.]

monolith [mon´ō-lith] *n* a single large block of stone, as one made into an obelisk; any massive, unyielding structure.—*adj* **monolith´ic**. [Gr *monos*, single, *lithos*, a stone.]

monologue, monolog [mol´ō-log] *n* a long speech; a soliloquy, a skit, etc. for one actor only. [Gr *monos*, single, *logos*, speech.]

monomania [mon-ō-mā´ni-a] *n* a craze confined to one subject.—*n* **monomā´niac**.—*adj* **mon´omaniàcal** [-mà-nī´àkl]. [Gr *monos*, single, *maniā*, madness.]

monomial [mon-ō´mi-àl] *n* an algebraic expression of one term only.—*adj* **monō´mial**. [Gr *monos*, single, L *nōmen*, name.]

mononucleosis [mo-nō-nōōk-lē-ōs´is] *n* an acute disease, esp of young people, with fever, swollen lymph glands, etc. [**mono-** + **nucle** (**us**) + **-osis**.]

monophonic [mon-ō-phon´ik] *adj* monaural.

monoplane [mon´ō-plān] *n* an airplane with only one main supporting surface. [**mono-**, + **plane**.]

monopoly [mon-op´o-li] *n* the sole right of dealing in any commodity; exclusive command or possession; that which is thus controlled; such control granted by a government.—*vt* **monop´olize**, to get, have, or exploit a monopoly of; to get full control of.—*ns* **monop´olizer, monop´olist**.—*adj* **monopolis´tic**. [L *monopōlium*—Gr *monos*, alone, *pōleein*, to sell.]

monorail [mon´ō-rāl] *n* a single rail that is a track for cars suspended from it or balanced on it. [**mono-**, + **rail**.]

monosyllable [mon-ō-sil´à-bl] *n* a word of one syllable.—*adj* **monosyllab´ic**. [**mono-**, + **syllable**.]

monotheism [mon´ō-thē-izm] *n* the belief in only one God.—*n* **mon´otheist**.—*adj* **monotheist´ic**. [Gr *monos*, single, *theos*, God.]

monotone [mon´ō-tōn] *n* a single, unvaried tone; a succession of sounds having the same pitch; a tiresome sameness of style, color, etc.—*adj* **monot´onous**.—*adv* **monot´-onously**.—*n* **monot´ony**. [Gr *monos*, single, *tonos*, a tone.]

Monotype [mon´ō-tīp] *n* trade name for a machine that casts and sets type letter by letter. [Gr *monos*, single, *typos*, type. Registered trade-mark.]

Monroe Doctrine [mon-rō´ dok´trin] the principle of the non-intervention of European powers in the affairs of the American continents. [President *Monroe's* Message to Congress, December 1823.]

Monsignor [mon-sē´nyör] *n* a title given to certain Roman Catholic prelates. [It,—Fr *monseigneur*.]

monsoon [mon-sōōn´] *n* a seasonal wind of the Indian Ocean and southern Asia; the rainy season during which this wind blows from the southwest. [Port *monção*—Malay *mūsim*—Ar *mausim*, a time, a season.]

monster [mon´stėr] *n* any greatly malformed plant or animal; a fabulous animal; a very wicked person; an animal or thing very large of its kind.—*adj* unusually large, huge.—*adj* **mon´strous**, abnormally developed; enormous; horrible.—*adv* **mon´strously**.—*n* **monstros´ity**, the state or fact of being monstrous. [Fr,—L *mōnstrum*, an omen, a monster—*monēre*, to warn.]

monstrance [mon´stràns] *n* the receptacle in which the consecrated Host is exposed for adoration. [Fr,—L *mōnstrāre*, to show, *mōnstrum*, an omen.]

montage [m•-täzh´] *n* a rapid sequence of movie scenes, often superimposed; assemblage, arrangements; a composite photograph; a picture made partly by sticking objects on the canvas. [Fr—*monter*, to mount.]

Montessori system [mon-tes-ōr´i sis´tem] a system of education, characterized by free discipline and informal, individual instruction. [Devised (c. 1900) by Dr Maria *Montessori*.]

Montezuma´s revenge [mon-tė-zōōm´às] *n* diarrhea contracted in Mexico, esp by tourists.

month [munth] *n* the period from new moon to new moon; a *lunar* month (=29.5306 days); one of the twelve divisions of the year; a calendar month.—*adj* **month´ly**, continuing for a month; done, happening, payable, etc. every month.—*n* a monthly periodical.—*adv* once a month; every month. [OE *mōnath*—*mōna*, moon.]

monument [mon´ū-mėnt] *n* anything that preserves the memory of a person or an event; a notable or enduring example.—*adj* **monument´al**, of or relating to or serving as a monument, tomb; memorial; impressive because of size or of lasting qualities.—*adv* **monument´ally**. [Fr,—L *monumentum*—*monēre*, to remind.]

moo [mōō] *vi* to low like a cow. [Imit.]

mooch [mōōch] *vti* (*slang*) to get (food, money, etc.) by begging, imposition, etc.—*n* **mooch´er**.

mood[1] [mōōd] *n* (*gram*) that aspect of verbs which indicates whether the action or state expressed is a fact (*indicative mood*), supposition (*subjunctive mood*) or command (*imperative mood*). [Partly through Fr *mode* from L *modus*, measure.]

mood[2] [mōōd] *n* temporary state of the mind or emotions; a predominant feeling or spirit.—*adj* **mood´y**, subject to changing moods; out of humor, sullen.—*adv* **mood´ily**.—*n* **mood´iness**, sullenness. [OE *mōd*, mind; cf Ger *mut*, courage.]

Moog synthesizer [mōōg, mōg] *n* trade name for electrophonic instrument operated by keyboard and pedals.

moon [mōōn] *n* the satellite which revolves round the earth and shines by reflected sunlight; anything (as an orb or a crescent) shaped like the moon; a satellite of any other planet.—*vi* to behave in an idle or abstracted way.—*ns* **moon´beam**, a ray of moonlight; **moon´light**, the light of the moon; **moon´light´ing**, the holding of a second job along with one's main job.—*adj* **moon´lit**, lit by the moon.—*ns* **moon´scape**, the surface of the moon, or a representation of it; **moon´shine, moonlight**; (*inf*) illegally-distilled whiskey; **moon´shot**, the launching of a spacecraft to the moon; **moon´stone**, an opalescent feldspar, used as a gemstone.—*adj* **moon´struck**, lunatic, crazed; romantically dreamy. [OE *mōna*; cf Ger *mond*, L *mēnsis*, Ger *mēn*.]

moor[1] [mōōr] *n* in Great Britain, a tract of open wasteland, usu. covered with heather and often marshy. [OE *mōr*.]

moor[2] [mōōr] *vt* to fasten by cable or anchor.—*vi* to moor a ship.—*ns* **moor´age**, an act of mooring; a place for mooring; **moor´ing**, act of mooring; place of mooring; (*pl*) the lines, cables, etc. by which a ship is moored; the place where a ship is moored. [Prob from an unrecorded OE word answering to Middle Du *mâren*.]

Moor [mōōr] *n* any of a Muslim people inhabiting northwest Africa.—*adj* **Moor´ish**. [Fr *More, Maure*—L *Maurus*.]

moose [mōōs] *n* the largest member of the deer family (**Alces alces**), native to Canada and northern US. [Indian *mus, moos*.]

moot [mōōt] *adj* debatable; hypothetical.—*n* **moot court**, a mock court where law students argue cases for practice. [OE *(ge)mōt*, (n), *mōtian* (vb), akin to *mētan*, to meet.]

mop [mop] *n* a bunch of rags, a sponge, etc. fixed on a handle, for washing floors, windows, etc.; a thick or bushy head of hair.—*vt* to rub or wipe with a mop.—*pr p* **mopp´ing**; *pt, pt p* **mopped**.—*n* **mopp´et** (*inf*), a little child.—**mop up**, to clear of remnants of defeated enemy forces; (*inf*) to finish. [OFr *mappe*—L *mappa*, a napkin.]

mope [mōp] *vi* to be gloomy and apathetic.—*n* **moper**.—*adj* **mopey**. [Origin obscure.]

moped [mō´ped] *n* a *mo*tor-power-assisted *ped*al bicycle.

moquette [mō´kėt] *n* an upholstery fabric with a velvety pile. [Fr]

moraine [mo-rān´] *n* a mass of rocks and gravel left by a glacier. [Fr.]

moral [mor´ȧl] *adj* of or relating to character or conduct; conformed to or directed towards right, virtuous; virtuous in matters of sex; capable of knowing right and wrong; subject to the moral law; supported by evidence of reason or probability.—*n* a moral lesson taught by a fable, event, etc.; (*pl*) principles or standards with respect to right and wrong in conduct.—*vt* **mor´alize**, to explain or interpret morally; to give a moral direction to; to improve the morals of.—*vi* to make moral reflections.—*ns* **mor´alizer; mor´alist**, one who teaches or is a student of morals; one concerned with the morals of others; **moral´ity**, that which renders an action right or wrong; virtue; moral principles.—*adv* **mor´ally**. [L *mōrālis*—*mōs, mōris*, custom, (esp in *pl* morals.]

morale [mo-, mö-rȧl´] *n* moral or mental condition with respect to courage, discipline, confidence, etc. [Fr]

morass [mo-ras´] *n* a bog, marsh. [Du *moeras*.]

moratorium [mor-a-tö´ri-um] *n* a legally authorized delay in the payment of money due; an authorized delay of any activity. [Neut of LL *morātōrius, adj*—*mora*, delay.]

morbid [mör´bid] *adj* diseased, resulting as from a diseased state of mind; gruesome.—*n* **morbid´ity**, the state of being morbid; the relative incidence of disease.—*adv* **mor´bidly**.—*n* **mor´bidness**.—*adj* **morbif´ic**, causing disease. [L *morbidus*—*morbus*, disease.]

mordacious [mör-dā´shùs] *adj* biting in style or manner; given to biting.—*adv* **mordā´ciously**.—*n* **mordac´ity** [-das´-].—*adj* **mor´dant**, biting and caustic in thought, style, or manner; acting as a mordant; pungent, burning.—*n* a corroding substance used in etching; a chemical that fixes a dye.—*vt* to treat with a mordant. [L *mordēre*, to bite.]

more [mör] *adj* (serves as comparative of **many** and **much**) in greater number or quantity; additional; other besides.—*adv* to a greater degree; again; further.—*superlative* **most** [mōst].—**and more**, with an additional number of amount; **the more fool he**, by which action he shows himself a greater fool, very foolish. [OE *māra*, greater.]

morel [mor-el´] *n* a genus (*Morchella*) of edible fungi. [Fr *morille*; cf OHG *morhela*, a mushroom.]

moreover [mōr-ō´vėr] *adv* in addition to what has been said before; besides. [**more + over**]

mores [mō´rēz] *n pl* folkways having the force of law. [L]

morganatic [mör-gȧn-at´ik] *adj* denoting a marriage of a king or prince in which neither the wife nor her children enjoy the rank or inherit the possessions of her husband, though the children are legitimate. [Low L *morganātica*, a gift from a bridegroom to his bride.]

morgue [mörg] *n* a place where the bodies of unknown dead or those dead of unknown causes are temporarily kept; in a newspaper office, a place where miscellaneous material is kept for reference; an artist's collection of reference materials. [Fr]

moribund [mor´i-bund] *adj* about to die; in a dying state. [L *moribundus*—*morī*, to die.]

Mormon [mör´mon] *n* member of the Church of Latter-Day Saints whose authority is the Bible and the Book of Mormon, revelations to Joseph Smith by the Angel Moroni in 1827 and certain pronouncements of the 1st Presidency.—Also **Latter-Day Saint**.—*n* **Mormonism**.

morn [mörn] *n* dawn; morning. [ME *morwen*—OE *mōrgen*; Ger *morgen*.]

Mornay sauce [mörn´ā] a cheese-flavored cream sauce.

morning [mörn´ing] *n* the first part of the day; the early part of anything.—*ns* **morning glory**, any of various twining plants (genus *Ipomoea*) with showy blue bell-shaped flowers; **morn´ing star**, a planet, as Venus, when it rises before the sun. [Contr of *morwening*; cf **morn**.]

morocco [mo-rok´ō] *n* a fine leather of goatskins. [*Morocco*.]

moron [mō´r-on] an adult mentally equal to a 8 to 12 year old child; (*inf*) a stupid person.—*adj* **moron´ic**. [Gr, neut of *mōros*, stupid.]

morose [mō-rōs´] *adj* sullen, surly; gloomy.—*adv* **morose´ly**.—*n* **morose´ness**. [L *mōrōsus*, peevish—*mōs, mōris*, manner.]

morphia [mör´fi-a] *n* morphine.—*n* **mor´phine** [-fēn] an alkoloid derived from opium. [Gr *Morpheus*, god of dreams.]

morphology [mö-fol´o-ji] *n* a branch of biology dealing with the form and structure of organisms; a study and description of wood formation in a language.—*adj* **morpholog´ical**.—*n* **morphol´ogist**.—*n* **morphēne**, the smallest meaningful language unit, as a base or affix. [Gr *morphē*, form, *logos*, discourse.]

morrow [mor´ō] *n* (*arch* or *poetic*) morning; the following day. [ME *morwe*.]

Morse code [mörs] *n* either of two codes consisting of dots and dashes or long and short sounds used for transmitting messages by visual or audible signals. [Sam F B *Morse* (1791–1872).]

morsel [mör´sėl] *n* a small piece of food; a small piece of anything. [OFr *morsel*, dim from L *morsus*—*mordēre, morsum*, to bite.]

mortal [mör´t(ȧ)l] *adj* liable to death; causing death, deadly, fatal; implacably hostile; very intense (*mortal terror*).—*n* a human being.—*n* **mortal´ity**, condition of being mortal; death on a large scale, as from war; frequency or number of deaths, esp in proportion to population.—*advs* **mor´tally**.—*n* **mortal sin**, a sin (as murder) of such consequence in Thomist theology that it deprives the soul of grace. [Fr—L *mortālis*—*mori*, to die.]

mortar [mör´tȧr] *n* a vessel in which substances are pounded with a pestle; a short piece of artillery for throwing a heavy shell; a cement of lime, sand, and water, used in building.—*n* **mor´tarboard**, an academic cap with a square flat top; a square board for carrying mortar. [OE *mortere*—L *mortārium*, a mortar.]

mortgage [mör´gij] *n* a transfer of rights to a piece of property usu. as security for the payment of a loan or debt that becomes void when the debit is paid.—*vt* to pledge as security for a debt; to put an advance claim on.—*ns* **mortgagee´**, one to whom a mortgage is made or given; **mort´gagor, -er**. [OFr *mort*, dead, *gage*, a pledge.]

mortify [mör´ti-fī] *vt* to subdue by severities and penance; to humiliate.—*vi* to practise mortification; to become gangrenous.—*pt, pt p* **mor´tified**.—*n* **mortificā´tion**, act of mortifying or state of being mortified; necrosis, gangrene; a bringing under of the passions and appetites by severe discipline; humiliation, vexation caused by something that injures one's self-respect or pride. [Fr—Low L *mortificāre*, to cause death to—*mors, mortis*, death, *facĕre*, to make.]

mortise, mortice [mör´tis] *n* a cavity cut into a piece of timber to receive a tenon.—*vt* to cut a mortise in; to join by a mortise and tenon. [Fr *mortaise*.]

mortuary [mört´ū-ȧr-i] *adj* connected with death or burial.—*n* a funeral home. [L *mortuārius*—*mortuus*, dead, *morī*, to die.]

mosaic [mō-zā´ik] *n* a surface decoration made by inlaying small pieces (as of colored glass or stone) to form figures or patterns; a design made in mosaic; an organism composed of cells of more than one genotype, a chimera; a virus disease of plants.—*adj* relating to, or composed of, mosaic.—*adv* **mosā´ically**. [Fr *mosaïque*—LL *mosaicum*—*mūsa*—Gr *mousa*, a muse.]

Mosaic [mō-zā´ik] *adj* pertaining to *Moses*, the great Jewish lawgiver.

moselle [mō-zel´] *n* a light wine from the *Moselle* valley, Germany.

Moslem [moz´lem] *n See* **Muslim**

mosque [mosk] *n* a Muslim place of worship. [Fr *mosquée*—It *moschea*—Ar *masjid*—*sajada*, to pray.]

mosquito [mos-kē´tō] *n* a two-winged insect (order Diptera) the females of which suck blood.—*pl* **mosqui´toes, -os**.—**mosquito fish**, either of two N American live-bearers (*Gambusia affinis* and *Heterandria formosa*) used to exterminate mosquito larvae. [Sp dim of *mosca*, a fly.—L *musca*.]

moss [mos] *n* a class (musci) of bryophytes, very small green plants that grow in clusters on rocks, moist ground, etc.; a piece of ground covered with moss.—*vt* to cover with moss.—*adj* **moss´grown**, covered with moss; antiquated.—*ns* **moss´ rose**, an old-fashioned variety of rose having a mosslike growth on and below the calyx.—*adj* **moss´y**, overgrown, or abounding, with moss.—*n* **moss´iness**. [OE *mōs*, bog; Du *mos*; Ger *moos*, moss.]

most [mōst] *adj* (superlative of **many** or **much**, of which **more** is the comparative) greatest in number; greatest in amount or degree; in the greatest number of instances.—*adv* in or to the greatest degree or extent.—*n* the greatest amount or degree; (with *pl*) the greatest number (of).—*adv* **most´ly**, for the most part; mainly, usually. [OE *mǣst*, cf Ger *meist*.]

MOT [em-ō-tē´] *n* (among Jews) Member of Our Tribe.

mot [mō] *n* a pithy or witty saying. [Fr.]

mote [mōt] *n* a particle of dust; a speck; anything very small. [OE *mot*; Du *mot*.]
motel [mō-tel´] *n* a hotel for motorists. [**mo(tor), (ho)tel**.]
motet [mō-tet´] *n* a choral composition without instrumental accompaniment having a sacred text. [Fr dim of *mot*, word.]
moth [moth] *n* a four-winged chiefly night-flying insect (order Lepidoptera) related to the butterfly, the larvae of one kind eat holes in woolens, furs, etc.,—*n* **moth´ball**, a small ball of camphor or naphthalene, the fumes of which repel clothes moths.—*adj* **moth´-eat´en**, eaten into by moths; dilapidated; outmoded.—**in mothballs**, put into storage or reserve. [OE *moththe, mohthe*; Ger *motte*.]
mother [muTH´ėr] *n* a female parent; an origin or source.—*adj* of or like a mother; native.—*vt* to be the mother of or a mother to.—*ns* **moth´er coun´try**, the country of one's birth; the country from which a colony has gone out; **moth´er-in-law**, the mother of one's husband or wife; **moth´erland**, the land of origin of something; mother country.—*adjs* **moth´erless**, without a mother; **moth´erly**, of, proper to a mother; like a mother.—*ns* **moth´erliness; moth´er-of-pearl´**, the internal layer of the shells of the pearl oyster; **moth´er superior**, a woman who is head of a religious establishment; **moth´er tongue**, one's native language; **moth´er wit**, natural intelligence; **Mother Carey's chicken**, Wilson's petrel (*Oceanites oceanicus*) a summer visitor in the N Atlantic. [OE *mōdor*; Du *moeder*; ON *mōthir*; Ger *mutter*; L *māter*; Gr *mētēr* etc.]
motif [mō-tēf´] *n* a theme or subject for development in a dramatic, musical, or literary composition; a design. [Fr—Low L *mōtivus*. See **motive**.]
motion [mō´shȯn] *n* act or state of moving, movement; a formal suggestion made in a meeting, law court, or legislative assembly.—*vt* to direct by a gesture.—*vi* to make a hand movement conveying a direction.—*adj* **mō´tionless**, without motion.—**motion picture**, a series of pictures thrown on a screen so rapidly that they produce a continuous picture in which persons and objects seem to move; a play, etc. in this form.—**motion sickness**, sickness induced by motion and characterized by vomiting.—Also *adj*. [Fr—L *mōtiō, -ōnis—movēre, mōtum*, to move.]
motive [mō´tiv] *adj* moving to action; of or relating to motion.—*n* something (as a need or desire) that causes a person to act; a recurrent theme in a musical composition.—*vt* **mō´tivāte**, to provide with a motive; to induce.—*ns* **motivā´tion**, motivating force, incentive; **motiv´ity**, power of moving or producing motion. [Low L *mōtīvus*—L *movēre, mōtum*, to move.]
motley [mot´li] *adj* of many colors; of many different or clashing elements.—*n* formerly, the dress of a professional buffoon; a mixture of incongruous elements. [Origin obscure.]
motor [mō´tȯr] *n* anything that produces motion; an engine, esp an internal-combustion engine; a machine for converting electrical energy into mechanical energy.—*adj* producing motion; of or powered by a motor; of, by or for motor vehicles; of or involving muscular movements.—*vi* to travel by automobile.—*ns* **mo´torbike**, a small lightweight motorcycle; **mot´orboat**, a boat propelled by an internal-combustion engine or an electric motor; **mo´torcade**, a procession of motor vehicles; **mo´torcar**, an automobile; **mo´tor court**, motel; **mo´torcycle**, a 2-wheeled automotive vehicle; **mo´tor home**, an automotive vehicle designed and equipped to serve as a traveling home for recreation; **mo´torist**, one who drives an automobile or travels by one.—*vt* **mo´torize**, to equip with a motor; to equip with motor-driven vehicles.—*ns* **mo´toriza´tion; mo´torman**, an operator of a motor driven vehicle (as a streetcar or subway train); **mo´tor scooter**, a low 2- or 3- wheeled automotive vehicle resembling a child's scooter but having a seat; **mo´tor vehicle**, an automotive vehicle not operated on rails, esp one with rubber tires for use on highways. [L *movēre, mōtum*, to move.]
mottle [mot´l] *vt* to mark with blotches of various colors. [Prob from **motley**.]
motto [mot´ō] *n* a short sentence or phrase adopted as a watchword or maxim; such a phrase attached to a coat-of-arms.—*pl* **mottoes** [mot´ōz]. [It—L *muttum*, a murmur.]
moue [mōō] *n* a little grimace. [Fr.]
moujik [mōō-zhik´, mōō´zhik] *See* **muzhik**.
mould [mōld] *See* **mold**.
moult [mōlt] *See* **molt**.
mound [mownd] *n* an artificial bank of earth or stones; the slight elevation on which a baseball pitcher stands; a heap or bank of earth.—*vt* to form into a mound.—*n* **Mound Builder**, a member of a prehistoric Amerindian people whose earthworks are found from the Great Lakes down the Mississippi valley to the Gulf of Mexico. [Origin obscure.]
mount[1] [mownt] *n* a high hill. [OE *munt*—L *mōns, montis*, mountain.]
mount[2] [mownt] *vi* to go up; to climb; to extend upward; to increase in amount.—*vt* to ascend; to get up on (a horse, platform, etc.); to provide with horses; to fix (a jewel, picture, etc.) on or in a proper support, etc.; to arrange (a dead animal, etc.) for exhibition; to place (a gun) into position ready for use.—*n* an act of mounting; a riding animal that upon which a thing is placed for use or display.—*adj* **mount´able**, that may be mounted. [Fr *monter*, to go up—L *mōns, montis*, mountain.]
mountain [mownt´in] *n* a landmass higher than a hill; a vast number or quantity.—*adj* of or in mountains.—*ns* **mount´ain ash**, a tree (*Pyrusaucuparia*) of the rose family with pinnate leaves and red or orange-red fruits; **mount´ain dew**, moonshine; **mountaineer´**, an inhabitant of a mountain; a climber of mountains; **mountaineer´ing**, the technique of climbing the high places of the earth.—*adj* **mount´ainous**, full of mountains; large as a mountain, huge.—*ns* **mount´ain goat**, a long-haired goatlike antelope (*Oreamnos americanus*) of the Rocky Mountains; **mount´ain lion**, a cougar; **mount´ain sick´ness**, sickness brought on by breathing rarefied air; **mount´ain time**, the 7th time zone west of Greenwich that includes the Rocky Mountain states of the US. [OFr *montaigne*—L *mōns, montis*, mountain.]
mountebank [mown´ti-bangk] *n* a quack; a charlatan. [It *montambanco—montare*, to mount, *in*, on, *banco*, a bench.]
mourn [mōrn, mörn] *vti* to grieve for (someone dead); to feel or express sorrow for (something regrettable).—*n* **mourn´er**.—*adj* **mourn´ful**, expressing grief or sorrow; causing sorrow.—*adv* **mourn´fully**.—*n* **mourn´fulness**.—*adj* **mourn´ing**, grieving, lamenting; of wear as a sign of mourning.—*n* the act of expressing grief; the dress, esp black clothes of mourners. [OE *murnan, meornan*; OHG *mornēn*, to grieve.]
mouse [mows] *n* any of numerous small rodents (as of the genus *Mus*) with pointed snout, long body, and slender tail; a timid person; a hand-held device moved in front of a computer terminal screen to position the lighted indicator; (*slang*) a black eye.—*pl* **mice** [mīs].—*vi* [mowz] to hunt for mice; to prowl.—*vt* to toy with roughly; to search for carefully (*with* **out**).—*ns* **mouser** [mowz´ėr] a cat that catches mice.—*adj* **mousy, mousey** [mows´i] like a mouse; grayish brown; quiet, stealthy; timid, retiring. [OE *mūs*, pl *mȳs*, Ger *maus*, L *mūs*, Gr *mȳs*.]
mousse [mōōs] *n* a chilled dessert containing eggs and whipped cream. [Fr.]
moussaka, mussaka [mōō-sä´ka] *n* a Middle Eastern dish of ground meat and eggplant, baked in a sauce.
mousseline [mōōs-ė-lēn] *n* a sheer fabric resembling muslin; a sauce to which whipped cream has been added.
moustache *See* **mustache**.
mouth [mowth] *n* the opening in the head of an animal by which it eats and utters sound; opening or entrance, as of a bottle, river, etc. —*pl* **mouths** [mowTHz].)—*vt* [mowTH] to say, esp insincerely; to rub with the mouth.—*vi* to declaim, rant; to grimace.—*ns* **mouth´er**, one who mouths; **mouth´ful**, as much as fills the mouth; a small quantity; (*slang*) a pertinent remark.—*pl* **mouth´fuls**.—*adj* **mouth´less**, without a mouth.—*ns* **mouth´ or´gan**, a harmonica; **mouth´piece**, the part of a musical instrument, or tobacco pipe, held in the mouth; a person, periodical, etc. who speaks for others; **mouth´wash**, a flavored, often antiseptic liquid for rinsing the mouth.—*adjs* **mouth´water´ing**, appetizing; tasty; **mouth´y**, talkative esp in a rude or bombastic way.—**down in the mouth** (*inf*) unhappy; **mouth-to-mouth resuscitation**, a method of artificial respiration in which the rescuer forces air into the victim's lungs. [OE *mūth*; Ger *mund*; Du *mond*.]
move [mōōv] *vt* to cause to change place; to set in motion; to excite (to action, or to emotion), to persuade; to arouse; to touch the feelings of; to propose formally in a meeting.—*vi* to go from one place to another; to change place; to walk, to carry oneself; to change residence; to make a motion as in an assembly; to evacuate the bowels.—*n* the act of moving; a movement, esp at chess; one's turn to move.—*adj* **movable** [mōōv´å-bl], that may be moved; **move´able**.—*n* (*pl*) (law) personal property, esp furniture; a portable piece of furniture or property.—*ns* **move´ment**, act or manner of moving; change of position; motion of the mind, emotion; activity; process; the moving parts in a mechanism, esp the wheelwork of a clock or watch; a main division of an extended musical composition; an agitation in favor of, concerted endeavor to further, an object or policy; **mov´er; mov´ie**, a motion picture; (*pl*) the showing of a motion picture; the motion-picture medium or industry.—*adj* **mov´ing**, causing motion; changing position; affecting the feelings.—*adv* **mov´ingly**. [OFr *movoir*—L *movēre*, to move.]
mow[1] [mow] *n* a pile of hay esp in a barn; the part of a barn where hay, etc. is stored. [OE *mūga*, heap; ON *mūgi*, swath.]
mow[2] [mō] *vti* to cut down (grass, etc.) from (a lawn, etc.) with a sickle or lawn mower.—*pr p* **mow´ing**; *pt* **mowed**; *pt p* **mowed** or **mown**.—*n* **mow´er**.—**mow down**, to cause to fall like cut grass. [OE *māwan*; Ger *mähen*; L *metēre*, to reap.]
mozzarella [mot-så-rel´å] *n* a cow's milk cheese notable for its elasticity when melted. [It]
Ms [miz] *n* a title put before the name of a woman instead of Miss or Mrs.
mu [myōō] *n* The Twelfth letter of the Greek alphabet.
much [much] *adj* (*comparative* **more**; *superlative* **most**) great in quantity.—*adv* to a great degree; by far; often.—*n* a great amount. [ME *muche, muchel*—OE *micel*.]
muck [muk] *n* moist manure; black earth with decaying matter, used as manure; mud, dirt, filth.—*vt* to clear of muck; to manure with muck.—*vi* to move or load muck (as in a mine); to engage in useless activity (*with* **about** *or* **around**).—*adj* **muck´y**.—*n* **muck´iness**. [Prob Scand; cf ON *myki*, Dan *mōg*, dung.]
mucus [mū´kus] *n* the slimy fluid secreted by the mucous membrane.—*n* **mucilage** [mū´sil-ij], adhesive.—*adjs* **mucilaginous** [-aj´-], pertaining to mucilage; slimy; **mucous**, like mucus; slimy.—**mucous membrane**, mucus-secreting lining of body cavities. [L cf L *mungēre*, wipe away.]

mud [mud] *n* wet soft sticky earth.—*vt* to treat or plaster with mud; to make turbid.—*adj* **mudd'y**, foul with mud; containing mud; covered with mud; confused, stupid.—*vti* to make or become muddy.—*pt, pt p* **mudd'ied**.—*adv* **mudd'ily**.—*n* **mudd'iness**.—*ns* **mud'guard**, a screen to catch mud splashes from wheels. [Old Low Ger *muddle*, Du *modder*.]
muddle [mud'l] *vt* to render muddy or foul, as water; to bungle.—*vi* to blunder.—*n* confusion, mess; bewilderment.—*n* **mudd'lehead**, a blockhead.—*adj* **muddle-head'ed**. [Freq of **mud**.]
Muenster [mun'ster, mōōn'ster] *n* a cylindrical whole-milk cheese with a brick-red rind. [*Muenster*, France.]
muesli [myōō'li] *ns* a mixture of rolled oats, dried fruit, nuts, etc. eaten with milk.
muezzin [mōō-ez'in] *n* a Muslim crier who calls the hour of daily prayer. [Ar]
muff[1] [muf] *n* a cylinder of fur or the like for keeping the hands warm. [Prob from Du *mof*; cf Ger *muff*, a muff.]
muff[2] [muf] *n* a bungling performance; failure to hold a ball when trying a catch.—*vti* to bungle; muff a ball. [Origin unknown.]
muffin [muf'in] *n* a quick bread baked in a muffin pan.—**muffin pan**, a baking pan formed of connected cups.
muffle [muf'l] *vt* to wrap up for warmth or concealment; to dull or deaden the sound of.—*n* **muff'ler**, a scarf for the throat; any means of muffling, esp the exhaust of a motor vehicle. [App Fr *mouffle*, mitten.]
mufti [muf'ti] *n* civilian clothes. [Ar]
mug [mug] *n* a cylindrical drinking cup, usu. of metal or earthenware; its contents; (*slang*) the face.—*vt* to assault, usu. with intent to rob.—*vi* (*slang*) to grimace, esp in overacting;
muggy [mug'i] *adj* hot, close, and damp.—**mugg'ish**. [Perh ON *mugga*, mist.]
mugwump [mug'wump] *n* an independent in politics. [Amer Indian.]
Muhammadan [mō-ham'a-dån] *adj* of, or relating to Muhammad or Islam. [Ar *Muhammad*, the great prophet of Arabia (570–632); lit 'praised'.]
mujik *See* **muzhik**.
mukluk [muk'luk'] *n* an Eskimo boot of sealskin or reindeer skin; heavy socks with soft leather soles. [Eskimo.]
mulatto [mū-lat'ō] *n* the offspring of a Negro and a person of European stock. [Sp *mulato*, dim of *mulo*, mule.]
mulberry [mul'bėr-i] *n* a genus (*Morus*) of trees on the leaves of some of which silkworms feed; a fruit of any of these. [Poss OHG *mulberi*.]
mulch [mulch, mulsh] *n* loose strawy dung, etc., laid down to protect the roots of plants.—*vt* to cover with mulch. [Cf Ger dial *molsch*, soft; OE *melsc*.]
mulct [mulkt] *n* a fine, a penalty.—*vt* to fine; to take (money, etc.) by fraud. [L *mulcta*, a fine.]
mule[1] [mūl] *n* the offspring of a male donkey and a mare; an instrument for spinning cotton; an obstinate person.—*n* **mule deer**, a long-eared deer (*Odocoileus hemionus*) of western N America; **mūleteer'**, one who drives mules.—*adj* **mūl'ish**, like a mule; obstinate.—*adv* **mūl'ishly**.—*n* **mūl'ishness**. [OE *mūl*—L *mūlus*.]
mule[2] [mūl] *n* a heelless slipper. [Fr]
mull[1] [mul] *n* a soft, fine, sheer fabric of cotton, silk, or rayon.
mull[2] [mul] *vti* (*inf*) to ponder (over).
mull[3] [mul] *vt* to warm, spice, and sweeten (wine, ale, etc.).—*adj* **mulled**.
mullah [mul'ä] *n* a Muslim of a quasi-clerical class trained in traditional law and doctrine. [Pers, Turk and Hindustani *mullā*—Ar *maulā*.]
mullet [mul'et] *n* any of a family (Mugilidae) of palatable fishes nearly cylindrical in form. [OFr *mulet*, dim—L *mullus*.]
mulligan stew [mul'ĭ-gån] *n* a stew made from whatever ingredients are available.
mulligatawny [mul-i-ga-tö'ni] *n* an East Indian curry-soup. [Tamil *milagutannīr*, pepper-water.]
mullion [mul'yon] *n* an upright division between the lights of windows, between panels, etc.—*adj* **mull'ioned**. [Apparently by metathesis from OFr *monial* of unknown origin.]
multi-, mult- in composition, much, many. [L *multus*];—eg **multiped**, [mul'ti-ped] an insect having many feet (L *pēs, pedis*, foot); **multilingual**, [mul-ti-ling'gwäl] in many languages; speaking many languages (L *lingua*, tongue); **mul'tinat'ional**, large business company which operates in several countries; **mul'ti-pur'pose; multiracial**, [mul-ti-rā'shl] including (people of) many races (as, a *multiracial society*.)
multifarious [mul-ti-fā'ri-us] *adj* having great diversity; manifold.—*adv* **multifā'riously**. [L *multifārius*—*multus*, many, and perh *fārī*, to speak.]
multiform [mul'ti-förm] *adj* having many forms.—*n* **multiform'ity**. [Fr *multiforme*—L *multiformis*—*multus*, many, *forma*, shape.]
multilateral [mul-ti-lat'ėr-ål] *adj* many-sided; with several parties or participants. [**multi-, lateral**.]
multimedia [mul'-ti-mē'di-a] *n, adj* the process of combining computer data, sound and video images to create an environment similar to television.
multinomial [mul-ti-nō'mi-ål] *n* (*math*) an expression that consists of the sum of several terms. [**multi-** + L *nōmen*, a name.]
multiple [mul'ti-pl] *adj* consisting of many elements; various; complex.—*n* the product of a quantity by an integer.—*adj* **multiple-choice**, having several answers given from which the correct one is to be chosen.—*n* **multiple sclerosis**, a disease of the nervous system with loss of muscular coordination, etc. [Fr—LL *multiplus*—L *multus*, many, and root of *plēre*, to fill.]
multiply [mul'ti-plī] *vti* to increase in number, degree, etc.; to find the product (of) by multiplication.—*pr p* **mul'tiplying**; *pt, pt p* **mul'tiplied**.—*ns* **multiplicand'**, a number to be multiplied by another; **multiplicā'tion**, the act of multiplying; the process of repeatedly adding a quantity to itself a certain number of times, or any other process which has the same result.—*adj* **mul'tiplicātive**, relating to the mathematical operation of multiplication.—*ns* **multiplic'ity**, a great number or variety (of); **mulitiplier**, the number by which another is to be multiplied. [Fr,—L *multiplex*.]
multitude [mul'ti-tūd] *n* a large number of people.—*adj* **multitud'inous**, consisting of innumerable elements. [Fr,—L *multitūdō, -inis*—*multus*, many.]
mum[1] [mum] *n* (*inf*) a chrysanthemum.
mum[2] [mum] *adj* silent, not speaking—*n* silence.—*interj* not a word!—*vi* to act in dumb show; to masquerade;—*pr p* **mumm'ing**; *pt p* **mummed**.—*ns* **mumm'er**, an actor in a pantomine; a masquerader; **mumm'ery**, mumming; a pretentious ceremony or performance. [An inarticulate sound, closing the lips; partly OFr *momer*, to mum.]
mumble [mum'bl] *vti* to utter or speak indistinctly—*n* a mumbled utterance.—*n* **mum'bler**.—*adv* **mum'blingly**. [Freq of **mum**.]
mumbo-jumbo [mum'bō-jum'bō] *n* an idol or fetish; meaningless ritual, talk, etc.
mummy [mum'i] *n* a carefully preserved dead body, esp an embalmed corpse of ancient Egypt.—*n* **mummificā'tion**.—*vt* **mumm'ify**, [OFr *mumie*—Low L *mumia*—Ar and Pers *mūmiyā*.]
mumps [mumps] *npl* an acute contagious virus disease characterized by swelling of the salivary glands. [Cf **mum**, and Du *mompen*, to cheat.]
munch [munch, -sh] *vti* to chew steadily, often with a crunching sound.—*n* **munch'er**. [Prob imit]
mundane [mun'dān] *adj* belonging to the world; ordinary, banal.—*adv* **mun'danely**. [Fr,—L *mundānus*—*mundus*, the world.]
mung bean [mung] *n* an annual bean (*Phaseolus aureas*) widely grown in warm regions, the usu. source of bean sprouts. [Hindi]
municipal [mū-nis'i-pål] *adj* of or concerning a city, town, etc. or its local government.—*n* **municipal'ity**, a town or city having corporate status and powers of self-government; the governing body of a municipality.—*adv* **munic'ipally**. [L *mūnicipālis*—*mūnicipium*, a free town—*mūnia*, official duties, *capĕre*, to take.]
munificence [mū-nif'i-sėns] *n* magnificent liberality in giving; bountifulness.—*adj* **munif'icent**.—*adv* **munif'icently**. [Fr,—L *mūnificentia*—*mūnus*, a present, *facĕre*, to make.]
munitions [mū-nish'ons] *npl* war supplies, esp weapons and ammunition. [L *mūnīre, mūnītum*, to fortify; *mūnitiō, -ōnis*, fortification; *mūnimentum*, fortification, title-deeds—*moenia*, walls.]
muon [myōō-on] *n* an unstable lepton common in cosmic radiation, and existing in positive and negative forms.
mural [mū'rål] *adj* of, on, attached to, or of the nature of, a wall.—*n* a painting on a wall. [L *mūrālis*—*mūrus*, a wall.]
murder [mûr'dėr] *n* the act of putting a person to death, intentionally and unlawfully; (*inf*) something unusually difficult or dangerous to do or deal with.—*vt* to kill unlawfully and with malice aforethought; to destroy; to spoil by performing badly.—*n* **mur'derer**;—*adj* **mur'derous**, of the nature of murder; bloody; cruel capable or guilty of, or intending, murder.—*adv* **mur'derously**. [OE *morthor*—*morth*, death; Ger *mord*; cf L *mors, mortis*.]
murex [mū'reks] *n* any of a genus (*Murex*) of a marine gastropod mollusk yielding a purple dye. [L]
muriatic acid [mū-ri-at'ik] *n* hydrochloric acid. [L *muriāticus*—*muria*, brine.]
murky [mûrk'i] *adj* dark, gloomy; darkly vague or obscure.—*adv* **murk'ily**.—*ns* **murk; murk'iness**. [OE *mirce*; ON *myrkr*, Dan and Swed *mörk*.]
murmur [mûr'mur] *n* a low, indistinct sound, continuous sound; a mumbled complaint; (*med*) an abnormal sound in the body, esp near the heart.—*vi* to make a murmur.—*vt* to say in a murmur.—*n* **mur'murer**.—*adj* **mur'murous**.—*adv* **mur'murously**. [Fr,—L; imit]
Murphy's law [mûr-fiz] the notion that if anything is liable to go wrong, it will.
muscatel [mus-ka-tel'] *n* a sweet fortified white wine made from the muscat.—*n* **mus'cat**, a sweet European grape used in making wine and raisins. [OFr *muscatel, muscadel*—Provençal, *muscat*, musky.]
muscle [mus'l] *n* an animal tissue by contraction of which bodily movement is effected; strength; brawn.—*vi* (*inf*) to force one's way (in).—*adj* **muscle-bound**, having some of the muscles abnormally enlarged and lacking in elasticity (as from too much exercise).—*n* **muscle pill**, (*inf*) anabolic steriod.—*adj* **muscular**, of or done by a muscle; consisting of muscles; brawny, strong.—*ns* **mus'culature**, the arrangement of the muscles of a body, limb, etc.; **muscular'ity**, state of being muscular.—*adv* **mus'cularly**.—**muscular dystrophy**, [dis'trō-fi], a disease in which muscles progressively deteriorate. [Fr,—L *mūsculus*, dim of *mūs*, a mouse, a muscle.]
Muscovy [mus'ko-vi] *n* (*hist*) the old principality of *Moscow*; extended to Russia in general.—*n, adj* **Mus'covite**, of Muscovy; Russian; a Russian.
muse [mūz] *vi* to meditate.—*vt* to say musingly.—*n* deep thought; contemplation.—*n* **mus'er**.—*adv* **mus'ingly**. [Fr *muser*, to loiter, in OFr to muse.]
muse [mūz] *n* one of the nine goddesses of poetry, music, and the other liberal arts; **muse**, poetic inspiration; poetry. [Fr,—L *mūsa*—Gr *mousa*.]

museum [mū-zē´um] *n* a repository for the collection, exhibition, and study of objects or artistic, scientific or historic interest;—*pl* **museums**. [L *mūsēum*—Gr *mouseion*.]

mush[1] [mush] *n* a thick porridge of boiled meal; any thick, soft mass; (*inf*) maudlin sentimentality. [Prob **mash**.]

mush[2] [mush] *vi* to travel on foot with dogs over snow.—*interj* a shout to urge on sled dogs. [Prob Fr *marcher*, to walk.]

mushroom [mush´rŏŏm] *n* a fleshy fungus with a capped stalk, esp such as are edible.—*vi* to gather mushrooms; to increase, spread with rapidity. [OFr *mousseron*, perh —*mousse*, moss.]

music [mū´zik] *n* the art of combining tones into a composition having structure and continuity; vocal or instrumental sounds having rhythm, melody, or harmony; an agreeable sound.—*adj* **mū´sical**, of or relating to music or musicians; having the pleasing tonal qualities of music; having an interest in or talent for music.—*n* a movie or theatrical production consisting of musical numbers and a dialogue based on a unifying plot.—*n* **musicale**, [myōō´zikal] a social affair featuring music.—*adv* **mū´sically**.—*ns* **musi´cian**, [-shȧn] one skilled in music; esp a performer **musicol´ogy**, the study of the history, forms etc. of music; **musicol´ogist**. [Fr *musique*—L *mūsica*—*Gr mousikē* (*technē*), musical (art)—*mousa*, a muse.]

musique concrète [mū-zēk kon-kret] music made up of scraps of natural sound recorded and then variously treated. [Fr]

musk [musk] *n* an animal secretion with a strong odor, used in fixing perfumes; the odor of musk; the musk plant.—*ns* **musk deer**, a small Asiatic deer (*Moschus moschiferous*) that produces musk in the male; **muskmelon**, any melon with a netted skin (genus *Cucumis*), the variety most widely cultivated in N America; **musk-ox**, a shaggy-coated wild ox (*Ovibos moschatus*) of Greenland and the barren northern lands of N America; **musk plant**, a yellow-flowered N American herb (*Mimulus moschatus*); **muskrat**, an aquatic rodent (*Ondatra zibethica*) of the US and Canada; its fur or pelt.—Also **musquash**.—*adj* **musky**. [Fr *musc*—L *muscus*.]

muskeg [mus´keg] *n* a mossy bog in Northern N America. [Algonquian.]

muskellunge, muskallonge [musk´e-lunj, lonj] *n* a large freshwater game and food fish (*Esox masquinongy*) found in eastern and midwestern N America.—Also **maskanonge, maskelonge, maskinonge**.

musket [mus´ket] *n* (*hist*) a smooth-bore military firearm.—*ns* **musketeer´**, a soldier, armed with a musket; **mus´ketry**, muskets in general; the art of using small arms. [OFr *mousquet*, a musket, formerly a hawk—It *moschetto*.]

Muslim [mus´lim] *n, adj* (of) an adherent of Islam; a Black Muslim.

muslin [muz´lin] *n* a fine soft cotton fabric resembling gauze in appearance. [Fr *mousseline*—It *mussolino*, from *Mosul* in Mesopotamia.]

musquash [mus´kwosh] *n* the muskrat. [Amer Indian.]

mussaka *See* **moussaka**.

mussel [mus´l] *n* any of several marine bivalve shellfish, used for food. [OE *mūs(c)le*; cf Ger *muschal*, Fr *moule*; L *mūsculus*.]

Mussulman [mus´ul-man] *n* a Muslim.—*pl* **Muss´ulmans**, [-manz]. [Pers *musulmān*—Ar *muslin, moslim*, Moslem.]

must[1] [must] an auxiliary verb expressing necessity (*I must go*); probability (*it must be Jack*); certainty (*all must die*).—*n* (*inf*) something that must be done, had, etc. [OE *mōste*, pa of *mōt*, may; cf Ger *müssen*.]

must[2] [must] *n* newly-pressed grape juice, unfermented or partially fermented wine; the pulp and skin of crushed grapes. [OE *must*—L *mustus*, new, fresh.]

mustache, moustache [mus-tash´, mus´tash] *n* hair on the upper lip. [Fr]

mustang [mus´tang] *n* the small wild horse of the western plains of N America;—Also **bronco**. [Sp]

mustard [mus´tȧrd] *n* any of several herbs (genus *Brassica*) with lobed leaves, yellow flowers, and long beaked pods; a pungent condiment made from the seeds of several common mustards; (*slang*) zest.—*n* **mustard gas**, the vapor from a poisonous blistering liquid. [OFr *mostarde*—L *mustum*, must (because the condiment was prepared with must). See **must** (2).]

muster [mus´tėr] *vt* to assemble, as troops for duty or inspection; to gather.—*vi* to be gathered together, as troops.—*n* an assembling of troops for inspection, etc.; a register of troops mustered. **mus´ter roll**, a register of the officers and men present at the time of muster. [OFr *mostre, monstre*—L *mōnstrum*—*monēre*, to warn.]

musty [must´i] *adj* moldy, spoiled by damp; stale; trite; antiquated.—*adv* **must´ily**.—*n* **must´iness**.

mutable [mū´ta-bl] *adj* that may be changed; inconstant.—*ns* **mūtabil´ity**, state of quality of being mutable.—*adv* **mū´tably**.—*n* **mutā´tion**, act or process of changing; change; a sudden variation in some inheritable characteristic of a plant or animal. [L *mūtabilis*—*mūtāre, -ātum*, to change—*movēre, mōtum*, to move.]

mute [mūt] *adj* dumb; silent.—*n* a deaf-mute; a device that softens the sound of a musical instrument.—*vt* to deaden the sound of a musical instrument.—*adj* **mut´ed**, silent; subdued.—*adv* **mute´ly**.—*n* **mute´ness**. [L *mūtus*.]

mutilate [mu´ti-lāt] *vt* to maim; to render defective; to remove a material part of.—*ns* **mutilā´tion; mūtilātor**. [L *mutilāre, -ātum*—*mutilus*—Gr *mytilos, mitulos*, curtailed.]

mutiny [mūti-ni] *vi* to rise against authority in army, navy, or air force; to revolt against rightful authority;—*pr p* **mu´tinying**; *pt, pt p* **mu´tinied**.—*n* insurrection, esp in armed forces;—*n* **mutineer´**,—*adj* **mū´tinous**,.—*adv* **mū´tinously**.—*n* **mū´tinousness**. [Fr *mutin*, riotous—L *movēre, mōtum*, to move.]

mutter [mut´ėr] *vi* to utter words in a low voice; to grumble.—*vt* to utter indistinctly.—*n* **mutt´erer**. [Prob imit like dial Ger *muttern*; L *muttire*.]

mutton [mut´n] *n* sheep's flesh as food.—*n* **mutt´onchops**, side-whiskers that are narrow at the temple and broad and round by the lower jaw. [OFr *moton*, a sheep—Low L *multō*.]

mutual [mū´tū-ȧl] *adj* given and received in equal amount; having the same feelings one for the other; shared in common.—*n* **mutual fund**, a corporation that invests its shareholders' funds in diversified securities.—*n* **mutual´ity**.—*adv* **mūtually**. [Fr *mutuel*—L *mūtuus*—*mūtāre*, to change.]

muumuu [mōō´mōō] *n* a long loose brightly patterned dress. [Hawaiian.]

Muzak [myōō´zak] trade name for recorded light music played in stores, restaurants, etc.

muzhik, moujik, mujik [mōō-zhik´, mōō´zhik] *n* a Russian peasant. [Russ *muzhik*.]

muzzle [muz´l] *n* the projecting jaws and nose of an animal; a fastening for the mouth to prevent biting; the extreme end of a gun, etc.—*vt* to put a muzzle on; to gag or silence. [OFr *musel* (Fr *museau*)—LL *mūsellum*, dim of *mūsum* or *mūsus*, beak.]

muzzy [muz´i] *adj* dazed, tipsy.—*n* **muzz´iness**.

my [mī] *poss adj* of or belonging to me. [**mine**—OE *mīn* (gen), of me.]

myasthenis gravis [mī´es-thēn´is gräv´is] *n* a disease marked by progressive muscle weakness without atrophy or loss of sensation in the muscles.

mycelium [mī-sē´li-um] *n* the thallus of a fungus when it consists of hyphae; mushroom spawn;—*pl* **myce´lia**. [Gr *mykēs*, a fungus, *ēlos*, a nail or wart.]

mycology [mīkol´o-ji] *n* the study of fungi. [Gr *mykēs*, fungus, *logos*, discourse.]

myopia [mī-ō´pi-a] *n* shortness of sight.—*adj* **myop´ic**.—*n* **my´ope**, a short-sighted person. [Gr *myōps*, short-sighted—*ōps*, the eye.]

myriad [mir´i-ad] *n* a great number of persons or things.—*adj* numberless. [Gr *mȳrias, -ados*, ten thousand.]

myriapod [mir´i-a-pod] *n* a group (Myriapoda) of animals with many jointed legs including the millipedes and centipedes. [Gr *myrios*, numberless, *pous*, gen *podos*, a foot.]

myrmidon [mûr´mi-don] *n* an unquestioning follower. [L,—Gr]

myrrh [mûr] *n* a fragrant gum resin of Arabia and east Africa used in perfume, incense, etc. [OE *myrra*—L and Gr *myrrha*; cf Ar *murr*.]

myrtle [mûr´tl] *n* a genus (*Myrtus communis*) of evergreen shrubs with beautiful and fragrant leaves; any of various other plants, as the periwinkle. [OFr *myrtil*, dim of *myrte*—L *myrtus*—Gr *myrtos*.]

myself [mī-self´] *pron* I, or me, in person—used for emphasis: (reflexively) me. [**me, self**.]

Mysost [mī´sost] *n* a hard, usu. brown, sweet goat's milk cheese.

mystery[1] [mis´tėr-i] *n* something unexplained and secret; a story about a secret crime, etc; secrecy.—*adj* **mystē´rious**,.—*adv* **mystē´riously**.—*n* **mystēriousness**.—[L *mystērium*—Gr *mystērion*—*mystēs*, one initiated—*myein*, to close the eyes.]

mystery[2] [mis´tėr-i] *n* (*arch*) a trade, handicraft; guild; mystery play.—*n* **mystery play**, a medieval drama based on scriptural events as the creation of the world, the Flood, or life life of Christ. [LL *misterium*—L *ministerium*-*minister*, servant. Properly *mistery*; the form *mystery* is due to confusion with **mystery** (1).]

mystic, -al [mis´tik, -ȧl] *adj* relating to, or containing, esoteric rites or doctrines; involving a sacred or a secret meaning revealed only to a spiritually enlightened mind.—*n* **mys´tic**, one who seeks for direct intercourse with God in elevated religious feeling or ecstasy.—*adv* **mys´tically**.—*n* **mys´ticism** [-sizm], the doctrine of the mystics; an effort to attain to direct spiritual communion with God.—*vt* **mys´tify**, to make mysterious, obscure, or secret; to puzzle, bewilder; to play on the credulity of;—*pr p* **mys´tifying**; *pt, pt p* **mys´tified**.—*n* **mystificā´tion**. [L *mysticus*—Gr *mystikos*; same root as **mystery**. (1).]

mystique [mis-tēk´, mēs-tēk] *n* incommunicable spirit, gift, or quality; secret (of an art) as known to its inspired practitioners; sense of mystery, remoteness from the ordinary, and power surrounding a person, activity, etc. [Fr]

myth [mith] *n* an ancient traditional story of gods or heroes, offering an explanation of some fact or phenomenon; a fable; a fictitious person or thing; a commonly-held belief that is untrue or without foundation; myths collectively.—*adjs* **my´thical, my´thic**, relating to myths; fabulous; imaginary.—*adv* **myth´ically**.—*n* **mythol´ogy**, a collection of myths; the study of myths.—*adjs* **mytholog´ical, mytholog´ic**—*adv* **mytholog´ically**.—*n* **mythol´ogist**, [Gr *mȳthos*, story.]

myxedema [mik-si-dēm´a] *n* illness caused by severe thyroxine deficiency.

myxomatosis [miks-ō-mȧ-tō´sis] *n* a severe contagious virus disease of rabbits. [Gr *myxa*, mucus.]

N

nabob [nā´bob] *n* any man of great wealth or importance. [Hindustani *nawwāb*. *See* **nawab**.]
nacre [nā´kėr] *n* mother-of-pearl. [Fr; prob of Eastern origin.]
nadir [nā´dēr, -dėr] *n* the point opposite the zenith, ie that directly under where the observer stands; the lowest point of anything. [Fr,—Ar *nadīr* (*nazīr*), opposite to.]
nag[1] [nag] *n* a horse, esp a small one. [ME *nagge*; origin obscure; cf Middle Du *negge, negghe* (mod Du *neg, negge*).]
nag[2] [nag] *vt* to find fault with constantly; to worry;—*pr p* **nagg´ing**; *pt p* **nagged**. [Cf Norw and Swed *nagga*, to gnaw.]
Nahum [nā´hum] *n* (*Bible*) 34th book of the Old Testament, written by the prophet Nahum, dealing with the judgment upon the city of Nineveh.
naiad [nī´ad] *n* a nymph, presiding over rivers and springs. [Gr *nāias, -ados*, pl *-adĕs*, from *naein*, to flow.]
nail [nāl] *n* a horny plate at the end of a finger or toe; a thin pointed piece of metal for fastening wood.—*vt* to fasten as with nails; (*inf*) to catch or hit.—**nail down**, to settle or establish clearly and unmistakably; to win decisively. [OE *nægel*; Ger *nagel*.]
nainsook [nān-sŏŏk] *n* a soft lightweight muslin. [Hindi.]
naive, naïve [nä-ēv´] *adj* with natural or unaffected simplicity in thought, speech, or manners; artless, ingenuous.—*n* **naïveté** [nä-ēv´tā]. [Fr, fem of *naïf*—L *nātivus*, natural.]
naked [nāk´id] *adj* without clothes; without covering; without a sheath or case (eg a sword, a light); undisguised (eg truth).—*n* **nakedness**. [OE *nacod*; Ger *nackt*.]
namby-pamby [nam´bi-pam´bi] *adj* insipid; weakly sentimental (of a person).—Also *n*. [Nickname for *Ambrose* Philips (1674–1749), whose writings include simple odes to children.]
name [nām] *n* that by which a person or a thing is known or called; a designation; reputed character (eg for honesty; of a miser); authority.—*vt* to give a name to; to speak of by name; to nominate; to appoint to an office; to specify (a date, price, etc.).—*ns* **name-calling**, the use of offensive names esp to win an argument; **name´-dropping**, casual mention of important persons as if they were one's friends, in order to impress; **name´-dropper**.—*adj* **name´less**, without a name; anonymous; unnamed; indefinable.—*adv* **name´ly**, videlicet, that is to say.—*n* **name´sake**, one bearing the same name as another.—**in the name of**, in appeal to; by the authority of; **name of the game**, the essential matter; the basic goal of an activity. [OE *nama*; Ger *name*; L *nōmen*.]
nankeen, nankin [nan-kēn´] *n* a buff-colored cotton cloth; trousers made from this cloth [first made at *Nanking* in China.]
nanny, nannie [nan´i] *n* (*Brit*) a child's nurse. [From *Nan—Ann(e)*.]
nanny goat [nan´i] *n* a female domestic goat. [Same as **nanny**.]
nano- [nān´ō-, nan´o-] in composition, one thousand millionth, as in **nan´osecond**; of microscopic size. [Gr *nanos*, a dwarf.]
nap[1] [nap] *vi* to take a short or casual sleep;—*pr p* **napp´ing**; *pt p* **napped**.—Also *n*. [OE *knappian*.]
nap[2] [nap] *n* a hairy surface on cloth or leather; such a surface.—*adjs* **nap´less, napped**. [ME *noppe*; app—Middle Du or Middle Low Ger *noppe*.]
napalm [nā´päm, na´] *n* a substance added to gasoline to form a jellylike compound, used in fire bombs and flamethrowers.—*vt* to attack or burn with napalm. [*na*phthenate *palm*itate.]
nape [nāp] *n* the back of the neck.
napery [nā´pėr-i] *n* household linen, esp for the table. [OFr *naperie*—Low L *napāria*—*napa*, a cloth—L *mappa*, a napkin.]
naphtha [naf´tha] *n* a flammable liquid distilled from coal tar, petroleum, etc.—*n* **naph´thalene**, a white, crystalline hydrocarbon produced from coal tar, used in moth repellents, dyes, etc. [Gr.]
Napierian, Naperian [nā-pēr´i-an] *adj* pertaining to John *Napier* of Edinburgh, Scotland (1550–1617), esp of the system of natural logarithms invented by him.
napkin [nap´kin] *n* a small square of linen, paper, etc. used while eating. [Dim of Fr *nappe*—L *mappa*.]
napoleon [na-pōl´yȯn, or i-on] *n* an oblong, many-layered pastry filled with cream or custard; a former French gold coin.
Napoleonic [na-pō-li-on´ik] *adj* of Napoleon (1769–1821), a French general, emperor of France 1804–15.
narcissus [när-sis´us] *n* a spring-flowering bulb plant (genus *Narcissus*) including daffodils and jonquils, esp one with a short trumpet and flowers borne separately.—*pl* **narciss´uses, -ciss´ī, -ciss´us**.—*n* **narciss´ism**, excessive interest in one's own body or self. [L,—Gr *Narkissos*, a youth who fell in love with his own image.]
narcotic [när-kot´ik] *adj* inducing sleep.—*n* any drug producing a narcotic effect.—*n* **nar´colepsy**, illness marked by sudden short spells of overpowering sleepiness. [Gr *narkōtikos*—*narkē*, numbness, torpor.]
nard [närd] *n* spikenard. [L *nardus*—Gr *nardos*; apparently an Eastern word.]
narrate [na-rāt´] *vt* to give a continuous account of (details of an event, or a series of events).—*n* **narrā´tion**, act of telling; that which is told; an orderly account of a series of events.—*adj* **narrative** [nar´a-tiv], narrating; giving an account of any occurrence; story-telling.—*n* that which is narrated; a story.—*n* **narrā´tor**, one who tells a story. [L *narrāre, -ātum*, prob—*gnārus*, knowing.]
narrow [nar´ō] *adj* of little breadth; of small extent; confining; limited (eg fortune or circumstances); with little to spare, little margin (eg escape, majority); careful (eg search, scrutiny); bigoted or illiberal in views.—*n* (usu. in *pl*) a narrow passage, channel, or strait.—*vti* to make narrower; to contract.—*adj*.—*adv* **narr´owly**.—*adj* **narr´ow-mind´ed**, of a narrow or illiberal mind.—*ns* **narr´ow-mind´edness; narr´owness**. [OE *nearu*.]
narwhal, narwhale [när´wȧl] *n* an arctic whale (*Mondon monoceros*) with a long twisted projecting ivory tusk in the male. [Dan *narhval*; ON *nāhvalr* is supposed to be from *nār*, corpse, *hvalr*, whale, from the creature's pallid color.]
nasal [nā´zȧl] *adj* belonging to the nose; affected by, or sounded through, the nose.—*n* a sound uttered through the nose.—*vi* **nā´salize**, to render nasal, as a sound.—*adv* **nā´sally**, by or through the nose. [L *nāsus*, the nose.]
nascent [nās´ent] *adj* coming into being, beginning to form or develop. [L *nāscens, -entis*, pr p of *nāscī, nātus*, to be born.]
nasturtium [nas-tûr´shȯm] *n* a genus (*Tropaeolum*) of plants with a pungent odor, widely cultivated as ornamentals. [L *nāsus*, nose, *torquēre*, to twist (from its pungency).]
nasty [nas´ti] *adj* disgustingly foul, nauseous; morally offensive; disagreeable, unpalatable, or annoying; difficult to deal with (eg problem); dangerous or serious (eg fall, illness).—*adv* **nas´tily**.—*n* **nas´tiness**. [Perh for earlier *nasky* (cf Swed dial *naskug, nasket*); or perh conn with Du *nestig*, dirty.]
natal [nā´tȧl] *adj* of or connected with birth; native. [L *nātālis*—*nāscī, nātus*, to be born.]
natation [nat-, or nāt-ā´sh(ȯ)n] *n* swimming.—*adj* **nā´tatory**. [L *natāns, -antis*, pr p of *natāre*, freq of *nāre*, to swim.]
nation [nā´sh(ȯ)n] *n* a body of people marked off by common descent, language, culture, or historical tradition; people united under a single government.—*adj* **national** [na´shȯnȧl], pertaining to a nation or nations; common to the whole nation; public (eg debt); attached to one's own country.—*n* a citizen or subject.—*vt* **na´tionalize**, to make national; to transfer ownership to the nation.—*n* **na´tionalist**, one who favors the unity, independence, interests, or domination of a nation.—*adj* **nationalis´tic**.—*ns* **na´tionalism; nationality** [-al´-iti], the status of belonging to a nation by birth or naturalization; a nation or national group.—*adv* **na´tionally**.—*adj* **na´tionwide**, covering the whole nation.—**national anthem**, an official song or hymn of a nation; **national bank**, central bank; a bank operating under federal charter and supervision; **national debt**, money borrowed by the government of a country and not yet paid back; **National Guard**, a militia recruited by each state, equipped by the federal government, and subject to the call of either; **national park**, an area owned by or for the nation by an act of the US Congress; **national socialism**, the doctrines of the **National Socialist party**, an extreme nationalistic fascist party in Germany, led by Adolf Hitler (d 1945).—Also **Nazism**. [L *nātiō, -ōnis*—*nāscī, nātus*, to be born.]
native [nā´tiv] *adj* natural to a person or thing, innate, inherent; of, pertaining to, or belonging to the place of one's birth (eg language); belonging to the people inhabiting a country originally or at the time of its discovery, indigenous; not exotic; occurring naturally.—*n* one born in the place indicated; an original inhabitant; an indigenous plant or animal.—*n* **Native American**, an American Indian, Amerindian.—*adj* **native-born**, born in a specified locality.—*n* **nativity** [na-tiv´i-ti], time, place, and manner of birth, esp **the Nativity**, the birth of Jesus; a horoscope at the time of one's birth; the place of origin. [L *nātīvus*—*nāscī, nātus*, to be born.]
natter [nat´er] *vi* to chatter.
natterjack [nat´ėr-jak] *n* a toad with a yellow stripe down the back. [Origin unknown.]
natty [nat´i] *adj* dapper, spruce.—*adv* **natt´ily**. [Possibly connected with **neat**.]
natural [na´chûr-ȧl] *adj* produced by, or according to, nature; not artificial; innate, not acquired; true to nature; lifelike; normal (*a natural result*); at ease; (*mus*) neither sharped nor flatted.—*n* one having a natural aptitude (for), or being an obvious choice (for); (*inf*) a thing assured of success by its very nature, a certainty.—*vt* **nat´uralize**, to confer citizenship upon (an alien); to adapt to a different climate (as plants).—*vi* to become

established as if native.—*ns* **naturalīzā´tion; nat´uralism**, practice of, or attachment to, what is natural; in art or literature, a close following of nature without idealization; **nat´uralist**, one who studies animals or plants esp in the field.—*adj* **naturalist´ic**, belonging to the doctrines of naturalism.—*adv* **nat´urally**.—*ns* **nat´uralness; natural history**, the study of the animal, mineral, and vegetable world; **natural logarithm**, a logarithm with *e* as the base; **e** being 1 + 1/1 + 1/1.2 + 1/1.2.3 . . ., or 2.71828 . . .; **natural resources**, those forms of wealth as supplied by nature, as coal, oil, water power, etc.; **natural science**, the science of nature, including biology, chemistry, physics, etc.; **natural selection**, evolution by the *survival of the fittest* (ie of those forms of plants and animals best adjusted to the conditions under which they live), with inheritance of their qualities by succeeding generation; **natural theology**, theology deriving its knowledge of God from the study of nature, without revelation.—*adv* **nat´urally** in a natural manner, by nature; of course. [L *nātūrālis*—*nātūra*, nature.]

nature [nā´chûr] *n* the power that regulates the world; the entire external world; the essential qualities of anything; constitution; kind or order; character, instinct, or disposition; a primitive undomesticated condition before society is organized; natural scenery.—*adj* **nā´tured**, having a certain temper or disposition (used in compounds, as *good-natured*).—**by nature**, inherently. [Fr,—L *nātūra*—*nāscī, nātus*, to be born.]

naught [nöt] *n* nothing; a zero.—Also **nought**. [OE *nāht, nāwiht*—*nā*, never, *wiht*, whit.]

naughty [nöt´i] *adj* mischievous or disobedient; indelicate.—*adv* **naught´ily**.—*n* **naught´iness**. [**naught**.]

nausea [nö´si-a, nö´shi-a] *n* a feeling of inclination to vomit; loathing.—*vi* **nau´seāte**, to feel nausea or disgust.—*vt* to loathe; to strike with disgust.—*adjs* **nau´seāting**, causing nausea or disgust; **nau´seous** [-shůs], producing nausea; loathsome.—*adv* **nau´seously**.—*n* **nau´seousness**. [L,—Gr *nautiā*, sea-sickness—*naus*, a ship.]

nautical [nöt´ik-ål] *adj* of ships, sailors, or navigation.—**nautical mile** (*see* **mile**). [L *nauticus*—Gr *nautikos*—*nautēs*, sailor—*naus*, a ship.]

nautilus [nö´ti-lus] *n* any of a genus (*Nautilus*) of cephalopod mollusks of the S Pacific and Indian oceans with a chambered external shell that is pearly on the inside.—*pl* **nau´tiluses**, or **nau´tili**. [L,—Gr *nautilos*, a sailor, a paper nautilus—*naus*, a ship.]

Navaho, Navajo [na´vå-hō] *n* member of an Amerindian people of northern New Mexico and Arizona.—*pl* **-ho, -jo**, or **-s**; the Athapascan language of this people.

naval [nā´vål] *adj* pertaining to warships or to a navy.—**naval architect**, one whose profession is designing ships. [L *nāvālis*—*nāvis*, a ship.]

nave[1] [nāv] *n* the main part of a church from the chancel to the principal entrance. [L *nāvis*, a ship.]

nave[2] [nāv] *n* the hub of a wheel. [OE *nafu*; cf Du *naaf*, Ger *nabe*.]

navel [nāv´ėl] *n* the small scar in the abdomen marking the position of former attachment of the umbilical cord.—*n* **navel orange**, a seedless orange with a navellike hollow at its apex. [OE *nafela*, dim of *nafu*, nave.]

navigate [nav´i-gāt] *vti* to steer a ship, aircraft, motor vehicle, etc.; to travel through or over (water, air, etc.) in a ship or aircraft; to find one's way and keep one's course; (*inf*) to walk.—*adj* **nav´igable**, sufficiently deep, wide, etc., to give passage to ships; that can be steered.—*ns* **navigabil´ity, nav´igableness**.—*ns* **navigā´tion**, the act, science, or art of directing the movement of ships or aircraft; **nav´igator**, one skilled in the navigation of a ship or aircraft. [L *nāvigāre, -ātum*—*nāvis*, a ship, *agĕre*, to drive.]

navy [nā´vi] *n* the whole of a nation's ships-of-war; (often **Navy**) a nation's entire sea force, including ships, men, stores, etc.; a very dark blue.—*ns* **navy bean**, a white-seeded small bean; **navy blue**, an almost black blue; **Navy Cross**, a US naval decoration awarded for heroism in combat. [OFr *navie*—L *nāvis*, a ship.]

nawab [nä-wäb´] *n* a nabob. [Hindustani *nawwāb*—Ar *nawwāb*, respectful pl of *nā-ib*, deputy.]

nay [nā] *adv* no; not only so but; and even more than that.—*n* a denial; a vote against (a motion). [ME *nay, nai*—ON *nei*; Dan *nei*; cog with **no**.]

Nazarene [naz´år-ēn] *n* a follower of Jesus of Nazareth; a native or resident of Nazareth; member of the Protestant denomination, Church of the Nazarene which shares Methodist doctrine.

Nazi [nä´tsē] *n, adj* for *Na*tional-so*zi*alist, National Socialist, Hitlerite.—*n* **Naz´ism**.—*vt* **Naz´ify**. [Ger.]

Neanderthal [ne-an´dėr-tal] *adj* of, or pertaining to, a Paleolithic (ie Old Stone Age) species of man whose remains were first found in 1857 in a cave in the *Neanderthal*, a valley in the Rhineland.

neap [nēp] *adj* either of the lowest high tides in the month.—*n* a neap tide. [OE *nēp*, apparently meaning helpless; *nēpflod*, neap tide.]

Neapolitan [nē-a-pol´i-tån] *adj* of the city of *Naples* or its inhabitants.—**Neapolitan ice cream**, brick ice cream in layers of different flavors. [L *Neapolītānus*—Gr *Neāpolis*, Naples—*neos*, new, *polis*, city.]

near [nēr] *adv* to or at a little distance; almost.—*prep* close to.—*adj* not far away in place or time; close in kin, friendship, or other relation; close in imitation or resemblance; approximate; narrow, barely missing or avoiding something.—*vti* to approach; to come nearer.—*adv* **near´ly**, almost.—*ns* **near´ness; near beer**, a beer with very low alcoholic content; **Near East**, countries near the eastern Mediterranean, including those of Arabia.—*adj* **near´sight´ed**, myopic.—*n* **near´sight´edness**. [OE *nēar*, comp of *nēah*, nigh (*adv*), and ON *nǣr*, comp (but also used as positive) of *nā*, nigh; cf Ger *näher*.]

neat[1] [nēt] *n* the common domestic bovine (*Bos taurus*).—*n* **neat´herd**, herdsman. [OE *nēat*, cattle, a beast—*nēotan, niotan*, to use.]

neat[2] [nēt] *adj* clean and tidy; adroit or skilful; skilfully made or done; well and concisely put; undiluted (of liquor); (*slang*) nice, pleasing, etc.—*adv* **neat´ly**.—*n* **neat´ness**. [Fr *net*—L *nitidus*, shining—*nitēre*, to shine.]

nebula [neb´ū-la] *n* a faint, misty appearance in the heavens produced either by a group of stars too distant to be seen singly, or by diffused gaseous matter;—*pl* **neb´ulae** [-lē].—*adjs* **neb´ular**, pertaining to nebulae; **neb´ulous**, unclear; vague.—*ns* **nebulos´ity, neb´ulousness**. [L *nebula*, mist; cf Ger *nephelē*, cloud, mist.]

necessary [nes´es-år-i] *adj* indispensable; required; inevitable.—*n* something necessary.—*adv* **nec´essarily**. [L *necessārius*.]

necessity [nė-ses´i-ti] *n* compulsion exerted by the nature of things; the constraining power of circumstances; something that cannot be done without; imperative need; poverty.—*n* **necessitā´rianism**, determinism.—*n* and *adj* **necessitā´rian**.—*vt* **necess´itāte**, to make necessary or unavoidable; *adj* **necess´itous**, urgent; pressing; very poor, destitute.—*adv* **necess´itously**.—*n* **necess´itousness**.—**of necessity**, necessarily. [L *necessitās, -ātis*.]

neck [nek] *n* the part connecting head and body; that part of a garment nearest the neck; a necklike part, esp a narrow strip of land; the narrowest part of a bottle; a strait.—*vti* (*slang*) to kiss and caress in making love.—*ns* **neck´erchief**, a kerchief for the neck; **neck´lace** [-lis], a chain, or string of beads or precious stones worn on the neck; **neck´tie**, a band tied round the neck under a collar and tied in front; **neck´wear** articles worn about the neck, as neckties, scarfs, etc.—**neck and neck**, very close, as in a contest; **stick one's neck out**, to act boldly, risking failure. [OE *hnecca*; Ger *nacken*.]

necro- [nek´rō-, -ro-] in composition, dead, dead body.—*ns* **necrŏl´ogy**, an obituary list; **nec´rōmancer**, a sorcerer; **nec´rōmancy**, divination by alleged communication with the dead; sorcery.—*adjs* **necrōman´tic**.—*adv* **necrōman´tically**.—*ns* **necrŏp´olis**, a cemetery; **nec´rŏpsy**, a post mortem examination; **necrō´sis**, death of part of the living body.—*adj* **necrŏt´ic**, affected by necrosis. [Gr *nekros*, dead body, dead.]

nectar [nek´tår], *n* the beverage of the gods; a delicious beverage; a sweetish liquid in many flowers, used by bees to make honey.—*adj* **nec´tarous**.—*n* **nec´tary**, the part of a flower that secretes nectar. [Gr *nektar*; ety uncertain.]

nectarine [nek-tår-ēn] *n* a smooth-skinned peach.

née, nee [nā] *adj* born (*Mrs Rebecca Crawley, née Sharp*). [Fr fem of *né*, pt p of *naître*, to be born—L *nāscī, nātus*, to be born.]

need [nēd] *n* necessity; a state that requires relief; want of the means of living.—*vt* to have need of; to require; to be obliged.—*vi* to be necessary; to be in want.—*adjs* **need´ful**, needy; necessary, requisite; **need´less**, uncalled for.—*adv* **need´lessly**.—*n* **need´lessness**.—*adj* **need´y**, very poor.—**have need to**, to be required to; **if need be**, if it is required. [OE *nēd, nīed, nȳd*; Du *nood*, Ger *noth*.]

needle [nēd´l] *n* a small, sharp piece of steel for sewing; any similar slender, pointed rod for knitting or crocheting; the short, pointed piece that moves in the groove of a phonograph record and transmits vibrations; the pointer of a compass, gauge, etc.; the thin, short leaf of the pine, spruce, etc.; the sharp, slender metal tube at the end of a hypodermic syringe.—*vt* (*inf*) to goad, prod, or tease.—*ns* **needle therapy**, acupuncture; **need´lewoman**, a seamstress; **need´lework**, work done with a needle. [OE *nǣdl*; Ger *nadel*; cog with Ger *nähen*, to sew, L *nēre*, to spin.]

ne´er [nār] *adv* (*poetic*) never.—*n* **ne´er-do-well**, a shiftless, irresponsible person.

nefarious [ni-fā´ri-us] *adj* extremely wicked.—*adv* **nefā´riously**.—*n* **nefā´riousness**. [L *nefārius*—*nefās*, wrong, crime—*ne-*, not, *fās*, divine law, prob from *fārī*, to speak.]

negate [ni-gāt´] *vt* to deny; to nullify.—*n* **negation** [negā´sh(ó)n], act of saying no; denial; the absence or opposite (of something that is actual, positive, or affirmative).—*adj* **negative** [neg´ātiv], expressing denial or refusal; lacking distinguishing features, devoid of positive attributes; (*math*) denoting a quantity less than zero, or one to be subtracted; (*photography*) reversing the light and shade of the original subject; (*elect*) at relatively lower potential; of, having, or producing, negative electricity; having an excess of electrons.—*n* a negative word, reply, etc.; refusal; something that is the opposite or negation of something else; the side that votes or argues for the opposition (as in a debate); the platelike part to which the current flows from the external circuit in a discharging storage battery; a negative photographic image on transparent material.—*vt* to refuse assent; to reject by vote.—*adv* **neg´atively**.—*n* **neg´ativeness**. [L *negāre, -ātum*, to deny.]

negatron [neg´å-tron] *n* electron.

neglect [ni-glekt´] *vt* to pay little or no respect or attention to; to ignore as of no consequence; to leave uncared for; to omit by carelessness.—*n* disregard; slight; omission.—*adj* **neglect´ful**, careless; accustomed to omit or neglect duties, etc.; slighting.—*adv* **neglect´fully**.—*n* **neglect´fulness**. [L *neglegĕre, neglectum*—*neg-* or *nec-*, not, *legĕre*, to gather.]

negligee [neg-li-jā´] *n* a woman's loosely fitting dressing gown. [Fr *négligé*, neglected.]

negligence [neg´li-jėns] *n* carelessness or want of attention; an act of carelessness; a carelessly easy manner.—*adj* **neg´ligent**.—*adv* **neg´ligently**.—

adj **neg´ligible**, such as may be ignored or left out of consideration; trifling. [L *negligentia* for *neglegentia—neglegĕre*, to neglect.]

negotiate [ni-gō´shi-āt] *vi* to bargain (with), to confer (with) for the purpose of coming to an agreement or arrangement.—*vt* to settle by agreement (eg a treaty, a loan); to transfer or exchange for value (eg a bill); to get past (eg an obstacle, a difficulty).—*adj* **nego´tiable** (of bills, drafts etc.), capable of being transferred or assigned in the course of business from one person to another.—*ns* **negotiabil´ity; negotiā´tion; negō´tiator**. [L *negōtiārī, -ātus—negōtium*, business—*neg-*, not, *ōtium*, leisure.]

Negrito [ne-grē´to] *n* a member of any of several diminutive Negroid races, esp in the Malayan region or in Polynesia.

Negro [nē´grō] *n* a member of the dominant group of mankind in Africa, characterized generally by a dark skin; a member of the Negroid group; any person with some Negro ancestors.—*adj* **Negroid**, denoting or of one of the major groups of mankind, including most of the peoples of Africa South of the Sahara. [Sp *negro*—L *niger, nigra, nigrum*, black.]

Nehemiah [nē-he-mī´a] *n* (*Bible*) 16th book of the Old Testament, completing the story of the return to Palestine after the exile.

neigh [nā] *vi* to utter the cry of a horse;—*pr p* **neigh´ing**; *pt, pt p* **neighed** [nād].—*n* the cry of a horse. [OE *hnǣgan*.]

neighbor [nā´bȯr] *n* a person who lives near another; a fellow man.—*adj* neighboring.—*vti* to live or be near.—*n* **neigh´borhood**, state of being neighbors; a particular community, area, or district.—*adjs* **neigh´boring**, adjoining; **neigh´borly**, friendly, sociable.—Also *adv*.—*n* **neigh´borliness.—in the neighborhood of**, (*inf*) about; approximately. [OE *nēahgebūr—nēah*, near, *gebūr* or *būr*, a farmer.]

neither [nē´THėr or nī´THėr] *adj* and *pron* not one or the other (of two); not either.—*conj* not either; also not. [OE *nāther, nāwther*, abbrev of *nāhwæther—nā*, never, *hwæther*, whether; the vowel assimilated to **either**.]

nematode [nėm-ȧ-tōd´] *n* any of a phylum (Nematoda) of elongated cylindrical worms parasitic in animals or plants or free-living in soil or water.

Nemesis [nem´e-sis] *n* (*myth*) the Greek goddess of retribution; **nemesis**, just punishment; one who imposes it; anyone or anything that seems to defeat one. [Gr *nemesis*, retribution—*nemein*, to deal out, dispense.]

neo- [nē´ō] in composition, new, as in **neoclassic**, belonging to a revival of classicism; **neonāt´al**, newly born. [Gr *neos*.]

neocolonialism [nē-ō-kol-ōn´i-al-izm] *n* the exploitation of a supposedly independent region, as by imposing a puppet government.

neoconservative [nē-ō-kȯn-sûrv´ȧ-tiv] *n* a former liberal advocating politically conservative views.—*n* **neoconserv´atism**.

neodymium [nē-ō-dim´i-ŭm] *n* a metallic element (symbol Nd; at wt 144.2; at no 60), a rare earth. [**neo-**, and *didymium*, a mixture of neodymium and praseodymium, formerly thought to be an element—Gr *didymos*, twin.]

neo-impressionism [nē-ō-im-presh-ȯn-izm] *n* a late 19th century French art movement reintroducing the idea (rejected by impressionists) that a picture should be deliberately planned.

neolithic [nē-ō-lith´ik] *adj* of the later Stone Age, marked by the use of polished stone implements. [Gr *neos*, new, *lithos*, a stone.]

neology [nē-ol´o-ji] *n* the introduction of new words, or of new senses of old words, into a language.—*n* **neol´ogism**, a new word, phrase, or doctrine; a meaningless word coined by a psychotic. [Gr *neos*, new, *logos*, word.]

neon [nē´on] *n* an inert gaseous element (symbol Ne; at wt 38.30; at no 10) found in the atmosphere.—**neon lamp**, an electric discharge lamp containing neon, giving a red glow. [Neuter of Gr *neos*, new.]

neonatal [nē-ō-nā´tl] *adj* of or relating to a newborn child, esp one less than a month old.—*n* **nē´onāte**.

neophyte [nē´ō-fīt] *n* a new convert; a novice, beginner. [Gr *neophytos*, newly planted—*phyein*, to produce.]

neoplasm [nē´o-plazm] *n* a tumor.

neoprene [nē´ō-prēn] *n* a tough synthetic rubber.

Neorican [nē´o-rē´kȧn] *n* A New Yorker of Puerto Rican origin or descent.—Also *adj*.—Also **Nuyorican, Newyorican**.

nepenthe [ni-pen´thē] *n* anything that causes forgetfulness of sorrow. [Gr *nepenthēs, es*—prefix *nē*, not, *penthos*, grief.]

nephew [nev´ū or nef´ū] *n* the son of a brother or sister. [OFr *neveu*—L *nepōs, nepōtis*, grandson; cf OE *nefa*, Ger *neffe*, nephew.]

nephrite [nef´rīt] *n* a less valuable form of jade, ranging in color from white to dark green.

nephro- [nef´rō], **nephr-**, in composition, kidney. [Gr *nephros*, a kidney];—eg *ns* **nephrec´tomy**, the surgical removal of a kidney; **nephrol´ogy**, a branch of medicine dealing with the kidneys.—*adj* **nephrit´ic**, of, or in, the kidneys.—*n* **nephrī´tis**, inflammation of the kidneys.

ne plus ultra [nā plus ul´tra] nothing further; the uttermost point or extreme perfection of anything. [L.]

nepotism [nep´o-tizm] *n* favoritism shown to relatives, esp in securing jobs.—*n* **nep´otist**. [L *nepōs, nepōtis*, a grandson.]

Neptune [nep´tūn] *n* the Roman god of the sea; the planet eighth in distance from the sun.—*adj* **Neptū´nian**, pertaining to Neptune or to the sea; (*geol*) formed by water. [L *Neptūnus*.]

neptunium [nep-tūn´i-ŭm] *n* a radioactive element (symbol Np; at wt 237; at no 93) (*See* **plutonium**). [L *Neptunus*.]

nerd [nûrd] *n* (*slang*) a foolish or ineffectual person.—Also **nurd**.

nereid [nē´rē-id] *n* (*Gr myth*) any of the sea nymphs fathered by Nereus. [Gr *nērēis* or *nērēis—Nēreus*.]

nereis [ner-ē´is] *n* any of a genus (*Nereis*) of greenish marine worms with paired, segmented appendages.

nerve [nûrv] *n* any of the fibers or bundles of fibers carrying impulses of sensation or of movement between the brain and spinal cord and all parts of the body; courage, coolness in danger; (*inf*) impudent boldness; (*pl*) nervousness, anxiety.—*vt* to give strength, courage, or vigor to.—*ns* **nerve cell**, a cell transmitting impulses to nerve tissue; **nerve center**, a group of closely connected cells; a center of control from which instructions are sent out; **nerve gas**, a poison gas that affects the nervous system.—*adjs* **nerve´less**, incapable of effort or movement; confident, not nervous; **nerve´racking, nerve´wracking**, inflicting great strain on the nerves; **ner´vous**, of the nerves or nervous system; excitable; easily agitated; timid; uneasy.—*ns* **nervous breakdown**, loss of mental and emotional stability, usu. to the extent of requiring hospitalization; **nervous system**, the brain, spinal cord, and nerves collectively.—*adj* **nervy** (*inf*) bold and presumptuous; cool and confident.—**get on one's nerves** (*inf*) to make one irritable; **nerve oneself**, to collect one's energy or courage for an effort. [L *nervus*, sinew; cf Gr *neuron*. *See* **neuro-**.]

nescience [nesh´(y)ėns] *n* ignorance; lack of knowledge.—*adj* **nes´cient**. [L *nescientia—nesеīre*, to be ignorant—*ne*, not, *scīre*, to know.]

ness [nes] *n* a promontory. [OE *næs, næss*.]

nest [nest] *n* a structure prepared for egg-laying, brooding, and nursing, or as a shelter; the place used by insects, fish, etc. for spawning or breeding; a comfortable residence; a place where anything teems, prevails, or is fostered; the occupants of a nest, as a brood, a swarm, a gang; a set of things (as boxes) fitting one within another.—*vi* to build or occupy a nest.—*ns* **nest egg**, money put aside as a reserve or to establish a fund; **nest´ling**, a young bird who has not abandoned the nest. [OE *nest*; Ger *nest*, L *nīdus*.]

nestle [nes´l] *vi* to lie close or snug as in a nest; to settle comfortably; to lie sheltered, as a house among trees.—*vt* to rest snugly. [OE *nestlian—nest*.]

net[1] [net] *n* an open fabric of twine, etc. knotted into meshes for catching birds, fishes, etc.; anything like a net; a snare; a difficulty.—*vt* to snare or enclose as with a net; to hit (a ball) into the net at racket games for the loss of a point or into the goal for a score (as in hockey or soccer).—*pr p* **nett´ing**; *pt, pt p* **nett´ed**.—*ns* **nett´ing**, a netted material; **net´work**, an arrangement or pattern with intersecting lines; a chain of interconnected people, operations, or broadcasting stations; **net´working**, the making of contacts and trading information, as for career advancement; the interconnection of computer systems. [OE *net, nett*; Du *net*, Ger *netz*.]

net[2] [net] *adj* clear of all charges, allowances, or deductions.—*n* a net amount, price, weight, profit, etc.—*vt* to clear as profit. [Fr; same word as **neat** (2).]

nether [neTH´ėr] *adj* lower or under.—*adj* **neth´ermost**, lowest.—*n* **neth´erworld**, the underworld; hell. [OE *neothera*, adj—*nither*, adv, from the root *ni-*, down; Ger *nieder*, low.]

netsuke [net´su-ki] *n* an intricately carved ivory toggle used in Japan. [Jap.]

nettle [net´l] *n* a genus (*Urtica*) of plants with stinging hairs.—*vt* to irritate, annoy, or vex.—*adj* **nett´lesome**, annoying, vexing. [OE *netele*; Ger *nessel*.]

Neufchatel [nyōō, -nōō-sha-tel´] *n* a soft, cow's-milk cheese with a mild flavor. [*Neufchâtel*, France.]

neur- [nūr-], **neuro-** [nū´rō-] in composition, nerve.—*adj* **neural** [nū´ral] of, or relating to, nerves.—*n* **neuralgia** [-ral´jȧ; Gr *algos*, pain] pain along a nerve.—*adj* **neural´gic**.—*n* **neurasthenia** [nū-ras-thē´ni-a; Gr *astheneia*, weakness] nervous debility.—*adj* **neurasthen´ic**.—*n* one suffering from neurasthenia.—*ns* **neuritis** [nū-rī´tis] inflammation of a nerve; **neurology** [nū-rol´o-ji] the branch of medicine dealing with the nervous system and its diseases.—*adj* **neurolog´ical**.—*ns* **neurol´ogist; neuron**, a nerve cell and its processes; **neu´roscience**, a science that deals with the anatomy, physiology, and biochemistry of the nervous system as it relates to learning and behavior; **neurō´sis**, functional derangement due to a disordered nervous system, generally not associated with any physical disease or injury; mental disturbance accompanied by anxiety and obsessional fears.—*adj* **neurotic** [-rot´ik] of the nature of, characterised by, or affected by, neurosis; of abnormal sensibility; (loosely) obsessive.—*n* a person with neurosis. [Gr *neuron*, a sinew, a nerve. *See* **nerve**.]

neuropteran [nū-rop´tėr-ȧn] *n* any of an order of insects that have generally four net-veined wings.—Also *adj*.—*adj* **neurop´terous**. [Gr *neuron*, a sinew, *pteron*, a wing.]

neuter [nū´tėr] *adj* (*gram*) neither masculine nor feminine; (*biol*) having no sexual organs; having undeveloped sex organs in the adult; a neuter word, plant, insect, or castrated animal.—*vt* to castrate or spay (an animal). [L *neuter*, neither—*ne*, not, *uter*, either.]

neutral [nū´trȧl] *adj* taking no part on either side; of no decided character; having no decided color; (*chem*) neither acid nor alkaline.—*n* a neutral person or nation; a neutral color; a position or gear in which no power is transmitted.—*n* **neutrality** [-tral´i-ti].—*adv* **neu´trally**.—*vt* **neu´tralize**, to declare neutral; to counteract, to render of no effect.—*ns* **neu´tralizer; neutralizā´tion**. [L *neutrālis—neuter*, neither.]

neutron [nū´tron] *n* an uncharged subatomic particle, of about the same mass as a proton.—*n* **neutrino** [-trē´nō] uncharged particle with approx zero mass. [L *neuter*, neither.]

never [nev´ėr] *adv* not ever, at no time; not at all; in no case.—*adv* **nev´ermore**, never again.—*n* **nev´er-nev´er land**, an imaginary place or situation.—*adv* **nevertheless´**, in spite of that; however. [OE *nǣfre*—*ne*, not, *ǣfre*, ever.]

nevus [nē´vus] *n* a birthmark or mole.—*pl* **nē´vī**. [L *naevus*.]

new [nū] *adj* lately made, invented, discovered; recently heard of, or experienced for the first time; different, changed (eg *turn over a new leaf, a new man*); recently grown, fresh; unused; starting as the repetition of a cycle, series, etc.; unaccustomed; having been in a position, relationship, etc., only a short time (eg a member, an assistant); recently commenced.—*adv* again; newly; recently.—*n* **new blood**, a recent arrival in an organization expected to bring new ideas and revitalize the system.—*adj* **new´born**, just born; reborn.—*ns* **new´comer**, a recent arrival; **New Deal**, the principles and policies adopted by President F D Roosevelt in the 1930s to advance economic recovery and social welfare; **New England**, the six northeastern States of the US.—*adj* **new´-fashioned**, recently come into fashion; new in form.—*adv* **newly**, recently; lately.—*ns* **new´lywed´**, a recently married person; **new math** (*inf*) mathematics based on the set theory; **new moon**, the moon when it is seen in the evening as a crescent after it has disappeared; **New Testament**, the part of the Bible that contains the life and teachings of Jesus and his followers; **New World**, the Western Hemisphere; **New Year's Day**, January 1, observed as a legal holiday in the US and many other countries; **Newyorican**, Neorican. [OE *nīwe, nēowe*; Ger *neu*, Ir *nuadh*, L *novus*, Gr *neos*.]

newel [nū´ėl] *n* the upright column about which the steps of a circular staircase wind; the post that supports the handrail of a flight of stairs. [OFr *nual* (Fr *noyau*), fruitstone—Low L *nucālis*, nut-like—L *nux, nucis*, a nut.]

newfangled [nū-fang´gld] *adj* (*contemptuous*) new; novel.—*n* **newfang´ledness**. [ME *newefangel*—*newe* (OE *nīwe*), new, *fangel*, ready to catch—*fang-*, the stem of OE *fōn*, to take.]

news [nūz] *n* (*pl*) a report of a recent event; something one had not heard before; **news agency** an organization that gathers news for newspapers and other news media such as television and radio (*also* **press agency**);—*ns* **news´boy**, a boy who delivers or sells newspapers; **news´cast**, a radio or television news broadcast; **news´caster; news´deal´er**, a retailer of newspapers, magazines, etc.; **news´group** on the Internet, a group of people who use an on-line service to discuss a particular topic; **news´letter**, a bulletin issued regularly, containing news, supplied to members of a particular group; **news´man**, newsdealer; one who gathers and reports news for a newspaper, TV station, etc.; **news´paper**, a paper published periodically for circulating news, etc.; **news´paperman**, a reporter, editor, etc. for a newspaper; a newspaper owner or publisher; **news´paper-woman; news´print**, cheap paper for printing newspapers.—*adjs* **news´worthy**, timely and important or interesting; **newsy**, (*inf*) containing much news. [Late ME *newes*, an imit of Fr *nouvelles*.]

newt [nūt] *n* any of various small amphibious salamanders (genus *Triturus*). [Formed with initial *n*, borrowed from the article *an*, from *ewt*, a form of *evet* or **eft**—OE *efeta, efete*.]

newton [nū´tȯn] *n* unit of force in the mks system which, acting on a mass of one kilogram, produces an acceleration of one meter per second per second.

next [nekst] *adj* (*superlative* of **nigh**) nearest; immediately preceding or following.—*adv* in the nearest time, place, rank, etc.; on the first subsequent occasion.—*prep* nearest.—*adj* **next´-door´**, in or at the next house, building, etc.—*adv* nearest; immediately after. [OE *nēhst* (*nīehst*), superlative of *nēh* (*nēah*), near; Ger *nächst*.]

nexus [nek´sus] *n* a link or connection. [L *nexus*, pl *-ūs*—*nectĕre*, to bind.]

Nez Perce [nez pers, nes pārs] *n* a member of an Amerindian people of Idaho, Washington and Oregon; Penutian language of this people.

niacin [nī´ȧ-sin] *n* nicotinic acid.

nib [nib] *n* a bird's beak; a pen point.—*adj* **nibbed**, having a nib. [Variant of **neb**.]

nibble [nib´l] *vti* to eat food by small bites; to bite (at) lightly and intermittently.—*n* **nibb´ler**. [Origin obscure; cf L Ger *nibbelen*, Du *knibbelen*.]

niblick [nib´lik] *n* a golf club with a heavy iron head with wide face, used for lofting.

nice [nīs] *adj* fastidious; able to make fine distinctions, minutely accurate (eg judgment, ear); displaying fine discrimination (eg a distinction); pleasant, attractive, kind, good, etc.—*adv* **nice´ly**.—*ns* **nice´ness**, exactness, scrupulousness; **nicety** [nīs´i-ti] fastidiousness; fineness of perception; exactness of treatment; intricate or subtle quality. [OFr *nice*, foolish, simple—L *nescius*, ignorant—*ne*, not, *scīre*, to know.]

Nicene [nī´sēn] *adj* of a church council (held in Nicaea in 325 AD or to the Nicene creed.—**Nicene Creed**, a Christian creed based on one issued by the 1st Nicene Council.

niche [nich] *n* a recess in a wall for a statue, etc.; a place, use, or work for which a person or thing is best suited. [Fr—It *nicchia*, a niche.]

nick [nik] *n* a small cut, chip, etc. made on a surface.—*vt* to make a nick in; to wound superficially.—**in the nick of time**, exactly when needed. [Possibly connected with **notch**.]

nickel [nik´ėl] *n* a metallic element (symbol Ni; at wt 58.7; at no 28); a US or Canadian coin, equal to five cents.—*n* **nick´el sil´ver**, an alloy of copper, zinc, and nickel.—*adj* **nickel-and-dime**, (*inf*) involving only a small amount of money.—*vt* **nickel and dime**, to pay close attention to petty spending; to treat stingily. [Ger *kupfernickel*, an ore from which nickel is obtained—*kupfer*, copper, *nickel*, a mischievous sprite, because the ore looked like copper ore but yielded no copper.]

nickname [nik´nām] *n* a substitute name, often descriptive, given in fun; a familiar form of a proper name.—*vt* to give a nickname to. [ME *nekename*, for **eke-name**, additional name, surname, with *n* from the indefinite article *an*. *See* **eke**; cf **newt**.]

nicotine [nik´ō-tēn] *n* a poisonous alkaloid got from tobacco leaves. [Jean *Nicot*, who introduced tobacco into France (1560).]

nicotinic acid [nik´ō-tin´ik] *n* a member of the Vitamin B complex.—Also **niacin**.

nictitate [nik´ti-tāt] *vi* to wink.—**nictitating membrane**, the third eyelid developed in birds, etc., a thin movable membrane that passes over the eye. [L *nictāre, -ātum*, and its LL freq *nictitāre*, to wink.]

nidification [nid-i-fi-kā´sh(ȯ)n] *n* the act or process of building a nest. [L *nīdus*, nest, *facĕre*, to make.]

niece [nēs] *n* the daughter of a brother or sister. [OFr—Low L *neptia*—L *nevtia*—L *neptis*, a granddaughter, niece.]

niello [nē-el´ō] *n* black alloy of lead, silver, copper, and sulfur used to decorate metal objects.

Nielsen rating [nēl´sėn] *n* the percentage of US households tuned into a specified radio or television program based on the automatic sampling by the AC Nielsen marketing research organization.

Nietzschean [nē´che-ȧn] *adj* pertaining to the philosophy of Friedrich *Nietzsche* (1844–1900), who denounced all religion, declared that moral laws cherished the virtues of the weak, and described as his ideal 'overman' one who ruthlessly sought his own power and pleasure.

nifty [nif´ti] *adj* (*slang*) smart; attractive, stylish, etc.

niggard [nig´ȧrd] *n* one who grudges to spend or give away.—*adj* niggardly.—*adj* **nigg´ardly**, stingy.—*adv* stingily; grudgingly.—*n* **nigg´ardliness**. [Origin obscure.]

niggle [nig´l] *vi* to work in a fussy way; be finicky.—*adj* **nigg´ling**. [Prob of Scand origin.]

nigh [nī] *adj* (*arch*) near.—*adv* nearly.—*prep* near to.—*n* **nigh´ness**. [OE *nēah, nēh*; Du *na*, Ger *nahe*.]

night [nīt] *n* the time from sunset to sunrise; nightfall; a specified or appointed evening.—*ns* **night blindness**, poor vision in near darkness; **night´cap**, a cap worn in bed; (*inf*) an alcoholic drink taken just before going to bed; **night´clothes**, clothes to be worn in bed, as pajamas; **night´club**, a place of entertainment for drinking, etc. at night; **night crawler**, a large earthworm that comes to the surface at night; **night´dress**, nightgown; **night´fall**, the close of the day; **night´gown**, a loose gown worn in bed by women and girls; **night´hawk**, any of several N American birds (genus *Chordeiles*) related to the whippoorwill; a night owl; **night´ie** (*inf*) a nightgown.—*adjs, advs* **night´long** (lasting) all night; **night´ly**, done or happening by night or every night.—*ns* **night owl**, a person who stays up late at night; **night´shirt**, a boy's or man's long shirt for sleeping in; **night´spot** (*inf*) a nightclub; **night stick**, a short club carried by a policeman or policewoman; **night´time**, night; **night´wear**, night clothes. [OE *niht*; Ger *nacht*, L *nox*, Gr *nyx*.]

nightingale [nīt´ing-gāl] *n* a small Old World bird of the thrush family (genus *Luscinia*) celebrated for its singing at night. [OE *nihtegale*—*niht*, night, *galan*, to sing; Ger *nachtigall*.]

nightmare [nīt´mār] *n* a frightening dream; any horrible experience. [OE *niht*, night, *mara*, a night-mare; cf OHG *mara*, incubus, ON *mara*, nightmare.]

nightshade [nīt´shād] *n* any of a genus (*Solanum*) of flowering plants related to the potato and tomato, esp belladonna. [OE *nihtscada*, apparently—*niht*, night, *scada*, shade.]

nihilism [nī´hil-izm] *n* belief in nothing, extreme scepticism; the rejection of customary beliefs in morality, religion, etc.—*n* **nī´hilist**. [L *nihil*, nothing.]

-nik [nik] *suffix* (*inf; often offensive*) denoting person associated with a specified state or quality (eg *beatnik, jognik, pornonik*).

nil [nil] *n* nothing. [L *nīl*, contracted form of *nihil*, nothing.]

nimble [nim´bl] *adj* light and quick in motion, active, swift.—*n* **nim´bleness**.—*adv* **nim´bly**. [App OE *nǣmel, numol*—*niman*, to take.]

nimbus [nim´bus] *n* a rain cloud; halo encircling the head of a saint as on a picture. [L.]

nincompoop [nin(g)´kom-pōōp] *n* a stupid, silly person. [Origin unknown.]

nine [nīn] *adj, n* one more than eight.—*ns* the symbol for this (9, IX, ix); the ninth in a series or set; something having nine units as members (as a baseball team or the first or last nine holes of a golf course).—**the Nine**, the Muses.—*adj* **ninefold** having nine units or members; being nine times as great or as many.—*adj, n* **ninth**, next after eighth; one of nine equal parts of a thing; **nine´teen´**, one more than eighteen; the symbol for this (19, XIX, xix); **nine´teenth´; ninety**, nine times ten; the symbol for this (90, XC, xc) —*pl* **nine´ties** (90s); the numbers for 90 to 99; the same numbers in a life or century.—*adj* **nine´tieth.—dressed to the nines**, dressed very elaborately; **nine days' wonder**, something newsworthy at first but soon forgotten; **to the nines**, to the highest degree; **Nineteenth Amendment** the woman's suffrage amendment to the US constitution; **nineteenth hole**, the convivial gathering place of golfers after a game; **talk nineteen to the dozen**, to talk continually. [OE *nigon*; Du *negen*, L *novem*, Gr *ennea*, Sans *nava*.]

ninny [nin´i] *n* a fool. [Possibly from **innocent**; poss—It *ninno*, child.]
ninon [nē´no•] *n* a smooth sheer fabric. [Fr *Ninon*, a woman's name.]
niobium [nī-ō´bi-ùm] *n* a metallic element (symbol Nb; at wt 92.9; at no 41), formerly Columbium. [L *Niobe*, who wept for her children until she was turned to stone.]
nip[1] [nip] *n* a small drink of liquor.—*vti* to drink in nips.
nip[2] [nip] *vt* to pinch; to press between two surfaces; to remove or sever shoots by pinching to check the growth of; to have a harmful effect on because of cold.—*pr p* **nipp´ing**, *pt, pt p* **nipped**.—*n* a pinch; a bite; a check of growth of plants due to cold; biting coldness of air.—*n* **nipp´er**, one who, or that which, nips; *(pl)* pliers, pincers, etc.—*adv* **nipp´ingly.—nip and tuck**, so close as to leave the outcome in doubt. [Prob related to Du *nijpen*, to pinch.]
nipple [nip´l] *n* the small protuberance on a breast or udder through which the milk passes, a teat; a teatlike rubber part on the cap of a baby's bottle. [A dim of **neb** or **nib**.]
Nippon [nip-pon´] *n* Japan. [Jap.]
nirvana [nir-vä´nä] *n* the cessation of individual existence by the absorption of the soul into the supreme spirit, the state to which a Buddhist aspires as the best attainable; loosely, a state of supreme happiness. [Sans *nirvāna*, 'a blowing out'.]
nisei [nē-sā´, nē´sā] *n* a person whose parents emigrated from Japan, esp to the US. [Jap.]
nit [nit] *n* the egg of a louse or other parasitic insect; the insect itself when young.—*n* **nit´-pick´ing**, petty criticism of minor details.—Also *adj*—*vi* **nit´-pick´**.—*n* **nit´wit**, a stupid person. [OE *hnitu*.]
niter *see under* **nitrogen**.
nitrogen [nītrō-jėn] *n* a gaseous element (symbol N; at wt 14.0; at no 7) forming nearly 4/5 of air.—*adj* **nitrog´enous**, containing, having the nature of, nitrogen.—*adjs* **nī´tric, nī´trous**, of, pertaining to, or containing nitrogen; of, pertaining to, or derived from niter. In the nitric compounds the nitrogen has a higher valency than in the nitrous;—*eg* **nitric oxide** (NO), a colorless, poisonous gas; **nitrous oxide** (N_2O), laughing gas, a gas used as an anesthetic; **nitric acid** (HNO_3), a colorless, fuming, corrosive liquid.—*n* **nī´trate**, a salt or ester of nitric acid.—*vt* to form a nitrate or organic nitro compound.—*vt* **nitrify**, to oxidize ammonium salts (as by bacteria) to nitrites and nitrates.—*ns* **nitrifi´er; nitrificā´tion; nī´trile**, an organic cyanide; **nitrite**, a salt or ester of nitrous acid; **nitrocell´ulose**, a substance obtained by treating cellulose with nitric acid, used in making explosives, lacquers, plastics, etc.; **nitrogenase**, an enzyme of nitrogen-fixing bacteria that catalyzes the reduction of nitrogen to ammonia; **niter** [nī´tėr] potassium nitrate, sodium nitrate, esp Chile saltpeter; **ni´troglyc´erine**, a powerful explosive, the chief constituent of dynamite, used in medicine as a vasodilator.—**nitrogen cycle**, the sum total of the transformations undergone by nitrogen and nitrogenous compounds in nature, from atmospheric nitrogen through soil bacteria, plant-tissues, and animal tissues back to bacteria and atmospheric nitrogen again; **nitrogen fixation**, the conversion (of nitrogen from the air) into nitrogen compounds either industrially or by nitrogen-fixing microorganisms; **nitrogen mustard**, a class of nitrogen compounds used in cancer chemotherapy. [Gr *nitron*, sodium carbonate (but taken as if meaning niter) and the root of *gennaein*, to generate.]
nitty-gritty [nit´i-grit´i] *n* the basic details, matters of fundamental importance.
nix[1] [niks] *n* in Germanic folklore, a male water spirit.—**nix´ie, nix´y**. [Ger *nix*.]
nix[2] [niks] *adv (slang)* no; not at all.—*interj (slang)* stop!; I forbid, disagree, etc.—*vt (slang)* to disapprove of or stop.—*n (slang)* nothing; short for 'nothing doing, you'll get no support from me'. [Inf Ger and Du for Ger *nichts*, nothing.]
nixie[1] [niks´ē] *n* in Germanic folklore, a female water/sprite.
nixie[2] [niks´ē] *n* a piece of undeliverable mail because incorrectly or illegibly addressed.—Also **nixy**.
no[1] [nō] *adv* not so; (with *comp*) in no degree, as *no sooner than, no less than*.—*n* a denial; a refusal; a vote or voter for the negative;—*pl* **noes, nos**. [OE *nā—ne*, not, *ā*, ever; cf **nay**.]
no[2] [nō] *adj* not any; not one; by no means properly called (eg *no lady*). [OE *nān*, none. *See* **none**.]
No[3] [no] (abbrev) number. [L *numero*.]
No[4], **Noh** [nō] *n* traditional Japanese drama with stylized song and dance. [Jap.]
Nobel prizes [nō-bel´] annual international prizes given for distinction in physics, chemistry, medicine, literature, and promoting peace.
nobelium [nō-bēl´i-um] *n* a transuranic element (symbol No; at wt 254; at no 102).
nobility [nō-bil´i-ti] *n* being noble; high rank in society; the class of people of noble rank. [See next word.]
noble [nō´bl] *adj* famous or renowned; high in character or quality; of high birth.—*n* a person of exalted rank.—*ns* **nō´bleman**, a man who is noble or of rank, a peer; **nō´bleness**.—*adv* **nō´bly**. [Fr *noble*—L *(g)nōbilis*—*(g)nōscĕre*, to know.]
noblesse oblige [nō-bles ō-blēzh] rank imposes obligations. [Fr.]
nobody [nō´bȯd-i] *n* no person, no one; a person of no account. [**no, body**.]
nocturnal [nok-tûr´nȧl] *adj* belonging to night; happening, done, or active by night.—*adv* **noctur´nally**.—*n* **nocturne** [nok´tûrn, or -tûrn´] a dreamy or pensive piece for the piano. [L *nocturnus—nox*, night.]
nocuous [nok´ū-us] *adj* harmful. [L *nocuus—nocēre*, to hurt.]
nod [nod] *vi* to give a quick forward motion of the head, esp in assent, or salutation; to let the head drop in weariness.—*vt* to signify by a nod;—*pr p* **nodd´ing**, *pt, pt p* **nodd´ed**.—*n* a quick bending forward of the head.—*n, adj* **nodd´ing**. [ME *nodde*.]
noddle [nod´l] *n* the crown of the head; the head. [ME *nodle*, back of the head or neck.]
noddy [nod´i] *n* a stupid person; any of several stout-bodied terns (genera *Anous* and *Micranous*) of warm seas. [Origin obscure.]
node [nōd] *n* a knot; a knob; a swelling; *(astron)* one of the two points in which the orbit of a planet intersects the plane of the ecliptic; a point or line of rest, or of comparative rest, in a vibrating body (such as a stretched string); *(bot)* the point of attachment of a leaf or leaves.—*adjs* **nōd´al**, of a node or nodes; **nodose** [nōd-ōs´, nōd´ōs] having nodes, knots, or swellings; knotty; **nod´ular**, of or like a nodule.—*n* **nŏd´ūle**, a little rounded lump. [L *nōdus; dim nōdulus*.]
no-fault [nō´fōlt´] *adj* of a form of automobile insurance in which the insured collects damages without blame being fixed; of a form of divorce without blame being charged.
Noel, Noël [nō-el] *n* Christmas. [OFr (Fr *noël*)—L *Nātālis*, belonging to a birthday.]
noggin [nog´in] *n* a small quantity of alcoholic drink; *(inf)* the head.
Noh *see* **No** (4).
no-good [nō-gŏŏd] *adj (inf)* contemptible.—Also *n*.
noise [noiz] *n* sound; an esp loud or disturbing sound, din.—*vt* to spread (a rumor, report, etc.).—*vi* to sound loud.—*adj* **noise´less**, without noise; silent.—*adv* **noise´lessly**.—*n* **noise´lessness**.—*adj* **nois´y**, making a loud sound; clamorous, turbulent.—*adv* **nois´ily**.—*n* **nois´iness**. [Fr *noise*, quarrel; perh from L *nausea*, disgust; but possibly from L *noxia*, hurt—*nocēre*, to hurt.]
noisome [noi´sùm] *adj* injurious to health; foul-smelling.—*n* **noi´someness**. [**noy**, a form of **annoy**.]
no-knock [nō´näk´] *adj (inf)* letting police with search warrants enter private dwellings by force without announcing or identifying themselves.
nomad [nōm´ad] *n* one of a wandering pastoral community; a rover.—*adj* **nomadic** [nōm-ad´ik].—*n* **nom´adism**. [Gr *nomās, -ados—nomos*, pasture—*nemein*, to drive to pasture.]
no-man's-land [nō´manz-land] *n* a waste region to which no one has a recognized claim; land, esp between entrenched hostile forces.
nom de guerre [näm dė gair] *n* a pseudonym.
nom de plume [näm dė plōōm] *n* a pen name. [Formed in Eng from Fr *nom*, name, *de*, of, *plume*, pen.]
nomenclature [nō´men-klā-chůr] *n* a system of names used in a science etc., or for parts of a device, etc. [L *nōmen*, a name, *calāre*, to call.]
nominal [nom´in-ȧl] *adj* of or like a name; existing only in name, not real or actual; inconsiderable, hardly more than a matter of form.—*adv* **nom´inally**.—*ns* **nom´inalism**, the doctrine that general terms have no corresponding reality either in or out of the mind, being mere words; **nom´inalist**. [L *nōminālis—nōmen, -inis*, a name.]
nominate [nom´in-āt] *vt* to appoint to an office or position; to propose (a candidate) for election.—*n* **nom´ination**, the act or power of nominating; state of being nominated.—*adj* **nominative** [nom´inȧ-tiv] naming; *(gram)* applied to the case of the subject.—*n* the case of the subject. [L *nōmināre, -ātum*, to name—*nōmen, -inis*, name.]
nominee [nom-in-ē´] *n* one who is nominated for an office, duty, or position. [L *nōmināre, -ātum*, to name, with *-ee* as if from Fr.]
non [non] *prefix* not.—*adj* **nonaligned** (-līnd) not in alliance with any side, esp in power politics.—*ns* **non´com** *(inf)* a noncommissioned officer; **noncom´batant**, a member of a military or naval force whose duties do not include fighting, as a doctor or chaplain; **nonconductor**, a substance that does not conduct heat or electricity; **nonconform´ist**, a person who does not conform to prevailing attitudes, behavior, etc.; in Britain, a Protestant who does not belong to the established church.—*adjs* **noncred´it**, of a course of study that does not fulfill a requirement for a degree; **nonferr´ous**, not containing iron; denoting or of metals other than iron; **nonflamm´able**, unable to be set on fire; **nonhēr´o**, antihero.—*ns* **noninterven´tion**, the policy of refusing to interfere in the affairs of others, esp nations; **nonmet´al**, an element lacking the characteristics of a metal.—*adj* **non´partisan**, without regard to political party interests or policies.—*n* **nonprescription drug**, a drug administered or sold legally without the need for a physician's order or prescription.—*adjs* **nonrestric´tive** *(gram)* (of a clause, phrase, etc.) describing the antecedent, but not essential to the sense; (of membership of a club, etc.) open to all; **nonsectar´ian**, not restricted to or not affiliated with any particular religion; **nonstan´dard** (of language) varying in usage from what is usually regarded as preferred or correct.—*n* **nonstart´er**, a person who does not assume the initiative; (of a race, a horse, racing car, etc.) scratched at the last moment.—*adj* **nonstop** (of a train or plane, etc.) not stopping at intermediate places; not ceasing.—*adv* without stopping or pausing.—*n* **nonsupport´**, failure to support a legal dependent.—*adj* **nonun´ion**, not

belonging to a labor union; not made or serviced under union conditions; refusing to recognize a labor union.—*ns* **nonvi´olence**, an abstaining from violence, as in the struggle for civil rights; **nonvōt´er**, a person who is eligible to vote but does not; **nonwhite´**, one not belonging to the white race. [L *non*, not.]

nonage [non´ij] *n* the state of being under full legal age. [OFr *nonage*—pfx *non*. (L *nōn*), and *age*, age.]

nonagenarian [non-a-jė-nā´ri-ȧn] *n* one who is ninety years old or between ninety and a hundred.—*adj* of that age. [L *nōnāgēnārius*, relating to ninety—*nōnāgintā*, ninety.]

nonagon [non´ȧ-gon] *n* a polygon with nine angles. [L *nōnus*, ninth, Gr *gōniā*, angle.]

nonce [nons] *n* (almost confined to the phrase **for the nonce**) the occasion; the moment, time being.—**nonce-word**, a word specially coined for use at the moment. [From 'for the nones', originally *for then ones*, for the once.]

nonchalance [non´shȧ-lȧns] *n* unconcern, coolness, indifference.—*adj* **nonchalant** [non´shȧ-lȧnt]. [Fr—*non*, not, *chaloir*, to matter, interest—L *calēre*, to be warm.]

nondescript [non´di-skript] *adj* not easily classified; not distinctive enough to be described; neither one thing nor another.—Also *n*. [L *nōn*, not, *dēscrībĕre*, *-scrīptum*, to describe.]

none [nun] *pron* no one; not anyone; (*pl verb*) not any; no one.—*adj* (*arch*) no (before vowel or *h*).—*adv* not at all (eg *none too soon*).—*n* not any; no part. [OE *nān*—*ne*, not, *ān*, one.]

nonentity [non-en´ti-ti] *n* a person or thing of no importance. [L *nōn*, not, and *entitās*. *See* **entity**.]

nonesuch [nun´such] *n* an unparalleled or extraordinary thing or person. [**none, such**.]

nonpareil [non-pȧ-rel´] *n* a person or thing without equal; a small printing type.—*adj* without an equal, matchless. [Fr,—*non*, not, *pareil*, from a LL dim of L *pār*, equal.]

nonplus [non´plus´] *vt* to cause to be so perplexed that one cannot go, speak, act further. [L *nōn*, not, *plūs*, more.]

nonsense [non´sėns] *n* language, actions, etc. that are absurd and without meaning.—*adj* **nonsensical** [-sens´-].—*n* **nonsens´icalness**.—*adv* **nonsens´ically**.—**nonsense verse**, verse deliberately written to convey an absurd meaning or to convey no obvious meaning at all. [Pfx *non-*, + **sense**.]

non sequitur [non sek´wit-ůr] *n* a statement in which the conclusion does not follow from the premises. [L, it does not follow.]

nonsuit [non´sūt] *n* a judgment against a plaintiff who has failed to make out cause of action or to bring sufficient evidence.—*vt* to subject to a nonsuit. [Anglo-Fr *no(u)nsute*, dares not pursue.]

non-U [nän-yōō] *adj* not characteristic of the upper classes.

noodle[1] [nōōd´l] *n* a simpleton, a blockhead. [Cf **noddy**.]

noodle[2] [nōōd´l] *n* pasta formed in ribbons. [Ger *nudel*.]

noodle[3] [nōōd´l] *vi* (*inf*) to improvise idly on an instrument, esp a piano.

nook [nŏŏk] *n* a corner; a recess; a secluded retreat. [ME *nok, noke*; prob Scand; Gael and Ir *niuc* is prob from the Northern form *neuk*.]

noon [nōōn] *n* midday; twelve o'clock; highest point.—*ns* **noon´day**, midday; time of greatest prosperity; **noon´tide**, the time of noon; the culminating point. [OE *nōn*—L *nōna* (*hōra*), the ninth (hour).]

noose [nōōs] *n* a loop with a running knot which ties the firmer the closer it is drawn; a snare like a noose.—*vt* to tie in a noose; to make a noose in or of. [Perh OFr *nous*, pl of *nou* (Fr *noeud*—L *nōdus*, knot.]

nor [nör] *conj* and not; neither—used esp in introducing the second part of a negative proposition (correlative to *neither*). [App from *nother*, a form of **neither**.]

Nordic [nör´dik] *adj* of a physical type characterized by tall stature, long head, light skin and hair, and blue eyes exemplified by Scandinavians; of competitive ski events consisting of ski jumping and cross-country ski racing. [Fr *nord*, north.]

norm [nörm] *n* a standard or model, esp the standard of achievement of a large group.—*adj* **nor´mal**, acording to rule; ordinary, average in intelligence.—*n* anything normal; the usual state, amount, etc.—*ns* **nor´malcy, normal´ity, nor´malness**.—*vti* **nor´malize**, to make or become normal.—*adv* **nor´mally**.—*adj* **norm´ative**, of or establishing a norm.—**normal school**, a training college for teachers. [L *norma*, a rule.]

Norman [nör´mȧn] *n* any of the people of Normandy who conquered England in 1066; a native or inhabitant of Normandy.—*adj* pertaining to the Normans or to Normandy. [OFr *Normanz, Normans* (nom sing and acc pl), Northman, from Scand.]

Norse [nörs] *adj* Scandinavian.—*n* the Norwegian language.—*n* **Norse´man**, any of the ancient Scandinavian people. [Prob Du *Noorsh*, Norwegian.]

north [nörth] *n* the direction to the left of a person facing the rising sun; the region lying in that direction; (often **North**) the northern part of the earth.—*adj* in, of, or toward the north; from the north.—*adv* in or toward the north.—*adj* **north´bound**, traveling northward.—*ns* **northeast´**, the direction midway between north and east; **Northeast´**, the northeast region of the US.—*adj, adv* toward or in the northeast; **northeast´wards**.—*adj* **northeastern**.—*adj, adv* **northeast´erly**.—*ns* **northeast´er**, a northeast wind or storm; **north´er**, a strong cold north wind blowing in fall and winter over the Gulf of Mexico.—*adj* **nor´therly** [TH] in, from or toward the north.—*n* a northerly wind.—*adj* **northern** [TH] of or in the north.—*ns* **nor´therner** [TH] a native or inhabitant of the north; **Nor´therner**, a Union supporter in the Civil War.—*adjs* **nor´thernmost** [TH] farthest north; **northward**, toward or in the north.—Also *adv*.—*adv* **north´wards**.—*ns* **northwest´**, the direction midway between north and west; **Northwest´**, the northwest region of the US.—*adj, adv* **northwest´ward**.—*adv* **northwestwards**.—*adj* **northwestern**.—*adj, adv* **northwesterly**.—**Northern Cross**, Cygnus; **Northern Hemisphere**, that half of the earth north of the equator; **northern lights**, aurora borealis; **North Pole**, the northern end of the earth's axis; **north pole** (of a magnet) the pole that points toward the north; **North Star**, Polaris, the star almost above the North Pole. [OE *north*; cf Ger *nord*.]

Norwegian [nör-wē´j(y)ȧn] *adj* of Norway, its people, or its language.—*n* a native of Norway; the language of Norway. [LL *Norvegia*, Norway—ON *Norvegr* (OE *Northweg*)—ON *northr*, north, *vegr*, way.]

nose [nōz] *n* the part of the face above the mouth, having two openings for breathing and smelling; the sense of smell; anything like a nose in shape or position.—*vt* to discover as by smell; to nuzzle; to push (away, etc.) with the front forward.—*vi* to sniff; to pry; to move nose first.—*ns* **nose´bleed**, a bleeding from the nose; **nose cone**, the foremost part of a rocket or missile; **nose dive**, a swift downward plunge of an airplane, nose first; any sudden, sharp drop, as in prices; **nos´ing**, the projecting rounded edge of the step of a stair.—**nose out**, to defeat by a very small margin; **on the nose** (*slang*) precisely; exactly; **pay through the nose**, to pay more for something than it is worth; **turn up one's nose at**, to sneer at; scorn; **under one's** (**very**) **nose**, in plain view. [OE *nosu*; Ger *nase*, L *nāsus*.]

nosegay [nōz´gā] *n* a small bunch of flowers. [**nose** + **gay**.]

nosh [nosh] *n* (*slang*) food.—*ns* **nosh´er**, one who eats between meals; **nosh´ery**, a restaurant. [Yiddish.]

no-show [nō´shō´] *n* (*inf*) a person who fails to appear, as for an appointment, or reserves an airline seat and neither cancels nor claims it; an instance of non-appearance.

noso- [nos-o-] in composition, of, or relating to, disease;—eg *n* **nosology** [nos-ol´o-ji], a list of diseases; the branch of medicine that treats of the classification of diseases.—*adj* **nosolog´ical**.—*n* **nosol´ogist**. [Gr *nosos*, disease, *logos*, discourse.]

nostalgia [nos-tal´ji-a] *n* longing for past times or places.—*adj* **nostal´gic**, feeling, showing, or expressing, nostalgia. [Gr *nostos*, a return, *algos*, pain.]

nostril [nos´tril] *n* one of the openings of the nose. [ME *nosethirl*—OE *nosthyr(e)l*—*nosu*, nose, *thyrel*, opening. Cf **drill**, to pierce, and **thrill**.]

nostrum [nos´trum] *n* a quack medicine; a panacea. [L *nostrum* (neut), our own—*nōs*, we.]

not [not] *adv* a word expressing denial, negation, or refusal. [*See* **naught, nought**.]

nota bene [nō´ta ben´i, nō´ta ben´e] mark well, take notice—often abbrev **NB**. [L.]

notable [nō´tȧ-bl] *adj* worthy of being known or noted; remarkable; distinguished.—*n* a person or thing worthy of note.—*ns* **notabil´ity**, the condition of being notable; a notable person or thing; **no´tableness**.—*adv* **not´ably**. [L *notābilis*—*notāre*, to mark.]

notaphily [nō´tȧ-fil-i] *n* the hobby of collecting bank notes.—*adj* **notaphil´ic**.—*n* **notaph´ilist**.

notary [nō´tȧ-ri] *n* an officer authorized to certify deeds or other formal writings; in full **notary public**.—*adj* **notā´rial**. [L *notārius*.]

notation [nō-tā´sh(ȯ)n] *n* a system of signs or symbols, esp in mathematics, music, etc. [L *notātiō*, *-ōnis*—*notāre*, *-ātum*, to mark.]

notch [noch] *n* a V-shaped cut in an edge or surface; a narrow pass with steep sides; (*inf*) a step, degree.—*vt* to cut notches in. [Supposed to be from Fr *oche* (now *hoche*) with *n* from the indefinite article.]

note [nōt] *n* a brief record of topics for speech, sermon, article, etc. set down provisionally for use afterwards; a comment (explanatory, illustrative, or critical) attached to a text; a paper acknowledging a debt and promising payment; a mark representing a musical sound; the sound itself; a key of a piano or other instrument; the song, cry, or utterance of a bird or other animal; a short informal letter; a diplomatic paper; a memorandum; notice, attention.—*vt* to make a note of; to notice; to annotate.—*n* **note´book**, a book with blank pages for writing in.—*adjs* **not´ed**, well-known; renowned; **note´worthy**, worthy of notice; remarkable.—**compare notes**, to exchange views. [Fr—L *nota*, to mark.]

nothing [nuth´ing] *n* no thing; nothingness; a zero; a thing or person of no significance or value; a trifle.—*adv* in no degree, not at all.—*n* **noth´ingness**, state of being nothing; worthlessness; unconsciousness.—**come to nothing**, to fail to develop or to show results, to be valueless; **for nothing**, in vain; free; without reason; **think nothing of**, to regard as easy to do; consider as of no importance. [**no, thing**.]

notice [nōt´is] *n* intimation; information; warning; a writing, placard, etc., conveying an announcement or warning; a short article about a book, play, etc.; attention, heed; a formal warning of intention to end an agreement at a certain time.—*vt* to observe; to mention.—*adj* **not´iceable**, likely to be noticed.—*adv* **not´iceably**. [Fr. *notifier*—L *nōtitia*—*nōscĕre*, *nōtum*, to know.]

notify [nō´ti-fī] *vt* to inform; to give notice to.—*pt, pt p* **nōtified**.—*adj* **nōtifiable**, (of diseases) that must be reported to public-health authorities.—*n* **notificā´tion**, the act of notifying; the notice given; the paper containing the notice. [Fr—L *nōtificāre, -ātum—nōtus*, known, *facĕre*, to make.]

notion [nō´sh(o)n] *n* a general idea; an opinion; a whim; (*pl*) small useful articles as thread, needles, etc. sold in a store.—*adj* **no´tional**, speculative; imaginary. [Fr—L *nōtiō, -ōnis—nōscĕre, nōtum*, to know.]

notorious [nō-tō´ri-us, -tö´] *adj* widely known, esp unfavorably.—*n* **notorī´ety**, state of being notorious.—*adv* **notō´riously**.—*n* **notō´riousness**. [Low L *nōtōrius—nōtus*, known.]

notwithstanding [not-with-stand´ing] *prep* in spite of.—*conj* although.—*adv* nevertheless. [Orig a participial phrase in nominative absolute = L ablative *non obstante*.]

nougat [nōō´gät] *n* a confection of sugar paste with nuts. [Fr (cf Sp. *nogado*, an almond-cake)—L *nux, nucis*, a nut.]

nought [nöt] *See* **naught**.

noun [nown] *n* (*gram*) a word that names a person, living being, object, action, etc. [Anglo-Fr *noun* (OFr *non*; Fr *nom*)—L *nōmen*, name.]

nourish [nur´ish] *vt* to feed; to help forward the growth of in any way; to bring up.—*adj* **nour´ishing**, affording nourishment.—*n* **nour´ishment**, the act of nourishing or the state of being nourished; food. [OFr *norir, norissant*—(Fr *nourrir*)—L *nūtrīre*, to feed.]

nouveau riche [nōō-vo rēsh] *n* a person who has recently become rich, esp one who has no social graces or culture;—*pl* **nouveaux riches** (pronounced as *sing*). [Fr.]

Novocain [nō´vō-kān] *n* trade name for procaine.

novel [nov´l, nuv´l] *adj* new and unusual.—*n* a relatively long fictitious prose narrative.—*n* **novelette´**, a short novel; a long short story.—*adj* **novelett´ish**, sentimental.—*ns* **nov´elist**, a writer of novels; **novella** [nō-vel´lä] a long story of about 10 to 15 thousand words.—*pl* **novel´las, novel´le** [-lē]; **nov´elty**, newness; anything new or unusual; (*pl*) a small, usu cheap, manufactured article. [Partly through OFr *novelle* (Fr *nouvelle*) partly through It *novella*, partly direct from L *novellus*, fem *novella—novus*, new.]

November [nō-vem´bėr] *n* the eleventh month, having 30 days. [L *November—novem*, nine.]

novice [nov´is] *n* a person on probation in a religious order before taking final vows; a beginner.—*n* **novi´tiate** [ish´i-ȧt] the state or period of being a novice. [Fr—L *novīcius—novus*, new.]

now [now] *adv* at the present time; by this time; at once; at that time, then; with things as they are.—*conj* since; seeing that.—*n* the present time.—*adj* of the present time.—**now and then, now and again**, sometimes; from time to time; **now . . . now**, at one time . . . at another time. [OE *nū*; Ger *nun*, L *nunc*, Gr *nȳn*.]

nowadays [now´a-dāz] *adv* in these days; at the present time. [Formerly two words, *adays* being OE *dæges*, gen of *dæg*, day, to which the prep *a* (OE *on*) was later added.]

noway, noways, nowise *adv* in no way.

nowhere [nō´hwār, wėr] *adv* not in, at, or to any place. [**no, where**.]

no-win [nō-win] *adj* not leading to victory; not played or engaged in to win; noncompetitive.

noxious [nok´shus] *adj* harmful, unwholesome.—*adv* **nox´iously**.—*n* **nox´iousness**. [L *noxius—noxa*, hurt—*nocēre*, to hurt.]

nozzle *noz´l n* the spout at the end of a hose, pipe, etc. [Dim of **nose**.]

nuance [nü-ãs, nwãs] *n* a delicate degree or shade of difference. [Fr,—L *nūbēs*, a cloud.]

nub [nub] *n* a lump or small piece; (*inf*) the point or gist. [Prob **knub**.]

nubile [nū´bil, -bīl] *adj* marriageable (of a girl). [L *nūbilis—nūbĕre*, to veil oneself, to marry.]

nucleus [nū´klė-us] *n* that around which something may grow, or be collected, or be concentrated; something established that will receive additions; the centrally positively charged portion of an atom; the part of an animal or plant cell containing genetic material; (*chem*) a stable group of atoms which is normally retained intact in chemical transformations (eg the benzine nucleus, a ring of six carbon atoms).—*pl* **nuclei** [nū´kli-ī], **nu´cleuses**.—*adjs* **nūclēar**, of a nucleus; pertaining to the nucleus of an atom or to the nuclei of atoms; pertaining to, or derived from, fission or fusion of atomic nuclei; **nū´cleate, -d**, having a nucleus.—*ns* **nuclē´olus**, a body observed within a cell nucleus; **nucleon**, a proton or neutron, esp in the atomic nucleus; **nucleonics**, nuclear physics dealing with nucleons; **nūc´lide**, species of atom of any element distinguished by number of neutrons and protons in its nucleus.—**nuclear energy**, energy released or absorbed during reactions taking place in atomic nuclei; **nuclear family**, father, mother, and children; **nuclear fission**, spontaneous or induced splitting of atomic nucleus; **nuclear fusion**, creation of new nucleus by merging two lighter ones; **nuclear physics**, the branch of physics dealing with forces and transformations within the nucleus of the atom; **nuclear reaction**, a reaction within the nucleus of an atom; **nuclear reactor**, an assembly in which a nuclear chain reaction can develop; **nucleic acid**, any of the complex acids which are important constituents of cell nuclei. [L *nucleus—nux, nucis*, a nut.]

nude [nūd] *adj* naked; bare.—*n* a nude human figure, esp in a work of art; the state of being nude. *ns* **nud´ism**, the practice of going nude esp in sexually mixed groups at designated places and times; **nud´ist**, supporter of nudism.—Also *adj*.—*n* **nū´dity**, the state of being nude. [L *nūdus*, naked.]

nudge [nuj] *n* a gentle poke, as with the elbow.—*vt* to poke gently to urge into action. [Origin obscure; perh conn with Norw dial *nugga*, to push, or with **knock**.]

nugatory [nū´ga-tȯr-i] *adj* trifling, worthless, inoperative, invalid. [L *nūgātōrius—nūgae*, trifles, trumpery.]

nugget [nug´et] *n* a lump, esp of native gold.

nuisance [nū´sȧns] *n* that which annoys or causes trouble; a person or thing that is troublesome or obtrusive. [Fr—L *nocēre*, to hurt.]

nuke [nūk] *vt* (*inf*) to use nuclear weapons on.

null [nul] *adj* of no legal force; void, invalid.—*n* **null´ity**, the state of being null; an act, document, etc., that is legally invalid.—**null and void**, amounting to nothing; of no value, effect, etc. [L *nūllus*, not any, from *ne*, not, *ūllus*, any.]

nullify [nul´i-fī] *vt* to make null, to cancel out.—*n* **nullificā´tion**. [Late L *nūllificāre—nūllus*, none, *facĕre*, to make.]

numb [num] *adj* deadened; insensible.—*vt* to make numb;—*pr p* **numbing** [num´ing]; *pt p* **numbed** [numd].—*n* **numb´ness**. [OE *nymen*, pa p of *niman*, to take.]

number [num´bėr] *n* a symbol or word indicating how many; a numeral identifying a person or thing by its position in a series; a single issue of a magazine; a song or piece of music, esp as an item in a performance; (*inf*) an object singled out (*a smart number*); a total of persons or things; (*gram*) the form of a word indicating singular or plural; (*pl*) arithmetic; (*pl*) numerical superiority; **Numbers** (*Bible*) the 4th book of the Old Testament, a part of which contains the census of the Israelites.—*vt* to count; to give a number to; to include as one of a group; to limit the number of; to total.—*vi* to be included.—*adj* **numberless**, too many to count.—**number cruncher** (*inf*), a computer designed to perform complicated and lengthy numerical calculations; **numbered account**, a bank account identified only by number; **number system**, the classification of numbers by their functions and properties of which the number systems in everyday use comprise positive and negative integers and fractions; **the numbers game**, an illegal lottery based on numbers published in newspapers, usu the results of races, etc.; **without number**, too many to be counted.—**a number of**, several or many; **by numbers**, following simple instructions identified by numbers; **do a number** (*inf*), to do a (specified) act, performance, or routine; **do a number on** (*slang*), to hurt or harm, esp by deception.—*adj* **num´erable**, capable of being counted.—*ns* **num´eracy**, state of being numerate; **num´eral**, a symbol or group of symbols used to express a number (eg two = 2, II, binary 10, beta, 4/2, etc.).—*adj* **num´erally**, expressing numbers; consisting of numbers.—*adj* **num´erate**, having the capacity for quantitive thought and expression.—*vt* [-rāt´] to count one by one.—*ns* **numera´tion**, act of numbering; the art of reading in words numbers expressed by symbols; **num´erator**, the number above the fraction line; **numer´ic**, numeral, number.—*adj* denoting a number or a system of numbers.—*adj* **numer´ical**, of or relating to numbers; expressed in numbers.—*n* **numerol´ogy**, divination by numbers; the study of the occult meaning of numbers.—*adj* **num´erous**, many, consisting of many items. [ME—OFr *nombre*—L *numerus*, number.]

numero uno [nōō-mer-´ō ōōn´ō] *n* the first, best, or most important of a kind; number one.—Also *adj*. [It or Sp.]

numismatic [nū-miz-mat´ik] *adj* of paper money, coins, or medals.—*n sing* **nūmismat´ics**, the study of coins, medals, etc.—*n* **numis´ma**. [L *numisma*—Gr *nomisma*, current coin—*nomizein*, to use commonly—*nomos*, custom.]

numskull, numbskull [num´skul] *n* a dunce. [**numb, skull**.]

nun [nun] *n* a woman belonging to a religious order.—*n* **nunn´ery**, a convent of nuns. [OE *nunne*—Low L *nunna, nonna*, a nun, an old maiden lady, orig mother.]

nunc dimittis [nungk di-mit´is] *n* the song of Simeon (Luke ii 29–32) in the RC Breviary and the Anglican evening service. [From L *nunc dimittis*, now lettest thou depart.]

nuncio [nun´shi-ō] *n* an ambassador from the Pope to a foreign state.—*n* **nun´ciātūre**, a nuncio's office or term of office. [It (now *nunzio*)—L *nūntius*, a messenger.]

nuptial [nup´shȧl] *adj* pertaining to marriage; (*zool*) pertaining to mating.—*n* (usu. in *pl*) marriage; wedding ceremony.—**nuptial plumage**, the brilliant plumage assumed by the males of many birds during the breeding season. [L *nuptiālis—nubĕre, nuptum*, to marry.]

nurd *see* **nerd**.

nurse [nûrs] *n* one who tends a child; one who has the care of the sick, feeble, or injured.—*vt* to suckle; to tend, as an infant or a sick person; to foster (the arts, a specified feeling—eg hatred); to manage with care and economy (resources).—*ns* **nurs´ery**, a room set aside for children; a place where children may be left in temporary care; a place where young trees and plants are raised for transplanting; **nurs´eryman**, one who owns or works in a tree nursery; **nurs´ling**, that which is nursed; a nursing child; **nursery school**, a school for very young children usu. under five; **nursery slopes**, slopes set apart for people learning to ski; **nursing home**, a residence providing care for the infirm, chronically ill, disabled, etc. [OFr *norrice* (Fr *nourrice*)—L *nūtrīx, -īcis—nūtrīre*, to nourish.]

nurture [nûr´chůr] *n* upbringing, rearing, training; food.—*vt* to nourish; to bring up, to educate.—*n* **nurt´urer**. [OFr *noriture*—Low L *nūtrītūra*—L *nūtrīre*, to nourish.]

nut [nut] *n* any fruit with one seed in a hard shell; (*bot*) a hard dry fruit that does not open at maturity, formed from a gynoecium consisting of two or more united carpels, and usu. containing one seed; a small threaded block, usu. of metal for screwing on the end of a bolt; (*slang*) a crazy person; (*slang*) a devotee, fan.—*vi* to gather nuts.—*ns* **nut´cracker**, a bird (genus *Nucifraga*) of the crow family; an implement for cracking nuts; **nut´hatch**, any of several small birds (genus *Sitta*) that go up and down on tree trunks and feed on insects.—*adj* **nuts** (*slang*) crazy; foolish.—*interj* exclamation of disgust, scorn, etc.—*adj* **nutt´y**, containing nuts; having the flavor of nuts; (*slang*) very enthusiastic; (*slang*) queer, crazy, etc.; **be nuts about** (*slang*) to be very enthusiastic about; (*slang*) to be greatly in love with; **in a nutshell**, expressed very concisely and exactly. [OE *hnutu*; ON *hnot*, Du *noot*, Ger *nuss*.]

nutmeg [nut´meg] *n* the aromatic seed produced by a tree (*Myristica fragrans*), grated and used as a spice. [ME *notemuge*, a hybrid word formed from *nut* and OFr *muge*, musk—L *muscus*, musk.]

nutria [nū´tri-a] *n* the coypu, a S American aquatic rodent (*Myocastor coypus*); its fur. [Sp *nutria*, otter—L *lūtra*.]

nutrient [nū´tri-ėnt] *adj* nourishing.—*ns* **nū´triment**, that which nourishes; food; **nūtri´tion**, act or process of nourishing.—*adjs* **nūtri´tious; nū´tritive**. [L *nūtrīre*, to nourish.]

nux vomica [nuks vom´ik-a] *n* a seed that yields strychnine; the Asian tree (*Strychnos nux-vomica*) that produces it. [L *nux*, a nut, *vomĕre*, to vomit.]

Nuyorican *see* **Neorican**.

nuzzle [nuz´l] *vti* to push (against) or rub with the nose or snout; to nestle, snuggle. [Freq vb from **nose**.]

nyctalopia [nik-ta-lō´pi-a] *n* night blindness. [Gr *nyktalōps*, night-blind, day-blind—*nyx, nyktos*, night, *alaos*, blind, *ōps*, eye, face.]

nylon [nī´lȯn] *n* any of numerous strong, tough, elastic, synthetic materials used esp in plastics and textiles; (*pl*) stockings made of nylon. [Coined word.]

nymph [nimf] *n* (*myth*) one of the divinities who inhabited mountains, rivers, trees, etc.; a young and beautiful maiden; an immature insect similar to the adult but with wings and sex-organs undeveloped; an insect pupa.—*n* **nymph´olepsy**, a species of ecstasy or frenzy said to have seized those who had seen a nymph; a frenzy of emotion; **nymphomā´nia**, uncontrollable sexual desire in women; **nymphomā´niac**. [L *nympha*—Gr *nymphē*, a bride, a nymph.]

O

O, oh [ō] *interj* an exclamation of wonder, pain, desire, fear, etc. The form *oh* is the more usual in prose.

o usually written **o'**, an abbrev for **of**, and **on**.

oaf [ōf] *n* a dolt; an awkward lout;—*pl* **oafs**.—*adj* **oaf'ish**. [ON *ālfr*, elf.]

oak [ōk] *n* a genus (*Quercus* or *Lithocarpus*) of trees of the beech family; their timber valued in shipbuilding, etc.—*n* **oak' apple**, a gall caused by a gall wasp (esp *Amphibolips concluentus* or *Andricus californicus*) on an oak leaf.—*adj* **oak'en**, consisting or made of oak. [OE *āc*; ON *eik*, Ger *eiche*.]

oakum [ōk'ùm] *n* tarry ropes untwisted and teased into loose hemp for caulking seams of (as of wooden ships) and packing joints (as of pipes). [OE *ācumba—cemban*, to comb.]

oar [ōr, ör] *n* a light pole with a flat blade for propelling a boat; an oarsman.—*vt* to impel as by rowing.—*vi* to row.—*adj* **oared**, furnished with oars.—*n* **oars'man**, one who rows with an oar.—**rest on one's oars**, to stop; to rest. [OE *ār*.]

oasis [ō-ā'sis, ō'ä-sis] *n* a fertile spot or tract in a desert;—*pl* **oases** [ō-ā'sēz]. [Gr *oasis*, an Egyptian word.]

oast [ōst] *n* a kiln to dry hops, malt or tobacco.—*n* **oast'-house**. [OE *āst*.]

oat [ōt] (oftener in *pl* **oats** [ōts]) *n* any of several grasses (genus *Avena*), esp a widely cultivated cereal grass (*A sativa*) whose seeds are much used as food; the seeds; (*arch*) a musical pipe of an oat straw.—*n* **oat'cake'**, a thin, hard cake of oatmeal.—*adj* **oat'en**, of an oat stem or straw; made of oatmeal.—*n* **oat'meal**, meal made of oats; a porridge of this. [OE *āte*, pl *ātan*.]

oath [ōth] *n* a solemn appeal to a god or to something holy or reverenced as witness of the truth of a statement or of the inviolability of a promise; an irreverent use of God's name; an ejaculation or imprecation;—*pl* **oaths** [ōTHZ]. [OE *āth*; Ger *eid*, ON *eithr*.]

Obadiah [ō-bȧ-dī'ȧ] *n* (*Bible*) 31st book of the Old Testament, written by the prophet Obadiah to show judgment on the nation of Edom.

obbligato [ob-li-gä'tō] *n* a musical accompaniment that is not to be omitted; a mere accompanying part. [It—L *obligātus*, bound, obliged.]

obdurate [ob'dū-rȧt] *adj* hardened in heart or in feelings; stubborn.—*n* **ob'dūracy**, state of being obdurate; invincible hardness of heart.—*adv* **ob'dūrately**.—*n* **ob'dūrateness**. [L *obdūrāre, -ātum—ob-*, against, *dūrāre*, to harden—*dūrus*, hard.]

obeah [ō'bē-ȧ] or **obi** [ō'bē] *n* a system of belief among Negroes chiefly of the British West Indies, the Guianas, and southeastern US, marked by the use of magic ritual and sorcery. [Of West African origin.]

obedience [ō-bē'-di-ėns] *n* state of being obedient; compliance with commands, instructions, etc.; dutiful submission to authority.—*adj* **obē'dient**, obeying; ready to obey.—*adv* **obē'diently**. [L *obēdientia—obēdiens*, pr p of *obēdire*. See **obey**.]

obeisance [ō'bā'sȧns] *n* a bow; homage; deference. [Fr *obéissance—obéir*. See **obey**.]

obelus [ob'ė-lus] *n* a symbol (– or ÷) used in ancient manuscript to mark a questionable passage;—*pl* **ob'eli** [-lī].—*n* **ob'elisk**, a tall, four-sided, tapering pillar, usu on one stone, finished at the top like a pyramid. [L *obelus*—Gr *obelos* (dim *obeliskos*), a spit.]

obese [ō'bēs] *adj* very fat; stout.—*n* **obes'ity**, abnormal fatness. [L *obēsus—ob-*, completely, *edĕre, ēsum*, to eat.]

obey [ō-bā'] *vi* to render obedience; to submit.—*vt* to do as told by; to comply with; to yield to. [Fr *obéir*—L *oboedīre, obēdīre—ob-*, toward, *audīre*, to hear.]

obfuscate [ob-fus'kāt] *vt* to darken; to bewilder.—*n* **obfuscā'tion**. [L *obfuscāre, -ātum—ob-*, inten, *fuscus*, dark.]

obi[1] [ō'bē] *n* a broad sash worn with a Japanese kimono, esp by women and girls. [Jap]

obi[2] *see* **obeah**.

obit [ō'bit] *n* an obituary.—*n* **obit'uary**, a short biographical account of a deceased person, or a notice of his death.—Also *adj*. [L *obitus—obīre, -itum*, to go to meet, to die—*ob*, in the way of, *īre*, to go.]

object [ob'jekt] *n* a thing capable of being presented to the senses, a thing observed, a material thing; a sight, a person or thing to which action, feeling, etc. is directed; an end or aim; (*gram*) part of a sentence denoting that upon which the action of a transitive verb is directed or which is similarly related to a preposition.—*vt* **object'**, to bring forward in opposition.—*vi* to be opposed (to); to feel or express disapproval; to refuse assent.—*ns* **ob'ject ball**, the ball first struck by the cue ball in pool or billiards; a ball hit by the cue ball; **objec'tion**, act of objecting; feeling or expression of disapproval; an argument against.—*adjs* **objec'tionable**, that may be objected to; displeasing, distasteful; **object'ive**, relating to an object; exterior to the mind; detached, impartial; that is real or exists in nature in contrast with what is ideal or exists merely in the thought of the individual; also, showing facts without obvious coloring due to the individual tastes and views of the artist (eg *objective treatment*); (*gram*) belonging to the case of the object of a preposition or verb.—*n* (*gram*) the case of the object; the point to which operations are directed.—*adv* **object'ively**.—*ns* **object'iveness, objectiv'ity; ob'ject less'on**, something that serves as a practical example of a principle or abstract idea; **objec'tor**, one who objects.—**objective correlative**, the image underlying a metaphor or literary symbol; the kind of artistic selectivity re-creating an experience through referent objects and images instead of subjective comment. [L *objectāre*, freq of *ob(j)icĕre—ob*, in the way of, *jacĕre*, to throw.]

objet d'art [ob-zhā där] an article with artistic value; **objet trouvé**, [trōō-vā] something that has been found and is considered to be of artistic value;—*pls* **objets d'art, trouvés**. [Fr.]

objurgate [ob'jûr-gāt] *vti* to upbraid severely; to rebuke.—*n* **objurgā'tion**.—*adj* **objur'gatory**. [L *objurgāre, -ātum*, to rebuke—*ob-*, intensive, *jurgāre*, to chide.]

oblate[1] [ob-lāt'] *adj* (of a spheroid) flattened or depressed at opposite poles.—*n* **oblate'ness**. [Formed on the analogy of **prolate**, with the pfx *ob-*.]

oblate[2] [ob-lāt'] *n* a layman living in a monastery under modified rule and without vows; a member of one of several Roman Catholic communities of men or women. [L *oblatus*, one offered up.]

oblation [ob-lā'sh(ȯ)n] *n* anything offered in worship; an offering. [L *oblātiō—oblātus*, pa p of *offerre*. See **offer**.]

oblige [ō-blij'] *vt* to compel by moral, legal, or physical force; to bind by some favor rendered; to do a favor for.—*vt* **ob'ligate**, to bind by a contract, promise, sense of duty, etc.—*n* **obligā'tion**, act of obliging; a moral or legal bond; a debt; a favor; a committment (as by a government) to pay a certain amount of money; the amount owed under such an obligation.—*adj* **oblig'atory**, binding, constraining of the nature of an obligation or duty, not subject to discretion or choice.—*adv* **oblig'atorily**, [or ob'lig-].—*n* **obligee**, [ob-lī-jē']. one who is protected by a surety bond;—*adj* **oblīg'ing**, disposed to confer favors, ready to do a good turn.—*adv* **oblīg'ingly**.—*ns* **oblīg'ingness; obligor**, [ob'lig-ȯr] (*law*) person who is bound by a legal obligation. [Fr *obliger*—L *obligāre, -ātum—ob*, down, *ligāre*, to bind.]

oblique [ob-lēk'] *adj* slanting; not perpendicular; not parallel; not straightforward, indirect; (*geom*) not at right angles.—*ns* **oblique'ness, obliquity**, [-lik'-] state of being oblique; a slanting direction; an obscure or confusing statement.—*adv* **oblique'ly**.—**oblique case**, (*gram*) any case other than the nominative and vocative; **oblique question**, an indirect question. [L *oblīquus—ob-*, intensive, *līquis*, slanting.]

obliterate [ob-lit'ėr-āt] *vt* to blot out, to efface, to destroy.—*n* **obliterā'tion**. [L *oblīterāre, oblitterāre, -ātum—ob*, over, *lītera, littera*, a letter.]

oblivion [ob-liv'i-ȯn] *n* forgetfulness; a state of being forgotten.—*adj* **obliv'ious**, forgetful; unaware (of); causing forgetfulness.—*n* **obliv'iousness**. [Fr,—L *oblīviō, -ōnis—oblīviscī*, to forget.]

oblong [ob'long] *adj* deviating from a square, circle, or sphere by being long in one direction.—*n* any oblong figure. [L *oblongus—ob-* (force obscure), *longus*, long.]

obloquy [ob'lo-kwi] *n* widespread censure or abuse; disgrace or infamy resulting from this. [L *obloquium—ob*, against, *loquī*, to speak.]

obnoxious [ob-nok'shùs] *adj* objectionable; highly offensive.—*adv* **obnox'iously**.—*n* **obnox'iousness**. [L *obnoxius—ob-*, exposed to, *noxa*, hurt.]

oboe [ō'bō] *n* an orchestral woodwind musical instrument, with a double reed and keys; having a high, penetrating tone. [It *oboe*—Fr *haut-bois—haut*, high, *bois*, wood.]

obscene [ob-sēn'] *adj* foul, disgusting, indecent, esp in a sexual sense; offending against an accepted standard of morals or taste.—*adv* **obscene'ly**.—*ns* **obscene'ness, obscen'ity** [-sen'i-ti]. [L *obscēnus*.]

obscure [ob-skūr'] *adj* dark, enveloped in darkness; not distinct; not clear or legible; not easily understood, doubtful; hidden; inconspicuous; lowly, unknown to fame.—*vt* to darken; to hide.—*n* **obscū'rant**, one who labors to prevent enlightenment or reform.—*adj* tending to make obscure.—*ns* **obscū'rantism**, opposition to inquiry or reform; a policy of withholding knowledge from the general public; a literary or artistic style marked by deliberate vagueness or abstruseness; **obscū'rantist**, an obscurant.—Also *adj*.—*adv* **obscūre'ly**.—*n* **obscū'rity**, state or quality of being obscure; darkness; a humble place or condition; unintelligibleness. [Fr *obscur*—L *obscūrus*.]

obsequies [ob'sė-kwiz] *n pl* funeral rites and solemnities. [LL *obsequiae*, a confusion of *exsequiae*, funeral rites and *obsequium*. See next word.]

obsequious [ob-sē'kwi-us] *adj* compliant to excess, fawning.—*adv*

obsē´quiously.—*n* **obsē´quiousness**. [LL *obsequiōsus*, compliant, *obsequium*, compliance.]

observe [ob-zûrv´] *vt* to keep in view; to notice; to regard attentively; to remark in words; to comply with; to keep with ceremony; to adhere to (a law, custom, etc.); to arrive at as a conclusion; to examine scientifically.—*vi* to take notice; to attend; to remark (on).—*adj* **observ´able**, discernible; noteworthy.—*adv* **observ´ably**.—*n* **observ´ance**, the keeping of, or acting according to, a law, duty, custom, ceremony; the keeping with ceremony or according to custom.—*adj* **observ´ant**, observing; taking notice; having acute powers of observing and noting; carefully attentive to rites, customs, laws, etc.—*adv* **observ´antly**.—*n* **observā´tion**, act of observing; habit, practice, or faculty of observing; the act of recognizing and noting phenomena as they occur, often involving measurement with instruments; that which is observed; fact of being observed; a remark.—*adj* **observā´tional**, consisting of, or containing, observations or remarks; derived from observation.—*ns* **observ´atory**, a place for making astronomical observations; an institution whose primary purpose is making such observations; a place or building commanding a wide view; **observ´er**, one engaged in scientifically exact observation; a representative sent to listen to formal discussions but not to take part; an expert analyst and commentator in a particular field, esp politics.—*adj* **observ´ing**, habitually following practices, customs, etc. esp of religion. [Fr,—L *observāre, -ātum—ob*, before, *servāre*, to keep.]

obsess [ob-ses´] *vt* to haunt; completely to engage the thoughts of.—*n* **obsession** [-sesh´-(ò)n], morbid persistence of an idea in the mind; a fixed idea. [L *obsidēre, obsessum*, to besiege.]

obsidian [ob-sid´i-àn] *n* a hard, usu. black volcanic glass. [From one *Obsidius* (properly *Obsius*), who, according to Pliny, discovered it in Ethiopia.

obsolescent [ob-so-les´ėnt] *adj* going out of use.—*n* **obsoles´cence**.—*adj* **ob´solete** [-lēt], gone out of use, antiquated; of a plant or animal part, indistinct or imperfect as compared with the corresponding part in related organisms, vestigial. [L *obsolēscĕre, obsolētum*, to decay.]

obstacle [ob´stà-kl] *n* anything that stands in the way of or hinders progress; an obstruction.—**obstacle course**, a military training course filled with obstacles (as hurdles, ditches, etc.) that must be negotiated; a series of obstacles that must be overcome. [Fr,—L *obstăculum—ob*, in the way of, *stāre*, to stand.]

obstetric, -al [ob-stet´rik, -àl] *adj* pertaining to the care and treatment of women during pregnancy and childbirth.—*ns* **obstetrician** [-rish´àn], one skilled in obstetrics; **obstet´rics**, the branch of medicine concerned with the care and treatment of women during pregnancy and childbirth. [L *obstetrīcius—obstetrīx, -īcis*, a midwife.]

obstinate [ob´sti-nàt] *adj* blindly or excessively firm, stubborn; unyielding; not easily remedied.—*ns* **ob´stinacy, ob´stinateness**, the condition of being obstinate.—*adv* **ob´stinately**. [L *obstināre, -ātum—ob*, in the way of, *stāre*, to stand.]

obstreperous [ob-strep´ėr-us] *adj* noisy, clamorous; unruly.—*adv* **obstrep´erously**. [L *obstreperus—ob-*, before, against, *strepĕre*, to make a noise.]

obstruct [ob-strukt´] *vt* to block up, make impassable; to hinder from passing; to hamper; to shut off (eg light, a view).—*n* **obstruc´tion**, act of obstructing; state of being obstructed; that which hinders progress or action; an obstacle.—*adj* **obstruct´ive**, tending to obstruct; hindering.—*adv* **obstruct´ively**. [L *obstruĕre, obstructum—ob*, in the way of, *struĕre, structum*, to build.]

obtain [ob´tān´] *vt* to get, to procure by effort, to gain.—*vi* to be established, prevalent; to hold good; to prevail.—*adj* **obtain´able**. [Fr,—L *obtinēre*, to occupy—*ob*, against, *tenēre*, to hold.]

obtrude [ob-trōōd] *vt* to thrust forward, or upon one, unduly or unwelcomely.—*vi* to thrust oneself forward.—*ns* **obtrud´ing, obtru´sion**, an unwanted thrusting in or forward.—*adj* **obtrusive** [ob-trōō´siv], disposed to thrust oneself forward; unduly prominent or noticeable.—*adv* **obtrus´ively**. [L *obtrūdĕre—ob*, before, *trūdĕre, trūsum*, to thrust.]

obtuse [ob-tūs´] *adj* blunt; not pointed; (*geom*) greater than a right angle; stupid; insensitive.—*adv* **obtuse´ly**.—*n* **obtuse´ness**. [L *obtūsus—obtundĕre*, to blunt—*ob*, against, *tundĕre*, to beat.]

obverse [ob-vûrs´] *adj* turned toward one; complemental, constituting the opposite aspect of the same fact; (*bot*) having the base narrower than the apex.—*n* **ob´verse**, the side of a coin containing the head or principal symbol; the side of anything normally presented to view.—*adv* **obverse´ly**. [L *obversus—ob*, towards, *vertĕre*, to turn.]

obviate [ob´vi-āt] *vt* to prevent, get round, avert (eg a necessity, a difficulty, a danger); make unnecessary. [L *obviāre, -ātum—ob*, in the way of, *viāre, viātum*, to go—*via*, a way.]

obvious [ob´vi-us] *adj* (*arch*) being in the way or in front; easily seen or understood; evident.—*adv* **ob´viously**.—*n* **ob´viousness**. [L *obvius—ob, via*. See **obviate**.]

ocarina [ok-ä-rē´na] *n* a small wind instrument with finger holes and a mouthpiece. [It, dim of *oca*, a goose.]

occasion [o-kā´zh(ò)n] *n* a special time or season; an event; an opportunity; a reason or excuse; an immediate but subsidiary cause; (usu. in *pl*) business.—*vt* to cause; to give occasion to.—*adj* **occā´sional**, occurring infrequently, irregularly, now and then; produced on or for a special event; subsidiary, secondary (eg *occasional cause*).—*adv* **occā´sionally**, now and then; at infrequent times. [Fr,—L *occāsiō, -ōnis*, opportunity—*occidĕre—ob*, in the way of, *cadĕre, cāsum*, to fall.]

Occident [ok´si-dėnt] *n* Europe and the Americas; **occident** (*poet*) the west.—*adj* **occiden´tal**, situated in the Occident; of or relating to Occidentals.—*n* **Occidental**, a member of the occidental peoples, esp one of European ancestry.—*n* **Occiden´talism**, the characteristic features of occidental peoples or culture.—*vti* **Occ´iden´talize**, to turn to the ways of the Occident.—[Fr,—L *occidēns, -entis*, pr p of *occidĕre*, to set.]

occiput [ok´si-put] *n* the back part of the head or skull.—*adj* **occip´ital**, pertaining to the back of the head. [L,—*ob* over against, *caput*, head.]

occlude [o-klōōd´] *vt* to shut in or out; to stop (as a passage, cavity, or opening); to absorb and retain.—*vi* (*dentistry*) to meet, with the cusps of the teeth fitting closely.—*n* **occlu´sion** [-zh(ò)n] the act of occluding; the front formed by a cold front overtaking a warm front and lifting the warm air above the earth's surface. [L *occlūdere, -clūsum—ob*, in the way of, *claudĕre*, to shut.]

occult [ok-ult´] *adj* hidden; beyond the range of sense; mysterious; magical; supernatural.—*ns* **occultā´tion**, a concealing, esp of one of the heavenly bodies by another; state of being hid; **occult´ism**, occult theory or practice; belief in the influence of supernatural or supernormal powers.—*adv* **occult´ly**.—*n* **occult´ness**. [Fr,—L *occulĕre, occultum*, to hide.]

occupy [ok´ū-pī] *vt* to take or seize; to hold possession of; to take up, as room, etc.; to fill, as an office; to employ (oneself, one's mind, etc.); take up (time, space, etc.);—*pt, pt p* **occupied**.—*ns* **occ´upancy**, the act or fact of occupying; possession; **occ´upant**, one who takes or has possession; **occupā´tion**, the act of occupying; possession; state of being occupied; profession; habitual employment, craft, or trade; **occ´upier**, an occupant.—*adj* **occupā´tional**.—**occupational therapy**, therapy by means of work in the arts and crafts, prescribed for its effect in promoting recovery or rehabilitation; **occupational therapist**. [Fr,—L *occupāre, -ātum—ob*, to, on, *capĕre*, to take.]

occur [o-kûr´] *vi* to come into the mind of a person (eg *it occurs to me that*); to happen; to be, to be found;—*pr p* **occurr´ing**; *pt p* **occurred´**.—*n* **occurr´ence**, act or fact of happening; an event.—*adj* **occurr´ent**, occurring at a particular time or place; incidental.—*n* something that occurs as distinguished from something that continues to exist. [L—*occurrĕre—ob*, in the way of, *currĕre*, to run.]

ocean [ō´shàn] *n* the vast expanse of salt water that covers the greater part of the surface of the globe; any one of its five great divisions; any immense expanse or vast quantity.—*adj* pertaining to the ocean.—*adj* **oceanic** [ō-shian´ik] pertaining to the ocean; found or formed in the ocean.—*ns* **oceanog´raphy**, the scientific description of the ocean; a science dealing with the oceans including the physics and chemistry of their waters, marine biology, and the exploitation of their resources; **oceanog´rapher**, one versed in oceanography.—*adj* **oceanograph´ic**.—*n* **oceanol´ogy**, oceanography; the science of marine resources and technology. [Fr,—L *Ōcĕānus*—Gr *Ōkĕānos*, the great river supposed to encircle the earth.]

ocelot [os´ė-lot] *n* a medium-sized spotted wildcat (*Felis pardalis*) of N and S America. [Mexican.]

ocher, ochre [ō´kėr] *n* a fine clay, mostly pale yellow, used as a pigment.—*adjs* **o´cherous, o´chreous**, consisting of, containing, or resembling ocher. [Fr,—L *ōchra*—Gr *ōchrā—ōchros*, pale yellow.]

ochlocracy [ok-lok´ra-si] *n* mob rule. [Gr *ochlokratiā—ochlos*, a crowd, *kratos*, power.]

octagon [ok´ta-gon] *n* a plane figure of eight sides and eight angles.—*adj* **octag´onal**. [Gr *oktō*, eight, *gōniā*, an angle.]

octahedron [ok-ta-hē´dron] *n* a solid bounded by eight plane faces.—*adj* **octahē´dral**. [Gr *oktō*, eight, *hedrā*, a base.]

octane [ok´tān] *n* C_8H_{18}, the eighth member of the paraffin series of hydrocarbons. So-called *iso*-octane serves as a standard of gasoline comparison, the **octane number** being the percentage by volume of this octane in a mixture with heptane C_7H_{16} which has the same knocking characteristics as the motor fuel under test. [Gr *oktō*, eight, and *-ane*, the termination used to denote a saturated hydrocarbon.]

octant [ok´tànt] *n* the eighth part of a circle; an instrument for observing altitudes of a celestial body from a moving ship or aircraft. [L *octāns, -antis*, an eighth.]

octave [oc´tiv, -tāv] *n* a set of eight; the last day of eight beginning with a church festival; (*mus*) the eighth full tone above or below a given tone, the interval of eight degrees between a tone and either of its octaves, or the series of tones within this interval; the first eight lines of a Petrarchan or Italian sonnet. [Fr,—L *octāvus*, eighth—*octo*, eight.]

octavo [ok-tā´vō] *adj* having eight leaves to the sheet.—*n* the page size (about 6 by 9 in) of a book printed on sheets folded into eight leaves, contracted 8vo;—*pl* **octā´vos**. [L *in octavo*, in the eighth.]

octet [ok-tet´] *n* a group of eight (performers, lines of a sonnet); a composition for eight instruments or voices. [From L *octo*, eight, on analogy of **duet**.]

October [ok-tō´bėr] *n* the tenth month of the year, having 31 days. [L *octō*, eight, eighth month of the Roman calendar.]

octogenarian [ok-tō-je-nā´ri-àn] *n* one who is between the ages of eighty and ninety.—Also *adj*. [L *octōgēnārius*, pertaining to eighty.]

octopod [ok´tō-pod] *adj* eight-footed or eight-armed.—*n* an octopus.—*n* **Octopoda** [oktop´o-da] cephalopods with eight arms, as octopusses (cf *Decapoda*). [See **octopus**.]

octopus [ok´tō-pus] *n* any of a genus (*Octopus*) of mollusks having a soft body and eight arms covered with suckers;—*pl* **oc´topusses, octopī´**. [Gr *okto*, eight, *pous*, gen *podos*, foot.]

octosyllabic [ok-tō-sil-ab´ik] *adj* consisting of eight syllables.—*n* **oc´tosyllable**, a word or line of eight syllables. [L *octo*, eight, + **syllable**.]

ocular [ok´ū-lȧr] *adj* pertaining to the eye; formed in, or known by the eye; received by actual sight; resembling an eye in form or function.—*n* eyepiece.—*adv* **oc´ularly**.—*n* **oc´ulist**, an obsolescent term for ophthamologist. [L *oculus*, the eye.]

odalisque [ō´da-lisk] *n* a female slave or concubine in a harem. [Fr,—Turk *ōdaliq*—*ōdah*, a chamber.]

odd [od] *adj* having a remainder of one when divided by two; with the other of the pair missing; unpaired; not one of a complete set; left over; extra; unusual, queer, eccentric; occasional.—*n pl* **odds** [odz] inequalities; difference in favor of one against another; more than an even wager; the amount or proportion by which the bet of one exceeds that of another; chances; dispute, strife; scraps, miscellaneous pieces, as in the phrase **odds and ends**.—*ns* **Odd Fellow**, a member of a major fraternal and benevolent society; **odd´ity**, the state of being odd or singular; strangeness; a singular person or thing.—*adv* **odd´ly**.—*ns* **odd´ man out´**, one that is unorthodox or eccentric; **odd´ment**, a scrap, remnant; **odd´ness**.—*adj* **odds´-on´**, of a chance, better than even.—**at odds**, at variance. [ON *oddi*, a point, triangle, odd number; cf OE *ord*, point.]

ode [ōd] *n* lyric poem generally addressed to some person or thing, marked by lofty feeling and dignified style. [Fr *ode*—Gr *ōidē*, contr from *aoidē*—*aeidein*, to sing.]

odium [ō´di-um] *n* a general hatred, the bad feeling naturally aroused by a particular action (eg *incurred the odium of telling the truth*).—*adj* **o´dious**, hateful, offensive, repulsive, causing hatred.—*adv* **o´diously**.—*n* **o´diousness**. [L *ŏdium*.]

odometer [ō-dom´ė-tėr] *n* an instrument for measuring the distance traveled by a vehicle.

odont- [od-ont´-, od´ont-], **odonto-** [-ō, -o] in composition, tooth.—*ns* **odontalgia** [-al´ji-a] toothache; **odontol´ogy**, the science of teeth. [Fr *odous*, gen *odontos*, a tooth.]

odor [ō´dȯr] *n* smell; scent; aroma; a characteristic or predominant quality.—*adj* **odorif´erous**, emitting a (usu. pleasant) smell; morally offensive.—*adv* **odorif´erously**.—*adj* **o´dorous**, emitting an odor or scent; smelly; fragrant.—*adv* **o´dorously**.—*adj* **o´dorless**, without odor. [Fr,—L *odor*.]

Odyssey [od´is-i] *n* a Greek epic poem, ascribed to Homer, describing ten years' wanderings of Odysseus (Ulysses) on his way home from Troy to Ithaca; **odyssey**, any adventurous journey; an intellectual or spiritual quest;—*pl* **od´ysseys**.

Oedipus complex [ē´di-pus kom´pleks] (*psych*) in a son, a complex involving undue attachment to his mother, hostility to his father. [*Oedipus*, king of Thebes, who unwittingly married his mother, + **complex**.]

o'er [ōr] contracted from **over**.

oersted [ûr´sted] *n* the centimeter-gram-second electromagnetic unit of magnetic field strength, about 80 amperes per meter. [Hans Christian *Oersted* (1777–1851), Danish physicist.]

œuvre [œvr´] *n* a substantial body of work, usu. consisting of the lifework of a writer, artist, or composer;—*pl* **œuvres**. [Fr.]

of [ov, ȯv] *prep* now has many shades of meaning in idiomatic phrases, including:—from (eg *within a week of, a yard of; upwards of*); belonging to; among; proceeding or derived from; owing to (cause or reason, as *to die of, sick of, proud of*); concerning (eg *to speak, think of*); indicating some form of deprivation (eg *rid of, destitute of, take leave of*); showing a possessive relation (eg *the son of the owner of the house*); showing an objective relation (eg *the care of the sick, loss of appetite*). [OE *of*; Du *af*, Ger *ab*, L *ab*, Gr *apo*.]

off [of] *adv* away; newly in motion; out of continuity; no longer available; in deterioration or diminution.—*adj* most distant; on the opposite or farther side; (*fig*) remote (eg *an off chance*); not devoted to usual business (eg *an off day*); not showing the usual activity; not up to the usual standard of quality or efficiency.—*prep* not on, away from.—*interj* away! depart!—*adv* **off´ and on´**, occasionally.—*n* **off´beat** (*mus*), a beat having a weak accent.—*adj* (*inf*) unconventional, strange, unusual, etc.—*adj* **off´-color**, varying from the standard color; improper; risque.—*n* **off´-day**, a day when one is not at one's best (see also **off**, *adj* above).—*adv* **off´hand**, extempore; without hesitating.—*adj* unceremonious, free and easy; ungraciously lacking in ceremony.—*n* **off´ing**, visible part of the sea at some distance from the shore; the near or foreseeable future (eg *promotion is in the offing*).—*adj* **off´key´**, out of tune; not in keeping.—*vt* **off´load**, to unload.—*adj* **off´-peak´**, not at (time of) highest demand.—*ns* **off´scouring**, matter scoured off, refuse, anything vile or despised; **off´set**, a thing or value set off against another as an equivalent or compensation; a horizontal ledge on the face of a wall; in surveying, a perpendicular from the main line to an outlying point.—*vt* to place (against) as an equivalent; to counterbalance, compensate for.—*n* **off´shoot**, that which shoots off from the main stem; anything growing out of another.—*adj, adv* **off´shore**, from the shore; at a distance from the shore.—*adj, adv* **off side**, illegally in advance of the ball or puck; **off´spring**, a child, or children; issue; production of any kind.—*adj* **off´-white´**, a yellowish or grayish white.—**well off**, rich, well provided. [See **of**.]

offal [of´ȧl] *n* the part of a carcase that is unfit for human food; entrails (eg heart, liver) eaten as food (*pl* **off´als**); refuse; anything worthless. [**off** + **fall**.]

offend [of-end´] *vt* to displease, to make angry; to affront.—*vi* to sin; to transgress (against).—*ns* **offense´**, any cause of anger or displeasure; an affront; an infraction of law; a sin; assault, aggressive action; **offend´er**, one who offends; a trespasser; a criminal.—*adj* **offens´ive**, causing offense, displeasure, or injury; disgusting; used in attack; making the first attack.—*n* the act of the attacking party; the posture of one who attacks; a sustained effort to achieve an end.—*adv* **offens´ively**.—*n* **offens´iveness**.—**give offense**, to cause displeasure; **take offense**, to be aggrieved. [L *offendĕre, offensum*—*ob*, against, *fendĕre*, to strike.]

offer [of´ėr] *vt* to present, esp as an act of devotion; to hold out for acceptance or rejection; to declare a willingness (to do); to lay before one; to present to the mind; to attempt, make a show of attempting (eg resistance).—*vi* to present itself, to be at hand; to declare a willingness.—*n* act of offering; that which is offered; proposal made.—*ns* **off´ering**, act of making an offer; that which is offered; a gift; presentation in worship; **off´ertory**, act of offering of the bread and wine to God in the Eucharist; money collected at a church service; the prayers or music during the collection. [L *offerre*—*ob*, towards, *ferre*, to bring.]

office [of´is] *n* an act of kindness or attention, a service; a function or duty; a position of trust or authority, esp in the government; act of worship; order or form of a religious service; a place where business is carried on; the people working there.—*ns* **off´iceholder**, a government official; **off´icer**, a person holding a position of authority, in a government, business, club, etc.; a policeman; a person holding a commission in the armed forces.—*vt* to furnish with officers; to command as officers.—*adj* **official** [ofish´ȧl], pertaining to an office; holding a public position; done by, or issued by, authority; formal.—*n* one who holds an office.—*adv* **offic´ially**.—*n* **officialese´** [-ēz] stilted, wordy, and obscure English alleged to be characteristic of official letters and documents.—*vi* **offic´iāte**, to perform the duties of an office; to perform the functions of a priest, minister, rabbi, etc. [Fr,—L *officium*, a favor, duty, service.]

officinal [of-is´in-ȧl] *adj* (of medicine) available without special preparation or compounding or described by the US Pharmacopeia. [Fr,—L *officina*, a workshop—*opus*, work, *facĕre*, to do.]

officious [of-ish´ùs] *adj* too forward in offering services; highhandedly meddlesome.—*adv* **offic´iously**.—*n* **offic´iousness**. [Fr,—L *officiōsus*—*officium*; cf **office**.]

off line, off-line (*when prenomial*) [off´līne] *adj* pertaining to a computer when it is disconnected from the Internet.

oft [oft], **often**, [of´n] *adv* frequently; many times.—*adv* **oft´entimes**, many times; frequently. [OE *oft*; Ger *oft*.]

ogham, ogam [ō´ȧm, äg´ȧm, ōg´ȧm] *n* an ancient Celtic alphabet; any one of its twenty characters. [OIr *ogam*, mod Ir *ogham*.]

ogee [ō´jē, ō-jē´] *n* a molding S-shaped in section; a pointed arch having a reversed curve near the apex on each side. [Fr *ogive*.]

ogive [ō´jīv, -jīv´] *n* (*archit*) a diagonal rib across a Gothic vault; a pointed arch. [Fr; perh Ar *auj*, summit.]

ogle [ō´gl] *vt* to look at fondly or impertinently, with side glances; to eye greedily.—*vi* to cast amorous glances.—*ns* **o´gle; o´gler; o´gling**. [Cf Low Ger *oegeln*, Ger *äugeln*, to leer.]

ogre [ō´gėr] *n* a man-eating monster or giant of fairy tales; an ugly, cruel, bad-tempered or stern person.—*fem* **o´gress**.—*adj* **o´gr(e)ish**. [Fr.]

ohm [ōm] *n* the practical meter-kilogram-second unit of electric resistance equal to the resistance of a circuit in which a potential difference of one volt produces a current of one ampere. [*Ohm*, German physicist (1787–1854).]

oil [oil] *n* any of various greasy, combustible liquid substances obtained from animal, vegetable, and mineral matter; petroleum; oil color; an oil painting.—*vt* to smear, lubricate, or supply with oil.—*n* **oil´ cake**, the solid residue after extracting the oil from seeds (as of cotton); **oil´can**, a spouted can designed to release oil drop by drop (as for lubricating machinery); **oil´cloth**, cloth made waterproof by being treated with oil or paint; **oil´ color**, paint made by grinding a pigment in oil; **oil´er**, one who, or that which, oils; an oil can; a producing oil well; a ship using oil as fuel; an oil-cargo ship; (*pl*) an oilskin suit; **oil´field**, a region that produces petroleum; **oil´ painting**, a picture painted in oil colors; the art of painting in oil colors; **oil´palm**, a pinnate-leaved palm (*Elaeis guineensis*), a native of Africa cultivated for its fruit whose flesh and seeds yield oil; **oil´skin**, cloth made waterproof by means of oil; a garment made of oilskin; **oil slick**, film of oil on the surface of water; **oil´ well**, a well from which petroleum is obtained.—*adj* **oil´y**, consisting of, containing, or having the qualities of oil; greasy; too suave or smooth, unctuous.—*n* **oil´iness**. [OFr *oile*—L *oleum*—Gr *elaion*—*elaiā*, the olive.]

ointment [oint´ment] *n* a fatty substance used on the skin for healing or cosmetic purposes; a salve. [Fr *oint*, pt p of *oindre*—L *unguĕre*, to anoint.]

Ojibwa [ō-jib´wā] *n* member of an Amerindian people of Michigan;—*pl* **Ojibwa, -s**; the Algonquian language of this people.—Also **Choppewa**.

okapi [o-kä´pē] *n* an animal (*Okapia johnstoni*) of Central Africa, related to the giraffe but with a much shorter neck. [African.]

OK, O.K. [o-kā´] *adj* all correct; all right; satisfactory.—*adv* yes, certainly.—*n* approval; sanction; endorsement.—*vt* to mark or pass as all right; to sanction;—*pr p* **OK´ing, O.K.´ing**; *pt, pt p* **OK'd, O.K.'d**; (*inf*) **o´kay´**. [Origin uncertain.]

old [ōld] *adj* advanced in years; having been long in existence; worn or worn out; former; of long standing; denoting the earlier or earliest of two or more; antique, ancient, early; having the age or duration of; long practiced.—*adjs* **old´en**, relating to a bygone era; **old-fash´ioned**, of a fashion like that used long ago; out of date.—*n* a cocktail made with whiskey, bitters, soda, and bits of fruit.—*n* **Old Glory**, the flag of the US.—*adjs* **old´ hat´**, out of date; lacking in freshness; trite; **old´ish**, somewhat old.—*n* **old´timer**, one who has lived in a place or kept a position for a long time; something that is old-fashioned.—*adj* **old´world**, belonging to earlier times, esp having the picturesque qualities of the old world.—**Old Bailey**, the Central Criminal Court in London; **Old English**, the language of the English people from the middle of the 5th to the beginning of the 12th century AD; English of any period before Modern English; black letter; **Old High German**, the High German language before the 12th century; **old lady**, (*slang*) one's mother or one's wife; **Old Low German**, the Low German language before the 12th century; **old maid**, a woman, esp an older woman who has never married; a prim, prudish, fussy person; **old man**, (*slang*) one's father or one's husband; **old master**, any of the great European painters before the 18th century; a painting by any of these; **Old Norse**, the Germanic language of the Scandinavians before the 14th century; **old school**, adherents of traditional or conservative ideas; **old school tie**, clannishness among members of an established clique.—*adj* **Old Style**, according to the Julian calendar.—*ns* **Old Testament**, Christian designation for the Holy Scriptures of Judaism, the first of the two general divisions of the Christian Bible; **Old World**, Europe, Asia, and Africa, often with reference to European culture, customs, etc.—**of old**, long ago. [OE *ald, eald*; Du *oud*; Ger *alt*.]

oleaginous [ō-lė-aj´in-us] *adj* oily.—*n* **oleag´inousness**. [L *oleāginus*—*oleum*, oil.]

oleander [ō-lė-an´dėr] *n* an evergreen shrub (*Nerium oleander*) with lance-shaped leaves and beautiful flowers. [LL, of doubtful origin.]

oleaster [ō-lė-as´tėr] *n* any of several plants (genus *Eleagnus*) of southern Europe with bitter olive-shaped fruit. [L,—*olea*, an olive-tree—Gr *elaiā*.]

oleo- [ō´lė-ō-] in composition, oil. [L *oleum*, oil.]

oleograph [ō´lė-ō-gräf] *n* a lithograph printed on cloth to imitate an oil painting. [L *oleum*, oil, Gr *graphein*, to write.]

olfactory [ol-fak´tȯr-i] *adj* pertaining to, or used in, smelling. [L *olfacĕre*, to smell—*olēre*, to smell, *facĕre*, to make.]

oligarchy [ol´i-gärk-i] *n* government by a small exclusive class; a state governed by such.—*n* **ol´igarch**, a member of an oligarchy.—*adjs* **oligarch´al, oligarch´ic, -ical**. [Gr *oligos*, few, *archē*, rule.]

Oligocene [ol´i-gō-sēn] *adj* pertaining to a period of the Tertiary geological era—between the Eocene and Miocene. [Gr *oligos*, little, *kainos*, new.]

olio [ō´li-ō] *n* a savory dish of different sorts of meat and vegetables; a mixture, a medley, a miscellany. [Sp *olla*—L *ōlla*, a pot.]

olive [ol´iv] *n* an Old World evergreen tree (*Olea europaea*) cultivated for its oily fruit; its fruit; peace, of which the olive was the emblem; a color like the unripe olive.—*adj* of a brownish-green color like the olive.—*adj* **olivāceous** [o-li-vā´shus] olive-colored.—*n* **ol´ive oil**, oil pressed from the fruit of the olive.—**olive branch**, a symbol of peace; (*pl*) children (Ps. cxxvii 4, *Pr Bk* version). [Fr,—L *olīva*.]

-ology *see* **-logy**.

Olympus [ol-im´pus] *n* a mountain on border of Thessaly and Macedonia, home of the gods.—*n* **Olym´piad**, in ancient Greece, a period of four years, being the interval from one celebration of the Olympic games to another, used in reckoning time (beginning of first Olympiad is 776 BC); a celebration of the modern Olympic games.—*adj* **Olym´pian**, pertaining to Olympus; godlike.—*n* a dweller in Olympus, one of the greater gods.—*adj* **Olym´pic**, of Olympia.—**Olym´pic games**, games celebrated every four years at Olympia, dedicated to Olympian Zeus; quadrennial international athletic contests, held at various centers since 1896. [Gr *Olympos*.]

ombudsman [om´bŏŏdz-man] *n* a public official appointed to investigate citizens' complaints. [Sw]

omega [ō-meg´a] *n* the last letter of the Greek alphabet (Ω, *φ*;); (*B*) the end. [Gr *ōmega*, great *O*.]

omelet, omelette [om´e-let] *n* eggs beaten and cooked flat in a pan. [OFr *amelette*, which through the form *alemette* is traced to OFr *alemelle*, a thin plate—L *lāmella, lāmina*.]

omen [ō´mėn] *n* a sign of some future event.—**of good, ill, omen**, foreshowing good, or ill, fortune. [L *ōmens, -inis*.]

omicron [ō´mi-kron] *n* the 15th letter of the Greek alphabet.

ominous [om´in-us] *adj* pertaining to, or containing, an omen; portending evil, inauspicious.—*adv* **om´inously**.—*n* **om´inousness**. [L *ōminōsus*—*ōmen*. See **omen**.]

omit [ō-mit´] *vt* to leave out; to fail (to); to fail to use, perform;—*pr p* **omitt´ing**; *pt, pt p* **omitt´ed**.—*adj* **omiss´ible**, that may be omitted.—*n* **omiss´ion**, act of omitting; a thing omitted.—*adj* **omiss´ive**, omitting or leaving out. [L *omittĕre, omissum*—*ob*, in front, *mittĕre*, to send.]

omnibus [om´ni-bus] *n* a bus, a large public vehicle for passengers by road; a book containing reprints of a number of works;—*pl* **om´nibuses**.—*adj* widely comprehensive; of miscellaneous contents. [Dat pl of L *omnis*, all.]

omnifarious [om-ni-fār´i-us] *adj* of all varieties or kinds. [L *omnifarius*—*omnis*, all; cf **multifarious**.]

omnipotent [om-nip´o-tėnt] *adj* all powerful, possessing unlimited power.—*n* **the Omnipotent**, God.—*ns* **omnip´otence, omnipotency**, unlimited power.—*adv* **omnip´otently**. [L *omnipotens*—*omnis*, all, *potens*, powerful.]

omnipresent [om-ni-prez´ėnt] *adj* always present everywhere.—*n* **omnipres´ence**. [L *omnis*, all *praesens*, present.]

omniscient [om-nish´ėnt] *adj* knowing all things.—*adv* **omnis´ciently**.—*n* **omnis´cience**. [L *omnis*, all, *sciens*, pr p of *scire*, to know.]

omnium-gatherum [om´nium-gaTH´er-um] *n* a miscellaneous collection of things or persons. [L *omnium*, gen pl of *omnis*, all + **gather**.]

omnivorous [om-niv´or-us] *adj* taking in everything indiscriminately; (*zool*) feeding on both animal and vegetable foods. [L *omnis*, all, *vorāre*, to devour.]

on [on] *prep* in contact with the upper or presented surface of; indicating position more generally (as, *on the far side, on the Continent*); to and toward the surface of; at or near; acting by contact with; not off; indicating position in time (eg *on the last day*); indicating direction or object (eg *money spent on provisions, to have pity on*); having for basis, principle, or condition (eg *on trust, on loan*); concerning, about (eg *to lecture on*); by the agency of, with (eg *to tear on barbed wire*); immediately after; (*inf*) at the expense of, to the disadvantage of; (*slang*) using; addicted to.—*adv* in or into a position on something; forward; in continuance; in progress; on the stage; not off.—*interj* go on! proceed!—**on and off**, intermittently; **on and on**, for a long time; continuously. [OE *on*; Du *aan*, ON *ā*, Ger *an*.]

onager [on´a-jėr] *n* the wild ass (*Equus onager*) of Central Asia. [L,—Gr *onagros*—*onos*, an ass, *agros*, wild.]

Onandaga [ŏn-an-däg´ȧ] *n* member of an Iroquoian-speaking Amerindian people of upper New York state.

once [ons] *n see* **ounce** (2).

once [wuns] *adv* a single time; at a former time; at some future time.—*n* **once´-ov´er**, (*inf*) a single, comprehensive survey.—**once in a while**, occasionally; rarely.—**at once**, without delay; **for once**, on one occasion only. [OE *ānes*, orig gen of *ān*, one, used as adv.]

oncology [on-köl´ó-ji] *n* the branch of medicine dealing with tumors.—*adj* **oncolog´ical**.—*n* **oncol´ogist**, one who studies cancer. [Gr *onkos*, mass.]

oncoming [on´kum-ing] *n* approach.—*adj* advancing, approaching. [**on** + pr p of **come**.]

one [wun] *adj* a single; of unit number; undivided; the same; a certain.—*n* the first and lowest cardinal number; an individual person or thing.—*pron* a person (indefinitely), as in 'one may say'; any one; some one.—*n* **one´ness**, singleness, unity.—*pron* **oneself´, one's self**, the emphatic and reflexive form of **one**.—*adj* **one´-sid´ed**, unfair, partial.—*ns* **one-step**, a ballroom dance of US origin; **one-up´manship**, the art of being one jump ahead of or going one better than a friend or competitor.—**one another**, each other; **one-armed bandit**, a slot machine; **one day**, at an indefinite time.—*adj* (*inf*) **one-track**, limited in scope.—**all one**, just the same, of no consequence; **at one**, agreed. [OE *ān*, ON *einn*, Ger *ein*, L *unus*.]

onerous [on´ėr-us] *adj* burdensome, oppressive.—*adv* **on´erously**.—*n* **on´erousness**. [L *onerōsus*—*onus, -eris*, a burden.]

ongoing [on´gō-ing] *n* a going on; progressing. [**on**, + pr p of **go**.]

onion [un´yȯn] *n* an edible bulb (*Allium cepa*) of the lily family. [Fr *oignon*—L *ūniō, -ōnis*, an onion.]

on line, on-line (*when prenomial*) [on´līne] *adj* pertaining to a computer when it is connected via a modem to an online service or Internet service provider. Using the computer in this way means the user is "online."

onlooker [on´look-ėr] *n* a looker on, observer.

only [ōn´li] *adj* single in number; without others of the kind; without others worthy to be counted.—*adv* not more than; exclusively; alone; merely; barely.—*conj* (*inf*) but; except that. [OE *ānlic* (adj)—*ān*, one, *-līc*, like.]

onomatopoeia [on-ō-mat-o-pē´ya] *n* the formation of a word in imitation of the sound of the thing meant; a word so formed, as 'click', 'cuckoo'.—*adjs* **onomatopoe´ic, onomatopoet´ic**. [Gr *onoma, -atos*, a name, *poieein*, to make.]

onrush [on´rush] *n* a rushing onward. [**on** + **rush**.]

onset [on´set] *n* violent attack, assault; beginning. [**on** + **set**.]

onslaught [on´slöt] *n* an attack, onset, assault. [Prob Du *aanslag* or Ger *anschlag*.]

ontology [on-tol´o-ji] *n* the science that treats of the principles of pure being, that part of metaphysics which treats of the nature of existence.—*adjs* **ontolog´ic, -al**.—*adv* **ontolog´ically**.—*n* **ontol´ogist**. [Gr *ōn, ontos*, pr p of *einai*, to be, *logos*, discourse.]

onus [ō´nus] *n* burden; responsibility. [L *onus*, burden.]

onward [on´wȧrd] *adj* going forward; advancing.—*adv* (also **on´wards**) toward a point on or in front; forward. [**on**, + suffx *-ward*.]

onyx [on´iks] *n* a variety of chalcedony with parallel layers of different colors used for making cameos. [Gr *onyx*, a finger-nail.]

oolite [ō´o-līt] *n* (*geol*) a kind of limestone, composed of grains like the eggs or roe of a fish.—*adj* **oölit´ic**. [Gr *ōion*, an egg, *lithos*, stone.]

ooze [ōōz] *n* slimy mud; a fine-grained, soft, deposit, composed of shells and fragments of organisms on the bottom of a body of water.—*vi* to flow gently; to percolate, as a liquid through pores.—*vt* to exude.—*adj* **ooz´y**, resembling ooze; slimy. [OE *wāse*, mud; OE *wōs*, juice.]

opacity *See* **opaque**.

opal [ō´pȧl] *n* a mineral consisting of silica with some water, usu. milky white with fine play of color, in some varieties semiprecious.—*n* **opales´cence**, a milky iridescence.—*adj* **opales´cent**. [Fr *opale*—L *opalus*.]

opaque [ō-pāk´] *adj* (*obs*) dark; impervious to light or other radiation; not transparent; obscure.—*adv* **opaque´ly**.—*ns* **opacity** [ō-pas´it-ti], **opaque´ness**. [L *opācus*.]

op art [op ärt] art using geometrical forms precisely executed and so arranged that movement of the observer's eye, or inability to focus, produces an illusion of movement in the painting.—Also **optical art**.—*n* **op artist**. [*op*tical.]

open [ō´pn] *adj* not shut; allowing passage; uncovered, unprotected; free from trees; not fenced; loose; widely spaced; not frozen up; not frosty; free to be used, etc.; public; without reserve; candid; undisguised; easily understood; liable (to); accessible (to suggestions, etc.); unrestricted; not restricted to any class of persons; of a consonant, made without stopping the breath stream; of a syllable, ending with a vowel.—*vt* to make open; to expose to view; to begin.—*vi* to become open; to have an opening; to begin to appear; to begin.—*n* a clear space.—*n* **o´pener**.—*adjs* **o´pen-hand´ed**, generous, liberal; **o´pen-heart´ed**, responsive to emotional appeal, frank.—*n* **o´pening**, an open place; a breach; an aperture; beginning; opportunity.—*adv* **o´penly**.—*adjs* **o´pen-mind´ed**, free to receive and consider new ideas; **o´penmouthed**, gaping; expectant; clamorous.—*ns* **o´penness; o´pen ses´ame**, a spell or other means of making barriers fly open; **o´pen work**, ornamental work showing openings.—**open circuit**, in television, the customary system in which the showing is for general, not restricted, viewing; **open house**, hospitality to all comers; a house or apartment open for inspection, esp by prospective buyers or tenants; **open secret**, a matter known to many but treated as a secret; **open shop**, an establishment where membership in a labor union is not a condition for employment, although there may be an agreement by which the union has sole bargaining rights on behalf of all of the employees. [OE *open*; cf Du *open*, ON *opinn*, Ger *offen*; prob related to **up**.]

opera [op´ėr-a] *n* musical drama; a musical drama.—*adj* used in or for an opera.—*ns* **op´era glass**, a small low-power binocular for use at operas, plays, etc.; **op´era hat**, a man's collapsible top hat.—*adj* **operat´ic**, pertaining to or resembling opera. [It,—L *opera*. Cf **operate**.]

opera bouffe [op´ėr-a-bōōf] *n* satirical comic opera. [Fr *opéra-bouffe*]—It *opera-buffa*. Cf **buffoon**.]

operate [op´ėr-āt] *vi* to work; to exert power or influence; to produce any effect; to perform a surgical operation.—*vt* to effect; to work (eg a machine); to conduct, carry on.—*ns* **op´erand**, something on which an operation is performed, eg a quantity in mathematics; the address in a computer instruction of data to be operated on; **operā´tion**, act, process, or result of operating; agency; influence; method of working; action or movements; surgical performance.—*adjs* **operā´tional**, relating to, connected with, operations; ready for action; engaged in, constituting, or forming part of, an operation; **op´erātive**, having the power of operating or acting; acting; efficacious.—*n* a mechanic; a secret agent; a private detective.—*adv* **op´erātively**.—*n* **op´erātor**, one who, or that which, operates or produces an effect. [L *operārī, -ātus*—*opera*, work, closely conn with *opus, operis*, work.]

operculum [ō-pėr´kū-lum] *n* (*bot*) a cover or lid; (*zool*) the plate over the entrance of a shell; the gill cover of fishes;—*pl* **oper´cula**.—*adjs* **oper´cular**, belonging to the operculum; **oper´culate, -d**, having an operculum. [L,—*operīre*, to cover.]

operetta [op-ėr-et´a] *n* a short, light musical drama. [It, dim of *opera*.]

operose [op´ėr-ōs] *adj* laborious; tedious.—*adv* **op´erosely**.—*n* **op´eroseness**. [L *operōsus*—*opus, operis*, work.]

ophidian [o-fid´i-ȧn] *adj* pertaining to snakes; having the nature of a snake. [Gr *ophidion*, dim of *ophis*, a serpent.]

ophthalm- [of-thalm´-, of´-] in composition, eye.—*n* **ophthalm´ia**, inflammation of the conjunctiva or the eyeball.—*adj* **ophthal´mic**, pertaining to or situated near the eye.—*ns* **ophthalmol´ogy**, the branch of medicine dealing with diseases of the eye; **ophthalmol´ogist; ophthal´moscope**, an instrument for examining the interior of the eye and esp the retina. [Gr,—*ophthalmos*, eye.]

opiate [ō´pi-ȧt] *n* a drug containing opium; that which dulls sensation, physical or mental.—*adj* inducing sleep.—*adj* **o´piated**, mixed with opiates; drugged. [**opium**.]

opine [ō-pīn´] *vti* (usu. humorous) to suppose; to form or express as an opinion. [Fr,—L *opīnārī*, to think.]

opinion [ō-pin´yȯn] *n* a belief based on what seems to one to be probably true; judgment; view; estimation, evaluation; a formal expert judgment.—*adjs* **opin´ionāted, opin´ionātive**, unduly attached to one's own opinions.—*adv* **opin´ionātively**.—*n* **opin´ionātiveness**.—**a matter of opinion**, a question open to dispute; **no opinion of**, a very low opinion or estimate of. [L *opīniō, -ōnis*.]

opium [ō´pi-um] *n* the bitter brownish addictive dried narcotic juice of the opium poppy.—*n* **opium poppy**, an annual Eurasian poppy (*Papaver somniferum*) cultivated since antiquity as the source of opium, for its edible oily seeds, or for its showy flowers. [L,—Gr *opion*, dim from *opos*, sap.]

opossum [o-pos´um] *n* any of various small American marsupial mammals (family Didelphidae), esp a common nocturnal and arboreal mammal (*Didelphus virginiana*) of the eastern and midwestern US; any of several Australian phalangers with prehensile tail. [West Indian.]

opponent [o-pō´nėnt] *adj* opposing; placed opposite or in front.—*n* an adversary; one who opposes a course of action, belief, person, etc. [L *oppōnens, entis*, pr p of *oppōnĕre*—*ob*, in the way of, *pōnĕre*, to place.]

opportune [op-ȯr-tūn´, op´-] *adj* occurring at a fitting time, timely; convenient.—*adv* **opportune´ly**.—*ns* **opportune´ness; opportun´ist**, one (eg a politician) who waits for events before declaring his opinions, or shapes his conduct or policy to circumstances of the moment; **opportun´ity**, an occasion offering a possibility or chance; a combination of favoring circumstances (eg *opportunity makes the thief*). [Fr,—L *opportūnus*—*ob*, before, *portus*, a harbor.]

oppose [o-pōz´] *vt* to place in front of or in the way of; to set in contrast (to); to balance against; to place as an obstacle; to resist; to contend with.—*adj* **oppos´able**, that may be opposed; capable of being placed against one or more of the remaining digits of the hand or foot.—*n* **oppos´er**. [Fr,—L *ob*, against, Fr *poser*, to place—LL *pausāre*, to rest, stop.]

opposite [op´o-zit] *adj* placed over against (*often with* **to**); face to face; (of foliage leaves) in pairs at each node with the stem between; opposed (eg *the opposite side in a dispute*); contrary (eg *in opposite directions*); diametrically different (*with* **to**).—*n* that which is opposed or contrary; an opponent.—*prep* across from.—*adv* **opp´ositely**.—*n* **opp´ositeness**.—**opposite number**, one who has a corresponding place in another set. [Fr,—L *oppositus*—*oppōnĕre*—*ob*, against, *pōnĕre, positum*, to place.]

opposition [op-o-zish´(ȯ)n] *n* state of being placed over against; position over against; contrast; contradistinction; act of setting opposite; act of opposing; resistance; that which opposes; (*astron*) the situation of heavenly bodies when 180 degrees apart; **Opposition**, political party that opposes the existing administration; [L *oppositiō, -ōnis*—*oppōnĕre*. See **opposite**.]

oppress [o-pres´] *vt* to press against or upon; to lie heavy upon; to overpower; to treat with tyrannical cruelty or injustice.—*n* **oppress´ion**, act of oppressing; tyranny; state of being oppressed; physical or mental distress.—*adj* **oppress´ive**, tending to oppress; overburdensome; tyrannical; heavy, overpowering (eg of weather).—*adv* **oppress´ively**.—*ns* **oppress´iveness; oppress´or**. [Fr,—LL *oppressāre*, freq of L *opprimĕre, oppressum*—*ob*, against, *premĕre*, to press.]

opprobrium [o-prō´bri-um] *n* the disgrace or reproach of shameful conduct; infamy.—*adj* **oppro´brious**, reproachful, insulting, abusive; disgraceful, infamous.—*adv* **opprō´briously**.—*n* **opprō´briousness**. [L,—*ob*, against, *probrum*, reproach.]

oppugn [o-pūn´] *vt* to assail, call in question; to attack or to resist.—*n* **oppugn´er**. [L *oppugnāre*, to attack—*ob, pugna*, fight.]

opt [opt] *vi* to choose.—**optative**, [op´ta-tiv] *adj* expressing desire or wish.—*n* (*gram*) a mood of the verb expressing wish.—**opt out** (**of**), to choose to take no part (in). [L *optāre, -ātum*, to wish.]

optic, -al [op´tik, -ȧl] *adj* relating to sight; (**optical**) constructed to help the sight; acting by means of light; visual.—*adv* **op´tically**.—*ns* **optician** [tish´ȧn] one who makes or sells eyeglasses, etc.; **op´tics** (*sing*), the branch of physics dealing with light and vision.—**optical art**, op art. [Gr *optikos*, optic—*optos*, seen.]

optimism [op´ti-mizm] *n* the belief that everything is ordered for the best; a disposition to take a hopeful view of things; (*loosely*) hopefulness.—*vt* **op´timize**, to make as perfect, effective, or functional as possible.—*n* **op´timist**, one given to optimism, a sanguine person.—*adj* **optimist´ic**.—*adv* **optimist´ically**. [L *optimus*, best.]

optimum [op´ti-mum] *n* that point at which any condition is most favorable;—*pl* **op´tima, optimums**.—*adj* (of conditions) best for the achievement of an aim or result; very best. [L neut of *optimus*, best.]

option [op´sh(ȯ)n] *n* act of choosing; power of choosing; an alternative for choice; the right to buy, sell, or lease at a fixed price within a specified time.—*adj* **op´tional**, left to one's choice.—*adv* **op´tionally**. [L *optiō, -ōnis*—*optāre*, to choose.]

optometry [op-tom´e-trē] *n* the profession of testing the vision and prescribing glasses to correct eye defects.—*n* **optom´etrist**. [Gr *optikos*, optic + *metron*, a measure.].

opulent [op´ū-lėnt] *adj* wealthy.—*n* **op´ulence**, riches.—*adv* **op´ulently**. [L *opulentus*.]

opus [op´us or ō´pus] *n* a work, a musical composition, esp any of the numbered musical works of a composer;—*pl* **opera** (op´ėr-a). [L 'work'.]

or[1] [ör] *conj* a coordinating conjunction introducing: an alternative; the last in a series of choices; a synonymous word or phrase. [ME *other*, either, or.]

or[2] [ör] (*her*) yellow or gold. [Fr,—L *aurum*, gold.]

oracle [or´a-kl] *n* a medium or agency, esp in ancient Greece, of divine revelation; a response by a god; a shrine where such responses are given; a person of great wisdom; a wise utterance.—*adj* **oracular** [or-ak´ū-lȧr], of the nature of an oracle; like an oracle (as in solemnity of delivery).—*adv* **orac´ularly**. [L *ōrāculum*—*ōrāre*, to speak.]

oral [ō´rȧl, ö´rȧl] *adj* relating to the mouth; uttered by the mouth; spoken, not written; taken through the mouth.—*n* (usu. *pl*) an oral examination.—*adv* **o´rally**. [L *ōs, ōris*, the mouth.]

orang [ō-rang´] *n* orangutan. [Clipped form.]

orange [or´inj] *n* the gold-colored fruit of certain trees (genus *Citrus*); the trees themselves; a color between red and yellow.—*adj* pertaining to an orange; orange-colored.—*ns* **orangeāde´**, a drink made with orange juice; **or´angery**, a protected place and esp a greenhouse for raising oranges in cool climates.—**orange stick**, a thin pointed stick, esp one of wood from an orange tree, used for manicuring. [Fr, ult from Ar *nāranj*; the loss of the *n* due to confusion with the indef art and the vowel changes to confusion with L *aurum*, Fr *or*, gold.]

Orangeman [or´inj-man] *n* a member of a society instituted in Ireland in 1795 to uphold Protestantism, or the cause of William of Orange.

orangutan [ō-rang´ōō-tan´] *n* a largely herbivorous anthropoid ape (*Pongo pygmaeus*), found only in the forests of Sumatra and Borneo, reddish-brown, arboreal in habit.—Also **orang´**. [Malay, 'man of the woods'—said not to be applied by the Malay to the ape.]

oration [ō-rā´sh(ȯ)n] *n* a formal speech, esp one given at a ceremony.—*vi* **orate´**, to make such a speech; to speak in a pompous or bombastic way. [L *ōrātiō, -ōnis—ōrāre*, to pray.]

orator [or´a-tȯr] *n* a public speaker; a man of eloquence.—*n* **or´atory**, the art of speaking well, or so as to please and persuade, esp publicly; the exercise of eloquence; a place of prayer, esp a private or institutional chapel.—*adj* **orator´ical**, pertaining to an orator or to oratory.—*adv* **orator´ically**. [L *ōrātor, -ōris—ōrāre*, to pray.]

oratorio [or-a-tō´ri-ō] *n* a story, usually Biblical, set to music, without scenery, costumes, or acting;—*pl* **orato´rios**. [It,—L *ōrātōrium*, an oratory, because they developed out of the singing in church oratories.]

orb [örb] *n* a sphere; a celestial body; the globe; a wheel; the eye; a sphere surmounted by a cross symbolizing regal power and justice.—*vt* to form into a disk or circle.—*adj* **orbic´ular**, spherical; circular.—*adv* **orbic´ularly**.—*adj* **orbic´ulate**, circular or nearly circular in outline. [L *orbis*, circle.]

orbit [ör´bit] *n* the path in which a heavenly body moves round another, or an electron round the nucleus of an atom, or the like; a path in space round a heavenly body; regular course; sphere of action; the hollow in which the eyeball rests.—*vt* to put into orbit; to circle round; to go round in orbit.—*adj* **or´bital**. [L *orbita*, wheel—*orbis*, a ring.]

orchard [ör´chȧrd] *n* a planting of fruit trees or nut trees; the trees of such a planting. [OE *ort-geard*, prob L *hortus*, garden, and OE *geard*. See **yard**.]

orchestra [ör´kės-tra] *n* in the Greek theater, the place where the chorus danced; now the part of a theater in which the musicians are placed (in full, **orchestra pit**); the seats on the main floor of a theater; a company of musicians playing together under a conductor; their instruments.—*adj* **orches´tral**, of or for an orchestra.—*vt* **or´chestrāte**, to arrange (music) for an orchestra; to organize so as to achieve the best effect. [L,—Gr *orchēstrā—orcheesthai*, to dance.]

orchid [ör´kid] *n* any of a family (Orchidaceae) of plants with rich, showy, often fragrant flowers.—*adj* **orchidā´ceous**, pertaining to the orchids.—*n* **or´chis**, an orchid, esp one (*Orchis spectabilis*) of N America with a spurred lip and fleshy roots. [Gr *orchis*, a testicle.]

ordain [ör-dān´] *vt* (*obs*) to arrange in order; (*obs*) to appoint (to a duty); to invest with the office of minister, priest, or rabbi; to decree, destine; to order.—*vi* to enact, command. [OFr *ordener*—L *ordināre—ordō, -inis*, order.]

ordeal [ör-dēl´] *n* an ancient form of referring a disputed question to the judgment of God, by lot, fire, water, etc.; any severe trial or examination. [OE *ordēl, ordāl*—pfx *or-*, out, *dǣl*, share; cf Du *oordeel*, Ger *urteil*.]

order [ör´dėr] *n* arrangement; method; sequence; suitable, normal, or fixed arrangement; regular government; an undisturbed condition; tidiness; a class of society; a body of persons of the same profession, etc.; a religious fraternity; a dignity conferred by a sovereign, etc.; an instruction or authorization; a rule, regulation; a command; state or condition, esp with regard to functioning; a request to supply something; the goods supplied; (*archit*) a style of building; (*biol*) a group above a family and below a class; (*pl*) the several degrees or grades of the Christian ministry.—*vti* to put or keep (things) in order; to arrange; to command; to request (something) to be supplied.—*adjs* **or´dered**, marked by regularity and discipline; having elements arranged or identified according to a rule; having elements labeled by ordinal numbers; **or´derly**, in good order; methodical; well regulated, quiet, peaceable, obedient.—*n* a soldier who carries official messages for his superior officer; a hospital attendant who does routine or heavy work.—*n* **or´derliness**.—**order of the day**, business set down for the day for an assembly; the characteristic or dominant feature or activity; **in order**, appropriate, desirable; **out of order**, not in accordance with regular procedure; **in order to**, for the end that; **in short order**, quickly; **on the order of**, similar to; **to order**, in accordance with the buyer's specifications. [Fr *ordre*—L *ordō, -inis*.]

ordinal [ör´din-ȧl] *adj* indicating order of sequence.—*n* an ordinal numeral (as first, second, etc.); a book of forms for ordination. [LL *ordinālis*—L *ordō, -inis*, order.]

ordinance [ör´din-ȧns] *n* that which is ordained by an authority; a law; an established rite.—*n* **ordinā´tion**, the act of ordaining; admission to the clergy. [L *ordināre, -ātum—ordō, -inis*, order.]

ordinary [ör´di-nȧ-ri] *adj* usual; of common rank; plain, undistinguished.—*n* something settled or customary; a judge of probate in some states of the US; (*her*) one of a class of armorial charges, figures of simple and geometrical form.—*adv* **or´dinarily**. [L *ordinārius—ordō, -inis*, order.]

ordinate [örd´nȧt or i-nȧt or i-nāt] *n* half of a chord of a conic section bisected by the diameter; for rectilineal axes, the distance of a point from the axis of abscissae (*x*-axis) measured in a direction parallel to the axis of ordinates (*y*-axis).—*adv* **ord´inately**. [L *ordinātus*, pa p of *ordināre—ordō, -inis*, order.]

ordnance [örd´nȧns] *n* military supplies; artillery. [Variant of **ordinance**.]

ordure [ör´dūr] *n* excrement; dung. [Fr,—OFr *ord*, foul—L *horridus*, rough.]

ore [ōr, ör] *n* a mineral aggregate from which one or more valuable constituents may be obtained; a source from which valuable matter is extracted. [OE *ār*, brass, influenced by *ora*, unwrought metal; cf L *aes, aeris*, bronze.]

oregano [ö-reg-ä´nō, ȯ-reg´ȧ-nō] *n* an aromatic culinary herb (*Origanum vulgare*) of the mint family; any of several plants (genera *Lippia* and *Coleus*) other than oregano of the vervain or mint families. [Amer Sp *orégano*, wild marjoram.]

organ [ör´gȧn] *n* an instrument, or means by which anything is done; a part of a plant or animal body fitted for carrying out a natural or vital function; a means of communicating information or opinions, as a periodical; a subordinate group or organization that performs specialized functions; a musical instrument consisting of pipes made to sound by compressed air or electronically, and played upon by means of keys; a musical instrument in some way resembling the pipe organ, as the barrel organ, etc.—*ns* **or´ganist**, one who plays an organ; **or´gan-pipe cactus**, saguro.—*adjs* **organ´ic**, pertaining to, derived from, of the nature of, a bodily organ or a living organism; systematically arranged (eg *an organic whole*); structural, inherent in the constitution; affecting the structure of an organ; (*chem*) containing or combined with carbon; concerned with carbon compounds.—*adv* **organ´ically**.—*vt* **or´ganize**, to form into an organized whole; to establish; to institute; to persuade to join a cause, group, etc.; to arrange for.—*adjs* **or´ganized**, having a formal organization to coordinate and carry out activities; affiliated by membership in an organization (as a union); **organiz´able**, that may be organized.—*ns* **organizā´tion**, the act of organizing; the state of being organized; a system or society; **or´ganīzer; or´ganism**, any living thing.—**organic chemistry**, the chemistry of carbon compounds. [L *organum*—Gr *organon—ergon*, work.]

organdy, organdie [ör´gan-di] *n* a fine transparent muslin with a stiff finish. [Fr *organdi*.]

orgasm [ör´gazm] *n* immoderate excitement or action, esp in the culmination of sexual excitement; an instance of it. [Gr *orgasmos*, swelling.]

orgy [ör´ji] *n* a riotous or drunken revel, esp with sexual activity; an excessive indulgence in any activity;—*pl* **or´gies**. [Fr *orgies*—L—Gr *orgia* (pl).]

oriel [ō´ri-ėl] *n* a recess with a window built out from a wall.—Also *adj*. [OFr *oriol*, a porch, recess.]

Orient [ō´ri-ėnt] *n* the East, or Asia, esp the Far East.—*adj* (*arch*) of the east; lustrous, sparkling.—*vti* to adjust (oneself) to a particular situation.—*vt* to arrange in a direction, esp in relation to the points of the compass; to cause the axes of molecules to assume the same direction.—*n* **Orien´tal**, a member of a people native to the Orient.—*adj* of the Orient, its people, languages.—*ns* **orien´talism**, an expression, custom, etc. characteristic of oriental peoples; scholarship or learning in oriental subjects; **orien´talist**.—*adv* **orien´tally**.—*vt* **o´rientāte**, to orient; to face or turn to the east.—*n* **orientā´tion**, arrangement; alignment; general usu lasting direction of thought or interest; change of position by living organisms in response to external stimuli.—*n* **orienteer´ing**, the sport of making one's way quickly across difficult country with the help of map and compass. [L *oriēns, -entis*, pr p of *orīrī*, to rise.]

orifice [or´i-fis] *n* a mouthlike opening. [Fr,—L *ōrificium—ōs, ōris*, mouth, *facěre*, to make.]

oriflamme [or´i-flam] *n* a banner, symbol, or ideal inspiring devotion or courage. [Fr,—Low L *auriflamma*—L *aurum*, gold, *flamma*, a flame.]

origami [or-i-gäm´ē] *n* the Japanese art of folding paper so as to make animal forms, etc.

origin [or´i-jin] *n* the rising or first existence of anything; that from which anything first proceeds, source; parentage; (*math*) the intersection of coordinate axes.—*adj* **orig´inal**, pertaining to the origin or beginning; existing from or at the beginning; innate; not derived or imitated; novel; having the power to originate; being that from which copies are made.—*n* a primary type that has given rise to varieties; an original work, as of art or literature.—*n* **original´ity**.—*adv* **orig´inally**.—*vt* **orig´ināte**, to give origin or beginning to; to bring into existence.—*vi* to have origin, to begin.—*n* **originā´tion**.—*adj* **orig´inātive**, having power to originate or bring into existence.—*n* **orig´inātor**. [Fr *origine*—L *orīgō, inis—orīrī*, to rise.]

oriole [ōri´ōl] *n* any of a family (Oriolidae) of Old World birds related to the crows; any of a family (Icteridae) of New World passerine birds in which the males are usu. bright yellow or orange and black and the females chiefly greenish or yellowish. [OFr *oriol*—L *aureolus*, dim of *aureus*, golden—*aurum*, gold.]

Orion [ō-rī´on] *n* (*astron*) one of the constellations, containing seven very bright stars, three of which form Orion's belt. [Gr *Ōrion*, celebrated giant and hunter.]

orison [or´i-zȯn] *n* a prayer. [OFr *orison*—L *ōrātiō, -ōnis—ōrāre*, to pray.]
orlop deck [ör´lop dek] *n* the lowest deck in a ship having four or more decks. [Du *overloop*, a covering to the hold—*overloopen*, to run over.]
ormolu [ör´mo-lōō] *n* an imitation gold made of a copper and tin alloy, used chiefly for decorative purposes (as in mounts for furniture). [Fr *or* (L *aurum*), gold, *moulu*, pt p of *moudre* (L *molĕre*), to grind.]
ornament [ör´na-mėnt] *n* anything that adds, or is meant to add, grace or beauty; one whose character or talent adds luster to his surroundings.—*vt* [or-na-ment´] to adorn, to furnish with ornaments.—*adjs* **ornament´al**, serving to adorn or beautify; like an ornament, decorative, beautiful.—*adv* **ornament´ally**.—*n* **ornamentā´tion**, act or art of ornamenting; (*archit*) ornamental work. [Fr *ornement*—L *ornāmentum—ornāre*, to adorn.]
ornate [ör-nāt´] *adj* decorated; much or elaborately ornamented.—*adv* **ornate´ly**.—*n* **ornate´ness**. [L *ornātus*, pt p of *ornāre*, to adorn.]
ornithology [ör-ni-thöl´ȯ-jē] *n* the branch of zoology dealing with birds; a treatise on ornithology.—*adj* **ornitholog´ical**, pertaining to ornithology.—*n* **ornithol´ogist**, one versed in ornithology. [Gr *ornis*, gen *ornīthos*, a bird.]
orography [or-og´ra-fi] *n* a branch of physical geography dealing with mountains.—*adjs* **orographic, -al**. [Gr *oros*, a mountain, *graphein*, to write.]
orphan [ör´fȧn] *n* a child whose parents are dead.—*adj* being an orphan; of or for orphans.—*vt* to cause to become an orphan.—*vt* **or´phanage**, an institution that is a home for orphans. [Gr *orphanos*, akin to L *orbus*, bereaved.]
Orphean [ör-fē´an] *adj* pertaining to Orpheus, who tamed wild beasts by the music of his lyre.
orpiment [ör´pi-mėnt] *n* arsenic trisulfide, a yellow mineral used as a pigment. [OFr,—L *auripigmentum—aurum*, gold, *pigmentum*, paint.]
orrery [or´ėr-i] *n* a clockwork model to illustrate the relative positions, motions, etc., of the heavenly bodies. [From Charles Boyle, Earl of *Orrery* (1676–1731), for whom one was made.]
orris [or´is] *n* a species of iris in the south of Europe, the dried root of which has the smell of violets, used in perfumery. [Perh **iris**.]
orthodontics, orthodontia [ör-thō-don´tiks, -don´-shi-ȧ] *ns* the branch of dentistry dealing with rectification of abnormalities of the teeth (as by using braces). [Gr *orthos*, right, *odous, ondontos*, teeth.]
orthodox [ör´thō-doks] *adj* sound in doctrine; holding the received or established opinions, esp in religion; according to such opinions.—*n* **or´thodoxy**, soundness of opinion or doctrine; holding of the commonly accepted opinions, esp in religion; **Orthodoxy**, Eastern Orthodox Christianity; Orthodox Judaism.—**Orthodox (Eastern) Church**, the dominant Christian Church in eastern Europe, western Asia, and north Africa; **Orthodox Judaism**, Judaism that adheres to the Torah and Talmud as interpreted in rabbinic law and applies their principles to modern living. [Through Fr and Late L from Gr *orthodoxos—orthos*, right, *doxa*, opinion—*dokeein*, to think.]
orthogonal [ör-thog´on-ȧl] *adj* intersecting or lying at right angles. [Gr *orthos*, right, *gōniā*, angle.]
orthographer [ör-thog´ra-fėr] *n* one skilled in orthography.—*n* **orthog´raphy** (*gram*), the art or practice of spelling words correctly.—*adjs* **orthograph´ic, -al**, of orthography; of orthographic projection; spelled correctly.—*adv* **orthograph´ically.—orthographic projection**, a projection of a single view of an object (as from the front) on a drawing surface that is perpendicular both to the view and the lines of projection; the representation of related views of an object as by orthographic projection. [Gr *orthographiā*, spelling—*orthos*, right, *graphein*, to write.]
orthopedic [ör-thȯ-pēd´ik] *adj* of, relating to, or used in orthopedics; marked by deformities or crippling.—*ns* **orthopedic surgery**, the branch of medicine dealing with disorders of the bones; **orthoped´ics**, orthopedic surgery; **orthope´dist**, one skilled in orthopedic surgery. [Gr *orthos*, straight, *pais*, gen *paidos*, a child.]
orthopteran [ör-thop´tėr-an] *n* any of an order (Orthoptera) of insects, including crickets, locusts, and grasshoppers having biting mouthparts, two pairs of wings or none and incomplete metamorphosis.—Also *adj*.—*ns* **orthop´terist; orthopteroid**.—Also *adj*. [Gr *orthos*, straight, *pteron*, wing.]
ortolan [ör´tō-lȧn] *n* a kind of bunting (*Emberiza hortulana*) common in Europe, and considered a great table delicacy. [Fr,—It *ortolano*—L *hortulānus*, belonging to gardens—*hortulus*, dim of *hortus*, a garden.]
Osage [ō-sāj] *n* member of an Amerindian people of Missouri;—*pl* **-s, Osage**; the Siouan language of this people.
Oscar [os´kȧr] *n* any of several small gold statuettes awarded annually by the US motion-picture industry for outstanding achievements; a word used in communications for the letter *o*.
oscillate [os´il-lāt] *vi* to swing to and fro like a pendulum; to vary between certain limits (eg between extremes of opinion, action, etc.); to vary above and below a mean value.—*ns* **oscillā´tion; os´cillator**, a device for producing alternating current.—*adj* **oscilla´tional**.—*ns* **oscill´ograph, oscill´oscope**, instruments for recording in visible form oscillatory motion, as electric oscillations. [L *ōscillāre, -ātum*, to swing.]
osculate [os´kū-lāt] *vt* to kiss (someone).—*n* **osculā´tion**.—*adj* **os´culatory**, of or pertaining to kissing or osculation. [L *osculārī, -ātus—osculum*, a little mouth, a kiss, dim of *os*, mouth.]
Osee [ō´zē or ō-zē´ē] *n* (*Bible*) Hosea in the Douay Version of the Old Testament.
osier [ōzh´(y)ėr, ōz´i-ėr, ōz´yėr] *n* any willow (esp *Salix viminalis*) whose twigs are used in making baskets; a willow rod used in basketry; any of several American dogwoods. [Fr *osier*, of unknown origin.]
osmium [os´mi-ùm] *n* a metallic element (symbol Os; at wt 192.2; at no 76). [Gr *osmē*, smell.]
osmosis [oz-mō´sis] *n* the passage of fluid through a semipermeable membrane from a low-to-high concentrate of solutions; a process of absorption or diffusion suggesting the flow of osmotic action.—*adj* **osmot´ic**. [Gr *ōsmos*, impulse—*ōtheein*, to push.]
osprey [os´prā] *n* a hawk (*Pandion haliaetus*) that feeds on fish; an egret or other plume used in millinery, not from the osprey. [Supposed to be from L *ossifraga* misapplied. See **ossifrage**.]
osseous [os´ė-us] *adj* bony; composed of, or resembling, bone.—*n* **oss´icle**, a small bone or bony structure.—*vt* **oss´ify**, to make into bone; to make rigidly conventional.—*vi* to become bone; to become callous or conventional;—*pt p* **oss´ified**.—*n* **ossificā´tion**, the process or state of being changed into a bony substance; state of being molded into a rigid, conventional condition. [L *os, ossis*, bone.]
Ossianic [os-i-an´ik] *adj* pertaining to *Ossian*, a legendary Gaelic poet whose poems James Macpherson (1736–1796) professed to translate.
ossifrage [os´i-frāj] *n* a large Eurasian vulture (*Gypaetus barbatus aureas*) of mountain regions. [L *ossifragus*, breaking bones—*os*, bone, *frag-*, root of *frangĕre*, to break.]
ossuary [os´ū-ȧr-i] *n* a charnel house or urn, etc., in which the bones of the dead are deposited. [L *ossuārium*, a charnel-house—*os*, a bone.]
ostensible [os-tens´i-bl] *adj* that may be shown; pretended, professed, apparent (eg of a reason).—*adv* **ostens´ibly**.—*adj* **ostens´ive**, showing, exhibiting.—*n* **ostentā´tion**, act of showing; a pretentious display; boasting.—*adj* **ostentā´tious**, given to show; fond of display; intended for display.—*adv* **ostentā´tiously**.—*n* **ostentā´tiousness**. [L *ostendĕre* (for *obstendĕre*), *ostensum*, to show.]
osteo- [os´tė-ō-], **oste-**, [os´tė-], in composition, bone.—*n* **osteol´ogy**, a branch of anatomy dealing with bones; the bony structure of an organism.—*adj* **osteolog´ical**, pertaining to osteology.—*adv* **osteolog´ically**.—*ns* **osteomyelitis** [-mī-ė-lī´tis], infectious inflammation of bone; **osteop´athy**, a therapeutic system which treats disease by manipulation and massage, often as an adjunct to medical and surgical measures; **os´teopath**, a practitioner of osteopathy; **osteoporosis** [os-te-ō-pȯ-rōs´is] a condition marked by decrease in bone mass and enlargement of bone spaces producing porosity and fragility. [Gr *osteon*, bone.]
-ostomy *see* **-stomy**.
ostracize [os´tra-sīz] *vt* in ancient Greece, to banish by the votes of the citizens without trial or special accusation; to exclude from society.—*n* **os´tracism** [-sizm], banishment by ostracizing; expulsion from society. [Gr *ostrakon*, an earthenware tablet.]
ostrich [os´trich] *n* a genus (*Struthio*) of the largest living birds, found in Africa, remarkable for their speed in running, and prized for their feathers. [OFr *ostruche*—L *avis*, a bird, LL *struthiō*—Gr *strouthiōn*, an ostrich, *strouthos*, a bird.]
other [uTH´ėr] *adj* second; alternate; different from or not the same as; remaining.—*pron* the other one; some other one.—*advs* **oth´erwhere**, elsewhere; **oth´erwise**, in another way or manner; by other causes; in other respects; under other conditions.—**every other**, each alternate; **the other day**, quite recently. [OE *ōther*; cf Ger *ander*, L *alter*.]
-otic[1] [ot´ik] in composition, characterized by a specified process or condition (*symbiotic*); having a diseased condition of a specified kind (*epizootic*).
-otic[2] [ō´tik] in composition, the ear.—*n* **otī´tis**, inflammation of the internal ear. [Gr *ous*, gen *ōtos*, ear.]
otiose [ō´shi-ōs] *adj* unoccupied, idle; functionless, superfluous. [L *ōtiōsus—ōtium*, leisure.]
ottava rima [ot-tä´va rēma] a stanza of eight lines of iambic pentameter rhyming *a b a b a b c c*. [It.]
Ottawa [ot´ȧ-wȧ] *n* member of a Siouan-speaking Amerindian people originally of Michigan and southern Ontario and now of Oklahoma.
otter [ot´ėr] *n* any of several aquatic fish-eating carnivores (genus *Lutra*) of the weasel family; the fur or the pelt of an otter. [OE *otor*; akin to **water**.]
otto [ot´ō], **ottar** [ot´ȧr]. Corrs of **attar**.
Ottoman [ot´ō-mȧn] *adj* pertaining to the Turks or Turkey; **ottoman**, an upholstered chair or couch usu without a back; an overstuffed footstool without a back. [Fr.]
oubliette [ōō-blē-et´] *n* a dungeon with an opening at the top. [Fr,—*oublier*, to forget—L *oblīviscī*.]
ouch[1] [owch] *n* (*arch*) a brooch; the setting for a precious stone; a buckle or brooch set with precious stones. [OFr *nouche*.]
ouch[2] [owch] *interj* expressing sudden pain. [Ger *autsch*.]
ought[1] [öt] *n* a variant of **aught**.
ought[2] [öt] *pt* of **owe**; now an auxiliary *v* (with either present or past sense) to be under obligation; to be proper or necessary.
Ouija [wē´ja] *n* (*trade name*) a board with an alphabet, used with a planchette. [Fr *oui*, Ger *ja*, yes.]
ounce[1] [owns] *n* a unit of weight, 1/16 pound avoirdupois or 1/12 pound troy; a unit of capacity 1/16 pint, a fluid ounce. [OFr *unce*—L *uncia*, the twelfth part; cf **inch**.]

ounce[2] [owns] *n* a snow leopard. [Fr *once*.]

our [owr] *possessive adj* (or *possessive pron*) pertaining or belonging to us.—**ours**, the possessive (*gen*) case of **we** (eg *the decision is ours*).—Also *possessive adj* (used without noun—eg *that is their share, this is ours*).—*pl* **ourselves** [-selvz´], we, not others (emphatic form of **we**); emphatic or reflexive form of **us**. [OE *ūre*, gen of *wē*, we.]

ousel *See* **ouzel**.

oust [owst] *vt* to eject, expel, dispossess.—*n* **oust´er** (*law*), ejection; a wrongful dispossession. [OFr *oster*, Anglo-Fr *ouster*, to remove.]

out [owt] *adv* not within; forth; abroad; in or into the open air; in, towards, or at the exterior; to the full stretch or extent; beyond bounds; in a state of exclusion; ruled out, not to be considered; no longer in concealment; no longer in office, in the game, in use, fashion, etc.; on strike; in error; loudly and clearly; (*slang*) into unconsciousness.—*adj* external; outlying; outward; exceeding the usual; in any condition expressed by the adverb *out*; (*inf*) having suffered a financial loss; (*baseball*) having failed to get on base.—*prep* out of; along the way of.—*n* something that is out; (*slang*) a way out; excuse.—*vi* to become known.—*interj*, away! begone!—*adj* **out-of-the-way´**, uncommon.—*n* **outpatient** [owt´pā-shėnt] a hospital patient who is not an inmate.—*adj* **out-and-out**, thorough, complete—**out of one's mind**, mad. [OE *ūte*, *ūt*, Ger *aus*, Sans *ud*.]

out- [owt-] *pfx* (1) meaning in, or toward, a position external to a position understood (eg *outline, outbuilding, outlying, outdoor, outgoing, outlook*); also (*fig*) with suggestion of openness, frankness, completeness (eg *outcry, outspoken, outworn*); (2) prefixed to verbs to express the fact that, in some action, the subject goes beyond a standard indicated (eg to *outbid, outshine*), and to nouns and adjectives to express the fact of exceeding a standard (eg *outsize*). [See above.]

outbalance [owt-bal´ȧns] *vt* to outweigh. [**out** (indicating fact of exceeding), **balance**.]

outbid [owt-bid´] *vt* to offer a higher price than. [**out** (indicating fact of exceeding), **bid**.]

outboard [owt´bōrd, -börd] *adj* outside of a ship or boat; having engines outside the boat; toward, or nearer, the ship's side. [**out, board**, ship's side.]

outbreak [owt´brāk] *n* a breaking out (eg of anger, strife, contagious or infectious disease); a disturbance. [**out, break**.]

outbuilding [owt´bild-ing] *n* a building separate from, but used in connection with, a main house. [**out, build**.]

outburst [owt´bûrst] *n* a bursting out (eg a vehement expression of feelings); an explosion. [**out, burst**.]

outcast [owt´käst] *n* one who is banished from society or home. [**out, cast**.]

outclass [owt´kläs´] *vt* to surpass so far as to seem in a different class. [**out** (indicating fact of exceeding or excelling), **class**.]

outcome [owt´kum] *n* the consequence, result. [**out, come**.]

outcrop [owt´krop] *n* the exposure of a stratum at the surface; the part of a stratum so exposed.—Also *vi* [**out, crop**.]

outcry [owt´krī] *n* a loud cry of protest, distress, etc.; noise; an auction. [**out, cry**.]

outdistance [owt-dis´tȧns] *vt* to leave far behind in any competition. [**out** (indicating fact of exceeding), **distance**.]

outdo [owt´dōō´] *vt* to surpass, excel. [**out** (indicating fact of exceeding), **do**, vb.]

outdoor [owt´dōr, -dör] *adj* outside the door or the house; in the open air.—*adv* **out´doors**, out of the house; in the open air. [**out, door**.]

outer [owt´ėr] *adj* further out or away.—*adjs* **out´ermost, out´most**, farthest out; most distant; **outer space**, space beyond the earth's atmosphere or the solar system. [OE *ūterra*, *ūtemest*, comp, superl *adjs*—*adv ūt(e)*, outside.]

outface [owt´fās´] *vt* to stare down; to bear down by bravery or impudence. [**out** (indicating the fact of exceeding), **face**.]

outfield [owt´fēld] *n* (*baseball*) the playing area beyond the infield and between the foul lines.—*n* **outfield´ers**, the players who occupy it. [**out, field**.]

outfit [owt´fit] *n* the equipment used in an activity; clothes worn together, an ensemble; a group of people associated in an activity.—*vt* to furnish with an outfit.—*ns* **out´fitter**, one who furnishes outfits. [**out, fit** (1).]

outflank [owt-flangk´] *vt* to extend beyond or pass round the flank of; to circumvent. [**out** (indicating fact of exceeding), **flank**.]

outflow [owt´flō] *n* a flowing out; something that flows out. [**out, flow**.]

outgeneral [owt-jen´ėr-ȧl] *vt* to surpass in generalship. [**out** (indicating fact of exceeding or excelling), **general**.]

outgoing [owt´gō-ing] *n* act or state of going out; extreme limit; expenditure.—*adj* departing—opp to *incoming*, as a tenant. [**out, go**.]

outgrow [owt-grō´] *vt* to surpass in growth; to grow out of.—*n* **out´growth**, that which grows out from anything; a consequence. [**out, grow**.]

outhouse [owt´hows] *n* a boothlike shelter outdoors, used as a toilet. [**out, house**.]

outing [owt´ing] *n* a pleasure trip; an outdoor excursion. [**out**.]

outlandish [owt-land´ish] *adj* foreign; strange; fantastic. [**out, land**.]

outlast [owt-läst´] *vt* to endure longer than. [**out** (indicating fact of exceeding), **last** (2).]

outlaw [owt´lö] *n* originally one deprived of the protection of the law; a habitual or notorious criminal.—*vt* originally, to place beyond the law, to deprive of the benefit of the law; to declare illegal.—*n* **out´lawry**, state of being an outlaw. [OE *ūtlaga*—ON *ūtlāgi*—*ūt*, out, *lög*, law.]

outlay [owt´lā] *n* a spending (of money); expenditure. [**out, lay** (2).]

outlet [owt´let] *n* the place or means by which anything is let out; a means of expression; a market for goods. [**out, let** (1).]

outline [owt´līn] *n* the line by which any figure is bounded; the line bounding a solid object seen as a plane figure; a sketch without shading; a general indication (eg of a plan); a rough draught; a systematic summary.—*vt* to draw the exterior line of; to delineate or sketch; to summarize, indicate, the main features of. [**out, line** (2).]

outlive [owt-liv´] *vt* to live longer than; to survive; to live through. [**out** (indicating fact of exceeding), **live** (vb).]

outlook [owt´lŏŏk] *n* a place for looking out from; a view, prospect; a prospect for the future; mental point of view. [**out, look**.]

outlying [owt´lī-ing] *adj* lying out or beyond; remote; on the exterior or frontier. [**out, lie** (2).]

outmaneuver [out-ma-nōō´vėr] *vt* to outwit by maneuvering. [**out** (indicating fact of exceeding), **maneuver**.]

outmoded [owt-mōd´id] *adj* no longer in fashion; no longer accepted. [**out, mode**.]

outmost [owt´mōst] *See* **outermost**.

outnumber [owt-num´bėr] *vt* to exceed in number. [**out** (indicating fact of exceeding), **number**.]

outpace [owt-pās´] *vt* to surpass in speed; to outdo. [**out** (indicating fact of exceeding), **pace**.]

outpost [owt´pōst] *n* (*mil*) a small group stationed at a distance from the main force, the station so occupied, or a foreign base; a frontier settlement. [**out, post** (2).]

outpour [owt-pōr´] *vt* to pour out.—*ns* **out´pour; out´pouring**, a pouring out; an outflow. [**out, pour**.]

output [owt´pŏŏt] *n* the quantity produced or turned out, esp over a given period; information delivered by a computer; (*electricity*) the useful voltage, current, or power delivered. [**out, put**.]

outrage [owt´rāj´] *n* an extremely vicious or violent act; a grave insult or offense; great anger, etc. aroused by this.—*vt* to commit an outrage upon or against; to cause outrage in.—*adj* **outrā´geous**.—*adv* **outrā´geously**.—*n* **outrā´geousness**. [OFr *oultrage*—L *ultrā*, beyond.]

outrance [ōō-trãs´] *n* the utmost extremity; the bitter end. [Fr.]

outré [ōōt´rā] *adj* eccentric, bizarre. [Fr pt p of *outrer*—*outre*—L *ultrā*, beyond.]

outride [owt´rīd´] *vt* to ride beyond; to ride better or faster than.—*n* **out´rider**, a rider on horseback who accompanies a stagecoach, etc.; a cowboy riding the range to keep cattle from straying; a forerunner. [**out, ride**.]

outrigger [owt´rig-ėr] *n* a projecting spar for extending sails or any part of the rigging; a timber rigged out from the side of a canoe to prevent topping; a canoe of this type; a projecting frame to support the elevator or tail of an aircraft or the rotor of a helicopter. [**out, rig** (1).]

outright [owt´rīt] *adj* out-and-out, downright, direct.—*adv* **outright´**, unreservedly; at once and completely. [**out, right** (adv).]

outrival [owt-rī´vȧl] *vt* to surpass, excel. [**out** (indicating fact of exceeding or excelling), **rival**.]

outrun [owt-run´] *vt* to go beyond in running; to exceed; to elude. [**out** (indicating fact of exceeding), **run**.]

outset [owt´set] *n* a setting out; beginning. [**out, set**.]

outshine [owt-shīn´] *vt* to surpass in brilliance; to shine longer and brighter than. [**out** (indicating fact of exceeding or excelling), **shine**.]

outside [owt´sīd] *n* the outer side; the surface, exterior; any area not inside.—*adj* on the outside; exterior; extreme; slight.—*adv* on or to the outside; not within.—*prep* outside of; beyond.—*n* **out´sider**, one not included in a particular group or set.—**outside of**, outside; (*inf*) other than. [**out, side**.]

outsize [owt´sīz] *n* an odd size, esp an unusually large size. [**out, size** (1).]

outskirt [owt´skûrt] *n* (*pl*) districts remote from the center, as of a city. [**out, skirt**.]

outsmart [owt-smärt] *vt* (*inf*) to show more cleverness or cunning than; to outwit.—**outsmart oneself**, to have one's cunning or cleverness result in one's own disadvantage. [**out** (indicating the fact of exceeding), **smart** (adj).]

outspoken [owt-spō´ken] *adj* frank or bold of speech; uttered with boldness. [**out**, + pt p of **speak**.]

outspread [owt-spred´] *vt* to spread out; to extend.—Also *adj*. [**out, spread**.]

outstanding [owt-stand´ing] *adj* projecting; distinguished, prominent; unpaid; still to be attended to or done; (of stocks and bonds) issued and sold. [**out, stand**.]

outstretch [owt-strech´] *vt* to spread out, extend; to stretch beyond. [**out, stretch**.]

outstrip [owt-strip´] *vt* to outrun; to leave behind. [**out** (indicating the fact of exceeding), and late ME *strip*, to move swiftly.]

outvie [owt-vī´] *vt* to compete with and surpass. [**out** indicating the fact of exceeding), **vie**.]

outvote [owt-vōt´] *vt* to defeat by votes. [**out** (indicating the fact of exceeding), **vote**.]

outward [owt´wȧrd] *adj* toward the outside; external; exterior; clearly apparent.—*adv* toward the exterior.—*adj* **out´ward-bound**, sailing outwards or to a foreign port.—*adv* **out´wardly**, in an outward manner; externally; in appearance.—*adv* **outward, out´wards**, in an outward direction. [**out** + suffx *-ward*.]

outweigh [owt-wā´] *vt* to exceed in weight or importance. [**out** (indicating the fact of exceeding), **weigh**.]

outwit [owt-wit´] *vt* to surpass in wit or ingenuity; to defeat by superior ingenuity;—*pr p* **outwitt´ing**; *pt, pt p* **outwitt´ed**. [**out** (indicating the fact of exceeding or excelling), **wit** (2).]

outwork [owt´würk] *n* a minor defensive position outside the principal wall or line of fortification. [**out, work**.]

outworn [owt-wōrn´, -wörn´] *adj* worn out; out of date; obsolete. [**out**, + pt p of **wear**.]

ouzel, ousel [ōō´zl] *n* the European blackbird (*Turdus merula*); the water ouzel. [OE *ōsle*; cog with Ger *amsel*.]

ova [ō´va] *pl* of **ovum**.—*adj* **o´val**, having the shape of an egg.—*n* anything oval.—*adv* **o´vally**. [Fr *ovale*—L *ōvum*, an egg.]

ovary [ō´vȧr-i] *n* either of two female reproductive glands producing eggs; (*bot*) the enlarged hollow part of the pistil, containing ovules.—*adjs* **ovar´ial, ovā´rian**, pertaining to an ovary. [Low L *ōvāria*—*ōvum*, egg.]

ovate [ō´vāt] *adj* egg shaped. [L *ōvātus*—*ōvum*, egg.]

ovation [ō-vā´sh(ȯ)n] *n* in ancient Rome, a lesser triumph; an outburst of popular applause or public welcome. [L *ŏvātiō, -ōnis*—*ŏvāre*, to exult.]

oven [uv´n] *n* a chamber for baking, heating, or drying. [OE *ofen*; Ger *ofen*.]

over [ō´vėr] *prep* higher than—in place, rank, value, etc.; across; above; upon the whole surface of; concerning; on account of; in study of or occupation with; more than.—*adv* on the top; above; across; from beginning to end, up and down; from one side, person, etc., to another; outward, downward, out of the perpendicular; above in measure; unduly; as surplus, or in an unfinished state (*left over*); again.—*interj* in telecommunications, indicates that the speaker now expects a reply.—*adj* upper or superior; surplus; excessive; finished, at an end.—**over again**, afresh, anew; **over against**, opposite; **over and above**, in addition to; besides; **over and over**, repeatedly.—**all over**, completely; at an end. [OE *ofer*; Ger *über*, L *super*, Gr *hyper*.]

over- [ō-vėr-] *prefix* meaning: (1) above in position (eg *overarch, overlord*), across (eg *overleap, overlook*), across the surface (*overrun, overflow, vt*), beyond (eg *overseas, overtime*), away from the perpendicular (eg *overbalance, overthrow*), across the edge or boundary (*overflow, vti*); (2) completely (eg *overawe*); (3) beyond the normal or desirable limit, excessively (eg *overheat*). Many words with prefix *over* have more than one meaning (see **overcharge, overgrow**). [See above.]

overact [ō´vėr-akt´] *vti* to overdo (any part).—*n* **overact´ing**, acting with exaggeration. [**over** (indicating excess), **act**.]

overactive [ō-vėr-ak´tiv] *adj* acting, working, too rapidly or energetically.—*n* **overactiv´ity**. [**over** (indicating excess), **active**.]

overall [ō´vėr-öl] *n* trousers of strong material, usu. with a bib and shoulder straps.—*adj* including the whole or everything; considering everything.—*adv* as a whole; generally. [**over, all**.]

overanxious [ō-vėr-angk´shu̇s] *adj* too anxious.—*n* **overanxī´ety**.—*adv* **overanx´iously**. [**over** (indicating excess), **anxious**.]

overarching [ō-vėr-ärch´ing] *adj* forming an arch overhead; dominating or embracing all else. [**over, arch** (1).]

overawe [ō-vėr-ö´] *vt* to restrain by fear or authority. [**over, awe**.]

overbalance [ō-vėr-bal´ȧns] *vt* to cause to lose balance; to outweigh.—*n* excess of weight or value. [**over, balance**.]

overbear [ō-vėr-bār´] *vt* to bear down or overpower; to overwhelm.—*adj* **overbear´ing**, haughty and dogmatical; imperious. [**over, bear** (1).]

overboard [ō-vėr-bōrd´] *adv* over the board or side of a ship, etc.; (*inf*) to extremes of enthusiasm; into discord. [**over, board**, ship's side.]

overburden [ō-vėr-bûr´dn] *vt* to burden too much. [**over** (indicating excess), **burden**.]

overcapitalize [ō-vėr-kap´it-ȧl-īz] *vt* to fix the capital to be invested in, or the capital value of, beyond what the profit making prospects warrant. [**over** (indicating excess), **capitalize**.]

overcast [ō-vėr-käst´] *vt* to cloud, cover with gloom; to sew over rough edges of (a piece of cloth).—*adj* clouded over. [**over, cast**.]

overcharge [ō-vėr-chärj´] *vti* to load with too great a charge, as of a battery; to charge (a person) too great a price; to charge too great a price for.—*n* **o´vercharge**, an excessive load or burden; an undue price. [**over** (indicating excess), **charge**.]

overcoat [ōvėr-kōt] *n* an outdoor coat worn over all the other dress for warmth. [**over, coat**.]

overcome [ō-vėr-kum´] *vt* to get the better of, to conquer or subdue.—*adj* helpless, overpowered by exhaustion or emotion.—*vi* to be victorious. [**over, come**.]

overconfident [ō-vėr-kon´fi-dėnt] *adj* too confident.—*n* **overcon´fidence**. [**over** (indicating excess), **confident**.]

overcrowd [ō-vėr-krowd´] *vt* to fill or crowd to excess. [**over** (indicating excess), **crowd**.]

overdo [ō-vėr-dōō´] *vt* to exaggerate, carry to excess; to cook too much.—*adj* **overdone´**. [**over** (indicating excess), **do** (vb).]

overdose [ō´vėr-dōs] *n* an excessive dose.—*vt* **overdose´**, to dose in excess.—*vi* to take an overdose. [**over, dose**.]

overdraw [ō-vėr-drö´] *vt* to draw beyond one's credit; to exaggerate.—*vi* to make an overdraft.—*n* **o´verdraft**, the excess of the amount drawn over the sum against which it is drawn; a current of air passing over a fire in a furnace. [**over** (indicating excess), **draw**.]

overdress [ō-vėr-dres´] *vti* to dress too warmly, too showily, or too formally. [**over** (indicating excess), **dress**.]

overdrive [ō-vėr-drīv´] *n* an automotive gearing device which transmits to the driving shaft a speed greater than engine crankshaft speed. [**over** (indicating excess), **drive**.]

overdue [ō-vėr-dū´] *adj* unpaid, unperformed, etc., though the time for payment, performance, etc., is past. [**over, due**.]

overestimate [ō-vėr-es´tim-āt] *vt* to set too high an estimate on or for.—*n* [-ȧt] an excessive estimate. [**over** (indicating excess), **estimate**.]

overexert [ō-vėr-eg-zûrt´] *vt* to exert too much.—*n* **overexer´tion**. [**over** (indicating excess), **exert**.]

overexpose [ō-vėr-eks-pōz´] *vt* to expose too much, esp to light.—*n* **overexpos´ure**. [**over** (indicating excess), **expose**.]

overflow [ō-vėr-flō´] *vt* to flow over; to flood; (of eg people) to fill and then spread beyond (eg a room).—*vi* to run over; to abound;—*pt, pt p* **overflowed´**.—*n* **o´verflow**, a flowing over; a pipe or receptacle for surplus water, etc.; an inundation; superabundance.—*adj* **overflow´ing**, exuberant, very abundant. [**over, flow**.]

overgrow [ō-vėr-grō´] *vt* to overspread, as with foliage, so as to cover.—*vi* to grow too fast or beyond the proper size.—*adj* **overgrown´**, grown beyond the natural size; covered with overgrowth. [**over, grow**.]

overhand [ō´vėr-hand] *adj, adv* with hand raised above the elbow or the arm raised above the shoulder.—*vt* to sew with short vertical stitches.—*n* an overhand stroke, as in handball. [**over, hand**.]

overhang [ō-vėr-hang´] *vti* to hang over; to project over; to impend over.—*n* the projection of one thing over another; an excess supply of a commodity that cannot readily be sold or converted. [**over, hang**.]

overhaul [ō-vėr-höl´] *vt* to turn over for examination; to examine; to catch up with.—*n* **o´verhaul**, examination; repair. [**over, haul**.]

overhead [ō-vėr-hed´] *adv* above the head; in the sky; on a higher level, with reference to related objects.—*n* the general, continuing costs of a business, as of rent, taxes, etc.—*adv* [o´vėr-hed´] above the head; aloft. [**over, head**.]

overhear [ō-vėr-hēr´] *vt* to hear by stealth or by accident. [**over, hear**.]

overheat [ō-vėr-hēt´] *vt* to heat to excess; to stimulate unduly.—*vi* to become overheated. [**over** (indicating excess), **heat**.]

overjoy [ō-vėr-joi´] *vt* to fill with great joy. [**over** (indicating completeness), **joy**.]

overland [ō´vėr-land´] *adj, adv* by, on, or across land. [**over, land**.]

overlap [ō-vėr-lap´] *vti* to extend over (a thing or each other) so as to coincide in part. [**over, lap** (2).]

overlay [ō-vėr-lā´] *vt* to cover by laying or spreading something over; to cover, as with a decorative layer.—*pt, pt p* **overlaid´**. [**over, lay** (2).]

overleaf [ō-vėr-lēf´] *adv* on the other side of the page. [**over, leaf**.]

overleap [ō-vėr-lēp´] *vt* to leap over; to defeat oneself by going too far. [**over, leap**.]

overlie [ō-vėr-lī´] *vt* to lie above or upon; to smother by lying upon;—*pr p* overly´ing; *pt* **overlay´**; *pt p* **overlain**. [**over, lie** (2).]

overlook [ō-vėr-lŏŏk´] *vt* to look over; to see from a higher position; to view carefully; to ignore, neglect; to fail to notice; to pass by without punishment; to excuse. [**over, look**.]

overlord [ō´vėr-lörd] *n* a lord ranking above other lords; an absolute or supreme ruler. [**over, lord**.]

overman[1] [ō´vėr-man] *n* a foreman; a superman. [**over, man** (n).]

overman[2] [ō-vėr-man´] *vt* to have or get too many men for the needs of. [**over** (indicating excess), **man** (vb).]

overmantel [ō´vėr-man-tl] *n* an ornamental structure (as a painting) above a mantelpiece. [**over, mantel**.]

overmuch [ō-vėr-much´] *adj, adv* too much. [**over** (indicating excess), **much**.]

overnight [ō-vėr-nīt´] *adv* in the course of the night; suddenly. [**over, night**.]

overpass [ō´vėr-päs] *n* a road crossing another highway, pedestrian path, or railroad crossing at a higher level; the upper level of such a crossing. [**over, pass**.]

overplus [ō´vėr-plus] *n* that which is more than enough; surplus. [**over, plus**.]

overpower [ō-vėr-pow´ėr] *vt* to overcome by force, to subdue; to overwhelm; to provide with more power than is needed. [**over, power**.]

overprint [ō´vėr-print] *vt* to print on an already printed surface (eg *to overprint a postage stamp*).—*n* overprinted surface; a word, device, etc., printed across eg a stamp. [**over, print**.]

overproof [ō´vėr-prōōf] *adj* containing more alcohol than proof spirit. [**over, proof**.]

overrate [ō-vėr-rāt´] *vt* to rate or value too highly. [**over** (indicating excess), **rate** (1).]

overreach [ō-vėr-rēch´] *vt* to reach or extend beyond; to outwit or get the better of; (*refl*) to defeat by attempting too much or by being oversubtle. [**over, reach**.]

override [ō-vėr-rīd´] *vt* to ride over; to set aside; prevail over. [**over, ride**.]

overrule [ō-vėr-rōōl´] *vt* to prevail over; to set aside (eg a decision) by greater power; to reject or declare invalid. [**over, rule**.]

overrun [ō-ver-run´] *vt* to swarm over as vermin; to grow over; to spread over and take possession of. [**over, run**.]
oversea [ō´vėr-sē] *adj, adv* overseas.—*adv* **o´verseas´**, over or beyond the sea.—*adj* foreign; over or across the sea. [**over, sea**.]
oversee [ō-vėr-sē´] *vt* to supervise; to superintend.—*n* **o´versēer**. [**over, see** (2).]
overset [ō-vėr-set´] *vt* to disturb mentally or physically; to turn or tip over; to set too much type matter for. [**over, set**.]
overshadow [ō-vėr-shad´ō] *vt* to throw a shadow over; to cast into the shade by surpassing; to shelter or protect. [**over, shadow**.]
overshoe [ō´vėr-shōō] *n* a shoe, esp of waterproof, worn over another. [**over, shoe**.]
overshoot [ō-vėr-shōōt´] *vt* to shoot over or beyond (a mark) so as to miss; to pass swiftly beyond; to excel in shooting.—*adj* **o´vershot´**, having the upper jaw extending above the lower; actuated by the weight of water passing over and flowing from above.—*n* a pattern featuring filling threads which pass at least two warp threads before reentering the fabric. [**over, shoot**.]
oversight [ō´vėr-sīt] *n* superintendence; failure to notice; an omission. [**over, sight**.]
oversleep [ō-vėr-slēp´] *vt* to sleep beyond one's usual time. [**over** (indicating excess), **sleep**.]
overspread [ō-vėr-spred´] *vt* to spread or cover over. [**over, spread**.]
overstate [ō-vėr-stāt´] *vt* to exaggerate.—*n* **overstate´ment**. [**over** (indicating excess), **state**.]
oversteer [ō-vėr-stēr´] *n* the tendency of an automobile to steer into a sharper turn than the driver intends; action or instance of an oversteer. [**over** (indicating excess), **steer**.]
overstep [ō-vėr-step´] *vt* to step beyond; to exceed. [**over, step**.]
overstrung [ō-vėr-strung´] *adj* too highly strung; too sensitive. [**over** (indicating excess), + pt p of **string**.]
overt [ō´vėrt, ō-vûrt´] *adj* open to view, public; (*law*) openly done with evident intent.—*adv* **o´vertly**. [Fr *ouvert*, pt p of *ouvrir*, to open.]
overtake [ō-vėr-tāk´] *vt* to come up with, to catch; to pass from behind; to come upon unexpectedly (eg *a storm overtook him*). [**over, take**.]
overtax [ō-vėr-taks´] *vt* to tax too highly; to make too great demands on (eg one's strength). [**over** (indicating excess), **tax**.]
overthrow [ō-vėr-thrō´] *vt* to throw over, overturn; to ruin, to subvert, to defeat utterly; to throw a baseball over or past (as a base).—*n* **o´verthrow**, act of overthrowing or state of being overthrown. [**over, throw**.]
overtime [ō´vėr-tīm] *n* time employed in working beyond the regular hours; work done in such time; pay for such work. [**over, time**.]
overtone [ō´vėr-tōn] *n* (*mus*) a harmonic, any of the components above the fundamental frequency of a tone; the color of light reflected (as by a paint); a subtle meaning additional to the main meaning, conveyed by a word or statement; implicit quality. [**over, tone**.]
overtop [ō-vėr-top´] *vt* to rise over the top of; to surpass. [**over, top**.]
overtrade [ō-vėr-trād´] *vi* to trade beyond one's capital. [**over** (indicating excess), **trade**.]
overture [ō´vėr-chůr] *n* an opening of negotiations; a proposal; (*mus*) an instrumental prelude to an opera, oratorio, etc.; an orchestral piece written esp as a single movement in sonata form. [OFr *overture*, an opening.]
overturn [ō-vėr-tûrn´] *vt* to throw down or over, to upset; to subvert.—*vi* to upset, turn over.—*n* **o´verturn**, state of being overturned; the sinking of surface water and the rise of bottom water in a lake that results from changes of temperature. [**over, turn**.]
overvalue [ō-vėr-val´ū] *vt* to assign an excessive or fictitious value to. [**over** (indicating excess), **value**.]
overweening [ō-vėr-wēn´ing] *adj* conceited, arrogant, presumptuous. [From rare verb *overween*, to think too highly (usu of oneself)—**over** (indicating excess), **ween**.]
overweigh [ō-vėr-wā´] *vt* to exceed in weight; to oppress.—*n* **o´verweight**, weight beyond what is required or allowed.—*vt* **overweight´**, to overburden. [**over** (indicating excess), **weigh**.]
overwhelm [ō-vėr-hwelm´] *vt* to overspread and crush; to overpower. [**over, whelm**.]
overwork [ō-vėr-wûrk´] *vt* to work or use to excess.—*vi* to work too hard or too long.—*n* [ō´vėr-wûrk´] severe or burdensome work. [**over** (indicating excess), **work**.]
overwrought [ō-vėr-röt´] *pt p* of **overwork**, worked too hard; excited, with highly strained nerves; worked or embellished all over.
oviduct [ō´vi-dukt] *n* (*zool*) the tube by which the egg passes from the ovary to the uterus. [L *ōvum*, egg, *dūcĕre, ductum*, to convey.]
ovine [ō´vīn] *adj, n* (of, or resembling) a sheep. [L *ŏvis*, sheep.]
oviparous [ō-vip´ȧ-rus] *adj* producing eggs that hatch after leaving the body. [L *ōvum*, egg, *parĕre*, to bring forth.]
ovipositor [ō-vi-poz´i-tȯr] *n* a special organ (as of an insect) for depositing eggs. [L *ōvum*, egg, *positor—pōnĕre*, to place.]
ovoid [ō´void] *adj* oval; egg-shaped.—*n* anything ovoid. [L *ōvum*, egg, Gr *eidos*, form.]
ovulate [ov´ūl-āt] *vt* to produce ova; to discharge ova from the ovary.—*n* **ovulā´tion**. [From L *ōvum*, an egg.]
ovule [ōv´ūl] *n* (*bot*) the body that upon fertilization becomes the seed; (*zool*) the immature ovum. [Dim from L *ōvum*, an egg.]
ovum [ō´vum] *n* a female germ cell.—*pl* **o´va**. [L.]
owe [ō] *vt* to be indebted to for (something—to someone or something; eg *we owe our lives to him, to his skill*; also *we owe him our lives, money*); to be under an obligation to pay, restore, etc.; to have the need to give, do, etc. as because of gratitude.—*vi* to be in debt;—*pt, pt p* **owed**. [OE *āgan*, pres indic *āh*, pt *āhte*, pt p *āgen*; ON *eiga*, OHG *eigan*, to possess.]
owing [ō´ing] *adj* due, to be paid; imputable, attributable (to).—**owing to**, in consequence of. [**owe**.]
owl [owl] *n* any of an order (Strigiformes) of predacious nocturnal birds having a large head and eyes and a short, hooked beak; a person of nocturnal habits, solemn appearance, etc.—*n* **owl´et**, a little or young owl.—*adj* **owl´ish**, like an owl; solemn. [OE *ūle*; Ger *eule*, L *ulula*; imit.]
own[1] [ōn] *vt* to possess; to acknowledge as one's own; to admit.—*vi* to confess (to).—*n* that which belongs to oneself.—*ns* **own´er**, possessor; **own´ership**. [OE *āgnian—āgen*, one's own; cf **own**, adj.]
own[2] [ōn] *adj* belonging to oneself or itself, often used with reflexive force, *my own, his own*.—**on one's own**, on one's own initiative, or by one's own efforts; set up in independence. [OE *āgen*, pa p of *āgan*, to possess; cf **owe**.]
ox [oks] *n* any of various cud-chewing mammals of the cattle family, esp a domestic bovine mammal (*Bos taurus*); a castrated bull;—*pl* **ox´en, ox**,—*ns* **ox´eye**, any of several composite plants (as of the genera *Chrysanthemum, Heliopsis*, or *Buphthalmum*) having heads with both disk and ray flowers; **oxeye daisy**, a composite herb (as of genera *Bellis* or *Chrysanthemum*) having a flowerhead with well-developed ray flowers; **ox´heart**, any of various large sweet cherries. [OE *oxa*, pl *oxan, oxen*; ON *uxi*; Ger *ochs*, Sans *uksan*.]
oxalis [oks´a-lis] *n* wood sorrel.—*n* **oxalic acid**, a poisonous strong acid that occurs in various plants as oxalates, used as a bleaching or cleaning agent and in making dyes.—*n* **ox´alate**, a salt or ester of oxalic acid. [Gr *oxalis—oxys*, sharp, acid.]
oxide [oks´īd] *n* a compound of oxygen and another element or radical.—*vt* **ox´idize**, to combine with oxygen as in burning or rusting; to add an electropositive atom or group to, or remove an electronegative atom or group from, a molecule.—*vi* to become oxidized.—*n* **oxidā´tion**.—*adj* **oxidiz´able**. [Fr (now *oxyde*)—*oxygène*, oxygen.]
oxlip [oks´lip] *n* a Eurasian primula (*Primula eliator*) resembling the cowslip. [OE *oxanslyppe*; cf **cowslip**.]
oxy- [oks´i-] in composition, sharp; acid; oxygen.—*adj* **ox´yacet´ylene**, involving, using, or by means of, a mixture of oxygen and acetylene. [Gr *oxys*, sharp.]
oxygen [oks´i-jėn] *n* a gaseous element (symbol O; at wt 16.0; at no 8) without taste, color, or smell, forming part of the air, water, etc., and supporting life and combustion.—*vt* **ox´ygenāte**, to impregnate, combine, or supply (as blood) with oxygen.—*n* **oxygenā´tion**, act of oxygenating.—*adj* **oxyhy´drogen**, involving or using a mixture of oxygen and hydrogen.—**oxygen mask**, a breathing apparatus through which oxygen is supplied in rarefied atmospheres to aviators, mountaineers, etc. from a storage tank; **oxygen tent**, a canopy which can be placed over a bedridden patient within which a flow of oxygen can be maintained. [Gr *oxys*, sharp, *gen-*, the root of *gennaein*, to generate.]
oxymoron [ok-si-mō´, (-mö´)ron] *n* a figure of speech in which contradictory terms are combined, as *falsely true*, etc. [Gr,—*oxys*, sharp, *mōros*, foolish.]
oyer and terminer [ō´yer-rȧn-ter´mi-nėr] *n* a royal commission conferring power on a British judge to hear and determine criminal cases; a high criminal court in some US states. [Anglo-Fr *oyer* (Fr *ouïr*)—L *audīre*, to hear.]
oyez, oyes [ō-yes´, ō´yes] *interj* the call of a public crier for attention. [OFr *oyez*, imper of *oïr*, to hear.]
oyster [ois´tėr] *n* any of various marine bivalve mollusks (family Ostreidae), used as food. [OFr *oistre*—L *ostrea*—Gr *ostreon*, an oyster—*osteon*, a bone.]
ozone [ō´zōn] *n* an allotropic form of oxygen, (O_3), with a peculiar smell, a powerful oxydizing agent. [Gr *ozein*, to smell.]

P

pabulum [pab´ū-lum] *n* easily assimilated food; nourishment for the mind; an insipid piece of writing. [L,—*pāscĕre*, to feed.]

pace[1] [pās] *n* a stride, step; the space between the feet in walking; rate of motion (of a man or a beast); a mode of stepping in horses in which the legs on the same side are lifted together, amble.—*vt* to measure by steps; to train in walking or stepping; to set the pace for in a race by example.—*vt* to measure by steps; to train in walking or stepping; to set the pace for in a race by example.—*vi* to walk with regular steps; (of a horse) to move at a pace.—*ns* **pace´mak´er**, one who sets the pace, as in a race; a small mass of cells in the heart which controls the heartbeat; an electronic device used to correct weak or irregular heart rhythms; **pac´er**, one who paces; a horse whose usual gait is a pace; pacemaker; **pace´setter**, a person, horse, or automobile who is a pacemaker. [Fr *pas*—L *passus*, a step—*pandĕre, passum*, to stretch.]

pace[2] [pās´ē] *prep* with all due respect to (so-and-so—accompanying the expression of an opinion contrary to his). [L abl of *pāx*, peace.]

pachyderm [pak´i-dûrm] *n* one of an order of nonruminant, hoofed mammals, thick-skinned, as the elephant, rhinoceros, or pig.—*adj* **pachyder´matous**, thick-skinned; of the pachyderms; insensitive. [Gr *pachys*, thick.]

pacify [pas´i-fī] *vt* to appease; to calm; to bring peace to.—*adj* **pacif´ic**, peacemaking; appeasing; peaceful (eg of disposition); **Pacific**, of the ocean between Asia and America (also *n*).—*n* **pacificā´tion**, peace-making; conciliation; peace treaty.—*ns* **pac´ifier**, a person or thing that pacifies; a nipple or teething ring for babies; **pac´ifist**, an adherent of pacifism; **pac´ifism**, opposition to the use of force under any circumstances, specifically the refusal to participate in war.—*vt* **pac´ify**, to make peaceful, calm, nonhostile, etc.—**Pacific time**, the time of the 8th time zone west of Greenwich that includes the Pacific coastal region of the US. [Partly through Fr *pacifier*—L *pācificus*, pacific—*pācificāre*—*pāx, pācis*, peace, *facĕre*, to make.]

pack[1] [pak] *n* a bundle (esp one for carrying on the back); a complete set of playing cards; a group or mass; a number of wild animals living together; an organized troop (as of Cub Scouts); a concentrated or compact mass (as of snow); a cosmetic paste; act or method of packing; a compact package, esp of something for sale.—*vt* to make into a bundle or pack; to prepare (food—eg meat) and arrange it compactly in boxes, etc., for transport; to put into a bag or other article of luggage; to press together closely; to crowd, to cram; to press tightly, as for prevention of leaks; to carry in a pack; to send (off); (*slang*) to carry (a gun, etc.); (*slang*) to deliver (a punch) with force.—*vi* to form into a pack; to settle or be driven into a firm mass; to put one's belongings together in bags or boxes (*often with* **up**); to take oneself off; to depart in haste; to be suitable for packing.—*adj* used for carrying packs, loads, etc.—*n* **pack´age**, a bundle, or parcel; a number of items, plans, etc. offered as a unit.—*vt* to make a parcel of.—*ns* **pack´er**, one who operates a packinghouse; **pack´et**, a small package; a ship or vessel employed in carrying letters, passengers, etc. plying regularly between one port and another (also **pack´et boat**).—*ns* **pack´horse**, a horse used to carry goods; **pack´ice**, sea ice formed into a mass by the crushing together of pans, floes, etc.; **pack´ing**, the act of putting into packs or of tying up for carriage; material for doing so; anything used to protect packed goods or making airtight or watertight; **packinghouse**, a plant where meats, etc. are processed and packed for sale; **pack´man**, a peddler; **pack rat**, a large bushy-tailed rodent (*Neotoma cinerea*) of the Rocky Mountain area with well-developed cheek pouches and hoards food, etc.; one who collects, esp unneeded items; **pack´ sadd´le**, a saddle adapted for supporting the load on a pack animal; **pack´thread**, a coarse thread used to sew up packages.—**package deal**, a bargain or deal which includes a number of clauses and has to be accepted as a whole, the less favorable items along with the favorable; **package store**, a store that sells alcohol in bottles or cans to be consumed off the premises; **send one packing**, to dismiss one summarily. [ME *packe, pakke*, app—Middle Flemish *pac*, or Du, or Low Ger *pak*.]

pack[2] [pak] *n* (*obs*) a secret arrangement.—*vt* to fill up (a jury, meeting, etc.) with persons of a particular kind for one's own purposes. [Probably **pact**.]

pact [pakt] *n* an agreement or compact, esp one informal and not legally enforceable. [L *pactum*—*paciscĕre, pactum*, to contract.]

pad[1] [pad] *n* the dull sound of a footstep.—*vi* to walk esp with a soft step;—*pr p* **padd´ing**; *pt, pt p* **padd´ed**. [Du *pad*, a path.]

pad[2] [pad] *n* anything stuffed with a soft material to prevent friction or pressure or injury, or for filling out; a number of sheets of paper glued together at one edge; the cushioned thickening of an animal's sole; the floating leaf of a water lily; a piece of folded absorbent material used as a surgical dressing; a section of an airstrip used for warm-ups, take-offs, landings, etc.; a flat concrete surface (as for parking a mobile home); (*inf*) bed; (*slang*) a bed, room or home, esp one's own.—*vt* to stuff with anything soft; to fill out to greater length with words or matter that add nothing to the meaning; to expand an expense account with fraudulent entries.—*pr p* **padd´ing**; *pt, pt p* **padd´ed**.—*n* **padd´ing**, stuffing; matter of less value introduced into a book or article to make it of the length desired. [Origin obscure; possibly connected with **pod**.]

paddle[1] [pad´l] *vi* to wade about or dabble in shallow water. [Cf **pad** (1), and Low Ger *paddeln*, to tramp about.]

paddle[2] [pad´l] *n* a short oar with a wide blade at one or both ends, used without an oarlock; an implement shaped like this, used to hit a ball (as in table tennis), to beat someone, to stir something, etc.—*vti* to propel (a canoe etc.) by a paddle; to beat as with a paddle; to spank.—*ns* **paddle tennis**, a game like tennis played on a small court with a wooden paddle and a sponge rubber ball; **padd´le wheel**, a wheel with paddles, floats, or boards around its circumference used to propel a boat; **paddle wheeler**, a steamer propelled by a paddle wheel.

paddock [pad´ók] *n* an enclosed field under pasture, near a stable; the saddling enclosure at a racetrack. [Apparently from earlier *parrock*—OE *pearroc*, park.]

paddy [pad´i] *n* threshed unmilled rice; a rice field. [Malay *pādī*.]

padlock [pad´lok] *n* a detachable lock with a link to pass through a staple or other opening.—*vt* to fasten with a padlock. [Possibly dial Eng *pad*, a basket, and **lock**.]

padre [pä´drā] *n* father, a title given to priests in Spain, Italy, etc.; (*slang*) a priest or chaplain.—*n* **padrō´ne**, the master of a Mediterranean trading vessel; in Italy, an innkeeper; one that secures employment for immigrants, esp of Italian extraction. [Port (also Sp and It) *padre*—L *pater*, a father.]

paean [pē´ân] *n* a song or hymn of triumph. [L *paeān, paeōn*—Gr *Paiān, -ānos*, name for Apollo.]

paed- *See* **ped-**.

paella [pī-el´a] *n* a stew containing saffron, shellfish, chicken, rice, vegetables, etc. [Sp.]

pagan [pā´gȧn] *n* a heathen; one who has no religion.—Also *adj*—*n* **pā´ganism**, heathenism. [L *pāgānus*, rustic, peasant, also civilian (because the Christians reckoned themselves soldiers of Christ)—*pāgus*, a district.]

page[1] [pāj] *n* a boy attendant; at a formal function (as a wedding); a boy in livery employed to do errands.—*vt* to seek (a person) out by sending a page around or by repeatedly calling aloud for him in order to give a message.—*ns* **pager**, device carried on a person so he or she can be summoned; **pageboy**, medium-length hairstyle with ends of hair turned under. [Fr *page*.]

page[2] [pāj] *n* one side of a leaf of a book.—*vt* to number the pages of; to make up into pages.—*n* **pagination** [paj-i-nā´sh(ó)n] the act of paging a book; the arrangement and number of pages. [Fr,—L *pāgina*.]

pageant [paj´ént] *n* a spectacle, esp one carried around in procession; a series of tableaux or dramatic scenes connected with local history or other topical matter held outdoors; a mere show.—*adj* of the nature of pageant.—*n* **page´antry**, splendid display; mere show.

pagoda [pa-gō´da] *n* in the Far East, a temple the form of a many-storied, tapering tower. [Port *pagode*—Pers *butkadah*, idol-house, or some other Eastern word.]

paid [pād] *pt, pt p* of **pay**.

pail [pāl] *n* an open vessel with a hooped handle, usu. for holding or carrying liquids.—*n* **pail´ful**, as much as fills a pail. [OE *pægel*, a gill measure, apparently combined with or influenced by O Fr *paele*, a pan—L *patella*, a pan.]

pain [pān] *n* bodily or mental suffering; anguish; threat of punishment (in *under pain of*); (*pl*) trouble (taken).—*vt* to cause suffering to.—*adjs* **pained**, showing or expressing pain; **pain´ful**, causing pain; distressing.—*adv* **pain´fully**.—*n* **pain´fulness**.—*n* **pain´killer**, (*inf*) a medicine that relieves pain;—*adj* **pain´less**, without pain.—*adv* **pains´taking**, taking pains or care; diligent.—**on pain of** or **under pain of**, subject to penalty or punishment. [Fr *peine*—L *poena*, satisfaction—Gr *poinē*, penalty.]

paint [pānt] *vt* to make (a picture) using oil pigments, etc.; to depict with paints; to cover or decorate with paint; to describe.—*vi* to practice painting.—*n* a coloring substance; a dried coat of paint.—*adj* **paint´able**, suitable for painting.—*ns* **paint´er**, one who paints; an artist who paints pictures; one whose work is covering surfaces, as walls, with paint; **paint´ing**, the act or employment of laying on colors; a painted picture. [O Fr *peint*, pt p of *peindre*, to paint—L *pingĕre*, to paint.]

painter [pānt´ėr] *n* a rope used to fasten a boat.—**cut the painter**, to sever ties.

pair [pãr] *n* two things equal, or suited to each other, or growing, grouped, or used together; a set of two equal or like things forming one instrument, garment, etc.; any two persons or animals regarded as a unit.—*vti* to form a pair (of); to mate. [Fr *paire*, a couple—L *paria*, neut pl of *pār*, equal, afterwards regarded as a fem sing.]

Paiute [pī´yōōt, pī´ōōt] *n* member of an Amerindian people of northeastern Arizona, southern Utah, and southwestern Nevada; the Shoshonean language of this people.

pajamas [pȧ-jam´äz] *n pl* a loosely fitting sleeping or lounging suit consisting of jacket and trousers. [Hindi *pāējāmah—pāē*, leg, *jāmah*, clothing.]

Pakistani [pä-ki-stän´ē] *adj* of or pertaining to Pakistan.—*n* a native or citizen of Pakistan.

pal [pal] *n* a close friend.—*n* **pal´imony**, a court-ordered allowance paid by one member of a couple formerly living together out of wedlock to the other. [Gypsy].

palace [pal´ás] *n* the official residence of a sovereign; a large stately house or public building; a gaudy place for amusement or refreshment. [Fr *palais*—L *Palātium*, the Roman emperor's residence on the *Palatine* Hill at Rome.]

paladin [pal´a-din] *n* a champion of a medieval prince; an eminent champion of a cause. [Fr—It *paladino*—L *palātīnus*, adj of the palace.]

palanquin [pal´-an-kēn´] *n* a covered litter, formerly used in the Orient, carried on the shoulders of four men. [Port *palanquim*; cf Hindustani *palang*, a bed—Sans *palyaṅka*, a bed.]

palate [pal´ȧt] *n* the roof of the mouth; taste; mental relish.—*adj* **palatable** [pal´ȧt-ȧ-bl] pleasant to the taste; acceptable (eg a truth, advice).—*adv* **pal´atably**.—*adj* **pal´atal**, pertaining to the palate; (*phonetics*) of a consonant, formed with the tongue touching or near the hard palate; of a vowel, formed at the front of the palate. [L *palātum*.]

palatial [pa-lā´sh(ȧ)l] *adj* of or like a palace. [From L as **palace**.]

palatine [pal´a-tīn] *adj* of the Palatine hill or of a palace of a Roman or Holy Roman Emperor.—*n* **Palatine**, a native or inhabitant of a Palatinate; one of the hills of Rome; a noble invested with royal privileges and jurisdiction; a subject of a palatinate.—*n* **palat´inate**, province ruled by a palatine. [L *palātīnus—Palātium*. See **palace**.]

palaver [pa-läv´er] *n* a conference, usu. between persons of different levels of sophistication; idle talk, talk intended to deceive.—Also *vt*. [Port *palavra*, word—L *parabola*, a parable, later a word, speech—Gr *parabolē*.]

pale[1] [pāl] *n* a stake of wood driven into the ground for fencing; anything that encloses; an enclosed or limited region or place; a district subject to a particular jurisdiction, as (*hist*) the *English Pale* in Ireland or in France; sphere of authority, influence, etc. as *the pale of civilisation*; a broad stripe from top to bottom of a shield in heraldry.—*n* **pāl´ing**, wood or stakes for fencing.—**beyond the pale**, (of a person or his conduct) beyond what is morally or socially tolerable. [Fr *pal*—L *pālus*, a stake.]

pale[2] [pāl] *adj* (of a complexion) whitish; wan; (of color, light) lacking in intensity; dim.—*vt* to make pale.—*vi* to turn pale; to appear or become pale in comparison with something else. [OFr *palle*, pale (Fr *pâle*)—L *pallidus*, pale.]

pale-, paleo- prefix meaning; old; concerned with the distant past. [Gr *palaios*.]

paleobotany [pal-i-ō-bot´ȧn-i] *n* the study of fossil plants. [**paleo- + botany**.]

paleography [pāl-i-og´ra-fi] *n* ancient modes of writing; study of ancient modes of handwriting. [Gr *palaios*, old, *graphein*, to write.]

Paleolithic [pal-i-ō-lith´ik] *adj* of the earlier Stone Age, marked by the use of primitive stone implements. [Gr *palaios*, old, *lithos*, stone.]

paleontology [pāl-i-on-tol´o-ji] *n* the study of fossils.—*adj* **paleontolog´ical**.—*n* **paleontol´ogist**. [Gr *palaios*, old, *onta*, neut pl of pr p of *einai*, to be, *logos*, discourse.]

Paleozoic [pal-i-ō-zō´ik or pāl-] *adj, n* (of) the geological era, beginning with the Cambrian period and lasting until the end of the Permian period; the system of rocks formed in this era. [Gr *palaios*, old, *zōē*, life.]

paleozoology [pāl-i-ō-zō-ol´o-ji] *n* the study of fossil animals. [**paleo- + zoology**.]

palette [pal´ėt] *n* a little board on which a painter mixes his colors. [Fr—It *paletta—pala*, spade—L *pāla*, a spade.]

palfrey [pöl´fri] *n* (*arch*) a saddle horse, esp for a lady. [OFr *palefrei*—Low L *paraverēdus*.]

palimpsest [pal´imp-sest] *n* a parchment or other piece of writing material on which old writing has been rubbed out to make room for new. [Gr *palimpsēston—palin*, again, *psāein* (contracted *psēn*), to rub, rub smooth.]

palindrome [pal´in-drōm] *n* a word, verse, or sentence that reads the same backwards and forward, as *madam*. [Gr *palindromos*, running back—*palin*, back, *dromos*, a running.]

paling *See* **pale** (1)

palingenesis [pal-in-jen´e-sis] *n* the passing of the soul at death into another (human or animal) body. [Gr *palin*, again, *genesis*, birth.]

palinode [pal´i-nōd] *n* a poem retracting something said in a former one; a recantation. [Gr *palinōidiā—palin*, back, *ōidē*, song.]

palisade [pal-i-sād´] *n* a fence of stakes; (*pl*) a line of steep cliffs.—*vt* to surround or defend with a palisade.—**palisade layer**, a layer of elongated cells (**palisade cells**), found under the surface of a foliage leaf. [Fr *palissade*, and Sp *palizada*—L *pālus*, a stake.]

pall[1] [pöl] *n* a rich cloth used as covering, esp for a coffin; a chalice cover; a mantle as of smoke, darkness.—*n* **pall´bear´er**, a person who helps to carry the coffin at a funeral; a member of the honor guard who does not actually help to carry it. [OE *pæll*, a rich robe—L *pallium*.]

pall[2] [pöl] *vi* to become insipid, or wearisome to appetite or interest; to become satiated. [Prob from **appal**.]

palladium[1] [pa-lā´di-um] *n* a statue of *Pallus*, on whose preservation the safety of Troy depended; any safeguard. [L—Gr *palladion—Pallas, -ados*, Pallas, Greek goddess identified with Roman Minerva.]

palladium[2] [pa-lā´di-um] *n* a metallic element (symbol Pd; at wt 106.4; at no 46) resembling platinum. [L *Pallas*, name of an asteroid + suffix *-ium*.]

pallet[1] [pal´ėt] *n* a flat wooden tool with a handle; a lever or escapement wheel in a timepiece; a portable platform for lifting and stacking goods. [**palette**.]

pallet[2] [pal´ėt] *n* a mattress of straw, usu. laid on the floor; a small bed. [Dial Fr *paillet*, dim of Fr *paille*, straw—L *palea*, chaff.]

palliasse [pal-i-as´, pal-yas´] *n* a thin straw mattress used as a pallet. [Fr *paillase—paille*, straw—L *palea*.]

palliate [pal´i-āt] *vt* to extenuate, to soften by favorable representations; to alleviate without curing (a disease).—*n* **palliā´tion**, extenuation; mitigation.—*adj* **pall´iātive**, serving to extenuate; alleviating.—Also *n*. [L *palliāre, -ātum*, to cloak—*pallium*, a cloak.]

pallid [pal´id] *adj* pale, wan. [L *pallidus*, pale.]

pall-mall [pel´-mel´ or pȯl´mȯl´] *n* an old game, in which a ball was driven through an iron ring with a mallet; an alley for the game (hence the street in London—now usu. pronounced *pal´-mal´*). [Obs Fr *pale-maille*—It *pallamaglio—palla*, a ball, *maglio*, a mallet (L *malleus*, a hammer).]

pallor [pal´ȯr] *n* paleness, esp of the face. [L *pallēre*, to be pale.]

palm[1] [päm] *n* the inner surface of the hand between wrist and fingers.—*vt* to touch or stroke with the palm; to conceal in the palm, as in a sleight-of-hand trick.—*adjs* **palmar** [pal´mȧr] relating to the palm; **palmate** [pal´-] **-d**, handshaped; (of leaves) having lobes radiating from one center; (*zool*) having the portion away from the point of origin broad, flat, and lobed, as an antler.—*ns* **palmist** [päm´ist] one who tells fortunes from the lines on the palm; **palm´istry.—palm off**, to pass off by fraud. [L *palma*; cf Gr *palamē*; OE *folm*.]

palm[2] [päm] *n* a tropical or subtropical tree, shrub or vine (family Palmae) of many varieties, bearing at the summit a crown of large fan-shaped leaves; a leaf of this tree borne in token of rejoicing or of victory; a symbol or token of triumph or preeminence.—*ns* **palmett´o** [pal-] any of several low-growing palms (genera *Thrinax* or *Coccothrinax*); strips of the leaf blade of a palmetto used in weaving; **palm´oil**, an oil or fat obtained from the pulp of the fruit of palms, used esp in soap, candles, and lubricating greases; **Palm´ Sun´day**, the Sunday before Easter, in commemoration of Jesus' entry into Jerusalem, when palm branches were strewn before him.—*adj* **palm´y**, bearing palms; prosperous. [OE *palm, palma, palme*—L *palma*, palm-tree, from the shape of its leaves. See **palm** (1).]

palmyra [pal-mī´rä] *n* a tall African palm (*Borassus flabellifer*) cultivated for its hard wood, fiber, and sugar-rich sap. [Port *palmeira*, palm tree, confused with *Palmyra* (a city now in ruins) in Syria.]

palpable [pal´pa-bl] *adj* that can be felt; readily perceived by any of the senses; readily perceived or detected by the mind (eg errors, lies.—*ns* **palpabil´ity, pal´pableness**.—*adv* **pal´pably**.—*vt* **pal´pāte**, to examine by touch, esp medically. [Low L *palpābilis*—L *palpāre, -ātum*, to touch softly, stroke, caress, flatter.]

palpitate [pal´pi-tāt] *vi* to throb, beat rapidly and strongly; pulsate.—*n* **palpitā´tion**, act of palpitating with abnormal force or rapidity. [L *palpitāre, -ātum*, freq of *palpāre*; cf **palpable**.]

palsy [pöl´zi] *n* paralysis; a condition marked by an uncontrollable tremor of a part of the body.—*pl* **palsies**.—*vt* to affect with palsy.—*pt, pp* **pal´sied**. [Through OFr from same root as **paralysis**.]

palter [pöl´tėr] *vi* to trifle (with a subject); to haggle, bargain (with a person about something); to shuffle, equivocate, play false. [Perh conn with **paltry**.]

paltry [pöl´tri] *adj* almost worthless; trifling.—*adv* **pal´trily**.—*n* **pal´triness**. [Cf Dan *pialter*, rags, Low Ger *paltrig*, ragged.]

pampa [pam´pä] a vast grass-covered plain of temperate S America esp in Argentina.—*n* **pam´pas grass**, a S American grass (*Cordateria argentea*) growing in thick tussocks and sending up stalks 6 to 12 feet high, extensively cultivated as an ornamental. [Sp—South Amer Indian *pampa, bamba*, plain.]

pamper [pam´pėr] *vt* to overindulge (eg a child, oneself, a taste, or an emotion). [A freq from obs *pamp, pomp*; cf Ger Dial *pampen*, to cram.]

pamphlet [pam´flet] *n* a thin, unbound booklet, usu. on some subject of the day.—*n* **pamphleteer´**, a writer of pamphlets attacking something or urging a cause.—*vi* to write and publish pamphlets; to engage in arguments indirectly in writings.—*n adj* **pamphleteer´ing**. [Possibly from a Latin poem *Pamphilus*, very popular in the Middle Ages.]

pan[1] [pan] *n* a usu. broad, shallow container for domestic use (as for cooking, etc.); any of various similar usu. metal receptacles used in a pair of scales or for separating metal (as gold) by washing; a basin or depression in land; (*slang*) a face; (*inf*) a harsh criticism.—*vti* to wash (gold-bearing gravel) in a pan; (*inf*) to criticize harshly.—*ns* **pan´cake**, a thin cake of eggs, flour, sugar, and milk cooked on a griddle; **pancake landing**, a landing of an airplane dropping from a relatively steep angle, with low forward speed.—

pan out (*inf*) to turn out, esp to turn out well; succeed. [OE *panne*, a word common to the West Germanic languages.]
pan[2] [pan] *vti* of a movie or television camera, to move while taking a picture so as to follow a particular object or to produce a panoramic effect.—Also *n*. [**pan(orama)**.]
Pan- in composition, all, eg **Pan-American**, involving the independent republics of N and S America; **Pan-Slavism**, a political and cultural movement originally emphasizing the cultural ties between the Slavic peoples, but later associated with Russian expansionist policies. [Gr *pān*, neut of *pās*, all.]
panacea [pan-a-sē´a] *n* a universal medicine. [Gr *panakeia—pās, pān*, all, *akos*, cure.]
panache [pä-näsh´] *n* a plume, esp on a helmet; swagger, display, sense of style. [Fr.]
panada [pa-nä´dä] *n* a paste of flour or bread crumbs and water or stock used as a base for sauce or a binder in stuffing. [Sp.]
panama [pan-a-mä´] *n* a hat made of plaited strips of the leaves of a S American plant; an imitation thereof. [Sp *Panamá*.]
panchromatic [pan-krō-mat´ik] *adj* equally sensitive to light of all colors in the spectrum. [Gr *pās*, neut *pān*, all, *chrōma, -atos*, color.]
pancreas [pan(g)´kré-as] *n* a large gland situated under and behind the stomach, secreting a digestive juice into the intestine and also producing insulin.—*adj* **pancreat´ic**. [Gr *pās, pān*, all, *kreas, -atos*, flesh.]
panda [pan´dä] *n* a long-tailed Himalayan carnivore (*Ailurus fulgens*) related to the raccoon, with a reddish coat, known as lesser panda; a large black-and-white mammal (*Ailuropoda melanoleuca*) of western China, resembling a bear but related to the raccoon, known as giant panda. [Orig uncertain.]
pandect [pan´dekt] *n* a treatise covering the whole of any subject; a complete code of the laws of a country or system of law. [L *pandecta*—Gr *pandektēs—pās*, neut, *pān*, all, *dechesthai*, to receive.]
pandemic [pan-dem´ik] *adj* epidemic over a large region. [Gr *pān*, all + *demos*, people.]
pandemonium [pan-dė-mō´ni-um] *n* tumultuous uproar. [Gr *pās, pān*, all, *daimōn*, a spirit.]
pander [pan´dėr] *n* one who procures for another the means of gratifying his base passions; a pimp.—*vi* to act as a pander (to). [*Pandarus*, the pimp in the story of Troilus and Cressida.]
pane [pān] *n* a sheet of glass in a frame of a window, door, etc.; one of the sections of a sheet of postage stamps.—*adj* **paned**, composed of panes. [Fr *pan*—L *pannus*, a cloth, a rag.]
panegyric [pan-ė-jir´ik] *n* a eulogy, a formal speech or writing in praise of some person, or achievement.—*adj* **panegyr´ic, -al**.—*n* **pan´egyrist**. [Gr *panēgyrikos*, fit for a national festival—*pās*, neut *pān*, all, *agyris* (form of *agorā*), an assembly.]
panel [pan´(ė)l] *n* a usu. rectangular section or division forming part of a wall, door, etc.; a board for instruments or controls; a lengthwise strip in a skirt, etc.; a list of names summoned for jury duty; a group of persons chosen for judging, discussing, etc..—*vt* to decorate or furnish with panels.—*pr p* **pan´elling**; *pt p* **pan´elled**.—*n* **pan´eling, pan´elling**, panels collectively; sheets of wood, plastic, etc. used for panels.—**panel heating**, indoor heating diffused from floors, walls or ceilings; **panel truck**, an enclosed pickup truck. [OFr—Low L *pannellus*—L *pannus*, a cloth.]
pang [pang] *n* a sudden sharp pain or feeling, as of hunger or regret. [Perh a form of **prong**.]
panhandle [pan´han-dl] *n* a strip of land projecting like the handle of a pan.—*vti* (*inf*) to beg (from) on the streets.
panic [pan´ik] *n* frantic or sudden fright; contagious fear; general alarm.—Also *adj*.—*vt* to affect with panic; (*slang*) to convulse (an audience) with delight.—*vi* to be struck by panic.—*adj* **pan´icky**, inclined to panic, or inspired by panic.—*n* **pan´ic button**, something setting off a precipitous emergency response.—*adjs* **pan´ic-strick´en, pan´ic-struck**, struck with a panic or sudden fear. [Gr *pānikos*, belonging to Pan; *pānikon* (*deima*), panic (fear), fear associated with the god Pan.]
panicle [pan´i-kl] *n* (*bot*) a raceme whose branches are themselves racemes; an inflorescence in which the cluster is shaped like a pyramid. [L *pānicum*, Italian millet.]
panjandrum [pan-jan´drum] *n* one who assumes grand airs; a burlesque potentate. [From the Grand *Panjandrum* in a string of nonsense made up by Samuel Foote, the 18th-century actor.]
pannier, panier [pan´yėr or pan´ē-ėr] *n* a large basket for carrying loads on the back of an animal or the shoulders of a person; one of a pair or packs of baskets slung over the rear wheel of a bicycle; a contrivance of whalebone, etc., for puffing out a woman's dress at the hips; an overskirt draped at the sides of a skirt for an effect of fulness. [Fr *panier*—L *pānārium*, a bread-basket—*pānis*, bread.]
panoply [pan´ō-pli] *n* a full suit of armour; full or brilliant covering or array.—*adj* **pan´oplied**, in panoply. [Gr *panopliā*, full armour—*pās, pān*, all, *hopla* (pl), arms.]
panorama [pan-ō-rä´ma] *n* a wide or complete view; a picture unrolled and made to pass before the spectator; a comprehensive presentation of a subject; a constantly changing scene.—*adj* **panoramic** [-ram´ik]. [Gr *pās*, neut *pān*, all, *horāma*, a view—*horaein*, to see.]
panpipe [pan´pīp] *n* a primitive musical instrument consisting of a row of parallel pipes of increasing length. [Gr god *Pan* + **pipe** (1).]
pansy [pan´zi] *n* a garden plant (*Viola tricolor hortensis*) derived chiefly from the wild pansy of Europe. [Fr *pensée—penser*, to think—L *pensāre*, to weigh.]
pant [pant] *vi* to gasp for breath; to run gasping; to throb; to wish ardently (for, after something).—*vt* to utter gaspingly. [Apparently related to OFr *pantoisier*, to pant.]
Pantaloon [pan-ta-lōōn] *n* a character in Italian comedy, and afterwards in pantomime, a lean old man (originally a Venetian) more or less a dotard; (*pl*) loose-fitting usu. shorter than ankle-length trousers. [Fr *pantalon*—It *pantalone*, from St *Pantaleone*, a favorite saint of the Venetians.]
pantheism [pan´thē-izm] *n* the doctrine that identifies God with the universe; worship of the gods of different creeds and peoples impartially; toleration of worship of all gods.—*n* **pan´thēist**.—*adjs* **panthēist´ic, -al**.—*n* **pantheon** [pan´thē-on] a temple of all the gods; a building in which the famous dead of a nation are entombed or commemorated; a group of illustrious poems. [Gr *pās*, neut *pān*, all, *theos*, a god, *pantheion*, a pantheon.]
panther [pan´thėr] *n* a leopard, esp a black one; a cougar or jaguar. [Gr *panthēr*.]
pantile [pan´tīl] *n* a tile whose cross section is S-shaped, one curve being much larger than the other. [**pan** (1) + **tile**.]
pantograph [pan´tō-gräf] *n* a jointed framework of rods for copying drawings, plans, etc., on the same, or a different, scale. [Gr *pās*, neut *pān*, all, *graphein*, to write.]
pantomime [pan´tō-mīm] *n* a drama without words, using only actions and gestures; action or gestures without words; a British theatrical entertainment, usu. around Christmas, in which some nursery story is acted, with showy scenery, topical allusions, songs, and dancing.—*vti* to express or act in pantomime.—*adjs* **pantomimic** [-mim´ik], **-al**.—*n* **pan´tomimist**, an actor in pantomime. [L *pantomīmus*—Gr *pantomīmos*, imitator of all—*mīmos*, an imitator.]
pantry [pan´tri] *n* a small room or closet off the kitchen for storing cooking ingredients and utensils etc.; a room (as in a hotel or hospital) for preparing foods to order. [Fr *paneterie*—Low L *pānitāria*—L *pānis*, bread.]
pants [pants] *n* trousers.—*n pl* **panties**, very short underpants for women and children.—Also **pant´ie, pant´y**.—*ns* **pantsuit**, matching jacket and trousers for women; **panty hose**, women's undergarment combining panties and hose. [**pantaloons**.]
panzer [pant´zėr] *n* a tank.—*adj* armoured. [Ger.]
pap [pap] *n* soft food for infants or invalids; any oversimplified or insipid writing, ideas, etc.; (*inf*) political patronage. [Imit.]
papa [pȧ-pä´] *n* father; **Papa**, word used in communications for the letter *p*. [Partly through Fr *papa*, partly directly from LL *pāpa*, Gr *papās, pappās*, father (used as petname.]
papacy [pā´pa-si] *n* the office of pope; a pope's tenure of office; papal system of government. [LL *pāpāia—pāpa*, pope, father.]
Papago [pä´pȧ-gō] *n* member of an Amerindian people of southern Arizona.—*pl* **Papago, Papagos**; the Uto-Aztecan language of the Papago.
papal [pā´pȧl] *adj* of the pope, the papacy, or the Roman Catholic Church. [LL *pāpālis—pāpa*, pope.]
papaw [pö´pö] *n* a tree (*Asimina triloba*) of the custard-apple family, native to the US, or its fruit; the papaya.—Also **paw´paw´**. [Prob variant of **papaya**.]
papaya [pa-pä´ya] *n* a tropical American tree (*Carica papaya*) with large oblong yellow edible fruit; its fruit.—*n* **papain** [pa-pā´in] an enzyme in the juice of unripe papaya used esp as a tenderizer for meat and in medicine. [Sp *papayo* (tree), *papaya* (fruit), apparently from Carib.]
paper [pā´pėr] *n* the material made from rags, wood, etc. on which we commonly write and print; similar material for wrapping and other purposes; a single sheet of this; an official document; (*pl*) documents proving identity, authorisation, etc.; a newspaper; an essay or literary contribution, esp to a learned journal or society; wallpaper; a newspaper.—*adj* consisting, or made, of paper.—*vt* to cover with wallpaper.—*ns* **pa´perback**, a book with a limp paper cover; **paper clip**, a flexible clasp for holding papers together; **pa´perhang´er**, one whose work is hanging wallpaper; **pa´perhang´ing**, the act of applying wallpaper; **pa´pering**, the operation of covering with paper; the paper so used; **pa´per knife**, a thin, flat blade for cutting open envelopes or uncut pages; **pa´per mon´ey**, pieces of paper stamped or marked by government or by a bank, as representing a certain value of money; **pa´per nau´tilus**, a cephalopod (genus *Argonanta*) whose female has a delicate papery shell; **pa´perweight**, a small weight for keeping loose papers from being displaced; **pa´perwork**, clerical work, often incidental to a more important task.—**paper tiger**, a person, organization, that appears to be powerful but is in fact the reverse; **on paper**, theoretically. [AF *papir*, OFr (Fr) *papier*—L *papȳrus*—Gr *papȳros*, papyrus.]
papier collé [pa´pyā kol´ā] *n* collage. [Fr, glued paper.]
papier-mâché [pap´yā-mä´shā] *n* a material consisting of paper pulp mixed with size, glue, etc. and molded into various objects when moist. [Would-be French. Fr *papier* is paper, *mâché*, chewed—L *masticātus*.]
papilla [pap-il´a] *n* a small nipple-like protuberance; a minute elevation on

the skin, esp on the upper surface of the tongue.—*pl* **papill´ae** [-ē].—*adjs* **papill´ary, pap´illose**. [L dim of *papula*, a pimple.]

papist [pā´pist] *n* an adherent of the pope; a name slightingly given to a Roman Catholic; pertaining to popery, or to the Church of Rome, its doctrines, etc. (usu. disparaging).—*n* **pā´pistry**, popery (in hostile sense). [LL *pāpa*, pope.]

papoose [pap-ōōs´] *n* an Amerindian baby. [Amer Indian *papoos*.]

pappus [pap´us] *n* downy appendage growing on the seeds of thistles, dandelions, and other plants.—*adj* **pappōse´**, having or being a pappus. L *pappus*—Gr *pappos*, down.]

paprika [pa-prē´kȧ, pap´ri-ka] *n* a mild red condiment ground from the fruit of certain peppers. [Gr *peperi*, a pepper.]

Pap smear [pap] *n* a method for the early detection of cancer employing exfoliated cells and a special staining technique that identifies precancerous changes, used esp for the cervix.—Also **Pap test**. [G N *Papanicolaou*, Amer medical scientist.]

papular [pap´ū-lȧr] *adj* consisting of or marked by papules.—*n* **pap´ule**, a small solid elevation of the skin. [L *papula*, a pimple.]

papyrus [pa-pī´rus] *n* a tall sedge (*Cyperus papyrus*); of the Nile Valley; its pith prepared as a writing material by the ancients; a manuscript on papyrus;—*pl* **papy´rī**. [L *papȳrus*—Gr *papȳros*, prob Egyptian.]

par [pär] *n* the established value of a currency in foreign-exchange rates; the face value of stocks, etc.; the normal level, the standard or norm; equality in value, condition, or circumstances; (*golf*) the number of strokes for a hole, or a round, that should be taken if play is perfect.—**on a par with**, on a level with; **at par**, at exactly the nominal, or face, value (used in speaking of stocks, shares, etc.); **above par**, at a premium, ie at more than the face value; **below par**, at a discount ie at less than the face value; (*inf*) not up to the normal standard (used esp of health); **par value**, value at par. [L *pār*, equal.]

para- [pa´ra-] in composition, beside; faulty; irregular, disordered; abnormal; associated in a subsidiary or accessory capacity, as **paralegal**, a paraprofessional who assists a lawyer; **paramedical** a paraprofessional who assists in medicine; **paraprofessional**, a trained aide who assists a profession person; closely resembling or patterned on, as **paramil´itary**, supplementing the military. [Gr *para*; beside.]

parable [par´a-bl] *n* a fable or story told to illustrate some doctrine, or to make some duty clear. [Same as **parabola**.]

parabola [par-ab´o-la] *n* a curve, one of the conic sections, being the intersection of a cone and a plane parallel to its side or slope;—*pl* **parab´olas**.—*adj* **parabolic** [par-a-bol´ik], of or like a parable or a parabola; expressed by a parable; belonging to, or of the form of, a parabola.—*adv* **parabol´ically**.—*n* **parab´oloid**, a surface or solid generated by the rotation of a parabola about its axis. [Gr *parabolē*, a placing alongside, comparison, parabola, etc.—*para*, beside, *ballein*, throw.]

parachute [par´a-shōōt] *n* an apparatus like an umbrella for descending safely from a height.—*vti* to descend by parachute.—*n* **par´chutist**. [Fr *parachute*—It *para* imper of *parare*, to ward (L *parāre*, to prepare), and Fr *chute*, fall.]

parade [pa-rād´] *n* display, ostentation; an assembling in order for exercise, inspection, etc.; a procession; a public promenade.—*vt* to march or walk through, as for display; to show off.—*vi* to march up and down as if for show; to march in procession. [Fr,—Sp *parada*—*parar*, to halt—L *parāre*, *-ātum*, to prepare.]

paradigm [par´a-dīm] *n* an example, exemplar; (*gram*) a table of the inflections of a word representative of a declension or conjugation.—*adjs* **paradigmatic** [-dig-mat´ik].—*adv* **paradigmat´ically**. [Fr *paradigme*—Gr *paradeigma*—*paradeiknynai*, to exhibit side by side—*deiknynai*, to show.]

paradise [par´a-dīs] *n* a park or pleasure ground, esp in ancient Persia; **Paradise**, the garden of Eden; the abode of the blessed dead; a place, or state, of bliss.—*adj* **paradisiacal** [-dis-ī´ȧ-kl]. [Fr *paradis*—L *paradīsus*—Gr *paradeisos*, a park—O Pers *pairidaēza*, park.]

paradox [par´a-doks] *n* that which is contrary to received opinion; a statement that is apparently absurd or self-contradictory, but is or may be really true; a self-contradictory statement that is false; something (as a person, condition, or act) with seemingly contradictory qualities or phases.—*adj* **paradox´ical**.—*adv* **paradox´ically**. [Gr *paradoxos*, (neut) *-on*, contrary to opinion—*doxa*, opinion.]

paraffin [par´a-fin] *n* a white, crystalline substance obtained from shale, petroleum, etc., used for making candles, sealing jars, and in pharmaceuticals and chemicals; any of various mixtures of similar hydrocarbons including mixtures that are semisolid or oily.—*vt* to coat or saturate with paraffin. [L *parum*, little, *affinis*, have affinity.]

paragon [par´a-gon] *n* a model of perfection or supreme excellence. [O Fr *paragon*—It *paragone*, touchstone; origin obscure.]

paragraph [par´a-gräf] *n* a distinct part of a discourse or writing, a short passage, or a collection of sentences with unity of purpose; a short separate item of news or comment in a newspaper; a sign (usu. ¶) marking off a section of a book, etc.—*vt* to write paragraphs about; to divide into paragraphs.—*vi* to write paragraphs.—*adj* **paragraphic** [-graf´ik]. [Gr *paragraphos*, written alongside—*para*, beside, *graphein*, to write.]

parakeet, parrakeet [par´a-kēt] *n* a small, long-tailed parrot (subfamilies Paleornithinae and Platycercinae) of various kinds. [Sp *periquito*, It *parrocchetto*, O Fr *paroquet*.]

Paralipomenon [par-ȧ-li-pom´ėn-ȯn] (*Bible*) chronicles in the Douay Version of the Old Testament.

parallax [par´a-laks] *n* an apparent change in the position of an object caused by change of position in the observer; (*astron*) the apparent change (measured angularly) in the position of a heavenly body when viewed from different points.—*adj* **parallac´tic**. [Gr *parallaxis*—*para*, beside, *allassein*, to change, *allos*, another.]

parallel [par´a-lel] *adj* extended in the same direction and equidistant in all parts; like in essential parts, analogous;—*n* a parallel line, surface, etc.; a line of latitude; a person, thing, etc., exactly analogous to another; a comparison to show resemblance; the arrangement of electrical devices on which all positive poles, electrodes, and terminals are joined to one conductor and all negative ones to another conductor so that each unit is on a parallelbranch.—*vt* to place so as to be parallel; to represent as similar; to match;—*pr p*, **par´alleling**; *pt p* **par´alleled**.—*n* **par´allelism**, state or fact of being parallel; resemblance; a balanced construction of a verse or sentence where one part repeats the form or meaning of the other; the development of similar new characteristics by two or more related organisms in response to similarity of environment, also called **parallel evolution**. [Gr *parallēlos*, as if *par'allēloin*, beside each other.]

parallelepiped [par-ȧ-lel´e-pī´-ped] *n* a solid figure bounded by six parallelograms, opposite pairs being identical and parallel. [L,—Gr *parallēlepipedon*—*parallēlos* and *epipedon*, a plane surface—*epi*, on, *pedon*, ground.]

parallelogram [par-a-lel´ō-gram] *n* a plane four-sided figure, the opposite sides of which are parallel and equal. [Gr *parallēlogrammon*—*grammē*, a line.]

paralogism [pär-al´o-jizm] *n* false reasoning. [Gr *paralogismos*—*para*, beside, *logismos*—*logos*, reason.]

paralysis [pa-ral´i-sis] *n* a partial or complete loss of power of motion or sensation in any part of the body; a condition of helpless inactivity.—*vt* **paralyze** [par´a-līz], to afflict with paralysis; to deprive of power of action.—*adj* **paralytic** [par-a-lit´ik], afflicted with paralysis.—*n* one who is affected with paralysis. [Gr *paralysis*, secret undoing, paralysis—*para*, beside, *lyein*, to loosen.]

paramagnetic [par-a-mag-net´ik] *adj* having, or capable of, greater magnetization than a vacuum. [Gr *para*, beside, and **magnetic**.]

paramatta [par-a-mat´ä] *n* a fine lightweight dress fabric of silk and wool or cotton and wool. [App from *Parramatta* in New South Wales.]

paramecium [par-ȧ-mē´shē-um] *n* an oval freshwater protozoan that moves by means of cilia. [Gr *paramēkēs*, oval.]

parameter [pa-ram´i-ter] *n* a line or quantity which serves to determine a point, line, figure, or quantity in a class of such things; quantity to which an arbitrary value may be given as a convenience in expressing performance or for use in calculations; a variable in terms of related variables which may then be regarded as being dependent upon the parameter. [Gr *para*, beside, *metron*, measure.]

paramnesia [par-am-nē´si-a] *n* a disorder of memory in which the proper meaning of words cannot be remembered or in which one has the illusion that one remembers things actually experienced for the first time. [Gr *para*, and the root of *mimnēskein*, to remind.]

paramount [par´a-mownt] *adj* superior to all others; supreme.—*n* **par´amountcy**. [O Fr *paramont*—*par* (L prep *per*), *à mont* (L *ad montem*). See **amount**.]

paramour [par´a-mōōr] *n* an illicit lover. [Fr *par armour*, by or with love—L *per amōrem*.]

paranoia [par-a-noi´ä] *n* a form of insanity characterised by fixed delusions, esp of grandeur or persecution.—*adj* **paranoi´ac**. [Gr *paranoiă*—*noos*, mind.]

parapet [par´a-pet] *n* a bank or wall, to protect soldiers from the fire of an enemy in front; a low wall along the side of a bridge, etc.—*adj* **par´apeted**, having a parapet. [It *parapetto*, from pfx *para-* (see **parachute**), and It *petto*—L *pectus*, the breast.]

paraph [par´af] *n* a mark or flourish under one's signature. [Fr *paraphe*. Same root as **paragraph**.]

paraphernalia [par-a-fėr-nāl´i-a] *n pl* property that remains under a married woman's own control (esp articles of jewelry, dress, personal belongings); personal belongings; equipment; miscellaneous accessories. [Late L *paraphernālia*—*parapherna*—Gr, from *para*, beyond, *phernē*, a dowry—*pherein*, to bring.]

paraphrase [par´a-frāz] *n* expression of the same thing in other words; an exercise in such expression, esp in studying or teaching composition.—*vt* to express in other words.—*vi* to make a paraphrase.—*ns* **par´aphraser, par´aphrast** [-frast], one who paraphrases.—*adj* **paraphrast´ic**, explaining or translating more clearly; having the nature of a paraphrase. [Gr *paraphrasis*—*para*, beside, *phrasis*, a speaking—*phrazein*, to speak.]

paraplegia [par-a-plē´je-a] *n* paralysis of the lower half of the body. [Gr *para*, beside, *plege*, a stroke.]

parapsychology [par-a-sī-kol´o-jē] *n* psychology dealing with psychic phenomena such as telepathy.]

paraquat [par-a-kwat] *n* an herbicide containing a salt of afcation $C_{19}H_{19}N_3O$ used esp as a weed killer.

paraselene [par-a-se-lē´nē] *n* a luminous appearance seen in conjunction with a lunar halo; a mock moon. [Gr *para*, beside, *selēnē*, moon.]

parasite [par´a-sīt] *n* one who lives at the expense of society or of others and contributes nothing; an organism that lives in or on another organism without rendering it any service in return.—*adj* **parasitic** [-sit´ik], **-al**, like a parasite.—*adv* **parasit´ically**.—*n* **par´asitism** [-sīt-izm]. [Gr *parasītos*—*para*, beside, *sītos*, corn, bread, food.]

parasol [par´a-sol] *n* a lightweight umbrella used as a sunshade. [Fr,—It *parasole*—*para*, imper of *parare*, to ward—L *parāre*, to prepare, and *sole*—L *sōl, sōlis*, the sun.]

parathyroid [par-a-thī´roid] *adj* denoting the small glands near the thyroid that regulate calcium and phosphorus metabolism.

paratroops [par´a-trōōps] *n pl* troops carried by an airplane to be dropped by parachute.—*n* **par´atrooper**, a member of a body of troops trained for this purpose.

paratyphoid [par-a-tī´foid] *adj* of a disease resembling typhoid fever.—*n* a salmonellosis, commonly contracted by eating contaminated food.

paravane [par´a-vān] *n* a fish-shaped rudder-steered device attached by a stout rough wire to a ship's bows for the purpose of cutting mines from their moorings. [Pfx *para-* (as in **parachute**), and **vane**.]

par avion [par av-y•] by airmail. [Fr.]

parboil [pär´boil] *vt* to boil briefly as a preliminary cooking procedure. [O Fr *parboillir*—LL *perbullīre*, to boil thoroughly; influenced by confusion with **part**.]

parbuckle [pär´buk´l] *n* an arrangement for raising or lowering a heavy object that will roll (eg a barrel), the middle of a rope being made fast to a post and both ends being passed under and over the object; a double sling made of a single rope (as for slinging a cask).—*vt* to hoist or lower by means of a parbuckle. [Earlier *parbunkel, parbuncle*, origin unknown.]

parcel [pär´sl] *n* a tract or plot of land; a wrapped bundle; a package; a collection or group of persons, animals or things; a caulked seam; a protective wrapping around rope.—*vt* to divide into portions; to make up into a parcel; to cover (as a rope) with strips of canvas, etc.—*pr p* **par´celling**; *pt, pt p*; **par´celled**.—**parcel post**, a mail service handling parcels; packages handled by parcel post; **parcel post zone**, a designated distance zone within which US parcel post is charged at a single rate. [Fr *parcelle* (It *particella*)—L *particula*, dim of *pars, partis*, a part.]

parch [pärch] *vt* to make hot and very dry (of the sun, fever, thirst, cold); to roast slightly.—*vt* to be scorched; to become very dry.—*adj* **parched**. [Origin unknown.]

parchment [pärch´mėnt] *n* the skin of a sheep, goat, or other animal prepared for writing on; a document on parchment; paper like parchment. [Fr *parchemin*—L *pergamēna* (*charta*), Pergamene (paper)—from Gr *Pergamos*, Bergamo, in Asia Minor.]

pard [pärd] *n* the leopard. [L *pardus* (masc), *pardalis* (fem)—Gr *pardos, pardalis*; prob of Eastern origin.]

pardon [pär´d(ȯ)n] *vt* to forgive (a person, an offense); to remit the penalty of; to make allowance for, excuse.—*n* forgiveness; remission of a penalty or punishment; a warrant declaring a pardon;—*adj* **par´donable**, that may be pardoned; excusable.—*adv* **par´donably**.—*n* **par´doner** (*hist*), one licensed to sell papal indulgences; one that pardons. [Fr *pardonner*—Low L *perdōnāre*—L *per*, through, away, *dōnāre*, to give.]

pare [pār] *vt* to cut or shave off the outer surface or edge of; to peel; to diminish by small quantities (*often with* **down**).—*ns* **pār´er; pār´ing**, the act of paring; that which is pared off. [Fr *parer*—L *parāre*, to prepare.]

paregoric [par-ė-gor´ik] a tincture of opium used to relieve pain and to treat diarrhea. [Gr *parēgorikos*—*parēgoreein*, to exhort, comfort.]

parent [pār´ėnt] *n* a father or a mother; a plant or an animal from which others are derived (also *adj*); an author, cause, source.—*n* **pār´entage**, descent from parents; extraction, lineage; derivation.—*adj* **parental** [pä-rent´ȧl].—*adv* **parent´ally**. [Fr *parent*, kinsman—L *parēns, -entis*, old pr p of *parĕre*, to bring forth.]

parenthesis [pä-ren´thė-sis] *n* a word or passage of comment or explanation inserted in a sentence that is grammatically complete without it; a figure of speech consisting of the use of such insertion; a digression; an interval, interlude; one or both of the curved marks () used to mark off a parenthesis or to group a symbolic unit in a logical or mathematical expression.—*pl* **paren´theses** [-sēz].—*adjs* **parenthetic** [par-ėn-thet´ik], **-al**.—*adv* **parenthet´ically**. [Gr,—*para*, beside, *en*, in, *thesis*, a placing.]

parhelion [pär-hē´li-ȯn] *n* a luminous appearance seen in conjunction with a solar halo, a mock sun;—*pl* **parhē´lia**. [Irregularly—Gr *parēlion*—*para*, beside, *hēlios*, sun.]

pariah [pa-rī´ä] *n* in south India, one of low caste; a social outcast. [Tamil, *paraiyar*.]

parietal [pä-rī´ė-tȧl] *adj* of, relating to, or forming the walls of an anatomical structure; of or relating to college dormitory living and its regulations.—*n* **parietal bone**, either of a pair of bones of the roof of the skull between the front bones and occipital bones. [L *parietālis*—*pariēs, parietis*, a wall.]

pari-mutuel [par´i-myōō´chōō-wėl] *n* a system of betting on races in which the winning bettors share the net of each pool in proportion to their wagers. [Fr.]

parish [par´ish] *n* an ecclesiastical area in the charge of one pastor; the congregation of a church; a civil division in Louisiana, like a county. [Anglo-Fr *paroche*—L *parochia*—Gr *paroikiā*, an ecclesiastical district.]

Paris green [par´is] *n* a very poisonous bright green powder prepared from arsenic trioxide and copper acetate that is used as an insecticide and pigment. [*Paris*, France.]

parity [par´i-ti] *n* equality in status; equality in quantity and kind; equality of value at a given ratio between different kinds of money, etc. [Fr *parité*—L *paritās*—*pār*, equal.]

park [pärk] *n* a tract of land kept as a game preserve or recreation area; a piece of ground in a town or city kept for ornament and recreation, with playgrounds, etc.; an enclosed stadium, esp for ball games.—*vti* to leave (a vehicle in a certain place temporarily; to maneuver (a vehicle) into a parking space.—*vt* (*inf*) to deposit and leave temporarily.—*ns* **parking lot**, an area used for the parking of motor vehicles; **parking meter**, a coin-operated meter that registers the purchase of parking time for a motor vehicle. [O Fr *parc*, of Gmc origin; cf O E *pearruc, pearroc*.]

parka [pär´ka] *n* a hooded fur pullover for arctic wear; a fabric pullover or jacket for sports or military wear. [Aleutian Eskimo word.]

Parkinson's disease [pär´kin-sȯnz] a chronic progressive nervous disease of later life characterized by tremor of resting muscles and by a peculiar gait.—*adj* **parkinsonian**.—*n* **parkinsonism**, condition resembling Parkinson's disease marked by rigidity of muscles without tremor. [Studied by James *Parkinson* (1755–1824.)

Parkinson's law [pär´kin-sȯz] (*humorous*), any of the laws propounded by C. Northcote *Parkinson*, esp the law that in office organization work expands so as to fill the time available for its completion.

parlance [pär´lȧns] *n* mode of speech, phraseology (eg *legal parlance*).—*vi* **par´ley**, to confer; to treat with an enemy.—*n* a conference, esp with an enemy. [Fr *parler*—L *parabola*—Gr *parabolē*, a parable, word.]

parliament [pär´li-mėnt] *n* a meeting for deliberation; a legislative body; **Parliament**, the legislature of Great Britain, House of Commons, the House of Lords and the Sovereign; the legislature of various other countries, as Canada, South Africa, Australia (Federal Parliament), etc.—*n* **parliamentā´rian**, one skilled in the ways of parliament; **Parliamentarian**, adherent of Parliament in opposition to Charles I.—*adj* **parliament´ary**, pertaining to parliament; enacted or done by parliament; according to the rules and practices of legislative bodies; (of language) civil, decorous.—**parliamentary government**, a system of government having real executive power vested in a cabinet composed of members of the legislature who are individually and collectively responsible to the legislature. [Fr *parlement*—*parler*, to speak.]

parlor [pär´lȯr] *n* a room in a house used primarily for conversation or for receiving guests; a room in a hotel or club for conversation or semiprivate use; any of certain business establishments.—*ns* **parlor car**, an extra-fare railroad passenger car for day travel equipped with individual chairs; **parlor grand**, a grand piano intermediate in length between a baby grand and a concert grand, about 7 or 8 feet long. [Anglo-Fr *parlur*—*parler*, to speak.]

parlous [pär´lus] *adj* full of danger or difficulty, very bad (as '*a parlous state*'). [Form of **perilous**.]

Parmesan [pär´mė-zän, -zan, -zȧn] *n* the hardest cheese, made from cow's milk, with mild flavor. [*Parma*, Italy.]

parochial [pär-ō´ki-ȧl] *adj* of or relating to a parish; restricted or confined within narrow limits—of sentiments, tastes, etc.—*n* **parō´chialism**, provincialism, narrowness of view.—*adv* **parō´chially**.—**parochial school**, a usu. elementary school supported and controlled by a church. [L *parochiālis*—*parochia*. See **parish**.]

parody [par´o-di] *n* a burlesque imitation of a literary or musical work or style.—*vt* to make a parody of;—*pr p* **par´odying**; *pt p* **par´odied**.—*n* **par´odist**, one who writes a parody. [Gr *parōidiā*—*para*, beside, *ōidē*, an ode.]

parole [pȧr-ōl´] *n* the release of a prisoner before his sentence has expired, on condition of future good behavior; (*linguistics*) the use of language by a given language in a given case.—*vt* to release on parole.—*n* **parol** [par´ol], word of mouth. [Fr *parole*, word—L *parabola*—Gr *parabolē*. See **parable**.]

paronomasia [par-on-o-mā´syä, -zyä, -zh(y)ä] *n* a play upon words, a pun.—*n* **paronym** [par´o-nim], a word formed from a word in another language; a word with a form similar to that of a cognate foreign word. [Gr *para*, beside, *onoma, onyma*, name.]

parotid [par-ot´id] *adj* of or relating to the parotid gland.—*n* **parotid gland**, a salivary gland situated below and in front of the ear. [Gr *parōtis, -idos*—*para*, beside, *ous, ōtos*, ear.]

paroxysm [par´oks-izm] *n* a sudden attack of a disease; fit of acute pain; a fit of passion, laughter, coughing, etc.—*adj* **paroxys´mal**. [Gr *paroxysmos*—*para*, beyond, *oxys*, sharp.]

parquet [pär´kā] *n* the main floor of a theater, the orchestra; a flooring of parquetry.—*vt* to make of parquetry.—*n* **par´quetry**, geometrically patterned inlaid work of wood. [Fr *parquet*, dim of *parc*, enclosure.]

parr [pär] *n* a young salmon in its first two years before it becomes a smolt and descends to the sea. [Orig uncertain.]

parrakeet *See* **parakeet**.

parricide [par´i-sīd] *n* the murder of a parent or near relative, or of anyone to whom reverence is considered to be due; one who commits such a crime.—*adj* **parricid´al**. [Fr,—L *parricīdium, pāricīdium* (the offense), *parricīda, pāricīda* (the offender)—*caedĕre*, to slay; the connection with *pater*, father, is apparently fanciful.]

parrot [par´ȯt] *n* any of numerous widely distributed tropical and subtropical birds (order Psittaciformes) with brilliant plumage, hooked bill, and toes arranged in pairs, two before and two behind, good imitators of human speech; a person who repeats words mechanically and without understanding.—*vt* to repeat by rote.—**parrot fever**, psittacosis. [Possibly Fr *Perrot*, a dim of *Pierre*, Peter.]

parry [par´i] *vt* to ward or keep off; to turn aside (blow, argument, question, etc.);—*pt, pt p* **parr´ied**. [Perh from Fr *parez*, imper of *parer*—L *parāre*, to prepare, in Low L to keep off.]

parse [pärz] *vt* (*gram*) to break (a sentence) down, giving the form and function of each part; to describe (a word) fully by stating the part of speech, inflection and relation to other words in the sentence.—*vi* to give a grammatical description of a word or a group of words.—*n* **pars´ing**. [L *pars* (*ōrātiōnis*), a part (of speech).]

parsec [pär´sec] *n* a unit of measure for interstellar space equal to 19.2 billion miles (19.2 x 10^{12} miles). [*par*allax, and *sec*ond.]

Parsi, Parsee [pär´sē, or -sē] *n* a descendant of the Zoroastrians (followers of the religious teacher Zoroaster) who emigrated from Persia to India; the Iranian dialect of Parsi religious literature. [Pers *Pārsī*—*Pārs*, Persia.]

parsimony [pär´si-mȯn-i] *n* sparingness in the spending of money; economy in the use of means to an end; niggardliness.—*adj* **parismonious** [-mō´ni-us].—*adv* **parsimō´niously**.—*n* **parsimō´niousness**. [L *parsimōnia*—*parcĕre, parsum*, to spare.]

parsley [pärs´li] *n* a bright green umbelliferous (*Petroselinum crispum*) annual or biennial herb used to flavor or garnish some foods. [OE *petersilie*, modified by Fr *persil*; both—L *petroselīnum*—Gr *petroselinon*—*petros*, a rock, *selīnon*, parsley.]

parsnip [pärs´nip] *n* an umbelliferous plant or its edible biennial herb (*Pastinaca sativa*); its long tapered root used as a vegetable in some cultivated varieties. [L *pastināca*—*pastinum*, a dibble.]

parson [pär´s(ȯ)n] *n* a clergyman, esp a Protestant pastor.—*n* **par´sonage**, the residence provided for a parson by his church. [OFr *persone*—L *persōna*, a person. See **person**.]

part [pärt] *n* something less than the whole;portion (of a thing), some out of a larger number (of things); an essential, separable piece of a machine; (*pl*) region; an inflected form (of a verb); words and actions of a character in a play; a copy of an actor's words; a voice or an instrument in a musical ensemble; that which is performed by such voice or instrument; a copy of the music for it; (*pl*) intellectual qualities, talents (eg *a man of parts*); share, duty (eg *do one's part*); side or party (eg *take his part*); one of the sides in a conflict; a dividing line formed in combing the hair.—*vt* to divide into parts or shares; to comb the hair so as to leave a part; to separate.—*vi* to become separated; to go different ways.—*adj* **part´ible**, separable, divisible.—*n* **part´ing**, a departure; a breaking or separating.—*adj* departing, esp dying; separating; dividing.—*adv* **part´ly**, in part; in some degree.—*ns* **part´song**, a melody, usu. unaccompanied, with parts in harmony.—*adj* **part´time**, for part of working time only.—Also *adv*; **for the most part**, in general; on the whole; **part of speech**, one of the various grammatical classes of words. [OE and Fr *part*—L *pars, partis*.]

partake [pär-tāk´, pȧr-tāk´] *vi* to take or have a part or share; to take some (esp of food or drink—*with* **of**); to have something of the nature or properties (of);—*pr p* **parta´king**; *pt* **partook´**; *pt p* **parta´ken**.—*n* **partā´ker**. [Back-formation from **partaker—part, taker**.]

parterre [pär-ter´] *n* an arrangement of flowerbeds; the orchestra of a theater esp under the galleries. [Fr,—L *per*, along, *terra*, the ground.]

parthenogenesis [pär-the-nō-jen´ė-sis] *n* reproduction from an unfertilized ovum, seed, or spore. [Gr *parthenos*, a virgin, *genesis*, production.]

Parthenon [pär-the-non] *n* the temple of Athēnē *Parthĕnos*, on the Acropolis at Athens. [Gr *Parthenōn*—*parthenos*, a virgin.]

partial [pär´shȧl] *adj* not total or complete; inclined to favor one person or party, biased; having a preference or liking for (*with* **to**).—*n* **partiality** [-shi-al´i-ti].—*adv* **par´tially**. [Fr,—Low L *partiālis*—L *pars*, a part.]

partible *See* **part**.

participate [pär-tis´i-pāt] *vi* to take a share or part with others (in some activity).—*ns* **partic´ipant**, one that participates; **participā´tion**, act of participating; the state of being related to a larger whole; **partic´ipātor**.—*adj* **partic´ipator´y**. [L *participāre, -ātum*—*pars, partis*, part, *capĕre*, to take.]

participle [pär´ti-si-pl] *n* a verbal form combining the functions of adjective and verb.—*adj* **particip´ial**. [Fr,—L *participium*—*particeps*—*pars, partis*, a part, *capĕre*, to take.]

particle [pär´ti-kl] *n* a minute piece of matter; any of the consistuents of an atom; a minute quantity of something immaterial (eg *a particle of truth*); a short, invariable part of speech, as a preposition, a conjunction, an interjection; a prefix or suffix; (*RC Church*) a small eucharistic wafer distributed to a layman at Communion.—*adj* **particular** [pȧr-tik´ū-lȧr], indicating a single definite person or thing as distinguished from others (eg *this particular critic, occasion*); individual (eg *my particular views*); special (eg *particular care*); concerned with things single or distinct; minutely attentive and careful; fastidious in taste.—*n* a single point, a detail.—*vti* **partic´ularize**, to mention the particulars of; to enumerate in detail.—*ns* **particularizā´tion; particularity** [-ar´i-ti], quality of being particular, as distinguished from universal; exactness; state of being fastidious in expression.—*adv* **partic´ularly**, in a particular manner; especially; specifically.—*adj* **partic´ulate**, of, or relating to minute, separate particles.—**in particular**, especially. [L *particular*, dim of *pars, partis*, a part.]

parti-colored. *See* **party**.

partisan[1] partizan [pär-ti-zan´, pär´ti-zan] *n* a strong supporter of a person, party, or cause; a guerrilla fighter.—Also *adj*.—*n* **par´tisanship** [or -zan´-]. [Fr *partisan*, from a dial form of It *partigiano*—*parte* (L *pars, partis*), part.]

partisan[2] partizan [pär´ti-zan] *n* a weapon of the 16th and 17th centuries with a long shaft and broad blade. [Fr *partizane* (now *pertiusane*)—It *partesana*.]

partite [pär´tīt] *adj* divided usu. in a specified number of parts; cleft nearly to the base.—*n* **partition** [-tish´(ȯ)n], act of dividing; state of being divided; separate part; that which divides; a wall between rooms.—*vt* to divide into shares; to divide into parts by walls.—*adj* **par´titive**, denoting division or the result of division.—*adv* **par´titively**. [L *partītus*, pa p of *partīrī* or *partīre*, divide.]

partner [pärt´nėr] *n* one of two or more persons owning jointly a business who shares the risks and profits of the company or firm; one who plays on the same side with, and along with, another in a game; one who dances with another; a husband or wife.—*vt* to act as partner to; to join as partners.—*n* **part´nership**, state of being partner; a contract between persons engaged in any business.—**sleeping partner**, one who has money invested in a business but takes no part in its management. [Prob a form of *parcener*, a coheir; through Anglo-Fr and LL—L *pars*, a part.]

partridge [pär´trij] *n* any of various medium-sized stout-bodied game birds (genera *Perdix* and *Alectoris*) of the old world of the grouse family; any of numerous gallinaceous N American birds (as the ruffed grouse) resembling the partridge in size, habits, or value as game.—*n* **partridgeberry**, an American trailing evergreen plant (*Mitchella repens*) with insipid scarlet berries; its fruit. [Fr *perdrix*—L *perdīx*—Gr *perdīx*.]

parturient [pär-tū´ri-ėnt] *adj* bringing, or about to bring, forth.—*n* **partūri´tion**, act of bringing forth. [L *parturīre*, desiderative from *parĕre*, to bring forth.]

party [pär´ti] *n* a side in a battle, game, lawsuit, etc.; a body of persons united for political or other action; a meeting or entertainment of guests; one concerned in a contract; a detachment; (*inf*) a single individual.—*vi* to attend social parties.—*vt* to give a party for.—*adj* pertaining to a party.—*adj* **par´ticol´ored**, variegated.—*ns* **par´ty line**, a telephone exchange used by a set of subscribers; the policies of a political party; **par´ty wall**, a wall between two properties, and in which each of the owners shares the rights. [Fr *parti(e)*, pt p of *partir*—L *partīre*, divide.]

parvenu [pär´ve-nū] *n* an upstart, one newly risen into wealth or power. [Fr, pt p of *parvenir*—L *pervenīre*, to arrive—*per*, through, *venīre*, to come.]

parvis, parvise [pär´vis] *n* an enclosed space before a church; a single colonnade or portico before a church. [OFr *parevis*.]

pas [pä] *n* a step or combination of steps; as in dancing.—**pas de deux** [pä dė d_], a dance for two performers; an intricate activity involving two parties or things; **pas seul** [sœl], a dance for one. [Fr]

pascal [pas´kal] *n* a unit of pressure in the meter-kilogram-second system, equal to one newton per square meter; **Pascal, PASCAL**, a computer programming language developed from Algol and designed to process both numerical and textual data. [Blaise *Pascal*, French scientist 1623–62.]

Pasch [päsk] *n* Passover; Easter.—*adj* **pasch´al**, of Passover or Easter; **paschal full moon**, the 14th day of a lunar month occurring on or next after March 21 according to ecclesiastical calendar rules disregarding the real moon. [L *pascha*—Gr,—Heb *pesach*, the Passover—*pāsach*, to pass over.]

pasha [pä´shä, pä-shä´] *n* a former Turkish title given to governors and high military and naval officers, placed after the name. [Turk *pāshā*.]

pasqueflower [päsk´flow´(ė)r] *n* any of several low-growing perennial herbs (genus *Anemone*) of the buttercup family with white or purple spring flowers. [Fr *passefleur*, apparently—*passer*, to surpass, modified after *pasque*, Pasch.]

pass [päs] *vi* to proceed; to go from one place or state to another; to go by; to be regarded as (*with* **for**); to go unheeded or neglected; to elapse; to go away; to die; to undergo an examination successfully; to be approved as by a legislative body; to happen; (*cards*) to abstain from making a bid; to withdraw from the current poker pot.—*vt* to go by, over, beyond, through, etc.; to spend (as time); to omit; to enact; to pronounce (eg judgment); to transfer; to excrete; to approve; to undergo (a test, course, etc.) successfully; to circulate;—*pt p* **passed**.—*n* a way by which one may pass; a narrow passage or defile; a ticket for free travel or admission; state or condition; in games, transference of the ball to another member of the team; a movement of the hand; (*slang*) unwelcome amorous approach; success in any test; (*mil*) a brief leave of absence.—*adj* **pass´able**, that may be passed, traveled over, or navigated; that may bear inspection; tolerable.—*adv* **pass´ably**.—*ns* **pass´book**, a bankbook; **pass´er; pass´erby**, one who passes by;—*pl* **pass´ersby; pass´key**, a key enabling one to enter a house; a key for opening several locks; **pass-fail**, a system of grading whereby the grades 'pass' and 'fail' replace the traditional letter grades; **pass´word**, a secret term by which a friend is recognized and allowed to pass; any means of admission; a sequence of characters required for access to a computer system.—**come to pass**, to happen; **pass the buck** (*slang*) to shift the responsibility (to someone else); **pass up** (*inf*) to refuse or let go by. [Fr *pas*, step, and *passer*, to pass—L *passus*, a step.]

passacaglia [päs-sä-käl´yä] *n* a slow old Italian or Spanish dance tune or dance. [From Sp *pasacalle*, a certain guitar tune.]

passage [pas´ij] *n* act of passing; crossing; transition; lapse, course; a journey (by sea or air); means of passing to and fro; a sum paid for a voyage; a corridor; a channel; enactment (of a law); occurrence, episode; a portion of a book, etc., or piece of music; incubation of a pathogen (as a virus) in any medium. [Fr *passager*—L *passus*, step.]

Passamaquoddy [pas-àm-a-kwod´i] *n* member of an Algonquian-speaking Amerindian people of Maine, a member of the Abnaki confederacy;—*pl* **-dy -s**.

passé [pas´ā, pas-ā´] *adj* past one's best; out-of-date; behind the times. [Fr]

passenger [pas´ėn-jėr] *n* one who travels in a private or public conveyance.—*n* **passenger pigeon**, an extinct but formerly abundant N American migratory pigeon (*Ectopistes migratorius*). [OFr *passagier*, with inserted *n*, as in *messenger, nightingale*.]

passe-partout [pas-pär-tōō´] *n* a method of framing, with glass front and pasteboard back, the picture being fixed by strips of paper pasted over the edges; strong paper, gummed on one side, used for this and other purposes. [Fr,—*passer*, to pass, *par*, over, *tout*, all.]

passerine [pas´er-in] *adj* relating to the largest order (Passeriformes) of birds which includes more than half of all living birds and consists of songbirds of perching habits; relating to a suborder (Passeres) of passerine birds comprising the true songbirds with specialized voice apparatus. [L *passer*, a sparrow.]

passim [pas´im] *adv* here and there. [L]

passing [pas´ing] *adj* going by; transient; surpassing; satisfying given requirements; current.—*adv* exceedingly, very.—*n* death.—**pass´ing shot**, a stroke (as in tennis) that drives the ball to one side and beyond the reach of an opponent. [**pass**.]

passion [pash´(ȯ)n] *n* the sufferings and death of Christ; a suffering or passive condition, as opposed to action; emotion or agitation of mind, esp rage; ardent love; eager desire; the object of any strong desire.—*adj* **pass´ionate**, easily moved to anger, or other strong feeling; intense; sensual.—*adv* **pass´ionately**.—*ns* **pass´ionateness; pass´ion flow´er**, any of a genus (*Passiflora*) of chiefly tropical climbing vines with usu. showy flowers and often edible berries; **passion fruit**, the edible fruit of a passion flower.—*adj* **pass´ionless**, free from passion, unemotional; calm.—*ns* **Pass´ion play**, a religious drama representing the sufferings and death of Christ; **Pass´ion Sun´day**, the fifth Sunday in Lent; **Pass´ion Week**, Holy Week; the week before Holy Week. [OFr *passiun*—L *passiō, -ōnis*—*pati, passus*, to suffer.]

passive [pas´iv] *adj* unresisting; lethargic; not reacting upon; (*gram*) denoting the voice of a verb whose subject receives the action.—*adv* **pass´ively**.—*ns* **pass´iveness, passiv´ity**.—**pass´ive immunity**, immunity acquired by transfer of antibodies (as by injection of serum from an individual who has active immunity); **pass´ive resis´tance**, opposition to a law, tax, etc. by refusal to comply or by nonviolent acts, as fasting. [L *passīvus*—*pati*, suffer.]

Passover [päs´ō-vėr] *n* (*Judaism*) a spring holiday, celebrating the liberation of the Jews from slavery in Egypt.—Also **Pesach**.

passport [päs´pōrt, -pört] *n* a government document carried by a citizen traveling abroad, certifying identity and citizenship; a document of identification required by law to be carried by persons residing or traveling within a country; something that secures admission or acceptance. [Fr *passeport*; cf **pass, port**.]

past [päst] *pt p* of **pass**.—*adj* bygone; ended; in time already passed.—*prep* farther than; beyond; beyond the possibility of.—*adv* by.—*n* that which has passed, esp time; the history of a person, group, etc.; a personal background that is hidden or questionable.—**past master**, a former holder of office in a Masonic Lodge, club, society, etc.; one who is expert.

pasta [päs´ta] *n* the flour paste of which spaghetti, noodles, etc. is made; any dish of cooked pasta. [It]

paste [pāst] *n* a soft plastic mass; dough for pies, etc. an adhesive made of flour, water, etc.; a fine kind of glass for making artificial gems.—*vt* to fasten with paste.—*n* **paste´board**, a stiff board made of sheets of paper pasted together, etc.—*adj* made of such; sham. [OFr *paste*—LL *pasta*—Gr *pasta*, porridge—*passein*, to sprinkle.]

pastel [pas´tėl] *n* chalk mixed with other materials and colored for crayons; a drawing made with such; a soft, pale, shade of color. [Fr *pastel*—It *pastello*—L *pasta*, paste.]

pastern [pas´tėrn] *n* the part of a horse's foot from the fetlock to the hoof; the corresponding part in an animal not an equine. [OFr *pasturon*—OFr *pasture*, pasture, a tether for a horse.]

Pasteur treatment [pas´tûr] *n* a method of aborting rabies by stimulating production of antibodies through successive inoculations.—*n* **pasteurizā´tion**, a method of destroying harmful organisms in beer, milk, etc., by heating to a prescribed temperature for a prescribed time; a partial sterilization of perishable food products with radiation.—*vt* **pas´teurize**. [Louis *Pasteur*, Fr chemist (1822–95).]

pastiche [pas-tēsh´] *n* a musical or literary composition made up of parts from other compositions; a work in literature or art in direct imitation of another; a jumble. [Fr—LL *pasta*. See **paste**.]

pastille [pas-tēl´] *n* a small cone of charcoal and aromatic substances, burned to perfume; an aromatic or medicated lozenge. [L *pastillus*, dim of *panis*, bread.]

pastime [päs´tīm] *n* that which serves to pass away the time; recreation. [**pass, time**.]

pastor [päs´tȯr] *n* a clergyman in charge of a congregation.—*adj* **pas´toral**, relating to shepherds or to shepherd life; rustic; of or pertaining to spiritual care or guidance, esp of a congregation.—*n* a poem or other composition that professes to depict the life of shepherds; a pastoral letter, esp one from a bishop.—*adv* **pas´torally**.—*ns* **pas´torate**, the office of a pastor; the whole body of pastors.—**Pastoral Epistle**, one of three New Testament letters including two addressed to Timothy and one to Titus that give advice on matters of church government and discipline. [L *pāstor*, a shepherd—*pāscĕre, pāstum*, to feed.]

pastry [pās´tri] *n* dough containing a high proportion of fat; sweet baked goods made of such a dough; all fancy baked goods. [**paste**.]

pasture [päst´chùr] *n* growing grass for grazing; grazing land; the feeding of livestock.—*vt* to put (cattle, etc.) out to graze in a pasture.—*n* **past´ūrage**, pasture. [OFr *pasture*—L *pāstūra*—*pāscĕre, pāstum*, to feed.]

pasty[1] [pās´ti] *adj* like paste, pallid and unhealthy in appearance.

pasty[2] [pas´ti] *n* a meat pie; a turnover. [OFr *pastée* (Fr *pâté*)—LL *pasta*. See **paste**.]

pat [pat] *n* a gentle tap, as with the palm of the hand; a small lump of butter molded by an instrument with flat surface; a light sound.—*vt* to strike gently; to shape or apply by patting.—*pr p* **patt´ing**; *pt p* **patt´ed**.—*adj* exactly to the purpose; ready to be given easily or fluently (eg *he had his answer, the story, pat*).—*adv* aptly; promptly.—**pat on the back**, a mark of approbation; to praise; **stand pat**, to refuse to change an opinion, etc. [Prob imit.]

patch [pach] *n* a piece put on to mend or cover a defect; any similar scrap of material; a plot of ground; a bandage; an area or spot; a small piece of black silk, etc., stuck on the face.—*vt* to mend with a patch; to join in patchwork; (usu. *patch up*) to mend or fashion clumsily or hastily.—*n* **patch´work**, work formed of patches or pieces sewed together; work patched up or clumsily executed.—*adj* **patch´y**, covered with, or consisting of, patches; varying in quality.—*n* **patch´iness**.—*adv* **patch´ily**.—**patch up**, to settle (a quarrel, etc.). [ME, perh conn with **piece**.]

patchouli, patchouly [pach´ŏŏ-lē, pä-chōō´lē] *n* a shrub (*Pogostemon cabuli*) of SE Asia; a perfume made from patchouli oil. [Tamil *pach*, green, *ilai*, leaf.]

pate [pāt] *n* (*humorous*) the head.

pâté [pa-tā] *n* a paste made of blended meat, herbs, etc.—**pâté de fois gras** [dė fwa grä] paste of fat goose liver and truffles. [Fr.]

patella [pa-tel´a] *n* the thick, flat, movable bone at the front of the knee that protects the joint.—*pl* **patell´ae** [-tel´ē], **patell´as**.—Also **kneecap**. [L dim of *patina*, a pan.]

paten [pat´ėn] *n* a plate for bread in the Eucharist. [Fr—L *patina*, a plate—Gr *patanē*.]

patent [pat´ėnt] *adj* [pā´tėnt] lying open; obvious; [pat´ėnt] open to public perusal; protected by patent.—*n* [pat´ėnt] an official document, granting the exclusive right to produce and sell an invention, etc. for a certain time; the right so granted; the thing protected by such a right.—*vt* to secure a patent for.—*adj* **pa´tentable**.—*n* **patentee´**, one who holds a patent.—*adv* **pā´tently**, openly, obviously.—**patent leather**, a leather with a hard, glossy finish; **patent medicine**, a trademarked medical preparation; **patent office**, a government office for examining patents and granting patents. [L *patēns, -entis*, pr p of *patēre*, to lie open.]

paterfamilias [pat´ėr-fa-mil´i-as, pät´-, or pāt-] *n* the male head of a household; the father of a family. [L *păter*, father, *familiās*, old. gen of *familia*, household.]

paternal [pa-tûr´nȧl] *adj* fatherly; showing the disposition of a father; derived from a father.—*adv* **pater´nally**.—*n* **pater´nity**, fatherhood; origin or descent from a father.—**paternity test**, a test to determine whether a given man could be the biological father of a given child. [L *pater* (Gr *patēr*), a father.]

paternoster [pat-ėr-nos´tėr or pä´tėr-nos-tėr] *n* the Lord's Prayer. [L *Pater noster*, Our Father, the first words of the Lord's Prayer in Latin.]

path [päth] *n* a way worn by footsteps; a way for people on foot; a track; course of action or conduct.—*pl* **paths** [päTHZ, paths].—*n* **path´finder**, one that discovers a way; one that explores untraveled regions to mark out a new route.—*n, adj* **path´finding**.—*adj* **path´less**, without a path; untrodden.—*n* **path´way**, a path, a sequence of enzyme-catalyzed reactions. [OE *pæth*; Gr *pfad*.]

pathetic [pȧ-thet´ik] *adj* affecting the tender emotions, touching.—*adv* **pathet´ically**.—**pathetic fallacy**, the tendency to impute human emotions to inanimate nature. [Gr *pathētikos*, subject to suffering.]

pathogenesis [path-ō-jen´ė-sis], **pathogeny** [path-oj´ė-ni] *ns* mode of production or development of disease.—*n* **path´ogen**, an organism (as a bacterium or virus) that causes disease.—*adj* **pathogen´ic**, causing disease. [Gr *pathos*, suffering, *genesis*, production.]

pathology [pa-thol´o-ji] *n* the branch of medicine that deals with the nature of disease, esp its functional and structural effects; any abnormal variation from a sound condition.—*adj* **patholog´ical**.—*adv* **patholog´ically**.—*n* **pathol´ogist**, a medical specialist who interprets and diagnoses the changes caused by disease in tissues and body fluids. [Gr *pathos*, suffering, *logos*, discourse.]

pathos [pā´thos] *n* the quality that excites pity. [Gr.]

patience [pā´shėns] *n* quality of being able calmly to wait or endure.—*adj* **pā´tient**, sustaining pain, etc., without repining; not easily provoked, long-suffering; waiting with calmness; persevering.—*n* a person under medical treatment.—*adv* **pā´tiently**. [Fr—L *patientia—patiens—patī*, to bear.]

patina [pat´in-a] *n* the green incrustation on ancient bronzes, etc. formed by oxidation; a surface appearance of something grown beautiful by age or use; a superficial covering or exterior.—Also *fig*. [L *patina*, a dish.]

patio [pat´i-ō] *n* a courtyard connected with a house, esp an inner court open to the sky; a paved area adjoining a house, for outdoor lounging, dining, etc. [Sp—L *spatium*, space.]

patois [pat´wä] *n* a dialect, esp a local dialect of the lower social strata. [Fr, origin unknown.]

patriarch [pā´tri-ärk] *n* the father and head of a family or a tribe as Abraham, Isaac, or Jacob in the Bible; a man of great age and dignity; a high-ranking bishop, as in the Orthodox Eastern Church.—*adj* **pātriarch´al**, pertaining to, or subject to, a patriarch.—*ns* **pā´triarchate**, the office, jurisdiction, or residence of a church patriarch; **pā´triarchy**, a social organization in which the father is the head of a family, descent being traced through the male line; ruled or dominated by men. [Gr *patriarchēs—patriā*, family—*patēr*, father, *archē*, rule.]

patrician [pä-trish´ȧn] *n* a member or descendant of one of the original families of citizens forming the Roman people; an aristocrat; a person of breeding and cultivation.—Also *adj*. [L *patricius—pater, patris*, a father.]

patricide [pat´ri-sīd] *n* the murder of one's own father; one who murders his father. [L *patricīda—pater, patris*, father, *caedĕre*, to kill.]

patrimony [pat´ri-mȯn-i] *n* an inheritance from a father or from ancestors; a church estate or revenue.—*adj* **patrimō´nial**.—*adv* **patrimō´nially**. [L *patrimōnium*, a paternal estate—*pater, patris*, a father.]

patriot [pā´tri-ot] *n* one who truly loves and serves his country.—*adj* devoted to one's country.—*adj* **patriotic** [pāt-riot´ik] like a patriot; actuated by a love of one's country; directed to the public welfare.—*adv* **patriot´ically**.—*n* **pa´triotism**. [Gr *patriōtēs*, fellow-countryman—*patrios—patēr*, a father.]

patristic, -al [pa-tris´tik, -ȧl] *adj* pertaining to the fathers of the Christian Church or their writings. [Gr *patēr*, a father.]

patrol [pa-trōl] *vti* to go the rounds of (eg a camp, town), perambulate (streets), in order to watch, protect, inspect.—*pr p* **patroll´ing**; *pt, pt p*, **patrolled´**.—*n* the act or service of going the rounds of an area; a unit of persons or vehicles employed for reconnaissance, security, or combat; a subdivision of a Boy Scout or Girl Scout troop.—*n* **patrol´man**, a police man who patrols a certain area.—**patrol wagon**, an enclosed truck used by police to carry prisoners.—Also **Black Maria, paddy wagon**. [OFr *patrouille*, a patrol, *patrouiller*, to patrol, orig to paddle in the mud.]

patron [pā´trȯn] a protector; one who countenances or encourages; customer; one who sponsors and supports some activity, person, etc.—*n* **pat´ronage**, the support given by a patron; clientele; business; trade; the power to grant political favors; such favors.—*vt* **păt´ronize**, to act as a patron toward; to assume the air of a patron toward; to treat condescendingly; to countenance, encourage; to give one's custom to, or to frequent habitually.—*adj* **patronī´zing**, who or that patronises, esp with condescension.—*adv* **pat´ronīzingly**.—**patron saint**, a saint chosen as a protector. [Fr—L *patrōnus—pater, patris*, a father.]

patronymic [pat-rō-nim´ik] *adj* derived from the name of a father or an ancestor.—*n* a name showing descent from a given person. [Gr *patrōnymikos—patēr*, a father, *onoma*, a name.]

patten [pat´n] *n* a clog, sandal, or overshoe with a wooden sole or a metal device to elevate the foot and increase the wearer's height or aid in walking in mud. [OFr *patin*, clog.]

patter[1] [pat´ėr] *vi* to strike against something with quick successive pats or taps; to run with light steps.—*n* the sound so produced. [Freq of **pat**.]

patter[2] [pat´ėr] *vi* to mumble; to talk rapidly.—*vt* to repeat hurriedly, to gabble.—*n* glib talk, chatter; the cant of criminals; words in a song sung or spoken very rapidly. [**paternoster**.]

pattern [pat´ėrn] *n* a person or thing to be copied; a model; a design or guide with the help of which something is to be made; an example of excellence; a sample; a decorative design; a regular way of acting or doing; a predictable route, movement, etc.—*vt* to make or do in imitation of a pattern. [Fr *patron*, patron, pattern; cf **patron**.]

patty [pat´i] *n* a little pie; a small flat cake of ground meat, fish, etc. usu. fried.—*pl* **patt´ies**.—**patty shell**, a pastry shell for a single portion of creamed food, etc. [Fr *pâté*; cf **pasty**, a pie.]

paucity [pö´sit-i] *n* fewness; smallness of number or quantity; scarcity. [L *paucitās, -ātis—paucus*, few.]

Pauline [pö´līn] *adj* of or belonging to the Apostle Paul.

paunch [pön(t)sh] *n* the belly and its contents; the first and largest stomach of a ruminant; a potbelly. [OFr *panche*—L *pantex, panticis*.]

pauper [pö´pėr] *n* a destitute person, esp one supported by charity or by some public provision.—*n* **pau´perism**, state of being a pauper.—*vt* **pau´perize**, to reduce to pauperism.—*n* **pauperisā´tion**. [L.]

pause [pöz] *n* a temporary ceasing, stop; cessation caused by doubt, hesitation; a mark for suspending the voice; (*mus*) continuance of a note or rest.—*vi* to make a pause. [Fr—L *pausa*—Gr *pausis—pauein*, to cause to cease.]

pavane, pavan [pav´an or -an´] *n* a slow stately dance; the music for it. [Fr *pavane*, peacock, from It or Sp.]

pave [pāv] *vt* to cover with concrete, etc., so as to form a level surface for travel.—*ns* **pave´ment**, a paved surface; that with which it is paved; **pa´ving**, pavement.—**pave the way**, to prepare a smooth easy way; to facilitate development. [Fr *paver*—L *pavīmentum—pavīre*, to beat hard; cog with Gr *paiein*, to beat.]

pavilion [pä-vil´yȯn] *n* a large and luxurious tent; an ornamental building often turreted or domed, as at a fair or park, for exhibitions; any of a group of related buildings.—*vt* to furnish with pavilions; to put in a pavilion. [Fr *pavillon*—L *pāpiliō, -ōnis*, a butterfly, a tent.]

paw [pö] *n* a foot with claws; (*inf*) a human hand.—*vti* to touch, dig, hit, etc. with paws; to handle clumsily or roughly. [OFr *poe, powe*, prob Gmc; cf Du *poot*, Ger *pfote*.]

pawl [pöl] *n* a catch falling into the notches of a toothed wheel, as on a windlass, etc., to prevent it from running back. [Origin obscure.]

pawn[1] [pön] *n* something deposited as a pledge for repayment or performance; state of being pledged.—*vt* to give in pledge; to wager or risk.—*ns* **pawn´broker**, a person licensed to lend money at interest on personal property left with him as security; **pawn´er**, one who gives a pawn or pledge as security for money borrowed. [OFr *pan*; cf Du *pand*.]

pawn[2] [pön] *n* a small piece in chess of lowest rank and range; a person used to advance another's purpose. [OFr *paon*, a foot-soldier—LL *pedō, -ōnis*, a walker—L *pēs, pedis*, the foot.]

Pawnee [pö-nē] *n* member of a Siouan-speaking Amerindian people originally of Kansas and Nebraska, now of Oklahoma.—*pl* **Pawnee, Pawnees**.

pax [paks] *n* the kiss of peace in the Mass; a tablet used in giving the kiss of peace at celebration of Mass. [L, peace.]

pay [pā] *vt* to discharge, as a debt, duty; to requite with what is due or deserved; to reward; to punish; to give, render (eg homage, attention); to be profitable to.—*vi* to hand over money or other equivalent; to yield a profit; be punished (for).—*pt, pt p* **paid**.—*n* money given for service; salary, wages.—*adj* **pay´able**, that may or should be paid on a specified date.—*ns* **pay´check**, a check in payment of wages or salary; **pay´day**, the day on which wages or salary is paid; **payee´**, one to whom money is paid; **pay´er**.—*adj* **pay´ing**, remunerative.—*ns* **payload**, a cargo; the part of an airplane's load for which revenue is obtained; the part of a rocket's equipment that is to fulfil the purpose of the rocket, as a warhead; **pay´master**, one in charge of paying employees; **pay´ment**, the act of paying; that which is paid; recompense, reward; **pay´off**, payment of what one has earned; (*inf*) a bribe; (*inf*) an unexpected climax; **pay phone, pay station**, a public, usu. coin-operated telephone; **payō´la**, a secret payment to secure a favor; **payroll**, list of employees to be paid, with amounts due to them; the money for paying wages.—**pay off**, to discharge; to take revenge upon; to requite; to yield good results; **pay out**, to let out (a rope, cable, etc.) (*pt* **payed**); **pay up**, to pay in full or on time. [Fr *payer*—L *pācāre*, to appease; cf **pax, pācis**, peace.]

pea [pē] *n* the variable seed of a climbing leguminous annual plant (*Pisum satirum*) used widely as a vegetable; the plant.—*ns* **pea´shoot´er**, a small tube for blowing peas through; **pea´ soup**, a thick purée made of dried peas; a thick fog. [See **pease**.]

peace [pēs] *n* a state of quiet; freedom from contention, disturbance, or war; a treaty that ends a war; ease (of mind or conscience); silence.—*interj* silence! be silent!—*adj* **peace´able**, disposed to peace; peaceful.—*n* **peace´ableness**.—*adv* **peace´ably**.—*adj* **peace´ful**, full of peace; tranquil; tending towards peace; inclined to peace.—*adv* **peace´fully**.—*ns* **peace corps**, a body of trained persons sent as volunteers, esp to assist underdeveloped nations; **peace´fulness; peace´maker**, one who makes or produces peace; one who reconciles enemies; **peace´offering**, a gift or service for procuring peace or reconciliation; **peace´pipe**, the calumet. [OFr *pais*—L *pax, pācis*, peace.]

peach[1] [pēch] *vi* to give information against an accomplice. [ME *apeche*; cf **impeach**.]

peach[2] [pēch] *n* a sweet, juicy, velvety-skinned stone fruit; the tree (*Prunus persica*) bearing it; (*slang* a well-liked person or thing; a color averaging a yellowish pink.—*adj* **peach´y**. [OFr *pesche*—L *Persicum* (*mālum*), the Persian (apple).]

peacock [pē´kok] *n* the male of a genus (*Pavo*) of large terrestial pheasants, **peafowl**, noted for gay plumage, esp the tail feathers; a man who is a show-off.—*ns* **pea´hen**, a female peafowl; **Pea´cock Throne**, the former throne of the kings of Delhi; formerly the Persian throne. [OE *pēa* (*pawa*)—L *pāvō* + **cock** (1).]

pea jacket [pē´-jak´ėt] *n* a coarse thick jacket worn esp by seamen.—Also **peacoat**. [Du *pîe* (now *pij*), a coat of coarse stuff, and **jacket**.]

peak[1] [pēk] *n* a point; the pointed end of anything; the top of a mountain, a summit; maximum value; the projecting front of a cap; (*naut*) the upper outer corner of a sail extended by a gaff or yard; the upper end of a gaff.—*vti* to reach or cause to reach the height of one's power, popularity, etc.; of prices, etc. to reach, and remain at, the highest level.—*adj* **peaked**, pointed. [App connected with **pike**.]

peak[2] [pēk] *vi* to grow thin or sickly.—*adj* **peaked**, having a pinched or sickly look. [Origin unknown.]

peal [pēl] *n* a loud sound as of thunder, laughter, etc.; a set of bells tuned to each other; the changes rung upon a set of bells.—*vti* to give forth in peals. [Prob short for **appeal** (perh through the idea of a summons).]

peanut [pē´nut] *n* a leguminous annual herb (*Arachis hypogaea*) with underground pods containing edible seeds; the pod or any of its seeds; (*pl*) (*slang*) a trifling sum.—*n* **peanut butter**, a food paste made by grinding roasted peanuts. [**pea, nut**.]

pear [pār] *n* a common fruit tapering towards the stalk and bulged at the end; the genus (*Pyrus*) of trees on which it grows, of the rose family. [OE *perer, peru*—L *pirum*, pear.]

pearl [pûrl] *n* a concretion of nacre found in an oyster or other mollusks, prized as a gem; mother-of-pearl; anything resembling a pearl intrinsically or physically; one that is choice and precious; a bluish medium gray.—*adj* made of, or belonging to, pearls; having medium size grains.—*vt* to set or adorn with pearls; to make into small round grains.—*vi* to fish or dive for pearls; to form into pearls.—*ns* **Pearl Harbor**, a sneak attack with devastating effect; **pearl onion**, a very small usu. pickled onion.—*adj* **pearl´y**, like pearl; rich in pearls.—*n* **pearl´iness**. [Fr *perle*, prob either from L *pirula*, a dim of *pirum*, a pear, or from L *pilula*, dim of *pila*, a ball.]

peasant [pez´ȧnt] *n* a small farmer or farm laborer, as in Europe or Asia; a person regarded as boorish, ignorant, etc.—*n* **peas´antry**, the body of peasants. [OFr *paisant* (Fr *paysan*)—*pays*—L *pāgus*, a district.]

pease [pēz] *n* (*obs*) a pea; peas collectively.—*ns* **pease´cod, peas´cod**, the pod of the pea. [ME *pēse*, pl *pēsen*—OE *pise*, pl *pisan*—L *pisum*—Gr *pison*.]

peat [pēt] *n* a shaped block dug from a bog and dried for fuel; the decayed vegetable matter from which such blocks are cut.—*n* **peat´ moss**, peat composed of residues of mosses (esp of the genus *Sphagnum*), used as a mulch.—*adj* **peat´y**, like peat; abounding in, or composed of, peat. [Anglo-Latin *peta*, a peat; possibly of British origin.]

pebble [peb´l] *n* a small roundish stone, esp waterworn; transparent and colorless quartz; rock crystal; an irregular, grainy surface.—*adjs* **pebb´led, pebb´ly**, full of pebbles. [OE *papol* (*-stān*), a pebble.]

pecan [pi-kan´] *n* a large hickory (*Carya illinoensis*) widely grown in the warmer parts of the US and Mexico for its edible nuts; its wood; the smooth, oblong thin-shelled nut. [Indian name.]

pecadillo [pek-ä-dil´ō] *n* a trifling fault.—*pl* **peccadill´os** (or **peccadill´oes**). [Sp *pecadillo*, dim of *pecado*—L *peccātum*, a sin.]

peccary [pek´ȧr-i] *n* either of two gregarious largely nocturnal American mammals (*Pecari tajacu*, the collared peccary, and *Tayassus pecari*; the white-lipped peccary) of warm regions. [Carib *pakira*.]

peck[1] [pek] *n* a measure of capacity for dry goods equal to 8 quarts or ¼ bushel; a large quantity or number. [ME *pekke, pek*—OFr *pek*, generally a horse's feed of oats.]

peck[2] [pek] *vt* to strike or pick up with the beak; to eat sparingly; to strike with anything pointed; to strike with repeated blows.—*n* a stroke so made; (*inf*) a quick, casual kiss.—*n* **peck´er**, that which pecks—**pecking order, peck order**, the basic pattern of social organization in a flock of poultry in which each bird pecks another lower in the scale without fear of retaliation and submits to pecking by one of higher rank; a social hierarchy. [App a form of **pick**.]

pectin [pek´tin] *n* any of certain carbohydrates found in the cell walls of fruits and vegetables yielding a gel that is the basis of jellies; a commercial product rich in pectin. [Gr *pēktos*, fixed, congealed.]

pectoral [pek´to-rȧl] *adj* relating to the breast or chest.—*n* something worn on the breast.—*adv* **pec´torally**.—**pectoral fin**, the anterior paired fins of fishes (corresponding to the forelimbs of an animal); **pectoral girdle**, the bony arch that supports the forelimbs of a vertebrate. [L *pectorālis*—*pectus, pectoris*, the breast.]

peculate [pek´ū-lāt] *vti* to appropriate dishonestly, to embezzle.—*ns* **peculā´tion; pec´ulātor**. [L *peculāri, -ātus*—*pecūlium*, private property, akin to *pecūnia*, money.]

peculiar [pi-kūl´yȧr] *adj* of one's own; belonging exclusively (to); characteristic; particular, special; strange.—*n* **peculiarity**, [pi-kū-li-ar´i-ti], that which is found in one and in no other; a characteristic; oddity.—*adv* **pecul´iarly**. [L *pecūlium*, private property.]

pecuniary [pi-kūn´i-ȧr-i] *adj* relating to money; consisting of money.—*adv* **pecū´niarily**. [L *pecūnia*, money, from the root that appears in L *pecudes* (pl), cattle.]

ped [pēd-] in composition, child, boy.—*adj* **pediat´ric**, [Gr *iātrikos*, medical], relating to the medical treatment of children.—*ns* **pediatrics**, the branch of medicine dealing with the treatment of children's diseases; **pediatric´ian**. [Gr *pais, paidos*, boy, child.]

pedagogue, pedagog [ped´ȧ-gog] *n* a teacher esp a pedantic one.—*adjs* **pedagog´ical, pedagogic**, [-goj´-] relating to teaching.—*ns* **pedagogics**, [-goj´iks], **pedagogy**, [-goj´i] the art or science of teaching. [Gr *paidagōgos*, a slave who led a boy to school—*pais*, gen *paidos*, a boy, *agōgos*, leader—*agein*, to lead.]

pedal [ped´ȧl] *adj* pertaining to the foot.—*n* a lever pressed by the foot.—*vt* to drive by pedals;—*pr p* **ped´aling**; *pt, pt p* **ped´aled**. [L *pedālis*—*pēs, pedis*, the foot.]

pedant [ped´ȧnt] *n* one who makes a vain and pretentious show of learning; one who attaches too much importance to minute details or to formal rules in scholarship.—*adjs* **pedant´ic**, of the character, or in the manner, of a pedant; a pedantic expression; unnecessarily rigorous formality. [It *pedante* (perh through Fr *pédant*); connection with **pedagogue**, not clear.]

peddle [ped´l] *vti* to go from place to place selling (small articles).—*n* **pedd´ler**, one who offers merchandise (as fresh produce for sale from door to door; one who deals in an intangible (as a personal asset or idea). [Perh **pedlar**.]

pederast [ped´ėr-ėst] *n* a man who has homosexual relations with boys.—*n* **ped´erasty**. [Gr *paiderastēs*, lover of boys.]

pedestal [ped´ės-tȧl] *n* the support of a column, statue, vase, etc. [Fr *piédestal*—It *piedistallo*—*piè* (L *pēs, pedis*), foot, *di* (L *dē*), of, *stallo*, stall.]

pedestrian [pi-des´tri-ȧn] *adj* on foot; of walking on foot; prosaic, commonplace.—*n* one who walks.—*n* **pedes´trianism**, walking or fondness for walking; the quality of being pedestrian. [L *pedester, -tris*—*pēs, pedis*, foot.]

pedicel [ped´i-sel] *n* the stalk of a plant supporting a fruiting or spore-bearing organ; a narrow basal attachment of an animal organ or part. [Botanists' L *pedīcellus*, dim of *pēs, pedis*, the foot.]

pediculosis [pi-dik-ū-lō´sis] *n* infestation with lice.—*adjs* **pedic´ulous**, lousy. [L *pedīculus*, dim of *pedis*, louse.]

pedicure [ped´i-kūr] *n* a chiropodist; cosmetic care of the feet, toes, and nails; a single treatment of these parts. [L *pēs, pedis*, foot, *cūra*, care.]

pedigree [ped´igrē] *n* a line of ancestors; a scheme or record of ancestry, a genealogy; lineage; distinguished or ancient lineage; succession, series, set, the recorded purity of breed of an individual, esp domestic animals.—*adj* of known descent, purebred and of good stock.—*adj* **ped´igreed**, having a pedigree. [App Fr *pied de grue*, crane's-foot, from the arrow-head figure used in depicting pedigrees.]

pediment [ped´i-mėnt] *n* (*archit*) a triangular structure crowning the front of a building; a similar structure, triangular or rounded, over a portico, etc.—*adj* **pediment´al**. [Earlier *periment*, prob for **pyramid**.]

pedlar [ped´lȧr] *n* (*Brit*) a peddler. [Ety uncertain; occurs earlier than **peddle**.]

pedometer [pi-dom´ėt-ėr] *n* an instrument for counting paces and so measuring distance walked. [L *pēs, pedis*, a foot, Gr *metron*, a measure.]

peduncle [pi-dung´kl] *n* a stalklike organ or process in some plants, animals, etc.—*adjs* **pedun´cular, pedun´culated, pedun´culate**. [Low L *pedunculus*—L *pēs, pedis*, the foot.]

peek [pēk] *vi* to look quickly or furtively.—*n* such a look. [ME *piken*.]

peel[1] [pēl] *vt* to strip off the skin or bark from; to bare.—*vi* to come off, as the skin.—*n* rind, esp that of oranges, lemons, etc.—*n* **peel´ing**, a peeled-off strip. [OE *pilian*—L *pilāre*, to deprive of hair—*pilus*, a hair; perh influenced by Fr *peler*, to skin.]

peel[2] [pēl] *n* a palisaded enclosure in medieval times along the Scottish-English border. [Anglo-Fr *pel*—L *pālus*, stake.]

peel[3] [pēl] *n* a shovel, esp a baker's wooden shovel. [OFr *pele*—L *pāla*, a spade.]

peep[1] [pēp] *vi* to cheep as a young bird.—*n* a peeping sound.—*n* **peep´er**, any of various tailless amphibious (esp *Hyla crucifer*) that peep in a shrill manner. [Imit]

peep[2] [pēp] *vi* to look through a narrow opening; to look stealthily or cautiously; (to begin) to appear; to be just showing.—*n* a sly look; a glimpse.—*ns* **peep´er**, one that peeps; **peep´hole**, a hole to peep through; **peep´ show**, a show viewed through a small hole, usually fitted with a magnifying glass.—**Peeping Tom**, one who gets sexual pleasure from furtively watching others. [Origin obscure.]

peer[1] [pēr] *n* an equal in rank, ability, etc.; a British nobleman.—*n* **peer´ess**, the wife or widow of a peer; a woman who holds the rank of a peer in her own right.—*n* **peer´age**, the rank or dignity of a peer; the body of peers; a book of the genealogy, etc., of the different peers.—*adj* **peer´less**, unequalled, matchless.—*adv* **peer´lessly**. [OFr (Fr *pair*)—L *pār, paris*, equal.]

peer[2] [pēr] *vi* to look narrowly or closely; to look with strain; to peep out, appear.

peevish [pēv´ish] *adj* fretful, querulous.—*adv* **peev´ishly**.—*n* **peev´ishness**.

peewit [pē´wit, pū´it] *n* the lapwing, so named for its cry. [Imit]

peg [peg] *n* a tapered piece (of wood) for hanging up or fastening things, or for marking a position; a predetermined level at which something (as a price) is fixed; something (as a fact or opinion) used as a support, pretext, or reason; one of the movable pegs for tuning the string of a musical instrument.—*vt* to fasten, mark, score, etc. with a peg.—*vi* to work assiduously;—*pr p* **pegg´ing**; *pt, pt p* **pegged**.—*n* **peg´board**, a board having holes into which pegs are placed, used for playing and scoring in games; **Pegboard**, trade name for a system of displaying or storing articles on a perforated board.—*adj* **pegged**, fashioned of, or furnished with pegs; of trousers or skirts, wide at the top and narrow at the bottom.—*ns* **peg´ leg**, a simple wooden leg; **peg´ top**, a top, with a metal point, spun by winding a string round it.—**off the peg**, ready-made; **take down a peg**, to humble. [Cf L Ger *pigge*; Du dial *peg*; Dan *pig*.]

peignoir [pen-wär] *n* a loose negligee or dressing gown worn by women. [Fr,—*peigner*—L *pectināre*, to comb.]

pejorative [pi-jor´a-tiv or pē´jor-] *adj* depreciatory, disparaging.—Also *n* [L *pējor*, worse.]

Pekingese, Pekinese [pē´kin-ez´] *n* the Chinese dialect of Peking; native or resident of Peking; a breed of small dog with long, silky hair, short legs, and a pug nose.—**Peking duck**, a Chinese dish consisting of crispy duck skin and roast duck meat enclosed in a thin pancake; **Peking man**, an extinct Pleistocene man now classified with the pithecan-thropines. [*Peking*, China.]

pekoe [pek´ō, pē´kō] *n* a tea made from the two youngest leaves and the end bud of the shoot. [Chinese.]

pelargonium [pel-är-gō´ni-um] *n* a genus (*Pelargonium*) of southern African flowering plants of the geranium family, including the plants grown in greenhouses and gardens and there known as '*geraniums*'. [Gr *pelārgos*, stork, the beaked capsules resembling a stork's head.]

pelecypod [pel-ėsipō-d] *n* lamelli-branch. [Formed from Gr *pelekys*, hatchet, and *poda—pous*, gen *podos*, foot.]

pelf [pelf] *n* money or wealth regarded with contempt. [OFr *pelfre*, booty; cf **pilfer**.]

pelican [pel´i-kȧn] *n* any of a genus (*Pelecanus*) of large waterbirds with an enormous pouched bill. [Low L *pelicānus*—Gr *pelekan, -ānos*, pelican; cf *pelekās, -āntos*, a woodpecker, and *pelekys*, an axe.]

pelisse [pe-lēs´] *n* a long cloak or coat made of fur or trimmed or lined with fur; a woman's loose lightweight cloak with wide collar and fur trimming. [Fr,—Low L *pellicea(vestis)*—L *pellis*, a skin.]

pellagra [pel-ag´rä or -äg´-] *n* a deficiency disease caused by lack of nicotinic acid in the diet, marked by skin eruptions and nervous disorders. [Gr *pella*, skin, *agrā*, seizure; or It *pella agra*, rough skin.]

pellet [pel´ėt] *n* a little ball; a small pill; a ball of shot. [OFr *pelote*—L *pīla*, a ball.]

pellicle [pel´i-kl] *n* a thin skin, membrane, or film.—*adj* **pellic´ūlar**. [L *pellicula*, dim of *pellis*, skin.]

pell-mell [pel´-mel´] *adv* confusedly; headlong, helterskelter.—*adj* disorderly; headlong. [OFr *pesle-mesle, -mesle* being from OFr *mesler*, to mix—Low L *mis-culāre*—L *miscēre*; and *pesle*, a rhyming addition, perh influenced by Fr *pelle*, shovel.]

pellucid [pe-l(y)ōō´sid] *adj* perfectly clear; transparent—*adv* **pellū´cidly**. [Fr,—L *pellūcidus—per*, through, *lūcidus*, clear—*lūcēre*, to shine.]

pelota [pel-ō´tä] *n* a court game related to jai alai; the ball used in jai alai. [Sp, a ball.]

pelt[1] [pelt] *n* a usu. undressed skin with its hair, wool, or fur; a stripped skin for tanning. **pelt´ry**, (often *pl*) raw, undressed skins. [App a back formation from *peltry*—OFr *pelleterie—pelletier*, a skinner—L *pellis*, a skin.]

pelt[2] [pelt] *vt* to assail with blows, missiles, or words.—*vi* to fall heavily, as rain; to speed.—*n* a blow; a downpour; a rapid pace.

pelvis [pel´vis] *n* the bony cavity forming the lower part of the abdomen; the bones forming this.—*pl* **pel´vises, pel´ves** [pel´vēz].—*adj* **pel´vic**. [L *pelvis*, a basin.]

pemmican, pemican [pem´i-kȧn] *n* a N American Indian preparation, consisting of lean meat, dried, pounded, and mixed with other ingredients; a concentrated food of dried beef, suet, dried fruit, etc. [Indian word.]

pen[1] [pen] *n* a small enclosure, esp for animals; a small place of confinement; a dock for reconditioning submarines.—*vt* to put or keep in a pen; to confine within a small space;—*pr p* **penn´ing**; *pt, pt p* **penned** or **pent**. [OE *penn*, pen.]

pen[2] [pen] *n* an instrument used for writing or drawing with ink or a similar fluid; a pen regarded as an instrument of expression; the horny internal shell of a squid.—*vt* to write;—*pr p* **penn´ing**; *pt, pt p* **penned**.—*ns* **pen´hold´er**, a rod on which a pen point may be fixed; **pen´knife**, a small pocketknife usu. with only one blade; **pen´man**, one skilled in the use of the pen; an author; **pen´manship**, handwriting as an art or skill; **pen´ name**, a name assumed by an author; **pen pal**, a friend made and kept through exchanging letters. [OFr *penne*—L *penna*, a feather.]

penal [pē´nȧl] *adj* pertaining to, liable to, imposing, constituting, used for, punishment; constituting a penalty; very severe.—*vt* **pē´nalize**, to make punishable; to put under a disadvantage.—*adv* **pē´nally**.—**penal code**, a code of laws concerning crimes and offenses and their punishment. [L *poenālis—poena*—Gr *poinē*, punishment.]

penalty [pen´ȧl-ti] *n* a punishment; suffering or loss imposed for a fault or breach of a law; a fine.—**penalty kick**, in soccer, a free kick awarded because a player on the opposite side has broken a rule. [LL *pownālitās, -ātis—poena*. See **penal**.]

penance [pen´ȧns] *n* a penalty voluntarily undertaken; a sacramental rite practiced in Roman, Eastern, and some Anglican churches consisting of private confession, absolution, and a penance directed by the confessor.—Also *fig*. [OFr Same root as **penitence**.]

Penates [pe-nā´tēz] *n pl* the household gods of a Roman family. See **lares**. [L, prob from root *pen-* in L *penes*, in the house of, etc.]

pence [pens] *n* (*Brit*) plural of **penny**.

penchant [pā-shā] *n* inclination, decided taste (for). [Fr, pr p of *pencher*, to incline—LL *pendicāre*—L *pendēre*, to hang.]

pencil [pen´sl] *n* a pointed rod-shaped instrument with a core of graphite or crayon for writing, drawing, etc.; any small stick of similar shape; a collection of rays of light, or of lines, converging to a point; (*rare*) the art or style of a painter.—*vt* to write, sketch, or mark with a pencil; to paint or draw;—*pr p* **pen´ciling, pen´cilling**; *pt, pt p* **pen´ciled, pen´cilled**.—*adj* **pen´cilled**, written or marked with a pencil; marked with fine lines, delicately marked.—*n* **pen´cilling**. [OFr *pincel*—L *pēnicillum*, a painter's brush, dim of *pēnis*, a tail.]

pendant, pendent [pen´dȧnt] *n* anything hanging, esp for ornament; anything attached to another thing of the same kind; an appendix; a companion picture, poem, etc.—*n* **pen´dency**, undecided state.—*adj* **pen´dent, pen´dant**, hanging; overhanging; not yet decided.—*adv* **pen´dently**. [Fr *pendant*, pr p of *pendre*, to hang—L *pendens, -entis*—pr p of *pendēre*, to hang.]

pending [pen´ding] *adj* impending; undecided.—*prep* during; until, awaiting. [Fr *pendre* or L *pendēre*, to hang.]

pendulum [pen´dū-lum] *n* any weight so hung from a fixed point as to swing freely; the swinging weight which regulates the movement of a clock; anything that swings or is free to swing to and fro.—*adj* **pen´dulous**, hanging loosely; swinging freely.—*adv* **pen´dulously**. [L neut of *pendulus*, hanging—*pendēre*, to hang.]

penetrate [pen´ė-trāt] *vti* to thrust or force a way into the inside of; to pierce into or through; to reach the mind or feelings of; to see into, or through, understand.—*adj* **pen´etrable**.—*n* **penetrabil´ity**.—*adj* **pen´etrating**, piercing; sharp; discerning.—*n* **penetrā´tion**, the act or power of penetrating; acuteness; discernment.—*adj* **pen´etrātive**, tending or able to penetrate; piercing; having keen or deep insight; reaching and affecting the mind. [L *penetrāre, -ātum—penes*, in the house, possession, or power of.]

penguin [peng´gwin, or pen´-] *n* any of a family (Spheniscidae) of seabirds of the southern hemisphere, unable to fly. [Ety uncertain.]

penicillin [pen-i-sil´in] *n* an antiobotic produced synthetically or from molds; (*Penicillium*, esp *notatum* or *P. chrysogenum*). [L *pēnicillus*, dim of *pēnis*, a tail.]

peninsula [pen-in´sū-lä] *n* a piece of land that is almost an island.—*adj* **penin´sular**, pertaining to a peninsula; in the form of a peninsula; inhabiting a peninsula. [L,—*paene*, almost, *insula*, an island.]

penis [pē´nis] *n* the external male organ. [L, orig a tail.]

penitent [pen´i-tėnt] *adj* sorry for sin, contrite, repentant.—*n* one who sorrows for sin; one under penance.—*n* **pen´itence**.—*adv* **pen´itently**.—*adj* **penitential** [-ten´shȧl], of the nature of, pertaining to, or expressive of, penitence.—*adv* **peniten´tially**.—*adj* **penitentiary** [-ten´shȧr-i], relating to penance; penitential.—*n* a penitent; **Penitentiary**, an office at Rome dealing with cases of penance; a state or federal prison in the US. [L *paenitēns, -entis*, pr p of *paenitēre*, to cause to repent.]

penknife, penman *See* **pen**.

pennant [pen´ȧnt] *n* a long narrow flag; such a flag symbolizing a championship. [A combination of **pendant** and **pennon**.]

pennon [pen´ȯn] *n* a medieval streamer attached to a lance; a long narrow flag; a wing; a pinion. [O Fr *penon*, a streamer, prob—L*penna*, feather.]

penny [pen´i] *n* a coin of the United Kingdom (orig silver, later copper, then, 1860, bronze) formerly 1/240 of £1 (abbrev *d*—L *denārius*), now (**new penny**) 1/100 of £1 (abbrev *p*); a small sum; (in *pl*) money in general.—*pl* **pennies** [pen´iz] as material objects, **pence** [pens] as units of value; a US or Canadian cent.—*adj* sold for a penny.—*adj* **penn´iless**, without a penny; without money; poor.—*n* **penny ante**, poker played for very low stakes.—*adj* two bit; small time.—*ns* **penny cress**, a Eurasian herb (*Thlaspi arvense*) with round or heart-shaped leaves that is widely naturalized in temperate N America; **penny dreadful**, a novel of violent adventure or crime; **penn´yweight**, a unit of weight, equal to 1/20 ounce troy weight.—*adj* **penny-wise**, intent on petty economies; **penn´yworth**, a penny's worth; value for money.—**a pretty penny**, a considerable sum of money. [OE *penig*, oldest form *pending*; cf Ger *pfenning* or *pfennig*; Du *penning*.]

pennyroyal [pen-i-roi´ȧl] *n* a European perennial mint (*Mentha pulegium*) with tiny aromatic leaves; an aromatic American mint (*Hedeoma pulegioides*) with blue flowers yielding an oil used in folk medicine or as a mosquito repellent. [ME *puliol real*—Anglo-Fr,—L *pūlēium*, pennyroyal, and *rēgālis*, royal.]

Penobscot [pė-nob´skot] *n* member of an Algonquian-speaking Amerindian people of Maine, member of the Abnaki confederacy;—*pl* **Penobscot, Penobscots**.

pension [pen´shȯn] *n* a stated allowance to a person for past services; an allowance to one who has retired or has been disabled or reached old age, or who has been widowed, orphaned, etc.—*vt* to grant a pension to; to dismiss or retire from service with a pension.—*adjs* **pen´ionable**, entitled, or entitling, to a pension; **pen´sionary**, receiving a pension; of the nature of a pension;—*n* one who receives a pension.—*n* **pen´sioner**, one who receives a pension; a dependent, a hireling. [Fr,—L *pēnsiō, -ōnis—pendĕre, pensum*, to weigh, pay.]

pensive [pen´siv] *adj* meditative; expressing thoughtfulness with sadness.—*adv* **pen´sively**.—*n* **pen´siveness**. [Fr *pensif, -ive—penser*, to think—L *pēnsāre*, to weigh—*pendĕre*, to weigh.]

penstock [pen´stok] *n* a sluice. [**pen** (1), **stock** (1).]

pent *pt, pt p* of **pen**, to shut up.

pentagon [pen´tȧ-gon] *n* (*geom*) a rectilineal plane figure having five angles and five sides; **Pentagon**, the US military leadership.—*adj* **pentagonal** [pen-tag´ȯn-ȧl]. [Gr *pentagōnon—pente* five, *gōniā*, angle.]

pentagram [pen´tä-gram] *n* a five-pointed star. [Gr *pente*, five, *gramma*, a letter.]

pentameter [pen-tam´ė-tėr] *n* a verse (line) of five measures or feet.—*adj* having five metrical feet. [Gr *pentametros—pente*, five, *metron*, a measure.]

Pentateuch [pen´tȧ-tūk] *n* the first five books of the Old Testament.—*adj* **pen´tateuchal**. [Gr *pente*, five, *teuchos*, tool, (later) book.]

pentathlon [pen-tath´lon] *n* an athletic contest involving participation by each contestant in five different events; a contest in wrestling, discus throwing, spear throwing, leaping, running, held in ancient Greece; a five-event contest at modern Olympic Games, 1906–1924; a five-event Olympic games contest for women; (**modern pentathlon**) an Olympic games contest consisting of swimming, cross-country riding and running, fencing, and revolver shooting.—*n* **pentath´lete´**, an athlete participating in a pentathlon. [Gr *pente*, five, *athlon*, contest.]

pentatonic scale [pen-tȧ-tön´ik] *n* a five-tone scale, specifically one like a major scale omitting the fourth and seven tones.

Pentecost [pent´ė-kost] *n* shabuoth; a Christian festival on the seventh Sunday after Easter commemorating the descent of the Holy Spirit on the apostles. Whit Sunday.—*adj* **Pentacostal**, denoting a mainly Protestant Christian movement, now with various organized forms, emphasizing the immediate presence of God in the Holy Spirit; of Pentocost or the influence of the Holy Ghost.—*n* a member of a Pentacostal Church.—*adj, n* **Pentecost´alist**. [Gr *pentēkostē* (*hēmerā*), the fiftieth (day).]

penthouse [pent´hows] *n* a shed or lean-to projecting from or adjoining a main building; a structure or dwelling on a roof. [ME *pentis*—Fr *appentis*—L *appendicium*, an appendage.]

penult [pė-nult´, pē´nult], **penult´ima**, *ns* the syllable last but one.—*adj* **penult´imate**, last but one.—*n* the last but one. [L *paenultima—paene*, almost, *ultimus*, last.]

penumbra [pen-um´bra] *n* a partial shadow round the perfect shadow of an eclipse; the part of a picture where the light and shade blend. [L *paene*, almost, *umbra*, shade.]

penury [pen´ū-ri] *n* want, great poverty.—*adj* **penū´rious**, showing penury; scanty, niggardly.—*adv* **penū´riously**.—*n* **penū´riousness**. [L *pēnūria*, want.]

peon [pē´on] *n* a member of the landless laboring class in Spanish America; one working off a debt by bondage; a drudge, a menial. [Sp,—Low L *pedō*—L *pēs, pedis*, a foot.]

peony [pē´o-ni] *n* a genus (*Paenia*) of plants with large showy flowers. [OFr *pione*—L *paeōnia*, healing—Gr *Paiōn* or *Paiān*. See **paean**.]

people [pē´pl] *n* the body of enfranchised citizens of a state; one's family, relatives; the persons of a certain place, group, or class; persons considered indefinitely; human beings; (*pl*) all the persons of a racial or ethnic group, typically having a common language, institutions, homes, and folkways.—*vt* to stock with people or inhabitants. [O Fr *people*—L *populus*.]

pep [pep] *n* (*inf*) vigor.—*ns* **pep pill**, a pill containing a stimulant drug; **pep talk**, a stongly-worded talk designed to arouse enthusiasm for a cause or course of action.—**pep up**, to put pep into. [**pepper**.]

pepper [pep´ėr] *n* a pungent condiment made from the fruit of various plants (genera *Piper* or *Capsicum*); the fruit of the pepper plant (genus *Capsicum*) which can be red, yellow, or green, sweet or hot, and is eaten as a vegetable.—*vt* to sprinkle with pepper; to hit or pelt with shot, etc.—*adj* **pepp´er-and-salt´**, mingled black and white.—*ns* **pepp´er-corn**, a dried berry of a woody vine (*Piper nigrum*) yielding white peppercorns when freed from the outer black skin; **pepp´ermint**, a pungent and aromatic mint (*Mentha piperata*) with dark green leaves and small pink flowers; any of several related mints; candy flavored with peppermint; the oil of the peppermint used for flavoring.—*adj* **pepp´ery**, possessing the qualities of pepper; hot, choleric. [OE *pipor*—L *piper*—Gr *peperi*—Sans *pippali*.]

pepsin [pep´sin] *n* a stomach enzyme, aiding in the digestion of proteins.—*adj* **pep´tic**, relating to or promoting digestion; of, or relating to, producing, or caused by pepsin (eg a peptic ulcer).—*n* **pep´tōne**, a product of the action of enzymes on proteins. [Gr *pepsis*, digestion—*peptein*, to digest.]

Pequot [pē´kwot] *n* member of an Algonquian-speaking Amerindian people of Connecticut.

per [pûr] *prep* for each, (eg fifty cents per yard); through, by, by means of; (*inf*) according to.—**per annum** [an´ùm] yearly; **per capita** [kap´i-ta] for each person; **per se** [sā] in itself, intrinsically. [L.]

peradventure [per-ad-vent´chùr] *adv* by chance; perhaps. [L *per*, by, **adventure**.]

perambulate [pėr-am´bū-lāt] *vt* to walk through, about, or over; to pass through for the purpose of surveying; to survey the boundaries of.—*ns* **perambulā´tion**, act of perambulating; official inspection on foot in order to define boundaries; **peram´bulātor**, one who perambulates; (*Brit*) a baby carriage. [L *perambulāre, -ātum—per*, through, *ambulāre*, to walk.]

perceive [pėr-sēv´] *vt* to become or be aware of through the senses; to see; to understand; to discern.—*n* **perceiv´er**. [OFr *percever*—L *percipĕre, perceptum—per-*, thoroughly, *capĕre*, to take.]

per cent [pėr sent´] *adv* in the hundred, for each hundred; (*inf*) percentage.—*n* **percent´age**, rate or amount per cent; a proportion; (*inf*) gain, rake-off. [L *per centum*, per hundred.]

percept [pûr´sept] *n* an object perceived by the senses.—*adj* **percep´tible**, that can be perceived; discernible.—*n* **perceptibil´ity**.—*adv* **percep´tibly**.—*n* **percep´tion**, act or power of perceiving; discernment; the combining of sensations into recognition of an object.—*adj* **percep´tive**, able, or quick to, perceive or discern.—*ns* **percep´tiveness, perceptiv´ity**. [From *perceptum*. See **perceive**.]

perch [pûrch] *n* a genus (*Perca*) of spiny-finned chiefly freshwater fishes; esp the American yellow perch (*P. florescens*), a food and game fish, and related species in Europe and Asia; any of various other spiny-finned fishes as of the families Percidae, Centrarchidae, Serranidae, many of them marine. [Fr *perche*—L *perca*—Gr *perkē*, a perch, perh conn with *perknos*, dusky.]

perch [pûrch] *n* a rod on which birds alight, sit, or roost; any high seat or position.—*vti* to rest or place on or as on a perch. [Fr *perche*—L *pertica*, a rod.]

perchance [pėr-chäns´] *adv* by chance; perhaps. [Anglo-Fr *par chance*.]

Percheron [pürch´ėr-on] *n* a powerful rugged draft horse (*Equus caballus*) outstandingly popular in the US. [*Perche* region, France.]

percipient [pėr-sip´i-ėnt] *adj* perceiving; having the faculty of perception.—*n* one who perceives or can perceive. [L *percipiens, -entis*, pr p of *percipĕre*; cf **perceive**.]

percolate [pür´kō-lāt] *vt* to pass (a liquid) through pores; to filter.—*vi* to ooze through a porous substance; to become percolated; to spread gradually.—*ns* **percolā´tion**, act of filtering; **per´colātor**, an apparatus for making coffee in which boiling water bubbles up through a tube and repeatedly filters back down through a perforated basket of ground coffee. [L *percōlāre, -ātum—per*, through, *cōlāre*, to strain.]

percussion [pėr-kush´(o)n] *n* impact; (*med*) tapping upon the body to find the condition of an organ by the sounds; instruments played by striking—cymbals, etc.—*ns* **percuss´ion cap**, a paper or metal case filled with material that explodes when struck; **percussion instrument**, a musical instrument whose sounding agent is a stretched membrane or some solid material as steel or wood; **percuss´ionist**, a musician who plays percussion instruments. [L *percussiō, -ōnis—percutĕre, percussum—per-*, thoroughly, *quatĕre*, to shake.]

per diem [pėr dē´ėm] *n* a daily allowance; a daily fee.—*adj* based on use or service by the day; daily; paid by the day.—*adv* by the day; for each day. [L.]

perdition [pėr-dish´(o)n] *n* utter loss or ruin; the utter loss of happiness in a future state, hell. [L *perditiō, -ōnis—perdĕre, perditum—per-*, entirely, *dăre*, to give up.]

peregrinate [per´ė-gri-nāt] *vi* to travel about, journey.—*n* **peregrinā´tion**, travel; pilgrimage.—*adj* **per´egrine**, foreign; migratory.—*n* a swift almost cosmopolitan falcon (*Falco peregrinus*) much used in falconry, also called **peregrine falcon**. [L *peregrīnārī, -ātus—peregrīnus*, foreign—*peregre*, abroad—*per*, through, *ager*, field.]

peremptory [perėm(p)´tòr-i] *adj* admitting no refusal; dogmatic; imperious.—*adv* **peremp´torily**.—*n* **peremp´toriness**. [Fr,—L *peremptōrius—perimĕre, peremptum—per-*, entirely, *emĕre*, to take, buy.]

perennial [pėr-en´yȧl] *adj* lasting through the year; perpetual; (*bot*) lasting more than two years.—*adv* **perenn´ially**. [L *perennis—per*, through, *annus*, a year.]

perfect [pûr´fekt] *adj* done thoroughly or completely; complete; faultless; having every moral excellence; completely skilled or versed; (of an insect) in the final adult stage of development;—*n* a verb form in the perfect tense.—*vt* [or pėr-fekt´] to make perfect; to finish; to make fully skilled in anything.—*adv* **per´fectly**.—*adj* **perfect´ible**, capable of becoming perfect.—*ns* **perfectibil´ity; perfec´tion, per´fectness**, state of being perfect; a perfect quality or acquirement; the highest state or degree; consummate excellence; **perfec´tionist**, one who claims to be perfect; one who thinks that moral perfection can be attained in this life; **perfec´tionism**.—*adj* **perfect´ive**, tending to make perfect.—*adv* **perfect´ively**.—**perfect binding**, a book binding in which a layer of adhesive holds the pages and cover together; **perfect game**, a baseball game in which a pitcher allows no hits, no runs, and no opposing batter to reach first base; a game in bowling in which a bowler gets twelve consecutive strikes; **perfect number**, a number equal to the sum of its divisors as 6=1 + 2 + 3, 28=1 + 2 + 4 + 7 + 14; **perfect tense**, tense signifying action completed or designating a present state which is the result of an action in the past. [L *perfectus*, pt p of *perficĕre—per-*, thoroughly, *facĕre*, to do.]

perfecta [pû-fek´tȧ] *n* a system of betting in which one wins if one picks the first and second place finishers in a race correctly. [Sp.]

perfervid [pėr-für´vid] *adj* excessively fervent. [L *perfervidus*, a misreading for *praefervidus—prae*, before, *fervidus*, fervid.]

perfidious [pėr-fid´i-us] *adj* treacherous, basely violating faith.—*adv* **perfid´iously**.—*ns* **perfid´iousness, per´fidy**, treachery. [L *perfidiōsus—perfidia*, faithlessness—pfx *per-*, implying destruction, *fidēs*, faith.]

perfoliate [pėr-fō´li-ȧt] *adj* (of a leaf) having the base joined round the stem so as to appear pierced by the stem. [L *per*, through, *folium*, a leaf.]

perforate [pûr´fō-rāt] *vt* to bore through or into, to pierce; to make a hole, or holes, or a row of holes, through.—*ns* **perforā´tion**, act of boring through; a hole, or row of holes, made by boring; **per´forātor**, one who bores; a boring instrument. [L *perforāre, -ātum—per*, through, *forāre*, to bore.]

perforce [pėr-fōrs´, -förs´] *adv* by force, of necessity. [O Fr *par force*.]

perform [pėr-förm´] *vt* to do; to carry out duly; to carry into effect (eg a promise, a command); to act.—*vi* to execute an undertaking; to act a part;

to play, as on a musical instrument.—*adj* **perform´able**, capable of being performed; practicable.—*ns* **perform´ance**, act of performing; a carrying out (of something); a piece of work; an exhibition in a theatre or a place of amusement; an act or action; manner of, or success in, working; **perform´er**, one who performs, esp one who makes a public exhibition of his skill.—**perform´ing arts**, arts, such as ballet and drama, for performance before an audience. [Anglo-Fr *parfourmer*, app—O Fr *parfournir*—*par* (L *per*), through, *fournir*, to furnish.]

perfume [pûr´fūm or pėr-fūm´] *n* a pleasing odor; fragrance; fluid containing fragrant essential oil and a fixative.—*vt* [pėr-fūm´] to scent; to put perfume on.—*ns* **perfū´mer**, a make or seller of perfumes; **perfū´mery**, perfume in general; the art of preparing perfumes, the place (in a shop) where perfumes are sold. [Fr *parfum*—L *per*, through, *fūmus*, smoke.]

perfunctory [pėr-fungk´tȯ-ri] *adj* done merely as a routine performed carelessly; hasty or superficial; acting without zeal or interest.—*adv* **perfunc´torily**.—*n* **perfunc´toriness**. [L *perfunctōrius*—*perfunctus*, pt p of *perfungī*, to execute—*per-*, thoroughly, *fungī*, to do.]

pergola, [pûr´go-la] *n* a latticework structure with climbing plants. [It,—L *pergula*, a shed.]

perhaps [pėr-haps´] *adv* it may be, possibly. [From the pl of **hap**, after the model of **perchance**.]

peri [pē´ri] *n* a Persian fairy; a beautiful and graceful girl. [Pers *parī*, a fairy.]

peri- in composition, around. [Gr *peri*, around], eg **periosteum** [pėr-i-os´tė-um], *n* a membrane forming the outer coating of a bone. [Gr *osteon*, bone.]

perianth [per´i-anth] *n* (*bot*) calyx and corolla together, esp when not clearly distinguishable. [Gr *peri*, around, *anthos*, a flower.]

pericardium [per-i-kär´di-um] *n* (*anat*) the membrane round the heart.—*adjs* **pericar´diac, pericar´dial**. [Latinised from Gr *perikardion*—*peri*, around, *kardiā*, heart.]

pericarp [per´i-kärp] *n* (*bot*) the wall of a fruit if derived from that of the ovary.—*adj* **pericarp´ial**. [Gr *perikarpion*—*peri*, around, *karpos*, fruit.]

pericranium [per-i-krā´ni-um] *n* the membrane that surrounds the cranium. [Latinised from Gr *perikrānion*—*peri*, around, *krānion*, skull.]

perigee [per´i-jē] *n* (*astron*) the point nearest a heavenly body, as the earth, in the orbit of a satellite around it. [Gr *peri*, near, *gē*, the earth.]

perihelion [per-i-hē´li-ȯn] *n* the point of the orbit of a planet or a comet or of a man-made satellite at which it is nearest to the sun. [Gr *peri*, near, *hēlios*, the sun.]

peril [per´il] *n* danger.—*vt* to expose to danger.—*pr p* **periling, per´illing**; *pt, pt p* **periled, per´illed**.—*adj* **per´ilous**, dangerous.—*adv* **per´ilously**.—*n* **per´ilousness**. [Fr *péril*—L *periculum*.]

perimeter [pėr-im´ė-tėr] *n* (*geom*) the circuit or boundary of any plane figure, or the sum of all its sides; (*mil*) the boundary of a fortified position; the outer edge of any area. [Gr *perimetros*—*peri*, around, *metron*, measure.]

period [pē´ri-ȯd] *n* the time in which anything runs its course; the time in which a heavenly body revolves through its orbit; a division of geological time, itself divided into epochs and forming part of an era; a stated and recurring interval of time as in an academic day, playing time in a game, etc., an age, a stage or phase in history; a complete sentence, esp one of elaborate construction; conclusion; (*gram*) a mark (.) at the end of a sentence; a pause in speaking; menstrual discharge;—*interj* an exclamation used for emphasis.—*adjs* **periodic** [pēr-i-od´ik] pertaining to a period; of revolution in an orbit; occurring at regular intervals; occurring from time to time; **period´ical**, periodic; published in numbers at stated intervals.—*n* a magazine or other publication that appears at regular intervals.—*adv* **period´ically**.—*n* **periodicity** [-dis´-], the fact or character of being periodic; rhythmic activity; tendency to recur at regular intervals.—**periodic law**, a law in chemistry; the elements when arranged in the order of their atomic numbers show a periodic variation in most of their properties; **periodic sentence**, in rhetoric, a sentence in which the most significant part occupies the final position; **periodic table**, an arrangement of the elements based on the periodic law; **period piece**, a piece (as of fiction, music, art, or furniture) whose special value lies in its evocation of the past. [Fr *période*—L *periodus*—Gr *periodos*—*peri*, around, *hodos*, a way.]

peripatetic [per-i-pȧ-tet´ik] *adj* walking about; going from place to place on business; **Peripatetic**, of or pertaining to the philosophy of Aristotle.—*n* a pedestrian; an itinerant; **Peripatetic**, an adherent of the philosophy of Aristotle.—*n* **Peripatet´icism** [-is-izm]. [Gr *peripatētikos*—*peri*, about, *patieen*, to walk.]

periphery [pėr-if´ėr-i] *n* the bounding line or surface, esp of a rounded object; the outside of anything.—*adj* **periph´eral**. [Gr *peri*, around, *pherein*, to carry.]

periphrasis [pėr-if´rȧ-sis] *n* the use of more words than are necessary to express an idea;—*pl* **periph´rases** [-sēz].—*adj* **periphrastic** [per-i-fras´tik], containing or expressed by periphrasis or circumlocution.—*adv* **periphras´tically**. [L,—Gr *periphrasis*—*peri*, about, *phrasis*, speech.]

periscope [per´i-skōp] *n* a tube with mirrors by which an observer in a trench, submarine, etc., can see what is going on above or around an obstacle. [Gr *peri*, about, *skopeein*, to look at, look about.]

perish [per´ish] *vi* to be destroyed or ruined; to die, esp violently.—*adj* per´ishable, that may perish; liable to spoil or decay.—*n* something perishable, esp food.—*n* **per´ishability**.—*adv* **per´ishably**. [O Fr *perir*, pr p *perissant*—L *perīre*, to perish—*per-*, 'to the bad', *īre*, to go.]

peristalsis [per´i-stal´sis] *n* contractions and dilations of the intestines, moving the contents onward.—*adj* **per´istal´tic**. [Gr *peri*-around, *stallein*, to place.]

peristyle [per´i-stīl] *n* a range of columns round a building or round a square; a court, square, etc., with columns all round. [L *peri-stȳl(i)um*—Gr *peristȳlon*—*peri*, around, *stȳlos*, a column.]

peritoneum [per-i-tȯn-ē´um] *n* a membrane that lines the abdomen.—*n* **peritonī´tis**, inflammation of the peritoneum. [Gr *peritonaion*—*peri*, around, *teinein*, to stretch.]

periwig [per´i-wig] *n* a peruke. [Earlier *perwyke, perwig*, etc.—*Fr perruque*. See **peruke, wig**.]

periwinkle[1] [per´i-wingk-l] *n* a creeping evergreen plant, (genus *Vinca*) with blue, white, or pink flowers.—Also **myrtle**. [ME *peruenke*—OE *peruince*, from L *pervinca*.]

periwinkle[2] [per´i-wingk-l] *n* a genus (Littorina) of edible marine snails; any related marine mollusks (genus *Thais* of America); any of several freshwater snails of N America. [OE (pl) *pinewinclan*.]

perjure [pûr-jùr] *vt* to forswear (oneself).—*ns* **per´jurer; per´jury**, false swearing; the breaking of an oath; (*law*) the crime of wilfully giving false evidence on oath. [O Fr *parjurer*—L *perjūrāre*—*per-*, *jūrāre*, to swear.]

perk[1] [pûrk] *vi* to bear oneself with self-confidence; to recover spirits or energy (*with* **up**).—*vt* to make smart or trim.—*adj* brisk.—*adj* **perk´y**, lively, spry.—*adv* **perk´ily**.—*n* **perk´iness**. [Origin unknown.]

perk[2] [pûrk] *n* (*usu. pl*) perquisite. [Clipped form.]

perk[3] [pûrk] *vti* (*inf*) to percolate (coffee). [Clipped form.]

perm [pûrm] *vt* to give (hair) a permanent wave.

permafrost [pûr´ma-frost] *n* permanently frozen subsoil. [*perma*nent *frost*.]

permanent [pûr´mȧ-nėnt] *adj* remaining, or intended to remain, indefinitely;—*n* a straightening or waving of hair by use of chemicals or heat lasting through many washings;—Also **permanent wave**.—*ns* **per´manence**, fact or state of being permanent; **per´manency**, permanence; a thing that is permanent.—*adv* **per´manently**.—**permanent magnet**, a magnet that retains its magnetism after removal of the magnetizing force; **permanent tooth**, any of the permanent teeth of a mammal that follow the milk teeth, the second set of teeth persisting into old age. [L *permanēre*—*per*, through, *manēre*, to continue.]

permanganate [pėr-mang´ga-nāt] *n* a dark purple crystalline compound that is a salt of permanganic acid ($HMnO_4$). [*per-*, indicating excess, and **manganese**.]

permeate [pûr´mė-āt] *vti* to pass through the pores, or interstices, of; to pervade; to diffuse.—*n* **permeā´tion**.—*adj* **per´meable**.—*n* **permeabil´ity**. [L *permeāre*—*per*, through, *meāre*, to pass.]

Permian [pûr-mi-ȧn] *n* the last period of the Palaeozoic geological era; the system of rocks formed during that period.—Also *adj*. [*Perm*, province in Russia.]

permit [pėr-mit´] *vt* to allow to be done; to authorize.—*vi* to give opportunity.—*pr p* **permitt´ing**; *pt, pt p* **permitt´ed**.—*n* [pėr´mit] a license.—*adj* **permiss´ible**, that may be permitted; allowable.—*adv* **permiss´ibly**.—*n* **permiss´ion**, act of permitting; leave.—*adj* **permiss´ive**, granting permission or liberty; not prohibited; allowing much freedom in social conduct.—*adv* **permiss´ively**. [L *permittĕre, -missum*, to let pass through—*per*, through, *mittĕre*, to send.]

permute [pėr-mūt´] *vt* to change the order or arrangement of, esp to arrange in all possible ways.—*adj* **permut´able**.—*n* **permuta´tion**, any radical alteration; any of the total number of groupings within a group; an ordered arrangement of a set of objects. [L *permūtāre*—*per-*, *mūtāre*, to change.]

pernicious [pėr-nish´ůs] *adj* destructive; highly injurious.—*adv* **perni´ciously**.—*n* **perni´ciousness**—**pernicious anemia**, a severe anemia marked by gastrointestinal and nervous disorders, weakness, etc. associated with the reduced ability to absorb Vitamin B_{12}. [L *perniciōsus*—*per-*, completely, *nex, necis*, death by violence.]

peroration [per-ō-rā´sh(ȯ)n] *n* the conclusion of a speech; a rhetorical performance. [L *perōrātiō*—*perōrāre*, to bring a speech to an end—*per*, through, *ōrāre*, to speak.]

peroxide [pėr-oks´id] *n* an oxide whose molecules contain two atoms of oxygen linked together; hydrogen peroxide.—*vt* to treat or bleach with hydrogen peroxide. [*per-*, indicating excess, and **oxygen**.]

perpend [pėr-pend´] *vt* to consider carefully.—*vi* to be attentive. [L *perpendĕre*—*per-*, thoroughly, *pendĕre*, to weigh.]

perpendicular [pėr-pėn-dik´ū-lȧr] *adj* upright; erect; vertical; (*geom*) at right angles to a given line or surface; (*archit*) of the latest style of English Gothic remarkable for the use of slender pillars and vertical lines.—*n* a perpendicular line or plane.—*n* **perpendicular´ity**, state of being perpendicular.—*adv* **perpendic´ularly**. [L *perpendicularīs*—*perpendiculum*, a plumb-line—*per-*, completely, *pendĕre*, to hang.]

perpetrate [pûr´pė-trāt] *vt* to do (something evil, criminal, etc.); to commit (a blunder, etc.).—*ns* **perpetrā´tion; per´petrātor**. [L *perpetrāre, -ātum*—*per-*, thoroughly, *patrāre*, to perform.]

perpetual [pėr-pet´ū-ȧl] *adj* never ceasing; everlasting; (of flowers) blooming continuously throughout the season.—*adv* **perpet´ually**—**perpetual calendar**, a table for finding the day of the week for any one of a wide range of dates; **perpetual check** (*chess*), an endless succession of checks to the opponents' king. [L *perpetuālis*—*perpetuus*, continuous.]

perpetuate [pėr-pet´ū-āt] *vt* to preserve from extinction or oblivion, give continued existence to; to pass on, cause to continue to be believed, known, etc.—*ns* **perpetuā´tion**, continuation or preservation for ever, or for a very long time; **perpetū´ity**, state of being perpetual; endless time; duration for an indefinite period; something lasting forever; an annuity payable forever. [L *perpetuāre, -ātum—perpetuus*, perpetual.]

perplex [pėr-pleks´] *vt* to embarrass, puzzle, bewilder; to complicate (eg a problem; a situation).—*n* **perplex´ity**, state of being perplexed; confusion of mind, doubt; intricacy. [Fr,—L *perplexus*, entangled—*per-*, completely, *plexus*, involved, pa p of *plectĕre*.]

perquisite [pûr´kwi-zit] *n* an expected or promised privilege, gain, or profit incidental to regular wages or salary; a tip, gratuity; something claimed as an exclusive right. [L *perquīsītum*, from perquīrĕre, to seek diligently—pfx *per-*, thoroughly, *quaerĕre*, to ask.]

perry [per´i] *n* fermented pear juice often made sparkling. [O Fr *peré*—L *pirum*, a pear.]

persecute [pûr´sė-kūt] *vt* to harass, afflict, hunt down, esp for reasons of race, religion, etc.; to worry continually, to importune.—*ns* **persecū´tion; per´secutor**. [L *persequī, persecūtus*—pfx *per-*, thoroughly, *sequī*, to follow.]

persevere [pėr-sė-vēr´] *vi* to continue steadfastly, esp in face of discouragement.—*n* **persevē´rance**, act or state of persevering.—*adv* **persevē´ringly**. [Fr *persévérer*—L *persevērāre—persevērus*, very strict—pfx *per-*, very, *sevērus*, strict.]

Persian [pûr´sh(y)ȧn, -zh(y)ȧn] *adj* of, from, or relating to Persia or modern Iran; its inhabitants, or language.—*n* a native of Persia; the language of Persia or Iran in any of its ancient or modern forms. **Persian carpet**, a handwoven or knotted one-piece carpet or rug made in Persia, valued for its workmanship and designs; **Persian cat**, a breed of domestic cat with long silky hair and bushy tail; **Persian lamb**, karakul.

persiflage [per-si-fläzh] *n* banter, flippancy. [Fr,—*persifler*, to banter—L *sībilāre*, whistle.]

persimmon [pėr-sim´ȯn] *n* any of a genus of trees (known also as *date-plum*) of the ebony family or their fruit, esp the Virginian date-plum; any of a genus (*Diospyrus*) of the ebony family with fine hard wood, esp an American tree (*D. Virginiana*); the orange, edible, usu. many-seeded fruit of the persimmon. [From an Amer Indian word.]

persist [pėr-sist´] *vi* to continue steadfastly or obstinately, in spite of opposition or warning; to persevere; to last, endure.—*ns* **persis´tence, persis´tency**, quality of being persistent; persistent methods; doggedness, obstinacy; duration, esp of an effect after the exciting cause has been removed.—*adj* **persis´tent**, persisting; constantly recurring or long-continued (eg efforts); (*zool* and *bot*) remaining after the usual time of falling off, withering, or disappearing.—*advs* **persis´tently; persis´tingly**. [L *persistĕre—per* through, *sistĕre*, to cause to stand, to stand—*stāre*, to stand.]

person [pûr´sȯn] *n* assumed character, as on the stage (*in the person of*); an individual human being; an individual (used slightingly); (*obs*) a personage; the outward appearance, living body (exclusive or inclusive of clothing) of a human being; a living soul; one of three modes of being of the God-head (Father, Son, and Holy Spirit); one (as a person, partnership, or corporation) that is recognized by law as the subject of rights and duties; (*gram*) a form of inflexion or use of a word according as it or its subject represents the person(s) or thing(s) speaking (*first person*), spoken to (*second*), or spoken about (*third*); used as suffix in to avoid discrimination on grounds of sex.—*n* **persona** [pėr-sōn´ȧ], a character who appears in fiction, esp in drama—*pl* **person´ae**; social façade or public image—*pl* **person´as**.—*adj* **personable** [pėr´sȯn-ȧ-bl], of good appearance.—*n* **per´sonage**, a person; an exalted or august person; a character in a play or story.—*adj* **per´sonal**, of the nature of a person as opposed to a thing or an abstraction; of, relating to, belonging to, or affecting the individual, the self (eg convenience, luggage); exclusively for a given individual (eg letter); performed, etc., in person (eg service, interview); pertaining to or affecting the person or body (eg charm, injury); aimed at a particular person or persons (eg abuse, remark); making, or given to making, personal remarks; (*law*) of property that is movable; (*gram*) indicating person.—*vt* **per´sonalize**, to personify; to give a mark to (something) so that it is identifiable as belonging to a particular person.—*adv* **per´sonally**, in person; as a person; in one's own opinion; as though directed to oneself.—*n* **personal´ity**, fact or state of being a person as opposed to a thing or an abstraction; (*psych*) the totality of an individual's characteristics (psychological, intellectual, emotional, and physical), esp as they are presented to other people; distinctive or well-marked character; excellence or distinction of social and personal traits; a person with such qualities; *pl* direct reference to, or an utterance aimed at, a particular person or persons, esp of a derogatory nature.—*n* **per´sonalty**, personal property.—*vt* **per´sonate**, to assume the likeness or character of, esp for fraudulent purposes; to play the part of.—*ns* **personā´tion; per´sonātor; personnel´**, persons employed in any work, enterprise, service etc.; a department for hiring employees, etc.—**in person**, by one's own act, not by an agent or representative; **personal equation**, variation (as in observation) as a result of the idiosyncrasies of the observer; a correction or allowance made for such variation. [L *persōna*, a player's mask, player, personage, person, perh from Etruscan *phersu*, masked figures commonly associated (in spite of difference of quantity) with *persŏnāre, -ātum—per*, through, *sŏnāre*, to sound; cf **parson**.]

persona grata [pėr-sō´na grat´a] *adj* personally acceptable or welcome. [L.]

personify [pėr-son´i-fī] *vt* to represent as a person; to ascribe personality to; to be the embodiment of;—*pt, pt p* **person´ified**.—*n* **personificā´tion**. [L *persōna*, a person, *facĕre*, to make. See **person**.]

personnel *See* **person**.

persona non grata [pėr-sō´na nōn grat´ȧ, – grät´a] *adj* personally unacceptable or unwelcome. [L]

perspective [pėr-spek´tiv] *n* the art or science of drawing solid objects on a plane or curved surface as they appear to the eye; appearance, or representation of appearance, of objects in space with effect of distance, solidity, etc.; just proportion in all the parts; ability to view things in just proportion; a picture in perspective; a vista; a mental view or prospect.—*adj* pertaining or according to perspective.—**in perspective**, according to the laws of perspective; in just relationship, with the important and the unimportant things in their proper places. [L (*ars*) *perspectīva*, perspective (art)—*perspicĕre, perspectum—per*, through, *specĕre*, to look.]

perspicacious [pėr-spi-kā´shůs] *adj* (*arch*) clear-sighted; having clear mental vision or discernment.—*adv* **perspicā´ciously**.—*n* **perspicacity** [-kas´i-ti]. [L *perspicāx, -ācis—perspicĕre*. See **perspective**.]

perspicuous [pėr-spik´ū-us] *adj* clearly expressed, clear; (of a person) lucid, expressing himself clearly.—*adv* **perspic´ūously**.—*ns* **perspic´ūousness, perspicū´ity**. [L *perspicuus—perspicĕre*. See **perspective**.]

perspire [pėr-spīr´] *vi* to sweat;—*n* **perspiration** [-spirā´sh(ȯ)n], act of perspiring; sweat.—*adj* **perspīr´atory**. [L *perspīrāre, -ātum—per*, through, *spīrāre*, to breathe.]

persuade [pėr-swād´] *vt* to induce by argument, advice, etc. (*to*, do, *into* doing something); to convince.—*n* **persuad´er**.—*adj* **persuas´ible**, capable of being persuaded.—*ns* **persuasion** [-swā´zh(ȯ)n], act of persuading; settled opinion; a system of religious beliefs; a group adhering to a particular system of beliefs.—*adj* **persuasive** [-swāz´-], having the power to persuade; influencing the mind or passions.—*adv* **persua´sively**.—*n* **persua´siveness**. [L *persuādēre, -suāsum*—pfx *per-*, throughly, *suādēre*, to advise.]

pert [pûrt] *adj* saucy, presumingly free in speech or conduct; sprightly.—*adv* **pert´ly**.—*n* **pert´ness**. [Shortened from *apert*—L *aperīre, apertum*, to open.]

pertain [pėr-tān´] *vi* to belong as a characteristic quality, function, concern, etc. (*with* **to**); to be appropriate (to); to relate (to).—*ns* **per´tinence, per´tinency**, state of being pertinent or to the point.—*adj* **per´tinent**, pertaining or related to a subject; relevant; apposite.—*n* (usu. in *pl*) appurtenances.—*adv* **per´tinently**. [OFr *partenir*—L *pertinēre*—pfx *per-*, thoroughly, *tenēre*, to hold.]

pertinacious [pėr-ti-nā´shůs] *adj* holding obstinately to an opinion or a purpose; hard to get rid of.—*adv* **pertinā´ciously**.—*ns* **pertinā´ciousness, pertinacity** [-nas´i-ti], quality of being pertinacious; obstinacy. [L *pertināx, -ācis*, holding fast—pfx *per-*, thoroughly, *tenāx*, tenacious—*tenēre*, to hold.]

perturb [pėr-tûrb´] *vt* to disturb greatly; to agitate.—*n* **perturbā´tion**, state of being perturbed; disquiet of mind; (*astron*) a deviation of a heavenly body from its regular orbit produced by some additional force. [L *perturbāre, -ātum*—pfx *per-*, thoroughly, *turbāre*, to disturb—*turba*, a crowd.]

peruke [pėr-ōōk´] *n* a wig of a type popular from the 17th to the early 19th century. [Fr *perruque*—It *parrucca*; connection with L *pīlus*, hair, very doubtful.]

peruse [pėr-ōōz´] *vt* to read attentively; to study; to read.—*ns* **perus´al**, a careful reading; **perus´er**. [L pfx *per-*, thoroughly, *ūtī, ūsus*, to use.]

pervade [pėr-vād´] *vt* to diffuse or extend through the whole of.—*adj* **perva´sive** [-vā´ziv], tending or having power to pervade. [L *pervādĕre—per*, through, *vādĕre*, to go.]

perverse [pėr-vûrs´] *adj* turned aside from right or truth; obstinate in the wrong; capricious and unreasonable in opposition.—*adv* **perverse´ly**.—*ns* **perverse´ness; perversion** [-vėr´sh(ȯ)n], a turning from truth or propriety; a diversion to a wrong end or use; a perverted or corrupted form of anything (eg of the truth); a misdirection of the sex instinct, which finds gratification in abnormal ways, eg in sadism; **pervers´ity**.—*vt* **pervert´**, to turn aside, derange (eg the ends of justice, the course of justice); to turn (a person) from truth or virtue; to misinterpret or misapply (eg words), esp on purpose.—*ns* **per´vert**. one suffering from derangement of the sex instinct; **pervert´er**. [Partly through Fr—L *pervertĕre, perversum*—pfx *per-*, thoroughly, wrongly, *vertĕre*, to turn.]

pervious [pûr´vi-us] *adj* accessible; permeable, penetrable.—*adv* **per´viously**.—*n* **per´viousness**. [L *pervius—per*, through, *via*, a way.]

Pesach [pā-säk] *n* Passover.

peseta [pe-sā´tä] *n* a Spanish silver coin. [Sp dim of *pesa*, weight.]

pesky [pes´ki] *adj* (*inf*) vexatious.

peso [pā´sō] *n* a unit of money in various Spanish-speaking countries. [Sp—L *pēnsum*, weight.]

pessimism [pes´i-mizm] *n* the doctrine that the world is bad rather than good; the doctrine that reality is essentially evil; a temper of mind that always expects the worse things;—*n* **pess´imist**. *adj* **pessimis´tic**. [L *pessimus*, worst.]

pest [pest] *n* (now *rare*) any deadly epidemic disease, esp plague; anything destructive like a pest, esp a plant or animal detrimental to man as rats, flies, weeds, etc.; one that pesters or annoys.—*ns* **pest´house**, a hospital or shelter for those infected with a contagious or pestilential disease. **pest´icide** [pes´ti-sīd], any chemical for killing pests.—*adj* **pestif´erous**.—*n* **pest´ilence**, any deadly epidemic disease; anything regarded as harmful.—*adjs* **pest´ilent**, hurtful to health and life; causing displeasure or annoyance; infectious, contagious. **pestilential** [-elen´shȧl], pestilent; morally harmful; pernicious. [Fr *peste* and *pestilence*—L *pestis, pestilentia*.]

pester [pes´tėr] *vt* (*arch*) to crowd thickly; to annoy persistently. [App from OFr *empestrer* (Fr *empêtrer*), to entangle, from L *in*, in, Low L *pāstōrium*, a foot-shackle for a horse—L *pāstus*, pt p of *pāscĕre*, to feed; influenced by **pest**.]

pestle [pes´l also pest´l] *n* a usu. club-shaped tool for pounding or grinding substances in a mortar.—*vt* to beat, pound, or pulverize with a pestle. *vi* to use a pestle. [OFr *pestel*—L *pistillum*, a pounder, *pinsĕre, pistum*, to pound.]

pet[1] [pet] *n* a domesticated animal kept as a companion; a person treated as an indulged favorite;—*adj* kept as a pet; indulged; cherished; particular (eg *a pet peeve*).—*vt* to stroke or pat gently; to caress.—*vi* (*inf*) to kiss, embrace, etc. in making love.—*vt pr p* **pett´ing**; *pt, pt p* **pett´ed**. [Origin unknown; not from Gael.]

pet[2] [pet] *n* a sulky mood.—*adj* **pett´ish**, peevish, sulky.—*adv* **pett´ishly**.—*n* **pett´ishness**.

petal [pet´ȧl] *n* a corolla leaf, any of the leaflike parts of a blossom.—*adjs* **pet´aled, pet´alled**, having petals; **pet´aloid**, having the appearance of a petal. [Gr *petalon*, a leaf.]

petard [pe-tär(d)´] *n* a case containing an explosive, used for blowing in doors, etc.—**hoist with one's own petard**, destroyed by the very thing with which one meant to destroy others. [OFr—*péter*, to crack or explode—L *pēdĕre*, to break wind].

Peter [pē´tėr] *n* (*Bible*) 21st and 22d books of the New Testament, written by St Peter to the Jews between 60 and 70 AD.

peter [pētėr] *vi* (*inf*) to dwindle away to nothing, (*with* **out**). [US mining slang; origin unknown.]

Peter Pan [pē´tėr pan´] a character in J M Barrie's play of that name (1904); the type of person who never grows up.

Peter principle [pē´tėr] *n* the notion that in every hierarchy each employee tends to rise to his level of incompetence, thus every post tends to be filled by a person incompetent to execute his duties.

petiole [pet´i-ōl] *n* (*bot*) a leaf stalk; (*zool*) a stalk-like structure. [L *petiolus*, a little foot, a petiole.]

petit [pė-tē´] *adj* little, used chiefly in legal compounds.

petite [pė-tēt] *adj* of a woman, small and trim in figure.—**petit bourgeois**, member of the **petite bourgeoisie**, the lower-middle class—**petit jury**, a group of usu. twelve citizens to decide the issues of a trial in court; **petit larceny**, larceny involving property of a value below a legally established minimum. [Fr]

petition [pe-tish´(ȯ)n] *n* a formal request to an authority; a written supplication signed by a number of persons;—*vt* to address a petition to; to ask someone (*for* something, *to* do something).—*adj* **petit´ionary**.—*ns* **petit´ioner; petit´ioning**. [L *petītiō, -ōnis—petĕre*, to ask.]

petrel [pet´rėl] *n* any of a number of dark-colored seabirds (families Procellariidae and Hydrobatidae), esp those flying far from land. [L *Petrus*, Peter, from its seeming to walk on water; see Matt xiv 29]

petrify [pet´ri-fī] *vt* to turn into stone; to make hard like a stone; to fix in amazement, horror, etc.—*vi* to become stone, or hard like stone;—*pr p* **pet´rifying**; *pt, pt p* **pet´rified**.—*n* **petrifac´tion**, turning or being turned into stone; a petrified object; a fossil. [L *petra*—Gr *petrā*, rock, L *facĕre, factum*, to make.]

petro-, in composition, stone; eg **petroglyph** [pet´rō-glif; Gr *glyphein*, to carve] *n* a carving or inscription on rock; **petrography** [petrog´-ra-fi; Gr *graphein*, to write] *n* the description and systematifc classification of rocks; **petrology** [pe-trol´ō-ji; Gr *logos*, discourse] *n* the science of the origin, chemical and mineral composition and structure, of rocks. [Gr *petrā*, rock.]

petrochemical [pet-rō-kem´i-kȧl] *n* any chemical obtained from petroleum or natural gas.

petroleum [pė-trō´lė-um] *n* an oily liquid solution of hydrocarbons occurring naturally in certain rock strata which yields kerosene, gasoline, etc.—*n* **petrolā´tum**, a greasy, jellylike substance derived from petroleum and used for ointments, etc.—Also **petroleum jelly**. [L *petra*, rock, *oleum*, oil.]

petticoat [pet´i-kōt] *n* an underskirt.—*adj* **pett´icoated**. [**petty, coat**.]

pettifogger [pet´i-fog-ėr] *n* a lawyer who handles petty cash, esp unethically; one given to quibbling over trifles.—*n* **pett´ifoggery**, mean tricks; quibbles.—*adj* **pett´ifogging**. [**petty**; origin of second part obscure.]

petty [pet´i] *adj* of small importance, trivial; of inferior status, minor; small-minded.—*adv* **pett´ily**.—*n* **pett´iness**.—**petty cash**, cash kept on hand for payment of minor items; **petty larceny** petit larceny; **petty officer**, a subordinate officer in the navy or coastguard appointed from among the enlisted men. [Fr *petit*, little, inconsiderable.]

petulant [pet´ū-lȧnt] *adj* showing peevish impatience, irritation, or caprice; forward, impudent in manner.—*ns* **pet´ulance, petu´lancy**.—*adv* **pet´ulantly**. [L *petulāns, -antis*, as from assumed *petulāre*, dim of *petĕre*, to seek.]

petunia [pe-tū´ni-ȧ] *n* a genus (*Petunia*) of tropical American herbs of the nightshade family with funnel-shaped corallas. [South American Indian *petun*, tobacco.]

pew [pū] *n* an enclosed compartment or fixed bench in a church;—*n* **pew´holder**, a renter or owner of a church pew. [OFr *puie*, raised place, balcony—L *podia*, pl of *podium*—Gr *podion*, dim of *pous*, gen *podos*, foot.]

pewit [pē´wit, pū´it] *See* **peewit**.

pewter [pū´tėr] *n* an alloy of tin and lead; sometimes tin with a little copper and antimony; vessels made of pewter.—Also *adj*—*n* **pew´terer**, one who works in pewter. [OFr *peutre*; cf It *peltro*, Low Ger *spialter*, Eng **spelter**.]

pH [pē-āch] *n* potential of hydrogen; a measure of the acidity or alkalinity of a solution on a logarithmic scale.

phaeton [fā´(i-)tn] *n* any of various light four-wheeled horse-drawn carriages; an early type of open automobile. [Gr *Phaethōn, -ontos*, lit shining; cf *phaos, phōs*, light.]

phage Short for **bacteriophage**.

phagocyte [fag´ō-sīt] *n* a white blood corpuscle that engulfs harmful bacteria and other particles. [Gr *phagein*, to eat, *kytos*, a vessel.]

phalanger [fal-an´jėr] *n* any one of a family (Phalangeridae) of small arboreal Australian marsupials. [Gr *phalangion*, spider's web, from their webbed toes.]

phalanx [fāl´angks] *n* a solid formation of ancient Greek heavily-armed infantry; a solid body of men, etc.;—*pl* **phal´anxes**; a massed arrangement of persons, animals, or things; an organized body of persons;—*n pl* **phalanges** [falan´jēz] the bones of the fingers and toes. [Gr *phalanx, -angos*, a roller, phalanx, spider.]

phalarope [fal´a-rōp] *n* any of various shorebirds (family Phaloropodidae) resembling sandpipers but good swimmers. [Gr *phalāris*, a coot, *pous*, a foot.]

phanerogam [fan´ėr-ō-gam] *n* a flowering plant, a plant producing seeds. [Gr *phaneros*, visible, *gamos*, marriage.]

phantasm [fan´tazm] *n* a product of fantasy; a spectre; a supposed vision of an absent person, living or dead; an illusive likeness (of).—*pl* **phantas´mata**.—*adjs*. [Gr *phantasma—phantazein*, to make visible—*phainein*, to bring to light—*phaein*, to shine.]

phantasmagoria [fan-taz-ma-gō´ri-a] *n* a fantastic series of images, produced by mechanical means, seen in a dream, or called up by the imagination; something that presents itself to the mind in the form of shifting scenes consisting of many elements.—*adj* **phantasmagŏr´ic**. [Gr *phantasma*, an appearance, *agorā*, assembly.]

phantasy, phantastic *See* **fantasy, fantastic**.

phantom [fan´tȯm] *n* an apparition, a specter; an immaterial form, a vision.—Also *adj* an illusion. [OE *fantosme*—Gr *phantasma*.]

pharaoh [fā´rō] *n* the title of the kings of ancient Egypt.

pharisee [far´i-sē] *n* one of a religious school among the Jews, marked by their strict observance of both the written and oral law; **pharisee**, a very self-righteous or hypocritical person.—*adjs* **pharisā´ic, -al**, pertaining to, or like, the Pharisees; hypocritical.—*adv* **pharisā´ically**.—*ns* **phar´isāism**. [OE *phariseus*—Late L *pharisaeus*—Gr *pharisaios*—Heb *pārūsh*, separated.]

pharmaceutical [fär-ma-sū´tik-ȧl] *adj* pertaining to the knowledge of pharmacy or drugs.—*ns* **pharmaceutical**, a medicinal drug, **pharmaceu´tics**, the science of preparing medicines. [Gr *pharmakeutikos*.]

pharmacopoeia, pharmacopeia [fär-ma-kō-pē´-(y)a] *n* a book or list of drugs with directions for their preparation, esp one issued by an official organization and serving as a standard. [Gr *pharmakopoiiā—pharmakon*, a drug, *poieein*, to make.]

pharmacy [fä´mȧ-si] *n* the art or profession of preparing drugs and medicines; a drug store.—*ns* **phar´macist**, one licensed to practice pharmacy; **pharmacol´ogy**, the science dealing with the effects of drugs on living organisms. [Gr *pharmakon*, a drug.]

pharynx [far´ingks] *n* the cavity leading from the mouth and nasal passages to the larynx and esophagus.—*adj* **pharyngeal** [fa-rin´ji-ȧl].—*n* **pharyngitis** [far-in-jī´tis], inflammation of the pharynx. [Gr *pharynx, -yngos*.]

phase [fāz] *n* the appearance of the moon or a planet at a given time according to the amount of illuminated surface exhibited; any transitory stage or stage in a regularly recurring cycle of changes; a separate and homogeneous part of a heterogeneous system (eg the solid, the liquid and the gaseous phase of water); a stage in a development (eg in a career); an aspect of a thing of varying appearance, or of a problem or situation.—*pl* **phases**.—*vt* to do by phases or stages.—*adj* **phased**, adjusted to be in the same phase at the same time; by stages.—**phase-contrast microscope**, a microscope that translates differences in phase of the light transmitted through or reflected by the object into differences of intensity in the image.—Also **phase microscope**.—**phase out**, to cease gradually to use, make, etc. [Gr *phasis—phaein*, to shine.]

pheasant [fez´(ȧ)nt] *n* a genus (*Phasianus*) of richly colored, gallinaceous, Old World birds raised as ornamental or game birds; any of various birds resembling a pheasant; the bird as food. [Anglo-Fr *fesant*—L *phāsiānus*—Gr *Phāsiānos* (*ornis*, bird), from the river Phasis (now Rioni) in Georgia, Asia.]

phenacetin [fen-as´it-in] *n* a colorless crystalline substance used to decrease fever and to dispel headaches and other pains [*phen(o)-* (Gr *phainos*, shining), used of substances derived from benzene, *acetyl*, the radical or acetic acid, and *-in*.]

phenobarbital [fē-nō-bär´bi-tal] *n* a crystalline barbituate $C_{12}H_{12}N_2O_3$ used as a hypnotic and sedative.

phenomenon [fė-nom´ė-nȯn] *n* anything directly apprehended by the senses or by one of them; any fact or event that can be scientifically described; a remarkable or unusual person, thing, or appearance; (*inf*) an extraordinary person; a prodigy.—*pl* **phenom´ena**.—*adj* **phenom´enal**, known through the senses, perceptible, sensible; dealing with observed data; (*inf*) very unusual or remarkable.—*adv* **phenom´enally**. [Gr *phainomenon*—*phainein*, to show.]

phenotype [fēn´ō-tīp] *n* the observable characteristics of an organism produced by the genes. [Gr *phainein*, to show, and **type**.]

phew [fū] *inter* exclamation of relief or fatigue.

phial [fī´ȧl] *n* a small glass bottle; a vial. [L *phiala*—Gr *phialē*, a broad shallow bowl.]

phil-, philo- [fil-, -ō-] in composition, loving, friend. [Gr *phileein*, to love, *philos*, loved, loving];—eg **philharmonic** [fil-här-mon´ik], *adj*, loving music; *n* a society sponsoring a symphony orchestra; (*inf*) such an orchestra; **philoprogenitive** [fil-ō-prō-jen´i-tiv], *adj* loving one's offspring. [L *progeniēs*, progeny.]

philander [fil-an´dėr] *vi* of a man, to make love, esp in a trifling manner; to be in the habit of so doing.—*n* **philan´derer**. [Gr *philandros*, fond of men or of a husband—*phileein*, to love, *anēr*, gen *andros*, a man, husband; misapplied as if meaning a loving man.]

philanthropy [fil-an´thrȯ-pi] *n* love of mankind, esp as shown in services to general welfare.—*n* **philan´thropist**, one who tries to benefit mankind.—*adjs* **philanthrop´ic** [-throp´ik], **-al**, doing good to others, benevolent.—*adv* **philanthrop´ically**. [Gr *philanthrōpiā*—*phileein*, to love, *anthrōpos*, a man.]

philately [fil-at´ė-li] *n* the study and collection of postage and imprinted stamps; stamp collecting.—*adj* **philatel´ic**.—*n* **philat´elist**. [Fr *philatélie*, invented in 1864—Gr *phileein*, to love, *atelēs*, tax-free—*a-* (privative), *telos*, tax.]

Philemon [fi-lē´mȯn or fī-] *n* (*Bible*) 18th book of the New Testament, epistle written by St Paul during his imprisonment addressed to Philemon.

Philippians [fi-lip-´i-ȧnz] *n* (*Bible*) 11th book of the New Testament, epistle written by St Paul to the Christians of Philippi in Macedonia.

philippic [fil-ip-´ik] *n* a bitter verbal attack. [Gr *philippikos, philippizein*—*Philippos*, Philip.]

Philistine [fil´is-tīn] *n* one of the ancient inhabitants of southwest Palestine, enemies of the Israelites; a person indifferent to culture, whose interests are material and whose ideas are ordinary and conventional.—*n* **Phil´istinism**. [*Philistinos*—Heb *P´lishtīm*.]

philology [fil-ol´ō-ji] *n* the science of language which concerns itself with the sounds of speech, the history of sound changes, etymology, grammar, the history of inflections, etc; an earlier term for linguistics, esp historical and comparative linguistics.—*n* **philol´ogist**, one versed in philology.—*adjs* **philolog´ic, -al**. [Gr *philologiā*—*philos*, loving, *logos*, word.]

Philomel [fil´ō-mel] *n* the nightingale. [Gr *Philomēla*, who was changed into a nightingale or swallow.]

philosopher [fil-os´o-fėr] *n* a lover of wisdom; one versed in or devoted to philosophy; a metaphysician; one who acts calmly and rationally in the affairs and changes of life.—*adjs* **philosoph´ical, philosoph´ic** [-sof´-], pertaining, or according, to philosophy; befitting a philosopher, rational, temperate, calm (of outlook, behaviour, etc.)—*adv* **philosoph´ically**.—*vi* **philos´ophize**, to reason like a philosopher; to moralize, express truisms, etc.—*ns* **philos´ophizer**.—*n* **philos´ophy**, the study of the principles underlying conduct, thought, and the nature of the universe; general principles of a field of knowledge; a particular system of ethics; composure; calmness. [Gr *phileein*, to love, *sophiā*, wisdom.]

philter, philtre [fil´tėr] *n* a magic potion, esp to excite love. [Fr *philtre*—L *philtrum*—Gr *philtron*—*phileein*, to love, suffx *-tron*, denoting the agent.]

phlebitis [flė-bī´tis] *n* inflammation of a vein.—*n* **phlebot´omy**, blood-letting. [Gr *phelps*, gen *phlebos*, a vein.]

phlegm [flem] *n* thick mucus discharged from the throat, as during a cold; sluggishness; apathy.—*adjs* **phlegmatic** [flegmat´ik]. [By later return to Greek spelling, from ME *fleme*, etc., through OFr from L *phlegma*—Gr *phlegma, -atos*, flame, inflammation, phlegm (regarded as produced by heat).]

phloem [flō´ėm] *n* the vascular tissue present in plants, chiefly concerned with the transport of food. [Gr *phloos*, bark.]

phlogiston [flo-jis´ton] *n* the hypothetical principle of fire regarded formerly as a material substance. [Gr neut of verbal adj *phlogistos*, burnt, inflammable,—*phlogizein*, to set on fire.]

phlox [floks] *n* a genus (*Phlox*) of American annual or perennial herbs having red, purple, white, or variegated flowers. [Gr *phlox*, flame, wallflower—*phlegein*, to burn.]

phobia [fō´bi-a] an irrational, excessive, and persistent fear of some thing or situation. [Gr *phobos*, fear.]

phoebe [fē´bē] *n* an American bird (sayornis phoebe) that catches insects in flight. [Gr *phoibos*, bright.]

phoenix [fē´niks] *n* a fabulous bird, the only one of its kind, that burned itself every 500 years or so and rose rejuvenated from its ashes; anything that rises from its own or its predecessor's ashes, the emblem of immortality. [OE *fenix*, later assimilated to L *phoenīx*—Gr *phoinix*.]

phone [fōn] *n vti* (*inf*) telephone.

phoneme [fōn´ēm] *n* a set of language sounds with slight variations but heard as the same sound by native speakers. [Gr *phōnēma*, a sound.]

phonetic, -al [fō-net´ik, -ȧl] *adj* of, concerning, according to, or representing, the sounds of spoken language.—*adv* **phonet´ically**.—*n* **phonetician** [fō-nė-tish´ȧn] one versed in phonetics.—*n* (*pl* in form, treated as *sing*) **phonet´ics**, the science that deals with pronunciation and the representation of the sounds of speech. [Gr *phōnētikos*—*phōnē*, voice.]

phonic [fōn´ik, or fon´ik] *adj* of sound or producing sound; acoustic; of, or relating to the sounds of language.—*n* **phon´ics** [fon´iks], a phonetic method of teaching reading; the science of sound. [Gr *phōnē*, voice, sound.]

phonogram [fō´no-gram] *n* a character representing a sound of speech; a succession of orthographic characters that occurs with the same phonetic value in several words (as ight in bright, light, etc.). [Gr *phōnē*, voice, *gramma*, that which is written—*graphein*, to write.]

phonograph [fō´nō-gräf] *n* an instrument for reproducing sound recorded in a spiral groove on a revolving disk.—*n* **phonography** [fō-nog´ra-fi], spelling based on pronunciation; a system of shorthand writing based on sound [Gr *phōnē*, voice, *graphein*, to write.

phonology [fō-nol´o-ji] *n* the phonetics and phonemes of a language at a particular time; the study of the system of sounds in a language and of the history of their changes, esp in two or more related languages.—*adj* **phonolog´ical**.—*n* **phonol´ogist**. [Gr *phōnē*, voice, *logos*, discourse.]

phony, phoney [fōn´i] *adj* (*int*) not genuine, counterfeit. [Origin unknown.]

phosgene [fos´jēn] *n* a colorless gas $COCl_2$ of unpleasant odor that is a severe respiratory irritant. [Gr *phōs*, light, and the root of *gignesthai*, to be produced.]

phosphorus [fos´fȯr-us] *n* a metalloid element (symbol P; at wt 31.0; at no 15); a phosphorescent substance or body, esp one that glows in the dark.—*n* **phos´phor**, a substance that emits light when excited by radiation.—*adjs* **phosphor´ic, phos´phorous**, of, pertaining to, or resembling phosphorus—used for compounds in which phosphorus has respectively its higher and its lower combining powers (usually a valency of 5 and a valency of 3);—eg **phosphoric acid** (H_3PO_4) and **phosphorous acid** (H_3PO_3; a reducing agent).—*ns* **phosphate** [fos´fāt] a salt of phosphoric acid; **phos´phite**, a salt of phosphorous acid; **phos´phide**, a compound of phosphorus and another element.—*adj* **phosphoro-**, in composition, phosphorus.—*vi* **phosphoresce´** [-es´] to exhibit phosphorescence.—*n* **phosphores´cence**, the property of giving off light without noticeable heat, as phosphorus does; such light.—*adj* **phosphores´cent**. [L *phōsphorus*—Gr *phōsphoros*, light-bearer—*phōs*, light, *phoros*, bearing, from *pherein*, to bear.]

photo- [fō´to-], **phot-**, *fōt-*, in composition, light; as in **photochemistry** [fō-tō-kem´is-tri] *n* the branch of chemistry concerned with the effect of radiant energy in producing chemical changes; photochemical properties; photochemical processes; **photoelectric cell** (or **photocell**), a cell whose electrical properties are modified by light; any device in which light controls an electric circuit which operates a mechanical device, as for opening doors; **photoelectron**, *n* electron ejected from the surface of a body by the action of ultraviolet rays or X-rays upon it; **photoemiss´ion**, *n* emission of electrons from the surface of a body on which light falls; **photo´phobia** [fō´bi-a], a shrinking from the light.—*adjs* **photophobic**, shunning or avoiding light; growing best under reduced illumination; **photosens´itive**; affected by light. [Gr *phōs*, gen *phōtos*, light.]

photo- [fō´to-] in composition, photographic; made by, or by the aid of, photographic means.—**photo**, *n*, *vt* and *adj* an *inf* abbrev of **photograph(ic); photocomposition** *n* in printing, setting of copy by projecting images of letters successively on a sensitive material (also **pho´tosetting**), **pho´tocopy** *n* a photographic reproduction of written matter made by a special device.—*vt* to make a photocopy; **pho´to finish**, *n* a finish of a race in which photography is used to show the winner, etc.; a neck and neck finish of any contest; **photomi´crograph**, photograph taken through a microscope. [**photograph**.]

photoengraving [fō´tō-en-grā´ving] *n* a process by which photographs are reproduced on relief printing plates; such a plate or a print made from it. [**photo**, + **engraving**.]

photogenic [fō-tō-jen´ik] *adj* likely to look attractive in photographs. [Gr *phōs*, gen *phōtos*, light, and *gen-*, root of *gignesthai*, to be produced.]

photography [fō-tog´ra-fi] *n* the art or process of producing permanent and visible images by the action of light on chemically prepared surfaces.—*ns* **phō´tograph** [-gräf], an image so produced; **phōtog´rapher**.—*adjs* **phōtographic** [-graf´ik].—*adv* **phōtograph´ically**.—*n* **photogravūre´**, a method of printing using plates, usually copper, on which the design etched is intaglio (ie consists of hollows below the surface), not relief; a picture so produced. [Gr *phōs*, *phōtos*, light, *graphein*, to draw.]

photolithography [fō´to-li-thog´ra-fi] *n* a process of lithographic printing in which the plates have been prepared photographically.—*n* and *vt* **photolith´ograph** [-o-gräf]. Abbrev **photoli´tho**. [**photo**, + **lithography**.]

photometer [fō-tom´ė-tėr] *n* an instrument for measuring the intensity of light. [Gr *phōs*, gen *phōtos*, light, *metron*, measure.]

photon [fō´ton] *n* a quantum of electromagnetic energy. [Gr *phōs*, gen *phōtos*, light, and suffx *-on*.]

photosphere [fō´tō-sfēr] *n* a sphere of light or radiance; the luminous surface layer of the sun or a star. [Gr *phōs, phōtos*, light, *sphaira*, a sphere.]

Photostat [fō´tō-stat] *n* a photographic apparatus for making facsimiles of writings, drawings, etc., directly upon prepared paper; a facsimile so made. [Gr *phōs*, gen *phōtos*, light, *statos*, set, placed; trade-mark.]

photosynthesis [fō-tō-sin´the-sis] *n* (*bot*) the process by which a green plant manufactures sugar from carbon dioxide and water in the presence of light.—*vi* **photosyn´thesize**.—*adj* **photosynthet´ic**. [Gr *phōs, phōtos*, light, *synthesis*—*syn*, with, together, *thesis*, a placing—*tithenai*, to place.]

phrase [frāz] *n* a group of words, not a full sentence or clause, expressing a single idea by themselves; a pithy expression; an empty or high-sounding expression; (*mus*) a short distinct musical passage; a series of dance movements comprising a section of a pattern.—*vt* to express in words; or in telling terms; to divide into melodic phrases.—*ns* **phrase book**, a book containing idiomatic expressions of a foreign language and their translation; **phrasemaker, phrase´-mong´er**, a user or maker of wordy or fine-sounding phrases; **phraseogram** [frā´zė-ō-gram], **phraseograph**, a symbol for a phrase in some shorthand systems; **phraseol´ogy**, style or manner of expression or arrangements of phrases; peculiarities of diction; **phrā´sing**, the wording of a speech or passage; (*mus*) the grouping and accentuation of the sounds in a melody. [Gr *phrăsis*—*phrazein*, to speak.]

phrenetic, frenetic [fren-et´ik] *adj* delirious; frenzied; proceeding from madness.—Also *n*.—*n* **phrenol´ogy**, a system, now rejected, of analyzing character from the shape of the skull.—*adjs* **phrenolog´ic, -al**.—*n* **phrenol´ogist**. [Gr *phrēn*, gen *phrenos*, midriff, supposed seat of passions, mind, will.]

phthisis [thī´sis, tī´-] *n* wasting disease, esp tuberculosis of the lungs.—*n* **phthisic** [tiz´ik] phthisis.—*adj* **phthisical** [tiz´-]. [Gr *phthisis*—*phthi(n)ein*, to waste away.]

phycology [fī-kol´ō-ji] *n* the study of seaweeds.—*n* **phycol´ogist**. [Gr *phȳkos*, seaweed, *logos*, discourse.]

phylactery [fi-lak´tė-ri] *n* among the Jews, a slip of parchment inscribed with certain passages of Scripture, worn in a box on the left arm or forehead during morning weekday prayers. [L,—Gr *phylaktērion*—*phylax*, a guard.]

phylloxera [fil-ok-sē´ra] *n* any of various plant lice (esp genus *Phylloxera*) that differ from aphids in wing structure and in being continually oviparous, seriously destructive to vines. [Gr *phyllon*, a leaf, *xēros*, dry.]

phylum [fī´lum] *n* a major taxonomic division of plants and animals containing one or more classes; any analogous group, as a group of related language families or linguistic stocks. [Gr *phylon*, race.]

physic [fiz´ik] *n* the science, art, or practice of medicine; a medicine, esp a cathartic.—*vt* to give medicine, esp a purgative, to;—*pr p* **phys´icking**; *pt, pt p* **phys´icked**.—*adj* **phys´ical**, pertaining to the world of matter and energy, or its study; material; bodily.—*n* a general medical examination.—*adv* **phys´ically**.—*ns* **physician** [fi-zish´ȧn] one skilled in the use of physic or in the art of healing; a doctor of medicine; (*arch*) a healer or healing influence; **phys´icist** [-sist], a specialist in physics; (*arch*) a person skilled in natural science.—**phy´sics**, a science that deals with matter and energy and their interactions in the fields of mechanics, acoustics, optics, heat, electricity, magnetism, radiation, atomic structure and nuclear phenomena; the physical processes and phenomena of a particular system.—**physical chemistry**, the study of the dependence of physical properties on chemical composition, and of the physical changes accompanying chemical reactions; **physical geography**, the study of the earth's natural features; **physical therapy**, the treatment of disorders and disease by physical and mechanical means (as massage, exercise, water, heat, etc.); **physical therapist**. [Gr *physikos*, natural—*physis*, nature.]

physiognomy [fiz-i-o(g)n´o-mē] *n* the art of judging character from appearance, esp from the face; the face as an index of the mind; the general appearance of anything. [Gr *physiognōmiă*, a shortened form of *physiognōmoniă* —*physis*, nature, *gnōmōn, -onos*, an interpreter.]

physiography [fiz-i-og´ra-fi] *n* physical geography. [Gr *physis*, nature, *graphein*, to describe.]

physiology [fiz-i-ol´o-ji] *n* the science of the processes of life in animals and plants.—*adjs* **physiologic** [-ō-loj´ik], **-al**.—*adv* **physiolog´ically**.—*n* **physiol´ogist**. [Gr *physis*, nature, *logos*, discourse.]

physiotherapy [fiz-i-ō-ther´ȧ-pi] *n* physical therapy.—*n* **physiother´apist**. [Gr *physis*, nature, *therapeiă*, treatment.]

physique [fiz-ēk´] *n* bodily type, build, or constitution. [Fr.]

phyto- [fī-tō-] in composition, plant. [Gr *phyton*, a plant.]

pi[1] [pī, pē] *n* the sixteenth letter (Π, π) of the Greek alphabet; (*math*) a symbol for the ratio of the circumference of a circle to the diameter, approximately 3.14159.—**pi-** (or **π meson**, particle providing nuclear force holding protons and neutrons together.—Also called **pion**. [Gr *pī*.]

pi[2] [pī] *n* jumbled printing type; any jumble;—*pl* **pies**.—*vt* to jumble.

pianoforte [pē-a´nō-fört or -ä or pē-an-e-fört´ē] *n* piano.—*n* **piano** (pē-a´nō, pya´nō), *n* a large stringed keyboard instrument in which each key operates a felt-covered hammer that strikes a corresponding steel wire or wires.—*pl* **pia´nofortes, pian´os**.—*adj, adv* **pianissimo** [pē-ä-nis´i-mō], very soft(ly).—*n* **pianist** [pē-an´ist, also pyan´-, pē-an´ist], one who plays the pianoforte, esp expertly.—*adj, adv* **piano** [pē-ä´nō, pyä´nō] soft, softly. [It—*piano*, soft (L *plānus*, level), *forte*, loud. (L *fortis*, strong).]

piaster, piastre [pi-as´tėr] *n* a unit of money in Egypt, Lebanon, Sudan, and Syria. [Fr,—It *piastra*, a leaf of metal.]

piazza [pē-ät´sä] *n* in Italy a place or square surrounded by buildings; a walk under a roof supported by pillars; a veranda. [It,—L *platea*—Gr *plateia*, a street (fem of *platys*, broad).]

pibroch [pē´broH] *n* bagpipe music consisting of variations on a theme, often martial. [Gael *piobaireachd*, pipe-music—*piobair*, a piper—*piob*, from Eng **pipe**.]

pica [pi´kä] *n* a size of printing type, 12 point; a typewriter type providing 10 characters to the linear inch and six lines to the vertical inch.

picador [pik´a-dör] *n* a horseman in a bullfight with a lance who uses it to jab the bull to weaken its neck and shoulder muscles. [Sp,—*pica*, a pike.]

picaresque [pik-a-resk´] *adj* resembling the characters or incidents of the *picaresque novels*, tales of Spanish rogue and vagabond life in the 17th century. [Sp *picaro*, rogue.]

picaroon [pik-a-rōōn´] *n* a rogue; a pirate; a bohemian. [Sp *picarón*. See **picaresque**.]

piccalilli [pik´a-lil´i] *n* chopped vegetables in pickle. [Origin uncertain.]

piccolo [pik´ō-lō] *n* a small flute an octave higher than the ordinary flute. [It, little.]

pick [pik] *n* a tool for breaking ground, rock, etc., with head pointed at one or both ends and handle fitted to the middle; an instrument of various kinds for picking as a toothpick or pectrum; an act, opportunity, or right of choice; a portion picked; the best or choicest.—*vt* to break up, dress, or remove with a pick; to pull apart; to poke or pluck at; to clear (as bones of flesh); to remove (from); to pluck; to peck, bite, or nibble; to select; to open (as a lock) by a sharp instrument; to steal from another's pocket.—*vi* to use a pick; to eat by morsels; to pilfer.—*ns* **pick´er; pick´-me-up**, a stimulating drink; a tonic; **pickpocket**, one who picks or steals from other people's pockets; **pickthank** (*arch*), one who seeks to ingratiate himself; **pickup**, an act of picking up; a thing or person picked up; a device for picking up an electric current; accelerating power; a transducer, activated by a sapphire or diamond stylus following the groove on a phonograph record, which transforms the mechanical into electric impulses; a light truck having an enclosed cab and an open body with low sides and tailgate.—*adj* using available or local personnel without formal organization.—**pick at**, to eat sparingly of; **pick faults** (**in**), to seek occasions of fault-finding or of criticizing adversely; **pick off**, to remove by picking; to hit with a carefully aimed shot; **pick on**, (*inf*) to single out for criticism or abuse; to annoy; to tease; **pick out**, to select from a number; **pick up**, to lift from the ground, etc.; to get, find, or learn, esp by chance; to stop for and take along; to gain (speed); to improve in health; (*inf*) to become acquainted casually esp for lovemaking. [Ety obscure.]

pickaback [pik´a-bak] *adv* piggy back.

pickax [pik´aks] *n* a tool used in digging, a pick. [ME *pikois*—OFr *picois*, a mattock, *piquer*, to pierce, *pic* a pick.]

picket [pik´ėt] *n* a pointed stake driven into the ground for fortification, tethering, surveying, etc.; a small outpost, patrol, or other body of men set apart for a special duty; a person as a member of a striking labor union, stationed outside a factory, etc. to demonstrate protest; a person posted for a demonstration or protest.—*vt* to tether to a stake; to enclose with a picket fence; to post as a military picket; to place pickets, or serve as a picket (at a factory, etc.).—*n* **picket line**, a cordon of people serving as pickets. [Fr *picquet*, dim of *pic*, a pickaxe.]

pickle [pik´l] *n* a liquid, esp brine or vinegar, in which food is preserved; anything so preserved, esp a cucumber; (*inf*) a plight.—*vt* to preserve with salt, vinegar, etc. [Me *pikkyll*, etc.; cf Du *pekel*; Ger *pökel*.]

picnic [pik´nik] *n* a usu. informal meal taken on an excursion and eaten outdoors; an outdoor snack; the food so eaten; a shoulder of pork with the butt removed; an easy or pleasant experience.—*vi* to have a picnic.—*pr p* **pic´nicking**; *pt, pt p*, **pic´nicked**. [Fr *pique-nique*.]

pico [pē-kō-, pī-kō-] in composition, 10^{-12}, one million millionth part.

picric acid [pik´rik a´sid] an acid used as a yellow dyestuff in medicine, and as the basis of high explosives. [Gr *pikros*, bitter.]

pictograph [pik´tō-gräf] *n* a picture or picturelike symbol used in a system of writing; a graph using pictures to give data. [L *pictus*, painted, Gr *graphein*, to write.]

pictorial [pik-tō´, tö´, ri-ȧl] *adj* of or relating to painting or drawing; consisting of, expressed in, or of the nature of, pictures; graphic.—*adv* **picto´rially**. [L *pictor, -ōris*, painter—*pingĕre, pictum*, to paint.]

picture [pik´tyůr, -chůr] *n* a representation on a surface, by painting, drawing, photography, etc., of an object or objects, or of a scene, esp when a work of art; a portrait; a person or a sight worthy of being painted; a person resembling another as closely as his portrait; a symbol or type (as, *a picture of health*); an image formed in the mind; a vivid verbal description; a motion picture; (an image on) a television screen.—*vt* to depict, represent in a picture; to form a likeness of in the mind; to describe vividly.—*ns* **pic´ture writ´ing**, the method of recording events or ideas, or conveying messages, by means of pictures.—**in the picture**, adequately informed about the situation; **put someone in the picture**, to give someone all the information necessary for understanding the situation. [L *pictūra—pingĕre, pictum*, to paint.]

picturesque [pik-tū-resk´] *adj* such as would make a striking picture, implying some beauty and much quaintness or immediate effectiveness; (of language) vivid and colorful, evoking mental images.—*adv* **picturesque´ly**.—*n* **picturesque´ness**. [It *pittoresco—pittura*, a picture—L *pictūra*.]

piddle [pid´l] *vi* to deal in trifles; to trifle.

pidgin [pij´in] *n* a jargon for trade purposes, using words and grammar from different languages.—**Pidgin English**, an English based pidgin, used in the Orient and Melanesia. [Chinese pron of **business**.]

pie[1] [pī] a magpie; a chatterer. [Fr,—L *pīca*.]

pie[2] [pī] *n* a baked dish of fruit, meat, etc. with an under or upper crust, or both.—**(as) easy as pie** (*inf*), extremely easy. [Origin unknown.]

piebald [pī´böld] *adj* covered with patches of two colors.—*n* a piebald horse, etc. [**pie** (1) + **bald**.]

piece [pēs] *n* a part or portion of anything; a single article; a definite length, as of cloth manufactured as a unit; a literary, dramatic, musical, or artistic composition; (*slang*) a firearm; a coin or token; a man in chess (excluding pawns); an opinion, view; a short distance; (*slang*) an act of copulation; (*slang; offensive*) the female partner in copulation.—*vt* to enlarge by adding a piece; to form from pieces.—*n pl* **piece´goods**, yard goods.—*adv* **piece´meal**, in pieces; to pieces; bit by bit.—*adj* done bit by bit; fragmentary.—*n* **piece´work**, work paid for by the piece.—**piece of eight**, an old Spanish peso worth eight reals; a **piece**, (of price) each; **a piece of one's mind**, a frank outspoken rebuke; **go to pieces**, to break into parts; to lose self-control; **of a piece**, of the same kind (eg *two of a piece*); of the same kind (with *with*); in keeping, consistent (with). [OFr *piece*—Low L *pecia, petium*, a fragment, a piece of land—thought to be of Celtic (Brythonic) origin.]

pièce de résistance [pyes dė rā-zēs-tās] the main dish of a meal; the most important article in a number of articles. [Fr.]

pied [pīd] *adj* spotted with various colors. [**pie** (1).]

pied-à-terre [pyād a ter] temporary lodging. [Fr.]

pier [pēr] *n* a structure supporting the spans of a bridge; a structure built out over the water and supported by pillars, used as a landing place, pavilion, etc.; (*architecture*) a heavy column used to support weight.—*ns* **pier glass**, a tall mirror occupying the space between windows.—Also **pier mirror**. [ME *pēr*, LL *pēra*.]

pierce [pērs] *vt* to thrust or make a hole through; to enter, or force a way into; to touch or move deeply; to penetrate, see right through (eg a mystery).—*vi* to penetrate—*adj* **pierc´ing**, penetrating; very acute (of cold, pain, etc.).—*adv* **pierc´ingly**. [OFr *percer*.]

Pierian [pī-ē´ri-àn] *adj* of *Pieria*, in Thessaly, the country of the Muses; of or relating to learning or poetry.

Pierrot [pē´ėr-ō, pyer-ō´] *n* a figure in old Italian comedy and old French pantomime, usu. having a whitened face and wearing baggy white clothes. [Fr, dim of *Pierre*, Peter.]

pietà [pyā-tä´] *n* a representation of the Virgin with the dead Christ across her knees. [It—L *pietās, -ātis*, dutifulness, piety.]

piety [pī´ė-ti] *n* the quality of being pious; devoutness; sense of duty towards parents, benefactors, etc.; dutiful conduct.—*ns* **Pī´etist**, adherent of a sect of German religious reformers of deep devotional feeling (end of 17th century); **pi´etist**, a person marked by strong devotional feeling; one affecting devotion. **Pī´etism, pi´etism**.—*adjs* **pietist´ic, -al**. [OFr *piete*—L *pietās, -ātis*.]

piezo- [pī-ē´zō-] in composition, pressure [Gr *piĕzein*, to press] **piezoelectricity**, electricity developed in certain crystals by mechanical strains—also, the effect of an electric field in producing in such crystals expansion along one axis and contraction along another; these effects are made use of in types of microphone, etc.

piffle [pif´l] *n* (*inf*) nonsense, worthless talk.

pig [pig] *n* a domesticated animal with a broad snout and a fat body raised for food; a swine; a hog, a young hog; a greedy or filthy person; an oblong casting of metal poured from the smelting furnace; (*slang*) a policeman.—*vi* to bring forth pigs; to live like pigs.—*pr p* **pigg´ing**; *pt, pt p* **pigged**—*adj*—**pigg´ery**, a place where pigs are kept.—*adjs* **pigg´ish**, like a pig; greedy; dirty; **pigg´yback**, on the shoulders or back; of or by a transportation system in which loaded truck trailers are carried on railroad cars; **pig´head´ed**, stupidly obstinate.—*n* **pig iron**, crude iron as it comes from the blast furnace.—*vi* **pig´stick**, to hunt wild boar on horseback with a spear.—*ns* **pig´sticker; pig´sty**, a pen for keeping pigs; **pig´tail**, a tight braid of hair; a roll of twisted tobacco.—**a pig in a poke**, something offered in such a way that its real nature or value is concealed; **make a pig of oneself**, (*inf*), to overindulge in food or drink. [ME *pigge*; cf Du *bigge*, big.]

pigeon [pij´in] *n* any bird of the dove family (Columbidae), birds with a small head, plump body, and short legs, esp the varieties existing in domestication and a feral state in towns and cities throughout most of the world; a young woman; an easy mark; an object of special concern. *ns* **pig´eon breast´**, a deformity with breastbone thrown forward; **pig´eonhole**, a niche for a pigeon's nest; a compartment for storing papers, etc.; a category usu. failing to reflect actual complexities.—*vt* to classify, arrange systematically; to file for reference; to put aside—*adjs* **pig´eonliv´ered**, meek, mild; **pig´eon-toed**, having the toes turned in.—*n* **clay pigeon**, a clay disk thrown from a trap and shot at as a substitute for a live pigeon. [OFr *pijon*—L *pīpiō, -ōnis—pīpīre*, cheep.]

piggin [pig´in] *n* a small wooden pail with one stave extendible as a handle.

pigment [pig´mėnt] *n* paint; any substance used for coloring; that which gives color to animal and vegetable tissues.—*n* **pigmentā´tion**, coloration or discoloration by pigments in the tissues. [L *pīgmentum—pingĕre*, to paint.]

pigmy *See* pygmy.

pike[1] [pīk] *n* a pikestaff; a sharp point or spike; the top of a spear; a long-snouted fish (*E sox lucius*) of lakes, rivers and streams widely distributed in cooler parts of the northern hemisphere, important as a food and game fish.—*ns* **pike´man**, a man armed with a pike; **pike´staff**, a spiked staff for use on slippery ground; a former weapon consisting of a metal spearhead on a long wooden shaft. [OE *pīc*, pick, spike; similar words occur in Fr, the Scand languages, etc.]

pike[2] [pīk] a turnpike; a railroad or a railroad line or system.

pilaf, pilaff [pi-läf´] or **pilau, pilaw** [pe-lō´ or pē´lō] *n* a dish of rice cooked in a seasoned liquid usu. containing meat. [Pers *pilāw*, Turk *pilāw, pilāf*.]

pilaster [pi-las´tėr] *n* a square column, partly built into, partly projecting from a wall. [Fr *pilastre*—It *pilastro*—L *pīla*, a pillar.]

pilau, pillau *See* **pilaf**.

pilchard [pil´chȧrd] *n* a fish (*Sardinia pilchardus*) of the herring family occurring in great schools along European coasts; any of several sardines, esp one in Pacific waters, related to the pilchard. [Origin unknown; poss Scand; cf Norw *pilk*, artificial bait.]

pile[1] [pīl] *n* a heap of more or less regular shape; a heap of combustibles, esp for burning dead bodies; a tall building (*elect*) a form of battery; (*inf*) a large amount; earlier term for nuclear reactor.—*vt* (*usu. with* **up** or **on**) to lay in a pile or heap; to heap up; to accumulate.—*vi* to become piled up; to move confusedly in a mass (*with* **in, out, on**, etc)—*n* **pileup**, an accumulation of tasks, etc.; (*inf*) a collision involving several motor vehicles. [Fr,—L *pīla*, a pillar.]

pile[2] [pīl] *n* a large stake or cylinder driven into the earth to support foundations.—*vt* to drive piles into.—*n* **pile´driv´er, pile engine**, an engine for driving in piles. [OE *pīl*—L *pīlum*, a javelin.]

pile[3] [pīl] *n* a covering of hair, esp soft, fine or furry; a raised surface on cloth, etc produced by an extra set of filling yarns forming raised loops which are sheared, as on a rug. [L *pīlus*, a hair.]

pile[4] [pīl] *n* a single haemorrhoid. [L *pīla*, a ball.]

pileated [pī´li-ātėd] *adjs* having a crest covering the pileum.—*n* **pileum**, the top of the head of a bird from the bill to the nape. [L *pīleum, pīleus*, for *pilleum, pilleus*, a felt cap; cf Gr *pīlos*, felt.]

pilfer [pil´fėr] *vi* and *vt* to steal esp in small quantities.—*n* **pil´ferage**, petty theft. [Prob connected with **pelf**.]

pilgrim [pil´grim] *n* (*arch* and *poet*) a wanderer, wayfarer; one who travels a distance to visit a holy place; **Pilgrim**, one of the band of English Puritans who founded the Plymouth colony in 1620.—*n* **pil´grimage**, the journeying of a pilgrim; a journey to a shrine or other holy place; any long journey. [OFr assumed *pelegrin* (later *pèlerin*)—L *peregrīnus*, foreigner, stranger.]

pill [pil] *n* a little ball of medicine; anything unpleasant or repugnant that must be accepted or endured; (*slang*) a disagreeable or tiresome person.—*n* **pillbox**, a box for pills, esp an ornamental one; a small concrete blockhouse; a small round brimless hat.—**the Pill, pill**, an oral contraceptive for women. [L *pĭla*, perh through OFr *pile*, or from a syncopated form of the dim *pilŭla*.]

pillage [pil´ij] *n* act of plundering; plunder.—*vti* to plunder.—*n* **pill´ager**. [OE *pylian* and OFr *peler*, both—L *pĭlāre*, to deprive of hair; cf **peel** (1).]

pillar [pil´ȧr] *n* a slender, vertical structure used as a support; a structure of like form erected as a monument, etc.; one who, or anything that, sustains.—*n* **pill´ar-box**, (*Brit*) a short hollow pillar for posting letters in.—**from pillar to post**, from one state of difficulty to another; hither and thither. [OFr *piler* (Fr *pilier*)—Low L *pīlāre*—L *pīla*, a pillar.]

pillau *See* **pilaf**.

pillion [pil´yȯn] *n* a pad or light saddle consisting chiefly of a cushion for a woman; a cushion behind a horseman for a second rider; an extra seat on a bicycle or motorcycle. [Prob Ir *pillín, pilliún*, Gael *pillean*, a pad, a pack-saddle—*peall*, a skin or mat, L *pellis*, skin.]

pillory [pil´ȯr-i] *n* a wooden frame, supported by an upright pillar or post, and having holes through which the head and hands of a criminal were put as a punishment.—*vt* to set in the pillory; to hold up to ridicule;—*pt, pt p* **pill´oried**. [OFr *pilori*; perh through Low L—L *speculāria*, windowpanes.]

pillow [pil´ō] *n* a cushion for a sleeper's head; any object used for the purpose; cushion for making lace with a bobbin; a support used to equalize or distribute pressure.—*vt* to lay for support (on); to serve as pillow for.—*ns* **pill´owcase, pillowslip**, a cover for a pillow.—*adj* **pill´owy**, like a pillow; soft. [OE *pyle*, also *pylu*—L *pulvīnus*.]

pilose [pī´lōs´] *adj* hairy.—*n* **pilos´ity**. [L *pīlōsus—pīlus*, hair.]

pilot [pī´lȯt] *n* a steersman; esp one licensed to conduct ships in and out of a harbor, along a dangerous coast, etc.; one qualified to operate the flying controls of an aircraft; a guide; a mechanical directing device; a television show produced as a sample of a proposed series.—*vt* to act as pilot to.—*ns* **pī´lotage**, piloting; pilot's fee; **pī´lot balloon´**, a small balloon sent up to find how the wind blows; **pī´lot en´gine**, a locomotive sent before a train to clear its way, **pī´lot fish**, a fish (*Naucratus ductor*) that accompanies a shark; **pīlot light**, a small gas light kept burning to light a larger jet; a small electric light to show where a switch is located or whether a motor is in operation or when the current is on. [Fr *pilotte*, now *pilote*—It *pilota*, perh—Gr *pēdon*, oar, in pl rudder.]

Pima [pē´mȧ] *n* member of an Amerindian people of southern Arizona;—*pl* **Pima, Pimas**; the Uto-Aztecan language of the Pima.—*n* **Pima cotton**, variety of cotton grown in the southern US, used esp for clothing.

pimento [pi-men´tō] *n* allspice or Jamaica pepper; the tree (*Pimenta officinalis*) producing it.—Also **pimien´to**, [-myen or -men]. [OFr *piment*, Sp *pi-miento*—L *pīgmentum*, paint.]

pimp [pimp] *n* a prostitute's agent.—Also *vi*

pimpernel [pim´pėr-nel] *n* a genus (*Anagallis*) of plants of the primrose family, with scarlet (or blue etc.) flowers. [OFr *pimpernelle*, mod Fr *pimprenelle*; origin doubtful.]

pimple [pim´pl] *n* a pustule; a small, elevated, inflamed swelling of the skin.—*adjs* **pim´pled, pim´ply**, having pimples.

pin [pin] *n* a piece of wood or metal used for fastening things together; a peg for various purposes; a small piece of pointed wire with a head; an ornament or badge with a pin or clasp for fastening to clothing; (*bowling*) one of the clubs at which the ball is rolled; anything of little value; (*pl*) (*inf*) leg.—*vt* to fasten with a pin; to transfix with a pin or a sharp weapon; to hold firmly in one position; to fix or fasten (to)—*pr p* **pinn´ing**; *pt, pt p* **pinn´ed**.—*n* **pin´ball machine, pinball game**, an amusement device in which a ball runs down a sloping board set with pins or other targets.—*ns* **pinfeath´er**, a young unexpanded feather, esp one just emerging from the skin; **pin mon´ey**, money allotted to a wife for private expenses; money set aside for incidental minor expenses; a trivial amount of money; **pin´point´**, the point of a pin; anything very sharp and very minute (*vt* **pin´point**, to locate, place, very exactly; to define exactly); **pin´prick´**, a small puncture as made by a pin; a trifling irritation; **pinstripe´**, a very narrow stripe in suit fabrics, etc.—**pin something on (someone)**, (*inf*) to lay the blame for (something) on someone; **pin (down)**, to get (someone) to commit himself as to his plans, etc.; to establish (a fact, etc.); **pins and needles**, a tingling feeling in arm, leg, etc. due to impeded circulation; **on pins and needles**, in agitated expectancy. [OE *pinn*, prob—L *pinna*, a feather, a pinnacle.]

pinafore [pin´a-fōr, -för] *n* a sleeveless garment worn over a dress, blouse, or sweater. [**pin**, + **afore**.]

pince-nez [pẽs´-nā] *n* pair of eyeglasses with a spring for catching the nose. [Fr, pinch nose.]

pincers [pin´sėrz] *n* a gripping tool, used for drawing out nails, etc; a grasping claw, as of a crab. [OFr *pincer*, to pinch.]

pinch [pinch] *vt* to compress a small part of between finger and thumb or between any two surfaces; to nip; to squeeze or compress painfully; to prune the tip of (a plant or shoot) to induce branching or to improve appearance; to stint (a person) of food, etc.; (*slang*) to steal; (*slang*) to catch or to arrest, take into custody.—*vi* to nip or squeeze; to be painfully tight; to be very economical or niggardly.—*n* an act or experience of pinching; a quantity that can be taken up between the finger and thumb; a critical time of difficulty or hardship; an emergency.—*adj* **pinched**, having the appearance of being tightly squeezed; hard pressed by want or cold.—*vi* **pinch-hit**, (*baseball*) to bat in place of the player whose turn it is; to substitute in an emergency (for).—*n* **pinch hitter**.—*adv* **pinch´ingly**.—**pinch pennies**, to practice strict economy. [OFr *pincier*; prob Gmc cf Du *pitsen*, to pinch.]

pinchbeck [pinch´bek] *n* a yellow alloy of copper with much less zinc than ordinary brass, simulating gold; something counterfeit or spurious. [invented by Chris *Pinchbeck*, a London watchmaker (*d* 1732).]

pine[1] [pīn] *n* any tree of the northern temperate coniferous genus (*Pinus*) with long needles growing two to five in a cluster and having large, well-formed cones; trees of the pine family (*Pinacca*) which include spruce, fir, and hemlock; the wood of the pine ranging from extreme softness in the white pine to hardness in the longleaf pine; a pineapple.—Also *adj*—*ns* **pine´apple**, a tropical plant, (*Ananas comosus*) and its fruit, shaped like a pine cone; **pine nut**, the edible seed of various pines; **pin´ery**, a hothouse where pineapples are grown; a grove or forest of pine.—*adj* **pī´ny**, of, like, or abounding in pine trees. [OE *pīn*—L *pīnus*.]

pine[2] [pīn] *vi* to waste away, esp under pain or mental distress; to long (*with* **for**.) [OE *pīnian*, to torment—L *poena*, punishment.]

ping [ping] *n* a whistling sound as of a bullet—*vti* to strike with a ping.—*n* **ping´ pong´**, a trade name for table tennis equipment. [Imit]

pinion[1] [pin´yȯn] *n* a wing; the last joint of a bird's wing; any wing feather.—*vt* to confine the wings of; to confine by binding the arms. [OFr *pignon*—L *pinna* (= *penna*), wing.]

pinion[2] [pin´yȯn] *n* a small toothed wheel, meshing with a larger toothed wheel, or with a rack; the smaller of a pair or the smallest of a train of gear wheels. [Fr *pignon*—OFr *penon*, a battlement—L *pinna*.]

pink[1] [pingk] *n* any plant or flower of the genus (*Dianthus*) that includes carnation and Sweet William; pale-red; the most perfect condition; the highest point.—*adj* pale-red; (*inf*) somewhat radical in political views.—*n* **pinkeye**, an acute highly contagious conjunctivitis of man and various domestic animals. [Prob a different word from the preceding.]

pink[2] [pingk] *vt* to stab, pierce; to wound by ridicule, etc.; to cut a saw-toothed edge on (cloth, etc.); to perforate in an ornamental pattern.—*n* **pinking shears**, shears with notched edges for pinking edges of cloth. [ME *pinkey*, to thrust.]

[Du *pinken*, to wink.]

pinnace [pin´ȧs] *n* a small vessel with oars and sails, esp one used as a ship's tender; any of various ship's boats. [Fr *pinasse*.]

pinnacle [pin´ȧ-kl] *n* a slender turret; a high pointed rock or mountain like a spire; the highest point. [Fr *pinacle*—Low L *pinnāculum*, dim from L *pinna*, a feather.]

pinnate [pin´āt] *adj* shaped like a feather, esp in having parts arranged in the opposite sides of an axis.—*adv* **pinn´ately**. [L *pinna*, feather.]

pint [pīnt] *n* measure of capacity equal to ½ quart. [Fr *pinte*.]

pintle [pin´tl] *n* a bolt or pin, esp one on which something turns. [OE *pintel*.]

Pinyin [pin´yin´] *n* the official system of romanizing Chinese.

pion [pī´on] *n* a pi- (π-) meson (see **pi**.)

pioneer [pī-ȯn-ēr´] *n* one who is among the first in new fields of enterprise, exploration, colonization, research, etc.; a plant or animal capable of establishing itself in a barren area and initiating an ecological cycle.—Also *vti*. [OFr *peonier*—*pion*, a foot-soldier—Low L *pedō, pedōnis*—L *pēs, pedis*, a foot.]

pious [pī´us] *adj* showing, having, or proceeding from piety; professing to be religious.—*adv* **pi´ously**. [L *pius*.]

pip[1] [pip] *n* a disease of a bird, marked by formation of a scale on the tongue; the scale; a slight nonspecific disorder of humans. [App—Middle Du *pippe*—LL *pipita*—L *pītuīta*, rheum.]

pip[2] [pip] *n* a small hard body (seed or fruitlet) in fleshy fruit. [App from **pippin**.]

pip[3] [pip] *vt* to break open (the shell of an egg) in hatching.—*vi* to break through the shell of an egg.

pip[4] [pip] *n* a spot on dice and dominoes to indicate numerical value; a single rootstock of the lily of the valley. [Orig unknown.]

pip[5] [pip] *n* a short high-pitched tone. [Imit.]

pipe[1] [pīp] *n* a tube of wood, metal, etc. for making musical sounds; (*pl*) the bagpipes; any tube; a tube with a bowl at the end for smoking tobacco; a long tube or hollow body for conveying water, gas, etc.—*vi* to play upon a pipe; to whistle.—*vt* to play on a pipe; to utter shrilly in speech or song; to lead, call, or accompany with a pipe; to supply with pipes; to ornament with piping.—*ns* **pipe´ clay**, fine white clay used for making tobacco pipes and for whitening belts, etc.; **pipe´ dream**, a hope or fancy as futile and unreal as an opium smoker's dream; **pipe´line**, a long continuous line of pipes to carry water from a reservoir, oil from an oilfield, finely divided solids; a direct channel for information; the processes through which supplies pass from source to user; **pipe´ organ**, an organ with pipes; **pip´er**, a player on a pipe, esp a bagpipe.—*adj* **pip´ing**, playing a pipe; whistling; thin and high pitched.—*n* pipeplaying; singing (of birds) or similar noise; a system of pipes; a pipelike fold of material used as trimming for clothes; **piping hot** hissing hot.—**in the pipeline**, waiting, ready to be considered or dealt with; **pipe down**, to subside into silence. [OE *pīpe*—*L pīpāre*, to cheep; cf Du *pijp*, Ger *pfeife*.]

pipe[2] [pīp] *n* a cask or butt of two hogsheads. [OFr *pipe*, cask, tube; cf **pipe** (1).]

pipette [pip-et´] *n* a tube for transferring and measuring fluids. [Fr dim of *pipe*.]

pipit [pip´it] *n* a larklike genus (*Anthus*) of birds. [Prob imit.]

pipkin [pip´kin] *n* a small earthenware or metal pot with a horizontal handle. [Perh a dim of **pipe**.]

pippin [pip´in] *n* a kind of apple, usu. green or yellow strongly flushed with red, esp used for cooking; a highly admired person or thing. [OFr *pepin*.]

pipsissewa [pip-sis´ė-waw] *n* any of a genus (*Chimaphila*, esp *C umbellata*) of evergreen herbs of the wintergreen family whose astringent leaves are used as a tonic and a diuretic.—Also **bittersweet**.

piquant [pē´kȧnt] *adj* stinging; pleasantly pungent; appetizing; kindling keen interest.—*n* **piq´uancy**.—*adv* **piq´uantly**. [Fr, *pr p* of *piquer*, to prick.]

pique [pēk] *n* animosity or ill-feeling; offense taken.—*vt* to wound the pride of; to nettle; to arouse (eg curiosity); to pride (*oneself on* or *upon*).—*pr p* **piquing** [pēk´ing]; *p t, pt p* **piqued** [pēkd]. [Fr *pique*, a pike, pique, *piquer*, to prick.]

piqué [pē-kā] *n* a stiff corded cotton fabric. [Fr pt p of *piquer*, to prick.]

piquet [pi-ket´] *n* a two-handed game played with a pack of 32 cards. [Fr; origin unknown.]

pirate [pī´rȧt] *n* one who practices piracy.—*vti* to take (something) by piracy; to publish or reproduce (a book, recording, etc.) in violation of a copyright.)—*n* **piracy** [pī´rȧ-si] robbery on the high seas; infringement of copyright or patented work.—*adj* **piratical** [pī-rat´ik-ȧl] pertaining to a pirate; practising piracy.—*adv* **pirat´ically**. [L *pīrāta*—Gr *peirātēs*—*peiraein*, to attempt.]

pirouette [pir-ōō-et´] *n* a spinning about on tiptoe.—*vi* to spin round on tiptoe. [Fr.]

Pisces [pis´ēz] *n* the Fishes, the twelfth sign of the zodiac in astrology, operative from February 19 to March 20.—*n* **piscator** [pis-kā-tȯr] an angler.—*adjs* **piscatorial** [pis-ka-tō´ri-ȧl], **piscatory** [pis´ka-tȯr-i] relating to fishing.—*n* **pis´ciculture**, the rearing of fish by artificial methods.—*adjs*

piscine [pis´īn] of fishes; **pisciv´orous**, feeding on fishes. [L *piscis*, a fish; *piscātor*, fishes.]
piscina [pis´ē´na, -ī´na] *n* a basin near the altar. [L *piscis*, a fish.]
pismire [pis´mīr] *n* an ant or emmet.
pistachio [pis-ta´(t)shi-ō] *n* a small tree (*Pistacia vera* of the sumac family related to the cashew; its edible greenish seed.—Also **pistachio nut**. [Sp *pistacho* and It *pistacchio*—forms in LL, Gr and Pers.]
piste [pēst] *n* a beaten track, esp a ski trail. [Fr.]
pistil [pis´til, -tl] *n* properly the gynaeceum of a flower, but, in cases where the carpels are separate, often used as meaning a single carpel.—*adj* **pis´tillāte**, having a pistil but no functional stamens, female. [L *pistillum*, a pestle.]
pistol [pis´tl] *n* a small handgun.—*vt* to shoot with a pistol.—*ns* **pistole** [pis-tōl´] an old Spanish gold coin; any of several old gold coins of Europe of approximately the same value. [OFr *pistole* prob from *Pistoia* province in Italy.]
piston [pis´tȯn] *n* a solid piece moving to and fro in a close-fitting hollow container as in engines and pumps.—*n* **pis´ton rod**, the rod to which the piston is fixed, and which moves with it. [Fr—It *pistone*—*pestāre*, to pound—L *pinsĕre, pistum*.]
pit [pit] *n* a hole in the earth; a scooped-out place for burning something (as charcoal); a sunken or depressed area below the adjacent floor area; a space at the front of the stage for the orchestra; an area in a securities or commodities exchange in which members do the trading; a place beside the course where cars in a race can be refuelled and repaired; the indentation left by smallpox, etc.; an enclosure for cockfights or the like.—*vt* to mark with little hollows; to lay in a pit; to set to fight (against another).—*vi* to become marked with pits; to make a pit stop.—*pr p* **pitt´ing**; *pt, pt p* **pitt´ed**.—*ns* **pit´fall**, a lightly covered hole as a trap for beasts; (*fig*) a hidden danger; **pit´ saw**, a handsaw worked by two persons one of whom stands on or above the log being sawed and the other below it usu. in a pit.—**the pit**, hell. [OE *pytt*—L *puteus*, a well.]
pit-a-pat [pit´a-pat] *adv* with palpitation or pattering. [Imit.]
pitch[1] [pich] *n* the black shining residue of distillation of tar, etc.; any of various bituminous substances; resin obtained from various conifers and often used medicinally; any of various artificial mixtures resembling resinous or bituminous pitches.—*vt* to smear, cover, or caulk with pitch.—*adj* **pitch´-black**, black or extremely dark.—*n* **pitch´blende**, a black mineral of resinous luster, chiefly composed of uranium oxides.—*adj* **pitch´-dark**, utterly dark.—*n* **pitch´ pine**, a name for several American pines that yield pitch, esp a 3-leaved pine (*Pinus rigida*) of eastern N America; the wood of a pitch pine.—*adj* **pitch´y**, like pitch; smeared with pitch; black. [OE *pic*—L *pix*.]
pitch[2] [pich] *vt* (*rare*) to thrust or fix in the ground; to fix in position by means of stakes, pegs, etc., driven into the ground, to erect (eg a tent); to place or lay out (wares) for sale; to arrange, to set in array; (*mus*) to set (in a particular key, high, low); (*fig*) to give this or that emotional tone to; to throw or toss, esp in such a manner as to cause to fall flat or in a definite position; to let one's choice fall (upon); (*golf*) to lift the ball so that it does not roll much on falling; (*baseball*) to deliver the ball to the batter.—*vi* to plunge or fall, esp forward; (of a ship) to plunge so that bow and stern alternately rise and fall in the water—opp to *roll*; to slope down.—*n* a throw or cast; the place at which one (eg a street trader) is stationed; (*cricket*) the ground between the wickets; the distance between two consecutive things or points in a series of corresponding things or points, eg between a point on a gear tooth and the corresponding points on the next, or between corresponding points on the thread of a screw; degree of slope; degree, esp of elevation or depression; any point, degree, or stage, esp the extreme; the degree of acuteness of sounds.—*n* **pitch´fork**, a fork for pitching hay, etc.—*vt* to lift with a pitchfork; to throw suddenly into (*lit* and *fig*).—**pitch into**, to assail vigorously; **pitch pipe**, a small tuning pipe, used to set the pitch especially for singers. [App conn with **pick, pike**.]
pitcher [pich´ėr] *n* a vessel for holding or pouring liquids.—*n* **pitch´er plants**, an insectivorous plant (esp family Sarraceniaccae) with modified leaves in pitcher form. [OFr *picher*—Low L *picārium*, a goblet—Gr *bīkos*, a wine-vessel.]
piteous [pit´ė-us] *adj* fitted to excite pity and compassion.—*adv* **pit´eously**.—*n* **pit´eousness**. [OFr *pitos*—root of **pity**.]
pith [pith] *n* the soft substance in the center of the stems of plants; similar material elsewhere, as the white inner skin of an orange; importance; the soft or spongy interior of a part of a body.—*adj* **pith´y**, full of pith; forcible; terse and full of meaning.—*adv* **pith´ily**.—*n* **pith´iness**. [OE *pitha*; Du *pit*, marrow.]
pithecanthropine [pith-i-kan(t)´thrȯ-pīn] *n* any of a group of pleistocene hominids (as Java man, Peking man, and Heidelberg man) having a smaller cranial capacity than modern man (*Homo sapiens*), formerly considered to comprise a genus (*Pithecanthropus*) but now grouped in a single species (*Homo erectus*).—*n* **pithecanthropus** [pith-ē-kan-thrō´pus] pithecanthropine. [Gr *pithēkos*, ape, *anthrōpos*, man.]
piton [pē-t•] *n* a steel peg to be driven into rock or ice, used in climbing. [Fr.]
pittance [pit´ȧns] *n* a special additional allowance of food or drink in a religious house, or a bequest to provide it; a dole; a very small portion or quantity, or remuneration. [OFr *pitance*—L *pietās*, pity.]
pity [pit´i] *n* a feeling for the sufferings and misfortunes of others; a cause or source of pity or grief; a regrettable fact.—*vt* to feel pity for;—*pt, pt p* **pit´ied**.—*adj* **pit´iable**, to be pitied; miserable, contemptible.—*n* **pit´iableness**.—*adv* **pit´iably**.—*adj* **pit´iful**, compassionate; sad; despicable.—*adv* **pit´ifully**.—*n* **pit´ifulness**.—*adj* **pit´iless**, without pity; cruel.—*adv* **pit´ilessly**.—*n* **pit´ilessness**. [OFr *pite*—L *pietās, pietātis*—*pius*, pious.]
pivot [piv´ȯt] *n* a pin on which anything turns; a key person upon whom, or position on which, a body wheels; (*fig*) that on which anything depends or turns.—*vi* to turn on, or as if on, a pivot.—*adj* **piv´otal**.—*n* **piv´oting**, the pivot-work in machines. [Fr *pivot*, perh related to It *piva*, a pipe, a peg, a pin.]
pixel [pik´sel] *n* one of the minute units which make up an image (as on a television screen).
pixy, pixie [pik´si] *n* a small fairy, esp a mischievous sprite.
pizza [pēt´sa] *n* an open pie of bread dough with tomatoes, cheese, etc.—*n* **pizzeria** [pēt´sė-rē-ȧ] a place where pizzas are made and sold. [It.]
pizzicato [pit-si-kä´tō] *adj* (*mus*) played by plucking the string, not with the bow.—*adv* by plucking.—*n* a tone so produced; a passage so played. [It twitched.]
placable [plak´ȧ-bl] *adj* that may be appeased, willing to forgive.—*n* **placabil´ity**.—*adv* **plac´ably**.—*vt* **plac´ate** [plāk-, plak´āte] to conciliate. [L *plācāre*, to appease, akin to *placēre*, to please.]
placard [plak´ärd] *n* a written or printed paper stuck upon a wall or otherwise displayed as an intimation.—*vt* [plakärd´] to publish by placard; to display as a placard; to stick placards on. [OFr *plackart, placard, etc*—*plaquier*, to lay flat, plaster.]
place [plās] *n* a court or short street in a city; space; room; a region; a particular point, part, position, etc.; the part of space occupied by a person or thing; a dwelling or home; a building, room, etc., assigned to some purpose (as, *place of business, worship*); a seat or accommodation in a theater, train, at table etc.; a position in space or on the earth's surface, or in any system, order or arrangement; the position held by anyone; the position of a figure in a series as indicating its value; a position attained as in a competition or assigned by criticism; proper position or dignity; rank; a step in the progression of an exposition (*in the first place* etc.).—*vt* to put in any place; to find a place for; to identify; to estimate; to rank; to give (an order) to a supplier.—*vi* to finish second or among the first three in a race.—*ns* **place mat**, a small mat serving as an individual table cover for a person at a meal; **placement**, a placing or being placed; location or arrangement; **placement test**, a test usu. given to a student entering a school, a college, etc. to determine his proficiency in various subjects; **place-name**, the name of a geographical locality.—**take place**, to occur. [Partly OE (Northumbrian) *plæce*, market-place, but mainly Fr *place*, both from L *platēa*—Gr *plateia* (*hodos*), broad (street).]
placebo [pla-sē´bō] *n* a pharmacologically inactive substance administered as a drug either to humor the patient in the treatment of psychological illness or in the course of drug trials. [L lit 'I shall please'.]
placenta [pla-sen´ta] *n* the structure that unites the unborn mammal, excepting monotremes and marsupials, to the womb of its mother; an analogous structure in other animals; (*bot*) the part of a plant to which the seeds are attached.—*pl* **placentas, placen´tae** [-tē].—*adj* **placen´tal**. [L *placenta*, a flat cake—Gr *plakoeis* (contr *plakous*), from *plax*, gen *plakos*, anything flat.]
placer [plas´ėr, plās´ėr] *n* a surface deposit of sand, gravel, etc., from which gold or other mineral can be washed. [Sp *placer*, sandbank—*plaza*, place.]
placid [plas´id] *adj* calm, serene.—*ns* **placid´ity, plac´idness**.—*adv* **plac´idly**. [L *placidus*—*placēre*, to please.]
placket [plak´ėt] *n* a slit at the waist of a skirt or dress to make it easy to put on or take off.
plagal [plāg´ȧl] *adj* of a church mode, having the key note on the 4th scale step; of a cadence, progressing from the subdominant chord to the tonic. [Mediaeval L *plagālis*—Gr *plagios*, sideways, aslant + **cadence**.]
plage [pläzh] *n* a beach at a seaside resort; a bright spot on the sun. [Fr.]
plagiary [plā´ji-ȧr-i] *n* one who takes the writings of others and gives them out as his own.—*vt* **pla´giarize**, to steal from the writings of another.—*ns* **pla´giarism**, the act or practice of plagiarizing; **pla´giarist**. [L *plăgiārius*, a kidnapper, plagiary—*plăga*, a net.]
plague [plāg] *n* a deadly epidemic or pestilence; any troublesome thing or person.—*vt* to afflict with a plague; to pester or annoy.—*pr p* **plāg´uing**; *pt, pt p* **plāgued**. [OFr *plague*—L *plāga*, a blow.]
plaice [plās] *n* any of various flatfishes, esp a large European flounder (*Pleuronectes platessa*). [OFr *plaïs* (Fr *plie*)—Low L *platessa*, a flatfish, perh—Gr *platys*, flat.]
plaid [plad] *n* a long piece of woolen cloth worn over the shoulder, usu. in tartan (as part of Highland dress) or checked (as formerly worn by Lowland shepherds); a cloth with a crossbarred pattern imitating tartan; any pattern imitating tartan.—*adj* **plaid´ed**, wearing a plaid. [Perh Gael *plaide*, a blanket; but that may be from the Scots word.]
plain [plān] *adj* flat, level; unobstructed (eg view); open to the mind, manifest, obvious; readily understood; outspoken, candid; without ornament; not intricate or elaborate; not colored; not rich or highly seasoned (of

food); not luxurious (eg *plain living*); not highly born, cultivated, or gifted; without beauty; pure; unmixed.—*n* an extent of level land.—*adv* clearly, distinctly.—*adv* **plain´ly**.—*adj* **plain´clothes**, wearing ordinary clothes while on duty.—*ns* **plain´clothes´man; plain sailing**, easy progress over an unobstructed course; **plains´man**, an American frontiersman on the western plains; **plain´song**, a very old, plain kind of church music chanted in unison.—*adj* **plain´spoken**, candid, frank. [Fr—L *plānus*, level, flat.]

plaint [plānt] *n* lamentation; complaint; a statement of grievance.—*n* **plaint´iff** (*law*) one who commences a suit against another.—*adj* **plaint´ive**, mournful.—*adv* **plaint´ively**.—*n* **plaint´iveness**. [OFr *pleinte* (Fr *plainte*)—L *plangĕre, planctum*, to beat the breast, lament.]

plait [plat] *n* a flat fold made by doubling cloth back upon itself; a pleat; three or more strands of straw, hair, etc., interlaced in a regular pattern; a pigtail, a braid.—Also *vt*.—*adj* **plait´ed**. [OFr *pleit, ploit* (Fr *pli*)—L *plicāre, -ĭtum, -ātum*, to fold.]

plan [plan] *n* a representation of anything projected on a plane or flat surface, esp that of a building as disposed on the ground; a scheme or project; a way of proceeding; any outline or sketch.—*vt* to make a plan of; to design; to lay plans for; to intend.—*vi* to make plans.—*pr p* **plann´ing**; *pt, pt p* **planned**.—**plan-position indicator** (*radar*) an apparatus in which the position of reflecting objects is shown on the screen of a cathoderay tube, as if on a plan;—abbrev **PPI**. [Fr—L *plānus*, flat.]

planchette [plā-shet´, plan-shet´] *n* a board mounted on two castors and on a vertical pencil point, used as a medium for automatic writing and supposed spirit messages. [Fr, dim of *planche*, a board.]

plane[1] [plān] *n* (*geom*) a surface on which, if any two points be taken, the straight line joining them will lie entirely on the surface; any flat or level surface; one of the main supporting surfaces of an airplane; (short for) airplane; any grade of life or of development, or level of thought or existence.—*adj* perfectly level; pertaining to, lying in, or confined to a plane.—*vi* to fly while keeping the wings motionless; to skim across the surface of the water; to travel by airplane.—*ns* **plane´ tā´ble**, an instrument consisting of a drawing board on a tripod with a ruler pointed at the object observed, used for plotting the lines of a survey directly from observation; **plane geometry**, the geometry of plane figures; **plane section**, the figure formed by the intersection of a plane and a solid. [L *plānum*, a flat surface, neut of *plānus*, flat; cf **plain** (2) and next word.]

plane[2] [plān] *n* a carpenter's tool for producing a smooth surface.—*vt* to make (a surface, as of wood) level by means of a plane. [Fr *plane*—LL *plāna*—*plānāre*, to smooth.]

plane[3] [plān] *n* any one of the genus (*Platanus*) of tall trees with large broad lobed leaves and flowers with globose heads.—Also **plane tree, sycamore**. [Fr *plane*—L *platanus*. See **platane**.]

planet [plan´ėt] *n* a body (other than a comet or meteor) that revolves about the sun or other fixed star, reflecting the latter's light and generating no heat or light of its own; a celestial body, esp one of the seven bodies known from ancient times held to influence the fate of human beings; a person or thing of great importance.—*n* **planeta´rium**, a model or a representation of the solar system; an optical device for showing the motions and orbits of the planets; a building housing such a projector.—*adj* **plan´etary**, of, or pertaining to, the planets; under the influence of a planet; wandering, erratic; terrestrial.—*n* **plan´etoid**, a minor planet.—*adjs* **plan´et-strick´en, plan´et-struck** (*arch*) affected by the influence of the planets, blasted. [Fr *planète*—Gr *planētēs*, wanderer—*planaein*, to make to wander.]

plangent [plan´jėnt] *adj* having a loud reverberating sound; clangorous; resounding mournfully. [L *plangens, -entis*, pr p of *plangĕre*, to beat.]

planish [plan´ish] *vt* to toughen and finish (metal) by hammering lightly.—*n* **plan´isher**, a tool for planishing, esp a flat-faced steel hammer. [Obs Fr *planir, -issant*—*plan*, flat.]

plank [plangk] *n* a long, broad, thick board; one of the principles or aims that form the platform of a political party.—*vt* to cover with planks; to set down to rest; to cook and serve on a board.—*n* **plank´ing**, the act of laying planks; a quantity of planks. [L *planca*, a board.]

plankton [plangk´tȯn] the drifting organisms in oceans, lakes, or rivers. [Neut of Gr *planktos, -ē, -on*, wandering.]

plant [plänt] *n* a living thing that cannot move voluntarily, has no sense organs, and synthesizes food from carbon dioxide; a soft-stemmed organism of this kind, as distinguished from a tree or shrub; the machinery, buildings, etc. of a factory, etc.; the buildings and other physical equipment of an institution; (*inf*) an act of planting; (*inf*) something or someone planted.—*vt* to put into the ground for growth; to furnish with plants; to set firmly in position; to implant, to cause to take root (eg an idea, a principle); to found, establish (eg a colony); (*slang*) to place (stolen goods, etc.) in another's possession so as to incriminate him; (*slang*) to place as evidence.—*vi* to plant something.—*ns* **plantā´tion**, a large cultivated planting of trees; an estate used for growing cotton, rubber, tea, or other product of warm countries, cultivated by resident laborers; **plant´er**, the owner of a plantation; **planting**, a machine that plants; a decorative container for plants; a plantation; an area where plants are grown for commercial or decorative purposes; **plant kingdom**, one of the three basic groups of natural objects that includes all living and extinct plants. [OE *plante* (n)—L *planta*, slip, cutting, and OE *plantian* (vb), and partly from or affected by Fr *plante*.]

plantain[1] [plan´tān] *n* the roadside plant (either *Plantago major* or *P rugelii*) that presses its leaves flat on the ground, any plant of the genus (*Plantago*). [L *plantāgō, -inis*—*planta*, the sole of the foot.]

plantain[2] [plan´tān] *n* a banana plant *Musa paradisiaca*); the greenish starchy fruit of the plantain that is a staple food of the tropics when cooked.

plantigrade [plant´i-grād] *adj* walking on the soles of the feet with the heel touching the ground.—*n* a plantigrade animal, as the bear. [L *planta*, the sole, *gradī*, to walk.]

plaque [pläk] *n* a plate, tablet, or slab hung on, applied to, or inserted in a surface as an ornament; a brooch worn as a badge of honor; a localized abnormal patch on a body part of surface; a film of mucus harboring bacteria formed on the teeth. [Fr]

plash[1] [plash] *n* a short plunge or pool. [OE *plæsc*.]

plash[2] [plash] *vt* to break the surface (of water); to splash.—*vi* cause a splashing or spattering effect. [Cf Middle Low Ger *plaschen*; perh conn with preceding.]

plasm [plazm] *n* plasma.—*n* **plas´ma**, protoplasm; the liquid part of blood, lymph, or milk; a collection of charged particles resembling gas but differing from it as it conducts electricity and is affected by a magnetic field.—*adj* **plas´mic**. [Gr *plasma, -atos*, a thing molded—*plassein*, to mold.]

plaster [pläs´tėr] *n* a fabric coated with a pasty substance for local application as a remedy, a pasty composition that sets hard, esp a mixture of lime, sand, and water, used for coating walls and ceilings, etc.—*vt* to cover as with plaster; to apply like a plaster; to make lie smooth and flat; to damage by a heavy attack.—*vi* to apply plaster.—*adj* **plas´tered** (*inf*) drunk, intoxicated.—*ns* **plas´terboard**, a thin board formed by layers of plaster and paper, used in wide sheets for walls, etc.; **plas´terer**, one who plasters, or one who works in plaster; **plas´tering**.—**plaster cast**, a sculptor's model in plaster of paris; a rigid dressing of gauze impregnated with plaster of paris; **plaster of paris**, gypsum quick-setting and water made into a paste. [OE *plaster* (in medical sense), and OFr *plastre* (builder's plaster), both—LL *plastrum*—L *emplastrum*—Gr *emplastron*—*plassein*, to mold.]

plastic [plas´tik] *adj* giving form to clay, wax, etc.; creative (eg of imagination); capable of being easily molded; made of plastic.—*n* any of various nonmetallic compounds synthetically produced, that can be molded, cast, extruded, drawn, or laminated into objects, films, or filaments.—*n* **plasticity** [-tis´i-ti], capacity for being molded or altered; the ability to retain a shape attained by pressure deformation; the capacity of organisms with the same genotype to vary in developmental patterns, esp of behavior in varying environmental conditions.—**plastic art**, the art of shaping (in three dimensions), as sculpture, modeling; art which is, or appears to be, three dimensional; one of the visual arts (as painting, sculpture, or film) esp as distinguished from those that are written (as poetry or music); **plastic surgeon**, a medical specialist in plastic surgery; **plastic surgery**, the branch of surgery concerned with the repair of deformed or destroyed parts of the body. [Gr *plastikos*—*plassein*, to mold.]

plastron [plas´tron] *n* a breastplate; a quilted pad worn in fencing practice to protect the chest, waist, and the side on which the weapon is held; the ventral part of the shell of a tortoise or turtle; a trimming like a bib for a woman's dress. [Fr *plastron*—It *piastrone*—*piastra*, breastplate, plate of metal.]

plat[1] [plat] *n* a plait.

plat[2] [plat] *n* a plot of ground; a map or plan, as of a subdivision. [**plot**.]

platan [plat´ȧn] *n* a plane tree. [L *platanus*—Gr *platanos*—*platys*, broad.]

plate [plāt] *n* a flat sheet of metal, specifically one on which an engraving is cut; a broad piece of armor; an engraved sheet of metal for printing from; an impression printed from it, esp a whole page, usu. separately printed and inserted as illustration in a book; a mold made from type, or a sheet of metal photographically prepared, for printing from; a sheet, usu. of glass, coated with an emulsion sensitive to light for use as a photgraphic negative; part of a denture fitting the mouth and carrying the teeth; (*hist*) precious metal, esp silver; wrought gold or silver; household utensils plated in gold or silver; plated ware; a shallow dish; contents of a plate; a helping (of food); a vessel used for church collection; (*baseball*) home plate; a horse race in which the competitors ride for a prize rather than stakes.—*vt* to overlay with metal; to cover with a thin film of another metal, mechanically, chemically, or electrically.—*adj* **plā´ted**, covered with metal; covered with a coating of another metal, esp gold or silver.—*ns* **plā´ting**; the act or process of plating; a coating of metal plates; a thin coating of metal; **plate´ glass**, rolled, ground, and polished sheet glass; **plate rail**, a narrow shelf along the upper part of a wall for holding plates or ornaments. [OFr *plate*, fem, and (for the dish) *plat*, masc, flat—Gr *platys*, broad.]

plateau [pla´tō, pla-tō´] *n* a tableland; a temporary stable state reached in the course of upward progress; the part of a graphic representation showing this;—*pl* **plateaus; plateaux** [-tōz]. [Fr,—OFr *platel*, dim of *plat*, flat.]

platen [plat´n] *n* the part of printing press that presses the paper against the type; the roller of a typewriter. [Fr *platine*—OFr *plate*—*plat*, flat.]

platform [plat´förm] *n* a raised level surface; a raised floor for speakers, musicians, etc.; a place or opportunity for public discussion; a public declaration of policy, esp of a political party, or a candidate for public office; a usu. thick layer (as of cork) between the inner and outer sole of a shoe; such a shoe. [Fr *plateforme*, lit, flat form.]

platinum [plat´in-um] *n* a noble metal (symbol Pt at wt 195.1; at no 78), grayish-white, very valuable, malleable and ductile, very heavy and hard to fuse.—*n* **plat´ina**, crude native platinum.—*adjs* **platinic** [pla-tin´ik], of, relating to, or containing platinum, esp with a valence of four; **platinous** [plat´in-us], of, relating to, or containing platinum, esp with a valence of two.—*vt* **plat´inize**, to cover, treat, or combine with platinum or a compound of platinum.—*platinum blond*, a woman with metallic silvery hair. [Sp *platina—plata*, silver.]

platitude [plat´i-tūd] *n* commonplaceness; a dull commonplace or truism; an empty remark made as if it were important.—*adj* **platitud´inous**. [Fr,—*plat*, flat.]

Platonic [plä-ton´ik] *adj* pertaining to *Plato* the Greek philosopher, or to his philosophy; **platonic**, of love, between soul and soul, without sensual desire; relating to or experiencing platonic love.—*adv* **platon´ically**.—*ns* **Plā´tonism**, the philosophy of Plato; stressing that actual things are copies of transcendant ideas and that these ideas are the objects of true knowledge accessible by recollection; **Plā´tonist**, a follower of Plato. [Gr *platōnikos—Platōn, -ōnos*, Plato.]

platoon [pla´tōōn´] *n* a military unit consisting of two or more squads; (*sports*) any of the specialized players making up a team.—*vt* (*sports*) to alternate (players) at a position. [Fr *peloton*, ball, knot of men—L *pila*, ball.]

platter [plat´ėr] *n* a large usu. oval flat plate for serving food. [Anglo-Fr *plater—plat*, a plate.]

platypus [plat´i-pus] *n* a small aquatic egg-laying mammal (*Ornithorhynchus anatinus*) with webbed feet, a bill like a duck's, dense fur, and a broad, flattened tail of eatern and southern Australia and Tasmania. [Gr *platys*, flat, *pous*, gen *podos*, a foot.]

plaudit [plöd´it] *n* (usu. *pl*) applause; praise bestowed emphatically.—*adj* **plaud´itory**. [Shortened from L *plaudite*, applaud, an actor's call for applause at the end of a play, pl imper of *plaudĕre, plausum*, to clap the hands.]

plausible [plöz´i-bl] *adj* seemingly worthy of approval or praise; specious, apparently reasonable or probable (eg of an explanation).—*ns* **plausibil´ity, plaus´ibleness.**—*ns* **plaus´ibly**. [L *plaudĕre*, to clap the hands.]

play [plā] *vi* to gambol, to frisk; to perform acts not part of the immediate business of life but in mimicry or rehearsal; to engage in pleasureable activity; to behave without seriousness; to amuse oneself (with), to trifle (with); to take part in a game or sport; (*card games*) to table a card; to gamble; to act on a stage; to perform on a musical instrument; to move, irregularly, lightly, or freely, to flicker, to flutter, to shimmer; to discharge or direct a stream or shower (eg of water, light); to move or function freely within prescribed limits; to act in a specified way; to impose unscrupulously (on another's feelings).—*vt* to act a part on the stage or in life (eg Hamlet, the woman); to engage in (a game); to contend against in a game; to perform music on; to do or execute for amusement (eg a trick); to bring about or work (eg havoc); to direct (**on, over, along**, of a light, a hose, etc.); to give a limited freedom of action to (eg *to play a fish*); to bet on.—*n* recreative activity; amusement; the playing of a game; manner of playing; gambling; a drama or dramatic performance; manner of dealing (as *fairplay*); activity, operation (as *come into play*); freedom of movement, scope for activity (eg *allow full play to*).—*adj* **play´able**, capable (by nature or by the rules of the game) of being played or of being played on.—*ns* **playacting**, performance, esp professional, of plays; pretence; **play´back**, act of reproducing a recording of sound or visual material, esp immediately after it is made; a device for doing this; **play´boy**, a lighthearted irresponsible person, esp rich and leisured; **play´girl; play´er**, one who plays a specified game or instrument; an actor.—*adj* **play´ful**, sportive; humorous.—*adv* **play´fully**.—*ns* **playbill**, a bill announcing a play; **Playbill**, tradename for a theater program; **play´book**, a book of plays; **play´fellow, play´mate**, a companion in play; **playgōer**, one who habitually attends the theater; **playhouse**, a theater; a small house for children to play in; **play´ing card**, one of a pack used in playing games; **playpen**, a portable usu. collapsible enclosure within which a young child may safely play; **play´thing**, a toy; **play´wright**, a dramatist.—**in, out of, play**, in, out of, such a position that the rules allow it to be played (of a ball used in a game); **play ball**, cooperate; **play down**, to treat as less important than is the case; **play hard to get**, to make a show of unwillingness to cooperate with a view to strengthening one's position; **play by ear**, to improvise a plan of action to meet the situation as it develops; **play off**, to complete the playing of (an interrupted contest); to break (a tie) by a play-off; to set in opposition for one's own gain; **play-off**, a final contest to determine the winner between contestants or teams that have tied; a series of contests after the end of the regular season to determine a championship; **play on**, to work upon and make use of (eg a person's fears, credulity); **play out**, to play to the end; to finish; to exhaust; **played out**, exhausted; no longer good for anything; **play the game**, to act strictly honorably. [OE *pleg(i)an*, vb, *plega*, n]

plea [plē] *n* (*law*); defendant's answer to a charge or claim; an excuse; a request; urgent entreaty.—**plea bargaining**, pretrial negotiations in which the defendant agrees to plead guilty to lesser charges if more serious charges are dropped. [OFr *plai, plaid, plait*—Low L *placitum*, a decision—L *placēre, -itum*, to please.]

pleach [plēch] *vt* to intertwine the branches of, as a hedge; to plait, as hair. [Allied to **plash**—from another form of OFr *pless(i)er*—L *plectĕre*, to plait; Gr *plekein*.]

plead [plēd] *vi* to present a plea in a lawsuit; to argue in support of a cause against another; to put forward an allegation or answer in court; to implore (*with* **with**).—*vt* to argue (a law case); to answer (guilty or not guilty) to a charge; to offer in excuse;—*pt, pt p* **plead´ed**, or **pled**.—*n* **plead´er**, one who pleads.—*adj* **plead´ing**, imploring.—*n* advocacy of a cause in a court of law; one of the allegations and counter allegations made alternately, usu. in writing, by the parties in a legal action; the act or instance of making a plea; a sincere entreaty.—*adv* **plead´ingly**. [OFr *plaidier*; cf **plea**.]

please [plēz] *vi* to give pleasure to; to delight; to satisfy; to have the wish.—*vt* to give pleasure; to seem good; to like, to think fit, to choose.—*adv* as a word to express politeness or emphasis in a request; an expression of polite affirmation.—*n* **pleasance** [plez´åns], (*arch*) enjoyment; a pleasure ground.—*adj* **pleas´ant**, pleasing; agreeable; cheerful; gay; facetious.—*adv* **pleas´antly**.—*ns* **pleas´antness; pleas´antry**, jocularity; a facetious utterance or trick.—*adj* and *n*; **pleas´ing**.—*adv* **pleas´ingly**.—*adj* **pleasureable** [plezh´ůr-å-bl], able to give pleasure, delightful.—*adv* **pleas´urably**.—*n* **pleasure** [plezh´ůr], agreeable emotions; gratification of the senses or of the mind; what the will prefers.—*vt* (*arch*) to give pleasure to.—*n* **pleasure principle**, a tendency for individual behavior to be directed toward immediate satisfaction of instinctual drives and immediate relief from pain or discomfort. [OFr *plaisir* (Fr *plaire*)—L *placēre*, to please.]

pleat [plēt] *n* a double fold of cloth, etc. pressed or stitched in place.—*vt* to lay and press (cloth) in a pleat or pleats.

plebeian [plė-bē´ån] *adj* of the common people; vulgar.—*n* one of the common people; a vulgar, coarse person.—*n* **pleb** (*inf*), a person of unpolished manners, of low rank in society. [L *plēbēius—plēbs, plēbis*, the common people.]

plebiscite [pleb´i-sit, also -sīt] *n* a direct vote of the whole nation, or of the people of a district, on a political issue such as annexation, independent nationhood, etc. [Partly through Fr *plébiscite*—L *plēbiscitum—plēbs*, the people, *scītum*, a decree—*scīscĕre*, to vote for.]

plectrum [plek´trum] *n* a thin piece of metal etc. for plucking the strings of a guitar, etc. [L *plēctrum*—Gr *plēktron—plēssein*, to strike.]

pledge [plej] *n* something given as a security; a token or assuring sign; a solemn promise; a promise to join a fraternity or a secret society; a person who has so promised.—*vt* to give as security; to pawn; to bind by solemn promise; to drink to the health of. [OFr *plege* (Fr *pleige*)—LL *plevium, plivium*, prob of Ger origin.]

Pleistocene [plīs´tō-sēn] *adj* of the earlier epoch of the *Quaternary* geological era. [Gr *pleistos*, most, *kainos*, recent.]

plenary [plē´når-ē, or plen´å-rē] *adj* full, entire, unqualified; fully attended (eg of an assembly).—*adv* **plē´narily.—plenary indulgence**, in the Roman Catholic Church, full remission of temporal penalties to a repentant sinner. [Low L *plēnārius*—L *plēnus*, full—*plēre*, to fill.]

plenipotentiary [plen-i-pō-ten´shår-i] *adj* having full powers.—*n* a person invested with full powers, esp a special ambassador or envoy. [L *plēnus*, full, *potentia*, power.]

plenitude [plen´i-tūd] *n* fullness, completeness; abundance; repletion. [L *plēnitūdō, -inis—plēnus*, full.]

plenty [plen´ti] *n* a full supply; abundance.—*adj* **plenteous** [plen´tyus], fully sufficient; abundant.—*adv* **plen´tiful**, copious; abundant; yielding abundance.—*adv* **plen´tifully**.—*n* **plen´tifulness**. [OFr *plente*—L *plēnitās—plēnus*, full.]

plenum [plē´num] *n* a space completely filled with matter; a general assembly of all members, esp of a legislative body. [L *plēnum* (*spatium*), full (space).]

pleonasm [plē´o-nazm] *n* redundancy, esp of words; a redundant expression.—*adj* **pleonas´tic**.—*adv* **pleonas´tically**. [Gr *pleonasmos—pleōn* (*pleiōn*), more.]

plesiosaur [ple´si-ō-sör] *n* any of a suborder (Plesiosaurus) of marine reptiles whose fossil remains are found in rocks of the Mesozoic systems. [Gr *plēsios*, near, *sauros*, lizard.]

plethora [pleth´ōr-a] *n* a bodily condition marked by an excessive fullness of blood; over abundance of any kind.—*adj* **plethoric** [-thor´ik; pleth´-]. [Ionic Gr *plēthōrē*, fullness—*pleos*, full.]

pleura [plōō´rä] *n* a delicate membrane that covers the lung and lines the cavity of the chest;—*pl* **pleu´rae** [-rē], **pleuras**.—*adj* **pleu´ral**.—*n* **pleurisy** [plōō´ri-si], inflammation of the pleura.—*adj* **pleurit´ic**, of; affected with, or causing, pleurisy.—*n* **pleuropneumo´nia**, combined inflammation of the pleura and the lungs. [Gr *pleurā* and *pleuron*, rib, side.]

Plexiglas [plek´si-glas] *n* trade name for a lightweight, transparent, thermoplastic substance.—*n*this material.—Also **plexiglass**.

plexus [pleks´us] *n* a network of veins, nerves, etc.; an interwoven combination of parts in a structure or system. [L *plexus, -ūs*, a weaving.]

pliable [plī´å-bl] *adj* easily bent or folded, flexible; easily persuaded; adaptable.—*ns* **pliabil´ity, plī´ableness, plī´ancy, plī´antness**.—*adj* **plī´ant**, bending easily, flexible; tractable, easily influenced.—*adv* **plī´antly**. [See **ply**.]

plicate [plī´kåt] *adj* folded like a fan; marked with parallel ridges. [L *plīca*, a fold.]

plied, pliers *See* **ply**.

plight[1] [plīt] *n* pledge; engagement; promise.—*vt* to pledge;—*pt p* **plighted**, also **plight**. [OE *pliht*, risk, *plēon*, to risk.]

plight[2] [plīt] *n* condition, state, now usu. bad (eg *a hopeless plight*). [Assimilated in spelling to the foregoing, but derived from OFr *plite*—L *plicāre, -itum, -ātum*, to fold.]

Plimsoll line or **mark** [plim´sòl, -sol] *n* a ship's load line, or set of load lines. [Samuel *Plimsoll*, MP].

plinth [plinth] *n* the square block under the base of a column; any of various bases or lower parts, often recessed. [L *plinthus*—Gr *plinthos*, a brick, squared stone, plinth.]

Pliocene [plī´ō-sēn] *adj* of the last period of the Tertiary geological era. [Gr *pleiōn*, greater, more numerous, *kainos*, recent.]

plod [plod] *vi* to walk heavily and laboriously; to study or work steadily and laboriously;—*pr p* **plodd´ing**; *pt, pt p* **plodd´ed**.—*n* **plodd´er**, one who plods on; one who gets on more by sheer toil than by inspiration or natural aptitude; a dull, heavy, laborious man.—*adj* and *n* **plodd´ing**. [Prob imit].

plop [plop] *n* the sound of a small object falling into water.—*vi* to make the sound of a plop. [Imit]

plosive [plō´siv, -ziv] *adj* and *n* stop, explosive—used of consonants formed by closing the breath passage completely. (eg *p, b, t, d*). [From **explosive**.]

plot [plot] *n* a small piece of ground; a plan of a field, etc.; the story or scheme of connected events running through a play, novel, etc.; a conspiracy, a stratagem or secret contrivance.—*vt* to lay out in plots; to make a plan of by means of a graph; to mark (points) on a graph; to conspire;—*pr p* **plott´ing**; *pt p* **plott´ed**.—*n* **plott´er**. [OE *plot*, a patch of ground; influenced by (or partly from) Fr *complot*, a conspiracy.]

plover [pluv´ėr] *n* any of numerous shorebirds (family Charadriidae) resembling the sandpiper but having a hard-tipped bill. [Fr *pluvier*—L *pluvia*, rain; possibly from their restlessness before rain; cf Ger *regenpfeifer*, lit rain-piper.]

plow [plow] *n* a farm implement for turning up the soil; any implement like this, as a snowplow.—*vt* to cut and turn up with the plow; to tear, force, or cut a way through, advance laboriously through.—*ns* **plowboy**, a boy who leads the team drawing a plow; a country youth; **plow´ing**, an act or instance of plowing; **plow´man**, a man who guides a plow; a farm laborer; **plow sole**, a layer of earth at the bottom of the furrow compacted by repeated plowing at the same depth; **plow back**, to reinvest (profits of a business) in that business; **plow under**, to cause to disappear. [Late OE *plōh, plōg*, a plowland; cf ON *plōgr*.]

plowshare [plow´shār] *n* the detachable part of a plow that cuts the under surface of the sod from the ground. [**plow**, and OE *scear*, plowshare—*scieran*, to shear, cut.]

ploy [ploi] *n* escapade, affair; method or procedure used to achieve a particular result; a maneuver in a game, conversation, etc. [Prob **employ**.]

pluck [pluk] *vt* to pull off, out, or away; to snatch; to strip, as a fowl of its feathers; to remove (a person) from one situation and transfer him to another situation in life.—*vi* to make a sharp pull or twitch.—*n* a single act of plucking; the heart, liver, and lungs of an animal; heart, courage, spirit; dogged resolution.—*adj* **pluck´y**, having courageous spirit and pertinacity.—*adv* **pluck´ily**.—*n* **pluck´iness**. [OE *pluccian*; akin to Du *plukken*, Ger *pflücken*.]

plug [plug] *n* a peg or any piece of wood, metal, or other substance stopping, or for stopping, a hole; a stopper; a wall fitting for making an electrical connection; a fireplug; a compressed cake of tobacco; a kind of fishing lure; (*inf*) a free boost, usu. incorporated in other matter; (*slang*) an old worn-out horse.—*vt* to stop with a plug; (*slang*) to shoot a bullet into; (*inf*) to advertise or publicize by frequent repetition (as a tune).—*vi* (*inf*) to work doggedly;—*pr p* **plugg´ing**; *pt p* **plugged**.—*n* **plugō´la** (*slang*) a bribe for underhanded promotion on radio or television. [App Du *plug*, a bung, a peg; cf Swed *plugg*, a peg, Ger *pflock*.]

plum [plum] *n* the oval smooth-skinned stone fruit or drupe of various species of temperate zone trees and shrubs (genus *Prunus*); any of various trees bearing similar edible fruit; its fruit; a raisin when used in cakes or puddings; a choice thing of its kind (eg of a position or post); the bluish-red color of some plums; **plum pudding**, a rich boiled or steamed dish made of flour and suet, with raisins, currants, and various species. [OE *plūme*—L *prūnum*—Gr *prou(m)non*.]

plumage [plōōm´ij] *n* a bird's feathers. [Fr,—*plume*—L *plūma*, a feather, down.]

plumb [plum] *n* a lead weight attached to a line used to determine how deep the water is or whether a wall is vertical; any of various weights (as a sinker for a fishing line).—*adj* perfectly vertical.—*adv* vertically; in a direct manner; (*inf*) entirely.—*vt* to test by a plumb line; to examine minutely and critically; to weight with lead; to seal with lead; to supply with or install as plumbing.—*vi* to work as a plumber.—*ns* **plumb´ bob**, the weight at the end of a **plumb line**, a line to show the vertical, a line directed to the center of gravity of the earth. *adjs* **plumbic**, [plum´bik]; combined with lead, esp with a valency of four; **plumbous**, of, relating to, or combine with lead, esp with a valency of two.—*ns* **plumber**, [plum´ėr], one who installs and mends pipes, cisterns, and other fittings for the distribution and use of water in a building. **plumbing**, [plum´ing], the craft of a plumber; installations fitted by a plumber. **plumber's helper, plumber's friend**, a plunger. [Fr *plomb*—L *plumbum*, lead.]

plumbago [plum-bā´gō] *n* any of a genus (*Plumbago*) of chiefly tropical plants cultivated for their showy flowers; graphite. [L *plumbāgō, -inis*—*plumbum*, lead.]

plumber *See* **plumb**.

plume [plōōm] *n* a feather, esp a large showy one; a group of these; something resembling a feather in structure or lightness (eg a *plume of smoke*); a feather or tuft of feathers, or anything similar, used as an ornament; a token of prowess.—*vt* to preen; to indulge (oneself) with an obvious display of self-satisfaction; to adorn with plumes—*adj* **plu´mose**, feathery; feathered. [Ofr,—L *plūma*, a small soft feather.]

plummet [plum´ėt] *n* a plumb; a plumb line.—*vi* to fall in a perpendicular manner; to drop sharply and abruptly. [OFr *plomet*, dim of plombe, lead. See **plumb**.]

plump[1] [plump] *vti* to fall, drop or sink, or come into contact suddenly and heavily; to favor or give support (to someone or something).—*n* the sound or act of plumping.—*adv* straight down; straight ahead; without hesitation, reserve, or qualification.—*n* **plump´er**, an object carried in the mouth to fill out the cheeks.—*adv* **plump´ly**. [L Ger *plumpen* or Du *plompen*.]

plump[2] [plump] *adj* pleasantly fat and rounded, chubby.—Also *vti*—*n* **plump´ness**. [App the same word as Du *plomp*, blunt, Low Ger *plump*.]

plumule [plōō´mūl] *n* (*bot*) the embryo shoot in a seed; a down feather. [L *plūmula*, dim of *plūma*, a feather, down-feather.]

plunder [plun´dėr] *vt* to carry off the goods of (another) by force; to pillage.—*n* pillage; booty.—*n* **plun´derer**. [Ger *plündern*, to pillage—*plunder*, household stuff, now trash.]

plunge [plunj] *vt* to thrust suddenly (into water, a cavity, a condition, etc.); to immerse (eg to *plunge* a person in *gloom, plunged* in *thought*) to sink (a potted plant) into the ground.—*vi* to fling oneself or rush impetuously, esp into water, downhill, or into danger; (*inf*) to gamble heavily.—*n* **plung´er**, one who plunges; a solid cylinder that operates in with a plunging motion, as a piston; a large rubber suction cup used to free clogged drains.—*adj*—*n* **plung´ing**. [OFr *plonger*—L *plumbum*, lead.]

pluperfect [plōō-pėr´fėkt or plōō´-] *adj* (*gram*) the past perfect tense. [L *plūs quam perfectum* (*tempus*), more than perfect (tense).]

plural [plōōr´l] *adj* numbering or expressing more than one; consisting of or containing more than one kind or class.—*n* (*gram*) the form denoting more than one,—*ns* **plur´alism**, the holding by one person of more than one office at a time, esp applied to ecclesiastical benefices; a theory that reality is composed of a plurality of entities; a theory that there are at least two levels of ultimate reality; a (condition of) society in which different ethnic, etc., groups preserve their own customs; a doctrine or policy advocating this condition. **plur´alist**, one who supports any theory or doctrine of pluralism. **plurality**, [-al´i-ti], the state of being plural; numerousness; the greater number, more than half; the excess of votes in an election that the leading candidate has over his leading rival; the holding of more than one benefice at one time.—*adv* **plur´ally**.—*vi* **plur´alize**, to make plural. [L *plūrālis*—*plūs, plūris*, more.]

plus [plus] *prep* added to; in addition to.—*adj* indicating addition; positive; somewhat higher than; involving extra gain; (*inf*) and more.—*n* the sign (+) prefixed to positive quantities, or set between quantities or numbers to be added together; an addition; an advantage; a benefit. [L *plūs*, more.]

plus fours [plus-fōrz´] *n pl* loose sports knickers made four inches longer than ordinary knickers. [**plus, four**, from the four additional inches of cloth required.]

plush [plush] *n* a fabric with an even and more open pile than velvet.—*adj* of plush (*inf*); pretentiously luxurious (also **plush´y**.). [Fr *pluche* for *peluche*—L *pilus*, hair; cf **pile**. (3).]

Pluto [plōō´tō] *n* the Greek god of the underworld; the planet furthest from the sun.—*adjs* **pluto´nian**, of Pluto; of the underworld; **plutonic**, [-ton´ik], of Pluto; (*geol*) formed by solidification of magona deep within the earth and crystalline throughout. [L *Plūtō, -ōnis*—Gr *Ploutōn, -ōnos*.]

plutocracy [plōō-tok´ra-si] *n* government by the wealthy; a ruling body or class of rich men.—*n* **plutocrat**, [plōō´tō-krat], one who is powerful because of his wealth. [Gr *ploutokratia*—*ploutis*, wealth, and *krateein*, to rule.]

plutonium [plōō´tō´ni-ùm] *n* a transuranic element (symbol Pu; at wt 242; at no 94). [L *Plūtō, -ōnis*, Pluto.]

pluvial [plōō´vi-àl] *adj* of or by rain; rainy.—*adj* rainy. [L *pluvia*, rain.]

ply[1] [plī] *n* a layer or thickness, as of cloth, plywood, etc.; any of the twisted strands in a yarn, etc.—*vt* to twist together.—*pr p* **ply´ing**; *pt p* **plied**.—*ns* **pli´er**, (*pl*) small pincers for bending or cutting wire, etc.; **ply´wood**, a construction material made of thin layers of wood glued together. [OFr *pli*, a fold, *plier*, to fold—L *plicāre*.]

ply[2] [plī] *vt* to work at steadily and energetically; to use or wield diligently or vigorously; to supply (a person) persistently (eg with food); to assail persistently (eg with questions) to sail back and forth across.—*vi* to keep busy; to make regular journeys over a route;—*pr p* **ply´ing**; *pt p* **plied**. [Shortened from **apply**.]

Plymouth Rock [plim´òth] *n* any of an American breed of medium-sized domestic fowl bred for laying eggs and for the table. [*Plymouth Rock*, on which the Pilgrims are suppose to have landed in 1620.]

pneumatic [nū-mat´ik] *adj* relating to wind, air, or gases; containing or inflated with air; filled with or worked by compressed air.—*adv* **pneumat´ically**.—*n pl* **pneumat´ics**, the branch of mechanics concerned with the mechanical properties of gases.—*ns* **pneumatol´ogy**, the study of spiritual beings; **pneumatol´ogist**. [Gr *pneuma, -atos*, breath—*pneein*, to breathe.]

pneumonia [nū-mō´ni-a] *n* inflammation of the lung.—*adj* **pneumonic**, [-mon´ik] pertaining to the lungs. [Gr *pneumōn, -ŏnos*, lung—*pneein*, to breathe.]
pneumoconiosis [nū-mō-kō-ni-ōs´is] *n* any of various diseases caused by habitually inhaling mineral or metallic dust. [Gr *pneumōn, -ŏnos*, lung, *konia*, dust.]
poach[1] [pōch] *vt* to cook (an egg without its shell, fish, etc.) in or over boiling water. [App Fr *pocher*, to pocket—*poche*, pouch, the white forming a pocket about the yolk.]
poach[2] [pōch] *vti* to intrude on another's preserves in order to hunt game or to catch fish; to take game or fish illegally.—*ns* **poach´er; poach´ing**. [A form of **poke**, (3), or from OFr *pocher*, to poke.]
pock [pok] *n* a small elevation of the skin containing pus, as in smallpox.—*ns* **pock´mark**, the mark, pit, or scar left by a pock. [OE *poc*, a pustule; Ger *pocke*, Du *pok*.]
pocket [pok´et] *n* a little pouch or bag, esp one attached to a garment for carrying small articles; a pouchlike hollow, a cavity, or a place of lodgement; a deposit (as of gold, water, or gas); a small body of ore; a portion of the atmosphere differing in pressure or in other condition from its surroundings; a small isolated area, as of military resistance, unemployment, etc.—*adj* for the pocket; of small size.—*vt* to put in the pocket; to envelop; to enclose; to take (money) dishonesty; to suppress (*to pocket one's pride*).—*pr p* **pock´eting**; *pt, pt p* **pock´eted**.—*ns* **pock´etbook**, a woman's purse; monetary resources; a small esp paperback book that can be carried in the pocket; **pock´et bor´ough**, an English constituency controlled before parliamentary reform by a single person or family; **pock´et mon´ey**, money carried for occasional expenses; **pocket veto**, an indirect veto of a legislative bill by an executive by not signing a bill until after the adjournement of a legislative. **in, out of, pocket**, with, or without, money; the richer or the poorer by a transaction. [Anglo-Fr *pokete* (Fr *pochette*, dim of *poche*, pouch).]
pod [pod] *n* a dry fruit or seed vessel, as of peas, beans, etc.; a grasshopper egg case; a protective container or housing; a detachable compartment on a spacecraft.—*vi* to form pods;—*pr p* **podd´ing**; *pt, pt p* **podd´ed**.
podgy [poj´i] *adj* squat; thickset.
podiatry [pō-dī´ȧ-trē] *n* the care and treatment of the human foot in health and disease.—*n* **pod´iatrist**.—Also **chiropody**.
poem [pō´ėm] *n* an arrangement of words, esp in meter, often rhymed, in a style more imaginative than ordinary speech; a creation, achievement, etc., marked by beauty or artistry suggesting a poem. [Fr *poème*—L *poēma*—Gr *poiēma*—*poieein*, to make.]
poesy [pō´e-si] *n* poetry, esp a body of poems; sentimentalized poetic writing; poetic inspiration. [Fr *poésie*—L *poēsis*—Gr *poiēsis*—*poieein*, to make.]
poet [pō´ėt, -it] *n* the author of a poem; one skilled in making poetry; one with a poetical imagination;—*ns* **pō´etess**, a girl or woman who writes poetry.—*n* **pōetas´ter**, an inferior poet.—*adj* **poetic, -al** [pō-et´ik, -ȧl] of the nature of, or pertaining to, poetry; expressed in poetry; in the language of poetry; imaginative.—*adv* **poet´ically**.—*n sing* **poet´ics**, a treatise on poetry or aesthetics; poetic theory or practice;—*vt* **poet´icize´**, to give a poetic quality to.—*ns* **pō´et lau´reate**, the official poet of a nation, appointed to write poems celebrating national events, etc.; **pō´etry**, the art of the poet; the essential quality of a poem; poetical compositions or writings collectively; poetical quality.—**poetic justice**, an outcome in which vice is punished and virtue rewarded in an appropriate manner; **poetic licence**, a departing from strict fact or rule by a poet for the sake of effect. [Fr *poète*—L *poēta*—Gr *poiētēs*—*poieein*, to make.]
pogo stick [pō´gō stik] a pole with a crossbar on a strong spring on which one stands in order to bounce along the ground. [*Pogo*, a trademark.]
pogrom [pog-rom´] *n* an organized massacre of helpless people; such a massacre of Jews in 19th century Russia [Yiddish from Russ devastation.] [Russ destruction.]
poi [poi] *n* a pastelike Hawaiian food made of taro root. [Hawaiian.]
poignant [poin´ȧnt] *adj* piercing; sharp, pungent, in taste or smell; affecting one's feelings sharply or keenly (eg a pathetic scene); painfully sharp (eg regret).—*adv* **poign´antly**. [OFr *poignant, poindre*—L *pungĕre*, to sting.]
poinsettia [poin-set´ē-ȧ] *n* a showy tropical American plant (*Euphorbia pulcherrima*) with tapering usu. scarlet bracts that suggest petals and surround small yellow flowers. [J R *Poinsett*, 19th century US ambassador to Mexico.]
point [point] *n* a dot or other small mark used in writing or printing; a mark of punctuation esp a period; a dot separating the integral from the fractional part of a decimal; (*geom*) that which has position but no magnitude; a place or station considered in relation to position only; a place in a scale (eg *boiling point*); course, or cycle; a moment of time, without duration; a unit in judging, scoring, or measurement; a unit of measurement of printing type; one of thirty-two divisions of the compass; a detail taken into account in judging; the most important element in an argument, discourse, etc.; that without which a story, joke, etc., is meaningless; a head, clause, or item in a discourse, etc.; a matter in debate, under attention, or to be taken into account; the head of a bow of a stringed musical instrument; a unit for measuring the strength of a bridge hand; a unit of academic credit; a unit used in quoting the prices of stocks, bonds, and commodities; the number thrown on the first roll of the dice in the game of craps which the player attempts to repeat before throwing a seven; one of the 12 spaces marked off on one side of a backgammon board; a railroad switch; the tapering end of anything; the tip; a nib; a cape or headland.—*vt* to give point to; to sharpen; to aim (at); to direct attention to (esp *with* **out**); to fill the joints of with mortar, as a wall; to give point, force, or piquancy to (eg a remark).—*vi* to direct the finger, the eye, or the mind (at or to); to call attention (to); to be directed (to or toward).—*adj* **point´ed**, having a sharp point; being an arch with a pointed crown; marked by the use of a pointed arch; pertinent; aimed at a particular person or group; conspicuous.—*adv* **point´edly**.—*ns* **point´edness; point´er**, one who points in any sense; a rod for pointing to a blackboard, etc.; (*inf*) a hint, tip, suggestion; an index hand of a balance, etc.; a breed of dogs that point on discovering game; (*pl*) the two stars in the Great Bear, a line through which points to the North Star; **point´ing**.—*adj* **point´less**.—*ns* **point´lace**, lace made with a needle over a paper pattern; **point man**, a soldier who goes ahead on patrol; one in the forefront (as in a political issue).—**point of no return**, that point on a flight after which one can only go on, for want of fuel to return; a critical point (as in a course of action) at which turning back is not possible; **point of view**, the position from which one looks at anything; **point set topology**, a branch of topology dealing with the properties and theory of topological spaces with emphasis on set theory; **beside the point**, irrelevant; **in point, to the point**, pertinent; apt. [Partly Fr *point*, point, dot, stitch, lace, partly Fr *pointe*, sharp point, pungency—L *punctum* and LL *puncta*, respectively—L *pungĕre, punctum*, to prick.]
point-blank [point´-blangk´] *adj* of a shot, fired horizontally, not allowing for any appreciable curve in its trajectory or path; direct, unqualified, blunt (eg of a refusal).—Also *adv*. [App from **point** (vb) and **blank** (of the target).]
pointillism [pwan´til-izm] *n* in painting, the practice of applying small strokes or dots of color to a surface so that from a distance they blend together.—*n* **point´illist**. [Fr *pointillisme*—*pointille*, dim of *point*, point.]
poise[1] [poiz] *vt* to hold or carry in equilibrium, to balance; to hold supported without motion; to hold (the head) in a particular way; to put into readiness.—*vi* to become drawn up into readiness; to hover.—*n* a balanced state; self-possessed assurance of manner; gracious tact; bearing, carriage. [OFr *poiser* (Fr *peser*)—L *pensāre*, freq of *pendĕre*, to weigh, and OFr *pois*—L *pensum*, weight.]
poise[2] [poiz] *n* a centimeter-gram-second unit of viscosity equivalent to 0.1 newton second per square meter. [Jean Louise Marie *Poiseuille* (1799–1869), Fr physician.]
poison [poi´zn] *n* a substance that through its chemical action usu. destroys life or impairs health; any malignant influence; an object of aversion or abhorrence; a substance that inhibits the activity of another substance or the course of a process or reaction.—*vt* to injure or to kill with poison; to taint; to put poison into; to influence wrongfully.—*ns* **poi´soner**.—*adj* **poi´sonous**, having the quality of poison.—*adv* **poi´sonously**.—**poison gas**, a poisonous gas or a liquid or solid giving off poisonous vapors, used in warfare to kill or harm; **poison hemlock**, a large branching biennial poisonous herb (*Conium maculatum*) of the carrot family; water hemlock; **poison ivy**, a climbing plant (*Rhus toxicodendron*) that is esp common in the eastern and central US having thee leaflets and ivory-colored berries and producing an acutely irritating oil causing an intensely itching skin rash; the rash caused by poison ivy; **poison oak**, any of several plants resembling poison ivy; poison sumac; a bushy plant (*Rhus diversiloba*) of the Pacific coast; a bushy plant (*Rhus quercifolia*) of the southeastern US; **poison sumac**, an American swamp shrub (*Rhus vernix*) having pinnate leaves, greenish flowers, and greenish white berries and producing an irritating oil.—Also **poison dogwood**.—**poison-pen letter**, a letter written in malice, usu. anonymously, intended to abuse or frighten the recipient. [OFr *puison*, poison—L *pōtiō, -ōnis*, a draught; cf **potion**.]
poke[1] [pōk] *n* (*dial*) a sack, a bag.—**a pig in a poke**, a blind bargain, as of a pig bought without being seen. [ME *poke*; of Gmc origin.]
poke[2] [pōk] *n* (*Brit*) a projecting brim of front of a bonnet; a poke bonnet.—*n* **poke´ bonnet**, a woman's bonnet with a projecting brim at the front. [Perh from foregoing, or from following word.]
poke[3] [pōk] *vt* to thrust or push the end of anything against or into; (*slang*) to hit; to make (a hole, etc.) by poking.—*vi* to jab (at); to pry or search (about or around); to move slowly (along).—*n* a jab; a thrust; (*slang*) a blow with the fist.—*n* **po´ker**, one who pokes; a rod for poking or stirring the fire.—*adj* **pō´ky**, slow; dull; small and uncomfortable, as a room.—**poke fun at**, to ridicule, mock. [ME *pōken*; app of Low Ger origin.]
poker [pō´kėr] *n* one of several card games in which a player bets that the value of his hand (determined by convention) is higher than that of the hands held by others.—*n* **poker´face**, an inscrutible face, concealing a person's thoughts or feelings.—*adj* **poker-faced**.
polar [pō´lȧr] *adj* of or near the North or South Pole; of a pole; having polarity.—*n* **polarity** [pō-lar´i-ti] the property possessed by certain bodies (eg a magnetized bar) of turning so that their opposite extremities point towards the magnetic poles of the earth; attraction toward a particular object or in a specific direction; the tendency to develop differently in different directions along an axis; the electrical condition, positive or negative, of a body; diametrical opposition; an instance of such opposition.—*vt* **polarize**

[pō´lārīz] to cause (as light waves) to vibrate in a definite pattern; to give physical polarity to; to break up into opposing factions; to concentrate.—*vi* to become polarized.—*ns* **polarization** [pō-lȧr-ī-zā´sh(ȯ)n] the act of polarizing; the state of being polarized; the restriction of the vibrations in light waves to one plane or direction; **Polaroid**, trade name for a transparent material capable of polarizing light used esp in eyeglasses and lamps to prevent glare; a camera that produces a print in seconds, in full **Polaroid (Land) Camera**.—**polar bear**, a large creamy-white bear (*Thalarctos maritimus*) that inhabits arctic regions; **polar circle**, one of the two parallels of latitude each at a distance from a pole to about 23 degrees 27 minutes; **pō´lar coor´dinates**, coordinates defining a point by means of a radius vector and the angle which it makes with a fixed line through the origin. [Low L *polāris—polus*. See **pole** (1).]

polder [pōl´dėr] *n* a piece of low-lying reclaimed land, esp in the Netherlands. [Du]

pole[1] [pōl] *n* the end of an axis, esp of the earth, or any rotating sphere; either of two opposed forces, parts, etc. as the ends of a magnet, the terminals of a battery, etc.; (*geom*) a fixed point in a system of polar coordinates that serves as the origin.—*n* **pole´star**, a star near the north pole of the heavens; a guide or director.—**poles apart**, as diametrically opposed as possible. [L *polus*]—Gr *polos*, pivot, axis, firmament.]

pole[2] [pōl] *n* a long, slender piece of wood, metal, etc.; a long staff of wood, metal, or fiberglass used in the pole vault; a measure of length, 5½ yards, or of area, 30¼ square yards.—*n* **pole´ vault**, a field event in which the competitor uses a pole to achieve great height in jumping over a crossbar.—Also *vi*. [OE *pāl* (Ger *pfahl*)—L *pālus*, a stake.]

Pole [pōl] *n* a native or citizen of Poland; a person of Polish descent.

poleax [pōl´aks] *n* a battle-ax consisting of an ax-head on a short handle; a battle-ax with a long handle used as an ornamental weapon; an ax used in slaughtering cattle. [Orig *pollax* from **poll**, head, and **ax**, confused later with **pole** (2).]

polecat [pōl´kat] *n* a European carnivorous mammal (*Mustela putorius*) of which the ferret is considered a domesticated variety; a skunk. [ME *polcat*; perh Fr *poule*, hen, and **cat**.]

polemic [po-lem´ik] *adj* given to disputing; controversial.—*n* a controversialist; a controversy; (*pl*) practice or art of controversy.—*adj* **polem´ical**.—*adv* **polem´ically**. [Gr *polemikos—polemos*, war.]

police [pol-ēs´] *n* the governmental department (of a city, state, etc.) for keeping order, detecting crime, law enforcement, etc.; the members of such a department; a private organization resembling a police force; its members; the process of cleaning and putting in order; military personnel assigned to perform this function.—*vt* to control, protect, etc. with police or a similar force; to keep (a military camp, etc.) clean and orderly.—*ns* **police action**, a localized military action undertaken without formal declaration of war usu. initiated by an international authority; **police court**, a court for trying small offenses and the power to bind over for trial in a superior court or a grand jury persons accused of more serious offenses; **police´ force**, a body of trained men and women entrusted by a government to maintain peace and order, enforce laws, and to prevent and detect crime; **police´man**, member of a police force; **police´stā´tion**, the headquarters of the police of a district; **police´off´icer**, a policeman or policewoman; **police´woman**, a woman member of a police force.—**police state**, a country in which secret police are employed to detect and stamp out any opposition to the government in power. [Fr—L *polītia*—Gr *politeiā—polītēs*, a citizen—*polis*, a city.]

policy[1] [pol´i-si] *n* prudence in the management of public or private affairs; a course of action selected from among alternatives; a high-level overall plan embracing the general principles and aims of an organization, esp a government. [OFr *policie*—L *polītia*. See **police**.]

policy[2] [pol´i-si] *n* a writing containing a contract of insurance.—*n* **pol´icyhold´er**, one who holds a contract of insurance. [Fr *police*, a policy, app—LL *apodissa*, a receipt—Gr *apodeixis*, proof.]

polio [pōl´i-ō] *n* short for *polio*myelitis.

poliomyelitis [pōl-i-ō-mī-ē-lī´tis] *n* an acute infectious virus disease marked by inflammation of nerve cells in the spinal cord causing paralysis and atrophy of the muscles.—Also **infantile paralysis**. [Gr *polios*, grey, *myelos*, marrow.]

Polish [pō´lish] *adj* of *Poland*, or its people.—*n* the Slavic language of Poland.

polish [pol´ish] *vt* to make smooth and glossy by rubbing; to impart culture and refinement to; to make elegant (eg a literary style).—*vi* to take a polish.—*n* an act of polishing; gloss; a substance used to produce a smooth surface; refinement.—*n* **pol´isher**.—**polish off** (*inf*) to finish (a meal, job, etc.) completely. [OFr *polir, polissant*—L *polīre*, to polish.]

politburo [pol´it-bū-rō] *n* the principal policy-making and executive committee of a Communist party. [Russ *politicheskoe*, political, *byuro*, bureau.]

polite [po-līt´] *adj* refined; of courteous manners.—*adv* **polite´ly**.—*n* **polite´ness**. [L *polītus*, pt p of *polīre*, to polish.]

politic [pol´i-tik] *adj* (of actions) in accordance with good policy, expedient, judicious; (of persons) prudent, discreet, shrewdly tactful; political.—*vi* to campaign in politics.—*adj* **polit´ical**, pertaining to politics or government; characteristic of political parties or politicians.—*adv* **polit´ically**.—*n* **politician** [-tish´ȧn] one engaged in political life, often used with implications of seeking personal or partisan gain, scheming, etc.—*n* (*pl* in form, treated as *sing*) **pol´itics**, the art or science of government; the management of a political party; political affairs; political opinions, etc.; factional scheming for power.—**political economy**, a 19th century social science comprising the modern science of economics; a modern social science concerned with interrelationship of political and economic process; **political science**, the science or study of government, as to its principles, aims, methods, etc. [Gr *polītikos—polītēs*, a citizen.]

politico [pō-lit´i-kō] *n* a person engaged in party politics as a profession. [It or Sp]

polity [pol´i-ti] *n* the form or constitution of the government of a state, etc.; political organization; a specific form of political organization; the form of government of a religious denomination. [Gr *polīteiā*.]

polka [pōl´ka] *n* a Bohemian dance or its tune, in 2–4 time with accent on the first note of the second beat.—*n* **polka dot**, any of a pattern of small round dots on cloth. [Perh Czech *pulka*, half, from the half-step prevalent in it; or from Polish *polka*, a Polish woman.]

poll [pōl] *n* the head; the top or back of the head; a counting, listing, etc. of persons, esp of voters; the number of votes recorded; (*pl*) a place where votes are cast; a canvassing of people's opinions on some question.—*vt* to cut off the hair, horns, of, or the top of (a tree); to register, the votes of; to receive (a specified number of votes); to cast, give (one's vote) to canvass or question in a poll; to test (as several computer terminals sharing a line) in sequence for messages to be transmitted.—*vi* to cast one's vote at a poll.—*adj* **polled**, shorn; pollarded; deprived of horns; hornless.—*ns* **poll´ster**, one who conducts a poll or compiles data obtained from a poll; **poll´ tax**, a tax of a fixed amount per person levied on adults. [Cf obs Du and L Ger *polle*.]

pollack [pol´ȧk] *n* a common food fish (*Pollachius virens*) of the north Atlantic of the cod family, with long lower jaw.—Also **poll´ock**. [Etymology obscure; connection with Gael *pollag* doubtful.]

pollard [pol´ȧrd] *n* a tree having the whole crown cut off to promote the growth of a dense head of foliage.—*vt* to make a pollard of (a tree). [**poll**, the head.]

pollen [pol´ėn] *n* the fertilizing powder formed in the anthers of flowers.—*vt* **poll´inate**, to convey pollen to.—*n* **pollinā´tion**, the transferring or supplying of pollen to the stigma of a flower, esp by aid of insects or other external agents, esp of ragweed, in a given volume of air at a specified time and place. [L *pollen, -inis*, fine flour.]

pollute [pol-(y)ōōt] *vt* to contaminate, make filthy; to make (any feature of the environment) offensive or harmful to human, animal, or plant life; to make unclean morally; to profane.—*ns* **pollut´er; pollū´tion**, act of polluting; state of being polluted; defilement. [L *polluĕre, pollūtus—pol-*, a form of *pro* or *per*, *luĕre*, to wash.]

polo [pō´lō] *n* a game played on horseback by two teams, using a wooden ball and long-handled mallets.—**polo neck**, a high, close-fitting collar with a part turned over at the top on a knitted garment; a sweater with such a collar. [From a word meaning ball.]

polonaise [pol-o-nāz´] *n* a Polish national dance; music for such a dance. [Fr, 'Polish'.]

polonium [po-lō´ni-ům] *n* a transuranic element (symbol Po; at wt 210.0; at no 84). [L *Polonia*, Poland.]

poltergeist [pol´tėr-gīst] *n* an alleged spirit said to move heavy furniture, etc., a noisy ghost. [Ger *poltern*, to make an uproar, *geist*, spirit.]

poltroon [pol-trōōn´] *n* a thorough coward.—*n* **poltroon´ery**, cowardice, want of spirit. [Fr *poltron*—It *poltro*, lazy.]

poly- [pol-i-] in composition, much, many, etc **polyphagus** [pol-if´a-gus] *adj* eating many kinds of food. [Gr *phagein*, aor, to eat]. [Gr *polys, poly*, much.]

polyandrous [po-li-an´drus] *adj* having several husbands or male mates at the same time.—*n* **polyan´dry**, the social usage by which a woman has more husbands than one at the same time. [Gr *polys*, many, *anēr*, gen *andros*, a man.]

polyanthus [pol-i-an´thus] *n* any of various hybrid primroses; a narcissus (*Narcissus tazette*) having small yellow or white flowers in clusters; a primrose with many flowers.—*pl* **polyan´thuses, -anthi**. [Gr *polys*, many, *anthos*, a flower.]

polychrome [pol´i-krōm] *adj* made with, or decorated in many colors. [Gr *polys*, many, *chrōma*, color.]

polyester [pol-i-es´ter] *n* any of a range of polymeric resins, some thermoplastic, some thermosetting, used in making plastics, films, etc. [**poly-, ester**.]

polyethylene [pol-i-eth´i-lēn] *n* a plastic made by polymerizing ethylene (ethylene is C_2H_4, an inflammable gas); thermoplastic materials widely used for many purposes, including wrappings.

polygamy [pol-ig´a-mi] *n* the practice of having more than one spouse at one time.—*n* **polyg´amist**.—*adj* **polyg´amous**, (*bot*) the occurrence of male, female, and hermaphrodite flowers on the same plant or on different plants. [Gr—*polys*, many, *gamos*, marriage.]

polyglot [pol´i-glot] *adj* using many languages; composed of numerous linguistic groups; containing matter in several languages; composed of elements from different languages.—*n* one who speaks or writes many languages; **Polyglot**, a collection of versions of the same work in different languages, esp a Bible of this kind; a confusion of languages or nomenclatures. [Gr *polys*, many, *glōtta*, tongue, language.]

polygon [pol´i-gon] *n* a plane figure bounded by straight lines, esp more than four. [L—Gr *polygōnon—polys*, many, *gōniā*, a corner.]

polygraph [pol´i-gräf] *n* a device measuring changes in respiration, pulse rate, etc. used on persons suspected of lying.—*n* **pol´ygrapher**, one who operates a polygraph.—*adj* **pol´ygraph´ic**. [Gr *polys*, many, *graphein*, to write.]

polygyny [pol-ij´i-ni or -ig´-] *n* the social usage by which a man has more wives than one at the same time. [Gr *polys*, many, *gynē*, woman.]

polyhedron [pol-i-hē´dron] *n* a solid figure with many (usu. more than six) faces.—*adjs* **polyhē´dral, polyhē´drous**. [Gr *polys*, many, *hedra*, a base.]

polymer [pol´i-mėr] *n* (*chem*) one of a series of substances alike in percentage composition, but differing in molecular weight.—*n* **polymerizā´tion**, the combination of several molecules to form a more complex molecule having the same empirical formula as the simpler ones, but having a greater molecular weight; a process by which many of the plastics are obtained; reduplication of parts in an organism.—*vt* **polym´erize**. [Gr *polys*, many, *meros*, part.]

polymorphism [pol-i-mörf´izm] *n* occurrence of the same thing in several different forms; the property of crystallizing in two or more forms with distinct structure.—*n* **pol´ymorph**, any one of several forms in which the same thing may occur.—*adjs* **polymorphous, -ic**. [Gr *polymorphos*, many-formed—*polys*, many, *morphē*, form.]

Polynesian [pol-i-nē´zi-àn] *adj* pertaining to Polynesia, the tropical islands in the Pacific Ocean.—*n* a native of Polynesia. [Gr *polys*, many, *nēsos*, an island.]

polynomial [pol-i-nō´mi-àl] *n* a mathematical expression consisting of a sum of terms each of which is product of a constant and one or more variables raised to a positive or zero integral power.—*adj* composed of or expressed as one or more polynomials. [Gr *polys*, many—L *nōmen*, a name.]

polyp [pol´ip] *n* a small water animal (Phylum Coelenterata) with tentacles at the top of a tubelike body; a growth on mucous membrane.—*adj* **polypoid´**. [L *polypus, -i*—Gr *polypous—polys*, many, *pous*, foot.]

polypetalous [pol-i-pet´al-us] *adj* with petals separated. [Gr *polys*, many, *petalon*, a leaf.]

polyphony [pol-if´on-i] *n* a style of musical composition in which two or more independent melodies are in harmony.—*adj* **polyphon´ic**. [Gr *polys*, many, *phōnē*, voice.]

polypody [pol´i-pōd-ē] *n* a widely distributed fern (*Polypodium vulgare*) having creeping roofstocks and feathery fronds. [Gr *polypous—polys*, many, *pous*, gen *podos*, a foot.]

polystyrene [pol-i-stī´rēn] *n* a plastic made by polymerizing styrene having good mechanical properties, resistant to moisture and to chemicals.

polysyllable [pol´i-sil-à-bl] *n* a word of many, or of more than four, syllables.—*adj* **polysyllab´ic**. [Gr *polys*, many, and **syllable**.]

polytechnic [pol-i-tek´nik] *adj* of or providing instruction in many applied sciences and technical subjects.—*n* a school in which such subjects are taught. [Gr *polys*, many, *technē*, an art.]

polytheism [pol´i-thē-izm] *n* belief in more than one god.—*n* **pol´ytheist**, a believer in many gods.—*adjs* **polytheist´ic, -al**. [Gr *polys*, many, *theos*, a god.]

polyunsaturated [pol-i-un-sach´ū-rāt´id] *n* denoting any of certain plant and animal fats and oils with a low cholesterol content.

polyurethane [pol-i-ur´ė-thān] *n* any of various polymers that contain NHC00 linkages and are used esp in flexible and rigid foams, resins, etc.

pomade [po-mād´, -mäd´] *n* a perfumed ointment for the hair. [Fr *pommade*—It *pomada, pomata*, lipsalve—L *pōmum*, an apple.]

pomander [pom-an´dėr or pom´àn-dėr] *n* a ball of perfumes, or a perforated globe or box in which it was carried. [OFr *pomme d'ambre*, apple of amber.]

pome [pōm] *n* a fleshy fruit consisting of a thickened outer layer and a central core with usu. five seeds enclosed in a capsule (eg an apple).—*adj* **pomaceous** [-ā´shùs]. [L *pōmum*.]

pomegranate [pom´gran-it] *n* a fruit with a thick rind and many seeds; a widely cultivated tropical tree (*Punica granatum*) bearing pomegranates. [OFr *pome grenate*—L *pōmum*, apple, *grānātum*, seeded.]

pomelo [pum´- or pom´el-o] *n* a shaddock; a grapefruit with pink flesh.

Pomeranian [pom-ė-rā´ni-àn] *adj* pertaining to Pomerania in Northern Prussia; a breed of very small compact dogs with a dense double coat.

pommel [pum´ėl] *n* the knob on the hilt of a sword; the rounded upward-projecting front part of a saddle.—*vt* to pummel. [OFr *pome*—L *pōmum*, an apple.]

pomp [pomp] *n* a splendid procession; ceremony; grandeur; ostentation; vain show.—*adj* **pomp´ous**, displaying pomp or grandeur; solemnly consequential; self-important.—*adv* **pomp´ously**.—*ns* **pomp´ousness, pompos´ity**. [Fr *pompe*—L *pompa*—Gr *pompē—pempein*, to send.]

pompadour [pom´pa-dōr] *n* a man's style of hairdressing in which the hair is brushed up high from the forehead; a woman's hairdo in which the hair is brushed into a loose full roll around the face.—*adj* **pompadoured´**. [Marquise de *Pompadour*, 1721–64.]

pom-pom[1] [pom´-pom] *n* an automatic gun of 20 to 40 millimeters mounted on ships in pairs, fours, or eights. [Imit.]

pom-pom[2] [pom´pom´] *n* an ornamental ball or tuft of fabric strands used on clothing as an ornament.

poncho [pon´chō] *n* a cloak like a blanket with a hole in the middle for the head; any similar garment, esp worn as a raincoat. [Sp—S Amer Indian.]

pond [pond] *n* a body of standing water smaller than a lake.—*vt* to block (as a stream) to create a pond.—*vi* to collect in or form a pond. [ME *ponde*; variant of **pound** (2).]

ponder [pon´dėr] *vti* to think deeply (about); to consider carefully.—*adj* **pon´derable**, sufficiently significant to be worth considering; **pon´derous**, weighty; massive; clumsy, unwieldy; oppressively dull; lifeless.—*adv* **pon´derously**.—*ns* **pon´derousness, ponderos´ity**. [L *ponderāre*, and *pondus, ponděris*, a weight.]

pongee [pon-jē] *n* soft unbleached washable silk woven from filaments of wild silkworms. [Chinese.]

poniard [pon´yård] *n* a small dagger with a slender blade of triangular or square cross section.—*vt* to stab with a poniard. [Fr *poignard—poing*—L *pugnus*, fist.]

pontiff [pon´tif] *n* (*RC*) a bishop, esp the Pope.—**pon´tifex**, a member of the council of priests in Ancient Rome.—*pl* **pontif´icēs**.—*adj* **pontif´ical**, of or belonging to a pontiff; splendid; authoritative; pompously dogmatic.—*adv* **pontif´ically**.—*n pl* **pontif´ical**, (*pl*) the dress of a priest, bishop, or pope.—*n* **pontif´icate**, the office and dignity or reign of a pope.—*vi* to perform the duties of a pontiff; to speak in a pompous manner. [L *pontifex, pontificis* (partly through Fr *pontife*), perh from *pons, pontis*, a bridge, *facěre*, to make.]

pontoon [pon-tōōn´] *n* a flat-bottomed boat; a float; such a boat or float used to support a bridge. [Fr *ponton*—L *pontō, -ōnis*, a pontoon—*pons*, a bridge.]

pony [pō´ni] *n* a small horse, esp one of various breeds of small stocky animals known for their gentleness and endurance; a bronco, mustang, etc. of the western US; a literal translation of a foreign language text, esp one used surreptiously by students.—*ns* **pony express**, a postal system that operated across the western US in 1860–61 by relays of horses and riders; **pony tail**, a style of arranging hair to resemble a pony's tail.—**pony up** (*inf*) to pay (money) in settlement of an account.—*vi* to pay. [From Scots *powny*, prob—OFr *poulenet*, dim of *poulain*—LL *pullānus*, a foal—L *pullus*, a young animal.]

poodle [pōō´dl] *n* a breed of dog with a solid-colored curly coat of many colors and sizes. [Ger *pudel*; Low Ger *pudeln*, to splash.]

pooh [pōō] *interj* of disdain.—*vt* **pooh-pooh´**, to express contempt. [Imit.]

Pooh-Bah, pooh-bah [pōō´bä] a person who holds many offices simultaneously; one giving himself airs. [Character in Gilbert and Sullivan's *The Mikado*.]

pool[1] [pōōl] *n* a small pond; a puddle; a small collection of liquid; a tank for swimming. [OE *pōl* (Du *poel*, Ger *pfuhl*.]

pool[2] [pōōl] *n* a game of billiards played on a table with six pockets; a combination of resources, funds, supplies, etc. for some common purpose; the parties forming such a combination; a group of people who may be called upon as required, eg a pool of secretaries.—*vti* to put into a common fund. [Fr *poule*, a hen, also stakes, associated in English with **pool** (1).]

poop [pōōp] *n* a high deck in the stern of a ship.—*vt* to break over the stern of. [Fr *poupe*—L *puppis*, the poop.]

poor [pōōr] *adj* possessing little, without means, needy; deficient; unproductive; inferior, paltry; feeble; humble; unfortunate, to be pitied.—Also as *n* (collective), those possessing little; those dependent on relief or charity.—*adv* **poor´ly**.—*adj* used predicatively) not in good health.—*ns* **poor´ness; poor´house**, a house established at the public expense for sheltering the poor.—*n* **poor´law**, a law providing for the support of the poor.—*vi* **poor´mouth´**, (*inf*) to complain about one's lack of money.—*adj* **poor´spir´ited**, lacking zest, confidence, or courage.—*n* **poor´spir´itedness**.—**the poor**, poor, or needy, people. [OFr *poure, povre*—L *pauper*, poor.]

pop[1] [pop] *n* a sharp, quick sound, a shot; any carbonated, nonalcoholic beverage.—*vi* to make a pop; to shoot; to come or go suddenly or quickly (in, out, etc.); said of the eyes, to bulge; (*baseball*) to hit the ball high into the infield.—*vt* to cause to pop, as corn by roasting; to put suddenly.—*pr p*, **popp´ing**; *pt, pt p* **popped**.—*adv* with a pop; suddenly.—*ns* **pop´corn**, a kind of corn which when heated pops or bursts open; the popped corn; **popgun**, a toy gun operated by compressed air.—**pop off**, to leave suddenly; (*inf*) to die; (*inf*) to talk thoughtlessly and often angrily. **pop the question**, (*inf*) to propose marriage. [Imit.]

pop[2] [pop] *adj* in a popular modern style.—*n* pop music; pop art; pop culture.—*ns* **pop art**, a realistic art style using techniques and subjects from commercial art, comic strips, posters, etc; **pop artist**.

Pope [pōp] *n* the bishop of Rome, head of the Roman Catholic Church.—*ns* **pope´dom**, office, dignity, or jurisdiction of the pope; **pop´ery**, a hostile term for Roman Catholicism.—*adv* **pop´ish**, (*disparaging*) relating to the pope or to popery. [OE *pāpa*—L *pāpa*—Gr *pappas*, a father.]

popinjay [pop´in-ja] *n* a strutting supericilious person. [OFr *papegai*; cf Low L *papagallus*; Late Gr *papagas*, a parrot; prob Eastern.]

poplar [pop´lår] *n* a genus (*Populus*) of trees of the willow family, common in the northern hemisphere. [OFr *poplier*—L *pōpulus*, poplar-tree.]

poplin [pop´lin] *n* a corded fabric with a silk warp and worsted weft; an imitation in cotton or other material. [Fr *popeline*—It *papalina*, papal, from the papal town of Avignon, where it was made.]

poppy [pop´i] *n* any of a genus (*Papaver*) of chiefly annual or perennial herbs with milky juice, showy flowers, and capsular fruits including one (*P. somniferum*) that is the source of opium and several that are cultivated as ornamentals; an extract of poppy used medicinally; a strong reddish orange.—*ns* **popp´yhead**, a carved ornament in wood, often finishing the end of a pew; **poppy seed**, the small dark seed of the poppy, used in baking. [OE *popig*—L *papāver*, poppy.]

populace [pop´ū-lȧs] *n* the common people; the masses; all the people in a country, region, etc. [Fr,—L *popolazzo*—L *pŏpulus*, people.]

popular [pop´ū-lȧr] *adj* of the people; pleasing to, enjoying the favor of, prevailing among, the people; liked by one's associates; suited to the understanding or to the means of ordinary people.—*vt* **pop´ularize**, to make generally known or widely approved; to present in a manner suited to ordinary people.—*n* **popular´ity**, quality or state of being popular.—*adv* **pop´ularly**.—*vt* **pop´ulāte**, to people; to furnish with inhabitants.—*ns* **populā´tion**, the inhabitants of any place or their number; group of persons, objects, etc. considered statistically; **pop´ulism**, any movement based on belief in the rights, wisdom, or virtue of the common people; **pop´ulist**, a member of a political party claiming to represent the common people.—*adj* **pop´ulous**, thickly inhabited.—*n* **pop´ulousness**.—**popular front**, an alliance, esp of leftist political parties against a common opponent; one dominated by Communists as a device to gain power; **population explosion**, the great and rapid increase in human population in modern times. [L *pŏpulus*, the people.]

porcelain [pör´sė´lin] *n* a hard, white, translucent variety of ceramic ware.—Also *adj*. [OFr *porcelaine*—It *porcellana*, cowrie.]

porch [pörch] *n* a covered entrance to a building; an open or enclosed gallery or room on the outside of a building. [OFr *porche*—L *porticus*—*porta*, a gate.]

porcine [pör´sīn] *adj* of or like pigs or hogs. [L *porcīnus*—*porcus*, a swine.]

porcupine [pör´kū-pīn] *n* a large rodent quadruped of several kinds, constituting of an Old World terrestial family (Hystricidae) and a New World arboreal family (Erethizontidae), bristling with quills. [OFr *porc espin*—L *porcus*, a pig, *spīna*, a spine.]

pore[1] [pōr, pör] *n* a tiny opening, as in plant leaves, stem, etc. for absorbing and discharging fluids.—*n* **poros´ity**.—*adj* **por´ous**, having pores; permeable by fluids, etc.—*n* **por´ousness**. [Fr,—L *porus*—Gr *poros*, a passage.]

pore[2] [pör] *vi* to study closely and attentively (with **over**); to ponder (*with* **over**).]

pork [pörk] *n* the flesh of a pig used as food; (*inf*) government money, jobs, or favors used by politicians as patronage.—*ns* **pork barrel**, (*inf*) government appropriations yielding benefits to a political district and its political representative; **pork belly**, an uncured side of pork; **pork´er**, a young hog; a pig fed for pork.—**pork-pie hat**, a soft felt hat with a round flat crown and brim turned up.—*adj* **pork´y**, of or like pork; (*inf*) saucy, cocky, etc. [Fr *porc*—L *porcus*, a hog.]

pornography [pör-nog´ra-fi] *n* writings, pictures, etc. intended primarily to arouse sexual desire.—Also **por´no**.—*adj* **pornograph´ic**.—*n* **pornog´rapher**. [Gr *pornē*, a whore, *graphein*, to write.]

porphyry [pör´fir-i] *n* any igneous rock with large, distinct crystals.—*adj* **porphyritic** [-it´ik], like, or of the nature of porphyry; having distinct crystals (as of feldspar) in a finegrained base. [Gr *porphyrītēs*—*porphyros*, purple.]

porpoise [pör´pùs] *n* any of several small whales (genus *Phocaena*), esp a black blunt-nosed whale (*P. phocaena*) of the north Atlantic and Pacific 5 to 8 feet long; any of several bottle-nosed dolphins. [OFr *porpeis*—L *porcus*, a hog, *piscis*, a fish.]

porridge [pör´ij] *n* a food usu. made by slowly stirring oatmeal in boiling water. [**pottage**, altered by influence of obs or dial *porray*, vegetable soup.]

porringer [por´in-jėr] *n* a small bowl for soup, porridge, etc.; a low metal bowl with a single flat usu. pierced handle. [See **porridge, pottage**; for inserted *n*, cf **passenger, messenger**.]

port[1] [pört] *n* the left side of a ship, or aircraft looking forward.—Also **larboard**.—*adj* **port**.—*vti*, to turn left. [Ety doubtful.]

port[2] [pört] *n* bearing, carriage of the body; the position in which a military weapon is carried at the command 'port arms'.—*adj* **port´able**, easily or conveniently carried or moved about.—*n* **port´age**, a carrying of boats and supplies overland between navigable rivers, lakes, etc.; any route over which this is done.—*vti* to carry (boats, etc.) over a portage.—**port arms**, a position in which the rifle is carried diagonally in front of the body with the muzzle pointing upward to the left. [Fr *port*—L *portāre*, to carry.]

port[3] [pört] *n* a harbor; a city with a harbor where ships load and unload cargo; airport; port of entry.—**port of call**, a port where vessels can call for stores or repairs; **port of entry**, a place where foreign goods may be cleared through a customhouse; a place where an alien may be permitted to enter a country. [OE *port*—L *portus, -ūs*; akin to *porta*, a gate.]

port[4] [pört] *n* a porthole; an opening, as in a valve face, for the passage of steam, etc.; a hole in an armored vehicle for firing a weapon. [Fr *porte*—L *porta*, gate.]

port[5] [pört] *n* a fortified sweet dark-red or tawny wine (sometimes white) of the type shipped from Portugal; a similar wine made elsewhere. [*Oporto*, Portugal.]

portal [pör´tȧl] *n* a gate or doorway, esp a great or magnificent one; any entrance; (*archit*) the arch over a gate; the lesser of two gates.—**portal vein**, vein conveying to the liver blood from intestines, spleen and stomach. [OFr *portal*—Low L *portāle*—L *porta*, a gate.]

portcullis [pört-kul´is] *n* a grating that can be let down to close a gateway. [OFr *porte coleïce*, sliding gate.]

portend [pör-tend´] *vt* to betoken, presage.—*n* **portent** [pör´tent], that which portends or foreshows; an evil omen.—*adj* **portent´ous**, of the nature of, or containing, a portent or warning; very great; impressive; pompous, self-important. [L *portendĕre, portentum*—*por-*, equivalent to *prō* or *per tendĕre*, to stretch.]

porter[1] [port´er] *n* a doorman or gatekeeper. [L *porta*, a gate.]

porter[2] [pört´ėr] *n* a man who carries luggage, etc. for hire; a man who sweeps, cleans, etc. in a bank, store, etc.; a railroad attendant for passengers as on a sleeper; a dark-brown beer.—*ns* **port´erage**, a porter's work; charge made by a porter for carrying goods; **port´erhouse**, (*arch*) a house where porter is sold; a large steak cut from the thick end of the short loin containing a T-shaped bone and a large piece of tenderloin. [OFr *porteour*—L *portātor, -ōris*—*portāre*, to carry.]

portfolio [pört-fōli-ō] *n* a portable case for loose papers, drawings, etc.; a collection of such papers; the office of minister of state; a list of investments held.—*pl* **portfo´lios**. [It *portafogli*—L *portāre*, to carry, *folium* a leaf.]

porthole [pört´hōl] *n* an opening (as a window) with a cover or closure esp in the side of a ship or aircraft; a port through which to shoot; an opening for intake or exhaust of a fluid. [**port** (4) + **hole**.]

portico [pör´ti-kō] *n* (*archit*) a range of columns with a roof forming a covered walk along the front or side of a building; a colonnade;—*pl* **por´ticoes, porticos**. [It,—L *porticus*, a porch.]

portière [por-tyer´] *n* a curtain hung over the door or doorway of a room. [Fr]

portion [pōr´sh(ȯ)n] *n* a part, esp an alloted part of a dowry; destiny.—*vt* to divide into portions; to allot as a share. **por´tionless**, having no portion, dowry. [OFr,—L *portiō, -ōnis*.]

portland cement [pört´land] *n* a cement that sets under water made by grinding and burning a mixture of limestone and clay. [*Isle of Portland*, England, because of its resemblance to the stone quarried there.]

portly [pört´li] *adj* having a dignified port or mien; corpulent.—*n* **port´liness**. [**port** (2).]

portmanteau [pört-man´tō] *n* a large traveling bag that folds back flat from the middle.—**portman´teau word**, a word (as *brunch, smog*) produced by combining other words or parts of words. [Fr,—*porter*, to carry, *manteau*, a cloak.]

portrait [pōr´trȧt] *n* a painting, photograph, etc. of a person, esp of the face; the likeness of a real person; a vivid description in words.—*n* **por´traiture**, the art or act of portraying.—*vt* **portray** [pōr-trā´], to paint or draw the likeness of; to describe in words; to play the part of in a play, movie, etc.—*ns* **portray´al**, the act of portraying; **portray´er**. [OFr *po(u)rtrait, po(u)rtaire*—L *prōtrahēere, -tractum*; see **protract**.]

Portuguese [pōr´tū-gēz´] *adj* of *Portugal*, its people, or its language.—*n* a native or citizen of Portugal; the Romance language of Portugal and Brazil.

pose [pōz] *n* a position or attitude, esp one held for an artist or photographer; an attitude of body or of mind assumed for effect.—*vt* to assume or maintain a pose; to set oneself up (as)—*vt* to put in a suitable attitude; to propound (a question).—*ns* **poser**, one who poses; **poseur** [pōz-œr´; Fr], an affected person, one who attitudinises. [Fr.—*poser*, to place—Low L *pausāre*, to cease—L *pausa*, pause—Gr *pausis*. Between Fr *poser* and L *pōnĕre, positum*, there has been confusion, influencing the derivatives of both words.]

pose [pōz] *vt* to puzzle, to perplex by questions.—*n* **pos´er**, a difficult question, a baffling problem. [Shortened from **oppose**, or *appose* (to put one thing to or opposite to another).]

posh [posh] *adj* (*inf*) elegant; fashionable; spruced up. [Origin unknown.]

posit [poz´it] *vt* to assume as true;—*pr p* **pos´iting**; *pt p* **pos´ited**. [L *pōnĕre, positum*, to lay down.]

position [poz-ish´(ȯ)n] *n* situation; place occupied; disposition, arrangement (with reference to other things); posture; state of affairs; ground taken in argument or dispute; principle laid down; place in society, esp high rank; a post of employment; a job.—*vt* to set in place; to determine the position of.—*adj* **posi´tional**; related to, or fixed by position; involving little movement; dependent on context, environment or position.—**positional notation**, a system of expressing numbers in which the position of each digit has a place value; **position paper**, a detailed report that recommends a course of action on a particular issue. [Fr—L *positiō, -ōnis*—*ponĕre, positum*, to place.]

positive [poz´i-tiv] *adj* definitely, formally, or explicitly laid down; express; downright; (*gram*) of an adjective or adverb, expressing a quality without comparison; characterized by the presence of some quality, not merely by the absence of its opposite; dealing with matters of fact, unqualified; expressed clearly, or in a confident or peremptory manner; constructive; empirical; (*math*) greater than zero; in the direction of increase, actual or conventional; (*photography*) having light and shade as in the original; (*elect*) charged with positive electricity; (of a point of electrode with respect to another point) at more positive electrical potential; having a deficiency of electrons.—*n* that which is positive; a positive quantity; (*gram*) the positive degree; a photograph or a print from a negative.—*adv* **pos´itively**.—*ns* **pos´itiveness**, state or quality of being positive; certainty; confidence; **pos´itivism**, a theory that positive knowledge is based on the properties and relations of natural phenomena as verified by the empirical sciences; the quality or state of being positive.—**positive electricity**, such as is developed in glass by rubbing with silk, arising from a deficiency of electrons on the glass; **positive electron**, positron. [L *positīvus*, fixed by agreement—*pōnĕre, positum*, to place.]

positron [poz´-itron] *n* a particle of same magnitude of charge and mass as an electron, and constituting the antiparticle of the electron.—Also **positive electron**.

posse [pos´ė] *n* a body of men summoned by a sheriff to assist him in keeping the peace, etc. [L *posse*, to be able.]

possess [poz-es´] *vt* to have or hold as owner; to have (a quality, faculty, etc.); to occupy and dominate the mind of; to take into one's possession.—*adj* **possessed´**, owned; controlled as if by a demon.—*n* **possession** [poz-esh´(ȯ)n], act, state, or fact of possessing or being possessed; a thing possessed; (*pl*) wealth; a subject foreign territory.—*adj* **possess´ive**, pertaining to or denoting possession; (*gram*) denoting or of a case, form or construction expressing possession; showing a desire or tendency to treat (a person or thing) as a possession.—*n* (*gram*) the possessive case, form, or construction.—*adv* **possess´ively**.—*ns* **possess´iveness**, extreme attachment to one's possessions; desire to dominate another emotionally; **possess´or**. [OFr *possesser*—L *possidēre, possessum*.]

posset [pos´ėt] *n* a drink, milk curdled, as with wine, or ale. [ME *poschote, possot*.]

possible [pos´i-bl] *adj* not contrary to the nature of things; that may be or happen; that may be done, practicable; that one may tolerate, accept, or get on with.—*n* **possibil´ity**, state of being possible; that which is possible; a contingency.—*adv* **poss´ibly**. [L *posibilis*—*posse*, to be able.]

post[1] [pōst] *n* a piece of wood, metal, etc. set upright to support a building, sign, etc.; the starting point of a horse race.—*vt* to put up (a poster, etc.) on (a wall etc.); to announce by posting notices; to warn against trespassing on by posted notices; to put (a name) on a posted or published list.—*n* **post´er**, a usu. decorative or ornamental bill or placard for posting in a public place. [OE *post*—L *postis*, a doorpost—*pōnĕre*, to place.]

post[2] [pōst] *n* a fixed place or station, esp a place where a soldier or body of soldiers is stationed; a trading post; a settlement; a trading station on the floor of a stock exchange; an office, employment or appointment—*vt* to station in a given place; to carry ceremoniously to a position; to put up (as a bond); (*bookkeeping*) to transfer (an entry) to the ledger; to supply with information.—*vi* to travel with post-horses, or with speed; to move up and down in the saddle, the movements synchronizing with a horse's trot.—*adv* with post-horses; with speed.—*ns* **post´age**, money charged for mailing a letter, etc. as represented by stamps; **postage stamp**, a government adhesive stamp or imprinted stamp used on mail as evidence of prepayment of postage; **postage-due stamp**, a special stamp applied by the post office to mail bearing insufficient postage that is paid for by the addressee.—*adj* **pos´tal**, of or pertaining to the mail service.—*ns* **postal card**, a card officially stamped and issued by the government for use in the mail; a postcard; **post´boy**, a postilion; **post´card**, a card on which a message may be sent by mail; **post´ chaise**, a carriage, usually four-wheeled, for two or four passengers with a postilion, once used in traveling; **post exchange**, a nonprofit general store at an army post or camp;—*adv* **post´haste**, with all possible speed.—*adj* (*obs*) speedy; immediate.—*ns* **post´ horn**, a horn blown by the driver of a mail coach in the 18th and 19th centuries; **post´-horse**, a horse for use esp by couriers or mail carriers; **post´man**, a mailman; **post´mark**, the mark impressed upon a letter at a post office cancelling the stamp or showing the date and place of posting or of arrival; **post´master**, the manager or superintendent of a post office; **post´master gen´eral**, an official in charge of a national post office department or agency; **post´ office**, a government department or agency handling the transmission of mail; a local branch of a national post office; a game in which a kiss is exacted as payment for delivery of an imaginary letter; **postal union**, an association of governments setting up uniform regulations and practices for international mail. [Fr *poste*—It *posta* and *posto*—L *pōnĕre, positum*, to place.]

post- [pōst-] *prefix* after, behind—as *postclassical, postnatal, postwar*, etc.—*adj* **post bellum**, of, or characteristic of the period following a war, esp the American Civil War.—*vt* **postdate´**, to date after the real time; to mark with a date (as for payment) later than the time of signing.—*adjs* **postdilu´vian**, of the period after the flood described in the Bible; **postexil´ic**, occurring after the Babylonian exile of the Jews (587–539 BC); **post´grad´uate**, belonging to study pursued after graduation.—Also *n*.—*n* **Post´impress´ionism**, a movement in painting at the end of the 19th century which rejected the naturalism and momentary effects of impressionism but adapted its use of pure color to paint subjects with greater subjective emotion.—*n, adj* **Post´impress´ionist**, of Paul Cézanne, Vincent Van Gogh, Paul Gauguin, and neo-impressionists.—*adjs* **post´merid´ian**, coming after the sun has crossed the meridian; in the afternoon; **post´nup´tial**, after marriage. [L *post*, after, behind.]

posterior [pos-tē-´ri-ȯr] *adj* coming after; later; at the rear.—*n* the buttocks.—*ns* **posteriority** [post-tē-ri-or´i-ti] the quality or state of being later; **posterity** [-ter´i-ti], succeeding generations; all of a person's descendants. [L *postĕrior*, comp of *posterus*, coming after—*post*, after.]

postern [pōst´ėrn] *n* a back door or gate; a private or side entrance.—*adj* back; private. [OFr *posterne, posterle*—L *posterula*, a dim from *posterus*.]

posthumous [post´ū-mus] *adj* born after the father's death; published after the author's or composer's death; arising or continuing after one's death.—*adv* **post´humously**. [L *posthumus, postumus*, superl of *posterus*, coming after—*post*, after; the *h* inserted from false association with *humāre*, to bury.]

postiche [pos-tēsh´] *n* a false hairpiece; a wig. [Fr,—It *posticio*—L *postīcus*, hinder.]

postilion, postillion [pōs-til´yȯn] *n* one who rides as a guide on the leading left-hand horse of a team drawing a carriage.—Also **postboy**. [Fr *postillion*—It *postiglione*—*posta*, post.]

postmortem [pōst-mör´tėm] *adj* after death; of a postmortem.—*n* a postmortem examination, autopsy; a discussion after an event—**postmortem examination**, an examination of the body after death to determine the cause of death or to discover the character and extent of changes produced by disease. [L *post mortem* (acc of *mors, mortis*, death.]

postpone [pōs(t)-pōn´] *vt* to put off to a future time, to defer, to delay.—*n* **postpone´ment**. [L *postpōnĕre, -positum*—*post*, after, *pōnĕre*, to put.]

postprandial [pōst-pran´di-ȧl] *adj* after a meal. [L *post*, after, *prandium*. See **prandial**.]

postscript [pōs(t)´skript] *n* a part added to a letter after the signature; an addition to an article or book following a completed text. [L *post*, after, *scrīptum*, written, pa p of *scrībĕre*, to write.]

postulate [pos´tū-lāt] *vt* to claim; to take for granted, assume.—*n* a position assumed as self-evident; (*math*) an unproved assumption taken as basic on a mathematical system; an axiom.—*ns* **pos´tulant**, a candidate on probation for admission to a religious order; a person on probation before being admitted as a candidate for holy orders in the Episcopal Church. **postulā´tion**. [L *postulāre, -ātum*, to demand—*poscĕre*, to ask urgently.]

posture [pos´tūr] *n* the position and carriage of the body as a whole; pose; state of affairs; condition, attitude of mind; an official stand or position; a conscious expression of attitude.—*vt* to place in a particular manner.—*vi* (*lit* and *fig*) to pose. [Fr,—L *positūra*—*pōnĕre, positum*, to place.]

posy [pō´zi] *n* a motto, as on a ring; a bunch of flowers. [**poesy**.]

pot [pot] *n* a deep round vessel for various purposes, esp cooking; an earthen vessel for plants; a framework for catching fish or lobsters; the quantity in a pot; (*inf*) a large amount (as of money); (*inf*) all the money bet at a single time; (*slang*) marijuana.—*vt* to put in a pot or pots, esp in order to preserve; to shoot by a potshot;—*vi* to take a potshot;—*pr p* **pott´ing**; *pt p* **pott´ed**.—*ns* **pot´-bell´y**, a protuberant abdomen.—*adj* **pot´bell´ied**.—*ns* **potboiler**, a work in art or literature produced merely to secure the necessaries of life; **potboy**, a boy who serves drinks in a tavern; **pot´ hat**, a hat with a stiff crown; **potherb**, an herb whose leaves or stems are cooked for use as greens; one (as mint) used to season food; **pothole**, a pot-shaped hole; a hole ground into rock by stones in an eddying current; a deep hole eroded in limestone; a round depression in a road surface; **pot´hook**, a hook for hanging a pot over a fire; a hooked stroke in writing; **pot´house**, a tavern; **pot´hunter**, one who hunts game for food; an amateur archeologist; **pot´luck´**, what may happen to be in the pot for a meal without special preparation for guests; whatever is available or offered in given circumstances at a given time; **pot marigold**, a calendula (*Calendula officinalis*) grown esp for ornament; **pot´shot**, a shot taken from ambush or at an easy target; (*inf*) a random critical remark.—*adj* **pott´ed**, planted or grown in a pot; (*slang*) drunk; (*slang*) under the influence of marijuana. [Lat OE *pott*; cf Ger *pott*; Fr *pot*; origin unknown.]

potable [pō´ta-bl] *adj* fit to drink.—*n* something drinkable. [L *pōtābilis*—*pōtāre*, to drink.]

potash [pot´ash] *n* potassium carbonate, originally got in a crude state by leaching woodash, an alkali; potassium hydroxide (*caustic potash*).—*ns* **potass´ium**, an alkali metal (symbol K, at wt 39.1; at no 19) dicovered in potash; **potassium-argon dating**, a method of estimating the age of prehistoric materials. [English **pot, ash**, or the corresponding Du *pot-asschen* (mod D *potasch*).]

potation [pō-tā´sh(ȯ)n] *n* a usu. alcoholic drink or brew; act of drinking or inhaling; portion taken in such an act. [L *pōtātiō, -ōnis*—*pōtāre, -ātum*, to drink.]

potato [pȯ-tā´tō] *n* a sweet potato; an erect American herb (*solanum tuberosum*) widely grown for food in temperate regions; its tuber;—*pl* **potā´toes**. [Sp *patata*—Haitian *batata*, sweet-potato.]

poteen, potheen [po-tyēn´, -chēn´] *n* whisky illicitly distilled in Ireland. [Ir *poitín*, dim of *pota*, pot, from Eng **pot**, or Fr *pot*.]

potent [pō´tėnt] *adj* powerful, mighty, strongly influential; cogent; chemically and medicinally effective; (of a male) able to have sexual intercourse.—*adv* **pō´tently**.—*ns* **pō´tency**, power; strength or effectiveness; **pō´tentate**, one who possesses great power; a ruler; a monarch.—*adj* **pōtential** [-ten´shl], (*rare*) powerful, efficacious; latent, existing in possibility; (*gram*) expressing power, possibility, or liberty.—*n* anything that may be possible; possibility; powers or resources not yet developed; the relative voltage at a point in an electric circuit with respect to some reference point in the same circuit.—*n* **pōtentiality** [pō-ten-shi-al´iti],.—*adv* **pōten´tially**.—**potential difference**, the voltage difference existing at two points which causes a current to tend to flow between them—measured by the work done in transferring a unit of electricity from one point to the other; **potential energy**, the power of doing work possessed by a body in virtue of its position (eg a vehicle at the top of a hill, or a body in a state of tension of compression). [L *potēns, -entis*, pr p of *posse*, to be able—*potis*, able, *esse*, to be.]

pother [poTH´ėr] *n* a choking smoke or dust; turmoil; fuss, commotion.—*vt* to fluster; to perplex.—*vi* to make a pother. [Origin unknown.]

potion [pō´sh(ȯ)n] *n* a mixture of liquids (as liquor or medicine). [Fr,—L *pōtiō, -ōnis—potāre*, to drink.]

potpourri [pō-pōō-rē´] *n* a mixture of sweet-scented materials, chiefly dried petals; a medley or miscellany. [Fr, *pot*, pot, *pourri*, rotten, pt p of *pourrir*—L *putrēre*, to rot.]

potsherd [pot´shėrd] *n* a piece of broken pottery. [**pot**, + **shard**.]

pottage [pot´ij] *n* a thick soup of meat and vegetables. [Fr *potage—pot*, jug, pot.]

potter[1] [pot´ėr] *n* one who makes articles of baked clay, esp earthenware vessels.—*n* **pott´ery**, earthenware vessels, esp as distinguished from stoneware or porcelain and brick or tile; a place where such goods are manufactured. [**pot**.]

potter[2] [pot´ėr] *vi* to be fussily engaged about trifles; to putter.—*n* **pott´erer**. [Obs *pote*, to push.]

pouch [powch] *n* a small bag or sack; a mailbag; a sacklike structure, as that on the abdomen of a kangaroo, etc. for carrying young. [O Norman Fr *pouche* (O Fr *poche*).]

pouf, pouff, pouffe [pōōf] *n* a soft loose roll of hair; a bouffant part of a garment; an ottoman. [Fr *pouf*.]

poult [pōlt] *n* a young fowl, esp a young turkey.—*ns* **poult´erer**, one that deals in poultry; **poult´ry**, domesticated birds kept for meat or eggs; **poulter's measure**, a meter in which lines of 12 and 14 syllables alternate. [Fr *poulet*, dim of *poule*—LL *pulla*, hen, fem of L *pullus*, young animal.]

poultice [pōl´tis] *n* a hot, soft mass applied to a sore part of the body.—*vt* to put a poultice on. [L *pultēs*, pl of *puls, pultis* (Gr *poltos*), porridge.]

pounce[1] [powns] *n* the claw of a bird of prey; a sudden spring or swoop with intent to seize.—*vi* to fix suddenly or eagerly (on, upon); to make a sudden assault or approach. [Derived in some way from L *punctiō, -ōnis—pungĕre, punctum*, to prick.]

pounce[2] [powns] *n* a fine powder formerly used to prevent ink from spreading; a fine powder for making stenciled patterns.—*vt* to prepare with pounce; to trace, transfer, or mark with pounce.—*n* **pounce´t-box**, (*arch*) a box for carrying pomander. [Fr *ponce*, pumice—L *pūmex, pūmicis*.]

pound[1] [pownd] *n* a unit of weight, equal to 16 ounces avoirdupois, or 12 ounces troy or apothecaries'; abbreviation **lb**; a unit of money in the United Kingdom and other countries, symbol **£**.—*ns* **pound´age**, a charge per pound of weight; weight in pounds; **pound´al**, a unit of force or that which gives an acceleration of one foot per second per second to a free mass of one pound; **pound´ cake**, a rich butter cake made with a high proportion of eggs and shortening; **pound´er**, in composition, he who has, or that which weighs, is worth, or carries, a specified number of pounds (eg a 12-*pounder*).—*adj* **pound´-fool´ish**, neglecting the care of large sums in attending to little ones. [OE *pund*—L (*libra*) *pondō*, (pound) by weight—*pondus*, a weight—*pendĕre*, to weigh.]

pound[2] [pownd] *n* a municipal enclosure for stray animals; a depot for holding impounded personal property until claimed by the owner (eg *a car pound*); a place or condition of confinement; the inner compartment of a fish trap.—*n* **pound´age**, the act of impounding; the state of being impounded. [OE *pund* (in compounds), enclosure.]

pound[3] [pownd] *vt* to beat into a powder or a pulp; to hit hard.—*vi* to deliver heavy blows repeatedly (at or on); to move with heavy steps; to throb; to work hard and continuously (*with* **away**). [OE *pūnian*, to beat; *d* excrescent.]

pour [pōr, pör] *vt* to cause or allow to flow in a stream; to send forth or emit in a stream or like a stream.—*vi* to stream; to rain heavily.—*n* **pour´er**. [ME *pouren*; original obscure.]

pourboire [pōō-bwär] *n* a tip. [Fr *pour*, for, *boire*, to drink.]

pourparler [pōōr-pär´lā] *n* an informal preliminary conference. [Fr.]

pout [powt] *vi* to push out the lips, in sullen displeasure or otherwise; (of lips) to protrude.—Also *vt*—*n* a protrusion, of the lips expressive of displeasure; (*pl*) a fit of pique.—*n* **pout´er**, one that pouts; a variety of pigeon, having a dilatable crop and an erect carriage. [ME *powte*.]

poverty [pov´ėr-ti] *n* the state of being poor; necessity, want; lack, deficiency.—*adj* **pov´erty-strick´en**, suffering from poverty. [OFr *poverte*—L *paupertās, -ātis—pauper*, poor.]

powder [pow´dėr] *n* any substance in fine particles; a specific kind of powder, esp for medicinal or cosmetic use; fine dry light snow.—*vt* to reduce to powder; to sprinkle, daub, or cover with powder; to hit (as a ball) very hard.—*vi* to crumble into powder; to use powder for the face.—*adj* **pow´dery**, like, of the nature of, powder; friable.—*adj* **pow´dered**, reduced to powder; sprinkled with powder;—*ns* **pow´der horn**, (*hist*) a flask for carrying gunpowder, esp one made from the horn of an ox or cow; **powder keg**, a keg for gunpowder; an explosive situation; **powder metallurgy**, a branch of science or an art concerned with preparing metals for use by reducing them, as a stage in the process, to powder form; **pow´der monk´ey**, one who carries or has charge of explosives (as in blasting operations); **pow´der puff**, a soft pad, etc., for dusting powder on the face; **pow´der room**, a lavatory for women. [OFr *poudre*—L *pulvis, pulveris*, dust.]

power [pow´ėr, powr] *n* ability to do anything: physical, mental, spiritual, legal, etc.; capacity for producing an effect; strength; authority; a wielder of authority, strong influence, or rule; a sovereign state, esp one with influence over other states; legal force or authority; a supernatural agent; an order of angels; (*arch*) an armed force; (*dial*) a great deal or great many; physical force or energy; (*math*) the product obtained by multiplying a number by itself a specified number of times; (*optics*) magnifying strength.—*adj* operated by electricity, a fuel engine, etc.; served by an auxiliary system that reduces effort; carrying electricity.—*vt* to supply with a source of power.—*adj* **pow´erful**, mighty; strong; influential.—*adv* **pow´erfully**.—*ns* **pow´erhouse**, a building where electric power is generated; (*inf*) a strong or energetic person, team, etc.; aplace where mechanical power (esp electric) is generated.—*adj* **pow´erless**, without power; weak; impotent.—*n* **pow´erlessness**.—**power plant**, an electric utility generating station; the assemblage of parts generating motive power in a self-propelled vehicle; **power politics**, politics based primarily on power as a coercive force; international politics in which the course taken by states depends upon their knowledge that they can back their decisions with military or economic force. [OFr *poer*—Low L *potēre* (for L *posse*), to be able.]

powwow [pow´wow] *n* an American Indian medicine man; an American Indian ceremony (as for victory in war); (*inf*) any conference or get-together.—*vi* to hold a powwow. [Amer Indian *powwaw, powah*.]

pox [poks] *n* a virus disease (as *chicken pox*) marked by pustules; (*arch* smallpox; syphilis; a plague; a curse.—*pl* **pox, poxes**.—*vt* (*arch*) to infect with pox.

practice [prak´tis] *n* actual doing; habitual action, custom; repeated performance to acquire skill; the exercise of a profession; a professional man's business.—*adj* **prac´ticable**, that may be practised, used, or is feasible.—*ns* **practicabil´ity, practicableness**.—*adj* **prac´tical**, in, relating to, concerned with or well adapted to actual practice; practising; efficient in action; inclined to action; virtual.—*n* **practical´ity**, practicalness; a practical matter or feature, aspect, of an affair.—*adv* **prac´tically**, in a practical way; to all intents and purposes.—*n* **prac´ticalness**.—*vt* **practice** [prak´tis] to put into practice; to perform; to do habitually; to exercise, as a profession; to exercise oneself in, or on, or in the performance of, in order to maintain or acquire skill; to train by practice.—*vi* to act habitually; to be in practice (esp medical or legal); to exercise oneself in any art, esp instrumental music.—*n* **practitioner** [-tish´ȯn-ėr] one who is in practice; one who practises.—**practical joke**, a prank intended to embarrass someone or to cause him physical discomfort; **practical nurse**, a nurse with less training than a registered nurse, often one licensed by the State (**licensed practical nurse**) for specified duties. [Obs Fr *practique*—L *practicus*—Gr *prāktikos*, fit for action—*prāssein*, to do.]

prae- *See* **pre-**.

praetor [prē´tȯr] *n* a magistrate of ancient Rome, next in rank to the consuls.—*adj* **praetorian** [-tō´ri-ȧn].—*n* **prae´torship**.—**Praetorian Guard**, the bodyguard of the Roman Emperor. [L *praetor*, for *praeitor—prae*, before, *ire, itum*, to go.]

pragmatic [prag-mat´ik] *adj* practical; testing the validity of all concepts by their practical results.—*adj* **pragmat´ical**, practical; matter of fact; (*arch*) officious, meddlesome, opinionative.—*ns* **prag´matism**, a practical approach to problems and affairs; an American movement in philosophy founded by C S Peirce and William James marked by the doctrine that each notion should be interpreted by tracing its respective practical consequences; **prag´matist**, a pragmatic person; a believer in pragmatism.—**pragmatic sanction**, a solemn decree issued by a sovereign on a matter of fundamental importance which has the force of law. [Gr *prāgma, -atos*, deed—*prāssein*, to do.]

prairie [prā´ri] *n* a land predominantly in grass, esp the large area of level or rolling land in the Mississippi Valley; one of the dry treeless plateaus into which the prairies proper merge in the western US.—*ns* **prai´rie chicken**, a grouse (*Tympanuchus cupido pinnatus*) of the Mississippi Valley; a closely related American grouse (*T pallidicinctus*); **prai´rie dog**, a colonial American burrowing rodent (*Cynomys ludovicianus*) of the prairies related to the marmots; **prai´rie schoon´er**, a covered wagon used by pioneers in cross-country travel.—Also **prairie wagon; prai´rie wolf**, the coyote. [Fr—L *prātum*, a meadow.]

praise [prāz] *vt* to speak highly of, to commend, to extol; to glorify, as in worship.—*vi* to express praise.—*n* commendation; glorifying.—*adj* **praise´worthy**, worthy of praise; commendable.—*n* **praise´worthiness**. [OFr *preisier*—LL *preciāre* for L *pretiāre*, to prize—L *pretium*, price.]

Prakrit [prä´krit] *n* any or all of the ancient Indo-Iranian dialects of India other than Sanskrit; any of the modern Indic languages. [Sans *prākrita*, natural, unrefined.]

praline [prä´lēn] *n* any of various soft or crisp candies made of nuts and sugar. [Fr *praline*, from Marshal Duplessis-*Praslin*, whose cook invented it.]
pram [pram] *n* a small light nearly flat-bottomed boat with a usu. squared-off bow. [Du *praam.*]
prance [präns] *vi* to bound from the hind legs; to go with a capering or dancing movement; to swagger; to ride a prancing horse.—*vt* to cause (a horse) to prance.—*adj, n* **pranc´ing**.—*adv* **pranc´ingly**. [ME *praunce.*]
prandial [pran´di-ȧl] *adj* relating to dinner. [L *prandium*, a morning or midday meal.]
prang [prang] *n* (*inf*) a crash.—*vt* (*inf*) to crash or smash.
prank[1] [prangk] *n* a malicious or mischievous trick; a ludicrous act. [Origin unknown.]
prank[2] [prangk] *vt* to dress or adorn showily.—*vi* to show oneself off. [Akin to Du *pronken*, Ger *prunken*, to show off.]
praseodymium [prā´zē-ō-dim´i-ům] *n* a metallic element (symbol Pr; at wt 140.9; at no 59), a member of the rare-earth group. [Gr *prasios*, leek-green and *didymium* (See **neodymium**).]
prate [prāt] *vi* to talk foolishly; to be loquacious.—*n* trifling talk.—*n* **pra´ter**.—*n, adj* **pra´ting**.—*adv* **pra´tingly**. [Cf Low Ger *praten*, Dan *prate*, Du *praaten.*]
pratique [prä´tēk, prat´ik] *n* permission for an incoming vessel to communicate with the shore after a clean bill of health. [Fr.]
prattle [prat´l] *vt* to say in a childish manner.—*vi* to talk much and idly; to utter child's talk.—*n* empty talk; a meaningless, repetitive sound suggestive of children's chatter.—*n* **pratt´ler**, one who prattles; a child. [Dim and freq of **prate**.]
prawn [prön] *n* any of numerous edible shrimplike crustaceans (as of genera *Pandalus* and *Peneus*).—*vi* to fish for prawns. [ME *prayne, prane*; origin unknown.]
praxis [praks´is] *n* exercise or practice of an art, science, or skill; customary practice or conduct. [Gr *prāxis—prāssein*, to do.]
pray [prā] *vi* to ask earnestly (*with* **to, for**); to speak and make known one's desires to God.—*vt* to implore; to ask earnestly and reverently, as in worship.—*pr p* **pray´ing**; pt, pt p **prayed**.—*ns* **pray´er**, the act of praying; entreaty; the words used; solemn giving of thanks and praise to God, and a putting forward of requests; (*pl*) devotional services; something prayed for; **pray´ing; pray´er book**, a book containing prayers or forms of devotion.—*adj* **pray´erful**, devout; earnest; sincere.—*adv* **pray´erfully**.—*ns* **pray´erfulness; pray´er meet´ing**, a Protestant worship service usu. held on a week night.—Also **prayer service; pray´er rug**, a small Oriental rug on which a Muslim kneels at prayer; **prayer wheel**, a cylinder that revolves on an axis and contains written prayers used in praying by Tibetan Buddhists. [OFr *preier*—L *precāri—prex, precis*, a prayer.]
pre- [prē-] (as living prefix), **prae-** (L spelling more common formerly), *prī-*, prefix before, previous to, in compound words such as *prewar, pre-Christian* (before the Christian era); with *vbs* and *verbal ns* denoting that the action is done before some other action, as in **predecease**; in front of; surpassingly, as preeminent. [L *prae-*.]
preach [prēch] *vi* to pronounce a public discourse on sacred subjects; to discourse earnestly; to give advice in an offensive or obtrusive manner.—*vt* to teach or publish in religious discourses; to deliver (a sermon); to advocate, inculcate (eg a quality, as patience).—*n* **preach´er**, one who preaches, esp a clergyman.—*vi* **preach´ify**, to preach tediously; to weary with lengthy advice.—*ns* **preach´ing; preach´ment**, (in contempt) a sermon; a discourse affectedly solemn.—*adj* **preach´y**, (*inf*) given to tedious moralizing. [Fr *prêcher*—L *praedicāre, ātum*, to proclaim.]
preamble [prē-amb´bl] *n* preface; introduction, esp one to a constitution, statute, etc. stating its purpose. [Fr *préambule*—L *prae*, before, *ambulāre*, to go.]
prearrange [prē-a-rānj´] *vt* to arrange beforehand.—*n* **prearrange´ment**. [L *prae*, before, and **arrange**.]
prebend [preb´ȩnd] *n* the share of the revenues of a cathedral or collegiate church allowed to a clergyman who officiates in it at stated times.—*n* **preb´endary**, a resident clergyman who enjoys a prebend, a canon. [LL *praebenda*, an allowance—L *praebēre*, to grant.]
Precambrian [prē-kam´brē-ȧn] *adj* of or being the earliest era of geological history equivalent to the Archeozoic and Proterozoic era or the corresponding system of rocks.—Also *n*.
precancerous [prē-kan´sėr-us] *adj* likely to become cancerous.
precarious [pri-kā´ri-us] *adj* depending on the will of another; depending on chance, uncertain; insecure, perilous.—*adv* **precā´riously**.—*n* **precā´riousness**. [L *precārius—precāri*, to pray.]
precatory [prek´a-tȯr-i] *adj* expressing a wish. [L *precāri*, to pray.]
precaution [pri-kö´sh(ȯ)n] *n* caution or care beforehand; a preventive measure.—*vt* to warn or advise beforehand.—*adj* **precau´tionary**, containing or proceeding from precaution. [Fr—L *prae*, before, *cautio*. See **caution**.]
precede [prē-sēd´] *vti* to be, come or go before in time, rank, or importance.—*ns* **precedence** [pres´i-dȩns, also pri-sēd´ȩns] the act of going before in time; the right of being before in rank; priority; the foremost place in ceremony.—Also **precedency** [pres´i-dȩn-si, also pre-sē´dȩn-si]; **precedent** [pres´ȩd-ȩnt] a past instance, that may serve as an example or rule in the future.—*adj* [prė-sēd´ent or pres´ȩd-ent] preceding.—*adj* **precē´ding**, going before in time, rank, etc.; antecedent; previous. [Fr *précéder*—L *praecēděre—prae*, before, *cēděre*, go.]
precentor [pri-sen´tȯr] *n* the leader of the singing in a church choir or congregation.—*n* **precen´torship**. [L *praecentor*—L *prae*, before, *caněre*, to sing.]
precept [prē´sept] *n* a rule of moral conduct; a maxim; an order issued by a legally constituted authority to a subordinate.—*adj* **precep´tive**, containing or giving precepts.—*n* **precep´tor**, a teacher; a tutor; the principal of a school; the head of a preceptory.—*adj* **precep´tory**, giving precepts.—*n* a community of Knights Templars. [Fr—L *praeceptum-praecipěre*, to give rules to—*prae*, before, *capěre*, to take.]
precession [pri-sesh´(ȯ)n] *n* the motion of a spinning body as a top, gyroscope, or planet, in which it wobbles so that the axis of rotation sweeps out a cone.—**precession of the equinoxes**, a slow westward motion of the equinoctial points along the ecliptic, caused by the greater attraction of the sun and moon on the excess of matter at the equator, such that the times at which the sun crosses the equator come at shorter intervals than they would otherwise do. [LL *praecessiō, -ōnis—praecēděre*. See **precede**.]
precinct [prē´singkt] *n* (usu. *pl*) an enclosure between buildings, walls, etc.; (*pl*) environs; a police district; a subdivision of a voting ward; a limited area. [LL *praecinctum*, neut pt p of *praecingěre—prae*, before, *cingěre*, to gird.]
precious [presh´ůs] *adj* of great price or worth; cherished; very fastidious; affected; thoroughgoing.—*adv* extremely.—*n* **prec´iousness**.—*adv* **prec´iously.—precious metal**, gold, silver, or platinum; **precious stone**, a jeweler's term for diamond, emerald, ruby, sapphire, pearl and sometimes black opal. [OFr *precios*—L *pretiōsus—pretium*, price.]
precipice [pres´i-pis] *n* a high vertical, or overhanging rock face.—*vt* **precip´itāte**, to hurl headlong; to force (into hasty action); to bring on suddenly or prematurely; (*chem*) to separate from a state of solution or suspension.—*vi* to condense and fall as rain, snow, hail, etc.; (*chem*) to come out of solution or suspension.—*adj* [-ȧt] headlong; hasty.—*n* (*chem*) a substance separated from solution or suspension; a product, result, or outcome of some action or process.—*adv* **precip´itately**.—*n* **precipitā´tion**, act of precipitating; rash haste; rain, snow, etc.; the amount of this.—*adj* **precip´itant**, falling headlong; rushing down with too great velocity; hasty.—*n* anything that causes the formation of a precipitate.—*adv* **precip´itantly**.—*ns* **precip´itance, precip´itancy**, quality of being precipitate; headlong haste or rashness.—*adj* **precip´itable** (*chem*), that may be precipitated.—*adj* **precip´itous**, like a precipice; sheer.—*adv* **precip´itously**.—*n* **precip´itousness**. [L *praecepts, praecipitis*, headlong—*prae*, before, *caput*, head.]
précis [prē´sē] *n* an abstract, a summary.—*pl* **précis** [-sēz]. [Fr.]
precise [pri-sīs´] *adj* definite, exact; very accurate; scrupulous; formal; distinguished from every other.—*adv* **precise´ly**.—*ns* **precise´ness; preci´sian**, a too precise person; **preci´sion**, quality of being precise; exactness; minute accuracy.—*adj* adapted to produce minutely accurate results; characterized by great accuracy. [Fr *précis, -e*—L *praecīsus*, pt p of *praecīděre—prae*, before, *caeděre*, to cut.]
preclude [pri-klōōd´] *vt* to rule out in advance; to make impossible.—*n* **preclusion** [pri-klōō´zh(ȯ)n].—*adj* **preclusive** [pri-klōō´siv] tending to preclude. [L *praeclūděre, -clūsum—prae*, before, *clauděre*, to shut.]
precocious [pri-kō´shůs] *adj* early in reaching some stage of development, eg. flowering, ripening, mental maturity.—*adv* **precō´ciously**.—*ns* **precō´ciousness, precoc´ity** [-kos´-], state or quality of being precocious; early development. [L *praecox, praecŏcis—prae*, before, *coquěre*, to cook, to ripen.]
precognition [prē-kog-nish´(ȯ)n] *n* the supposed extrasensory perception of a future event; clairvoyance. [L *praecognoscěre—prae*, before, and *cognoscere*. See **cognition**.]
pre-Columbian [prē-kȯ-lum´bē-ȧn] *adj* preceding the time before the arrival of Columbus in America.—**pre-Columbian art**, the indigenous art of the New World before 1492.
preconceive [prē-kon-sēv´] *vt* to conceive or form a notion of before having actual knowledge.—**preconcep´tion**, act of preconceiving; previous opinion formed without actual knowledge. [L *prae*, before, *concipěre*. See **conceive**.]
precondition [prē-kȯn-dish´ȯn] *n* a condition that must be satisfied beforehand.—*vt* to prepare to behave or react in a certain way under certain conditions.
preconcert [prē-kon-sûrt´] *vt* to settle, arrange beforehand. [L *prae*, before + **concert**.]
precursor [prē-kûr´sȯr] *n* a forerunner, a predecessor; a substance from which another substance is formed.—*adj* **precur´sory**. [L *prae*, before, *cursor—currěre, cursum*, to run.]
predator [pred´ȧ-tȯr] *n* one that preys, destroys or devours; an animal that lives by predation.—*n* **predā´tion**, the act of preying or plundering; a way of life in which food is chiefly obtained by killing animals.—*adj* **pred´atory**, relating to, or characterized by, predation. [L *praeda*, booty.]
predate [prē-dāt´] *vt* to date before the true date, to antedate. [Pfx **prē-** + **date** (1).]
predecease [prē-di-sēs´] *n* death before another's death.—*vt* to die before (someone else).—*vi* to die first. [Pfx **pre-** + **decease**.]

predecessor [prē-di-ses´ȯr] *n* one who has been before another in any office; (*arch*) an ancestor. [L *prae*, before, *dēcessor*, a retiring officer—*dēcēdĕre, dēcessum*, to withdraw—*dē*, away, *cēdĕre*, to go.]

predestine [prē-des´tin] *vt* to destine or decree beforehand, to foreordain.—*vt* **predes´tinate**, to determine beforehand; to preordain by an unchangeable purpose.—*adj* [-ȧt] fore-ordained; fated.—*n* **predestinā´tion** (*theology*) God's decree fixed unalterably from all eternity whatever is to happen, esp the souls destined for salvation or damnation; destiny.—*adj* **predestinā´rian**, pertaining to predestination.—*n* one who holds the doctrine of predestination.—*n* **predestinā´rianism**. [L *praedestināre—prae*, before, *destināre*. See **destine**.]

predetermine [prē-di-tûr´min] *vt* to determine or settle beforehand.—*n* **predeterminā´tion**. [L *prae*, before, *dēterminăre*. See **determine**.]

predicable [pred´i-kȧ-bl] *adj* that may be asserted.—*n* anything that can be predicated or asserted, esp the general attributes on traditional logic: genus, species, difference, property, and accident. [Fr *prédicable*—L *praedicābilis*, praiseworthy—*praedicāre*. See **predicate**.]

predicament [pri-dik´ȧ-mėnt] *n* (*logic*) any one of the categories in which predicables are arranged; an unfortunate or embarrassing position. [Low L *praedicāmentum*, something predicated or asserted.]

predicate [pred´i-kāt] *vt* to affirm as a quality or attribute; to base (on facts, conditions, etc.).—*n* [-ȧt] (*logic, gram*) that which is stated of the subject.—*n* **predicā´tion**, act of predicating. [L *praedīcāre, -ātum*, to proclaim.]

predict [pri-dikt´] *vt* to foretell; to state (what one believes will happen).—*adj* **predic´table**.—*n* **predic´tion**, act of predicting; that which is foretold; prophecy.—*adj* **predic´tive**, foretelling; prophetic.—*n* **predic´tor, predic´ter**, one who, or that which, predicts. [L *praedictus*, pt p of *praedīcĕre—prae*, before, *dīcĕre*, to say.]

predilection [prē-di-lek´sh(ȯ)n] *n* favorable prepossession of mind; preference. [L *prae*, before, *dīlectiō, -ōnis*, choice—*dīligĕre, dīlectum*, to love—*dis*, apart, *legĕre*, to choose.]

predispose [prē-dis-pōz´] *vt* to dispose or incline beforehand; to render favorable (toward); to render liable (to).—*n* **predisposi´tion**. [L *prae*, before + **dispose**.]

predominate [prē-dom´in-āt] *vi* to be dominant, to surpass in strength or authority; to prevail, be most obvious because most numerous or in greatest quantity.—*adj* **predom´inant**, ruling; ascendant; preponderating, prevailing.—*adv* **predom´inantly**.—*ns* **predom´inance, predom´inancy**. [L *prae*, before, *dominārī*. See **dominate**.]

preeminent [prē-em´in-ėnt] *adj* eminent above others; surpassing others in good or bad qualities; outstanding.—*n* **prēem´inence**.—*adv* **prēem´inently**. [L *praeēminens*, pr p of *praeēminēre—prae*, before, *ēminēre*. See **eminent**.]

preemption [prē-em(p)´sh(ȯ)n] *n* a preempting; action taken to check other action beforehand.—*vt* **prēempt´**, to gain the right to buy (public land) by settling on it; to seize before anyone else can; (*radio, TV*) to replace (a scheduled program).—*adj* **prēemp´tive**, preempting. [L *prae*, before, *emptiō, -ōnis*, a buying—*emĕre*, to buy.]

preen [prēn] *vt* to arrange or trim as birds do their feathers; to pride (oneself) for achievement.—*vi* to make oneself sleek; to gloat. [App **prune** (1).]

preexist [prē-ėg-zist´] *vi* to exist beforehand.—*adj* **prēexist´ent**, existent or existing beforehand. [L *prae*, before + **exist**.]

prefabricate [prē-fab´ri-kāt] *vt* to build (a house, etc.) in standardized sections for shipment and quick assembly; to produce artificially.—*n* **pre´fab** (*inf*) a prefabricated building.—*n* **prefabricā´tion**. [L *prae*, before, *fabricārī*. See **fabricate**.]

preface [pref´is] *n* something said or written by way of introduction or preliminary explanation; anything preliminary or immediately antecedent.—*vt* to introduce by a preface; to precede (*with* **with**).—*adj* **pref´atory**, pertaining to a preface; introductory. [Fr *préface*—L *praefātiō—prae*, before, *fārī, fātus*, to speak.]

prefect [prē´fekt] *n* one set in authority over others; a student monitor in a private school; in France, the governor of a department.—*n* **prē´fecture**, the office or district of a prefect. [Fr *préfet*—L *praefectus*, pt p of *praeficĕre*, to set over—*prae, facĕre*, to make.]

prefer [pri-fûr´] *vt* (*arch*) to put forward, submit for acceptance or consideration; to promote, advance; to regard or hold in higher estimation; to put before a court, etc. for consideration; to like better.—*pr p* **preferr´ing**; *pt, pt p* **preferred´**.—*adj* **pref´erable** [pref´-] to be preferred, more desirable.—*n* **preferabil´ity**.—*adv* **pref´erably**, by choice, in preference.—*n* **pref´erence**, the act of choosing, liking, or favoring one above another; higher estimation; the state of being preferred; that which is preferred; advantage given to one person, country, etc. over others.—*adj* **preferential** [pref-ėr-en´shl] having, or giving, allowing, a preference.—*adv* **preferen´tially**.—*n* **prefer´ment**, advancement in rank, etc.; promotion.—**preferred stock**, stock guaranteed by a corporation's charter over common stock in the payment of dividends and often in the distribution of assets. [Fr *préférer*—L *praeferre—prae*, before, *ferre*, to bear.]

prefigure [prē-fig´ūr] *vt* to imagine beforehand; to represent beforehand (eg *these types or symbols prefigured Christ*); to foreshadow.—*ns* **prefigūrā´tion, prefig´urement** [-fig´ūr-].—*adj* **prefig´ūrātive**. [LL *praefigūrāre—prae*, before, *figūrāre*—L *figūra*. See **figure**.]

prefix [prē-fiks´] *vt* to put before, or at the beginning.—*n* **prē´fix**, a syllable or group of syllables put before a word to affect its meaning (usu. joined to it). [L *praefigĕre—prae*, before, *figĕre*. See **fix**.]

pregnant [preg´nȧnt] *adj* having a child or young in the womb; mentally fertile; inventive (*with* **with**) about to produce; momentous, significant; implying more than is actually expressed; filled (with) or rich (in).—*n* **preg´nancy**.—*adv* **preg´nantly**. [OFr—L *praegnans,—antis*—earlier *praegnās, -ātis*, app—*prae*, before, and the root *gnāscī*, to be born.]

prehensile [pri-hen´sīl] *adj* capable of grasping, esp by wrapping around. [L *praehendĕre, -hensum*, to seize.]

prehistoric, -al [prē-his-tor´ik, -ȧl] *adj* of a time before extant historical records.—*n* **prēhis´tory**. [L *prae*, before + **historic**.]

prejudge [prē-juj´] *vt* to judge or decide upon before hearing the whole case; to condemn unheard.—*n* **prejudg´ment**. [L *praejūdicāre, -ātum—prae*, before, *jūdicāre*, to judge.]

prejudice [prej´ŏŏ-dis] *n* a judgment or opinion formed beforehand for or against due examination; prepossession for or against anything, bias; injury, or harm; intolerance or hatred of other races, etc.—*vt* to fill with prejudice, to bias the mind of; to injure, hurt, or to impair the validity of.—*adj* **prejudicial** [-dish´ȧl] causing prejudice or injury, detrimental.—*adv* **prejudi´cially**. [Fr *préjudice*, wrong + L *praejūdicium—prae*, before, *jūdicium*, judgment.]

prelate [prel´ȧt] *n* an ecclesiastic (as a bishop or abbot) of high rank.—*n* **prel´acy**, the office of a prelate; episcopal church government. [Fr *prélat*—L *praelātus—prae*, before, *lātus*, borne.]

prelect [pri-lekt´] *vi* to discourse in public.—*ns* **prelec´tion**, a lecture. [L *praelegĕre—prae*, before, *legĕre, lectum*, to read.]

prelibation [prē-lī-bā´sh(ȯ)n] *n* a foretaste. [L *praelībātiō, -ōnis—prae*, before, *lībāre*, to taste.]

preliminary [pri-lim´in-ȧr-i] *adj* introductory; preparatory.—*n* that which precedes or prepares for; a preliminary scholastic examination. [L *prae*, before, *līmināris*, relating to a threshold—*līmen, līminis*, a threshold.]

prelude [prel´(y)ūd] *n* a preliminary performance; an event preceding and leading up to another of greater importance; (*mus*) an introductory passage or movement; a short independent composition such as might be the introduction to another.—*vt* to precede as a prelude to play as a prelude.—*vi* to play a musical introduction.—*adjs* **prelu´sive** [or -lū´-] [Fr *prélude*—LL *praelūdium*—L *prae*, before, *lūdĕre*, to play.]

premature [prē´mȧ-tūr or chūr or tyūr] *adj* unduly early; overhasty.—*adv* **prē´mature´ly**,—*ns* **pre´mature´ness, prematur´ity**. [L *praemātūris—prae*, before, *mātūrus*, ripe.]

premeditate [prē-med´i-tāt] *vt* to meditate upon beforehand; to design, intend, beforehand.—*n* **premeditā´tion**. [L *praemeditārī, -ātus—prae*, before, *meditārī*, to meditate.]

premier [pre´mi-ėr, pre´myėr] *adj* prime or first; chief;—*n* the first or chief; a prime minister.—*ns* **prem´iership; première**, [prė-myer´ or prė-mir´] first performance of a play, etc.; the chief actress of a theatrical cast.—*vt* to give a first performance.—*vi* to have a first public performance; to appear for the first time as a star performer.—**premier danseur**, the principle male dancer in a ballet company. [Fr,—L *prīmārius*, the first rank—*prīmus*, first.]

premise [prem´is] *n* (*logic*) one of the two propositions in a syllogism from which the conclusion is drawn; something assumed or taken for granted; (*pl*) a piece of real estate.—*vt* **premise**, [or pri-mīz´] to mention or state by way of introduction; to postulate; to base on certain assumptions. [Fr *prémisse*—L (*sententia*) praemissa, (a sentence) put before—*prae*, before, *mittĕre, missum*, to send.]

premium [prē´mi-um] *n* a reward, a prize, esp as an inducement to buy; payment made for insurance; excess over the original price; something given free or at a reduced price with the purchase of a product or service; a high value or value in excess of expectation.—**at a premium**, very valuable because of scarcity. [L *praemium—prae*, above, *emĕre*, to buy.]

premolar [prē-mō´lȧr] *n* a tooth between the canine and the molars. [L *prae*, before, + **molar**.]

premonition [prē-mȯn-ish(ȯ)n] *n* a forewarning; a feeling that something is going to happen.—*adj* **prēmon´itory**, giving warning or notice beforehand.—*adv* **prēmon´itorily**. [Through Fr from LL *prae-monitiō—praemonēre*, to forewarn—*prae*, before, *monēre*, to warn.]

prenatal [prē-nāt´l] *adj* before birth. [**pre** + **natal**.]

prentice [pren´tis] *n, adj, vt* Short for **apprentice**.

preoccupy [prē-ol´ū-pī] *vt* to occupy or fill beforehand or before others; to fill the mind of.—*n* **prēocc´upancy**, the act or the right of occupying beforehand.—*adj* **prēocc´upied**, already occupied; lost in thought, abstracted; having one's attention wholly taken up by (*with* **with**).—*n* **prēoccupā´tion**. [L *praeoccupāre, -ātum—prae*, before, and *occupāre*. See **occupy**.]

preordain [prē-ör-dān´] *vt* to ordain, appoint, determine, beforehand. [L *prae*, before, *ordināre*. See **ordain**.]

prepaid *See* **prepay**.

prepare [prī-pār´] *vt* to make ready; to equip, train; to make (someone) ready or fit (to bear a shock, etc.); to put together.—*vi* to make oneself ready; to make things ready.—*n* **preparation**, [prep-a-rā´sh(ȯ)n] the act or process of preparing; a preparatory measure; something prepared, as a medicine, cosmetic, etc.—*adj* **preparative**, [pripar´ȧ-tiv] serving to prepare.—*n* that which prepares; a preparation.—*adj* **prepar´atory**, preparing for something coming; introductory.—*adv* by way of preparation; in a prepatory manner.—*adj* **prepared´**, subjected to a special process or treatment.—*ns* **prepā´redness**, the state of being prepared, esp for waging war. **prepā´rer**.—**preparatory school**, a private school that prepares students for college.—Also **prep school**.—*adj* **preppy, preppie**, denoting one who apparently has a preparatory school background.—*n* one who is a student at or a graduate of a preparatory school. [Fr *préparer*—L *praeparāre*—*prae*, before, *parāre*, to make ready.]

prepay [prē´pā´] *vt* to pay before or in advance;—*pt, pt p* **pre´paid´**.—*n* **prepay´ment**. [L *prae*, before, + **pay**.]

prepense [pri-pens´] *adj* premeditated, intentional, chiefly in the phrase 'malice prepense' = malice aforethought. [Fr,—L *prae*, before, *pensāre*—*penděre*, *pensum*, to weigh.]

preponderate [pri-pon´dėr-āt] *vi* to weigh more, to turn the balance; to prevail or exceed in any respect, as number, quantity, importance, influence.—*adj* **prepon´derant**, superior in number, weight, influence, etc.—*n* **prepon´derance**.—*adv* **prepon´derantly**. [L *praeponderāre, -ātum*—*prae*, before, *pondus*, a weight.]

preposition [prep-ȯ-zish´(ȯ)n] *n* a word placed before a noun or pronoun to show its relation to another word.—*adj* **preposi´tional**.—*adv* **preposi´tionally**. [Fr,—L *praepositiō, -ōnis*—*prae*, before, *pōněre*, *positum*, to place.]

prepossess [prē-poz-es´] *vt* (*obs*) to take possession of beforehand; to caused to be preoccupied; to bias or prejudice, esp favorably (eg *I was not prepossessed by, with, her*).—*adj* **prepossess´ing**, tending to prepossess; making a favorable impression; pleasing.—*n* **prepossess´ion**, an impression or opinion formed beforehand, usu favorable. [Pfx **pre-**, + **possess**.]

preposterous [pri-pos´tėr-us] *adj* ridiculous; laughable; utterly absurd.—*adv* **prepos´terously**.—*n* **prepos´terousness**. [L *praeposterus*—*prae*, before, *posterus*, after—*post*, after.]

Pre-Raphaelite [prē-raf´ā-ėl-īt] *n* one of a school of English artists, formed about 1850, who sought inspiration in the works of painters before *Raphael* (1483–1520); a modern artist dedicated to restoring early Renaissance ideals or methods.—Also *adj*

prerecord [prē´re-körd] *vt* (radio, TV) to record (a program etc.) in advance, for later broadcasting.

prerequisite [prē-rek´wi-zit] *n* a condition or requirement that must be fulfilled beforehand.—*adj* required as a condition of something else. [L *prae*, before, *requīrěre, requīsītum*, to need.]

prerogative [pri-rog´ȧ-tiv] *n* a special right or privilege belonging to a particular rank or station. [L *praerogātīvus*, asked first for his vote, as a richer Roman citizen in an assembly consisting of both patricians and plebeians—*prae*, before, *rogāre, -ātum*, to ask.]

presage [pres´ij] *n* an omen, an indication of the future; a presentiment.—*vt* **presage**, [pri-sāj´] to portend, to forebode; to predict.—*adj* **presage´ful**.—*n* (*obs*) **presag´er**. [L *praesāgium*, a foreboding—*prae*, before, and *sāgus*, prophetic.]

presbyopia [pres-bi-ō´pi-a] *n* longsightedness, difficulty in accommodating the eye to near vision (common in old age). [Gr *presbys*, old, *ōps*, gen *ōpos*, the eye.]

presbyter [prez´bi-tėr] *n* an elder of the early Christian church; in the Presbyterian Church, an elder; in the Episcopal Church, a priest or minister.—*adjs* **presbytē´rial**, [-tē´ri-ȧl] of a presbytery; **presbytē´rian**, characterized by a graded system of representative ecclesiastical bodies (as presbyteries) excercising legislative and judicial powers; **Presbyterian**, of a Protestant Christian church emphasizing the sovereignity and justice of God in a highly structural representational system of ministers and lay persons.—*ns* **Presbytē´rian**, a member or adherent of such a church; **Presbytē´rianism**, the form of church government by presbyters; **pres´bytery**, a ruling body in presbyterian churches consisting of the ministers and representative elders from congregations within a district; that part of a church reserved for the officiating priests; (*RC*) a priest's house. [L,—Gr *presbyteros*, comp of *presbys*, old; cf **priest**.]

preschool [prē´skōōl] *adj* of or for a child between infancy and school age.

prescience [prē´shē-ėns] *n* knowledge of events beforehand; foresight.—*adj* **pre´scient**.—*adv* **pre´sciently**. [L *prae-sciens, -entis, pr p* of *praescīre*—*prae*, before, *scīre*, to know.]

prescribe [pri-skrīb´] *vt* to lay down as a rule or direction; (*med*) to order, advise, the use of (a remedy).—*ns* **prescrib´er; prē´script**, a prescribed ordinance or rule; **prescrip´tion**, act of prescribing or directing; (*med*) a written direction for the preparation of a medicine; (*law*) custom continued until it becomes a right or has the force of law.—*adj* **prescrip´tive**, prescribing, laying down rules; consisting in, or acquired by, custom or long continued use, customary.—*n* **prescription drug**, drug that can only be obtained by means of a physician's prescription. [L *praescrīběre, -scrīptum*—*prae*, before, *scrīběre*, to write.]

preselect [prē-si-lekt´] *vt* to select beforehand; usu. on the basis of a particular criterion.—*n* **preselec´tion**.—*adj* **preselect´ive**. [**pre-, select**.]

presence [prez´ėns] *n* fact or state of being present; immediate surroundings; personal appearance and manner; impressive bearing, personality, etc.; something (as a spirit) felt or believed to be present.—**presence of mind**, coolness and readiness in emergency, danger, or surprise; ability to say the right thing. [OFr,—L *praesentia*—*praesens*. See following word.]

present[1] [prez´ėnt] *adj* being at the specified place; (*arch*) instant; immediate; now under consideration; now existing, not past or future (*gram*) denoting action or state now or action that is always true.—*n* the present time; the present tense; (*pl*) the present words or statements, specifically the legal instrument in which these words are used.—*adv* **pres´ently**, now, without delay; soon.—**present participle**, a participle used to express present or continuing action or existence, as in 'he is growing'. [OFr,—L *praesens, -sentis*.]

present[2] [prez´ėnt´] *n* a gift. [OFr *present*, orig presence, hence gift (from the phrase *mettre en present à*, put into the presence of, hence offer as a gift to).]

present[3] [pri-zent´] *vt* to set before, to introduce into the presence of someone, esp socially; to bring before the public (eg a play, a performer, exhibition etc.); to make a gift to; to give or bestow formally; to lay a charge before a court or tribunal; to bring a formal public charge against; to nominate to a benefice; to show; to perform; to aim, point or direct (as a weapon) in a particular direction.—*vi* to present a weapon; to become manifest; to come forward as a patient.—*adj* **present´able**, fit to be presented; fit to be seen;—*ns* **presentation**, [prez-ėn-tā´sh(ȯ)n] act of presenting; an exhibition, display; a setting forth; manner of presenting; something offered or given; a description or persuasive account (as by an advertising agency or a salesman); the position of a fetus in the uterus; the act or the right of presenting to a benefice; **presentee**, [prez-ėn-tē´] one who is presented or to whom something is presented; **present´er; present´ment**, act of presenting; the thing presented or represented; (*law*) notice taken or statement made by the grand jury of an offense from their own knowledge without a bill of indictment laid before them.—**present arms**, a position in the manual of arms in which the rifle be held vertically in front of the body; a command to assume this position or to give a hand salute. [OFr *presenter*—L *praesentāre, -ātum*—*praesens*, present.]

presentiment [pri-zent´i-mėnt] *n* a vague foreboding, esp of evil. [Obs Fr,—*pre-* (L *prae*, before), + **sentiment**.]

preserve [pri-zûrv´] *vt* to keep safe from injury; to save from danger; to keep from decay; to can, pickle, or prepare (food) for future use; to keep up and reserve for personal or special use.—*vi* to make preserves; to raise and protect game for purposes of sport.—to keep in existence;—*n* (usu. *pl*) fruit preserved by cooking in sugar; an area restricted for the preservation and protection of natural resources (as trees and game), esp one used for regulated hunting and fishing; something regarded as reserved for certain persons.—*ns* **preservā´tion**, act of preserving or keeping safe; state of being preserved; safety; **preservāt´ionist**, a person who is interested in preservation (as of a biological species or a historic landmark).—*adjs* **preservative**, tending to preserve; having the quality of preserving.—*n* something that preserves or has the power of preserving, esp an additive used to protect against decay, discoloration or spoilage.—*n* **preserv´er**. [Fr *préserver*—L *prae*, beforehand, *servāre*, to keep.]

preside [pri´zīd´] *vi* to sit in the chair or chief seat (eg at a meeting, at table); to exercise authority or control (over); to occupy a position of featured instrumental performer (usu. with at) (eg *presided at the organ*).—*ns* **presidency** [prez´i-dėn-si], the office of president, his dignity, or term of office; the office of president of the US; the American governmental institution comprising the office of president and associated policy-making and administrative agencies; a Mormon executive council of the church; **president**, the highest officer of a company, club, etc.; **President**, the chief executive (as in the US), or the nominal head in a republic having a parliamentary government.—*adj* **presiden´tial** [-sh(ȧ)l], pertaining to a president.—*n* **pres´identship**.—**President's Day**, Washington's birthday. [Fr *présider*—L *praesidēre*—*prae*, before, *sedēre*, to sit.]

presidium [pre-sid´i-ům] *n* in the Soviet Union, an administrative committee, usu. permanent. [L *presidium*, a presiding over.]

press[1] [pres] *vt* to act on with steady force or weight; to push against, squeeze, compress, etc.; to squeeze (juice, etc.) from; to iron (clothes, etc.); to embrace closely; to force, compel; to entreat; to try to force; to emphasize; to trouble; to urge on; to make (a phonograph record) from a matrix.—*vi* to weigh down; to crowd closely; to go forward with determination; to take or hold a press.—*n* pressure, urgency, etc.; a crowd; a machine for crushing, stamping, etc.; a printing press; a printing or publishing establishment; the gathering, publishing, and broadcasting of news and the persons who perform these functions; any of various pressure devices (as one for keeping sporting gear from warping); an upright closet for storing clothes, etc.—*ns* **press agent**, one whose work is to get publicity for his client; **press box**, a place for reporters at sports events, etc.; **press conference**, a group interview granted to newsmen as by a celebrity; **presser**, one that presses, esp in a laundry or drycleaner, etc.—*adj* **pressing**, urgent; calling for immediate attention.—*ns* **press kit**, a collectional of promotional materials for distribution to the press; **press´room**, a room in a printing plant containing the printing presses; a room (as at the White House) for the use of members of the press; **press secretary**, a person officially in charge of press relations for a usu. prominent public figure.—**press the flesh**, to greet and shake hands with people, esp when campaigning for political office; **press of sail**, as much sail as can be spread. [Fr *presser*—L *pressāre*—*preměre*, *pressum*, to squeeze.]

press[2] [pres] *vt* (*hist*) to carry off and force into service in the navy; to commandeer; to compel, force (a person or thing into the service of).—*n* **press´-gang** (*hist*), a gang or body of men under command of an officer empowered to force men into naval or military service.—Also *vt.* [From obs *prest*, to engage by paying earnest—OFr *prester*—L *praestāre*, to offer, etc.]

pressure [presh´ůr] *n* act of pressing; the state of being pressed; constraining force; that which presses or afflicts; urgency; strong demand; (*physics*) force directed over a surface measured by so much weight on a unit of area.—*vt* to exert pressure on.—*ns* **press´ure ca´bin**, a pressurized cabin in an aircraft; **press´ure cooker**, a strong container in which food can be cooked quickly by steam under pressure; (*inf*) a situation fraught with emotional or social pressure.—*vt* **press´urize**, to keep nearly normal atmospheric pressure inside (an airplane, etc.) as at high altitudes.—*ns* **pressure group**, an interest group organized to influence public opinion and esp governmental policy, but not to elect candidates to office; **pressure point**, a point where a blood vessel can be compressed (as to check bleeding) by the application of pressure; **pressure suit**, an inflatable suit for high-altitude or space flight to protect the body from low pressure. [L *pressura*—*premĕre*, to press.]

prestidigitation [pres-ti-dij-i-tā´sh(ȯ)n] *n* sleight of hand.—*n* **prestidig-itātor**. [Fr,—*preste*, nimble, and L *digitus*, a finger.]

prestige [pres-tēzh´] *n* standing in the eyes of people; commanding position in people's minds.—**presti´gious**, imparting prestige or distinction. [Fr,—L *praestigium*, delusion—*praestinguĕre*, to dazzle.]

presto [pres´tō] *adv* quickly; at once; (*mus*) at a rapid tempo. [It,—L *praestō*, at hand.]

presume [pri-zūm´] *vt* to take as true without examination or proof; to take for granted.—*vi* to venture without right (to do); to count unduly (on, upon), take advantage of (*with* **on, upon**); to act without due regard to the claims of others.—*adj* **presūm´able**, that may be presumed or supposed to be true.—*adv* **presūm´ably**.—*adj* **presūm´ing**, venturing without permission, unreasonably bold.—*adv* **presūm´ingly**.—*n* **presumption** [-zump´sh(ȯ)n], act of presuming; a supposition; strong probability; conduct going beyond proper bounds; (*law*) an assumption made from known facts; an assumption made failing evidence to the contrary.—*adj* **presump´tive**, grounded on probable evidence; that may be assumed as true, accurate, etc.; giving grounds for presuming.—*adv* **presump´tively**.—*adj* **presumptuous** [-zum(p)´tū-ůs], too bold or forward.—*adv* **presump´tuously**.—*n* **presump´tuousness**. [Fr *présumer*—L *praesūmĕre*, *-sumptum*—*prae*, before, *sūmĕre*, to take—*sub*, under, *emĕre*, to buy.]

presuppose [prē-sů-pōz´] *vt* to assume or take for granted; to involve as a necessary antecedent.—*n* **presupposi´tion**. [Fr *présupposer*—L *prae*, before, *suppōnĕre*. See **suppose**.]

pretend [pri-tend´] *vt* to profess falsely that; to feign, to sham, claim, represent, or assert falsely.—*vi* to put in a claim; to make-believe.—*ns* **pretense´**, an act of pretending; a claim; a pretext; something pretended; appearance or show to hide reality; sham; make-believe; **preten´der**, one who makes a false hypocritical show; a claimant to a throne who is held to have no just title; **preten´sion**, claim; aspiration; show; pretentiousness.—*adj* **preten´tious** [-shůs], claiming more than is warranted; showy, ostentatious.—*adv* **preten´tiously**.—*n* **preten´tiousness**. [Fr *prétendre*—L *praetendĕre*—*prae*, before, *tendĕre, tentum, tensum*, to stretch.]

preter- [prē´tėr-] in composition, beyond, as *adj* **preter-human**, more than human. [L *praeter*.]

preterit(e) [pret´ėr-it] *adj* past.—*n* a verbal tense that indicates action in the past without reference to duration, continuance, or repetition. [L *praeteritus*—*praeter*, beyond, *īre, itum*, to go.]

pretermit [prē-tėr-mit´] *vt* to omit; to desist from for a time; to neglect; to suspend; to break off;—*pr p* **prētermitt´ing**; *pt, ptp* **prētermitt´ed**.—*n* **pretermiss´ion**. [L*praetermittĕre*—*praeter*, past, *mittĕre, missum*, to send.]

preternatural [prē-tėr-na´chůr-ål] *adj* beyond what is natural; abnormal; supernatural.—*adv* **preternat´urally**. [L *praeter*, beyond, and *nātūra*, nature.]

pretest [prē´test´] *vti* to test in advance.

pretext [prē´tekst] *n* an ostensible motive or reason put forward to conceal the real one, or as an excuse. [L *praetextum*—*praetexĕre*—*prae*, before, *texĕre*, to weave.]

pretty [prit´i] *adj* artful; clever; apt; attractive in a dainty, graceful way but not strikingly beautiful; beautiful without dignity; miserable; terrible; considerable in amount.—*adv* in some degree; moderately.—*vt* **prett´ify**, to make pretty.—*adv* **prett´ily**, pleasingly; neatly.—*n* **prett´iness**. [OE *prættig*, tricky—*prætt*, trickery.]

pretzel [pret´s'l] *n* a hard, brittle, salted biscuit, often formed in a loose knot.

prevail [pri-vāl´] *vi* to gain the mastery (with *over, against*); to succeed; to be usual or customary; to predominate.—*adjs* **prevail´ing**, having great power; controlling; very general or common, most common; **prev´alent**, prevailing.—*n* **prevalence** [prev´ål-ėns], the state of being prevalent; widespread diffusion; the percentage of a population that is affected with a particular disease at a particular time. [L *praevalēre*—*prae*, before, *valēre*, to be powerful.]

prevaricate [pri-var´i-kāt] *vi* to evade the truth, to quibble.—*ns* **prevaricā´tion; prevar´icātor**. [L *praevāricārī, -ātus*, to walk crookedly—*prae*, inten, *vāricus*, straddling—*vārus*, bent.]

prevent [pri-vent´] *vt* (*arch*) to anticipate, forestall; to hinder; to keep from coming to pass, make impossible.—*adjs* **prevent´able, preventible**.—*n* **preven´tion**, act of preventing.—*adjs* **preven´tive, preven´tative**, tending to prevent or hinder.—*n* something used to prevent disease; that which prevents or averts. [L *praevenīre, -ventum*—*prae*, before, *venīre*, to come.]

preview [prē´vū] *n* an advance, restricted showing, as of a movie; a showing of scenes from a movie to advertise it.—Also **prevue**, an advance statement, sample, or survey.—*vt* to view or show in advance of public presentation; to give a preliminary survey of. [**pre-**, + **view**.]

previous [prē´vi-ůs] *adj* going before in time; former; acting too soon.—*adv* previously (*with* **to**).—*adv* **prē´viously**, beforehand; at an earlier time.—*n* **prē´viousness**.—**previous question**, in parliamentary procedure, to put the pending question to an immediate vote that if defeated has the effect of allowing resumption of debate on the question; **previous to**, before. [L *praevius*—*prae*, before, *via*, a way.]

prevision [prē-vizh´(ȯ)n] *n* foresight; foreknowledge. [Through Fr *prévision*, or direct from L *praevidēre, -vīsum*, to foresee—*prae*, before, *vidēre*, to see.]

prevue *See* **preview**.

prey [prā] *n* an animal that is, or may be, killed and eaten by another; a victim; the act or habit of preying on other animals.—*vi* to make depredations to take plunder; to seize and devour prey; to commit violence or robbery or fraud; to have a destructive or wasting effect. [OFr *preie* (Fr *proie*)—L *praeda*, booty.]

price [prīs] *n* the amount, usu. in money, for which a thing is sold or offered; the cost, as in life, labor, etc. of obtaining some benefit; value or worth.—*vt* to fix the price of; (*inf*) to ask the price of; to drive by raising prices excessively.—*adjs* **price´less**, beyond price, invaluable; (*inf*) amusing, odd, or absurd; **prīc´ey** (*inf*), expensive.—*ns* **price-cutter**, one that reduces prices esp to a level to cripple competitors; **price-cutting; price-fixing**, artificially setting of prices (as by producers or government) contrary to free market operations; **price support**, maintenance of prices (as of a raw material) at some predetermined level through government action; **price war**, a period of commercial competition marked by repeated cutting of prices among competitors.—**price-earnings ratio**, a measure of the value of a common stock; the ratio of its market price to its earnings per share. [OFr *pris*—L *pretium*, price.]

prick [prik] *n* a sharp point; the act or experience of piercing or puncturing with a small sharp point; the wound or mark so made.—*vt* to affect with anguish, grief, or remorse; to pierce with a fine point; to indicate by a prick or dot; to spur or goad, to incite; (of a dog) to stick up (the ears); to remove a young seedling from one seedbed to another (*with* **out**).—*vi* to ride with spurs;—*pt, pt p* **pricked**.—*ns* **prick´er**, that which pricks; a military light horseman; a rider of horse; a prickle, a thorn; **prickle** [prik´l], a sharp point growing from the bark or epidermis of a plant.—*adj* **prick´ly**, full of prickles; easily annoyed.—*ns* **prick´liness; prickly heat**, a skin eruption caused by inflammation of the sweat glands; **prick´ly pear**, a genus (*Opuntia*) of plants with clusters of prickles and edible pear-shaped fruit.—**prick up one's ears**, to listen intently. [OE *prica*, point; cf Du *prik*.]

pride [prīd] *n* state or feeling of being proud; too great self-esteem; haughtiness; a proper sense of what is becoming to oneself; a feeling of pleasure in achievement; that of which one is proud; splendour, magnificence; a group, herd (of lions).—*vt* (*reflex*) to feel proud.—**pride of place**, the highest or first position. [OE *prȳde*—*prūd*, proud.]

priest [prēst] *n* one with special rank who offers sacrifices or performs sacred rites; an Anglican, Eastern Orthodox, or Roman Catholic clergyman ranking below a bishop.—*ns* **priest´ess**, a woman authorized to perform the sacred rites of a religion; a woman regarded as a leader (as of a movement); **priest´hood**, the office or character of a priest; the priestly order.—*adj* **priest´ly**, pertaining to or like a priest.—*n* **priest´liness**.—*adj* **priest´-ridd´en**, controlled by priests. [OE *prēost*—L *presbyter*—Gr *presbyteros*, elder.]

prig[1] [prig] *n* a person whose smug and scrupulous behavior offends others.—*adj* **prigg´ish**.

prig[2] [prig] *n* (*obs*) (*slang*) a thief. [Origin unknown.]

prim [prim] *adj* exact and precise in manner; demure.—*vt* to deck with great nicety; to give a prim and demure expression to;—*pr p* **primm´ing**; *pt, pt p* **primmed**.—*adv* **prim´ly**.—*n* **prim´ness**. [Late 17th century slang.]

prima ballerina [prē´mȧ bal-ėr-ēn´a] *n* the principal female dancer in a ballet company. [It]

primacy [prī´mȧ-si] *n* state of being first; the chief place; the office or dignity of a primate. [L *primus*, first.]

prima donna [prē´mä don´(n)ä] *n* the leading lady in opera;—*pl* **prī´ma donn´as**. [It,—L *prīma domina*.]

prima facie [prī´ma fā´shi-ē] *adv* at first view or sight.—*adj* true, valid, or sufficient at first impression; self evident; legally sufficient to establish a fact unless disproved. [L *prīmā*, abl fem of *prīmus*, first, *faciē*, abl of *faciēs*, a face.]

primal *See* **prime**.

primary [prī´mår-i] *adj* first; original; fundamental; chief; primitive; elementary;—*n* that which is highest in rank or importance; a preliminary election at which candidates are chosen for the final election.—*adv*

prī´marily.—**primary colors**, those from which all others can be derived; red, blue, yellow; **primary school**, a school usu including the first three grades of elementary school and sometimes including kindergarten; an elementary school. [L *prīmārius—prīmus*, first.]

primate [prī´māt, -mȧt] *n* an archbishop; or the highest ranking bishop in a province, etc; any of an order (Primates) of mammals, including man, the anthropoid apes, monkeys, and related forms (as lemurs and tarsiers).—*ns* **pri´mateship**, the office and dignity of an archbishop, etc.; **primatol´ogy**, the study of primates excepting modern man. [L *prīmās, -ātis—primus*, first.]

prime[1] [prīm] *adj* first in order of time, rank, or importance; chief; of the highest quality; (*arith*) divisible by no whole number except one and itself.—*n* the beginning; the spring; the height of perfection; full health and strength; the first note or tone of a musical scale.—*adj* **prī´mal**, first; original; fundamental.—**prime meridian**, the meridian at Greenwich, England from which longitude is measured east and west; **prime minister**, in some countries, the chief executive of the government; **prime mover**, the self-moved being that is the source of all motion; a machine that transforms energy from such a natural source into motive power; **prime time**, (radio, TV) the hours when the largest audience is available. [L *prīmus*, first.]

prime[2] [prīm] *vt* to charge, fill; to supply (a firearm) with powder; to bring into activity or working order by a preliminary charge (as an internal-combustion engine by injecting gas or oil); to fill (a person with liquor); to prepare for painting by laying on a first coat of paint or oil; to post up, instruct, prepare beforehand.—*ns* **prī´mer; prī´ming**. [Ety obscure.]

primer [prī´mėr, prim´ėr] *n* simple book for teaching, reading a small introductory book on a subject. [L *prīmārius*, primary.]

primeval [prī-mē´vȧl] *adj* belonging to the first ages.—*adv* **primē´vally**. [L *prīmaevus—prīmus*, first, *aevum*, an age.]

primitive [prim´i-tiv] *adj* belonging to the beginning, or to the first times; original; ancient; crude; simple; basic.—*n* that from which other things are derived; a root word; a primitive person or thing.—*adv* **prim´itively**.—*n* **prim´itiveness**. [Fr,—L *prīmitīvus*, an extension of *prīmus*, first.]

primogenitor [prī-mō-jen´i-tȯr] *n* an ancestor; a forefather.—*n* **primogen´iture**, the state or fact of being first-born; of the same parents; the right of inheritance by the eldest son. [L *prīmō*, first (adv) *genitor*, begetter.]

primordial [prī-mör´di-ȧl] *adj* existing from the beginning; original; rudimentary; primitive. [L *prīmus*, first, *ordīrī*, to begin.]

primrose [prim´rōz] *n* any of a genus (*Primula*) of perennial herbs with tube-like, often yellow flowers.—**primrose path**, the path of pleasure, self-indulgence, etc.; a course that seems easy but could lead to disaster; **primrose yellow**, a light to moderate greenish yellow; a light to moderate yellow. [OFr *primerose*, as if—L *prīma rosa*; perh really through ME and OFr *primerole*—Low L *prīmula—prīmus*, first.]

primula [prim´ū-la] *n* primrose. [L *primula veris*, firstling of spring.]

primus [prī´mus] *n* the presiding bishop in the Scottish Episcopal Church.

prince [prins] *n* a ruler ranking below a king; head of a principality; the son of a sovereign; any preeminent person; a nobleman of varying rank and status.—*ns* **prin´cess**, a daughter of a sovereign; the wife of a prince; one outstanding in a specified respect; **prince con´sort**, the husband of a reigning queen; **prince´dom**, the estate, jurisdiction, sovereignty, or rank of a prince; **prince´ling**, a petty prince.—*adj* **prince´ly**, becoming a prince; splendid.—*ns* **prince´liness; prin´cess roy´al**, a title conferred upon the eldest daughter of a sovereign.—**Prince of Wales**, a title conferred upon the eldest son of the British sovereign. [Fr,—L *princeps—prīmus*, first, *capĕre*, to take.]

principal [prin´si-pl] *adj* highest in rank, character, or importance; chief.—*n* a principal person; the head of a school; one who takes a leading part; money on which interest is paid; the main beam in a piece of framing; (*law*) the perpetrator of a crime; one for whom another acts as agent;—*n* **principal´ity**, the position or responsibility of a principal (as of a school); territory of a prince or the country that gives him title; an order of angels.—*adv* **prin´cipally**, chiefly, for the most part.—*n* **prin´cipalship**, position of a principal.—**principal diagonal**, (*math*) the diagonal in a square matrix that runs from upper left to lower right; **principal parts**, (*gram*) the principal inflected forms of a verb; in English, the infinitive, the past tense, and present and past participles. [L *principālis—princeps, -ipis*, chief.]

principle [prin´si-pl] *n* a fundamental truth on which others are founded or from which they spring; a law or doctrine from which others are derived; a settled rule or action; consistent regulation of behavior according to moral law; a basic part; an ingredient (as a chemical) that exhibits or imparts a characteristic quality; the scientific law explaining a natural action; the method of a thing's working.—*adj* **prin´cipled**, holding specified principles; having, or behaving in accordance with, good principles.—**in principle**, with respect to fundamentals. [L *principium*, beginning—*princeps*.]

prink [pringk] *vti* to primp. [App conn with **prank**. (2).]

print [print] *n* a mark made on a surface by pressure; the impression of letters, designs, etc. made from inked type, a plate, or block; an impression made by a photo mechanical process; cloth printed with a design; a photographic or motion-picture copy, esp from a negative.—*vti* to stamp (a mark, letter, etc.) on a surface; to produce (on paper, etc.) the impressions of inked type, etc.; to produce (a book, etc.); to write in letters resembling printed ones; to make (a photographic print).—*ns* **printer**, a person engaged in printing; a machine for printing from photographic negatives; a device that produces printout; **print´ing**, act, art, or practice of printing; **print´ing press**, a machine for producing printed copies;—**printed circuit**, a circuit for electronic apparatus, formed by printing the design of the wire on copper foil bonded to a flat base and etching away the unprinted foil. **printed manner**, matter printed by various processes that is elegible for mailing at a special rate; **printmaking**, the design and production of prints by an artist; **printout**, a printed record produced automatically (as by a computer).—*vt* **print out**, to make a printout of.—**in print**, procurable from the publisher; **out of print**, not procurable from the publisher. [ME *print, prente*—OFr *preinte, priente—preindre*—L *premĕre*, to press.]

prior [prī´ȯr] *adj* previous; taking precedence (as in importance).—*n* the superior ranking below an abbot in a monastery; the head of a house or group of houses in a religious community.—*ns* **pri´oress**, a nun corresponding in rank to a prior; **pri´orāte, pri´orship**, the government or office of a prior; **prior´ity**, state of being prior or first in time, place, or rank, preference; a person, thing, entitled to preferential treatment or requiring early attention; **prī´ory**, a religious house under a prior or prioress. [L *prior*, former.]

prism [prizm] *n* (*geom*) a solid whose ends are similar, equal, and parallel polygons, and whose sides are parallelograms; a triangular prism of transparent glass or the like for resolving light into the spectrum.—*adjs* **prismat´ic**, resembling or pertaining to a prism; formed by a prism.—*adv* **prismat´ically**.—*n* **pris´moid**, a figure like a prism but with unequal ends so that the faces are trapezords instead of parallelograms. [Gr *prīsma, -atos*, a piece sawn off—*prīein*, to saw.]

prison [priz´n] *n* a building for the confinement of persons while on trial for safe custody or after a trial for punishment; an institution for the confinement of persons convicted of serious crimes.—*n* **pris´oner**, one under arrest or confined in prison; a captive; anyone involuntarily kept under restraint.—**prison camp**, a camp for confining trustworthy prisoners usu. working on government projects; a camp for prisoners of war; **prisoner of war**, a member of an armed force taken prisoner by the enemy during combat. [OFr *prisun*—L *prensiō, -ōnis*, for *praehensiō*, a seizing—*praehendĕre, -hensum*, to seize.]

pristine [pris´tīn] *adj* belonging to the earliest time; unspoiled. [L *pristinus*; cf *priscus*, antique, *prior*, former.]

privacy [prīv´ȧ-si] *n* seclusion; avoidance of notice or display; secrecy; one's private life. [From **private**.]

private [prī´vȧt] *adj* of or concerning a particular person or group; not open to or controlled by the public; for an individual person; not holding public office; secret.—*n* (*pl*) the genitals; an enlisted man of the lowest rank either in the US Army or the US Marine Corps.—*adv* **prī´vately**.—*n* **privateness. private enterprise**, free enterprise, economic system in which individual private firms operate and compete freely; **private eye**, (*inf*) a private detective; **private treaty**, a sale of property determined in discussion by the seller and buyer.—**go private**, to restore private corporate ownership by buying back publicly owned stock; **in private**, not publicly, in secret. [L *prīvātus*, pa p of *prīvāre*, to separate.]

privateer [prī-vȧ-tēr´] *n* a private vessel commissioned in war to capture enemy ships; a commander or crew of a privateer. [From **private**.]

privation [prī-vā´sh(ȯ)n] *n* state of being deprived of something, esp of what is necessary for comfort.—*adj* **privative**, [priv´ȧ-tiv] expressing the absence of a quality (eg a-, un-, non- are privative prefixes; blind is a privative term).—*n* a genetic term for suffixes, prefixes and other elements forming words to indicate lack, absence, etc.—*adv* **priv´atively**. [L *prīvātiō, -ōnis, prīvātīvus—prīvāre*, to deprive.]

privet [priv´et] *n* a half-evergreen shrub (*Ligustrum vulgare*) used for hedges; any of various similar shrubs of the same genus. [Origin unknown.]

privilege [priv´i-lij] *n* an advantage granted to or enjoyed by an individual or a few; prerogative.—*vt* to grant a privilege to.—*adj* **priv´ileged**, having or enjoying privileges; not subject to disclosure in a court of law; having a plenary indulgence attached to an altar. [Fr,—L *prīvilēgium—prīvus*, private, *lex, lēgis*, a law.]

privy [priv´i] *adj* private; having knowledge of (something secret).—*n* (*law*) a person having an interest in an action; a small building with a bench having holes through which the user may urinate or defecate.—*pl* **privies**.—*adv* **priv´ily**, privately, secretly.—*n* **priv´ity**, knowledge, shared with another, of something private or confidential; knowledge implying concurrence.—**Privy Council**, a body of dignatories and officials chosen by the British monarch as an advisory council to the Crown usu. functioning through its committees; **privy councillor; privy purse**, an allowance for the private or personal use of the British sovereign. [Fr *privé*—L *prīvātus*, private.]

prize[1] [prīz] *vt* to force (esp up or open) with a lever. [Fr *prise*, hold, grip.]

prize[2] [prīz] *n* anything taken from an enemy in war, esp a ship.—*n* **prize´ mon´ey**, share of the money or proceeds from any prizes taken from an enemy; money offered in prizes. [Fr *prise*, capture, thing captured—L *prehendĕre*, to seize.]

prize[3] [prīz] *n* a reward or symbol of success offered or won in competition by contest or by chance; anything well worth striving for; a highly valued acquisition.—*adj* awarded, or worthy of, a prize.—*vt* to set a prize on, to value; to value highly.—*ns* **prize´fight**, a professional boxing match; **prize´fighting; prize´fighter**. [OFr *pris* (n), *prisier* (vb)—L *pretium*, price.]

pro- [prō] *prefix* from Latin prep meaning before (as in *proceed, proposition*), in place of or as the substitute of, in favor of, for.—eg **procathedral**, a parish church used as a cathedral; **pro-**, favoring, a partisan of.—**pro and con** [L *prō et contrā*), for and against.—*n pl* **pros and cons**, arguments for and against an opinion, a plan etc.

pro [prō] *adj, n* Abbrev for **professional**.

probable [prob´à-bl] *adj* having more evidence for than against; that may be expected, likely.—*n* **probabil´ity**, quality of being probable; appearance of truth; likelihood; likelihood estimated mathematically; that which is probable.—*adv* **prob´ably**, without much doubt.—**probable cause**, a reasonable ground for supposing that a criminal charge is well-founded. [Fr—L *probābilis—probāre, -ātum*, to prove.]

probate [prō´bāt] *n* the action or process of proving before a competent court that a written paper purporting to be the will of a person who has died is indeed his lawful act; the judicial determination of the validating of a will; the official copy of a will, with the certificate of its having been proved.—**probate court**, a court that has jurisdiction chiefly over the probate of wills and the administration of the estates of deceased persons. [L *probātus*, tested—*probāre*. See **probable**.]

probation [prō-bā´sh(ò)n] *n* testing; proof; a preliminary time or condition appointed to allow fitness or unfitness to appear; suspension of prison sentence with liberty (depending on good behavior) under the supervision of a probation officer; the state or period of being under probation.—*adjs* **probā´tional**, relating to, or serving the purpose of, probation or trial; **probā´tionary**, probational; on probation.—*ns* **probā´tioner**, one (as a newly admitted student nurse or teacher) whose fitness is being tested during a trial period; a convicted offender on probation; **probation officer**, an official who watches over prisoners on probation.—*adj* **probative** [prō´bà-tiv] testing; affording proof. [L *probātiō, -ōnis*, trial—*probāre, -ātum*, to test, prove.]

probe [prōb] *n* an instrument for exploring a wound, locating a bullet, etc.; an investigation; a device, as an instrumented spacecraft, used to get information about an environment.—*vt* to examine with, or as with, a probe; to examine searchingly. [L *proba*, a proof—*probāre*, to test.]

probity [prōb´i-ti or prob´-] *n* uprightness, moral integrity. [L *probitās—probus*, good.]

problem [prob´lèm] *n* a matter difficult to arrange, or in which it is difficult to decide the best course of action; a person, thing, or matter difficult to deal with; a question propounded for solution; a proposition in mathematics and physics stating something to be done; an intricate unsettled question.—*adjs* **problemat´ic, -al**, of the nature of a problem; questionable, doubtful.—*adv* **problemat´ically**. [Gr *problēma, -atos—pro*, before, *ballein*, to throw.]

proboscis [prō-bos´is] *n* the trunk of the elephant or any similar long, flexible snout. [L—Gr *proboskis*, a trunk—*pro*, in front, *boskein*, to feed.]

procaine [prō´kān] *n* a synthetic compound used as a local anesthetic. [*pro*, for + **(co)caine**.]

proceed [prō-sēd´] *vi* to go on, esp after stopping; to continue; to come forth, issue (from); to take legal action (against).—*n pl* **prō´ceeds**, the total amount of money brought in; the net amount received.—*adj* **procedural** [-sēd´yù-ràl].—*ns* **procē´dure**, method of conducting business, esp in a law case or in a meeting; prescribed or traditional course of action; a step taken as part of an established order of steps; **proceed´ing**, a going forward, continuance, advance; an action; (*pl*) steps in a legal action; (in *pl*) a record of the transactions of a society. [Fr *procéder*—L *prōcēdere—prō*, before, *cēdere, cessum*, to go.]

process [pros´es] *n* state of being in progress or of being carried on; course (eg of time); a series of actions or events; a sequence of operations, or of changes undergone; (*law*) a court summons; the whole course of proceedings in a legal action; (*biol*) a projecting part, esp on a bone.—*vt* to subject to a special process, eg, in manufacturing food; to prepare by a special process; to proceed against by law by prosecuting, taking out a summons against, or serving a summons on. [Fr *procès*—L *prōcessus—prōcēdere*. See **proceed**.]

procession [prō-sesh´(ò)n] *n* the act of proceeding; a large company advancing in order, as in a parade.—*adj* **process´ional**, pertaining to a procession.—*n* a hymn sung at the beginning of a church service during the entrance of the clergy. [L *prōcessiō, -ōnis—prōcēdere*. See **proceed**.]

proclaim [prō-klām´] *vt* to publish abroad; to announce or declare officially.—*ns* **proclaim´er; proclamation** [prok-là-mā´sh(ò)n] the act of proclaiming; official notice given to the public. [Fr *proclamer*—L *prōclāmāre—prō*, out, *clāmāre*, to cry.]

proclivity [prō-kliv´i-ti] *n* inclination, tendency, or propensity. [L *prōclīvis—prō*, forward, *clīvus*, a slope.]

proconsul [prō-kon´sùl] *n* a governor or military commander of an ancient Roman province; an administrator in a modern colony, dependency, or occupied area with usu. wide powers.—*adj* **procon´sular** [-sū-làr].—*ns* **procon´sulate, procon´sulship**, the office, or term of office, of a proconsul. [L.]

procrastinate [prō-kras´ti-nāt] *vti* to put off action, to delay.—*ns* **procrastinā´tion**, a putting off till a future time; dilatoriness; **procras´tinātor**. [L *prōcrastināre—prō*, onward, *crastinus—crās*, tomorrow.]

procreate [prō´krē-āt] *vt* to bring into being, to beget off-spring.—*n* **procreā´tion**, generation; production.—*adj* **prō´creātive**, having the power to procreate; generative; productive.—*n* **prō´creātor**, a parent. [L *prōcreāre, -ātum—prō*, forth, *creāre*, to produce.]

procrustean [prō-krus´tė-àn] *adj* violently making conformable to a standard.—**procrustean bed**, a scheme or pattern into which someone or something is arbitrarily forced. [From *Procrustes*, a robber who by lopping or stretching fitted his victims to the same bed.]

proctor [prok´tòr] *n* one appointed to supervise students (as at an examination).—Also *vti*.—*n* **proc´torship**. [Syncopated form of **procurator**.]

procumbent [prō-kum´bėnt] *adj* lying face down; (*bot*) lying along the ground without rooting. [L *prōcumbens, -entis*, pr p of *prōcumbĕre—pro*, forward, *cumbĕre*, to lie down.]

procurator [prok´ū-rā-tòr] *n* a financial agent in a Roman imperial province; one who manages affairs for another. [L *prōcūrātor—prōcūrāre*. See **procure**.]

procure [prō-kūr´] *vt* to obtain by effort; to get and make available for promiscuous sexual intercourse; to bring about.—*vi* to procure women.—*adj* **procur´able**.—*ns* **procure´ment**, the act of procuring; management; agency; **procur´er**, one who procures; a pander. [Fr *procurer*—L *prōcūrāre*, to manage—*prō*, for, *cūrāre, -ātum*, to care for.]

prod [prod] *vt* to poke; as with a pointed stick; to goad into activity.—*pt p* **prodd´ed**.—*n* an act of prodding; a sharp instrument. [Origin unknown.]

prodigal [prod´i-g(à)l] *adj* wasteful; lavish.—*n* a waster; a spendthrift.—*n* **prodigal´ity**, state or quality of being prodigal; extravagance; profusion.—*adv* **prod´igally**, profusely; wastefully. [Fr *prōdigĕre*, to squander—pfx *prōd-* (early form of *prō-*), away, *agĕre*, to drive.]

prodigy [prod´i-ji] *n* an extraordinary person, thing, or act; a child of precocious genius or virtuosity.—*adj* **prodig´ious**, astonishing; enormous.—*adv* **prodig´iously**.—*n* **prodig´iousness**. [Fr *prodige*—L *prōdigium*, a prophetic sign.]

produce [prō-dūs´] *vt* to bring forward or out; to bring into being, to yield; to bring about, cause; to make, manufacture; to put on the stage; to prepare for exhibition to the public; to extend.—*vi* to yield something.—*ns* **produce** [prod´ūs] that which is produced, esp fruit and vegetables; **produc´er**, one who produces; a farmer or a manufacturer; one who finances or supervises the presentation of a play or motion picture, etc.; an apparatus that makes gas to be used for fuel; any of various organisms (as a green plant) which produce their own organic compounds which are food sources for other organisms.—*adj* **produc´ible**.—*ns* **product** [prod´ukt] a thing produced by nature, industry, or art; a result; an outgrowth; (*math*) the number obtained by multiplying two or more numbers together; **produc´tion**, act or process of producing; that which is produced; a work presented on the stage or screen or over the air.—*adj* **produc´tive**, having the power to produce; generative; fertile, producing richly.—*n* **productiv´ity**.—**producer gas**, made in a producer consisting chiefly of carbon monoxide, hydrogen, and nitrogen; **producer goods**, goods, such as tools and raw materials, used in the production of other goods and satisfy human wants only indirectly. [L *prōdūcĕre, -ductum—prō*, forward, *dūcĕre*, to lead.]

proem [prō´em] *n* an introduction, preface; a preliminary comment.—*adj* **proē´mial**. [Fr *proème*—L *prooemium*—Gr *prooimion—pro*, before, *oime*, a song.]

profane [prō-fān´] *adj* not sacred, secular; heathen; showing contempt of sacred things, impious; not possessing esoteric or expert knowledge.—*vt* to violate, desecrate; to debase by a wrong, unworthy, or vulgar use.—*adv* **profāne´ly**.—*ns* **profāne´ness; profān´er; profan´ity**, irreverence; that which is profane; profane language or conduct. [L *profānus*, outside the temple, not sacred.—*prō*, before, *fānum*, a temple.]

profess [prō-fes´] *vt* to make open declaration of; to declare in strong terms; to declare in words or appearance only; to claim to be expert in.—*adj* **professed´**, openly avowed, acknowledged; alleged, pretended.—*adv* **profess´edly**.—*n* **profession** [-fesh´(ò)n] the act of professing; open declaration; religious belief; avowal; pretence; an occupation requiring specialized knowledge and often long and intensive academic preparation; the collective body of persons engaged in any profession; entrance into a religious order.—*adj* **profess´ional**, pertaining to a profession; conforming to the technical or ethical standards of a profession; earning a livelihood in an activity or field often engaged in by amateurs; having a specified occupation as a permanent career; engaged in by persons receiving financial return; pursuing a line of conduct as though it were a profession; (abbrev **pro**).—*adv* **profess´ionally**.—*n* **profess´or**, one who professes, avows, or declares; a faculty member of the highest academic rank at a university; a teacher at a university, college, and sometimes secondary school; one teaching or professing special knowledge of an art, sport, or occupation requiring skill.—*adj* **professō´rial**.—*ns* **professō´rate**, office of a professor; his period of office; body of professors; **profess´orship**, the office, duties, or position of an academic professor. [L *professus*, perf p of *profitērī—prō*, publicly, *fatērī*, to confess.]

proffer [prof´ėr] *vt* to tender, to offer, usu. something intangible, for acceptance.—*pr p* **proff´ering**; *pt, pt p* **proff´ered**.—*n* an offer made.—*n* **proff´erer**. [Anglo-Fr *proffrir*—L *prō*, forward, *offerre*. See **offer**.]

proficient [prō-fish´ėnt] *adj* competent, skilled, thoroughly qualified (in, at).—*n* an adept, an expert.—*n* **profi´ciency**.—*adv* **profi´ciently**. [L *prōficiens, -entis*, pr p of *prōficĕre*, to make progress.]

profile [prō´fīl] *n* a head or portrait in a side view; the outline of any object without foreshortening; a vertical section of soil from the ground to underlying rock; a graph representing a person's abilities as determined by tests; a short biographical sketch.—*vt* to represent in profile; to produce (as by writing, drawing, or graphing) a profile of; to shape the outline of by passing a cutter around. [It *profilo*—L *prō*, before, *filum*, a thread.]

profit [prof´it] *n* gain; the excess of returns over expenditure in a transaction; the compensation to entrepreneurs resulting from the assumption of risk as distinct from wages or rent; advantage, benefit.—*vti* to benefit; to be of advantage (to).—*adj* **prof´itable**, yielding or bringing profit or gain; advantageous.—*n* **prof´itableness**.—*adv* **prof´itably**.—*n* **profiteer´**, one who exacts exorbitant profits.—Also *vi, adj*; **prof´itless**, without profit.—*adv* **prof´itlessly**.—*n* **prof´it shār´ing**, a system under which the employee receives a share in the profits of a business.—**profit and loss**, a summary account and the end of an accounting period showing the net profit and loss of a business. [Fr—L *prōfectus*, progress—*prōficĕre, prōfectum*, to make progress.]

profligate [prof´li-gāt] *adj* abandoned to vice, dissolute; prodigal, extravagant.—*n* one leading a profligate life.—*n* **prof´ligacy** [-ȧs-i] state or quality of being profligate; a vicious course of life.—*adv* **prof´ligately**. [L *prōfligatus*, pt p of *prōfligāre*—*prō*, forward, *fligĕre*, to dash.]

pro forma [prō fōr´ma] *adj* made or carried out as a formality; provided in advance to prescribe form or describe items. [L.]

profound [prō-fownd´] *adj* deep; far below the surface; intense; penetrating deeply into knowledge; abstruse.—*n* the depths of the ocean.—*adv* **profound´ly**.—*ns* **profound´ness, profund´ity**, the state or quality of being profound; depth of place, of knowledge, etc.; that which is profound. [Fr *profond*—L *profundus*—*prō*, forward, *fundus*, bottom.]

profuse [prō-fūs´] *adj* liberal to excess, lavish (*with* **in, with**); excessively abundant (eg *profuse thanks*).—*adv* **profūse´ly**.—*ns* **profūse´ness, profusion** [-fū´zh(ȯ)n] state of being profuse; extravagance; prodigality. [L *prōfūsus*, pa p of *prōfundĕre*—*prō*, forth, *fundĕre*, to pour.]

progenitor [prō-jen´i-tȯr] *n* a precursor, originator; an ancestor in a direct line.—*n* **prog´eny**, that which is brought forth; descendants; offspring of animals or plants; a body of followers, disciples, or successors. [L *prōgenitor*—*prō*, before, *gignĕre, genitum*, to beget.]

progesterone [prō-jes´tėr-ōn] *n* one of the female sex hormones.

prognosis [prog-nō´sis] *n* a forecast, esp of the course of a disease.—*n* **prognost´ic**, a foretelling; an indication, a presage.—*adj* indicating what is to happen by signs or symptoms.—*vt* **prognos´ticate**, to foretell; to indicate (what is to come).—*ns* **prognosticā´tion; prognos´ticātor**, one who predicts the future. [Gr *prognōsis*—*pro*, before, *gignōskein*, to know.]

program, programme [prō´gram] *n* a sheet or booklet giving the details of proceedings arranged for any occasion or ceremony; the items of an entertainment, etc.; a scheduled radio or television broadcast; a curriculum or syllabus for a course of study; a scheme or plan; the sequence of actions to be performed by an electronic computer in dealing with data of a certain kind; course of instruction (by book or teaching machine) in which subject matter is broken down into a logical sequence of short items of information.—*vt* to provide with, enter in, a program; to prepare a program for (an electronic computer, etc.).—*adj* **pro´grammed**.—**program music**, music that seeks to depict a scene or tell a story. [Gr *programma*, proclamation—*pro*, before, *graphein*, to write.]

progress [prog´res] *n* forward movement; advance; improvement, gain in proficiency; passage from place to place; a journey of state, or a circuit.—*vi* **progress´**, to go foward; to go on, continue; to advance; to improve.—*n* **prōgression** [-gresh´(ȯ)n] motion onward; progress; movements by successive stages; a series of numbers or magnitudes increasing or decreasing according to a fixed law; (*mus*) a regular succession of tones or chords.—*adjs* **prōgress´ional; prōgress´ive**, moving forward; advancing by successive stages; tending to improvement; favoring reforms, or encouraging the adoption of new methods and inventions; increasing as the base increases; (*gram*) a verb form expressing that the action is, was, or will be in progress at the time indicated.—*n* one believing in moderate political change, esp social improvement by governmental action.—**Progress´ive**, a member of various US political parties of the 20th century.—*adv* **prōgress´ively**.—*n* **prōgress´iveness**.—**in progress**, going on, taking place. [Fr *progresse* (now *progrès*)—L *prōgressus*—*prō*, forward, *gradī*, to step.]

prohibit [prō-hib´it] *vt* to forbid; to prevent.—*n* **prohibition** [prō-i-bi´sh(ȯ)n] the act of prohibiting, forbidding, or interdicting; an interdict; the forbidding by law of the manufacture and sale of alcoholic drinks.—*adj* **prohibitive** [-hib´-] prohibitory; having the effect of restricting the sale, use, etc., of something (eg *prohibitive price, tax*).—*adv* **prohib´itively**.—*adj* **prohib´itory**, that prohibits or forbids; forbidding. [L *prohibēre, prohibitum*—*prō*, before, *habēre*, to have.]

project [proj´ekt] *n* a scheme, plan, proposal for an undertaking; a definitely formulated piece of research; a large usu. government-supported undertaking; a task engaged in usu. by a group of students to supplement or apply classroom studies; a group of houses or apartments built and arranged according to a single plan.—*vt* **project** [pro-jekt´] to throw, impel, out or foward; to contrive or plan; to cast (as a light, a shadow, an image) upon a surface or into space; to throw an image of; to externalize, make objective; to show outlined against a background; (*theat*) to speak or sing in such a way as to aim the voice at the back of the auditorium; to reproduce (as a print, line, or area) on a surface by motion in a prescribed direction; to attribute (something in one's own mind) to a person or group; to estimate, plan, or figure for the future.—*vi* to jut out; to come across vividly; to make oneself heard clearly.—*adj* **projec´tile**, projecting or throwing forward; impelling; capable of being thrown forward.—*n* a body projected by force; a missile.—*ns* **projec´tion**, an act or method of projecting; the fact or state of being projected; that which is projected; planning; a jutting out; a method of representing geographical detail on a plane; a projected image; an estimation of future possibilities based on a current trend; the reading of one's own emotions and experience into a particular situation; (*geom*) a figure formed by projection; **projec´tor**, one who promotes enterprises; an apparatus for projecting, esp an image or a beam of light. [L *prōicĕre, prōjectum*—*prō*, forth, *jacĕre*, to throw.]

prolapse [prō-laps´] *vi* (*med*) to fall or slip out of place.—*n* **pro´lapse**, a prolapsed condition.

prolate [prō´lāt] *adj* elongated in the direction of a line joining the poles. [L *prōlātus*, pt p of *prōferre*—*prō*, forth, *ferre*, to bear.]

prolegomen [prō-le-gom´ėn] *n* an introduction, esp to a treatise;—(*pl*) **prolegom´ena**. [Gr *prolegomenon*, pl *-a*, pt p neut of *prolegein*—*pro*, before, *legein*, to say.]

prolepsis [prō-lep´sis] *n* a rhetorical figure of anticipation, use of a word, such as an adjective, not literally applicable till a later time; a figure of speech by which objections are anticipated and answered.—*adj* **prolep´tic**. [Gr—*pro*, before, *lambanein*, to take.]

proletarian [prō-le-tā´ri-ȧn] *adj* of the proletariat.—*n* a member of the proletariat.—*n* **proletā´riat** [-ȧt] the lowest social or economic class of a community; the laboring class, esp the industrial working class. [L *prōlētārius* (in ancient Rome) citizen of sixth and lowest class, who served the state not with property, but with his *prōles* (children).]

prolific [prō-lif´ik] *adj* bringing forth much offspring; fruitful, fertile; marked by inventiveness or productivity.—*vi* **prolif´erate**, to grow by multiplication of parts (cells, buds, etc.); increase rapidly and abundantly.—*n* **proliferā´tion**. [L *prōles*, offspring, *facĕre*, to make.]

prolix [prō´liks or -liks´] *adj* long and wordy; long-winded (eg of a writer).—*n* **prolix´ity**.—*adv* **prolix´ly**. [L *prōlixus*—*prō*, forward, *liquī*, to flow.]

prolocutor [prō-lok´ū-tȯr] *n* a spokesman; a presiding officer. [L *prō*, before, *loquī, locūtus*, to speak.]

prologue [prō´log] *n* in a Greek play, the part before the entry of the chorus; an introduction to a poem, etc.; an introductory event or action. [Fr—L *prologus*—Gr *prologos*—*pro*, before, *logos*, speech.]

prolong [prō-long´] *vt* to lengthen in time or space.—*n* **prolongātion** [prō-long-gā´sh(ȯ)n] act of prolonging in space or time; a piece added in continuation. [L *prōlongāre*—*prō*, forward, *longus*, long.]

prom [prom] *n* (*inf*) a dance, as of a particular school class.

promenade [prom-ė-näd´ or -nād´] *n* a walk for pleasure, show, or gentle exercise; an esplanade; a ball or dance.—*vti* to take a promenade (along or through). [Fr from (*se*) *promener*, to walk—L *prōmināre*, to drive forwards—*prō*, forward, *mināre*, to drive (with threats).]

Promethean [prō-mē´thė-ȧn] *adj* relating to or resembling Prometheus, his experiences, or his art, esp daringly original or creative. [*Prometheus*, a Titan punished for stealing fire from heaven and giving it to man.]

promethium [prō-mēth´i-ům] *n* a rare-earth element (symbol Pm; at wt 147; at no 61). [*Prometheus*, see above.]

prominent [prom´i-nėnt] *adj* projecting; conspicuous; widely and favorably known; distinguished.—*n* **prom´inence**, state or quality of being prominent; a prominent point or thing.—*adv* **prom´inently**. [L *prōminens, -entis*, pr p of *prōminēre*, to jut forth.]

promiscuous [prȯ-mis´kū-us] *adj* confusedly or indiscriminately mixed; collected together without order; indiscriminate, esp in sexual liaisons.—*ns* **promiscū´ity** [prom], **promis´cuousness**.—*adv* **promis´cuously**. [L *prōmiscuus*—*prō*, pfx (of obscure force here), *miscēre*, to mix.]

promise [prom´is] *n* an engagement to do or keep from doing something; a thing promised; indication, as of a successful future.—*vti* to make an engagement (to do or not to do something); to afford reason to expect.—*ns* **prom´iser, prom´isor**.—*adj* **prom´ising**, affording ground for hope or expectation of good results.—*adv* **prom´isingly**.—*adj* **prom´issory**, containing or being a promise.—**promised land**, a place or condition believed to fulfill realization of hopes; **promissory note**, a written promise to pay a sum of money to another, or to bearer, at a certain date, or at sight, or on demand. [L *prōmissum*, neut pt p of *prōmittĕre*, to send forward—*prō*, forward, *mittĕre*, to send.]

promontory [prom´ȯn-tȯr-i] *n* a headland; a peak of high land that juts out into a body of water. [LL *prōmontōrium* (L *prōmuntūrium*)—*prō*, forward, *mons, montis*, a mountain.]

promote [prō-mōt´] *vt* to further the growth or improvement of, to encourage; to raise to a higher position; to encourage the sales of by advertising, publicity, or discounting; to advance (a student) from one grade to the next higher grade; (*chess*) to change a pawn into a piece by advancing to the eighth rank; (*slang*) to obtain (something) by doubtful means.—*ns* **promō´ter**, one who promotes, esp one who organizes and finances a sporting event (as a boxing match); a substance in varying amounts that increases the activity of a catalyst.; **promotion**, a being raised in position or rank; the furtherance of the sale of merchandise through advertising, publicity, or discounting.—*adj* **promō´tive**. [L *prōmovēre, -mōtum—prō*, forward, *movēre*, to move.]

prompt [prompt] *adj* ready in action; performed at once; immediate, unhesitating; of or relating to prompting actors.—*n* something that reminds; a time limit for payment of an account for goods purchased; the contract by which this time is fixed.—*vt* to incite; to inspire (eg an action); to supply forgotten words, or elusive words, facts or ideas, to.—*ns* **promptbook**, a copy of a play with directions for performance used by a theater prompter; **prompt´itūde, prompt´ness**, quickness, immediateness; quickness in decision and action.—*adv* **prompt´ly**.—**prompt side**, the side of the stage from which prompting is done—usu. to the actor's left. [L *promptus—prōmĕre*, to bring forward.]

promulgate [prom´ul-gāt] *vt* to proclaim, publish abroad, make widely known the terms of (a proposed law); to put (a law) into action or force.—*ns* **promulgā´tion; prom´ulgātor**. [L *prōmulgāre, -ātum*.]

prone [prōn] *adj* with the face, ventral surface, downward; disposed inclined (to).—*n* **prone´ness**. [L *prōnus*.]

prong [prong] *n* the spike of a fork or forked object.—*adj* **pronged**, having prongs—*n* **pronghorn**, a ruminant mammal (*Antilopa americana*) of treeless parts of western N America that resembles an antelope.—Also **pronghorn antelope**. [ME *prange*; origin obscure.]

pronominal *See* **pronoun**.

pronoun [prō´nown] *n* a word used instead of a noun, to indicate without naming.—*adj* **pronom´inal**, belonging to, or of the nature of, a pronoun.—*adv* **pronom´inally**. [L *prō*, before, (hence) instead of, and **noun**.]

pronounce [prō-nowns´] *vt* to utter formally (eg a sentence, judgement); to declare (eg a decision); to utter; to articulate.—*adsj* **pronounce´able**, capable of being pronounced; **pronounced´**, marked, decided, noticeable.—*adv* **pronoun´cedly**.—*ns* **pronounce´ment**, a confident or authoritative assertion; proclamation; **pronoun´cer**.—*adj* **pronoun´cing**, giving or making pronunciation. [Fr *prononcer—*L *prōnuntiāre—prō*, forth, *nuntiāre*, to announce—*nuntius*, a messenger.]

pronucleus [prō-nū´klē-ùs] *n* the nucleus of a germ cell after completion of meiosis but before fusion with the other genetic nucleus. [Pfx **pro-**, + **nucleus**.]

pronunciamento [prō-nun-si-ä-men´tō] *n* a pronouncement a formal proclamation. [Sp]

pronunciation [pro-nun-si-ā´sh(ò)n] *n* mode of pronouncing; articulation. [L *pronuntiātiō, -ōnis—pronuntiāre*. See **pronounce**.]

proof [prōōf] *n* that which proves; evidence that convinces the mind; the fact, act, or process of proving or showing to be true; test; demonstration; ability to stand a test; (*print*) an impression taken for correction; (*photography*) a trial print from a negative; the relative strength of an alcoholic liquor.—*adj* impervious, invulnerable (*often with* **against** or as suffix, as in **fireproof**). **proof´read´er**, one who reads printed proofs to discover and correct errors; **proof´ spir´it**, a mixture containing fixed proportions of alcohol and water. [OFr *prove* (Fr *preuve*)—L *probāre*, to prove.]

prop[1] [prop] *n* a rigid support; a supporter, upholder, on whom one depends.—*vt* to hold up by means of something placed under or against; to sustain;—*pr p* **propp´ing**; *pt, pt p* **propped**. [ME *proppe*; cf Du *proppe*, wine-prop.]

prop[2] [prop] *n* abbrev for property used on a stage.

prop[3] [prop] *n* abbrev for **propeller**.

propagate [prop´a-gāt] *vt* to cause (a plant or animal) to reproduce itself; of a plant or animal, to reproduce (itself); to spread (ideas, customs, etc.).—*vi* to reproduce, as plants or animals.—*ns* **propagan´da**, a committee (*congregatio de propaganda fide*) at Rome charged with the management of the RC missions; any concerted action for the spread of ideas, doctrines, etc.; the ideas, etc. so spread. **propagand´ist**, one engaged in propaganda.—Also *adj—ns* **propagā´tion**, act of propagating; **prop´agātor**. [L *propāgāre, -ātum*, conn with *propāgō*, a layer.]

propane [prō´pān] *n* a colorless imflammable gas occurring naturally or obtained from petroleum, used as fuel or in chemical synthesis.

propel [prō-pel´] *vt* to drive onward or forward;—*pr p* **propell´ing**; *pt, pt p* **propelled´**—*ns* **propellant, propellent**, the fuel for a rocket; **propell´er**, one who, or that which, propels; a driving mechanism; a device having two or more blades in a revolving hub for driving a ship or aircraft. [L *prōpellĕre—prō*, forward, *pellĕre*, to drive.]

propensity [pro-pens´i-ti] *n* a natural inclination, tendency, disposition (*with* **to, for**). [L *prōpensus*, inclined, pt p of *prōpendēre, -pensum—prō*, forward, *pendēre*, to hang.]

proper [prop´ėr] *adj* natural, characteristic, appropriate; pertaining characteristically (to); fitting; suitable (to); correct; decorous; conforming strictly to convention; in the most restricted sense (*Chicago proper*, not including the suburbs).—*adv* **prop´erly**, in a proper manner; strictly;—**proper fraction**, a fraction that is less than 1 in value; **proper noun, name**, a noun, name, designating a particular person, animal, town, etc. [Fr *propre—*L *prōprius*, own.]

property [prop´ėr-ti] *n* a quality that is always present, a characteristic; any quality; that which is one's own; land or buildings; ownership; a movable article used in a stage setting.—*adj* **prop´ertied**, possessed of property —*n* **prop´erty tax**, a tax levied on real or personal property, [OFr *properte—*L *proprietās. See* **propriety**.]

prophecy, prophesy [prof´ė-si] *n* inspired utterance of divine will and purpose; a predicition of something to come. [OFr *prophecie—*L *prophētia—*Gr *prophēteiā—prophētēs*, prophet.]

prophesy [prof´ė-si] *vi* to utter prophecies; to predict with assurance or on the basis of mystic knowledge.—*vt* to foretell;—*pt, pt p* **proph´esied**. [A variant of **prophecy**.]

prophet [prof´ėt] *n* a religious leader regarded as, or claims to be divinely inspired; **Prophet**, the writer of one of the Prophetic books of the Old Testament an inspired poet; one who predicts the future; **Prophets**, the second part of the Jewish scripture, a division of the Old Testament.—*n* **proph´etess**, a woman who is a prophet.—*adjs* **prophet´ic, -al**, pertaining to a prophet; containing prophecy; foreseeing or foretelling events.—*adv* **prophet´ically**. [Fr *prophète—*L *prophēta—*Gr *prophētēs—pro*, for (another), *phanai*, to speak.]

prophylactic [prof-i-lak´tik] *adj* guarding against disease.—*n* a prophylactic medicine, device, etc.—*n* **prophylaxis**, preventive treatment esp a cleaning of the teeth to remove plaque and tartar. [Gr *propylaktikos—pro*, before, *phylax*, a guard.]

propinquity [prō-ping´kwi-ti] *n* nearness in place, time, blood relationship, quality—proximity, similarity. [L *propinquitās—propinquus*, near—*prope*, near.]

propitiate [prō-pish´i-āt] *vt* to render (a person) favorable; to appease (one who is angry or resentful).—*adj* **propitiable** [prō-pish´i-à-bl], that may be propitated.—*ns* **propitiā´tion**, act of propitiating; atonement; atoning sacrifice; **propi´tiātor**.—*adj* **propi´tiatory**, having power to, or intended to, propitiate.—*adj* **propi´tious**, favorable, of good omen; favorable (for, to); disposed to be gracious.—*adv* **propi´tiously**.—*n* **propi´tiousness**. [L *propitiāre, -ātum*, to make favourable—*propitius*, well-disposed.]

proportion [prò-pōr´sh(ò)n] *n* the relation of one thing to another, or of a part to the whole, in regard to magnitude; ration; (*math*) the equality of two ratios; due relation (in respect of accuracy, or of harmony or rhythm); an equal or just share; (*pl*) dimensions.—*vt* to put in proper relation with something else; to adjust or fashion in due proportion (to)—*adjs* **propor´tionable**, that may be proportioned; having a due or definite relation (to); **propor´tional**, having a due proportion; relating to proportion; (*math*) having the same or a constant ratio.—*n* (*math*) a number or quantity in a proportion.—*n* **proportional´ity**.—*adv* **propor´tionally**.—*adj* **propor´tionate**, in fit proportion, proportional.—*adv* **propor´tionately**.—**proportional representation**, a system intended to give parties in an elected body a representation as nearly as possible proportional to their voting strength. [L *prōportiō, -ōnis—prō*, in comparison with, *portiō*, part, share.]

propose [prō-pōz´] *vt* to put forward for consideration, to propound; to suggest; to put before one as an aim; to nominate (a person); to invite the company to drink (a health); to purpose or intend.—*vi* to form or put forward an intention; to make an offer, esp of marriage.—*ns* **propō´sal**, an act of proposing anything proposed; an offer, esp of marriage; **propō´ser**. [Fr,—pfx *pro-* (L *prō*), and *poser*, to place.]

proposition [prop-o-zish´(ò)n] *n* an act of proposing; the thing propounded; a request for sexual intercourse; (*inf*) a proposed deal, as in business; (*inf*) an undertaking to be dealt with; (*logic*) a form of statement in which a predicate is affirmed or denied of a subject; (*math*) a problem to be solved.—*vt* to make a proposition to someone.—*adj* **proposi´tional**, pertaining to a proposition; considered as a proposition. [Fr,—L *prōpositiō, -ōnis—prō*, before. See **position**.]

propound [prō-pownd´] *vt* to offer for consideration.—*n* **propound´er**. [Orig *propone—*L *prō*, forth, *pōnĕre*, to place.]

proprietor [prō-prī´ė-tòr] *n* an owner;—*ns* **proprī´etress**, a woman who is a proprietor; **proprī´etary**, an owner of an exclusive right to something, specifically one granted ownership of a colony and full prerogatives of establishing a government and distributing land (as of the original American colonies); a drug (as a patent medicine) protected by secrecy, patent, or copyright against free competition; a business secretly owned and run as a cover for an intelligence organization.—*adj* characteristic of a proprietor; legally made only by a person or body of persons having special rights (eg a medicine); privately owned and managed and run as a profit-making organization.—*n* **proprī´etorship**. [LL *proprietārius—proprius*, own.]

propriety [prō-prī´ė-ti] *n* conformity with accepted standards of conduct; appropriateness; fear of offending against rules of behavior, esp between the sexes; (*pl*) the customs and manners of polite society. [Fr *propriété—*L *proprietās—proprius*, own.]

propulsion [prō-pul´sh(ò)n] *n* act of propelling; something that propels.—*adj* **propul´sive**, tending or having power to propel. [L *prōpellĕre, prōpulsum*, to push forward. See **propel**.]

pro rata [prō rā´ta, rä´ta] in proportion.—*vti* **prōrate´**, to divide or assess proportionately. [L]

prorogue [prō-rōg´] *vt* to terminate a session (as a British parliament) by royal prerogative.—*vi* to suspend or end a legislative session.—*pr p* **prorog´uing**; *pt, pt p* **prorogued´**.—*n* **prorogā´tion**, act of proroguing. [L *prorogāre, -ātum—prō*, forward, *rogāre*, to ask.]

prosaic [prō-zā´ik] *adj* like prose; commonplace; dull.—*adv* **prosā´ically**. [**prose**.]

proscenium [prō-sē´ni-um] *n* the front part of the stage; the curtain and its framework, esp the arch that frames the stage. [L,—Gr *proskēnion—pro*, before, *skēnē*, the stage.]

proscribe [prō-skrīb´] *vt* to outlaw; to refuse to tolerate, to prohibit the use of; to publish the name of (a person) condemned to death with his property forfeited to the state.—*ns* **prōscrib´er; prōscrip´tion**.—*adj* **prōscrip´tive**. [L *prōscrībĕre—prō*, before, publicly, *scrībĕre, scriptum*, to write.]

prose [prōz] *n* ordinary spoken and written language with words in direct straightforward arrangement; all writings not in verse.—*adj* of or in prose; not poetical; plain; dull.—*vi* to write prose; to speak or write tediously.—*adj* **prōs´y**, dull, tedious. [Fr—L *prōsa—prorsus*, straightforward—*prō*, forward, *vetĕre, versum*, to turn.]

prosecute [pros´ė-kūt] *vt* to pursue until finished; to engage in, practice (eg a trade); to bring legal action against.—*vi* to institute and carry on a legal suit or prosecution; to be prosecutor in a lawsuit.—*ns* **prosecū´tion**, the act of prosecuting or pursuing, esp by litigation; the prosecuting party in legal proceedings; **pros´ecūtor**, one instituting a lawsuit; a prosecuting attorney.—**prosecuting attorney**, an attorney who conducts proceedings in court on behalf of the government; a district attorney. [L *prōsequī—prō*, onwards, *sequī, secūtus*, to follow.]

proselyte [pros´e-līt] *n* one who has come over from one religion to another; a convert, esp to Judaism.—*vti* to proselytize.—*vti* **pros´elytīze**, to try to make a convert (of).—*n* **pros´elytism**. [Gr *prosēlytos*, a new-comer.]

prosody [pros´o-di] *n* the study of versification, esp that of metrical structure; a particular style, system, or theory of versification.—*adjs* **prosō´dial, prosod´ic, -al.**—*n* **pros´odist**, one skilled in prosody. [L *prosōdia*—Gr *prosōidia—pros*, to, *ōidē*, a song.]

prosopopoeia [pros-ō-po-pē´ya] *n* personification. [Gr *prosōpopoiiā—prosōpon*, a person, *poieein*, to make.]

prospect [pros´pekt] *n* a wide view; a scene; outlook for the future, (*pl*) measure of success to be expected by one; expectation; a likely customer, candidate, etc.—*vti* **prospect´**, to explore or search (for).—*n* **prospec´tor**.—*adj* **prospec´tive**, likely; expected.—*adv* **prospec´tively**.—*n* **prospec´tus**, a statement of the features of a new work, enterprise, etc.; something (as a condition or statement) that forecasts the course or nature of a situation. [L *prospectus—prōspicĕre, prōspectum—prō*, forward, *specĕre*, to look.]

prosper [pros´pėr] *vi* to thrive, to succeed; to turn out well.—*vt* to cause to thrive or succeed.—*n* **prosper´ity**, the state of being prosperous; success, good fortune.—*adj* **pros´perous**, thriving; successful.—*adv* **pros´perously**. [L *prosper*, or *prosperus*, successful.]

prostaglandins [pros-tȧ-gland´inz] *n pl* a group of chemical substances secreted by various parts of the body into the bloodstream and which act on the smooth muscle of the vascular and reproductive systems. [*prostate gland*, one of the parts of the body where they are found.]

prostate [pros´tāt] *n* a gland in males at the neck of the bladder. [Fr *prostatēs—pro*, before, *sta*, root of *histanai*, to set up.]

prosthesis [pros´thē-sis] *n* an artificial part to replace a missing part of the body.—*n* **prosthet´ics**, the surgery or dentistry involved in supplying artificial parts to the body. [Gr *pros*, to, *thesis*, putting.]

prostitute [pros´ti-tūt] *vt* to offer indiscriminately for sexual intercourse, esp for money; to devote to corrupt or unworthy purposes.—*adj* devoted to vice.—*n* a woman who offers herself to indiscriminate sexual intercourse for money; a person (as a writer or painter) who deliberately debases himself or his talents (as for money).—*ns* **prostitū´tion**, the act or practice of prostituting; lewdness for hire; the state of being prostituted; **pros´titūtor**. [L *prostituĕre, -ūtum*, to set up for sale—*prō*, before, *statuĕre*, to place.]

prostrate [pros´trȧt´] *adj* lying with face on the ground; reduced to helplessness; completely exhausted; lying prone or supine.—*vt* [-āt] to throw forwards on the ground; to lay flat; to overthrow; to reduce to impotence or exhaustion; to bow (oneself) in humble reverence.—*n* **prostrā´tion**. [L *prōstrātus*, pa p of *prōsternĕre—prō*, forwards, *sternĕre, strātum*, to spread.]

protactinium [prōt-ak-tin´i-ùm] *n* a metallic element (symbol Pa; at wt 231.0; at no 91). [Pfx **prot(o)-**, and **actinium**.]

protagonist [prō-tag´on-ist] *n* the main character in a drama, novel, etc.; a champion (of a cause). [Gr *prōtos*, first, *agōnistēs*, a combatant.]

protasis [prot´a-sis] *n* the introductory part of a play or narrative poem; the subordinate clause of a conditional sentence. [Gr *—pro*, before, *tasis*, a stretching—*teinein*, to stretch.]

protean [prō´tė-ȧn, prō-tē´ȧn] *adj* readily assuming different shapes; displaying great variety or diversity. [**Proteus**, sea-god who assumed any form he pleased.]

protect [prō-tekt´] *vt* to shield from danger, injury, capture, loss, change; to defend; to maintain the status and integrity of, esp through financial guarantees; to foster or shield from infringement or restriction; to restrict competition through tariffs and trade controls.—*ns* **protec´tion**, act of protecting; state of being protected; defense; that which protects; a guard, shield; the freeing of home producers from foreign competition by restrictions on foreign goods; immunity from prosecution purchased by payment of bribes; money extorted by racketeers posing as a protective association; **protec´tionist**, one who favors the protection of trade by taxing imports.—Also *adj.*—*adj* **protec´tive**, affording protection, defensive, sheltering; intended to protect.—*n* **protec´tor**, one who protects from injury or oppression; a guard, shield; a regent; **protec´tress**, a woman who is a protector.—*adj* **protec´toral**, pertaining to a protector or a regent.—*ns* **protec´torate**, the rule of a protector; authority over a vassal state; relation assumed by a state over territory which it governs without annexing it; **protec´torship**.—**protective tariff**, a tariff intended primarily to protect domestic producers rather than to raise revenue. [L *prōtegĕre, -tectum*.]

protégé [prō´tā-zhā] *n* a person guided and helped in his career by another person. [Fr, pt p of *protéger*, to protect—L *prōtegĕre*.]

protein [prō´tēn] *n* any one of a group of complex nitrogenous substances that play an important part in the bodies of plants and animals and are an essential food item. [Gr *prōteus*, primary.]

pro tempore [prō tem pō-rē] for the time being; temporarily.—Abbrev **pro tem**. [L]]

Proterozoic [prot´ė-rō-zō´ik] *adj* of an era of geological history including the interval between the Archezoic and Paleozoic, perhaps exceeding in length all of subsequent geologic time; relating to the system of rocks formed in this era. [Gr *proteros*, earlier, *zōē*, life.]

protest [prȯ-test or prō-, prō-test´] *vi* to express or record dissent or objection (*often with* **against**).—*vt* to make a solemn declaration or affirmation of; to execute or have executed a formal protest against; to make a statement or gesture in objection to.—*ns* **prō´test**, a declaration of objection or dissent; remonstrance; affirmation, protestation; a formal statement of objection. **Prot´estant**, a member or adherent of one of the Christian churches deriving from the Reformation; a Christian not of the Orthodox or Roman Catholic Church.—**Protestant ethic**, an ethic that stresses the virtues of hard work, thrift, and self-discipline.—*adj* pertaining to Protestants or their doctrine.—*ns* **Prot´estantism; protestation**, [pro-testā´sh(ȯ)n], the act of protesting; a solemn declaration or avowal; **protest´er**. [Fr,—L *prōtestārī, -ātus*, to bear witness in public.]

protium [prō´ti-ùm, -shi-ùm] *n* ordinary hydrogen of atomic weight 1. [Gr *prōtos*, first.]

proto- [prō-tō-], **prot-**, in composition, first in time, most primitive or earliest, chief. [Gr *prōtos*, first];—eg **protolanguage**, an assumed ancestral language; **protomartyr**, (see below).

protocol [prō´tō-kol] *n* an original note, minute, or draft of an instrument or transaction; the ceremonial forms accepted as correct in official dealings, as between heads of state or diplomatic officials; the formatting of data in an electronic communications system; the plan of a scientific experiment or treatment. [Fr *protocole*, through LL—Late Gr *prōtokollon*, the glued-on descriptive first leaf of a MS—Gr *prōtos*, first, *kolla*, glue.]

protomartyr [prō´tō-mär-tėr] *n* the first martyr in any cause. [Gr *prōtos*, first, + **martyr**.]

proton [prō´ton] *n* an elementary particle in the nucleus of all atoms, carrying a unit positive charge of electricity. [Gr neut of *prōtos*, first.]

protoplasm [prō´tō-plazm] *n* a semifluid viscous colloid, the essential living matter of all plant and animal cells. [Gr *prōtos*, first, *plasma*, form—*plassein*, to form.]

prototype [prō´tō-tīp] *n* the first or original type or model from which anything is copied. [Fr,—Gr *prōtos*, first, *typos*, a type.]

protozoan [prō-tō-zō´ȧn] *n* any of a phylum (Protozoa) of mostly microscopic, single-celled animals which are found in almost every kind of habitat, some of which are serious parasites of man and animals.—Also *adj.*—*n* **protozo´on**, protozoa;—*pl* **protozo´a**.—*n* **pro´tozool´ogy**, a branch of zoology dealing with protozoans. [Gr *prōtos*, first, *zōion*, an animal.]

protract [prō-trakt´] *vt* to draw out or lengthen in time or space; to lay down the lines and angles of with scale and protractor; to extend forward and outward.—*n* **protrac´tion**.—*adj* **protrac´tive**, drawing out in time, prolonging, delaying.—*n* **protrac´tor**, one who, or that which, protracts; an instrument for laying down angles on paper; a muscle whose contraction extends a part. [L *prōtrahĕre, -tractum—prō*, forth, *trahĕre*, to draw.]

protrude [prō-trōōd´] *vt* to thrust or push on or forward; to obtrude.—*vi* to stick out, project.—*n* **protru´sion**, the act of protruding; the state of being protruded; that which protrudes.—*adj* **protru´sive**, thrusting or impelling forward; protruding. [L *protrūdĕre, -trūsum—prō*, forward, *trūdĕre*, to thrust.]

protuberance [prō-tūb´ėr-ȧns] *n* a bulging out; a swelling.—*adj* **protū´berant**.—*adv* **protū´berantly**. [L *prōtūberāre, -ātum—prō*, forward, *tūber*, a swelling.]

proud [prowd] *adj* having excessive self-esteem; haughty; ostentatious; having a proper sense of self-respect; having an exultant sense of credit or gratification; giving reason for pride or boasting.—*n* **proud flesh**, a growth or excrescence of flesh around a healing wound.—*adv* **proud´ly**.—**proud of**, highly pleased with. [OE *prūd*.]

prove [prōōv] *vt* to establish or ascertain as true or genuine; to demonstrate (the correctness of any result); to show (oneself) to be worthy or capable.—*vi* to turn out, esp after trial or test.—*n* **prov´er**.—*adj* **prov´able**.—*adv* **provably**.—**proving ground**, a place for testing (as of vehicles or weapons); a place where something is developed or tried out. [OFr *prover*—L *probāre—probus*, excellent; perh partly OE *prōfian*, to assume to be.]

provenance [prov´ė-nȧns] *n* origin; source. [Fr,—L *prō*, forth, *venīre*, to come.]

Provençal [prov-ä-säl] *adj* of or pertaining to *Provence* in France; cooked with garlic, onion, mushrooms, olive oil, and herbs.—*n* a native or inhabitant of Provence; the Romance language spoken in southeastern France.

provender [prov´ėn-dėr] *n* dry food for domestic animals, esp livestock; (*inf*) food. [LL *praebenda*, later *provenda*, a daily allowance of food; cf **prebend**.]

proverb [prov´ėrb] *n* a short familiar sentence expressing a supposed truth or moral lesson; a byword; **Proverbs**, (*Bible*) 20th book of the Old Testament, written by Solomon, a guide for moral practice outside of the place of worship.—*adj* **prover´bial**, like or of the nature of a proverb; mentioned in a proverb; widely known.—*adv* **prover´bially**. [Fr *proverbe*—L *prōverbium*—*prō*, before, publicly, *verbum*, a word.]

provide [prō-vīd´] *vt* to make ready beforehand; to supply; to furnish (a person with).—*vi* to procure supplies, means, etc.; to make provision (for, against); to prescribe as a necessary condition (that).—*conj* **provi´ded, providing**, (*often with* **that**) on the condition or understanding.—*n* **provi´der**. [L *prōvidēre*—*prō*, before, *vidēre*, to see.]

providence [prov´i-dėns] *n* foresight; timely preparation; prudent management and thrift; **Providence**, God considered as the power sustaining and guiding human destiny; an event in which God's care is clearly shown.—*adj* **prov´ident**, seeing beforehand, and providing for the future; prudent; thrifty.—*adv* **prov´idently**.—*adj* **providential**, [-den´sh(à)l], as if effected by, or proceeding from, divine providence.—*adv* **providen´tially**. [L *prōvidens, -entis*, pr p of *prōvidēre*—*prō*, before, *vidēre*, to see.]

province [prov´ins] *n* an administrative district or division of a country; an administrative division of Canada; the jurisdiction of an archbishop or metropolitan; (*pl*) the parts of a country removed from the major cities; a department of knowledge or activity.—*adj* **provincial**, [prō-vin´sh(à)l], relating to a province; having the way, speech, etc of a certain province; countrylike; rustic; unsophisticated; of a style of furniture marked by plainness and informality.—*n* an inhabitant of a province or country district; (*RC*) the superior of a religious house in a province; a person lacking urban polish or refinement.—*n* **provin´cialism**, a manner, a turn of thought, or a word or idiom peculiar to a province or a country district; state or quality of being provincial.—*adv* **provin´cially**. [Fr,—L *prōvincia*, a province.]

provision [prō-vizh´(ò)n] *n* act of providing (for, against); something provided for the future; a stipulation, previous agreement; (*pl*) a stock of food,—*vt* to supply with provisions.—*adj* **provi´sional**, temporary.—*adv* **provi´sionally**. [Fr,—L *prōvisiō, -ōnis*—*prōvidēre*. See **provide**.]

proviso [prō-vī´zō] *n* a provision or condition in a deed or other writing; the clause containing it;—*pl* **provī´sos; provisoes** [-zōz].—*adj* **provī´sory**, containing a proviso or condition, conditional. [From the L law phrase *prōvisiō quod*, it being provided that.]

Provō [prō´vō] *n* a member of the provisional Irish Republican Army.

provoke [prō-vōk´] *vt* to call forth, give rise to, result in (eg a protest, laughter, an attack); to excite (a person) to action; to excite with anger; to annoy, exasperate.—*n* **prǒ vocā´tion**, act of provoking; incitement; that which provokes.—*adj* **provǒc´ative**, tending or designed to provoke or excite (*often with* **of**); such as to stimulate thought or discussion.—*n* anything that stirs up or provokes.—*adj* **provō´king**, irritating.—*adv* **provō´kingly**. [L *prōvocāre, -ātum*—*prō*, forth, *vocāre*, to call.]

provost [prōv´ōst] *n* a high executive official, as in some churches, colleges, or universities.—*ns* **provost court**, a military court usu. for the trial of minor offences within a hostile territory; **provost guard**, a police detail of soldiers under the authority of the provost marshall; **provost marshall**, an officer who supervises the military police of a command. [OE *profast* and OFr *provost*—L *praepositus*, pt p of *praepōnĕre*—*prae*, over, *pōnĕre*, to place.]

prow [prow] *n* the forward part of a ship. [Fr *proue*—L *prōra*.]

prowess [prow´es,] *n* bravery, esp in war; achievement through valor; skill. [From OFr *prou* (Fr *preux*), valiant.]

prowl [prowl] *vi* to move about stealthily; to rove in search of prey or plunder.—*n* the act of prowling; a roving for prey.—*n* **prowl´er**,—*n* **prowl car**, a squad car.—**on the prowl**, engaged in prowling.

proximate [proks´i-màt] *adj* nearest or next; without anything between, immediate as in a chain of events, causes, or effects.—*adv* **prox´imately**.—*n* **proxim´ity**, immediate nearness in time, place, relationship, etc.—*adv* **prox´imo**, next month.—**proximity fuze**, a device for activating an explosive device when it comes near the object. [L *proximus*, next, superl—*prope*, near.]

proxy [prok´si] *n* the agency of one who acts for another; one who acts or votes for another; the writing by which he is authorized to do so.—**proxy marriage**, a marriage celebrated in the absence of one of the contracting parties who authorizes a proxy to represent him at the ceremony. [Contr form of *procuracy*, office of a **procurator**.]

prude [prōōd] *n* one who is overly modest or proper in behavior, speech, etc.—*n* **pru´dery**, manners of a prude.—*adj* **pru´dish**.—*adv* **pru´dishly**. [OFr *prode*, excellent.]

prudent [prōō´dėnt] *adj* cautious and wise in conduct; discreet, dictated by forethought; managing carefully.—*adv* **pru´dently**.—*n* **pru´dence**, quality of being prudent; wisdom applied to practice, caution.—*adj* **pruden´tial**, using or practicing prudence.—*adv* **pruden´tially**. [Fr,—L *prūdens, prūdentis*, contr of *prōvidens*, pr p of *prōvidēre*, to foresee.]

prune[1] [prōōn] *vt* to trim dead or living parts from (a plant); to divest of anything superfluous; to remove by pruning.—*vi* to cut away what is unwanted or superfluous.—*ns* **pru´ner; pru´ning hook**, a pole bearing a curved blade for pruning plants. [OFr *proignier*; origin unknown.]

prune[2] [prōōn] *n* a plum dried or capable of drying without fermentation. [Fr,—L *prūnum*; cf Gr *prou(m)non*.]

prunella [prōō-nel´a] *n* a strong silk or woolen stuff, generally black—also **prunell´e**. [App from Fr *prunelle*, a sloe, dim of Fr *prune*, a plum.]

prurient [prōō´ri-ėnt] *adj* tending to excite lust; having lascivious thoughts.—*ns* **pru´rience, pru´riency**.—*adv* **pru´riently**. [L *prūriens*, pr p of *prūrīre*, to itch.]

Prussian [prush´àn] *adj* of or pertaining to Prussia.—**Prussian blue**, a cyanide of iron, used as a pigment, first discovered in Berlin.

pry[1] [prī] *n* a lever or crowbar.—*vt* to raise or move with a pry; to obtain with difficulty. [See **prize** (1).]

pry[2] [prī] *vi* to peer or peep (into what is closed or into what is not divulged); to try curiously or impertinently to find out about other people's affairs;—*pt, pt p* **pried**.—[ME *prien*; origin unknown.]

psalm [säm] *n* a devotional song or hymn; **Psalms** (*Bible*) 19th book of the Old Testament, collection of 150 psalms, many of which were written by David for worship.—*ns* **psalmist** [säm´ist], a composer of psalms, applied to David; **psalmody** [säm´o-di, or sal´mo-di], the singing of psalms, esp in public worship; psalms collectively. [OE *(p)salm, (p)sealm*—Low L *psalmus*—Gr *psalmos*, music of or to a stringed instrument—*psallein*, to pluck.]

Psalter [söl´tėr] *n* the Book of Psalms, esp when separately printed.—*n* **psal´tery, psal´try**, an ancient and medieval stringed instrument resembling the zither. [OE *saltere*—L *psaltērium*—Gr *psaltērion*, a psaltery.]

psephology [sē-fol´ò-ji] *n* the scientific study of elections.—*n* **psephol´ogist**. [Gr *psēphos*, a pebble (used in the same way as a voting paper), *logos*, discourse.]

pseudo- [sū-dō-] in composition, false or spurious; deceptively resembling, eg **pseu´doclass´icism**, imitated representation of classicism in literature and art.—*adj* **pseudo**, false, sham. [Gr *pseudo-*, false, seeming, pretended.]

pseudomorph [sū´dō-mörf] *n* a portion of a mineral showing the outward form of another; a deceptive of irregular form. [Gr *pseudo-*, false, *morphē*, form.]

pseudonym [sū´dō-nim] *n* a fictitious name assumed, as by an author.—*adj* **pseudon´ymous**, bearing a fictitious name. [Gr *pseudo-*, false, *onoma*, name.]

psi [sī] *n* the 23d letter of the Greek alphabet.

psyche [sī´kē] *n* the soul, spirit; the mind, esp as a functional entity governing the total organism and its interactions with the environment.—*vt* **psych, psyche**, [sīk] (*inf*) to defeat or intimidate by psychological means; to get oneself psychologically prepared for (*usu. with* **up**).—*adjs* **psych´ic, -al**, pertaining to the psyche; spiritual; sensitive to, or in touch with, that which cannot be explained physically.—*n* **psych´ic**, a person apparently sensitive to nonphysical forces; a medium; psychic phenomena.—*adj* **psychedel´ic**, of or causing extreme changes in the conscious mind; of or like the auditory or visual effects produced by drugs (as LSD).—*ns* **psychī´atrist**, one who practices psychiatry; **psychiatry**, the branch of medicine dealing with disorders of the mind, including psychoses and neuroses; **psychoanalysis**, a method of treating neuroses, phobias, and some other mental disorders by analyzing emotional conflicts, repressions, etc. through the use of free association, dream analysis, etc.; **psych´o-an´alyst**.—*vt* **psych´o-an´alyze**.—*adj* **psychogen´ic**, having origin in the mind or in mental conflicts.—*n* **psychol´ogy**, the science that investigates the phenomena of mental and emotional life.—*adjs* **psycholog´ical, psycholog´ic**, pertaining to psychology.—*adv* **psycholog´ically**.—*ns* **psychol´ogist**, one who studies psychology; **psychomet´rics**, the branch of psychology dealing with measurable factors; statistical treatment of mental test results; **psy´chopath**, one suffering from a behavioral disorder resulting in indifference to or ignorance of his obligations to society, often shown in a moral or a social behavior, as acts of violence.—*adj* **psychopath´ic**, pertaining to psychopathy or psychopath.—*ns* **psychopathol´ogy**, the branch of psychology that deals with the abnormal workings of the mind; **psychopathol´ogist; psychop´athy**, extreme derangement of mental functions; **psychōs´is**, a serious mental disorder in which the personality is very seriously disorganized and contact with reality is usu. impaired.—*adj* **psychosomat´ic**, of mind and body as a unit; concerned with physical diseases that have an emotional origin.—*n* **psychother´apy**, the treatment of disease by hypnosis, psychoanalysis and similar means.—*adj* **psychot´ic**, pertaining to a psychosis.—**psychological moment**, the best, most appropriate, moment. [Gr *psychē*, the soul.]

ptarmigan [tär´mi-gan] *n* any of various grouses (genus *Lagopus*) or northern regions with completely feathered feet. [Gael *tàrmachan*.]

pterodactyl [ter-ō-dak´til] *n* an order (Pterosauria) of fossil flying reptiles with a featherless wing membrane attached to an elongated finger. [Gr *pteron*, wing, *daktylos*, finger.]

Ptolemaic [tol-e-mā´ik] *adj* pertaining to the *Ptolemies*, Greek kings of Egypt, or to *Ptolemy* the astronomer (of the 2d century AD).—**Ptolemaic system**, the theory by which Ptolemy explained the motions of the heavenly bodies on the assumption that the earth is the center of the solar system with the sun, moon, and planets revolving around it.

ptomaine [tō-mān´] *n* substances, often poisonous, formed from putrefying tissues. [Gr *ptōma*, a corpse—*piptein*, to fall.]

puberty [pū´bėr-ti] *n* the beginning of sexual maturity.—*n* **pūbescence** [-es´ėns] quality or state of being pubescent; a pubescent covering or surface.—*adj* **pūbes´cent**, arriving at or having reached puberty; of or relating to puberty; covered with fine soft short hairs; **pubic**, related to or situated near the pubis.—*n* **pubis**, the front part of the bones composing either half of the pelvis. [Fr *puberté*—L *pūbertās*—*pūbēs*, grown up.]

public [pub´lik] *adj* of, belonging to, or concerning, the people; pertaining to a community or a nation; engaged in the affairs of the community; common to, or shared in by, all; generally known; acting officially for the people.—*n* the general body of mankind; the people, indefinitely; a specified section of the community (eg *an author's public*); public view, or a public place, society, or the open.—*adv* **pub´licly**.—*ns* **publican**, a Jewish tax collector for the ancient Romans; (*Brit*) the licensee of a public house; **public assistance**, government aid to needy, blind, aged, or disabled persons and to dependent children; **publication**, public notification; the printing and distribution of books, magazines, etc.; something published as a periodical, book, etc.; **public defender**, a lawyer, usu. holding public office, whose duty is to defend accused persons unable to pay for legal assistance; **public domain**, land owned directly by the government; the condition of being free from copyright or patent; **public health**, the art and science of dealing with the protection and improvement of community health by organized effort including sanitation, social science, preventive medicine; **public house**, an inn, hostelry; (*Brit*) a licensed tavern or bar; **pub´licist**, a person whose business is publicity; **publicity**, any information or action that brings a person, cause to public notice; work concerned with such promotional matter; notice by the public.—*vt* **pub´licize´**, to give publicity to.—*ns* **public relations**, relations of a company, firm, institution, etc. with the general public as through publicity; **public school**, an elementary or secondary school maintained by public taxes and supervised by local authorities; (*Brit*) a private secondary usu. boarding school whose heads are members of an organization which includes school overseas; **public servant**, a government official or a civil-service employee; **public service**, the business of supplying a commodity (as electricity or gas) or service (as transportation) to a community; a service rendered in the public interest; governmental employment, esp civil service; **public-service corporation**, a quasi-public corporation;—*adj* having or showing zeal for the public welfare.—*ns* **public television**, television that provides cultural, instructional, etc. programs without commercials; **public utility**, a business corporation (as an electric company) performing a public service and subject to special government regulations; **public works**, works (as schools, highways, docks) constructed for public use and enjoyment, esp when financed and owned by the government.—**public-address system**, a system that enables groups of people to be addressed clearly in an auditorium or out of doors. —**in public**, openly. [L *pūblicus*—*populus*, the people.]

publish [pub´lish] *vt* to make public, to divulge; to announce formally, to proclaim; to put forth and offer for sale (as a book).—*vi* to put out an edition; to have one's work accepted for publication.—*ns* **pub´lisher**, one that published, esp a person or corporation whose business is publishing; **publishing**, the business or profession of the usu. commercial production and issuance of literature, information, musical stores, and sometimes recordings, or art. [Fr *publier*—L *pūblicāre*.]

puce [pūs] *n, adj* a dark red. [Fr *puce*—L *pūlex, -icis*, a flea.]

puck[1] [puk] *n* a goblin or mischievous sprite. [OE *pūca*; cf ON *pūki*, Ir *puca*, W *pwca*.]

puck[2] [puk] *n* a vulcanized rubber disk used in ice hockey; the ball used in field hockey.

pucker [puk´ėr] *vti* to wrinkle.—*n* a fold or wrinkle. [Prob from the same root as **poke**, a bag.]

pudding [po͝od´ing] *n* a boiled or baked soft food usu. with a cereal base; a dessert of a soft, spongy or thick, creamy consistency.—*n* **pudding´stone**, conglomerate. [ME *poding*; origin unknown.]

puddle [pud´l] *n* a small pool of water, esp stagnant, spilled, or muddy water; a mixture of clay, sand, and water and gravel that becomes watertight when dry; a thin mixture of soil and water for puddling plants.—*vt* to make a puddle or puddles; to subject (iron) to puddling; to compact (soil) when too wet to work.—*vi* to dabble in mud.—*ns* **pudd´ler; puddling**, to process of converting pig iron to wrought iron or rarely steel. [App dim of OE *pudd*, ditch.]

pueblo [pweb´lō] *n* a type of communal Indian village on the southwestern US, consisting of terraced structures, as of adobe, housing many families;—*pl* **pueblos; Pueblo**, a group of Amerindian peoples of the southwest; a member of any of these peoples. [Sp, town—L *populus*, people.]

puerile [pū´ėr-īl] *adj* juvenile; childish.—*n* **pū´erilism**, childish behavior, esp as a symptom of mental disorder. [L *puerīlis*—*puer*, a boy.]

puerperal [pū´ûr´pėr-ȧl] *adj* relating to childbirth, or the period immediately following it. [L *puerpera*, a woman in labour—*puer*, a child, *parĕre*, to bear.]

puff [puf] *vt* to blow or issue in whiffs; to pant; to swell (up, out).—*vt* to blow, smoke, etc. in or with puffs; to inflate; to praise in exaggerated terms.—*n* a sudden, forcible breath; a gust or whiff.a light pastry—*ns* **puff´adder**, a harmless stout-bodied N American snake (*Heterodon platyrhinos*) found in sandy gardens and sunny roadsides.—Also **hognose snake**.—**puff´ball**, a round, white-fleshed often edible fungus (class Basidiomycetes) that discharges ripe spores in a smokelike cloud when touched; **puff´er**, one that puffs; any of a family (Tetraodontidæ) of usu. highly poisonous marine tropical fish which can assume a globular form; any of various spiny-finned fish or the same order (Plectognathi) as the puffers; **puff´ery**, exaggerated commendation, esp for purpose of promotion.—*adj* **puff´y**, puffed out with air or any soft matter; swollen; out of breath.—*adv* **puff´ily**.—*ns* **puff´iness; puff´ paste**, a rich dough containing many alternating layers of butter and flour paste used for making light flaky pastries. [OE *pyffan*; cf Ger *puffen*, etc.]

puffin [puf´in] *n* any of several seabirds (genera *Fratercula* and *Lunda*) having a short neck and a parti-colored laterally compressed bill.

pug[1] [pug] *n* a breed of small, short-haired dog with a snub nose; a pug nose; a close coil of hair.—*n* **pug´ nose**, a nose having a slightly concave bridge and flattened nostrils.

pug[2] [pug] *vt* to work and mix (as clay) when wet, esp to make more homogenous and easier to handle (as in throwing or molding wares, making clay figures, etc.); to line or pack with sawdust, plaster, etc., put between floors to deaden sound. [Origin unknown.]

pug[3] [pug] *n* a footprint, esp of a wild animal. [Hindi *pag*, foot.]

pugilism [pū´jil-izm] *n* the sport of boxing.—*ns* **pug, pū´gilist**, one who fights with his fists.—*adj* **pūgilist´ic**. [L *pugil*, a boxer.]

pugnacious [pug-nā´shůs] *adj* fond of fighting, combative, quarrelsome.—*adv* **pugnā´ciously**.—*n* **pugnacity** [-nas´-]. [L *pugnax, -ācis*, fond of fighting—*pugnāre*, to fight.]

puissant [pwis´ȧnt, pū´is-ȧnt] *adj* powerful.—*n* **puiss´ance**, power; strength.—*adv* **puiss´antly**. [Fr, apparently from a vulgar Latin substitute for L *potens*, powerful.]

puke [pūk] *vti* (*inf*) to vomit. [Perh conn with Flemish *spukken*, Ger *spucken*.]

pukka [puk´a] *adj* first-rate; genuine, real. [Hindustani *pakkā*, ripe.]

pulchritude [pul´kri-tūd] *n* beauty.—*adj* **pulchritud´inous**. [L *pulchritudiō, -inis*—*pulcher*, beautiful.]

pule [pūl] *vi* to whimper or whine as a sick or fretful child.—*n* **pū´ler**. [Imit; cf Fr *piauler*.]

Pulitzer Prize [po͝o´litsėr] *n* any of the annual prizes awarded for achievement in American journalism, letters, and music. [Joseph *Pulitzer*, whose will established them.]

pull [po͝ol] *vt* to pluck, to cull; to move, or try or tend to move, towards oneself (or in a direction so thought of); to draw; to drag; to attract; to extract; to rip; to tear; to strain (a muscle); (*inf*) to carry out, perform; (*inf*) to restrain; (*inf*) to draw out (a gun, etc.).—*vi* to perform the action of pulling anything; to be capable of being pulled; to move (away, ahead, etc.).—*n* the act of pulling; a pulling force; a struggle or effort; an apparatus for pulling; (*inf*) influence; (*inf*) drawing power.—*n* **pull´over**, a jersey, a jumper, a body garment put on over the head.—**pull a fast one** (*inf*), to take advantage of by fraud or a trick; **pull down**, to take down or apart; to demolish; *inf* to draw as wages or salary **pull for** (*inf*) to cheer on; **pull off** (*inf*) to gain or achieve by effort; **pull oneself together**, to regain one's self-control; to collect oneself, preparing to think or act; **pull out**, to abandon a place or situation which has become too difficult to cope with; **pull through** (*inf*) to get safely to the end of a difficult or dangerous experience; **pull up**, to bring to a stop; to move ahead. [OE *pullian*, to pluck, draw.]

pullet [po͝ol´et] *n* a young hen. [Fr *poulette*, dim of *poule*, a hen—Low L *pulla*, a hen, fem of L *pullus*, a young animal.]

pulley [po͝ol´i] *n* a wheel turning about on axis, and having a groove on its rim in which runs a rope, chain, or band, used for raising weights, changing direction of pull, etc.;—*pl* **pull´eys**. [ME *poley, puly*—OFr *polie*.]

Pullman [po͝ol´mȧn] *n* a railroad car with private compartments or berths for sleeping.—Also **Pullman car**; a large suitcase.—Also **Pullman case**. [George M *Pullman* (1831–97), US inventor.]

pulmonary [pul´mȯn-ȧr-i] *adj* pertaining to, or affecting, the lungs. [L *pulmōnārius*—*pulmō, pulmōnis*, a lung.]

pulp [pulp] *n* a soft, moist, sticky mass; the soft, juicy part of a fruit or soft pith of a plant stem; the sensitive substances under the dentine of a tooth; ground-up, moistened fibers of wood, rags, etc. used to make paper; a book or magazine printed on cheap paper (as newsprint) and often dealing with sensational material.—*vi* to become pulp or pulpy.—*vt* to reduce to pulp; to deprive of pulp; to produce or reproduce (written matter) in pulp form.—*adj* **pulp´y**.—*n* **pulp´iness**. [L *pulpa*, flesh, pulp.]

pulpit [po͝ol´pit] *n* a raised structure, esp in a church, occupied by a preacher; preachers or preaching collectively.—*adj* belonging to the pulpit. [L *pulpitum*, a stage.]

pulsar [pul´sär] *n* any of several small heavenly objects on the Milky Way that emit radio pulses at regular intervals.

pulsate [pul´sāt] *vi* to beat or throb rhythmically; to vibrate, quiver.—*n* **pulsā´tion**.—*adj* **pul´satile**, marked by pulsation. [L *pulsāre, -ātum*, to beat, freq of *pellĕre, pulsum*, to drive.]

pulse[1] [puls] *n* a measured beat or throb; the beating in the arteries; an underlying opinion or sentiment of an indiction of it; (*radio*) a signal of very short duration.—*vt* to drive by pulsation; to produce or cause to be emitted, in the form of pulses.—*vi* to throb. [L *pulsus pellĕre, pulsum*, to drive.]

pulse[2] [puls] *n* the edible seed of beans, peas, and other leguminous plants; the plants bearing them. [L *puls*, porridge; cf Gr *poltos*, and **poultice**.]

pulverize [pul´vėr-īz] *vt* to reduce to dust or fine powder.—*adj* **pul´verizeable**.—*ns* **pulverizā´tion; pul´verizer**, one who pulverizes; a machine for pulverizing. [L *pulvis, pulveris*, powder.]

puma [pū´ma] *n* a cougar; the fur or pelt of a cougar. [Peruvian *puma*.]

pumice [pum´is] *n* a light, porous volcanic rock, used for removing stains, polishing, etc.—*adj* **pumiceous** [pūmish´ūs], of or like pumice. [ME *pomis*, pumice—L *pūmex, -icis—spuma*, foam.]

pummel [pum´l] *vt* to beat, pound, thump, esp repeatedly;—*pr p* **pumm´elling**; *pt p* **pumm´elled**. [**pommel**.]

pump[1] [pump] *n* a machine that forces a liquid or gas into, or draws it out of, something.—*vt* to move (fluids) with a pump; to remove water, etc.from; to drive air into with a pump; to draw out, move up and down, pour forth, etc. as a pump does; (*inf*) to draw information from (a person) by artful questions.—Also *vi*.—**pump iron**, to lift weights. [Origin obscure.]

pump[2] [pump] *n* a low-cut shoe without fastening. [Origin unknown.]

pumpkin [pum(p)´kin] *n* a large, round, orange fruit of a vine (*Curcubita pepo*) of the gourd family widely cultivated as food. [OFr *pompon*—L *pepō*—Gr *pepōn*, ripe.]

pun [pun] *vi* to play humorously upon words alike or nearly alike in sound but different in meaning;—*pr p* **punn´ing**; *pt, pt p* **punned**.—*n* a play upon words. [Origin unknown.]

punch[1] [punch] *n* a sweet drink made with fruit juices, sherbet, etc. often mixed with wine or liquor. [Traditionally from the five original ingredients—Hindi pāc, five—Sans *pañcha*.]

punch[2] [punch] *vt* to prod; to strike with a forward thrust; to stamp, pierce by a thrust of a tool (or with a machine); to drive (cattle).—*n* a vigorous thrust; striking power, vigor; a tool or machine for punching.—*n* **punch´ card**, in date processing, a card with perforations representing data.—*adj* **punch-drunk**, (of a boxer) stupefied with blows.—*ns* **punch´ line**, the last line or conclusion of a joke, in which the point lies; the last part of a story giving it meaning or an unexpected twist.—**to the punch**, to the first blow or to decisive action. [**pounce**; or shortened from **puncheon** (1); possibly in some senses for **punish**.]

puncheon[1] [pun´-sh(ȯ)n] *n* a tool for piercing or working on stone; a tool for piercing or stamping metal plates. [OFr *poinçon*—L *pungĕre, punctum*, to prick.]

puncheon[2] [pun´-sh(ȯ)n] *n* a large cask; any of various units of liquid capacity. [OFr *poinçon*, a cask.]

punctate [pungk´tāt] *adj* marked with minute spots or depressions; characterized by dots or points.—*n* **puncta´tion**. [L *punctum*, point—*pungĕre, punctum*, to prick.]

punctilio [pungk-til´i-ō, -yō] *n* a nice point in behavior or ceremony; nicety in forms; exact observance of forms;—*pl* **punctilios**.—*adj* **punctil´ious**, attentive to punctilios, scrupulous and exact.—*adv* **punctil´iously**.—*n* **punctil´iousness**. [It *puntiglio*, Sp *puntillo*, dims of *punto*—L *punctum*, a point.]

punctual [pungk´tū-ȧl] *adj* being on time; prompt.—*n* **punctual´ity**.—*adv* **punc´tually**. [LL *punctuālis—punctum*, a point.]

punctuate [pungk´tū-āt] *vt* to use certain standardized marks in (written matter) to clarify meaning; to interrupt; to emphasize.—*vi* to use punctuation marks; the act of punctuating; the state of being punctuated; a system of punctuation.—*n* **punctuā´tion, punctuation marks**, standardized symbols used in punctuation as the comma, semicolon, colon, period, etc. [LL *punctuāre, -ātum*, to prick—L *punctum*, a point.]

puncture [pungk´-chūr] *n* a small hole made with a sharp point; to make useless or ineffective as if by a puncture; to deflate.—*vi* to become punctured. [L *punctūra—pungĕre, punctum*, to prick.]

pundit [pun´dit] *n* a learned man; a critic, esp one who writes in a daily newspaper. [Hindi *pandit*—Sans *panedeita*.]

pungent [pun´jėnt] *adj* pricking or acrid to taste or smell; keen, sarcastic (eg of a comment).—*n* **pun´gency**.—*adv* **pun´gently**. [L *pengens, -entis*, pr p of *pungĕre*, to prick.]

Punic [pū´nik] *adj* of ancient Carthage; of, pertaining to, characteristic of, the Carthaginians; faithless, treacherous, deceitful (as the Romans alleged the Carthaginians to be).—*n* the Phoenician dialect of ancient Carthage. [L *Pūnicus—Poenī*, the Carthaginians.]

punish [pun´ish] *vt* to cause (a person) to suffer for an offense; to cause one to suffer for (eg *to punish one's carelessness*); to chastise; to treat severely.—*adj* **pun´ishable**, that may be punished—said both of persons and of crimes.—*n* **pun´isher**.—*adj* **pun´ishing**, causing suffering or retribution; (*inf*) severe, testing.—*n* **pun´ishment**, act or method of punishing; judical penalty imposed for an offense; severe treatment.—*adj* **punitive**, [pū´ni-tiv] pertaining to punishment; inflicting, or with the purpose of inflicting, punishment (eg measures, an expedition)—**punitive damages**, damages awarded in excess of normal compensation to the plaintiff to punish a defendant for a serious wrong. [Fr *punir, punissant*—L *pūnīre*, to punish—*poena*, penalty.]

punk[1] [punk] *n* decayed wood used as tinder; a fungous substance that smolders when ignited, used to light fireworks, etc.

punk[2] [punk] *adj* (*slang*) worthless, of poor quality;—*n* (*slang*) a young hoodlum; a young person regarded as insignificant, inexperienced, etc. **punk rock**, a form of rock music usu performed in a hostile, coarse, offensive way.

punkah [pung´kä] *n* a large mechanical fan for cooling a room. [Hindi *pākhā* fan.]

punster [pun´stėr] *n* one who makes puns. [**pun**.]

punt[1] [punt] *n* a flat-bottomed boat with square ends, usu propelled with a pole.—*vt* to propel by pushing a pole against the bottom of a river.—*n* **punter**. [OE *punt*—L *pontō*.]

punt[2] [punt] *vi* to play at a gambling game against the banker. [Fr *ponter*.]

punt[3] [punt] *n* the act of kicking a dropped football before it touches the ground.—Also *vti*

puny [pū´ni] *adj* of inferior size, strength, or importance; feeble.—*n* **pun´iness**. [*puisne*—OFr *puis*, after, *né*, born.]

pup [pup] *n* a young dog, a puppy; a young fox, seal, rat, etc.—*vi* to give birth to pups. [a shortened form of **puppy**.]

pupa [pu´pa] *n* the stage that intervenes between the larva (eg caterpillar) and the imago (eg butterfly) in the life cycle of certain insects (as a bee, moth, or beetle).—*pl* **pupae**, [pū´pē]. [L *pūpa*, a girl, a doll.]

pupil[1] [pū´pil] *n* a child or young person taught under the supervision of a teacher or tutor; one who has been taught or influenced by a famous or distinguished person.—*n* **pū´pilage, pū´pillage**, state of being a pupil; the time during which one is a pupil. [Fr *pupille*—L *pūpillus*, dim of *pūpus*, boy.]

pupil[2] [pū´pil] *n* the round opening, apparently black, in the middle of the eye through which the light passes.—*adj* **pū´pillary**. [L *pupilla*, pupil of the eye, orig the same as the preceding, from the small image to be seen in the eye.]

puppet [pup´ėt] *n* a doll or image moved by wires or hands in a show; one who acts just as another tells him.—*adj* behaving like a puppet; actuated by others.—*ns* **pupp´eteer´**, an operator, designer, of puppets; **pupp´etry**, puppets collectively; the art of producing puppet shows; **puppet show**, a dramatic performance, usu grotesque or burlesque, carried on by means of puppets. [OFr *poupette*, dim from L *pūpa*, a girl, doll.]

puppy [pup´i] *n* a young domestic dog less than a year old. [OFr *poupée*, a doll or puppet—L *pūpa*.]

purblind [pûr´blind] *adj* partly blind; lacking in vision, insight, or understanding.—*adv* **pur´blindly**.—*n* **pur´blindness**. [**pure**, (or perh OFr intensive pfx *pur-*), + **blind**.]

purchase [pûr´chȧs] *vt* to buy; to obtain by labor, danger, etc.;—*n* act of purchasing; that which is purchased; any mechanical advantage in raising or moving bodies; means of exerting force advantageously.—*adj* **pur´chasable**, that may be purchased.—*n* **pur´chaser**. [OFr *porchacier*, to seek eagerly, pursue.]

purdah [pûr´dä] *n* the seclusion of women from public observation among Muslims and some Hindus, esp in India. [Hindi and Pers *pardah*, a curtain.]

pure [pūr] *adj* clean, unsoiled; unmixed; not adulterated; free from guilt or defilement; chaste, modest; mere; that and that only; utter; abstract and theoretical; (*mus*) clear and smooth in tone; perfectly in tune; of a vowel, marked by no appreciable alteration of articulation in utterance.—*adjs* **pure-blooded, pure-blood**, of unmixed ancestry; purebred; **purebred**, bred from members of a recognized breed or strain without admixture of other blood over many generations.—*adv* **pure´ly**, chastely; unmixedly; wholly, entirely; solely.—*n* **pure´ness**. See also **purity**. [Fr *pur*—L *pūrus*, pure.]

purée [pū-rā] *n* cooked food passed through a sieve, or reduced to pulp by a blending machine; a thick soup of this. [Fr]

purfle [pûr´fl] *vt* to ornament the edge of, as with embroidery.—*n* a decorated border. [Fr *pourfiler*—L *prō*, before, *filum*, a thread.]

purge [pûrj] *vt* to purify; to cleanse of sin; to rid (a nation, party, etc.) of undesirable persons; to remove (an impurity); to clear from accusation; to evacuate (bowels).—*vi* to become pure by clarifying; to have frequent evacuations.—*n* act of purging; a medicine that purges; removing persons believed to be disloyal or treacherous to an organization, esp a political party.—*n* **purgā´tion**, the act or result of purging.—*adj* **pur´gative**, cleansing; having the power of evacuating the intestines.—*n* a medicine that evacuates.—*adj* **purgatō´rial**, pertaining to purgatory;—*n* **pur´gatory**, (*RC Church*) a place or state in which souls are after death purified from venial sins; a place or state of suffering for a time. [Fr *purger*—L *purgāre, -ātum—pūrus*, pure, *agĕre*, to do.]

purify [pū´ri-fī] *vt* to make pure; to cleanse from foreign or hurtful matter; to free from guilt or ritual uncleanness; to free from improprieties or barbarisms in language.—*vi* to become pure;—*pr p* **pu´rifying**; *pt, pt p* **pu´rified**.—*n* **purificā´tion**, act or instance of purifying.—*adj* **pū´rificātory**, tending to purify or cleanse.—*n* **pū´rifier**. [Fr *purifier*—L *pūrificāre—pūrus*, pure, *facĕre*, to make.]

Purim [pŏŏ´rim] *n* (*Judaism*) Feast of Lots commemorating the rescue of the Persian Jews from Haman's plot to exterminate them. [Heb]

purism [pūr´izm] *n* fastidious insistence upon purity of language, style, etc.—*n* **pūr´ist**. [L *pūrus*, pure.]

Puritan [pūr´i-tȧn] *n* one of a religious and political party in the 16th and 17th century England which desired greater purity and simplicity of doctrine and ceremony in the Church of England; **puritan**, a person professing strict morality in conduct and opinions.—*adj* in sympathy with the Puritans or puritans.—*adjs* **pūritan´ic, -al**.—*adv* **pūritan´ically**.—*n* **Pūr´itanism**. [L *pūrus*, pure.]

purity [pūr´i-ti] *n* condition of being pure; freedom from stain, fault, or taint; chastity. [L *pūrus*, pure.]

purl[1] [pûrl] *vi* to flow with a murmuring sound; to flow in eddies.—*n* a soft murmuring sound, as of a stream. [Cf Norw *purla*, to babble; Swed *porla*, to ripple.]

purl[2] [pûrl] *vt* to fringe with a waved edging, as lace; to knit in purl stitch.—*n* an embroidered border; knitting in purl stitch—**purl stitch**, a knitting stitch drawn through its base loop from front to back of the fabric, leaving the bight of the base loop on the front of the fabric. [Origin unknown.]

purlieu [pûr´lū] *n* borders or outskirts; *(pl)* environs, neighborhood; a frequently visited place; *(pl)* confines; bounds. [Anglo—Fr *puralee*, land severed by perambulation—OFr *pur* (L *prō*), *allee*, a going; app influenced by Fr *lieu*, place.]

purloin [pûr-loin´] *vt* to filch, steal.—*n* **purloin´er**. [Anglo-Fr *purloigner*, to remove to a distance—*pur-* (L *prō*), for, *loin* (L *longē*), far.]

purple [pûr´pl] *n* a dark, bluish red; crimson cloth or clothing, esp as a former emblem of royalty.—*adj* dark bluishred; imperial; ornate; offensively strong.—*vt* or *vi* to make or to become purple. **Purple Heart**, a US military decoration awarded to any member of the armed forces wounded or killed in action; **purple heart**, *(slang)* an amphetamine pill. [L *purpura*—Gr *porphyrā*, a shellfish yielding purple dye.]

purport [pûr´pōrt] *n* meaning conveyed; substance, gist.—*vt* [pûr-port´] to profess or claim as its meaning; to give the appearance, often falsely, of being, intending, etc. [OFr from *pur* (L *prō*), forward, *porter* (L *portāre*), to carry.]

purpose [pûr´pus] *n* the end or object towards which effort is directed; intention; function.—*vt* to intend.—*vi* to have an intention.—*adj* **pur´poseful**, directed towards, serving, a purpose; actuated by purpose, conscious of purpose, determined.—*adv* **pur´posefully**.—*adj* **pur´poseless**.—*adv* **pur´poselessly**.—*adv* **pur´posely**, with purpose; intentionally.—*adj* **pur´posive**, having an aim.—**on purpose**, intentionally. [OFr *pourpos, propos*—L *prōpositum*, a thing intended—*prō*, forward, *pōnĕre, positum*, to place. Cf **propose**.]

purr [pûr] *vti* to utter a low, murmuring sound, as a cat when pleased.—*ns* **purr; purr´ing**. [Imit]

purse [pûrs] *n* a small bag for carrying money; finances, money; a sum of money for a present or a prize; a woman's handbag.—*vt* to put into a purse; to pucker.—*adj* **purseproud**, proud of one's wealth.—*ns* **purs´er**, an official on a passenger ship, in charge of accounts, tickets, etc.; an official on an airline responsible for the comfort and welfare of the passengers. **purs´ership**.—*n pl* **purse´ strings**, financial resources. [Low L *bursa*—Gr *byrsa*, a hide.]

purslane [pûrs´lin] *n* a fleshy-leaved trailing plant (*Portulaca oleracea*) that is a common weed but sometimes eaten as a potherb or in salads. [OFr *porcelaine*—L *porcilāca, portulāca*.]

pursue [pûr-sōō´] *vt* to follow in order to overtake and capture; to seek to attain; to be engaged in; to proceed with.—*vi* to go in pursuit;—*n* **pursū´ance**, act of following, or of carrying out.—*prep* **pursū´ant**, in carrying out; in conformity with; according to.—*n* **pursū´er**, one who pursues. [Anglo-Fr *pursuer, pursiwer*—L *prōsequī, persequī*—*prō, per-*, and *sequī*, to follow.]

pursuit [pûr-s(y)ōōt´] *n* the act of pursuing; endeavor to attain; occupation, employment. [Anglo-Fr *purseute*, fem pa p of *pursuer*. See **pursue**.]

pursy [pûrs´i] *adj* short-winded, esp because of corpulence; fat.—*n* **purs´iness**. [OFr *poulsif*, broken—OFr *poulser*—L *pulsāre*, to drive.]

purulent [pū´r(y)ŏŏ-lėnt] *adj* consisting of, full of, or discharging pus.—*n* **pū´rulence**. [L *pūrulentus*—*pūs, pūris*, pus.]

purvey [pûr-vā´] *vt* to provide or supply (esp food).—*vi* to furnish provisions or meals as one's business.—*ns* **purvey´ance**, the act of purveying; that which is supplied; **purvey´or**, one whose business is to provide victuals. [Anglo-Fr *purveier*—L *prōvidēre*. See **provide**.]

purview [pûr´vū] *n* the body or enacting part of a statute; scope or extent, as of control activity, etc. [Anglo-Fr *purveu*, provided, pt p of *purveier*. See **purvey**.]

pus [pus] *n* a thick yellowish fluid exuded from infected tissues. [L *pūs, pūris*, matter; cf Gr *pyon*.]

push [pŏŏsh] *vt* to thrust or press against so as to move; to drive by pressure; to thrust (out); to advance, carry to a further point; to press forward (*with* **on**); to urge the use, sale, etc. of; *(inf)* to come near an age or number.—*vi* to make a thrust; to make an effort; to press forward.—*n* a thrust; an impulse; effort; enterprising or aggressive pertinacity; an advance against opposition; *(inf)* aggressiveness and drive.—*ns* **push´er**, one who, or that which, pushes; esp *(inf)* one that pushes illegal drugs; **push´ button**, a knob which when pressed puts on or cuts off an electric current, as for bells, etc.—*adjs* **push´ful**, energetically or aggressively enterprising; **push´ing**, pressing forward in business, enterprising, vigorous; self-assertive.—*n* **push´over** *(slang)*, an easy task; *(slang)* a person or side easily overcome; *(slang)* a person easily persuaded.—*adj* **pushpull**, of any piece of apparatus in which two electrical or electronic devices act in opposition to each other, as, eg of an amplifier in which two thermionic valves so acting serve to reduce distortion.—**push-button**, using or dependent on complex and often self-operating mechanisms that are put into operation by a simple act. [Fr *pousser*—L *pulsāre*, freq of *pellĕre, pulsum*, to beat.]

pusillanimous [pū-si-lan´i-mus] *adj* lacking firmness of mind; cowardly.—*adv* **pusillan´imously**.—*n* **pusillanim´ity**. [L *pusillanimis*—*pusillus*, very little, *animus*, mind.]

puss [pŏŏs] *n* a familiar name for a cat.—*n* **puss´y**, a dim of **puss**—also **puss´ycat**.—*vi* **puss´yfoot**, to go stealthily; to act timidly or cautiously. [Cf Du *poes*, puss; Ir and Gael *pus*, a cat.]

pustule [pus´tūl] *n* a blister or pimple containing pus.—*adjs* **pus´tūlar, pus´tūlous**. [L *pustula*.]

put [pŏŏt] *vt* to push or thrust; to cast, throw; to constrain (to a specified action), to compel to go (to); to set, lay, or deposit; to apply (to); to add (to); to bring into any state or position; to propose (a question); to express, state.—*vi* to start in motion; to go (in, out, etc.); *(naut)* to proceed, make one's way;—*pr p* **putting**; *pt, pt p* **put**.—*adj* fixed.—**put across**, to cause to be understood, accepted, etc.; **put aside** (or **by**), to reserve for later use; **put down**, to crush, repress; to write down; *(slang)* to belittle or humiliate; **put in for**, to apply for; **put it** (or **something**) **over on** *(inf)*, to deceive, trick; **put off**, to delay, postpone; to evade; to divert; **put on**, to clothe oneself with; to pretend; to stage (a play, etc.); *(slang)* to hoax; **put out**, to expel, dismiss; to extinguish (a fire or light); to inconvenience; *(baseball)* to retire a batter or runner; **put the arm on** or **put the bite on**, to ask for money; **put through**, to carry out; to cause to do or undergo; **put up**, to offer; to preserve (fruits, etc.); to build; to provide lodgings for; to provide (money); to arrange (the hair) with curlers; etc.; *(inf)* to incite to some action; **put up with**, to tolerate. [ME *puten*; cf Dan *putte*, Swed *putta*.]

putative [pū´ta-tiv] *adj* supposed, reputed. [L *putātīvus*—*putāre, -ātum*, to suppose.]

putrefy [pū´tre-fī] *vti* to make or become putrid.—*vi* to rot;—*pt, pt p* **pu´trefied**.—*n* **putrefac´tion**, rotting.—*adjs* **putrefac´tive; putres´cent** [-tres´ėnt], rotting.—*n* **putres´cence** [-tres´ėns], rottenness.—*adj* **pū´trid**, rotten and foul-smelling.—*ns* **pūtrid´ity**. [L *putrefacĕre, putrescĕre, putridus*—*puter, putris*, rotten.]

putsch [pŏŏch] *n* a secretly plotted sudden revolutionary outbreak. [Swiss Ger dialect.]

putt [put] *vti* to hit (a ball) with a putt;—*pr p* **putt´ing** [put´-]; *pt, pt p* **putt´ed**.—*n* *(golf)* a gentle stroke intended to make the ball roll into the hole.—*n* **putt´er** *(golf)* a straightfaced club used in putting. [A Scottish form of **put**.]

puttee [put´i] *n* a cloth strip wound round the legs from ankle to knee, as a legging; a usu. leather legging secured by laces or a strap or catch. [Hindi *paṭṭī*.]

putter [put´ėr] *vi* to busy oneself in an aimless way (with along, around, etc.).—*vt* to fritter (away).

putty [put´i] *n* a soft, plastic mixture of powdered chalk and linseed oil, used to fill small cracks, etc.—*vt* to fix or fill with putty;—*pt, pt p* **putt´ied**. [Fr *potée*, potful—*pot*.]

puzzle [puz´l] *vt* to bewilder; to perplex.—*vi* to be perplexed; to exercise one's mind, as over a problem.—*n* perplexity; a cause of perplexity; a toy or problem for testing skill or ingenuity.—*ns* **puzz´lement, puzz´ler**.—*adj* **puzzling**, baffling, perplexing.—**puzzle out**, to discover, by persevering mental effort. [Ety obscure.]

pyemia [pī-ē´mi-a] *n* a poisoning of the blood by bacteria from a part of the body that has become septic, resulting in the formation of abscesses in other parts. [Gr *pyon*, pus, *haima*, blood.]

pye-dog [pī-dog] *n* an ownerless or pariah dog, common in Asian villages. [From Hindi *pāhī*, outsider.]

Pygmy, Pigmy [pig´mi] *n* any of a small people of equatorial Africa ranging under five feet in height; any of a race of dwarfs described by ancient Greek authors;—*pl* **Pygmies; pygmy**, a short, insignificant person; a dwarf.—*adj* **pig´moid**, resembling or having the characteristics of Pygmies. [Gr *pygmaios*, measuring a *pygmē* (13½ inches, distance from elbow to knuckles).]

pylon [pī´lon] *n* a gateway to an Egyptian temple; a towerlike structure supporting electric lines, marking a flight course, etc. [Gr *pylōn*—*pylē*, a gate.]

pylorus [pi-lō´rus] *n* the lower opening from the stomach to the duodenum.—*adj* **pylor´ic**. [L,—Gr *pylōros*—*pylē*, an entrance, *ouros*, a guardian.]

pyorrhoea [pī-ō-rē´a] *n* an infection of the gums and tooth suckers, with formation of pus. [Gr *pyon*, pus, *rheein*, to flow.]

pyramid [pir´a-mid] *n* a three-dimensional geometric figure having a polygon as base, and whose sides are triangles sharing a common vertex; a huge structure with a square base and four triangular sides meeting at the top, as a royal tomb of ancient Egypt; an immaterial structure built on a broad supporting base and narrowing gradually to an apex (eg the socio-economic pyramid).—*vti* to speculate (as on a commodity exchange) by using paper profits as margin for additional transactions; to build up as in a pyramid.—*vt* to use (as profits) in speculative pyramiding; to increase the impact of price to the consumer by treating an assessed tax as a cost subject to markup.—*adjs* **pyram´idal, pyramid´ical**, having the form of a pyramid.—*adv* **pyram´idally**. [Gr *pyramis, -idos*.]

pyre [pīr] *n* a pile of wood, etc., for burning a dead body. [L *pyra*—Gr *pyr*, fire.]

pyretic [pī-ret´ik] *adj* of, of the nature of, fever.—*n* **pyrex´ia**, fever. [Gr *pȳretikos—pȳretos*, fever—*pȳr*, fire.]

Pyrex [pī´reks] *n* a registered trademark applied to glassware resistant to heat. [Gr *pȳr*, fire, and L *rex*, king.]

pyrexia *See* **pyretic**.

pyrites [pīr-ī´tēz] *n* a yellow mineral compound of iron and sulphur (also **iron pyrites**), so called because it strikes fire like a flint; extended to a large class of mineral compounds of metals with sulphur or arsenic.—*adjs* **pyrit´ic, -al**. [Gr *pȳritēs—pȳr*, fire.]

pyro- [pīr-o-] in composition, fire; also (*chem*) obtained by, or as if by, heating. [Gr *pȳr*, fire]; **pyrogenic** [-jen´-], **pyrogenetic** [-jėn-et´ik], *adjs* produced by or producing fire or fever (see **genetic**).

pyroelectricity [pī-rō-el-ek-tris´i-ti] *n* a state of electric polarization produced (as in a crystal) by a change of temperature. [Gr *pȳr*, fire, + **electricity**.]

pyrolysis [pī-rol´is-is] *n* chemical change brought about by the action of heat. [Gr *pȳr*, fire, *lysis*, loosing—*lyein*, to loose.]

pyrometer [pī-rom´ė-tėr] *n* an instrument for measuring temperatures, esp when beyond the range of mercurial thermometers.—*adjs* **pyromet´ric, -al**. [Gr *pȳr*, fire, *metron*, a measure.]

pyrotechnics [pī-rō-tek´niks] *n* a display of fireworks; showy display in talk, music, etc.—*adjs* **pyrotech´nic, -al**. [Gr *pȳr*, fire, *technikos*, skilled—*technē*, art.]

Pyrrhic victory [pir´ik vik´tȯr-i] a victory gained at too great a cost, such as those gained (esp 279 BC) by King *Pyrrhus* of Epirus (Greece) over the Romans.

Pythagorean [pī-thag-ȯ-rē´ȧn] *adj* pertaining to *Pythagoras* (6th cent BC), a celebrated Greek philosopher, or to his philosophy.—*n* a follower of Pythagoras.

Pythian [pith´i-ȧn] *adj* pertaining to the *Pythia* or priestess of Apollo at Delphi, or to the Delphic oracles, or to the national games held there.—*n* **Pythiad**, the 4-year period between the celebrations of the Pythian games in ancient Greece.

python [pī´thȯn] *n* a large, nonpoisonous snake that kills by constriction (as a boa or anaconda); any of a genus (*Python*) that includes the largest of living snakes.—*n* **py´thoness**, the priestess of the oracle of Apollo at Delphi; a witch. [Gr *pȳthōn*, a great snake killed by Apollo at Delphi.]

pyx [piks] *n* a box; (*RC*) a vessel in which the host is kept after consecration, now usu. that in which it is carried to the sick; a box used in a mint containing sample coins for testing. [L *pȳxis*, a box—Gr *pȳxis—pȳxos*, a box-tree.]

Q

quack[1] [kwak] *n* the cry of a duck.—*vi* to make such a sound. [Imit.]

quack[2] [kwak] *n* a shortened form of **quack´salver**, a charlatan, an untrained person who practices medicine fraudulently; one who pretends to have knowledge and skill he does not have.—Also *adj*—*ns* **quack´ery**, the pretensions or practice of a quack, esp in medicine; **quack´salver**. [Du *quacksalver* (now *kwakzalver*).]

quack grass [kwak] *n* a European grass (*Agropyron repens*) that is naturalized throughout N America as a weed and spreads very rapidly by means of trailing underground stems.—Also **quick grass, twitch grass, witch grass**.

quad [kwod] *n* quadrangle; quadruplet. [Clipped form.]

quadrangle [kwod´rang-gl] *n* (*geom*) a plane figure with four angles (and therefore four sides); an object or space of that form; an open space, usu rectangular, enclosed by buildings.—*adj* **quadrang´ular**. [Fr—L *quadrangulum*—*quattuor*, four, *angulus*, an angle.]

quadrant [kwod´rȧnt] *n* (*geom*) the fourth part of the circumference of a circle, an arc of 90°; a sector bounded by a quadrant and two radii, the fourth part of the area of a circle; any of the four regions marked off on a surface by rectangular axes; an instrument with an arc of 90° for taking altitudes in astronomy and navigation. [L *quadrāns, -antis*, a fourth part—*quattuor*, four.]

quadraphonic [kwod-rȧ-fon´ik] *adj* using four channels to record and reproduce sound. [**quadri-**, + **phonics**.]

quadrate [kwod´rāt] *adj* square or nearly square; of a bony or cartilaginous element of each side of the skull to which the lower jaw is articulated in most vertebrates below mammals.—*n* an almost square or cubical area, space or body; a quadrate bone.—*adj* **quadrat´ic**, involving terms of the second degree at most.—*ns* **quadratic equation**, an equation in which the highest power of the unknown is the second degree (square).—*n* **quad´rature**, the finding of a square equal to a given figure of some other shape; an angular distance of 90°; the position of a heavenly body at such an angular distance from another, or the time of its being there. [L *quadrātus*, pt p of *quadrāre*, to square—*quattuor*, four.]

quadrennial [kwod-ren´yȧl] *adj* lasting four years; once in four years.—*adv* **quadrenn´ially**. [L *quadrennis*—*quattuor*, four, *annus*, a year.]

quadri- [kwod-ri-] in composition, of or with four, as in **quadriplēgia**, *n* paralysis of all four limbs; **quadrisyllable**, *n* a word of four syllables.—*adj* **quadrivālent** (*chem*), having four valencies. [L *quadri*—*quattuor*, four.]

quadrilateral [kwod-ri-lat´ėr-ȧl] *adj* four-sided.—*n* (*geom*) a plane figure bounded by four lines; a combination or group that involves four parts or individuals. [L *quadrilaterus*—*quattuor*, four, *latus, lateris*, a side.]

quadrille [kwȯ-dril´, or kȧ-] *n* a square dance for four couples; music for such a dance. [Fr,—Sp *cuadrilla*, a troop, app—L *quadra*, a square.]

quadrillion [kwod-ril´yȯn] *n* in the US, a number represented as one followed by 15 zeros (10^{15}); in Britain, France, and Germany, one followed by 24 zeros (10^{24}). [Modelled on **million**—L *quarter*, four times.]

quadrivium [kwod-riv´i-um] *n* in medieval times, the more advanced part of the university course of seven liberal arts, namely, the four subjects of arithmetic, music, geometry and astronomy. [L crossroads.]

quadroon [kwod-rōōn] *n* one whose blood is one-quarter Negro. [Sp *cuarterón*—*cuarto*, a fourth.]

quadrumanous [kwod-rōō´mȧn-us] *adj* of, related to, or being the primates, excepting man, which are distinguished by hand-shaped feet. [L *quatuor*, four, *manus*, a hand.]

quadruped [kwod´rŏŏ-ped] *n* a four-footed animal. [L *quattuor*, four, *pēs, pedis*, a foot.]

quadruple [kwod´rŏŏ-pl] *adj* four times as much or as many; consisting of four; having four parts or divisions.—*vti* to make or become four times as much or as many.—*n* **quad´ruplet**, a set of four things, usu of one kind; one of four born at a birth [also kwod-rōō´plet]. [L *quadruplus*—*quattuor*, four.]

quadruplicate [kwod-rŏŏ-pli-kȧt] *adj* fourfold; being the last of four identical copies.—*vt* to make four such copies of.—**in quadruplicate**, in four identical copies. [L *quadruplex, -icis*, fourfold—*quattuor*, four, *plicāre, -ātum*, to fold.]

quaestor [kwēs´tȯr] *n* a Roman magistrate with financial responsibilities. [L—*quaerĕre, quaesitum*, to seek.]

quaff [kwäf, kwof] *vti* to drink (a beverage) deeply.—*n* **quaff´er**. [Origin obscure.]

quag [kwag] *n* a marsh, a bog.

quagga [kwag´a] *n* an extinct wild ass (*Equus quagga*), of southern Africa related to the zebra. [Hottentot.]

quagmire [kwag´mīr] *n* wet, muddy ground.

quahog, quahaug [kō´hȯg or kwȯ´-, or kwō-, or -häg´] *n* a thick-shelled American clam (*Mercenaria mercenaria*).—Also **hard-shell clam, littleneck clam**. [Amer Indian.]

Quai d'Orsay [kā dör-sā] the French Foreign Office. [Name of a quay on the Seine faced by the French Ministry of Foreign Affairs.]

quail[1] [kwāl] *vi* to cower, to flinch. [ME *quayle*.]

quail[2] [kwāl] *n* any of various small American game birds (family Perdicidae). [OFr *quaille*; prob Gmc.]

quaint [kwānt] *adj* odd, whimsical (eg *a quaint conceit*); pleasantly odd or strange, esp because old-fashioned.—*adv* **quaint´ly**.—*n* **quaint´ness**. [OFr *cointe*—L *cognitus*, known.]

quake [kwāk] *vi* to tremble, esp with cold or fear; to quiver;—*pr p* **quā´king**; *pt, pt p* **quāked**.—*n* a shaking or tremor; an earthquake. [OE *cwacian*.]

Quaker [kwā´kėr] *n* a popular name for a member of the Society of Friends, founded by George Fox (1624–91).—*ns* **Quā´kerism**, the tenets of the Quakers; **Quaker gun**, a dummy piece of artillery, usu made of wood. [The nickname Quakers was given them because Fox bade a judge before whom he was summoned *quake*, at the word of the Lord.]

qualify [kwol´i-fī] *vt* to ascribe a quality to (eg *an adjective qualifies a noun*); to describe (as—eg *he qualified his rival's action as dishonest*); to render capable or suitable; to furnish with legal power; to limit by modifications (eg *he now qualified his first statement; qualified approval*); to mitigate.—*vi* to prove oneself fit for a certain position, or activity; to reach an accepted standard of attainment, esp academic;—*pr p* **qual´ifying**; *pt, pt p* **qual´ified**.—*ns* **qualificā´tion**, that which qualifies; a quality or attainment that fits a person for a place, etc.; limitation; **qual´ifier**, one that qualifies; an adjective or adverb. [Fr,—Low L *quālificāre*—L *quālis*, of what sort, *facĕre*, to make.]

quality [kwol´i-ti] *n* that which makes a thing what it is, nature; kind or degree of goodness or worth; attribute; degree of excellence; excellence; (*logic*) the character of a proposition as affirmative or negative.—*adj* of high quality.—*adj* **qual´itātive**, relating to quality.—**qualitative analysis**, chemical analysis designed to identify the components of a substance or mixture; **quality circle**, any of the small group of workers that meet regularly to suggest improvements in production. [OFr *qualité*—L *quālitās, -ātis*—*quālis*, of what kind.]

qualm [kwäm] *n* a sudden sensation of faintness or sickness; a doubt; a misgiving; an uneasiness, as of conscience.

quandary [kwon´dȧ-rē] *n* a state of perplexity; a predicament; a dilemma.

quantity [kwon´ti-ti] *n* an amount that can be counted or measured; an indefinite amount; a large amount; (*pl*) a great amount; that property by which a thing can be measured; a number or symbol expressing this property; the length or shortness of the duration of a sound or syllable; (*logic*) the character of a proposition as universal, particular, or singular.—*adj* **quan´titātive**, measurable in quantity; (*chem*) determining the relative proportions of components.—**quantitative analysis**, chemical analysis designed to determine the amounts or proportions of the components of a substance. [OFr *quantité*—L *quantitās, -ātis*—*quantus*, how much.]

quantum [kwon´tum] *n* quantity; amount; a fixed, elemental unit of energy.—*pl* **quan´ta**.—*adj* large, significant.—**quantum jump, quantum leap**, an abrupt transition (as of an electron, an atom, or a molecule) from one discrete energy state to another; an abrupt change, sudden increase, or dramatic advance; **quantum mechanics**, a general mathematical theory dealing with the interactions of matter and radiation in terms of observable quantities only; **quantum number**, any of a set of integers or half-integers which together describe the state of a particle or system of particles; **quantum theory**, a theory in physics stating that energy is radiated discontinuously in quanta. [L *quantum*, neut of *quantus*, how great.]

quarantine [kwor´ȧn-tēn] *n* a period (orig for a ship forty days) of compulsory isolation or detention to prevent contagion or infection; isolation or detention for such a purpose; the place in which the period is spent.—*vt* to put in quarantine. [It *quarantina*—*quaranta*, forty—L *quadrāgintā*, forty—*quattuor*, four.]

quarrel[1] [kwor´ėl] *n* a square-headed arrow for a crossbow. [OFr,—Low L *quadrellus*—*quadrus*, a square—L *quattuor*, four.]

quarrel[2] [kwor´ėl] *n* a dispute; a breach of friendship; a ground of dispute.—*vi* to dispute violently; to disagree; to find fault (with);—*pr p* **quarr´elling**; *pt, pt p* **quarr´elled**.—*n* **quarr´eller**.—*adj* **quarr´elsome**, disposed to quarrel.—*n* **quarr´elsomeness**. [OFr *querele*—L *querēla*—*querī, questus*, to complain.]

quarry[1] [kwor´i] *n* an excavation from which stone is taken, by cutting, blasting, etc.—*vt* to excavate from a quarry; to cut into or cut away.—*vi* to make, or dig in, a quarry;—*pr p* **quarr´ying**; *pt, pt p* **quarr´ied**.—*ns* **quarrier**, a worker in a stone quarry; **quarr´yman**, a quarrier. [LL *quareia*, for *quadrāria*—L *quadrāre*, to square.]

quarry[2] [kwor´i] *n* (*obs*) a deer's entrails given to the dogs after the chase; a hunted animal; esp game hunted with hawks; a prey, victim. [OFr *cuirée, curée—cuir*—L *corium*, hide.]

quart [kwört] *n* a liquid measure, equal to ¼ gallon; a dry measure, equal to 1/8 peck. [Fr *quarte*—L *quartus*, fourth—*quattuor*, fourth.]

quartan [kwör´tȧn] *adj* occurring every third day or recurring at 72-hour intervals. [Fr *quartaine*—L *quārtānus*, of the fourth.]

quarter [kwör´ter] *n* a fourth of something; one fourth of a year; one fourth of an hour; one fourth of a dollar; 25 cents, or a coin of this value; any leg of a four-legged animal with the adjoining parts; a certain district or section; (*pl*) lodgings; a particular source; an unspecified person or group; a compass point other than the cardinal points; mercy.—*vt* to divide into four equal parts; to divide (a human body) into four parts; to provide with lodging or shelter; to separate into fewer or more than four parts; to crisscross (an area) in many directions.—*vi* to lodge, dwell; to crisscross a district.—*adj* constituting a quarter.—*n* **quar´tering** (*her*), the bearing of two or more coats-of-arms on a shield divided by horizontal and perpendicular lines; one of the divisions so formed.—*adj* **quar´terly**, computed for or payable at 3-month intervals; recurring, issued, or spaced at 3-month intervals; divided into heraldic quarters or compartments.—*adv* once a quarter; (*her*) in quarters or quarterings.—*n* a periodical published four times a year.—*n* **quar´terback´** (*football*), the back who calls the signals.—*adj* **quar´ter-bound**, of a book, bound in two materials, of two qualities with the better quality material on the back only.—*ns* **quar´terdeck**, the stern area of a ship's upper deck; a part of a deck on a naval vessel set aside by the captain for ceremonial and official use.—*adj* **quarterfinal**, coming just before the semifinals in a tournament.—*ns* **quarterfinal**, a quarterfinal match; **quarter horse**, any of a breed of thickset, muscular horse capable of sprinting speed up to ¼ mile; **quar´termaster** (*mil*), an officer who looks after the quarters of the soldiers, and attends to the supplies; (*naut*) a petty officer who attends to the helm, signals, etc.; **quarter note** (*mus*), a note having one fourth the duration of a whole note; **quarter section**, a tract of land that is half a mile square and contains 160 acres in the US government system of land surveying.—**at close quarters**, very near; hand to hand. [OFr *quarter*—L *quartārius*, a fourth part—*quārtus*, fourth.]

quartern [kwör´tėrn] *n* a fourth part. [Anglo-Fr *quartrun*, OFr *quarteron—quart(e)*, fourth part.]

quartet, quartette [kwör-tet´] *n* a set of four; a composition for four voices or instruments; a set of performers for such compositions; a group of four persons or things. [It *quartetto*, dim—*quarto*—L *quārtus*, fourth.]

quarto [kwör´tō] *n* the page size (about 9 by 12 in) of a book made up of sheets each of which is folded twice to form four leaves, or eight pages; a book of this size of page. [L (*in*) *quarto*, (in) one-fourth.]

quartz [kwörts] *n* a crystalline mineral, a form of silica, usu. colorless and transparent.—*adj* **quart´zose.—quartz glass**, vitreous silica prepared from pure quartz and noted for its transparency to ultraviolet radiation. [Ger.]

quasar [kwā´sar] *n* a distant, starlike, celestial object that emits much light and powerful radio waves.

quash [kwosh] *vt* to crush; to annul. [OFr *quasser* (Fr *casser*)—L *quassāre*, inten of *quatĕre*, to shake.]

quasi [kwā´sī, kwä´sē] *adv* as if; in composition, **quasi-**, in a certain manner or sense; in appearance only, as *quasihistorical*, etc. [L.]

quassia [kwosh´(y)a] *n* a drug from the heartwood of various tropical trees (family Simaroubaceae) used as a bitter tonic, a remedy for roundworms, and an insecticide. [Named from *Quassi*, a Negro, who used it against fever.]

quatercentenary [kwot-er-sen-ten´ȧr-i, -sen´tin-ȧr-i] *n* a 400th anniversary. [L *quater*, four times, + **centenary**.]

quaternary [kwo-tûr´nȧr-i] *adj* consisting of four; by fours; **Quater´nary**, pertaining to the geological era which followed the Tertiary and includes the present time and the corresponding system of rocks.—*n* a member of a group fourth in rank;—*pl* **quaternaries; Quater´nary**, the Quaternary era.—*n* **quater´nion**, a set or group of four. [L *quaternī*, four by four.]

quatrain [kwot´rān] *n* a stanza or poem of four lines. [Fr.]

quattrocento [kwät-rō-chen´tō] *n* the 15th century in Italian art and literature. [It 'four-hundred', used for dates beginning with fourteen hundred.]

quaver [kwā´vėr] *vi* to speak or sing with tremulous modulations.—*n* a trembling, esp of the voice. [Frequentative—obs or dial *quave*, ME *cwavien*, to shake; akin to **quake**.]

quay [kē] *n* a wharf for the loading or unloading of vessels.—*n* **quay´age**, payment for use of a quay; provision or space of quays. [OFr *kay, cay*, perh Celtic; assimilated to mod Fr spelling *quai*.]

quean [kwēn] *n* a prostitute. [OE *cwene*, woman; cf **queen** (OE *cwēn*).]

queasy, quezy [kwē´zi] *adj* sick, squeamish; over-fastidious; causing nausea.—*adv* **quea´sily**.—*n* **quea´siness**. [Perh OFr *coisier*, to hurt; or ON *kveisa*, a boil.]

Quebec [kwė-bek´ or ki-] communications code word for the letter *q*.

quebracho [kā-brä´chō] *n* the name of several S American trees as one (*Aspidosperma quebracho*) occurring in Argentina and Chile, and another (*Schinopsis lorentzii*) of Argentina, yielding very hard wood. [Sp *quebrar*, to break, *hacha*, axe.]

Quechua [ke´chōō-ȧ or kė-chū-ȧ] *n* the language of the Quechua people widely spoken by other peoples in Peru, Bolivia, Ecuador, Chile, and Argentina; language family comprising Quechua; an Indian people of central Peru; the peoples forming the dominant element of the Inca Empire.

queen [kwēn] *n* the wife of a king; a female monarch; a woman, or anything, of surpassing beauty, excellence, etc.; the sexually functional (egg-laying) female of bees and other social insects; a playing card with a picture of a queen; (*chess*) the most powerful piece.—*vt* to promote (a pawn) to a queen in chess.—*vi* to act like a queen, esp to put on airs (*usu. with* **it**).—*adj* **Queen Anne**, of architecture, furniture and silverware in the reign of Queen Anne of England (1702–14); of an American architectural style of the late 19th century combining many materials and styles.—*ns* **Queen Anne's Lace**, wild carrot; **queen´ con´sort**, the wife of a reigning sovereign.—*adj* **queen´ly**, like a queen; becoming or suitable to a queen.—*ns* **queen´mother**, a queen dowager who is the mother of the reigning king or queen; **queen´ reg´nant**, a queen reigning as monarch. [OE *cwēn*.]

queer [kwēr] *adj* odd, strange; (*inf*) eccentric; arousing suspicion; sick or faint (eg *to feel queer*).—*n* (*slang*) a strange person.—*vt* (*slang*) to spoil the success of.—*adv* **queer´ly**.—*n* **queer´ness**. [Perh Ger *quer*, across.]

quell [kwel] *vt* to subdue; to quiet; to allay.—*n* **quell´er**. [OE *cwellan*, to kill, causal of *cwelan*, to die.]

quench [kwench] *vt* to put out, extinguish, as a flame; to cool; to slake (thirst); to subdue, suppress (eg enthusiasm); to cool (hot steel, etc.) suddenly by plunging into water, etc.—*vi* to become extinguished; to become calm.—*adjs* **quench´able; quench´less**, unquenchable. [OE *cwencan*, found only in *ācwencan*, to quench.]

querist [kwe´rist] *n* one who enquires. [**query**.]

quern [kwûrn] *n* a primitive stone handmill for grinding grain. [OE *cwyrn, cweorn*; ON *kwern*.]

querulous [kwer´ū-lu̇s, -ŏŏ-lu̇s] *adj* complaining, peevish.—*adv* **quer´ulously**.—*n* **quer´ulousness**. [Low L *querulōsus*—L *querī*, to complain.]

query [kwē´ri] *n* a question; a question mark; doubt.—*vti* to question;—*pt, pt p* **quē´ried**. [L *quaere*, imper of *quaerĕre, quaesītum*, to seek, ask.]

quest [kwest] *n* the act of seeking; a journey for adventure.—*vt* to search for; to ask for.—*vi* (of a dog) to search a trail; to go on a quest. [OFr *queste*—L (*rēs*) *quaesīta*, a thing sought—*quaerĕre, quaesitum*, to seek.]

question [kwes´ch(ȯ)n] *n* an enquiry; an interrogative sentence; a problem; a subject of doubt or controversy; a point being debated before an assembly; an individual part of a test of knowledge.—*vt* to ask questions of; to interrogate intensively; to dispute; to subject to analysis.—*vi* to ask questions.—*adj* **quest´ionable**, doubtful; suspicious; morally unjustifiable.—*n* **quest´ionableness**.—*adv* **quest´ionably**.—*ns* **quest´ion mark**, a mark of punctuation (?) put after a sentence or word to indicate a direct question, or to express doubt, uncertainty, etc.; something unknown, unknowable, or uncertain; **questionnaire** [kwes-tyȯn-ār], a prepared set of written questions to obtain statistically useful or personal information from individuals; a survey made by the use of a questionnaire.—**in question**, under consideration; in dispute, open to question; **out of the question**, not to be regarded as feasible. [OFr,—L *quaestiō, -ōnis—quaerĕre*, to ask.]

queue [kū] *n* a pendent braid of hair at the back of the head, a pigtail; stored computer data or programs waiting to be processed. [Fr,—L *cauda*, a tail.]

quibble [kwib´l] *n* an evasive turning away from the point in question; a minor objection or criticism.—*vi* to evade a question by caviling about words.—*n* **quibb´ler**. [Perh dim of obs *quib*, quibble; or a variant of *quip*.]

quiche [kēsh] *n* a shell of unsweetened pastry filled with egg custard, cheese, etc. [Fr.]

quick [kwik] *adj* speedy; nimble; readily responsive; prompt in perception, learning, or repartee; hasty.—*adv* in a quick manner.—*n* the living (in **the quick and the dead**); the sensitive area of flesh lying under a fingernail or toenail; the inmost sensibilities.—*adv* **quick´ly**.—*vt* **quick´en**, to make alive; to invigorate, reinvigorate; to sharpen; to accelerate.—*vi* to come to life, esp to enter into a phase of active growth and development (as the stage when fetal motion is felt).—*ns* **quick´ener**.—**quick assets**, cash, accounts receivable, and other current assets excluding inventory; **quick bread**, any biscuit, bread, cake, doughnut, pancake, or waffle leavened with baking powder.—*vt* **quick-freeze**, to freeze (food) rapidly enough so that the ice crystals formed are too small to rupture cells.—*ns* **quick fix** (*inf*) an expedient, often inadequate, solution to a problem; **quick grass**, quack grass; **quick´ie** (*inf*) anything done rapidly or in haste; **quick´lime**, calcium oxide; **quickness; quick´sand**, loose wet sand easily yielding to pressure and engulfing persons, animals, etc.; something that entraps or frustrates; **quick´silver**, mercury; **quick´step**, a march, step, dance, or tune in quick time.—*adj* **quick´tempered**, irascible.—*n* **quick time**, a rate of marching in which 120 steps are taken in one minute.—*adj* **quick´-witt´ed**, alert and quick in mind; quick in repartee.—**a quick one** (*inf*), a quick drink. [OE *cwic*; ON *kvikr*, living.]

quid [kwid] *n* a piece of something chewable. [A variant of **cud**.]

quiddity [kwid´i-ti] *n* the essence of anything; a trifling point; a quibble; an eccentricity; a crotchet. [Schoolmen's L *quidditās, -tātis*.]

quidnunc [kwid´nungk] *n* a gossiping busybody. [L *quid nunc*? what now?]

quid pro quo [kwid prō quō] *n* something given, or taken, as equivalent to, a just return for, something else. [L, something for something.]

quiescent [kwī-es´ėnt] *adj* resting; dormant; inactive; causing no trouble or symptoms.—*n* **quies´cence**.—*adv* **quies´cently**. [L *quiēscēns, -entis*, pr p of *quiēscĕre*, to rest.]

quiet [kwī´ėt] *adj* at rest, calm; peaceable; gentle, unobtrusive, inoffensive; silent; undisturbed.—*n* rest, repose, calm, stillness, peace.—*vti* to make or become quiet.—*ns* **quī´etism**, the doctrine that religious perfection consists in passive and uninterrupted contemplation of the Deity and divine things; a passive attitude toward the world and worldly things; a state of calmness; **quī´etist**, one who believes in this doctrine.—*adv* **quī´etly**.—*ns* **quī´etness, quī´etude**. [L *quiētus*—*quiēscĕre*, to rest.]

quietus [kwī-ē´tus] *n* a discharge from debt, etc.; death. [L *quiētus est*, he is quiet.]

quill [kwil] *n* the hollow basal part of a feather; anything made from this, as a pen; a spine, of a porcupine or hedgehog.—*vt* to pierce with quills; to make a series of small round ridges in (cloth). [Ety obscure.]

quilt [kwilt] *n* a decorative, often intricately patterned bedcover of two thicknesses of material, with padding between held in place by stitching; any material so treated.—*vt* to stitch like a quilt.—*vi* to make a quilt. [OFr *cuilte*—L *culcita*, a cushion.]

quince [kwins] *n* the fruit of an Asian tree (*Cydonia oblonga*) that resembles a hard-fleshed yellow apple used in preserves; the tree it grows on. [Pl of *quine*—OFr *coin*—L *cotōneum*—Gr *kydōnion*—*Kydōniā*, in Crete.]

quin *See* **quintuplet**.

quincunx [kwin´kungks] *n* an arrangement of five things (eg trees) with one at each corner and one in the middle of a square or rectangle. [L, five-twelfths of a pound—*quinque*, five, *uncia*, ounce.]

quinine [kwī´nīn, kwin´īn, kwin-īn, kwė´n-ēn´] *n* a bitter crystalline alkaloid made from cinchana bark and used in medicine; one of its salts used esp as an antipyretic, antimalarial, and bitter tonic. [Fr,—Sp *quina*—Peruvian *kina, kinakina*, bark.]

Quinquagesima [kwin-kwä-jes´i-ma] the Sunday before Lent, being the fiftieth day before Easter. [L *quinquāgēsimus, -a, -um*, fiftieth.]

quinquennial [kwin-kwen´yȧl] *adj* occurring once in five years; consisting of, lasting five years.—*n* a fifth anniversary or its celebration.—*n* **quinquenn´ium** [-ē-um], a period of five years. [L *quinquennium*, a period of five years.—*quinque*, five, *annus*, a year.]

quinsy [kwin´zi] *n* a severe infection of the throat or adjacent parts with swelling and fever. [LL *quinancia*—Gr *kynanchē*—*kyōn*, a dog, *anchein*, to throttle.]

quintain [kwin´tin, -tȧn] *n* a post for tilting at, with a revolving crosspiece having a target at one end and a sandbag at the other end. [Fr,—L *quintāna via*, the place of recreation in the Roman camp.]

quintal [kwin´t(ȧ)l] *n* a hundredweight; 100 kilograms. [Fr and Sp *quintal*—Ar *qintār*—L *centum*, a hundred.]

quintessence [kwin-tes´ėns] *n* the purest concentrated essence of anything; the most typical example of anything.—*adj* **quintessen´tial** [-shȧl]. [Fr,—L *quinta essentia*, fifth essence, orig a fifth entity (esp that considered as composing the heavenly bodies) in addition to the four ancient elements.]

quintet, quintette [kwin´tet´] *n* a musical composition for five voices or instruments; a set of performers or instruments for such compositions; a group of five persons or things. [It *quintetto*, dim of *quinto*—L *quintus*, fifth.]

quintillion [kwin-til´yȯn] *n* in the US, a number represented as one followed by 18 zeros (10^{18}); in Britain, France, and Germany, one followed by 30 zeros (10^{30}). [Modelled on **million**—L *quintus*, fifth.]

quintuple [kwin´tū-pl] *adj* fivefold; having five parts or divisions.—*vti* to increase fivefold.—*n* **quin´tūplet**, a set of five things; one of five born at a birth [also kwin-tōō´plet]—abbrev **quin**. [L *quintus*, fifth, on the model of **quadruple**.]

quip [kwip] *n* a short, clever remark; a repartee; a gibe; a fanciful jest or action. [Perh L *quippe*, forsooth.]

quipu [kē´pōō] *n* a device consisting of cord with attached strings of various colors used by ancient Peruvians for recording events and for calculating. [Quechua.]

quire[1] [kwīr] *n* a set of 24 or 25 sheets of paper of the same size and quality; one twentieth of a ream. [OFr *quaier* (Fr *cahier*), prob from Low L *quaternum*, a set of four sheets—L *quattuor*, four.]

quire[2] [kwīr] *n See* **choir**.

quirk [kwûrk] *n* a quick turn or twist; an oddity of character, or behavior.—*vti* to curl, twist.—*adj* **quirk´y**, having sudden turns; tricky, difficult. [Origin unknown.]

quisling [kwiz´ling] *n* a traitor who takes office under a government formed by an enemy who has occupied his country.—Also *adj*. [Vidkun *Quisling*, who thus acted during the German occupation of Norway (1940–45).]

quit [kwit] *vt* to pay, requite; to release from obligation; to acquit; to depart from; to cease to occupy; to rid (oneself of).—*vi* to cease; to desert one's job or task; to admit defeat.—*pr p* **quitt´ing**; *pt, pt p* **quitt´ed**.—*adjs* **quit**, set free; acquitted; rid (of); **quits**, even; neither debtor nor creditor.—*ns* **quit´claim**, a deed relinquishing a claim, as to property; **quitt´ance**, a release, discharge from debt; **quitt´er** (*inf*), one who gives up easily. [OFr *quiter*—Low L *quiētāre*, to pay—L *quiētāre*, to make quiet—*quiētus*, quiet.]

quite [kwīt] *adv* completely; really; positively; very or fairly.—**quite a few**, more than a few. [A form of **quit**.]

quiver[1] [kwiv´ėr] *n* a case for arrows. [OFr *cuivre*; prob Gmc; cf OHG *kohhar* (Ger *köcher*), OE *cocer*.]

quiver[2] [kwiv´ėr] *vi* to shake with slight and tremulous motion; to tremble, to shiver.—*n* **quiv´er**, a tremulous motion, shiver. [Perh OE *cwifer*, seen in adv *cwiferlīce*, eagerly.]

qui vive [kē vēv] *n* alert. [From the French sentry's challenge, meaning (long) live who? ie whose side are you on?]

quixotic [kwiks-ot´ik] *adj* like Don *Quixote*, the knight-errant in the romance of Cervantes (1547–1616), extravagantly chivalrous; idealistic but impracticable (eg a project).—*adv* **quixot´ically**.—*n* **quix´otism**, absurdly romantic or magnanimous notions or conduct.

quiz [kwiz] *n* an eccentric person; a practical joke; a short written or oral test.—*vt* to make fun of; to tease; to eye with mockery; to interrogate.—*pr p* **quizz´ing**; *pt, pt p* **quizzed**.—*adj* **quizz´ical**.—*ns* **quiz´master**, a person who puts the questions to a contestant in a quiz show; **quiz show, quiz program**, an entertainment program (as on radio or television) in which contestants answer questions. [Origin obscure.]

quoin [koin] *n* the external corner of a building; any of the large stones at such a corner; a wedge-shaped block. [See **coin**.]

quoit [koit] *n* a heavy flat ring thrown in quoits; (*pl*) a game somewhat like horseshoes, in which rings are thrown at a peg.—*vt* to throw like a quoit.

quondam [kwon´dam] *adj* former. [L, formerly.]

quorum [kwō´rum, kwö´-] *n* the fixed minimum attendance necessary for the transaction of business at an assembly. [The first word of a commission formerly issued in Latin to certain magistrates.]

quota [kwō´ta] *n* a proportional share; a part or number assigned. [L *quŏta* (*pars*), the howmanieth (part)—*quŏtus*, of what number?—*quŏt*, how many?]

quote [kwōt] *vt* to refer to; to cite; to give the actual words of; to adduce for authority or illustration; to set off by quotation marks; to state the price of (something).—*n* (*inf*) something quoted; a quotation mark.—*vi* to inform the hearer or reader that what follows immediately is a quotation.—*adj* **quō´table**.—*ns* **quōtā´tion**, act of quoting; that which is quoted; a price quoted; **quōtā´tion mark**, one of the marks used to note the beginning and the end of a written or printed quotation. [OFr *quoter*, to number—Low L *quotāre*, to divide into chapters and verses—L *quŏtus*, of what number?—*quŏt*, how many?]

quoth [kwōth] *vt* said (1st and 3rd persons sing past tense of the otherwise obs verb *quethe*), followed by its subject. [OE *cwæthan*, pa t *cwæth*, to say.]

quotidian [kwō-tid´i-ȧn] *adj* occurring every day; belonging to each day; commonplace, routine, everyday. [L *quotīdiānus*—*quotīdiē*, daily—*quot*, how many, *diēs*, a day.]

quotient [kwō´shėnt] *n* (*math*) the number of times one quantity is contained in another; a ratio, usu. multiplied by 100, used in giving a numerical value to ability, etc. [L *quotiens, quoties*, how often?—*quot*, how many?]

qwerty, QWERTY [kwer´ti] *n* (*inf*) a standard typewriter or computer keyboard. [From the letters at the top lefthand corner of the keyboard.]

R

rabbet [rab´ėt] *n* a groove cut in the edge of a board so that another piece may be fitted into it.—*vti* to cut, or be joined by, a rabbet.—**rabbet joint**, a joint made by fitting together rabbeted boards or timbers.—*pr p* **rabb´eting**; *pt p* **rabb´eted**. [Fr *rabat—rabattre*, to beat back.]

rabbi [rab´ī] an ordained Jewish clergyman, spiritual leader of a congregation; [reb´ė] the revered leader, not necessarily ordained, of a Hasidic sect.—*pl* **rabbis, rabbies.**—*adjs* **rabbin´ic, -al**, pertaining to the rabbis or to their opinions, learning. [Heb *rabbi*, my great one—*rabh*, great, master.]

rabbit [rab´it] *n* a small burrowing animal of the hare family (Leporidae) with long ears, a short tail, and long hind legs; a hare; their flesh (as food); their fur; a figure of a rabbit sped mechanically along the edge of a dog track as an object of pursuit; a runner on a track team who sets the pace in a long-distance race.—*n* **rabbit punch** (*boxing*), a short, sharp blow to the back of the neck. [ME *rabet*.]

rabble[1] [rab´l] *n* a disorderly, noisy crowd, a mob; the lowest class of people.—*vt* to assault by a mob.—*ns* **rabb´lement**, a rabble; tumult. [Cf Old Du *rabbelen*, to gabble, Ger *rabbeln*.]

rabble[2] [rab´l] *n* an iron bar with a bent end used like a rake in puddling iron; a similar device used in a smelting or refining furnace. [F *râble*.]

Rabelaisian [rab-ė-lā´zi-ȧn] *adj* marked by the broad humor and indecency in which the writings of *Rabelais* (d 1553) abound.

rabid [rab´id] *adj* violent (of a feeling); fanatical; (of a mammal) affected with rabies.—*adv* **rab´idly**.—*ns* **rab´idness; rabies** [rā´-bez] a disease, also called hydrophobia, due to a virus usu. transmitted by the bite of an infected animal. [L *rabidus* (adj), *rabiēs* (n).—*rabĕre*, to rave.]

raccoon [ra-kōōn´] *n* a small nocturnal carnivore (*Procyon lotor*) of N America that lives in trees, having yellowish gray fur and a black-ringed tail; its fur. [Amer Indian.]

race[1] [rās] *n* any of the three primary divisions of mankind distinguished esp by color of skin; any geographical, national, or tribal ethnic grouping; any distinct group of plants or animals having the potential to interbreed; a distinctive flavor, taste, or strength.—*adj* **racial** [rā´sh(i-ȧ)l] of, relating to race.—*n* **ra´cialism**, hatred, rivalry or prejudice accompanying difference of race; belief in inherent superiority of some races over others, usu. with implication of right to rule; discriminative treatment based on that belief; **ra´cialist; rac´ism**, racialism; **rac´ist**.—*adj* **rac´y**, having the taste or quality of the genuine type; lively; spirited; pungent; risqué.—*adv* **rā´cify**.—*n* **raciness**. [Fr—Ital *razza*; of doubtful origin.]

race[2] [rās] *n* a strong and rapid current of water or its channel; a competitive trial of speed, as in running; any contest like a race; the course of life.—*vi* to run at top speed or out of control; to compete in a trial of speed; to revolve too fast under a diminished load.—*vt* to cause to race; to oppose in a race; to rush; to run (eg an engine) without a working load or with the transmission disengaged.—*ns* **race´course, racetrack**, the course over which races are run, esp an oval track for horse racing; **race´horse**, a horse bred for racing; **ra´cer**, one who or that which races; **race´way**, a channel for a current of water or for loosely holding electric wires in a building; a racetrack for harness racing. [ON *rās*; OE *rǣs*.]

raceme [rā-sēm´] *n* a cluster of flowers attached by stalks to a central stem. [L *racēmus*, a cluster of grapes.]

racial, racialism *see* **race** (1).

rack[1] [rak] *n* an instrument for racking or stretching, esp an instrument of torture; extreme pain, anxiety, or doubt; a framework on which articles are arranged, as tie rack, etc.; the grating above a manger for hay; a bar with teeth to work into those of a wheel pinion, or worm gear; a pair of antlers; a triangular frame used to set up balls in a game of pool.—*vt* to stretch forcibly; to arrange in or on a rack; to torture, torment.—*ns* **rack´ railway**, a railway having between its rails a rack that meshes with a pinion of the locomotive for traction on steep grades; **rack´ rent**, an excessively high rent. [The radical sense is to stretch, closely allied to **reach**.]

rack[2] [rak] *n* destruction.—**rack and ruin**, a state of neglect and collapse. [Alteration of **wrack**.]

rack[3] [rak] *n* a wind-driven mass of high often broken clouds. [App ON *rek*, drifting wreckage; OE *wrecan*, to drive.]

rack[4] [rak] *n* the neck and spine of a forequarter of veal, pork, or lamb.

rack[5] [rak] *n* either of two gaits of a horse: a pace or a showy 4-beat gait.

racket[1], **racquet** [rak´ėt] *n* a bat strung with catgut or nylon, for playing tennis, etc.—*pl* a game for two or four players played in a 4-walled court with ball and racket. [Fr *raquette* perh—Ar *rāhat*, coll form of *rāha*, the palm of the hand.]

racket[2] [rak´ėt] *n* din, clamor; an obtaining money illegally; (*inf*) any fraudulent activity.—*n* **racketeer´**, one who extorts money by threats or makes profit by illegal action. [Prob imit.]

raconteur [ra-k•-tœr] *n* one who excels in relating anecdotes. [Fr.]

racquet *See* **racket** (1).

racy *See* **race** (1).

rad [rad] *n* a unit of absorbed dose of ionizing radiation. [*r*adiation *a*bsorbed *d*ose.]

radar [rā´där] *n* a system or device for using reflection of radio waves for locating objects (aircraft, ships, landmarks, etc.). [*ra*dio *d*etecting *a*nd *r*anging.]

raddle[1] [rad´l] *vt* to interweave. [Anglo-Fr *reidele*, rail.]

raddle[2] [rad´l] *n* red ocher. [Akin to **red**.]

radial [rā´di-ȧl] *adj* pertaining to or like a ray or radius; characterized by divergence from a center; relating to or adjacent to a bodily radius.—**radial** (*ply*) **tire**, an automobile tire with ply cords nearly at right angles to the center of the tread. [LL *radiālis*—L *radius*. See **radius**.]

radian [rā´di-ȧn] *n* a unit of angular measurement; the central angle of a circle which is determined by an arc equal in length to the radius of the circle. [L *radius*. See **radius**.]

radiant [rā´dē-ȧnt] *adj* emitting rays; issuing in rays; glowing; shining; beaming with joy.—*n* luminous point from which rays emanate; the center from which meteoric showers seem to proceed.—*ns* **rā´diance, rā´diancy**, quality of being radiant; brilliancy; splendor.—*adv* **rā´diantly**. [L *radians, -antis*, pr p of *radiāre, -ātum*, to radiate—*radius*. See **radius**.]

radiate [rā´di-āt] *vt* to emit rays; to shine; to issue in rays; to proceed in divergent lines from any central point or surface.—*adj* [-āt] having ray flowers; spreading like a ray or rays; having a form showing symmetrical divergence from a center.—*vt* to send out in or by rays; to spread around as if from a center; to give forth (happiness, love, etc.).—*ns* **rādiā´tion**, act of radiating; the emission and diffusion of rays; that which is radiated, esp energy emitted in the form of electromagnetic waves (as light, radio, waves); **rādiātor**, an apparatus for emitting heat, as for warming a room, or from an automobile engine; a wireless transmitting aerial.—**radiation sickness**, an illness caused by excessive exposure to the rays from radioactive substances. [L *radiātus*, rayed.]

radical [rad´ik(ȧ)l] *adj* pertaining to the root or origin; fundamental; favoring basic change, as in the economic or social structure; relating to, or constituting a linguistic root; designed to remove the root of a disease or all diseased tissue.—*n* (*math*) the sign (√) used with a quantity to show that its root is to be extracted; (*chem*) an uncharged group of atoms passing unchanged from one compound to another; an advocate of drastic political reform.—*n* **rad´icalism**, the principles or spirit of a radical.—*adv* **rad´ically**. [L *rādix, -īcis*, a root.]

radicle [rad´i-kl] *n* a little root; the part of a seed that becomes the root. [L *rādicula*, a little root; dim of *rādīx*.]

radio- [rā´di-ō, -o] in composition denotes radial, by radio, using radiant energy as **radiotho´rium**, a radioactive isotope of thorium.—*n* **ra´dio**, the transmission of sounds or signals by electromagnetic waves through space, without wires, to a receiving set; such a set; broadcasting by radio as an industry, entertainment, etc.—*adj* of, using, used in, or sent by radio.—*vti* to transmit, or communicate with, by radio.—*n* **radioactiv´ity**, a giving off of radiant energy in the form of particles or rays by the disintegration of atomic nuclei.—*adj* **radioact´ive**.—*ns* **radio astron´omy**, astronomy dealing with radio waves in space in order to obtain information about the universe; **radiobiol´ogy**, a branch of biology dealing with the interaction of biological systems and radiant energy or radioactive materials; **radiocar´bon**, a radioactive carbon, specifically carbon-14; **ra´dioel´ement**, a radioactive element; **radio frequency**, a frequency intermediate between audio frequencies and infrared frequencies used esp in radio and television transmission.—*adj* **radiogen´ic**, produced by or determined from radioactivity.—*ns* **ra´diogram**, radiograph; a message transmitted by radio telegraphy; **rā´diograph**, an X-ray or gamma ray photograph.—*vt* to make a radiograph of; to send a radiogram to.—*ns* **rādiog´raphy**, the technique, or practice, of making radiographs; **rad´ioīs´otope**, a radioactive isotope; **rādiolocā´tion**, the detection and determination of the location of distant objects by radar; **rādiol´ogy**, a branch of medicine concerned with the use of radiant energy (as X-rays and radium) in the diagnosis and treatment of disease; **radiol´ogist**, a physician specializing in radiology; **radiosonde**, a miniature radio transmitter carried aloft (as by an unmanned balloon) to broadcast information on humidity, temperature, and pressure; **radio star**, a cosmic radio source of very small dimensions and relatively strong radiation; **radiostrontium**, strontium-90, a radioactive isotope of strontium; **radiotelegraph, radiotelephone**, wireless telegraph, telephone; **radio telescope**, a radio-antenna combination used for observation in radio astronomy; **rādiother´apy**, treatment of disease by X-rays or by radioactive substances; **radio wave**, an electromagnetic wave with radio frequency. [L *radius*, a spoke, radius, ray.]

radish [rad´ish] *n* a plant (*Raphanus sativa*) of the mustard family whose pungent root is eaten as a salad. [Fr *radis*—Provençal *raditz*—L *rādīx, rādīcis*, a root.]

radium [rā´di-um] *n* a radioactive metallic element (symbol Ra; at wt 226.1; at no 88). [L *radius*, a ray.]

radius [rā´di-us] *n* (*geom*) a straight line from the center to the circumference of a circle and a straight line extending from the center to a point on the surface of a sphere; anything like a radius, as the spoke of a wheel; (*anat*) the bone on the thumb side of the forearm;—*pl* **rā´diī**. [L *radius*, a spoke, radius, ray.]

radix [rā´diks] *n* the base of a number system or of logarithms; the primary source;—*pl* **radices** [rā´di-sēz], **radixes**. [L *rādīx, rādīcis*.]

radon [rā´don] *n* a gaseous element (symbol Rn; at wt 222.0; at no 86). [*Radium*, with suffx *-on*.]

raff [raf] *n* riffraff.—*adj* **raff´ish**, disreputable, rakish; flashy.—*adv* **raff´ishly**.—*n* **raff´ishness**. [See **riff-raff**.]

raffia [raf´i-a] *n* strips of the pliant fiber of the leaves of the raffia palm (*Raphia raffia*) of Madagascar. [Malagasy.]

raffle [raf´l] *n* a lottery to decide which of the subscribers shall receive a certain article.—*vt* to offer as a prize in a raffle; *vi* to engage in a raffle. [Fr *rafle*, a winning throw of the dice.]

raft[1] [raft] *n* a flat structure of logs or planks for support or conveyance on water; an inflatable boat. [ON *raptr*, a rafter.]

raft[2] [raft] *n* (*inf*) a large quantity.

rafter [räft´ėr] *n* any of the inclined beams supporting the roof of a house.—*vt* to furnish with rafters. [OE *ræfter*, a beam.]

rag [rag] *n* worn, torn, or waste scrap of cloth; a tatter or shred; a worthless piece of any material; (*pl*) tattered clothing.—*adj* made of rags.—*n* **rag´bag**, a bag for scraps; a miscellaneous collection.—*adj* **ragg´ed**, shaggy; jagged; uneven; irregular; torn into rags; wearing ragged clothes.—*adv* **ragg´edly**.—*ns* **ragg´edness; rag´man**, a man who deals in rags; **rag´time**, music of American Negro origin, having more or less continuous syncopation in the melody, merged into jazz after about 1915.—*ragtag and bobtail*, riff-raff. [OE *ragg*, inferred from the adj *raggig*, shaggy.]

ragamuffin [rag´a-muf-in] *n* an ill-clad dirty person, esp a boy. [Per *rag*.]

rage [rāj] *n* overmastering passion of any kind, as desire or (esp) anger; frenzy; vogue; a thing in the vogue; violence (eg of the wind).—*vi* to behave with passion, esp with furious anger; to storm; to be prevalent and violent.—*adj* **rā´ging**, violent, furious.—*adv* **rā´gingly**. [Fr,—L *rabiēs*—*rabĕre*, to rave.]

raglan [rag´lȧn] *n* an overcoat, with the sleeve in one piece with the shoulder.—*adj* of a sleeve, in one piece with the shoulder. [From Lord *Raglan* (1788–1855).]

ragout [ra-gōō´] *n* a highly seasoned stew of meat and vegetables. [Fr *ragoût*—*ragoûter*, to restore the appetite.]

ragtime *see* **rag**.

ragweed [rag´wēd] *n* any of various N American weedy composite herbs (genus *Ambrosia*) that produce highly allergenic pollen.

ragwort [rag´wûrt] *n* any of several composite herbs (genus *Senecio*) with a yellow flower. [**rag**, and OE *wyrt*, a plant.]

raid [rād] *n* a sudden swift inroad, orig of horsemen, for assault or seizure; an air attack.—*vt* to make a raid on; (*inf*) to help oneself to things from.—*vi* to go on a raid.—*n* **raid´er**, one who raids; an aircraft over enemy territory. [OE *rād*, a riding.]

rail[1] [rāl] *n* a bar extending from one support to another, as in fences, staircases, etc.; one of the steel bars used to form a track for wheeled vehicles; the railway as a means of travel or transport.—*vt* to enclose or separate by rails.—*ns* **rail´bus**, a passenger car with an automotive engine for operation on rails; **rail´car**, a railroad car; a single railway car operating as a unit with a light engine; **rail´head**, a point on a railroad at which traffic may originate or terminate; **rail´ing**, a fence of posts and rails; material for rails; **rail´road**, a road laid with parallel steel rails along which cars are drawn by locomotives; a complete system of such roads.—*vt* to push forward (a bill) unduly; to get rid of, esp by sending to prison on a false charge.—*ns* **rail´splitt´er**, one who splits logs into rails for a fence; **rail´way**, a line of track providing a runway for wheels; a railroad operating with light equipment or within a small area; (*Brit*) railroad. [OFr *reille*—L *rēgula*, ruler.]

rail[2] [rāl] *vi* to utter angry taunts or bitter reproaches (at, against).—*n* **raillery** [rāl´ėr-i], mockery, good-natured banter, playful satire. [Fr *railler*.]

rail[3] [rāl] *n* any of numerous wading birds (family Rallidae) related to the cranes. [OFr *rasle* (Fr *râle*).]

raiment [rā´mėnt] *n* (*arch*) clothing. [Contr of obs *arrayment*—**array**.]

rain [rān] *n* water from the clouds in drops; a shower; a fall of anything in the manner of rain; (*pl*) the rainy season.—*vi* (of rain) to fall; to fall like rain.—*vt* to pour down (rain, etc.); to give in large quantities.—*ns* **rain´bow**, the arc containing the colors of the spectrum formed in the sky by the refraction of the sun's rays in falling rain or in mist; **rain´ check**, a ticket stub to a ball game, etc., allowing future admission if the event is rained out; a token for future use given by retailers when they are temporarily out of a special offer; a promise to accept an invitation at a later date; **rain´coat**, a light waterproof overcoat; **rain´fall**, a fall of rain; the amount of rain that falls in a given time; **rain forest**, a dense, evergreen forest in a tropical area with much rainfall; **rain´ gauge**, an instrument for measuring rainfall.—*adjs* **rain´less**, without rain; **rain´ proof**, impervious to rain; **rain´y**, characterized by rain.—**rain cats and dogs**, to rain very heavily.—**a rainy day**, a future time of need. [OE *regn*; Du and Ger *regen*, ON *regn*.]

raise [rāz] *vt* to cause to rise; to lift up; to set up or upright; to increase in size, amount, degree, intensity, etc; to rear, grow or breed; to put prominently forward (eg an objection, a question); to get, collect, or levy; (*phonet*) to pronounce (a vowel sound) with some part of the tongue closer to the palate (eg *to raise 'a' as in 'hat', to 'e', as in 'bell'*).—*n* a rising road; (*inf*) an increase in wages or salary. [ME *reisen*—ON *reisa*, causative of *rīsa*, to rise. Cf **rise, rear**.]

raisin [rā´z(i)n] *n* a sweet dried grape. [Fr grape—L *racēmus*, a bunch of grapes.]

raison d'être [rā-z• detr'] justification for being, purpose of existence. [Fr.]

raj [räj] *n* rule, sovereignty.—*n* **ra´ja(h)**, an Indian or Malay prince or chief; the bearer of a title of nobility among the Hindus. [Hindustani *rāj, rājā*.]

rake[1] [rāk] *n* a toothed bar on a handle for scraping, gathering together, smoothing, etc.—*vt* to draw a rake over; to gather as with a rake; to sweep with gunfire from stem to stern, or in the direction of the length; to scrape, gather (together); to search minutely.—*n* **rake-off** (*slang*), pecuniary gain, esp a commission illegally exacted.—**rake in**, to gather a great amount rapidly; **rake up**, to detect and bring to notice (usu. something scandalous). [OE *raca*; Ger *rechen*, rake, ON *reka*, shove.]

rake[2] [rāk] *n* a dissolute, debauched man.—*adj* **rak´ish**.—*adv* **rak´ishly**. [**rakehell**.]

rake[3] [rāk] *n* (*naut*) the projection of the stem and stern of a ship beyond the extremities of the keel; the slope or slant (of a mast); the slope of a stage, auditorium, etc.—*vi* to slope from the perpendicular.—*adj* **rā´kish**, having a rake; dashing, jaunty.—*adv* **ra´kishly**.

rakehell [rāk´hel] *n* an utterly vicious character. [Prob **rake** (1) and **hell**—ie one such as might be found by searching hell.]

rallentando [ral-ėn-tan´do] *adj, adv* (*mus*) becoming slower.—*n* a passage or movement so played. [It pr p of *raellentare*, to slacken.]

rally[1] [ral´i] *vti* to reassemble; to gather for renewed and united effort; to muster by an effort (as the faculties); to recover to some degree of health or vigor;—*pr p* **rall´ying**; *pt, pt p* **rallied** [ral´id].—*n* act of rallying; a gathering to promote a common purpose; a temporary or partial recovery; (*tennis*, etc.) a sustained exchange of strokes; a competition to test skill in driving and ability to follow an unknown route, or to test the quality of an automobile. [OFr *rallier*—pfx *re-* + *allier*. See **ally**.]

rally[2] [ral´i] *vti* to tease or banter;—*pr p* **rall´ying**; *pt, pt p* **rall´ied**. [Fr *railler*; cf **rail** (2).]

ram [ram] *n* a male sheep; a battering ram; a hydraulic ram or water-ram; (*hist*) an iron beak on the stem of a warship for piercing the hull of a hostile vessel.—*vt* to push or press hard, to cram; to drive by hard blows; to strike, batter, pierce, with a ram; to strike (esp a ship) head-on;—*pr p* **ramm´ing**; *pt, pt p* **rammed**.—**the Ram**, Aries, the 1st sign of the zodiac. [OE *ram, rom*; Ger *ramm*.]

Ramadan [ram´-a-dän] *n* the ninth month of the Islamic year throughout which Muslims are required to fast from dawn to sunset. [Ar *Ramadān*.]

ramble [ram´bl] *vi* to wander at will for pleasure; to straggle; to wander in mind or discourse; to be incoherent.—*n* a leisurely walk with no fixed goal.—*n* **ram´bler**, one who rambles; a climbing rose.—*adj* **ram´bling**, desultory; incoherent. [ME *romblen*; app conn with **roam**.]

ramie [ram´ē] *n* an Asian plant (*Boehmeria nivea*) of the nettle family; the strong lustrous fiber of this plant. [Malay *rami*.]

ramify [ram´i-fī] *vt* to divide into branches;—*pr p* **ram´ifying**; *pt, pt p* **ram´ified**.—*n* **ramification** [ram-i-fi-kā´sh(ȯ)n], division into branches; a branch, esp a remote branch, offshoot, or link (of a division or part of a subject, a plot, a consequence that must be taken into account, etc.). [Fr *ramifier*—L *rāmus*, a branch, *facĕre*, to make.]

ramjet engine [ram´jet´] *n* a jet engine having in its forward end a continuous inlet of air that depends on the speed of flight for the compressing effect.

ramose [rā´mōs] *adj* branched. [L *rāmōsus*—*rāmus*, a branch.]

ramp [ramp] *vi* to grow rankly; to stand or advance menacingly with forelegs or arms raised.—*n* a sloping walk or runway joining different levels; a wheeled staircase for boarding a plane; a sloping runway for launching boats, as from trailers.—*n* **rampāge´**, aggressively agitated behavior or rushing about.—*vi* to rush about wildly.—*adjs* **rampā´geous**, unruly; boisterous; **ramp´ant**, unrestrained; prevalent; (*her*) standing upon the hindlegs with forelegs extended.—*n* **rampancy**.—*adv* **ramp´antly**. [Fr *ramper*, to creep, to clamber.]

rampart [ram´pärt] *n* a flat topped defensive mound; a protective barrier. [Fr *rempart*—OFr *rempar*—*remparer*, to defend—L pfx *re-*, again, *ante*, before, *parāre*, to prepare.]

ramrod [ram´rod] *n* a rod for ramming down the charge in a muzzle-loading firearm.—*adj* denoting a stern, inflexible person. [**ram** + **rod**.]

ramshackle [ram´shak´l] *adj* tumbledown; rickety. [Ety doubtful.]

ran *pt* of **run**.

ranch [ränch] *n* a large farm, esp in western US, for raising cattle, horses, or sheep; a style of house with all the rooms on one floor.—Also **ranch house**.—*vi* to own, manage, or work on a ranch.—*ns* **ranch´er, ranch´man**, one who owns or works on a ranch. **ran´cho**, a ranch. [Sp *rancho*, small farm.]

rancid [ran´sid] *adj* rank in smell and taste, as stale fats or oil.—*ns* **rancid´ity, rancidness**. [L *rancidus*.]

rancor [rang´kůr] *n* bitter deep-seated enmity.—*adj* **ran´corous**.—*adv* **ran´corously**. [L *rancor*, old grudge—*rancēre*, to be rancid.]

rand [rand] *n* a unit of money in South Africa; a former unit of money in Botswana, Lesotho, and Swaziland. [OE, Du.]

random [ran´dȯm] *n* a haphazard course.—*adj* haphazard; chance.—**random-access**, in computers, direct access to any data in any desired order.—**at random**, aimlessly; haphazardly. [OFr *randon*—*randir*, to gallop.]

ranee *see* **rani**.

rang [rang] *pt* of **ring**.

range [rānj] *vt* to set in a row; to place in proper order; to make level (with); to traverse in all directions; to sail along; to determine the range of; to graze (livestock) on a range.—*vi* to lie in a certain direction; to extend; to take or have position in line or alongside; to move freely; to vary (within limits).—*n* a system of points in a straight line; anything extending in line, as a chain of mountains; variety; area within which movement takes place; position in relation to a person taking aim; distance to which a projectile can be thrown; ground on which shooting is practiced; a place for testing rockets in flight; a large open area for grazing livestock; a cooking stove.—*ns* **range´ find´er**, an instrument for finding the range of a target; a camera attachment serving a similar purpose; **rang´er**, officer who superintends a forest or park; a member of a body of mounted troops policing an area; a soldier specially trained for raiding combat.—**to range oneself with**, to side, to take sides with. [Fr *ranger*, to range—*rang*, a rank.]

rani, ranee [rän´ē] *n* a Hindu queen; a rajah's wife. [Hindustani *rānī*—Sans *rājñī*, queen, fem of *rājan*.]

rank[1] [rangk] *n* a row or line; a line of soldiers standing side by side; order, grade, or degree; high standing; (*pl*) the army, esp enlisted soldiers.—*vt* to place in a line; to assign to a definite class or grade; to outrank.—*vi* to have a specified place in a scale, or a place in a specified class.—*n* **rank´er**, an officer promoted from the ranks.—**rank and file**, enlisted soldiers; ordinary members, as distinguished from their leaders. [OFr *renc* perh—OHG *hring, hrinc*, ring.]

rank[2] [rangk] *adj* growing high and luxuriantly; coarsely overgrown; excessive; offensive in odor or flavor; arrant, utter.—*adv* **rank´ly**.—*n* **rank´ness**. [OE *ranc*, proud, strong.]

rankle [rangk´l] *vi* to fester; to cause persistent pain, vexation, or bitterness. [OFr *rancler, raoncler*—*draoncler*, app—LL *dra(cu)nculus*, an ulcer, dim of L *dracō*—Gr *drakōn*, dragon.]

ransack [ran´sak] *vt* to search thoroughly; to plunder, to pillage. [ON *rannsaka*—*rann*, house, *sækja*, seek.]

ransom [ran´sȯm] *n* redemption from captivity; price of redemption; a huge sum.—*vt* to pay ransom.—*n* **ran´somer**.—[Fr *rançon*—L *redemptiō*, -*ōnis*, redemption.]

rant [rant] *vti* to use vehement or extravagant language.—*n* loud, wild declamation, bombast.—*n* **rant´er**, one who rants. [Obs Du *ranten*, to rave; Low Ger *randen*, Ger *ranzen*.]

ranunculus [rȧ-nung´kū-lus] *n* any of a large widely distributed genus (*Ranunculus*) of herbs (as a buttercup) having usu. yellow flowers.—*pl* **ranun´culuses, ranun´culī**. [L a dim of *rāna*, a frog—name for a medicinal plant, perh a buttercup.]

rap[1] [rap] *n* a sharp blow; a sound made by knocking.—*vt* to hit sharply; (*slang*) to criticize sharply.—*vi* to knock or tap;—*pr p* **rapp´ing**; *pt, pt p* **rapped**.—**take the rap**, (*slang*) to take the blame or punishment. [Imit.]

rap[2] [rap] *vt* to snatch away; to transport with rapture;—*pr p* **rapp´ing**; *pt p* **rapped**, or **rapt**. [Partly akin to Middle Low Ger *rappen*, Swed *rappa*, to snatch; influenced by **rapt**.]

rap[3] [rap] *n* (*inf*) talk, conversation. [Perhaps **repartee**.]

rapacious [ra-pā´shůs] *adj* given to plunder; ravenous; greedy of gain.—*adv* **rapā´ciously**.—*ns* **rapā´ciousness, rapac´ity**. [L *rapāx, rapācis*—*rapĕre*, to seize and carry off.]

rape[1] [rāp] *n* the plundering (of a city, etc.) as in warfare; sexual intercourse with a woman without her consent.—*vt* to commit rape upon.—*vi* to commit rape. [Prob L *rapĕre*, to snatch, confused with **rap** (2).]

rape[2] [rāp] *n* a plant (*Brassica napus*) of the mustard family cultivated for its leaves and oily seeds. [L *rāpa, rāpum*, a turnip.]

rapid [rap´id] *adj* swift; quickly accomplished; steeply sloping.—*n* (usu *pl*) a swift-flowing, steeply-descending part of a river, often with broken water.—*ns* **rapid´ity, rap´idness**.—*adv* **rap´idly**.—**rapid transit**, a system of rapid public transportation in an urban area, using electric trains along an unimpeded right of way. [L *rapidus*—*rapĕre*, to seize.]

rapier [rā´pi-ėr] *n* a straight 2-edged sword with a narrow pointed blade. [Fr *rapière*.]

rapine [rap´in] *n* act of seizing forcibly; plunder, robbery. [L *rapīna*—*rapĕre*, to seize.]

rapparee [rap-a-rē´] *n* an Irish irregular soldier; a plunderer. [Ir *rapaire*, a robber.]

rapper [rap´ėr] *n* one who raps; a door knocker. [**rap** (1).]

rapport [rä-pör´] *n* relation, connection, sympathy, accord. [Fr.]

rapprochement [rä-prosh´mã] *n* a drawing together, establishment or state of cordial relations. [Fr.]

rapscallion [rap-skal´yȯn] *n* a rascal, a ne'er-do-well. [From *rascallion*—**rascal**.]

rapt [rapt] *adj* carried away; transported, enraptured; wholly engrossed. [L *raptus*, pt p of *rapĕre*, to seize and carry off; but partly also pt p of **rap** (2).]

raptorial [rap-tō´ri-ål] *adj* predatory; of, relating to, or being a bird of prey. [L *raptor, -ōris*, a plunderer—*rapĕre*, to seize.]

rapture [rap´chůr] *n* state of being carried away with love, joy, etc.; extreme delight, transport, ecstasy.—*adj* **rap´tūrous**.—*adv* **rap´tūrously**. [L *rapĕre, raptum*, to seize.]

rare[1] [rar] *adj* thin, not dense; uncommon; excellent.—*adv* **rāre´ly**, seldom; remarkably well.—*ns* **rāre´ness; rarity** [rar´i-ti], state of being rare; thinness; uncommonness; something valued for its scarcity.—*vt* **rarefy, rarify** [rar´ifī], to make or become less dense; to expand without the addition of matter; to make more spiritual, abstruse, or refined.—*vi* to become less dense.—*pt, pt p* **rar´efied**.—*ns* **rarefac´tion** [rār-i- or rar-i-], rarefying; **rāre´bit**, Welsh rabbit.—**rare earth**, any oxide of lanthanide; any element of the lanthanide series which include the elements with atomic numbers 58 through 71.—Also **rare earth element**. [Fr,—L *rārus*.]

rare[2] [rar] *adj* not completely cooked, partly raw, esp of meat. [OE *hrēr*.]

raree-show [rār´ē-shō] *n* a show carried about in a box; an unusual or amazing spectacle. [App a Savoyard showman's pron of **rare show**.]

raring [rar´ing] *adj* eager; full of enthusiasm. [**rear** (2).]

rascal [ras´kål] *n* a knave, rogue, scamp.—*ns* **rascality** [-kal´-], the rabble; the character or conduct of rascals.—*adj* **ras´cally**. [OFr *rascaille*, scum of the people.]

rase [rāz] *vt* to erase; to demolish.

rash[1] [rash] *adj* overhasty, wanting in caution.—*adv* **rash´ly**.—*n* **rash´ness**. [Cognate with Dan and Swed *rask*; Du and Ger *rasch*, rapid.]

rash[2] [rash] *n* a slight eruption on the skin; a large number of instances at the same time or in the same place. [Perh OFr *rasche*.]

rasher [rash´ėr] *n* a thin slice of bacon or ham broiled or fried; a portion consisting of several such slices. [Perh from *rash*, to slash, a variant of **raze**.]

rasp [räsp] *n* a coarse file; a grating sound or feeling.—*vt* to grate as with a rasp; to utter gratingly.—*vi* to scrape; to produce a grating sound.—*n* **rasper**.—*adj* **ras´py**, rough. [OFr *raspe*; perh Gmc.]

raspberry [räz´bėr-i] *n* any of various edible usu. black or red berries that are aggregate fruits consisting of small drupes, rounder and smaller than the related blackberry; a plant (genus *Rubus*) that bears raspberries; (*inf*) a sign of disapproval, esp a noise produced by blowing hard with the tongue between the lips. [*rasp*, earlier *raspis* (origin unknown), + **berry**.]

raster [ras´tėr] *n* a complete set of television scanning lines appearing at the receiver as a rectangular patch of light on which the image is produced. [Perh—L *rāstrum*, rake.]

rasure [rā´zh(y)ůr] *n* erasure; obliteration. [L *rāsūra*.]

rat [rat] *n* any of numerous rodents (*Rattus* and related genera) closely allied to mice but larger; (*slang*) a sneaky, contemptible person, esp an informer; a scab; a pad over which a woman's hair is arranged.—*vi* to hunt or catch rats; to betray, desert, or inform on one's associates; to work as a scab; to use a rat in the hair.—*pr p* **ratt´ing**; *pt, pt p* **ratt´ed**.—*ns* **rat fink**, (*slang*) an informer; a strike breaker; **rat race**, continual hectic competitive activity; **ratt´er**, a dog or cat that catches and kills rats; **rattail cactus**, a commonly cultivated tropical American cactus (*Aporcactus flagelliformis*) with creeping stems and showy red flowers; **rat´trap**, a trap for rats; (*inf*) a dirty, rundown building.—*adj* **ratt´y**, of a rat, like a rat; full of rats; (*slang*—of a person) mean, rather despicable.—**smell a rat**, have a suspicion of something afoot. [OE *ræt*; cf Ger *ratte*.]

ratable, rateable [rā´tȧ-bl] *adj* See **rate**.

ratafia [rat-ȧ-fē´a] *n* a flavoring essence made with the essential oil of almonds; a cordial or liqueur flavored with fruit; an almond biscuit or cake. [Fr; origin unknown.]

rataplan [rat-a-plan´] *n* the beat of a drum. [Fr.]

ratch [rach] *n* a ratchet; a ratched wheel.—*n* **ratch´et wheel**, a wheel with inclined teeth with which a pawl engages. [History obscure; cf Ger *ratsche*, Fr *rochet*.]

rate[1] [rāt] *n* the amount, degree, etc. of something in relation to units of something else; price, esp per unit; a class or rank.—*vt* to estimate the value of; to settle the relative rank, scale, or position of; to esteem, regard as; (*inf*) to deserve.—*vi* to have value or status.—*adjs* **ratable, rateable**.—*ns* **rat(e)abil´ity; rāt´ing**, classification according to grade, as of military personnel; an evaluation, an appraisal, as of credit worthiness; (radio, TV) the relative popularity of a program according to sample polls.—**at any rate**, in any case, anyhow. [OFr,—LL (*pro*) *ratā* (*parte*), according to a calculated part—*rērī, rătus*, to think, judge.]

rate[2] [rāt] *vt* to scold, to chide, to reprove. [ME *raten*; origin obscure.]

rather [rä´THėr] *adv* more willingly; in preference; somewhat, in some degree; more accurately; on the contrary. [Comp of **rath**, adv; OE *hrathor*.]

ratify [rat´i-fī] *vt* to approve, esp by official sanction; to confirm.—*pr p* **rat´ifying**; *pt, pt p* **rat´ified**.—*n* **ratificā´tion**. [Fr *ratifier*—L *rătus*, pt p of *rērī* (see **rate**), *facĕre*, to make.]

ratio [rā´shi-ō] *n* the measurable relation of one thing to another; the relation of quantities as shown by their quotient; proportion. [L *rătiō, -ōnis*, reason—*rēri, rătus*, to think.]

ratiocination [rash-i-os-i-nā´sh(ò)n] *n* the process of reasoning; deduction from premises.—*vi* **ratio´cinate**, to reason, esp using formal logic.—*adj* **ratioc´inative** [-os´-]. [L *ratiōcinārī, -ātus*, to reason.]

ration [ra´sh(ò)n or rā´-] *n* a fixed allowance or portion of food, as a daily allowance for one soldier; (*pl*) food supply.—*vt* to supply with rations; to restrict the supply of to so much for each. [Fr,—L *ratiō, -ōnis*, reckoning, reason, etc.]

rational [ra´shòn-àl] *adj* of or based on reason; endowed with reason; agreeable to reason; sane; (*math*) involving only multiplication, division, addition, and subtraction and only a finite number of times.—*n* **rationale** [rash´ō-nal], the reasons or rational basis for something; an explanation of principles.—*vt* **ra´tionalize**, to make rational, to conform to reason; to substitute a natural for a supernatural explanation; to explain or justify by reason (thoughts or actions motivated by emotion); (*math*) to free (a mathematical expression) from irrational quantities.—*vi* to provide plausible but untrue reasons for conduct.—*ns* **rationaliza´tion; ra´tionalism**, (*phil*) a system which regards reasoning as the source of knowledge; a disposition to apply to religious doctrines the same critical methods as to science and history, and to attribute all phenomena to natural rather than miraculous causes; **ra´tionalist**.—*adj* **rationalist´ic**.—*adv* **rationalist´ically**.—*n* **rationality** [ra-shòn-al´i-ti], quality of being rational; the possession, or due exercise, of reason; reasonableness.—*adv* **ra´tionally**.—**rational number**, any number that can be expressed as a ratio of two integers, providing the second number is not zero. [L *ratiōnālis, -e*—*ratiō*, reason.]

ratline [rat´lin] *n* one of the small lines or ropes forming steps of the rigging of ships. [Origin obscure.]

rattan [ra-tan´] *n* any of a number of climbing palms (esp genera *Calamus* and *Daemonorops*) with very long thin stem; a cane made from part of a stem. [Malay *rōtan*.]

rattle [rat´l] *vi* to clatter; to move along rapidly with a clatter; to chatter briskly and emptily.—*vt* to cause to rattle; to utter glibly, as by rote; to disturb the equanimity of.—*n* the sound of rattling; a sound in the throat of a dying person; an instrument or toy for rattling; the rings of a rattlesnake's tail.—*ns* **ratt´lebrain**, a shallow, volatile person; **ratt´ler**, a rattlesnake; **ratt´lesnake**, any of several venomous American snakes (genera *Sistrurus* and *Crotalus*) with rattling bony rings on the tail; **rattle trap**, a rickety, old car.—*adj* **ratt´ling**, lively, vigorous; excellent.—*adv* to an extreme degree; very. [ME *ratelen*.]

ratty *See* **rat**.

raucous [rö´kus] *adj* hoarse, harsh; loud and rowdy.—*adv* **rauc´ously**. [L *raucus*, hoarse.]

raunchy [rönch´i] (*slang*) *adj* coarse, earthy, rather obscene; carelessly untidy.

ravage [rav´ij] *vt* to lay waste, to pillage; to despoil (of).—*n* devastation; ruin.—*n* **rav´ager**. [Fr *ravager*—*ravir*, to carry off by force—L *rapĕre*.]

rave [rāv] *vi* to rage; to talk as if mad, delirious, or enraptured.—*n* (*inf*) infatuation; extravagant praise.—*adj* **rā´ving**. [Per OFr *raver*, which may be—L *rabĕre*, to rave.]

ravel [rav´l] *vti* to separate into its parts, esp thread; fray; untwist;—*pr p* **rav´elling**; *pt, pt p* **rav´elled**.—*n* a ravelled part or thread. [App Du *ravelen*.]

raven[1] [rā´vèn] *n* a large glossy black crow (*Corvus corax*) of northern Europe, Asia, and America.—*adj* of the color or glossy sheen of a raven. [OE *hræfn*.]

raven[2] [rav´en] *vt* to devour hungrily or greedily.—*vi* to prey rapaciously; to prowl for food; to plunder.—*adj* **rav´enous**, rapacious; voracious; intensely hungry.—*adv* **rav´enously**.—*n* **rav´enousness**. [OFr *ravine*, plunder—L *rapīna*, plunder.]

ravin [rav´in] *n* plunder; pillage; act or habit of preying; something seized as prey. [Same as foregoing.]

ravine [ra-vēn´] *n* a deep, narrow gorge. [Fr,—L *rapīna*, rapine, violence.]

ravioli [rav-i-ōl´ē] *n* small cases of pasta filled with highly seasoned chopped meat or vegetables. [It.]

ravish [rav´ish] *vt* to seize or carry away by violence; to snatch away from sight or from the world; to rape; to enrapture.—*n* **rav´isher**.—*adj* **rav´ishing**, charming, enrapturing.—*n* **rav´ishment**. [Fr *ravir*—L *rapĕre*, to seize and carry off.]

raw [rö] *adj* not altered from its natural state; not cooked; having the skin abraded or removed; unrefined; untrained, immature, inexperienced; chilly and damp; (*inf*) harsh or unfair.—*adj* **raw´boned**, with little flesh on the bones, gaunt.—*n* **raw´hide**, an untanned cattle hide; a whip of untanned leather.—*n* **raw´ness**.—**raw material**, crude material that can be converted into a new and useful product by processing, manufacture, or combination with another material; something with a potential for development, improvement, etc. [OE *hrēaw*; Du *rauw*, ON *hrār*, Ger *roh*.]

ray[1] [rā] *n* a line along which light comes from a bright source; a moral or intellectual light; any of several lines radiating from a center; a beam of radiant energy, radioactive particles, etc.; a tiny amount.—*n* **ray flower**, one of the marginal flowers on a composite herb that also has disk flowers. [OFr *rais* (acc *rai*)—L *radius*. See **radius**.]

ray[2] [rā] *n* any of various fishes (order Hypotremata) with a flattened body and the eyes on the upper surface. [Fr *raie*—L *raia*.]

rayon [rā´on] *n* a textile fiber made from a cellulose solution; a fabric of such fibers. [From **ray** (1).]

raze [rāz] *vt* to graze; scrape off; to erase; to lay level with the ground. [Fr *raser*—L *rādĕre, rāsum*, to scrape.]

razor [rā´zòr] *n* a sharp-edged implement for shaving.—*ns* **rā´zorbill**, a N Atlantic auk (*Alca torda*) with black plumage above and white below and having a compressed bill.—Also **razor billed auk**. [OFr *rasour*—*raser*. See **raze**.]

re[1] [rā or rē] *prep* in the matter of, concerning. [L *in rē* (abl of *rēs*, thing), in the matter.]

re[2] [rā] *n* the 2d tone of the diatonic scale in solmization.

rē- [rē-] prefix meaning: again or anew; back. *re-* is sometimes hyphenated, as before a word beginning with *e* or to distinguish such forms as re-cover (to cover again) and recover.

reach [rēch] *vt* to stretch forth; to hand, pass; to succeed in touching or getting; to arrive at; to extend to; to attain to; to get in touch with, as by telephone.—*vi* to stretch out the hand; to extend in influence, space, etc.; to carry, as sight, sound, etc.; to attain; to try to get something.—*n* act or power of reaching; extent of stretch; range, scope; a continuous extent, esp of water. [OE *rǣcan*, Ger *reichen*, to reach.]

react [rē-akt´] *vi* to act reciprocally or in return to respond to a stimulus; to have a reciprocatory effect; to undergo chemical change.—*ns* **reac´tance**, (*elect*) the component of impedance due to inductance or capacitance; **reac´tant**, any substance involved in a chemical reaction; **reac´tion**, action resisting other action; backward tendency from revolution, reform, or progress; response to stimulus; mutual effect; a chemical change.—*adj* **reac´tionary**, of, or favoring, reaction.—*n* one who attempts to revert to past political conditions.—*adj* **reac´tive**, of, pertaining to, reaction; responsive to stimulus; produced by emotional stress.—*n* **reac´tor**, one who or that which undergoes a reaction; a container in which a chemical reaction takes place; a nuclear reactor. [LL *reagĕre, -actum*—*agĕre*, to do.]

read [rēd] *vt* to utter aloud, or go over with silent understanding (written or printed words); to observe and interpret (signs, or from signs, other than letters (eg *to read the clock, the time*; eg *to read one's face, one's thoughts, meaning*)); to study; to foretell (the future); to register, as a gauge; (of a computer) to obtain (information) from (punch cards, tapes, etc.); (*slang*) to hear and understand (a radio communication, etc.).—*vi* to perform the act of reading; to learn by reading (*with* **about** *or* **of**); to be phrased in certain words;—*pt, pt p* **read** [red].—*adjs* **read** [red], versed in books, learned; **read´able** [rēd´-], legible; interesting and attractively written.—*ns* **readabil´ity, read´ableness**.—*adv* **read´ably**.—*ns* **read´er**, one selected to read aloud to others, esp in a Christian Science church or society; a proofreader; one who evaluates manuscripts; a book for instruction and practice, esp in reading; a unit that scans material (as on punch cards) for storage or computation.—**readership**, all the readers of a certain publication, author, etc.; **read´ing**, the act of one who reads; any material to be read; the amount measured by a barometer, electric meter, etc.; a particular interpretation or performance; **read´ing desk**, a desk for holding a book in position for a standing reader; **read-only memory**, a small computer memory that cannot be changed by the computer and that contains a special purpose program; **read´-out**, output unit of a computer; data from it, printed, or registered on magnetic tape or punched paper tape.—**read between the lines**, to detect a meaning not expressed; **read out of**, to expel (from a group); **read the riot act**, to order a mob to disperse; to warn to cease something; to protest vehemently; to reprimand severely. [OE *rǣdan*, to discern, read—*rǣd*, counsel; Ger *raten*, to advise.]

ready [red´i] *adj* prepared; willing; inclined; liable; dexterous; prompt; quick, esp in repartee; handy; immediately available.—*vt* to make ready.—*n* the state of being ready, esp the position of a firearm ready to be fired.—*adv* **read´ily**.—*n* **read´iness**.—*adj* **read´y-made**, made before sale, not made to order.—Also (of clothing) **ready-to-wear**.—*n* a ready-made garment. [OE *(ge)rǣde*; cf Ger *bereit*.]

reagent [rē-ā´jènt] *n* (*chem*) a substance used to detect, measure, or react with other substances. [From same root as **react**.]

real[1] [rē´àl] *adj* actually existing; not counterfeit or assumed; true, genuine, sincere; (*law*) consisting of immovable things.—*adv* (*inf*) very.—*vt* **rē´alize**, to make real or as if real; to bring into being or fact, to accomplish, achieve; to convert into money; to obtain, bring (a specified price); to feel strongly, or to comprehend completely.—*adj* **rēalī´zable**.—*ns* **realīzā´tion**, the action of realizing; something realized; **rē´alism**, the doctrine that general terms, or universals, have an equal or superior reality to actual physical particulars; the tendency to look at, to accept, or to represent, things as they really are and be practical; precision in representing the details of actual life, in art or literature; **realist**.—*adj* **rēalis´tic**, pertaining to the realists or to realism; lifelike.—*n* **reality** [rē-al´i-ti], the state or fact of being real; truth.—*adv* **rē´ally**, in reality; actually; in truth.—*interj* indeed.—*n* **rē´alty**, (*law*) real estate.—**real estate**, property in buildings and land; **real number**, one of the numbers that have no imaginary parts and comprise rational and irrational numbers; **real presence**, the doctrine that Christ is actually present in the Eucharist. [Low L *reālis*—L *rēs*, a thing.]

real[2] [rā-äl´] *n* a former monetary unit and coin of Spain and its possessions; a former monetary unit and coin of Brazil and Portugal. [Sp,—L *rēgālis*, royal.]

realign [rē-a-līn´] *vt* to align afresh; to group or divide on a new basis.—*n* **realign´ment**. [Pfx **re-**, + **align**.]

realm [relm] *n* a kingdom; a domain, province, region; sphere (of action). [OFr *realme*—hypothetical LL *rēgālimen*—L *rēgālis*, royal.]

ream[1] [rēm] *n* a quantity of paper varying from 480 to 516 sheets; (*pl*) (*inf*) a great amount. [Ar *rizmah*, a bundle.]

ream[2] [rēm] *vt* to enlarge (a hole) with a reamer.—*n* **ream´er**, a sharp-edged tool for enlarging or tapering holes; a juicer. [OE *reman*, widen.]

reap [rēp] *vti* to cut down, as grain; to clear by cutting a crop; to derive (an advantage or reward).—*ns* **reap´er**, one who reaps; a reaping machine; **reap´hook**, a sickle. [OE *rīpan*, or *ripan*.]

rear[1] [rēr] *n* the back or hindmost part or position; a position behind; the part of an army, etc. farthest from the battle front.—*adj* of, at, or in the rear.—*ns* **rear ad´miral**, a commissioned officer in the navy who ranks above a commodore and in the coast guard who ranks above a captain; **rear´ guard**, the rear of an army; troops protecting it.—*adj* **rear´most**, last of all.—*n* **rear´ward**, the part of an army in the rear.—*adv* backward; at the back.—*adj* located at, near, or toward the rear; directed toward the rear. [Contracted from **arrear**; also partly from OFr *rere* (Fr *arrière*).]

rear[2] [rēr] *vt* to raise; to bring up, breed and foster; to set up; to educate, nourish, etc.—*vi* to rise on the hind legs, as a horse. [OE *rǣran*, to raise, causative of *rīsan*, to rise.]

reason [rē´zn] *n* ground, support, or justification (of an act or belief); a cause; a motive or inducement; the mind's power of drawing conclusions and determining truth; the exercise of this power; conformity to what is fairly to be expected or called for; moderation; sanity.—*vti* to think logically (about); analyze; to argue or infer.—*adj* **rea´sonable**, endowed with reason, rational; acting according to reason; agreeable to reason; just, not excessive, moderate.—*n* **rea´sonableness**.—*adv* **rea´sonably**.—*adj* **rea´soned**, argued out, logical.—*ns* **rea´soner; rea´soning**.—**stand to reason**, to be logical. [Fr *raison*—L *ratiō, -ōnis*—*rērī, rătus*, to think.]

reassure [rē-a-shōōr´] *vt* to assure anew; to reinsure; to give confidence to.—*n* **reassur´ance**. [Pfx **re-**, + **assure**.]

Réaumur [rā-ō-mür] *adj* of a thermometer or thermometer scale, having the freezing point of water marked 0° and the boiling point 80°. [RAF *de Réaumur* (1683–1757).]

reave *vti* to plunder; to rob;—*pt, pt p* **reaved, reft**.—*n* **reav´er**. [OE *rēafian*, to rob; cf Ger *rauben*, to rob.]

rebate [ri-bāt´] *vt* to reduce, abate; to dull, to blunt.—*vi* to give rebates.—*n* abatement; a return of part of a payment.—*n* **rēbat´er**. [Fr *rabattre*, to beat back—pfx *re-*, *abbatre*, to abate.]

rebec [rē´bek] *n* a medieval instrument of the viol class. [OFr *rebec*—Ar *rabāb, rebāb*.]

rebel [reb´(ė)l] *n* one who rebels.—*adj* rebellious.—*vi* [ribel´] to renounce the authority of the laws and government, or to take up arms and openly oppose them; to oppose any authority;—*pr p* **rebell´ing**; *pt, pt p* **rebelled´**.—*n* **rebell´ion** [-yȯn], act of rebelling; revolt.—*adj* **rebell´ious** [-yûs], engaged in rebellion; characteristic of a rebel or rebellion; inclined to rebel; refractory.—*adv* **rebell´iously**.—*n* **rebell´iousness**. [Fr *rebelle*—L *rebellis*, insurgent—pfx *re-*, against, *bellum*, war.]

rebound [ri-bownd´] *vi* to bound or start back from collision; to spring back; to recover quickly after a setback.—*n* act of rebounding; recoil.—**on the rebound**, after bouncing back; after being jilted. [Fr *rebondir*.]

rebuff [ri-buf´] *n* a repulse, unexpected refusal, snub.—*vt* to repulse, to snub. [OFr *rebuffe*—It *ribuffo*, a reproof—It *ri-* (=L *re-*), back, *buffo*, puff.]

rebuke [ri-būk´] *vt* to check, beat back; to put to shame; to reprove sternly.—*n* a reproach; stern reproof, reprimand.—*n* **rebūk´er**. [Anglo-Fr *rebuker* (OFr *rebucher*)—pfx *re-*, *bucher*, to strike.]

rebus [rē´bus] *n* an enigmatical representation of a name, etc., by pictures or signs punningly representing parts of a word or phrase, as in a puzzle, or a coat of arms;—*pl* **re´buses**. [L *rēbus*, by things, ablative pl of *rēs*, thing.]

rebut [ri-but´] *vt* to drive back; to repel; to refute in a formal manner by argument, proof, etc.—*vi* (*law*) to return an answer;—*pr p* **rebutt´ing**; *pt, pt p* **rebutt´ed**.—*ns* **rebutt´al, rebutt´er**. [OFr *reboter, rebouter, rebuter*, to repulse.]

recalcitrance [ri-kal´si-trans] *n* the state of being recalcitrant.—*adj* **recal´citrant**, refusing to obey authority, etc.; refractory; obstinate in opposition. [L *recalcitrāre, -ātum*, to kick back—*calx, calcis*, the heel.]

recall [ri-köl´] *vt* to call back; to command to return; to revoke; to call back to mind.—*n* act, power, or possibility of recalling or revoking; remembrance of things learned or experienced; the removal of, or right to remove, an official by popular vote. [Pfx **re-**, + **call**.]

recant [ri-kant´] *vti* to revoke a former declaration; to declare one's renunciation of one's former religious or political belief or adherence.—*n* **recantā´tion**. [L *recantāre*, to revoke—*cantāre*, to sing, to charm.]

recap[1] [rē-kap´] *n* to put a new tread on (a worn tire).—*n* [rē´kap] such a tire.

recap[2] [rē-´kap] *n* a recapitulation or summary.—*vti* to recapitulate.

recapitulate [rē-ka-pit´ū-lāt] *vt* to go over again the chief points of; to repeat in one's own life history (the process of development of the species).—*n* **recapitūlā´tion**. [L *recapitulāre, -ātum*—*re-*, again, *capitulum*, heading, chapter—*caput*, head.]

recapture [rē-kap´chùr] *vt* to capture back or retake; to regain, or to bring back to memory.—*n* act of retaking; a thing recaptured. [Pfx **re-**, + **capture**.]

recast [rē-käst´] *vt* to cast again; to reconstruct;—*pt, pt p* **recast´**. [Pfx **re-**, + **cast**.]

recede [ri-sēd´] *vi* to go, draw, or fall back, or to appear to do so; to bend or slope backward; to withdraw (from); to grow less; decline.—*vt* **recede**, [rē´-sēd´] to yield back.—*adj* **reced´ing**, sloping backward. [L *recēdĕre, recessum*—*re-*, back, *cēdĕre*, to go, yield.]

receipt [ri-sēt´] *n* receiving; place of receiving; a written acknowledgement of anything received; that which is received; (*pl*) amount of money received from business transactions.—*vt* to mark (a bill) as paid; to write a receipt for. [OFr *receite, recete* (Fr *recette*)—L (*rē*) *recepta*, fem pt p of *recipĕre*, to receive.]

receive [ri-sēv´] *vt* to take, get, or catch, usu. more or less passively; to have given or delivered to one; to admit, take in, or serve as receptacle of; to meet or welcome on entrance; to give audience to, or acknowledge socially; to give a specified reception to; to accept as authority or as truth; to be acted upon by, and transform, electrical signals.—*vi* to be a recipient; to hold a reception for visitors; to convert incoming radio waves in perceptible signals; to catch or gain possession of a kicked ball in football.—*adj* **receiv´able**, that can be received; due.—*adj* **received´**, generally accepted.—*ns* **receiv´er**, one who receives; one who knowingly accepts stolen goods; an instrument which transforms electrical signals into audible or visual form, as a telephone, radio, television set, etc.; (*football*) the player designated to receive a forward pass; (*law*) one appointed to administer or hold in trust property in bankruptcy or in a lawsuit; **receiv´er gen´eral**, a public officer in charge of the treasury (as of Massachusetts); **receiving blanket**, a small lightweight blanket used to wrap an infant (as after bathing); **receiving line**, a group of people who stand in line and individually welcome guests (as at a wedding reception). [Anglo-Fr *receivre*—L *recipĕre, receptum*—*re-*, back, *capĕre*, to take.]

recension [ri-sen´sh(ȯ)n] *n* a critical revision of a text; a text established by critical revision; a review. [L *recēnsēre*—*re-, cēnsēre*, to value.]

recent [rē´sėnt] *adj* of late origin or occurrence; relatively near in past time; modern; **Recent**, of the present or post-Pleistocene geological epoch.—*adv* **rē´cently**.—*n* **rē´centness**. [L *recēns, recentis*.]

receptacle [ri-sep´tȧ-kl] *n* that in which anything is or may be received or stored; the enlarged end of an axis bearing the parts of a flower or the crowded flowers of an inflorescence; a mounted female electrical fitting that contains the live parts of the circuit. [L *recipĕre, receptum*, to receive.]

reception [ri-sep´sh(ȯ)n] *n* the act, fact, or manner of receiving or of being received; a formal receiving, as of guests; response, reaction, the quality of the receiving of a radio or television broadcast; a social gathering often for the purpose of extending a formal welcome.—*n* **recep´tionist**, one employed to greet telephone callers, visitors, patients, or clients.—*adj* **recept´ive**, quick to receive impression, able to take in and absorb.—*ns* **recept´iveness, receptiv´ity**. [L *recipĕre, receptum*, to receive.]

recess [ri-ses´] *n* temporary halting of work, a session, school, etc.; a hidden or inner place; a niche or alcove.—*vt* to place in a recess; to form a recess in.—*vi* to take a recess.—*ns* **recession** [ri-sesh´ȯn], act of receding; withdrawal; the state of being set back; in trade, a temporary decline; [rē´sesh´ȯn], a ceding back; **recessional** [risesh´ȯn-ȧl], a hymn sung during recession or retirement of clergy and choir.—*adj* **recess´ive**, tending to recede; of an ancestral character, apparently suppressed in crossbred offspring in favor of the alternative contrasted character from the other parent, though it may be transmitted to later generations.—*n* a recessive character or gene; an organism having one or more recessive characteristics. [See **recede**.]

réchauffé [rā-shō´fā] *n* a warmed-over dish of food; a fresh concoction of old material. [Fr.]

recherché [rė-sher´shā] *adj* carefully chosen; particularly choice, select, peculiar and refined, rare. [Fr.]

recidivism [ri-sid´i-vizm] *n* the habit of relapsing into crime.—*n* **recid´ivist**. [Fr *récidivisme*—L *recidīvus*, falling back.]

recipe [res´i-pi] *n* directions for making something, esp a food or drink; a method laid down for achieving a desired end;—*pl* **rec´ipes**. [L *recipe*, take, imper, of *recipĕre*.]

recipient [ri-sip´i-ėnt] *adj* receiving.—*n* one who or that which receives. [L *recipiēns, -entis*, pr p of *recipĕre*, to receive.]

reciprocal [ri-sip´ro-k(ȧ)l] *adj* acting in return; mutual; giving and receiving or given and received; related inversely, complementary; (*gram*) expressing mutual action or relation (eg the pronouns *each other* and *one another*).—*n* that which is reciprocal; (*math*) the multiplier that gives unity (eg *b/a is the reciprocal of a/b*); unity divided by any quantity (eg *l/a*).—*adv* **recip´rocally**.—*vt* **recip´rocāte**, to give and receive mutually; to return, repay in kind.—*vi* to make a return; (*mech*) to move alternately to and fro.—*ns* **recip´rocating-en´gine**, an engine in which the to-and-fro motion of a piston is transformed into the circular motion of the crankshaft; **reciprocā´tion**.—*adj* **recip´rocātive**, characterized by or inclined to reciprocation.—*ns* **recip´rocātor**, one who or that which reciprocates; **reciprocity** [res-i-pros´it-i] mutual exchange of privileges, specifically, a recognition of two countries or institutions of the validity of licenses or privileges granted by the other. [L *reciprocus*.]

recision [ri-sizh´(ȯ)n] *n* cancellation. [L *recisiō, -ōnis*—*recidere*, to cut off.]

recite [ri-sīt´] *vt* to repeat from memory; to declaim; to read aloud publicly; to narrate, to give the particulars of.—*vi* to give a recitation.—*ns* **recī´tal**, act of reciting; setting forth; enumeration, narration; a public performance given by an individual musician or dancer or by a dance troupe; a concert given by music or dance pupils; **recitation** [resi-tā´sh(ò)n], a poem or passage for repeating from memory before an audience; the act of repeating it; a student's oral reply to questions; a class period; **recitative** [-tȧ-tēv´], a vocal style designed for the speechlike declamation of narrative episodes in operas, oratorios, or cantatas, marked by a strictly syllabic treatment of the text with careful attention to word accent.—*adj* in the style of recitative.—*n* **recit´er**. [L *recitāre—citāre, -ātum*, to call.]

reck [rek] *vt* (*arch*) to care for, heed; to matter.—*vi* to care; to worry.—*adj* **reck´less**, careless, rash; heedless (of consequences).—*adv* **reck´lessly**.—*n* **reck´lessness**. [OE *reccan, rēcan*; cf OHG *ruoh*, care, Ger *ruchlos*, regardless.]

reckon [rek´òn] *vt* to count, compute; to regard as being; to estimate; (*inf*) to think, believe, suppose or expect.—*vi* to calculate; (*inf*) to rely (on).—*ns* **reck´oner, reck´oning**, count or computation; the settlement of an account.—**reckon with**, to take into consideration. [OE *gerecenian*, to explain; Ger *rechnen*.]

reclaim [ri-klām´] *vt* to win back; to win from evil, wildness; to make (wasteland) fit for cultivation; to drain and use (land submerged by the sea, etc.); to obtain from waste material or from byproducts; [rē-klām´] to claim back.—*vi, adj* **reclaim´able**. [OFr *reclamer*—L *reclāmāre*.]

reclamation [rek-lȧ-mā´sh(ò)n] *n* act of reclaiming; state of being reclaimed. [L *reclāmatiō, -ōnis—reclāmāre—clāmāre*, to cry out.]

recline [ri-klīn´] *vt* to cause or permit to incline or bend backwards.—*vi* to lean in a recumbent position, on back or side. [L *reclīnāre, -ātum—clīnāre*, to bend.]

recluse [ri-klōōs´] *adj* enclosed, as an anchorite; secluded, retired, solitary.—*n* a religious devotee who lives shut up in a cell; one who lives retired from the world. [L *reclūsus*, pt p of *reclūdĕre*, to open, in later Latin, shut away—*re-*, back, away, *claudĕre*, to shut.]

recognize [rek´og-nīz] *vt* to know again, to identify by means of characteristics, or as known or experienced before; to show signs of knowing (a person); to acknowledge, admit, realize (eg *to recognize one's obligations; recognized as the ablest surgeon; to recognize that it was necessary*); to acknowledge formally; to acknowledge the status or legality of (eg a government); to show appreciation of, reward.—*adj* **rec´ogniz´able**.—*n* **recognizance** [ri-kog´nizȧns], a legal obligation entered into before a court or magistrate to do, or not do, some particular act, usu. under penalty of a money forfeiture; the sum liable to forfeiture. [OFr *reconiss-*, stem of *reconoistre*—L *recognoscĕre*, with *g* restored from L and ending assimilated to the suffx *-ise, -ize*.]

recognition [rek-og-nish´(ò)n] *n* act of recognizing; state of being recognized; acknowledgement; formal acknowledgement of status; sign of recognizing; the sensing and encoding of printed and written data by a machine. [L *recognoscĕre—re-*, again, *cognoscĕre, -nitum*, to know.]

recoil [ri-koil´] *vti* to rebound; to shrink (in horror, etc.); to kick back, as a gun.—*n* [rē´koil´] a starting or springing back, rebound; the kick of a gun; reaction. [Fr *reculer—cul*—L *cūlus*, the hinder parts.]

recollect [rek-òl-ekt´] *vt* to remember, esp with effort; to remind (oneself) of something temporarily forgotten.—*vi* to call something to mind.—*n* **recollec´tion**, act or power of recollecting; a memory, reminiscence; a thing remembered; tranquility of mind; religious contemplation. [L *re-*, again, and **collect**.]

recombinant [rē-kom´bi-nȧnt] *adj* exhibiting genetic recombination.—Also *n*.—*n* **recombinant DNA**, DNA prepared in the laboratory by breaking up and splicing together DNA from several different sources (as different species of organism).

recommend [rek-o-mend´] *vt* to commend, commit (eg to God's care); to introduce as worthy of confidence or favor; to advise; to make acceptable.—*adj* **recommend´able**.—*n* **recommendā´tion**.—*adj* **recommend´atory**. [L *re-*, again, + **commend**.]

recommit [rē-kom-it´] *vt* to commit again; to send back (eg a bill) to a committee.—*ns* **recommit´ment, recommitt´al**. [L *re-*, again, + **commit**.]

recompense [rek´om-pens] *vt* to return an equivalent for; to repay (eg *to recompense one's losses, one's efforts*;).—*n* that which is so returned; repayment. [OFr *récompenser*—L *re-*, again, *compensāre*, to compensate.]

recompose [rē-kom-pōz´] *vt* to compose again, rearrange; to form anew; to soothe or quiet.—*n* **recomposi´tion**. [L *re-*, again, + **compose**.]

reconcile [rek´on-sīl] *vt* to restore to friendship or union (persons; also a person to, with, another); to bring to regard with resignation or submission (eg *to reconcile oneself to hardship*); to make or prove consistent; to adjust, settle (eg differences); to check (a financial account) with another for accuracy.—*vi* to become reconciled.—*adj* **rec´oncīl´able**.—*ns* **rec´oncilement; rec´onciler; reconciliā´tion** [sil-], act of reconciling; state of being reconciled; the Roman Catholic sacrament of penance. [Fr *réconcilier*—L *re-*, again, *conciliāre, -ātum*, to call together.]

recondite [rek´on-dīt, ri-kon´dīt] *adj* obscure, abstruse, profound (of subject, style, author). [L *recondĕre, -itum*, to put away—*re-*, again, *condĕre*, to establish, store.]

recondition [rē-con-dish´(ò)n] *vt* to repair and refit; to restore to sound condition. [L *re-*, again, + **condition**.]

reconnaissance [ri-kon´i-sȧns] *n* the survey of a region, esp for obtaining military information about an enemy. [Fr.]

reconnoiter [rek-ò-noi´tėr] *vti* to make a reconnaisance (of);—*pr p* **reconnoitering**, [-tėr-]; *pt, pt p* **reconnoitered**, [-tėrd]. [Fr *reconnoître* (now *reconnaître*)—L *recognoscĕre*, to recognize.]

reconsider [rē-kon-sid´ėr] *vti* to consider again, esp with a view to altering a decision.—*n* **reconsiderā´tion**. [L *re-*, again, and **consider**.]

reconstitute [rē-kon´sti-tūt] *vt* to constitute again, esp to restore (a dried or condensed substance) to its original form by adding water.—*n* **reconstitu´tion**. [L *re-*, again, and **constitute**.]

reconstruct [rē-kon-strukt´] *vt* to construct again, to rebuild; to build up, as from remains, an image of the original.—*n* **reconstruc´tion**, a reconstructing; **Reconstruction**, the period or process, after the Civil War, of reestablishing the Southern States in the Union. [L *re-*, again, and **construct**.]

record [ri-körd´] *vt* to set down in writing for future reference; (of an instrument) to indicate, show as a reading; to state as if for a record; to register permanently by mechanical means; to register (sound or visual images) on a disc, tape, etc. for later reproduction.—*vi* to record something.—*adj* being the best, largest, etc.—*n* **record** [rek´örd], a register; a formal account in writing of any fact or proceedings; the known facts about anything or anyone; a performance or event that surpasses all others previously noted; a grooved disc for playing on a phonograph; the sounds so recorded.—*ns* **record´er**, an official who keeps records; a machine or device that records; a tape recorder; a flute of the earlier style blown through a mouthpiece at the upper end, not through a hole in the side; **record´ing**, what is recorded, as on a disc or tape; the record; **record player**, an instrument for playing phonograph records through a loudspeaker.—**for the record**, for public knowledge; on the record; **off the record**, not for publication; **of record**, being documented or attested; **on record**, recorded in a document, etc.; publicly known; **on the record**, for publication. [OFr *recorder*—L *recordārī*, to call to mind, get by heart.]

recount [ri-kownt´] *vt* to narrate the particulars of; to detail; **recount, re-count** [rē-kownt´], to count over again.—*n* a second count, as of votes. [OFr *reconter—re-*, again, *conter*, to tell.]

recoup [ri-kōōp´] *vt* to make good (losses); to recover expenses or losses; to regain.—*vi* to make good or make up for something lost. [Fr *recouper*, to cut again—*re-*, again, *couper*, to cut.]

recourse [rē´körs or ri-kors´] *n* a turning for aid or protection; that to which one turns seeking aid, etc. [Fr *recours*—L *recursus—re-*, back, *currĕre, cursum*, to run.]

re-cover [rē-kuv´ėr] *vt* to cover again. [Pfx **re-**, + **cover**.]

recover [ri-kuv´ėr] *vt* to get back or find again; to retrieve; (*arch*) to rescue; to regain (health, etc.); to make up for; to save (oneself) from a fall, etc.; to reclaim (land from the sea, etc.); (*sports*) to regain control of (a wild ball, etc.); (*reflex*) to bring back to normal condition, as after stumbling, losing control of feelings, etc.; to obtain as compensation.—*vi* to regain health or any former state or position; (*sports*) to recover a ball, etc.—*adj* **recov´erable**.—*n* **recov´ery**, the act, fact, process, possibility, or power of recovering, or state of having recovered; a retrieval of a capsule, etc. after a space flight.—*n* **recovery room**, a hospital room where postoperative patients are kept for close observation or care. [OFr *recovrer*—L *recuperāre*. See **recuperate**.]

recreant [rek´ri-ȧnt] *adj* surrendering, craven; false, apostate.—*n* a craven; a deserter; a renegade. [OFr, pr p of *recroire*, to yield in combat—LL *recrēdĕre*, to surrender—L *crēdĕre*, to entrust.]

recreate [rek´rē-āt] *vt* to reinvigorate, to refresh, esp to indulge, gratify, or amuse by sport or pastime.—*vi* to take recreation, amuse oneself.—*vt* (**re-create**) [rē´-], to create again, anew, esp in the mind.—*n* **recreā´tion**, any refreshment of the body or mind after toil, sorrow, etc.; pleasurable occupation of leisure time; an amusement or sport; (**recreation**) [rē-], a new creation.—*adjs* **recreā´tional** [rek-], **re-c´reātive** [rē-].—*n* **recreation room**, a room (as a rumpus room) used for relaxation and recreation; a public room (as in a hospital) for recreation and social activities. [L *re-*, again, and **create**.]

recriminate [ri-krim´in-āt] *vi* to charge an accuser.—*n* **recriminā´tion**.—*adjs* **recrim´inative, recrim´inatory**. [Through Low L—L *re-*, again, *crīmināri*, to accuse.]

recrudesce [rē-krōō-des´] *vi* to break out afresh after a period of inactivity.—*n* **recrudes´cence**.—*adj* **recrudes´cent**. [L *recrūdēscens, -entis*, pr p of *recrūdēscĕre—crūdus*, raw.]

recruit [ri-krōōt´] *n* a newly enlisted soldier, etc. or member.—*vti* to enlist (personnel) into an army or navy; to enlist (new members) for an organization; to increase or maintain the numbers of.—*n* **recruit´er**.—*n* **recruit´ment**, a recruiting. [Obs Fr *recrute*, reinforcement, dial pt p fem of *recroître*—L *recrēscĕre*, to grow again.]

rectangle [rek´tang-gl] *n* a four-sided plane figure with all its angles right angles.—*adj* **rectang´ūlar**, of the form of a rectangle; crossing, meeting, or lying at a right angle; having faces or surfaces shaped like right angles.—*n* **rectangular´ity**. [LL *rēct(i)angulum*—L *angulus*, an angle.]

rectify [rek´ti-fī] *vt* to set right, to correct, to adjust; (*chem*) to purify (as alcohol) by distillation; to change (an electric current) from alternating to direct;—*pr p* **rec´tifying**; *pt, pt p* **rec´tified**.—*adj* **rec´tifiable**, having finite length.—*ns* **rectificā´tion**; **rec´tifier**, a device for converting alternating current into direct current. [Fr *rectifier*—LL *rēctificāre*—L *rēctus*, straight, *facĕre*, to make.]

rectilin´ear [rek-ti-lin´ē-ȧr] *adj* moving in or forming a straight line; characterized by straight lines; corrected for distortion so that straight lines are imaged correctly. [L *rēctus*, straight, *līnea*, a line.]

rectitude [rek´ti-tūd] *n* straightness; uprightness; integrity; being correct in judgement or procedure. [Fr,—LL *rēctitūdo*—L *rectus*, straight.]

rector [rek´tȯr] *n* in some churches, a clergyman in charge of a parish; the head of certain schools, colleges, etc.—*n* **rec´torate**, a rector's office or term of office.—*adj* **rectorial** [-tō´ri-ȧl], of a rector.—*ns* **rec´torship; rec´tory**, the house of a minister or priest. [L *rēctor, -ōris*—*regĕre, rēctum*, to rule.]

rectum [rek´tum] *n* the terminal part of the large intestine;—*pl* **rec´ta**.—*adj* **rectal**, of, for, or near the rectum. [L neut of *rēctus*, straight.]

recumbent [ri-kum´bėnt] *adj* leaning, resting; lying down; (*anat*) tending to rest on the surface from which it extends.—*ns* **recum´bence, recum´bency**.—*adv* **recum´bently**. [L *recumbĕre*—*re-*, back, *cubāre*, to lie down.]

recuperate [ri-kū´pėr-āt] *vti* to get well again; to recover (losses, etc.).—*n* **recuperā´tion**. [L *recuperāre*, to recover.]

recur [ri-kûr´] *vi* to come back in thought, talk, etc.; to occur again or at intervals;—*pr p* **recurr´ing**; *pt, pt p* **recurred´**.—*n* **recurr´ence**.—*adjs* **recurr´ent**, (*anat*) of various nerves and blood vessels in arms and legs, turning back in an opposite direction; returning at intervals; **recur´sion**, of a mathematical formula, enabling a term in a sequence to be computed from one or more of the preceding terms; **recur´sive**, constituting a procedure that can repeat itself indefinitely or until a specified condition is met; involving mathematical recursion.—**recurring decimal**, repeating decimal. [L *recurrĕre*—*re-*, back, *currĕre*, to run.]

recusant [rek´ū-zȧnt or ri-kū-zȧnt] *n* a Roman Catholic who refused to attend the Church of England when it was legally compulsory (from about 1570 till 1791).—*adj* **rec´usancy** (or rė-kū´). [L *recūsāre*—*re-*, against, *causa*, a cause.]

recycle [rē-sī´kl] *vt* to pass through a cycle again; to process (as liquid body waste, glass, or cans) in order to regain material for human use; to save from loss and restore to usefulness; to make ready for reuse.—*vi* to return to an earlier point in a countdown; (of an electronic device) to return to an original condition. [L *re-*, **cycle**.]

red [red] *adj* (*comparative* **redd´er**; *superlative* **redd´est**) of a color like blood; (often) **Red**, politically left-wing, esp a communist.—*n* the color of blood; any red pigment; (often) **Red**, a communist, esp in the former USSR.—*vt* **redd´en**, to make red.—*vi* to grow red; to blush.—*adj* **redd´ish**.—*n* **red´ness**.—*ns* **red´ ad´miral**, a common butterfly of Europe and America (*Vanessa atalanta*) having broad orange-red bands on the forewings; **red blood cell**, any of the hemoglobin-containing cells that carry oxygen to the tissues and are responsible for the red color of vertebrate blood.—Also **red blood corpuscle, red cell, red corpuscle**.—*adj* **red´blood´ed**, high-spirited and strong-willed; vigorous; **red´breast**, a bird (as a robin) with a reddish breast; a reddish-bellied sunfish (*Leponis auritis*) of the eastern US.—Also **red-breasted bream**.—*adj* **red´brick**, built of red brick; (often) **Redbrick**, of the English universities founded in the 19th and early 20th centuries.—*ns* **red´cap**, a porter in a railroad station, etc.; **red carpet**, a very grand or impressive welcome or entertainment.—*adj* marked by ceremonial courtesy.—*ns* **red´coat**, a British soldier, esp in America during the Revolutionary War; **Red Cross**, an international society for the relief of suffering in time of war and disaster; **red currant**, any of numerous cultivated currants derived from two natural forms (*Ribus sativum* and *R rubrum*); **red deer**, the common Eurasian deer (*Cervuselaphus*) of temperate regions, related to the elk of N America; the whitetail in its summer coat; **red-´eye**, cheap whiskey; a late night or overnight flight; **red-eye gravy**, gravy made from ham juices; **red flag**, something that incites to vexation or anger; **Red Guard**, member of a teenage activist organization in China in the late 1960s.—*adj, adv* **red-´hand´ed**, in the act of committing a crime or misdeed.—*ns* **red´head**, a person having red hair; an American duck (*Aythya americana*); **red heat**, the state of being red-hot; **red herring**, a herring cured to a dark brown color; something used to divert attention from the main issue; **red-hot**, one who shows intense partisanship or emotion; a hot dog; a small red candy strongly flavored with cinnamon.—*adj* glowing with heat; extremely hot; very excited, angry, etc.; very new.—*adj* **red-letter**, of special significance.—*ns* **red light**, a warning signal, esp a red traffic signal; a cautionary sign; a deterrent; **red light district**, an area containing many prostitutes or brothels; **red´line**, a recommended safety limit; the red line which marks this point on a gauge.—*vi* to withhold home-loan funds or insurance from neighborhoods considered poor risks.—*vt* to discriminate against in housing or insurance.—*ns* **red pepper**, cayenne pepper; **redpoll**, any of several small finches (genus *Carduelis* or *Acanthus*), esp one (*C flammea*) of the northern regions of the New and Old World; **red´skin**, (*offensive*) an Amerindian; **red snapper**, any of various food fishes (genus *Lutjanus* and *Sebastodes*); **red squirrel**, a common N American squirrel (*Tamiasciurus hudsonicus* or *Sciuris hudsonicus*) having red upper parts and smaller than the gray squirrel; **red tape**, rigid adherence to routine and regulations, causing delay; **red tide**, sea water discolored by red protozoans poisonous to marine life; **redwood**, an important timber tree (*Sequoia sempervivens*) of California that can reach the height of 360 feet; any of various trees yielding a red dye or reddish wood. [OE *rēad*; cf Ger *rot*, L *ruber, rūfus*, Gr *erythros*, Gael *ruadh*.]

redact [ri-dakt´] *vt* to edit, work into shape; to select or adapt for publication.—*ns* **redac´tion, redac´tor**. [L *redigĕre, redactum*, to bring back—pfx *red-, re-*, back, *agĕre*, to drive.]

redeem [ri-dēm´] *vt* to buy back, recover by payment, etc.; to pay off (a mortgage, etc.); to turn in (coupons for premiums); to deliver from sin; to ransom; to pay the penalty of; to atone for; to fulfil (a promise); to restore (oneself) to favor.—*adj* **redeem´able**.—*ns* **redeem´ableness, redeem´er; Redeemer**, Jesus. [L *redimĕre*—*red-, re-*, back, *emĕre*, to buy.]

redemption [ri-dem(p)´sh(ȯ)n] *n* act of redeeming.—*adjs* **redemp´tive**, bringing about redemption; **re demp´tory**, serving to redeem. [L *redimĕre, redemptum*; cf **redeem**.]

redeploy [rē-di-ploi´] *vti* to transfer (eg military forces, supplies, industrial workers) from one area to another.—*n* **redeployment**. [L *re-*, again, + **deploy**.]

redingote [red´ing-gōt] *n* a long double-breasted overcoat worn by men in the 18th century; a woman's lightweight coat open at the front, usu. matching a dress; a dress with a front gore of contrasting material. [Fr,—Eng **riding-coat**.]

redintegrate [red-in´tė-grāt] (*arch*) *vt* to restore to wholeness; to renew.—*n* **redintegrā´tion**. [L *redintegrāre, -ātum*—*red-, re-*, again, *integrāre*, to make whole—*integer*.]

redirect [rē-di-rekt´] *vt* to change the course or direction of. [L *re-*, again, + **direct**.]

redolent [red´ō-lėnt] *adj* fragrant; smelling (of); suggestive (of).—*ns* **red´olence, red´olency**. [L *redolēns, -entis*—*red-, re-*, again, *olēre*, to emit smell.]

redouble [ri-dub´l] *vti* to double again; to make or become twice as much. [Fr *redoubler*. See **double**.]

redoubt [ri-dowt´] *n* a fieldwork enclosed on all sides, its ditch not flanked from the parapet; an inner last retreat. [Fr *redoute*—It *ridotto*—L *reductus*, retired—*redūcĕre*; the *b* from confusion with **redoubt** (2).]

redoubt´able [ri-dowt´ȧ-bl] *adj* formidable; valiant. [OFr *redouter*, to fear greatly—L *re-*, back, *dubitāre*, to doubt.]

redound [ri-downd´] *vi* to flow back, or to become swollen; to have an effect for good or ill; to become transferred or added; to come back; react (upon). [OFr *redonder*—L *redundāre*—*red-, re-*, back, *undāre*, to surge—*unda*, a wave.]

redress [ri-dres´] *vt* to set right (a wrong, a grievance); to reform (an abuse, a fault); to readjust (the balance); to remedy.—*n* relief; reparation. [Fr *redresser*. See **dress**.]

reduce [ri-dūs´] *vt* to change to another form; to express in other terms (*with* **to**); to put into (eg *to reduce to writing, practice*); to degrade; to impoverish; to subdue; to lessen; to diminish in size, amount, extent, or number; to weaken; to drive to (eg *reduce to tears*); to extract (a metal from ore); (*photog*) to make (a negative) less dense; (*surgery*) to restore (a dislocated part) to proper position; (*chem*) to convert (oxide, etc.) to metal; (*chem*) to remove oxygen from or to add hydrogen or electrons to.—*vi* to resolve itself; to slim.—*adj* **reduced´**, in a state of reduction; weakened; impoverished; diminished; simplified.—*adj* **reduc´ible**.—*n* **reduction**, [-duk´sh(ȯ)n] act of reducing or state of being reduced; diminution; subjugation; meiosis; (*arith*) changing of numbers or quantities from one denomination to another.—**reducing agent**, a substance capable of bringing out chemical reduction, usu. by donating electrons; **reductio ad absurdum**, proof of the falsity of an assumption by pointing out its logical, but obviously false, inferences; carrying out the application of a principle to absurd lengths. [L *redūcĕre, reductum*—*re-*, back, *dūcĕre*, to lead.]

redundant [ri-dun´dȧnt] *adj* superfluous, excessive, wordy; (of words) unnecessary to the meaning.—*n* **redun´dancy**.—*adv* **redun´dantly**. [L *redundāns, -antis*, pr p of *redundāre*, to overflow.]

reduplicate [ri-dū´pli-kāt] *vt* to double; to repeat; (*gram*) to show, have reduplication.—*adj* doubled.—*n* **reduplicā´tion**, a folding or doubling; (*gram*) the complete or partial repetition of an element or elements, as a method of tense formation or forming a plural, etc.—*adj* **redu´plicātive**. [L *reduplicāre, -ātum*—*duplicāre*, to double.]

reecho [rē-ek´ō] *vt* to echo back; to repeat as or like an echo.—*vi* to give back echoes; to resound. [L *re-*, back, + **echo**.]

reed [rēd] *n* a tall stiff hard-culmed grass, esp the ditch reed (*Phragmites communis*), found in marshes throughout temperate and warm regions of the world; a musical instrument made from a hollow stem; a person or thing too weak to rely on; one easily swayed or overcome; the vibrating tongue of an organ pipe or woodwind instrument; the part of a loom by which the warp threads are separated.—*ns* **reed´or´gan**, a keyboard instrument with free reeds, as the harmonium; **reed´pipe**, a pipe, esp of a pipe-organ, whose tone is produced by the vibration of a reed.—*adj* **reed´y**, abounding with reeds; resembling a reed in slenderness and fragility; having the tone quality of a reed instrument. [OE *hrēod*; cf Du and Ger *riet*.]

reef[1] [rēf] *n* a chain of rocks at or near the surface of water; a hazardous obstruction; a lode or vein of ore. [Du *rif*—ON *rif*.]

reef[2] [rēf] *n* a portion of a sail that may be rolled or folded up.—*vti* to reduce the exposed surface (of a sail); to lower or bring inboard (a spar).—*ns* **reef´er**, one who reefs; a short jacket worn by sailors; any similar close-fitting, double-breasted coat; (*inf*) a marijuana cigarette; **reef knot**, a square knot used in reefing a sail. [ON *rif*.]

reek [rēk] *n* (*dial*) smoke; vapor; fume.—*vi* emit smoke, fumes, or strong or offensive smell.—*vt* to subject to the action of smoke or vapor; to give off; to exude smell.—*adj* **reek´y**, smoky. [OE *rēc*; ON *reykr*, Ger *rauch*, Du *rook*, smoke.]

reel [rēl] *n* a cylinder, drum, or spool on which wire, cables, films, etc., may be wound; a lively dance, esp Scottish Highland or Irish; a tune for it; a length of material wound on a reel.—*vt* to wind on a reel.—*vi* to dance the reel; to stagger; to waver.—**reel in**, to wind on a reel; to pull in (a fish) by winding a reel; **reel off**, to tell, write, etc. with fluency; **reel out**, to unwind from a reel. [OE *hrēol*, but possibly partly of other origin; Gael *righil* (the dance) may be from English.]

reelect [rē-ė-lekt´] *vt* to elect again.—*n* **reelec´tion**. [L *re-*, again, + **elect**.]

reenact [rē-en-akt´] *vt* to enact again.—*n* **reenact´ment**. [L *re-*, again, + **enact**.]

reenter [rē-en´tėr] *vti* to enter again or anew.—*adj* **reen´trant**, pointing inward.—*n* one that reenters or is reentrant; an indentation in a landform.—*n* **reen´try**, an entering again; resumption of possession; a playing card that will enable a player to regain the lead; the action of reentering the earth's atmosphere after travel in space. [L *re-*, again, + **enter**.]

reeve[1] [rēv] *n* (*hist*) a high official, chief magistrate of a district; the council president in some Canadian municipalities; a local official responsible for the enforcement of specific regulations. [OE *gerēfa*.]

reeve[2] [rēv] *vt* to pass the end of a rope through any hole, as the channel of a block;—*pt, pt p* **reeved, rove**. [Origin obscure.]

refection [ri-fek´sh(ȯ)n] *n* refreshment of mind, spirit, or body; a meal or repast.—*n* **refectory** [ri-fek´tȯr-i], a dining hall, esp monastic.—**refectory table**, a long table with heavy legs. [L *reficĕre, refectum—re-*, again, *facĕre*, to make.]

refer [ri-fûr] *vt* to assign (to class, a cause or source, etc.); to hand over for consideration; to direct for information (to a person or place).—*vi* to have recourse (to, eg, a dictionary) for information; to make mention or allusion (*with* **to**); to direct attention (to);—*pr p* **referr´ing**; *pt, pt p* **referred´**.—*adj* **referable** [ref´ėr-å-bl; ri-fer´i-bl], to be referred or assigned.—*ns* **referee** [ref-ė-rē´], one to whom anything is referred; an arbitrator, umpire, or judge; **ref´erence**, the act of referring; a submitting for information or decision; relation; allusion; one who is referred to; a testimonial; a book or passage referred to; **ref´erence mark**, a conventional mark (as *, †, or ‡) placed in a written or printed text to direct the reader's attention, esp to a footnote; **referen´dum**, the principle or practice of submitting a law directly to the vote of entire electorate (*pl* **-da, -dums**); **ref´erent**, the thing that a sign or symbol stands for; the thing referred to, esp by a word or expression; **referr´al**, act or instance of referring or being referred, esp to another person, etc. for eg consideration, treatment. [L *referre*, to carry back—*re-*, back, *ferre*, to carry.]

refill [rē´fil´] *vt* to fill again.—*n* [rē´-], a duplicate for refilling purposes; a refilling of a medical prescription. [L *re-*, again, + **fill**.]

refine [ri-fīn´] *vt* to purify; to clarify; to free from coarseness, vulgarity, crudity; to make more cultured.—*vi* to become more fine, pure, subtle, or cultured; to affect nicety; to improve by adding refinement or subtlety (*with* **on** *or* **upon**).—*adj* **refined´**, polished, well-mannered; cultured; affectedly well-bred.—*ns* **refine´ment**, act or practice of refining; state of being refined; culture in feelings, taste, and manners; an improvement; a subtlety; **refin´er; refin´ery**, a place for refining eg sugar, oil; **refin´ing**. [L *re-*, denoting change of state, + **fine** (1).]

refit [rē-fit´] *vti* to make or become fit again by repairing, reequiping, etc.—*ns* **refit´, refit´ment, refitt´ing**. [L *re-*, again, + **fit** (1).]

reflation [rē-flā´shȯn] *n* the restoration of deflated prices to a desirable level.—*adj* **reflā´tionary**. [L *re-*, again, + **inflation**.]

reflect [rī-flekt´] *vt* to bend back or aside; to throw back after striking; to give an image of in the manner of a mirror; to cast, shed (as credit, discredit); to express, exemplify.—*vi* to bend or turn back or aside; to mirror; to meditate; to consider meditatively (*with* **upon**); to cast reproach (*with* **on, upon**).—*adj* **reflect´ed**, cast or thrown back; turned or folded back; mirrored.—*adj* **reflect´ing**.—*n* **reflection**, a turning, bending, or folding aside, back or downwards; change of direction when a ray strikes upon a surface and is thrown back; reflected light, color, heat, etc.; an image in a mirror; the action of the mind by which it is conscious of its own operations; attentive consideration; contemplation; a thought or utterance resulting from contemplation; censure or reproach.—*adj* **reflect´ive**, reflecting; reflected; meditative.—*adv* **reflect´ively**.—*ns* **reflect´iveness; reflect´or**, a reflecting surface, instrument, or body.—*adj* **reflex** [rē´fleks], bent or turned back; reflected; reactive; of an angle, more than 180°; involuntary, produced by, or concerned with, the response from a nerve center to a stimulus from without.—*n* a reflection, reflected image; reflected light; a reflex action; a linguistic element derived from a prior element or system.—*adj* **reflex´ive** (*gram*), referring back to the subject.—*adv* **reflex´ively**.—**reflecting telescope**, one in which the principal means of focusing the light is a mirror. [L *reflectĕre, reflexum—flectĕre*, to bend.]

refluent [ref´lŏŏ-ėnt] *adj* flowing back, ebbing.—*ns* **ref´luence, reflux** [rē´fluks], flowing back, ebb. [L *refluens, -entis*, pr p of *refluĕre—re-*, back, *fluĕre, fluxum*, to flow.]

re-form [rē-förm´] *vti* to form again.—*vt* **reform´** [ri-], to remove defects from (eg a political institution, a practice); to put an end to (eg an abuse); to bring (a person) to a better way of life.—*vi* to abandon evil ways.—*n* amendment or transformation, esp of a system or institution; removal of political or social abuses.—*ns* **re-formation** [rē´förmā´sh(ȯ)n], the act of forming again; **reformation** [ref-ȯrmā´sh(ȯ)n], the act of reforming; amendment, improvement; **Reformation**, the great religious revolution of the 16th century, which gave rise to the various Protestant churches.—*adjs* **reformative** [ri-förm-a-tiv], tending to produce reform; **refor´matory**, reforming; tending to produce reform.—*n* an institution for reforming young law offenders.—*adjs* **rē-formed´**, formed again, anew; **reformed** [rī-formd´], amended, improved; **Reformed´**, Protestant, esp Calvinistic in doctrine or polity.—*ns* **reform´er**, one who reforms; one who advocates political reform; an apparatus for cracking oils or gases to form specialized products; **Reform´er**, one of those who took part in the Reformation of the 16th century. [L *refōrmāre, -ātum—fōrmāre*, to shape—*fōrma*, form; partly from *re-*, + **form**.]

refract [ri-frakt´] *vt* to cause (a ray of light, etc.) to undergo refraction.—*ns* **refrac´tion**, the bending of a ray or wave of light, heat, or sound as it passes from one medium into another; **refractor**, refracting telescope.—*adj* **refrac´tive**.—**refracting telescope**, one in which the principal means of focusing the light is a lens. [L *refringĕre, refractum—re-*, back, *frangĕre*, to break.]

refractory [ri-frak´tȯr-i] *adj* unruly, unmanageable, obstinate, perverse; not yielding to treatment; difficult to fuse, corrode, or draw out, esp capable of withstanding high temperature.—*n* a material suitable for lining furnaces.—*n* **refrac´toriness**. [L *refractārius*, stubborn.]

refrain[1] [ri-frān´] *n* a line or phrase recurring, esp at the end of a stanza; the music of such a refrain. [OFr *refrain—refraindre*—L *refringĕre—frangĕre*, to break.]

refrain[2] [ri-frān´] *vt* (*arch*) to curb, restrain.—*vi* to keep from action; to abstain (from). [OFr *refrener*—Low L *refrēnāre—re-*, back, *frēnum*, a bridle.]

refrangible [ri-fran´ji-bl] *adj* that may be refracted.—*n* **refrangibil´ity**. [For *refringible*—root of **refract**.]

refresh [ri-fresh´] *vt* to make fresh again; to give new vigor, spirit, brightness, etc., to.—*vi* to become fresh again; to take refreshment, esp drink.—*adj* **refresh´ing**, reviving, invigorating; pleasing or stimulating by a lack of sophistication.—*n* **refresh´er**, something (as a drink) that refreshes; a reminder; a course of study or training to maintain the standard of one's knowledge or skill.—*n* **refresh´ment**, the act of refreshing; state of being refreshed; renewed strength or spirit; that which refreshes, as food or rest; (*pl*) food or drink, or both. [L *re-*, again, + **fresh**.]

refrigerate [ri-frij´er-āt] *vt* to make cold; to expose to great cold, as (food) for preservation.—*n* **refrigerā´tion**.—*n* **refrig´erator** [-ėr-ā-tȯr], something that refrigerates; a cabinet, room or appliance for keeping food and other items cool; an apparatus for rapidly cooling heated liquids or vapors in a distilling process. [L *refrīgerāre, -ātum—re-*, denoting change of state, *frīgerāre—frīgus*, cold.]

reft [reft] *pt, pt p* of **reave**.

refuge [ref´ūj] *n* a shelter or protection from danger or trouble; an asylum or retreat.—*n* **refugēē´**, one who flees for refuge to another country, esp from religious or political persecution. [Fr,—L *refugium—re-*, back, *fugĕre*, to flee.]

refulgent [ri-ful´jėnt] *adj* casting a flood of light, radiant, beaming.—*n* **reful´gence**. [L *refulgens, -entis*, pr p of *refulgēre—re-*, inten, *fulgēre*, to shine.]

refund [rē-fund´] *vti* to repay; to restore what was taken.—*n* [rē´fund], a refunding or the amount refunded. [L *refundĕre—re-*, back, *fundĕre*, to pour.]

refuse[1] [ri-fūz´] *vt* to decline to take or accept; to renounce; to decline to give.—*vi* to make refusal.—*n* **refū´sal**, the act of refusing; the option of taking or refusing; **refuse´nik**, a Soviet citizen, esp a Jew, refused permission to emigrate. [Fr *refuser*—L *refundĕre, refūsum—fundĕre*, to pour.]

refuse[2] [ref´ūs] *adj* rejected as worthless.—*n* waste, that which is rejected or left as worthless. [Prob OFr *refus*, refusal—*refuser*; see foregoing.]

refute [ri-fūt´] *vt* to disprove.—*adj* **refutable** [ref´ūt-å-bl, or ri-fūt´-].—*adv* **ref´utably** [or ri-fūt´-].—*n* **refutā´tion** [ref-]. [L *refūtāre*.]

regain [rē-gān´] *vt* to gain back; to get back to (eg *to regain the shore*). [Fr *regaigner* (now *regagner*.]

regal [rē´gål] *adj* royal; kingly.—*n* **regality** [rē-gal´i-ti], state of being regal; royalty; sovereignty.—*adv* **rē´gally**. [L *rēgālis—rex*, a king—*regĕre*, to rule.]

regale [ri-gāl´] *vt* to entertain, as with a feast; to give pleasure or amusement to.—*vi* to feast oneself; to feed.—*n* a feast; a choice dish. [Fr *régaler*—It *regalare*, perh—*gala*, a piece of finery.]

regalia [ri-gā´li-a] *n pl* royal privileges or powers; the insignia of royalty, crown, scepter, etc., insignia or decorations of an office or membership; finery. [Neut pl of L *rēgālis*, royal.]

regard [ri-gärd´] *vt* to look at, to observe; to look on (with eg affection); to esteem highly, to respect; to consider (as); to take into account.—*n* look; attention with interest; concern; esteem, respect; relation; reference; (*pl*) good wishes.—*n* **regar´der**.—*adj* **regard´ful**, heedful; respectful.—*prep* **regar´ding**, concerning.—*adj* **regard´less**, heedless; inconsiderate.—*adv* (*inf*) despite expense; without regard to consequences; **regardless of**, in spite of; **with regard to**, with respect to, as far as (the thing specified) is concerned. [Fr *regarder—re-, garder*, to keep watch.]

regatta [ri-gat´a] *n* a boat race; a series of boat races. [It (Venetian) *regata*.]

regelation [rē´jė-lā´sh(ȯ)n] *n* (of ice melted under pressure) the act of freezing anew when pressure is removed. [L *re-*, again, *gelāre*, to freeze.]

regency [rē´jėn-si] *n* the office, term of office, jurisdiction, or dominion of a regent or body or regents.—**the Regency**, in Eng hist, 1810–1820, when the Prince of Wales (later George IV) was Prince Regent. [Formed from **regent**.]

regenerate [ri-jen´ėr-āt] *vt* to produce anew; to renew spiritually; to reform completely; to reproduce (a part anew; the body); (*chem*) to produce again in a changed form; to increase the amplification of (an electron current) by causing part of the output circuit to act upon the input circuit.—*vi* to be regenerated.—*adj* [-ȧt] regenerated, renewed; spiritually reborn or converted; restored to a better or more worthy state; **regenerā´tion**, renewal of lost parts; spiritual rebirth; utilization of products (as heat) that would ordinarily be lost.—*adj* **regen´erative**.—*adv* **regen´eratively**. [L *regenerāre, -ātum*, to bring forth again—*re-*, again, *generāre*, to generate.]

regent [rē´jėnt] *adj* invested with interim or vicarious sovereign authority.—*n* one invested with interim authority on behalf of another; a member of a governing board (as of a state university). [L *regens, -entis*, pr p of *regĕre*, to rule.]

regicide [rej´i-sīd] *n* the killing or killer of a king. [L *rēx, rēgis*, a king, *caedĕre*, to kill.]

regime, régime [rā-zhēm´] *n* regimen; a political or ruling system. [Fr,—L *rĕgimen*.]

regimen [rej´i-men] *n* government; rule; a system of diet, exercise, etc. for improving the health; a regular course of strenuous training. [L *rĕgimen, -inis—regĕre*, to rule.]

regiment [rej´i-mėnt] *n* a military unit, smaller than a division, consisting usu. of a number of battalions.—*vt* [rej´imėnt´], to systematize, organize; to subject to excessive control; to subject to order or conformity.—*n* **regimentation** [-i-mėn-tā´-sh(ȯ)n].—*adj* **regimental** [-i-ment´(ȧ)l], of a regiment. [LL *rĕgimentum*—L *regĕre*, to rule.]

region [rē´jȯn] *n* a large, indefinite part of the earth's surface; one of the zones in which the atmosphere is divided; a part of the body.—*adj* **rē´gional**.—*n* **re´gionalism**, regional quality in life or literature; a word, etc. peculiar to some geographic region.—**in the region of**, near; about, approximately. [Anglo-Fr *regiun*—L *rĕgiō, -ōnis—regĕre*, to rule.]

register [rej´is-tėr] *n* a written record, regularly kept; the book containing such a record; a recording apparatus; an opening into a room by which the amount of air passing through can be controlled; a variety of language that is appropriate to a subject or occasion; a device in a computer in which data can both be stored and operated on; the set of pipes controlled by an organ stop; the compass of a voice or instrument; (*printing*) exact correspondence in position.—*vt* to enter in a register; (of an instrument) to record on a scale; to indicate by bodily expression (eg *to register astonishment*); to pay a special fee for (a letter, etc.) in order that it may have special care in transit.—*vi* to enter one's name in a list, as of voters; to enroll formally as a student; to be in correct alignment; to make or convey an impression; correspond.—*adj* **reg´istered**, recorded, entered, or enrolled, eg as a voter; recorded as to ownership or designation, as of luggage or a letter requiring special precautions for security, etc.; recorded in the studbook of a breeding association; qualified formally or officially.—*ns* **reg´istrar** [-trär], one who keeps records, esp the officer of an educational institution in charge of student records; an admitting officer at a hospital; **registrā´tion**, act of registering; record of having registered; the act or art of combining stops in organ-playing; **reg´istry**, registration; a list or book of names, etc.; the nationality of a ship according to its entry in a register; a place of registration; an official record book; an entry in it.—**registered nurse**, a trained nurse who has passed a State examination. [OFr *registre*, or Low L *registrum*, for L pl *regesta*, things recorded—*re-*, back, *gerĕre*, to carry.]

regnant [reg´nȧnt] *adj* reigning; having the chief power; prevalent. [L *rēgnāns, -antis*, pr p of *rēgnāre*, to reign.]

regress [rē´gres] *n* passage back; return; right or power of returning.—*vi* [ri-gres´], to go back; to return to a former place or state.—*n* **regression** [ri-gresh(ȯ)n], act of regressing; reversion; return towards the mean; return to an earlier stage of development.—*adj* **regressive** [ri-gres´iv]. [L *regressus, -ūs—regredī, regressus—re-*, perh *gradī, gressus*, to go.]

regret [ri-gret´] *vt* to remember with sense of loss or of having done amiss; to feel sorrow or dissatisfaction because (*with* **that**), or because of;—*pr p* **regrett´ing**; *pt, pt p* **regrett´ed**.—*n* sorrowful wish that something had been otherwise; compunction; an intimation of regret or refusal.—*adjs* **regret´ful**, feeling regret; **regrett´able**, to be regretted.—*advs* **regret´fully, regrett´ably**. [OFr *regreter, regrater*; perh conn with **greet** (2).]

regular [reg´ū-lȧr] *adj* belonging to a religious order; governed by or according to rule, law, order, habit, custom, established practice, mode prescribed, or the ordinary course of things; uniform; periodical; (*gram*) inflected in the usual way (esp of weak verbs); (*geom*) having all the sides and angles equal; (of soldier, army) permanent, professional, or standing; (*inf*) thorough, complete; (*inf*) pleasant, friendly.—*n* a regular soldier or player; (*inf*) one who is regular in attendance; (*politics*) one loyal to the party.—*vt* **reg´ularize**, to make regular.—*n* **regularity** [-ar´i-ti], state, character, or fact of being regular.—*adv* **reg´ularly**.—*vt* **reg´ulāte**, to control according to a rule; to adapt or adjust continuously; to adjust so as to make work accurately.—*n* **regulā´tion**, act of regulating; state of being regulated; a rule prescribed, esp in the interests of order or discipline.—*adj* prescribed by regulation (eg *regulation dress*).—*adj* **reg´ulātive**, tending to regulate.—*ns* **reg´ulātor**, one who, or that which, regulates; a regulatory gene; **regulatory gene, regulator gene**, a gene controlling the production of a genetic repressor. [L *rēgula*, a rule—*regĕre*, to rule.]

regulus [reg´ū-lus] *n* an impure metal, an intermediate product in smelting of ores; **Regulus**, a first-magnitude star in the constellation Leo. [L *rēgulus*, dim of *rex*, king.]

regurgitate [rē-gûr´ji-tāt] *vt* to cast out again, to pour back; to bring back into the mouth after swallowing.—*vi* to gush back.—*n* **regurgitā´tion**. [Low L *regurgitāre, -ātum—re-*, back, *gurges, gurgitis*, a whirlpool, gulf.]

rehabilitate [rē-(h)a-bil´i-tāt] *vt* to reinstate, restore to former privileges, rights, etc.; to clear the character of; to put back in good condition; to restore, by opportunity for gradual adjustment or specialized training (after illness or absence), fitness for living or making a living in normal or contemporary conditions.—*n* **rehabilitā´tion**. [LL *rehabilitāre, -ātum—habilitāre*, to enable—L *habilis*, able.]

rehash [rē-hash´] *n* something (esp a book or an article) made up of materials formerly used.—Also *vt*. [L *re-*, again, + **hash**.]

rehearse [ri-hürs´] *vt* to repeat, to recount, narrate in detail; to practice (a play, etc.) for public performance.—*vi* to take part in rehearsal.—*ns* **rehears´al**, the act of rehearsing; repetition; narration; enumeration; a performance for trial or practice; **rehear´ser**. [OFr *rehercer, reherser—re-*, again, *hercer*, to harrow—*herce* (Fr *herse*)—L *hirpex, -icis*, a rake, a harrow.]

reheat [rē-hēt´] *vt* to heat again. [L *re-*, again, + **heat**.]

rehouse [rē-howz´] *vt* to provide with a new or substitute house or houses.—*n* **rehous´ing**. [L *re-*, + **house**.]

reign [rān] *n* rule of a monarch; predominating influence; time of reigning.—*vi* to be a monarch; to be predominant.—**reign of terror**, a period marked by violence often committed by those in power that produces widespread terror. [OFr *regne*—L *rēgnum—regĕre*, to rule.]

reimburse [rē-im-bûrs´] *vt* to repay; to pay an equivalent to (for loss or expense).—*n* **reimburse´ment**. [LL *imbursāre—in*, in, *bursa*, purse.]

rein [rān] *n* the strap of a bridle; (*pl*) any means of curbing or governing.—*vt* to govern with the rein; to restrain or control.—*adj* **rein´less**, without rein or restraint.—**draw rein**, to pull up, stop riding; **give rein to**, to leave unchecked. [OFr *reine, resne, rene*, perh from L *retinēre*, to hold back.]

reindeer [rān´dēr] *n* any of several large deer (subspecies of *Rangifer tarandus*), wild and domesticated, of northern regions, antlered in both sexes, grouped with the caribou in a single species.—*n* **rein´deer moss**, a lichen (*Cladonia rangiferina*), the winter food of the reindeer, sometimes eaten by man. [ON *hreinndȳri*, or ON *hreinn* (OE *hrān*), + **deer**.]

reinforce [rē-in-förs´] *vt* to enforce again; to strengthen with new force or support.—*n* **reinforce´ment**, the act of reinforcing; additional force or assistance, esp (*pl*) of troops.—**reinforced concrete**, concrete strengthened by embedded steel bars. [L *re-*, again, + **enforce**.]

reins [rānz] *n pl* the kidneys; the seat of emotion; the loins. [OFr *reins*—L *rēnēs*.]

reinstate [rē-in-stāt´] *vt* to restore or re-establish in a former station, condition, or employment.—*n* **reinstāte´ment**. [L *re-*, again, + obs *instate*, to install.]

reinvest [rē-in-vest´] *vt* to invest again or anew; to invest (as income from investments) in additional securities; to invest (as earnings) in a business instead of distributing as dividends or profits.—*n* **reinvest´ment**. [L *re-*, again, + **invest**.]

reissue [rē-ish´ū] *vt* to issue again. [L *re-*, again, + **issue**.]

reiterate [rē-it´ė-rāt] *vt* to repeat; to repeat again and again.—*n* **reiterā´tion**.—*adj* **reit´erative**. [L *re-*, again, + **iterate**.]

reject [ri-jekt´] *vt* to throw out; to refuse to adopt, to have, to believe, to grant (eg a request), etc.—*n* [rē´jekt], a person or thing put aside as unsatisfactory.—*n* **rejec´tion**. [L *rejicĕre, rejectum—re-*, back, *jacĕre*, to throw.]

rejoice [ri-jois´] *vt* to make joyful, to gladden.—*vi* to feel joy, to exult; to make merry.—*n* **rejoic´ing**, act of being joyful; expression, subject, or experience of joy.—**rejoice in**, to possess; to have. [OFr *resjoir, resjoiss-* (Fr *réjouir*)—L *re-, ex, gaudēre*, to rejoice.]

rejoin [ri-join´] *vi* (*law*) to reply to a charge or pleading.—*vt* to say in answer; [rē-] to join again.—*n* **rejoin´der** [ri-], (*law*) the defendant's answer to a plaintiff's *replication*; an answer to a reply, an answer. [L *re*, again, + **join**.]

rejuvenate [ri-jōō´vė-nāt] *vt* to make, feel or seem young again.—*n* **rejuvenā´tion**.—*vi* **rejuvenesce** [-es´], to grow young again.—*n* **rejuvenes´cence**.—*adj* **rejuvenes´cent**. [L *re-*, again, *juvenis*, young, *juvenēscĕre*, to become young.]

relapse [ri-laps´] *vi* to slide, sink or fall back; to return to a former state or practice, to backslide.—*n* a falling back into a former bad state; return of an illness after partial recovery. [L *relābī, relapsus—re-*, back, *lābī*, to slide.]

relate [ri-lāt´] *vt* to recount, narrate, tell; to ally by connection or kindred.—*vi* to have reference or relation (to).—*adj* **relā´ted**, recounted; referred; connected; allied by kindred or marriage.—*n* **relā´tion**, act of relating; recital; a narrative; state or mode of being related; way in which one thing is connected with another; connection by blood or marriage; a relative; (*pl*) the connections between or among persons, nations, etc.—*adj* **relā´tional**, expressing relation; of the nature of relation.—*n* **relā´tionship**, state or mode of being related; relations.—*adj* **relative** [rel´a-tiv], in or having relation; corresponding; relevant; comparative, not absolute or independent; meaningful only in relationship; (*gram*) referring to an antecedent.—*n* that which is relative; a relative word, esp a relative pronoun; one who is related by blood or marriage.—*adv* **rel´atively**.—*n* **relativ´ity**, state or fact of being relative; (*physics*) the theory of the relative, rather than absolute, character of motion, velocity, mass, etc. and the interdependence of time, matter, and space.—**relative adverb**, an adverb which introduces a subordinate clause and serves as both an adverb and a conjunction; **relative clause**, any subordinate clause introduced by a relative pronoun or relative adverb; **relative humidity**, the ratio of the amount of moisture in the air to the top amount possible at the temperature; **relative pronoun**, any pronoun used to connect a dependent clause to a main clause and refers to a substantive in that main clause.—**in** (or **with**) **relation to** concerning; regarding. [L *relātus, -a, -um*, used as a pt p of *referre*, to bring back—*re-, ferre*.]

relax [ri-laks´] *vt i* to loosen (eg one's hold); to make or become less close, tense, rigid, strict or severe.—*n* **rēlaxā´tion**, act of relaxing; state of being relaxed; recreation; the lengthening that characterizes inactive muscles; **relaxant**, a drug that relieves muscular tension.—Also *adj*. [L *relaxāre, -ātum—laxus*, loose.]

relay [rē´lā] a fresh set of dogs, horses, etc., to relieve others; a relieving shift of men; a device whereby a weak electric current can control or operate one or more currents; a race between teams, each member of which goes a part of the distance.—Also **relay race**.—*vt* [also ri-lā´] to convey as by relays;—*pt, pt p* **relayed**. [OFr *relais*, relay of dogs or horses.]

release [ri-lēs´] *vt* to let loose; to set free; to relieve (from); to give up to another (eg a legal right); to make available, permit the publication of or public exhibition.—*n* a setting free, as from prison, work, etc.; a device to release a catch, etc. as on a machine; a book, news item, etc. released to the public; (*law*) a written surrender of a claim. [OFr *relaissier*—L *relaxāre*. See **relax**.]

re-lease [rē´lēs´] *vt* to lease again.—Also *n*. [Pfx **re-**, + **lease**.]

relegate [rel´ė-gāt] *vt* to banish; to consign (usu. to an inferior position); to assign (eg to a class); to refer to an authority for decision.—*n* **relegā´tion**. [L *relēgāre, -ātum—re*, away, *lēgāre*, to send.]

relent [ri-lent´] *vi* to soften or grow less severe.—*adj* **relent´less**, without relenting; without tenderness or compassion, merciless.—*adv* **relent´lessly**.—*n* **relent´lessness**. [L *re-*, back, *lentus*, sticky, sluggish, pliant.]

relevant [rel´ė-vȧnt] *adj* bearing upon, or applying to, the matter in question, pertinent.—*ns* **rel´evance, rel´evancy**. [L *relevāns, -antis*, pr p of *relevāre*, to raise up, relieve; from the notion of helping.]

reliable, etc. *See* **rely**.

relic [rel´ik] *n* that which is left after loss or decay of the rest; (usu. in *pl*) a corpse; (*RC*) any personal memorial of a saint; a memorial of antiquity; a souvenir; a survival (eg of a custom) from the past. [Fr *relique*—L *reliquiae—relinquěre, relictum*, to leave behind.]

relict [rel´ikt] *n* a survivor or surviving trace; widow. [L *relictus, -a, -um*, left, pt p of *relinquěre*, to leave.]

relief [ri-lēf] *n* the lightening or removal of any discomfort, stress, or evil; release from a post or duty; one who releases another by taking his place; that which relieves or mitigates; aid; assistance to the poor; projection or standing out from the general surface; a sculpture, carving or impression so made; appearance of standing out solidly; distinctness by contrast.—*adj* providing relief in cases of distress, danger, or difficulty.—*ns* **relief´ map**, a map representing topographic relief; **relief pitcher**, (*baseball*) a pitcher who replaces another during a game. [OFr *relef—relever*. See **relieve**; cf **relievo**.]

relieve [ri-lēv´] *vt* to bring, give, or afford relief to; to release; to ease, to mitigate; to discharge the bladder or bowels of (oneself).—*vi* to bring or give relief; to stand out in relief; to serve as a relief pitcher.—*adjs* **reliev´ing; relieved**, having or showing relief, esp from anxiety or pent-up emotions. [OFr *relever*—L *relevāre*, to lift, relieve—*re-*, again, *levāre*, to raise—*levis*, light.]

relievo [ri-lē´vō, also rē-lyā´vō] *n* (in art) relief; a work in relief. [It *rilievo*.]

religion [ri-lij´ȯn] *n* belief in, acceptance of God or gods, with the emotion and morality connected therewith; rites or worship; any system of such belief or worship.—*ns* **relig´ionist**, one attached to a religion; **religiosity** [-i-os´i-ti], sentimental religious feeling or observance.—*adj* **relig´ious** [-us], of, concerned with, devoted to, or imbued with, religion; scrupulously and conscientiously faithful.—*n* one bound by monastic vows.—*adv* **relig´iously**. [L *religiō, -ōnis*, n, *religiōsus*, adj, perh conn with *religāre*, to bind, perh with *relegěre*, to read again.]

relinquish [ri-ling´kwish] *vt* to give up; to renounce or surrender (property, a right, etc.).—*n* **relin´quishment**. [OFr *relinquir, relinquissant*—L *relinquěre, relictum—re-, linquěre*, to leave.]

relish [rel´ish] *n* an appetizing flavor; zest-giving quality; zestful enjoyment; pickles, etc. served with a meal or as an appetizer.—*vt* to like the taste of; to be pleased with; to appreciate discriminatingly.—*vi* to have an agreeable taste. [OFr *reles, relais*, remainder—*relaisser*, to leave behind; perh with idea of after-taste.]

reluctance [ri-lukt´ȧns] *n* unwillingness; the ratio of the magnetic potential difference to the corresponding flux.—Also **reluct´ancy**.—*adj* **reluct´ant**, unwilling; resisting. [L *reluctans, -antis*, pr p of *reluctāri—re-*, against, *luctāri*, to struggle.]

rely [ri-lī] *vi* to depend confidently;—*pr p* **rely´ing**; *pt, pt p* **relied´**.—*adj* **relī´able**, to be relied on, trustworthy.—*ns* **relīabil´ity, relī´ableness**.—*adv* **relī´ably**.—*n* **relī´ance**, trust; that in which one trusts; dependence.—*adj* **relī´ant**. [OFr *relier*—L *religāre*, to bind back.]

REM [rem] *n* the rapid, jerky movements of the eyeballs during stages of sleep associated with dreaming;—*pl* **REMs**. [*r*apid *e*ye *m*ovement.]

rem [rem] *n* a unit of radiation dosage, the amount which has the same effect as one rad of X-ray or gamma-ray dosage. [*r*öntgen *e*quivalent *m*an or *m*ammal.]

remain [ri-mān´] *vi* to stay or be left behind; to continue in the same place; to be left after or out of a greater number; to continue in one's possession, mind; to continue unchanged.—*n* (*pl*) what is left; relics; a corpse.—*n* **remain´der**, that which remains after the removal of a part; an interest in an estate to come into effect after a certain other event happens; what is left when a smaller number is subtracted from a larger number; residue of an edition when the sale of a book has fallen off.—*vt* to sell (book) as a remainder. [OFr *remaindre*—L *remanēre—re-*, back *manēre*, to stay.]

remake [rē´māk´] to make anew or in a different form. [Pfx **re-**, + **make**.]

remand [ri-mand´] *vt* to send back (esp a prisoner into custody to await further evidence). [OFr *remander*, or LL *remandāre—re-*, back, *mandāre*, to order, commit.]

remark [ri-märk´] *vti* to notice; to observe; to comment, utter as an observation.—*n* a brief comment.—*adj* **remark´able**, noteworthy; unusual, strange, or distinguished.—*n* **remark´ableness**.—*adv* **remark´ably**. [OFr *remarquer—re-*, inten, *marquer*, to mark.]

remedy [rem´ė-di] *n* any means of curing a disease, redressing, counteracting or repairing any evil or loss.—*vt* to put right, repair, counteract;—*pr p* **rem´edying**; *pt, pt p* **rem´edied**.—*adjs* **remē´diable**, that may be remedied, curable; **remē´dial**, tending or intended to remedy; corrective, as some courses of study. [Anglo-Fr *remedie*, OFr *remede*—L *remedium—re-*, back, *medērī*, to restore.]

remember [ri-mem´bėr] *vt* to keep in, or recall to, memory or mind; to be careful not to forget; mention (a person) to another, as sending regards.—*vi* to exercise or have the power of memory; to have a recollection or remembrance.—*ns* **remem´brance**, memory; that which serves to bring to or keep in mind; a souvenir, a memorial; the reach of memory; a greeting or gift recalling or expressing friendship or affection; **remem´brancer**, one who or that which reminds. [OFr **remembrer**—L *re-*, again, *memor*, mindful.]

remind [ri-mīnd´] *vt* to put in mind (of), to cause to remember.—*n* **remind´er**, that which reminds. [Pfx **re-**, + **mind**.]

reminiscence [rem-i-nis´ėns] *n* the recurrence to the mind of the past; a recollection; (*pl*) an account of something remembered.—*vi* **reminisce** [-nis], to think, talk, or write about past events.—*adj* **reminis´cent**. [L *reminiscens, -entis*, pr p of *reminiscī*, to remember.]

remiss [ri-mis´] *adj* negligent, slack, lax (of a person or action).—*adv* **remiss´ly**.—*n* **remiss´ness**.—*adj* **remiss´ible**, that may be remitted.—*n* **remissibil´ity**.—*n* **remission** [ri-mish´(ȯ)n], act of remitting; slackening; abatement (of a pain, disease, etc.); relinquishment (of a claim); cancellation; forgiveness.—*adj* **remiss´ive**, remitting; forgiving. [L *remittěre, remissum*. See **remit**.]

remit [ri-mit´] *vt* to relax; to pardon; to refrain from exacting or inflicting; to transmit, as money, etc., in payment; to refer for decision (to another committee, court, etc.).—*vi* to abate, to relax;—*pr p* **remitt´ing**; *pt, pt p* **remitt´ed**.—*n* the act, or an instance, of referring for decision, to another authority.—*ns* **remitt´ance**, the sending of money, etc., to a distance; a sum or thing sent; **remitt´ance man**, a person living abroad depending on remittances from home.—*adj* **remitt´ent**, of a disease, marked by alternating periods of abatement and increase of symptoms.—*n* **remitt´er**, one who makes a remittance. [L *remittěre, remissum—re-*, back, *mittěre*, to send.]

remnant [rem´nȧnt] *n* a fragment or a small number remaining after destruction, removal, sale, etc., of the greater part; an unsold or unused end of piece goods. [L *re-*, back, *manēre*, to remain.]

remonstrance [ri-mon´strȧns] *n* a strong or formal protest; expostulation.—*adj* **remon´strant**, remonstrating.—*n* one who remonstrates.—*vi* **remon´strāte** [or rem´], to make a remonstrance; to expostulate (with). [L *re-*, again, *mōnstrāre*, to point out.]

remorse [ri-mörs´] *n* the gnawing pain of conscience; compunction.—*adj* **remorse´ful**, penitent; compassionate.—*adv* **remorse´fully**.—*adj* **remorse´less**, without remorse; cruel, relentless.—*adv* **remorse´lessly**.

—*n* **remorse´lessness**. [OFr *remors* (Fr *remords*)—Low L *remorsus*—L *remordēre, remorsum,* to bite again.]

remote [ri-mōt´] *adj* far removed in place, or time; widely separated (from); out-of-the-way, not quickly reached; slight (eg *a remote resemblance*); very indirect; aloof in manner.—*adv* **remote´ly**.—*n* **remote´ness**.—**remote control**, control of a device from a distance by the making or breaking of an electric circuit or by means of radio waves. [L *remōtus*, pt p of *removēre*. See **remove**.]

remount [rē-mownt´] *vt* to mount (something) again; to furnish remounts to.—*vi* to mount again.—*n* a fresh horse to replace one no longer available. [L *re-*, again, + **mount** (2).]

remove [ri-mōōv´] *vt* to put or take away; to dismiss, as from office; to get rid of; to kill.—*vi* to go away; to change abode.—*n* a step or degree away.—*adj* **remov´able**.—*ns* **removabil´ity; remov´al**, the act or process of removing; the fact of being removed.—*adj* **removed´**, remote; distant by specified degrees, as in a relationship; of a younger or older relationship. [OFr *remouvoir*—L *removēre, remōtum*—*re*, away, *movēre*, to move.]

remunerate [ri-mū´nė-rāt] *vt* to recompense; to pay.—*adj* **remū´nerable**.—*n* **remunerā´tion**, recompense; payment.—*adj* **remū´nerative**, profitable. [L *remūnerārī* (late *-āre*), *-ātus*—*mūnus, -ĕris*, a gift.]

renaissance [ren´i-säns´] *n* a new birth or revival; **Renaissance**, revival of arts and letters, under classical influence, marking the transition from the Middle Ages to the modern world; period of this revival beginning in the 14th century in Italy, and lasting into the 17th century.—*adj* of the period, or in the style, of the Renaissance.—**Renaissance man**, a person who has wide interests and is expert in several areas. [Fr,—L *renasci*. See **renascent**.]

renal [rē´n(à)l] *adj* of or near the kidneys. [L *rēnālis*—*rēnēs* (sing *rēn*, rare), the kidneys.]

renascent [ri-nas´ėnt, also -nās´-] *adj* coming into renewed life or vitality.—*n* **renas´cence**, being born anew; Renaissance. [L *renāscēns, -entis*, pr p of *renāscī*—*re-*, again, *nāscī*, to be born.]

rend [rend] *vt* to tear asunder with force; to split;—*pt, pt p* **rent**.—*vi* to become torn. [OE *rendan*, to tear.]

render [ren´dėr] *vt* to submit, as for approval, payment, etc.; to give back; to give in return; to pay; to represent as by drawing; to play (music), act (a role); to translate; to cause to be; to melt down (fat).—*ns* **ren´dering**, the act of rendering; version; translation; performance; **rendi´tion**, surrender; translation; performance, interpretation. [OFr *rendre*—LL *rendĕre*, app formed by influence of *prendĕre*, to take—L *reddĕre*—*re-*, back, *dăre*, to give.]

rendezvous [rändā-vōō] *n* an appointed meeting place; a meeting by appointment; such a meeting; a place of popular resort, a haunt; the process of bringing two spacecraft together.—*vi* to assemble at any appointed place.—*vt* to bring together at a rendezvous; to meet at a rendezvous. [Fr *rendez-vous*, render yourselves—*rendre*, to render.]

renegade [ren´ė-gād] *n* one faithless to principle or party, an apostate, a turncoat. [LL *renegātus*—L *re-*, inten, *negāre, -ātum*, to deny; partly through Sp *renegado*.]

renew [ri-nū´] *vt* to renovate; to transform to new life, revive; to begin again; to repeat; to grant or obtain an extension of (eg a lease).—*vi* to become new; to begin again; to make a renewal.—*adj* **renew´able**.—*n* **renew´al**, renewing. [L *re-*, again, and **new**.]

reniform [ren´i-förm] *adj* suggesting a kidney in outline. [L *rēnēs* (sing *rēn*), the kidneys, *forma*, form.]

rennet [ren´it] *n* an extract from the stomach of calves, etc., used to curdle milk; rennin; a substitute for rennin.—*n* **rennin**, an enzyme that coagulates milk and is used in making cheese and junkets, esp one from the mucous membrane of the stomach of a calf. [OE *rinnan*, to run.]

renounce [ri-nowns´] *vt* to disclaim, repudiate; to reject publicly and finally; to abandon (eg one's faith).—*ns* **renounce´ment; renounc´er**. [OFr *renuncer*—L *renuntiāre*—*re-*, away, *nuntiāre, -ātum*, to announce.]

renovate [ren´ō-vāt] *vt* to make new again; to make as if new.—*ns* **renovā´tion; ren´ovātor**. [L *re-*, again, *novāre, -ātum*, to make new—*novus*, new.]

renown [ri-nown´] *n* fame.—*adj* **renowned´**, famous. [OFr *renoun* (Fr *renom*)—L *re-*, again, *nōmen*, a name.]

rent[1] [rent] *n* an opening or hole made by rending; fissure.—Also *pt, pt p* of **rend**.

rent[2] [rent] periodical payment for use of another's property, esp houses and lands; revenue.—*vt* to hold or occupy by paying rent; to let or hire out for a rent.—*vi* to be let at a rent.—*ns* **ren´tal**, an amount paid or received as rent; a house, car, etc., for rent; an act of renting; a business that rents something; **rent´er**, a tenant who pays rent; **rentier** [rã-tyā], one who has a fixed income from land, bonds, stocks and the like.—**rent control**, government regulation of the amount charged as rent for housing; **rent strike**, a refusal of a group of tenants to pay rent (as in protest against high rates).—**for rent**, available to be rented. [Fr *rente*—L *reddita* (*pecūnia*), money paid—*reddĕre*, to pay.]

renunciation [ri-nun-si-ā´sh(ȯ)n] *n* act of renouncing; ascetic self-denial. [L *renūntiāre*, to proclaim.]

rep[1], **repp** [rep] *n* a corded cloth. [Fr *reps*, perh—Eng **ribs**.]

rep[2] [rep] *n* an abbreviation for **repertory** (theater), **representative** and **reputation**.

repaid [rē-pād´] *pt, ptp* of **repay**.

repair[1] [ri-pār´] *vi* to betake oneself, to go, to resort.—*n* a resort, haunt. [OFr *repairer*, to return to a haunt—L *re-*, back, *patria*, native country.]

repair[2] [ri-pār´] *vt* to mend; to remedy; to make amends for.—*n* (usu. *pl*) restoration after injury, decay, or loss; sound condition.—*n* **repair´er**.—*adj* **reparable** [rep´ár-a-bl], capable of being made good.—*adv* **rep´arably**.—*n* **reparā´tion**, repair; amends; (*pl*) compensation, as for war damage.—*adj* **reparative** [ri-par´a-tiv]. [OFr *reparer*—L *reparāre*—*re-*, again, *parāre*, to prepare.]

repartee [rep-ȧr-tē´] *n* a ready and witty retort; skill in making such retorts. [OFr *repartie*—*repartir*—*re-*, back, *partir*, to set out—L *partīri*, to divide.]

repartition [rep-ȧr-tish´(ȯ)n] *n* distribution; [rē-pär-] a second or additional dividing or distribution. [L *re-*, + **partition**.]

repast [ri-päst´] *n* a meal; food and drink. [OFr *repast* (Fr *repas*)—LL *repastus*—L *re-*, inten, *pascĕre, pastum*, to feed.]

repatriate [rē-pāt´ri-āt, or -pat´-] *vt* to restore or send back to one's country of origin, allegiance, or citizenship.—*n* **repatriā´tion**. [LL *repatriāre, -ātum*, to return to one's country—L *patria*.]

repay [rē-pā´] *vt* to pay back; to make return for; to recompense;—*pr p* **repay´ing**; *pt, pt p* **repaid´**.—*adj* **repay´able**, that is to be repaid.—*n* **repay´ment**. [L *re-*, back, + **pay**.]

repeal [ri-pēl´] *vt* to revoke, to annul.—*n* abrogation, annulment.—*adj* **repeal´able**.—*n* **repeal´er**, a legislative act that abrogates an earlier act. [OFr *rapeler*—pfx *re-, appeler*, to appeal.]

repeat [ri-pēt´] *vt* to say, do, perform, again; to quote from memory; to recount; to divulge; to say or do after another.—*vi* to say, do, or accomplish something again, esp to vote illegally by casting more than one ballot in an election.—*n* a repetition, anything said or done again, as a rebroadcast of a television program; (*mus*) a passage repeated or marked for repetition; the sign directing repetition.—*adjs* **repeat´able**, fit to be repeated; **repeat´ed**, done, appearing, etc., again.—*adv* **repeat´edly**, many times, again and again.—*n* **repeat´er**, one who, or that which, repeats; a watch or clock with a striking mechanism; a firearm having a magazine that reloads by action of the piece; a habitual violator of the laws; a student enrolled in a course for the second time; a device for receiving and amplifying electronic communication signals.—*adj* **repeat´ing**, of a firearm, designed to load cartridges from a magazine.—**repeating decimal**, a nonterminating decimal which consists of an initial pattern of digits followed by continuous repetition of a single digit or pattern of digits. [Fr *répéter*—L *repetĕre, -itum*—*re-*, again, *petĕre*, to seek.]

repel [ri-pel´] *vt* to drive back; to repulse; to hold off; to be repulsive or distasteful to; to be resistant to (water, dirt, etc.).—*pr p* **repell´ing**; *pt, pt p* **repelled´**.—*adj* **repell´ent**, driving back; able or tending to repel; distasteful.—*n* that which repels.—*n* **repell´er**. [L *repellĕre*—*re*, back, *pellĕre*, to drive.]

repent [ri-pent´] *vi* to regret, sorrow for, or wish to have been otherwise, what one has done or left undone (*with* **of**); to change from past evil; to feel contrition.—*vt* to regret.—*n* **repent´ance**, act of repenting; penitent state of mind.—*adj* **repent´ant**, experiencing or expressing repentance. [OFr *repentir*—L *paenitēre*, to cause to repent.]

repercussion [rē-pėr-kush´(ȯ)n] *n* driving back; reverberation, echo; a far-reaching, often indirect reaction to some event.—*adj* **repercussive** [-kus´iv], driving back; reverberating, echoing. [L *repercutĕre, -cussum*—*re-, per, quatĕre*, to strike.]

repertory [rep´ėr-tȯr-i] *n* a repertoire; the system of alternating several plays throughout a season with a permanent acting group.—*n* **repertoire** [rep´ėr-twär], the stock of plays, songs, etc., that a company, singer, etc., is prepared to perform. [LL *repertōrium*—L *reperire*, to find again—*parĕre*, to bring forth.]

repetition [rep-i-tish´(ȯ)n] *n* act of repeating; something repeated.—*adj* **repetitive** [re-pet´-i-tiv], given to repetition. [L *repetĕre, -itum*, to seek again, repeat—*petĕre*, to seek.]

repine [ri-pīn´] *vi* to express or feel discontent; to long for something.—*n* **repī´ner**. [App from **pine** (2).]

replace [ri- or rē-plās´] *vt* to put back; to provide a substitute for; to take the place of.—*adj* **replace´able**.—*n* **replace´ment**, act of replacing; person or thing that replaces another. [L *re-*, back, again, + **place**.]

replenish [ri-plen´ish] *vt* to fill again; to fill completely; to stock abundantly.—*n* **replen´ishment**. [OFr *replenir, -issant*, from *replein*, full—L *re-*, again, *plēnus*, full.]

replete [ri-plēt´] *adj* full, well stored; completely filled; filled to satiety.—*n* **replē´tion**, superabundant fullness; satisfaction. [L *replētus*, pt p of *replēre*—*re-*, again, *plēre*, to fill.]

replica [rep´li-ka] *n* a duplicate, esp one by the original artist; a facsimile. [It,—L *replicāre*, to repeat.]

replicate [rep´li-kāt] *vt* to repeat; to duplicate.—*vi* to undergo replication; to produce a replica of itself.—*adj* repeated.—*n* one of several identical experiments, procedures, or samples.—*n* **replicā´tion**, a reply; (*law*) the plaintiff's reply to the defendant's counterstatement of facts (plea, answer, defence); reproduction. [L *replicāre, -ātum*, to fold back—*plicāre*, to fold.]

reply [ri-plī´] *vi* to say or write in answer.—*vt* to give as an answer.—*pr p* **reply´ing**; *pt, pt p* **replied´**.—*n* an answer.—*n* **replī´er**. [OFr *replier*—L *replicāre*, to repeat.]

report [ri-pōrt´, -pört´] *vt* to bring back, as an answer, news, or account of anything; to announce; to give a formal statement of; to circulate publicly; to write down or take notes of, esp for a newspaper; to make a complaint about, against.—*vi* to make a formal statement (on); to write an account of occurrences; to present oneself (for duty).—*n* a statement of facts; a newspaper account of an event or the words of a speech; a formal or official statement, as of results of an investigation; rumor, hearsay; repute; explosive noise.—*ns* **report´age** [-ij], accurately observed and vividly written account of contemporary events (eg *a piece of brilliant reportage*); journalistic style of writing; **report card**, a report on a student that is periodically submitted to a student's parent or guardian; an evaluation of performance; **report´er**, one who reports, as one who makes authorized statements of law decisions or legislative proceedings or makes a shorthand account of such a proceeding; one employed by a newspaper, magazine, or broadcasting company to gather and report news; one who broadcasts news. [OFr *reporter*—L *reportāre*—*re-*, back, *portāre*, to carry.]

repose [ri-pōz´] *vt* to lay at rest; to place at rest; to place (trust, etc.) in someone; to place (power) in control of some person or group.—*vi* to rest; to lie at rest; to lie dead.—*n* rest; stillness; ease of manner; serenity.—*adj* **repōsed´**, calm; settled. [Fr *reposer*—Low L *repausāre*—*re-, pausāre*. See **pose** (1).]

repository [ri-poz´i-tȯr-i] *n* place or receptacle in which anything is stored; a confidant. [L *repōnĕre, repositum*, to put back, lay aside—*pōnĕre*, to put; confused with foregoing.]

repossess [rē-poz-es´] *vt* to regain possession of; to take back because payment has not been made; to restore to possession.—*n* **repossession** [-esh´(ȯ)n]. [L *re-*, again, and **possess**.]

repoussé [rė-pōō´sā´] *adj* raised in relief by hammering from behind or within.—*n* repoussé work. [Fr.]

repp *See* **rep** (1).

reprehend [rep-rė-hend´] *vt* to find fault with, to reprove.—*adj* **reprehen´sible**, blameworthy.—*adv* **reprehen´sibly**.—*n* **reprehen´sion**, reproof, censure.—*adj* **reprehen´sive**. [L *reprehendĕre, -hensum*—*re-*, inten, *prehendĕre*, to lay hold of.]

represent [rep-rė-zent´] *vt* to present to, bring before, the mind; to point out (eg *he represented to him the danger of this course*); to make to appear (as), to allege (to be); to depict; to act the rôle of on the stage; to serve as a symbol for; to correspond to; to be a substitute agent, or delegate for, esp by conferred authority; to serve as a specimen, example, etc., of.—*vt* **re-present´** [rē-], to present again, anew.—*adj* **represent´able**.—*n* **representation** [-zėntā´sh(ȯ)n], act of representing or being represented as in a legislative assembly; legislative representatives, collectively; that which represents; an image, picture; (*pl*) a presentation of a view of facts or arguments, claims, protests, etc.—*adj* **representative** [rep-rė-zent´a-tiv], representing; consisting of or based on representation of the people by elected delegates; typical.—*n* an example or type; one authorized to act for others; a delegate, agent, salesman, etc.; **Representative**, a member of the lower house of Congress or of a State legislature. [L *repraesentāre, -ātum*—*re-*, again, *praesentāre*, to place before.]

repress [ri-pres´] *vt* to restrain; to keep under; (*psychiatry*) to confine to the unconscious mind; [rē] to press again.—*adj* **repress´ible**.—*n* **repression** [-presh´(ȯ)n].—*adj* **repress´ive**. [L *reprimĕre, repressum*—*premĕre*, to press.]

reprieve [ri-prēv´] *vt* to delay or commute the execution of; to give a respite to; to rescue, redeem.—*n* a suspension of a criminal sentence; interval of ease or relief. [Supposed to be from Anglo-Fr *repris*, pt p of *reprendre*, to take back (see **reprisal**); the *v* app by confusion.]

reprimand [rep´ri-mänd´] *n* a severe or formal reproof.—*vt* to reprove severely, esp publicly or officially from a position of authority. [Fr *réprimande*—L *preprimĕre, repressum*, to press back—*re-*, back, *premĕre*, to press.]

reprint [rē-print´] *vt* to print again; to print a new impression of.—*n* **rē´print**, a later impression; matter (as an article) that has appeared in print before. [L *re-*, again, and **print**.]

reprisal [ri-prī´zȧl] *n* seizure in retaliation; an act of retaliation. [Fr *reprise*—*reprendre*—L *reprehendĕre*. See **reprehend**.]

reproach [ri-prōch´] *vt* to accuse of a fault; to censure, upbraid; to bring into discredit.—*n* upbraiding, reproof, censure; a source or matter of disgrace or shame.—*adjs* **reproach´able; reproach´ful**, reproving.—*adv* **reproach´fully**. [Fr *reprocher*, perh from L *prope*, near; cf **approach**.]

reprobate [rep´rō-bāt] *adj* given over to sin, depraved, unprincipled; condemnatory.—*n* an abandoned or profligate person.—*vt* to reject; to disapprove, express disapproval, of; to exclude from salvation.—*n* **reprobā´tion**, the act of reprobating; disapproval; rejection; predestination to eternal punishment. [L *reprobāre, -ātum*, to reprove, contrary of *approbāre*—*probāre*, to prove.]

reproduce [rē-prō-dūs´] *vt* to produce a copy of; to form anew; to propagate.—*vi* to produce offspring; to undergo reproduction.—*n* **reproduction** [-duk´sh(ȯ)n], the act of reproducing; the process by which plants and animals produce new individuals; a copy, facsimile; a representation.—*adj* **reproduc´tive**. [L *re-*, again, + **produce**.]

reproof [ri-prōōf´] *n* a reproving; rebuke, censure, reprehension.—*n* **reproval** [ri-prōō´v(ȧ)l], reproof.—*vt* **reprove´**, to rebuke, to censure.—*n* **repro´ver**.—*adv* **repro´vingly**. [OFr *reprover* (Fr *réprouver*)—L *reprobāre*. See **reprobate**.]

reptile [rep´tīl] *adj* creeping; like a reptile in nature.—*n* any of a class (Reptilia) of cold-blooded, air-breathing vertebrates with horny scales or plates, as turtles, alligators and crocodiles, lizards, snakes, etc.; a groveling or despised person.—*adj* **reptilian** [-til´i-ȧn]. [LL *reptilis, -e*—*repĕre*, to creep.]

republic [ri-pub´lik] *n* a form of government headed by a president, in which the supreme power is vested in the people and their elected representatives; a state or country so governed; a body of persons freely engaged in a specified activity; a constituent political or territorial unit.—*adj* **repub´lican**, of or favoring a republic.—*n* one who advocates a republican form of government; of the Republican party; one of the two major US political parties.—*n* **repub´licanism**. [L *rēspublica*, commonwealth—*rēs*, affair, *publica* (fem), public.]

republish [rē-pub´lish] *vt* to publish again.—*n* **republicā´tion**. [L *re-*, again, + **publish**.]

repudiate [ri-pū´di-āt] *vt* to disown; to refuse to recognize (eg authority), acknowledge or pay (eg a debt); to deny as unfounded (a charge, etc.); to disavow (a treaty, etc.).—*ns* **repudiā´tion; repū´diator**. [L *repudiāre, -ātum*—*repudium*, divorce—*re-*, away, and the root of *pudēre*, to be ashamed.]

repugnance [ri-pug´nȧns] *n* inconsistency; aversion.—*adj* **repug´nant**, inconsistent; incompatible; distasteful, disgusting; opposing, resisting. [L *repugnāre*—*re-*, against, *pugnāre*, to fight.]

repulse [ri-puls´] *vt* to drive back, to beat off (eg an attack); to rebuff (an overture, a person).—*n* a driving back, a beating off; a check; a refusal, a rebuff.—*n* **repulsion** [-pul´sh(ȯ)n], driving off; (*physics*) the mutual action by which bodies tend to repel each other; strong distaste.—*adj* **repul´sive**, that repulses or drives off; repelling; cold, reserved, forbidding; causing aversion and disgust.—*adv* **repul´sively**.—*n* **repul´siveness**. [L *repulsus*, pt p of *repellĕre*—*re-*, back, *pellĕre*, to drive.]

repurchase agreement [rē-pûr´chȧs] *n* a contract giving the seller of securities (as treasury bills) the right to repurchase after a designated period and the buyer to retain the interest earned.

repute [ri-pūt´] *vt* to consider, deem.—*n* general opinion or impression; attributed character; widespread or high estimation.—*adj* **reputable** [rep´ūt-ȧ-bl], in good repute, respectable.—*adv* **rep´ūtably**.—*n* **repūtā´tion** [rep-], repute; estimation, character generally ascribed; good report, fame; good name.—*adj* **reputed** [ri-pūt´id], supposed; of high repute.—*adv* **repūt´edly**, in common repute or estimation. [L *reputāre, -ātum*—*re-*, again, *putāre*, to reckon.]

request [ri-kwest´] *n* an asking for something; a petition; a favor asked for; the state of being sought after.—*vt* to ask as a favor; to ask politely; to ask for. [OFr *requeste* (Fr *requête*)—L *requīsitum*, pt p of *requīrĕre*—*re-*, away, *quaerĕre*, to seek.]

requiem [rek´wi-em] *n* (*RC Church*) a mass for the rest of the soul of the dead; music for it; any music of similar character. [L acc of *requiēs*— (*re-*, inten, *quiēs*, rest); first word of the mass.]

requiescat [re-kwi-es´kät] *n* a prayer for the repose of a dead person. [L *requiescere*, may he (or she) rest.]

require [ri-kwīr´] *vt* to demand, to exact; to direct, order; to need.—*n* **require´ment**, a need; a thing needed; a necessary condition; a demand. [L *requīrĕre*; partly through OFr *requerre*, later assimilated to L.]

requisite [rek´wi-zit] *adj* required, needful, indispensable.—*n* that which is required, necessary, or indispensable.—*n* **requisi´tion**, the act of requiring; a formal demand, request, or order, as for the supply of anything for military purposes.—*vt* to demand or take by requisition; to make such a demand upon (for). [L *requīsītus*, pt p of *requīrĕre*. See **require**.]

requite [ri-kwīt´] *vt* to repay (an action); to avenge, to repay (a person, for).—*n* **requī´tal**, the act of requiting; payment in return, retribution, recompense, reward. [Pfx **re-**, + **quit**.]

reredos [rēr´dos] *n* an ornamental wood screen, a stone screen, or partition wall behind an altar; the back of a fireplace or open hearth. [OFr, *rere*, rear, *dos*—L *dorsum*, back.]

rescind [ri-sind´] *vt* to annul, abrogate.—*n* **rescission** [-sizh´(ȯ)n], abrogation.—*adj* **rescissory** [-sis´ȯr-i], annulling. [L *rescindĕre, rescissum*—*re-*, back, *scindĕre*, to cut.]

rescript [rē´skript] *n* the official answer of a pope or a Roman emperor to any legal question; an edict or decree; a rewriting. [L *rescriptum*—*re-*, back, *scrībĕre, scrīptum*, to write.]

rescue [res´kū] *vt* to free from danger, captivity, or evil plight; to deliver forcibly from legal custody;—*pr p* **res´cūing**; *pt, pt p* **res´cūed**.—*n* the act of rescuing; deliverance from danger or evil; forcible recovery (of property); forcible release from arrest or imprisonment.—*n* **res´cuer**.—**rescue mission**, a city religious mission seeking to convert and rehabilitate the down-and-out. [OFr *rescourre*—L *re-*, away, *executĕre*—*ex*, out, *quatĕre*, to shake.]

research [ri-sėrch´] *n* a careful search or investigation; systematic investigation towards increasing the sum of knowledge.—*vi* to make researches.—*n* **research´er**. [OFr *recerche*. See **search**.]

resect [ri-sekt´] *vt* to perform a resection.—*n* **resect´ion**, the surgical removal of part of an organ or structure. [L *resecāre, -sectum*, to cut off—*secāre*, to cut.]

resemble [ri-zem´bl] *vt* to be like; (*arch*) to represent as like.—*n* **resem´blance**, likeness. [OFr *resembler* (Fr *ressembler*)—*re-*, again, *sembler*, to seem—L *simulāre*, to make like.]

resent [ri-zent´] *vt* to take badly, to consider as an injury or affront.—*adj* **resent´ful**.—*adv* **resent´fully**.—*n* **resent´ment**. [OFr *ressentir*—L *re-*, in return, *sentīre*, to feel.]

reserve [ri-zûrv´] *vt* to hold back, to save up for future use or emergency; to retain (for one's own use); to set apart or destine (for); to have set aside to save one's energies (for).—*n* that which is reserved; a reservation; (*pl*) a military force not usually serving but liable to be called up when required; part of assets kept readily available for ordinary demands; restrained manner; reticence; a mental reservation.—*adj* **reserv´able**.—*n* **reservā´tion** [rez-], the act of reserving or keeping back or keeping for oneself; an expressed, or tacit, proviso, limiting condition, or exception; something withheld; safe keeping; a tract of public land reserved for some special purpose; a holding of a hotel room, etc., until called for.—*adj* **reserved´**, reticent, uncommunicative; aloof in manner.—*adv* **reservedly** [-id-li].—*ns* **reservedness** [rizervd´nės]; **reser´vist**, a member of a military reserve force. [OFr *reserver*—L *reservāre*—*re-*, back, *servāre*, to save.]

reservoir [rez´ėr-vwär] *n* a receptacle; a store; a receptacle for fluids, esp an artificial lake or tank for storing water; a large supply or store of something. [Fr.]

reset [rē-set´] *vt* to set again; to change the reading of. [Pfx **re-**, + **set**.]

reside [ri-zīd´] *vi* to dwell permanently; to be vested (in); to inhere (in).—*ns* **residence** [rez´i-dėns], act of dwelling in a place; period of dwelling; a house where one lives permanently; the status of a legal resident; a building used as a home; **res´idency**, a usu. official place of residence; a period of advanced training in a medical specialty.—*adj* **res´ident**, dwelling in a place; residing at the place of one's duties; not migratory.—*n* one who resides; **Resident**, a representative of a governor in a protected state; a doctor who is serving a residency; **resident commissioner**, a nonvoting representative of a dependency in the US House of Representatives.—*adj* **residential** [-den´shål], of, for, connected with, residence; (of a quarter) suitable for, occupied by residences.—**in residence**, engaged to live and work at a particular place often for a specified time (eg *writer in residence at a university*); at official abode. [L *residēre*—*re-*, back, *sedēre*, to sit.]

residue [rez´i-dū] *n* that which is left, remainder.—*adjs* **resid´ual**, remaining as residue; **resid´uary**, of, or of the nature of, a residue, esp of an estate; to whom the residue of an estate is willed (eg *residuary legatee*).—*n* **resid´uum**, a residue. [L *residuum*—*residēre*, to remain behind.]

resign [ri-zīn´] *vt* to yield up, to relinquish; to submit calmly; to entrust (to).—*vi* to give up office, employment, etc.—*n* **resignation** [rez-ig-nā´sh(ȯ)n], act of giving up; formal statement that one is giving up (a post); the document conveying it; state of being resigned or quietly submissive.—*adj* **resigned** [ri-zīnd´], calmly submissive. [OFr *resigner*—L *resignāre*, *-ātum*, to unseal, annul—*re-*, signifying reversal, *signāre*, to seal—*signum*, a mark.]

re-sign [rē-sīn] *vt* to sign again. [**re**, + **sign**.]

resile [ri-zīl´] *vi* to recoil, to rebound, to spring back into shape or position.—*ns* **resilience** [ri-zil´i-ėns], recoil; elasticity, physical or mental; the stored energy of a strained material, or the work done per unit volume of an elastic material by any force in producing strain; **resil´iency**, elasticity.—*adj* **resil´ient**, elastic, buoyant (physically or in spirits). [L *resilīre*, to leap back—*re-*, back, *salīre*, to leap.]

resin [rez´in] *n* any of a number of substances, products obtained from the sap of certain plants and trees, used in varnishes, printing inks, sizes, plastics, and in medicine; rosin; any of a large class of synthetic products that have the physical properties of resins but are different chemically and are used chiefly in plastics; any of various products made from resin.—*adj* **res´inous**, of, like, containing, of the nature of, resin.—*adv* **res´inously**. [Fr *résine*—L *rēsīna*.]

resist [ri-zist´] *vt* to strive against; to oppose with success; to be little affected by.—*vi* to oppose or withstand something.—*n* **resis´tance**, act or power of resisting; power to resist, as to ward off disease; opposition, or a party continuing opposition to a foreign occupying power after the country has nominally capitulated; the opposition of a body to the motion of another; to opposition offered by a body or substance to the passage through it of a steady electric current.—*adj* **resis´tant**, making resistance; (*with* **to**) habitually unaffected by.—*adj* **resis´tible**.—*n* **resistibil´ity**.—*adj* **resis´tive**.—**resistiv´ity**, capacity for resisting; a property of a conducting material expressed as resistance X cross-sectional area over length.—*adj* **resist´less**, irresistible; unresisting, unable to resist.—*adv* **resist´lessly**.—*ns* **resist´lessness; resist´or**, a piece of apparatus used to offer electric resistance. [L *resistĕre*—*re-*, against, *sistĕre*, to make to stand.]

resoluble [rez´ol-ū-bl] *adj* capable of being resolved.—*adj* **resolute** [rez´ol-ūt, -ōōt], having a fixed purpose, constant in pursuing a purpose, determined.—*adv* **res´olutely**.—*ns* **res´oluteness; resolution** [rez-ol-ōō´sh(ȯ)n], act of resolving; analysis; solution; state of being resolved; fixed determination; that which is resolved; (*mus*) progression from discord to concord; formal proposal in a public assembly; the definition of a picture in TV or facsimile; (*phys, electronics*) the process or capability of making distinguishable closely adjacent optical images or sources of light.—*vt* **resolve** [ri-zolv´], to separate (into components), to analyze; to solve, to free from doubt or difficulty, to explain; to determine; to decide by vote; (*mus*) to make to pass into a concord.—*vi* to undergo resolution; to melt; to come to a decision (*with* **on**).—*n* anything resolved or determined; resolution, fixed purpose.—*adj* **resol´vable**.—*adj* **resolved´**, fixed in purpose.—*adv* **resolvedly** [ri-zol´-vid-li], resolutely. [L *resolvĕre*, *resolūtum*—*re-*, inten, *solvĕre*, to loose.]

resonance [rez´on-åns] *n* resounding; sympathetic vibration; sonority; the sound heard in auscultation; (*phys*) (the state of a system in which) a large vibration (is) produced by a small stimulus of approx the same frequency as that of the system.—*adj* **res´onant**, resounding, ringing; vibrating.—*n* **res´onā´tor**, a device that produces, or increases sound by, resonance. [L *resonāre*, *-ātum*—*re-*, back, *sonāre*, to sound.]

resort [ri-zört´] *vi* to have recourse; to turn (to) for help, etc.—*n* a place to which people go often, as on vacation; a source of help, support, etc.; recourse.—**in the last resort**, as a last expedient. [OFr *resortir* (Fr *ressortir*), to rebound, retire—*sortir*, to go out.]

resound [ri-zownd´] *vt* to echo; to sound with reverberation; to sound or spread (the praises of).—*vi* to echo; to reecho; reverberate; to sound sonorously.—*adj* **resound´ing**, echoing; thorough, decisive. [Pfx **re-**, + **sound**.]

resource [ri-sōrs´, -sörs´] *n* source or possibility of help; an expedient; (*pl*) wealth; assets; resourcefulness.—*adj* **resource´ful**, able to deal effectively with problems, etc.—*n* **resource´fulness**. [OFr *ressource*—*resourdre*—L *resurgĕre*, to rise again.]

respect [ri-spekt´] *vt* to feel or show esteem, deference or honor to; to refrain from violating, treat with consideration (eg a person's privacy, innocence, desire not to discuss).—*n* honor or esteem; consideration; regard; (*pl*) a greeting or message of esteem; reference; relation.—*adj* **respec´table**, worthy of respect; proper, correct; of moderate quality or size; decent and well-behaved.—*adv* **respec´tably**.—*n* **respectabil´ity**.—*adj* **respect´ful**, showing or feeling respect.—*adj* **respect´fully**.—*prep* **respec´ting**, concerning.—*adj* **respec´tive**, particular or several, relating to each distributively (eg *in their respective places; the respective claims, merits, of*).—*adv* **respec´tively**, in the order indicated (eg *Books I, II, and III have yellow, red, and blue covers respectively*). —**in respect of**, in the matter of. [L *respicĕre*, *respectum*—*re-*, back, *specĕre*, to look.]

respire [ri-spīr´] *vti* to breathe.—*adj* **respirable** [res´pir-å-bl, ri-spīr´å-bl], fit for breathing; capable of being taken in by breathing.—*ns* **respiration** [res-pir-ā´sh(ȯ)n], act or process of breathing; any of various energy-yielding oxidative reactions in living matter; **res´pirātor**, a mask, as of gauze, to prevent the inhaling of harmful substances; an apparatus to maintain breathing by artificial means.—*adj* **respiratory** [ri-spir´a-tȯr-i, res´pir-ā-tȯr-i, ri-spīr´a-tȯr-i], of or for respiration. [L *respīrāre*, *-ātum*—*re-*, signifying repetition, *spīrāre*, to breathe.]

respite [res´pit] *n* temporary cessation of something that is tiring or painful; postponement requested or granted; (*law*) temporary suspension of the execution of a criminal.—*vt* to grant a respite to; to relieve by a pause; to delay, postpone (something disagreeable, eg punishment); to grant postponement to. [OFr *respit* (Fr *répit*)—L *respectus*, respect.]

resplendent [ri-splen´dėnt] *adj* very splendid, gorgeous, shining brilliantly.—*ns* **resplen´dence, resplen´dency**.—*adv* **resplen´dently**. [L *resplendēre*—*re-*, inten, *splendēre*, to shine.]

respond [ri-spond´] *vi* to answer; to show a favorable reaction; to be answerable.—*vt* to reply.—*adj* **respon´dent**, answering; corresponding; responsive.—*n* one who answers; one who maintains a thesis in reply; a defendant; a person who responds to a poll; a reflex that occurs in response to a specific stimulus.—*ns* **respond´er**, one who or that which responds; the part of a transponder which replies automatically to the correct interrogation signal; **response´**, an answer; oracular answer; answer made by the congregation to the choir or clergyman during divine service; any reaction to stimulus; an action or feeling incited by the request, action, etc., of another person or by an occurrence.—*adj* **respon´sible**, liable to be called upon to answer (to); answerable (for); deserving the blame or credit of (*with* **for**); morally answerable (for); governed by a sense of responsibility; trustworthy; involving responsibility.—*n* **responsibil´ity**, state of being responsible; what one is responsible for.—*adv* **respon´sibly**.—*adj* **respon´sive**, ready to respond; answering; correspondent.—*adv* **respon´sively**. [L *respondēre*, *responsum*—*re-*, back, *spondēre*, to promise.]

rest[1] [rest] *n* repose, refreshing inactivity; intermission of, or freedom from, motion; tranquillity; a place for resting; a prop or support (eg for a billiard cue, etc.); a pause in speaking or reading; an interval of silence in music, or a mark indicating it.—*vi* to repose; to be at ease; to be still; to be supported, to lean (on); to put trust (in); to have foundation (in, on); to remain.—*vt* to give rest to; to place or hold in support; to lean; to base.—*adj* **rest´ful**, at rest; giving rest, tranquil.—*adv* **rest´fully**.—*ns* **rest´fulness; rest home**, an establishment for those who need special care and attention, eg invalids, old people, etc.; **rest house**, a building used for shelter by travelers; **rest´room**, a room in a public building equipped with toilets, washbowls, etc.—*adj* **rest´less**, without rest, unresting; uneasily active, impatient of inactivity.—*adv* **rest´lessly**.—*n* **rest´lessness**.—**at rest**, stationary, motionless, free from disquiet; **lay to rest**, bury. [OE *rest*, *ræst*; Ger *rast*, Du *rust*, converging and merging in meaning with the following word.]

rest[2] [rest] *n* remainder; the others.—*vi* to remain. [Fr *reste*—L *restāre*, to remain—*re-*, back, *stāre*, to stand.]

restaurant [res´tà-rànt] *n* a place where meals can be bought and eaten.—*n* **restaurateur** [res-tör-a-tœr´], the keeper of a restaurant. [Fr—*restaurer*, to restore.]

restitution [res-ti-tū´sh(ȯ)n] *n* act of restoring what was lost or taken away; a reimbursement, as for loss. [L *restituĕre, -ūtum—re-*, again, *statuĕre*, to make to stand.]

restive [res´tiv] *adj* unwilling to go forward; obstinate, refractory, uneasy, as if ready to break from control.—*adv* **res´tively**.—*n* **res´tiveness**. [OFr *restif*—L *restāre*, to rest.]

restore [ri-stōr´] *vt* to bring, put, or give back; to reestablish (eg peace); to reinstate (eg a ruler); to repair; to bring back to a known or conjectured former state; to supply (a part) by conjecture; to cure (a person).—*n* **restoration** [res-tō-rā´sh(ȯ)n], act of restoring; renovation and reconstruction of a building, painting, etc.; a model, etc., of a conjectured original form; **Restoration**, the reestablishing of the monarchy in England under Charles II in 1660.—*adj* **restorative** [ris-tor´a-tiv], tending to restore, esp to strength and vigor.—*n* something that restores.—*adv* **restor´atively**.—*n* **restōr´er**. [OFr *restorer*—L *restaurāre, -ātum*.]

restrain [ri-strān] *vt* to hold back (from); to control; to subject to forcible repression.—*adj* **restrained´**, controlled; self-controlled; free from excess.—*n* **restraint´**, act of restraining; state of being restrained; a restraining influence; want of liberty; artistic control or reticence; control of emotions, impulses, etc.; reserve. [OFr *restraindre, restrai(g)nant*—L *restringĕre, restrictum—re-*, back, *stringĕre*, to draw tightly.]

restrict [ri-strikt´] *vt* to keep within limits.—*adj* **restrict´ed**.—*n* **restric´tion**, act of restricting; limitation; confinement; a limiting or restraining regulation.—*adj* **restric´tive**, restricting; tending to restrict; (*gram*) denoting a subordinate clause or phrase felt as limiting the application of the word it modifies, and not set off by commas.—*adv* **restric´tively**. [L *restringĕre, restrictum*.]

result [ri-zult´] *vi* to issue as an effect (*with* **in**); to follow as a consequence.—*n* consequence; effect; quantity obtained by calculation; (*pl*) a desired effect.—*adj* **resul´tant**, derived from or resulting from something else.—*n* an outcome; a single vector that is the sum of a given set of vectors. [L *resultāre*, to leap back—*saltāre*, to leap.]

resume [ri-zōōm´] *vt* to take or occupy again; to take up again; to begin again, continue after interruption.—*vi* to proceed after interruption.—*ns* **résumé** [rez´ū-mā, rā-zümā], a summary, esp of employment experience; **resumption** [ri-zump´sh(ȯ)n, or -zum-], act of resuming. [L *resūmĕre, -sūmptum—re-*, back, *sumĕre*, to take.]

resurge [ri-sûrj´] *vi* to rise again into life, activity, or prominence.—*n* **resur´gence**.—*adj* **resur´gent**. [L *resurgĕre, resurrectum—re-*, again, *surgĕre*, to rise.]

resurrect [rez-ůr-ekt´] *vt* to restore to life.—*ns* **Resurrection**, the rising of Jesus from the dead; **resurrec´tion**, rising from the dead of all humans before the final judgment; resuscitation; **resurrectionist**, one that steals corpses from graves. [Same root as **resurge**.]

resuscitate [ri-sus´i-tāt] *vti* to revive when apparently dead or in a faint, etc.—*n* **resuscitā´tion**.—*adj* **resus´citātive**, tending to resuscitate, reviving, revivifying, reanimating.—*n* **resusc´itātor**, one who, or that which resuscitates; an apparatus used to induce breathing after partial asphyxiation. [L *resuscitāre, -ātum—re-, sus-* (*sub-*), from beneath, *citāre*, to put into quick motion—*ciēre*, to make to go.]

ret [ret] *vt* to soak (as flax) to loosen the fiber from woody tissue.—*vi* to become retted.—*pr p* **rett´ing**; *pt, pt p* **rett´ed**. [App akin to **rot**.]

retail [rē´tāl] *n* sale to consumer in small quantities.—*adj* pertaining to such sale.—*adv* at a retail price.—*vti* to sell or be sold by retail.—*ns* **retail´er; retailing**, the activities involved in selling goods for personal or household consumption direct to the customer. [OFr *retail*, piece cut off—*re-*, again, *tailler*, to cut.]

retain [ri-tān´] *vt* to keep; to hold back; to continue to keep, to hold secure; to reserve the services of, by a preliminary fee.—*ns* **retain´er**, one who or that which retains; a person attached to, and owing service to, a family; a fee paid to retain a lawyer's services; **retaining wall**, a wall built to hold back earth or water. [Fr *retenir*—L *retinēre—re-*, back, *tenēre*, to hold.]

retaliate [ri-tal´i-āt] *vt* to repay in kind (usu an injury).—*vi* to return like for like, esp to get revenge.—*n* **retaliā´tion**, return of like for like; imposition of counter-tariffs.—*adjs* **retal´iātive, retal´iatory** [-āt-ȯr-i, -at-ȯr-i], [L *retāliāre, -ātum—re-*, in return, *tāliō, -ōnis*, like for like—*tālis*, such.]

retard [ri-tärd´] *vt* to slow, to delay.—Also *vi*.—*n* **retard´ant**, something that retards, esp a substance that delays a chemical reaction.—*adj* that retards.—*ns* **retar´date**, a mentally retarded person; **retardā´tion** [rē-], slowing; delay; lag.—*adj* **retar´ded**, slow in development, mental or physical, or having made less than normal progress in learning. [L *retardāre, -ātum—re-*, inten, *tardāre*, to slow.]

retch [rech] *vi* to strain as if to vomit.—*vt* to vomit. [OE *hrǣcan*.]

retention [ri-ten´sh(ȯ)n] *n* act or power of retaining; memory; capacity for retaining; abnormal retaining of a fluid or secretion in a body cavity.—*adj* **reten´tive**, retaining; tenacious.—*adv* **reten´tively**.—*n* **reten´tiveness**. [L *retentiō, -ōnis*; Fr *retentif*. See **retain**.]

rethink [rē-thingk´] *vt* to consider again.—Also *n*. [L *re-*, again, and **think**.]

reticent [ret´i-sėnt] *adj* reserved or sparing in communication.—*ns* **ret´icence, ret´icency**. [L *reticēns, -ēntis*, pr p of *reticēre—re-, tacēre*, to be silent.]

reticle [ret´i-kl] *n* a system of lines, dots, cross hairs, or wires in the focus of the eyepiece of an optical instrument.—*adj* **reticular** [rė-tik´ū-lȧr], netted; netlike; reticulated.—*vt* **retic´ulate**, to form into, or mark with, a network; to distribute (eg water, electricity) by a network.—*adj* netted; marked with network.—*ns* **reticulā´tion**, network; netlike structure; **reticule** [ret´i-kūl], a reticle; a woman's drawstring bag used esp as a carryall. [L *rēticulum*, dim of *rēte*, net.]

retina [ret´i-na] *n* the innermost coat of the back part of the eye, on which the image is formed. [LL *rētina*, app—L *rēte*, net.]

retinue [ret´i-nū] *n* a body of retainers or attendants. [Fr *retenue*, pt p of *retenir*. See **retain**.]

retire [ri-tīr´] *vi* to withdraw; to retreat; to recede; to withdraw from office, business, profession, etc. (esp on reaching a certain age); to go to bed.—*vt* to withdraw (troops); to cause to retire from a position, office, etc.; to pay off (bonds, etc.); to withdraw from use; (*baseball*) to put out (a batter, side, etc.).—*adj* **retired´**, withdrawn; reserved in manner; secluded; withdrawn from business.—*n* **retire´ment**, act of retiring; state of being retired; solitude; privacy.—*adj* **retī´ring**, reserved, unobtrusive, modest. [Fr *retirer—re-*, back, *tirer*, to draw.]

retort [ri-tört´] *vt* to throw back; to return upon an assailant or opponent; to answer in retaliation, sharply, or wittily.—*vi* to make a sharp reply.—*n* retaliation; a ready and sharp or witty answer; a vessel used in distillation, typically a flask with a long straight beak. [L *retorquēre, retortum—re-*, back, *torquēre*, to twist.]

retouch [rē-tuch´] *vt* to touch up details (in a picture, writing, etc.) so as to improve or change it; to alter (as a photographic negative); to color (new growth of hair) to match previously dyed, tinted, or bleached hair.—*n* an act of touching up, esp a new growth of hair.—*n* **retouch´er**. [L *re-*, again, + **touch**.]

retrace [rē-trās´] *vt* to trace again or back. [L *re-*, back, + **trace** (1).]

retract [ri-trakt´] *vt* to draw back or in; to withdraw, to revoke, to unsay.—*vi* to take back, or draw back from, what has been said or granted.—*adj* **retrac´table**, able to be drawn back or withdrawn.—*n* **retractā´tion** [rē-], revoking, recantation.—*adj* **retrac´tile** [-tīl], that may be drawn back or in.—*n* **retrac´tion**, drawing back; retractation. [Mainly from L *retrahĕre, retractum*; partly from *retractāre, retractātum*; both from *re-*, back, *trahĕre*, to draw.]

retread [rē-tred´] *vt* to put a new tread on (a worn tire); to make over as if new.—*n* [rē´tred] a new tread or a retreaded tire; something made or done again in a new form; one (as a retired person) retrained for work; one (as an athlete) who has held the same position. [Pfx **re-**, + **tread**.]

retreat [ri-trēt´] *n* withdrawal; an orderly withdrawal before an enemy, or from a position of danger or difficulty; a signal for withdrawal or retirement; seclusion; place of privacy, seclusion, refuge or quiet.—*vi* to draw back; to retire. [OFr *retret, -e*, pt p of *retraire*—L *retrahĕre*, to draw back.]

retrench [rē-trench´] *vti* to cut down (esp expenses); to economize.—*n* **retrench´ment**, an act of retrenching; reduction; curtailment. [OFr *retrencher* (Fr *retrancher*)—*re-*, off, *trencher*, to cut. See **trench**.]

retribution [ret-ri-bū´sh(ȯ)n] *n* deserved reward; something given or exacted in compensation, esp punishment.—*adj* **retrib´ūtive** [ri-], involving retribution, punishing suitably. [L *retribuĕre, -būtum*, to give back—*re-*, back, *tribuĕre*, to give.]

retrieve [ri-trēv´] *vt* to recover, repossess; to restore (eg one's fortunes, credit); to make good, (eg a loss); to recover (information) from data stored in a computer; of dogs, to find and bring back (killed or wounded game).—*vi* to retrieve game.—*adj* **retriev´able**.—*ns* **retriev´al**, retrieving; **retriev´er**, any of several breeds of dogs capable of being trained to find and fetch game that has been shot. [OFr *retroev-, retreuv-*, stressed stem of *retrover* (Fr *retrouver*)—*re-*, again, *trouver*, to find.]

retro- [ret´ro-] *pfx* backwards; behind. [L *retrō-*, backward.]

retroactive [ret-rō-akt´iv] *adj* having an effect on things that are already past.—*ns* **retroac´tion**, retroactive operation (as of a law or tax); a reciprocal action; a reaction; **retroactiv´ity**.—*adv* **retroac´tively**. [L *retroagĕre, -actum—retrō*, backward, *agĕre*, to do.]

retrocession [ret-rō-sesh´(ȯ)n] *n* a giving back.—*vi* **retrocede´**, to cede back (as a territory). [L *retrōcēdĕre, -cessum—cēdĕre*, to go, yield; partly from *retrō*, backward, and **cede**, or Fr *céder*.]

retrograde [ret´rō-grād] *adj* going backward; falling from better to worse.—*vi* to go back or backwards; to become worse.—*ns* **retrogradation** [-grȧdā´sh(ȯ)n], the action or process of retrograding; **retrogression** [-gresh´(ȯ)n], a going backward; return to a former usu. less complex level of development or organization.—*adj* **retrogress´ive**.—*adv* **retrogress´ively**. [L *retrōgradus*, going backward, *retrōgressus*, retrogression—*retrō*, backward, *gradī, gressus*, to go.]

retro-rocket [ret´-rō-rok´ėt] *n* a rocket whose function is to slow down, fired in a direction opposite to that in which a body eg a spacecraft, an artificial satellite, is traveling. [L *retrō*, back, and **rocket**.]

retrospect [ret´rō-spekt] *n* a looking back; a contemplation of the past.—*n* **retrospec´tion**.—*adj* **retrospec´tive**, looking back in time.—*n* a representative show of an artist's lifetime work.—*adv* **retrospec´tively**. [L *retrō*, back, *specĕre, spectum*, to look.]

retroussé [rė-trōōs´ā] *adj* turned up (esp of the nose). [Fr *retrousser* (pt p *retroussé*), to turn up.]

retry [rē-trī´] *vt* to try again;—*pr p* **retry´ing**; *pt, pt p* **retried´**.—*n* **retrī´al**. [L *re-*, again, + **try**.]

return [ri-tûrn´] *vi* to come or go back; to recur; to reply.—*vt* to give, put, cast, bring or send back; to answer, to retort; to report officially; to do in reciprocation; to yield (a profit, etc.); to elect or reelect.—*n* the act of returning; something returned; a recurrence; that which comes in exchange; (*pl*) proceeds, profit, yield; recompense; requital; an answer; an official report; a form for computing (income) tax.—*adj* **retur´nable**, legally required to be returned, delivered, or argued at a specified time or place; capable of being returned (as for reuse); permitted to be returned. [Fr *retourner—re-*, back, *tourner*, to turn.]

reunion [rē-ūn´yȯn] *n* a meeting after separation. [Fr *réunion—re-*, again, *union*, union.]

reunite [rē-ū-nīt´] *vti* to join after separation. [L *re-*, again, + **unite**.]

rev [rev] *vt* (*inf*) to increase the speed of an engine (*with* **up**);—*vi* to operate at an increase in speed of revolution (*with* **up**);—*pr p* **revv´ing**; *pt, pt p* **revved**. [From **revolution**.]

revanche [ri-vänch´] *n* revenge; policy directed towards recovery of territory lost to an enemy.—*n* **revanch´ist**. [Fr.]

reveal [ri-vēl´] *n* to make known (something hidden or secret); to disclose; to make visible.—*adj* **reveal´ing**. [OFr *réveler* (Fr *révéler*)—L *revēlāre—re-*, the reverse of, *vēlāre*, to veil.]

reveille [rev´ė-lē] *n* the sound of the drum or bugle at daybreak to awaken soldiers. [Fr *réveillez*, awake, imper of *réveiller*—L *re-*, *vigilāre*, to watch.]

revel [rev´l] *vi* to feast or make merry in a riotous or noisy manner; to take intense delight (*with* **in**);—*pr p* **rev´elling**; *pt, pt p* **rev´elled**.—*n* a riotous feast; (often in *pl*) merry-making.—*ns* **rev´eller; rev´elry**, revelling. [OFr *reveler*—L *rebellāre*, to rebel.]

revelation [rev-ė-lā´sh(ȯ)n] *n* the act or experience of revealing; that which is revealed; an illuminating experience; (*theology*) divine communication; **Revelation**, (*Bible*) the 27th book of the New Testament, the last book of the Bible, written by St John the Divine, considered a book on prophecy about the world to come: **Apocalypse**, in the Douay Version of the New Testament. [L *revēlāre, -ātum*. See **reveal**.]

revenant [rėv´nã, rev´ė-nȧnt] *n* one who returns from the dead, or a long absence. [Fr.]

revenge [ri-venj´] *vt* to inflict injury in retribution for; to avenge (as oneself) by retaliating.—*n* (act of inflicting) a malicious injury in return for an injury received; the desire for retaliation; its satisfaction.—*adj* **revenge´ful**, ready to seek revenge.—*adv* **revenge´fully**.—*ns* **revenge´fulness; reveng´er**. [OFr *revenger, revencher* (Fr *revancher*)—L *re-*, in return, *vindicāre*, to lay claim to.]

revenue [rev´ėn-ū] *n* the total income produced by a given source; the income from taxes, licenses, etc., as of a city, state, or nation.—*ns* **revenue bond**, a bond issued by a public agency authorized to provide a revenue-producing property (as a toll road) and payable out of the revenue derived; **revenue stamp**, a stamp (as on a cigar box) for use as evidence of payment of a tax. [Fr *revenue*, pt p of *revenir*, to return—L *revenīre—re-*, back, *venīre*, to come.]

reverberate [ri-vûr´bėr-āt] *vt* to send back, to reflect, (heat, esp sound); to heat in a reverberatory furnace.—*vi* to recoil, rebound, be reflected; to reecho, resound.—*adj* **rever´berant**, reverberating.—*n* **reverberā´tion**.—*adj* **rever´beratory** [-ȧt-ȯr-i, or -āt-].—*n* **reverberatory**, a furnace or kiln in which heat is radiated from the roof onto the material treated. [L *reverberāre, -ātum—re-*, back, *verberāre*, to beat—*verber*, a lash.]

revere [ri-vēr´] *vt* to regard with high respect, to venerate.—*n* **reverence** [rev´ėr-ėns], high respect; respectful awe; state of being held in high respect; a gesture or observance of respect.—*vt* to venerate, regard with respect; to treat with respect.—*adjs* **rev´erend**, worthy of reverence; of or relating to the clergy; **Reverend**, used as a title for a member of the clergy, preceded by *the* and followed by a title or full name (eg the Reverend Dr Nancy Nelson); **rev´erent**, feeling or showing reverence; **reverential** [-en´sh(ȧ)l], proceeding from reverence; reverent; respectful.—*advs* **reveren´tially, rev´erently**. [OFr *reverer* (Fr *révérer*)—L *reverērī—re-*, inten, *verērī*, to feel awe.]

reverie, revery [rev´ė-ri] *n* an undirected train of thoughts or fancies in meditation; mental abstraction; a waking dream. [Fr *rêverie—rêver*, to dream.]

revers [ri-vēr] *n* a lapel, esp on a woman's garment.—*pl* **revers** [-vērz´]. [Fr,—L *reversus*.]

reverse [ri-vûrs´] *vt* to turn the other way about, as upside down, outside in, etc.; to invert; to set moving backwards; (*law*) to revoke or annul (a decision, etc.).—*vi* to move in the opposite direction.—*n* the contrary, opposite; the back, esp of a coin or medal; a change from good fortune to bad; a mechanism for reversing, as a gear on a machine.—*adj* contrary, opposite; turned about; causing movement in the opposite direction.—*n* **revers´al**, act or fact of reversing or being reversed.—*adj* **rever´sible**, capable of going through a series of changes either backward or forward (eg a reversible chemical reaction); having two finished usable sides; wearable with either side out.—*n* a reversible cloth or article of clothing.—*n* **rever´sion**, the act or fact of reverting or returning; that which reverts or returns; the return, or the future possession (of any property) after some particular event; the right to future possession; a throwback.—*adj* **rever´sionary**, of the nature of a reversion; involving reversion. [L *reversāre*, to turn round, and *reversus*, turned round; partly through Fr.]

revert [ri-vûrt´] *vi* to fall back (to a former state); to recur (to a former subject); (*biology*) to return to a former or primitive type; (*law*) to go back to a former owner or his heirs.—*adj* **rever´tible**. [L *re-, vertěre*, to turn.]

review [ri-vū´] *n* a viewing again, a reconsideration; a general survey (*to take a review of, pass in review*); (*law*) a reexamination, as of the decision of a lower court; a descriptive and critical account (of eg a book, play), a critique; a periodical with critiques of books, etc.; a display and inspection of troops or ships.—*vt* to reexamine; to examine critically; to write a critique on; to inspect, as troops.—*n* **review´er**, a writer of critiques. [Partly pfx **re-**, + **view**; partly Fr *revue*, fem. of *revu*, pt p of *revoir*—L *revidēre—vidēre*, to see.]

revile [ri-vīl´] *vti* to use abusive language (to or about).—*ns* **revile´ment; revil´er**. [OFr *reviler*—L *re-*, inten, *vīlis*, worthless.]

revise [ri-vīz´] *vt* to examine and correct; to make a new, improved version of; to study anew.—*n* a revision; a later printing proof embodying previous corrections.—*ns* **revis̄´al**, revision; **revi´ser, revisor; revision** [-vizh´(ȯ)n], act, or product, of revising; **revi´sionist**, an advocate of revision (as of a policy, doctrine or in historical analysis); a movement in revolutionary Marxism favoring an evolutionary approach.—**Revised Standard Version**, a revision of the American Standard Version of the Bible, originally published in 1901, published in 1946 and 1952; **Revised Version**, a British revision of the Authorized Version of the Bible, issued 1881–5. [Fr *reviser* and L *revīsěre—re-, vīsěre*, inten of *vidēre*, to see.]

revive [ri-vīv´] *vti* to return to life, vigor, memory, notice, use, the stage, etc.—*ns* **revī´val**, act or fact of reviving; recovery from languor, neglect, depression, etc.; renewed performance of, as of a play; renewed interest or attention; a time of extraordinary religious awakening; **revī´valist**, one who promotes religious or other revivals; **revī´valism; revī´ver**, one who, or that which, revives; a renovating preparation.—**Revival of Learning**, the Renaissance. [L *revīvěre*, to live again—*vīvěre*, to live.]

revivify [ri-viv´i-fī] *vt* to put vigor or new life into.—*vi* to revive.—*pr p* **reviv´ifying**; *pt, pt p* **reviv´ified**.—*n* **revivificā´tion**. [LL *revivificāre—re-, vīvus*, alive, *facěre*, to make.]

revoke [ri-vōk´] *vt* to annul; to retract.—*vi* to neglect to follow suit (at cards).—*n* act of revoking at cards.—*adj* **revocable** [rev´ō-kȧ-bl].—*adv* **rev´ocably**.—*n* **revocā´tion**, act of revoking. [L *revocāre—re-*, back, *vocāre*, to call.]

revolt [ri-vōlt´] *vi* to renounce allegiance, to rise in opposition; to experience disgust or shock; to turn away with disgust.—*vt* to cause to turn away or shrink with disgust.—*n* rebellion; insurrection; secession.—*n* **revol´ter**.—*adj* **revol´ting**, extremely offensive.—*adv* **revol´tingly**. [Fr *révolter*—L *re-, volūtāre*, freq of *volvěre, volūtum*, to turn.]

revolution [rev-ol-ōō´sh(ȯ)n] *n* act or condition of revolving; motion round a center; a complete turn by an object or figure, about an axis; a cycle of phenomena or of time; a great upheaval; a complete change, eg in outlook, social habits or circumstances; overthrow of a government, social system, etc.—*adj* **revolu´tionary**, of, favoring, or of the nature of, revolution, esp in government or conditions; **Revolutionary**, relating to the American Revolution or to the period in which it occurred.—*n* **revolutionary**, one who takes part in, or favours, revolution.—*vt* **revolu´tionize**, to cause radical change in.—*n* **revolu´tionist**, one who favors revolution. [LL *revolūtiō, -ōnis*—L *revolvěre*; see **revolt**.]

revolve [ri-volv´] *vt* to ponder; to travel or cause to travel in a circle or orbit; to rotate or cause to rotate.—*adj* **revolute** [rev´ol-ūt], rolled backward or downward.—*n* **revol´ver**, a handgun with a rotating magazine. [L *revolvěre, revolūtum—re-*, back, *volvěre*, to roll.]

revue [ri-vū´] *n* a musical show with skits, dances, etc., often parodying recent events. [Fr.]

revulsion [ri-vul´sh(ȯ)n] *n* disgust; a sudden change or reversal, esp of withdrawal with a sense of utter distaste or repugnance.—*adj* **revul´sive**. [L *revellěre, revulsum*, to pluck back, *vellěre*, to pluck.]

reward [ri-wÖrd´] *n* that which is given in return for something done; money offered, as for the capture of a criminal.—*vt* to give a reward to (someone) for (service, etc.).—*adj* **reward´ing**, of an activity, study, etc., giving pleasure or profit. [OFr *rewarder, regarder— re-*, again, *warder, garder*, to guard; cf **regard, guard, ward**.]

rhabdomancy [rab´dō-man-si] *n* divination by rod or wands. [Gr *rhabdos*, rod, *manteiā*, divination.]

rhadamanthine [rad-a-man´thīn] *adj* rigorously just and severe, like *Rhadamanthus* (Gr *-os*) a judge of the lower world.

Rhaeto-Romanic [rē´tō-rō-man´ik] *n* a Romance language of eastern Switzerland and northeastern Italy. [From L *Rhaetia*, a province of the Roman Empire, and *Rōmānicus*, Roman.]

rhapsody [raps´o-di] *n* a portion of an epic poem adapted for recitation; (*arch*) a miscellaneous collection; any ecstatic or enthusiastic speech or writing; an instrumental composition of an epic, heroic, or national character having a free, irregular form.—*adjs* **rhapsodic** [-od´ik] of the nature of rhapsody; **rhapsod´ical**, rhapsodic; emotionally enthusiastic.—*adv* **rhapsod´ically**.—*vi* **rhap´sodize**, to write or utter in a rhapsodic manner.—*n* **rhap´sodist**, a professional reciter of epic poems; one who speaks or writes rhapsodically. [Gr *rhapsōidiā*, an epic, a rigmarole—*rhaptein*, to sew, *ōide*, a song.]

rhea [rē´a] *n* a genus (*Rhea*) of S American ostriches. [Gr *Rhĕā*, mother of Zeus.]

rhenium [rē´ni-ùm] *n* a metallic element (symbol Re; at wt 186.2; at no 75). [L *Rhēnus*, Rhine.]

rheology [rē-ol´o-ji] *n* the science of the deformation and flow of matter; the quality or state of elasticity, viscosity, and plasticity. [From Gr *rheos*, flow, *logos*, discourse.]

rhesus monkey [rē´sùs] *n* a pale brown Indian monkey (*Macaca mulatta*) often used in medical research.—**Rh factor**, a genetically determined substance present in the red blood cells of most persons and of higher animals and capable of inducing severe antigenic reactions; **Rh-negative**, lacking Rh in the blood.

rhetoric [ret´ȯr-ik] *n* the theory and practice of effective speaking and writing, esp as formulated by critics of ancient times; skill in using speech; false, showy, or declamatory expression.—*adj* **rhetor´ical**, pertaining to rhetoric; oratorical; ornate or insincere in style.—*adv* **rehetor´ically**.—*n* **rhetorician** [ret-ȯr-ish´(à)n], one who teaches the art of rhetoric; an orator.—**rhetorical question**, a question in form, for rhetorical effect, not calling for an answer. [Gr *rhētōr*, a public speaker.]

rheum [rōōm] *n* mucous discharge.—*adj* **rheumat´ic**, of the nature of, pertaining to, affected with, rheumatism.—*n* one who suffers from rheumatism.—*n* **rheum´atism**, disease causing inflammation and pain in muscles, joints.—*adj* **rheum´atoid**, resembling rheumatism.—*n* **rheumatol´ogy**, the study of rheumatism.—*adj* **rheum´y**.—**rheumatic fever**, an acute disease occurring chiefly in children and young adults, characterized by fever, inflammation and pain around the joints, and inflammation of the pericardium and heart valves; **rheumatoid arthritis**, a usu. chronic disease marked by inflammation, pain, and swelling of the joints. [Gr *rheuma*, gen *-atos*—*rheein*, to flow.]

Rh factor *See* **rhesus monkey**.

rhinal [rī´nàl] *adj* of the nose.—*n* **rhinī´tis**, inflammation of the mucous membrane of the nose. [Gr. *rhīs*, gen *rhīnos*, nose.]

rhinoceros [rī-nos´ėr-os] *n* a family (Rhinocerotidae) of large animals in Africa and southern Asia, having a very thick skin, and one or two horns on the nose;—*pls* **rhinoc´eroses, rhinoc´eros**, or **rhinoc´eri**. [Gr *rhīnokerōs*, gen *-ōtos*—*keras*, horn, *rhīs*, gen *rhīnos*, nose.]

rhizome [rī´zōm] *n* a rootstock; an underground stem producing roots and leafy shoots. [Gr *rhizōma*, a root mass—*rhizā*, root.]

Rhodes scholar [rōdz] *n* a student from the US or British Commonwealth holding a Rhodes scholarship to study at Oxford University, England. [Cecil J *Rhodes*, 1853–1902, Brit financier in S Africa.]

rhodium [rō´di-ùm] *n* a metallic element (symbol Rh; at wt 102.9; at no 45), resembling platinum. [From Gr *rhodon*, rose—some of its salts are rose-colored.]

rhododendron [rō-dō-den´dron] *n* a genus (*Rhododendron*) of trees and shrubs of the heath family, with evergreen leaves and large, beautiful flowers. [Gr *rhodon*, rose, *dendron*, tree.]

rhodomontade *See* **rodomontade**.

rhomb [rom(b)] *n* a rhombus; a rhombohedron;—*pl* **rhombuses, rhombi** [-bī or -bē].—*adjs* **rhombic** [rom´bik], shaped like a rhombus; **rhomboid**, like a rhombus or rhomboid.—*n* a parallelogram whose adjacent sides are unequal and whose angles are not right angles.—*adjs* **rhomboid, rhomboidal**, more or less like a rhomboid.—*ns* **rhombohedron**, a parallelepiped whose faces are rhombuses; a parallelogram having its sides equal but its angles usu. not right angles. [Gr *rhombos*, bull-roarer, magic wheel, rhombus.]

rhubarb [rōō´bärb] *n* a genus (*Rheum*) of plants, the leafstalks of which are used as food, and the root in medicine; (*inf*) a heated dispute. [OFr *reubarbe*, through Low L—Gr *rhā*, rhubarb (*Rhā*, the Volga), and L *barbarum* (neut; Gr *barbaron*), foreign.]

rhumb [rum] *n* a line or course on a single bearing; any point of the compass.—*n* **rhumb line**, a line which cuts all the meridians at the same angle. [Fr *rumb*, or Sp or Port *rumbo*—L *rhombos*—Gr *rhombos*. See **rhomb**.]

rhyme, rime [rīm] *n* the repetition of sounds usu at the ends of lines in verse; such poetry or verse or such correspondence of sound; a word corresponding with another in end sound.—*vi* to make (rhyming) verse; to form a rhyme.—*vi* to put into rhyme; to use as a rhyme.—*ns* **rhy´mer**, a versifier, a poetaster; a minstrel; **rhyme´ roy´al**, a seven-line stanza in iambic pentameter with a rhyme scheme of *a b a b b c c*; **rhyme´ster**, a poetaster, a would-be poet. [OFr *rime*—L *rhythmus*—Gr *rhythmos*. See **rhythm**; associated and confused with OE *rīm*, number.]

rhythm [riTHm] *n* regular recurrence of beat, accent or silence, in the flow of sound; pattern of recurring stresses in music; movement, course of change, showing regular recurrence of features or phenomena.—*adjs* **rhyth´mic, -al**.—*adv* **rhyth´mically**.—**rhythm and blues**, the form of black American popular music from which rock-and-roll derives; **rhythm method**, a method of birth control requiring the avoidance of sexual intercourse during the time in which conception is most likely to occur. [L *rhythmus*—Gr *rhythmos*—*rheein*, to flow; cf **rhyme**.]

rib[1] [rib] *n* one of the bones attached to the spine that curve around and forward enclosing the chest cavity; a curved member of the side of a ship running from keel to deck; a vein of a leaf; a vein of an insect's wing; a light fore-and-aft member in an airplane's wing; one of the stiff strips supporting an umbrella's fabric; an arch in Romanesque and Gothic vaulting; one of the ridges in a knitted or woven fabric.—*vt* to furnish, form, cover, or enclose with ribs; to form vertical ridges in knitting;—*pr p* **ribb´ing**; *pt, pt p* **ribbed**.—*n* **ribb´ing**, an arrangement of ribs. [OE *ribb*, rib; Ger *rippe*, rib.]

rib[2] *vt* (*inf*) to tease, ridicule, make fun of. [Perh **rib** (1).]

ribald [rib´àld] *n* a loose, low character.—*adj* low, licentious, foul-mouthed (eg *a ribald jest*).—*n* **rib´aldry**, obscenity, scurrility. [OFr *ribald, ribaut* (Fr *ribaud*); origin doubtful.]

riband [rib´ànd] *n* a ribbon used esp as a decoration.

ribband [rib´ànd] *n* a long narrow strip or bar used in shipbuilding.

ribbon [rib´ȯn] *n* material woven in narrow bands or strips; (*pl*) torn shreds; a strip of cloth, etc., inked for use, as in a typewriter.—*vt* to adorn with ribbons; to divide into ribbons; to rip into shreds.—*n* **ribb´on development**, siting buildings side by side along a road. [OFr *riban*; origin obscure.]

riboflavin [rī´bȯ-flā´vin] *n* a factor of the Vitamin B complex found in milk, eggs, fruits, etc.

ribonucleic acids [rī´bō-nū-klē´ik as´ids] nucleic acids containing **ribose**, a pentose, $C_5 H_{10} O_5$, present in living cells, where they play an important part in the development of proteins—abbrev **RNA**.

rice [rīs] *n* an annual cereal grass (*Oryza sativa*) grown in warm climates; its grain, a valuable food.—*ns* **rice´ pā´per**, sliced and flattened pith of a small Asian tree or shrub (*Tetrapanax papyriferum*); **ricer**, a kitchen utensil in which soft foods are pressed through perforations to produce strings the diameter of rice grains. [OFr *ris*—L *oryza*—Gr *oryza*, a word of Oriental origin.]

rich [rich] *adj* abounding in possessions, wealthy; abounding (in, with); costly, splendid, elaborately decorated; sumptuous; abundant; fertile; deep in color; full-toned; full-flavored; abounding in oily ingredients; (*inf*) full of absurdities; ridiculous, very amusing.—*adv* **rich´ly**.—*n* **rich´ness**.—**the rich**, wealthy people collectively. [OE *rīce*, great, powerful; Ger *reich*, Du *rijk*.]

riches [rich´iz] *n pl* wealth. [OFr *richesse*—*riche*, rich, powerful; of Gmc origin.]

Richter scale [rik´tėr] *n* a logarithmic scale ranging from one to ten for expressing the intensity of earth-quake (eg 2 indicates the slightest earthquake that can be felt; 4.5 causes slight damage, and 8.5 is devastating). [From its inventor, Charles *Richter* (1900-).

rick [rik] *n* a stack of hay in the open; a heap of short logs. [OE *hrēac*; ON *hraukr*.]

rickets [rik´ėts] *n sing* a disease of children, caused by Vitamin D deficiency, characterized by softness of the bones.—*adj* **rick´ety, rick´etty**, affected with rickets; feeble; tottery, unsteady. [First recorded in SW England in the 17th cent, perh ME *wrikken*, to twist; or Gr *rhachītis*.]

ricksha, rickshaw [rik´shö] *n* a small, two-wheeled, hooded vehicle drawn by a man, orig used in Japan. [Abbrev of **jinricksha(w), jinrik´isha**; Jap *jin*, man, *riki*, power, *sha*, a vehicle.]

ricochet [rik´ō-shā´] *n* a glancing rebound or skip, as an object striking a surface at an angle.—*vi* to make a ricochet;—*pr p* **ricocheting** [-shā´ing], **ricochetting** [-shet´ing]; *pt, pt p* **ricocheted** [-shād], **ricochetted** [-shet´id]. [Fr]

rid [rid] *vt* to free from, clear of, disencumber (of); (*arch*) to deliver (from, out of);—*pr p* **ridd´ing**; *pt, pt p* **rid** or **ridd´ed**.—*n* **ridd´ance**, clearance; deliverance.—**a good riddance**, a welcome relief; **get rid of**, to disencumber oneself of. [ON *rythja*, to clear.]

riddle[1] [rid´l] *n* an obscure description of something which the hearer is asked to name; a puzzling question; anything puzzling.—*vt* to solve as a riddle; to set a riddle for.—*vi* to make riddles; to speak obscurely. [OE *rǣdelse*—*rǣdan*, to guess, to read—*rǣd*, counsel.]

riddle[2] [rid´l] *n* a coarse sieve.—*vt* to separate with a riddle; to make full of holes like a riddle, as with shot; to spread through, permeate. [OE *hriddel*, earlier *hridder*.]

ride [rīd] *vi* to travel or be borne on the back of an animal, on a bicycle, or in a vehicle; to float or move on the water; to lie at anchor; to be supported in motion (*with* **on**); to travel over a surface; to move on the body; (*inf*) to continue undisturbed.—*vt* to traverse on horseback, on bicycle, etc.; to perform on horseback, bicycle, etc. (eg a race); to sit on and control (eg a horse); to control at will or oppressively; (*inf*) to torment, harass;—*pt* **rōde**; *pt p* **ridd´en**.—*n* a journey on horseback, on bicycle, or in a vehicle; a thing to ride at an amusement park.—*ns* **rī´der**, one who rides or can ride; an addition to a document, often on a separate sheet of paper; a clause attached to a legislative bill to secure a distinct object; something used to move along another piece; **ri´dership**, the passengers of a particular transport system.—**ride for a fall**, to court disaster; **ride herd on**, to keep a check on; **ride high**, to experience success. [OE *rīdan*; Du *rijden*, Ger *reiten*.]

ridge [rij] *n* the back of an animal; the earth thrown up by the plough between the furrows; a long narrow top or crest; the horizontal line formed by the meeting of two sloping surfaces; a narrow elevation; a hill range.—*vti* to form into ridges.—*n* **ridgepole**, the horizontal beam at the ridge of a roof, to which the rafters are attached; the horizontal pole at the top of a tent.—*adj* **ridg´y**, having ridges. [OE *hrycg*; ON *hryggr*, Ger *rücken*, back.]

ridicule [rid´i-kūl] *n* derision, mockery.—*vt* to laugh at, to expose to merriment, to mock.—*adj* **ridic´ūlous**, deserving or exciting ridicule, absurd.—*adv* **ridic´ūlously**.—*n* **ridic´ūlousness**. [L *rīdiculus—rīdēre*, to laugh.]
riding *See* **ride**.
rife [rīf] *adj* prevalent; abounding.—*adv* **rife´ly**.—*n* **rife´ness**. [OE *rȳfe, rīfe*; Du *rijf*, ON *rifr*.]
riffraff [rif´-raf] *n* disreputable persons; refuse, rubbish. [ME *rif and raf*—OFr *rif et raf*.]
rifle[1] [rī´fl] *vt* to plunder (a person, place) thoroughly; to steal, carry away.—*vi* to engage in ransacking and stealing.—*n* **rī´fler**. [OFr *rifler*.]
rifle[2] [rī´fl] *vt* to groove spirally within.—*n* a shoulder gun with spirally grooved barrel.—*n* **rī´fling**, the act or process of making spiral grooves; a system of spiral grooves in the surface of the bore of a gun. [OFr *rifler*, to scratch; cf Ger *riefeln*, and preceding word.]
rift [rift] *n* a cleft; a fissure.—*vti* to cleave, split.—*n* **rift´valley**, valley formed by subsidence of a portion of the earth's crust between two faults.—**rift in the lute**, beginning of disagreement or discord. [Cf Dan and Norw *rift*, a cleft.]
rig [rig] *vt* (*naut*) to fit with sails and tackle; to fit up or fit out; to set in working order; (*inf*) to dress (*with* **out**);—*pr p* **rigg´ing**; *pt, pt p* **rigged**.—*n* the way sails etc., are rigged; equipment, gear; a tractor-trailer.—*ns* **rigg´ing**, tackle; the system of cordage which supports a ship's masts and extends the sails; a similar network (as in theater scenery) used for support and manipulation; clothing. [Origin obscure; perh conn with Norw *rigga*, to bind.]
right [rīt] *adj* straight, direct; perpendicular; forming one-fourth of a revolution; (*arch*) true, genuine; truly judged or judging; in accordance, or identical, with what is true and fitting; not mistaken; just, normal, sane; at or toward that side at which, in most persons, is the better developed hand (of a river, as referred to a person going downstream); conservative; designating the side meant to be seen.—*adv* straight; directly; exactly; in a right manner; justly; correctly; very; to or on the right side.—*n* that which is right or correct; equity; truth; justice; just or legal claim; what one has a just claim to; due; the right side; the right wing; **Right**, those members of certain of the legislative assemblies of Europe (eg France) who have seats to the right of the presiding officer—conservatives, monarchists, etc.—*vt* to set right; to set in order; to do justice to.—*vi* to recover an erect position.—*n* **right´angle**, an angle equal to a fourth of a revolution.—*adj* **right´ful**, having a just claim; according to justice; belonging by right.—*adv* **right´fully**.—*n* **right´fulness**, righteousness; justice.—*adv* **right´ly**.—*n* **right´ness**.—*adj* **right´wing´**, of or on the right wing; conservative.—**right off**, right away, without delay; **right-of-way**, the right of the public to pass over a piece of ground; a track over which there is such a right; precedence in passing other traffic.—**all right** (see **all**); **by rights**, rightfully; **in one's own right**, by absolute and personal right, not through another; **in the right**, maintaining a justifiable position. [OE *riht* (n and adj) *rihte* (adv), *rihtan* (vb); cf Ger *recht*, L *rēctus*.]
righteous [rī´chùs] *adj* just, upright.—*adv* **right´eously**.—*n* **right´eousness**, rectitude; a righteous act. [OE *rihtwis—riht*, right, *wīs*, wise, prudent, or *wīse*, wise, manner.]
rigid [rij´id] *adj* stiff, unbending; rigorous, strict; of an airship, having a rigid structure to maintain shape.—*adv* **rig´idly**.—*ns* **rig´idness, rigid´ity**. [L *rigidus—rigēre*, to be stiff.]
rigmarole [rig´ma-rōl] *n* nonsense; a foolishly involved procedure. [A corr of *ragman-roll*, a document with a long list of names, or with numerous seals pendent.]
rigor [ri´gòr] *n* harsh inflexibility; severity; strict precision; a tremor caused by a chill.—*adj* **rigorous** [rig´ōr-us], rigidly strict or scrupulous; exact; very harsh, severe.—*adv* **rig´orously**.—*ns* **rig´orousness**.—**rigor mortis**, temporary stiffening of the body after death. [L *rigor—rigēre*, to be stiff.]
rile [rīl] *vt* (*inf*) to irritate, make angry. [A form of *roil*, to make turbid.]
rill [ril] *n* a very small brook.—*vi* to flow like a rill. [Cf Du *ril*, Ger (orig Low Ger) *rille*, channel, furrow.]
rim [rim] *n* a border, brim, edge, or margin, esp of something circular; the outer part of a wheel.—*vt* to form or furnish a rim to;—*pr p* **rimm´ing**; *pt, pt p* **rimmed**.—*adj* **rim´less**. [OE *rima* (found in compounds).]
rime[1] [rīm] *n* a hoarfrost or frozen dew.—*adj* **rī´my**. [OE *hrīm*; Du *rijm*, Ger *reif*.]
rime[2] *See* **rhyme**.
rind [rīnd] *n* bark; peel; crust; skin. [OE *rinde*; Du and Ger *rinde*.]
rinderpest [rin´dėr-pest] *n* a contagious virus disease of cattle. [Ger, cattle-plague.]
ring[1] [ring] *n* a circlet or small hoop, esp one of metal, worn on the finger, in the ear, nose, or elsewhere; any object, mark, group, etc., circular but hollow in form; a space set apart for sport, as boxing, wrestling, amusement, display, etc.; a clique organized to control the market or for other gain; (*math*) a system of elements in which addition is associative and commutative and multiplication is associative and distributive with respect to addition.—*vt* to encircle; to put a ring on or in.—*vi* to move in rings; to gather or be in a ring;—*pt, pt p* **ringed**.—*n* **ring´dove**, a common European pigeon (*Columba palumbus*) with a whitish patch on each side of the neck; a small dove (*Streptopelia risoria*) of southeastern Europe and Asia.—*adj* **ringed**, surrounded by, or marked with, a ring or rings; ringshaped.—*ns* **ring´ finger**, the third finger, esp of the left hand, on which the wedding ring is worn; **ring´leader**, one who takes the lead in mischief; **ring´let**, a little ring; a fairy ring; a long curl of hair; **ring´master**, one who has charge of performances in a ring as of a circus; **ring´worm**, a contagious skin disease characterized by ring-shaped patches, caused by infection with certain fungi.—**a ringside seat**, a position which allows one to have a clear view. [OE *hring*; ON *hringr*, Ger, Dan, and Swed *ring*.]
ring[2] [ring] *vi* to give a metallic or bell-like sound; to sound aloud and clearly; to resound; to be filled (with sound, or a sensation like sound, or report, or renown); to have a sound suggestive of a quality indicated (eg *his words ring true*).—*vt* to cause to give a metallic or bell-like sound; to summon or announce by a bell or bells; to resound, proclaim; to call on the telephone.—*pt* **rang** (*dialect* **rung**); *pt p* **rung**.—*n* a sounding of a bell; a characteristic sound or tone; a set of bells.—*n* **ring´er**.—*n, adj* **ring´ing**.—**ring a bell**, to begin to arouse a memory; **ring in, out**, to usher in, out (esp the year) with bell-ringing; **ring up**, to total and record esp by means of a cash register; to achieve; **ring the changes**, to proceed through all the permutations in ringing a chime of bells; to do a limited number of things repeatedly in varying order; to run through all possible variations. [OE *hringan*; ON *hringja*; Ger *ringen*; Dan *ringe*.]
rink [ringk] *n* an expanse of ice for skating; a smooth floor for roller-skating; an alley for lawn bowling. [Orig Scots.]
rinse [rins] *vt* to wash lightly by pouring, shaking, or dipping; to wash in clean water to remove soap traces.—*n* an act of rinsing; liquid used for rinsing; a solution used in hairdressing, esp one to tint the hair slightly and impermanently. [OFr *rinser* (Fr *rincer*).]
riot [rī´ôt] *n* tumult; a disturbance of the peace by a crowd; an exuberance (eg of color, emotion); (*inf*) something very funny.—*vi* to take part in a riot.—*ns* **rī´oter, rī´oting**.—*adj* **rī´otous**.—*adv* **rī´otously**.—*n* **rī´otousness**.—**read the riot act to**, to give very strict orders to so as to make obey; **run riot**, to act or grow wild without restraint or control. [OFr *riot, riotte*.]
rip [rip] *vt* to cut or tear apart roughly; to remove in this way (*with* **off, out**); to sever the threads of (a seam); to saw (wood) along the grain.—*vi* to become ripped; (*inf*) to rush, speed.—*pr p* **ripp´ing**; *pt, pt p* **ripped**.—*n* a tear; a rent.—*ns* **rip´ cord**, a cord for opening a parachute or a balloon's gasbag; **rip´-off**, (*slang*) the act or a means of stealing; plagiarizing, cheating, etc.; **ripp´er**, a ripsaw; a machine for breaking up solid material (as rock or ore); (*inf*) an excellent example or instance of its kind; **rip´saw**, a saw for cutting along the grain.—**rip into** (*inf*) to attack, esp verbally. [Precise origin uncertain; cf Frisian *rippe*, Flemish *rippen*, Norw *rippa*.]
riparian [rī-pā´ri-àn] *adj* of, or inhabiting, a river bank, sometimes of a lake or tidewater. [L *rīpārius—rīpa*, a river bank.]
ripe [rīp] *adj* ready for harvest; fully developed; mature; arrived at perfection, consummate (eg scholarship, wisdom); in best condition for use (eg *a ripe cheese*); mature.—*adv* **ripe´ly**.—*vt* **rī´pen**, to make or grow ripe or riper.—*n* **ripe´ness**. [OE *rīpe*, ripe, *rīpian*, to ripen; conn with *rīp*, harvest, and perh **reap**.]
riposte [ri-pōst´] *n* a quick return thrust after a parry; a repartee; a retaliatory maneuver. [Fr—It *risposta*, reply.]
ripple [rip´l] *n* light fretting of the surface of a liquid; a little wave; a sound as of rippling water.—*vti* to have or form little waves on the surface (of).—**ripple effect**, the spreading effects caused by a single event. [Origin obscure.]
rise [rīz] *vi* to get up; to stand up; (*theology*) to come back to life; to become excited or hostile; to revolt; to move upward; to come up to the surface; to come above the horizon; to come (into view, notice, or consciousness); to grow upward; to attain (to); to advance in rank, fortune, etc.; to swell; to increase in price; to become more acute in pitch; to take origin; to tower; to slope up; to respond as to provocation, or to a situation calling forth one's powers.—*pt* **rose** [rōz]; *pt p* **risen** [riz´n].—*n* rising; ascent; vertical difference or amount of elevation; origin; an increase of salary, price, etc.; progress upward; a sharpening of pitch.—*ns* **rī´ser**, one who rises, esp from bed; that which rises; the upright portion of a step; **rī´sing**, act of rising; a revolt; a prominence; a swelling; a hill.—*adj, pr p* ascending; increasing; coming above the horizon.—**rise to it** (from fishing), to take the lure. [OE *rīsan*.]
risible [riz´i-bl] *adj* able or inclined to laugh; of laughter; ludicrous.—*n* **risibil´ity**, laughter; inclination to laugh; (often in *pl*) faculty of laughter. [L *rīsibilis—rīdēre, rīsum*, to laugh.]
risk [risk] *n* hazard; chance of loss or injury; degree of probability of loss; person, thing, or factor likely to cause loss or danger.—*vt* to expose to hazard; to venture.—*adj* **risk´y**, dangerous.—**run a risk**, to expose oneself to, or to involve, the possibility of loss, injury, or failure. [Fr *risque*—It *risco*.]
risotto [ri-sot´to] *n* dish of rice cooked in meat stock, mixed with savory ingredients, as chicken, onions. [It.]
risqué [rēs´kā] *adj* bordering on the improper. [Fr, risky.]
ritardando [rē-tär-dan´dō] *adj* and *adv* (*mus*) with diminishing speed. [It.]
rite [rīt] *n* a ceremonial form or observance, esp religious; a liturgy. [L *rītus*.]
ritual [rit´ū-àl] *adj* relating to, or of the nature of, rites.—*n* manner of performing divine service, or a book containing it; a body or code of ceremonies; performance of rites.—*ns* **rit´ūalism**, attachment of importance to ritual, esp with the implication of undue importance; **rit´ūalist**, one exces-

sively devoted to a ritual.—*adj* **ritūalist´ic.**—*advs* **ritūalist´ically, rit´ūally.** [L *rituālis—rītus*, rite.]

ritzy [rit´zi] *adj* (*slang*) stylish, elegant, ostentatiously rich. [The *Ritz* hotels.]

rival [rī´vȧl] *n* one pursuing an object in competition with another, one who strives to equal or excel another; one for whom, or that for which, a claim to equality might be made.—*adj* standing in competition; of like pretensions or comparable claims.—*vt* to try to gain the same object as; to try to equal or excel; to be worthy of comparison with.—*pr p* **rī´valling**; *pt, pt p* **rī´valled**.—*n* **rī´valry**, state of being a rival; competition, emulation. [L *rīvālis*, said to be from *rīvus*, river, as one who draws water from the same river.]

rive [rīv] *vt* to tear asunder; to split.—*vi* to tug, tear; to split.—*pt* **rīved**; *pt p* **riven** [riv´n], **rived** [rīvd]. [ON *rīfa*.]

river [riv´ėr] *n* a natural stream of water flowing into an ocean, lake, etc.; something resembling a river; large quantities.—*ns* **river basin**, the area drained by a river and its tributaries; **riv´erbed**, the channel in which a river flows; **riv´erfront**, the land, or area along a river; **riv´er horse**, a hippopotamus; **riv´erside**, the bank of a river.—Also *adj*.—*adj* **riv´erine** [-īn, -ēn], of, on, or dwelling near or in a river.—**up the river**, (*inf*) to or in prison. [OFr *rivere* (Fr *rivière*)—L *rīpārius*, adj—*rīpa*, bank; cf It *riviera*.]

rivet [riv´et] *n* a bolt fastened by hammering the end.—*vt* to fasten with rivets; to fix immovably;—*pr p* **riv´eting**; *pt, pt p* **riv´eted**.—*ns* **riv´eter**, one who rivets; a machine for riveting; **riv´eting**. [OFr *rivet—river*, to clinch.]

rivulet [riv´ū-let] *n* a little stream. [L *rīvulus*, dim of *rīvus*, a stream, perh through It *rivoletto—rivolo—rivo*.]

roach[1] [rōch] *n* cockroach; (*slang*) butt of a marijuana cigarette. [Clipped form.]

roach[2] [rōch] *n* a silvery freshwater fish (*Rutilis rutilis*) of Europe; any of several American freshwater sunfishes (family Centrarchidae). [OFr *roche*.]

road [rōd] *n* a way made for traveling; a highway; (often *pl*) a roadstead; a path (eg *the road to ruin*).—*ns* **road´bed**, the foundation laid for railroad tracks or for a highway, etc.; **road´block**, an obstruction set up across a road; **road´ hog**, a car driver who obstructs another vehicle by encroaching on the other's traffic lane; **road´house**, a tavern usu. outside the city limits providing meals, alcoholic drinks, dancing and often gambling; **road metal**, broken stones and cinders used in making and repairing roads or ballasting railroads; **road´runner**, a long-tailed, swift-running bird (*Geococcyx califorianus*) of the cuckoo family of the southwestern US; **road´side**, border of a road (also *adj*); **road´stead**, a place near a shore where ships may ride at anchor; **road´ster**, a horse for riding or driving on roads; a light carriage; an automobile with an open body that seats two, has a folding fabric top and a luggage compartment in the rear; **road test**, a test of a vehicle under practical operating conditions; a test on the road as part of the requirement for a driving license; **road´way**, the strip of land over which a road passes; a roadbed; a railroad right-of-way; the part of a bridge used by vehicles; **road´work**, conditioning for an athletic contest consisting mainly of long runs.—*adj* **road´worthy**, fit for the road.—**down the road**, in the future. [OE*rād*, a riding, raid; cf **raid, ride**.]

roam [rōm] *vi* to rove about; to ramble.—*vt* to wander over.—*n* **roam´er**. [ME *romen*.]

roan [rōn] *adj* having a base color (as red, black, or brown) thickly sprinkled with white or gray.—*n* an animal (as a horse) with a roan coat; a roan horse, esp when the base is red; a tanned sheepskin finished to imitate morocco. [OFr *roan* (Fr *rouan*).]

roar [rōr, rör] *vi* to make a full, loud, hoarse, low-pitched sound, as a lion, fire, wind, the sea; to bellow; to bawl; to guffaw.—*vt* to utter, say, very loudly.—*n* a sound of roaring.—*n* **roar´ing**. [OE *rārian*; but partly from Middle Du *roer*, stir, disturbance.]

roast [rōst] *vt* to cook (meat, etc.) with little or no moisture, as before an open fire or in an oven; to process (coffee, etc.) by exposure to heat; to expose to great heat; (*inf*) to criticize harshly;—*pt p* **roast´ed**.—*adj* **roast**.—*vi* to undergo roasting.—*n* roasted meat; cut of meat for roasting; a picnic at which food is roasted.—*ns* **roaster**, one that roasts; a device for roasting; a suckling pig; a young chicken; **roasting ear**, an ear of young corn suitable for roasting, usu in the husk. [OFr *rostir* (Fr *rôtir*); of Gmc origin.]

rob [rob] *vt* to deprive (of), esp wrongfully and forcibly; to steal from (a person); to plunder (a place); to take as plunder.—*vi* to commit robbery;—*pr p* **robb´ing**; *pt, pt p* **robbed**.—*ns* **robb´er**, one who robs; **robb´ery**, (*law*) theft from the person, aggravated by violence or intimidation; plundering.—**robber baron**, an American capitalist of the late 19th century who became wealthy through exploitation (as of natural resources, governmental influence, or low wage scales).—**rob Peter to pay Paul**, to satisfy or benefit one person by depriving another. [OFr *rober*, of Gmc origin; cf **reave**, OHG *roubōn*, Ger *rauben*.]

robe [rōb] *n* a long loose outer garment; a dress of office, dignity, or state; a bathrobe or dressing gown; a covering or wrap.—*vti*, to dress in a robe. [Fr *robe*, orig booty; cf **rob**.]

robin [rob´in] *n* a large N American thrush (*Turdus migratorius*) with a dull-red breast; a small European thrush (*Erithacus rubecula*) with a yellowish-red throat and breast. [A familiar form of **Robert**; cf *Jack*daw, *Mag*pie.]

robot [rō´bot] *n* a mechanical device acting in a seemingly human way; a mechanism guided by automatic controls; an efficient, insensitive often brutalized person. [Name of artificially made persons in Karel Čapek's play *R.U.R.* (1920)—Czech *robota*, statute labor.]

robust [rō-bust´] *adj* stout, strong, and sturdy; constitutionally healthy; having strength and vigor; (eg of style, humor, intelligence) vigorous, sane, not inclined to subtlety.—*adv* **robust´ly**.—*n* **robust´ness**. [L *rōbustus—rōbur*, strength, oak.]

roc [rok] *n* a fabulous bird of great size and strength believed to inhabit the Indian Ocean area. [Pers *rukh*.]

rochet [roch´ėt] *n* a white linen vestment worn esp by bishops and privileged prelates. [OFr; of Gmc origin; cf Ger *rock*, OE *rocc*.]

rock[1] [rok] *n* a large outstanding natural mass of stone; (*geol*) a natural mass of one or more minerals, consolidated or loose; (*inf*) a diamond; a flavored stick candy with color running through; a sure foundation or support.—*n* **rock´ bott´om**, the lowest or most fundamental part or level.—*adj* being the lowest possible.—*ns* **rock´ crys´tal**, transparent quartz; **rock´ dove**, a bluish gray wild pigeon (*Columba livia*) of Europe and Asia that is the ancestor of many domestic pigeons and of the feral pigeons found throughout the world.—Also **rock pigeon; rock garden**, a garden among rocks for alpine plants; **rock´ oil**, petroleum; **rock´ pi´geon**, the rock dove; **rock´ salt**, common salt in large crystals or masses; **rock wool**, a fibrous material made from molten rock, used for insulation.—*adj* **rock´y**, full of rocks; like rock.—**on the rocks**, in or into a state of wreckage or destruction; (of whiskey, etc.) on ice. [OFr *roke*—Low L *rocca*.]

rock[2] [rok] *n* a distaff; the wool or flax on a distaff. [ME *roc*; cf ON *rokkr*; Ger *rocken*.]

rock[3] [rok] *vti* to move to and fro, tilt from side to side; to sway strongly; to shake.—*n* a rocking motion; rock and roll.—*ns* **rock´er**, either of the curved pieces on which a cradle, etc., rocks; a chair mounted on such pieces; **rock´ing**, a swaying backward and forward; **rock´ing chair**, a rocker; **rock´ing horse**, a toy horse mounted on rockers or springs.—*adj* **rock´y**, disposed to rock; shaky; unsteady.—**rock and roll**, popular music usu. played on electronically amplified instruments with a heavily accented beat and country, folk, and blues elements.—**off one's rocker**, in a state of extreme confusion or insanity; **rock the boat**, to do something to disturb the equanimity of a situation. [OE *roccian*.]

rocket [rok´ėt] *n* any device driven forward by gases escaping through a rear vent as a firework, projectile, or the propulsion mechanism of a spacecraft.—*vi* to move in or like a rocket; soar.—*n* **rock´etry**, the science of building and launching rockets. [It *rocchetta*; of Gmc origin.]

rococo [rō-ko´kō, rō-kō-kō´] *n* a style of architecture, decoration, and furniture-making, prevailing in Louis XV's time, marked by endless multiplication of ornamental details (a lighter, freer, frivolous development of the baroque); any art in this style.—Also *adj*. [Fr, prob—*rocaille*, rockwork.]

rod [rod] *n* a long straight shoot; a slender stick; a slender bar of metal or other matter; an emblem of authority; a wand for magic, divination; a fishing-rod; a pole or perch (5½ yards); a rod-shaped photosensitive receptor in the retina responsive to faint light; a rod-shaped bacterium; (*slang*) a pistol. [OE *rodd*; cf ON *rudda*, club.]

rode [rōd] *pt* of **ride**.

rodent [rō´dėnt] *n* any of an order (*Rodentia*) of relatively small gnawing mammals (as a mouse, rat, squirrel, or a beaver) that have a single pair of incisors with a chisel-shaped edge; a small mammal (as a rabbit or a shrew).—Also *adj*.—*n* **rodent´icide**, an agent that kills, repels, or controls rodents. [L *rōdēns, -entis*, pr p of *rōděre*, to gnaw.]

rodeo [rō-dā´ō] *n* a round-up of cattle; an exhibition of cowboy skill; a contest suggestive of a rodeo. [Sp—*rodear*, to go round—L *rotāre*, to wheel.]

rodomontade [rod-ō-mon-tād´] *n* extravagant boasting; vain bluster.—Also *adj*. [*Rodomonte* in Ariosto's *Orlando Furioso* (1516).]

roe [rō] *n* the eggs or spawn of fishes. [ME *rowe*; cf ON *hrogn*, Ger *rogen*.]

roe deer [rō] *n* a species of small deer (*Capreolus capreolus*) of Europe and Asia, very graceful and agile; sometimes applied to the female red deer.—*n* **roe´buck**, the male roe deer. [OE *rā, rāha*; Ger *reh*, Du *ree*.]

roentgen, röntgen [rent´gėn] *n* the unit for measuring X-rays or gamma rays.—Also *adj*. [W. K. *Roentgen* (1845–1923), Ger physicist.]

rogation [rō-gā´sh(ȯ)n] *n* an asking; supplication.—**Rogation days**, the three days before Ascension Day, when (RC Church) supplications are recited. [L *rogātiō, -ōnis—rogāre*, to ask.]

rogue [rōg] *n* a vagrant; a rascal; a wag, a mischievous person; a sport, or variation from type.—*vt* to cheat; to eliminate rogues from.—*n* **roguery** [rōg´ėr-i], knavish tricks; fraud; mischievousness, waggery.—*adj* **roguish** [rōg´ish], knavish; mischievous, waggish.—*adv* **rog´uishly**.—*n* **rog´uishness**.—**rogue elephant**, a savage elephant cast out or withdrawn from the herd; **rogues' gallery**, a police collection of photographs of criminals. [Cant.]

roister [rois´tėr] *vi* to bluster, swagger, revel noisily.—*n* **rois´terer**. [OFr *rustre*, a rough, rude fellow—OFr *ruste*—L *rusticus*, rustic.]

role, rôle [rōl] *n* a part played by an actor or other; a function assumed by someone else.—*n* **role model**, a person so effective or inspiring in some social role, job, etc. as to be a model for others. [Fr.]

roll [rōl] *n* a scroll; a sheet of paper or other material wound upon itself into cylindrical form; a revolving cylinder; a register; a list, esp of names; a small cake of bread; a part turned over in a curve; act of rolling; a swaying or rotary motion about an axis in the direction of advance (eg of a ship, aircraft); a continuous reverberatory sound (eg of drums, cannon, thunder); a trill of some birds, esp a canary.—*vi* to move like a ball, a wheel, a wheeled vehicle, or a passenger in one; to turn on an axis; to turn over or from side to side; to move in, on, or like waves; to flow; to sound with a roll; to undulate; to curl.—*vt* to cause to roll; to turn on an axis; to wrap round on itself; to enwrap; to drive forward; to move upon wheels; to press or smooth with a roller or between rollers; to beat rapidly, as a drum.—*ns* **roll´ call**, the calling of a list of names to ascertain attendance; **roll´er**, one who or that which rolls; a revolving or rolling cylinder used for grinding, rolling, etc.; a long heavy wave; **roller-blades** [rō´lėr-blād] roller skates that have a row of wheels down the middle of the boot; **roller blading**; **roll´er coast´er**, an amusement ride in which small cars move on tracks that curve and dip sharply; **roll´er skate**, a skate with wheels instead of a blade; **roll´er skating; roll´er towel**, a towel with joined ends hung over a roller.—*n* and *adj* **roll´ing**.—*ns* **roll´ing pin**, a long cylinder for rolling dough; **roll´ing stock**, all the vehicles of a railroad or trucking company; **roll´top desk**, a writing desk with a sliding cover, often of parallel slats fastened to a flexible backing.—**be rolling in**, to have large amounts of (eg money); **rolled gold**, metal having a gold coating of 1/30th to 1/40th of the thickness of the metal. [OFr *rolle*, n, *roller*, vb—L *rotula*, dim of *rota*, a wheel.]

rollicking [rol´ik-ing] *adj* careless, swaggering, exuberantly gay or jovial. [Origin unknown.]

roly-poly [rōl´i-pōl´i] *n* a dessert made of a sheet of paste, covered with jam or fruit, and rolled up; a round podgy person. [Prob **roll**.]

Rom [rom] *n* a gypsy man. [Romany, man, husband.]

Romaic [rō-mā´ik] *n, adj* modern Greek vernacular. [Modern Gr *Rhōmaikos*, Roman (ie of the Eastern Roman Empire)—*Rhōmē*, Rome.]

Roman [rō-mȧn] *adj* pertaining to Rome, esp ancient Rome, its people, or the empire founded by them; pertaining to the Roman Catholic Church or the see of Rome; of or relating to the Latin alphabet; **roman** (of type) of the ordinary upright kind, as opposed to *italic, Gothic*, or *black letter*.—*n* a native or citizen of Rome; a Roman Catholic.—*adj* **Roman´ic**, Romance.—*vt* **Ro´manize**, to make Roman or Roman Catholic; **romanize**, to print or write (as a language) in the Latin alphabet.—*n* **romaniza´tion**.—*vi* to accept Roman or Roman Catholic ways, laws, doctrines, etc.—*ns* **Rō´manism**, (*offensive*) Roman Catholicism; **Rō´manist**, (*offensive*) a Roman Catholic; one versed in Romance philology or in Roman law or antiquities.—*adj* (*offensive*) Roman Catholic.—**Roman Catholic**, a Christian church recognizing the spiritual supremacy of the Pope or Bishop of Rome; a member of the Roman Catholic Church; **Roman Catholicism**, doctrines and polity of the Roman Catholic Church; **Roman Empire**, that established in 27 BC by Augustus, divided in 395 AD by Theodosius into Western or Latin and Eastern or Greek; **Roman law**, the legal code developed by ancient Romans and forming the bases of many modern codes; **Roman numerals**, the letters I, V, X, L, C, D, and M used to represent numbers in the manner of the Romans. [L *Rōmānus*—*Rōma*, Rome.]

roman [ro-mã] *n* a medieval romance, tale of chivalry; novel.—**roman à clef** [nä klā], a novel in which the characters are real persons more or less disguised; **roman-fleuve** [flœv], a novel in the form of a long chronicle of a social group (as a family or community).

Romance [rō-mans´] *adj* of the languages that developed out of popular Latin: French, Provençal, Italian, Spanish, Portuguese, Rumanian, Romansch and Catalan, with their various dialects.—Also —*n* **romance**, a tale of chivalry, orig one in verse, written in one of the Romance tongues; any fictitious and wonderful tale; a fictitious narrative in prose or verse which passes beyond the limits of ordinary life; a love story, romantic fiction as a branch of literature; a love affair or a career involving social difficulties or other vicissitudes successfully overcome; a love affair; a romantic habit of mind; romantic quality; an imaginative lie.—*vi* to write or tell romances; to talk extravagantly; to lie.—*n* **roman´cer**. [OFr *romanz*—(hypothetical) LL *rōmānicē* (adv), in (popular) Roman language.]

Romanesque [rō-mȧn-esk´] *adj* of the transition from Classical to Gothic architecture, characterized by round arches and vaults.—*n* the Romanesque style, art, or architecture. [Fr.]

Romansh, Romansch [rō-mansh´] *n* Rhaeto-Romanic. [Romansch.]

Romans [rō´mȧnz] *n* (*Bible*) 6th book of the New Testament, an epistle written by St Paul to the Christians of Rome and considered the foundation of Christian theology.

romantic [rō-man´tik] *adj* pertaining to, inclining toward, or suggesting, romance; fictitious; extravagant, fantastic.—Also *n*.—*adv* **roman´tically**.—*vt* **roman´ticize**, to make seem romantic.—*vi* to have or express romantic ideas.—*ns* **roman´ticism** [-sizm], in English literature, a 19th century poetic movement characterized by the desire to bring nature and man into unity through the shaping power of the imagination; romantic quality, tendency, or spirit; **roman´ticist**. [Fr *romantique*—OFr *romant*, romance.]

Romany [rom´ȧ-ni] *n* a gypsy; the language of the gypsies.—*adj* gypsy. [Romany, *rom*, man.]

Romeo [rōm´i-ō] *n* a young man very much in love; a communications code word for the letter *r*. [Shakespearian character.]

Romish [rōm´ish] *adj* (*offensive*) Roman Catholic. [L *Rōma*, Rome.]

romp [romp] *vi* to frolic actively; to move (along, home) easily and quickly.—*n* a child or girl who romps; a vigorous frolic; a swift, easy run.—*n* **rom´per**, one who romps; (*pl*) a child's one-piece garment consisting of a blouse or shirt with attached shorts or trousers; a jumpsuit.—*adj* **romp´ish**.—*adv* **romp´ishly**.—*n* **romp´ishness**. [**ramp**.]

rondeau [ron´dō] *n* a French verse form freely adapted by many English poets, the traditional rondeau consisting of 15 tetrameter lines divided into three stanzas, with lines 9 and 15 being short refrains; (*mus*) an instrumental form of the 17th century, consisting of a recurring section alternating with three or more varying sections.—*pl* **ron´deaux** [-dōz].—*ns* **ron´del**, a similar form of French verse, consisting of thirteen or fourteen lines in iambic pentameter, with the first two and last two lines refrains and having two rhymes; **round´el**, a variation of the rondeau and rondel, running on two rhymes, with the refrain taken from the first line; **ron´do**, a musical form often used for the final movement of classical sonatas, string quartets, symphonies, and concertos, as well as for independent pieces developed from the rondeau. [Fr *rondeau*, earlier *rondel*—*rond*, round.]

röntgen *See* **roentgen**.

rood [rōōd] *n* Christ's cross, esp a cross or crucifix, esp at the entrance to the chancel of a medieval church; (*Brit*) a rod, pole, or perch, linear or square (with variations in value). [OE *rōd*, gallows, cross.]

roof [rōōf] *n* the top covering of a building or vehicle; a ceiling; the upper covering of any cavity; a dwelling; an upper limit.—*pl* **roofs**.—*vt* to cover with a roof; to be the roof of.—*n* **roof´ing**, covering with a roof; materials for a roof; a roof.—*adj* for roofing.—*adj* **roof´less**.—*ns* **roof´garden**, a restaurant or nightclub at the top of a building in connection with or decorated to suggest an outdoor garden; **roof´tree**, a ridgepole. [OE *hrōf*; Du *roef*.]

rook[1] [rŏŏk] *n* a gregarious species of crow (*Corvus frugilegus*) of the Old World about the size and color of the related American crow.—*vt* to fleece.—*n* **rook´ery**, a breeding place of rooks in a group of trees; a breeding ground or haunt of other gregarious birds, or mammals; a crowded dilapidated tenement. [OE *hrōc*.]

rook[2] [rŏŏk] *n* (*chess*) a piece with the power to move horizontally or vertically.—Also **castle**. [OFr *roc*—Pers *rukh*.]

rookie [rŏŏk´i] *n* (*slang*) an inexperienced army recruit; any novice.—Also *adj*. [App from **recruit**.]

room [rōōm] *n* space; necessary or available space; space unoccupied; opportunity, scope, or occasion; stead; a compartment of a house, a chamber; the people in a room; (*pl*) lodgings.—*ns* **room´er**, one who rents a room or rooms to live in; a lodger; **roomette´**, a small compartment in a railroad sleeping car; **room´mate**, a person with whom one shares a room or rooms.—*adj* **room´y**, having ample room, wide, spacious.—*n* **room´iness**. [OE *rūm*; Ger *raum*, Du *ruim*.]

roost [rōōst] *n* a perch or place for a sleeping bird; a sleeping place; a set of fowls resting together.—*vi* to settle or sleep on a roost or perch; to settle down, as for the night.—*n* **roost´er**, an adult male domestic fowl; an adult male of other birds; a vain or cocky person. [OE *hrōst*; Du *roest*.]

root[1] [rōōt] *n* the part of a plant, usu. underground, that anchors the plant, draws water from the soil, etc.; the embedded part of a tooth, a hair, etc.; a supporting or essential part; something that is an origin or source; (*math*) the factor of a quantity which multiplied by itself a specified number of times produces that quantity.—*vi* to take root; to be firmly established.—*vt* to fix the roots of in the earth; to implant deeply.—*adj* **root´ed**, firmly planted; fixed by roots.—*ns* **root beer**, a carbonated drink made of root extracts from certain plants; **root canal**, the part of the pulp cavity lying in the root of a tooth; **root´let**, a little root; **root´stock**, (*bot*) a rhizome or underground creeping part of a plant; a stock for grafting consisting of a root or a piece of root.—**take root**, to begin growing by putting out roots; to become fixed, settled, etc. [Late OE *rōt*—ON *rōt*; Dan *rod*; OE *wyrt*.]

root[2] [rōōt] *vt* to turn up with the snout.—*vi* to grub; to search about; (*inf*) to encourage a team (*usu. with* **for**). [OE *wrōtan*—*wrōt*, a snout.]

rope [rōp] *n* a thick twisted cord of fibers or wires; a row or string of things united by braiding, twining, or threading.—*vt* to fasten, enclose, or mark off, with a rope.—*ns* **ropedanc´er**, a tightrope performer; **rō´pery**, (*arch*) roguish tricks; **rope´walk**, a long narrow shed or alley where ropes are manufactured; **rope´walker**, an acrobat that walks on a rope high in the air.—*adj* **rō´py**, stringy; glutinous; wrinkled; (*slang*) bad of its kind.—*n* **rō´piness.**—**know the ropes**, (*inf*) to be acquainted with a procedure; **on the ropes**, to be in a helpless and defensive position; **rope in**, (*slang*) to trick into doing something. [OE *rāp*; cf ON *reip*, Du *reep*, Ger *reif*.]

rorqual [rör´kwȧl] *n* any of several large whalebone wales (genus *Balaenoptera* or *Sibbaldus*) esp the blue whale (*B musculus*), the largest animal that ever lived. [Fr,—Norw *röyrkval*, lit red whale.]

rosaceous [rō-zā´shủs] *adj* of the rose family; like a rose, esp in having a 5-petalled regular corolla. [L *rosāceus*—*rōsa*, a rose.]

Rorschach test [ror´shäk] *n* (*psychology*) a personality test in which the subject's interpretations to standard inkblots are analyzed. [H *Rorschach* 1884–1922, Swiss psychiatrist.]

rosary [rō´zȧr-i] *n* a string of beads used in counting prayers, esp by Roman Catholics; similar beads used for the same purpose in other religions. [L *rosārium*, rose-garden—*rōsa*, a rose.]

rose *pt* of **rise**.

rose [rōz] *n* the flower of a plant of many species (genus *Rosa*, family Rosaceae), emblem of the US; white, yellow, pink, or red, with five petals in the wild state but double or semi-double in many cultivated forms; the shrub bearing it, generally prickly; a rosette; a perforated nozzle; pinkish red or purplish red; (*pl*) a comfortable situation or an easy task.—*adjs* **roseāte** [rō´zė-āt], rosy; overly optimistic; viewed favourably; **rose´-**

col´ored, rosy; seeing or representing things in too favorable a light, optimistic.—*ns* **rō´sery**, a place where roses are grown; **rose water**, water distilled from rose petals, used as a perfume.—*adj* **rosewater**, affectedly delicate; having the odor of rose water.—*ns* **rose window**, a circular window filled with tracery; **rose´wood**, heavy dark-colored wood streaked with black of various tropical trees (genus *Dalbergia*) yielding valuable cabinet wood.—*adj* **rō´sy**, of the color of roses; blooming; blushing; bright, hopeful.—*n* **rō´siness**.—rose of Sharon, a widely cultivated small shrub (*Hibiscus syriacus*) having showy flowers; **under the rose**, sub rosa; in confidence; secretly. [OE *rōse*—L *rŏsa*.]

rosé [rō-zā] *n* a pinkish table wine in making which grape skins are removed early in fermentation. [Fr lit, pink.]

rosemary [rōz´mȧ-ri] *n* a fragrant shrubby mint (*Rosmarinus officinalis*) used in cookery and in perfumery. [L *rōs marīnus*, sea dew.]

rosette [rō-zet´] *n* a knot of radiating loops of ribbon or the like; a rose-shaped ornament. [Fr, dim of *rose*.]

Rosh Hashanah [rōsh hȧ-shōn´ȧ or rosh hȧ-shän´ȧ] *n* Jewish New Year. [Heb.]

rosin [roz´in] *n* a resin obtained eg when turpentine is prepared from dead pine wood.—*vt* to rub (a violin, etc., bow) with rosin.—*adj* **ros´iny**. [Formed from **resin**.]

roster [rōs´tėr, ros´-] *n* a list or roll, as of military personnel. [Du *rooster*, orig gridiron (from the ruled lines)—*roosten*, to roast.]

rostrum [ros´trum] *n* a beak; *pl* **rostrums, rostra**, a platform for public speaking.—*adjs* **ros´tral**, of or like a rostrum; having a rostrum; **ros´trāte**, rostral; located toward the nasal or oral region of either a part of the brain or of the spinal cord. [L *rōstrum*, beak—*rōdĕre, rōsum*, to gnaw.]

rot [rot] *vti* to putrefy; to decay;—*pr p* **rott´ing**; *pt, pt p* **rott´ed**.—*n* decay; putrefaction; corruption; various diseases of sheep, timber, etc., characterized by decay; (*slang*) nonsense. [OE *rotian*, pt p *rotod*; cf **rotten**.]

Rota [rō´ta] *n* a tribunal of the papal curia exercising jurisdiction esp in matrimonial cases appealed from diocesan courts.—*ns* **Rotarian** [rō-tā´ri-ȧn], a member of a Rotary club, an international system of clubs with a wheel as badge, each member being of a different occupation from the rest of his club.—*adj* **rotary** [rō´tȧr-i], turning like a wheel; having parts that rotate; resembling the motion of a wheel.—*vti* **rōtāte´**, to turn like a wheel; to put, take, go, or succeed in rotation.—*ns* **rotā´tion**, a turning round like a wheel; succession in definite order, as of crops; **rotā´tor**.—*adj* **rotatory** [rō´tȧ-tȯr-i], rotary. [L *rota*, a wheel—*rotāre, -ātum*, to turn, roll.]

rote [rōt] *n* a fixed, mechanical way of doing something.—**by rote**, by memory alone, without regard to the meaning. [L *rota*, wheel, and OFr *rote*, road, have been conjectured.]

rotor [rō´tȯr] *n* a rotating part, esp of a dynamo, motor, or turbine; a system of rotating airfoils producing lift, as in a helicopter. [For **rotator**.]

rotten [rot´n] *adj* putrefied; decaying; corrupt; unsound; disintegrating; (*slang*) very bad, unpleasant, etc.—*ns* **rott´enness; rott´enstone**, a decomposed silicious limestone, used for polishing.—**rotten borough**, an election district that has many fewer inhabitants than other election districts with the same voting power. [ON *rotinn*; cf **rot**.]

rotter [rot´ėr] *n* a thoroughly depraved or worthless person. [**rot**.]

rotund [rō-tund´] *adj* round; rounded; nearly spherical.—*ns* **rotund´a**, a round (esp domed) room, building, or hall; **rotund´ity**, roundness; a round mass. [L *rotundus*—*rota*, a wheel.]

rouble *see* **ruble**.

roué [rōō´ā] *n* a profligate, rake, debauchee. [A name given by Philippe, Duke of Orléans, Regent of France 1715–23, to his dissolute companions—Fr *roué*, broken on the wheel—pt p of *rouer*—*roue*, a wheel—L *rota*.]

rouge [rōōzh] *n* a powder used to color the cheeks or lips; a red polishing powder for jewelry, etc.—*vti* to use cosmetic rouge (on). [Fr *rouge*—L *rubeus*, red.]

rough [ruf] *adj* uneven; rugged; unshorn; unpolished; harsh; crude; unfinished; coarse in texture; unrefined; ungentle; turbulent; approximate; (*inf*) difficult.—*n* untended ground; (*golf*) any part of the course with grass, etc. left uncut; difficulty, hardship; a rowdy person; a preliminary sketch.—*vt* to make rough; to shape or depict roughly.—*n* **rough´age**, rough or coarse food or fodder, as bran, straw, etc.—*adjs* **rough-and-read´y**, easily improvised, and serving the purpose well enough; **rough-and-tum´ble**, haphazard and scrambling.—*n* a scuffle.—*vt* **rough´cast**, to shape roughly; to cover with roughcast.—*n* plaster mixed with small stones, used to coat buildings; a rough surface finish (as of a plaster wall).—*vti* **rough´en**, to make or become rough.—*n* **roughhouse**, (*slang*) a disturbance, a brawl; boisterous play.—*vti* (*slang*) to treat or act roughly or boisterously.—*adv* **rough´ly**.—*ns* **roughneck**, (*slang*) an unmannerly lout; a hooligan; a worker of an oil-well-drilling crew other than the driller; **rough´ness**, the quality of being rough; **roughrid´er**, a rider of untrained horses; **Rough Rider**, a member of the 1st Volunteer Cavalry regiment in the Spanish-American War commanded by Theodore Roosevelt.—*adj* **rough´shod**, shod with calked shoes; marked by main force without justice or consideration.—**rough it**, to live without the ordinary comforts of civilization. [OE *rūh*, rough.]

rouleau [rōō-lō] *n* a little roll, esp a roll of coins put up in paper. [Fr.]

roulette [rōōl-et´] *n* a game of chance in which a ball rolls from a rotating disk into one or other of a set of compartments answering to those on which the players place their stakes; any of various toothed wheels or disks used for producing perforations to facilitate division; the slits so made on a sheet of stamps. [Fr.]

round [rownd] *adj* having a curved outline or surface; circular, globular, or cylindrical in form; plump; full; considerable (eg a sum of money); approximate (number), in whole tens, hundreds, etc.; unqualified; pronounced with lips contracted to a circle; brisk, vigorous.—*adv* about; on all sides; in a ring; from one to another successively; through a recurring period of time; in circumference; in a roundabout way; about; near; here and there; with a rotating movement; in the opposite direction.—Also **around**.—*prep* on every side of; so as to encircle; in the vicinity of; in a circuit through.—Also **around**.—*n* a round thing or part; a ring, circumference, circle, or globe; a ladder rung; a dance in a ring, or its tune; a canon sung in unison; a complete revolution; a recurring series of events or doings; an accustomed walk; a prescribed circuit; a cut of beef between the rump and the lower leg; a volley, as a shot or of applause; a unit of ammunition; a successive or simultaneous action of each member of a company or player in a game; a part of a competition complete in itself; a bout, part of a contest of prearranged duration, as in boxing; (*golf*) play over the whole course once.—*vt* to make round; to make plump; to express as a round number; to complete; to go or pass around.—*vi* to make a circuit; to turn; to reverse direction; to become plump.—*adj* **round´about**, circuitous; indirect.—*n* (*Brit*) a merry-go-round; a circuitous route.—*adjs* **round´ed**, round, flowing rather than angular; finished, complete, developed.—*ns* **Round´head**, a Puritan; a member of the Parliamentary party in England at the time of Charles I and Cromwell; **roundhouse**, a circular building with a turntable for housing and repairing locomotives; a cabin on the afterpart of the quarterdeck; a blow delivered with a wide swing.—*adj* **round´ish**.—*adv* **round´ly**.—*ns* **round´ness; rounds´man**, one that makes rounds; a supervisory police officer of the grade of sergeant or just below.—*adj* **roundta´ble**, meeting on equal terms, like the inner circle of King Arthur's knights who sat at a round table.—*n* **round trip**, a trip to a place and back again.—*adj* **roundtrip**.—*n* **roundup**, a driving together, as all the cattle in a ranch, a set of persons wanted by the police, etc.; a summary, as of news; **round robin**, a paper with signatures in a circle, that no one may seem to be a ringleader; a tournament in which every contestant meets every other contestant in turn.—**round the clock**, for twenty-four hours on end; **round up**, gather in, collect; **in the round**, in an arena theater; (of sculpture) in full, rounded form; in full detail. [OFr *rund-, rond-* (Fr *rond*—L *rotundus*—*rota*, a wheel.]

roundel [rown´dl] *n* a round figure or object (as a circular panel, window, or niche); a rondeau, a rondel.—*n* **roun´delay**, a song with a refrain; a dance in a ring. [OFr *rondel, rondele, rondelet*, dim of *rond*, round.]

rouse[1] [rowz] *vt* to start (as game from cover or lair); to stir up; to awaken; to excite, to anger; to put in action.—*vi* to awake; to be excited to action.—*adj* **rous´ing**, awakening; stirring, vigorous, violent.—*vt* **roust**, to stir up; to rout out.—*n* **roustabout** [rowst´ ȧ-bowt], an unskilled, transient laborer, as on wharves.

rouse[2] [rowz] *n* a carousal. [Prob shortened form of **carouse**.]

rout[1] [rowt] *n* a tumultuous crowd, a rabble; a pack, herd, flock; a large party, a fashionable assembly; a defeated body; an utter defeat; disorderly flight; (*arch*) disturbance.—*vt* to defeat utterly; to put to disorderly flight. [OFr *route*, from the pt p of L *rumpĕre, ruptum*, to break.]

rout[2] [rowt] *vt* to grub up, as a pig; to search haphazardly.—*vi* to gouge out or make a furrow in (as wood or metal); to cause to emerge, esp from bed; to come up with; to uncover. [An irregular variant of **root** (2).]

route [rōōt, rowt] *n* a course to be traversed.—*vt* to fix the route of; to send (by a particular route). [Fr,—L *rupta* (*via*), broken way.]

routine [rōō-tēn´] *n* regular, unvarying, or mechanical course of action or round; the set series of movements gone through in a dancing, skating, or other performance.—Also *adj*.—*vt* **routinize** [rōō-tēn´-īz], to make or bring into a routine. [Fr.]

rove[1] [rōv] *vti* to roam.—*n* **rō´ver**, a wanderer; (*usu pl*) a random or long-distance target in archery; a player on a team who plays wherever needed.—*n, adj* **rō´ving**. [Partly from Du *rooven*, to rob.]

rove[2] [rōv] *vt* to twist (textile fibers) slightly in preparation for spinning. [Origin obscure.]

row[1] [rō] *n* a line or rank of persons or things as spectators, houses, turnips; a series in line, or in ordered succession.—**in a row**, in unbroken sequence. [OE *rāw*; Ger *reihe*, Du *rij*.]

row[2] [rō] *vti* to impel with an oar; to transport by rowing.—*n* an act or instance of rowing.—*ns* **row´boat**, a small boat made for rowing; **row´er**. [OE *rōwan*.]

row[3] [row] a noisy squabble, a brawl; a din, hubbub; a chiding. [A late 18th-century word; possibly a back-formation from **rouse** (2).]

rowan [row´ȧn, also rō´ȧn] *n* an American mountain ash (*Sorbus americana*) with flat corymbs of white flowers followed by small red berries; a related Eurasian tree (*S aucuparia*); the fruit of the rowan. [Cf Norw *raun*, Swed *rönn*.]

rowdy [row´di] *n* a noisy turbulent person.—Also *adj*.—*ns* **rowd´iness; rowd´yism**.

rowel [row´ėl] *n* a little spiked wheel on a spur. [Fr *rouelle*—Low L *rotella*, dim of L *rota*, a wheel.]

royal [roi´ȧl] *adj* of a king or queen; like, or fit for, a king or queen; magnificent; founded, chartered, or patronized by a king or queen; of a kingdom, its government, etc.—*n* a sail immediately above the topgallant sail; a stag having antlers with twelve points.—*ns* **roy´alism**, attachment to monarchy; **roy´alist**, an adherent of royalism.—*adv* **roy´ally**.—*n* **roy´alty**, the rank or power of a king or queen; a royal person or persons; royal quality; a share of the proceeds from a patent, book, song, etc. paid to the owner, author, composer, etc.—**royal blue**, a bright deep blue. [Fr,—L *rēgālis*, regal.]

royster *See* **roister**.

rub [rub] *vt* to move something with pressure along the surface of; to clean, polish, or smooth, by friction; to remove, erase, or obliterate by friction (*usu with* **away, off, out**); to irritate, fret.—*vi* to move with friction, to chafe, to grate; to make shift to get along somehow (*with* **along**);—*pr p* **rubb´ing**; *pt, pt p* **rubbed**.—*n* process or act of rubbing; a difficulty, a hitch, an irritating experience.—*n* **rubb´er**, one who, or that which, rubs or massages; an eraser; an elastic substance made from the milky sap of various tropical plants (genus *Ficus* or *Hevea*) or synthetically; a rubber overshoe.—*n* **rubb´erneck**, one who cranes or twists his neck in curiosity; a sightseer.—*vi* to behave as a rubber-neck (of a driver); looking around in traffic.—*n* **rubb´er stamp**, an instrument for stamping by hand with ink, the characters being in flexible vulcanized rubber; (*inf*) a person, bureau, etc., that gives automatic approval; (*inf*) such approval.—*n* **rubb´ing**, an impression of a raised, incised, or textured surface obtained by placing paper over it and rubbing the paper with a colored substance; **rubdown**, a brisk rubbing of the body; **rub in**, to be unpleasantly insistent in emphasizing; **rub the wrong way**, to irritate; **rub elbows, rub shoulders**, to associate closely; **rub up**, to freshen one's memory of. [Cf Low Ger *rubben*.]

rubato [rōō-bä´tō] *adj* and *adv* (*mus*) intentionally and temporarily not in strict tempo.—*n* a phrase so played. [It pt p of *rubare*, to steal.]

rubber[1] *See* **rub**.

rubber[2] [rub´ėr] *n* a contest consisting of an odd number of games won by the side that takes a majority (as two out of three); an odd game played to decide the winner of a tie. [Origin obscure.]

rubbish [rub´ish] *n* waste matter; litter; trash; nonsense.—*adj* **rubb´ishy**, worthless. [Origin obscure; app conn with **rubble**.]

rubble [rub´l] *n* loose fragments of rock of ruined buildings; undressed irregular stones used in rough masonry; masonry of such a kind.—*n* **rubb´lework**, coarse masonry. [Origin obscure; cf **rubbish**.]

rubella [rŏŏ-bel´a] *n* a mild contagious virus disease which may cause severe damage to an unborn child; German measles. [Dim from L *rubeus*, red.]

Rubicon [rŏŏb´i-kon] *n* a bounding or limiting line, esp that when crossed commits a person irrevocably. [A stream of Central Italy, separating Caesar's province of Gallia Cisalpina from Italia proper—its crossing by Caesar (49 BC) being thus a virtual declaration of war against the republic.] [L *Rubicō, -ōnis*.]

rubicund [rōō´bi-kund] *adj* ruddy.—*n* **rubicun´dity**. [L *rubicundus*—*rubēre*, to be red.]

rubidium [rōō-bid´i-ům] *n* a metallic element (symbol Rb; at wt 85.5; at no 37). [Formed from L *rubidus*, red.]

ruble, rouble [rōō´bl] *n* the unit of money in Russia. [Russ *rubl'*, perh—*rubit'*, to cut; or Pers *rūpīya*, a rupee.]

rubric [rōō´brik] *n* a heading, entry, or liturgical direction often in red; any rule, explanatory comment, etc.—*adj* in red; ruddy.—*adj* **ru´brical**. [L *rubrīca*, red ochre—*ruber*, red.]

ruby [rōō´bi] *n* a highly-prized precious stone of a deep red color.—*adj* red as a ruby. [OFr *rubi* and *rubin*—L *rubeus*—*ruber*, red.]

ruche [rōōsh] *n* a pleated, gathered, or fluted piece of fabric used as trimming.—*adj* **ruched**. [Fr; prob Celt.]

ruck[1] [ruk] *n* a wrinkle, fold, or crease.—*vti* to wrinkle. [ON *hrukka*, a wrinkle.]

ruck[2] [ruk] *n* the usual run of persons or things; the persons or things following the vanguard. [Probably Scand.]

rucksack [ruk´-sak] *n* a bag carried on the back by hikers. [Ger dial *ruck* (Ger *rücken*), back and Ger *sack*, bag.]

ruction [ruk´sh(ȯ)n] *n* a disturbance, a rumpus; an uproar. [Perh for **insurrection**.]

rudder [rud´ėr] *n* a steering apparatus; a flat structure hinged to the stern of a ship or boat for steering; a similar movable surface in a vertical plane for steering an airplane left or right. [OE *rōthor*, oar; Ger *ruder*, oar.]

ruddle [rud´l] *n* red ocher.—*vt* to mark with ruddle; to rouge coarsely.—Also **redd´le**. [Prob from obs *rud*, red.]

ruddy [rud´i] *adj* red; reddish; of the color of the skin in health.—*adv* **rudd´ily**.—*n* **rudd´iness**. [OE *rudig*; cf **red**.]

rude [rōōd] *adj* uncultured; unskilled; discourteously unmannerly; ungentle, harsh; crude, coarse.—*adv* **rude´ly**.—*n* **rude´ness**. [L *rudis*, rough.]

rudiment [rōōd´i-mėnt] *n* a first principle or element; a first slight beginning of something.—*adjs* **rudimental** [-ment´ȧl], rudimentary; **rudiment´ary**, of rudiments; elementary; imperfectly developed or represented only by a vestige. [L *rudīmentum*—*rudis*, rough, raw.]

rue[1] [rōō] *n* a strong-smelling Mediterranean shrub (*Ruta graveolens*) with bitter leaves and greenish-yellow flowers. [Fr *rue*—L *rūta*—Peloponnesian Gr *rhȳtē*.]

rue[2] [rōō] *n* (*arch*) sorrow.—*vti* feel remorse for (a sin, fault, etc.); to regret (an act, etc.;—*pr p* **rue´ing, ru´ing**; *pt, pt p* **rued**.—*adj* **rue´ful**, sorrowful; mournful; exciting sympathy and pity.—*adv* **rue´fully**.—*n* **rue´fulness**. [OE *hrēow*, n, *hrēowan*, vb; cf Ger *reue*, OHG *hriuwa*, mourning.]

ruff[1] [ruf] *n* a frill, usu. starched and pleated, worn round the neck, esp in the 16th and 17th centuries; a frilled appearance on the neck of a bird or animal. [Perh from **ruffle**.]

ruff[2] [ruf] *n* the act of trumping.—*vti* to trump. [Perh conn with OFr *roffle*, It *ronfa*, a card game.]

ruffian [ruf´i-ȧn, -yȧn] *n* a brutal, violent person; a bully.—*adj* brutal; violent.—*n* **ruff´ianism**.—*adj* **ruff´ianly**. [OFr *ruffian*.]

ruffle [ruf´l] *vt* to make uneven, disturb the smoothness of; to wrinkle; to disorder; to agitate, to disturb the equanimity of.—*vi* to grow rough; to flutter.—*n* a frill, esp at the wrist or neck; annoyance; a quarrel; agitation. [Origin uncertain. Cf Low Ger *ruffelen*.]

rufous [rōō´fus] *adj* reddish. [L *rūfus*, akin to *ruber*, red.]

rug [rug] *n* a thick heavy fabric used as a floor covering. [Cf Norw dial *rugga, rogga*, coarse coverlet, Swed *rugg*, coarse hair.]

rugby [rug´bi] *n* a game for two teams of 15 players from which American football developed. [From *Rugby* school, England.]

rugged [rug´id] *adj* rough; uneven, massively irregular; unpolished; strong, robust.—*adv* **rugg´edly**.—*n* **rugg´edness**. [Prob rel to **rug**.]

rugose [rōō´gōs´] *adj* wrinkled, covered with sunken lines. [L *rūgōsus*—*rūga*, a wrinkle.]

ruin [rōō´in] *n* (*pl*) the remains of something destroyed, decayed, etc.; downfall, collapse, overthrow; complete destruction; irrevocable loss of position or reputation; cause of ruin.—*vt* to reduce or bring to ruin; destroy; spoil; bankrupt.—*vi* to come to ruin.—*n* **ruinā´tion**, act of ruining; state of being ruined.—*adj* **ru´inous**, fallen to ruins, decayed; bringing ruin. [L *ruīna*—*ruĕre*, to tumble down.]

rule [rōōl] *n* an instrument used in drawing straight lines; a ruler; government; a principle, a standard, maxim or formula for conduct, procedure, usage, etc.; a straight line; that which is normal; a regulation, an order.—*vt* to mark with straight lines; as with a ruler; to govern, to manage; to determine or declare authoritatively to be; to determine, decree (that).—*vi* to exercise power (*with* **over**); to be prevalent.—*n* **ru´ler**, one who governs; a strip of wood, etc. with a straight edge, used in drawing lines, measuring, etc.—*adj* **ru´ling**, predominant; prevailing; reigning.—*n* an authoritative decision.—**as a rule**, usually; **rule of the road**, the regulations to be observed in traffic by land, water, or air; **rule of thumb**, any rough-and-ready practical method; **rule out**, to exclude, to eliminate; to make impossible. [OFr *reule* (Fr *règle*)—L *rēgula*—*regĕre*, to rule.]

rum [rum] *n* a spirit distilled from fermented sugarcane juice, molasses, etc. [Perh from *rumbullion*; or kindred form.]

rumba [rum´ba] *n* a dance of Cuban Negro origin or the music for it.—*vi* to dance the rumba. [Sp.]

rumble [rum´bl] *vti* to make or cause to make a low heavy grumbling or rolling noise; to move with such a sound.—*n* a sound of rumbling; (*slang*) a fight between teenage gangs.—*n* **rum´bling**.—**rum´ble seat**, a folding seat at the back of a car (as a coupe or roadster) not covered by the top. [Perh Low Ger; cf Du *rommelen*, Ger *rummeln*.]

ruminant [rōō´mi-nȧnt] *n* an animal, as cattle, deer, camels, etc., that chews the cud.—*adj* cud-chewing; meditative.—*vi* **ru´mināte**, to chew the cud; to meditate.—*vt* to chew over again; to muse on.—*n* **ruminā´tion**. [L *rūmināre, -ātum*—*rūmen, -inis*, the gullet.]

rummage [rum´ij] *n* odds and ends; a thorough search.—*vti* to search through (a place) thoroughly.—**rummage sale**, a sale of contributed miscellaneous articles, as for charity. [Fr *arrumage* (now *arrimage*), stowage.]

rummer [rum´ėr] *n* a large footed drinking glass. [Du *roemer*; Ger *römer*.]

rummy [rum´i] *n* any of certain card games whose object is to form sets and sequences.

rumor [rōō´mȯr] *n* hearsay, general talk not based on definite knowledge; an unconfirmed report, story, etc., in general circulation.—*vt* to put about by rumor. [OFr,—L *rūmor, -ōris*, a noise.]

rump [rump] *n* the hind part of an animal's body, the root of the tail with parts adjoining; the buttocks. [Scand.]

rumple [rum´pl] *n* a fold or wrinkle.—*vti* to crush out of shape, crumple, crease. [Du *rompel*; cf OE *hrimpan*, to wrinkle.]

rumpus [rum´pus] *n* an uproar, a disturbance.

run [run] *vi* to go swiftly; to flee; to go by moving the legs faster than in walking; to hurry; to ply (from, to, between); to proceed through a sequence of operations, or go, as a machine; to follow a course; to flow; to spread, diffuse; to discharge; to have a course, stretch, or extent; to pass into a specified condition; to be current; to be valid; to compete in a race, election, etc.; to recur repeatedly or remain persistently (in the mind).—*vt* to cause to run; to drive into a specified condition, place, etc.; to drive (an object) into or against (something); to manage (a business, etc.); to undergo (a fever, etc.); to publish (a story, etc.) in a newspaper;—*pr p* **runn´ing**; *pt* **ran**; *pt p* **run**.—*n* an act, spell, or manner of running; a trip; distance or time of running; a continuous stretch or series; a rush for payment, as upon a bank; a brook; ravel, as in a stocking; course; prevalence; the usual kind; a spell of being in general demand; (*baseball*) a scoring point, made by a successful circuit of the bases; an enclosure for chickens, etc.; freedom of access to all parts.—*ns* **run´about**, a stray; a light open wagon, roadster, or motorboat; **run´away**, a fugitive; a horse that is out of control; an overwhelming victory.—*adj* fleeing; easily won, as a race; rising rapidly, as prices.—*adj* **run´-down´**, not wound and therefore not running, as a watch; in poor health, as from overwork; fallen into disrepair.—*n* **run´down**, a concise summary.—*ns* **runn´er**, one who, or that which, runs; a racer; a messenger; a long narrow cloth or rug; a ravel, as in hose; a long, trailing stem, as of a strawberry; either of the long, narrow pieces on which a sled or ice skate slides; **runn´er-up**, the competitor next after the winner or winners.—*adj* **runn´ing**, that runs (in various senses); measured in a straight line; continuous.—*adv* in succession.—*n* the act of one that runs; racing, managing, etc.—*ns* **runn´ing board**, a footboard along the side of an automobile; **runn´ing gear**, wheels, axles and frame of a motor vehicle; **runn´ing knot**, one that slips along the rope or line round which it is tied; an overhand slip knot; **runn´ing light**, the light that a ship or aircraft must display at night.—**running mate**, a horse entered in a race to set the pace for the horse of the same owner or stable; a candidate running for a subordinate place on a ticket, esp for vice-president; a companion.—*adj* **run-of-the-mill**, constituting an ordinary fair sample, not selected; mediocre.—*n* **run´way**, track or channel along which something moves, esp a strip of leveled ground used by airplanes in taking off and landing.—**run down**, pursue to exhaustion or capture; collide with and knock over or sink; to disparage; to become unwound or exhausted; to trace the source of; (*baseball*) to tag out (a base runner) between bases on a rundown; **run in**, pay a casual visit; to arrest for a minor offense; to operate (a new machine carefully) until there is efficient running; **run-in** (*inf*) an altercation, quarrel, etc.; (*printing*) matter added without a break or new paragraph; **run off**, to cause to flow out; to decide (as a race) by a runoff; **runoff**, a final, deciding contest; **run on**, to continue without a break; **run out**, to leak; to run short (of); to cause to leave by force or coercion; **runover**, matter for publication that exceeds the space allotted; **run over**, to overflow; to exceed a limit; to go over, rehearse quickly; to collide with, knock down, and often drive over; **run up**, to make or mend hastily; to build hurriedly; to incur increasingly.—**in the long run**, ultimately. [OE *rinnan, irnan, iernan*, to run.]

runagate [run´à-gāt] *n* a vagabond. [**renegade**, influenced by **run**, and adv *agate*, away.]

rune [rōōn] *n* a letter of the ancient Germanic alphabet; a secret, a mystic symbol, sentence, spell, or song; a Finnish or Old Norse poem.—*adj* **ru´nic**. [OE and ON *rūn*, mystery, rune.]

rung[1] [rung] *n* a spoke; a crossbar or rail; a ladder round or step. [OE *hrung*; Ger *runge*.]

rung[2] *pt p* of **ring** (2).

runnel [run´l] *n* a little stream; a brook. [OE *rynel*, dim of *ryne*, a stream—*rinnan*, to run.]

runner, running. *See* **run**.

runt [runt] *n* an unusually small animal, esp the smallest of a litter of pigs; a person of small stature. [Origin obscure.]

rupee [rōō-pē´] *n* the unit of money in India, Pakistan, Sri Lanka, Seychelles, Mauritius, and Nepal. [Hindustani *rūpiyah*.]

rupture [rup´-chùr] *n* a breach, breaking, or bursting; the state of being broken; breach of harmony, relations, or negotiations; hernia.—*vti* to cause or suffer a rupture. [LL *ruptūra*—L *rumpĕre, ruptum*, to break.]

rural [rōō´räl] *adj* of the country (as opposed to the town).—*adv* **ru´rally**. [L *rūrālis*—*rūs, rūris*, the country.]

ruse [rōōz] *n* a trick, stratagem, artifice. [OFr *ruse*—*ruser*, to get out of the way, double on one's tracks; cf **rush** (1).]

rush[1] [rush] *vti* to move, push, drive, etc. swiftly or impetuously; to make a sudden attack (on); to pass, go, send, do, act, etc. with unusual haste; to hurry.—*adj* requiring or marked by special speed or urgency; haste suggesting this; a hurry; an unedited print of a motion picture scene or series of scenes for immediate viewing by the film makers.—**rush hour**, a time of maximum activity or traffic. [Anglo-Fr *russher*, OFr *ruser* (Fr *ruser*); cf **ruse**.]

rush[2] [rush] *n* a grasslike marsh-growing plant; a stalk of such a plant; any of various marsh plants (genus *Juncus* or *Scirpus*) with cylindrical often hollow stems used in bottoming chairs and making plaited mats.—*ns* **rush´cand´le, rush´light**, a candle consisting of the pith of a rush dipped in grease. [OE *risce*; Ger *risch*.]

rusk [rusk] *n* a sweet or plain bread baked, sliced, and baked again until dry and crisp. [Sp *rosca*, a roll; origin unknown.]

russet [rus´ėt] *n* a coarse homespun usu. reddish brown cloth; a reddish-brown color; a winter apple having a russet rough skin.—*adj* reddish brown.—*adj* **russ´ety**. [OFr *rousset*—rare L *russus*, red.]

Russo- [rus´ō-] *adj* in composition, Russian, as **Russ´ophile** (*n, adj*), favoring or friendly towards Russia; **Russ´ophobe**, afraid of or hostile towards Russia.

rust [rust] *n* the reddish-brown coating on iron or steel exposed to moisture; any stain resembling this; any plant disease characterized by rusty blotches caused by fungi; the color of rust.—*vti* to form rust (on); to deteriorate, as through disuse.—*adj* **rust´y**, covered with rust; impaired by inactivity or disuse; discolored through age.—*n* **rust´iness**.—*adjs* **rust´less; rust´proof**. *rūst*; Ger *rost*.]

rustic [rus´tik] *adj* of, or characteristic of, the country; simple or artless; rough or uncouth.—*n* a country person.—*adv* **rust´ically**.—*vti* **rust´icate**, to go or to send into the country; to become or make rustic.—*ns* **rusticā´tion; rusticity** [-tis´i-ti], rustic manner; simplicity; rudeness. [L *rusticus*—*rūs*, the country.]

rustle[1] [rus´l] *vti* to make a soft, whispering sound, as of dry leaves.—*n* a quick succession of small sounds, as that of dry leaves. [Imit; cf Flemish *ruysselen*.]

rustle[2] [rus´l] *vi* to act energetically.—*vt* to steal, esp cattle.—*n* **rust´ler**, a hustler; a cattle thief.—**rustle up**, (*inf*) to collect or get together. [**rustle** (1).]

rut[1] [rut] *n* a furrow made by wheels; a fixed course difficult to depart from.—*vt* to furrow with ruts;—*pr p* **rutt´ing**; *pt, pt p* **rutt´ed**.

rut[2] [rut] *n* sexual excitement in male deer; also in other animals.—*vi* to be in heat. [OFr *ruit, rut*—L *rugītus*—*rugīre*, to roar.]

ruth [rōōth] *n* pity, sorrow, remorse.—*adj* **ruth´ful**.—*adv* **ruth´fully**.—*adj* **ruth´less**, pitiless; unsparing.—*adv* **ruth´lessly**.—*n* **ruth´lessness**. [ME *ruthe, reuth*. From **rue** (2); with ending *-th*.]

Ruth [rōōth] *n* (*Bible*) 8th book of the Old Testament, the story of the Moabite woman who remained loyal to her mother-in-law, Naomi, after the death of her husband.

ruthenium [rŏŏ-thē´ni-ùm] *n* a metallic element (symbol Ru; at wt 101.1; at no 44). [From Low L *Ruthenia*, Russia.]

rutherfordium *See* **kurchatovium**.

rye[1] [rī] *n* a hardy annual grass (*Secale cereale*); its grain, used for making bread, etc.; rye whiskey.—*ns* **rye´grass**, any of several grasses (genus *Lolium*) esp two (*L perenne* and *L multiflorum*) used widely as pasture and as cover crops; **rye´ whiskey**, whiskey made from rye. [OE *ryge*; ON *rugr*, Ger *roggen*.]

rye[2] [rī] *n* a male gypsy. [Romany *rei, rai*, lord.]

S

Sabbath [sab´ath] *n* among the Jews, Saturday, set apart for rest from work; among most Christians, Sunday; a time of rest.—*adj* of, or appropriate to, the Sabbath.—*n* **sabbat**, midnight meeting of diabolists held in medieval and Renaissance times to renew allegiance to the devil.—*n* **Sabbatā´rian**, a very strict observer of the Sabbath on Saturday **Sabbath** in conformity with the Fourth commandment.—*adj* pertaining to the Sabbath or to Sabbatarians.—*n* **Sabbatā´rianism**.—*adjs* **sabbat´ical, sabbat´ic**, relating to the Sabbath or a sabbatical year.—**sabbatical year** (*hist*) among the Jews, every seventh year, in which the ground was left untilled; a year's leave from a teaching post, often with pay, for rest, travel, or research. [Heb *Shabbāth*.]

saber, sabre [sā´bėr] *n* a heavy one-edged sword, slightly curved towards the point, used by cavalry; a light fencing sword with an arched guard covering the back of the hand and a tapering flexible blade with a full cutting edge along one side; the sport of fencing with the saber.—*vt* to wound or kill with a saber.—*ns* **saber rattling**, ostentatious display of military might; **saber-toothed tiger**, any of numerous extinct cats (genus *Smilodon*) characterized by having swordlike upper canine teeth. [Fr *sabre*—Ger *säbel*.]

Sabin vaccine [sā´bin] *n* a polio vaccine taken orally. [Dr A B *Sabin* (1906-).]

sable [sā´bl] *n* a carnivorous mammal (*Martes zibellina*) of arctic regions of the Old World valued for its glossy fur; its fur; the color black; (usu *pl*) black clothing worn in mourning.—*adj* of the color black; dark. [OFr *sable*; prob from Slav.]

sabot [sab´ō] *n* a wooden shoe, worn in various European countries; a strap across the instep of a sandal; a shoe with a sabot strap.—*n* **sabotage** [-täzh´] deliberate destruction of machinery, etc., in the course of a dispute with an employer; similar destruction intended to slow down production for political or other reasons; action taken to prevent the achievement of any aim.—*vt* to practice sabotage on.—*n* **saboteur** [-tœr´] one who sabotages. [Fr *sabot*.]

sac [sak] *n* (*biol*) a pouch within a plant or animal. [Fr—L *saccus*, a bag.]

saccharine [sak´a-rin, -rēn] *adj* pertaining to, or having the qualities of, sugar; yielding or containing sugar; sickly-sweet (eg *a saccharine smile*).—*vt* **sacchar´ify**, to convert into simple sugars.—*ns* **saccharom´eter**, an instrument for measuring the quantity of sugar in a liquid; **sacch´arin**, an intensely sweet crystalline solid, used as a calorie-free substitute for sugar. [Fr *saccharin*—L *saccharum*, sugar.]

sacerdotal [sas-ėr-dō´tål] *adj* priestly.—*ns* **sacerdō´talism**, religious belief emphasizing the powers of priests as essential mediators between God and man; **sacerdō´talist**, a supporter of sacerdotalism.—*adv* **sacerdō´tally**. [L *sacerdōs, -ōtis*, a priest—*sacer*, sacred, *dăre*, to give.]

sachem [sach´em] *n* a N American Indian chief, esp of a confederation of Algonquian tribes of the north Atlantic coast; a Tammany leader. [Native word.]

sachet [sa´shā] *n* a small bag or packet; a small perfumed packet used to scent clothes. [Fr.]

sack[1] [sak] *n* a large bag of coarse cloth material for holding grain, flour, etc.; the contents of a sack, esp a fixed amount used as a unit of measure; a woman's loose-fitting dress; a short loose-fitting coat for women and children; (*slang*) dismissal (*with* **the**); (*slang*) a bed; (*baseball*) a base; (*football*), an instance of tackling a quarterback.—*vt* to put into a sack; (*slang*) to dismiss (a person).—*ns* **sack´cloth**, cloth for sacks; coarse cloth formerly worn in mourning or penance; **sack´ing**, coarse cloth, as burlap, for sacks, etc.; **sack race**, a race in which the legs of each competitor are confined by a sack.—**get the sack**, to be dismissed from a post, esp summarily; **give the sack**, to dismiss. [OE *sacc*—L *saccus*—Gr *sakkos*.]

sack[2] [sak] *n* the plunder or devastation of a town.—*vt* to plunder; to strip of valuables.—*n* **sack´ing**, the storming and pillaging of a town. [Fr *sac*, a sack, plunder (*saccager*, to sack)—L *saccus*, a sack.]

sack[3] [sak] *n* a dry white Spanish wine popular in England during the 16th and 17th centuries. [Fr *sec*—L *siccus*, dry.]

sackbut [sak´but] *n* the medieval and Renaissance trombone. [Fr *saquebute*.]

sacrament [sak´rå-mėnt] *n* any of certain Christian rites, as baptism, the Eucharist, marriage, etc.—*adj* **sacramen´tal**, belonging to or constituting a sacrament.—*adv* **sacramen´tally**.—*n* **Sacramentā´rian**, one who holds a high or extreme view of the efficacy of the sacraments. [L *sacrāmentum*, an oath, pledge—*sacrāre*, to consecrate—*sacer*, sacred.]

sacred [sā´krid] *adj* holy; dedicated to a god or God; having to do with religion; worthy of religious veneration; not to be violated; (*arch*) accursed.—*adv* **sā´credly**.—*n* **sā´credness**.—**sacred cow**, an institution, custom, etc. so venerated that it is above criticism; **sacred mushroom**, any of various New World hallucinogenic fungi (genus *Psilocype*) used esp in some Indian ceremonies. [OFr *sacrer*—L *sacrāre*—L *sacer*, sacred.]

sacrifice [sak´ri-fīs] *n* the act of sacrificing or offering to a deity, esp a victim on an altar; that which is sacrificed or offered; destruction or surrender of anything to gain an important end; that which is surrendered or destroyed for such an end; loss of profit.—*vti* [-fīs] to offer up in sacrifice; to make a sacrifice of; to give up for a higher good or for mere advantage; to disregard or neglect the interests of; to sell at less than the supposed value.—*n* **sac´rificer**.—*adj* **sacrifi´cial** [-fish´ål] relating to, or consisting in, sacrifice; of a metal that serves as an anode and is electrolytically consumed instead of another metal that is present.—*adv* **sacrifi´cially**.—**sacrifice hit** (*baseball*) a bunt that allows a runner to advance one base while the batter is put out. [L *sacrificium*—*sacer*, sacred, *facĕre*, to make.]

sacrilege [sak´ri-lėj] *n* profanation of anything holy.—*adj* **sacrilegious** [-lēj´ūs or -lij´-] guilty of sacrilege; profane.—*adv* **sacrileg´iously**.—*n* **sacrileg´iousness**. [Fr *sacrilège*—L *sacrilegium*—*sacer*, sacred, *legĕre*, to gather.]

sacristan [sak´ris-tån] *n* an officer in a church who has charge of the sacred vessels and other movables; a sexton.—**săc´risty**, a room in a church where the sacred utensils, vestments, etc., are kept. [Low L *sacrista, sacristānus*, a sacristan, *sacristia*, a vestry—L *sacer*, sacred.]

sacroiliac [sā´krō-il´ē-ak or sak´rō] *n* the joint between the top part of the hipbone and the sacrum.

sacrosanct [sak´rō-sang(k)t] *adj* inviolable, that must not be profaned; holy and worthy of reverence. [L *sacrōsanctus*—*sacer*, sacred, *sanctus*, pt p of *sancīre*, to hallow.]

sacrum [sā´krum] *n* the five united vertebrae situated at the lower part of the vertebral column. [L (*os*) *sacrum*, holy (bone).]

sad [sad] *adj* expressing grief or unhappiness; sorrowful, dejected; regrettable, calamitous; deplorable; of a dull somber color.—*vt* **sadd´en**, to make sad.—*vi* to grow sad.—*adv* **sad´ly**.—*n* **sad´ness**. [OE *sæd*, sated, weary.]

saddle [sad´l] *n* a seat for a rider on a horse, bicycle, etc. usu padded and of leather; a ridge connecting two higher elevations; a cut of lamb, etc. including part of the backbone and the two loins; a piece of leather across the instep of a shoe.—*vt* to put a saddle on, to load; to encumber (with); to fix the responsibility for (something, upon a person).—*ns* **sadd´lebag**, a bag carried at or attached to the saddle; **sadd´lebow** [-bō] the arched front of a saddle or the pieces forming it; **sadd´le horse**, a horse suitable for riding; **sadd´ler**, a maker or seller of saddles; **sadd´lery**, occupation of a saddler; his shop or stock in trade; materials for saddles; **sadd´le shoe**, white Oxford shoe with a contrasting band across the instep; **sadd´le soap**, a mild soap used for cleaning and conditioning leather; **sadd´letree**, the frame of a saddle.—**in the saddle**, in control. [OE *sadol, sadel*; cf Du *zadel*, Ger *sattel*.]

Sadducee [sad´ū-sē] *n* one of an ancient Jewish priesthood that accepted only the doctrines in the written Law.—*n* **Sadduceeis´m**. [Gr *Saddoukaios*—Heb *Tsaddūqim* (pl).]

sadism [sad´- or sād´izm] *n* a perversion in which pleasure is obtained by mistreating others; pleasure in inflicting or watching cruelty.—*n* **sad´ist**.—*adj* **sadis´tic**.—*ns* **sad´omas´ochism**, obtaining pleasure by inflicting pain on oneself and receiving it from another; **sadomasochist**.—*adj* **sadomasochistic**. [Marquis de *Sade* (1740–1814), who died insane, depicted this perversion in his novels.]

safari [sa-fä´ri] *n* the caravan and equipment of a hunting expedition, esp in eastern Africa; a journey or hunting expedition, esp in Africa.—**safari jacket**, a belted shirt jacket with pleated expansible pockets; **safari suit**, a safari jacket with matching pants. [Swahili.]

safe [sāf] *adj* unharmed; free from danger; secure; not involving risk; trustworthy; giving protection; cautious (eg *a safe driver*).—*n* a locking metal container for valuables.—*ns* **safe´-con´duct**, a writing, passport, or guard granted to a person to enable him to travel with safety, esp through hostile territory; **safe-deposit box**, a box (as in the vault of a bank) for safe storage of valuables; **safe´guard**, anything that increases security or averts danger; a guard, passport, or warrant to protect a traveler.—*vt* to protect.—*n* **safe´keep´ing**, protection; custody.—*adv* **safe´ly**.—*ns* **safe´ness; safety**, freedom from danger or loss; **safe´ty belt**, a belt for fastening a workman, etc. to a fixed object while he carries out a dangerous operation; a belt for fastening a passenger to his seat as a precaution against injury in a crash; **safe´ty glass**, shatterproof glass; **safe´ty island**, an area within a roadway from which vehicular traffic is excluded (as by pavement markings or curbings); **safe´ty lamp**, a lamp, used in mines, that will not ignite flammable gases, usu. by enclosing the flame in fine wire gauze; **safe´ty match**, a match which can be ignited only on a surface specially prepared for the purpose; **safe´ty net**, a net suspended as beneath aerialists; any protection against loss, esp financial loss; **safe´ty pin**, a pin in the form of a clasp with a guard covering its point; **safe´ty razor**, a razor with a detachable blade held in a guard or guards; **safe´ty valve**, a valve that opens when pressure becomes too great for safety; any outlet that gives relief; **safe´ty zone**, a safety island for pedestrians or for streetcar or bus passengers.—**safe and sound**, unharmed, uninjured. [OFr *sauf*—L *salvus*.]

safflower [saf´low-ėr] *n* a thistlelike plant (*Carthamus tinctorius*) whose seeds yield an edible oil. [Cf Du *saffloer*—OFr *saffleur*.]

saffron [saf´ròn] *n* a species of crocus (*Crocus sativus*) with purple flowers; a coloring and flavoring substance prepared from its yellow stigmas; orange yellow. [OFr *safran*—Ar *za'farān*.]

sag [sag] *vi* to bend, sink or droop, esp in the middle; to hang down unevenly; to yield or give way as from weight or pressure.—*pr p* **sagg´ing**; *pt, pt p* **sagged**.—*n* a droop. [Cf Low Ger *sacken*, to sink.]

saga [sä´ga] *n* a medieval Scandinavian story of battles, legends, etc.; any long story of heroic deeds.—**saga novel**, a roman-fleuve. [ON.]

sagacious [sa-gā´shùs] *adj* keen in perception or thought, discerning and judicious; shrewd, having practical wisdom; arising from or showing judiciousness or shrewdness.—*adv* **sagā´ciously**.—*ns* **sagā´ciousness, sagacity** [sa-ga´si-ti]. [L *sagāx, sagācis*.]

sage[1] [sāj] *n* a plant (*Salvia officinalis*) of the mint family with leaves used for seasoning meats, etc.; sagebrush.—*ns* **sage´brush**, a plant (*Artemisia tridentata*) with aromatic leaves, common in the dry areas of the western US. [OFr *sauge* (It *salvia*)—L *salvia*—*salvus*, safe.]

sage[2] [sāj] *adj* wise through reflection and experience.—*n* a man of great wisdom.—*adv* **sage´ly**.—*n* **sage´ness**. [Fr *sage*—L *sapĕre*, to be wise.]

Sagittarius [saj-i-tār´i-us] *n* the Archer, the 9th sign of the zodiac; in astrology, operative November 22 to December 20. [L *sagittārius*—*sagitta*, an arrow.]

sago [sā´gō] *n* a starch produced from the pith of a sago palm used in foods and as textile stiffening.—*n* **sago palm**, a plant (genus *Metroxylan*) that yields sago. [Malay *sāgū*.]

saguaro [sȧ-wär´ō] *n* a giant cactus (*Carnegia gigantea*) of the southwestern US and northern Mexico. [Mex Sp.]

sahib [sä´ib] *n* a term of respect given in colonial India to Europeans of rank. [Ar, friend.]

said [sed] *pt, pt p* of **say**.—*adj* aforesaid (eg *the said witness*.]

sail [sāl] *n* a sheet of canvas, etc., spread to catch the wind, by which a ship is driven forward; sails collectively; anything like a sail; a trip in a vessel.—*vi* to be moved by sails; to go by water; to begin a trip by water; to manage a sailboat; to glide or move smoothly, like a ship in full sail.—*vt* to move upon (a body of water) in a vessel; to manage (a vessel).—*ns* **sail´boat**, a boat that is propelled by means of a sail or sails; **sail´cloth**, a strong cloth for sails, tents, etc.; **sail´er**, a boat or ship with respect to its mode of sailing, or its speed; **sail´ing**, act of sailing; motion of a vessel on water; act of directing a ship's course; a departure from a port; **sail´or**, one who sails in a ship; a mariner; a seaman; a stiff straw hat with a low flat crown and straight circular brim.—**under sail**, in motion, having the sails spread. [OE *segel*; cf Du *zeil*, Ger *segel*.]

sainfoin [sān´foin] *n* a leguminous forage plant (*Onobrychia viciaefolia*) [Fr, prob *sain*, wholesome, *foin*, hay—L *sānum fēnum*.]

saint [sānt] *n* a holy person; a person who is exceptionally patient, charitable, etc.; one canonized by the RC Church; (*pl*) Christians generally.—*adjs* **saint´ed**, holy, virtuous; gone to heaven, dead; much admired; **saint´ly**, like or becoming a saint.—*n* **saint´liness**.—**St Bernard**, a breed of large dog, formerly kept at the hospice of the Great St Bernard pass in the Swiss Alps to rescue lost travelers; **St Elmo's fire**, a glow that appears at the end of masts and spars of ships and at prominent points on an airplane during thunderstorms at night; **Saint-John's-wort**, a herb or shrub (genus *Hypericum*) widely cultivated for its showy yellow flowers; **saint's day**, a day in a church calendar on which a saint is commemorated; **St Patrick's Day**, March 17, observed by the Irish in honor of the patron saint of Ireland; **St Martin's summer**, Indian summer when occurring in November; **St Valentine's Day**, February 14, observed in honor of a 3d century martyr and as a day for sending valentines; **Saint Vitus's dance**, chorea. [Fr,—L *sanctus*, holy.]

saith [seth] *vt* and *vi* (*arch*) 3d pers sing pres indic of **say**.

sake[1] [sāk] *n* purpose, motive (eg *for the sake of peace, argument*); behalf, advantage (eg *for my, pity's, sake*). [OE *sacu*, strife, a lawsuit; Du *zaak*, Ger *sache*; OE *sacan*, to strive. **seek** is a doublet.]

sake[2] [sä´ki] *n* an alcoholic beverage made by the Japanese from fermented rice. [Jap.]

sal [sal] *n* (*chem, pharmacy*) salt.—*ns* **sal ammō´niac**, ammonium chloride; **sal soda**, crystallized sodium carbonate.—Also washing soda; **sal volatile** [vol-at´i-li] ammonium carbonate. [L.]

salaam [sä-läm´] *n* a word and gesture of salutation in the Middle East; an obeisance made by bowing very low and placing the right palm on the forehead. [Ar *salām*, peace; Heb *shālōm*.]

salacious [sal-ā´shùs] *adj* lustful, lecherous; obscene. [L *salax, -ācis*—*salīre*, to leap.]

salad [sal´ȧd] *n* a dish, usu. cold, of fruits, vegetables (esp lettuce), meat, eggs, etc. usu. mixed with salad dressing.—*ns* **sal´ad bar**, a buffet in a restaurant at which diners make their own salads; **sal´ad dressing**, a cooked or uncooked preparation of oil, vinegar, and spices, etc. put on a salad; **sal´ad oil**, an edible vegetable oil (as olive oil) suitable for use in salad dressings.—**salad days**, days of youthful inexperience. [Fr *salade*—L *sāl*, salt.]

salamander [sal´a-man-dėr or -man´-] *n* any of numerous scaleless, tailed amphibians (order Caudata); a mythological animal having the power to endure fire without harm; any of various cooking devices used to glaze or brown food.—*adj* **salaman´drine**, like a salamander; enduring fire. [Fr *salamandre*—L—Gr *salamandra*; prob of Eastern origin.]

salami [sa-lä´mi] *n* a highly seasoned sausage of dried or fresh pork or beef. [It.]

sal ammoniac *See* **sal**.

salary [sal´ȧ-ri] *n* periodical payment at a fixed rate for services.—*adj* **sal´aried**, receiving a salary. [OFr *salarie*—L *salārium*, salt-money (which formed a part of the Roman soldier's pay)—*sal*, salt.]

sale [sāl] *n* act of selling; the exchange of anything for money; power or opportunity of selling; an auction; a public offer of goods to be sold, esp at reduced prices.—*adj* **sāl´able, saleable**, fit to be sold; easy to sell; in good demand.—*n* **salabil´ity**.—*ns* **sales´clerk**, a person employed to sell goods in a store; **sales´man**, one who sells either in a given territory or in a store; **sales´manship**, the art of selling; skill in presenting wares in the most attractive light or in persuading purchasers to buy; **sales´room**, a place where goods are displayed for sale, esp an auction room; **sales talk**, talk aimed at selling something; any talk to persuade; **sales tax**, a tax on the sale of goods; **sales´woman**, a woman employed to sell merchandise, esp in a store. [Late OE *sala*, perh—ON *sala*.]

salep [sal´ep] *n* the dried tubers of various Old World orchids (genus *Orchis*) used for food and in medicine. [Ar.]

Salic law [sāl´ik lö] a rule limiting succession to males.

salicin [sal´i-sin] *n* a bitter crystalline substance with medicinal properties, obtained from the bark of several willows (genus *Salix*).—**salicylic** [sal-i-sil´ik] **acid**, a colorless crystalline acid occurring in many plants and fruits, formerly obtained from salicin but now made from carbolic acid and used as an analgesic and antipyretic, as in aspirin. [L *salix, salicis*, a willow.]

salient [sā´li-ėnt] *adj* leaping or springing; (*fort*) projecting outwards, as an angle; outstanding, prominent, striking.—*n* an outward pointing angle, esp in a line of defense.—*adv* **sā´liently**. [Fr—L *saliēns, -entis*, pr p of *salīre*, to leap.]

saline [sā´lēn or sā´līn] *adj* consisting of, or containing, salt; partaking of the qualities of salt.—*n* a metallic salt; a saline solution. [Fr—L *salīnus*—*sāl*, salt.]

saliva [sa-lī´va] *n* the watery fluid secreted by glands in the mouth which aids in digestion.—*adj* **sa´livary**, pertaining to saliva or the glands that produce it, esp secreting or conveying saliva.—*vt* **sal´ivāte**, to produce, or discharge, saliva, esp in excess.—*n* **salivā´tion**, a flow of saliva. [L *salīva*.]

salk vaccine [sawk] *n* a vaccine consisting of poliomyelitis virus inactivated with formaldehyde. [Jonas *Salk*, Amer physician.]

sallow[1] [sal´ō] *n* a willow (*as Salix caprea*) esp of the broad-leaved kind with comparatively brittle twigs. [OE *salh, sealh*; cf L *salix*.]

sallow[2] [sal´ō] *adj* of a grayish, greenish, yellow color.—*n* **sall´owness**. [OE *salo, salu*; cf Du *zaluw*, and OHG *salo*.]

sally [sal´i] *n* a leap; a sudden rush forth to attack besiegers; excursion; outburst (of fancy, wit, etc.)—*vi* to rush out suddenly; to set forth, issue;—*pt, pt p* **sall´ied**.—*n* **sall´y port**, a passage by which a garrison may make a sally. [Fr *saillie*—*saillir* (It *salire*)—L *salīre*, to leap.]

Sally Lunn [sal´i lun´] *n* a sweet yeast-leavened bread. [From the name of a girl who sold them in the streets of Bath about the close of the 18th century.]

salmon [sam´òn] *n* a large game and food fish (*Salmo salar*), with silvery sides and delicate flesh, that lives in salt water and spawns in fresh water.—*n* **salmon, salmon pink**, yellowish pink. [OFr *saumon*—L *salmō, -ōnis*—*salīre*, to leap.]

salmonella [sal-mò-nel´ȧ] *n* a large genus (*Salmonella*) of bacteria pathogenic for man and other warm-blooded animals, causing food poisoning, gastrointestinal inflammation, and diseases of the genital tract;—*pl* **-ae**.—*n* **salmonellō´sis**, infection with or disease caused by salmonellae. [Daniel *Salmon*, veterinarian.]

salon [sal´•] *n* a large reception hall or drawing room; a fashionable reception, esp a periodic gathering of notable persons, in the house of an eminent hostess; a hall for exhibition of art; **Salon**, an annual exhibition of works of art; stylish shop or business establishment (eg *beauty salon*). [Fr.]

saloon [sa-lōōn´] *n* a large public room for holding salons, receptions, etc.; a large cabin for the social use of a ship's passengers; a room or establishment where alcoholic drinks are sold and consumed; a tavern. [Fr *salon*.]

salsa [sal´sa] *n* (the music for) a type of Puerto Rican dance; a spicy tomato sauce.

salsify [sal´si-fi] *n* a biennial plant (*Tragopogon porrifolius*) whose long and tapering root has a flavor resembling oysters.—Also **vegetable oyster**. [Fr *salsifis*, prob It *sassefrica*, goat's-beard—L *saxum*, a rock, *fricāre*, to rub.]

sal soda *See* **sal**.

salt [sölt] *n* a white crystalline substance, sodium chloride, or common salt, used for seasoning, either found in natural beds or obtained by evaporation from brine, etc.; seasoning; piquancy, esp pungent wit; that which preserves from corruption; (*chem*) a compound formed by the replacement of one or more hydrogen atoms of an acid by metal atoms or radicals; (*pl*) a mixture of salts used as a medicine; (*inf*) a sailor, esp an old sailor.—*adj* containing salt; seasoned or cured with salt; pungent.—*vt* to sprinkle, season, cure, impregnate with salt; to give flavor or piquancy to (as a story); to enrich (as a mine) artificially by secretly placing valuable minerals in some of the working places.—*adv* **salt´ly**.—*ns* **salt lick**, a place where salt is found or where a block of salt has been left and to which animals go to lick it up; **salt pan**, a pan, basin, or pit where salt is obtained by evaporation.—*adjs* **saltwat´er**, of, pertaining to, or living or growing in, salt water; **salt´y**, seasoned with or containing salt; smacking of the sea or nautical life; piquant; earthy.—**salt away**, to store away, to hoard; **salt of the earth**, the most worthy people.—**above, below, the salt**, (*hist*) among those of high, or low, social rank, the saltcellar marking the boundary when all dined at the same table; **lay, put, salt on the tail of**, to catch; **take with a grain of salt**, to believe with some reserve; **worth one's salt**, worth one's salary. [OE *salt, sealt*, cf Ger *salz*, also L *sāl*, Gr *hals*.]

saltcellar [sölt´sel-ăr] *n* a small vessel for holding salt at the table; a saltshaker. [**salt**, and OFr *saliere*—L *salārium*—*sāl*, salt; spelling influenced by **cellar**.]

saltire [sal´tīr, söl´-] *n* a diagonal cross, also called a St Andrew's Cross. [OFr *saultoir, sautoir*—Low L *saltātōrium*, a stirrup—L *saltāre*, to leap.]

saltpeter [sölt-pē´tėr] *n* potassium nitrate, niter. [OFr *salpetre*—Low L *salpetra*—L *sāl*, salt, *petra*, a rock.]

saltshaker [sölt´shā´kėr] *n* a small container for salt, with a perforated top.

salubrious [sa-lōō´bri-ůs] *adj* healthful; wholesome.—*adv* **salu´briously**.—*ns* **salu´briousness, salu´brity**. [L *salūbris*—*salūs, salūtis*, health.]

salutary [sal´ū-tȧr-i] *adj* promoting health; beneficial.—*adv* **sal´ūtarily**.—*n* **sal´ūtariness**. [L *salūtāris*—*salūs*, health.]

salute [sal-ūt´] *vt* to greet with words or (now esp) a gesture (eg of the hand), or with a bow or kiss; to honor by performing a prescribed act, such as raising the hand to the head, in military and naval practice; to commend; to honor (as a person, nation, or event) by a conventional naval or military ceremony.—*vi* to perform the act of saluting.—*n* act or attitude of saluting.—*n* **salūtā´tion**, act, or words, of greeting. [L *salūtāre, -ātum*—*salūs, salūtis*.]

salvage [sal´vij] *n* reward paid for saving or rescuing a ship or cargo from danger or loss; the act of saving a ship or cargo, or of saving goods from fire, etc.; goods so saved; waste material saved for further use.—*vt* to save from loss or destruction; to recover (wreckage). [Fr,—Low L *salvāre*, to save.]

salvation [sal-vā´sh(ȯ)n] *n* the act of saving; means of preservation from evil; (*theol*) the saving of man from the power and penalty of sin.—*n* **Salvā´tionist**, a soldier or officer of the Salvation Army; **salvationist**, an evangelist.—**Salvation Army**, an international religious and charitable group organized in military lines founded by William Booth in 1865 for evangelization and social betterment (as of the poor). [Low L *salvāre*, to save.]

salve[1] [salv] *vt* to salvage. [Low L *salvāre*, to save.]

salve[2] [säv, also salv] *n* an ointment; a remedy; anything to soothe the feelings or conscience.—*vt* to anoint; to heal; to soothe. [OE *sealf*; Ger *salbe*, Du *zalf*.]

salver [sal´vėr] *n* a tray, esp for serving food or drink. [Sp *salva*, a salver—*salvar*, to save—Low L *salvāre*.]

salvo[1] [sal´vō] *n* a mental reservation; a means of safeguarding one's honor or allaying one's conscience. [L, in phrase, *salvo jure*, one's right being safe.]

salvo[2] [sal´vō] *n* a simultaneous discharge of artillery, or of bombs; a sudden burst; a spirited verbal attack.—*pl* **salvo(e)s** [sal´vōz]. [It *salva*, salute—L *salvē*, hail!]

sal volatile *See* **sal**.

samara [sam´ȧr-a, sa-mä´ra] *n* a dry, indehiscent, usually one-sided, fruit with a wing. [L *samara, samera*, elm seed.]

Samaritan [sa-mar´i-tȧn] *adj* pertaining to *Samaria* in ancient Palestine.—*n* an inhabitant of Samaria; the language of Samaria which was a dialect of Aramaic; one ready and generous in helping those in distress.

samarium [sa-mā´ri-ům] *n* a metallic element (symbol Sm; at wt 150.4; at no 62), a member of the rare earth group. [From *samarskite* (named after a Russian mine official), the mineral in which it was first observed.]

samba [sam´ba] *n* a Brazilian dance of African origin or the music for it.—*vi* to dance the samba.

Sam Browne belt [sam brown] *n* a military officer's leather belt with shoulder strap. [General Sir *Samuel Browne* (1824–1901).]

same [sām] *adj* identical; not different; unchanged; mentioned before.—*pron* the same person or thing.—*adv* in like manner.—*n* **same´ness**, the being the same; tedious monotony.—**all the same; just the same**, despite everything; nevertheless. [OE *same*.]

samite [sam´īt] *n* a heavy medieval silk fabric interwoven with gold and silver. [OFr *samit*—Low L *examitum*—Gr *hexamiton*—*hex*, six, *mitos*, thread.]

samizdat [sam´iz-dat] *n* in the former USSR the secret printing and distribution of literature banned by the government. [Russ.]

samovar [sam´ō-vär, -vär´] *n* an urn with a spigot at its base and an internal tube for heating water used esp in Russia to boil water for tea; a similar urn with a heating device. [Russ.]

Samoyed, Samoyede [sam´ō-yed] *n* a people of north west Siberia; their language; a breed of sled dog developed in Siberia.—Also *adj*. [Russ.]

sampan [sam´pan] *n* a flat-bottomed Chinese skiff propelled by two short oars. [Chinese *san*, three, *pan*, board.]

samphire [sam´fīr] *n* a European plant (*Chrithmum maritimum*) found chiefly on rocky cliffs near the sea, used in pickles and salads. [Fr (*herbe de*) *Saint Pierre*, Saint Peter's herb.]

sample [säm´pl] *n* a specimen; a small portion to show the quality of the whole; an example.—*vt* to make up samples of; to test or estimate by taking a sample.—*n* **sam´pler**, one that collects, prepares or examines samples; something containing representative selections (as a book or box of chocolates); an assortment. [L *exemplum*, example.]

sampler [säm´plėr] *n* a piece of ornamental embroidery, containing names, figures, texts, etc. in different stitches as an example of skill. [OFr *essemplaire*—L *exemplar*, a pattern.]

Samuel [sam´yŏŏ-ėl] *n* (*Bible*) 9th and 10th books of the Old Testament telling of the reunification of the people of Israel and Samuel's yielding to their demand for a king. As a result, Saul was established on the throne and David anointed as a future king.

samurai [sam´ŏŏ-rī] *n sing* (also *pl*) a member of the military class in the old feudal system of Japan, including both territorial nobles and their military retainers. [Jap.]

sanative [san´ȧ-tiv] *adj* tending, or able, to heal, healing.—*n* **sanator´ium**, (*Brit*) a sanitarium.—*pl* **sanatar´ia, -iums**.—*adj* **san´atory**, healing; conducive to health. [L *sānāre, -ātum*, to heal.]

sanctify [sang(k)´ti-fī] *vt* to make sacred or holy, to set apart to sacred use; to free from sin or evil; to make efficient as the means of holiness;—*pt, pt p* **sanc´tified**.—*ns* **sanctificā´tion**, act of sanctifying; state of being sanctified; **sanc´tifier**.—*adj* **sanctimō´nious**, simulating or pretending holiness.—*adv* **sanctimō´niously**.—*ns* **sanctimō´niousness, sanc´timony**, affected devoutness, show of sanctity; **sanctity** [sang(k)´ti-ti], quality of being sacred or holy, purity, godliness; inviolability (eg of an oath); (*pl* **sanc´tities**) holy feelings, obligations, or objects; **sanc´tūary**, a sacred place; a place of worship; the most sacred part of a temple or church; a consecrated place which affords immunity from arrest or violence; the privilege of refuge therein; an animal or plant reserve; **sanc´tum**, a sacred place; a private room where one is not to be disturbed. [Fr—L *sanctificāre, -ātum*—*sanctus*, sacred, *facĕre*, to make.]

sanction sang(k)´sh(ȯ)n] *n* a law, decree; act of ratifying, or giving authority to; permission, countenance (eg of social custom); motive for obedience to any moral or religious law; penalty expressly attached to breach of a law or treaty; a coercive measure applied eg to a nation taking a course of action disapproved by others.—*vt* to give validity to, usu. by a formal procedure (as ratification); to authorize; to countenance. [L *sanctiō, -ōnis*—*sancīre, sanctum*, to hallow, ratify.]

Sanctus [sang(k)´tus] *n* an ancient Christian hymn of adoration. [The hymn *Holy, holy, holy*, from Isa vi, L holy.]

sand [sand] *n* a mass of fine particles of crushed or worn rocks; (*pl*) land covered with sand; a sandy beach; moments of a lifetime.—*vt* to sprinkle or fill with sand; to smooth or polish, as with sandpaper.—*n* **sand´bag**, a bag filled with sand used for ballast, to protect levees, etc.—*vt* to protect with sandbags; to stun with a sandbag; (*inf*) to force into doing something.—*ns* **sand´bank**, a sand bar; a large deposit of sand forming a hill or mound; **sand bar**, a ridge of sand built up in a river, a lake, or coastal waters by currents; **sandblast**, a steam of sand projected by air or steam at high velocity (as for cleaning stone, engraving, etc.).—*vt* to affect with sandblast.—*ns* **sand´erling**, a small sandpiper (*Calidris alba*) with largely gray-and-white plumage; **sand´glass**, a glass instrument for measuring time by the running of sand; **sand´hog**, a laborer in underwater or underground construction.—*adj* **sand´lot**, denoting games, esp baseball, played by amateurs.—*ns* **sand´man**, a mythical person supposed to make children sleepy by dusting sand in their eyes; **sand painting**, a Navaho and Pueblo Indian ceremonial design made of colored sands on a flat surface of sand; **sand´paper**, a paper coated on one side with sand or another abrasive, used for smoothing and polishing.—*vt* to rub with sandpaper.—*ns* **sand´piper**, a small shore bird (suborder Charadrii) with a long, soft-tipped bill; **sand´stone**, a sedimentary rock composed of sand grains cemented together, as by silica or calcium carbonate; **sand´storm** a windstorm (as in a desert) driving clouds of sand before it.—*adj* **sand´y**, of, like, or sprinkled with sand; yellowish-gray.—*ns* **sand´iness**. [OE *sand*; Du *zand*, Ger *sand*, ON *sandr*.]

sandal [san´d(ȧ)l] *n* a sole bound to the foot by straps; any of various low slippers or shoes.—*adj* **san´daled**, wearing sandals. [L *sandalium*—Gr *sandalion*, dim of *sandalon*.]

sandalwood [san´d(ȧ)l-wŏŏd] *n* the compact, close-grained, fragrant heartwood of a parasitic tree (*Santalum album*) of southern Asia; the tree or various other trees yielding a fragrant wood.—**sandalwood oil**, an essential oil obtained from sandalwood. [Low L *santalum*; cf Late Gr *sandanon*.]

sandwich [san(d)´-wich] *n* two slices of bread with any sort of food between; anything in like arrangement.—*vt* to lay or place (between two layers or between two things of another kind); to make a place for (*with* **in** *or* **between**).—*n* **sand´wich man**, one who advertizes or pickets a place of business by wearing a sandwich board; **sandwich board**, two usu hinged boards hanging from the shoulders, one in front and one in back, carried by a sandwich man. [Earl of *Sandwich* (1718–1792).]

sane [sān] *adj* sound in mind; rational, sensible.—*adv* **sane´ly**. [L *sānus*, healthy.]

sang *pt* of **sing**.

sangfroid [sā-frwä´] *n* coolness, composure, absence of excitement. [Fr *sang*, blood, *froid*, cold.]

Sangreal [san(g)´-grāl´], the holy grail. [**saint, grail**.]

sanguinary [sang´gwin-ȧr-i] *adj* attended with much bloodshed; bloodthirsty. [L *sanguinārius*—*sanguis, sanguinis*, blood.]

sanguine [sang´gwin] *adj* bloodred; ruddy; ardent, hopeful, cheerfully confident.—*adv* **san´guinely**, hopefully, confidently.—*n* **san´guineness**.—*adj* **sanguin´eous**, bloodred; involving bloodshed, bloodthirsty; containing blood. [Fr,—L *sanguineus*—*sanguis, sanguinis*, blood.]

Sanhedrin [san´i-drin] *n* the supreme ecclesiastical and judicial tribunal of the ancient Jews. [Heb *sanhedrīn*—Gr *synedrion*—*syn*, together, *hedra*, a seat.]

sanitary [san´i-tȧr-i] *adj* pertaining to the promotion of health; of drainage and sewage disposal; characterized by or readily kept in cleanliness.—*ns* **sanitary napkin**, an absorbent cotton pad for use in menstruation, etc.; **san´itary ware**, ceramic plumbing fixtures (as sinks, lavatories, or toilet bowls); **sanitā´tion**, the science and practice of effecting hygienic conditions; drainage and disposal of sewage; **sanitār´ium**, an establishment for the treatment of convalescents or the chronically ill, formerly esp those suffering from tuberculosis. [Fr *sanitaire*—L *sānitās*, health.]

sanity [san´i-ti] *n* state of being sane; soundness of judgment. [L *sānitās*—*sānus*, sane.]

sank [sangk] *pt* of **sink**.

Sanskrit [sans´krit] *n* an ancient Indo-European language which was the literary language also used by educated persons about the 4th century BC; the sacred language of the Hindu religion; classical Sanskrit together with its later modifications.—*adj* **Sanskrit´ic**. [Sans *saṁskṛta*, perfected—*sam*, together, *karoti*, he makes, cog with L *creāre*, to create.]

Santa Claus [san´ta klöz] *n* a fat white-bearded old fellow who brings good children Christmas presents. [US modification of Du dial *Sante Klaas*, St Nicholas.]

sap[1] [sap] *n* juice, esp the vital juice of plants, an aqueous solution of mineral salts, sugars and other organic substances; a body fluid (as blood) essential to life, health, or vigor; energy and health; (*inf*) a fool; a bludgeon.—*vt* to drain or withdraw the sap from; to knock out with a sap.—*n* **sap green**, a strong yellow green.—*adj* **sap´less**, wanting sap; lacking vitality or worth.—*n* **sap´ling**, a young tree, not more than four inches in diameter at breast height; a youth.—*adj* **sappy**, abounding with sap; consisting largely of sapwood; immaturely sentimental; lacking in good sense, silly.—*ns* **sapp´iness; sapwood**, the living outer portion of wood lying between the cambium and heartwood. [OE *sæp*; Low Ger *sap*, juice, Ger *saft*.]

sap[2] [sap] *n* the extension of a trench from within the trench itself to a point within the enemy's fortifications.—*vt* to dig beneath; to undermine; to weaken or exhaust.—*pr p* **sapp´ing**; *pt, pt p* **sapped**.—*n* **sapp´er**, a military specialist in field fortifications or one who lays, detects, and disarms mines. [It *zappa* and Fr *sappe* (now *sape*); cf LL *sapa*, a pick.]

sapid [sap´id] *adj* perceptible by taste; having a strong agreeable flavor; agreeable to the mind.—*n* **sapid´ity**. [L *sapidus*—*sapĕre*, to taste.]

sapience [sā´pi-ėns] *n* discernment, judgment, wisdom.—*adj* **sā´pient**, wise, sagacious.—*adv* **sā´piently**. [L *sapientia*—*sapiens, sapientis*, pr p of *sapĕre*, to be wise.]

sapling [sap´ling] *n See* **sap** (1).

sapodilla [sap-ō-dil´a] *n* a large evergreen tree, (*Achras zapota*) native of tropical America, yielding chicle; its edible fruit. [Sp *zapotilla*.]

saponaceous [sap-o-nā´shůs] *adj* soapy; resembling soap. [L *sāpō, sāpōnis*, soap.]

sapper [sap´ėr] *n See* **sap** (2).

Sapphic [saf´ik] *adj* pertaining to *Sappho*, a Greek lyric poet (*c* 600 BC), or to her poetry; denoting female homosexuality.—*n* a quatrain with eleven syllables in the first three lines, and five in the fourth.—*n* **Sapph´ism**, lesbianism, of which she was accused.

sapphire [saf´īr] *n* a brilliant precious stone, a variety of corundum, of deep clear blue; the color of sapphire.—*adj* of sapphire; deep pure blue. [Fr,—L *sapphīrus*—Gr *sappheiros*.]

saprophagous [sap-rof´ȧ-gůs] *adj* feeding on decaying organic matter. [Gr *sapros*, rotten, and *phagein*, to eat.]

saprophyte [sap´rō-fīt] *n* any plant that feeds upon decaying organic matter.—*adj* **saprophytic** [sap-ro-fit´ik], obtaining nourishment osmotically from the products of organic breakdown and decay.—*adv* **saprophyt´ically**. [Gr *sapros*, rotten, *phyton*, a plant.]

saraband, sarabande [sar´a-band] *n* a stately court dance of the 17th and 18th centuries resembling the minuet; the music, in slow triple time with the accent on the second beat. [Sp *zarabanda*.]

Saracen [sar´a-sėn] a member of a nomadic people of the deserts between Syria and Arabia; (*loosely*) an Arab, esp formerly during the Crusades. [L *Saracēnus*—Late Gr *Sarakēnos*.]

Saran [sȧ-ran´] *n* a transparent thermoplastic substance used in various fabrics, wrapping materials, etc. [A coinage.]

Saratoga trunk [sar-a-tōg´a trungk] *n* a large traveling trunk, usu. with a rounded top. [Prob from *Saratoga* Springs, NY State.]

sarcasm [sär´kazm] *n* a satirical remark in scorn or contempt, esp one worded ironically; the tone or language of such sayings; the use of such.—*adj* **sarcas´tic**, containing sarcasm; given to sarcasm.—*adv* **sarcas´tically**. [L *sarcasmus*—G *sarkasmos*—*sarkazein*, to tear flesh like dogs, to speak bitterly—*sarx*, gen *sarkos*, flesh.]

sarcenet, sarsenet [sär´snėt] *n* a soft thin silk in plain or twill weaves. [Anglo-Fr *sarzinett*, prob—*Sarzin*, Saracen.]

sarcoma [sär-kō´ma] *n* a tumor arising in connective tissue, bone, cartilage, or striated muscle.—*pl* **sarcomas, sarcō´mata**. [Gr *sarkōma*—*sarx*, flesh.]

sarcophagus [sär-kof´a-gus] *n* a stone coffin; a tomb;—*pl* **sarcoph´agi, sarcoph´aguses**. [L,—Gr *sarkophagos*—*sarx*, flesh, *phagein* (aor), to eat.]

sard [särd] *n* a deep-red chalcedony, sometimes classed as carnelian. [Gr *sardios* (*lithos*), the Sardian (stone)—*Sardeis*, Sardis in Lydia.]

sardine [sär-dēn´] *n* a young pilchard (*Sardinia pilchardus*) commonly tinned in oil; any of various small fishes (as an anchovy) resembling the true sardines or similarly preserved for food. [Fr, (It *sardina*)—L *sardīna*—Gr *sardīnē*.]

sardonic [sär-don´ik] *adj* forced, heartless, or bitter (said of a laugh, smile, etc.).—*adv* **sardon´ically**. [Fr *sardonique*—L *sardonius*—Late Gr *sardonios*, doubtfully referred to *sardonion*, a plant of Sardinia (Gr *Sardō*), which was said to screw up the face of the eater.]

sardonyx [sär´do-niks] *n* an onyx with layers of cornelian or sard. [Gr]

sargasso [sär-gas´ō] *n* a mass of floating vegetation and esp sargassum.—*n* **sargassum**, any of a genus (*Sargassum*) of brown algae with lateral outgrowths; gulfweed. [Port *sargaço*.]

sari, saree [sär´ē] *n* a Hindu woman's chief garment, wrapped round the waist and passed over the shoulder. [Hindustani.]

sarong [sä-rong´] *n* a loose skirt made of a long strip of cloth wrapped around the body, worn by men and women of the Malay archipelago and the Pacific islands; cloth for sarongs. [Malay.]

sarsaparilla [sär-sä-pȧr-il´a] *n* any tropical American species of *Smilax*; its dried root; a carbonated drink flavored with it. [Sp *zarzaparilla*—*zarza*, bramble (prob Basque, *sartzia*), *parilla*, a dim of *parra*, a vine.]

sarsenet [särs´net] *n See* **sarcenet**.

sartorial [sär-tō´ ri-ȧl] *adj* pertaining to a tailor or tailoring; of men's dress. [L *sartor*, a patcher.]

sash[1] [sash] *n* a band or scarf worn round the waist or over the shoulder. [Ar *shāsh*.]

sash[2] [sash] *n* a frame, esp a sliding frame, for panes of glass. [Fr *châsse*—L *capsa*, a case.]

sassafras [sas´ȧ-fras] *n* a tall N American tree (*Sassafras albidum*) of the laurel family; the dried root bark used for flavoring. [Sp *sasafrás*.]

sat [sat] *pt, pt p* of **sit**.

Satan [sā´tȧn] *n* the adversary of God and lord of evil in Judaism and Christianity.—*adj* **sătan´ic**, pertaining to, or like Satan; marked by viciousness or extreme cruelty.—*adv* **satan´ically**. [OFr,—Heb *sātān*, enemy—*sātan*, to be adverse.]

satchel [sach´ėl] *n* a small bag for carrying clothes, books, etc. [OFr *sachel*—L *saccellus*, dim of *saccus*, a sack.]

sate [sāt] *vt* to satisfy fully; to glut. [ME *sade*—OE *sadian*, to become satisfied, influenced by L *satis*, enough.]

sateen [sa-tēn´] *n* a glossy fabric of cotton made to imitate satin. [**satin**.]

satellite [sat´ėl-īt] *n* an attendant of some important person; a small planet revolving round one of the larger planets; a man-made object put into orbit around the earth, moon, etc.; a small state economically dependent on a larger one. [Fr,—L *satelles, satellitis*, an attendant.]

satiate [sā´shi-āt] *vt* to provide with more than enough, so as to weary or disgust; to glut.—*adj* **sā´tiable**, that may be satiated.—*n* **satiety** [sa-tī´ėt-i], state of being satiated; surfeit. [L *satiāre, -ātum*—*satis*, enough.]

satin [sat´in] *n* a closely woven silk with a lustrous and unbroken surface on one side.—*adj* made of satin; resembling satin.—*ns* **sat´inet**, a thin silk or imitation satin; **sat´in stitch**, an embroidery stitch, repeated in parallel lines, giving a satiny appearance and making both sides alike; **sat´inwood**, a smooth yellowish brown wood, esp from an East Indian tree (*Chloroxylon swietenia*); any of various trees yielding such a wood.—*adj* **sat´iny**, like satin in being smooth and lustrous. [Fr *satin*, app—LL *sēta*, silk.]

satire [sat´īr] *n* a literary composition, orig in verse, essentially a criticism of folly or vice, which it holds up to ridicule or scorn; cutting comment; ridicule.—*adjs* **satir´ic, -al**, pertaining to, or conveying, satire; (**satirical**) using, or given to using, satire.—*adv* **satir´ically**.—*vt* **sat´irize**, to make the object of satire, to ridicule by sarcasm.—*n* **sat´irist**, a writer of satire. [Fr,—L *satira, satura* (*lanx*), a dish of mixed fruit, a poem dealing with various subjects, or a poem in which vices and follies are ridiculed or denounced.]

satisfy [sat´is-fī] *vt* to give enough to; to supply fully and hence appease (eg hunger, a desire, curiosity); to pay (a creditor) in full; to meet (a claim) in full; to atone for (eg *to satisfy guilt*); to answer (a question) adequately, or dispel (a doubt); to be in accordance with (a hypothesis), or to fulfil (a condition); to come up to (an idea, preconception); to convince (eg oneself) by investigation or production of evidence.—*vi* to give content, leave nothing to be desired;—*pt, pt p* **sat´isfied**.—*n* **satisfac´tion**, the act of satisfying; state of being satisfied; gratification, comfort; that which satisfies; amends, atonement, payment of debt.—*adj* **satisfactory**, satisfying, giving contentment; making amends or payment; atoning; convincing.—*adv* **satisfac´torily**.—*n* **satisfac´toriness**. [OFr *satisfier*—L *satisfacĕre*—*satis*, enough, *facĕre*, to make.]

satrap [sat´rap or sā´trap] *n* a viceroy or governor of an ancient Persian province; a despot; a provincial governor, esp if powerful and ostentatiously rich; a petty tyrant.—*n* **sat´rapy**, a satrap's province, office, or period of office. [Gr *satrapēs*, from Pers *khshatrapā* or Zend *shōithra-paiti*—lit 'chief of a district.']

satsuma [sat-sōō´ma, sat´sōō-ma] *n* a thin-skinned seedless type of mandarin orange or its tree. [*Satsuma*, name of a former province in south-west Japan.]

saturate [sat´ū-rāt] *vt* to impregnate (with); to unite with till no more can be absorbed; to soak; to charge with a maximum quantity of magnetism, electricity, heat, etc.; to fill completely; to pervade; to surfeit.—*adjs* **sat´ūrable**, that may be saturated; **sat´ūrate, sat´ūrated**, charged to the fullest extent; pure in color.—*n* **saturā´tion**, act of saturating; state of being saturated; the purity of a color, its degree of freedom from mixture with white or gray; the supplying of a market with all the goods it will absorb; an overwhelming concentration of military forces or fire power. [L *saturāre*, -*ātum*—*satur*, full, akin to *satis*, enough.]

Saturday [sat´ur-dā] *n* the seventh and last day of the week.—**Saturday night special**. (*slang*) any small, cheap handgun. [OE *Sæterdæg, Sætern(es)dæg*, Saturn's day—L *Sāturnus*.]

Saturn [sat´urn] *n* the ancient Roman god of agriculture; the second largest planet in the solar system, with three rings revolving about it.—*n pl* **Saturnā´lia**, the annual festival in honor of Saturn in ancient Rome; **saturnālia**, an orgy; a celebration of unrestrained licence.—*adjs* **Saturnā´lian**, pertaining to the Saturnalia; riotously merry; dissolute; **Satur´nian**, (*arch*) pertaining to Saturn, whose fabulous reign was called 'the golden age'; of, or influenced by the planet Saturn; **sat´urnine**, born under or influenced astrologically by the planet Saturn; cold or steady in mood; slow to act; gloomy, surly. [L *Sāturnus*—*serĕre*, *setum*, to sow.]

satyr [sat´ėr] *n* a sylvan deity, represented as part man and part goat, and extremely wanton; a lecherous man; one having satyriasis.—*n* **satyriasis**, abnormal sexual craving in the male.—*adj* **satyr´ic**, pertaining to satyrs. [L *satyrus*—Gr *satyros*.]

sauce [sös] *n* a liquid or soft dressing poured over food; anything that gives relish; stewed or preserved fruit eaten with other food or as a dessert; (*inf*) impudence.—*vt* to add or give sauce to; to make piquant or pleasant.—*ns* **sauce´boat**, a low boat-shaped pitcher for serving sauces or gravies; **sauce´pan**, a small deep cooking pan with a handle. [Fr *sauce*—L *salsa*—*sallĕre, salsum*, to salt—*sāl*, salt.]

saucer [sö´sėr] *n* a shallow dish, esp one placed under a tea or coffee cup; anything of like shape. [OFr *saussiere*—Low L *salsārium*—L *salsa*, sauce.]

saucy [sö´si] *adj* (*comparative* **sau´cier**, *superlative* **sau´ciest**) pert, bold, forward; rude, impudent.—*adv* **sau´cily**.—*n* **sau´ciness**. [**sauce**.]

sauerkraut [sowr´krowt] *n* chopped cabbage fermented in brine. [Ger 'sour cabbage.']

sauna [sow´na, sö´na] *n* (a building or room equipped for) a Finnish bath with exposure to hot, dry air. [Finn.]

saunter [sön´tėr] *vi* to wander about idly, to loiter, to stroll.—*n* a leisurely stroll.—*n* **saun´terer**.

saurian [sö´ri-ȧn] *n* a group (Sauria) of scaly reptiles including the lizards; formerly including the crocodile and certain extinct reptiles, as the dinosaur.—*adj* pertaining to, or of the nature of a saurian. [Gr *sauros*, a lizard.]

sausage [sos´ij] *n* chopped meat, esp pork, seasoned and stuffed in a tube of gut or other casing. [Fr *saucisse*—Low L *salsīcia*—L *salsus*, salted.]

sauté [sō´tā] *adj* fried lightly and quickly.—*vt* to fry in a small amount of fat.—*n* a sautéed dish. [Fr.]

sauterne [sō-tûrn´] *n* a sweet, full-bodied white wine from the Bordeaux region of France; a semidry to semisweet American white wine that is a blend of various grapes. [*Sauternes*, in France.]

savage [sav´ij] *adj* in a state of nature; wild (of an animal); uncivilized; ferocious; primitive.—*n* a member of a primitive society; a brutal, fierce, or cruel person.—*adv* **sav´agely**.—*ns* **sav´ageness; sav´agery**, the condition of a savage; an act of cruelty or violence; an uncivilized state. [OFr *salvage*—L *silvāticus*, pertaining to the woods—*silva*, a wood.]

savanna, savannah [sa-van´a] *n* a treeless plain, esp in Florida; a tropical or subtropical grassland having scattered trees and drought-resistant undergrowth. [Sp *zavana* (now *sabana*).]

savant [sa´vā] *n* a learned man. [Fr, obs pr p of *savoir*, to know.]

save [sāv] *vt* to bring safe out of evil or danger; to rescue; to rescue (from); to protect, prevent the loss of; to keep, preserve (from); (*theol*) to deliver from the power of sin and from its consequences; to prevent waste of (eg time, energy); to use thriftily with a view to future need; to set aside for future use; to obviate the necessity of.—*vi* to avoid expense, waste, etc.; to store up money or goods; (*sports*) an action that keeps an opponent from scoring or winning.—*n* (*sports*) a saving play; (*baseball*) the action of a relief pitcher in successfully protecting a team's lead.—*prep* except; but.—*n* **sā´ver**, one who saves.—*adj* **sā´ving**, thrifty; making a reservation; redeeming; (*theol*) securing salvation.—*prep* excepting; without disrespect to.—*n* that which is saved; (*pl*) money kept for future use; the excess of income over expenditure.—*ns* **savings account**, a bank account on which interest is paid from which withdrawals can be made only by prescribed forms; **savings and loan association**, a cooperative association organized to hold savings of members in the form of dividend bearing shares and to invest chiefly in home mortgage loans; **savings bank**, a bank organized to hold funds of depositors in interest bearing accounts and to make long-term investments (as in property); **savings bond**, a nontransferable registered US bond issued in denominations of $50 to $10,000. [Fr *sauver*—Low L *salvāre*—L *salvus*, safe.]

savior, saviour [sā´vyȯr] *n* one who saves from destruction or danger; **Savior, Saviour**, Jesus Christ. [ME *sauveur*—OFr *sauvëour*—L *salvātor*—*salūs*, -*ūtis*, health, well-being, safety.]

savoir faire [sav-wär-fer´] *n* the faculty of knowing just what to do and how to do it in any situation. [Fr.]

savor, savour [sā´vȯr] *n* taste or smell of something; characteristic flavor; distinctive quality.—*vi* to have a specified taste, smell, or quality.—*vt* to give flavor to; to enjoy; to discern or appreciate the distinctive quality of.—*adj* **sā´vory, sā´voury**, having savor, of good savor or relish.—*n* **sā´voriness**. [Fr *saveur*—L *sapor*—*sapĕre*, to taste.]

savoy cabbage [sa-voi´] *n* a cabbage with large close head and wrinkled leaves.—*n* **Savoyard** [sav´oi-ärd] a devotee, performer, or producer of the comic operas of W S Gilbert and A S Sullivan. [Fr *Savoie, Savoyard.*]

savvy [sav´ē] *n* (*slang*) shrewdness or understanding. [Sp *sabe* (*usted*), do (you) know?]

saw[1] [sö] *pa t* of **see**.

saw[2] [sö] *n* an instrument for cutting, formed of a blade, band, or disk of thin steel, with a toothed edge.—*vt* to cut with a saw.—*vi* to use a saw.—*pt* **sawed**; *pt p* **sawed** or **sawn**.—*n* **saw´dust**, dust or fine particles of wood, etc., made in sawing.—*adj* **sawed´ off´**, short or shortened.—*ns* **saw´fish**, any of several rays (family Pristidae) with a flattened bony beak toothed on the edges; **saw´horse**, a support for wood while it is being sawn; **saw´mill**, a mill or machine for sawing logs.—*adj* **saw´-toothed**, having notches along the edge like the teeth of a saw.—*n* **saw´yer**, one who saws timber. [OE *saga*; Ger *säge*.]

saw[3] [sö] *n* a saying; a proverb. [OE *sagu*—*secgan*, to say.]

saxhorn [saks´hörn] *n* a family of brass instruments with three upright valves standing in a tube of various lengths according to range, having a conical tube and cup-shaped mouthpiece.—*n* **saxtuba**, the bass saxhorn. [Invented by Antoine or Adolphe *Sax* (1814–1894), Belgian maker of musical instruments.]

saxifrage [sak´si-frij] *n* a genus (*Saxifraga*) of chiefly perennial herbs with often showy flowers and usu. basal, tufted leaves. [L *saxifraga*, spleenwort—*saxum*, a stone, *frangĕre*, to break.]

Saxon [saks´ȯn] *n* one of a North German people that conquered part of Britain in the 5th and 6th centuries.—*adj* pertaining to the Saxons. [L *Saxŏnēs* (pl), of Gmc origin; cf OE *Seaxe*; Ger *Sachsen*.]

saxophone [sak´sō-fōn] *n* a metal woodwind instrument with a conical bore, using a single reed, available in six sizes, played in bands. [*Sax* (see **saxhorn**), the inventor, Gr *phōnē*, the voice.]

say [sā] *vt* to utter (a word, etc., eg *to say Yes*); to state in words; to assert, affirm, declare; to tell (eg *to say one's mind*); to go through in recitation or repetition (eg prayers); to estimate; to assume.—*vi* to make a statement; to affirm.—*pt, pt p* **said** [sed]; 2d sing pr indic **sayst** [sāst], **sayest** [sā´ist]; 3d sing **says** [sez], (*arch*) **saith** [seth].—*n* a remark; a speech; what one wants to say; opportunity of speech; a voice, part, or influence, in decision; authority, as to make a final decision, often with *the*.—*n* **say´ing**, an expression; a maxim, proverb, or adage; **say-´so´** (*inf*) (one's) word, assurance, etc.; (*inf*) right of decision.—**that is to say**, in other words. [OE *secgan* (*sægde, gesægd*); ON *segja*, Ger *sagen*.]

scab [skab] *n* a crust formed over a sore; any of various diseases of plants caused by bacteria or fungi, characterized by crustaceous spots; one of the spots; scabies of domestic animals; a worker who refuses to join a union or who replaces a striking worker.—*adjs* **scabb´ed**, affected or covered with scabs; diseased with the scab; **scabb´y**, scabbed. [App from an ON equivalent of OE *sceabb*, influenced by association with L *scabiēs*—*scabĕre*, to scratch.]

scabbard [skab´ärd] *n* the case in which the blade of a sword is kept; a sheath. [ME *scauberc*, prob through OFr—OHG *scala*, a scale, *bergan*, to protect.]

scabies [skā´bi-ēz] *n* a contagious, itching skin disease caused by a mite (*Sarcoptes scabei*) that burrows under the skin to lay its eggs.—*adj* **scab´ious**, scabby, resembling scabs. [L *scabiēs*—*scabĕre*, to scratch.]

scabious [skā´bi-ùs] *n* any plant of a genus (*Scabiosa*) of the teasel family, some of which were long thought to cure scaly eruptions. [L *scabiōsus*—*scabiēs*, the itch.]

scabrous [skab´rùs] *adj* bristly, rough; indecent; shocking. [L *scaber*, rough.]

scaffold [skaf´old] *n* a temporary erection for men at work on a building; a raised platform, esp for the execution of a criminal; a platform at a height above ground or floor level; a supporting framework.—*n* **scaff´olding**, a system of scaffolds; materials for scaffolds. [OFr *escadafault* (Fr *échafaud*).]

scalar *See* **scale** (1).

scalawag, scallywag [skal´ē-wag] *n* a rascal. [Ety unknown.]

scald [sköld] *vt* to injure with hot liquid; to heat almost to boiling point; to use boiling liquid on; to heat short of boiling.—*n* a burn caused by hot liquid. [OFr *escalder* (Fr *échauder*)—Low L *excaldāre*, to bathe in warm water—*ex*, from, *calidus*, warm, hot.]

scale[1] [skāl] *n* (*obs*) a ladder; a graduated measure; any instrument so marked; (*mus*) a sequence of tones, rising or falling in pitch, according to a system of intervals; the proportion that a map, etc bears to the thing it represents; a series of degrees classified by size, amount, etc.; relative scope of an activity or size, grandeur, of a production.—*vt* to go up or over; to change in fixed ratio or proportion (*often with* **up** *or* **down**).—*adjs* **scā´lable**, that can be scaled or climbed; **scāl´ar**, having an uninterrupted series of steps; graduated; capable of being represented by a point on a scale; of a scalar or scalar product.—*n* (*physics*) a quantity, such as mass or time, which has magnitude, but does not involve any concept of direction; (*math*) a quantity fully described by a number; (*math*) in vector analysis, an undirected quantity.—*n* **scalar product**, a real number that is the product of the lengths of two vectors and the cosine of the angle between them. [L *scāla*, a ladder—*scandĕre*, to mount.]

scale[2] [skāl] *n* a small, thin plate on a fish or reptile; a thin layer.—*vt* to clear of scales; to peel off in thin layers.—*vi* to come off in thin layers or flakes.—*adjs* **scaled**, having scales; covered with scales; **scale´less**, without scales; **scal´y**, covered with scales; like scales; formed of scales.—*n* **scal´iness**. [ME *scāle*—OFr *escale*, husk, of Gmc origin.]

scale[3] [skāl] *n* either pan or tray of a balance; (*pl*) a beam supported freely in the center having two pans of equal weight suspended at each end; an instrument or machine for weighing; **Scales**, the constellation Libra, one of the signs of the zodiac.—*vt* to weigh in scales.—*vi* to have a specified weight on scales.—**turn the scales**, to decide or settle. [ON *skāl*, bowl; cf OE *sceale*, shell, Du *schaal*, Ger *schale*.]

scalene [skālēn´, skā´lēn] *adj* (*geom*) having three unequal sides.—*n* a scalene triangle. [Gr *skalēnos*, uneven.]

scall [sköl] *n* a scabby disorder of the scalp. [ON *skalli*, bald head.]

scallop [skal´ọp, skol´ọp] *n* a marine bivalve mollusk (family Pectinidae) having the edge of its shell in the form of a series of curves; one of a series of curves in the edge of anything.—*vt* to cut into scallops or curves; to cook by baking in a scallop shell, or utensil of comparable shape, with a milk sauce, breadcrumbs, etc. [OFr *escalope*; of Gmc origin.]

scalp [skalp] *n* the outer covering of the skull, usu covered with hair.—*vt* to cut or tear the scalp from; (*inf*) to buy (theater tickets, etc.) and resell them at higher prices.—*n* **scalp lock**, a long tuft of hair left unshorn by some No American Indians. [ME *scalp*; perh Scand; cf ON *skālpr*, sheath.]

scalpel [skalp´ėl] *n* a small straight, thin knife used esp for surgery. [L *scalpellum*, dim of *scalprum*, a knife—*scalpĕre*, to engrave.]

scaly *See* **scale** (2).

scamp[1] [skamp] *n* a rascal; a playful young person.—*vi* **scam´per**, to run in alarm or haste; to run gaily.—*n* a hurried or playful run or movement.—*adj* **scam´pish**, rascally. [OFr *escamper*, or It *scampare*, to decamp—L *ex*, from, *campus*, field; cf **decamp**.]

scamp[2] [skamp] *vt* to do, execute, perfunctorily, without thoroughness. [Perh ON *skemma*, to shorten.]

scampi [skam´pē] *n* a large shrimp or prawn, often prepared with a garlic-flavored sauce. [It, pl of *scampo*.]

scan [skan] *vt* to analyze the structure of (verse) by marking the metrical feet; to examine carefully, to scrutinize; to cast an eye quickly over; (*television*) to pass a beam over every part of in turn; (*radar*) to detect by rotating the beam; to check (as a magnetic tape or punch card) for recorded data by means of a mechanical or electronic device; to examine successive small portions of (as an object) with a sensing device (as a photometer or a beam of radiation); to make a scan of (as the human body).—*vi* to scan verse; to conform to a metrical pattern.—*pr p* **scann´ing**; *pt, pt p* **scanned**.—*n* **scann´er**, a device that monitors a process or condition and may initiate corrective action; a device for sensing recorded data; a device used for scanning (as in television, facsimile, or radar); a device (as a CAT scanner) for making scans of the human body; **scan´sion**, the analysis of verse to show its meter. [Fr *scander*, to scan—L *scandĕre, scansum*, to climb.]

scandal [skan´d(à)l] *n* anything that brings discredit on the agent or agents by offending the moral feelings of the community; a feeling of moral outrage, or the talk it gives rise to; ignominy, disgrace; malicious gossip, slander.—*vt* **scan´dalize**, to give scandal or offense to, to shock; to disgrace.—*vi* to talk scandal.—*ns* **scan´dalmong´er**, one who spreads stories of scandal; **scan´dalmongering**.—*adj* **scan´dalous**, causing scandal; shameful; spreading slander.—*adv* **scan´dalously**.—*n* **scan´dalousness**. [L *scandalum*—Gr *skandalon*, a stumbling-block.]

Scandinavian [skan-di-nā´vi-ȧn] *adj* of Scandinavia, the region comprising Norway, Sweden, and Denmark, and sometimes, Iceland; of the North Germanic languages.—*n* a native of Scandinavia; a person of Scandinavian descent; the North Germanic languages. [L *Scandināvia* (from Gmc word which did not have *n* before *d*), applied to the southern part of the peninsula and its shortened form *Scandia*.]

scandium [skan´di-ųm] *n* a metallic element (symbol Sc; at wt 45.0; at no 21). [L *Scandia*; see **Scandinavian**.]

scansion *See* **scan**.

scant [skant] *adj* not full or plentiful, scarcely sufficient, deficient.—*adj* **scan´ty**, scant; meager, deficient.—*adv* **scant´ily**.—*n* **scant´iness**. [ON *skamt*, neut of *skammr*, short.]

scape[1] [skāp] *vti* to escape. [A contr of **escape**.]

scape[2] [skāp] *n* a peduncle, quite or nearly leafless, arising from the middle of a rosette of leaves, and bearing a flower, several flowers, or a crowded inflorescence; the shaft of an animal part (as an antenna or feather).—*adj* **scāp´ose**, bearing a scape; like a scape. [L *scāpus*, a shaft.]

scapegoat [skāp´gōt] *n* (*Bible*) a goat on which, once a year, the Jewish high-priest laid symbolically the sins of the people, and which was then allowed to escape into the wilderness; one who is made to bear the misdeeds of another; one that is the object of irrational hostility. [**scape** (1) + **goat**.]

scapegrace [skāp´grās] *n* an incorrigible scamp. [**scape** (1) + **grace**.]

scapula [skap´ū-la] *n* the shoulder blade.—*adj* **scap´ūlar**, pertaining to the shoulder; the scapula, or scapulars.—*n* a long strip of cloth with an opening for the head, worn hanging before and behind over a monastic habit; a pair of small cloth squares joined by shoulder tapes worn under the clothing on the breast and back as a sacramental garment; a scapula; one of the feathers covering the base of a bird's wing. [L *scapulae*, the shoulder-blades.]

scar[1] [skär] *n* the mark left by a wound, sore or injury; any mark or blemish resulting from damage or wear.—*vt* to mark with a scar.—*vi* to become scarred.—*pr p* **scarr´ing**; *pt, pt p* **scarred**. [OFr *escare*—L *eschara*—Gr *escharā*, a scar produced by burning.]

scar[2] [skär] *n* a protruding or isolated rock; a steep rocky eminence; a bare place on the side of a mountain. [App ON *sker*—*skera*, to cut.]

scarab [skar´ab] *n* any of a family (Scarabaedae) of stout-bodied beetles (as a dung beetle), esp the sacred beetle of the ancient Egyptians; a gem, cut in the form of a beetle. [L *scarabaeus*.]

scaramouch, scaramouche [skar´ȧ-mowch] *n* a bragging, cowardly buffoon. [Fr,—It *Scaramuccia*, a stock character in Italian comedy.]

scarce [skārs] *adj* not plentiful; hard to get; rare, not common.—*adv* **scarce´ly**, hardly, only just; probably not or certainly not.—*ns* **scarce´ness; scarc´ity**, state of being scarce; deficiency; rareness; want, famine.—**make oneself scarce**, to go or stay away. [OFr *escars*, niggardly—L *excerptus*, pt p of *excerpere*—*ex*, out of, *carpĕre*, to pick.]

scare [skār] *vt* to startle, to affright; to drive or keep (off) by frightening.—*vi* to become frightened.—*n* a sudden fear.—*ns* **scare´crow**, something frightening but harmless; a human figure made with sticks, old clothes, etc. put in a field to scare birds from crops; a skinny and ragged person; **scare´monger**, one who habitually causes panic by spreading or initiating alarming rumors.—**scare up** (*inf*) to produce or gather quickly. [ME *skerre*—ON *skirra*, to avoid—*skiar*, shy.]

scarf[1] [skärf] *n* a light piece of material worn loosely on the shoulders or about the neck or head; a long, narrow covering for a table, etc. [Perh OFr *escarpe* (Fr *écharpe*), sash.]

scarf[2] [skärf] *vt* to join two pieces of timber endwise, so that they may appear to be used as one. [Perh Scand.]

scarfskin [skärf´skin] *n* skin, esp that forming the cuticle of a nail.

scarify [skar´i-fī] *vt* to make a number of scratches or slight cuts in (as the skin); to lacerate the feelings of; to break up the surface of (ground); to soften the wall (of a hard seed) to hasten germination.—*pt, pt p* **scar´ified**.—*n* **scarificā´tion**, act of scarifying. [L *scarīficāre, -ātum*—Gr *skarīphaesthai*—*skarīphos*, an etching tool.]

scarlatina [skär-là-tē´na] *n* scarlet fever. [It *scarlattina*.]

scarlet [skär´lėt] *n* a brilliant red; a brilliant red cloth or garb.—*adj* of the color called scarlet; glaringly offensive; whorish.—*ns* **scar´let fē´ver**, an acute contagious disease caused by streptococci marked by fever, sore throat and a scarlet rash; **scar´let runn´er**, a bean (*Phaseolus coccineus*) with scarlet flowers which runs up any support grown widely as an ornamental and in Great Britain as a preferred food bean. [OFr *escarlate* (Fr *écarlate*), thought to be from Pers *saqalāt*, scarlet cloth.]

scarp [skärp] *n* the inner side of a ditch below a fortification; a line of cliffs produced by faulting or erosion; a low steep slope along a beach caused by wave erosion.—*vt* to cut into a scarp. [It *scarpa*.]

scathe [skāTH] *n* damage, injury.—*vt* to scorch, sear; to denounce witheringly.—*adj* **scā´thing**, damaging; vehement, bitter (eg of criticism).—*adv* **scā´thingly**. [ON *skathe*; cf OE *sceatha*, an injurer; Ger *schade*, injury.]

scatter [skat´ėr] *vt* to disperse widely; to throw loosely about, to strew, to sprinkle; to dispel; to reflect or disperse irregularly (waves or particles).—*vi* to disperse; to occur at random.—*n* scattering; a sprinkling; extent of scattering.—*adj* **scatt´ered**, dispersed irregularly, widely, or here and there.—*ns* **scatt´ering**, dispersion; the deflection of particles as a result of collisions with other particles; **scatt´erbrain**, one incapable of sustained attention or thought.—*adj* **scatt´er-brained**, erratic.—*n* **scatt´er rug**, a small rug. [Origin obscure.]

scavenger [skav´en-jėr] *n* one who gathers things discarded by others; any animal that eats refuse and decaying matter; a chemical substance that acts to make innocuous or remove an unwanted substance.—Also *vti*. [Orig *scavager*, an inspector of goods for sale, and also of the streets; from *scavage*, duty on goods for sale.]

scenario [sė-ner´ē-ō] *n* the working script of a motion picture, television play, etc.; an outline of future development or of a plan to be followed, real or imagined. [It,—L *scēna*, Gr *skēnē*, a tent, a background.]

scene [sēn] *n* the place of action in a play, or a story, or that of an actual occurrence; a division of a play; an episode; a dramatic or stagy incident, esp an uncomfortable, untimely, or unseemly display of hot feelings; a landscape, picture or a place of action; a view, spectacle; (*inf*) the locale for a specified activity.—*ns* **scē´nery**, painted screens, backdrops, etc., used on the stage to represent places, as in a play; prospects of beautiful, picturesque, or impressive country; general aspect of a landscape; **scene´shift´er**, one employed to set and remove the scenery in a theater.—*adj* **scenic** [sē´nik], pertaining to scenery.—*n* **scenog´raphy**, the art of representation in perspective, esp as applied to stage scenery.—*adjs* **scēnograph´ic**, drawn in perspective.—**scenic railway**, a railway on a small scale, running through representations of picturesque scenery.—**behind the scenes**, out of public view; in secret; in a position to see the hidden workings. [L *scēna*—Gr *skēnē*, a tent, a stage.]

scent [sent] *vt* to discern by the sense of smell; to have some suspicion of; to perfume.—*n* a perfume; an odor; the sense of smell; an odor left by an animal, by which it is tracked; a mixture prepared for use as a lure in hunting or fishing; a course of pursuit or discovery.—*adjs* **scent´ed**, perfumed; having or exhaling an odor; **scent´less**, having no scent or smell. [Fr *sentir*—L *sentīre*, to feel, perceive.]

scepter [sep´tėr] *n* the staff or baton borne by kings as an emblem of authority; royal power.—*adj* **scep´tered**, bearing a scepter; regal. [L *scēptrum*—Gr *skēptron*—*skēptein*, to lean.]

schedule [sked´ūl] *n* (*obs*) a slip or scroll with writing; a list, inventory, or table; (*obs*) a supplementary, explanatory, or appended document; a timetable, plan, program or scheme; a timed plan for a project.—*vt* to form into, or place in, a schedule or list; to plan, appoint, arrange for a certain time.—**Scheduled Castes**, the groups of people in India formerly untouchables. [OFr *cedule*—LL *sc(h)edula*, dim of *scheda*, a strip of papyrus—Gr *schedē*.]

scheme [skēm] *n* (*arch*) a diagram of positions, esp of planets; a diagram; a system; a plan of proposed action, a project; a plan pursued secretly, insidiously or by intrigue.—*vti* to devise or plot.—*adj* **schēmat´ic**, of or like a scheme, diagram.—*n* **schē´mer**, one who forms schemes, esp a habitual plotter, intriguer.—*adj* **schē´ming**, given to forming schemes, intriguing. [Gr *schēma*, form, from root of *echein* (fut *schēsein*), to have.]

scherzo [skėr´tsō] *n* (*mus*) a lively busy movement in triple time. [It,—Gmc; cf Ger *scherz*, jest.]

schipperke [ship´ėr-kė] *n* a Belgian breed of dogs with a solid black, short heavy coat, originally watchdogs on barges. [Du, "little boatman".]

schism [sizm skizm], *n* division, separation; discord, disharmony; a breach or division, esp in the unity of a church because of a difference of opinion, doctrine, etc.; the offense of promoting schism.—*n* **schismat´ic**, one who creates or takes part in schism.—*adjs* **schismat´ic, -al**, tending to, or guilty of schism.—*adv* **schismat´ically**. [Gr *schisma*, a cleft—*schizein*, to split.]

schist [shist] *n* a metamorphic crystalline rock easily split into layers.—*adj* **schist´ose**, like schist. [Fr *schiste*—Gr *schistos*—*schizein*, to split.]

schizocarp [ski´zō-kärp] *n* a dry fruit, formed from more than one carpel, and separating when ripe into a number of one-seeded parts which do not dehisce. [Gr *schizein*, to split, *karpos*, fruit.]

schizoid [skit´soid] *adj* showing qualities of a schizophrenic personality. [Gr *schizein*, to cleave, *eidos*, form.]

schizophrenia [skit-zō-frē´ni-a] *n* a mental disorder marked by introversion, loss of connection between thoughts, feelings and actions, and by delusions; the presence of mutually contradictory parts or qualities.—*adj, n* **schizophrenic** [-fren´ik]. [Gr *schizein*, to split, *phrēn*, mind.]

schmaltz, schmalz [shmölts] *See* **shmalz**.

schnapps [shnaps] *n* a strong alcoholic liquor, esp Holland gin, Hollands. [Ger *schnapps*, a dram.]

schnorkel [shnör´kėl] *See* **snorkel**.

scholar [skol´ȧr] *n* a pupil, a disciple, a student; an educated person; one whose learning is extensive and exact; the holder of a scholarship.—*adj* **schol´arly**, of, characteristic of, suitable to learned persons; learned, academic.—*n* **schol´arship**, the quality of knowledge a student shows; the systematized knowledge of a scholar; a gift of money to a student (as by a foundation, college, etc.). [OE *scōlere*—LL *scholāris*—L *schŏla*; see **school** (1).]

scholastic [skol-as´tik] *adj* pertaining to schools or scholars, esp to high school or secondary school; **Scholastic**, relating to Scholasticism; suggesting a scholastic, esp in subtlety, aridity, or pedantry.—*n* a schoolman; one who adheres to the method of subtleties of the medieval schools.—*n* **scholas´ticism** [-tis-izm] a close adherence to the traditional teachings of a school or sect or pedantic adherence to scholarly methods; **Scholasticism**, all the intellectual activity carried out in the medieval schools, based on the concept of a Christian society, its method of reasoning derived from the Greek philosophers, esp Aristotle. [Gr *scholastikos*—*schŏlē*, leisure, school.]

scholium [skō´li-um] *n* an explanatory note such as grammarians wrote in ancient manuscripts; an observation subjoined but not essential to a train of reasoning;—*pl* **schō´lia, schō´liums**.—*n* **schō´liast**, a writer of scholia, an annotator, a commentator.—*adj* **scholias´tic**. [Gr *schŏlion, schŏliastēs*—*schŏlē*, leisure, school.]

school[1] [skōōl] *n* a place or institution, with its buildings, for instruction and learning; all of its teachers and students; a regular session of teaching; formal education, schooling; a particular division of a university; a group following the same beliefs, methods, etc.—*vt* to train; to teach; to discipline or control.—*ns* **school´board**, a group of people in charge of local public schools; **school´boy**, a boy attending a school; **school´fell´ow**, a schoolmate; **schoolgirl**, a girl attending school; **school´house**, a building used as a school, esp as an elementary school; **school´ing**, instruction in school; the teaching and exercise of horse and rider in the formal techniques of equitation; **school´man**, a medieval philosopher or theologian; a scholastic; esp one skilled in disputation; **school´master**, a man who teaches school; an edible snapper (*Lutjanus apodus*) of the tropical Atlantic and the Gulf of Mexico; **school´mate**, a companion at school; **school´mistress**, a woman who teaches school; **school´room**, a room in which pupils are taught, as in a school. [OE *scōl*—L *schŏla*—Gr *schŏlē*, leisure, school.]

school[2] [skōōl] *n* a shoal of fish, whales, or other aquatic animals of one kind swimming together. [Du *school*; cf **shoal** (1).]

schooner [skōōn´ėr] *n* a sailing vessel, generally two-masted, rigged with fore-and-aft sails on both masts; a large beer glass; a large sherry glass. [Early 18th century (Massachusetts) *skooner, scooner*, said to be from a dial Eng word *scoon*, to skim.]

schottische [shot´ish, sho-tēsh´] *n* a round dance, or dance tune, like the polka. [Ger (*der*) *schottische* (*tanz*), (the) Scottish (dance).]

schuss [shŏŏs] *vi* to ski directly down a slope at high speed.—Also *n*.—*n* **schuss´bōōmer**, a skier, esp one who schusses expertly. [Ger.]

sciatic [sī-at´ik] *adj* of, or in the region of, the hip.—*n* **sciat´ica**, pain along the sciatic nerve, esp in the back of the thigh; (*loosely*) pain in the lower back, buttocks, hips, or adjacent parts.—*n* **sciatic nerve**, either of the pair of the largest nerves in the body arising from the pelvic region and passing down the back of the thigh. [Low L *sciaticus*—Gr *ischion*, hip-joint.]

science [sī´ens] *n* knowledge ascertained by observation and experiment, critically tested, systematized, and brought under general principles; a branch of such knowledge; skill or technique.—*adj* **scientif´ic**, of or dealing with science; based on, or using the principles and methods of science; systematic and exact.—*adv* **scientif´ically**.—*n* **sci´entist**, a specialist in science, as in chemistry, biology, etc.—**science fiction**, highly imaginative fiction typically involving some actual or projected scientific phenomena. [Fr,—L *scientia*—*sciēns, -entis*, pr p of *scīre*, to know.]

sci-fi [sī´fī] science fiction. [Clipped form.]

scilicet [sil´i-set] *adv* to wit, namely. [L = *scīre licet*, it is permitted to know.]

scilla [sil´a] *n* any of a genus (*Scilla*) of Old World bulbous herbs of the lily family with narrow basal leaves and pink, blue, or white racemes. [Gr *skilla*, a sea-onion, squill.]

scimitar [sim´i-tȧr] *n* a short, single-edged curved sword, broadset at the point end, used by the Turks and Persians. [Perh through Fr *cimeterre* or It *scimitarra*—Per *shamshīr*.]

scintilla [sin-til´a] *n* a spark; a trace.—*vi* **scin´tillate**, to spark; to sparkle, twinkle; to talk wittily.—*vt* to throw off as a spark or as sparkling flashes.—*ns* **scintillā´tion**. [L, a spark.]

sciolism [sī´ō-lizm] *n* superficial pretentious knowledge.—*n* **sci´olist**. [L *sciolus*, dim of *scius*, knowing—*scīre*, to know.]

scion [sī´ón] *n* a cutting or twig for grafting; a young member of a family; a descendant. [OFr *sion, cion*.]

scirrhus [s(k)ir´us or sir´us] *n* a scirrhous tumor.—*adj* **scirr´hous**, of a hard, slow-growing malignant tumor having much fibrous tissue. [Gr *skirros, skīros*, a tumour, *skīrōs*, hard.]

scissors [siz´órz] *n pl* a cutting instrument with two blades, whose cutting edges slide past each other; a gymnastic feat in which the leg movements resemble the opening and closing of scissors.—*vt* **scissor**, to cut, cut off, or cut out with scissors. [OFr *cisoires*—LL *cīsōrium*, a cutting instrument—L *caedĕre, caesum*, to cut.]

sclerosis [sklėr-ō´sis] *n* pathological hardening of body tissue; a disease marked by sclerosis; hardening of plant cell walls.—*n* **scler´a**, the dense white coat enclosing the eyeball except that part covered by the cornea.—*adjs* **scler´al**, of the sclera; affected with sclerosis.—*adj* **sclerŏt´ic**.—*n* the sclera. [Gr *sklēros*, hard.]

scoff[1] [skof] *vti* to mock or jeer (at).—*n* an expression of scorn; mockery; an object of derision.—*ns* **scoff´er; scoff´law**, (*inf*) one who flouts traffic laws, liquor laws, etc.—*adv* **scoff´ingly**. [Cf obs Dan *skof*, jest.]

scoff[2] [skof] *vt* (*dial* and *slang*) to devour; to plunder. [Scot scaff, food, riff-raff.]

scold [skōld] *n* one who scolds habitually; a woman who disturbs the public peace by noisy, quarrelsome, abusive behavior.—*vi* to find fault noisily.—*vt* to censure angrily.—*ns* **scold´er; scold´ing**, a harsh reprimand. [App ON *skāld*, poet (through an intermediate sense, lampooner). See **scald** (2).]

scollop *See* **scallop**.

sconce[1] [skons] *n* a detached defensive work. [Du *schans*.]

sconce[2] [skons] *n* a candlestick with a handle or on a bracket fixed to a wall; an electric light fixture patterned on a candle sconce. [OFr *esconse*—Low L *absconsa*, a dark-lantern—*abscondĕre*, to hide.]

scone [skōn] a rich quick bread cut int usu. triangular shapes and cooked on a griddle or baked on a sheet. [Perh from Du *schoon* (*brot*), fine (bread).]

scoop [skōōp] *n* any of various small, shovellike utensils, as for taking up flour, ice cream, etc.; the deep bucket of a dredge, etc.; the act of scooping or the amount scooped up at one time; (*inf*) advantage gained by being first in publishing a news item; (*inf*) such a news item.—*vt* to take up or out with a scoop; to hollow (out); (*inf*) to publish news before (a rival). [Prob partly Middle Du *schôpe*, bailingvessel, partly Middle Du *schoppe*, shovel.]

scoot [skōōt] *vti* (*inf*) to hurry (off).—*n* **scoot´er**, a child's two-wheeled vehicle with steering handle, propelled by kicking the ground; a development of it driven by a motor (also motor scooter). [Prob conn **shoot**.]

scope [skōp] *n* extent of the mind's grasp; range, field of activity, extent of field covered; room for action or opportunity (for activity—eg *his instructions gave him no scope, gave no scope for originality*); any of various instruments for viewing (eg microscope, telescope, oscilloscope, etc.). [Gr *skopeein*, to look at.]

scopolamine [sko-pol´ȧ-mēn (also -min)] *n* a poisonous alkaloid obtained from various plants (esp genus *Scopolia*) of the nightshade family, used as a truth serum and with morphine as a sedative in surgery and obstetrics.—Also **hyoscine**. [*Scopoli* (1723–88), Italian naturalist.]

scorbutic [skör-bū´tik] *adj* pertaining to, resembling, or affected by, scurvy. [Low L *scorbūticus*—*scorbūtus*, scurvy; of Gmc origin.]

scorch [skörch] *vt* to burn slightly; to parch; to singe; to wither with scorn, censure, etc.—*vi* to be burned on the surface; to travel at great and usu. excessive speed; to cause intense heat or mental anguish.—*n* a superficial burn; a browning of plant tissues usu. from disease or heat.—*n* **scorch´er**, a very hot day.—*adj* **scorch´ing**, burning superficially; bitterly sarcastic, scathing. [Perh—ME *skorken*; cf ON *skorpna*, to shrivel; prob affected by OFr *escorcher*, to flay.]

score [skōr, skör] *n* a notch; an incised line; a line drawn to indicate deletion or to define a position; a copy of a musical composition, showing all the parts for the instruments or voices; a grievance one wishes to settle; a reason or motive; (*inf*) the real facts; an account of charges; the total or record of points in a game or examination; a point gained; a set of twenty; (*pl*) an indefinitely large number.—*vt* to mark with notches or lines; to gain, or record, as points in a game; to evaluate, as in testing; (*mus*) to arrange in a score.—*vi* to make points, as in a game; to keep the score of a game; to gain an advantage, a success, etc.—*n* **scōr´er**, one who makes or keeps a score. [Late OE *scoru*—ON *skor, skora*; cf OE *scor*—*sceran* (pt p *scoren*), to shear.]

scoria [skō´ri-a] *n* dross or slag left after smelting ore; a piece of lava with steam holes;—*pl* **sco´riae**. [L,—Gr *skōriā*—*skōr*, dung.]

scorn [skörn] *n* extreme contempt; object of contempt.—*vt* to feel or express scorn for; to refuse with scorn.—*n* **scorn´er**.—*adj* **scorn´ful**.—*adv* **scorn´fully**. [OFr *escarn*, mockery; of Gmc orig; cf OHG *skern*, mockery.]

scorpion [skör´pi-ȯn] *n* any one of an order (Scorpionada) of animals belonging to the same class (arachnids) as spiders, with head and thorax united, pincers, four pairs of legs, and a segmented abdomen including a tail with a sting; something that incites to action like the sting of an insect.—*n* **Scor´pio**, a constellation and the 8th sign of the zodiac in astrology, operative from October 23 to November 21. [L *scorpiō, -ōnis*—Gr *skorpios*.]

scot [skot] *n* a payment; a share of a reckoning. [OE *scot, sceot*—*scēotan*, to shoot.]

Scot [skot] *n* a native or inhabitant of Scotland; one of a Celtic people who migrated from Ireland before the end of the 5th century; a person of Scotch descent. [OE *Scottas*, the Scots—LL *Scottus*.]

Scotch [skoch] *adj* a form of **Scottish**, or **Scots**, in common use though disapproved by many Scotsmen; the generally accepted form when applied to certain products or articles associated with Scotland as *Scotch whisky*; inclined to frugality.—*n* Scotch whisky.—*n* **Scotch broom**, a deciduous shrub (*Cytisus scoparius*) of western Europe, cultivated for its bright yellow or partly red flowers, which has become a pest in some areas. [From **Scottish**.]

scotch [skoch] *vt* to maim; stamp out (eg a rumor). [Origin unknown.]

Scotland Yard [skot´lȧnd yärd] *n* (strictly, *New* Scotland Yard) the headquarters of the London police, esp its detective bureau, the Criminal Investigation Department.

Scots [skots] *adj* Scottish (almost always used of money, manners, and law; preferably also of language and persons).—*n* the dialect of Lowland Scotland developed from the northern form of Middle English.—*n* **Scots´man**, a native or inhabitant of Scotland, the preferred term in Scotland. [Shortened form of ME *Scottis*, Scottish.]

Scottish [skot´ish] *adj* of Scotland, its people, or its English dialect.—*n* **Scottish terrier**, a breed of terrier with a large head and wiry hair.

scoundrel [skown´drėl] *n* a low mean blackguard, an utter rascal.—Also *adj.*—*adj* **scoun´drelly**, fit for or like a scoundrel. [Origin unknown.]

scour[1] [skowr] *vt* to clean by hard rubbing, as with abrasives; to clear out by a current of water.—*n* a place scoured by running water; scouring action (as of a glacier); (*inf*) dysentery, diarrhea; damage done by scouring action.—*n* **scour´er**. [OFr *escurer*—L *ex*, inten, and *cūrāre*, to take care of.]

scour[2] [skowr] *vt* to move quickly, esp in search.—*vt* to pass over quickly, or range over, as in search. [Perh ON *skūr*, storm; cf **shower**.]

scourge [skûrj] *n* a whip made of leather thongs; an instrument of punishment; a cause of widespread and great affliction.—*vt* to whip severely; to afflict or punish severely.—*n* **scour´ger**. [OFr *escorge*—L *excoriāre*, to flog—*corium*, leather.]

scouse [skows] *n* a native of Liverpool, England; the northern English dialect spoken in and around Liverpool. [Short for *lobscouse*.]

scout [skowt] *n* a person, plane, etc. sent to spy out the enemy's strength, actions, etc.; a person sent out to find new talent, survey a competitor, etc.; a Boy Scout or Girl Scout.—*vti* reconnoiter; to go in search of (something).—*ns* **scout´ing**, the act of one who scouts; the activities of the Boy Scouts or Girl Scouts; **scout´master**, the leader of a troop of Boy Scouts. [OFr *escoute*—*escouter*—L *auscultāre*, to listen—*auris*, the ear.]

scout[2] [skowt] *vt* to mock; to scorn.—*vi* to scoff. [Cf ON *skūta*, a taunt.]

scow [skow] *n* a large flat-bottomed boat, used chiefly to transport bulk materials, often towed by a tug. [Du *schouw*.]

scowl [skowl] *vi* to contract the brows in displeasure; to look gloomy.—*n* the contraction of the brows in displeasure. [Cf Du *skule*, to cast down the eyes, look sidelong.]

scrabble [skrab´l] *vt* to scramble; to scribble.—*vi* to scrape, scratch, etc. as though looking for something; to struggle.—*n* a scribble; a repeated scratching or clawing; a scramble. [Du *schrabbelen*, freq of *schrabben*, to scratch.]

scrag [skrag] *n* a scrawny person or animal; the lean end of a neck of mutton or veal; (*loosely*) neck.—*vt* to put to death by hanging; to throttle.—*adjs* **scragg´ed, scragg´y**, lean and gaunt.—**scragg´ly**, uneven, ragged, etc. in growth or form. [Cf Du *kragg*, Ger *kragen*, the neck.]

scram [skram] *vi* (*slang*) to get out, to go away at once.

scramble [skram´bl] *vi* to move or climb hastily on all fours; to scuffle or struggle for something; to move with urgency or panic.—*vt* to mix haphazardly; to stir (slightly beaten eggs) while cooking; to make (transmitted signals) unintelligible in transit.—*n* a hard climb or advance; a disorderly struggle as for something prized; a rapid emergency takeoff of fighter-interceptor planes; a jumble.—*n* **scram´bler**. [Cf the dialect word *scramb*, to rake together with the hands.]

scrap[1] [skrap] *n* a small piece; a fragment of discarded material; (*pl*) bits of food.—*adj* in the form of pieces, leftovers, etc.; used and discarded.—*vt* to consign to the scrapheap; to make into scraps;—*pr p* **scrapp´ing**; *pt, pt p* **scrapped**.—*ns* **scrap´book**, a book in which to mount clippings, etc.; **scrap´ heap**, a pile of discarded material or things.—*adj* **scrapp´y**, fragmentary; disconnected.—*n* **scrapp´iness**.—**not a scrap**, not in the least. [ON *skrap*, scraps.]

scrap[2] [skrap] *n* (*inf*) a fight or quarrel.—Also *vi*. [Origin unknown.]

scrape [skrāp] *vt* to rub with something sharp; to remove by drawing a sharp edge over; to gain or collect by laborious effort.—*vi* to scratch the ground or floor.—*n* an act or process of scraping; a mark made by scraping; backward movement of one foot in making a bow; a predicament that threatens disgrace or penalty.—*ns* **scrap´er**, an instrument used for scraping, esp the soles of shoes; **scrap´ing**, a piece scraped off.—**scrape a leg**, to make a low bow. [OE *scrapian*, or ON *skrapa*.]

scratch [skrach] *vt* to draw a sharp point over the surface of; to leave a mark on by so doing; to tear or dig with the claws; to write hurriedly; to withdraw (a contestant, etc.) from a competition; to strike out (writing, etc.).—*vi* to use the claws or nails in tearing or digging; to scrape.—*n* a mark or tear made by scratching; a slight wound; the line from which competitors start in a race.—*adj* improvised (as a *scratch crew*); receiving no handicap.—*n* **scratch´er**.—*adj* **scratch´y**, like scratches; likely to scratch; uneven; grating.—**from scratch**, from nothing; without advantage; **scratch someone's back**, to do someone a favor, esp in expectation of return; **scratch the surface**, to make a modest start; **up to scratch**, (*inf*) up to standard. [Perh ME *cracchen*, to scratch.]

scrawl [skröl] *vti* to mark or write irregularly or hastily, to scribble.—*n* irregular, often illegible handwriting.—*n* **scrawl´er**. [Origin obscure.]

scrawny [skrö´ni] *adj* gaunt and lean. [Cf Norw *skran*, lean.]

scream [skrēm] *vti* to cry out in a loud shrill voice, as in fear, pain, or immoderate mirth, to shriek.—*n* a shrill, sudden cry, as in fear or pain, a shriek; (*inf*) a very funny person or thing. [ME *scræmen*.]

scree [skrē] *n* loose debris on a rocky slope. [ON *skritha*, a landslip—*skrītha*, to slide.]

screech [skrēch] *vti* to utter (with) a harsh, shrill, and sudden cry.—*n* a harsh, shrill, and sudden cry.—*n* **screech´ owl**, any of numerous New World owls (genus *Otus*), esp a small N American owl (*O. asio*) with tufted feathers resembling ears. [ME *scrichen*.]

screed [skrēd] *n* a long and tedious discourse; an informal piece of writing; a leveling device drawn over freshly poured concrete. [OE *screade*.]

screen [skrēn] *n* that which shelters from danger or observation; that which protects from heat, cold, or the sun; a surface on which motion pictures, etc. are projected; the motion-picture industry or medium; a coarse mesh of wire used as a sieve; a frame covered with wire mesh; the surface on which an image appears in an electronic display (as in a television set, computer terminal, or radar receiver).—*vt* to shelter or conceal; to sift through a screen; to separate according to skills, etc.; to provide with a screen to keep out pests (as insects); to show (a motion picture) on a screen.—*vi* to appear on a motion-picture screen; to provide a screen in a game or sport.—*n* **screen´ing**, the refuse matter after sifting; metal or plastic mesh (as for window screens); a showing of a motion picture.

—*ns* **screen´play**, a story written in a form suitable for a motion picture; **screen´writer**, a writer of screenplays. [App related to OFr *escren* (Fr *écran*); cf Ger *schirm*.]

screw [skrōō] *n* a cylindrical or conical metal piece threaded in an advancing spiral, for fastening things by being turned; any spiral thing like this; anything having a helical thread or groove; a screw propeller; a turn of a screw; a twist; a wornout horse.—*vt* to fasten, tighten, compress, force, adjust, extort, by a screw or thumbscrew; a screwing motion, or as if by a screw; to summon up (courage, etc.; *with* **up**); to deprive or cheat out of something due.—*vi* to go together or come apart by being turned like a screw; to twist or turn with a writhing movement.—*ns* **screw´ball** (*baseball*) a pitch that spins and breaks in an opposite direction to a curve; a whimsical, eccentric or crazy person; **screw´driv´er**, an instrument for driving or turning screws; vodka and orange juice served with ice; **screw´ propell´er**, a propeller.—*adj* **screw´y** (*slang*), eccentric, slightly mad.—**put the screws on**, to coerce; **screw up** (*slang*), to bungle. [Earlier *scrue*; app—OFr *escroue*, of obscure origin.]

scribble [skrib´l] *vt* to scrawl, to write badly or carelessly (as regards handwriting or substance); to fill with worthless writing.—*vi* to write carelessly; to make meaningless marks suggestive of writing.—*n* careless writing; marks suggestive of writing; a hastily written letter, etc.—*n* **scribb´ler**, a petty author. [A freq of **scribe**.]

scribe [skrīb] *n* a public or official writer; (*Bible*) an expounder, jurist and teacher of the Mosaic and traditional law; a journalist.—*vt* to mark a line on by cutting or scratching with a pointed instrument.—*n* **scriber**, a sharp-pointed instrument used esp for marking off material (as wood or metal) to be cut. [L *scrība*—*scrībĕre*, to write.]

scrim [skrim] *n* a light, sheer, loosely woven cotton or linen cloth; such a cloth used as a stage backdrop.

scrimmage [skrim´ij] *n* (*football*) the play that follows the pass from center or a practice game.—*vi* to take part in a scrimmage.—**line of scrimmage**, an imaginary line along which the teams line up for play. [Prob corr of **skirmish**.]

scrimp [skrimp] *vti* to be sparing or frugal (with).—*adj* **scrimp´y**. [Cf Swed and Dan *skrumpen*, OE *scrimman*, to shrink.]

scrip[1] [skrip] *n* a short writing; a certificate of a right to receive something, as money. [A variant of **script**, but partly perh from **scrap**.]

scrip[2] [skrip] *n* (*arch*) a small bag, a satchel, a pilgrim's pouch. [Cf ON *skreppa*, a bag.]

script [skript] *n* an original document; a manuscript; the text of a stage play, screenplay or broadcast used in production or performance; a plan of action; print in imitation of handwriting; a set of characters used in writing a language.—*vt* to write a script for or from.—*n* **script´writer**. [L *scrīptum*—*scrībĕre*, to write.]

scriptorium [skrip-tō´, -tö´, ri-ùm] *n* a copying room, esp in a monastery. [L *scrīptōrium*—*scrībĕre*, to write.]

scripture [skrip´chùr] *n* any sacred writing; something written; **Scripture**, (often *pl*) the Jewish Bible or Old Testament; the Christian Bible or Old and New Testaments.—*adj* **scrip´tural**, contained in, or according to scripture, or the Bible. [L *scrīptūra*—*scrībĕre*.]

scrivener [skriv´nėr] *n* a scribe, a copyist; a notary public. [OFr *escrivain* (Fr *écrivain*)—LL *scrībānus*—L *scrība*, a scribe.]

scrod [skröd] *n* a young codfish or haddock, filleted for cooking.

scrofula [skrof´ū-la] *n* tuberculosis of the lymphatic glands, esp of the neck.—*adj* **scrof´ulous**. [L *scrōfulae*—*scrōfa*, a sow.]

scroll [skrōl] *n* a roll of paper or parchment; a writing in the form of a roll; a list; a riband partly coiled or curved, often bearing a motto; anything shaped more or less like a scroll; the curved head of a violin, etc.—*vi* to move text across a display screen as if by unrolling a scroll.—*adj* **scrolled**, formed into a scroll; ornamented with scrolls. [Earlier *scrowl(e)*—ME *scrow*—Anglo-Fr *escrowe*.]

scrotum [skrōt´ùm] *n* the pouch of skin containing the testicles;—*pl* **scrot´a, scrotums**. [L.]

scrub[1] [skrub] *vti* to rub hard in order to clean; to rub hard;—*pr p* **scrubb´ing**; *pt, pt p* **scrubbed**.—*n* act or process of scrubbing.—*ns* **scrubb´er**, one that scrubs, esp an apparatus for removing impurities from gases; **scrub´woman**, a woman who does cleaning, as at an office. [Perh obs Du *schrubben*.]

scrub[2] [skrub] *n* a stunted tree; stunted trees and shrubs collectively; country covered with bushes or low trees; an undersized or inferior animal or person; (*sports*) a substitute player.—*adj* small, stunted, inferior, etc.—*n* **scrub typhus**, a disease caused by a rickettsia transmitted to humans by mite larva, widespread in the Pacific area.—*adj* **scrubb´y**, stunted; covered with scrub; shabby. [A variant of **shrub**.]

scruff [skruf] *n* the nape of the neck.—*adj* **scruff´y**, shabby; unkempt. [Perh ON *skopt, skoft*, the hair.]

scrum [skrum] *n* (*Rugby football*) a play consisting of a closing-in of rival forwards around the ball in readiness for its being inserted into the compact, pushing mass.—*vi* **scrumm´age**, to form a scrum. [Abbreviation of *scrummage*, variant spelling of **scrimmage**.]

scruple [skrōō´pl] *n* a small weight—in apothecaries' weight, 20 grains; a very small quantity; a doubt or hesitation, usu. moral, restraining one from action, esp a difficulty turning on a fine point of right or wrong.—*vti* to hesitate (at) from doubt.—*adj* **scru´pūlous**, influenced by scruples, conscientious; exact, very careful (eg *scrupulous honesty, cleanliness*).—*adv* **scru´pūlously**.—*ns* **scru´pūlousness, scrupūlos´ity**, state of being scrupulous. [L *scrūpulus*, dim of *scrūpus*, a sharp stone, anxiety.]

scrutiny [skrōō´ti-ni] *n* close, careful, or minute investigation; a searching look.—*n* **scrutineer´**, one who makes a scrutiny.—*vt* **scru´tinize**, to examine carefully or critically; to investigate.—*vi* to make a scrutiny. [OFr *scrutine*—L *scrūtinium*—*scrūtārī*, to search even to the rags—*scrūta*, rags, trash.]

scuba [skōō´bȧ] *n* a diver's equipment with compressed-air tanks for breathing under water. [*s*elf-*c*ontained *u*nderwater *b*reathing *a*pparatus.]

scud [skud] *vi* to move or run swiftly; to be driven before the wind;—*pr p* **scudd´ing**; *pt, pt p* **scudd´ed**.—*n* act of moving quickly; clouds, etc. driven by wind. [Origin obscure.]

scuffle [skuf´l] *vi* to struggle closely; to fight confusedly; to drag the feet.—*n* a confused fight; a shuffling of feet.—*vti* **scuff**, to wear or get a rough place on the surface (of); to drag (the feet).—*n* a worn or rough spot; a flat-heeled house slipper with no back upper part. [Cf Swed *skuffa*, to shove, Du *schoffelen*; cf **shove, shovel, shuffle**.]

scull [skul] *n* an oar worked from side to side over the stern of a boat; a light rowboat for racing.—*vti* to propel with a scull.—*n* **scull´er**, one who sculls.

scullery [skul´ėr-i] *n* a room for rough kitchen work, as cleansing of utensils. [OFr *escuelerie*—Low L *scutellārius*—L *scutella*, a tray.]

scullion [skul´yȯn] *n* (*arch*) a servant for drugery, a menial. [OFr *escouillon*, a dishclout—L *scōpa*, a broom.]

sculpt *vt* to sculpture; to carve. [Fr *sculpter*—L *sculpĕre*, to carve.]

sculptor [skulp´tȯr] *n* an artist in carving; **sculp´tress**, a woman who sculptures.—*adj* **sculp´tūral**, pertaining to sculpture; resembling, having the quality of, sculpture.—*n* **sculp´ture**, the act or art of forming stone, clay, wood, etc. into statues, figures, etc.; a three-dimensional work of art; the work of a sculptor.—*vt* to carve; to shape in relief; to mold or form like sculpture; to modify the form of the earth's surface as by erosion or depositing.—*adj* **sculp´tured**, carved; engraved; (of features) fine and regular. [L *sculptor, sculptūra*—*sculpĕre, sculptum*, to carve.]

scum [skum] *n* a thin layer of impurities on top of a liquid; refuse; despicable people.—*vi* to become covered by scum;—*pr p* **scumm´ing**; *pt, pt p* **scummed**. [Cf Dan *skum*, Ger *schaum*, foam.]

scupper [skup´ėr] *n* a hole in a ship's side to drain the deck. [Ety uncertain.]

scurf [skûrf] *n* small flakes or scales of dead skin, esp on the scalp (as dandruff); any scaly coating.—*adj* **scurf´y**. [OE *scurf, sceorf*.]

scurrilous [skur´il-ùs] *adj* vulgarly evil; grossly abusive.—*adjs* **scurr´il, scurr´ile**, scurrilous.—*n* **scurril´ity**, buffoonery, low or obscene jesting; indecency of language; vulgar abuse.—*adv* **scurr´ilously**.—*n* **scurr´ilousness**. [L *scurrīlis*—*scurra*, a buffoon.]

scurry [skur´i] *vi* to hurry along, to scamper.—*n* a flurry, bustle. [From **hurry-scurry**, reduplication of **hurry**, or from **scour** (2).]

scurvy [skûr´vi] *adj* vile, contemptible.—*n* a disease marked by general debility, due to a lack of Vitamin C.—*adv* **scur´vily**, in a scurvy manner; meanly, basely.—*n* **scur´viness**, state of being scurvy; meanness. [**scurf**.]

scut [skut] *n* a short erect tail, like a hare's. [Origin obscure.]

scutage [skū´tij] *n* (*hist*) a tax paid instead of the personal service which a vassal or tenant owed to his lord. [LL *scūtāgium*—L *scūtum*, shield.]

scutcheon [skuch´ȯn] *n* escutcheon.

scuttle[1] [skut´l] *n* a shallow basket; a bucket with a lip for holding coal. [OE *scutel*—L *scutella*, a tray.]

scuttle[2] [skut´l] *n* an opening in a ship's deck or side; its lid.—*vt* to make a hole in the lower hull of a ship, esp in order to sink; to destroy, ruin.—*n* **scutt´lebutt**, a drinking fountain on shipboard; (*inf*) rumor. [OFr *escoutille*, a hatchway.]

scuttle[3] [skut´l] *vi* to scamper, to withdraw in haste.—*n* a short swift run; a quick shuffling pace.

scythe [sīTH] *n* an instrument with a large curved blade for mowing grass, etc.—*vti* to mow with a scythe. [OE *sithe*; cf ON *sigthr*, Ger *sense*.]

sea [sē] *n* the ocean; any great expanse of salt water less than an ocean; a large body of fresh water; the state of the surface of the ocean; a heavy wave or swell; something like the sea in vastness; the seafaring life.—*adj* of the sea, marine.—*ns* **sea´ anem´one**, any of numerous, usu. solitary, polyps (order Actiniara) whose form and bright colors resemble a flower; **sea´board**, land bordering on the sea.—*adj* bordering on the sea.—*adj* **sea´borne**, carried on the sea.—*ns* **sea´breeze**, a breeze blowing from the sea toward the land, **sea´ change**, (*arch*) a change effected by the sea; a transformation; **sea´coast**, the land adjacent to the sea; **sea cow**, a manatee, dugong; a nebulous arc of light sometimes seen in fog; **sea dog**, a veteran sailor; **sea eagle**, any of various fish-eating eagles (esp genus *Haliaeetus*); **sea´fārer**, a sailor.—*adj* **sea´fāring**.—*ns* **sea´food**, edible marine fish and shellfish; **sea front**, the waterfront of a seaside place.—*adjs* **sea´girt**, surrounded by seas; **sea´going**, (of a ship) made for use on the open sea; **sea´green**, a moderate green or bluish green; a moderate yellow green.—*ns* **sea´ gull**, a gull; **sea´horse**, a hippocampus; **sea´ kale**, a fleshy plant (*Crambe maritima*) used as a potherb; **sea´ king´**, a Norse pirate chief; **sea´lab**, any of a series of US Navy undersea laboratories for research in oceanography; **sea´ law´yer**, a captious, verbose sailor.—*n pl* **sea´ legs**, ability to walk on a ship's deck when it is pitching or rolling;

resistance to seasickness.—*ns* **sea´level´**, the mean level of the surface of the sea; **sea´ lī´on**, any of several large seals (genus *Zalophus* or *Otaria*) of the Pacific Ocean with external ears, so called from their roar and the mane of the male; **sea´man**, a sailor; a mariner; one of the three ranks below petty officer in the navy or coast guard; **sea´manship**, the art of handling, working, and navigating a ship; **sea´mark**, a mark of tidal limit; an object serving as a guide to those at sea; **sea´ mew**, a European gull (*Larus canus*); **sea´ mile**, a nautical mile; **sea´piece**, a picture representing a scene at sea; **sea´plane**, an airplane that can alight on, or rise from, water; **sea´port**, a port, harbor, or town accessible to oceangoing ships; **sea power**, national strength in naval armaments; a nation with a notably strong navy; **sea´room**, room for maneuver at sea; **sea´ rōver**, a pirate; **sea´scape**, a seapiece; **sea´ ser´pent**, an enormous marine animal of serpent-like form, whose existence is frequently alleged but has never been proved; **sea´shore´**, the land immediately adjacent to the sea; the foreshore.—*adj* **sea´sick´**, affected with sickness through the rolling of a vessel at sea.—*ns* **sea´sickness; sea´side**, seashore; **sea´ trout**, any of various chars and trouts that live in the sea but ascend rivers to spawn; **sea´ ur´chin**, any of a class (Echinoidea) of small marine animals, with a round body in a shell covered with sharp spines; **sea´wall**, a wall or embankment to protect the shore from erosion or to act as a breakwater.—*adj* **sea´ward**, toward the sea.—*adv* (also **sea´wards**) toward or in the direction of the sea.—*n* **sea´way**, a regular route taken by ocean traffic; an inland waterway on which oceangoing vessels can sail; **sea´weed**, a mass of plants growing in or under water; a sea plant, esp a marine alga (as kelp).—*adj* **sea´worthy**, fit for sea, able to endure stormy weather.—*ns* **sea´worthiness; sea´ wrack**, seaweed, esp that cast ashore in masses.—**at sea**, on an ocean voyage; lost, bewildered; **to sea**, to or on the open waters of the ocean. [OE *sǣ*; Du *zee*, Ger *see*, ON *sǣr*.]

seal[1] *n* a piece of wax, lead, or other material, stamped with a device and attached as a means of authentication or attestation; an engraved stone or other stamp for impressing a device; a closure that must be broken to be opened and thus reveal tampering; a tight or perfect closure to prevent the passage or return (as of gas or water in a pipe); an ornamental paper stamp; anything that pledges.—*vt* to attach a seal to; to mark, fasten, or close with a seal; to attest, authenticate, confirm; to close securely, keep closed; to decide irrevocably (eg *this sealed his fate*).—*ns* **seal´ant**, something that seals a place where there is a leak; **seal´ing wax**, a resinous compound that is plastic when warm for sealing letters, etc.—**seal off**, to close tightly; **under seal**, with an authenticating seal attached. [OFr *seel*—L *sigillum*, dim of *signum*, a mark.]

seal[2] [sēl] any of numerous carnivorous aquatic mammals (families Phocidae and Otariidae) with a torpedo-shaped body and limbs modified into webbed flippers; the fur of some seals; a dark brown;—*pl* **seals, seal**.—*vi* to hunt seal.—*ns* **seal´er**, a man or a ship engaged in hunting seals; **seal´skin**, the prepared fur of the fur seal; a garment made of this. [OE *seolh*; ON *selr*.]

Sealyham [sē´li(h)àm] *n* a breed of white terrier with short legs. [*Sealyham*, in Pembrokeshire, Wales.]

seam [sēm] *n* the line formed by the sewing together of two pieces; a line of union; a wrinkle, furrow; (*geol*) a stratum of ore, coal, etc.—*vt* to unite by a seam; to mark by a seamlike line.—*adj* **seam´less**, without a seam.—*n* **seamstress** [sēm´stres], a woman whose occupation is sewing.—*adj* **seamy** [sēm´i], (*arch*) having or showing a seam or seams; unpleasant or sordid. [OE *sēam*—*sīwian*, to sew; Du *zoom*, Ger *saum*.]

séance [sā´ãs] *n* a meeting at which spiritualists try to communicate with the dead. [Fr,—L *sedēre*, to sit.]

sear [sēr] *See* **sere**.

search [sûrch] *vt* to survey inquiringly, to examine or inspect closely; to probe.—*vi* to make a search.—*n* inquisition; investigation; quest.—*n* **search´er**, one who searches.—*adj* **search´ing**, penetrating; examining thoroughly.—*adv* **search´ingly**.—*ns* **search´light**, a strong beam of electric light projected by an apparatus on a swivel; the apparatus; **search´ warr´ant**, a legal document authorizing a police search.—**in search of**, making a search for. [OFr *cerchier*—L *circāre*, to go about—*circus*, a circle.]

search engine [serch´ en´jin] *n* a tool that is used to look for and retrieve information on the world wide web.

season [sē´z(ò)n] *n* one of the four divisions of the year: spring, summer, fall or winter; the usual or appropriate time; any particular time; any brief period of time; seasoning, relish.—*vt* to make (food) more tasty by adding salt, spices, etc.; to mature; to accustom, inure (to); to give relish, or zest, to; (*arch*) to moderate by admixture (eg *to season justice with mercy*); to dry (timber) until the moisture content is brought down to a suitable amount; to make fit by experience.—*vi* to become seasoned.—*adj* **sea´sonable**, happening in due season; timely, opportune.—*n* **sea´sonableness**.—*adv* **sea´sonably**.—*adj* **sea´sonal**, belonging to a particular season.—*n* **sea´soning**, that which is added to food to give relish; the process by which anything is seasoned.—**in season**, ripe, fit and ready for use; opportune; **out of season**, not in season; **season ticket**, a ticket or set of tickets valid for repeated use during a specified period, as for a series of concerts, baseball games, etc. [OFr *seson*—L *satiō, -ōnis*, a sowing.]

seat [sēt] *n* a chair, bench, etc.; the part of a chair on which the body rests; that part of the body or of a garment on which one sits; the manner in which one sits on a horse; a place where anything is settled or established; the right to sit as a member; the chief location, or center; a part at or forming the base of something.—*vt* to install in a seat of dignity or office; to cause to sit down; to assign a seat to; to place in any situation, site, etc.; to establish, to fix; to furnish with a seat, or with seats; to have seats for (a specified number).—*vi* to fit correctly on a seat.—*adj* **seat´ed**, fixed, confirmed; situated, located; furnished with a seat or seats.—*ns* **seat´ belt**, an anchored belt which can be fastened to hold a person in his seat in a car or aircraft; **seat´ing**, provision or arrangement of seats. [ON *sæti*, seat; cf OE *sǣt*, ambush.]

sebaceous [se-bā´shùs] *adj* secreting sebum; pertaining to, producing, or containing fatty material.—*n* **sē´bum**, fatty matter secreted by sebaceous glands of the skin. [LL *sēbāceus*—*sēbum*, tallow.]

secant [sē´kant, ànt] *n* (*geom*) a straight line that intersects a curve in two or more points; (*trigonometry*) one of the six trigonometrical functions of an angle, the reciprocal of the cosine, identical with the cosecant of the complementary angle.—*abbrev* **sec** [sek]. [L *secāns, -antis*, pr p of *secāre*, to cut.]

secede [si-sēd´] *vi* to withdraw formally from a society, federation or organization, esp a religious communion or political party.—*ns* **secē´der**, one who secedes; **secess´ion**, the act of seceding; withdrawal into privacy or solitude. [L *sēcēdĕre, sēcessum*—*sē-*, apart, *cēdĕre*, to go.]

seclude [si-klōōd´] *vi* to shut off, esp from association or influence (*with* **from**).—*adj* **seclud´ed**, withdrawn from observation or society.—*adv* **seclud´edly**.—*n* **seclusion** [siklōō´zh(ò)n], the act of secluding; the state of being secluded; retirement, privacy, solitude. [L *sēclūdĕre, sēclūsum*—*sē-*, apart, *claudĕre*, to shut.]

second [sek´ònd] *adj* next after the first in time, place, power, quality, etc.; other, alternate (eg *every second day*); another of the same kind; next below the first in rank, value, etc.—*n* one who, or that which, is second; an article of merchandise not of first quality; an aid or assistant, as to a boxer; the gear after low gear; (*mus*) an interval embracing two diatonic degrees; 1/60th of a minute of time or of angular measure.—*vt* to act as second (to); to support, back up; to further, encourage; to indicate formal support of (a motion) before discussion or a vote.—*adv* in the second place, group, etc.—*adj* **sec´ondary**, subordinate; of a second stage; of a second order in importance (eg *a secondary consideration*); derived, not primary; relating to a secondary school.—*n* that which is secondary; (*football*) the defensive backfield.—*adv* **sec´ondarily**.—*adj* **second-best**, next to the best.—*n* **second best**, next to the best.—*adv* in second place.—*n* **sec´ond class**, the class next to the first in a classification; a class of US mail comprising periodicals sent to regular subscribers.—*adj* **second-class**, relating to a second class; inferior, mediocre; socially, politically or economically deprived.—*adj* **sec´ondhand´**, derived from another; not new, that has been used by another; dealing in secondhand merchandise.—*adv* **sec´ondly**, in the second place.—*adj* **sec´ond-rate**, inferior, mediocre.—**Second Coming**, the coming of Christ as judge on the last day; **secondary school**, a school intermediate between elementary school and college; **second childhood**, mental weakness in old age; **second cousin**, a child of one's parent's first cousin; **second lieutenant**, a commissioned officer of the lowest rank in the army, airforce, or marine corps; **second nature**, an acquired habit, etc., deeply fixed in one's nature; **second person**, that form of a pronoun (as *you*) or verb (as *are*) which refers to the person spoken to; **second sight**, a gift of prophetic vision, attributed to certain persons; **second thought**, a change in thought after reconsideration. [Fr,—L *secundus*—*sequī, secūtus*, to follow.]

secret [sē´kret] *adj* concealed from others, guarded against discovery or observation; not avowed; constructed, carried out, so as to escape discovery or notice (eg *secret drawer*); recondite; secluded; keeping secrets, secretive.—*n* a fact, purpose, or method that is kept undivulged; anything unrevealed or unknown; something taken to be a key to a desired end.—*n* **sē´crecy**, the state of being secret; concealment; privacy; the power or habit of keeping secrets.—*adj* **secretive** [sē´krė-tiv, si-krē´tiv], given to secrecy, very reticent; indicative of secrecy.—*adv* **sē´cretly**, in a secret manner; unknown to others; inwardly.—**Secret Service**, a US agency of the Treasury Department chiefly dealing with the suppression of counterfeiting and protecting the president. [L *sēcrētus*—*sēcernĕre, sēcrētum*—*sē-*, apart, *cernĕre*, to separate.]

secretary [sek´rė-tà-ri] *n* one employed to conduct correspondence and transact business for an individual, society, etc.; the head of a government department; an officer of a business concern who may keep records of directors' and stockholders' meetings and of stock ownership, etc.; an officer of an organization responsible for its records and correspondence; a writing desk, often with a top section for books.—*adj* **secretā´rial**, pertaining to a secretary or his duties.—*ns* **secretariat** [sek-rė-tā´ri-àt], a secretarial staff, esp an administrative staff, as in a government; **sec´retary bird**, a long-legged bird of prey (*Sagittarius serpentarius*) that feeds largely on reptiles; **sec´retaryship**, the office or duties of a secretary.—**Secretary of State**, in the US federal government, the cabinet officer at the head of the Department of State, which has charge of all foreign relations; in state governments, the official whose chief duty is the keeping of records. [LL *sēcrētārius*, a confidential officer, from same root as **secret**.]

secrete [si-krēt´] *vt* to appropriate secretly; to hide; to form and release (a substance) as a gland, etc., does.—*n* **secrē´tion**, the act, or process, of secreting; a substance secreted by an animal or plant.—*adj* **secrē´tive**, tending to, or causing, secretion.—*adv* **secrē´tively**.—*adj* **secrē´tory**, having the function of secreting, as a gland. [L *sēcernere, sēcrētum*. See **secret**.]

sect [sekt] *n* a religious denomination; a body of persons who unite in holding some particular views, esp those who dissent from an established religion.—*adj* **sectā´rian**, of a sect; devoted to a sect; narrow, exclusive.—*n* a member of a sect; one strongly imbued with the characteristics of a sect.—*ns* **sectā´rianism**, excessive devotion to a sect; **sec´tary**, a member of a sect. [L *secta*, a school of philosophy—*sequī, secūtus*, to follow; influenced by *secāre*, to cut.]

section [sek´sh(ȯ)n] *n* act of cutting; a division; a portion; one of the parts into which anything may be considered as divided, or of which it may be built up; a thin slice for microscopic examination; a drawing of any object cut through, as it were, to show its interior; the line of intersection of two surfaces; the surface formed when a solid is cut by a plane; one of the classes formed by dividing the students taking a course; one of the discussion groups into which a conference is divided; a division of an orchestra composed of one class of instruments.—*vt* to cut or separate into sections; to represent in sections.—*vi* to become separated or cut into parts.—*adjs* **sec´tile**, capable of being cut with a knife; **sec´tional**, of a section; in section; built up by sections; local or regional rather than general in character.—*n* **sec´tionalism**, an exaggerated devotion to the interests of a region.—*adv* **sec´tionally**. [L *sectiō, -ōnis—secāre*, to cut.]

sector [sek´tȯr] *n* a plane figure bounded by two radii and an arc; a length or section of a fortified line or army front; a distinctive part (as of an economy); a mathematical instrument consisting of two graduated rulers hinged together. [L *secāre, sectum*, to cut.]

secular [sek´ū-lȧr] *adj* pertaining to an age or generation; occurring or observed only once in a century; becoming appreciable only in the course of ages; of a long term of indefinite duration; not religious; not connected with a church; not bound by monastic rules.—*n* a layman; an ecclesiastic not bound by monastic rules.—*vt* **sec´ularize**, to change from religious to civil use or control.—*ns* **seculariz ā´tion**, the state or process of being secularized; **sec´ularism**, the belief that politics, morals, education, etc., should be independent of religion; **sec´ularist**, one who believes in secularism; **secular´ity**, state of being secular; worldliness. [L *saeculāris—saeculum*, an age, a generation.]

secure [si-kūr´] *adj* (*arch*) without care or anxiety; confident in expectation, assured; free from danger, safe; affording safety; firmly fixed or held.—*vt* to make safe; to guarantee against loss as with a pledge; to fasten; to seize and guard; to gain possession of, to obtain.—*adj* **secūr´able**, that may be secured.—*adv* **secūre´ly**.—*ns* **secūre´ness; secūr´ity**, state of being secure; freedom from fear or anxiety; something given as a pledge of repayment, etc.; protection; safeguard; (*pl*) bonds, stocks, etc.—**Security Council**, a body of the United Nations consisting of five permanent members (China, France, UK, USA, Russia—each with the right of veto) and six elected two-yearly members, charged with the maintenance of international peace and security; **security police**, police whose duty it is to prevent espionage; the military police of an air force. [L *sēcūrus—sē-*, without, *cūra*, care.]

sedan [si-dan´] *n* a covered chair for one, carried on two poles by two men; an enclosed automobile with front and rear seats and two or four doors; a motorboat having one passenger compartment.

sedate [si-dāt´] *adj* quiet; composed; serious and unemotional.—*adv* **sedāte´ly**.—*ns* **sedāte´ness; sedā´tion**, act of calming, or state of being calmed, by means of sedatives; use of sedatives to calm a patient.—*adj* **sed´ative**, tending to calm, soothe; allaying excitement, irritation, etc.—*n* a soothing medicine. [L *sēdātus*, pt p of *sēdāre*, to still.]

sedentary [sed´(ė)n-tȧ-ri] *adj* not migratory; passed chiefly in sitting, requiring much sitting (eg of occupation); permanently attached. [L *sedentārius—sedēre*, to sit.]

Seder [sā´dėr] *n* (*Judaism*) the feast of Passover as observed in the home on the eve of the first (by some also of the second) day of the holiday. [Heb.]

sederunt [si-dē´runt] *n* a prolonged sitting (as for discussion). [L 'they sat'—*sedēre*, to sit.]

sedge [sej] *n* any of several coarse grasslike plants (family Cyperaceae) growing in wet ground.—*adj* **sedg´y**, overgrown with sedge. [OE *secg*; cf Low Ger *segge*.]

sediment [sed´i-mėnt] *n* matter that settles at the bottom of a liquid; (*geol*) matter disposited by water or wind.—*adj* **sedimen´tary**, pertaining to, consisting of, or formed by sediment.—**sedimentary rock**, rock formed by deposit of fragments of rock, precipitation or solution (as gypsum) or inorganic remains (as shells and skeletons) of organisms. [L *sedimentum—sedēre*, to sit.]

sedition [si-dish´(ȯ)n] *n* stirring up of rebellion against the government.—*adj* **sedi´tious**, pertaining to, or exciting, sedition.—*adv* **sedi´tiously**.—*n* **sedi´tiousness**. [Fr,—L *sēditiō, -ōnis—sēd-*, away, *īre, itum*, to go.]

seduce [si-dūs´] *vt* to draw aside from right conduct or belief; to entice into unlawful sexual intercourse, esp for the first time.—*ns* **sedūce´ment**, act of seducing; allurement; **sedū´cer; seduc´tion**, act of enticing from virtue by promises; allurement, attraction.—*adj* **seduc´tive**, tending to seduce; attractive. [L *sēdūcere—sē-*, apart, *dūcere, ductum*, to lead.]

sedulous [sed´ū-lu̇s] *adj* diligent, assiduous.—*n* **sed´ulousness**.—*adv* **sed´ulously**. [L *sēdulus—sedēre*, to sit.]

sedum [sē´dum] *n* a large genus (*Sedum*) of plants, often with tufted stems; the stonecrop. [L *sėdum*, house-leek.]

see[1] [sē] *n* the seat or jurisdiction of a bishop or archbishop. [OFr *se, siet*—L *sēdēs—sedēre*, to sit.]

see[2] [sē] *vt* to perceive by the eye; to observe, to discern; to perceive with the understanding; to ascertain (eg *I'll see what has been arranged*); to ensure (eg *see that he does what he has promised*); to escort (a person to a specified place); to meet; to visit; to consult; to undergo, experience (eg *to see trouble*); to receive.—*vi* to have power of vision; to look, inquire (into); to consider (eg *let me see*); to understand.—*pt* **saw**; *pt p* **seen**.—*n* **see´ing**, sight, vision.—*adj* having sight or insight; observant.—*conj* since, in view of the fact that.—**see after**, to take care of; **see eye to eye**, to have a common viewpoint; **see out**, to conduct to the door; to see to the end; to outlast; **see over**, to be conducted all through; **see things**, to have hallucinations; **see through**, to discern the secret of; **see to**, to attend to; to care for. [OE *sēon*; Ger *sehen*, Du *zien*.]

seed [sēd] *n* a cellular structure containing the embryo of a flowering plant together with stored food, the whole protected by a seed coat; such seeds collectively; the source of anything; sperm or semen; progeny; condition of having or proceeding to form seed; a seeded tournament player.—*vi* to sow seed; to shed seed.—*vt* to sow; to remove the seeds from; to cause to form granules or crystals, esp to treat (a cloud) with solid particles in an attempt to produce rain; to arrange (the draw for a tournament) in such a way that the best players will not meet in the early rounds.—*adj* **seed´y**, abounding in seed; shabby; rundown.—*adv* **seed´ily**.—*ns* **seed´iness**, the state of being seedy; **seed´bed**, a piece of ground for receiving seed; a place or source of growth or development; **seed´cake**, a cake or cookie containing aromatic seeds; **seed´ coat**, the outer covering of a seed; **seed leaf**, a cotyledon; **seed´ling**, a plant reared from the seed; a young tree before it becomes a sapling; a nursery plant not yet transplanted; **seed money**, money to begin a long-term project or get more funds for it; **seed´ pearl**, a very small pearl; **seeds´man**, one who deals in seeds;—*pl* **seeds´men; seed´ vessel**, a dry fruit; the ovary of a flower. [OE *sæd*; cf *sāwan*, to sow, ON *sath*, Ger *saat*.]

seek [sēk] *vt* to look for; to try to find, get, or achieve; to resort to (eg *to seek the shade*).—*vi* to make a search or inquiry; to be sought; to be lacking;—*pt, pt p* **sought**.—*n* **seek´er**.—**seek after**, to go in quest of; **sought after**, in demand. [OE *sēcan* (pt *sōhte* pt p *gesōht*); cf Du *zoeken*, Ger *suchen*.]

seem [sēm] *vi* to appear to be; to appear (to be, or to do); to have the impression (*with an infinitive*).—*adj* **seem´ing**, that seems real, true; apparent; ostensible.—*n* appearance; semblance.—*adv* **seem´ingly**.—*adj* **seem´ly** (*comparative* **seem´lier**, *superlative* **seem´liest**), proper; suitable; decent.—*n* **seem´liness**. [OE *sēman*, to satisfy, to suit; or prob direct from ON *sœma*, to conform to.]

seen [sēn] *pt p* of **see**.

seep [sēp] *vi* to ooze gently, to percolate.—*n* **seep´age**, act or process of seeping; liquid that has percolated; the quantity of liquid that has done so. [OE *sipian*, to soak.]

seer [sē´er] *n* one who sees; [sēr] one who sees into the future, a prophet. [**see** (2).]

seesaw [sē´sö or -sö´] *n* alternate up-and-down or back-and-forth motion; repeated alternation in a contest or struggle; a plank balanced so that its ends may move up and down alternately, on which children play, riding the ends.—*adj, adv* like a seesaw.—*vi* to move like a seesaw. [Prob a reduplication of **saw**, from a sawyer's jingle.]

seethe [sēTH] *vt* (*arch*) to boil; to soak or saturate in liquid.—*vi* (*arch*) to boil; to be violently agitated;—*pr p* **seeth´ing**; *pt, pt p* **seethed**. [OE *sēothan*; ON *sjōtha*, Ger *sieden*.]

segment [seg´mėnt] *n* a part cut off; a portion; of a line, that portion bound by two points; of a circle, that portion of a plane bound by an arc of the circle and its chord; of a sphere, the solid formed between two parallel planes that cut through a sphere; any one of the more or less distinct sections into which the bodies of many animals are divided.—*vti* [also -ment´] to divide into segments.—*n* **segmentā´tion**, the act or process of dividing into segments; the state of being divided thus; the early divisions of the nucleus of a fertilized ovum. [L *segmentum—secāre*, to cut.]

segregate [seg´rė-gāt] *vt* to separate from others, to group apart.—*vi* to separate, withdraw; to practice or enforce a policy of segregation; to undergo genetic segregation.—*n* **segregā´tion**, act of segregation; state of being segregated; a segregated group; the policy of compelling racial groups to live apart and use separate schools, facilities, etc. [L *sēgregāre, -ātum—sē*, apart, *grex, gregis*, a flock.]

seguidilla [seg-i-dēl´ya] *n* a Spanish dance with many regional variations; the music for it; a Spanish stanza of four or seven verses. [Sp—L *sequī*, to follow.]

Seidlitz powders [sed´lits] applied to an aperient medicine consisting of an effervescent solution of sodium bicarbonate, tartaric acid, etc. [The mineral water of *Se(i)dlitz* in Bohemia, named from a fancied resemblance.]

seignior [sē´nyėr], **seigneur** [sen´yœr] *n* a title of respectful address; a feudal lord; **seigneur**, a member of the landed gentry of Canada.—*adjs* **seignorial** [sē-nyō´ri-ȧl], **seigneu´rial** [sē-nū´-] manorial.—*n* **seign´iory**, the power or authority of a seignior. [Fr *seigneur*—L *senior*, comp of *senex*, old. In Late L *senior* is sometimes equivalent to *dominus*, lord.]

seine [sān or sēn] *n* a large fishing net weighted along the bottom.—*vti* to fish with a seine. [OE *segne*—L *sagēna*—Gr *sagēnē*, a fishing net.]

seismograph [sīs´mō-gräf] *n* an instrument for registering the direction, intensity, and time of earthquakes.—*adj* **seis´mic**, belonging to an earthquake.—*n* **seismol´ogy**, the science of earthquakes and of artificially produced vibrations of the earth. [Gr *seismos*, an earthquake, *graphein*, to write, *logos*, discourse.]

seize [sēz] *vt* to take legal possession of; to take possession of suddenly, eagerly, or forcibly; to snatch, to grasp; to attack or afflict suddenly.—*vi* (of machinery) to jam, become stuck; (of an engine) to fail to operate due to the seizing of a part.—*adj* **seiz´able**.—*ns* **seiz´er; seiz´ure**, the act of seizing; capture; grasp; the thing seized; a fit or attack of illness, eg of apoplexy. [OFr *saisir*—LL *sacire*; cf OHG *sazzan*, to set, Ger *setzen*, Eng *set*.]

seldom [sel´dȯm] *adv* rarely, not often. [OE *seldum*, altered (on the analogy of *hwīlum*, whilom) from *seldan*.]

select [si-lekt´] *vti* to choose or pick out.—*adj* picked out; choice; careful in choosing; exclusive.—*n* **selec´tion**, act of selecting; thing, or a collection of things, selected.—*adj* **selec´tive**, exercising power of selection; (*radio*—of a circuit or apparatus) able to respond to a specific frequency without interference; highly specific in activity or effect.—*ns* **selectiv´ity**, quality of being selective; **select´man**, one of a board of governing officers in New England towns; **select´or**, one that selects.—**selective service**, a system under which men are called up for military service. [L *sēligĕre, sēlectum*—*sē-*, aside, *legĕre*, to choose.]

selenium [se-lē´ni-ŭm] *n* a metalloid element (symbol Se; at wt 79.0; at no 34). [Coined from Gr *selēnē*, the moon, as *tellurium* is from L *tellūs*, earth.]

selenography [se-lēn-og´raf-i] *n* study of the moon's physical features; the physical geography of the moon. [Gr *selēnē*, moon, *graphein*, to write.]

self [self] *n* the identity, character, etc. of any person or thing; one's own person as distinct from all others; what one is; personal advantage;—*pl* **selves** [selvz].—*adj* (*obs*) very same; having one color only; of the same kind (as in color, material, etc.) as something with which it is used.—*adj* **self´ish**, chiefly or wholly regarding oneself, heedless of others.—*adv* **self´ishly**.—*n* **self´ishness**.—*adj* **self´less**, regardless of self, utterly unselfish. [OE *self*; Du *zelf*; Ger *selbe*.]

self- [self-] in composition, indicating that the agent is also the object of the action; by, of, for, in, in relation to, oneself or itself; automatic;—eg **self´-pleas´ing**, pleasing oneself; **self´-condemned´**, condemned by oneself; **self´-pit´y**, pity for oneself; **self´-trust**, trust in oneself; **self´-sat´isfied**, satisfied with oneself; **self´-right´eous**, righteous in one's own esteem; **self´-clō´sing**, closing of itself.—*adj* **self´-absorbed´**, wrapped up in one's own thoughts or affairs.—*n* **self-advert´isement**, calling, or a means of calling, public attention to oneself.—*adjs* **self´-assert´ing, self´-assert´ive**, given to asserting one's opinion, or to putting oneself forward.—*n* **self´-bind´er**, a harvesting machine with automatic binding apparatus.—*adj* **self´-col´ored**, of a single color.—*n* **self´-conceit´**, an over-high opinion of one's merits, abilities, etc., vanity.—*adj* **self´conceit´ed**.—*n* **self´-con´fidence**, confidence in one's own powers; self-reliance.—*adjs* **self´-con´fident; self´-con´scious**, conscious of one's own mind and its acts and states; conscious of being observed by others; ill at ease.—*n* **self´-con´sciousness**.—*adj* **self´contained´**, absorbed in oneself, reserved; showing self-control; complete in itself.—*n* **self´-control´**, control of one's emotions, desires, etc.—*adj* **self´-defeat´ing**, that defeats its own purpose.—*ns* **self´-defense´**, a plea of justification for the use of force or for homicide; the act of defending one's own person, rights, etc.; **self´-denī´al**, denial or sacrifice of one's own desires or pleasures.—*adj* **self´-deny´ing**.—*n* **self´-determinā´tion**, free will; choice of action without external compulsion; the right of a territorial unit to choose their political status.—*adj* **self´-ed´ucated**, educated by one's own efforts with little formal schooling.—*n* **self´-efface´ment**, keeping oneself in the background out of sight.—*adjs* **self´-effac´ing**, reserved, shy; **self´-employed´**, working independently in one's own business, trade, or profession; **self´-ev´ident**, evident without explanation or proof; **self´-exist´ent**, existing of or by oneself or itself, independent of any other cause.—*n* **self´-expression** [-presh´(ȯ)n] a giving expression to one's personality, as in art.—*adj* **self´-gov´erning**.—*ns* **self´-gov´ernment**, government without external interference; government administered and controlled by citizens; **self´-help´**, providing for one's needs by personal effort without help from others; **self´-import´ance**, an absurdly high sense of one's own importance; pomposity.—*adj* **self´-import´ant**.—*n* **self´-indul´gence**, undue gratification of one's appetites, desires or whims.—*adj* **self´-indul´gent**.—*n* **self´-int´erest**, personal advantage; exaggerated concern for one's own private aims.—*adjs* **self´-made´**, made by one's own effort; risen to a high position from poverty or obscurity by unaided personal exertions; **self´-possessed´**, calm or collected in mind or manner.—*ns* **self´-possess´ion**, ability to use one's faculties in a crisis, presence of mind; calm, composure; **self´-realizā´tion**, the attainment of such development as one's mental and moral nature is capable of.—*adj* **self´-regard´ing**, concerned with one's own self, or with the promotion of one's own interests.—*n* **self´-relī´ance**, healthy confidence in one's own abilities.—*adj* **self´-relī´ant**.—*n* **self´-respect´**, due regard and concern for one's character and reputation.—*adjs* **self´-respect´ing; self´-righteous**, righteous in one's own estimation.—*ns* **self´-right´eousness; self´-sac´rifice**, the act of seeking the welfare of others at the cost of one's own.—*adjs* **self´-sac´rificing; self´-same**, the very same.—*n* **self´-seek´er**, one who pursues only selfish aims.—*adj* **self´-ser´vice**, of restaurants, stores, etc. in which goods are displayed on shelves for customers to help themselves, paying at a cashier's desk or by means of a coin-operated mechanism.—*ns* **self´-ser´vice; self´-start´er**, a device for starting an internal-combustion engine automatically.—*adjs* **self-styled´**, so called by oneself; **self´-suffi´cient**, requiring nothing from without; independent.—*ns* **self´-suffi´ciency; self´-support´** independent support of oneself or itself.—*adj* **self´-support´ing**.—*n* **self-will´**, one's own will; persistence in attempts to do as one chooses.—*adj* **self-willed´**, governed by self-will, obstinate.—**self-rising flour**, a commercially prepared mixture of flour, salt, and a leavening agent. [**self**.]

sell [sel] *vt* to exchange (goods, services, etc.) for money, etc.; to offer for sale; to promote the sale of; to make (an idea, a course of action, etc.) seem desirable (to a person).—*vi* to make sales; to be sold (for or at); to attract buyers;—*pt, pt p* **sold**.—*n* an act or instance of selling; a fraud.—*ns* **sell´er; sellout**, a show for which all seats are sold; (*inf*) a betrayal.—*vt* **sell out**, to sell the goods of (a debtor) to satisfy creditors; to sell security or commodity holdings to satisfy an uncovered margin.—**be sold on**, to be keen on, in favor of; **sell down the river**, to play false, betray; **sellers' market**, one in which sellers control the price, demand exceeding supply; **sell off**, to sell cheaply in order to dispose of. [OE *sellan*, to hand over; ON *selja*.]

seltzer [selt´zėr] *n* an artificially prepared carbonated mineral water. [Nieder-*Seltsers*, Germany.]

selvage, selvedge [sel´vij] *n* the firm edge of a woven piece of cloth; a border. [**self**, + **edge**.]

selves [selvz] *pl* of **self**.

semantic [si-man´tik] *adj* pertaining to meaning, esp of words.—*n* (*pl*) the study of the development of the meaning of words. [Gr *sēmantikos*.]

semaphore [sem´à-fōr, -för] *n* a signaling apparatus, consisting of an upright with arms that can be turned up and down; a system of visual signaling using the signaler's own body and arms with flags. [Gr *sēma*, a sign, *pherein*, to bear.]

semblance [sem´blȧns] *n* likeness, image, guise; a deceptive appearance; a faint indication. [Fr—*sembler*, to seem, resemble—L *similis*, like.]

semen [sē´men] *n* the fluid that carries spermatozoa. [L *sēmen*, seed.]

semester [si-mes´tėr] *n* either of the two terms usu. making up a school year. [L *sēmestris*—*sex*, six, *mēnsis*, a month.]

semi- [sem´i-] *prefix* half; not fully; twice in a (specified period).—*adj* **sem´iann´ual**, half-yearly; lasting half a year.—*n* **sem´icircle**, half a circle; the figure bounded by the diameter and half the circumference.—*adj* **semicir´cular**.—*n* **sem´icōlon**, the point (;) marking a division more strongly than a comma.—*n* **sem´idiam´eter**, the apparent radius of a generally spherical celestial body.—*adj* **semifīn´al**, immediately before the final in an elimination tournament; participating in a semifinal.—*n* a semifinal match or round.—*adjs* **sem´ipre´cious**, denoting gems, as the garnet, turquoize, etc. of lower value than precious stones; **sem´iprivate**, of a hospital room with two, three or sometimes four beds.—*ns* **sem´iprofessional**, one who engages in sport for pay but not as a regular occupation; **sem´itone**, half a tone.—*adj* **sem´i-transpa´rent**, imperfectly transparent. [L *sēmi-*, half-.]

semiconductor [sem-i-kon-dukt´ȯr] *n* a substance, as germanium or silicon, used in transistors to control current flow. [**semi-**.]

seminal [sem´in-ȧl] *adj* pertaining to, or of the nature of, seed or of semen; that is a source; generative, originative. [L *sēmen, sēminis*, seed—*serĕre*, to sow.]

seminar [sem´in-är] *n* a group of advanced students working under a teacher in some specific branch of study; a course for such a group.—*n* **sem´inary**, a private school for young women; a school where priests, ministers, etc. are trained. [L *sēminārium*, a seed-plot—*sēmen*.]

Seminole [sem´i-nōl] *n* a member of an Amerindian people of southern Florida and Oklahoma;—*pl* **-noles, -nole**.

Semite [sem´- or sēm´īt] *n* a member of any of the peoples now inhabiting the Middle East including Arabs and Jews.—*adj* **Semit´ic**, of an Afro-Asian language group including Amharic, Arabic, and Hebrew and speakers of these languages; Jewish. [Gr *Sēm*, Shem.]

semolina [sem-o-lē´na] *n* the milled product of hard wheat used esp for pasta. [It *semolino*, dim of *semola*, bran—L *simila*, fine flour.]

sempiternal [sem-pi-tûr´nȧl] *adj* everlasting. [L *sempiternus*—*semper*, ever, always.]

senary [sēn´-, sen´ȧr-i] *adj* of, involving, based on, six. [L *sēnārius*—*sēnī*, six each—*sex*, six.]

senate [sen´ȧt] *n* a legislative or deliberative body; **Senate**, the upper branch of the US Congress or of most of the State legislatures; a governing body of some universities charged with maintaining academic standards.—*n* **sen´ator**, a member of a senate.—*adj* **senatō´rial**, pertaining to, or becoming, a senate or a senator.—*n* **sen´atorship**.—**senatorial district**, a territorial district from which a senate is elected. [L *senātus*—*senex, senis*, an old man.]

send [send] *vt* to cause or direct to go; to cause to be conveyed, to dispatch, to forward; to propel; to commission (to do); to cause to happen, come, etc.; (*slang*) rouse (a person) to ecstasy.—*vi* to dispatch a message or messenger (*often with* **out**); to dispatch a request or order (*often with* **away**); to transmit;—*pt, pt p* **sent**.—*ns* **sen´der**, one who sends; **send´-off**, (*inf*) a farewell demonstration; (*inf*) a start given to someone or something; **send-up**, (*inf*) a process of making fun of someone.—**send down**, to expel from a university or college; **send up**, (*inf*) to send to prison; to make fun of. [OE *sendan*: ON *senda*, Ger *senden*.]

senescent [sen-es´ėnt] *adj* growing old.—*n* **senes´cence**. [L *senēscēns, -entis*, pr p of *senēscĕre*, to grow old.]

seneschal [sen´ė-shȧl] *n* (*hist*) a steward of a lord's estate. [OFr (Fr *sénéchal*), of Gmc origin, lit old servant.]

senile [sē´nīl] *adj* pertaining to, or attendant on, old age; showing the feebleness or imbecility of old age.—*n* **senility** [se-nil´i-ti]. [L *senīlis*—*senex, senis*, old.]

senior [sēn´yȯr] *adj* older, written *Sr* after a father's name if his son's name is the same; older in office or higher in standing; of or for seniors.—*n* one who is senior; a student in the last year of high school or college.—*n* **seniority** [sēni-or´i-ti] state or fact of being senior; status, priority, etc. achieved by length of service in a given job.—**senior citizen**, an elderly person, esp one who is retired; **senior high school**, high school usu. grades 10, 11, and 12. [L, comp of *senex*, old.]

senna [sen´a] *n* any of a genus (*Cassia*) of leguminous trees, shrubs, or herbs of warm regions, esp one used medicinally; the purgative dried leaflets or pods of various sennas (esp *C acutifolia* and *C angustifolia*). [Ar *sanā*.]

senor, señor [se-nyör´] *n* a gentleman; prefixed to a name, Mr.—*ns* **señora** [se-nyö´ra] a married woman; **senorita** [se´nyo-rē´tä] an unmarried woman or girl; as a title, equivalent to *Miss*. [Sp.]

sensation [sen-sā´sh(ȯ)n] *n* awareness of a physical experience; awareness by the senses generally; an effect on the senses; a thrill; a state, or matter, of general and excited interest; melodramatic quality or method.—*adj* **sensā´tional**, pertaining to sensation; tending to excite violent emotions; melodramatic.—*ns* **sensā´tionalism**, the doctrine that our ideas originate solely in sensation; a striving after wild excitement and melodramatic effects; **sensā´tionalist**, a believer in sensationalism; a sensational writer. [LL *sensātiō, -ōnis*—L *sēnsus*. See **sense**.]

sense [sens] *n* a faculty by which objects are perceived (sight, hearing, smell, taste, or touch); immediate consciousness; consciousness (of eg shame, responsibility); impressions (of eg strangeness); appreciation (of eg the ridiculous, the fitness of things); quality of intellect or character expressed in such appreciation (eg *sense of humor, honor*); soundness of judgment; (*pl*) conscious awareness; that which is reasonable; meaning, as of a word; general feeling, opinion (*the sense of the meeting*).—*vt* to perceive; to detect, as by sensors; to grasp, understand; to become conscious of.—*adj* **sense´less**, deficient in good sense, foolish; meaningless, purposeless.—*adv* **sense´lessly**.—*n* **sense´lessness**.—*adj* **sen´sible**, perceptible by sense; easily perceived; appreciable; cognisant, aware (of); prudent, judicious; having power of sensation.—*ns* **sen´sibleness; sensibil´ity**, state or quality of being perceptible by sense, or of feeling readily; readiness and delicacy of emotional response, sensitiveness; sentimentality.—(*often pl* **sensibil´ities**) delicate, sensitive awareness or feelings.—*adv* **sen´sibly**, prudently, appreciably.—*vt* **sen´sitize**, to render sensitive.—*ns* **sensitizā´tion**, the action or process of sensitizing; quality or state of being sensitized (as to an antigen); **sen´sitizer**.—*adj* **sen´sitive**, having power of sensation; ready and delicate in response to outside influences; feeling readily, acutely, or painfully; easily offended; touchy.—*adv* **sen´sitively**—*ns* **sen´sitiveness; sensitiv´ity**, state of being sensitive; ability to register minute changes or differences; degree of responsiveness to stimuli; abnormal responsiveness; **sen´sor** [-sȯr] a device to detect, measure, or record physical phenomena, as heat, pulse, etc.; sense organ.—*adj* **sensō´rial**, sensory.—*ns* **sensō´rium**, the parts of the brain dealing with sensory stimuli; (*loosely*) the entire sensory apparatus.—*adj* **sen´sory** of the sensorium; of sensation.—*adj* **sensual** [sench´ů-ȧl, sen´shōō-ȧl] of the senses as distinct from the mind, not intellectual or spiritual; connected or preoccupied with sexual pleasures.—*vt* **sen´sualize**, to make sensual.—*ns* **sen´sualism**, sensual indulgence; **sen´sualist**, a debauchee; **sensual´ity**, indulgence in sensual pleasures; lewdness.—*adv* **sen´sually**.—*adj* **sen´suous**, pertaining to sense; having strong sensory appeal; easily affected through the medium of the senses.—*adv* **sen´suously**.—*n* **sen´suousness**.—**sensitive plant**, any of several mimosas (esp *Mimosa pudica*) with leaves that fold or drop when touched; (*loosely*) a plant that responds with movement to touch.—**in a sense**, in one aspect; **make sense**, to be understandable or logical. [Fr,—L *sēnsus*—*sentīre*, to feel.]

sent [sent] *pt, pt p* of **send**.

sentence [sen´tėns] *n* (*obs*) opinion; a judgment; determination of punishment pronounced by a court or judge; the punishment; (*arch*) a maxim; (*gram*) a number of words making a complete grammatical structure.—*vt* to pronounce punishment upon (a convicted person); to cause to suffer something.—*adj* **senten´tious** [-shůs], ponderously trite; fond of moralizing.—*adv* **senten´tiously**.—*n* **senten´tiousness**. [Fr,—L *sententia*—*sentīre*, to feel.]

sentient [sen´sh(y)ėnt] *adj* conscious; capable of sensation, responsive to stimulus.—*ns* **sen´tience**.—*adv* **sen´tiently**, in a sentient or perceptive manner. [L *sentiēns, -entis*, pr p of *sentīre*, to feel.]

sentiment [sen´ti-mėnt] *n* a thought, or body of thought, tinged with emotion; an opinion; a thought expressed in words; feeling bound up with some object or ideal (eg *patriotic sentiment*); appeal to the emotions, or sensitivity to this; maudlin emotion.—*adj* **sentimen´tal**, having or showing delicate feelings; maudlin, mawkish; of or resulting from sentiment; affectedly tender.—*ns* **sentimen´talism, sentimental´ity**, quality of being sentimental; affectation of fine feeling; **sentimen´talist**, one who delights in sentiment or fine feeling; one who regards sentiment as more important than reason.—*adv* **sentimen´tally**. [Fr,—LL *sentimentum*—L *sentīre*, to feel.]

sentinel [sen´ti-nėl] *n* one posted on guard, a sentry. [Fr *sentinelle*—It *sentinella*, a watch, sentinel.]

sentry [sen´tri] *n* a sentinel, a soldier on guard to prevent or announce the approach of an enemy.—*n* **sen´try box**, a box to shelter a sentry.

sepal [sep´ȧl] *n* one of the leaflike members forming the calyx of a flower. [Fr *sépale*.]

separate [sep´ȧ-rāt] *vt* to divide, part; to sever; to disconnect; to set apart; to keep apart; to sort into different sizes, divide into different constituents, etc.—*vi* to part, go different ways; to cease to live together as man and wife; to become isolated from a mixture.—*adj* [sep´ȧ-rȧt] divided; apart from another; distinct; not shared.—*n* [sep´a-rȧt] a separately printed excerpt (as a magazine article); an article of clothing designed to be worn interchangeably with others to form various outfits.—*adj* **sep´arable**, that may be separated or disjointed.—*n* **separabil´ity**.—*advs* **sep´arably; sep´arately**.—*ns* **separā´tion**, act of separating or disjoining; state of being separate; termination of a contractual relationship; **sep´aratism**, the action or policy of a separatist; withdrawing esp from an established church; the advocacy of separation, racially, politically, etc.; **sep´aratist**, one who withdraws or advocates separation, esp from an established church, federation, organization, etc.; a dissenter.—*adj* **sep´arative**, tending to separate.—*n* **sep´arātor**, one who, or that which, separates; a machine for separating liquids of different specific gravities (as cream from milk) or liquids from solids. [L *sēparāre, -ātum*—*sē*, aside, *parāre*, to put.]

Sephardi [sė-fär´di] *n* a Spanish or Portuguese Jew or descendant of Sephardim; a member of Ashkenazic Hasidim who use part of the Sephardic liturgy;—*pl* **Sephar´dim**.—*adj* **Sephar´dic**. [Heb.]

sepia [sē´pi-a] *n* a cuttlefish; the ink of a cuttlefish; a pigment made from it; its color, a dark reddish brown.—*adj* of the color sepia. [L,—Gr *sēpiā*, the cuttlefish.]

sepoy [sē´poi] *n* a native of India in European military service. [Hindustani and Pers *sipāhī*, a horseman.]

sepsis [sep´sis] *n* septicemia. [Gr.]

sept [sept] *n* in ancient Ireland, a division of a tribe; a similar division elsewhere, as a division of a Scottish clan; a branch of a family. [Prob for **sect**; influenced by **septum**.]

September [sep-tem´bėr] *n* the ninth month of the year, having 30 days. [L,—*septem*, seven.]

septennial [sep-ten´i-ȧl] *adj* lasting seven years; happening every seven years.—*adv* **septenn´ially**. [L *septennis*—*septem*, seven, *annus*, a year.]

septet [sep-tet´] *n* a musical composition for seven voices or instruments; a company of seven (esp musicians). [L *septem*, seven.]

septic [sep´tik] *adj* putrefactive; suppurating.—**septic tank**, an underground tank in which sewage is partially purified by the action of certain bacteria. [Gr *sēptikos*—*sēpein*, to rot.]

septicemia [sep-ti-sē´mi-a] *n* presence of poisonous bacteria in the blood. [**septic**, + Gr *haima*, blood.]

septuagenarian [sep-tū-ȧ-je-nā´ri-ȧn] *n* a person over seventy and under eighty years of age.—Also *adj*. [L *septuāgēnārius*—*septuāgēni*, seventy each—*septum*, seven.]

Septuagesima [sep-tū-ȧ-jes´i-ma] *n* the third Sunday before Lent. [L *septuāgēsimus*, seventieth.]

Septuagint [sep´tū-ȧ-jint] *n* a pre-Christian Greek version of the Old Testament, said to have been made by 72 Jewish scholars at Alexandria in the 3d century BC and adapted by Greek-speaking Christians. [L *septuāgintā*, seventy—*septum*, seven.]

septum [sep´tum] *n* (*biol*) partition separating two cells or cavities as in the nose, fruit, etc.;—*pl* **sep´ta**. [L,—*saepīre, sēpīre*, to enclose.]

sepulcher, sepulchre [sep´ul-kėr] *n* a place of burial, tomb.—*adj* **sepul´chral**, pertaining to a sepulcher; funereal, dismal; (of sound) deep, hollow in tone.—*n* **sep´ulture**, interment, burial. [L *sepulcrum*—*sepelīre, sepultum*, to bury.]

sequel [sē´kwėl] *n* that which follows, the succeeding part; result, consequence; a resumption of a story begun in an earlier literary work.—*n* **sequela** [si-kwē´la] morbid affection following disease or injury;—*pl* **sequē´lae** [-lē]. [L *sequēla*—*sequī*, to follow.]

sequence [sē´kwėns] *n* state of being sequent or following; order of succession; a series of things following in order; (*mus*) a succession of repetitions of a harmonic pattern or melodic phrase each in a new position; a single, uninterrupted episode, as in a movie.—*adjs* **sē´quent**, following; successive; **sequen´tial**, arranged in a sequence; following a sequence; based on a method of testing a statistical hypothesis involving examination of a sequence of samples. [L *sequēns, -entis*, pr p of *sequī*, to follow.]

sequester [si-kwes´tėr] *vt* to set aside; to seclude; (*law*) to remove from one's possession until a dispute be settled, creditors satisfied, or the like.—*adj* **seques´tered**, retired, secluded.—*vt* **seques´trate**, to sequester.—*ns* **sequestrā´tion**, the act of sequestering; a legal writ authorizing a sherriff to take into custody the property of a defendant who is in contempt of court until he complies with its orders; a deposit held by a neutral depository of property in litigation; **sequestrā´tor**. [Low L *sequestrāre, -ātum*—L *sequester*, a depositary—*secus*, apart.]

sequin [sē´kwin] *n* an old Italian or Turkish gold coin; a spangle. [Fr,—It *zechino*—*zecca*, the mint; of Ar origin.]

sequoia [si-kwoi´a] *n* a genus (*Sequoia*) consisting of two species, the 'big tree' (*S gigantea*) or giant sequoia or the redwood (*S sempervirens*). [After the name of an American Indian scholar.]

sera [sēr´a] *pl* of **serum**.

seraglio [se-ral´yō] *n* formerly, a palace or residence of the Sultan of Turkey; a harem; its occupants. [It *serraglio*—L *sera*, a door-bar. The word was confused with Turk *serāī*, a palace.]

serape [se-räp´ē] *n* a bright-colored woolen blanket used as a garment by men in Mexico, etc. [Mex Sp.]

seraph [ser´áf] *n* an angel of the highest rank; one of the 6-winged angels standing in the presence of God;—*pl* **seraphs** [ser´afs], **seraphim** [ser´af-im].—*adj* **seraph´ic**, like a seraph, angelic, pure, sublime.—*adv* **seraph´ically**. [Heb *Serāphīm* (pl).]

Serb [sûrb] *n* a native or citizen of Serbia, formerly a kingdom, now part of Yugoslavia.—*adj* **Serbian**, of Serbia, its people, or their language.—*n* a Serb; the Serbo-Croatian language as spoken in Serbia; a literary form of Serbo-Croatian using the Cyrillic alphabet.—*n* **Serbo-Crōāt´ian, Serbo-Cro´at**, the Slavic language which is the chief official language of Yugoslavia, of which Serbian is written in the Cyrillic alphabet and Croatian in the Roman alphabet.—Also *adj.* [Serbian *Srb.*]

sere, sear [sēr] *adj* (*poetical*) dried up, withered; (*arch*) threadbare. [OE *sēar*, dry, *sērian*, to dry up; Low Ger *soor*, Du *zoor.*]

serenade [ser-ė-nād´] *n* evening music in the open air; music played or sung by a lover under his lady's window at night; a piece of music suitable for such an occasion.—*vt* to entertain with a serenade. [Fr *sérénade*, and It *serenata*—*sereno*, serene—L *serēnus*, clear; meaning influenced by L *sērus*, late.]

serendipity [ser-ėn-dip´i-ti] *n* the faculty of making happy chance finds. [*Serendip*, a former name for Ceylon. Horace Walpole coined the word (1754) from title of fairy tale, 'Three Princes of Serendip', whose heroes 'were always making discoveries, by accidents and sagacity, of things they were not in quest of'.]

serene [si-rēn´] *adj* calm (eg of sea); unclouded; tranquil; august, used as an adjunct to a title.—*adv* **serēne´ly**, calmly, tranquilly.—*n* **seren´ity**, state or quality of being serene, calmness, tranquillity. [L *serēnus*, clear.]

serf [sûrf] *n* a person in feudal service attached to his master's land and transferred with it to a new owner;—*pl* **serfs**.—*n* **serf´dom**, condition of a serf. [Fr,—L *servus*, a slave.]

serge [sûrj] *n* a strong twilled fabric. [Fr,—L *sērica*, silk—*Sēres*, the Chinese.]

sergeant [sär´jánt] *n* a noncommissioned officer next above a corporal in the army and marine corps; a police officer ranking next below a captain or a lieutenant.—*ns* **ser´geancy**, office or rank of a sergeant; **ser´geant at arms**, an officer of a legislative body or court of law who preserves order and executes commands; **ser´geant mā´jor**, a noncommissioned officer in the army, air force, or marine corps serving as chief administrative assistant in a head-quarters; a bluish green to yellow perchlike fish (*Abudefduf saxatilis*) that is common in the tropical Atlantic Ocean. [Fr *sergent*—L *serviēns, -entis*, pr p of *servīre*, to serve.]

seriatim *see* **series**.

series [sē´rēz] *n sing* and *pl* a set of things of the same class coming one after another in spatial or temporal succession; a set of things having something in common; a set of things differing progressively; a succession of quantities each derivable from its predecessor by a law; (*geol*) the rocks formed during an epoch; a group of chemical compounds related in composition and structure; an arrangement in an electric circuit whereby the current passes through without branching; a number of games (as of baseball) played usu. on consecutive days between two teams.—*adj* **sē´rial**, forming a series; in series; in a row; of publications, films, or broadcasts, in installments at regular intervals.—*n* a publication, film, or broadcast, in installments.—*vt* **se´rialize**, to arrange in series; to publish serially.—*n* **serializa´tion**.—*adv* **sē´rially**.—*adj* **sēriate**, arranged in rows.—*adv* **sēriātim**, one after another.—**serial number**, one of a series of numbers given for identification. [L *seriēs*—*serĕre*, to join.]

serin [ser´in] *n* a small European finch (*Serinus serinus*) related to the canary. [Fr, canary.]

serious [sē´ri-ùs] *adj* solemn, grave; in earnest; demanding close attention; important; dangerous.—*adj* **sē´riocom´ic**, partly serious and partly comic.—*advs* **seriocom´ically; sēriously**.—*n* **sē´riousness**. [LL *sēriōsus*—L *sērius*, earnest.]

sermon [sûr´mòn] *n* a speech on religion or morals, esp by a clergyman; any serious admonition or reproof, esp a tedious one.—*vi* **ser´monize**, to compose sermons.—*vt* to preach to or on at length.—**Sermon on the Mount**, the sermon delivered by Jesus to his disciples. [L *sermō, -ōnis*—*serĕre*, to join.]

serous *See* **serum**.

serpent [sûr´pėnt] *n* (*arch*) any reptile or creeping thing, esp if venomous; a snake; the Devil; a treacherous person.—*adj* **ser´pentine**, resembling a serpent; winding, coiled; cunning, tortuous.—*n* a soft mineral, some forms of which are fibrous, composed of magnesium silicate, yielding asbestos. [L *serpēns, -entis*, pr p of *serpĕre*, to creep; akin to Gr *herpein.*]

serrate [ser´āt] *adj* notched like a saw.—*vt* to notch.—*n* **serrā´tion**, state of being serrated; a formation resembling the toothed edge of a saw; one of the teeth in a serrate margin. [L *serrātus*—*serra*, a saw.]

serried [ser´id] *adj* crowded, dense, set close together (eg *serried ranks*); marked by ridges. [Fr *serrer*, to crowd—L *sera*, a door-bar.]

serum [sē´rum] *n* any watery fluid from an animal, esp that which separates from coagulating blood; blood serum used as an antitoxin, taken from an animal inoculated for a specific disease;—*pl* **sē´rums, sēr´a**.—*adj* **sē´rous**, resembling serum; thin, watery.—*n* **sē´rum sickness**, an allergic reaction to the injection of foreign serum manifested by urticaria, swelling, eruption, arthritis, and fever. [L *sĕrum*, whey.]

servant [sûr´vánt] *n* one hired to work for another, esp to perform duties about the house or person of a personal employer. [Fr, pr p of *servir*—L *servīre, to serve.*]

serve [sûrv] *vt* to be a servant to, to work for; to do military or naval service for; to provide (customers) with (goods or services); to be of use to or for; to suffice for; to help to food, etc.; to distribute (food) at table; (*law*) to deliver (a summons, etc.) to; to undergo (a prison sentence); to strike (a ball or shuttlecock) to start play in tennis, etc.; (of male animals) to copulate with; to wind yarn or wire tightly around (a rope or stay) for protection.—*vi* to be employed as a servant; to perform appointed duties; to be used (for); to suffice, to avail; (of weather) to be favorable.—*n* the act of serving in tennis, etc.—*n* **ser´ver**, one who serves, esp at meals, mass or tennis; something used in serving food and drink; one that serves legal processes on another; the celebrant's assistant at low mass.—**serve one right**, to be deserved. [Fr *servir*—L *servīre*, to serve.]

service [sûr´vis] *n* occupation of a servant; public employment; a branch of this, specifically the armed forces; work done for others; any religious ceremony; benefit, advantage; (*pl*) friendly help or professional aid; a system of providing people with some utility, as water, gas, etc.; a facility providing some public demand (as of telephones, buses, etc.); a branch of a hospital medical staff devoted to a particular specialty; waiting at table; order of dishes at table; a set, as of dishes for a particular meal; act or mode of serving a ball.—*vt* to furnish with a service; to make fit for service, as by repairing; to perform business functions in support of production and distribution of goods.—*adj* **ser´viceable**, durable; useful; durable or useful.—*adv* **ser´viceably**.—*ns* **serviceabil´ity, ser´viceableness; ser´vice book**, a book of forms of religious service; **ser´viceman**, a member of the armed forces; a person whose work is repairing something; **service mark**, a word, etc. used like a trademark by a supplier of services; **service road**, a local street that parallels an expressway or through street and that provides access to property near to the expressway; **service station**, a place selling gasoline, oil, etc. for motor vehicles; a place at which some service is offered; **ser´vicewoman**, a female member of the armed forces. [Fr—L *servitium*—*servus*, slave.]

serviceberry [sûr´vis-ber-ē] *n* a small tree or shrub (*Amelanchior arborea*) of N America cultivated for its showy flowers and edible fruits; any of numerous related species.

servile [sûr´vīl] *adj* pertaining to slaves; suitable to a slave; meanly submissive, cringing.—*adv* **ser´vilely**.—*n* **servil´ity**, state or quality of being servile; slavery; obsequiousness. [L *servīlis*—*servus.*]

servitor [sûr´vi-tòr] *n* a male servant. [L *servīre*, to serve.]

servitude [sûr´vi-tūd] *n* bondage or slavery; work imposed as punishment for crime. [L *servitūdō*—*servus*, slave.]

servomechanism [sûr´vō-mek´án-izm] *n* an automatic control system of low power, used to exercise remote but accurate mechanical control. [L *servus*, slave.]

sesame [ses´á-me] *n* annual herb (*Sesamum indica*) of Southern Asia, whose seed yields valuable oil; its small seeds also used as a flavoring agent.—**open sesame**, charm by which door of robbers' cave flew open in 'Ali Baba and the Forty Thieves'; a magic key. [Fr—L—Gr.]

sesquipedalian [ses-kwi-pė-dā´li-án] *adj* having many syllables; given to the use of long words. [L *sēsquipedālis*—*sēsqui*, one-half more, *pēs, pedis*, a foot.]

sessile [ses´īl] *adj* having no stalk or peduncle, attached directly (as a leaf without petiole to a branch, or certain marine animals to rock, mud, etc.). [L *sessilis*, low, dwarf.]

session [sesh´(ò)n] *n* the meeting of a court, legislature, etc.; a series of such meetings; a period of these; a period of study, classes, etc.; a period of time spent engaged in any one activity.—**session man**, a studio musician who backs up a performer at a recording session. [Fr—L *sessiō, -ōnis*—*sedēre, sessum*, to sit.]

sestet, sestette [ses-tet´] *n* a stanza or poem of six lines, specifically, the last six lines of an Italian sonnet. [It *sestetto*—*sesto*—L *sextus*, sixth.]

set [set] *vt* to seat; to put in a specified place, condition, etc.; to fix (a trap for animals), adjust (a clock or dial), arrange (a table for a meal), fix (hair) in a desired style, put (a broken bone, etc.) into normal position, etc.; to make settled, rigid, or fixed; to mount (gems); to direct; to appoint, establish, fix (a boundary, the time for an event, a rule, a quota, etc.); to furnish (an example) for others; to fit (words to music or music to words); to arrange (type) for printing.—*vi* (of a fowl) to sit on eggs; to become firm, hard, or fixed; to begin to move (out, forth, off, etc.); to sink below the horizon; to have a certain direction;—*pr p* **sett´ing**; *p t, pt p* **set**.—*adj* fixed, established; intentional; rigid, firm; obstinate; ready.—*n* a setting or being set; the way in which a thing is set; direction; the scenery for a play, etc.; a group of persons or things classed or belonging together; assembled equipment for radio or television reception, etc.; (*math*) the totality of points, numbers, or objects that satisfy a given condition; (now usu. **sett**), a badger's burrow; (or **sett**), a sandstone or granite rectangular paving stone; (or **sett**), a rooted cutting or young plant ready for transplanting; (*tennis*) a group of games in which the winning side wins six by a margin of two or by winning a tiebreaker.—*ns* **set´back**, a check, reverse, or relapse; **set´off**, a claim set against another; a counterbalance; an ornament; **set´ piece**, a piece of theatrical scenery standing by itself; **sett´er**, one who or that which sets; a breed of dog trained to point game; **sett´ing**, the manner, position, or direction in which something is set; a mounting, as of a gem; scene; environment; music composed for a song, etc.; **set´-to´**, (*inf*) a bout, an argument; **set´up**, bodily carriage and physique; the plan, makeup, etc. of equipment used in an organization; the details of a situation, plan, etc.; (*inf*) a contest, etc. arranged to result in an easy victory.—**set about**, to begin; to do; **set forth**, to publish; to give an account of; to start on a journey; **set in**, to stitch (a small part) within a large article; to become established; to blow toward shore; **set off**, to show up by contrast; to set in motion; to cause to explode; **set on**, to urge (as a dog) to attack or pursue; to go on, advance; **set one's hand to**, to become engaged in; **set one's heart on**, to resolve; **set someone straight**, to correct someone by providing accurate information; **set store by**, to consider trustworthy, valuable, or worthwhile; **set the stage**, to provide the basis; **set up**, to erect; to establish, found; **set upon**, to attack, usu. with violence. [OE *settan*; cog with Ger *setzen*, ON *setja; settan* is the weak causative of *sittan*, to sit.]

sett *see* **set**

settee [se-tē´] *n* a long seat with a back esp a sofa for two. [Prob **settle**.]

setter, setting *See* **set**.

settle [set´l] *n* a long high-backed bench.—*vt* to place at rest or in comfort; to establish, install; to colonize; to restore to order; to quiet, compose; to determine, decide; to put beyond doubt or dispute; to cause to sink and become more compact; to free (the nerves, etc.) from disturbance; to pay (a debt, etc.).—*vi* to come to rest; to subside; to sink to the bottom; to take up permanent abode; to grow more stable; to come to a decision or agreement; to become localized, as pain.—*ns* **settle´ment**, act of settling; state of being settled; arrangement; a village; a community center for the underprivileged esp in large cities; a colony newly established; a settling of property, etc.; an instrument by which it is settled, or the sums, income, etc. settled; **sett´ler**, one who settles; a colonist.—**settle for**, to agree to accept; **settle someone's hash**, (*inf*) to subdue someone by decisive action; **settle the stomach**, to relieve the distress of indigestion. [OE *setl*, seat, *setlan*, to place.]

seven [sev´n] *adj, n* one more than six.—*n* the symbol for this (7, VII, vii); the seventh in a series or set; something having seven units as members.—*adj* **sevenfold**, having seven units as members; being seven times as great or as many.—*n* **seventh** (*mus*) an interval of seven diatonic degrees; the leading note.—Also *adj, adv*.—**seven seas**, the oceans of the world; **seven liberal arts**, in medieval classification, grammar, logic, rhetoric, arithmetic, music, geometry, and astronomy; **seventh chord**, (*mus*) a chord comprising a fundamental note with its third, fifth, and seventh; **Seventh-Day**, advocating or practicing the observance of the Sabbath on Saturday; **seventh heaven**, perfect happiness. [OE *seofon*; Du *zeven*, Ger *sieben*, Gr *hepta*, L *septem*.]

seventeen [sev´n-tēn] *adj, n* one more than sixteen; the symbol for this (17, XVII, xvii).—*adj, n* **seventeenth**.—*n* **seventeen-year locust**, a cicada (*Magicicada septendecim*) of the US that lives underground (in the North for 17 years, in the South for 13 years) as a nymph and only a few weeks as a winged adult. [OE *seofontēne, seofontīene*.]

seventy [sev´n-ti] *adj, n* seven times ten; the symbol for this (70, LXX, lxx];—*pl* **seventies** (70s) the numbers from 70 to 79; the same numbers in a life or a century.—*adj* **seventieth**.—*n* **sev´enty-eight**, a phonograph record designed to be played at seventy-eight revolutions per minute—usu. written 78. [OE *seofontig—seofon*, seven.]

sever [sev´ėr] *vti* to separate, to divide; to cut or break, or be broken, off, away from.—*n* **sev´erance**, act of severing; separation. [Fr *sevrer*, to wean—L *sēparare*, to separate.]

several [sev´ėr-ål] *adj* particular, distinct; respective; various; more than two but not very many.—*n* (with *pl v*) a small number (of).—*pron* (with *pl v*) a few.—*adv* **sev´erally**, separately. [OFr—L *sēparāre*, to separate.]

severe [sė-vēr´] *adj* rigorous, very strict; unsparing; inclement; hard to endure; austerely restrained or simple (eg style); rigidly exact (eg reasoning).—*adv* **severe´ly**.—*n* **severity** [sė-ver´i-ti] quality of being severe. [L *sevērus*.]

sew [sō] *vti* to join or fasten together with a needle and thread; to make, mend, etc. by sewing;—*pt* **sewed** [sōd]; *pt p* **sewn** [sōn] or **sewed** [sōd].—*ns* **sew´er**; **sew´ing**, act of sewing; what is sewn; **sew´ing machine**, any of numerous machines for sewing or stitching.—**sew up**, to get full control of; (*inf*) to make sure of success in. [OE *sīwian, sēowian*.]

sewer [sū´ėr] *n* a pipe or drain, usu. underground, used to carry off liquid waste matter and sometimes surface water (as from rainfall).—*ns* **sew´age**, refuse carried off by sewers; **sew´erage**, system of sewers; sewage. [OFr *seuwiere*, a canal—L *ex*, out, *aqua*, water.]

sex [seks] *n* the total characteristics, structural and functional, which distinguish male and female organisms, esp with regard to the part played in reproduction; either of the divisions of organisms according to this distinction, or its members collectively; the attraction between the sexes; sexual intercourse.—*ns* **sex´ism**, exploitation and domination of one sex by the other, esp of women by men; **sex´ist**.—*adjs* **sex´less**, of neither sex; without sex; without sexual feelings; **sex´ūal**, pertaining to sex; distinguished by, founded on, sex; relating to the distinct organs of the sexes.—*n* **sexūal´ity**, sexual activity; expression of sexual interest, esp when excessive.—*adv* **sex´ūally**.—*ns* **sex´appeal´**, power of attracting the other sex; **sex´ chrō´mosome**, a chromosome that is inherited differently in the two sexes and that is the seat of factors governing the inheritance of sex-linked and sex-limited characteristics.—*adjs* **sexed** [sekst] having sex; having sexual character or feelings to a specified degree (as in **over-, under-, highly sexed**); **sex-limited**, expressed in the phenotype of only one sex; **sex´-link´ed**, inherited along with sex, that is by a factor located in the sex chromosome; **sexy**, (*inf*) exciting or intended to excite sexual desire. [Fr *sexe*—L.]

sex- [seks-], **sexi-** [seks-i-] in composition, six. [L *sex*, six.]

sexagenarian [sek-så-je-nā´ri-ån] *n* a person over sixty and under seventy years of age.—Also *adj*. [L *sexāgēnārius—sexāgintā*, sixty.]

Sexagesima [sek-så-jes´i-ma] *n* the second Sunday in Lent. [*sexāgēsimus, -a, -um*, approximately sixtieth day before Easter.]

sextant [seks´tånt] *n* an instrument for measuring the angular distance of the sun, a star, etc. from the horizon, as to determine position at sea. [L *sextāns, -antis*, the sixth part.]

sextet [seks-tet´] *n* (*mus*) a work for six voices or instruments; the performers of a sextet; a hockey team. [Variant of **sestet**.]

sexton [seks´tón] *n* a church officer or employee in charge of the maintenance of church property. [Through OFr from root of **sacristan**.]

sextuple [seks´tū-pl] *adj* sixfold. [LL *sextuplus*—L *sex*, six.]

sforzando [sför-tsän´dō] *adj, adv* (*mus*) played with prominent stress or accent.—*n* an accented tone or chord. Abbrevs *sf, fz* and *sfz*, or marked >, △. [It, pr p and pt p of *sforzare*, to force.]

Shabbat [shå-bät´ or shäb´ås] *n* the Jewish Sabbath. [Heb.]

shabby [shab´i] *adj* threadbare or worn, as clothes; run down, dilapidated; mean, shameful.—*adv* **shabb´ily**.—*n* **shabb´iness**. [From obs or dial *shab*, scab.]

shack [shak] *n* a small, crudely built house or cabin; a shanty. [Origin obscure.]

shackle [shak´l] *n* a metal fastening, usu. in pairs, for the wrists or ankles of a prisoner; anything that restrains freedom, as of expression; a device for coupling; (*pl*) fetters, manacles.—*vt* to fetter; to join or couple by a shackle; to impede in freedom of action or expression. [OE *sc(e)acul*.]

shad [shad] *n* an important saltwater food fish (genus *Alosa*) related to the herring but spawning in rivers. [OE *sceadd*.]

shaddock [shad´ók] *n* the largest citrus fruit (*Citrus maxima*), native to the East Indies, similar to the grapefruit. [Introduced to the W Indies, *c* 1700, by Captain *Shaddock*.]

shade [shād] *n* a partial or relative darkness; interception of light; obscurity; a shady place; (*pl*) the abode of the dead, Hades; shelter from light or heat; a screen; degree of darkness of a color; a very minute amount (of difference); (*poet*) a ghost; a device used to screen from light; (*pl*) (*slang*) sunglasses.—*vt* to screen; to overshadow; to mark with gradations of color or shadow; to darken.—*vi* to change slightly or by degrees.—*n* **shā´ding**, a shielding against light; the effect of light and shade, as in a picture; fine gradations, nuances; toning down, modification.—*adj* **shā´dy**, having, or in, shade; sheltered from light or heat; (*inf*) disreputable.—*adv* **shā´dily**.—*n* **shā´diness**.—**on the shady side of**, beyond (a given age). [OE *sceadu*. See **shadow**.]

shadoof, shaduf [sha-dōōf´] *n* a contrivance for raising water by a bucket on a counterpoised pivoted rod, used since ancient times, esp in Egypt. [Egyptian Ar *shādūf*.]

shadow [shad´ō] *n* shade due to interception of light by an object; the dark shape of that object so projected on a surface; protective shade; the dark part, eg of a picture; gloom, affliction; an inseparable companion; a ghost, spirit; one (as a spy or detective) that shadows; a remnant, a trace.—*vt* to shade; to cloud or darken; to represent as by a shadow; to hide; to follow closely and watch, esp in secret.—*adj* having an indistinct pattern; having darker sections of a design; (of the opposition party in a parliamentary system of government) inactive but ready for the time when opportunity or need arises (eg *shadow minister of defense*).—*adj* **shad´owy**, shady; like a shadow; dim, vague; unsubstantial.—**shadow-box** (*boxing*) to spar with an imaginary opponent. [OE *sceadwe*, gen, dat, acc of *sceadu* (**shade** representing the nom).]

shaft [shäft] *n* an arrow or spear, or its stem; anything hurled like a missile; a stem; a narrow beam (of light); an arrow, esp for a longbow; a bar, usu. cylindrical, used to support rotating parts of machinery; a pole; the part of a column between the base and capital; the main upright part of anything; a long handle; a long, narrow passage sunk into the earth; a vertical opening passing through a building, as for an elevator; a pithily critical remark or attack; (*slang*) harsh or unfair treatment (*usu. with* **the**).—*vt* to fit with a shaft; (*slang*) to treat harshly or unfairly.—*n* **shaft´ing**, shafts or material for shafts. [OE *sceaft*; perh partly Ger *schacht*, pit.]

shag[1] [shag] *vt* to chase after and retrieve (baseballs hit in batting practice). [Origin unknown.]

shag[2] [shag] *n* a ragged mass of hair, or the like; a long coarse nap; a kind of tobacco cut into shreds; the green cormorant.—*adj* **shagg´y**, covered with rough hair, wool, or other growth; rough, rugged; untidy.—*n* **shagg´iness.**— **shaggy-dog story**, a long-drawn-out story about a trivial happening that is funny to the teller but boring and pointless to the hearer. [OE *sceaga.*]

shagreen [sha-grēn´] *n* an untanned leather covered with small round granulations and usu. dyed green; the skin of shark, ray, etc., covered with small nodules.—*adj* of, or covered with, shagreen. [Fr *chagrin*—Turk *saghrī*, etc., horse's rump, shagreen.]

shah [shä] *n* a title of a sovereign of Iran. [Pers.]

Shahaptian [shȧ-hap´ti-ȧn] *n* Amerindian linguistic family of Oregon, Washington, and Iowa.

shake [shāk] *vti* to move with quick, short motions, to agitate; to tremble or cause to tremble; to become or cause to become unsteady; to unnerve or become unnerved; to clasp (another's hand) as in greeting;—*p t* **shook**; *pt p* **shāk´en.**—*n* a shaking; a wood shingle; a milkshake; (*pl*) (*inf*) a convulsive trembling (*usu. with* **the**); (*inf*) deal (*a fair shake*).—*n* **shake´down**, an improvised bed (as one made on the floor); (*slang*) an extortion of money, as by blackmail; a thorough search.—*adj* for testing new equipment.—*ns* **Shaker**, a member of a religious sect that lived in celibate communities in the US; **shake-'up**, an extensive reorganization.—*adj* **shāk´y**, shaking or inclined to shake; loose; tremulous; precarious; unreliable.—*adv* **shāk´ily.**—*n* **shak´iness.**—**no great shakes**, not outstanding; **shake down**, to cause to fall by shaking; (*slang*) to extort money from; **shake off**, to get rid of. [OE *sc(e)acan.*]

Shakespearean [shāk-spē´ri-ȧn] *adj* of or relating to, or in the style of, *Shakespeare*, or his works.—Also **Shakespē´rian, Shakspear´ean, Shakspē´rian.**—**Shakespearean sonnet**, a sonnet having three quatrains and a couplet with the rhyme scheme *abab cdcd efef gg.* [William *Shakespeare* (1564–1616), Eng poet and dramatist.]

shako [shak´ō] *n* a military cap of cylindrical shape with a flat top and a plume. [Hungarian *csákó.*]

shale [shāl] *n* a rock formed by the consolidation of clay, mud, or silt, splitting readily into thin laminae.—**shale oil**, oil obtained from some shales by heating. [Ger *schale*, a scale.]

shall [sh(a)l] *vt* an auxiliary verb used in formal speech to express futurity in the 1st person, and determination, obligation or necessity in the 2d and 3d persons.—*vi* (*arch*) will go.—*infin* obsolete; no participles; 2d pers sing (*arch*) **shalt**; 3d **shall**; *pt* **should** [shŏŏd]. [OE *sculan*, pr t (orig a preterite) *sceal, scealt, sceal*; pt *sceolde*; cf Ger *soll*, ON *skal*, to be in duty bound.]

shallop [shal´ȯp] *n* a usu. 2-masted sloop with secondary sails attached to the mainsails; a small open boat propelled by oars or sails and used chiefly in shallow waters. [OFr *chalupe*; cf **sloop**.]

shallot [shȧ-lot´] *n* a bulbous perennial herb (*Allium ascolonicum*) resembling an onion having small clustered bulbs used in seasoning; a green onion. [OFr *eschalote.*]

shallow [shal´ō] *adj* not deep; not profound; not wise; superficial. —*n* a place where the water is not deep; a shoal.—*n* **shall´owness**. [ME *schalowe*, perh related to **shoal** (2).]

Shalom aleichem [shaw´lȯm ȧ-lā´kėm or shō] used as a traditional Jewish greeting.—**shalom´**, used as a greeting and farewell. [Heb *shālōm 'alēkhem* peace unto you.]

shalt [shalt] 2d pers sing of **shall**.

sham [sham] *n* a pretense; a person or thing that is a fraud.—*adj* not real, pretended, false.—*vti* to pretend, to feign;—*pr p* **shamm´ing**; *pt, pt p* **shammed**. [First found as slang, late 17th cent.]

shaman [shä´mȧn] *n* a priest of Shamanism; a medicine man of a similar religion.—*n* **Sha´manism**, the religion of certain peoples of northern Asia, based on the belief that good and evil spirits can only be controlled by shamans. [Russian.]

shamble [sham´bl] *vi* to walk with an awkward, unsteady gait.—*n* a shambling gait. [Perh from next word, in allusion to trestle-like legs.]

shambles [sham´blz] *n pl* a slaughterhouse; a scene of great slaughter, destruction, or disorder. [OE *scamel*, a stool—Low L *scammellum*, dim of *scamnum*, a bench.]

shame [shām] *n* the sense of humiliation due to fault or failure; modesty; dishonor, disgrace; a cause or source of disgrace; a thing to be ashamed of.—*vt* to make ashamed; to disgrace; to put to shame by greater excellence; to drive by shame (into doing).—*adj* **shame´faced**, very modest or bashful; showing shame; ashamed.—*adv* **shame´facedly**.—*n* **shame´facedness.**—*adj* **shame´ful**, disgraceful.—*adv* **shame´fully**.—*n* **shame´fulness.**—*adj* **shame´less**, immodest; brazen; done without shame or compunction.—*adv* **shame´lessly**.—*n* **shame´lessness.**—**put to shame**, to cause to feel shame; to surpass. [OE *sc(e)amu*; Ger *scham.*]

shammy [sham´i] *See* **chamois**.

shampoo [sham-pōō´] *vt* (*arch*) to massage; to wash (the hair); to clean (carpet, etc.) by rubbing with a special preparation;—*pt, pt p* **shampooed´**.—*n* act of shampooing; a soap or other preparation for this purpose. [Hindustani *cā~pna*, to squeeze.]

shamrock [sham´rok] *n* a cloverlike plant with leaflets in groups of three, the national emblem of Ireland; a yellow-flowered clover (*Trifolium dubium*), often regarded as the true shamrock; wood sorrel; white clover. [Ir *seamróg*, Gael *seamrag*, dim of *seamar*, trefoil.]

shamus [shäm´us] *n* the sexton of a synagogue; (*slang*) a detective or private eye; an unimportant menial; an informer; the center candle of the Menorah which is used to light the others.

shandy [shan´di] *n* shandygaff; a mixture of beer with lemonade.—*n* **shandygaff**, beer diluted with a nonalcoholic drink (as ginger beer).

shanghai [shang´hī´] *vt* to drug or make drunk and ship as a sailor; to trick into performing an unpleasant task;—*pr p* **shanghai´ing**; *pt, pt p* **shanghaied´**. [*Shanghai* in China.]

Shangri-la [shang´gri-lä] *n* an imaginary place where life approaches perfection; a remote usu. idyllic hideaway. [An earthly paradise, described in James Hilton's novel, *Lost Horizon* (1933).]

shank [shangk] *n* the leg from knee to foot in man, or a corresponding part in animals; the whole leg; the part between the handle and the working part (of a tool, etc.). [OE *sc(e)anca*, leg; Du *schonk*, Low Ger *schanke.*]

shan't [shänt] a contraction of **shall not**.

shantung [shan-tung´] *n* a plain rough cloth of wild silk. [*Shantung*, province of China.]

shanty[1] [shan´ti] *n* a roughly built hut; a ramshackle dwelling.—*n* **shant´ytown**, a town, or an area of one, where housing is makeshift and ramshackle. [Canadian Fr *chantier*, a workshop.]

shanty[2] [shant´i] a song sung by sailors in rhythm with their work. [Said to be from Fr *chanter*, to sing.]

shape [shāp] *vt* to form, to fashion, to frame; to model, to mold; to regulate, direct, to determine; to adapt.—*vi* to take shape, to develop; to happen; to befall.—*pt p* **shāped**.—*n* form or figure; external appearance; condition (eg *in good shape; in no shape to do it*); that which has form or figure; an apparition; a pattern; (*cookery*) a jelly, or the like, turned out of a mold.—*adjs* **shā´pable, shape´able**, capable of being shaped; **shape´less**, having no shape or regular form; lacking symmetry.—*n* **shape´lessness.**—*adj* **shape´ly**, having shape or regular form; well-proportioned.—*n* **shape´liness.**—**shape up**, to develop to a definite or satisfactory form; **take shape**, to show distinct development. [OE *scieppan*, to form, make; ON *skapa*, Ger *schaffen.*]

shard [shärd] *n* a fragment, as of an earthen vessel. [OE *sceard.*]

share[1] [shār] *n* a part shorn or cut off; a division, section, portion; a fixed and indivisible section of the capital of a company.—*vt* to divide into shares; to apportion; to give or take a share of; to have in common.—*vi* to have a share.—*n* **share´holder**, one who owns a share in property, esp a stockholder. [OE *scearu*; cf **shear**.]

share[2] [shār] *n* a plowshare. [OE *scear*; cf foregoing word, and **shear**.]

shark [shärk] *n* any of a class (Elasmobranchii) of large voracious fishes of warm seas, some of which are dangerous to man and are of economic importance for oil from their livers and leather from their hides; an extortioner, a swindler, a sponging parasite; (*slang*) an expert in a given activity.—*n* **shark´skin´**, a smooth, silky cloth of wool, rayon, etc. [Origin doubtful.]

sharp [shärp] *adj* cutting, piercing; having a thin edge or fine point; not rounded; not gradual; severe; harsh; pungent; high in pitch; raised a semitone; sarcastic; of keen or quick perception; alert; abrupt; clear-cut; well-defined; crafty; underhanded; intense, as a pain; nippy, as a wind; (*slang*) smartly dressed.—*adv* too high in pitch; attentively; punctually; precisely; abruptly.—*n* a note raised a semitone; the symbol for it.—*vti* (*mus*) to make or become sharp.—*vti* **shar´pen**, to make or become sharp.—*n* **sharp´er**, a trickster, a swindler.—*adv* **sharp´ly**.—*n* **sharp´ness.**—*adj* **sharp´-set**, eager in appetite or desire; set at a sharp angle or to present a sharp edge.—*n* **sharp´-shoot´er**, a good marksman.—*adjs* **sharp´-sight´ed**, having acute sight; shrewd; **sharp´-witt´ed**, thinking quickly and effectively. [OE *scearp*; ON *skarpr*, Ger *scharf.*]

shatter [shat´ėr] *vti* to break into fragments suddenly; to damage or be damaged severely.—*adj* **shatt´erproof**, that will resist shattering. [Perh Low Ger; cf **scatter**.]

shave [shāv] *vt* to scrape or pare off a superficial slice, hair (esp of the face), or other surface material from; to graze the surface of.—*vi* to remove hair by a razor;—*pt p* **shāved** or (*arch*) **shā´ven.**—*n* the act or process of shaving; a paring;—*ns* **shave´ling**, a monk or friar; (*used disparagingly*) an adolescent youth; **shā´ver**, one who shaves; an instrument used in shaving, esp one with electrically-operated cutters; (*inf*) a boy; **shā´ving**, the act of scraping or using a razor; a thin piece of wood, metal, etc. shaved off. [OE *sc(e)afan*; Du *schaven*, Ger *schaben.*]

Shavian [shā´vi-ȧn] *adj* pertaining to the British critic and dramatist George Bernard *Shaw* (1856–1950).

shaw [shö] *n* a thicket, a small wood. [OE *sc(e)aga*; ON *skōgr*, Dan *skov.*]

shawl [shöl] *n* an oblong or square cloth worn as a covering for the head or shoulders.—*vt* to wrap in a shawl. [Pers *shāl.*]

shawm [shöwm] *n* an early double-reed woodwind instrument. [OFr *chalemie*—L *calamus*, a reed-pipe.]

Shawnee [shö-nē´] *n* a member of an Amerindian people originally of the central Ohio valley;—*pl* **-ee, -s**; the language of this people.

shay [shā] *n* (*dial*) a chaise. [Formed from **chaise**, mistaken as a pl.]

she [shē] *pron fem* the female (or thing spoken of as a female) named before, indicated or understood.—*n* a woman, girl, or female animal, often used in combination. [OE *sēo*, orig the fem of the definite article; in the 12th century it began to replace *hēo*, the old fem pron.]

sheaf [shēf] *n* a bundle of things bound side by side, esp stalks of grain, etc.; a collection of papers, etc. bound in a bundle;—*pl* **sheaves** [shēvz]. [OE *scēaf*; cf Ger *schaub*, Du *schoof.*]

shear [shēr] *vt* to cut, esp to clip with shears; to divest.—*vi* to separate;—*pt* **sheared**; *pt p* **sheared** or **shorn**.—*n* a machine for cutting metal; a type of deformation in which parallel planes in a body remain parallel but are relatively displaced in a direction parallel to themselves (also **shearing force**).—*ns* **shear´er; shear´ling**, skin from a recently sheared sheep that has been tanned and dressed with the wool left on.—*n pl* **shears**, large scissors; a large tool or machine with two opposed blades, used to cut metal, etc. [OE *sceran*; ON *skera*, to clip, Ger *scheren*, to shave.]

sheath [shēth] *n* a case for a blade; a covering (esp tubular or long); a woman's closefitting dress usu. worn without a belt;—*pl* **sheaths** [shēTHZ].—*vt* **sheathe** [shēTH] to put into, or cover with, a sheath or case; to withdraw (a claw) into a sheath.—*ns* **sheath´ing** [TH] that which sheathes, as boards, etc. forming the base for roofing or siding; **sheath´ knife**, a knife with a fixed blade encased in a sheath. [OE *scēath, scǣth*; Ger *scheide*, ON *skeithir.*]

sheave [shēv] *n* a grooved wheel or pulley (as of a pulley block). [ME *shefe, shive*; cf Ger *scheibe*, a flat thin piece.]

shed[1] [shed] *vt* (*dial*) to set apart, segregate; to pour out; to cause to flow; to radiate; to cause to flow off; to cast off (a natural growth, as hair, etc.)—*vi* to shed hair, etc;—*pr p* **shedd´ing**; *pt, pt p* **shed**.—*n* something (as the skin of a snake) that is discarded in shedding; a divide of land. [OE *scēadan*, to separate; Ger *scheiden.*]

shed[2] [shed] *n* a structure, often with one or more sides not enclosed, for storing or shelter; (*arch*) a hut. [App a variant of **shade**.]

sheen [shēn] *n* a shine, luster; brightness. [OE *scēne*, beautiful; Du *schoon*, Ger *schön.*]

sheep [shēp] *n* a genus (*Ovis*) of beardless, woolly, wild or domesticated, cud-chewing animals closely allied to goats, with edible flesh called mutton; a silly, helpless submissive person;—*pl* **sheep**.—*ns* **sheep´-dip**, a liquid preparation into which sheep are plunged, esp to destroy parasites; **sheep´dog**, a dog trained to tend, drive, or guard sheep; **sheep´fold**, a pen or enclosure for sheep.—*adj* **sheep´ish**, like a sheep; bashful, foolishly diffident or embarrassed.—*adv* **sheep´ishly**.—*ns* **sheep´ishness; sheep´shank**, a knot for temporarily shortening a rope; **sheep´shearer**, one who shears sheep; **sheep´shearing; sheep´skin**, the skin of a sheep; leather or parchment prepared from it; a garment made of or lined with sheepskin; (*inf*) a diploma. [OE *scēap*; Ger *schaf.*]

sheer[1] [shēr] *adj* absolute, utter (eg *sheer folly*); extremely steep; (of fabric) very thin, diaphanous.—*adv* vertically; outright.—*n* a sheer fabric or garment. [ME *schere*, perh from a lost OE equivalent of ON *skærr*, bright.]

sheer[2] [shēr] *vti* to deviate or cause to deviate from a course; to swerve.—*n* the fore-and-aft upward curve of a ship's deck as shown in a side elevation; the position of a ship riding to a single anchor and heading toward it; a change in course (of a ship). [Partly at least another spelling of **shear**; perh partly from the Low Ger or Du equivalent, *scheren*, to cut, withdraw.]

sheet[1] [shēt] *n* a broad thin piece of any material, as glass, plywood, metal, etc.; a large piece of cloth for a bed; a single piece of paper; (*inf*) a newspaper; a wide expanse; a suspended or moving expanse (as of fire or rain).—*vt* to cover with, or as with, a sheet; to furnish with sheets; to form into sheets.—*vi* to fall, spread, or flow in a sheet.—*ns* **sheet´ glass**, glass made in large sheets directly from the furnace or by making a cylinder and then flattening it; **sheet´ing**, cloth for sheets; material used to cover or line a surface; **sheet´ light´ning**, diffused appearance of lightning due to reflection and diffusion by the clouds and sky; **sheet metal**, metal rolled in the form of a thin sheet; **sheet music**, music printed on unbound sheets of paper. [OE *scēte*; cf next word.]

sheet[2] [shēt] *n* a rope for controlling the set of a sail. [OE *scēata*, corner; akin to **sheet** (1).]

sheet anchor [shēt´-angk´ȯr] *n* an anchor for an emergency; chief support, last refuge. [Formerly *shut-, shot-, shoot-anchor.*]

sheikh, sheik [shāk, shēk] *n* an Arab chief; (*slang*) a young man considered by girls to be irresistibly fascinating. [Ar *shaikh*—*shākha*, to be old.]

shekel [shek´l] *n* the unit of money in Israel; a gold or silver coin of the ancient Hebrews; (*pl*—*slang*) money. [Heb *sheqel*—*shāqal*, to weigh.]

sheldrake [shel´drāk] *n* a merganser; a shelduck.—*n* **shelduck** [shel-duk´] any of various Old World ducks (genus *Tadorna*), esp a common black-and-white European duck (*T. tadorna*). [Prob dial *sheld*, variegated, + **drake, duck**.]

shelf [shelf] *n* a board fixed in a cupboard, on a wall, etc., for laying things on; a flat layer of rock, a ledge; a shoal, a sandbank;—*pl* **shelves** [shelvz].—*n* **shelf life**, the period of time during which a material may be stored and remain suitable for use.—**off the shelf**, available from stock, not made to order; **on the shelf**, shelved; laid aside from duty or service. [OE *scylf*, shelf, ledge.]

shell [shel] *n* a hard outer covering, esp of a shellfish, a tortoise, an egg, or a nut; something like a shell in being hollow, empty, a covering, etc.; a light, narrow racing boat rowed by a team; a small-arms cartridge; a sleeveless blouse or sweater; an explosive projectile shot from a cannon.—*adj* of, with, or like, shell or shells.—*vt* to separate from the shell; to bombard with shells.—*ns* **shellac, shell´ack**, a resin usu. produced in thin, flaky layers or shells; a thin varnish containing this resin and alcohol.—*vt* to apply shellac to; (*slang*) to beat or defeat decisively; **shell´back**, an old sailor; **shell´fish**, any aquatic animal with a shell, esp an edible one as the clam, lobster, etc.—*adj* **shell´proof**, able to resist shells or bombs.—*n* **shell´shock**, any of numerous hysterical psychoneurotic conditions appearing in soldiers under fire.—**shell out**, (*inf*) to pay out (money). [OE *scel*; Du *schel*, ON *skel.*]

shelter [shel´tėr] *n* a structure that shields or protects, esp against weather; a place of refuge, retreat, or temporary lodging in distress; protection.—*vt* to take shelter. [Orig *sheltron*—OE *scyld-truma*, shield-troop.]

shelve [shelv] *vt* to furnish with shelves; to place on a shelf; to put aside.—*vi* to slope, incline.—*n pl* **shelves**, *pl of* **shelf**.—*n* **shelv´ing**, material for shelves; shelves collectively. [See **shelf**.]

shepherd [shep´ėrd] *n* one who tends sheep; a clergyman.—*n* **shep´herdess** a woman or girl who tends sheep; a rural girl or woman.—*vt* to tend, or to guide, as a shepherd.—*ns* **shepherd's check, shepherd's plaid**, a small black and white checked pattern; **shepherd's pie**, a dish of meat cooked with a mashed potato crust. [OE *scēaphirde*. See **sheep, herd**.]

Sheraton [sher´ȧ-tȯn] *adj* applied to a style of furniture characterized by straight lines and graceful proportions. [Thomas *Sheraton* (1751–1806).]

sherbet [shûr´bėt] *n* a frozen dessert like an ice, but with gelatin and, often, milk added. [Turk and Pers *sherbet*, from Ar]

sheriff [sher´if] *n* (*hist*) the king's representative in a shire, with wide judicial and executive powers; the chief law-enforcement officer of a county.—*n* **sher´iffdom**. [OE *scīrgerēfa*—*scīr*, shire, *gerēfa*, a reeve.]

sherlock [shûr´lok] *n* a detective. [Sherlock Holmes, in the stories of Conan Doyle (1859–1930).]

Sherpa [shûr´pȧ] *n sing* and *pl* one or more of an eastern Tibetan people living high on the south side of the Himalayas, skilled in mountain climbing. [Tibetan *shar*, east, *pa*, inhabitant.]

sherry [sher´i] *n* a fortified wine made in the neighborhood of Jerez de la Frontera in Spain; a similar wine produced elsewhere. [*Xeres*, earlier form of Jerez.]

Shetland pony [shet´land pō´ni] a small sturdy and shaggy horse, originally bred in the *Shetland* Islands.—**Shetland wool**, a fine yarn spun from the wool of the sheep in the Shetland Islands.

shewbread, showbread [shō´bred] *n* consecrated unleavened bread ritually placed by Jewish priests of ancient Israel in the Tabernacle on the Sabbath. [Ger.]

sheygets [shā´gėts or -gits] *n* a Gentile boy or young man; a clever Jewish or Gentile lad, esp one with good looks and charm; a boy with no intellectual ambitions. [Heb.]

shibboleth [shib´ȯ-leth] *n* (*Bible*) the test word used to distinguish the enemy; the use of language to distinguish a particular group; any password; a commonplace idea or saying. [Heb *shibbōleth*, an ear of corn, or a stream.]

shield [shēld] *n* a piece of armor carried for defense against weapons and missiles; anything that protects; a person who protects; defense; the escutcheon used for displaying arms; a trophy shaped like a shield.—*vti* to protect; to defend. [OE *sceld*; Ger *schild*; ON *skjöldr*, protection.]

shift [shift] *vi* to manage, get on, do as one can; to change position.—*vt* to move from one person or place to another; to replace by another or others; to change the arrangement of (gears).—*n* a shifting; a transfer; a plan of conduct, esp for an emergency; an evasion; a trick; a gearshift; a group of people working in relay with another; their regular work period.—*n* **shift´er**, one who shifts; a trickster.—*adj* **shift´less**, without resource; inefficient, feckless.—*adv* **shift´lessly**.—*n* **shift´lessness**.—*adj* **shift´y**, full of, or ready with, shifts or expedients, esp evasive, tricky; indicating evasivenes or trickery (eg *shifty eyes*); tending to shift.—*n* **shift´iness**.—**shift gears**, to make a change; **make shift**, to manage with the means at hand. [OE *sciftan*, to divide, ON *skipta.*]

Shih Tzu [shēd´dzōō] *n* a Chinese breed of small dog with long, silky hair and short legs. [Chinese.]

shikse [shik´sȧ] *n* a girl or woman who is not Jewish; (among Orthodox Jews) a Jewish housewife who does not keep a kosher kitchen; a Jewish woman who does not respect the Jewish faith. [Yiddish, from Heb.]

shilelagh, shillelah [shi-lā´la] *n* the oak or blackthorn cudgel of the conventional Irishman. [*Shillelagh*, an oak-wood in County Wicklow.]

shill [shill *n* (*slang*) a confederate, as of a gambler, who acts as a decoy.

shilling [shil´ing] *n* a former monetary unit of the United Kingdom, and of various Commonwealth countries; a coin at first silver, later cupronickel, worth £1/20; its value. [OE *scilling*; Ger *schilling.*]

shilly-shally [shil´i-shal´i] *n* a vacillation, indecision.—*vi* to hesitate feebly. [A reduplication of **shall I?**]
shim [shim] *n* a thin wedge of wood, metal, etc. as for filling space.
shimmer [shim´ėr] *vi* to gleam tremulously, to glisten.—*n* **shimm´er**, a tremulous gleam. [OE *scimerian—scīmian*, to shine; Ger *schimmern*.]
shimmy [shim´i] *n* a marked vibration or wobble, as in a car's front wheels.—*vi* to vibrate or wobble. [From **chemise**.]
shin [shin] *n* the forepart of the leg below the knee.—*vti* to climb (a pole, etc.) by gripping with hands and legs.—*n* **shin´bone**, tibia. [OE *scin*, the shin (*scin-bān*, shin-bone); Du *scheen*, Ger *schiene*.]
shindig [shin´dig] *n* (*inf*) a dance, party or other lively celebration. [Cf **shindy**.]
shindy [shin´di] *n* (*inf*) shindig; uproar, a row, disturbance. [Perh **shinty**.]
shine [shīn] *vi* to give or reflect light; to beam with steady radiance, to glow, to be bright; to excel, or to appear preeminent.—*vt* to cause to shine by polishing; to direct the light of;—*pt, pt p* **shone** [shon], **shīned**.—*n* brightness, luster, sheen.—*n* **shiner**, a silvery minnow (esp genus *Notropis*); a discoloration around the eye from bruising.—*adj* **shī´ny**, glossy.—**take a shine to**, (*slang*) to take a liking to; **shine up to (someone)**, (*slang*) to curry favor. [OE *scīnan*; Ger *scheinen*.]
shingle[1] [shing´gl] *n* a thin, wedge-shaped piece of wood, slate, etc. laid in overlapping rows to cover the sides or roof of a building; (*inf*) a small signboard, as of a doctor, etc.; a mode of haircutting showing the form of the head at the back.—*vt* to cover with shingles; to cut in the manner of a shingle. [Low L *scindula*, a wooden tile—L *scindĕre*, to split.]
shingle[2] [shing´gl] *n* coarse waterworn gravel as on a beach; an area covered with this.—*adj* **shing´ly**. [Origin obscure.]
shingles [shing´glz] *n pl* a virus disease marked by a painful eruption of clusters of firm vesicles along the course of a nerve. [L *cingulum*, a belt—*cingĕre*, to gird.]
Shinto [shin´tō] *n* the indigenous religion of Japan, characterized by the veneration of nature and of ancestors. [Jap, = Chinese *shin tao—shin*, god, *tao*, way, doctrine.]
ship [ship] *n* any large vessel navigating deep water; a ship's officers and crew; an aircraft.—*vt* to put, receive, or take on board; to send or convey by any carrier; to take in (water) over the side in a heavy sea; to put in place on a vessel (eg *to ship the oars*).—*vi* to embark; to go or travel by ship;—*pr p* **shipp´ing**; *pt, pt p* **shipped**.—*ns* **ship´ bis´cuit**, hardtack; **ship´board**, a ship's side; a ship; **ship´builder** one who designs or constructs ships; **ship´building; ship´master**, the captain of a ship other than a warship; **ship´mate**, a fellow sailor; **ship´ment**, act of putting on board ship; consignment by ship; that which is shipped; **ship´owner**, the owner of, or owner of a share in a ship; **shipp´er; shipp´ing**, the act or business of transporting goods; ships collectively, as of a nation, port, etc.—*adj* **ship´shape**, in a seamanlike condition; trim, neat, orderly.—ns **ship´way**, a support for ships under examination or repair; a ship canal; **ship´wreck**, the remains of a wrecked ship; the loss of a ship through storm, etc.; ruin, disaster.—*vt* to cause to undergo shipwreck.—*ns* **ship´wright**, a carpenter skilled in ship construction and repair; **ship´yard**, a yard, place, or enclosure where ships are built or repaired. [OE *scip*; ON *skip*, Ger *schiff*.]
shire [shīr (in composition, -shėr)] *n* (*Brit*) a county; applied also to certain smaller districts in England, as Richmondshire, Hallamshire.—*ns* a large, strong draft horse, once bred chiefly in the Midland shires in England; **shire town**, in New England, a town where a court of superior jurisdiction sits. [OE *scīr*, office, authority.]
shirk [shûrk] *vti* to evade or neglect duties or obligations.—*n* **shir´ker**. [shark.]
shirr [shûr] *vt* to make shirrings in cloth; to bake (eggs) in buttered dishes.—*n* **shirring**, a gathering made in cloth by drawing the material up on parallel rows of short stitches.
shirt [shûrt] *n* a man's loose sleeved garment for the upper body; typically with fitted collar and cuffs; an undershirt; (*inf*) all or most of one's money or resources.—*ns* **shirt´dress**, a tailored dress patterned on a shirt and having buttons down the front; **shirt´ing**, cloth for shirts; **shirt´tail**, the part of a shirt extending below the waist.—*adj* very young; immature; distantly and indefinitely related (eg *a shirttail cousin*).—*n* **shirt´waist**, a woman's blouse tailored like a shirt.—**keep one's shirt on**, (*slang*) to keep calm. [OE *scyrte*; cf **short**.]
shittimwood, shittim [shit´imwŏŏd] *n* the wood of the shittah tree; any of several trees (genus *Bumelia*) of the southern US; their hard dense wood.—*n* **shitt´àh**, a tree of certain indentity but probably an acacia (as *Acacia seyal*), the wood from which the Hebrew tabernacle was made. [Heb *shittāh*, pl *shittīm*.]
shiver[1] [shiv´ėr] *n* a splinter, a chip, a small fragment.—*vti* to break into splinters.—*adj* **shiv´ery**, brittle. [Early ME *scifre*; cf **sheave**; Ger *schiefer*.]
shiver[2] [shiv´ėr] *vi* to quiver or tremble, to make an involuntary movement as with cold or fear.—*vt* to cause to quiver.—*n* a shivering movement.—*adj* **shiv´ery**, inclined to shiver or tremble. [ME *chivere*.]
shlemiel [shle-mēl´] *n* (*inf*) a clumsy or unlucky person; a foolish person; a social misfit. [Yiddish.]
shlep [shlep] *vti* to drag, pull, lag behind; to delay or cause to delay.—*n* an unkempt person; a petty thief; a hobo, a bum.
shlock [shlok] *n* (*inf*) any article of poor quality; kitsch; dope, narcotics. [Yiddish.]
shmalz [shmölts, shmälts] *n* (*inf*) excessive sentimentality; rendered chicken fat.—*vi* to express inappropriate emotion.—*adj* corny; mawkish; trite.—Also **schmaltz**. [Ger Yiddish.]
shmeer [shmēr] *n* (*inf*) a bribe; the entire deal.—*vt* to spread, smear; to bribe (someone). [Yiddish.]
shmo [shmō] *n* (*inf*) a foolish, ineffectual person; a natural victim. [Yiddish.]
shmoos [shmus, shmōōz] *n* (*inf*) aimless, friendly chat.—*vi* to engage in a heart-to-heart talk. [Yiddish.]
schnook [shnŏŏk] *n* (*inf*) a shlemiel; a timid, unassertive person. [Yiddish.]
shnorer [shnor´er] *n* (*inf*) a professional beggar; a compulsive bargainer.—*vi* **shnor**, to beg; to try to get for nothing. [Yiddish.]
shoal[1] [shōl] *n* a large crowd; a multitude of fishes swimming together.—*vi* to crowd. [OE *scolu*, troop; cf **school**. (2).]
shoal[2] [shōl] *adj* shallow.—*n* a shallow; a sandbar.—*vi* to become shallow.—*vt* to come to a shallow or less deep part. [OE *sceald*, shallow.]
shock[1] [shok] *n* a violent impact, a collision; a sudden jarring or shaking as if by a blow; an alarming and disconcerting experience; the cause of this; a convulsive excitation of nerves, as by electricity; a disorder of the blood circulation, produced by hemorrhage, disturbance of heart function, etc.—*vt* to give a shock to; to startle; to dismay, to horrify.—*vi* to be horrified; to collide.—*n* **shock´er**, a sensational tale, play, etc.; anything that shocks.—*adj* **shock´ing**, causing horror or dismay, highly offensive.—*adv* **shock´ingly**.—*ns* **shock´ absorber**, a device, as on the springs of a car, that absorbs the force of bumps and jars; **shock´ troops**, troops trained to lead attacks; **shock´ wave**, the violent effect produced in the vicinity of an explosion as a result of a change in atmospheric pressure; a compressional wave formed when the speed of a body or fluid in a medium exceeds that at which the medium can transmit sound; **shock therapy**, the treatment of certain severe mental illnesses by using electricity, drugs, etc. to produce convulsions or coma. [App Fr n *choq*, vb *choquer*, or perh directly from a Gmc source.]
shock[2] [shok] *n* bundles of grain stacked together. [ME *schokke*.]
shock[3] [shok] *n* a shaggy mass (of hair). [Perh a variant of **shag**.]
shod [shod] *pt, pt p* of **shoe**.
shoddy [shod´i] *n* wool from shredded rags; cloth made of it, alone or mixed; any inferior article seeking to pass for better than it is.—*adj* of shoddy; cheap and nasty; sham.
shoe [shōō] *n* a stiff outer covering for the foot, not coming above the ankle; a horseshoe; the part of a brake that presses against a wheel; the casing of a pneumatic tire; any device to guide movement, provide contact, or protect against wear, damage, or slipping; a dealing box designed to hold several decks of cards;—*pl* **shoes**, [shōōz].—*vt* to furnish with a shoe; to cover for strength or protection;—*pr p* **shoe´ing**; *pt, pt p* **shod**.—*ns* **shoe´black**, one who blacks shoes or boots; **shoe´horn**, a curved piece of horn or metal used to help the heel into a shoe; **shoelace**, a string passed through the eyelet holes to fasten a shoe; **shoe´string**, a shoelace; a small amount of capital.—*adj* at or near the ankles.—**fill someone's shoes**, take someone's place. [OE *scōh* (pl *scōs*—weak pl in *-n* appears in ME); Ger *schuh*.]
shone [shon] *pt, pt p* of **shine**.
shook [shŏŏk] *pt* of **shake**.
shoot [shoot] *vt* to move swiftly over, by, etc.; to variegate (with another color, etc.); to thrust or put forth; to discharge or fire (a bullet, arrow, gun, etc.); to send forth swiftly, esp with force; to wound with a bullet, arrow, etc.; to photograph; (*sports*) to throw or drive (a ball, etc.) toward the objective or to score (a goal, points, etc.).—*vi* to move swiftly; to feel suddenly, as pain; to grow rapidly; to jut out; to send forth a missile; to use guns, etc. as in hunting;—*pt, pt p* **shot**.—*n* a contest, shooting trip, etc.; a new growth or sprout.—*ns* **shoot´er**, one who, or that which, shoots; a marble shot from the hand; **shoot´ing**, act of discharging firearms or an arrow; **shoot´ing gall´ery**, a long room used for practice in the use of firearms; (*slang*) a place where one can obtain narcotics and shoot up; **shoot´ing star**, a meteor; any of several N American perennial herbs (genus *Dodecathon*, esp *D meadia*) with showy flowers with reflex petals; **shoot´ing stick**, a walking stick with a head that opens out into a seat.—**shoot up**, to attack, injure or kill by shooting, esp indiscriminately; (*slang*) to inject a narcotic into a vein. [OE *scēotan*; Du *schieten*, Ger *schiessen*, to dart.]
shop [shop] *n* a place in which goods are sold, esp a small store; a place where mechanics work, or where any kind of industry is carried on; details of one's own work, business, or profession, or talk about these; a school laboratory equipped for manual training.—*vi* to visit shops to examine or buy goods; to hunt through a market looking for the best buy.—*vt* to examine the stock or offerings of;—*pr p* **shopp´ing**; *pt p* **shopped**.—*ns* **shop´keeper**, one who owns or operates a small store; **shop´keeping; shoplift´ing**, stealing from a store during shopping hours; **shoplift´er; shopp´er**, one who shops; one hired by a store to shop for others; one hired by a store to compare competitor's prices, etc.; **shop´ stew´ard**, a union member elected as the union representative of a shop or department

in dealings with the management; **shop´talk**, the specialized words and idioms of those in the same work or sharing a special area of interest; talk about work, esp after hours.—**shopping center**, a complex of stores, restaurants, and service establishments with a common parking area.—Also **shopping plaza**. [OE *sceoppa*, a treasury, perh booth.]

shore[1] [shōr, shör] *n* land bordering on the sea or an expanse of water.—*adv* **shore´ward, shorewards**, towards the shore.—*n* **shore patrol**, a detail of the navy, coast guard, or marine corps acting as military police on shore. [ME *schore*; cf Du *schoor, schor.*]

shore[2] [shōr, shör] *n* a prop or beam used for support.—*vt* to prop (up). [Cf Du *schoor.*]

shorn [shörn, shōrn] *pt p* of **shear**.

short [shört] *adj* not measuring much from end to end in space or time; not great in range or scope; not tall; brief; concise; not retentive; curt; abrupt; less than a correct amount; crisp or flaky, as rich pastry; denoting a sale of securities, etc. which the seller does not yet own but expects to buy later at a lower price.—*n* something short; (*pl*) short trousers; (*pl*) a man's undergarment like these; a shortstop; a short circuit.—*adv* abruptly; concisely; so as to be short in length.—*vti* to give less than what is needed; to shortchange; to short-circuit.—*adv* **short´ly**, in a short time, soon; briefly; curtly.—*ns* **short´ness; short´age**, deficiency; **short´bread**, a rich, crumbly cake or cookie made with much shortening; **short´cake**, a light biscuit or sweet cake served with fruit.—*vt* **short´change´** (*inf*) to give less than the correct change to.—*n* **short´ cir´cuit**, a connection between two points in an electric circuit resulting in a side circuit that deflects current or in excessive current flow causing damage; popularly, an interrupted electric current caused by this.—*vti* **short-circuit**.—*ns* **short´coming**, a defect or deficiency; **short´cut**, a shorter route; any way of saving time, effort, etc.—*vt* **short´en**, to make or become shorter.—*ns* **short´ening** [shört´ning], act of making, or becoming, short, or shorter; fat suitable for making pastry, etc., friable; **short´hair**, a domestic cat with a short thick coat, esp a breed with a plushy coat; **short´hand**, a method of swift writing (by signs for sounds and groups of sounds) to keep pace with speaking; writing of such a kind.—Also *adj.*—*adj* **short´hand´ed**, not having the proper number of people, etc.—*ns* **short´horn**, any of a breed of cattle having short curved horns.—*adjs* **short´lived**, living or lasting only for a short time; **short´sight´ed**, having clear sight only of near objects; lacking foresight.—*ns* **short´sight´edness; short´stop**, (*baseball*) the infielder between second and third base.—*adjs* **short´-tem´pered**, easily put into a rage; **short´-term**, extending over a short time.—*ns* **short ton**, 2,000 pounds; **shortwave**, a radio wave 60 meters or less in length.—*adj* **short´wind´ed**, easily put out of breath by exertion.—**in short**, in a few words; **run short**, to have less than enough; **short of**, less than; poorly provided with. [OE *sc(e)ort*; cf OHG *scurz*.]

Shoshone [shō-shōn´i, shō-shōn, shō´shōn], **Shoshoni** [shō-shōn-i] *n* a group of Amerindian peoples originally ranging through California, Colorado, Utah, Nebraska, and Kansas; a member of any of these peoples;—*pl* **-s, -ne, ni**.—*n* **Shoshon´ean**, a language family of the Uto-Aztecan phylum.

shot[1] *pt, pt p* of **shoot**.—*adj* hit or killed by shooting; (*inf*) ruined or worn out.

shot[2] [shot] *n* the act of shooting; range, scope; an attempt; a pointed, critical remark; the path of a thrown object, etc.; a projectile for a gun; projectiles collectively; small pellets of lead for a shotgun; the heavy metal ball used in the shot put; a marksman; a photograph or a continuous film sequence; a hypodermic injection, as of vaccine; a drink of liquor.—*n* **shot´gun**, a gun for firing small shot at close range; (*football*) an offensive formation in which the quarterback stands a few yards behind the line to receive the ball.—*adj* pertaining to a shotgun; involving force (eg *a shotgun marriage*); covering a wide field with hit-or-miss effectiveness.—**shot put**, a field event in which a heavy metal ball is propelled with an overhand thrust from the shoulder; **a shot in the arm** (*slang*) a hypodermic injection of a narcotic; (*inf*) a reviving injection, as of money, fresh talent; **a shot in the dark**, a wild guess; an attempt that has little chance of success; **shot of**, rid of. [OE *sc(e)ot*; cf **shoot**.]

should [shŏŏd] *pt* of **shall**, an auxiliary used to express obligation, duty, expectation or probability, or a future condition. [OE *sceolde*.]

shoulder [shōl´dėr] *n* the part of the trunk between the neck and the forelimb in mammals; the joint making this connection; a cut of meat including this joint; (*pl*) the capacity to bear a task or blame; a bulge, a prominence; either edge of a road.—*vti* to thrust with the shoulder; to take upon the shoulder, to sustain; to undertake; to take responsibility for.—*ns* **shoul´der belt**, an automobile safety belt that passes across the shoulder; **shoul´der blade**, the scapula; **shoulder harness**, shoulder belt; **shoul´der knot**, a knot worn as an ornament on the shoulder.—**straight from the shoulder**, without reserve; **give** or **turn a cold shoulder to**, to snub or shun. [OE *sculdor*; Ger *schulter*, Du *schouder*.]

shout [showt] *n* a loud cry; a call.—*vti* to utter or cry out in a shout.—*ns* **shout´er; shout song**, a rhythmic religious song used esp in Afro-American congregations marked by responsive singing. [Origin unknown.]

shove [shuv] *vti* to thrust; to push along; to jostle.—*n* act of shoving; a push. [OE *scūfan*; Du *schuiven*, Ger *schieben*.]

shovel [shuv´l] *n* a broad tool, like a scoop with a long handle for moving loose material.—*vt* to move with, or as if with, a shovel.—*vi* to use a shovel;—*pr p* **shov´elling**; *pt, pt p* **shov´elled**.—*n* **shov´el hat**, a hat with a broad brim, turned up at the sides, and projecting in front. [OE *scofl*, from *scūfan*, to shove.]

show [shō] *vt* to exhibit, to display; to cause or allow to be seen or known; to prove; to manifest; to usher or conduct (in, out, over, round, etc.); to bestow (favor, mercy, etc.).—*vi* to appear; to come into sight; to finish third in a horse race;—*pt p* **shōwn** or **shōwed**.—*n* act of showing; display; a spectacle, an entertainment; a theatrical performance; a radio or television program; third place at the finish (as a horse race).—*ns* **show´ bill; show´bread**, shewbread; **show´ business**, the entertainment business.—Also (*inf*) **show´-biz; show´down**, exposure of cards, esp in poker, or of intentions; open conflict; **show´er; show´man**, one whose business is producing plays or theatrical shows; a person skilled at presenting anything in a striking manner; **show´manship**, skillful display, or a talent for it; **show´room**, a room where goods or samples are displayed for advertising or sale.—*adj* **showy** [shō´i], making a show, ostentatious, gaudy; given to show.—*adv* **show´ily**.—*n* **show´iness**.—**show-and-tell**, a classroom exercise in which children display an item and talk about it; a public display; **show off**, to display or behave ostentatiously; to try to make an impression by one's possessions or talents; **show one's hand**, to display one's cards faceup; to declare one's intentions or reveal one's resources; **show up**, to expose to blame or ridicule; to be present; to appear to advantage or disadvantage. [OE *scēawian*; Du *schouwen*, Ger *schauen*, to behold.]

shower [show´ėr] *n* a short fall, as of rain or hail; a fall, flight of many things together, as of meteors, arrows, etc.; a copious supply; a shower bath; a party at which gifts are presented to the guest of honor, esp a prospective bride or mother.—*vt* to wet with rain; to pour, bestow (upon).—*vi* to drop in showers; to take a shower bath.—*n* **shower´ bath**, a bath in which the body is sprayed by fine streams of water.—*adj* **shower´y**, marked by showers; raining intermittently. [OE *scūr*; ON *skūr*, Ger *schauer*.]

shrank [shrangk] *pt* of **shrink**.

shrapnel [shrap´n(ė)l] *n* an artillery shell filled with small metal balls and a bursting charge; fragments scattered by such a shell on explosion. [Invented by General *Shrapnel* (1761–1842).]

shred [shred] *n* a strip cut or torn off; a scrap, fragment.—*vt* to cut or tear into shreds. [OE *scrēad*; cf **screed**.]

shrew [shrōō] *n* any of numerous small nocturnal mouselike animals (family Soricidae) with a long snout, very small eyes, and velvety fur; a brawling, troublesome woman, a scold.—*adj* **shrewd**, (*obs*) ill-natured; having, or showing, an acute judgment; biting, keen (eg pain, cold).—*adv* **shrewd´ly**.—*n* **shrewd´ness**.—*adj* **shrew´ish**, having the qualities of a shrew or scold, ill-natured and troublesome.—*adv* **shrew´ishly**.—*n* **shrew´ishness**. [OE *scrēawa*.]

shriek [shrēk] *vti* to utter with or make a loud, piercing cry; to screech.—*n* a shrill outcry; a wild, piercing scream. [Cf **screech**.]

shrieval [shrē´vål] *adj* pertaining to a sheriff. [From *shrieve*, obs form of **sheriff**.]

shrift [shrift] *n* (*arch*) a confession made to a priest; (*obs*) time granted to a condemned criminal to make such a confession before execution. [OE *scrift—scrīftan*, to shrive.]

shrike [shrīk] *n* any of numerous songbirds (family Laniidae) of prey with a hooked beak, some kinds of which impale small animals on thorns. [App OE *scrīc*, perh thrush.]

shrill [shril] *adj* high pitched and piercing; strident.—*vti* to sound or cry shrilly.—*n* **shrill´ness**.—*adv* **shril´ly**. [Cf Low Ger *schrell*, whence prob Ger *schrill*.]

shrimp [shrimp] *n* any of numerous small edible marine crustaceans (suborder Natantia); other similar crustaceans valued as food; (*inf*) any small person.—*vi* to fish for or catch shrimps. [Cf **scrimp** and OE *scrimman*, to shrink.]

shrine [shrīn] *n* a case for sacred relics; a saint's tomb; a place of worship; a place hallowed by its associations. [OE *scrīn*—L *scrīnium*, a case for paper—*scrībĕre*, to write.]

shrink [shringk] *vi* to contract as from cold, wetting, etc.; to give way, to draw back, to recoil (from).—*vt* to cause to shrink or contract;—*pt* **shrank, shrunk**; *pt p* **shrunk**.—*n* **shrink´age**, a contraction into a less compass; the extent of such diminution.—*vt* **shrink-wrap**, to wrap (as a book or meat) in plastic film that is then shrunk by heat to form a tightly fitting package.—*adj* **shrunk´en**, contracted, reduced; shrivelled.—**shrinking violet**, a very shy person. [OE *scrincan*.]

shrive [shrīv] *vt* (*arch*) to hear a confession from and give absolution to.—*vi* (*arch*) to receive, or make, confession;—*pt* **shrōve** or **shrīved**; *pt p* **shriv´en**. [OE *scrīfan*, to write, to prescribe penance—L *scrībĕre*.]

shrivel [shriv´l] *vti* to contract into wrinkles;—*pr p* **shriv´elling**; *pt, pt p* **shriv´elled**. [Ety uncertain.]

shroud [shrowd] *n* the dress of the dead; that which clothes or covers; any of the ropes from the masthead to a ship's sides.—*vt* to enclose in a shroud; to cover; to hide; to shelter. [OE *scrūd*; ON *skrūth*, clothing.]

Shrovetide [shrōv´tīd] *n* the period, usu. three days, immediately preceding Ash Wednesday.—*n* **Shrove Tuesday**, the last day before Lent. [Of obscure origin; related to OE *scrīfan*, to shrive.]

shrub[1] [shrub] *n* a low woody plant with several stems; a bush.—*n* **shrubb´ery**, a plantation of shrubs.—*adj* **shrubb´y**, full of shrubs; like a shrub; consisting of shrubs. [OE *scrybb*, scrub.]

shrub[2] [shrub] *n* a drink prepared from the juice of lemons, or other acid fruit, with spirits; a beverage made by adding an acid fruit juice to iced water. [Ar *sharab* for *shurb*, drink.]

shrug [shrug] *vti* to draw up (the shoulders) as an expression of doubt, indifference, etc.;—*pr p* **shrugg´ing**; *pt, pt p* **shrugged**.—*n* an expressive drawing up of the shoulders.—**shrug off**, to brush aside; to shake off; to remove (a garment) by wriggling out.

shrunk, shrunken *See* **shrink**.

shtetl [shtet´l] *n* any of the former Jewish village communities of eastern Europe, esp in Czarist Russia;—*pl* **shtet´lack** [shtet´läk]. [Yiddish.]

shuck [shuk] *n* a shell, pod, or husk.—*vt* to remove the shucks of; to lay aside (*with* **off**).

shucks [shuks] *interj* an exclamation of disappointment, disgust, etc.

shudder [shud´ėr] *vi* to shiver from cold or horror; to vibrate.—*n* a tremor as from cold or horror; a vibration. [Cf Ger *schaudern*.]

shuffle [shuf´l] *vti* to mix at random, as playing cards; to shove (the feet) along without lifting them; to slip or move surreptitiously or evasively.—*n* act of shuffling; a shuffling gait; an evasion or artifice.—*n* **shuff´ler**. [A byform of *scuffle*.]

shun [shun] *vt* to avoid scrupulously; to keep clear of;—*pr p* **shunn´ing**; *pt, pt p* **shunned**—*ns* **shun´pīke´**, a side road used to avoid the toll on or the speed and traffic of a super highway; **shun´pīker**. [OE *scunian*.]

shunt [shunt] *vti* to turn or move to one side; to switch, as a train, from one track to another.—*n* a shunting; a railroad switch; a bypass in surgery.—*n* **shunt´er**. [Per conn with **shun**.]

shut [shut] *vt* to close the opening of; to lock, bar, fasten; to forbid entrance into; to confine; to catch or pinch (in a fastening).—*vi* to become closed; to admit of closing;—*pr p* **shutt´ing**; *pt, pt p* **shut**.—*n* **shutt´er**, one who, or that which, shuts; a movable cover for a window; a device for opening and closing the aperture of a camera lens.—*vt* to close or furnish with shutters.—**shut down**, to (cause to) stop operating.—*ns* **shutdown**, a stoppage of work or activity, as in a factory; **shut eye** (*slang*), sleep; **shut-in**, an invalid who is shut in.—*adj* confined indoors by illness.—*n* **shutout**, (*sports*) a preventing of the opposing side from scoring.—**shut up**, to confine; (*inf*) to cease speaking; (*inf*) to silence. [OE *scyttan*, to bar; cf *scēotan*, to shoot.]

shuttle [shut´l] *n* an instrument used for shooting the thread of the woof between the threads of the warp in weaving, or through the loop of thread in a sewing machine; a bus, etc. making back-and-forth trips over a short route.—*vti* to move back and forth rapidly.—*adj* running, or run, backwards and forwards (eg *shuttle service, race*).—*n* **shutt´lecock**, a cork stuck with feathers, or a plastic imitation, used in badminton. [OE *scytel*, bolt, *scēotan*, to shoot; Dan and Swed *skyttel*.]

shy[1] [shī] *adj* timid, shrinking from notice or approach; bashful; warily reluctant to (eg *shy of committing himself*); doubtful, suspicious (of); (*slang*) lacking.—*comparative* **shy´er** (or **shi´er**); *superlative* **shy´est** (or **shi´est**).—*vi* to move suddenly as when startled; to be or become cautious, etc.—*n* a sudden start aside.—*pt, pt p* **shīed**.—*advs* **shy´ly, shi´ly**.—*ns* **shy´ness; shy´ster** (*slang*), a lawyer who uses unethical or tricky methods. [OE *scēoh*; Ger *sheu*, Dan *sky*.]

shy[2] [shī] *vti* to fling, toss, esp sideways.—*n* a throw; a verbal fling; a thing to shy at.

shylock [shī´lok] *n* a ruthless creditor.—*vi* to lend money at high rates of interest. [From Shylock in *The Merchant of Venice*.]

Siamese [sī-am-ēz´] *adj* of Siam.—**Siamese cat**, a domestic fawn or gray cat with darker ears, paws, tail and face, blue eyes and a small head; **Siamese twins**; any pair of twins born with bodies joined together [Chinese twins (1811–74) born in Siam joined from birth by a fleshy ligature].

sib [sib] *adj* related by blood.—*n* a blood relation; any plant or animal of a group sharing a corresponding degree of relationship; a group of persons unilaterally descended from a real or supposed ancestor.—*n* **sib´ling**, one who has a parent, or parents, in common with another. [OE *sibb*, relationship.]

sibilate [sib´i-lāt] *vti* to hiss.—*adj* **sib´ilant**, hissing.—*n* hissing consonant sound, as of *s* or *z*.—*ns* **sib´ilance, sibilā´tion**, a hissing sound. [L *sibilāre, ātum*, to hiss.]

Sibyl [sib´il] *n* (*myth*) one of several ancient prophetesses; (**sibyl**) a prophetess, sorceress, or witch, or an old crone.—*adj* **sibylline** [sib´i-līn, or sibil´īn], pertaining to sibyls; prophetical; oracular. [Gr *Sybylla*.]

sic[1] [sik] *adv* so, thus; printed within brackets [*sic*] in quoted matter to show that the original is being faithfully reproduced, even though incorrect or seemingly so. [L.]

sic[2] [sik] *vt* to incite (a dog) to attack.—Also **sick**.

siccative [sik´ȧ-tiv] *adj* drying.—*n* a drying agent. [Through LL—L *siccus*, dry.]

sick [sik] *adj* unwell, ill; having nausea; out of condition; suffering the effects (of); thoroughly wearied (of); disgusted by an excess; (*inf*) of humor, comedy, macabre, gruesome.—*n* **sick´ness**.—*adj* **sick´ly**, inclined to be ailing; feeble; pallid; suggestive of sickness (eg a smile); slightly sickening; mawkish.—*ns* **sick´liness; sick´bay**, a compartment in a ship used as a dispensary and hospital; (*loosely*) a place for the care of the sick and injured; **sick´bed**, a bed on which one lies sick.—*vti* **sick´en**, to make or become sick.—*adj* **sick´ening**.—*adv* **sick´eningly**.—*ns* **sick´ leave**, leave of absence because of sickness; **sick´room**, a room to which one is confined by sickness. [OE *sēoc*; Ger *siech*, Du *ziek*.]

sickle [sik´l] *n* a tool with a crescent-shaped blade for cutting tall grasses and weeds. [OE *sicol, sicel*, perh L *secula*, a sickle—*secāre*, to cut.]

side [sīd] *n* a line or surface forming part of a boundary; the part near such a boundary; the margin; a surface or part turned in a certain direction, esp one more or less upright, or one regarded as right or left (not front or back, top or bottom); the left or right half of the body; half of a carcass divided along the backbone; a direction; an aspect; the slope (of a hill); the wall (of a vessel or cavity); either of the surfaces of anything in the form of a sheet; the father's or the mother's line in a genaology; any party team, interest, or opinion opp to another.—*adj* at or towards the side; indirect; subsidiary.—*vi* to embrace the opinion or cause of one party against another.—*adj* **sid´ed**, having sides (of a specified kind).—*n pl* **side´arms**, weapons worn at the side or waist, as swords, pistols, etc.—*ns* **side´board**, a piece of dining room furniture for holding dishes, etc.; **side´burns**, the hair growing on the sides of a man's face, just in front of the ears; **side´car**, a small car attached to the side of a motor cycle; a cocktail consisting of a liqueur with lemon juice and brandy; **side´ effect**, a secondary and usu. adverse effect (as of a drug); **side´-glance**, a sidelong glance; a passing allusion; **side´kick** (*slang*), a confederate; a partner; a close friend; **side´light**, light coming from the side; a light carried on the side of a vessel or vehicle; a bit of incidental information or knowledge; **side´line**, either of two lines marking the side limits of a playing area, as in football; a subsidiary activity.—*adj* **side´long**, oblique, not straight.—*adv* in the direction of the side; obliquely;—*ns* **side reaction**, a side effect; **side´saddle**, a saddle for riding with both feet on one side; **side´show**, an exhibition, show, attached to and subordinate to a larger one; any subsidiary or incidental activities or happenings; **side´slip**, a skid or slip to the side.—*vi* to slip or skid sideways.—*vt* to make a sideslip.—*vi* to skid.—*adj* **side´splitting**, provoking uncontrollable laughter.—*n* **side´step**, a step taken to one side.—*vti* to avoid as by a step aside.—*n* **side´track**, a siding.—*vt* to divert into a siding; to prevent action on by diversionary tactics.—*n* **side´walk**, a path for pedestrians, usu. paved, at the side of a street.—*adj, adv* **side´ways**, toward or on one side.—*ns* **side´winder**, a heavy swinging blow from the side; a small desert rattlesnake (*Crotalus cerastes*) of the South Western US that moves forward in a series of S-shaped loops; **sid´ing**, a covering as of overlapping boards, for the outside of a frame building; a short railway track for unloading, etc., connected with a main track by a switch.—**side by side**, together; **side with**, to support (a faction, etc.); **take sides**, to support a faction, etc. [OE *sīde*; Ger *seite*, Du *zijde*.]

sidereal [sī-dē´ri-ȧl] *adj* relative to a star or stars; of, like, or measured by, the apparent motion of the stars.—**sidereal day**, approximately 24 hours; **sidereal year**, approximately 365 days. [L *sidus, sīderis*, a star.]

siding *See* **side**.

sidle [sī´dl] *vi* to move sideways, esp to edge along. [Backformation from obs adv *sidling*, now **sidelong**.]

siege [sēj] *n* (*obs*) a seat, throne; an attempt to take a fortified place by keeping it surrounded by an armed force; a persistent attempt to gain possession or control (of).—**lay siege to**, to besiege, beleaguer, invest, to surround with armed forces in order to force to surrender; to pursue diligently and persistently. [OFr *sege* (Fr *siège*), seat—L *sēdēs*, seat.]

siemens [sē´mėnz] *n* unit of electrical conductance in the meter-kilogram-second system equal to one ampere per volt. Abbrev. **S**. [William *Siemens*, 1823–83.]

sienna [sē-en´a] *n* an earthy substance that is brownish yellow when raw and orange red or reddish brown when burnt and is used as a pigment. [It *terra di Siena*, Sienna earth.]

sierra [si-er´a] *n* a jagged ridge of mountain peaks; **Sierra**, communication code word for the letter *s*. [Sp,—L *serra*, a saw.]

siesta [si-es´ta] *n* a short sleep or rest usu taken in the afternoon. [Sp,—L *sexta* (*hōra*), the *sixth* (hour) after sunrise, the hour of noon.]

sieve [siv] *n* a vessel with many small holes to separate the fine part of anything from the coarse or for straining liquids. [OE *sife*; Ger *sieb*.]

sift [sift] *vt* to separate as by passing through a sieve; to examine closely; to separate (eg to sift fact from fable).—*vi* to pass as through a sieve.—*n* **sift´er**. [OE *siftan*—*sife*, a sieve.]

sigh [sī] *vi* to inhale and respire with a sigh; to yearn (for); to grieve; to sound like a sigh.—*vt* to express by sighs; to spend in sighing.—*n* a long, deep, audible respiration, expressive of yearning, dejection, relief, etc. [Prob from the weak pt of ME *sichen*—OE (strong) *sīcan*.]

sight [sīt] *n* act of seeing; faculty of seeing; an opportunity of seeing, view; that which is seen; a spectacle; space within vision; a small opening for observing objects; a device in a gun, or optical or other instrument, to guide the eye; (*inf*) anything that looks unpleasant, odd, etc.—*vt* to descry, discern; to look at through a sight; to adjust the sights of (a gun, etc.).—*adjs* **sight´ed**, having sight of a specified character (eg *short´sighted*); **sight´less**, blind.—*n* **sight´lessness**.—*adj* **sight´ly**, pleasing to the sight or eye, comely.—*ns* **sight´liness; sight´read´er**, one who can perform music at first sight of the notes; **sight´read´ing; sight´see´ing**, visiting scenes or objects of interest; **sight´sē´er**.—**at sight**, as soon as seen; **out of sight**, not in sight; far off; (*inf*) beyond reach; (*slang*) excellent, wonderful. [OE *siht, gesiht*—*gesegen*, pt p of *sēon*, to see; Ger *sicht*.]

sigma [sig´mȧ] *n* the 18th letter of the Greek alphabet; (*math*) the symbol Σ, indicating summation.

sign [sīn] *n* a gesture expressing a meaning; a signal; a mark with a meaning; a symbol, an emblem; a token, proof, outward evidence; a portent; a miracle; (*math*) a conventional mark used as part of the description of a quantity (eg √, +, -), or to indicate an operation to be performed (eg +, ÷, Σ); a device marking an inn, etc.; a board or panel giving a shopkeeper's name or trade, etc.; (*astron*) one of the twelve parts of the zodiac; a placard, etc. bearing information, etc.; any trace or indication; an objective evidence of plant or animal disease.—*vt* to mark with a sign; to indicate, convey, communicate (a meaning or message), or direct (a person), by a sign or signs; to engage by written contract; to write as a signature.—*vi* to sign one's name.—*ns* **sign´board**, a board bearing a notice or sign, **sign´er; signet** [sig´-], a small seal; the impression of such a seal; a seal used officially to give personal authority to a document instead of a signature; **sign´post**, a post (as at a fork of a road) with signs on it to direct travelers; a beacon, guide.—*vt* to furnish with signposts or guides.—**sign of the cross**, a gesture of tracing the form of a cross; to profess Christian faith or to invoke divine blessing, esp by Catholics; **sign in, out**, to sign one's name on coming in, going out; **sign on**, to engage (*vt* or *vi*) by signature; to record arrival at work; **sign off**, to leave off broadcasting. [Fr *signe*—L *signum*.]

signal [sig´n(ȧ)l] *n* a, usu visible or audible, intimation, eg of warning, conveyed to a distance; in radio, etc. the electrical impulses transmitted or received; a sign or event that initiates action.—*vti* to make a signal or signals (to); to communicate by signals;—*pr p* **sig´naling**; *pt, pt p* **sig´naled**.—*adj* remarkable, notable; used as a signal.—*adv* **sig´nally**, in a signal way; notably.—*vt* **sig´nalize**, to mark or distinguish; to make known or draw attention to.—*ns* **sig´naling; sig´nalman**, one who transmits signals; one who works with signals. [Fr,—through LL—L *signum*.]

signature [sig´na-chūr] *n* a person's name written by himself; a signing of one's own name; a signed name; an indication of key, also of time, at the beginning of a line of music; a letter or numeral at the foot of a page to indicate sequence of sheets; a folded sheet that is one unit of a book.—*n* **sig´natory**, a signer with another or others, esp a government bound with others by a signed convention. [LL *signātūra*—L *signāre, -ātum*, to sign.]

signet *See* **sign**.

signify [sig´ni-fī] *vt* to be a sign of; to mean; to indicate or declare (eg *to signify one's approval*).—*vi* to have importance.—*pt, pt p* **sig´nified**.—*n* **significance** [sig-nif´ik-ȧns] meaning (esp disguised or implicit); import; importance.—*adj* **signif´icant**, having, or conveying, meaning, esp a special or hidden one; expressive of much; important; indicative (of).—*adv* **signif´icantly**.—*n* **significā´tion**, act of signifying; accepted meaning.—*adj* **signif´icative**, indicative; significant. [L *significāre, -ātum*—*signum*, a sign, *facĕre*, to make.]

Signor [sē´nyor] *n* an Italian word of address equivalent to *Mr* or *Sir*.—*ns* **Signora** [sē-nyō´ra], a title equivalent to *Mrs* or *Madam*; **Signorina** [sē-nyō-rē´na] the Italian equivalent of *Miss*. [It *signore*.]

Sikh [sēk] *n* one of an Indian monotheistic sect founded about 1500 by a Hindu under Islamic influence and marked by rejection of idolatry and caste. [Hindustani, 'disciple'.]

silage [sī´lij] *n* green fodder preserved in a silo. [**ensilage**.]

silence [sī´lens] *n* absence of sound; forbearance from sounding, or from speech; abstention from mentioning or divulging something; a time characterized by absence of sound; a time of abstention from communication by speech or other means; taciturnity.—*vt* to cause to be silent.—*interj* be silent!.—*n* **sī´lencer**, a device to muffle the sound of a gun.—*adj* **sī´lent**, noiseless; unaccompanied by sound; refraining from speech, or from mentioning or divulging; taciturn; not pronounced.—*adv* **sī´lently.—silent butler**, a receptacle with a hinged lid for collecting table crumbs and emptying ashtrays; **silent partner**, secret partner. [L *silēre*, to be silent.]

silhouette [sil-ōō-et´] *n* a solid outline drawing, usu. filled in with black, esp of a profile; an outline showing an object against a contrasting background.—*vt* to represent or display in silhouette. [Etienne de *Silhouette* (1709–67), French minister of finance in 1759, after whom, because of his injudicious parsimony, anything cheap was named.]

silica [sil´i-ka] *n* a compound of silicon and oxygen, a white or colorless substance, the most abundant solid constituent of our globe, existing both in the crystalline amorphous and impure forms (as in quartz, opal, and sand respectively), and present in animal and plant tissue.—*ns* **sil´icate**, a salt of silicic acid; **silicōs´is**, a condition of massive fibrosis of the lungs due to the inhalation of silica dust.—*adj* **silic´ic** [-is´ik] pertaining to, or obtained from, silica; **silic´eous, -ious** [-ish´ůs] pertaining to, containing, silica.—*vt* **silic´ify** [-is´-] to render silicious, to impregnate with, or turn into, silica.—*vi* to become silicified.—*ns* **sil´icon** [-kon] a metalloid element (symbol Si; at wt 28.1; at no 14); **sil´icone**, any of various organic derivatives of silicon obtained as oils, greases, or plastics (used esp as heat-resisting plastics, lubricants, polishes, etc.). [L *sīlex, sīlicis*, flint.]

silicon, silicone, silicosis *See* **silica**.

silk [silk] *n* a fiber produced by various insect larvae, usu. for cocoons, esp a lustrous tough elastic fiber produced by silkworms and used for textiles; a thread, yarn, cloth, or garment, or attire, made from silk; (*pl*) the colors representing a stable worn by a jockey or harness horse driver; a filament resembling silk (as that produced by a spider); the styles of an ear of corn.—*adj* pertaining to, or consisting of, silk.—*adj* **silk´en**, made of silk; dressed in silk; resembling silk; soft, delicate.—*ns* **silk screen**, a stencil method of printing a color design through the meshes of a fabric, as silk; **silk´worm**, a moth whose larva spins a large amount of strong silk in constructing a cocoon, esp an Asian moth (*Bombyx mori*) whose caterpillar produces the silk of commerce.—*adj* **silk´y**, like silk in texture, soft, smooth; glossy.—*n* **silk´iness**. [OE *seolc*—L *sēricum*—Gr *sērikon*, neut of adj *sērikos*, silken, (*cap*) pertaining to the *Sēres*—*Sēr*, prob a native of China.]

sill [sil] *n* a heavy, horizontal timber or line of masonry supporting a house wall, etc.; the timber, stone, etc., at the foot of an opening, as for a door or window. [OE *syl*; ON *sylla*, Ger *schwelle*.]

sillabub *See* **syllabub**.

silly [sil´i] *adj* simple; witless; foolish; lacking in sense or judgment; being stunned or dazed.—*n* a silly person.—*adj* **silly; sill´ily**.—*n* **sill´iness.—silly season**, a season, usu. late summer, when newspapers fill up with trivial matter for want of more newsworthy material. [Orig 'blessed', and so 'innocent', 'simple', OE *sǣlig, gesǣlig*, happy, prosperous—*sǣl*, time, due time, happiness; Ger *selig*, blest, happy.]

silo [sī´lō] *n* an airtight pit or tower in which green fodder is preserved; a deep bin for storing material (as cement or coal); an underground structure for housing a guided missile. [Sp,—L *sīrus*—Gr *sīros*, a pit.]

silt [silt] *n* a fine-grained sandy sediment carried or deposited by water.—*vti* to fill or choke up with silt. [ME *sylt*; cf Dan and Norw *sylt*, salt-marsh.]

Silurian [sil-(y)ōō´ri-ȧn] *adj* of the Silures, a British tribe of South Wales.—*n* the period of the Paleozoic era between the Ordovician and the Devonian; the system of rocks formed during this period.

silvan *See* **sylvan**.

silver [sil´vėr] *n* a metallic element (symbol Ag; at wt 107.9; at no 47), capable of a high polish; money made of silver; silverware; anything having the appearance of silver; a lustrous, grayish white.—*adj* made of silver; plated with, or containing silver; silvery; clear and ringing in tone.—*vt* to cover with silver (as by electroplating); to coat with a substance resembling silver; to make silvery.—*ns* **sil´verfish**, any of various silvery fishes (as a tarpon or silversides); a small wingless insect (*Lepisma saccharina*) found in houses; **silver fox**, a genetically determined color phase of the common red fox in which the black pelt is tipped with white.—*adj* **sil´vern**, made of silver.—**sil´ver pap´er**, a metallic paper with a coating or lamination resembling silver; **sil´ver plate´**, a plating of silver; domestic flatware and hollowware of silver or of a silver-plated base metal; **silverside, silversides**, any of various small fishes (family Atherindae) with a silver stripe on each side of the body; **sil´versmith**, a smith who works in silver; **silver spoon**, wealth, esp inherited wealth; **Silver Star Medal**, a US military decoration awarded for gallantry in action.—*adj* **sil´ver-tongued**, eloquent, persuasive.—*n* **silverware**, flatware; silver plate.—*adj* **sil´very**, covered with silver; resembling silver in color; clear and musical in tone.—*n* **sil´veriness**. [OE *silfer, seolfor*; ON *silfr*, Ger *silber*.]

silviculture [sil´vi-kul-chūr] *n* a branch of forestry dealing with the care and development of forests. [Fr,—L *silva*.]

simian [sim´i-ȧn] *adj* of or like an ape or monkey.—Also *n*. [L *sīmia*, ape.]

similar [sim´i-lȧr] *adj* somewhat like, resembling; having resemblance (to); (*geom*) exactly corresponding in shape, without regard to size.—*n* **similar´ity**.—*adv* **sim´ilarly**. [Fr *similaire*—L *similis*, like.]

simile [sim´i-le] *n* a figure of speech likening one thing to another by the use of *like, as*, etc. (eg *in controversy he is like a tiger*);—*pl* **sim´iles**.—*n* **simil´itude**, the state of being similar or like; semblance, likeness; comparison. [Fr *similaire*—L neut of *similis*, like.]

simmer [sim´ėr] *vi* to remain at or just below boiling point; to be about to break out, as in anger.—*vt* to cause to simmer.—*n* a simmering. [Imit.]

simnel [sim´n(ė)l] *n* a fine wheat-flour roll or bread. [OFr *simenel*—L *simila*, fine flour.]

simony [sī´mȯn-i, sim´ȯn-i] *n* the buying or selling of a church office.—*n* **simō´niac**, one guilty of simony.—*adj* **simonī´ac, -al**, pertaining to, guilty of, or involving simony. [*Simon* Magus (Acts viii, 18, 19).]

simoom [si-mōōm´] *n* a hot suffocating wind from African and Asian deserts.—Also **simoon´**. [Ar *samūm*—*samm*, to poison.]

simper [sim´pėr] *vi* to smile in a silly, affected manner.—*n* a silly or affected smile. [Norw *semper*, smart.]

simple [sim´pl] *adj* consisting of one thing or element; not complex or compound; easy; plain, unornate; unpretentious; mere, sheer; ordinary; of humble rank or origin; unlearned or unskilled; unaffected, artless; unsuspecting, credulous; weak in intellect, silly.—*n* a simple person; a vegetable drug of one constituent.—*adj* **sim´ple-mind´ed**, having a mind of less than normal ability; unsuspecting, undesigning.—*ns* **sim´pleness; sim´pleton**, a foolish person; **simplic´ity**, the state or quality of being simple; lack of complication; easiness; freedom from excessive adornment, plainness; artlessness; credulity, silliness, folly; **simplificā´tion**, the act, or result, of making simple.—*vt* **sim´plify**, to make simple, simpler, less difficult;—*pr p* **sim´plifying**; *pt, pt p* **sim´plified**.—*adj* **simplis´tic**, making complex problems unrealistically simple.—*adv* **sim´ply**, in a simple manner; considered by itself; merely; veritably, absolutely (eg *simply magnificent*). [Fr,—L *simplex*—*semel*, once, *plicāre*, to fold.]

simulate [sim´ū-lāt] *vt* to feign; to have or assume a false appearance of.—*n* **simulā´tion**, the act of simulating or putting on a character or appearance which is not true.—*adj* **sim´ulative**.—*n* **sim´ulātor**, a device that enables the operator to reproduce under test conditions phenomena likely to occur in actual performance. [L *simulāre, -ātum*, to make (something) similar to (another thing)—*similis*, like.]

simulcast [sī´mul-kast] *vt* to broadcast (a program) simultaneously by radio and television.—*n* a program so broadcast. [*simul*taneous broad*cast*.]

simultaneous [sim-ul-tā´nyůs] *adj* being, or happening, at the same time; (*math*) of equations, satisfied by the same values of the variables.—*adv* **simultā´neously**. [Formed from L *simul*, at the same time.]

sin [sin] *n* moral offense or shortcoming, esp from the point of view of religion; condition of so offending; an offense generally; transgression of the law of God.—*vi* to commit a sin;—*pr p* **sinn´ing**; *pt, pt p* **sinned**.—*adj* **sin´ful**, tainted with sin; wicked.—*adv* **sin´fully**.—*n* **sin´fulness**.—*adj* **sin´less**.—*adv* **sin´lessly**.—*ns* **sin´lessness; sinn´er**. [OE *syn, sinn*; Ger *sünde*; perh L *sons, sontis*, guilty.]

since [sins] *adv* from then until now; at some time between then and now; before now, ago.—*prep* continuously from (then) until now; during the period between (then) and now.—*conj* from the time that; seeing that, because. [ME *sins, sithens*—OE *sīth-thām*, lit 'after that'—*sīth*, late, *thām*, dat of *thæt*, that.]

sincere [sin-sēr´] *adj* pure, unadulterated, unmixed; unfeigned, genuine, the same in reality as in appearance.—*adv* **sincēre´ly**.—*n* **sincer´ity** [ser´-] state or quality of being sincere; honesty of mind; freedom from pretence. [Fr,—L *sincērus*, clean.]

sinciput [sin´si-put] *n* the forehead; the upper half of the skull. [L,—*sēmi-*, half, *caput*, the head.]

sine [sīn] *n* (*math*) one of the six trigonometrical functions of an angle, the ratio of the perpendicular to the hypotenuse—identical with the cosine of the complementary angle—*abbrev* **sin** [sīn]. [L *sinus*, a bay.]

sine die [sī´nē dī´ē] *adv* without an appointed day, ie indefinitely; **sine qua non** [quā non] an indispensable condition; a necessity. [L *sine*, without, *diē*, abl sing of *diēs*, day, *quā* (*causā*), fem abl sing of *qui*, which (*causa*, cause, circumstance), *nōn*, not.]

sinecure [sī´nė-kūr (or sin´-)] *n* any position that provides an income without involving much work. [L *sine*, without, *cūra*, care.]

sinew [sin´ū] *n* a tendon, esp one dressed for use as a thread or cord; (*obs*) nerve; strength; the chief supporting force.—*vt* to strengthen as if with sinews.—*adjs* **sin´ewed; sin´ewy**, having sinews; tough, stringy; strong. [OE *sinu*, gen *sinwe*.]

sing [sing] *vi* to utter melodious sounds in successive musical notes; to emit songlike sounds; to compose poetry; to give a cantabile or lyrical effect; to ring (as the ears).—*vt* to utter, perform by voice, musically; to celebrate; to relate in verse;—*pt* **sang** or (now rarely) **sung**; *pt p* **sung**.—*ns* **sing-along**, a songfest; **sing´er; sing´ing**, the act or art of singing.—**singing game**, a children's game in which a narrative song is accompanied by gestures. [OE *singan*; Ger *singen*.]

singe [sinj] *vt* to burn on the surface, to scorch, esp to remove feathers, etc. by passing rapidly over a flame.—*pr p* **singe´ing**; *pt, pt p* **singed**.—*n* a burning of the surface, a slight burn. [OE *sen(c)gan*.]

Singhalese *See* **Sinhalese**.

single [sing´gl] *adj* consisting of one only, individual, unique; uncombined; unmarried; for one person or family; consisting of one part, undivided; between two persons only; whole, unbroken.—*n* a single person or thing; a phonograph record (as a 45) having one short tune on each side; (*baseball*) a hit by which the batter reaches first base; (*pl*) (*tennis*, etc.) a match with only one player on each side.—*vt* to select, pick (out).—*vi* (*baseball*) to hit a single.—*ns* **sin´gle en´try**, a system of bookkeeping in which each entry appears only once on one side or other of an account; **single file**, a single column of persons or things, one behind another.—*adjs* **sin´gle-hand´ed**, by oneself, unassisted; **sing´le-heart´ed**, sincere, without duplicity; **sing´le-mind´ed**, sincere, bent upon one sole purpose.—*ns* **sing´leness; sing´lestick**, a fighting stick for one hand; a fight or game with singlesticks; **sing´let** (*Brit*) an undershirt; **sing´leton**, a single card of its suit.—*adv* **sing´ly**, one by one; alone. [OFr—L *singulī*, one by one.]

single-tree *See* **swingle-tree**.

singsong [sing´song] *n* monotonous up-and-down intonation; verse with regular, marked rhythm and rhyme.—*adj* of the nature of singsong. [**sing, song**.]

singular [sing´gū-lȧr] *adj* (*gram*) denoting one person or thing; unique; preeminent, exceptional; unusual, extraordinary, strange, odd.—*n* (*gram*) the singular number or form of a word.—*n* **singular´ity**, the state of being singular; peculiarity; anything curious or remarkable.—*adv* **sing´ularly**, unusually; strangely. [Fr,—L *singulāris*.]

Sinhalese [sin´hȧ-lēz´], **Singhalese** [sing´gȧ-lēz´] *n* a member of a people living chiefly in Sri Lanka; the language of this people which is descended from sanskrit.—*adj* of this people or their language. [Sans *Sinhalam*, Ceylon.]

sinicize, *See* **Sino-**.

sinister [sin´is-tėr] *adj* left; on the left side (eg of the bearer of a shield); unlucky, inauspicious, threatening harm, disaster; wicked, evil.—*adj* **sin´istral**, turning to the left; (of a shell) coiled counterclockwise down the spine when viewed with the apex toward the observer.—*adv* **sin´istrally**. [L.]

sink [singk] *vi* to become submerged, wholly or partly; to subside; to fall slowly; to pass to a lower level or state; to slope away, dip; to subside, as wind or sound; to become hollow, as the cheeks; to approach death.—*vt* to cause or allow to sink; to lower; to keep out of sight, to suppress; to make by digging, cutting, engraving, etc.; to invest.—*p t* **sank** (now rarely) **sunk**; *pt p* **sunk, sunk´en** (*obs* except as *adj*).—*n* a drain to carry off dirty water; a cesspool; a kitchen basin with a drainpipe; an area of sunken land.—*ns* **sink´er**, one that sinks; a lead weight used in fishing; **sink´ing; sink´ing fund**, a fund set up for paying off the principal of a debt when it falls due, as of a corporation.—**sink in** (*inf*) to be understood in full. [OE *sincan* (*intrans*); Ger *sinken*, Du *zinken*.]

Sinn Fein [shin fān] an Irish Society formed in 1905 to promote economic prosperity in Ireland; the revolutionary movement that led to the establishment of the Irish Free State (later Eire, later again Irish Republic) in 1921.—*n* **Sinn Fein´er**, a supporter of Sinn Fein. [Ir, 'ourselves'.]

Sino- (also **Sin-**) [sin´ō-, sīn´ō-] in composition, Chinese.—*ns* **sinol´ogy**, knowledge of Chinese history, customs, language, etc.; **sinol´ogist, sin´ologue**.—*vti* **sin´icize** [sīz] to make or become Chinese. [Gr *Sīnai*, Chinese (*pl*).]

sinter [sin´tėr] *n* a deposit formed by the evaporation of spring or lake water.—*vt* to cause to coalesce into a single mass under heat without actually liquefying.—*vi* to undergo sintering. [Ger.]

sinus [sī´nus] *n* an indentation, a notch; a cavity, specifically, any of the air cavities in the skull which open in the nasal cavities.—*pl* **sīn´uses**.—*adjs* **sinuate** [sin´ū-åt], **-d** [-id], wavy-edged; winding.—*adv* **sin´uately**.—*ns* **sinuā´tion**, winding; **sīnusī´tis**, inflammation of a sinus of the skull.—*adj* **sĭn´uous**, wavy; winding; bending with suppleness; devious; crooked.—*adv* **sĭn´uously**.—*n* **sinuos´ity**. [L *sĭnus, -ūs*, a bend, fold, bay.]

Siouan [sōō-ȧn] *n* an Amerindian language family spoken in the northern Midwest, Montana, and Oklahoma.

Sioux [sōō] *n* a member of an Amerindian people of the northern Mississippi Valley; the Siouan language of this people.

sip [sip] *vti* to drink in small quantities.—*pr p* **sipp´ing**; *pt, pt p* **sipped**.—*n* an act of sipping; the quantity sipped at once. [Cf **sup**; OE *sypian*.]

siphon [sī´fȯn] *n* a bent tube full of water, connecting two reservoirs so that flow can take place over an intervening barrier under atmospheric pressure.—*n* **syphon**, a glass bottle for containing and discharging aerated liquid, fitted with a glass tube reaching nearly to the bottom and bent like a siphon at the outlet. [Fr,—Gr, *sīphōn*.]

sir [sûr] *n* a word of respect used in addressing a man; a word of address to a man in a formal letter; **Sir**, prefixed to the Christian name of a knight or baronet.—*vt* to address as 'sir'. [OFr *sire*, from L *senior*, an elder.]

sirdar [sėr-där´ or sėr´-] *n* a hereditary noble in India; (*hist*) the commander of the Anglo-Egyptian army; a foreman in India. [Hindustani *sardār*.]

sire [sīr] *n* a term of address to a king; (*poetical*) a father or forefather; the male parent of a four-legged animal.—*vt* to beget. [**sir**.]

siren [sī´ren] *n* (*Gr myth; cap*) one of certain fabulous nymphs in south Italy who lured sailors to destruction by their sweet music; a charming temptress; a warning device, etc., producing a loud wailing sound; a genus (*Siren*) of eel-like, amphibious animals with small forelimbs but neither hind legs nor pelvis. [L *sīrēn*—Gr *seirēn*, prob—*seira*, a cord.]

Sirius [sir´i-us] *n* the Dog Star which is the brightest star in the sky. [L,—Gr *Seirios*.]

sirloin [sûr´loin] *n* a choice cut of beef from the loin end in front of the rump. [Fr *surlonge*—*sur*, over, and *longe* (OFr *loigne*; cf **loin**).]

sirocco [si-rok´ō] *n* a hot, oppressive wind blowing from the deserts of North Africa into southern Europe. [It *s(c)irocco*—Ar *sharq*, the east.]

sirrah, sirra [sir´a] *n* sir, used in anger or contempt. [**sir**.]

siree [sir-ē] *n* emphatic form of sir, usu. after yes or no.

sirup, sirupy *See* **syrup, syrupy**.

sisal [sīs´-, sis´(ȧ)l] *n* the fiber of a West Indian agave (*Agave sisalana*) supplying cordage, etc.; similar fiber from related plants. [From *Sisal*, a Yucatan port.]

siskin [sis´kin] *n* a yellowish-green Eurasian finch (*Carduelis spinus*). [Ger dial.]

sister [sis´tėr] *n* the name applied to a female by other children of the same parents; a friend who is like a sister; a female fellow member of the same race, creed, etc.; a nun; one of the same kind, model, etc.—*adj* closely related, akin.—*ns* **sis´terhood**, fact or state of being a sister; the relationship of sister; a society, esp a religious community, of women; **sis´ter-in-law**, a husband's or wife's sister, or a brother's wife.—*adj* **sis´terly**, like or befitting a sister, kind, affectionate. [ON *systir*; OE *sweostor*; Du *zuster*, Ger *schwester*.]

sit [sit] *vi* to rest oneself upon the buttocks, as on a chair; to rest on the haunches with the forelegs braced, as a dog; to perch, as a bird; to cover eggs for hatching, as a hen; to occupy a seat as a judge, legislator, etc.; to be in session, as a court; to pose, as for a portrait; to be located; to rest or lie; to take an examination; to take care of a child, pet, or house while the parents or owners are away.—*vt* to cause to sit; to keep one's seat (as on a horse, etc.); to provide seats or seating room for.—*pr p* **sitt´ing**; *pt, pt p* **sat**.—*ns* **sit´-down**, a strike in which the strikers refuse to leave the premises; civil disobedience in which demonstrators sit down in streets, etc., and refuse to leave voluntarily; **sit´-in**, a sit-down inside a public place, as by a civil-rights group; **sitt´er**, one who sits, esp a baby, dog, or house; **sitting**, the act or position of one that sits; a session, as of a court; a period of being seated.—*adj* that is sitting; being in a judicial or legislative seat; used in or for sitting; performed while sitting.—*ns* **sitting duck**, (*inf*) a person or thing easily attacked; an easy target; **sit´-up, sit´up´**, an exercise of sitting up from a lying position without using hands or legs.—**sit in** (**on**), to be a visitor at a session of discussion or music; to participate in a sit-in; **sit on**, to repress, squelch; to delay action or decision concerning; **sit pretty**, to be in a highly favorable situation; **sit tight**, to maintain one's position without change; to remain quiet as if in hiding; **sit under**, to attend the lectures or instructions of (esp a religious leader); **sit up**, to sit erect; to postpone going to bed; (*inf*) to become suddenly alert. [OE *sittan*; Ger *sitzen*, L *sedēre*.]

sitar [si-tär´] *n* an Indian lute with a long neck. [Hind *sitār*.]

site [sīt] *n* situation, esp of a building; ground occupied by, or set apart for, a building, etc.; the place or scene of something.—*vt* to locate. [Fr,—L *situs*—*sinĕre, situm*, to set down.]

situate [sit´ū-āt] *vt* to place in a site, situation, or category.—*adj* having a site; located.—*adj* **sit´uated**, situate; provided with money or possessions.—*n* **situā´tion**, position; temporary state; condition; a set of circumstances, a juncture; office, employment.—**situation comedy**, a comic television series made up of episodes involving the same group of stock characters. [Low L *situātus*—L *situs*, site.]

sitz bath [sits-bäth] *n* a therapeutic bath in a sitting position, with the hips and buttocks immersed; a tub adapted for such. [Ger *sitz-bad*.]

SI units [es ī ūnits] a system of units to describe quantities based on six arbitrary defined units, adopted officially by many, esp European countries. [*S*ystème *I*nternational d'Unités.]

Siva [sē´va, shē´va], **Shiva** [shē´va] *n* the destroyer and restorer, one of the triad of Hindu gods. [Sans *siva*, happy.]

six [siks] *adj, n* one more than five.—*n* the symbol for this (6, VI, vi); the sixth in a series or set; something having six units as members as an ice hockey team or a 6-cylinder engine or automobile.—*adj* **sixfold**, having six units or members; being six times as great or as many.—**sixth**, (*mus*) an interval of 6 diatonic degrees; the submediant.—Also *adj, adv*.—*ns* **six-pack**, a package of six units, as of six cans or bottles of beer, etc.; **six-shooter**, (*inf*) a revolver firing six shots without reloading; **sixth sense**, intuitive power.—**at sixes and sevens**, being in disorder. [OE *siex*; Ger *sechs*, Gael *sé*.]

sixteen [siks´tēn] *adj, n* one more than fifteen; the symbol for this (16, XVI, xvi).—*adj, n* **sixteenth**.—*n* **sixteen´mo**, the size of a piece of paper cut 16 from a sheet; a book of this size, 4½ inches by 6 3/4 inches high. [OE *sixtēne, sixtīene*.]

sixty [siks´tē] *adj, n* six times ten; the symbol for this (60, LX, lx);—**sixties** (60s), the numbers from 60 to 69; the same numbers in a life or a century.—*adj* **sixtieth**. [OE *sixtig*.]

size[1] [sīz] *n* magnitude; (*obs*) a portion of food and drink; an allotted portion; one, or belonging to one, of a series of classes according to standard dimensions, esp of merchandise.—*vt* to arrange according to size; to measure.—*adjs* **sī´zable, size´able**, of considerable size; **sized**, having a size of specified kind (eg *middle-sized*).—**size up**, (*inf*) to make an estimate or judgement of; to meet requirements. [Contr of **assize**.]

size[2] [sīz], **sizing** [sī´zing] *n* a pasty substance used as a glaze or filler on paper, cloth, etc.—*vt* to cover with size. [Perh same as **size** (1).]

sizzle [siz´l] *vi* to make a hissing sound of frying; to be extremely hot.—*vt* to fry, scorch, sear with a sizzling sound.—*n* a hissing sound. [Imit.]

skate[1] [skāt] *n* a metal runner in a frame, fastened to a shoe for gliding on ice; a boot with such a runner attached (Also **ice skate**); a similar frame or shoe with two pairs of small wheels for gliding on a floor, sidewalk, etc. (Also **roller skate**).—*vi* to move on skates.—*ns* **skā´ter; skā´ting**.—*n* **skate´board**, a short, oblong board with two wheels at each end, ridden as down an incline.—*vi* to ride on a skateboard. [Du *schaats*; Low Ger *schake*, shank, bone (skates orig being made of bones).]

skate[2] [skāt] *n* a fish (esp genus *Raja*) of the ray family with a broad, flat body and short, spineless tail. [ON *skata*.]

skean, skene [skēn´] *n* a dirk, dagger. [Gael *sgian*, knife.]

skein [skān] *n* a loosely tied coil of yarn; anything suggesting such a coil; thread wound on a reel; a flight of geese. [OFr *escagne*.]

skeleton [skel´e-tòn] *n* the bony framework of an animal; the framework or outline of anything; a very lean and emaciated person or animal; something shameful and kept secret (as in a family).—*adj* (of a set of persons, eg a staff) reduced to lowest strength.—**skeleton key**, a key with a slender bit that can open many simple locks. [Gr *skeleton* (*sōma*), a dried (body)—*skellein*, to dry.]

skep [skep] *n* a beehive, esp one made of straw. [ON *skeppa*.]

skeptic [skep´tik] *n* an adherent of skepticism; one who habitually questions matters generally accepted; one who doubts religious doctrines.—*adj* **skeptical**, doubting; questioning.—*n* **skep´ticism**, the doctrine that the truth of all knowledge must always be in question; a skeptical attitude; doubt about religious doctrines. [L *scepticus*—Gr *skeptikos*, thoughtful—*skeptesthai*, to consider.]

skerry [sker´i] *n* a reef of rock; a rocky isle. [ON *sker*.]

sketch [skech] *n* a drawing, slight, rough, or without detail, esp as a study towards a more finished work; an outline or short account; a short and slightly constructed play, dramatic scene, musical entertainment, etc.; a short descriptive essay.—*vti* to make a sketch.—*adj* **sketch´y**, like a sketch; incomplete, slight; imperfect, inadequate.—*adv* **sketch´ily**.—*n* **sketch´iness**. [Du *schets*, prob—It *schizzo*—L *schedium*, an extempore—Gr *schedios*, off-hand.]

skew [skū] *adj* oblique.—*adv* awry.—*vti* to slang or set at a slant.—*adj* **skewed**, distorted. [Prob O Norman Fr *eskiu(w)er*—OFr *eschiver, eschever*. See **eschew**.]

skewbald [skū´böld] *adj* of an animal, marked with patches of white and any other color but black.

skewer [skū´ėr] *n* a long pin of wood or metal, used for keeping meat together while roasting.—*vt* to fasten or pierce with a skewer. [**shiver** (1).]

ski [skē, shē] *n* a long narrow runner orig of wood, now also of metal, etc., fastened to the foot to enable the wearer to slide across snow, etc.;—*pl* **ski**, or **skis**.—*vi* to travel on skis;—*pt* **skied**, ski'd.—*ns* **ski´er; ski´ing**.—*ns* **ski lift, ski tow**, motor-driven devices for taking skiers uphill. [Norw.]

skid [skid] *n* a support on which something rests, is brought to the desired level, or slides; a ship's wooden fender; a runner on an aircraft landing gear; a sliding wedge used to brake a wheel; the act of skidding; (*pl*) (*slang*) a route to defeat or downfall.—*vti* to slide or slip, as a vehicle on ice.—*adj* **skidd´y**, having a slippery surface on which vehicles are liable to skid.—**skid row**, a city area where chronic drunks and other derelicts gather. [Of Scand origin.]

skiff [skif] *n* a small light rowboat, often with sails or a motor. [Akin to **ship**.]

skill [skil] *n* expertness; expert knowledge; a craft accomplishment (eg *manual skills*); a complex movement or action carried out with facility as a result of practice; a developed aptitude or ability.—*adj* **skill´ful, skil´ful**.—*adv* **skill´fully, skil´fully**.—*n* **skill´fulness, skil´fulness**.—*adj* **skilled**, expert. [ON *skil*, a distinction, *skilja*, to separate.]

skillet [skil´et] *n* a shallow metal vessel with a long handle, used in cooking, etc. [Origin doubtful.]

skim [skim] *vti* to remove (floating matter) from the surface of; to glide lightly over; to read superficially, skipping portions;—*pr p* **skimm´ing**; *pt, pt p* **skimmed**.—*ns* **skimm´er**, a utensil for skimming milk; **skim´ milk; skimmed milk**, milk from which the cream has been skimmed. [App related to **scum**.]

skimp [skimp] *vti* (*inf*) to be sparing or frugal (with).—*adj* (*inf*) scanty, spare.—*adj* **skim´py**.—*adv* **skim´pily**. [Perh **scamp** combined with **scrimp**.]

skin [skin]*n* the natural outer covering of an animal; a hide; an integument; a thin outer layer or covering; a vessel for containing wine or water made of an animal's skin; the physical well-being of a person; a casing forming the outside surface of a structure.—*vt* to strip the skin from; to injure by scraping (one's knee, etc.); (*inf*) to swindle.—*vi* to become covered with skin; (*inf*) to slip through or away;—*pr p* **skinn´ing**; *pt, pt p* **skinned**.—*adj* **skin´-deep**, no deeper than the skin; superficial.—*ns* **skin´ diving**, the sport of swimming under water with a face mask and flippers without a portable breathing device; underwater swimming with air supplied by scuba equipment; **skin´flick** (*slang*) a pornographic motion picture; **skin´flint**, a very niggardly person; **skin´head**, one with a very short haircut; (*Brit*) a young working-class hoodlum.—*adj* **skinned**, having skin (of a specified kind).—*n* **skinn´er**.—*adj* **skinn´y**, thin; emaciated.—*vi* **skinn´y-dip** (*inf*) to swim nude.—*n* (*inf*) a swim in the nude.—*n* **skinn´iness**.—*adj* **skin´tight**, fitting close to the skin.—**by the skin of one's teeth**, very narrowly; **under one's skin**, (*inf*) to annoy one greatly; to interest one deeply; **under the skin**, beneath apparent differences; at heart. [OE *scinn*; ON *skinn*, skin, Ger *schinden*, to flay.]

skip [skip] *vti* to spring or hop lightly over; to pass from one point to another, omitting or ignoring (what lies between); to leave (town) hurriedly;—*pr p* **skipp´ing**; *pt, pt p* **skipped**.—*n* an act of skipping; specifically, a gait alternating light hops on each foot.—**skip bail**, to jump bail; **skip rope**, to jump rope. [ME *skippen*; perh of Scand origin.]

skipper [skip´ėr] *n* the master of a fishing, small trading, or pleasure boat; the captain or first pilot of an airplane.—*vt* to act as skipper (as of a boat); to act as coach of (as a team). [Du *schipper*; Dan *skipper*.]

skirmish [skûr´mish] *n* a brief fight between small parties.—*vi* to take part in a skirmish.—*n* **skir´misher**. [OFr *escarmouche*.]

skirt [skûrt] *n* a garment, generally a woman's, that hangs from the waist; the lower part of a dress, coat or other garment; something like a skirt, esp for a piece of furniture; (*pl*) outlying parts (as of a town or city); a rim, border, margin.—*vti* to border; to pass along the edge (of).—*n* **skir´ting**, material for skirts; a border, an edging. [ON *skyrta*, a shirt, kirtle; cf **shirt**.]

skit [skit] *n* a short humorous sketch, as in the theater. [Perh related to ON *skjōta*, to shoot.]

skittish [skit´ish] *adj* shy, nervous, easily frightened; frivolous, frisky; lively; coquettish, coy.—*adv* **skitt´ishly**.—*n* **skitt´ishness**. [Dial *skit*, to caper.]

skittle [skit´l] *n* (*Brit*) a pin, or wooden object set on end, for the game of **skittles** (English ninepins); a wooden ball being used to knock the pins down.—*vt* **skitt´le**, to knock down.

skua [skū´a] *n* any one of several large birds (genus *Stercorarius*) of northern seas that tend to harass weaker birds until they drop or disgorge their prey. [Norw.]

skulk [skulk] *vi* to move in a stealthy manner; to conceal (oneself) out of cowardice, fear, or with sinister intent.—*n* **skulk´er**. [Scand, as in Dan *skulke*, to sneak.]

skull [skul] *n* the bony case that encloses the brain; the head.—*n* **skull´cap**, a cap that fits closely to the head, usu. worn indoors.—**skull and crossbones**, a representation of a skull over crossbones, used as a warning of danger to life. [ME *scolle*; perh Scand.]

skunk [skungk] *n* a small bushy-tailed N American mammal (*Mephitis mephitis*, the common skunk, or *Spilogale putorius*, the little spotted skunk), having a black-and-white coat and a pair of glands emitting a foul-smelling liquid when molested; the fur of a skunk; (*inf*) an obnoxious or despicable person.—*n* **skunk cabbage**, an eastern N American perennial herb (*Symplocarpus foetidus*) whose spring-flowering spathe emits a foul odor; a related plant (*Lysichitum americanum*) of the Pacific coast region. [Algonquian.]

sky [skī] *n* the upper atmosphere that constitutes an apparent vault over the earth; heaven; the weather in the upper atmosphere; the climate.—*vt* to hang (as a painting) above the line of sight.—*ns* **sky blue**, a variable color ranging from a pale to a light blue; **sky´cap**, a porter at an air terminal; **sky diving**, parachute jumping involving free-fall maneuvers.—*adj, adv* **sky´high**, very high; in an enthusiastic manner; exorbitantly expensive.—*vt* **sky´jack**, (*inf*) to hijack (an aircraft).—*ns* **sky´jacker; Sky´lab**, US earth-orbiting laboratory (1973–79) housing alternating crews of astronauts; **sky´lark**, a Eurasian lark (*Alauda arvensis*) famous for the song it utters as it soars.—*vi* to romp or frolic.—*n* **sky´light**, a window in a roof or ceiling; **sky´line**, the visible horizon; the outline, as of a city, seen against the sky; **sky marshal**, a Federal officer assigned to guard against skyjacking; **sky´rocket**, a firework rocket that explodes high in the sky.—*vti* to rise or make rise rapidly.—*ns* **sky´scraper**, a very tall building; **sky´walk**, an enclosed aerial walkway connecting two buildings.—*adj, adv* **sky´ward**, toward the sky.—*adv* **sky´wards**. [ON *skȳ*, a cloud.]

Skye terrier [skī ter´i-ėr] *n* a breed of small long-haired Scottish terrier. [*Skye* in the Inner Hebrides.]

slab [slab] *n* a flat, broad, and fairly thick piece (as of stone, wood, or bread, etc.); something that resembles a slab in size.—*vt* to divide or form into slabs; to cover or support with slabs; to put on thickly. [ME; origin obscure.]

slabber [slab´er] *vti* to slaver, to drool; to slobber.—*n* **slabb´er**. [Allied to Low Ger and Du *slabberen*.]

slack[1] [slak] *adj* loose, not tight; slow, sluggish; not busy; dull; careless; lacking in completeness, finish, or perfection.—*vti* to slacken.—*n* a part that hangs loose; a lack of tension; a dull period; a lull; (*pl*) trousers for men or women.—*adv* **slack´ly**.—*vti* **slack´en**, to make or become less active, brisk, etc.; to loosen or relax, as a rope.—*n* **slack´er**, an idler, shirker.—*adv* **slack´ly**.—*n* **slack´ness**.—*n, adj* **slack´ening**.—*n* **slack´ wa´ter**, the turn of the tide; a stretch of still water, slow-moving water.—Also **slack tide**.—**slack off**, to slacken; **slack up**, to go more slowly. [OE *sleac*; Swed *slak*, ON *slakr*.]

slack[2] [slak] *n* coal dross. [Cf Ger *schlacke*, dross.]

slag [slag] *n* vitrified cinders from smelting; scoriae from a volcano. [Cf Ger *schlacke*, dross.]

slain [slān] *pt p* of **slay**.

slake [slāk] *vi* to quench, satisfy (eg thirst); to hydrate (lime). [OE *sleacian*, to grow slack—*slæc, sleac*, slack.]

slalom [slä´lom] *n* downhill skiing in a zigzag course between upright obstacles (as flags); a timed race (as on skis or in an automobile or kayak) over a wavy course past a series of flags or markers.—*vi* to move over a zigzag course. [Norw.]

slam[1] [slam] *vti* to shut with violence and noise, to bang; to put forcibly, noisily, hurriedly (down on, against, etc.); (*inf*) to criticize severely.—*pr p* **slamm´ing**; *pt, pt p* **slammed**.—*n* the act or sound of slamming; (*inf*) a severe criticism; (*slang*) slammer.—*n* **slamm´er**, (*slang*) a prison or jail. [Cf Norw *slemma*.]

slam[2] [slam] *n* grand slam; little slam. [Origin unknown.]

slander [slän´dėr] *n* the utterance of a falsehood that damages another's reputation; such a statement.—*vt* to utter such a statement about.—*n* **slan´derer**.—*adj* **slan´derous**.—*adv* **slan´derously**.—*n* **slan´derousness**. [OFr *esclandre*—L *scandalum*—Gr *skandalon*. See **scandal**.]

slang [slang] *n* cant, jargon peculiar to a social class, or age group; words or phrases common in colloquial speech (eg new coinages, abreviations, fantastic or violent metaphors) which are not accepted for dignified use.—*adj* pertaining to slang.—*vt* to abuse with harsh or coarse language.—*vi* to use slang or vulgar abuse.—*adj* **slang´y**.—*n* **slang´iness**. [Ety uncertain.]

slant [slänt] *vti* to slope; to tell so as to express a particular bias.—*n* a slope; obliquity; a sloping surface, line, ray, or movement; a divergence from a direct line; a point of view or way of looking at a thing.—*adj* sloping, oblique, inclined from a direct line.—*adj* **slanted**, sloping; biased, prejudiced. *advs* **slant´ly, slant´wise**. [ME *slent*; cf Norw *slenta*, Swed *slinta*, to slope, slip.]

slap [slap] a blow with the hand or anything flat; an insult; a rebuff.—*vt* to strike with something flat; to put, hit, etc. with force.—*pr p* **slapp´ing**; *pt, pt p* **slapped**.—*adv* directly; suddenly, violently.—*adv* **slapdash**, in a bold, careless way.—*adj* hurried; careless; haphazard.—*n* **slap´stick**, knockabout low comedy or farce. [Allied to Low Ger *slapp*, Ger *schlappe*; imit.]

slash [slash] *vt* to cut by striking with sweeping strokes, as of a knife; to make long cuts in; to slit so as to show a color underneath; to criticize very harshly; to reduce drastically or suddenly, as prices.—*vi* to strike violently. and at random with an edged instrument.—*n* a long cut made by slashing; a slashing.—*n* **slash pocket**, a pocket (in a garment) with a finished diagonal opening. [Perh OFr *eslachier*, to break.]

slat [slat] *n* a thin strip of wood, etc.—*adj* **slatt´ed**, having slats. [OFr *esclat*.]

slate[1] [slāt] *n* a piece of construction material (as laminated rock) prepared as a shingle for roofing or siding; a dense fine-grained metamorphic rock that cleaves in thin, smooth layers; a tablet of material (as slate) for writing on; a list of proposed candidates.—*adj* of slate.—*vt* to cover with slate; to designate for action or appointment.—*ns* **slā´ter**, one who covers roofs with slates; a wood louse; any of various marine isopods; **slā´ting**, the work of a slater; to designate, as for candidacy.—*adj* **slā´ty**, of, or like, slate.—**a clean slate**, a record that shows no faults, mistakes, etc. [OFr *esclate*; cf **slat**.]

slate[2] [slāt] *vt* to thrash severely. [From the ON word corresponding to OE *slǣtan*, to bait.]

slattern [slat´ėrn] *n* a slut, a dirty woman; a prostitute.—*adj* **slatt´ernly**, sluttish.—*n* **slatt´ernliness**. [App obs *slat*, to strike, splash.]

slaughter [slö´tėr] *n* the killing of animals for food; killing of great numbers, carnage (as in a battle or massacre).—*vt* to slay in large numbers; to butcher; to kill in a violent manner.—*ns* **slaugh´terer; slaugh´terhouse**, a place where animals are butchered for food.—*adj* **slaugh´terous**, given to slaughter, destructive, murderous. [ON *slātr*, butchers' meat, whence *slātra*, to slaughter cattle.]

Slav [släv] *n* a member of any of the peoples of eastern Europe or Soviet Asia who speak a Slavonic language.—*ns* **Slavon´ic, Slavic**, a branch of the Indo-European family of languages including Russian, Ukrainian, Polish, Czech, Slovak, Bulgarian, etc.—*adj* of this group of languages. [Medieval L *Sclavus*—Late Gr *Sklabos*, from the stem of the Slavonic words *slovo*, word, *sloviti*, to speak.]

slave [slāv] *n* a person owned by another; one who is submissive under domination; one who works like a slave, a drudge; a device (as the typewriter unit of a computer) that is directly responsive to another.—*vi* to work like a slave, to drudge.—*ns* **slave drī´ver**, one who superintends slaves at their work; any cruel taskmaster; **slā´ver**, a person engaged in the slave trade; a shop used in the slave trade; a white slaver; **slā´very**, the state of being a slave; the institution of ownership of slaves; drudgery; **slave state**, a state of the US in which Negro slavery was legal until the Civil War; a nation subjected to totalitarian rule; **slave trade**, traffic in slaves, esp the buying and selling of Negroes for profit before the American Civil War.—*adj* **slā´vish**, befitting a slave, servile, abject; servilely following guidance or conforming to pattern or rule (eg *slavish adherence to the text*).—*adv* **slā´vishly**.—*n* **slā´vishness**. [OFr *esclave*, orig a **Slav**, the slaves of the Germanic races being usually captive Slavs.]

slaver [slav´ėr] *n* saliva running from the mouth.—*vi* to let the saliva run out of the mouth; to drivel; to fawn.—*vt* (*arch*) to smear with saliva. [Allied to **slabber**.]

slay [slā] *vt* to kill violently, wantonly, or in great numbers; (*slang*) to overwhelm, to affect in a powerful way.—*vi* to kill, murder.—*pt* **slew** [slōō]; pt p **slain** [slān].—*n* **slay´er**. [OE *slēn*; ON *slā*, Ger *schlagen*, to strike.]

sled [sled] *n* a vehicle with runners made for sliding upon snow; a rocket sled.—*vti* to carry or travel in a sled. [Middle Du *sleedse*.]

sledge[1] [slej] *n* a sled or sleigh.

sledge[2] [slej] *n* a large heavy hammer.—Also **sledgehammer**. [OE *slecg*—*slēan*, to strike.]

sleek [slēk] *adj* smooth, glossy, and soft; having a well-fed or well-groomed appearance; insinuating, plausible.—*vt* to make sleek.—*adv* **sleek´ly**.—*n* **sleek´ness**. [A later form of **slick**.]

sleep [slēp] *n* a natural, regularly recurring rest for the body, during which there is little or no conscious thought; any state like this; death; a trance; a coma; a period spent sleeping; a state of numbness followed by tingling.—*vi* to rest in a state of sleep; to be in a state resembling sleep; to have sexual relations.—*vt* to be slumbering in; to get rid of by sleep; to provide sleeping accommodation for;—*pt, pt p* **slept**.—*n* **sleep´er**, one who sleeps; a horizontal beam supporting and spreading a weight; a sleeping car; something that suddenly attains prominence or value; (*pl*) pajamas, usu. for children, with feet.—*ns* **sleep´ing bag**, a bag for sleeping in used by travelers, campers, etc.; **sleep´ing car**, a railroad car with berths for sleeping in; **sleep´ing pill**, a pill to induce sleep; **sleep´ing part´ner**, a secret partner; **sleep´ing sick´ness**, a serious infectious disease, esp of tropical Africa, marked by lethargy, prolonged coma, etc., caused by trypanosomes transmitted by the tsetse fly; any of various forms of encephalitis characterized by lethargy, etc.—*adj* **sleep´less**, without sleep; unable to sleep.—*adv* **sleep´lessly**.—*ns* **sleep´lessness; sleepwalk´er**, one who walks in sleep, a somnambulist; **sleepwalk´ing**.—*adj* **sleep´y**, inclined to sleep; drowsy; inducing, or suggesting, sleep.—*adv* **sleep´ily**.—*n* **sleep´iness**.—*n* **sleepy´head**, a lazy person.—**sleep off**, to recover from by sleeping. [OE *slǣpan*; Ger *schlafen*.]

sleet [slēt] *n* partly frozen rain; rain mixed with snow.—*vi* to shower in the form of sleet.—*adj* **sleet´y**. [ME; prob conn with Ger *schlosse*, hail.]

sleeve [slēv] *n* the part of a garment which covers the arm; a tubelike part fitting around another part; an open-ended flat or tubular packaging or cover, esp a paperboard envelope for a phonograph record.—*vt* to furnish with sleeves.—*adj* **sleeve´less**, without sleeves.—**up one's sleeve**, hidden but ready at hand. [OE (Anglian) *slēfe*, a sleeve.]

sleigh [slā] *n* a light vehicle on runners, as for travel on snow.—*vi* to drive or travel in a sleigh. [Du *slee.*]

sleight [slīt] *n* cunning, dexterity; an artful trick.—*n* **sleight of hand´**, legerdemain; expert manipulation; skill in tricks depending on such. [ON *slægth*, cunning, *slægr*, sly.]

slender [slen´dėr] *adj* thin or narrow; slim; slight.—*adv* **slen´derly**.—*n* **slen´derness**.—*vti* **slen´derize**, to make or become slender.

slept [slept] *pt, pt p* of **sleep**.

sleuth [slōōth] *n* (*inf*) a detective.—*n* **sleuthhound**, a detective. [ON *slōth*, track.]

slew[1] [slōō] *pt* of **slay**.

slew[2] [slōō] *vti* to turn, swing, round.

slew[3] [slōō] *n* a large number. [Ir Gael *sluagh.*]

slice [slīs] *n* a thin flat piece cut from something; a wedge-shaped piece (as of pie or cake); a spatula for spreading paint or ink; a serving knife with a wedge-shaped blade; a portion, a share.—*vt* to cut into slices; to stir or spread with a slice; to hit (a ball) so that it curves to the right if right-handed or to the left if left-handed.—*vi* to slice something; to move with a cutting action.—*n* **sli´cer**.—*n, adj* **slīc´ing**. [OFr *esclice*—OHG *slīzan*, to split.]

slick [slik] *adj* sleek, smooth, trim; adroit, dexterous; wily; (*inf*) smooth but superficial, tricky, etc.—*n* a smooth area on the water, as from a film of oil.—*adv* smoothly; glibly; deftly.—*vt* to polish, make glossy; (*inf*) to make smart, neat, etc. (*with* **up**).—*ns* **slick´er**, a loose waterproof coat; (*inf*) a tricky person; one of natty appearance and sophisticated manner.—*adv* **slick´ly**.—*n* **slick´ness**. [OE *slician*, smooth.]

slid pt, pt p of **slide**.

slide [slīd] *vi* to move along in constant contact with a smooth surface, as on ice; to coast over snow and ice; (*baseball*) to approach a base by gliding along the ground; to slip; to glide.—*vt* to cause to glide or slip; to traverse by sliding; to put unobtrusively.—*pt, pt p* **slid**.—*n* a sliding; a smooth, inclined surface for sliding; something that works by sliding; a photographic transparency for use with a projector or viewer; a small glass plate on which objects are mounted for microscopic study; the fall of a mass of rock, snow, etc., down a slope.—*n* **slī´der**, one who, or that which, slides; (*baseball*) a curve ball that breaks only slightly.—*ns* **slide´ rule**, mechanical device for multiplying, dividing, etc., consisting of two logarithmic graduated rules sliding one against the other; **slide valve**, a valve that opens and closes a passageway, esp in a steam engine; **slī´ding scale**, a schedule of costs, wages, etc. that varies with different conditions; a system for raising or lowering tariffs in accord with price changes; a flexible scale (as of fees or subsidies) adjusted to the needs or incomes of individuals.—**let slide**, to take no action over. [OE *slīdan*, to slide.]

slight [slīt] *adj* frail, flimsy—lacking solidity, massiveness, weight; slim; trifling, insignificant.—*vt* to ignore or overlook disrespectfully.—*n* discourteous disregard; an affront by showing neglect or want of respect.—*adv* **slight´ly**, slenderly, flimsily; in a small degree.—*n* **slight´ness**, slenderness or frailness; inadequacy, lack of thoroughness; small degree (of).—*adv* **slight´ingly**, in a neglectful, discourteous, or disparaging, manner. [Cf OE *eorthslihtes*, close to the ground.]

slily [slī´li] *adv See* **slyly**.

slim [slim] *adj* small in girth, slender; small in amount, degree, etc.—*vti* to make or become slim.—*ns* **slim´ness; slimm´ing**. [Du, Low Ger *slim*, crafty; Ger *schlimm*, bad.]

slime [slīm] *n* ooze, very fine, thin, slippery, or gluey mud; any viscous organic secretion, as mucus secreted by various animals (as slugs and catfishes); (*inf*) one that is odious.—*adj* **slīm´y**.—*n* **slim´iness**. [OE *slīm*; Ger *schleim.*]

sling[1] [sling] *n* a strap or pocket with a string attached to each end, for hurling a stone; a loop for hoisting, lowering, or carrying, a weight; a hanging support for an injured arm.—*vt* to throw (as) with a sling.—*pt, pt p* **slung**.—*ns* **sling-back**, a shoe, having the back absent except for a strap representing the top edge; **sling´shot´**, a Y-shaped piece of wood, etc., with an elastic band attached to it for shooting stones, etc.—*n* **sling´er**. [Prob from several sources; cf ON *slyngva*, to fling, OE *slingan*, to wind, twist.]

sling[2] [sling] *n* a hot or cold alcoholic drink consisting of liquor, sugar, lemon juice and plain or carbonated water. [Perh **sling** (1) in sense of toss off; perh Ger *schlingen*, to swallow.]

slink [slingk] *vi* to move stealthily, to sneak;—*pt, pt p* **slunk**.—*adj* **slink´y**, slinking; (*inf*) sinuous in line or movement. [OE *slincan*, to creep.]

slip[1] [slip] *vi* to slide or glide along; to move out of position; to lose foothold; to escape; to slink; to move unobserved; to make a slight mistake; to lapse morally; to lose one's grip on things, one's control of the situation; to become worse.—*vt* to cause to slide; to convey quietly or secretly; to put, pass, etc., quickly or deftly; to escape from; to elude (the memory).—*pr p* **slipp´ing**; *pt, pt p* **slipped**.—*n* a space between piers for docking ships; a woman's undergarment the length of a dress with shoulder straps; a pillowcase; a slipping or falling down; an error or mistake.—*ns* **slip´case**, a boxlike container for a book or books, open at one end; **slip´cover**, a removable, fitted cloth cover for a sofa, chair, etc.; **slip´knot**, a knot that will slip along the rope around which it is tied; **slip noose**, a noose made with a slip knot; **slippage**, a slipping, as of one gear past another; **slipped disk**, a ruptured cartilaginous disk between vertebrae; **slipp´er**, a light, low shoe easily slipped on the foot.—*adj* **slipp´ery**, liable to cause slipping, as a wet surface; tending to slip away, as from a grasp; unreliable; deceitful; **slip´shod**, careless or slovenly.—*ns* **slip´stick**, a slide rule; **slip stitch**, a concealed stitch for sewing folded edges (as hems); an unworked knitting stitch transferred from one needle to another without knitting or purling; **slip´stream**, a stream of fluid (as air or water) driven aft by a propeller; an area of forward suction immediately behind a rapidly moving racing car.—*vi* to drive in the slipstream of a racing car.—*ns* **slip´-up**, (*inf*) an error; **slip´way**, an inclined surface for a ship being repaired or built; a space between docks.—**let slip**, to say without intending to. [Perh Low Ger or Du; OE has *slipor*, slippery.]

slip[2] [slip] *vt* to take cuttings from (a plant); to divide into slips.—*n* a stem, root, etc., of a plant, used for planting or grafting; a descendant, offspring; a small piece of paper; a young, slim person; a long seat or narrow pew. [ME *slippen.*]

slit [slit] *vt* to cut open lengthwise; to cut into strips.—*pr p* **slitt´ing**; *pt, pt p* **slit**.—*n* a long cut; a narrow opening.—**slit trench**, a deep narrow trench, esp for shelter in battle. [OE *slītan*; Ger *schlitzen.*]

slither [sliTH´ėr] *vi* to slide, as on mud or scree; to slip or slide like a snake.—*vt* to cause to slide. [OE *slidderian*, to slip.]

sliver [sliv´ėr] *vti* to split or cut into slivers.—*n* a long thin piece cut or rent off; a splinter. [OE (*tō-*) *slīfan*, to cleave.]

slob [slob] *n* (*inf*) a coarse or sloppy person. [Ir *slab*, mud.]

slobber [slob´ėr] *vt* to smear with dribbling saliva or food.—*vi* to drool; to speak in a maudlin way.—*n* saliva drooled; driveling or incoherent utterance.

sloe [slō] *n* a small sour plum, the fruit of the blackthorn; the blackthorn.—*adj* **sloe´-eyed**, having large dark eyes; having almond-shaped eyes.—*n* **sloe gin**, a red liqueur made of dry gin flavored with sloes. [OE *slā*; Du *slee.*]

slog [slog] *vti* to hit hard; to make (one's way) laboriously; to toil (at).—*n* a strenuous spell of work; a hard dogged march or tramp.—*n* **slogg´er**, a hard worker.

slogan [slō´gȧn] *n* a war cry among the ancient Highlanders of Scotland; a catchword or motto associated with a political party, etc.; an advertising catch phrase. [Gael *sluagh*, army, *gairm*, cry.]

sloop [slōōp] *n* a small sailing vessel with a single mast and a jib. [Du *sloep.*]

slop[1] [slop] *n* slush; spilled liquid; a puddle; unappetizing liquid or semiliquid food; (*pl*) liquid refuse; gush; effusive sentiment in speech or writing.—*vti* to spill or splash.—*pr p* **slopp´ing**; *pt p* **slopped**.—*adj* **slopp´y**, wet; muddy; slipshod; (*inf*) disagreeably effusive.—*ns* **sloppy joe**, ground beef cooked with tomato sauce, etc., and served on a bun; a long, loose girl's sweater; **slop sink**, a deep sink for filling scrub pails, washing out mops, etc.—*n* **slopp´iness**. [OE *(cu-)sloppe*, (cow-)droppings.]

slop[2] [slop] *n* a loose smock or overall; (*pl*) wide breeches worn in the 16th century; (*pl*) clothing sold to sailors. [Cf OE *oferslop*, loose outer garment.]

slope [slōp] *n* rising or falling ground; an inclined surface; the amount or degree of this.—*vt* to cause to slope.—*vi* to have a slope or slant; (*inf*) to go; to travel. [From **aslope**.]

slot[1] [slot] *n* the track of an animal (as a deer). [Fr *esclot*, track.]

slot[2] [slot] *n* a long narrow depression or opening to receive a coin, or part of a mechanism, etc.; a slit; (*inf*) a niche in an organization, etc.—*vt* to make a slot in; (*inf*) to place in a series.—*n* **slot machine**, a machine, specifically a gambling machine worked by inserting a coin in a slot. [Low Ger or Du *slot*, a lock.]

sloth [sloth or slōth] *n* laziness, sluggishness; any of several sluggish arboreal quadrupeds (genus *Bradypus* or *Choleopus*) of tropical America.—*adj* **sloth´ful**, given to sloth, inactive, lazy.—*adv* **sloth´fully**.—*n* **sloth´fulness**. [ME *slawthe*, altered from OE *slæwth—slāw*, slow.]

slouch [slowch] *n* a loose, ungainly, stooping posture; a lazy or incompetent person; a lout.—*vi* to go or bear oneself with a slouch.—*vt* to cause to droop.—*n* **slouch hat**, a soft hat with a broad flexible brim. [Cf ON *slōkr*, a slouching fellow.]

slough[1] [slow] *n* a hollow filled with mud: deep, hopeless dejection.—*vt* to engulf in a slough.—*vi* to plod through mud; to slog.—*adj* **slough´y**, full of sloughs; miry.—**slough of despond**, a state of extreme depression. [OE *slōh.*]

slough[2] [sluf] *n* castoff skin of a snake; dead tissue in a sore; something that may be shed or cast off.—*vi* to come away as a slough (*with* **off**); to cast the skin.—*vt* to cast off, as a slough. [ME *sloh*; origin uncertain.]

sloven [sluv´n] *n* a person carelessly or dirtily dressed.—Also *adj.*—*adj* **slov´enly**.—*n* **slov´enliness**. [Cf ODu *slof, sloef*, Low Ger *sluf*, slow, indolent.]

slow [slō] *adj* not quick in understanding; not swift; not hasty; not progressive; dull; behind in time.—*adv* slowly.—*vti* to make or become slow or slower (*often with* **up** or **down**).—*adv* **slow´ly**.—*n* **slow´ness**.—*ns* **slow burn**, (*slang*) a gradual working up of anger; **slow´down**, a slowing down, as of production.—*adj* **slow-motion**, moving slowly; denoting a filmed or taped scene with the original action slowed down.—*ns* **slow-pitch**, a form of softball with 10 players on each side and in which the pitch has a limited arc and base stealing is not allowed; **slow´poke´** (*slang*), a person who acts or moves slowly.—*adj* **slow´-witt´ed**, mentally slow; dull.—*n* **slow´worm**, a blindworm. [OE *slāw*; Du *slee*, ON *sljōr*.]

sludge [sluj] *n* soft mud or mire; any heavy, slimy deposit, sediment, etc.; partly melted snow. [Cf **slush**.]

slug[1] [slug] *n* a habitually lazy fellow; a terrestrial mollusk (family Limacidae) resembling a land snail but having no outer shell; a smooth soft larvae of a moth that creeps like a mollusk.—*n* **slugg´ard**, one habitually idle or inactive.—*adj* **slugg´ish**, habitually lazy; having little motion; having little or no power.—*adv* **slugg´ishly**.—*n* **slugg´ishness**. [Prob Scand.]

slug[2] [slug] *n* a lump of metal, esp one for firing from a gun; (*print*) a solid line of type cast by a composing machine; unit of mass to which a pound force can impart an acceleration of one foot per second per second; a disk for insertion in a slot machine, esp one used illegally instead of a coin; (*inf*) a hard blow, with the fist or a bat.—*vt* (*inf*) to hit hard with the fist or a bat. [Perh **slug** (1).]

sluice [slōōs] *n* a structure with a gate for stopping or regulating the flow of water; a drain, channel; a regulated outlet or inlet; a trough for washing gold from sand, etc.; a sluicing, quick wash.—*vt* to draw off through a sluice; to wash with water from a sluice.—*vi* to pour as from a sluice. [OFr *escluse*—Low L *exclūsa* (*aqua*), a sluice, ie (water) shut out—pt p of L *exclūděre*, to shut out.]

slum [slum] *n* an overcrowded area characterized by poverty, etc.—*vi* to visit slums in a condescending way.—*n* **slum´lord** (*slang*), an absentee landlord who exploits slum property. [Cant.]

slumber [slum´bėr] *vi* to sleep; to be inactive.—*n* sleep; a light sleep; lethargy; torpor.—*n* **slum´berer**.—*adjs* **slum´berous, slum´brous**, inviting or causing slumber; sleepy.—**slumber party**, an overnight gathering esp of teenage girls, usu. at one of their homes. [ME *slūmeren*—OE *slūma*, slumber.]

slump [slump] *vi* to fall or sink suddenly; to drop or slide suddenly; to collapse; to have a drooping posture; to go into a slump.—*n* a sudden or serious fall in business activity; a period of poor or losing play by a team or individual; a downward slide of a mass of land or rock. [Prob imit.]

slung *pt, pt p* of **sling**.

slunk *pt, pt p* of **slink**.

slur [slûr] *vt* to disparage, asperse; to sound indistinctly; to glide (over) quickly and carelessly; (*mus*) to produce (successive notes) by gliding without a break;—*pr p* **slurr´ing**; *pt, pt p* **slurred**.—*n* an aspersion, stain, imputation of blame; (*mus*) a curved line indicating that notes are to be sung to one syllable or with a smooth gliding effect; a running together resulting in indistinctness in speech.—*n* **slurr´y**, a thin watery mixture of insoluble matter (as mud, lime, or plaster of paris). [Origin obscure.]

slurp [slûrp] *vti* (*slang*) to drink or eat noisily.—*n* (*slang*) a loud sipping or sucking sound.

slush [slush] *n* liquid mud; melting snow; worthless sentimental drivel; grout made of portland cement, sand, and water; unsolicited writings submitted (as to a magazine) for publication.—*vt* to wet or splash with slush; to fill in (joints) with slush or grout.—*vi* to go through slush; to make a splashing sound.—*adj* **slush´y**.—**slush fund**, a fund raised from the sale of refuse to buy small luxuries for a warship's crew; a fund of money set aside for secret and corrupt use, eg in a political campaign.

slut [slut] *n* a dirty, untidy woman; a lewd woman; a prostitute.—*adj* **slutt´ish**.—*adv* **slutt´ishly**.—*n* **slutt´ishness**. [Ety uncertain.]

sly [slī] *adj* skillful in doing anything so as to be unobserved; cunning, wily, secretive; done with artful dexterity; with hidden meaning.—*n* **sly´boots**, a sly or cunning person esp one with an engaging manner.—*adv* **sly´ly** (or **sli´ly**).—*n* **sly´ness** (or **slī´ness**).—**on the sly**, surreptitiously. [ON *slægr*; cf **sleight**.]

smack[1] [smak] *n* taste; a distinctive or distinguishable flavor; small quantity, a trace, tinge.—*vi* to have a taste (of). [OE *smæc*.]

smack[2] [smak] *n* a fishing vessel fitted with a well to keep fish alive. [Du *smak*.]

smack[3] [smak] *vt* to strike smartly, to slap loudly; to kiss roughly and noisily; to make a sharp noise with, as the lips by separation.—*n* a sharp sound; a loud slap or blow; a hearty kiss.—*adv* with a smack; directly.—*n* **smack´er**, one that smacks; (*slang*) a dollar bill. [Prob imit; Du *smakken*, to smite, Ger *schmatzen*, to smack.]

small [smöl] *adj* little in size, extent, quantity, or degree; fine in grain, texture, gauge, etc.; of little value, power, or importance; operating on no great scale; unimposing, humble; petty (eg *it was small of him to do that*); dilute; young.—*adv* in a low tone, gently; in small pieces; in a small manner.—*n* the slenderest part, esp of the back; (*pl*) small-sized products.—*ns* **small´ arm**, a hand-held firearm; **small´ beer**, a kind of weak beer; trivial matters.—*n pl* **small´clothes**, close-fitting knee breeches, esp those worn in the 18th century; minor articles of clothing (as underwear).—*n pl* **small´ hours**, the hours immediately following midnight.—*adj* **small´ish**, somewhat small.—*ns* **small´ness; small´pox**, a contagious, febrile disease, characterized by pocks or eruptions on the skin; **small screen**, television; **small´sword**, a light thrusting sword for fencing or duelling; **small talk**, light conversation.—*adj* **small´time**, (*inf*) unimportant.—**feel small**, to feel shame. [OE *smæl*; Ger *schmal*.]

smarmy [smärm´-ē] *adj* fawning, ingratiatingly and fulsomely. [Origin obscure.]

smart [smärt] *n* a quick, stinging pain; (*pl*) (*slang*) intelligence.—*vi* to cause sharp, stinging pain (as by a slap); to feel such pain; to feel distress or irritation.—*adj* sharp and stinging; vigorous, brisk; acute, witty; vivacious; keen, quick, and efficient in business; trim, spruce, fine; fashionable, stylish.—*vti* **smart´en**, to make or become smart.—*adv* **smart´ly**.—*n* **smart´ness**.—**smart aleck, smart alec**, (*inf*) an offensively conceited person; **smart ass**, (*inf*) an aggressively knowledgeable usu. young person. [OE *smeortan*; Du *smarten*, Ger *schmerzen*.]

smash [smash] *vti* to break into pieces with noise or violence; to hit, collide, or move with force; to destroy or be destroyed.—*n* a hard, heavy hit; a violent, noisy breaking; a violent collision; total failure, esp in business; a popular success.—*n* **smash´up**, a complete collapse; a motor vehicle collision. [Imit; cf Swed dial *smaske*, to smack.]

smattering [smat´ėr´ing] *n* a scrappy superficial knowledge; a small number. [ME *smateren*, to rattle, to chatter.]

smear [smēr] *vt* to cover with anything sticky or oily, as grease; to rub in such a way as to make a smear; to defame, slander.—*vi* to be or become smeared.—*n* a mark or patch of, anything sticky or oily; something smeared on a slide for examination under the microscope; a preparation made by smearing material on a surface; a usu. unsubstantiated charge against a person or organization.—*adj* **smear´y**, ready to smear; showing smears. [OE *smeru*, fat, grease; ON *smjör*, butter.]

smell [smel] *n* the sense by which odors are perceived; the specific sensation excited by an odor; the property of exciting it; a perfume, scent, odor, or stench; an act of instance of smelling; a pervading, characteristic quality; a very small amount.—*vi* to have an odor; to use the sense of smell.—*vt* to perceive, detect, find, by smell; to sense the presence of.—*pt, pt p* smelled, smelt.—*ns* **smell´ing salts**, a preparation of ammonium carbonate with lavender, etc., used as a stimulant in faintness, etc.—*adj* **smell´y**, having a bad smell.—**smell a rat**, to have a suspicion of something wrong. [Very early ME *smel*, prob OE but not recorded.]

smelt[1] [smelt] *n* a small, silvery food fish (*Osmerus mordax*) shaped like a salmon, found in northern seas and in N American lakes. [OE.]

smelt[2] [smelt] *vt* to melt (ore) in order to separate metal; to refine (metal) in this way.—*ns* **smel´ter**, one whose work is smelting; a smeltery; **smel´tery**, a place for smelting. [Swed *smälta*.]

smew [smū] *n* a Eurasian merganser (*Mergus albellus*).

smilax [smī´laks] *n* a prickly vine (*Smilax rotundifolia*) of the eastern US; a tender twining plant (*Asparagus asparagoides*) with ovate bright green leaves. [L,—Gr *smīlax*, bindweed.]

smile [smīl] *vi* to express amusement, slight contempt, favor, pleasure, etc., by a slight drawing up of the corners of the lips; to look joyous; to be favorable toward.—*vt* to indicate by smiling; to affect with or by smiling.—*n* act of smiling; the expression of the features in smiling; favor. [ME *smīlen*; perh from Low Ger.]

smirch [smûrch] *vt* to dishonor; to soil, stain, or sully.—*n* a stain on reputation; a smudge, smear. [Earlier *smorch*, prob.—OFr *esmorcher*, to hurt; influenced by **smear**.]

smirk [smûrk] *vi* to put on a complacent, conceited, or foolish smile.—*n* an affected or foolish smile. [OE *smercian*.]

smite [smīt] *vt* to strike, to beat; to kill or injure; to strike, affect suddenly and powerfully (eg of pain, an idea, charms); to afflict.—*vi* to strike.—*pt* **smōte**; *pt p* **smitt´en**, or **smōte**.—*n* **smī´ter**. [OE *smītan*, to smear.]

smith [smith] *n* a worker in metals; one who makes anything; a blacksmith.—*n* **smith´y**, the workshop of a smith, esp a blacksmith. [OE *smith*; Ger *schmied*.]

smithereens [smiTH-ėr-ēnz´] *n pl* (*inf*) fragments. [Ir *smidirīn*.]

smitten [smit´n] *pt p* of **smite**.

smock [smok] *n* (*arch*) a chemise; a loose shirtlike outer garment to protect the clothes.—*ns* **smock frock**, a shirtlike outer garment of coarse white linen with smocking worn by workmen, esp in Europe; **smock´ing**, ornamental gathering made by embroidering cloth in regularly spaced tucks. [OE *smoc*.]

smog [smog] *n* a mixture of fog and smoke. [*sm*oky f*og*.]

smoke [smōk] *n* the gases, vapors, and small particles that come off from a burning substance; any similar vapor; a cigar or cigarette; an act of smoking tobacco, etc.—*vi* to give off smoke; to draw in and puff out the smoke of tobacco, etc.—*vt* to fumigate; to dry or cure by smoke; to draw in and puff out the smoke from.—*adj* **smoke´less**, having or producing no smoke.—*ns* **smō´ker**, one who smokes tobacco; a railroad car in which smoking is permitted; an informal party for men; **smoke´ screen**, a dense cloud of smoke raised to conceal movements; something designed to hide one's motives; **smoke´stack**, a pipe for discharging smoke.—*adj* **smoking-room**, marked by indecency or obscenity.—*n* **smoking room**, a room (as in a hotel or club) set apart for smokers.—*adj* **smō´ky**, giving out smoke; like smoke; colored like or by smoke; filled with smoke.—*adv* **smō´kily**.—*n* **smō´kiness**.—**smoke out**, to destroy or expel by diffusion of smoke; to bring to public view or knowledge. [OE *smoca* (n), *smocian* (vb); Ger *schmauch*.]

smolder, smoulder [smōl´dėr] *vi* to burn slowly or without flame; to persist, linger on, in a suppressed state; to show suppressed feeling, as anger, jealousy. [ME *smolderen*; origin obscure.]

smolt [smōlt] *n* a young salmon or sea trout about two years old, when it assumes the silvery color of the adult.

smooch [smōōch] *vti* (*slang*) to kiss.

smooth [smōōTH] *adj* having an even surface; not rough; evenly spread; glossy; slippery; hairless; of even consistency; gently flowing in rhythm or sound; easy; bland, agreeable; polished or ingratiating, esp in an insincere way.—*vt* to make smooth; to free from obstruction, difficulty, harshness; to remove by smoothing; to calm, soothe; to gloss (over).—*vi* to become smooth; to flatter, behave ingratiatingly.—*n* the smooth part.—*adj* **smooth´bore**, not rifled.—*n* a gun with a smoothbore barrel.—*adv* **smooth´ly**.—*n* **smooth´ness**.—**smooth breathing**, the mark (') over an initial vowel indicating absence of aspiration; **smooth muscle**, muscle tissue made up of spindle-shaped cells found in vertebrate visceral structures (as the stomach and bladder) performing functions not under conscious control by the mind. [OE *smōth*, usually *smēthe*.]

smorgasbord [smör´gȧs-börd] *n* a wide variety of appetizers, cheeses, meats, etc. served buffet style; a restaurant serving these. [Sw.]

smote [smōt] *pt* of **smite**.

smother [smuTH´ėr] *vt* to suffocate by excluding the air, esp by means of a thick covering; to cover over thickly; to stifle (a yawn).—*vi* to undergo suffocation.—*n* dense, stifling smoke, dust, spray, etc.; a state of being suppressed; a jumble. [ME *smorther*—OE *smorian*, to smother.]

smoulder *See* **smolder**.

smudge [smuj] *n* a dirty spot; a fire made to produce dense smoke; such smoke, used to protect plants from frost, etc.—*vti* to make or become dirty; to smear.—*adj* **smud´gy**. [Scand, Swed *smuts*, dirt, Dan *smuds*, smut.]

smug [smug] *adj* neat, spruce; complacent, self-satisfied.—*adv* **smug´ly**.—*n* **smug´ness**. [Low Ger; cf Ger *schmuck*, fine.]

smuggle [smug´l] *vt* to import or export illegally or without paying duties imposed by law; to convey secretly.—*adj* **smugg´led**.—*ns* **smugg´ler**, one who smuggles; **smugg´ling**. [Low Ger *smuggeln*; Ger *schmuggeln*.]

smut [smut] *n* soot; a flake or spot of dirt, soot, etc; indecent talk or writing; any of various fungous diseases of plants, esp one caused by parasitic fungi (order Ustilaginales) affecting cereal grasses; a fungus causing a smut.—*vt* to soil, spot, or affect with smut;—*pr p* **smutt´ing**; *pt, pt p* **smutt´ed**.—*adj* **smutt´y**, stained with smut; obscene, filthy.—*adv* **smutt´ily**.—*n* **smutt´iness**. [Cf Low Ger *schmutt*, Ger *schmutz*, dirt.]

smutch [smuch] *n* a dirty mark.—Also *vt*.—*adj* **smutch´y**. [**smudge**.]

snack [snak] *n* a light meal between regular meals.—**snack´bar**, a counter in a restaurant where snacks are served. [**snatch**.]

snaffle [snaf´l] *n* a jointed bit for a horse's mouth having no curb.—*vt* to get possession of, esp by devious or irregular means. [Du *snavel*, the muzzle.]

snag [snag] *n* a sharp point or projection; an underwater tree stump or branch; a tear, as in cloth, made by a snag, etc.; an unexpected or hidden difficulty.—*vt* to catch or tear on a snag; to impede with a snag. [Cf ON *snagi*, peg.]

snail [snāl] *n* a gastropod mollusk having a wormlike body and a spiral protective shell; a slow-moving or sluggish person or thing.—*vi* to move, act, or go slowly or lazily.—*adj* **snail-paced**, moving very slowly. [OE *snegl*, *snægl*.]

snake [snāk] *n* any of numerous limbless, scaly reptiles (suborder Serpentes or Ophidia) with a long, tapering body and with salivary glands often modified to produce venom; anything snakelike in form or movement; a treacherous person.—*vi* to move, curve, twist, etc. like a snake.—*adj* **snak´y**, of or like a snake or snakes; winding; twisting; cunningly treacherous.—**snake in the grass**, a person who furtively does one an injury. [OE *snaca*.]

snap [snap] *vti* to bite or grasp suddenly (*with* **at**); to speak or utter sharply (*with* **at**); to break suddenly; to make or cause to make a sudden, cracking sound; to close, fasten, etc. with this sound; to move or cause to move suddenly and sharply; to take a snapshot (of).—*n* a sudden bite, grasp, etc.; a sharp cracking sound; a short, angry utterance; a brief period of cold weather; a fastening that closes with a click; a hard, thin cookie; (*inf*) alertness or vigor; (*slang*) an easy job, problem, etc.—*adj* made or done quickly; that fastens with a snap; (*slang*) easy.—*ns* **snap bean**, a bean that is grown primarily for its pods that are usu. broken in pieces and cooked as a vegetable; **snap´dragon**, any of several garden plants (genus *Antirrhinum*, esp *A majus*) having showy saclike, two-lipped flowers; **snap fastener**, a metal or plastic fastener consisting of a ball and socket; **snapper**, something (as a remark) that changes the direction of a situation; a snapping turtle; any of numerous carnivorous fishes (family Lutjanidae) of warm seas important as food and sport fishes; **snapping turtle**, a large, dangerous, edible turtle (*Chelydra serpentina*) of N America.—*adj* **snappish**, given to curt irritable speech; arising from annoyance; inclined to bite.—*adv* **snapp´ishly**.—*n* **snapp´ishness**.—*adj* **snapp´y**, given to curt speech; quickly made or done; marked by liveliness; briskly cold; stylish.—*adv* **snapp´ily**.—*ns* **snapp´ishness; snap´shooter**, a person who takes snapshots; **snap´shot´**, an informal photograph usu. taken by an amateur with a hand-held camera; an impression of something transitory.—**snap out of it**, to improve or recover quickly. [Du *snappen*, to snap; Ger *schappen*.]

snare [snār] *n* a running noose of string or wire, etc., for catching an animal; a trap; an allurement, temptation, moral danger, entanglement; a length of wire or gut across the bottom of the drum.—*vt* to catch. [OE *sneare*, or ON *snara*.]

snarl[1] [snärl] *vi* to make a surly resentful noise with show of teeth; to speak in a surly manner.—*vt* to utter snarlingly.—*n* an unnatural growl; a surly malicious utterance.—*n* **snar´ler**. [Prob imit; Low Ger *snarren*.]

snarl[2] [snärl] *vti* to twist, entangle.—*n* a tangle; disorder. [**snare**.]

snatch [snach] *vt* to seize suddenly; to pluck away quickly; to take as opportunity occurs.—*vi* to try to seize; to grab (at); to take advantage of a chance, etc., eagerly (*with* **at**).—*n* an attempt to seize; a seizure; a spell; a fragment. [Perh related to **snack**.]

snazzy [snaz´i] *adj* (*slang*) very attractive or fashionable; flashy.

sneak [snēk] *vti* to move, act, give, put, take, etc., secretly or stealthily.—*n* one who sneaks; an act of sneaking.—*adj* without warning.—*n* **sneak´er**, one who sneaks; a shoe with a cloth upper and a soft rubber sole.—*adj* **sneak´ing**, mean; underhand, not openly avowed; lurking under other feelings.—*ns* **sneak preview**, an advance showing of a movie, as to get audience reactions; **sneak´ thief**, a thief who steals without using violence or forcibly breaking into buildings. [Connection with OE *snīcan*, to crawl, is obscure.]

sneer [snēr] *vi* to show cynical contempt by the expression of the face, as by drawing up the lip; to show harsh derision and contempt in speech or writing.—*vt* to utter sneeringly.—*n* a sneering expression of face; a remark conveying contemptuous ridicule; an act of sneering.—*n* **sneer´er**.—*n, adj* **sneer´ing**.—*adv* **sneer´ingly**. [Perh related to Frisian *sneere*, to scorn.]

sneeze [snēz] *vi* to eject air violently through the nose with an explosive sound.—*n* an act of sneezing.—**sneeze at**, to make light of. [ME *snesen*, *fnesen*—OE *fnēosan*, to sneeze; Du *fniezen*.]

snick [snik] *vt* to cut, snip, nick.—*n* a small cut or nick.—*n* **snick´ersnee**, a large knife. [Orig uncertain.]

snicker [snik´ėr] *vti* to laugh or utter with a sly, partly stifled manner.—*n* a snickering.

snide [snīd] *adj* base, mean, cheap; sham, insincere; superior in attitude; sneering; derogatory in an insinuating manner.

sniff [snif] *vti* to draw in by the nose with the breath; to express (disdain, etc.) by sniffing; to smell by sniffing.—*n* an act or sound of sniffing; something sniffed.—*vi* **sniffle**, to sniff repeatedly, as in checking mucus running from the nose.—*n* an act or sound of sniffing.—*adj* **sniffy**, disdainful.—**the sniffles**, (*inf*) a head cold. [Imit; cf **snuff**.]

snigger [snig´ėr] *vti* to snicker.—*n* a snicker. [Imit.]

snip [snip] *vti* to sever instantaneously, esp by a single cut with scissors;—*pr p* **snipp´ing**; *pt, pt p* **snipped**.—*n* a small piece cut off; (*inf*) a small or young person.—*n* **snipp´et**, a little piece snipped off; a scrap specifically, of information, writing, etc.—*adj* **snipp´y**, (*inf*) unduly brief or curt; (*inf*) short-tempered; putting on airs. [Du *snippen*; Ger *schnippen*.]

snipe [snīp] *n* birds (genus *Capella* or *Gallinago*) with long straight flexible bills, frequenting marshy places; a contemptible person.—*vi* to hunt snipe; to shoot at individuals from a hidden position.—*n* **snip´er**. [Prob Scand; ON *snīpa*.]

snivel [sniv´l] *vi* to whimper and sniffle; to whine tearfully; to make a tearful, often false display of grief, etc;—*pr p* **sniv´elling**; *pt, pt p* **sniv´elled**.—*n* (*pl*) (*dial*) a cold in the head; an affected tearful state; cant.—*n* **sniv´eller**.—*adj* **sniv´elling**. [OE *snofl*, mucus.]

snob [snob] *n* one animated by obsequious admiration for those of higher social rank or by a desire to dissociate himself from those whom he regards as inferior.—*n* **snobb´ery**, the quality of being snobbish.—*adj* **snobb´ish**, having the feelings of, or acting like, a snob; characteristic of, or befitting, a snob.—*adv* **snobb´ishly**.—*n* **snobb´ishness**. [Origin slang.]

snood [snōōd] *n* a conspicuous net supporting the back hair; a short line by which a fishhook is fixed to the line. [OE *snōd*.]

snooker [snōōk´ėr] *n* a variation of pool played with 15 red balls and 6 variously colored balls.—*vt* to hoodwink. [Ety unknown.]

snoop [snōōp] *vi* (*inf*) to pry about in a sneaking way.—*n* **snoop´er**, (*inf*) one who snoops. [Du *snoepen*.]

snooze [snōōz] *vi* (*inf*) to doze.—*n* (*inf*) a nap.—*n* **snooz´er**. [Origin obscure; perh orig slang.]

snore [snör] *vi* to breathe roughly and hoarsely in sleep with vibration of uvula and soft palate.—*n* the act or a noisy breathing of this kind.—*ns* **snōr´er; snōr´ing**. [Imit; cf **snort**.]

snorkel [snör´kėl] *n* a breathing tube extending above the water, used in swimming just below the surface.

snort [snört] *vi* to force the air with violence and noise through the nostrils; to make a like noise, esp as a token of displeasure.—*vt* to express by a snort; to utter with a snort.—*n* an act of snorting; a sound of snorting; (*slang*) a quick drink of liquor.—*n* **snort´er**. [Imit.]

snot [snot] *n* mucus of the nose.—*adj* **snott´y**, like, or foul with, snot; irritatingly unpleasant. [ME *snotte*; cf Du *snot*; allied to **snout**.]

snout [snowt] *n* the projecting nose of an animal as of a swine; any similar projection as of a prow or nozzle; the terminal face of a glacier. [ME *snūte*; cf Swed *snut*; Ger *schnauze*, Du *snuit*.]

snow [snō] *n* the frozen atmospheric vapor, in crystalline form, which falls as light, white flakes; a snowfall; a mass or expanse of snow; a dessert made of stiffly beaten egg whites, sugar, and fruit pulp; transient light or dark specks on a television screen; (*slang*) cocaine or heroin.—*vi* to fall in snowflakes.—*vt* to pour abundantly, as if snow; (*inf*) to deceive, persuade, or charm glibly; to whiten like snow.—*n* **snow´ball**, a ball made of snow pressed hard together; shaved ice molded into a ball and flavored with a syrup; a cultivated shrub (genus *Viburnum*) with clusters of white sterile flowers.—Also **snowball bush**.—*vti* to increase or cause to increase at a rapidly accelerating rate.—*vt* to pelt with snowballs.—*vi* to throw snowballs.—*ns* **snow´bank**, a large mass of snow; **Snow´belt**, the Midwest and northeast US as having cold, snowy winters; **snow´ blind´ness**, impaired eyesight caused by the reflection of light from snow.—*adjs* **snow´bound**, confined to a restricted space by snow; **snow´capped**, crowned with snow.—*ns* **snow´drift**, a bank of drifted snow; **snow´drop**, a bulbous plant (*Galanthus nivalis*) with drooping bell-shaped flower, often seen while snow still lies on the ground; **snow´fall**, a fall of snow; the amount falling in a given time; **snow fence**, a light fence of lath and wire to control the drifting of snow; **snow´field**, a wide expanse of snow, esp where permanent; **snow´flake**, a single snow crystal; **snow´line**, the line upon a mountain that marks the limit of perpetual snow; **snow´man**, a human figure shaped from snow; **snow´mobile**, any of various automotive vehicles for travel on snow; **snow´plow**, a machine for clearing away snow; **snow´shoe**, a strung frame or other contrivance attached to the feet for walking on the surface of snow; **snowshoe rabbit**, a large rabbit (*Lepus americanus*) of northern N America with a coat that is usu. brown in summer and white in winter; **snow´storm**, a storm with falling snow.—*adjs* **snow´white**, as white as snow; **snow´y**, abounding or covered with snow; white, like snow; pure.—**snow under**, to overwhelm with work, etc.; to defeat decisively. [OE *snāw*; Ger *schnee*, L *nix, nivis*.]

snowboard [snō´bōrd] *n* a board shaped like a large ski which a person can stand on to slide across snow.

snub [snub] *vt* to check, curb (a rope, etc.); to humiliate by an intentional rebuff or crushing retort;—*pr p* **snubb´ing**; *pt, pt p* **snubbed**.—*n* an act of snubbing.—*adjs* short and turned up, as a nose; **snub´-nosed**. [ON *snubba*, to chide, snub.]

snuff[1] [snuf] *vti* to sniff or smell.—*n* a powdered preparation of tobacco; the amount taken at one time.—*ns* **snuff´box**, a small box for snuff; **snuff´er**, one who snuffs.—*adj* **snuff´y**, soiled with, or smelling of, snuff.—**up to snuff** (*inf*) up to the usual standard. [Du *snuffen*; Ger *schnaufen*, to snuff.]

snuff[2] [snuf] *n* the charred portion of a wick.—*vt* to crop or pinch the snuff from, as a burning candle.—*n* **snuff´er**, an instrument for taking the snuff off a candle.—**snuff out**, to extinguish; to destroy. [ME *snoffe*; connection with **snuff** (1) is obscure.]

snuffle [snuf´l] *vi* to breathe hard or in an obstructed manner through the nose; to sniff; to speak through the nose.—*vt* to test by repeated sniffs.—*n* an act or sound of snuffling; a nasal twang; (*pl*) sniffles. [Frequentative of **snuff** (1).]

snug [snug] *adj* lying close and warm; neat; trim; sheltered; not exposed to view or notice; tight in fit; offering safe concealment.—*n* **snugg´ery**, a cosy little room.—*vi* **snugg´le**, to cuddle, nestle.—*adv* **snug´ly**.—*n* **snug´ness**. [Origin obscure.]

so [sō] *adv* in this way; as shown; as stated; to such an extent; very; (*inf*) very much; therefore; more or less; also, likewise; then.—*conj* in order (that); (*inf*) with the result that.—*pron* that which has been specified or named.—*interj* an exclamation of surprise, triumph, etc.—*adj* true.—*n* **so-and-so**, (*inf*) an unspecified person or thing, often euphemistic; *pl* **so-and-sos**.—*adj* **so-called**, known by this term; inaccurately or questionably designated as such.—*adj, adv* **so-so, so so**, just passably or passable; fair.—**and so on** (or **forth**), and the rest; et cetera; so as with the purpose or result; **so far as**, to the extent or degree that; **so what**? (*inf*) even if so, what then? [OE *swā*; ON *svā*, Ger *so*.]

soak [sōk] *vt* to steep in a fluid; to take in; to absorb (*with* **up**); (*inf*) to overcharge.—*vi* to be steeped in a liquid; to penetrate; to drink alcohol to excess.—*n* (*slang*) a habitual drunkard; a soaking or being soaked.—*adj* **soak´ing**, drenching; drenched. [ME *soke*—OE *socian*, a weak verb, related to *sūcan*, to suck.]

soap [sōp] *n* a substance used with water to produce suds for washing, made by the action of an alkali on a fat; (*slang*) a soap opera.—*vt* to rub with soap.—*ns* **soap´box**, a street orator's improvised platform; **soap´ bubb´le**, a globe of air enclosed in a film of soapsuds formed by blowing (as from a pipe); **soap opera**, (*inf*) a daytime radio or television serial melodrama; **soap´stone**, steatite.—*n pl* **soapsuds**, soapy water, esp when worked into a foam.—*adj* **soap´y**, like soap; covered with soap; containing soap; (*inf*) having the qualities of a soap opera; unctuous.—*n* **soap´iness**. [OE *sāpe*; Du *zeep*, Ger *seife*.]

soar [sōr] *vi* to mount high in the air; to glide along high in the air; to rise high. [O Fr *essorer*, to expose to air—L *ex*, out, *aura*, air.]

sob [sob] *vi* to catch the breath convulsively in distress or other emotion; to make a similar sound.—*vt* to utter with sobs;—*pr p* **sobb´ing**; *pt, pt p* **sobbed**.—*n* a convulsive catch of the breath; any similar sound.—*ns* **sob sister**, a journalist who specializes in writing or editing sob stories; an impractical person usu. engaged in good works; **sob´ story**, a sentimental story told to arouse sympathy. [Imit.]

sober [sō´bėr] *adj* not drunk; temperate, esp in use of intoxicants; moderate; without excess or extravagance; serious; sedate; quiet in color.—*vt* to make or become sober (*often with* **up** *or* **down**).—*adv* **sō´berly**.—*ns* **sō´berness**; **sō´bersides**, a sedate and solemn person; **sōbrī´ety**, state or habit of being sober, esp in the use of liquor; calmness; gravity. [Fr *sobre*—L *sōbrius*—*sē-*, apart, not, *ēbrius*, drunk.]

sobriquet [sō´brē-kā] *n* a nickname; an assumed name.—Also **sou´briquet** [sōō´]. [Fr.]

socage, soccage [sok´ij] *n* (*hist*) tenure of lands by service fixed and determinate in quality. [OE *sōc*, a right of holding a court.]

soccer [sok´ėr] *n* a football game played on a field by two teams of 11 players with a round inflated ball. [Abbrev of **association**.]

sociable [sō´shȧ-bl] *adj* inclined to society; companionable; favorable to social intercourse.—*n* an informal party.—*n* **sōciabil´ity**, quality of being sociable.—*adv* **sō´ciably**.—*adv* **sō´cial**, pertaining to society or companionship; pertaining to an organized community, or to fashionable circles; growing or living in communities or societies (eg *social insects*); gregarious; convivial; of or doing welfare work.—*n* an informal gathering.—*adv* **sō´cially**.—*vt* **sō´cialize**, to train or adapt to fit social environment; to subject to government ownership or control.—*vi* to behave in a sociable manner.—*ns* **sō´cialism**, a theory, principle, or scheme of social organization which places the means of production and distribution in the hands of the community; a political movement for establishing such a system; **sō´cialist**, an adherent of socialism.—*adj* **sōcialis´tic**.—*ns* **sō´cialite**, a person who has a place in fashionable society; **society** [sō-sī´it-i], fellowship, companionship; company; any organized association; a community; the body of mankind; the wealthy, dominant class.—**Society of Friends**, a Christian religious sect that believes in plain worship, pacifism, etc.; the Quakers.—**social disease**, any venereal disease; a disease (as tuberculosis) whose incidence is directly related to social and economic factors; **socialized medicine**, a system of giving complete medical and hospital care to all through public funds; **Social Register**, trade name for a directory of eminent persons in a community; **social science**, sociology, history, or any study of social structure and culture; **social security**, a Federal system of old-age, unemployment, or disability insurance; **social service**, welfare work. [Fr—L *sociabilis*—*sociāre*, to associate—*socius*, a companion.]

Socinian [sō-sin´i-ȧn] *adj* pertaining to *Socinus*, who in the 16th century denied the doctrine of the Trinity, the deity of Christ, etc.—*n* a follower of Socinus; a Unitarian.—*n* **Socin´ianism**, the doctrines of Socinus.

sociology [sō-shi-ol´o-ji] *n* the science that treats of the development and structure of society and social relationships.—*n* **sociol´ogist**. [A hybrid from L *socius*, a companion, and Gr *logos*, discourse—*legein*, to speak.]

sock[1] [sok] *n* a light shoe worn by Greek and Roman actors of comedy; a kind of short stocking. [OE *socc*—L *soccus*.]

sock[2] [sok] *vt* (*slang*) to strike hard.—*n* (*slang*) a violent blow.

socket [sok´et] *n* a cavity into which something is inserted, as the receptacle of the eye, of a bone, a tooth, an electric light bulb, etc.—*vt* to provide with or support in or by a socket. [OFr *soket*.]

sockeye [sok´ī] *n* a red salmon (*Onchorhynchus nerka*) of the north Pacific that is an important food fish. [Amer Ind *sukai*, the fish of fishes.]

Socratic [sō-krat´ik] *adj* pertaining to the Greek philosopher Socrates (469–399 BC), to his philosophy, or to his method of teaching, which was to elicit and test the opinions of others by a series of questions.—*adv* **Socrat´ically**.

sod [sod] *n* any surface of earth grown with grass turf; a piece of this; one's native land.—*vt* to cover with sod. [Low Ger *sode*; Ger *sode*.]

soda [sō´da] *n* sodium bicarbonate; sodium carbonate; soda water; a confection of soda water, syrup, and ice cream.—*ns* **soda biscuit**, a biscuit made with baking soda and sour milk or buttermilk; **soda cracker**, a light, crisp cracker, usu. salted, made from flour, water, and leavening, originally baking soda; **soda fountain**, a counter for making and serving soft drinks, sodas, etc.; **soda pop**, a flavored, carbonated soft drink; **soda water**, water charged under pressure with carbon dioxide. [It and LL *soda*.]

sodality [sō-dal´i-ti] *n* a fellowship or sorority, esp of Roman Catholic laity. [L *sodālitās*—*sodālis*, a comrade.]

sodden [sod´n] soaked thoroughly; boggy; doughy, not well baked; dull or stupefied, as from liquor.

sodium [sō´di-um] *n* a metallic element (symbol Na; at wt 23.0; at no 11).—*ns* **sodium bicarbonate**, a white crystalline compound $NaHCO_3$, used in baking powder, as an antacid, etc.—Also **bicarbonate of soda; sodium carbonate**, a hydrated carbonate of sodium, used in washing; **sodium chloride**, common table salt; **sodium hydroxide**, a white, strongly alkaline substance.—Also **lye; sodium nitrate**, a clear, crystalline salt used in explosives, fertilizers, etc.; **sodium pentothal**, a substance injected as a general anesthetic. [Latinized from **soda**.]

soever [sō-ev´ėr] *adv* in any way; of any kind; at all; used to extend or render indefinite the sense of *who, what, where, how*, etc.

sofa [sō´fa] *n* long upholstered seat with fixed back and arms.—*n* **sofa bed**, a sofa that can be opened into a double bed. [Ar *suffah*.]

soft [soft] *adj* easily yielding to pressure; easily cut, shaped, etc.; not as hard as normal, desirable, etc.; smooth to the touch; of a diet, easy to digest; of drinks, nonalcoholic; having few of the mineral salts that keep soap from lathering; mild, as a breeze; weak, not vigorous; easy; of color or light, not bright; of sound, gentle, low; of currency, not readily convertible; of a drug, considered less detrimental than other mood-altering substances; (*phonet*) of a voiced consonant; of an X-ray, having relatively low energy.—*n* a soft object, material, or part.—*advs* **soft, softly**, in a soft or gentle manner.—*vti* **soften** [sof´n] to make or become soft or softer.—*n* **soft´ener**.—*n* **soft´ball**, a game like baseball played with a larger and softer ball, for seven innings; this ball.—*n pl* **soft´ goods**, goods that are not durable, esp textiles.—*adjs* **soft´-headed**, having a weak, uncritical, or unrealistic mind; **soft´hearted**, kindhearted, gentle.—*adv* **soft´ly**.—*n* **soft´ness**.—*adj* **soft´-spō´ken**, having a mild or gentle voice; affable; suave, plausible in speech.—*ns* **soft´ware**, the programs, data, etc., for a digital computer; **soft´wood**, timber of a coniferous tree.—Also *adj*.—**soft drink**, a nonalcoholic, usu. carbonated, beverage; **soft palate**, the back part of the palate; **soft pedal**, a pedal for reducing volume in the piano.—*vt* **soft´-ped´al**, to play with the soft pedal down; (*inf*) to make less emphatic; to tone down; **soft sell**, that relies on subtle inducement or suggestion; **soft soap**, a semiliquid soap; (*inf*) flattery or smooth talk.—*vt* to soothe or persuade with blarney.—*n* **soft´y**, (*inf*) one who is too sentimental or trusting. [OE *sōfte, sēfte*; Du *zacht*, Ger *sanft*.]

soggy [sog´i] *adj* soaked with water; moist and heavy. [Origin unknown.]

soi-disant [swä-dē-zã] *adj* self-styled; so-called; pretended. [Fr.]

soigné, soignée [swä-nyā] *adj* very well groomed; elegantly designed or maintained. [Fr.]

soil[1] [soil] *n* the surface layer of the earth in which plants grow; country. [OFr *soel, suel, seuil*—L *solum*, ground.]

soil[2] [soil] *n* dirt; dung; sewage; a spot or stain.—*vt* to make dirty; to stain.—*vi* to become dirty.—*n* **soil´ pipe**, a pipe for carrying off wastes from toilets. [OFr *soil, souil*, wallowing-place.]

soiree, soirée [swär-ā, swor´ā] *n* an evening social meeting. [Fr,—*soir*, evening—L *sērus*, late.]

sojourn [sō´jùrn, sō-jùrn´] *vi* to stay for a short time.—*n* a temporary stay.—*n* **so´journer**. [OFr *sojourner*—L *sub*, under, and Low L *jornus*—L *diurnus*, of a day—*diēs*, a day.]

Sol [sol] *n* the Roman god of the sun; the sun personified. [L *sōl*.]

sol [sōl] *n* (*mus*) the fifth tone of the diatonic scale.

sola *pl* of **solum**.

solace [sol´ȧs] *n* consolation, comfort in distress; a source of comfort or pleasure.—*vt* to comfort in distress; to divert, amuse (oneself); to allay (eg *to solace grief*). [OFr *solas*—L *sōlātium*—*sōlārī, -ātus*, to comfort in distress.]

solan goose [sō´lan gōōs] *n* a very large white gannet (*Sula bassanus* or *Morus bassanus*) with black wing tips. [ON *sūla*.]

solar [sō´lȧr] *adj* of, from, like, or pertaining to, the sun; measured by the progress of the sun; influenced by the sun; powered by energy for the sun's rays.—*n* **sōlā´rium**, a glass-enclosed room or porch; a place, in a hospital, for sunning or sunbathing.—**solar plexus**, in higher mammals a central network of nerves, situated in the abdomen behind the stomach; the pit of the stomach; **solar system**, the sun and the attendant bodies moving about it under the attraction of gravity. [L *sōl*, the sun, *sōlāris*, pertaining to the sun.]

solatium [sō-lā´shi-um] *n* compensation for disappointment, inconvenience, or wounded feelings. [L *sōlātium*. See **solace**.]

sold [sōld] *pt, pt p* of **sell**.

solder [sod´ėr] something that unites; a metal alloy used when melted to join or patch metal parts, etc.—*vti* to join with solder. [OFr *soud-, souldure—souder, soulder*, to consolidate—L *solidāre*, to make solid.]

soldier [sōl´jėr] *n* a man engaged in military service; an enlisted man, as distinguished from an officer; one who works for a specified cause.—*vi* to serve as a soldier.—*n* **sol´diering**.—*adj* **sol´dierly**, like a soldier; martial; brave.—*ns* **sol´dier of for´tune**, one ready to serve under any flag if there is a good prospect of pay or advancement; any adventurer; **sol´diership**, state or quality of being a soldier; military qualities; martial skill; **sol´diery**, soldiers collectively; the profession or technique of soldiering. [OFr *soldier*—L *solidus*, a piece of money, the pay of a soldier.]

sole[1] [sōl] *n* the underside of the foot; the bottom of a boot or shoe; the bottom, understructure, floor, or undersurface of various things.—*vt* to put a sole on (a shoe). [OE *sole*—L *solea*, a sandal, a sole (fish).]

sole[2] [sōl] *n* any of various elliptical flatfish (family Soleidae) with small twisted mouth and teeth on the underside only, esp the superior food fishes. [Fr *sole*—L *solea*. See **sole** (1).]

sole[3] [sōl] *adj* not married, esp of a woman; (*arch*) alone; only (eg *the sole heir*); acting without another (eg *the sole author*); belonging to one person, or group exclusively (eg *his sole responsibility, the sole rights*).—*adv* **sole´ly**, alone; only; exclusively.—*n* **sole´ness**. [Fr,—L *sōlus*, alone.]

solecism [sol´ė-sizm] *n* a flagrant grammatical error; any conspicuous breach of the rules of usage of language.—*n* **sol´ecist**, one who commits solecisms.—*adjs* **solecis´tic**, pertaining to, or involving, a solecism; incorrect; incongruous. [Gr *soloikismos*, said to come from the corruption of the Attic dialect among the Athenian colonists (*oikizein*, to colonise) of *Soloi* in Cilicia (in Turkey).]

solemn [sol´em] *adj* attended with, or marked by, special (esp religious) ceremonies, pomp, or gravity; attended with an appeal to God, as an oath; in serious earnestness; awed, grave; glum; awe-inspiring; somber; stately; pompous.—*vt* **sol´emnize**, to perform the ceremony of (marriage, etc.); to celebrate with rites.—*ns* **solenmizātion; solem´nity**, a solemn ceremony; seriousness; affected gravity.—*adv* **sol´emnly**.—*n* **sol´emness**. [OFr *solempne, solemne* (Fr *solennel*)—L *sollemnis, solennis*, perh—*sollus*, all, every, *annus*, a year.]

solenoid [sōle-noid] *n* a coil of wire that acts like a bar magnet when carrying a current. [Gr *sōlēn*, tube, *eidos*, a form.]

sol-fa [sol-fä] *n* (*mus*) sol-fa syllables; solmization; an exercise thus sung; tonic sal-fa.—*adj* belonging to this system.—*vti* to sing to sol-fa syllables.—*n pl* **sol-fa syllables**, the syllables *do, re, mi, fa, sol, la, ti* used in singing the tones of the scale. [It.]

solicit [sō-lis´it] *vti* to petition, importune (a person for something); to entice or lure.—*ns* **sol- ic´itant**, one who solicits; **solicitā´tion**, act of soliciting; earnest request; invitation; **solic´itor**, an agent that solicits (as contributions to charity); a British lawyer who advises clients, represents them in lower courts, and prepares cases for barristers to try in higher courts; the chief law officer of a municipality, county or government department; **solic´itor gen´eral**; a law officer appointed to assist an attorney general; **solic´itorship**.—*adj* **solic´itous**, soliciting or earnestly asking or desiring; very desirous (to); anxious (about, for, of).—*adv* **solic´itously**.—*n* **solic´itude**, state of being solicitous; anxiety or uneasiness of mind. [Fr,—L *sōlicitāre, sollicitāre—sō-, sollicitus—sollus*, whole, *citus*, aroused—*ciēre*, to cite.]

solid [sol´id] *adj* resisting change of shape, having the parts firmly cohering; distinguished from liquid and gaseous; hard; compact; full of matter, not hollow; strong, strongly constructed; having three dimensions; of uniform undivided substance, color, etc.; unanimous, standing together in close union; financially sound (eg *a solid business man*); sensible; genuine (eg *solid comfort*); of a compound word, joined without a hyphen.—*n* a solid substance, not a liquid or gas; an object having length, breadth, and thickness.—*n* **solidar´ity**, firm union in sentiment and action.—*vti* **solid´ify**, to make or become solid, compact, hard, etc.—*pt p* **solid´ified**.—*ns* **solidificā´tion**, act of making, becoming, solid; **solid´ity**, the state of being solid; fullness of matter; strength or firmness, moral or physical; soundness; volume.—*adv* **sol´idly**.—*n* **sol´idness**.—*adj* **solid-state**, of the branch of physics dealing with the structure, properties, etc., of solids; equipped with transistors, etc. [L *solidus*, solid.]

soliloquy [sȯ-lil´ȯ-kwi] *n* talking to oneself when no one else is present; a discourse uttered with none to hear; a speech of this nature made by a character in a play, etc.—*vti* **solil´oquize**, to speak to oneself, to utter a soliloquy. [L *sōliloquium*—*sōlus*, alone, *loquī*, to speak.]

solitaire [sol-i-tār´] *n* a card game for one; a gem, esp a diamond, set by itself. [Fr.]

solitary [sol´i-tȧr-i] *adj* alone; without company; only; single (eg *not a solitary example*); living alone, not social or gregarious.—*n* one who lives alone; a hermit; solitary confinement in prison.—*adv* **sol´itarily**.—*n* **sol´itariness**. [Fr *solitaire*—L *sōlitārius*—*sōlus*, alone.]

solmization [sol-mi-zā´sh(ȯ)n] *n* a system of designating the degrees of the scale by syllables) rather than by letters (as by sol-fa syllables). [*sol* (or *so*), *mi*. See **sol-fa**.]

solo [sō´lō] *n* a piece or passage for one voice or instrument; a piece by two or more performers if one is featured (eg *violin solo with piano accompaniment*). (*pl* **sō´lōs, soli** [sō´lē]).—*vi* to perform by oneself, esp to fly an airplane without one's instructor.—*adv* without a companion.—*adj* performed, or for performance, as a solo; for one; performing a solo.—*n* **sō´lōist**. [It,—L *sōlus*, alone.]

Solomon's seal, Solomon seal [sol´ȯ-mȯn's sēl] *n* any of a genus (*Polygonatum*) of perennial herbs of the lily family with guarded rhizomes; an emblem consisting of two interlaced triangles forming a 6-pointed star. [King *Solomon* (1 Kings).]

solstice [sol´stis] *n* either of the two points in the ecliptic at which the sun is farthest from the equator and consequently appears to pause and turn in its course; the time when the sun reaches these two points in its orbit farthest north (June 21 or 22) or farthest south (December 21 or 22) in the Northern Hemisphere.—*adj* **solstitial** [-sti´sh(ȧ)l], pertaining to, or happening at, a solstice, esp at the summer solstice. [Fr,—L *solstitium*—*sōl*, the sun, *sistěre*, to make to stand—*stāre*, to stand.]

soluble [sol´ū-bl] *adj* capable of being dissolved in a fluid; capable of being solved.—*n* **solubil´ity**. [L *solūbilis*—*solvěre*, to loosen.]

solum [sō´lum] *n* the altered layer of soil above the parent material;—*pl* **so´la, solums**.

solus [sō´lus] *adj* alone (in dramatic directions). [L *sōlus, -a, -um*.]

solution [sol-ūsh(ȯ)n] *n* the act or process of discovering the answer to a problem; the answer discovered; the dispersion of one substance in another, usu. a liquid, so as to form a homogenous mixture; the mixture so produced.—*n* **sol´ute**, a substance which is dissolved in another.—*adj* dissolved; in solution. [L *solūtiō*—*solvěre, solūtum*, to loosen.]

solve [solv] *vt* to discover the answer to; to clear up, explain; to pay (as a debt) in full.—*vi* to solve something.—*adj* **sol´vable**, capable of being solved or explained.—*n* **sol´vency**, state of being solvent, or able to pay all debts.—*adj* **sol´vent**, able to solve or to dissolve; able to pay all debts.—*n* anything that dissolves another substance.—*n* **sol´ver**, one who solves. [L *solvěre*, to loosen, prob from *sē*, aside, *luěre*, to loosen.]

soma [sō´mȧ] *n* the body of an organism; all of an organism except the germ cells;—*pl* **somata, somas**.—*adj* **somatic**. [Gr *sōma*, body.]

somber, sombre [som´bėr] *adj* dark and gloomy or dull; dismal; sad.—Also **som´brous**.—*adv* **som´berly**.—*n* **som´berness**. [Fr *sombre*—L *sub*, under, *umbra*, a shade.]

sombrero [som-brā´rō] *n* a broad-brimmed hat, tall-crowned hat worn in Mexico, southwestern US, etc. [Sp,—*sombra*, a shade.]

some [sum] *adj* certain but not specified or known; of a certain unspecified quantity, degree, etc.; about; (*inf*) remarkable, striking, etc.—*pron* a certain unspecified quantity, number, etc.—*adv* approximately; (*inf*) to some extent; somewhat; (*inf*) to a great extent or at a great rate.—*pron* **some´body**, a person unknown or not named; some person.—*n* a person of importance.—*advs* **some´day**, at some future day or time; **some´how**, in a way or by a method not known or stated.—*ns* **some´one´**, somebody; **some´thing**, a thing not definitely known, understood, etc.; a definite but unspecified thing; a bit; a little; (*inf*) an important or remarkable person or thing.—*adv* somewhat; (*inf*) really; quite.—*adv* **some´time´**, (*arch*) formerly; (*arch*) occasionally; at some time in the future; at some not specified or definitely known time.—*adj* having been formerly; being so occasionally or in only some respects.—*adv* **some´times´**, at times; now and then.—*adj* **sometime**.—*advs* **some´way; some´ways**, somehow.—**some´what´**, some degree, amount, part, etc.—*adv* to some extent, degree, etc.; a little.—*adv* **some´where**, in, to or at some place not known or specified; at some time, degree, figure, etc. (*with* **about, around, between**, etc.).—**and then some**, (*inf*) and more than that. [OE *sum*; ON *sumr*.]

somersault [sum´ėr-sölt] *n* a leap in which a person turns with his heels over his head.—*vi* to turn a somersault.—Also **som´erset; summ´ersault**. [OFr *sombre saut* (Fr *soubresaut*)—L *suprā*, over, *saltus*, a leap—*salīre*, to leap.]

somnambulate [som-nam´bū-lāt] *vi* to walk while asleep.—*ns* **somnambūlā´tion; somnam´bulism**, act or practice of walking while asleep; **somnam´būlist**, a sleepwalker. [L *somnus*, sleep, *ambulāre, -ātum*, to walk.]

somniferous [som-nif´ėr-us] *adj* bringing or causing sleep. [L *somnus*, sleep, *ferre*, to bring.]

somnolence [som´nō-lens] *n* sleepiness; inclination to sleep.—Also **som´nolency**.—*adj* **som´nolent**, sleepy; drowsy.—*adv* **som´nolently**. [L *somnolentia*—*somnus*, sleep.]

son [sun] *n* a male child or offspring, or a descendant, or one so treated; a disciple; a native or inhabitant.—*ns* **son´-in-law**, a daughter's husband;—*pl* **sons´-in-law; sonn´y**, a little son; a familiar mode of address to a boy; **son´ship**, the relationship of son to father. [OE *sunu*; Du *zoon*, Ger *sohn*.]

sonant [sō´nant] *adj* (*phonet*) uttered by vocal cord vibration.—*n* a voiced sound. [L *sonāns, -antis*, pr p of *sonāre*, to sound.]

sonata [sȯ-, sō-nä´ta] *n* (*mus*) a composition usu. of three or more movements for a solo instrument in contrasting forms and keys.—*n* **sonatina** [so-nȧ-tē´na], a short or simplified sonata.—*n* **sonata form**, a musical form consisting of an exposition, a development, and recapitulation, used esp for the first movement of a sonata. [It,—L *sonāre*, to sound.]

sonde [sond] *n* any device for obtaining information about atmospheric and weather conditions at high altitudes. [Fr.]

son et lumière [son ā lüm-yėr] a dramatic spectacle presented after dark, involving lighting effects, esp on a historical monument or at an historic site, with recorded sound. [Fr.]

song [song] *n* that which is sung; a short poem or ballad for singing, or set to music; the melody to which it is sung; an instrumental composition of like form and character; singing; the melodious outburst of a bird; any sound; a fuss.—*ns* **song´bird**, a bird that sings; a passerine bird; (*inf*) a female singer; **song´book**, a book containing vocal music, esp hymns; **song´ cy´cle**, a sequence of songs forming a musical entity; **song´fest**, an informal gathering of people to sing songs, esp folk songs; **song´ster**, a singer; **song´stress**, a female singer.—**Song of Solomon**, (*Bible*) 22d book of the Old Testament, written by Solomon, depicting the perfect picture of true love. [OE *sang*—*singan*, to sing; Du *zang*, Ger *gesang*, ON *söngr*.]

sonic [son´ik] *adj* pertaining to sound or the speed of sound.—**sonic barrier**, the large increase of air resistance met by some aircraft flying near the speed of sound; **sonic boom**, the explosive sound of supersonic jets passing overhead. [L *sonus*, sound, and suffx, *-ic*.]

sonnet [son´et] *n* a poem in which one thought is developed in a single stanza of fourteen lines, usu. iambic pentameters rhyming according to a fixed pattern.—*ns* **sonneteer´**, a composer of sonnets; **sonn´et sē´quence**, a connected series of sonnets. [It *sonetto*, dim of *suono*—L *sonus*, a sound.]

sonorous [sȯ-nō´rus] *adj* sounding or ringing when struck (eg *sonorous metal*); full, rich, or deep in sound; imposing in style or effect.—*adv* **sonō´rously**.—*n* **sonō´rousness**, sonorous quality or character. [L *sonōrus*—*sonor, -ōris*, a sound—*sonāre*, to sound.]

soon [sōōn] *adv* immediately or in a short time; without delay; early (eg *can you come as soon as that*?); readily, willingly (eg *I would as soon go as stay*).—**sooner or later**, eventually. [OE *sōna*.]

soot [sŏŏt] *n* a black deposit from imperfect combustion of carbonaceous matter; a smut.—*adj* **soot´y**, of, foul with, or like, soot. [OE *sōt*; Dan *sod*.]

sooth [sōōth] *n* (*arch*) truth, reality.—*adj* (*arch*) true; (*poet*) pleasant.—*ns* **sooth´-sayer**, one who divines or foretells events, esp a pretender to the power; **sooth´saying**, divination, prediction. [OE *sōth*, true; ON *sannr*.]

soothe [sōōTH] *vt* to calm, comfort, compose, tranquillize; to relieve (pain, etc.).—*adj* **sooth´ing**.—*adv* **sooth´ingly**. [OE (*ge*)*sōthian*, to confirm as true—*sōth*, true.]

sop [sop] *n* (*dial*) bread or other food dipped or soaked in liquid; something given to appease; a bribe.—*vti* to steep in liquor; to take (up) by absorption;—*pr p* **sopp´ing**; *pt, pt p* **sopped**.—*adj* **sopp´ing**.—*adj* **sopp´y**, drenched, thoroughly wet; (*inf*) mawkishly sentimental. [OE *sopp* (n), *soppian* (vb); prob conn with *sūpan*, to sup.]

sophism [sof´izm] *n* a clever and plausible but fallacious argument.—*n* **Sophist**, one of a class of teachers of rhetoric, philosophy, etc., in 5th century Greece known for their subtle, adroit and allegedly often specious reasoning; **sophist**, a captious or fallacious reasoner.—*adjs* **sophis´tic, -al**, pertaining to a sophist or to sophistry; fallaciously subtle.—*adv* **sophis´tically**.—*vt* **sophis´ticāte**, to imbue (a person) with superficial knowledge and subtlety, or make dissatisfied with simplicity of thought and manners; to give a fashionable air of worldly wisdom to.—*n* a sophisticated person.—*adj* **sophis´ticāted**, adulterated, falsified; not simple or natural; worldly-wise and disillusioned; very refined and subtle; of equipment, highly complex or developed in form, technique, etc.—*ns* **sophisticā´tion**, act of sophisticating; state of being sophisticated; **soph´istry**, specious but fallacious reasoning. [Fr *sophisme*—Gr *sophisma*—*sophizein*, to make wise—*sophos*, wise.]

sophomore [sof´ȯ-mōr] *n* a second-year student at college or secondary school.—*adj* **sophomor´ic**, poorly informed and immature, but conceited and overconfident. [Prob from *sophom* (obs form of *sophism*) and *-or*, as if from *sophos*, wise, *mōros*, foolish.]

soporific [sop-, sōp-or-if´ik] *adj* inducing sleep.—*n* anything that causes sleep. [L *sopor*, deep sleep, and *facĕre*, to make, *ferre*, to bring.]

soprano [sȯ-prä´no] *n* the highest singing voice of females or boys; a singer with such a voice; a part for such a voice.—*pl* **sopra´nos**. [It from *sopra*—L *suprā*, or *super*, above.]

sorcery [sör´ser-i] *n* divination by the assistance of evil spirits; enchantment; magic.—*n* **sor´cerer**, one who practices sorcery; **sor´ceress**, a woman who practices sorcery. [OFr *sorcerie*—L *sors, sortis*, a lot.]

sordid [sör´did] *adj* dirty, squalid; meanly avaricious, mercenary; of low or unworthy ideals, ignoble.—*adv* **sor´didly**.—*n* **sor´didness**. [L *sordidus*, dirty.]

sore [sōr, sör] *n* a painful or tender injured or diseased spot; an ulcer or boil; grief; an affliction.—*adj* wounded; tender; painful; grievous; (*inf*) angry; offended.—*adv* (*arch*) greatly.—*adv* **sore´ly**, painfully; grievously; urgently.—*ns* **sore´head** (*inf*) a person easily angered or made resentful, etc.; **sore´ness**, a feeling of discomfort, pain, or grievance. [OE *sār*; Ger *sehr*, very, ON *sārr*, sore.]

sorghum [sör´gum] *n* a tropical Old World genus (*Sorghum*) of grasses grown for grain, syrup, fodder, etc.; syrup made from its juices. [It *sorgo*, prob from an East Indian word.]

sorites [sō-rī´tēz] *n* (*logic*) a string of propositions in which the predicate of one is the subject of the next, the conclusion consisting of the subject of the first and the predicate of the last. [From Gr *sōros*, a heap.]

Soroptimist [sor-opt´i-mist] *adj* of an international organization of women's clubs.—*n* a member of one of these clubs. [L *soror*, sister, and **optimist**.]

sorority [sȯ-rör´i-tē] *n* a group of women or girls joined together for fellowship, as in some colleges. [L *soror*, sister.]

sorrel[1] [sor´ėl] *n* any of several plants with sour juice, esp the common sorrel (*Rumex acetosa*); wood sorrel. [OFr *sorele, surele*—*sur*, sour—OHG *sûr* (Ger *sauer*).]

sorrel[2] [sor´ėl] *n* a reddish-brown color; a sorrel horse. [OFr *sorel*.]

sorrow [sor´ō] *n* pain of mind, grief; an affliction, misfortune; an expression of grief.—*vi* to feel sorrow or pain of mind, grieve.—*adj* **sorr´owful**, causing or expressing sorrow; sad, dejected.—*adv* **sorr´owfully**.—*n* **sorr´owfulness**. [OE *sorg, sorh*; Ger *sorge*, ON *sorg*.]

sorry [sor´i] *adj* regretful; regretful in sympathy with another (eg *sorry for her, for her disappointment*); poor, worthless, contemptible.—*adv* **sorr´ily**.—*n* **sorr´iness**. [OE *sārig*, wounded—*sār*, pain; Du *zeerig*.]

sort [sört] *n* (*arch*) a company, group; a class, kind, or species (eg *people of this sort, this sort of person*); quality or type; an instance of a kind; (*arch*) way, fashion.—*vt* to separate into lots or classes, to group, classify; to examine in order to clarify; to free of confusion.—*vi* to be joined (with others of the same sort); to associate; agree (with).—*n* **sort´er**, one who separates and arranges, as letters.—**after a sort**, in a rough or haphazard way; **of a sort, of sorts**, inferior; **out of sorts**, (*inf*) slightly unwell, grouchy, irritable; **sort of**, (*inf*) somewhat. [Partly through OFr, from L *sors, sortis*, a lot.]

sortie [sör´tē] *n* a sally of besieged to attack the besiegers; one mission by a single military plane.—Also *vi*. [Fr,—*sortir*, to go out, to issue.]

SOS [es-ō-es´] *n* a radio code signal (in Morse . . . — — — . . .) calling for help; an urgent summons for help or rescue.

sostenuto [sos-te-nōō´tō] *adj* (*mus*) sustained.—*adv* beyond the full time allowed for each note. [It.]

sot [sot] *n* a habitual drunkard.—*adj* **sott´ish**, foolish; stupid with drink.—*adv* **sott´ishly**.—*n* **sott´ishness**. [OFr *sot*.]

sotto voce [sot´tō vō´chē] *adv* in an undertone, aside. [It, 'below the voice'.]

sou [sōō] *n* a French five-centime piece. [Fr,—L *solidus*, a piece of money.]

soubrette [sōō-bret´] *n* a pert, intriguing, coquettish maid in comedies, an actress who plays such a part; a soprano who sings supporting roles in comic opera. [Fr.]

soubriquet *See* **sobriquet**.

souchong [sōō-shong´, -chong´] *n* tea made from the larger leaves. [Chinese *siao*, small, *chung*, sort.]

soufflé [sōō´flā] *n* a baked dish made light and puffy by adding beaten egg whites before baking.—*adj* prepared thus. [Fr pt p of *souffler*—L *sufflāre*, to blow.]

sough [sow, suf] *vi* to sigh, as the wind in trees.—*n* a moaning or sighing sound. [OE *swōgan*, to rustle.]

sought [söt] *pt, pt p* of **seek**.]

soul [sōl] *n* that which thinks, feels, desires, etc.; a spirit, embodied or disembodied; innermost being or nature; nobleness of spirit or its sincere expression; embodiment or exemplification; essence; the moving spirit, inspirer, leader, a person, a human being; *(inf)* a feeling of US blacks of racial pride and solidarity.—*adj (inf)* of, for, or by Afro-Americans.—*adjs* **souled**, having a soul (esp in compounds—eg *high-souled*); **soul´ful**, having or expressive of elevated feeling or yearning, sentiment; **soul´less**, without nobleness of mind, mean; spiritless.—**soul food**, *(inf)* certain food (as chitterlings, ham hocks, and greens) traditionally eaten by southern black Americans; **soul music**, music derived from Afro-American gospel singing marked by intensity of feeling and closely related to rhythm and blues. [OE *sāwol*; Ger *seele*.]

sound[1] [sownd] *adj* healthy; uninjured, unimpaired, in good condition; deep (as sleep); solid; thorough (as a thrashing); well-founded, well-grounded (eg of reasoning); trust-worthy, dependable; of the right way of thinking, orthodox.—*adv* soundly.—*adv* **sound´ly**, deeply; thoroughly; in a manner accordant with logic or common sense.—*n* **sound´ness**. [OE *gesund*; Ger *gesund*.]

sound[2] [sownd] *n* a narrow passage of water connecting, eg two seas or separating a mainland from an island; a long arm of the sea; the swimming bladder of a fish. [OE *sund*, swimming.]

sound[3] [sownd] *n* sensation of hearing; a transmitted disturbance perceived by, or perceptible by, the ear; a noise, report; range of audibility; mental impression produced by wording.—*vi* to give out a sound; to resound; to be audible; to give an impression on hearing that it is, to seem to be (eg *that sounds like the train; it sounds like Mary; it sounds like an attempt to blackmail you*).—*vt* to cause to make a sound; to produce, utter, make, the sound of; to pronounce; to announce, publish, proclaim (eg *to sound his praises*); to examine by percussion and listening.—*adj* **sound´ing**, sonorous, resounding.—*ns* **sound´board**, a thin plate of wood (as the belly of a violin) so placed as to reinforce its tones by sympathetic vibration; a structure behind a platform, etc., to give sonority to sound; **sound´ing board**, the horizontal board or structure over a pulpit, etc., carrying the speaker's voice towards the audience; a person used to test ideas on.—*adj* **sound´proof**, impenetrable by sound.—*ns* **sound´ track**, on a motion-picture film, the strip on which sounds are recorded; **sound´ wave**, a longitudinal disturbance propagated through air or other medium.—**sound barrier**, sonic barrier; **sound effects**, sounds imitative of sounds called for in the script of a play, radio or television program, or motion picture, produced by various means. [ME *sound* (n), *sounen* (vb)—L *sonāre*, to sound.]

sound[4] [sownd] *vt* to measure the depth of; to probe; to try to discover the thoughts and intentions of.—*vi* to take soundings; to investigate the possibility; of a fish or whale, to dive down suddenly.—*ns* **sound´ing**, a measurement of depth, esp with a sounding line; an ascertained depth; *(pl)* a place in the water where a hand sounding line will reach bottom; a measurement of atmospheric conditions; a probe, sampling, etc., of opinions or intentions; **sound´ing line**, a line with a plummet at the end for soundings.—**sound off**, *(inf)* to speak loudly and freely, esp in complaint; to boast. [OE *sund-* (in compounds), or perh—OFr *sonder*, to sound.]

soup [sōōp] *n* the nutritious liquid obtained by boiling meat, vegetables, etc., in water, milk, etc.; something having the consistency or nutrient qualities of soup; *(inf)* an unfortunate predicament.—*n* **soup´ kitch´en**, a place supplying minimum dietary needs (as soup and bread) to the needy.—**soup up** *(slang)* to increase the capacity for speed of (an engine, etc.).—*adj* **soup´y**, like soup; *(inf)* foggy. [OFr *soupe*; cf **sop**.]

soupçon [sŏŏp-so•] *n* a hardly perceptible quantity. [Fr, suspicion, a trace.]

sour [sowr] *adj* having an acid taste or smell; spoiled by fermentation; cross; bad-tempered; distasteful or unpleasant; of soil, acid in reaction.—*vti* to make or become sour.—*adv* **sour´ly**.—*ns* **sour cream**, a commercial cream product produced by using lactobacilli; **sour´dough**, a leaven consisting of actively fermenting dough; a lone prospecter, as in Alaska and the Old West; **sour grapes**, a scorning of something only because it cannot be had or done; **sour´ness**. [OE *sūr*; Ger *sauer*, ON *sūrr*.]

source [sōrs, sörs] *n* a spring; the head of a stream; that from which anything rises or originates; a person, book, etc., that provides information. [OFr *sorse* (Fr *source*), from *sourdre*—L *surgĕre*, to rise.]

souse [sows] *n* pickled meat, esp pig's feet or ears; pickling liquid; a plunge in pickling or other liquid; a ducking; *(slang)* a drunkard; a heavy blow or fall.—*vti* to pickle; to plunge, immerse, duck in a liquid; to make or become soaking wet. [Partly OFr *sous, souce*, from the root of salt; partly imit; partly **source**.]

south [sowth] *n* the direction in which the sun appears at noon to people north of the Tropic of Cancer; the region lying in that direction; a part of a country, continent, etc., lying relatively in that direction.—*adj* situated in, facing toward the south; blowing from the south.—Also *adv*.—*vi* [sowTH] to veer toward the south; to cross the meridian.—*adjs* **south´erly** [suTH´ėr-li] (also *adv*); **Southern, south´ern** [suTH´-]; **south´ernmost** [suTH´-]; **south´ward** [sowth´-] (also *adv*), toward the south.—*adv* **south´wards**, southward.—*adj* **south´bound**, traveling southwards.—*ns* **south´erner**, [suTH´-], a native of, or resident in, the south; **south´ing** [sowTH-], southward progress or deviation in sailing.—*n* **southeast´**, the direction midway between south and east; the region lying in that direction; *(poet)* the wind blowing from that direction.—Also *adj, adv*.—*ns* **southwest´; south´er** [sowTH´-], **southeast´er, southwest´er**, winds blowing from these directions.—*adjs* **southeast´ern; southwest´ern**.—*advs* **southeast´ward; southwest´ward**.—*n* **southernwood** [suTH´-], an aromatic plant (*Artemesia abrotanum*) of southern Europe.—*ns* **southron** [suTH´-], a native or inhabitant of the southern US; **southwest´er**, a strong southwest wind; a storm with southwest winds.—**Southern Cross**, a constellation in the Southern Hemisphere of which the four brightest stars form the extremities of a Latin cross; **Southern Hemisphere**, the half of the earth south of the equator; **southern lights**, aurora australis; **south´paw**, *(slang)* a left-handed person; **South Pole**, the end of the earth's axis in Antarctica.—**the South**, the part of the US south of Pennsylvania, the Ohio River, and northern Missouri. [OE *sūth*; Ger *süd*, ON *sudhr*.]

souvenir [sōō-vė-nēr´] *n* a memento, a keepsake. [Fr,—L *subvenīre*, to come up, to come to mind—*sub*, under, *venīre*, to come.]

sovereign [sov´(ė)rin] *adj* supreme, possessing absolute authority within a given sphere; superior to all rivals; invariably efficacious; extreme, utter (eg *sovereign contempt*).—*n* a supreme ruler; a monarch; *(Brit)* formerly a gold coin = £1.—*n* **sov´ereignty**, supreme power; dominion. [OFr *sovrain*—L *super*, above.]

Soviet [sō´vi-et or so´-] *n* a council, esp one of those forming (since 1917) the machinery of local and national government in Russia (the Union of Soviet Socialist Republics); a similar council in a socialist governing system.—*adj* of or connected with the Soviet Union. [Russ *sovet*.]

sow[1] [sow] *n* an adult female pig; a female bear, etc.; a channel for molten iron, leading to pig beds; metal solidified there. [OE *sū, sugu*; Ger *sau*, ON *sȳr*; L *sūs*, Gr *hȳs*.]

sow[2] [sō] *vt* to scatter or put in the ground, as seed; to plant by strewing; to scatter seed over; to spread, disseminate.—*vi* to scatter seed for growth.—*pt* **sowed** [sōd]; *pt p* **sown** [sōn] or **sowed** [sōd].—*n* **sow´er**. [OE *sāwan*; Ger *säen*, ON *sā*.]

soy, soya [sō´yȧ, soi´a] a dark, salty sauce made from fermented soybeans; the soybean.—*n* **soybean, soya bean**, a leguminous plant (*Glycine max*) native to China and Japan, now largely cultivated elsewhere, the nutritious beans of which are used for fodder and human consumption and yield an oil which has many important uses; its seed. [Jap *shō-yu*; Chin *shî-yau*.]

spa [spä] *n* a mineral spring; a resort where there is a mineral spring; a fashionable resort or hotel; a commercial establishment with facilities for exercise, sauna baths, etc. [From *Spa* in Belgium.]

space [spās] *n* that in which material bodies have extension; extension in one, two, or three dimensions; room; an intervening distance; an open or empty place; regions remote from the earth; an interval between lines or words; an interval between the lines of the stave; a portion or interval of time; opportunity, leisure.—*vt* to make or arrange intervals between.—*ns* **space´craft**, vehicle, manned or unmanned, designed for putting into space, orbiting the earth or reaching other planets.—*adj* **spaced´-out´**, *(slang)* under the influence of a drug, marijuana, etc.—**space´flight**, a flight through outer space; **space heater**, a small heating unit for a room or small area; **space´man**, a traveler in interplanetary space; **space´ship**, a spacecraft; **space´ suit**, a suit devised for use in space travel.—*adjs* **spā´cial**, same as **spatial; spā´cious** [spā´shůs], large in extent; roomy, wide.—*adv* **spā´ciously**.—*n* **spā´ciousness**.—*adj* **spaceage**, befitting the age of space exploration; modern. [Fr *espace*—L *spatium*; Gr *spaein*, to draw.]

spade[1] [spād] *n* a broad-bladed tool with a handle, used for digging.—*vti* to dig, work, or to remove, with a spade.—*ns* **spade´ful**, as much as a spade will hold; **spade´work**, toilsome preparation for a projected operation.—**call a spade a spade**, to speak out plainly without euphemism. [OE *spadu, spædu*; akin to Gr *spathē*. See **spade** (2).]

spade[2] [spād] *n* a black figure resembling a stylized spear-head marking one of the four suits of playing cards; a card of this suit.—**in spades** *(inf)* in the extreme. [Sp *espada*, sword—L *spatha*—Gr *spathe*, a broad blade.]

spadix [spā´diks] *n* *(bot)* a spike with a swollen fleshy axis, enclosed in a spathe.—*pl* **spadices** [spā-dī´sēz]. [Gr *spādix, -īkos*, a torn-off (palm) branch.]

spaghetti [spa-get´i] *n* pasta made in thin, solid strings; insulating tubing for covering bare electric wires or holding insulating wires together.—**spaghetti western**, a cowboy movie produced by Italians. [It, pl of *spaghetto*, dim of *spago*, a cord.]

spahi [spä´hē] *n* formerly a Turkish or French Algerian cavalryman. [Turk (from Pers) *sipāhī*.]

spake [spāk] old *pt* of **speak**.

spam [spam] *n* the term given to junk mail in e-mail transmissions.

span[1] [span] *n* the space from the end of the thumb to the end of the little finger when the fingers are extended (about nine inches); the full extent between any two limits; the full duration of; the distance between abutments, piers, supports, etc., or the portion of a structure (eg a bridge) between.—*vt* to measure by spans or otherwise; to form an arch or bridge across;—*pr p* **spann´ing**; *pt, pt p* **spanned**. [OE *spann*; Cf Ger *spanne.*]

span[2] [span] *n* a pair of horses or a team of oxen.—*vt* to yoke. [Du and Low Ger *span.*]

spandrel, spandril [span´drėl] *n* the space between the curve of an arch and an enclosing right angle; the irregular space beneath the string of a stair. [Poss connected with **expand**.]

spangle [spang´gl] *n* a thin glittering plate of metal; a sparkling speck, flake, or spot.—*vt* to glitter. [OE *spange*; Cf Ger *spange, spängel.*]

Spaniard [span´yȧrd] *n* a native or citizen of Spain.

spaniel [span´yėl] *n* any of several breeds of dogs with large drooping ears, a silky wavy coat, and short legs, comprising gun dogs (eg field spaniels, springers, cockers), water spaniels, and toy dogs (eg King Charles and Blenheim spaniels); one who fawns. [OFr *espaigneul* (Fr *épagneul*)—Sp *español*, Spanish.]

Spanish [span´ish] *adj* of or pertaining to Spain.—*n* the Romance language of Spain and Spanish Americans.—**Spanish American**, a resident of the US whose native language is Spanish and whose culture is of Spanish origin; a native or inhabitant of one of the countries of America in which Spanish is the national language; **Spanish fly**, a green blister beetle (*Lytta vesicatoria*) of southern Europe; **Spanish moss**, an epiphytic plant (*Tillindsia usneoides*) that grows in long, graceful strands from tree branches in the southern US.

spank[1] [spangk] *vi* and *vt* to move, or drive, with speed or spirit.—*n* **spank´er**, the fore-and-aft sail on the aftermost mast.—*adj* **span´king**, spirited, speedy; striking. [Poss back-information from **spanking**.]

spank[2] [spangk] *vt* to strike with the flat of the hand, to smack.—*n* a loud slap, esp on the buttocks.—*n* **span´king**. [Imit.]

spanking [spangk´ing] *adj* remarkable of its kind; being fresh and strong, brisk.—*adv* (*inf*) completely; very. [Origin unknown.]

spanner [span´ėr] *n* a wrench with a hole, projection, or hook that corresponds to a device on the object to be turned. [Ger; cf **span** (1).]

spar[1] [spär] *n* a pole, as a mast or yard supporting the rigging of a ship; one of the main longitudinal members of the wing of an airplane. [OE *gesparrian*, to bar; cf ON *sparri*, Du *spar.*]

spar[2] [spär] *n* any of various nonmetallic minerals, usu. cleavable and lustrous. [Middle Low Ger *spar*, related to OE *spærstān*, gypsum.]

spar[3] [spär] *vi* to fight with spurs, as cocks; to box, or make the motions of boxing; to exchange provocative remarks;—*pr p* **sparr´ing**; *pt, pt p* **sparred**.—*n* a defensive or offensive movement in boxing; a sparring match or session.—**sparring partner**, one with whom a boxer practices. [OFr *esparer*, to kick out; prob Gmc.]

SPAR [spär] *n* a member of the women's reserve of the US Coast Guard.

spare [spär] *vt* to use frugally; to refrain from using; to do without or afford (eg *I cannot spare her, spare the time*); to forbear to hurt, injure, kill, etc.; to treat mercifully; to forebear to inflict (something) on (a person).—*vi* to be frugal; to forbear, to be merciful.—*adj* sparing, frugal, scanty; lean; extra, not in actual use; kept or available for others or for such purposes as may occur.—*n* a spare tire; a spare part; a duplicate kept or carried for emergencies; (*bowling*) a knocking down of all the pins with two rolls of the ball.—*adv* **spare´ly**.—*n* **spare´ness**.—*n pl* **spare´ribs**, a cut of pork, consisting of the thin end of the ribs.—*adj* **spā´ring**, scanty; frugal, economical.—*adv* **spā´ringly**, frugally; not abundantly or frequently. [OE *sparian*, to spare—*spær*, sparing.]

spark [spärk] *n* a glittering or glowing particle of matter thrown off by an incandescent substance; anything of like appearance or character, as anything easily extinguished, ready to cause explosion, burning hot; a flash; an electric discharge across a gap; a latent particle capable of growth or development; (*pl*) a radio operator on a ship.—*vt* to stir up; to activate.—*vi* to emit sparks.—*n* **spark plug**, a plug screwed into the cylinder head of an internal-combustion engine and carrying wires between which an electric spark passes and fires the explosive mixture of gases. [OE *spearca*; Du *spark.*]

sparkle [spärk´l] *n* a little spark; emission of sparks; bright effervescence, as in wines; vivacity; coruscation of wit.—*vi* to emit sparks; to shine, glitter; to effervesce with glittering bubbles, as certain wines; to be bright, animated, vivacious, or witty.—*n* **spark´ler**, one who, or that which, sparkles; a diamond; a small firework which can be held in the hand.—*n, adj* **spark´ling**. [Inten and freq. of **spark**.]

sparrow [spar´ō] *n* an Old World genus (*Passer*) of birds related to the finches; any of various finches (genus *Spizella* or *Melospiza* resembling the true sparrows.—*n* **sparr´ow hawk**, any of various small hawks or falcons as the N American *Falco sparverius*. [OE *spearwa*; ON *spörr*, Ger *sperling*.]

sparse [spärs] *adj* thinly scattered; scanty.—*adv* **sparse´ly**.—*n* **sparse´ness**. [L *sparsus*, pt p of *spargĕre*, to scatter; Gr *speirein*, to sow.]

Spartan [spär´tȧn] *adj* of or pertaining to Sparta in ancient Greece; rigorously severe; trained to endure privation or hardship.—*n* a native or inhabitant of ancient Sparta; a person of great courage and self-discipline.

spasm [spazm] *n* a sudden, involuntary contraction of muscles; any sudden strong short burst (of feeling or activity).—*adj* **spasmod´ic**, relating to, or consisting in, spasms; intermittent.—*adv* **spasmod´ically**.—*adj* **spastic** [spas´-], of the nature of, characterized by muscle spasm.—*n* one having a spastic condition.—**spastic paralysis**, a form of paralysis in which the patient suffers from permanent muscle constriction or involuntary jerky muscle movement. [Gr *spasma, -atos*, convulsion, and *spastikos—spaein*, to draw, pull, convulse.]

spat[1] [spat] *pt* of **spit** (2).

spat[2] [spat] *n* a young bivalve (as an oyster). [Perh from root of **spit** (2).]

spat[3] [spat] *n* a short gaiter covering the ankle and instep. [**spatterdash**.]

spat[4] [spat] *n* (*inf*) a brief, petty quarrel.—*vi* (*inf*) to engage in a spat.

spate [spāt] *n* a freshet; a large amount; a sudden outburst (as of words).

spathe [spāTH] *n* (*bot*) a sheathing bract, usu. one enclosing a spadix (eg the white part of the arum lily). [Gr *spathē*, a broad blade.]

spatial [spā´sh(ȧ);] *adj* relating to space.—Also **spā´cial**.—*adv* **spā´tially**. [L *spatium*, space.]

spatter [spat´ėr] *vti* to scatter or spurt out in drops; to splash.—*n* the act of spattering; a mark caused by spattering. [Cf Du and Low Ger *spatten.*]

spatula [spat´ū-la] *n* an implement with a broad, flexible blade for spreading or blending foods, paints, scooping, lifting, etc.—*adj* **spat´ulate**, shaped like a spatula; broad and rounded at the tips and tapering at the base. [L *spatula, spathula*, dim of *spatha*—Gr *spathē*, a broad blade.]

spavin [spav´in] *n* a disease of the hock joint of a horse.—*adj* **spav´ined**, affected with spavin. [OFr *espa(r)vain.*]

spawn [spön] *n* a mass of eggs, as of fishes, mollusks, or other aquatic animals; something produced, esp in great quantity, as offspring; mushroom mycelium.—*vti* to produce or deposit (eggs, sperm, or young); to bring forth or produce prolifically. [OFr *espandre*, to shed—L *expandĕre*, to spread out.]

spay [spā] *vt* to sterilize (a female animal) by removing the ovaries. [OFr *espeier—espee*, a sword.]

speak [spēk] *vi* to utter words; to talk; to hold a conversation (*with—or with* **to**); to make a speech; to sound; to convey an impression (of), be evidence (of).—*vt* to pronounce; to converse, or be able to converse, in (a specified language); to voice, to make known (eg *to speak one's thoughts, the truth*); to utter (eg *to speak sense*); to hail, or to communicate with.—*pt* **spōke**, (*arch*) **spāke**; *pt p* **spōken**.—*ns* **speak´eas´y**, a place where alcoholic beverages are illegally sold; **speak´er**, one who speaks; a loudspeaker; **Speaker**, the person who presides in the US House of Representatives; **Speak´ership**, the office of Speaker.—*adj* **speak´ing**, seeming to speak; expressive, or lifelike; used to assist the voice.—*n* **speak´ing tube**, a tube for speaking through, communicating from one room to another.—**speak well for**, to say or indicate something favorable about; **speak up**, to express an opinion freely; to speak loudly and distinctly. [OE *specan* (for *sprecan*); Du *spreken*, Ger *sprechen.*]

spear [spēr] *n* a weapon used in war and hunting, having a long shaft pointed with iron; a lance with barbed prongs used for catching fish; a spearsman; a long blade or shoot (eg of a grass).—*vt* to pierce or kill with a spear.—*ns* **spear´head**, the iron point of a spear; the leading person or group, as in an attack.—*vt* to take the lead in (a drive, attack, etc.); **spear´man**, a man armed with a spear; **spear´mint**, a common garden mint (*Mentha spicata*) grown for flavoring and esp for its aromatic oil. [OE *spere*; Ger *speer.*]

spec [spek] *vt* to write specifications for.

special [spesh´(ȧ)l] *adj* exceptional, uncommon, marked; peculiar to one person or thing; limited (to one person or thing); designed, appointed, arranged, run, etc., for a particular purpose (eg *special envoy, performance, train*); additional to ordinary.—*n* any person or thing set apart for a particular duty or purpose.—*adv* **specially** [spesh´ȧl-i].—*vt* **spec´ialize**, to narrow and intensify (eg one's studies); to become or be a specialist in (*with* **in**); to differentiate; to develop (a part of an organism) in such a way that it becomes adapted for a particular function; to specify, particularize.—*vi* to give particular attention to a single branch of study or business; to go into details or particulars; to become differentiated.—*adj* **spec´ialized**, adapted to a particular function, or limited purpose; restricted and made more exact (eg *specialized meaning*); appropriate to a specialist (eg *specialized knowledge*).—*ns* **specializā´tion**, the act or process of specializing; **spec´ialist**, one who applies himself to a special study or pursuit; any of the four enlisted ranks in the army corresponding to the grades of corporal through sergeant first class; **specialty** [spesh´ȧl-ti], a special activity or object of attention; a special product.—**special delivery**, mail delivery by a special messenger, for an extra fee; **Special Forces**, a branch of the army composed of men specially trained in guerrilla warfare. [L *speciālis*, particular—*speciēs*. See **species**.]

specie [spē´shi] *n* money in coin.—**in specie**, in the same kind; in coin. [L *in speciē*, in (the required) kind.]

species [spē´shēz] *n* a group of individuals having common characteristics, a kind or sort of human beings; a category of biological classification immediately below the genus potentially capable of inter-breeding; an individual belonging to a biological species; a particular kind of atomic nucleus, molecule, or atom;—*pl* **spe´cies**.—*adj* belonging to a biological species as distinguished from a horticultural variety. [L *speciēs*, kind or sort.]

specify [spes´i-fī] *vt* to mention particularly; to mention in detail; to set down as a requisite;—*pt, pt p* **spec´ified**.—*n* **specif´ic**, a remedy regarded as a certain cure for a particular disease.—*adj* **specif´ic**, distinctive, peculiar; precise; specially indicated as a cure for some disease.—*n* **specificā´tion**, the act of specifying; any point or particular specified; (usu. *pl*) a comprehensive statement of details.—**specific gravity**, the ratio of the weight of a given volume of a substance to that of an equal volume of another substance (as water) used as a standard. [OFr *specifier*—LL *specificāre*—L *speciēs*, kind, *facĕre*, to make.]

specimen [spes´i-mėn] *n* an object or portion serving as a sample, esp for purposes of study or collection; (*inf*) an individual, person. [L *specimen*—*specĕre*, to see.]

specious [spē´shùs] *adj* that looks well at first sight; deceptively attractive; plausible.—*ns* **speciosity** [spē-shi-os´i-ti], **spē´ciousness**.—*adv* **spē´ciously**. [L *speciōsus*, showy, plausible—*speciēs*, form, kind—*specĕre*, to look at.]

speck [spek] *n* a small spot; the least morsel or quantity.—*vt* to mark with specks. [OE *specca*.]

speckle [spek´l] *n* a little speck.—*vt* to mark with speckles.—*adj* **speck´led**.—*adv* **speck´lessly**. [**speck**.]

specs [speks] *n pl* (*inf*) eyeglasses; (*inf*) specifications.

spectacle [spek´tȧ-kl] *n* a sight; a large public show; (*pl*) an old-fashioned term for eyeglasses.—*adjs* **spec´tacled**, having markings suggesting a pair of spectacles; **spectacular** [-tak´ū-lȧr], of the nature of, or marked by, unusual display; remarkable, extraordinary.—*n* a theatrical show, or any display, that is large-scale and elaborate.—*adv* **spectac´ularly**. [L *spectăculum*—*spectāre, -ātum*, intensive of *specĕre*, to look at.]

spectator [spek-tā´tȯr] *n* one who looks on. [L,—*spectāre*. See **spectacle**.]

specter, spectre [spek´tėr] *n* a ghost.—*adj* **spec´tral**, relating to, or like, a specter.—*adv* **spec´trally**. [L *spectrum*, a vision—*specĕre*, to look at.]

spectrum [spek´trum] *n* the range of color produced by passing a white light through a prism, etc.; violet, indigo, blue, green, yellow, orange, red (the colors of the rainbow); any analogous range of radations in order of wavelength; a continuous sequence or range; kinds of organisms associated with a particular environment or susceptible to an agent;—*pl* **spec´tra, spectrums**.—*ns* **spectrom´eter**, an instrument for measuring refractive indices; a spectroscope that can measure the spectra produced; **spec´troscope**, an instrument for producing and observing spectra.—*adj* **spectroscop´ic**.—*adv* **spectroscop´ically**. [L,—*specĕre*, to look at.]

speculate [spek´ū-lāt] *vi* to reflect (on); to theorize, make conjectures or guesses (about); to engage in business transactions that offer huge profits.—*n* **speculā´tion**, act of speculating; meditation; conjecture; any more or less risky investment of money for the sake of profits.—*adj* **spec´ulātive**, of the nature of, based on, speculation; given to speculation or theory; engaging in speculation in business, etc.—*adv* **spec´ulātively**.—*n* **spec´ulātor**. [L *speculātus*, pt p of *speculārī*—*specula*, a lookout—*specĕre*, to look at.]

speculum [spek´ū-lum] *n* a reflector in an optical instrument; an ancient mirror usu. of bronze or metal; an instrument for bringing into view body parts otherwise hidden;—*pl* **spec´ula, speculums**. [L,—*specĕre*, to look at.]

sped *pt, pt p* of **speed** (also *adj*).

speech [spēch] *n* that which is spoken; language; the power of speaking; manner of speaking; oration, discourse.—*vi* **speech´ify**, to make speeches, harangue.—*adj* **speech´less**, unable to speak; silent, as from shock.—*adv* **speech´lessly**.—*ns* **speech´lessness; speech community**, a group of people sharing patterns of vocabulary, grammar, and pronunciation. [OE *spǣc*, *sprǣc*; Ger *sprache*.]

speed [spēd] *n* quickness, velocity; rate of motion; good progress; (*slang*) any of various amphetamine compounds; the sensitivity of a photographic film, plate, or paper expressed numerically.—*vi* to move quickly, to hurry; (*arch*) to succeed, fare; to drive at high, or at dangerously or illegally high, speed.—*vt* to further, help; to send forth with good wishes; to push forward; to regulate the speed of;—*pr p* **speed´ing**; *pt, pt p* **sped**.—*n* **speedom´eter**, an instrument attached to a vehicle for measuring speed.—*adj* **speed´y**, swift; prompt; soon achieved.—*adv* **speed´ily**.—*ns* **speed´iness; speed´boat**, a swift motorboat; **speed limit**, the maximum speed at which motor vehicles may be driven legally on certain roads; **speed´way**, a road for fast traffic; **speed up**, to quicken the rate of.—*n* **speed´-up**, an acceleration; an employer's demand for accelerated output without an increase in pay. [OE *spēd*; Du *spoed*.]

speedwell [spēd´wel] *n* a perennial European herb (*Veronica officinalis*) with small blue flowers; a plant resembling this. [**speed, well**.]

spell[1] [spel] *n* any form of words supposed to possess magical power; fascination.—*n* **spell´binder**, an orator, usu. political or evangelical, who holds his audience spellbound.—*adj* **spell´bound**, entranced, fascinated. [OE *spell*, a narrative; ON *spjall*, a tale.]

spell[2] [spel] *vt* to name or set down in order the letters of; to represent in letters (eg *c-a-t spells 'cat'*); to read laboriously, letter by letter; to make out, decipher, laboriously; to mean.—*vi* to spell words;—*pr p* **spell´ing**; *pt, pt p* **spelled**.—*ns* **spell´er**, one who spells; a book with exercises to teach spelling; **spell´ing**, the act of one who spells words; orthography; a sequence of letters forming a word; **spell´ing bee**, a competition in spelling in which each contestant is eliminated when he misspells a word.—Also **spell´down**.—**spell out**, to be specific in explaining something. [OFr *espeller* (Fr *épeler*), of Gmc origin. See **spell** (1).]

spell[3] [spel] *vt* (*inf*) to take the place of (another) for an interval; to relieve;—*pr p* **spell´ing**; *pt, pt p* **spelled**.—*n* a turn at work; a period at anything; (*inf*) a fit of illness. [OE *spelian*, to act for another; cf Du *spelen*, Ger *spielen*, to play.]

spelt [spelt] *n* a wheat (*Triticum spelta*) the grains of which are firmly enclosed in the chaff. [OE *spelt*—LL *spelta*.]

spelter [spel´tėr] *n* zinc cast in slabs for commercial use. [Low Ger *spialter*.]

spencer [spens´ėr] *n* a short waist-length jacket. [After Earl *Spencer*.]

spencerian [spen-sir´ē-ȧn] *adj* denoting a form of slanting hand writing. [P R *Spencer*, Am calligrapher.]

spend [spend] *vt* to expend, pay out (money); to give, bestow, employ (eg one's energies) for any purpose; to exhaust; to pass, as time.—*vi* to expend money;—*pr p* **spend´ing**; *pt, pt p* **spent**.—*n* **spen´der**.—*adj* **spent**, physically exhausted; used up; worn out; (of fish) exhausted by spawning. [OE *spendan*—L *expendĕre* or *dispendĕre*, to weigh out.]

spendthrift [spend´thrift] *n* one who wastes money; a prodigal.—*adj* excessively lavish. [**spend + thrift**.]

Spenserian stanza [spen-sē´ri-ȧn] *n* a nine-line stanza comprising eight lines in iambic pentameter and the last line in iambic hexameter with the rhyme scheme *ababbcbcc*. [Edmund *Spenser* (1552–99), Eng poet.]

spent [spent] *pt, pt p* of **spend**.

sperm [spûrm] *n* semen; a spermatozoon; a product of the sperm whale.—*adj* **spermat´ic**, pertaining to, consisting of, conveying, sperm; relating to sperm or a spermary.—*ns* **sperm´ary**, an organ in which male gametes are developed; **spermatozō´on, spermatazo´an**, one of the male reproductive cells of animals, a male gamete;—*pl* **spermatozō´a; sperm´ oil**, oil from the sperm whale; **sperm whale**, a large whale (*Physeter catadon*) with a large closed cavity in the head containing spermaceti and oil. [Fr,—L *sperma*, seed—Gr *sperma, -atos*—*speirein*, to sow.]

spermaceti [spėr-ma-sēt´i, or -sē´tī] *n* a waxy matter obtained mixed with oil from the head of the sperm whale and other cetaceans, used for candles and ointment.—Also *adj*. [L *sperma*, seed, *cētī*, gen of *cētus*, a whale—Gr *kētos*.]

spew [spū] *vti* to vomit; to flow or gush forth.—*n* something spewed. [OE *spīwan*; Du *spuwen*, Ger *speien*; also L *spuĕre*, Gr *ptyein*.]

sphagnum [sfag´num] *n* a genus (*Sphagnum*) of mosses that grow only in wet acid areas where their remains, compacted with other plant debris, form peat; a mass of sphagnum plants.—*adj* **sphag´nous**. [Gr *sphagnos*, moss.]

sphenoid, sphenoidal [sfē´noid, -noid´ȧl] *adj* wedge-shaped, esp a set of bones at base of the skull.—*n* a sphenoid bone. [Gr *sphēn, sphēnos*, wedge, *eidos*, form.]

sphere [sfēr] *n* a solid body bounded by a surface of which all points are equidistant from a center; its bounding surface; a ball or other spherical object; the apparent sphere of the heavens in which the stars seem to be placed; any one of the concentric spherical shells once supposed to carry the planets in their revolutions; the place, range, or extent of action, existence, knowledge, experience, etc.; any one of the celestial bodies.—*adjs* **sphēr´al; spheric** [sfer´ik], **-al**, of a sphere or spheres; having the form of a sphere or one of its segments.—*adv* **spher´ically**.—*ns* **sphericity** [sfer-is´i-ti], state or quality of being spherical; **sphē´roid**, a body or figure of a form differing very slightly from that of a sphere.—*adj* **sphēroi´dal**, having the form of a spheroid.—*n* **sphēr´ūle**, a little sphere.—*adj* **sphē´ry**, spherical, round; belonging to the celestial spheres.—**spherical geometry**, the geometry of figures on a sphere. [Fr,—L *sphaera*—Gr *sphaira*.]

sphincter [sfingk´tėr] *n* (*anat*) a ring-shaped muscle whose contraction narrows or shuts an orifice. [Gr *sphinktēr*—*sphingein*, to bind tight.]

Sphinx [sfingks] *n* a monster of Greek mythology, with the head of a woman and the body of a lioness, that strangled all wayfarers who could not solve the riddle she proposed; the gigantic image of the Sphinx near the Pyramids in Egypt; **sphinx**, an enigmatic or inscrutable person. [Gr,—*sphingein*, to bind tight, throttle.]

spica [spi´ka] *n* a bandage that is applied in successive V-shaped crossings used to immobilize a joint.—*adj* **spī´cāte**, forming a spike. [L *spīca*, an ear of corn.]

spice [spīs] *n* an aromatic and pungent vegetable substance used as a condiment and for seasoning food (eg pepper, ginger, nutmeg, cinnamon); such substances collectively or generally; anything that adds piquancy or interest.—*vt* to season with spice; to add zest to.—*n* **spī´cery**, spices in general; a spicy quality. [OFr *espice*—Late L *speciēs*, kinds of goods, spices—L *speciēs*, a kind.]

spick´-and-span, spic-and-span [spik and span] *adj* perfectly new, spotlessly clean. [**spike**, a nail.]

spicy [spī´si] *adj* producing or abounding with spices; fragrant; pungent; piquant, pointed, racy, sometimes with a touch of indecency.—*adv* **spī´cily**.—*n* **spī´ciness**. [**spice**.]

spider [spī´der] *n* any of an order (Araneida) of arachnids with a body of two main divisions, four pairs of walking legs, and abdominal spinnerets for spinning silk threads to make cocoons, nests, or webs; a cast-iron frying pan; a frame with radiating arms for drying clothes, etc.—*ns* **spider monkey**, a genus (*Ateles*) of New World monkeys with long slender limbs and an extremely long prehensile tail; **spider web**, the often symmetrical web spun by most spiders used as a resting place and as a trap for prey.—*adj*

spīd´ery, like a spider; composed of fine threads or lines in a weblike arrangement; infested with spiders. [ME *spither*—OE *spinnan*, to spin; cf Dan *spinder*, Ger *spinne*.]

spiel [spēl] *n* (*slang*) eloquent talk; sales talk; a long story.—*vi* (*slang*) to talk glibly.—*n* **spiel´er**, (*slang*) one who talks glibly and persuasively. [Ger, play, game.]

spigot [spig´ot] *n* a small pointed peg or bung; a faucet. [Conn with root of **spike**, a nail.]

spike [spīk] *n* an ear of grain; an inflorescence in which sessile flowers, or spikelets are arranged on a long axis.—*n* **spike´let**, in grasses, etc., a small spike itself forming part of a greater inflorescence. [L *spīka*, an ear of corn.]

spike [spīk] *n* long heavy nail; a sharp-pointed projection, as on a shoe to prevent slipping.—*vt* to fasten, set, or pierce with a spike or spikes; to pierce with, or impale on a spike; to thwart (a scheme, etc.); (*slang*) to add alcoholic liquor (to a drink).—*adj* **spiked**, furnished, fastened, or stopped with spikes.—*adj* **spī´ky**, furnished with spikes; having a sharp point.—**spike heel**, a very narrow high heel on a woman's shoe. [OE *spīcing*, a spike, nail; perh.—L *spīca*, an ear of corn.]

spikenard [spik´närd] *n* (*hist*) a fragrant ointment; an East Indian plant (*Nardostachys jatamansi*) from which spikenard is believed to be obtained; an American herb (*Avalia racemosa*) with an aromatic root and panicled umbels. [L *spica nardī*. See **nard**.]

spill[1] [spil] *vt* to allow, esp unintentionally, to run out of a container; to shed (blood); (*inf*) to throw off (a rider, etc.).—*vi* to be shed; to be allowed to fall, be lost, or wasted;—*pt, pt p* **spilled, spilt**.—*n* a fall, a tumble; something spilled; a spillway.—*ns* **spill´age**, the act of spilling; that which is spilt; **spill´way**, a passage for surplus water from a dam.—**spill the beans**, (*inf*) to divulge information, esp indiscreetly. [OE *spillan*; Du *spillen*, ON *spilla*, to destroy.]

spill[2] [spil] *n* a small peg or pin to stop a hole; a thin strip of wood or twisted paper for lighting a pipe, etc.; a roll or cone of paper serving as a container. [Ety uncertain.]

spin [spin] *vt* to draw out and twist into threads; to shape into threadlike form (usu. in *pt p*—eg *spun glass*); to draw out as a thread, as spiders do; to form by spinning; to twirl, revolving rapidly; to draw out (a story) to a great length.—*vi* to practice the art or trade of spinning; to perform the act of spinning; to whirl; to seem to be spinning from dizziness; to go swiftly, esp on wheels; *pr p* **spinn´ing**; *pt, pt p* **spun**.—*n* a rotatory motion; a ride in a motor vehicle; the movement of an aircraft in a steep continuous helical dive.—*ns* **spinn´er**, one that spins; a fisherman's lure that revolves when drawn through the water; a movable arrow mounted on a dial used in board games; **spinn´eret**, a spinning organ in spiders, etc.; **spinn´erette**, device used in the spinning of man-made filaments (as rayon or nylon) by forcing a chemical solution through fine holes; **spinn´ing jenn´y**, a machine by which a number of threads can be spun at once; **spinn´ing wheel**, a machine for spinning yarn, consisting of a wheel driven by the hand or by a treadle, which drives one or two spindles; **spin´off**, a byproduct that proves profitable on its own account. [OE *spinnan*, Ger *spinnen*.]

spinach [spin´ij] *n* a plant (*Spinacia oleracea*) whose young leaves are eaten as a vegetable; the leaves; something unwanted, insubstantial, or spurious; an unwanted growth. [OFr *espinage, espinache*; of doubtful origin.]

spinal [spīn´ål] *adj See* **spine**.

spindle [spin´dl] *n* the pin by which thread is twisted in spinning; a pin on which anything turns; a spindlelike thing; the part of an axle on which a vehicle wheel turns.—*vi* to grow long and slender.—*vt* to impale or perforate on the spike of a spindle; to make or equip (as a piece of furniture) with spindles.—*adjs* **spin´dle-legged, -shanked**, having long slender legs; **spin´dly**, disproportionally long and slender, frail in appearance or structure. [OE *spinel*—*spinnan*, to spin; Ger *spindel*.]

spindrift [spin´drift] *n* the spray blown from the crests of waves; spoondrift. [Scot form of *spoon* (arch and of uncertain ety), to scud, and **drift**.]

spine [spīn] *n* a sharp, stiff projection, as a thorn of the cactus; anything like this; a spinal column; the backbone of a book; a sharp process on an animal.—*adj* **spīn´al**, of the spine or spinal column.—*adjs*, **spine´less**, having no spine or spines; unable to make a firm stand; irresolute; **spī´nose** [or -nos´], **spī´nous**, full of spines; thorny; **spī´ny**, full of spines; thorny; troublesome, perplexed.—**spīna bifida** [bif´i-da], a condition in which two parts of the bony spinal canal fail to unite perfectly; **spinal canal**, a canal that contains the spinal cord; **spinal column**, the axial skeleton of the trunk and tail of a vertebrate comprising a series of vertebrae and protecting the spinal cord; the backbone; **spinal cord**, the thick cord of nerve tissue in the spinal column that connects the brain to the rest of the body. [OFr *espine*—L *spīna*, a thorn.]

spinet [spin´et, spin-et´] *n* an early harpsichord having a single keyboard and only one string for each note; a compactly built small piano; a small electronic organ. [It *spinetta*.]

spinnaker [spin´å-kėr] *n* a jib-shaped sail sometimes carried by racing yachts. [Said to be from a yacht, the *Sphinx*, that carried it.]

spinneret, spinnerette *See* **spin**.

spinster [spin´stėr] *n* an unmarried woman, esp an old maid.—*ns* **spin´sterhood**. [**spin**, + suffx *-ster*.]

spiracle [spīr´å-kl] *n* a breathing hole, a vent, (*zool*) a breathing aperture, ranging from the minute orifices of insects to the blowhole of whales, etc. [L *spīrāculum*—*spīrāre*, to breathe.]

spiral [spīr´ål] *adj. See* **spire** (1) and (2).

spirant [spī´rånt] *n* a consonant (as *f, s*, and *sh*) produced with a narrowing of the air passages; fricative. [L *spīrans, -antis*, pr p of *spīrāre*, to breathe.]

spire[1] [spīr] *n* a tapering or conical body, esp a tree-top; a tall, slender architectural structure tapering to a point.—*vi* to sprout; to shoot up.—*adjs* **spīr´al**, towering and tapering; **spī´ry**, tapering like a tall spire. [OE *spīr*, shoot, sprout.]

spire[2] [spīr] *n* a coil; a spiral; the spiral part of a shell, excluding the whorl in contact with the body.—*vi* to wind, mount, or proceed, in spirals.—*adj* **spī´ral**, circling around a point in constantly increasing (or decreasing) curves, or in constantly changing planes.—*n* a spiral curve or coil.—*vti* to move in or form (into) a spiral.—*adv* **spir´ally**.—*n* **spīr´ochete** [-kēt], any of an order (Spirochaeteles) of slender spirally undulating bacteria including those causing syphilis. [Gr *speira*, a coil.]

spirea, spiraea [spī-re´a] *n* any of a genus (*Spiraea*) of shrubs of the rose family with small, perfect pink or white flowers in dense clusters; a shrub (*Astilbe japonica*) resembling the spirea. [L,—Gr *speiraiā*, meadowsweet—*speira*, a coil.]

spirit [spir´it] *n* an entity without material reality; life, will, thought, etc., regarded as separate from matter; a supernatural being, as a ghost, angel, etc.; an individual; (*pl*) disposition; mood; vivacity, courage, etc.; enthusiastic loyalty; real meaning; a pervading animating principal; essential quality; (*usu. pl*) distilled alcoholic liquor; an alcoholic solution of a volatile substance.—*vt* to carry (away, off, etc.) secretly and swiftly.—*adj* **spir´ited**, full of spirit, life, or fire; animated.—*adv.* **spir´itedly**.—*ns.* **spir´itedness**—*adj.* **spir´itless**, without spirit, cheerfulness, or courage; dead.—*adv* **spir´itlessly**.—*ns* **spir´it lev´el**, a glass tube filled with a liquid and containing a small bubble of air which indicates by its position variation from perfect level.—*adj* **spir´itual**, of, of the nature of, relating to, a spirit or spiritualism; of, of the nature of, relating to, spirit or the soul; not corporeal; religious; sacred.—*n* a religious folk song of Afro-American origin.—*vt* **spir´itūalize**, to imbue with spirituality; to free from sensuality; to give a spiritual meaning to.—*ns* **spiritualizā´tion; spir´itualism**, the doctrine that spirit has a real existence apart from matter; the belief that the dead survive as spirits, which can communicate with the living usu. through a medium; **Spiritualism**, a movement comprising religious organizations emphasizing spiritualism; **spir´itūalist**, one who holds any doctrine of spiritualism.—*adj* **spiritūalist´ic**, relating to, or connected with, spiritualism.—*n* **spiritūal´ity**, state of being spiritual; essence distinct from matter.—*adv* **spir´itūally**.—*adjs* **spirituel, spirituelle** [spirit-ū-el´], showing refined, witty, grace and delicacy; **spir´itūous**, containing distilled alcohol.—**spirits of wine**, alcohol; **in spirits**, cheerfully vivacious; **out of spirits**, depressed; **the Spirit**, in Christian Science, God. [L *spīritus*, a breath—*spīrāre*, to breathe.]

spirochete *See* **spire** (2).

spirt [spûrt] *See* **spurt**.

spit[1] [spit] *n* a prong, usu. iron, on which meat is roasted; a long narrow strip of land extending into the water.—*vt* to fix as on a spit.—*pr p* **spitt´ing**; *pt, pt p* **spitt´ed**. [OE *spitu*; Du *spit*, Ger *spiess*.]

spit[2] [spit] *vt* to throw out from the mouth; to eject with violence; to utter with scorn.—*vi* to throw out saliva from the mouth; to rain in scattered drops;—*pr p* **spitt´ing**; *pt, pt p* **spit, spat**.—*n* saliva; a light fall of rain or snow; an exact replica (eg *the spit of him*).—*ns* **spit´ball**, paper chewed up into a wad for throwing; (*baseball*) an illegal pitch made to curve by wetting one side of the ball, as with spit; **spit´fire**, a hot-tempered person; **spittle**, spit, saliva; **spittoon´**, receptacle for spittle.—**spit and polish**, extreme attention to cleanliness, tidiness, etc., esp at the expense of efficiency in operation; **spit it out**, to say what is in the mind without further delay. [Northern OE *spittan*; ON *spȳta*.]

spite [spīt] *n* a grudge; ill will; malice.—*vt* to annoy spitefully, to thwart out of hatred.—*adj* **spite´ful**, showing spite, desirous to vex or injure; arising from spite, malignant.—*adv* **spite´fully**.—*n* **spite´fulness**.—**in spite of**, notwithstanding; regardless of. [Short for **despite**.]

spitz [spits] *n* a Pomeranian dog. [Ger.]

splash [splash] *vt* to spatter with liquid or mud; to throw (about), as liquid; to dash liquid on or over; to variegate as if by splashing.—*vi* to dabble; to dash liquid about; to fall into liquid with a splash.—*n* a dispersion of liquid suddenly disturbed, as by throwing something onto it or throwing it about; a wet or dirty mark; a bright patch; ostentation, display, publicity; a sensation.—**splash´board**, a dashboard; a panel to protect against splashes; a plank used to close a sluice or spillway of a dam; **splash´down**, the landing of a spacecraft on the sea.—*adj* **splash´y**, splashing; likely to splash; wet and muddy; (*inf*) getting much attention; (*inf*) spectacular. [**plash**.]

splatter [splat´ėr] *vti* to splatter, splash. [**spatter**,]

splay [splā] *vt* (*archit*) to slope, slant or bevel; to turn out at an angle; to spread out.—*vi* to slope, slant; be spread out.—*n* a slant or bevel, as of the side of a doorway, window, etc.—*adj* spreading outward.—*n* **splay´foot**, a flat foot turned outward.—*adj* **splay´footed**. [Short for **display**.]

spleen [splēn] *n* a large lymphatic organ in the upper left part of the abdomen which modifies the blood structure; (*obs*) the seat of emotions or passions;

(*arch*) melancholy; mingled ill will and bad temper.—*adjs* **splenet´ic**, affected with spleen; peevish; (*arch*) melancholy.—*n* a splenetic person. —*adv* **splenet´ically**.—*adj* **splēn´ic**, pertaining to the spleen. [L *splēn*—Gr *splēn*.]

splendid [splen´did] *adj* brilliant; magnificent; (*inf*) excellent.—*adj* **splen´dent**, brightly shining.—*adv* **splen´didly**.—*ns* **splen´didness, splen´dor**, brilliance; magnificence. [L *splendidus*—*splendēre*, to shine.]

splice [splīs] *vt* to unite (two ends of a rope) by separating and interweaving the strands; to join together (two pieces of timber) by overlapping; to fasten the ends of (wire, film, etc.) together as by soldering, etc.; to combine (genetic information) from two or more organisms.—*n* act of splicing; joint made by splicing; (*slang*) marriage, a wedding. [Du (now dial) *splissen*.]

splint [splint] *n* a thin strip of wood, etc. woven with others to make baskets, etc.; a thin piece of padded wood, etc., for keeping a fractured limb in its proper position; a hard excrescence on the cannon bone of a horse.—*vt* to put in splints.—*n* **splint´er**, a thin, sharp piece of wood, split off.—*vti* to split into splinters.—*adj* **splint´ery**, made of, or like, splinters; apt to splinter. [Middle Du or (Middle) Low Ger *splinte*.]

split [split] *vti* to cleave lengthwise; to break in pieces, asunder; to divide into shares; to disunite; to break (a molecule) into atoms; to produce nuclear fission in (an atom);—*pr p* **splitt´ing**; *pt, pt p* **split**.—*n* a splitting; a break; a crack; a division in a group, etc.; act of lowering oneself to the floor or leaping in the air with legs at right angles to the trunk; a wine bottle holding about 6 ounces; a confection of sliced fruit (as a banana), ice cream, nuts, etc.—*adj* **splitt´ing**, rending; cleaving; (of a headache) very severe.—**split hairs**, to make exceedingly fine distinctions; **split infinitive**, an infinitive in which an adverb separates 'to' from the verb (eg *be sure to carefully place it in position*); **split-level**, (denoting) a building having adjacent floor levels about a half-story apart; **split personality**, schizophrenia; **split second**, a fraction of a second; **split ticket**, a ballot cast by a voter who votes for candidates of more than one party; **split one's sides**, to laugh immoderately. [Du *splitten*; related to Ger *spleissen*.]

splurge [splûrj] *n* (*inf*) any very showy display or effort; (*inf*) a spell of extravagant spending.—*vi* (*inf*) to show off; (*inf*) to spend money freely.

splutter [splut´ėr] *vi* to eject drops of liquid with spitting noises; to articulate confusedly and hurriedly.—*vt* to utter in a spluttering manner.—*n* a spluttering.—*n* **splutt´erer**, one who splutters. [Variant of **sputter**.]

Spode [spōd] *n* a kind of porcelain made with addition of bone ash by Josiah *Spode* (1754–1827) in England.

spoil [spoil] *vt* to damage as to make useless, etc.; to impair the enjoyment, etc., of; to cause to expect too much by overindulgence; (*arch*) to rob; to plunder.—*vi* to become spoiled; to decay, etc., as food;—*pt, pt p* **spoiled, spoilt**.—*n* (*usu. pl*) plunder; booty.—*ns* **spoil´age**, the act or process of spoiling; something spoiled or wasted; loss by spoilage; **spoil´er**, one that spoils; a long narrow plate along the upper surface of an airplane wing for reducing lift and increasing drag; an air deflector on a racing car to reduce the tendency to lift off the road; **spoil´sport**, one whose actions ruin the pleasure of others.—**spoils system**, the treating of public offices as the booty of a successful political party. [OFr *espoilee*—L *spolium*, plunder.]

spoke[1] [spōk] *pt* of **speak**.

spoke[2] [spōk] *n* any of the braces extending from the hub to the rim of a wheel. [OE *spāca*; Du *speek*, Ger *speiche*.]

spoken [spōk´n] *pt p* of **speak**.

spokeshave [spōk´shāv] *n* a small transverse plane with end handles for planing convex or concave surfaces. [**spoke** (2) and **shave**.]

spokesman [spōks´mȧn] *n* one who speaks for another, or for others;—*pl* **spok´esmen**;—*fem* **spok´eswoman**. [**spoke** (1) and **man**.]

spoliate [spō´li-āt] *vti* to despoil, to plunder.—*n* **spōliā´tion**, act of despoiling; robbery. [L *spoliāre, -ātum*—*spolium*, spoil.]

spondee [spon´dē] *n* in poetry, a foot of two long or stressed syllables.—*adj* **spondā´ic**. [Fr,—L *spondēus* (*pēs*)—Gr *spondeios* (*pous*), (a foot) used in the slow solemn hymns at a *spondē* or drink-offering.]

sponge [spunj] *n* a plantlike marine animal (phylum Porifera) with an internal skeleton of elastic interlacing horny fibers; the highly absorbent skeleton of such animals, used for washing surfaces, etc.; any substance like this, as spongy rubber, etc.—*vt* to wipe, wipe out, soak up, remove, with a sponge; (*inf*) to get as by begging, imposition, etc.—*vi* (*inf*) to be dependent on others, as a parasite.—*ns* **sponge bath**, a bath taken by using a wet sponge or cloth without getting into water; **sponge´ cake**, a very light cake of flour, eggs, and sugar; **sponge´ rubber**, rubber processed into spongelike form.—*adj* **spongy** [spun´ji], like a sponge, absorptive; of open texture, porous; wet and soft.—*n* **spong´iness**. [OFr *esponge*—L *spongia*—Gr *spongiā*.]

sponsor [spon´sȯr] *n* one who promises solemnly for another, a surety; a godfather or godmother; a business firm etc. that pays for a radio or TV program advertising its product.—*vt* to act as sponsor for.—*adj* **sponsō´rial**.—*n* **spon´sorship**. [L,—*spondēre, sponsum*, to promise.]

spontaneous [spon-tā´nė-ůs] *adj* uttered, offered, done, etc., of one's free will; natural, unforced; involuntary; acting by its own impulse or natural law; produced of itself or without interference.—*ns* **spontanē´ity, spontā´neousness**, the state or quality of being spontaneous; naturalness, unforced quality.—*adv* **spontā´neously**.—**spontaneous combustion**, combustion due to heat caused by chemical action within a flammable substance; **spontaneous generation**, also known as *abiogenesis*, the origination of living by nonliving matter. [L *spontāneus*—*sponte*, of one's own accord.]

spoof [spōōf] *n* (*slang*) a hoax or joke; a light satire.—*vti* (*slang*) to hoax.

spook [spōōk] *n* a ghost; (*inf*) an undercover agent.—*adjs* **spook´ish, spook´y**. [App Low Ger; cf Ger *spuk*, Du *spook*.]

spool [spōōl] *n* a cylinder, bobbin, or reel, for winding thread, photographic film, etc., upon; the material wound.—*vt* to wind on a spool; to wind. [Low Ger *spôle*, Du *spoel*; Ger *spule*.]

spoon [spōōn] *n* utensil with a shallow bowl and a handle, for eating, stirring, etc.; something like a spoon in shape, as a curved metal fishing lure.—*vt* to propel (a ball) with a weak, lifting stroke; to transfer with, or as with, a spoon.—*vi* to court in an excessive and ridiculous manner; to spoon a ball.—*ns* **spoon´bill**, a wading bird (family Plataleidae) with a long, flat, broad bill, spoon-shaped at the tip.—**spoon bread**, a soft bread made of cornmeal mixed with milk, eggs, and shortening and served with a spoon.—*vt* **spoon-feed**, to feed with a spoon; to present (information) so completely as to preclude independent thought; to present information in this manner.—*n* **spoon´ful**, as much as fills a spoon; a small quantity;—*pl* **spoon´fuls**.—*adjs* **spoon´y, spoon´ey**, foolishly and demonstratively fond. [OE *spōn*, silver, chip, shaving; Ger *span*, chip, ON *spānn*, chip, spoon.]

spoondrift [spōōn´drift] *n* spray blown from waves during a gale at sea.

spoonerism [spōōn´ėr-izm] *n* transposition of the initial sounds of spoken words—eg 'shoving leopard' for 'loving shepherd'. [Rev W A *Spooner* (1844–1930), who was prone to this error.]

spoor [spōōr] *n* a track, trail, scent, or droppings of a wild animal.—*vti* to track (something) by a spoor. [Du *spoor*, a track; cf OE and ON *spor*.]

sporadic [spo-rad´ik] *adj* occurring here and there and now and then; occurring casually.—*adv* **sporad´ically**. [Gr *sporadikos*—*sporas, -ados*, scattered—*speirein*, to sow.]

spore [spōr, spör] *n* a unicellular asexual reproductive body produced by mosses, ferns, and some invertebrates and capable of giving rise to new individuals.—*n* **sporangium** [spor-an´ji-ům], a case in which spores are produced;—*pl* **sporan´gia**.—*adj* **sporan´gial**.—*n* **spō´rophyte** [-fit], the asexual generation or individual in the life cycle of a plant.—*adj* **sporophy´tic** [-fitik]. [Gr *sporos*, a sowing, a seed—*speirein*, to sow.]

sporran [spor´ȧn] *n* an ornamental pouch worn in front of the kilt by the Highlanders of Scotland. [Gael *sporan*.]

sport [spört] *vi* to play, to frolic; to trifle; (of a plant bud) to deviate from the normal.—*vt* (*inf*) to display, flaunt.—*n* a pastime, amusement; a game, esp one involving bodily exercise; a field diversion (eg hunting, fishing, athletics); a thing joked about; (*inf*) a sportsmanlike person; (*inf*) a showy, flashy fellow; (*biol*) an individual differing markedly from the normal.—*adj* of or for sports; suitable for casual wear.—Also **sports**.—*adj* **sport´ful**, entertaining; playful; done in sport.—*adv* **sport´fully**.—*n* **sport´fulness**.—*adj* **sport´ing**, used or suitable for sport; calling for sportsmanship; involving such risk as a contender in sports may expect to encounter; relating to dissipation, esp gambling; tending to mutate freely.—*adv* **sport´ingly**.—*adj* **sport´ive**, playful; wanton; relating to sports, esp field sports.—*adv* **sport´ively**.—*ns* **sport´iveness; sporting house**, a brothel; **sports car**, a low usu. small two-passenger automobile designed for quick response and easy maneuvering at high speed; **sports´cast**, a radio or television program dealing with news about sports; **sports´man**, a man who takes part in sports, esp hunting, fishing, etc.; one who plays fair and can lose without complaint or win without gloating; **sports´manship**, conduct becoming to a sportsman; **sports´wear**, clothing suitable for recreation; **sports´woman**, a woman who engages in sports; **sports´writer**, one who writes about sports esp for a newspaper.—*adj* **sport´y**, sporting or like a sportsman; notably dissipated; flashy, showy; capable of giving good sport. [Shortened from **disport**.]

spot [spot] *n* a small area differing in color, etc., from the surrounding area; a stain, speck, etc.; a taint on character or reputation; a small quantity or amount; a locality; a place on an entertainment program; a brief announcement or advertisement.—*vt* to mark with spots; to tarnish (reputation); to recognize, identify, to espy, detect; (*inf*) to allow as a handicap;—*pr p* **spott´ing**; *pt, pt p* **spott´ed**.—*adj* **spot´less**, without a spot; untainted, pure.—*adv* **spot´lessly**.—*n* **spot´lessness**.—*adjs* **spott´ed, spott´y**, marked with spots.—*n* **spot-check**, a check on the spot without warning; a check of random samples to serve in place of a general check.—Also *vt*.—**spot´light**, a circle of light thrown upon one actor or a small part of the stage; apparatus for projecting it; public notice.—*vt* to turn the spotlight on.—*n* **spott´er**, one who spots or detects.—**in a spot** (*slang*) in a difficult situation; **on the spot**, at once; in the place required; alert, equal to any emergency; (*slang*) in a position of extreme difficulty or danger. [Cf obs Du, Low Ger *spot*, ON *spotti*.]

spouse [spowz] *n* (one's) husband or wife.—*adj* **spous´al**, nuptial; matrimonial.—*n* usu. *pl* nuptials; marriage. [OFr *espous*, fem *espouse* (Fr *époux*, fem *épouse*)—*espouser*. See **espouse**.]

spout [spowt] *vti* to throw out as from a spout; to declaim.—*n* a projecting lip or tube for discharging liquid from a vessel, a roof, etc.; a gush, discharge, or jet; a waterspout.—*n* **spout´er**, one who, or that which, spouts. [ME *spouten*; cf Du *spuiten*, to spout, ON *spȳta*, to spit.]

sprag [sprag] *n* a bar inserted to stop a wheel.
sprain [sprān] a wrenching of a joint with tearing or stretching of ligaments.—*vt* to wrench so as to cause a sprain. [Connection with OFr *espreindre*, to squeeze out, is disputed.]
sprang *pt* of **spring**.
sprat [sprat] *n* a small European herring (*Clupea sprattus*). [OE *sprot*; Ger *sprotte*.]
sprawl [spröl] *vi* to stretch the body carelessly when lying; to spread ungracefully, as handwriting.—*n* sprawling posture.—*n* **sprawl´er**. [OE *sprēawlian*, to move convulsively.]
spray[1] [sprā] *n* a cloud of small flying drops; such a cloud applied as a disinfectant, insecticide, etc.; an atomizer or other apparatus for dispersing it.—*vti* to direct a spray (on); to sprinkle or squirt in a spray.—*n* **spray´ gun**, a device for applying paint, etc., in the form of a spray. [Middle Du *sprayen*.]
spray[2] [sprā] *n* a shoot or twig, esp one spreading out in branches or flowers; an ornament, casting, etc., of similar form. [Perh conn with **sprig**, or with OE *spræc*, twig.]
spread [spred] *vt* to cause to extend more widely or more thinly; to scatter abroad or in all directions; to extend (over time, or over a surface); to overlay; to shoot out (branches); to circulate (news); to convey to others, as a disease; to set with provisions, as a table.—*vi* to extend or expand in all directions; to be extended or stretched; to be propagated or circulated.—*pt, pt p* **spread**.—*n* act or process of spreading; extent, compass, expansion; a cover for a bed or a table; jam, butter, etc., used on bread; (*inf*) a meal with many different foods.—*n* **spread´ ea´gle**, a heraldic eagle with wings and legs stretched out; a skating figure resembling this.—*adj* bombastic, boastful, esp of the greatness of the US.—*vi* to execute a spread eagle, as in skating; to sprawl.—*vt* to stretch out into the position of a spread eagle. [OE *sprǣdan*; Du *spreiden*, Ger *spreiten*.]
spree [sprē] *n* a merry frolic; a drunken bout; a period of uninhibited activity. [Orig slang.]
sprig [sprig] *n* a small shoot or twig; a scion, a young person; a small nail with little or no head.—*vt* to drive sprigs into; to mark or decorate with drawings of sprigs; to propagate (a grass) by means of small divisions;—*pr p* **sprigg´ing**; *pt, pt p* **sprigged**. [Origin obscure.]
sprightful [sprīt´fùl] *n* full of life or spirit; sprightly.—*adv* **spright´fully**.—*n* **spright´fulness**.—*adjs* **spright´less**, destitute of spirit or life; **spright´ly**, vivacious, animated; lively; brisk.—*n* **spright´liness**.
spring [spring] *vi* to move suddenly, as by elastic force; to bound, to leap; to start up suddenly, to break forth; to appear, to issue; to take origin; to sprout; to become warped, split, etc.—*vt* to cause to spring up, to start; to release the elastic force of; to let off, allow to spring; to cause (a trap, etc.) to snap shut; to produce suddenly (eg a surprise), to make known suddenly (*with* **on, upon** a person); to open, as a leak; to crack, as a mast; to bend by force, strain; to leap over; to set with springs; (*slang*) to procure the escape of from jail.—*pt* **sprang** (*now rarely* **sprung**); *pt p* **sprung**.—*n* a leap; a sudden movement; a recoil or rebound; elasticity; an elastic device or appliance used eg for setting in motion, or for reducing shocks; a source (of action or life); a motive; rise, beginning; cause or origin; a source; an outflow of water from the earth; the season after winter when plants spring up and grow; any period of beginning.—*adj* having or supported on springs; of the season of spring; sown, appearing, or used in, spring; coming from a spring.—*ns* **spring´ald, springal**, a young man; a youth; **spring´bok**, a graceful southern African gazelle (*Antidorcus euchore*) noted for its habit of springing lightly and suddenly into the air; **spring´-clean´ing**, a thorough cleaning of a place.—*vt* **spring´-clean´**.—*ns* **spring´er**, one who springs; a springer spaniel; a cow nearly ready to calve; **springer spaniel**, either of two breeds of sporting dogs used to find and flush small game; **spring´-house**, a small building located over a spring and formerly used for cool storage (as of dairy products and meat); **spring´tide**, very low tide occurring about new and full moon, when sun and moon pull together; **spring´tide, spring´time**, the season of spring; **spring´wa´ter**, water of or from a spring.—*adj* **spring´y**, elastic; resilient.—*n* **spring´iness**.—**spring a leak**, to begin to leak suddenly. [OE *springan*; Ger *springen*.]
springe [sprinj] *n* a noose fastened to an elastic body to catch small game; a snare, trap. [Earlier *sprenge*, from a prob OE *sprencg*.]
sprinkle [spring´kl] *vt* to scatter in small drops or particles (on something); to scatter (something with something); to strew, dot, diversify.—*vi* to scatter in drops; to rain lightly.—*ns* **sprin´kle, sprin´kling**, a small quantity sprinkled; **sprin´kler**. [Frequentative from OE *sprengan*, the causative of *springan*, to spring; cf Ger *sprenkeln*.]
sprint [sprint] *n* a short run, row, or race, at full speed.—*vi* to run at full speed.—*n* **sprin´ter**. [Scand.]
sprit [sprit] *n* (*naut*) a spar set diagonally to extend a fore-and-aft sail. [OE *sprēot*, a pole; Du and Ger *spriet*, sprit.]
sprite [sprīt] *n* (*arch*) a soul; a goblin, elf, imp, impish or implike person. [OFr *esprit*; cf **spright, spirit**.]
sprocket [sprok´ėt] *n* a tooth on the rim of a wheel or capstan for engaging the chain.—*n* **sprock´et wheel**, a toothed wheel used for a chain drive, as on the pedal shaft and rear hub of a bicycle. [Origin unknown.]
sprout [sprowt] *n* a new growth; a young shoot; a side bud; a scion, descendant; a sprouting condition.—*vi* to push out new shoots; to begin to grow.—*vt* to cause to sprout; to put forth, grow (a sprout, a bud, etc.). [OE *sprūtan* (found in compounds); cf Du *spruiten*, Ger *spriessen*.]
spruce[1] [sprōōs] *adj* smart, neat, dapper; over-fastidious, finical.—*vt* to smarten.—*vi* to become spruce or smart (*often with* **up**).—*adv* **spruce´ly**.—*n* **spruce´ness**. [Prob from **spruce** (2), from the vogue of Spruce (ie Prussian) leather in the 16th century.]
spruce[2] [sprōōs] *n* any of a genus (*Picea*) of evergreen trees of the pine family with a conical head and soft light wood; any of several coniferous trees of the same habit.—*n* **spruce´ beer´**, a beverage made from spruce twigs and leaves boiled with molasses or sugar and fermented with yeast. [ME *Spruce*, Prussia—OFr *Pruce*.]
sprung *pt, pt p* of **spring**.—**sprung rhythm**, a poetic rhythm closer to that of ordinary speech than is the 'running rhythm' of classical English poetry, consisting of mixed feet, each stressed on the first syllable.
spry [sprī] *adj* nimble, agile, esp though elderly. [Origin uncertain.]
spud [spud] *n* a small narrow digging tool; (*inf*) a potato.
spume [spūm] *n* foam; scum.—*vi* to foam, froth.—*adjs* **spū´mous, spū´my**. [L *spūma*—*spuĕre*, to spew.]
spun *pt, pt p* of **spin**.—**spun sugar**, sugar spun into fine fluffy threads, as in candy floss.
spunk [spungk] *n* touchwood, tinder; any fungi used to make tinder; (*inf*) spirit, mettle, courage.—*adj* **spunk´y**. [Cf Ir *sponc*, tinder, sponge—L *spongia*, a sponge—Gr *spongiā*.]
spur [spûr] *n* an instrument on a rider's heel, with sharp point for goading the horse; incitement, stimulus; a hard sharp projection; a projection at the back of a cock's or other bird's leg; a short, usu. flowering or fruit-bearing, branch; a lateral root; a tubular pouch at the base of a petal; a small range of mountains extending laterally from a larger range; a short railroad track connected with the main track.—*vt* to apply the spur to; to urge on; to put spurs on.—*vi* to press forward with the spur; to hasten.—*pr p* **spurr´ing**; *pt, pt p* **spurred**. [OE *spora*; ON *spori*, Ger *sporn*.]
spurge [spûrj] *n* a genus (*Euphorbia*) of plants with a bitter milky juice and tiny flowers. [OFr *espurge*—L *expurgāre*, to purge—*ex*, off, *purgāre*, to clear.]
spurious [spūr´i-ùs] *adj* bastard, illegitimate; not genuine, sham; forged; (*bot*) simulating but essentially different.—*adv* **spūr´iously**.—*n* **spūr´iousness**. [L *spurius*, false.]
spurn [spûrn] *vt* to reject with contempt.—*n* disdainful rejection. [OE *spornan*, *spurnan*, related to **spur**.]
spurt, spirt [spûrt] *vt* to spout, or send out in a sudden stream or jet.—*vi* to gush out suddenly; to flow out forcibly or at intervals; to make a sudden, short, intense effort.—*n* a sudden or violent gush; a jet; a short spell of intensified effort, speed, etc.
Sputnik [spŏŏtnik] *n* any of a series of Soviet manmade satellites. [After the Russian *Sputnik* ('traveling companion') 1, the first such satellite, put in orbit in 1957.]
sputter [sput´ėr] *vi* to spit or throw out moisture in scattered drops; to speak rapidly and indistinctly; to make a noise of sputtering, as frying fat.—*vt* to spit out or throw out in or with small drops; to utter hastily and indistinctly.—*n* sputtering; matter sputtered out. [Imit; cf Du *sputteren*.]
sputum [spū´tum] *n* matter composed of secretions from the nose, throat, bronchi, lungs, which is spat out.—*pl* **spū´ta**. [L *spūtum*—*spuĕre*, to spit.]
spy [spī] *n* agent employed to watch others secretly or to collect information, esp of a military nature; act of spying.—*vt* to descry, make out; to discover by close search; to inspect secretly.—*vi* to play the spy.—*pt, pt p* **spied** [spīd].—*n* **spy´glass**, a small telescope. [OFr *espie* (n), *espier* (vb).]
squab [skwob] *adj* fat, clumsy; newly hatched.—*n* a four-week-old pigeon.
squabble [skwob´l] *vi* to dispute noisily, to wrangle.—*n* a noisy, petty quarrel.—*n* **squabb´ler**. [Scand; prob imit.]
squad [skwod] *n* a small group of soldiers drilled or working together; any working party; a set or group.—**squad car**, a police patrol car. [Fr *escouade*.]
squadron [skwod´ròn] *n* a unit of warships, cavalry, military aircraft, etc.; a military flight formation. [It *squadrone*—*squadra*, a square.]
squalid [skwol´id] *adj* filthy, foul; neglected, sordid and dingy.—*adv* **squal´idly**.—*ns* **squal´idness; squal´or**, state of being squalid; dirtiness. [L *squālidus* (adj), stiff, rough, dirty, *squālor, -ōris* (n).]
squall [skwöl] *vi* to cry out violently; to sing loudly and unmusically.—*n* a loud cry or scream; a violent gust of wind.—*n* **squall´er**.—*adj* **squall´y**, abounding with, or disturbed with, squalls or gusts of wind; gusty. [Prob imit.]
squama [skwā´ma] *n* a scale; a scalelike structure.—*pl* **squā´mae** [-ē].—*adjs* **squā´mous, squā´mose**, covered with, or consisting of, scales; scaly. [L *squāmōsus*—*squāma*, a scale.]
squander [skwon´dėr] *vt* to spend lavishly or wastefully.—*n* **squan´derer**. [Origin obscure.]
square [skwār] *n* an equilateral rectangle; an object, piece, space, figure of approximately that shape; an open space—commonly but not necessarily of that shape—in a town, with its surrounding buildings; a body of troops drawn up in that form; an instrument for drawing or testing right angles; the product of a number or quantity multiplied by itself; (*slang*) one of square tastes or outlook.—*adj* having the form of a square; relatively broad; right-angled; fair, honest; even, leaving no balance, settled, as accounts;

equal in score; unequivocal, uncompromising; solid, satisfying (eg *a square meal*); (*inf*) of taste in music, etc., traditional and orthodox; (*slang*) bourgeois in outlook.—*vt* to make square or rectangular, esp in cross section; to straighten (the shoulders), bend (the elbows) to form right angles; to form into squares; to convert into an equivalent square; to multiply by itself; to regulate (by, according to—*also with* **on**) any given standard; to adjust (to), harmonize (with); (*naut*) to place at right angles with the mast or keel.—*vi* to suit, fit; to accord or agree.—*adv* at right angles; solidly; directly; fairly, honestly.—*adv* **square´ly**.—*n* **square´ness**.—*adj* **square´-rigged**, rigged chiefly with square sails.—*ns* **square´ root**, that number or quantity which being multiplied by itself produces the given quantity (eg 4 is √16, ie the square root of 16); **square´ sail**, a foursided sail extended by yards suspended by the middle at right angles to the mast.—*adj* **square´-toed**, an old-fashioned, puritanical, punctilious person.—**square foot, inch**, etc., an area equal to that of a square whose side measures one foot, inch, etc.—**square off** (or **away**), to adopt the posture of a boxer; **square oneself**, (*inf*) to make amends. [OFr *esquarre*—L *ex* and *quadra*, a square.]

squash[1] [skwosh] *vt* to press into pulp; to crush flat; to put down, suppress; to snub.—*vi* to form a soft mass as from a fall; to become crushed or pulpy; to squelch; to crowd.—*n* something squashed; the act or sound of squashing; a game played in a walled court with rackets and rubber ball.—*adj* **squash´y**, like a squash; muddy. [OFr *esquacer, esquasser*—*es-* (L *ex-*) and *quasser*. See **quash**.]

squash[2] [skwosh] *n* any of several species (genus *Cucurbita*) of gourd eaten as a vegetable. [From Amer Indian name.]

squat [skwot] *vi* to sit down upon the heels; to sit close, as an animal; to settle on land or in occupied property, without permission or title; to settle on public land in order to get title to it;—*pr p* **squatt´ing**; *pt, pt p* **squatt´ed**.—*adj* short and thick, dumpy.—*n* the act of squatting.—*n* **squatt´er**, one who occupies land or property without permission or title; one that settles on public land under government regulation with the purpose of acquiring title. [OFr *esquatir*, to crush; cf **squash** (1).]

squaw [skwö] *n* an American Indian woman; a woman, wife, usu. disparaging. [Amer Indian word.]

squawk [skwök] *n* a croaky call or cry; (*inf*) a raucous complaint.—*vti* to utter a squawk or with a squawk. [Imit.]

squeak [skwēk] *vi* to utter, or to give forth, a high-pitched cry, or note.—*n* a squeaky sound; or bare chance.—*n* **squeak´er**.—*adj* **squeak´y**, squeaking or given to squeaking; of the nature of a squeak.—*adv* **squeak´ily**.—*n* **squeak´iness**.—**narrow squeak** (*inf*) a narrow escape; **squeak through** (or **by**), (*inf*) to succeed with difficulty. [Imit; cf Swed *sqväka*, croak, Ger *quieken*.]

squeal [skwēl] *vi* to utter a shrill and prolonged sound; (*slang*) to be an informer.—*vt* to utter, to express, etc., with squealing.—*n* a shrill loud cry. [Imit; cf Swed dial *sqväla*, to cry out.]

squeamish [skwēm´ish] *adj* inclined to nausea; easily shocked or disgusted; fastidious; reluctant from scruples or compunction.—*adv* **squeam´ishly**.—*n* **squeam´ishness**. [ME *scoymous*—Anglo-Fr *escoymous*; origin obscure.]

squeegee [skwē´jē] *n* a wooden implement edged with rubber for clearing water away from decks, floors, windows, etc.; a photographer's roller for squeezing the moisture from a print. [Perh **squeeze**.]

squeeze [skwēz] *vt* to crush, press hard, compress; to grasp tightly; to embrace; to force (through, into) by pressing; to force liquid, juice, from by pressure; to force to discard winning cards; to fleece, extort from.—*vi* to press; to force a way.—*n* act of squeezing; pressure; an embrace; a close grasp; a portion withheld and appropriated by a middleman; a few drops got by squeezing; a restriction or time or restriction (usually financial or commercial).—*n* **squeez´er**. [ME *queisen*—OE *cwisan*.]

squelch [skwel(t)sh] *n* (*inf*) a crushing retort, rebuke, etc.; a heavy blow on, or fall of, a soft and moist body; the sound of such an impact; the sound made by wet mud under pressure.—*vt* (*inf*) to suppress or silence completely.—*vi* to take heavy steps in water or on moist ground. [Imit.]

squib [skwib] *n* a paper tube filled with combustibles, used as firework; a petty lampoon. [Perh imit.]

squid [skwid] *n* any of various ten-armed cephalopods (esp genus *Loligo* or *Ommastrephes*) often, but not always, confined to those in which the internal shell, the *pen*, is not calcified and is hence flexible; also called *calamary*. [L *calamus*, a reed pen—Gr *kalamos*.]

squill [skwil] *n* any flower of the genus *Scilla*, esp the sea onion, a Mediterranean species which is used as a diuretic. [Fr *squille*—L *squilla, scilla*—Gr *skilla*.]

squint [skwint] *adj* looking obliquely; squinting; oblique.—*vi* to look obliquely; to be strabismic; to have a side reference or allusion to (*with* **at**, *etc.*); to hint disapprobation of (*with* **at, on**).—*vt* to cause to squint; to direct or divert obliquely.—*n* act or habit of squinting; an oblique look; a glance, a peep; an oblique reference, hint, tendency; a hagioscope; strabismus, distortion of vision due to an infirmity whereby the line of vision of the eye affected is not parallel to that of the other; (*inf*) a quick look or sidelong glance. [Shortened from *asquint*, probably of Du origin.]

squire [skwīr] *n* an esquire, an aspirant to knighthood attending a knight; an attendant, esp a man escorting a woman; an English landed gentleman, esp of old family; a title of respect for a judge, lawyer, justice of the peace, etc.—*vt* (of a man) to escort or attend (a woman).—*n* **squir(e)´archy**, the rule of squires; squires as a body. [Shortened from **esquire**.]

squirm [skwûrm] *vi* to writhe; to go writhing; to feel or show distress. [Prob imit.]

squirrel [skwir´ėl] *n* any of a family (Sciuridae) of rodents, of arboreal habit, which have a bushy tail and strong hind legs; the pelt of such an animal. [OFr *escurel*—Low L *scurellus*, dim of L *sciūrus*—Gr *skiouros*—*skia*, shade, *oura*, tail.]

squirt [skwûrt] *vt* to throw out liquid in a jet.—*vi* to spurt.—*n* an instrument for squirting; a jet; (*inf*) an insignificant person. [Cf Low Ger *swirtjen*.]

stab [stab] *vt* to wound or pierce with a pointed weapon; to pain suddenly and deeply; to injure secretly, or by slander; to aim (at).—Also *vi*.—*pr p* **stabb´ing**; *pt; pt p* **stabbed**.—*n* an act of stabbing; a wound, as with a pointed weapon; a sharp pain; an attempt.—*n* **stabb´er**.—**stab in the back**, to injure in a treacherous manner. [Perh variant of *stob*, a stake.]

stable[1] [stā´bl] *adj* standing firm; firmly established; durable; firm in purpose or character, constant; not decomposing readily; not radioactive (eg *stable isotopes*).—*ns* **stabil´ity**, state of being stable; steadiness; **stā´bleness**.—*vt* **stab´ilize**, to render stable or steady; to limit the fluctuations of; to maintain the stability of (as an airplane) by means of a stabilizer.—*ns* **stabilization** [stāb-il-īz-ā´sh(ȯ)n]; **stab´ilizer**, a substance added to another substance to prevent or retard an unwanted alteration; a gyroscope device to keep ships steady in a heavy sea; the fixed horizontal member of the tail assembly on an airplane. [Fr,—L *stabilis*—*stāre*, to stand.]

stable[2] [stā´bl] *n* a building for housing horses or cattle; a group of racehorses under one ownership; a group of athletes (as boxers) or performers under one management.—*vt* to put or keep in a stable.—*vi* to be accommodated in a stable or as in a stable.—*n* **stā´bling**, act of putting into a stable; accommodation for horses, etc.—**stablemate**. [OFr *estable*—L *stabulum*—*stāre*, to stand.]

staccato [stȧ-kä´tō, stäk-kä´to] *adj, adv* (*mus*) with each note detached. [It pt p of *staccare*, for *distaccare*, to separate.]

stack [stak] *n* a large neatly arranged pile of hay, straw, etc.; a group or cluster of chimneys or flues; a smokestack; (*pl*) a series of bookshelves; a computer memory consisting of arrays of stacked memory elements.—*vt* to pile into a stack; to arrange (cards) for cheating.—**stack up**, to stand in comparison (with or against); **stackup**, an arrangement of aircraft awaiting their turn to land. [ON *stakkr*, a stack of hay.]

stadium [stā´di-ŭm] *n* a Greek measure of length, 600 Greek, or 606 3/4 English, feet; a large structure for football, baseball, etc. surrounded by tiers of seats.—*pl* **stā´dia**. [L,—Gr *stadion*.]

staff [stäf] *n* a stick carried in the hand as a symbol of authority; (*pl* **stāves**); a prop; a pole; a flagstaff; the long handle of an instrument; a stick or ensign of authority; lines and spaces on which music is written or printed; (*pl* **stāves**); a body of officers who help a commanding officer, or perform special duties; a body of persons employed in an establishment—business, professional, or domestic;—*pl* **staffs**.—*vt* to provide with a staff.—*ns* **staff´-off´icer**, a commissioned officer assigned to a military commander's staff; **staff´ ser´geant**, a noncommissioned officer ranking in the army above a sergeant and below a platoon sergeant or sergeant first class, in the air force above a sergeant and below a technical sergeant, and in the marine corps above a sergeant and below a gunnery sergeant.—**staff of life**, staple food, esp bread. [OE *stæf*; ON *stafr*, Ger *stab*.]

stag [stag] *n* a full-grown male deer.—*adj* for men only.—*adv* unaccompanied by a woman.—*ns* **stag´ beetle**, any of a family (Lucanidae) of beetles, the males of which have large antler-like mandibles; **stag´hound**, a hound formerly used in hunting deer; **stag´-party**, a party without women. [OE *stagga*; cf ON *steggr*, cock-bird, gander.]

stage [stāj] *n* an elevated platform, esp for acting on; the theater, theatrical representation, the theatrical calling (*with* **the**); any field of action, scene; a place of rest on a journey or road; the portion of a journey between two such places; a point reached in, or a section of, life, development, or any process; a subdivision of a geological series or formation; a stagecoach.—*vt* to represent, or to put, on the stage; to organize and bring off.—*ns* **stage´coach**, a coach that ran regularly with passengers from stage to stage; **stage´craft**, skill in, knowledge of, the technicalities of the dramatist's and of the actor's art; **stage´ direction**, in a copy of a play, an instruction to the actor to do this or that; **stage´ fright**, nervousness before an audience, **stage´ hand**, a stage worker who looks after scenery, etc.; **stage´ man´ager**, one who superintends the production of plays, with general charge behind the curtain.—*vt* **stage´man´age**, to arrange or exhibit so as to achieve a desired effect; to arrange and direct from behind the scenes; to act as stage manager; **stā´ger**, one long engaged in any occupation.—*adj* **stage´struck**, intensely eager to become an actor or actress.—*ns* **stage´ whis´per**, audible utterance conventionally understood by the audience to represent a whisper; a loud whisper meant to be heard by people other than the person addressed; **stā´ging**, a scaffold-like structure, eg for workmen; putting on the stage.—*adj* **stagy, stagey**, [stā´ji] theatrical, artificial, melodramatic.—*n* **stā´giness**. [OFr *estage*, a storey of a house, through LL from L *stāre*, to stand.]

stagger [stag´ėr] *vi* to reel; to go reeling or tottering; to waver.—*vt* to cause to reel; to give a shock to; to nonplus, confound; to cause to waver; to arrange on each side of a line, at equal distances and symmetrically, or otherwise; to arrange (opening of businesses, hours of work, etc.) so that sets of workers alternate with each other on the job, or are free at different times.—*n* a staggering; a wavering; a staggered arrangement; (in *pl* form, often trated as *sing*) giddiness—also a disease of various kinds causing horses, etc., to stagger.—*adj* **stagg´ering**, disconcerting, overwhelming.—*adv* **stagg´eringly**. [ON *stakra*, to push, freq of *staka*, to push.]

stagnant [stag´nȧnt] *adj* not flowing, motionless; impure through lack of inflow and outflow; inactive, dull.—*ns* **stag´nancy, stagnā´tion**.—*adv* **stag´nantly**.—*vi* **stag´nate**, to be, or become, stagnant; to exist, pass one's time, in dullness and inactivity. [L *stagnans, -antis*, pr p of *stagnāre*—*stagnum*, a pool, swamp.]

staid [stād] *adj* steady, sober, grave; sedate.—*adv* **staid´ly**.—*n* **staid´ness**. [Archaic pt p of **stay**.]

stain [stān] *vt* to impart a new color to with a dye; to tinge, to discolor, spot, sully; in microscopy, to impregnate (plant or animal material) with a substance that colors some parts, so as to pick out certain tissue elements, or to make transparent tissues visible, etc.—*vi* to take or impart a stain.—*n* a dye or coloring matter; a discoloration, a spot; taint of guilt; cause of reproach or shame.—*adj* **stain´less**, free from stain; not liable to stain, rust, or tarnish.—**stained glass**, glass with certain pigments fused into its surface; **stain´less steel**, an alloy of steel and another element, usu. nickel, that does not corrode easily. [Short for *distain* (*arch* and *obs*), to take away the color; through OFr—L *dis-*, private, *tingĕre*, to color.]

stair [stār] *n* a series of steps from landing to landing; one of such steps.—*ns* **stair´case**, the structure enclosing a stair; stairs with banisters, etc.; **stair´way**, one or more flights of stairs usu. with landings to pass from one level to another.—**below stairs**, among the servants. [OE *stǣger*—*stīgan*, to ascend.]

stake[1] [stāk] *n* a strong stick pointed at one end; one of the upright pieces of a fence; a post to which one condemned to be burned was tied, hence, death or martyrdom by burning.—*vt* to fasten to or with, to protect, shut, support with, a stake or stakes; to mark the bounds of with stakes.—**stake a claim (for, to)**, to intimate one's right or desire to possess. [OE *staca*, a stake.]

stake[2] [stāk] *vt* to bet, hazard; (*inf*) to furnish with money or resources.—*n* anything pledged as a wager; anything to gain or lose; (often *pl*) money risked as in a wager; (often *pl*) the winner's prize in a race, etc.—**at stake**, hazarded, in danger, at issue. [Perh Middle Du *staken*, to place.]

Stakhanovite [stȧ-kan´ō-vīt] *n* a Soviet industrial worker who has received recognition for his part in increasing the rate of production in the factory, etc., where he works. [*Stakhanov*, a Russian worker.]

stalactite [sta-lak´tīt] *n* an icicle-like pendant of calcium carbonate (carbonate of lime), formed by evaporation of water percolating through limestone, as on a cave roof; the material it is composed of; anything of similar form.—*adj* **stalactit´ic**. [Gr *stalaktos* (adj)—*stalassein*, to drip.]

stalag [stä´läg, -läH] *n* a German prisoner-of-war camp for noncommissioned officers and enlisted men. [Ger,—*stamm*, base, *lager*, camp.]

stalagmite [sta-lag´mīt] *n* a deposit on the floor of a cavern, usually cylindrical or conical in form, caused by the dripping from the roof, or from a stalactite, of water holding calcium carbonate in solution.—*adj* **stalagmit´ic**, [Gr *stalagmos* (n), dropping—*stalassein*, to drip.]

stale[1] [stāl] *adj* altered for the worse by age; tainted; vapid or tasteless from age; having lost its novelty or piquancy through repetition, trite; out of condition.—*vti* to make or become stale.—*n* **stale´ness**. [Perh from the root *sta-*, as in **stand**.]

stale[2] [stāl] *n* urine of a domestic animal (as a horse).—*vi* to urinate, used chiefly of camels and horses. [Cf Du *stalle*, Ger *stall*, OFr vb *estaler*.]

stalemate [stāl´māt] *n* (*chess*) a situation in which the person to play, while not actually in check, cannot move without getting into check; a deadlock.—Also *vt*. [Anglo-Fr *estale*, with the addition of *mate* as in check*mate*.]

stalk[1] [stök] *n* the stem of a plant; the stem on which a flower or fruit grows; anything resembling the stem of a plant.—*adj* **stalk´less**, having no stalk. [Dim from the root of OE *stæla, stalu*, stalk.]

stalk[2] [stök] *vi* to stride stiffly or haughtily; to go after game, keeping under cover.—*vt* to approach under cover; to walk stiffly or haughtily over or through.—*n* an act of stalking; stalking gait.—*n* **stalk´er**.—*n* and *adj* **stalk´ing**.—*n* **stalk´ing-horse**, a horse, or substitute, behind which a sportsman hides while stalking game; a person, thing, or ostensible motive, used to divert attention from one's doings or real aims. [OE *(bi)stealcian*, frequentative of **steal**.]

stall[1] [stöl] *n* a compartment for one animal in a stable; a bench, table, booth, or stand, for display or sale of goods; a space marked off for parking a motor vehicle; a pew in a church; a small compartment; a stop, esp due to malfunction; a covering for a finger.—*vt* to put or keep in a stall; to bring to a standstill.—*vi* (of aircraft) to lose flying speed and so fall temporarily out of control; (of an engine) to stop owing to mired wheels or engine failure; to experience a stall in flying.—*adj* **stalled**, kept or fed in a stall; stopped.—*vt* **stall´-feed**, to feed and fatten in a stall or stable. [OE *stall, steall*; ON *stallr*, Ger *stall*.]

stall[2] [stöl] *vti* to play for time, avoid a decision or decisive action.—*n* (*inf*) any action used in stalling. [From obs *stale*, a decoy—root of **stall** (1).]

stallion [stal´yȯn] *n* a male horse, esp one kept for breeding. [OFr *estalon*—OHG *stal*, stall.]

stalwart [stöl´wȧrt] *adj* stout, sturdy; staunch, resolute.—*n* a resolute person.—*n* **stal´wartness**. [Orig Scot form (popularized by Sir Walter Scott) of *stalworth*—OE *stælwierthe*—*stǣl*, place, *wierthe*, worth.]

stamen [stā´mėn] *n* the pollen-producing part of a flower, consisting of anther and filament;—*pl* **stā´mens**.—*n pl* (generally treated as *sing*.) **stam´ina** [stam´-], constitutional strength; staying power.—*adjs* **stam´inal**, of stamens or stamina; **stam´inate**, having stamens but no carpels. [L *stāmen* (pl *stāmina*), a warp thread (upright in an old loom)—*stāre*, to stand.]

stammer [stam´ėr] *vi* to falter in speaking; to stutter.—*vt* to utter falteringly or with a stutter.—*n* hesitation in speech; a stammering mode of utterance.—*n* **stamm´erer**.—*adv* **stamm´eringly**. [OE *stamerian*; Du *stameren*.]

stamp [stamp] *vt* to trample; to bring (the foot) forcibly down; to impress, imprint, or cut with a downward blow, as with a die or cutter; to mint, make, shape, by such a blow; to fix or mark deeply; to affix an adhesive stamp to; to characterize.—*vi* to step or set down the foot forcibly and noisily.—*n* the act of stamping; an impression; a stamped device, mark, imprint; an adhesive paper with a device used to show that a fee, as for postage, has been paid; any similar seal; kind, form, character; distinguishing mark, imprint, sign, evidence; an instrument or machine for stamping.—*ns* **stamp´er**, a worker who performs an industrial stamping operation; an implement for pounding or stamping; a stamping machine; **stamping ground**, (*inf*) an animal's or person's usual place of resort.—**stamp out**, to crush by treading on forcibly; to suppress, or put down. [From an inferred OE *stampian*, from the same root as OE *stempan*; Ger *stampfen*.]

stampede [stam-pēd´] *n* a sudden rush of a panic-stricken herd; any impulsive action of a large number of people; an extended festival combining a rodeo with exhibitions, contests, and social events.—*vi* to rush in a stampede.—*vt* to send rushing into a stampede. [Sp *estampido*, a crash—*estampar*, to stamp.]

stance [stans] *n* manner of standing, esp the placement of the feet; the attitude taken in a given situation. [Fr *stance*, now meaning only 'stanza'.]

stanch [stän(t)sh], **staunch** [stön(t)sh] *vt* to stop the flow of, as blood; to allay.—*vi* to cease to flow. [OFr *estanchier*, perh—L *stagnāre*, to be or make stagnant.]

stanch *See* **staunch**.

stanchion [stan´sh(ȯ)n] *n* an upright iron bar of a window or screen; a device to confine a cow. [OFr *estançon*—*estance*, prop—L *stāre*, to stand.]

stand [stand] *vi* to be, become, or remain, upright, erect, rigid, or still; to be on, or rise to one's feet; to be supported on a base, pedestal, etc.; to have a (specified) height when standing; to gather and remain, as water; to make resistance; to halt or be stationary; to have or take a position; to be or remain; to be set or situated; to come from a specified direction; to endure, continue; to hold good.—*vt* to set upright; to endure, bear, tolerate; to endure the presence of (a person); to withstand; to undergo.—*pt, pt p* **stood**.—*n* an act, manner, or place, of standing; a taking up of a position for resistance; resistance; a standing position; a standstill; a post, station; a place for vehicles awaiting hire; (*pl*) an erection for spectators; the place taken by a witness for testifying in court; a base or structure for setting things on; a piece of furniture for hanging things from; a stop on tour to give one or more theatrical performances, or the place where it is made; a small often open-air structure for a small retail business; a group of plants, esp trees, growing in a continuous area.—*ns* **stand´by**, that which, or one whom, one relies on or readily resorts to; **stand´-in**, a temporary substitute.—*adj* **stand´ing**, erect, on one's feet; established, accepted (eg *a standing rule, objection, joke*); permanent (eg *standing army*); stagnant.—*n* status or reputation; derivation of position or condition; a place to stand in.—*n pl* **stand´ing or´der**, an instruction in force until specifically changed or cancelled, esp any of the rules governing parliamentary procedure.—*n* **stand´ing room**, room for standing without, a seat; esp for spectators or passengers.—*adj* **stand´off**, used for holding something at a distance from a surface; aloof, reserved—also **stand´off´ish**.—*ns* **stand´off´ishness; stand´point**, viewpoint; **stand´still**, a complete stop.—*adj* **stand´-up**, erect; done or taken in a standing position; of a fight, in earnest.—**stand by**, to stand close to; to adhere to, to abide by (eg a decision); to support; to hold oneself in readiness; **stand for**, to represent; (*inf*) to tolerate; **stand in with**, to be in a specially favored position with; **stand off**, to remain at a distance; to sail away from shore; to keep from advancing, repel; to put off, stall; **stand off and on**, to sail away from shore and then toward it; **stand one's ground**, to maintain one's position; **stand on one's own feet**, to manage one's own affairs unaided; **stand out**, to project, to be prominent; to refuse to comply or yield; **stand pat**, to play one's poker hand as it was dealt without drawing any cards; to oppose or resist change; **stand up**, to get to one's feet; (*inf*) to be clad (in); (*inf*) to fail to keep an appointment with; **stand up for**, to defend against attack or criticism; **stand up to**, to face boldly; to meet fairly and fully; **stand up with**, to be best man or maid or matron of honor at a wedding. [OE *standan*; Ger *stehen*; cf Gr *histanai*, to place, L *stāre*, to stand.]

standard [stand´ȧrd] *n* a flag, banner, etc., as an emblem of a military unit, etc., formerly used to mark a rallying point; a flag generally; the uppermost petal of a papilionaceous flower; that which stands or is fixed; an upright post, pillar; a standing shrub or tree not trained on an espalier or a wall; a basis of measurement, esp a specimen weight or measure preserved for reference; the legally fixed fineness of coinage metal, or weight of a new coin; a criterion; an established or accepted model; a definite level of excellence or adequacy required, aimed at, or possible.—*adj* serving as, or conforming to, a standard; growing as a standard.—*ns* **stand'ard-bear'er**, one who carries a standard or banner; the leader of a political party, movement, etc.; **stand'ard gauge**, a railroad gauge of 4 feet 8½ inches; **standard time**, the official civil time for any given region, the earth being divided into 24 time zones, one hour apart.—*vt* **stand'ardize**, to make, or keep, of uniform size, shape, etc.—*n* **standardizā'tion.—** **Standard English**, the form of English which has gained literary and cultural supremacy over the other dialects and is accepted by the users of the other dialects as the proper form of English. [OFr *estandart*; prob connected either with **extend** or with **stand**.]

stank [stangk] *pt* of **stink**.

stannary [stan'ăr-i] *n* a tin mining district in England.—*n* **stann'ate**, a salt of stannic acid.—*adjs* **stann'ic**, denoting a compound in which tin has a valency of 4; **stann'ous**, denoting a compound in which tin has a valency of 2 (eg *stannic chloride*, Sn Cl_4; *stannous chloride*, sn Cl_2); **stannif'erous**, tin-bearing. [L *stannum*, tin.]

stanza [stan'za] *n* a group of lines which form a division of a poem (following a definite pattern as regards lengths of line, accentuation, and rhyme scheme).—*adj* **stanzā'ic**. [It *stanza*, a stop—L *stāre*, stand.]

staple[1] [stā'pl] *n* a leading commodity of trade or industry, main element (eg of diet, reading, conversation); wool or other raw material; textile fiber or its length or quality.—*adj* constituting a staple; leading, main.—*vt* to grade according to staple; one who grades and deals in wool. [OFr *estaple*—Low Ger *stapel*, a heap, mart.]

staple[2] [stā'pl] *n* a bent rod or wire, both ends of which are driven into a wall, post, etc., to form a fastening or through papers as a binding.—*vt* to fasten with a staple. [OE *stapol*, a prop.]

star [stär] *n* any one of the heavenly bodies, esp of those visible by night whose places in the firmament are relatively fixed, sometimes (*loosely*) including planets, comets, meteors, less commonly the sun and moon, or even the earth; a planet as a supposed influence, hence (usu. in *pl*) one's luck or destiny; an object or figure with pointed rays, most commonly five; a representation of a star worn as a badge of rank or honor; (*print*) an asterisk (*); a preeminent or exceptionally brilliant person; a leading performer, or one supposed to draw the public.—*adj* of stars; marked by a star; leading, preeminent, brilliant.—*vt* to mark with a star; to set with stars, to bespangle; to make a star of; (*inf*) to have (a specified person) as a star performer.—*vi* to shine, as a star; to appear as a star performer;—*pr p* **starr'ing**; *pt, pt p* **starred**.—*ns* **star'dom**, the state of being, the status of, a star or leading performer on stage or screen; **star'dust**, cosmic dust, meteoric matter in fine particles; distant stars seen like dust grains; **star'fish**, a class of invertebrate marine animals (class Asteroida) so named because the body consists of a central disk, from which the arms, most commonly five in number, radiate; **star'gāz'er**, an astrologer; an astronomer; any of several marine fish (family Uranoscopidae) with the eyes on top of the head; **star'gaz'ing**, act or practice of being a stargazer; absorption in impractical ideas; quality or state of being absentminded; **star' shell**, a shell that explodes high in the air scattering burning chemicals to illuminate the scene.—*adj* **star'less**, having no stars visible; having no light from stars.—*n* **star'light**, light from the stars.—*adj* **star'lit**, lighted by the stars.—*n* **star'-of-Beth'lehem**, a bulbous herb (genus *Ornithogalum*) of the lily family, with starlike flowers.—*adjs* **starred**, adorned or studded with stars; marked with a star, as specially distinguished; **starr'y**, abounding or adorned with stars; consisting of, or proceeding from, the stars; like, or shining like, the stars; **starr'y-eyed**, innocently idealistic; out of touch with reality; radiantly happy.—*n* **starr'iness**.—*adj* **star'-spang'led**, spangled or studded with stars.—**Stars and Bars**, the first flag of the Confederate States of America having three bars of red, white, and red and a blue union with white stars in a circle.—**Stars and Stripes**, the flag of the United States of America, with thirteen horizontal stripes alternately red and white, and a blue field containing as many white stars as there are states; **Star-Spangled Banner**, the US flag; the US national anthem. [OE *steorra*; Ger *stern*, L *stella* (for *sterula*), Gr *astēr*.]

starboard [stär'bȯ(r)d, -bōrd] *n* the right side of a ship or aircraft looking forward, when one is looking towards the bow.—*adj* of, to, towards, on, the right side of a ship. [OE *stēorbord*—*stēor*, steering, *bord*, a board, the side of a ship.]

starch [stärch] *n* a white, tasteless, odorless food substance found in potatoes, cereal, etc., chemically a carbohydrate, used in the laundry as a stiffener; stiffness, formality.—*vt* to stiffen with starch.—*adj* **starched**, stiffened with starch; stiff, formal.—*adj* **starch'y**, of, or like, starch; stiff, precise.—*n* **star'chiness**. [OE *stercan*, to stiffen (inferred from *stercedferhth*, stiff-spirited); cf **stark**.]

star-chamber [stär' chām'bėr] *adj* marked by secrecy and often arbitrary and oppressive. [Prob named from the gilt stars on the ceiling of the Star Chamber, an English court.]

stare [stār] *vi* to look with a fixed gaze, as in horror, astonishment, etc.; to glare; to be insistently or obtrusively conspicuous, or obvious to (eg *to stare one in the face*).—*vt* to look fixedly at.—*n* a fixed look.—*n* **stā'rer**. [OE *starian*, from a Gmc root seen in Ger *starr*, rigid; also in Eng **stern**.]

stark [stärk] *adj* stiff, as a corpse; sharply outlined; bleak; downright.—*adv* utterly.—*adv* **stark'ly**.—*n* **stark'ness**. [OE *stearc*, hard, strong, cog with ON *sterkr*, Ger *stark*.]

starling [stär'ling] *n* any of a family (Sturnidae) of usu. dark gregarious birds, esp the common starling (*Sturnis vulgaris*) with iridescent summer plumage, naturalized in N America. [OE *stærling*, dim of *stær*, a starling.]

start [stärt] *vi* to shoot, dart, move, suddenly forth or out; to spring up or forward; to break away, become displaced; to make a sudden involuntary movement, as of surprise or becoming aware; to begin; to set forth on a journey, race, career.—*vt* to begin; to set going; to set on foot; to set up (eg in business); to drive from lair or hiding place; to cause, or to undergo, displacement or loosening of (eg of tooth, a nail, a bolt, timbers).—*n* a sudden involuntary motion of the body; a startled feeling; a spurt; an outburst or fit; a beginning of movement, esp of a journey, race, or career; a beginning; a setting in motion; a help in, or opportunity of, beginning; an advantage in being early or ahead; the extent of such an advantage in time or distance.—*ns* **start'er**, one who, or which, sets out on a race or journey; one who gives the signal to begin a race or game; that which sets machinery in motion; material containing micro-organisms used to induce a desired fermentation; something that is the beginning of a process, activity, or series, esp an appetizer.—*n* **start-up**, act or instance of setting in operation or motion. [ME *sterten*; closely akin to Du *storten*, to plunge, Ger *stürzen*.]

startle [stärt'l] *vi* to start, to feel sudden alarm.—*vt* to cause (a person) surprise mingled with alarm, outrage to sense of propriety or fitness, or similar emotion; to cause (a person) to start with surprise and alarm. [OE *steartlian*, to stumble, struggle, kick; or from **start**.]

starve [stärv] *vi* to die of hunger; to suffer extreme hunger; to be in want; to feel a great longing (for).—*vt* to cause to starve; to force (into) by want of food; to deprive (of) anything needful.—*n* **starvā'tion**.—*adj* **starving**.—*n* **starve'ling**, a thin, weak, pining person or animal. [OE *steorfan*, to die; Du *sterven*, Ger *sterben*, to die.]

stasis [stas'is] *n* stoppage, esp of blood circulation or of the contents of the bowels. [Gr.]

state [stāt] *n* condition; circumstances at any time; a phase or stage; station in life; high station; pomp, display, ceremonial dignity; an estate, order, or class in society or the body politic; the civil power; **State**, a body of people politically organized and independent; **State**, any of the members of a federation as in the US; the territory of such.—*adj* of, belonging to, relating to, the state or State; public; ceremonial.—*vt* to set forth, express the details of; to set down fully and formally; to assert, affirm; to fix, settle.—*ns* **state' aid**, public monies appropriated by a state government for the support of a public local institution; **state'craft**, the art of managing state affairs.—*adjs* **stāt'ed**, settled, fixed, regular; **stāte'ly**, showing state or dignity; majestic, very impressive.—*ns* **State'house**, the building in which the legislature of a State meets; **state'liness; state'ment**, the act of stating; that which is stated; a formal account; a financial record; **state'room**, a private cabin on a ship; a private room in a train; **states'man**, one skilled, wise, and experienced in government.—*adj* **states'manlike**, befitting a statesman—judicious, sagacious.—*ns* **states'manship; states' rights**, all rights not vested by the Constitution of the US in the Federal government nor forbidden by it to the separate States.—**State Department**, the US executive branch dealing with foreign affairs headed by a member of the cabinet; **lie in state**, of a corpse, to be laid out in a place of honor before being buried; **the States**, the United States. [L *status, -ūs—stāre, statum*, to stand; partly through OFr.]

static [stat'ik] *adj* pertaining to statics; pertaining to bodies, forces, charges, etc., in equilibrium; stationary; stable; acting by mere weight.—*n* statics; atmospheric disturbances causing noise on radio or TV; (*slang*) adverse criticism.—*n* **stat'ics**, the science of forces in equilibrium among material bodies. [Gr *statikē* (fem of adj), bringing to a standstill—*histanai*, to cause to stand.]

station [stā'sh(ȯ)n] *n* the place or building where one stands or is located; a standing place, fixed stopping place as on a bus line or railroad; a local office, headquarters, or depôt (eg *police station*); one of a series, esp one of (usu.) fourteen representative of stages in Christ's way to Calvary, disposed around a Roman Catholic church interior or elsewhere; an assigned place or post; a place for specialized observation and study of scientific phenomenon; an Australian stock farm; position in life, or in the scale of nature; exalted position or status.—*adj* of a station.—*vt* to assign a station to; to appoint to a post, place, of office.—*adj* **stā'tionary**, standing, not moving; fixed; permanently located.—*ns* **sta'tioner**, a dealer in stationery, office supplies, etc.; **stā'tionery**, writing materials, esp paper and envelopes; **stā'tionmas'ter**, one in charge of a railroad station; **station wagon**, an automobile with folding or removable rear seats and a back end that opens. [Fr,—L *statiō, -ōnis—stāre*, to stand.]

statist [stā'tist] *n* an advocate of statism.—*n* **statism**, concentration of all economic power in the hands of a highly centralized government.—*n* **statis'tic**, a single term in a collection of statistics; an estimate compiled from a sample; a random variable; (*pl*) numerical data assembled and classified so as to yield significant information; the science of compiling such data.—*adj* **statist´ical**, of, concerned with, of the nature of, statistics.—*adv* **statist´ically**.—*n* **statistician** [stat-is-tish´ȧn] one skilled in statistics; a compiler or student of statistics. [It *statista* and Ger *statistik*—L *status*, state.]

stator [stā´tȯr] *n* a stationary part within which a part rotates, as the fixed part of an electrical machine. [L *stātor*, stander.]

statue [stat´ū] *n* a representation of a human or animal form in the round.—*adj* **stat´ūary**, of, or suitable for, sculpture; sculptured.—*n* statues collectively.—*adj* **statuesque** [statū-esk´]; like a statue.—*adv* **statuesquely**.—*n* **statuette´**, a small statue, figurine. [L *statua*—*statuĕre*, to cause to stand—*stāre*.]

stature [stat´yu̇r] *n* the standing height of the body; level of attainment.—*adj* **stat´ured**, of a specified stature (eg *low statured*). [L *statūra*.]

status [stā´tus] *n* social position; standing in profession, in society, or in any organization of persons; condition, description from the point of view of the law, determining capacity to sue, etc.; position of affairs.—**status quo**, the state, condition of affairs, existing before a certain event, date. [L *stătus*.]

statute [stat´ūt] *n* a law enacted by a legislature; an established rule or law; the act of a corporation or its founder, intended as a permanent rule or law; an international instrument setting up an agency and regulating its authority.—*adj* **stat´ūtable**, prescribed, permitted, recognized by, or according to, statute.—*n* **stat´ute book**, (usu. *pl*) the whole body of statutes or enacted laws.—*adj* **stat´ūtory**, enacted by statute; required by statute; depending on statute for its authority.—**statute of limitations**, a statute limiting the time for legal action. [L *statūtum*, that which is set up—*statuĕre*.]

staunch [stönch, stanch], **stanch** [stanch, -sh] *adj* seaworthy; firm in principle; trusty, constant, zealous. [OFr *estanche*—*estanchier*. See **stanch** (1).]

stave [stāv] *n* one of the shaped side pieces of a cask or barrel; a staff, rod, bar, shaft; (*mus*) a staff; a stanza, verse of a song.—*vt* to break a stave or the staves of, to break, to burst (often with *in*); to drive (off), keep at bay, as with a staff; to delay (eg *to stave off the evil day*); to put together, or repair, with staves.—*pt, pt p* **stāved** or **stōve**. [By-form of **staff**.]

staves [stāvz] *pl* of **staff** and of **stave**.

stay [stā] *n* a rope supporting a mast; a guy; a prop, support; a brace, connecting piece to resist tension; a strip of stiffening material used in a corset, shirt collar, etc.; a stopping, bringing or coming to a standstill; a suspension of legal proceedings; delay; a sojourn; staying power.—*vt* to support or incline with a stay or stays; to support, prop, sustain; to endure; to endure to the end; to stop; to detain; to hold, restrain, check the action of; to allay; (*obs*) to await.—*vi* to stop; to remain, to tarry; to wait (for); to sojourn; to dwell; to hold out, last, endure.—*pt, pt p* **stayed**, (*arch*) **staid** (see **staid**, *adj*).—*ns* **stay´er**, one who, or that which, stops, or that holds or supports; **stay´ing power**, ability to go on long without flagging; **staysail** [stā´sl], a sail extended on a stay; **stay put**, (*inf*) to remain in the same place or unchanged. [Partly OE *stæg*, stay (rope); partly OFr *estayer*, to prop, from the same Gmc root; partly OFr *ester*—*stāre*, to stand.]

stead [sted] *n* the place which another had, or might have; service, advantage.—*vt* to avail, help.—*pt, pt p* **stead´ed, stead** [sted].—*n* **stead´ing**, a small farm.—**stand one in good stead**, prove of good service to one in time of need. [OE *stede*, place; cf Ger *stadt*, town, *statt*, place.]

steadfast [sted´fast] *adj* firmly fixed or established; firm, constant, resolute.—*adv* **stead´fastly**.—*n* **stead´fastness**. [OE *stedefæst*—*stede*, a place (see **stead**, *fæst*, firm.]

steady [sted´i] *adj* (*comparative* **stead´ier**, *superlative* **stead´iest**) firm in standing or in place; stable; unshaking, unfaltering; constant, consistent (eg *a steady supporter*); regular (eg *steady work*); uniform (eg *steady flow*); sober, industrious.—*vt* to make steady, to make or keep firm.—*pr p* **stead´ying**; *pt, pt p* **stead´ied**.—*n* (*inf*) a regular boy friend or girl friend.—*adv* **stead´ily**.—*n* **stead´iness**.—**go steady**, (*inf*) to be sweethearts; **steady-state theory**, a theory that as the universe is expanding new matter is continuously being created. [**stead** + suffx *-y*.]

steak [stāk] *n* a slice of meat, esp beef or fish, for broiling or frying; ground meat prepared for cooking in the manner of a steak. [ON *steik; steikja*, to roast on a spit.]

steal [stēl] *vt* to take by theft, esp secretly; to take, gain, or win, by address, by contrivance, unexpectedly, insidiously, or gradually; to take (a look, etc.) slyly; to move, put, etc., stealthily (in, from, etc.); (*baseball*) to gain (a base) as by running to it from another base while a pitch is being delivered.—*vi* to practice theft; to take feloniously; to pass quietly, unobtrusively, gradually, or surreptitiously.—*pt* **stōle**; *pt p* **stōl´en**.—*n inf* an extraordinary bargain.—*n* **steal´er.**—**steal a march on**, to gain an advantage over unperceived; **steal one's thunder**, (*inf*) to grab attention from another by anticipating an idea, plan, etc.; to claim credit for another's idea. [OE *stelan*; Ger *stehlen*, Du *stelen*.]

stealth [stelth] *n* secret procedure or manner, furtiveness.—*adj* **stealth´y**, acting, or acted, with stealth, furtive.—*n* **stealth´iness**.—*adv* **stealth´ily**. [**steal**.]

steam [stēm] *n* the vapor into which water is converted by boiling; the condensation of this vapor; the power of steam under pressure; (inf) energy, force, spirit.—*vi* to rise or pass off in steam or vapor; to become covered with condensed vapor; to move by steam power.—*vt* to expose to steam; to cook by means of steam.—*ns* **steam´ boil´er**, a boiler for generating steam; **steam´ chest**, a chamber from which steam is distributed to a cylinder of a steam engine; **steam´er**, a ship propelled by steam, a steamship; an engine or machine worked by steam; a cooking vessel in which things are steamed; a soft-shell clam; **steam´ iron**, an electric iron having a compartment in which water is heated to provide steam; **steam´roll´er**, a heavy, steam-driven roller used in building roads, etc.; a crushing force, esp when ruthlessly used to overcome opposition.—*vti* to move, crush, override, etc., as (with) a steamroller.—*ns* **steam´ship**, a ship driven by steam power;—*n* **steam shovel**, a large, mechanically-operated digger, powered by steam.—*adj* **steam´y**, of, like, full of, covered with, as if covered with, emitting steam; (*inf*) erotic.—*n* **steam´iness.**—**steamed up**, (*inf*) indignant; **let off steam**, to release steam into the atmosphere; to work off energy, or to give vent to anger or annoyance; **under one's own steam**, by one's own unaided efforts. [OE *stēam*; Du *stoom*.]

stearin [stē´a-rin] *n* an ester of stearic acid, being a white crystalline solid found in many vegetable and animal fats, esp hard fats; (also **stearine**) the solid part of any fat; (also **stearine**) a mixture of stearic acid and other fatty acids.—**stearic acid**, a fatty acid. [Gr *stĕār*, gen *stĕātos*, suet.]

steatite [stē´a-tīt] *n* a coarse, massive, or granular variety of talc, soft and greasy to the touch. [Gr *steatitēs*—*stĕār*, gen *stĕātos*, suet.]

stedfast *see* **steadfast**.

steed [stēd] *n* a horse, esp a spirited horse. [OE *stēda*, stallion; cf OE *stōd*, stud.]

steel [stēl] *n* iron containing a little carbon, with or without other substances; a cutting tool or weapon; an instrument, object, or part, made of steel, eg a steel knife sharpener, a skate; a piece of steel as for stiffening a corset, striking fire from a flint; extreme hardness, staying power, trustworthiness; (*pl*) shares of stock in steel companies.—*adj* of, or like, steel.—*vt* to cover or edge with steel; to harden, make obdurate; to nerve (oneself).—*ns* **steel band**, a percussion band, beating on steel oil drums; **steel´ engrav´ing**, engraving on steel plates; an impression or print so obtained; **steel wool**, long, thin, shavings of steel used for scouring, smoothing, and polishing.—*adj* **steel´y**, of, or like, steel. [OE *stēle* (WS *stīele*); Ger *stahl*.]

steelyard [stēl´yärd] *n* a weighing machine consisting of a metal arm suspended from above in which a single weight is moved along a graduated scale on a beam. [From the *Steelyard* or *Stālhof* (Low Ger 'sample yard'—*stāl*, sample), the headquarters of Hanseatic traders in London.]

steep[1] [stēp] *adj* rising or descending with great inclination, precipitous, headlong; (*inf*) excessive, exorbitant.—*n* a precipitous place.—*vti* **steep´en**, to make or become steep.—*n* **steep´ness**.—*adv* **steep´ly**. [OE *stēap*; cf **stoop**.]

steep[2] [stēp] *vt* to dip or soak in a liquid; to wet thoroughly; to saturate; to imbue.—*vi* to undergo soaking or thorough wetting.—*n* a soaking process; a liquid, for steeping anything in.—*n* **steep´er**, a vessel in which articles are steeped. [ME *stepen*; perh conn with **stoup**.]

steeple [stēp´l] *n* a tower of a church or other building, with or without, including or excluding, a spire; the spire alone.—*adj* **steep´led**, having a steeple or steeples, or appearance of steeples.—*ns* **steep´lechase**, a horse-race over a course with obstacles; a race of like kind on foot (as over hurdles); (*inf*) a course of action obstructed by obstacles; **steep´lejack**, one who builds or repairs steeples, smokestacks, etc. [OE *stēpel*, *stȳpel*; from root of *stēap*, steep.]

steer[1] [stēr] *n* a castrated male of the cattle family; (*loosely*) any male of beef cattle. [OE *stēor*; Ger *stier*.]

steer[2] [stēr] *vt* to direct with, or as with, the helm; to guide; to direct (one's course).—*vi* to direct a ship, cycle, etc., in its course; to be directed or guided; to move (for, toward).—*n* **steer´age**, act or practice of steering; formerly, a section in a ship occupied by passengers paying the lowest fare.—Also *adj*.—*ns* **steer´ageway**, sufficient rate of progress to bring a vessel under the control of the helm; **steer´ing wheel**, a handwheel by means of which one steers; **steers´man**, one who steers a ship.—**steering committee**, a group of members of the majority party in a legislative assembly who decide what measures shall be brought forward and in what order. [OE *stēoran*, *stȳran*, to steer.]

stele [stē´lē] *n* the central vascular portion of the axis of a vascular plant.—*pl* **stē´lae** [-ē]. [Gr *stēlē*—*histanai*, to set, stand.]

stellar [stel´ȧr] *adj* of the stars; of the nature of a star; composed of stars; relating to a theatrical or film star; chief; excellent.—*adj* **stell´āte**, resembling a star (as in shape). [L *stellāris*—*stella*, a star.]

stem[1] [stem] *n* the leaf-bearing axis of a plant, a stalk, anything like a stalk, as the upright slender part of a note, of a wineglass, etc.; the main line (or sometimes a branch) of a family; the prow of a ship; the forepart of a ship; (*linguistics*) the base of a word, to which inflectional suffixes are added.—*vt* to provide with a stem; to deprive of stalk or stem; (of a ship) to make headway against, breast.—*vi* to grow a stem; to spring, take rise (from);—*pr p* **stemm´ing**; *pt, pt p* **stemmed**.—*adj* **stem´less**.—**from stem to stern**, from one end of a vessel to the other; completely, throughout. [OE *stefn*, *stemn*; Ger *stamm*; perh conn with **stand**.]

stem[2] [stem] *vt* to stop, check, to dam, to staunch; to tamp; to turn (skis) in stemming.—*vi* to become checked or staunched; to retard oneself by forcing the skis away from the line of progress.—*pr p* **stemm´ing**; *pt, pt p* **stemmed**. [ON *stemma*.]

stench [stench] *n* stink.—*adj* **stench´y**. [OE *stenc*, smell (good or bad); Ger *stank*.]

stencil [sten´s(i)l] *vti* to paint by brushing over a perforated plate or sheet; to make a stencil for producing copies of typewriting, etc.—*pr p* **sten´cilling**; *pt, pt p* **sten´cilled**.—*n* a thin sheet, as of paper, cut through so that when ink, paint, etc. is applied, designs, letters, etc., form on the surface underneath; a design, etc., so made.—*ns* **sten´ciler; sten´ciling**. [OFr *estinceller*, to spangle—*estincelle*—L *scintilla*, a spark.]

stenography [sten-og´rȧ-fi] *n* the art, or any method, of writing very quickly, shorthand.—*n* **stenog´rapher**.—*adj* **stenographic**. [Gr *stenos*, narrow, *graphein*, to write.]

stentorian [sten-tö´ri-ȧn] *adj* very loud or powerful, like the voice of *Stentor*, a herald celebrated by Homer.

step [step] *n* a pace; a movement of the leg in walking, running, or dancing; the distance so covered; a footstep; a footfall, a footprint; gait; a small space; a short journey; a degree; a degree of a scale; a stage upward or downward; one tread of a stair, rung of a ladder; a rest for the foot; a move towards an end or in the course of proceeding; coincidence in speed or phase; a support for the end of a mast, pivot, or the like.—*vi* to advance, retire, mount, or descend, by taking a step or steps; to pace; to walk; to walk slowly or gravely.—*vt* to perform by stepping; to measure by pacing; to arrange or shape stepwise; to place (the foot); to fix (a mast);—*pr p* **stepp´ing**; *pt, pt p* **stepped**.—*ns* **step´ dance**, a dance emphasizing steps rather than gesture or posture; **step´-in**, an article of clothing put on by being stepped into (as a shoe resembling a pump but having a higher, elasticized, vamp); (*pl*) a woman's short panties; **stepp´ing-stone**, a stone rising above water to afford a passage; a means to gradual progress.—*adj* **step´wise**, marked by or proceeding in steps; moving step by step to adjacent musical tones.—**step in**, or **into**, to enter easily or unexpectedly; **step out**, to go out a little way; to increase the length of the step and so the speed; to die; to lead an active social life; to be unfaithful; **step up**, to increase in intensity, amount, etc.; **step on it**, (*inf*) hurry, increase the speed; **in step**, with simultaneous putting forward of the right (or left) feet in marching, etc.; **out of step**, not in step; **keep step**, to continue in step. [OE (Mercian) *steppe* (WS *stæpe*); Du *stap*, Ger *stapfe*.]

step- [step-] in composition denotes the mutual relationship between children who, in consequence of a subsequent marriage, have only one parent in common (as **step´sister**) or between such children and the later husband or wife of the mother or father (as **step´mother, step´son**). [OE *stēop* (as in *stēopmōdor*), orig meaning orphan.]

steppe [step] *n* a vast generally treeless and uncultivated plain, as in the southeast of Europe and in Asia. [Russ *step*.]

stercoraceous [stėrk-ȯ-rā´shủs] *adj* of, of the nature of, dung. [L *stercus, -ŏris*, dung.]

stereo *See* **stereophonic**.

stereograph [ster´i-ō-gräf] *n* a pair of photographs for viewing in a stereoscope or special eyeglasses.—*n* **ste´reogram**, a stereograph; a diagram or picture giving an impression of solidity or relief.—*adjs* **stereograph´ic, -al**.—*adv* **stereograph´ically**.—*n* **stereog´raphy**, the art of showing solids on a plane. [Gr *stereos*, solid, *graphein*, to write.]

stereophonic [ster-i-ō-fon´ik] *adj* giving the effect of sound coming from different directions.—*n* **ster´eo**, a stereophonic record player, radio, system, etc.; a stereoscopic system, effect, picture, etc. [Gr *stereos*, solid, *phōnē*, sound.]

stereoscope [ster´i-ō-skōp] *n* an instrument by which the images of two pictures differing slightly in point of view are seen one by each eye and so give an effect of solidity.—*adv* **stereoscop´ically**, pertaining to the stereoscope; producing such an effect.—*n* **stereos´copy**. [Gr *stereos*, solid, *skopeein*, to look at.]

stereotype [ster´i-ō-tīp] *vt* a solid metallic plate for printing, cast from a mold (of papier-mâché or other substance) from movable types; the art, method, or process, of making such plates; a fixed conventionalized representation.—*adj* pertaining to, or done with, stereotypes.—*vt* to make a stereotype of; to print with stereotypes; to make in one unchangeable form.—*adj* **ste´reotyped**, fixed, unchangeable (eg patterns, opinions); conventionalized.—*n* **ste´reotyper**, one who makes stereotype plates for printing. [Gr *stereos*, solid + **type**.]

sterile [ster´īl] *adj* unfruitful, barren; not producing, or unable to produce, offspring, fruit, seeds, or spores; (of a flower) without pistils; sterilized; destitute of ideas or results; free from living microorganisms.—*vt* **ster´ilize**, to cause to be fruitless; to deprive of power of reproduction; to destroy microorganisms in.—*ns* **sterilīzā´tion; ster´ilizer**, anything which sterilizes; an apparatus for sterilizing objects by boiling water, steam, or dry heat; **steril´ity**, quality of being barren. [L *sterilis*, barren.]

sterling [stûr´ling] *n* sterling silver; British money of standard value.—*adj* of silver that is at least 92.5% pure; of standard British money; made of sterling silver; of thoroughly good character, thoroughly good.—**sterling area**, a group of countries with currencies tied to the British pound sterling. [Prob a coin with a star—OE *steorra*, a star.]

stern[1] [stûrn] *adj* severe of countenance, manner, or feeling—austere, harsh, unrelenting; rigorous.—*adv* **stern´ly**.—*n* **stern´ness**. [OE *styrne*.]

stern[2] [stûrn] *n* the hind part of a vessel; the rump or tail.—*n* **stern´ chase**, a chase in which one ship follows directly in the wake of another.—*adj* **stern´most**, farthest astern.—*ns* **stern´post**, the aftermost timber of a ship, supporting the rudder; **stern sheets**, the part of an open boat not occupied by the thwarts.—*advs* **stern´ward; stern´wards**, aft. [On *stjōrn*, a steering; cog with **steer** (2).]

sternum [stûr´num] *n* the breastbone.—*adj* **ster´nal**. [Gr *sternon*, chest.]

sternutation [stûr-nū-tā´sh(ȯ)n] *n* sneezing.—*n* **sternū´tator**, a substance that causes sneezing. [L *sternūtātiō, -ōnis—sternūtāre, -ātum*, inten of *sternuĕre*, to sneeze.]

stertorous [stûr´tȯ-rus] *adj* with a snoring sound.—*adv* **ster´torously**. [L *stertĕre*, to snore.]

stet [stet] *vt* to restore after marking for deletion;—*pr p* **stett´ing**; *pt, pt p* **stett´ed**. [L 'let it stand', 3rd sing pres subj of *stāre*, to stand; written on a proofsheet with dots under the words to be retained.]

stethoscope [steth´ō-skōp] *n* an instrument used in auscultation.—*adj* **stethoscop´ic** [-skop´ik]. [Gr *stēthos*, chest, *skopeein*, to look at, examine.]

stevadore [stēv´e-dör] *n* one who loads and unloads vessels. [Sp *estivador*, packer—*estivar*, to stow—L *stīpāre*, to press.]

stew [stū] *n* (*obs*) a utensil used for boiling; a hot bath; mental agitation; (*pl*) a brothel, or a prostitutes' quarter; a dish of stewed food, esp meat with vegetables.—*vt* to simmer or boil slowly.—*vi* to swelter; to undergo stewing; to be in a state of worry or agitation. [OFr *estuve*, stove; prob conn with *stove*.]

steward [stū´ärd] *n* one who manages the domestic concerns of a family or institution; one who superintends another's affairs, esp on an estate or farm; the manager of the provision department, or an attendant on passengers, in a ship, aircraft; one who actively directs affairs; a manager.—**stewardess**, a woman airline attendant.—*n* **stew´ardship**, office of a steward; management. [OE *stigweard—stig*, a hall (cog with **sty**), *weard*, a ward.]

stick[1] [stik] *vt* to pierce, transfix; to stab; to spear; to thrust; to fasten by piercing; to insert; to set in position; to set or cover (with things fastened on); to cause to adhere; to bring to a standstill; (*inf*) to put, set, etc.; (*inf*) to puzzle, baffle; (*slang*) to impose a burden, etc., upon; to defraud.—*vi* to be fixed by means of something inserted; to adhere; to become or remain fixed; to remain; to be detained by an impediment; to jam; to fail to proceed or advance; to hold fast, keep resolutely (to); to hesitate, scruple; to protrude or project (out, up, etc.);—*pt, pt p* **stuck**.—*ns* **stick´er**, one that pierces with a point; one that adheres or causes adhesion; an adhesive label; **stick´ing plas´ter**, an adhesive plaster for covering superficial wounds; **stick´-in-the-mud**, (*inf*) an absolutely unprogressive person.—*adj* **stick´y**, adhesive; tenacious; (*inf*) hot and humid; (*inf*) troublesome.—*n* **stick´iness**.—**stick around**, (*inf*) to wait about; **stick by**, to be firm in supporting, to adhere closely to; **stick out**, to project; to continue to resist; to endure, last; **stick to**, to adhere to; to persevere in; **stick up for** (*inf*), to speak or act in defense of; **stick with**, to remain with; **sticky end**, an unpleasant end, disaster; **sticky wicket**, a difficult or delicate problem or situation. [OE *stician*; cf **stick** (2).]

stick[2] [stik] *n* a small shoot or branch of a tree, broken or cut off; a walking stick; a piece of firewood; an instrument for beating a percussion instrument; an instrument for playing hockey or other game; a control rod of an airplane; anything in the form of a stick or rod; a support for a candle; a group of bombs, or of paratroops, released at one time from an airplane; a person of stiff or wooden manner; (*slang*) a marijuana cigarette.—**the sticks**, remote areas, backwoods. [OE *sticca*; ON *stika*.]

stickle [stik´l] *vi* to be scrupulous or obstinately punctilious.—*n* **stick´ler**, one who insists on scrupulous exactness, punctilious observance of rules, etc. (*with* **for**); (*inf*) something difficult to solve. [Prob ME *stightle*—OE *stihtan*, to set in order.]

stickleback [stik´l-bak] *n* any of a family (Gasterosteidae) of small spiny-backed freshwater fish of streams, the male of which builds a nest for the female's eggs. [OE *sticel*, sting, prick, + **back**.]

stiff [stif] *adj* not easily bent; rigid; wanting in suppleness; moved or moving with difficulty or friction; approaching solidity of joints and muscles, sore or limited in movement; harsh, severe (eg a stiff penalty); difficult, toilsome; stubborn, pertinaceous (eg *a stiff resistance*); strong (eg *a stiff breeeze*); potent, concentrated and strong (eg *a stiff drink*); (*inf*—of price) high; not natural and easy, constrained, formal.—*adv* stiffly; stark; (*inf*) extremely.—*n* (*slang*) a corpse; (*slang*) a tramp, bum; (*slang*) a laborer, hand; (*slang*) a flop, failure.—*vt* **stiff´en**, to make stiff.—*vi* to become stiff; to become less impressible or more obstinate.—*ns* **stiff´ener**, one who, or that which, stiffens; **stiff´ening**, something used to make a substance stiff.—*adv* **stiff´ly**.—*adj* **stiff´-necked**, obstinate, hard to move; haughty; formal and unnatural.—*n* **stiff´ness**. [OE *stīf*; stiff; Du *stijf*, Ger *steif*.]

stifle [stī´fl] *vt* to suffocate; to make breathing difficult for; to smother or extinguish; to suppress, hold back; to stop.—*vi* to suffocate.—*adj* **stī´fling**, impeding respiration, close, oppressive.

stigma [stig´ma] *n* a brand, a mark of infamy; any special mark; a place on the skin which bleeds periodically; the part of a carpel that receives pollen;—*pl* **stig´mas**, or **stig´mata**.—*n pl* **stig´mata**, the marks of the wounds on Christ's body, or marks resembling them claimed to have been miraculously impressed on the bodies of certain persons, as Francis of Assisi in 1224.—*adj* **stig´matic**, having or conveying a social stigma; of or relating to supernatural stigma; of a bundle of light rays intersecting at a single point.—*n* one marked with stigmata.—*adv* **stigmat´ically**.—*vt* **stig´matize**, to mark with a stigma or with stigmata; to describe abusively (as). [Gr *stigma, -atos*, tattoomark, brand, *stigmē*, a point.]

stilbestrol [stil-bes´trōl] *n* a synthetic estrogen.

stile[1] [stīl] *n* a step, or set of steps, for climbing over a wall or fence. [OE *stigel*; cf OE *stīgan*, Ger *steigen*, to mount.]

stile[2] [stīl] *n* an upright member in framing or panelling. [Origin uncertain.]

stiletto [sti-let´ō] *n* a dagger with a narrow blade; a pointed instrument for making holes for eyelets or embroidery.—*pl* **stilett´os**. [It, dim of *stilo*, a dagger—L *stilus*, a stake.]

still[1] [stil] *adj* motionless; silent; calm; not carbonated; designating or of a single photograph taken from a motion-picture film.—*vti* to make or become still.—*adv* at or up to the present time or time in question; nevertheless, for all that; yet, even.—*n* calm; a still photograph.—*conj* nevertheless, yet.—*n* **still´birth**, birth of a stillborn fetus.—*adj* **still´born**, dead when born.—*ns* **still´life**, a picture representing inanimate objects; *pl* **still lifes; still´ness**, silence; calm.—*adj* **still´y**, still, quiet, calm. [OE *stille*, quiet, calm. stable; Du *stil*, Ger *still*.]

still[2] [stil] *vt* to distill.—*n* an apparatus for distilling liquids.—*n* **still´room**, (*Brit*) a room where liquors, preserves, and the like are kept, and where tea, etc., is prepared for the table, a housekeeper's pantry. [From **distil**.]

stilt [stilt] *n* one of a pair of poles with a rest for the foot, mounted on which one can walk, as in play; any of a number of long posts used to hold a building, etc., above the ground or out of the water.—*vt* to raise on stilts.—*adj* **stilt´ed**, stiff and pompous. [ME *stilte*; cf Du *stelt*, Ger *stelze*.]

Stilton [stil´tȯn] *n* a semihard, double cream, inoculated blue-mold cheese made from cow's milk. [*Stilton* in Huntingdonshire, England.]

stimulant [stim´ū-lȧnt] *adj* stimulating; increasing or exciting vital action.—*n* anything that stimulates or excites; a stimulating drug; alcoholic liquor, not in a technical sense.—*vt* **stim´ulāte**, to incite; to produce increased action in; to excite.—*n* **stimulā´tion**, act of stimulating, or condition of being stimulated.—*adj* **stim´ulātive**, tending to stimulate.—*n* that which stimulates or excites.—*n* **stim´ūlus**, an action, influence, or agency, that produces a response in a living organism; anything that rouses to action or increased action;—*pl* **stim´ulī**. [L *stimulāre, ātum*, to goad—*stimulus* (for *stigmulus*)—Gr *stizein*, to prick.]

sting [sting] *n* in some plants and animals a weapon (hair, tooth, etc.) that pierces and injects poison; the act of inserting a sting; the pain or the wound caused; any sharp tingling or irritating pain or its cause; an elaborate confidence game, esp one worked by undercover police in order to trap criminals.—*vt* to pierce, wound, with a sting; to pain or incite as if with a sting; to cause to suffer mentally; to stimulate suddenly and sharply; (*slang*) to cheat.—*vi* to have a sting; to give pain; to have a stinging feeling;—*pt, pt p* **stung**.—*n* **sting´er**, one who, or that which, stings, specifically, a sharp blow or remark; a sharp organ (as of a bee, scorpion, or stingray) designed to wound by piercing and inoculating a poisonous secretion; a cocktail consisting of brandy, white crème de menthe, and sometimes lime juice.—*adj* **sting´less**, having no sting.—*n* **sting´ray**, any of a large number of cartilaginous fishes, rays (family Dasytidae), with tail bearing a long spine capable of giving an ugly wound. [OE *stingan*; ON *stinga*.]

stingy [stin´ji] *adj* niggardly, parsimonious.—*adv* **stin´gily**.—*n* **stin´giness**. [**sting** and adj suffx. *-y*.]

stink [stingk] *vi* to give out a strong smell; to be of bad repute; (*inf*) to possess something to an offensive degree; (*inf*) to be extremely bad in quality.—*pt, pt p* **stunk**.—*n* a disagreeable smell.—*ns* **stink´pot**, a jar filled with a stinking combustible mixture, formerly used in boarding an enemy's vessel; one that stinks; **stink´er**, one who, or that which stinks; an offensive person; (*slang*) something extremely difficult. [OE *stincan*.]

stint [stint] *vt* (*arch*), to cease (to do); to give (a person) a niggardly allowance (eg *to stint him in food and drink*); to supply (something) in a niggardly manner; to assign a task to (a person).—*vi* (*arch*) to cease, stop; to be saving.—*n* limitation, restriction (eg *praised him without stint; worked without stint*); task, share of task, alloted; a period of time spent at a specified activity.—*n* **stint´er**. [OE *styntan*—*stunt*, stupid.]

stipe [stīp] *n* (*bot*) the stalk of a mushroom or similar fungus; the petiole of a fern frond up to the lowest leaflet. [Fr,—L *stīpes*, a stem.]

stipend [stī´pėnd] *n* a salary paid for services, settled pay.—*n* **stipend´iary**, one who performs services for a salary. [L *stīpendium*—*stips*, donation, *pendĕre*, weight.]

stipple [stip´l] *vt* to engrave, paint, draw, etc., in small dots;—*pr p* **stipp´ling**; *pt p* **stipp´led**.—*n* any process in which an effect (eg of shade or of gradation of color) is produced by separate touches; the effect itself.—*n* **stipp´ler**, one who stipples. [Du *stippelen*, dim of *stippen*, to dot.]

stipulate [stip´ū-lāt] *vt* to specify or require as a condition or essential part of an agreement; to give a guarantee of.—*vi* to make an agreement or covenant to do or forbear something (*with* **for**).—*ns* **stipulā´tion**, act of stipulating; a condition of agreement; **stip´ulātor**. [L *stipulārī, -ātus*, conn with *stīpāre*, to press firm.]

stipule [stip´ūl] *n* (*bot*) one of the two appendages, often present at the base of a leaf. [L *stipula*, a stalk, dim of *stīpes*.]

stir[1] [stûr] *vt* to change the position of; to set in motion; to move around; to rouse, to move to activity, to excite.—*vi* to move oneself; to be active;—*pr p* **stirr´ing**; *pt, pt p* **stirred**.—*n* tumult; bustle; sensation.—*n* **stirr´er**.—*adj* **stirr´ing**, putting in motion; active; bustling; exciting.—*vt* **stir-fry**, to fry quickly over high heat in a wok, with a little oil, stirring constantly. [OE *styrian*; Du *storen*, Ger *stören*, to disturb.]

stir[2] [stûr] *n* (*slang*) prison. [Perh OE *stēor, stȳr*, punishment.]

stirrup [stir´ûp] *n* a flat-bottomed ring suspended by a strap (**stirr´up leath´er**) from the saddle, for a rider's foot while mounting or riding.—*ns* **stirr´up cup**, a cup drunk by a guest who is departing on horseback; a farewell cup; **stirr´up pump**, a portable hand pump, held in position by pressing the foot on the bracket at its base and used for throwing a jet or spray of liquid. [OE *stigrāp*—*stīgan*, to mount, *rāp*, a rope.]

stitch [stich] *n* a single in-and-out movement of a threaded needle in sewing, embroidery, or suturing; a portion of thread left in the material or tissue after one stitch; a single loop of a yarn in knitting or crocheting; a sudden, sharp pain, esp in the side; a least part, esp of clothing; a stitch formed in a specified way.—*vti* to make stitches (in); sew.—*ns* **stitch´ing**, a regular line of sewing; **stitch´wort**, any of several chickweeds (genus *Stellaria*).—**in stitches**, in a state of uncontrollable laughter. [OE *stice*; a prick; Ger *sticken*, to embroider.]

stithy [stiTH´i, stith´i] *n* an anvil; a smith's shop. [ON *stethi*, Swed *städ*, an anvil.]

stiver [stī´vėr] *n* a Dutch coin; any small coin. [Du *stuiver*.]

stoat [stōt] *n* a large European weasel (*Mustela erminea*), in its brown summer coat; called the ermine when in its winter coat. [ME *stote*.]

stock [stok] *n* (*arch*) a log, a block of wood; a stupid person; the trunk or main stem of a plant; raw material; shares of corporate capital, or the certificates showing such ownership; any of a genus (*Matthiola*) of herbs or subshrubs with racemes of sweet-scented flowers; a part into which another is fixed, as the handle of a whip, the wood holding the barrel of a rifle; the original progenitor; family, race; a store, supply (eg of goods); the cattle, horses, etc., kept on a farm; the liquor obtained by boiling meat or bones, a foundation for soup, etc.; a band worn as a cravat; (*pl*) an instrument in which the legs of offenders were confined; (*pl*) the frame for a ship while building.—*vi* to send out new shoots; to put in stocks or supplies.—*vt* to store; to keep for sale; to fill; to supply with domestic animals or stock; to fit with a stock.—*adj* kept in stock; usual, trite; that deals with stock; related to a stock company.—*ns* **stockbreed´er**, one who raises livestock; **stock´broker**, a broker who deals in securities; **stock car**, a standard automobile modified for racing; **stock company**, a company whose capital is in shares; a permanent repertory company attached to a theater; **stock exchange**, premises where stocks are bought and sold in an organized system; an association of people organized to provide an auction market for the purchase and sale of securities among themselves; **stock´holder**, one who owns corporate stock; **stock´-in-trade**, all the goods a shopkeeper keeps for sale; a person's equipment for any enterprise; a person's basic intellectual and emotional resources; **stock´jobb´ing**, speculative exchange dealings; **stock´jobb´er**, disparaging term for stockbroker; **stock´man**, one occupied as an owner or worker in the raising of livestock (as sheep or cattle); **stock´ market**, a market for the sale of stocks, the stock exchange; **stock´pile**, a reserve supply of essentials; a gradually accumulated reserve of something.—*vt* to accumulate reserve supplies; **stock´pot**, the pot in which the stock for soup is kept; **stock´room**, a storage place for supplies or goods used in business.—*adj* **stock´-still**, perfectly motionless.—*ns* **stock´tak´ing**, a periodical inventory made of the stock or goods in a shop or warehouse; the action of estimating a situation at a given moment; **stock´yard**, a yard where cattle are kept for slaughter, market, etc.—**off, on, the stocks**, (of a ship) launched, in process of building; hence (of a piece of work) finished, in the course of being done; **take stock**, to make an inventory of goods on hand; to make an estimate (of); **take stock in**, to trust to, attach importance to. [OE *stocc*, a stick; Ger *stock*.]

stockade [stok-ād´] *n* a palisade formed of stakes fixed in the ground.—*vt* to fortify with such. [Fr *estocade*—*estoc*—Ger *stock*, stick.]

stockfish [stok´fish] *n* fish (as cod, haddock, or hake) dried hard in the open air without salt. [Du *stokvisch*, Ger *stockfisch*.]

stocking [stok´ing] *n* a close covering for the foot and lower leg.—*n* **stockinette, stockinet**, a soft elastic knitted fabric for bandages and infant's wear. [From (*arch*) *stock*, hose, the stockings being the *nether-stocks* when the long hose came to be cut at the knee.]

stocky [stok´i] *adj* short and stout, thickset; having a strong stem.—*adv* **stock´ily**. [**stock** (1) and adj suffx *-y*.]

stodgy [stoj´i] *adj* heavy and indigestible; heavy and uninteresting.—*vt* **stodge**, to stuff full, esp with food.—*n* a thick filling food (as oatmeal or stew).—*n* **stodg´iness**. [Perh imit.]

stoic [stō´ik] *n* a disciple of the school founded by the philosopher Zeno (died c 261 BC), who taught in the *Stoa Poikilē* ('painted porch') at Athens; one indifferent to pleasure or pain.—*adjs* **stō´ic, -al**, pertaining to the Stoics, or to their opinions; indifferent to pleasure or pain.—*adv* **stō´ically**.—*n* **stō´icism** [-sizm], the doctrines of the Stoics holding that the wise man should be free from passion, unmoved by joy or grief, and submissive to natural law; **stoicism**, impassiveness. [Gr *Stōikos*—*stoa*, a porch.]

stoke [stōk] *vt* to feed (a fire) with fuel.—*ns* **stoke´hold**, the hold containing the boilers of a ship; one of the spaces in front of a ship's boilers from which the furnaces are fed; **stoke´hole**, the space about the mouth of a furnace; a stokehold; **stōk´er**, one who, or that which, feeds a furnace with fuel, esp one that tends a marine steam boiler; a machine for feeding a fire. [Du *stoker*, stoker—*stōken*, to stoke.]

stole[1] [stōl] *pt* and *obs pt p* of **steal**.

stole[2] [stōl] *n* a long robe; a narrow vestment worn on the shoulders, hanging down in front; a woman's outer garment, of similar form. [L *stŏla*, a Roman matron's long robe—Gr *stolē*, equipment, garment—*stellein*, to array.]

stolen [stōl´ėn] *pt p* of **steal**.

stolid [stol´id] *adj* dull, heavy, impassive; unemotional.—*ns* **stolid´ity**.—*adv* **stol´idly**. [L *stolidus*.]

stolon [stō´lon] *n* a shoot from the base of a plant that produces new plants from buds at its tip; an extension of the body wall (as of a hydrozoan) that gives rise to new individuals.—*adj* **stōlonif´erous**. [L *stolō, -ōnis*, a sucker, twig.]

stoma [stō´ma] *n* (*bot*) a minute opening, by which gases pass through the leaf of a plant; (*zool*) any of various small bodily openings, esp in a lower animal; an artificial permanent opening, esp in the abdominal wall, made in surgical procedures;—*pl* **stō´mata**. [Gr *stoma, -atos*, a mouth.]

stomach [stum´āk] *n* the strong muscular bag into which the food passes when swallowed, and where it is principally digested; (in ruminants, etc.) one of several digestive cavities; the belly; appetite, or inclination generally; (*arch*) courage, pride.—*vt* to brook or put up with.—*n* **stomacher** [stum´ak-ėr, -ach-ėr; *hist*], a part of a woman's dress covering the front of the body, generally forming the lower part of the bodice in front, sometimes richly ornamented.—*adj* **stomach´ic**, pertaining to the stomach; strengthening or promoting the action of the stomach.—*n* a medicine for this purpose. [OFr *estomac*—L *stomachus*—Gr *stomachos*, the throat, later stomach—*stoma*, a mouth.]

stomp [stomp] *vti* (*inf*) to stamp; to dance.—*n* an early jazz dance with foot stamping. [Variant of **stamp**.]

-stomy [stŏm-i] in composition, indicating a new surgical opening into an organ. [Gr *stoma*, a mouth.]

stone [stōn] *n* a detached piece of rock; a piece of such material fashioned for a particular purpose, as a *grindstone*; a precious stone or gem; a tombstone; a concretion formed in the kidney or gallbladder; a hard shell containing the seed, eg of a drupe; a standard weight of 14 lb avoirdupois (in *pl* **stone**) in Great Britain; a round playing piece used in various games (as backgammon or go).—*adj* made of, consisting of, containing, stone; made of stoneware; of the Stone Age.—*vt* to pelt with stones; to free from stones; to wall with stones.—*adv* entirely, utterly, used as an intensive, often in combination.—*n* **Stone Age**, the first known period of prehistoric human culture identified by the use of stone tools.—*adj* **stone´-blind**, completely blind.—*ns* **stone's´ throw**, a short distance; **stone´ chat**, a common European songbird (*Saxicola torquata*); **stone´crop**, a mossy evergreen creeping sedum (*Sedum acre*) with pungent fleshy leaves; any of several related plants; **stone´cutt´ing**, the business of hewing and carving stones for walls, monuments, etc.; **stone´cutt´er**, one that cuts, carves, or dresses stone; a machine for dressing stone.—*adj* **stone´deaf**, totally deaf.—*n* **stone´fruit**, a fruit whose seeds are enclosed in a stone or hard shell, a drupe.—*vi* **stone´wall** (*inf*), to obstruct by various tactics, as by withholding information, by denials, etc.—*vt* to refuse to comply or cooperate with.—*ns* **stone´waller, stone´walling; stone´ware**, a coarse kind of potter's ware baked hard and glazed.—*adj* **stō´ny**, abounding with stones; hard, pitiless, obdurate.—*adv* **ston´ily**, in a cold, hard, unrelenting manner. [OE *stān*, Ger *stein*, Du *steen*.]

stood [stŏŏd] *pt, pt p* of **stand**.

stooge [stōōj] *n* (*inf*) a comedian's assistant and foil; anyone who plays a subordinate or compliant role to a principal; a stool pigeon.—*vi* to act as a stooge. [Slang; origin uncertain.]

stool [stōōl] *n* a seat without a back; a low support for the feet when sitting, or the knees when kneeling; the seat used in evacuating the bowels; the act of evacuating the bowels; feces; a plant crown from which shoots grow out.—*n* **stool´ pigeon**, a decoy pigeon; (*inf*) a spy or informer, esp for the police. [OE *stōl*; Ger *stuhl*; cf Ger *stellen*, to place.]

stoop[1] [stōōp] *vi* to bend the body forward; to lean forward; to submit; to descend from rank or dignity (to do something); to degrade oneself; (*arch*) to swoop down on the wing, as a bird of prey.—*vt* to debase, degrade; to bend (a part of the body) downward and forward.—*n* the act of stooping; inclination forward; a swoop.—*adj* **stooped**, having a stoop, bent. [OE *stūpian*; ON *stūpa*.]

stoop[2] [stōōp] *n* a small porch at the door of a house. [Du *stoep*.]

stop [stop] *vt* to stuff up and so close or partially close; to obstruct, to render impassable, to close; to bring to a standstill, prevent the motion of; to prevent (from); to put an end to; to discontinue; to keep back (eg *to stop payment of a check*); (*mus*) of woodwind and stringed instruments, to alter the pitch of by means of a stop.—*vi* to cease going forward, halt; to cease from any motion; to leave off, desist; to come to an end; to stay;—*pr p* **stopp´ing**; *pt, pt p* **stopped**.—*n* act of stopping; state of being stopped; a cessation; a halt; a stay; an obstacle; in machinery, a device for arresting movement or for limiting scope of action; a screen having a circular aperture, used eg. to limit the effective aperture of a lens in a camera; (*mus*) a method of, or device for, altering pitch, as pressing a string with the fingers, closing a hole; a set of organ pipes graduated in pitch, or a knob operating a lever for bringing them into use; (*phonet*) a sound requiring complete closure of the breath passage, as (voiced) *b, d, g* and (voiceless) *p, t, k*.—*ns* **stop´cock**, a short pipe in a cask, etc., opened and stopped by turning a valve; **stop´gap**, that which fills a gap or supplies a deficiency, esp. an expedient of emergency.—*ns* **stop´over**, a short break in a journey; **stopp´age**, act of stopping; state of being stopped; an obstruction; **stopp´er**, one who stops; that which closes a vent or hole, as the cork or glass mouthpiece for a bottle; (*baseball*) an effective relief pitcher.—*vt* to close or secure with a stopper.—*n* **stopple** [stop´l], that which stops or closes the mouth of a vessel, a cork or plug.—*vt* to close with a stopple; **stopwatch**, a watch with hands that can be started and stopped, used in timing a race, etc. [OE *stoppian*, found in the compound *forstoppian*, to stop up, from L *stūpa*, tow.]

store [stōr, stör] *n* a hoard or quantity gathered; (in *pl*) supplies of food, clothing, etc.; abundance; a storehouse; a retail establishment where goods are offered for sale.—*vt* to accumulate and put in a place for keeping; to put in a storehouse, warehouse, etc.; to furnish (with supplies); to put (data) into a computer memory.—*ns* **stō´rage**, the act of placing in a store; the safekeeping of goods in a store; the price paid or charged for keeping goods in a store; **sto´rage batt´ery**, a battery of cells generating electric current and capable of being recharged; **storefront**, a front room on the ground floor of a building, designed for use as a retail store; **store´house**, a house for storing goods of any kind, a repository;—eg book, mind—where things of value are stored, a treasury; **store´keeper**, a man who manages or owns a store; **stō´rer**, one who stores; **store´room**, a room in which things are stored; **store´ship**, a vessel used for transporting supplies.—**in store**, destined, about to come; in readiness (for a person); **set (great) store by**, to value greatly; **storefront church**, a city church that uses storefront quarters as a meeting place and whose services are highly emotional. [OFr *estor, estoire—L instaurāre*, to provide.]

storied *see* **story**.

stork [störk] *n* any of various long-necked and long-legged wading birds (family Ciconiidae) allied to the herons.—*n* **stork´sbill**, any of several plants of the geranium family; a pelargonium or related plant. [OE *storc*; Ger *storch*.]

storm [störm] *n* a violent commotion of the atmosphere producing wind, rain, etc., a tempest; a violent commotion or outbreak of any kind; a paroxysm; wind having a speed of 64 to 72 miles an hour; (*mil*) an assault on a fortified place.—*vi* to blow, rain, etc., with violence (eg *it stormed all night*); to be in, show, a violent passion; to rage (at).—*vt* to attack and take by storm.—*adj* **storm´bound**, delayed by storms; cut off by storm from communication with the outside.—*ns* **storm cellar**, a cellar or covered excavation designed for refuge during dangerous windstorms (as tornadoes); **storm door**, an additional door placed outside an ordinary door for protection against severe weather; **storm´pet´rel, storm´y pet´rel** any of various small petrels, esp a black white-marked one (*Hydrobates pelagiens*) of the north Atlantic and Mediterranean; **storm trooper**, member of a private Nazi army notorious for violence and brutal aggressiveness; one that resembles a Nazi storm trooper; **storm win´dow**, an additional outer casement.—*adj* **storm´y**, having many storms; agitated with furious winds; boisterous; violent; passionate.—*n* **storm´iness**.—**take by storm**, to take by assault; to captivate totally and instantly. [OE *storm*; ON *stormr*; from root of **stir**.]

story[1] [stō´ri] *n* a narrative of consecutive events; an anecdote; an account, allegation; a fictitious narrative; the plot of a novel, etc.; (*inf*) an untruth; a news article.—*adj* **stō´ried**, told or celebrated in a story; having a history; interesting from the stories belonging to it; adorned with scenes from history.—*n* **sto´ry book**, a book of tales true or fictitious, esp one for children.—*adj* luckier or happier than is usual in real life. [Anglo-Fr. *estorie*—L *historia*.]

story[2] [stō´ri] *n* a horizontal division of a building, from a floor to the ceiling above it; a set of rooms in such a space; a unit of measure equal to the number of stories in a building.

stoup [stōōp] *n* a flagon, or its contents; a small measure for liquids; a basin for holy water. [Cf ON *staup*, Du *stoop*; OE *stēap*.]

stout [stowt] *adj* strong, robust; corpulent; of strong material; resolute; staunch; forceful; (*Bible*) stubborn.—*n* type of strong dark beer.—*adj* **stoutheart´ed**, having a brave heart; courageous; stubborn.—*adv* **stout´ly**.—*n* **stout´ness**. [OFr *estout*, bold—Old Du *stolt, stout*; Ger *stolz*, bold.]

stove[1] [stōv] *n* a closed heating or cooking apparatus; a kiln.—*n* **stove´pipe**, a metal pipe for carrying smoke and gases from a stove to a chimney; a tall silk hat. [OE *stofa*, a hot air bath; cf Ger *stube*.]

stove[2] [stōv] —*pt, pt p* of **stave**.

stow [stō] *vt* to place, arrange, pack, in an orderly way; to put away in a convenient place; (*slang*) to put aside; to cease.—*ns* **stow´age**, act of placing in order; state of being stowed; capacity for articles to be laid away; **stow´away**, one who hides himself in an outward bound vessel in order to get a passage for nothing, evade port officials, etc. [ME *stowen*, to place—OE *stōw*, a place; cf Du *stuwen*, to stow, to push, Ger *stauen*, to pack.]

strabismus [stra-biz´mus] *n* a squint in the eye. [Gr *strābos* and *strabismos*, squinting; cf *strephein*, to twist.]

straddle [strad´l] *vi* to part the legs wide; to stand or walk with the legs far apart; (of legs) to spread apart.—*vt* to stand or sit astride of; to shoot a missile beyond and another short of (a target) in order to determine the range; to cover the area containing (a target) with bombs.—*n* act or posture of straddling. [Freq of OE *stræd*, pt of *strīdan*, stride.]

Stradivarius [strad-i-vā'ri-us] *n* a stringed instrument of the violin family made by Antonio *Stradivari* (1644–1737) of Cremona.

straggle [strag'l] *vi* to stray from the course or line of march; to wander beyond, or to escape from, proper limits; to move in an irregular way, not as a compact body (eg *the crowd straggled over the park*); to grow irregularly and untidily.—*n* **stragg'ler**, one who strays from, or is left behind by, the body of persons or animals to which he, she, belongs; a plant, etc., out of its proper place or required position.

straight [strāt] *adj* (of a line) invariable in direction, determined by the position of two points; not curved or bent; direct (eg *the straight way to the churchyard*); going directly and honestly to the point (as in *a straight talk, straight thinking*); honest, fair (eg *straight dealings, a straight race*); placed levelly or symmetrically (eg. *the pictures, mats, are not straight*); in order (*put the room, your accounts, straight*); unmixed, undiluted (eg *a straight whiskey*).—*adv* in the most direct line or manner (*arch*) without delay; honestly, fairly.—*ns* **straight angle**, an angle of 180° or two right angles; **straight'edge**, a narrow board or piece of metal having one edge perfectly straight for applying to a surface to ascertain whether it is exactly even; *straightjacket*, straitjacket.—*vt* **straight'en**, to make straight.—*ns* **straight face**, a sober, unsmiling face.—*adj* **straightfor'ward**, going forward in a straight course; honest, open, downright.—*advs* **straightfor'wardly; straight'ly**, evenly; tightly, closely.—*ns* **straight'ness**, evenness; narrowness; tightness; **straight talk**, a candid outspoken talk; **straight thinking**, clear, logical, thinking not confused by emotion, predispositions, or preconceived ideas; **straight tip**, a racing tip that comes straight from the owner; inside information that can be relied on.—*adv* **straight'way**, directly, without loss of time.—**go straight**, to give up criminal activities. [OE *streht*, pt p of *streccan*, to stretch.]

strain[1] [strān] *vt* to stretch tight; to make tight; to stretch beyond due limits, make cover too much (eg *to strain credulity, the meaning, the law*); to exert to the utmost (eg *to strain every nerve*); to injure by overtaxing; to constrain, make uneasy or unnatural; to separate the solid from the liquid part of by a filter.—*vi* to make violent efforts; to trickle through a filter.—*n* the act of straining; over-stretching, over-exertion, tension; a violent effort; an injury inflicted by straining, esp a wrenching of the muscles; (*mech*) any change in form or in volume of a portion of matter either solid or fluid due to system of forces.—*adj* **strained**, having been strained; forced or unnatural.—*n* **strain'er**, one who, or that which, strains, esp a utensil to separate solid from liquid.—**strain a point**, to go beyond an accepted limit or rule; **strain at**, to strive after; to balk at. [OFr *straindre*—L *stringĕre*, to stretch tight.]

strain[2] [strān] *n* race, stock, generation; (in domestic animals) individuals of common descent; hereditary character; natural tendency, element in character; a passage of a song, a poem, a flight of the imagination; mood, temper, prevailing note. [App OE *(ge)strēon*, gain, getting, begetting, with altered vowel by confusion with **strain** (1).]

strait [strāt] *adj* difficult; distressful; (*arch*) strict, rigorous; (*arch*) narrow.—*n* a narrow pass in a mountain (*arch*), or in the ocean (often in *pl*) between two portions of land; (usu. *pl*) difficulty, distress.—*vt* **strait'en**, to make strait, narrow, difficult (esp in *pt p*, as *straitened circumstances, means*); to hem in, distress, put into difficulties (eg *he was straitened in circumstances*).—*adj* **strait'laced**, (*orig*) laced tightly, in tightly laced stays, etc.; (*now*) rigid in adherence to a narrow code of morals and manners.—*adv* **strait'ly**, narrowly; (*arch*) strictly.—*ns* **strait'jacket**, a coatlike device to restrain violent persons.—Also **straightjacket**. [OFr *estreit, estrait* (Fr *étroit*)— L *strictus*, pt p of *stringĕre*, to draw tight.]

strand[1] [strand] *n* the margin or beach of the sea.—*vt* to run aground.—*vi* to drift or be driven ashore.—*adj* **strand'ed**, driven on shore; friendless and helpless. [OE *strand*; Ger *strand*, ON *strönd*, border.]

strand[2] [strand] *n* one of the strings or parts that compose a rope; a tress of hair.—*vt* to break a strand; to form by uniting strands, compose of strands. [Origin obscure.]

strange [strānj] *adj* foreign, alien; from elsewhere; not of one's own place, family, or circle; not one's own; not formerly known or experienced; unfamiliar; interestingly unusual; odd; estranged; distant or reserved; unacquainted, unversed.—*adv* **strange'ly**.—*ns* **strange'ness; strān'ger**, a foreigner; one whose home is elsewhere; one unknown or unacquainted; a guest or visitor; one not admitted to communion or fellowship; one ignorant of, or with no experience of (eg *a stranger to your thoughts, to truth, to fear*). [OFr *estrange*—L *extrāneus*—*extrā*, beyond.]

strangle [strang'gl] *vt* to kill by compressing the throat, to choke; to suppress, stifle.—*ns* **strangle'hold**, a choking hold in wrestling; an influence strongly repressing development or freedom of action or expression; **strang'ler** [OFr *estrangler*—L *strangulāre*; see next word.]

strangulate [strang'gū-lāt] *vt* to strangle; to compress so as to suppress or suspend the function of.—*n* **strangulā'tion**, act of strangling; compression of the throat and partial suffocation; the state of an organ abnormally constricted. [L *strangulāre, -ātum*—Gr *strangalaein*, to strangle, *strangos*, twisted.]

strap [strap] *n* a narrow strip of leather or cloth, esp one with a buckle or other fastening; a razor-strop; an iron plate secured by screw-bolts, for connecting two or more timbers.—*vt* to beat with a strap; to bind with a strap; to strop, as a razor;—*pr p* **strapp'ing**; *pt, pt p* **strapped**.—*ns* **strap'hang'er**, a passenger in a crowded vehicle who stands and steadies himself by holding a strap suspended from the roof; **strapp'ing**, the act of fastening with a strap; materials for straps; a thrashing.—*adj* tall, handsome. [Form of **strop**.]

strata [strā'ta] *pl* of **stratum**.

stratagem [strat'à-jem] *n* action planned to outwit an enemy; an artifice.—*adjs* **strategic** [strat-ē'jik], **-al**, pertaining to strategy; dictated by strategy (eg *strategic withdrawal*); of value for strategy.—*n* **strat'egy**, generalship, the act of managing armed forces in a campaign (cf **tactics**); artifice or finesse generally.—*adv* **stratēg'ically**.—*n* **strat'ĕgist**, one skilled in strategy. [Gr *stratēgēma*—*stratēgos*, a general—*stratos*, an army, *agein*, to lead.]

strathspey [strâth-spā'] *n* a Scottish dance, allied to the reel. [*Strathspey*, valley of the *Spey*.]

stratify [strat'i-fī] *vt* to form or lay in strata or layers;—*pr p* **strat'ifying**; *pt, pt p* **strat'ified**.—*n* **stratificā'tion**, act of stratifying; state of being stratified; process of being arranged in layers. [Fr *stratifier*—L *strātum* (see **stratum**) and *facĕre*, to make.]

stratosphere [strāt'- or strat'ō-sfēr] *n* a layer of the earth's atmosphere, beginning about 4½ to 10 miles up, in which temperature does not fall as height increases. [**stratum + sphere**.]

stratum [strā'tum] *n* a bed of sedimentary rock, consisting usually of a series of layers; level (of society);—*pl* **strā'ta**.—*adj* **strat'iform**, formed like strata; in layers. [L *strātum*, a bed-cover, a horse-cloth, a pavement—*sternĕre, strātum*, to spread out.]

stratus [strā'tus] *n* a long, low, gray cloud layer.—*pl* **strā'tī**. [L *strātus*, a coverlet—*sternĕre, strātum*, to spread out.]

straw [strö] *n* the stalk on which grain grows, and from which it is thrashed; a quantity of dried stalks of corn, etc.; a tube for sucking up a beverage; a straw hat; a trifle, a whit.—*ns* **straw'berry**, the fruit (botanically, the enlarged receptacle) of a genus of perennial plants of the rose family, with long creeping shoots; the plant (genus *Fragaria*) itself; **straw'berry mark**, a soft reddish birthmark.—*adj* **straw'y**, made of, or like, straw.—*ns* **straw boss**, (*inf*) a person having subordinate authority; **straw hat**, a hat made of plaited straw; **straw vote**, an unofficial vote taken to get some idea of the general trend of opinion; **straw in the wind**, a slight sign of possible future developments. [OE *strēaw*; Ger *stroh*.]

stray [strā] *vi* to wander; to wander (from eg the proper place, the company to which one belongs); to deviate from duty or rectitude.—*n* a domestic animal that has strayed or is lost; a waif, a truant; anything occurring casually, isolatedly, out of place.—*adj* wandering, lost; casual (eg *a stray remark*), isolated (eg *a stray example*). [OFr *estraier*, to wander—L *extrā*, beyond, *vagārī*, to wander.]

streak [strēk] *n* a line or long mark different in color from the surface on which it is traced; a stripe; a flash; a slight characteristic, a trace; (*min*) the appearance presented by the surface of a mineral when scratched.—*vt* to form streaks in; to mark with streaks.—*vi* to move swiftly, rush; to have a streak (as of winning performances).—*adj* **streak'y**, marked with streaks, striped; (of bacon) fat and lean in alternate layers; uneven in quality. [OE *strica*, a stroke—*strīcan*, to go, Ger *strich*.]

stream [strēm] *n* a current (of water, air, light, etc.); running water; a river, brook, etc.; anything flowing out from a source; anything flowing and continuous; a large quantity coming continuously.—*vi* to flow in a stream; to gush abundantly; to be covered with a flow of (*with* **with**); to issue in rays; to stretch in a long line.—*vt* to discharge in a stream; to wave (eg a pennant).—*ns* **stream'er**, an ensign or flag streaming or flowing in the wind; a long ribbon for decorative purposes; a luminous beam shooting upward from the horizon; **stream'let**, a little stream; **streamline**, the line followed by a streaming fluid.—Also *vt* to make streamlined.—*adjs* **stream'lined**, shaped so as to offer least possible resistance to air or water; having flowing lines; modernized; **streamy**.—**stream of consciousness**, the continuous succession of thoughts, emotions, and feelings, both vague and well-defined, that forms an individual's conscious experience. [OE *strēam*; Ger *strom*, ON *straumr*.]

street [strēt] *n* a public road in a town or city lined with houses; such a road with its buildings and sidewalks; the people living, working, etc., along a given street.—*ns* **street'car**, a car on rails for public transportation along the street; **street'-walker**, a prostitute.—*adj* **street'wise'**, (*inf*) experienced in dealing with people in urban poverty areas where crime is common.—**not in the same street**, not comparable, of an entirely different (usu. inferior) quality; **on the streets**, idle, homeless, or out of a job; out of prison; **up one's street**, in the region in which one's tastes, knowledge, abilities, etc., lie. [OE *strǣt* (Du *straat*, Ger *strasse*, It *strada*)—L *strāta* (*via*), a paved (way), from *sternĕre, strātum*, to spread out, level.]

strength [strength] *n* quality of being strong; power of any kind, active or passive—force, vigor, solidity or toughness, power to resist; degree in which a person or thing is strong (eg *he has the strength of a horse; the enemy's strength*); intensity (eg *the strength of his hatred*); the proportion of the essential ingredient in any compound or mixture; vigor (of style or expression); validity (of an argument); a source of power or firmness.—*vt* **strength´en**, to make strong or stronger; to confirm; to encourage; to increase the power or security of.—*vi* to become stronger.—**go from strength to strength**, to move forward successfully, having one triumph after another; **on the strength of**, in reliance on, encouraged by. [OE *strengthu*—*strang*, strong.]

strenuous [stren´ū-ůs] *adj* vigorous, urgent, zealous; necessitating exertion.—*adv* **stren´uously**.—*n* **stren´uousness**. [L *strēnuus*, akin to Gr *strēnēs*, strong.]

streptococcus [strep-tō-kok´us] *n* a group of spherical bacteria that form chains, some species of which are associated with diseases such as scarlet fever;—*pl* **streptococci**. [-kok´sī]. [Gr *streptos*, pliant, twisted, *kokkos*, a grain.]

stress [stres] *n* pressure, urgency, strain, violence (eg *stress of circumstance, weather*), emphasis; (*mech*) a system of forces operating over an area, esp a combination producing or sustaining a strain.—*vt* to put pressure on; to emphasise. [Abbrev for **distress**; prob also partly from OFr *estrece*—L *strictus*—*stringěre, strictum*, to draw tight.]

stretch [strech] *vt* to extend, to draw out; to lay at full length; to reach out; to exaggerate, strain, or carry further than is right.—*vi* to be drawn out; to extend, reach; to be extensible without breaking; to straighten and extend fully one's body and limbs.—*n* act of stretching; state of being stretched; reach; extension; utmost extent; strain; undue straining; exaggeration; extensibility; a single spell; a continuous journey; a straight part of a course; a term of imprisonment.—*adj* capable of being stretched.—*n* **stretch´er**, anything for stretching; a frame on which anything is stretched; a frame for carrying the sick or wounded; a brick or stone laid along a wall lengthwise.—**at a stretch**, without interruption, continuously. [OE *streccan*.]

strew [strōō] *vt* to scatter loosely; to cover by scattering (with);—*pt p* **strewed** or **strewn**. [OE *strewian, streowian*.]

stria [strī´a, strē´a] *n* a fine streak, furrow, or threadlike line usu. parallel to others;—*pl* **strī´ae** [-ē].—*adjs* **strī´āted**, marked with striae or small parallel channels.—*n* **striā´tion**. [L *stria*, a furrow, flute of a column.]

stricken [strik´n] *pt p* of **strike**.—*adj* struck or wounded; afflicted, as by something painful.

strict [strikt] *adj* exact (eg *in the strict meaning of the term*); allowing of no exception, irregularity, laxity (eg *strict confidence, orders, obedience, honesty*); rigorous, severe (eg *strict laws, regulations*); enforcing rigorous discipline, usu. in conformity with a narrow code of behavior (eg *their parents were very strict*).—*adv* **strict´ly**, narrowly, closely, rigorously, exclusively.—*ns* **strict´ness; stric´ture** [-chůr], an abnormal contraction of a duct or passage in the body; something that restrains and limits; an unfavorable criticism. [L *strictus*, pt p of *stringěre*, to draw tight.]

stride [strīd] *vi* to walk with long steps; to take a long step.—*vt* to stride over; to bestride;—*pt* **strōde** [obs strid]; *pt p* **stridden** [strid´n].—*n* a long step; the space stepped over; (*pl*) progress.—**make great strides**, to make rapid progress; **take in one's stride**, to accomplish without undue effort or difficulty. [OE *strīdan*.]

strident [strī´dėnt] *adj* loud and grating.—*adv* **strīdently**.—*ns* **strī´dence, -cy**. [L *strīdens, -entis*, pr p of *strīdēre*, to creak.]

stridulate [strid´ū-lāt] *vi* (of insects) to make a chirping or scraping sound (eg as a grasshopper does by rubbing its forewings).—*ns* **stridulā´tion; strid´ulātor**, an insect that makes a sound by scraping; the organ it uses. [L *strīdēre*. See **strident**.]

strife [strīf] *n* contention; fight, quarrel; struggle. [OFr *estrif*. See **strive**.]

strike [strīk] *vt* to hit with force, to smite; to stab, pierce (eg to the heart); to move in a specified direction by hitting; to dash (against, on); to cause to pierce; to collide with, knock against; to attack, punish; to hook (a fish) by a quick turn of the wrist; to give (a blow); to ignite (a match) by friction; to produce by friction (eg a light, sparks); to cause to sound; to mint; (of a tree, etc.) to thrust (roots) down in the earth; to lower, let down (a flag, sail, or tent); (*theat*) to dismantle a stage set, etc. (also *n*); to impress, or to affect in a specified way, with force or suddenness like that of a blow (eg *I was struck by the resemblance; a thought struck me; it strikes one with astonishment; to strike dumb; to strike terror into*); to light upon, to come upon, esp unexpectedly; to make (a compact or agreement); to assume (eg an attitude); to cancel, erase (*with* **off, out, from**); to arrive at by calculation (eg an average); to cause (a cutting) to take root; to propagate by cuttings.—*vi* to give a quick or sudden blow; to stab, penetrate (to); to make an attack; to fight; (of a fish) to seize the bait; to knock (against); to fall (eg *the light strikes her hair*); (of a clock) to sound; to take a course (eg *to strike across the field, through the wood; to strike for home*); to happen (on) suddenly; to cease work in support of a demand for higher wages or improved conditions of service, or as a protest against a grievance;—*pt* **struck**; *pt p* **struck** [*arch* **strick´en**].—*n* act of striking for higher wages, etc.; (*geol*) the direction of a horizontal line at right angles to the dip of a bed; a find (as of oil, ore, etc.); rooting (of cuttings); an attack, esp by aircraft; (*baseball*) a pitched ball that is in the strike zone or is swung at and not hit fair; (*baseball*) a perfectly thrown ball; an instance of knocking down all the bowling pins with one ball.—*n* **strik´er**.—*adj* **strik´ing**, that strikes; for hitting, smiting, attacking; surprising; impressive.—*adv* **strīk´ingly**.—*n* **strikebreak´er**, one hired to replace a striking worker; **strike´breaking**, action designed to break up a strike.—**on strike**, taking part in a strike; **strike a balance**, to calculate the difference between the debtor and creditor sides of an account; **strike camp**, to dismantle a camp and continue the march; **strike off**, to produce in an effortless manner; to depict clearly and exactly; **strike out**, to enter on a course of action; to set out vigorously; to make an out in baseball by a strikeout; to bowl three strikes in the last frame in bowling; (of a baseball pitcher) to retire a batter by a strikeout; **strike´out**, an out in baseball as a result of three strikes against the batter; **strike zone**, (*baseball*) the area over home plate through which a pitched ball must pass to be called a strike (as between the armpits and tops of the knees of the batter); **strike up**, to begin to beat, sing, or play; to cause to begin; **striking price**, an agreed-upon price at which an option contract can be exercised. [OE *strīcan*, to stroke, go, move.]

Strine [strīn] *n* (*inf*) Australian speech. [Alleged pron of *Australian*.]

string [string] *n* coarse material in very narrow and relatively long pieces, made by twisting threads, used for tying, fastening, etc.; a portion of this; a piece of anything for tying; anything of like character as a nerve, tendon, fiber; a stretched piece of catgut, silk, wire, or other material in a musical instrument; (*pl*) the stringed instruments played by a bow in an orchestra; their players; a cord on which things are filed (eg a string of beads); a line or series of things.—*vt* to supply with strings; to put on a string; to remove the strings from, as beans; to stretch out in a long line; *pt, pt p* **strung**.—*adjs* **stringed**, having strings; **string´less**, having no strings; **string´y**, consisting of strings or small threads; fibrous; capable of being drawn into strings.—**have strings attached**, (*inf*—of a gift or benefit) to be limited by an obligation of some kind; **pull the strings**, to control the actions of others, be the real instigator of an action; **string along**, to go along, agree; to keep waiting; **strung out**, debilitated from long-term drug addiction; addicted to a drug; intoxicated by a drug. [OE *streng*; cf Ger *strang*, ON *strengr*.]

stringent [strin´jėnt] *adj* binding strongly, exact and strictly enforced (eg *stringent regulations*).—*n* **strin´gency**, state or quality of being stringent; severe pressure.—*adv* **stri´gently**. [L *stringens, -entis*, pr p of *stringěre*, to draw tight.]

strip [strip] *vt* to pull off in strips; to tear off; to deprive of a covering—to skin, to peel, to remove fruit or leaves from; to make bare by taking away removable parts; to break the thread of (a bolt, screw, etc.) or the teeth of (a gear); to deprive (of).—*vi* to undress; to come off (eg leaves);—*pr p* **stripp´ing**; *pt, pt p* **stripped**.—*n* a long narrow piece of anything; a runway for airplanes.—*n* **strip´tease**, an act of undressing slowly and seductively in a place of entertainment. [OE *strȳpan*; Ger *streifen*.]

stripe [strīp] *n* a line, or long narrow division of a different color from the ground; a chevron on a sleeve, indicating noncommissioned rank, years served, etc.; a distinct variety or sort.—*vt* to make stripes on; to form with lines of different colors. [Old Du *strijpe*, a stripe in cloth; Low Ger *stripe*, Ger *streif*.]

stripling [strip´ling] *n* a lad who has not reached full growth. [Dim of **strip**.]

strive [strīv] *vi* to endeavor earnestly, labor hard (to do, for); to struggle, contend (with, against);—*pt* **strōve**; *pt p* **strĭven**.—*n* **strīv´er**. [OFr *estriver*; perh of Gmc origin.]

strode [strōd] *pt* of **stride**.

stroke [strōk] *n* an act of striking; a blow; an attempt to hit; a sudden attack of apoplexy; the sound of a clock; a dash in writing; the sweep of an oar in rowing; the rower who sets the pace for the crew; one complete movement, eg of the piston of a mechanical part having a reciprocating motion; a movement in one direction of a pen, pencil, or paintbrush; a method of striking in games, etc.; an effective action, a feat, achievement.—*vti* to act as stroke for, to set the stroke for a rowing crew; to hit (a ball or shuttlecock).—*n* **stroke play**, a golf competition scored by total number of strokes. [OE (inferred) *strāc*; cf Ger *streich*.]

stroke [strōk] *vt* to rub gently in one direction; to do so as a sign of affection. [OE *strācian*; cf Ger *streichen*, to rub.]

stroll [strōl] *vi* to ramble idly, to saunter; to wander on foot.—*n* a leisurely walk; a ramble on foot.—*n* **stroll´er**, one who strolls; a light chairlike baby carriage. [Origin unknown; perh conn with Ger *strolch*, a vagrant.]

strong [strong] *adj* able to endure—eg firm, solid, well fortified, having wealth or resources; hale, healthy; having great physical power; having great vigor, as the mind; forcible; energetic; convincing (eg *a strong argument*); powerfully affecting the sense of smell or taste, pungent; having a quality in a great degree—eg very bright, loud, intense, rich in alcohol; (*gram*) inflecting by a change of radical vowel, as *sing, sang, sung*, instead of by syllabic addition.—*adv* **strong´ly**.—*adj* **strong-arm**, (*inf*) by, having, or using physical force.—*vt* (*inf*) to use physical force on.—*n* **strong´hold**, a place strong to hold out against attack, a fastness; a fortress; a place where doctrine is strongly held or a cause strongly supported.—*adj* **strong´-mind´ed**, having a vigorous mind, strong powers of reasoning; determined to make one's views known and effective; **strong´ room**, a room, constructed to be fireproof and burglarproof, used as a safe for the storage of valuables. [OE *strang*, strong; ON *strangr*, Ger *streng*, tight.]

strontium [stron´shi-ům] *n* a metallic element (symbol Sr; at wt 87.6; at no 38).—**strontium 90**, a radioactive isotope of strontium, an important element in nuclear fallout.

strop [strop] *n* a strip of leather, or of wood covered with leather, etc., for sharpening razors.—*vt* to sharpen on a strop;—*pr p* **stropp´ing**; *pt, pt p* **stropped**. [Older form of **strap**.]

strophe [strōf´e] *n* in ancient Greek drama, a stanza of an ode sung by the chorus while dancing towards one side of the orchestra; (*loosely*) a stanza.—*adj* **stroph´ic**. [Gr *strŏphē*, a turn.]

strove [strōv] *pt* of **strive**.

struck *See* **strike**.

structure [struk´chůr] *n* manner of building or putting together, construction; arrangement of parts or of particles in a substance, or of atoms in a molecule; manner of organization (eg *the structure of society*); an erection; a building, esp one of large size; an organic form.—*vt* to organize, build up; to construct a framework for.—*adj* **struc´tūral**, of, pertaining to, affecting, produced by, structure.—*adv* **struc´tūrally**, in, as regards, structure. [L *structūra*—*struĕre, structum*, to build.]

strudel [s(h)trōōdl] *n* very thin pastry rolled up enclosing fruit and baked. [Ger.]

struggle [strug´l] *vi* to make great efforts with contortions of the body; to make great exertions (to); to contend (with, for, against); to make one's way (along, through, up, etc.) with difficulty.—*n* a violent effort with contortions of the body; great labor; agony.—*n* **strugg´ler**. [ME *strogelen*.]

strum [strum] *vt* to play on (a guitar, etc.), in an inexpert manner.—Also *vi;*—*pr p* **strumm´ing**; *pt, pt p* **strummed**. [Imit; cf **thrum**.]

strumpet [strum´pet] *n* a prostitute. [OFr *strupe, stupre*—L *stuprum*, dishonor, *stuprāre*, to debauch.]

strung [strung] *pt, pt p* of **string**.

strut[1] [strut] *vi* to walk in a pompous manner, with affected dignity;—*pr p* **strutt´ing**; *pt, pt p* **strutt´ed**.—*n* a step or walk suggesting vanity or affected dignity. [OE *strutian* or kindred form.]

strut[2] [strut] *n* any light structural part or long column that resists pressure in the direction of its length; a prop.—*vt* to brace.

strychnine [strik´nin, -nēn] *n* a poisonous alkaloid obtained from the seeds of nux vomica, a plant (genus *Strychnos*). [Gr *strychnos*, a kind of nightshade.]

stub [stub] *n* the stump left after a tree is cut down; a short piece left after the larger part has been used (as a cigarette, pencil, etc.,); the part of a ticket, bank check, etc. kept as a record; anything short and thick.—*vt* to take the stubs or roots of from the ground; to grub (up); to strike (eg the toe) against a stub or other object; to put (out), to extinguish (a cigarette) by pressure on the end;—*pr p* **stubb´ing**; *pt, pt p* **stubbed**.—*adjs* **stubbed**, short and thick like a stump, blunt, obtuse; **stubb´y**, abounding with stubs or stubble; short and dense; short and thickset.—*n* **stubb´iness**. [OE *stubb, stybb*.]

stubble [stub´l] *n* the stubs or stumps of corn left in the ground when the stalks are cut; any short, bristly growth, as of beard.—*adj* **stubb´ly**. [OFr *estuble*—L *stipula*, dim of *stīpes*, a stalk.]

stubborn [stub´ȯrn] *adj* immovably fixed in opinion, obstinate; persevering; stiff, inflexible.—*adv* **stubb´ornly**.—*n* **stubb´ornness**. [Connection with **stub** is obscure.]

stucco [stuk´ō] *n* a plaster of lime and fine sand, etc., used as a coating for walls, for decorations, etc.; work done in stucco.—*vt* to face or overlay with stucco; to form in stucco. [It *stucco*; from OHG *stucchi*, a crust, a shell.]

stuck [stuk] *pt, pt p* of **stick**.—*adj* **stuck´-up´**, (*inf*) self-importantly aloof.

stud[1] [stud] *n* a male animal, esp a horse; a collection of breeding horses and mares, also the place where they are kept; (*inf*) a young man who is virile and promiscuous.—*ns* **stud´book**, a record of the pedigrees of purebred animals, esp horses and dogs.—**at stud**, for breeding as a stud. [OE *stōd*; Ger *gestüt*.]

stud[2] [stud] *n* a nail with a large head; a headless bolt; a double-headed button worn eg in a shirt; an ornamental knob or boss; an upright piece in a building frame, to which laths, etc., are nailed.—*vt* to adorn with knobs; to set thickly, as with studs;—*pr p* **studd´ing**; *pt, pt p* **studd´ed**. [OE *studu*, a post.]

student [stū´dėnt] *n* one who studies or investigates; one who is enrolled for study at a school, college, etc. [L *studēns, -entis*, pr p of *studēre*, to be zealous.]

studio [stū´di-ō] *n* the workshop of a painter, sculptor, or of a photographer; a place where dancing lessons are given; a building or (also in *pl*) place where motion pictures are made; a room or rooms from which radio or television programs are broadcast.—Also *adj;*—*pl* **stūdios**.—**studio couch**, a couch, usu. without a back, that can be converted into a bed. [It.]

studious [stū´di-ůs] *adj* fond of study; careful (to do, of); studied, deliberately planned or consistently carried out; suitable for, conducive to, study.—*adv* **stū´diously**.—*n* **stū´diousness**. [L *studiōsus*, assiduous—*studium*, zeal.]

study [stud´i] *vt* to observe (eg phenomena) closely; to examine (information) thoroughly so as to understand, interpret, select data from, etc.; to give attention to (a branch of learning—eg *to study mathematics*); to ascertain and act in accordance with (eg *to study his wishes, convenience*; hence, *to study him*, to consult, consider, indulge his wishes, convenience, etc.); to aim at achieving, producing (eg *you should study variety in the menu*).—*vi* to apply the mind closely to a subject, to books; (*dial*) to meditate; to try hard, take pains (eg *study to be quiet, to avoid controversy*);—*pt, pt p* **stud´ied**.—*n* application of the mind to a subject, to books; (*pl*) education, schooling; any object of attentive consideration; a branch of learning; earnest endeavour (eg *to make it his study to please*); a room devoted to study; an artist's preliminary sketch from nature, a student's exercise in painting or sculpture; a composition in music intended to help in acquiring mechanical facility; in theatrical language, one who commits a part to memory (usu. with a qualifying adjective).—*adv* **stud´ied**, deliberate, premeditated (eg *a studied insult*); prepared by careful study. [OFr *estudie* (Fr *étude*)—L *studium*, zeal.]

stuff [stuf] *n* material of which anything is made; essence, elemental part; textile fabrics; cloth, esp when woolen; something consumed or taken into the body by humans, as food or drugs; worthless matter; possessions generally, esp household furniture, etc.; (*inf*) ability, skill, etc.—*vt* to fill by crowding; to cram; to cause to bulge (out) by filling; to fill with seasoning, as of fowl; to fill the skin of, as in taxidermy; to fill by intellectual effort; to thrust (into a bag).—*vi* to feed gluttonously.—*ns* **stuff´ing**, material used to stuff or fill anything.—**do one's stuff**, to do what is expected of one; **know one's stuff**, to have a thorough knowledge of the field in which one is concerned; **that's the stuff**! that's what (ie the substance, object, action, attitude, etc., that) is wanted. [OFr *estoffe*, prob—L *stuppa*, tow.]

stuffy [stuf´i] *adj* badly ventilated, musty; causing difficulty in breathing; (*inf*) obstinate, ungracious, sulky.—*n* **stuff´iness**. [OFr *estouffer*, to choke—*estoffe*, stuff.]

stultify [stul´ti-fī] *vt* to cause to appear foolish, or absurd; hence, to make of no effect, value, or weight (eg *to stultify oneself by inconsistent actions, one's argument by self-contradiction, one's efforts by an ill-judged step*); to dull the mind;—*pt, pt p* **stul´tified**.—*n* **stultificā´tion**, act of stultifying, showing in a foolish light, depriving of weight or effect; state of being stultified. [L *stultus*, foolish, *facĕre*, to make.]

stumble [stum´bl] *vi* to strike the feet against something and trip or lose balance; to falter; to light (on) by chance; to slide into crime or error.—*vt* to cause to trip or stop; to puzzle.—*n* a trip in walking or running; a faltering; a blunder, a failure.—*ns* **stum´bling block**, a block or stone over which one would be likely to stumble; a cause of error; an obstacle, impediment. [ME *stomblen, stomelen, stumlen*; cf **stammer**.]

stump [stump] *n* the part of a tree left in the ground after the trunk is cut down; the part of a limb, tooth, remaining after a part is cut off or destroyed; a similar remnant, eg of a pencil.—*vt* to reduce to a stump, to truncate, to cut off a part of; to baffle, thwart, make helpless (*slang*) to pay (up; also *vi*).—*vi* to walk along heavily; to make stump-speeches.—*n* **stump´er**,—*adj* **stum´py**, full of stumps; short and thick. [Late ME *stompe*; Du *stomp*, Ger *stumpf*.]

stun [stun] *vt* to stupefy with a loud noise, or with a blow; to surprise completely, to amaze;—*pr p* **stunn´ing**; *pt, pt p* **stunned**.—*n* **stunn´er**, a person or an action that strikes with amazement or admiration; a very attractive person. [OFr *estoner*, to astonish; cf Ger *staunen*.]

stung [stung] *pt, pt p* of **sting**.

stunk [stungk] *pt p* of **stink**.

stunt[1] [stunt] *vt* to check the growth of, to dwarf, check.—*adj* **stunt´ed**, dwarfed, checked in development. [OE *stunt*, dull, stupid; ON *stuttr*, short.]

stunt[2] [stunt] *n* a spectacular feat; a project designed to attract attention.—*vi* to perform stunts.—*n* **stunt´man**, one paid to perform dangerous and showy feats (esp a stand-in for a film actor). slang.]

stupefy [stū´pe-fī] *vt* to make stupid or insensible (with drink, drugs, misery, etc.), to deaden the perceptive faculties of;—*pt, pt p* **stū´pefied**.—*n* **stūpefac´tion**, the act of making stupid or senseless; insensibility; (*inf*) dazed condition caused by astonishment and intense disapproval. [L *stupēre*, to be struck senseless, *facĕre*, to make.]

stupendous [stū-pen´důs] *adj* wonderful, amazing, astonishing for its magnitude; often used loosely as a coll term of approbation or admiration.—*adv* **stūpen´dously**.—*n* **stūpen´dousness**. [L *stupendus*—*stupēre*. See **stupefy**.]

stupid [stū´pid] *adj* struck senseless; deficient or dull in understanding; formed or done without reason or judgement, foolish.—*ns* **stūpid´ity, stū´pidness**.—*adv* **stū´pidly**. [Fr,—L *stupidus*—*stupēre*. See **stupefy**.]

stupor [stū´pȯr] *n* suspension of sense either complete or partial, dazed condition; excessive amazement or astonishment. [L,—*stupēre*. See **stupefy**.]

sturdy [stûr´di] *adj* (*comparative* **stur´dier**, *superlative* **stur´diest**) resolute, firm, forcible; strong, robust.—*adv* **stur´dily**.—*n* **stur´diness**. [OFr *estourdi*, pt p of *estourdir*, to stun.]

sturgeon [stûr´jȯn] *n* a genus (*Acipenser*) of large fishes with head and body partly covered by cartilaginous shields, esteemed for its palatable flesh, and for the caviar it yields. [OFr *esturgeon*.]

stutter [stut´ėr] *vi* to hesitate in utterance, repeating initial consonants, to stammer.—*vt* to say or utter in this way.—*n* the act of stuttering; a hesitation in utterance.—*n* **stutt´erer**, one who stutters.—*adv* **stutt´eringly**. [A frequentative of obs *stut*, to stutter.]

sty[1] [stī] *n* a small inflamed swelling on rim of an eyelid. [Obs or dial *stian, styan*—OE *stīgend*, perh—*stīgan*, to rise.]

sty[2] [stī] *n* a pen for swine; any extremely filthy place;—*pl* **sties**. [OE *sti*; cog with *stig*, hall. See **steward**.]

Stygian [stij´i-ȧn] *adj* relating to *Styx*, a river of the lower world; hellish, infernal (eg *Stygian darkness*). [L *Stygius*—Gr *Stygios*—*stygeein*, to hate.]

style [stīl] *n* a stylus; anything long and pointed; mode of expressing thought in language (eg *the matter was excellent but the style was poor*); ideas in the visual arts, etc.; manner of performing an action or of playing a game (eg *he got the results he wanted, but his style was ugly*); the distinctive manner peculiar to an author, painter, etc. or to a period; manner, method; form (*good style, bad style*); fashion; air of fashion, elegance, consequence; title, mode of address; the pin of a sundial; (*bot*) the middle portion of the pistil, between the ovary and the stigma; a convention with respect to spelling, punctuation, capitalization, and typographic arrangement and display followed in writing or printing.—*vt* to entitle in addressing or speaking of; to name or designate; to arrange, dictate the fashion or style of.—*adjs* **sty´lar**, pertaining to the style of a plant ovary; **sty´lish**, conforming to current style, as in dress; fashionable.—*adv* **sty´lishly**.—*ns* **sty´lishness; sty´list**, one with a distinctive and fine literary style; one who develops, designs, or advises on style.—*adj* **stylis´tic**.—*adv* **stylist´ically**. [Partly from L *stilus*; perhaps some meanings from Gr *stȳlos*, a pillar, (erroneously) a style.]

stylite [stī´līt] *n* any of an early class of ascetics who live unsheltered on the tops of pillars—St Simeon Stylites [stīlī´tēz] (c 390–459) is said to have lived thirty years on one. [Gr *stȳlītēs*—*stȳlos*, pillar.]

stylus [sti´lùs] *n* a sharp, pointed marking device, as an instrument used by the ancients in writing on clay or waxed tablets; a pen-shaped instrument used for marking on stencils; a cutting tool used to produce a record groove during disc recording; a phonograph needle. [Root as **style**.]

stymie [stī´mi] *n* in golf, a position when an opponent's ball lies on the direct line between the player's ball and the hole, and blocks the line of play.—*vt* to block; to impede. [Ety obscure.]

styptic [stip´tik] *adj* astringent; that stops bleeding.—*n*. an astringent agent for application to bleeding. [Fr,—L *stypticus*—Gr *styptikos*—*styphein*, to contract.]

suasion [swā´zh(ò)n] *n* the act of persuading, persuasion.—*adj* **suā´sive**, tending to persuade. [Fr,—L *suāsiō, -ōnis*—*suādēre*, to advise.]

suave [swäv] *adj* pleasant, agreeable, polite; bland, mollifying.—*adv* **suave´ly**.—*n* **suav´ity** [swav´-]. [Fr,—L *suāvis*, sweet.]

sub- [sub-] *pfx* (by assimilation before *c, f, g, m, p, r, s*, **suc-**, as *suc*ceed, **suf-**, as *suf*fuse, **sug-**, as *sug*gest, **sum-**, as *sum*mon, **sup-**, as *sup*port, **sur-**, as *sur*reptitious, **sus-**, as *sus*pend—also as **s-**, in *s*ombre and **so-**, in *so*journ) denotes:—

(1) under, below, as **subterranean**, *substratum, substructure, subway*;

(2) below the level of, less than, as **subconscious**, *subhuman, subnormal*;

(3) slightly less than, almost, as **subacute**, *subarctic, subtemperate, subtorrid, subtropical*;

(4) formed by subdivision, as **subtype**, *subphylum, subclass, sub order, subfamily, subgenus, subspecies, subgrade, subgroup, subsection, subvariety*;

(5) under the control of, subordinate, as **subagent**, *subcontract, suboffice, substation*;

(6) next in rank to, under (*fig*) as **subdeacon**, *subdean, subinspector, sublibrarian*. [L *sub*, under (which in OFr became *so-*).]

sub [sub] *n* a submarine; a substitute.—*vi* (*inf*) to be a substitute for someone.

subacid [sub-as´id] *adj* somewhat sharp or biting (eg *a subacid manner*). [L *subacidus*—*sub*, under, somewhat, *acidus*, sour.]

subacute [sub-a-kūt´] *adj* having a tapered but not sharply pointed form; (of a disease) between acute and chronic, moderately acute. [**sub-**, less than, + **acute**.]

subaltern [sub-öl´tėrn] *adj* subordinate; particular with reference to a related universal proposition.—*n* a particular proposition that follows immediately from a universal; an officer in the British army under the rank of captain. [Fr,—L *sub*, under, *alternus*, one after the other—*alter*, the other.]

subaqueous [sub-ā´kwe-ùs] *adj* lying under water; formed under water; living under water.—*adj* **subaquat´ic**, subaqueous; partially aquatic. [**sub-**, + **aqueous, aquatic**.]

subatomic [sub-à-tom´ik] *adj* smaller than an atom; occurring within an atom. [**sub-**, less than, + **atom**.]

subclinical [sub-klin´i-kal] *adj* of a slightness not detectable by usual clinical means. [**sub-**, below the level of, + **clinical**.]

subcommittee [sub´ko-mit´i] *n* a committee exercising powers delegated to it by a larger committee by which it is appointed. [**sub-**, subordinate, + **committee**.]

subconscious [sub-kon´shùs] *adj* of, pertaining to, mental operations just below the level of consciousness; active beneath consciousness.—*n* subconscious mental operations.—*adv* **subcon´sciously**.—*n* **subcon´sciousness**. [**sub-**, below the level of, + **conscious**.]

subcontinent [sub-con´tinent] *n* a land mass having great size (as Greenland) but smaller than any of the usu. recognized continents; a vast subdivision of a continent (as India, Pakistan, and Bangladesh.) [**sub-**, almost, + **continent**.]

subcontract [sub-kon´tràkt] *n* a secondary contract undertaking some or all obligations of another contract.—*vti* to make a subcontrast (for).—*n* **subcon´tractor**.

subcutaneous [sub-kū-tā´ne-ùs] *adj* under the skin. [**sub-**, under, **cutaneous**.]

subdeacon [sub-dē´kòn] *n* a cleric next in rank below deacon. [**sub-**, under, + **deacon**.]

subdivide [sub-di-vīd´] *vt* to divide into smaller divisions, esp to divide (a tract of land) into building lots; to divide again.—*vi* to be subdivided; to separate into smaller divisions.—*n* **subdivi´sion**, the act of subdividing; a part made by subdividing. [**sub-**, under, + **divide**.]

subdominant [sub-dom´i-nànt] *n* (*mus*) the fourth tone of a diatonic scale; an ecologically important life form subordinate in influence to the dominant forms in a habitat. [**sub-**, under, + **dominant**.]

subdue [sub-dū´] *vt* to conquer; to render submissive, to tame; to overcome (eg a desire, impulse), discipline (eg the flesh); to soften, tone down (often in *pt p*—eg color, light, mood or manner, emotion or feeling).—*adj* **subdū´able**.—*n* **subdū´er**. [ME *soduen*—OFr *so(u)duire*—L *sēdūcere*, to seduce; meaning influenced by confusion with L *subdĕre*, to put under—*sub* under, *dăre*, to put.]

subjacent [sub-jā´sėnt] *adj* lying under or below, being in a lower situation. [L *subjacēns, -entis*, pr p of *subjacēre*—*sub*, under, *jacēre*, to lie.]

subject [sub´jekt] *adj* under the power of, owing allegiance to, another; not independent; liable, prone (to—eg *subject to temptation, to colds*); dependent on (a condition) for validity, being put into effect, etc. (eg *the treaty is subject to ratification; this plan is subject to your approval*).—*n* one under the power of another; one under allegiance to a sovereign; the person or thing on which any operation or experiment is performed; (*anat*) a dead body for dissection; that which the artist is trying to express, the scheme or idea of a work of art, as a painting, poem, etc.; a principal theme of a piece of music; the topic or theme of a discourse, etc.; hence, material (eg circumstances) suitable for specified treatment (eg *not a subject for mirth, a subject for congratulation*); something dealt with in discussion, study, etc.; theme; the mind, regarded as the thinking power, in contrast with the *object*, that about which it thinks; (*gram*) the word or words in a sentence about which something is said.—*vt* **subject´**, to bring under the power of; (*with* **to**) to expose or make liable (to—eg *such an indiscretion would subject you to widespread criticism*); to cause to undergo (eg *to subject to great pressure*).—*n* **subjec´tion**, the act of subjecting; the state of being subjected.—*adj* **subjec´tive**, relating to the subject (eg *the nominative case*); determined by, derived from, one's own mind or consciousness; (in literature and other arts) showing clearly the individual tastes, views, prejudices, of the artist (eg *subjective treatment*; cf *objective*).—*adv* **subject´ively**.—*ns* **subject´iveness; subjectiv´ity**, state of being subjective; that which is treated subjectively; **sub´ject matt´er**, the material (facts, ideas) dealt with in a book, etc. [Fr *sujet*—L *subjectus*—*subjicĕre, -jectum*—*sub*, under, *jacĕre*, to throw.]

subjoin [sub-join´] *vt* to add at the end or afterwards. [Through Fr—L *subjungĕre*—*sub*, under, *jungĕre*, to join.]

subjugate [sub´jŏŏ-gāt] *vt* to bring under the yoke, under power or dominion; to conquer.—*ns* **subjugā´tion; sub´jugātor**. [L *subjugāre, -ātum*—*sub*, under, *jugum*, a yoke.]

subjunctive [sub-jungk´tiv] *adv* denoting that mood of a verb which expresses condition, hypothesis, or contingency.—*n* the subjunctive mood. [L *sugjunctīvus*—*sub*, under, *jungĕre, junctum*, to join.]

subkingdom [sub-king´dòm] *n* a primary division of a taxonomic kingdom. [**sub-**, under, + **kingdom**.]

sublease [sub-lēs´] *n* a lease by a tenant to another, the subtenant.—Also *vt*. [**sub-**, under, + **lease**.]

sublet [sub-let´] *vt* to let to another (property which one is renting); to let out (work) to a subcontractor.—Also *n*. [**sub-**, under, and **let**.]

sublimate [sub´lim-āt] *vt* to refine and exalt; to sublime; (*psych*) to use the energy of (a primitive impulse) for purposes of a high nature such as artistic creation.—*n* [-àt], the product of sublimation.—*n* **sublimā´tion**, the act or process of sublimating. [L *sublīmāre, -ātum*, to lift up.]

sublime [sub-līm´] *adj* lofty, majestic, awakening feelings of awe or veneration; (*ironically*) great in a degree that would befit worthier conduct, a finer feeling, etc. (eg *sublime indifference*).—*n* that which is sublime; the lofty or grand in thought or style.—*vt* to exalt, dignify, ennoble; to purify (a solid) by heating to a gaseous state and condensing the vapor back into solid form.—*vi* to be sublimed or sublimated.—*adv* **sublime´ly**.—*n* **sublim´ity**, loftiness, elevation, grandeur. [L *sublīmis*, high; origin uncertain.]

subliminal [sub-lim´i-nàl] *adj* beneath the level of consciousness; too weak or small to produce a conscious sensation or perceptible effect. [L *sub*, under, *līmen, līminis*, the threshold.]

sublunar [sub-lū´nàr] *adj* earthly, belonging to this world; *also* **sub´lunary, sublunary** [sub-lū´nar-i]. [**sub-**, under, + **lunar**.]

submachine gun [sub-ma-shēn´ gun] *n* a lightweight type of machine gun, usu. one for firing from the shoulder. [**sub-**, slightly less than, + **machine-gun**.]

submarine [sub-mà-rēn´] *adj* underwater, esp under the sea.—*n* [sub´-] a submersible boat, capable of being propelled under water, esp for firing torpedoes; a large sandwich on a long split roll with any of a variety of fillings.—Also **hero**. [**sub-**, under, + **marine**.]

submediant [sub-mēd´i-ànt] *n* the sixth tone of a diatonic scale.

submerge [sub-merj´], **submerse** [sub-mėrs´] *vt* to plunge under water; to flood with water; to make obscure or subordinate.—*vi* to sink under water.—*ns* **submerg´ence, submer´sion**.—*adj* **submers´ible**. [L *submergĕre, -mersum*—*sub*, under, *mergĕre*, to plunge.]

submit [sub-mit´] *vt* to surrender (oneself) to another; to offer to another for consideration or criticism (eg *he submitted the manuscript to a friend; I* *have only one suggestion to submit*); to offer as an opinion.—*vi* to yield, to surrender; to yield one's opinion; to be resigned; to consent;—*pr p* **submitt'ing**; *pt, pt p* **submitt'ed.**—*n* **submission** [submish'(ȯ)n], act of submitting; that which is submitted; acknowledgement of inferiority or of a fault; humble behavior; resignation.—*adj* **submiss'ive**, willing or ready to submit, yielding; humble, obedient.—*adv* **submiss'ively**, humbly.—*n* **submiss'iveness**. [L *submittĕre—sub*, under, *mittĕre, missum*, to send.]

submultiple [sub-mul'ti-pl] *n* a number or quantity which is contained in another an exact number of times, an aliquot part. [**sub-**, under, + **multiple**.]

subnormal [sub-nör'mȧl] *adj* lower or smaller than normal; less than normal, esp of a person with less intelligence. [**sub-**, below the level of, + **normal**.]

subordinate [sub-ör'di-nȧt] *adj* lower in order, rank, nature, power, etc.; of less authority, weight, or importance than (*with* **to**).—*n* one in a lower order or rank; an inferior.—*vt* [-āt] to consider, treat, as of less importance than (*with* **to**); to make subject (to).—*adv* **subor'dinately**.—*n* **subordinā'tion**, act of subordinating; state of being subordinate; inferiority of rank or importance. [L *sub*, under, *ordō, ordinis*, order.]

suborn [sub-örn'] *vt* to procure, persuade (a person) eg by bribery, to commit a perjury or other unlawful act.—*ns* **subornā'tion; suborn'er**. [L *subornāre—sub*, under, *ornāre*, to fit out.]

subpoena [sub-pē'na] *n* a written legal order commanding the attendance of a person in court under a penalty.—*vt* to summon by a subpoena;—*pt, pt p* **subpoe'naed**. [L *sub*, under, *poena*, punishment.]

sub rosa [sub rō'zȧ] *adv* secretly; in confidence.—*adj* **subrosa**, secretive, private. [L.]

subscribe [sub-skrīb'] *vt* to write (usu. one's name) underneath, eg a document; to give consent to (something written) by writing one's name underneath; to authenticate (a document) officially in this way; to sign; to promise to give or pay by attaching one's name to a list; to assent to; to support.—*vi* to promise a certain sum by signature; to contribute (to, for); to enter one's name for a publication or service; to receive a periodical or service regularly on order; to agree to purchase and pay for securities, esp of a new offering; to feel favorably disposed.—*ns* **subscrīb'er; sub'script**, a figure, letter, or symbol written below and to the side of another.—Also *adj*.—*n* **subscript'ion**, act of subscribing; a name subscribed; consent as by signature; sum subscribed; a method of offering a series of public performances. [L *subscrībĕre—sub*, under, *scrībĕre, scriptum*, to write.]

subsequent [sub'sė-kwėnt] *adj* following or coming after.—*adv* **sub'sequently**. [L *subsequens, -entis*, pr p of *subsequī—sub*, under, after, *sequī*, to follow.]

subserve [sub-sûrv'] *vt* to promote the welfare or purposes of; to serve subordinately or instrumentally, to help forward (eg a purpose, plan).—*ns* **subser'vience, subser'viency**, state of being subservient; undue deference.—*adj* **subser'vient**, subserving, serving to promote; submissive, obsequious.—*adv* **subser'viently**. [L *subservīre—sub*, under, *servīre*, to serve.]

subside [sub-sīd'] *vi* to sink or fall to the bottom; to flatten out so as to form a depression; to let oneself settle down; to fall into a state of quiet (eg *the storm, the fever, subsided*).—*n* **subsī'dence** (or *sub'si-dėns*), act or process of subsiding, settling, or sinking. [L *subsīdĕre—sub*, down, *sīdĕre*, to settle.]

subsidy [sub'si-di] *n* (*hist*) a sum of money formerly granted by the British parliament to the sovereign raised by special taxes; a sum of money paid by one state to another; money granted by the government to a private person or company to assist an enterprise considered to be of public benefit.—*adj* **subsid'iary**, of, pertaining to, constituting, a subsidy; furnishing help or additional supplies; aiding but secondary; subordinate.—*n* one that is subsidiary, specifically a company controlled by another company.—*adv* **subsid'iarily**.—*vt* **sub'sidīze**, to furnish with a subsidy by purchasing the assistance of through payment of a subsidy or promoting (as a private enterprise) with public money. [Fr,—L *subsidium*, orig troops stationed behind in reserve, aid—*sub*, under, *sīdĕre*, to settle.]

subsist [sub-sist'] *vi* to have existence; to remain, continue; to keep oneself alive (on).—*vt* to provide food for.—*n* **subsist'ence**, state of being subsistent; (*philos*) real being; inherence; means of supporting life, livelihood.—*adj* of wage, allowance, etc., providing the bare necessities of living.—*adj* **subsist'ent**, subsisting; having real being; inherent. [Fr,—L *subsistĕre*, to stand still—*sub*, under, *sistĕre*, to stand.]

subsoil [sub'soil] *n* the under soil, the bed or stratum of earth lying immediately beneath the surface soil. [**sub-**, under, + **soil** (1).]

subsonic [sub-son'ik] *adj* of speed, less than that of sound. [**sub-**, below the level of, + **sonic**.]

substance [sub'stȧns] *n* that which underlies outward manifestation, the essential nature; the essential part, purport, meaning (eg *the substance of his discourse was as follows*); material; a material object; solidity, worth (eg *this cloth has no substance*); property, possessions (eg *a man of substance, to waste one's substance*); a particular kind of matter; an element, compound, or mixture.—**controlled substance**, a legally regulated drug. [L *substantia—substāre*, to stand under—*sub*, under, *stāre*, to stand.]

substantial [sub-stan'sh(ȧ)l] *adj* consisting of, of the nature of, substance; real, not merely seeming; virtual, in total effect though not in all details (eg *this is the substantial truth; in substantial agreement*); considerable, important (eg *a substantial sum, argument*); strong, stout, bulky; having property or estate.—*n* something having actual existence, value, or importance.—*n* **substantial'ity**.—*adv* **substan'tially**, in essence, in total effect, to all intents and purposes.—*vt* **substantiate** [-stan'shi-āt], to make substantial; to prove, to show the validity of, grounds for (eg *a statement, a charge, a claim*).—*n* **substantiā'tion**.—*adj* **sub'stantive**, expressing existence; real; of real, independent importance.—*n* (*gram*) any noun, as well as any other word or group of words used as a noun or instead of a noun, in contradistinction to an adjective.—*adv* **sub'stantively**. [Fr *substantiel*—L *substantiālis—substantia*. See **substance**.]

substitute [sub'sti-tūt] *vt* to put in place of another person or thing (*with* **for**); to replace (by).—*n* one who, or that which, is put in place of, or used instead of, for want of, another.—*adj* put instead of another.—*ns* **substit'uent**, something that may be, or is, substituted; an atom or radical taking the place of an atom or radical removed from a molecule; **substitū'tion**, act of substituting; the replacement of one mathematical entity by another of equal value; one that is substituted for another.—*adj* **substitū'tional**. [L *substituĕre, -ūtum—sub*, under, *statuĕre*, to set.]

subsume [sub-sūm'] *vt* to include (eg a particular, an instance) under a universal, a rule, class.—*n* **subsump'tion**. [L *sub*, under, *sumĕre*, to take.]

subtenant [sub-ten'ȧnt] *n* a tenant who leases from one who is also a tenant. [**sub-**, under, + **tenant**.]

subtend [sub-tend'] *vt* to extend under or be opposite to, as a hypotenuse a right angle, or a chord an arc. [L *subtendĕre—sub*, under, *tendĕre*, to stretch.]

subterfuge [sub'tėr-fūj] *n* an artifice to escape censure or the force of an argument, evasion. [Fr,—L *subterfugĕre—subter*, under, *fugĕre*, to flee.]

subterranean [sub-te-rā'nė-ȧn] *adj* under the earth or ground; hidden, secret.—also **subterrā'neous**. [L *subterrāneus—sub*, under, *terra*, the earth.]

subtile [sut'il or sub'til] *adj* subtle, elusive; cunning, crafty; sagacious, discerning.—*adv* **sub'tilely**.—*ns* **sub'tileness; subtilty** [sut'il-ti or sub'til-ti]. See **subtle**. [L *subtīlis—sub*, under, *tēla*, a web.]

subtitle [sub'tī-tl] *n* an explanatory, usu. secondary, title to a book; a line or lines as of dialogue shown on a TV or movie screen. [**sub-**, subordinate, + **title**.]

subtle [sut'l] *adj* pervasive but difficult to describe (eg *a subtle perfume, a subtle feeling of horror*); difficult to define, put into words (eg *a subtle distinction, subtle variations*); acute (of mind); showing acuteness of mind (eg *a subtle analysis of the situation*); insinuating, sly, artful; delicately skillful; cunningly made or contrived.—*ns* **subt'leness, subt'lety**, quality of being subtle; tenuousness, indefinableness; acuteness (of mind); quality of being discerning and penetrative (eg *the subtlety of the analysis*); a fine distinction.—*adv* **subt'ly**. [Contr of **subtile**.]

subtract [sub-trakt'] *vti* to take away or deduct, as one quantity from another.—*n* **subtrac'tion**, the operation of finding the difference between two quantities.—*adj* **subtract'ive**, subtracting; tending to subtract or lessen.—*n* **sub'trahend**, the number to be subtracted from another. [L *subtrahĕre, -tractum—sub*, under, *trahĕre*, to draw away.]

subtropical [sub-trop'ik-ȧl] *adj* of, characteristic of, the regions bordering on the tropics.

suburb [sub'ùrb] *n* a district, town, etc., on the outskirts of a large city; (*pl*) the residential area on the outskirts of a city; (*pl*) the near vicinity.—*adj* **subur'ban**, of a suburb.—*ns* **subur'banite**, a person living in a suburb; **subur'bia**, suburbanites and suburbs collectively. [L *suburbium—sub*, under, near, *urbs*, a city.]

subvention [sub-ven'sh(ȯ)n] *n* a subsidy. [L *sub*, under, *venīre, ventum*, to come.]

subvert [sub-vûrt'] *vt* to overthrow, to ruin utterly (something established); to corrupt, as in morals.—*n* **subver'sion**, act of subverting; entire overthrow, ruin.—*adj* **subver'sive**, tending to subvert (eg *subversive of morality*).—*n* **subvert'er**. [L *subvertĕre—sub*, under, *vertĕre, versum*, to turn.]

subway [sub'wā] *n* a passage under a street (as for pedestrians, power cables, or water or gas mains); an underground metropolitan electric railway. [**sub-**, under, + **way**.]

succeed [suk-sēd'] *vt* to come after, to follow in order; to follow, take the place of (eg *Henry III succeeded John; he succeeded him in office*).—*vi* to follow in order; to take the place of; to accomplish one's aim; to prosper.—*n* **success'**, the gaining of wealth, fame, etc.; the prosperous termination (of anything attempted); a successful person or affair.—*adj* **success'ful**, having, achieving, the desired end or effect, gaining the prize aimed at; prosperous.—*adv* **success'fully**.—*n* **success'ion**, act of following after; series (of persons or things following each other in time or place); right of succeeding; series of persons having this; order of succeeding.—*adj* **success'ive**, following in succession or in order.—*adv* **success'ively**.—*n* **success'or**, one who succeeds another, as to an office.—**in succession**, one after another, running. [L *succēdĕre—sub*, up, *cēdĕre*, to go.]

succès d'estime [sük-se des-tēm] *n* something (as a work of art) that wins critical respect but not popular success; **succès fou** [fōō], extraordinary success; **succès de scandale** [dė scā-dal], success of a book, play, etc. due not to merit but to its scandalous nature; the reception accorded such a work. [Fr.]

succinct [suk-singkt'] *adj* short, concise.—*adv* **succinct'ly**.—*n* **succinct'ness**. [L *succinctus—sub*, up, *cingĕre*, to gird.]

succory [suk´ȯr-i] *n* chicory.

succor [suk´ȯr] *vt* to assist, to relieve.—*n* aid, relief. [L *succurrĕre*, to run up to—*sub*, up, *currĕre*, to run.]

succotash [suk´ō-tash] *n* a dish of lima beans and corn kernels cooked together. [Amer Indian.]

succulent [suk´ū-lėnt] *adj* full of juice, juicy; moist and tasty; of a plant, having fleshy tissue designed to conserve moisture; rich in interest.—*n* a succulent plant (as a cactus).—*n* **succ´ūlence**.—*adv* **succ´ūlently**. [L *succulentus*—*succus*, juice—*sūgĕre*, to suck.]

succumb [su-kum´] *vi* to yield to superior strength or over-powering desire; to die. [L *succumbĕre*—*sub*, under, -*cumbĕre* (found only in compounds), to lie down.]

such [such] *adj* of this or that kind (eg *such people, such a man*); of the quality or character mentioned or implied; used to give emphasis (as in *such a fine day*!); of the kind (that, as—followed by explanatory clause or infinitive; eg *his absorption was such that he lost all sense of time, such as to make him unconscious of time*).—**such and such**, a demonstrative phrase vaguely indicating a person or thing not named—some (eg *such and such a person may say*); **such as**, of the same kind as; for example; those who; **suchlike**, persons or things of such a kind; of like kind, similar.—**as such**, in itself, intrinsically considered. [OE *swylc*—*swa*, so, *līc*, like.]

suck [suk] *vt* to draw into the mouth; to draw milk or other liquid from with the mouth; to lick, squeeze, and roll about in the mouth; to draw in as if by sucking (*with* **in, up**, etc.); to drain, exhaust (eg *to suck dry*).—*vi* to suck something; (*slang*) to be extremely objectionable or inadequate.—*n* act of sucking; a sucking movement.—*n* **suck´er**, one who, or that which, sucks; the organ by which an animal adheres to other bodies; a shoot rising from a subterranean stem; a lollipop; (*slang*) a gullible person.—*adj* **suck´ing**, still nourished by milk; young and inexperienced.—**suck in**, to tighten the abdomen by inhaling deeply; (*inf*) to dupe. [OE *sūcan, sūgan*; Ger *saugen*.]

suckle [suk´l] *vt* to feed at the breast or udder.—*n* **suck´ling**, a young child or animal still being fed on its mother's milk.—*adj* sucking. [Dim of **suck**.]

sucrose [sū´krōs] *n* the form of sugar obtained from sugarcane and sugar beet. [Fr *sucre*, sugar, and suffix *-ose*.]

suction [suk´sh(ȯ)n] *n* act, or power, of sucking; act or process of exhausting the air and creating a vacuum into which fluids are pushed by atmospheric pressure or, more generally, of exerting a force on a body (solid, liquid, or gas) by reducing the air pressure on part of its surface.—*n* **suc´tion pump**, the common pump, in which liquid rises to fill a partial vacuum produced by a simple mechanism of piston and valves. [L *suctiō, -ōnis*—*sūgĕre, suctum*, to suck.]

sudatory [sū´da-tȯr-i] *n* a sweat room in a bath.—Also **sudator´ium**. [L *sūdātōrius*—*sūdāre, -ātum*.]

sudden [sud´ėn] *adj* unexpected (eg *a sudden call; sudden death*), hasty (eg *a sudden departure*), abrupt (eg *a sudden bend in the road*).—*adv* **sudd´enly**.—*n* **sudd´enness**.—**all of a sudden**, suddenly.—**sudden death** (*sports*) an extra period added to a tied game, the game ending as soon as one side scores. [OFr *sodain*—L *subitāneus*, sudden—*subitus*, coming stealthily—*sub*, up, *īre, ĭtum*, to go.]

sudorific [sū-dor-if´ik] *adj* causing sweat.—*n* a medicine producing sweat, a diaphoretic.—*n* **sū´dor**, sweat. [L *sūdor*, sweat, *facĕre*, to make.]

suds [sudz] *n pl* soapy water; the froth and bubbles of stirred soapy water; foam, froth; beer. [OE *soden*, pt p of *sēothan*, to seethe; cog with Ger *sod*—*sieden*.]

sue [sōō] *vt* to entreat, make petition to; to prosecute at law.—*vi* to make legal claim; to petition, to entreat, to demand (*to* a person *for* a thing); to pay court to, to woo. [ME *suen*—OFr *(il)siut, suit*, 3d sing pres indic of *sevre* (Fr *suivre*)—L *sequī, secūtus*, to follow.]

suede, suède [swād] *n* skins used for gloves and for shoe uppers, made from sheep or lamb skins dressed on the flesh side and finished without glaze; a cloth like this.—Also *adj*. [Fr *Suède*, Sweden.]

suet [sū´ėt, sōō´ėt] *n* the hard fat, accumulating about the loins and kidneys of the ox, sheep, etc.—*adj* **su´ety**. [OFr *seu* (Fr *suif*)—L *sēbum*, fat.]

suffer [suf´ėr] *vt* to undergo (eg *to suffer a change*); to endure (eg pain, martyrdom); to permit (to do); to tolerate (eg *he would not suffer any interference*).—*vi* to feel pain; to undergo punishment (for); to sustain loss or injury.—*adj* **suff´erable**, that may be suffered; endurable; allowable.—*ns* **suff´erance**, state of suffering; endurance; permission, esp when tacit or unwilling, tolerance (usu. in phrase **on sufferance**—eg *he was there on sufferance*, his presence was tolerated but not desired or approved, or, he was there subject to good behavior); **suff´erer; suff´ering**, distress, pain, loss, or injury. [L *sufferre*—*sub*, under, *ferre*, to bear.]

suffice [su-fīs´] *vi* to be enough; to be equal (to do), adequate (for the end in view).—*vt* to satisfy.—*adj* **suffi´cient** [-fi´shėnt], enough; equal to any end or purpose.—*adv* **suffi´ciently**.—*n* **sufficiency** [sů-fi´shėn-si], an adequate quantity (of); adequate resources; state of being sufficient; competence, ability, capacity. [Fr,—L *sufficĕre*, to put in the place of—*sub*, under, *facĕre*, to make.]

suffix [suf´iks] *n* a letter, syllable, or syllables added to the end of a word to modify its meaning or to form a new derivative.—*vt* **suffix´**, to add a letter or syllable at the end of a word for such a purpose. [L *suffixus*—*sub*, under, *figĕre*, to fix.]

suffocate [suf´ō-kāt] *vt* to kill by stopping the breath, to stifle; to cause to feel unable to breathe freely; to deprive of conditions necessary for growth or expression, to destroy (eg aspirations).—*adj* **suff´ocāting**, choking, hindering respiration; hindering self-expression.—*adv* **suff´ocātingly**.—*n* **suffocā´tion**, act of suffocating; state of being suffocated. [L *suffōcāre, -ātum*—*sub*, under, *fauces*, the throat.]

suffragan [suf´ra-gȧn] *n* originally a bishop who might be required by his metropolitan to attend a synod and give a vote; a bishop who is an assistant to another bishop. [OFr *suffragan*—L *suffrāgans*, pr p of *suffrāgāri*, to vote for—*suffrāgium*, to vote.]

suffrage [suf´rij] *n* a vote; a vote in approbation or assent; the right to vote.—*n* **suffragette´**, a woman who advocates female suffrage. [L *suffrāgium*, a vote.]

suffuse [su-fūz´] *vt* to overspread or cover, as with a fluid (eg *eyes suffused with tears*), or with color or light.—*n* **suffū´sion**, act or operation of suffusing; state of being suffused; that which suffuses. [L *suffundĕre*—*sub*, underneath, *fundĕre, fūsum*, to pour.]

sugar [shŏŏg´ȧr] *n* a sweet substance obtained chiefly from sugarcane and the sugar beet, and also from maple and palm trees, etc.; any of a number of similar sweet soluble carbohydrates, eg fructose, glucose, lactose; excessive flattery or compliment.—*vt* to sprinkle or mix with sugar.—*vi* to form sugar crystals.—*ns* **sug´ar beet**, a variety of white beet, grown for sugar; **sug´arcane**, a stout tall perennial grass (*Saccharum officinarum*) that is widely grown in warm regions as a source of sugar.—*vt* **sug´arcoat´**, coat with sugar.—*n* **sug´ar daddy**, an elderly man who spends much money on a mistress or girlfriend; a generous benefactor of a cause.—*adj* **sug´ared**, sweetened with sugar; delightful, charming; too sweet.—*ns* **sug´arloaf**, a loaf or mass of sugar, usu. in the form of a truncated cone; a hill or mountain shaped like a sugarloaf (also *adj*); **su´garplum**, a species of sweetmeat made up in small lumps like a plum.—*adj* **sug´ary**, sweetened with, tasting of, or like, sugar; sickly sweet.—*n* **sug´ariness**.—**sugar of lead**, an acetate of lead, used as a mordant in dyeing, etc. [Fr *sucre*—Sp *azucar*—Ar *sukkar*—Pers *shakar*—Sans *sarkarā*, sugar, orig grains of sand, applied to sugar because occurring in grains.]

suggest [sug-jest´] *vt* to put into one's mind; to bring to one's mind; to bring to one's mind by association of ideas; to imply or seem to imply; to propose; to hint (to).—*adj* **suggest´ible**, that may be suggested; easily influenced by, susceptible to, suggestion.—*n* **suggestion** [sug-jes´ch(ȯ)n], act of suggesting; the mental process by which one thought or idea calls up another; the process by which an individual accepts an idea presented by another person or thing and acts in accordance with it; (*psychoanalysis*) such acceptance of an idea or attitude induced by an unconscious emotional tie with another person—used as a method of treatment in psychotherapy; a proposal; a hint; a slight trace.—*adj* **suggestive**, containing a hint; fitted to bring to one's mind the idea (of); of, pertaining to, suggestion; rather indecent.—*adv* **sugges´tively**.—*n* **sugges´tiveness**. [L *suggerĕre*—*sub*, under, *gerĕre, gestum*, to carry.]

suicide [sū´i-sīd, or sōō´-] *n* one who dies by his own hand; the act of killing oneself intentionally; ruin of one's own interests.—*adj* **sūicī´dal**, of, pertaining to, suicide; directed towards, or with an impulse towards, suicide; destructive of one's own interests.—*adv* **suicī´dally**. [Coined from L *sui*, of himself, *caedĕre*, to kill.]

suit [sūt, sōōt] *n* act of suing; an action at law; petition; a courtship; a set of playing cards of one kind (eg of hearts); all the dominoes bearing the same number; a number of things made to be worn together, esp a jacket and skirt (or trousers).—*vt* to fit, accommodate (to, eg *he suited his views to his audience*); to become (eg *the hat, sarcasm, does not suit you*); to please (eg *suit yourself*); to be convenient to (eg *the hour chosen did not suit him*); to agree with (eg *the climate did not suit her*).—*vi* to go well (with).—*pt p* **suit´ed**, fitted (to, for).—*adj* **suit´able**, fitting; agreeable (to), convenient (to, for).—*ns* **suitabil´ity, suit´ableness**.—*adv* **suit´ably**.—*ns* **suitcase**, an easily portable oblong traveling-bag for carrying suits and clothes, etc.; **suit´ing**, material for suits of clothes; **suit´or**, one who sues in love or law; **strong suit**, one's forte. [Through OFr,—L *sequī, secūtus*, to follow.]

suite [swēt] *n* a train of followers or attendants; a regular set, esp of rooms, furniture, pieces of music. [Fr; cf **suit**.]

sukiyaki [sōō´kē-yä-kē] *n* thinly sliced beef and vegetables, quickly cooked together, often at table. [Jap.]

sulcate [sul´kāt] *adj* furrowed, grooved. [L *sulcāre, -ātum*—*sulcus*, a furrow.]

sulfonamide. See **sulfur**.

sulfur [sul´fůr] *n* a yellow nonmetallic element (symbol S; at wt 32.1; no 16), very brittle, fusible, and inflammable.—*ns* **sul´fate**, a salt of sulfuric acid; **sul´fide**, a compound of sulfur with another element or radical; **sul´fite**, a salt of sulfurous acid.—*adj* **sulfū´reous**, consisting of, containing, or having the qualities of, sulfur.—*adjs* **sul´fūretted**, having sulfur in combination; **sul´fūrous**, sulfureous; **sulfūr´ic** and **sul´fūrous** are used for compounds in which sulfur has respectively a higher and a lower valency or combining power, eg *sulfuric acid* (H_2SO_4); *sulfurous acid* (H_2SO_3—known only as an aqueous solution of sulfur dioxide, but forming sulfites); **sulfonic** denotes compounds containing an acid group (SO_2OH) of valency 1, and appears in composition as **sulfon-**, eg **sulfon´amide**, any of a group of drugs with powerful antibacterial action.—**sulfur dioxide**, (SO_2)

a colorless gas formed when sulfur burns in air—**flowers of sulfur**, a yellow powder obtained by distilling other forms of sulfur. [L *sulphur*.]

sulk [sulk] *vi* to be sulky.—*n pl* **sulks**, a fit of sulkiness.—*adj* **sulk´y**, silently sullen, withdrawn and unresponsive because of (usu. petty) resentment.—*n* a light vehicle, consisting of a single seat, mounted on two wheels.—*n* **sulk´iness**, quality or state of being sulky.—*adv* **sulk´ily**, in a morose, sullen manner. [OE *solcen*, slow—*seolcan*, to be slow.]

sullen [sul´ėn] *adj* gloomily angry and silent; dark, dull (eg *a sullen sky*).—*adv* **sull´enly**.—*n* **sull´enness**. [OFr *solain*—L *sōlus*, alone.]

sully [sul´i] *vt* to soil, to spot, to tarnish.—*vi* to be soiled;—*pt t* and *pt p* **sull´ied**. [Fr *souiller*.]

sultan [sul´tan] *n* a sovereign, esp of a Muslim state.—**sultana** [sul-tä´na], the mother, a wife, or a daughter of a sultan; a pale yellow seedless grape grown for raisins and wine; the raisin of a sultana. **sul´taness**, (*arch*) **sultana**.—*n* **sul´tanate**. a state or country governed by a sultan; the office or dignity of a sultan. [Ar *sultān*, victorious, a ruler.]

sultry [sul´tri] *adj* sweltering, very hot and oppressive, close; hot with rage; passionate.—*adv* **sul´trily**.—*n* **sul´triness**. [Earlier **sweltry**; see **swelter**.]

sum [sum] *n* the amount of two or more things taken together; the whole amount, aggregate; a quantity of money; a problem in arithmetic; the substance or result of reasoning; summary, gist (also **sum and substance**).—*vt* to collect into one amount or whole; to add; (usu. **sum up**) to give the gist of;—*pr p* **summ´ing**; *pt, pt p* **summed**.—*ns* **sum´mand**, [or -and´] an addend; part of a sum; **summ´ing-up**, a recapitulation or review; a judge's summary survey of the evidence for the information and guidance of the jury; **sum total**, the aggregate of various smaller sums; total result.—**in sum**, in short. [OFr *summe*—L *summa*—*summus, suprēmus*, highest, superl of *superus*, on high—*super*, above.]

sumac, sumach [sū´mak] *n* any of a genus (*Rhus*) of small trees and shrubs, the leaves and shoots of which yield tannin and are used in dyeing; any of several related poisonous plants. [Fr *sumac*—Sp *zumaque*—Ar *summāq*.]

Sumerian [sū-mē´ri-ȧn] *adj* pertaining to *Sumer*, one of the two divisions of ancient Babylonia (the plain watered by the lower streams of the Tigris and Euphrates).—*n* a native of Sumer; the language of the Sumerians that has no known linguistic affinities.

summa cum laude [sům-ȧ kům lowd´ė] *adj, adv* with the highest distinction. [L.]

summary [sum´ȧ-ri] *adj* short, brief, compendious; quick, without waste of time or words, without formalities.—*n* an abstract, abridgment, or compendium.—*adv* **summ´arily**.—*vt* **summ´arize**, to present in a summary, to state briefly.—*vi* to make a summary. [L *summārium*—*summa*. See **sum**.]

summation [sum-ā´sh(ȯ)n] *n* act of forming a total or sum; cumulative action or effect; a final part of an argument expressing conclusions, as in a trial. [**sum**.]

summer [sum´ėr] *n* the second and warmest season of the year, following the spring—in northern temperate regions from May or June to July or August; astronomically, from the summer solstice to the autumn equinox.—*vi* to pass the summer.—*adj* of or like summer.—*ns* **summ´er-house**, a structure in a garden, park, etc., for sitting in; **summ´ertime**, the summer season.—*adj* **sum´mery**, like summer; suitable for summer. [OE *sumer, sumor*; Du *zomer*, Ger *sommer*.]

summersault *See* **somersault**.

summit [sumit] *n* the highest point, the top.—*n* **summ´itry**, the practice or technique of holding summit conferences.—**summit conference**, a conference between heads of states. [OFr *sommette*, dim of *som*, the top of a hill—L *summum*, highest.]

summon [sum´ȯn] *vt* to call with authority; to command to appear, esp in court; (also **summon up**) to rouse to activity (eg *to summon energy, courage to do this*).—*ns* **summ´oner; summ´ons**, an authoritative call; a call to appear, esp in court; a call to surrender.—*vt* to serve with a legal summons. [OFr *somoner*—L *summonēre*—*sub*, secretly, *monēre*, to warn.]

sump [sump] *n* a small pit at the lowest point of a mine or excavation into which water can drain and out of which it can be pumped; a pit for used metal; the oil container in a motor vehicle. [Du *somp*; Ger *sumpf*.]

sumpter [sump´tėr] *n* a pack animal [OFr *sommetier*, a pack-horse driver—L *sagmārius*—Gr *sagma*, a pack-saddle, *sattein*, to pack.]

sumptuary [sumpt´ū-ȧr-i] *adj* pertaining to or regulating personal expenditures and esp preventing extravagance, usu. by imposing taxes on luxuries. [L *sumptuārius*—*sumptus*, cost.]

sumptuous [sumpch´ū-ȯs] *adj* costly; magnificent.—*n* **sumpt´ūousness**.—*adv* **sumpt´ūously**. [L *sumptuōsus*, costly—*sumptus*, cost.]

sun [sun] *n* the star which gives light and heat to the solar system; a body which, like the earth's sun, forms the center of a planetary system; that which resembles the sun in position of importance or in brightness; the sunshine.—*vt* to expose to the sun's rays.—*vi* to sun oneself;—*pr p* **sunn´ing**; *pt, pt p* **sunned**.—*n* **sun´bath**, exposure of the body to the sun's rays or a sunlamp.—*vi* **sun´bathe**, to take a sunbath.—*ns* **sun´bather; sun´beam**, a ray of sunlight; **sun´bird**, a family (*Nectariniidae*) of small Old World tropical birds, the males with resplendent metallic plumage; **Sun´belt´**, the southern and southwestern states of the US; **sun´bonn´et**, a bonnet shading the face and neck from the sun; **sun´burn**, inflammation of the skin from exposure to sunlight or to a sunlamp.—*vti* to get or cause to get a sunburn; **sun´dew**, a genus (*Drosera*) of small insectivorous plants found in bogs and moist ground; **sun´dī´al**, an instrument for measuring time by means of the shadow cast by a pointer erected on its surface; **sun´down**, sunset.—*ns* **sun´fish**, any of numerous N American freshwater fish (genus *Lepomis*) usu. with a deep compressed body and metallic luster; a large sluggish marine fish (*Mola mola*); **Sunfish**, trade name for a light sailboat; **sun´flower**, any of a genus (*Helianthus*) of plants whose seeds yield oil and whose flower is a large disk with yellow rays; **sun´glasses**, tinted eyeglasses to protect the eyes from strong light; **sun´lamp**, an electric lamp designed to emit wavelengths of light from ultraviolet to infrared.—*adj* **sun´less**, without sun; dark, cheerless.—*n* sun´light, the light of the sun.—*adjs* **sun´lit**, lighted by the sun; **sunn´y**, exposed to, filled with, warmed by, the sun's rays; like the sun or sunshine, esp in brightness; cheerful.—*ns* **sun´rise**, the daily appearance of the sun above the eastern horizon; the time of this rising; **sun´set**, the daily disappearance of the sun below the western horizon; the time of this; **sun´shade**, a parasol, a kind of umbrella used as protection against the sun; an awning; **sun´shine**, sunlight; the light and heat from the sun; warmth and brightness.—*adjs* **sun´shine**, prohibiting closed meeting of legislative or executive bodies and sometimes providing access to public records; **sun´shiny**, bright with sunshine; pleasant; bright like the sun.—*ns* **sunroof**, a car roof having a panel that can be opened; **sun´spot**, one of the temporarily cooler regions appearing as dark irregular spots on the surface of the sun; **sun´stroke**, a condition of fever, convulsions, coma, caused by excessive exposure to sunshine; **sun´tan**, a browning of the skin as a result of exposure to the sun; (*pl*) a tan-colored summer uniform.—*adj* **sun´tanned**.—*n* **sun´up´**, sunrise.—*adv* **sun´ward**, toward the sun.—**in the sun**, in the public eye; **under the sun**, in the world, on earth. [OE *sunne*; ON *sunna*, Old Ger *sunne*.]

sundae [sun´dā] *n* a serving of ice cream covered with a topping (as of crushed fruit, syrup, nuts, etc.) [**Sunday**.]

Sunday [sun´dā] *n* the first day of the week, now regarded as the Sabbath by most Christians.—*adj* **Sunday-go-to-meeting**, clothes appropriate for churchgoing.—*n* **Sun´day school**, a school for religious instruction of children, held on Sunday; the teachers and pupils of such a school. [OE *sunnan dæg*; Ger *sonntag*.]

sunder [sun´dėr] *vti* to separate, to divide. [OE *syndrian*, to separate—*sundor*, separate; ON *sundr*, asunder.]

sundry [sun´dri] *adj* miscellaneous, various.—*pron* (plural in construction) an indeterminate number.—*n pl* **sun´dries**, various small things. [OE *syndrig*—*syndrian*, to separate.]

sung [sung] *pt p* of **sing**.

sunk [sungk], **sunken** [sungk´n] *pt p* of **sink**.

sup [sup] *vt* to take into the mouth in small quantities, as with a spoon.—*vi* to have supper;—*pr p* **supp´ing**; *pt, pt p* **supped**.—*n* a small mouthful, as of liquid. [OE *sūpan*; ON *sūpa*, Ger *saufen*, to drink.]

super- [sōō´pėr-] *pfx* [L *super*, prep and pfx, above, etc.] conveys meanings such as the following:—(1) above, on the top of, eg **superstructure, superimpose**; (2) superior to, eg **superintendent**; (3) beyond, beyond the normal, eg **supernormal, supersaturate**; (4) greater than others of its kind, eg **superman, supermarket**; (5) additional, eg **supertax**.

super [sōō´pėr] *n* a supernumerary actor; superintendant, supervisor, esp the superintendant of an apartment building; a superfine grade or large size; a fabric used for reinforcing books.—*vt* to reinforce (as a book backbone) with super.—*adj* outstanding; great, extreme, or excessive.—*adv* very, extremely; to an excessive degree.

superable [sōō´pėr-ȧ-bl] *adj* able to be surmounted. [L *superāre*, to overcome—*super*, above.]

superabundant [sōō-pėr-ab-und´ȧnt] *adj* abundant to excess, more than enough.—*vi* **superabound´**, to abound exceedingly, to be more than enough.—*n* **superabund´ance**.—*adv* **superabund´antly**. [L *superabundans, -antis*, pr p of *superabundāre*. See **super**, and **abound**.]

superannuate [sōō-pėr-an´ū-āt] *vt* to make, declare or prove obsolete or out-of-date; to pension on account of old age or infirmity.—*n* **superannuā´tion**, state of being superannuated. [L *super*, above, *annus*, a year.]

superb [sōō-pûrb´] *adj* proud, magnificent, stately; of the highest, most impressive, quality.—*adv* **superb´ly**. [L *superbus*, proud—*super*, above.]

supercalender [sōō-pėr-kal´ėn-dėr] *vt* to give (paper) an extra smooth surface by means of supercalenders.—*n* a stack of highly polished calender rolls used to give an extra finish to paper. [**super-**, beyond the normal, + **calender**.]

supercargo [sōō´pėr-kär´go] *n* an officer on a merchant ship placed in charge of the cargo and superintending all the commercial transactions of the voyage. [**super-**, over, + **cargo**.]

supercharger [sōō´pėr-chär´jėr] *n* a compressor used to supply air or combustible mixture to an internal-combustion engine at a pressure greater than atmospheric.—*vt* **supercharge´**, to supply air, etc., to by means of a supercharger; to give an additional charge to, or to charge in excess. [**super-**, beyond the normal, + **charger** (see **charge**).]

supercilious [sōō´pėr-sil´i-us] *adj* prone to despise others; haughty, disdainful.—*adv* **supercil´iously**.—*n* **supercil´iousness**. [L *superciliōsus*—*supercilium*, an eyebrow—*super*, above, *cilium*, eyelid.]

superconductivity [sōō´pėr-kon-duk-tiv´i-ti] *n* the property possessed by many metals at near absolute zero temperature of having no resistance to the flow of electricity. [**super-**, beyond the normal, + **conductivity**.]

supercool [sōō´pėr-kōōl] *vt* to cool below the freezing point without solidification or crystallization. [**super-**, beyond the normal, + **cool**.]

superdominant [sōō´pėr-dom´i-nȧnt] *adj* the tone next above the dominant; submediant. [**super-**, above, + **dominant**.]

superego [sōō´pėr-ē´-gō] *n* in psychoanalytic theory, that part of the psyche which enforces moral standards.

supererogation [sōō´pėr-er-ō-gā´sh(ȯ)n] *n* performance of good deeds beyond those which the Church requires as necessary for salvation, hence anything superfluous or uncalled for.—*adj* **supererog´atory**. [L *super*, above, *ērogāre, -ātum*, to pay out.]

superficies [sōō´pėr-fish-i-ēz] *n* the upper surface, outer face; the external area; external features, appearance.—*adj* **superficial** [-fi´-sh(ȧ)l], of, or near, the surface; not going deeper than the surface; slight, not thorough; (of a person) shallow in nature or knowledge.—*adv* **superfi´cially**.—*n* **superficial´ity**. [L *superficiēs—super*, above, *faciēs*, face.]

superfine [sōō´pėr-fīn] *adj* finer than ordinary. [**super-**, beyond the normal, + **fine** (1).]

superfluous [sōō´pėr´flōō-ủs] *adj* beyond what is enough; unnecessary.—*n* **superflū´ity**, a superfluous quantity or more than enough, superabundance; state of being superfluous; something unnecessary.—*adv* **super´fluously**. [L *superfluus—super*, above, *fluĕre*, to flow.]

superheat [sōō´pėr-hēt] *vt* to heat (a liquid) beyond its boiling point without converting it into vapor; to heat (steam, etc.) out of contact with the liquid from which it was formed so as to cause to remain free from suspended liquid droplets. [**super-**, above the normal, + **heat**.]

superhighway [sōō´pėr-hī´wā] *n* an expressway or turnpike. [**super-**, beyond the normal, + **highway**.]

superhuman [sōō´pėr-hū´mȧn] *adj* above what is human; divine. [**super-**, of higher quality than, + **human**.]

superimpose [sōō´pėr-im-pōz´] *vt* to put or lay upon something else. [**super-**, above, + **impose**.]

superincumbent [sōō´pėr-in-kum´bėnt] *adj* resting or lying, esp heavily (on a person or thing). [**super-**, above, + **incumbent**.]

superinduce [sōō´pėr-in-dūs´] *vt* to bring in over and above, in addition to, something else. [L *superindūcĕre*, to draw over—*super*, above, *in*, on, *dūcĕre*, to lead.]

superintend [sōō´pėr-in-tend´] *vt* to have the oversight or charge of, to control, manage.—*ns* **superinten´dence, superinten´dency**, oversight, direction, management.—*adj* **superinten´dent**.—*n* a person in charge of a department, institution, etc.; a director; a person responsible for the maintenance of a building. [L *superintendĕre—super*, above, *in*, on, *tendĕre*, to stretch.]

superior [sōō´pē´ri-ȯr] *adj* upper; higher in place; higher in rank; higher in excellence; greater in number, power; above the common in quality or rank (eg *a superior article, person*); implying a sense of greater importance, knowledge, etc. (eg *a superior air, smile*); beyond the influence of; too courageous, self-controlled, etc., to yield (to—eg *superior to temptation*); supercilious or uppish.—*n* one superior to others; the chief of a religious community.—*n* **supĕrior´ity**, quality or state of being superior.—**superiority complex**, overvaluation of one's worth. [L comp of *superus*, high—*super*, above.]

superlative [sōō´pėr´lȧ-tiv] *adj* of the highest degree or quality (eg *a superlative example, superlative insolence, skill*); (*gram*) denoting the extreme degree of comparison of adjectives and adverbs.—*n* (*gram*) the superlative or highest degree of adjectives and adverbs (eg kindest, best, most beautiful; most readily, worst); an adjective or adverb in the superlative degree.—*adv* **super´latively**. [L *superlātīvus—superlātus*, pt p of *superferre—super*, above, *ferre*, to carry.]

superman [sōō´pėr-man] *n* a superior man, according to Nietzsche, who has learned to forgo fleeting pleasures and attains happiness by the exercise of creative power; an apparently superhuman man. [**super-**, of higher quality than, + **man**.]

supermarket [sōō´pėr-mär-kėt] *n* a large, usu. self-service, retail store selling food and other domestic goods. [**super-**, beyond the normal, + **market**.]

supernal [sủ-pür´nȧl] *adj* (*poet*) that is above or in a higher place or region; celestial. [L *supernus—super*, above.]

supernatural [sōō-pėr-nach´ū-rȧl] *adj* not according to the usual course of nature; miraculous; involving God or ghosts, spirits, etc.—*adv* **supernat´urally**. [**super-**, beyond, + **natural**.]

supernova [sōō-pėr-nōv´ȧ] *n* the explosion of a very large star in which it may reach the luminous intensity of one billion suns. [**super-**, above, + L *nova* (*stella*), new (star).]

supernumerary [sōō-pėr-nūm´ėr-ȧr-i] *adj* over and above the number stated, or which is usual or necessary.—*n* a person or thing beyond the usual, necessary, or stated number; one who appears on stage or screen without a speaking part. [L *supernūmerārius—super*, over, *nŭmerus*, a number.]

superphosphate [sōō-pėr-fos´fāt] *n* an acid phosphate; a fertilizer made from insoluble mineral phosphates treated with sulfuric acid. [**super-**, beyond the normal, + **phosphate**.]

superpose [sōō-pėr-pōz´] *vt* to place over or upon; (*geom*) to lay a figure upon another so as to make all parts alike. [L *super*, over, and Fr *poser* (see **pose**, n).]

supersaturation [sōō-pėr-sat-ū-rā´sh(ȯ)n] *n* a metastable state in which the concentration of a solution or a vapor is greater than that corresponding to saturation.—*vt* **supersat´urate**. [**super-**, beyond the normal, + **saturation**.]

superscribe [sōō-pėr-skrīb´] *vt* to write or engrave (an inscription) on the outside or top; to write the name on the outside or cover of.—*n* **superscrip´tion**, act of superscribing; that which is written or engraved above or on the outside. [L *superscrībĕre—super*, above, *scrībĕre, scriptum*, to write.]

supersede [sōō-pėr-sēd´] *vt* to take the place of by reason of superior right, power, etc.; to displace, set aside, render unnecessary; to put in the room of, to replace (by). [L *supersedēre*, to desist—*super*, above, *sedēre*, to sit.]

supersensitive [sōō-pėr-sen´si-tiv] *adj* extremely, or unduly, sensitive; specially treated to increase sensitivity. [**super-**, beyond the normal, + **sensitive**.]

supersonic [sōō-pėr-son´ik] *adj* faster than the speed of sound; ultrasonic.—*n* a supersonic wave or frequency; a supersonic airplane; (*pl*) the science of supersonic phenomena. [**super-**, beyond, + **sonic**.]

superstition [sōō-pėr-sti´sh(ȯ)n] *n* excessive reverence or fear, based on ignorance; false worship or religion; an ignorant and irrational belief in supernatural agency; belief in what is absurd or without evidence.—*adj* **supersti´tious**, pertaining to, or proceeding from, superstition; holding, influenced by, superstitions.—*adv* **supersti´tiously**. [L *superstitiō, -ōnis*, excessive religious belief—*super*, over, above, *sistĕre—stāre*, to stand.]

superstructure [sōō´pėr-struk´-chủr] *n* a structure above or on something else, as above the main deck of a ship; that part of a building above a foundation. [**super-**, above, + **structure**.]

supertanker [sōō´pėr-tangk-ėr] *n* an extremely large oil tanker, of 300,000 tons or more.

supertonic [sōō-pėr-ton´ik] *n* (*mus*) the note next above the keynote, the second tone of a diatonic scale. [**super-**, above, + **tonic**.]

supervene [sōō-pėr-vēn´] *vi* to come or happen as something additional or unexpected.—*n* **superven´tion**. [L *supervenīre*, to follow—*super*, above, *venīre, ventum*, come.]

supervise [sōō´pėr-vīz] *vti* to oversee, to superintend.—*ns* **supervĭ´sion**, act of supervising; inspection, control; **supervī´sor**, one who supervises, an overseer, an inspector. [L *super*, over, *vidēre, vīsum*, to see.]

supine [sōō-pīn´] *adj* lying on the back; negligent, indolent, lacking in energy and initiative.—*n* **sū´pine**, a verbal noun usu. incapable of complete inflection.—*adv* **sūpine´ly**.—*n* **sūpine´ness**. [*supinus—sub*, under.]

supper [sup´ėr] *n* a meal taken at the close of the day, esp when dinner is eaten at midday; an evening social, esp for raising funds; the food served at a supper; a light meal served late in the evening.—*n* **supper club**, an expensive nightclub. [OFr *soper*—Low Ger *supen*, to sup.]

supplant [su-plänt´] *vt* to displace by guile; to remove in order to replace with something else.—*n* **supplant´er**. [L *supplantāre*, to trip up one's heels—*sub*, under, *planta*, the sole of the foot.]

supple [sup´l] *adj* pliant; lithe; yielding to others; of the mind, adaptable.—*vt* to make supple; to make soft or compliant.—*vi* to become supple.—*n* **supp´leness**.—*adv* **supp´ly**. [Fr *souple*—L *supplex*, bending the knees—*sub*, under, *plicāre*, to fold.]

supplement [sup´lė-mėnt] *n* that which completes or brings closer to completion; a special part of a periodical publication accompanying an ordinary part; the quantity by which an angle or an arc falls short of 180° or a semicircle.—*vt* **supp´lement**, to add to.—*adjs* **supplemen´tal, supplement´ary**, added to supply what is wanting, additional. [L *supplēmentum—supplēre*, to fill up.]

suppliant [sup´li-ȧnt] *adj* supplicating, asking earnestly, entreating.—*n* a humble petitioner.—*adv* **supp´liantly**. [Fr *suppliant*, pr p of *supplier*—L *supplicāre*. See **supplicate**.]

supplicate [sup´li-kāt] *vt* to entreat earnestly; to address in prayer.—*n* **supplicā´tion**, act of supplicating; earnest prayer or entreaty.—*adj* **supp´licātory**, containing supplication or entreaty, imploring. [L *supplicāre, -ātum*, to beseech—*supplex*, bending the knee—*sub*, under, *plicāre*, to fold.]

supply [su-plī´] *vt* to fill up, meet (a deficiency, a need); to furnish; to fill (a vacant place);—*pt, pt p* **supplied´**.—*n* that which is supplied, or which supplies a want; (*pl*) needed materials, provisions, etc.; the amount available for use or sale at a particular time; a clergyman filling a vacant place temporarily. [Fr,—L *supplēre—sub*, up, *plēre*, to fill.]

support [su-pōrt´] *vt* to hold up, bear part of the weight of; to give power of resistance, enable to endure; to supply with means of living; to subscribe to; to uphold by advocacy (a cause, policy); to take the side of; to endure, tolerate; to tend to confirm (eg a statement); to have a role subordinate to (a star) in a play, motion picture, etc.—*n* act of supporting or upholding; that which supports, sustains, or maintains; a means of support.—*adj* **support´able**, capable of being supported; endurable; capable of being maintained.—*n* **support´er**, one who, or that which, supports; an adherent; a backer, a defender; (*her*) a figure, usu. animal, on each side of an escutcheon.—*adj* **support´ive**, giving support or help. [L *supportāre—sub*, up, *portāre*, to bear.]

suppose [su-pōz´] *vt* to assume, state as true, for the sake of argument; to presume, think probable; to believe without sufficient proof; to consider as a possibility; to expect.—*vi* to conjecture.—*adjs* **suppō´sable**, that may be supposed; **supposed´**, believed on insufficient evidence to exist or have reality (eg *the once supposed indestructibility of the atom*); wrongly believed to be, bear the character specified (*his supposed partner, interests, benevolence*); considered probable or certain, expected; understood; made by intent (*pills that are supposed to kill pain*); required by authority (*soldiers are supposed to obey their officers*); give permission (*not supposed to have visitors*).—*adv* **suppō´sedly**, according to supposition.—*n* **supposi´tion**, act of supposing; that which is supposed, assumption. [Fr *supposer*—L *suppōnĕre, -positum*—*sub*, under, *pōnĕre*, to place.]

supposititious [su-poz-i-tish´ùs] *adj* put by trick in the place of another, spurious; of the nature of a supposition.—Also **supposit´ious** [su-pò-zish´us].—*adv* **suppositi´tiously**. [L *supposititius*—*suppōnĕre, suppositum*, to put in the place of another—*sub*, under, *pōnĕre*, to place.]

suppository [su-poz´i-tòr-i] *n* a conical or cylindrical plug of medicated soluble material for insertion into the rectum or vagina. [LL *suppositōrium* (*neut*), that is placed underneath—L *suppōnĕre*. See **suppose**.]

suppress [su-pres´] *vt* to crush, put down (eg a rebellion, rebels, freedom of speech); to restrain (a person); to keep in (eg a sigh, an angry retort); to keep from publication or circulation or from being known (eg a book, a name, evidence, the truth); (*psychiatry*) to consciously dismiss from the mind.—*ns* **suppress´or**, one that suppresses, esp a gene that suppresses the expression of another gene when both are present; **suppress´ion**, act of suppressing; stoppage; concealment.—*adj* **suppress´ive**, tending to suppress. [L *supprimĕre, suppressum*—*sub*, under, *premĕre*, to press.]

suppurate [sup´ū-rāt] *vi* to form or discharge pus.—*n* **suppurā´tion**.—*adj* **supp´urătive**, tending to suppurate; promoting suppuration. [L *suppūrāre, -ātum*—*sub*, under, *pūs, pūris*, pus.]

supra- [s(y)ōō´pra-] *prefix* above, situated above; over; beyond. [L *supra*, above]:—eg **supramundane**, *supranasal, supramaxilla*.

supranational [s(y)ōō-prà-nash´òn-àl] *adj* transcending national boundaries, authority, or interests; of, for or above a number of or all nations. [**supra-**, above, + **national**.]

supreme [s(y)ōō-prēm´] *adj* highest; greatest; final; ultimate.—*n* **suprĕm´acy**, state of being supreme; highest authority or power.—*adv* **suprēme´ly**.—*ns* **Supreme Being**, God; **Supreme Court**, the highest Federal court; the highest court in most States; **Supreme Soviet**, the highest legislative body of the Soviet Union. [L *suprēmus*, superl of *superus*, high—*super*, above.]

surcease [sûr-sēs´] *vti* to cease, or cause to cease.—*n* cessation, esp a temporary respite or end. [OFr *sursis*, pt p of *surseoir*—L *supersedēre*, to refrain from.]

surcharge [sûr-chärj´] *vt* to overcharge (a person); to charge in addition; to overload; to fill excessively (with); to mark (a postage stamp) with a surcharge.—*n* **sur´charge**, an additional or abnormal tax or charge; an excessive load; an imprint on a postage stamp altering its original value. [Fr *sur*—L *super*, over, and **charge**.]

surcoat [sûr´kōt] *n* the tuniclike robe worn by knights over their armor. [OFr *surcote, surcot*—*sur*, over, *cote*, a garment.]

surd [sûrd] *n* an irrational number (as $\sqrt{2}$); an expression that cannot be reduced to a whole number; a decimal that terminates, or a repeating decimal.—*adj* lacking sense. [L *surdus*, deaf.]

sure [shōōr] *adj* secure, safe; firm, strong; reliable, to be depended on, certain; certain (to do); certain, having apparently adequate grounds for belief, or for expectation; convinced (of, that).—*advs* **sure**, (*inf*) surely; **surely**, firmly, safely; certainly, assuredly.—*adjs* **sure´fire**, (*inf*) sure to be successful or as expected; **sure´footed**, not liable to slip, stumble, or err.—*adv* **surefoot´edly**.—*ns* **surefoot´edness; sure´ness**.—**sure enough**, (*inf*) without doubt; **be sure**, see to it that; **for sure**, certain(ly); **to be sure**, it must be acknowledged. [OFr *seur* (Fr *sûr*)—L *sēcūrus*—*sē-*, apart from, *cūra*, care.]

surety [shōōr´ti] *n* sureness, certainty; security against loss or for payment; a guarantee; one who undertakes responsibility for the default of another.—*ns* **surety bond**, a bond guaranteeing performance of a contract or obligation; **sure´tyship**, state of being surety; obligation of one person to answer for another. [Doublet **security**.]

surf [sûrf] *n* the waves of the sea breaking on the shore or a reef; the foam made by the dashing of waves.—*adj* **surf´y**.—*ns* **surf´board**, a long narrow board used in the sport of surfing; **surf´ing**, the sport of riding in toward shore on the crest of a wave, esp on a surfboard. [Earlier *suffe*. Origin unknown.]

surface [sûr´fis] *n* the exterior part of anything; any of the faces of a solid; superficial features.—*adj* of, on, or near a surface.—*vt* put a surface on, as in paving.—*vi* to rise to the surface of the water; (*inf*) to come into public view.—*ns* **sur´face ten´sion**, in liquids, that property in virtue of which a liquid surface behaves as if it were a stretched membrane. [Fr *sur*, above, *face*, face.]

surfeit [sûr´fit] *v* to fill to satiety and disgust.—*n* excess in eating and drinking; sickness or satiety caused by such excess; excess. [OFr *surfait*, excess—*sur-*, *sorfaire*, to augment—L *super*, above, *facĕre, factum*, to make.]

surge [sûrj] *n* the rising or swelling of a large wave; a sudden, strong increase, as of power; a movement (as a slipping) of a rope or cable or the strain or jerk caused by this movement.—*vi* to move (forward) like a wave. [L *surgĕre*, to rise.]

surgeon [sûr´jòn] *n* a medical specialist who practices surgery.—*n* **sur´gery**, act and art of treating diseases or injuries by manual or instrumental operations; the operating room of a surgeon or hospital; alterations made as if by surgery.—*adj* **sur´gical**, pertaining to surgeons, or to surgery; done by surgery.—*adv* **sur´gically**. [OFr *serurgien*.]

surly [sûr´li] *adj* ill-natured, growling, morose, uncivil; gloomy, angry.—*adv* **sur´lily**.—*n* **sur´liness**. [Earlier *sirly*, for **sir, like**—like a domineering or ungracious master.]

surmise [sûr-mīz´] *n* a conjecture.—*vt* to infer the existence of from slight evidence. [OFr—*surmettre*, to accuse—L *super*, upon, *mittĕre, missum*, to send.]

surmount [sûr-mownt´] *vt* to mount above, surpass; to top, be the top of; to climb over; get past, to get the better of (eg a difficulty, temptation).—*adj* **surmount´able**, that may be surmounted. [Fr—*sur* (L *super*), above, *monter*, to mount.]

surname [sûr´nām] *n* the family name.—*vt* to give a surname to. [Formed from Fr *sur* (L *super*), over and above, and Eng **name**, on the analogy of Fr *surnom*.]

surpass [sûr-pas´] *vt* to exceed, to excel, outdo; to be beyond the reach or capacity of (eg *to surpass understanding, description, one's skill*).—*adj* **surpass´able**, that may be surpassed. [Fr *surpasser*—*sur* (L *super*), beyond, *passer*, to pass.]

surplice [sûr´plis] *n* a white linen garment worn over the cassock by the clergy and choir in some churches. [Fr *surplis*—Low L *superpellicium*, an over-garment—*pellis*, skin.]

surplus [sûr-plùs] *n* the excess above what is required. [Fr, from *sur* (L *super*), over, *plus*, more.]

surprise [sûr-prīz´] *n* act of taking unawares; the emotion caused by anything sudden and/or unexpected; something that surprises.—*vt* to come upon suddenly or unawares; to attack without warning; to amaze, astonish.—*adj* **surprīs´ing**.—*adv* **surprīs´ingly**. [Fr,—*surpris*, pt p of *surprendre*—L *super*, over, *prehendĕre*, to catch.]

surrealism [su-rē´àl-izm] *n* a form of art claiming to express activities of the unconscious mind, escaping the control of reason and all preconceptions.—*adj* **surreal** [su-rē´àl or surēl´], surrealistic; bizarre; fantastic.—*n, adj* **surrē´alist**.—*adj* **surrealist´ic**. [Fr *surréalisme*—*sur*, above, *réalisme*, realism.]

surrender [su-ren´dèr] *vt* to deliver over, yield (to another); to give up, relinquish (eg a right a claim); to abandon (oneself to, eg grief).—*vi* to yield up oneself to another.—*n* act or fact of surrendering. [OFr *surrendre*, from *sur* (L *super*), over, *rendre* (L *reddĕre*), *to render*.]

surreptitious [sûr-ep-ti´shùs] *adj* done by stealth or fraud; enjoyed secretly.—*adv* **surrepti´tiously**. [L, from *surripĕre, surreptum*, to take away secretly—*sub*, under, *rapĕre*, to seize.]

surrogate [sûr´ō-gāt] *n* a substitute, deputy; a person or thing standing for another person or thing; a thing, substance used as a substitute; in some States, a probate court judge. [L *surrogāre, -ātum*—*sub*, in the place of, *rogāre*, to ask.]

surround [su-rownd´] *vt* to encircle on all or nearly all sides; to form or be the member of the entourage of; to constitute part of the environment.—*n* something that surrounds, as a border or ambient environment.—*adj* **surround´ing**, encompassing; neighboring.—*n* an encompassing; (*pl*) things which surround, external circumstances, environment. [OFr *suronder*—L *superundāre*, to overflow; meaning influenced by confusion with **round**.]

surtax [sûr´taks] *n* an additional tax on top of the regular tax. [Fr *sur*, over, + **tax**.]

surtout [sûr-tōō´] *n* a man's close-fitting overcoat. [Fr,—*sur*, over, *tout*, all.]

surveillance [sûr-vāl´àns] *n* watch kept over a person, esp a suspect. [Fr,—*surveiller*—*sur* (L *super*), over, *veiller* (L *vigilāre*), to watch.]

survey [sûr-vā´] *vt* to see or look over; to take a general view of; to inspect, examine; to measure and estimate the position, extent, contours of (eg a piece of land).—*ns* **sur´vey**, a detailed study, as by gathering information and analyzing it, a general view; the process of surveying an area; a written description of the area; **survey´ing**, the science or work of making land surveys; **survey´or**, a measurer of land surfaces, etc. [O Fr *surveoir*—L *super*, over, *vidēre*, to see.]

survive [sûr-vīv´] *vt* to live longer than, to out-live; to come through alive.—*vi* to remain alive.—*n* **survi´val**, the state of surviving; anything that survives; a relic.—*adj* designed to help one to survive exposure or other dangerous condition.—*n* **survī´vor**, one who lives on after another's death; one who survives (eg a disaster); **survī´vorship**, the legal right of the survivor of persons having joint interest in property to take the interest of the person who has died; the state of being a survivor.—**survival of the fittest**, natural selection. [Fr,—L *super*, beyond, *vīvĕre*, to live.]

susceptible [su-sep´ti-bl] *adj* liable to be affected by (*with* **to**; eg *susceptible to colds, flattery, feminine charm*); easily affected, impressionable; capable (of), admitting (of—eg *susceptible of proof, of a specified interpretation*).—*n* **susceptibil´ity**, quality of being susceptible; sensibility; (in *pl*) feelings.—*adv* **suscep´tibly**.—*adj* **suscep´tive**, receptive, susceptible. [Fr,—L *suscipĕre, susceptum*, to take up—*sub*, up, *capĕre*, to take.]

suspect [sus-pekt´] *vt* to mistrust (eg *to suspect one's motives*); to imagine to be guilty; to conjecture, be inclined to think (that).—*n* [sus´pekt] a person suspected.—*adj* [sus´pekt] suspected, open to suspicion. [L *suspicĕre, suspectum*, to look at secretly—*sub*, up, *specĕre*, to look.]

suspend [sus-pend´] *vt* to hang; to hold floating in a fluid, hold in suspension; to discontinue, or discontinue the operation of, for a time (eg *to suspend publication, a law*); to debar for a time from a privilege, etc.; to defer, postpone.—*ns* **suspen´ded animā´tion**, the temporary cessation of some of the functions of life (as in persons nearly drowned); **suspen´der**, one who, or that which, suspends; one of a pair of straps to support trousers; **suspense´**, state of being suspended; temporary cessation; anxious uncertainty; **suspense account**, an account for temporary entry of charges and credits pending determination of their ultimate disposition; **suspen´sion**, act of suspending; state of being suspended; a system in which denser particles, which are at least microscopically visible, are distributed through a less dense liquid or gas, settling being hindered either by the viscosity of the fluid or by the impact of its molecules on the particles; temporary privation of office or privilege; in a vehicle, the system of springs, etc., supporting the chassis on the axles; **suspen´sion bridge**, a bridge in which the roadway is supported from chains or cables stretched between elevated piers; **suspension points**, usu. three spaced periods to show the omission of a word or words from a written context.—*adj* **suspen´sory**, that suspends.—*n* that which suspends; a supporting bandage. [L *suspendĕre—sub*, beneath, *pendĕre, pensum*, to hang.]

suspicion [sus-pi´sh(ȯ)n] *n* act of suspecting; an opinion formed or entertained on slender evidence; mistrust; a very slight amount.—*adj* **suspi´cious**, showing suspicion; inclined to suspect; exciting suspicion (eg actions).—*adv* **suspi´ciously**.—*n* **suspi´ciousness**. [Through OFr from LL *suspectiō*—L *suspicĕre* (see **suspect**); influenced by L *suspiciō, -ōnis*, distrust.]

sustain [sus-tān´] *vt* to hold up, bear the weight of, support; to maintain (eg *to sustain the deception; a sustained effort*); to prolong (eg a musical note); to give strength to, enable to endure (eg *sustained by the belief that*); to nourish; to endure, bear up under (an affliction of any kind); to uphold the legality or rightness of; to corroborate, confirm.—*adjs* **sustain´able**, that may be sustained; **sustained´**, kept up at one uniform pitch.—*ns* **sustain´er**, one who, or that which, sustains; **sus´tenance**, that which sustains; maintenance; nourishment; food and drink; **sustentā´tion**, support, maintenance. [L *sustinēre—sub*, up, *tenēre*, to hold.]

sutler [sut´lėr] *n* a person who followed an army and sold liquor or provisions, a camp-hawker. [ODu *soeteler* (now *zoetelaar*), a small trader.]

suttee [sut´ē, sut-ē´] *n* a Hindu custom in which the faithful widow burned herself on the funeral pyre along with her husband's body; a Hindu widow who died thus. [Sans *satī*, a true wife.]

suture [s(y)ōō´chůr] *n* a line of junction of two structures; an immovable articulation between bones as between the various bones of the cranium and face; (*bot*) a line of union between two adjacent edges, or of dehiscence; (*surg*) the sewing up of a wound and the thread, etc., and the stitches so used.—*vt* to unite, close or secure with sutures. [L *sūtūra—suĕre*, to sew.]

suzerain [s(y)ōō´ze-rān] *n* a feudal lord; a state in relation to another over which it has some political control.—*n* **su´zerainty**, the dominion of a suzerain. [OFr,—L *sursum* (*sub-vorsum*), on high.]

svelte [svelt] *adj* slender, supple and graceful. [Fr.]

swab [swob] *n* a mop for cleaning or drying floors or decks, or for cleaning out the bore of a cannon; a wad of absorbent material usu. wound around the end of a small stick used to medicate or clean the throat, mouth, etc.; a specimen of morbid secretion taken on a swab for bacteriological examination.—*vt* to use a swab on;—*pr p* **swabb´ing**; *pt, pt p* **swabbed**.—*n* **swabb´er**, one who, or that which, swabs. [Du *zwabber*, a swabber, *zwabberen*, to swab.]

swaddle [swod´l] *vt* formerly, to swathe or bind tight with clothes, as an infant.—*n pl* **swadd´ling clothes**, bands of cloth, swathed round an infant; restrictions imposed on the immature. [OE *swæthel, swethel*, a bandage; cf **swathe**.]

swag [swag] *vt* to hang in a swag.—*n* a valance, garland, etc. hanging decoratively in a curve; (*slang*) loot. [Related to **sway**.]

swagger [swag´ėr] *vi* to swing the body proudly or defiantly; to brag noisily, to bully.—*n* boastfulness; insolence of manner; a self-confident, swinging gait.—*adj* very fashionable.—*n* **swagg´erer**. [A frequentative of **swag**.]

Swahili [swä-hē´li] *n* (a member of) a people of Zanzibar and the adjacent coast; the Bantu language widely used as a lingua franca throughout east and central Africa.—*pl* **Swahili**, also **-lis**.

swain [swān] *n* a shepherd; an admirer, suitor. [ON *sveinn*, young man, servant, Dan *svend*, servant.]

swallow[1] [swol´ō] *n* any of numerous migratory birds (family Hirundinadae) with long wings and a forked tail, which seize their insect food on the wing.—*n* **swall´owtail**, a forked and tapering tail; a tailcoat; any of numerous butterflies (esp genus *Papilio*) having a taillike process on each of the hind wings. [OE *swalewe*; Ger *schwalbe*.]

swallow[2] [swol´ō] *vt* to receive through the gullet into the stomach; to engulf; to absorb (*often with* **up**); to retract (words said); to accept without protest; (*inf*) to accept as true.—*n* a swallowing; the amount swallowed. [OE *swelgan*, to swallow; cog with Ger *schwelgen*.]

swam [swam] *pt* of **swim**.

swamp [swomp] *n* wet, spongy land, low ground saturated with water.—*vt* to sink in, or as in, a swamp; to cause to fill with water, as a boat; to overwhelm; to flood as with water.—*adj* **swamp´y**, consisting of swamp; wet and spongy.—**swamp buggy**, a vehicle for traveling over swampy land, often amphibious. [Prob of Low German origin.]

swan [swon] *n* a group of large, usu. white, birds constituting a distinct section of the duck family (Anatidae), having a very long neck and noted for grace and stateliness of movement on the water.—*ns* **swann´ery**, a place where swans are bred and kept; **swan dive**, a front dive made with the head back, back arched, and arms spread sideways and brought together above the head just before entering the water; **swan's´down**, the down of a swan used as trimming on articles of dress; a heavy cotton flannel having a thick nap on the face; **swan´ song**, the fabled song of a swan just before its death; last work of any kind; final appearance. [OE *swan*; Ger *schwan*, Du *zwaan*.]

swank [swangk] *n* (*inf*) ostentatious display.—*adj* (*inf*) ostentatiously stylish.—*vi* (*inf*) to show off.—*adj* (*inf*) **swank´y**, boastful, ostentatious; stylish. [OE *swancer*, pliant; Ger *schwank*.]

swap [swäp, swop] *vti* (*inf*) trade, barter.—*n* (*inf*) the act of exchanging one thing for another.

sward [swörd] *n* the grassy surface of land; turf.—*adj* **sward´ed**, covered with sward. [OE *sweard*, skin, rind; Du *zwoord*, Ger *schwarte*.]

swarm[1] [swörm] *n* a number of bees migrating under the guidance of a queen to establish a new colony; a colony of bees in a hive; a moving mass, crowd, or throng.—*vi* of bees, to fly off in a swarm; to move, be present, etc. in large numbers; to be crowded. [OE *swearm*; Ger *schwarm*.]

swarm[2] [swörm] *vti* to climb by scrambling up by means of arms and legs (*often with* **up**). [Origin uncertain.]

swarthy [swörTH´i] *adj* dark-skinned—also **swart**.—*n* **swarth´iness**. [OE *sweart*; ON *svartr*, Ger *schwarz*, black.]

swash [swosh] *vt* to dash or splash.—*n* **swash´buck´ler**, a blustering, swaggering fighting man.—*vi* **swash´buckle**, to act the part of a swashbuckler.—**swash´buckling** (also *n*). [Imit.]

swastika [swas´ti-ka] *n* a widespread symbol of the form of a cross with equal arms and a limb of the same length projecting at right angles from the end of each arm; the form with counterclockwise arms used as an emblem by Amerindians and in the Orient; the form with clockwise arms the official symbol of the Nazi Party and the Third Reich. [Sans *svastika*, fortunate.]

swat [swot] *vt* (*inf*) to hit smartly.—*n* (*inf*) a quick sharp blow.—*n* **swatt´er**. [**squat**.]

swath [swöth] *n* the width cut by a scythe or other mowing device; a strip, row, etc., mowed. [OE *swathu*, a track.]

swathe [swāTH] *vt* to bind, wrap round, with a band or with loose material as if with a bandage; to envelop, enclose.—*n* a band used in swathing; an enveloping medium. [OE *swethian*; cf **swaddle**.]

sway [swā] *vi* to swing or move from one side to the other or to and fro; to lean to one side; to incline in judgment or opinion.—*vt* to cause to sway; to influence or divert.—*n* the motion of swaying; the power that moves; controlling influence; jurisdiction.—*adj* **sway´backed**, having a sagging spine, as some horses. [ME *sweyen*, from Scand or Low Ger.]

swear [swār] *vi* to make a solemn declaration, promise, etc., calling God to witness; to give evidence on oath; to utter the name of God or of sacred things profanely.—*vt* to utter (an oath), calling God to witness; to administer a legal oath to; to declare on oath;—*pt* **swōre**; *pt p* **sworn**.—*n* **swear´er**.— **swear by**, to put complete confidence in; **swear in**, to inaugurate by oath; **swear for**, to answer for; **swear off**, to renounce, abstain from. [OE *swerian*; Du *zweren*, Ger *schwören*.]

sweat [swet] *n* the moisture from the skin, perspiration; moisture in drops on any surface; the state of one who sweats; a state of eagerness, anxiety.—*vi* to give out sweat or moisture; to toil, drudge; to suffer penalty, smart.—*vt* to give out (sweat or other moisture); to cause to sweat or give out moisture; to get rid of by sweating (*with* **out**); to produce laboriously (*with* **out**); to squeeze money or extortionate interest from; to oppress by exacting incessant and unhealthy labor for shamefully inadequate wages.—*ns* **sweat´er**, one who sweats, or that which causes sweating; a knitted or crocheted jacket or pullover; **sweat´pants**, pants having a drawstring waist and elastic cuffs at the ankles worn esp by athletes on warming up; **sweat´shirt**, a loose collarless jersey of heavy cotton jersey; **sweat´shop**, a factory or shop where the employees work long hours at low wages under poor conditions; **sweat suit**, a sweatshirt and matching sweatpants.—*adj* **sweat´y**, wet with sweat; causing sweat.—*n* **sweat´iness**. [OE *swāt*, sweat, *swætan*, to sweat; Du *zweet*; Low Ger *sweet*, Ger *schweiss*.]

Swede [swēd] *n* a native or inhabitant of Sweden; a person of Swedish descent; **swede**, a yellow turnip (*Brassica napobrassica*), rutabaga.—*adj* **Swēd´ish**, pertaining to Sweden.—*n* the Scandinavian language of Sweden.

sweep [swēp] *vt* to brush dirt, etc., from with a broom; to carry (away, down, off, along) by a long brushing stroke; to strike with a long, esp light, stroke; to rid of, make free from, by vigorous action; to remove by force, or by strong measures, or in a high-handed manner; to pass rapidly (over); to win an overwhelming victory in or on; to win all the games of; to cover the entire range of.—*vi* to clean a floor, etc. as with a broom; to pass swiftly and forcibly; to move with a long reach; to curve widely;—*pt, pt p* **swept**.—

n act of sweeping; extent of a stroke, or of anything turning or in motion; a sweeping movement; compass, range; a curve; a chimney sweep; a very long oar; a sweepstake.—*adj* **sweep´ing**, that sweeps; comprehensive, complete (eg changes, victory); marked by wholesale and indiscriminate inclusion; having a curving line or form.—*n* **sweep´er**.—*adv* **sweep´ingly**, in a sweeping manner.—*n pl*, **sweep´ings**, things collected by sweeping; refuse.—*n* **sweep´stakes**, a race or contest in which the entire prize may be awarded to the winner; a contest; a competition; any of various lotteries.—**sweep off one's feet**, to gain immediate acceptance by a person; **sweep the board**, to win all the bets on the table; to win everything over the competition. [OE *swāpan*; Ger *schweifen*, cf **swoop**.]

sweet [swēt] *adj* pleasing to the taste; tasting like sugar; pleasing to other senses, fragrant, melodious, beautiful; not rancid or sour; not salty or salted; amiable, kindly, gracious.—*n* a sweet food.—*n* **sweet´ness**.—*adj* **sweet´-and-sour´**, seasoned with a sauce containing sugar, and vinegar or lemon juice.—*ns* **sweet´bread**, the thymus or pancreas of an animal used for food; **sweet´-brī´er**, a rose with many prickles, having a single flower and scented leaves; **sweet corn**, an Indian corn (esp. *Zea mays saccharata*) eaten unripe and uncooked as a table vegetable.—*vt* **sweet´en**, to make sweet; to make pleasing and agreeable.—*vi* to become sweet.—*ns* **sweet´ener**, a sweetening agent, esp a synthetic one, as saccharin; **sweet´ening**, act of sweetening; that which sweetens; **sweet´heart**, a lover, darling; **sweet´ie**, a sweetheart.—*adj* **sweet´ish**, somewhat sweet to the taste.—*adv* **sweet´ly**.—*ns* **sweet´meat**, a confection made wholly or chiefly of sugar; **sweet´pea**, a garden plant (*Lathyrus odoratus*) cultivated for its fragrance and beauty; **sweet´ potā´to**, a tropical vine (*Ipomoea batatas*) related to the morning glory; its large, fleshy orange root used as a vegetable; an ocarina; **sweet´ will´iam**, a species of pink (*Dianthus barbatus*) of many colors and varieties.—**sweet on**, enamored of. [OE *swēte*; Ger *süss*, Gr *hēdys*, L *suāvis*, Sans *svādu*, sweet.]

swell [swel] *vi* to expand, to be inflated; to rise into waves; to heave; to bulge out; to become elated, arrogant, or angry; to grow louder.—*vt* to increase the size of, or number of; to increase the sound of; to raise to arrogance;—*pt p* **swelled** or **swollen** [swōln, swōl´ėn].—*n* act of swelling; a bulge; increase in size; an increase and a succeeding decrease in the volume of a tone; a gradual rise of ground; a wave or succession of waves rolling in one direction, as after a storm; a piece of mechanism in an organ to producing a swell of tone; (*inf*) a dandy, one elaborately and fashionably dressed, an important person.—*adj* (*inf*) befitting a swell; (*slang*) excellent.—*n* **swell´ing**, an increase in size, volume, etc.; a protuberance; **swell-head**, a conceited person. [OE *swellan*; Ger *schwellen*.]

swelter [swelt´ėr] *vi* to be oppressed by great heat.—*n* a condition of oppressive heat; an overwrought state of mind.—*adj* **swelt´ering**, oppressively hot.—*adv* **swelt´eringly**. [OE *sweltan*, to die.]

swept [swept] *pt, pt p* of **sweep**.

swerve [swürv] *v* to turn aside from a line or course, etc.—*n* an act of swerving. [ME; origin uncertain.]

swift [swift] *adj* moving, or able to move, quickly—fleet or fast; rapid, taking only a short time; not long delayed; speedy; quick in action.—*n* a family (Apodidae) of birds with long pointed wings, a short tail, and remarkable powers of rapid and prolonged flight, superficially resembling swallows.—*adv* **swift´ly**.—*n* **swift´ness**. [OE *swift*, from same root as **swoop**.]

swig [swig] *n* (*inf*) a deep draft, as of liquor.—*vti* (*inf*) to drink in gulps.

swill [swil] *vti* to drink greedily or copiously; to feed swill to (pigs, etc.)—*n* liquid garbage fed to pigs; garbage.—*n* **swill´er**. [OE *swilian*, to wash.]

swim [swim] *vi* to move on or in water by using limbs or fins; to move with a gliding motion; to be dizzy; to be drenched, overflow, abound (with).—*vt* to cross by swimming; to make to swim or float;—*pr p* **swimm´ing**; *pt* **swam**; *pt p* **swum**.—*n* act of swimming; any motion like swimming; a dizziness; (*inf*) the main current of activity.—*ns* **swimm´er**, one who swims; **swim-bladder**, a fish's air bladder; **swimm´ing**, the act, art or sport of one that swims and dives.—*adv* **swimm´ingly**, in a gliding manner, as if swimming; smoothly, successfully.—*ns* **swimm´ing pool**, a tank (as of concrete or plastic) for swimming in; **swim´suit**, a garment worn for swimming.—**in the swim**, in the main current of affairs, business, fashion, etc. [OE *swimman*; Gr *schwimmen*.]

swindle [swin´dl] *vti* to cheat (another) of money or property.—*n* the act of swindling or defrauding; a fraud;—*n* **swin´dler**. [Ger *schwindler*, a cheat—*schwindeln*, to be giddy.]

swine [swīn] *n sing* and *pl* a quadruped with bristly skin and long snout, reared for its flesh, a pig or hog, usu. used collectively; a vicious contemptible person.—*n* **swine´herd**, a herd or keeper of swin. [OE *swīn*, a pig; Ger *schwein*, L (adj) *suīnus*—*sūs*, Gr *hȳs*.]

swing [swing] *vi* to sway or wave to and fro, as a body hanging in air; to oscillate; to hang (from); to move forward with swaying rhythmical gait; to turn round on some fixed center, as a ship at anchor, a door on its hinges; to turn quickly; to move to and fro on a swinging seat; to be hanged; to attract, excite; (*inf*) to be full of vitality; to be up-to-date.—*vt* to move to and fro, to cause to wave or vibrate; to whirl, to brandish; to cause to wheel or turn as about some point; to influence the result of (eg a doubtful election) in favor of an individual or party; to play (music) as swing;—*pt, pt p* **swung**.—*n* the act of swinging; motion to and fro; a vigorous swinging motion; a seat suspended for swinging in; the sweep or compass of a swinging body; influence or force of anything put in motion; vigorous sweeping rhythm; jazz music (about 1935–45) played by large bands in which the basic melody and rhythm are overlaid with impromptu variation etc.—*n* **swing´ing**, the act of moving back and forth, esp the pastime of moving in a swing.—*adj* (*inf*) fully alive to, and appreciative of, the most recent trends and fashions in living; (*inf*) up-to-date. [OE *swingan*; Ger *schwingen*.]

swinish [swī´nish] *adj* like or befitting swine; gross, sensual, bestial.—*adv* **swin´ishly**.—*n* **swin´ishness**. [**swine**.]

swipe [swīp] *n* (*inf*) a hard, sweeping blow.—*vt* (*inf*) to hit with a swipe; (*slang*) to steal. [OE *swipe*, a whip.]

swirl [swûrl] *vti* to sweep along with a whirling motion.—*n* a whirl, an eddy; a twist; a curl. [Orig Scot; cf Norw *svirla*, to whirl round.]

swish[1] [swish] *vt* to brandish, or to strike, with a whistling sound; to flog.—*vi* to move with a hissing sound.—*n* a swishing sound. [Imit.]

swish[2] [swish] *adj* (*inf*) smart, fashionable.

Swiss [swis] *adj* of or belonging to Switzerland.—*n* a native of Switzerland; one that is of Swiss descent; **swiss**, any of various fine sheer fabrics of cotton. [Middle High Ger *swiz*.]

switch [swich] *n* a small flexible twig; a whip; a separate tail of hair attached to supplement the wearer's own hair; a device which, by means of movable sections of rails, transfers rolling stock from one track to another; a mechanical device for opening or closing an electric circuit; an act of switching, a changing, change(-over).—*vt* to strike with a switch; to swing, whisk; to transfer from one line of rails to another by a switch; to divert (eg the conversation—*with* **to**); to change over; to divert (on to another circuit) by means of a switch; to turn (off, on, eg current, light) by means of a switch; (*inf*) to change or exchange.—*vi* to change over (from, to).—*ns* **switch´back**, a zigzag road in a mountainous region, esp a zigzag railroad, so arranged that a train making a steep ascent runs into a siding, from which it passes out along another line at an acute angle to the first; **switch´board**, an apparatus consisting of a frame or panel controlling a complex system of electric circuits, as in a telephone exchange; **switch-hitter**, a baseball player who bats left-handed or right-handed. [Old Du *swick*, a whip.]

swivel [swiv´l] *n* something fixed in another body so as to turn round it; a ring or link that turns round on a pin or neck.—*vi* to turn on a pin or pivot. [OE *swīfan*, to move quickly, to turn round.]

swollen *pt p* of **swell**.

swoon [swōōn] *vt* to faint, fall into a faint.—*n* the act of swooning; a faint. [OE *geswōgen*, fainted, pt p of a lost verb.]

swoop [swōōp] *vt* to carry off abruptly.—*vi* to make a sudden attack (*usu. with* **down**) as a bird in hunting.—*n* the act of swooping; a seizing, as of its prey by a bird. [OE *swāpan*, to sweep.]

swop [swop] *vt* to exchange, to barter.—*pr p* **swopp´ing**; *pt, pt p* **swopped**.—*n* an exchange.—Also **swap**. [Perh connected with obs *swap*, a blow.]

sword [sörd] *n* a hand weapon with a long blade, sharp on one or both edges, set in a hilt for cutting or thrusting; destruction by the sword or by war; military force; coercive power; something that resembles a sword.—*ns* **sword´cane**, a cane containing a sword; **sword´ dance**, a dance over and between crossed swords, or one in which there is a display of naked swords; **sword´fish**, a large oceanic fish (*Xiphias gladius*) with a swordlike prolongation of the upper jaw; **sword´ knot**, a ribbon tied to the hilt of a sword; **sword´play**, fencing; **swords´man**, a man skilled in the use of a sword, esp a saber fencer; **swords´manship**. [OE *sweord*; Ger *schwert*.]

swore, sworn *See* **swear**.

swum [swum] *pt p* of **swim**.

swung [swung] *pt, pt p* of **swing**.

Sybarite [sib´a-rīt] *n* an inhabitant of *Sybaris*, a Greek city in ancient Italy, noted for the effeminacy and luxury of its inhabitants; one devoted to luxury.—*adjs* **sybarit´ic, -al**.

sycamine [sik´a-mīn] *n* a mulberry. [Gr *sȳkaminos*.]

sycamore [sik´a-mōr, -mör] *n* a tree (*Ficus sycomorus*) of Egypt and Asia Minor that is the sycamore of the Bible; a Eurasian maple (*Acer pseudoplatanus*) widely planted as a shade tree; a large spreading tree (*Platanus occidentalis*) of eastern and central N America. [Gr *sȳkomoros*—*sȳkon*, a fig, *moron*, black mulberry.]

sycophant [sik´ō-fânt] *n* a servile flatterer.—*n* **syc´ophancy**, the behavior of a sycophant; obsequious flattery.—Also **sycophant´ism**.—*adjs* **sycophant´ic, sycophant´ish**, like a sycophant, obsequiously flattering, parasitic. [Gr *sȳkophantēs*, usually said to mean one who informed against persons exporting figs from Attica or plundering the sacred fig-trees; but more prob one who brings figs to light by shaking the tree, hence one who makes rich men yield up their fruit—*sȳkon*, a fig, *phainein*, to show.]

syllable [sil´â-bl] *n* word or part of a word uttered by a single effort of the voice; one or more letters written to represent a spoken syllable.—*vt* to give a number or arrangement of syllables to (a word or verse); to pronounce syllable by syllable; to utter.—*adj* **syllab´ic**, consisting of, constituting, a syllable; articulated in syllables.—*adv* **syllab´ically**.—*vs t* **syllab´icate, syllab´ify** (*pt, pt p* **syllab´ified**), to form into syllables.—*ns* **syllabicā´tion, syllabificā´tion**. [L *syllaba*—Gr *syllabē*—*syn*, with, *lambanein*, to take.]

syllabub [sil´â-bub] *n* a drink made by curdling milk or cream with an acid beverage (as wine or cider); a dessert made of milk or cream beaten with wine or liquor, often further thickened with gelatin.

syllabus [sil´à-bus] *n* a summary or outline of a course of study or of examination requirements.—*pl* **syll´abuses, syll´abī**. [L.]

syllogism [sil´ō-jizm] *n* a logical form of argument, consisting of three propositions, of which the first two are called the premises (major and minor), and the last, which follows from them, the conclusion, eg 'all men are fallible, James is a man, therefore James is fallible'. The truth of the conclusion depends on the truth of the premises; for instance, an argument having as major premise 'all dogs bark', or one having as minor premise 'Gelert was a wolf', might lead to a conclusion not in accordance with fact.—*vi* **syll´ogīze**, to reason by syllogisms.—*adjs* **syllogis´tic**, pertaining to a syllogism; in the form of a syllogism.—*adv* **syllogis´tically**. [Gr *syllogismos—syllogizesthai—syn*, together, *logizesthai*, to reckon—*logos*, speech.]

sylph [silf] *n* according to the system or view of the universe set forth by Paracelsus (1493–1541), one of the elemental spirits of the air, intermediate between immaterial and material beings, occasionally holding intercourse with human creatures; a slender woman or girl. [Fr *sylphe*, of Celtic origin.]

sylvan [sil´vȧn] *adj* of, characteristic of, or living in the woods or forests; wooded.

symbiosis [sim-bī-ō´sis] *n* the living together in close association or union of two organisms of different kinds to their mutual advantage, eg the union of algae and fungi to form lichen.—*n* **sym´bīont**, an organism living with another in symbiosis.—*adj* **symbiot´ic**. [Gr *symbioein—syn*, together, *bioein*, to live—*bios*, life.]

symbol [sim´bȯl] *n* an authoritative summary of faith or doctrine; an object used to represent something abstract; an arbitrary or conventional sign standing for a quality, process, relation, etc. as in music, chemistry, mathematics, etc.; an object representing something in the unconscious mind that has been repressed; something having cultural significance and the capacity to excite response.—*adjs* **symbol´ic, -al**, pertaining to, or of the nature of, a symbol; representing by signs; figurative; serving as a symbol (of).—*adv* **symbol´ically**.—*vi* **sym´bolize**, to use symbols or symbolism.—*vt* to represent by symbols; to serve as symbol of.—*ns* **sym´bolist**, one who uses symbols; one of a school of French writers in the late 19th and early 20th century who reacted against what had come to be known as realism in favor of idealism and the mystical (treating the actual as an expression of something underlying), and sought to make verse more subtle and musical; **sym´bolism**, representation by symbols or signs; a system of symbols; use of symbols in literature or art; the theory or practice of the symbolists. [Gr *symbolon*, from *symballein—syn*, together, *ballein*, to throw.]

symmetry [sim´e-tri] *n* the state in which one part exactly corresponds to another in size, shape, and position; balance or beauty of form resulting from this.—*adjs* **symmet´rical, symmet´ric**, having symmetry or due proportion in its parts.—*adv* **symmet´rically**, with symmetry.—*vt* **symm´etrize**, to make symmetrical. [L and Ger *symmetria—syn*, together, *metron*, a measure.]

sympathy [sim´pa-thi] *n* a state of conformity of tastes and inclinations, or of understanding of one another's tastes and inclinations, or the goodwill based on such conformity or understanding; an association or relationship which produces the same or a similar reaction or response to a particular phenomenon; compassion, pity; condolences; conformity of parts in the fine arts.—*adj* **sympathet´ic**, showing, or inclined to, sympathy; compassionate; produced by sympathy; congenial; inclined to support or favor (*with* **to, towards**, eg a scheme).—*adv* **sympathet´ically**.—*vi* **sym´pathīze**, to feel with or for another; to express sympathy (with).—*n* **sym´pathizer**. [Gr *sympatheia—syn*, with, *pathos*, suffering.]

symphony [sim´fȯ-ni] *n* (*mus*) a composition for a full orchestra in several movements; a large orchestra for playing symphonic works; in full **symphony orchestra**; (*inf*) a symphony concert; harmony of any kind (eg of color, emotion); something which, by its harmony and/or grandeur, suggests a symphony.—*adjs* **symphon´ic**, relating to, or resembling, a symphony; symphonious; **symphō´nious**, agreeing or harmonizing in sound, accordant, harmonious.—*n* **sym´phonist**, a member of a symphony orchestra; a composer of symphonies.—**symphonic poem**, an extended programmatic composition for a symphony orchestra, usu. in a freer form than a symphony. [Gr *symphōnia—syn*, together, *phōnē*, a sound.]

symposium [sim-pō´zi-um] *n* in ancient Greece, a banquet with philosophic conversation; a conference at which several specialists deliver short addresses on a topic; a collection of essays on a single subject by various writers. [L,—Gr *symposion—syn*, together, *posis*, a drinking—*pīnein*, to drink.]

symptom [sim(p)´tȯm] *n* that which attends and indicates the existence of a disease or disorder, not as a cause, but as a constant effect.—*adj* **symptomat´ic**, pertaining to symptoms; indicating the existence (of something else); characteristic, indicative.—*adv* **symptomat´ically**. [Gr *symptōma—sympiptein*, to coincide—*syn*, with, *piptein*, to fall.]

synagogue, synagog [sin´a-gog] *n* an assembly of Jews for worship and religious study; a building or place for such assembly.—*adj* **syn´agogal** [-goj´-). [Fr,—Gr *synagōgē—synagein*, to assemble—*syn*, together, *agein*, to lead.]

syncarpous [sin-kär´pus] *adj* (*bot*) of a gynaeceum consisting of two or more united carpels.—*n* **syn´carp**. [Gr *syn*, together, *karpos*, a fruit.]

synchromesh [sing´krō-mesh] *adj* designed for effecting synchronized shifting of gears.—Also *n*. [**synchronous**, + **mesh**.]

synchronous [sing´krȯ-nus] *adj* happening or being at the same time, simultaneous; having the same period, or period and phase.—Also **syn´chronal**.—*vi* **syn´chronīze**, to be simultaneous (eg *B's arrival synchronized with A's departure*); to agree in time (eg *the movements of the lips in the picture did not synchronize with the sound of the words*).—*vt* to cause to happen at the same time; to tabulate (eg events) so as to show coincidence in time; to cause (clocks, etc.) to agree in time; to add (sound, dialogue, etc.) in time with the action to a motion picture.—*ns* **synchronīzā´tion; synchronīzer; syn´chronism**, concurrence of events in time; the tabular arrangement of contemporary events, etc., in history; the state of being synchronous; synchronized operation.—*adj* **synchronis´tic**, showing synchronism.—*adv* **synchronis´tically**.—**synchronized swimming**, exhibition swimming in which the movements of one or more swimmers are synchronized with a musical accompaniment so as to form changing patterns. [Gr *synchronismos—synchronizein*, to agree in time—*syn*, together, *chronos*, time.]

syncopate [sing´kō-pāt] *vt* to contract a word by taking away letters from the middle; (*mus*) to alter rhythm by transferring the accent to a normally unaccented beat.—*ns* **syncopā´tion**, act of syncopating; state of being syncopated; **syn´cope**, the loss of a sound, letter or syllable from the middle of a word, resulting in contraction (eg fo'c'sle for forecastle); (*med*) a faint in which the breathing and circulation are suspended. [Low L *syncopāre, -ātum*—L *syncopē*—Gr *syn*, together, *koptein*, to cut off.]

syndic [sin´dik] *n* a municipal magistrate in some countries; an agent of a university or corporation.—*adj* **syn´dical**, relating to a syndic or a committee that assumes the power of a syndic; of or relating to syndicalism.—*n* **syn´dicāte**, an association of individuals or corporations formed for a project requiring much capital; any group, as of criminals, organized for some undertaking; an organization selling articles or features to many newspapers, etc.—*vt* to manage as or form into a syndicate; to sell (an article, etc.) through a syndicate.—*vi* to form a syndicate.—*ns* **syn´dicalism**, a theory of government based on functional rather than territorial representation; a system of economic organization whereby the workers own and manage industries; a revolutionary doctrine advocating direct means (as a general strike) to seize control of the government and economy. **syn´dicalist**.—*adj* **syndicalist´ic**. [L *syndicus*—Gr *syndikos—syn*, with, *dikē*, justice.]

syndrome [sin´drōm] *n* a characteristic pattern or group of symptoms of a disease. [Gr *syndromē—syn*, together, *dramein*, to run.]

synecdoche [sin-ek´dȯ-kē] *n* a figure of speech, in which a part represents the whole object or idea. [Gr *synekdochē—syn*, together, *ekdechesthai*, to receive.]

synod [sin´od] *n* an ecclesiastical council; the governing assembly of an Episcopal province; a Presbyterian governing body ranking between the presbytery and the general assembly; a regional or national organization of Lutheran congregations; the ecclesiastical district governed by a synod. [L *synodus*—Gr *synodos—syn*, together, *hodos*, a way.]

synonym [sin´o-nim] *n* a word having the same, or very nearly the same, meaning as another or others in the same language.—*adj* **synon´ymous**, pertaining to synonyms; expressing the same thing; having the same implications, connotations, or reference.—*n* **synon´omy** [mē] the study of synonyms; a list of synonyms defined and discriminated from each other; the scientific names, or a list of them, that have been used in different publications to denote a taxonomic group (as a species); the state of being synonymous.—*adv* **synon´ymously**. [Gr *synōnymon—syn*, with, *onoma*, a name.]

synopsis [si-nop´sis] *n* a collective or general view of any subject, a summary;—*pl* **synop´sēs**.—*adjs* **synop´tic, -al**, affording a general view of the whole.—*ad* **synop´tically**.—**the Synoptic Gospels**, the first three Gospels of the New Testament, of Matthew, Mark, and Luke, which have such a similarity in matter and form that they readily admit of being brought under one and the same combined view or *synopsis*. [Gr *synopsis—syn*, with, together, *opsis*, a view.]

synovial [sin-ō´vi-ȧl] *adj* of, pertaining to, **synō´via**, a lubricating fluid occurring typically within tendon sheaths surrounding moveable joints.—*n* **synovī´tis**, inflammation of the membrane lining a tendon sheath.

syntax [sin´taks] *n* (*gram*) the arrangement of words in a sentence; the rules governing this.—*adjs* **syntac´tic, -al**, pertaining to syntax; according to the rules of syntax.—*adv* **syntac´tically**. [Gr *syntaxis—syn*, together, *taxein*, fut of *tassein*, to put in order.]

synthesis [sin´the-sis] *n* the process of making a whole by putting together its separate component parts; the combination of separate elements of thought into a whole, as opposed to analysis; reasoning from principles to a conclusion; the dialectical combination of thesis and antithesis into a higher stage of truth; (*chem*) the uniting of elements, groups, or simpler compounds or the degradation of a complex compound to form a compound;—*pl* **syn´theses** [-sēz].—*n* **synthesiz´er**, an electronic device producing sounds unobtainable from ordinary musical instruments.—*adj* **synthet´ic**, pertaining to synthesis; produced by chemical synthesis, rather than of natural origin; not real; artificial.—*n* something synthetic.—*adv* **synthet´ically**.—**synthetic language**, a language in which grammatical relationships of words are expressed principally by means of inflections. [Gr *synthesis*—*syn*, with, together, *thesis*, a placing—*thēsein*, fut of *tithenai*, to place.]

syphilis [sif´i-lis] *n* a contagious, infectious venereal disease.—*adj* **syphilit´ic**. [Fr—the title of a Latin poem by Fracastoro, an Italian physician and astronomer (1483–1553).]

syphon *See* **siphon**.

Syriac [sir´i-ak] *adj* relating to *Syria*, or to its language.—*n* a literary language based on an Eastern Aramaic dialect used in the liturgy of several eastern Christian churches; an Aramaic language spoken in Iraq, Turkey, and Iran.

syringa [si-ring´gȧ] *n* a genus (*Syringa*) of Old World plants, the lilacs; commonly applied to various shrubs of a different genus, including the mock-orange. [Gr *syrinx*, gen *syringos*, a musical pipe.]

syringe [sir-inj´] *n* a tube with a piston or a rubber bulb, by which liquids are sucked up and ejected, used to inject or withdraw fluids, esp in medicine and surgery.—*vt* to inject, or to clean, with a syringe. [L *syrinx*—Gr *syrinx*, gen *syringos*, a musical pipe.]

syrup [sir´up] *n* a solution made by boiling sugar with water, often flavored or medicated; the concentrated juice of a fruit or plant; cloying sweetness.—Also **sir´up**.—*adjs* **syr´upy, sirupy**. [Fr *syrop*—Ar *sharāb*.]

system [sis´têm] *n* anything formed of parts placed together to make a regular and connected whole working as if one machine (eg *a system of pulleys, the solar system*); the body regarded as functioning as one whole; a set of organs that together perform a particular function (eg *digestive system*); a set of facts, rules, etc. arranged to show a plan; rocks formed during a geological period; a form of social, economic, or political organization or practice (eg *the feudal system*); a customary plan, method of procedure; regular method or order; a method of scheme of classification; a full and connected view of some department of knowledge.—*adj* **systemat´ic**, constituting or based on a system; according to a system.—*adv* **systemat´ically**.—*vt* **sys´tematize**, to reduce to a system.—*adj* **system´ic**, of or affecting the body as a whole; acting through the bodily systems after ingestion to make the organism toxic to a pest.—*n* a systemic pesticide.—**systems analyst**, one who studies an activity typically by mathematical means in order to define its goals and to discover operations and procedures for accomplishing them most efficiently. [Gr *systēma*—*syn*, together, and the root of *histanai*, to set.]

systole [sis´to-lē] *n* rhythmical contraction, esp of the heart.—*adj* **systol´ic** [-tol´ik]. [Gr *systolē*—*syn*, together, *stellein*, to place.]

T

T´-square a ruler shaped like the letter T, used in mechanical and architectural drawing.—**to a T**, with perfect exactness.

Taal [täl] (**the**) *n* Afrikaans. [Du, 'speech'.]

tab [tab] *n* a small tag, flap, or strap; (*inf*) a bill, as for expenses; (*inf*) total cost.—*vt* to fix a tab on; to tabulate.—**keep tabs on** (*inf*) to keep under observation.

tabard [tab´ärd] *n* a short outer garment of the 15th and 16th centuries, worn by knights often over armor; a loose short-sleeved or sleeveless coat worn by heralds; a sleeveless tunic. [OFr,—LL *tabardum*; perh conn with L *tapēte*, tapestry.]

tabasco [tȧ-bas´kō] *n* trade name for a hot pepper sauce. [From trademark—*Tabasco* state in Mexico.]

tabby [tab´i] *n* (*arch*) a coarse kind of waved or watered silk; a domestic cat, esp a female—also **tabb´y-cat**.—*adj* brindled, or similarly diversified in color. [Fr *tabis*—Ar *'attābiy*, a quarter in Baghdad where it was made.]

tabernacle [tab´ėr-na-kl] *n* (*Bible*) **Tabernacle**, the movable tent carried by the Jews through the desert, and used as a temple; a tent; the human body as the abode of the soul; a place of worship; (*RC*) the place in which the consecrated elements of the Eucharist are kept. [L *tabernāculum*, double dim of *taberna*, a hut, shed of boards.]

table [tā´bl] *n* a smooth, flat slab or board, with legs, used as an article of furniture; supply of food, entertainment; the company at a table; a surface on which something is written or inscribed; that which is cut or written on a flat surface (*the tables of the law*); a syllabus or index; a list of facts, figures, reckonings, etc., systematically arranged, esp in columns.—*adj* of, on, at, a table.—*vt* to enter in a table.—*n* **table d'hôte** [tab´l-dōt], a meal at a fixed total price, not paid for according to the dishes or items.—Also *adj*.—*ns* **tā´blecloth**, a cloth for covering a table; **tā´bleland**, an extensive region of elevated land with a plain-like or undulating surface; a plateau; **tā´ble lin´en**, tablecloths, napkins, etc.; **tā´blespoon**, a unit of measure used in cookery equal to ½ fluidounce or 15 milligrams; a spoon holding this amount; a large spoon for serving; **tā´blespoon´ful**, as much as will fill a tablespoon; **tā´ble talk**, familiar conversation, as that round a table, during and after meals; **tā´ble tennis**, a game like tennis played on a table with small bats and light balls; **tā´ble wine**, an unfortified wine usually drunk with a meal. [OFr *table*—L *tabula*, a board.]

tableau [tab´lō] *n* a picture; a striking and vivid scene or representation;—*pl* **tableaux** [tab´lōz].—**tableau vivant** [tab´lō vē´vã], a 'living picture', a motionless representation of a well-known character, painting, scene, etc., by one or more living persons in costume;—*pl* **tableaux vivants** [as sing]. [Fr,—L *tabula*, a board, painting.]

tablet [tab´let] *n* a small flat surface; something flat on which to write, paint, etc.; a small mass of medicated material. [Dim of **table**.]

tabloid [tab´loid] *n* a digest, summary; a newspaper of half-size sheets, consisting mostly of pictures, and news in condensed form.—*adj* in the form of tabloids; concentrated. [**table**, and *-oid*; cf **tablet**.]

taboo, tabu [tȧ-bōō] *n* an institution among the Polynesians, whose penal system is based on religious sanctions, the use of certain things held sacred or consecrated being prohibited; any prohibition, interdict, restraint, ban, exclusion, ostracism.—*adj* prohibited (orig because sacred); (by transference of ideas) unholy.—*vt* to forbid approach to; to forbid the use of;—*pr p* **tabōō´ing**; *pt, pt p* **tabōōed´**. [Polynesian *tapu*—prob *ta*, to mark, *pu* expressing intensity.]

tabour, tabor [tā´bȯr] *n* a small drum, played by a person accompanying himself on a pipe or fife.—*ns* **tab´oret, tab´ouret**, a low stool; a portable stand. [OFr *tabour* (Fr *tambour*); an Oriental word.]

tabu *See* **taboo**.

tabular [tab´ū-lȧr] *adj* of the form of a table; having the form of laminae or plates; arranged in a table or schedule; computed from tables.—*vt* **tab´ulāte**, to reduce to tables or synopses; to shape with a flat surface.—*n* **tabulā´tion**. [L *tabulāris*—*tabula*, a board.]

tacit [tas´it] *adj* implied, but not expressed by words; silent.—*adv* **tac´itly**.—*adj* **tac´iturn**, habitually reserved in speech.—*n* **taciturn´ity**.—*adv* **tac´iturnly**. [L *tacitus*, silent—*tacēre*, to be silent.]

tack[1] [tak] *n* a short, sharp nail with a broad head; the course of a ship in reference to the position of her sails; a temporary change of course; a course of policy; a strategical move; adhesiveness, sticky condition, as of varnish, etc.—*vt* to attach or fasten, esp in a slight manner, as by tacks.—*vi* to change the course or tack of a ship, orig by shifting the position of the sails; to shift one's position, to veer.—*adj* **tack´y** adhesive, sticky, not yet dry. [OFr *tache, taque*, a nail, a stain.]

tack[2] [tak] *n* stuff, substance; food, fare, as *hard-tack*. [App from **tackle**.]

tackle [tak´l] [*naut* tāk´l] *n* ropes, rigging, etc., of a ship; tools, gear, weapons, equipment (for fishing, etc.); ropes, etc., for raising heavy weights; a pulley; the act of grasping and stopping, or of obstructing and depriving of the ball (an opponent in football, etc.); a grasp.—*vt* to grapple with (eg a heavier man, a problem).—*vi* to make a tackle in football. [ME *takel*—Low Ger.]

tact [takt] *n* adroitness in managing the feelings of persons dealt with; nice perception in seeing and doing exactly what is best in the circumstances.—*adjs* **tact´ful; tact´less**.—*ns* **tact´fulness; tact´lessness**. [L *tactus*—*tangĕre, tactum*, to touch.]

tactics [tak´tiks] *n sing* the science or art of maneuvering fighting forces in the presence of the enemy; way or method of proceeding.—*adjs* **tac´tic, -al**, pertaining to tactics.—*adv* **tac´tically**.—*n* **tactician** [tak-tish´ȧn], one skilled in tactics. [Gr *taktikē* (*technē*) (art of) arranging men in a field of battle—*tassein*, to arrange.]

tactile [tak´tīl] *adj* capable of being touched or felt; concerned with touching or the sense of touch.—*adj* **tact´ual**, concerned with touch. [L *tactilis*—*tangĕre, tactum*, to touch.]

tadpole [tad´pōl] *n* a young toad or frog in its first state, during which the poll or head is prominent. [**toad, poll**.]

tael [tāl] *n* a small Chinese measure of weight; a money of account (but not normally a coin) formerly in China, orig a tael weight of pure silver. [Port,—Malay *taïl*, weight.]

taffeta [taf´e-ta] *n* a thin glossy silk, etc., having a luster. [It *taffetà*—Pers *tāftah*, woven.]

taffrail [taf´rāl] *n* the upper part of a ship's timbers; the rail round the stern of a vessel. [Du *tafereel*, a panel—*tafel*, a table—L *tabula*, a table.]

taffy [taf´i] *n* a pulled candy made usu. of boiled down molasses or sugar; (*inf*) flattery; cajolery.

tag[1] [tag] *n* a tack or point of metal at the end of a string or lace; any small thing tacked or attached to another—eg a luggage label; a trite quotation.—*vt* to fit a tag or point to, to furnish with tags; to tack, fasten, or hang (to).—*vi* to string words or ideas together; to attach oneself to (a person—*with* **on to, after**); *pr p* **tagg´ing**; *pt, pt p* **tagged**.—*n* **tag´ end**, the last part; a miscellaneous or random bit.—*n, adj* **tag´rag**, ragtag. [A weaker form of **tack** (1).]

tag[2] [tag] *n* a children's game in which one player chases the rest till he touches one, who then takes his place—also **tig**. [Perh **tack** (1).]

tail[1] [tāl] *n* the prolonged hindmost extremity of an animal, generally hanging loose; anything resembling a tail in appearance, position, etc.; the back, lower, or hinder part of anything; anything long and hanging, as a trail of a comet; (*inf*) one who follows another and keeps constant watch on him; (*pl*) (*inf*) full evening dress for a man.—*vt* to furnish with a tail; to follow like a tail; to shadow.—*ns* **tail´back**, the offensive football back farthest from the line of scrimmage; **tail´ end**, buttocks; rump; the hindmost end; the concluding period; **tail´gate**, the hinged or removable gate at the back of a truck, etc.—*vti* to drive too closely behind (another vehicle).—*n pl* **tail´ings**, refuse, dregs.—*adj* **tail´less**, having no tail.—*ns* **tail´light**, a light carried at the end of a vehicle; **tail´piece**, an ornamental design at the end of a chapter in a book. [OE *tægel*.]

tail[2] [tāl] *n* entail.—*adj* limited as to tenure; entailed. [Fr *taille*, cutting.]

tailor [tāl´ȯr] *n* one whose business is to cut out and make outer garments, as coats, suits.—*vi* to work as a tailor.—*vt* to fashion by tailor's work; to make or adapt so as to fit a special need.—*adj* **tail´ored**, tailor-made.—*n* **tail´oring**, the business or work of a tailor.—*adj* **tail´or-made**, made by a tailor (esp of plain, close-fitting garments for women); exactly adapted. [Fr *tailleur*—*tailler*, to cut.]

taint [tānt] *vt* to tinge, moisten, or impregnate with anything noxious, to infect.—*vi* to be affected with something corrupting; to begin to putrefy (of meat).—*n* a stain or tincture; infection or corruption; a source of corruption; a blemish in nature, character, or morals. [O Fr *taint*, pt p of *teindre*, to dye—L *tingĕre, tinctum*, to wet.]

take [tāk] *vt* to lay hold of; to get into one's possession; to capture; to receive (eg a prize); to choose; to accept; to captivate; to lead or carry with one; to travel by; to subtract (from); to appropriate and use (eg *to take a chair*); to use or require (eg *that takes time*); to deprive one of, steal from one; to employ (eg *to take pains, strong measures*); to choose and range oneself on (a side); to feel, experience (eg *to take umbrage*); to experience, enjoy (eg *to take a rest*); to understand; to assume, *take on*; to have room for; to swallow; to allow, agree to, accept; to infer (*with* **it**); to become infected with; to endure calmly; (*slang*) to cheat, trick; (*gram*) to be used with (eg *the verb 'hit' takes an object*).—*vi* to root, begin to grow; to become effective; to gain reception, to please; to catch; to gain favor, success, etc.; to go; (*inf*) to become (*to take ill*); to betake oneself (to; eg *he took to the hills*); to have recourse to;—*pt* **took**; *pt p* **tā´ken**.—*n* a taking; the amount taken; a portion of a scene filmed or televised at one time without stopping the camera; (*slang*) receipts or profit.—*n* **tā´ker**.—*adj* **tā´king**, captivating, alluring.—*n* the act of one that takes; (*pl* earnings; profits.—*adv* **tā´kingly**.—**take advantage of**, to employ to advantage; to make use of circumstances to the prejudice of (someone else); **take after**, to resemble; **take breath**, to stop in order to breathe or be refreshed; **take down**, to reduce; to bring down from a higher place, to humble; to pull down; to write down; **take for**, to mistake for; **take in**, to receive, admit; to draw in a smaller compass, to make smaller; to comprehend; to cheat, trick; **take in vain**, to use (a name) lightly or profanely; **take it**, to endure punishment or misfortune without giving way; **take it out on**, to vent one's anger, spite on; **take it out of**, to extort reparation from; to exhaust the strength or energy of; **take off**, of an airplane, to leave the ground, etc., in flight; (*inf*) to start; (*inf*) to imitate in a burlesque manner; (*n* **takeoff**, the act of leaving the ground, as in jumping or flight; (*inf*) a ridiculous imitation); **take on**, to acquire, assume; to employ; to undertake (a task, etc.); **take one up on (something)**, to accept a person's (challenge or offer); to put a person's statement to the test; **take over**, to assume control of; to acquire control of (a business) by purchase of a majority of its shares; (*n* **take´o´ver**, the usurpation of power in a nation, organization, etc.); **take part**, to share (in); assist (in); **take place**, to happen; **take the field**, to go upon the playing field, as a football team; **take the floor**, to rise to make an address, motion, or the like at a formal meeting; **take to**, to become fond of, to care for; **take to heart**, to feel deeply about; **take up**, to make tighter or shorter; to become interested in (an occupation, sturdy, etc.); **take up arms**, to prepare for combat; **take upon**, to assume; **take up with**, (*inf*) to form a connection with, to fall in love with; **taken with**, pleased with. [Scand; ON *taka* (pt *tōk*, pt p *tekinn*.]

talc [talk] *n* a mineral occurring in thin flakes, used to make talcum powder, etc.—*n* **talcum powder**, a powder for the body made of purified talc.—*adj* **talc´ose**. [Fr *talc*—Sp *talco*—Ar *talq*.]

tale [tāl] *n* a narrative or story; an invented account, a lie; idle or malicious gossip.—*n* **tale´bear´er**, one who maliciously and officiously gives information about others.—*adj* and *n* **tale´bear´ing**.—**old wives' tale**, any marvellous story that makes demands on one's credulity. [OE *talu*, a reckoning, a tale, also speech.]

talent [tal´ėnt] *n* an ancient weight for money and commodities—in the Attic system of money (*NT*) the talent weighed 58 lb avoirdupois; any natural or special gift or aptitude; eminent ability; people, or a person, with talent.—*adj* **tal´ented**, possessing mental gifts.—**talent scout**, one whose business is to discover and recruit talented people, esp on behalf of the entertainment industry. [L *talentum*—Gr *talanton*, a weight, a talent.]

talisman [tal´iz-man, or -is-] *n* a species of charm, engraved on metal or stone, supposed to exert some protective influence over the wearer; an amulet;—*pl* **tal´ismans**. [Fr,—Ar *tilsam*—Late Gr *telesma*, consecration, incantation.]

talk [tök] *vi* to speak; to converse; to communicate ideas (eg by signs); to speak to little purpose; to gossip; to divulge information.—*vt* to utter, express (eg nonsense, treason); to use in communication (eg *to talk German*).—*n* familiar conversation; a discussion; a lecture; subject of discourse (eg *she is the talk of the town*); rumor.—*adj* **talk´ative**, given to much talking, prating.—*adv* **talk´atively**.—*ns* **talk´ativeness; talk´er; talking book**, a book, etc., recorded for use on a phonograph or magnetic tape for the blind; **talk´ing point**, something that lends support to an argument; **talk´ing-to**, a reprimand, lecture; **talk down**, to disparage or speak in a condescending manner to; **talk into**, to persuade. [ME *talken*, freq of **tell**.]

talkie [tö´ki] *n* (*inf*) a motion picture with a synchronized sound track. [From **talk**.]

tall [töl] *adj* high, esp in stature; lofty; (*arch*) sturdy; hardly to be believed (*a tall story*).—*ns* **tall´ness; tall´boy**, a high chest of drawers. [App OE *getæl*, prompt.]

tallow [tal´ō] *n* the hard fat of animals melted, used to make soap, candles, etc. [Old Du *talgh, talch*, ON *tōlgr, tolg*.]

tally [tal´i] *n* a stick cut or notched to match another stick, used to mark numbers or keep accounts by; anything made to correspond with, duplicate another; a score or account; a label;—*pl* **tall´ies**.—*vt* to score with corresponding notches; to make to fit, agree; to estimate, count (up).—*vi* to correspond; to agree (with);—*pt, pt p* **tall´ied**. [Fr *taille*—L *talea*, a cutting.]

tally-ho [tal´i-hō] *interj* the huntsman's cry betokening that a fox has gone away.

Talmud [tal´mōōd] *n* the fundamental code of the Jewish civil and canonical law, comprising the written law and the traditions and comments of the Jewish doctors.—*adj* **Talmud´ic**.—*n* the language of the Talmud. [Heb *talmūd*, instruction—*lāmad*, to learn.]

talon [tal´ȯn] *n* the claw of a bird of prey. [Fr *talon*, through LL,—L *tālus*, the heel.]

tamarind [tam´ȧ-rind] *n* a tropical tree (*Tamarindus indica*) with edible leaves and flowers, and pods filled with pulp used to make a cooling drink, etc. [*tamarindus*, Latinized from Ar *tamr Hindī*, 'date of India'.]

tamarisk [tam´ȧr-isk] *n* a genus (*Tamarix*) of Mediterranean evergreen shrubs with small white or pink flowers. [L *tamariscus*.]

tambour [tam´bōōr] *n* a small, shallow drum; a frame on which muslin or other material is stretched for embroidering; a rich kind of gold and silver embroidery; a flexible top or front (as of a cabinet) made of narrow strips of wood fixed closely together on canvas, the whole sliding in grooves. [Fr *tambour*; cf **tabour**.]

tambourine [tam-bōō-rēn´] *n* a shallow drum (with one skin and jingles) played with the hand. [Fr *tambourin*, dim of *tambour*. See **tabour**.]

tame [tām] *adj* having lost native wildness and shyness; domesticated; gentle; spiritless, without vigor; dull.—*vt* to reduce to a domestic state; to make gentle, to humble (eg spirit, pride).—*adv* **tāme´ly**.—*ns* **tāme´ness; tā´mer**, one who tames.—*adjs* **tām´able, tāme´able**, that may be tamed; **tāme´less**, untamable. [OE *tam*.]

Tamil [tam´il] *n* a Dravidian language of southeast India, and north, east and central Ceylon (Sri Lanka); one of the people speaking it.

tam-o'-shanter [tam-ō-shan´tėr] *n* a usu. woolen cap with a flat round top.—*contr* **tamm´y**. [From the hero of Robert Burns's poem of that name.]

tamper [tam´pėr] *vi* to meddle (with); to make changes in without necessity or authority (*with* **with**); to practice upon, influence secretly and unfairly (*with* **with**). [A byform of **temper**.]

tampon [tam´pȯn] *n* a plug of cotton or other material inserted in a wound or orifice to control or absorb bleeding. [Fr.]

tan [tan] *n* bark of the oak, etc., bruised and broken for tanning hides; a yellowish-brown color; suntan.—*vt* to convert skins and hides into leather by steeping in vegetable solutions containing tannin or by impregnation with various mineral salts, or by treatment with oils and fats; to make brown, to suntan; (*inf*) to beat severely.—*vi* to become tanned;—*pr p* **tann´ing**; *pt, pt p* **tanned**.—*ns* **tann´er**, one whose occupation is tanning; **tann´ery**, a place for tanning; **tan´yard**, a yard or enclosure where leather is tanned. [OE *tannian*; cf Du *tanen*, or prob OFr *tan*—Breton *tann*, an oak.]

tandem [tan´dem] *adv* applied to the position of horses harnessed singly one before the other instead of abreast; in single file.—*n* a team of horses (usually two) so harnessed; a bicycle on which two ride one before the other. [Orig university slang, a play on the L adv *tandem*, at length.]

tang [tang] *n* a prong or tapering part of a knife or tool that goes into the haft; a strong or offensive taste, esp of something extraneous; specific flavor. [ON *tange*; cog with **tongs**.]

Tang [tang] *n* a Chinese dynasty (618–907 AD) noted for great wealth, strength of Buddhism, flourishing of art, and the invention of printing.

tangent [tan´jėnt] *n* a line which touches a curve; one of the six trigonometrical functions of an angle, the ratio of the perpendicular to the base—identical with the cotangent of the complementary angle.—*abbrev* **tan**.—*n* **tan´gency**, state of being tangent; a contact or touching.—*adj* **tangential** [-jen´shȧl], of or pertaining to, of the nature of, a tangent; in the direction of a tangent; digressive.—*adv* **tangen´tially.—go off**, or **fly off, at a tangent**, to break off suddenly into a different line of thought, etc. [L *tangēns, -entis*, pr p of *tangĕre*, to touch.]

tangerine [tan-je-rēn] *n* a mandarin orange, a small, flattish, loose-skinned variety.

tangible [tan´ji-bl] *adj* perceptible by the touch; capable of being realized by the mind (eg a distinction); real, substantial (eg *tangible benefits*).—*n* **tangibil´ity**.—*adv* **tan´gibly**. [L *tangibilis*—*tangĕre*, to touch.]

tangle [tang´gl] *n* a knot of things united confusedly; a large seaweed; a complication; conflict.—*vt* to unite together confusedly; to ensnare, entangle; to make complicated.—*vi* to become tangled or complicated; to become involved in conflict or argument (*with* **with**). [Scand; Dan *tang*, ON *thang*, seaweed.]

tango [tang´gō] *n* a dance of Argentine origin; music in tango rhythm.—Also *vi*.—**Tango**, communications code word for the letter *t*. [Sp.]

tank [tangk] *n* a large basin or cistern; a reservoir of water, oil, etc.; an armored motor vehicle, with caterpillar wheels, mounted with guns.—*ns* **tank´age**, the act of storing oil, etc., in tanks; the capacity of a tank or series of tanks; **tank´er**, a ship, or heavy vehicle, for carrying oil or other liquids in bulk; an aircraft that refuels others. [Port *tanque* (Sp *estanque*, OFr *estang*)—L *stagnum*, a stagnant pool.]

tankard [tangk´ȧrd] *n* a tall, one-handled drinking vessel, often with a hinged lid. [OFr *tanquard*.]

tanner, tannery *See* **tan**.

tannin [tan´in] *n* an astringent substance found in plant material used in tanning.—*adj* **tann´ic**, of or from tannin. [Fr *tannin*.]

tansy [tan´zi] *n* a bitter, aromatic plant (genus *Tanacetum*) with small yellow flowers, common on old pasture. [OFr *tanasie*, through Late L—Gr *athanasia*, immortality.]

tantalize [tan´ta-līz] *vt* to torment by presenting something to excite desire, but keeping it out of reach.—*n* **tan´talus**, a case for wines, etc., that locks. [*Tantalus*, who was punished by having to stand up to his chin in water, with branches of fruit hung over his head, the water receding when he wished to drink, and the fruit when he desired to eat.]

tantalum [tan´tal-ùm] *n* a metallic element (symbol Ta; at wt 181.0; at no 73). [*Tantalus*. See **tantalize**.]

tantalus *see* **tantalize**.

tantamount [tan´ta-mownt] *adj* amounting (to), equivalent (to), in effect or meaning. [OFr *tant* (L *tantum*, so much, so great), and *amunter*, to amount.]

tantivy [tan-tiv´i] *n* a hunting cry; a gallop. [Imit.]

tantrum [tan´trùm] *n* a capricious fit of ill temper. [Prob W *tant*, a passion.]

Taoism [dow´izm or tow´izm] *n* a Chinese philosophy and religion advocating simplicity, selflessness, etc., founded by Lao-tzu in the 6th century BC.—*n* **Ta´oist**, an adherent of this system.—*adj* **Tâoist´ic**. [Chin *tao*, a road.]

tap[1] [tap] *n* a gentle blow or touch, esp with something small.—*vt* to strike lightly, touch gently.—*vi* to give a gentle knock;—*pr p* **tapp´ing**; pt, pt p **tapped**.—*n* **tap´dance**, a step dance in syncopated rhythm in which the rapid tapping of the dancer's toes or heels on the floor is made clearly audible by the use of special shoes. [OFr *tapper*—Low Ger *tappen*.]

tap[2] [tap] *n* a hole or short pipe through which fluid is drawn; a faucet or spigot; a tool used to cut threads in a female screw; a place in an electrical circuit where a connection can be made.—*vt* to open (a cask) and draw off liquor, to broach; to pierce, so as to let out fluid (eg an organ of the body, a tree); to draw on (any source of wealth of, profit); (*inf*) to ask for a loan or gift of money from; secretly to attach a receiver to telephone wire in order to overhear a conversation;—*pr p* **tapp´ing**; *pt, pt p* **tapped**.—*ns* **tap´room**, a barroom; **tap´root**, a root of a plant striking directly downward and giving off lateral roots; **tap´ster**, a barman.—**on tap**, ready to be drawn upon. [OE *tæppa*, seen in *tæppere*, one who taps casks.]

tape [tāp] *n* a strong, narrow strip of cloth, paper, etc., used for tying, binding, etc.; tape measure; magnetic tape.—*vt* to furnish, or tie up, with tape; to record on magnetic tape.—*ns* **tape´meas´ure**, a tape marked with inches, etc.; **tape´ recorder**, an instrument for recording sound on magnetic tape and subsequently reproducing it; **tape´ recording**, a magnetic tape on which sound has been recorded (*vt* **tape´-record**). [OE *tæpe*, a fillet—L *tapēte*. See **tapestry**.]

taper [tā´pėr] *n* a long, thin candle.—*adj* narrowed towards the point, like a taper; long and slender.—*vi* to become gradually smaller towards one end.—*vt* to make to taper.—*adj* **tā´pering**, growing gradually thinner. [OE *tapor*.]

tapestry [tap´es-tri] *n* a woven fabric with wrought figures, used for the covering of walls and furniture, and for curtains and hangings. [OFr *tapisserie*—*tapis*, a carpet—L *tapētium*—Gr *tapēs, -ētos*—prob Iranian.]

tapeworm [tāp´wûrm] *n* any one of numerous tape-like parasitic worms (*Taenia* and allied genera), often of great length, found in the intestines of men and animals. [**tape, worm**.]

tapioca [tap-i-ō´ka] *n* a glutinous, granular, farinaceous substance obtained from roots of the cassava. [Brazilian *tipioka*—*tipi*, residue, *ok*, to press out.]

tapir [tā´pėr] *n* a family (Tapiridae) of thick-skinned, short-necked quadrupeds with a short flexible proboscis, all but one species of which are found in South America. [Brazilian.]

tapis [tap´ē´ or ta-pē] *n* (*obs*) tapestry, carpeting.—**on the tapis**, on the table, under consideration. [Fr. See **tapestry**.]

tar [tär] *n* a dark, viscous, resinous mixture obtained from wood, coal, peat, etc. (varying in constituents according to source and method used); a natural bituminous substance of like appearance (*mineral tar*); a sailor, so called from his tarred clothes.—*vt* to smear with tar;—*pr p* **tarr´ing**; *p t, pt p* **tarred**.—**tar and feather**, to humiliate and punish by smearing with tar and then covering with feathers. [OE *teoro, teru*.]

tarantella [tar´an-tel´a] *n* a lively Neapolitan dance for one couple, once believed to cure the effects of a tarantula's bite; music for such a dance. [From **tarantula**.]

tarantula [tar-an´tū-la] *n* any of several large, hairy spiders (family Theraphosidae) of southern Europe and tropical America that are somewhat poisonous. [It *tarantola*—*Taranto*—L *Tarentum*, a town in South Italy where the spider abounds.]

taraxacum [tar-aks´a-kum] *n* the root of the dandelion, used in medicine. [A botanical Latin word, prob of Ar origin.]

tarboosh, tarbush [tär-bōōsh´] *n* a cap (usually red) with dark tassel worn by Muslim men—the *fez* is the Turkish form. [Ar *tarbūsh*.]

tardy [tär´di] *adj* slow, late, sluggish; out of season.—*adv* **tar´dily**.—*n* **tar´diness** [Fr *tardif*—*tard*—L *tardus*, slow.]

tare[1] [tār] *n* any of several vetches (esp *Vicia hirsuta* and *V sativa*); (*pl*) an undesirable element.

tare[2] [tār] *n* the weight of the vessel or package in which goods are contained; an allowance made for it, the remainder being the *net* weight. [Fr,—Sp, *tara*—Ar *tarhah*, thrown away.]

target [tär´gėt] *n* a mark to aim at; any object of desire or ambition; a standard of quantity set for output, etc.; an object against which marks of hostile feeling (eg of scorn) are directed. [OE *targe*; OHG *zarga*, a frame, wall; Fr *targe* is of Gmc origin.]

tariff [tar´if] *n* a list of the taxes, etc., fixed by law on merchandise; a list of charges, fees, or prices; (*inf*) any bill, charge, etc. [Fr,—Sp,—Ar *ta'rīf*, giving information, from *'arafa*, to explain.]

tarlatan [tär´lȧ-tȧn] *n* a kind of transparent muslin.—Also **tar´letan**. [Ety uncertain.]

tarmacadam [tär-mak-ad´ȧm] *n* a road surfacing formed of broken stone which has been covered with tar and rolled.—**Tar´mac**, trade name for a bituminous binder for roads.

tarn [tärn] *n* a small lake among mountains. [ON *tjörn*.]

tarnish [tär´nish] *vt* to diminish the luster or purity of (a metal) by exposure to the air, etc.; to stain, sully (eg one's reputation).—*vi* to become dull, to lose luster. [Fr *ternir* (pr p *ternissant*)—*terne*, dull, wan.]

tarpaulin [tär-pö´lin] *n* canvas cloth coated with tar, pitch, etc. to render it waterproof; a sailor. [From **tar**, and dial Eng *pauling*, a cart cover.]

tarragon [tar´a-gon] *n* a bitter herb (*Artemesia dracunculus*) used for flavoring vinegar, sauces, etc. [Sp *taragona*—Ar *tarkhun*—Gr *drakōn*, a dragon.]

tarry[1] [tär´i] *adj* consisting of, covered with, or like tar. [**tar**.]

tarry[2] [tar´i] *vi* to be tardy or slow; to stay, lodge; to wait (for); to delay;—*p t, pt p* **tarr´ied**. [ME *targen*, to delay (confused in form with *tarien*, to irritate)—OFr *targer*—L *tardus*, slow.]

tarsus [tär´sus] *n* the ankle;—*pl* **tar´sī**.—*adj* **tar´sal**. [Gr *tarsos*, the flat part of the foot.]

tart[1] [tärt] *adj* sharp or sour to the taste; sharp, severe.—*adv* **tart´ly**.—*n* **tart´ness**. [OE *teart*—*teran*, to tear.]

tart[2] [tärt] *n* a fruit pie; a small, uncovered pastry cup, containing fruit or jelly; a prostitute.—*n* **tart´let**, a small tart.—*adj* **tart´y**, like a prostitute. [OFr *tarte*.]

tartan [tär´tȧn] *n* a woolen or worsted stuff checked with various colors, once the distinctive dress of the Scottish Highlanders; different patterns are now ascribed to different clans. [Perh conn with Fr *tiretaine*, linsey-woolsey.]

tartar [tär´tȧr] *n* a salt formed on the sides of wine casks; a concretion which forms on the teeth.—*adj* **tartar´ic**, pertaining to, or obtained from, tartar.—*ns* **tartar´ic acid**, an organic acid from grapes and many other fruits; **tar´trate**, a salt or ester of this acid. [Fr *tartre*—LL *tartarum*—Ar *durd*, dregs.]

Tartar [tär´tȧr] *n* a native of Tatary—in the Middle Ages a belt of territory extending from eastern Europe right across central Asia—noted for their ferocity as invaders of medieval Europe; one too strong for his assailant (*to catch a Tartar*); a person of irritable or intractable temper.—Also *adj*. [Orig *Tatar*; see **Tatar**.]

tartare sauce [tär´tȧr sös] *n* a mayonnaise dressing with chopped pickles, olives, capers, etc., added, usu. served with fish. [Fr *sauce tartare*.]

Tartarus [tar´tȧ-rus] *n* the lower world, esp the place of punishment for the wicked.—*adj* **Tartā´rean**. [L,—Gr *Tartaros*.]

Tarzan [tär´zan] *n* a man of great strength and agility. [From hero of stories by Edgar Rice Burroughs about a man brought up by apes.]

task [täsk] *n* a set amount of work, esp of study, given by another; work; drudgery.—*vt* to impose a task on; to burden with severe work, to tax, strain.—*n* **task´master**, one who imposes a task.—**task force**, a group brought together temporarily, under one leader, for the purpose of accomplishing a definite objective.—**take to task**, to reprove. [O Norman Fr *tasque*—LL *tasca, taxa*—L *taxāre*. See **taste**.]

Tasmanian devil [taz-mā´nē-ȧn] *n* a carnivorous marsupial (*Sarcophilus ursinus*) of Australia, about the size of a large cat; **Tasmanian wolf**, a carnivorous mammal (*Thylacinus cynocephalus*) now only of Tasmania that resembles a dog.—Also **Tasmanian tiger**.

tassel [tas´l] *n* a hanging ornament consisting of a bunch of silk or other material.—*adj* **tass´elled**, adorned with tassels. [OFr *tassel*, an ornament of a square shape, attached to the dress—L *taxillus*, dim of *tālus*, a die.]

taste [tāst] *vt* to perceive (a flavor) by the touch of the tongue or palate; to try by eating or drinking a little; to eat or drink a little of; to experience.—*vi* to try or perceive by the mouth; to have a flavor (of).—*n* the act or sense of tasting; the particular sensation caused by a substance on the tongue; the quality or flavor of anything; a small portion; intellectual relish or discernment, the faculty of recognizing what is seemly, fitting, beautiful, excellent in its kind; arrangement or choice resulting from the exercise of that faculty; liking, predilection.—*adj* **taste´ful**, having a high relish; showing good taste.—*adv* **taste´fully**.—*n* **taste´fulness**.—*adj* **taste´less**, without taste, insipid; unsuitable; ugly.—*adv* **taste´lessly**.—*ns* **taste´lessness; tāst´er**, one skilful in distinguishing flavors by the taste, esp one employed in judging tea, wine, etc.; (*hist*) one whose duty it was to test the quality of food by tasting it before serving it to his master; a device for tasting or sampling.—*adj* **tast´y**, having a good taste, highly flavored.—**to one's taste**, to one's liking. [OFr *taster*, prob—L *taxāre*, to touch repeatedly, to estimate—*tangĕre*, to touch.]

Tatar [tät´ėr] *n* a member of any of numerous Turkic peoples mainly in the Tatar Republic of Russia, and adjacent regions; their Turkic language. [Turk and Per.]

tatter [tat´ėr] *n* a torn piece; a loose hanging rag.—*adj* **tatt´ered**, in tatters or rags; torn. [Cf Icel *tötturr*, rags, a torn garment.]

tatting [tat´ing] *n* knotted thread work used for trimmings; the act of making it.—*vi* **tat**, to do tatting. [Prob Icel *tæta*, shreds, *tæta*, to tease or pick wool.]

tattle [tat´l] *n* trifling talk or chat.—*vi* to talk idly or triflingly; to tell tales or secrets.—*n* **tatt´ler**. [ME *tatelen*; Low Ger *tateln*, to gabble; an imit word.]

tattoo[1] [ta-tōō´] *n* a beat of drum and a bugle call to call soldiers to quarters; a drumming, rapping, etc.—**the devil's tattoo**, drumming absent-mindedly or impatiently with the fingers on a table, etc. [Du *taptoe*—*tap*, a tap, and *toe*, which is the prep, Eng *to*, Ger *zu*, in the sense of 'shut'.]

tattoo[2] [ta-tōō´] *vt* to mark permanently (as the skin) with figures, by pricking in coloring matter, or by making symmetrical scars.—*n* marks or figures made on the skin in these ways. [*tatu*, native word in Tahiti.]

taught [töt] *pt, pt p* of **teach**.

taunt [tönt] *vt* to reproach or upbraid jeeringly or contemptuously.—*n* upbraiding, sarcastic, or insulting words.—*n* **taunt´er**.—*adv* **taunt´ingly**. [OFr *tanter*—L *tentāre*, to assail.]

Taurus [tö´rus] *n* the Bull, the 2d sign of the zodiac; in astrology, operative April 21 to May 20.—*adjs* **Tau´rīne; tau´rine**, bull-like, bovine. [L,—Gr *tauros*.]

taut [töt] *adj* tightly drawn; trim, tidy; tense.—*vt* **taut´en**, to draw tightly.—*vi* to become tight or tense. [A form of **tight**.]

tautology [tö-tol´o-ji] *n* needless repetition of the same thing in different words.—*adjs* **tautolog´ical**, containing tautology.—*adv* **tautolog´ically**. [Gr *tautologia*—*tauto*, the same, *legein*, to speak.]

tavern [tav´ėrn] *n* a saloon, bar; an inn. [Fr *taverne*—L *taberna*.]

taw[1] [tö] *n* a special marble chosen to be aimed with; a game at marbles; the line from which to play. [Origin obscure.]

taw[2] [tö] *vt* to prepare and dress, as skins into white leather. [OE *tawian*, to prepare; OHG *zoujan*, make, Du *touwen*, curry.]

tawdry [tö´dri] *adj* showy, cheap, and tasteless; gaudily dressed.—*adv* **taw´drily**.—*n* **taw´driness**. [Said to be corr from *St Awdrey=St Ethelreda*, at whose fair, at Ely, laces and gay toys were sold.]

tawny [tö´ni] *adj* of the color of things tanned, a yellowish brown.—*n* **taw´niness**. [Fr *tanné*, pt p of *tanner*, to tan.]

tax [taks] *n* a rate imposed on property or persons for the benefit of the state; a strain, a burdensome duty.—*vt* to lay a tax on; to burden, strain; to accuse of (*with* **with**); (*law*) to assess (costs).—*adj* **tax´able**, capable of being, or liable to be, taxed.—*n* **taxā´tion**, act of taxing.—*adj* **tax-exempt**, exempt from taxation.—*n* **tax´pay´er**. [Fr *taxe*, a tax—L *taxāre*. See **task**.]

taxi [tak´si] *n* **tax´icab**, an automobile usu. fitted with a taximeter, licensed to ply for hire.—*vi* to go by taxi; (of an airplane) to run along the ground under its own power;—*pr p* **tax´iing**; *pt, pt p* **tax´ied**. [Contr of **taximeter**.]

taxidermy [taks´i-dėr-mi] *n* the art of preparing and stuffing the skins of animals.—*n* **tax´idermist**. [Fr,—Gr *taxis*, arrangement, *derma*, skin.]

taximeter [tak-sim´e-tėr] *n* an instrument fitted to cabs to indicate the fare due for the distance traveled. [Fr *taxe*, price, and Gr *metron*, a measure.]

taxis [tak´sis] *n* arrangement; (*biol*) movement of a whole organism in response to a stimulus. [Gr—*tassein*, to arrange.]

tea [tē] *n* a shrub (*Camellia sinensis*, family Theaceae) growing in China, India, Ceylon, etc.; its dried leaves; an infusion of the leaves in boiling water; any vegetable infusion (eg *senna tea*); an afternoon snack at which tea is generally served; a reception at which tea is served; (*slang*) marijuana.—*ns* **tea cadd´y**, an airtight box or jar for holding tea; **tea´cup; tea´-gar´den**, a public garden, restaurant, where tea and other refreshments are served; a tea plantation; **tea´ gown**, a loose gown for wearing at afternoon tea at home; **tea´kett´le**, a covered kettle with a handle in which to boil water; **tea´pot**, a vessel in which the beverage tea is made; **tea´ rose**, any of numerous garden bush roses descended from a Chinese rose (*Rosa odorata*) valued for their large tea-scented blooms; **tea´ service**, a matching teapot, sugar bowl, and pitcher, usu. in silver or silverplate; **tea´spoon**, a small spoon used at meals, holding about 5 milliliters; **tea´ towel**, a cloth for drying crockery, etc. [From South Chinese *te* (pron *tā*).]

teach [tēch] *vt* to impart knowledge to; to impart knowledge of (eg *to teach arithmetic*); to explain, show (that, how to); train in, show the desirability of (eg *experience teaches patience*); to make aware of the penalty attached (to an action—eg *that'll teach you to meddle*).—*vi* to give instruction, esp as a profession;—*pt, pt p* **taught** [tawt].—*adj* **teach´able**, capable of being taught; apt or willing to learn.—*ns* **teach´er**, one who teaches or instructs, esp as an occupation; one who instructs skilfully; **teach´ing**, the act, practice, or profession of giving instruction.—**teach´-in**, long public debate, usu. on a college campus, consisting of a succession of speeches by well-informed persons holding different views on a matter of general importance; **teaching machine**, any mechanical device capable of presenting an instructional program. [OE *tǣcan*, to show, teach.]

teak [tēk] *n* a tree of the East Indies (*Tectona grandis*) widely grown in southeast Asia; the very hard wood. [Dravidian *tēkka*.]

teal [tēl] *n* any of several river duck (genus *Anas*) of Europe and America. [Du *teling, taling*.]

team [tēm] *n* a number of animals moving together or in order; two or more oxen or other animals harnessed to the same vehicle; a number of persons associated for doing anything conjointly, playing a game, etc.—*vi* to join in cooperative activity (*with* **up**).—*ns* **team´ster**, one whose work is hauling loads with a truck or team; **team´work**, the subordination of the individual's task to the common purpose of the team; the ability of a team so to work together.—**team up with**, to join forces with. [OE *tēam*, offspring; prob *tēon*, to draw.]

tear[1] [tēr] *n* a drop of the fluid secreted by the lachrymal gland, appearing in the eyes; anything like a tear.—*adj* **tear´ful**, shedding tears; mournful.—*adv* **tear´fully**.—*ns* **tear´fulness; tear´ gas**, a gas that temporarily blinds the eyes with tears; **tear´jerk´er**, an extravagantly sentimental song, book, etc., inviting pity, sorrow.—*adjs* **tear´less; tear´-stained**. [OE *tēar*.]

tear[2] [tār] *vt* to draw asunder with violence; to make a violent rent in; to lacerate; to pull violently (away from) or separate violently (from).—*vi* to move or act with speed or impetuosity; to rage;—*pt* **tōre**; *pt, pt p* **tōrn** [or törn].—*n* act of tearing; a rent. [OE *teran*.]

tease [tēz] *vt* to separate into single fibers; to comb or card, as wool; to scratch, raise a nap on with a teasel, as cloth; to vex with importunity, jests, etc., esp playfully; to torment, irritate.—*n* one who teases or torments. [OE *tǣsan*, to pluck.]

teasel, teazel, teazle [tēz´l] *n* a plant (*Dipsacus fullonum*) with large burs or heads covered with stiff, hooked awns, used, attached to revolving cylinder, in raising a nap on cloth (**fuller's teasel**); any other plant of the same genus. [OE *tǣsel, tǣsl*—*tǣsan*, to pluck.]

teat [tēt] *n* the nipple on a breast or udder through which the young suck the milk. [OE *tit*; or perh through OFr *tete*, from Gmc.]

teazel, teazle [tēz´l] *see* **teasel**.

technetium [tek-nē´shi-ům] *n* a metallic element (symbol Tc; at wt 99; at no 43). [Gr *technētos*, artificial—*technē*, art.]

technical [tek´nik-ål] *adj* pertaining to skill in the arts; concerned with the mechanical or applied arts; belonging to, peculiar to, a particular art or profession (eg of a term or expression); concerned with, or abounding in, terms, methods, fine distinctions, etc., important to the expert practitioner of an art; so called in strict legal or technical language; (sometimes) technological.—*n* **technical´ity**, state or quality of being technical; a technical expression or its strict interpretation.—*adv* **tech´nically**.—*n* **technician** [tek-nish´ån], one skilled in the practical arts or in the practice of any art.—*n pl* **tech´nics**, applied science.—*n* **Technicolor**, a trade name of a process of color photography in motion pictures.—*ns* **technique** [tek-nēk], method of performance, manipulation, or execution, as in music or art; individualized execution; formal construction (eg of poetry); **technoc´racy** [-nok´]; government by technical experts; a state, etc. so governed; a body of ruling technical experts; **tech´nocrat**, a member of a technocracy; a believer in technocracy; **technol´ogy**, the practice of any or all of the applied sciences that have practical value and/or industrial use; technical method(s) in a particular field of industry or art; technical means and skills characteristic of a particular group, period, etc.; technical nomenclature.—*adjs* **technolog´ic, -al**, relating to technology.—*n* **technol´ogist**, one skilled in technology. [Gr *technikos*—*technē*, art, akin to *tiktein*, to produce.]

ted [ted] *vt* to spread or turn, as new-mown grass, for drying;—*pr p* **tedd´ing**; *pt, pt p* **tedd´ed**.—*n* **tedd´er**, an implement for spreading hay. [Scand; ON *tedhja*, spread manure.]

teddy bear [ted´i-bār] *n* a stuffed toy bear, usu. of yellow plush—often abbreviated to **tedd´y**. [Named in allusion to the fondness of Theodore (popularly *Teddy*) Roosevelt, President of the US 1901–09, for hunting big game.]

teddy boy [ted´i-boi] an unruly English adolescent (1950s) wearing clothes reminiscent of those worn by dandies in *Edward* VII's time.—Also **Ted**.

Te Deum [tē dē´um] *n* a famous Latin hymn of the Western Church, beginning with the words *Te Deum laudamus*, 'We praise thee, O God'.—**sing the Te Deum**, exult, rejoice.

tedious [tē´di-ůs] *adj* wearisome, tiresome.—*n* **tē´diousness**.—*adv* **tē´diously**.—*n* **tē´dium**, wearisomeness, irksomeness. [L *taedium*—*taedet*, it wearies.]

tee [tē] *n* (*golf*) the place from which the ball is first played at each hole; a small peg from which the ball is driven.—*vti* to place (the golf ball) on the tee. [Prob from *T*.]

teem[1] [tēm] *vi* to be full or prolific of (*with* **with**). [OE *tēam*, offspring.]

teem[2] [tēm] *vt* to pour, empty. [ON *tœma*, to empty.]

teens [tēnz] *n pl* the years of one's age from thir*teen* to nine*teen*.—*adj* **teen´age**, suitable for people between these ages.—*n* any age within the teens; (in *pl*) people in the teens.—*n* **teen´ager**, (*inf*) a person in the teens.

tee-shirt *See* **T-shirt**.

teeth *See* **tooth**.

teething [tēTH´ing] *n* the first growth of teeth, or the process by which they make their way through the gums.—*vi* **teethe**, to grow or cut the teeth.—**teething troubles**, pain caused by cutting of teeth; difficulties encountered in the early stages of any undertaking or when first using a new machine, etc. [**teeth**.]

teetotaler, teetotaller [tē-tō´tal-ėr] *n* one pledged to entire abstinence from intoxicating drinks.—*adj* **teetō´tal**.—*n* **teetō´talism**. [Prob from a stammering pronunciation of the word **total**.]

teetotum [tē-tō´tům] *n* a small top, orig four-sided and marked with letters for use in a game of chance. [From *T* the letter on one side, standing for L *totum*, all (the stakes).]

tegument [teg´ū-mėnt] *n* an integument, skin.—*adjs* **tegumen´tal, tegumen´tary**. [L *tegumentum*—*tegěre*, to cover.]

tele- [tel´i-] in composition, distant; television. [Gr *tēle*, at a distance.]

telecast [tel´i-käst] *n* a television broadcast.—Also *vt* and *vi*.

telecommunication [tel´i-kò-mū-ni-kā´shòn] *n* communication of information, in verbal, written, coded, or pictorial form, by telephone, telegraph, cable, radio, television; (usu. *pl*) the science of communication at a distance. [Gr *tēle*, at a distance, and **communication**.]

telegram [tel´i-gram] *n* a message sent by telegraph.—*n* **tel´egraph**, an apparatus for transmitting, or means of transmitting, coded messages to a distance, formerly applied to any kind of signals (eg **bush telegraph**, a system of signals used by primitive peoples in the bush, now the obscure and rapid transmission of news through a population), now confined to communication using electricity, wires, and a code.—*vt* to convey or announce by telegraph, to signal.—*n* **teleg´raphist**, one who works a telegraph.—*adj* **telegraphic**, pertaining to, or communicated by, a telegraph;

shortened.—*n* **teleg´raphy**, the science or art of constructing or using telegraphs. [Gr *tēle*, at a distance, *graphein*, to write.]

teleology [tel-e-ol´ö-ji] *n* the doctrine that natural processes are determined by an end to which they are directed—which seeks to explain the universe in the light of final purposes.—*adjs* **teleolog´ic, -al**.—*adv* **teleolog´ically**. [Gr *telos*, issue, *logos*, a discourse.]

telepathy [te-lep´a-thi] *n* a communication between mind and mind otherwise than through the senses, the persons concerned in the communication being not necessarily in the same place.—*adj* **telepath´ic**.—*adv* **telepath´ically**. [Gr *tēle*, at a distance, *pathos*, feeling.]

telephone [tel´e-fōn] *n* an instrument for reproducing sound, esp speech, at a distance, esp by means of electricity.—*vt* to communicate by telephone.—*adj* **telephon´ic**.—*n* **teleph´ony**, the use of a telephone system for transmitting sounds. [Gr *tēle*, far, *phōnē*, a sound.]

telephotography [tel-e-fō-tog´ra-fi] *n* photography which involves the use of a camera with a telephoto lens.—*n* **tele´pho´tograph**, a photograph taken with a telephoto lens; a photograph transmitted by telegraph or radio.—**telephoto lens**, a lens of long focal length for obtaining large images of distant objects. [Gr *tēle*, at a distance, + **photography**.]

teleprinter [tel´e-print-ėr] *n* a form of telegraph transmitter having a typewriter keyboard and a printing telegraph receiver. [Gr *tēle*, at a distance, and **printer**.]

teleprocessing [tel´e-prō´ses-ing] *n* the use of a computer to process data transmitted from distant points. [**tele-** + **process**.]

telescope [tel´e-skōp] *n* an optical instrument for viewing objects at a distance.—*vt* to drive or slide one into another like the movable joints of a spyglass.—*vi* to be forced into each other in such a way.—*adj* **telescop´ic**, pertaining to, performed by, or like a telescope; seen only by a telescope.—*adv* **telescop´ically**. [Fr,—Gr *tēle*, at a distance, *skopeein*, to look at.]

teletext [tel´e-tekst] *n* written data, such as business news, etc., transmitted by television companies in the form of coded pulses which can be decoded by a special adaptor for viewing on a regular television set. [**tele-** + **text**.]

television [tel-e-vizh´(ȯ)n] *n* the wireless transmission and reproduction on a screen of a view of objects, etc. at a place distant from the beholder; a television receiving set; television broadcasting.—*vt* **tel´evise**, to transmit by television. [Gr *tēle*, at a distance, + **vision**.]

telex [tel´eks] *n* a communication service whereby subscribers hire teleprinters which are connected by telephone lines through automatic exchanges. [*tel*etypewriter (teleprinter) *ex*-change.]

tell [tel] *vt* to number, count; to utter (eg a lie); to narrate; to disclose; to inform; to discern (eg *I can't tell what it is*); to distinguish (eg *to tell one from the other*).—*vi* to produce or have a marked effect; to tell tales, play the informer;—*pt, pt p* **tōld**.—*n* **tell´er**, one who tells; a bank clerk whose duty it is to receive and pay money; one who counts votes in an election, etc.—*adj* **tell´ing**, having great effect.—*n* **tell´tale**, one who officiously tells the private concerns of others; any of various signaling and warning devices in games, railroad safety, etc.—*adj* revealing what is meant to be hidden.—**tell on**, to affect obviously (eg *the strain told on him*); **tell off**, to count off; to detach on some special duty; (*inf*) to rebuke. [OE *tellan*.]

tellurium [te-lū´ri-ùm] *n* a metalloid element (symbol Te; at wt 127.6; at no 52).—*adj* **tellū´ric**, pertaining to the earth; of or from tellurium. [L *tellūs, tellūris*, the earth.]

Telugu [tel´oo-goo] *n* a Dravidian language of India; one of the people speaking it.

temerity [te-mer´i-ti] *n* rashness. [Fr *témérité*—L *temeritās*—*temere*, by chance, rashly.]

temper [tem´pėr] *vt* (*arch*) to mix in due proportion; to bring to a proper degree of hardness and elasticity by repeated heating and cooling, as steel; to moderate; to moderate by blending.—*n* due mixture or balance of different or contrary qualities; state of a metal as to hardness, etc.; constitutional state of mind, esp with regard to feelings, disposition, mood; passion, irritation; a disposition, proneness, to anger.—*adj* **tem´pered**, having a certain specified disposition or temper (eg *even-tempered*); brought to a certain temper, as steel.—**to keep one's temper**, to restrain oneself from showing one's anger or losing one's temper; **to lose one's temper**, to show anger. [L *temperāre*, to combine properly, allied to *tempus*, time.]

tempera [tem´pe-ra] *n* a painting medium in which pigment is dissolved with egg-white and combined with egg yolk; a painting done in tempera; opaque watercolor used for posters. [It.]

temperament [tem´pėr-a-mėnt] *n* in ancient physiology, the combination of the four humors by the relative proportions of which a man's natural disposition was determined; disposition, characteristic mental and emotional reactions as a whole; passionate disposition; (*mus*) the adjustment of the intervals between the notes of a piano (which does not contain a large enough number of notes to allow a sufficient number of exact distinctions of pitch) so that it is possible to modulate from one key to another—the inaccuracies of pitch being distributed according to a definite plan; the system on which this is done; the act of tempering.—*adj* **temperamen´tal**, pertaining to temperament; displaying alternation of moods, inclined to be swayed by emotion.—*adv* **temperamen´tally**. [L *temperāmentum*—*temperāre*. See **temper**.]

temperance [tem´pėr-àns] *n* moderation, esp in the indulgence of the natural appetites and passions; moderation in the use of alcoholic liquors, and even entire abstinence from such. [L *temperantia*.]

temperate [tem´pėr-at] *adj* moderate in degree of any quality, esp in the appetites and passions, calm; cool, mild, moderate in temperature; abstemious.—*adv* **tem´perately**.—*ns* **tem´perateness; tem´perature**, degree of any quality, esp of hotness or coldness measured with respect to an arbitrary zero; measured degree of the heat of a body or of the atmosphere, recorded on a thermometer; body heat above the normal. [L *temperātus*, pt p of *temperāre*. See **temper**.]

tempest [tem´pest] *n* wind rushing with great velocity, usually with rain or snow, a violent storm; any violent commotion.—*adj* **tempes´tūous**, resembling, or pertaining to, a tempest; very stormy; turbulent.—*adv* **tempes´tūously**.—*n* **tempes´tūousness**. [OFr *tempeste*—L *tempestās*, a season, tempest.]

Templar [tem´plȧr] *n* one of a religious military order, the **Knights Templars**, founded in 1119 for the protection of the Holy Sepulchre and pilgrims going thither; a student or lawyer living in the Temple, London.—**Good Templar**, a member of a teetotal society whose organization is modelled on that of the Freemasons. [Orig called 'Poor fellow-soldiers of Christ and of the *Temple* of Solomon', from their first headquarters in Jerusalem, on the site of the temple of Solomon.]

template [tem´plāt] *n* a pattern, in the form of a thin plate cut to the shape required, by which a surface of an article being made is marked out.—Also **tem´plet**. [L *templum*, small timber.]

temple[1] [tem´pl] *n* an edifice erected to a deity; a place of worship; anything regarded as sanctified by divine presence. [L *templum*.]

temple[2] [tem´pl] *n* the flat portion of either side of the head above the cheekbone.—*adj* **tem´poral**. [OFr *temple*—L *tempora*, the temples, pl of *tempus*, time.]

templet *See* **template**.

tempo [tem´pō] *n* (*mus*) time, rhythmic speed; rate of any activity. [It.]

temporal [tem´por-ȧl] *adj* pertaining to time, esp to the period of the history of this world, hence to this life or world, secular or civil.—*n* **tempo´ral´ity**, temporalness or temporariness; (in *pl*—**temporal´ities**) secular possessions, revenues of an ecclesiastic from lands, tithes, and the like.—*adj* **tem´porary**, lasting, used, for a time only; transient.—*n* a person employed temporarily.—*adv* **tem´porarily**.—*n* **tem´porariness**.—*vi* **tem´porize**, to act according to expediency; to yield temporarily to circumstances; to play for time, avoid committing oneself definitely.—*ns* **tem´poriziser; tem´porizing**. [Fr,—L *temporālis*—*tempus*, time.]

temporal *See* **temple** (2).

tempt [temt] *vt* (*obs*) to test; to try to persuade, esp to evil; to attract, pull strongly towards a course of action; to entice, induce.—*ns* **temptā´tion**, act of tempting; state of being tempted; that which tempts; enticement to evil; trial; **temp´ter**, one who tempts, esp (*with* **the**) the devil;—*fem* **temp´tress**.—*adj* **temp´ting**, adapted to tempt or entice, attractive.—*adv* **temp´tingly**. [OFr *tempter, tenter*—L *tentāre*, to feel, test, try.]

ten [ten] *adj* and *n* the cardinal number next above nine.—*n* a symbol for this (10, X, x).—*adjs* **ten´fold**, ten times; ten times more; **tenth** (see below).—**Ten Commandments**, the ten laws of moral and religious conduct given to Moses by God on Mt Sinai. [ME *ten*, shortened form of *tēne*—OE *tēn*, earlier *tīen*; Ger *zehn*.]

tenable [ten´a-bl] *adj* capable of being retained, held, or defended against attack.—*ns* **tenabil´ity, ten´ableness**. [Fr *tenable*, from *tenir*—L *tenēre*, to hold.]

tenacious [ten-ā´shùs] *adj* retaining or holding fast; sticky; retentive; stubborn; persevering.—*adv* **tenā´ciously**.—*ns* **tenā´ciousness, tenac´ity** [-as´-], quality of being tenacious; the quality of bodies which makes them stick to others. [L *tenāx, -ācis*—*tenēre*, to hold.]

tenant [ten´ȧnt] *n* one who holds or possesses land or property under another; one who has, on certain conditions, temporary possession of any place; an occupant.—*vt* (usu. in *pt p*) to hold as a tenant.—*n* **ten´ancy**, a temporary holding or occupying of land or buildings by a tenant; the period of this.—*n* **ten´antry**, tenancy; a body of tenants. [Fr *tenant*—L *tenēns, -entis*, pr p of *tenēre*, to hold.]

tench [tench, -sh] *n* a freshwater fish (*Tinca tinca*) noted for its ability to survive outside water. [OFr *tenche*—L *tinca*.]

tend[1] [tend] *vt* to take care of, look after.—*n* **ten´der**, a small craft that attends a larger with stores, etc.; one plying between a larger vessel and the shore; a vehicle attached to locomotives to carry fuel and water. [Contracted from **attend**.]

tend[2] [tend] *vi* to be directed, move, or incline, in a specified direction; to be directed (to any end or purpose); to contribute or conduce (to a result).—*n* **ten´dency**, direction, object, or result to which anything tends; inclination; drift.—*adj* **tenden´tious** [-shùs], having a deliberate tendency or bias, written or uttered with set purpose. [L *tendĕre*; Gr *teinein*, to stretch.]

tender[1] [ten´dėr] *vt* to offer for acceptance; to offer as payment.—*vi* to make an offer (for a contract—eg to offer to supply certain commodities for a certain period at rates specified).—*n* an offer or proposal, esp of some service; the thing offered, esp money offered—payment.—**legal tender**, currency which the creditor may not refuse to accept in payment. [L *tendĕre*, to stretch.]

tender[2] [ten´dėr] *adj* soft, delicate; succulent; not hardy, fragile; easily moved to pity, love, etc.; careful not to injure (*with* **of**); unwilling to cause pain; apt to feel pain, sensitive; expressive of the softer passions; young and inexperienced; delicate, requiring careful handling; apt to lean over under sail.—*n* **ten´derfoot**, a newcomer to ranching in the West, unused to hardship; an inexperienced beginner.—*adj* **ten´der-hear´ted**, full of feeling.—*vt* **ten´derize**, to break down the connective tissue (of meat) by pounding or by applying a chemical.—*adv* **ten´derly**.—*n* **ten´derness**. [Fr *tendre*—L *tener*.]

tendon [ten´don] *n* a cord, band, or sheet of fibrous tissue by which a muscle is attached to a bone and transmits the force which the muscle exerts. [Fr *tendon*—L *tendĕre*, to stretch; cf Gr *tenōn*—*teinein*, to stretch.]

tendril [ten´dril] *n* a slender, spiral shoot of a plant by which it attaches itself for support.—*adj* clasping or climbing. [App L *tendĕre*, to stretch.]

tenebrous [ten´e-brus] *adj* dark, gloomy. [L *tenebrōsus*—*tenebrae*, darkness.]

tenement [ten´e-ment] *n* (*law*) anything held, or that may be held, by a tenant, in the widest sense of the word; a dwelling or habitation, or part of it; a building divided into apartments, each occupied by a separate tenant, but with certain communal facilities. [LL *tenementum*—L *tenēre*, to hold.]

tenet [ten´et, tēn´-] *n* any opinion, principle, or doctrine that a person holds or maintains as true. [L *tenet*, he holds—*tenēre*, to hold.]

tennis [ten´is] *n* an ancient game for two to four persons, played with ball and rackets within a building specially constructed for the purpose; lawn tennis.—*n* **tenn´is-court**, a place or court for playing tennis. [Prob Fr *tenez*, imper of *tenir*, to take, receive.]

tenon [ten´on] *n* a projection at the end of a piece of wood inserted into the socket or mortise of another, to hold the two together.—*vt* to fit with tenons. [Fr,—*tenir*, to hold—L *tenēre*.]

tenor [ten´or] *n* a general run or course, prevailing direction; purport; the highest regular adult male voice; the part for a tenor; one who sings tenor.—*adj* pertaining to the tenor in music. [L,—*tenēre*, to hold.]

tense[1] [tens] *n* (*gram*) the form of a verb which indicates the time of the action, or the existence of a state or condition. [OFr *tens* (Fr *temps*)—L *tempus*, time.]

tense[2] [tens] *adj* tightly strained, hence rigid; critical, exciting; nervous and highly strained (eg *he was tense with emotion*); (*linguistics*) of a sound, pronounced with great muscular tension in those parts of the speech organs involved in its articulation.—*adv* **tense´ly**.—*n* **tense´-ness**.—*adjs* **ten´sible, ten´sile**, capable of being stretched.—*ns* **ten´sion**, act of stretching; state of being stretched or strained; strain, effort; mental strain; a state of barely suppressed emotion, as excitement, suspense, anxiety; strained relations (between persons); opposition (between conflicting ideas or forces); **ten´sor**, a muscle that stretches a part. [L *tensus*, pt p of *tendĕre*, to stretch.]

tent [tent] *n* a portable lodge or shelter, generally of canvas stretched on poles; anything like a tent.—*adj* **ten´ted**, covered with tents; shaped like a tent. [Fr *tente*—LL *tenta*—L *tendĕre*, to stretch.]

tentacle [ten´ta-kl] *n* a long, slender flexible growth of certain animals for feeling or motion, etc.—*adj* **tentac´ūlar**. [Fr *tentacule*—L *tentāre*, to feel—*tendĕre*, to stretch.]

tentative [ten´ta-tiv] *adj* of the nature of an attempt; experimental; provisional.—*adv* **ten´tatively**. [Fr,—L *tentāre*, to feel, try—*tendĕre*, to stretch.]

tenter [ten´tėr] *n* a machine on which cloth is extended or stretched by hooks.—*vt* to stretch on hooks.—*n* **ten´terhook**, a sharp, hooked nail.—**be on tenterhooks**, to be tortured by suspense or anxiety. [Fr *tenture*—L *tendĕre, tentum*, to stretch.]

tenth [tenth] *adj* the last of ten; being one of ten equal parts.—*n* one of ten equal parts.—*adv* **tenth´ly**, in the tenth place. [**ten**.]

tenuity [te-nū´i-ti] *n* thinness; slenderness; rarity; meagerness; faintness.—*adj* **ten´ūous**.—*n* **ten´uousness**. [L *tenuitās*—*tenuis*, thin, slender; cf *tendĕre*, to stretch.]

tenure [ten´ūr] *n* act or conditions of holding property or office; a tenant's rights, duties, etc.; the period during which office or property is held. [Fr *tenure*—LL *tenura*—L *tenēre*, to hold.]

tepee [tē´pē, tep´ē] *n* an American Indian tent formed of skins, etc., stretched over a frame of converging poles. [Amer Indian.]

tepid [tep´id] *adj* moderately warm, lukewarm.—*ns* **tepid´ity, tep´idness**, lukewarmness. [L *tepidus*—*tepēre*, to be warm.]

teraphim [ter´a-fim] *n pl* images of a Semitic household god.—*sing* **ter´aph**. [Heb.]

teratogen [tėr-at´ó´gėn] *n* an agent that raises the incidence of congenital malformations.—*adj* **terat´ogenic**, producing monsters. [Gr *teras, -atos*, a monster.]

terbium [tûr´bi-ům] *n* a metallic element (symbol Tb; at wt 158.9; at no 65. [*Ytterby*, a Swedish quarry.]

terce [tûrs] *n* the office of the third hour, which should be said between sunrise and noon.

tercentenary [tėr-sen-ten´a-ri or tėr-sen´te-nȧ-ri] *adj* including or relating to an interval of three hundred years.—*n* the 300th anniversary of anything.—*adj* **tercentenn´ial**. [L *ter*, thrice, and **centenary**.]

tercet [tûr´set] *n* a group of three lines of verse. [Fr,—L *tertius*, third.]

terebinth [ter´e-binth] *n* the tree (*Pistacia terebinthus*) from which turpentine is obtained.—*adj* **terebinth´ine**. [L,—Gr *terebinthos*.]

teredo [tė-rē´dō] *n* any of the shipworms, marine clams (esp family Teredinidae) that burrow into submerged wood and are very destructive of it. [L,—Gr *terēdōn*, from *teirein*, to wear away.]

tergiversation [ter-ji-ver-sā´sh(ȯ)n] *n* a shuffling or shifting, subterfuge; fickleness of conduct; flight, desertion.—*vi* **ter´giversate**, to use evasion; to desert one's party or principles.—*n* **ter´giversātor**. [L *tergum*, the back, *versārī*, to turn.]

term [tûrm] *n* a limit; any limited period; the time for which anything lasts; that by which a thought is expressed, a word or expression; one of the three elements in a syllogism; (*pl*) mutual relationship between persons; (*pl*) conditions of a contract, etc.; (*pl*) words, speech; (*math*) either quantity of a fraction or ratio; (*math*) each quantity in a series or algebraic expression.—*vt* to apply a term to, to name or call.—*n* **terminol´ogy**, the terms used in any art, science, etc.—*adj* **terminolog´ical**.—*advs* **terminolog´ically; term´ly**, term by term.—**be on good, bad**, etc., **terms with**, to have friendly, unfriendly, etc., relations with; **bring to terms**, to compel to the acceptance of conditions (with); **come to terms (with)**, to come to an agreement (with); to submit (to); to find a way of living (with some personal trouble or difficulty); **in terms of**, in the language peculiar to; (*math*) by an expression containing (eg *express x in terms of y*); **make terms**, to come to an agreement. [Fr *terme*—L *terminus*, a boundary.]

termagant [tûr´ma-gȧnt] *n* a boisterous, bold woman; a scold.—*adj* boisterous, brawling, quarrelsome, scolding. [*Termagant* or *Tervagant*, a supposed Mohammedan idol, represented in mediaeval plays as violent.]

terminate [tûr´min-āt] *vt* to set a limit to; to set the boundary to; to put an end to, to finish.—*vi* to be limited; to come to end either in space or in time.—*adjs* **ter´minable**, that may be, or is liable to be, terminated; limitable; **ter´minal**, pertaining to, or growing at, the end or extremity; ending a series or part; occurring in every term; close to, or causing death, as cancer; of or at the end of a transportation line.—*n* an end; a point of connection in an electric circuit; a point where the supply to an electrical machine is taken; either end of a transportation line, or a main station on it; a device usu. with a keyboard and video display, for putting data in, or getting it from, a computer.—*n* **terminā´tion**, act of terminating or ending; limit; end; the ending of words as varied by their signification.—*adjs* **terminā´tional**, pertaining to, or forming, a termination; **ter´minative**, tending to terminate, or to determine. [L *terminus*, a boundary.]

terminus [tûr´mi-nus] *n* the end or extreme point; a limit; either end of a transportation line.—*pl* **ter´mini** [-ī]. [L, a boundary.]

termite [tûr´mīt] *n* an order of social insects (order Isoptera) pale in color and superficially resembling the ants—hence known as *white ants*. [L *termes, -itis*, a wood-worm.]

tern [tûrn] *n* a seabird (*Sterna*, or related genera) allied to the gulls. [ON *therna*; OE *tearn*.]

ternary [tûr´nȧ-ri] *adj* proceeding by, or consisting of, threes.—*n* the number three.—*adj* **ter´nāte**, threefold, or arranged in threes. [L *terni*, three each—*trēs*, three.]

terpsichorean [tûrp-sik-ō-rē´ȧn] *adj* concerned with dancing. [Gr *Terpsichorē*, the muse of dancing.]

terrace [ter´ȧs] *n* a raised level bank of earth; an unroofed paved area between a house and a lawn; a row of houses.—*vt* to form into a terrace, or terraces. [Fr *terrasse*—It *terrazza*—L *terra*, the earth.]

terra cotta [ter´a-cot´a] *n* a composition of clay and sand used for statues, hardened like bricks by fire; the brown-red color of terra cotta. [L *terra*, earth, *cocta*, pt p of *coquĕre*, to cook.]

terra firma [ter´a fûr´ma] *n* dry land; solid ground. [L.]

terrain [ter´ān] *n* a tract of land; any tract considered in relation to its fitness for some purpose; field of activity. [Fr,—L *terrēnum*—*terra*, the earth.]

terrapin [ter´a-pin] *n* any of several edible tortoises (family Testudinidae) living in fresh or brackish water. [Prob Amer Indian.]

terraqueous [ter-ā´kwė-us] *adj* consisting of land and water. [L *terra*, earth, *aqua*, water.]

terrene [te-rēn´] *adj* pertaining to the earth; earthy; earthly. [L *terrēnus*—*terra*, the earth.]

terrestrial [te-res´tri-ȧl] *adj* pertaining to, or existing on, the earth; earthly; living on the ground; representing the earth. [L *terrestris*—*terra*, the earth.]

terrible [ter´i-bl] *adj* fitted to excite terror or awe, awful, dreadful; (*inf*) very unpleasant.—*n* **terr´ibleness**, state of being terrible; dreadfulness.—*adv* **terr´ibly**, frighteningly; (*inf*) extremely. [L *terribilis*—*terrēre*, to frighten.]

terrier [ter´i-ėr] *n* a name originally applied to any breed of dog used to burrow underground but now applied to many dogs. [Fr *terrier*—*terre*, the earth—L *terra*.]

terrify [ter´i-fī] *vt* to cause terror in, to frighten greatly, to alarm;—*pt, pt p* **terr´ified**.—*adj* **terrif´ic**, creating or causing terror, dreadful; (*inf*) huge, impressive; (*inf*) loosely, very good, enjoyable, attractive, etc.—*adv* **terrif´ically**. [L *terrēre*, to terrify, *facĕre*, to make.]

territory [ter´i-tȯ-ri] *n* the extent of land around or under the jurisdiction of a city or state; domain; a part of a country or empire that does not have full status; a wide tract of land; scope; field of activity.—*adj* **territō´rial**, pertaining to territory; limited to a district.—*n* a member of a territorial unit.—*adv* **territō´rially**.—**territorial waters**, the waters under the jurisdiction of a sovereign nation or state including both marginal sea and inland waters. [L *territōrium*—*terra*, the earth.]

terror [ter´or] *n* extreme fear; an object of fear or dread.—*vt* **terr´orize**, to terrify; to govern by terror.—*ns* **terrorizā´tion; terr´orism**, a state of terror; an organized system of intimidation; **terr´orist**, one who practices terrorism. [L,—*terrēre*, to frighten.]

terse [tûrs] *adj* compact or concise, with smoothness or elegance (eg of style).—*adv* **terse´ly**.—*n* **terse´ness**. [L *tersus*—*tergēre, tersum*, to rub clean.]

tertian [tûr´shi-ȧn] *adj* recurring approximately every 48 hours.—*n* an ague or fever with paroxysms every other day, esp malaria. [L *tertiānus*—*tertius*, third—*trēs*, three.]

tertiary [tûr´shi-ȧr-i] *adj* of the third degree, order, or formation; **Tertiary**, of the first period of the Cenozoic era or corresponding system of rocks marked by the formation of high mountains and the dominance of mammals on land.—*n* a member of a monastic third order, usu. of lay people; **Tertiary**, the Tertiary period or system of rocks. [L *tertiārius*—*tertius*.]

terza-rima [ter´tsa-rē´ma] *n* a three-line verse form, usu. in iambic pentameter with an interlacing rhyme scheme (as *aba, bcb, cdc*). [It *terza*, fem of *terzo*, third, *rima*, rhyme.]

tesla [tes´lȧ] *n* a unit of magnetic flux density, in the meter-kilogram-second system equal to one weber per square meter. Abbrev T. [N. *Tesla*, U.S. inventor.]

tessera [tes´e-ra] *n* one of the small square tiles or cut stones used in forming tessellated pavements;—*pl.* **tess´erae** [-ē].—*vt* **tess´ellate**, to form into squares or lay with mosaic work.—*n* **tessellā´tion**, tessellated or mosaic work: the operation of making it. [L *tessella*, dim. of *tessera*, a square piece.]

test [test] *n* any critical trial; means of trial; (*chem*) anything used to distinguish substances or detect their presence, a reagent; a standard; a series of questions or exercises.—*vt* to put to proof; to examine critically.—*n* **testability, test´case**, a legal case whose decision may serve as an example for others of the same kind.—*vt* **test´-fly**, to subject to a flight test.—*ns* **test´ match**, in cricket, one of a series of international matches (esp between England and Australia); **test pilot**, one whose job it is to take up new types of aircraft to test their quality; **test´ tube**, a cylinder of thin glass closed at one end, used in testing substances chemically. [OFr *test*—L *testa*, an earthen pot, a broken piece of earthenware, a skull, a shell.]

testa [tes´ta] *n* the seed coat, several layers of cells in thickness. [L. See **test**.]

testaceous [tes-tā´shūs] *adj* consisting of, or having, a hard shell. [L *testāceus*—*testa*. See **test**.]

testament [tes´ta-mėnt] *n* that which testifies, or in which an attestation is made; the solemn declaration in writing of one's will; a will; a covenant made by God with men; **Testament**, one of the two great divisions of the Bible: **Old Testament** and **New Testament**, dealing respectively with the covenant made by God with Moses and that made by God through Christ.—*adjs* **testamen´tal, testamen´tary**, pertaining to a testament or will; bequeathed or done by will; **tes´tāte**, having made and left a will.—*n* **testā´tor**, one who leaves a will; *fem* **testā´trix**. [L *testāmentum*—*testāri*, to be a witness—*testis*, a witness.]

tester [tes´tėr] *n* a flat canopy, esp over the head of a bed. [OFr *teste*, the head—L *testa*. See **test**.]

testicle [tes´ti-kl] *n* a gland that secretes spermatozoa in males.—Also **testis**.—*adj* **testic´ular**. [L *testiculus*, dim of *testis*, a testicle.]

testify [tes´ti-fī] *vi* to give evidence; to bear witness (to); to protest or declare a charge (against); (*with* **to**) to be evidence of.—*vt* to affirm or declare solemnly or on oath (eg one's determination that); to be evidence of;—*pt, pt p* **tes´tified**.—*n* **tes´tifier**. [L *testificārī*—*testis*, a witness, *facēre*, to make.]

testimony [tes´ti-mō-ni] *n* evidence; declaration to prove some fact; the two tables of the law; the whole divine revelation; a public profession of religious experience.—*adj* **testimō´nial**, containing testimony.—*n* a writing or certificate bearing a testimony to one's character or abilities. [L *testimōnium*—*testāri*, to witness.]

testudo [tes-tū´dō] *n* a cover for the protection of Roman soliders attacking a fortified place, formed by overlapping their oblong shields above their heads, or consisting of a fixed or movable shed of various kinds. [L *testūdō, -inis*, testudo, tortoise.]

testy [tes´ti] *adj* touchy, easily irritated, peevish.—*adv* **tes´tily**.—*n* **tes´tiness**. [OFr *teste*, head, shell; cf **test**.]

tetanus [tet´a-nus] *n* an intense and painful spasm of more or less extensive groups of the voluntary muscles caused by poison due to a bacillus (*Clostridium tetani*), usu. introduced through a wound; lockjaw.—*adj* **tetan´ic**. [L,—Gr, *tetanos*—*teinein*, to stretch.]

tête-à-tête [tet´-a-tet´] *n* a private conversation between two people.—*adj* confidential, secret.—*adv* in private conversation. [Fr *tête*, head.]

tether [teTH´ėr] *n* a rope or chain for tying an animal, while feeding, within certain limits.—*vt* to confine with a tether; to restrain within certain limits.—**at the end of one's tether**, desperate, having no further strength, resources, etc. [App ON *tjōthr*.]

tetragon [tet´ra-gon] *n* a figure of four angles.—*adj* **tetrag´onal**. [Gr *tetragōnon*—*tetra-*, four, *gōnia*, an angle.]

tetrahedron [tet-ra-hē´dron] *n* a solid figure enclosed by four triangles.—*adj* **tetrahē´dral**, having four sides; bounded by four triangles. [Gr *tetra-*, four, *hedrā*, a base.]

tetralogy [te-tral´o-ji] *n* a group of four related dramatic or literary works. [Gr *tetralogia*—*tetra-*, four, *logos*, discourse.]

tetrameter [te-tram´e-ter] *n* a verse line of four measures. [Gr *tetrametros*—*tetra-*, four, *metron*, measure.]

tetrarch [tet´rärk, tē´trärk] *n* under the Romans, the ruler of the fourth part of a province; a subordinate prince.—*ns* **tet´rarchate, tet´rarchy**, office or jurisdiction of a tetrarch; the fourth part of a province. [Gr *tetrarchēs*—*tetra-*, four, *archēs*, a ruler.]

tetter [tet´ėr] *n* any of various eruptive diseases of the skin (as ringworm, eczema, and herpes). [OE *teter*.]

Teuton [tū´ton] *n* one of ancient probably Germanic or Celtic people; a member of a people speaking a language of the Germanic branch of the Indo-European language family, esp German.—*adj* **Teuton´ic**, belonging to the race called Teutons, or to the Germanic group of languages. [L *Teutones*; from the same root as Ger *Deutsch*, German, and Eng *Dutch*.]

text [tekst] *n* the original words of an author; a passage of Scripture on which a sermon is based; a short quotation from the Bible used as a motto or a moral maxim; any concise phrase or statement on which a written or spoken discourse is based; a theme; the main printed part of a book as distinguished from preliminaries, index, illustrations.—*n* **text´book**, a book containing the leading principles of a subject (*adj* of operation, exactly as planned in perfect accordance with theory or calculation).—*adj* **tex´tūal**, pertaining to, or contained in, the text; serving for a text.—*adv* **tex´tually**.—**textual criticism**, criticism with a view to establishing the actual words of a book as originally written; a critical study of literature emphasizing a close reading and analysis of the text. [L *textus*—*texēre, textum*, to weave.]

textile [teks´tīl, -tl] *adj* woven, or capable of being woven.—*n* a knitted or woven fabric; raw material suitable for this. [L *textilis*—*texēre, textum*, to weave.]

texture [teks´-chůr] *n* the manner in which threads, etc., in a material, etc., are interwoven or combined; the manner of arrangement of particles in a substance; structural impression resulting from the manner of combining or interrelating the parts of a whole, as in music, art, etc.; the quality conveyed to the touch by woven fabrics, etc.—*adj* **tex´tūral**. [L *textūra*—*texēre, textum*, to weave.]

thalidomide [tha-lid´ō-mīd] *n* a sedative discovered to cause malformation in the fetus if taken during pregnancy.

thalassaemia [tha-lȧ-sē´mi-ȧ] *n* a serious kind of inherited blood disease found in Mediterranean countries, etc. [Gr *thalassa*, the sea.]

thallium [thal´i-ům] *n* a metallic element (symbol Tl; at wt 204.4; at no 81). [Gr *thallos*, a green shoot (from the bright green line in its spectrum).]

thallus [thal´ůs] *n* a plant body that is not differentiated into root, stem, leaves. [Gr *thallos*, a young shoot.]

than [THan] *conj* a word placed after the comparative of an adjective or adverb to introduce the second part of a comparison. [OE *thonne*, used after comparatives to introduce the standard of comparison; closely allied to *thone*, acc masc of definite article.]

thane [thān] *n* a member of a class in the old English community that stood below the old nobility, but above the ordinary freeman.—*n* **thane´dom**, the jurisdiction or the dignity of a thane. [OE *thegan, thegn*, a servant, nobleman—*thīhan*, to grow.]

thank [thangk] *vt* to express gratitude to (someone) for a favor; to acknowledge indebtedness to (eg *he has to thank the calm weather for his safe return*; often ironically, meaning to blame).—*n* (usually in *pl*) expression of gratitude, often used elliptically, meaning 'My thanks to you'.—*adj* **thank´ful**, full of thanks; grateful.—*adv* **thank´fully**.—*n* **thank´fulness**.—*adj* **thank´less**, unthankful; not expressing thanks for favors; not winning thanks.—*adv* **thank´lessly**.—*ns* **thank´lessness**, state of being thankless; ingratitude; **thanks´giving**, act of giving thanks; a public acknowledgement of divine goodness and mercy; **Thanks-giving Day**, a US legal holiday observed on the fourth Thursday of November.—*adj* **thank´worthy**, worthy of, or deserving, thanks.—**thank you**, polite formula to express thanks. [OE *thanc, thonc*, will, thanks; akin to **think**.]

that [THat] as a *demons pron* or *adj* (*pl* **those**), points out a person or thing—the former or more distant thing, not this but the other.—*rel pron* who or which.—*conj* used to introduce a noun clause, and various types of adverbial clauses, expressing the following:—because (eg *it is not that I mind*); in order that; that as a result (following *so* and *such*). [OE *thæt*, neut of the article *the*. Cf **the**.]

thatch [thach] *vt* to cover, as a roof, with straw, reeds, etc.—*n* straw, etc., used to cover the roofs of buildings and stacks.—*ns* **thatch´er; thatch´ing**, the act or art of covering with thatch; the materials used for thatching. [OE *thæc*, thatch, whence *theccan*, to cover.]

thaumaturgy [thö´ma-tûr-ji] *n* the art of working wonders or miracles, esp magic.—*adjs* **thaumatur´gic**. [Gr *thaumatourgia*—*thauma, -atos*, a wonder, *ergon*, work.]

thaw [thö] *vi* to melt or grow liquid, as ice; to become so warm as to melt ice; to relax stiffness or unfriendly reserve.—*vt* to cause to melt.—*n* the melting of ice or snow by heat; the change of weather which causes it. [OE *thawian*.]

the[1] [THe or (when emphatic) THē], *demons adj* usu. called the definite article, used to denote a particular person or thing; also to denote a species.

[OE *the*, rarely used as nom masc of definite article, but common as an indeclinable relative; cf **that**.]

the[2] [THė] *adv* used before comparatives, as, 'the more the better'. [OE *thȳ*, by that much, the instrumental case of the definite article.]

theater, theatre [thē-a-tėr] *n* a place where public representations as plays, motion pictures, etc. are seen; any place rising by steps like the seats of a theater; scene of action, field of operations; dramatic literature; the stage; dramatic effect; material lending itself to effective production on the stage.—*adjs* **theat´ric, -al**, relating to, or suitable to, a theater, or to actors; pompous, melodramatic, affected.—*adv* **theat´rically**.—*n pl* **theat´ricals**, dramatic performances; showy or extravagant gestures.—**theater-in-the-round**, a theater with central stage and audience on all sides; the style of staging plays in such a theater; **theater of the absurd**, branch of drama dealing with fantastic deliberately unreal situations, in reaction against the tragedy and irrationality of life. [Gr *theātron*—*theaesthai*, to see.]

thee [THē] *pron* objective case (*acc* or *dat*) of **thou**. [OE *the*, dat, acc of *thu* (cf **thou**).]

theft [theft] *n* act of thieving. [OE *thēofth, thȳfth*—*thēof*, thief.]

their [THār, THer] *possessive adj* (also called *possessive pron*) of or belonging to them. [ON *theirra*; OE *thǣra*, gen pl of the definite article.]

theirs [THārz, THers] *pron* the possessive (*gen*) case of **they** (eg *the furniture is theirs*).—Also *possessive adj* (used without noun—eg *that is my car at the door, not theirs*). [Like *hers, ours, yours*, a double genitive containing a plural suffix *-r* + a sing *-s*. These forms were confined in the 13th and 14th centuries to the Northern dialects, and are probably due to Scandinavian influence.]

theism [thē´izm] *n* belief in the existence of a god or gods; monotheism.—*n* **thē´ist**, one who believes in a god or gods.—*adjs* **thēist´ic, -al**, pertaining to theism, or to a theist; according to the doctrines of theists. [Gr *theos*, God.]

them [THem] *pron* the objective case (*accusative* or *dative*) of **they**. [ON *theim*; OE *thǣm*, dat pl of the definite article (this replaced the older *heom, hem*).]

theme [thēm] *n* a subject set or proposed for discussion, or on which a person speaks or writes; (*mus*) subject, a short melody developed with variations or otherwise.—*adj* **themat´ic**, (*mus*) pertaining to a theme; (*gram*) pertaining to a word stem.—**theme song**, a melody that is repeated often in a musical drama, film, or radio or television series, and is associated with a certain character, idea, emotion, etc. [Fr *thème*—L *thĕma*—*tithĕnai*, to place, set.]

themselves [THem-selvz´] *pron pl* of **himself, herself**, and **itself**. [**them** and **self**.]

then [THen] *adv* at that time; afterwards; immediately; at another time.—*conj* for that reason, therefore; in that case. [OE *thanne, thonne, thænne*, acc sing from stem of definite article *the*. Doublet of **than**.]

thence [THens] *adv* from that time or place; for that reason.—*advs* **thence´forth, thencefor´ward**, from that time forward. [ME *thennes* (*thenne* with the gen ending *-s*)—OE *thanon*. Cf **hence** and **whence**.]

theocracy [thē-ok´rȧ-si] *n* a state, usu. controlled by priests, in which a god is regarded as the sole sovereign, and the laws of the realm as divine commands rather than human ordinances.—*adjs* **theocrat´ic, -al**. [Gr *theokratiā*—*theos*, a god, *krateein*, to rule.]

theodicy [thē-od´i-si] *n* an exposition of Divine Providence, designed to vindicate the holiness and justice of God in creating a world in which evil seems so largely to prevail. [Gr *theos*, a god, *dikē*, justice.]

theodolite [thē-od´ō-līt] *n* an instrument used in surveying for the measurement of angles horizontal and vertical. [Ety unknown.]

theogony [thē-og´o-ni] *n* the birth and genealogy of the gods, esp as told in ancient poetry.—*n* **theog´onist**, a writer on theogony. [Gr *theogoniā*—*theos*, a god; *gonē*, race.]

theology [thē-ol´o-ji] *n* the study of God and of religious doctrine and matters of divinity.—*n* **theolō´gian**, one well versed in theology; a divine, a professor of divinity.—*adjs* **theolog´ic, -al**, pertaining to theology or divinity.—*adv* **theolog´ically**.—*vt* **theol´ogize**, to render theological.—*vi* to make a system of theology. [Gr *theologiā*—*theos*, a god, *logos*, a treatise.]

theorem [thē´o-rem] *n* a proposition that can be proved from accepted principles; law or principle; a proposition embodying something to be proved.—*adjs* **theoret´ic, -al**, concerned with theory, not with its applications; not derived from experience; hypothetical; arrived at by calculation, not by experiment (eg of a result).—*adv* **theoret´ically**.—*vi* **thē´orize**, to form a theory; to form opinions solely by theories; to speculate.—*ns* **thē´orizer; thē´orist**, a theorizer; one given to theory and speculation; **thē´ory**, an explanation or system of anything; an exposition of the abstract principles of a science or art; speculation as opposed to proof; a hypothesis; reasoned expectation as opposed to practice. [Gr *theōrēma*—*theōreein*, to view—*theaesthai*, to see.]

theosophy [thē-os´o-fi] *n* immediate divine illumination or inspiration claimed to be possessed by specially gifted persons, who are also held to possess abnormal control over natural forces; the doctrines of various sects, including a modern school founded in 1875, which profess to attain knowledge of God by inspiration.—*adjs* **theosoph´ic, -al**, pertaining to theosophy.—*n* **theos´ophist**, one who believes in theosophy. [Gr *theosophia*—*theos*, a god, *sophiā*, wisdom.]

therapeutic [ther-a-pū´tik] *adj* pertaining to healing, curative.—*adv* **therapeu´tically**.—*n sing* **therapeu´tics**, that part of medicine concerned with the treatment and cure of diseases.—*ns* **therapeu´tist; ther´apy**, the curative and preventive treatment of disease or an abnormal condition. [Gr *therapeuein*, to take care of, to heal.]

there [THār, THėr] *adv* in that place; at that point; to that place or point; in that respect; in that matter.—Also used pronominally as an anticipatory subject when the real subject follows the verb (eg *there is no one at home*).—*n* that place; that point.—*advs* **thereabout´** or **-abouts´**, about or near that place; near that number, quantity or degree; **thereaft´er**, from then on; **thereat´**, at that place or occurrence; on that account; **thereby´**, by that means; in consequence of that; **therefor´**, for that, this, or it; **therefore** [THār´fōr], for that or this reason; consequently; **therefrom´**, from that or it; **therein´**, in that or into that place; in that matter, detail, etc.; **thereof´**, of that; from that as a cause, reason, etc.; **thereon´**, on that or it; immediately following that; **thereto´**, to that or it; **thereupon´**, upon, or in consequence of, that or this; immediately following that; **therewith´**, along with that; immediately thereafter. [OE *thǣr, thēr*; conn with the stem of definite article *the*.]

therm [thûrm] *n* any of several units of energy; a small calorie, or gram calorie; a large calorie or kilogram calorie; 100,000 British thermal units (105.5 megajoules), that unit being the amount of heat necessary to raise the temperature of 1 1b of water at maximum density 1° Fahrenheit.—*adjs* **ther´mal**, of or marked by the presence of hot springs; having to do with heat; denoting a loosely knitted material with air spaces for insulation; **ther´mic**, pertaining to heat; warm; due to heat.—*ns* **ther´mal**, an ascending column of air; **ther´modynam´ics**, the branch of physics concerned with energy utilization and transfer; **ther´moelectric´ity**, electricity produced by the direct action of heat, as by the unequal heating of bodies.—*adj* **ther´monuc´lear**, pertaining to the fusion of atomic nuclei as seen in a **thermonuclear reaction**, a reaction produced by the fusion of nuclei at extremely high temperatures, as in the hydrogen bomb.—*n* **ther´mopile**, an apparatus used for generating currents or for determining intensities of radiation.—*adj* **thermoplastic** [thėr-mō-plas´tik], becoming plastic on heating.—*n* any resin that can be melted by heat and then cooled, an unlimited number of times, without appreciable change in properties.—*n* **ther´mostat**, an automatic device for regulating temperatures.—*adj* **thermostat´ic**.—*adv* **thermostat´ically**.—**thermal springs**, natural springs of hot water. [Gr *thermos*, hot—*thermē*, heat—*therein*, to heat.]

thermionics [thûr-mi-on´iks] *n sing* the science dealing with the emission of electrons from hot bodies.—**thermion´ic tube**, a vacuum tube containing a heated cathode from which electrons are emitted, an anode for collecting some or all of these electrons, and generally, additional electrodes for controlling their flow to the anode. [**therm** + **ion**, with *-ics* on the analogy of *mathematics*, etc.]

thermometer [thûr-mom´e-tėr] *n* an instrument for measuring temperature.—*adjs* **thermomet´ric, -al**, pertaining to a thermometer; ascertained by means of a thermometer.—*adv* **thermomet´rically**.—**maximum thermometer**, one that registers the maximum temperature to which it is exposed; **minimum thermometer**, one that registers the minimum temperature to which it is exposed. [Gr *theramē*, heat, *metron*, a measure.]

thermoplastic *See* **therm**.

thermosetting [thûr´mō-set´ing] compositions in which a chemical reaction takes place while they are being molded under heat and pressure, causing hardening. [**thermo-**, combining form of **therm, setting, composition**.]

thermos [thûr´mos] *n* a vacuum bottle or jug for keeping liquids at almost their original temperature. [Trade mark—Gr *thermos*, hot.]

thermostat *See* **therm**.

thesaurus [thē-sö´rus] *n* a treasury or repository, esp of knowledge, words, quotations, etc., a lexicon or cyclopaedia. [L,—Gr *thēsauros*—*tithenai*, to place.]

these [THēz] *demons adj* and *pron pl* of **this**. [OE *thǣs*, pl of *thēs*, this. Doublet **those**.]

thesis [thē´sis] *n* a position, or that which is set down or advanced for argument; a subject for a scholastic exercise; an essay on a theme;—*pl* **theses** [thē´sēs]. [L,—Gr *tithenai*, to set, place.]

Thespian [thes´pi-ȧn] *adj* pertaining to tragedy; tragic. [Gr *Thespis*, founder of Greek tragedy.]

Thessalonians [thes-ȧ-lōn´yȧns] *n* (*Bible*) 13th and 14th books of the New Testament, epistles written by St Paul to the church at Thessalonica.

theta [thā´tȧ or thē´tȧ] *n* the 8th letter in the Greek alphabet.

theurgy [thē´ûr-ji] *n* that kind of magic which claims to work by supernatural agency, as distinguished from natural magic and necromancy.—*adjs* **theur´gic, -al**. [Gr *theourgiā*—*theos*, a god, *ergein*, to work.]

thew [thū] *n* (used chiefly in *pl*) muscle or sinews; strength; resolution. [OE *thēaw*, manner.]

they [THā] *pers pron, pl* of **he, she**, or **it**. [The form *thei, tha* (meaning 'that') came into use in the north of England in the 13th cent, replacing the older *hī, hīe*. It is the OE *thā*, nom pl of the definite article, prob modified by Scandinavian influence.]

thick [thik] *adj* dense; firm (of a paste); crowded; closely set, abundant;

frequent, in quick succession; having considerable depth of circumference, usu. solid; not transparent or clear; misty; (*inf*) dull, stupid; indistinct (of speech); (*inf*) intimate.—*n* the thickest or densest part of anything (eg *in the thick of the fight*).—*adv* closely; frequently; fast; to a great depth.—*vt* **thick´en**, to make thick or close; to strengthen.—*vi* to become thick or obscure; to crowd or press.—*ns* **thick´ening**, something put into a liquid or mass to make it thick; **thick´et**, a collection of trees or shrubs thickly or closely set, a close wood or copse.—*adjs* **thick´-head´ed**, having a thick head or skull; stupid; **thick´ish**, somewhat thick.—*adv* **thick´ly**.—*n* **thick´ness**.—*adjs* **thickset**, closely planted; having a short, thick body; **thick´-skinned**, having a thick skin, insensitive, as to insult.—**through thick and thin**, in spite of all obstacles, without wavering. [OE *thicce*.]

thief [thēf] *n* one who steals or takes unlawfully what is not his own;—*pl* **thieves**. [OE *thēof*; ON *thjōfr*, Ger *dieb*.]

thieve [thēv] *vi* to practice theft, to steal.—*n* **thiev´ery**, the practice of thieving.—*adj* **thiev´ish**, addicted to theft; like theft; characteristic of a thief.—*adv* **thiev´ishly**.—*n* **thiev´ishness**. [OE *thēofian*.]

thigh [thī] *n* the thick fleshy part of the leg from the knee to the trunk. [OE *thēo, thēoh*; ON *thjō*, OHG *dioh*.]

thimble [thim´bl] *n* a cap or cover to protect the finger and push the needle in sewing.—*ns* **thim´bleful**, as much as a thimble will hold; a small quantity; **thim´blerig**, a sleight-of-hand trick in which the performer conceals, or pretends to conceal, a pea or small ball under one of three thimblelike cups.—*vi* to cheat by such means. [OE *thӯmel*, a thumbstall—*thūma*, a thumb.]

thin [thin] *adj* having little thickness; slim; lean; (of material) fine or transparent; lacking strength or substance (eg *thin soup*); rarefied; not dense; not close or crowded; inadequate, flimsy; not full or well grown, meager; lacking in volume or resonance; unduly full of hardships or misfortunes.—*adv* not thickly, not closely, in a scattered state.—*vt* to make thin; to make less close or crowded (*with* **away, out**, etc.); to make rare or less thick or dense.—*vi* to grow or become thin;—*pr p* **thinn´ing**; *pt, pt p*, **thinned**.—*adv* **thin´ly**.—*ns* **thinn´er**, a substance added to paint, shellac, etc., to thin it; **thin´ness**.—*adjs* **thinn´ish**, somewhat thin; **thin´-skinned**, having a thin skin; sensitive.—**into thin air**, into nothing or nothingness. [OE *thynne*.]

thine [THīn] *pron*, (*arch*) possessive (*gen*) case of **thy** (eg *the fault is thine*).—Also *possessive adj* (now used without noun—eg *that was my responsibility, but this is thine*); (*arch*) thy, used before a following vowel. [OE *thīn*, thy—*thīn*, gen of *thū*, thou.]

thing [thing] *n* an inanimate object; a living being (in tenderness or in contempt); whatever may exist independently in space and time, as opposed to an idea; an event; an action; a production of hand or brain, esp spoken or written; (*pl*) possessions, esp clothes or wraps; any distinct and individual fact, object, action, event, series, quality, or idea of which one may think or to which one may refer; (*inf*) that which is wanted or is appropriate; (*inf*) a slight obsession or phobia; (*inf*) a liking or dislike.—**do one's (own) thing**, (*inf*) to behave as is natural to or characteristic of oneself; to do something in which one specializes; **see things**, to imagine one sees things that are not there. [OE *thing, thinc*.]

think [thingk] *vi* to exercise the mind; to revolve ideas in the mind; to consider; to purpose or design (*with* **of**).—*vt* to imagine; to judge, to believe or consider.—*pt, pt p* **thought** [thawt].—*n* **think´er**, esp one who is capable of deep and fruitful thought.—*adj* **think´ing**, having the faculty of thought.—**think tank** (*slang*), a group or center organized to do intensive research and problem-solving; **think up**, to concoct, devise. [OE *thencan*, pt *thōhte*; cog with Ger *denken*.]

third [thûrd] *adj* the last of three; being one of three equal parts.—*n* one of three equal parts; (*mus*) a note two (conventionally, three) diatonic degrees above or below a given note, or the interval between the two notes (eg C to E).—*adv* **third´ly**, in the third place.—*adjs* **third par´ty**, of, involving, a third person or party (eg *third party risks*, those incurred by a third party—the insured person, i.e. the owner of vehicle, etc., being the first party, and the insurance company the second party); **third´-rate**, of the third order; inferior.—**third degree**, (*inf*) cruel treatment and questioning to force confession; **Third Reich**, Germany as a totalitarian state from 1933–45; **Third World**, the undeveloped countries of the world. [OE *thridda*—*thrēo*, three.]

thirst [thûrst] *n* the uneasiness caused by lack of drink; vehement desire for drink; eager desire (for anything).—*vi* to feel thirst; to have vehement desire.—*adj* **thirst´y**, suffering from thirst; dry, parched; vehemently desirous.—*adv* **thirst´ily**.—*n* **thirst´iness**. [OE *thurst, thyrst*.]

thirteen [thûr´tēn] (when used absolutely, thûrtēn´) *adj, n* three and ten.—*adj* **thirteenth**, the last of thirteen; being one of thirteen equal parts.—Also *n*.—**Thirteen Colonies**, the colonies of British North America that joined in the American Revolution and became the US. [OE *thrēotēne*—*thrēo*, three, *tēn*, ten.]

thirty [thûr´ti] *adj* and *n* three times ten.—*adj* **thir´tieth**, the last of thirty; being one of thirty equal parts.—Also *n*. [OE *thrītig*—*thrī*, three, *tig*, ten, related to *tien, tēn*.]

this [THis] *demons pron* or *adj* denoting a person or thing near, just mentioned, or about to be mentioned;—*pl* **these**. [OE the neut of the demons pron *thes* (masc), *thēos, thīos* (fem); pl *thās*, which gave **those**, later pl *thǣs*, which gave **these**; ON *thessi*, Ger *dieser*.]

thistle [this´l] *n* any of various composite prickly plants (esp genera *Carduus, Cirsium*, and *Onopordon*).—*n* **this´tledown**, the tufted feathery bristles of the seeds of a thistle.—*adj* **this´tly**, overgrown with thistles. [OE *thistel*.]

thither [THiTH´ėr] *adv* to that place; to that end or result.—*adv* **thith´erward**, toward that place. [OE *thider*.]

tho' [THō] abbreviation for **though**.

thole [thōl] *n* a pin in the side of a boat to keep the oar in place. [OE *thol*.]

Thomism [tō´mizm] *n* the doctrines of the scholastic theologian *Thomas* Aquinas (1226–1274), esp as these are set forth in his *Summa Theologiae*, which still represent, with few exceptions, the general teaching of the RC Church.—*n* **Thō´mist**, a follower of Aquinas.

thong [thong] *n* a piece or strap of leather to fasten anything; the lash of a whip. [OE *thwang*.]

thorax [thō´raks] *n* the part of the body between the neck and belly, the chest; in insects, the middle one of the three chief divisions of the body.—*adj* **thoracic** [-ras´-].—**thoracic duct**, the main trunk of the vessels conveying lymph in the body. [L,—Gr.]

thorium [thō´ri-ům] *n* a radioactive metallic element (symbol Th; at wt 232.0; at no 90). [*Thor*, the Norse deity.]

thorn [thörn] *n* a sharp, woody projection (a sharp-pointed, leafless branch) on the stem of a plant; (*loosely*) a prickle (as on roses) or a spine; a shrub or small tree having thorns, esp hawthorn and blackthorn; anything prickly or troublesome; (also **thorn letter**) þ, an early English symbol for *th*, orig a rune used by the scribes both for *th* in *thin* and for TH in *THen*, interchangeable with another symbol, ð, a crossed *d*; these signs are distinguished by modern phoneticians and used for the breath and the voiced consonant respectively.—*adj* **thorn´y**, full of thorns; prickly; troublesome; harassing.—**thorn in the flesh**, any cause of constant irritation, from 2 Cor xii 7. [OE *thorn*.]

thorough [thûr´ō] *adj* complete, consummate (eg *a thorough rogue, master of his art*); very exact and painstaking (of a person, his methods, or his work)—whole-hearted, or exhaustive.—*prep* (*obs.*) through.—*n* **thor´oughbass**, (*mus*) a bass line throughout a piece, to which harmonies, etc., have to be added (harmonies often being indicated by numbers).—*adj* **thor´oughbred**, bred from a dam and sire of the best blood, as a horse; aristocratic—well-bred, spirited, having distinction.—*n* an animal, esp a horse, of pure blood; a thoroughbred person.—*n* **thor´oughfare**, a place or passage for going through; a public way or street; right of passing through.—*adj* **thor´oughgō´ing**, going all lengths, complete, out-and-out, uncompromising.—*adv* **thor´oughly**, completely, entirely.—*n* **thor´oughness**.—*adj* **thor´ough-paced**, thoroughly or perfectly paced or trained; complete, thoroughgoing. [A longer form of **through**.]

those [THōz] *adj* and *pron, pl* of **that**. [OE *thās*, the old pl of *thes*, this. Cf **this**. Doublet **these**.]

thou[1] [THow] *pron* of the second person sing, the person spoken to (now generally used only in solemn address). [OE *thū*; cog with Gr *ty*, L *tu*, Sans *tvam*.]

thou[2] [thow] *n* (*inf*) 1/1000 in. [**thousand**.]

though [THō] *conj* admitting, allowing, even if; (used absolutely) however. [ON *thauh, thō*; OE *thēah, thēh*.]

thought [thöt] *pt, pt p* of **think**. [OE *thoht*—*thencan*, to think.]

thought [thöt] *n* the act of thinking; power of reasoning; conception; deliberation; that which one thinks; an idea; opinions collectively; consideration; meditation; design, intention (often *pl*); care.—*adj* **thought´ful**, full of thought; employed in meditation; marked by or showing thought; attentive, considerate.—*adv* **thought´fully**.—*n* **thought´fulness**.—*adj* **thought´less**, without thought or care; careless; inconsiderate; inattentive; stupid.—*adv* **thought´lessly**.—*ns* **thoughtlessness**; —**on second thoughts**, after further consideration. [OE *gethōht*; cf **think**.]

thousand [thow´zȧnd] *adj* ten hundred; denoting any great number.—*n* the number ten hundred; any large number.—*adjs* **thou´sandfold**, repeated a thousand times; multiplied by a thousand; **thou´sandth**, the last of a thousand or of any great number.—*n* one of a thousand equal parts of a whole.—**one in a thousand**, rare and excellent. [OE *thūsend*.]

thrall [thröl] *n* a slave, serf; slavery, servitude.—*vt* to enslave.—*n* **thrall´dom, thral´dom**, the condition of a thrall or slave; slavery, bondage. [ON *thræll*, a slave.]

thrash [thrash] *vt* to beat out grain from the straw by means of eg a flail or machinery; to beat soundly; (*with* **out**) to discuss thoroughly, so as to reach agreement.—*vi* to thresh grain; to move, stir, or toss violently (*with* **about**).—*ns* **thrash´er; thrashing**. [From a northern form of OE (WS) *therscan*.]

thread [thred] *n* a very thin line of any substance twisted and drawn out; a filament of any fibrous substance; a fine line of yarn; anything resembling a thread; the prominent helical part of a screw; a line (of reasoning); sequence (of ideas).—*vt* to pass a thread through the eye of (as a needle); to pass or pierce through, as a narrow way; to furnish with a thread.—*adjs* **thread´bare**, worn to the bare thread, having the nap worn off; hackneyed; **thread´y**, like thread; slender; containing, or consisting of, thread. [OE *thrǣd*—*thrāwan*, to wind, to twist.]

threat [thret] *n* a declaration of an intention to inflict punishment or other evil upon another; a menace (to).—*vti* **threat´en**, to declare an intention (to do, of doing); to declare the intention of inflicting (punishment or other evil upon another); to terrify by menaces; to suggest the approach of (evil or something unpleasant).—*n* **threat´ener**.—*adj* **threat´ening**, indicating a threat or menace; indicating something approaching or impending.—*adv* **threat´eningly**. [OE *thrēat—thrēotan*, to afflict.]

three [thrē] *adj* and *n* the cardinal number next above two.—*n* the symbol 3, III, iii denoting this.—*adj* **third** (see separate article); **three´fold**, thrice repeated; consisting of three; **three´score**, three times a score, sixty (also *n*). [OE *thrēo*, fem and neut of *thrī*; ON *thrīr*, Gael *tri*, Ger *drei*, L *trēs*, Gr *treis*, Sans *tri*.]

threnody [thren´ō-dē] *n* an ode or song of lamentation. [Gr *thrēnōidiā—thrēnos*, a lament, *ōidē*, a song.]

thresh [thresh] *vti* to beat out (grain) from (husks) as with a flail; thrash.

threshold [thresh´ōld, -hōld] *n* the piece of timber or stone under the door of a building; doorway, entrance; the place or point of entering or beginning; the point, limit at which a physiological or psychological experience begins (eg *the threshold of consciousness, threshold of pain*). [OE *therscwald—therscan*, to thresh, *wald*, wood.]

threw [thrōō] *pt* of **throw**.

thrice [thrīs] *adv* three times. [OE *thrīwa*.]

thrift [thrift] *n* careful management, frugality; (*obs*) prosperity; a plant (*Ameria maritima*) with pink or white flower heads; a mutual savings and loan association.—Also **thrift institution**.—*adj* **thrift´y**, showing thrift or economy; thriving by frugality.—*adv* **thrift´ily**.—*n* **thrift´iness**.—*adj* **thrift´less**, not thrifty, extravagant; not thriving.—*adv* **thrift´lessly**.—*n* **thrift´lessness**.—**thrift shop**, a shop, usu. run on behalf of a charity, which sells secondhand clothes and other articles. [Same root as **thrive**.]

thrill [thril] *vt, vi* to tingle with excitement; to throb or pulse.—*n* a thrilling sensation; vibration.—*n* **thrill´er**, an exciting (usu. detective) novel or play.—*adj* **thrill´ing**, exciting. [OE *thyrlian*, to bore a hole—*thyrel*, a hole.]

thrive [thrīv] *vi* to prosper, to increase in goods; to be successful; to grow vigorously, to flourish.—*pt* **thrōve** and **thrīved**; *pt p* **thriv´en**.—*adj* **thrī´ving**, flourishing, successful.—*adv*. [ON *thrīfa*, to grasp.]

throat [thrōt] *n* the forepart of the neck, in which are the gullet and windpipe; an entrance; a narrow part of anything.—*adj* **throat´y**, formed in the throat, guttural in sound; hoarse. [OE *throte*.]

throb [throb] *vi* to beat, as the heart or pulse, with more than usual force; to vibrate.—*pr p* **throbb´ing**; *pt, pt p* **throbbed**.—*n* a beat or strong pulsation. [Imit.]

throe [thrō] *n* (usu *pl*) suffering, pain; the pains of childbirth; distressing effort or struggle. [OE *thrēa, thrēaw*, suffering—*thrēowan*, to suffer.]

thrombosis [throm-bō´sis] *n* a coagulation of blood, forming a clot in a blood-vessel.—*n* **throm´bōem´bolism**, a blocking of a blood-vessel by a blood clot, causing illness/death. [Gr *thrombos*, a clot.]

throne [thrōn] *n* a chair of state richly ornamented and raised; seat of a bishop in the church of his diocese; sovereign power.—*vt* to place on a royal seat; to exalt;—*pr p* **thrōn´ing**; *pt, pt p* **thrōned**. [OFr,—L *thronus*—Gr *thronos*, a seat.]

throng [throng] *n* a crowd; a great multitude.—*vt* to press or crowd upon (a person); to fill with a crowd; (of a crowd) to fill very full.—*vi* to crowd (together); to come in multitudes. [OE *gethrang—thringan*, to press.]

throstle [thros´l] *n* the song thrush. [OE *throstle*; Ger *drossel*.]

throttle [throt´l] *n* the throat or windpipe; a valve controlling the flow of steam or other gas to an engine.—*vt* to choke by pressure on the windpipe; to shut off the steam from by a valve. [Dim of **throat**.]

through [thrōō] *prep* from end to end, or from side to side, of; into and then out of; over the whole extent of; from beginning to end of; by means of; in consequence of; up to and including.—*adv* from one end or side to the other; from beginning to end.—*adj* clear, unobstructed; going from starting point to destination without break or change.—*adv* **through´-and-through**, thoroughly.—*prep* **throughout´**, in every part of; from one end to the other of.—*adv* in every part, everywhere; from beginning to end.—*n* **throughput**, the amount of material put through a process.—**through with**, finished with. [OE *thurh*.]

throve [thrōv] *pt* of **thrive**.

throw [thrō] *vt* to hurl, to fling; to wind or twist together as yarn in knitting; to form on a wheel, as pottery; to venture at dice; to shed, cast off; (*inf*) to lose (a contest) deliberately; to put on or spread carelessly (*with* **on**); to cast down in wrestling; to put in position, or to offer, in such a way as to suggest throwing (eg *to throw a bridge across a river*); (*inf*) to hold, give (a party); (*inf*) to confuse or disconcert.—*vi* to cast or hurl; to cast dice;—*pt* **threw** [thrōō]; *pt p* **thrōwn**.—*n* the act of throwing; a cast, esp of dice; the distance to which anything may be thrown; a spread for a bed, etc.—*ns* **throwaway**, a leaflet, handbill, etc. given out on streets, at houses, etc.—*adj* for discarding after use.—*ns* **throw´er; throw´back**, a reversion to an ancestral or more primitive type; **throw´-in**, (*soccer*) a throw from the touch-line to put the ball back into play.—**throw in**, to add, give, gratuitously; to make (a comment) casually, to interpose; **throw off**, to cast off hastily, abruptly; get rid of (eg a disease, depression); to produce extempore (eg *to throw off epigrams*); **throw oneself at**, to make a determined and obvious attempt to captivate; **throw oneself into**, to engage heartily in; **throw oneself (up)on the mercy of**, to appeal to, rely on, for leniency; **throw up (something) against someone**, to reproach him with (something). [OE *thrāwan*, to turn, to twist.]

thrum[1] [thrum] *n* the end of a weaver's thread; any loose thread or fringe; coarse yarn.—*vt* to tuft; to fringe; to insert short pieces of rope yarn in a mat or piece of canvas; to make a mat for wrapping around the rigging to prevent chafing;—*pr p* **thrumm´ing**; *pt, pt p* **thrummed**. [OE *thrōmr*, the edge; Ger *trumm*, a fragment.]

thrum[2] [thrum] *vi* to strum. [Imit.]

thrush[1] [thrush] *n* a genus (*Turdinae*) (in a wider sense, a family (Turdidae) of passerine birds, including the robin. [OE *thrysce*, a thrush.]

thrush[2] [thrush] *n* a disease of the mouth and throat, characterized by white patches and caused by a yeast, usu. affecting infants. [Scand, ON *thurr*, dry.]

thrust [thrust] *vt* to push or drive with force; to press (in); to stab, pierce; to force (oneself, one's company, on).—*vi* to make a push, esp with a pointed weapon; to squeeze (in), to intrude;—*pt, pt p* **thrust**.—*n* a stab; pressure; stress between two parts of a structure, esp the equal horizontal forces acting on the abutments of an arch, due to the loading carried by it; the driving force of a propeller; the forward force produced by a jet or rocket engine; forward movement; the basic meaning, point. [ON *thrȳsta*, to press.]

thud [thud] *n* a dull, hollow sound, caused by a blow or a heavy body falling.—*vi* to make such a sound. [OE *thōden*, noise.]

thug [thug] *n* one of a class of professional robbers and assassins in India (extirpated 1826–35) whose violent deeds had a religious motive; a man who lives by violence.—*n* **thugg´ery**, organized robbery and violence. [Hindustani *thag*, cheat.]

Thule [thū´lē] *n* the name given by the ancients to the most northerly part of Europe of which they had heard—perh Scandinavia, or Iceland, or the Orkney and Shetland groups.—Also **Ultima** [ul´ti-ma] **Thule**. [L. *Thūlē*.]

thulium [thū´li-ům] *n* a metallic element (symbol Tm; at wt 168.9; at no 69). [L *Thūlē*. See **Thule**.]

thumb [thum] *n* the short, thick finger of the human hand; the corresponding member in other animals.—*vt* to handle awkwardly; to turn over, or to soil, with the thumb or fingers; (*inf*) to solicit or get (a ride) in hitchhiking by signaling with the thumb.—*adj* **thumbed**, marked by the thumb, worn by use.—*ns* **thumb´ index**, one arranged as indentations on the outer margins of pages of books; **thumb´-screw**, a screw that can be turned by the thumb and forefinger; an old instrument of torture for compressing the thumb by means of a screw; **thumb´nail**, the nail of the thumb (*adj* small but complete—eg *a thumbnail sketch*); **thumb´tack**, a tack with a wide, flat head that can be pressed into a board, etc. with the thumb.—**all thumbs**, clumsy; **rule of thumb**, a rough-and-ready practical method, found by experience to be convenient; **under one's thumb**, under one's influence. [With intrusive *b*, OE *thūma*.]

thump [thump] *n* a heavy blow.—*vt* to beat with something heavy.—*vi* to strike or fall with a dull heavy blow.—*n* **thump´er**, one who, or that which, thumps.—*adj* **thump´ing**, (*inf*) unusually big. [Prob imit, like ON *dumpa*, to thump.]

thunder [thun´dėr] *n* the deep rumbling sound after a flash of lightning; any similar sound.—*vi* to sound as thunder.—*vt* to utter loudly and emphatically.—*ns* **thun´derbolt**, a bolt or shaft of lightning and a peal of thunder; anything sudden and shocking.—*adjs* **thun´dering**, unusually big, tremendous; **thun´derous**, giving forth a sound like thunder; angry-looking; **thun´derstruck**, astonished, struck dumb; **thun´dery**, indicative of thunder, or attended by it.—**steal one's thunder**, to deprive one of the chance to make an impression or produce a startling effect by appropriating one's idea or material and using it first—a method of representing thunder invented by John Dennis (1657–1734) was used first in a rival's play. [With intrusive *d*, OE *thunor*, thunder, *Thunor*, thunder-god Thor.]

thurible [thū´ri-bl] *n* a censer.—*n* **thū´rifer**, the server who carries the thurible. [L *thūribulum—thūs*, gen *thūris*, frankincense; akin to Gr *thyos*, a sacrifice.]

Thursday [thûrz´dā] *n* the fifth day of the week, so called because originally sacred to *Thunor*, the English god of thunder. [OE *Thunres dæg*, Thunor's day; ON *Thōrsdagr*, Thor's day.]

thus [THus] *adv* in this or that manner; to this degree or extent; so; therefore.—*adv* **thus´wise**, in this manner. [OE *thus*, prob *thȳs*, instrumental case of *thes*, this.]

thwack [thwak] *vt* to strike with something blunt and heavy, to thrash.—*n* a heavy blow. [Perh **whack**, or OE *thaccian*, to smack.]

thwart [thwört] *adj* cross, lying crosswise.—*vt* to baffle, to frustrate (eg a purpose, a person).—*n* a seat across a rowboat. [ON *thvert*, neut of *thverr*, perverse.]

thy [THī] *possessive adj* (*arch, pretic*) your. of or pertaining to thee. [Short for *thine*, OE *thīn*, gen of *thū*, thou.]

thyme [tīm] *n* a genus (*Thymus*) of aromatic herbs.—the common garden thyme, used for seasoning, wild thyme, etc.—*adj* **thy´my**. [Fr,—L *thymum*—Gr *thyein*, to fill with sweet smells, to burn in sacrifice.]

thymus [thī-můs] *n* a ductless gland near the root of the neck.—*n* **thymine** [thī´mēn], one of the four bases in deoxyribonucleic acids. [Gr *thymos*, thymus gland.]

thyroid [thī´roid] *adj* denoting a ductless gland located near the trachea, secreting a hormone which regulates growth.—*n* the thyroid gland; an animal extract of this gland, used in treating goiter, etc. [Gr *thyreos*, a shield, *eidos*, form.]

thyself [THī-self´] *pron* thou or thee in person—used for emphasis. [**thy, self.**]

ti [tē] *n* (*mus*) the seventh tone of the diatonic scale.

tiara [ti-ä´ra] (*inf*) *n* the lofty ornamental headdress of the ancient Persians; the miter of the Jewish high priest; the Pope's triple crown; a circular or semicircular head ornament, often of jewels. [Fr *tiare*—L *tiāra*—Gr *tiāra*.]

tibia [tib´i-a] *n* the larger of the two bones between the knee and the ankle. [L, the shinbone, hence a flute, originally made from it.]

tic [tik] *n* any involuntary, regularly repeated, spasmodic contraction of a muscle.—*n* **tic doul´oureux** [-dol-ȯ-rōō´; Fr tek dōō-lōō-r_], painful convulsive motion of a nerve, usu. in the face. [Fr *tic*, a twitching.]

tick[1] [tik] *n* any of numerous bloodsucking arachnids that form a superfamily (Ixodoidea) that infest men and animals. [ME *teke*; Du *teek*.]

tick[2] [tik] *n* the cover in which feathers, etc., are put for bedding.—*n* **tick´ing**, the cloth of which ticks are made. [L *thēca*—Gr *thēkē*, a case.]

tick[3] [tik] *vi* to make a small, quick noise; to beat, as a watch; (*inf*) to work, function.—*n* the sound of a watch; a moment.—*n* **tick´er**, anything which ticks, a watch; a telegraphic device that records stock market quotations, etc. on paper tape **ticker tape**; (*slang*) the heart. [Imit.]

tick[4] [tik] *n* credit, trust. [**ticket**.]

tick[5] [tik] *vt* (*often with* **off**) to mark off lightly, as items in a list.—*n* a light mark.—**tick off**, (*inf*) to rebuke sharply. [ME *tek*, a touch; Du *tik*.]

ticket [tik´et] *n* a printed card, etc., that gives one a right, as to attend a theater; a license or certificate; a label on merchandise giving size, price, etc.; (*inf*) a court summons for a traffic violation; a list of candidates put forward by a party for election.—*vt* to label with a ticket; to give a ticket to.—**the ticket**, the correct thing. [Short for OFr *e(s)tiquet(te)*, a label (Fr *étiquette*), from Gmc; Ger *stecken*, to stick.]

tickle [tik´l] *vt* to touch lightly and provoke to laughter; to please or amuse.—*n* **tick´ler**, something difficult, a puzzle.—*adj* **tick´lish**, easily tickled; easily affected; nice, critical, difficult to handle (eg a problem).—*adv* **tick´lishly**.—*n* **tick´lishness**.—*adj* **tick´ly**, ticklish. [Freq of **tick** (5).]

tide [tīd] *n* time, season; the regular ebb and flow of the seas, oceans, etc. usu. twice a day; something that rises and falls like the tide; a stream, flood; trend.—*vt* to help along temporarily (*with* **over**).—*vi* to work in or out of a river or harbor with the tide.—*adj* **ti´dal**, pertaining to, or having, tides; flowing and ebbing periodically.—*adj* **tide´less**, having no tides.—*ns* **tide´mark**, high-water mark left by tidal water or a flood; the point to which something has attained; **tide´ tā´ble**, a table giving the time of high tide at any place; **tide´wa´ter**, the water overflowing land at flood tide; water that is affected by the tide; low-lying coastal land; **tide´way**, the channel in which the tide runs.—**tidal wave**, a great wave caused by the tide or an earthquake; something overwhelming. [OE *tīd*, time, tide.]

tidings [tī´dingz] *n pl* news, intelligence. [ON *tīthindi*—*tīth*, time; cf Ger *zeitung*, news, from *zeit*, time.]

tidy [tī´di] *adj* neat; in good order; (*inf*) considerable (eg *a tidy sum of money*).—*n* a cover for chairs, etc.; a receptacle for small odds and ends.—*vt* to make neat; to put in good order;—*pt, pt p* **ti´died**.—*adv* **ti´dily**.—*n* **ti´diness**. [ME *tidy*, seasonable—OE *tīd*, time, tide.]

tie [tī] *vt* to bind; to fasten with a cord; to make a bow or knot in; to unite; to constrain, bind (a person to); (*mus*) to unite (notes) with a tie.—*vi* to score the same number of points;—*pr p* **ty´ing**; *pt, pt p*, **tied** [tīd].—*n* a knot, bow, etc.; a bond; something for tying; necktie; a beam, etc., fastening parts together; an equality in numbers, as of votes, or of points in a game; one of a series of matches or games in a competition; (*mus*) a curved line drawn over two or more consecutive notes of the same pitch to show they are to be played continuously.—*n* **tie´-dye´ing**, a method of dyeing textiles in which parts of the material are bound or knotted so as to resist the dye.—**tie in**, to be associated with; **tie up**, to wrap up and tie; to moor to a dock; to obstruct, hinder; to cause to be already in use, committed, etc. [OE *tēag, tēah, tȳge*, a rope.]

tier [tēr] *n* a row or rank, especially when several rows are placed one above another. [OFr *tire*, sequence—*tirer*, to draw.]

tierce [tērs] *n* a cask containing one-third of a pipe—that is, 42 gallons; a sequence of three cards of the same suit; (*mus*) a third; a position in fencing. [OFr *tiers, tierce*—L *tertia* (*pars*), a third (part)—*trēs*, three.]

tiff [tif] *n* a slight quarrel or disagreement. [Perh orig a *sniff*; cf Norw *tev*, a drawing in the breath, *teva*, to sniff.]

tiger [tī´gėr] *n* a large, fierce Asiatic quadruped (*Felis tigris*) of the cat genus.—*fem* **tī´gress**.—*ns* **tī´ger cat**, any of several wild-cats; **tī´ger lily**, a Mexican plant (*Lilium tigrinum*) cultivated in gardens for its streaked flowers. [Fr *tigre*—L *tigris*—Gr *tigris*—O Pers *tighri*, an arrow, whence the river Tigris.]

tight [tīt] *adj* close; compact; rigid; taut; not loose; fitting closely; snug, trim; allowing little space or time for deviation from plan; not leaky; concise; strict; of a contest, close; (*inf*) tipsy; scarce, not easy to obtain (as money); difficult (eg *a tight place*); (*inf*) stingy.—*vt* **tight´en**, to make tight or tighter; to straiten.—*vi* to grow tight or tighter.—*adv* **tight´ly**.—*ns* **tight´ness; tight´rope**, a tightly stretched rope on which rope-dancers perform.—*n pl* **tights**, a close fitting garment covering the body from the neck down or the lower part of the body and the legs. [Scand,—ON *thēttr*.]

tiki [tē´kē] *n* a wood or stone image of a Polynesian super-natural power.

tilde [til´de] *n* in Spanish, a mark over *n* when pronounced *ny*, as in *señor*. [Sp *titulo*—L *titulus*. See **title**.]

tile [tīl] *n* a piece of baked clay used for covering roofs, floors, etc.; a tube or pipe of baked clay used in drains; a similar piece of plastic.—*vt* to cover with tiles.—*ns* **tī´ler**, one who makes or who lays tiles; **tī´lery**, a place where tiles are made; **tī´ling**, tiles collectively.—**on the tiles**, on a spree. [OE *tigele*—L *tegula*—*tegĕre*, to cover.]

till[1] [til] *n* a drawer for keeping money. [ME *tillen*, to draw out—OE *tyllan*, seen in *fortyllan*, to draw aside.]

till[2] [til] *prep* until.—*conj* until. [ON *til*.]

till[3] [til] *vt* to cultivate (land) for raising crops, as by plowing.—*ns* **till´age**, act or practice of tilling; cultivation; a place tilled; **till´er**. [OE *tilian*, to till.]

till[4] [til] *n* an unstratified mixture of glacial drift consisting of sand, clay, gravel, and boulders. [Ety obscure.]

tiller [til´ėr] *n* the handle or lever for turning a rudder. [OE *tyllan*, to draw.]

tilt[1] [tilt] *n* the canvas covering of a stall or wagon; an awning in a boat.—*vt* to cover with an awning. [OE *teld*—*teldan*, to cover.]

tilt[2] [tilt] *vi* to ride against another and thrust with a lance (*often with* **at**); to attack (*with* **at**); to fall into a sloping posture, to heel over; to be raised at an angle.—*vt* to slant; to raise one end of.—*n* a thrust; in the Middle Ages, an exercise in which combatants rode against each other with lances; any comparable encounter; an altercation (with); inclination, dip, slant.—*ns* **tilt´er**.—**full tilt**, at full speed, with full force. [OE *tealt*, tottering; ON *tölta*, to trot.]

tilth [tilth] *n* cultivation; cultivated land; the depth of soil turned up in cultivation. [From **till** (3).]

timber [tim´bėr] *n* wood for construction purposes; trees suitable for this; woods; one of the larger pieces of the framework of a house, ship, etc.; trees collectively.—*vt* to furnish with timber or beams.—*adj* **tim´bered**, built of wood; (of country) wooded.—*ns* **timberline**, on a mountain or in cold regions, the line beyond which there are no trees. [OE *timber*, building, wood.]

timbre, timber [tēbr´ or tim´bėr] *n* character or quality of a musical sound. [OFr,—L *tympanum*, a drum.]

timbrel [tim´brėl] *n* a small hand drum or tambourine. [OFr *timbre*—L *tympanum*, a drum.]

time [tīm] *n* a point at which, or period during which, things happen; hour of the day (eg *what time is it*?); an appropriate season or moment; an opportunity; duration; an interval; a period in the past; the duration of one's life; allotted or measured period or its completion; occasion; a repeated instance of anything or mention with reference to repetition; musical measure, or rate of movement; period of gestation; hour of travail; hour of death; the state of things at any period, usually in *pl*; the history of the world, as opposed to eternity; system of reckoning the passage of time.—*vt* to do at the proper season; to regulate as to time; to measure or record the duration of; to measure rate of movement.—*n* **time bomb**, a bomb made to explode at a predetermined time; something with a potentially dangerous delayed reaction.—*adj* **time´hon´ored**, venerable on account of antiquity.—*ns* **time´keep´er**, a clock, watch, or other instrument for keeping or marking time; one who keeps the time of workmen, etc.; **time lag**, the interval of the delay between two connected phenomena.—*adj* **time´ly**, in good time; opportune.—*adv* (*arch*) early.—*ns* **time´liness; time´out**, (*sports*) any temporary suspension of play; **time´piece**, a clock, watch, chronometer; **time´serv´er**, one who suits his opinions to the occasion or circumstances; **time´share**, joint ownership of a vacation lodging by several persons with each occupying the premises in turn for short periods; **time´tā´ble**, a table or list showing the times of certain things, as arrival or departure of trains, steamers, etc.; a schedule showing a planned order or sequence.—*adj* **time´worn**, worn or decayed by time.—*n* **time´zone**, a geographical region of the US having a standard time throughout its area.—*adj* **tim´eous**, timely.—**all in good time**, in due course; soon enough; **at times**, at intervals; occasionally; **do time**, (*inf*) serve a prison sentence; **have little, no, time for**, to have little, no interest in or patience with; **in time**, sufficiently early; eventually; in correct tempo; **the time being**, the present time, **time and again**, repeatedly; **time out of mind**, from time immemorial. [OE *tima*; cf ON *timi*.]

timid [tim´id] *adj* timorous, shy; wanting courage, faint-hearted.—*n* **timid´ity**, quality or state of being timid.—*adv* **tim´idly**. [Fr,—L *timidus*—*timēre*, to fear.]

timorous [tim´ȯr-ůs] *adj* timid, easily frightened.—*adv* **tim´orously**.—*n* **tim´orousness**. [LL *timorōrus*—L *timor*, fear.]

Timothy [tim´ō-thi] *n* (*Bible*) 15th and 16th books of the New Testament, epistles written by St Paul to the minister in charge of the churches at Ephesus.

timpani, tympani [tim´pȧn-ē] *n pl* kettledrums; the set of kettledrums used in an orchestra and usu. played by one performer.—*n* **tim´panist, tympanist**. [It.]

tin [tin] *n* a metallic element (symbol Sn; at wt 118.7; at no 50); a vessel of tin or tinplate, etc.—*adj* made of tin or tinplate.—*vt* to cover or overlay with tin, tinfoil, or solder; to pack in tins;—*pr p* **tinn´ing**; *pt, pt p* **tinned**.—*ns* **tin´plate**, thin sheets of iron or steel plated with tin; **tin´smith**, a worker in tin or tinplate; **tin´ware**, articles, esp utensils, made of tin.—**tin´foil**, a tin sheet of tin or a tin alloy used as wrapping.—**Tin Pan Alley**, the realm of popular music production, the world of its composers, publishers, record-makers, etc. [OE.]

tincture [tingk´-chůr] *n* a tinge, shade (of color); a slight taste added to anything; *(med)* an alcoholic solution of any substance.—*vt* to tinge; to imbue. [L *tinctūra—tingěre*, to tinge.]

tinder [tin´dėr] *n* anything used for kindling fire from a spark. [OE *tynder*.]

tine [tīn] *n* a slender projecting point, as a spike of a fork or harrow, or of a deer's antler.—*adj* **tīned**, furnished with spikes. [OE *tind*, a tooth, ON *tindr*, a tooth, a prickle.]

tinge [tinj] *vt* to tint or color; to modify by admixture;—*pr p* **ting(e)´ing**.—*n* a slight tint or flavor. [L *tingěre, tinctum*.]

tingle [ting´gl] *vi* to feel a thrilling sensation, as in hearing a shrill sound; to feel a prickling or stinging sensation.—*vt* to cause to tingle.—*n* a tingling sensation. [ME *tinglen*, a variant of *tinklen*, itself a freq of *tinken*, to tinkle.]

tinker [tingk´ėr] *n* a mender of brazen or tin kettles, pans, etc; a bungler.—*vi* to do tinker's work; to work ineffectively (with). [ME *tinkere—tinken*, to tinkle, to make a sharp, shrill sound.]

tinkle [tingk´l] *vi* to make small, sharp sounds, to clink, to jingle; to clink repeatedly or continuously.—*vt* to cause to make quick, sharp sounds.—*n* a sharp, clinking sound. [A freq of ME *tinken*.]

tinsel [tin´sel] *n* a stuff for ornamental dresses etc., consisting of cloth overlaid with a thin coating of glittering metal; anything showy, but of little value.—*adj* like tinsel; gaudy; superficial.—*vt* to adorn with, or as with, tinsel;—*pr p* **tin´selling**; *pt, pt p* **tin´-selled**.—*adj* **tin´selly**, like tinsel, gaudy, showy. [OFr *estincelle*—L *scintilla*, a spark.]

tint [tint] *n* a variety of any color, esp diluted; a slight admixture of color other than the main one, a tinge; a hair dye.—*vt* to give a slight coloring to; to tinge. [L *tinctus—tinguěre*, to tinge.]

tintinnabulation [tin-tin-ab-ū-lā´sh(ȯ)n] *n* the tinkling sound of bells. [L *tintinnābulum*, a bell—*tintinnāre*, to jingle, reduplicated from *tinnīre*, to jingle.]

tiny [tī´ni] *adj* (*comparative* **tī´nier**, *superlative* **tī´niest**) very small. [Ety uncertain.]

tip[1] [tip] *n* the small top or point of anything; the end, as of a billiard cue, etc.—*vt* to form a point to; to cover the tip or end of;—*pr p* **tipp´ing**; *pt, pt p* **tipped**. [A variant of **top**.]

tip[2] [tip] *vt* to strike lightly; to cause to slant; to overturn; to empty (out, into, etc.); *(inf)* to give private information to, about betting, etc.; to give a hint to; to give a small gift of money to, as a waiter, etc.—*vi* to slant; to give tips.—*n* a tap or light stroke; private information about horse-racing, stock speculations, etc.; a small gratuity.—*ns* **tip´-cat**, a game in which a pointed piece of wood called a cat is made to spring up from the ground by being struck on the tip with a stick, and is then driven as far as possible; **tip´-off**, a hint or warning in advance.—**tip off**, to give a tip-off to.—*n* **tip´ster**, one whose business is to give private hints about racing, the rise and fall of stocks, etc.—**straight tip**, a reliable hint about betting, etc.; **tip the scales**, to register weight; to shift the balance of power. [Scand,—Swed *tippa*, to tap.]

tippet [tip´et] *n* the cape of a coat; a cape of fur, etc. [OE *tæppet*—L *tapēte*, cloth—Gr *tapēs, -ētos*, a carpet.]

tipple [tip´l] *vi* to drink in small quantities; to drink strong liquors often or habitually.—*vt* to drink (strong liquors) to excess.—*n* **tipp´ler**, a constant toper. [Cf Norw dial *tipla*.]

tipstaff [tip´stäf] *n* a staff tipped with metal, or an officer who carries it; a constable. [**tip** (1) + **staff**.]

tipsy [tip´si] *adj* partially intoxicated.—*ns* **tip´siness**. [**tipple**.]

tiptoe [tip´tō] *n* the end of the toe.—*adv* on tiptoe, literally or figuratively, through excitement, expectation, etc.—*vi* to walk on tiptoe, to go lightly and slyly. [**tip** (1) + **toe**.]

tiptop [tip´top] *adj* first-rate. [**tip** (1) + **top** (1).]

tirade [tī-räd´] *n* a long vehement speech of censure or reproof. [Fr,—It *tirata*, a volley—*tirare*, to pull, to fire.]

tire[1] [tīr] *n* *(arch)* attire, apparel; *(arch)* a head-dress.—*vt* to dress, as the head. [Short for **attire**.]

tire[2] [tīr] *n* the hoop of iron, rubber band, cushion or tube round a wheel rim. [Prob **attire**.]

tire[3] [tīr] *vt* to exhaust the strength of, to weary.—*vi* to become weary; to have the patience exhausted.—*adj* **tired**, wearied; (*with* **of**) bored with.—*n* **tired´ness** [tīrd´-].—*adj* **tire´less**, unwearying, indefatigable.—*n* **tire´lessness**.—*adj* **tire´some**, fatiguing; tedious; annoying.—*adv* **tire´somely**.—*n* **tire´someness**. [App OE *tēorian*, to be tired.]

Tirolean, Tirolese *See* **Tyrolean, Tyrolese**.

tissue [tish´ū] *n* cloth interwoven with gold or silver, or with figured colors; a very finely woven fabric; the substance of which the organic body is composed; a connected series; a piece of soft, absorbent paper, used as a disposable handkerchief, etc.; tissue paper.—*n* **tiss´ue pā´per**, a thin, soft, unsized kind of paper. [Fr *tissu*, woven—L *texěre*, to weave.]

tit[1] [tit] *n* a titmouse; *(loosely)* any of various plump, long-tailed birds. [ON *tittr*, a little bird, Norw *tita*.]

tit[2] [tit] *n* in phrase **tit for tat**, properly *tip for tap*, blow for blow—an equivalent of any kind of retaliation.

Titan [tī´tån] *n* one of the giants of Greek mythology; the sun, son of one of these giants; **titan**, a person of great power or ability.—*adj* **titan´ic**, enormous in size and strength. [Gr.]

titanium [tī-tā´ni-ům] *n* a strong light metallic element (symbol Ti; at wt 47.9; at no 22). [From **Titan**.]

titbit [tit´bit] *See* **tidbit**.

tithe [tīTH] *n* a tenth part, hence any indefinitely small part; the tenth of the produce of land and stock, allotted for the maintenance of the clergy and other church purposes.—*vti* to pay a tithe (of one's income, etc.).—*n* **tī´ther**, one who pays tithes; one that collects or advocates the payment of tithes.—**tī´thing**, *(hist)* a district containing ten householders, each responsible for the behavior of the rest. [OE *tēotha*, tenth; cog with *tīen, tēn*, ten.]

titian [tish´ån] *n* a red-yellow color used by *Titian*, Venetian painter (1477–1576).—*adj* (chiefly of hair) of this color, or *(loosely)* of other shade of red or reddish-brown.

titillate [tit´il-lāt] *vt* to tickle; to excite pleasurably.—*n* **titillā´tion**, act of titillating; state of being titillated; a pleasant feeling. [L *titillāre, -ātum*.]

titlark [tit´lärk] *n* pipit (*Anthus pratensis*). [**tit** + **lark**.]

title [tī´tl] *n* an inscription placed over, or at the beginning of a thing, by which that thing is known; an epithet; a name denoting nobility or rank, or office held, or formally attached to personal name without implying any distinction (Mr, Mrs, Miss); *(law)* that which gives a just right (to possession); the writing that proves a right; a subtitle, credit, etc. in motion pictures and television productions; *(sports)* a championship.—*adj* **tī´tled**, having a title.—*ns* **tī´tle deed**, a deed or document that proves a title or right to exclusive possession; **tī´tle page**, the page of a book containing its title and usually the author's and publisher's names; **tī´tle rôle**, the part in a play which gives its name to it, as 'Macbeth'. [OFr *title* (Fr *titre*)—L *titulus*.]

titmouse [tit´mous] *n* a genus (*Parus*, or allied genera, family Paridae) of little birds that feed on insects, etc.;—*pl* **titmice** [tit´mīs]. [Obs Eng *tit*, anything small; OE *māse*, a titmouse.]

titrate [tīt´-, tit´rāt] *vt* to subject to titration.—*ns* **titrā´tion**, the addition of a solution from a graduated vessel (burette) to a known volume of a second solution, until the chemical reaction between the two is just completed—a knowledge of the volume of liquid added, and of the strength of one of the solutions, enabling that of the other to be calculated; **titer** [tī´tėr], the concentration of a substance in a solution as determined by titration. [Fr *titrer—titre*, title.]

titter [tit´ėr] *vi* to giggle, laugh restrainedly.—*n* a restrained laugh. [Prob imit.]

tittle [tit´l] *n* a small mark, point or sign, as the dot over *i* or *j*, or a vowel point in Hebrew or Arabic; a small particle. [OFr *title—titulus*, a title.]

tittle-tattle [tit´l-tat´l] *n* idle, empty gossip.—*vi* to prate idly.—*ns* **titt´le-tatt´ler; titt´le-tatt´ling**, the act of talking idly. [Variant of **tattle**.]

tittup [tit´ůp] *vi* to walk springily or jerkily. [Imit.]

titular [tit´ū-lår] *adj* held by virtue of a title; existing in name of title only; having the title without the duties of an office.—*adv* **tit´ularly**.—*adj* **tit´ulary**, consisting in, or pertaining to, a title.—*n* one having the title of an office whether he performs its duties or not. [From L *titulus*, as **title**.]

tizzy [tiz´i] *n* state of agitation, nervousness, confusion, dither.

TNT Abbrev for **trinitrotoluene**.

to [tōō, tŏŏ, tȯ] (according to word or sentence stress), *prep* in the direction of; as far as; expressing the end or purpose of an action; the sign of the infinitive mood; introducing the indirect object of a verb; in comparison with, with reference to, etc. (*this is nothing to what he has done already; true to life, etc.*—*adv* to a place or condition required, or understood (eg *to lie to, come to*.)—**to and fro**, backward and forward. [OE *tō*; Ger *zu*.]

toad [tōd] *n* a family (esp Bufonidae) of amphibious reptiles, like the frogs mostly living on moist land.—*ns* **toad´eater**, *(arch)* a fawning sycophant; **toad´stool**, any of various umbrella-shaped mushrooms, esp a poisonous or inedible one. **toad´y**, a hanger-on and flatterer.—*vt* to fawn upon as a sycophant.—*vi* to fawn upon (*usu. with* **to**);—*pt, ptp* **toad´ied**.—*n* **toad´yism**, the practice of a toady. [OE *tādige, tādie*, a toad.]

toast [tōst] *vt* to brown by means of the heat of fire, gas flame, or electricity; to warm; to name when a health is drunk; to drink to the health of.—*vi* to drink toasts.—*n* bread toasted; *(arch)* a slice of it dipped in liquor; the person or thing whose health is drunk; *(arch)* much-admired young woman; a proposal of health.—*ns* **toast´er**, one who, or that which, toasts, esp an electrical appliance for toasting; **toast´master**, the announcer of toasts at public dinners. [OFr *toster*—L *tostus*, roasted, pt p of *torēre*.]

tobacco [to-bak´ō] *n* any plant of the genus *Nicotiana*, native to America, the dried leaves of which are used for smoking, chewing, or as snuff.—*n* **tobacc´o pipe**, a pipe used for smoking tobacco. [Through Sp *tabaco*, from native word in Haiti.]

toboggan [tȯ-bog´ån] *n* a kind of sled without runners turned up at the front for sliding down snow-covered slopes.—*vi* to slide down over snow on such a sled:—*pr p* **tobogg´aning**; *pt, pt p* **tobogg´aned**. [Amer Indian.]

toccata [to-kä´tä] *n* *(mus)* a work for keyboard instrument in a free style and marked by full chords and rapid runs. [It,—*toccare*, to touch.]

tocsin [tok´sin] *n* an alarm bell, or the ringing of it. [OFr *toquesin—toquer*, to strike, *sing*, a sign, signal.]

today [tȯ-dā´] *n* this day; the present time.—*adv* on the present day; nowadays. [OE *tōdæge*.]

toddle [tod´l] *vi* to walk with short feeble steps, as a child.—*n* **todd´ler**, a young child. [Prob a by-form of **totter**.]

toddy [tod´i] *n* drink of whiskey, sugar, and hot water. [Hindustani *tārī—tār*, a palm-tree.]

to-do [tö-dōō´] *n* (*inf*) bustle, stir. [Infin of **do**.]

toe [tō] *n* one of the five small members at the point of the foot; the corresponding member of an animal's foot; the forepart of the foot; the front of an animal's hoof, or a shoe, a golf club, etc.—*vt* to touch or strike with the toe(s); to provide with a toe or toes.—*n* **toe´ cap**, a cap of leather, etc., covering the toe of a shoe.—*adj* **toed** [tōd], having toes, usu. of a specified kind (eg *square-toed.*)—*n* **toe´hold**, just enough to support the toe in climbing, etc.; a small established position.—**on one's toes**, poised for a quick start; alert, eager; **toe the line**, come into rank; to accept a rule, standard, or convention; to fulfill one's obligations; **tread on the toes of**, to offend. [OE *tā* (pl *tān*).]

toffee, toffy [tof´i] *n* a candy of brittle but tender texture made by boiling sugar and butter together.

tofu [tō´fōō] *n* a Chinese custardlike food made from soybeans. [Chinese.]

tog [tog] *n* (*slang*) a garment—generally in *pl*—*vt* to dress up in fine clothing. [Prob L *tŏga*, a robe.]

toga [tō´ga] *n* the mantle or outer garment of a Roman citizen. [L *tŏga—tegĕre*, to cover.]

together [tö-geтн´ėr] *adv* gathered to one place; in the same place, time, or company; in or into union; in concert.—*n* **togeth´erness**, unity; closeness. [OE *tōgædere—tō*, to, *geador*, together.]

toil[1] [toil] *n* a net or snare (esp in *pl; fig*). [OFr *toile*, cloth—L *tēla*, from *texĕre*, to weave.]

toil[2] [toil] *vi* to labor; to work with fatigue; to move with great effort.—*n* labor, esp of a fatiguing kind.—*n* **toil´er**.—*adj* **toil´some**, causing fatigue, wearisome.—*adv* **toil´somely**.—*n* **toil´someness**.—*adj* **toil´worn**, worn, or worn out, with toil. [OFr *touiller*, to entangle; of uncertain origin.]

toilet [toil´et] *n* mode or process of dressing; any particular costume; a room with a bowl-shaped fixture for defecation or urination; such a fixture.—*ns* **toil´etry**, any article or preparation used in washing and dressing oneself; **toilette** [twalet´], the process of grooming oneself; dress, attire. [Fr *toilette*, dim of *toile*, cloth.]

Tokay [tō-kā´] *n* a white wine with an aromatic flavor, produced at *Tokay* in Hungary; a blend of Angelica, port, and sherry made in California.

token [tō´kėn] *n* something representing another thing or event; a symbol, sign, a memorial (of friendship, etc.); a metal disk to be used in place of currency, for transportation fares, etc.—*adj* serving as a symbol, hence being a mere show or semblance, not effective reality (eg *token raid, resistance*).—*n* **tok´enism**, the practice of doing something once to give an impression of doing it regularly, eg employing one black person to avoid a charge of racialism.—**by the same token**, as corroboration. [OE *tācen*.]

told [tōld] *pt, pt p* of **tell**.

tolerable [tol´ėr-ȧ-bl] *adj* that may be endured; moderately good or agreeable.—*n* **tolerabil´ity**.—*adv* **tol´erably**.—*n* **tol´erance**, endurance of, or permitting liberty to, uncongenial persons, or opinions differing from one's own; (*med*) ability to resist the action of a drug, poison, etc.; allowable variation in dimension of a machine or part.—*adj* **tol´erant**, showing tolerance, indulgent (of); favoring toleration; (*biol*) able to endure adverse environmental and other conditions.—*adv* **tol´erantly**.—*vt* **tol´erāte**, to endure; to allow by not hindering.—*n* **tolerā´tion**, act or practice of tolerating; allowance of what is not approved; liberty given to a minority to hold and express their own political or religious opinions, and to be admitted to the same civil privileges as the majority. [L *tolerāre, -ātum—tollĕre*, to lift up.]

toll[1] [tōl] *n* a tax for the liberty of passing over a bridge or road; a charge for a service, as for a long-distance telephone call; any exaction, esp of human lives.—*ns* **toll´booth**, a booth where tolls are collected; **toll´bridge, toll´gate, toll´house**, a bridge, gate, house, where toll is taken.—**take toll of**, to inflict loss, hardship, pain, etc. on. [OE *tol, toll*.]

toll[2] [tōl] *vi* to sound, as a large bell, esp with a measured sound, as a funeral bell.—*vt* to ring a bell with slow, measured strokes; to announce, summon, etc. by this.—*n* the sound of a bell when tolling. [ME *tollen*, to pull—OF *tyllan*.]

tomahawk [tom´a-hök] *n* a light ax used by N American Indians as a tool or weapon.—*vt* to cut or kill with a tomahawk. [Amer Indian.]

tomato [tö-mä´tō] *n* a plant (*Lycopersicum esculentum*) with red (or yellow) pulpy edible fruit; used as a vegetable, native to South America, earlier called the 'love apple';—*pl* **toma´toes**. [Sp *tomate*—Aztec *tomatl*.]

tomb [tōōm] *n* a pit or vault in the earth, in which a dead body is placed; a memorial sarcophagus; (*with* **the**) death.—*n* **tomb´stone**, a stone erected over a tomb to preserve the memory of the dead. [Fr *tombe*—L *tumba*—Gr *tymbos*.]

tomboy [tom´boi] *n* a girl who prefers boyish games and activities to those generally considered more suitable for her sex. [*Tom* (dim of Thomas), a common male name, and **boy**.]

tomcat [tom´kat] a male cat. [*Tom* (see **tomboy**) and **cat**.]

Tom, Dick, and Harry [tom´ dik´ ȧn har´ē] *n* any person taken at random; the common man.

tome [tōm] *n* a book, a volume, esp a large heavy one; a book, esp a learned one. [Fr,—L *tomus*—Gr *tomos—temnein*, to cut.]

tomfool [tom´fōōl´] *n* a great fool; a blockhead.—*adj* foolish.—*n* **tomfool´ery**, foolish trifling or jesting; buffoonery. [*Tom* (see **tomboy**) and **fool**.]

Tommy [tom´i] *n* (*inf*) a British soldier. [*Thomas Atkins*, the fictitious name used as a model in army forms.]

tommy gun [tom´i gun] a submachine gun invented by US General John Thompson (1860–1940).

tomography [tō-mog´rȧ-fi] *n* radiography of a layer in the body by moving the X-ray tube and photoplate in such a way that only the chosen plane appears in clear detail.—*adj* **tom´ograph**. [Gr *tomos*, slice, *graphein*, to draw.]

tomorrow [tö-mor´ō] *n* and *adv* the day after today. [OE *tō morgen*.]

tomtit [tom´tit] *n* a small, active bird. [*Tom* (see **tomboy**) and **tit** (1).]

tom-tom [tom´-tom] *n* a primitive drum, usu. beaten with the hands. [Imit.]

-tomy [-tö-mi] in composition used to denote surgical incision in an organ. [Gr adj *tomos*, cutting, sharp.]

ton [tun] *n* a unit of weight equivalent to 2,000 pounds, a **short ton**; in Great Britain, a unit of weight equal to 2,240 pounds, a **long ton**; a unit of internal capacity for ships equal to 100 cubic feet, **register ton**; (*inf*) (often *pl*) a great quantity. [OE **tunne**, a vat, tub.]

tone [tōn] *n* the character of a sound; quality of the voice; inflection of the voice which conveys the speaker's feeling or attitude; harmony of the colors of a painting, also its prevailing effect as due to the combination of light and shade; tint, shade of color; character or style; stylishness; state of mind; mood; a healthy state of the body; (*mus*) a sound of distant pitch or any of the full intervals of the diatonic scale.—*vt* to give tone to; to alter or modify the color of.—*vi* to harmonize (with).—*n* **tonal´ity**, the type of scale and key in which a musical work is written; the principle of having a key; the tone interrelationship of a picture.—**tone down**, to moderate, to soften; **tone poem**, (*mus*) a symphonic poem. [L *tonus*—Gr *tonos*, a sound—*teinein*, to stretch.]

tonga [tong´ga] *n* a light two-wheeled cart or carriage, in use in India. [Hindustani.]

tongs [tongz] *n pl* a domestic instrument, consisting of two shafts of metal jointed, pivoted, or sprung, used for grasping and lifting. [OE *tange*.]

tongue [tung] *n* the fleshy organ in the mouth, used in tasting, swallowing, and speech; power of speech; manner of speaking; a language; an animal's tongue served as food; anything like a tongue in shape; a jet of flame; a strip of leather under the lacing in a boot or shoe; the catch of a buckle; the pointer of a balance; a point of land.—*adjs* **tongued**, having a tongue; **tongue´less**, having no tongue; mute; **tongue´-tied**, having an impediment, as if the tongue were tied; unable to speak freely.—*n* **tongue´ twister**, a word, phrase, or sentence difficult to enunciate clearly because of a sequence of similar consonants.—**hold one's tongue** (see **hold**); **lose one's tongue**, to become speechless; **with tongue in cheek**, ironically or whimsically, not sincerely or seriously. [OE *tunge*.]

tonic [ton´ik] *adj* relating to tones or sounds; (*med*) giving tone and vigor to the system; giving or increasing strength.—*n* a medicine that gives tone and vigor to the system; (*music*) a keynote, the first note of a scale; a quinine-flavored beverage served with gin, vodka, etc.—**tonic solfa** [sol-fä], a system of musical notation, in which the notes are indicated by letters, and time and accent by dashes and colons. [Fr *tonique*—Gr *tonikos—tonos*. See **tone**.]

tonight [tö-nīt´] *n, adv* this night; the night after the present day. [OE *tōniht*.]

tonnage [tun´ij] *n* total weight in tons of the amount of shipping of a country or port; the cubic capacity of a ship measured by a scale in which 100 cubic feet=1 ton; ships collectively, esp merchant ships; a duty on ships, estimated per ton. [**ton**.]

tonne [tön] *n* metric ton.

tonneau [ton´ō] *n* the rear seating compartment of an automobile; the entire seating compartment. [Fr.]

tonsil [ton´sil] *n* either of two bodies consisting of lymphoid tissue and situated one on each side of the throat.—*n* **tonsillī´tis**, inflammation of the tonsils. [L *tonsilla*, a stake, a tonsil, dim of *tonsa*, an oar.]

tonsure [ton´shür] *n* act of clipping the hair, or of shaving the head; the shaving of the head as a sign of dedication to the special service of God; the part of the head so shaven.—*adj* **ton´sured**, having the crown of the head shaven as a priest; shaven; bald. [L *tonsūra*, a shearing—*tondēre*, to shave.]

tontine [ton-tēn´] *n* a financial arrangement in which a number of participants usu. contribute equally to a prize that is eventually awarded to the last survivor. [From Lorenzo *Tonti*, its inventor.]

too [tōō] *adv* over, extremely; also, likewise.—*adj* **too-too**, quite too; extreme, superlative; (*inf*) going beyond the bounds of good taste and common sense. [A form of *to*, signifying lit 'added to'.]

took [tŏŏk] *pt* and obsolete *pt p* of **take**.

tool [tōōl] *n* an implement for manual work; an instrument for achieving any purpose; one who acts as the mere instrument of another.—*vt* to mark with a tool, esp (of book-binders) to ornament or imprint designs upon.—*vi* to install tools, equipment, etc. needed (*often with* **up**). [OE *tōl, tohl*.]

toot [tōōt] *vi* to sound a horn, whistle, etc. in short blasts.—Also *vt*.—*n* a sound, as of a horn, a blast; the sound of a horn. [Prob imit.]

tooth [tōōth] *n* one of the hard bodies in the mouth, attached to the skeleton but not forming part of it, used in biting and chewing; the taste or palate; anything toothlike, as one of the projections on a comb, saw, or wheel; (*pl*) effective means of enforcing;—*pl* **teeth**.—*vt* to furnish with teeth; to cut into teeth.—*n* **tooth´ache**, an ache or pain in a tooth.—*adjs* **toothed**, having teeth; (*bot*) having toothlike projections on the edge, as a leaf; **tooth´less**, having no teeth.—*n* **tooth´pick**, an instrument for picking out anything in or between the teeth.—*adj* **tooth´some**, pleasant to the taste.—**tooth and nail**, with all possible vigor and fury.—**a sweet tooth**, a relish for sweet things; **in the teeth of**, in defiant opposition to; **show one's teeth**, to threaten, to show one's anger and power to injure; **take the teeth out of**, to render harmless or powerless; **throw, cast, in one's teeth**, to fling at one, as a taunt, or in challenge. [OE *tōth* (pl *tēth*).]

tootle [tōōt´l] *vi* to toot gently, repetitively, or continuously; to drive along in a leisurely manner.—*vi* to toot continuously on. [Freq **toot**.]

top[1] [top] *n* the highest part of anything; the upper end or surface; the part of a plant above ground; the crown of the head; the highest place, rank, or crown, consummation; the chief or highest person; (*naut*) a small platform at the head of the lower mast; (*pl*) aces and kings in a hand in a card game.—*adj* highest, foremost, chief; good, capital.—*vt* to cover on the top; to rise above; to surpass; to reach the top of; to take off the top of;—*pr p* **topp´ing**; *pt, pt p* **topped**.—*n pl* **top´ boots**, long-legged boots with a showy band of leather round the top.—*ns* **top´coat**, an overcoat; **topdress´ing**, a dressing of manure etc. laid on the surface of land; any superficial covering.—*adj* **top´gallant**, being a part next above the topmast and below the royal mast.—*n* **top´hat´**, a tall silk hat (*adj* upper class; designed to benefit high executives or the rich, as *top hat budget*).—*adj* **top´heav´y**, having the upper part too heavy for the lower; tipsy.—*ns* **top´knot**, a crest, tuft of hair, or knot of ribbons, etc., on the top of the head; **top´mast**, the mast that is next above the lower mast and is topmost in a fore-and-aft rig.—*adj* **top´most**, next to the top, highest.—*n* **topsail, tops´l** [top´sāl, or -sl], a sail across the topmast.—*adj* **top´sec´ret**, of information, very secret, because of the highest importance.—**top dog**, the winner; the leader or dominant person (*adj* (used predicatively) in the dominant position, most favorably placed); **top drawer**, the highest level, esp of society. [OE *top*.]

top[2] [top] *n* a child's toy, with a point on which to spin, set whirling by means of a string, a whip, or a spring.

topaz [tō´paz] *n* any of various yellow gems, esp a variety of aluminum silicate. [OFr *topase, topaze*—Gr *topazion*, also *topazos*.]

tope[1] [tōp] *n* a Buddhist tumulus for the preservation of relics. [Corr from Sans *stūpa*, a heap.]

tope[2] [tōp] *vi* to drink hard.—*n* **top´er**, a drunkard.

topee [tō-pē´] *n* a helmet of pith or cork worn by Europeans in India—also **topi** [tō´pē]. [Hindustani *topī*, hat.]

topiary [tō´pi-à-ri] *n* the art and practice of clipping trees and shrubs into ornamental shapes. [L *topia* (*opera*), mural decorations depicting landscapes—Gr *topos*, a place.]

topic [top´ik] *n* a subject of discourse or argument.—*adj* **top´ical**, relating to a topic or subject; of current interest; (*med*) for local application.—*adv* **top´ically**. [Fr,—Gr *ta topika*, the general principles of argument—*topos*, a place.]

topographer [to-pog´raf-ėr] *n* one who describes a place, etc.; one skilled in topography.—*n* **topog´raphy**, the description of a place; a detailed account of the superficial features of a tract of country; the art of describing places.—*adjs* **topograph´ic, -al**, pertaining to topography.—*adv* **topograph´ically**. [Gr *topos*, a place, *graphein*, to describe.]

topple [top´l] *vi* to fall forward, to tumble (down, over).—*vt* to cause to overbalance and fall. [Freq of **top**.]

topsy-turvy [top´si-tûr´vi] *adv* bottom upwards.—*adj* turned upside down; disordered, in confusion. [Prob *top* + *so* (adv) + *tervy*, overturned—ME *terven*, to roll—OE *torfian*, to throw.]

toque [tōk] *n* a closs-fitting brimless hat for women. [Fr, prob Celt; Breton *tok*, W *toc*, a hat.]

tor [tör] *n* a high, craggy hill. [OE *torr*; W *tor*, a knob.]

Torah [tō´rȧ] *n* the body of Jewish scriptures; the Pentateuch;—*pl* **Toroth** [tō-rȯs], **torot** [tōrōt], a scroll containing it. [Heb.]

torch [törch] *n* a light formed of twisted tow dipped in pitch or other inflammable material; a large candle or a small flambeau.—*vt* (*slang*) to set fire to, as in arson.—**carry the torch (for)**, to suffer unrequited love (for). [Fr *torche*—L *tortum*, pt p of *torquēre*, to twist.]

tore [tōr] *pt* of **tear**.

torment [tör´ment] *n* torture, anguish; that which causes pain.—*vt* **torment´**, to torture, to put to extreme pain, physical or mental; to distress, to afflict; to tease.—*adv* **tormen´tingly**, in a tormenting manner.—*n* **tormen´tor, -er**, one who, or that which, torments. [OFr,—L *tormentum*, an engine for hurling stones—L *torquēre*, to twist.]

torn [törn, tōrn] *pt p* of **tear**.]

tornado [tör-nā´dō] *n* a violently whirling column of air seen as a funnel-shaped cloud that usu. destroys everything in its narrow path;—*pl* **tornā´does**.—*adj* **tornăd´ic**. [Prob Sp *tronada*, thunderstorm, altered as if from *tornada*, a turning.]

torpedo [tör-pē´dō] *n* a family (Torpedinidae) of fishes related to skates and rays, with organs on the head that give an electric shock; self-propelled submarine offensive weapon (usu. cigar-shaped), carrying explosive charge;—*pl* **torpe´does**.—*vt* to attack, hit or destroy, with torpedo(es); to wreck (a plan).—*ns* **torpē´do boat**, a small swift warship, designed to attack by discharging torpedoes; **torpē´do boat destroy´er** (now usu. **destroyer**), a swifter and more powerful type of torpedo boat. [L *torpēre*, to be stiff.]

torpid [tör´pid] *adj* stiff, numb, having lost the power of motion and feeling; sluggish.—*ns* **torpid´ity; tor´por**, state of being torpid; numbness; inactivity; dullness. [L *torpidus*—*torpēre*, to be stiff.]

torque [törk] *n* a necklace of metal rings interlaced, worn by the ancient Gauls, Germans, and Britons; the turning effect of a tangential force acting at a distance from the axis of rotation or twist (expressed in lbf ft or newton meters). [L *torquēs*, necklace, and *torquēre*, to twist.]

torr [tör] *n* the pressure which will support 1 millimeter of mercury—a unit used in expressing very low pressures. [E *Torr*icelli (1608–47), Italian mathematician.]

torrent [tor´ėnt] *n* a rushing stream (of water, lava, etc.); a violent and copious flow (eg of abuse, words, rain).—*adj* **torren´tial**, like a torrent. [L *torrēns, -entis*, burning, boiling, rushing, pr p of *torrēre*, to burn.]

torrid [tor´id] *adj* burning hot; dried with heat.—*ns* **torrid´ity, torr´idness**.—**torrid zone**, the broad belt round the earth between the tropics of Cancer and Capricorn, on either side of the equator. [L *torridus*—*torrēre*, to burn.]

torsion [tör´sh(ȯ)n] *n* act of twisting or turning a body; the force with which a thread or wire tends to return when twisted.—*n* **tor´sion bal´ance**, an instrument for measuring very small forces, such as those due to gravitation, magnetism, or electric charges, by a delicate horizontal bar or needle suspended by a very fine thread or wire. [L *torsiō, -ōnis*—*torquēre, tortum*, to twist.]

torso [tör´sō] *n* the trunk of a statue without head or limbs; the trunk of the body;—*pl* **tor´sos**.—Also **torse**. [It.]

tortilla [tor-tē´-yȧ] *n* a round thin maize pancake usually eaten hot

tortoise [tör´tůs, or -toiz] *n* an order (*Testudinata*) of reptiles, distinguished esp by the dorsal and ventral shields which protect the body—sometimes synonymous with *turtle*, sometimes restricted to land species.—*n* **tor´toiseshell** [tör´tȯ-shel], the shell of a species of turtle.—*adj* of the color of this shell, mottled in yellow, red, and black. [OFr *tortis*—L *tortus*, twisted.]

tortuous [tör´tū-us] *adj* twisting, winding; not straightforward; deceitful.—*adj* **tor´tuōse**, twisted; wreathed; winding.—*ns* **tor´tuousness, tortuos´ity**.—*adv* **tor´tuously**. [Fr,—L *tortuōsus*—*torquēre, tortum*, to twist.]

torture [tör´-chůr] *n* subjection to the rack or severe pain to extort a confession, or as a punishment; anguish of body or mind.—*vt* to put to torture; to pain excessively; to torment; to twist or wrench out of the natural shape, position, meaning, etc.—*n* **tor´turer**.—*adv* **tor´turingly**.—*adj* **tor´turous**, causing torture. [LL *tortūra*—*torquēre*, to twist.]

Tory [tō´ri, tö´ri] *n* a Conservative in English politics; often applied derogatorily to an extreme Conservative; an American upholding the cause of the British Crown during the American Revolution.—*n* **Tō´ryism**, the principles of the Tories. [Ir *toiridhe*, a pursuer; first applied to the 17th century Irish highway robbers; next, about 1680, to the most hot-headed supporters of James II, and, after the Revolution, to one of the two great political parties.]

toss [tos] *vt* to throw up, esp suddenly or violently; to throw back (one's head); to throw (eg oneself) restlessly about; to pass (from one to another) lightly; to toss up with (someone; eg *I'll toss you for the seat*).—*vi* to be tossed, to be agitated violently; to tumble about.—*n* act of throwing upward; a throwing up (of the head); a toss-up.—*ns* **toss´er; toss´pot**, (*arch*) a drunkard.—**toss off**, to drink off; to produce rapidly and easily (eg verses); **toss up**, to throw up a coin for deciding something according to which side lands uppermost.—*n* **toss´-up**, something that offers no clear basis for choice; an even chance or hazard.—**argue the toss**, to dispute a decision. [Celt, as W *tosio*, to jerk, *tos*, a quick jerk.]

tot[1] [tot] *n* anything little, esp a child; a small dram. [Cf ON *tottr*, a dwarf.]

tot[2] [tot] *vt* to add or sum up (usu. **tot up**).—*n* an addition of a long column. [Coll abbrev of **total**.]

total [tō´tȧl] *adj* whole, complete; unqualified, absolute.—*n* the sum; the entire amount.—*vt* to bring to a total, add up; to amount to.—*n* **tōt´alizāt´or**, a machine for registering bets and computing the odds and payoffs, as at a horse race.—*adj* **totalitā´rian**, belonging to a system of government in which one political group maintains complete control, esp under a dictator.—*n* **tōtal´ity**, the whole sum, quantity, or amount.—*adv* **tō´tally**.—**total abstinence**, abstinence from all alcoholic beverages; **total theater**, dramatic entertainment comprising in one performance all or most of the following—acting, dancing, gymnastics, singing, instrumental music, elaborate costumes and visual effects. [Fr,—LL *tōtālis*—L *tōtus*, whole.]

tote[1] [tōt] *vt* to add, total (*usu. with* **up**).

tote[2] [tōt] *vt* (*inf*) to carry or haul.

totem [tō´tem] *vt* (*inf*) a type of animal, plant, or object chosen as the badge of a primitive clan or group and treated with superstitious respect as the symbol of an intimate and mysterious relationship.—*adj* **totem´ic**.—*n* **tō´temism**, the use of totems as the foundation of a social system of alternate obligation and restriction.—*adj* **tō´temistic**.—**totem pole**, a pole, set up by the Indians in northwest N America, on which totems were carved and painted. [Amer Indian.]

totter [tot´ėr] *vi* to walk unsteadily; to be unsteady, to shake as if about to fall.—*n* **tott´erer**.—*adv* **tott´eringly**, in a tottering manner.—*adj* **tott´ery**, shaky. [For *tolter*—OE *tealtrian*, to totter, *tealt*, unsteady.]

toucan [tōō-kan´, or tōō´-] *n* a family (*Ramphastidae*) of South American birds, with an immense beak. [Fr,—Brazilian.]

touch [tuch] *vt* to be, or to come, in contact with; to strike, handle, gently or slightly; to reach; to approach in some good quality; to border on; to strike lightly; to give a light tint, aspect to; to stop at (a port); to handle; to treat of (a subject) in passing; to relate to; to concern; to affect slightly; to move or soften; (*slang*) to persuade to a gift or loan of money.—*vi* to be in contact; to make a passing call (at); to speak of (*usu. with* **on**).—*n* act of touching; any impression conveyed by contact; sense of feeling or contact; sympathy, understanding (eg *out of touch with*); a slight degree of a thing; distinctive handling of a musical instrument, skill or nicety in such; a special quality or skill; a subtle change or addition in a story, painting, etc.; a slight attack; (*slang*) the act of seeking or getting a gift or loan of money.—*adj* **touch´ing**, affecting, moving, pathetic.—*prep* concerning with regard to.—*adv* **touch´ingly**.—*adj* **touch´y**, irritable, sensitive, apt to take offense; very risky or precarious.—*adv* **touch´ily**.—*n* **touch´iness**.—*n* **touch and go**, a precarious situation or condition.—*adj* **touch´-and-go**.—*n* **touch´down**, the moment at which an aircraft or spacecraft lands; (*football*) a play, scoring six points, in which a player grounds the ball on or past the opponent's goal line.—*adj* **touched**, mentally disturbed; emotionally affected; moved.—*n* **touch´stone**, a compact silicious or other stone for testing gold or silver by the streak of the touchneedle; any test of genuineness.—*vti* **touch´-type**, to type without looking at the keys of the typewriter.—*n* **touch´wood**, soft combustible material, used as tinder.—**touch down**, of aircraft, to alight; **touch off**, to cause to explode, or burst forth or become active; to sketch, describe, in a few quick strokes but effectively; **touch up**, to improve by a series of small touches, to embellish; to sting somewhat as if by whip or sarcasm; **touch wood**, to put one's fingers on something made of wood as a supposed means of averting evil when one has spoken boastfully of one's good fortune.—**in touch with**, in direct relation with (by personal intercourse, correspondence, sympathy). [Fr *toucher*—OHG *zucchen*, to move, to draw.]

touché [tōō-shā´] *interj* said when touched by the opponent's weapon in fencing or to acknowledge a point in debate or a witty retort. [Fr.]

tough [tuf] *adj* not easily broken; stiff, viscous, tenacious; difficult; not easily cut or chewed; strong; brutal or rough; stubborn; able to endure hardship, physical or spiritual.—*n* a tough person; a thug.—*vti* **tough´en**, to make or become tough or tougher.—*adv* **tough´ly**.—*n* **tough´ness**. [OE *tōh*.]

toupee [tōō-pā´] *n* a little tuft or lock of hair; (*hist*) a wig with a topknot; a wig or section of hair to cover a bald spot, esp worn by men. [Fr *toupet*.]

tour [tōōr´] *n* a turn, period, etc. as of military duty; a long trip, as for sightseeing; any trip, as for inspection, giving performances, etc.—*vti* to go on a tour (through).—*ns* **tour´ing**, being on tour; cross-country skiing for pleasure; **tour´ism**, touring, traveling for pleasure; business of catering for tourists; the encouragement of touring. **tour´ist**, one who makes a tour, a sightseeing traveler.—Also *adj* **tourist class**, economy accommodation (as on a ship or airplane). [Fr,—L *tornus*, a turn.]

tour de force [tōō de fōrs] *n* an unusually skillful or ingenious performance or creation, sometimes a merely clever one. [Fr.]

tourmaline [tōōr´ma-lin] *n* a beautiful mineral, some varieties of which are used as gems. [Fr—Sinhalese *tòramalli*, carnelian.]

tournament [tûr´na-mėnt] *n* a military sport of the Middle Ages in which combatants engaged one another to display their courage and skill in arms; any contest in skill involving a number of competitors and a series of games.—*n* **tour´ney** [tŏŏr´-, or tûr´-]. [OFr *tournoiement, tornoi—torner*—L *tornāre*, to turn.]

tournedos [tōōr-nė-dō] *n* small beef fillet served with some kind of garnish. [Fr.]

tourniquet [tûr´ni-ket] *n* a device for compressing a blood vessel to stop bleeding, as a bandage, etc. twisted about a limb and released at intervals. [Fr,—L *tornāre*, to turn.]

tousle [tow´zl] *vt* to make untidy, disarrange, make tangled (esp hair). [ME *tusen*; cf dog's name, Towzer.]

tout [towt] *vti* (*inf*) to praise highly; (*inf*) to sell betting tips on (race horses).—*n* (*inf*) one who does so. [OE *tōtian*, to look out.]

tow[1] [tō] *n* the coarse part of flax or hemp.—*adj* **towheaded**, having flaxen or tousled hair. [OE *tow*, spinning; ON *to*, a tuft or wool for spinning.]

tow[2] [tō] *vt* to pull (a vessel) through the water with a rope; to pull along with a rope.—*n* a rope for towing with; the act of towing; two vessels or vehicles joined for towing.—*ns* **tow´age**, act of towing; money for towing; **tow´boat**, a boat that is towed, or one used for towing others; **tow´line**, a line used in towing.—**have, take, in tow**, have, take, under one's guidance or protection; to be accompanied by. [OE *togian*, to pull.]

toward [tōrd or tò-wård] *prep* in the direction of; facing; along a likely course to; concerning; just before; for.—Also **towards**. [OE *tōweard*, adj—*tō*, to, *ward*, signifying direction.]

towel [tow´ėl] *n* a cloth for wiping the skin after it is washed, and for other purposes.—*n* **tow´eling**, cloth for towels; a rubbing with a towel.—**throw** (or **toss**) **in the towel**, to admit defeat. [Fr *touaille*—OHG *twahilla*—*twahan*, to wash.]

tower [tow´ėr] *n* a lofty building, standing alone or forming part of another; a fortress.—*vi* to rise into the air, to be lofty; overtop the surrounding things or people (*with* **over**).—*adjs* **tow´ered**, having towers; **tow´ering**, very high. [OFr *tur*—L *turris*, a tower.]

town [town] *n* a place larger than a village; a city; the inhabitants of a town; a township; the business center of a city; the people of a town.—*ns* **town´clerk**, an official who keeps the records of a town; **town´ crier**, formerly one who cried public proclamations in a town; **town´ hall**, a public hall for the official business of a town; **town house**, a two-story dwelling, a unit in a complex of such buildings.—*n pl* **towns´folk**, the folk or people of a town.—*ns* **town´ship**, a division of a county, constituting a unit of local government; in the US land survey, a unit generally 6 miles square; **towns´man**, an inhabitant, or fellow-inhabitant, of a town.—*n pl* **towns´people**, townsfolk.—**go to town**, (*slang*) to act fast and efficiently; **on the town**, (*inf*) out for a good time. [OE *tūn*, an enclosure, town.]

toxicology [tok-si-kol´o-ji] *n* the science of poisons.—*n* **toxē´mia**, a type of blood poisoning, a condition caused by the absorption into the tissues and blood of toxins formed by microorganisms.—*adjs* **tox´ic**, pertaining to poisons, toxicological; caused by acting as, or affected by, a poison; **toxicolog´ical**, pertaining to toxicology.—*ns* **toxicol´ogist**, one versed in toxicology; **tox´in**, a poison produced by microorganisms and causing certain diseases; any poison secreted by plants or animals. [Gr *toxikon*, arrow-poison (*toxikos*, for the bow—*toxon*, a bow), and *logica* (*legein*, to say).]

toy [toi] *n* a child's plaything; a trifle; a thing only for amusement; an occupation of no importance; (*obs*) amorous sport.—*vi* to trifle; to dally amorously.—*n* **toy dog**, a very small pet dog. [Du *tuig*, tools.]

trace[1] [trās] *n* a mark etc. left by a person, animal or thing; a barely perceptible footprint; a small quantity.—*vt* to follow by tracks; to discover the whereabouts of; to follow with exactness; to sketch; to copy (a map or drawing) by the following lines on transparent paper.—*adj* **trace´able**, that may be traced.—*adv* **trace´ably**.—*ns* **trace element**, a chemical element, as copper, zinc, etc. essential in nutrition, but only in minute amounts; **trā´cer**, a person engaged (esp in the transportation services) in tracing missing articles; (*med*) an element having a peculiarity (as radioactivity) whereby it can be traced through biological processes; **trā´cery**, ornamentation traced in flowing outline; the beautiful forms in stone with which the arches of Gothic windows are filled for the support of the glass; **tra´cing**, a copy made by tracing. [Fr,—L *tractus*, pt p of *trahĕre*, to draw.]

trace[2] [trās] *n* either of two straps, etc. connecting a draft animal's harness to the vehicle.—**kick over the traces**, to throw off restraint. [OFr *trays, trais*, same as *traits*, pl of *trait*; cf **trait**.]

trachea [trā´ke-a] *n* the windpipe;—*pl* **trachē´ae** [-ē´ē].—*adj* **trā´chēal**, pertaining to the trachea.—*ns* **tracheo´stomy**, surgical formation of an opening into the trachea; **trāchēot´omy**, cutting into the trachea to aid breathing in an emergency. [L *trāchia*—Gr *trācheia* (*artēriā*), rough (artery; because formed of rings of gristle).]

track [trak] *vt* to follow by marks or footsteps; to find by so doing; to tread (a path, etc.); to follow the movement of (satellite, etc.) by radar, etc. and record its position.—*n* a mark left; footprint; a beaten path; course laid out for races; sports performed on a track, as running, hurdling, etc.; those sports along with other contests in jumping, throwing, etc,; a parallel line of rails; the endless band on which the wheels of a caterpillar tractor or tank move; the groove cut in a phonograph record by the recording instrument; sound-track; one of several items recorded on a phonograph record.—*adj* **track´less**, without a path; untrodden; without tracks.—*n* **track´suit**, a type of garment worn by athletes before and after eg a race or when training.—**make tracks for**, to go off towards, esp hastily; **the beaten track**, frequented roads; the normal conventional routine.—**track-and-field**, denoting various competitive athletic events (as running, jumping, and weight throwing) performed on a running track and on the adjacent field. [Fr *trac*—Du *trek*, draught, *trekken*, to draw.]

tract [trakt] *n* a region, area; a part of a bodily system or organ; (*arch*) a period of time; a short treatise, esp on a religious subject.—*adj* **trac´table**, easily worked or managed; easily taught; docile.—*ns* **trac´tableness, tractabil´ity**, quality or state of being tractable; docility.—*ns* **trac´tion**, act of drawing or state of being drawn; (*med*) pulling on a muscle, organ, etc. by means eg of weights to correct an abnormal condition; **trac´tor**, a motor vehicle used for haulage or for working plows and other agricultural implements. [L *tractus*, pa p of *trahĕre*, to draw.]

Tractarian [trakt-ār´i-ȧn] *n* one of the writers of the famous *Tracts for the Times*, published at Oxford during the years 1833–41 to assert the authority and dignity of the Anglican Church.—*n* **Tractar´ianism**. [**tract**.]

trade [trād] *n* buying and selling; commerce; occupation, craft; men engaged in the same occupation.—*vi* to buy and sell; to traffic (with a person, for something); to carry goods (to a place); to deal (in); (*inf*) to be a customer (*at* a certain store).—*vt* to barter.—*ns* **trade´mark**, name or distinctive device warranting goods for sale as the production of any individual or firm; **trade´-off**, the giving up of one thing in return for another considered more desirable; **trā´der**, one who trades; a merchant vessel; **trade´ un´ion (trades´)**, an organized association of workmen of any trade or industry for the protection of their common interests; **trade´ un´ionism; trade´-un´ionist; trade´ wind**, a wind blowing steadily toward the equator at either side of it; **trading stamp**, a stamp which may be exchanged for articles given as a premium by some merchants.—**trade in**, to give in part payment (*n* **trade´-in**); **trade on**, to take advantage of, presume on unscrupulously. [ME a trodden path; akin to OE *tredan*, to tread.]

tradition [tra-dish´(ȯ)n] *n* the handing down in unwritten form of opinions or practices to posterity; a belief or practice thus handed down; a convention established by habitual practice.—*adjs* **tradi´tional, tradi´tionary**, delivered by tradition.—*adv* **tradi´tionally**.—*n* **tradi´tionist**, one who adheres to tradition. [L *trāditiō, -ōnis—trāns*, over, *dăre*, to give.]

traduce [tra-dūs´] *vt* to calumniate, to defame.—*n* **tradū´cer**. [L *trādūcĕre*, to lead along—*trāns*, across, *dūcĕre*, to lead.]

traffic [traf´ik] *n* trade; dealings (with someone); the movement or number of automobiles, pedestrians, etc. along a street, etc.; the business done by a transportation company.—*vi* to carry on traffic (in a commodity); to have dealings (with someone).—*pr p* **traff´icking**; *pt, pt p* **traff´icked**.—*n* **traff´icker; traff´ic light**, light of changing color to regulate traffic at street crossings; **traff´ic man´ager**, a supervisor of the traffic functions of a commercial or industrial organization; the director of a large telegraph office. [OFr *trafique*.]

tragedy [traj´e-di] *n* a species of drama in which the action and language are elevated, and the climax a catastrophe; one such drama; any mournful and dreadful event.—*ns* **tragē´dian**, a writer of tragedy; an actor in tragedy; **tragēdienne´**, an actress of tragic rôles.—*adjs* **trag´ic, -al**, pertaining to tragedy; sorrowful; calamitous.—*adv* **trag´ically**.—*n* **trag´icom´edy**, a dramatic piece in which grave and comic scenes are blended; a play in the manner of a tragedy but with a happy ending.—*adjs* **trag´i-com´ic, -al**.—*adv* **trag´i-com´ically**. [Lit 'goat-song'—L *tragoedia*—Gr *tragōidiā—tragos*, a he-goat, *aoidos, ōidos*, a singer—*aeidein, āidein*, to sing.]

trail [trāl] *vt* to draw along the ground; to have in one's, its, wake; to follow behind; to hunt by tracking.—*vi* to hang or drag loosely behind; to lag; to run or climb as a plant; to grow weaker or dimmer (*with* **off** *or* **away**).—*n* anything drawn out in length; something long left stretching in the wake of anything (eg *a trail of smoke*); a continuous track left by something drawn or moving over a surface; a track followed by a hunter; a beaten path in unsettled country.—*ns* **trail´er**, one who trails; a wagon, van, etc. designed to be pulled by an automobile, truck, etc.; such a vehicle designed to be lived in; **trailer park, trailer camp, trailer court**, an area usu. with piped water, electricity, etc. for trailers, esp mobile homes. [Ety dub; poss OFr *traillier*, to tow—L *tragula*, sledge.]

train [trān] *vt* to educate, to discipline; to tame for use, as animals; to cause to grow properly; to prepare men for athletic feats, or horses for racing; to aim, a gun, etc.—*vi* to undergo systematic exercise or preparation.—*n* that which is drawn along after something else; the part of a dress that trails behind the wearer; a retinue; any connected order; a sequence; a line of connected railroad cars pulled by a locomotive.—*ns* **train´band** (*hist*), band of citizens trained to bear arms in 17th or 18th century England or America; **train´bear´er**, one who holds up a train, as of a robe or gown on ceremonial occasions.—*adj* **trained**, disciplined by training; skilled.—*ns* **trainee´**, one who is being trained; **train´er**, one who prepares men for athletic feats, horses for a race, or the like; something (as a machine or vehicle) used in training; a person who treats the ailments and minor injuries of the members of an athletic team; **train´ing**, practical instruction in any profession, art, or handicraft; a course of systematic physical exercise in preparation for an athletic event; **training table**, a table where athletes under a training regimen eat meals planned to help their conditioning. [Fr *train, trainer*—L *trahĕre*, to draw.]

trait [trāt] *n* a feature, lineament; a distinguishing feature of character or mind; a touch (of a quality). [Fr,—L *tractus—trahĕre*, to draw.]

traitor [trā´tȯr] *n* one who, being trusted, betrays his country, friends, etc.; one guilty of treason;—*fem* **trait´ress**.—*adj* **trait´orous**, like a traitor, perfidious, treasonable.—*adj* **trait´orously**. [Fr *traître*—L *trāditor—trādĕre*, to give up.]

trajectory [tra-jek´tȯ-ri] *n* the curve described by a body (as a planet or a projectile) under the action of given forces. [From L *trājicĕre, -jectum—trāns*, across, *jacĕre*, to throw.]

tram [tram] *n* an open railway car used in mines; (*Brit*) a streetcar.—*vt* to haul in a tram or over a tramway.—*n* **tramway**, a way for trams. [Dial Eng *tram*, a beam, a coal wagon, is prob cog with Swed dial *tromm*, a log.]

trammel [tram´l] *n* a net used in fowling and fishing; shackles for making a horse amble; anything that hampers movement.—*vt* to shackle, hamper;—*pr p* **tramm´eling**; *pt, pt p* **tramm´eled**. [OFr *tramail*, a net—Low L *tramacula*—L *tres*, three, *macula*, a mesh.]

tramp [tramp] *vt* to travel over on foot; to tread on heavily.—*vi* to walk, to go on foot; to wander about as a vagrant; to tread heavily.—*n* a journey on foot; a heavy tread; a vagrant; a freight ship that picks up cargo wherever it may be. [Ger *trampen*.]

trample [tramp´l] *vt* to tread under foot; to treat arrogantly or unfeelingly.—*vi* to tread in contempt (on, over); to tread forcibly and rapidly.—*n* **tramp´ler**. [A freq of **tramp**.]

trampoline [tram´pō-lēn] *n* a sheet of strong canvas stretched tightly on a frame, used in acrobatic tumbling. [It *trampolino*, springboard.]

trance [trans] *n* a state of unconsciousness, as under hypnosis, in which some of the powers of the waking body may be retained; complete abstraction from one's surroundings, the unconscious state into which spiritualistic mediums relapse; a daze; stupor. [Fr *transe*—L *transitum—transīre*, to go across, in Late L to die.]

tranquil [trang´kwil] *adj* quiet, serene, peaceful.—*vt* **tran´quillize**, to make tranquil.—*ns* **tran´quillizer**, a sedative drug; **tranquill´ity, tran´quilness**, state of being tranquil.—*adv* **tran´quilly**. [Fr,—L *tranquillus*.]

trans- [tranz-, trans-] prefix meaning across, through, on the other side of—eg *adj* **trans-Andean**, across, or beyond, the Andes. [L.]

transact [trans-akt´, tranz-akt´] *vt* to carry through, perform.—*vi* to carry through a piece of business (with someone).—*ns* **transac´tion**, act of transacting; management of any affair; a mutual arrangement, esp a business deal; (*pl*) a record of the proceedings of a society.—**transac´tional analysis**, a form of popular psychotherapy dealing with hypothetical states of the ego. [L *transactum—trāns*, through, *agĕre*, carry on.]

transalpine [trans-al´pīn] *adj* north of the Alps (considered from the point of view of Rome). [L *trānsalpīnus—trāns*, beyond, *Alpīnus*, pertaining to the Alps.]

transatlantic [trans-at-lan´tik] *adj* crossing the Atlantic; beyond, or across, the Atlantic Ocean. [L *trāns*, across, and **Atlantic**.]

transceiver [tran-sēv´ėr] *n* a radio *trans*mitter and *receiver* in a single housing.

transcend [tran-send´] *vt* to rise above, to surpass; to be outside the range of.—*adj* **transcen´dent**, supreme in excellence; surpassing others; beyond human knowledge.—*adv* **transcen´dently**.—*ns* **transcen´dence, transcen´dency**.—*adj* **transcenden´tal**, concerned with what is independent of experience, intuitive; supernatural.—*ns* **transcenden´talism**, the investigation of what, in human knowledge, is known by reasoning alone, independent of experience; that which is vague and illusive in philosophy; **transcenden´talist**.—*adv* **transcenden´tally**. [L *trāns*, beyond, *scandĕre*, to climb.]

transcribe [tran´skrīb´] *vt* to write over from one book into another, to copy; to write, type (shorthand notes) in full in ordinary letters; to make an arrangement of (a musical composition); to record for future broadcasting or the like; to broadcast a transcription of.—*ns* **transcrib´er; trans´cript**, that which is transcribed, a copy; an official copy of proceedings, etc.; **transcrip´tion**, the act of copying; a transcript; an arrangement of a piece of music for some other instrument or voice; a recording made for radio or television broadcasting. [L *transcrībĕre, -scriptum—trāns*, over, *scrībĕre*, to write.]

transducer [trans-dū´sėr] *n* a device that transforms power from one system to another in the same or in different form. [L *transdūcĕre, -ductum*, to lead across.]

transept [tran´sept] *n* one of the wings or cross-aisles of a church, at right angles to the nave. [L *trāns*, across, *saeptum*, an enclosure.]

transfer [trans-fûr´] *vt* to carry, convey, to another place; to give, hand over, to another person, esp legally; to convey (eg a picture) to another surface.—*vi* to change to another school, etc. or to another bus, etc.;—*pr p* **transferr´ing**; *pt, pt p* **transferred´**.—*n* **trans´fer**, the act of transferring; the conveyance of anything from one person or place to another; that which is transferred; a ticket entitling the bearer to change to another bus, etc.—*adj* **trans´ferable** [or -fer´-], that may be transferred from one place or person to another.—*ns* **transferabil´ity; transferēē**, the person to whom a thing is transferred; **trans´ference**, the act of conveying from one person or place to another; **transfer´or, -ferr´er**. [L *trāns*, across, *fĕrre*, to carry.]

transfiguration [trans-fig-ūr-ā´sh(ȯ)n] *n* a change of form or appearance; glorifying; idealization.—*vt* **transfig´ure** [-fig´ėr], to change the form of; to change the appearance of; to glorify.—**the Transfiguration**, the supernatural change in the appearance of Christ, described in the book of Mathew; a festival on August 6 in commemoration of it. [L *trāns*, across, and **figure**.]

transfix [trans-fiks´] *vt* to pierce through; to paralyze with emotion. [L *trāns*, through.]

transform [trans-fōrm´] *vt* to change the shape, appearance, character, or disposition of; to change the form of a mathematical expression in accordance with a rule.—*vi* to be changed in form or substance.—*adj* **transform´able**.—*ns* **transformā´tion**, change of form or substance; **transform´er**, a device for converting electrical energy received at one voltage to electrical energy sent out at a different voltage. [L *trāns*, across, + **form**.]

transfuse [trans-fūz´] *vt* to pour out into another vessel; to transfer blood from one to another.—*n* **transfū´sion**, the act of transfusing, esp blood from one living being into another. [L *trāns*, over, *fundĕre, fūsum*, to pour.]

transgress [trans-gres´] *vt* to pass beyond (a boundary, limit); to break (eg a law, commandment).—Also *vi*.—*ns* **transgress´ion**, the act of transgressing; violation of a law or command; fault; sin; **transgress´or**, one who transgresses; one who violates a law or command; a sinner. [L *trāns*, across, *gradī, gressus*, to step.]

tranship *See* **transship**.

transient [tran´shėnt] etc., *adj* passing, not lasting; of short duration, momentary.—*n* a transient person; a transient current or voltage.—*adv* **tran´siently**.—*n* **transience** [tran´shėns]. [L *transiēns, -entis*, pr p of *transīre—trāns*, across, *īre, itum*, to go.]

transistor [trans-sis´tȯr] *n* piece of semiconductor material so treated with impurities that a small current flowing from one electrode to another causes a large change in current between one of those electrodes and a third one, thus amplifying the current. Used frequently to replace thermionic valves.—*vt* **transis´torize**, to fit with a transistor.—**transistor (radio)**, small portable radio. [*trans*fer and res*istor*.]

transit [tran´zit or -sit] *n* a passing over; act or duration of conveyance; (*astron*) the passage of a heavenly body over the meridian of a place; the passage of a planet over the sun's disk; a theodolite with the telescope mounted so that it can be transited.—*ns* **trans´it-dū´ty**, a duty chargeable on goods passing through a country; **transi´tion**, passage from one place or state to another; change; (*mus*) a change of key.—*adjs* **transi´tional**, characterized by or denoting transition; **trans´itive**, passing over; having the power of passing; (*gram*) denoting a verb that has a direct object.—*adv* **trans´itively**,—*n* **trans´itiveness**.—*adj* **trans´itory**, going or passing away; lasting for a short time.—*adv* **trans´itorily**.—*ns* **trans´itoriness**. [L, 3d sing pres indic of *transire*, to cross over—*trāns*, across, *īre*, to go.]

translate [trans-lāt´] *vt* to remove to another place or office; to convey to heaven, esp without death; to render into another language; to express (an idea) in a different artistic medium from that in which it was originally expressed; to explain, interpret (eg a gesture, a remark).—*ns* **translā´tion**, the act of translating; removal to another place; the rendering into another language; a version; **translā´tor**. [OFr *translater*—L *trāns*, over, *ferre, lātum*, to carry.]

transliterate [trans-lit´e-rāt] *vt* to express the words of one language in the alphabetic characters of another.—*ns* **transliterā´tion; translit´erātor**. [L *trāns*, across, *litera, littera*, a letter.]

translucent [trans-lū´sėnt] *adj* allowing light to pass, but not transparent; clear.—*ns* **translū´cence, translū´cency**.—*adv* **translū´cently**. [L *translūcēns, -entis*—*trāns*, across, *lūcēre*, to shine—*lux, lūcis*, light.]

transmarine [trans-ma-rēn´] *adj* across or beyond the sea. [L *trans*, across, and **marine**.]

transmigrate [trans´mī´grāt] *vi* to migrate across, esp to another country; (of a soul) to pass into another body.—*ns* **transmigrā´tion**, the act of removing to another country; the passage of the soul after death into another body; **transmigrātor**.—*adj* **transmi´grātory**, passing to another place, body or state. [L *trāns*, across, + **migrate**.]

transmit [trans-mit´] *vt* to pass on to another person or place; to cause (eg heat, electricity, news) to pass through; to convey (force, movement, etc.); to send out (radio or television signals);—*pr p* **transmitt´ing**; *pt, pt p* **transmitt´ed**.—*adj* **transmiss´ible**, that may be transmitted from one to another, or through any body or substance.—*ns* **transmissibil´ity; transmiss´ion, transmitt´al**, act of transmitting; the sending from one place or person to another; passage through; **transmitt´er**, one who transmits; an apparatus for converting sound waves into electrical waves and thus transmitting a message or signal; (*radio*) a set or station sending out radio waves. [L *trāns*, across, *mittĕre, missum*, to send.]

transmute [trans-mūt´] *vt* to change to another form or substance.—*adj* **transmū´table**, that may be transmuted.—*ns* **transmū´tableness, transmūtabil´ity**.—*adv* **transmū´tably**.—*n* **transmūtā´tion**, a changing into a different form, nature, or substance; (*chem*) the conversion of one element into another, either spontaneously or artificially. [L *trāns*, over, *mūtāre, -ātum*, to change.]

transoceanic [trans-, tranz-ō-shē-an´ik] *adj* crossing the ocean; lying or dwelling beyond the ocean. [L *trāns*, across, + **ocean**.]

transom [tran´sȯm] *n* a horizontal beam or lintel across a window or the top of a door; a small window just above a door or window. [App L *transtrum*, a cross-beam.]

transpacific [trans´pȧ-sif´ik] *adj* crossing the Pacific; on the other side of the Pacific.

transparency [trans-par´en-si] *n* quality of being transparent; that which is transparent; a picture on semi-transparent material seen by means of light shining through.—*adj* **transpar´ent**, that may be distinctly and easily seen through; clear.—*adv* **transpar´ently**.—*n* **transpar´entness**. [L *trāns*, through, *pārēre*, to appear.]

transpierce [trans-pērs´] *vt* to breathe out or pass through the pores of the skin.—*vi* to exhale; (*bot*) to exhale watery vapor through the stomata; to become public, to come to light; to occur.—*n* **transpirā´tion**, act or process of transpiring; an exhalation through pores or stomata. [L *trāns*, through, *spīrāre*, to breathe.]

transplant [trans-plänt´] *vt* to remove and plant in another place; to remove and resettle; to remove (skin, a part, an organ) from its normal place in an individual and graft it into another position in the same or another individual.—*ns* **trans´plant**, a part, etc., so grafted; **transplantā´tion**. [L *trāns*, across, and **plant**.]

transponder [trans-pon´dėr] *n* a radio or radar device which, on receiving a signal, transmits a signal of its own. [*trans*mitter res*ponder*.]

transport [trans-pört´] *vt* to carry from one place to another; to banish oversea, esp to a penal colony; (of strong emotion) to carry (one) away.—*n* **trans´port**, carriage from one place to another; the conveyance of troops and their necessaries by sea or land; a ship, truck, etc., for this purpose; the system organized for transporting goods or passengers; ecstasy.—*adj* **transport´able**, that may be carried across.—*n* **transportā´tion**, removal; banishment of convicts beyond seas; means of transport. [L *trāns*, across, *portāre*, to carry.]

transpose [tranz-poz´] *vt* to put each in the place of the other; (*mus*) to change the key of.—*ns* **transpō´sal**, a change of place or order; **transposi´tion**, act of putting one thing in place of another; state of being transposed; a change of the order of words; (*mus*) a change of key. [Fr,—L *transpōnĕre*—*trāns*, across, *pōnĕre, positum*, to place.]

transship [tran´ship] *vt* to convey from one ship or conveyance to another. [L *trans*, across + **ship**.]

transubstantiation [tran-sub-stan-shi-ā´sh(ȯ)n] *n* a change into another substance; (*RC*) the conversion, in the consecration of the elements of the Eucharist, of the whole substance of the bread and wine into Christ's body and blood, only the appearances of bread and wine remaining. [L *trāns*, across, *substantia*, a substance.]

transuranic or **transuranium** [tranz-ū-ran´ik, tranz-ū-rā´niùm] an element (as neptunium, plutonium) of atomic number greater than uranium (92), the last of the series of elements occurring naturally. [*trans-*, beyond, + **uranium**.]

transverse [tranz-vûrs´] *adj* turned or lying, or acting, crosswise.—*vt* to cross; to thwart; to reverse; to transform.—*n* **transver´sal**, a line drawn across several others so as to cut them all.—*adv* **transverse´ly**, in a transverse or cross direction. [L *trāns*, across, *vertĕre, versum*, to turn.]

transvest [tranz-vest´] *vti* to dress oneself in the clothes of another, esp of the opposite sex.—*n* and *adj* **transvestite** [-vest´īt], one given to the practice of this. [L *trāns*, across, *vestīre, vestītum*, to dress.]

trap[1] [trap] *n* an instrument for snaring animals; an ambush; a trick to catch someone out; a bend in a pipe so arranged as to be always full of water, in order to imprison air within the pipe; a trapdoor; a carriage, a gig; (*pl*) percussion devices, as in a band.—*vt* to catch in a trap;—*pr p* **trapp´ing**; *pt, pt p* **trapped**.—*ns* **trap´door**, a hinged or sliding door in a roof, ceiling, or floor; **trapp´er**, one who traps animals for their fur, etc. [OE *træppe*; OHG *trapa*, a snare (whence Fr *trappe*, by which the Eng word has been modified).]

trap[2] [trap] *n* dark-colored igneous rock, used in road making. [Swed *trapp*—*trappa*, a stair.]

trap[3] [trap] *vt* to drape or adorn with trappings;—*pr p* **trapp´ing**; *pt, pt p* **trapped**.—*ns pl* **traps**, personal luggage; **trapp´ings**, colorful clothes; ornaments, esp those put on horses. [Fr *drap*—LL *drappus*, cloth.]

trapezium [tra-pē´zi-um] *n* a quadrilateral with no sides parallel.—*pl* **-ziums, trapē´zia**.—*n* **trapēze´**, a gymnastic apparatus consisting of a horizontal bar suspended by two parallel ropes.—*n* **trapē´zoid**, a quadrilateral with two sides parallel.—*adj* **trapezoid´al**, having the form of a trapezoid. [Gr *trapezion*, dim of *trapeza*, a table—*tetra*, four, *pous*, gen *podos*, a foot.]

Trappist [trap´ist] *n* a member of a monastic body, a branch of the Cistercians, noted for the extreme austerity of the rule—so named from the abbey of La *Trappe* in France.]

trash [trash] *vt* to vandalize, to destroy; to attack, assault.—*n* refuse, matter unfit for food; rubbish.—*adj* **trash´y**, like trash, worthless.—*n* **trash´iness**. [Prob Scand; ON *tros*, fallen twigs.]

trass [tras] *n* a volcanic earth used to give additional strength to lime mortars and plasters. [Du *tras*.]

trauma [trö´ma] *n* bodily condition arising from physical injury; disturbing experience that may be the origin of a neurosis.—*adj* **traumat´ic**, pertaining to, or caused by, a physical injury or emotional shock (often used loosely). [Gr, a wound.]

travail [trav´āl] *n* excessive labor, toil; labor in childbirth.—*vi* to labor; to suffer the pains of childbirth. [OFr *travailler*.]

trave [trāv] *n* a traverse beam. [OFr *traf, tref*—L *trabs*, a beam.]

travel [trav´ėl] *vi* to walk; to journey; to move; to offer (a commodity) for sale in various places (with *in*).—*vt* to journey along, through;—*pr p* **trav´eling**; *pt, pt p* **trav´eled**.—*n* act of passing from place to place; journey; (*often pl*) distant journeys in foreign lands; written account of such journeys.—*adj* **trav´eled**, experienced in traveling.—*ns* **trav´eler**, one who travels; a wayfarer; one who travels for a mercantile house; a ring that slides along a rope or spar; **travelogue, travelog** [trav´ė-log], a talk, lecture, or article about travels, esp one in the form of a motion picture with commentary.—**travel agency**, an agency providing information, brochures, tickets, etc. relating to travel; **traveler's check**, a draft purchased from a bank, etc. signed at the time of purchase and signed again at the time of cashing. [A form of **travail**.]

traverse [trav´ėrs] *adj* lying across; denoting drapes drawn by pulling a cord across.—*n* anything laid or built across; a work for protection from the fire of an enemy; sideways course in rock climbing, skiing, etc.; the place where this is done; a journey over or across (usu. a mountain).—*vt* to cross; to pass over, across, or through; to survey.—*vi* to climb at an angle; to ski across; to survey by using traverses.—*adv* athwart, crosswise.—*adj* **trav´ersable**, that may be traversed.—*n* **trav´erser**. [L *trāns, vertĕre, versum*, to turn.]

travesty [trav´es-ti] *n* a kind of burlesque in which the original characters are preserved, the situations parodied; any grotesque or misrepresentative imitation.—*vt* to turn into burlesque; to imitate badly or grotesquely. [Fr *travestir*, to disguise—L *trāns*, over, *vestīre*, to clothe.]

trawl [tröl] *vi* to fish (for sole, etc., which frequent the bottom of the sea) by dragging a trawl along.—*vt* to catch with a trawl.—*n* a large conical net drawn along the sea bottom.—*n* **traw´ler**, one who trawls; a vessel used in trawling. [Cf *trail*, and MDu *traghel*, drag-net.]

tray [trā] *n* a flat board, or sheet of metal, etc., surrounded by a rim, used for carrying or containing sundry articles; a salver. [OE *trēg*.]

treachery [trech´ėr-i] *n* faithlessness, betrayal of trust.—*adj* **treach´erous**, faithless; liable to deceive, betray confidence (eg of friend, memory, ice, bog).—*adv* **treach´erously**.—*n* **treach´erousness**. [OFr *tricherie*—*tricher*. **Trick** is a doublet.]

treacle [trē´kl] *n* formerly, a medicinal compound used against poison; (*Brit*) the dark, viscous liquid that drains from sugar at various stages in the process of manufacture.—*adj* **trea´cly**, composed of, or like, treacle. [OFr *triacle*—L *thēriacum*—Gr *thēriaka* (*pharmaka*), antidotes against the bites of wild beasts—*thērion*, a wild beast.]

tread [tred] *vi* to set the foot down; to walk or go; to copulate, as fowls.—*vt* to walk on; to press with the foot; to trample (under foot) in contempt; to step in dancing (eg *to tread a measure*);—*pr p* **trod** or **trodd´en**.—*n* pressure with the foot; a step, way of stepping; the part of a shoe, wheel, or tire that touches the ground.—*ns* **tread´er; tread´le**, the part of any machine which the foot moves; **tread´mill**, a mill in which a rotary motion is produced by the weight of a person or persons treading or stepping from one to another of the steps of a cylindrical wheel, formerly used as an instrument of prison discipline; any monotonous routine.—**tread on one's toes**, to give offense (as by encroaching); **tread water**, to maintain upright position in deep water. [OE *tredan*.]

treason [trē´zn] *n* betraying of the government or an attempt to overthrow it; disloyalty.—*adj* **trea´sonable**, pertaining to, consisting of, or involving treason.—*adv* **trea´sonably**.—**high treason**, treason against the sovereign or the state, the highest civil offense. [OFr *traïson* (Fr *trahison*)—*trahir*—L *trādĕre*, to betray.]

treasure [trezh´ůr] *n* wealth stored up; riches; anything much valued.—*vt* to hoard up; to value greatly.—*ns* **treas´urer**, one who has the care of a treasure or treasury; one who has charge of collected funds; **treas´urership; treas´ury**, a place where treasure is deposited; **Treasury**, a department of a government which has charge of the finances; **treasury note**, a US government bond usu. with a maturity of one to seven years. [Fr *trésor*—L *thēsaurus*—Gr *thēsauros*.]

treasure trove [trezh´ůr-trōv] *n* treasure or money found in the earth, the owner unknown. [**treasure** + OFr *trové*, pt p of *trover*, to find.]

treat [trēt] *vt* to handle, use, deal with, act towards (in a specified manner—eg *to treat unkindly*); to apply remedies to, prescribe remedies for (a person for an ailment); to subject to the action of a chemical; to discourse on; to entertain, as with food or drink, etc., take one's turn at being host.—*vi* to negotiate; to entertain, act as host; to deal with (*with* **of**).—*n* an entertainment; turn at being host; a pleasure seldom indulged; an unusual cause of enjoyment.—*ns* **treat´ise** [-is], a written composition in which a subject is treated systematically, a formal essay; **treat´ment**, act, or manner, of treating; behavior to (anyone—*with* **of**); remedies and manner of applying them; **treat´y**, a formal agreement between states.—**Dutch treat**, a treat at which each is his own host and pays his own expenses. [OFr *traitier*—L *tractāre*, to manage—*trahĕre, tractum*, to draw.]

treble [treb´l] *adj* triple, threefold; (*mus*) denoting the treble; that plays or sings the treble.—*n* the highest of the four principal parts in singing, soprano; a shrill, high-pitched voice; a singer or instrument taking the soprano part.—*vt* to make three times as much.—*vi* to become threefold;—*pr p* **treb´led** [-ld].—*adv* **treb´ly**. [OFr,—L *triplus*.]

tree [trē] *n* a perennial plant having a single trunk, woody, branched, and of a large size; anything like a tree, esp a diagram of family descent.—*vt* to drive up a tree.—*adj* **tree´less**.—*ns* **tree´nail, tre´nail** [trē´nāl, tren´l], a long wooden pin or nail to fasten the planks of a ship to the timbers.—**at the top of the tree**, in the highest position in eg a profession; **up a tree**, in a predicament. [OE *trēo, trēow*.]

trefoil [trē´foil, tre´-] *n* any plant of the genus *Trifolium* (the clovers), whose leaves are divided into three leaflets; (*archit*) an ornament like trefoil. [L *trifolium*—*trēs*, three, *folium*, a leaf.]

trek [trek] *vi* to travel slowly or laboriously; (*inf*) to go on foot (to).—*n* a journey; a migration; a long or wearisome journey.—*n* **trekk´er**. [Du *trekken*, to draw.]

trellis [trel´is] *n* a structure of lattice work, for supporting plants, etc.—*adj* **trell´ised**, having a trellis, or formed as a trellis. [OFr *treillis*; origin obscure.]

tremble [trem´bl] *vi* to shake, shiver, as from fear, cold, or weakness; to be alarmed, fear greatly (to think, for a person, at something); to quiver, vibrate (eg of sound, leaves, one's fate).—*n* the act of trembling; a fit of trembling.—*n* **trem´bler**.—*adv* **trem´blingly**.—*adj* **trem´ūlous**, trembling, affected with fear; quivering.—*adv* **trem´ūlously**.—*n* **trem´ūlousness**. [OFr *trembler*—L *tremulus*, trembling—*tremĕre*, to shake.]

tremendous [trė-men´důs] *adj* such as astonishes or terrifies by its force or greatness; very large or great; (*inf*) wonderful, amazing.—*adv* **tremen´dously**, (*inf*) very. [L *tremendus*, fit to be trembled at—*tremĕre*, to tremble.]

tremolo [trem´o-lō] *n* (*mus*) a tremulous effect; the device in an organ by which this is produced. [It.]

tremor [trem´ȯr] *n* a quivering; a vibration; an involuntary shaking. [L,—*tremĕre*, to shake.]

trench [trench] *vt* to dig a ditch in; to dig deeply with the spade or plow; to cut a groove in.—*vi* to make a trench; to encroach (on).—*n* a long narrow cut in the earth; such an excavation made for military purposes.—*n* **tren´cher**.—**trench coat**, a lined waterproof overcoat, originally military; **trench fever**, a fever, spread by lice, to which soldiers serving in trenches are subject; **trench foot**, a painful foot disorder resembling frostbite. [OFr *trenchier* (Fr *trancher*), prob—L *truncāre*, to maim—*truncus*, maimed.]

trenchant [tren´chȧnt] *adj* sharp, cutting; incisive, vigorous, to the point.—*n* **tren´chancy**. [OFr, pr p of *trenchier*, to cut.]

trencher [tren´chėr] *n* a wooden plate for serving food.—*n* **tren´cher-man**, a hearty eater. [O.E. *trendan*.]

trend [trend] *vi* to tend, to run, to go in a particular direction (with eg *toward, away from, southward*); to show a drift or tendency (toward, etc.).—*n* tendency; a current style.—*n* **trend´sett´er**, one who helps to give a new direction to follow.—*adj* **trend´y**, (*inf*) in the forefront of fashion in any sphere. [OE *trendan*.]

trepan [tri-pan´] *n* (*surg*) an early form of the trephine.—*vt* to use a trephine on (the skull); to remove a disk or cylindrical core (as metal for testing). [Fr,—Low L *trepanum*—Gr *trypănon*—*trȳpaein*, to bore.]

trephine [trē-fīn´ or tre-fēn] *n* a surgical instrument for cutting out circular sections (as of bone or corneal tissue).—*vt* to operate on with the trephine. [Dim of **trepan**.]

trepidation [trep-i-dā´sh(ȯ)n] *n* a state of confused hurry or alarm; an involuntary trembling. [L *trepidāre, -ātum*, to hurry with alarm—*trepidus*, restless.]

trespass [tres´pȧs] *vi* to enter unlawfully upon another's land; to encroach upon another's rights; to make too great a claim (on, eg another's generosity); to injure or annoy another; to sin.—*n* act of trespassing; any injury to another's person or property; a sin.—*n* **tres´passer**. [OFr *trespasser*—L *trāns*, across, *passus*, a step.]

tress [tres] *n* a lock, braid, or ringlet of hair, esp a woman's or girl's; (*pl*) hair, usu. long.—*vt* to form into tresses, to braid.—*adj* **tressed**, having tresses. [Fr *tresse*, through Low L *tricia, trica*, from Gr *tricha*, threefold—*treis*, three.]

trestle [tres´l] *n* a movable support (eg for a platform).—Also **tress´el**. [OFr *trestel*; ety uncertain; perh through Low L—L *transtrum*, a beam.]

trews [trōōz] *n pl* trousers, esp of tartan cloth. [Ir *trius*, Gael *triubhas*.]

tri- [trī] *pfx* having, consisting of, three or three parts; every third. [Gr and L];—eg **tricycle, triad; triennial**.

triad [trī´ad] *n* a group or union of three; a group of three short aphorisms, a common Welsh literary form; (*mus*) the three fundamental notes of a consonance. [Gr *trias, -ados*—*treis*, three.]

trial [trī´ȧl] *n* the act of trying; the state of being tried; examination by a test; experimental use; judicial examination; an attempt; a preliminary race, game, etc.; suffering, hardship; a source of suffering or of annoyance.—**trial run**, any introductory test, rehearsal, etc.; any experiment.—**trial and error**, trying out several methods and discarding those which prove unsuccessful; **on trial**, undergoing proceedings in a court of law; on probation, as an experiment. [From **try**.]

triangle [trī´ang-gl] *n* (*math*) a plane figure with three angles and three sides; a musical instrument of percussion, formed of a steel rod bent in the shape of a triangle; an emotional situation in which three people (usu. man and wife and another man or another woman) are involved.—*adjs* **tri´angled, triang´ūlar**, having three angles.—*adv* **triang´ūlarly**.—*vt* **triang´ulāte**, to survey by means of a series of triangles.—*n* **triangūlā´tion**, act of triangulating; the series of triangles so used. [Fr,—L *triangulum*—*trēs*, three, *angulus*, an angle.]

Triassic [trī-as´ik] *n* the earliest period of the Mesozoic era or the corresponding system of rocks.—Also *adj*. [So called by the German geologists, from their threefold grouping of the system, from Gr *trias*, union of three.]

tribe [trīb] *n* a race or family descended from the same ancestor; an aggregate of families, forming a community usually under the government of a chief; a political division in ancient Rome; a number of things having certain common qualities; a set of people associated in some way; a natural group of plants or animals.—*adj* **trib´al**.—*n* **trib´alism**, condition of existing as a separate tribe; tribal feeling.—*adv* **trib´ally**.—*n* **tribes´man**. [L *tribus*, one of the three (later increased to as many as thirty-five) tribes of Rome.]

tribology [trib-ol´ȯ-ji] *n* a science and technology embracing all subjects involved when surfaces in contact move in relation to each other. [Gr *tribein*, to rub, *logos*, a discourse.]

tribrach [trī´brak] *n* (*poet*) a foot of three short syllables, eg. *rĕgĕre*. [L,—Gr *tribrachys*—*tri-*, root of *treis*, three, *brachys*, short.]

tribulation [trib-ū-lāsh(ȯ)n] *n* severe affliction, distress, trial, hardship. [L *trībulātiō, -ōnis*—*trībulāre, -ātum*, to afflict—*trībulum*, a sledge for rubbing out corn—*terĕre*, to rub.]

tribunal [trī-bū´nȧl] *n* a court of justice; something that decides or determines. [L.]

tribune[1] [trib´ūn] *n* in ancient Rome, a magistrate appointed to protect the rights of plebeians; a champion of the people. [L *tribūnus*—*tribus*, a tribe.]

tribune[2] [trib´ūn] *n* the raised platform from which speeches are delivered. [Fr,—It *tribuna*.]

tribute [trib´ūt] *n* a fixed amount paid at certain intervals by one nation to another for peace or protection; any forced payment; an expression of respect or gratitude.—*adj* **trib´ūtary**, paying tribute; subject; yielding supplies of anything, subsidiary; making additions; flowing into a larger one.—*n* one who pays tribute; a tributary river. [L *tribūtum—tribuěre*, to give, assign—*tribus*, a tribe.]

trice [trīs] *vt* (*naut*) to haul or lift up by means of a rope;—*pr p* **tric´ing**; *pt p* **triced**.—*n* a haul or tug (*obs*); hence a single effort; an instant. [Middle Low Ger *trissen*.]

trichina [tri-kī´na] *n* a parasitic worm (*Trichinella spiralis*) which in its mature state infests the intestinal canal, and in its larval state the muscular tissue of man and certain animals, esp the hog;—*pl* **trichī´nae** [-ē].—*n* **trichinō´sis**, the disease caused by the presence of trichinae in the body. [Gr *trichinos*, small like a hair—*thrix*, gen *trichos*, hair.]

trick[1] [trik] *vt* to dress, to decorate (*with* **out, up**). [Same as **trick** (2).]

trick[2] [trik] *n* any fraud or stratagem to deceive; an illusion (eg *a trick of the imagination*); a clever contrivance to puzzle, amuse, or annoy; skill, knack; a habit, mannerism; cards falling to a winner at one turn.—*adj* using fraud or clever contrivance to deceive (eg the eye—as in *trick photography*).—*vt* to deceive, to cheat.—*ns* **trick´er; trick´ery**, act or practice of playing fraudulent tricks; artifice, stratagem.—*adj* **trick´y**, given to trickery; requiring skill or dexterity, difficult to handle or do successfully.—*adv* **trick´ily**.—*n* **trick´iness**.—*adj* **trick´ish**, addicted to tricks; artful in making bargains; tricky, difficult.—*n* **trick´ster**, one given to trickery, a cheat. [OFr *trichier*, to beguile.]

trickle [trik´l] *vi* to flow gently or in a small stream; to drip; to come or go very gradually or in very small quantities.—*n* a trickling flow. [ME *triklen*, prob for *striklen*, freq of *striken*, to go.]

tricolor, tricolore [trī´kul-ȯr or trī´-] a flag of three colors, esp the flag of France; having three colors. [Fr *tricolore*—L *trēs*, three, *color*, color.]

tricycle [trī´si-kl] *n* a child's vehicle with three wheels. [Gr *tri-*, root of *treis*, three, *kyklos*, circle, wheel.]

trident [trī´dėnt] *n* the three-pronged spear or scepter of Neptune, god of the ocean; any three-pronged spear. [Fr,—L *trēs*, three, *dēns, dentis*, tooth.]

tridimensional [trī-di-men´shȯn-ȧl] *adj* having three dimensions—length, breadth, thickness. [L *tri-, trēs*, three + **dimension**.]

tried *see* **try**.

triennial [trī-en´yȧl] *adj* continuing three years; happening every third year.—*adv* **trienn´ially**. [L *triennis—trēs*, three, *annus*, a year.]

trier [trī´ėr] *n* one who tests by experiment; an implement used to obtain samples. [From **try**.]

trifle [trī´fl] *vi* to act, or to talk, lightly, without seriousness; to toy, play, dally (with).—*vt* to waste (time, etc.).—*n* anything of little value; a dessert of whipped cream or white of egg, sponge cake, wine, etc.—*n* **trī´fler**.—*adj* **trī´fling**, of small value or importance; acting or talking without seriousness.—*adv* **trī´flingly**. [OFr *trufle*, mockery, deception.]

trifocal [trī-fōk´ȧl] *adj* of a lens, giving separately near, intermediate, and far vision. [L *tri-*, three, and focal.]

trifoliate [trī-fō´li-āt] *adjs* having three leaflets. [L *trēs*, three, *folium*, leaf.]

triforium [trī-fō´ri-um] *n* an arcaded gallery above nave, choir, or transept arches of a church. [L *tri-, trēs*, three, *foris*, a door.]

triform [trī´fȯrm] *adj* having a triple form. [L *trifōrmis—trēs*, three, *fōrma*, form.]

trig [trig] *n* trigonometry. [Clipped form.]

trigger [trig´ėr] *n* a catch which when pulled looses the hammer of a gun in firing.—*vt* to initiate (an action).—*adj* **trigg´er-happy**, aggressively belligerent. [Du *trekker—trekken*, to pull.]

triglyph [trī´glif or tri´-] *n* three-grooved tablet repeated at equal distances along the frieze in Doric architecture. [L *trīglyphus*—Gr *triglyphos—treis*, three, *glyphein*, to carve.]

trigonometry [trig-o-nom´ė-tri] *n* the branch of mathematics which treats of the relations between the sides and angles of triangles—*adjs* **trigonomet´ric, -al**, pertaining to trigonometry; done by the rules of trigonometry.—*adv* **trignonomet´rically**.—**trigonometric function**, any of six ratios determining, and determined by, the size of an angle—each ratio expressing the relation between a pair of sides in a right-angled triangle (see **sine, cosine, tangent, cotangent, secant, cosecant**). [Gr *trigōnon*, a triangle, *metron*, a measure.]

trihedral [trī-hē´drȧl] *adj* having three faces. [Gr *treis*, three, *hedrā*, a seat.]

trilateral [trī-lat´ėr-ȧl] *adj* having three sides or parties. [L *trēs*, three, *latus, lateris*, side.]

trilinear [trī-lin´ė-ȧr] *adj* consisting of three lines. [L *trēs*, three, and **linear** (see **line**).]

trilingual [trī-ling´gwȧl] *adj* consisting of, or using, three tongues or languages. [L *trēs*, three, *lingua*, tongue.]

trill [tril] *vti* to utter with a tremulous vibration; to pronounce with a quick vibration of one speech organ against another.—*n* (*mus*) a shake; a sound suggestive of tongue against the teeth ridge; a letter (eg a trilled *r*) so made. [It *trillare*, to shake; imit.]

trillion [tril´yȯn] *n* in US, ten thousand raised to the third power, represented by a unit and 12 ciphers; in Great Britain, France, and Germany, a million raised to the third power, or multiplied twice by itself, represented by a unit and 18 ciphers.—*adj* **trill´ionth**. [Fr,—L *trēs*, three, LL *millio*, a million.]

trilobite [trī´lō-bīt] *n* any of a group (Trilobita) of fossil marine animals. [Gr *tri-*, three, and *lobos*, a lobe.]

trilogy [tril´o-ji] *n* the name given by the Greeks to a group of three tragedies, each complete in itself, yet mutually related as parts of a larger whole; any series of three related dramatic or literary works. [Gr *trilogiā—tri, tris*, thrice, *logos*, discourse.]

trim [trim] *adj* in good order, tidy, neat.—*vt* to make trim; to put in due order; to decorate; to clip; to arrange (sails, a ship in regard to disposition of cargo) for sailing; (*inf*) to beat, punish, defeat, cheat, etc.—*vi* to balance or fluctuate between parties;—*pr p* **trimm´ing**; *pt, pt p* **trimmed**.—*n* dress (eg *hunting trim*); state of a ship as to readiness for sailing; state, degree of readiness or fitness.—*adv* **trim´ly**.—*ns* **trimm´er**, one who trims; one who fluctuates between parties, a time-server; **trimm´ing**, that which trims; ornamental parts, esp of a garment, dish, etc.; (*pl*) fittings; **trim´ness**. [OE *trymian*, to strengthen, set in order—*trum*, firm.]

trimeter [trim´e-tėr] *n* a verse line consisting of three measures. [Gr *trimetros—metron*, measure.]

trinitrotoluene [trī-nī-trō-tol´ū-ēn] *n* a highly explosive agent, commonly known as TNT. [Named from its chemical structure.]

trinity [trin´i-ti] *n* a group of three; **Trinity**, the union of three in one Godhead; the persons of the Godhead.—*adj* **Trinitā´rian**, pertaining to the Trinity, or to the doctrine of the Trinity.—*n* one who holds the doctrine of the Trinity.—*ns* **Trinitā´rianism**, the tenets of Trinitarians; **Trin´ity Sun´day**, the Sunday next after Whitsunday, the Festival of the Holy Trinity. [L *trīnitās*, a triad—*trīnī*, three each.]

trinket [tring´kėt] *n* a small ornament for the person; anything of little value.

trinomial [trīnō´mi-ȧl] *n* a polynomial of three terms; a trinomial name. [L *trēs*, three, *nōmen*, name.]

trio [trē´o, trī´o] *n* a set of three; (*mus*) a composition for, or company of, three performers;—*pl* **tri´os**. [It.]

triode [trī´ōd] *n* an electron tube with an anode, a cathode, and a controlling grid. [Gr *hodos*, way.]

triolet [trī´ō-let, or trē´-] *n* a stanza of eight lines on two rhymes—viz, *a, b, a, a, a, b, a, b*; lines 1, 4, 7 are identical, and 8 is the same as 2. [Fr.]

trip [trip] *vi* to move with short, light steps; to stumble and fall; to err.—*vt* to cause (a person) to stumble by impeding his feet (*often with* **up**); to catch in a fault;—*pr p* **tripp´ing**; *pt, pt p* **tripped**.—*n* a light, short step; a catch by which an antagonist is thrown; a false step, a mistake; a short voyage or journey, an excursion; (*slang*) a hallucinatory experience under the influence of a drug.—*ns* **tripp´er**, one who makes a popular trip or excursion; **tripp´ing**, the act of tripping; a light kind of dance.—*adv* **tripp´ingly**, with a light, quick step; in a quick, gay manner. [OFr *treper, trip(p)er*; akin to OE *treppan*, to tread.]

tripartite [trī-pär´tīt] *adj* divided into three parts; having three corresponding parts; relating to, or binding, three parties (as *a tripartite agreement*). [L *ter*, thrice, *partītus*, pt p of *partīrī*, to divide—*pars*, a part.]

tripe [trīp] *n* (*pl*) entrails; parts of compound stomach of a ruminant, esp of sheep or horned cattle, prepared as food; (*inf*) rubbish, poor stuff. [Fr; ety uncertain.]

triple [trip´l] *adj* consisting of three united; three times repeated.—*vti* to treble.—*n* **trip´let**, three of a kind, or three united; three lines rhyming together; (*mus*) a group of three notes occupying the time of two, indicated by a slur and the figure 3; one of three children born at one birth.—*adjs* **trip´lex**, consisting of three parts; threefold; **trip´licate** [-ȧt], threefold; made thrice as much.—*n* a third copy or thing corresponding to two others of the same kind.—*vt* to make threefold.—*n* **triplicā´tion**, act of making threefold or adding three together.—*adv* **trip´ly**.—**triple time** (*mus*), time or rhythm of three beats, or three times three beats, in a bar.—**in triplicate**, in three identical copies. [Fr,—L *triplus, triplex*, threefold—*trēs*, three.]

tripod [trī´pod] *n* anything on three feet or legs, as a stool, etc. [Gr *tripous, -podos—tri-, treis*, three, *pous*, foot.]

tripoli [trip´o-li] *n* a mineral substance employed in polishing metals, marble, glass, etc. [Orig brought from *Tripoli* in Africa.]

triptych [trip´tik] *n* a set of tablets consisting of three leaves, each painted with a distinct but related subject, joined together by hinges, the smaller outside leaves folding over the center one; a set of three hinged writing tablets. [Gr *tri-*, thrice, *ptyx*, gen *ptychos*, a fold, a leaf.]

trireme [trī´rēm] *n* an ancient galley—esp a war galley—having three banks of oars. [Fr,—L *trirēmis—tri-, trēs*, three, *rēmus*, an oar.]

trisect [trī-sekt´] *vt* to cut or divide into three, usu. equal parts.—*n* **trisec´tion**, the division of anything, as an angle, into three (equal) parts. [L *tri-*, thrice, *secāre, sectum*, to cut.]

trisyllable [trī-, or tri-sil´ȧ-bl] *n* a word of three syllables.—*adjs* **trisyllab´ic**, pertaining to a trisyllable; consisting of three syllables.—*adv* **trisyllab´ically**. [Gr *treis*, three, *syllabē*.]

trite [trīt] *adj* worn by use; used till novelty and interest are lost, hackneyed (eg of a figure of speech, a remark).—*adv* **trite´ly**.—*n* **trite´ness**. [It *trito*—L *trītus*, rubbed, pt p of *terěre*, to rub.]

triticale [tri´ti-kāl] *n* a hybrid cereal grass, a cross between wheat and rye grown as a food. [LL *Triticum*, wheat, *secale*, rye.]

tritium [trit´i-um, trish´-] *n* a heavy isotope of hydrogen, radioactive, of mass number 3.—*n* **trīt´on**, the nucleus of tritium. [Gr *tritos*, third.]

triturate [trit´ū-rāt] *vt* to rub or grind to a fine powder.—*adj* **trit´urable**, that may be reduced to a fine powder by grinding.—*n* **triturā´tion**. [LL *trītūrāre, -ātum*—L *terĕre*, to rub.]

triumph [trī´umf] *n* in ancient Rome, a solemn procession in honor of a victorious general; victory; success; a great achievement; joy for success.—*vi* to celebrate a victory with pomp; to obtain victory or success; to rejoice for victory; to boast; to exult (over a rival).—*adjs* **trium´phal**, pertaining to triumph; used in celebrating victory or success; **trium´phant**, celebrating, or rejoicing for, a triumph, expressing joy for success; victorious.—*adv* **trium´phantly**. [L *triumphus*—Gr *thriambos*, a hymn to Bacchus.]

triumvir [trī-um´vėr] *n* one of three men in the same office or with the same authority;—*pl* **trium´virs, trium´virī**.—*n* **trium´virate**, an association of three men in office or government, or for any political ends. [L *trium-* (from *trēs*), three, *vir*, a man.]

triune [trī´ūn] *adj* being three in one. [Coined from L *tri-*, root of *trēs*, three, *ūnus*, one.]

trivet [triv´ėt] *n* a stool or the like supported on three feet; a movable iron frame for hooking to a grate for supporting kettles, etc. [OFr *trpied*—L *tripēs, tripedis*—*trēs*, three, *pēs*, a foot.]

trivia [tri´vi-à] *n pl* trifles, trivialities, unimportant details.—*adj* **tri´vial**, of little importance; trifling; commonplace; (of a name) popular, not scientific.—*n* **trivial´ity**, the state or quality of being trivial; that which is trivial, a trifle.—*adv* **triv´ially**.—*n* **triv´ialness**. [L *triviālis*, 'at the crossroads or in public streets'—*trivium*, a place where three ways meet—*trēs*, three, *via*, a way.]

trivium [tri´vi-ùm] *n* in medieval schools, the name given to the first three liberal arts—grammar, rhetoric, and logic—which combined with the *quadrivium* to make up a complete system of education. [L *tri-*, three, *via*, a way.]

trochee [trō´kē] *n* a metrical foot of two syllables, so called from its tripping or joyous character—in Latin verse, consisting of a long and a short, as *dūlcĕ*; in English verse, of an accented and unaccented syllable, as *laugh´ing wa´ter*.—*n* **trochā´ic**, a trochaic verse or measure.—*adj* **trochā´ic**, consisting of trochees. [Gr *trochaios (pous)*, running, tripping (foot)—*trochos*, a running—*trechein*, to run.]

trod [trod] *pt* of **tread**.

trodden [trod´n] *pt p* of **tread**.

troglodyte [trog´lō-dīt] *n* a cave dweller; a genus of anthropoid apes, a gorilla or a chimpanzee; a hermit. [Fr,—Gr *trōglodytēs*—*trōglē*, a cave, *dyein*, to enter.]

Trojan [trō´jàn] *adj* pertaining to ancient *Troy*.—*n* an inhabitant of ancient Troy.—**Trojan horse**, the gigantic wooden horse inside which the Greeks entered Troy; a person, organization, placed within a country, group, etc., with the purpose of destroying it.

troll[1] [trōl] *n* a supernatural being, sometimes a giant, sometimes a dwarf, dwelling in a cave, hill, etc. [ON *troll*.]

troll[2] [trōl] *vt* to sing the parts of in succession, as of a catch or round; to sing loudly and light-heartedly; to fish for in a certain way; to fish (water).—*vi* to move, stroll, ramble; to sing a catch; to fish.—*n* a moving round, repetition; a round song.—*ns* **troll´er; trolley** [trol´i], **troll´y**, an overhead current collector for trolley cars, having a small grooved wheel running under the contact wire; **troll´eybus** (or **car**), an electric bus (or streetcar) powered from an overhead wire by means of a trolley. [OFr *troller, trauler*, to stroll; OHG *trollen*, to run.]

trollop [trol´op] a prostitute. [From **troll** (2), in the sense of 'to run about'.]

trombone [trom-bōn´ or trom´bōn] *n* a deep-toned brass musical wind instrument of the trumpet kind, consisting of a tube whose length is varied with a U-shaped sliding section. [It; augmentative of *tromba*, a trumpet.]

troop [trōōp] *n* a crowd or collection of people; *(pl)* soldiers taken collectively; a subdivision of a cavalry regiment, a unit of Boy Scouts or Girl Scouts.—*vi* to collect in numbers; to go in a crowd.—*ns* **troop´er**, a cavalryman; a mounted policeman; *(inf)* a State policeman; **troop´-ship**, a vessel for conveying soldiers. [Fr *troupe*.]

trope [trōp] *n* a figurative use of a word or expression, a figure of speech. [Fr,—L *tropus*—Gr *tropos*—*trepein*, to turn.]

trophy [trō´fi] *n* (Gr *hist*) a memorial of a victory, consisting of a pile of arms erected on the field of battle; anything taken from an enemy and preserved as a memorial of victory; a possession that is evidence of achievement in any sphere. [Fr *trophée*—L *tropaeum*—Gr *tropaion*—*tropē*, a rout—*trepein*, to turn.]

tropic [trop´ik] *n* one of the two imaginary circles on the celestial sphere, 23° 28´ on each side of the celestial equator, where the sun turns, as it were, after reaching its greatest declination north or south; one of two imaginary circles on the terrestrial globe corresponding to these—the tropics of Cancer and Capricorn; *(pl)* the regions lying between these circles.—*adjs* **trop´ic, -al**, pertaining to the tropics; within or near the tropics; very hot; luxuriant.—*adv* **trop´ically**. [L *tropicus*—Gr *tropikos*, relating to a turning—*tropos*, a turning.]

tropism [trō´pizm] *n* (*bot* and *zool*) a reflex response to an external stimulus that involves movements of the whole body. [Gr *tropos*, a turning, and suffx *-ism*.]

troposphere [trop´ō-sfēr] *n* the lowest layer of the atmosphere, in which temperature falls as height increases. [Gr *tropos*, a turning, *sphaira*, a sphere.]

trot [trot] *vi* (of a horse) to go, lifting the feet quicker and higher than in walking, moving them in diagonal pairs; to walk or move fast, esp with small steps; to run.—*vt* to ride at a trot;—*pr p* **trott´ing**; *pt, pt p* **trott´ed**.—*n* the pace of a horse, etc., when trotting; *(inf)* a literal translation of a foreign text; *(pl) (inf)* diarrhea. [OFr *trotter, troter*.]

troth [troth or trōth] *n* faith, fidelity (*to plight one's troth*). [OE *trēowth*. Doublet **truth**.]

troubadour [trōō´ba-dōōr] *n* one of a class of poets and poet-musicians of chivalric love, who first appeared in Provence, and flourished from the 11th to the 13th century. [Fr,—Provençal *trobador*—*trobar* (Fr *trouver*), to find, compose.]

trouble [trub´l] *vt* to agitate; to disturb; to worry; to pain, afflict; to put to inconvenience.—*vi* to take pains (to).—*n* disturbance; uneasiness; affliction; that which disturbs or afflicts; the taking of pains; a person, event, etc. causing annoyance, distress, etc.; public disturbance.—*n* **troub´ler**.—*adj* **troub´lesome**, causing or giving trouble or inconvenience; vexatious; importunate.—*adv* **troub´lesomely**.—*n* **troub´lesomeness**.—*adj* **troub´lous**, full of trouble or disorder, agitated, tumultuous.—*n* **troub´leshooter**, one whose work is to locate and eliminate the source of trouble in any flow of work. [OFr *tourbler*—Low L *turbulāre*—L *turbāre*, to disturb—*turba*, a crowd.]

trough [trof, or trōf] *n* a long, hollow vessel for water or other liquid; a long tray; a long narrow channel; a hollow; an elongated area of low barometric pressure. [OE *trog*; Ger *trog*.]

trounce [trowns] *vt* to punish or beat severely; *(inf)* to defeat.

troupe [trōōp] *n* a company, esp of actors, dancers or acrobats. [Fr. See **troop**.]

trousers [trow´zėrs] *n pl* a two-legged garment worn on the lower limbs and trussed or fastened up at the waist by suspenders or belt.—*adjs* **trouser**, of, or designed for trousers; denoting a male dramatic part played by a woman; **trou´sered**, wearing trousers.—**wear the trousers**, of a wife, to be the dominant partner in marriage. [OFr *trousses*, breeches worn by pages; allied to **trews**.]

trousseau [trōō´sō] *n* a bride's outfit;—*pl* **-seaux** [-sōz]. [Fr, a dim of *trousse*, a bundle.]

trout [trowt] *n* a common name for certain fish of the salmon family (Salmonidae), genera *Salmo, Salvelinus* and *Cristivomer*, smaller than salmon and in most cases living practically exclusively in fresh water. [OE *truht*—L *tructa, tructus*—Gr *trōktēs*, a sea-fish with sharp teeth—*trōgein*, to gnaw.]

trouvère [trōō-ver´] *n* one of a school of medieval French poets (11th–14th century) whose works were chiefly narrative. [Same root as **troubadour**.]

trove *See* **treasure trove**.

trover [trō´vėr] *n* (*law*) an action to recover goods wrongfully detained. [OFr *trover*, to find.]

trowel [trow´el] *n* a tool used in spreading mortar, paint, etc., and in gardening. [OFr *truelle*—L *trulla*, dim of *trua*, a ladle.]

troy weight [troi´-wāt] *n* a system of weights for gold, silver, gems, etc., based on a pound of 12 oz. [From *Troyes*, in France, the pound weight of which was adopted in England in the 14th century.]

truant [trōō´ànt] *n* pupil who, without excuse, absents himself from school; anyone who absents himself from his work without reason.—*adj* wandering from duty; loitering, idle.—*n* **tru´ancy**. [OFr *truand*—Celt; W *truan*, wretched, Breton *truek*, a beggar.]

truce [trōōs] *n* a suspension of hostilities between two armies, states, or disputants for a period specially agreed upon; a temporary cessation. [ME *trewes, treowes*, pl of *trewe*, a truce—OE *trēow*, faith; allied to *trēowe*, true.]

truck[1] [truk] *vti* to exchange or barter.—*n* small articles of little value; vegetables raised for market; *(inf)* dealings; payment in goods instead of cash wages.—**truck farm**, a farm where vegetables are grown to be marketed; **truck´system**, the practice of paying workmen in goods instead of money.—**have no truck with**, to have nothing to do with. [OFr *troquer*.]

truck[2] [truk] *n* a two-wheeled barrow or a low, wheeled frame, for carrying heavy articles; an automotive vehicle for hauling goods; a swiveling, wheeled frame under each end of a railroad car, etc.—*vt* to carry on a truck.—*vi* to drive a truck.—*n* **truck´age**, conveyance by truck; charge for carrying articles on a truck. [L *trochus*, a wheel—Gr *trochos*—*trechein*, to run.]

truckle [truk´l] *vi* to submit slavishly.—*n* **truckle bed**, a low bed on wheels that could be pushed under another, such as servants formerly used.—Also **trundle bed**. [Gr *trochlea*, a pulley.]

truculent [truk´ū-lent] *adj* very fierce; threatening and overbearing in manner.—*ns* **truc´ulence, truc´ulency**.—*adv* **truc´ulently**. [L *truculentus*—*trux*, wild, fierce.]

trudge [truj] *vti* to travel on foot, esp with labor or weariness.—*n* a weary walk.

trudgen stroke [truj´èn] *n* a swimming stroke in which each hand alternately is raised above the surface, thrust forward and pulled back through the water. [John *Trudgen*, who popularized the stroke in England.]

true [trōō] *adj* agreeing with fact (eg *a true story*); correct, accurate (eg *a true estimate, idea*); properly so called, genuine (eg *a true reptile*); placed, fitted accurately; perfectly in tune; rightful (eg *the true heir*); (*arch*) honest; (of persons—*rare*) in the habit of telling the truth, truthful; sincere;

faithful, loyal.—*adj* **true-heart´ed**, loyal.—*ns* **true´love**, a sweetheart; **true´love knot, true´ lov´er's knot**, lines interwoven with many involutions, fancifully held as an emblem of interwoven affection; **true´ness**.—*adv* **tru´ly**.—**true bill**, a bill of indictment endorsed, after investigation, by a grand jury, as warranting prosecution of the accused; **true rib**, a rib attached to spine and sternum, in man the first seven pairs.—**come true** (see **come**). [OE *trēowe*; ON *tryggr*, Ger *treu*.]

truffle [truf´l, trŏŏf´l] *n* a round underground fungus used in cookery; a candy made of chocolate, butter, and sugar.—*adj* **truff´led**, cooked with truffles. [OFr *truffle*—prob L *tūber*.]

truism [trōō´izm] *n* a plain or self-evident truth, esp one too obvious to mention. [**true**, + suffx *-ism*.]

trumpery [trump´ė-ri] *n* something showy but worthless; nonsense, idle talk.—*adj* showy and worthless.—**trump up**, to devise falsely, to fabricate. [Fr *tromper*, to deceive, orig to play on the trump.]

trump[1] [trump] *n* a trumpet; a sound of trumpeting. [OFr *trompe* (It *tromba*); cf Ger *tromme*, Eng *drum*.]

trump[2] [trump] *n* a card of the suit (determined each deal by chance or by choice) which takes precedence of any card of any other suit; (*inf*) a good, trusty fellow.—*vt* to play a trump card on.—Also *vi*.—*n* **trump card**, means of triumph, a victorious expedient. [From *triumph*, confused with **trump**, to deceive.]

trumpet [trum´pet] *n* a brass wind instrument with a clear ringing tone, consisting of a long narrow tube usu. bent once or twice upon itself and tapering into a bell at the end; in organs, a powerful reed-stop with a trumpet-like sound; one who praises.—*vt* to publish by trumpet, to proclaim; to sound the praises of.—*vi* to sound a trumpet, or to make a sound suggestive of one.—*ns* **trum´peter**, one who sounds on the trumpet the regimental calls and signals; one who proclaims, praises, or denounces; a loud-voiced, cranelike South American bird (genus *Psophia*); a kind of domestic pigeon; any of several large Australian or New Zealand food fishes; **trumpeter swan**, a rare pure white N American wild swan (*Olar buccinator*) noted for its sonorous voice. [OFr *trompette*, dim of *trompe*.]

truncate [trungk-āt´] *vt* to cut the top or end off, to lop, to maim.—*n* **truncā´tion**.—**truncated cone, pyramid**, a cone, pyramid, having the vertex cut off by plane. [L *truncāre, -ātum*—*truncus*, maimed.]

truncheon [trun´ch(ȯ)n] *n* a cudgel; a baton or staff of authority. [OFr *tronçon*.]

trundle [trun´dl] *n* a wheel; a truck.—*vt* to roll, as on wheels.—*vi* to roll, bowl along.—*n* **trun´dle bed**, a bed moving on trundles or low wheels that can be slid under a higher bed when not in use; a truckle bed. [OE *trendel*, a circle, wheel.]

trunk [trungk] *n* the stem of a tree; the body of a man or an animal apart from the limbs; the main body of anything; anything long and hollow; the proboscis of an elephant; the shaft of a column; a portable box or chest for clothes, etc., esp on a journey; (*pl*) men's short, light pants, eg for running, swimming; a circuit between two telephone exchanges for making connections between subscribers; (*loosely*) a usu. electronic path over which information is transmitted (as between computer memories); a compartment in an automobile usu. in the rear, for a spare tire, luggage, etc.—*ns* **trunk´ hose**, breeches formely worn over the lower part of the body and the upper part of the thigh; **trunk´ line**, a transportation system handling through traffic (as an airline, railroad, or highway); a main supply channel; a communications system. [OFr *tronc*—L *truncus*, a stock—*truncus*, maimed.]

trunnion [trun´yȯn] *n* a knob on each side of a cannon, on which it rested on the carriage; similar pivots, supported in bearings, forming part of machinery. [Fr *trognon*, a stalk—*tronc*, a stump—L *truncus*, maimed.]

truss [trus] *n* a bundle; timbers fastened together for binding a beam or supporting a roof; in ships, the rope or iron for keeping the lower yard to the mast; a bandage or apparatus used in ruptures.—*vt* to bind (up); to skewer in cooking; to support with a truss. [OFr *trosser*, orig *torser*, to bind together—L *tortus*, pt p of *torquēre*, to twist.]

trust [trust] *n* confidence in the truth of anything, as in the integrity, friendship, etc., of another; faith; confident expectation; credit (esp sale on credit or on promise to pay); he who, or that which, is the ground of confidence; that which is given or received in confidence; charge, keeping; an arrangement by which property is transferred to a person, in the trust or confidence that he will use and dispose of it for a specified purpose; the property so transferred; in modern commerce, an arrangement for the control of several companies under one direction.—*adj* held in trust.—*vt* to place confidence in; to give credit to, to sell to on credit; to commit (to) the care of; to believe; to expect confidently.—*vi* to be confident or confiding.—*ns* **trustēē´**, one to whom anything is entrusted; one to whom the management of a property is committed in trust for the benefit of others; member of a board managing the affairs of a college, hospital, etc.; **trustee´ship**.—*adj* **trust´ful**, trusting.—*adv* **trust´fully**.—*n* **trust´fulness**.—*adj* **trust´worthy**, worthy of trust or confidence, dependable.—*n* **trust´worthiness**.—*adj* **trust´y**, deserving confidence; honest; strong, firm.—*n* a convict granted special privileges as a trustworthy person.—*adv* **trust´ily**.—*n* **trust´iness**.—**trust fund**, money, stock, etc. held in trust; **trust territory**, a territory placed under the administrative authority of the United Nations. [Scand, ON *traust*, trust; Ger *trost*, consolation.]

truth [trōōth] *n* that which is true or according to the facts of the case; agreement with reality; practice of saying or telling, or disposition to say or tell, what is in accordance with the facts; fidelity; a true statement; an established principle;—*pl* **truths** [trōōths].—*adj* **truth´ful**, according to, or adhering to, truth, veracious.—*adv* **truth´fully**.—*n* **truth´fulness**. [OE *trēowthu*—*trēowe*, true. Doublet **troth**.]

try [trī] *vt* to put to the test or proof, to test by experiment; to examine judicially; to examine carefully; to experiment with, use experimentally, or seek to use as means; to attempt; to put to severe trial, cause suffering to; to subject to strain; to annoy greatly; to melt out or render (fat, etc.).—*vi* to endeavor, attempt; to make an effort;—*pt, pt p* **tried** [trīd].—*n* an effort, an attempt.—*adjs* **tried**, proved, experienced; **try´ing**, testing; causing strain or suffering.—**try on**, to put on for trial, as a garment; **try out**, to test by putting to use; to test one's fitness, as for a place on a team.—*n* **try´out**, (*inf*) a test to determine qualifications, fitness, etc.—**try it on**, to attempt to do something risky or audacious to see how far one can go unscathed. [OFr *trier*, to cull (grain from straw).]

trypanosome [trip´ȧ-nō-sōm] *n* any of a genus (*Trypanosom´a*) of protozoan parasites, usu. transmitted by the bite of an insect, some of which cause serious or deadly disease (eg sleeping sickness) in vertebrates, including man. [Formed from Gr *trypanon*, an auger, *soma*, a body.]

trysail [trī´sāl or trī´sl] *n* a small fore-and-aft sail set with a boom and gaff. [**try, sail**.]

tryst [trist] *n* an appointment to meet; an appointed place of meeting.—*vi* to agree to meet. [A variant of **trust**.]

tsar *see* **czar**.

tsetse fly [tset´si] *n* a dipterous insect (genus *Glossina*) found in southern and central Africa, whose bite conveys protozoan parasites (as trypanosomes). [Native word.]

tub [tub] *n* a vessel, made of staves and hoops, to hold water; any large open container, as of metal; a bathtub; an old slow boat.—*vt* to give or take a bath or store in a tub.—*adj* **tubb´y**, like a tub, plump. [Low Ger *tubbe*.]

tuba [tū´ba] *n* a large, low-pitched valved brass musical instrument.—*pl* **tūbae** [-ē], **tū´bas**. [L.]

tube [tūb] *n* a pipe, a long hollow cylinder for the conveyance of fluids, etc.; a tubelike part, organ, etc.; a pliable cylinder with a screw cap, for holding paste, etc.; (*Brit*) (*inf*) a subway, esp in London.—*vt* to furnish with, enclose in, a tube.—*n* **tū´bing**, the act of making tubes; tubes collectively; material for tubes.—*adjs* **tū´būlar**, having the form of a tube; **tū´būlate**. [Fr,—L *tubus*, a pipe.]

tuber [tū´bėr] *n* a swelling in the root of a plant where reserves of food are stored up, as a potato.—*adjs* **tū´berous**, having, or consisting of, tubers. [L *tūber*, a swelling—*tumēre*, to swell.]

tubercle [tū´bėr-kl] *n* a small swelling; a small tuber; a small mass or nodule of cells resulting from infection with the bacillus of tuberculosis.—*adj* **tuber´cular**, of, pertaining to, resembling, or affected with tubercles or nodules; tuberculous; **tuber´culous**, affected with, or caused by, tuberculosis.—*ns* **tuber´culin**, a solution injected into the skin as a test for tuberculosis; **tuberculō´sis**, a wasting disease, esp of the lungs, induced by the invasion of a bacillus and characterized by the presence of tubercles or other tubercular formations.—**tubercle bacillus**, the microorganism (*Mycobacterium tuberculosis*) that causes tuberculosis; **tuber´culin test**, a test for hypersensitivity to tuberculin as in indication of past or present tuberculosis infection. [L *tūberculum*, dim of *tūber*. See **tuber**.]

tuberose [tū´be-rōs, tūb´rōz] *n* a bulbous plant with creamy white, fragrant flowers. [From *tūberōsa*, fem of *tūberōsus*, tuberous.]

tuck [tuk] *vt* to draw or press (in or together); to fold (under); to gather (up); to enclose by pressing bedclothes closely around (*with* **up**).—*vi* (*inf*) (*with* **into**) to eat greedily or with enjoyment.—*n* a horizontal or vertical fold stitched in a garment; a body position, as in diving or skiing; an act or instance of tucking.—*n* **tuck´er**, a piece of cloth or lace in the neckline of a dress.—*vt* (*inf*) to weary. [OE *tucian*, to pull.]

tucket [tuk´et] *n* a trumpet fanfare. [It *toccata*; see **toccata**.]

Tudor [tū´dȯr] *adj* pertaining to the royal line of the *Tudors* (1485–1603), or to that historical period, or to the style of architecture common in that period.

Tuesday [tūz´dā] *n* the third day of the week. [OE *Tīwes dæg*, the day of Tiw (the god of war); Ger *dienstag*; cf L *dies Martis*.]

tufa [tū´fa] *n* a porous rock, usu. deposited from springs. [It *tufa*—L *tōfus*, a soft stone.]

tuff [tuf] *n* a rock formed of compacted volcanic fragments. [Fr *tuf, tuffe*—It *tufo, tufa*—L *tōfus*.]

tuft [tuft] *n* a crest of hair or feathers; a small bunch or knot of fragments, wool, etc.; a cluster; a dense head of flowers.—*vt* to separate into tufts; to adorn with tufts.—*adjs* **tuft´ed, tuft´y**. [OFr *tuffe*—Gmc; cf Low Ger *topp*, Ger *zopf*.]

tug [tug] *vt* to pull with effort; to drag along.—*vi* to pull with great effort;—*pr p* **tugg´ing**; *pt, pt p* **tugged**.—*n* a strong pull; a vessel for towing ships.—*ns* **tug´boat**, a strongly built powerful boat for towing and pushing vessels.—Also **towboat; tug-of-war**, a contest in which opposing teams tug at the ends of a rope in an effort to pull one another over a line marked on the ground; a struggle for supremacy between two opponents. [Conn with **tuck** and **tow** (vb).]

tuition [tū-ish´(ȯ)n] *n* (*arch*) care over a young person; teaching, private coaching; instruction; the price or payment for instruction. [L *tuitiō, -ōnis—tuērī.* See **tutor**.]

tulip [tū´lip] *n* a genus (*Tulipa*) of bulbous plants with highly-colored cup-shaped flowers. [OFr *tulipe, tulippe, tulipan*—Turk *tulbend*, a turban.]

tulle [tūl, or tōōl] *n* a delicate kind of thin silk, rayon, nylon, etc. net used for scarves and veils. [Fr, from *Tulle*, in south central France.]

tumble [tumb´l] *vi* to fall, to come down suddenly and violently; to roll; to move in a blundering manner; to twist the body, as an acrobat.—*vt* to throw headlong; to turn over; to throw carelessly; to toss about while examining; to disorder, dishevel.—*n* a fall; a rolling over, a somersault.—*adj* **tum´ble-down**, dilapidated.—*n* **tum´bler**, one who performs any feats or tricks of the acrobat or contortionist; a large drinking glass, so called because formerly, having a pointed base, it could not be set down without tumbling; a machine which dries clothes by tumbling. [Freq from OE *tumbian*.]

tumbril, tumbrel [tum´bril, tum´brėl] *n* a cart with two wheels that can be tilted for emptying; the name given to the carts which conveyed victims to the guillotine during the French Revolution. [OFr *tomberel*—*tomber*, to fall, because the body of the cart could be tipped up without unyoking.]

tumid [tū´mid] *adj* swollen or enlarged, inflated; falsely sublime, bombastic.—*ns* **tūmid´ity, tū´midness**.—*adv* **tū´midly**. [L *tumidus*—*tumēre*, to swell.]

tummy [tum´i] *n* childish form of the word **stomach**.

tumour [tū´mȯr] *n* a new swelling in any part of the body, of independent growth. [L *tumor*—*tumēre*, to swell.]

tumult [tōō´mult] *n* uproar of a multitude, violent agitation with confused sounds; high excitement.—*adjs* **tumult´ūary**, acted by, or acting in, a mob or a disorderly multitude; chaotic; haphazard; **tumult´uous**, disorderly; agitated, noisy.—*adv* **tumult´uously**.—*n* **tumult´ūousness**. [L *tumultus*—*tumēre*, to swell.] **tumulus** [tū´mū-lus] *n* a mound of earth over a grave, a barrow.—*pl* **tū´mūlī**. [L,—*tumēre*, to swell.]

tun [tun] *n* a large cask; any of various liquid measures of capacity, esp one equal to 252 gallons.—*n* **tunn´age**, (*hist*) a duty on imported wines. [OE *tunne*.]

tuna [tōō´na] *n* a large ocean fish of the mackerel group; the albacore; the canned flesh of the tuna, used for human food. [Amer Sp.]

tundra [tundra] *n* a level treeless plain of arctic or subarctic regions, with lichens, mosses, and dwarfed vegetation. [Lapp.]

tune [tūn] *n* a melodious succession of notes or chords, a melody; state of giving a sound or sounds of the correct pitch (eg *to be in tune*); state of giving a sound or sounds of exactly the same pitch; exact correspondence of vibrations other than sound vibrations; harmony (*in tune with*); frame of mind, temper (eg *not in good tune*).—*vt* to adjust the tones of, as a musical instrument; to adjust the resonant frequency of a circuit or circuits to a particular value.—*adjs* **tūn´able; tune´ful**, melodious.—*adv* **tune´fully**.—*n* **tune´fulness**.—*adj* **tune´less**, without tune; silent.—*ns* **tū´ner**, one who tunes instruments; **tū´ning-fork**, a steel two-pronged instrument, designed when set in vibration to give a musical sound of a certain pitch.—**tune in**, (*radio*) to adjust the circuit settings of a radio receiver so as to produce maximum response to particular signal.—**change one's tune**, to alter one's attitude, or way of talking; **in tune**, true in pitch; in accord; **out of tune**, not true in pitch; not agreeing; **to the tune of**, of the amount of. [A doublet of **tone**.]

tungsten [tung´sten] *n* a metallic element (symbol W; at wt 183.9; at no 74). [Swed—*tung*, heavy, *sten*, stone.]

tunic [tū´nik] *n* a short, loose, usu. belted blouselike garment; a loose, gownlike garment worn by men and women in ancient Greece and Rome; a close-fitting jacket worn by soldiers and policeman, etc.; (*anat*) a membrane that covers an organ; (*bot*) a covering, as of a seed.—*adjs* **tū´nicate, -ed**, (*bot*) covered with a tunic or with layers. [Fr *tunique*—L *tunica*, an undergarment worn by both sexes.]

tunnel [tun´ėl] *n* an underground passage, esp one by which a road or railway is carried under an obstacle; any tunnel-like passage.—*vt* to make a passage through.—*vi* to make a tunnel. [OFr *tonnel* (Fr *tonneau*), a cask; also OFr *tonnelle*, an arched vault.]

tunny [tun´i] *n* tuna, esp bluefin tuna. [L *thunnus*—Gr *thynnos*—*thynein*, to dart along.]

turban [tûrbȧn] *n* a headdress consisting of cloth wound in folds around the head worn by men, esp Muslims in Eurasia, and by Sikhs; a similar headdress worn by women.—*adj* **tur´banned**, wearing a turban. [Earlier forms *turbant, tulipant* (Fr *turban*)—Pers *dulband*.]

turbid [tûr´bid] *adj* muddy, thick; disordered, muddled.—*adv* **tur´bidly**.—*n* **tur´bidness**. [L *turbidus*—*turba*, tumult.]

turbine [tûr´bin, or tûrbīn] *n* a machine in which the forced passage of steam, water, air, etc. through a tube containing a close-fitting rotor with shaped vanes causes the rotor to rotate. [Fr,—L *turbō, turbinis*, a whirl—*turbāre*, to disturb—*turba*, disorder.]

turbojet [tûr´bo-jet], **turboprop** [tûr´bo-prop] *n* a jet aircraft engine which also operates a turbine-driven air compressor.

turbot [tûr´bot] *n* a large, flat, round fish (*Psetta maxima*), highly esteemed, and abundant in the North Sea. [OFr *turbot*, prob—L *turbō*, a whirl, a spinning-top.]

turbulent [tûr´bū̇lėnt] *adj* tumultuous, disturbed, in violent commotion; producing commotion; having an exciting, disturbing effect; inclined to insubordination or unrest.—*n* **tur´bulence**, disturbed state (*arch* **tur´bulency**); irregular movement of large volumes of air; irregular eddying motion of particles in a fluid.—*adv* **tur´bulently**. [Fr,—L *turbulentus*—*turba*, a crowd.]

tureen [tū-rēn´] *n* a large dish for holding soup, etc. at table. [Fr *terrine*—L *terra*, earth.]

turf [tûrf] *n* the surface of land matted with the roots of grass, etc.; a cake of turf cut off, a sod; horse racing (*with* **the**); a racetrack;—*pl* **turfs**.—*vt* to cover with sod.—*adj* **tur´fy**, resembling or abounding in turf. [OE *turf*; ON *torf*.]

turgid [tûr´jid] *adj* swollen; extended beyond the natural size; pompous, bombastic.—*ns* **turgid´ity, tur´gidness**.—*adv* **tur´gidly**.—*n* **turgor** [tûr´gȯr], state of being full, the normal condition of the capillaries. [L *turgēns, -entis*, pr p of *turgēre*, to swell.]

Turk [tûrk] *n* a native of Turkey, an Ottoman; (*arch*) a savage person.—*n* **Turk´ey red**, a fine durable red dye.—*adjs* **Turkic**, denoting a subfamily of languages, including Turkish, Tatar, etc.; **Turk´ish**, pertaining to the Turks or to Turkey, Ottoman.—*n* the language of the Turks.—*ns* **Turk´ish bath**, a bath with steam rooms, showers, massage, etc.; **Turk´ish delight´**, a gelatinous sweetmeat, orig Turkish.

turkey [tûrk´i] *n* a large gallinaceous bird (*Meleagris gallopavo*), a native of America; its flesh, used as food.—*n* **turk´ey buzz´ard**, a vulture (*Cathartes aura*) common in S and Central America and in the southern US.—Also **turkey vulture**. [From similarity to a fowl formerly imported from Turkey.]

Turkoman, Turcoman [tûrk´o-mȧn] *n* a member of a group of formerly nomadic tribes of Central Asia, speaking a Turkic language, now mainly found in the Turkmenistan and NE Iran. [Pers *Turkmān*, Turk-like.]

turmeric [tûr´mėr-ik] *n* the rootstock or rhizome of a herbaceous plant (*Curcuma longa*) cultivated all over India, used as a yellow dye, in curry powder, and as a chemical test for the presence of alkalis. [Cf Fr *terre-mérite*—as if from L *terra*, earth, and *merita*, deserved; both prob corr from an Oriental name.]

turmoil [tûr´moil] *n* physical or mental agitation; disturbance, confusion.

turn [tûrn] *vi* to revolve; to move through an arc of a circle; to go in the opposite direction; to turn one's head; to take a different direction (eg *his thoughts then turned to supper*); to become by a change, to change (to, into—eg *the ice turned to water*); to hinge (on), or to depend on; to be shaped on the lathe; (of milk, etc.) to sour; (of head, brain) to become giddy; to change from ebb to flow or from flow to ebb.—*vt* to cause to revolve; to reverse; to change the position or direction of; to reach and go round; to direct, apply; to transfer; to convert (into); to transform; to translate (into); to sour; to make giddy; to nauseate; to form into a lathe; to shape; to have just passed (a certain age, hour, etc.).—*n* act of turning; new direction or tendency; a walk to and fro; a turning point, crisis; a spell of work; performer's act, or performer; opportunity, alternating with that of others; requirement of the moment (eg *this will serve our turn*); (*with* **good** *or* **ill**) act of kindness or of malice; form, style, fashion; a natural aptitude (for); a nervous shock; a winding; a bend; (*mus*) an ornament of the form EDCD (where D is the principal note).—*ns* **turn´-coat**, one who abandons his principles or party; **turn´er**, one that is used for turning; one who uses a lathe; **turn´ery**, art of shaping by a lathe; things made by a turner; **turn´ing**, a winding; deviation from the proper course; a street corner; turnery; (*pl*) chips; act or manner of shaping or fashioning; **turn´ing point**, the point at which a significant change occurs; **turn´key**, a jailer; **turn´out**, a crowd, a large gathering for a special purpose; a wider part of a narrow road, for vehicles to pass; **turn´over**, act of turning over, upset, overthrow; a fruit or meat pasty; the total amount of the sales in a business for a specified time; the rate of replacement of workers; **turn´pike**, a toll road, esp one that is an expressway; **turn´spit**, one who turns a spit; a dog employed to drive a wheel by which roasting-spits were turned; **turn´stile**, a revolving frame across a footpath or entrance which admits only one person at a time; **turn´-tā´ble**, a circular revolving platform for turning wheeled vehicles; a lazy Susan; a circular rotating platform that carries a phonograph record.—**turn down**, to double or fold down; to reject; **turn in**, bend inward; enter; to surrender, hand over voluntarily; (*inf*) to go to bed; **turn off**, to shut off; to make (an electrical device) stop functioning; (*slang*) to make (a person) unenthusiastic, less aware and less vital; **turn on**, to set running (as water); to make (an electrical device) start functioning; (*slang*) to excite, to give (a person) a sense of heightened awareness and vitality as do psychedelic drugs; **turn one's head**, or **brain**, to make one giddy; to fill with pride or conceit; **turn out**, to put out (a light, etc.); to put outside; to dismiss; to come or go out; to produce; to result; to prove to be; to become; **turn over**, to ponder; to hand over; to transfer; **turn the edge of**, to blunt; **turn the tables**, to bring about a reversal in the fortunes of two contending parties; to show that an argument actually supports the other side; **turn to**, to have recourse to; to change to; to set to work; **turn turtle**, of a vessel, to capsize bottom upward; (*loosely*) to overturn; **turn up**, to appear, arrive; to find or be found; to happen.—**by turns**, one after another; alternately; **have turned, be turned**, to have gone, or to be, beyond (eg *he has turned 30*); **in turn**, in order of succession; **not to turn a hair**, to be quite undisturbed or unaffected; **on the turn**, at the turning point, changing; **take one's turn**, to take one's part, alternately with others, eg in a task; **take turns**, to do (eg to work) in rotation; **to a turn**, exactly, perfectly. [OE *tyrnan*; Ger *turnen*; Fr *tourner*; all from L *tornāre*, to turn in a lathe.]

turnip [tûr´nip] *n* a plant (*Brassica rapa*) with swollen and fleshy root—cultivated as a vegetable and for feeding cattle and sheep. [Perh orig *turnnep—turn*, implying something round, and *nep*—OE *nǣp*, a turnip.]

turpentine [tûr´pen-tīn] *n* a semi-solid resinous substance secreted by coniferous trees; the oil or spirit of turpentine, used for making paint and varnish, and in medicine. [OFr *terbentine*—L *terebinthina* (*rēsina*), (the resin) of the terebinth—Gr *terebinthos*.]

turpitude [tûr´pi-tūd] *n* baseness, extreme depravity or wickedness. [L *turpitūdō—turpis*, base.]

turquoise [tûr´koiz, or tûr´kwoiz] *n* an opaque greenish-blue mineral, a phosphate of aluminum and copper, valued as a gem. [OFr; because first brought through *Turkey* or from *Turkestan*.]

turret [tûr´et] *n* a small tower on a building or structure, rising above it; a dome or revolving structure for guns as on a warship, tank, or airplane; a rotating attachment for a lathe, etc. holding cutting tools for successive use.—*adj* **turr´eted**, furnished with turrets. [OFr *touret*, dim of *tour*, a tower.]

turtledove [tûr´tl-duv] *n* a genus (*Streptopelia*) of Old World doves noted for their soft cooing and their affection toward each other and their young. [OE *turtle*; Ger *turtel*, Fr *tourtereau, tourterelle*—L *turtur*.]

turtle [tûr´tl] *n* any of an order (Testudinata) of land, freshwater, or marine reptiles having a soft body encased in a hard shell.—*ns* **tur´tleback**, a raised convex surface; **tur´tleneck**, (a garment having) a high close-fitting neckline (*adj* **tur´tle-necked**); **turn turtle**, to turn upside down. [A corr of *tortoise*, or of Sp *tortuga*, or Port *tartaruga*, a tortoise.]

Tuscan [tus´kȧn] *adj* of or belonging to *Tuscany* in Italy; denoting the simplest of the five classic orders of Roman architecture. [L *Tuscānus*.]

tusk [tusk] *n* a long, protruding tooth on either side of the mouth, as of the elephant.—*adjs* **tusked, tusk´y**. [OE *tusc, tux*; ON *toskr*.]

tussle [tus´l] *n* a struggle.—*vi* to struggle. [Frequentative of ME *tusen*, to treat roughly.]

tussock [tus´ȯk] *n* a tuft of grass or sedge. [Perh conn with Swed dial, *tuss*, a wisp of hay.]

tutelage [tū´te-lij] *n* guardianship; state of being under a guardian; instruction.—*adjs* **tū´telar, tū´telary**, protecting; having the charge of a person or place. [L *tūtēla—tūtārī*, to guard—*tuērī*, to look at; cf **tutor**.]

tutor [tū´tȯr] *n* one who has charge of the education of another, esp a private teacher; one who directs the studies of students in a British university.—*vt* to instruct; to treat with authority or sternness; to direct the studies of.—*n* **tutō´rial**, a meeting for study between a tutor and a student or students.—*n* **tū´torship**, instruction of an individual; a guiding influence; the work of a tutor. [L *tūtor*, a guardian—*tuērī, tuitus*, to look at, to watch, guard.]

tutti [tŏŏ´ti] (*mus*) for all voices or instruments playing together.—*n* a passage so sung or played. [It.]

tutu [tōō´tōō] *n* a ballet dancer's short, stiff, spreading skirt. [Fr.]

tuxedo [tuk-sē´dō] *n* a man's semiformal suit with a tailless jacket. [*Tuxedo* Park, NY.]

twaddle [twod´l] *vi* to talk in a silly manner.—*n* silly talk.—*n* **twadd´ler**. [Earlier form *twattle*, a variant of **tattle**.]

twain [twān] *n* two, a couple, pair. [OE *twēgen* (masc), two.]

twang [twang] *n* a sharp, quick sound, as of a tight string when pulled and let go; a nasal tone of voice.—*vi* to sound as a tight string pulled and let go; to have a nasal sound.—*vt* to make to sound with a twang. [Imit.]

twayblade [twā´blād] *n* one of several kinds of orchid (genus *Listera* or *Liparis*) with green or purple flowers and a single pair of leaves. [Obs *tway*, two, + **blade**.]

tweak [twēk] *vt* to twitch, to pull to pull with sudden jerks.—*n* a sharp pinch or twitch. [A by-form of **twitch**.]

tweed [twēd] *n* a kind of woolen twilled cloth of various patterns.—*adj* made of tweed. [From a mistaken reading of '*tweels*' (see **twill**) on an invoice; not, as supposed, from the *Tweed* valley, Scotland.]

'tween Abbreviation for **between**.

tweezers [twēz´ėrz] *n sing* nippers; small pincers for pulling out hairs, etc. [Obs *tweeze*, a surgeon's case of instruments—*etuis*, pl of *etui*—Fr *étui*, a case.]

twelfth [twelfth] *adj* the last of twelve; being one of twelve equal parts.—Also *n*.—*ns* **Twelfth´ Day**, the twelfth day after Christmas, the Epiphany; **Twelfth´ Night**, the eve of Twelfth Day or evening before Epiphany.—**twelve-tone music**, music based on a pattern formed from the twelve notes of the chromatic scale, esp as developed by Arnold Schönberg (1874–1951) and his pupils. [OE *twelfta; th* on the analogy of *fourth*.]

twelve [twelv] *adj, n* the cardinal number next after eleven.—*n* the symbols 12, XII, xii denoting this.—*n* **twelve´-month**, twelve months, a year.—**the Twelve**, the twelve apostles; the books of the Minor Prophets in the Jewish Scriptures. [ME inflected form *twelve*—OE *twelf*; Ger *zwölf*.]

twenty [twen´ti] *adj, n* two times ten.—*adj* **twen´tieth**, the last of twenty; being one of twenty equal parts.—Also *n*. [OE *twēntig—twēn* (*-twēgen*), two, and *tig*, related to *tien, tēn*.]

twerp [twûrp] *n* (*slang*) a contemptible, insignificant, etc. person.

twice [twīs] *adv* two times, once and again; doubly.—**twice over**, twice (emphatically). [OE *twiges—twiwa—twā*; see **two**.]

twiddle [twid´l] *vt* to twirl idly, to play with.—**twiddle one's thumbs**, to be idle.

twig[1] [twig] *n* a small shoot or branch of a tree.—*adj* **twigg´y**, abounding in twigs. [OE *twig—twī-*, double.]

twig[2] [twig] *vti* (*inf*) to notice; to understand, grasp the meaning.

twilight [twī´līt] *n* the faint light after sunset and before sunrise; partial darkness; a period of decay following a period of success, greatness, etc.—*adj* of twilight; faintly illuminated, obscure. [Lit 'tween light', OE *twi—twā* (see **two**) + **light**.]

twill [twil] *ns* woven fabric, in which the warp is raised one thread, and depressed two or more threads for the passage of the weft—thus giving a curious appearance of diagonal lines; a fabric with a twill.—*vt* to weave in this way. [Low Ger *twillen*, to make double, *twill*, a forked branch.]

twin [twin] *n* one of a pair; one of two born at a birth; one very like another.—*adj* twofold, double; being one of two born at a birth; very like another; consisting of two parts nearly alike.—*n* **twin´ bed**, one of a matching pair of single beds.—**the Twins**, the constellation Gemini. [OE *getwinn, twinn*, double—*twī*, two.]

twine [twīn] *n* a cord composed of two or more threads twisted together; an intertwining.—*vt* to twist together; to form by twisting together; to wind (about something), encircle.—*vi* to unite closely; to make turns (eg of a river); to ascend spirally round a support. [OE *twīn*, double-thread. (Du *twijn*)—*twi-*, double.]

twinge [twinj] *vt* to affect with a sharp, sudden pain.—*n* a sudden, sharp pain. [OE *twengan*.]

twinkle [twing´kl] *vi* to shine with a trembling, sparkling light, to sparkle; to move rapidly (as toes or eyes).—*ns* **twink´le, twink´ling**, a quick motion of the eye; the time occupied by a wink, an instant; the scintillation of the fixed stars; **twink´ler**. [OE *twinclian*.]

twirl [twûrl] *vt* to turn round rapidly, esp with the fingers.—*vi* to turn round rapidly; to be whirled round.—*n* a whirl, a rapid circular motion; a flourish, a coil, or an eddy.—**twirl one's thumbs**, to be idle. [OE *thwirel*, a whisk for whipping milk—*thweran*, to churn, stir.]

twist [twist] *vt* to twine; to unite or form by winding together; to encircle (with); to wreathe; to wind spirally; to bend; to wrest, wrench; to turn from the true form or meaning, to distort.—*vi* to be united by winding; to be bent or to move spirally, to revolve, to writhe; to turn deviously.—*n* that which is twisted; a cord; a single thread; manner of twisting; a contortion; a roll of tobacco or bread; a wrench, strain; a peculiar bent, perversion.—*n* **twist´er**, one who, or that which, twists; a tornado or cyclone. [OE *twist*, a rope—*twi*, two; Ger *zwist*, discord.]

twit [twit] *vt* to remind of some fault, etc., to tease;—*pr p* **twitt´ing**; *pt, pt p* **twitt´ed**.—*n* **twitt´er**. [OE *ætwītan*, to reproach—*æt*, against, *wītan*, to blame.]

twitch [twich] *vt* to pull with a sudden jerk, to pluck, to snatch.—*vi* to be suddenly jerked; to move spasmodically.—*n* a sudden, quick pull; a spasmodic contraction of the muscles. [OE *twiccian*, to pluck.]

twitter [twit´ėr] *n* a chirp, as of a bird; a tremulous broken sound; nervous excitement.—*vi* to make a succession of small tremulous noises, to chirp; to be excited, to palpitate.—*n* **twitt´ering**, act of twittering; the sound of twittering; nervous excitement. [Imit.]

twixt Abbreviation for **betwixt**.

two [tōō] *adj and n* the cardinal number next above one.—*n* the symbols 2, II, ii denoting this.—*adjs* **two´-edged**, having two edges; that can be taken two ways, as a remark; **two´-faced**, having two faces; deceitful, hypocritical; **two´-fold**, multiplied by two; double.—*adv* doubly.—*adj* **two´-hand´ed**, having, or used with, two hands; to be used, played, by two persons.—*n* **twopence** [tup´ėns], the sum of two British pennies.—*adj* **twopenny** [tup´ėn-i], of the value of twopence; cheap, worthless.—*adj* **two´-ply**, consisting of two thicknesses or of two strands.—*n* **two´some**, a tête-à-tête; (*loosely*) in golf, a single, a match between two players.—*vt* **two´-time**, (*slang*) to deceive, esp a spouse or lover by secret lovemaking with another; to double-cross (*n* **two-tim´er**).—**in two**, asunder. [OE *twā*, fem and neut of *twēgen*; cf **twain**.]

tycoon [tī-kōō´] *n* a powerful industrialist, etc. [Jap *taikun*, a great prince.]

tympanic [tim´pan-ik] *adj* of, relating to, or being a tympanum.—*n* **tympanum**, (*anat*) the membrane that separates the external from the internal ear; the drum of the ear; (*archit*) the triangular space between sloping and horizontal cornices, or in the corners or sides of an arch; the panel of a door;—*pl* **tym´pana**.—*adjs* **tym´panal, tym´panic**, like a drum; pertaining to the tympanum.—*ns* **tympani, tympanist**, timpani, timpanist; **tympanites** [tim-pan-ī´tez], distension of the abdomen caused by accumulation of gas. [L,—Gr *tympanon, typanon*, a kettledrum—*typtein*, to strike.]

type [tīp] *n* the characteristic form, plan, style, etc. of a class or group; an examplar, pattern; (*bot, zool*) that which combines the characteristics of a group; a particular kind, sort (of anything); a rectangular piece of metal or of wood on one end of which is cast or engraved a character, sign, etc., used in printing; a set of these; the general effect of printing in one set of types or of the types chosen.—*vt* to reproduce by means of a typewriter; to classify.—*vt* **type´cast**, to cast (an actor) repeatedly for the same kind of part.—*ns* **type´found´er**, one engaged in the design and production of metal printing type for hand composition; **type´script**, a copy of a book, document, etc., produced by means of a typewriter, esp one intended as use for printer's copy; **type´sett´er**, a compositor; a machine that combines types in proper order for printing; **type´sett´ing**, the act or process of setting type (also *adj*).—*vti* **type´write**, to produce by means of a typewriter, now usu. **type**.—*ns* **type´writer**, a machine for producing characters resembling printed ones on paper by mechanical means; **type´writing**.—*adj* **typ´ical** [tip´-] pertaining to, or constituting, a type; emblematic; characteristic; (*biol*) combining the characteristics of a group.—*adv* **typ´ically**.—*vt* **typ´ify** [tip´-] to serve as a type of; to represent by an image or resemblance;—*pt p* **typ´ified**.—*ns* **tȳ´pist**, one who uses a typewriter; **typog´rapher**, a person (as a compositor, printer, or designer) who specializes in the design, choice, or arrangement of printed matter; **typog´raphy**, the art of printing; the general appearance of printed matter.—*adjs* **typograph´ic, -al**, pertaining to typography or printing.—*adv* **typograph´ically**. [Fr *type*—L *typus*—Gr *typos*—*typtein*, to strike.]

typhoid [tȳ´foid] *adj* pertaining to typhus or typhoid.—*n* an acute infectious disease acquired by ingesting contaminated food or water. [Gr *typhōdēs*—*typhos*, smoke (see **typhus**), *eidos*, likeness.]

typhoon [tī-fōōn´] *n* a violent tropical cyclone originating in the western Pacific.—*adj* **typhon´ic**. [Per Ar, Pers, Hindustani *tūfān*, a cyclone—Gr *tȳphōn, tȳphōs*, a whirlwind; or Chinese *t'ai fung*, a great wind, *pao fung*, fierce wind.]

typhus [tī´fus] *n* an extremely contagious and often fatal fever, transmitted by body lice, caused by a rod-shaped microorganism (*Rickettsia prowazekii*). [LL,—Gr *typhos*, smoke, hence stupor arising from fever—*typhein*, to smoke.]

typical, typify, typist, etc. *See* **type**.

tyrant [tī´rȧnt] *n* one who uses his power arbitrarily and oppressively; an absolute ruler.—*adjs* **tyrann´ic, -al, tyr´-annous** [tir´-], pertaining to or suiting a tyrant; unjustly severe; despotic.—*advs* **tyrann´ically, tyr´annously** [tir´-].—*n* **tyrann´icide**, act of killing a tyrant; one who kills a tyrant.—*vi* **tyr´annize** [tir´-], to act as a tyrant; to rule (over) with oppressive severity.—*n* **tyr´anny** [tir´-], the government or authority of a tyrant; absolute monarchy cruelly administered; oppression, harshness. [OFr *tirant* (Fr *tyran*)—L *tyrannus*—Gr *tyrannos*.]

Tyrian [tir´i-ȧn] *adj* of, pertaining to, ancient Tyre or its people; of **Tyrian purple**, a crimson or purple dye made by the ancients. [L *Tyrius*—*Tyrus*, Tyre—Gr *Tyros*.]

tyro [tī´rō] *n* one learning an art or skill; one not yet well acquainted with a subject;—*pl* **ty´ros**. [L *tīrō*, a young recruit.]

Tyrolean [tir-ol-ē´ȧn], **Tyrolese** [-ēz´] *adj* of the Tirol or its inhabitants.—*n* a native or inhabitant of the Tirol.—Also **Tirolē´an, Tirolēse´**.

tzar *see* **czar**.

U

U: U-boat [ū´bōt], a German submarine; **U´-turn**, a turn made by a vehicle which reverses its direction of travel.

ubiquity [ū-bi´kwi-ti] *n* existence everywhere at the same time, omnipresence.—*adj* **ubi´quitous**, present everywhere. [Fr *ubiquité*—L *ubīque*, everywhere—*ubi*, where.]

udder [ud´ėr] *n* a large, pendulous, milk-secreting organ containing two or more mammary glands each provided with a single nipple, as in cows. [OE *ūder*; cog with Ger *euter*; L *ūber*, Gr *outhar*.]

ugli [ug´li] *n* an odd-shaped fruit that is a cross between the grapefruit, tangerine and orange. [From the fruit's unattractive appearance.]

ugly [ug´li] *adj* offensive to the eye; hateful to refined taste or to moral feeling; (*inf*) ill-natured; very discreditable; dangerous.—*n* **ug´liness**.—*vt* **ug´lify**, to make ugly.—*n* **uglificā´tion**.—**ugly duckling**, despised member of family or group who later proves the most successful. [ON *uggligr*, frightful, *uggr*, fear.]

uhlan [u´lȧn] *n* a mounted lancer in the Polish, later in the Prussian, army. [Polish *ulan*, orig a light Tatar horseman—Turk *oglān*, a young man.]

Uitlander [āit´lȧn-dėr] *n* in S Africa a name once given to British and other residents in the old Transvaal and Orange Free State. [Du *uit*, out, *land*, land.]

ukase [ū-kās´, -kāz´] *n* a Russian imperial decree having the force of law; any comparable edict. [Russ *ukaz*, an edict.]

ukelele [ū-ku-lā´lė] *n* a small, four-stringed musical instrument. [Hawaiian=flea, from the movement of the fingers.]

ulcer [ul´sėr] *n* an open sore due to localized destruction of the surface of skin or mucous membrane—usu. a result of infection; a continuing source of evil.—*vti* **ul´cerate**, to make or become ulcerous.—*n* **ulcerā´tion**, the inflammatory process by which an ulcer is formed; an ulcer.—*adj* **ul´cerous**. [Fr *ulcère*—L *ulcus*, *ulcĕris*; Gr *helkos*, a wound.]

ulna [ul´na] *n* the outer and larger of the two bones of the forearm;—*pl* **ul´nae** [-ē].—*adj* **ul´nar**. [L *ulna*. See **ell**.]

ulster [ul´stėr] *n* a long and loose kind of overcoat worn by men and women, sometimes having a hood and belt. [*Ulster*, in Ireland.]

ulterior [ul-tē´ri-ȯr] *adj* situated on the further side; in the future; remoter, beyond what is seen or avowed (eg *ulterior motives*). [L *ulterior*, comp adj *ultrā*, beyond.]

ultimate [ul´ti-mȧt] *adj* furthest; final; fundamental (eg *ultimate truths*); maximum.—*adv* **ul´timately**.—*n* **ultimā´tum**, the final proposition or terms whose rejection will end a negotiation;—*pl* **ultimā´ta**.—*adj* **ul´timo**, in the last (month). [L *ultimus*, the last—*ultrā*, beyond.]

Ultima Thule *See* **Thule**.

ultra- [ul´trȧ-] *prefix* meaning beyond, as *ultramontane*; beyond in degree, as *ultramicroscopic* (too small to be seen with an ordinary microscope); extreme, as *ultraconservative, ultrahigh*. [L *ultrā*, beyond.]

ultramarine [ul-trȧ-ma-rēn´] *adj* deep blue.—*n* a blue pigment prepared by powdering lapis lazuli; a similar pigment made from kaolin, soda ash, sulfur and charcoal; any of several related pigments; a vivid, deep blue. [L *ultrā*, beyond, and **marine**.]

ultramontane [ul-trȧ-mon´tān] *adj* being beyond the mountains (ie the Alps); favoring the absolute supremacy of papal over national or diocesan authority in the Roman Catholic church.—*ns* **ultramon´tanism**, extreme support of the Pope's supremacy; **ultramon´tanist**. [L *ultrā*, beyond, *montānus*—*mons, montis*, a mountain.]

ultrasonic [ul-trȧ-son´ik] *adj* of waves and vibrations, having a frequency above the human ear's audibility limit of about 20,000 cycles per second.—*n* **ultrason´ics**, ultrasonic vibrations or waves; the study of ultrasonic vibrations and their effects; ultrasonic devices. [Pfx **ultra-**, + **sonic**.]

ultrasound [ul´trȧsound] *n* sound vibrations too rapid to be audible. [Pfx **ultra-**, + **sound**.]

ultraviolet [ul´trȧ-vī´o-let] *adj* of light waves shorter than the wavelengths of visible light and longer than X-rays, beyond the violet end of the visible spectrum.—**ultraviolet light**, ultraviolet radiation. [**ultra-**, + **violet**.]

ululate [ul´ū-lāt] *vi* to hoot or screech; to wail in lamentation.—*n* **ululā´tion**, howling, wailing. [L *ululāre*, to hoot.]

umbel [um´bėl, um´bl] *n* an inflorescence in which a number of stalks, each bearing a flower, radiate from one center.—*adj* **umbelif´erous**, bearing or producing umbels. [L *umbella*, dim of *umbra*, a shade.]

umber [um´bėr] *n* a kind of earth used as a reddish-brown pigment; a reddish-brown color. [*Umbria*, in Italy.]

umbilical [um-bil´i-kȧl] *adj* pertaining to the navel; relating to the central region of the abdomen.—**umbilical cord**, the vascular cord connecting the fetus with the placenta; a cable conveying power to a rocket or spacecraft before takeoff; a tethering or supply line for an astronaut or an underwater worker. [L *umbilīcus*, the navel; Gr *omphalos*.]

umbles *See* **humble-pie**.

umbra [um´bra] *n* a shade or shadow; (*astron*) the dark cone projected from a planet or satellite on the side opposite to the sun. [L.]

umbrage [um´brij] *n* suspicion of injury, sense of injury, offense (*take, give, umbrage*); (*poet*) shade.—*adj* **umbrā´geous**, shady or forming a shade.—*adv* **umbrā´geously**. [Fr *ombrage*—L *umbra*, a shadow.]

umbrella [um-brel´a] *n* a covered collapsible frame carried in the hand, as a screen from rain or sun; a protective force of aircraft covering land or sea operations; a protection, a general cover.—*ns* **umbrell´a-bird**, a fruit-crow of South America, so called from its radiating crest; **umbrell´a grass**, an Australian grass with millet-like seeds; **umbrell´a-tree**, a small magnolia of the United States. [It *ombrella*, dim of *ombra*, a shade—L *umbra*.]

umiak [ōōm´yak] *n* a large skin boat of the Eskimo. [Eskimo.]

umlaut [ōōm´lowt] *n* vowel mutation, esp the change of vowel sound brought about by its assimilation to another vowel; the mark () placed over such a vowel. [Ger *um*, about, *laut*, sound.]

umpire [um´pīr] *n* a third person called in to decide a matter on which arbitrators disagree; an impartial person chosen to enforce the rules, and decide disputes in certain sports.—Also *vti*. [For *numpire*; ME *nompere*—OFr *nompair*—*non*, not, *pair*, a peer. From the sense of 'unequal' the meaning passes to an odd man, an arbitrator.]

un- [un-] *pfx* attached to verbs to denote reversal of an action implied by the simple verb, as **unfasten, unpack, unwind**, and to nouns to denote release from, removal or deprivation of, as **unchain, uncork, unfrock**. Occasionally, as in **unloose**, 'un-' serves to intensify the sense of deprivation implied by the word to which it is prefixed. [OE *un-, on-*; cf Ger *ent-*.]

un- [un-] *negative pfx* denoting the opposite of the word to which it is attached, as **unbleached** (not bleached), **unconsciousness** (lack of consciousness). The new word formed with *un-* often means something more than the simple reverse of the original word. Thus, the sense of **unkind** is stronger than 'not showing gentleness or sympathy'; it is 'harsh, cruel'. [OE *un-*; cf L *in-*.]

unable [un-ā´bl] *adj* without sufficient strength, power, skill or opportunity. [OE *un-*, negative, + **able**.]

unaccountable [un-ȧ-kown´tȧ-bl] *adj* not to be explained or accounted for; not responsible; of a person, puzzling in character.—*adv* **unaccount´ably**, inexplicably. [OE *un-*, negative + **accountable**.]

unadulterated [un-ad-ul´tėr-ā-tid] *adj* unmixed; without reservation. [OE *un-* negative, + **adulterated**.]

unadvised [un-ȧd-vīzd´] *adj* not advised; not prudent or discreet, rash.—*adv* **unadvīs´edly**. [OE *un-*, negative, + **advised**.]

unaffected [un-ȧ-fek´tid] *adj* not affected or influenced; without affectation, simple, direct; genuine, sincere.—*adv* **unaffect´edly**. [OE *un-*, negative, + **affected**. See **affect** (2).]

unalloyed [un-ȧ-loid´] *adj* not alloyed or mid; pure. [OE *un-*, negative, + **alloyed**.]

unanimity [ū-nȧ-nim´i-ti] *n* state of being unanimous.—*adj* **unan´imous**, agreeing, one and all, in opinion or will; having the agreement, support, consent, of all.—*adv* **unan´imously**. [L *unus*, one, *animus*, mind.]

unanswerable [un-an´sėr-ȧ-bl] *adj* that cannot be refuted, conclusive. [OE *un-*, negative, + **answer**.]

unapproachable [un-ȧ-prōch´ȧ-bl] *adj* inaccessible; forbiding intimacy; that cannot be rivalled. [OE *un-*, negative, + **approach**.]

unarmed [un-ärmd´] *adj* without weapons, defenseless. [OE *un-*, deprivation of, + **arm** (2).]

unassuming [un-ȧ-sōōm´ing] *adj* not forward or arrogant, modest. [OE *un-*, negative, + **assuming**.]

unattached [un-ȧ-tacht´] *adj* not attached; not seized for debt; not engaged to be married or not married. [OE *un-*, negative, + **attached**.]

unattended [un-ȧ-tend´id] *adj* not accompanied; not attended to; without occupier and not in the care of an attendant. [OE *un-*, negative, + **attended**.]

unauthorized [un-öth´ȯr-īzd] *adj* not sanctioned by authority. [OE *un-*, negative, + **authorized**.]

unavailing [un-ȧ-vāl´ing] *adj* of no avail or effect, useless. [OE *un-*, negative, + **availing**.]

unaware [un-ȧ-wār´] *adj* not aware, ignorant (*usu. with* **of**).—*adv* (also **unawares´**) without warning; unexpectedly. [OE *un-*, negative, + **aware**.]

unbalanced [un-bal´ȧnst] *adj* not in a state of equipoise; mentally unstable; (*bookkeeping*) not adjusted so as to make credits equal to debits; erratic. [OE *un-*, negative, + **balance**.]

unbar [un-bär´] *vt* to unfasten, to open. [OE *un-*, release from, + **bar**.]

unbecoming [un-bi-kum´ing] *adj* not suited to the wearer or not showing him, her, to advantage; of behavior, etc., inappropriate, unseemly, improper. [OE *un-*, negative, + **becoming**.]

unbeknown [un-bē-nōn´] *adv* without the knowledge of (*with* **to**).—Also **unbeknown´st**. [OE *un-*, negative, *be-*, about, + **known**.]
unbelief [un-bi-lēf´] *n* want of belief, or disbelief, esp in divine revelation.—*n* **unbeliev´er**, one who does not believe, esp in divine revelation; an incredulous person. [OE *un-*, lack of, + **belief** (see **believe**).]
unbend [un-bend´] *vti* to free from being in a bent state, to make straight; to free from strain or exertion; to relax, as from formality.—*adj* **unbend´ing**, that unbends; becoming relaxed or informal.—Also *n*. See also next article. [OE *un-*, reversing action, + **bend**.]
unbending [un-bend´ing *adj* not bending; unyielding, resolute.—*adv* **unbend´ingly**. See also above. [OE *un-*, negative, + **bending** (see **bend**).]
unbiased [un-bī´ȧst] *adj* free from bias or prejudice, impartial. [OE *un*, negative, + **biased**.]
unbidden [un-bid´n] *adj* not commanded; uninvited. [OE *un-*, negative, + **bidden** (see **bid**).]
unbind [un-bīnd´] *vt* to remove a binding from; to set free. [OE *un-*, reversing action, + **bind**.]
unblessed [un-blest] *adj* having received no blessing; wretched; evil.—Also **unblest´**. [OE *un-*, not, + **blessed**.]
unblushing [un-blush´ing] *adj* without shame. [OE *un-*, negative, + **blush**.]
unbolt [un-bōlt´] *vti* to remove a bolt from; to open.—*adj* **unbolt´ed**, not fastened by bolts. [OE *un-*, release from, + **bolt** (1).]
unbolted [un-bolt´id] *adj* not sifted (see **bolt** (2)), coarse (eg *unbolted flour*). See also above.
unbosom [un-bōōz´ȯm] *vti* to disclose (one's thoughts or secrets).—**unbosom oneself**, to reval one's feelings, secrets, etc. [OE *un-*, removal from, + **bosom**.]
unbound [un-bownd´] *adj* not bound; loose, wanting a cover; not held in physical or chemical composition. [OE *un-*, negative, + **bound** (see **bind**).]
unbounded [un-bown´did] *adj* not limited, boundless; having no check or control. [OE *un-*, negative, + **bound** (2).]
unbridle [un-brī´dl] *vt* to free from the bridle; to free from restraint.—*adj* **unbri´dled**, of a horse, having no bridle; unrestrained; licentious. [OE *un-*, removal of, + **bridle**.]
unbuckle [un-buk´l] *vt* to undo the buckle or buckles of, to unfasten.—*vi* to loosen buckles; to relax. [OE *un-*, release from, + **buckle**.]
unburden [un-bûr´dn] *vt* to take a burden off; to free from any weight or anxiety; tell one's secrets or anxieties freely. [OE *un-*, removal of, + **burden** (1).]
unbutton [un-but´n] *vt* to loose the buttons of.—*adj* **unbutt´oned**, not buttoned; not under constraint; free and unrestricted in action. [OE *un-*, release from, + **button**.]
uncalled-for [un-köld´-för] *adj* quite unnecessary, gratuitous; unnecessary and out of place. [OE *un-*, negative, **called**, + **for**.]
uncanny [un-kan´i] *adj* weird, unearthly;' suggestive of supernatural powers, inexplicable on rational grounds. [OE *un-*, negative, + **canny**, in sense of 'safe to meddle with, of good omen'.]
uncertain [un-sûr´t(i)n] *adj* not knowing with certainty, doubtful; not definitely known; such as cannot be definitely forecast; subject to chance; not to be depended on; changeable. [OE *un-*, negative, + **certain**.]
unchain [un-chān´] *vt* to free from chains; to set loose. [OE *un-*, release from, + **chain**.]
uncharted [un-chärt´id] *adj* not marked on a chart or map; unexplored or unknown. [OE *un-*, negative, + **charted**.]
unchurch [un-chûrch´] *vt* to deprive of the rights of membership in a church; to refuse the name of church to. [OE *un-*, deprivation of, + **church**.]
uncial [un-shȧl] *adj* written in the large round characters used in Greek and Latin manuscripts between 300 and 900 AD.—*n* uncial script or letter. [Lit 'an *inch* long'—L, from *uncia*, a twelfth part, an inch.]
unciform [un´si-förm] *adj* hook-shaped.—*adj* **un´cinate**, hooked at the end. [L *uncus*, a hook, + suffx *-form*.]
uncircumcision [un-sėr-kum-sizh´(ȯ)n] *n* want of circumcision.—*adj* **uncir´cumcised**, not circumcised; gentile; (*arch*) heathen. [OE *un-*, lack of, + **circumcision**.]
uncivil [un-siv´il] *adj* not courteous, rude. [OE *un-*, negative, + **civil**.]
unclasp [un-kläsp´] *vt* to loose the clasp of (eg a necklace, the hands). [OE *un-*, release from, + **clasp**.]
unclassified [un-klas´i-fīd] *adj* not placed or belonging in a class; not subject to a security classification. [OE *un-*, negative, + **classified**.]
uncle [ung´kl] *n* the brother of one's father or mother; an aunt's husband; one who helps, advises, or encourages; used as a cry of surrender.—**Uncle Sam**, (*inf*) the personification of the US (government or people) as a tall man with whiskers; **Uncle Tom**, a term of contempt for a Negro regarded as servile toward whites or a person in a low position overly subservient to his superiors. [OFr (Fr *oncle*)—L *avunculus*.]
unclean [un-klēn´] *adj* not clean, foul; ceremonially impure; lacking in clarity and precision of conception or execution. [OE *un-*, negative, + **clean**.]
unclose [un-klōz´] *vt* to open; to disclose, reveal. [OE *un-*, reversing action, + **close**, vb.]
unclothe [un-klōTH´] *vt* to take the clothes off; to divest, uncover. [OE *un-*, reversing action, + **clothe** (see **cloth**).]
uncoil [un-koil´] *vti* to unwind. [OE *un-*, reversing action, + **coil** (1).]
uncommitted [un-kom-it´id] *adj* not pledged to support any party, policy or action; not taking a stand. [OE *un-*, negative, + **committed**.]
uncommon [un-kom´ȯn] *adj* rare; exceptional, remarkable in quality.—*adv* **uncomm´only**. [OE *un-*, negative, + **common**.]
uncompromising [un-kom´prō-mīz-ing] *adj* not willing to compromise, intractable, unyielding. [OE *un-*, negative, + **compromise**.]
unconcern [un-kon-sûrn´] *n* absence of concern or anxiety; indifference.—*adj* **unconcerned´**, not solicitous or anxious; indifferent. [OE *un-*, lack of, + **concern**.]
unconditional [un-kon-di´sh(ȯ)n-ȧl] *adj* unqualified, unreserved, made without conditions, absolute.—*adv* **uncondi´tionally**. [OE *un-*, negative, + **conditional**.]
unconfirmed [un-kon-fûrmd´] *adj* without final proof or ratification; not yet having received the rite of confirmation. [OE *un-*, negative, + **confirm**.]
unconscionable [un-kon´sh(ȯ)n-ȧ-bl] *adj* not conformable to conscience; conscienceless, or unscrupulous; unreasonable or excessive. [OE *un-*, negative, + *conscionable* (rare), regulated by **conscience**.]
unconscious [un-kon´shus] *adj* not aware (of); deprived of perception by the senses, insensible; not present to, or a part of, the conscious mind, esp (*psych*) prevented by repression from rising to the conscious mind.—*n* the deepest level of mind, frequently providing motives for conscious action otherwise inexplicable.—*adv* **uncon´sciously**.—*n* **uncon´sciousness**. [OE *un-*, negative, + **conscious**.]
uncork [un-körk´] *vt* to draw the cork from. [OE *un-*, removal of, + **cork**.]
uncouple [un-kup´l] *vt* to loose from being coupled, to disjoin, to set loose. [OE *un-*, reversing action, + **couple**.]
uncouth [un-kōōth´] *adj* awkward, ungraceful, esp in manners or language, grotesque, odd.—*n* **uncouth´ness**. [OE *uncūth*—*un-*, not, *cūth, gecūth*, known—*cunnan*, to know.]
uncoordinated [un-kō-ör´di-nāt-id] *adj* not coordinated; having clumsy movements. [OE *un-*, negative, + **coordinated**.]
uncover [un-kuv´ėr] *vt* to disclose; to remove the cover of; to remove the hat, etc. from (the head).—*vi* to bare the head, as in respect.—*adj* **uncov´ered**, not covered by insurance or included in a social insurance or welfare program; not covered by collateral. [OE *un-*, removal of, + **cover**.]
uncrown [un-krown´] *vt* to deprive of a crown, depose, dethrone.—*adj* **uncrowned´**. [OE *un-*, deprivation of, + **crown**.]
unction [ungk´sh(ȯ)n] *n* an anointing as for medical or religious purposes; that which is used for anointing; ointment; anything that soothes or comforts; superficial earnestness of language or manner.—*adj* **unctuous** [ungk´tū-ùs], oily, greasy; ostentatiously holy or fervent; offensively smug; too suave.—*adv* **unc´tūously**.—*ns* **unc´tūousness, unctūos´ity**, state or quality of being unctuous. [L *unctiō, -ōnis*—*unguĕre, unctum*, to anoint.]
uncurl [un-kûrl´] *vt* to straighten out, free from curls or ringlets.—*vi* to relax, unwind, from a curled state. [OE *un-*, reversing action, + **curl**.]
undated [un-dā´tid] *adj* having no date. [OE *un-*, negative, + **date** (1).]
undaunted [un-dön´tid] *adj* fearless; unsubdued; intrepid.—*adv* **undaun´tedly**.—*n* **undaun´tedness**. [OE *un-*, negative, + **daunt**.]
undeceive [un-di-sēv´] *vt* to free from deception or mistake; to inform of the truth. [OE *un-*, reversing action, + **deceive**.]
undecided [un-di-sī´did] *adj* not having the mind made up, irresolute; not yet settled or determined. [OE *un-*, negative, + **decided**.]
undefiled [un-di-fīld´] *adj* unstained, pure, innocent. [OE *un-*, negative, + **defile** (2).]
under [un´dėr] *prep* in a lower position than; beneath the surface of; below and to the other side of; covered by; below; less than, falling short of; in subjection, subordination to; during the time of; undergoing; subject to, bound by, in accordance with (eg *under this agreement*); with the disguise of; in (the designated category); being the subject of; because of; authorized by.—*adv* in, or to, a lower place or condition; below, lower down, in subjection.—*adj* lower in position, rank, or degree; subject, subordinate.—**underage**, still a minor; not yet of the age required by law; **underarm**, of, for, in, or used on the area under the arm, or armpit; done with the hand below the level of the elbow or shoulder; **under way**, (of a ship) not at anchor or aground, in motion; into motion from a standstill; in progress. [OE *under*; ON *undir*, Ger *unter*, L *infrā*].]
under- [un´dėr-] *prefix* meaning beneath, below, as **underlie**; too little, as **underfed**; lower in position, as **undercurrent, underclothes**; less in rank or attainments, as **undergraduate**; subordinate, as **underplot**. [**under**.]
underbid [un-dėr-bid´] *vti* to bid or offer less than, as at an auction; to bid less than the value of (a hand at bridge). [**under-, bid**.]
underbred [un-dėr-bred´] *adj* of inferior breeding or manners. [**under-, bred**.]
undercarriage [un´dėr-kar-ij] *n* the supporting framework (as of an automobile); the landing gear of an airplane. [**under-, carriage**.]
underclothes [un´dėr-klōTHz] *n pl* underwear.—Also **under´clothing**.
undercoat [un´der-kōt] *n* a tarlike coating applied to the underside of an automobile to retard rust, etc.; a coat of paint, etc. applied as a base for another coat; a growth of short hair or fur partly concealed by a longer growth.—Also **un´dercoating**.—*vt* to apply an undercoat to.
undercover [un´dėr-kuv´ėr] *adj* working, or done, in secret.
undercurrent [un´dėr-kur-ėnt] *n* a current under the surface of the water; any hidden influence or tendency, esp of feeling contrary to that shown on the surface. [**under-, current**.]

undercut [un-dėr-kut´] *vt* to cut below or under; to sell at a price lower than (a competitor); to accept (wages) lower than the standard.—*n* **un´dercut**, the action or result of cutting away from the lower part of something; a notch cut in a tree at the base before felling to direct the place of falling or to prevent splitting. [**under-, cut.**]

underdeveloped [un-dėr-dė-vel´opt] *adj* insufficiently developed; of a country, with resources inadequately used, having a low standard of living (as from lack of capital). [**under-, developed.**]

underdone [un´dėr-dun] *adj* incompletely cooked. [**under-, do.**]

underdog [un´dėr-dog] *n* a loser or predicted loser in a contest; a victim of persecution or injustice. [**under-, dog.**]

underestimate [un-dėr-es´ti-māt] *vti* to set too low an estimate on or for.—*n* an estimate that is too low. [**under-, estimate.**]

underexposed [un-dėr-eks-pōzd´] *adj* (*photography*) not exposed to the light long enough to make a good negative. [**under-, expose.**]

underfeed [un-dėr-fēd´] *vt* to feed inadequately.—*adj* **underfed´**.—*n* **underfeed´ing**. [**under-, feed.**]

underfoot [un-dėr-fŏŏt´] *adv* under the foot or feet; in the way. [**under-, foot.**]

undergarment [un´dėr-gär-mėnt] *n* a piece of underwear. [**under-, garment.**]

undergo [un-dėr-gō´] *vt* to experience; to be subjected to; to endure or suffer. [**under-, go.**]

undergraduate [un-dėr-grad´ū-āt] *n* a student at a college or university who does not have a first degree. [**under-, graduate.**]

underground [un´dėr-grownd] *adj* under the surface of the ground; secret; of noncommercial newspapers, movies, etc. that are unconventional, radical, etc.—*n* a secret movement working for the overthrow of the government or the expulsion of a foreign power in control of the country.—*adv* **underground´**, beneath the surface of the earth; in or into secrecy.—**Underground Railroad**, a system by which fugitive slaves were secretly helped to reach the North or Canada by antislavery people in the US before 1863. [**under-, ground.**]

undergrowth [un´dėr-grōth] *n* seedlings, saplings, herbs and shrubs growing on the floor of a forest. [**under-, growth.**]

underhand [un´dėr-hand´] *adj* done with the hand brought forward and up from below the shoulder level; underhanded.—*adv* with an underhand motion; underhandedly.—*adj* **un´derhand´ed**, sly, deceitful, etc.—*adv* **un´derhand´edly**. [**under-, hand.**]

underlay [un-dėr-lā´] *vt* to lay under; to support by something laid under.—*n* **un´derlay**, something that is or designed to be laid under. [**under-, lay** (2).]

underlie [un-dėr-lī´] *vt* to lie under or beneath; to be the foundation of; to exist as a prior claim.—*adj* **underly´ing**, lying under or lower in position; supporting, fundamental; present though not immediately obvious. [**under-, lie** (2).]

underline [un-dėr-līn´] *vt* to draw a line under or below; to emphasize.—*n* a horizontal line placed underneath something. [**under-, line** (2).]

underling [un´dėr-ling] *n* an agent of inferior rank; a subordinate, esp one of servile character. [**under-**, + suffx *-ling*.]

undermine [un-dėr-mīn´] *vt* to make a passage under so as to form a tunnel or mine; to wear away at the foundation; to injure or weaken, esp by subtle or insidious means. [**under-, mine** (2).]

undermost [un´dėr-most] *adj, adv* lowest in place, condition, rank, etc. [**under-**, + suffx *-most*.]

underneath [un-dėr-nēth´] *adv* beneath, below, in a lower place.—*prep* under, beneath. [**under-**, + OE *neothan*, beneath.]

underpass [un´dėr-päs] *n* a road passing under another road, a railway, etc. [**under-, pass.**]

underpay [un-dėr-pā´] *vt* to pay insufficiently.—*adj* **underpaid´**.—*n* **underpay´ment**. [**under-, pay** (1).]

underpin [un-dėr-pin´] *vt* to form part of, strengthen, or replace the foundation of; to support, substantiate.—*n* **un´derpinn´ing**, a support or prop; (*pl*) (*inf*) the legs. [**under-, pin.**]

underplot [un´dėr-plot] *n* a plot under or subordinate to the main plot in a play or tale. [**under-, plot** (2).]

underprivileged [un-dėr-priv´i-lijd] *adj* not enjoying normal social and economic rights. [**under-, privileged.**]

underrate [un-dėr-rāt´] *vt* to rate at less than the real value. [**under-, rate** (1).]

under secretary [un-dėrsek´rė-tȧ-ri] *n* a secretary immediately subordinate to a principal secretary. [**under-, secretary.**]

undersell [un-dėr-sel´] *vt* to sell at lower prices than. [**under-, sell.**]

undershoot [un-dėr-shōōt´] *vt* to shoot below or short of a target; to fall short of (a runway) in landing an airplane.—*adj* **un´dershot**, having the lower teeth protruding beyond the upper when the mouth is closed; driven by water flowing along the lower part. [**under-, shoot.**]

undershrub [un´dėr-shrub] *n* a sub-shrub. [**under-, shrub** (1).]

undersigned [un-dėr-sīnd´] *adj* signed at the end; whose name is signed at the end.—*n* one who signs his name at the end of a document.—**the undersigned**, the person or persons whose signatures are below, at the end of the document. [**under-, sign.**]

undersized [un´dėr-sīzed] *adj* below the usual size. [**under-, size** (1).]

understand [un-dėr-stand´] *vt* to comprehend, to have just ideas of; to grasp without explanation; to know thoroughly; to be informed, or, more usually, to gather (that);' to take as the meaning of (eg *what are we to understand by that remark*?); to take for granted as part of an agreement; to take as meant though not expressed; to be sympathetic with.—*vi* to have the use of the intellectual faculties; to be informed; to believe;—*pt, pt p* **understood´**.—*n* **understan´ding**, the act of comprehending; the faculty of the mind by which it understands or thinks; the power to understand; exact comprehension; agreement of minds, harmony; informal arrangement for mutual convenience; conditional agreement; implicit bond.—*adj* knowing, skillful; sympathetically discerning. [OE *understandan*, to perceive, etc.]

understate [un-dėr-stāt´] *vt* to state too weakly; to state without emphasis or embellishment.—*n* **understate´ment**. [**under-, state.**]

understood [un-dėr-stŏŏd´] *pt, pt p* of **understand**.

understrapper [un´dėr-strap-ėr] *n* an inferior agent, an underling, a petty fellow. [**under-, strap** (vb).]

understudy [un´dėr-stud-i] *vti* to study a dramatic part so as to be able to take the place of (the actor playing it); to prepare to act as a substitute for.—*n* an actor who prepares a part in the above way; one who is ready to act as a substitute. [**under-, study.**]

undertake [un-dėr-tāk´] *vt* to attempt, enter upon, engage in; to take upon onself; to promise; to guarantee.—*vi* (*arch*) to take upon onself.—*ns* **un´dertāker**, one who undertakes a surety; one who manages funerals; **undertā´king**, that which is undertaken; any business or project engaged in; a pledge; the business of an undertaker. [**under-, take.**]

undertone [un´dėr-tōn] *n* a low tone of voice; hidden or suppressed feeling, an undercurrent of feeling; subdued color. [**under-, tone.**]

undertook [un-dėr-tŏŏk´] *pt* of **undertake**.

undertow [un´dėr-tō] *n* a current of water moving beneath the surface in a different direction from that at the surface. [**under-, tow**, (2).]

undervalue [un-dėr-val´ū] *vt* to value below the real worth; to esteem too lightly.—*n* a value or price under the real worth.—*n* **undervaluā´tion**, an undervaluing; rate below the worth. [**under-, value.**]

underwater [un-dėr-wö´tėr] *adj* existing, acting, carried out, etc., below the surface of the water; below the waterline of a ship. [**under-, water.**]

underwear [un´edėr-wār] *n* clothing worn under one's outer clothes, usu. next to the skin. [**under-, wear.**]

underwent [un-dėr-went´] *pt* of **undergo**.

underwood [un´dėr-wŏŏd] *n* low wood or trees growing under large ones, coppice. [**under-, wood.**]

underworld [un´dėr-wûrld *n* Hades; criminals as an organized group. [**under-, world.**]

underwrite [un-dėr-rīt´] *vt* to agree to market (an issue of securities, and to buy any part remaining unsubscribed); to agree to finance (an undertaking, etc.); to sign one's name to (an insurance policy), thus assuming liability.—*vi* to work as an underwriter.—*n* **un´derwriter**. [**under-, write.**]

undesirable [un-di-zī´rȧ-bl] *adj* not to be wished for; reprehensible.—*ns* **undesir´abil´ity, undesir´ableness**.—*adv* **undesir´ably**.—*adjs* **undesired´; undesir´ing; undesir´ous**. [OE *un-*, negative, + **desire.**]

undid [un-did´] *pt* of **undo**.

undies [un´diz] *n pl* (*inf*) women's or girls' underwear. [Abbreviation for **underclothes.**]

undistinguished [un-dis-ting´gwisht] *adj* not distinguished; without conspicuous qualities; ordinary, commonplace. [OE *un-*, negative, + **distinguished.**]

undistributed [un-dis-trib´ūt-id] *adj* not distributed; (*logic*) having the character in a term that does not convey information about every member of the class that the term denotes. [OE *un-*, negative, + **distributed.**]

undo [un-dōō´] *vt* to reverse (what has been done); to open; to loose; to unravel; to bring to ruin.—*n* **undo´ing**, an annulling; a bringing to ruin; the cause of ruin.—*adj* **undone´**, not done; ruined; untied; unfastened. [OE *un-*, reversing action, + **do.**]

undoubted [un-dowt´id] *adj* not doubted; unquestioned; certainly genuine. [OE *un-*, negative, + **doubted.**]

undress [un-dres´] *vt* to take the dress or clothes off; to bare.—*vi* to take off one's clothes.—*n* a loose robe or dressing gown; informal dress; the state of being undressed.—*adj* **undressed´**, not dressed; informally dressed; not trimmed or tidied; not bandaged; not prepared for serving; not fully processed or finished, as hides. [OE *un-*, removal of, + **dress.**]

undue [un-dū´] *adj* not appropriate; improper, immoderate, excessive. [OE *un-*, negative, + **due.**]

undulate [un´dū-lāt] *vti* to move or cause to move like waves; to have or cause to have a wavy form or surface.—*adjs* **un´dulant, un´dulating**.—*n* **undulā´tion**, a waving motion; a wavy appearance.—*adj* **un´dulātory**, moving like waves.—**undulatory theory**, a theory in physics: that light is transmitted from luminous bodies to the eye, etc. by an undulatory movement.—Also called **wave theory**. [LL *undulāre, -ātum*—L *unda*, a wave.]

unduly [un-dū´li] *adv* in undue measure, too, excessively; improperly. [OE *un-*, negative, and **duly.**]

unearned [un-ûrnd´] *adj* not gained by labor, service, or skill.—**unearned increment**, an increase in the value of property (as land) that is due to natural causes (as the increase in population) that create a demand for it. [OE *un-*, negative, + **earn.**]

unearth [un-ûrth´] *vt* to dig up from the earth; to bring to light; to discover, to disclose. [OE *un-*, removal from, + **earth.**]

unearthly [un-ûrth´li] *adj* supernatural, weird; mysterious; (*inf*) fantastic, outlandish, etc. [OE *un-*, negative, + **earthly**.]
uneasy [un-ē´zi] *adj* not at ease; restless; feeling pain; feeling anxiety, disquieted; not comfortable; constraining or precarious.—*n* **uneas´iness**.—*adv* **uneas´ily**. [OE *un-*, negative, + **easy**.]
unemployed [un-em-ploid´] *adj* not put to use; out of work, without a job.—Also *n* **unemploy´ment**. [OE *un-*, negative, + **employed**.]
unequal [un-ē´kwål] *adj* not equal or alike in quality, extent, duration, etc.; unfair, unjust, varying, not uniform; having insufficient strength, ability, etc., for (eg *unequal to the task*).—*adj* **une´qualed**, unrivaled; unparalleled, unprecedented.—*adv* **une´qually**. [OE *un-*, neg, + **equal**.]
unequivocal [un-ė-kwiv´o-kål] *adj* unambiguous; explicit; clear and emphatic. [OE *un-*, negative, + **equivocal**.]
Unesco [ū-nes´kō] *n* the *U*nited *N*ations *E*ducational *S*cientific and *C*ultural *O*rganization.
uneven [un-ē´vn] *adj* not even, smooth, straight, or uniform; odd, not divisible by two without remainder.—*adv* **unē´venly**. [OE *un-*, negative, and **even**.]
unexceptionable [un-ek-sep´sh(ȯ)n-å-bl] *adj* not liable to exception or objection; faultless. [OE *un-*, negative, and **exceptionable**.]
unfailing [un-fāl´ing] *adj* never running short or giving out (eg supplies); unceasing; unflagging (eg efforts); certain.—*adv* **unfail´ingly**. [OE *un-*, negative, and **failing**.]
unfair [un-fâr´] *adj* not fair; not just; dishonest; inequitable.—*adv* **unfair´ly**.—*n* **unfair´ness**. [OE *un-*, negative, and **fair** (1).]
unfaithful [un-fāth´fo͝ol, -fl] *adj* not holding the true faith, disloyal; treacherous; inexact, not true to the original; guilty of adultery.—*n* **unfaith´fulness**, disloyalty; adultery. [OE *un-*, negative, + **faithful**.]
unfasten [un-fäs´n] *vt* to loose, as from a fastening; to unfix. [OE *un-*, reversing action, + **fasten**.]
unfathomable [un-faTH´om-å-bl] *adj* too deep to be fathomed or to be understood; immeasurable.—*adj* **unfath´omed**, not plumbed. [OE *un-*, negative, + **fathom**.]
unfeeling [un-fē´ling] *adj* without feeling; without kind feelings, hardhearted. [OE *un-*, negative, + **feeling**.]
unfetter [un-fet´ėr] *vt* to take the fetters from; to set at liberty.—*adj* **unfett´ered**, unrestrained. [OE *un-*, removal of, + **fetter**.]
unfilial [un-fil´yål] *adj* not observing the obligations of a child, undutiful. [OE *un-*, negative, + **filial**.]
unfinished [un-fin´isht] *adj* not finished or completed; showing lack of finish. [OE *un-*, negative, + **finished**.]
unfit [un-fit´] *adj* unsuitable, improper.—*vt* to make unsuitable (for); to make unable (to, for).—*n* **unfit´ness**. [OE *un-*, negative, + **fit** (1).]
unfix [un-fiks´] *vt* to make not fixed, to loose the fixing of; to unsettle. [OE *un-*, reversing action, + **fix**.]
unflagging [un-flag´ing] *adj* not flagging or drooping; untiring. [OE *un-*, negative, and **flag** (1).]
unflappable [un-flap´å-bl] *adj* (*inf*) imperturbable, never agitated or alarmed. [OE *un-*, negative, + **flap**.]
unfold [un-fōld´] *vt* to open the folds of; to spread out; to tell.—*vi* to spread open, expand, develop. [OE *un-*, reversing action, + **fold** (1).]
unformed [un-förmed´] *adj* structureless, amorphous; not fully formed, immature; not arranged in order. [OE *un-*, negative, + **formed**.]
unfortunate [un-för´tū-nåt] *adj* not fortunate, auspicious, or successful—unlucky.—*n* one who is unfortunate.—*adv* **unfor´tunately**, unhappily, unluckily. [OE *un-*, negative, + **fortunate**.]
unfounded [un-fown´did] *adj* not founded; baseless, without foundation in reality (eg of fears, hopes). [OE *un-*, negative, + **founded**. See **found** (2).]
unfreeze [un-frēz´] *vt* to cause thaw; to remove from a freeze. [OE *un-*, reversing action, + **freeze**.]
unfrock [un-frok´] *vt* to deprive of the rank of priest or minister. [OE *un-*, removal of, + **frock**.]
unfurl [un-fûrl´] *vti* to loose from being furled; to unfold, display; to spread. [OE *un-*, reversing action, + **furl**.]
ungainly [un-gān´li] *adj* awkward; clumsy.—*n* **ungain´liness**. [ME *ungein*, inconvenient—OE *un-*, negative, ON *gegn*, ready, serviceable.]
ungirt [un-gûrt´] *adj* having the girdle or belt off or loose; lacking in discipline or compactness; loose; slack. [OE *un-*, negative, *girt*, pt p of **gird** (2).]
ungodly [un-god´li] *adj* not godly or religious; (*inf*) outrageous.—*n* **ungod´liness**, the quality of being ungodly; wickedness. [OE *un-*, negative, + **godly**.]
ungrammatical [un-gra-mat´i-kål] *adj* not according to the rules of grammar. [OE *un-*, negative, + **grammatical**.]
ungual [ung´gwål] *adj* relating to, like, or resembling a nail, claw, or hoof. [L *unguis*, a nail.]
unguarded [un-gär´did] *adj* without guard or protection; not on one's guard, incautious; careless, inadvertent.—*adv* **unguar´dedly**.—*n* **unguar´dedness**. [OE *un-*, negative, + **guarded**.]
unguent [ung´gwėnt] *n* a salve or ointment. [L *unguentum*—*unguĕre*, to anoint.]
ungulate [ung´gū-lāt] *adj* having hoofs; of or relating to the ungulates.—*n* any of the group (Ungulata) of hoofed animals (as a ruminant, swine, horse, tapir, rhinoceros, elephant, or hyrax). [L *ungula*, a hoof.]
unhallowed [un-hal´ōd] *adj* unholy; profane; very wicked. [OE *un-*, negative, + **hallow**.]
unhand [un-hand´] *vt* to take the hands off; to let go of. [OE *un-*, release from, + **hand**.]
unhappy [un-hap´i] *adj* not happy, miserable; not fortunate; sad; wretched; not suitable.—*adv* **unhapp´ily**.—*n* **unhapp´iness**. [OE *un-*, negative, + **happy**.]
unhealthy [un-hel´thi] *adj* not healthy, weak, sickly; morally harmful or undesirable; unsafe.—*n* **unhealth´iness**.—*adv* **unhealth´ily**. [OE *un-*, negative, + **healthy**.]
unhinge [un-hinj´] *vt* to take from the hinges; to render unstable, to upset; to derange (the mind). [OE *un-*, removal from, + **hinge**.]
unholy [un-hō´li] *adj* not sacred or hallowed; wicked, sinful; mischievous; (*inf*) shocking, outrageous. [OE *un-*, negative, + **holy**.]
unhook [un-ho͝ok´] *vt* to loose from a hook; to unfasten the hooks of (eg a dress); (*inf*) to free from a habit or dependency. [OE *un-*, release from, + **hook**.]
unhorse [un-hörs´] *vt* to cause to come off, or to throw from, a horse. [OE *un*, removal from, + **horse**.]
Uniate, uniat [ū´ni-åt] *n* a member of any community of Oriental Christians that acknowledges the papal supremacy but adheres to the discipline, rites, and liturgy of the Greek Church.—Also **U´niate**. [Russian *uniyat*—*uniya*, union—L *ūnus*, one.]
unicameral [ūni-kam´ėr-ål] *adj* of a legislature, consisting of one chamber. [L *ūnus*, one, *camera*, a vault; see **chamber**.]
Unicef [ū´ni-sef] *n U*nited *N*ations *I*nternational *C*hildren's *E*mergency *F*und.
unicellular [ū-ni-sel´u-lår] *adj* having one cell. [L *ūnus*, one, + **cellular**.]
unicorn [ū´ni-körn] *n* a fabulous animal with a body like that of a horse and one straight horn on the forehead. [L *ūnus*, one, *cornu*, a horn.]
uniform [ū´ni-förm] *adj* having one or the same form; not varying, always of the same quality, character, degree, etc. (eg *a uniform temperature*); undiversified in appearance; consistent; agreeing, conforming to the same standard.—*n* the distinctive clothes of the same kind for persons (eg soldiers) who belong to the same organization.—*vt* to supply with a uniform.—*n* **uniform´ity**, state of being uniform; agreement with a pattern or rule; sameness; likeness between the parts of a whole.—*adv* **u´niformly**. [L *ūnus*, one.]
unify [ū´ni-fī] *vt* to make into one; to make consistent.—*n* **unificā´tion**. [L *ūnus*, one, *facĕre*, to make.]
unilateral [ū-ni-lat´ė-rål] *adj* one-sided; on one side only; involving one only of several parties; not reciprocal.—*adv* **unilat´erally**. [L *ūnus*, one, + **lateral**.]
unimpeachable [un-im-pēch´å-bl] *adj* not liable to be doubted or discredited; blameless. [OE *un-*, negative, + **impeachable**.]
uninhibited [un-in-hib´i-tid] *adj* not repressed, natural, unrestrained; boisterously informal. [OE *un-*, negative, + **inhibited**.]
uninterrupted [un-in-tė-rup´tid] *adj* not interrupted; continuous.—*adv* **uninterrup´tedly**. [OE *un-*, negative, + **interrupted**.]
union [ūn´yȯn] *n* act of uniting or state of being united; a whole formed by the combination of individual parts or persons; concord, agreement; marriage; an association between those in the same or kindred employment to safeguard wages and conditions; a device for uniting parts; (*math*) the set formed from all the elements present in two (or more) sets.—*ns* **un´ionist**, an advocate or supporter of union or unionism; **un´ionism**, the policy of adhering to a union; the principles, theory, advocacy, or system of trade unions; **Unionism**, adherence to the policy of a firm federal union between the states of the US, esp during the civil war period; **Union Jack**, the national flag of the United Kingdom, consisting of a union of the crosses of St George, St Andrew, and St Patrick.—**the Union**, the US. [Fr *union*—L *ūniō, -ōnis*—*ūnus*, one.]
unique [ū-nēk] *adj* without a like or equal. [Fr,—L *ūnicus*—*ūnus*.]
unisex [ū´ni-seks] (*inf*) of a style suitable for both sexes. [L *unus*, one, + **sex**.]
unison [ū´ni-sȯn] *n* identity of musical pitch; agreement.—**in unison**, with all the voices or instruments performing the same part. [L *ūnus*, one, *sonus*, a sound.]
unit [ū´nit] *n* the smallest whole number, one; a single thing or person; a known determinate quantity by which other quantities of the same kind are measured; (*education*) an amount of work used in calculating credits; (*pharmacy*) an amount of a biologically active agent (as a drug, vitamins, etc.); part of a school course dealing with a central theme; a distinct part or object with a specific purpose; a group forming a constituent part of a larger body divided eg for administrative purposes.—*adj* **u´nitary**, pertaining to unity or to a unit.—*ns* **un´it pric´ing**, a system of showing prices in terms of standard units; **unit trust**, an investment company whose portfolio consists of long-term bonds that are held to maturity. [L *ūnus*, one.]
unite [ū-nīt´] *vti* to join (two or more parts, etc.) into one; to make to agree, feel as one, or act in concert.—*adj* **unī´ted**, joined, made one; acting in concert; harmonious.—*adv* **unī´tedly**.—**United Nations**, an international organization of nations for world peace and security formed in 1945; **United Nations Day**, October 24 observed in commemoration of the founding of the United Nations; **United States**, a federation of states esp when forming a nation in a usu. specified territory. [L *ūnīre, ūnītum*.]
unity [ū´ni-ti] *n* oneness, state of being one or at one; the arrangement of all

the parts to one purpose or effect; harmony; continuity of purpose, action, etc.; (*math*) any quantity taken as one.—*n* **Unitā´rian**, a member of a religious sect holding that God is a single being.—*adj* pertaining to Unitarians or their doctrine.—*n* **Unita´rianism**, a monotheistic religion stressing individual freedom of belief, the use of reason in religion, a united world community, and liberal social action. [L *ūnitās—ūnus*, one.]

univalent [ū-ni-vāl´ėnt] *adj* (*chem*) having a valency of one, capable of combining with one atom of hydrogen or its equivalent; of a chromosome during meiosis, not paired with its homologue. [L *unus*, one, **valent** (see **valency**).]

univalve [ū´ni-valv] *adj* having one shell only.—*n* a shell of one valve only; a mollusk whose shell is composed of a single piece, as a snail.—*adj* **unival´vūlar**. [L *ūnus*, one, + **valve**.]

universal [ū-ni-vûr´sȧl] *adj* comprehending, affecting, or extending to the whole; comprising all the particulars; applied to a great variety of uses; affecting, including, or applicable to all mankind; (*logic*) affirming or denying something of every member of a class (eg *all horses are herbivorous*).—*n* a universal proposition, a general concept, or that in reality to which it corresponds; a behavior pattern or institution (as the family) existing in all cultures; a trait, characteristic of all normal adult members of a culture.—*ns* **univer´salism**, something that is universal in scope; the state of being universal; **Universalism**, (*theology*) the doctrine or belief of universal salvation, or the ultimate salvation of all mankind, now united with Unitariansim; **Univer´salist**, a believer in Universalism; **universal´ity**, state or quality of being universal; universal comprehensiveness in range.—**universal joint, universal coupling**, a joint or coupling that permits a swing of limited angle in any direction; **Universal Product Code**, a bar code used on consumer products to identify type and price, read by computerized scanners.—*adv* **univer´sally**. [L *ūniversālis—ūniversus*. See **universe**.]

universe [ū´ni-vûrs] *n* the whole system of existing things; all existing things viewed as one whole; the world. [L *ūniversum*, neut sing of *ūniversus*, whole—*ūnus*, one, *vertĕre, versum*, to turn.]

university [ū-ni-vûr´si-ti] *n* an educational institution with an undergraduate college which confers bachelor's degrees and graduate and professional schools each of which may confer master's degrees and doctorates; the physical plant of a university. [L *ūniversitās*, a corporation—*ūniversus*. See **universe**.]

unjust [un-just´] *adj* not just or controlled by justice; unfair. [[OE *un-*, negative, + **just**.]

unkempt [un-kemt´] *adj* uncombed; untidy, slovenly. [OE *un-*, negative, *cemban*, to comb—*camb*, a comb.]

unkind [un-kīnd´] *adj* lacking in kindness or sympathy; harsh; severe, cruel, etc.—*n* **unkind´ness**.—*adj* **unkind´ly**, not kind.—*adv* in an unkind manner, cruelly.—*n* **unkind´liness**. [OE *un-*, negative, + **kind**.]

unknown [un-nōn] *adj* not known or well-known; having an unknown value.—*n* something that requires to be discovered, identified or clarified as a symbol in a mathematical equation or specimen (as of bacteria or mixed chemicals).—**Unknown Soldier**, an unidentified soldier whose body represents those who died for his nation in the same war and esp in one of the world wars.

unlace [un-lās´] *vt* to undo the lace in (a boot, shoe, corset, etc.). [OE *un-*, reversing action, + **lace**.]

unlade [un-lād´] *vi* to unload; to take out the cargo of. [OE *un-*, reversing action, + **lade**.]

unlatch [un-lach´] *vt* to open by lifting the latch.—*vi* to become loose or opened. [OE *un-*, release from, + **latch**.]

unleaded [un-led´ėd] *adj* of gasoline, not mixed with tetraethyl lead.

unlearn [un-lûrn´] *vti* to seek to forget (something learned). [OE *un-*, reversing action, + **learn**.]

unlearned [un-lûr´nid] *adj* having no learning; ignorant; [un-lûrnd] not learned or mastered. [OE *un-*, negative, + **learned**.]

unleash [un-lēsh´] *vt* to free from a leash; to allow uncontrolled action to. [OE *un-*, release from, + **leash**.]

unless [un-les´] *conj* if not, supposing that not.—*prep* save; except. [formerly *on les, on lesse*, in phrase *on lesse that* (followed by clause), in a less case than.]

unlettered [un-let´ėrd] *adj* unlearned; illiterate. [OE *un-*, negative, + **letter**.]

unlike [un-līk´] *adj* not like or similar, different; not characteristic of.—*prep* not like; different from. [OE *un-*, negative, + **like**.]

unlikely [un-līk´li] *adj* not likely, improbable; not likely to succeed. [OE *un-*, negative, + **likely**.]

unload [un-lōd´] *vti* to take the load or cargo from, to discharge, to disburden; to get rid of; to dump. [OE *un-*, removal of, + **load**.]

unlock [un-lok´] *vt* to unfasten what is locked; to let loose; to release; to reveal. [OE *un-*, release from, + **lock**.]

unlooked-for [un-lŏŏkt´-fōr] *adj* not anticipated. [OE *un-*, negative, + **look**.]

unloose [un-lōōs´] *vt* to make loose; to set free.—*vt* **unloos´en**, to unloose. [OE *un-*, intensive, + **loose**.]

unlucky [un-luk´i] *adj* not lucky or fortunate; likely to bring misfortune; producing dissatisfaction.—*adv* **unluck´ily**. [OE *un-*, negative, + **lucky**.]

unmake [un-māk´] *vt* to destroy the form and qualities of; to depose from a position, rank, or authority; to change the nature of.—*adj* **unmade´**, not made. [OE *un-*, reversing action, + **made**.]

unman [un-man´] *vt* to deprive of the powers of a man, as courage, virility, etc.; to castrate, emasculate.—*adj* **unmanned´**, overcome or incapacitated by emotion; not manned and operating by remote control. [OE *un-*, deprivation of, **man**.]

unmanly [un-man´li] *adj* not becoming to a man; cowardly; effeminate. [OE *un-*, negative, + **manly**.]

unmask [un-mäsk´] *vti* to take a mask or disguise off, to expose. [OE *un-*, removal of, + **mask**.]

unmeaning [un-mē´ning] *adj* lacking intelligence; having no meaning, not intelligible.—*adv* **unmean´ingly**. [OE *un-*, negative, + **mean** (3).]

unmentionable [un-men´sh(ȯ)n-ȧ-bl] *adj* unfit to be mentioned in polite conversation; (*pl*) (*inf*) underwear.

unmitigated [un-mit´i-gā-tid] *adj* not mitigated; unqualified, out-and-out. [OE *un-*, negative, + **mitigate**.]

unmoor [un-mōōr´] *vt* to loose from being moored or anchored.—*vi* to cast off moorings. [OE *un-*, reversing action, + **moor** (2).]

unmoved [un-mōōvd´] *adj* not moved, firm; not affected by emotion, calm. [OE *un-*, negative, + **move**.]

unmuffle [un-muf´l] *vt* to free from something that muffles. [OE *un-*, reversing action, + **muffle**.]

unnatural [un-na´chùr-ȧl] *adj* not following the course of nature; artificial; strange; cruel, wicked, without natural affection. [OE *un-*, negative, + **natural**.]

unnerve [un-nûrv´] *vt* to cause to lose one's courage, strength, or vigor; to weaken; to frighten. [OE *un-*, deprivation of, + **nerve**.]

unnumbered [un-num´bėrd] *adj* not to be counted, innumerable; not provided with a number. [OE *un-*, negative, + **number**.]

unobtrusive [un-ob-trōō´siv] *adj* not obvious; modest, unassuming.—*adv* **unobtru´sively**.—*n* **unobtru´siveness**. [OE *un-*, negative, + **obtrusive**.]

unpack [un-pak´] *vti* to remove (the contents of a trunk, package, etc.); to take things out of (a trunk, etc.). [OE *un-*, reversing action, + **pack**.]

unparalleled [un-par´ȧ-leld] *adj* without precedent or equal. [OE *un-*, negative, + **parallel**.]

unparliamentary [un-pär-li-men´tȧr-i] *adj* contrary to the practice of parliamentary bodies. [OE *un-*, negative, + **parliamentary**.]

unperson [un-pûr´sȯn] *n* an individual whose influence usu. for political or ideological reasons has ceased so completely that he might never have existed. [OE *un-*, negative, + **person**.]

unpick [un-pik´] *vt* to undo (as sewing) by taking out stitches. [OE *un-*, intensive, + **pick**.]

unpin [un-pin´] *vt* to take pins out of. [OE *un-*, removal of, + **pin**.]

unpleasant [un-plez´ȧnt] *adj* not pleasant, disagreeable.—*adv* **unpleas´antly**.—*n* **unpleas´antness**, quality of being unpleasant; a disagreeable experience or situation, as an outburst, or a state, of anger or ill-feeling. [OE *un-*, negative, + **pleasant**.]

unpopular [un-pop´ū-lȧr] *adj* disliked; not winning general approval.—*n* **unpopular´ity**. [OE *un-*, negative, + **popular**.]

unprecedented [un-pres´i-den-tid] *adj* having no precedent; novel. [OE *un-*, negative, + **precedent**.]

unprepossessing [un-prē-pȯ-zes´ing] *adj* unattractive, not enlisting favor by its appearance. [OE *un-*, negative, + **prepossess**.]

unpretending [un-pri-ten´ding] *adj* unpretentious.—*n* **unpretent´ious**, free from affectation or ostentation; modest. [OE *un-*, negative, + **pretend**.]

unprincipled [un-prin´si-pld] *adj* without settled principles; not restrained by conscience. [OE *un-*, negative, + **principled**.]

unprofessional [un-prȯ-fesh´ȯn-ȧl] *adj* violating the ethical code of a given profession.—*adv* **unprofess´ionally**. [OE *un-*, negative, + **professional**.]

unpromising [un-prom´i-sing] *adj* affording little prospect of success, etc. [OE *un-*, negative, + **promise**.]

unqualified [un-kwol´i-fīd] *adj* not possessing recognized qualifications; not competent; not modified, complete. (eg *unqualified praise, support*). [OE *un-*, negative, + **qualify**.]

unquestionable [un-kwesh(ȯ)n-ȧ-bl] *adj* that cannot be questioned, indisputable; not doubtful, certain.—*adv* **unques´tionably**. [OE *un-*, negative, + **question**.]

unquiet [un-kwī´ėt] *adj* not at rest, disturbed; restless; anxious. [OE *un-*, negative, + **quiet**.]

unquote [un-kwōt´] *n* used orally to indicate the end of a quotation.—*interj* I end the quotation. [OE *un-*, release from, + **quote**.]

unravel [un-rav´ėl] *vt* to take out of a raveled state, to disentangle; to elucidate.—*vi* to become unraveled. [OE *un-*, reversing action, + **ravel**, to entangle.]

unread [un-red´] *adj* not read, as a book; having little or nothing.—*adj* **unreadable** [un-rē´dȧ-bl] illegible; too boring or too unpleasant to read. [OE *un-*, negative, + **read**.]

unreasonable [un-rēz´ȯn-ȧ-bl] *adj* not agreeable to reason; exceeding the bounds of reason, immoderate; not influenced by reason.—*ns* **unrea´son**, lack of reason; **unrea´sonableness**.—*adv* **unrea´sonably**.—*adjs* **unrea´soned**, not based on reason; **unreasoning**, not using reason. [OE *un-*, negative, + **reasonable**.]

unredeemed [un-ri-dēmd´] *adj* not ransomed or recovered; not fulfilled; unmitigated; not taken out of pawn. [OE *un-*, negative, + **redeem**.]

unregenerate [un-ri-jen´ė-rȧt] *adj* not spiritually reborn; stubbornly defiant.—*n* an unregenerate person. [OE *un-*, negative, + **regenerate**.]

unremitting [un-ri-mit´ing] *adj* not relaxing or lessening; incessant. [OE *un-*, negative, + **remit**.]
unrequited [un-rē-kwīt-ėd] *adj* not repaid, not returned. [OE *un-*, negative, + **requited**.]
unreserved [un-ri-zûrvd´] *adj* not reserved; withholding nothing, frank, open; complete, entire (eg *unreserved approval*).—*adv* **unreser´vedly** [-vid-li], without reservation; frankly. [OE *un-*, negative, + **reserved**.]
unrest [un-rest´] *n* want of rest; disquiet of mind or body; angry discontent verging on revolt. [OE *un-*, negative, + **rest**.]
unriddle [un-rid´l] *vt* to explain the riddle of; to solve. [OE *un-*, removal of, + **riddle**.]
unrivaled, unrivalled [un-rī´vȧld] *adj* surpassing the efforts of any rival; matchless. [OE *un-*, negative, + **rival**.]
unroll [un-rōl´] to roll down, to open out.—*vi* to become uncoiled or opened out. [OE *un-*, reversing action, + **roll**.]
unroof [un-rōōf´] *vt* to strip the roof or covering off. [OE *un-*, removal of, + **roof**.]
unruly [un-rōō´li] *adj* hard to control, restrain, or keep in order; disobedient. [OE *un-*, negative, + **rule**.]
unsaddle [un-sad´l] *vt* to take the saddle off (a horse, etc.). [OE *un-*, removal of or from, + **saddle**.]
unsaid [un-sed´] *adj* not said, esp not spoken aloud. [OE *un-*, negative, + **say**.]
unsavory [un-sā´vȯr-i] *adj* not savory, tasteless; unpleasant, disgusting; immoral. [OE *un-*, negative, + **savory**.]
unsay [un-sā´] *vt* to withdraw, retract. [OE *un-*, reversing action, + **say**.]
unscathed [un-skāTHd´] *adj* not harmed or injured. [OE *un-*, negative, + **scathe**.]
unscramble [un-skram´bl] *vt* to separate (as a tangle) into original parts; to decode (a message) or make (a telephone message) intelligible. [OE *un-*, reversing action, + **scramble**.]
unscrew [un-skrōō´] *vt* to unfasten by loosening screws; to loosen and take off by turning. [OE *un-*, removal of, + **screw**.]
unseal [un-sēl´] *vt* to remove the seal of; to open. [OE *un-*, removal of, + **seal** (1).]
unseasonable [un-sē´z(ȯ)n-ȧ-bl] *adj* not at the proper season; not suitable for the time of year; inopportune. [OE *un-*, negative, + **seasonable**.]
unseat [un-sēt´] *vt* to throw from or deprive of a seat; to remove or oust from an official position. [OE *un-*, removal from, + **seat**.]
unseen [un-sēn´] *adj* not seen; invisible; not previously read or studied. [OE *un-*, negative, + **see** (2).]
unsettle [un-set´l] *vti* to move from being settled; to disturb, displace, or disorder.—*adj* **unsett´led**, changeable; undecided; unpaid; having no settlers. [OE *un-*, reversing action, + **settle**.]
unsex [un-seks´] *vt* to deprive of sex or sexual power; to make unmanly or unwomanly. [OE *un-*, deprivation of, + **sex**.]
unshackle [un-shak´l] *vt* to loose from shackles; to set free. [OE *un-*, removal of, + **shackle**.]
unsheathe [un-shēTH´] *vt* to draw from the sheath or scabbard. [OE *un-*, removal from, + **sheathe**.]
unship [un-ship´] *vt* to take out of a ship or other vessel; to remove (as an oar or tiller) from the place where it is fixed or fitted. [OE *un-*, removal from, + **ship**.]
unsightly [un-sīt´li] *adj* not pleasing to the eye, ugly. [OE *un-*, negative, + **sightly**.]
unsocial [un-sō´shȧl] *adj* lacking a desire for society or close association; characterized by such a lack. [OE *un-*, negative, + **social**.]
unsophisticated [un-so-fis´ti-kā-tid] *adj* genuine; artless, simple, not worldly-wise. [OE *un-*, negative, + **sophisticated**.]
unsound [un-sownd´] *adj* not in perfect condition; not solid or firm; not correct; not clearly reasoned; (of mind) not functioning normally, not sane. [OE *un-*, negative, + **sound** (1).]
unsparing [un-spār´ing] *adj* not sparing; liberal, profuse; not merciful; severe.—*adv* **unspar´ingly**. [OE *un-*, negative, + **spare**.]
unspeakable [un-spē´kȧ-bl] *adj* incapable of being spoken, uttered or described; indescribably bad, evil, etc.—*adv* **unspea´kably**, in an unspeakable or inexpressible manner. [OE *un-*, negative, + **speak**, + suffx *-able*.]
unstop [un-stop´] *vt* to free from a stopper; to clear (a pipe, etc.) of obstruction. [OE *un-*, removal of, + **stop**.]
unstring [un-string´] *vt* to take from a string; to take the strings off; to make disordered, weak, or unstable.—*adj* **unstrung´**, nervous or upset; with the strings loosened or detached, as a bow, racket, etc. [OE *un-*, removal of, + **string**.]
unstudied [un-stud´id] *adj* done without premeditation, natural, easy; not acquired by study. [OE *un-*, negative, + **study**.]
unsung [un-sung´] *adj* not celebrated in song or verse; not sung. [OE *un-*, negative, + **sing**.]
unthinkable [un-thingk´ȧ-bl] *adj* inconceivable; improbable in the highest degree; (of an occurrence) not possible to imagine. [OE *un-*, negative, **think**, + suffix *-able*.]
untie [un-tī] *vt* to loose from being tied; to unbind; to loosen.—*adj* **untied´**. [OE *un-*, reversing action, + **tie**.]
until [un-til´] *prep* up to the time of; before.—*conj* up to the time when or that; to the point, degree, etc. that; before. [ME *untill*—**unto**, and **till** (prep).]
untimely [un-tīm´li] *adj* premature; immature; inopportune.—Also *adv*. [OE *un-*, negative, + **timely**.]
untiring [un-tīr´ing] *adj* not interrupted by weariness; diligent, assiduous.—*adv* **untir´ingly**. [OE *un-*, negative, + **tire** (3).]
unto [un´tŏŏ] *prep* (*arch*) to or until; used as a function word to indicate reference or concern. [Modelled on **until**.]
untold [un-tōld´] *adj* not told or related; too great to be counted; vast. [OE *un-*, negative, + **tell**.]
untouchable [un-tuch´ȧ-bl] *adj* not to be touched or handled; exempt from criticism or control; lying beyond reach; disagreeable to the touch.—*n* in India, formerly, a member of the lowest caste. [OE *un-*, negative, + **touchable**.]
untoward [un-tō´ȧrd, un-tȯrd´] *adj* not easily guided, perverse; unseemly; not favorable; adverse. [OE *un-*, negative, + **toward**.]
untried [un-trīd´] *adj* not tested by experience; not tried in court. [OE *un-*, negative, + **try**.]
untrod, untrodden [un-trod´n] *adj* seldom or never trodden, unfrequented. [OE *un-*, negative, + **trodden**.]
untroubled [un-trub´ld] *adj* not troubled or anxious; calm, tranquil. [OE *un-*, negative, + **troubled**.]
untrue [un-trōō´] *adj* not true, false; not faithful, disloyal; not in accordance with a standard; not level, not straight.—*n* **untruth´**, falsehood; falsity; (*arch*) disloyalty. [OE *un-*, negative, + **truth**.]
untutored [un-tūtȯrd] *adj* uninstructed; lacking refinement or elegance, rough. [OE *un-*, negative, + **tutor**.]
untwine [un-twīn´] *vt* to untwist, unwind.—*vi* to become untwisted. [OE *un-*, reversing action, + **twine**.]
untwist [un-twist´] *vti* to separate, as something twisted together; to unwind. [OE *un-*, reversing action, + **twist**.]
unutterable [un-ut´ėr-ȧ-bl] *adj* inexpressible, incapable of being uttered or expressed. [OE *un-*, negative, **utter** (2) + suffx *-able*.]
unvarnished [un-vär´nisht] *adj* not varnished; plain, simple, unadorned. [OE *un-*, negative, + **varnish**.]
unveil [un-vāl´] *vt* to remove a veil from; to disclose, reveal.—*vi* to become unveiled, to reveal oneself. [OE *un-*, removal of, + **veil**.]
unwary [un-wā´ri] *adj* not cautious, not on one's guard; heedless, gullible.—*adv* **unwā´rily**. [OE *un-*, negative, + **wary**.]
unweave [un-wēv´] *vt* to undo what is woven. [OE *un-*, reversing action, + **weave**.]
unwelcome [un-wel´kȯm] *adj* received with regret; causing grief or disappointment. [OE *un-*, negative, + **welcome**.]
unwell [un-wel´] *adj* not in perfect health, sick. [OE *un-*, negative, + **well** (2).]
unwieldy [un-wēl´di] *adj* not easily moved or handled, as because of large size.—*adv* **unwield´ily**.—*n* **unwield´iness**. [OE *un-*, negative, and obs *wieldy*, manageable—**wield**.]
unwilling [un-wil´ing] *adj* not willing, disinclined, reluctant; reluctantly done or said.—*adv* **unwill´ingly**.—*n* **unwill´ingness**. [OE *un-*, negative, + **willing**.]
unwind [un-wīnd´] *vt* to wind off or undo (something wound); to untangle (something involved).—*vi* to become unwound; to become relaxed. [OE *un-*, reversing action, + **wind** (2).]
unwise [un-wīz´] *adj* not wise; injudicious; foolish. [OE *un-*, negative, + **wise** (1).]
unwitting [un-wit´ing] *adj* not aware, ignorant; unintentional (eg *gave him unwitting aid*).—*adv* **unwitt´ingly**. [OE *un-*, negative, + **wit** (1).]
unwonted [un-won´tėd or -wōn´-] *adj* unaccustomed; unusual; rare. [OE *un-*, negative, + **wonted**.]
unworthy [un-wûr´THi] *adj* not worthy; not deserving (of); not in keeping with, unbecoming to (eg *unworthy of your high talents*). [OE *un-*, negative, + **worthy**.]
unwrap [un-rap´] *vt* to open what is wrapped.—*vi* to become unwrapped. [OE *un-*, reversing action, + **wrap**.]
unwritten [un-rit´n] *adj* not written; not committed to writing or record, traditional; oral.—**unwritten law**, law based on custom or mores rather than legislative enactment. [OE *un-*, negative, + **written** (see **write**).]
unyoke [un-yōk´] *vt* to loose from a yoke; to disjoin. [OE *un-*, removal of, + **yoke**.]
up [up] *adv* towards a higher place; aloft, on high; from a lower to a higher position, as out of bed, above the horizon, etc.; to a later period; so as to be even with in time, degree, etc.; so as to be tightly bound, closed, etc.; (*baseball*) to one's turn at batting; in a higher position; completely; at an end, over.—*prep* from a lower to a higher place on or along.—*adj* inclining up, upward.—*vt* to raise; to lift or haul up; to move up.—*vi* to set up; to move up; to intervene boldly, to start into activity or speech.—*n* in phrase **ups and downs**, rises and falls, vicissitudes.—*adjs* **up´-and-com´ing**, alert and pushful; likely to succeed (in a career, etc.); **upmar´ket**, appealing to wealthy consumers.—**up against**, (*inf*) confronted with; **up in** (or **on**), (*inf*) having a knowledge of; **up to**, (*inf*) about, engaged in doing; capable of and ready for; incumbent upon; as many as; as far as; **up to date**; to the present time; in touch with or in possession of the latest ideas, practices or devices; **up to the minute**, right up to the present time; right up to date.

—**on the up and up** (*slang*) honest; **what's up**, (*inf*) what's the matter, what's wrong? [OE *up, upp*; Ger. *auf.*]

upas [ū´pas] *n* the juice of the upas, a tall Asian tree (*Antiaris toxicaria*) or a shrub or tree (*Strychnos tieuté*) yielding a powerful vegetable poison, used for arrows; a poisonous or harmful influence. [Malay, *ūpas*, poison.]

upbraid [up-brād´] *vt* to rebuke severely; to reproach. [OE *upbregdan, upgebrēdan.*]

upbringing [up´bring-ing] *n* the process of nourishing and training (a child). [**up, bring**.]

upcast [up´käst] *n* something cast up. [**up, cast**.]

upcountry [up´kun-tri] *adv* toward the interior, inland.—*adj* belonging to the interior of a country.—*n* the interior of a country. [**up, country**.]

update [up´dāt´] *vt* to bring up to date. [**up, date**.]

upgrade [up´grād] *n* a rising slope or grade; an increase or rise.—*vt* [up-grād´] to improve (livestock) by using purebred sires; to advance to a job requiring a higher level of skill; to raise the quality of (as a manufactured product); to extend the usefulness of (as a device). [**up, grade**.]

upheave [up-hēv´] *vt* to heave or lift up; to move upward, esp with power.—*n* **upheav´al**, the raising of surface formations by the action of internal forces, esp of the earth's crust; radical change; extreme agitation or disorder. [**up, heave**.]

upheld [up-held´] *pt, pt p* of **uphold**.

uphill [up´hil] *adj* ascending; difficult.—*adv* [up-hil´] up a hill; against difficulties. [**up, hill**.]

uphold [up-hōld´] *vt* to hold up; to sustain; to countenance; to defend; to maintain, confirm (a decision).—*n* **uphōl´der**. [**up, hold**.]

upholster [up-hōl´stėr] *vt* to furnish (furniture) with stuffing, springs, etc.—*ns* **uphōl´sterer**, one who does this; **uphōl´stery**, materials (as fabric, padding, springs, etc.) used to make a soft covering esp for a seat; the work of an upholsterer. [**up, hold**, + suffx *-ster.*]

upkeep [up´kēp] *n* maintenance; state of repair; cost of maintenance. [**up, keep**.]

upland [up´lȧnd] *n* land elevated above other land, esp distant from the sea.—*adj* of or located in upland. [**up, land**.]

uplift [up-lift´] *vt* to lift up; to raise to a higher moral, social, or cultural level.—*n* [up´lift´]. [**up, lift**.]

upmost *See* **upper**.

upon [ůp-on´] *prep* on, on the top of. [**up, on**.]

upper [up´ėr] *adj* (*comparative* of **up**) farther up; higher in position, dignity, etc.; superior;—*superl* **upp´ermost, up´most**.—*ns* **upp´er**, the part of a boot or shoe above the sole and welt; (*slang*) any drug that is a stimulant; **upp´er hand**, the position of superiority, advantage, control.—**upper atmosphere**, the region of the atmosphere above about 20 miles from the earth; **upper class**, the people of the highest social rank (*adj* **upp´er-class´**); **upp´erclassman**, a junior or senior, as in a college; **upper crust**, the highest circle of the upper class.—*adj* **upp´ish** (*inf*) haughty, arrogant, affecting superiority.—*n* **upp´ishness**.—*adj* **upp´ity**, uppish.

upright [up´rīt] *adj* straight up, in an erect position; possessing moral integrity—honest, just.—*n* a vertical post or support.—*adv* vertically.—*adv* **up´rightly**.—*n* **up´rightness**.—**upright piano**, one with vertical rectangular body. [**up, right**.]

uprising [up´rīz-ing] *n* an insurrection, revolt. [**up, rising**.]

uproar [up´rōr] *n* noise and tumult, bustle and clamor.—*adj* **uproar´ious**, making or accommodated by great uproar.—*adv* **uproar´iously**. [Du *oproer*, revolt—*op*, up, *roeren* (Ger *rühren*, OE *hrēran*), to stir; the form due to confusion with *roar.*]

uproot [up-rōōt´] *vt* to tear up by the roots; to destroy or remove utterly. [**up, root** (1).]

upset [up-set´] *vt* to turn upside down; to overthrow; to put out of order; to distress; to affect temporarily the health of.—*n* **up´set**, an overturning; an unexpected defeat; distress or its cause.—*adj* relating to what is set up for sale, in phrase **upset price**, the minimum sum fixed for a bid at a sale by auction. [**up, set**.]

upshot [up´shot] *n* (*orig*) the last shot in an archery match; the conclusion; the result. [**up, shot**.]

upside down [up´sīd down] *adj* with the upper part undermost; in complete confusion.—**upside-down cake**, a cake baked with its batter covering an arrangement of fruit and served fruit side up. [**up, side**.]

upsilon [yōōp´si-lŏn] *n* the 20th letter of the Greek alphabet.

upstage [up´stāj´] *adv* toward or at the back of the stage.—Also *adj*.—*vt* to draw attention away from (another), as by moving upstage; (*inf*) to steal the stage from; (*inf*) to treat snobbishly. [**up, stage**.]

upstairs [up-stārz´] *adv* up the stairs, on or to an upper story.—*adj* **up´stairs** on an upper floor.—*n* an upper floor. [**up, stair**.]

upstanding [up-stan´ding *adj* erect; honorable; worthy, honest. [**up, stand**.]

upstart [up´stärt] *n* one who has suddenly risen from poverty or obscurity to wealth or power but who does not appear to have the appropriate dignity or ability. [**up, start**.]

upstream [up´strēm´] *adv* in the direction against the current of a stream. [**up, stream**.]

upstroke [up´strōk] *n* a stroke made in an upward direction. [**up, stroke** (1).]

uptake [up´tāk] *n* a taking up.—**quick** (or **slow**) **on the uptake** (*inf*) quick (or slow) to comprehend. [**up, take**.]

upthrust [up´thrust] *n* a thrust upward, esp an upheaval of a mass of rock. [**up, thrust**.]

uptight [up´tīt] *adj* (*slang*) very tense, nervous, etc. [**up, tight**.]

upward [up´wȧrd] *adj* directed up or to a higher place.—*advs* **up´ward, up´wards**, in a higher direction.—**upward mobility**, movement to a higher social and economic status. [**up**, + suffx. *-ward.*]

uranium [ū-rā´ni-ům] *n* a metallic element (symbol U, at wt 238.0; at no 92). [Gr *ouranos*, heaven.]

Uranus [ū-rā´nus] *n* a Greek god, grandfather of Zeus; one of the most distant of the major planets. [Gr *ouranos*, heaven.]

urban [ûr´bȧn] *adj* of or belonging to a city.—*adj* **urbāne**, pertaining to, or influenced by, city life, civilized, polished, suave.—*adv* **urbāne´ly**.—*vt* **ur´banize**, to make (a district) urban as opposed to rural in character.—*n* **urbanizā´tion**.—*n* **urbăn´ity**, the quality of being urbane.—**urban renewal**, rehabilitation of dilapidated urban areas, as by slum clearance and housing construction; **urban sprawl**, the spread of urban construction into surrounding areas. [L *urbānus—urbs*, a city.]

urchin [ûr´chin] *n* a hedgehog; a pert or mischievous child; a sea urchin. [OFr *(h)eriçun*, etc. (Fr *hérisson*)—L *ēricius*, a hedgehog.]

Urdu [ŏŏr´dōō] *n* the official language of Pakistan, belonging to the Indic branch of the Indo-European family of languages, closely related to Hindi. [Hindustani, 'camp (language)'.]

urea [ū-rē´ȧ] a substance found in mammalian urine, the end product of protein decomposition; synthesized urea (as from carbon dioxide and ammonia) used in making resins and plastics and for fertilizers and animal feed. [Gr *ouron*, urine.]

ureter [ū-rē´tėr] *n* the duct which conveys the urine from the kidneys to the bladder. [Gr,—*ouron*, urine.]

urethra [ū-rē´thra] *n* the canal by which the urine is discharged from the bladder;—*pl* **urē´thrae** [-ē]. [Gr,—*ouron*, urine.]

urge [ûrj] *vt* to drive forward, make to move faster; to press, entreat (a person) earnestly; to advocate earnestly (an action, course).—*vi* to insist; to press (on, etc.).—*n* an impulse, inner prompting.—*n* **ur´gency**, quality of being urgent; insistence; pressing necessity.—*adj* **ur´gent**, impelling; pressing with importunity; calling for immediate attention.—*adv* **ur´gently**. [L *urgēre*, to press.]

urine [ū´rin] *n* the yellowish fluid which is secreted or separated by the kidneys from the blood and conveyed to the bladder.—*n* **u´rinal**, a vessel for urine; accommodation provided for discharging urine.—*adjs* **u´rinary**, pertaining to, or like, urine; **urinogen´ital**, urogenital; **urogen´ital**, relating to or being the organs or functions of excretion and reproduction.—*n* **urology**, the branch of medicine dealing with the urogenital functions. [Fr,—L *ūrīna*; Gr *ouron*, Sans *vāri*, water.]

urn [ûrn] *n* a vase with a pedestal; such a vessel used for preserving the ashes of the dead; a metal container with a faucet, for making or serving hot coffee, tea, etc. [L *urna*, an urn—*urĕre*, to burn.]

ursine [ûr´sīn, ûr´sin] *adj* of or resembling a bear.—*n* **Ur´sa Major**, an extensive conspicuous constellation in the Northern Hemisphere, the seven brightest stars forming the Great Bear or Big Dipper; **Ursa Minor**, a constellation of seven stars whose stars include the Pole Star. [L *ursus*, a bear.]

us [us] *pron* the objective (accusative or dative) case of **we**. [OE.]

usage [ū´zij] *n* act of using; mode of using, treatment; customary use; practice, custom; the way in which a word, phrase, etc. is used to express a particular idea. [Fr,—L *usūs.*]

use[1] [ūz] *vt* to put to some purpose; to avail oneself of; to employ as an instrument; make use of (a person); to exercise; to deal with; treat; to consume; expend (*often with* **up**).—*vi* to be accustomed (used only in the past, with **to**) and pronounced *ūst*.—*adj* **used**, not new; second-hand.—**use up**, to consume, use completely; to exhaust, as of land. [Fr *user*—L *ūtī, ūsus*, to use.]

use[2] [ūs] *n* act of using or putting to a purpose; usage (eg *this book has seen much use*); employment; need (for), opportunity of employing; advantage, suitability, effectiveness; practice, custom.—*adj* **use´ful**, convenient, advantageous, serviceable, helpful, able to do good.—*adv* **use´fully**.—*n* **use´fulness**.—*adj* **use´less**, having no use; answering no good purpose; ineffective.—*adv* **use´lessly**.—*n* **use´lessness**.—**have no use for**, have no admiration or liking for; **in use**, in employment or practice; **make use of**, to use, to employ; to treat (another) as a means to one's own gain; **of no use**, useless; **of use**, useful. [L *ūsus—ūtī*, to use.]

usher [ush´ėr] one who shows people to their seats in a theater, church, etc.; a bridegroom's attendant.—*vt* to escort (others) to seats, etc.; to be a forerunner of (*often with* **in**).—*n* **usherette´**, a female usher as in a theater. [OFr *ussier* (Fr *huissier*)—L *ostiārius*, a door-keeper—*ostium*, a door.]

usual [ū´zhū-ȧl] *adj* customary; occurring in ordinary use, common, most frequent.—*adv* **u´sually**. [L *ūsuālis.*]

usufruct [ū´zū-frukt] *n* the use and profit, but not the property, of a thing; the right to use or enjoy something. [L *ūsusfructus—ūsus*, use, *fructus*, fruit.]

usurp [ū-zûrp´] *vt* to take possession of by force without right; to assume (eg a right) that properly belongs to another.—*ns* **usurpā´tion**, act of usurping; unlawful seizure and possession; **usur´per**. [Fr,—L *ūsurpāre, -ātum.*]

usury [ū´zhū-ri] *n* the taking of excessive interest on a loan; an excessive interest rate.—*n* **u´surer**, one who practices usury. [L *ūsūra—ūtī, ūsus*, to use.]

ut [ŏŏt] *n* (*mus*) do, formerly the keynote in the diatonic scale. [From the initial syllable of the first line of a medieval Latin hymn, successive phrases of which began on successive notes of the major scale.]

Ute [yōo7t] *n* a member of an Amerindian people originally ranging through Utah, Colorado, Arizona, and New Mexico;—*pl* **Ute, Utes**; the Uto-Aztecan language of this people.

utensil [ū-ten´sil] *n* an implement or container, esp one for use in a kitchen. [Fr *utensile*—L *ūtensilis*, fit for use—ūtī, to use.]

uterine [ū´tė-rin, -rīn] *adj* pertaining to the womb; born of the same mother by a different father.—*n* **ū´terus**, a womb. [Fr *uterin*—L *uterīnus*—*uterus*, the womb.]

utilize [ū´ti-līz] *vt* to make use of; put to profitable use.—*n* **utilizā´tion**. [Fr *utiliser*—L *ūtī*, to use.]

utility [ū-til´i-ti] *n* usefulness, profit; something useful, as the service to the public of gas, water, etc.; a company providing such a service.—*adj* of a serviceable type of article, capable of serving as a substitute; kept for production rather than show (as of animals); of a company providing utilities; utilitarian.—*adj* **ūtilitā´rian**, consisting in, or pertaining to, utility or to utilitarianism.—*n* one who holds utilitarianism.—*n* **utilitā´rianism**, the ethical theory which finds the basis of moral distinctions in the utility of actions, ie their fitness to produce happiness of the greatest number.—**utility room**, a room containing laundry appliances, heating equipment, etc. [L *ūtilitās, -ātis*—*ūtī*, to use.]

utmost [ut´mōst] *adj* most extreme; farthest; of the greatest degree, amount, etc.—*n* the most possible. [OE *ūtemest*, formed with double superlative suffx. *-m-est* from *ūt*, out.]

Uto-Aztecan [yōō-tō-az´tėk-ȧn] *n* an Amerindian language family spoken throughout the American Southwest and Mexico.

Utopian [ū-tō´pi-ȧn] *adj* ideally perfect.—*n* one that believes in the perfectibility of human society; one proposing or advocating utopian schemes.—*n* **Utopia**, any idealized place; any visionary scheme for a perfect society. [From *Utopia*, lit 'nowhere' (Gr *ou*, not, *topos*, place), an imaginary island represented by Sir Thomas More (1478–1535) as enjoying perfection in politics, laws, etc.]

utricle [ū´tri-kl] *n* a cell or bladder; a more or less inflated, bladderlike envelope surrounding the fruits of various plants. [L *ūtriculus*, dim of *ūter*, a bag.]

utter[1] [ut´ėr] *adj* extreme; complete (eg *utter wretchedness*).—*adv* **utt´erly**, completely. [OE *ūtor*, outer—*ūt*, out.]

utter[2] [ut´ėr] *vt* to emit; to put into circulation; to speak, give voice to.—*adj* **utt´erable**, that may be uttered or expressed.—*ns* **utt´erance**, act of uttering; manner of speaking; expression in speech, or in other sound, of a thought or emotion; words spoken, a saying; **utt´erer**. [OE *ūtian*, to put out—*ū*, out.]

uttermost [ut´ėr-mōst] *adj* farthest out; utmost.—*n* the greatest degree. [Same as *utmost*, the *r* being intrusive, and *t* being doubled on the analogy of *utter*.]

uvula [ū´vū-la] *n* the fleshy conical body suspended from the palate over the back part of the tongue.—*adj* **ū´vūlar**. [L *ūva*, a bunch of grapes.]

uxorious [uk-sō´ri-ůs] *adj* excessively or submissively fond of a wife.—*adv* **uxō´riously**.—*n* **uxō´riousness**. [L *uxōrius*—*uxor*, a wife.]

V

V-sign [vē´sīn] *n* a sign made with the index and middle fingers in the form of a V, with palm turned outwards in token of victory, with palm inwards as a sign of derision.

vacant [vā´kȧnt] *adj* empty; free, unoccupied; unreflecting (eg *vacant mood*); inane.—*n* **vā´cancy**, emptiness; empty space, gap between bodies; an unoccupied situation or office; (*rare*) idleness.—*adv* **vā´cantly**.—*vt* **vȧ-cāte´**, to leave empty; to quit possession of.—*n* **văcā´tion**, a vacating or making void; (time of) freedom from regular duties and engagements; a holiday, esp from academic or legal duties. [Fr,—L *vacāns, -antis*, pr p of *vacāre, -ātum*, to be empty.]

vaccinate [vak´si-nāt] *vt* to inoculate with *vaccine* as a preventive against certain diseases.—*n* **vaccinā´tion**.—*adj* **vaccine** [vak´sēn], pertaining to, derived from, cows; of, relating to, vaccination.—*n* a modified and hence harmless virus or other microorganism for inoculation to produce immunity to a disease by stimulating antibody production; cowpox virus similarly used against smallpox in man; a process to combat a computer virus. [L *vaccīnus—vacca*, a cow.]

vacillate [vas´i-lāt] *vi* to sway to and fro; to waver, show indecision.—*n* **vacillā´tion**. [L *vacillāre, -ātum*.]

vacuous [vak´ū-us] *adj* empty, void; lacking intelligence, inane.—*ns* **vacū´ity**, emptiness; an unoccupied space; idleness, listlessness; **vac´uōle**, a very small cavity in the tissue of organisms; **vac´ūum**, (theoretically—*perfect vacuum*) a space empty or devoid of all matter; (in practice) a region in which the gas pressure is considerably lower than atmospheric; a vacuum cleaner;—*pl* **vac´ūa; vac´uum clean´er**, an apparatus for removing dust from carpets, etc., by suction.—*adj* **vac´uum-packed´**, sealed in a container from which most of the air has been removed.—*n* **vac´ūum tube**, a sealed glass tube in which a vacuum has been made, eg. a thermionic valve. [L *vacuus*, empty.]

vade-mecum [vā´di-mē´kum] *n* a handbook carried for reference. [L 'go with me'—*vadĕre*, to go, *me*, abl of *ego*, I, *cum*, with.]

vagabond [vag´ȧ-bond] *adj* wandering; having no settled home; driven to and fro; unsettled.—*n* one who has no settled abode; a vagrant; a rascal.—*n* **vag´abondage**. [Fr,—LL,—L *vagārī*, to wander—*vagus*, wandering.]

vagary [vā´gȧ-ri, vȧ-gā´ri] *n* a wandering of the thoughts; a whim; an aberration;—*pl* **vagaries**. [Prob L *vagārī*, to stray.]

vagina [vȧ-jī´na] *n* (*anat*) the canal or passage which leads from the external orifice to the uterus;—*pl* **-as, -ae** [-ē]. [L *vāgina*, a sheath.]

vagrant [vā´grȧnt] *adj* without a settled abode; wandering, erratic.—*n* one who has no settled home; an idle and disorderly person, as one who has no means of livelihood but begging or stealing.—*n* **va´grancy**, the act of wandering; the condition of a vagrant; the offense of being a vagrant. [ME *vagraunt*, perh Anglo-Fr *wackerant*, influenced by L *vāgārī*, to wander.]

vague [vāg] *adj* indefinite (eg *vague statements*); indistinct, lacking precision (eg *he saw a vague figure*); (of a person) lacking character and purpose, or addicted to haziness of thought.—*adv* **vague´ly**.—*n* **vague´ness**. [Fr,—L *vagus*, wandering.]

vail [vāl] *vt* to lower, let fall (eg. crest, pride). [Contr from obs vb *avale*—Fr *avaler*; cf **avalanche**.]

vain [vān] *adj* unsatisfying; fruitless, unavailing, ineffectual; empty, worthless (eg threats, boasts, promises); conceited; showy.—*adv* **vain´ly**.—*ns* **vain´ness, van´ity**, worthlessness, futility; empty pride or ostentation; idle show, or empty pleasure.—**Vanity Fair**, the world depicted as a scene of vanity and folly in Bunyan's *Pilgrim's Progress*.—**in vain**, ineffectually, to no end; **take in vain**, to use (one's name) in an irreverent or profane manner. [Fr,—L *vānus*, empty.]

vainglory [vān-glō´ri, -glö´-] *n* boastful pride.—*adj* **vain´glō´rious**, given to vainglory; proceeding from vanity.—*adv* **vainglō´riously**. [**vain, glory**.]

valance [val´ȧns] *n* hanging drapery for a bed; a short curtain forming a border, esp across the top of a window. [Poss A Fr *valer*, to descend.]

vale [vāl] *n* a tract of low ground, esp between hills, a valley. [Fr *val*—L *vallis*, a vale.]

valediction [val-e-dik´sh(ȯ)n] *n* a farewell.—*adj* **valedic´tory**, saying farewell; taking leave.—*n* a farewell speech. [L *valedīcĕre, -dictum—valē*, farewell, *dīcĕre*, to say.]

valence [vā´len-si] *n* (*chem*) the combining power of an atom or group in terms of hydrogen atoms or their equivalent.—Also **vā´lency.-vāl´ent**, in composition, having a (specified) valence. [From L *valēre*, to be strong.]

valentine [val´en-tīn] *n* a lover or sweetheart chosen on St *Valentine's* Day, February 14; a love letter or other token sent on that day. [So named from the notion that birds choose their mates on that day.]

valerian [va-lē´ri-ȧn] *n* a genus (*Valeriana*) of dicotyledons, certain species of which have an edible root with medicinal properties. [OFr,—L *valēre*, to be strong.]

valet [val´et, or val´ā] *n* a manservant, esp one who attends on a gentleman's person.—*vt* to act as a valet to;—*pr p* **val´eting**; *pt, pt p* **val´eted** [or val´ād]. [OFr,—*vaslet*, later also *varlet*. See **varlet, vassal**.]

valetudinarian [val-e-tū-di-nā´ri-ȧn] *adj* pertaining to ill health; sickly, weak.—Also **valetū´dinary**.—*n* a person of weak health; a person preoccupied with his health.—*n* **valetūdinā´rianism**, weak health. preoccupation with health. [L *valētūdinārius—valētūdō*, state of health—*valēre*, to be strong.]

valiant [val´yȧnt] *adj* (*obs*) strong; brave, heroic (of a deed, etc.); intrepid in danger.—*adv* **val´iantly**.—*n* **val´iantness**, valor, courage. [Fr *vaillant—L valēns, valentis*, pr p of *valēre*, to be strong.]

valid [val´id] *adj* (*arch*) strong; having sufficient strength or force, founded in truth, sound (eg of an argument, objection); fulfilling all the necessary conditions; (*law*) executed with the proper formalities, legal.—*n* **valid´ity**.—*adv* **val´idly**. [Fr,—L *validus—valēre*, to be strong.]

valise [va´lēs´] *n* a traveling bag, generally of leather, opening at the side. [Fr—LL *valisia*.]

Valium [val´i-um] *n* trade name for a tranquilizing drug.

valley [val´i] *n* low land between hills or mountains; a low, extended plain, usu. watered by a river;—*pl* **vall´eys**. [OFr *valee—val*, a vale.]

valor [val´ȯr] *n* stoutness of heart, intrepidity; prowess.—*adj* **val´orous**, intrepid, valiant.—*adv* **val´orously**. [OFr *valour*—Low L *valor*—L *valēre*, to be strong.]

valse [völs, vals] *n* a concert waltz. [Fr.]

value [val´ū] *n* worth, that which renders anything useful or estimable; efficacy, importance, excellence; (*pl*) beliefs or standards; relative worth (eg *a sense of values*); estimated worth (eg *a high value*); price; purchasing power; an equivalent, fair return (eg *value for one's money*); precise meaning (of a word); quality of sound (as expressed by a phonetic symbol); duration (of a musical note); (*painting*) relation of one part of a picture to the others with reference to light and shade; amount indicated by a mathematical term or expression.—*vt* to estimate the worth of; to rate (at a price); to esteem; to prize.—*adj* **val´uable**, having considerable value or worth.—*n* a thing of value (esp an article of small bulk)—often in *pl*.—*ns* **val´uableness; valuā´tion**, the act of valuing; estimated worth; **val´uātor**, one who sets a value on goods, esp one licensed to do so, an appraiser.—Also **val´uer**.—*adj* **val´ueless**.—**value-added tax**, a tax on the rise in value of a product due to the manufacturing and marketing processes and included in the cost to the consumer; **value judgement**, a personal estimate of merit in a particular respect. [OFr *value*, properly fem of Fr *valu*, pt p of *valoir*, to be worth—L *valēre*.]

valve [valv] *n* (*arch*) one of the leaves of a folding door; a lid that opens in one direction and not in the other for controlling the flow of liquid or gas in a pipe; a membranous fold or other structure that performs the same function in a tube or organ of the body; one of the separable pieces forming a mollusk shell; a term used in electronics and thermionics, strictly applicable to a *rectifier*, but generally applied to all forms of thermionic and gas discharge tubes.—*adj* **val´vūlar**. [Fr,—L *valva*, a folding door.]

vamp[1] [vamp] *n* front upper part of a boot or shoe; a patch; (*mus*) an improvised accompaniment.—*vt* to repair with a new vamp; to patch old with new; give a new appearance to; (*mus*) to improvise; to play (such an accompaniment).—**vamp up**, to patch up, concoct, improvise. [Corr of Fr *avant-pied*, the forepart of the foot—*avant*, before, *pied*—L *pēs, pedis*, foot.]

vamp[2] [vamp] *n* (*slang*) a seductive type of woman who allures and exploits men.—*vt* to allure. [Abbrev of **vampire**.]

vampire [vam´pīr] *n* in the superstition of eastern Europe, a corpse which by night leaves its grave to suck the blood of sleeping men; an extortioner; a vampire bat.—*n* **vam´pire bat**, any of various bats (genus *Desmoda* or *Diphylla*) found in Central and South America which suck the blood of sleeping men and animals; other species erroneously believed to do so. [*vampir* is common in the Slavonic languages.]

van[1] [van] *n* the front; the front of an army or a fleet; the pioneers of any movement. [Abbrev of **vanguard**.]

van[2] [van] *n* covered wagon for conveying goods, etc., by road or rail. [Short for **caravan**.]

vanadium [van-ā´di-ŭm] *n* a metallic element (symbol V; at wt 51.0; at no 23). [*Vanadis*, a Scandinavian goddess.]

Van Allen belt zone of intense particle radiation surrounding the earth at a distance of from 2000 to 12000 miles. [J A *Van Allen*, American physicist, born 1914.]

Vandal [van´dȧl] *n* one of a fierce race who overran and barbarously devastated provinces of the Roman Empire in the 5th century; **vandal**, one who wantonly damages property; one who destroys what is beautiful.—*n* **van´dalism**, behavior of a vandal. [LL *Vandali, Vinduli*—Gmc.]

Vandyke [van´dīk´] *n* a painting by *Vandyke*; a small round cape, an elaborately bordered lace collar, or a pointed beard, as seen in paintings by Vandyke.—*n* **Vandyke brown**, a natural brown-black or synthetic brown pigment. [Anthony *Van Dyck or Vandyke*, a great Flemish painter (1599–1641).]

vane [vān] *n* a thin slip of wood or metal at the top of a spire, etc., to show which way the wind blows, a weathercock; the thin web of a feather; one of the blades of a windmill or propeller, etc. [Older form *fane*—OE *fana*; Ger *fahne*; akin to L *pannus*, Gr *pēnos*, a cloth.]

vanguard [van´gärd] *n* the part of an army preceding the main body; the front line. [Formerly *vantgard*—Fr *avant-garde*—*avant*, before, *garde*, guard.]

vanilla [va-nil´a] *n* the dried aromatic sheathlike pod or fruit of a tropical American climbing orchid (genus *Vanilla*) used in confectionery, etc. [Latinized from Fr *vanille*—Sp *vainilla*—*vaina*—L *vāgīna*, a sheath.]

vanish [van´ish] *vi* to pass suddenly out of sight, to disappear; to become gradually less, to fade away; (*math*) to become zero.—**vanishing cream**, cosmetic cream that, when rubbed over the skin, virtually disappears; **vanishing point**, the point at which a diminishing object or quantity seems to disappear. [Through Fr from L *vānescĕre*, to pass away—*vānus*, empty.]

vanity *See* **vain**.

vanquish [vangk´wish] *vt* to conquer, to defeat in any contest.—*n* **vanq´uisher**. [Late OFr *vainquir* (Fr *vaincre*, pt *vainquis*)—L *vincĕre*, to conquer.]

vantage [vän´tij] *n* a favorable position; a position allowing a clear view or understanding.—Also **van´tage point**. [ME,—OFr *avantage*. See *advantage*.]

vapid [vap´id] *adj* flat, insipid, without zest (eg of wine, beer, conversation).—*adv* **vap´idly**.—*ns* **vap´idness, vapid´ity**. [L *vapidus*.]

vapor [vā´pòr] *n* the gaseous state of a substance normally liquid or solid; water or other matter (eg smoke) suspended in the atmosphere; an exhalation; anything vain or transitory; hysterical fainting fit, or temporary depression of spirit; a fanciful idea.—*vi* to pass off in vapor; to emit vapors; to indulge in vapors—ie express oneself extravagantly or utter empty boasts.—*vt* **vā´porize**, to convert into vapor—ie to pass off in vapor.—*ns* **vāporizā´tion; vā´porizer** [or-īz´-], an apparatus for discharging liquid in a fine spray.—*adjs* **vā´porish**, full of vapors; hypochondriacal; peevish; **vā´porous**, full of or like vapor; affected with the vapors; unsubstantial, vainly imaginative.—*n* **vapor trail**, a white trail of condensed vapor left in the sky from the exhaust of an aircraft.—*adj* **vā´pory**, vaporous; misty. [Fr,—L *vapor*.]

variable [vā´ri-à-bl] *adj* that may be varied; liable to change, unsteady.—*n* (*math*) a quantity that may have any one of a set of values.—*ns* **vāriabil´ity, vā´riableness**.—*adv* **vā´riably**.—*ns* **vāriā´tion**, act or process of varying or being varied; an instance of it; extent to which a thing varies; (*mus*) a transformation of a melody by melodic, harmonic, contrapuntal, and rhythmic changes; (*astron*) deviation from the mean orbit of a heavenly body; **vā´riance**, state of being varied; a change of condition; discrepancy; difference that arises from, or produces, dispute; **vā´riant** (*linguistics*) a related but not identical form or an alternative form; a different form or version.—*adj* diverse.—**at variance**, in disagreement. [L *variābilis*—*variāre, -ātum*, to vary—*varius*, various.]

varicose [var´i-kōs] *adj* abnormally swollen and dilated. [L *varicōsus*, full of dilated veins—*varix*, a dilated vein—*vārus*, bent, crooked.]

variegate [vā´ri-e-gāt] *vt* to mark with different colors; to diversify.—*n* **variegā´tion**. [L *variegātus*—*varius*, various, *agĕre*, to make.]

variety [va-rī´e-ti] *n* the quality of being various; absence of uniformity or monotony; many-sidedness; a collection (of different things, or of similar things differing slightly); one or more individuals of a species, which, owing to accidental causes, differ from the normal form in minor points; a variety show;—*pl* **varī´eties**.—*n* **varī´ety show**, a theatrical entertainment comprising dances, songs, farces, etc. [L *varietās*—*varius*, various.]

variorum [vā-ri-ō´rùm, -ö-] *adj* a term applied to an edition in which the notes of various commentators are inserted. [From Latin 'editio cum notis *variōrum*', an edition with annotations of various persons.]

various [vā´ri-ùs] *adj* varied, different, unlike each other; changeable, uncertain; several (eg *various people said it*).—*adv* **vā´riously**.—*n* **vā´riousness**. [L *varius*.]

varlet [vär´let] *n* a footman; a low fellow, a scoundrel. [OFr *varlet*, formerly *vaslet*, from a dim of Low L *vassālis*. See **vassal**.]

varnish [vär´nish] *vt* to cover with a liquid so as to give a glossy surface to; to give a fair appearance to.—*n* a sticky liquid which dries and forms a hard, lustrous coating; a glossy, lustrous appearance; an attractive surface which serves to hide blemishes; gloss or palliation. [Fr *vernis*—LL *vitrinus*, glassy—L *vitrum*, glass.]

varsity [vär´si-ti] *n* the principal squad representing a university, college, school, or club, esp in a sport. [**university**; spelling and pronunciation are due to the 18th-century pronunciation of *e* before *r*; cf **clerk, parson** (*orig* same as **person**).]

varve [värv] *n* a seasonal layer of clay deposited in still water, useful in fixing Ice Age chronology. [Sw *varv*, layer.]

vary [vā´ri] *vt* to make different, to diversify, modify; to free from monotony.—*vi* to alter, to be or become different; to deviate (from); to differ (from); *pt, pt p* **vā´ried**.—**vary directly**, or **inversely, as**, to increase, or to decrease, in proportion to increase in—or the other way round. [Fr *varier*—L *variāre*—*varius*.]

vas [vas] *n* (*anat*) a vessel, duct, or tube for carrying fluid;—*pl* **va´sa**.—*adj* **vas´cūlar**, pertaining to, or provided with, such vessels.—*ns* **vascular´ity; vasectomy**, excision of the vas deferens or part of it, esp in order to produce sterility.—**vascular bundle** (*bot*) a strand of conducting tissue, consisting chiefly of xylem and phloem; **vas deferens**, a sperm-carrying duct. [L *vās*.]

vasculum [vas´kū-lùm] *vt* a botanist's specimen-box. [L dim of *vās*, a vessel.]

vase [väz or vāz] *n* a vessel of greater height than width, anciently used for domestic purposes and in sacrifices; an ornamental vessel; a sculptured, vaselike ornament. [Fr,—L *vāsum* or *vās*.]

Vaseline [vas´i-lēn] *n* trade name for petrolatum. [Ger *wasser*, water, and Gr *elaion*, oil.]

vassal [vas´àl] *n* one who holds land from, and renders homage to, a superior; a dependant, retainer.—*n* **vass´alāge**, state of being a vassal, dependence, subjection. [Fr,—Low L *vassālis*—Breton *gwaz*, a servant; cf W *gwas*, a youth.]

vast [väst] *adj* of great extent; very great in amount or degree.—*adv* **vast´ly**.—*n* **vast´ness**. [L *vastus*, waste, vast; cf OE *wēste*, waste.]

vat [vat] *n* a large vessel or tank, esp one for holding liquors. [Older form *fat*—OE *fæt*; Du *vat*, ON *fat*, Ger *fass*.]

Vatican [vat´i-kan] *n* the part of Rome, built on the Vatican hill, in which the Pope resides and which is an independent city under his temporal jurisdiction; the papal authority. [Fr,—It *Vaticano*—L *Mons Vāticānus*, Vatican hill.]

vaticinate [va-tis´i-nāt] *vt* to prophesy.—*n* **vaticinā´tion**. [L *vāticinārī, -ātus*, to prophesy—*vātes*, a seer, *canĕre*, to prophesy.]

vaudeville [vōd´vil] *n* a stage show consisting of various acts. [From *vau* (*val*) *de Vire*, the valley of the Vire, in Normandy, where popular songs were composed about 1400 AD.]

vault [völt] *n* an arched roof; a chamber with an arched roof, esp one underground; a cellar; anything like a vault; a leap or spring in which the weight of the body is supported by the hands, or by a pole; the bound of a horse.—*vt* to arch; to roof with an arch; to form vaults in; to leap over by performing a vault.—*vi* to curvet or leap, as a horse; to leap (over).—*adj* **vaul´ted**, arched; covered with a vault.—*ns* **vaul´ter**, one who vaults or leaps; **vaul´ting horse**, a wooden horse used in a gymnasium for vaulting over. [OFr *volte*—L *volvĕre, volūtum*, to roll.]

vaunt [vönt or vänt] *vti* to make a vain display, or display of; to boast.—*n* vain display; a boast. [OFr *vanter*—LL *vanitāre*—L *vānitās*, vanity—*vānus*, vain.]

veal [vēl] *n* the flesh of a calf. [OFr *veël*—L *vitellus*, dim of *vitulus*, a calf.]

vector [vek´tòr] *n* (*math*) a straight line of definite length drawn from a given point in a given direction, usu. representing a quantity (as a velocity or a force) that has both magnitude and direction; the course of an aircraft, missile, etc.—*adj* **vectō´rial**.—**vector quantity**, one that has direction as well as magnitude. [L,—*vehĕre, vectum*, to convey.]

Veda [vā´dä, vē´dä] *n* one or all of the four holy books, collections of hymns, prayers, etc., of the Hindus—written in ancient Sanskrit;—*pl* **Vedas**.—*adj* **Ve´dic**.—*n* the Sanskrit of the Vedas. [Sans *veda*, knowledge—*vid*, to know.]

vedette [ve-det´] *n* a mounted sentry stationed at the out-posts of an army to watch an enemy. [Fr,—It *vedetta*—*vedere*, to see—L *vidēre*, to see.]

veer[1] [vēr] *vi* (of the wind) to change direction clockwise; (*loosely*) to change direction; to change course, as a ship; to pass from one mood or opinion to another.—*vt* to turn (a ship's head) away from the wind. [Fr *virer*—LL *virāre*, to turn.]

veer[2] [vēr] *vt* to slacken, let out (as a rope). [Middle Du *vieren*, to slacken.]

vegetable [vej´e-tà-bl] *n* an organized body without sensation and voluntary motion, usu. nourished by roots fixed in the ground; a plant grown for food.—*adj* belonging to plants; consisting of or having the nature of plants; derived from vegetables.—*n* **vegan** [veg-an´ or vē´gan] a strict vegetarian who consumes no animal or dairy products.—*adjs* **veg´etal**, of the nature of a vegetable; pertaining to the vital functions of plants and animals, as growth, reproduction, etc.; **vegetā´rian**, consisting of vegetables; pertaining to a diet confined to vegetables.—*n* one who holds that vegetables are the only proper food for man and abstains from animal-derived food.—*n* **vegetā´rianism**.—*vi* **veg´etāte**, to grow by roots and leaves; to sprout; to lead an idle, aimless life.—*n* **vegetā´tion**, process of growing, as a plant; vegetable growth; plants in general.—*adj* **veg´etātive**, of reproduction by asexual processes; growing, as plants; having power to produce growth; pertaining to unconscious or involuntary bodily functions (eg digestion); without intellectual activity, unprogressive (eg of a manner of life).—*adv* **veg´etātively**.—*n* **veg´etativeness**.—**vegetable marrow**, a smooth-skinned elongated summer squash with creamy white to deep green skin. [OFr,—LL *vegetābilis*, animating—L *vegetāre*, to quicken.]

vehement [vē´e-mènt] *adj* passionate; very eager or urgent; violent, furious.—*n* **vē´hemence**, the quality of being vehement; violence; great ardor or fervor.—*adv* **vē´hemently**. [OFr,—L *vehemēns, -entis*.]

vehicle [vē´i-kl] *n* any kind of carriage or conveyance; that which is used to convey; (**space vehicle**) a structure for carrying burdens through air or space, or a rocket used to launch a spacecraft; (*med*) a substance in which a medicine is taken; the liquid substance which, when mixed with pigments, forms a paint.—*adj* **vehicular** [vė-hik´ū-lȧr] pertaining to, or serving as, a vehicle. [L *vehiculum—vehĕre*, to carry.]

veil [vāl] *n* a curtain; anything that hides an object; a piece of fabric worn by ladies to shade or hide the face; the headdress of a nun; a disguise, mask.—*vt* to cover with a veil; to cover; to conceal.—*n* **veil´ing**, the act of concealing with a veil; material for making veils.—**take the veil**, to become a nun. [OFr *veile* (Fr *voile*)—L *vēlum*, a curtain—*vehĕre*, to carry.]

vein [vān] *n* one of the vessels or tubes that convey the blood back to the heart; one of the horny tubes forming the framework of an insect's wings; (*bot*) one of the small branching ribs in a leaf; a seam of mineral through a rock of different formation; a streak of different quality, eg of different color, in wood, stone, etc.; mood or humor (eg *he was not in the vein for jesting*); a recurrent characteristic, streak, strain (*a vein of irony runs throughout the story*).—*vt* to form veins or the appearance of veins in.—*n* **vein´ing**, formation or disposition of veins; streaking. [Fr *veine*—L *vēna*, perh from *vehĕre*, to carry.]

Velcro [vel´krō] *n* trade name for a nylon material for fastenings, made up of matching strips of tiny hooks and pile, that are easily pressed together or pulled apart.

veld [velt, felt] *n* in S Africa, open, unforested, or thinly forested grassland.—Also **veldt**, but never so written in S Africa. [Du *veld*, field.]

vellum [vel´ȯm] *n* a superior kind of parchment prepared from the skins of calves, kids, or lambs; strong paper resembling this. [OFr *velin*—LL *(c(h)arta) vitulina* (writing material—see **chart**), of a calf—L *vitulus*.]

velocipede [ve-los´i-pēd] *n* a vehicle propelled by the feet of the rider, of which the bicycle is a development. [Fr,—L *vēlox, vēlōcis*, swift, *pēs, pedis*, foot.]

velocity [ve-los´i-ti] *n* quickness of motion. [L *vēlō-citās—vēlox*, swift.]

velodrome [vel´ō-drōm] *n* a track designed for cycling. [Fr *vélodrome*.]

velour, velours [ve-lōōr´] *n* any of several materials with a velvety nap; a hat of such material.—Also **velure** [vel´yůr, vel-ür´].—*adj* **velū´tinous**, velvety. [OFr *velours, velous*—L *villōsus*, shaggy.]

velvet [vel´vėt] *n* a cloth made from silk, rayon, etc. with a soft, thick pile; anything like velvet in texture.—*adj* made of velvet; soft like velvet.—*n* **velveteen´**, a cotton cloth with a pile like velvet.—*adj* **vel´vety**, made of or like velvet; soft in taste or touch. [From LL *velluetum*—LL *villutus*—L *villus*, shaggy hair.]

vena [vē´na] *n* a vein.—**vena cava**, in man, either of the large veins entering the right auricle of the heart. [L *vēna*.]

venal [vē´nȧl] *adj* (of a person or his services) that may be sold or got for a price; (of conduct) mercenary, corrupt.—*n* **vēnal´ity**, quality of being venal.—*adv* **vē´nally**. [Fr,—L *vēnālis—vēnus*, sale.]

venation [vē-nā´sh(ȯ)n] *n* the way in which the veins of plants are arranged; in insects, the distribution of the veins of the wings. [Same root as **vein**.]

vend [vend] *vt* to give for sale, to sell; to make an object of trade.—*n* **ven´dor, -der**, one who sells.—*adj* **vend´ible**, that may be sold; that may be disposed of as an object of trade.—*n* **vendibil´ity**.—*adv* **ven´dibly**.—**vending machine**, a coin-operated machine for selling certain small articles. [Fr *vendre*—L *vendĕre—vēnus*, sale, *dăre*, to give.]

vendetta [ven-det´a] *n* a sanguinary feud in pursuit of private vengeance for the death of a kinsman; inveterate hostility. [It,—L *vindicta*, revenge—*vindicāre*, to claim.]

vendeuse [ve-dœz] *n* a saleswoman. [Fr.]

veneer [ve-nēr´] *vt* to overlay or face with another and superior wood, or with a thin coating of another substance; to disguise with superficial polish.—*n* a thin coating, as of wood; false show or charm.—*n* **veneer´ing**, the act or art of overlaying an inferior wood with thin leaves of a more valuable kind; the thin leaf thus laid on. [Formerly *fineer*; corruption of Ger *furniren*—OFr *fornir*, It *fornire*, to furnish.]

venerate [ven´e-rāt] *vt* to honor or reverence with religious awe; to reverence, to regard with the greatest respect.—*n* **venerā´tion**, the act of venerating; the state of being venerated; the highest degree of reverence, respect mingled with awe.—*adj* **ven´erable**, that may be venerated, rendered sacred by religious or other associations; aged.—*n* **ven´erableness**.—*adv* **ven´erably**. [L *venerārī, -ātus*.]

venereal [ve-nē´re-ȧl] *adj* pertaining to, or arising from, sexual intercourse; exciting desire for sexual intercourse; curing venereal diseases.—*n* **ven´ery**, sexual intercourse.—**venereal disease**, a contagious disease characteristically transmitted by sexual intercourse. [L *venereus—Venus, Venĕris*, the goddess of love; conn with L *venerārī*.]

venery [ven´ėr-i] *n* the art, act, or practice of hunting; animals that are hunted. [OFr *venerie*—L *vēnārī*, to hunt.]

venesection [ve-ne-sek´sh(ȯ)n] *n* the operation of cutting open a vein for letting blood. [L *vēna*, a vein, *sectio*, cutting.]

Venetian [ve-nē´sh(ȧ)n] *adj* of or belonging to Venice.—*n* a native or inhabitant of Venice.—*n* **Venē´tian blind**, a blind for a window formed of thin slips of wood or other material, so hung as to admit of being set either edgewise or overlapping. [L *Venetia*, Venice.]

venge [venj] *vt* (*arch*) to avenge.—*n* **vengeance** [venj´ȧns] the infliction of punishment upon another in return for an injury or offense, retribution.—*adj* **venge´ful**, vindictive, revengeful.—*adv* **venge´fully**.—**with a vengeance** (*inf*) with excessive force; in excessive measure. [OFr *venger*—L *vindicāre*.]

venial [vē´ni-ȧl] *adj* pardonable, excusable; of a sin that can be remitted.—*adv* **vē´nially**.—*n* **vē´nialness**. [Fr,—L *veniālis*, pardonable—*venia*, pardon.]

venison [ven´i-sn, or ven´i-zn] *n* the flesh of animals taken in hunting, esp the deer. [Fr *venaison*—L *vēnātio*, a hunting, game—*vēnārī*, to hunt.]

Venn diagram [ven dī´a-gram] *n* a diagram using overlapping circles to show the relationships between sets. [John *Venn*, Eng logician.]

venom [ven´ȯm] *n* any liquid injurious or fatal to life, poison; spite, malice.—*adj* **ven´omous**, poisonous; spiteful, malignant.—*adv* **ven´omously**.—*n* **ven´omousness**. [Fr *venin* (It *veneno*)—L *venēnum*.]

venous [vē´nůs] *adj* pertaining to, or containing veins; (of blood) having passed through the capillaries and become charged with carbon dioxide. [L *vēnōsus—vēna*, a vein.]

vent¹ [vent] *n* a small opening, slit, or outlet; the anus of birds and fishes; outlet, expression.—*vt* to provide with vent or opening; to give vent to; to utter. [Altered form of *fent*, ME *fente*—OFr *fente*, a slit; confused with Fr *vent*—L *ventus*, wind.]

vent² [vent] *n* a vertical slit in a garment. [L *findere*, to split.]

ventilate [ven´ti-lāt] *vt* to admit fresh air to; to provide with duct(s) for circulating air, or for escape of air; to oxygenate, aerate; to supply air to (lungs); to expose to examination and discussion.—*n* **ventilā´tion**, act or art of ventilating; state of being ventilated.—*adj* **ven´tilātive**.—*n* **ven´tilātor**, that which ventilates; a contrivance for introducing fresh air. [L *ventilāre, -ātum—ventus*, the wind.]

ventral [ven´trȧl] *adj* belonging to the belly; on the anterior surface.—*n* in fishes, one of the pelvic fins.—*n* **ventricle** [ven´tri-kl] a small cavity as in the heart or brain.—*adj* **ventric´ular**. [L *ventrālis—venter*, the belly.]

ventriloquism [ven-tril´o-kwizm] *n* the act or art of speaking in such a way that the hearer imagines the voice to come from a source other than the actual speaker—also **ventril´oquy**.—*vi* **ventril´oquize**, to practice ventriloquism.—*n* **ventril´oquist**, one who practices ventriloquism.—*adj* **ventrilo´quial**. [L *ventriloquus*, speaking from the belly—*venter*, the belly, *loquī*, to speak.]

venture [ven´chůr] *n* (*obs*) chance, luck, hazard; that which is put to hazard (esp goods sent by sea at the sender's risk); an undertaking whose issue is uncertain or dangerous.—*vt* to send on a venture; to expose to hazard, to risk.—*vi* to run a risk; to dare.—*adjs* **ven´tūrous, ven´tūresome**.—*advs* **ven´tūrously, ven´tūresomely**.—*ns* **ven´tūrousness, ven´tūresomeness**.—**at a venture**, at random. [Short for **adventure**.]

venturi [ven-tŏŏr´ē] a tube or duct, wasp-waisted and expanding at the ends, used in eg measuring flow rate of fluids. [G B *Venturi*, Italian physicist.]

venue [ven´ū] *n* the scene of an action or event; (*law*) the area within which a crime is alleged to have been committed and from which a jury is summoned to try a question of fact. [OFr,—L *venīre*, to come, but confused with OFr *visne*, neighborhood—L *vīcīnia*, neighborhood.]

Venus [vē´nus] *n* Roman goddess of beauty and love; the most brilliant of the planets, second in order from the sun. [L *Venus*.]

veracious [ve-rā´shůs] *adj* truthful; true.—*adv* **verā´ciously**.—*n* **veracity** [ve-ras´i-ti], truthfulness, esp habitual; truth, conformity with truth or fact. [L *vērax, vērācis—vērus*, true.]

veranda, verandah [ve-ran´da] *n* a kind of covered balcony or open portico, with a roof sloping beyond the main building, supported by light pillars. [Hindustani *varandā*.]

verb [vûrb] *n* (*gram*) the part of speech which expresses an action, a process, state or condition or mode of being.—*adj* **ver´bal**, relating to or consisting in words; spoken (as opposed to written); literal, word for word; pertaining to or characteristic of verbs; derived from a verb.—*n* a word that combines characteristics of a verb with those of a noun or adjective.—*vt* **ver´balize**, to turn (another part of speech) into a verb; to put into words, to express in words.—*advs* **ver´bally; verbā´tim**, word for word.—*n* **ver´biāge**, abundance of words, wordiness, verbosity.—*adj* **verbōse´**, containing more words than are necessary, wordy; (of a person) prolix.—*adv* **verbōse´ly**.—*ns* **verbōse´ness, verbos´ity**.—**verbal noun**, a noun derived directly from a verb or verb stem and in some uses having the sense and construction of a verb; **verb-phrase**, an auxiliary with another verb-form. [Fr *verbe*—L *verbum*.]

verbatim *See* **verb**.

verbena [vėr-bē´na] *n* vervain, esp garden plants of hybrid origin. [L *verbēnae*, leaves.]

verbiage, verbose etc. *See* **verb**.

verdant [vûr´dȧnt] *adj* green; fresh (as grass or foliage); flourishing; inexperienced.—*n* **ver´dancy**.—*adv* **ver´dantly**.—*n* **ver´dūre**, greenness, freshness of growth; green vegetation. [Fr *verdoyant*—L *viridāns, -antis*, pr p of *viridāre*, to grow green.]

verdict [vûr´dikt] *n* the finding of a jury on a trial; decision, opinion pronounced. [OFr *verdit*—Low L *veredictum*—L *vērē*, truly, *dictum*, a saying.]

verdigris [vûr´di-grēs] *n* the greenish poisonous pigment resulting from the action of acetic acid on copper; the greenish or bluish deposit formed on copper, brass, or bronze surfaces.—Also **ver´degris**. [ME—OFr *verd* (*vert*) *de gris—verd*, green, *de*, of, *Grèce*, Greece.]

verge[1] [vûrj] *n* a rod, staff, or mace, or the like, used as an emblem of authority; extent of jurisdiction; the brink, extreme edge or margin (of something).—*vi* to be on the verge; to border (*with* **on**).—*n* **ver´ger**, a church official who keeps order during services or serves as an usher.—**on the verge of**, on the point of. [L *virga*, a slender branch.]

verge[2] [vûrj] *vi* (of the sun) to incline toward the horizon; to move or extend in some direction or toward some condition; to be in transition. [L *vergĕre*, to incline.]

veriest *See* **very**.

verify [ver´i-fī] *vt* to establish as true by evidence; to confirm as true by research;—*pt, pt p* **ver´ified**.—*adj* **ver´ifiable**, that may be verified, proved, or confirmed.—*n* **verificā´tion**, the process of verifying; the state of being verified. [L *vērus*, true, *facĕre*, to make.]

verily [ver´i-li] *adv* truly, certainly, really. [L *vērus*, true. See **very**.]

verisimilar [ver-i-sim´i-lȧr] *adj* having the appearance of truth, likely, probable.—*n* **verisimil´itude**, likeness to truth; a thing probably true. [L *vērisimilis*—*vērus*, true, *similis*, like.]

verity [ver´i-ti] *n* the quality of being true or real; truth; a true assertion or tenet;—*pl* **ver´ities**.—*adj* **ver´itable**, true, real, actual.—*adv* **ver´itably**. [L *vēritās*—*vērus*, true.]

verjuice [vûr´jōōs] *n* the sour juice of unripe fruit; the liquor made from verjuice; acidity of manner. [Fr *verjus*—*vert*, green, *jus*, juice.]

vermicelli [ver-mi-sel´i, or -chel´i] *n* a pasta like spaghetti, but in thinner strings. [It, pl of *vermicello*—L *vermiculus*, dim of *vermis*, worm.]

vermicide [vûr´mi-sīd] *n* an agent that destroys worms.—*adj* **vermic´ūlar**, pertaining to, or like, a worm (esp in its motion); or caused by worms.—*vt* **vermic´ūlate**, to decorate with inlaid work like the motion or track of worms.—*n* **vermiculā´tion**.—*adj* **ver´miform**, having the form of a worm.—*n* **ver´mifuge**, (*med*) a substance that destroys intestinal worms or expels them from the digestive canal. [L *vermis*, a worm.]

vermiculite [vûr-mik-y-līt] *n* a lightweight highly water-absorbent material made from expanded mica. [L *vermiculus*, little worm.]

vermilion [vėr-mil´yȯn] *n* a bright red pigment generally made artificially from mercury and sulfur; any beautiful red color; a variable color averaging a vivid reddish orange. [OFr *vermilion*—*vermeil*—L *vermiculus* (in LL a scarlet color, from an insect or a berry used in dyeing), dim of *vermis*, a worm.]

vermin [vûr´min] *n* (*collectively*) loathsome parasites on the body, as fleas, lice, bedbugs; domestic pests, as rats, mice; birds or animals destructive to preserved game; any contemptible and obnoxious person or persons.—*adj* **ver´minous**, consisting of vermin; like vermin; infested with parasitic or other vermin. [Fr *vermine*—L *vermis*, a worm.]

vermouth [vûr´-mōōth] *n* a fortified white wine flavored with herbs, used in cocktails and as an aperitif. [Ger *wermut(h)*, wormwood; cf OE *wermōd*.]

vernacular [vėr-nak´ū-lȧr] *adj* native, belonging to the country of one's birth.—*n* the current spoken daily language of a people or of a geographical area, as distinguished from the literary language used primarily in schools and in literature.—*adv* **vernac´ularly**. [L *vernāculus*—*verna*, a home-born slave.]

vernal [vûr´nȧl] *adj* belonging to the spring; appearing in spring; belonging to youth.—*adv* **ver´nally**.—*n* **vernā´tion**, the particular manner of arrangement of leaves in the bud. [L *vernālis*—*vēr*, spring.]

vernier [vėr´ni-ėr] *n* a contrivance consisting of a short scale made to slide along a graduated instrument and measure very small intervals. [So called from Pierre *Vernier* (1508–1637) of Brussels, its inventor.]

veronica[1] [ve-ron´ik-a] *n* a portrait of Christ's face on a handkerchief—from the legend that, on the way to Calvary, St *Veronica* wiped the sweat from His face with her handkerchief, whereupon His features were impressed on the cloth.

veronica[2] [ve-ron´ik-a] *n* speedwell.

veronica[3] [ve-ron´ik-a] *n* a posture in bullfighting in which the cape is swung slowly away from the charging bull while the matador keeps his feet in the same position. [Sp *veronica*, from St *Veronica*.]

verruca [ve-rōō´ka] *n* a wart. [L.]

versatile [vûr´sa-til] *adj* capable of moving or turning freely; able to turn easily and successfully to new tasks, etc.; changeable; of a material, capable of being used for many purposes.—*n* **versatil´ity**. [Fr,—L *versātilis*—*versāre*, freq of *vertĕre*, to turn.]

verse [vûrs] *n* a line of poetry; metrical arrangement and language; poetry; a short division of the chapters of the Bible.—*ns* **ver´sicle**, a little verse; in liturgy, the verse said or sung by a leader in public worship and followed by a response by the people; **versificā´tion**, the act, art or practice of composing metrical verses; prosody; metrical scheme; individual metrical style.—*vi* **ver´sify**, to make verses.—*vt* to relate in verse; to turn into verse;—*pt, pt p* **ver´sified**.—*ns* **ver´sifier; ver´sion**, the act of translating from one language into another, esp the Bible or parts of it; that which is translated from one language into another. [OE *fers*—L *versus, vorsus*, a line, furrow, turning—*vertĕre*, to turn; influenced by OFr *vers*.]

versed [vûrst] *adj* skilled or learned on a subject. [L *versari*, be busy.]

versicle, versify, version etc. *See* **verse**.

vers libre [ver´lē´br] *n* free verse—verse lacking usual metrical rules. [Fr.]

verso [vûr´sō] *n* a left-hand page. [L *verso (folio)*, with the page turned—*versus*, pt p of *vertĕre*, to turn, *folium*, a leaf or page.]

versus [vûr´sus] *prep* against; in contrast to. [L.]

vertebra [vûr´te-bra] *n* one of the segmented portions of the spinal column;—*pl*, **vertebrae** [vėr´te-brē].—*adj* **ver´tebral**.—*n* **ver´tebrāte**, an animal with a backbone.—Also *adj*. [L,—*vertĕre*, to turn.]

vertex [vûr´teks] *n* the top or summit; the point of a cone, pyramid, or angle; (*astron*) the zenith; the top of the head;—*pl* **vertices** [vûr´ti-sēz].—*adj* **ver´tical**, pertaining to the vertex; placed in the zenith; perpendicular to the plane of the horizon; straight up and down.—*n* a vertical line.—*adv* **ver´tically**.—*n* **vertical´ity**, quality of being vertical. [L, eddy, summit—*vertĕre*, to turn.]

vertigo [vûr´ti-gō] *n* a sensation of giddiness, dizziness.—*adj* **vertig´inous** [-tij´-], causing, or tending to cause, dizziness; like vertigo. [L,—*vertĕre*, to turn.]

vertu *See* **virtu**.

vervain [vûr´vān] *n* any of several plants of the genus *Verbena*, esp one with small spicate flowers. [OFr *verveine*—L *verbēna*.]

verve [vûrv] *n* the enthusiasm that animates a poet or artist; animation, energy. [Fr.]

very [ver´i] *adj* complete; absolute; same; being just what is needed; even; actual.—*adv* extremely; truly; really.—**very high frequency**, any radio frequency between 30 and 300 kilohertz; **very low frequency**, any radio frequency between 10 and 30 kilohertz. [Older form *veray*—OFr *verai*—L *vērax, vērācis*, speaking truly—*vērus*, true.]

Very light [ver´i līt] *n* a small colored flare fired from a pistol—used for signaling. [From Samuel *Very*, the inventor.]

vesical [ve-sī´kal] of or relating to a bladder and esp the urinary bladder.—*n* **vesicā´tion**, a blister; an instance or the process of blistering; **ves´icant**, a substance that vesicates, esp a war gas causing blistering and destruction of tissues, eg. mustard gas; **ves´icle**, a small bladder or blister; a small usu. fluid-filled pouch (as a sac or cyst) in a plant or animal body.—*adjs* **vesic´ular**, having the structure of a vesicle, esp the alveoli of the lungs. [L *vēsīca*, bladder.]

Vesper [ves´pėr] *n* the evening star, Venus; **vesper**, a vesper bell; (*arch*) evening; (*pl*) an evening prayer or service. [Fr,—L; Gr *hesperos*.]

vessel [ves´ėl] *n* a vase or utensil for holding something, as a bowl, kettle, etc; a ship or boat; a tube or duct of the body in which fluids, as blood, etc., are contained; a person considered as an agent of God.—**the weaker vessel**, woman. [OFr *vessel* (Fr *vaisseau*)—L *vascellum,—vās*, vase.]

vest [vest] *n* a short, sleeveless garment, esp one worn under a suit coat by men; a protective garment usu. sleeveless that extends to the waist (as a life preserver).—*vt* to clothe; to invest (with—eg authority); to grant to or confer on (with *in*—eg *power is vested in him*).—*vi* to become vested (in a person) as property.—**vested interest**, a particular interest in the continuance of an existing system, institution, etc., for personal reasons, often financial; one having such an interest. [Fr *veste*—L *vestis*.]

Vesta [ves´ta] *n* the Roman goddess of the hearth.—*n* **ves´ta**, a short wooden match;—*pl* **ves´tas**.—*adj* **Ves´tal**, pertaining to or consecrated to the service of Vesta; chaste, pure.—*n* a chaste virgin. [L *Vesta*, goddess of household fire and domestic life.]

vestibule [ves´ti-būl] *n* formerly an open court before a house; a hall next to the entrance to a building; (*anat*) a small bony cavity forming part of the ear. [Fr,—L *vestibulum*.]

vestige [ves´tij] *n* a track or footprint; a trace, esp one that serves as a clue; (loosely) a scrap, particle; (*biol*) an organ or tissue which survives without performing the function it fulfils in an organism of lower type.—*adj* **vestig´ial** [-tij´-]. [Fr,—L *vestīgium*—*vestīgāre*, to track.]

vestment [vest´ment] *n* a garment; a long outer robe worn by the clergy during divine service. [L *vestimentum*—*vestīre*, to clothe—*vestis*, a garment.]

vestry [ves´tri] *n* a room adjoining a church in which the vestments are kept and parochial meetings held, any small room attached to a church; a group of church members who manage temporal affairs.—*n* **ves´tryman**, a member of a vestry. [Fr,—L *vestiārium*—*vestiārius*, belonging to clothes—*vestis*, a garment.]

vesture [ves´tyûr] *n* clothing, dress; a robe; a covering. [OFr (Fr *vêture*)—L *vestīre*, to clothe—*vestis*, a garment.]

vet [vet] *n* (*inf*) a clipped form for veterinarian or veteran.—*vt* to subject (an animal or person) to a physical examination; to provide therapeutic treatment for a person or animal; to evaluate.

vetch [vech] *n* a genus (*Vicia*) of plants, mostly climbing, some cultivated for fodder, esp a tare. [OFr *veche* (Fr *vesce*)—L *vicia*, akin to *vincīre*, to bind.]

veteran [vet´ė-rān] *adj* old, experienced, long exercised, esp in military life; pertaining to a veteran; consisting of veterans.—*n* one long exercised in any service, esp in war; a person who has served in the military forces.—**Veterans Day**, a legal holiday in the US honoring all veterans of the armed forces, observed November 11; **veteran's preference**, special consideration given to veterans (as by allowance of points) on a civil service examination. [L *veterānus*—*vetus, veteris*, old.]

veterinary [vet´e-ri-nȧ-ri] *adj* pertaining to the art of treating the diseases of animals; a veterinarian.—*n* **vet´erinari´an**, one who practices veterinary medicine or surgery. [L *veterīnārius*—*veterīnae*, beasts of burden.]

veto [vē´tō] *n* any authoritative prohibition; the power of rejecting or forbidding, specif, the right of one branch of a government to reject bills passed by another; the exercise of this right.—*pl* **vetoes** [vē´tōz].—*vt* to reject by a veto; to withhold assent to. [L *vetāre*, to forbid.]

vex [veks] *vt* to irritate by small provocations, to annoy; to pain, grieve; to disturb, trouble.—*n* **vexā´tion**, act of vexing; state of being vexed; something causing vexation.—*adj* **vexā´tious**, causing annoyance; full of trouble; harassing.—*adv* **vexā´tiously**.—*n* **vexā´tiousness**. [Fr *vexer*—L *vexāre*, to shake, annoy.—*vehěre* to carry.]

via [vī´a, or vē´à] *prep* by way of.—**via media** [mēd´i-a], a middle course. [L.]

viable [vī´à-bl] *adj* capable of living; capable of growing or developing; of plan, project, of such a kind that it has a prospect of success. [Fr,—*vie*, life—L *vīta*.]

viaduct [vī´a-dukt] *n* a road or railroad carried by a structure over a valley, river, etc.; a steel bridge made up of short spans carried on high steel towers. [L *via*, a way, *dūcěre, ductum*, to lead, bring.]

vial [vī´al] *n* a small vessel or bottle for liquids.

viand [vī´ànd] *n* an article of food. [Fr *viande*—LL *vivanda* (for *vivenda*), food necessary for life—L *vīvěre*, to live.]

viaticum [vī-at´ik-ùm] *n* provisions for the way; the Christian eucharist given to persons in danger of death. [L,—*via*, a way.]

vibes [vībz] (*slang*) *n pl* feelings or sensations experienced or communicated. [**vibrations**.]

vibrate [vi´brāt] *vi* to shake; to move, swing, backwards and forwards, to oscillate; to produce an oscillating effect; to be thrilled.—*vt* to cause to shake; to move to and fro; (of a pendulum) to measure (eg seconds) by moving to and fro.—*adj* **vi´brant**, vibrating; sonorous.—*ns* **vibrā´tion**, act of vibrating; state of being vibrated; tremulousness, quivering motion; **vibrato**, a pulsating effect produced by alternation of a given tone.—*adj* **vi´brātory**, vibrating; consisting in vibrations; causing vibrations.—*n* **vibrātor**. [L *vibrāre, -ātum*, to tremble.]

vicar [vik´àr] *n* (*Anglican Church*) a parish priest who receives a stipend instead of the tithes; (*RC Church*) a bishop's assistant who exercises jurisdiction in his name.—*ns* **vic´arage**, the benefice, or residence, of a vicar; **vic´arapostol´ic**, a titular bishop of the Roman Catholic church who administers a territory not organized as a diocese; **vic´ar-gen´eral**, an administrative deputy of a Roman Catholic or Anglican bishop or of the head of a religious order.—*adjs* **vicā´rial**, pertaining to a vicar; substituted; **vicā´riāte**, having vicarious or delegated power.—*n* delegated power.—*adj* **vicā´rious**, filling the place of another; performed or suffered in place of or for the sake of another; imagined through the experiences of others.—*adv* **vicā´riously**.—**Vicar of Christ**, a title assumed by the Pope. [L *vicārius*, supplying the place of another—*vicis* (genitive), change, alternation.]

vice [vīs] *n* an evil action or habit, a blemish or fault; immoral conduct, depravity; prostitution.—*adj* **vicious** [vish´ùs], having a vice or defect; depraved; faulty, incorrect (eg of style); unsound (eg of argument); fierce, refractory; malicious (eg *vicious remarks*); intense, forceful.—*adv* **vic´iously**.—*n* **vic´iousness**.—**vice squad**, a police squad whose task is to see that the laws dealing with prostitution, gambling, etc., are observed; **vicious circle**, a chain of actions in which every step taken to improve the situation creates new difficulties which in the end returns to the difficulty of the original situation; reciprocal aggravation. [Fr,—L *vitium*, a blemish.]

vice- [vīs-] *prefix* forming compounds denoting one who acts in place of, or ranks second to, another, eg *vice´-ad´miral, vice´-pres´ident*.—*prep* [vī´se] in place of.—**vice versa** [vī´se vûr´sa], the terms being exchanged the other way round. [L, 'in place of,' abl of *vicis* (gen), change.]

vicegerent [vīs-je´rĕnt] *n* one acting in place of a superior.—*n* **viceger´ency**. [L *vice*, in place of, *gerens, -entis*, pr p of *gerěre*, to act.]

viceroy [vīs´roi] *n* a deputy ruling a province in name of his sovereign. [L *vice*, in place of, Fr *roi* a king.]

vicinage [vis´i-nij] *n* neighborhood; the places near.—**vicin´ity**, a nearby area; proximity; nearness. [OFr *veisinage*—*veisin*—L *vīcīnus*, neighbouring—*vīcus*, a row of houses.]

vicious *See* **vice**.

vicissitudes [vi-sisi-tūds] *n pl* ups and downs; successive changes of fortune. [L *viscissitūdō*—*vicis* (*gen*), change.]

victim [vik´tim] *n* a living creature offered as a sacrifice; one injured by others who pursue selfish aims, or by lack of self-control; anyone who incurs loss or harm (eg by mischance); a dupe.—*vt* **vic´timize**, to make a victim; to cause to suffer for something that is not essentially a fault; to cheat.—*n* **victimīzā´tion**. [Fr,—L *victima*, a beast for sacrifice, adorned with the fillet—*vincīre*, to bind.]

victor [vik´tòr] *n* one who conquers in battle or other contest, a winner.—*adjs* **vic´tor, victō´rious**, relating to victory; superior in contest; successful, triumphant.—*adv* **victō´riously**.—*n* **vic´tory**, success in battle or other contest; a battle gained. [L,—*vincěre, victum*, to conquer.]

Victorian [vik-tō´ri-àn -tö´-] *adj* pertaining to Queen Victoria, or to her reign; conventional, prudish, sentimental, and narrow—like the fashion in social conduct of Queen Victoria's time.

victual [vit´l] *n* food usable by man; (*pl*) (*dial* and *inf*) articles of food; (*pl*) supplies of food.—*vt* to supply with food.—*vi* to eat; to lay in provisions;—*pr p* **victualling** [vit´l-ing]; *pt, pt p* **victualled** [vit´ld].—*n* **victualler** [vit´lèr], one who supplies provisions. [OFr *vitaille*—LL *victualia*—L *victuālis*, relating to living—*vivěre, victum*, to live.]

vicuña, vicuna [vi-kōō´nya] *n* an undomesticated South American quadruped (*Lama vicugna*), allied to the llama; cloth made from the fine silky wool of the vicuña; a sheep's wool imitation of this. [Sp, from Quechua.]

video [vid´i-ō] *adj* pertaining to television; of the picture portion of a television broadcast; of data display on a computer terminal.—*n* television; videocassette; videotape or other clipped forms.—*ns* **video´cassette´**, a cassette containing videotape; **videocassette recorder**, a device for the playback or recording of videocassettes;—also **video recorder**.—**vid´eotape´**, a magnetic tape on which images and sounds can be recorded for reproduction on TV. [L *vidēre*, to see.]

vie [vī] *vi* to strive for superiority (followed by **with**);—*pr p* **vy´ing**; *pt, pt p* **vied**. [ME *vien*, by aphaeresis from *envien*, to vie, through Fr from L *invītāre*, to invite.]

view [vū] *n* sight; reach of the sight; whole extent seen; direction in which a thing is seen; scene, natural prospect; the picture of a scene; a sketch; inspection, examination; a mental survey; mode of looking at; opinion; intention, object (*with a view to, of*).—*vt* to see; look at attentively; examine intellectually.—*ns* **view´er**, one who views; one who watches television; a person legally appointed to inspect and report on property; an optical device used in viewing; **viewfinder**, a camera attachment or part for determining the field of view; **view halloo´**, huntsman's cry when the fox breaks cover.—*adj* **view´less**, invisible; having no view.—*n* **view´point**, point of view.—**in view**, in sight; under consideration; as a goal or hope; **in view of**, having regard to; **on view**, open to inspection; **with a view to**, with the purpose or hope of. [Fr *vue*—*vu*, pt p of *voir*, to see.]

vigil [vij´il] *n* watching; keeping awake for religious exercises; the eve before a church festival, originally kept by watching through the night.—*n* **vig´ilance**, wakefulness, watchfulness, circumspection.—*adj* **vig´ilant**, watchful, on the lookout for danger, circumspect.—*n* **vigilan´te**, a member of an unauthorized organization to look after the interests, threatened in some way, of a group.—*adv* **vig´ilantly**.—**vigilance committee**, a committee of vigilantes. [Fr,—L *vigilia*—*vigil*, awake, watchful—*vigēre*, to be lively.]

vignette [vin-yet´] *n* any small ornamental engraving, design, or photograph, not enclosed by a definite border; an ornamental flourish of vine leaves and tendrils on manuscripts and books; a portrait with background shaded off; a short delicate literary sketch; a brief incident or scene (as in a play or movie). [Fr,—*vigne*—L *vīnea*, a vine.]

vigor [vig´òr] *n* active strength, physical force; vital strength in animals or plants; strength of mind; energy.—*adj* **vig´orous**, strong, either in mind or in body; showing such strength, energetic, forceful.—*adv* **vig´orously**.—*n* **vig´orousness**. [Fr,—L *vigor*—*vigēre*, to be strong.]

Viking [vī´king, also vik´ing], *n* one of the Norse invaders who in the 8th, 9th, and 10th centuries ravaged the coasts of western Europe. [ON *vīkingr*, prob from OE *wīcing*—*wīc*, a camp.]

vile [vīl] *adj* worthless, mean; morally impure, wicked; very bad.—*adv* **vile´ly**.—*n* **vile´ness**.—*vt* **vil´ify** [vil´-], to make vile; to slander, to defame;—*pt, pt p* **vil´ified**.—*ns* **vilificā´tion** [vil-], act of vilifying; defamatory speech; abuse; **vil´ifier** [vil´-]. [Fr,—L *vīlis*.]

villa [vil´a] *n* a country residence or retreat.—*ns* **vill´age** [-ij], any small assemblage of houses, less than a town; the people of a village, collectively; **vill´ager**, an inhabitant of a village. [OFr *ville*—L *villa*, a country-house, prob reduced from *vicla*, dim of *vīcus*, a village; Gr *oikos*, a house.]

villain [vil´àn] *n* a man of base or evil character; such a person in a play, etc.—*adj* **vill´ainous**, like or suited to a villain, base, depraved, infamous.—*adv* **vill´ainously**.—*n* **vill´ainy**, extreme depravity; atrocious misconduct. [OFr *villain*—Low L *villānus*—L *villa*.]

villein [vil´àn] *n* an English serf in the late Middle Ages who was a freeman in some ways.—*n* **vill´enage**, in feudal times, the tenure of land (by a villein) by base or menial services.

villus [vil´us] *n* a small slender process of the mucous membrane of the small intestine that serves in the absorption of nutrient;—*pl* **vill´i**. [L, pl of *villus*, hair, wool.]

vim [vim] *n* energy, force. [Acc of L *vis*, strength.]

vinaigrette [vin-ā-gret´] *n* a small box of silver or gold for holding an aromatic preparation (as smelling salts); a mixture of oil, vinegar and seasoning used as a salad dressing. [Fr,—*vinaigre*, vinegar.]

vinculum [ving´kū-lùm] *n* a bond; (*math*) a horizontal line placed over two or more members of a compound mathematical expression and equivalent to parentheses or brackets about them. [L,—*vincīre*, to bind.]

vindicate [vin´di-kāt] *vt* to justify, to defend with success; to clear from blame.—*adj* **vin´dicable**.—*n* **vindicā´tion**, act of vindicating; defence; justification.—*adj* **vin´dicātive**, vindicating; tending to vindicate.—*n* **vin´dicātor**, one who vindicates.—*adjs* **vin´dicātory**, tending to vindicate; (of laws) inflicting punishment; **vindic´tive**, revengeful.—*adv* **vindic´tively**.—*n* **vindic´tiveness**. [L *vindicāre, -ātum*.]

vine [vīn] *n* any climbing or trailing plant, or its stem; a grape.—*ns* **vine´dress´er**, one who prunes and cultivates grapevines; **vī´nery**, an area or building in which vines are grown; **vineyard** [vin´yàrd], a plantation of grapevines; an area or category of physical or mental occupation; **vin´iculture**, the cultivation of the vine.—*adj* **vī´nous**, pertaining to wine; caused by wine. [OFr,—L *vīnea*, a vine—*vīnum*, wine; Gr *oinos*.]

vinegar [vin´e-gàr] *n* a liquor containing acetic acid, made by fermentation from malt, or from fruit juices.—*adjs* **vin´egary**, sour; disagreeable, bitter, irascible in manner; **vin´egarish**, having a disagreeable character or behavior, sour. [Fr *vinaigre*—*vin* (L *vinum*), wine, *aigre* (L *ācer*) sour.]

vingt-et-un [vē̃-tā-œ̃´] *n* a game of cards the aim in which is to hold cards the sum of whose pips is nearest to, but not exceeding, twenty-one. Also **blackjack**. [Fr, twenty-one.]

vintage [vin´tij] *n* the produce of grapes, or of wine, for one season; wine, esp of good quality; a wine of a particular season or region; the product of a particular period; a period of origin.—*adj* pertaining to the grape vintage; of wine, of a specified year and of good quality; generally, eg of a play by an author, among the best and most characteristic; old-fashioned and out of date and no longer admired; **vintage year**, one in which a particular wine reaches an exceptionally high standard; a year of outstanding distinction or success. [Fr *vendange*—L *vindēmia*—*vinum*, wine, grapes, *dēmĕre*, to remove—*dē*, out of, *emĕre*, to take, buy.]

vintner [vint´nėr] *n* a wine merchant. [OFr *vinetier*, through LL—L *vīnētum*, a vineyard—*vīnum*, wine.]

vinyl [vīn´il] *n* an organic radical CH_2:CH; loosely, polymerized vinyl chloride.—**vinyl chloride**, CH_2CHCl, a substance which, when polymerized, produces a widely used plastic—abbrev **PVC; vinyl resins, plastics**, thermoplastic resins, polymers or copolymers of vinyl compounds.

viol [vī´ol] *n* a musical instrument which was the immediate precursor of the violin, having six strings, frets, and a flat back and played by means of a bow. [OFr *viole*—LL *vīdula*—L *vītulārī*, to make merry.]

viola[1] [vē-ō´la, vi´ō-la] *n* a stringed instrument of the violin family, larger than a violin, and tuned a fifth below it.—*n* **viol´ist**, a viola player. [Same as **viol**.]

viola[2] [vī´ō-la] *n* the genus (*Viola*) of plants of which the pansy is a species; a plant, common in garden beds, resembling the pansy but of another species. [L *vĭŏla*.]

violate [vī´ō-lāt] *vt* to profane, treat with disrespect; to break, to transgress (eg a promise, a law); to abuse; to rape, ravish.—*adj* **vi´olable**, that may be violated.—*ns* **violā´tion**, the act of violating; profanation; infringement, transgression; rape; **vī´olātor**. [L *violāre, -ātum*—*vīs*, strength.]

violent [vī´ō-lėnt] *adj* acting with, or characterized by, physical force or strength; forcible, esp unlawfully so; produced by force (eg a death, end); moved by strong feeling; passionate; intense (eg of pain, a contrast).—*n* **vī´olence**, quality of being violent; force, intensity, vehemence; unjust force; outrage, profanation, injury.—*adv* **vī´olently**. [Fr,—L *violentus*—*vīs*, force.]

violet [vī´ō-let] *n* any plant of genus *Viola*, of many species, with a flower, generally blue, sometimes white or yellow, and most often fragrant; the color of the violet, a bluish or light purple. [Fr *violette*, dim of OFr *viole*—L *vĭŏla*.]

violin [vī-ō-lin´ or vī´-] *n* any instrument of the modern family of four-stringed instruments played with a bow, esp the smallest and highest pitched instrument of this family.—*n* **vī´olinist**, a player on the violin. [It *violino*—*viola*. Same root as **viol**.]

violoncello [vē-ō-lon-chel´ō] *n* a large four-stringed instrument of the violin family held between the knees in playing;—*pl* **violoncell´os**.—abbrev **cello**. [It, dim of *violone*, a bass violin.]

VIP Abbrev for **very important person**.

viper [vī´pėr] *n* common European venomous snake (*Vipera berus*); a base, malicious person. —*adjs* **vī´perish, vī´perous**, having the qualities of a viper; venomous, malignant. [Fr,—L *vipera* (contr of *vivipara*)—*vīvus*, living, *parĕre*, to bring forth.]

virago [vi-rä´gō] *n* a masculine woman; a bold, shrewish woman, a termagant. [L,—*vir*, a man.]

virelay [vir´e-lā] *n* ancient kinds of poem, esp French, in short lines, often with only two rhymes to the stanza. [Fr *virelai*—*virer*, to turn, *lai*, a song.]

virgin [vûr´jin] *n* a maiden, a woman who has had no sexual intercourse; a person of either sex who has not known sexual intercourse; **Virgo** [vûr´gō] the Virgin, the 6th sign of the zodiac; in astrology operative August 22 to September 21.—*adj* (also **vir´ginal**) becoming a maiden, maidenly, pure, chaste, unsullied, undefiled; fresh, new, unused (eg *virgin soil*).—*n* **virgin´ity**, the state of a virgin.—**the Virgin**, the Virgin Mary, the mother of Christ. [OFr,—L *virgō, virginis*.]

virginal [vûr´jin-ål] *n* an old keyed musical instrument, oblong in shape, one of the three forms of harpsichord. [OFr,—L *virginālis*—*virgō, -inis*, a maiden. Perh as played by young ladies.]

viridity [vi-rid´i-ti] *n* greenness; freshness. [L *viridis*, green—*virēre*, to be green.]

virile [vir´īl] *adj* having the qualities of, or belonging to, a man or to the male sex; of a man, sexually potent; (of style, etc.) manly, forceful.—*n* **viril´ity**, state or quality of being a man; the power of procreation; manhood; manly vigor. [L *virīlis*—*vir*, a man.]

virtu [vûr´tōō] *n* a love of the fine arts; taste for curiosities; objects of art of antiquity; the artistic quality they show.—*ns* **virtuos´ity** [-tū-] exceptional technical skill in the fine arts; **virtuō´sō**, one skilled in the fine arts, in antiquities, curiosities, and the like; a skillful musician, painter, etc.;—*pl* **virtuō´sōs, virtuō´sī**. [It; a doublet of *virtue*.]

virtual *See* **virtue**.

virtue [vûr´tū] *n* worth; moral excellence; the practice of duty; a moral excellence; sexual purity, esp female chastity; inherent power, efficacy.—*adj* **vir´tual**, in effect, though not in fact or strict definition.—*adv* **vir´tually**, in effect, though not in fact; loosely, almost, nearly.—*adj* **vir´tuous**, animated by virtue, obedient to the moral law (of person or action); chaste (of a woman).—*adv* **vir´tuously**.—**by, in, virtue of**, through the power inherent in; on the ground of. [OFr,—L *virtūs*, bravery, moral excellence—*vir*, a man; cf Gr *hērōs*, Sans *vīra*, a hero.]

virulent [vir´ū-lent] *adj* full of poison; very active in injury; deadly; bitter in enmity, malignant.—*ns* **vir´ulence, vir´ulency**.—*adv* **vir´ulently**. [L *vīrulentus*—*vīrus*, poison.]

virus [vī´rus] *n* a very simple, frequently pathogenic, microorganism capable of replicating within living cells; a transmissible disorder of computer function; a harmful influence.—*n* **virol´ogy**, the study of viruses and virus diseases. [L *vīrus*; cog with Gr *ios*, Sans *visha*, poison.]

visa [vēz´a] *n* an endorsement on a passport denoting that it has been officially examined and that the bearer may travel to a particular country.—Also **visé**. [Fr,—LL *visāre*, freq of L *vidēre, visum*, to see.]

visage [viz´ij] *n* the face or look.—*adj* **vis´aged**. [Fr,—L *vīsus*, seen—*vidēre*, to see.]

vis-à-vis [vēz´-a-vē´] *adj, adv* face to face, opposite.—*prep* opposite to; in relation to. [Fr,—*vis* (L *vīsus*; see **visage**), face, *à*, to, *vis*, face.]

viscera [vis´e-ra] *n pl* the inner parts of the animal body, the entrails;—*sing* **viscus** [vis´kus]. [L *viscera* pl, *viscus*, sing.]

viscount [vī´kownt] *n* an officer (the *vice-comes*) who formerly acted as deputy to an earl; a title of nobility next below an earl; **viscountess** [vī´kownt-es] the wife, ex-wife, or widow of a viscount; a noblewoman ranking below a countess and above a baroness. [OFr *viscomte*—L *vice*, in place of, *comes*, a companion. See **count**.]

viscous [vis´kus] *adj* sticky, tenacious.—*n* **viscos´ity**, the property of being viscous; (*phys*) internal friction due to molecular cohesion in fluids.—*adj* **viscid** [vis´id] sticky, viscous.—*ns* **viscid´ity; viscose** [vis´kōs] a solution obtained from cellulose with sodium hydroxide and dissolving in carbon disulfide—used in the manufacture of rayon, etc. [LL *viscōsus*, sticky—L *viscum*, bird-lime, mistletoe; cog with Gr *ixos*, mistletoe.]

vise [vīs] *n* an iron or wooden clamping device, usu. consisting of two jaws that can be brought together by means of a screw, lever, etc., for holding work that is to be operated on. [Fr *vis* (It *vite*), screw)—L *vītis*, tendril of a vine.]

visé [vē-zā´] *n See* **visa**.

Vishnu [vish´nōō] *n* 'the Preserver', who with Brahma and Siva makes up the triad or trinity of Hindu gods; in his numerous avatars (eg as Krishna) he showed himself the friend and benefactor of men. [Sans *Visnu*.]

visible [viz´i-bl] *adj* that may be seen; obvious.—*ns* **visibil´ity**, state or quality of being visible, or perceivable by the eye; clearness of the atmosphere; range of vision in the atmospheric conditions at a particular time; **vis´ibleness**.—*adv* **vis´ibly**. [L *visibilis*—*vidēre, vīsum*, to see.]

vision [vizh´(ò)n] *n* the act or sense of seeing, sight; anything seen; anything imagined to be seen; a supernatural appearance, an apparition; anything imaginary; imaginative perception; foresight.—*adj* **vis´ionary**, affected by visions; imaginative; unpractical; existing in imagination only, not real.—*n* one who sees visions; one who forms schemes that are impracticable or difficult to put into effect. [Fr,—L *vīsiō, vīsiōnis*—*vidēre, visum*, to see.]

visit [viz´it] *vt* to go to see or inspect; to pay a call upon; to stay with; to go to see professionally; to enter, appear in; to punish, or reward, bless; to punish or reward (with); to afflict (with).—*vi* to be in the habit of seeing or meeting each other at home.—*n* act of going to see.—*adj* **vis´itant**, visiting.—*n* a visitor, esp one thought to come from a spirit world; a migrating bird that appears at intervals.—*ns* **visitā´tion**, act of visiting; a formal visit by a superior; a dispensation of divine favor or displeasure; **Visitation**, the visit of the Virgin Mary to Elizabeth, celebrated July 2 by a Christian feast; **vis´iting card**, a small card bearing the name and address, left in paying visits, and sometimes sent as an act of courtesy or in token of sympathy; **vis´itor**, one who visits, calls on, or makes a stay with a person; a person authorized to visit for purpose of inspection or supervision. [Fr *visiter*—*vīsitāre*, freq of *vīsĕre*, to go to see, visit—*vidēre*, to see.]

visor [vīz´ȯr] *n* a part of a helmet covering the face, movable, and with openings through which the wearer can see; a mask; the peak of a cap; a movable sunshade attached at the top of an automobile windshield.—*adj* **vis´ored**, wearing a visor; masked. [Fr *visière*—*vis*, countenance.]

vista [vis´ta] *n* a view or prospect through or as through an avenue; the trees, etc., that form the avenue. [It *vista*, sight, view—L *vidēre*, to see.]

visual [viz´ū-ål] *adj* belonging to vision or sight; produced by sight; used in sight.—*vt* **vis´ualīze**, to make visible; to picture, call up a clear mental image of.—Also *vi*.—*n* **visualizā´tion**.—*adv* **vis´ually**.—**visual aid**, a picture, photograph, film, diagram, etc., used as an aid in teaching. [L *vīsuālis*—*vidēre, vīsum*, to see.]

vita [vēt´à or vīt´à] *n* a brief autobiographical sketch; a curriculum vitae.

vital [vī´tål] *adj* contributing to, or necessary to, life; manifesting or containing life; fatal (eg *a vital wound*); essential, in the highest degree important.—*vt* **vī´talīze**, to make alive, to give life to; to animate, give vigor to.—*ns* **vītalizā´tion; vītal´ity**, quality of being vital; capacity to endure and flourish.—*adv* **vī´tally**.—*n pl* **vī´tals**, the interior organs essential for life; the part of any whole necessary for its existence.—**vital statistics**,

statistics dealing with population, esp the number of births, deaths, and marriages; woman's bust, waist, and hip measurements. [L *vītālis—vīta*, life—*vīvĕre*, to live; cog with Gr *bios*, life.]

vitamin [vīt´a-min] *n* organic substance, present in minute quantities in nutritive foods, which is essential for the health of the animal organism—*accessory food factors*, named provisionally Vitamin A, B, B_2, C, etc., but later given names as their chemical nature was determined. [Coined in 1906 from L *vīta*, life, and (inappropriately) Eng *amine* (which denotes a class of compounds formed from ammonia).]

vitiate [vish´i-āt] *vt* to render faulty or defective; to make less pure, to deprave, to taint.—*n* **vitiā´tion**. [L *vitiāre, -ātum—vitium*. See **vice**.]

viticulture [vit´i-kul-tyůr, -chůr] *n* the cultivation of grapes. [L *vītis*, a vine, *colĕre, cultum*, to cultivate.]

vitreous [vit´ri-ůs] *adj* glassy; pertaining to, consisting of, glass.—*adj* **vitres´cent**, tending to become glass.—*vt* **vit´rify**, to make into glass.—*vi* to become glass.—*n* **vitrificā´tion**, act, process, or operation of converting into glass.—*adj* **vit´rifiable**, that may be vitrified or turned into glass. [L *vitrum*, glass—*vidēre*, to see.]

vitriol [vit´ri-ol] *n* sulfuric acid; a soluble sulfate of a metal—*green vitriol*=sulfate of iron, *blue vitriol*=sulfate of copper, *white vitriol*=sulfate of zinc.—*adj* **vitriol´ic**, pertaining to or having the qualities of vitriol; biting, scathing. [Fr,—Low L *vitriolum*—L *vitreus*, of glass.]

vituperate [vī-tū´pė-rāt or vi-] *vt* to assail with abusive reproaches, revile.—*vi* to use abusive language.—*n* **vitūperā´tion**, act of vituperating; censure, abuse.—*adj* **vitū´perātive**, containing vituperation or censure.—*adv* **vitū´erātively**. [L *vituperāre, -ātum—vitium*, a fault, *parāre*, to prepare, furnish.]

vivace [vē-vä´che] *adj* (*mus*) lively.—Also *adv*. [It.]

vivacious [vi-vā´shůs (or vī-)] *adj* lively or full of vitality, sportive.—*adv* **vivā´ciously**.—*ns* **vivā´ciousness, vivacity** [vi-vas´i-ti] state of being vivacious; animation, liveliness or sprightliness of temper or behavior. [L *vīvax, vīvācis—vīvĕre*, to live.]

vivarium [vī-vā´ri-ům] *n* an artificial enclosure for keeping or raising living animals indoors. [L *vīvārium—vīvere*, to live.]

viva voce [vī´va vō´sē] *adv* by word of mouth, orally.—Also *adj*.—*n* an examination conducted viva voce. [L, with living voice—*vīvus*, living, *vox, vōcis*, voice.]

vivid [viv´id] *adj* lively or lifelike, having the appearance of life; forming brilliant images (eg *a vivid imagination*); striking; intense.—*adv* **viv´idly**.—*n* **viv´idness**.—*vt* **viv´ify**, to make vivid, endue with life. [L *vīvidus—vīvĕre*, to live.]

viviparous [vī-vip´å-rus] *adj* producing young alive. [L *vīvus*, alive, *parăre*, to produce.]

vivisection [viv-i-sek´sh(ò)n] *n* the practice of performing surgical operations on living animals, for the purposes of research or demonstration. [L *vīvus*, alive, *sectiō, -ōnis—secāre*, to cut.]

vixen [vik´sn] *n* a female fox; an ill-tempered woman.—*adj* **vix´enish**, ill-tempered, shrewish. [A form of *fixen*—OE *fyxen*, a she-fox.]

viz [viz] *adv* namely (usu. so read). [Contr for *vidēlicet*—L *vidēre licet*, it is permissible to see.]

vizier [vi-zēr´, viz´i-ėr] *n* an oriental minister or councillor of state. [Ar *wazīr*, a porter.]

vocable [vō´kå-bl] *n* a word; a name.—*n* **vocab´ūlary**, a list of words explained in alphabetical order; the words of a language; any list of words; the words known to or used by a particular person (eg *his vocabulary is very limited*); the words used in a (particular) science or art; the signs or symbols used in any nonverbal type of communication, eg in computer technology. [L *vocābulum—vocāre*, to call.]

vocal [vō´kål] *adj* having a voice; uttered or modulated by the voice; talkative; having a vowel function.—*vt* **vō´calize**, to give utterance to; to form into voice, sing; to use as a vowel; (*phonet*) to voice, make voiced.—*ns* **vōcalizā´tion; vō´calist**, a vocal musician, a singer.—*adv* **vō´cally**.—**vocal cords**, two elastic membranous folds of the larynx which vibrate and produce sound. [L *vōcālis—vox, vōcis*, the voice.]

vocation [vō-kā´sh(ò)n] *n* call or act of calling (eg to a religious mission); talent; calling, occupation.—*adj* **vocā´tional**, pertaining to a trade or occupation; in preparation for a trade or occupation; pertaining to the act of calling.—*n* **vŏc´ative**, the case of a word when a person or thing is addressed—also *adj*. [L *vocātiō, -ōnis, vocātīvus—vocāre*, to call.]

vociferate [vō-sif´e-rāt] *vi* to cry with a loud voice.—*adj* **vocif´erous**, making a loud outcry, noisy.—*adv* **vocif´erously**. [L,—*vox, vōcis*, voice, *ferre*, to carry.]

vodka [vod´ka] *n* a Russian spirit distilled from rye, potatoes, etc. [Russ, 'brandy', dim of *voda*, water.]

vogue [vōg] *n* the prevalent mode or fashion; prevalency, popularity. [Fr *vogue*, course of a ship—*voguer*, to row, from OHG.]

voice [vois] *n* sound from the mouth; sound given out by anything; power of, or mode of, utterance; medium of expression; expressed opinion, vote; mode of inflecting verbs, as being active, passive or middle.—*vt* to give utterance to; to regulate the tone of (organ pipes).—*adjs* **voiced** (*phonet*) of a consonant pronounced with a vibration of the vocal cords; **voice´less**, having no voice; having no vote; (*phonet*) of a consonant pronounced without any vibration of the vocal cords.—*n* **voice´-over**, the background voice of an unseen narrator in a motion picture or television program.—**in voice**, in good condition for singing or speaking; **give voice to**, to express. [Fr *voix*—L *vox, vōcis*.]

void [void] *adj* unoccupied, empty; not valid or binding; nullified; lacking in.—*n* an empty space.—*vt* to make vacant; to quit; to emit; to render of no effect, to nullify.—*adj* **void´able**, that may be voided or evacuated.—*n* **void´ance**, act of voiding or emptying; state of being void; ejection. [OFr *voide, void*.]

voile [voil] *n* a thin semi-transparent dress material. [Fr, veil.]

volant [vō´lånt] *adj* flying, able to fly; nimble.—*adj* **vŏl´atile**, evaporating very quickly; gay or capricious in emotion.—*ns* **vol´atileness, volatil´ity**, quality of being volatile; tendency to evaporate rapidly; sprightliness; fickleness.—*vt* **vol´atilize**, to make volatile; to cause to evaporate.—*n* **volatilizā´tion**.—**volatile oil**, an oil that vaporizes readily; an essential oil. [Fr,—L *volans, -antis*, pr p of *volāre*, to fly.]

Volapük [vō-la-pük] *n* an artificial language created by Johann Martin Schleyer in 1880. [Lit 'world-speech'—*vol*, shortened from Eng *world*, *pük*, for Eng *speak*.]

volcano [vol-kā´no] *n* a hill or mountain formed by ejection of lava, ashes, etc. through an opening in the earth's crust which may or may not continue to emit volcanic materials, usu. through a central crater; a state suggestive of a volcano because an upheaval or outburst seems imminent.—*adj* **volcan´ic**, pertaining to, produced or affected by, a volcano. [It *volcano*—L *Volcānus, Vulcānus*, god of fire.]

vole [vōl] *n* any of various small rodents (esp genus *Microtus*) having a stout body and short ears inhabiting both moist meadows and dry uplands, which do much damage to crops. [For *vole-mouse*, field-mouse; *vole* from the same root as **wold**.]

volition [vō-li´sh(ò)n] *n* act of willing or choosing, the exercise of the will; the power of determining. [Low L *volitō*—L *volo, velle*, to will, be willing.]

volkslied [folks´lēt] *n* a folk song. [Ger.]

volley [vol´i] *n* a flight of missiles; the discharge of many missiles or small arms at once; a vehement outburst; in tennis and volleyball, the flight of the ball before it reaches the ground;—*pl* **voll´eys**.—*vt* to discharge in a volley; to return (a ball) before it bounces.—*vi* to fly in a volley, as missiles; to sound loudly, as firearms.—*n* **volleyball**, a team game played by volleying a large inflated ball over a net; the ball used. [Fr *volée*, a flight—*voler*—L *volāre*, to fly.]

volt[1] [vōlt] *n* (*fencing*) a sudden movement or leap to avoid a thrust; the gait of a horse going sideways round a center.—Also **volte**. [Fr *volte*—It *volta*—L *volvĕre*; see **voluble**.

volt[2] [vōlt] *n* the unit of electromotive force.—*n* **vōl´tage**, potential difference reckoned in volts.—*adj* **voltā´ic**, of or producing electricity by chemical action; pertaining to Alessandro *Volta* (1745–1827), who developed the theory of current electricity, or to his discoveries and inventions.—*n* **vōlt´meter**, an instrument for measuring potential difference directly, calibrated in volts.

volte-face [vōlt-fäs] *n* a turning round; a sudden and complete change in opinion or in views expressed. [Fr.]

voluble [vol´ū-bl] *adj* overwhelmingly fluent in speech.—*n* **volubil´ity**, excessive fluency of speech.—*adv* **vol´ubly**. [L *volūbilis—volvĕre, volūtum*, to roll, turn.]

volume [vol´ūm] *n* a roll or scroll of papyrus or the like, on which ancient books were written; any book; cubical content; dimensions; fullness (of voice or other sound).—*adjs*, **volumet´ric, -al**, pertaining to the measurement of volume; **volū´minous**, consisting of many volumes or books; of great bulk; copious; producing many books, as an author.—*adv* **volū´minously**.—*n* **volū´minousness**.—**speak, tell, volumes**, to signify much. [Fr,—L *volūmen*, a roll—*volvĕre, volūtum*, to roll.]

voluntary [vol´ůn-tå-ri] *adj* acting by choice; proceeding from the will; subject to the will; done by design or without compulsion; brought about by, proceeding from, free action.—*n* one who does anything of his own free will; a piece of music to be played at will on a church organ.—*adv* **vol´untarily**.—*n* **vol´untariness**. [L *voluntārius—voluntās*, choice—*volo*, I am willing.]

volunteer [vol-ůn-tēr´] *n* one who enters any service, or undertakes any task, esp military, voluntarily.—*adj* entering into service voluntarily.—*vt* to offer voluntarily.—*vi* to enter into any service of one's own free will or without being asked. [Fr *volontaire*—L *voluntārius*. See **voluntary**.]

voluptuary [vo-lup´tū-å-ri] *n* a person excessively given to bodily enjoyments or luxury, a sensualist.—*adj* **volup´tuous**, inducing, or filled with, pleasure; given to excess of pleasure, esp sensual.—*adv* **volup´tuously**.—*n* **volup´tuousness**. [L *voluptuārius, voluptuōsus—voluptās*, pleasure.]

volute [vo-lūt´] *n* in Greek architecture, a spiral scroll in capitals; a kind of spiral shell, chiefly tropical; whorl of a spiral shell.—*adj* (*bot*) rolled up in any direction.—*adj* **volū´ted**, having a volute.—*n* **volū´tion**, a convolution; a whorl. [Fr,—L *volvĕre, volūtum*, to roll.]

vomit [vom´it] *vi* to throw up the contents of the stomach by the mouth, to spew.—*vt* to throw out with violence.—*n* matter ejected from the stomach; something that excites vomiting.—*adj* **vom´itory**, causing to vomit.—*n* (*hist*) a door of a large building by which the crowd is let out. [L *vomĕre, -itum*, to throw up; Gr *emein*.]

voodoo [vōō´doo] *n* a primitive religion in the West Indies, based on a belief in sorcery, etc.; a charm, fetish, etc. used in voodoo.—*vt* to affect by voodoo magic.—*n* **voo´dooism** [or -doo´-] voodoo superstitions. [Creole Fr *vaudoux*, a Negro sorcerer.]

voracious [vo-rā´shůs] *adj* eager to devour; very greedy.—*adv* **vorā´ciously**.—*n* **vorac´ity** [-as´]. [L *vorax, vorācis—vorāre*, to devour.]

vortex [vör´teks] *n* a whirlpool; a whirlwind; a pursuit, way of life, etc., which, by its attraction or power, irresistibly engulfs one, taking up all one's attention or energies;—*pl* **vor´tices** [-tis-ēz], **vor´texes**.—*adj* **vor´tical**, whirling.—*ns* **vor´ticism** [-ti-sizm] a British movement in painting, a development from futurism, blending cubism and expressionism; **vor´ticist**. [L *vortex, vertex—vortěre, vertěre*, to turn.]

votary [vō´tȧ-ri] *adj* bound or consecrated by a vow.—*n* one devoted as by a vow to some service, worship, or way of life; one enthusiastically addicted to a pursuit, study, etc.;—*fem* **vō´taress**. [LL *votārius*—L *vōtum*, a vow.]

vote [vōt] *n* expression of a wish or opinion as to a matter on which one has a right to be consulted; the token by which a choice is expressed, as a ballot; decision by a majority; something granted by the will of the majority.—*vi* to express choice by a vote.—*vt* to resolve (that), express a desire (that); to suggest (that); to pronounce, adjudge to be (eg *it was voted a great success*); to grant by a vote; to bring about a result by voting (eg *they had voted him into power*).—*n* **vō´ter**. [L *vōtum*, a vow, wish—*vovēre, vōtum*, to vow.]

votive [vō´tiv] *adj* given by vow; vowed.—*adv* **vō´tively**. [L *vōtīvus—vōtum*, a vow, wish.]

vouch [vowch] *vt* (*arch*) to call upon to witness; to maintain by repeated affirmations, to warrant.—*vi* to bear witness (for), answer (for).—*n* **vouch´er**, one who vouches or gives witness; a paper that vouches or confirms the truth of anything, as of accounts, or that money has been paid. [OFr *voucher, vocher*, to call to defend—L *vocāre*, to call.]

vouchsafe [vowch-sāf´] *vt* to condescend to grant (eg a reply); to condescend (to).—*vi* to condescend. [**vouch, safe**.]

vow [vow] *n* a voluntary promise solemnly made to God; a solemn or formal promise.—*vt* to give by solemn promise; to devote; to threaten solemnly (eg vengeance); to maintain solemnly (eg *he vowed he had done so*). [OFr *vou* (Fr *vœu*)—L *vōtum—vovēre*, to vow.]

vowel [vow´ėl] *n* a simple vocal sound produced by continuous passage of the breath; a letter representing such a sound, as *a, e, i, o, u* (in English, each of these letters is used to represent more than one vowel sound).—*adj* **vocal**, pertaining to a vowel. [Fr *voyelle*—L *vōcālis—vox, vōcis*, the voice.]

vox [voks] *n* voice.—**vox populi**, voice of the people. [L.]

voyage [voi´ij] *n* a journey, esp a passage by water or by air.—*vi* to make a voyage.—*n* **voy´ager**.—*n pl* **voyageurs** [vwä-ya-zhœr] name given to the boatmen who kept up communication between the trading stations on the rivers and lakes of Canada. [Fr,—L *viāticum*, traveling-money—L *via*, a way.]

voyeur [vwä-yœr] *n* a sexual pervert who derives pleasure from secretly watching sexual acts or objects; a peeping Tom. [Fr, one who sees.]

vulcanize [vul´kan-īz] *vt* to convert latex to rubber by heating with sulfur.—*n* **vul´canite**, vulcanized rubber. [L *Vulcānus*, Vulcan, the Roman god of fire.]

vulgar [vul´gȧr] *adj* pertaining to the common people; vernacular (*the vulgar tongue*); public; common, usual; prevalent; low, unrefined; coarse.—*vt* **vul´garize**, to make vulgar.—*ns* **vul´garism**, a vulgar phrase; coarseness; **vulgar´ity**, quality of being vulgar; crudity of manner or language; an instance of this.—*adv* **vul´garly**.—*ns* **vulgar´ian**, a vulgar person; **Vul´gate**, an ancient Latin version of the Scriptures, made by St Jerome and others in the 4th century, and later twice revised—so called from its common use in the RC Church. [L *vulgāris—vulgus*, the people.]

vulnerable [vul´nė-ra-bl] *adj* capable of being wounded, liable to injury or hurt; exposed to attack; (*contract bridge*—of a side that has won a game) liable to have doubled the points scored against it.—*ns* **vulnerabil´ity, vul´nerableness**.—*adj* **vul´nerary**, useful in healing wounds.—Also *n*. [L *vulnerābilis—vulnerāre*, to wound—*vulnus, vulneris*, a wound.]

vulpine [vul´pīn] *adj* relating to or like the fox; cunning. [L *vulpes*, a fox.]

vulture [vul´-chůr] *n* any of a number of large rapacious birds of prey, temperate and tropical, living chiefly or entirely on carrion, constituting two families (Aegypiidae or Cathartidae) and allied to the hawks and eagles; one who or that which resembles or behaves like a vulture.—*adjs* **vul´tūrine, vul´tūrish**, like the vulture; rapacious. [OFr *voutour*—L *vultur*; perh from *vellěre*, to pluck, to tear.]

vulva [vul´va] *n* the external genital opening of a female mammal. [L *volva, vulva*, integument, womb.]

vying [vī´ing] *pr p* of **vie**.

W

wad [wod] *n* a small, soft mass, as of cotton or paper; a lump or small, compact roll; a disk of felt or paper, to keep the charge in a gun; a bundle of paper money.—*vt* to form into a wad; to pad, stuff out; to stuff a wad into;—*pr p* **wadd´ing**; *pt, pt p* **wadd´ed**.—*n* **wadd´ing**, any soft material for use in padding, packing, etc. [Cf Swed *vadd*, wadding; Ger *watte*.]
waddle [wod´l] *vi* to take short steps and move from side to side in walking.—*n* a clumsy, rocking gait.—*n* **wadd´ler**. [Perh freq of **wade**.]
wade [wād] *vi* to walk through any substance that yields to the feet, as water; to pass (through) with difficulty or labor; (*inf*) to attack with vigor (*with* **in** *or* **into**).—*vt* to cross by wading.—*n* **wa´der**, one who wades; a bird that wades, eg the heron; (*pl*) high waterproof boots used by anglers. [OE *wadan*, to move; Ger *waten*.]
Wade-Giles [wād-jīlz] *n* a system of transliterating the Chinese language into the English alphabet, now superseded by Pinyin in many countries.
wadi [wod´i] *n* the dry bed of a torrent, esp in northern Africa. [Ar *wādī*, a ravine (Sp *guad-*, first syllable of many river-names).]
wafer [wā´fėr] *n* a thin crisp cracker or cookie; a thin round cake of unleavened bread, used in the Eucharist; any small, thin, flat disklike thing. [OFr *waufre* (Fr *gaufre*)—Old Du *waefel*, a cake of wax; Ger *wabe*, a honeycomb.]
waffle[1] [wof´l] *n* a kind of batter cake cooked in a **waff´le iron**, a metal utensil with hinged halves having projecting studs on the insides. [Du *wafel*, wafer.]
waffle[2] [wof´l] *vi* (*inf*) to talk incessantly or nonsensically; to waver, vacillate.—Also *n*.
waft [wäft] *vt* to bear lightly through a fluid medium, as air or water.—*vi* to float or drift lightly.—*n* a breath, puff, slight odor or sound carried through the air; a gust of wind; a wafting movement. [From the same root as **wave**.]
wag[1] [wag] *vti* to move from side to side, to shake to and fro or up and down;—*pr p* **wagg´ing**; *pt, pt p* **wagged**.—*n* a single wagging movement. [OE *wagian*, to wag, *wegan*, to carry, move; conn with **weigh** and **wagon**.]
wag[2] [wag] *n* a droll, mischievous fellow, a habitual joker, a wit.—*n* **wagg´ery**, mischievous merriment.—*adj* **wagg´ish**, characteristic of a wag; roguish.—*adv* **wagg´ishly**.—*n* **wagg´ishness**. [Prob Eng (*obs*) *waghalter*, one who deserves hanging.]
wage [wāj] *vt* (*arch*) to pledge; to carry on (esp war).—*n* (*obs*) a gage or stake; payment for work, wages.—*n pl* **wā´ges** (also used as *sing*), that which is paid for services; what is given in return.—*n* **wā´ger**, (*arch*) a pledge; something staked on the issue of anything, a bet; that on which bets are laid; (*law*) an offer to make oath.—*vti* to bet. [OFr *wager* (Fr *gager*), to pledge. A doublet of **gage**.]
waggle [wag´l] *vti* to wag, esp in an uncertain or unrhythmical way. [Freq of **wag** (1).]
Wagnerian [väg-nē´ri-ȧn] *adj* pertaining to, or characterized by, the ideas or style of Richard *Wagner* (1813–83), German composer of operas.—*n* **Wag´nerite**, an adherent of Wagner's musical methods, or an admirer of his work.
wagon [wag´ȯn] *n* a four-wheeled vehicle for carrying heavy goods; a station wagon.—*ns* **wag´oner**, one who drives a wagon; **wagonette´**, a kind of open carriage with one or two seats crosswise in front and two back seats arranged lengthwise and facing inwards. [Du *wagen*; OE *wægn*; cf **wain**.]
wagtail [wag´tāl] *n* any of numerous small birds of a family (Motacillidae) that also includes the pipits; they have very long tails which they constantly move up and down. [**wag** (1), **tail**.]
waif [wāf] *n* anything found astray without an owner; a homeless wanderer, esp a child; (*pl*) stolen goods thrown away by a thief in flight. [OFr *waif*, *wef*—ON *veif*, any flapping or waving thing.]
wail [wāl] *vi* to lament or sorrow audibly.—*vt* to bemoan, to grieve over.—*n* a cry of woe; loud weeping.—*n* **wail´ing**.—*adv* **wailingly**. [ME *weilen*—ON *vaela*, *vāla*, to wail—*væ*, *vei*, woe.]
wain [wān] *n* a wagon esp a heavy one for farm use. [OE *wægen*, *wǣn*—*wegen*, to carry; cf Ger *wagen*, L *vehĕre*.]
wainscot [wān´skȯt] *n* a wooden lining, usu. paneled, applied to the walls of rooms.—*vt* to line with, or as if with, boards or panels.—*n* **wain´scoting**, materials for making a wainscot. [App Du *wagenschot*, oakwood, beechwood.]
waist [wāst] *n* the smallest part of the human trunk, between the ribs and the hips; the part of a garment that covers the body from the shoulder to the waistline; a blouse; the narrow part of anything that is wider at the ends.—*ns* **waist´band**, the band or part of a garment that encircles the waist; **waist´coat**, (*Brit*) a short coat, usu. sleeveless, worn immediately under the coat, and fitting the waist tightly.—*adj* **waist´ed**, having a waist, often of specified type.—*n* **waist´line**, a line thought of as marking the waist; the measurement of a waist. [ME *wast*; conn with OE *wæstm*, growth, *weaxan*, to grow.]
wait [wāt] *vi* to stay, or to be, in expectation (*often with* **for**); to tarry, remain; to remain undone; to serve food at a meal (*with* **at** *or* **on**).—*vt* to stay for, to await; (*inf*) to delay serving (a meal).—*n* act or period of waiting.—**to lie in wait** (for), to wait so as to catch after planning a trap (for).—*ns* **wait´er**, one who waits, esp a man who serves at table; **wait´ing list**, a list of applicants, in order of their application; **wait´ing room**, a room for the convenience of persons waiting; **wait´ress**, a female waiter.—**wait upon, on**, to serve as attendant to; to serve (a customer) at table. [OFr *waiter* (Fr *guetter*), to watch, attend—OHG *wahta* (Ger *wacht*), a watchman.]
waive [wāv] *vt* to give up, not insist upon (eg a claim, a right); to relinquish voluntarily; to neglect, disregard (eg an opportunity, scruples).—*n* **waiver**, (*law*) a waiving of a right, claim, etc. [OFr *guever*, to refuse, resign, perh—ON *veifa*, to move to and fro; cf L *vibrāre*.]
wake[1] [wāk] *vi* to cease from sleep; to be awake; to be roused up, active, or vigilant.—*vt* to rouse from sleep; to revive; to reanimate.—*pt* **waked** [wākt] or **woke** [wōk], pt p **waked, wo´ken**, (*rare*) **woke**.—*n* act of waking; a watch or vigil beside a corpse, sometimes with revelry.—*adj* **wake´ful**, not asleep; indisposed to sleep; vigilant.—*adv* **wake´fully**.—*n* **wake´fulness**.—*vti* **wā´ken**, to wake or awake; to be awake.—**wake up to**, to become conscious of, alive to. [OE has verbs *wacan*, to be born, *wacian, wæcnan, wæcnian*, to waken.]
wake[2] [wāk] *n* the streak of smooth or foamy water left in the track of a ship.—**in the wake of**, following immediately after. [Cf ON *vök*, a hole in the ice, *vökr*, moist. The root is seen in L *humēre*, to be moist, Gr *hygros*, moist.]
wale [wāl] *n* a welt raised by a whip, etc.; a ridge on the surface of cloth; (*pl*) planks along the outer timbers of ships.—*vt* to mark (as the skin) with welts. [OE *walu*, the mark of a stripe; ON *völr*, a rod.]
walk [wök] *vi* to move along on foot with alternate steps; to travel on foot; to follow a certain course; (*baseball*) to go to first base on four balls.—*vt* to pass through or upon; to pace; to cause (a horse, etc.) to walk; (*baseball*) to advance (a batter) to first base by pitching four balls; to accompany on a walk or stroll.—*n* act of walking; gait; distance walked over; place for walking, path, etc.; regular beat; conduct; sphere of action (**walk of life**).—*adv* **walk´about**, (orig *Austr slang*) on the move.—*n* a journey; a walk around.—*ns* **walk´er; walk´ie-talk´ie**, a compact radio set for sending out and receiving messages, carried on the person; **walk´ing stick**, a stick carried when walking; a cane; **walkout**, a labor strike; **walkō´ver**, a horse race with only one starter; an easy victory; **walk´way**, road, path, etc., constructed for pedestrians only.—**walk away with**, to win with ease; to steal. [OE *wealcan*, to roll, turn.]
wall [wöl] *n* an erection of brick, stone, etc. for enclosing, dividing or protecting; something like a wall as in function.—*vt* to enclose with, or as with, a wall; to close up (an opening) with a wall (*usu. with* **up**).—*ns* **wall´flower**, a plant of the *Cruciferae*, with fragrant flowers, yellow when wild, found on old walls; any other plant of the same genus (*Cheiranthus*); (*inf*) a person who remains a spectator at a dance, usu. a woman who cannot obtain partners; **wall´pā´per**, paper, usu. colored or decorated, for pasting on the walls of a room.—**drive** (or **push**) **to the wall**, to place in a desperate position; **off the wall**, (*slang*) insane, crazy; (*slang*) odd, unconventional; **to go to the wall**, to be hard pressed; to become bankrupt. [OE *weall, wall*; Ger *wall*, both from L *vallum*, a rampart.]
wallaby [wol´ab-i] *n* any of various small kangaroos (family Macropodidae). [From Australian native name.]
wallah [wol´a] *n* in India under British rule, (often in combination) one employed in, or concerned with, a specific type of work; one who occupies an eminent position in an organization, etc. [Hindi *-wālā*.]
wallaroo [wol-ȧ-rōō] *n* any of several large kangaroos, esp a formerly common species (*Macropus robustus*). [From Australian native name.]
wallet [wol´ėt] *n* a flat pocketbook for paper money, cards, etc. [ME *walet*, possibly from *watel*, a bag.]
walleye [wöl´-ī] *n* an eye that turns outward, showing much white; any of various American fishes having large, staring eyes, esp the freshwater walleyed pike or perch (*Stizostedion vitreum*).—*adj* **wall´-eyed**, very light grey in the eyes, esp of horses; having a blank or staring appearance or glaring eyes. [The adj is the earlier, prob from ON *vagleygr*—*vagl*, a disease of the eye, and *eygr*, eyed—*auga*, an eye.]
Walloon [wal-ōōn´] *adj* of or pertaining to a population of mixed Celtic and Romanic stock akin to the French, occupying the tract along the frontiers of France and Belgium.—*n* a native or inhabitant of that region; the Romance dialect of the Walloons. [OFr *Wallon*; cog with **Welsh**.]
wallop [wol´op] *vt* (*inf*) to beat or defeat soundly; (*inf*) to strike hard.—*n* (*inf*) a hard blow; (*inf*) a thrill. [Orig uncertain.]
wallow [wol´ō] *vi* to roll about in mud, etc., as an animal (implying enjoy-

ment); to indulge oneself fully (in a specified thing).—*n* a wallowing; a muddy or dusty place. [OE *wealwian*—L *volvĕre*.]

Wall Street [wöl strēt] a street in New York, the chief financial center in the United States; American financial interests.

walnut [wöl´nut] *n* a genus (*Fuglans*) of beautiful trees, the wood of which is much used for furniture; its nut or fruit. [OE *wealh*, foreign, *hnut*, a nut.]

walrus [wöl´rus or wol´-] *n* a large aquatic animal (*Odobenus rosmarus*), allied to the seals, having long canine teeth—also called the *morse* or the *seahorse*. [Du,—Swed *vallross* (ON *hross-hvalr*)—*vall*, a whale, ON *hross*, a horse.]

waltz [wöl(t)s] *n* a whirling or slowly circling dance performed by couples; music for such; a piece of instrumental music in triple time.—*vi* to dance a waltz.—*vti* to move as in a waltz. [Ger *walzer*—*walzen*, to roll.]

wampum [wom´pum] *n* the American Indian name for shell beads used as money.

wan [won] *adj* lacking color, pale and sickly; feeble or weak.—*adv* **wan´ly**.—*n* **wan´ness**. [OE *wann*, dark, lurid.]

wand [wond] *n* a rod of authority, or of conjurers. [ON *vöndr*, a shoot of a tree.]

wander [won´dėr] *vi* to ramble with no definite object; to go astray; to leave home; to depart from the subject; to be delirious; to lose one's way.—*vt* to traverse.—*n* **wan´derer**.—**Wandering Jew**, a legendary Jew who must wander till the Day of Judgement, for an insult offered to Christ on the way to the Crucifixion; **wandering jew**, any of several plants (genus *Zebrina* or *Tradescantia*), esp two trailing or creeping plants (*Z pendula* and *Z flumenensis*) cultivated for their showy foliage. [OE *wandrian*; Ger *wandern*; allied to **wend**, and to **wind** (*wīnd*).]

wanderlust [vän´der-lŏŏst, won´dėr-lust] *n* a craving for change of place, thirst for travel. [Ger.]

wane [wān] *vi* to decrease, esp of the moon; to decline, to fail.—*n* decline, decrease. [OE *wanian* (ON *vana*), to decrease—*wan*, deficient, lacking.]

wangle [wang´gl] (*inf*) *vti* to achieve (something) by trickery.

want [wont] *n* state of privation; lack of what is needful or desired; poverty; scarcity.—*vt* to be destitute of; to lack; to wish for.—*vi* (*arch*) to be deficient or lacking; to be in need; to be without something desired or necessary (eg *never to want for help*).—*adjs* **want´ed**, sought after; desired; **want´ing**, absent; deficient. [Scand, ON *vant*, neut of *vanr*, lacking; cog with **wane**.]

wanton [won´tȯn] *adj* sportive; licentious; wilful; running to excess, or unrestrained (eg of vegetation); motiveless (eg destruction); unprovoked (eg an assault).—*n* a wanton or lewd person, esp a female.—*vi* to frolic; to play lasciviously.—*adv* **wan´tonly**.—*n* **wan´tonness**. [ME *wantowen*, from pfx *wan-*, signifying want, OE *togen*, educated, pt p of *tēon*, to draw, lead.]

wapiti [wop´i-ti] *n* the N American elk (*Cervus canadensis*). [N American Indian.]

war [wör] *n* a state of opposition or contest; a contest between states carried on by arms; open hostility; the profession of arms.—*vi* to make war; to contend, fight (against);—*pr p* **warr´ing**; *pt, pt p* **warred**.—*ns* **war´ cry**, a cry or signal used in war; **war´ dance**, a dance engaged in by some savage tribes before going to war; **war´fāre**, armed contest, hostilities; conflict, struggle; **war´head**, section of torpedo, or other missile, containing the explosive; **war´horse**, a horse used in battle.—*adj* **war´like**, fond of war; pertaining to or threatening war; martial, military.—*ns* **warmonger** [wör´-mung-gėr], one who encourages war, esp for personal gain; **war´ paint**, paint applied to the face and person by savages, indicating that they are going to war; (*slang*) cosmetics for a woman's face; **war´path**, the path taken by Amerindians on a warlike expedition; the expedition itself; **warr´ior**, a veteran soldier; a fighting man; a redoubtable person; **war´ship**, a vessel for war; **war´time**, time of war (also *adj*).—**war of nerves**, systematic attempts to undermine morale by means of threats, rumors etc. [OE *werre*, influenced by OFr *werre* (Fr *guerre*), which is from OHG *werra*, quarrel.]

warble [wör´bl] *vi* to sing in a quavering way, or with variations; to sing sweetly as birds do.—Also *vt*.—*n* **war´bler**, a songster; a songbird; any of various kinds of small birds (esp family Compsothlypidae), not all fine singers, eg the **reedwarbler**. [O Norman Fr *werbler*—OFr *guerbler*; of Gmc origin.]

ward [wörd] *vt* to guard or take care of; to keep away, fend off (*with* **off**).—*n* act of warding; state of being guarded; means of guarding; one who is under a guardian; a division of a city, town, jail or hospital, etc.—*ns* **ward´en**, one who guards or has charge of something; the chief official of a prison; **ward´er**, a watchman; **ward´robe**, a cupboard or piece of furniture for clothes; wearing apparel; **ward´room**, a room used for eating and lounging by the commissioned officers, except the captain, of a warship; **ward´ship**, the office of a ward or guardian; state of being under a guardian. [OE *weardian*; Ger *warten*, to watch in order to protect; doublet of **guard**.]

ware[1] [wār] *n* (*pl*) merchandise, commodities, goods for sale; pottery.—*n* **ware´house**, a building for wares or goods.—*vt* to deposit in a warehouse. [OE *waru*, wares; Ger *ware*.]

ware[2] [wār] *adj* aware. [See **wary**.]

warily, wariness *See* **wary**.

warlock [wör´lok] *n* a sorcerer, a wizard. [OE *wǣrloga*, a breaker of an agreement—*wǣr*, a compact, *lēogan*, to lie.]

warm [wörm] *adj* having moderate heat, hot; violent; zealous, enthusiastic, ardent; excited; angry; having a warm color; (*inf*) close to discovering something.—*vt* to make warm; to interest; to excite.—*vi* to become warm or ardent.—*n* **war´ming pan**, (*hist*) covered pan, with long handle, for holding live coals to warm a bed.—*adv* **warm´ly**.—*ns* **warmth**, moderate heat; geniality; earnestness; growing anger; the bright effect of warm colors.—*adj* **warm´-blood´ed**, having body temperature constantly maintained at a point independent of the environmental temperature; generous, passionate.—*ns* **war´mer; warm front**, the advancing front of a mass of warm air.—*adj* **warm´heart´ed**, having warm affections; affectionate; hearty.—*n* **warm´-up**, a practice exercise before an event. [OE *wearm*; Ger *warm*.]

warn [wörn] *vt* to give notice of danger to; to caution (against); to admonish.—*vi* to give warning (that).—*ns* **war´ner; war´ning**, caution against danger, etc.; admonition; previous notice. [OE *warnian*; cf ON *varna*, to warn, forbid, Ger *warnen*; allied to **ward, beware, wary**.]

warp [wörp] *vt* to twist out of shape; to pervert; to haul (a ship) by warps or ropes attached to posts on a wharf, etc.—*vi* to be twisted out of the straight; to swerve.—*n* the threads stretched out lengthwise in a loom to be crossed by a weft or woof; a rope used in towing.—*adj* **warped**, twisted by shrinking; perverted, embittered and biased in outlook (eg *he had a warped nature*). [OE *weorpan, werpan*; Ger *werfen*, to cast.]

warrant [wor´ȧnt] *vt* to guarantee; to justify, constitute adequate grounds for.—*n* that which warrants or authorizes, esp a document; a commission giving authority; a writ for arresting a person or for carrying a judgment into execution; justification.—*adj* **warr´antable**, authorized by warrant or right; justifiable.—*n* **warr´antableness**.—*adv* **warr´antably**.—*ns* **warr´anter, -or**, one who warrants; **warr´ant off´icer**, a military officer ranking above enlisted men but below a commissioned officer; **warr´anty**, a pledge to replace something if it is not as represented. [OFr *warant* (Fr *garant*)—OHG *weren*.]

warren [wor´ėn] *n* an area in which rabbits breed or are numerous; any crowded building or buildings. [OFr *warenne* (Fr *garenne*)—*warir*, to defend.]

warrior *See* **war**.

wart [wört] *n* a small, hard excrescence on the skin; a small protuberance.—*adj* **wart´y**, like a wart; overgrown with warts. [OE *wearte*; Ger *warze*; prob allied to L *verrūca*.]

wary [wā´ri] *adj* warding or guarding against deception, etc.; cautious.—*adv* **wā´rily**.—*n* **wā´riness**. [Longer form of **ware** (2)—OE *wær*, cautious.]

was [woz] used as *pt* of **be**. [OE *wæs, wære*—*wesan*, to remain, be; ON *vera*, pt *var*.]

wash [wosh] *vt* to cleanse with water or other liquid; to overflow; to flow against; to waste (away), or to sweep (along, etc.), by the action of water; to cover with a thin coat of metal or paint; in mining, to separate from earth by means of water.—*vi* to be engaged in cleansing with water.—*n* a washing; the break of waves on the shore; the rough water left behind by a boat; the shallow part of a river or arm of the sea; a marsh or fen; alluvial matter; waste liquor, refuse of food, etc.; that with which anything is washed; a lotion; a thin coat of paint, metal, etc.; a liquid for cosmetic or toilet use.—*ns* **wash´bowl,-bā´sin**, a bowl, esp a bathroom fixture, for use in washing one's hands, etc.; **wash´er**, one who washes; a washing machine; a flat ring of metal, rubber, etc., to keep joints or nuts secure; **wash´er woman**, a woman whose job is to wash clothes; **wash´house**, a room or building for washing clothes in; **wash´ing**, the act of cleansing by water; clothes washed, or to be washed; **wash´ing machine**, maching for washing clothes; **wash´out**, a washing away of soil, etc. by water; (*slang*) a failure.—**wash out**, to cause to fade by laundering; to rain out; **washed out**, cancelled; pale; exhausted; **wash up**, to sweep up (something, eg on to a shore). [OE *wascan*; ON *vaska*, Ger *waschen*.]

wasp [wosp] *n* any of a large number of winged insects (order Hymenoptera) with biting mouth parts, slender waist, and usu. (in the case of females and workers) a sting—of the same order as ants and bees.—*adj* **was´pish**, like a wasp; spiteful.—*adv* **was´pishly**.—*n* **was´pishness**. [OE *wæsp, wæsps*; Ger *wespe*, L *vespa*.]

WASP, Wasp [wosp] *n* an American of northern European and esp British stock and of Protestant background; one considered to be a member of the dominant privileged class in the US. [*W*hite *A*nglo-*S*axon *P*rotestant.]

wassail [wos´(ā)l] *n* festive occasion; a drunken bout; the ale used on such occasions.—*vi* to hold a wassail or merry drinking meeting.—*n* **wass´ailer**, a reveler. [ON *ves heill*, 'be in health', the salutation used in pledging another, which the Normans transferred to mean 'a carousal'.]

wast [wost] *pt* 2d pers sing of the verb **be**.

waste [wāst] *adj* empty, desert, desolate; uncultivated or uninhabited; left over or superfluous; excreted from the body; used for waste.—*vt* to lay waste or make desolate; to destroy; to wear out gradually; to squander; to impair.—*vi* to lose strength, etc. as by disease; to be diminished, to dwindle.—*n* act of wasting; uncultivated or uninhabited land; a devastated area; discarded material, as ashes; excretions from the body, as urine.—*n* **was´tage**, loss by use, natural decay; wasteful or avoidable loss of something valuable.—*adj* **waste´ful**, characterized by, leading to, waste; given to waste, very extravagant.—*adv* **waste´fully**.—*ns* **waste´fulness; was´ter**, a ne'er-do-well; **wās´trel**, a profligate.—**go to waste**, to be wasted; **lay waste (to)**, to destroy. [OFr *wast, gaste*—L *vastus*, waste; cf ON *wēste*, Ger *wüst*, desolate.]

watch [woch] *n* act of looking out; close observation; guard; one who watches or those who watch; a sentry; any of the periods of duty (usu. four hours) on shipboard; the crew on duty during such a period; a small timepiece for carrying in a pocket, wearing on the wrist, etc.—*vi* to look with attention; to be awake, to keep vigil; to be on one's guard, be vigilant; to keep guard.—*vt* to keep one's eyes fixed on; to observe closely; to follow and note the movements of (a person); to wait for (eg one's opportunity, chance).—*n* **watch´er**.—*adj* **watch´ful**, careful to watch or observe; on the alert to further or to prevent; circumspect, cautious.—*adv* **watch´fully**.—*ns* **watch´fulness; watch´māk´er**, one who makes and repairs watches; **watch´man**, a man who watches or guards, esp premises; **watch´night**, a religious service held to usher in the New Year; **watch´tow´er**, a tower on which a sentinel keeps watch, as for forest fires; **watch´word**, formerly, the password to be given to a watch or sentry; a maxim, rallying cry.—**watch and ward**, uninterrupted vigilance; **watch out**, to look out, be careful. [OE *wæcce*—*wacan*, to wake.]

water [wö´tėr] *n* the substance H_2O, a clear transparent liquid, neutral in its reaction, and devoid of taste or smell; any body of it, as the ocean, a lake, river, etc.; mineral water; tears; saliva; urine; luster, as of a diamond.—*vt* to wet, overflow, or supply with water; to dilute with water.—*vi* to shed water; to gather saliva; to take in water.—*ns* **wa´ter bed**, a rubber mattress filled with water; **wa´ter buffalo**, an often domesticated Asiatic buffalo (*Bubalis bubalis*); **wa´ter cannon**, a high-pressure hose used to disperse crowds; **wa´ter chestnut**, the edible tuber of a Chinese sedge (*Eleochans tuberosa*); the nutlike fruit of an aquatic herb (genus *Trapa*); **wa´ter clock**, an instrument designed to measure time by the fall or flow of a quantity of water; a clepsydra; **wa´ter clos´et**, a room with a bowl-shaped fixture for urination or defecation; such a fixture; **wa´tercol´or**, a color or pigment diluted with water; a painting done with such pigments; **wa´tercourse**, a course or channel for water, as a stream, river, etc. or canal; **wa´tercress**, a plant (*Roripa nasturtium aquaticum*) growing in watery places, esteemed as a salad; **wa´terfall**, a fall or perpendicular descent of a stream of water; a cataract or cascade; **wa´terfowl**, birds that live on and beside water; **Watergate**, a scandal involving criminal abuses of power by officials; **wa´ter gauge**, an instrument for measuring the quantity or height of water; **wa´ter glass**, a drinking glass; a silicate of sodium or potassium, dissolved in water to form a syrupy liquid used as a preservative for eggs, etc.; **wa´ter hen**, any of various birds related to the rail, including the coots; **wa´tering can**, a vessel used for watering plants; **wa´tering place**, a place where livestock come to drink; a place to which people resort to drink mineral water, for bathing, etc.; a nightclub, bar, or tavern.—*adjs* **wa´terish**, somewhat watery; **wa´terless**, lacking water; not requiring water (as for cooling or cooking).—*ns* **wa´ter lev´el**, the level formed by the surface of still water; a waterline; **wa´ter lil´y**, any of a genus (*Nymphaea*) of aquatic plants, with showy flowers and floating leaves; **wa´terline**, the line on a ship to which the water rises.—*adj* **wa´terlogged**, soaked or filled with water so as to be heavy and sluggish.—*ns* **wa´ter main**, a pipe or conduit carrying water; **wa´terman**, a man who plies a boat on water for hire, a boatman, a ferryman; **wa´termark**, a mark showing the height to which water has risen; a mark in paper produced by the impression of a design, as in the mold; **wa´termelon**, a native of the warm parts of the Old World, a plant (*Citrullus vulgaris*) having large round fruits with dark green spotted rind and a juicy, red pulp; **wa´ter mill**, a mill driven by water; **wa´ter moccasin**, a venomous semiaquatic snake (*Agkistrodon piscivorus*) of the southern US; an American water snake (genus *Natrix*); **wa´ter pō´lo**, a goal game played by teams of swimmers; **wa´terpow´er**, the power of water, employed to move machinery, etc.—*adj* **wa´terproof**, proof against water.—*vt* to make impervious to water.—*ns* **wa´ter rat**, the muskrat; **wa´tershed**, the ridge that separates two river basins; the area drained by a river system; a crucial point or dividing line between two phases, conditions, etc.; **wa´terskiing**, the sport of being towed at speed on skilike boards behind a speedboat; **wa´terspout**, a pipe from which water spouts; a tornado occurring over water, and appearing as a rotating column of air full of spray; **wa´ter supply´**, the source, means, or process of supplying water to a community; **wa´ter table**, the upper limit of the portion of the ground saturated with water.—*adj* **wa´tertight**, so tight as not to let water pass through; completely separate; such that no flaw or weakness can be found in it.—*ns* **wa´terway**, a navigable body of water; a way or channel for water; **wa´terwheel**, a wheel moved by water; an engine for raising water; **wa´terworks**, the system of reservoirs, channels, mains, and pumping and purifying equipment by which a supply of water is obtained and distributed (as to a city); an ornamental fountain or cascade; the shedding of tears.—*adj* **wa´tery**, pertaining to or like water; thin, containing too much water; tearful; weak.—**water down**, to make less strong; **water of crystallization**, the water present in some crystalline compounds, eg the five molecules of water in hydrated copper sulfate, $CuSO_4.5H_2O$.—**first water** (see **first**); **heavy water** (see **heavy**); **hold water**, to be correct or well-grounded, to bear examination; **like water**, copiously. [[OE *wæter*; Du *water*, Ger *wasser*; Gr *hydōr*, L *ūdus*, wet, *unda*, a wave, Sans *udan*, water.]

watt [wot] *n* a unit of electrical power corresponding to the power dissipated by an electric current of one ampere flowing across a potential difference of one volt; a unit of power equal to a rate of working of 1 joule per sec. [James *Watt* (1736–1819).]

wattle [wot´l] *n* a twig or flexible rod; a hurdle; the fleshy excrescence under the throat of a cock or turkey; any Australian species of acacia.—*vt* to bind with wattles or twigs; to form by plaiting twigs. [OE *watel*, a hurdle.]

wave [wāv] *n* a surge traveling on the surface of water; (*poet*) the sea; a state of vibration propagated through a system of particles; inequality of surface; a line or streak like a wave; an undulation; one of an undulating succession of curves in hair; a rush of anything, eg of prosperity; a gesture; a movement of the raised hand, expressing greeting, farewell, etc.—*vi* to move like a wave; to move backward and forward; to flutter, as a signal; to undulate; to move the raised hand in greeting, farewell, etc.—*vt* to move backward and forward, to brandish, to flourish; to direct by, or to express by, a wave of the hand; to raise into inequalities of surface; to give an undulating appearance to (hair).—*ns* **wave´ band**, a range of wavelengths occupied by transmission of a particular type; **wave´length**, the distance between the crests (or other corresponding points) of successive waves (including electromagnetic and sound waves).—*adj* **wave´less**, free from waves; undisturbed.—*n* **wave´let**, a little wave.—*vi* **wa´ver**, to move uncertainly or unsteadily to and fro, to shake; to falter, to be irresolute.—*n* **wa´verer**.—*adj* **wa´vy**, full of, or rising in, waves; undulating.—*n* **wa´viness**. [OE *wafian*, to weave; cf ON *vafra*, to waver.]

wax[1] [waks] *n* beeswax; this substance used to make candles, etc.; any substance like it in some respect, as that in the ear.—*vt* to rub, polish, cover or treat with wax.—*adj* **wax´en**, made of wax; like wax; pale, plastic, etc.—*ns* **wax´light**, a candle or taper made of wax; **wax´work**, work made of wax, esp figures or models formed of wax; (*pl*) an exhibition of wax figures.—*adj* **wax´y**, resembling wax; soft; pallid, pasty.—*n* **wax´iness**. [OE *weax*; ON *vax*, Du *was*, Ger *wachs*.]

wax[2] [waks] *vi* to increase in strength, size, etc.; of the moon, to become gradually full; to become. [OE *weaxan*; ON *vaxa*, Ger *wachsen*, L *augēre*, to increase, Gr *auxanein*.]

way[1] [wā] *n* passage; road; length of space, distance; room to advance; direction; condition, state (eg *he is in a bad way*); general manner of acting (eg *as is his way*; also in *pl*); means; manner of living; (*naut*) progress or motion through the water, headway.—*ns* **way´bill**, list of passengers and goods carried by a conveyance; **way´fārer**, a traveler or passenger, esp on foot.—*adj, n* **way´fāring**.—*vt* **way´lay**, to watch or lie in ambush for (a person), now usu. in order to converse with him against his inclination.—*n* **way´side**, the side of a way, path, or highway.—*adj* growing or lying near the wayside.—*adj* **way´ward**, wilful, capricious; perverse; irregular.—*n* **way´wardness**.—**ways and means**, resources; methods eg of raising money for the carrying on of government.—**be under way**, to be in motion, as a vessel; **by the way**, incidentally, in passing; while traveling; **by way of**, as a kind of (eg *he said this by way of apology*); as for the purpose of (*by way of making matters better*); **be by way of**, to be supposed, alleged (inaccurately) to be, do (eg *she was by way of tidying the room*); **get one's own way**, to get what one wants; **have a way with one**, to have a fascinating or a persuasive manner; **have one's way**, to get what one wants; **in a small way**, on a small scale; **in the way**, on the way; impeding, obstructing; **make one's way**, to push forward; **make way**, to give place; to advance; **out of the way**, so as not to hinder or obstruct; unusual; **take one's way**, to proceed; to follow one's own inclination or plan. [OE *weg*; Ger *weg*, L *via*, Sans *vaha*, akin to L *vehĕre*, to carry, draw.]

way[2] [wā] *adv* abbrev form of **away**, far; at a considerable distance or interval of time.—*adj* **way´-out** (*inf*) eccentric, unusual; excellent.—**from way back**, of long standing.

we [wē] *pron pl* of I; I and others. [OE *wē*, cog with Ger *wir*.]

weak [wēk] *adj* wanting strength; not able to sustain a great weight; easily overcome or subdued; wanting health; frail; having little of the important ingredient (eg *weak tea; a weak solution*); impressible, easily led; inconclusive (eg *a weak argument*); (*gram*) of a verb which forms *pt* and *pt p* by addition of **-ed**.—*vt* **weak´en**, to make weak; to reduce in strength or spirit.—*vi* to grow weak or weaker.—*adj* **weak´-kneed**, lacking firm will.—*n* **weak´ling**, one lacking physical or moral strength.—*adv* **weak´ly**.—*adj* **weak´minded**, having feeble intelligence; having, or showing, lack of resolution; too easily convinced or persuaded.—*n* **weak´ness**, state of being weak; infirmity; inability to resist. [OE *wāc*, pliant—*wīcan*, to yield; Du *week, veikr*, Ger *weich*.]

weal[1] [wēl] *n* (*arch*) state of being well, a sound or prosperous state; welfare. [OE *wela*, wealth, bliss; Ger *wohl*.]

weal[2] [wēl] *n* a raised streak left by a blow with a lash, etc; welt. [**wale**.]

weald [wēld] *n* a heavily wooded area; a wild or uncultivated, usu. upland, region. [OE *weald*, a forest, wold. There has been some confusion with **wild**. Cf **wold**.]

wealth [welth] *n* possessions of any kind; riches; an abundance (of).—*adj* **wealth´y**, rich; prosperous.—*adv* **wealth´ily**.—*n* **wealth´iness**. [**weal** (1).]

wean [wēn] *vt* to accustom to nourishment other than the mother's milk; to estrange the affections of (a person from any object or habit).—*n* **wean´ling**, a child or animal newly weaned. [OE *wenian*; ON *venja*, Ger *gewöhnen*, to accustom, *entwöhnen*, to wean.]

weapon [wep´ȯn] *n* any instrument or means of offense or defense. [OE *wæpen*; Ger *waffen* and *wappen*.]

wear[1] [wār] *vt* to carry on the body; to arrange (clothes, hair) in a specified way; to have, show, display (eg *she wears a pleased expression*); (of a ship) to fly (eg a flag); to consume, waste, damage, by use or exposure; to make by friction (eg a hole, a path); to exhaust, tire (out); to tolerate.—*vi* to be wasted by use or time; to be spent tediously; to consume slowly; to last under use (eg *corduroy is a material that wears well*);—*pt* **wōre**; *pt p* **wōrn**.—*n* act of wearing; lessening or injury by use or friction; articles worn.—*adj* **wear´able**, fit to be worn.—*n* **wear´er**.—*adj* **wear´ing**, made or designed for wear; consuming, exhausting.—**wear and tear**, damage by wear or use. [OE *werian*, to wear; ON *verja*, to cover.]

wear[2] [wār] *vti* (*naut*) to bring, or be brought, to another course by turning the helm to windward;—*pt, pt p* **wore**. [Prob **veer** (1).]

weary [wē´ri] *adj* tired, having the strength or patience exhausted; tedious.—*vt* to wear out or make weary, to reduce the strength or patience of; to harass.—*vi* to become weary or impatient.—*n* **wea´riness**.—*adj* **wea´risome**, making weary, tedious.—*adv* **wea´risomely**.—*n* **wea´risomeness**. [OE *wērig*, weary.]

weasand [wē´zȧnd] *n* the gullet; the throat; the windpipe. [OE *wǣsend, wāsend*.]

weasel [wē´zl] *n* a genus (*Mustela*) of small carnivores with long slender body, active, furtive, and bloodthirsty, eating frogs, birds, mice, etc.—*vi* to be evasive or deliberately misleading. [OE *wesle*; Ger *wiesel*.]

weather [weTH´ėr] *n* atmospheric conditions as to heat or cold, wetness, cloudiness, etc.; storm, rain, etc.—*vt* to affect by exposing to the air; to sail to the windward of; to come safely through (a storm).—*vi* to become discolored, disintegrated (as rocks), etc., by exposure.—*adj* (*naut*) toward the wind, windward.—*adjs* **weath´er-beat´en**, distressed by, or seasoned by, the weather; **weath´er-bound**, delayed by bad weather.—*ns* **weather´cock**, a weather vane in the form of a cock to show the direction of the wind; one who changes his opinions, allegiance, etc., easily and often; **weath´erglass**, (*loosely*) a barometer; **weath´ering**, the action of the elements in altering the form, color, texture, or composition of rocks, etc.; **weather vane**, a vane for showing which way the wind is blowing.—**keep one's weather eye open**, to be alert; **make heavy weather of**, to find excessive difficulty in; **under the weather**, indisposed; drunk. [OE *weder*; ON *vedhr*, Ger *wetter*.]

weave[1] [wēv] *vt* twine threads together; to interlace threads in a loom to form cloth; to work (into a fabric, story, etc.); to construct, contrive.—*vi* to practice weaving;—*pt* **wōve**, (rarely) **weaved**; *pt p* **wōv´en**.—*ns* **weav´er; weav´ing**, the act or the art of forming a web or cloth by the intersecting of two distinct sets of fibers, threads, or yarns—the *warp* and the *weft* or *woof*. [OE *wefan*; ON *vefa*, Ger *weben*.]

weave[2] [wēv] *vi* to move to and fro, or in and out; (in boxing) to move back or forward with sinuous movements of the body; (in flying) to fly with a weaving motion. [ME *weve*; ety dub.]

web [web] *n* that which is woven; the fine texture spun by the spider as a snare for flies; the membrane joining the digits of various water birds, animals, etc.—*ns* **webb´ing**, a strong woven fabric used for belts, etc.; **web´foot**, a foot the toes of which are united with a web or membrane. [OE *webb*; ON *vefr*, Ger *gewebe*; from root of **weave**.]

weber [vā´bėr, wē´bėr] *n* a unit of magnetic flux equal to 10^8 maxwells; formerly, a coulomb. [Wilhelm *Weber*, German physicist (1804–91).]

wed [wed] *vt* to marry; to join in marriage; to unite closely.—*vi* to marry;—*pr p* **wedd´ing**;—*pt, pt p* **wedd´ed** or **wed**.—*ns* **wedd´ing**, marriage; marriage ceremony.—**silver, golden, diamond wedding**, the 25th, 50th and 60th anniversaries of a wedding. [OE *weddian*, to engage, to marry (Ger *wetten*, to wager)—*wedd*, a pledge; Ger *wette*, a bet.]

wedge [wej] *n* a piece of wood or metal, thick at one end and sloping to a thin edge at the other, used in splitting or in fixing tightly; anything shaped like a wedge; any act serving to open the way for change.—*vt* to fasten, or to fix, with a wedge or wedges; to press, thrust (in), tightly (a person, eg oneself, or a thing).—*vi* to become fixed or jammed by, or as if by, a wedge.—**the thin**, or **small, end of the wedge**, a small beginning that is bound to be followed by important developments and results. [OE *wecg*; ON *veggr*, Ger *weck*, a wedge; prob from the root of *weigh*.]

Wedgwood [wej´wŏŏd] *n* a trade name for ceramic ware (as bone china or jasper) invented by Josiah *Wedgwood* (1730–1795).]

wedlock [wed´lok] *n* matrimony; married state, esp in the phrase **out of wedlock**, with the natural parents not married to each other. [OE *wedlāc*—*wedd, lāc*, a gift.]

Wednesday [wenz´dā] *n* fourth day of the week. [OE *Wōdenes dæg*, the day of *Woden* or *Odin*, the king of gods and men in Scandinavian myth.]

wee [wē] *adj* small, tiny, very early. [ME *we*, a bit.]

weed[1] [wēd] *n* any undesired plant, esp one that crowds out desired plants; (*inf*) tobacco; (*inf*) marijuana; an obnoxious thing, growth, or person.—*vt* to free (a garden, etc) from weeds; to remove anything troublesome or useless (often *with* **out**).—*vi* to remove weeds.—*n* **weed´er**, any of various devices for freeing an area from weeds.—*adj* **weed´y**, consisting of weeds; full of weeds: very thin and scrawny. [OE *wēod*, a herb.]

weed[2] [wēd] *n* (used in *pl*) a widow's mourning apparel. [OE *wæd*, clothing.]

week [wēk] *n* the space of seven days, esp from Sunday to Sunday; the working days of the week.—*ns* **week´day**, any day of the week except Sunday; **weekend**, a period from Friday night or Saturday morning to Monday morning.—*adj* **week´ly**, coming, happening, or done once a week.—*adv* once a week.—*n* a publication appearing once a week.—[OE *wice*; Du *week*, Ger *woche*.]

weep [wēp] *vi* to express grief by shedding tears; to wail or lament; to drip, ooze.—*vt* to lament; to pour forth (eg *to weep bitter tears*); to express while or by weeping; to exude;—*pt, pt p* **wept**.—*n* **weep´er**, one who weeps; (*hist*) a long black hatband worn by a mourner, or a white border around the sleeve of a mourning dress.—*adj* **weep´ing**, of trees, drooping the branches. [OE *wēpan*—*wēp*, clamor.]

weevil [wēv´il] *n* one of a group of beetles (suborder Rhynch-ophora) having an elongated snout.—*adjs* **weev´ily, weev´illy**, infested by weevils. [Conn with OE *wifel*, beetle.]

weft [weft] *n* the threads woven into and crossing the warp.—Also **woof**. [OE *weft*—*wefan*, to *weave*.]

weigh[1] [wā] *vt* to find the heaviness of; to have (a specified weight); to raise a ship's anchor; to ponder, consider (eg arguments, probabilities).—*vi* to have weight; to be considered of importance; to press heavily.—*n* **weight**, the heaviness of a thing when weighed, or the amount which anything weighs; (*physics*) the force exerted on a mass by gravity, measured by product of mass and acceleration; any unit of heaviness; any system of such units; a piece of standard heaviness used in weighing; any body used for its heaviness; a burden, as of sorrow; influence; importance; power.—*vt* to attach or add a weight or weights to; to hold down in this way; to make more heavy.—*n* **weight´lessness**, the condition where little or no reaction to the force due to gravity is experienced, as eg in free fall through thin air at high altitude, or in space travel.—*adj* **weigh´ty**, heavy; important; being the fruit of judicious consideration and hence worthy of attention.—*adv* **weigh´tily**.—*n* **weigh´tiness**.—**weigh in**, to weigh (a jockey or a boxer) before a contest; to have one's possessions (as baggage) weighed; (*inf*) to enter as a participant; **weigh one's words**, to choose one's words carefully before speaking. [OE *wegan*, to carry; Ger *wiegen*; L *vehĕre*, to carry.]

weigh[2] [wā] *n* way, used in the phrase 'under way'.

weir [wēr] *n* a dam across a river; a fence of stakes set in a stream for catching fish. [OE *wer*, an enclosure, allied to *werian*, to protect.]

weird [wērd] *n* fate; that which comes to pass.—*adj* skilled in witchcraft; unearthly, mysterious; odd, very queer.—*n* **weirdie, weir´do**, (*slang*) an eccentric; someone unconventional in dress, etc.—**the Weird Sisters**, the Fates. [OE *wyrd*, fate—*weorthan*, to become; Ger *werden*.]

welcome [wel´kȯm] *adj* received with gladness, admitted willingly; causing gladness; free to enjoy; under no obligation.—*n* (kindly) reception.—*vt* to receive with kindness; to receive (anything) with pleasure or enthusiasm. [OE *wilcuma*, influenced by ON *velkominn*.]

weld [weld] *vt* to join together, as metal by heating until fused or soft enough to hammer together; to join closely.—*n* a welded joint. [Conn with OE *weallan*, to boil; Ger *wallen*.]

welfare [wel´fār] *n* state of faring or doing well; those government agencies which grant aid to the poor, the unemployed, etc.—**welfare state**, a social system based on a political state assuming primary responsibility for the individual and social welfare of its citizens; a nation characterized by the operation of the welfare state system; **welfare work**, organized efforts by a community or organization for the social betterment of a group in society.—**on welfare**, receiving government aid because of poverty, etc. [**well, fare**.]

welkin [wel´kin] *n* (*arch*) the sky or region of clouds. [OE *wolcnu*, pl of *wolcen*, cloud, air, sky; Ger *wolke*, cloud.]

well[1] [wel] *n* a spring; a source; a lined shaft made in the earth whence a supply of water, oil, etc., is obtained; any similar walled space, eg the open space in the middle of a staircase; a container for a liquid, as an inkwell.—*vi* to issue forth, as water from the earth.—*n* **well´-spring**, a fountain. [OE *wella*—*weallan*, to boil; cf ON *vella*, to boil.]

well[2] [wel] *adj comparative* **bett´er**, *superlative* **best**; fortunate; comfortable; in health.—*adv* in a proper, satisfactory, or excellent manner; thoroughly; prosperously; with good reason; to a considerable degree; definitely; familiarly.—*interj* expressing surprise, etc.—*adjs* **well´-advised´**, wise, prudent; **well´-appoint´ed**, finely equipped.—*n* **well´-bē´ing**, state of being well, welfare.—*adjs* **well´born**, born of a good or respectable family; **well´-bred**, of polished manners; of good stock; **well´-disposed´**, friendly (toward a person) or receptive (to an idea); *adjs* **well´-done**, peformed with skill; thoroughly cooked, as meat; **well´-earned**, thoroughly deserved; **well´-fāv´ored**, good-looking; handsome; **well´-heeled**, (*inf*) prosperous; **well´-informed**, having considerable knowledge of a subject or many subjects; **well´-knit**, strongly framed; sturdy in body build; **well´-known**, familiar; celebrated; thoroughly known; **well-mannered**, polite; courteous; **well´-mean´ing**, having good intentions; rightly intended.—*adv* **well´-nigh**, nearly, almost.—*adjs* **well´-off**, in good circumstances; prosperous; **well-preserved**, in good condition or looking good, in spite of age; **well´-read**, widely acquainted with books, etc.; **well´-timed**, opportune; **well´-to-do**, prosperous; **well-turned**, gracefully shaped; expressed well; **well´-worn**, much worn or used.—**as well (as)**, in addition (to); equally (with). [OE *wel*; cog with Ger *wohl.*]

Wellington [wel´ing-tȯn] *n* a leather boot having a loose top with the front usu. coming above the knee. [Named after the Duke of *Wellington* (1769–1852).]

Welsh [welsh] *adj* pertaining to *Wales*, or its inhabitants.—*n pl* the inhabitants of Wales;—*sing* their Celtic language.—*n* **Welsh´-man**, a native of Wales.—**Welsh rabbit**, cheese melted on toasted bread.—Also **Welsh rarebit**. [OE *wealas*, foreigners; Anglo-Saxon invaders' name for Welsh and native Britons.]

welsh [welsh] *vi* (*slang*) to fail to pay a debt, fulfill an obligation, etc. (*often with* **on**).—*n* **welsh´er**.

welt [welt] *n* a band or strip fastened to an edge to give strength or for ornament; a narrow strip of leather used in one method of sewing the upper to the sole of a shoe; a ridge raised on the skin by a slash or blow.—*vt* to furnish with a welt; (*inf*) to lash, beat. [W *gwald*, a hem.]

welter [wel´tėr] *vi* to roll or wallow, esp in dirt.—*n* a turmoil.—*adj* **wel´tering**. [ME *walten*, to roll over—OE *wealtan*, to roll.]

welterweight [wel´tėr-wāt] *n* a boxer or wrestler weighing 136–247 lb.

wen [wen] *n* a benign skin tumor, most commonly on the scalp. [OE *wen*, a swelling, a wart; Du *wen*.]

wench [wench] *n* a derogatory term for a girl; (*arch*) a maidservant; a harlot.—*vi* to frequent the company of harlots. [OE *wencel*, a child.]

wend [wend] *vi* to go, to wind or turn.—*vt* in **wend one's way**, follow the road in a leisurely fashion. [OE *wendan*, the causative of *windan*, to turn round.]

went [went] *pt* of **go**.

wept [wept] *pt, pt p* of **weep**.

were [wûr] *vi* the *pl* of **was**, used as *pt* of **be**. [OE *wǣre*; Ger *war*, ON *vera*, to be. Cf **was**.]

werewolf [wēr´wŏŏlf] *n* a person supposed to be able to change himself for a time into a wolf. [OE *werwulf*—*wer*, man (L *vir*), *wulf*, a wolf.]

wert [wûrt] (*arch*) the 2nd pers sing of **be**.

Wesleyan [wes´le-ȧn] *adj* pertaining to Wesleyanism.—*n* adherent of Wesleyanism.—*n* **Wes´leyanism**, the system of doctrine and church polity of the Wesleyan Methodists. [Named from John *Wesley* (1703–91).]

west [west] *n* the quarter where the sun sets; one of the four chief points of the compass; the region in the west of any country; **West**, Europe and the Western Hemisphere.—*adj* situated toward, or (of wind) coming from, the west.—*adv* in or toward the west.—*adj, adv* **wes´terly**, toward the west; from the west.—*adj* **wes´tern**, situated in the west; belonging to the west; toward the west; **Western**, of the West.—*n* a story or motion picture about cowboys, etc. in the western US.—*n* **wes´terner**, a person belonging to the west.—*adj, adv* **west´ward**, toward the west.—*advs* **west´wardly, west´wards**, toward the west.—**Western Hemisphere**, that half of the earth including N and S America. [OE *west* (Fr *ouest*, ON *vestr*).]

wet [wet] *adj* covered or saturated with water or other liquid; rainy; misty; not yet dry; permitting the sale of alcoholic liquor.—*n* water or other liquid; rain or rainy weather; one who favors the sale of alcoholic liquor.—*vti* to make or become wet;—*pr p* **wett´ing**, *pt, pt p* **wet, wett´ed**.—*ns* **wet´back**, (*inf*) a Mexican who illegally enters the US to work; **wet´ness; wet nurse**, a nurse who suckles a child for its mother; **wet suit**, a closefitting suit worn by skindivers, etc. for warmth.—*adj* **wett´ish**, somewhat wet.—**a wet blanket**, any cause of discouragement or depression; a depressing companion; **all wet** (*slang*) wrong. [OE *wǣt*; ON *vātr*; from root of **water**.]

wether [weTH´ėr] *n* a male sheep castrated before maturity. [OE *wither*; Ger *widder*.]

whack [hwak] *vti* (*inf*) to strike smartly, esp making a sound.—*n* (*inf*) a blow; a stroke; an attempt; a share.—*adj* **whack´ing**, (*inf*) very large.—*n* a beating. [**thwack**.]

whale [hwāl] *n* any of numerous cetaceous mammals (order Cetacea), esp the larger kinds; (*slang*) something very large or impressive of its kind.—*vi* to catch whales.—*ns* **whaleback**, a freight steamer having rounded upper deck; **whale´-bone**, a light flexible substance from the upper jaw of certain whales.—*adj* made of whalebone; **whaler**, a ship or a person employed in whaling.—**a whale of a** (*slang*) something very large of its kind. [OE *hwæl* (ON *hvalr*, Ger *walfisch*); orig unknown.]

wharf [hwörf] *n* a landing stage, for loading and unloading ships;—*pl* **wharfs, wharves**.—*vt* to secure beside a wharf; to place on a wharf.—*ns* **wharf´age**, the dues paid for using a wharf; accommodation at a wharf; **wharfinger** [whörf´injėr], one who has the care of, or owns, a wharf. [OE *hwerf*, a dam; prob conn with *hweorfan* (ON *hverfa*), to turn.]

what [hwot] *interrog pron* neuter of **who**—also used elliptically and as an interjection of astonishment.—*interrog adj* of what sort, how much, how great.—*rel pron* that which (eg *give me what you have*).—*rel adj* such . . . as (eg *give me what money you have*).—*prons* **whatev´er, whate'er´**, any thing which.—*adj* any or all that, no matter what.—*adjs* **whatsoev´er, whatsoe'er´**, of whatever kind.—**what have you**, (*inf*) anything else of the kind; **what's-his, -its, -name**, the person or thing indicated or understood; **what's what**, the true position of affairs; **what time**, at the very time when. [OE *hwæt*, neut of *hwā*, who; Ger *was*, L *quid*.]

whatnot [hwot´not] *n* a piece of furniture with shelves for books, etc., so-called because used to hold anything. [**what, not**.]

wheat [hwēt] *n* a cereal grass (*Triticum aestivum*), the grain furnishing a nutritious flour for bread.—*adj* **wheat´en**, made of wheat. [OE *hwǣte*—*hwīt*, white; Ger *weizen*; allied to *white*, its color.]

wheatear [hwēt´ēr] *n* a small white-rumped northern bird (*Oenanthe oenanthe*). [Corr from *white-arse*, white-rump.]

wheedle [hwēd´l] *vt* to entice by soft words, flatter, cajole (into); to coax (something out of a person); to cheat (a person out of something) by cajolery.—*n* **wheed´ler**. [Perh from OE *wǣdlian*, to be in want, to beg.]

wheel [hwēl] *n* a circular frame turning on an axle; an old instrument of torture; a steering wheel; (*pl*) (*slang*) an automobile; (*pl*) the moving forces; a turning movement; (*slang*) an important person.—*vt* to cause to whirl; to convey on wheels.—*vi* to turn round or on an axis; to be provided with wheels on which to be propelled; to change direction.—*ns* **wheelbarrow**, a barrow with one wheel in front and two handles and legs behind; (loosely) any other hand cart; **wheel´base**, the distance between the front and rear axles of a vehicle.—*adj* **wheeled**, having wheels.—*ns* **wheel´er**, one who wheels; a horse nearest the wheels of a carriage; a maker of wheels; **wheelhouse**, the shelter in which a ship's steering wheel, etc., is placed; **wheel´wright**, one who makes and repairs wheels and wheeled vehicles.—**wheel and deal**, to pursue one's interests, esp in a shrewd and unscrupulous manner. [OE *hwēol*; ON *hjōl*.]

wheeze [hwēz] *vi* to breathe with a hissing sound; to breathe audibly or with difficulty.—*n* the act of wheezing.—*adj* **wheez´y**. [OE *hwēsan*; ON *hvæsa*, to wheeze, to hiss.]

whelk [hwelk] *n* any of numerous edible mollusks (*Buccinum* and allied genera) with spiral shell. [OE *wiloc, weoluc*.]

whelm [hwelm] *vt* to cover completely, to submerge; to overpower. [ME *whelmen*.]

whelp [hwelp] *n* the young of the dog and of lions, etc.—a puppy, a cub; a young man (in contempt).—*vti* of animals, to bring forth young. [OE *hwelp*; ON *hvelpr*.]

when [hwen] *adv, conj* at what time? at which time? at or after the time that; while; even though.—*rel pron* at which (eg *at the time when I said that I believed it was so*).—*adv, conj* **whence** (also **from whence**), from what place; from which things; wherefore.—*conjs* **whencesoev´er**, from what place, cause, or source, soever; **whenev´er**, at every time when; **whensoev´er**, at what time soever; whenever. [OE *hwænne, hwonne* (Ger *wann, wenn*); orig acc of interrog pron *hwā*, who.]

where [hwār] *adv, conj* at which place; at what place? to which place; to what place?—*rel pron* in which, to which (eg *he could not find the place where he had left it*).—*adv, conj* **whereabouts** about where; near what?—*n* **where´abouts**, situation, location, esp approximate.—*conj* **whereas´**, when in fact; but on the other hand.—*advs, conjs* **whereat´**, (*arch*) at which; at what? **whereby´**, by which; **where´fore**, (*arch*) for which reason; for what reason? why?—*n* the cause.—*advs, conjs* **wherein´**, in which respect; **whereof´**, of which; of what; of whom; **whereon´**, on which; **wheresoev´er**, in or to what place soever; **whereto´**, to which; to what? **whereun´to** [-un´tōō´] (*arch*) whereto; for what purpose? **whereupon´**, upon or in consequence of which; **wherev´er** (*inf*) at, to, whatever place; **wherewith´, wherewithal´**, with which; with what?—*adv, n* **wherewithal**, the means (*usu with* **the**).—*advs* **whereat**, at or toward which; **whereby´**, by or through which; by the help of which. [OE *hwǣr, hwār*; from stem of **who**.]

wherry [hwer´i] *n* a racing scull for one person; a light rowboat.

whet [hwet] *vt* to sharpen by rubbing; to make keen; to excite;—*pr p* **whett´ing**; *pt, pt p* **whett´ed**.—*n* act of sharpening; something that sharpens the appetite.—*ns* **whet´stone**, a stone for sharpening edged instruments; **whett´er**. [OE *hwettan*—*hwæt*, sharp; Ger *wetzen*.]

whether [hweTH´ėr] *conj* introducing the first of two alternative words, phrases, clauses, the second being introduced by *or*, or (in the case of clauses) sometimes by *or whether*—used similarly as *interrog adv*. [OE *hwæther*, from *hwā*, who, with the old comp suffx *-ther*; cog with Ger *weder*; also with L *uter*, Sans *katara*. Cf **other** and **alter**.]

whew [hwū] *interj* expressing wonder or dismay.

whey [hwā] *n* the watery part of milk, separated from the curd, esp in making cheese.—*adj* **whey´-faced**, pale with terror. [OE *hwæg*; Low Ger *wey*.]

which [hwich] *interrog pron* what one of a number?—also used adjectivally.—*rel pron* (*obs*) who, whom; now used of things only.—*prons* **whichev´er, whichsoev´er**, every one which; any one, no matter which.—**which is which**? which is the one, which is the other? [OE *hwilc, hwelc*, from *hwī*, instrumental case of *hwā*, who, and *līc*, like; Ger *welch, welcher*; L *quālis*. Cf **such** and **each**.]

whiff [hwif] *n* a sudden puff of air or smoke from the mouth; a slight blast; a slight inhalation; a puff of smell.—*vt* to throw out in whiffs; to puff (along, away).—Also *vi*.—*vi* **whiff´le**, to veer about, blow in gusts; to be fickle; to prevaricate. [Imit.]

Whig [hwig] *n* a member of a former English political party which championed reform and parliamentary rights; a supporter of the American Revolution; a member of a US political party (about 1836–1856). [Prob short for *whiggamore*, one of a group of 17th century Scottish Presbyterian rebels.]

while [hwīl] *n* space of time.—*conj* during the time that; at the same time that; although; whereas.—*vt* to cause to pass without irksomeness (*with* **away**).—*adj* **whī´lom**, former.—**the while**, (*arch*) while; meantime. [OE *hwīl*; Ger *weile.*]

whim [hwim] *n* a caprice, a fancy.—*adj* **whim´sical**, full of whims, odd, fantastical.—*ns* **whimsical´ity, whim´sicalness.**—*adv* **whim´sically.**—*n* **whim´sy, whim´sey**, a whim, freak; whimsical behavior. [ON *hvima*, to have the eyes wandering.]

whimper [hwim´pėr] *vi* to cry with a low, whining voice.—*n* a peevish cry. [From *whimmer*; Ger *wimmern*; perh from the root of **whine.**]

whin [hwin] *n* gorse, furze.—*adj* **whinn´y**, covered with whins. [Prob of Scand origin.]

whine [hwīn] *vi* to utter a plaintive cry; to complain in an unmanly way.—*n* a plaintive cry; an affected nasal tone of utterance.—*n* **whī´ner.**—*adv* **whī´ningly**. [OE *hwīnan*, to whine; ON *hvīna*, to whistle through the air.]

whinny [hwin´i] *vt* to neigh;—*pt, pt p* **whinn´ied.**—*n* a neigh. [Freq of **whine.**]

whinstone [hwin´stōn] *n* trap; any of various dark resistant rocks. [**whin** (ety uncertain), **stone.**]

whip [hwip] *n* a flexible lash with a handle for punishing or driving; a stroke administered as by a whip; an officer of a political party in a legislature who maintains discipline, etc.; a whipping motion.—*vt* to move, pull, throw, etc. suddenly; to strike, as with a lash; to wind (cord, etc.) around a rope to prevent fraying; to beat into a froth; (*inf*) to defeat.—*vi* to move nimbly; to flap about.—*pr p* **whipp´ing**; *pt, pt p* **whipped, whipt.**—*ns* **whip´cord**, cord for making whips; a strong worsted material with ribs; **whip´hand**, control or advantage; **whip´lash**, the lash of a whip; a sudden, severe jolting of the neck back and forth, as caused by the impact of an automobile collision; **whipp´er; whipp´er-in**, one who whips the hounds to keep them to the line of chase; **whipp´ersnapp´er**, a pretentious but insignificant person; **whipp´ing**, act of whipping; punishment with the whip or lash; a defeat; **whipp´ing boy**, a boy who was educated with a prince and whipped for the royal pupil's faults; a scapegoat; **whipp´ing post**, a post to which offenders are tied to be legally whipped.—**whip up**, to rouse, raise to greater intensity. [ME *whippen*; prob a form of *wippen*—Old Du *wippen*, to shake.]

whippet [hwip´et] *n* a small dog like a greyhound, developed from a cross between the Italian greyhound and a terrier; a small tank used in World War I by the Allied armies. [Perh **whip.**]

whippoorwill [hwip-pȯr-wil´] *n* a nocturnal bird (*Caprimulgus vociferus*) of eastern N America. [From its notes.]

whir, whirr [hwûr] *n* a sound from rapid whirling.—*vti* to whirl round with a noise;—*pr p* **whirr´ing**; *pt, pt p* **whirred.** [Imit; cf Dan *hvirre*, to whirl.]

whirl [hwûrl] *n* a turning with rapidity; anything that turns with velocity; a great or confusing degree (of activity or emotion); commotion, agitation.—*vi* to revolve rapidly.—*vt* to turn (round) rapidly; to carry (away) rapidly, as on wheels.—*ns* **whirl´igig**, a child's toy which is spun or whirled rapidly round; anything whirling; **whirl´pool**, a circular current in a river or sea, produced by opposing tides, winds, or currents; an eddy; **whirl´wind**, a violent aerial current, with a whirling, rotary, or spiral motion; **whir´lybird**, (*inf*) a helicopter. [Cf ON *hvirfla*, freq of *hverfa*, to turn round; Ger *wirbeln.*]

whisk [hwisk] *vt* to move with a quick motion; to sweep, or stir, rapidly.—*vi* to move nimbly and rapidly.—*n* a rapid sweeping motion; a brushing with such a motion.—*ns* **whisk broom**, a small short-handled broom for brushing clothes, etc.—*n* **whis´ker**, (*pl*) the hair growing on a man's face, esp the cheeks; any of the long bristles on the face of a cat, etc.—*adj* **whis´kered.** [Scand, ON *visk*, a wisp of hay; Swed *viska*, to wipe, Ger *wischen*; prob conn with **wash.**]

whiskey [hwis´ki] *n* a strong alcoholic beverage distilled from grain;—*pl* **whiskeys, whiskies.**—Also **whisk´y**, in British and Canadian usage; **Whiskey**, a communications code word for the letter *w*. [Gael *uisge beatha* (lit, water of life).]

whisper [hwis´pėr] *vi* to speak with a low sound; to speak covertly, spread rumors; to make a rustling sound.—*vt* to utter in a low voice or under the breath, or covertly, or by way of gossip.—*n* a low hissing voice or sound; cautious or timorous speaking; a secret hint; a rumor.—*ns* **whis´perer**, one who whispers.—**whispering campaign**, an attack by means of derogatory rumors or charges, esp against a candidate for public office. [OE *hwisprian*; Ger *wispern*, ON *hvīskra*; allied to **whistle.**]

whist [hwist] *n* a card game, played by two against two, a forerunner of bridge. [Orig *whisk*; ety uncertain.]

whistle [hwis´l] *vi* to make a sound by forcing the breath through the lips or teeth; to make a like sound with an instrument; to sound shrill; to move with a shrill sound, as the wind.—*vt* to form or utter by whistling; to call by a whistle.—*n* the sound made in whistling; an instrument for whistling.—*ns* **whis´tler; whis´tle stop**, a small town; a brief stop in a small town on a tour.—*vi* of a political candidate, to make an electioneering tour with many brief personal appearances in small communities. [OE *hwistlian.*]

whit [hwit] *n* the smallest particle imaginable; a bit. [By-form of **wight**, a creature.]

white [hwīt] *adj* of the color of milk or pure salt; stainless; pure; bright; light-colored, as of Caucasoid skin; pallid.—*n* the color of anything white; the albuminous part of an egg; the white part of the eyeball; a white pigment.—*vt* to make white.—*vti* **whit´en**, to make or become white or whiter.—*ns* **white´ness; whit´ing**, a small fish (*Merlangus merlangus*) allied to the cod, so called from its white color; the silver hake; the northern whiting (*Menticirrhus saxatilis*) and related species; ground chalk used in paints, etc.—*adj* **whit´ish**, somewhat white.—*ns* **white ant**, a termite; **white´bait**, the fry of the herring and sprat.—*adj* **white´coll´ar**, pertaining to, or designating office and professional workers.—*ns* **white corpuscle**, a leucocyte; **white elephant**, an albino elephant, held as sacred in southeast Asia; a thing of little use, but expensive to maintain; any object not wanted by its owner, but useful to another; **white feather**, a symbol of cowardice; **white flag**, an emblem of truce or of surrender; **White Friar**, one of the Carmelite order of friars, so called from their white dress; **white goods**, household items, as sheets, towels, etc.; large household appliances, as refrigerators; **white heat**, the degree of heat at which certain metals become white (*adj* **white-hot**); **White House**, official residence of the President of the US in Washington, DC; the executive branch of the US government; **white lead**, a carbonate of lead used in painting white.—*adj* **white´-livered**, cowardly.—*ns* **white metal**, any of several light-colored alloys used for type metals, bearing, etc., or as a base for plated silverware and ornaments and novelties; **white noise**, a mixture of sound waves covering a wide frequency range; **white race**, (loosely) the Caucasoid group of mankind; **white sale**, a sale of household linens; **white slave**, a woman forced into prostitution for others' profit; **white slavery; white´wash**, a mixture of whiting or lime and water, used for whitening walls and as a disinfectant; anything that conceals a stain.—*vt* to cover with whitewash; to give a fair appearance to; to attempt to conceal the faults of; (*inf*) to defeat (an opponent) without letting him score. [OE *hwīt*, ON *hvītr.*]

whither [hwiTH´ėr] *adv* to what place? to which place; to what.—*adv* **whithersoev´er**, to whatever place. [OE *hwider.*]

whitlow [hwit´lō] *n* a painful inflammation of a finger or toe, esp near the nail, tending to suppurate. [A corr of *whick-flaw*, quick-flaw. Cf **quick**, living flesh, and **flaw** (2).]

Whitsun [hwit´sun] *adj* pertaining to, or observed at Whitsuntide.—*ns* **Whit´sunday**, the seventh Sunday after Easter, commemorating the day of Pentecost, when the converts in the primitive Church wore white robes; **Whit´suntide**, the season of Pentecost. [**white, Sunday.**]

whittle [hwit´l] *vt* to pare or cut thin shavings from (wood) with a knife; to shape with a knife; to diminish gradually (*with* **away, down**). [ME *thwitel*—OE *thwītan*, to cut.]

whiz, whizz [hwiz] *vi* to make a hissing sound, like an arrow or ball flying through the air; to move rapidly;—*pr p* **whizz´ing**; *pt, pt p* **whizzed.**—*n* a hissing sound; (*slang*) an expert.—*n* **whizbang, whizz´bang**, one that is conspicuous for noise, speech, or startling effect. [Imit.]

who [hōō] *pron* (both *rel* and *interrog*) what person? which person.—*pron* **whoev´er**, every one who; whatever person.—Also **whosoev´er**, emphatic form of whoever. [OE *hwā*; cog with ON *hver*, Ger *wer*; also with Sans *ka*, L *quis.*]

whodunit, whodunnit [hōō-dun´it] *n* (*inf*) a story concerned with a crime mystery.

whole [hōl] *adj* not broken, unimpaired; containing the total amount, number, etc.; all complete; sound, as in health; (*math*) not a fraction.—*n* the entire amount; a thing complete in itself.—*adj* **whole´-hearted**, zealous and sincere.—*ns* **whole´ness, whole´sāle**, selling of goods, usu. at lower prices and in quantity, to a retailer.—*adj* buying and selling thus; extensive and indiscriminate.—*adv* at wholesale prices; extensively or indiscriminately.—*vti*, to sell wholesale.—*adj* **whole´some**, healthy; sound; salutary.—*adv* **whole´somely.**—*n* **whole´someness.**—*adv* **wholly** [hōl´li, hōl´i], completely, altogether.—**on the whole**, taking everything into account; **go the whole hog**, (*slang*) to do completely, go to the limit. [OE *hāl*, Ger *heil.* By-form of **hale** (1).]

whom [hōōm] *pron* objective case (*acc* or *dat*) of **who.**—*pron* **whomsoev´er**, objective case of **whoever, whosoever.** [OE *hwām*, which was orig dat of *hwā*, who, and replaced as acc the older acc *hwone.*]

whoop [hwōōp] *n* a loud eager cry; the long noisy inspiration heard in whooping cough.—*vi* to give a loud cry of triumph or scorn.—*ns* **whoop´er**, a whooping crane; **whoop´ing cough**, an infectious and epidemic disease, esp of children, causing a convulsive cough; **whoop´ing crane**, a large white nearly extinct N American crane (*Grus americana*) noted for its loud whooping note. [OFr *houper*, to shout.]

whoopee [hwōōp´ē] *interj* an exclamation of delight. [**whoop.**]

whore [hör] *n* a prostitute; any unchaste woman.—*vi* to practice lewdness.—*ns* **whore´dom**, unlawful sexual intercourse; idolatry; **whore´monger** (*arch*) a lecher; a pander.—*adj* **who´rish.**—*adv* **who´rishly.**—*n* **who´rishness.** [ON *hōra*, an adulteress.]

whorl [hwörl, hwûrl] *n* a number of leaves in a circle round the stem; a turn in a spiral shell; any of the circular ridges forming the design of a fingerprint.—*adj* **whorled**, having whorls. [By-form of **whirl.**]

whortleberry [hwûr´tl-ber-i] *n* a European heath plant with a dark blue edible berry, called also the **bilberry** (*Vaccinium myrtillus*); the huckleberry. [Earlier *hurtleberry*; cf OE *hortan*, whortleberries.]

whose [hōōz] *pron* the possessive case of **who** or **which.**—*pron* **whosesoev´er**, (*Bible*) of whomsoever. [ME *hwas*—OE *hwæs*, gen of *hwā*, who.]

why [hwī] *adv, conj* for what cause or reason (?).—*rel pron* on account of which (eg *the reason why I came*).—*interj* expressing sudden realization, or protest, or impatience.—*n pl* **whys**, the reason, cause, etc.—**the why and wherefore**, the whole reason. [OE *hwī hwȳ*, instrumental case of *hwā*, who.]

wick [wik] *n* the twisted threads of cotton or other substance in a candle, lamp, etc., that absorbs the fuel and, when lighted, burns. [OE *wēoce*.]

wicked [wik´id] *adj* evil in principle or practice, deviating from morality, sinful, ungodly; mischievous, spiteful; (*slang*) showing great skill.—*adv* **wick´edly**.—*n* **wick´edness**. [ME *wicked, wikked*; perh conn with OE *wicca*, wizard.]

wicker [wik´ėr] *n* a long, thin, flexible twig; such twigs or long, woody strips woven together, as in making baskets.—*n* **wick´erwork**, things made of wicker, esp baskets. [ME *wiker*—OE *wīcen*, p p of *wīcan*, to bend.]

wicket [wik´et] *n* a small door or gate, esp one forming part of a larger one; a small window, as in a box office; (croquet) any of the small wire arches through which the balls must be hit. [OFr *wiket* (Fr *guichet*); of Germanic origin.]

wide [wīd] *adj* extending far; having a considerable distance between the sides; of a specified extent from side to side; open fully; far from the point aimed at (*with* **of**); extending or fluctuating considerably between limits; comprehensive, inclusive.—*adv* over a relatively large area; to a large or full extent; so as to miss the point aimed at; astray.—*adv* **wīde´ly**.—*adjs* **wīde´-angle**, (*phot*) pertaining to a lens having an angle of view of 60° or more and a short focal length; **wīde´-awake´**, fully awake; on the alert; ready.—*vti* **wī´den**, to make or grow wide or wider.—*n* **wīde´ness**.—*adj* **wīde´spread**, widely extended or diffused.—*n* **width**, wideness, breadth. [OE *wīd*; ON *vīthr*, Ger *weit*.]

widgeon [wij´ȯn] *n* a genus (*Mareca*) of freshwater duck between the teal and mallard in size. [OFr *vigeon*—L *vipiō, vipiōnis*, a small crane.]

widow [wid´ō] *n* a woman who has lost her husband by death and has not remarried.—*vt* to cause to become a widow.—*ns* **wid´ower**, a man whose wife is dead and has not remarried; **widowerhood**, the state of being a widower; **wid´owhood**, state of being a widow.—**widow's walk**, a railed observation platform atop a coastal house. [OE *widewe, wuduwe*; Ger *witwe*, L *vidua*.]

wield [wēld] *vt* to use with full command; to manage, to use.—*n* **wiel´der**.—*adj* **wiel´dy**, capable of being wielded, manageable. [OE *getweldan*—*wealdan*; Ger *walten*.]

wiener [wē´ner] a smoked link sausage; a frankfurter.—*n* **wie´niē**, (*inf*) a wiener. [Ger.]

Wiener schnitzel [vē´ner shnit´sėl] a veal cutlet dressed with egg and breadcrumbs. [Ger.]

wife [wīf] *n* a married woman; the woman to whom one is married; a woman;—*pl* **wīves**.—*adj* **wife´less**, without a wife; **wife´like, wife´ly**. [OE *wīf*; ON *vīf*, Ger *weib*.]

wig [wig] *n* an artificial covering of real or synthetic hair for the head.—*vt* to furnish with a wig; to censure or rebuke; (*slang*) to annoy, upset, craze, etc.—*vi* (*slang*) to be or become excited, etc.—*adj* **wigged**, wearing a wig. [Short for **periwig**.]

wight [wīt] *n* a creature or a person—used chiefly in sport or irony. [OE *wiht*, a creature, prob from *wegan*, to move, carry.]

wigwam [wig´wom, -wam] *n* a N American Indian shelter consisting of a framework of arched poles covered with bark, leaves, branches, etc. [Algonquin.]

wild [wīld] *adj* being in a state of nature; not tamed or cultivated; uncivilized; lawless; violent; distracted; licentious; tempestuous (eg *a wild night*); haphazard; rash; wide of the mark; enthusiastic; of a card in certain card games, having any desired value.—*n* (usu. *pl*) wilderness or wasteland.—*adj* **wild´cat**, of business, scheme, etc., unreliable, unsound; illegal or unauthorized.—*n* any fierce, undomesticated, medium-sized animal of the cat family; a fierce, aggressive person; a productive oil well in an area not previously known to have oil.—*vi* to drill for oil in such an area.—*ns* **wil´derness**, a wild or waste place; an uncultivated part of a garden; a vast dreary extent, a large number, a confused collection; **wild´fire**, a fire that spreads fast and is hard to put out; **wild-goose chase**, a fruitless search or pursuit; **wild´life**, wild animals, birds, etc., regarded collectively; **wild oats**, a wild grass (*Avena fatua*) common in meadows and pastures, esp in the western US; **wild rice**, a tall aquatic grass (*Zizania aquatica*) yielding a grain used for food.—*adv* **wild´ly**.—*n* **wild´ness**.—**sow one's wild oats**, to be promiscuous and dissolute in youth. [OE *wild*; Ger *wild*.]

wile [wīl] *n* a trick, a sly artifice.—*vt* to beguile, inveigle. [OE *wīl, wīle*; ON *vēl, væl*, a trick. Prob same root as **guile**.]

will [wil] *n* power of choosing or determining; act of using this power, volition; choice or determination; pleasure; arbitrary disposal; feeling towards, as in *good* or *ill will*; a legal document directing the disposal of one's property after death; a particular desire, choice, etc. of someone; a mandate.—*vi* to be accustomed, ready, or sure to (do, etc.); used as an auxiliary in future constructions in 2d and 3d persons; in formal speech, used to express determination, obligation, etc. in the 1st person; to exercise the will; to decree;—*pt* **would** [wŏŏd].—*vt* to desire; to be resolved; to command; to seek to force, influence (oneself or another to perform a specified action) by silent exertion of the will; to dispose of by will, to bequeath;—*pt* **willed** [wild].—*adj* **wil´ful**, governed only by one's will; obstinate; done intentionally.—*adv* **wil´fully**.—*n* **wil´fulness**.—*adj* **will´ing**, not reluctant (to), disposed (to); eager.—*adv* **will´ingly**.—*n* **will´ingness; will´power**, the ability to control one's impulses, emotions, actions, etc.—**at will**, as one chooses; **with a will**, heartily. [OE *willa*, will—*willan*, to wish; Ger *wollen*, L *velle*.]

will-o'-the-wisp [wil´-o-the-wisp´] *n* a luminous marsh gas, the ignis fatuus; an elusive person or thing.

willow [wil´ō] *n* a genus (*Salix*) of trees or shrubs with slender, pliant branches; the wood of the willow.—*adj* **will´owy**, abounding in willows; flexible, graceful.—**willowware**, a blue design of Chinese character used on plates, cups, etc. featuring a large willow tree by a small bridge. [OE *welig*; Low Ger *wilge*, Du *wilg*.]

willy-nilly [wil´i-nil´i] *adv* whether one wishes it or not. [**will** (vb) and obs *nill* (neg of **will**).]

wilt[1] [wilt] *vi* to become limp, as from heat; of a plant, to droop; to become weak or faint, or lose strength or courage.—*vt* to cause to wilt. [Cf Ger *welk*, withered.]

wilt[2] [wilt] (*arch*) 2d pers sing of **will**.

wily [wī´li] *adj* full of *wiles* or tricks; using craft or stratagem, artful, sly.—*adv* **wī´lily**.—*n* **wī´liness**, cunning.

wimp [wimp] *n* (*inf*) an ineffectual fellow.

wimple [wim´pl] *n* (*hist*) a wrapping folded round neck and face (still part of a nun's dress). [OE *wimpel*, a neck-covering; cf Ger *wimpel*, a pennon, Fr *guimpe*, a nun's veil, Eng **gimp**.]

win [win] *vt* to get to with effort; to gain in contest; to gain eg by luck; to gain influence over; to induce (to); to obtain the favor of.—*vi* to gain a victory; to gain favor; to make one's way; to finish first in a race, etc.—*pr p* **winn´ing**; *pt, pt p* **won** [wun].—*n* a victory, success.—*ns* **winn´er; winn´ing**, the act of one who wins; that which is won (usually in *pl*).—*adj* prepossessing, persuasive, attractive.—*adv* **winn´ingly**.—**win by a head**, to win very narrowly; **win through**, to be successful after overcoming difficulties. [OE *winnan*, to suffer, to struggle; ON *vinna*, to accomplish, Ger *gewinnen*, to win.]

wince [wins] *vi* to shrink or start back; to make an involuntary movement (as in pain). [OFr *guinc(h)ir*, to wince—Gmc; cf OHG *wenken* (Ger *wanken*), to wince. Allied to Eng **wink**, and Ger *winken*, to nod.]

winch [winch] *n* a crank with a handle for transmitting motion; a kind of hoisting machine. [OE *wince*, prob orig 'a bent handle'.]

wind[1] [wind] *n* air in motion; a current of air; air bearing the scent eg of game; air regarded as bearing information, etc.; breath; flatulence; empty, insignificant words; (*pl*) the wind instruments of an orchestra.—*vt* to put out of breath; to perceive by scent.—*ns* **wind´age**, the difference between the size of the bore of a gun and that of the ball or shell; the influence of the wind in deflecting a missile; **wind´bag**, an excessively talkative person; **wind´breaker**, trade name for an outer jacket made of wind-resistant material; **wind´fall**, fruit blown off a tree; any unexpected gain or advantage; **wind´flower**, wood anemone; **wind´ in´strument**, musical instrument sounded by means of the breath; **wind´jammer**, large sailing vessel; **wind´mill**, a machine driven by the force of the wind acting on a set of sails; **wind´pipe**, the passage for the breath between the mouth and lungs, the trachea; **wind´screen**, a screen that protects against the wind; (*Brit*) a windshield; **windshield**, in automobiles, etc., a transparent screen (as of glass) in front of the occupants.—*adj* **wind´swept**, exposed to, or swept by, the wind.—*n* **wind tunnel**, an experimental apparatus for producing a uniform steady airstream past a model for aerodynamic investigation work.—*adv, adj* **wind´ward**, toward where the wind blows from.—*n* the point from which the wind blows.—*adj* **wind´y**, consisting of or resembling wind; exposed to the winds; tempestuous, empty, pretentious.—**in the wind**, astir, afoot; **to have (in) the wind of**, to be on the scent of; **sail close to the wind**, to keep the boat's head so near to the wind as to fill but not shake the sails; to be in danger of transgressing an approved limit; to manage economically; **up the wind**, in a direction counter to the wind; **second wind**, power of respiration recovered after breathlessness; the energy necessary for a renewal of effort. [OE *wind*; ON *vindr*, Ger *wind*, L *ventus*, Gr *aētēs*, Sans *vāta*, wind.]

wind[2] [wīnd] *vt* to turn (a crank); to coil into a ball around something else; to encircle; to tighten the mechanism of (eg a timepiece); to make (one's way) by turning and twisting.—*vi* to turn completely or often; to turn round something, to twist, to move spirally; to meander;—*pr p* **wīnd´ing**; *pt, pt p* **wound** [wownd].—*n* **wīnd´er**, one who winds; an instrument for winding.—*adj* **wīnd´ing**, curving, full of bends; spiral.—*n* a turning; a twist.—*ns* **wīnd´ing-sheet**, a sheet enwrapping a corpse; **wīndup**, the close.—**wīnd up**, to bring or come to a conclusion; to adjust for final settlement; to arrive in a situation, place, or condition as a result of a course of action; to give a preliminary swing to the arms (as before pitching a baseball). [OE *windan*; Ger *winden*, ON *vinda*; cf **wend, wander**.]

windlass [wind´las] *n* a winch, esp one worked by winding a rope round a revolving cylinder. [ME *windas*, a windlass—ON *vindāss*—*vinda*, to wind, *āss*, pole.]

window [win´dō] *n* an opening in a wall of a building, etc., for air and light; the frame in the opening; any opening, or any enclosed area consisting of a different material, that suggests a window.—**window dressing**, the art of arranging effectively, or the arrangement of, goods in a store window; that which is meant to make something seem better than it really is; **win-**

dow shopping, considering the goods in shop windows without intending to buy. [ME *windowe—*ON *vingauga—vindr*, wind, *auga*, eye.]

Windsor [win´zọr] *adj* pertaining to Windsor, England, as in **Wind´sor chair**, a kind of strong, plain, polished chair, made entirely of wood.

wine [wīn] *n* the fermented juice of grapes used as an alcoholic beverage; the fermented juice of other fruits or plants.—*adj* **wine-colored**, having the color of red wine; dark purplish-red.—*ns* **winepress**, a vat in which grapes are pressed in the manufacture of wine; **wine´skin**, a bag made of skin for holding wine. [OE *wīn*, Ger *wein—*L *vīnum*; cog with Gr *oinos*.]

wing [wing] *n* the organ of a bird, bat or insect, by which it flies; something like a wing in function or position, as the main lateral surface of an airplane, a subordinate, projecting part of a building, either side of a stage beyond the sight of the audience; a section of a political party with reference to its conservation or radicalism; a unit in an air force; a flying, or manner of flying.—*vt* to furnish or transport with wings; to lend speed to; to traverse by flying; to wound (as with a bullet) without killing.—*vi* to soar.—*adj* **winged** [wingd or wing´id], furnished with wings; swift; [wingd] wounded in the wing, shoulder, or arm.—**on the wing**, flying, in motion; departing; **under the wing**, or **wings of**, under one's protection, guidance; **wing it**, (*inf*) to improvise in acting, speaking, etc. [ON *vængr*, a wing; Swed *vinge*.]

wink [wingk] *vi* to move the eyelids quickly; to give a hint by winking; to flicker, twinkle.—*vt* to close and open quickly.—*n* act of winking; a hint given by winking.—**wink at**, to pretend not to see. [OE *wincian* (Ger *winken*).]

winkle [wing´kl] *n* any of various whelks (esp genus *Busycon*) that destroy oysters and clams by drilling their shells and rasping out their flesh; periwinkle (perh derived from Ger *winkel*, corner).

winning, winner *See* **win**.

winnow [win´ō] *vt* to separate the chaff from (the grain) by wind; to fan; to sift.—Also *vi*.—*n* **winn´ower**. [OE *windwian*, to winnow.]

winsome [win´sọm] *adj* cheerful; pleasant, attractive.—*adv* **win´somely**.—*n* **win´someness**. [OE *wynsum*, pleasant—*wyn*, joy (Ger *wonne*).]

winter [win´tėr] *n* the cold season of the year—in northern temperate regions, from November or December to January or February; astronomically, from the winter solstice to the vernal equinox; any season of cheerlessness.—*adj* pertaining to winter.—*vi* to pass the winter.—*vt* to feed, or to maintain, during winter.—*n* **win´tergreen**, a low evergreen herb (*Gaultheria procumbens*) with white bell-shaped flowers and spicy red berries, one source of oil of wintergreen used in medicine and confectionery.—*n pl* **win´ter quar´ters**, a winter residence or station (as of a military unit, a circus or a sports team).—*adj* **win´try, win´tery**, resembling, or suitable to, winter; stormy. [OE *winter*; Ger *winter*; of uncertain origin; not conn with **wind**.]

wipe [wīp] *vt* to clean or dry by rubbing with a cloth, etc.; to rub (a cloth, etc.) over something; to apply or remove by wiping.—*n* a wiping.—*n* **wī´per**, one who, or that which, wipes.—**wipe out**, to remove; to erase; to kill off; to destroy. [OE *wīpian*.]

wire [wīr] *n* a thread of metal; a length of this; the finish line of a race; telegraph; a telegram.—*adj* formed of wire.—*vt* to fasten, furnish, connect, etc. with wire; to telegraph.—*vi* to telegraph.—*adjs* **wire´drawn**, spun out into needless fine distinctions; **wire´less**, wireless telegraphy; radio telephony.—*n* wireless telegraphy or telephony.—*vti* to send (a message) by wireless.—*ns* **wire´ service**, a news agency that sends out syndicated news copy by wire to subscribers; **wire´less tele´graphy, teleph´ony**, telegraphy, telephony, by means of electric waves without the use of conducting wires between transmitter and receiver; **wire´-pull´er**, one who uses secret or underhand means to influence the acts of an organization or person; **wire´-pull´ing; wi´ry**, made of, or like, wire; flexible and strong; (of a person) being lean and supple and vigorous. [OE *wīr*; ON *vīrr*; per conn with L *viriae*, bracelets.]

wisdom [wiz´dọm] *n* quality of being wise; ability to make right use of knowledge; (*Bible*) spiritual perception.—*n* **wis´dom tooth**, the last tooth of the full set on each side of the jaw in human beings. [OE *wīsdōm*, wisdom; cf **wise**.]

wise[1] [wīz] *adj* having knowledge; learned; able to use knowledge well, judging rightly, discreet; skilful, dictated by wisdom; containing wisdom.—*adv* **wise´ly**.—**wise guy**, a conceited, overconfident person; **wisewoman**, a witch; a midwife. [OE *wīs*; Ger *weise*; from root of **wit** (1) and (2).]

wise[2] [wīz] *n* way, manner.—**in any wise, in no wise**, in any way, in no way; **on this wise**, in this way. [OE *wīse*, orig wiseness; Ger *weise*; akin to **wise** and **wit** (1) and (2). Doublet **guise**.]

wisent [vē-zent´] *n* a European bison (*Bison bonasus*).—Also **aurochs**.

wiseacre [wīz´ā-kėr] *n* one who unduly assumes an air of superior wisdom. [Perh through the medium of Middle Du from OHG *wīzago*, a prophet.]

wish [wish] *vi* to have a desire (for); to long (so in *Bible*); to express a desire.—*vt* to desire or long for; to express a desire (that, to do, etc.); to pray or hope for on behalf of (someone).—*n* desire, longing; thing desired; expression of desire.—*n* **wish´er**.—*adj* **wish´ful**, having a wish or desire; eager.—*adv* **wish´fully**.—*n* **wish´fulness**.—**wishful thinking**, a belief that a particular thing will happen, engendered by desire that it should; (loosely) thinking about and wishing for an event or turn of fortune that may not take place; **wish fulfilment**, (*psych*) the satisfaction of a desire in dreams, daydreams, etc. [OE *wȳscan—wūsc*, a wish; Ger *wünschen*, Swed *önska*.]

wishy-washy [wish´i-wosh´i] *adj* thin and weak, diluted, feeble. [Formed from **wash**.]

wisp [wisp] *n* a small tuft or thin strand. [ME *wisp*; of doubtful origin.]

wistful [wist´fŏŏl -fl] *adj* pensive; yearning with little hope.—*adv* **wist´fully**.—*n* **wist´fulness**. [Most prob for *wistly*, intently—*whistly*, silently; and not conn with **wish**.]

wit[1] [wit] *vti* (*arch*) to know; (*arch*) to come to know.—**to wit**, that is to say, used esp in legal language to call attention to what has preceded. [OE *witan*, to know; Ger *wissen*; cf L *vidēre*, Gr *idein* (aor), to see.]

wit[2] [wit] *n* understanding; a mental faculty (chiefly in *pl*); common sense; facility in combining ideas with a pointed verbal effect; the product of this power; a person endowed with such power.—*adj* **wit´less**, without wit or understanding; thoughtless.—*adv* **wit´lessly**.—*ns* **wit´lessness; wit´ling**, one who has little wit.—*adj* **witt´ed**, having wit or understanding—usu. in composition, as *quick-witted*.—*n* **witticism** [wit´i-sizm], a witty remark.—*adv* **witt´ingly**, knowingly, by design.—*adj* **witt´y**, possessed of wit—amusing, droll, sarcastic; (*Bible*) ingenious.—*adv* **witt´ily**.—*n* **witt´iness**.—**at one's wits' end**, utterly perplexed; **live by one's wits**, to gain a livelihood by ingenious expedients rather than by honest labor. [OE *(ge)wit*—**wit** (1).]

witch [wich] *n* a woman regarded as having supernatural or magical power and knowledge through compact with the devil; a hag, crone; (*inf*) a fascinating woman.—*vt* to bewitch.—*ns* **witch´craft**, the craft or practice of witches, sorcery, supernatural power; **witch´ery**, witchcraft; fascination; **witch grass**, quack grass; **witch´-hunt**, the searching out and harassment of those (as political opponents) with unpopular views; a searching out for persecution of those accused of witchcraft. [ME *wicche* (both masc and fem)—OE *wicca* (masc), *wicce* (fem), wizard, witch.]

witch´ hā´zel [wich´hā´zėl] *n* a N American shrub or tree (*Hamamelis virginiana*) with yellow flowers appearing after the leaves have fallen, which supplies bark for making a supposed remedy for bruises, etc. [OE *wice*, the service-tree—*wican*, to bend.]

with [wiTH, with] *prep* denoting nearness, agreement, or connection—eg in competition; in contrast; on the side of; in the same direction as; in company with; among; possessing; in respect of, in the regard of; by, by means of, through.—*adv* **withal´** (*obs*), with all or the rest; likewise; moreover.—*prep* an emphatic form of **with** (used after its object).—**feel**, or **be**, or **think, with**, to feel as, or be of the same opinion as, the other person specified; **in with**, (*inf*) friendly with; **with it**, (*slang*) aware of and abreast of current trends in popular taste. [OE *with*, against; ON *vith*, Ger *wider*. It ousted the OE *mid*, with (Ger *mit*).]

withdraw [wiTH-drö´ or -th] *vt* to draw back or away; to take back or away; to recall, retract, unsay.—*vi* to retire; to go away.—*ns* **withdraw´al**.—*adj* **withdrawn´**, secluded (of place); remote, detached (of manner). [Pfx *with-*, against, and **draw**.]

withe [wiTH, with or wīTH], **withy** [wiTH´i] *n* a flexible twig, esp of willow; a band of twisted twigs. [OE *withthe*, or *wīthig*; ON *vidhir*, Ger *weide*, willow.]

wither [wiTH´ėr] *vi* to fade or become dry; to lose freshness; to decay, waste.—*vt* to cause to dry up, fade, or decay; to blight; to cause to feel very unimportant or despicable (eg *withered her with a look*). [OE *wederen*, to expose to weather.]

withers [wiTH´ėrz] *n pl* the part of a horse's back between the shoulder blades. [OE *wither*, against, an extension of *with*, against.]

withhold [wiTH-hōld´ or with-] *vt* to restrain; refuse to give;—*pt, pt p* **withheld´**.—**withholding tax**, the amount of income tax withheld from wages, etc. [Pfx *with-*, against, and **hold**.]

within [wiTH-in´] *prep* in the inner part of, inside; indoors; in the limits of, not going beyond.—*adv* in the inner part; inwardly.—**within reach**, obtainable without difficulty. [OE *withinnan—with*, against, with, *innan*, in.]

without [wiTH-owt´] *prep* outside or out of, beyond; out-of-doors; not with, in absence of, not having, free from.—*adv* on the outside; (*arch*) out of doors. [OE *withūtan—with*, against, *ūtan*, outside.]

withstand [wiTH-stand´ or with-] *vt* to stand against, to oppose or resist, esp successfully.—*pt, pt p* **withstood´**. [Pfx *with-*, against, and **stand**.]

witness [wit´nes] *n* knowledge brought in proof; testimony (of a fact); that which furnishes proof; one who sees or has personal knowledge of a thing; one who gives evidence or attests to a signing, etc.—*vt* to have direct knowledge of; to see; to be the scene of; to testify to, or (that); to show.—*vi* to give evidence; to attest.—*n* **witness stand**, the stand or enclosure from which a witness gives evidence in a court of law.—**bear witness**, to provide evidence or proof, give testimony. [OE *witnes*, testimony—*witan*, to know.]

wives [wīvz] *pl* of **wife**.

wizard [wiz´ȧrd] *n* one (usu. a man) who practices witchcraft or magic; one who works wonders. [ME *wysard—wys, wis*, wise, and suffx *-ard*.]

wizen [wiz´n], **wizened** [wiz´nd] *adj* dried up, thin, shriveled.—*vti* to become or make dry. [OE *wisnian*, to wither; cog with ON *visinn*, wizened, *visna*, to wither.]

woad [wōd] *n* a genus of plants (*Isatis tinctoria*) yielding a blue dye; the dyestuff made from their leaves. [OE *wād*; Ger *waid*.]

wobble [wob´l] *vi* to rock unsteadily from side to side; to waver, to vacillate.—*adj* **wobb´ly**. [Low Ger *wabbeln*; cog with **waver**.]

woe [wō] *n* grief, misery; a heavy calamity; a curse; an exclamation of grief.—*adjs* **woe´begone**, beset with woe (*begone* is pt p of OE *begān*, to go round, beset); **woe´ful**, sorrowful; bringing calamity; wretched.—*adv* **woe´fully**.—*n* **woe´fulness.—woe worth the day** (see **worth** (2)). [OE (interj) *wā*; Ger *weh*; L *vae*; cf **wail**.]

wok [wäk] *n* a bowl-shaped cooking utensil used esp in the preparation of Chinese food. [Chinese.]

woke *pt* and (*rare*) *pt p* of **wake; woken**, *pt p* of **wake**.

wold [wōld] *n* a usu. upland area of open country.

wolf [wŏŏlf] *n* a gregarious beast of prey of the dog genus (*Canis*, esp *C lupus*; anything very ravenous; a greedy and cruel person; (*slang*) a man who flirts with many women;—*pl* **wolves**.—*vt* to devour ravenously.—*n* **wolf´ dog**, any of various large dogs formerly kept for hunting wolves; the offspring of a wolf and a domestic dog; **wolf´hound**, a breed of large dog, developed from hunting dogs.—*adjs* **wol´fish**, like a wolf either in form or quality; rapacious.—*adv* **wol´fishly**.—*ns* **wolfs´bane**, a yellow-flowered Eurasian herb (*Aconitum lycoctonum*); **wolf´ whistle**, a two-note male whistle emitted at the sight of a woman.—**cry wolf**, to give a false alarm; **keep the wolf from the door**, to keep hunger or want from the home. [OE *wulf*; Ger *wolf*; L *lupus*; Gr *lykos*.]

wolfram [wŏŏl´fràm] *n* an ore containing iron, manganese, and tungsten, from which tungsten is obtained; tungsten. [Ger.]

wolverine [wŏŏl-ve-rēn´] *n* a carnivorous quadruped (*Gulo gulo*) of N America, of the same genus as the weasel; a glutton. [Extension of **wolf**.]

woman [wŏŏm´àn] *n* the female of man, an adult female of the human race; the female sex, women collectively; a female attendant;—*pl* **women** [wim´ėn].—*n* **wom´anhood**, the state, character or qualities of a woman.—*adj* **wom´anish**, like or befitting a woman (used disparagingly); effeminate.—*adv* **wom´anishly**.—*ns* **wom´anishness; wom´ankind, womenkind; wom´enkind**, female human beings, esp as distinguished from males.—*adj, adv* **wom´anlike**.—*adj* **wom´anly**, (of conduct, feelings) like or befitting a woman.—*ns* **wom´anliness; women's rights**, legal, political, and social rights for women equal to those of men; organized activity on behalf of women's rights and interests. [OE *wimman, wīfman*, a compound of *wīf*, a woman, *man*, man.]

womb [wōōm] *n* the organ in which the young of mammals are developed and kept till birth; the place where anything is produced; any deep cavity. [OE *wamb*; Ger *wamme*, paunch.]

wombat [wom´bat] *n* any of several Australian marsupial mammals (family Vombatidae) resembling small bears. [Native name.]

won [wun] *pt, pt p* of **win**.

wonder [wun´der] *n* the state of mind produced by something new, unexpected, or extraordinary; a strange thing; a prodigy; quality of being strange, unexpected.—*vi* to feel wonder; to be amazed (*with* **at**); to speculate; to feel doubt.—*vt* to speculate (with noun clause or direct quotation).—*adj* **won´derful**, full of wonder, exciting wonder, strange.—*adv* **won´derfully**.—*n* **won´derfulness**.—*adv* **won´deringly**, with wonder.—*n* **won´derland**, a land of wonders.—*adj* **won´drous**, such as may excite wonder, strange.—*adv* **won´drously**.—*n* **won´drousness.—Seven Wonders of the World**, in the ancient world, the Pyramids, the Hanging Gardens of Babylon, the Temple of Artemis at Ephesus, Phidias's statue of Zeus at Olympia, the Mausoleum at Halicarnassus, the Colossus of Rhodes, and the Pharos of Alexandria. [OE *wundor*; Ger *wunder*, ON *undr*.]

wont [wunt, wōnt] *adj* accustomed.—*n* habit.—*vi* to be accustomed.—*adj* **won´ted**, accustomed; usual.—*n* **won´tedness**. [Orig pt p of *won*, to dwell—OE *wunian*; Ger *wohnen*.]

won't [wōnt] will not. [Contr of ME *wol not*.]

woo [wōō] *vt* to ask in marriage; to court, to solicit eagerly; to seek to gain.—Also *vi*.—*n* **woo´er**. [OE *wōgian*, to woo—*wōg, wōh*, bent.]

wood [wŏŏd] *n* the hard part of trees; trees cut or sawn, timber; a kind of timber; a collection of growing trees (also used in *pl*); a cask, barrel.—*vt* to cover with trees.—*ns* **wood anemone**, a common anemone (*Anemone quinque folia*) of the eastern US with solitary pink-tinged flowers;—also **mayflower, wind flower; wood´bine, wood´bind**, the honeysuckle (*Lonicera periclymenum* and related genera), applied also to other climbers, such as some kinds of ivy, the Virginia-creeper, etc.; **wood´-coal**, coal like wood in texture, lignite or brown coal; charcoal; **wood´cock**, a genus of bird (the American *Philohela minor* or the European *Scopolax rusticola*) allied to the snipes; **wood´craft**, skill in the chase and everything pertaining to life in the forests; skill in shaping or constructing articles from wood; **wood´cut**, an engraving cut on wood; an impression from it; **wood´cutter**.—*adjs* **wood´ed**, covered with trees; **wood´en**, made of, or like, wood; lacking ease or flexibility; awkwardly stiff.—*ns* **wood´ engrā´ving**, an engraving on or print from wood; **wood´ hy´acinth**, the wild hyacinth or English bluebell (*Scilla nonscripta*); **wood´land**, land covered with wood; **wood louse** (*pl* **wood lice**), any of numerous small crustaceans (suborder Oniscoidea) usu. grayish or brownish, and usu. living under stones, etc.; **wood´man**, a man who cuts down trees; **wood´pecker**, any of a family (*Picidae*) of birds that peck holes in the wood or bark of trees and extract the insects on which they feed; **wood´ pig´eon**, the ringdove (*Columba palumbus* or in US also *C fasciata*); **wood´pulp**, wood reduced to a pulp, used in making paper and rayon; **wood´ruff**, a genus (*Asperula odorata*) of scented herbs; **wood sorrel**, any herb of the genus *Oxalis* having delicate white flowers, a source of oxalic acid; **wood spirit**, a spirit living among trees; methanol, wood alcohol, an alcohol obtained from wood or synthetically, used as a solvent, etc.; **woodwind**, section of an orchestra in which wind instruments, originally made of wood (flute, clarinet, oboe, English horn, and bassoon) are played; *pl*) the woodwind section of a band or orchestra. **wood´work**, work done in wood, esp the interior fittings as the moldings, stairways and doors of a house; **woŏd´worm**, a larva that bores in wood.—*adj* **wood´y**, abounding with woods; (*rare*) pertaining to woods; consisting of wood or woody fiber. [OE *wudu*; cog with ON *vithr*, wood; akin to Ir *fiodh*, timber.]

woodchuck [wŏŏd´chuk] *n* a thickset marmot (*Marmota monax*) of northeastern N America and Canada.—Also **ground hog**. [Corr of an Amer Indian name.]

wooer, wooing, etc. *See* **woo**.

woof [wōōf] *n* the horizontal threads crossing the warp in a woven fabric. [OE *ōwef, ōwebb—āwefan*, to weave—*ā-*, inten; *wefan*, to weave.]

wool [wŏŏl] *n* the soft hair of sheep and other animals; thread or yarn made of wool; fabric of wool; short, thick hair; any light, fleecy substance resembling wool; any substance with a fibrous texture resembling wool.—*n* **wool´gath´ering**, absentminded dreaming.—*adj* dreamy.—*adj* **woolen**, made of, or pertaining to, wool.—*n* cloth made of wool.—*adj* **wooll´y**, consisting of, or like, wool; clothed with wool; vague, hazy.—*ns* **wooll´iness; wool´pack**, a bale of wool weighing 240 lb; fleecy cloud; **wool´sack**, (*Brit*) the seat of the Lord Chancellor in the House of Lords, a large square sack covered with scarlet. [OE *wull*; Ger *wolle*.]

woozy [wōō´zi] *adj* fuddled; dazed; blurred, vague; sick.

wop [wop] *n* a derogatory term for an Italian. [It (dial) *guappo*.]

word [wûrd] *n* an oral or written sign denoting a thing or an idea; talk, discourse; a message; a promise; a declaration; a password; a watchword; a signal or sign; news; information; a brief conversation; (*pl*) talk, speech; (*pl*) lyrics, text; (*pl*) a quarrel or dispute.—*vt* to express in words.—*ns* **word´book**, a vocabulary; a dictionary; **wor´ding**, act or manner of expressing in words; choice of words, phrasing.—*adj* **wor´dy**, using or containing many words.—*adv* **wor´dily**.—*n* **wor´diness.—word for word**, literally, verbatim; **good word**, favorable mention, praise; **in a word**, briefly; **take at one's word**, to accept one's statements as being true; **the Word**, the Scripture. [OE *word*; ON *orth*, Ger *wort*; also conn with L *verbum*, a word, Gr *eirein*, to speak.]

wore [wōr, wör] *pt* of **wear**.

work [wûrk] *n* effort directed to an end; employment; that on which one works; the product of work, anything made or done; needlework; deed; doings; a literary composition; a book; (*pl*) collected writings; management, manner of working (as good, skillful, bad, etc.); (*pl*) engineering structures; (*pl*) a manufactory; workshop; (*phys*) the act of producing an effect by means of a force (F) whose point of application moves through a distance (s) in its own line of action—measured by the product of the force and the distance (W=Fs).—*vi* to make efforts (to achieve or attain anything); to be in action; to be occupied in business or labor; to produce effects; to make one's way slowly and labori-ously; to strain or labor; to ferment, to seethe.—*vt* to make by labor; to bring (into any state) by action; to effect; to solve a mathematical problem; to fashion; to manipulate; to cause to ferment; to keep going, eg a machine; to embroider;—*pt, pt p* **worked** or **wrought**.—*adjs* **work´able**, that may be worked; **work´aday**, fit for a working day; dull, prosaic.—*ns* **workahol´ic**, a person having a compulsive need to work; **work´bag**, a bag for holding materials for work, esp needlework; **work´box**, a box for holding materials for work; **work´day**, a day on which work is done; the part of the day in which work is done; **work´er**, one who works for a living; one who works for a cause; a sterile ant, bee, etc. that does work for the colony; **work´force**, the number of workers who are engaged in particular industry; the total number of workers who are potentially available; **work´house**, a house of correction for petty offenders, as drunkards or vagrants; **work´ing**, the act of one that works; (*pl*) the manner of functioning or operating; **work´ing class**, the class of people who work for wages, usu. at manual work; **work´ing day**, workday; **wor´king man**, one who works for wages, usu. at manual labor; **work´-man**, a workingman; an artisan.—*adj* **work´man-like**, befitting a skillful workman; well performed.—*ns* **work´manship**, the skill of a workman; manner of making; that which is made or produced by one's hands; **work´room**, a room for manual work; **work´shop**, a room or building where work is done; a seminar for specified intensive study, work, etc.—**work in**, to insert by repeated and continued effort; to interpose gradually or unobtrusively; **work off**, to get rid of; **work out**, to effect by continued labor; to solve or study fully; to come out by degrees; to turn out in the end; to test or improve one's fitness, esp for athletic competition or performance (*n* **work´out**, a session of physical exercises or any strenuous work); **work up**, to excite, rouse; to create by degrees (*n* **work´up**, a complete medical study of a patient, including tests); **out of work**, without employment. [OE *weorc*; conn with Gr *ergon*.]

world [wûrld] *n* the earth and its inhabitants; the universe; present state of existence; individual experience, outlook, etc.; public life or society; sphere of interest or activity; the public; a secular life; course of life; (often *pl*) very much or a great deal.—*n* **world´ling**, one who is devoted to worldly pursuits and temporal possessions.—*adj* **world´ly**, pertaining to the world, esp as distinguished from the world to come; devoted to this life and its enjoyments; bent on gain.—*adjs* **world´ly-mind´ed**, having the mind set on the present world; **world´ly-wise**, sophisticated, showing the earthly wisdom of those experienced in, and affected by, the ways of the world.—*ns* **world´liness; World War**, one of the international conflicts which ultimately involved the principal nations of the world; specifically World War I (1914–18) and World War II (1939–45).—*adj* **world´wide**, extending over, or found everywhere in, the world.—**all the world**, everybody; everything; **for all the world**, precisely, entirely; **in the world**, among innumerable possibilities; ever (an intensive phrase); **on top of the world**, in a state of great elation or happiness; **out of this world**, wonderful, good beyond all experience; **the best (worst) of both worlds**, to have the advantage (disadvantage) of both alternatives when a choice is presented; **the New World**, the western hemisphere, the Americas; **the Old World**, the eastern hemisphere, comprising Europe, Africa, and Asia; **the other world**, the non-material sphere, the spiritual world; **the world is his oyster**, the world lies before him, ready to yield him profit or success; **the world's end**, the most distant point possible. [OE *woruld, world, weorold*, (*lit*) 'a generation of men', from *wer*, a man, and *yldo*, a signifying an age.]

worm [wûrm] *n* an earthworm, loosely applied to invertebrate animals which more or less resemble the earthworm; anything helical; the thread of a screw; anything that corrupts, or that torments; remorse; a mean, groveling creature; (*pl*) any intestinal disease arising from the presence of parasitic worms.—*vi* to make one's way like a worm; to work slowly or secretly.—*vt* to treat for, rid of, worms; to work (oneself into a position) slowly or secretly; to elicit by slow and indirect means (eg *to worm the information out of him*).—*adj* **worm´-eat´en**, eaten into by wood-worms; old; worn-out.—*n* **worm´-hole**, a hole or a passage made by a worm.—*adj* **worm´y**, like a worm; having many worms. [OE *wyrm*, dragon, snake, creeping animal; cog with ON *ormr*, Ger *wurm*; also with L *vermis*.]

wormwood [wûrm´wood] *n* a plant (of the southernwood genus, *Artemisia*) with a bitter taste, formerly used as a vermifuge, with which absinth is flavored; bitterness. [OE *wermōd* (Ger *wermuth*), wormwood; influenced by **wormwood**.]

worn [wörn, wōrn] *pt p* of **wear**.

worn-out [wörn´owt´] *adj* much injured or rendered useless by wear; wearied. [**worn, out**.]

worry [wur´i] *vt* to tear with the teeth; to harass; to tease.—*vi* to be unduly anxious; to fret;—*pt, pt p* **worr´ied**.—*n* trouble, perplexity, vexation. [OE *wyrgan*, found in compound *āwyrgan*, to harm; cf Du *worgen*, Ger *würgen*, to choke.]

worse [wûrs] *adj* (used as comp of **bad**) bad or evil in a greater degree; not so well as before.—*adv* badly in a higher degree.—*vti* **wor´sen**, to grow or make worse.—**none the worse for**, not harmed by. [OE *wyrsa*, from *wirsiza*, formed with comp suffx *-iz* from a Gmc root *wers*, found in Ger *verwirren*, to confuse.]

worship [wûr´ship] *n* a religious service; fervent esteem; adoration paid to God.—*vt* to show religious reverence for; to adore or idolize.—*vi* to perform acts of adoration; to take part in a religious service;—*pr p* **wor´shipping**; *pt, pt p* **wor´shipped**.—*n* **wor´shipper**. [OE *weorthscipe*—*weorth, wurth*, worth, *-scipe*, -ship.]

worst [wûrst] *adj* (used as *superl* of **bad**; see also **worse**) bad or evil in the highest degree; of the lowest quality.—*adv* to a very bad or very evil degree.—*n* the highest degree of badness; the least good part (esp of news).—*vt* to get the advantage over in a contest, to defeat.—**(in) the worst way**, (*slang*) very much or greatly. [OE *wyrst, wyrrest, wyrresta*, from the same source as **worse**.]

worsted[1] [wŏŏst´id, or wûrst´id] *n* twisted thread or yarn spun out of long, combed wool.—*adj* made of worsted yarn. [From *Worstead*, a village near Norwich in England.]

worsted[2] [wûrst´id] *pt, pt p* of *vt* **worst**.

wort[1] [wûrt] *n* an herbaceous plant, usu. based in combination; (*arch*) potherb. [OE *wyrt*; Ger *wurz, wurzel*, a root.]

wort[2] [wûrt] *n* a liquid prepared with malt which, after fermenting, becomes beer, ale, etc. [OE *wyrte*, new beer—*wyrt*, root.]

worth[1] [wûrth] *n* value; that quality which renders a thing valuable; price; moral excellence; importance.—*adj* equal in value to (eg *worth a penny*); deserving of.—*adj* **worth´less**, of no value, virtue, excellence.—*adv* **worth´lessly**.—*n* **worth´lessness**.—*adjs* **worthwhile´**, such as to repay trouble and time spent on it; good; estimable; **worthy** [wûr´THi], having worth; valuable; estimable; deserving (of); deserving of; suited to, in keeping with; of sufficient merit (to do).—*n* a notability, esp local;—*pl* **wor´thies**.—*adv* **worth´ily** [TH], in a worthy manner.—*n* **worth´iness** [TH]. [OE *weorth, wurth* (Ger *wert*), value.]

worth[2] [wûrth] *vi* to be, happen, as in the archaic phrase **woe worth (the day)** = *woe be to*. [OE *weorthan*, to become; cf Ger *werden*.]

wot [wot] (*archaic, dial*) 1st and 3rd pers sing of **wit** (1).

would [wŏŏd] *pt p* of **will**.—*adj* **would´-be**, aspiring, trying, or merely professing, to be. [OE *wolde*, pt of *willan*.]

wound[1] [wownd] *pt, pt p* **wind** [wīnd], (1) and (2).

wound[2] [wŏŏnd] *n* any cut, bruise, hurt, or injury caused by external force.—*vt* to make a wound in; to injure. [OE *wund* (Ger *wunde*, ON *und*).]

wove, woven *pt, pt p* of **weave**.

wrack [rak] *n* seaweed cast up on the shore, kelp; destruction (see **rack** (2)). [Doublet of **wreck**.]

wraith [rāth] *n* a specter, an apparition, esp of a living person; a thin, pale person.

wrangle [ran´gl] *vi* (*arch*) to dispute; to dispute noisily or peevishly.—Also *vt*.—*n* a noisy dispute. [A freq of **wring**.]

wrang´ler [rang´glėr] *n* a cowboy who herds livestock, esp saddle horses. [Amer Sp.]

wrap [rap] *vt* to roll or fold together; to enfold; to cover by folding or winding something round (*often with* **up**);—*pr p* **wrapp´ing**; *pt, pt p* **wrapped**.—*n* a covering, as a shawl, etc.—*ns* **wrapp´er**, one who, or that which, wraps; a woman's dressing gown. **wrap-up** (*inf*) a concluding, summarizing statement, report, etc. [ME *wrappen*, also *wlappen*. (vt to wrap) and **envelop**.]

wrath [rath] *n* intense anger; rage; fury; any action of vengeance.—*adj* **wrath´ful**, full of wrath, very angry; springing from, or expressing, wrath.—*adv* **wrath´fully**.—*n* **wrath´fulness**. [Old Northumbrian *wræththu*—OE *wrāth*, adj wroth; ON *reithi*.]

wreak [rēk] *vt* to give full play or effect to (anger, resentment, etc.); inflict or execute (eg vengeance). [OE *wrecan*, orig to drive, and so to punish, avenge; ON *reka*, to drive, pursue, Ger *rächen*; conn with L *urgēre*.]

wreath [rēth] *n* a twisted ring of leaves, flowers, etc.; something like this in shape.—*pl* **wreaths** [rēTHz].—*vt* **wreathe** [rēth], to form into a wreath; to twine about or encircle.—*vi* to twine. [OE *writha*; allied to *wrīthan*, to writhe.]

wreck [rek] *n* destruction of a ship; a badly damaged ship; remains of anything ruined; a run-down person.—*vt* to destroy or disable; to ruin.—*vi* to suffer wreck or ruin.—*ns* **wreck´age**, the act of wrecking; wrecked material; **wreck´er**, a person who purposely causes a wreck; one that salvages or removes wrecks. [OE *wræc*, expulsion—*wrecan*, to drive, Low Ger *wrak*, Du *wrak*, ON *reki*, a thing drifted ashore; a doublet of *wrack*.]

wren [ren] *n* any of numerous small brownish songbirds, esp a European one (*Troglodytes troglodytes*) with a short erect tail. [OE *wrenna, wrænna*.]

wrench [rench] *vt* to wring or pull with a jerk; to injure with a twist; to distort (a meaning).—*n* a violent twist; a sprain; an instrument for turning nuts, etc.; emotional pain at parting. [OE *wrencan* (Ger *renken*)—*wrenc*, fraud; root of **wring**.]

wrest [rest] *vt* to twist by force (from); to get by toil. [OE *wrǣstan*—*wræst*, firm—*wrāth*, pt of *wrīthan*, to writhe.]

wrestle [res´l] *vti* to contend with another by grappling and trying to throw down; to struggle.—*n* a bout of wrestling; a struggle between two to throw each other down.—*n* **wrest´ler**. [OE *wrǣstlian*; a freq of *wrǣstan*, to wrest.]

wretch [rech] *n* a most miserable person; a despised and scorned person.—*adj* **wretch´ed**, very miserable; distressingly bad; despicable, worthless.—*adv* **wretch´edly**.—*n* **wretch´edness**. [OE *wrecca*, an outcast—*wræc*, pt of *wrecan*, to drive, punish, exile.]

wriggle [rig´l] *vi* to twist to and fro; to move with a twisting or sinuous motion; to use evasive tricks.—*vt* to cause to wriggle.—*n* the motion of wriggling.—*n* **wrigg´ler**. [A freq of obs *wrig*, to move about, itself a variant of *wrick*, ME *wrikken*, to twist; cf Du *wriggelen*, to wriggle.]

wright [rīt] *n* a maker (chiefly used in compounds, as *shipwright*, etc.). [OE *wyrhta*—*wyrht*, a work—*wyrcan*, to work.]

wring [ring] *vt* to twist; to force by twisting; to expel moisture from material by hand twisting or roller pressure; to pain; to extort;—*pt, pt p* **wrung**, (*Bible*) **wringed**.—*n* **wring´er**, one who wrings; a machine for forcing water from wet clothes. [OE *wringan*, to twist; Du *wringen*, Ger *ringen*; cf **wreak, wry**.]

wrinkle[1] [ring´kl] *n* (*inf*) a clever tip, valuable hint. [Perh from OE *wrenc*, a trick; cf **wrench**.]

wrinkle[2] [ring´kl] *n* a small crease or furrow on a surface.—*vti* to contract into wrinkles.—*adj* **wrink´ly**, full of wrinkles. [ME *wrinkel*, conn with OE *wringan*, to twist.]

wrist [rist] *n* the joint by which the hand is united to the arm.—*ns* **wrist´band**, the band or part of a sleeve that covers the wrist; **wrist´let**, a band on the wrist, esp a close-fitting knitted band attached to the top of a glove or the end of a sleeve. [OE *wrist*—*wrīthan*, to twist.]

writ[1] [rit] obsolete *pt, pt p* of **write**.

writ[2] [rit] *n* a writing; (*law*) a written document by which one is summoned or required to do something.—**Holy Writ**, the Scriptures. [**write**.]

write [rīt] *vt* to form letters as with a pen or pencil; to express in writing; to compose (eg a poem); to record; to communicate by letter.—*vi* to perform the act of writing; to compose; to send a letter (to a person);—*pr p* **wrī´ting**; *pt* **wrōte**; *pt p* **writt´en**.—*ns* **wrī´ter**, one who writes; a professional scribe or clerk; an author; **wrī´ter's cramp**, cramp of the muscles of the hand caused by much writing; **wrī´ting**, the act of forming letters as with a pen; that which is written; literary production.—*adj* **writt´en**, expressed in writing.—**write down**, to set down in writing; to depreciate, to write disparagingly of; to reduce in status, rank, or value, esp to reduce the book value of; to write so as to be intelligible (to), or attractive (to), people of lower intelligence or inferior taste; **write in**, to insert in a document or text; to insert (a name not listed on a ballot or voting machine) in an appropriate place; to cast (a vote in this manner) (*n* **write-in**); **write-in campaign**, a political campaign to encourage writing in a candidate's name; **write off**, to cancel, esp in bookkeeping, to take (eg a bad debt) off the books; to regard, accept, as an irredeemable loss (*n* **write´-off**; *adj* **writt´en-off**); **write out**, to transcribe; **write up**, to bring (a writing) up to date; to write a full description of; to write a summons for; to increase the book value of; **write-up**, (*inf*) a written report, specifically a favorable one. [OE *wrītan*; ON *rīta*; the original meaning being 'to scratch'; cf the cog Ger *reissen*, to tear.]

writhe [rīTH] *vt* to twist violently.—*vt* to twist this way and that; to squirm (under, at). [OE *wrīthan*, to twist; ON *rītha*; cf **wreath, wrest, wrist**.]

wrong [rong] *adj* not according to rule, incorrect; not in accordance with moral law, wicked; not that (thing) which is required, intended, advisable, or suitable; amiss; mistaken, misinformed; not functioning properly; not meant to be seen.—*n* whatever is not right or just; any injury done to another.—*adv* not correctly; not in the right way; astray (*to go wrong*).—*vt* to do wrong to, to deprive of some right; to impute fault to unjustly.—*ns* **wrong´do´er**, an offender, transgressor; **wrong´do´ing**.—*adj* **wrong´ful**, wrong; unjust; unlawful.—*adv* **wrong´fully**.—*n* **wrong´fulness**.—*adj* **wrong´head´ed**, obstinate and perverse, adhering stubbornly to wrong principles or policy.—*n* **wrong´head´edness**.—*adv* **wrong´ly**, in a wrong manner.—**in the wrong**, guilty of error, immorality, etc. [OE *wrang*, a wrong; most prob ON *rangr*, unjust; allied to OE *wringan*, to wring, like Fr *tort*, from L *tortus*, twisted.]

wrote [rōt] *pt* of **write**.

wroth [roth, rōth] *adj* highly incensed; wrathful. [OE *wrāth*, angry; cf ON *reithr*.]

wrought [röt] *pt, pt p* of **work**.—*adj* formed; made; of metals, shaped by hammering, etc.—*n* **wrought´ iron**, iron containing very little carbon.—*adj* **wrought-up**, very disturbed or excited. [OE *worhte, geworht*, pt, pt p of *wyrcan, wircan*, to work.]

wrung [rung] *pt, pt p* of **wring**.

wry [rī] *adj* twisted or turned to one side; distorted in a grimace; ironic, sardonic, etc.—*ns* **wry´neck**, a genus (*Fynx*) of small woodpeckers, which twist round their heads strangely; **wry´ness**. [OE *wrīgian*, to drive, bend. Conn with **wriggle** and **writhe**.]

WWW [abbrev] World Wide Web

wyvern [wī´vėrn] *n* (*her*) a fictitious monster, winged and two-legged, allied to the dragon and the griffin. [O. Norman Fr. *wivre*, a viper—L *vīpera*.]

X

X chromosome [ex krō´mō-sōm] a chromosome associated with femaleness, occurring paired in the female cell and alone in the male cell. **x-axis** [eks-aks´is] in a plane Cartesian coordinate system, the horizontal axis along which the abscissa is measured; in a 3-dimensional Cartesian coordinate, the axis along which values of x are measured and at which both y and z equal zero; **Xmas**, written abbreviation for Christmas. **x-ray, X-ray** [eks-rā] radiation of very short wavelengths, capable of penetrating solid bodies, and printing on a photographic plate a shadow picture of objects not permeable by light rays; a communications code word for the letter x.—*vt* to photograph by x-rays.—**x-ray astronomy**, astronomy dealing with heavenly bodies by means of the x-rays they emit; **x-ray crystallography**, the study and practice of determining the structure of a crystal by using x-rays; **x-ray therapy**, medical treatment using x-rays.

xenon [zen´on] *n* a gaseous element (symbol Xe; at wt 131.3; at no 54) present in the atmosphere in minute quantities. [Gr *xenos*, a stranger.]

xenophobia [zen-ō-fō´bi-à] *n* fear or hatred of strangers or things foreign. [Gr *xenos*, guest, stranger, *phobos*, fear.]

xerography [zē-rog´rà-fi] *n* a reprographic process in which the plate is sensitized electrically and developed by dusting with electrically-charged fine powder.—**Xer´ox**, trade name for a xerographic copying process or machine.—*vti* to reproduce by this process. [Gr *xēros*, dry, *graphein*, to write.]

xerophyte [zē´ro-fīt] *n* a plant able to grow in any conditions.

xi [zī, ksī] *n* the 14th letter in the Greek alphabet.

xylem [zī´lem] *n* plant tissue that conducts water and mineral salts from roots to other parts. [Gr *xylon*, wood.]

xylography [zī-log´rà-fi] *n* the art of engraving on wood.—*ns* **xy´lograph**, a wood engraving; the print made; **xylog´rapher**.—*adjs* **xylograph´ic, -al.** [Gr *xylon*, wood, *graphein*, to write.]

xylophone [zī´lo-fōn] *n* an orchestral musical instrument consisting of a series of bars tuned in a chromatic scale mounted on a horizontal frame and struck by hammers. [Gr *xylon*, wood, *phōnē*, sound.]

Y

Y: y-axis [wi-aks´is] *n* the reference axis of a graph or 2- or 3-dimensional Cartesian coordinate system along which the y-coordinate is measured; **Y chromosome**, a sex chromosome that occurs as one of a pair with the X chromosome in the germ cells of the males of many animals.

yacht [yot] *n* a sailing or mechanically driven vessel—generally of light tonnage, fitted for pleasure trips or racing.—*vi* to race or cruise in a yacht.—*ns* **yacht´ club**, a club of yachtsmen; **yachts´man**, one who keeps or sails a yacht. [Du *jacht* (formerly *jaght*), from *jagen*, to chase; Ger *jagen*, to hunt.]

yahoo [ya-hōō´] *n* a name given by Swift in *Gulliver's Travels* to a class of animals which have the forms of men but the understanding and passions of the lowest brutes; a boorish or stupid person.

Yahweh [yä´wä or vä] *n* the God of the Hebrews. [Heb.]

yak [yak] *n* a species (*Bos grunniens*) of ox found in Tibet, and domesticated there. [Tibetan.]

Yakima [yäk´i-mȧ] *n* a member of a group of Shaptian peoples, of the lower Yakima valley in south central Washington;—*pl* **Yakima, Yakimas**; the language of this people.

yam [yam] *n* the edible, starchy tuberous root of a tropical climbing plant (genus *Discorea*); a plant producing yams; a moist-fleshed, usu. orange-fleshed, sweet potato. [Port *inhame*.]

yang *See* **yin and yang**.

yank [yangk] *vti* (*inf*) to jerk. [Origin uncertain.]

Yankee [yang´ki] *n* a New Englander; a native of a Northern State; a citizen of the US; a communications code word for the letter *y*. [Prob *Janke*, a diminutive of Dutch *Jan*, John.]

yanqui [yängk´ē] *n* a citizen of the US who is not a Hispano-American. [Sp.]

yap [yap] *vi* to yelp, bark sharply; (*slang*) to speak constantly, esp in a noisy or foolish manner.—*n* a yelp; shrill insistent talk; a bumpkin; (*slang*) the mouth. [Imit.]

Yaqui [yak´ē] *n* a member of an Amerindian people of southern Arizona originally from Sonora, Mexico;—*pl* **Yaqui, Yaquis**.

yard[1] [yärd] *n* a unit of measure of 3 feet or 36 inches, and equivalent to 0.9144 meters; a unit of volume equal to a cubic yard; a great length or quantity; (*slang*) one hundred dollars; a long beam on a mast for spreading sails.—*ns* **yard´arm**, either end of a yard of a square-rigged ship; **yard´stick**, a graduated measuring stick one yard in length; any standard used in judging, etc. [OE *gyrd, gierd*, a rod, measure; Du *garde*, Ger *gerte*; further conn with L *hasta*, a spear.]

yard[2] [yärd] *n* an enclosed place, esp near a building; an enclosure for a special purpose; a rail center where trains are switched, etc. [OE *geard*, hedge, enclosure; Ger *garten*; conn with *hortus*, Gr *chortos*.]

yarmulke [yä´mu̇-kė, or yä´mul-kė] *n* (*Judaism*) a man's skullcap worn at prayer, and by strongly religious Jews at all times. [Yiddish.]

yarn [yärn] *n* fibers of wool, cotton, etc. spun into strands for weaving, knitting, etc.; (*inf*) a tale or story.—*vi* to tell a yarn. [OE *gearn*, thread; ON and Ger *garn*.]

yarrow [yar´ō] *n* a strongly scented plant (*Achillea millefolium*) with finely dissected leaves and a nearly flat-topped cluster of small, usu. white, flowers. [OE *gearwe*; Ger *garbe*.]

yashmak, yasmak [yash´mak´] *n* the veil worn by Muslim women, covering the face so that only the eyes are exposed to public view. [Ar *yashmaq*.]

yataghan [yat´a-gan] *n* a long dagger or short saber, common among Muslims, without guard, usu. curved. [Turk.]

yaw [yö] *vi* to deviate from a set course as a ship, spacecraft, etc.—Also *n*. [Origin obscure.]

yawl [yöl] *n* a small two-masted sailboat rigged fore-and-aft. [Du *jol*.]

yawn [yön] *vi* to open the jaws involuntarily from drowsiness; to gape.—*n* the opening of the mouth from drowsiness.—*adj* **yawn´ing**, gaping; opening wide; drowsy. [OE *gānian*, to yawn—*gīnan*, pt *gān*, to gape widely; ON *gīna*, to gape, Gr *chainein*, to gape.]

yaws [yöz] *n* a tropical contagious skin disease.

yclept, or **ycleped** [i-klept´] *pt p* (*obs*) called, named. [OE *clipian*, to call.]

ye[1] [yē] *pron* the nom pl of the 2d person. [OE *gē* (nom), ye; *ēower* (gen); *ēow* (dat and acc). See **you**.]

ye[2] [THė or THi or THē, now often erroneously yē] (*arch*) the.

yea [yā] *adv* yes; verily. [OE *gēa*; Du and Ger *ja*, ON *jā*; cf **yes**.]

year [yēr] *n* a period of time determined by the revolution of the earth around the sun (365 days, 5 hours, 48 minutes, 46 seconds); the period beginning with January 1 and ending with December 31, consisting of 365 days (except in leap year, when one day is added to February, making the number 366); a space of twelve calendar months reckoned from any date; an annual period of less than 365 days, as a school year; (*pl*) period of life, esp age or a long time.—*ns* **year´book**, an annual book, review of the events of the past year; **year´ling**, an animal a year old or in its second year.—*adj* **year´ly**, happening every year; lasting a year; of a year, or each year.—*adv* once a year; from year to year.—**year after year**, every year. [OE *gēar, gēr*; Ger *jahr*, ON *ār*, Gr *hōrā*, season.]

yearn [yûrn] *vi* to feel earnest desire (for); to feel uneasiness, from longing or pity.—*n* **yearn´ing**, earnest desire, tenderness, or pity.—*adj* longing.—*adv* **yearn´ingly**. [OE *giernan, giernian*, to desire—*georn*, desirous, eager.]

yeast [yēst] *n* a substance, consisting of certain minute fungi, which causes alcoholic fermentation, used in brewing and baking; yeast dried in flakes or granules or compressed into cakes; foam; froth; ferment; agitation.—*adj* **yeast´y**, containing yeast; frothy, foamy. [OE *gist, gyst*; Ger *gäscht, gischt*.]

yell [yel] *vti* to howl or cry out with a sharp noise; to scream.—*n* a sharp outcry; a rhythmic cheer in unison. [OE *gellan*; Ger *gellen*; conn with OE *galan*, to sing.]

yellow [yel´ō] *adj* of the color of ripe lemons; having a somewhat yellow skin; (*inf*) cowardly; sensational, as a newspaper.—*n* the color of the rainbow between orange and green; an egg yolk; (*pl*) jaundice; (*pl*) any of several plant diseases marked by yellowing foliage.—*vi* to become or turn yellow.—*vt* to make yellow or give a yellow tinge or color to.—*ns* **yellow fever**, a pestilential tropical fever caused by a virus transmitted by certain mosquitoes—also known as **yellow jack; yell´ow hamm´er**, a common European finch (*Emberiza citrinella*) bright yellow in the male, also called **yellow bunting**.—*adj* **yell´owish**, somewhat yellow.—**yellow peril**, a danger to western civilization held to arise from the expansion of Oriental power and influence; a threat to western living standards from the influx of Orientals willing to work for low wages. [OE *geolo*; Ger *gelb*; cog with L *helvus*, light bay.]

yelp [yelp] *vti* to utter a sharp bark.—*n* a sharp, quick cry or bark. [OE *gilpan*, to boast, exult; ON *giālpa*, to yelp.]

yen[1] [yen] *n* a unit of money in Japan. [Jap,—Chinese *yüan*, round, a dollar.]

yen[2] [yen] *n* (*inf*) an intense desire, longing, urge. [Chinese *yeen*, opium.]

yenta [yen´tȧ] *n* (*inf*) a vulgar, ill-tempered woman who gossips. [Yiddish.]

yeoman [yō´mȧn] *n* a naval petty officer assigned to clerical duties; in early English history, a common menial attendant; after the fifteenth century, one of a class of small farmers, the next grade below gentlemen; an officer of the British royal household;—*pl* **yeo´men**.—*n* **yeo´manry**, the collective body of yeomen.—**yeomen of the guard**, a member of a military corps attached to the British royal household and serves as ceremonial attendants of the sovereign and as warders of the Tower of London. [ME *yoman, yeman*, doubtless from an OE *gāman*, not found, but seen in Old Frisian *gāman*, villager—*gā*, a village (Ger *gau*, district), *man*, man.]

yerba maté [yûr´ba mä-tā] *n* maté. [Sp,—L *herba*. See also **maté**.]

yes [yes] *adv* ay; a word of affirmation or consent.—*n* **yes´man**, (*slang*) one who agrees with everything that is said to him, an obedient follower with no initiative. [OE *gīse, gēse*—*gēa*, yea, *sȳ*, let it be.]

yeshiva [yė-shē´vȧ] *n* a rabbinical seminary; a school for talmudic study; a Jewish day school providing secular and religious instruction. [Heb.]

yester [yes´tėr] *adj* relating to yesterday last.—*n* **yes´terday**, the day last past; a recent day of time.—*adv* on the day last past; recently.—*n* **yes´teryear**, last year; the recent past. [OE *geostran-, giestran-* (only in compounds); Ger *gestern*; cf L *hesternus*, Gr *chthes*.]

yet [yet] *adv* in addition, besides; still; up to the present time; before the matter is finished (eg *will get even with him yet*); even (eg *a yet more terrible experience*).—*conj* nevertheless; however.—**as yet**, up to now. [OE *giet, gīeta*; Ger *jetzt*.]

yeti [yet´i] *n* the abominable snowman. [Native Tibetan name.]

yew [ū] *n* an evergreen tree or shrub (genus *Taxus*) with needle leaves; its wood; (*arch*) an archery bow made of yew. [OE *īw, ēow, ēoh*; Ger *eibe*.]

Yiddish [yid´ish] *n* a language derived from medieval High German, written in the Hebrew alphabet, and spoken esp by eastern European Jews and their descendants.—*n* **yidd´icism**, a borrowing from Yiddish. [Ger *jüdisch*, Jewish.]

yield [yēld] *vt* to resign; to grant; to give out, to produce, as a crop, result, profit, etc.—*vi* to submit; to give place (*often with* **to**); to give way to physical force; to produce.—*n* amount yielded; the return on a financial investment.—*adj* **yield´ing**, inclined to give or to give way; compliant. [OE *gieldan, gildan*, to pay; Ger *gelten*; ON *gjalda*.]

yin and yang [yin and yang] *n* the two opposing principles of Chinese philosophy and religion influencing destiny, the former negative, feminine and dark, the latter positive, masculine and light. [Chin.]

yodel [yō´dl] *vti* to sing, changing frequently from the ordinary voice to falsetto and back again.—*n* a yodeling.—*n* **yō´deler**. [Ger dial *jodeln*.]

yoga [yō´ga] *n* a system of exercises for attaining bodily or mental control and well-being; **Yoga**, a Hindu theistic philosophy teaching the suppression of all activity of body, mind, and will so that the self may be liberated.—*n* **yō´gi**, a person who practices yoga; **Yō´gi**, an adherent of yoga philosophy. [Hindustani—Sans *yoga*, union.]

yogurt, yoghurt [yog´ėrt] *n* a semi-liquid food made from fermented milk. [Turk *yōghurt.*]

yoke [yōk] *n* that which joins together; the frame of wood joining oxen for drawing together; such a harnessed pair; any similar frame, as one for carrying pails; a mark of servitude; slavery; part of a garment which fits the shoulders.—*vt* to put a yoke on; to harness (an animal) to (a plow, etc.); to join together.—*ns* **yoke´-fellow, -mate**, a comrade, partner. [OE *geoc, iuc, ioc*; Ger *joch*; L *jugum*, Gr *zygon.*]

yokel [yō´kl] *n* (*offensive*) a country bumpkin.

yolk [yōk] *n* the yellow part of an egg. [OE *geolca, geoleca—geolo*, yellow.]

yom kippur [yōm ki-pŏŏ´er, or yȯm] *n* a Jewish holiday celebrated as a day of fasting, when prayers of penitence are recited in a synogogue. [Heb.]

yon [yon], **yonder** [yon´dėr] *advs* in that place (referring to somewhere specified or relatively distant).—*adj* that (referring to something at a distance within view). [OE *geon*; Ger *jener*, that.]

yore [yōr, yör] *n* old time, time long past.—**of yore**, formerly. [OE *geāra*, formerly, apparently connected with *gēar*, a year.]

you [ū] *pron* (*gram*) 2d person singular or plural; the person or persons spoken to; a person or people generally. [OE *ēow* (perh through a later form *eōw*), orig only dat and acc; cf **ye**.]

young [yung] *adj* not long born; in early life; in the first part of growth; inexperienced.—*n* young people; offspring, esp young offspring.—*adj* **young´ish**, somewhat young.—*ns* **young´ling**, a young person or animal; **young´ster** (*offensive*) a young person; a lad. [OE *geong*; Ger *jung*; also conn with L *juvenis*, Sans *yuvan*, young.]

younker [yung´kėr] *n* a young man; a child. [Old Du *joncker* (Du *jonker*), from *jonk-heer*, 'young master' or 'lord'; Ger *junker*.]

your [ūr] *possessive adj* (also called *possessive pron*) of or belonging to or done by you; used before some titles; relating to one or oneself; used almost as an equivalent to the definite article *the*. [OE *ēower*; cf **ye**.]

yours [ūrz] *pron* that or those belonging to you.—**yours truly**, a phrase used in ending a letter; (*inf*) I or me; cf **theirs** for uses and derivation.

yourself [ūr-self´] *pron* the intensive form of **you**; the reflexive form of **you**; your true self;—*pl* **yourselves´**.

youth [yōōth] *n* state of being young; early life; a young person, esp a young man; young persons collectively.—*adj* **youth´ful**, pertaining to youth or early life; young; suitable to youth; new; early; fresh.—*adv* **youth´fully**.—*n* **youth´fulness**.—**youth hostel**, a supervised lodging for usu. young travelers. [OE *geogoth—geong*, young; Ger *jugend.*]

yowl [yowl] *vi* to cry mournfully, as a cat; to yell, bawl.—*n* a loud, long, mournful cry. [ME *yowlen.*]

ytterbium [i-tûr´bi-ùm] *n* a metallic element (symbol Yb; at wt 173.0; at no 70). [*Ytterby*, a Swedish quarry.]

yttrium [it´ri-ùm] *n* a metallic element (symbol Y; at wt 88.9; at no 39). [*Ytterby*, a Swedish quarry.]

yuan [yōō-än´] *n* the unit of money of the People's Republic of China; the dollar of the Republic of China (Taiwan).

yucca [yuk´a] *n* a large desert plant (genus *Yucca*) of the lily family, native to subtropical America. [Sp.]

yule [yōōl] *n* the season or feast of Christmas.—*n* **yule´tide**, the Christmas season. [OE *gēol*; ON *jōl.*]

Yuma [yōō´mȧ] *n* an Amerindian language family of southwestern US and northern Mexico.—*adj, n* **Yu´man**.

yuppie [yup´ē] *n* (*inf*) any of those young professionals regarded as affluent, ambitious, materialistic, etc. [young *u*rban *p*rofessional + pie.]

yurt [yŏŏrt] *n* a light tent of skins, etc., used by nomads in Siberia. [From Russ.]

Z

Zacharias [zak-ė-rī´as] *n* (*Bible*) Zechariah in the Douay Version of the Old Testament.

zany [zā´ni] *n* a clown, a buffoon; a fool.—*adj* crazy, clownish. [Fr *zani*—It *zani*, a corr of *Giovanni*, John.]

zareba, zariba [za-rē´ba] *n* a stockade; a camp protected by a stockade. [Ar *zarībah*.]

zeal [zēl] *n* intense or passionate ardor, enthusiasm.—*n* **zealot** [zel´ot], one full of zeal, an enthusiast, a fanatic.—*adj* **zealous** [zel´-], full of zeal, warmly engaged or ardent in anything.—*adv* **zealously** [zel´-]. [OFr *zele*—L *zēlus*—Gr *zēlos*—*zeein*, to boil.]

zebra [zē´bra] *n* any of several beautifully striped animals (genus *Equus*) related to the horse, peculiar to the African continent. [Of African origin.]

zebu [zē´bū] *n* the humped domestic ox (*Bos indicus*) found in many parts of India, China, the east coast of Africa, etc. [Fr *zébu*, ultimately Asiatic.]

Zechariah [zek-ė-rī´a] *n* (*Bible*) 38th book of the Old Testament, written by the prophet Zechariah in the 5th century BC about the coming of Christ.

zeitgeist [tsīt´gīst] *n* the spirit of the age. [Ger.]

Zen [zen] *n* a Japanese Buddhist sect which holds that the truth is not in scriptures but in man's own heart if he will but strive to find it by meditation and introspection. [Jap—Chin *ch´an*, Sans *dhyāna*, religious contemplation.]

zenana [ze-nä´na] *n* the apartments in which women are secluded in upper crust families in India and Pakistan; a lightweight quilted fabric used mainly for housecoats. [Pers *zanāna*—*zan*, a woman.]

Zend-Avesta [zend avest´a] the ancient sacred writings of the Parsees. [Pers *zend, zand*, commentary.]

zenith [zen´ith] *n* that point of the heavens which is exactly overhead; greatest height, summit of ambition, etc. [Fr through Sp *zenit*, from Ar *samt*, short for *samt-ar-ras*, lit 'way, direction, of the head'.]

Zephaniah [zef-e-nī´a] *n* (*Bible*) 36th book of the Old Testament, written by the prophet Zephaniah about the 5th century BC concerning the Day of the Lord.

zephyr [zef´ir] *n* a soft, gentle breeze, esp from the west; any of various lightweight fabrics and articles of clothing. [Gr *zephyros*—*zophos*, darkness, the west.]

zeppelin [zep´el-in] *n* a rigid, dirigible, cigar-shaped airship. [Count *Zeppelin* (about 1900).]

zero [zē´ro] *n* the symbol 0; cipher; nothing; the point from which the reckoning begins in scales, such as those of the barometer, etc.; the lowest point.—**zero hour**, exact time (hour, minute and second) fixed for launching an attack or beginning an operation.—**zero in on**, to focus one's attentions or energies on. [Fr,—Ar *sitr*. Doublet **cipher**.]

zest [zest] *n* a piece of the peel or the outer part of the skin of an orange or lemon used to give flavor; something that gives a relish; relish. [Fr *zeste*—Gr *schizein*, to cleave.]

zeta [zāt´å] *n* the 6th letter of the Greek alphabet.

zeugma [zūg´ma] *n* a figure of speech by which an adjective or verb is applied to two nouns, although strictly appropriate to only one of them. [Gr,—*zeugnynai*, to yoke.]

zigzag [zig´zag] *n* a series of short, sharp angles in alternate directions; a design path, etc. in this form.—*adj* having sharp turns.—*vti* to move or form in a zigzag.—*pr p* **zig´zagging**; *pt p* **zig´zagged**.—*adv* with frequent sharp turns. [Fr *zigzag*—Ger *zick-zack*.]

zinc [zingk] *n* a bluish-white metallic element (symbol Zn; at wt 65.4; at no 30). [Ger *zink*, prob allied to *zinn*, tin.]

zinjanthropus [zin-jan´thrȯ-pùs] *n* a fossil hominid (*Australopithecus boisei* or *Zinjanthropus boisei*) characterized by a very low brow and large molars.

zinnia [zin´i-a] *n* a tropical American plant (genus *Zinnia*) having colorful, composite flowers. [From J G *Zinn* (1727–59).]

Zion [zī´on] *n* a hill in Jerusalem; the site of Solomon's temple; Jerusalem; Israel; heaven.—*ns* **Zi´onism**, a movement that re-established, and now supports, the state of Israel; **Zi´onist**. [Heb *Tsīyōn*.]

zip [zip] *n* a whizzing sound; (*inf*) energy, vigor.—*vi* to make or move with, a zip; (*inf*) to move with speed.—*vt* to fasten with a zipper.—*n* **zipp´er**, a device consisting of interlocking tabs worked by a sliding part.—*adj* **zipp´y**, (*inf*) full of energy or zip. [From the sound.]

zip code [zip kōd] *n* a system combining a two-letter abbreviation for a State and a five-figure number identifying each postal delivery area in the US.—*vt* to furnish with a zip code. [Zone *I*mprovement *P*lan.]

zircon [zir´kon] *n* a tetragonal mineral, zirconium, silicate, sometimes used as a gem.—*n*. **zirconium** [zėr-kō´ni-ùm] a metallic element (symbol Zr; at wt 91.2; at no 40). [Ar *zarqūn*, vermilion—Pers *zargūn*, gold-colored.]

zither [zith´ėr] *n* a flat many-stringed musical instrument of ancient origin, played with a pick and fingers. [Ger.]

zloty [zlot´ē] *n* the unit of money in Poland.

zodiac [zō´di-ak] *n* an imaginary belt in the heavens along which the sun, moon, and chief planets appear to move, divided crosswise into twelve equal areas, called 'signs of the zodiac', each named after a constellation; a diagram representing this. [Fr *zodiaque*—L *zōdiacus*—Gr *zōidiakos*, of figures—*zōidion*, a small carved or painted figure—*zōion*, an animal.]

zombie, zombi [zombi] *n* orig in Africa, the deity of the python; in West Indian superstition, a supernatural power by which a corpse may be reanimated; a corpse reanimated by sorcery; a person held to resemble the walking dead; a drink made of a mixture of rums, liqueur and fruit juice. [W African *zumbi*, fetish.]

zone [zōn] *n* a girdle, a belt; one of the five great belts in which the surface of the earth is divided; any area with reference to a specified use or restriction.—*vt* to encircle as with a zone; to divide into zones; to assign to a zone.—*adj* **zoned**, wearing a zone, having zones. [L *zōna*—Gr *zōnē*, a girdle—*zōnnynai*, to gird.]

zoo [zōō] *n* a place where a collection of wild animals is kept for public showing. [*zoo*logical garden.]

zoology [zō-ol´o-ji] *n* the science that deals with animals and animal life and is a branch of biology.—*adj* **zoolog´ical**.—*adv* **zoolog´ically**.—*n* **zool´ogist**, one versed in zoology.—**zoological garden**, a garden or park where live wild animals are exhibited. [Gr *zōion*, an animal, *logos*, discourse.]

zoom [zōōm] *vi* to make a loud, deep, persistent buzzing noise; to climb in an airplane sharply; to rise rapidly; to focus with a zoom lens.—*vt* to cause to zoom.—*n* the act of zooming.—**zoom lens**, a system of lenses, as in a motion-picture camera, that can be rapidly adjusted for close or distance shots while keeping the image in focus. [Imit.]

zoophyte [zō´o-fīt] *n* any animal, as a sponge, that looks and grows somewhat like a plant. [Gr *zōion*, an animal, *phyton*, a plant.]

Zoroastrianism [zor-ō-as´tri-ån-izm] *n* the ancient Persian religion founded or reformed by *Zoroaster*, set forth in the Zend-Avesta, and still adhered to by the Parsees in India.—*adj* **Zoroas´trian**, of or pertaining to Zoroaster or to Zoroastrianism.—*n* a follower of Zoroaster.

Zouave [zōō´äv] *n* a member of a former French military unit with colorful uniforms; of any similar military group. [From the *Zwawa*, an Algerian tribe.]

zucchini [zōō-kē´nē] *n* a cucumberlike summer squash. [It.]

Zulu [zōō´lōō] *n* a member of a people of South Africa; their language; a communications code word for the letter *z*.—*adj* of the Zulus, their language, etc. [South African.]

zuni [zōō´nē], **Zuñi** [zōōn´yē] *n* an Amerindian people of western New Mexico; a member of this people;—*pl* **Zuni, Zunis**; the language of this people.—*adjs* **Zu´nian, Zuñ´ian**. [Amer Sp.]

zwieback [swē´bak, or swi] *n* a kind of biscuit that is sliced and toasted after baking. [Ger *zwie*, twice, *backen*, baked.]

zygote [zī´gōt] *n* the cell formed by the union of two gametes; the developing individual from such a cell. [Gr *zygōtos*, yoked.]

zymurgy [zī´mur-jē] *n* the chemistry of fermentation processes.

THE WORLD

Countries of the World

Afghanistan
Area: 652,090 sq km, 251,773 sq miles
Population: 20,883,000
Capital: Kabul
Other major cities: Herat, Kandahar, Mazar-e-Sharif
Government: The Islamic State of Afghanistan has no functioning government at this time.
Religions: Sunni Islam, Shia Islam
Currency: Afghani

Albania
Area: 28,748 sq km, 11,009 sq miles
Population: 3,670,000
Capital: Tirane
Other major cities: Durrès, Shkodèr, Vlorë
Government: Socialist Republic
Religion: Constitutionally atheist but mainly Sunni Islam
Currency: Lek

Algeria
Area: 2,381,741 sq km, 919,595 sq miles
Population: 29,168,000
Capital: Algiers (Alger)
Other major cities: Oran, Constantine, Annaba
Government: Republic
Religion: Sunni Islam
Currency: Algerian Dinar

American Samoa
Area: 199 sq km, 77 sq miles
Population: 56,000
Capital: Pago Pago
Government: Unincorporated Territory of the USA
Religion: Christianity
Currency: US Dollar

Andorra
Area: 453 sq km, 175 sq miles
Population: 65,877
Capital: Andorra la Vella
Government: Republic
Religion: R. Catholicism
Currency: Franc, Peseta

Angola
Area: 1,246,700 sq km, 481,354 sq miles
Population: 11,185,000
Capital: Luanda
Other major cities: Huambo, Lobito, Benguela, Lubango
Government: People's Republic
Religions: R. Catholicism, Animism
Currency: Kwanza

Anguilla
Area: 96 sq km, 37 sq miles
Population: 12,394
Capital: The Valley
Government: British Overseas Territory
Religion: Christianity
Currency: East Caribbean Dollar

Antigua and Barbuda
Area: 442 sq km, 171 sq miles
Population: 66,000
Capital: St John's
Government: Constitutional Monarchy
Religion: Christianity (mainly Anglicanism)
Currency: East Caribbean Dollar

Argentina
Area: 2,780,400 sq km, 1,073,518 sq miles
Population: 35,220,000
Capital: Buenos Aires
Other major cities: Cordoba, Rosario, Mar del Plata, Mendoza, La Plata, Salta
Government: Federal Republic
Religion: R. Catholicism
Currency: Peso

Armenia
Area: 29,800 sq km, 11,506 sq miles
Population: 3,893,000
Capital: Yerevan
Other major city: Kunmayr (Gyumri)
Government: Republic
Religion: Armenian Orthodox
Currency: Dram

Aruba
Area: 193 sq km, 75 sq miles
Population: 87,000
Capital: Oranjestad
Government: Self-governing Dutch Territory
Religion: Christianity
Currency: Aruban Florin

Australia
Area: 7,741,220 sq km, 2,988,902 sq miles
Population: 18,871,800
Capital: Canberra
Other major cities: Adelaide, Brisbane, Melbourne, Perth, Sydney
Government: Consitutional Monarchy
Religion: Christianity
Currency: Australian Dollar

Austria
Area: 83,859 sq km, 32,378 sq miles
Population: 8,106,000
Capital: Vienna
Other major cities: Graz, Linz, Salzburg, Innsbruck
Government: Federal Republic
Religion: R. Catholicism
Currency: Schilling

Azerbaijan
Area: 86,600 sq km, 33,436 sq miles
Population: 7,625,000
Capital: Baku
Other major city: Sumqayit
Government: Republic
Religions: Shia Islam, Sunni Islam, Russian Orthodox
Currency: Manat

Bahamas
Area: 13,878 sq km, 5,358 sq miles
Population: 284,000
Capital: Nassau
Other important city: Freeport
Government: Constitutional Monarchy
Religion: Christianity
Currency: Bahamian Dollar

Bahrain
Area: 694 sq km, 268 sq miles
Population: 599,000
Capital: Manama (Al Manamah)
Government: Hereditary Monarchy
Religions: Shia Islam, Sunni Islam
Currency: Bahrain Dinar

Bangladesh
Area: 143,998 sq km, 55,598 sq miles
Population: 120,073,000
Capital: Dhaka

Other cities: Chittagong, Khulna, Narayanganj, Saidpur
Government: Republic
Religion: Sunni Islam
Currency: Taka

Barbados
Area: 430 sq km, 166 sq miles
Population: 265,000
Capital: Bridgetown
Government: Constitutional Monarchy
Religions: Anglicanism, Methodism
Currency: Barbados Dollar

Belarus
Area: 207,600 sq km, 80,155 sq miles
Population: 10,203,000
Capital: Minsk
Other major cities: Homyel (Gomel), Vitsyebsk, Mahilyov
Government: Republic
Religions: Russian Orthodox, R. Catholicism
Currency: Rouble

Belgium
Area: 30,519 sq km, 11,783 sq miles
Population: 10,159,000
Capital: Brussels
Other major cities: Antwerp, Charleroi, Ghent, Liège, Oostende
Government: Constitutional Monarchy
Religion: R. Catholicism
Currency: Belgian Franc

Belize
Area: 22,696 sq km, 8,763 sq miles
Population: 222,000
Capital: Belmopan
Other major city: Belize City
Government: Constitutional Monarchy
Religions: R. Catholicism, Protestantism
Currency: Belize Dollar

Benin
Area: 112,622 sq km, 43,484 sq miles
Population: 5,563,000
Capital: Porto Novo
Other major city: Cotonou
Government: Republic
Religions: Animism, Roman Catholicism, Sunni Islam, Christianity
Currency: CFA Franc

Bermuda
Area: 53 sq km, 20 sq miles
Population: 64,000
Capital: Hamilton
Government: British Overseas Territory
Religions: Protestantism, R. Catholicism
Currency: Bermuda Dollar

Bhutan
Area: 47,000 sq km, 18,147 sq miles
Population: 1,812,000
Capital: Thimphu
Government: Constitutional Monarchy
Religions: Buddhism, Hinduism
Currency: Ngultrum

Bolivia
Area: 1,098,581 sq km, 424,165 sq miles
Population: 8,140,000
Capital: La Paz (administrative), Sucre (legal)
Other major cities: Cochabamba, Santa Cruz, Oruro, Potosi
Government: Republic
Religion: R. Catholicism
Currency: Boliviano

Bosnia-Herzegovina
Area: 51,129 sq km, 19,735 sq miles
Population: 4,510,000
Capital: Sarajevo
Other major cities: Banja Luka, Mostar, Tuzla
Government: Republic
Religions: Eastern Orthodox, Sunni Islam, R. Catholicism
Currency: Dinar

Botswana
Area: 581,730 sq km, 224,607 sq miles
Population: 1,490,000
Capital: Gaborone
Other cities: Francistown, Molepolole, Mahalapye
Government: Republic
Religions: Animism, Christianity
Currency: Pula

Brazil
Area: 8,547,403 sq km, 3,300,171sq miles
Population: 157,872,000
Capital: Brasília
Other major cities: Belem, Belo Horizonte, Curitiba, Porto Alegre, Recife, Rio de Janeiro, Salvador, São Paulo
Government: Federal Republic
Religion: R. Catholicism
Currency: Cruzeiro

Brunei
Area: 5,765 sq km, 2,226 sq miles
Population: 300,000
Capital: Bandar Seri Begawan
Other major cities: Kuala Belait, Seria
Government: Monarchy (Sultanate)
Religion: Sunni Islam
Currency: Brunei Dollar

Bulgaria
Area: 110,912 sq km, 42,823 sq miles
Population: 8,356,000
Capital: Sofiya
Other major cities: Burgas, Plovdiv, Ruse, Varna
Government: Republic
Religion: Eastern Orthodox
Currency: Lev

Burkina Faso
Area: 274,000 sq km, 105,792 sq miles
Population: 10,780,000
Capital: Ouagadougou
Other major cities: Bobo-Dioulasso, Koudougou
Government: Republic
Religions: Animism, Sunni Islam
Currency: CFA Franc

Burundi
Area: 27,834 sq km, 10,747 sq miles
Population: 6,088,000
Capital: Bujumbura
Government: Republic
Religion: R. Catholicism
Currency: Burundi Franc

Cambodia
Area: 181,035 sq km, 69,898 sq miles
Population: 10,273,000
Capital: Phnom-Penh
Other major cities: Battambang, Kampong Cham
Government: People's Republic
Religion: Buddhism
Currency: Riel

Cameroon
Area: 475,442 sq km, 183,569 sq miles
Population: 13,560,000
Capital: Yaoundé
Other major city: Douala
Government: Republic
Religions: Animism, R. Catholicism, Sunni Islam
Currency: CFA Franc

Canada
Area: 9,970,610 sq km, 3,849,674 sq miles
Population: 29,964,000
Capital: Ottawa
Other major cities: Calgary, Toronto, Montréal, Vancouver, Québec City, Winnipeg
Government: Federal Parliamentary State
Religions: R. Catholicism, United Church of Canada, Anglicanism
Currency: Canadian Dollar

Cape Verde
Area: 4,033 sq km, 1,557 sq miles
Population: 396,000
Capital: Praia
Government: Republic
Religion: R. Catholicism
Currency: Cape Verde Escudo

Cayman Islands
Area: 264 sq km, 102 sq miles
Population: 38,000
Capital: George Town
Other main town: West Bay
Government: British Overseas Territory
Religion: Christianity
Currency: Cayman Islands Dollar

Central African Republic
Area: 622,984 sq km, 240,535 sq miles
Population: 3,344,000
Capital: Bangui
Other major cities: Bambari, Bangassou
Government: Republic
Religions: Animism, R. Catholicism
Currency: CFA Franc

Chad
Area: 1,284,000 sq km, 495,755 sq miles
Population: 6,515,000
Capital: N'Djamena
Other major cities: Sarh, Moundou, Abéché
Government: Republic
Religions: Sunni Islam, Animism
Currency: CFA Franc

Chile
Area: 756,626 sq km, 292,135 sq miles
Population: 14,419,000
Capital: Santiago
Other major cities: Arica, Concepcion, Valparaiso, Viña del Mar
Government: Republic
Religion: R. Catholicism
Currency: Chilean Peso

China, or **The People's Republic of China**
Area: 9,596,961 sq km, 3,705,408 sq miles
Population: 1,246,871,951
Capital: Beijing (Peking)
Other major cities: Chengdu, Guangzhou, Harbin, Shanghai, Tianjin, Wuhan
Government: People's Republic
Religions: Buddhism, Confucianism, Taoism
Currency: Yuan

Colombia
Area: 1,138,914 sq km, 439,737 sq miles
Population: 35,626,000
Capital: Bogotá
Other major cities: Barranquilla, Cali, Cartagena, Medellin
Government: Republic
Religion: R. Catholicism
Currency: Colombian Pesov

Comoros
Area: 1,865 sq km, 720 sq miles (excluding Mayotte)
Population: 538,000
Capital: Moroni
Other towns: Dornoni, Fomboni, Mutsamudu, Mitsamiouli
Government: Federal Islamic Republic
Religion: Sunni Islam
Currency: Comorian Franc

Congo
Area: 342,000 sq km, 132,047 sq miles
Population: 2,668,000
Capital: Brazzaville
Other major city: Pointe-Noire
Government: Republic
Religions: Christianity, Animism
Currency: CFA Franc

Congo, The Democratic Republic of (DRC)
Area: 2,344,858 sq km, 905,355 sq miles
Population: 46,812,000
Capital: Kinshasa
Other major cities: Bukavu, Lubumbashi, Mbuji-Mayi, Kananga, Kisangani
Government: Republic
Religions: R. Catholicism, Protestantism, Islam
Currency: Congolese Franc

Costa Rica
Area: 51,100 sq km, 19,730 sq miles
Population: 3,398,000
Capital: San José
Other major cities: Alajuela, Límon, Puntarenas
Government: Republic
Religion: R. Catholicism
Currency: Colon

Côte D'Ivoire
Area: 322,463 sq km, 124,504 sq miles
Population: 14,781,000
Capital: Yamoussoukro
Other major cities: Abidjan, Bouaké, Daloa
Government: Republic
Religions: Animism, Sunni Islam, R. Catholicism
Currency: CFA Franc

Croatia
Area: 56,538 sq km, 21,824 sq miles
Population: 4,501,000
Capital: Zagreb
Other major cities: Osijek, Rijeka, Split
Government: Republic
Religions: R. Catholicism, Eastern Orthodox
Currency: Kuna

Cuba
Area: 110,861 sq km, 42,804 sq miles
Population: 11,019,000
Capital: Havana
Other major cities: Camaguey, Holguin, Santa Clara, Santiago de Cuba
Government: Socialist Republic
Religion: R. Catholicism
Currency: Cuban Peso

Cyprus
Area: 9,251 sq km, 3,572 sq miles
Population: 756,000
Capital: Nicosia
Other major cities: Famagusta, Limassol, Larnaca
Government: Republic
Religions: Greek Orthodox, Sunni Islam
Currency: Cyprus Pound

Czech Republic
Area: 78,864 sq km, 30,450 sq miles
Population: 10,315,000
Capital: Prague (Praha)
Other major cities: Brno, Olomouc, Ostrava, Plzen
Government: Republic
Religions: R. Catholicism, Protestantism
Currency: Koruna

Denmark
Area: 43,094 sq km, 16,639 sq miles
Population: 5,262,000 (excluding the Faeroe Islands)
Capital: Copenhagen (København)
Other major cities: Ålborg, Århus, Odense
Government: Constitutional Monarchy
Religion: Lutheranism
Currency: Danish Krone

Djibouti
Area: 23,200 sq km, 8,958 sq miles
Population: 3,280,000
Capital: Djibouti
Government: Republic
Religion: Sunni Islam
Currency: Djibouti Franc

Dominica
Area: 751 sq km, 290 sq miles
Population: 74,000

Capital: Roseau
Government: Republic
Religion: R. Catholicism
Currency: East Caribbean Dollar

Dominican Republic
Area: 48,734 sq km, 18,816 sq miles
Population: 8,052,000
Capital: Santo Domingo
Other cities: Barahona, Santiago, San Pedro de Macoris
Government: Republic
Religion: R. Catholicism
Currency: Dominican Peso

Ecuador
Area: 283,561 sq km, 109,484 sq miles
Population: 11,698,000
Capital: Quito
Other major cities: Guayaquil, Cuenca
Government: Republic
Religion: R. Catholicism
Currency: Sucre

Egypt
Area: 1,001,449 sq km, 386,662 sq miles
Population: 60,603,000
Capital: Cairo (El Qâhira)
Other major cities: Giza (El Gîza), Suez Alexandria (El Iskandarîya), Port Said,
Government: Republic
Religions: Sunni Islam, Christianity
Currency: Egyptian Pound

El Salvador
Area: 21,041 sq km, 8,124 sq miles
Population: 5,796,000
Capital: San Salvador
Other major cities: Santa Ana, San Miguel,
Government: Republic
Religion: R. Catholicism
Currency: Colón

Equatorial Guinea
Area: 28,051 sq km, 10,831 sq miles
Population: 410,000
Capital: Malabo
Other major town: Bata
Government: Republic
Religion: R. Catholicism
Currency: CFA Franc

Eritrea
Area: 28,051 sq km, 10,831 sq miles
Population: 410,000
Capital: Malabo
Other major town: Bata
Government: Republic
Religion: R. Catholicism
Currency: CFA Franc

Estonia
Area: 45,227 sq km, 17,413 sq miles.
Population: 1,453,844
Capital: Tallinn
Other major cities: Narva, Pärnu
Government: Republic
Religions: Eastern Orthodox, Lutheranism
Currency: Kroon

Ethiopia
Area: 1,104,300 sq km, 426,373 sq miles
Population: 58,506,000
Capital: Addis Ababa (Adis Abeba)
Other major towns: Dire Dawa, Gonder, Jima
Government: Federation
Religions: Ethiopian Orthodox, Sunni Islam
Currency: Ethiopian Birr

Falkland Islands
Area: 12,173 sq km, 4,700 sq miles
Population: 2,221
Capital: Stanley
Government: British Crown Colony
Religion: Christianity
Currency: Falkland Islands Pound

Faeroe (Faroe) Islands
Area: 1,399 sq km, 540 sq miles
Population: 47,000
Capital: Tørshavn
Government: Self-governing Region of Denmark
Religion: Lutheranism
Currency: Danish Krone

Fiji
Area: 18,274 sq km, 7,056 sq miles
Population: 797,000
Capital: Suva
Government: Republic
Religions: Christianity, Hinduism
Currency: Fijian Dollar

Finland
Area: 338,145 sq km, 130,559 sq miles
Population: 5,125,000
Capital: Helsinki (Helsingfors)
Other major cities: Turku, Tampere
Government: Republic
Religion: Lutheranism
Currency: Markka

France
Area: 551,500 sq km, 212,935 sq miles
Population: 58,375,000
Capital: Paris
Other major cities: Bordeaux, Marseille, Lyon, , Nantes, Nice, Toulouse, Strasbourg
Government: Republic
Religion: R. Catholicism
Currency: Franc

French Guiana or Guyane
Area: 90,000 sq km, 34,749 sq miles
Population: 153,000
Capital: Cayenne
Government: French Overseas Department
Religion: R. Catholicism
Currency: Franc

French Polynesia
Area: 4,000 sq km, 1,544 sq miles
Population: 223,000
Capital: Papeete
Government: Overseas Territory of France
Religions: Protestantism, R. Catholicism
Currency: Franc

Gabon
Area: 267,668 sq km, 103,347 sq miles
Population: 1,106,000
Capital: Libreville
Other major city: Port Gentil
Government: Republic
Religions: R. Catholicism, Animism
Currency: CFA Franc

Gambia
Area: 11,295 sq km, 4,361 sq miles
Population: 1,141,000
Capital: Banjul
Government: Republic
Religions: Sunni Islam, Christianity
Currency: Dalasi

Georgia
Area: 69,700 sq km, 26,911 sq miles
Population: 5,411,000
Capital: T'bilisi
Other major cities: Sukhumi, Batumi
Government: Republic
Religions: Georgian and Russian Orthodox, Islam
Currency: Lari

Germany
Area: 356,733 sq km, 137,735 sq miles
Population: 81,912,000
Capital: Berlin, Bonn (seat of government)
Other major cities: Cologne (Köln), Dortmund, Düsseldorf, Essen, Frankfurt, Hamburg, Leipzig, Munich (München), Stuttgart
Government: Republic
Religions: Lutheranism, R. Catholicism
Currency: Deutsche Mark

Ghana
Area: 238,537 sq km, 92,100 sq miles
Population: 17,459,350
Capital: Accra
Other major cities: Sekondi-Takoradi, Kumasi, Tamale
Government: Republic
Religions: Protestantism, Animism, R. Catholicism
Currency: Cedi

Gibraltar
Area: 6.5 sq km, 2.5 sq miles
Population: 27,192
Capital: Gibraltar
Government: Self-governing British Colony
Religion: Christianity
Currency: Gibraltar Pound

Greece
Area: 131,957 sq km, 50,949 sq miles
Population: 10,475,000
Capital: Athens (Athínai)
Other major cities: Iráklion, Lárisa, Patras (Patrai), Piraeus (Piraiévs), Thessaloníki
Government: Republic
Religion: Greek Orthodox
Currency: Drachma

Greenland
Area: 2,175,600 sq km, 840,000 sq miles
Population: 58,200
Capital: Godthåb (Nuuk)
Government: Self-governing Region of Denmark
Religion: Lutheranism
Currency: Danish Krone

Grenada
Area: 344 sq km, 133 sq miles
Population: 92,000
Capital: St George's
Government: Independent State within the Commonwealth
Religions: R. Catholicism, Anglicanism, Methodism
Currency: East Caribbean Dollar

Guadelope
Area: 1,705 sq km, 658 sq miles
Population: 431,000
Capital: Basse-Terre
Other main town: Pointe-à-Pitre
Government: French Overseas Department
Religion: R. Catholicism
Currency: Franc

Guam
Area: 549 sq km, 212 sq miles
Population: 153,000
Capital: Agana
Government: Unincorporated Territory of the USA
Religion: R. Catholicism
Currency: US dollar

Guatemala
Area: 108,889 sq km, 42,042 sq miles
Population: 10,928,000
Capital: Guatemala City
Other cities: Cobán, Puerto Barrios, Quezaltenango
Government: Republic
Religion: R. Catholicism Currency: Quetza

Guinea
Area: 245,857 sq km, 94,926 sq miles
Population: 7,518,000
Capital: Conakry
Other major cities: Kankan, Kindia, Labé
Government: Republic
Religion: Sunni Islam
Currency: Guinea Franc

Guinea-Bissau
Area: 36,125 sq km, 13,948 sq miles
Population: 1,091,000
Capital: Bissau
Government: Republic
Religions: Animism, Sunni Islam
Currency: Peso

Guyana
Area: 214,969 sq km, 83,000 sq miles
Population: 838,000
Capital: Georgetown
Other cities: Linden, New Amsterdam
Government: Cooperative Republic
Religions: Hinduism, Protestantism, R. Catholicism
Currency: Guyana Dollar

Haiti
Area: 27,750 sq km, 10,714 sq miles
Population: 7,336,000
Capital: Port-au-Prince
Other towns: Cap-Haïtien, Les Cayes, Gonaïves
Government: Republic
Religions: R. Catholicism, Voodooism
Currency: Gourde

Honduras
Area: 112,088 sq km, 43,277 sq miles
Population: 6,140,000
Capital: Tegucigalpa
Other cities: San Pedro Sula, La Ceiba, Puerto Cortés
Government: Republic
Religion: R. Catholicism
Currency: Lempira

Hong Kong
Area: 1,075 sq km, 415 sq miles
Population: 6,687,200
Government: Special Autonomous Province of China
Religions: Buddhism, Taoism, Christianity
Currency: Hong Kong Dollar

Hungary
Area: 93,032 sq km, 35,920 sq miles
Population: 10,193,000
Capital: Budapest
Other major cities: Debrecen, Miskolc, Pécs, Szeged
Government: Republic
Religions: R. Catholicism, Calvinism, Lutheranism
Currency: Forint

Iceland
Area: 103,000 sq km, 39,769 sq miles
Population: 275,277
Capital: Reykjavík
Other major cities: Akureyri, Kópavogur
Government: Republic
Religion: Lutheranism
Currency: Icelandic Króna

India
Area: 3,287,590 sq km, 1,269,346 sq miles
Population: 970,930,000
Capital: New Delhi
Other major cities: Ahmadabad, Bangalore, Bombay, Calcutta, Delhi, Madras, Hyderabad, Kanpur
Government: Federal Republic, Secular Democracy
Religions: Hinduism, Islam, Sikkism, Christianity, Jainism, Buddhism
Currency: Rupee

Indonesia
Area: 1,904,569 sq km, 735,358 sq miles
Population: 196,813,000
Capital: Jakarta
Other major cities: Bandung, Medan, Palembang, Semarang, Surabaya
Government: Republic
Religions: Sunni Islam, Christianity, Hinduism
Currency: Rupiah

Iran, Islamic Republic of
Area: 1,648,195 sq km, 634,293 sq miles
Population: 61,128,000
Capital: Tehran
Other major cities: Esfahan, Mashhad, Tabriz

Government: Islamic Republic
Religion: Shia Islam
Currency: Rial

Iraq
Area: 438,317 sq km, 169,235 sq miles
Population: 20,607,000
Capital: Baghdad
Other major cities: Al-Basrah, Al Mawsil
Government: Republic
Religions: Shia Islam, Sunni Islam
Currency: Iraqi Dinar

Ireland, Republic of
Area: 70,284 sq km, 27,137 sq miles
Population: 3,626,087
Capital: Dublin
Other major cities: Cork, Galway, Limerick, Waterford
Government: Republic
Religion: R. Catholicism
Currency: Punt = 100 Pighne

Israel
Area: 21,056 sq km, 8,130 sq miles
Population: 6,100,000
Capital: Tel Aviv (Tel Aviv-Yafo)
Other major cities: Jerusalem, Haifa
Government: Republic
Religions: Judaism, Sunni Islam, Christianity
Currency: New Israeli Shekel

Italy
Area: 301,268 sq km, 116,320 sq miles
Population: 57,339,000
Capital: Rome (Roma)
Other major cities: Milan (Milano), Naples (Napoli), Turin (Torino), Genoa (Genova), Palermo, Florence (Firenze)
Government: Republic
Religion: R. Catholicism
Currency: Lira

Jamaica
Area: 10,990 sq km, 4,243 sq miles
Population: 2,491,000
Capital: Kingston
Other town: Montego Bay
Government: Constitutional Monarchy
Religions: Anglicanism, R. Catholicism, Protestantism
Currency: Jamaican Dollar

Japan
Area: 377,801 sq km, 145,870 sq miles
Population: 125,761,000
Capital: Tokyo
Other major cities: Osaka, Nagoya, Sapporo, Kobe, Kyoto, Yokohama
Government: Constitutional Monarchy
Religions: Shintoism, Buddhism, Christianity
Currency: Yen

Jordan, Hashemite Kingdom of
Area: 97,740 sq km, 37,738 sq miles
Population: 5,581,000
Capital: Amman
Other major cities: Aqaba, Zarqa, Irbid
Government: Constitutional Monarchy
Religion: Sunni Islam
Currency: Jordanian Dinar

Kazakhstan
Area: 2,717,300 sq km, 1,049,156 sq miles
Population: 15,671,000
Capital: Astana
Other major city: Almaty
Government: Republic
Religion: Sunni Islam
Currency: Tenge

Kenya
Area: 580,367 sq km,
Population: 31,806,000
Capital: Nairobi
Other towns: Mombasa, Eldoret, Kisumu, Nakuru
Government: Republic
Religions: R. Catholicism, Protestantism, other Christianity, Animism
Currency: Kenya Shilling

Kiribati
Area: 726 sq km, 280 sq miles
Population: 80,000
Capital: Tarawa
Government: Republic
Religions: R. Catholicism, Protestantism
Currency: Australian Dollar

Korea or Democratic People's Republic of Korea
Area: 120,538 sq km, 46,540 sq miles
Population: 22,466,000
Capital: Pyongyang
Other cities: Chongjin, Wonsan, Hamhung
Government: Socialist Republic
Religions: Buddhism, Confucianism, Chondogyo (a combination of Taoism and Confucianism)
Currency: Won

Korea, Republic of
Area: 99,373 sq km, 38,368 sq miles
Population: 46,430,000
Capital: Seoul (Soul)
Other major cities: Pusan, Taegu
Government: Republic
Religions: Buddhism, Christianity, Confucianism, Chondogyo (a combination of Taoism and Confucianism) Unification Church
Currency: Won

Kuwait
Area: 17,818 sq km, 6,880 sq miles
Population: 1,866,104
Capital: Kuwait City (Al Kuwayt)
Government: Constitutional Monarchy
Religions: Sunni Islam, Shia Islam
Currency: Kuwaiti Dinar

Kyrgyzstan
Area: 198,500 sq km, 76,641 sq miles
Population: 4,575,000
Capital: Bishkek
Other major city: Osh
Government: Republic
Religion: Sunni Islam
Currency: Som

Laos
Area: 236,800 sq km, 91,429 sq miles
Population: 5,035,000
Capital: Vientiane
Other major cities: Luang Prabang, Savannakhét, Paksé
Government: People's Republic
Religion: Buddhism
Currency: New Kip

Latvia
Area: 64,600 sq km, 24,942 sq miles
Population: 2,491,000
Capital: Riga
Other cities: Liepaja, Daugavpils
Government: Republic
Religion: Lutheranism
Currency: Lat

Lebanon
Area: 10,400 sq km, 4,015 sq miles
Population: 3,084,900
Capital: Beirut (Beyrouth)
Other important cities: Tripoli (Trablous), Sidon (Saïda),
Government: Republic
Religions: Shia Islam, Sunni Islam, Christianity
Currency: Lebanese Pound

Lesotho
Area: 30,355 sq km, 11,720 sq miles
Population: 2,078,000
Capital: Maseru
Government: Constitutional Monarchy
Religions: R. Catholicism, other Christianity
Currency: Loti

Liberia
Area: 111,369 sq km, 43,000 sq miles
Population: 2,820,000
Capital: Monrovia
Other major city: Buchanan
Government: Republic
Religions: Animism, Sunni Islam, Christianity
Currency: Liberian Dollar

Libya
Area: 1,759,540 sq km, 679,362 sq miles
Population: 4,389,739
Capital: Tripoli (Tarabulus)
Other major cities: Banghazi, Misrãtah
Government: Socialist People's Republic
Religion: Sunni Islam
Currency: Libyan Dinar

Liechtenstein, Principality of
Area: 160 sq km, 62 sq miles
Population: 31,320
Capital: Vaduz
Government: Constitutional Monarchy (Principality)
Religion: R. Catholicism
Currency: Swiss Franc

Lithuania
Area: 65,200 sq km, 25,174 sq miles
Population: 3,701,300
Capital: Vilnius
Other major cities: Kaunas, Klaipeda, Siauliai,
Government: Republic
Religion: R. Catholicism
Currency: Litas

Luxembourg, Grand Duchy of
Area: 2,586 sq km, 998 sq miles
Population: 412,000
Capital: Luxembourg City
Other cities: Esch-sur-Algette, Differdange, Dudelange
Government: Constitutional Monarchy (Duchy)
Religion: R. Catholicism
Currency: Luxembourg Franc

Macao or Macau
Area: 18 sq km, 7 sq miles
Population: 440,000
Capital: Macao
Government: Special Adminstrative Region under Chinese Sovereignity
Religions: Buddhism, R. Catholicism
Currency: Pataca

Macedonia, Former Yugoslav Republic of (FYROM)
Area: 25,713 sq km, 9,928 sq miles
Population: 2,174,00
Capital: Skopje
Other cities: Kumanovo, Ohrid
Government: Republic
Religions: Eastern Orthodox, Islam
Currency: Dinar

Madagascar
Area: 587,041 sq km, 226,658 sq miles
Population: 15,353,000
Capital: Antananarivo
Other major cities: Fianarantsoa, Mahajanga, Toamasina, Toliara
Government: Republic
Religions: Animism, R. Catholicism, Protestantism
Currency: Franc Malgache

Malawi
Area: 118,484 sq km, 45,747 sq miles
Population: 10,114,000
Capital: Lilongwe
Other cities: Blantyre, Zomba
Government: Republic
Religions: Animism, R. Catholicism, Presbyterianism
Currency: Kwacha

Malaysia
Area: 329,758 sq km, 127,320 sq miles
Population: 20,581,000
Capital: Kuala Lumpur
Other major cities: Ipoh, George Town, Johor Baharu
Government: Federal Constitutional Monarchy
Religion: Islam
Currency: Ringgit or Malaysian Dollar

Maldives
Area: 298 sq km, 115 sq miles
Population: 263,000
Capital: Malé
Government: Republic
Religion: Sunni Islam Currency: Rufiyaa

Mali
Area: 1,240,192 sq km, 478,841 sq miles
Population: 11,134,000
Capital: Bamako
Other towns: Gao, Kayes, Ségou, Mopti, Sikasso
Government: Republic
Religions: Sunni Islam, Animism
Currency: CFA Franc

Malta
Area: 316 sq km, 122 sq miles
Population: 376,513
Capital: Valletta
Government: Republic
Religion: R. Catholicism
Currency: Maltese Pound

Marshall Islands
Area: 181 sq km, 70 sq miles
Population: 58,000
Capital: Dalap-Uliga-Darrit (on Majuro Atoll)
Government: Republic in free association with the USA
Religion: Protestantism
Currency: US Dollar

Martinique
Area: 1,102 sq km, 425 sq miles
Population: 384,000
Capital: Fort-de-France
Government: Overseas Department of France
Religion: R. Catholicism
Currency: French Franc

Mauritania or the Islamic Republic of Mauritania
Area: 1,025,520 sq km, 395,956 sq miles
Population: 2,351,000
Capital: Nouakchott
Other major cities: Kaédi, Nouadhibou
Government: Republic
Religion: Sunni Islam
Currency: Ouguiya

Mauritius
Area: 2,040 sq km, 788 sq miles
Population: 1,160,000
Capital: Port Louis
Government: Republic
Religions: Hinduism, R. Catholicism, Sunni Islam
Currency: Mauritian Rupee

Mexico
Area: 1,958,201 sq km, 756,066 sq miles
Population: 96,578,000
Capital: Mexico City
Other major cities: Guadalajara, León, Monterrey, Puebla, Tijuana
Government: Federal Republic
Religion: R. Catholicism
Currency: Mexican Peso

Micronesia, Federated States of
Area: 702 sq km, 271 sq miles
Population: 109,000
Capital: Palikir
Government: Republic
Religion: Christianity
Currency: US Dollar

Moldova (Moldavia)
Area: 33,700 sq km, 13,012 sq miles

Population: 4,327,000
Capital: Chisinau
Other cities: Tiraspol, Tighina, Bel'tsy
Government: Republic
Religion: Russian Orthodox
Currency: Leu

Monaco
Area: 1 sq kilometre or 0.4 sq miles
Population: 32,000
Capital: Monaco
Government: Constitutional Monarchy
Religion: R. Catholicism
Currency: French Franc

Mongolia
Area: 1,566,500 sq km, 604,829 sq miles
Population: 2,354,000
Capital: Ulaanbaatar
Other cities: Altay, Saynshand, Hovd, Choybalsan, Tsetserleg
Government: Republic
Religions: Buddhism, Shamanism, Islam
Currency: Tughrik

Montserrat
Area: 102 sq km, 39 sq miles
Population: 4,500
Capital: Plymouth
Government: British Overseas Territory
Religion: Christianity
Currency: East Caribbean Dollar

Morocco
Area: 446,550 sq km, 172,414 sq miles
Population: 27,623,000
Capital: Rabat
Other major cities: Casablanca (Dar el Beida), Fès, Marrakech, Tanger
Government: Constitutional Monarchy
Religion: Sunni Islam
Currency: Dirham

Mozambique
Area: 799,380 sq km, 309,496 sq miles
Population: 16,916,000
Capital: Maputo
Other towns: Beira, Nampula
Government: Republic
Religions: Animism, R. Catholicism, Sunni Islam
Currency: Metical

Myanmar, Union of
Area: 676,578 sq km, 261,228 sq miles
Population: 45,922,000
Capital: Rangoon (Yangon)
Other major cities: Mandalay, Moulmein, Pegu
Government: Republic
Religion: Buddhism
Currency: Kyat

Namibia
Area: 824,292 sq km, 318,261 sq miles
Population: 1,575,000
Capital: Windhoek
Other cities: Swakopmund, Lüderitz
Government: Republic
Religions: Lutheranism, R. Catholicism, other Christianity
Currency: Namibian Dollar

Nauru
Area: 21 sq km, 8 sq miles
Population: 11,000
Capital: Nauru
Government: Republic
Religions: Protestantism, R. Catholicism
Currency: Australian Dollar

Nepal, Kingdom of
Area: 147,181 sq km, 56,827 sq miles
Population: 21,127,000
Capital: Kathmandu
Other city: Biratnagar
Government: Constitutional Monarchy
Religions: Hinduism, Buddhism
Currency: Nepalese Rupee

Netherlands
Area: 40,844 sq km, 15,770 sq miles
Population: 15,517,000
Capital: Amsterdam
Seat of government: The Hague (s'Gravenhage)
Other major cities: Rotterdam, Eindhoven
Government: Constitutional Monarchy
Religions: R. Catholicism, Dutch Reform, Calvinism
Currency: Guilder

Netherlands Antilles
Area: 800 sq km, 309 sq miles
Population: 207,333
Capital: Willemstad
Government: Self-governing Dutch Territory
Religion: R. Catholicism
Currency: Netherlands Antilles Guilder

New Caledonia or Nouvelle Calédonie
Area: 18,575 sq km, 7,172 sq miles
Population: 189,000
Capital: Noumea
Government: French Overseas Territory
Religion: R. Catholicism
Currency: Franc

New Zealand
Area: 270,534 sq km, 104,454 sq miles
Population: 3,681,546
Capital: Wellington
Other major cities: Auckland, Christchurch, Dunedin, Hamilton
Government: Constitutional Monarchy
Religions: Anglicanism, R. Catholicism, Presbyterianism
Currency: New Zealand Dollar

Nicaragua
Area: 130,668 sq km, 50,193 sq miles
Population: 4,663,000
Government: Republic
Capital: Managua
Other cities: Matagalpa, León, Granada
Religion: R. Catholicism
Currency: Córdoba Oro

Niger
Area: 1,267,000 sq km, 489,191 sq miles
Population: 9,465,000
Capital: Niamey
Other major cities: Agadez, Maradi, Tahoua, Zinder
Government: Republic
Religion: Sunni Islam
Currency: CFA Franc

Nigeria
Area: 923,768 sq km, 356,669 sq miles
Population: 115,120,000
Capital: Abuja
Other major cities: Lagos, Onitsha, Enugu, Ibadan, Kano, Ogbomosho
Government: Federal Republic
Religions: Sunni Islam, Christianity
Currency: Naira

Northern Mariana Islands
Area: 464 sq km, 179 sq miles
Population: 49,000
Capital: Saipan
Government: Commonwealth in union with the USA
Religion: R. Catholicism
Currency: US Dollar

Norway, Kingdom of
Area: 323,877 sq km, 125,050 sq miles
Population: 4,445,460
Capital: Oslo
Other major cities: Bergen, Trondheim, Stavanger, Kristiansand, Tromsö
Government: Constitutional Monarchy
Religion: Lutheranism
Currency: Norwegian Krone

Oman, or the Sultanate of Oman
Area: 309,500 sq km, 119,498 sq miles
Population: 2,302,000
Capital: Muscat (Masqat)
Other towns: Salalah, Al Khaburah, Matrah
Government: Monarchy
Religions: Ibadi Islam, Sunni Islam
Currency: Rial Omani

Pakistan, or the Islamic Republic of Pakistan
Area: 796,095 sq km, 307,374 sq miles
Population: 134,146,000
Capital: Islamabad
Other major cities: Faisalabad, Hyderabad, Karachi, Lahore, Rawalpindi
Government: Federal Islamic Republic
Religions: Sunni Islam, Shia Islam
Currency: Pakistan Rupee

Palau
Area: 459 sq km, 177 sq miles
Population: 17,000
Capital: Koror
Government: Free Associated Republic (USA)
Religions: R. Catholicism and Modekngei
Currency: US Dollar

Palestine
Area:
Gaza 360 sq km,146 sq miles
Jericho 70 sq km, 27 sq miles
West Bank 5,860 sq km, 2,269 sq miles
Population:
Gaza 924,200
Jericho 20,600
West Bank 2,050,000
Government: Republic with limited powers
Religions: Sunni Islam, Shia Islam, Eastern Catholicism
Currency: None (Israeli and Jordanian currency used)

Panama
Area: 75,517 sq km, 29,157 sq miles
Population: 2,674,000
Capital: Panama City
Other major cities: Colón, Puerto Armuelles, David
Government: Republic
Religion: R. Catholicism
Currency: Balboa

Papua New Guinea
Area: 462,840 sq km, 178,704 sq miles
Population: 4,400,000
Capital: Port Moresby
Government: Republic
Religions: Protestantism, R. Catholicism
Currency: Kina

Paraguay
Area: 406,752 sq km, 157,048 sq miles
Population: 4,955,000
Capital: Asunción
Other major cities: Concepción, Ciudad del Este, Encarnación
Government: Republic
Religion: R. Catholicism
Currency: Guaraní

Peru
Area: 1,285,216 sq km, 496,225 sq miles
Population: 25,015,000
Capital: Lima
Other major cities: Arequipa, Callao, Chiclayo, Cuzco, Trujillo
Government: Republic
Religion: R. Catholicism
Currency: Nuevo Sol

Philippines
Area: 300,000 sq km, 115,831 sq miles
Population: 71,899,000
Capital: Manila
Other cities: Cebu, Davao, Quezon City, Zamboanga
Government: Republic
Religions: Sunni Islam, R. Catholicism, Animism
Currency: Philippine Peso

Pitcairn Islands
Area: 5 sq km, 2 sq miles
Population: 54
Government: British Overseas Territory
Religion: Seventh Day Adventism
Currency: New Zealand Dollar

Poland
Area: 323,250 sq km, 124,808 sq miles
Population: 38,628,000
Capital: Warsaw (Warszawa)
Other major cities: Gdansk, Kraków, Lódz, Poznan, Wroclaw
Government: Republic
Religion: R. Catholicism
Currency: Zloty

Portugal
Area: 91,982 sq km, 35,514 sq miles
Population: 9,920,760
Capital: Lisbon (Lisboa)
Other major cities: Braga, Coimbra, Faro, Porto, Setúbal
Government: Republic
Religion: R. Catholicism
Currency: Escudo

Puerto Rico
Area: 8,875 sq km, 3,427 sq miles
Population: 3,736,000
Capital: San Juan
Government: Self-governing Commonwealth (in association with the USA)
Religions: R. Catholicism, Protestantism
Currency: US Dollar

Qatar
Area: 11,000 sq km, 4,247 sq miles
Population: 558,000
Capital: Doha (Ad Dawhah)
Government: Absolute Monarchy
Religion: Wahhabi Sunni Islam
Currency: Qatar Riyal

Réunion
Area: 2,510 sq km, 969 sq miles
Population: 664,000
Capital: St Denis
Government: French Overseas Department
Religion: R. Catholicism
Currency: Franc

Romania
Area: 238,391 sq km, 92,043 sq miles
Population: 22,520,000
Capital: Bucharest (Bucuresti)
Other major cities: Brasov, Constanta, Galati, Iasi, Timisoara, Craiova, Brâila, Arad, Ploiesti
Government: Republic
Religions: Romanian Orthodox, R. Catholicism
Currency: Leu

Russia or the Russian Federation
Area: 17,075,400 sq km, 6,592,850 sq miles
Population: 146,100,000
Capital: Moscow (Moskva)
Other major cities: St Petersburg (Sankt Peterburg), Nizhniy Novgorod, Novosibirsk, Samara
Government: Republic
Religions: Russian Orthodox, Sunni Islam, Shia Islam, Roman Catholicism
Currency: Rouble

Rwanda
Area: 26,338 sq km, 10,169 sq miles
Population: 5,397,000
Capital: Kigali
Other major city: Butare
Government: Republic
Religions: R. Catholicism, Animism
Currency: Rwanda Franc

St Helena
Area: 122 sq km, 47 sq miles
Population: 5,157
Capital: Jamestown
Government: British Overseas Territory
Currency: St Helena Pound

St Kitts and Nevis
Area: 261 sq km, 101 sq miles
Population: 41,000
Capital: Basseterre
Other major city: Charlestown
Government: Constitutional Monarchy
Religions: Anglicanism, Methodism
Currency: East Caribbean Dollar

St Lucia
Area: 622 sq km, 240 sq miles
Population: 144,000
Capital: Castries
Government: Constitutional Monarchy
Religion: R. Catholicism
Currency: East Caribbean Dollar

St Vincent and the Grenadines
Area: 388 sq km, 150 sq miles
Population: 113,000
Capital: Kingstown
Government: Constitutional Monarchy
Religions: Anglicanism, Methodism, R. Catholicism
Currency: East Caribbean Dollar

San Marino
Area: 61 sq km, 24 sq miles
Population: 25,000
Capital: San Marino
Other towns: Borgo Maggiore, Serravalle
Government: Republic
Religion: R. Catholicism
Currency: Lira

Saõ Tomé and Príncipe
Area: 964 sq km, 372 sq miles
Population: 135,000
Capital: São Tomé
Government: Republic
Religion: R. Catholicism
Currency: Dobra

Saudi Arabia
Area: 2,149,690 sq km, 830,000 sq miles
Population: 18,836,000
Capital: Riyadh (Ar Riyãd)
Other major cities: Ad Dammam, Mecca (Makkah), Jeddah(Jiddah), Medina (Al Madinah)
Government: Monarchy
Religions: Sunni Islam, Shia Islam
Currency: Riyal

Senegal
Area: 196,722 sq km, 75,955 sq miles
Population: 8,572,000
Capital: Dakar
Other major cities: Kaolack, Thiès, St Louis
Government: Republic
Religions: Sunni Islam, R. Catholicism
Currency: CFA Franc

Seychelles
Area: 455 sq km, 175 sq miles
Population: 76,000
Capital: Victoria
Government: Republic
Religion: R. Catholicism
Currency: Seychelles Rupee

Sierra Leone
Area: 71,740 sq km, 27,699 sq miles
Population: 4,297,000
Capital: Freetown
Other city: Bo
Government: Republic
Religions: Animism, Sunni Islam, Christianity
Currency: Leone

Singapore
Area: 618 sq km, 239 sq miles
Population: 3,044,000
Capital: Singapore
Government: Parliamentary Democracy
Religions: Buddhism, Sunni Islam, Christianity, Hinduism
Currency: Singapore Dollar

Slovakia or the Slovak Republic
Area: 49,035 sq km, 18,928 sq miles
Population: 5,374,000
Capital: Bratislava
Other major cities: Kosice, Zilina, Nitra
Government: Republic
Religion: R. Catholicism
Currency: Slovak Koruna

Slovenia
Area: 20,256 sq km, 7,821 sq miles
Population: 1,991,000
Capital: Ljubljana
Other major cities: Maribor, Kranj
Government: Republic
Religion: R. Catholicism
Currency: Tolar

Solomon Islands
Area: 28,896 sq km, 11,157 sq miles
Population: 391,000
Capital: Honiara
Government: Parliamentary Democracy within the Commonwealth
Religion: Christianity
Currency: Solomon Islands Dollar

Somalia
Area: 637,657 sq km, 246,201 sq miles
Population: 9,822,000
Capital: Mogadishu (Muqdisho)
Other major towns: Hargeysa, Burco
Government: Republic
Religion: Sunni Islam
Currency: Somali Shilling

South Africa
Area: 1,221,037 sq km, 471,445 sq miles
Population: 42,393,000
Capital: Pretoria (administrative), Cape Town (legislative)
Other major cities: Johannesburg, Durban, Port Elizabeth, Soweto
Government: Republic
Religions: Christianity, Hinduism, Islam
Currency: Rand

Spain
Area: 505,992 sq km, 195,365 sq miles
Population: 39,270,400
Capital: Madrid
Other major cities: Barcelona, Valencia, Sevilla, Zaragoza, Malaga, Bilbao
Government: Constitutional Monarchy
Religion: R. Catholicism
Currency: Peseta

Sri Lanka
Area: 65,610 sq km, 25,332 sq miles
Population: 18,354,000
Capital: Colombo
Other major cities: Trincomalee, Jaffna, Kandy, Moratuwa
Government: Republic
Religions: Buddhism, Hinduism, Christianity, Sunni Islam
Currency: Sri Lankan Rupee

Sudan
Area: 2,505,813 sq km, 967,500 sq miles
Population: 27,291,000
Capital: Khartoum (El Khartum)
Other major cities: Omdurman, Khartoum North, Port Sudan
Government: Republic
Religions: Sunni Islam, Animism, Christianity
Currency: Sudanese Dinar

Suriname
Area: 163,265 sq km, 63,037 sq miles
Population: 423,000
Capital: Paramaribo
Government: Republic
Religions: Hinduism, R. Catholicism,

Sunni Islam
Currency: Suriname Guilder

Swaziland
Area: 17,364 sq km, 6,704 sq miles
Population: 938,700
Capital: Mbabane
Other towns: Big Bend, Manzini, Mankayane, Lobamba
Government: Monarchy
Religions: Christianity, Animism
Currency: Lilangeni

Sweden
Area: 449,964 sq km, 173,732 sq miles
Population: 8,843,000
Capital: Stockholm
Other major cities: Göteborg, Malmö, Uppsala, Örebro, Linköping
Government: Constitutional Monarchy
Religion: Lutheranism
Currency: Krona

Switzerland
Area: 41,284 sq km, 15,940 sq miles
Population: 7,076,000
Capital: Bern
Other major cities: Zürich, Basle (Basel), Geneva (Genève), Lausanne
Government: Federal Republic
Religions: R. Catholicism, Protestantism
Currency: Swiss franc

Syria or the Syrian Arab Republic
Area: 185,180 sq km, 71,498 sq miles
Population: 14,619,000
Capital: Damascus (Dimashq)
Other cities: Halab, Hims, Dar'a
Government: Republic
Religion: Sunni Islam
Currency: Syrian Pound

Taiwan, Republic of China
Area: 35,742 sq km, 13,800 sq miles
Population: 21,854,273
Capital: T'ai-pei
Other major cities: Kao-hsiung, T'ai-nan, Chang-hua, Chi-lung
Government: Republic
Religions: Taoism, Buddhism, Christianity
Currency: New Taiwan Dollar

Tajikistan
Area: 143,100 sq km, 55,251 sq miles
Population: 5,919,000
Capital: Dushanbe
Other major city: Khujand
Government: Republic
Religion: Shia Islam
Currency: Tajik Rouble

Tanzania
Area: 938,000 sq km, 362,162 sq miles
Population: 30,799,100
Capital: Dodoma
Other towns: Dar es Salaam, Zanzibar, Mwanza, Tanga
Government: Republic
Religions: Sunni Islam, R. Catholicism, Anglicanism, Hinduism
Currency: Tanzanian Shilling

Thailand
Area: 513,115 sq km, 198,115 sq miles
Population: 60,206,000
Capital: Bangkok (Krung Thep)
Other major cities: Chiang Mai, Nakhon Ratchasima, Ubon Ratchathani
Government: Constitutional Monarchy
Religions: Buddhism, Sunni Islam
Currency: Baht

Togo
Area: 56,785 sq km, 21,925 sq miles
Population: 4,201,000
Capital: Lomé
Other major city: Sokodé
Government: Republic
Religions: Animism, R. Catholicism, Sunni Islam
Currency: CFA Franc

Tonga
Area: 747 sq km, 288 sq miles
Population: 99,000
Capital: Nuku'alofa
Government: Constitutional Monarchy
Religions: Methodism, R. Catholicism
Currency: Pa'anga

Trinidad and Tobago
Area: 5,130 sq km, 1,981 sq miles
Population: 1,297,000
Capital: Port of Spain
Other towns: San Fernando, Arima
Government: Republic
Religions: R. Catholicism, Hinduism, Anglicanism, Sunni Islam
Currency: Trinidad and Tobago Dollar

Tunisia
Area: 162,155 sq km, 62,592 sq miles
Population: 9,092,000
Capital: Tunis
Other major cities: Sfax, Bizerte, Sousse
Government: Republic
Religion: Sunni Islam
Currency: Dinar

Turkey
Area: 774,815 sq km, 299,158 sq miles
Population: 62,697,000
Capital: Ankara
Other major cities: Istanbul, Izmir, Adana, Bursa
Government: Republic
Religion: Sunni Islam
Currency: Turkish Lira

Turkmenistan
Area: 488,100 sq km, 188,456 sq miles
Population: 4,569,000
Capital: Ashkhabad (Ashgabat)
Other cities: Chardzhou, Mary, Turkmenbashi
Government: Republic
Religion: Sunni Islam
Currency: Manat

Turks and Caicos Islands
Area: 430 sq km, 166 sq miles
Population: 23,000
Capital: Grand Turk
Government: British Crown Colony
Religion: Christianity
Currency: US Dollar

Tuvalu
Area: 26 sq km, 10 sq miles
Population: 10,000
Capital: Funafuti
Government: Constitutional Monarchy
Religion: Protestantism
Currency: Tuvalu Dollar/Australian Dollar

Uganda
Area: 241,038 sq km, 93,065 sq miles
Population: 19,848,000
Capital: Kampala
Other cities: Entebbe, Jinja, Soroti, Mbale
Government: Republic
Religions: R. Catholicism, Protestantism, Animism, Sunni Islam
Currency: Uganda Shilling

Ukraine
Area: 603,700 sq km, 233,090 sq miles
Population: 51,094,000
Capital: Kiev (Kiyev)
Other major cities: Dnepropetrovsk, Donetsk, Khar'kov, Odessa, Lugansk, Sevastopol (in the Crimea)
Government: Republic
Religions: Eastern Orthodox, R. Catholicism
Currency: Rouble

United Arab Emirates (UAE)
Area: 83,600 sq km, 32,278 sq miles
Population: 2,260,000
Capital: Abu Zabi (Abu Dhabi)

Other major cities: Dubai (Dubayy), Sharjah, Ras al Khaymah
Government: Monarchy
Religion: Sunni Islam
Currency: Dirham

United Kingdom of Great Britain and Northern Ireland (UK)
Area: 244,101 sq km, 94,248 sq miles
Population: 58,784,000
Capital: London
Other major cities: Birmingham, Manchester, Glasgow, Liverpool, Edinburgh, Cardiff, Belfast
Government: Constitutional Monarchy
Religions: Anglicanism, R. Catholicism, Presbyterianism, Methodism
Currency: Pound Sterling

United States of America (USA)
Area: 9,158,960 sq km, 3,536,278 sq miles
Population: 270,298,524
Capital: Washington DC
Other major cities: New York, Chicago, Detroit, Houston, Los Angeles, Philadelphia, San Diego, San Francisco
Government: Federal Republic
Religions: Protestantism, R. Catholicism, Judaism, Eastern Orthodox
Currency: US Dollar

Uruguay
Area: 177,414 sq km, 68,500 sq miles
Population: 3,203,000
Capital: Montevideo
Other major cities: Salto, Melo
Government: Republic
Religions: R. Catholicism, Protestantism
Currency: Peso Uruguayos

Uzbekistan
Area: 447,400 sq km, 172,742 sq miles
Population: 24,000,000
Capital: Tashkent
Other cities: Urgench, Nukus, Bukhara, Samarkand
Government: Republic
Religions: Sunni Islam, Eastern Orthodox
Currency: Soum

Vanuatu
Area: 12,189 sq km, 4,706 sq miles
Population: 169,000
Capital: Vila
Government: Republic
Religion: R. Catholicism
Currency: Vatu

Vatican City
Area: 0.44 sq km, 0.2 sq miles
Population: 1000
Capital: Vatican City
Government: Papal Commission
Religion: R. Catholicism
Currency: Vatican City Lira

Venezuela
Area: 912,050 sq km, 352,145 sq miles
Population: 22,710,000
Capital: Caracas
Other major cities: Maracaibo, Valencia, Barquisimeto
Government: Federal Republic
Religion: R. Catholicism
Currency: Bolívar

Vietnam
Area: 331,689 sq km, 128,066 sq miles
Population: 75,181,000
Capital: Hanoi
Other major cities: Ho Chi Minh City, Haiphong, Hué, Dà Nang
Government: Socialist Republic
Religions: Buddhism, Taoism, Roman Catholicsm
Currency: New Dong

Virgin Islands, British
Area: 151 sq km, 58 sq miles
Population: 19,000
Capital: Road Town
Government: British Overseas Territory
Religion: Protestantism
Currency: US Dollar

Virgin Islands, US
Area: 347 sq km, 134 sq miles
Population: 106,000
Capital: Charlotte Amalie
Government: Self-governing US Territory
Religion: Protestantism
Currency: US Dollar

Wallis and Futuna Islands
Area: 200 sq km, 77 sq miles
Population: 15,000
Capital: Mata-Uru
Government: French Overseas Territory
Religion: R. Catholicism
Currency: Franc

Western Sahara
Area: 266,000 sq km, 102,703 sq miles
Population: 266,000
Capital: Laâyoune (El Aaiún)
Government: Republic (de facto controlled by Morocco)
Religion: Sunni Islam
Currency: Moroccan Dirham

Western Samoa
Area: 2,831 sq km, 1,093 sq miles
Population: 166,000
Capital: Apia
Government: Constitutional Monarchy
Religion: Protestantism
Currency: Tala

Yemen
Area: 527,968 sq km, 203,850 sq miles
Population: 15,919,000
Capital: San'a
Commercial capital: Aden (Adan)
Other cities: Al Hudaydah, Ta'izz
Government: Republic
Religions: Zaidism, Shia Islam, Sunni Islam
Currency: Riyal

Yugoslavia (FRY)
Area: 102,173 sq km, 39,449 sq miles
Population: 10,574,000
Capital: Belgrade (Beograd)
Other cities: Nis, Novi Sad, Pristina
Government: Federal Republic
Religions: Eastern Orthodox, Islam
Currency: New Dinar

Zambia
Area: 752,618 sq km, 290,587 sq miles
Population: 8,275,000
Capital: Lusaka
Other cities: Kitwe, Ndola, Mufulira
Government: Republic
Religions: Christianity, Animism
Currency: Kwacha

Zimbabwe
Area: 390,757 sq km, 150,872 sq miles
Population: 11,908,000
Capital: Harare
Other cities: Bulawayo, Mutare, Gweru
Government: Republic
Religions: Animism, Anglicanism, R. Catholicism
Currency: Zimbabwe Dollar

THE WORLD

Map Index

C

G

H

L

M

N

O

P

Q

R

S

U

V

W

Roads – *at scales larger than 1:3 million*

Motorway/Highway
Other Main Road

– *at scales smaller than 1:3 million*

Principal Road: Motorway/Highway
Other Main road
Main Railway

Towns & Cities

Population > 5,000,000
1–5,000,000
500,000–1,000,000
< 500,000
Paris National Capital
Airport
International Boundary
International Boundary – not defined or in dispute
Internal Boundary
River
Canal
Marsh or Swamp

Relief

▲ 1510 Peak (meters)

5,000 meters (16,405 feet)
4,000 (13,124)
3,000 (9,843)
2,000 (6,562)
1,000 (3,281)
500 (1,641)
200 (656)
100 (328)
0
Land below sea level

Note:
The 0–100 contour layer appears only at scales larger than 1:3 million

Scale 1:97 150 000

OCEAN
RUSSIAN FEDERATION
CANADA
Arctic Circle
Alaska (U.S.A.)
Bering Strait
GULF OF ALASKA
BERING SEA
Aleutian Is.
SEA OF OKHOTSK
KAZAKHSTAN
Astana
Ulaanbaatar
MONGOLIA
UZBEKISTAN
Bishkek
KYRGYZSTAN
Tashkent
TURKMENISTAN
Ashkhabad
TAJIKISTAN
Dushanbe
Tehrān
IRAN
Kābul
AFGHANISTAN
Islāmabād
PAKISTAN
New Delhi
NEPAL
Kathmandu
Thimphu
BHUTAN
Dhākā
BANG.
INDIA
CHINA
Beijing
Pyongyang
N. KOREA
SEA OF JAPAN
Sŏul
S. KOREA
JAPAN
Tōkyō
EAST CHINA SEA
T'ai-pei
TAIWAN
HONG KONG
Hanoi
MYANMAR (BURMA)
Vientiane
LAOS
Rangoon
THAILAND
VIETNAM
Bangkok
CAMB.
Phnom Penh
SOUTH CHINA SEA
Manila
PHILIPPINES
U.A.E.
Masqat
OMAN
YEMEN
ARABIAN SEA
BAY OF BENGAL
Colombo
SRI LANKA
MALDIVES
BRUNEI
Kuala Lumpur
MALAYSIA
SINGAPORE
INDONESIA
Jakarta
EAST TIMOR
TIMOR
SEYCHELLES
INDIAN OCEAN
Rodrigues
Antananarivo
MAURITIUS
Réunion
PACIFIC OCEAN
Tropic of Cancer
Hawaii (U.S.A.)
NORTHERN MARIANAS IS. (U.S.A.)
MARSHALL ISLANDS
FEDERATED STATES OF MICRONESIA
PALAU
KIRIBATI
Equator
NAURU
PAPUA NEW GUINEA
Port Moresby
SOLOMON ISLANDS
TUVALU
SAMOA
CORAL SEA
VANUATU
FIJI
Nouvelle Calédonie (Fr)
TONGA
Tropic of Capricorn
AUSTRALIA
Canberra
TASMAN SEA
Tasmania
Wellington
NEW ZEALAND
Is. Kerguelen (Fr.)
Antarctic Circle
ANTARCTICA

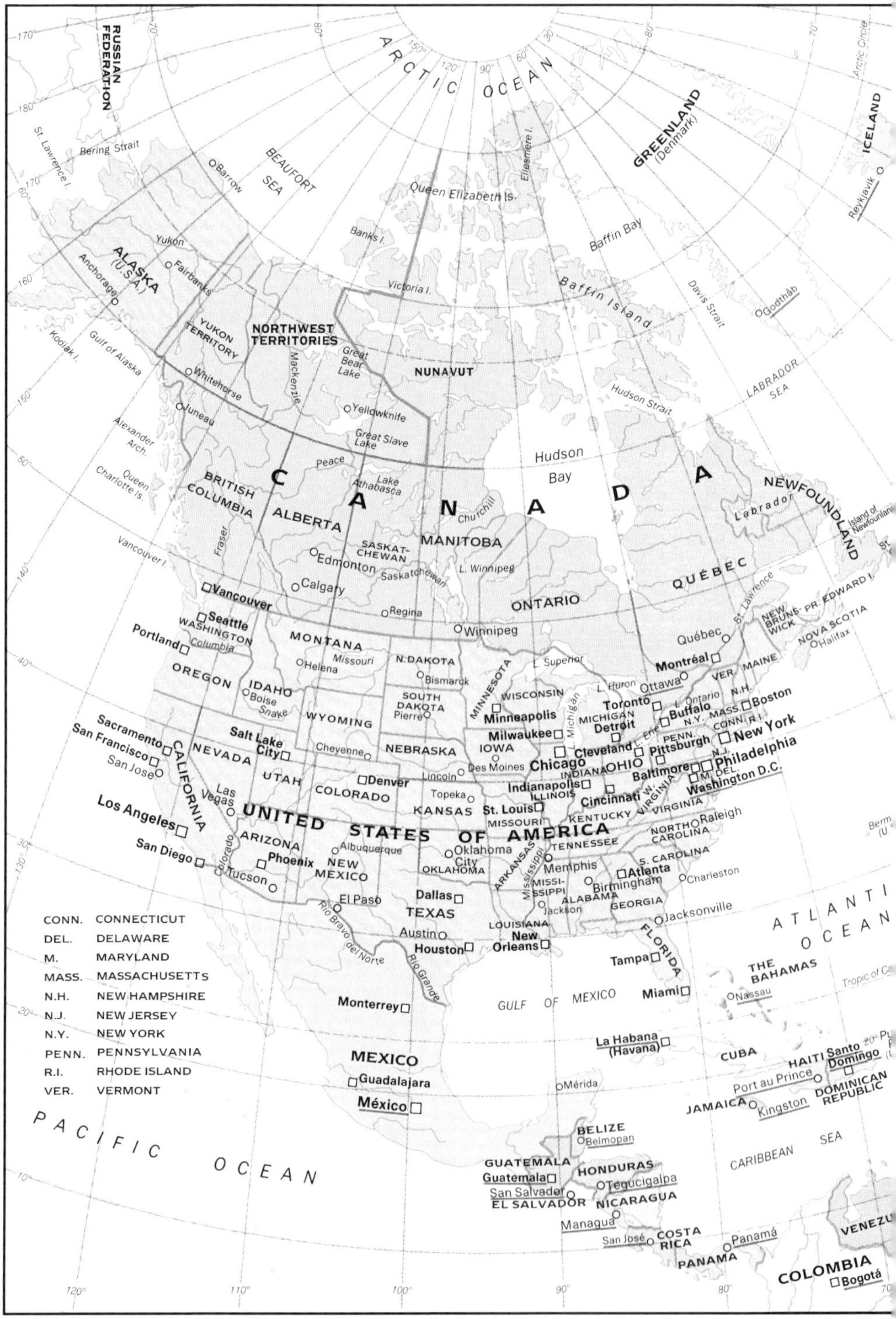

Scale 1:47 270 000

0 500 1000 1500 km

0 250 500 750 1000 miles

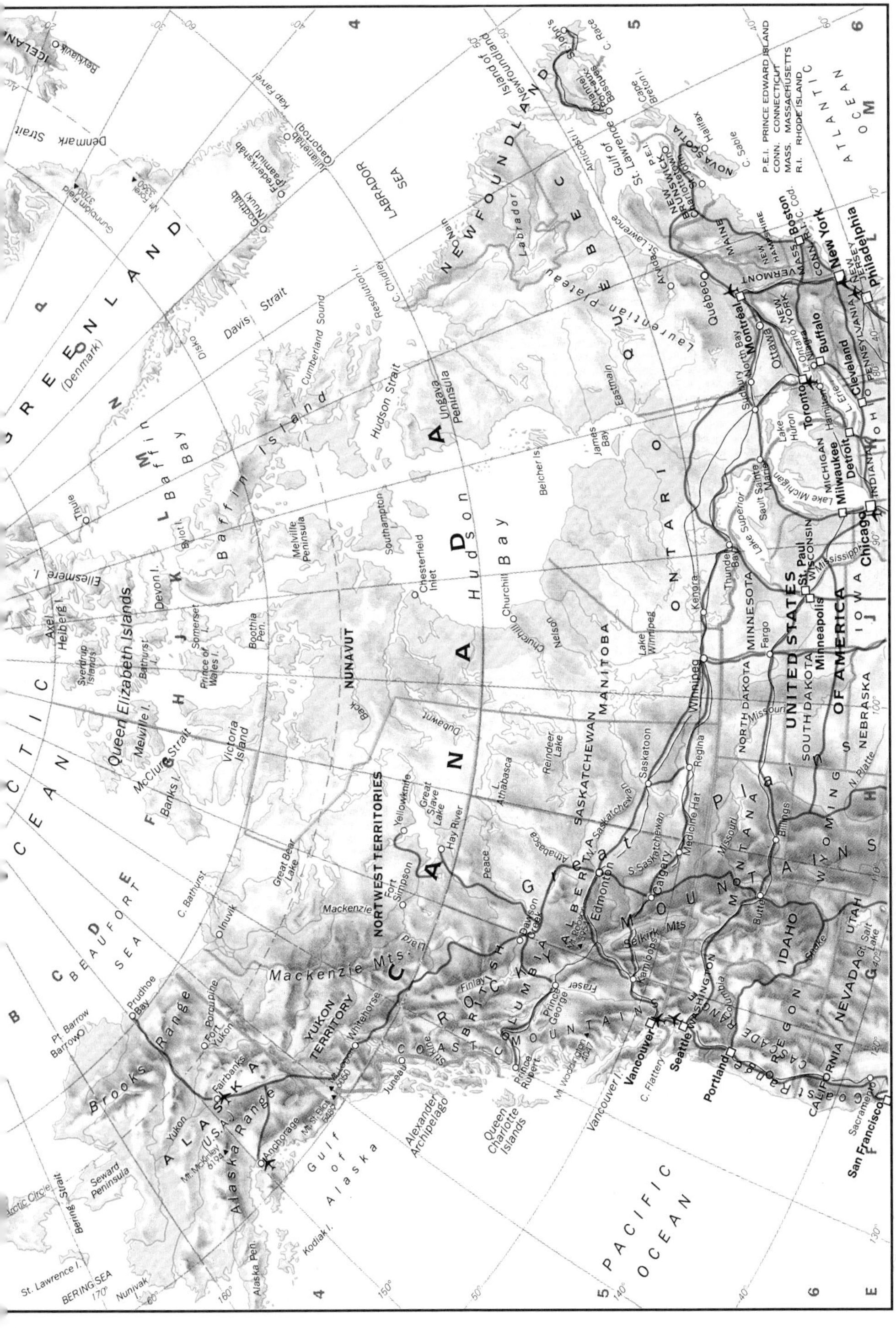

Scale 1:34 000 000

0 250 500 750 1000 km

0 150 300 450 600 miles

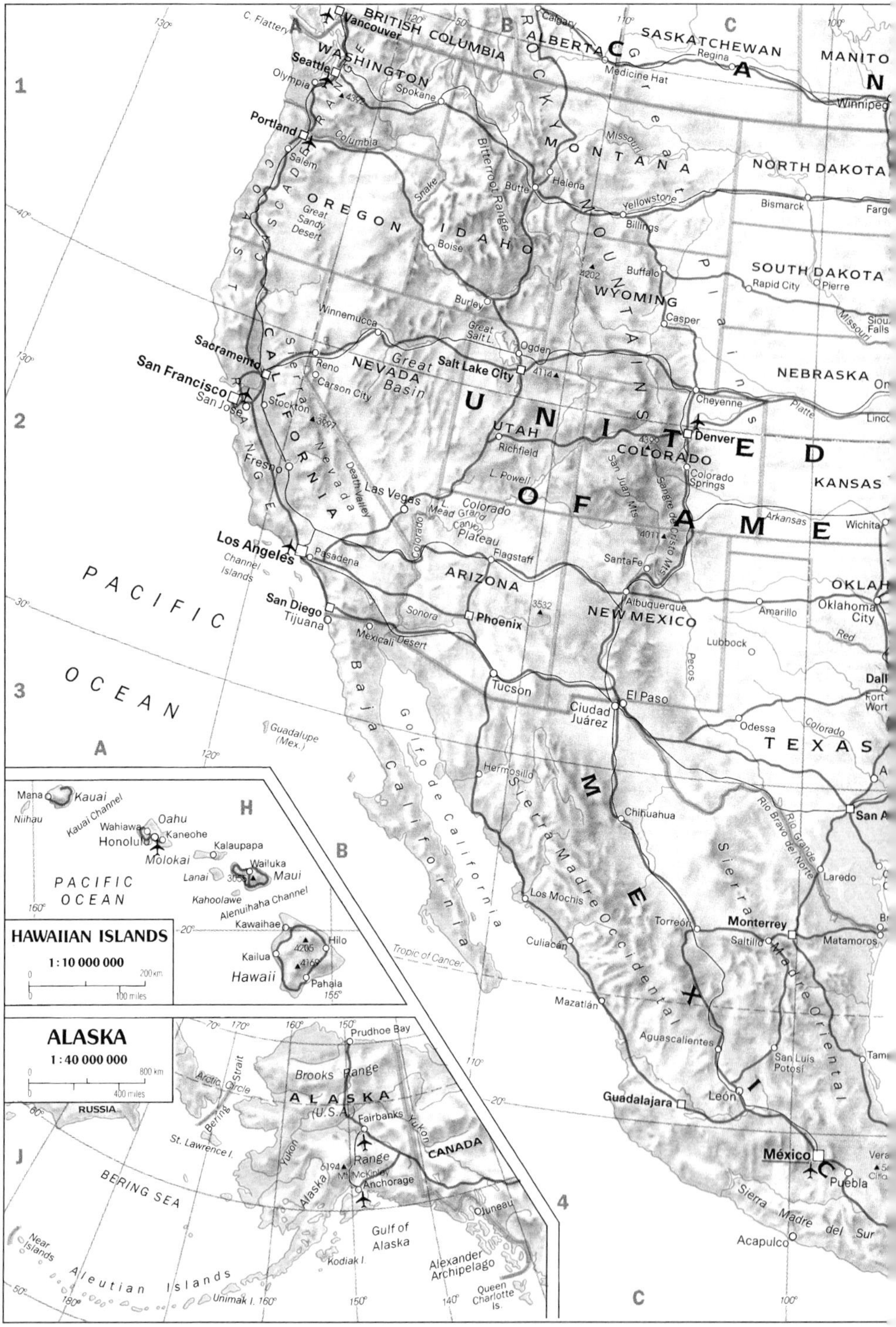

Scale 1:22 700 000

0 250 500 750 1000 km

0 200 400 600 miles

CONN. CONNECTICUT
MASS. MASSACHUSETTS
R.I. RHODE ISLAND
N.J. NEW JERSEY
DEL. DELAWARE
ATLANTIC OCEAN
GULF OF MEXICO
CARIBBEAN SEA
QUÉBEC
ONTARIO
NEW BRUNSWICK
NOVA SCOTIA
Prince Edward I.
Halifax
Bay of Fundy
Québec
Montréal
Ottawa
Sudbury
North Bay
Sault Ste. Marie
Thunder Bay
Lake Superior
Lake Huron
Lake Michigan
L. Ontario
Lake Erie
St. Lawrence
MICHIGAN
WISCONSIN
MAINE
VERMONT
NEW HAMPSHIRE
Augusta
Montpelier
Concord
Boston
C. Cod
Providence
Long Island
Hartford
New York
Albany
Syracuse
Toronto
Hamilton
Niagara Falls
Buffalo
NEW YORK
Grand Rapids
Milwaukee
Madison
Lansing
Detroit
Chicago
Rockford
Toledo
Cleveland
Akron
PENNSYLVANIA
Pittsburgh
Harrisburg
Newark
Philadelphia
Trenton
Camden
Baltimore
Dover
Annapolis
Washington D.C.
MARYLAND
OHIO
Colombus
Dayton
Cincinnati
INDIANA
Ft. Wayne
Indianapolis
ILLINOIS
Springfield
St. Louis
WEST VIRGINIA
Charleston
VIRGINIA
Richmond
Norfolk
Frankfort
Louisville
Evansville
KENTUCKY
Greensboro
Durham
Raleigh
Roanoke
NORTH CAROLINA
Charlotte
Wilmington
Nashville
Knoxville
TENNESSEE
Chattanooga
Memphis
Huntsville
SOUTH CAROLINA
Columbia
Charleston
Atlanta
Augusta
Savannah
Birmingham
ALABAMA
MISSISSIPPI
Macon
Columbus
Montgomery
GEORGIA
Jackson
Jacksonville
Mobile
Tallahassee
Apalachee Bay
LOUISIANA
New Orleans
FLORIDA
Daytona Beach
Orlando
Tampa
St. Petersburg
Lake Okeechobee
Fort Lauderdale
Miami
Key West
Straits of Florida
Bermuda (U.K.)
Grand Bahama I.
Great Abaco I.
Eleuthera I.
THE BAHAMAS
Nassau
Cat I.
Andros I.
Long I.
Acklins I.
Great Inagua I.
Tropic of Cancer
La Habana (Havana)
Pinar del Rio
Camaguey
CUBA
Guantánamo
Santiago de Cuba
HAITI
Port au Prince
DOMINICAN REPUBLIC
Santo Domingo
Yucatán Channel
Mérida
Puerto Juárez
Yucatan
Cayman Is. (U.K.)
Kingston
JAMAICA
Belmopan
BELIZE
GUATEMALA
Guatemala
San Pedro Sula
HONDURAS
NICARAGUA
Aruba (Neth.)
Curaçao (Neth.)
COLOMBIA
VENEZUELA
ARKANSAS
Little Rock
MISSOURI
Springfield
Des Moines
Shreveport
de Campeche
UNITED STATES
CANADA

Scale 1:9 770 000

0 100 200 300 km

0 100 200 miles

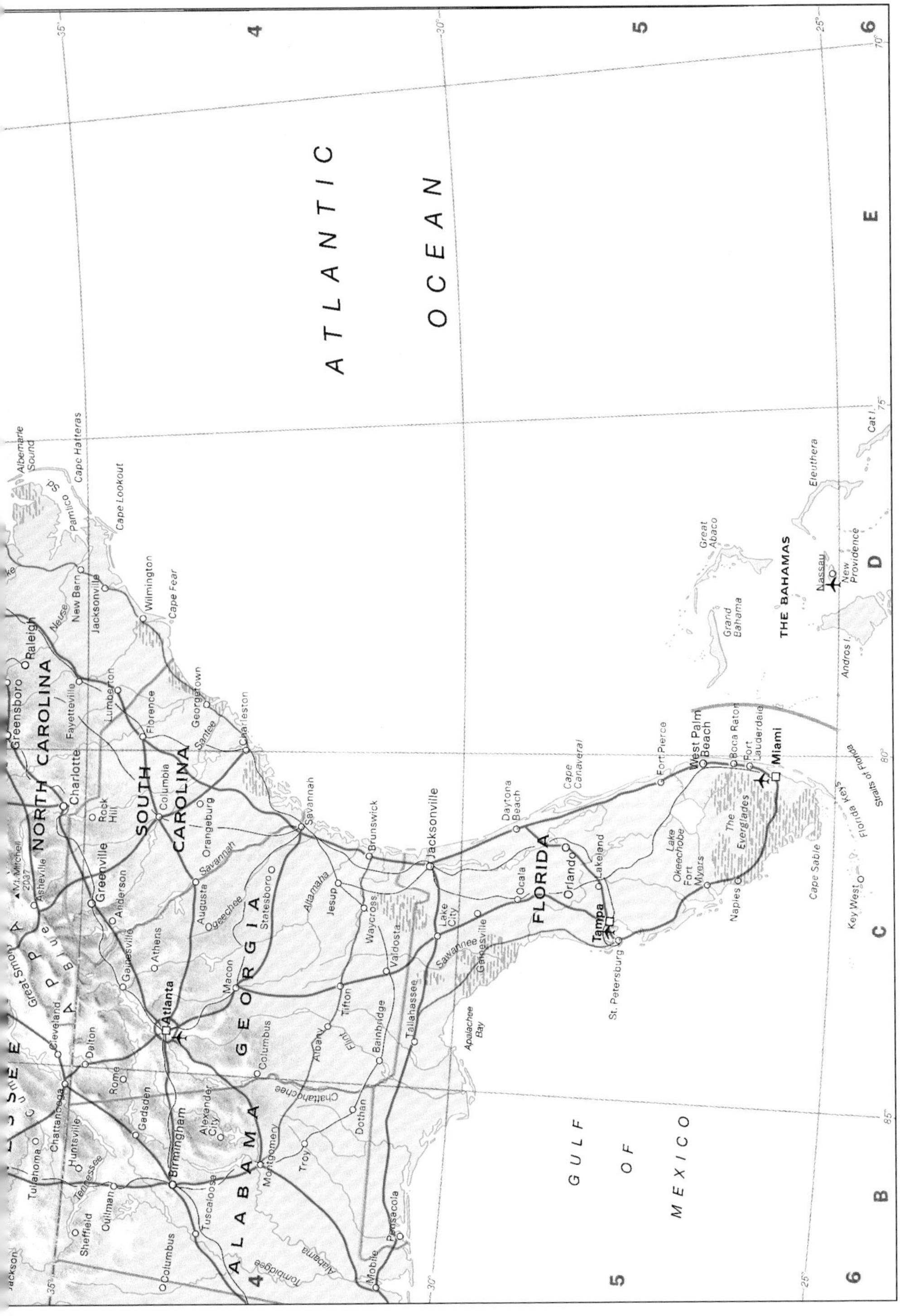
ATLANTIC
OCEAN
GULF
OF
MEXICO
NORTH CAROLINA
SOUTH CAROLINA
GEORGIA
ALABAMA
FLORIDA
THE BAHAMAS
Albemarle Sound
Pamlico Sd
Cape Hatteras
Cape Lookout
Cape Fear
Greensboro
Raleigh
Neuse
New Bern
Jacksonville
Wilmington
Fayetteville
Lumberton
Charlotte
Rock Hill
Florence
Georgetown
Santee
Charleston
Columbia
Orangeburg
Greenville
Anderson
Asheville
Mt. Mitchell 2037
Savannah
Augusta
Ogeechee
Statesboro
Gainesville
Athens
Atlanta
Macon
Altamaha
Jesup
Brunswick
Waycross
Valdosta
Tifton
Albany
Flint
Bainbridge
Columbus
Dalton
Rome
Cleveland
Chattanooga
Huntsville
Gadsden
Birmingham
Alexander City
Montgomery
Troy
Dothan
Chattahoochee
Tuscaloosa
Tennessee
Cullman
Sheffield
Tullahoma
Columbus
Tombigbee
Alabama
Mobile
Pensacola
Tallahassee
Apalachee Bay
Jacksonville
Lake City
Suwannee
Gainesville
Ocala
Daytona Beach
Cape Canaveral
Orlando
Lakeland
Tampa
St. Petersburg
Fort Pierce
West Palm Beach
Lake Okeechobee
Fort Myers
The Everglades
Naples
Boca Raton
Fort Lauderdale
Miami
Cape Sable
Key West
Florida Keys
Straits of Florida
Grand Bahama
Great Abaco
Andros I.
Nassau
New Providence
Eleuthera
Cat I.
Great Smoky
Blue Ridge
A B C D E
4 5 6

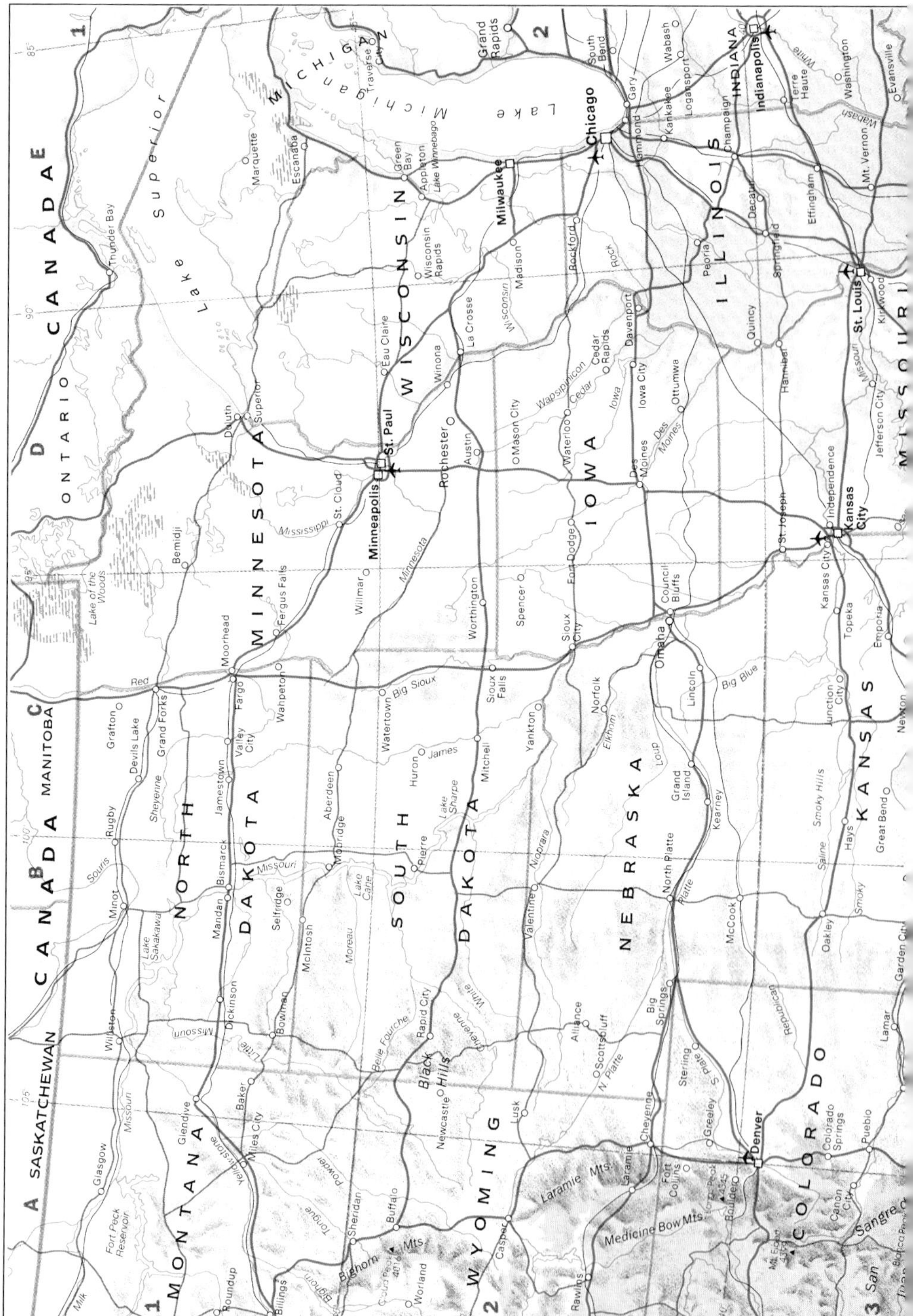

Scale 1:9 770 000

0 100 200 300 km

0 100 200 miles

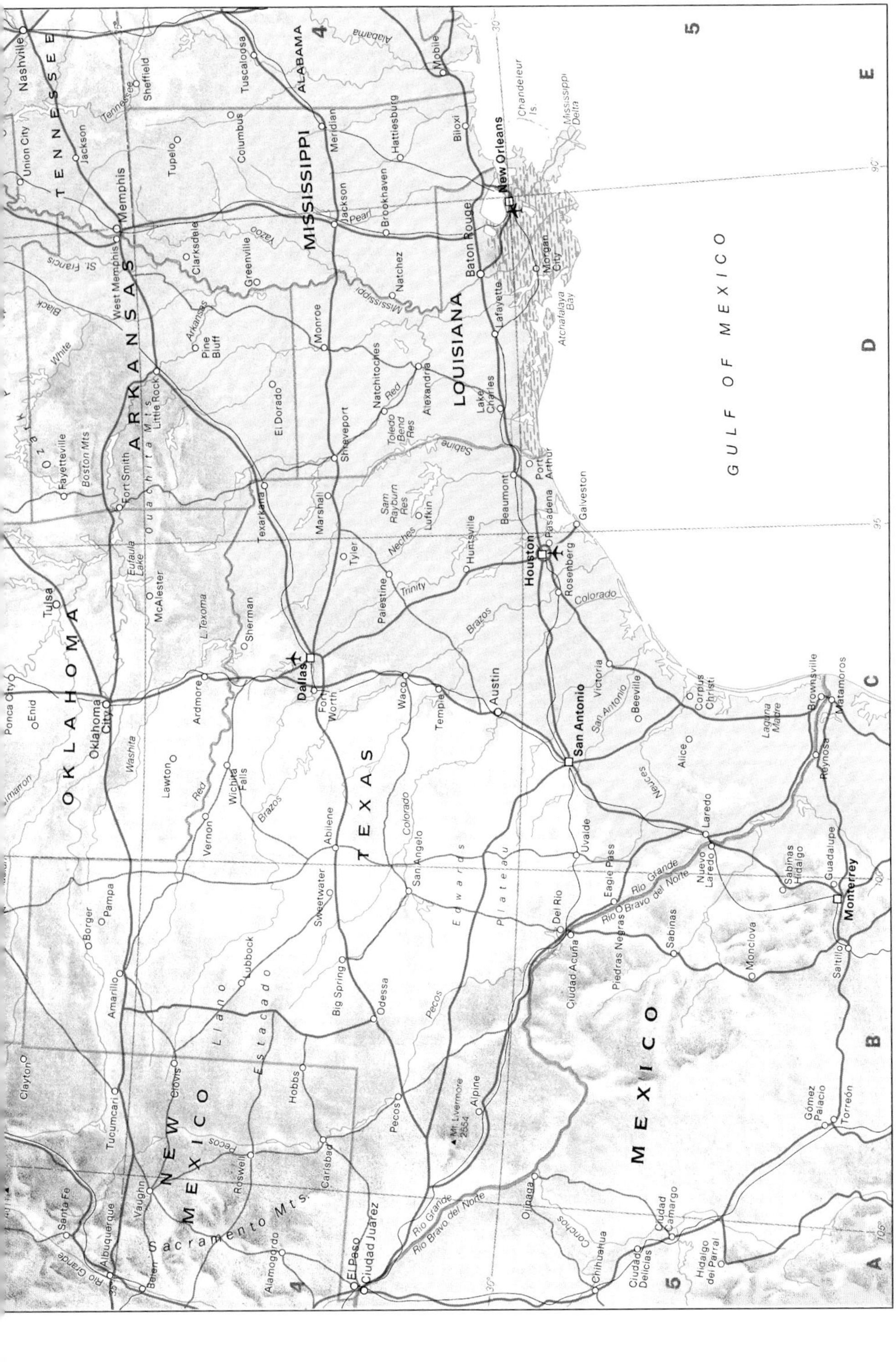
TENNESSEE
Nashville
Union City
Jackson
Memphis
Tennessee
Sheffield
Tuscaloosa
ALABAMA
Alabama
Mobile
Tupelo
Columbus
MISSISSIPPI
Meridian
Hattiesburg
Biloxi
Jackson
Pearl
Brookhaven
Clarksdale
Greenville
Yazoo
Natchez
Mississippi
Chandeleur Is.
Mississippi Delta
New Orleans
Baton Rouge
Morgan City
Atchafalaya Bay
Lafayette
LOUISIANA
Monroe
Alexandria
Natchitoches
Red
Toledo Bend Res
Lake Charles
Shreveport
El Dorado
Sabine
ARKANSAS
West Memphis
St. Francis
Black
White
Arkansas
Pine Bluff
Little Rock
Ouachita Mts
Ozark
Fayetteville
Boston Mts
Fort Smith
Texarkana
Marshall
Sam Rayburn Res
Lufkin
Beaumont
Port Arthur
Galveston
Pasadena
Houston
Rosenberg
Huntsville
Tyler
Neches
Palestine
Trinity
Colorado
Brazos
GULF OF MEXICO
OKLAHOMA
Tulsa
Eufaula Lake
McAlester
L. Texoma
Sherman
Dallas
Fort Worth
Ponca City
Enid
Oklahoma City
Ardmore
Waco
Temple
Austin
Victoria
San Antonio
Beeville
Corpus Christi
Laguna Madre
Brownsville
Matamoros
Reynosa
Alice
Nueces
Laredo
Nuevo Laredo
Washita
Lawton
Red
Wichita Falls
Brazos
Vernon
Abilene
TEXAS
Colorado
San Angelo
Edwards Plateau
Uvalde
Eagle Pass
Rio Grande
Rio Bravo del Norte
Sabinas Hidalgo
Guadalupe
Monterrey
Pampa
Borger
Sweetwater
Del Rio
Piedras Negras
Ciudad Acuña
Sabinas
Monclova
Saltillo
Amarillo
Lubbock
Llano Estacado
Big Spring
Odessa
Pecos
MEXICO
Clayton
Tucumcari
Clovis
NEW MEXICO
Hobbs
Pecos
Mt. Livermore 2554
Alpine
Roswell
Carlsbad
Vaughn
Santa Fe
Albuquerque
Rio Grande
Belen
Sacramento Mts.
Alamogordo
El Paso
Ciudad Juárez
Ojinaga
Conchos
Chihuahua
Ciudad Delicias
Ciudad Camargo
Hidalgo del Parral
Gómez Palacio
Torreón
A
B
C
D
E
4
5

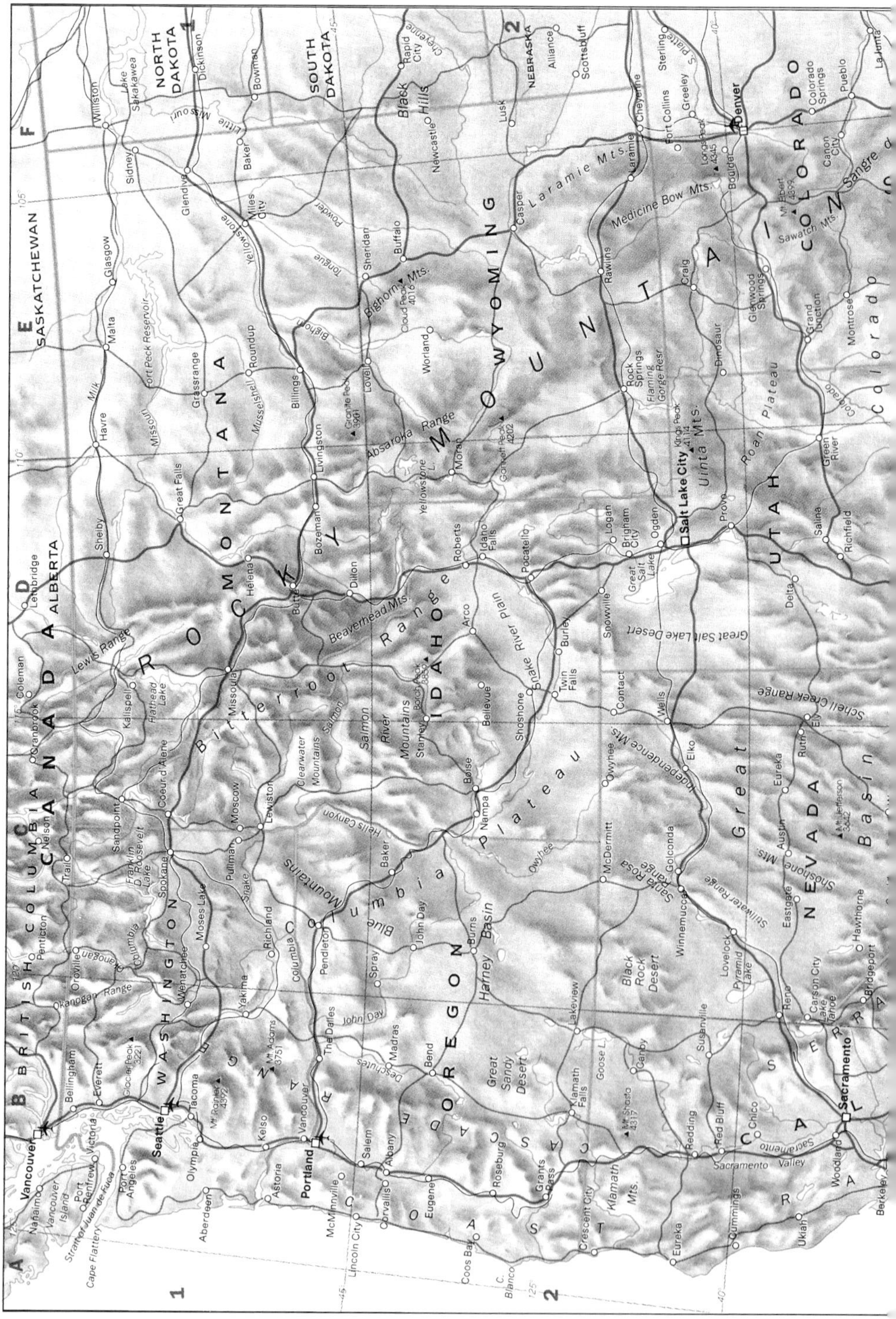

Scale 1:9 770 000

0 100 200 300 km

0 100 200 miles

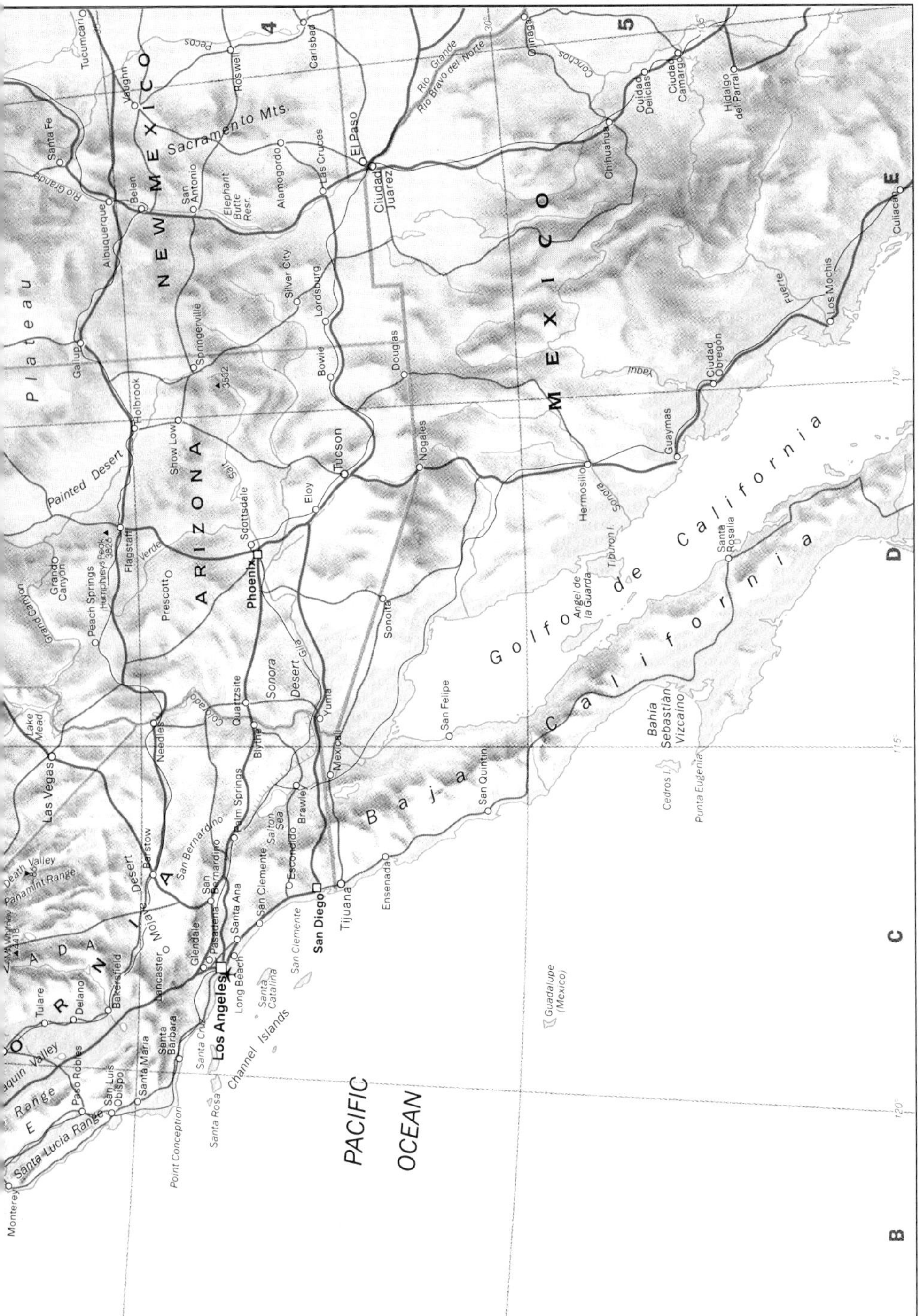

Tucumcari
Santa Fe
Rio Grande
Vaughn
Pecos
Roswell
Carlsbad
NEW MEXICO
Sacramento Mts.
Albuquerque
Belen
San Antonio
Elephant Butte Resr.
Alamogordo
Las Cruces
El Paso
Ciudad Juárez
Silver City
Lordsburg
Gallup
Springerville
Holbrook
Bowie
Douglas
Tucson
Nogales
Show Low
ARIZONA
Salt
Eloy
Scottsdale
Phoenix
Flagstaff
Humphreys Peak
Verde
Prescott
Grand Canyon
Peach Springs
Painted Desert
Plateau
Sonoita
Gila
Sonora Desert
Quartzsite
Yuma
Blythe
Colorado
Needles
Lake Mead
Las Vegas
Mexicali
Brawley
Salton Sea
Palm Springs
San Bernardino
Barstow
Mojave Desert
Death Valley
Panamint Range
San Bernardino
Santa Ana
San Clemente
Escondido
San Diego
Tijuana
Ensenada
Glendale
Pasadena
Los Angeles
Long Beach
Lancaster
Bakersfield
Delano
Tulare
Santa Catalina
San Clemente
Channel Islands
Santa Cruz
Santa Rosa
Santa Barbara
Santa Maria
San Luis Obispo
Paso Robles
Santa Lucia Range
Point Conception
Monterey
PACIFIC OCEAN
Guadalupe (Mexico)
San Quintín
Baja California
San Felipe
Golfo de California
Bahía Sebastián Vizcaíno
Cedros I.
Punta Eugenia
Angel de la Guarda
Tiburón I.
Hermosillo
Sonora
Santa Rosalía
Guaymas
Ciudad Obregón
Yaqui
MEXICO
Los Mochis
Fuerte
Culiacán
Chihuahua
Ciudad Delicias
Ciudad Camargo
Hidalgo del Parral
Conchos
Ojinaga
Rio Grande
Río Bravo del Norte
B
C
D
E
4
5

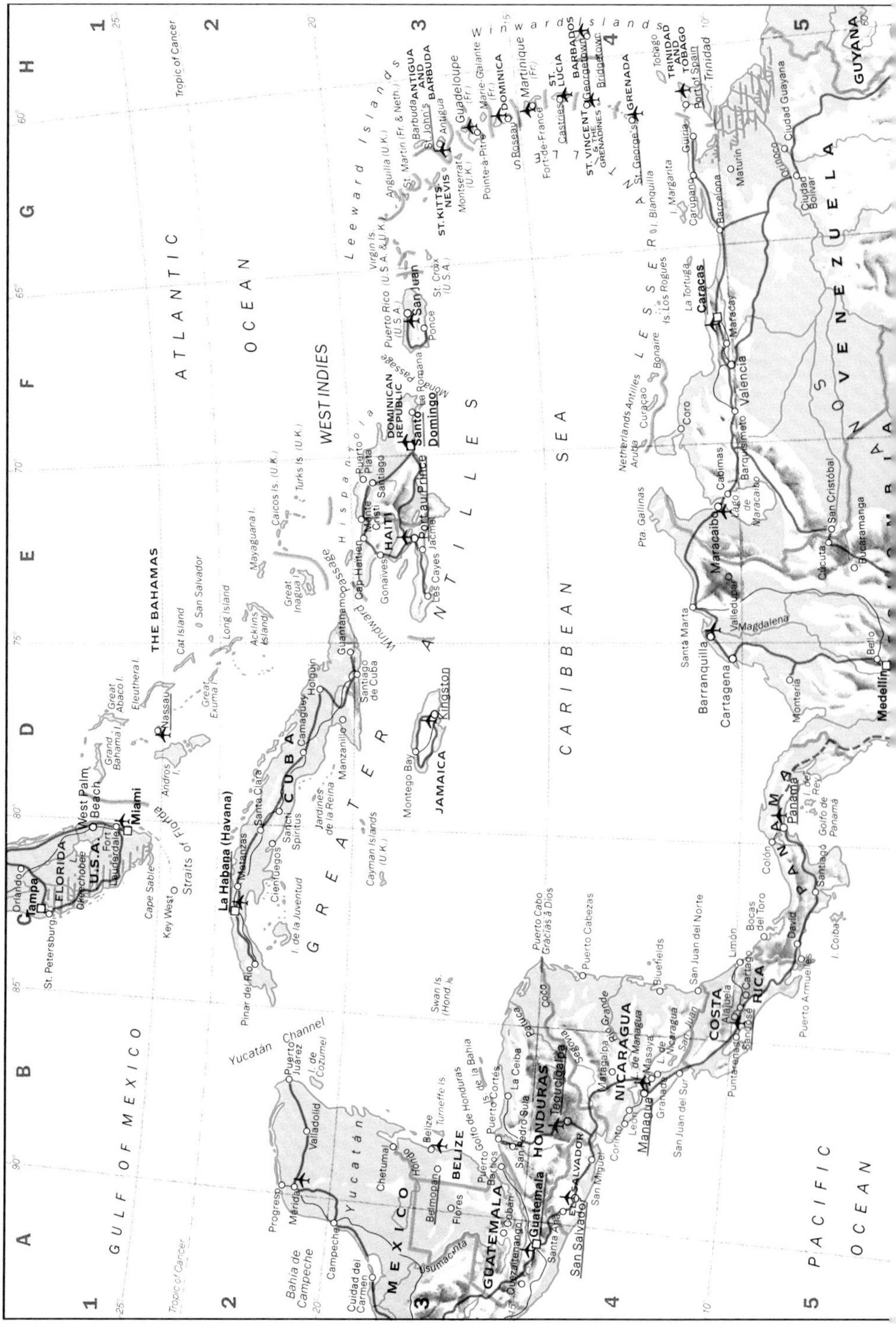

Scale 1:19 300 000

0 200 400 600 800 km

0 250 500 miles

Scale 1:42 000 000

0 400 800 1200 1600 km

0 200 400 600 800 1000 miles

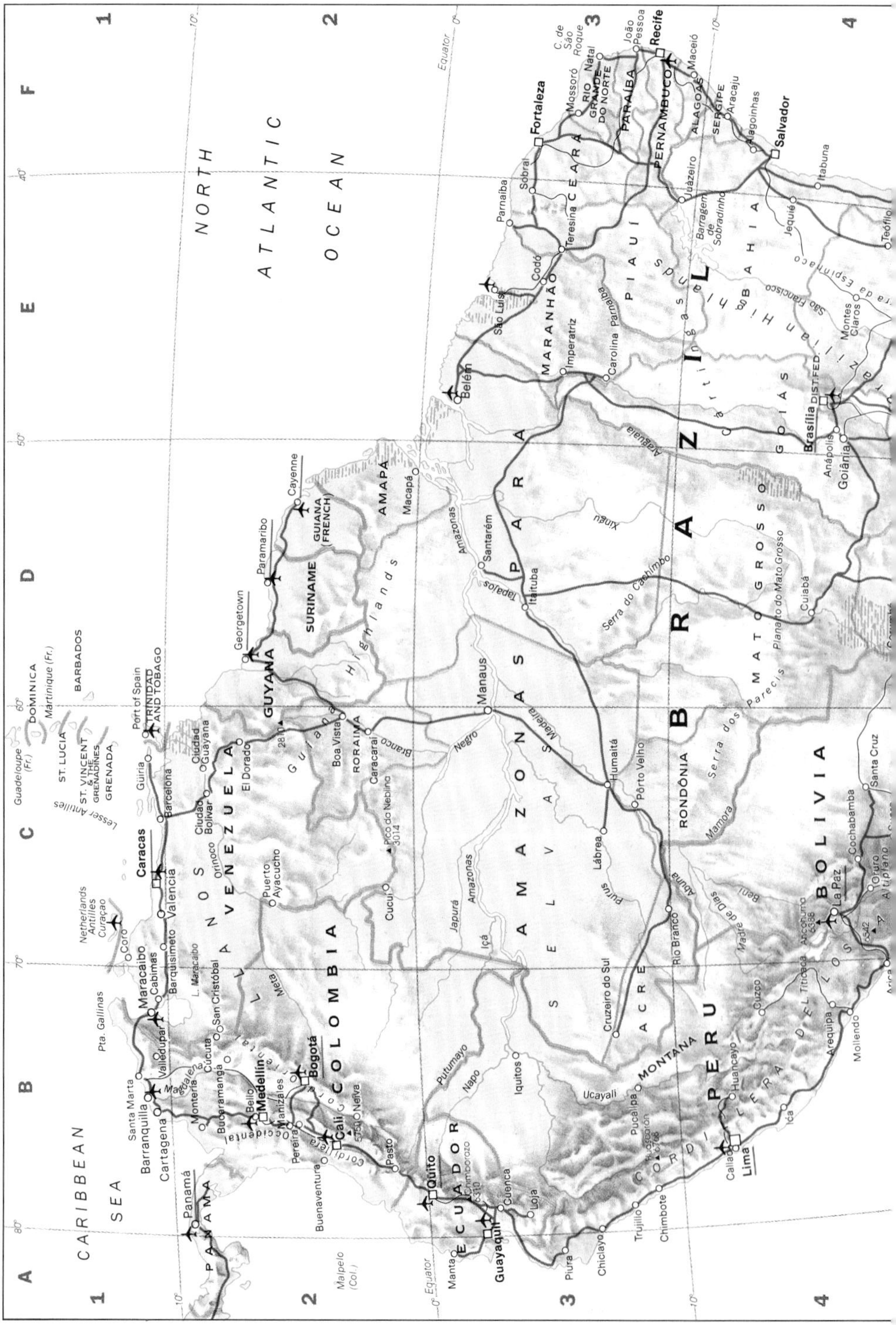

Scale 1:29 000 000

0 200 400 600 800 1000 km

0 150 300 450 600 miles

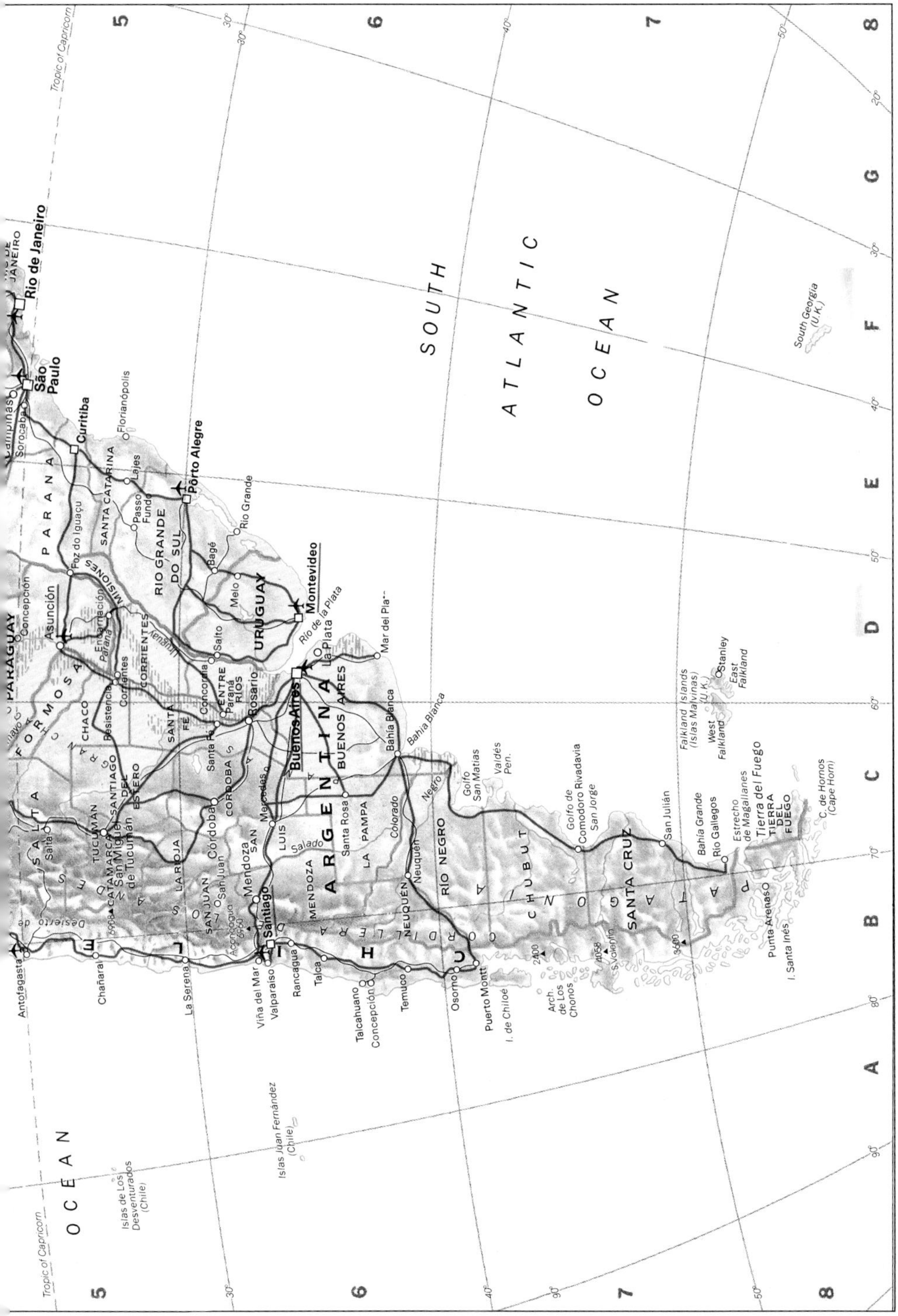
SOUTH ATLANTIC OCEAN
OCEAN
Tropic of Capricorn
Rio de Janeiro
São Paulo
Curitiba
Florianópolis
Pôrto Alegre
Rio Grande
Montevideo
URUGUAY
Buenos Aires
La Plata
Mar del Plata
Bahía Blanca
Rosario
Córdoba
Mendoza
Santiago
Valparaíso
Viña del Mar
Rancagua
Talca
Talcahuano
Concepción
Temuco
Osorno
Puerto Montt
I. de Chiloé
Arch. de Los Chonos
Comodoro Rivadavia
Golfo San Jorge
San Julián
Río Gallegos
Bahía Grande
Estrecho de Magallanes
Tierra del Fuego
Punta Arenas
I. Santa Inés
C. de Hornos (Cape Horn)
Falkland Islands (Islas Malvinas) (U.K.)
West Falkland
East Falkland
Stanley
South Georgia (U.K.)
Islas Juan Fernández (Chile)
Islas de Los Desventurados (Chile)
Antofagasta
Chañaral
La Serena
Salta
San Miguel de Tucumán
Santiago del Estero
Corrientes
Resistencia
Asunción
PARAGUAY
Encarnación
Posadas
Foz do Iguaçu
Santa Fe
Paraná
Concordia
Salto
Melo
Bagé
Passo Fundo
Lajes
Sorocaba
Neuquén
Santa Rosa
Golfo San Matías
Valdés Pen.
ARGENTINA
CHILE
SANTA CRUZ
CHUBUT
RÍO NEGRO
NEUQUÉN
LA PAMPA
BUENOS AIRES
MENDOZA
SAN LUIS
SAN JUAN
LA RIOJA
CÓRDOBA
SANTA FE
ENTRE RÍOS
CORRIENTES
MISIONES
CHACO
FORMOSA
SALTA
TUCUMÁN
CATAMARCA
SANTIAGO DEL ESTERO
RIO GRANDE DO SUL
SANTA CATARINA
PARANÁ
TIERRA DEL FUEGO
Aconcagua 6960
A B C D E F G
5 6 7 8

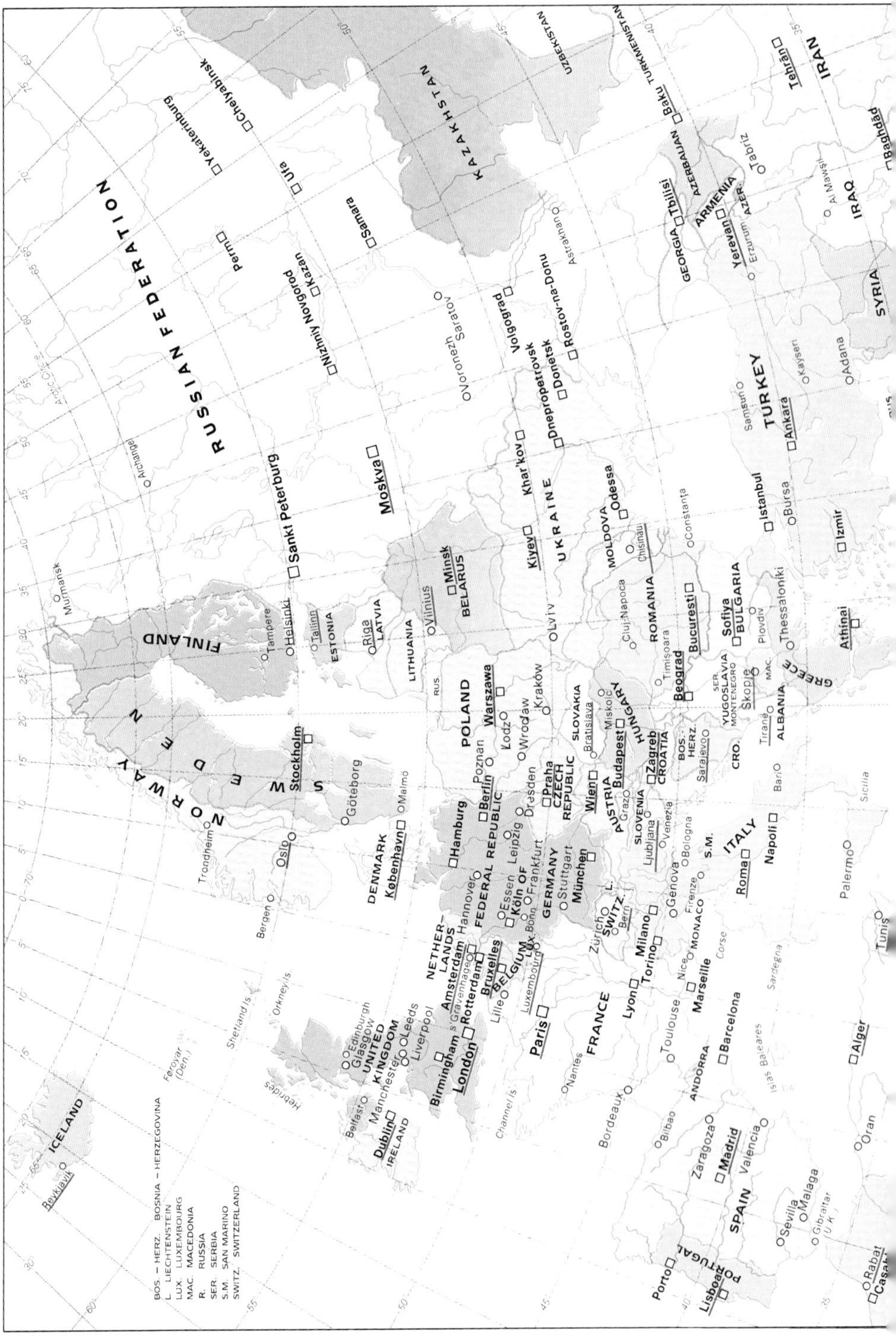

Scale 1:29 000 000

0 200 400 600 800 1000 km

0 150 300 450 600 miles

Scale 1:9 000 000

0 100 200 300 km

0 100 200 miles

Scale 1:2 950 000

0 20 40 60 80 100 km

0 15 30 45 60 miles

WALES
London
Birmingham
Cambridge
Ely
Thetford
Bury St. Edmunds
Ipswich
Felixstowe
Harwich
Clacton-on-Sea
Saxmundham
Colchester
Chelmsford
Basildon
Southend-on-Sea
Margate
Canterbury
Dover
Hythe
Ashford
Maidstone
Rochester
Hastings
Eastbourne
Lewes
Brighton
Worthing
Bognor Regis
Chichester
Horsham
Crawley
Guildford
Tonbridge
Royal Tunbridge Wells
Harlow
St. Albans
Watford
Luton
Bedford
Northampton
Corby
Milton Keynes
Aylesbury
Chesham
Windsor
Reading
Aldershot
Basingstoke
Winchester
Southampton
Portsmouth
Havant
Fareham
Cowes
Newport
ISLE OF WIGHT
Bournemouth
Poole
Ringwood
Salisbury
Warminster
Trowbridge
Chippenham
Swindon
Didcot
Oxford
Banbury
Buckingham
Rugby
Coventry
Warwick
Stratford-on-Avon
Worcester
Cheltenham
Gloucester
Stroud
Kingswood
Bristol
Bath
Weston-super-Mare
Hereford
Dudley
Warley
Church Stretton
Llandrindod Wells
Builth Wells
Abergavenny
Cwmbran
Newport
Cardiff
Barry
MID GLAMORGAN
Merthyr Tydfil
Brecon Beacons
Swansea
Port Talbot
Carmarthen
Carmarthen Bay
Aberystwyth
Cardigan
Fishguard
St. Davids
Milford Haven
Pembroke
St. George's Channel
Bristol Channel
Lundy
Ilfracombe
Barnstaple
Bideford
Bude
Bude Bay
Exmoor
Bridgwater
Taunton
Yeovil
Axminster
Dorchester
Weymouth
Portland Bill
Lyme Bay
Exeter
Okehampton
Dartmoor
Torquay
Start Pt.
Plymouth
Tamar
Bodmin
St. Austell
Truro
Falmouth
Newquay
St. Ives
Penzance
Sennen
Land's End
Lizard Pt.
English Channel
Cotswold Hills
Chiltern Hills
North Downs
South Downs
Thames
Severn
Wye
Avon
Kennet
Exe
Stour
Waveney
The Solent
Strait of Dover
Channel Tunnel
Calais
Boulogne
Dieppe
Rouen
Seine
Le Havre
Baie de la Seine
Caen
Cherbourg
Alderney
Guernsey
St. Peter Port
Sark
CHANNEL ISLANDS
Jersey
St. Helier
FRANCE
West from Greenwich
East from Greenwich
Isles of Scilly
St. Martin's
St. Mary's

Scotland

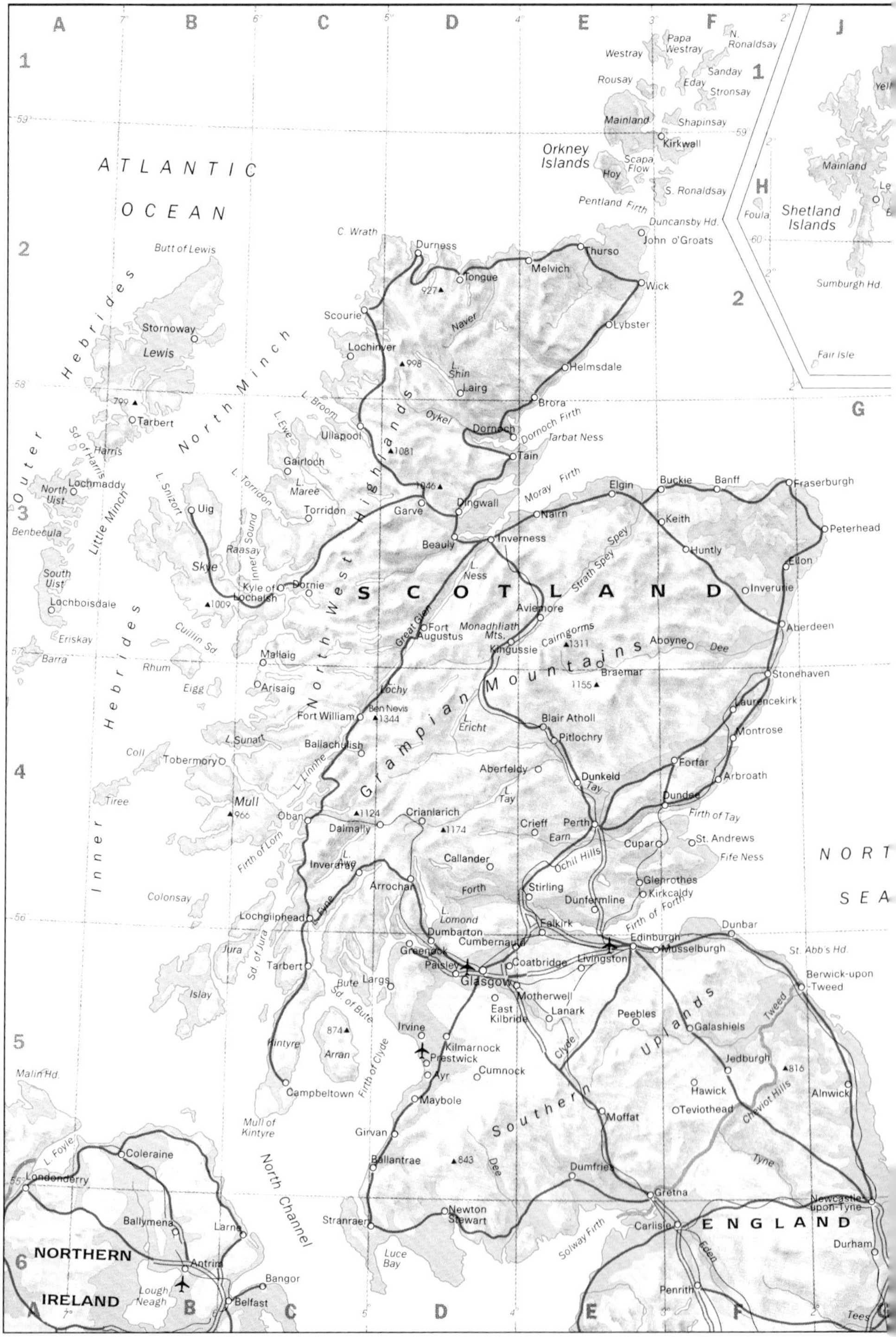

Scale 1:2 950 000

0 20 40 60 80 100 km

0 15 30 45 60 miles

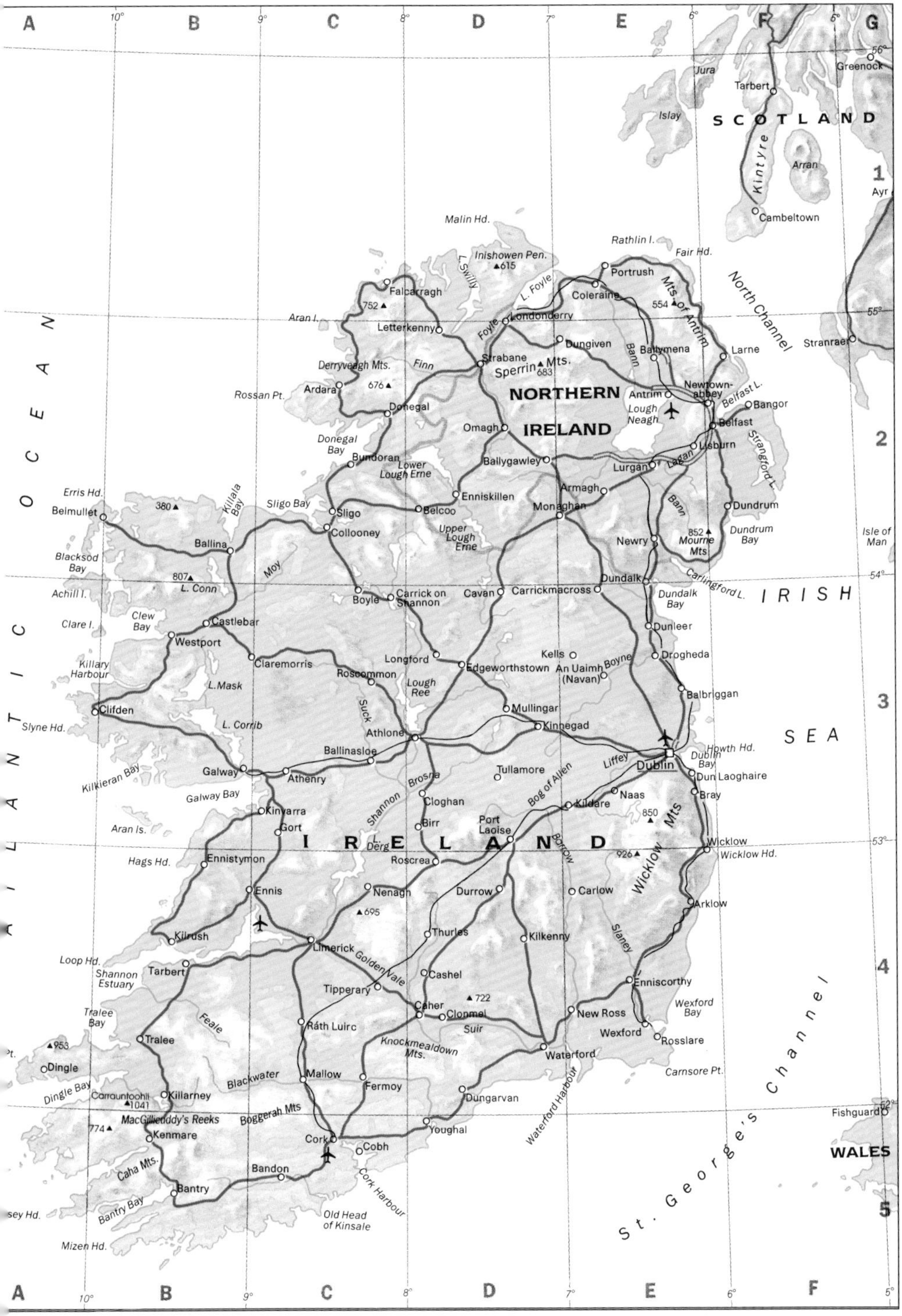

Scale 1:2 950 000

0 20 40 60 80 100 km

0 15 30 45 60 miles

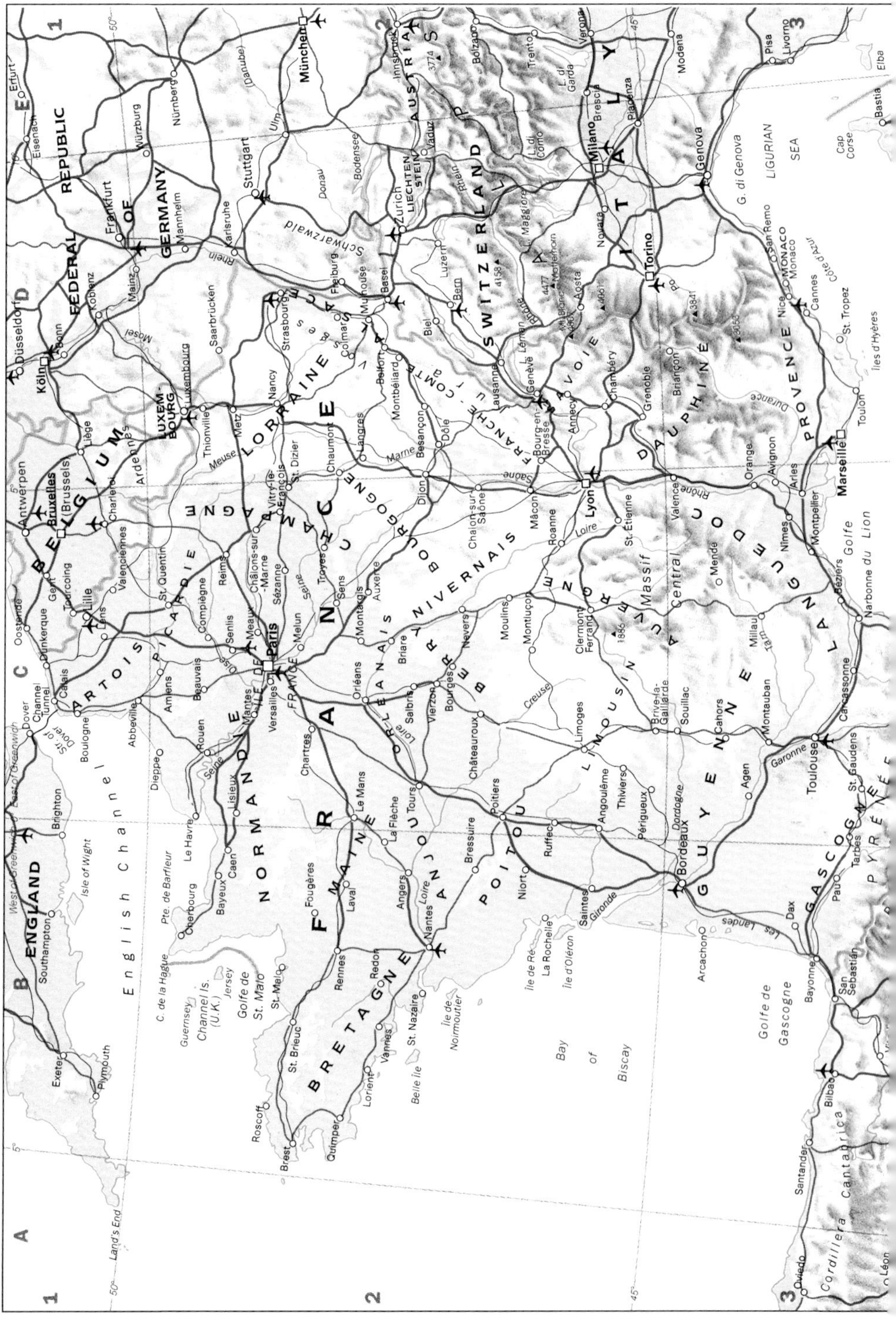

Scale 1:7 250 000

0 100 200 300 km

0 100 200 miles

Scale 1:7 250 000

0 100 200 300 km

0 100 200 miles

Scale 1:7 400 000

0 100 200 300 km

0 100 200 miles

Budapest
Debrecen
Karcag
Szolnok
Kecskemet
Kiskunfelegyháza
Szeged
Makó
Subotica
VOJVODINA
Osijek
Novi Sad
Ruma
Vršac
Beograd
(Belgrade)
Šabac
Tuzla
Loznica
Sarajevo
Kragujevac
Jagodina
Paraćin
Čačak
YUGOSLAVIA
Kruševac
SERBIA
Niš
Pirot
Novi Pazar
Leskovac
Kosovska-Mitrovica
Priština
Ivangrad
Peć
KOSOVO
Uroševac
Vranje
MONTENEGRO
Podgorica
Kotor
Shkodër
Kumanovo
Skopje
Titov Veles
MACEDONIA
Gevgelija
Bitola
Tiranë (Tirana)
Durrës
Berat
Vlorë
Korçe
Kastoria
Brindisi
Gallipoli
C. Sta Maria di Leuca
Strait of Otranto
Kérkira (Corfu)
Igoumenítsa
Ioannina
Kalabáka
Lárisa
Vólos
Árta
Amfilokhía
Lamía
Levkás
Mesolóngion
Kefallinia
Pátrai
Kórinthos
Piraiévs
Athínai (Athens)
Thívai
Khalkís
Livanátais
Pelopónnisos
Pírgos
Zákinthos
Argos
Tripolis
Kalámai
Pilos
Neápolis
Kíthira
IONIAN SEA
IÓNIOI NÍSOI
GREECE
ALBANIA
Thessaloníki
Khalkidhikí
Kateríni
Olimbos 2917
Sérrai
Dráma
Kaválla
Xánthi
Komotini
Alexandroúpolis
Thásos
Samothráki
Límnos
Áyios Evstrátios
Skíathos
Skópelos
Évvoia
Skíros
AEGEAN SEA
Lésvos
Khíos
Sámos
Ikaría
Ándros
Tínos
Kéa
Síros
Míkonos
Kíthnos
Sérifos
Sífnos
Páros
Náxos
KIKLÁDHES
Mílos
Síkinos
Íos
Amorgós
Thíra
Astipálaia
Anáfi
DHODHEKÁNISOS
Léros
Kálimnos
Kós
Tílos
Ródhos (Rhodes)
Kárpathos
Kásos
Akr. Sídheros
Mirtoan Sea
Sea of Crete
Kríti (Crete)
Khaniá
Iráklion
Timbákion
ROMANIA
Oradea
Salonta
Arad
Cluj-Napoca
Turda
Tirgu Mureş
Sebeş
Deva
Timişoara
Caransebes
Sibiu
TRANSYLVANIA
Braşov
Carpathian Mts
Carpaţii Meridionali
Rimnicu-Vilcea
Piteşti
Cimpina
Ploieşti
Buzău
Urziceni
Focşani
Bacău
Roman
Iaşi
Bîrlad
Tecuci
Galaţi
Brăila
Hîrşova
Medgidia
Constanţa
Mangalia
Bucureşti (Bucharest)
Dobreta-Turnu-Severin
Filiaşi
Slatina
Craiova
Caracal
Videle
Giurgiu
Chisinau
MOLDOVA
UKRAINE
Odessa
Izmail
BLACK SEA
BULGARIA
Vidin
Lom
Pleven
Vratsa
Ruse
Razgrad
Ludogorie
Tolbukhin
Šumen
Varna
Byala
Veliko Turnovo
Stara Planina
Kazanlŭk
Sliven
Burgas
Michurin
Sofiya (Sofia)
Stara Zagora
Dimitrovgrad
Plovdiv
Blagoevgrad
Rodopi Planina
Kulata
Edirne
Babaeski
Çorlu
Istanbul
Üsküdar
Keşan
Sea of Marmara
Marmara
Bandirma
Bursa
Gelibolu
Eceabat
Çanakkale
Gökçeada
Balikesir
Edremit
Ayvalik
Akhisar
Manisa
Izmir
Selçuk
TURKEY
Denizli
Muğla
Bodrum
Marmaris
Dunav
Tisza
Mureş
Morava
Drina
Sava
Drin
Struma
Mesta
Néstos
Olt
Jiu
Prut
Siret
Dunărea
Simav
Gediz
Pindhos
Aliakmon
Piniós
Vijose
Thermaikos Kólpos
K. Strimonikós
K. Singitikós
K. Toronaíos
Messiniakós Kólpos
Lakonikós Kólpos
Parnon
Ohridsko ezero
Prespansko ezero
Skadarsko Jez.
Ohrid
Konjic
Mostar
Gallipoli

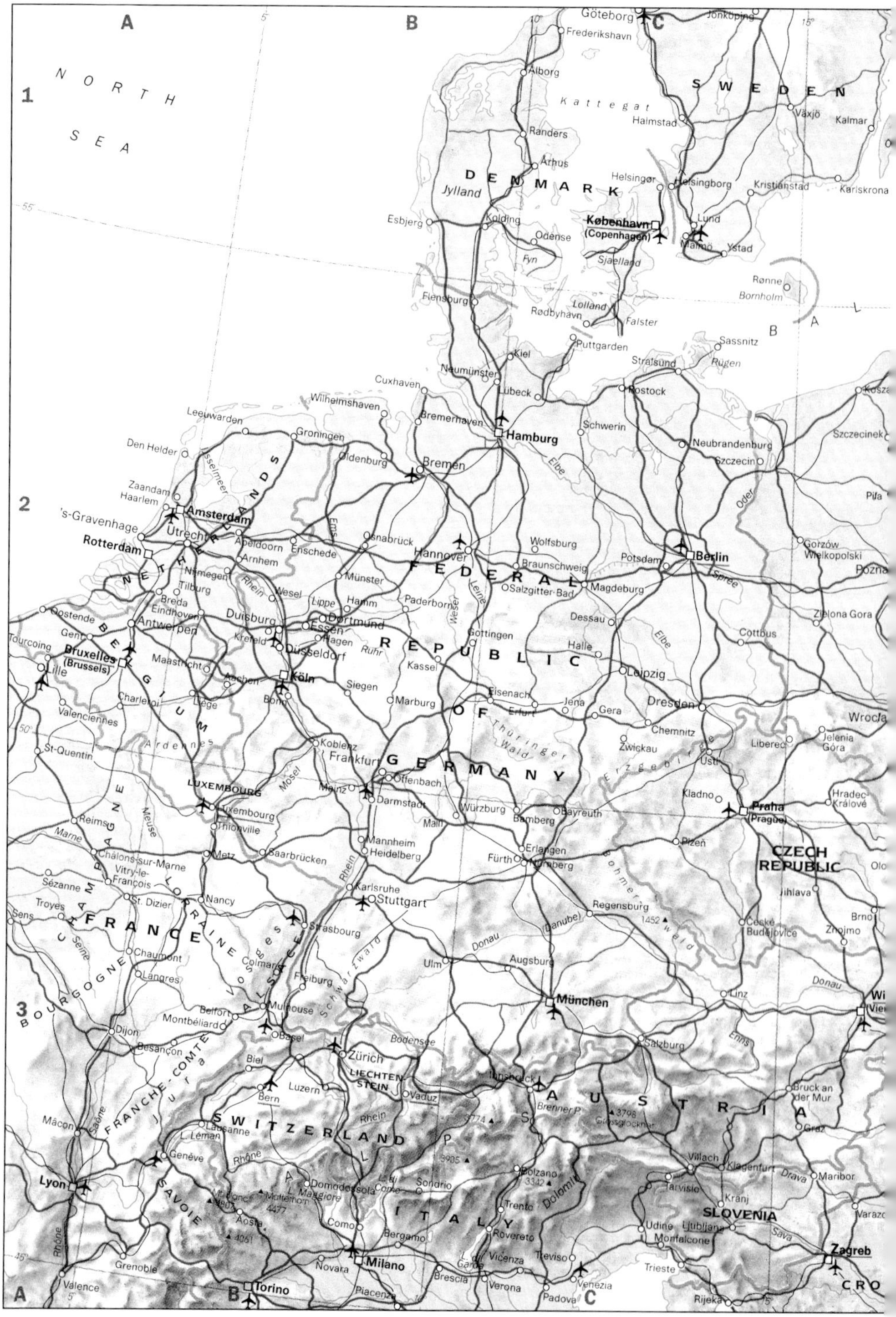

Scale 1:7 400 000

0 100 200 300 km

0 100 200 miles

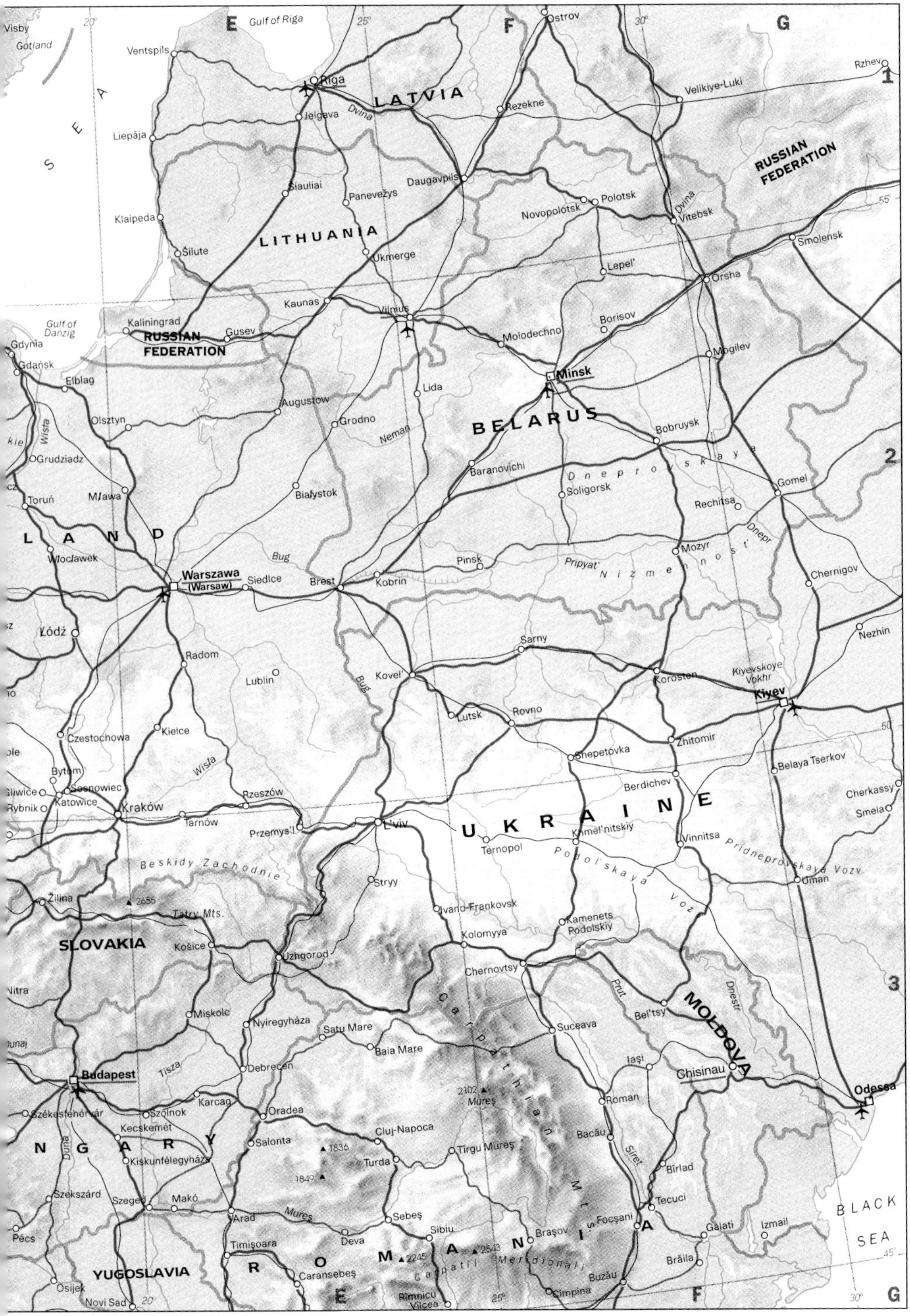
Visby
Gotland
Gulf of Riga
Ventspils
Riga
LATVIA
Dvina
Jelgava
Liepāja
Rezekne
Ostrov
Velikiye-Luki
Rzhev
RUSSIAN FEDERATION
SEA
Siauliai
Panevežys
Daugavpils
Polotsk
Novopolotsk
Vitebsk
Dvina
Klaipeda
Šilute
LITHUANIA
Ukmerge
Smolensk
Lepel'
Orsha
Kaunas
Vilnius
Borisov
Gulf of Danzig
Kaliningrad
RUSSIAN FEDERATION
Gusev
Molodechno
Mogilev
Gdynia
Gdańsk
Minsk
Elblag
Augustow
Lida
Olsztyn
Grodno
Neman
BELARUS
Bobruysk
Wisła
Grudziadz
Dneprovskaya
Baranovichi
Gomel
Soligorsk
Toruń
Mława
Białystok
Rechitsa
LAND
Dnepr
Bug
Mozyr
Pinsk
Włocławek
Warszawa
(Warsaw)
Siedlce
Brest
Kobrin
Pripyat'
Nizmennost'
Chernigov
Łódź
Nezhin
Sarny
Radom
Lublin
Kovel'
Korosten
Kiyevskoye Vokhr
Kiyev
Bug
Lutsk
Rovno
Kielce
Czestochowa
Zhitomir
Shepetovka
Wisła
Bytom
Belaya Tserkov
Gliwice
Sosnowiec
Rzeszów
Berdichev
Cherkassy
Katowice
Rybnik
Kraków
Smela
Tarnów
Przemyśl
L'viv
UKRAINE
Khmel'nitskiy
Ternopol
Vinnitsa
Pridneprovskaya Vozv.
Podol'skaya Voz
Beskidy Zachodnie
Stryy
Uman
Žilina
2655
Tatry Mts.
Ivano-Frankovsk
Kamenets Podolskiy
SLOVAKIA
Košice
Kolomyya
Uzhgorod
Chernovtsy
Nitra
Carpathian Mts
Prut
Dnestr
MOLDOVA
Miskolc
Nyiregyháza
Bel'tsy
Satu Mare
Suceava
Dunaj
Baia Mare
Iaşi
Chisinau
Budapest
Tisza
Debrecen
Odessa
2102
Mureş
Roman
Székesfehérvár
Szolnok
Karcag
Oradea
Kecskemét
Cluj-Napoca
Bacău
HUNGARY
Salonta
1836
Tirgu Mureş
Duna
Kiskunfélegyháza
Turda
Siret
Bîrlad
1849
Szekszárd
Szeged
Makó
Tecuci
Mureş
Arad
Sebeş
BLACK SEA
Pécs
Sibiu
Focşani
Galati
Izmail
Timişoara
Deva
ROMANIA
2245
2543
Braşov
Brăila
Carpatii Meridionali
YUGOSLAVIA
Caransebeş
Osijek
Buzău
Novi Sad
Rîmnicu Vîlcea
Cîmpina
E
F
G
1
2
3
20°
25°
30°
45°
50°
55°

Scale 1:10 900 000

0 100 200 300 km

0 100 200 miles

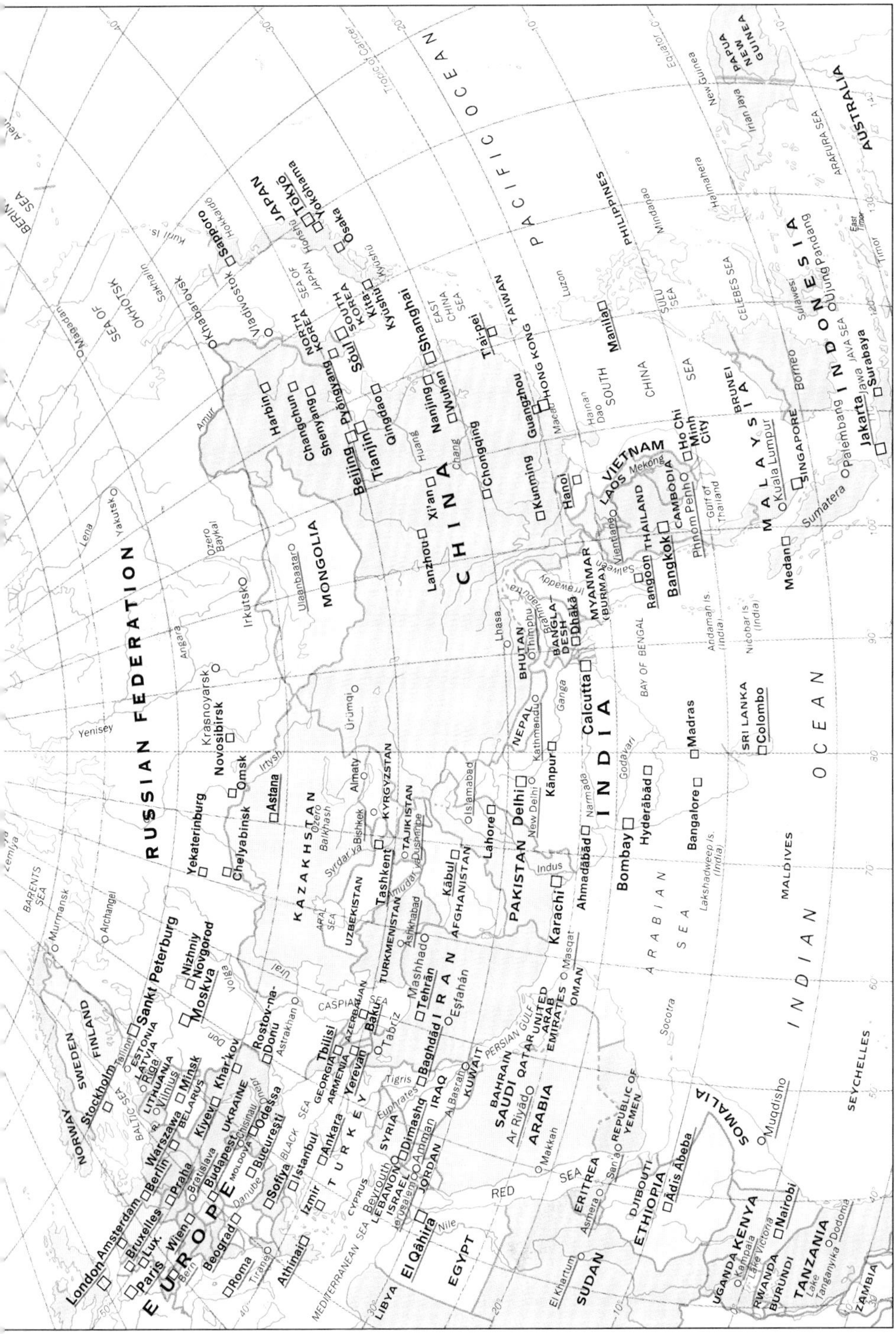

Scale 1:69 200 000

0 400 800 1200 1600 km

0 200 400 600 800 1000 miles

NORWEGIAN SEA
ARCTIC
BARENTS SEA
KARA SEA
NORTH SEA
BALTIC SEA
BLACK SEA
CASPIAN SEA
ARAL SEA
PERSIAN GULF
Gulf of Bothnia
Arctic Circle
West from Greenwich
East from Greenwich
Spitsbergen
Svalbard (Norway)
Edgeøya
Nordaustlandet
Zemlya Frantsa Iosifa
Novaya Zemlya
O. Kolguyev
O. Vaygach
Poluostrov Yamal
Gydanskiy Poluostrov
Obskaya Guba
Kol'skiy Poluostrov
Beloye More
UNITED KINGDOM
Glasgow
Aberdeen
DENMARK
København (Copenhagen)
NORWAY
Bergen
Oslo
Trondheim
Narvik
SWEDEN
Göteborg
Malmö
Stockholm
FINLAND
Turku
Tampere
Helsinki
Oulu
ESTONIA
Tallinn
LATVIA
Riga
LITHUANIA
Vilnius
Kaliningrad
Klaipeda
FEDERAL REPUBLIC OF GERMANY
Hamburg
Berlin
POLAND
Poznan
Łódź
Wrocław
Kraków
Warszawa (Warsaw)
BELARUS
Minsk
Brest
Vitebsk
Gomel
Moglilev
Daugavpils
Pskov
Sankt Peterburg (St Petersburg)
Ladozhskoye Ozero
Onezhskoye Ozero
Petrozavodsk
Murmansk
Kandalaksha
Severodvinsk
Archangel
Cherepovets
Vologda
Rybinsk
Yaroslavl'
Tver'
Moskva (Moscow)
Smolensk
Serpukhov
Tula
Bryansk
Kolomna
Vladimir
Ivanovo
Ryazan'
Orel
Kursk
Tambov
Voronezh
UKRAINE
Kiyev
Chernigov
Zhitomir
Vinnitsa
Chernovtsy
Lvov
Dnestr
Pripyat
Desna
Dnepr
Sumy
Poltava
Khar'kov
Dnepropetrovsk
Donetsk
Krivoy Rog
Nikolayev
Odessa
Zaporozh'ye
Melitopol'
Mariupol'
Lugansk
Sevastopol'
Kerch
Azovskoye More
MOLDOVA
Chişinău
ROMANIA
Novorossiysk
Krasnodar
Rostov-na-Donu
Shakhty
Don
Volgograd
Saratov
Penza
Syzran'
Ul'yanovsk
Samara
Nizhniy Novgorod
Cheboksary
Kazan
Volga
Stavropol'
Astrakhan'
Ural'sk
Orenburg
Gur'yev
Ural
Sukhona
Kotlas
Sev. Dvina
Syktyvkar
Kirov
Ukhta
Pechora
Nar'yan Mar
Vorkuta
Labytnangi
G. Narodnaya 1894
URAL'SKIY KHREBET
Perm
Izhevsk
Ufa
Zlatoust
Magnitogorsk
Yekaterinburg
Chelyabinsk
Nizhniy Tagil
Serov
Sergino
Surgut
Tyumen'
Tobol'sk
Irtysh
Tobol
Ishim
Petropavlovsk
Omsk
Novosibirsk
Prokop'yevsk
Barnaul
Ob
Orsk
RUSSIA
Zapadno Sibirskaya Nizmennost
KAZAKHSTAN
Astana
Pavlodar
Semipalatinsk
Karaganda
Balkhash
Ozero Balkhash
Oz. Zaysan
Zaysan
Kzyl Orda
Syrdar'ya
Plato Ustyurt
Nukus
Urgench
Kyzylkum
Karakumy
Krasnovodsk
TURKMENISTAN
Ashkhabad
Chardzhou
Mary
Murgab
Amudar'ya
UZBEKISTAN
Bukhara
Samarkand
Karshi
Termez
Tashkent
Chimkent
Aulie-Ata
Bishkek
Almaty
KYRGYZSTAN
Namangan
Andizhan
Fergana
Oz. Issyk Kul'
Pik Pobedy 7439
TIAN SHAN
TAJIKISTAN
Dushanbe
Pik Kommunizma 7495
Pamir
Kashi
Tarim
Tarim Pendi
AFGHANISTAN
Mazar-e Sharif
Herat
Samsun
Sukhumi
Batumi
GEORGIA
Tbilisi
Kavkaz
Elbrus 5642
ARMENIA
Yerevan
AZERBAIJAN
Baku
Grozny
Makhachkala
Gyandzha
Araks
TURKEY
Erzurum
Diyarbakir
Ararat
SYRIA
IRAQ
Al Mawşil
Baghdād
Al Başrah
KUWAIT
IRAN
Tabrīz
Tehrān
Eşfahān
Mashhad
Scale 1:30 700 000
0 200 400 600 800 1000 km
0 150 300 450 600 miles

CHUKCHI SEA
EAST SIBERIAN SEA
BERING SEA
LAPTEV SEA
SEA OF OKHOTSK
SEA OF JAPAN
YELLOW SEA
Bo Hai
O. Vrangelya
Chukotskiy Poluostrov
St. Lawrence (U.S.A.)
Novosibirskiye Ostrova
O. Kotel'nyy
Khrebet Cherskogo
Khrebet Kolymskiy
Koryakskiy Khrebet
Kamchatka
Sredinnyy Khrebet
Ust'Kamchatsk
Petropavlovsk Kamchatskiy
Verkhoyanskiy Khrebet
Khrebet Dzhugdzhur
Stanovoy Khrebet
Indigirka
Kolyma
Lena
Aldan
Ust'Nera
Magadan
Okhotsk
Yakutsk
Suntar
Tunguska
Sredne Sibirskoye Ploskogorye
FEDERATION
Angara
Bratsk
Ozero Baykal
Irkutsk
Cheremkhovo
Angarsk
Tulun
Ulan Ude
Chita
Borzya
Skovorodino
Amur
Shilka
Belogorsk
Blagoveshchensk
Birobidzhan
Khabarovsk
Komsomol'sk na-Amure
Sovetskaya Gavan'
Sakhalin
Aleksandrovsk-Sakhalinskiy
Yuzhno-Sakhalinsk
Kuril'skiye Ostrova
Sikhote-Alin'
Ussuri
Ussuriysk
Nakhodka
Vladivostok
Oz. Khanka
Xiao Hinggan Ling
Da Hinggan Ling
Qiqihar
Harbin
Jilin
Changchun
Fushun
Shenyang
Anshan
Jinzhou
Lüda
Manzhouli
Choybalsan
Ulaanbaatar (Ulan Bator)
Tsetserleg
MONGOLIA
Hövsgöl Nuur
Altay
Saynshand
GOBI
Hohhot
Baotou
Beijing
Tianjin
Shijiazhuang
Jinan
Qingdao
Taiyuan
Yumen
Huang
CHINA
NORTH KOREA
SOUTH KOREA
Ch'ŏngjin
Hamhŭng
Wŏnsan
P'yŏngyang
Sŏul (Seoul)
Taegu
Pusan
Taejŏn
Kwangju
Mokp'o
JAPAN
Hokkaidō
Wakkanai
Sapporo
Hakodate
Aomori
Sendai
Niigata
Honshū
Tōkyō
Yokohama
Nagoya
Kyōto
Ōsaka
Kōbe
Shikoku
Kita-Kyūshū
Fukuoka
Kyūshū
Kagoshima
OCEAN

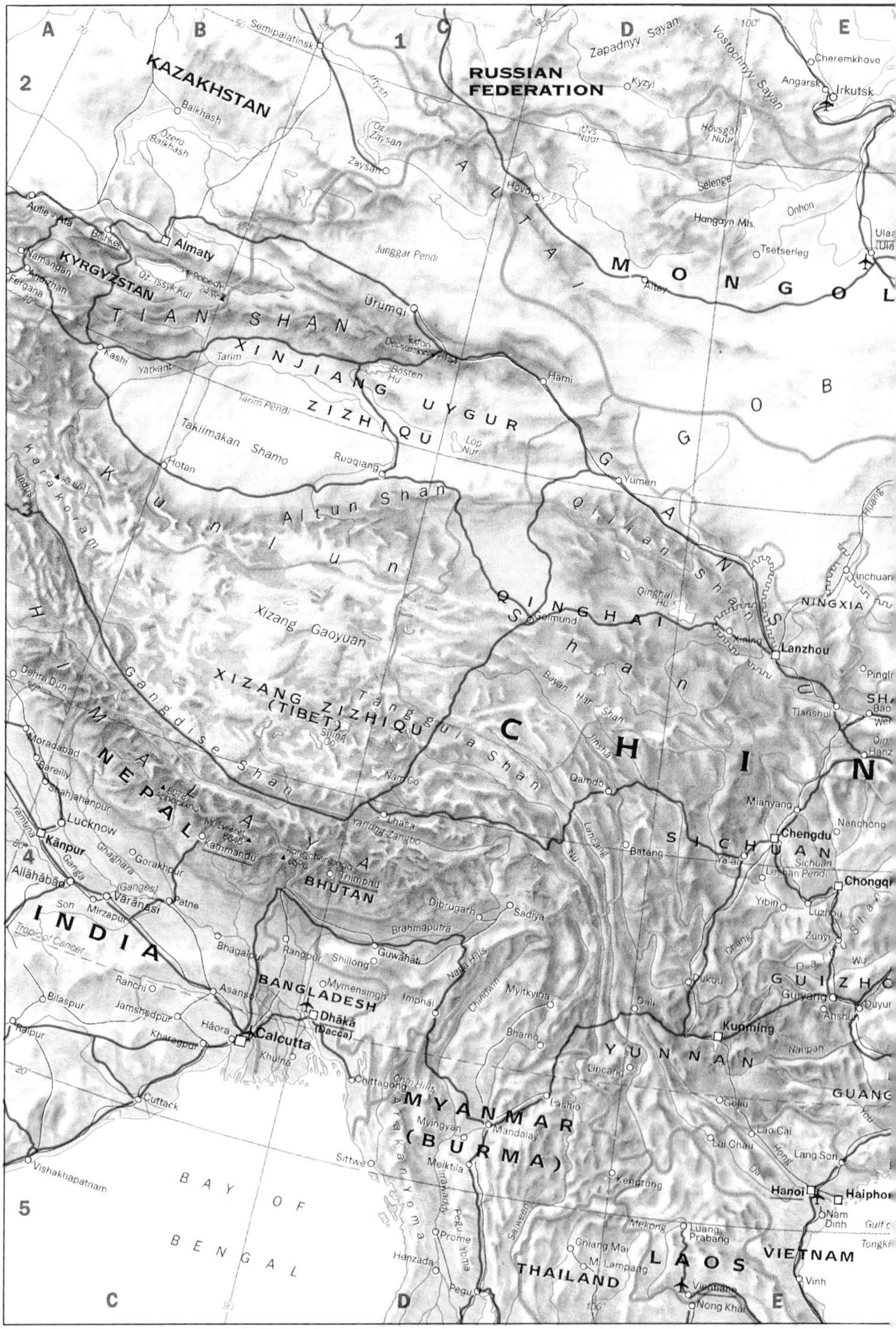

Scale 1:22 150 000

0 200 400 600 800 km

0 100 200 300 400 500 miles

F
G
H
J
K
RUSSIAN FEDERATION
Skovorodino
Chita
Borzya
Manzhouli
Hailar
Choybalsan
Belogorsk
Blagoveshchensk
Komsomol'sk na-Amure
Aleksandrovsk-Sakhalinskiy
Sovetskaya Gavan
Birobidzhan
Khabarovsk
Sakhalin
Yuzhno-Sakhalinsk
Kuril Islands
Iturup
Kunashir
La Perouse Strait
Wakkanai
Asahikawa
Sapporo
Kushiro
Hokkaidō
Otaru
Hakodate
Amur
Shilka
Ergun
Nen
Ussuri
Xiao Hinggan Ling
Da Hinggan Ling
Sikhote-Alin
HEILONGJIANG
Hegang
Jiamusi
Shuangyashan
Qiqihar
Songhua
Harbin
Khanka
Mudanjiang
Ussuriysk
Nakhodka
Vladivostok
Baicheng
JILIN
Changchun
Jilin
Siping
Liaoyuan
Tonghua
Ch'ŏngjin
NEI MONGOL ZIZHIQU (INNER MONGOLIA)
Chifeng
Shenyang
Fushun
Fuxin
Benxi
Liaoyang
Anshan
LIAONING
Jinzhou
Yingkou
Liaodong
Dandong
Hamhŭng
NORTH KOREA
Wŏnsan
Pyŏngyang
Kaesŏng
Sŏul (Seoul)
SOUTH KOREA
Taejŏn
Taegu
Kwangju
Pusan
Mokp'o
Korea Strait
Cheju do
SEA OF JAPAN
Aomori
Hachinohe
Morioka
Akita
Ishinomaki
Sendai
Yamagata
Niigata
Honshū
Nagaoka
Utsunomiya
JAPAN
Nagano
Tōkyō
Chiba
Kawasaki
Yokohama
Kanazawa
Fukui
Gifu
Nagoya
Shizuoka
Hamamatsu
Tottori
Kyōto
Ōsaka
Kōbe
Sakai
Wakayama
Matsue
Okayama
Hiroshima
Tokushima
Matsuyama
Kōchi
Shikoku
Kita-Kyūshū
Fukuoka
Sasebo
Nagasaki
Kumamoto
Kyūshū
Miyazaki
Kagoshima
Ōsumi-shotō
PACIFIC OCEAN
Zhangjiakou
Hohhot
BEIJING
Beijing (Peking)
Qinhuangdao
Tangshan
Tianjin
Lüda
Bo Hai
Baoding
HEBEI
Cangzhou
Shijiazhuang
Yangquan
Xingtai
Dezhou
Handan
Huang
Jinan
Zibo
Weifang
Qingdao
Yantai
SHANDONG
YELLOW SEA
Anyang
Jining
Xinxiang
Zhengzhou
Kaifeng
Xuzhou
Lianyungang
JIANGSU
Qingjiang
Xuchang
HENAN
Luohe
Bengbu
Huainan
Yangzhou
Nantong
Xiangfan
Xinyang
Nanjing
Zhenjiang
Wuxi
Hefei
Lu'an
ANHUI
Wuhu
Suzhou
Shanghai
Wuhan
Huangshi
Tongling
Hangzhou
Ningbo
Shashi
Jiujiang
Anqing
Shaoxing
EAST CHINA SEA
ZHEJIANG
Poyang Hu
Jingdezhen
Jinhua
Qu Xian
Yiyang
Nanchang
Shangrao
Wenzhou
Zhuzhou
Fuzhou
JIANGXI
Ji'an
Nanping
Hengyang
FUJIAN
Ganzhou
Quanzhou
Zhangzhou
Xiamen
Shaoguan
Taiwan Strait
Chi-lung
T'ai-pei
TAIWAN
Chang-hua
T'ai-nan
Kao-hsiung
GUANGDONG
Shantou
Guangzhou
Foshan
Kowloon
Macau (Macao)
Hong Kong
Nansei-shotō (Ryūkyū Is.)
Amami Ō-shima
Okinawa
Sakishima -shoto
Batan Is.
Luzon Strait
Babuyan Is.
C. Engano
Aparri
Laoag
PHILIPPINES
Luzon
SOUTH CHINA SEA
2
3
4
5
6
7
8
9
10
L
M
N
P
CENTRAL JAPAN
1 : 10 000 000
0 100 200 km
0 50 100 150 miles
Hachinohe
Morioka
Miyako
Akita
Hanamaki
Mizusawa
Kamaishi
Sakata
Tsuruoka
Furukawa
Ishinomaki
Yamagata
Sendai
Niigata
Fukushima
Sado-ga-shima
Sanjō
Aizu-Wakamatsu
Nagaoka
Kōriyama
Noto hantō
Takada
Iwaki
Takaoka
Nagano
Utsunomiya
Hitachi
Kanazawa
Toyama
Komatsu
Ashikaga
Mito
Fukui
Matsumoto
Takasaki
Tsuchiura
Wakasa wan
Tsuruga
Okaya
Tottori
Kōfu
Tōkyō
Chiba
Maizuru
Gifu
Fuji-san 3776
Kawasaki
Yokohama
Ōgaki
Shimizu
Yokosuka
Himeji
Kyōto
Nagoya
Okazaki
Odawara
Numazu
Bōsō-hantō
Kōbe
Yokkaichi
Toyohashi
Shizuoka
Ōsaka
Sakai
Matsusaka
Hamamatsu
Ise
Tokushima
Wakayama
Kii-sanchi
Kii-suidō
Shikoku
Shingū

South-East Asia

Scale 1:23 850 000

0 200 400 600 800 km

0 100 200 300 400 500 miles

EAST
CHINA
SEA
Okinawa
Nansei-shotō (Ryūkyū Is.)
Sakishima guntō
Ogasawara-shotō (Jap.)
Kazan-rettō (Jap.)
Iwo Jima
Tropic of Cancer
NORTHERN MARIANA IS. (U.S.A.)
PACIFIC
OCEAN
Guam (U.S.A.)
FEDERATED STATES OF MICRONESIA
Yap
PALAU
Caroline Islands
Batan Is.
Babuyan Is.
C. Engaño
Aparri
Luzon
Quezon City
PHILIPPINES
Naga
Legaspi
Masbate
Samar
Iloilo
Cebu
Leyte
Bacolod
Bohol
Butuan
Cagayan de Oro
Mindanao
Davao
Moro Gulf
Cotabato
General Santos
Kep. Talaud
Kep. Sangihe
Morotai
Manado
Halmahera
MOLUCCA SEA
Kep. Togian
Waigeo
Manokwari
Biak
Sorong
Yapen
Obi
MALUKU (MOLUCCAS)
Kep. Sula
Kep. Banggai
SERAM SEA
Misoöl
Teluk Cenderawasih
Jayapura
Wewak
Admiralty Is.
Bismarck Archipelago
BISMARCK SEA
Fakfak
IRIAN
Seram
Buru
Ambon
Kendari
Pegunungan Maoke
Pk. Jaya 5029
JAYA
Sepik
Central Range
PAPUA
Mt. Hagen
4508 Mt. Wilhelm
Madang
Lae
New Britain
NEW GUINEA
New Guinea
Butung
E S I A
Kep. Kai
Wokam
Kep. Aru
BANDA SEA
Wau
Fly
D'Entrecasteaux Is.
Owen Stanley Range
Yamdena
Trangan
Kepulauan Tanimbar
P. Dolak
Babar
Wetar
Alor
Tg. Vals
Merauke
Daru
Port Moresby
Alotau
Ende
Dili
East Timor
Kep. Leti
ARAFURA SEA
Torres Strait
C. York
AUSTRALIA
CORAL SEA
Timor
Kupang
Roti
E
F
G
H
1
2
3
4
5
130°
140°
150°
20°
10°
0°
Equator

Scale 1:23 850 000

0 200 400 600 800 km

0 100 200 300 400 500 miles

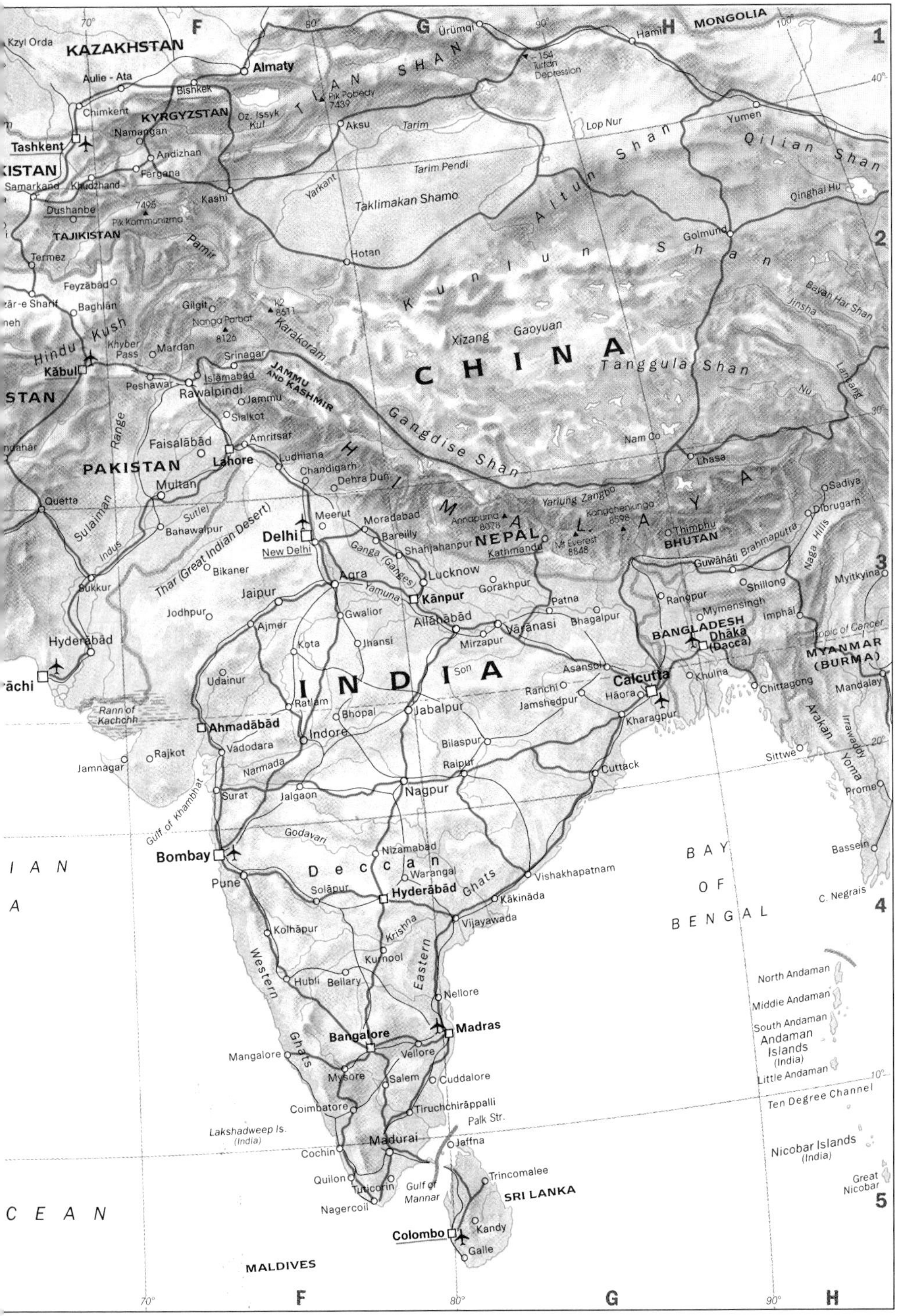
F
G
H
1
2
3
4
5
70°
80°
90°
100°
40°
30°
20°
10°
KAZAKHSTAN
Kzyl Orda
Aulie - Ata
Almaty
Bishkek
KYRGYZSTAN
Chimkent
Namangan
Tashkent
Andizhan
Fergana
Samarkand
Khudzhand
Dushanbe
TAJIKISTAN
Termez
7495
Pik Kommunizma
Kashi
Oz. Issyk Kul
Pik Pobedy 7439
T I A N S H A N
Ürümqi
Hami
MONGOLIA
-154 Turfan Depression
Aksu
Tarim
Lop Nur
Yumen
Tarim Pendi
Yarkant
Taklimakan Shamo
Hotan
Qilian Shan
Altun Shan
Qinghai Hu
Golmud
Kunlun Shan
Bayan Har Shan
Jinsha
Pamir
Feyzābād
Baghlān
Gilgit
K2 8611
Nanga Parbat 8126
Karakoram
Hindu Kush
Khyber Pass
Mardan
Kābul
Srinagar
Islāmābād
Peshawar
Rawalpindi
JAMMU AND KASHMIR
Jammu
Sialkot
Xizang Gaoyuan
CHINA
Tanggula Shan
Lancang
Nu
Gangdise Shan
Nam Co
Lhasa
Range
Faisalābād
Amritsar
Lahore
PAKISTAN
Ludhiana
Chandigarh
Dehra Dun
HIMALAYA
Multan
Quetta
Sulaiman
Sutlej
Bahawalpur
Indus
Thar (Great Indian Desert)
Meerut
Moradabad
Bareilly
Delhi
New Delhi
Bikaner
Sukkur
Ganga (Ganges)
Shahjahanpur
NEPAL
Kathmandu
Annapurna 8078
Mt Everest 8848
Kangchenjunga 8598
Yarlung Zangbo
Thimphu
BHUTAN
Sadiya
Dibrugarh
Guwāhāti
Brahmaputra
Naga Hills
Myitkyina
Shillong
Agra
Lucknow
Gorakhpur
Jaipur
Yamuna
Kānpur
Patna
Rangpur
Mymensingh
Imphāl
Jodhpur
Gwalior
Allahābād
Bhagalpur
BANGLADESH
Dhāka (Dacca)
Tropic of Cancer
MYANMAR (BURMA)
Ajmer
Vārānasi
Mirzapur
Hyderābād
Kota
Jhansi
Son
INDIA
Asansol
Khulna
Chittagong
Mandalay
Karāchi
Udaipur
Ranchi
Calcutta
Hāora
Jamshedpur
Rann of Kachchh
Ratlam
Bhopal
Jabalpur
Kharagpur
Arakan
Irrawaddy
Yoma
Ahmadābād
Indore
Vadodara
Bilaspur
Sittwe
Rajkot
Jamnagar
Narmada
Raipur
Cuttack
Prome
Surat
Jalgaon
Nagpur
Gulf of Khambhat
Godavari
Nizamabad
BAY OF BENGAL
Bassein
I A N
A
C E A N
Bombay
Deccan
Warangal
Pune
Vishakhapatnam
Solāpur
Hyderābād
Ghats
Kākināda
C. Negrais
Vijayawada
Kolhāpur
Krishna
Kurnool
Eastern
Western
Hubli
Bellary
Nellore
North Andaman
Middle Andaman
South Andaman
Andaman Islands (India)
Little Andaman
Madras
Bangalore
Vellore
Mangalore
Ghats
Mysore
Salem
Cuddalore
Ten Degree Channel
Coimbatore
Tiruchchirāppalli
Palk Str.
Lakshadweep Is. (India)
Madurai
Jaffna
Nicobar Islands (India)
Cochin
Trincomalee
Quilon
Tuticorin
Gulf of Mannar
SRI LANKA
Great Nicobar
Nagercoil
Kandy
Colombo
Galle
MALDIVES

Scale 1:3 700 000

0 25 50 75 100 km

0 15 30 45 60 miles

Scale 1:54 500 000

0 400 800 1200 1600 km

0 250 500 750 1000 miles

Scale 1:26 700 000

0 200 400 600 800 km

0 100 200 300 400 500 miles

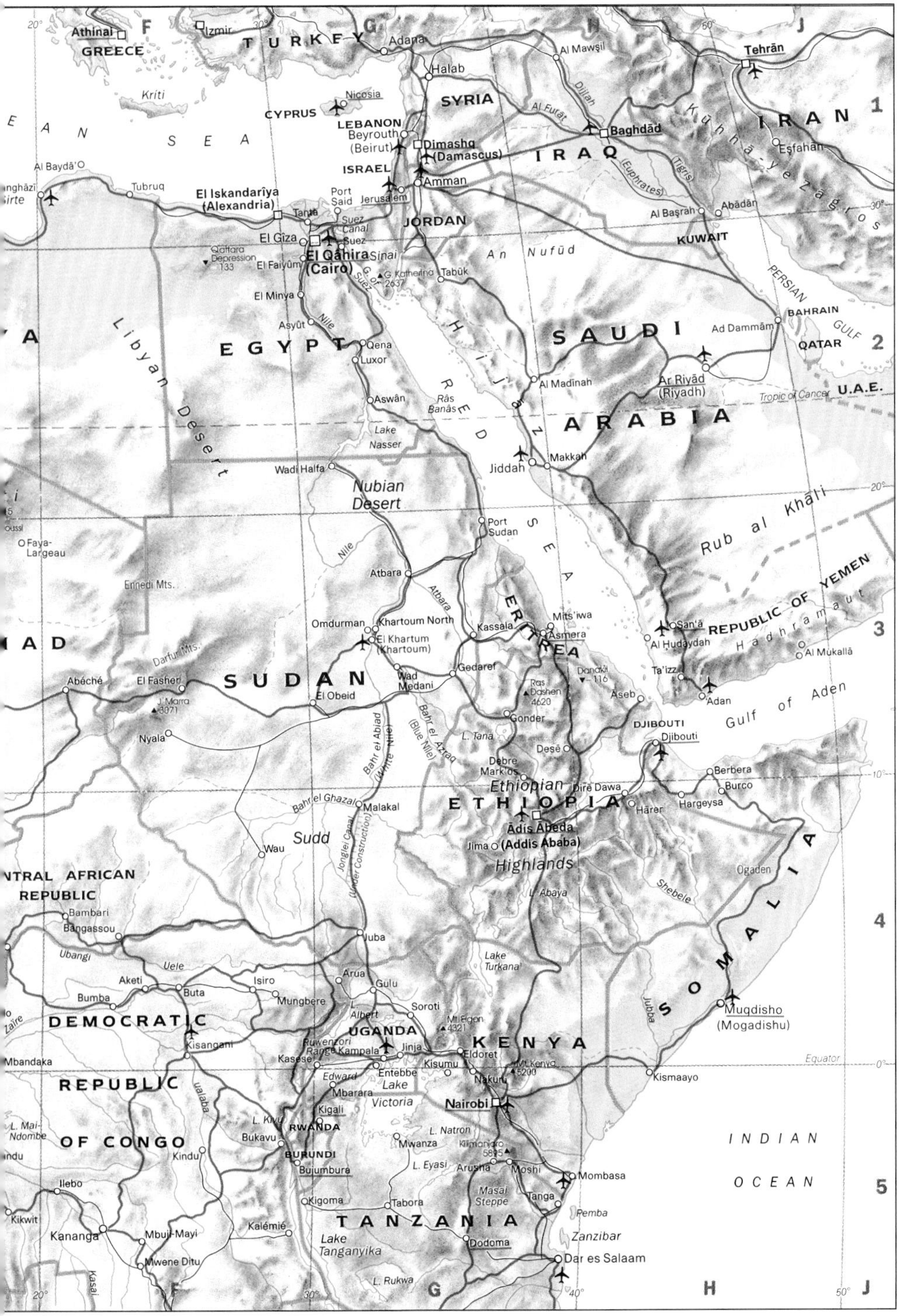

Athinai
GREECE
Izmir
TURKEY
Adana
Al Mawşil
Tehrān
Halab
Kríti
Nicosia
CYPRUS
SYRIA
IRAN
LEBANON
Beyrouth
(Beirut)
Dimashq
(Damascus)
Baghdād
IRAQ
Eşfahān
Al Furāt
Dijlah
(Tigris)
(Euphrates)
Kūhhā-ye Zāgros
SEA
Al Baydā'O
ISRAEL
Amman
Tubruq
El Iskandarîya
(Alexandria)
Port Said
Jerusalem
Al Başrah
Abādān
Tanta
Suez Canal
JORDAN
KUWAIT
El Gîza
Suez
Qattara Depression 133
El Faiyûm
El Qâhira
(Cairo)
Sinai
An Nufūd
G. of Suez
G. Katherina 2637
Tabūk
PERSIAN GULF
El Minya
BAHRAIN
Libyan Desert
Asyût
Nile
SAUDI ARABIA
Ad Dammām
QATAR
EGYPT
Qena
Luxor
HIJAZ
Al Madīnah
Ar Riyāḍ
(Riyadh)
U.A.E.
Tropic of Cancer
Aswân
Râs Banâs
RED SEA
Lake Nasser
Jiddah
Makkah
Wadi Halfa
Nubian Desert
Rub al Khālī
Faya-Largeau
Port Sudan
Nile
Atbara
Ennedi Mts.
ERITREA
REPUBLIC OF YEMEN
Hadhramaut
Omdurman
Khartoum North
Kassala
Mits'iwa
Asmera
Şan'ā
Al Ḩudaydah
Al Mukallā
El Khartum
(Khartoum)
Darfur Mts.
Gedaref
Wad Medani
Danakil 116
Ta'izz
Abéché
El Fasher
SUDAN
Ras Dashen 4620
Aseb
Adan
J. Marra 3071
El Obeid
Gulf of Aden
Nyala
Gonder
DJIBOUTI
Djibouti
Bahr el Abiad
(White Nile)
Bahr el Azraq
(Blue Nile)
L. Tana
Desē
Debre Mark'os
Berbera
Ethiopian Highlands
Dire Dawa
Burco
Bahr el Ghazal
Malakal
ETHIOPIA
Hārer
Hargeysa
Ādīs Ābeba
(Addis Ababa)
Jima
Sudd
Wau
Jonglei Canal
(Under Construction)
CENTRAL AFRICAN REPUBLIC
Ogaden
Shebele
L. Abaya
Bambari
Bangassou
Juba
SOMALIA
Ubangi
Uele
Lake Turkana
Aketi
Isiro
Arua
Gulu
Bumba
Buta
Mungbere
Jubba
DEMOCRATIC REPUBLIC OF CONGO
L. Albert
Soroti
Mt. Elgon 4321
Muqdisho
(Mogadishu)
Zaïre
UGANDA
Kisangani
Ruwenzori Range
Kampala
Jinja
KENYA
Eldoret
Mbandaka
Kasese
Kisumu
Mt. Kenya 5200
Equator
Entebbe
Nakuru
Kismaayo
Edward
Lake Victoria
Mbarara
Lualaba
Kigali
Nairobi
L. Kivu
RWANDA
L. Natron
INDIAN OCEAN
L. Mai-Ndombe
Bukavu
Mwanza
Kilimanjaro 5895
BURUNDI
Kindu
Bujumbura
L. Eyasi
Arusha
Moshi
Ilebo
Mombasa
Masai Steppe
Kigoma
Tabora
Tanga
Kikwit
Pemba
Kalémié
TANZANIA
Kananga
Mbuji-Mayi
Lake Tanganyika
Dodoma
Zanzibar
Mwene Ditu
Dar es Salaam
Kasai
L. Rukwa
20°
30°
40°
50°
60°
30°
20°
10°
0°
F
G
H
J
1
2
3
4
5

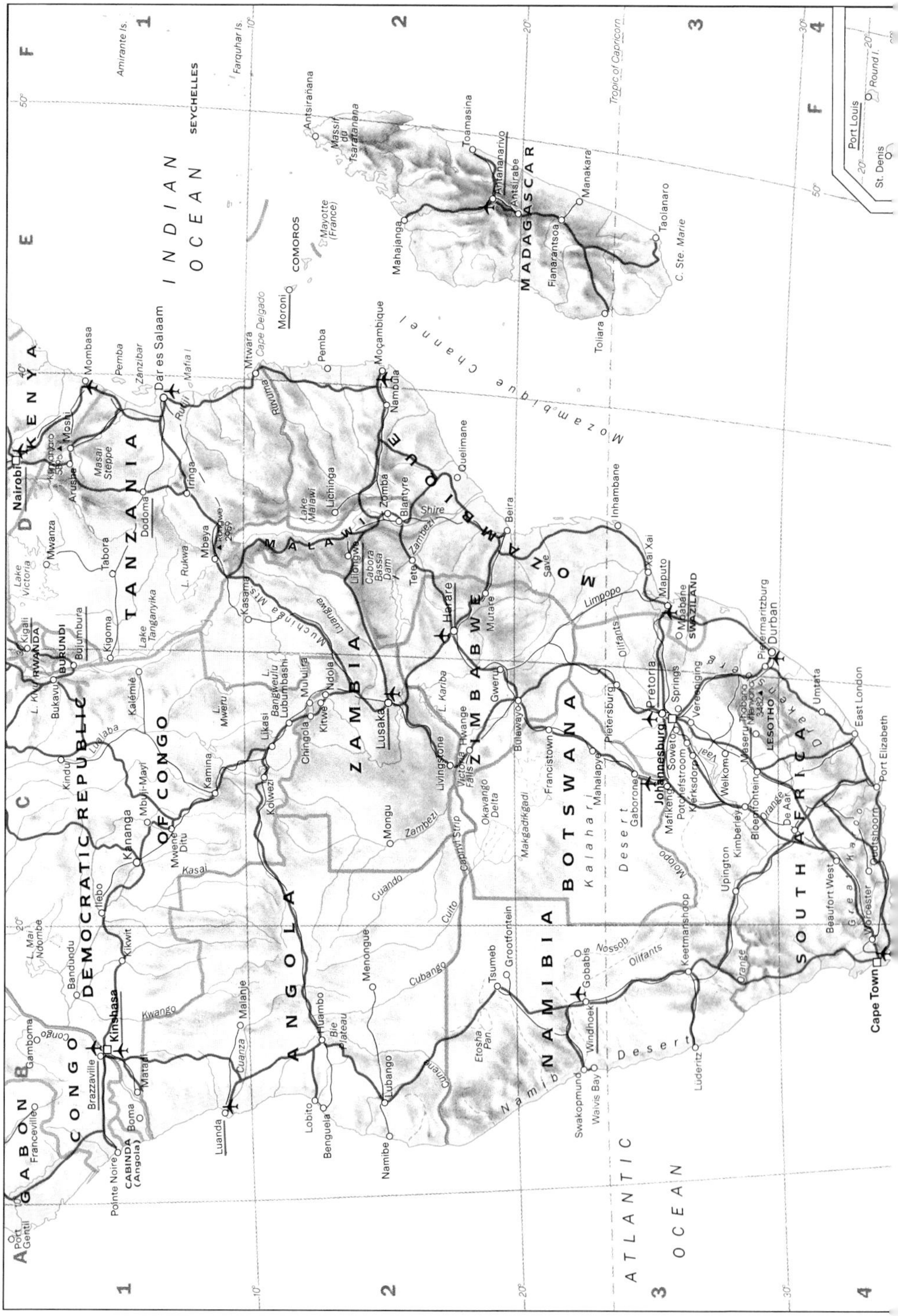

Scale 1:26 700 000

0 200 400 600 800 km

0 100 200 300 400 500 miles

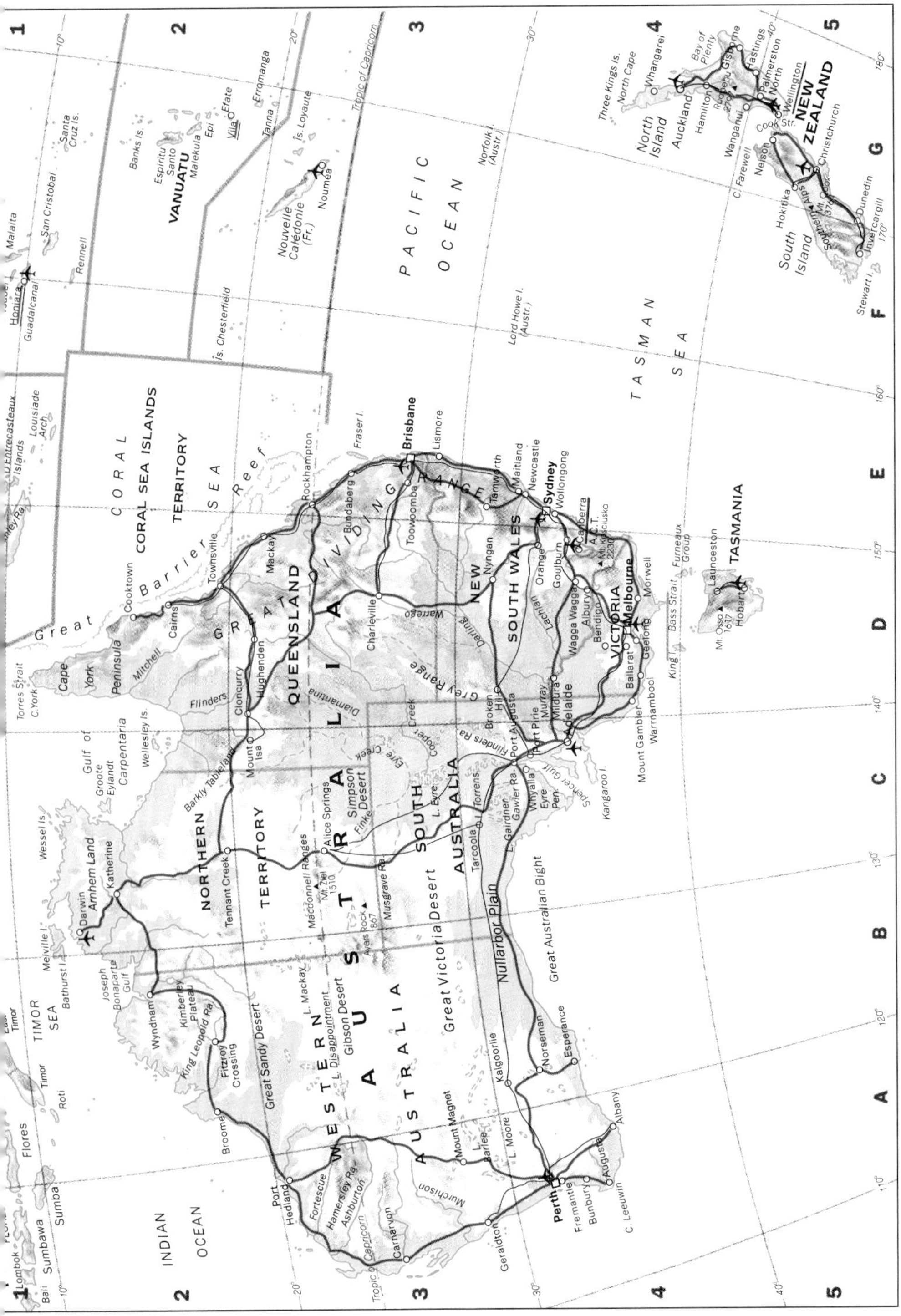

Scale 1:32 950 000

0 200 400 600 800 1000 km

0 200 400 600 miles

Scale 1:81 800 000

0 1000 2000 3000 km

0 500 1000 1500 2000 miles

CANADA
Edmonton
Calgary
Regina
Winnipeg
Vancouver
Seattle
Portland
Hudson Bay
L. Athabasca
L. Winnipeg
Great Bear Lake
Great Slave Lake
Mackenzie
Anchorage
Gulf of Alaska
Kodiak I.
Alexander Arch.
Queen Charlotte Is.
Vancouver I.
GREENLAND (Den.)
ICELAND
Reykjavik
Davis Str.
LABRADOR SEA
Newfoundland
St Lawrence
L. Superior
L. Huron
L. Michigan
L. Ontario
L. Erie
Montréal
Ottawa
Toronto
Detroit
Boston
New York
Philadelphia
Baltimore
Washington
Pittsburgh
Cincinnati
Chicago
Minneapolis
Missouri
Snake
UNITED STATES OF AMERICA
Denver
St. Louis
San Francisco
Los Angeles
San Diego
Dallas
Atlanta
New Orleans
Houston
Colorado
Ohio
Mississippi
Rio Grande
Rio Bravo del Norte
Guadalupe (Mex.)
ATLANTIC OCEAN
Bermuda (U.K.)
GULF OF MEXICO
Miami
THE BAHAMAS
Tropic of Cancer
Monterrey
MEXICO
La Habana
CUBA
Guadalajara
México
DOMINICAN REPUBLIC
HAITI
Greater Antilles
JAMAICA
BELIZE
Puerto Rico (U.S.A.)
Lesser Antilles
Revillagigedo (Mex.)
GUATEMALA
Guatemala
HONDURAS
Tegucigalpa
CARIBBEAN SEA
San Salvador
EL SALVADOR
NICARAGUA
Managua
COSTA RICA
San José
Clipperton I. (Fr.)
Panamá
PANAMA
Caracas
VENEZUELA
Medellín
Bogotá
COLOMBIA
de Coco (C.R.)
Honolulu
Hawaii
OCEAN
Tabuaeran
Kiritimati
Jarvis I. (U.S.A.)
Malden I.
Starbuck I.
Caroline I.
Flint I.
Îs. Marquises (Fr.)
Îs. de la Société (Fr.)
Tahiti
Îs Tuamotu (Fr.)
FRENCH POLYNESIA
Îs. Gambier
Îs. Tubuai (Fr.)
Pitcairn I. (U.K.)
Ducie I.
Equator
Islas Galápagos (Ecuador)
Quito
Guayaquil
ECUADOR
Amazonas
BRAZIL
Trujillo
PERU
Callao
Lima
Arequipa
L. Titicaca
La Paz
BOLIVIA
Sucre
PAR.
Tropic of Capricorn
Antofagasta
Asunción
Sala-y-Gomez (Ch.)
I. de Pascua (Ch.)
CHILE
Córdoba
URUGUAY
Montevideo
Rosario
Santiago
Is. Juan Fernández (Ch.)
Buenos Aires
ARGENTINA
Concepción
Bahía Blanca
Puerto Montt
Patagonia
Punta Arenas
Tierra del Fuego
Falkland Is. (Islas Malvinas) (U.K.)
South Georgia (U.K.)
West of Greenwich

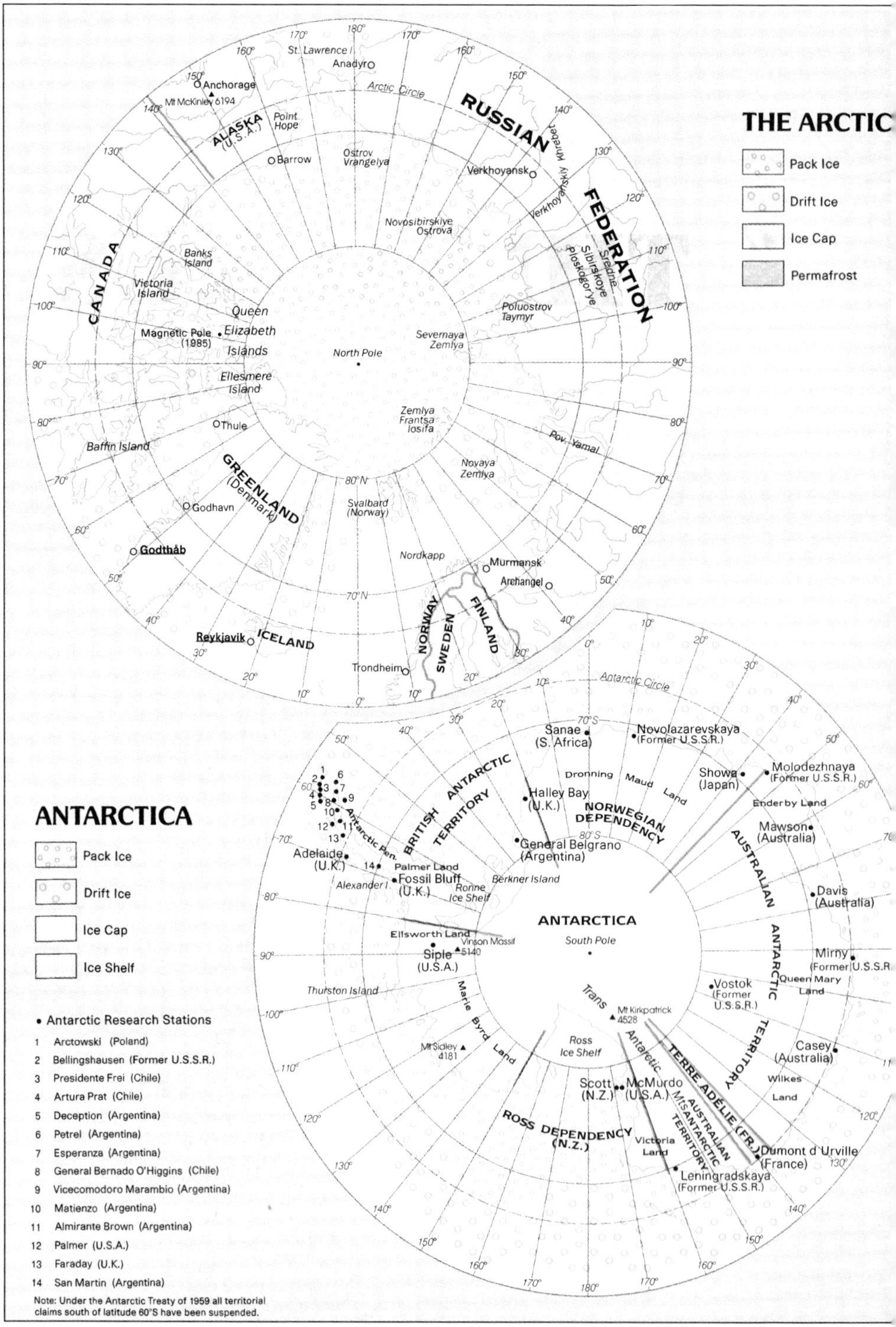

Scale 1:68 200 000

0 400 800 1200 1600 km

0 200 400 600 800 1000 miles

THESAURUS

A

abandon *v.* abdicate, back-pedal, cede, chuck, desert, desist, discontinue, ditch, drop, evacuate, forgo, forsake, give up, jilt, leave, leave behind, leave in the lurch, quit, relinquish, renounce, repudiate, resign, scrap, sink, surrender, vacate, waive, withdraw from, yield.
antonyms continue, persist, support.
n. dash, recklessness, unrestraint, wantonness, wildness.
antonym restraint.

abandoned *adj.* cast aside, cast away, cast out, corrupt, debauched, depraved, derelict, deserted, desolate, discarded, dissipated, dissolute, dropped, forlorn, forsaken, jilted, left, neglected, outcast, profligate, rejected, relinquished, reprobate, scorned, sinful, unoccupied, vacant, wanton, wicked.
antonyms cherished, restrained.

abase *v.* belittle, cast down, debase, degrade, demean, discredit, disgrace, dishonor, downgrade, humble, humiliate, lower, malign, mortify, reduce, vitiate.
antonyms elevate, honor.

abashed *adj.* affronted, ashamed, astounded, bewildered, chagrined, confounded, confused, cowed, discomfited, discomposed, disconcerted, discountenanced, discouraged, dismayed, dum(b)founded, embarrassed, floored, humbled, humiliated, mortified, nonplused, perturbed, shamefaced, taken aback.
antonyms at ease, audacious, composed.

abate *v.* alleviate, appease, attenuate, bate, decline, decrease, deduct, diminish, discount, dull, dwindle, ease, ebb, fade, fall off, lessen, let up, mitigate, moderate, mollify, pacify, quell, rebate, reduce, relieve, remit, sink, slacken, slake, slow, subside, subtract, taper off, wane, weaken.
antonyms increase, strengthen.

abbreviate *v.* abridge, abstract, clip, compress, condense, contract, curtail, cut, digest, epitomize, lessen, précis, reduce, shorten, shrink, summarize, trim, truncate.
antonyms amplify, extend.

abbreviation *n.* abridgment, abstract, abstraction, clipping, compendium, compression, condensation, conspectus, contraction, curtailment, digest, epitome, précis, reduction, résumé, shortening, summarization, summary, summation, synopsis, trimming, truncation.
antonyms expansion, extension.

abdicate *v.* abandon, abjure, abnegate, cede, demit, forgo, give up, quit, relinquish, renounce, repudiate, resign, retire, surrender, vacate, yield.

abduct *v.* abduce, appropriate, carry off, kidnap, lay hold of, make off with, rape, run away with, run off with, seduce, seize, snatch, spirit away.

abduction *n.* appropriation, enlevement, kidnap, rape, seduction, seizure, theft.

aberrant *adj.* abnormal, anomalous, atypical, corrupt, corrupted, defective, degenerate, depraved, deviant, different, divergent, eccentric, egregious, erroneous, incongruous, irregular, odd, peculiar, perverse, perverted, queer, quirky, rambling, roving, straying, untypical, wandering, wrong.
antonyms normal, straight.

aberration *n.* aberrancy, abnormality, anomaly, defect, delusion, deviation, divergence, eccentricity, freak, hallucination, illusion, irregularity, lapse, nonconformity, oddity, peculiarity, quirk, rambling, rogue, straying, vagary, wandering.
antonym conformity.

abet *v.* aid, assist, back, condone, connive, egg on, encourage, goad, help, incite, promote, prompt, sanction, second, spur, succor, support, sustain, uphold, urge.
antonym discourage.

abeyance *n.* adjournment, deferral, discontinuation, inactivity, intermission, lull, postponement, recess, remission, reservation, suspension, waiting.
antonyms activity, continuation.

abhor *v.* abominate, despise, detest, execrate, hate, loathe, recoil from, shrink from, shudder at, spurn.
antonyms adore, love.

abhorrent *adj.* abominable, absonant, despiteful, detestable, disgusting, distasteful, execrable, hated, hateful, heinous, horrible, horrid, loathsome, nauseating, obnoxious, odious, offensive, repellent, repugnant, repulsive, revolting.
antonym attractive.

abide *v.* accept, bear, brook, continue, endure, last, outlive, persist, put up with, remain, stand, stay, stomach, submit to, suffer, survive, tarry, tolerate.
antonyms dispute, quit.

ability *n.* adeptness, adroitness, aptitude, capability, capacity, competence, competency, deftness, dexterity, endowment, energy, expertise, expertness, facility, faculty, flair, forte, genius, gift, knack, know-how, long suit, nous, potentiality, power, proficiency, qualification, savoir-faire, savvy, skill, strength, talent, touch.
antonyms inability, incompetence.

abject *adj.* base, contemptible, cringing, debased, degenerate, degraded, deplorable, despicable, dishonorable, execrable, fawning, forlorn, groveling, hopeless, humiliating, ignoble, ignominious, low, mean, miserable, outcast, pathetic, pitiable, servile, slavish, sordid, submissive, vile, worthless, wretched.
antonym exalted.

able *adj.* accomplished, adept, adequate, adroit, capable, clever, competent, deft, dexterous, effective, efficient, experienced, expert, fit, fitted, gifted, ingenious, masterful, masterly, powerful, practiced, proficient, qualified, skilful, skilled, strong, talented.
antonyms incapable, incompetent.

able-bodied *adj.* firm, fit, hale, hardy, healthy, hearty, lusty, powerful, robust, sound, stalwart, staunch, stout, strapping, strong, sturdy, tough, vigorous.
antonyms delicate, infirm.

abnegation *n.* abandonment, abjuration, abstinence, acquiescence, continence, disallowance, eschewal, forbearance, giving up, refusal, rejection, relinquishment, renunciation, sacrifice, self-denial, submission, surrender, temperance.
antonyms acceptance, support.

abnormal *adj.* aberrant, anomalous, atypical, curious, deviant, different, divergent, eccentric, erratic, exceptional, extraordinary, irregular, monstrous, odd, paranormal, peculiar, queer, singular, strange, uncanny, uncommon, unexpected, unnatural, untypical, unusual, wayward, weird.
antonyms normal, straight.

abode *n.* domicile, dwelling, dwelling-place, habitat, habitation, home, house, lodging, pad, place, quarters, residence.

abolish *v.* abrogate, annihilate, annul, blot out, cancel, destroy, do away with, eliminate, end, eradicate, expunge, exterminate, extinguish, extirpate, get rid of, invalidate, kibosh, nullify, obliterate, overthrow, overturn, put an end to, put the kibosh on, quash, repeal, repudiate, rescind, revoke, sink, stamp out, subvert, suppress, terminate, vitiate, void, wipe out.
antonyms continue, retain.

abolition *n.* abolishment, abrogation, annihilation, annulment, cancellation, destruction, dissolution, elimination, end, ending, eradication, expunction, extermination, extinction, extirpation, invalidation, nullification, obliteration, overthrow, overturning, quashing, repeal, repudiation, rescission, revocation, subversion, suppression, termination, vitiation, voiding, withdrawal.
antonyms continuance, retention.

abominable *adj.* abhorrent, accursed, appalling, atrocious, base, beastly, contemptible, despicable, detestable, disgusting, execrable, foul, hateful, heinous, hellish, horrible, horrid, loathsome, nauseating, nauseous, nefast, obnoxious, odious, repellent, reprehensible, repugnant, repulsive, revolting, terrible, vile, villainous, wretched.
antonyms delightful, desirable.

abomination *n.* abhorrence, anathema, animosity, animus, antipathy, aversion, bête noire, bugbear, curse, detestation, disgrace, disgust, distaste, evil, execration, hate, hatred, horror, hostility, loathing, odium, offence, plague, repugnance, revulsion, torment. *antonyms* adoration, delight.

abort *v.* arrest, call off, check, end, fail, frustrate, halt, miscarry, nullify, stop, terminate, thwart.
antonym continue.

abortion *n.* aborticide, disappointment, failure, feticide, fiasco, freak, frustration, misadventure, misbirth, miscarriage, monster, monstrosity, termination, thwarting.
antonyms continuation, success.

abortive *adj.* barren, bootless, failed, failing, fruitless, futile, idle, ineffective, ineffectual, misborn, miscarried, sterile, unavailing, unproductive, unsuccessful, useless, vain.
antonym successful.

abound *v.* be plentiful, brim over, crowd, exuberate, flourish, increase, infest, luxuriate, overflow, proliferate, run riot, superabound, swarm, swell, teem, thrive.
antonym be in short supply.

about *prep.* adjacent to, all over, anent, around, as regards, beside, busy with, circa, close to, concerned with, concerning, connected with, encircling, encompassing, engaged on, in respect to, in the matter of, near, nearby, on, over, re, referring to, regarding, relating to, relative to, respecting, round, surrounding, through, throughout, touching, with reference to, with regard to, with respect to.
adv. active, almost, approaching, approximately, around, astir, close to, from place to place, here and there, hither and thither, in motion, in the region of, more or less, nearing, nearly, present, roughly, stirring, to and fro.

about-turn *n.* about-face, apostasy, backtrack, enantiodromia, reversal, right-about (face), switch, turnabout, turn(a-)round, U-turn, volte-face.

above *prep.* atop, before, beyond, exceeding, higher than, in excess of, on top of, over, prior to, superior to, surpassing, upon.
antonyms below, under.
adv. aloft, atop, earlier, heavenwards, in heaven, on high, overhead, supra.
antonym below.
adj. above-mentioned, above-stated, aforementioned, aforesaid, earlier, foregoing, preceding, previous, prior.

above-board *adj.* candid, fair, fair and square, forthright, frank, guileless, honest, honorable, legitimate, on the level, open, overt, reputable, square, straight, straightforward, true, trustworthy, truthful, upright, veracious.
antonyms shady, underhand.

abrasion *n.* abrading, chafe, chafing, erosion, friction, grating, graze, grinding, levigation, rubbing, scouring, scrape, scraping, scratch, scratching, scuff, scuffing, trituration, wearing away, wearing down.

abrasive *adj.* abradant, annoying, attritional, biting, caustic, chafing, erodent, erosive, frictional, galling, grating, hurtful, irritating, nasty, rough, scraping, scratching, scratchy, scuffing, sharp, unpleasant.
antonyms pleasant, smooth.

abreast *adj.* acquainted, au courant, au fait, conversant,

familiar, in the picture, in touch, informed, knowledgeable, on the ball, up to date.
antonyms out of touch, unaware.

abridge *v.* abbreviate, abstract, circumscribe, clip, compress, concentrate, condense, contract, curtail, cut, cut down, decrease, digest, diminish, dock, epitomize, lessen, lop, précis, prune, reduce, shorten, summarize, synopsize, trim, truncate.
antonyms amplify, pad.

abridgment *n.* abbreviation, abrégé, abstract, compendium, compression, concentration, condensation, conspectus, contraction, curtailment, cutting, decrease, digest, diminishing, diminution, epitome, lessening, limitation, outline, précis, pruning, reduction, restriction, résumé, shortening, summary, synopsis, truncation.
antonyms expansion, padding.

abroad *adv.* about, at large, away, circulating, current, elsewhere, extensively, far, far and wide, forth, in circulation, in foreign parts, out, out of the country, out-of-doors, outside, overseas, publicly, widely.

abrupt *adj.* blunt, brief, brisk, broken, brusque, curt, direct, disconnected, discontinuous, discourteous, gruff, hasty, headlong, hurried, impolite, irregular, jerky, precipitate, precipitous, prerupt, quick, rapid, rough, rude, sharp, sheer, short, snappy, steep, sudden, surprising, swift, terse, unannounced, unceremonious, uncivil, uneven, unexpected, unforeseen, ungracious.
antonyms ceremonious, expansive, leisurely.

abscond *v.* absquatulate, beat it, bolt, clear out, decamp, disappear, do a bunk, escape, flee, flit, fly, hightail it, make off, quit, run off, scram, skedaddle, skip, take French leave, vamoose.

absence *n.* absenteeism, absent-mindedness, abstraction, dearth, default, defect, deficiency, distraction, inattention, lack, need, non-appearance, non-attendance, non-existence, omission, paucity, preoccupation, privation, reverie, scarcity, truancy, unavailability, vacancy, vacuity, want.
antonyms existence, presence.

absent *adj.* absent-minded, absorbed, abstracted, away, bemused, blank, day-dreaming, distracted, distrait(e), dreamy, elsewhere, empty, faraway, gone, heedless, inattentive, lacking, missing, musing, non-existent, not present, oblivious, out, preoccupied, truant, unavailable, unaware, unconscious, unheeding, unthinking, vacant, vague, wanting, withdrawn, wool-gathering.
antonyms aware, present.

absent-minded *adj.* absent, absorbed, abstracted, bemused, distracted, distrait(e), dreaming, dreamy, engrossed, faraway, forgetful, heedless, impractical, inattentive, musing, oblivious, otherwordly, pensive, preoccupied, scatterbrained, unaware, unconscious, unheeding, unthinking, withdrawn, wool-gathering.
antonyms matter-of-fact, attentive, practical.

absolute *adj.* absolutist, actual, almighty, arbitrary, autarchical, autocratic, autonomous, categorical, certain, complete, conclusive, consummate, decided, decisive, definite, definitive, despotic, dictatorial, downright, entire, exact, exhaustive, final, flawless, free, full, genuine, independent, indubitable, infallible, omnipotent, out-and-out, outright, peremptory, perfect, positive, precise, pure, sheer, sovereign, supreme, sure, terminative, thorough, total, totalitarian, tyrannical, unadulterated, unalloyed, unambiguous, unbounded, unconditional, uncontrolled, undivided, unequivocal, unlimited, unmitigated, unmixed, unqualified, unquestionable, unrestrained, unrestricted, utter.
antonyms conditional, partial.

absolutely *adv.* actually, arbitrarily, autocratically, autonomously, bang, categorically, certainly, completely, conclusively, consummately, dead, decidedly, decisively, definitely, despotically, diametrically, dictatorially, entirely, exactly, exhaustively, finally, fully, genuinely, indubitably, infallibly, peremptorily, perfectly, positively, precisely, purely, sovereignly, supremely, surely, thoroughly, totally, truly, tyrannically, unambiguously, unconditionally, unequivocally, unmitigatedly, unquestionably, unrestrainedly, utterly, wholly.

absolution *n.* acquittal, acquittance, amnesty, compurgation, deliverance, discharge, dispensation, emancipation, exculpation, exemption, exoneration, forgiveness, forgiving, freeing, indulgence, liberation, mercy, pardon, purgation, redemption, release, remission, shriving, vindication.
antonym condemnation.

absolve *v.* acquit, clear, deliver, discharge, emancipate, exculpate, excuse, exempt, exonerate, forgive, free, justify, let off, liberate, loose, pardon, ransom, redeem, release, remit, set free, shrive, vindicate.
antonym charge.

absorb *v.* apprehend, assimilate, captivate, consume, coopt, devour, digest, drink in, engage, engross, engulf, enthral(l), enwrap, exhaust, fascinate, fill (up), fix, grip, hold, imbibe, immerse, incorporate, ingest, involve, monopolize, occupy, osmose, preoccupy, receive, retain, rivet, soak up, sorb, submerge, suck up, take in, understand, utilize.
antonyms dissipate, exude.

absorbing *adj.* amusing, arresting, captivating, compulsive, diverting, engrossing, entertaining, enthralling, fascinating, gripping, interesting, intriguing, preoccupying, riveting, spellbinding, unputdownable.
antonyms boring, off-putting.

abstain *v.* avoid, cease, decline, deny, desist, eschew, forbear, forgo, give up, keep from, refrain, refuse, reject, renounce, resist, shun, stop, swear off, withhold.
antonym indulge.

abstemious *adj.* abstinent, ascetic, austere, continent, disciplined, frugal, moderate, restrained, self-denying, self-disciplined, sober, sparing, temperate.
antonyms gluttonous, intemperate, luxurious.

abstinence *n.* abstemiousness, abstinency, asceticism, avoidance, continence, forbearance, frugality, moderation, nephalism, non-indulgence, refraining, self-denial, self-discipline, self-restraint, soberness, sobriety, teetotalism, temperance.
antonym self-indulgence.

abstract *adj.* abstruse, academic, arcane, complex, conceptual, deep, discrete, general, generalized, hypothetical, indefinite, intellectual, metaphysical, non-concrete, occult, philosophical, profound, recondite, separate, subtle, theoretic, theoretical, unpractical, unrealistic.
antonym concrete.
n. abbreviation, abridgment, abstractive, compendium, compression, condensation, conspectus, digest, epitome, essence, outline, précis, recapitulation, résumé, summary, synopsis.
v. abbreviate, abridge, compress, condense, detach, digest, dissociate, epitomize, extract, isolate, outline, précis, purloin, remove, separate, shorten, steal, summarize, withdraw.
antonyms expand, insert.

abstraction *n.* absence, absent-mindedness, absorption, bemusedness, concept, conception, dissociation, distraction, dream, dreaminess, formula, generalization, generality, hypothesis, idea, inattention, notion, pensiveness, preoccupation, remoteness, separation, theorem, theory, thought, withdrawal, wool-gathering.

abstruse *adj.* abstract, arcane, complex, cryptic, dark, deep, devious, difficult, enigmatic, esoteric, hermetic, hidden, incomprehensible, mysterious, mystical, obscure, occult, perplexing, profound, puzzling, recondite, subtle, tortuous, unfathomable, unobvious, vague.
antonyms concrete, obvious.

absurd *adj.* anomalous, comical, crazy, daft, derisory, fantastic, farcical, foolish, funny, humorous, idiotic, illogical, implausible, incongruous, irrational, laughable, ludicrous, meaningless, nonsensical, paradoxical, preposterous, ridiculous, risible, senseless, silly, stupid, unreasonable, untenable.
antonyms logical, rational, sensible.

absurdity *n.* comicality, craziness, daftness, farce, farcicality, farcicalness, fatuity, fatuousness, folly, foolery, foolishness, idiocy, illogicality, illogicalness, incongruity, irrationality, joke, ludicrousness, meaninglessness, nonsense, nonsensicality, preposterousness, ridiculousness, senselessness, silliness, stupidity, unreasonableness.

abundance *n.* affluence, ampleness, amplitude, bonanza, bounty, copiousness, exuberance, fortune, fullness, glut, heap, lavishness, luxuriance, luxuriancy, milk and honey, munificence, oodles, opulence, plenitude, plenteousness, plenty, pleroma, plethora, prodigality, profusion, riches, richness, scads, uberty, wealth.
antonyms dearth, scarcity.

abundant *adj.* ample, bounteous, bountiful, copious, exuberant, filled, full, generous, in plenty, lavish, luxuriant, overflowing, plenteous, plentiful, prodigal, profuse, rank, rich, superabundant, teeming, uberous, unstinted, well-provided, well-supplied.
antonyms scarce, sparse.

abuse *v.* batter, calumniate, castigate, curse, damage, deceive, defame, denigrate, disparage, exploit, harm, hurt, ill-treat, impose on, injure, insult, inveigh against, libel, malign, maltreat, manhandle, mar, misapply, miscall, misemploy, misuse, molest, objurgate, oppress, oppugn, revile, scold, slander, slate, smear, spoil, swear at, take advantage of, traduce, upbraid, vilify, violate, vituperate, wrong.
antonyms cherish, compliment, praise.
n. affront, blame, calumniation, calumny, castigation, censure, contumely, curses, cursing, damage, defamation, denigration, derision, diatribe, disparagement, execration, exploitation, flyting, harm, hurt, ill-treatment, imposition, injury, insults, invective, libel, malediction, maltreatment, manhandling, misapplication, misconduct, misdeed, misuse, obloquy, offence, oppression, opprobrium, reproach, revilement, scolding, sin, slander, spoiling, swearing, tirade, traducement, upbraiding, vilification, violation, vitriol, vituperation, wrong, wrong-doing.
antonyms attention, care.

abusive *adj.* brutal, calumniating, calumnious, castigating, censorious, contumelious, cruel, defamatory, denigrating, derisive, derogatory, destructive, disparaging, harmful, hurtful, injurious, insulting, invective, libelous, maligning, objurgatory, offensive, opprobrious, pejorative, reproachful, reviling, rough, rude, scathing, scolding, slanderous, traducing, upbraiding, vilifying, vituperative.
antonym complimentary.

abysmal *adj.* abyssal, bottomless, boundless, complete, deep, endless, extreme, immeasurable, incalculable, infinite, profound, thorough, unending, unfathomable, vast, yawning.

academic *adj.* abstract, bookish, collegiate, conjectural, donnish, educational, erudite, highbrow, hypothetical, impractical, instructional, learned, lettered, literary, notional, pedagogical, scholarly, scholastic, speculative, studious, theoretical, well-read.
n. academe, academician, don, fellow, lecturer, man of letters, master, pedant, professor, pundit, savant, scholar, scholastic, schoolman, student, tutor.

accede *v.* accept, acquiesce, admit, agree, assent, assume, attain, capitulate, comply, concede, concur, consent, defer, endorse, grant, inherit, submit, succeed (to), yield.
antonyms demur, object.

accelerate *v.* advance, antedate, dispatch, expedite, facilitate, festinate, forward, further, hasten, hurry, pick up speed, precipitate, promote, quicken, speed, speed up, spur, step on the gas, step on the juice, step up, stimulate.
antonyms delay, slow down.

accent *n.* accentuation, arsis, articulation, beat, cadence,

emphasis, enunciation, force, ictus, inflection, intensity, intonation, modulation, pitch, pronunciation, pulsation, pulse, rhythm, stress, thesis, timbre, tonality, tone.
v. accentuate, emphasize, stress, underline, underscore.

accept *v.* abide by, accede, acknowledge, acquiesce, acquire, admit, adopt, affirm, agree to, approve, assume, avow, bear, believe, bow to, brook, concur with, consent to, co-operate with, defer to, gain, get, have, jump at, obtain, put up with, receive, recognize, secure, stand, stomach, submit to, suffer, swallow, take, take on, tolerate, undertake, wear, yield to.
antonyms demur, reject.

acceptable *adj.* adequate, admissible, agreeable, all right, conventional, correct, delightful, desirable, done, grateful, gratifying, moderate, passable, pleasant, pleasing, satisfactory, standard, suitable, tolerable, unexceptionable, unobjectionable, welcome.
antonyms unsatisfactory, unwelcome.

access *n.* adit, admission, admittance, approach, avenue, course, door, entering, entrance, entrée, entry, gateway, increase, ingress, key, onset, passage, passageway, path, road, upsurge, upsurgence.
antonyms egress, outlet.

accessible *adj.* achievable, affable, approachable, at hand, attainable, available, come-at-able, conversable, cordial, exposed, friendly, get-at-able, handy, informal, liable, near, nearby, obtainable, on hand, open, possible, procurable, reachable, ready, sociable, subject, susceptible, vulnerable, wide-open.
antonym inaccessible.

accessory *n.* abettor, accompaniment, accomplice, addition, adjunct, adjuvant, adornment, aid, appendage, assistant, associate, attachment, colleague, component, confederate, conniver, convenience, decoration, embellishment, extension, extra, frill, help, helper, particeps criminis, partner, supplement, trim, trimming.
adj. abetting, additional, adjuvant, adventitious, aiding, ancillary, assisting, auxiliary, contributory, extra, incidental, secondary, subordinate, subsidiary, supplemental, supplementary.

accident *n.* blow, calamity, casualty, chance, collision, contingency, contretemps, crash, disaster, fate, fluke, fortuity, fortune, happenstance, hazard, luck, misadventure, miscarriage, mischance, misfortune, mishap, pile-up, prang, serendipity, shunt.

accidental *adj.* adventitious, adventive, casual, chance, contingent, fluky, fortuitous, haphazard, inadvertent, incidental, random, serendipitous, unanticipated, uncalculated, uncertain, unexpected, unforeseen, unintended, unintentional, unlooked-for, unplanned, unpremeditated, unwitting.
antonyms intentional, premeditated.

acclaim *v.* announce, applaud, approve, celebrate, cheer, clap, commend, crown, declare, eulogize, exalt, extol, hail, honor, laud, praise, salute, welcome.
antonym demean.
n. acclamation, applause, approbation, approval, celebration, cheering, clapping, commendation, eulogizing, eulogy, exaltation, honor, laudation, ovation, plaudits, praise, welcome.
antonyms brickbats, criticism, vituperation.

accommodate *v.* acclimatize, accustom, adapt, adjust, afford, aid, assist, attune, billet, board, cater for, comply, compose, conform, domicile, entertain, fit, furnish, harbor, harmonize, help, house, lodge, modify, oblige, provide, put up, quarter, reconcile, serve, settle, shelter, supply.

accommodating *adj.* complaisant, considerate, co-operative, friendly, helpful, hospitable, indulgent, kind, obliging, polite, sympathetic, unselfish, willing.
antonym disobliging.

accommodation[1] *n.* adaptation, adjustment, assistance, compliance, composition, compromise, conformity, fitting, harmonization, harmony, help, modification, reconciliation, settlement.

accommodation[2] *n.* bed and breakfast, billet, board, digs, domicile, dwelling, harboring, house, housing, lodgings, quartering, quarters, residence, shelter, sheltering.

accompany *v.* attend, belong to, chaperon, co-exist, coincide, complement, conduct, consort, convoy, escort, follow, go with, occur with, squire, supplement, usher.

accomplice *n.* abettor, accessory, ally, assistant, associate, coadjutor, collaborator, colleague, confederate, conspirator, helper, helpmate, henchman, mate, particeps criminis, participator, partner, practisant.

accomplish *v.* achieve, attain, bring about, bring off, carry out, compass, complete, conclude, consummate, discharge, do, effect, effectuate, engineer, execute, finish, fulfil, manage, obtain, perform, produce, realize.

accomplished *adj.* adept, adroit, consummate, cultivated, expert, facile, gifted, masterly, polished, practiced, professional, proficient, skilful, skilled, talented.
antonym inexpert.

accomplishment *n.* ability, achievement, act, aptitude, art, attainment, capability, carrying out, completion, conclusion, consummation, coup, deed, discharge, doing, effecting, execution, exploit, faculty, feat, finishing, forte, fruition, fulfilment, futurition, gift, management, perfection, performance, production, proficiency, realization, skill, stroke, talent, triumph.

accord *v.* agree, allow, assent, bestow, concede, concur, confer, conform, correspond, endow, fit, give, grant, harmonize, jibe, match, present, render, suit, tally, tender, vouchsafe.
antonym disagree.
n. accordance, agreement, assent, concert, concurrence, conformity, congruence, congruity, consort, correspondence, harmony, rapport, symmetry, sympathy, unanimity, unity.
antonym discord.

accordingly *adv.* appropriately, as a result, as requested, consequently, correspondingly, ergo, fitly, hence, in accord with, in accordance, in consequence, properly, so, suitably, therefore, thus.

according to after, after the manner of, agreeably to, commensurate with, consistent with, in accordance with, in compliance with, in conformity with, in keeping with, in line with, in obedience to, in proportion, in relation, in the light of, in the manner of, obedient to.

account[1] *n.* advantage, basis, benefit, cause, chronicle, communiqué, concern, consequence, consideration, description, detail, distinction, esteem, estimation, explanation, ground, grounds, history, honor, import, importance, interest, memoir, merit, motive, narration, narrative, note, performance, portrayal, presentation, profit, rank, reason, recital, reckoning, record, regard, relation, report, reputation, repute, sake, score, significance, sketch, standing, statement, story, tale, use, value, version, worth, write-up.
v. adjudge, appraise, assess, believe, consider, count, deem, esteem, estimate, explain, gauge, hold, judge, rate, reckon, regard, think, value, weigh.

account for answer for, clarify, clear up, destroy, elucidate, explain, illuminate, incapacitate, justify, kill, put paid to, rationalize, vindicate.

account[2] *n.* balance, bill, book, books, charge, check, computation, inventory, invoice, journal, ledger, reckoning, register, score, statement, tab, tally, tick.

accountable *adj.* amenable, answerable, blamable, bound, charged with, liable, obligated, obliged, responsible.

accredit *v.* appoint, approve, ascribe, assign, attribute, authorize, certificate, certify, commission, credit, depute, empower, enable, endorse, entrust, guarantee, license, okay, qualify, recognize, sanction, vouch for.

accrue *v.* accumulate, amass, arise, be added, build up, collect, emanate, enlarge, ensue, fall due, flow, follow, gather, grow, increase, issue, proceed, redound, result, spring up.

accumulate *v.* accrue, agglomerate, aggregate, amass, assemble, build up, collect, cumulate, gather, grow, hoard, increase, multiply, pile up, stash, stockpile, store.
antonyms diffuse, disseminate.

accumulation *n.* accretion, aggregation, assemblage, augmentation, backlog, build-up, collection, conglomeration, gathering, growth, heap, hoard, increase, mass, pile, reserve, stack, stock, stockpile, store.

accurate *adj.* authentic, careful, close, correct, exact, factual, faithful, faultless, just, letter-perfect, mathematical, meticulous, minute, nice, perfect, precise, proper, regular, right, rigorous, scrupulous, sound, spot-on, strict, true, truthful, unerring, veracious, veridical, well-aimed, well-directed, well-judged, word-perfect.
antonyms inaccurate, wrong.

accursed *adj.* abominable, anathematized, bedeviled, bewitched, blighted, condemned, cursed, damned, despicable, detestable, doomed, execrable, foredoomed, hateful, hellish, hopeless, horrible, ill-fated, ill-omened, jinxed, luckless, ruined, star-crossed, undone, unfortunate, unholy, unlucky, wretched.
antonym blessed.

accusation *n.* accusal, allegation, arraignment, attribution, charge, citation, complaint, crimination, delation, denunciation, gravamen, impeachment, imputation, incrimination, indictment, plaint, recrimination.

accuse *v.* allege, arraign, attaint, attribute, blame, censure, charge, cite, criminate, delate, denounce, impeach, impugn, impute, incriminate, indict, inform against, recriminate, tax.

accustom *v.* acclimatize, acculturate, acquaint, adapt, adjust, discipline, exercise, familiarize, habituate, harden, inure, season, train.

ache *v.* agonize, covet, crave, desire, grieve, hanker, hunger, hurt, itch, long, mourn, need, pain, pine, pound, rack, smart, sorrow, suffer, throb, twinge, yearn.
n. anguish, craving, desire, grief, hankering, hunger, hurt, itch, longing, misery, mourning, need, pain, pang, pining, pounding, smart, smarting, soreness, sorrow, suffering, throb, throbbing, yearning.

achieve *v.* accomplish, acquire, attain, bring about, carry out, compass, complete, consummate, do, earn, effect, effectuate, execute, finish, fulfil, gain, get, manage, obtain, perform, procure, produce, reach, realize, score, strike, succeed, win.
antonyms fail, miss.

achievement *n.* accomplishment, acquirement, act, attainment, completion, deed, effort, execution, exploit, feat, fruition, fulfilment, magnum opus, performance, production, qualification, realization, stroke, success.

acid *adj.* acerbic, acidulous, acrid, astringent, biting, bitter, caustic, corrosive, cutting, harsh, hurtful, ill-natured, incisive, mordant, morose, pungent, sharp, sour, stinging, tart, trenchant, vinegarish, vinegary, vitriolic.

acid test crucial test, touchstone, verification.

acknowledge *v.* accede, accept, acquiesce, address, admit, affirm, agree to, allow, answer, attest, avouch, concede, confess, confirm, declare, endorse, grant, greet, hail, notice, own, profess, react to, recognize, reply to, respond to, return, salute, vouch for, witness, yield.

acme *n.* apex, apogee, climax, crest, crown, culmination, height, high point, maximum, optimum, peak, pinnacle, sublimation, sublimity, summit, top, vertex, zenith.
antonym nadir.

acquaint *v.* accustom, advise, announce, apprize, brief, disclose, divulge, enlighten, familiarize, inform, notify, reveal, tell.

acquaintance *n.* associate, association, awareness, chum, cognizance, colleague, companionship, confrère, consociate, contact, conversance, conversancy, experience, familiarity, fellowship, intimacy, knowledge, relationship, understanding.

acquiesce *v.* accede, accept, agree, allow, approve,

assent, comply, concur, conform, consent, defer, give in, submit, yield.
antonyms disagree, object.

acquire *v.* achieve, amass, appropriate, attain, buy, collect, cop, earn, gain, gather, get, net, obtain, pick up, procure, realize, receive, secure, win.
antonyms forfeit, forgo, relinquish.

acquirements *n.* accomplishments, achievements, acquisitions, attainments, attributes, culture, erudition, knowledge, learning, mastery, qualifications, skills.

acquisition *n.* accession, achievement, acquest, acquirement, appropriation, attainment, buy, gain, gaining, learning, obtainment, possession, prize, procurement, property, purchase, pursuit, securing, take-over.

acquisitive *adj.* avaricious, avid, covetous, grabbing, grasping, greedy, insatiable, mercenary, possessive, predatory, rapacious, voracious.
antonym generous.

acquit *v.* absolve, bear, behave, clear, comport, conduct, deliver, discharge, dismiss, exculpate, excuse, exonerate, free, fulfil, liberate, pay, pay off, perform, release, relieve, repay, reprieve, satisfy, settle, vindicate.
antonym convict.

acrid *adj.* acerbic, acid, acrimonious, astringent, biting, bitter, burning, caustic, cutting, harsh, incisive, irritating, malicious, mordant, nasty, pungent, sarcastic, sardonic, sharp, stinging, tart, trenchant, venomous, virulent, vitriolic.

acrimonious *adj.* abusive, acerbic, astringent, atrabilious, biting, bitter, caustic, censorious, churlish, crabbed, cutting, ill-tempered, irascible, mordant, peevish, petulant, pungent, rancorous, sarcastic, severe, sharp, spiteful, splenetic, tart, testy, trenchant, virulent, waspish.
antonyms irenic, kindly, peaceable.

acrobat *n.* aerialist, balancer, contortionist, equilibrist, funambulist, gymnast, somersaulter, stunt-girl, stuntman, tumbler, voltigeur.

act *n.* accomplishment, achievement, action, affectation, attitude, bill, blow, counterfeit, decree, deed, dissimulation, doing, edict, enactment, enterprise, execution, exertion, exploit, fake, feat, feigning, front, gest, gig, law, make-believe, maneuver, measure, move, operation, ordinance, performance, pose, posture, pretense, proceeding, resolution, routine, sham, show, sketch, spiel, stance, statute, step, stroke, transaction, turn, undertaking. *v.* acquit, act out, affect, assume, bear, behave, carry, carry out, characterize, comport, conduct, counterfeit, dissimulate, do, enact, execute, exert, feign, function, go about, imitate, impersonate, make, mime, mimic, move, operate, perform, personate, personify, play, portray, pose, posture, pretend, put on, react, represent, seem, serve, sham, simulate, strike, take effect, undertake, work.

act up carry on, cause trouble, give bother, give trouble, horse around, make waves, malfunction, mess about, misbehave, muck about, play up, rock the boat.

act (up)on affect, alter, carry out, change, comply with, conform to, execute, follow, fulfil, heed, influence, modify, obey, sway, transform, yield to.

acting *adj.* interim, pro tem, provisional, reserve, stand-by, stop-gap, substitute, supply, surrogate, temporary. *n.* affectation, assuming, bluff, characterization, counterfeiting, dissimulation, dramatics, enacting, feigning, histrionicism, histrionics, histrionism, imitating, imitation, impersonation, imposture, melodrama, performance, performing, play-acting, playing, portrayal, portraying, posing, posturing, pretense, pretending, putting on, seeming, shamming, stagecraft, theatre, theatricals.

action *n.* accomplishment, achievement, act, activity, affray, agency, battle, case, cause, clash, combat, conflict, contest, deed, effect, effort, encounter, endeavor, energy, engagement, enterprise, exercise, exertion, exploit, feat, fight, fighting, force, fray, functioning, influence, lawsuit, litigation, liveliness, mechanism, motion, move, movement, operation, performance, power, proceeding, process, prosecution, skirmish, sortie, spirit, stop, stroke, suit, undertaking, vigor, vim, vitality, warfare, work, working, works.

actions *n.* address, air, bearing, behavior, comportment, conduct, demeanor, deportment, manners, mien, port, ways.

activate *v.* actuate, animate, arouse, bestir, energize, excite, fire, galvanize, impel, initiate, mobilize, motivate, move, prompt, propel, rouse, set in motion, set off, start, stimulate, stir, switch on, trigger.
antonyms arrest, deactivate, stop.

active *adj.* acting, activist, aggressive, agile, alert, ambitious, animated, assertive, assiduous, astir, bustling, busy, committed, deedy, devoted, diligent, doing, effectual, energetic, engaged, enterprising, enthusiastic, forceful, forward, full, functioning, hard-working, in force, in operation, industrious, involved, light-footed, live, lively, militant, moving, nimble, occupied, on the go, on the move, operate, quick, running, sedulous, spirited, sprightly, spry, stirabout, stirring, strenuous, through-going, vibrant, vigorous, vital, vivacious, working, zealous.
antonyms dormant, inactive, inert, passive.

activity *n.* act, action, activeness, animation, avocation, bustle, commotion, deed, endeavor, enterprise, exercise, exertion, hobby, hurly-burly, hustle, industry, interest, job, kerfuffle, labor, life, liveliness, motion, movement, occupation, pastime, project, pursuit, scheme, stir, task, undertaking, venture, work.

actor *n.* actress, agent, artist, comedian, doer, executor, factor, functionary, guiser, ham, hamfatter, histrio, histrion, impersonator, masquerader, mime, mummer, operative, operator, participant, participator, performer, perpetrator, personator, play-actor, player, practitioner, Roscius, Thespian, tragedian, trouper, worker.

actual *adj.* absolute, authentic, bona fide, categorical, certain, concrete, confirmed, corporeal, current, de facto, definite, existent, extant, factual, genuine, indisputable, indubitable, legitimate, live, living, material, physical, positive, present, present-day, prevailing, real, realistic, substantial, tangible, thingy, true, truthful, unquestionable, verified, veritable.
antonyms apparent, imaginary, theoretical.

actuality *n.* corporeality, fact, factuality, historicity, materiality, reality, realness, substance, substantiality, truth, verity.

acute[1] *adj.* astute, canny, clever, critical, crucial, cutting, dangerous, decisive, discerning, discriminating, distressing, essential, excruciating, exquisite, extreme, fierce, grave, important, incisive, ingenious, insightful, intense, intuitive, judicious, keen, lancinating, observant, overpowering, overwhelming, penetrating, perceptive, percipient, perspicacious, piercing, poignant, pointed, powerful, racking, sagacious, sapient, sensitive, serious, severe, sharp, shooting, shrewd, shrill, smart, stabbing, subtle, sudden, urgent, violent, vital.
antonyms chronic, mild, obtuse.

acute[2] *adj.* acicular, apiculate, cuspate, cuspidate, needle-shaped, peaked, pointed, sharp, sharpened.
antonym obtuse.

adamant *adj.* adamantine, determined, firm, fixed, flinty, hard, immovable, impenetrable, indestructible, inexorable, inflexible, infrangible, insistent, intransigent, obdurate, resolute, rigid, rock-like, rocky, set, steely, stiff, stony, stubborn, tough, unbending, unbreakable, uncompromising, unrelenting, unshakable, unyielding.
antonyms flexible, pliant, yielding.

adapt *v.* acclimatize, accommodate, adjust, alter, apply, attemper, change, comply, conform, contemper, convert, customize, familiarize, fashion, fit, habituate, harmonize, match, metamorphose, modify, prepare, proportion, qualify, refashion, remodel, shape, suit, tailor.

add *v.* adjoin, affix, amplify, annex, append, attach, augment, combine, compute, count, include, join, reckon, subjoin, sum up, superimpose, supplement, tack on, tot up, total.
antonym subtract.

add up add, amount, be consistent, be plausible, be reasonable, come to, compute, count, count up, hang together, hold water, imply, indicate, make sense, mean, reckon, reveal, ring true, signify, stand to reason, sum up, tally, tot up, total.

addict *n.* acid-head, adherent, buff, devotee, dope-fiend, enthusiast, fan, fiend, follower, freak, head, hop-head, junkie, mainliner, nut, pot-head, tripper, user.

address[1] *n.* abode, department, direction, domicile, dwelling, home, house, inscription, location, lodging, place, residence, situation, superscription, whereabouts.

address[2] *n.* adroitness, air, allocution, application, art, bearing, declamation, deftness, dexterity, discourse, discretion, dispatch, disquisition, dissertation, expedition, expertise, expertness, facility, harangue, ingenuity, lecture, manner, oration, sermon, skilfulness, skill, speech, tact, talk.
v. accost, address (oneself) to, apostrophize, apply (oneself) to, approach, attend to, bespeak, buttonhole, concentrate on, devote (oneself) to, discourse, engage in, focus on, greet, hail, harangue, invoke, lecture, orate, salute, sermonize, speak, speak to, take care of, talk, talk to, turn to, undertake.

adept *adj.* able, accomplished, ace, adroit, deft, dexterous, experienced, expert, masterful, masterly, nimble, polished, practiced, proficient, skilful, skilled, versed.
antonyms bungling, incompetent, inept.
n. ace, dab hand, dabster, deacon, don, expert, genius, maestro, mahatma, master, old hand, pastmaster, wizard.
antonyms bungler, incompetent.

adequate *adj.* able, acceptable, capable, commensurate, competent, condign, efficacious, enough, fair, fit, passable, presentable, requisite, respectable, satisfactory, serviceable, sufficient, suitable, tolerable.
antonyms inadequate, insufficient.

adhere *v.* abide by, accrete, agree, attach, cement, cleave, cleave to, cling, coalesce, cohere, combine, comply with, fasten, fix, follow, fulfil, glue, heed, hold, hold fast, join, keep, link, maintain, mind, obey, observe, paste, respect, stand by, stick, stick fast, support, unite.

adherent *n.* admirer, advocate, aficionado, devotee, disciple, enthusiast, fan, follower, freak, hanger-on, henchman, nut, partisan, satellite, sectary, supporter, upholder, votary.

adhesive *adj.* adherent, adhering, attaching, clinging, cohesive, emplastic, gluey, glutinous, gummy, holding, mucilaginous, sticking, sticky, tacky, tenacious.
n. cement, glue, gum, mountant, mucilage, paste, tape.

adjacent *adj.* abutting, adjoining, alongside, beside, bordering, close, conterminant, conterminate, conterminous, contiguous, juxtaposed, near, neighboring, next, proximate, touching, vicinal.

adjoin *v.* abut, add, affix, annex, append, approximate, attach, border, combine, communicate with, connect, couple, impinge, interconnect, join, juxtapose, link, meet, neighbor, touch, unite, verge.

adjourn *v.* continue, defer, delay, discontinue, interrupt, postpone, prorogue, put off, recess, stay, suspend.
antonym convene.

adjust *v.* acclimatize, accommodate, accustom, adapt, alter, arrange, balance, change, coapt, compose, concert, conform, convert, dispose, fine-tune, fit, fix, harmonize, jiggle, measure, modify, order, proportion, reconcile, rectify, redress, refashion, regulate, remodel, reshape, set, settle, shape, square, suit, temper, tune.
antonyms derange, disarrange, upset.

administer *v.* adhibit, apply, assign, conduct, contribute, control, direct, disburse, dispense, dispose, distribute, dole out, execute, give, govern, head, impose, lead, manage, measure out, mete out, officiate, organize, oversee, perform, preside over, provide, regulate, rule, run, superintend, supervise, supply.

administration *n.* adhibition, administering, application, conduct, control, direction, directorship, disbursement, dispensation, disposal, distribution, execution, executive, governing, governing body, government, leadership, management, ministry, organization, overseeing, performance, provision, regime, regulation, rule, ruling, running, settlement, superintendence, supervision, supply, term of office.

admirable *adj.* choice, commendable, creditable, deserving, estimable, excellent, exquisite, fine, laudable, meritorious, praiseworthy, rare, respected, superior, valuable, wonderful, worthy.
antonym despicable.

admiration *n.* adoration, affection, amazement, appreciation, approbation, approval, astonishment, awe, delight, esteem, fureur, idolism, pleasure, praise, regard, respect, reverence, surprise, veneration, wonder, wonderment, worship.
antonym contempt.

admire *v.* adore, applaud, appreciate, approve, esteem, iconize, idolize, laud, praise, prize, respect, revere, value, venerate, worship.
antonym despise.

admissible *adj.* acceptable, allowable, allowed, equitable, justifiable, lawful, legitimate, licit, passable, permissible, permitted, tolerable, tolerated.
antonyms illegitimate, inadmissible.

admission *n.* acceptance, access, acknowledgment, adhibition, admittance, admitting, affirmation, allowance, avowal, concession, confession, declaration, disclosure, divulgence, entrance, entrée, entry, exposé, granting, inclusion, ingress, initiation, introduction, owning, profession, revelation.
antonyms denial, exclusion.

admit *v.* accept, acknowledge, adhibit, affirm, agree, allow, allow to enter, avow, concede, confess, declare, disclose, divulge, give access, grant, initiate, introduce, intromit, let, let in, permit, profess, receive, recognize, reveal, take in.
antonyms exclude, gainsay.

admittance *n.* acceptance, access, admitting, allowing, entrance, entrée, entry, ingress, letting in, passage, reception.

admonish *v.* advise, berate, caution, censure, check, chide, counsel, enjoin, exhort, forewarn, rebuke, reprehend, reprimand, reproach, reprove, scold, upbraid, warn.

admonition *n.* advice, berating, caution, censure, counsel, pi-jaw, rebuke, reprehension, reprimand, reproach, reproof, scolding, warning.

ado *n.* agitation, bother, business, bustle, ceremony, commotion, confusion, delay, disturbance, excitement, ferment, flurry, fuss, hassle, hurly-burly, kerfuffle, labor, pother, stir, to-do, trouble, tumult, turmoil.
antonyms calm, tranquility.

adolescence *n.* boyhood, boyishness, childishness, development, girlhood, girlishness, immaturity, juvenescence, juvenility, minority, puberty, puerility, teens, transition, youth, youthfulness.
antonym senescence.

adopt *v.* accept, affect, appropriate, approve, assume, back, choose, embrace, endorse, espouse, follow, foster, maintain, ratify, sanction, select, support, take in, take on, take up.
antonyms disown, repudiate.

adoration *n.* admiration, esteem, estimation, exaltation, glorification, honor, idolatry, idolization, love, magnification, reverence, veneration, worship.
antonyms abhorrence, detestation.

adore *v.* admire, cherish, dote on, esteem, exalt, glorify, honor, idolatrize, idolize, love, magnify, revere, reverence, venerate, worship.
antonyms abhor, hate.

adorn *v.* adonize, apparel, array, beautify, bedeck, bedight, bedizen, begem, bejewel, bestick, crown, deck, decorate, dight, doll up, embellish, emblazon, enhance, enrich, furbish, garnish, gild, grace, impearl, miniate, ornament, tart up, trick out, trim.

adrift *adj.* aimless, amiss, anchorless, astray, at sea, directionless, goalless, insecure, off course, purposeless, rootless, rudderless, unsettled, wrong.
antonyms anchored, stable.

adroit *adj.* able, adept, apt, artful, clever, cunning, deft, dexterous, expert, habile, ingenious, masterful, neat, nimble, proficient, quick, resourceful, skilful, skilled, slick.
antonyms clumsy, inept, maladroit.

adult *adj.* developed, full-grown, fully grown, grown-up, mature, of age, ripe, ripened.
antonym immature.

advance *v.* accelerate, adduce, allege, ameliorate, assist, benefit, bring forward, cite, elevate, expedite, facilitate, foster, furnish, further, go ahead, go forward, grow, hasten, improve, increase, lend, move on, multiply, offer, pay beforehand, present, press on, proceed, proffer, profit, progress, promote, prosper, provide, raise, send forward, speed, submit, suggest, supply, thrive, upgrade.
antonyms impede, retard, retreat.
n. advancement, amelioration, betterment, breakthrough, credit, deposit, development, down payment, furtherance, gain, growth, headway, improvement, increase, loan, preferment, prepayment, profit, progress, promotion, retainer, rise, step.
antonym recession.
adj. beforehand, early, foremost, forward, in front, leading, preliminary, prior.

advantage *n.* account, aid, ascendancy, asset, assistances, avail, benefit, blessing, boon, boot, convenience, dominance, edge, expediency, fruit, gain, good, help, hold, interest, lead, leverage, precedence, pre-eminence, profit, purchase, service, start, superiority, sway, upper hand, use, usefulness, utility, welfare.
antonyms disadvantage, hindrance.

adventure *n.* chance, contingency, enterprise, experience, exploit, gest, hazard, incident, occurrence, risk, speculation, undertaking, venture.

adventurous *adj.* adventuresome, audacious, bold, dangerous, daredevil, daring, dauntless, doughty, enterprising, foolhardy, game, hazardous, headstrong, impetuous, intrepid, perilous, plucky, rash, reckless, risky, spunky, swashbuckling, temerarious, venturesome.
antonyms cautious, chary, prudent.

adversary *n.* antagonist, assailant, attacker, competitor, contestant, enemy, foe, foeman, opponent, opposer, rival.
antonyms ally, supporter.

adverse *adj.* antagonistic, conflicting, contrary, counter, counter-productive, detrimental, disadvantageous, hostile, hurtful, inauspicious, inexpedient, inimical, injurious, inopportune, negative, noxious, opposing, opposite, reluctant, repugnant, uncongenial, unfavorable, unfortunate, unfriendly, unlucky, unpropitious, untoward, unwilling.
antonyms advantageous, propitious.

adversity *n.* affliction, bad luck, blight, calamity, catastrophe, contretemps, disaster, distress, hard times, hardship, ill-fortune, ill-luck, mischance, misery, misfortune, mishap, reverse, sorrow, suffering, trial, tribulation, trouble, woe, wretchedness.
antonym prosperity.

advertise *v.* advise, announce, apprize, blazon, broadcast, bruit, declare, display, flaunt, herald, inform, make known, notify, plug, praise, proclaim, promote, promulgate, publicize, publish, puff, push, tout, trumpet.

advertisement *n.* ad, advert, announcement, bill, blurb, circular, commercial, display, handbill, handout, hype, leaflet, notice, placard, plug, poster, promotion, propaganda, propagation, publicity, puff, puffery.

advice *n.* admonition, caution, communication, conseil, counsel, direction, do's and don'ts, guidance, help, information, injunction, instruction, intelligence, memorandum, notice, notification, opinion, recommendation, rede, suggestion, view, warning, wisdom, word.

advisable *adj.* advantageous, appropriate, apt, beneficial, correct, desirable, expedient, fit, fitting, judicious, meet, politic, profitable, proper, prudent, recommended, seemly, sensible, sound, suggested, suitable, wise.
antonyms inadvisable, injudicious.

advise *v.* acquaint, apprize, bethink, caution, commend, counsel, enjoin, forewarn, guide, inform, instruct, make known, notify, recommend, report, suggest, teach, tell, tutor, urge, warn.

adviser *n.* admonitor, aide, authority, coach, confidant, consultant, counsel, counselor, éminence grise, guide, helper, instructor, lawyer, mentor, monitor, preceptor, righthand man, solicitor, teacher, therapist, tutor.

advocate *v.* adopt, advise, argue for, campaign for, champion, countenance, defend, encourage, endorse, espouse, favor, justify, patronize, plead for, press for, promote, propose, recommend, subscribe to, support, uphold, urge.
antonyms deprecate, disparage, impugn.
n. apologist, apostle, attorney, backer, barrister, campaigner, champion, counsel, counselor, defender, interceder, intercessor, lawyer, mediator, paraclete, patron, pleader, promoter, proponent, proposer, solicitor, speaker, spokesman, supporter, upholder, vindicator.
antonyms critic, opponent.

affable *adj.* agreeable, amiable, amicable, approachable, benevolent, benign, civil, congenial, cordial, courteous, expansive, free, friendly, genial, good-humored, good-natured, gracious, kindly, mild, obliging, open, pleasant, sociable, suave, urbane, warm.
antonyms cool, reserved, reticent, unfriendly.

affair *n.* activity, adventure, amour, amourette, business, circumstance, concern, connection, episode, event, happening, incident, interest, intrigue, liaison, matter, occurrence, operation, organization, party, proceeding, project, question, reception, relationship, responsibility, romance, subject, topic, transaction, undertaking.

affect[1] *v.* act on, agitate, alter, apply to, attack, bear upon, change, concern, disturb, grieve, grip, impinge upon, impress, influence, interest, involve, melt, modify, move, overcome, penetrate, pertain to, perturb, prevail over, regard, relate to, seize, soften, stir, strike, sway, touch, transform, trouble, upset.

affect[2] *v.* adopt, aspire to, assume, contrive, counterfeit, fake, feign, imitate, pretend, profess, put on, sham, simulate.

affected[1] *adj.* afflicted, agitated, altered, changed, concerned, damaged, distressed, gripped, hurt, impaired, impressed, influenced, injured, melted, moved, perturbed, smitten, stimulated, stirred, swayed, touched, troubled, upset.

affected[2] *adj.* alembicated, artificial, assumed, bogus, chichi, conceited, contrived, counterfeit, debby, euphuistic, fake, feigned, fussy, greenery-yallery, hyperaesthesic, hyperaesthetic, insincere, lah-di-dah, literose, mannered, mincing, minikin, namby-pamby, niminy-piminy, phoney, pompous, precious, pretended, pretentious, put-on, sham, simulated, spurious, stiff, studied, unnatural.
antonyms genuine, natural.

affection *n.* amity, attachment, care, desire, devotion,

favor, feeling, fondness, friendliness, good will, inclination, kindness, liking, love, partiality, passion, penchant, predilection, predisposition, proclivity, propensity, regard, tenderness, warmth.
antonyms antipathy, dislike.

affectionate *adj.* amiable, amorous, attached, caring, cordial, devoted, doting, fond, friendly, kind, loving, passionate, responsive, solicitous, tender, warm, warm-hearted.
antonyms cold, undemonstrative.

affirm *v.* assert, asseverate, attest, aver, avouch, avow, certify, confirm, corroborate, declare, depose, endorse, maintain, pronounce, ratify, state, swear, testify, witness.

afflict *v.* beset, burden, distress, grieve, harass, harm, harrow, hurt, oppress, pain, plague, rack, smite, strike, torment, torture, trouble, try, visit, wound, wring.
antonyms comfort, solace.

affliction *n.* adversity, calamity, cross, curse, depression, disaster, disease, distress, grief, hardship, illness, misery, misfortune, ordeal, pain, plague, scourge, sickness, sorrow, suffering, torment, trial, tribulation, trouble, visitation, woe, wretchedness.
antonyms comfort, consolation, solace.

affluent *adj.* comfortable, flourishing, flush, loaded, moneyed, opulent, pecunious, prosperous, rich, wealthy, well-heeled, well-off, well-to-do.
antonyms impecunious, impoverished, poor.

afford *v.* bear, bestow, cope with, engender, furnish, generate, give, grant, impart, manage, offer, produce, provide, render, spare, stand, supply, sustain, yield.

affront *v.* abuse, anger, annoy, displease, gall, incense, insult, irritate, nettle, offend, outrage, pique, provoke, slight, snub, vex.
antonyms appease, compliment.
n. abuse, discourtesy, disrespect, facer, indignity, injury, insult, offense, outrage, provocation, rudeness, slap in the face, slight, slur, snub, vexation, wrong.
antonym compliment.

afraid *adj.* aghast, alarmed, anxious, apprehensive, cowardly, diffident, distrustful, faint-hearted, fearful, frightened, intimidated, nervous, regretful, reluctant, scared, sorry, suspicious, timid, timorous, tremulous, unhappy.
antonyms confident, unafraid.

after *prep.* afterwards, as a result of, behind, below, following, in consequence of, later, post, subsequent to, subsequently, succeeding, thereafter.
antonym before.

again *adv.* afresh, also, anew, another time, au contraire, besides, bis, conversely, da capo, de integro, de novo, ditto, encore, furthermore, in addition, moreover, on the contrary, on the other hand, once more.

against *prep.* abutting, across, adjacent to, athwart, close up to, confronting, contra, counter to, facing, fronting, hostile to, in contact with, in contrast to, in defiance of, in exchange for, in opposition to, in the face of, on, opposed to, opposing, opposite to, resisting, touching, versus.
antonyms for, pro.

age *n.* aeon, agedness, anility, caducity, date, day, days, decline, decrepitude, dotage, duration, elderliness, epoch, era, generation, lifetime, majority, maturity, old age, period, senescence, senility, seniority, span, the sere and yellow, time, years.
antonyms salad days, youth.
v. decline, degenerate, deteriorate, grow old, mature, mellow, obsolesce, ripen, season.

aged *adj.* advanced, age-old, ancient, antiquated, antique, decrepit, elderly, geriatric, gray, hoary, old, patriarchal, senescent, sere, superannuated, time-worn, venerable, worn-out.
antonyms young, youthful.

agency *n.* action, activity, bureau, business, department, effect, effectuation, efficiency, finger, force, handling, influence, instrumentality, intercession, intervention, means, mechanism, mediation, medium, office, offices, operation, organization, power, work, workings.

agent *n.* actor, agency, author, cause, channel, delegate, deputy, doer, emissary, envoy, executor, factor, force, functionary, go-between, instrument, intermediary, legate, means, middleman, mover, negotiator, operative, operator, organ, performer, power, practisant, rep, representative, substitute, surrogate, vehicle, vicar, worker.

aggravate *v.* annoy, exacerbate, exaggerate, exasperate, harass, hassle, heighten, incense, increase, inflame, intensify, irk, irritate, magnify, needle, nettle, peeve, pester, provoke, tease, vex, worsen.
antonyms alleviate, appease, mollify.

aggregate *n.* accumulation, agglomeration, aggregation, amount, assemblage, body, bulk, collection, combination, entirety, generality, heap, herd, lump, mass, mixture, pile, sum, throng, total, totality, whole.
adj. accumulated, added, assembled, collected, collective, combined, complete, composite, corporate, cumulative, mixed, total, united.
antonyms individual, particular.
v. accumulate, add up, agglomerate, amass, amount to, assemble, cluster, collect, combine, conglomerate, heap, mix, pile, total.

aggression *n.* aggressiveness, antagonism, assault, attack, bellicosity, belligerence, combativeness, destructiveness, encroachment, hostility, impingement, incursion, injury, intrusion, invasion, jingoism, militancy, offence, offensive, onslaught, provocation, pugnacity, raid.

aggressive *adj.* argumentative, assertive, bellicose, belligerent, bold, butch, combative, contentious, destructive, disputatious, dynamic, energetic, enterprising, forceful, go-ahead, hostile, intrusive, invasive, jingoistic, militant, offensive, provocative, pugnacious,

pushful, pushing, pushy, quarrelsome, scrappy, vigorous, zealous.
antonyms peaceable, submissive.

aghast *adj.* afraid, amazed, appalled, astonished, astounded, awestruck, confounded, dismayed, frightened, horrified, horror-struck, shocked, startled, stunned, stupefied, terrified, thunder-struck.

agile *adj.* active, acute, adroit, alert, brisk, clever, fleet, flexible, limber, lissome, lithe, lively, mobile, nimble, prompt, quick, quick-witted, sharp, smart, sprightly, spry, supple, swift.
antonyms clumsy, stiff, torpid.

agility *n.* activity, acuteness, adroitness, alertness, briskness, cleverness, flexibility, lissomeness, litheness, liveliness, mobility, nimbleness, promptitude, promptness, quickness, quick-wittedness, sharpness, sprightliness, spryness, suppleness, swiftness.
antonyms sluggishness, stiffness, torpidity.

agitate *v.* alarm, arouse, beat, churn, confuse, convulse, discompose, disconcert, disquiet, distract, disturb, excite, ferment, flurry, fluster, incite, inflame, perturb, rattle, rock, rouse, ruffle, shake, stimulate, stir, toss, trouble, unnerve, unsettle, upset, work up, worry.
antonyms calm, tranquilize.

agitated *adj.* anxious, discomposed, distracted, feverish, flurried, flustered, in a lather, insecure, jumpy, nervous, perturbed, restive, restless, ruffled, tumultuous, twitchy, uneasy, unnerved, unsettled, upset, wrought-up.
antonyms calm, composed.

agony *n.* affliction, anguish, distress, misery, pain, pangs, paroxysm, spasm, suffering, throes, torment, torture, tribulation, woe, wretchedness.

agree *v.* accede, accord, acquiesce, admit, allow, answer, assent, chime, coincide, comply, concede, concord, concur, conform, consent, consort, contract, correspond, cotton, covenant, engage, fadge, fit, fix, get on, grant, harmonize, homologate, jibe, match, permit, promise, see eye to eye, settle, side with, square, suit, tally, yield.
antonyms conflict, disagree.

agreeable *adj.* acceptable, acquiescent, amenable, amicable, appropriate, approving, attractive, befitting, compatible, complying, concurring, conformable, congenial, consenting, consistent, d'accord, delectable, delightful, enjoyable, fitting, gemütlich, gratifying, in accord, likable, palatable, pleasant, pleasing, pleasurable, proper, responsive, satisfying, suitable, sympathetic, well-disposed, willing.
antonyms disagreeable, distasteful, incompatible, nasty.

agreement[1] *n.* acceptance, accord, accordance, adherence, affinity, analogy, closing, compact, compatibility, complaisance, compliance, concert, concord, concordat, concurrence, conformity, congruence, congruity, consentience, consistency, consonance, consort, convention, correspondence, harmony, modus vivendi, preconcert, resemblance, respondence, similarity, suitableness, sympathy, unanimity, union, unison.
antonym disagreement.

agreement[2] *n.* arrangement, bargain, compact, concordat, contract, covenant, deal, pact, settlement, treaty, understanding.

agriculture *n.* agribusiness, agronomics, agronomy, cultivation, culture, farming, geoponics, husbandry, tillage.

ahead *adj., adv.* advanced, along, at an advantage, at the head, before, earlier on, forwards, in advance, in front, in the forefront, in the lead, in the vanguard, leading, onwards, superior, to the fore, winning.

aid *v.* abet, accommodate, adminiculate, assist, befriend, boost, ease, encourage, expedite, facilitate, favor, help, oblige, promote, prop, rally round, relieve, second, serve, subsidize, succor, support, sustain.
antonyms impede, obstruct.
n. a leg up, adminicle, aidance, assistance, assistant, benefit, contribution, donation, encouragement, favor, help, helper, patronage, prop, relief, service, sponsorship, subsidy, subvention, succor, support, supporter.
antonyms impediment, obstruction.

ail *v.* afflict, annoy, be indisposed, bother, decline, distress, droop, fail, irritate, languish, pain, pine, sicken, trouble, upset, weaken, worry.
antonyms comfort, flourish.

ailing *adj.* debilitated, diseased, feeble, frail, ill, indisposed, infirm, invalid, languishing, off-color, out of sorts, peaky, poorly, sick, sickly, suffering, under the weather, unsound, unwell, weak, weakly.
antonyms flourishing, healthy.

ailment *n.* affliction, complaint, disability, disease, disorder, illness, indisposition, infection, infirmity, malady, sickness, weakness.

aim *v.* address, aspire, attempt, beam, design, direct, draw a bead, endeavor, essay, head for, intend, level, mean, plan, point, propose, purpose, resolve, seek, set one's sights on, sight, strive, take aim, target, train, try, want, wish, zero in on.
n. ambition, aspiration, course, desideratum, design, desire, direction, dream, end, goal, hope, intent, intention, mark, motive, object, objective, plan, purpose, scheme, target, telos, wish.

aimless *adj.* chance, desultory, directionless, erratic, feckless, frivolous, goalless, haphazard, irresolute, pointless, purposeless, rambling, random, stray, undirected, unguided, unmotivated, unpredictable, vagrant, wayward.
antonyms determined, positive, purposeful.

air *n.* ambience, ambient, appearance, aria, atmosphere, aura, bearing, blast, breath, breeze, character, demeanor, draught, effect, ether, feeling, flavor, heavens, impression, lay, look, manner, melody, mood, motif, oxygen, puff, quality, sky, song, strain, style, theme, tone, tune, waft, whiff, wind, zephyr.

v. aerate, broadcast, circulate, communicate, declare, disclose, display, disseminate, divulge, exhibit, expose, express, freshen, give vent to, make known, make public, parade, proclaim, publicize, publish, reveal, tell, utter, vaunt, ventilate, voice.

airy *adj.* aerial, blithe, blowy, bodiless, breezy, buoyant, cheerful, cheery, debonair, delicate, disembodied, drafty, ethereal, fanciful, flimsy, fresh, frolicsome, gay, graceful, gusty, happy, high-spirited, illusory, imaginary, immaterial, incorporeal, insouciant, insubstantial, jaunty, light, light-hearted, lively, lofty, merry, nimble, nonchalant, off-hand, open, roomy, spacious, spectral, sportive, sprightly, trifling, uncluttered, unreal, unsubstantial, vaporous, visionary, weightless, well-ventilated, windy.
antonyms close, heavy, oppressive, stuffy.

aisle *n.* alleyway, ambulatory, corridor, deambulatory, division, gangway, lane, passage, passageway, path, walkway.

akin *adj.* affiliated, agnate, alike, allied, analogous, cognate, comparable, congenial, connected, consanguineous, consonant, corresponding, kin, kindred, like, parallel, related, similar.
antonym alien.

alarm *v.* affright, agitate, daunt, dismay, distress, frighten, give (someone) a turn, panic, put the wind up (someone), scare, startle, terrify, terrorize, unnerve.
antonyms calm, reassure, soothe.
n. alarm-bell, alert, anxiety, apprehension, bell, consternation, danger signal, dismay, distress, distress signal, fear, fright, horror, larum, larum-bell, nervousness, panic, scare, siren, terror, tocsin, trepidation, unease, uneasiness, warning.
antonym composure.

alarming *adj.* daunting, direful, dismaying, distressing, disturbing, dreadful, frightening, ominous, scaring, shocking, startling, terrifying, threatening, unnerving.
antonym reassuring.

alcoholic *adj.* ardent, brewed, distilled, fermented, hard, inebriant, inebriating, intoxicating, spirituous, strong, vinous.
n. bibber, boozer, dipso, dipsomaniac, drunk, drunkard, hard drinker, inebriate, lush, piss artist, soak, sot, sponge, tippler, toper, tosspot, wino.

alert *adj.* active, agile, attentive, brisk, careful, circumspect, heedful, lively, nimble, observant, on the ball, on the lookout, on the qui vive, perceptive, prepared, quick, ready, sharp-eyed, sharp-witted, spirited, sprightly, vigilant, wary, watchful, wide-awake.
antonyms listless, slow.
n. alarm, signal, siren, tocsin, warning.
v. alarm, forewarn, inform, notify, signal, tip off, warn.

alias *n.* allonym, anonym, assumed name, false name, nick-name, nom de guerre, nom de plume, pen name, pseudonym, soubriquet, stage name.
adv. alias dictus, also, also called, also known as, formerly, otherwise, otherwise called.

alibi *n.* cover-up, defence, excuse, explanation, justification, plea, pretext, reason, story.

alien *adj.* adverse, antagonistic, conflicting, contrary, estranged, exotic, extraneous, foreign, inappropriate, incompatible, incongruous, inimical, opposed, outlandish, remote, repugnant, separated, strange, unfamiliar.
antonym akin.
n. emigrant, foreigner, immigrant, metic, newcomer, outlander, outsider, stranger.
antonym native.

alight[1] *v.* come down, come to rest, debark, descend, detrain, disembark, disentrain, dismount, get down, get off, land, light, perch, settle, touch down.
antonyms ascend, board, rise.

alight[2] *adj.* ablaze, afire, aflame, blazing, bright, brilliant, burning, fiery, flaming, flaring, ignited, illuminated, illumined, lighted, lit, lit up, on fire, radiant, shining.
antonym dark.

alive *adj.* active, alert, animate, animated, awake, breathing, brisk, cheerful, eager, energetic, existent, existing, extant, functioning, having life, in existence, in force, life-like, live, lively, living, operative, quick, real, spirited, sprightly, spry, subsisting, vibrant, vigorous, vital, vivacious, zestful.
antonyms dead, lifeless.

alive with abounding in, bristling with, bustling with, buzzing with, crawling with, crowded with, infested with, lousy with, overflowing with, overrun by, stiff with, swarming with, teeming with, thronged with.

allay *v.* allege, alleviate, appease, assuage, blunt, calm, check, compose, diminish, dull, ease, lessen, lull, mitigate, moderate, mollify, pacify, quell, quiet, reduce, relieve, slake, smooth, soften, soothe, subdue, tranquilize.
antonyms exacerbate, intensify.

allege *v.* adduce, advance, affirm, assert, asseverate, attest, aver, avow, charge, claim, contend, declare, depose, hold, insist, maintain, plead, profess, put forward, state.

allegiance *n.* adherence, constancy, devotion, duty, faithfulness, fealty, fidelity, friendship, homage, loyalty, obedience, obligation, support.
antonyms disloyalty, enmity.

allegory *n.* analogy, apologue, comparison, emblem, fable, metaphor, myth, parable, story, symbol, symbolism, tale.

alleviate *v.* abate, allay, assuage, blunt, check, cushion, deaden, diminish, dull, ease, lessen, lighten, mitigate, moderate, modify, mollify, palliate, quell, quench, quiet, reduce, relieve, slacken, slake, smooth, soften, soothe, subdue, temper.
antonym aggravate.

alley *n.* alleyway, back street, close, entry, gate, lane, mall, passage, passageway, pathway, walk.

alliance *n.* affiliation, affinity, agreement, association, bloc, bond, cartel, coalition, combination, compact, concordat, confederacy, confederation, conglomerate, connection, consociation, consortium, faction, federation, guild, league, marriage, pact, partnership, syndicate, treaty, union.
antonyms divorce, enmity, estrangement, hostility.

allot *v.* allocate, apportion, appropriate, assign, budget, designate, dispense, distribute, earmark, grant, mete, render, set aside, share out.

allow *v.* accord, acknowledge, acquiesce, admeasure, admit, allocate, allot, apportion, approve, assign, authorize, bear, brook, concede, confess, deduct, endure, give, give leave, grant, let, own, permit, provide, put up with, remit, sanction, spare, stand, suffer, tolerate.
antonyms deny, forbid.

allow for arrange for, bear in mind, consider, foresee, include, keep in mind, keep in view, make allowances for, make concessions for, make provision for, plan for, provide for, take into account.
antonym discount.

allowance *n.* admission, allocation, allotment, amount, annuity, apportionment, concession, deduction, discount, emolument, grant, lot, measure, pension, portion, quota, ration, rebate, reduction, remittance, sanction, share, stint, stipend, subsidy, sufferance, tolerance, weighting, X-factor.

allude *v.* adumbrate, advert, cite, glance, hint, imply, infer, insinuate, intimate, mention, refer, remark, speak of, suggest, touch upon.

allure *v.* attract, beguile, cajole, captivate, charm, coax, decoy, disarm, enchant, enrapture, entice, entrance, fascinate, interest, inveigle, lead on, lure, persuade, seduce, tempt, win over.
antonym repel.
n. appeal, attraction, captivation, charm, enchantment, enticement, fascination, glamor, lure, magnetism, persuasion, seductiveness, temptation.

ally *n.* abettor, accessory, accomplice, associate, coadjutor, collaborator, colleague, confederate, confrere, consort, coworker, friend, helper, helpmate, leaguer, partner, sidekick.
antonyms antagonist, enemy.
v. affiliate, amalgamate, associate, band together, collaborate, combine, confederate, conjoin, connect, fraternize, join, join forces, league, marry, team up, unify, unite.
antonym estrange.

almighty *adj.* absolute, all-powerful, awful, desperate, enormous, excessive, great, intense, invincible, loud, omnipotent, overpowering, overwhelming, plenipotent, severe, supreme, terrible, unlimited.
antonyms impotent, insignificant, weak.

almost *adv.* about, all but, approaching, approximately, as good as, close to, just about, nearing, nearly, not far from, not quite, practically, towards, virtually, well-nigh.

alms *n.* benefaction, beneficence, bounty, charity, donation, gift, largess(e), offerings, relief.

alone *adj., adv.* abandoned, apart, by itself, by oneself, deserted, desolate, detached, discrete, forlorn, forsaken, incomparable, isolated, just, lonely, lonesome, matchless, mere, nonpareil, on one's own, only, peerless, separate, simply, single, single-handed, singular, sole, solitary, unaccompanied, unaided, unassisted, unattended, uncombined, unconnected, unequaled, unescorted, unique, unparalleled, unsurpassed.

aloof *adj.* chilly, cold, cool, detached, distant, forbidding, formal, haughty, inaccessible, indifferent, offish, remote, reserved, reticent, stand-offish, supercilious, unapproachable, uncompanionable, unforthcoming, unfriendly, uninterested, unresponsive, unsociable, unsympathetic.
antonyms concerned, sociable.

also *adv.* additionally, along with, and, as well, as well as, besides, ditto, further, furthermore, in addition, including, moreover, plus, therewithal, to boot, too.

alter *v.* adapt, adjust, amend, bushel, castrate, change, convert, diversify, emend, metamorphose, modify, qualify, recast, reform, remodel, reshape, revise, shift, take liberties with, transform, transmute, transpose, turn, vary.
antonym fix.

alteration *n.* adaptation, adjustment, amendment, castration, change, conversion, difference, diversification, emendation, interchanging, metamorphosis, modification, reciprocation, reformation, remodeling, reshaping, revision, rotation, shift, transfiguration, transformation, transmutation, transposition, variance, variation, vicissitude.
antonym fixity.

altercation *n.* argument, bickering, clash, contention, controversy, debate, disagreement, discord, dispute, dissension, fracas, logomachy, quarrel, row, sparring, squabble, wrangle.

alternate *v.* alter, change, fluctuate, follow one another, interchange, intersperse, oscillate, reciprocate, rotate, substitute, take turns, transpose, vary.
adj. alternating, alternative, another, different, every other, every second, interchanging, reciprocal, reciprocating, reciprocative, rotating, second, substitute.

alternative *n.* back-up, choice, option, other, preference, recourse, selection, substitute.
adj. alternate, another, different, fall-back, fringe, other, second, substitute, unconventional, unorthodox.

although *conj.* admitting that, albeit, conceding that, even if, even supposing, even though, granted that, howbeit, notwithstanding, though, while.

altitude *n.* elevation, height, loftiness, stature, tallness.
antonym depth.

altogether *adv.* absolutely, all in all, all told, as a whole, collectively, completely, entirely, fully, generally, holusbolus, in all, in general, in sum, in toto, on the whole, perfectly, quite, thoroughly, totally, utterly, wholesale, wholly.

altruism *n.* considerateness, disinterestedness, generosity, humanity, philanthropy, public spirit, self-abnegation, self-sacrifice, social conscience, unself, unselfishness.
antonym selfishness.

always *adv.* aye, consistently, constantly, continually, endlessly, eternally, ever, everlastingly, evermore, every time, forever, in perpetuum, invariably, perpetually, regularly, repeatedly, sempiternally, unceasingly, unfailingly, without exception.
antonym never.

amalgamate *v.* alloy, ally, blend, coalesce, coalize, combine, commingle, compound, fuse, homogenize, incorporate, integrate, intermix, merge, mingle, synthesize, unify, unite.
antonym separate.

amass *v.* accumulate, agglomerate, agglutinate, aggregate, assemble, collect, compile, foregather, garner, gather, heap up, hoard, pile up, rake up, scrape together.

amateur *n.* buff, dabbler, dilettante, do-it-yourselfer, fancier, ham, layman, non-professional.
antonym professional.

amaze *v.* alarm, astonish, astound, bewilder, confound, daze, disconcert, dismay, dumbfound, electrify, flabbergast, floor, shock, stagger, startle, stun, stupefy, surprise, wow.

ambiguous *adj.* ambivalent, amphibolic, amphibological, amphibolous, confused, confusing, cryptic, Delphic, double-barrelled, double-meaning, doubtful, dubious, enigmatic, enigmatical, equivocal, inconclusive, indefinite, indeterminate, louche, multivocal, obscure, oracular, puzzling, uncertain, unclear, vague, woolly.
antonyms clear.

ambition *n.* aim, aspiration, avidity, craving, design, desire, dream, drive, eagerness, end, enterprise, goal, hankering, hope, hunger, ideal, intent, longing, object, objective, purpose, push, striving, target, wish, yearning, zeal.
antonyms apathy, diffidence.

ambitious *adj.* arduous, aspiring, assertive, avid, bold, challenging, demanding, desirous, difficult, driving, eager, elaborate, energetic, enterprising, enthusiastic, exacting, fervid, formidable, go-ahead, grandiose, hard, hopeful, impressive, industrious, intent, keen, pretentious, purposeful, pushy, severe, strenuous, striving, zealous.
antonym unassuming.

amble *v.* dawdle, drift, meander, mosey, perambulate, promenade, ramble, saunter, stroll, toddle, walk, wander.
antonyms march, stride.

ambush *n.* ambuscade, concealment, cover, emboscata, hiding, hiding-place, retreat, shelter, snare, trap, waylaying.
v. ambuscade, bushwhack, ensnare, entrap, surprise, trap, waylay.

amend *v.* adjust, alter, ameliorate, better, change, correct, emend, emendate, enhance, fix, improve, mend, modify, qualify, rectify, redress, reform, remedy, repair, revise.
antonyms impair, worsen.

amends *n.* atonement, compensation, expiation, indemnification, indemnity, mitigation, quittance, recompense, redress, reparation, requital, restitution, restoration, satisfaction.

amiable *adj.* accessible, affable, agreeable, approachable, attractive, benign, biddable, charming, cheerful, companionable, complaisant, congenial, conversable, delightful, engaging, friendly, gemütlich, genial, good-humored, good-natured, good-tempered, kind, kindly, likable, lovable, obliging, pleasant, pleasing, sociable, sweet, winning, winsome.
antonyms hostile, unfriendly.

amid *conj.* amidst, among, amongst, in the middle of, in the midst of, in the thick of, surrounded by.

amiss *adj.* awry, defective, erroneous, fallacious, false, faulty, improper, inaccurate, inappropriate, incorrect, out of order, unsuitable, untoward, wonky, wrong.
adv. ill, imperfect, imprecise, out of kilter.
antonyms right, well.

among *prep.* amid, amidst, amongst, between, in the middle of, in the midst of, in the thick of, midst, mongst, surrounded by, together with, with.

amorous *adj.* affectionate, amatory, ardent, attached, doting, enamored, erotic, fond, impassioned, in love, lovesick, loving, lustful, passionate, randy, tender, uxorious.
antonyms cold, indifferent.

amount *n.* addition, aggregate, bulk, entirety, expanse, extent, lot, magnitude, mass, measure, number, quantity, quantum, quota, sum, sum total, supply, total, volume, whole.

amount to add up to, aggregate, approximate to, be equivalent to, be tantamount to, become, come to, equal, grow, mean, purport, run to, total.

ample *adj.* abundant, big, bountiful, broad, capacious, commodious, considerable, copious, expansive, extensive, full, generous, goodly, great, handsome, large, lavish, liberal, munificent, plenteous, plentiful, plenty, profuse, rich, roomy, spacious, substantial, sufficient, unrestricted, voluminous, wide. *antonyms* insufficient, meager.

amplify *v.* add to, augment, boost, broaden, bulk out, deepen, develop, dilate, elaborate, enhance, enlarge, expand, expatiate, extend, fill out, heighten, increase, intensify, lengthen, magnify, raise, strengthen, supplement, widen.
antonym reduce.

amuse *v.* absorb, beguile, charm, cheer, cheer up, delight, disport, divert, engross, enliven, entertain, enthral, gladden, interest, occupy, please, popjoy, recreate, regale, relax, slay, tickle.
antonym bore.

amusement *n.* beguilement, delight, disportment, distraction, diversion, enjoyment, entertainment, fun, game, gladdening, hilarity, hobby, interest, joke, lark, laughter, merriment, mirth, pastime, pleasure, prank, recreation, regalement, sport.
antonyms bore, boredom.

amusing *adj.* amusive, charming, cheerful, cheering, comical, delightful, diverting, droll, enjoyable, entertaining, facetious, funny, gladdening, hilarious, humorous, interesting, jocular, jolly, killing, laughable, lively, ludicrous, merry, pleasant, pleasing, risible, sportive, witty.
antonym boring.

analogous *adj.* agreeing, akin, alike, comparable, correlative, corresponding, equivalent, homologous, like, matching, parallel, reciprocal, related, resembling, similar.
antonym disparate.

analysis *n.* anatomization, anatomy, assay, breakdown, dissection, dissolution, division, enquiry, estimation, evaluation, examination, exegesis, explanation, explication, exposition, interpretation, investigation, judgment, opinion, reasoning, reduction, resolution, review, scrutiny, separation, sifting, study, test.

analyze *v.* anatomize, assay, break down, consider, dissect, dissolve, divide, estimate, evaluate, examine, interpret, investigate, judge, reduce, resolve, review, scrutinize, separate, sift, study, test.

ancestral *adj.* atavistic, avital, familial, genealogical, genetic, hereditary, lineal, parental.

ancestry *n.* ancestors, antecedents, antecessors, blood, derivation, descent, extraction, family, forebears, forefathers, genealogy, heredity, heritage, house, line, lineage, origin, parentage, pedigree, progenitors, race, roots, stirps, stock.

anchor *n.* grapnel, kedge, killick, mainstay, mud-hook, pillar of strength, prop, security, staff, support.
v. affix, attach, fasten, fix, make fast, moor.

ancient *adj.* aged, age-old, antediluvian, antiquated, antique, archaic, bygone, démodé, early, fossilized, hoary, immemorial, obsolete, old, olden, old-fashioned, original, outmoded, out-of-date, preadamic, prehistoric, primeval, primordial, pristine, superannuated, timeworn, venerable, world-old.
antonym modern.

anecdote *n.* exemplum, fable, reminiscence, sketch, story, tale, yarn.

anemic *adj.* ashen, bloodless, chalky, characterless, colorless, dull, enervated, exsanguine, exsanguin(e)ous, feeble, frail, ineffectual, infirm, insipid, pale, pallid, pasty, sallow, sickly, spiritless, toneless, wan, weak, whey-faced.
antonyms full-blooded, ruddy, sanguine.

anesthetic *n.* analgesic, anodyne, narcotic, opiate, painkiller, palliative, sedative, soporific, stupefacient, stupefactive.

anesthetize *v.* benumb, deaden, desensitize, dope, dull, etherize, lull, mull, numb, stupefy.

angel *n.* archangel, backer, benefactor, cherub, darling, divine messenger, fairy godmother, guardian spirit, ideal, paragon, principality, saint, seraph, supporter, treasure.
antonyms devil, fiend.

angelic *adj.* adorable, beatific, beautiful, celestial, cherubic, divine, entrancing, ethereal, exemplary, heavenly, holy, innocent, lovely, pious, pure, saintly, seraphic, unworldly, virtuous. *antonyms* devilish, fiendish.

anger *n.* annoyance, antagonism, bad blood, bile, bitterness, choler, dander, displeasure, dudgeon, exasperation, fury, gall, indignation, ire, irritability, irritation, monkey, outrage, passion, pique, rage, rancor, resentment, spleen, temper, vexation, wrath.
antonym forbearance.
v. affront, aggravate, annoy, antagonize, bother, bug, displease, enrage, exasperate, fret, frustrate, gall, incense, infuriate, irk, irritate, madden, miff, needle, nettle, offend, outrage, pique, provoke, rile, ruffle, vex.
antonyms appease, calm, please.

angry *adj.* aggravated, annoyed, antagonized, bitter, burned up, choked, choleric, chuffed, disgruntled, displeased, enraged, exasperated, furious, heated, hot, incensed, indignant, infuriated, irascible, irate, ireful, irked, irritable, irritated, mad, miffed, needled, nettled, outraged, passionate, piqued, provoked, raging, rancorous, ratty, red-headed, resentful, riled, shirty, splenetic, stomachful, tumultuous, uptight, waxy, wrathful, wroth.
antonyms calm, content.

anguish *n.* agony, angst, anxiety, desolation, distress, dole, dolor, grief, heartache, heartbreak, misery, pain, pang, rack, sorrow, suffering, torment, torture, tribulation, woe, wretchedness.
antonyms happiness, solace.

animal *n.* barbarian, beast, brute, creature, critter, cur, hound, mammal, monster, pig, savage, swine.
adj. bestial, bodily, brutish, carnal, faunal, feral, ferine, fleshly, gross, inhuman, instinctive, physical, piggish, savage, sensual, wild, zoic.

animate *v.* activate, arouse, embolden, encourage, energize, enliven, excite, fire, galvanize, goad, impel, incite, inspire, inspirit, instigate, invest, invigorate, irradiate, kindle, move, quicken, reactivate, revive, revivify, rouse, spark, spur, stimulate, stir, suffuse, urge, vitalize, vivify.
antonyms dull, inhibit.
adj. alive, breathing, conscious, live, living, sentient.
antonyms dull, spiritless.

animated *adj.* active, airy, alive, ardent, brisk, buoyant,

eager, ebullient, energetic, enthusiastic, excited, fervent, gay, glowing, impassioned, lively, passionate, quick, radiant, spirited, sprightly, vehement, vibrant, vigorous, vital, vivacious, vivid, zestful.
antonyms inert, sluggish.

animosity *n.* acrimony, animus, antagonism, antipathy, bad blood, bitterness, enmity, feud, feuding, hate, hatred, hostility, ill-will, loathing, malevolence, malice, malignity, odium, rancor, resentment, spite.
antonym goodwill.

annex *v.* acquire, add, adjoin, affix, append, appropriate, arrogate, attach, connect, conquer, expropriate, fasten, incorporate, join, occupy, purloin, seize, subjoin, tack, take over, unite, usurp.
n. addendum, additament, addition, adjunct, appendix, attachment, supplement.

annihilate *v.* abolish, assassinate, destroy, eliminate, eradicate, erase, exterminate, extinguish, extirpate, liquidate, murder, nullify, obliterate, raze, rub out, thrash, trounce, wipe out.

announce *v.* advertise, blazon, broadcast, declare, disclose, divulge, intimate, leak, make known, notify, preconize, proclaim, promulgate, propound, publicize, publish, report, reveal, state.
antonym suppress.

announcement *n.* advertisement, broadcast, bulletin, communiqué, declaration, disclosure, dispatch, divulgation, divulgence, intimation, notification, proclamation, promulgation, publication, report, revelation, statement.

annoy *v.* aggravate, anger, badger, bore, bother, bug, chagrin, contrary, displease, disturb, exasperate, fash, gall, get, give the pigs, harass, harm, harry, hip, hump, incommode, irk, irritate, madden, molest, needle, nettle, peeve, pester, pique, plague, provoke, rile, ruffle, tease, trouble, vex. *antonyms* gratify, please.

annulment *n.* abolition, abrogation, cancellation, cassation, countermanding, disannulment, invalidation, negation, nullification, quashing, recall, repeal, rescindment, rescission, retraction, reversal, revocation, suspension, voiding.
antonyms enactment, restoration.

anoint *v.* anele, bless, consecrate, daub, dedicate, embrocate, grease, hallow, lard, lubricate, oil, rub, sanctify, smear.

answer *n.* acknowledgment, apology, comeback, counter-buff, countercharge, defence, explanation, outcome, plea, reaction, rebuttal, reciprocation, refutation, rejoinder, reply, report, resolution, response, retaliation, retort, return, riposte, solution, vindication.
v. acknowledge, agree, balance, conform, correlate, correspond, do, echo, explain, fill, fit, fulfil, match up to, meet, pass, qualify, react, reciprocate, refute, rejoin, reply, resolve, respond, retaliate, retort, return, satisfy, serve, solve, succeed, suffice, suit, work.

antagonism *n.* animosity, animus, antipathy, competition, conflict, contention, discord, dissension, friction, hostility, ill-feeling, ill-will, opposition, rivalry.
antonyms rapport, sympathy.

antagonist *n.* adversary, competitor, contender, contestant, disputant, enemy, foe, opponent, opposer, rival.
antonyms ally, supporter.

anthology *n.* analects, choice, collection, compendium, compilation, digest, divan, florilegium, garland, miscellany, selection, spicilegium, treasury.

anticipate *v.* antedate, apprehend, await, bank on, beat to it, count upon, earlierize, expect, forecast, foredate, foresee, forestall, foretaste, foretell, forethink, hope for, intercept, look for, look forward to, predict, preempt, prevent.

anticipation *n.* apprehension, awaiting, expectancy, expectation, foresight, foretaste, forethought, forewarning, hope, preconception, premonition, prescience, presentiment, prodrome, prolepsis.

antics *n.* buffoonery, capers, clownery, clowning, didoes, doings, escapades, foolery, foolishness, frolics, larks, mischief, monkey tricks, playfulness, pranks, silliness, skylarking, stunts, tomfoolery, tricks, zanyism.

antipathy *n.* abhorrence, allergy, animosity, animus, antagonism, aversion, bad blood, contrariety, disgust, dislike, distaste, enmity, hate, hatred, hostility, ill-will, incompatibility, loathing, odium, opposition, rancor, repugnance, repulsion, resentment.
antonyms rapport, sympathy.

antiquated *adj.* anachronistic, ancient, antediluvian, antique, archaic, dated, démodé, elderly, fogeyish, fossilized, obsolete, old, old hat, old-fashioned, old-fogeyish, outdated, outmoded, out-of-date, outworn, passé, quaint, superannuated, unfashionable.
antonyms forward-looking, modern.

antique *adj.* aged, ancient, antiquarian, archaic, elderly, obsolete, old, old-fashioned, outdated, quaint, superannuated, vintage.
n. antiquity, bibelot, bygone, curio, curiosity, heirloom, knick-knack, museum-piece, object of virtu, period piece, rarity, relic.

anxiety *n.* angst, anxiousness, apprehension, care, concern, craving, desire, disquiet, disquietude, distress, dread, dysthymia, eagerness, foreboding, fretfulness, impatience, keenness, misgiving, nervousness, presentiment, restlessness, solicitude, suspense, tension, torment, torture, unease, uneasiness, watchfulness, willingness, worriment, worry.
antonym composure.

anxious *adj.* afraid, angst-ridden, apprehensive, avid, careful, concerned, desirous, disquieted, distressed, disturbed, eager, expectant, fearful, fretful, impatient, in suspense, intent, itching, keen, nervous, on tenterhooks, overwrought, restless, solicitous, taut, tense, tormented, tortured, troubled, uneasy, unquiet, watchful, worried, yearning.
antonym composed.

apartment *n.* accommodation, chambers, compartment, condominium, flat, living quarters, lodgings, maisonette, pad, penthouse, quarters, room, rooms, suite, tenement.

apathy *n.* accidie, acedia, coldness, coolness, emotionlessness, impassibility, impassivity, incuriousness, indifference, inertia, insensibility, lethargy, listlessness, passiveness, passivity, phlegm, sluggishness, torpor, unconcern, unfeelingness, uninterestedness, unresponsiveness.
antonyms concern, warmth.

aperture *n.* breach, chink, cleft, crack, eye, eyelet, fissure, foramen, gap, hole, interstice, opening, orifice, passage, perforation, rent, rift, slit, slot, space, vent.

apex *n.* acme, apogee, climax, consummation, crest, crown, crowning point, culmination, fastigium, height, high point, peak, pinnacle, point, summit, tip, top, vertex, zenith.
antonym nadir.

apologetic *adj.* compunctious, conscience-stricken, contrite, excusatory, penitent, regretful, remorseful, repentant, rueful, sorry.
antonym defiant.

apology *n.* acknowledgment, apologia, confession, defence, excuse, explanation, extenuation, justification, palliation, plea, semblance, substitute, travesty, vindication.
antonym defiance.

apostate *n.* defector, deserter, heretic, recidivist, recreant, renegade, renegado, runagate, tergiversator, traitor, turncoat.
antonyms adherent, convert, loyalist.
adj. disloyal, faithless, false, heretical, perfidious, recreant, renegate, traitorous, treacherous, unfaithful, unorthodox, untrue.
antonym faithful.

apostle *n.* advocate, champion, crusader, evangelist, exponent, herald, messenger, missionary, pioneer, preacher, promoter, propagandist, propagator, proponent, proselytizer.

appal *v.* alarm, astound, daunt, disconcert, disgust, dishearten, dismay, frighten, harrow, horrify, intimidate, outrage, petrify, scare, shock, terrify, unnerve.
antonyms encourage, reassure.

appalling *adj.* alarming, astounding, awful, daunting, dire, disheartening, dismaying, dreadful, fearful, frightening, frightful, ghastly, grim, harrowing, hideous, horrible, horrid, horrific, horrifying, intimidating, loathsome, petrifying, scaring, shocking, startling, terrible, terrifying, unnerving, wretched.
antonym reassuring.

apparatus *n.* appliance, bureaucracy, contraption, device, equipment, framework, gadget, gear, gismo, hierarchy, implements, machine, machinery, materials, means, mechanism, network, organization, outfit, setup, structure, system, tackle, tools, utensils.

apparel *n.* accouterments, array, attire, clothes, clothing, costume, dress, equipment, garb, garments, garniture, gear, guise, habiliments, habit, outfit, raiment, rig-out, robes, suit, trappings, vestiture, vestments, wardrobe, weeds.

apparent *adj.* clear, conspicuous, declared, discernible, distinct, evident, indubitable, manifest, marked, noticeable, obvious, on paper, open, ostensible, outward, overt, patent, perceptible, plain, seeming, specious, superficial, unmistakable, visible.
antonyms obscure, real.

apparition *n.* chimera, eidolon, ghost, manifestation, materialization, phantasm, phantom, presence, revenant, shade, specter, spirit, spook, umbra, vision, visitant, visitation, wraith.

appeal[1] *n.* adjuration, application, entreaty, imploration, invocation, orison, petition, plea, prayer, request, solicitation, suit, supplication.
v. address, adjure, apply, ask, beg, beseech, call, call upon, entreat, implore, invoke, petition, plead, pray, refer, request, resort to, solicit, sue, supplicate.

appeal[2] *n.* allure, attraction, attractiveness, beauty, charisma, charm, enchantment, fascination, interest, magnetism, winsomeness.
v. allure, attract, charm, draw, engage, entice, fascinate, interest, invite, lure, please, tempt.

appear *v.* act, arise, arrive, attend, be published, bob up, come into sight, come into view, come out, come to light, crop up, develop, emerge, enter, issue, leak out, look, loom, materialize, occur, perform, play, rise, seem, show, show up, surface, take part, transpire, turn out, turn up.
antonym disappear.

appearance *n.* advent, air, appearing, arrival, aspect, bearing, brow, cast, character, coming, début, demeanor, emergence, expression, face, facies, favor, figure, form, front, guise, illusion, image, impression, introduction, look, looks, manner, mien, physiognomy, presence, pretense, seeming, semblance, show, the cut of one's jib.
antonyms disappearance, reality.

appease *v.* allay, assuage, blunt, calm, compose, conciliate, diminish, ease, give a sop to, humor, lessen, lull, mitigate, mollify, pacify, placate, propitiate, quell, quench, quiet, reconcile, satisfy, soften, soothe, subdue, tranquilize.
antonym aggravate.

append *v.* add, adjoin, affix, annex, attach, conjoin, fasten, join, subjoin, tack on.

appendage *n.* accessory, addendum, addition, adjunct, affix, ancillary, annexe, appendix, appurtenance, attachment, auxiliary, excrescence, extremity, limb, member, projection, prosthesis, protuberance, supplement, tab, tag.

appertaining *adj.* applicable, applying, belonging, characteristic, connected, germane, pertinent, related, relevant.

appetite *n.* appetence, appetency, craving, demand, desire, eagerness, hankering, hunger, inclination, keenness, liking, limosis, longing, orexis, passion, predilection, proclivity, propensity, relish, stomach, taste, willingness, yearning, zeal, zest.
antonym distaste.

appetizer *n.* antipasto, apéritif, bonne bouche, canapé, cocktail, foretaste, hors d'oeuvre, preview, sample, taste, taster, tidbit, whet.

applaud *v.* acclaim, approve, cheer, clap, commend, compliment, congratulate, encourage, eulogize, extol, laud, ovate, praise.
antonyms censure, disparage.

appliance *n.* apparatus, contraption, contrivance, device, gadget, gismo, implement, instrument, machine, mechanism, tool.

applicable *adj.* apposite, appropriate, apropos, apt, befitting, fit, fitting, germane, legitimate, pertinent, proper, related, relevant, suitable, suited, useful, valid.
antonym inapplicable.

apply[1] *v.* adhibit, administer, appose, assign, bring into play, bring to bear, direct, employ, engage, execute, exercise, implement, ply, practice, resort to, set, use, utilize, wield.

apply[2] *v.* appertain, be relevant, fit, have force, pertain, refer, relate, suit.

apply[3] *v.* anoint, cover with, lay on, paint, place, put on, rub, smear, spread on, use.

apply[4] *v.* appeal, ask for, claim, indent for, inquire, petition, put in, request, requisition, solicit, sue.

apply[5] *v.* address, bend, buckle down, commit, concentrate, dedicate, devote, direct, give, persevere, settle down, study, throw.

appoint *v.* allot, arrange, assign, charge, choose, command, commission, constitute, co-opt, decide, decree, delegate, designate, destine, detail, determine, devote, direct, elect, engage, enjoin, equip, establish, fit out, fix, furnish, install, name, nominate, ordain, outfit, plenish, provide, select, set, settle, supply.
antonyms dismiss, reject.

appointment *n.* allotment, arrangement, assignation, assignment, choice, choosing, commissioning, consultation, date, delegation, election, engagement, installation, interview, job, meeting, naming, nomination, office, place, position, post, rendezvous, selection, session, situation, station, tryst.

appraise *v.* assay, assess, estimate, evaluate, examine, gauge, inspect, judge, price, rate, review, size up, survey, valuate, value.

appreciate[1] *v.* acknowledge, admire, be sensible of, be sensitive to, cherish, comprehend, dig, do justice to, enjoy, esteem, estimate, know, like, perceive, prize, realize, recognize, regard, relish, respect, savor, sympathize with, take kindly to, treasure, understand, value.
antonyms despise, overlook.

appreciate[2] *v.* enhance, gain, grow, improve, increase, inflate, mount, rise, strengthen.
antonym depreciate.

apprehend[1] *v.* arrest, bust, capture, catch, collar, detain, get, grab, nab, nick, pinch, run in, seize, take.

apprehend[2] *v.* appreciate, believe, comprehend, conceive, consider, discern, grasp, imagine, know, perceive, realize, recognize, see, twig, understand.

apprehension[1] *n.* arrest, capture, catching, seizure, taking.

apprehension[2] *n.* alarm, anxiety, apprehensiveness, awareness, belief, comprehension, concept, conception, concern, conjecture, discernment, disquiet, doubt, dread, fear, fore-boding, grasp, idea, impression, intellect, intellection, intelligence, ken, knowledge, misgiving, mistrust, nervousness, notion, opinion, perception, premonition, presentiment, qualm, sentiment, suspicion, thought, understanding, unease, uneasiness, uptake, view, worry.

apprehensive *adj.* afraid, alarmed, anxious, concerned, disquieted, distrustful, disturbed, doubtful, fearful, mistrustful, nervous, solicitous, suspicious, uneasy, worried.
antonym confident.

apprentice *n.* beginner, cub, learner, neophyte, newcomer, novice, probationer, pupil, recruit, starter, student, trainee, tyro.
antonym expert.

approach *v.* advance, anear, appeal to, apply to, approximate, be like, begin, broach, catch up, come close, come near to, commence, compare with, draw near, embark on, gain on, introduce, make advances, make overtures, meet, mention, near, reach, resemble, set about, sound out, undertake.
n. access, advance, advent, appeal, application, approximation, arrival, attitude, avenue, course, doorway, entrance, gesture, invitation, landfall, likeness, manner, means, method, mode, modus operandi, motion, nearing, offer, overture, passage, procedure, proposal, proposition, resemblance, road, semblance, style, system, technique, threshold, way.

appropriate *adj.* applicable, apposite, appurtenant, apropos, apt, becoming, befitting, belonging, condign, congruous, correct, felicitous, fit, fitting, germane, meet, merited, opportune, pertinent, proper, relevant, right, seasonable, seemly, spot-on, suitable, timely, to the point, well-chosen, well-suited, well-timed.
antonym inappropriate.
v. allocate, allot, annex, apportion, arrogate, assign, assume, commandeer, confiscate, devote, earmark, embezzle, expropriate, filch, impound, impropriate, misappropriate, pilfer, pocket, possess oneself of, preempt, purloin, seize, set apart, steal, take, usurp.

approval *n.* acclaim, acclamation, acquiescence, admiration, adoption, agreement, applause, appreciation, approbation, approof, assent, authorization, blessing,

certification, commendation, compliance, concurrence, confirmation, consent, countenance, endorsement, esteem, favor, go-ahead, good opinion, green light, honor, imprimatur, leave, licence, liking, mandate, OK, permission, plaudits, praise, ratification, recommendation, regard, respect, sanction, support, validation.
antonym disapproval.

approve *v.* accede to, accept, acclaim, admire, adopt, advocate, agree to, allow, applaud, appreciate, assent to, authorize, back, bless, commend, comply with, concur in, confirm, consent to, countenance, dig, endorse, esteem, favor, homologate, like, mandate, OK, pass, permit, praise, ratify, recommend, regard, respect, rubber-stamp, sanction, second, support, take kindly to, uphold, validate.
antonym disapprove.

approximate *adj.* close, comparable, conjectural, estimated, extrapolated, guessed, inexact, like, loose, near, relative, rough, similar, verging on.
antonym exact. *v.* approach, be tantamount to, border on, resemble, verge on.

apt *adj.* accurate, adept, applicable, apposite, appropriate, apropos, astute, befitting, bright, clever, condign, correct, disposed, expert, fair, fit, fitting, germane, gifted, given, inclined, ingenious, intelligent, liable, likely, meet, pertinent, prompt, prone, proper, quick, ready, relevant, seasonable, seemly, sharp, skilful, smart, spot-on, suitable, talented, teachable, tending, timely.
antonym inapt.

aptitude *n.* ability, aptness, bent, capability, capacity, cleverness, disposition, facility, faculty, flair, gift, inclination, intelligence, knack, leaning, penchant, predilection, proclivity, proficiency, proneness, propensity, quickness, talent, tendency.
antonym inaptitude.

aptness *n.* ability, accuracy, applicability, appositeness, appropriateness, aptitude, becomingness, bent, capability, capacity, cleverness, condignness, congruousness, correctness, disposition, facility, faculty, felicitousness, felicity, fitness, fittingness, flair, germaneness, gift, inclination, intelligence, knack, leaning, liability, likelihood, likeliness, opportuneness, pertinence, predilection, proclivity, proficiency, proneness, propensity, properness, quickness, readiness, relevance, rightness, seemliness, suitability, talent, tendency, timeliness.

arbitrary *adj.* absolute, autocratic, capricious, chance, despotic, dictatorial, discretionary, dogmatic, domineering, erratic, fanciful, high-handed, imperious, inconsistent, instinctive, magisterial, optional, overbearing, peremptory, personal, random, subjective, summary, tyrannical, tyrannous, unreasonable, unreasoned, unsupported, whimsical, wilful.
antonyms circumspect, rational, reasoned.

architecture *n.* architectonics, arrangement, building, composition, construction, design, framework, make-up, planning, structure, style.

ardent *adj.* amorous, avid, devoted, eager, enthusiastic, fervent, fervid, fierce, fiery, hot, hot-blooded, impassioned, intense, keen, lusty, passionate, perfervid, spirited, vehement, warm, zealous.
antonym dispassionate.

ardor *n.* animation, avidity, devotion, eagerness, earnestness, empressement, enthusiasm, feeling, fervor, fire, heat, intensity, keenness, lust, passion, spirit, vehemence, warmth, zeal, zest.
antonyms coolness, indifference.

arduous *adj.* backbreaking, burdensome, daunting, difficult, exhausting, fatiguing, formidable, grueling, hard, harsh, herculean, laborious, onerous, punishing, rigorous, severe, strenuous, taxing, tiring, toilsome, tough, troublesome, trying, uphill, wearisome.
antonym easy.

area *n.* arena, bailiwick, ball-park, breadth, canvas, compass, department, district, domain, environs, expanse, extent, field, locality, neighborhood, part, patch, portion, province, range, realm, region, scope, section, sector, size, sphere, stretch, terrain, territory, tract, width, zone.

argue *v.* altercate, argufy, assert, bicker, chop logic, claim, contend, convince, debate, demonstrate, denote, disagree, discuss, display, dispute, evidence, evince, exhibit, expostulate, fall out, fence, feud, fight, haggle, hold, imply, indicate, join issue, logicize, maintain, manifest, moot, persuade, plead, prevail upon, prove, quarrel, question, reason, remonstrate, show, squabble, suggest, talk into, wrangle.

argument *n.* abstract, altercation, argumentation, assertion, barney, beef, bickering, case, claim, clash, contention, controversy, debate, defence, demonstration, dialectic, difference, disagreement, discussion, dispute, exposition, expostulation, feud, fight, gist, ground, lemma, logic, logomachy, outline, plea, pleading, plot, polemic, quarrel, questioning, quodlibet, reason, reasoning, remonstrance, remonstration, row, set-to, shouting-match, squabble, story, story line, subject, summary, synopsis, theme, thesis, wrangle.

arid *adj.* baked, barren, boring, colorless, desert, desiccated, dreary, droughty, dry, dull, empty, flat, infertile, jejune, lifeless, moistureless, monotonous, parched, spiritless, sterile, tedious, torrid, torrefied, uninspired, uninteresting, unproductive, vapid, waste, waterless.
antonyms fertile, lively.

arise *v.* appear, ascend, begin, climb, come to light, commence, crop up, derive, emanate, emerge, ensue, flow, follow, get up, go up, grow, happen, issue, lift, mount, occur, originate, proceed, result, rise, set in, soar, spring, stand up, start, stem, tower, wake up.

aristocrat *n.* eupatrid, grand seigneur, grande dame, grandee, lady, lord, lordling, nob, noble, nobleman,

noblewoman, optimate, patrician, peer, peeress, swell, toff.
antonym commoner.

arm[1] *n.* appendage, authority, bough, brachium, branch, channel, department, detachment, division, estuary, extension, firth, inlet, limb, offshoot, projection, section, sector, sound, strait, sway, tributary, upper limb.

arm[2] *v.* accouter, ammunition, array, brace, empanoply, equip, forearm, fortify, furnish, gird, issue with, munition, outfit, prepare, prime, protect, provide, reinforce, rig, steel, strengthen, supply.

army *n.* armed force, array, arrière-ban, cohorts, gang, horde, host, land forces, legions, military, militia, mob, multitude, pack, soldiers, soldiery, swarm, the junior service, throng, troops.

aroma *n.* bouquet, fragrance, fumet(te), odor, perfume, redolence, savor, scent, smell.

arouse *v.* agitate, animate, awaken, bestir, call forth, disentrance, enliven, evoke, excite, foment, foster, galvanize, goad, incite, inflame, instigate, kindle, move, prompt, provoke, quicken, rouse, sharpen, spark, spur, startle, stimulate, stir up, summon up, wake up, waken, warm, whet, whip up.
antonyms calm, lull, quieten.

arraign *v.* accuse, attack, call to account, charge, denounce, impeach, impugn, incriminate, indict, prosecute.

arrange[1] *v.* adjust, align, array, categorize, class, classify, collocate, concert, construct, contrive, co-ordinate, design, determine, devise, dispose, distribute, fettle, file, fix, form, group, lay out, marshal, methodize, order, organise, plan, position, prepare, project, range, rank, regulate, schedule, set out, settle, sift, sort, sort out, stage-manage, style, swing, systematize, tidy, trim.

arrange[2] *v.* adapt, harmonize, instrument, orchestrate, score, set.

arrangement[1] *n.* adjustment, agreement, alignment, array, Ausgleich, battery, classification, compact, compromise, construction, deal, design, display, disposition, form, grouping, layout, line-up, marshaling, method, modus vivendi, order, ordering, organization, plan, planning, preconcert, preparation, provision, ranging, rank, schedule, scheme, settlement, set-up, spacing, structure, system, tabulation, taxis, terms.

arrangement[2] *n.* adaptation, harmonization, instrumentation, interpretation, orchestration, score, setting, version.

array *n.* apparel, arrangement, assemblage, attire, battery, clothes, collection, display, disposition, dress, equipage, exhibition, exposition, finery, formation, garb, garments, line-up, marshaling, muster, order, parade, raiment, regalia, robes, show, supply.
v. accouter, adorn, align, apparel, arrange, assemble, attire, bedeck, bedizen, caparison, clothe, deck, decorate, display, dispose, draw up, dress, equip, exhibit, form up, garb, group, habilitate, line up, marshal, muster, order, outfit, parade, range, rig out, robe, show, supply, trick out, wrap.

arrest *v.* absorb, apprehend, block, bust, capture, catch, check, collar, delay, detain, divert, end, engage, engross, fascinate, grip, halt, hinder, hold, impede, inhibit, interrupt, intrigue, lay, nab, nick, nip, obstruct, occupy, pinch, prevent, restrain, retard, run in, seize, slow, stall, stanch, stay, stem, stop, suppress.
n. apprehension, blockage, bust, caption, capture, cessation, check, cop, delay, detention, end, halt, hindrance, inhibition, interruption, obstruction, prevention, restraint, seizure, stalling, stay, stoppage, suppression, suspension.

arrival *n.* accession, advent, appearance, approach, caller, comer, coming, débutant(e), entrance, entrant, happening, incomer, landfall, newcomer, occurrence, visitant, visitor.
antonym departure.

arrive *v.* alight, appear, attain, befall, come, enter, fetch, get to the top, happen, land, make it, materialize, occur, reach, show, show up, succeed, turn up.
antonyms depart.

arrogance *n.* airs, conceit, conceitedness, condescension, contempt, contemptuousness, contumely, disdain, disdainfulness, haughtiness, hauteur, high-handedness, hubris, imperiousness, insolence, loftiness, lordliness, morgue, presumption, presumptuousness, pretension, pretentiousness, pride, scorn, scornfulness, superciliousness, superiority, uppishness.
antonym humility.

arrogant *adj.* assuming, conceited, condescending, contemptuous, contumelious, disdainful, fastuous, haughty, high and mighty, high-handed, hubristic, imperious, insolent, lordly, on the high ropes, overbearing, overweening, presumptuous, proud, scornful, supercilious, superior, uppish.
antonym humble.

art *n.* address, adroitness, aptitude, artfulness, artifice, artistry, artwork, astuteness, contrivance, craft, craftiness, craftsmanship, cunning, deceit, dexterity, draughtsmanship, drawing, expertise, facility, finesse, guile, ingenuity, knack, knowledge, mastery, method, métier, painting, profession, sculpture, skill, slyness, subtlety, trade, trick, trickery, virtu, virtuosity, visuals, wiliness.

artful *adj.* adept, adroit, canny, clever, crafty, cunning, deceitful, designing, devious, dexterous, fly, foxy, ingenious, masterly, politic, resourceful, rusé, scheming, sharp, shrewd, skilful, sly, smart, subtle, tricksy, tricky, vulpine, wily.
antonyms artless, ingenuous, naïve.

article *n.* account, bit, clause, commodity, composition, constituent, count, detail, discourse, division, element, essay, feature, head, heading, item, matter, object, paper, paragraph, part, particular, piece, point, portion, report, review, section, story, thing, unit.

artifice *n.* adroitness, artfulness, chicanery, cleverness, contrivance, cozenage, craft, craftiness, cunning, deception, deftness, device, dodge, duplicity, expedient, facility, finesse, fraud, guile, hoax, invention, machination, maneuver, manipulation, ruse, scheme, shift, skill, slyness, stratagem, strategy, subterfuge, subtlety, tactic, trick, trickery, wile.

artificial *adj.* affected, assumed, bogus, contrived, counterfeit, ersatz, factitious, fake, false, feigned, forced, hyped up, imitation, insincere, made-up, man-made, mannered, manufactured, meretricious, mock, non-natural, phony, plastic, pretended, pseudo, sham, simulated, specious, spurious, stagey, synthetic, unnatural.
antonyms genuine, natural.

artisan *n.* artificer, craftsman, expert, handicraftsman, journeyman, mechanic, operative, technician, workman.

artist *n.* colorist, craftsman, draughtsman, expert, maestro, master, painter, portraitist, portrait-painter, sculptor, water-colorist.

artless *adj.* candid, childlike, direct, frank, genuine, guileless, honest, humble, ingenuous, innocent, naïf, naïve, naked, natural, open, plain, primitive, pure, simple, sincere, straightforward, true, trustful, trusting, unadorned, unaffected, uncontrived, undesigning, unpretentious, unsophisticated, unwary, unworldly.
antonym artful.

ascend *v.* climb, float up, fly up, go up, lift off, mount, move up, rise, scale, slope upwards, soar, take off, tower.
antonym descend.

ascertain *v.* confirm, detect, determine, discover, establish, find out, fix, identify, learn, locate, make certain, settle, verify.

ascribe *v.* accredit, arrogate, assign, attribute, chalk up to, charge, credit, impute, put down.

ashamed *adj.* abashed, apologetic, bashful, blushing, chagrined, confused, conscience-stricken, crestfallen, discomfited, comfited, discomposed, distressed, embarrassed, guilty, hesitant, humbled, humiliated, modest, mortified, prudish, red in the face, redfaced, reluctant, remorseful, self-conscious, shamefaced, sheepish, shy, sorry, unwilling, verecund.
antonyms defiant, shameless.

ask *v.* appeal, apply, beg, beseech, bid, catechize, claim, clamor, crave, demand, enquire, entreat, implore, importune, indent, interrogate, invite, order, petition, plead, pray, press, query, question, quiz, request, require, seek, solicit, sue, summon, supplicate.

askance *adv.* contemptuously, disapprovingly, disdainfully, distrustfully, doubtfully, dubiously, indirectly, mistrustfully, obliquely, sceptically, scornfully, sideways, suspiciously.

askew *adv., adj.* aglee, agley, aslant, asymmetric, awry, cock-eyed, crooked, crookedly, lopsided, oblique, offcenter, out of line, skew, skew-whiff, squint.

asleep *adj.* benumbed, comatose, dead to the world, dormant, dormient, dozing, fast asleep, inactive, inert, napping, numb, reposing, sleeping, slumbering, snoozing, sound asleep, unconscious.

aspect *n.* air, angle, appearance, attitude, bearing, condition, countenance, demeanor, direction, elevation, exposure, expression, face, facet, feature, look, manner, mien, outlook, physiognomy, point of view, position, prospect, scene, side, situation, standpoint, view, visage.

aspersion *n.* abuse, animadversion, calumny, censure, criticism, defamation, denigration, derogation, detraction, disparagement, mud-slinging, obloquy, reproach, slander, slur, smear, traducement, vilification, vituperation.
antonyms commendation, compliment.

asphyxiate *v.* burke, choke, garrotte, smother, stifle, strangle, strangulate, suffocate, throttle.

aspirant *n.* applicant, aspirer, candidate, competitor, contestant, hopeful, postulant, seeker, striver, suitor.

aspire *v.* aim, crave, desire, dream, ettle, hanker, hope, intend, long, purpose, pursue, seek, wish, yearn.

aspiring *adj.* ambitious, aspirant, eager, endeavoring, enterprising, hopeful, keen, longing, optimistic, striving, wishful, would-be.

ass[1] *n.* blockhead, bonehead, cretin, dolt, dope, dunce, fool, half-wit, idiot, moron, nincompoop, ninny, nitwit, numskull, schmuck, simpleton, twerp, twit.

ass[2] *n.* burro, cardophagus, cuddy, donkey, hinny, jackass, jenny, Jerusalem pony, moke, mule.

assail *v.* abuse, assault, attack, belabor, berate, beset, bombard, charge, criticize, encounter, fall upon, impugn, invade, lay into, malign, maltreat, pelt, revile, set about, set upon, strike, vilify.

assassinate *v.* dispatch, eliminate, hit, kill, liquidate, murder, rub out, slay.

assault *n.* aggression, attack, blitz, charge, incursion, invasion, offensive, onset, onslaught, raid, storm, storming, strike.
v. assail, attack, beset, charge, fall on, hit, invade, lay violent hands on, set upon, storm, strike.

assemble *v.* accumulate, amass, build, collect, compose, congregate, construct, convene, convocate, convoke, erect, fabricate, flock, forgather, gather, group, join up, levy, make, manufacture, marshal, meet, mobilize, muster, muster (up), piece, rally, round up, set up, summon, together.
antonym disperse.

assembly *n.* agora, assemblage, ball, body, building, caucus, collection, company, conclave, concourse, conference, congregation, congress, consistory, construction, convention, convocation, council, crowd, diet, divan, ecclesia, erection, fabrication, fitting, flock, gathering, group, indaba, joining, levy, manufacture, mass, meeting, moot, multitude, panegyry, rally, reception, setting up, soirée, synod, throng.

assent *v.* accede, accept, acquiesce, agree, allow, approve, comply, concede, concur, consent, grant, permit, sanction, submit, subscribe, yield.
antonym disagree. *n.* acceptance, accession, accord, acquiescence, agreement, approval, capitulation, compliance, concession, concurrence, consent, permission, sanction, submission.

assert *v.* advance, affirm, allege, asseverate, attest, aver, avouch, avow, claim, constate, contend, declare, defend, dogmatize, insist, lay down, maintain, predicate, press, profess, promote, pronounce, protest, state, stress, swear, testify to, thrust forward, uphold, vindicate.
antonym deny.

assertion *n.* affirmance, affirmation, allegation, asservation, attestation, averment, avowal, claim, constatation, contention, declaration, dictum, gratis dictum, ipse dixit, predication, profession, pronouncement, statement, vindication, vouch, word.
antonym denial.

assess *v.* appraise, compute, consider, demand, determine, estimate, evaluate, fix, gauge, impose, investigate, judge, levy, rate, reckon, review, size up, tax, value, weigh.

asset *n.* advantage, aid, benefit, blessing, help, plus, resource, service, strength, virtue.
antonym liability.

assign *v.* accredit, adjudge, allocate, allot, apart, appoint, apportion, arrogate, ascribe, attribute, choose, consign, delegate, designate, determine, dispense, distribute, fix, give, grant, name, nominate, put down, select, set, specify, stipulate.

assignment *n.* allocation, allotment, appointment, apportionment, ascription, attribution, charge, commission, consignment, delegation, designation, determination, dispensation, distribution, duty, errand, giving, grant, imposition, job, mission, nomination, position, post, responsibility, selection, specification, task.

assimilate *v.* absorb, accept, acclimatize, accommodate, acculturate, accustom, adapt, adjust, blend, conform, digest, fit, homogenize, imbibe, incorporate, ingest, intermix, learn, merge, mingle, take in, tolerate.
antonym reject.

assist *v.* abet, accommodate, aid, back, benefit, bestead, boost, collaborate, co-operate, enable, expedite, facilitate, further, help, rally round, reinforce, relieve, second, serve, succor, support, sustain.
antonym thwart.

assistance *n.* a leg up, abetment, accommodation, adjutancy, aid, backing, benefit, boost, collaboration, comfort, co-operation, furtherance, help, reinforcement, relief, succor, support, sustainment.
antonym hindrance.

assistant *n.* abettor, accessory, accomplice, adjutant, aide, ally, ancillary, associate, auxiliary, backer, coadjutor, collaborator, colleague, confederate, co-operator, Girl Friday, helper, helpmate, henchman, Man Friday, partner, Person Friday, right-hand man, second, subordinate, subsidiary, supporter.

associate *v.* accompany, affiliate, ally, amalgamate, combine, company, confederate, conjoin, connect, consort, correlate, couple, fraternize, hang around, hobnob, identify, join, league, link, mingle, mix, pair, relate, socialize, unite, yoke.
n. affiliate, ally, assistant, bedfellow, coadjutor, collaborator, colleague, companion, compeer, comrade, confederate, confrère, co-worker, fellow, follower, friend, leaguer, mate, partner, peer, side-kick.

association *n.* affiliation, alliance, analogy, band, blend, bloc, bond, cartel, clique, club, coalition, combination, combine, companionship, company, compound, comradeship, concomitance, confederacy, confederation, connection, consociation, consortium, conspiracy, co-operative, corporation, correlation, familiarity, federation, fellowship, fraternization, fraternity, friendship, Gesellschaft, group, intimacy, joining, juxtaposition, league, linkage, mixture, organization, pairing, partnership, relation, relations, relationship, resemblance, society, syndicate, syndication, tie, trust, union, Verein.

assortment *n.* arrangement, array, assemblage, categorization, choice, classification, collection, disposition, distribution, diversity, farrago, grading, grouping, hotchpotch, jumble, medley, mélange, miscellany, mishmash, mixture, olio, olla-podrida, pot-pourri, ranging, salad, salmagundi, selection, sift, sifting, sorting, variety.

assuage *v.* allay, alleviate, appease, calm, dull, ease, lessen, lighten, lower, lull, mitigate, moderate, mollify, pacify, palliate, quench, quieten, reduce, relieve, satisfy, slake, soften, soothe, still, temper, tranquilize.
antonym exacerbate.

assume *v.* accept, acquire, adopt, affect, appropriate, arrogate, believe, commandeer, counterfeit, deduce, don, embrace, expect, expropriate, fancy, feign, guess, imagine, infer, opine, postulate, pre-empt, premise, presume, presuppose, pretend to, put on, seize, sham, shoulder, simulate, strike, suppose, surmise, suspect, take, take for granted, take on, take over, take up, think, understand, undertake, usurp.

assumption *n.* acceptance, acquisition, adoption, appropriation, arrogance, arrogation, audacity, belief, bumptiousness, conceit, conjecture, expectation, expropriation, fancy, guess, guesswork, hypothesis, impudence, inference, postulate, postulation, pre-emption, premise, premiss, presumption, presumptuousness, presupposition, pride, seizure, self-importance, supposition, surmise, suspicion, theory, understanding, undertaking, usurpation.

assurance *n.* affirmation, aplomb, assertion, asseveration, assuredness, audacity, boldness, certainty, certitude, chutzpah, confidence, conviction, coolness, courage, declaration, firmness, gall, guarantee, nerve, oath, pledge, plerophory, poise, positiveness, profession,

promise, protestation, security, self-confidence, self-reliance, sureness, vow, word.
antonym uncertainty.

assure *v.* affirm, attest, boost, certify, clinch, comfort, confirm, convince, embolden, encourage, ensure, guarantee, hearten, persuade, pledge, promise, reassure, seal, secure, soothe, strengthen, swear, tell, vow, warrant.

astonish *v.* amaze, astound, baffle, bewilder, confound, daze, dumbfound, electrify, flabbergast, floor, nonplus, shock, stagger, startle, stun, stupefy, surprise, wow.

astound *v.* abash, amaze, astonish, baffle, bewilder, confound, daze, dumbfound, electrify, flabbergast, overwhelm, shake, shock, stagger, stun, stupefy, surprise, wow.

astute *adj.* acute, adroit, artful, astucious, calculating, canny, clever, crafty, cunning, discerning, fly, foxy, intelligent, keen, knowing, penetrating, perceptive, percipient, perspicacious, politic, prudent, sagacious, sharp, shrewd, sly, subtle, wily, wise.
antonym stupid.

asunder *adv.* apart, in half, in pieces, in twain, in two, into pieces, to bits, to pieces.

asylum *n.* bedlam, bughouse, cover, funny farm, harbor, haven, hospital, institution, loony-bin, madhouse, mental hospital, nuthouse, preserve, refuge, reserve, retreat, safety, sanctuary, shelter.

athletic *adj.* active, brawny, energetic, fit, husky, muscular, powerful, robust, sinewy, strapping, strong, sturdy, thewy, vigorous, well-knit, well-proportioned, wiry.
antonym puny.

atone *v.* aby(e), compensate, expiate, make amends, make up for, offset, pay for, propitiate, recompense, reconcile, redeem, redress, remedy.

atrocious *adj.* abominable, barbaric, brutal, cruel, diabolical, execrable, fell, fiendish, flagitious, ghastly, grievous, heinous, hideous, horrible, horrifying, infamous, infernal, inhuman, monstrous, piacular, ruthless, savage, shocking, terrible, vicious, vile, villainous, wicked.

attach *v.* add, adhere, adhibit, affix, annex, append, articulate, ascribe, assign, associate, attract, attribute, belong, bind, captivate, combine, connect, couple, fasten, fix, impute, join, link, place, put, relate to, secure, stick, tie, unite, weld.
antonyms detach, unfasten.

attachment *n.* accessory, accouterment, adapter, addition, adhesion, adhibition, adjunct, affection, affinity, appendage, appurtenance, attraction, bond, codicil, cohesion, confiscation, connection, connector, coupling, devotion, esteem, extension, extra, fastener, fastening, fidelity, fitting, fixture, fondness, friendship, joint, junction, liking, link, love, loyalty, partiality, predilection, regard, seizure, supplement, tenderness, tie.

attack *n.* abuse, access, aggression, assailment, assault, battery, blitz, bombardment, bout, broadside, censure, charge, convulsion, criticism, fit, foray, impugnment, incursion, inroad, invasion, invective, kamikaze, offensive, onset, onslaught, paroxysm, raid, rush, seizure, spasm, spell, strike, stroke.
v. abuse, assail, assault, belabor, berate, blame, censure, charge, chastise, criticize, denounce, do over, fake, fall on, flay, have one's knife in, impugn, invade, inveigh against, lash, lay into, light into, make at, malign, mob, put the boot in, raid, rate, revile, rush, set about, set on, snipe, storm, strafe, strike, vilify, visit, wade into.

attain *v.* accomplish, achieve, acquire, arrive at, bag, compass, complete, earn, effect, fulfil, gain, get, grasp, net, obtain, procure, reach, realize, reap, secure, touch, win.

attainment *n.* ability, accomplishment, achievement, acquirement, acquisition, aptitude, art, capability, competence, completion, consummation, facility, feat, fulfilment, gift, mastery, procurement, proficiency, reaching, realization, skill, success, talent.

attempt *n.* assault, assay, attack, bash, bid, coup d'essai, crack, effort, endeavor, essay, experiment, go, move, push, shot, shy, stab, struggle, trial, try, undertaking, venture. *v.* aspire, endeavor, essay, experiment, have a bash, have a crack, have a go, have a shot, seek, strive, tackle, try, try one's hand at, try one's luck at, undertake, venture.

attend *v.* accompany, appear, arise from, assist, be all ears, be present, care for, chaperon, companion, convoy, escort, follow, frequent, give ear, guard, hear, hearken, heed, help, lend an ear, listen, look after, mark, mind, minister to, note, notice, nurse, observe, pay attention, pay heed, pin back one's ears, regard, result from, serve, squire, succor, take care of, tend, usher, visit, wait upon, watch.

attendant *n.* accompanier, acolyte, aide, assistant, auxiliary, batman, bed captain, chaperon, companion, custodian, equerry, escort, famulus, flunkey, follower, ghillie, guard, guide, helper, jäger, lackey, lady-help, lady-in-waiting, lady's-maid, livery-servant, marshal, menial, page, poursuivant, retainer, servant, steward, underling, usher, waiter.
adj. accessory, accompanying, associated, attached, concomitant, consequent, incidental, related, resultant, subsequent.

attention *n.* advertence, advertency, alertness, attentiveness, awareness, care, civility, concentration, concern, consciousness, consideration, contemplation, courtesy, deference, ear, gallantry, heed, heedfulness, intentness, mindfulness, ministration, notice, observation, politeness, recognition, regard, respect, service, thought, thoughtfulness, treatment, vigilance.
antonyms disregard, inattention.

attentive *adj.* accommodating, advertent, alert, awake,

careful, civil, concentrating, conscientious, considerate, courteous, deferential, devoted, gallant, gracious, heedful, intent, kind, mindful, obliging, observant, polite, regardant, studious, thoughtful, vigilant, watchful.
antonyms heedless, inattentive, inconsiderate.

attest *v.* adjure, affirm, assert, authenticate, aver, certify, confirm, corroborate, declare, demonstrate, depose, display, endorse, evidence, evince, exhibit, manifest, prove, ratify, seal, show, substantiate, swear, testify, verify, vouch, warrant, witness.

attire *n.* accouterments, apparel, array, clothes, clothing, costume, dress, finery, garb, garments, gear, getup, habiliments, habit, outfit, raiment, rig-out, robes, togs, uniform, vestment, wear, weeds.
v. accouter, adorn, apparel, array, caparison, clothe, costume, deck out, dress, equip, garb, habilitate, outfit, prepare, rig out, robe, turn out.

attitude *n.* affectation, air, Anschauung, approach, aspect, bearing, carriage, condition, demeanor, disposition, feeling, manner, mien, mood, opinion, outlook, perspective, point of view, pose, position, posture, stance, view, Weltanschauung.

attractive *adj.* agreeable, alluring, appealing, appetible, beautiful, beddable, captivating, catching, catchy, charming, comely, enchanting, engaging, enticing, epigamous, fair, fascinating, fetching, glamorous, good-looking, gorgeous, handsome, interesting, inviting, jolie laide, lovely, magnetic, nubile, personable, pleasant, pleasing, prepossessing, pretty, seductive, snazzy, stunning, taky, tempting, toothsome, voluptuous, winning, winsome.
antonyms repellent, unattractive.

attribute *v.* accredit, apply, arrogate, ascribe, assign, blame, charge, credit, impute, put down, refer.
n. affection, aspect, character, characteristic, facet, feature, idiosyncrasy, mark, note, peculiarity, point, property, quality, quirk, sign, symbol, trait, virtue.

auction *n.* cant, roup, sale, vendue.

audacious *adj.* adventurous, assuming, assured, bold, brave, brazen, cheeky, courageous, dare-devil, daring, dauntless, death-defying, der-doing, disrespectful, enterprising, fearless, forward, impertinent, impudent, insolent, intrepid, pert, plucky, presumptuous, rash, reckless, risky, rude, shameless, unabashed, valiant, venturesome.
antonyms cautious, reserved, timid.

audacity *n.* adventurousness, assurance, audaciousness, boldness, brass neck, bravery, brazenness, cheek, chutzpah, courage, daring, dauntlessness, defiance, derring-do, disrespectfulness, effrontery, enterprise, fearlessness, foolhardiness, forwardness, gall, guts, impertinence, impudence, insolence, intrepidity, nerve, pertness, presumption, rashness, recklessness, rudeness, shamelessness, valor, venturesomeness.
antonyms caution, reserve, timidity.

audible *adj.* appreciable, clear, detectable, discernible, distinct, hearable, perceptible, recognizable.
antonym inaudible.

augment *v.* add to, amplify, boost, dilate, eke out, enhance, enlarge, expand, extend, grow, heighten, increase, inflate, intensify, magnify, multiply, raise, reinforce, strengthen, supplement, swell.
antonym decrease.

auspicious *adj.* bright, cheerful, encouraging, favorable, felicitous, fortunate, happy, hopeful, lucky, opportune, optimistic, promising, propitious, prosperous, rosy, white.
antonyms inauspicious, ominous.

austere *adj.* abstemious, abstinent, ascetic, astringent, bitter, bleak, chaste, cold, conservative, continent, Dantean, Dantesque, economical, exacting, forbidding, formal, grave, grim, hard, harsh, plain, puritanical, restrained, rigid, rigorous, self-denying, self-disciplined, serious, severe, simple, sober, solemn, sour, spare, Spartan, stark, stern, strict, stringent, unadorned, unembellished, unornamented, unrelenting.
antonyms elaborate, extravagant, genial.

authentic *adj.* accurate, actual, authoritative, bona fide, certain, dependable, dinkum, factual, faithful, genuine, honest, kosher, legitimate, original, pure, real, reliable, simon-pure, true, true-to-life, trustworthy, valid, veracious, veritable.
antonyms counterfeit, inauthentic, spurious.

authenticate *v.* accredit, attest, authorize, avouch, certify, confirm, corroborate, endorse, guarantee, validate, verify, vouch for, warrant.

author *n.* architect, begetter, composer, creator, designer, fabricator, fashioner, father, forger, founder, framer, initiator, inventor, maker, mover, originator, paperstainer, parent, pen, penman, penwoman, planner, prime mover, producer, volumist, writer.

authoritative *adj.* accepted, accurate, approved, assured, authentic, authorized, cathedratic, commanding, confident, convincing, decisive, definitive, dependable, factual, faithful, learned, legitimate, magisterial, magistrial, masterly, official, reliable, sanctioned, scholarly, sound, sovereign, true, trustworthy, truthful, valid, veritable.
antonym unreliable.

authority[1] *n.* administration, ascendancy, attestation, authorization, avowal, charge, command, control, declaration, domination, dominion, evidence, force, government, imperium, influence, jurisdiction, justification, licence, management, might, officialdom, permission, permit, power, prerogative, profession, right, rule, sanction, sovereignty, statement, strength, supremacy, sway, testimony, textbook, warrant, weight, word.

authority[2] *n.* arbiter, bible, connoisseur, expert, judge, master, professional, pundit, sage, scholar, specialist.

autocrat *n.* absolutist, authoritarian, Caesar, cham, despot, dictator, fascist, Hitler, panjandrum, totalitarian, tyrant.

automatic *adj.* automated, certain, habitual, inescapable, inevitable, instinctive, involuntary, mechanical, mechanized, natural, necessary, perfunctory, push-button, reflex, robot, robot-like, routine, self-acting, self-activating, self-moving, self-propelling, self-regulating, spontaneous, unavoidable, unbidden, unconscious, unthinking, unwilled, vegetative.

automobile *n.* armored car, convertible, coupe, fastback, gocart, hot rod, jeep, land-rover, limousine, racing car, roadster, sedan, sports car, station wagon.

auxiliary *adj.* accessory, adjuvant, adminicular, aiding, ancillary, assistant, assisting, back-up, emergency, helping, reserve, secondary, subsidiary, substitute, supplementary, supporting, supportive.
n. accessory, accomplice, adminicle, ally, ancillary, assistant, associate, companion, confederate, foederatus, helper, partner, reserve, subordinate, supporter.

avail *v.* advance, advantage, aid, assist, benefit, boot, dow, exploit, help, make the most of, profit, serve, work.
n. advantage, aid, assistance, benefit, boot, good, help, profit, purpose, service, use, value.

available *adj.* accessible, at hand, attainable, convenient, disengaged, free, handy, obtainable, on hand, on tap, procurable, ready, to hand, vacant, within reach.
antonym unavailable.

avarice *n.* acquisitiveness, cheese-paring, covetousness, cupidity, greed, greediness, meanness, miserliness, niggardliness, parsimoniousness, parsimony, penny-pinching, penuriousness, predatoriness, rapacity, stinginess, tight-fistedness.
antonym generosity.

average *n.* mean, mediocrity, medium, midpoint, norm, par, rule, run, standard.
antonyms exception, extreme.
adj. common, commonplace, everyday, fair, general, indifferent, intermediate, mean, medial, median, mediocre, medium, middle, middling, moderate, normal, ordinary, passable, regular, run-of-the-mill, satisfactory, so-so, standard, tolerable, typical, undistinguished, unexceptional, unremarkable, usual.
antonyms exceptional, extreme.

averse *adj.* antagonistic, antipathetic, disapproving, disinclined, hostile, ill-disposed, inimical, loath, opposed, reluctant, unfavorable, unwilling.
antonyms sympathetic, willing.

aversion *n.* abhorrence, abomination, anathema, animosity, antagonism, antipathy, detestation, disapproval, disgust, disinclination, dislike, distaste, hate, hatred, horror, hostility, loathing, odium, opposition, phobia, phobism, reluctance, repugnance, repulsion, revulsion, unwillingness.
antonyms liking, sympathy.

avert *v.* avoid, deflect, evade, fend off, forestall, frustrate, obviate, parry, preclude, prevent, stave off, turn, turn aside, turn away, ward off.

avid *adj.* acquisitive, ardent, avaricious, covetous, dedicated, devoted, eager, earnest, enthusiastic, fanatical, fervent, grasping, greedy, hungry, insatiable, intense, keen, passionate, rapacious, ravenous, thirsty, voracious, zealous.
antonym indifferent.

avocation *n.* business, calling, distraction, diversion, employment, hobby, interest, job, occupation, pastime, profession, pursuit, recreation, relaxation, sideline, trade, vocation, work.

avoid *v.* abstain from, avert, balk, bypass, circumvent, dodge, duck, elude, escape, eschew, evade, evite, funk, get out of, obviate, prevent, refrain from, shirk, shun, side-step, steer clear of.

award *v.* accord, adjudge, allot, allow, apportion, assign, bestow, confer, determine, dispense, distribute, endow, gift, give, grant, present.
n. adjudication, allotment, allowance, bestowal, conferment, conferral, decision, decoration, dispensation, endowment, gift, grant, judgment, order, presentation, prize, trophy.

aware *adj.* acquainted, alive to, appreciative, apprized, attentive, au courant, cognizant, conscient, conscious, conversant, enlightened, familiar, heedful, hep, hip, informed, knowing, knowledgeable, mindful, observant, on the ball, on the qui vive, sensible, sensitive, sentient, sharp, shrewd.
antonyms insensitive, unaware.

awe *n.* admiration, amazement, apprehension, astonishment, dread, fear, respect, reverence, terror, veneration, wonder, wonderment.
antonym contempt.
v. amaze, astonish, cow, daunt, frighten, horrify, impress, intimidate, overwhelm, stun, terrify.

awful *adj.* abysmal, alarming, amazing, atrocious, august, awe-inspiring, awesome, blood-curdling, dire, dread, dreadful, eldritch, fearful, fearsome, frightful, ghastly, gruesome, harrowing, hideous, horrendous, horrible, horrific, horrifying, majestic, nasty, portentous, shocking, solemn, spine-chilling, terrible, tremendous, ugly, unpleasant.

awkward *adj.* annoying, bloody-minded, blundering, bungling, chancy, clownish, clumsy, coarse, compromising, cubbish, cumbersome, delicate, difficult, disobliging, embarrassed, embarrassing, exasperating, farouche, fiddly, gauche, gawky, graceless, ham-fisted, ham-handed, hazardous, ill at ease, inconvenient, inelegant, inept, inexpedient, inexpert, inopportune, intractable, intransigent, irritable, left-handed, maladroit, obstinate, painful, perplexing, perverse, prickly, risky, rude, spastic, sticky, stubborn, thorny, ticklish, touchy, troublesome, trying, uncomfortable, unco-operative, unco-ordinated, uncouth, ungainly, ungraceful, unhandy, unhelpful, unmanageable, unpleasant,

unrefined, unskilful, untimely, untoward, unwieldy, vexatious, vexing.
antonyms amenable, convenient, elegant, graceful, straightforward.

awry *adv., adj.* aglee, amiss, askew, asymmetrical, cock-eyed, crooked, misaligned, oblique, off-center, out of kilter, skew-whiff, twisted, uneven, unevenly, wonky, wrong.
antonyms straight, symmetrical.

axiom *n.* adage, aphorism, apophthegm, byword, dictum, fundamental, gnome, maxim, postulate, precept, principle, truism, truth.

B

babble *v.* blab, burble, cackle, chatter, gabble, gibber, gurgle, jabber, mumble, murmur, mutter, prate, prattle, purl, twattle.
n. burble, clamor, drivel, gabble, gibberish, lallation, lalling, murmur, purl, purling, twattle.

baby *n.* babe, bairn, child, infant, nursling, papoose, suckling, tiny, toddler, wean, weanling, youngling.
adj. diminutive, dwarf, Lilliputian, little, midget, mini, miniature, minute, pygmy, small, small-scale, tiny, toy, wee.
v. cocker, coddle, cosset, humor, indulge, mollycoddle, overindulge, pamper, pander to, pet, spoil, spoon-feed.

babyish *adj.* baby, childish, foolish, immature, infantile, jejune, juvenile, naïve, namby-pamby, puerile, silly, sissy, soft, spoilt.
antonyms mature, precocious.

back[1] *v.* advocate, assist, boost, buttress, champion, countenance, countersign, encourage, endorse, favor, finance, sanction, second, side with, sponsor, subsidize, support, sustain, underwrite.
antonym discourage.

back up aid, assist, bolster, champion, confirm, corroborate, endorse, reinforce, second, substantiate, support.
antonym let down.

back[2] *n.* backside, end, hind part, hindquarters, posterior, rear, reverse, stern, tail, tail end, tergum, verso.
adj. end, hind, hindmost, posterior, rear, reverse, tail.

back[3] *v.* backtrack, recede, recoil, regress, retire, retreat, reverse, withdraw.

back[4] *adj.* delayed, earlier, elapsed, former, outdated, overdue, past, previous, prior, superseded.

backbiting *n.* abuse, aspersion, bitchiness, calumniation, calumny, cattiness, criticism, defamation, denigration, detraction, disparagement, gossip, malice, revilement, scandalmongering, slagging, slander, spite, spitefulness, vilification, vituperation.
antonym praise.

backbone *n.* basis, bottle, character, core, courage, determination, firmness, foundation, grit, hardihood, mainstay, mettle, nerve, pluck, power, resolution, resolve, spine, stamina, staunchness, steadfastness, strength, support, tenacity, toughness, vertebral column, will.
antonyms spinelessness, weakness.

backbreaking *adj.* arduous, crushing, exhausting, grueling, hard, heavy, killing, laborious, punishing, strenuous, tiring, toilsome, wearing, wearisome.
antonym easy.

backer *n.* advocate, benefactor, bottle-holder, champion, patron, promoter, second, seconder, sponsor, subscriber, supporter, underwriter, well-wisher.

backfire *v.* boomerang, come home to roost, fail, flop, miscarry, rebound, recoil, ricochet.

background *n.* breeding, circumstances, credentials, culture, dossier, education, environment, experience, fond, grounding, history, milieu, preparation, record, surroundings, tradition, upbringing.

backing *n.* accompaniment, advocacy, aid, assistance, championing, championship, encouragement, endorsement, favor, funds, grant, helpers, moral support, patronage, sanction, seconding, sponsorship, subsidy, support.

backlash *n.* backfire, boomerang, counterblast, kickback, reaction, recoil, repercussion, reprisal, resentment, response, retaliation.

backlog *n.* accumulation, excess, hoard, leeway, mountain, reserve, reserves, resources, stock, supply.

backslide *v.* apostatize, default, defect, fall from grace, lapse, regress, relapse, renegue, retrogress, revert, sin, slip, stray, weaken.
antonym persevere.

backward *adj.* bashful, behind, behindhand, diffident, dull, hesitant, hesitating, immature, late, reluctant, retarded, shy, slow, sluggish, stupid, subnormal, tardy, underdeveloped, unwilling, wavering.
antonyms forward, precocious.

bad *adj.* adverse, ailing, base, blameworthy, consciencestricken, contrite, corrupt, criminal, damaging, dangerous, decayed, defective, deficient, deleterious, delinquent, despondent, detrimental, disastrous, discouraged, discouraging, diseased, disobedient, distressed, distressing, evil, fallacious, faulty, gloomy, grave, grim, grotty, guilty, harmful, harsh, ill, illaudable, immoral, imperfect, inadequate, incorrect, inferior, injurious, mean, melancholy, mischievous, mouldy, naughty, noxious, off, offensive, onkus, painful, piacular, poor, putrid, rancid, regretful, remorseful, ropy, rotten, rueful, ruinous, sad, serious, severe, shoddy, sick, sinful, somber, sorry, sour, spoilt, stormy, substandard, terrible, troubled, unfortunate, unhealthy, unpleasant, unruly, unsatisfactory, unwell, upset, vile, wicked, wrong.

badger *v.* bait, bully, bullyrag, chivvy, goad, harass, harry, hassle, hound, importune, nag, pester, plague, torment.

baffle *v.* amaze, astound, balk, bamboozle, bemuse, bewilder, check, confound, confuse, daze, defeat, disconcert, dumbfound, flabbergast, floor, flummox, foil, frustrate, hinder, mystify, nonplus, perplex, puzzle, stump, stun, stymie, thwart, upset. *antonyms* enlighten, help.

bag *v.* acquire, appropriate, capture, catch, commandeer, corner, gain, get, grab, kill, land, obtain, reserve, shoot, take, trap.
n. carrier, container, dorlach, Dorothy bag, dressing-case, Gladstone bag, grab-bag, grip, gripsack, handbag, haversack, hold-all, holder, pack, poke, reticule, rucksack, sack, satchel, satchet, scrip, shoulder-bag, tote-bag, valise.

bail *n.* bond, guarantee, guaranty, pledge, security, surety, warranty.

bait *n.* allurement, attraction, bribe, carrot, decoy, enticement, inducement, lure, temptation.
antonym disincentive.
v. annoy, gall, goad, harass, hound, irk, irritate, needle, persecute, provoke, tease, torment.

balance *v.* adjust, assess, calculate, compare, compute, consider, counteract, counterbalance, counterpoise, deliberate, equalize, equate, equilibrate, equipoise, equiponderate, estimate, evaluate, level, librate, match, neutralize, offset, parallel, poise, settle, square, stabilize, steady, tally, total, weigh.
antonyms overbalance, unbalance.
n. composure, correspondence, difference, equality, equanimity, equilibrium, equipoise, equity, equivalence, evenness, parity, poise, remainder, residue, rest, self-possession, stability, stasis, steadiness, surplus, symmetry.
antonyms imbalance, instability.

bald *adj.* bald-headed, baldpated, bare, barren, bleak, depilated, direct, downright, exposed, forthright, glabrate, glabrous, hairless, naked, outright, peeled, plain, severe, simple, stark, straight, straightforward, treeless, unadorned, uncompromising, uncovered, undisguised, unvarnished.
antonyms adorned, hirsute.

baleful *adj.* deadly, destructive, evil, fell, harmful, hurtful, injurious, malevolent, malignant, menacing, mournful, noxious, ominous, pernicious, ruinous, sad, sinister, venomous, woeful.
antonyms auspicious, favorable.

balk, baulk *v.* baffle, bar, boggle, check, counteract, defeat, demur, disconcert, dodge, evade, flinch, foil, forestall, frustrate, hesitate, hinder, jib, make difficulties, obstruct, prevent, recoil, refuse, resist, shirk, shrink, stall, thwart.

ball[1] *n.* bauble, bobble, bullet, clew, conglomeration, drop, globe, globule, orb, pellet, pill, shot, slug, sphere, spheroid.

ball[2] *n.* assembly, carnival, dance, dinner-dance, fandango, hop, masquerade, party, ridotto, rout, soirée.

ballad *n.* carol, composition, ditty, folk-song, lay, poem, pop-song, shanty, song.

ballet *n.* ballet-dancing, dancing, leg-business.

balloon *v.* bag, belly, billow, blow up, bulge, dilate, distend, enlarge, expand, inflate, puff out, swell.

ballot *n.* election, plebiscite, poll, polling, referendum, vote, voting.

balmy[1] *adj.* clement, gentle, mild, pleasant, soft, summery, temperate.
antonym inclement.

balmy[2] *adj.* barmy, crazy, daft, dippy, dotty, foolish, idiotic, insane, loony, mad, nuts, nutty, odd, round the bend, silly, stupid.
antonyms rational, sane, sensible.

ban *v.* anathematize, banish, bar, debar, disallow, exclude, forbid, interdict, ostracize, outlaw, prohibit, proscribe, restrict, suppress.
antonym permit.
n. anathematization, boycott, censorship, condemnation, curse, denunciation, embargo, interdiction, outlawry, prohibition, proscription, restriction, stoppage, suppression, taboo.
antonyms dispensation, permission.

banal *adj.* boring, clichéd, cliché-ridden, commonplace, corny, empty, everyday, hackneyed, humdrum, jejune, old hat, ordinary, pedestrian, platitudinous, stale, stereotyped, stock, threadbare, tired, trite, unimaginative, unoriginal, vapid.
antonym original.

band[1] *n.* bandage, bandeau, belt, binding, bond, chain, cincture, cord, fascia, fetter, fillet, ligature, manacle, ribbon, shackle, strap, strip, swath, tape, tie, vitta.

band[2] *n.* association, body, clique, club, combo, company, coterie, crew, ensemble, flock, gang, group, herd, horde, orchestra, party, range, society, troop, waits.
v. affiliate, ally, amalgamate, collaborate, consolidate, federate, gather, group, join, merge, unite.
antonyms disband, disperse.

bandit *n.* brigand, buccaneer, cowboy, dacoit, desperado, footpad, freebooter, gangster, gunman, highwayman, hijacker, marauder, outlaw, pirate, racketeer, robber, ruffian, thief.

bang *n.* blow, boom, box, bump, clang, clap, clash, collision, crash, cuff, detonation, explosion, hit, knock, noise, peal, pop, punch, report, shot, slam, smack, stroke, thud, thump, wallop, whack.
v. bash, boom, bump, burst, clang, clatter, crash, detonate, drum, echo, explode, hammer, knock, peal, pound, pummel, rap, resound, slam, stamp, strike, thump, thunder.
adv. directly, hard, headlong, noisily, plumb, precisely, right, slap, smack, straight, suddenly.

banish *v.* ban, bar, blacklist, debar, deport, discard, dislodge, dismiss, dispel, eject, eliminate, eradicate, evict, exclude, excommunicate, exile, expatriate, expel, get rid of, ostracize, oust, outlaw, remove, shut out, transport.
antonyms recall, welcome.

bank[1] *n.* accumulation, cache, depository, fund, hoard, pool, repository, reserve, reservoir, savings, stock, stockpile, store, storehouse, treasury.

v. accumulate, deposit, keep, save, stockpile, store.
antonym spend.

bank[2] *n.* acclivity, banking, brink, bund, earthwork, edge, embankment, fail-dike, heap, margin, mass, mound, pile, rampart, ridge, rivage, shallow, shoal, shore, side, slope, tilt.
v. accumulate, aggrade, amass, camber, cant, drift, heap, incline, mass, mound, pile, pitch, slant, slope, stack, tilt, tip.

bank[3] *n.* array, bench, echelon, file, group, line, rank, row, sequence, series, succession, tier, train.

banner *n.* banderol(e), bannerol, burgee, colors, ensign, fanion, flag, gonfalon, labarum, oriflamme, pennant, pennon, standard, streamer, vexillum.

banquet *n.* binge, dinner, feast, meal, repast, revel, treat, wayzgoose.

banter *n.* badinage, chaff, chaffing, cross-talk, derision, dicacity, jesting, joking, kidding, mockery, persiflage, pleasantry, quiz, raillery, repartee, ribbing, ridicule, word play.

bar[1] *n.* barricade, barrier, batten, check, cross-piece, deterrent, deterrment, hindrance, impediment, obstacle, obstruction, overslaugh, paling, pole, preventive, rail, railing, rod, shaft, stake, stanchion, stick, stop.
v. ban, barricade, blackball, bolt, debar, exclude, fasten, forbid, hinder, latch, lock, obstruct, preclude, prevent, prohibit, restrain, secure.

bar[2] *n.* bierkeller, boozer, canteen, counter, dive, doggery, dram-shop, estaminet, exchange, gin-palace, ginshop, groggery, grogshop, honky-tonk, howff, inn, joint, lounge, nineteenth hole, pub, public house, saloon, tavern, vaults, watering-hole.

bar[3] *n.* advocates, attorneys, barristers, bench, counsel, court, courtroom, dock, law court, tribunal.

bar[4] *n.* block, chunk, ingot, lump, nugget, slab, wedge.

barbarian *n.* ape, boor, brute, clod, hooligan, hottentot, hun, ignoramus, illiterate, lout, lowbrow, oaf, philistine, ruffian, savage, tramontane, vandal, vulgarian, yahoo. *adj.* boorish, brutish, coarse, crude, lowbrow, philistine, rough, tramontane, uncivilized, uncouth, uncultivated, uncultured, unsophisticated, vulgar.

barbarous *adj.* barbarian, barbaric, brutal, brutish, coarse, crude, cruel, ferocious, heartless, heathenish, ignorant, inhuman, monstrous, philistine, primitive, rough, rude, ruthless, savage, uncivilized, uncouth, uncultured, unlettered, unrefined, vicious, vulgar, wild.
antonyms civilized, cultured, educated.

bare *adj.* austere, bald, barren, basic, blank, defoliate, defoliated, denudated, denuded, disfurnished, empty, essential, explicit, exposed, hard, lacking, literal, mean, naked, napless, nude, open, peeled, plain, poor, scanty, scarce, severe, sheer, shorn, simple, spare, stark, stripped, unadorned, unarmed, unclad, unclothed, uncovered, undisguised, undressed, unembellished, unforested, unfurnished, unprovided, unsheathed, untimbered, unvarnished, unwooded, vacant, void, wanting, woodless.

barefaced *adj.* arrant, audacious, bald, blatant, bold, brash, brazen, flagrant, glaring, impudent, insolent, manifest, naked, obvious, open, palpable, patent, shameless, transparent, unabashed, unconcealed.

barely[1] *adv.* almost, hardly, just, scarcely, sparingly, sparsely.

barely[2] *adv.* explicitly, nakedly, openly, plainly.

bargain *n.* agreement, arrangement, compact, contract, discount, giveaway, negotiation, pact, pledge, promise, reduction, snip, steal, stipulation, transaction, treaty, understanding.
v. agree, barter, broke, buy, chaffer, contract, covenant, deal, dicker, haggle, higgle, negotiate, promise, sell, stipulate, trade, traffic, transact.

bargain for anticipate, consider, contemplate, expect, foresee, imagine, include, look for, plan for, reckon on.

baroque *adj.* bizarre, bold, convoluted, elaborate, extravagant, exuberant, fanciful, fantastic, flamboyant, florid, grotesque, ornate, overdecorated, overwrought, rococo, vigorous, whimsical.
antonym plain.

barren *adj.* arid, boring, childless, desert, desolate dry, dull, empty, flat, fruitless, infecund, infertile, jejune, lackluster, pointless, profitless, stale, sterile, unbearing, unfruitful, uninformative, uninspiring, uninstructive, uninteresting, unproductive, unprolific, unrewarding, useless, vapid, waste.
antonyms fertile, productive, useful.

barricade *n.* barrier, blockade, bulwark, fence, obstruction, palisade, protection, rampart, screen, stockade.
v. bar, block, blockade, defend, fortify, obstruct, palisade, protect, screen.

barrier *n.* bail, bar, barricade, blockade, boom, boundary, bulkhead, check, difficulty, ditch, drawback, fence, fortification, handicap, hindrance, hurdle, impediment, limitation, obstacle, obstruction, railing, rampart, restriction, stop, stumbling-block, transverse, wall.

barter *v.* bargain, chaffer, deal, dicker, exchange, haggle, higgle, negotiate, sell, swap, switch, trade, traffic, truck.

base[1] *n.* basis, bed, bottom, camp, center, core, essence, essential, foot, foundation, fundamental, groundwork, headquarters, heart, home, key, origin, pedestal, plinth, post, principal, rest, root, settlement, socle, source, stand, standard, starting-point, station, substrate, substructure, support, underpinning, understructure.
v. build, construct, depend, derive, establish, found, ground, hinge, locate, station.

base[2] *adj.* abject, contemptible, corrupt, counterfeit, depraved, disgraceful, disreputable, dog, evil, groveling, humble, ignoble, ignominious, immoral, infamous, low, lowly, low-minded, low-thoughted, mean, menial, miserable, paltry, pitiful, poor, scandalous, servile, shameful, slavish, sordid, sorry, valueless, vile, villainous, vulgar, wicked, worthless, wretched.

base[3] *adj.* adulterated, alloyed, artificial, bastard, counterfeit, debased, fake, forged, fraudulent, impure, inferior, pinchbeck, spurious.

bashful *adj.* abashed, backward, blushing, confused, coy, diffident, embarrassed, hesitant, inhibited, modest, nervous, reserved, reticent, retiring, self-conscious, self-effacing, shamefaced, sheepish, shrinking, shy, timid, timorous, unforthcoming, verecund.
antonym confident.

basic *adj.* central, elementary, essential, fundamental, important, indispensable, inherent, intrinsic, key, necessary, primary, radical, root, underlying, vital.
antonyms inessential, peripheral.

basis *n.* approach, base, bottom, core, essential, fond, footing, foundation, fundamental, ground, groundwork, heart, keynote, pedestal, premise, principle, support, thrust.

bask *v.* apricate, delight in, enjoy, laze, lie, lounge, luxuriate, relax, relish, revel, savor, sunbathe, wallow.

bastion *n.* bulwark, citadel, defence, fastness, fortress, mainstay, pillar, prop, redoubt, rock, stronghold, support, tower of strength.

batch *n.* amount, assemblage, assortment, bunch, collection, consignment, contingent, group, lot, pack, parcel, quantity, set.

bath *n.* ablution, bathtub, cleaning, douche, douse, hamman, Jacuzzi®., scrubbing, shower, soak, tub, wash.
v. bathe, clean, douse, lave, shower, soak, tub, wash.

bathe *v.* cleanse, cover, dook, dunk, encompass, flood, immerse, moisten, rinse, soak, steep, stew, suffuse, swim, wash, wet.
n. dip, dook, rinse, soak, swim, wash.

bathos *n.* anticlimax, comedown, let-down.

battalion *n.* army, brigade, company, contingent, division, force, herd, horde, host, legion, mass, multitude, phalanx, platoon, regiment, squadron, throng.

batten *v.* barricade, board up, clamp down, fasten, fix, nail down, secure, tighten.

batter *v.* abuse, assault, bash, beat, belabor, bruise, buffet, crush, dash, deface, demolish, destroy, disfigure, distress, hurt, injure, lash, maltreat, mangle, manhandle, mar, maul, pelt, pound, pummel, ruin, shatter, smash, thrash, wallop.

battery *n.* artillery, assault, attack, barrage, beating, cannon, cannonry, emplacements, guns, mayhem, onslaught, progression, sequence, series, set, thrashing, violence.

battle *n.* action, affray, attack, campaign, clash, combat, conflict, contest, controversy, crusade, debate, disagreement, dispute, encounter, engagement, fight, fray, hostilities, row, skirmish, strife, struggle, war, warfare.
v. agitate, argue, campaign, clamor, combat, contend, contest, crusade, dispute, feud, fight, strive, struggle, war.

bauble *n.* bagatelle, flamfew, gewgaw, gimcrack, kickshaw, knick-knack, plaything, tinsel, toy, trifle, trinket.

bawd *n.* brothel-keeper, madam, panderess, pimp, procuress.

bawdy *adj.* blue, coarse, dirty, erotic, gross, improper, indecent, indecorous, indelicate, lascivious, lecherous, lewd, libidinous, licentious, lustful, obscene, pornographic, prurient, ribald, risqué, rude, salacious, smutty, suggestive, vulgar.
antonyms chaste, clean.

bawl *v.* bellow, blubber, call, caterwaul, clamor, cry, halloo, howl, roar, shout, sob, squall, vociferate, wail, waul, weep, yell.

bay[1] *n.* arm, bight, cove, embayment, fjord, gulf, inlet, reach.

bay[2] *n.* alcove, booth, carrel, compartment, cubicle, embrasure, niche, nook, opening, recess, stall.

bay[3] *v.* bark, bawl, bell, bellow, cry, holler, howl, roar.

bazaar *n.* agora, alcaicería, alcázar, bring-and-buy, exchange, fair, fête, market, market-place, mart, sale.

beach *n.* coast, foreshore, lido, littoral, margin, plage, riviera, sand, sands, seaboard, seashore, seaside, shingle, shore, strand, water's edge.

beachcomber *n.* Autolycus, forager, loafer, loiterer, scavenger, scrounger, wayfarer. **beacon** *n.* beam, bonfire, fanal, flare, lighthouse, pharos, rocket, sign, signal, watch-fire.

bead *n.* blob, bubble, dot, drop, droplet, glob, globule, pearl, pellet, pill, spherule.

beak *n.* bill, bow, mandibles, neb, nib, nose, nozzle, proboscis, projection, prow, ram, rostrum, snout, stem.

beam *n.* arbor, bar, boom, girder, gleam, glimmer, glint, glow, joist, plank, radiation, rafter, ray, shaft, spar, stanchion, stream, support, timber.
v. broadcast, effulge, emit, fulgurate, glare, glimmer, glitter, glow, grin, laugh, radiate, shine, smile, transmit.

beaming *adj.* beautiful, bright, brilliant, cheerful, effulgent, flashing, gleaming, glistening, glittering, glowing, grinning, happy, joyful, lambent, radiant, refulgent, scintillating, shining, smiling, sparkling, sunny.
antonyms lowering, sullen.

bear[1] *v.* abide, admit, allow, beget, bring, brook, carry, cherish, convey, endure, entertain, exhibit, hack, harbor, have, hold, maintain, move, permit, possess, put up with, shoulder, stomach, suffer, support, sustain, take, tolerate, tote, transport, undergo, uphold, weather, weigh upon.

bear[2] *v.* breed, bring forth, develop, drop, engender, generate, give birth to, give up, produce, propagate, yield.

bearable *adj.* acceptable, endurable, livable(-with), manageable, sufferable, supportable, sustainable, tolerable.

bearing *n.* air, application, aspect, attitude, behavior, carriage, comportment, connection, course, demeanor, deportment, direction, import, manner, mien, pertinence, poise, posture, presence, reference, relation, relevance, significance.

bearings *n.* aim, course, direction, inclination, location, orientation, position, situation, tack, track, way, whereabouts.

beast *n.* animal, ape, barbarian, brute, creature, devil, fiend, monster, pig, sadist, savage, swine.

beastly *adj.* barbarous, bestial, brutal, brutish, coarse, cruel, depraved, disagreeable, foul, inhuman, mean, monstrous, nasty, repulsive, rotten, sadistic, savage, sensual, swinish, terrible, unpleasant, vile.

beat[1] *v.* bang, bash, baste, bastinade, bastinado, batter, belabor, bethump, bethwack, bless, bludgeon, bruise, buffet, cane, contuse, cudgel, curry, ding, drub, dunt, fashion, flog, forge, form, fustigate, hammer, hit, impinge, knobble, knock, knout, knubble, lam, lash, lay into, malleate, maul, mill, model, nubble, pelt, pound, punch, shape, slat, strap, strike, swipe, tan, thrash, thwack, trounce, vapulate, verberate, warm, welt, whale, wham, whip, work.
n. blow, hit, lash, punch, shake, slap, strike, swing, thump.
adj. exhausted, fatigued, jiggered, tired, wearied, worn out, zonked.

beat[2] *v.* best, conquer, defeat, excel, hammer, outdo, outrun, outstrip, overcome, overwhelm, slaughter, subdue, surpass, trounce, vanquish.

beat[3] *v.* flutter, palpitate, patter, pound, pulsate, pulse, quake, quiver, race, shake, throb, thump, tremble, vibrate.
n. accent, cadence, flutter, measure, meter, palpitation, pulsation, pulse, rhyme, rhythm, stress, throb, time.

beat[4] *n.* circuit, course, journey, path, round, rounds, route, territory, way.

beaten[1] *adj.* baffled, cowed, defeated, disappointed, disheartened, frustrated, overcome, ruined, surpassed, thwarted, vanquished, worsted.

beaten[2] *adj.* fashioned, forged, formed, hammered, malleated, shaped, stamped, worked.

beaten[3] *adj.* blended, foamy, frothy, mixed, pounded, stirred, tenderized, whipped, whisked.

beating *n.* belting, caning, chastisement, conquest, corporal punishment, defeat, downfall, dressing, drubbing, flogging, lamming, overthrow, rout, ruin, slapping, smacking, thrashing, vapulation, verberation, warming, whaling, whipping.
adj. pounding, pulsatile, pulsating, pulsative, pulsatory, pulsing, racing, throbbing, thumping.

beau *n.* admirer, Adonis, boyfriend, cavalier, coxcomb, dandy, escort, fancy man, fiancé, fop, gallant, Jack-a-dandy, ladies' man, lover, popinjay, suitor, swain, sweetheart, swell.

beautiful *adj.* alluring, appealing, attractive, beau, beauteous, belle, charming, comely, delightful, exquisite, fair, fine, good-looking, gorgeous, graceful, handsome, lovely, pleasing, pulchritudinous, radiant, ravishing, stunning.
antonyms plain, ugly.

beauty[1] *n.* allure, attractiveness, bloom, charm, comeliness, elegance, excellence, exquisitness, fairness, glamor, grace, handsomeness, loveliness, pleasure, pulchritude, seemliness, symmetry.
antonym ugliness.

beauty[2] *n.* belle, charmer, corker, cracker, femme fatale, goddess, good-looker, knockout, lovely, siren, stunner, Venus.
antonym frump.

becalmed *adj.* at a standstill, idle, motionless, still, stranded, stuck.

because *conj.* as, by reason of, for, forasmuch, forwhy, in that, inasmuch as, on account of, owing to, since, thanks to.

beckon *v.* allure, attract, bid, call, coax, decoy, draw, entice, gesticulate, gesture, invite, lure, motion, nod, pull, signal, summon, tempt, waft.

become *v.* befit, behove, embellish, enhance, fit, flatter, grace, harmonize, ornament, set off, suit.

becoming *adj.* appropriate, attractive, befitting, charming, comely, comme il faut, compatible, congruous, decent, decorous, enhancing, fit, fitting, flattering, graceful, maidenly, meet, neat, pretty, proper, seemly, suitable, tasteful, worthy.
antonym unbecoming.

bed[1] *n.* bedstead, berth, bunk, cot, couch, divan, kip, mattress, pallet, palliasse, sack, the downy.

bed[2] *n.* base, border, bottom, channel, foundation, garden, groundwork, layer, matrix, patch, plot, row, stratus, strip, substratum, wadi, watercourse.
v. base, embed, establish, fix, found, ground, implant, insert, plant, settle.

bedeck *v.* adorn, array, beautify, bedight, bedizen, decorate, embellish, festoon, garnish, ornament, trick out, trim.
antonym strip.

bedevil *v.* afflict, annoy, besiege, confound, distress, fret, frustrate, harass, irk, irritate, pester, plague, tease, torment, torture, trouble, vex, worry.

bedlam *n.* anarchy, babel, chaos, clamor, commotion, confusion, furore, hubbub, hullabaloo, madhouse, noise, pandemonium, tumult, turmoil, uproar.
antonym calm.

bedraggled *adj.* dirty, disheveled, disordered, messy, muddied, muddy, scruffy, slovenly, sodden, soiled, stained, sullied, unkempt, untidy.
antonym tidy.

beef[1] *n.* beefiness, brawn, bulk, flesh, fleshiness, heftiness, muscle, robustness, sinew, strength.

beef[2] *n.* complaint, criticism, dispute, dissatisfaction, grievance, gripe, grouse, grumble, objection, protest.
v. complain, criticize, gripe, grumble, moan, object.
antonym approve.

beefy *adj.* brawny, bulky, burly, corpulent, fat, fleshy, heavy, hefty, hulking, muscular, plump, podgy, pudgy, rotund, stalwart, stocky, strapping, sturdy.
antonym slight.

befall *v.* arrive, betide, chance, ensue, fall, follow, happen, materialize, occur, supervene, take place.

before *adv.* ahead, earlier, formerly, in advance, in front, previously, sooner.
antonyms after, later.
prep. ahead of, earlier than, in advance of, in anticipation of, in front of, in preparation for, previous to, prior to, sooner than.
conj. in case, rather than.

befriend *v.* aid, assist, back, benefit, comfort, encourage, favor, help, patronize, stand by, succor, support, sustain, take a liking to, take under one's wing, uphold, welcome.
antonym neglect.

befuddled *adj.* baffled, bewildered, confused, dazed, fuddled, groggy, hazy, inebriated, intoxicated, muddled, woozy.
antonym lucid.

beg *v.* beseech, cadge, crave, desire, entreat, fleech, implore, importune, petition, plead, pray, prog, request, require, schnorr, scrounge, shool, skelder, solicit, sponge on, supplicate, touch.

beget *v.* breed, bring, cause, create, effect, engender, father, gender, generate, get, give rise to, occasion, procreate, produce, propagate, result in, sire, spawn.

beggar[1] *n.* Abraham-man, bankrupt, beadsman, besognio, bluegown, cadger, canter, derelict, down-and-out, hobo, lazzarone, mendicant, pauper, schnorrer, scrounger, sponger, starveling, supplicant, toe-rag, toe-ragger, tramp, vagrant.

beggar[2] *v.* baffle, challenge, defy, exceed, surpass, transcend.

begin *v.* activate, actuate, appear, arise, commence, crop up, dawn, emerge, happen, inaugurate, initiate, instigate, institute, introduce, originate, prepare, set about, set in, spring, start.
antonyms end, finish.

beginner *n.* abecedarian, alphabetarian, amateur, apprentice, cheechako, cub, fledgling, freshman, greenhorn, initiate, Johnny-raw, learner, neophyte, novice, recruit, rookie, rooky, starter, student, tenderfoot, tiro, trainee.
antonyms expert, old hand, veteran.

beginning *n.* birth, commencement, embryo, establishment, fons et origo, fountainhead, germ, inauguration, inception, inchoation, initiation, introduction, onset, opening, origin, outset, preface, prelude, prime, rise, root, rudiments, seed, source, start, starting point.
antonyms end, finish.
adj. early, elementary, inaugural, inauguratory, inceptive, inchoative, incipient, initial, introductory, nascent, primal, primary, primeval.

begrudge *v.* covet, envy, grudge, mind, resent, stint.
antonym allow.

beguiling *adj.* alluring, appealing, attractive, bewitching, captivating, charming, diverting, enchanting, entertaining, enticing, interesting, intriguing.
antonyms offensive, repulsive.

behalf *n.* account, advantage, authority, benefit, defense, good, interest, name, part, profit, sake, side, support.

behave *v.* acquit, act, bear, comport, conduct, demean, deport, function, operate, perform, react, respond, run, work.

behavior *n.* action, actions, bearing, carriage, comportment, conduct, dealings, demeanor, deportment, doings, functioning, habits, manner, manners, operation, performance, reaction, response, ways.

behead *v.* decapitate, decollate, execute, guillotine, unhead.

behest *n.* authority, bidding, charge, command, commandment, decree, dictate, direction, fiat, injunction, instruction, mandate, order, ordinance, precept, wish.

behind *prep.* after, backing, causing, following, for, initiating, instigating, later than, responsible for, supporting.
adv. after, afterwards, behindhand, en arrière, following, in arrears, in debt, in the wake of, next, overdue, subsequently.
n. ass, backside, bottom, butt, buttocks, derrière, fanny, posterior, prat, rear, rump, seat, sit-upon, tail, tush.

behold *v.* consider, contemplate, descry, discern, espy, eye, look at, note, observe, perceive, regard, scan, survey, view, watch, witness.
interj. ecce, lo, look, mark, observe, see, voici, voilà, watch.

being[1] *n.* actuality, animation, entity, essence, existence, haecceity, life, living, nature, quiddity, reality, soul, spirit, substance.

being[2] *n.* animal, beast, body, creature, human being, individual, mortal, sentient, thing.

belabor *v.* attack, bash, batter, beat, belt, berate, castigate, censure, chastise, criticize, flay, flog, lambast, lay into, thrash, whip.

belated *adj.* behind-hand, delayed, late, overdue, retarded, tardy, unpunctual.
antonyms punctual, timely.

belch *v.* burp, discharge, disgorge, emit, eruct, eructate, erupt, gush, hiccup, spew, vent.
n. burp, eructation, eruption, hiccup.

beleaguered *adj.* badgered, beset, besieged, bothered, harassed, hedged about, hedged in, persecuted, plagued, surrounded, vexed, worried.

belie *v.* conceal, confute, contradict, deceive, deny, disguise, disprove, falsify, gainsay, mislead, misrepresent, negate, refute, repudiate, run counter to, understate.
antonym attest.

belief *n.* assurance, confidence, conviction, credence, credit, credo, creed, doctrine, dogma, expectation, faith, feeling, ideology, impression, intuition, ism, judgment,

notion, opinion, persuasion, presumption, principle, principles, reliance, sureness, surety, tenet, theory, trust, view.
antonym disbelief.

believe *v.* accept, assume, be under the impression, conjecture, consider, count on, credit, deem, depend on, gather, guess, hold, imagine, judge, maintain, postulate, presume, reckon, rely on, speculate, suppose, swallow, swear by, think, trust, wear.
antonym disbelieve.

believer *n.* adherent, catechumen, convert, devotee, disciple, follower, proselyte, supporter, upholder, votary, zealot.
antonyms apostate, sceptic, unbeliever.

belittle *v.* decry, deprecate, depreciate, deride, derogate, detract, diminish, dismiss, disparage, downgrade, lessen, minimize, ridicule, run down, scorn, underestimate, underrate, undervalue, vilipend.
antonym exaggerate.

belligerent *adj.* aggressive, antagonistic, argumentative, bellicose, bullying, combative, contentious, forceful, militant, pugnacious, quarrelsome, violent, warlike, warring.
antonym peaceable.

bellow *v.* bell, call, clamor, cry, howl, roar, scream, shout, shriek, troat, yell.

belly *n.* abdomen, bowels, bread-basket, corporation, gut, guts, insides, paunch, pot, sound-board, stomach, tummy, uterus, venter, vitals, womb.
v. bag, balloon, billow, blow up, bulge, dilate, distend, expand, fill out, inflate, swell.
antonyms deflate, shrink.

belonging *n.* acceptance, affinity, association, attachment, closeness, compatibility, fellow-feeling, fellowship, inclusion, kinship, link, linkage, loyalty, rapport, relationship.
antonym antipathy.

belongings *n.* accouterments, chattels, effects, gear, goods, impedimenta, paraphernalia, possessions, stuff, things, traps.

beloved *adj.* admired, adored, cherished, darling, dear, dearest, favorite, loved, pet, precious, prized, revered, sweet, treasured.
n. adored, darling, dear, dearest, favorite, inamorata, inamorato, lover, pet, precious, sweet, sweetheart.

below *adv.* beneath, down, infra, lower, lower down, under, underneath.
prep. inferior to, lesser than, 'neath, subject to, subordinate to, under, underneath, unworthy of.

belt[1] *n.* area, band, ceinture, cincture, cingulum, cummerbund, district, girdle, girth, layer, region, sash, strait, stretch, strip, swathe, tract, waistband, zone, zonule, zonulet.
v. circle, encircle, girdle, ring, surround.

belt[2] *v.* bolt, career, charge, dash, hurry, race, rush, speed.

bemoan *v.* bewail, deplore, grieve for, lament, mourn, regret, rue, sigh for, sorrow over, weep for.
antonym gloat.

bend *v.* aim, bow, brace, buckle, compel, constrain, contort, couch, crankle, crimp, crouch, curve, deflect, direct, dispose, diverge, embow, fasten, flex, incline, incurvate, incurve, influence, lean, mold, nerve, persuade, shape, stoop, string, subdue, submit, sway, swerve, turn, twist, veer, warp, yield.
n. angle, arc, bight, bought, bow, corner, crank, crook, curvature, curve, elbow, flexure, genu, hook, incurvation, incurvature, incurve, inflexure, loop, turn, twist, zigzag.

beneath *adv.* below, lower, lower down, under, underneath.
prep. below, inferior to, infra dig(nitatem), lower than, 'neath, subject to, subordinate to, unbefitting, under, underneath, unworthy of.

benediction *n.* beatitude, Benedictus, benison, blessing, consecration, favor, grace, invocation, orison, prayer, thanksgiving.
antonyms anathema, curse, execration.

beneficial *adj.* advantageous, benign, benignant, edifying, favorable, gainful, healthful, helpful, improving, nourishing, nutritious, profitable, restorative, rewarding, salubrious, salutary, serviceable, useful, valuable, wholesome.
antonym harmful.

benefit *n.* advantage, aid, asset, assistance, avail, betterment, blessing, boon, favor, gain, good, help, interest, profit, service, use, weal, welfare.
antonym harm.
v. advance, advantage, aid, ameliorate, amend, assist, avail, better, enhance, further, improve, profit, promote, serve.
antonyms harm, hinder, undermine.

benevolence *n.* altruism, benignity, bounty, charity, compassion, fellow-feeling, generosity, goodness, goodwill, humanity, kind-heartedness, kindliness, kindness, munificence, sympathy.
antonym meanness.

benevolent *adj.* altruistic, beneficent, benign, bounteous, bountiful, caring, charitable, compassionate, considerate, generous, good-will, humane, humanitarian, kind, kind-hearted, kindly, liberal, loving, philanthropic, solicitous, well-disposed.
antonym mean.

bent *adj.* angled, arched, bowed, coudé, criminal, crooked, curved, dishonest, doubled, falcate, folded, homosexual, hunched, inbent, inflexed, retorted, retroverted, stolen, stooped, twisted, untrustworthy.
antonym straight.
n. ability, aptitude, capacity, facility, faculty, flair, forte, gift, inclination, knack, leaning, penchant, preference, proclivity, propensity, talent, tendency.

berate *v.* castigate, censure, chastise, chide, criticize, flyte, jump down the throat of, rail at, rate, rebuke,

reprimand, reproach, reprove, revile, scold, tell off, upbraid, vituperate.
antonym praise.

beseech *v.* adjure, ask, beg, call on, conjure, crave, desire, entreat, implore, importune, obsecrate, petition, plead, pray, solicit, sue, supplicate.

beset *v.* assail, attack, badger, bamboozle, bedevil, besiege, embarrass, encircle, enclose, encompass, entangle, environ, faze, harass, hassle, hem in, perplex, pester, plague, surround.

beside *prep.* abreast of, abutting on, adjacent, bordering on, close to, near, neighboring, next door to, next to, overlooking, upsides with.

besides *adv.* additionally, also, as well, extra, further, furthermore, in addition, into the bargain, moreover, otherwise, to boot, too, withal.
prep. apart from, in addition to, other than, over and above.

besiege *v.* assail, badger, belay, beleaguer, beset, blockade, bother, confine, dun, encircle, encompass, environ, harass, harry, hound, importune, nag, pester, plague, surround, trouble.

bespeak *v.* attest, betoken, demonstrate, denote, display, evidence, evince, exhibit, forebode, foretell, imply, indicate, predict, proclaim, reveal, show, signify, suggest, testify to.

best *adj.* advantageous, apt, correct, excellent, finest, first, first-class, first-rate, foremost, greatest, highest, incomparable, largest, leading, makeless, matchless, nonpareil, optimal, optimum, outstanding, perfect, preeminent, preferable, principal, right, superlative, supreme, transcendent, unequaled, unsurpassed.
antonym worst.
adv. excellently, exceptionally, extremely, greatly, superlatively, surpassingly.
antonym worst.
n. choice, cream, crème de la crème, élite, favorite, finest, first, flower, hardest, nonpareil, pick, prime, the tops, top, utmost.
antonym worst.
v. beat, conquer, defeat, get the better of, have the laugh of, lick, outclass, outdo, outwit, surpass, thrash, trounce, vanquish, worst.

bestial *adj.* animal, barbaric, barbarous, beastly, brutal, brutish, carnal, degraded, depraved, feral, gross, inhuman, savage, sensual, sordid, subhuman, swinish, vile.
antonyms civilized, humane.

bestow *v.* accord, allot, apportion, award, bequeath, commit, confer, donate, dower, endow, entrust, give, grant, impart, lavish, lend, present, transmit, wreak.
antonym deprive.

bet *n.* accumulator, ante, bid, flutter, gamble, hazard, pledge, risk, speculation, stake, venture, wager.
v. ante, bid, chance, gamble, hazard, lay, pledge, punt, risk, speculate, stake, venture, wager.

betray *v.* abandon, beguile, corrupt, deceive, delude, desert, disclose, discover, divulge, dob in, double-cross, dupe, ensnare, entrap, evince, expose, forsake, give away, grass, inform on, jilt, manifest, mislead, reveal, seduce, sell, sell down the river, sell out, shop, show, tell, testify against, turn state's evidence, undo.
antonyms defend, fulfil, protect.

betrothal *n.* engagement, espousal, fiançailles, handfast, plight, promise, troth, vow.

better *adj.* bigger, cured, finer, fitter, greater, healthier, improving, larger, longer, on the mend, preferable, progressing, recovered, recovering, restored, stronger, superior, surpassing, worthier.
antonym worse.
v. advance, ameliorate, amend, beat, cap, correct, enhance, exceed, excel, forward, further, go one further than, improve, improve on, increase, meliorate, mend, outdo, outstrip, overtake, overtop, promote, raise, rectify, redress, reform, strengthen, surpass, top, transcend.
antonyms deteriorate, worsen.

between *prep.* amidst, among, amongst, betwixt, inter-, mid.

beware *v.* avoid, give a wide berth to, guard against, heed, look out, mind, shun, steer clear of, take heed, watch out.
antonyms brave, dare.

bewilder *v.* baffle, bamboozle, befuddle, bemuse, buffalo, confound, confuse, daze, disconcert, disorient, fuddle, maze, muddle, mystify, perplex, puzzle, stupefy, tie in knots.

bewitch *v.* allure, attract, beguile, captivate, charm, elfshoot, enchant, enrapture, ensorcell, entrance, fascinate, forspeak, hex, hoodoo, hypnotize, jinx, obsess, possess, spellbind, voodoo, witch.

beyond *prep.* above, across, apart from, away from, before, further than, out of range, out of reach of, over, past, remote from, superior to, yonder.

bias *n.* angle, bent, bigotry, distortion, editorialization, favoritism, inclination, intolerance, leaning, one-sidedness, parti pris, partiality, penchant, predilection, predisposition, prejudice, proclivity, proneness, propensity, slant, tendency, tendentiousness, turn, unfairness, viewiness.
antonyms fairness, impartiality.
v. angle, distort, earwig, editorialize, influence, jaundice, load, load the dice, predispose, prejudice, slant, sway, twist, warp, weight.

bibulous *adj.* alcoholic, crapulous, dipsomaniac, drunken, inebriate, intemperate, sottish, thirsty, tipsy.
antonyms sober, temperate.

bicker *v.* altercate, argue, clash, disagree, dispute, feud, fight, quarrel, row, scrap, spar, squabble, wrangle.
antonym agree.

bid *v.* ask, call, charge, command, desire, direct, enjoin, greet, instruct, invite, offer, proclaim, propose, request, require, say, solicit, summon, tell, wish.
n. advance, amount, ante, attempt, crack, effort,

endeavor, go, offer, price, proposal, proposition, submission, sum, tender, try, venture.

bidding *n.* behest, call, charge, command, demand, dictate, direction, injunction, instruction, invitation, order, request, requirement, summons.

big *adj.* adult, altruistic, beefy, benevolent, boastful, bombastic, bulky, burly, buxom, colossal, considerable, corpulent, elder, elephantine, eminent, enormous, extensive, gargantuan, generous, gigantic, gracious, great, grown, grown-up, heroic, huge, hulking, immense, important, influential, large, leading, lofty, magnanimous, main, mammoth, man-sized, massive, mature, mighty, momentous, noble, paramount, plonking, ponderous, powerful, prime, principal, prodigious, prominent, serious, significant, sizable, spacious, stout, substantial, titanic, tolerant, unselfish, valuable, vast, voluminous, weighty.
antonyms little, small.

bigot *n.* chauvinist, dogmatist, fanatic, racist, religionist, sectarian, sexist, verkrampte, zealot.
antonyms humanitarian, liberal.

bigoted *adj.* biased, blinkered, chauvinist, closed, dogmatic, illiberal, intolerant, narrow, narrow-minded, obstinate, opinionated, prejudiced, sectarian, twisted, verkrampte, warped.
antonyms broad-minded, enlightened, liberal.

bilious *adj.* choleric, crabby, cross, crotchety, grouchy, grumpy, irritable, liverish, nauseated, out of sorts, peevish, queasy, sick, sickly, testy.

bilk *v.* balk, bamboozle, cheat, con, cozen, deceive, defraud, do, do out of, fleece, foil, rook, sting, swindle, thwart, trick.

bill[1] *n.* account, advertisement, battels, broadsheet, broadside, bulletin, card, catalog, charges, check, chit, circular, greenback, handbill, hand-out, inventory, invoice, leaflet, legislation, list, listing, measure, note, notice, placard, playbill, poster, program, proposal, reckoning, roster, schedule, score, sheet, statement, syllabus, tab, tally.
v. advertise, announce, charge, debit, invoice, list, post, reckon, record.

bill[2] *n.* beak, mandible, neb, nib, rostrum.

billow *v.* balloon, belly, expand, fill out, heave, puff out, roll, seethe, spread, surge, swell, undulate.

bind *v.* astrict, astringe, attach, bandage, border, cinch, clamp, colligate, compel, complain, confine, constipate, constrain, cover, detain, dress, edge, encase, engage, fasten, finish, force, glue, hamper, harden, hinder, hitch, indenture, lash, necessitate, obligate, oblige, prescribe, require, restrain, restrict, rope, seal, secure, stick, strap, swathe, thirl, tie, trim, truss, wrap.
n. bore, difficulty, dilemma, embarrassment, hole, impasse, nuisance, predicament, quandary.

binding *adj.* compulsory, conclusive, imperative, indissoluble, irrevocable, mandatory, necessary, obligatory, permanent, requisite, strict, unalterable, unbreakable.
n. bandage, border, covering, deligation, edging, stricture, syndesis, tape, trimming, wrapping.

birth *n.* ancestry, background, beginning, birthright, blood, breeding, childbirth, delivery, derivation, descent, emergence, extraction, family, fell, genealogy, genesis, geniture, line, lineage, nativity, nobility, origin, parentage, parturition, pedigree, race, rise, source, stirps, stock, strain.

biscuit *n.* cake, cookie, cracker, hardtack, rusk, wafer.

bit *n.* atom, chip, crumb, fragment, grain, instant, iota, jiffy, jot, mammock, minute, mite, moment, morsel, part, period, piece, scrap, second, segment, sippet, slice, snippet, speck, spell, tick, time, tittle, while, whit.

bite *v.* burn, champ, chew, clamp, corrode, crunch, crush, cut, gnaw, knap, masticate, nibble, nip, pierce, pinch, rend, seize, smart, snap, sting, tear, tingle, wound.
n. edge, food, grip, kick, morsel, morsure, mouthful, nip, piece, pinch, piquancy, prick, punch, pungency, refreshment, smarting, snack, spice, sting, taste, wound.

biting *adj.* astringent, bitter, blighting, caustic, cold, cutting, cynical, freezing, harsh, hurtful, incisive, mordant, nipping, penetrating, piercing, raw, sarcastic, scathing, severe, sharp, stinging, tart, trenchant, withering.
antonyms bland, mild.

bitter *adj.* acerb, acerbic, acid, acrid, acrimonious, astringent, begrudging, biting, calamitous, crabbed, cruel, cynical, dire, distressing, embittered, fierce, freezing, galling, grievous, harsh, hateful, heartbreaking, hostile, intense, ironic, jaundiced, merciless, morose, odious, painful, poignant, rancorous, raw, resentful, ruthless, sarcastic, savage, severe, sharp, sore, sour, stinging, sullen, tart, unsweetened, vexatious, vinegary, waspish.
antonyms contented, genial, sweet.

bizarre *adj.* abnormal, comical, curious, deviant, eccentric, extraordinary, extravagant, fantastic, freakish, grotesque, ludicrous, odd, off-beat, outlandish, outré, peculiar, quaint, queer, ridiculous, strange, unusual, way-out, weird.
antonym normal.

black *adj.* angry, atrocious, bad, begrimed, coal-black, coaly, dark, darksome, depressing, dingy, dirty, dismal, doleful, dusky, ebony, evil, filthy, funereal, furious, gloomy, grim, grimy, grubby, hopeless, horrible, hostile, inky, jet, jet-black, jetty, lugubrious, menacing, moonless, morel, mournful, murky, nefarious, ominous, overcast, pitchy, raven, resentful, sable, sad, sloe, soiled, somber, sooty, stained, starless, Stygian, sullen, swarthy, threatening, thunderous, villainous, wicked.
v. ban, bar, blacklist, boycott, taboo.

blackball *v.* ban, bar, blacklist, debar, exclude, expel, ostracize, oust, pip, reject, repudiate, snub, veto.

blacken *v.* befoul, begrime, besmirch, calumniate, cloud, darken, decry, defame, defile, denigrate, detract, dishonor, malign, revile, slander, smear, smirch, smudge, soil, stain, sully, taint, tarnish, traduce, vilify.
antonyms enhance, praise.

blackmail *n.* blood-sucking, chantage, exaction, extortion, hush money, intimidation, milking, pay-off, protection, ransom.
v. bleed, bribe, coerce, compel, demand, force, hold to ransom, lean on, milk, put the black on, squeeze, threaten.

blackout *n.* censorship, coma, concealment, cover-up, faint, oblivion, power cut, secrecy, suppression, swoon, syncope, unconsciousness.

bladder *n.* aveole, bag, bursa, cecum, capsule, cell, cyst, pocket, pouch, receptacle, sac, theca, utricle, vesica, vesicle, vesicula.

blade *n.* dagger, edge, knife, rapier, scalpel, sword, vane.

blame *n.* accountability, accusation, animadversion, castigation, censure, charge, complaint, condemnation, criticism, culpability, discommendation, fault, guilt, incrimination, liability, obloquy, onus, rap, recrimination, reprimand, reproach, reproof, responsibility, stick, stricture.
v. accuse, admonish, censure, charge, chide, condemn, criticize, disapprove, discommend, dispraise, find fault with, rebuke, reprehend, reprimand, reproach, reprove, tax, upbraid.
antonym exonerate.

blameless *adj.* above reproach, clean, clear, faultless, guiltless, immaculate, impeccable, inculpable, innocent, irreprehensible, irreproachable, irreprovable, perfect, sinless, stainless, unblamable, unblemished, unimpeachable, unspotted, unsullied, untarnished, upright, virtuous.
antonym guilty.

blanch *v.* bleach, blench, drain, etiolate, fade, pale, wan, whiten.
antonyms blush, color, redden.

bland *adv.* affable, amiable, balmy, boring, calm, characterless, congenial, courteous, demulcent, dull, fair-spoken, flat, friendly, gentle, gracious, humdrum, hypoallergenic, impassive, inscrutable, insipid, mild, mollifying, monotonous, nondescript, non-irritant, smooth, soft, soothing, suave, tasteless, tedious, temperate, unexciting, uninspiring, uninteresting, urbane, vapid, weak.
antonyms piquant, sharp.

blandishments *n.* blarney, cajolery, coaxing, compliments, enticements, fawning, flattery, inducements, ingratiation, inveiglement, lip-salve, persuasiveness, soft soap, sweet talk, sycophancy, wheedling.

blank *adj.* apathetic, bare, bewildered, clean, clear, confounded, confused, deadpan, disconcerted, dull, dumbfounded, empty, expressionless, featureless, glazed, hollow, immobile, impassive, inane, inscrutable, lifeless, muddled, nonplused, plain, poker-faced, sheer, spotless, staring, uncomprehending, unfilled, unmarked, unrhymed, vacant, vacuous, vague, void, white.
n. break, emptiness, gap, nothingness, space, tabula rasa, vacancy, vacuity, vacuum, void.

blanket *n.* carpet, cloak, coat, coating, cover, covering, coverlet, envelope, film, housing, layer, mackinaw, manta, mantle, rug, sheet, wrapper, wrapping.
adj. across-the-board, all-embracing, all-inclusive, comprehensive, inclusive, overall, sweeping, wide-ranging.
v. cloak, cloud, coat, conceal, cover, deaden, eclipse, hide, mask, muffle, obscure, surround.

blare *v.* blast, boom, clamor, clang, honk, hoot, peal, resound, ring, roar, scream, shriek, toot, trumpet.

blasphemous *adj.* execrative, godless, hubristic, impious, imprecatory, irreligious, irreverent, profane, sacrilegious, ungodly.

blasphemy *n.* curse, cursing, defilement, desecration, execration, expletive, hubris, impiety, impiousness, imprecation, irreverence, outrage, profanation, profaneness, profanity, sacrilege, swearing, violation.

blast[1] *n.* blare, blow, boom, honk, hoot, peal, roar, scream, shriek, sound, wail.

blast[2] *n.* bang, bluster, burst, clap, crack, crash, detonation, discharge, draught, eruption, explosion, flatus, gale, gust, hail, outburst, salvo, squall, storm, tempest, volley.
v. assail, attack, blight, blow up, burst, castigate, demolish, destroy, explode, flay, kill, lash, ruin, shatter, shrivel, storm at, wither.

blasted *adj.* blighted, desolated, destroyed, devastated, ravaged, ruined, scorched, shattered, wasted, withered.

blatant *adj.* arrant, bald, barefaced, brazen, clamorous, conspicuous, egregious, flagrant, flaunting, glaring, harsh, loud, naked, noisy, obtrusive, obvious, ostentatious, outright, overt, prominent, pronounced, sheer, unmitigated.

blather *n.* blether, chatter, chatterbox, chatterer, chitchat, claptrap, drivel, gibberish, gibble-gabble, gobbledegook, jabbering, loquacity, moonshine, nonsense, prattle, prattler, twaddle.
v. blabber, chatter, gab, gabble, haver, jabber, prattle.

bleach *v.* blanch, decolorise, etiolate, fade, lighten, pale, peroxide, whiten.

bleak *adj.* bare, barren, blae, blasted, cheerless, chilly, cold, colorless, comfortless, delightless, depressing, desolate, discouraging, disheartening, dismal, dreary, empty, exposed, gaunt, gloomy, grim, hopeless, joyless, leaden, loveless, open, raw, somber, unsheltered, weather-beaten, windswept, windy.
antonyms cheerful, congenial.

bleary *adj.* blurred, blurry, cloudy, dim, fogged, foggy, fuzzy, hazy, indistinct, misty, muddy, murky, obscured, rheumy, watery.

bleed *v.* blackmail, deplete, drain, exhaust, exploit, extort, extract, extravasate, exude, fleece, flow, gush, hemorrhage, leech, milk, ooze, reduce, run, sap, seep, spurt, squeeze, suck dry, trickle, weep.

blemish *n.* birthmark, blot, blotch, blur, botch, defect, deformity, disfigurement, disgrace, dishonor, fault, flaw, imperfection, mackle, macula, maculation, mark, naevus, smudge, speck, spot, stain, taint.
v. besmirch, blot, blotch, blur, damage, deface, disfigure, flaw, impair, injure, maculate, mar, mark, smirch, smudge, spoil, spot, stain, sully, taint, tarnish.

blend *v.* amalgamate, coalesce, combine, complement, compound, contemper, fit, fuse, harmonize, intermix, meld, merge, mingle, mix, synthesize, unite.
antonym separate.
n. alloy, amalgam, amalgamation, combination, composite, compound, concoction, fusion, interunion, meld, mix, mixture, synthesis, union.

bless *v.* anoint, approve, bestow, consecrate, countenance, dedicate, endow, exalt, extol, favor, glorify, grace, hallow, magnify, ordain, praise, provide, sanctify, thank.
antonyms condemn, curse.

blessed *adj.* adored, beatified, blissful, contented, divine, endowed, favored, fortunate, glad, hallowed, happy, holy, joyful, joyous, lucky, prosperous, revered, sacred, sanctified.
antonym cursed.

blessing *n.* advantage, approbation, approval, authority, backing, benedicite, benediction, benefit, benison, boon, bounty, commendation, concurrence, consecration, consent, countenance, dedication, favor, fortune, gain, gift, godsend, grace, help, invocation, kindness, leave, permission, profit, sanction, service, support, thanksgiving, windfall.
antonyms blight, condemnation, curse.

blight *n.* affliction, bane, cancer, canker, check, contamination, corruption, curse, decay, depression, disease, evil, fungus, infestation, mildew, pest, pestilence, plague, pollution, rot, scourge, set-back, woe.
antonyms blessing, boon.
v. annihilate, blast, crush, dash, destroy, disappoint, frustrate, injure, mar, ruin, shatter, shrivel, spoil, undermine, wither, wreck.
antonym bless.

blind *adj.* amaurotic, beetle-eyed, blinkered, careless, closed, concealed, dark, dim, eyeless, hasty, heedless, hidden, ignorant, impetuous, inattentive, inconsiderate, indifferent, indiscriminate, injudicious, insensate, insensitive, irrational, mindless, neglectful, oblivious, obscured, obstructed, prejudiced, purblind, rash, reckless, sand-blind, senseless, sightless, stone-blind, thoughtless, unaware, uncontrollable, uncritical, undiscerning, unobservant, unobserving, unreasoning, unseeing, unsighted, unthinking, violent, visionless, wild.
antonyms aware, clear, sighted.
n. camouflage, cloak, cover, cover-up, distraction, façade, feint, front, mask, masquerade, screen, smokescreen.

blink *v.* bat, condone, connive at, disregard, flash, flicker, flutter, gleam, glimmer, glimpse, ignore, nictate, nictitate, overlook, peer, pink, scintillate, shine, sparkle, squint, twinkle, wink.

bliss *n.* beatitude, blessedness, blissfulness, ecstasy, euphoria, felicity, gladness, happiness, heaven, joy, nirvana, paradise, rapture.
antonyms damnation, misery.

blister *n.* abscess, bleb, boil, bubble, bulla, canker, carbuncle, cyst, furuncle, papilla, papula, papule, pimple, pompholyx, pustule, sore, swelling, ulcer, vesicle, vesicula, welt, wen.

blithe *adj.* animated, buoyant, carefree, careless, casual, cheerful, cheery, debonair, gay, gladsome, happy, heedless, jaunty, light-hearted, lightsome, lively, merry, mirthful, nonchalant, sprightly, sunny, thoughtless, unconcerned, untroubled, vivacious.
antonym morose.

bloated *adj.* blown up, bombastic, dilated, distended, dropsical, edematous, enlarged, expanded, inflated, sated, swollen, tumescent, tumid, turgid.
antonyms shriveled, shrunken, thin.

blob *n.* ball, bead, bobble, bubble, dab, dew-drop, drop, droplet, glob, globule, gob, lump, mass, pearl, pellet, pill, spot.

block *n.* bar, barrier, blockage, brick, cake, chunk, cube, delay, hang-up, hindrance, hunk, impediment, ingot, jam, let, lump, mass, obstacle, obstruction, piece, resistance, square, stoppage, tranche.
v. arrest, bar, check, choke, clog, close, dam up, deter, halt, hinder, impede, obstruct, obturate, oppilate, plug, scotch, stonewall, stop, stop up, thwart, trig.

blockade *n.* barricade, barrier, beleaguerment, closure, encirclement, obstruction, restriction, siege, stoppage.

blockhead *n.* bonehead, boodle, chump, dolt, dullard, dunce, fool, idiot, ignoramus, jobernowl, klutz, leatherhead, loggerhead, log-head, noodle, numskull, pigsconce, pinhead, pot-head, thickhead, thick-skull.
antonyms brain, genius.

blood *n.* ancestry, anger, birth, bloodshed, consanguinity, descendants, descent, extraction, family, kindred, kinship, lineage, murder, relations, relationship, temper, temperament.

bloodcurdling *adj.* appalling, chilling, dreadful, eldritch, fearful, frightening, hair-raising, horrendous, horrible, horrid, horrifying, scaring, spine-chilling, terrifying, weird.

bloodshed *n.* bloodletting, butchery, carnage, gore, killing, massacre, murder, slaughter, slaying.

bloodthirsty *adj.* barbaric, barbarous, brutal, cruel, ferocious, inhuman, murderous, ruthless, sanguinary, savage, slaughterous, vicious, warlike.

bloody *adj.* bleeding, bloodstained, blooming, brutal, cruel, ferocious, fierce, gaping, murderous, raw, sanguinary, sanguine, sanguineous, sanguinolent, savage.

bloom *n.* beauty, blossom, blossoming, blow, blush, bud, efflorescence, florescence, flourishing, flower, flush, freshness, glaucescence, glow, health, heyday, luster, perfection, prime, radiance, rosiness, vigor.
v. blossom, blow, bud, burgeon, develop, flourish, grow, open, prosper, sprout, succeed, thrive, wax.
antonym wither.

blooming *adj.* blossoming, bonny, florescent, flowering, healthful, healthy, rosy, ruddy.
antonym ailing.

blossom *n.* bloom, bud, floret, flower, flowers.
v. bloom, blow, burgeon, develop, effloresce, flourish, flower, grow, mature, progress, prosper, thrive.
antonym wither.

blot *n.* blemish, blotch, defect, disgrace, fault, flaw, mackle, macula, mark, patch, smear, smudge, speck, splodge, spot, stain, taint.
v. bespatter, blur, disfigure, disgrace, maculate, mar, mark, smudge, spoil, spot, stain, sully, taint, tarnish.

blow[1] *v.* bear, blare, blast, breathe, buffet, drive, exhale, fan, fling, flow, flutter, mouth, pant, pipe, play, puff, rush, sound, stream, sweep, toot, trumpet, vibrate, waft, whirl, whisk, wind.
n. blast, draft, flurry, gale, gust, puff, squall, tempest, wind.

blow[2] *n.* affliction, bang, bash, bat, belt, biff, bombshell, bop, box, buff, buffet, calamity, catastrophe, clap, clip, clout, clump, comedown, concussion, counterbluff, crack, disappointment, disaster, douse, haymaker, hit, jab, jolt, knock, knuckle sandwich, misfortune, oner, poke, punch, rap, reverse, setback, shock, siserary, slap, slat, slosh, smack, sock, sockdologer, souse, stroke, swash, swat, swipe, thump, upset, wallop, wap, welt, whack, whang, winder.

blue[1] *adj.* aquamarine, azure, cerulean, cobalt, cyan, indigo, navy, sapphire, turquoise, ultramarine, watchet.

blue[2] *adj.* black, bleak, dejected, depressed, despondent, dismal, dispirited, doleful, down in the dumps, downcast, down-hearted, fed up, gloomy, glum, low, melancholy, miserable, morose, sad, unhappy.
antonym cheerful.

blue[3] *adv.* bawdy, coarse, dirty, improper, indecent, lewd, naughty, near the bone, near the knuckle, obscene, offensive, pornographic, risqué, smutty, vulgar.
antonym decent.

blueprint *n.* archetype, design, draft, guide, model, outline, pattern, pilot, plan, project, prototype, sketch.

blues *n.* blue devils, dejection, depression, despondency, doldrums, dumps, gloom, gloominess, glumness, melancholy, miseries, moodiness.
antonym euphoria.

bluff[1] *n.* bank, brow, cliff, crag, escarp, escarpment, foreland, headland, height, knoll, peak, precipice, promontory, ridge, scarp, slope.
adj. affable, blunt, candid, direct, downright, frank, genial, good-natured, hearty, open, outspoken, plainspoken, straightforward.
antonyms diplomatic, refined.

bluff[2] *v.* bamboozle, blind, deceive, defraud, delude, fake, feign, grift, hoodwink, humbug, lie, mislead, pretend, sham.
n. bluster, boast, braggadocio, bravado, deceit, deception, fake, fanfaronade, feint, fraud, grift, humbug, idle boast, lie, pretence, sham, show, subterfuge, trick.

blunder *n.* bêtise, bevue, bloomer, boner, boob, booboo, bungle, clanger, clinker, error, fault, faux pas, floater, fluff, gaffe, gaucherie, goof, howler, impropriety, inaccuracy, indiscretion, mistake, oversight, pratfall, slip, slip-up, solecism.
v. blow it, botch, bumble, bungle, err, flounder, flub, fluff, fumble, goof, miscalculate, misjudge, mismanage, muff it, slip up, stumble.

blunt *adj.* abrupt, bluff, brusque, candid, curt, direct, discourteous, downright, dull, dulled, edgeless, explicit, forthright, frank, honest, impolite, insensitive, obtuse, outspoken, plain-spoken, pointless, retuse, rounded, rude, straightforward, stubbed, stumpy, tactless, thick, trenchant, unceremonious, uncivil, unpolished, unsharpened.
antonyms sharp, tactful.
v. abate, allay, alleviate, anesthetize, bate, dampen, deaden, disedge, dull, hebetate, numb, obtund, palliate, rebate, retund, soften, stupefy, unedge, weaken.
antonyms intensify, sharpen.

blur *v.* becloud, befog, blear, blemish, blot, blotch, cloud, darken, dim, fog, mask, obfuscate, obscure, scumble, smear, smutch, soften, spot, stain.
n. blear, blot, blotch, cloudiness, confusion, dimness, fog, fuzziness, haze, indistinctness, muddle, obscurity, smear, smudge, spot, stain.

blush *v.* color, crimson, flush, glow, mantle, redden.
antonym blanch.
n. color, erubescence, flush, glow, reddening, rosiness, ruddiness, suffusion.

board[1] *n.* beam, clapboard, deal, lath, panel, plank, sheet, slab, slat, timber, two-by-four.

board[2] commons, food, grub, meals, provisions, rations, repasts, table, victuals.
v. accommodate, bed, billet, feed, house, lodge, put up, quarter, room, table.

board[3] *n.* advisers, chamber, commission, committee, conclave, council, directorate, directors, jury, panel, trustees.

board[4] *v.* catch, embark, embus, emplane, enter, entrain, mount.

boast *v.* be all mouth, blazon, blow, bluster, bounce, brag, claim, crow, exaggerate, exhibit, gasconade, possess, puff, rodomontade, show off, strut, swagger, talk big, trumpet, vaunt.
antonym deprecate.

n. avowal, brag, claim, fanfaronade, gasconade, gem, joy, pride, rodomontade, swank, treasure, vaunt.

body[1] *n.* being, bod, build, bulk, cadaver, carcass, consistency, corpse, corpus, creature, density, essence, figure, firmness, form, frame, human, individual, mass, material, matter, mortal, opacity, person, physique, relics, remains, richness, shape, solidity, stiff, substance, substantiality, tabernacle, torso, trunk.

body[2] *n.* association, band, bevy, bloc, cartel, collection, company, confederation, congress, corporation, crowd, group, horde, majority, mass, mob, multitude, society, syndicate, throng.

bogus *adj.* artificial, counterfeit, dummy, ersatz, fake, false, forged, fraudulent, imitation, phony, pinchbeck, pseudo, sham, spoof, spurious, unauthentic.
antonym genuine.

boil[1] *v.* agitate, brew, bubble, churn, decoct, effervesce, erupt, explode, fizz, foam, froth, fulminate, fume, gurgle, mantle, parboil, rage, rave, seethe, simmer, sizzle, spume, steam, stew, storm, wallop.

boil down abridge, abstract, concentrate, condense, decrease, digest, distil, epitomize, reduce, summarize, synopsize.

boil[2] *n.* abscess, anthrax, bleb, blister, carbuncle, furuncle, gathering, gumboil, inflammation, papule, parulis, pimple, pock, pustule, tumor, ulcer, whelk.

boisterous *adj.* blusterous, blustery, bouncy, clamorous, disorderly, exuberant, gusty, impetuous, loud, noisy, obstreperous, rackety, raging, rambunctious, riotous, roisting, rollicking, rough, rowdy, rumbustious, squally, tempestuous, termagant, tumultous, turbulent, unrestrained, unruly, uproarious, vociferous, wild.
antonyms calm, quiet, restrained.

bold *adj.* adventurous, audacious, brash, brave, brazen, bright, cheeky, colorful, confident, conspicuous, courageous, daring, dauntless, enterprising, extrovert, eye-catching, fearless, flamboyant, flashy, forceful, forward, fresh, gallant, heroic, impudent, insolent, intrepid, jazzy, lively, loud, malapert, outgoing, pert, plucky, prominent, pronounced, saucy, shameless, showy, spirited, striking, strong, unabashed, unashamed, unbashful, valiant, valorous, venturesome, vivid.
antonyms diffident, restrained.

bolt *n.* arrow, bar, bound, catch, dart, dash, elopement, escape, fastener, flight, flit, latch, lock, missile, peg, pin, projectile, rivet, rod, rush, shaft, sneck, sprint, thunderbolt.
v. abscond, bar, bound, cram, dart, dash, devour, discharge, elope, escape, expel, fasten, fetter, flee, fly, gobble, gorge, gulp, guzzle, hurtle, jump, latch, leap, lock, run, rush, secure, spring, sprint, stuff, wolf.

bomb *n.* A-bomb, bombshell, charge, egg, explosive, grenade, mine, missile, mortar-bomb, petrol bomb, projectile, rocket, shell, torpedo.
v. attack, blow up, bombard, collapse, come a cropper, come to grief, destroy, fail, flop, misfire, shell, strafe, torpedo.

bond *n.* affiliation, affinity, agreement, attachment, band, binding, chain, compact, connection, contract, copula, cord, covenant, fastening, fetter, ligament, ligature, link, manacle, obligation, pledge, promise, relation, shackle, tie, union, vinculum, word.
v. bind, connect, fasten, fuse, glue, gum, paste, seal, unite.

bondage *n.* captivity, confinement, durance, duress, enslavement, enthralment, imprisonment, incarceration, restraint, serfdom, servitude, slavery, subjection, subjugation, subservience, thraldom, vassalage, yoke.
antonyms freedom, independence.

book *n.* album booklet, codex, companion, diary, hornbook, incunable, incunabulum, jotter, lectionary, manual, manuscript, notebook, pad, paperback, publication, roll, scroll, textbook, tome, tract, volume, work.
v. arrange, arrest, bag, charter, engage, enter, insert, list, log, note, organize, post, procure, program, record, register, reserve, schedule.
antonym cancel.

boom[1] *v.* bang, blare, blast, crash, explode, resound, reverberate, roar, roll, rumble, sound, thunder.
n. bang, blast, burst, clang, clap, crash, explosion, reverberation, roar, rumble, thunder.

boom[2] *v.* develop, escalate, expand, explode, flourish, gain, go from strength to strength, grow, increase, intensify, prosper, spurt, strengthen, succeed, swell, thrive.
antonyms collapse, fail.
n. advance, boost, development, escalation, expansion, explosion, gain, growth, improvement, increase, jump, spurt, upsurge, upturn.
antonyms collapse, failure.

boon *n.* advantage, benefaction, benefit, blessing, donation, favor, gift, godsend, grant, gratification, gratuity, kindness, petition, present, windfall.
antonyms blight, disadvantage.

boor *n.* barbarian, brute, bumpkin, churl, clodhopper, goop, Goth, hayseed, hedgehog, hick, hog, lout, oaf, peasant, philistine, rube, rustic, vulgarian, yokel.
antonyms aesthete, charmer.

boorish *adj.* awkward, barbaric, bearish, churlish, clodhopping, clownish, coarse, crude, gross, gruff, ill-bred, inconsiderate, loutish, lubberly, lumpen, oafish, rude, ruffianly, rustic, slobbish, uncivilized, uncouth, uneducated, unrefined, vulgar.
antonyms cultured, polite, refined.

boost *n.* addition, advancement, ego-trip, encouragement, enhancement, expansion, fillip, heave, help, hoist, hype, improvement, increase, increment, jump, lift, praise, promotion, push, rise, supplement, thrust.
antonyms blow, setback.

v. advance, advertise, aid, amplify, assist, augment, bolster, develop, elevate, encourage, enhance, enlarge, expand, foster, further, heave, heighten, hoist, improve, increase, inspire, jack up, lift, plug, praise, promote, push, raise, supplement, support, sustain, thrust.
antonyms hinder, undermine.

boot[1] *n.* bootee, galosh, gumshoe, jackboot, loafer, moccasin, mule, overshoe, platform, pump, riding-boot, rubber, sneaker, top-boot, wader, wellington.
v. bounce, dismiss, eject, expel, fire, give the bum's rush, give the heave, kick, kick out, knock, oust, punt, sack, shove.

boot[2] *v.* advantage, aid, avail, benefit, help, profit, serve.

bootless *adj.* barren, fruitless, futile, ineffective, on a hiding to nothing, pointless, profitless, sterile, unavailing, unproductive, unsuccessful, useless, vain, worthless.
antonyms profitable, useful.

bootlicking *n.* ass-licking, back-scratching, crawling, cringing, deference, faggery, fagging, fawning, flattery, groveling, heepishness, ingratiation, lackeying, obsequiousness, servility, sycophancy, toadying.

booty *n.* boodle, bunce, gains, haul, loot, pickings, pillage, plunder, spoil, spoils, swag, takings, winnings.

border *n.* borderline, bound, boundary, bounds, brim, brink, circumference, confine, confines, demarcation, edge, fringe, frontier, hem, limit, limits, lip, list, march, margin, perimeter, periphery, rand, rim, screed, selvage, skirt, surround, trimming, valance, verge.
adj. boundary, circumscriptive, dividing, frontier, limitary, limitrophe, marginal, perimeter, separating, side.

borderline *adj.* ambivalent, doubtful, iffy, indecisive, indefinite, indeterminate, marginal, problematic, uncertain.
antonyms certain, definite.

bore[1] *v.* burrow, countermine, drill, gouge, mine, penetrate, perforate, pierce, sap, sink, thrill, tunnel, undermine.

bore[2] *v.* annoy, bother, bug, fatigue, irk, irritate, jade, pester, tire, trouble, vex, weary, worry.
antonyms charm, interest.
n. annoyance, bind, bother, drag, dullard, headache, nuisance, pain, pain in the neck, pest, schmo, terebrant, trial, vexation, vieux jeu, yawn.
antonym pleasure.

boredom *n.* acedia, apathy, doldrums, dullness, ennui, flatness, irksomeness, listlessness, monotony, sameness, tediousness, tedium, vapors, weariness, wearisomeness, world-weariness.
antonym interest.

boring *adj.* commonplace, dead, dreary, dry, dull, ennuying, flat, ho-hum, humdrum, insipid, irksome, monotonous, repetitious, routine, stale, stupid, tedious, tiresome, tiring, trite, unamusing, undiverting, unedifying, uneventful, unexciting, unfunny, unimaginative, uninspired, uninteresting, unvaried, unwitty, vapid, wearisome.
antonyms interesting, original.

borrow *v.* adopt, ape, appropriate, cadge, copy, crib, derive, draw, echo, filch, imitate, list, mimic, obtain, pilfer, pirate, plagiarize, scrounge, sponge, steal, take, use, usurp.

bosom *n.* breast, bust, center, chest, circle, core, heart, midst, protection, sanctuary, shelter.
adj. boon, cherished, close, confidential, dear, favorite, inseparable, intimate.

boss[1] *n.* administrator, baron, captain, chief, director, employer, executive, foreman, gaffer, governor, head, leader, manager, master, overseer, owner, superintendent, supervisor, supremo.
v. administrate, command, control, direct, employ, manage, oversee, run, superintend, supervise.

boss[2] *n.* knob, knub, knubble, nub, nubble, omphalos, point, protuberance, stud, tip, umbo.

bossy *adj.* arrogant, authoritarian, autocratic, demanding, despotic, dictatorial, domineering, exacting, hectoring, high-handed, imperious, insistent, lordly, oppressive, overbearing, tyrannical.
antonyms unassertive.

botch *v.* blunder, bungle, butcher, cobble, corpse, do carelessly, flub, fudge, fumble, goof, louse up, mar, mend, mess, mismanage, muff, patch, ruin, screw up, spoil.
antonyms accomplish, succeed. *n.* balls-up, blunder, bungle, cock-up, failure, farce, hash, mess, miscarriage, muddle, shambles.
antonyms success.

bother *v.* alarm, annoy, bore, chivvy, concern, dismay, distress, disturb, dog, harass, harry, hassle, inconvenience, irk, irritate, molest, nag, pester, plague, pother, pudder, trouble, upset, vex, worry.
n. aggravation, annoyance, bustle, consternation, difficulty, flurry, fuss, hassle, inconvenience, irritation, kerfuffle, molestation, nuisance, palaver, perplexity, pest, pother, problem, pudder, strain, trouble, vexation, worry.

bothersome *adj.* aggravating, annoying, boring, distressing, exasperating, inconvenient, infuriating, irksome, irritating, laborious, tedious, tiresome, troublesome, vexatious, vexing, wearisome.

bottom *n.* ass, backside, base, basis, behind, bum, butt, buttocks, core, depths, derrière, essence, floor, foot, foundation, fundament, fundus, ground, groundwork, heart, nadir, origin, pedestal, plinth, posterior, principle, rear, rear end, root, rump, seat, sit-upon, socle, sole, source, substance, substratum, substructure, support, tail, underneath, underside, understratum.

bounce *v.* bob, bound, bump, dap, dismiss, eject, expel, jounce, jump, kick out, leap, oust, rebound, recoil, resile, ricochet, spring, throw out.
n. animation, bound, dap, dynamism, ebullience, elasticity, energy, exuberance, give, go, life, liveliness, pep,

rebound, recoil, resilience, spring, springiness, vigor, vitality, vivacity, zip.

bound[1] *adj.* bandaged, beholden, cased, certain, chained, committed, compelled, constrained, destined, doomed, duty-bound, fastened, fated, fixed, forced, held, liable, manacled, obligated, obliged, pinioned, pledged, required, restricted, secured, sure, tied, tied up.

bound[2] *v.* bob, bounce, caper, frisk, gallumph, gambol, hurdle, jump, leap, lope, loup, lunge, pounce, prance, skip, spring, vault.
n. bob, bounce, caper, dance, frisk, gambado, gambol, jump, leap, lope, loup, lunge, pounce, prance, scamper, skip, spring, vault.

boundary *n.* abuttal, barrier, border, borderline, bounds, bourne, brink, confines, demarcation, edge, extremity, fringe, frontier, junction, limes, limits, line, march, margin, mete, perimeter, termination, verge.
adj. border, demarcation, frontier, limitary, limitrophe, perimeter.

boundless *adj.* countless, endless, illimitable, immeasurable, immense, incalculable, indefatigable, inexhaustible, infinite, interminable, interminate, limitless, measureless, prodigious, unbounded, unconfined, unending, unflagging, unlimited, untold, vast.
antonym limited.

bounty *n.* allowance, almsgiving, annuity, assistance, beneficence, benevolence, bonus, charity, donation, generosity, gift, grace, grant, gratuity, kindness, largesse, liberality, philanthropy, premium, present, recompense, reward.

bourgeois *adj.* Biedermeier, circumscribed, commonplace, conformist, conservative, conventional, dull, hide-bound, humdrum, kitsch, materialistic, middle-class, pedestrian, tawdry, traditional, trite, trivial, unadventurous, unimaginative, uninspired, unoriginal, vulgar.
antonyms bohemian, original, unconventional.
n. conformist, petit bourgeois, philistine, plebeian, stick-in-the-mud.
antonyms bohemian, nonconformist.

bout *n.* battle, competition, contest, course, encounter, engagement, fight, fit, go, heat, match, period, round, run, session, set-to, spell, spree, stint, stretch, struggle, term, time, turn, venue.

bow[1] *v.* accept, acquiesce, bend, bob, capitulate, comply, concede, conquer, consent, crush, curtsey, defer, depress, droop, genuflect, give in, incline, kowtow, nod, overpower, stoop, subdue, subjugate, submit, surrender, vanquish, yield.
n. acknowledgment, bending, bob, curtsey, genuflexion, inclination, kowtow, nod, obeisance, salaam, salutation.

bow out abandon, back out, bunk off, chicken out, defect, desert, give up, opt out, pull out, quit, resign, retire, stand down, step down, withdraw.

bow[2] *n.* beak, head, prow, rostrum, stem.

bowels *n.* belly, center, core, depths, entrails, guts, heart, hold, innards, inside, insides, interior, intestines, middle, viscera, vitals.

bowl[1] *n.* basin, container, cruse, dish, pan, porringer, receptacle, sink, tureen, vessel.

bowl[2] *n.* jack, wood.
v. fling, hurl, pitch, revolve, roll, rotate, spin, throw, trundle, whirl.

bowl over amaze, astonish, astound, dumbfound, fell, flabbergast, floor, stagger, startle, stun, surprise, topple, unbalance.

bowl[3] *n.* amphitheater, arena, auditorium, coliseum, field, ground, hall, hippodrome, stadium.

box[1] *n.* bijou, carton, case, casket, chest, coffer, coffin, coffret, consignment, container, coop, fund, pack, package, portmanteau, present, pyx, pyxis, receptacle, trunk.
v. case, embox, encase, pack, package, wrap.

box[2] *v.* buffet, butt, clout, cuff, fight, hit, punch, slap, sock, spar, strike, thwack, wallop, whack, wham, whang.
n. blow, buffet, clout, cuff, punch, slap, stroke, thump, wallop, wham, whang.

boy *n.* callant, cub, dandiprat, fellow, gamin, gossoon, halfling, imp, junior, kid, lad, loon, loonie, man-child, nipper, puppy, schoolboy, spalpeen, stripling, urchin, whippersnapper, youngster, youth.

boycott *v.* ban, bar, black, blackball, blacklist, cold-shoulder, disallow, embargo, exclude, ignore, ostracize, outlaw, prohibit, proscribe, refuse, reject, spurn.
antonyms encourage, support.

boyfriend *n.* admirer, beau, date, fancy man, fellow, inamorato, lover, man, steady, suitor, swain, sweetheart, young man.

brace[1] *n.* binder, bracer, bracket, buttress, cleat, corset, nogging, prop, reinforcement, shoring, stanchion, stay, strap, strut, support, truss. *v.* bandage, bind, bolster, buttress, fasten, fortify, prop, reinforce, shore (up), steady, strap, strengthen, support, tie, tighten.

brace[2] *n.* couple, doubleton, duo, pair, twosome.

bracing *adj.* brisk, crisp, energetic, energizing, enlivening, exhilarating, fortifying, fresh, invigorating, refreshing, restorative, reviving, rousing, stimulating, strengthening, tonic, vigorous.
antonym debilitating.

brag *v.* bluster, boast, crow, fanfaronade, rodomontade, swagger, talk big, trumpet, vapor, vaunt.
antonym deprecate.

braid *v.* entwine, interlace, intertwine, interweave, lace, plait, ravel, twine, twist, weave, wind.
antonyms undo, untwist.

brain[1] *n.* boffin, egghead, expert, genius, highbrow, intellect, intellectual, mastermind, prodigy, pundit, sage, savant, scholar, wizard.
antonym simpleton.

brain[2] *n.* cerebrum, gray matter, intellect, mind, sensorium, sensory.

brake *n.* check, constraint, control, curb, drag, rein, restraint, restriction, retardment.
v. check, decelerate, drag, halt, moderate, pull up, retard, slacken, slow, stop.
antonym accelerate.

branch *n.* arm, bough, chapter, department, division, grain, limb, lodge, office, offshoot, part, prong, ramification, ramus, section, shoot, sprig, subdivision, subsection, whip, wing, witty.

branch out bifurcate, broaden out, develop, divaricate, diversify, enlarge, expand, extend, increase, move on, multiply, proliferate, ramify, vary.

brand *n.* brand-name, class, emblem, grade, hallmark, kind, label, line, logo, make, mark, marker, marque, quality, sign, sort, species, stamp, symbol, trademark, type, variety.
v. burn, censure, denounce, discredit, disgrace, label, mark, scar, stain, stamp, stigmatize, taint, type.

brave *adj.* audacious, bold, courageous, daring, dauntless, doughty, fearless, fine, gallant, game, glorious, hardy, heroic, indomitable, intrepid, plucky, resolute, resplendent, splendid, stalwart, stoic, stoical, stout-hearted, unafraid, undaunted, unflinching, valiant, valorous.
antonyms cowardly, timid.
v. accost, bear, beard, challenge, confront, dare, defy, encounter, endure, face, face up to, stand up to, suffer, withstand.
antonyms capitulate, crumple.

brawl *n.* affray, altercation, argument, bagarre, battle, broil, bust-up, clash, disorder, dispute, dog-fight, Donnybrook, dust-up, fight, fracas, fray, free-for-all, mêlée, punch-up, quarrel, row, ruckus, rumpus, scrap, scuffle, squabble, tumult, uproar, wrangle.
v. altercate, argue, battle, come to blows, dispute, fight, flyte, quarrel, row, scrap, scuffle, squabble, tussle, wrangle, wrestle.

brawn *n.* beef, beefiness, brawniness, bulk, bulkiness, flesh, meat, might, muscle, muscles, muscularity, power, robustness, sinews, strength, thews.

brazen *adj.* assured, audacious, barefaced, blatant, bold, brash, brassy, defiant, flagrant, forward, immodest, impudent, insolent, malapert, pert, saucy, shameless, unabashed, unashamed.
antonym shamefaced.

breach *n.* alienation, aperture, break, break-up, chasm, cleft, contravention, crack, crevice, difference, disaffection, disagreement, discontinuity, disobedience, disruption, dissension, dissociation, division, estrangement, fissure, gap, hole, infraction, infringement, lapse, offence, opening, parting, quarrel, rent, rift, rupture, schism, scission, scissure, secession, separation, severance, split, transgression, trespass, variance, violation.

break *v.* abandon, absorb, announce, appear, bankrupt, batter, beat, better, breach, burst, bust, contravene, cow, crack, crash, cripple, cushion, cut, dash, defeat, degrade, demolish, demoralize, destroy, diminish, discharge, disclose, discontinue, disintegrate, disobey, dispirit, disregard, divide, divulge, emerge, enervate, enfeeble, erupt, escape, exceed, excel, explode, flee, flout, fly, fract, fracture, fragment, go phut, happen, humiliate, impair, impart, incapacitate, inform, infract, infringe, interrupt, jigger, knacker, knap, lessen, moderate, modify, occur, outdo, outstrip, part, pause, proclaim, reduce, rend, rest, retard, reveal, ruin, separate, sever, shatter, shiver, smash, snap, soften, splinter, split, stave, stop, subdue, surpass, suspend, tame, tear, tell, transgress, undermine, undo, violate, weaken, worst.
n. abruption, advantage, alienation, breach, breather, chance, cleft, crack, crevice, disaffection, discontinuity, dispute, disruption, divergence, division, estrangement, fissure, fortune, fracture, gap, gash, halt, hiatus, hole, interlude, intermission, interruption, interval, lapse, letup, lull, opening, opportunity, pause, quarrel, recess, rent, respite, rest, rift, rupture, schism, separation, split, suspension, tear, time-out.

breed *v.* arouse, bear, beget, bring forth, bring up, cause, create, cultivate, develop, discipline, educate, engender, foster, generate, hatch, induce, instruct, make, multiply, nourish, nurture, occasion, originate, procreate, produce, propagate, raise, rear, reproduce, train.
n. family, ilk, kind, line, lineage, pedigree, progeny, race, sort, species, stamp, stock, strain, type, variety.

breeze *n.* air, breath, cat's-paw, draft, flurry, gale, gust, waft, whiff, wind, zephyr.
v. flit, glide, hurry, sail, sally, sweep, trip, wander.

breezy *adj.* airy, animated, blithe, blowing, blowy, blustery, bright, buoyant, carefree, careless, casual, cheerful, debonair, easy-going, exhilarating, fresh, gusty, informal, insouciant, jaunty, light, light-hearted, lively, nonchalant, sprightly, squally, sunny, untroubled, vivacious, windy.
antonyms calm, staid.

brevity *n.* abruptness, briefness, brusqueness, conciseness, concision, crispness, curtness, economy, ephemerality, evanescence, fugacity, impermanence, incisiveness, laconicism, laconism, pithiness, shortness, succinctness, summariness, terseness, transience, transitoriness.
antonyms longevity, permanence, verbosity.

brew *v.* boil, build up, concoct, contrive, cook, decoct, develop, devise, excite, ferment, foment, gather, hatch, infuse, mix, plan, plot, prepare, project, scheme, seethe, soak, steep, stew.
n. beverage, blend, bouillon, brewage, broth, concoction, distillation, drink, fermentation, gruel, infusion, liquor, mixture, potion, preparation, stew.

bribe *n.* allurement, back-hander, baksheesh, boodle, dash, enticement, graft, grease, hush money, incentive,

inducement, kickback, pay-off, payola, protection money, refresher, slush fund, sweetener.
v. buy off, buy over, corrupt, reward, square, suborn.

bridle *v.* check, contain, control, curb, govern, master, moderate, rein in, repress, restrain, subdue.

brief *adj.* abrupt, aphoristic, blunt, brusque, capsular, compendious, compressed, concise, crisp, cursory, curt, ephemeral, fast, fleeting, fugacious, fugitive, hasty, laconic, limited, momentary, passing, pithy, quick, sharp, short, short-lived, succinct, surly, swift, temporary, terse, thumbnail, transient, transitory.
antonyms long, long-lived, verbose.
n. advice, argument, briefing, case, contention, data, defense, demonstration, directions, directive, dossier, instructions, mandate, orders, outline, précis, remit, summary.
v. advise, direct, explain, fill in, gen up, guide, inform, instruct, prepare, prime.

brigand *n.* bandit, cateran, dacoit, desperado, footpad, freebooter, gangster, haiduk, heister, highwayman, klepht, marauder, outlaw, plunderer, robber, ruffian.

bright *adj.* ablaze, acute, astute, auspicious, beaming, blazing, brainy, breezy, brilliant, burnished, cheerful, clear, clear-headed, clever, cloudless, dazzling, effulgent, encouraging, excellent, favorable, flashing, fulgent, gay, genial, glad, glaring, gleaming, glistening, glittering, glorious, glowing, golden, happy, hopeful, illuminated, illustrious, ingenious, intelligent, intense, inventive, jolly, joyful, joyous, keen, lambent, lamping, light-hearted, limpid, lively, lucent, lucid, luculent, luminous, lustrous, magnificent, merry, observant, optimistic, pellucid, perceptive, percipient, perspicacious, polished, prefulgent, promising, propitious, prosperous, quick, quick-witted, radiant, resplendent, rosy, scintillating, sharp, sheeny, shimmering, shining, smart, sparkling, splendid, sunny, translucent, transparent, twinkling, unclouded, undulled, untarnished, vivacious, vivid, wide-awake.
antonyms depressing, dull, stupid.

brilliant *adj.* ablaze, accomplished, adroit, animated, astute, blazing, brainy, bright, celebrated, clever, coruscating, dazzling, effulgent, eminent, exceptional, expert, famous, gemmy, gifted, glaring, glittering, glorious, glossy, illustrious, ingenious, intellectual, intelligent, intense, inventive, lambent, luminous, magnificent, masterly, outstanding, quick, refulgent, scintillating, shining, showy, skilful, sparkling, splendid, star, star-like, superb, talented, vivacious, vivid, witty.
antonyms dull, restrained, stupid, undistinguished.

brim *n.* border, brink, circumference, edge, lip, marge, margin, perimeter, periphery, rim, skirt, verge.

bring *v.* accompany, accustom, add, attract, bear, carry, cause, command, conduct, convey, convince, create, deliver, dispose, draw, earn, effect, engender, escort, fetch, force, gather, generate, get, gross, guide, induce, inflict, influence, introduce, lead, make, move, net, occasion, persuade, produce, prompt, return, sway, take, transfer, transport, usher, wreak, yield.

brink *n.* bank, border, boundary, brim, edge, extremity, fringe, limit, lip, marge, margin, point, rim, skirt, threshold, verge, waterside.

brisk *adj.* active, agile, alert, allegro, bracing, bright, brushy, bustling, busy, crank, crisp, effervescing, energetic, exhilarating, expeditious, fresh, galliard, invigorating, keen, lively, nimble, nippy, no-nonsense, prompt, quick, refreshing, sharp, snappy, speedy, spirited, sprightly, spry, stimulating, vigorous.
antonym sluggish.

briskly *adv.* abruptly, actively, allegro, brightly, decisively, efficiently, energetically, expeditiously, incisively, nimbly, promptly, quickly, rapidly, readily, smartly, vigorously.
antonym sluggishly.

bristle *n.* barb, hair, prickle, spine, stubble, thorn, vibrissa, whisker.
v. bridle, draw oneself up, horripilate, prickle, react, rise, seethe, spit.

brittle *adj.* anxious, breakable, crackly, crisp, crumbling, crumbly, curt, delicate, edgy, fragile, frail, frangible, friable, frush, irritable, nervous, nervy, shattery, shivery, short, tense.
antonyms durable, resilient, sturdy.

broach *v.* crack open, introduce, launch into, mention, pierce, propose, puncture, raise, start, suggest, tap, uncork, utter.

broad *adj.* all-embracing, ample, beamy, blue, capacious, catholic, coarse, comprehensive, eclectic, encyclopedic, enlightened, expansive, extensive, far-reaching, general, generous, gross, improper, inclusive, indecent, indelicate, large, latitudinous, roomy, spacious, square, sweeping, tolerant, universal, unlimited, unrefined, vast, voluminous, vulgar, wide, wide-ranging, widespread.
antonym narrow.

broadcast *v.* advertise, air, announce, beam, cable, circulate, disseminate, proclaim, promulgate, publicize, publish, radio, relay, report, show, spread, televise, transmit.
n. program, relay, show, telecast, transmission.

broaden *v.* augment, branch out, develop, diversify, enlarge, enlighten, expand, extend, increase, open up, spread, stretch, supplement, swell, thicken, widen.

broad-minded *adj.* catholic, cosmopolitan, dispassionate, enlightened, flexible, free-thinking, indulgent, liberal, open-minded, permissive, receptive, tolerant, unbiased, unprejudiced, verligte.

brochure *n.* advertisement, booklet, broadsheet, broadside, circular, folder, handbill, hand-out, leaflet, pamphlet.

broil *n.* affray, altercation, argument, brawl, brouhaha, dispute, disturbance, fracas, fray, imbroglio, quarrel, scrimmage, scrum, stramash, strife, tumult, wrangle.

broken *adj.* bankrupt, beaten, betrayed, browbeaten, burst, crippled, crushed, defeated, defective, demolished, demoralized, destroyed, disconnected, discontinuous, dishonored, disjointed, dismantled, dispersed, disregarded, disturbed, down, dud, duff, erratic, exhausted, faulty, feeble, forgotten, fracted, fractured, fragmentary, fragmented, halting, hesitating, humbled, ignored, imperfect, incoherent, incomplete, infirm, infringed, intermittent, interrupted, isolated, jiggered, kaput, knackered, oppressed, out of order, overpowered, prerupt, rent, retracted, routed, ruined, run-down, ruptured, separated, severed, shattered, shivered, spasmodic, spent, stammering, subdued, tamed, traduced, transgressed, uncertain, vanquished, variegated, weak.

broken-hearted *adj.* crestfallen, dejected, desolate, despairing, despondent, devastated, disappointed, disconsolate, grief-stricken, hard-hit, heartbroken, heartsick, heartsore, inconsolable, miserable, mournful, prostrated, sorrowful, unhappy, wretched.

bromide *n.* anodyne, banality, cliché, commonplace, platitude, stereotype, truism.

brooch *n.* badge, breastpin, clasp, clip, pin, prop.

brood *v.* agonize, cover, dwell on, fret, go over, hatch, incubate, meditate, mope, mull over, muse, ponder, rehearse, repine, ruminate.
n. birth, chicks, children, clutch, family, hatch, issue, litter, nide, offspring, progeny, spawn, young.

brook[1] *n.* beck, burn, channel, freshet, gill, inlet, mill, rill, rivulet, runnel, stream, streamlet, watercourse.

brook[2] *v.* abide, accept, allow, bear, countenance, endure, permit, stand, stomach, submit to, suffer, support, swallow, thole, tolerate, withstand.

brother *n.* associate, blood-brother, brer, chum, colleague, companion, compeer, comrade, confrère, cousin, fellow, fellow-creature, friar, friend, kin, kinsman, mate, monk, pal, partner, relation, relative, religieux, religious, sibling.

brotherhood *n.* affiliation, alliance, association, clan, clique, community, confederacy, confederation, confraternity, confrèrie, coterie, fraternity, guild, league, society, union.

brotherly *adj.* affectionate, amicable, benevolent, caring, concerned, cordial, fraternal, friendly, kind, loving, neighborly, philanthropic, supervisory, sympathetic.
antonyms callous, unbrotherly.

brow *n.* appearance, aspect, bearing, brink, cliff, countenance, crown, edge, eyebrow, face, forehead, front, mien, peak, ridge, rim, summit, temples, tip, top, verge, visage.

browbeat *v.* awe, batter, bludgeon, bulldoze, bully, coerce, cow, domineer, dragoon, hector, hound, intimidate, oppress, overbear, threaten, tyrannize.
antonym coax.

brown *adj.* auburn, bay, brick, bronze, bronzed, browned, brunette, chestnut, chocolate, coffee, dark, donkey, dun, dusky, fuscous, ginger, hazel, mahogany, russet, rust, rusty, sunburnt, tan, tanned, tawny, titian, toasted, umber, vandyke brown.

brown study absence, absent-mindedness, absorption, abstraction, contemplation, meditation, musing, pensiveness, preoccupation, reflection, reverie, rumination.

browse *v.* crop, dip into, eat, feed, flick through, graze, leaf through, nibble, pasture, peruse, scan, skim, survey.

bruise *v.* blacken, blemish, contund, contuse, crush, discolor, grieve, hurt, injure, insult, mar, mark, offend, pound, pulverize, stain, wound.
n. blemish, contusion, discoloration, injury, mark, rainbow, shiner, swelling.

brunt *n.* burden, force, impact, impetus, pressure, shock, strain, stress, thrust, violence, weight.

brush[1] *n.* besom, broom, sweeper.
v. buff, burnish, caress, clean, contact, flick, glance, graze, kiss, paint, polish, rub, scrape, shine, stroke, sweep, touch, wash.

brush[2] *n.* brushwood, bushes, frith, ground cover, scrub, shrubs, thicket, undergrowth, underwood.

brush[3] *n.* clash, conflict, confrontation, dust-up, encounter, fight, fracas, incident, run-in, scrap, set-to, skirmish, tussle.

brush-off *n.* cold shoulder, discouragement, dismissal, go-by, rebuff, refusal, rejection, repudiation, repulse, slight, snub.
antonym encouragement.

brusque *adj.* abrupt, blunt, curt, discourteous, gruff, hasty, impolite, sharp, short, surly, tactless, tart, terse, uncivil, undiplomatic.
antonyms courteous, tactful.

brutal *adj.* animal, barbarous, bearish, beastly, bestial, bloodthirsty, boarish, brute, brutish, callous, carnal, coarse, crude, cruel, doggish, ferocious, gruff, harsh, heartless, impolite, inhuman, inhumane, insensitive, merciless, pitiless, remorseless, rough, rude, ruthless, savage, sensual, severe, uncivil, uncivilized, unfeeling, unmannerly, unsympathetic, vicious.
antonyms humane, kindly.

brute *n.* animal, barbarian, beast, bête, boor, creature, devil, fiend, lout, monster, ogre, sadist, savage, swine.
antonym gentleman.
adj. bestial, bodily, carnal, coarse, depraved, fleshly, gross, instinctive, mindless, physical, senseless, sensual, unthinking.
antonym refined.

bubble[1] *n.* ball, bead, bladder, blister, blob, drop, droplet, globule, vesicle.
v. babble, boil, burble, effervesce, fizz, foam, froth, gurgle, murmur, percolate, purl, ripple, seethe, sparkle, trickle, trill, wallop.

bubble[2] *n.* bagatelle, delusion, fantasy, fraud, illusion, sting, toy, trifle, vanity.

buccaneer *n.* corsair, filibuster, freebooter, pirate, privateer, sea-robber, sea-rover, sea-wolf.

buck[1] *n.* beau, blade, blood, coxcomb, dandy, fop, gallant, playboy, popinjay, spark, swell.

buck[2] *v.* bound, cheer, dislodge, encourage, gladden, gratify, hearten, inspirit, jerk, jump, leap, please, prance, spring, start, throw, unseat, vault.

bucket *n.* bail, barrel, basin, can, cask, kibble, pail, pan, pitcher, vessel.

buckle *n.* bend, bulge, catch, clasp, clip, contortion, distortion, fastener, hasp, kink, twist, warp.
v. bend, bulge, catch, cave in, clasp, close, collapse, connect, contort, crumple, distort, fasten, fold, hitch, hook, secure, twist, warp, wrinkle.

bud *n.* embryo, germ, knosp, shoot, sprig, sprout.
v. burgeon, develop, grow, pullulate, shoot, sprout.
antonyms waste away, wither.

budge *v.* bend, change, convince, dislodge, give (way), inch, influence, move, persuade, propel, push, remove, roll, shift, slide, stir, sway, yield.

budget *n.* allocation, allotment, allowance, cost, estimate, finances, fonds, funds, means, resources.
v. allocate, apportion, cost, estimate, plan, ration.

buff[1] *adj.* fawn, fulvid, fulvous, khaki, sandy, straw, tan, yellowish, yellowish-brown.
v. brush, burnish, polish, polish up, rub, shine, smooth.

buff[2] *n.* addict, admirer, aficionado, bug, cognoscente, connoisseur, devotee, enthusiast, expert, fan, fiend, freak.

buffet[1] *n.* café, cafeteria, counter, snack-bar, snack-counter.

buffet[2] *v.* bang, batter, beat, box, bump, clobber, clout, cuff, flail, hit, jar, knock, pound, pummel, push, rap, shove, slap, strike, thump, wallop.
n. bang, blow, box, bump, clout, cuff, jar, jolt, knock, push, rap, shove, slap, smack, thump, wallop.

buffoon *n.* clown, comedian, comic, droll, fool, goliard, harlequin, jester, joker, merry-andrew, mountebank, scaramouch, schmuck, tomfool, vice, wag, zany.

bug *n.* addict, admirer, bacterium, blemish, buff, catch, craze, defect, disease, enthusiast, error, fad, failing, fan, fault, fiend, flaw, freak, germ, gremlin, imperfection, infection, mania, micro-organism, obsession, rage, snarl-up, virus.
v. annoy, badger, bother, disturb, get, harass, irk, irritate, needle, nettle, pester, plague, vex.

bugbear *n.* anathema, bane, b&eced;te noire, bloody-bones, bogey, bugaboo, devil, dread, fiend, horror, Mumbo-jumbo, nightmare, pet hate, poker, rawhead.

build *v.* assemble, augment, base, begin, big, constitute, construct, develop, edify, enlarge, erect, escalate, establish, extend, fabricate, form, formulate, found, improve, inaugurate, increase, initiate, institute, intensify, knock together, make, originate, raise, strengthen.
antonyms destroy, knock down, lessen, weaken.
n. body, figure, form, frame, physique, shape, size, structure.

building *n.* architecture, construction, domicile, dwelling, edifice, erection, fabric, fabrication, house, pile, structure.
antonym destruction.

build-up *n.* accretion, accumulation, ballyhoo, development, enlargement, escalation, expansion, gain, growth, heap, hype, increase, load, mass, plug, promotion, publicity, puff, stack, stockpile, store.
antonyms decrease, reduction.

bulge *n.* belly, boost, bump, distension, hump, increase, intensification, lump, projection, protrusion, protuberance, rise, surge, swelling, upsurge.
v. bag, belly, bulb, dilate, distend, enlarge, expand, hump, project, protrude, sag, strout, swell.

bulk *n.* amplitude, bigness, body, dimensions, extensity, extent, generality, immensity, largeness, magnitude, majority, mass, most, plurality, preponderance, size, substance, volume, weight.

bulky *adj.* big, colossal, cumbersome, enormous, heavy, hefty, huge, hulking, immense, large, lumping, mammoth, massive, massy, ponderous, substantial, unmanageable, unwieldy, volumed, voluminous, weighty.
antonyms handy, insubstantial, small.

bulldoze *v.* browbeat, buffalo, bully, clear, coerce, cow, demolish, drive, flatten, force, hector, intimidate, knock down, level, propel, push, push through, raze, shove, thrust.

bulletin *n.* announcement, communication, communiqué, dispatch, dope, message, newsflash, notification, report, sitrep, statement.

bully *n.* bouncer, browbeater, bucko, bully-boy, bully-rook, coercionist, harasser, intimidator, killcrow, oppressor, persecutor, rowdy, ruffian, termagant, tormentor, tough, tyrant.
v. bluster, browbeat, bulldoze, bullyrag, coerce, cow, domineer, haze, hector, intimidate, oppress, overbear, persecute, push around, swagger, terrorize, tyrannize.
antonyms coax, persuade.

bulwark *n.* bastion, buffer, buttress, defense, embankment, fortification, guard, mainstay, outwork, partition, rampart, redoubt, safeguard, security, support.

bumbling *adj.* awkward, blundering, botching, bungling, clumsy, footling, foozling, incompetent, inefficient, inept, lumbering, maladroit, muddled, stumbling.
antonyms competent, efficient.

bump *v.* bang, bounce, budge, collide (with), crash, dislodge, displace, hit, jar, jerk, jolt, jostle, jounce, knock, move, rattle, remove, shake, shift, slam, strike.
n. bang, blow, bulge, collision, contusion, crash, hit, hump, impact, jar, jolt, knob, knock, knot, lump, node, nodule, protuberance, rap, shock, smash, swelling, thud, thump.

bumptious *adj.* arrogant, boastful, brash, cocky, conceited, egotistic, forward, full of oneself, impudent,

overbearing, over-confident, pompous, presumptuous, pushy, self-assertive, self-important, showy, swaggering, vainglorious, vaunting.
antonyms humble, modest.

bumpy *adj.* bouncy, choppy, irregular, jarring, jerky, jolting, jolty, knobbly, knobby, lumpy, rough, rutted, uneven.
antonym smooth.

bunch *n.* assortment, band, batch, bouquet, bundle, clump, cluster, collection, crew, crowd, fascicle, fascicule, flock, gang, gathering, group-knot, heap, lot, mass, mob, multitude, number, parcel, party, pile, quantity, sheaf, spray, stack, swarm, team, troop, tuft.
v. assemble, bundle, cluster, collect, congregate, crowd, flock, group, herd, huddle, mass, pack.
antonyms scatter, spread out.

bundle *n.* accumulation, assortment, bag, bale, batch, box, bunch, carton, collection, consignment, crate, drum, fascicle, fascicule, group, heap, mass, Matilda, pack, package, packet, pallet, parcel, pile, quantity, roll, shock, shook, stack, stook, swag, truss.
v. bale, bind, fasten, pack, palletize, tie, truss, wrap.

bungle *v.* blunder, bodge, boob, botch, bumble, cock up, duff, flub, footle, foozle, foul up, fudge, goof, louse up, mar, mess up, miscalculate, mismanage, muff, mull, ruin, screw up, spoil.
n. blunder, boob, boo-boo, botch-up, cock-up, foul-up, mull.

buoyant *adj.* afloat, animated, blithe, bouncy, breezy, bright, bullish, carefree, cheerful, debonair, floatable, floating, happy, jaunty, joyful, light, light-hearted, lively, peppy, rising, sprightly, sunny, weightless.
antonym depressed.

burden *n.* affliction, anxiety, bear, care, cargo, clog, dead weight, encumbrance, grievance, load, millstone, obligation, obstruction, onus, responsibility, sorrow, strain, stress, trial, trouble, weight, worry.
v. bother, encumber, handicap, lade, lie hard on, lie heavy on, load, oppress, overload, overwhelm, strain, tax, worry.
antonyms disburden, lighten, relieve.

burdensome *adj.* crushing, difficult, distressing, exacting, heavy, irksome, onerous, oppressive, taxing, troublesome, trying, wearisome, weighty.
antonyms easy, light.

bureau *n.* agency, branch, counter, department, desk, division, office, service.

bureaucrat *n.* administrator, apparatchik, bureaucratist, chinovnik, civil servant, functionary, mandarin, minister, office-holder, officer, official.

burglar *n.* cat-burglar, cracksman, house-breaker, picklock, pilferer, robber, thief, yegg.

burial *n.* burying, entombment, exequies, funeral, inhumation, interment, obsequies, sepulcher, sepulture.

burly *adj.* athletic, beefy, big, brawny, bulky, heavy, hefty, hulking, husky, muscular, powerful, stocky, stout, strapping, strong, sturdy, thickset, well-built.
antonyms puny, slim, small, thin.

burn *v.* bite, blaze, brand, calcine, cauterize, char, combust, conflagrate, consume, corrode, deflagrate, desire, expend, flame, flare, flash, flicker, fume, glow, hurt, ignite, incinerate, kindle, light, oxidize, pain, parch, scorch, seethe, shrivel, simmer, singe, smart, smoke, smolder, sting, tingle, toast, use, wither, yearn.

burnish *v.* brighten, buff, furbish, glaze, polish, polish up, rub, shine.
antonym tarnish.
n. gloss, luster, patina, polish, sheen, shine.

burrow *n.* den, earth, hole, lair, retreat, set(t), shelter, tunnel, warren.
v. delve, dig, earth, excavate, mine, tunnel, undermine.

burst *v.* barge, blow up, break, crack, dehisce, disintegrate, erupt, explode, fragment, gush, puncture, run, rupture, rush, shatter, shiver, split, spout, tear.
n. bang, blast, blasting, blow-out, blow-up, breach, break, crack, discharge, eruption, explosion, fit, gallop, gush, gust, outbreak, outburst, outpouring, rupture, rush, spate, split, spurt, surge, torrent.
adj. broken, flat, kaput, punctured, rent, ruptured, split, torn.

bury *v.* absorb, conceal, cover, embed, enclose, engage, engross, engulf, enshroud, entomb, hide, immerse, implant, inearth, inhume, inter, interest, lay to rest, occupy, secrete, sepulcher, shroud, sink, submerge.
antonyms disinter, uncover.

business *n.* affair, assignment, bargaining, calling, career, commerce, company, concern, corporation, craft, dealings, duty, employment, enterprise, establishment, firm, function, industry, issue, job, line, line of country, manufacturing, matter, merchandising, métier, occupation, organization, palaver, point, problem, profession, pursuit, question, responsibility, selling, subject, task, topic, trade, trading, transaction(s), venture, vocation, work.

bustle *v.* dash, flutter, fuss, hasten, hurry, rush, scamper, scramble, scurry, scuttle, stir, tear.
n. activity, ado, agitation, commotion, excitement, flurry, fuss, haste, hurly-burly, hurry, palaver, pother, stir, to-do, toing and froing, tumult.

bustling *adj.* active, astir, busy, buzzing, crowded, energetic, eventful, full, humming, lively, restless, rushing, stirring, swarming, teeming, thronged.
antonym quiet.

busy *adj.* active, assiduous, brisk, diligent, eident, employed, energetic, engaged, engrossed, exacting, full, fussy, hectic, industrious, inquisitive, interfering, lively, meddlesome, meddling, nosy, occupied, officious, persevering, prying, restless, slaving, stirabout, stirring, strenuous, tireless, tiring, troublesome, unleisured, versant, working.
antonyms idle, quiet.

v. absorb, bother, concern, employ, engage, engross, immerse, interest, occupy.

busybody *n.* eavesdropper, gossip, intriguer, intruder, meddler, nosey parker, pantopragmatic, pry, scandal-monger, snoop, snooper, troublemaker.

butcher *n.* destroyer, killcow, killer, murderer, slaughterer, slayer.
v. assassinate, botch, carve, clean, cut, destroy, dress, exterminate, joint, kill, liquidate, massacre, mutilate, prepare, ruin, slaughter, slay, spoil, wreck.

butt[1] *n.* base, end, foot, haft, handle, hilt, shaft, shank, stock, stub, tail, tip.

butt[2] *n.* dupe, laughing-stock, mark, object, point, subject, target, victim.

butt[3] *v., n.* buck, buffet, bump, bunt, hit, jab, knock, poke, prod, punch, push, ram, shove, thrust.

buttocks *n.* ass, backside, beam end, behind, bottom, breach, bum, cheeks, derrière, fanny, haunches, hinderend, hinderlin(g)s, hindquarters, natch, nates, posterior, prat, rear, rump, seat, tush.

buttress *n.* abutment, brace, mainstay, pier, prop, reinforcement, shore, stanchion, stay, strut, support.
v. bolster up, brace, hold up, prop up, reinforce, shore up, strengthen, support, sustain, uphold.
antonyms weaken.

buxom *adj.* ample, bosomy, busty, chesty, comely, debonair, hearty, jocund, jolly, lively, lusty, merry, plump, robust, voluptuous, well-rounded, winsome.
antonyms petite, slim, small.

buy *v.* acquire, bribe, corrupt, fix, get, obtain, procure, purchase, square, suborn.
antonym sell.
n. acquisition, bargain, deal, purchase.

buzz *n.* bombilation, bombination, buzzing, drone, gossip, hearsay, hiss, hum, murmur, news, purr, report, ring, ringing, rumor, scandal, susurration, susurrus, whir(r), whisper, whizz.
v. bombilate, bombinate, drone, hum, murmur, reverberate, ring, susurrate, whir(r), whisper, whizz.

by *prep.* along, beside, near, next to, over, past, through, via.
adv. aside, at hand, away, beyond, close, handy, near, past.

bygone *adj.* ancient, antiquated, departed, erstwhile, forepast, forgotten, former, lost, olden, past, previous.
antonyms modern, recent.
n. antique, grievance, oldie.

bypass *v.* avoid, circumvent, ignore, neglect, outflank.
n. detour, ring road.

by-product *n.* after-effect, consequence, epiphenomenon, fall-out, repercussion, result, side-effect.

bystander *n.* eye-witness, looker-on, observer, onlooker, passer-by, spectator, watcher, witness.

C

cab *n.* hack, minicab, taxi, taxicab, vettura.
cabin *n.* berth, bothy, chalet, compartment, cot, cot-house, cottage, crib, deck-house, hovel, hut, lodge, quarters, room, shack, shanty, shed.
cabinet *n.* almirah, case, chiffonier, closet, commode, cupboard, dresser, escritoire, locker.
cable *n.* chain, cord, hawser, line, mooring, rope.
cache *n.* accumulation, fund, garner, hoard, repository, reserve, stockpile, store, storehouse, supply, treasure-store.
v. bury, conceal, hide, secrete, stash, store, stow.
cad *n.* blackguard, bounder, caitiff, churl, cur, dastard, heel, knave, oik, poltroon, rat, rotter, skunk, swine, worm.
antonym gentleman.
café *n.* cafeteria, coffee bar, coffee shop, estaminet, greasy spoon, restaurant, snack bar, tea-room.
cag(e)y *adj.* careful, chary, circumspect, discreet, guarded, non-committal, secretive, shrewd, wary, wily.
antonyms frank, indiscreet, open.
calamity *n.* adversity, affliction, cataclysm, catastrophe, desolation, disaster, distress, downfall, misadventure, mischance, misfortune, mishap, reverse, ruin, scourge, tragedy, trial, tribulation, woe, wretchedness.
antonyms blessing, godsend.
calculate *v.* aim, cipher, compute, consider, count, determine, enumerate, estimate, figure, gauge, intend, judge, plan, rate, reckon, value, weigh, work out.
calculating *adj.* canny, cautious, contriving, crafty, cunning, designing, devious, Machiavellian, manipulative, politic, scheming, sharp, shrewd, sly.
antonyms artless, naïve, open.
calculation *n.* answer, caution, ciphering, circumspection, computation, deliberation, estimate, estimation, figuring, forecast, foresight, forethought, judgment, planning, precaution, reckoning, result.
call *v.* announce, appoint, arouse, assemble, awaken, bid, christen, collect, consider, contact, convene, convoke, cry, declare, decree, denominate, designate, dub, elect, entitle, estimate, gather, hail, halloo, invite, judge, label, muster, name, ordain, order, phone, proclaim, rally, regard, rouse, shout, style, summon, telephone, term, think, waken, yell. *n.* announcement, appeal, cause, claim, command, cry, demand, excuse, grounds, hail, invitation, justification, need, notice, occasion, order, plea, reason, request, right, ring, scream, shout, signal, summons, supplication, urge, visit, whoop, yell.
calling *n.* business, career, employment, field, job, line, line of country, métier, mission, occupation, profession, province, pursuit, trade, vocation, work.
callous *adj.* case-hardened, cold, hard-bitten, hard-boiled, hardened, hard-hearted, heartless, indifferent, indurated, insensate, insensible, insensitive, inured, obdurate, soulless, thick-skinned, uncaring, unfeeling, unresponsive, unsouled, unsusceptible, unsympathetic.
antonyms kind, sensitive, sympathetic.
calm *adj.* balmy, collected, composed, cool, dispassionate, equable, halcyon, impassive, imperturbable, laid back, mild, pacific, passionless, peaceful, placid, quiet, relaxed, restful, sedate, self-collected, self-possessed, serene, smooth, still, stilly, tranquil, unapprehensive, unclouded, undisturbed, unemotional, uneventful, unexcitable, unexcited, unflappable, unflustered, unmoved, unperturbed, unruffled, untroubled, windless.
antonyms excitable, rough, stormy, wild, worried.
v. compose, hush, mollify, pacify, placate, quieten, relax, soothe.
antonyms excite, irritate, worry.
n. calmness, dispassion, hush, peace, peacefulness, quiet, repose, serenity, stillness.
antonyms restlessness, storminess.
campaign *n.* attack, crusade, drive, excursion, expedition, jihad, movement, offensive, operation, promotion, push.
v. advocate, attack, crusade, fight, promote, push.
can *n.* canister, cannikin, container, jar, jerrycan, pail, receptacle, tin.
canal *n.* waterway, zanja.
cancel *v.* abolish, abort, abrogate, adeem, annul, compensate, counterbalance, countermand, delete, efface, eliminate, erase, expunge, neutralize, nullify, obliterate, offset, quash, redeem, repeal, repudiate, rescind, revoke, scrub, strike.
candid *adj.* blunt, clear, fair, forthright, frank, free, guileless, ingenuous, just, open, outspoken, plain, shining, sincere, straightforward, truthful, unbiased, uncontrived, unequivocal, unposed, unprejudiced.
antonyms cagey, devious, evasive.
candidate *n.* applicant, aspirant, claimant, competitor, contender, contestant, doctorand, entrant, nominee, possibility, pretendant, pretender, runner, solicitant, suitor.
candor *n.* artlessness, directness, fairness, forthrightness, franchise, frankness, guilelessness, honesty, ingenuousness, naïvety, openness, outspokenness, plain-dealing, simplicity, sincerity, straightforwardness, truthfulness, unequivocalness.
antonyms cageyness, deviousness, evasiveness.
canny *adj.* acute, artful, astute, careful, cautious,

circumspect, clever, comfortable, gentle, harmless, innocent, judicious, knowing, lucky, perspicacious, prudent, sagacious, sharp, shrewd, skilful, sly, subtle, wise, worldly-wise.
antonyms foolish, imprudent.

canopy *n.* awning, baldachin, covering, dais, shade, sunshade, tabernacle, tester, umbrella.

cant[1] *n.* argot, humbug, hypocrisy, insincerity, jargon, lingo, pretentiousness, sanctimoniousness, slang, thieves' Latin, vernacular.

cant[2] *n.* angle, bevel, incline, jerk, rise, slant, slope, tilt, toss.

cantankerous *adj.* bad-tempered, captious, carnaptious, choleric, contrary, crabbed, crabby, cranky, crotchety, crusty, difficult, disagreeable, feisty, grouchy, grumpy, ill-humored, ill-natured, irascible, irritable, peevish, perverse, piggish, quarrelsome, testy.
antonyms good-natured, pleasant.

canyon *n.* box-canyon, cañon, coulée, gorge, gulch, gully, ravine.

cap *v.* beat, better, complete, cover, crown, eclipse, exceed, excel, finish, outdo, outstrip, surpass, top, transcend.
n. beret, bonnet, chapka, cowl, fez, glengarry, hat, shako, skullcap, yarmulka.

capability *n.* ability, capacity, competence, facility, faculty, means, potential, potentiality, power, proficiency, qualification, skill, talent.

capable *adj.* able, accomplished, adept, adequate, apt, clever, competent, disposed, efficient, experienced, fitted, gifted, intelligent, liable, masterly, predisposed, proficient, qualified, skilful, suited, susceptible, talented.
antonyms incapable, incompetent, useless.

capacity *n.* ability, amplitude, appointment, aptitude, aptness, brains, caliber, capability, cleverness, compass, competence, competency, dimensions, efficiency, extent, facility, faculty, forte, function, genius, gift, intelligence, magnitude, office, position, post, power, province, range, readiness, role, room, scope, service, size, space, sphere, strength, volume. **cape**[1] *n.* foreland, head, headland, ness, peninsula, point, promontory, tongue.

cape[2] *n.* cloak, coat, cope, mantle, pelerine, pelisse, poncho, robe, shawl, wrap.

caper *v.* bounce, bound, capriole, cavort, dance, frisk, frolic, gambol, hop, jump, leap, romp, skip, spring.
n. affair, antic, business, capriole, dido, escapade, gambado, gambol, high jinks, hop, jape, jest, jump, lark, leap, mischief, prank, revel, sport, stunt.

capital[1] *adj.* cardinal, central, chief, controlling, essential, excellent, fine, first, first-rate, foremost, great, important, leading, main, major, overruling, paramount, pre-eminent, primary, prime, principal, splendid, superb, upper-case.
antonyms minor, sad, unfortunate.

capital[2] *n.* assets, cash, finance, finances, financing, fonds, funds, investment(s), means, money, principal, property, resources, stock, wealth, wherewithal.

capricious *adj.* changeable, crotchety, erratic, fanciful, fickle, fitful, freakish, humorous, impulsive, inconstant, mercurial, odd, queer, quirky, uncertain, unpredictable, variable, wayward, whimsical.
antonyms sensible, steady.

captain *n.* boss, chief, chieftain, commander, head, leader, master, officer, patron, pilot, skip, skipper.

captivate *v.* allure, attract, beguile, besot, bewitch, charm, dazzle, enamor, enchain, enchant, enrapture, enslave, ensnare, enthrall, entrance, fascinate, hypnotize, infatuate, lure, mesmerize, seduce, win.
antonyms appal, repel.

captive *n.* convict, detainee, hostage, internee, prisoner, slave.
adj. caged, confined, enchained, enslaved, ensnared, imprisoned, incarcerated, restricted, secure, subjugated.
antonym free.

captivity *n.* bondage, confinement, custody, detention, durance, duress, enchainment, enthralment, imprisonment, incarceration, internment, restraint, servitude, slavery, thraldom, vassalage.
antonym freedom.

capture *v.* apprehend, arrest, bag, catch, collar, cop, feel someone's collar, lift, nab, secure, seize, snaffle, take.
n. apprehension, arrest, catch, imprisonment, seizure, taking, trapping.

car *n.* auto, automobile, caboose, diner, freight car, handcar, Pullman, sleeper, smoker, streetcar.

carcass *n.* body, cadaver, corpse, framework, hulk, relics, remains, shell, skeleton, stiff.

cardinal *adj.* capital, central, chief, essential, first, foremost, fundamental, greatest, highest, important, key, leading, main, paramount, pre-eminent, primary, prime, principal.

care *n.* affliction, anxiety, attention, burden, carefulness, caution, charge, circumspection, concern, consideration, control, custody, direction, disquiet, forethought, guardianship, hardship, heed, interest, keeping, leading-strings, management, meticulousness, ministration, pains, perplexity, pressure, protection, prudence, regard, responsibility, solicitude, stress, supervision, tribulation, trouble, vexation, vigilance, ward, watchfulness, woe, worry.
antonyms carelessness, inattention, thoughtlessness.

career *n.* calling, course, employment, job, life-work, livelihood, occupation, passage, path, procedure, progress, pursuit, race, vocation, walk.
v. bolt, dash, gallop, hurtle, race, run, rush, shoot, speed, tear.

carefree *adj.* airy, blithe, breezy, buoyant, careless, cheerful, cheery, easy-going, happy, happy-go-lucky, insouciant, jaunty, laid-back, light-hearted, lightsome, radiant, sunny, untroubled, unworried.
antonyms anxious, worried.

careful *adj.* accurate, alert, attentive, cautious, chary, circumspect, concerned, conscientious, discreet, fastidious, heedful, judicious, meticulous, mindful, painstaking, particular, precise, protective, prudent, punctilious, scrupulous, softly-softly, solicitous, thoughtful, thrifty, vigilant, wary, watchful.
antonyms careless, inattentive, thoughtless.

careless *adj.* absent-minded, casual, cursory, derelict, forgetful, heedless, hit-or-miss, inaccurate, incautious, inconsiderate, indiscreet, irresponsible, lackadaisical, messy, neglectful, negligent, nonchalant, offhand, perfunctory, regardless, remiss, slap-dash, slipshod, sloppy, thoughtless, uncaring, unconcerned, unguarded, unmindful, unstudied, untenty, unthinking.
antonyms accurate, careful, meticulous, thoughtful.

caress *v.* canoodle, cuddle, embrace, fondle, hug, kiss, lallygag (lollygag), nuzzle, paw, pet, rub, stroke, touch.
n. cuddle, embrace, fondle, hug, kiss, pat, stroke.

cargo *n.* baggage, consignment, contents, freight, goods, haul, lading, load, merchandise, pay-load, shipment, tonnage, ware.

caricature *n.* burlesque, cartoon, distortion, farce, lampoon, mimicry, parody, Pasquil, Pasquin, pasquinade, representation, satire, send-up, take-off, travesty.
v. burlesque, distort, lampoon, mimic, mock, parody, pasquinade, ridicule, satirize, send up, take off.

carnage *n.* blood-bath, bloodshed, butchery, havoc, holocaust, massacre, murder, shambles, slaughter.

carnal *adj.* animal, bodily, corporeal, earthly, erotic, fleshly, human, impure, lascivious, lecherous, lewd, libidinous, licentious, lustful, mundane, natural, physical, profane, prurient, salacious, secular, sensual, sensuous, sexual, sublunary, temporal, unchaste, unregenerate, unspiritual, voluptuous, wanton, worldly.
antonyms chaste, pure, spiritual.

carnival *n.* celebration, fair, Fasching, festival, fête, fiesta, gala, holiday, jamboree, jubilee, Mardi Gras, merrymaking, revelry, wassail, wassail-bout, wassailry.

carol *n.* canticle, canzonet, chorus, ditty, hymn, lay, noel, song, strain, wassail.

carp *v.* cavil, censure, complain, criticize, hypercriticize, knock, nag, quibble, reproach, ultracrepidate.
antonym praise.

carpet *n.* Axminster, kali, mat, Navaho, Persian, rug, Wilton.

carping *adj.* biting, bitter, captious, caviling, critical, fault-finding, grouchy, hypercritical, nagging, nit-picking, picky, reproachful, Zoilean.
n. censure, complaints, criticism, disparagement, knocking, reproofs, Zoilism.
antonyms compliments, praise.

carriage *n.* air, bearing, behavior, cab, carrying, chaise, coach, comportment, conduct, conveyance, conveying, delivery, demeanor, deportment, four-wheeler, freight, gait, manner, mien, posture, presence, transport, transportation, vehicle, vettura, voiture, wagon, wagonette.

carry *v.* accomplish, bear, bring, broadcast, capture, chair, communicate, conduct, convey, display, disseminate, drive, effect, fetch, gain, give, haul, hip, impel, influence, lift, lug, maintain, motivate, move, offer, publish, relay, release, secure, shoulder, spur, stand, stock, suffer, support, sustain, take, tote, transfer, transmit, transport, underpin, uphold, urge, win.

carve *v.* chip, chisel, cut, divide, engrave, etch, fashion, form, grave, hack, hew, incise, indent, make, mold, sculp(t), sculpture, slash, slice, tool, whittle.

case[1] *n.* box, cabinet, canister, capsule, carton, cartridge, casing, casket, chest, compact, container, cover, covering, crate, envelope, étui, folder, holder, integument, jacket, receptacle, sheath, shell, showcase, suit-case, tray, trunk, wrapper, wrapping.
v. encase, enclose, skin.

case[2] *n.* argument, circumstances, condition, context, contingency, dilemma, event, example, illustration, instance, occasion, occurrence, plight, point, position, predicament, situation, specimen, state, thesis.
v. investigate, reconnoiter.

case[3] *n.* action, argument, cause, dispute, lawsuit, proceedings, process, suit, trial.

cash *n.* bank-notes, bread, bucks, bullion, change, coin, coinage, currency, dough, funds, hard currency, hard money, money, notes, payment, readies, ready, ready money, resources, specie, wherewithal.
v. encash, liquidate, realize.

casserole *n.* pot-au-feu, stew-pan.

cast[1] *v.* abandon, add, allot, appoint, assign, bestow, calculate, categorize, choose, chuck, compute, deposit, diffuse, distribute, drive, drop, emit, figure, fling, forecast, form, found, give, hurl, impel, launch, lob, model, mold, name, pick, pitch, project, radiate, reckon, reject, scatter, select, set, shape, shed, shy, sling, spread, throw, thrust, toss, total.
n. air, appearance, complexion, demeanor, fling, form, lob, look, manner, mien, quality, semblance, shade, stamp, style, throw, thrust, tinge, tone, toss, turn.

cast[2] *n.* actors, artistes, characters, company, dramatis personae, entertainers, performers, players, troupe.

caste *n.* class, degree, estate, grade, lineage, order, position, race, rank, species, station, status, stratum.

castle *n.* casbah (kasba, kasbah), château, citadel, donjon, fastness, fortress, keep, mansion, motte and bailey, palace, peel, schloss, stronghold, tower.

casual *adj.* accidental, apathetic, blasé, chance, contingent, cursory, fortuitous, incidental, indifferent, informal, insouciant, irregular, lackadaisical, negligent, nonchalant, occasional, offhand, perfunctory, random, relaxed, serendipitous, stray, unceremonious, uncertain, unconcerned, unexpected, unforeseen, unintentional, unpremeditated.
antonyms deliberate, painstaking, planned.

casualty *n.* death, injured, injury, loss, sufferer, victim, wounded.

catalog *n.* directory, gazetteer, index, inventory, list, litany, record, register, roll, roster, schedule, table.
v. accession, alphabetize, classify, codify, file, index, inventory, list, record, register.

catastrophe *n.* adversity, affliction, blow, calamity, cataclysm, conclusion, culmination, curtain, debacle (débâcle), dénouement, devastation, disaster, end, failure, fiasco, finale, ill, mischance, misfortune, mishap, reverse, ruin, termination, tragedy, trial, trouble, upheaval, upshot, winding-up.

catch *v.* apprehend, arrest, benet, bewitch, captivate, capture, charm, clutch, contract, cop, delight, detect, develop, discern, discover, enchant, enrapture, ensnare, entangle, entrap, expose, fascinate, feel, follow, grab, grasp, grip, hear, incur, nab, nail, perceive, recognize, seize, sense, snare, snatch, surprise, take, twig, unmask.
antonyms drop, free, miss.
n. bolt, clasp, clip, detent, disadvantage, drawback, fastener, hasp, hitch, hook, latch, obstacle, parti, snag, sneck, snib, trap, trick.

catching *adj.* attractive, captivating, charming, communicable, contagious, enchanting, fascinating, fetching, infectious, infective, taking, transferable, transmissible, transmittable, winning, winsome.
antonyms boring, ugly, unattractive.

catchy *adj.* attractive, captivating, confusing, deceptive, haunting, memorable, popular.
antonyms boring, dull.

category *n.* chapter, class, classification, department, division, grade, grouping, head, heading, list, order, rank, section, sort, type.

cater *v.* furnish, humor, indulge, outfit, pander, provide, provision, purvey, supply, victual.

cause *n.* account, agency, agent, aim, attempt, basis, beginning, belief, causation, consideration, conviction, creator, end, enterprise, genesis, grounds, ideal, impulse, incentive, inducement, mainspring, maker, motivation, motive, movement, object, origin, originator, producer, purpose, reason, root, source, spring, stimulus, undertaking.
antonyms effect, result.
v. begin, compel, create, effect, engender, generate, give rise to, incite, induce, motivate, occasion, precipitate, produce, provoke, result in.

caustic *adj.* acidulous, acrid, acrimonious, astringent, biting, bitter, burning, corroding, corrosive, cutting, escharotic, keen, mordant, pungent, sarcastic, scathing, severe, stinging, trenchant, virulent, waspish.
antonyms mild, soothing.

caution *n.* admonition, advice, alertness, care, carefulness, circumspection, counsel, deliberation, discretion, forethought, heed, heedfulness, injunction, prudence, via trita, via tuta, vigilance, wariness, warning, watchfulness.
v. admonish, advise, urge, warn.

cautious *adj.* alert, cagey, careful, chary, circumspect, discreet, guarded, heedful, judicious, politic, prudent, scrupulous, softly-softly, tentative, unadventurous, vigilant, wary, watchful.
antonyms heedless, imprudent, incautious.

cavalcade *n.* array, march-past, parade, procession, retinue, spectacle, train, troop.

cavalier *n.* attendant, beau, blade, chevalier, equestrian, escort, gallant, gentleman, horseman, knight, partner, royalist.
adj. arrogant, cavalierish, condescending, curt, disdainful, free-and-easy, gay, haughty, insolent, lofty, lordly, misproud, off-hand, scornful, supercilious, swaggering.

cave *n.* antre, cavern, cavity, den, grotto, hole, hollow, mattamore, pothole.

cavity *n.* antrum, belly, caries, crater, dent, gap, hole, hollow, pit, pot-hole, sinus, vacuole, ventricle, well, womb.

cavort *v.* caper, caracole, dance, frisk, frolic, gambol, hop, prance, romp, skip, sport.

cease *v.* call a halt, call it a day, conclude, culminate, desist, die, discontinue, end, fail, finish, halt, pack in, poop out, refrain, stay, stop, terminate.
antonyms begin, start.

cede *v.* abandon, abdicate, allow, concede, convey, give up, grant, relinquish, renounce, resign, surrender, transfer, yield.

celebrate *v.* bless, commemorate, commend, emblazon, eulogize, exalt, extol, glorify, honor, keep, laud, live it up, observe, perform, praise, proclaim, publicize, rejoice, reverence, solemnize, toast, wassail, whoop it up.

celebrated *adj.* acclaimed, big, distingué, distinguished, eminent, exalted, famed, famous, glorious, illustrious, lionized, notable, outstanding, popular, pre-eminent, prominent, renowned, revered, well-known.
antonyms obscure, unknown.

celebrity *n.* big name, big shot, bigwig, dignitary, distinction, éclat, eminence, fame, glory, honor, lion, luminary, name, notability, personage, personality, popularity, pre-eminence, prestige, prominence, renown, reputation, repute, star, stardom, superstar, VIP.
antonyms nobody, obscurity.

celestial *adj.* angelic, astral, divine, elysian, empyrean, eternal, ethereal, godlike, heavenly, immortal, paradisaic(al), seraphic, spiritual, starry, sublime, supernatural, transcendental.
antonyms earthly, mundane.

cement *v.* attach, bind, bond, cohere, combine, fix together, glue, gum, join, plaster, seal, solder, stick, unite, weld.
n. adhesive, concrete, glue, gum, mortar, paste, plaster, sealant.

censure *n.* admonishment, admonition, blame, castigation, condemnation, criticism, disapproval, obloquy,

rebuke, remonstrance, reprehension, reprimand, reproach, reprobation, reproof, stricture, telling-off, vituperation.
antonyms approval, compliments, praise.
v. abuse, admonish, animadvert, berate, blame, castigate, chide, condemn, criticize, decry, denounce, jump on, rebuke, reprehend, reprimand, reproach, reprobate, reprove, scold, slam, tell off, upbraid.
antonyms approve, compliment, praise.

center *n.* bull's-eye, core, crux, focus, heart, hub, Mecca, mid, middle, mid-point, nave, nucleus, omphalos, pivot.
antonyms edge, outskirts, periphery.
v. cluster, concentrate, converge, focus, gravitate, hinge, pivot, revolve.

central *adj.* chief, essential, focal, fundamental, important, inner, interior, key, main, mean, median, mid, middle, pivotal, primary, principal, vital.
antonyms minor, peripheral.

ceremonious *adj.* civil, courteous, courtly, deferential, dignified, exact, formal, grand, polite, pompous, precise, punctilious, ritual, solemn, starchy, stately, stiff.
antonyms informal, relaxed, unceremonious.

ceremony *n.* celebration, ceremonial, commemoration, decorum, etiquette, event, form, formality, function, niceties, observance, parade, pomp, propriety, protocol, rite, ritual, service, show, solemnities.

certain *adj.* ascertained, assured, bound, conclusive, confident, constant, convinced, convincing, decided, definite, dependable, destined, determinate, established, express, fated, fixed, incontrovertible, individual, indubitable, ineluctable, inescapable, inevitable, inexorable, irrefutable, known, one, particular, plain, positive, precise, regular, reliable, resolved, satisfied, settled, some, special, specific, stable, steady, sure, true, trustworthy, undeniable, undoubted, unequivocal, unfailing, unmistakable, unquestionable, valid.
antonyms doubtful, hesitant, uncertain, unsure.

certainly *adv.* doubtlessly, naturally, of course, questionless.

certainty *n.* assurance, authoritativeness, certitude, confidence, conviction, fact, faith, indubitableness, inevitability, nap, plerophoria, plerophory, positiveness, reality, sure thing, sureness, surety, trust, truth, validity.
antonyms doubt, hesitation, uncertainty.

certificate *n.* attestation, authorization, award, credentials, diploma, document, endorsement, guarantee, license, pass, qualification, testimonial, validation, voucher, warrant.

certify *v.* ascertain, assure, attest, authenticate, authorize, aver, avow, confirm, corroborate, declare, endorse, evidence, guarantee, notify, show, testify, validate, verify, vouch, witness.

certitude *n.* assurance, certainty, confidence, conviction, plerophoria, plerophory.
antonym doubt.

cessation *n.* abeyance, arrest, arresting, break, ceasing, desistance, discontinuance, discontinuation, discontinuing, end, ending, halt, halting, hiatus, intermission, interruption, interval, let-up, pause, recess, remission, respite, rest, standstill, stay, stoppage, stopping, suspension, termination.
antonym commencement.

chafe *v.* abrade, anger, annoy, enrage, exasperate, fret, fume, gall, get, grate, heat, incense, inflame, irritate, offend, provoke, rage, rasp, rub, scrape, scratch, vex, wear, worry.

chagrin *n.* annoyance, discomfiture, discomposure, displeasure, disquiet, dissatisfaction, embarrassment, exasperation, fretfulness, humiliation, indignation, irritation, mortification, peevishness, spleen, vexation.
antonyms delight, pleasure.
v. annoy, displease, disquiet, dissatisfy, embarrass, exasperate, humiliate, irk, irritate, mortify, peeve, vex.

chain *n.* bond, catena, concatenation, coupling, fetter, fob, link, manacle, progression, restraint, sequence, series, set, shackle, string, succession, train, union, vinculum.
v. bind, confine, enslave, fasten, fetter, gyve, handcuff, manacle, restrain, secure, shackle, tether, trammel.
antonyms free, release.

chairman *n.* chair, chairperson, chairwoman, convenor, director, master of ceremonies, MC, president, presider, speaker, spokesman, toastmaster.

challenge *v.* accost, beard, brave, confront, dare, defy, demand, dispute, impugn, provoke, query, question, stimulate, summon, tax, test, throw down the gauntlet, try.
n. confrontation, dare, defiance, gauntlet, hurdle, interrogation, obstacle, poser, provocation, question, test, trial, ultimatum.

chamber *n.* apartment, assembly, bed-chamber, bedroom, boudoir, camera, cavity, closet, compartment, council, cubicle, enclosure, hall, legislature, parliament, room, vault.

chance *n.* accident, act of God, coincidence, contingency, destiny, fate, fortuity, fortune, gamble, happenstance, hazard, jeopardy, liability, likelihood, luck, misfortune, occasion, odds, opening, opportunity, peril, possibility, probability, prospect, providence, risk, speculation, time, uncertainty, venture.
antonyms certainty, law, necessity.
v. befall, gamble, happen, hazard, occur, risk, stake, transpire, try, venture, wager.
adj. accidental, casual, contingent, fortuitous, inadvertent, incidental, random, serendipitous, unforeseeable, unforeseen, unintended, unintentional, unlooked-for.
antonyms certain, deliberate, intentional.

change *v.* alter, alternate, barter, convert, denature, displace, diversify, exchange, fluctuate, interchange, metamorphose, moderate, modify, mutate, reform, remodel,

remove, reorganize, replace, restyle, shift, substitute, swap, take liberties with, trade, transfigure, transform, transmit, transmute, transpose, vacillate, vary, veer.
n. alteration, break, chop, conversion, difference, diversion, exchange, innovation, interchange, metamorphosis, metanoia, modification, mutation, novelty, permutation, revolution, satisfaction, sea-change, shift, substitution, trade, transformation, transition, transmutation, transposition, upheaval, variation, variety, vicissitude.

changeable *adj.* capricious, chameleonic, changeful, erratic, fickle, fitful, fluid, inconstant, irregular, kaleidoscopic, labile, mercurial, mobile, mutable, protean, shifting, uncertain, unpredictable, unreliable, unsettled, unstable, unsteady, vacillating, variable, vicissitudinous, volatile, wavering, windy.
antonyms constant, reliable, unchangeable.

chaos *n.* anarchy, bedlam, confusion, disorder, disorganization, entropy, lawlessness, pandemonium, snafu, tohu bohu, tumult, unreason.
antonym order.

chaotic *adj.* anarchic, confused, deranged, disordered, disorganized, lawless, purposeless, rampageous, riotous, shambolic, snafu, topsy-turvy, tumultous, tumultuary, uncontrolled.
antonyms organized, purposive.

character[1] *n.* attributes, bent, caliber, cast, complexion, constitution, disposition, feature, honor, individuality, integrity, kidney, make-up, nature, peculiarity, personality, physiognomy, position, quality, rank, rectitude, reputation, stamp, status, strength, temper, temperament, type, uprightness.

character[2] *n.* card, customer, eccentric, fellow, guy, individual, joker, oddball, oddity, original, part, person, persona, portrayal, role, sort, type.

character[3] *n.* cipher, device, emblem, figure, hieroglyph, ideogram, ideograph, letter, logo, mark, rune, sign, symbol, type.

characteristic *adj.* discriminative, distinctive, distinguishing, idiosyncratic, individual, peculiar, representative, singular, special, specific, symbolic, symptomatic, typical, vintage.
antonyms uncharacteristic, untypical.
n. attribute, faculty, feature, hallmark, idiosyncrasy, lineament, mannerism, mark, peculiarity, property, quality, symptom, thing, trait.

charitable *adj.* accommodating, beneficent, benevolent, benign, benignant, bountiful, broad-minded, clement, compassionate, considerate, eleemosynary, favorable, forgiving, generous, gracious, humane, indulgent, kind, kindly, lavish, lenient, liberal, magnanimous, mild, philanthropic, sympathetic, tolerant, understanding.
antonyms uncharitable, unforgiving.

charity *n.* affection, agape, alms-giving, altruism, assistance, benefaction, beneficence, benevolence, benignity, benignness, bountifulness, bounty, clemency, compassion, endowment, fund, generosity, gift, goodness, hand-out, humanity, indulgence, love, philanthropy, relief, tender-heartedness.

charm *v.* allure, attract, becharm, beguile, bewitch, cajole, captivate, delight, enamor, enchant, enrapture, entrance, fascinate, mesmerize, please, win.
n. abraxas, allure, allurement, amulet, appeal, attraction, attractiveness, desirability, enchantment, fascination, fetish, grisgris, idol, ju-ju, magic, magnetism, medicine, obeah, obi, phylactery, porte-bonheur, sorcery, spell, talisman, trinket, weird.

charming *adj.* appealing, attractive, bewitching, captivating, delectable, delightful, engaging, eye-catching, fetching, honeyed, irresistible, lovely, pleasant, pleasing, seductive, sweet, winning, winsome.
antonyms ugly, unattractive.

chart *n.* abac, alignment chart, blueprint, diagram, graph, map, nomograph, plan, table, tabulation.
v. delineate, draft, draw, graph, map out, mark, outline, place, plot, shape, sketch.

charter *n.* accreditation, authorization, bond, concession, contract, deed, document, franchise, indenture, license, permit, prerogative, privilege, right.
v. authorize, commission, employ, engage, hire, lease, rent, sanction.

chase *v.* course, drive, expel, follow, hunt, hurry, pursue, rush, track.
n. coursing, hunt, hunting, pursuit, race, run, rush, venery.

chasm *n.* abysm, abyss, breach, canyon, cavity, cleft, crater, crevasse, fissure, gap, gorge, gulf, hiatus, hollow, opening, ravine, rent, rift, split, void.

chaste *adj.* austere, decent, decorous, elegant, immaculate, incorrupt, innocent, maidenly, modest, moral, neat, pure, refined, restrained, simple, unaffected, undefiled, unsullied, unvulgar, vestal, virginal, virginly, virtuous, wholesome.
antonyms indecorous, lewd.

chasten *v.* admonish, afflict, castigate, chastise, correct, cow, curb, discipline, humble, humiliate, repress, reprove, soften, subdue, tame.

chastise *v.* beat, berate, castigate, censure, correct, discipline, flog, flyte, lash, punish, reprove, scold, scourge, smack, spank, upbraid, whip.

chat *n.* chatter, chinwag, confab, coze, crack, gossip, heart-to-heart, natter, rap, talk, tête-à-tête, visit.
v. chatter, chew the fat, crack, gossip, jaw, natter, rabbit (on), talk, visit, yackety-yak.

chatter *n.* babble, blather, blether, chat, gab, gabfest, gossip, jabber, prate, prattle, prattlement, tattle, tonguework, twaddle.
v. babble, blab, blather, blether, chat, clack, clatter, gab, gossip, jabber, prate, prattle, prittle-prattle, talk like a pengun, tattle, twaddle, yackety-yak.

cheap *adj.* à bon marché, bargain, base, budget, common, contemptible, cut-price, despicable, dirt-cheap, dog-

cheap, economical, economy, inexpensive, inferior, jitney, keen, knock-down, low, low-cost, low-priced, mean, paltry, poor, reasonable, reduced, sale, scurvy, second-rate, shoddy, sordid, tatty, tawdry, uncostly, vulgar, worthless.
antonyms costly, excellent, noble, superior.

cheat *v.* baffle, bam, bamboozle, beguile, bilk, check, chisel, chouse, cog, con, cozen, deceive, defeat, defraud, deprive, diddle, do, double-cross, dupe, finagle, fleece, fob, foil, fool, frustrate, fudge, grift, gudgeon, gull, gyp, hand (someone) a lemon, hoax, hocus, hoodwink, mislead, prevent, queer, rip off, screw, short-change, skin, smouch, swindle, thwart, touch, trick, trim, victimize.
n. artifice, bilker, charlatan, cheater, chouse, cogger, con man, cozener, deceit, deceiver, deception, dodger, double-crosser, extortioner, fraud, grifter, impostor, imposture, knave, picaroon, rip-off, rogue, shark, sharp, sharper, short-changer, snap, swindle, swindler, trickery, trickster, welsher.

check[1] *v.* compare, confirm, examine, give the once-over, inspect, investigate, monitor, note, probe, research, scrutinize, study, test, verify.
n. audit, examination, inspection, investigation, research, scrutiny, tab, test.

check[2] *v.* arrest, bar, blame, bridle, chide, control, curb, damp, delay, halt, hinder, impede, inhibit, limit, obstruct, pause, rebuke, repress, reprimand, reprove, restrain, retard, scold, stop, thwart.
n. blow, constraint, control, curb, damp, damper, disappointment, frustration, hindrance, impediment, inhibition, limitation, obstruction, rejection, restraint, reverse, setback, stoppage.

check[3] *n.* bill, counterfoil, token.

cheek[1] *n.* audacity, brass, brass neck, brazenness, brazenry, disrespect, effrontery, face, gall, impertinence, impudence, insolence, nerve, sauce, temerity.

cheek[2] *n.* buttock, face, gena, jowl.

cheer *v.* acclaim, animate, applaud, brighten, clap, comfort, console, elate, elevate, encheer, encourage, enhearten, enliven, exhilarate, gladden, hail, hearten, hurrah, incite, inspirit, solace, uplift, warm.
antonyms boo, dishearten, jeer.
n. acclamation, animation, applause, bravo, buoyancy, cheerfulness, comfort, gaiety, gladness, glee, hoorah, hopefulness, hurrah, joy, liveliness, merriment, merrymaking, mirth, optimism, ovation, plaudits, solace.

cheerful *adj.* animated, blithe, bobbish, bright, bucked, buoyant, canty, cheery, chipper, chirpy, chirrupy, contented, enlivening, enthusiastic, eupeptic, gay, gaysome, genial, glad, gladsome, happy, hearty, jaunty, jolly, jovial, joyful, joyous, light-hearted, lightsome, light-spirited, merry, optimistic, perky, pleasant, sparkling, sprightly, sunny, upbeat, winsome.
antonym sad.

cherish *v.* comfort, cosset, encourage, entertain, foster, harbor, make much of, nourish, nurse, nurture, prize, shelter, support, sustain, tender, treasure, value.

chest *n.* ark, box, case, casket, coffer, crate, kist, strongbox, trunk.

chew *v.* champ, crunch, gnaw, grind, manducate, masticate, munch.

chic *adj.* à la mode, chichi, elegant, fashionable, modish, smart, stylish, trendy.
antonyms out-moded, unfashionable.

chide *v.* admonish, berate, blame, censure, check, criticize, lecture, objurgate, rate, rebuke, reprehend, reprimand, reproach, reprove, scold, tell off, upbraid.
antonym praise.

chief *adj.* capital, cardinal, central, especial, essential, foremost, grand, highest, key, leading, main, outstanding, paramount, predominant, pre-eminent, premier, prevailing, primal, primary, prime, principal, superior, supreme, uppermost, vital.
antonyms junior, minor, unimportant.
n. boss, captain, chieftain, cock of the loft, commander, coryphaeus, director, duke, governor, head, kaid, kingpin, leader, lord, manager, master, paramount, paramount chief, principal, ringleader, ruler, superintendent, superior, supremo, suzerain.

chiefly *adv.* especially, essentially, for the most part, generally, mainly, mostly, predominantly, primarily, principally, usually.

childish *adj.* boyish, foolish, frivolous, girlish, hypocoristic, hypocoristical, immature, infantile, juvenile, puerile, silly, simple, trifling, weak, young.
antonyms adult, sensible.

chill *adj.* aloof, biting, bleak, chilly, cold, cool, depressing, distant, freezing, frigid, hostile, parky, raw, sharp, stony, unfriendly, unresponsive, unwelcoming, wintry.
antonyms friendly, warm.
v. congeal, cool, dampen, depress, discourage, dishearten, dismay, freeze, frighten, refrigerate, terrify.
n. bite, cold, coldness, coolness, coolth, crispness, frigidity, nip, rawness, sharpness.

chilly *adj.* aloof, blowy, breezy, brisk, cold, cool, crisp, draughty, fresh, frigid, hostile, nippy, parky, penetrating, sharp, stony, unfriendly, unresponsive, unsympathetic, unwelcoming.
antonyms friendly, warm.

chirp *v., n.* cheep, chirrup, peep, pipe, tweet, twitter, warble, whistle.

chivalrous *adj.* bold, brave, chivalric, courageous, courteous, courtly, gallant, gentlemanly, Grandisonian, heroic, honorable, knightly, polite, true, valiant.
antonyms cowardly, ungallant.

chivalry *n.* boldness, bravery, courage, courtesy, courtliness, gallantry, gentlemanliness, knight-errantry, knighthood, politeness.

choice *n.* alternative, choosing, decision, dilemma, discrimination, election, espousal, opting, option, pick, preference, say, selection, variety.

adj. best, dainty, elect, élite, excellent, exclusive, exquisite, hand-picked, nice, plum, precious, prime, prize, rare, select, special, superior, uncommon, unusual, valuable.
antonym inferior.

choke *v.* asphyxiate, bar, block, clog, close, congest, constrict, dam, gag, obstruct, occlude, overpower, reach, retch, smother, stifle, stop, strangle, suffocate, suppress, throttle.

choose *v.* adopt, cull, designate, desire, elect, espouse, fix on, opt for, pick, plump for, predestine, prefer, see fit, select, settle on, single out, take, vote for, wish.

chop *v.* cleave, cut, divide, fell, hack, hew, lop, sever, shear, slash, slice, truncate.

chore *n.* burden, duty, errand, fag, job, stint, task, trouble.

chronic *adj.* appalling, atrocious, awful, confirmed, deep-rooted, deep-seated, dreadful, habitual, incessant, incurable, ineradicable, ingrained, inveterate, persistent, terrible.
antonym temporary.

chronicle *n.* account, annals, chanson de geste, diary, epic, gest(e), history, journal, narrative, record, register, saga, story.
v. enter, list, narrate, record, recount, register, relate, report, tell, write down.

chuckle *v.* chortle, crow, exult, giggle, laugh, snigger, snort, titter.

chummy *adj.* affectionate, close, friendly, intimate, matey, pally, sociable, thick.

chunk *n.* block, chuck, dod, dollop, hunk, lump, mass, piece, portion, slab, wad, wodge.

chunky *adj.* beefy, brawny, dumpy, fat, square, stocky, stubby, thick, thickset.
antonym slim.

cinema *n.* big screen, filmhouse, flicks, movies, picturehouse, picture-palace.

circle *n.* area, assembly, band, bounds, circuit, circumference, class, clique, club, coil, company, compass, cordon, coterie, crowd, cycle, disc, domain, enclosure, fellowship, field, fraternity, globe, group, gyre, lap, loop, orb, orbit, perimeter, periphery, province, range, realm, region, revolution, ring, round, roundance, roundel, roundlet, rundle, scene, school, set, society, sphere, turn.
v. belt, circumambulate, circumnavigate, circumscribe, coil, compass, curl, curve, encircle, enclose, encompass, envelop, gird, girdle, hem in, loop, pivot, revolve, ring, rotate, surround, tour, whirl.

circuit *n.* ambit, area, boundary, bounds, circumference, compass, course, district, eyre, journey, limit, orbit, perambulation, range, region, revolution, round, route, tour, track, tract.

circuitous *adj.* ambagious, anfractuous, cagey, devious, indirect, labyrinthine, meandering, oblique, periphrastic, rambling, roundabout, tortuous, winding.
antonyms direct, straight.

circular *adj.* annular, discoid(al), disc-shaped, hoop-shaped, ring-shaped, round.
n. advert, announcement, handbill, leaflet, letter, notice, pamphlet.

circumference *n.* border, boundary, bounds, circuit, edge, extremity, fringe, limits, margin, outline, perimeter, periphery, rim, verge.

circumspection *n.* canniness, care, caution, chariness, deliberation, discretion, guardedness, prudence, wariness.

circumstance *n.* accident, condition, contingency, detail, element, event, fact, factor, happening, happenstance, incident, item, occurrence, particular, position, respect, situation.

circumstances *n.* conditions, galère, lifestyle, means, position, resources, situation, state, state of affairs, station, status, times.

cite *v.* accite, adduce, advance, call, enumerate, evidence, extract, mention, name, quote, specify, subpoena, summon.

citizen *n.* burgess, burgher, city-dweller, denizen, dweller, freeman, inhabitant, oppidan, ratepayer, resident, subject, townsman, urbanite.

city *n.* conurbation, megalopolis, metropolis, municipality, town.

civil *adj.* accommodating, affable, civic, civilized, complaisant, courteous, courtly, domestic, home, interior, internal, internecine, lay, municipal, obliging, polished, polite, political, refined, secular, temporal, urbane, well-bred, well-mannered.
antonym uncivil.

civilization *n.* advancement, cultivation, culture, development, education, enlightenment, kultur, progress, refinement, sophistication, urbanity.
antonyms barbarity, primitiveness.

civilize *v.* ameliorate, cultivate, educate, enlighten, humanize, improve, meliorate, perfect, polish, refine, sophisticate, tame.

claim *v.* affirm, allege, arrogate, ask, assert, challenge, collect, demand, exact, hold, insist, maintain, need, profess, request, require, state, take, uphold.
n. affirmation, allegation, application, assertion, call, demand, insistence, petition, pretension, privilege, protestation, request, requirement, right, title.

clamor *n.* agitation, babel, blare, brouhaha, commotion, complaint, din, exclamation, hubbub, hue, hullabaloo, katzenjammer, noise, outcry, racket, shout, shouting, uproar, vociferation.
antonym silence.

clan *n.* band, brotherhood, clique, confraternity, coterie, faction, family, fraternity, gens, group, house, phratry, race, sect, sept, set, society, sodality, tribe.

clandestine *adj.* backroom, behind-door, cloak-and-dagger, closet, concealed, covert, fraudulent, furtive, hidden, private, secret, sly, sneaky, stealthy, subreptitious, surreptitious, underground, underhand, under-the-counter.
antonym open.

clarify *v.* cleanse, define, elucidate, explain, gloss, illuminate, purify, refine, resolve, shed/throw light on, simplify.
antonym obscure.

clash *v.* bang, clang, clank, clatter, conflict, crash, disagree, feud, fight, grapple, jangle, jar, quarrel, rattle, war, wrangle.
n. brush, clank, clatter, collision, conflict, confrontation, disagreement, fight, jangle, jar, noise, show-down.

clasp *n.* agraffe, brooch, buckle, catch, clip, embrace, fastener, fastening, grasp, grip, hasp, hold, hook, hug, pin, snap, tach(e).
v. attach, clutch, concatenate, connect, embrace, enclasp, enfold, fasten, grapple, grasp, grip, hold, hug, press, seize, squeeze.

class[1] *n.* caliber, caste, category, classification, collection, denomination, department, description, division, genre, genus, grade, group, grouping, ilk, kidney, kind, kingdom, league, order, phylum, quality, rank, section, set, sort, species, sphere, status, style, taxon, type, value.
v. assort, brand, categorize, classify, codify, designate, grade, group, rank, rate.

class[2] *n.* course, lecture, seminar, teach-in, tutorial.

classic *adj.* abiding, ageless, archetypal, Augustan, best, characteristic, chaste, consummate, deathless, definitive, enduring, established, excellent, exemplary, finest, first-rate, ideal, immortal, lasting, master, masterly, model, paradigmatic, quintessential, refined, regular, restrained, standard, time-honored, traditional, typical, undying, usual.
antonym second-rate.
n. chef d'oeuvre, exemplar, masterpiece, masterwork, model, paradigm, pièce de résistance, prototype, standard.

classification *n.* analysis, arrangement, cataloging, categorization, codification, digestion, grading, pigeonholing, sorting, taxis, taxonomy.

classify *v.* arrange, assort, catalog, categorize, codify, digest, dispose, distribute, file, grade, pigeon-hole, rank, sort, systematize, tabulate.

clause *n.* article, chapter, condition, demand, heading, item, paragraph, part, passage, point, provision, proviso, section, specification, stipulation, subsection.

claw *n.* griff(e), gripper, nail, nipper, pincer, pounce, talon, tentacle, unguis.
v. dig, graze, lacerate, mangle, maul, rip, scrabble, scrape, scratch, tear.

clean *adj.* antiseptic, chaste, clarified, complete, conclusive, decent, decisive, decontaminated, delicate, elegant, entire, exemplary, faultless, final, flawless, fresh, good, graceful, guiltless, honest, honorable, hygienic, immaculate, innocent, laundered, moral, natural, neat, perfect, pure, purified, respectable, sanitary, simple, spotless, sterile, sterilized, thorough, tidy, total, trim, unblemished, unadulterated, uncluttered, uncontaminated, undefiled, unimpaired, unpolluted, unsoiled, unspotted, unstained, unsullied, upright, virtuous, washed, whole.
antonyms dirty, indecent, polluted, unsterile.
v. bath, cleanse, deodorize, deterge, disinfect, dust, launder, lave, mop, purge, purify, rinse, sanitize, scour, scrub, sponge, swab, sweep, vacuum, wash.
antonyms defile, dirty.

clean up sanitize, tidy, wash.

cleanse *v.* absolve, absterge, catharize, clean, clear, deterge, detoxicate, detoxify, lustrate, purge, purify, rinse, scavenge, scour, scrub, wash.
antonyms defile, dirty.

clear *adj.* apparent, audible, bright, certain, clean, cloudless, coherent, comprehensible, conspicuous, convinced, crystalline, decided, definite, diaphanous, disengaged, distinct, eidetic, empty, evident, explicit, express, fair, fine, free, glassy, guiltless, halcyon, hyaline, immaculate, incontrovertible, innocent, intelligible, light, limpid, lucid, luculent, luminous, manifest, obvious, open, palpable, patent, pellucid, perceptible, perspicuous, plain, positive, pronounced, pure, recognizable, resolved, satisfied, see-through, serene, sharp, shining, smooth, stainless, sunny, sure, translucent, transparent, unambiguous, unblemished, unclouded, undefiled, undimmed, undulled, unequivocal, unhampered, unhindered, unimpeded, unlimited, unmistakable, unobstructed, unquestionable, untarnished, untroubled, well-defined.
antonyms cloudy, fuzzy, guilty, vague.
v. absolve, acquire, acquit, brighten, clarify, clean, cleanse, decode, decongest, deoppilate, disengage, disentangle, earn, emancipate, erase, excuse, exonerate, extricate, fix, free, gain, jump, justify, leap, liberate, lighten, loosen, make, miss, open, pass over, purify, reap, refine, rid, secure, strip, tidy, unblock, unclog, uncloud, unload, unpack, unscramble, vault, vindicate, wipe.
antonyms block, condemn, defile, dirty.

clearly *adv.* distinctly, evidently, incontestably, incontrovertibly, manifestly, markedly, obviously, openly, plainly, undeniably, undoubtedly.
antonyms indistinctly, vaguely.

clemency *n.* compassion, forebearance, forgiveness, generosity, humanity, indulgence, kindness, lenience, leniency, lenity, magnanimity, mercifulness, mercy, mildness, moderation, soft-heartedness, tenderness.
antonyms harshness, ruthlessness.

clerical *adj.* ecclesiastical, pastoral, priestly, sacerdotal.

clerk *n.* account-keeper, assistant, copyist, official, pen-driver, pen-pusher, protocolist, quill-driver, quillman, receptionist, shop-assistant, writer.

clever *adj.* able, adroit, apt, astute, brainy, bright, canny, capable, cunning, deep, dexterous, discerning, elegant, expert, gifted, gleg, good-natured, habile, ingenious, intelligent, inventive, keen, knowing, knowledgeable,

quick, quick-witted, rational, resourceful, sagacious, sensible, shrewd, skilful, smart, talented, witty.
antonyms foolish, naïve, senseless.

clever dick smart alec, smart-ass, smartypants, wiseling, witling, wit-monger.

cleverness *n.* ability, adroitness, astuteness, brains, brightness, canniness, cunning, dexterity, flair, gift, gumption, ingenuity, intelligence, nous, quickness, resourcefulness, sagacity, sense, sharpness, shrewdness, smartness, talent, wit.
antonyms foolishness, naïvety, senselessness.

client *n.* applicant, buyer, consumer, customer, dependant, habitué, patient, patron, protégé, shopper.

cliff *n.* bluff, crag, escarpment, face, overhang, precipice, rock-face, scar, scarp.

climate *n.* ambience, atmosphere, clime, country, disposition, feeling, milieu, mood, region, setting, temper, temperature, tendency, trend, weather.

climax *n.* acme, apogee, culmination, head, height, high point, highlight, orgasm, peak, summit, top, zenith.
antonyms bathos, low point, nadir.

climb *v.* ascend, clamber, mount, rise, scale, shin up, soar, swarm (up), top.

clip[1] *v.* crop, curtail, cut, dock, pare, poll, pollard, prune, shear, shorten, snip, trim.

clip[2] *v.* box, clobber, clout, cuff, hit, knock, punch, skelp, slap, smack, sock, thump, wallop, whack.
n. blow, box, clout, cuff, hit, knock, punch, skelp, slap, smack, sock, thump, wallop, whack.

clip[3] *n.* gallop, lick, rate, speed.

clip[4] *v.* attach, fasten, fix, hold, pin, staple.

cloak *n.* blind, cape, coat, cover, front, mantle, mask, pretext, shield, wrap.
v. camouflage, conceal, cover, disguise, hide, mask, obscure, screen, veil.

clog *v.* ball, block, burden, congest, dam up, gaum, hamper, hinder, impede, jam, obstruct, occlude, shackle, stop up, stuff.
antonym unblock.
n. burden, dead-weight, drag, encumbrance, hindrance, impediment, obstruction.

cloistered *adj.* cloistral, confined, enclosed, hermitic, insulated, protected, reclusive, restricted, secluded, sequestered, sheltered, shielded, withdrawn.
antonyms open, urbane.

close[1] *v.* bar, block, cease, choke, clog, cloture, complete, conclude, confine, connect, cork, couple, culminate, discontinue, end, fill, finish, fuse, grapple, join, lock, mothball, obstruct, plug, seal, secure, shut, stop, terminate, unite, wind up.
n. cadence, cessation, completion, conclusion, culmination, denouement, end, ending, finale, finish, junction, pause, stop, termination, wind-up.

close[2] *adj.* accurate, adjacent, adjoining, airless, alert, approaching, approximative, assiduous, at hand, attached, attentive, careful, compact, concentrated, confidential, confined, congested, conscientious, cramped, cropped, crowded, dear, dense, detailed, devoted, dogged, earnest, exact, faithful, familiar, fixed, frowsty, fuggy, handy, hard by, heavy, hidden, humid, illiberal, imminent, impending, impenetrable, inseparable, intense, intent, intimate, jam-packed, keen, literal, loving, mean, mingy, minute, miserly, muggy, narrow, near, near-by, neighboring, niggardly, nigh, oppressive, packed, painstaking, parsimonious, penurious, precise, private, reserved, reticent, retired, rigorous, searching, secluded, secret, secretive, short, solid, stale, stifling, stingy, strict, stuffy, suffocating, sweltering, taciturn, thick, thorough, tight, tight-fisted, uncommunicative, unforthcoming, ungenerous, unventilated.
antonyms careless, cool, far, unfriendly.

cloth *n.* dish-cloth, duster, fabric, face-cloth, material, rag, stuff, textiles, tissue, towel.

clothe *v.* accouter, apparel, array, attire, bedizen, caparison, cover, deck, drape, dress, enclothe, endow, enwarp, equip, garb, habilitate, habit, invest, outfit, rig, robe, swathe, vest.
antonyms unclothe, undress.

clothes *n.* apparel, attire, clobber, clothing, costume, dress, duds, ensemble, garb, garments, garmenture, gear, getup, habiliments, habit(s), outfit, raiment, rig-out, threads, toggery, togs, vestiture, vestments, vesture, wardrobe, wear, weeds.

cloud *n.* billow, crowd, darkness, flock, fog, gloom, haze, horde, host, mist, multitude, murk, nebula, nebulosity, obscurity, shower, swarm, throng, vapor, water-dog, weft, woolpack.
v. becloud, confuse, darken, defame, dim, disorient, distort, dull, eclipse, impair, muddle, obfuscate, obscure, overcast, overshadow, shade, shadow, stain, veil.
antonym clear.

cloudy *adj.* blurred, blurry, confused, dark, dim, dismal, dull, emulsified, hazy, indistinct, leaden, lightless, lowering, muddy, murky, nebulous, nubilous, obscure, opaque, overcast, somber, sullen, sunless.
antonyms clear, sunny.

club[1] *n.* bat, bludgeon, cosh, cudgel, mace, mere, stick, truncheon, waddy.
v. bash, baste, batter, beat, bludgeon, clobber, clout, cosh, hammer, hit, pummel, strike.

club[2] *n.* association, bunch, circle, clique, combination, company, fraternity, group, guild, lodge, order, set, society, sodality, union.

clue *n.* clavis, evidence, hint, idea, indication, inkling, intimation, lead, notion, pointer, sign, suggestion, suspicion, tip, tip-off, trace.

clumsy *adj.* awkward, blundering, bumbling, bungling, cack-handed, chuckle, clumping, crude, gauche, gawky, ham-fisted, ham-handed, heavy, hulking, ill-made, inept, inexpert, lubber, lubberly, lumbering, maladroit, ponderous, rough, shapeless, squab, unco-ordinated,

uncouth, ungainly, ungraceful, unhandy, unskilful, unwieldy.
antonym graceful.

cluster *n.* assemblage, batch, bunch, clump, collection, gathering, glomeration, group, knot, mass.
v. assemble, bunch, collect, flock, gather, group.

clutch *v.* catch, clasp, embrace, fasten, grab, grapple, grasp, grip, hang on to, seize, snatch.

coalition *n.* affiliation, alliance, amalgam, amalgamation, association, bloc, coadunation, combination, compact, confederacy, confederation, conjunction, federation, fusion, integration, league, merger, union.

coarse *adj.* bawdy, blowzy, boorish, brutish, coarse-grained, crude, earthly, foul-mouthed, homespun, immodest, impolite, improper, impure, indelicate, inelegant, loutish, mean, offensive, Rabelaisian, ribald, rough, rude, smutty, Sotadic, uncivil, unfinished, unpolished, unprocessed, unpurified, unrefined, vulgar.
antonyms fine, polite, refined, sophisticated.

coast *n.* coastline, littoral, seaboard, seaside, shore.
v. cruise, drift, free-wheel, glide, sail.

coax *v.* allure, beguile, cajole, decoy, entice, flatter, inveigle, persuade, soft-soap, sweet-talk, wheedle, whilly, whilly-wha(w), wile.
antonym force.

coddle *v.* baby, cocker, cosset, humor, indulge, mollycoddle, nurse, pamper, pet, spoil.

code *n.* canon, cipher, convention, cryptograph, custom, ethics, etiquette, manners, maxim, regulations, rules, system.
v. encipher, encode.

coerce *v.* bludgeon, browbeat, bulldoze, bully, compel, constrain, dragoon, drive, drum, force, intimidate, pressgang, pressurize.
antonyms coax, persuade.

coercion *n.* browbeating, bullying, compulsion, constraint, direct action, duress, force, intimidation, pressure, threats.
antonym persuasion.

cognizance *n.* acknowledgment, apprehension, cognition, knowledge, notice, perception, percipience, recognition, regard.
antonym unawareness.

cognizant *adj.* acquainted, aware, conscious, conversant, familiar, informed, knowledgeable, versed, witting.
antonym unaware.

coherent *adj.* articulate, comprehensible, consistent, intelligible, logical, lucid, meaningful, orderly, organized, rational, reasoned, sensible, systematic.

coincide *v.* accord, agree, co-exist, concur, correspond, harmonize, match, square, tally.

coincidence *n.* accident, chance, concomitance, concurrence, conjunction, correlation, correspondence, eventuality, fluke, fortuity, luck, synchronism.

coincidental *adj.* accident, casual, chance, coincident, concomitant, concurrent, fluky, fortuitous, lucky, simultaneous, synchronous, unintentional, unplanned.
antonyms deliberate, planned.

cold *adj.* agued, algid, aloof, apathetic, arctic, benumbed, biting, bitter, bleak, brumal, chill, chilled, chilly, cold-blooded, cool, dead, distant, freezing, frigid, frosty, frozen, gelid, glacial, icy, inclement, indifferent, inhospitable, lukewarm, numbed, parky, passionless, phlegmatic, raw, reserved, shivery, spiritless, stand-offish, stony, undemonstrative, unfeeling, unfriendly, unheated, unmoved, unresponsive, unsympathetic, wintry.
antonyms friendly, warm.
n. catarrh, chill, chilliness, coldness, frigidity, frostiness, hypothermia, iciness, inclemency.
antonyms friendliness, warmth.

cold fish iceberg.

collapse *v.* crumple, fail, faint, fall, fold, founder, peg out, sink, subside.
n. breakdown, cave-in, crash, debacle (débâcle), detumescence, disintegration, downfall, exhaustion, failure, faint, flop, subsidence.

colleague *n.* aide, aider, ally, assistant, associate, auxiliary, bedfellow, coadjutor, collaborator, companion, comrade, confederate, confrère, helper, partner, teammate, workmate.

collect *v.* accumulate, acquire, aggregate, amass, assemble, cluster, congregate, convene, converge, forgather, gather, gather together, heap, hoard, muster, obtain, raise, rally, save, secure, stockpile, uplift.

collected *adj.* assembled, calm, composed, confident, cool, efficient, gathered, imperturbable, placid, poised, self-possessed, serene, together, unperturbed, unruffled.
antonyms disorganized, dithery, worried.

collection *n.* accumulation, anthology, assemblage, assembly, assortment, caboodle, cluster, company, compilation, congeries, conglomerate, conglomeration, congregation, convocation, crowd, festschrift, gathering, group, harvesting, heap, hoard, ingathering, inning, jingbang, job-lot, mass, pile, set, spicilege, stockpile, store, whip-round.

collective *adj.* aggregate, combined, common, composite, concerted, congregated, co-operative, corporate, cumulative, joint, shared, unified, united.
n. aggregate, assemblage, corporation, gathering, group.

collision *n.* accident, bump, clash, clashing, conflict, confrontation, crash, encounter, impact, opposition, pile-up, prang, rencounter, skirmish, smash.

collusion *n.* artifice, cahoots, coactivity, complicity, connivance, conspiracy, craft, deceit, fraudulent, intrigue.

color[1] *n.* animation, appearance, bloom, blush, brilliance, chroma, colorant, coloration, complexion, disguise, dye, façade, flush, glow, guise, hue, liveliness, paint, pigment, pigmentation, plausibility, pretense, pretext,

race, reason, rosiness, ruddiness, semblance, shade, timbre, tincture, tinge, tint, variety, vividness, wash, water-color.
v. blush, burn, colorwash, disguise, distort, dye, embroider, encolor, exaggerate, falsify, flush, misrepresent, paint, pervert, prejudice, redden, slant, stain, strain, taint, tinge, tint.

color[2] *n.* colors, ensign, flag, standard.

color-blind *adj.* dichromatic.

colorful *adj.* bright, brilliant, distinctive, graphic, intense, interesting, jazzy, kaleidoscopic, lively, motley, multicolored, parti-colored, picturesque, psychedelic, rich, stimulating, unusual, variegated, vibrant, vivid.
antonyms colorless, drab, plain.

coma *n.* catalepsy, drowsiness, hypnosis, insensibility, lethargy, oblivion, somnolence, sopor, stupor, torpor, trance, unconsciousness.

combat *n.* action, battle, bout, clash, conflict, contest, duel, encounter, engagement, fight, hostilities, j(i)u-jitsu, judo, karate, kendo, kung fu, skirmish, struggle, war, warfare.
v. battle, contend, contest, defy, engage, fight, oppose, resist, strive, struggle, withstand.

combination *n.* alliance, amalgam, amalgamation, association, blend, cabal, cartel, coalescence, coalition, combine, composite, composition, compound, confederacy, confederation, conjunction, connection, consortium, conspiracy, federation, meld, merger, mix, mixture, syndicate, unification, union.

combine *v.* amalgamate, associate, bind, blend, bond, coadunate, compound, conjoin, connect, cooperate, fuse, incorporate, integrate, join, link, marry, meld, merge, mix, peace, pool, sythesize, unify, unite.
antonym separate.

come *v.* advance, appear, approach, arrive, attain, become, draw near, ejaculate, enter, happen, materialize, move, near, occur, originate, reach.
antonyms depart, go, leave.

comedian *n.* card, clown, comic, droll, funny man, gagster, humorist, jester, joker, jokesmith, laugh, wag, wit.

comely *adj.* attractive, beautiful, becoming, blooming, bonny, buxom, callipygian, callipygous, decent, decorous, fair, fit, fitting, gainly, good-looking, graceful, handsome, lovely, pleasing, pretty, proper, pulchritudinous, seemly, suitable, wholesome, winsome.

come-uppance *n.* chastening, deserts, dues, merit, punishment, rebuke, recompense, requital, retribution.

comfort *v.* alleviate, assuage, cheer, console, ease, encheer, encourage, enliven, gladden, hearten, inspirit, invigorate, reassure, refresh, relieve, solace, soothe, strengthen.
n. aid, alleviation, cheer, compensation, consolation, cosiness, ease, easy street, encouragement, enjoyment, help, luxury, opulence, relief, satisfaction, snugness, succor, support, well-being.
antonyms distress, torment.

comfortable *adj.* adequate, affluent, agreeable, ample, canny, commodious, contented, convenient, cosy, delightful, easy, enjoyable, gemütlich, gratified, happy, homely, loose, loose-fitting, pleasant, prosperous, relaxed, relaxing, restful, roomy, serene, snug, well-off, well-to-do.
antonyms poor, uncomfortable.

comical *adj.* absurd, amusing, comic, diverting, droll, entertaining, farcical, funny, hilarious, humorous, laughable, ludicrous, priceless, ridiculous, risible, side-splitting, silly, whimsical.
antonyms sad, unamusing.

command *v.* bid, charge, compel, control, demand, direct, dominate, enjoin, govern, head, lead, manage, order, reign over, require, rule, supervise, sway.
n. authority, behest, bidding, charge, commandment, control, decree, dictation, diktat, direction, directive, domination, dominion, edict, fiat, government, grasp, injunction, instruction, management, mandate, mastery, order, power, precept, requirement, rule, supervision, sway, ukase, ultimatum.

commandeer *v.* appropriate, confiscate, expropriate, hijack, requisition, seize, sequester, sequestrate, usurp.

commanding *adj.* advantageous, assertive, authoritative, autocratic, compelling, controlling, decisive, dominant, dominating, forceful, imposing, impressive, peremptory, superior.

commando *n.* fedayee, Green Beret, soldier.

commence *v.* begin, embark on, inaugurate, initiate, open, originate, start.
antonyms cease, finish.

commend *v.* acclaim, applaud, approve, commit, compliment, confide, consign, deliver, entrust, eulogize, extol, praise, recommend, yield.
antonym criticize.

commendable *adj.* admirable, creditable, deserving, estimable, excellent, exemplary, laudable, meritorious, noble, praiseworthy, worthy.
antonyms blameworthy, poor.

commendation *n.* acclaim, acclamation, accolade, applause, approbation, approval, credit, encomium, encouragement, panegyric, praise, recommendation.
antonyms blame, criticism.

commensurate *adj.* acceptable, adequate, appropriate, coextensive, comparable, compatible, consistent, corresponding, due, equivalent, fitting, just, meet, proportionate, sufficient.
antonym inappropriate.

comment *v.* animadvert, annotate, criticize, descant, elucidate, explain, gloss, interpose, interpret, mention, note, observe, opine, remark, say.
n. animadversion, annotation, commentary, criticism, elucidation, explanation, exposition, footnote, illustration, marginal note, marginalia, note, observation, remark, statement.

commerce *n.* business, communication, dealing(s), exchange, intercourse, merchandising, relations, trade, traffic.

commission *n.* allowance, appointment, authority, board, brokerage, brok(er)age, charge, committee, compensation, cut, delegation, deputation, duty, employment, errand, fee, function, mandate, mission, percentage, rake-off, representative, task, trust, warrant.
v. appoint, ask for, authorize, contract, delegate, depute, empower, engage, nominate, order, request, select, send.

commit *v.* align, bind, commend, compromise, confide, confine, consign, deliver, deposit, do, enact, endanger, engage, entrust, execute, give, imprison, involve, obligate, perform, perpetrate, pledge.

commitment *n.* adherence, assurance, dedication, devotion, duty, engagement, guarantee, involvement, liability, loyalty, obligation, pledge, promise, responsibility, tie, undertaking, vow, word.

committee *n.* advisory group, board, cabinet, commission, council, jury, panel, table, task force, think-tank, working party.

commodious *adj.* ample, capacious, comfortable, expansive, extensive, large, loose, roomy, spacious.
antonym cramped.

commodities *n.* goods, merchandise, output, produce, products, stock, things, wares.

common *adj.* accepted, average, coarse, collective, commonplace, communal, conventional, customary, daily, everyday, familiar, flat, frequent, general, habitual, hackneyed, humdrum, inferior, low, mutual, obscure, ordinary, pedestrian, plain, plebby, plebeian, popular, prevailing, prevalent, public, regular, routine, run-of-the-mill, simple, social, stale, standard, stock, trite, tritical, undistinguished, unexceptional, universal, usual, vulgar, widespread, workaday.
antonyms noteworthy, uncommon.

commonplace *adj.* common, customary, everyday, humdrum, obvious, ordinary, pedestrian, quotidian, stale, threadbare, trite, uninteresting, widespread, worn out.
antonyms exceptional, rare.
n. banality, cliché, platitude, truism.

common-sense *adj.* astute, common-sensical, down-to-earth, hard-headed, judicious, level-headed, matter-of-fact, practical, pragmatical, realistic, reasonable, sane, sensible, shrewd, sound.
antonym foolish.

commotion *n.* ado, agitation, ballyhoo, bobbery, brouhaha, burst-up, bustle, bust-up, carfuffle, disorder, disturbance, excitement, ferment, fracas, furore, fuss, hubbub, hullabaloo, hurly-burly, perturbation, pother, pudder, racket, riot, rumpus, to-do, toss, tumult, turmoil, uproar.

communicable *adj.* catching, contagious, conveyable, impartible, infectious, infective, spreadable, transferable, transmittable.

communicate *v.* acquaint, announce, bestow, connect, contact, convey, correspond, declare, diffuse, disclose, disseminate, divulge, impart, inform, intimate, notify, proclaim, promulgate, publish, report, reveal, signify, spread, transmit, unfold.

communication *n.* announcement, bulletin, communiqué, connection, contact, conversation, converse, correspondence, disclosure, dispatch, dissemination, information, intelligence, intercourse, intimation, message, news, promulgation, report, statement, transmission, word.

communicative *adj.* candid, chatty, conversable, conversational, expansive, extrovert, forthcoming, frank, free, friendly, informative, loquacious, open, outgoing, sociable, talkative, unreserved, voluble.
antonym reticent.

communion *n.* accord, affinity, agreement, closeness, communing, concord, converse, empathy, Eucharist, fellow-feeling, fellowship, harmony, Holy Communion, housel, intercourse, Lord's Supper, Mass, participation, rapport, Sacrament, sympathy, togetherness, unity.

community *n.* affinity, agreement, association, body politic, brotherhood, coincidence, colony, commonness, commonwealth, company, concurrence, confraternity, confrèrie, correspondence, district, fellowship, fraternity, identity, kibbutz, kindredness, likeness, locality, nest, people, populace, population, public, residents, sameness, similarity, society, state.

compact[1] *adj.* brief, close, compendious, compressed, concise, condensed, dense, firm, impenetrable, solid, stocky, succinct, thick, well-knit.
antonyms diffuse, rambling, rangy.
v. compress, condense, consolidate, cram, flatten, ram, squeeze, tamp.

compact[2] *n.* agreement, alliance, arrangement, bargain, bond, concordat, contract, covenant, deal, entente, pact, settlement, treaty, understanding.

companion *n.* accomplice, aide, ally, assistant, associate, attendant, attender, buddy, chaperon, cohort, colleague, compeer, complement, comrade, confederate, confidant, confidante, consort, counterpart, crony, duenna, escort, fellow, follower, friend, intimate, mate, partner, satellite, shadow, squire, twin.

companionship *n.* camaraderie, companionhood, company, comradeship, confraternity, consociation, conviviality, esprit de corps, fellowship, fraternity, friendship, rapport, support, sympathy, togetherness.

company[1] *n.* assemblage, assembly, association, band, body, business, cartel, circle, collection, community, concern, concourse, consociation, consortium, convention, corporation, coterie, crew, crowd, ensemble, establishment, firm, fraternity, gathering, group, house, league, line, partnership, party, set, set-out, syndicate, throng, troop, troupe.

company[2] *n.* attendance, callers, companionhood,

companionship, fellowship, guests, party, presence, society, support, visitors.

comparable *adj.* akin, alike, analogous, cognate, commensurate, correspondent, corresponding, equal, equivalent, kindred, parallel, proportionate, related, similar, tantamount.
antonym unlike.

compare *v.* balance, collate, confront, contrast, correlate, emulate, equal, equate, juxtapose, liken, match, parallel, resemble, similize, vie, weigh.

comparison *n.* analogy, collation, comparability, contrast, correlation, distinction, juxtaposition, likeness, parallel, parallelism, resemblance, similarity, similitude.

compartment *n.* alcove, area, bay, berth, booth, box, carrel, carriage, category, cell, chamber, cubby-hole, cubicle, department, division, locker, niche, pigeonhole, section, stall, subdivision.

compassion *n.* charity, clemency, commiseration, concern, condolence, fellow-feeling, heart, humanity, kindness, loving-kindness, mercy, pity, ruth, sorrow, sympathy, tenderness, understanding, weltschmerz, yearning.
antonym indifference.

compassionate *adj.* benevolent, caring, charitable, clement, humane, humanitarian, indulgent, kind-hearted, kindly, lenient, merciful, piteous, pitying, supportive, sympathetic, tender, tender-hearted, understanding, warm-hearted.
antonym indifferent.

compatibility *n.* accord, affinity, agreement, amity, concord, congeniality, consistency, consonance, correspondence, empathy, fellowship, harmony, like-mindedness, rapport, reconcilability, sympathy, understanding, unity.
antonyms antagonism, antipathy, incompatibility.

compatible *adj.* accordant, adaptable, agreeable, conformable, congenial, congruent, congruous, consistent, consonant, harmonious, kindred, like-minded, reconcilable, suitable, sympathetic.
antonyms antagonistic, antipathetic, incompatible.

compel *v.* browbeat, bulldoze, bully, coact, coerce, constrain, dragoon, drive, enforce, exact, force, hustle, impel, make, necessitate, obligate, oblige, press-gang, pressurize, strongarm, urge.

compensate *v.* atone, balance, cancel, counteract, counterbalance, countervail, expiate, guerdon, indemnify, offset, recompense, recover, recuperate, redeem, redress, refund, reimburse, remunerate, repay, requite, restore, reward, satisfy.

compensation *n.* amends, atonement, comfort, consolation, damages, guerdon, indemnification, indemnity, payment, quittance, recompense, redress, refund, reimbursement, remuneration, reparation, repayment, requital, restitution, restoration, return, reward, satisfaction, solatium.

compete *v.* battle, challenge, contend, contest, duel, emulate, fight, oppose, rival, strive, struggle, tussle, vie.

competence *n.* ability, adequacy, appropriateness, aptitude, capability, capacity, competency, experience, expertise, facility, fitness, proficiency, skill, suitability, technique.
antonym incompetence.

competent *adj.* able, adapted, adequate, appropriate, belonging, capable, clever, efficient, endowed, equal, fit, legitimate, masterly, pertinent, proficient, qualified, satisfactory, strong, sufficient, suitable, trained, well-qualified.
antonym incompetent.

competition *n.* challenge, challengers, championship, combativeness, competitiveness, competitors, contention, contest, corrivalry, cup, emulation, event, field, match, opposition, quiz, race, rivalry, rivals, series, strife, struggle, tournament, tourney, trial.

competitor *n.* adversary, agonist, antagonist, challenger, competition, contender, contestant, corrival, emulator, entrant, opponent, opposition, rival.

complain *v.* beef, belly-ache, bemoan, bewail, bind, bitch, bleat, carp, deplore, fuss, girn, grieve, gripe, groan, grouse, growl, grumble, kvetch, lament, moan, squeal, whine, whinge.

complaint[1] *n.* accusation, annoyance, beef, belly-ache, bitch, bleat, censure, charge, criticism, dissatisfaction, fault-finding, girn, gravamen, grievance, gripe, grouse, grumble, lament, moan, nit-picking, plaint, querimony, remonstrance, squawk, stricture, wail, whinge, winge.

complaint[2] *n.* affliction, ailment, disease, disorder, illness, indisposition, malady, malaise, sickness, trouble, upset.

complement *n.* aggregate, capacity, companion, completion, consummation, counterpart, entirety, fellow, quota, sum, supplement, total, totality, wholeness.

complete *adj.* absolute, accomplished, achieved, all, concluded, consummate, ended, entire, equipped, faultless, finished, full, intact, integral, integrate, out-and-out, perfect, plenary, root-and-branch, self-contained, thorough, thoroughgoing, thorough-paced, total, unabbreviated, unabridged, unbroken, uncut, undivided, unedited, unexpurgated, unimpaired, utter, whole, whole-hog.
antonyms imperfect, incomplete.
v. accomplish, achieve, cap, clinch, close, conclude, consummate, crown, discharge, do, effect, end, execute, finalize, finish, fulfil, perfect, perform, realize, settle, terminate, wind up.

completion *n.* accomplishment, achievement, attainment, close, conclusion, consummation, crowning, culmination, discharge, end, expiration, finalization, finish, fruition, fulfilment, perfection, plenitude, realization, settlement, telos, termination.

complex *adj.* ambagious, Byzantine, circuitous, complicated, composite, compound, compounded, convoluted, Daedalian, devious, diverse, elaborate, heterogeneous, intricate, involved, knotty, labyrinthine, manifold,

mingled, mixed, multifarious, multipartite, multiple, plexiform, polymerous, ramified, tangled, tortuous.
antonym simple.
n. aggregate, composite, establishment, fixation, hang-up, idée fixe, institute, network, obsession, organization, phobia, preoccupation, scheme, structure, syndrome, synthesis, system.

complexion *n.* appearance, aspect, cast, character, color, coloring, composition, countenance, disposition, guise, hue, kind, light, look, make-up, nature, pigmentation, rud, skin, stamp, temperament, type.

compliant *adj.* accommodating, acquiescent, agreeable, amenable, biddable, complaisant, conformable, deferential, docile, obedient, obliging, passive, submissive, tractable, yielding.
antonyms disobedient, intractable.

complicated *adj.* ambivalent, baroque, Byzantine, complex, convoluted, devious, difficult, elaborate, entangled, intricate, involved, labyrinthine, perplexing, problematic, puzzling, rigmarole, tangled, tortuous, troublesome.
antonyms easy, simple.

compliment *n.* accolade, admiration, bouquet, commendation, congratulations, courtesy, douceur, encomium, eulogy, favor, felicitation, flattery, honor, plaudit, praise, tribute.
antonyms criticism, insult.
v. admire, applaud, commend, congratulate, eulogize, extol, felicitate, flatter, laud, praise, salute.
antonyms condemn, insult.

complimentary *adj.* admiring, appreciative, approving, commendatory, congratulatory, courtesy, encomiastic, eulogistic, favorable, flattering, free, gratis, honorary, laudatory, panegyrical.
antonyms critical, insulting, unflattering.

comply *v.* accede, accommodate, accord, acquiesce, agree, assent, conform, consent, defer, discharge, fall in, follow, fulfil, obey, oblige, observe, perform, respect, satisfy, submit, yield.
antonyms disobey, resist.

component *n.* bit, constituent, element, factor, ingredient, item, part, piece, spare part, unit.

comport *v.* acquit, act, bear, behave, carry, conduct, demean, deport, perform.

compose *v.* adjust, arrange, build, calm, collect, compound, comprise, constitute, construct, contrive, control, create, devise, fashion, form, frame, govern, imagine, indite, invent, make, meditate the muse, pacify, produce, quell, quiet, recollect, reconcile, regulate, resolve, settle, soothe, still, structure, tranquilize, write.

composed *adj.* calm, collected, complacent, confident, cool, imperturbable, level-headed, placid, poised, relaxed, self-possessed, serene, together, tranquil, unflappable, unruffled, unworried.
antonym agitated.

composer *n.* arranger, author, bard, creator, maker, originator, poet, songsmith, songwriter, tunesmith, writer.

composition *n.* arrangement, balance, combination, compilation, compromise, concord, confection, configuration, congruity, consonance, constitution, creation, design, essay, exaration, exercise, form, formation, formulation, harmony, invention, lay-out, lucubration, make-up, making, mixture, opus, organization, piece, placing, production, proportion, structure, study, symmetry, work, writing.

composure *n.* aplomb, assurance, calm, calmness, confidence, cool, coolness, dignity, dispassion, ease, equanimity, impassivity, imperturbability, placidity, poise, sang-froid, savoir-faire, sedateness, self-assurance, self-possession, serenity, tranquility.
antonym discomposure.

compound *v.* aggravate, alloy, amalgamate, augment, blend, coalesce, combine, complicate, compose, concoct, exacerbate, fuse, heighten, increase, intensify, intermingle, magnify, mingle, mix, synthesize, unite, worsen.
n. alloy, amalgam, amalgamation, blend, combination, composite, composition, confection, conglomerate, conglomeration, fusion, medley, mixture, synthesis.
adj. complex, complicated, composite, conglomerate, intricate, mixed, multiple.

comprehend *v.* appreciate, apprehend, assimilate, compass, comprise, conceive, cover, discern, embrace, encompass, fathom, grasp, include, know, penetrate, perceive, see, see daylight, tumble to, twig, understand.
antonym misunderstand.

comprehension *n.* appreciation, apprehension, capacity, conception, discernment, grasp, intellection, intelligence, intension, judgment, knowledge, perception, realization, sense, understanding.
antonym incomprehension.

comprehensive *adj.* across-the-board, all-embracing, all-inclusive, blanket, broad, catholic, compendious, complete, encyclopedic, exhaustive, extensive, full, general, inclusive, omnibus, sweeping, thorough, wide.
antonyms incomplete, selective.

compress *v.* abbreviate, astrict, astringe, compact, concentrate, condense, constrict, contract, cram, crowd, crush, flatten, impact, jam, précis, press, shorten, squash, squeeze, stuff, summarize, synopsize, telescope, wedge.
antonyms diffuse, expand, separate.

comprise *v.* comprehend, consist of, contain, cover, embody, embrace, encompass, include, incorporate, involve, subsume.

compromise[1] *v.* adapt, adjust, agree, arbitrate, bargain, concede, make concessions, negotiate, retire, retreat, settle.
antonyms differ, quarrel.
n. accommodation, accord, adjustment, agreement,

bargain, concession, co-operation, settlement, trade-off, via media.
antonyms disagreement, intransigence.

compulsion *n.* coercion, constraint, demand, distress, drive, duress, exigency, force, impulse, necessity, need, obligation, obsession, preoccupation, pressure, urge, urgency.
antonyms freedom, liberty.

compulsory *adj.* binding, de rigueur, forced, imperative, mandatory, obligatory, required, requisite, stipulated, stipulatory.
antonyms optional, voluntary.

compute *v.* assess, calculate, count, enumerate, estimate, evaluate, figure, measure, rate, reckon, sum, tally, total.

computer *n.* adding machine, analog computer, calculator, data processor, digital computer, mainframe, processor, word processor.

comrade *n.* Achates, ally, associate, brother, buddy, bully-rook, butty, china, cobber, colleague, companion, compatriot, compeer, confederate, co-worker, crony, fellow, frater, friend, mate, pal, partner, sidekick.

con *v.* bamboozle, beguile, bilk, bluff, bunko, cheat, cozen, deceive, defraud, double-cross, dupe, fiddle, grift, gull, hoax, hoodwink, humbug, inveigle, mislead, racket, rip off, rook, swindle, trick.
n. bluff, deception, fraud, grift, kidology, scam, swindle, trick.

conceal *v.* bury, camouflage, cloak, cover, disguise, dissemble, hide, keep dark, mask, obscure, screen, secrete, shelter, sink, smother, submerge, suppress, veil.
antonym reveal.

concede *v.* accept, acknowledge, admit, allow, cede, confess, forfeit, grant, own, recognize, relinquish, sacrifice, surrender, yield.
antonyms deny, dispute.

conceit[1] *n.* arrogance, assumption, cockiness, complacency, conceitedness, egotism, narcissism, pride, self-assumption, self-conceit, self-importance, self-love, self-pride, self-satisfaction, swagger, vainglory, vainness, vanity.
antonyms diffidence, modesty.

conceit[2] *n.* belief, caprice, concetto, fancy, fantasy, freak, humor, idea, image, imagination, impulse, jeu d'esprit, judgment, notion, opinion, quip, quirk, thought, vagary, whim, whimsy, wit.

conceited *adj.* arrogant, assuming, bigheaded, cocky, complacent, egotistical, highty-tighty, hoity-toity, immodest, narcissistic, overweening, self-important, self-satisfied, stuck-up, swell-headed, swollen-headed, toffee-nose(d), uppist, uppity, vain, vainglorious, windy.
antonyms diffident, modest.

conceive *v.* appreciate, apprehend, believe, comprehend, contrive, create, design, develop, devise, envisage, fancy, form, formulate, germinate, grasp, ideate, imagine, invent, originate, produce, project, purpose, realize, suppose, think, understand, visualize.

concentrate *v.* absorb, accumulate, attend, attract, center, cluster, collect, condense, congregate, converge, crowd, draw, engross, focus, foregather, gather, huddle, intensify.
antonyms disperse, distract, separate.
n. apozem, decoction, decocture, distillate, distillation, elixir, essence, extract, juice, quintessence.

concentrated *adj.* all-out, compact, condensed, deep, dense, evaporated, hard, intense, intensive, reduced, rich, thickened, undiluted.
antonyms desultory, diffuse, diluted.

concept *n.* abstraction, conception, conceptualization, construct, hyphothesis, idea, image, impression, invention, notion, pattern, picture, plan, theory, type, view, visualization.

conception *n.* appreciation, apprehension, beginning, birth, clue, comprehension, concept, design, envisagement, fertilization, formation, germination, idea, image, impregnation, impression, inauguration, inception, initiation, inkling, insemination, invention, knowledge, launching, notion, origin, outset, perception, picture, plan, understanding, visualization.

concern *v.* affect, bother, disquiet, distress, disturb, interest, involve, pertain to, perturb, refer to, regard, relate to, touch, trouble, upset, worry.
n. affair, anxiety, apprehension, attention, bearing, burden, business, care, charge, company, consideration, corporation, disquiet, disquietude, distress, enterprise, establishment, field, firm, heed, house, importance, interest, involvement, job, matter, mission, occupation, organization, perturbation, reference, relation, relevance, responsibility, solicitude, stake, task, transaction, unease, uneasiness, worry.
antonym unconcern.

concerning *prep.* about, anent, apropos of, as regards, germane to, in regard to, in the matter of, re, regarding, relating to, relevant to, respecting, touching, with reference to, with regard to.

concerted *adj.* collaborative, collective, combined, co-ordinated, joint, organized, planned, prearranged, shared, united.
antonyms disorganized, separate, unco-ordinated.

concession *n.* acknowledgment, adjustment, admission, allowance, assent, boon, compromise, exception, favor, grant, indulgence, permit, privilege, relaxation, sacrifice, surrender, yielding.

concise *adj.* abbreviated, abridged, aphoristic, brief, compact, compendious, compressed, condensed, epigrammatic, gnomic, laconic, pithy, short, succinct, summary, synoptic, terse, thumbnail.
antonyms diffuse, expansive.

conclude *v.* accomplish, assume, cease, clinch, close, complete, consummate, culminate, decide, deduce, determine, effect, end, establish, finish, fix, gather, infer, judge, opine, reckon, resolve, settle, suppose, surmise, terminate.

concluding *adj.* closing, epilogic, epilogistic, final, last, perorating, terminal, ultimate.
antonym introductory.

conclusion *n.* answer, assumption, clincher, close, come-off, completion, consequence, consummation, conviction, culmination, decision, deduction, end, explicit, finale, fine, finis, finish, illation, inference, issue, judgment, opinion, outcome, resolution, result, settlement, solution, termination, upshot, verdict.

conclusive *adj.* clear, clinching, convincing, decisive, definite, definitive, final, incontrovertible, irrefragable, irrefutable, manifest, ultimate, unanswerable, unappealable, unarguable, undeniable.
antonym inconclusive.

concord *n.* accord, agreement, amicability, amity, brotherliness, compact, concert, concordat, consensus, consonance, convention, diapason, entente, friendship, harmony, peace, protocol, rapport, treaty, unanimity, unison.
antonym discord.

concrete *adj.* actual, calcified, compact, compressed, conglomerated, consolidated, definite, explicit, factual, firm, material, perceptible, petrified, physical, real, seeable, sensible, solid, solidified, specific, substantial, tactile, tangible, touchable, visible.
antonym abstract.

concur *v.* accede, accord, acquiesce, agree, approve, assent, coincide, combine, comply, consent, co-operate, harmonize, join, meet, unite.
antonym disagree.

condemn *v.* ban, blame, castigate, censure, convict, damn, decry, denounce, disapprove, disparage, doom, pan, proscribe, reprehend, reproach, reprobate, reprove, revile, sentence, slam, slate, upbraid.
antonyms approve, praise.

condense *v.* abbreviate, abridge, capsulize, coagulate, compact, compress, concentrate, contract, crystallize, curtail, decoct, distil, encapsulate, epitomize, evaporate, inspissate, precipitate, précis, reduce, shorten, solidify, summarize, synopsize, thicken.
antonyms dilute, expand.

condition *n.* ailment, arrangement, article, case, caste, circumstances, class, complaint, defect, demand, diathesis, disease, disorder, estate, fettle, fitness, grade, health, infirmity, kilter, level, liability, limitation, malady, modification, nick, obligation, order, plight, position, predicament, prerequisite, problem, provision, proviso, qualification, rank, requirement, requisite, restriction, rule, shape, situation, state, status, stipulation, stratum, terms, trim, understanding, weakness.
v. accustom, adapt, adjust, attune, determine, educate, equip, groom, habituate, hone, indoctrinate, inure, limit, prepare, prime, ready, restrict, season, temper, train, tune.

conditional *adj.* contingent, dependent, limited, provisional, qualified, relative, restricted, tied.
antonym unconditional.

condolence *n.* commiseration, compassion, condolences, consolation, pity, support, sympathy.
antonym congratulation.

conduct *n.* actions, administration, attitude, bearing, behavior, carriage, comportment, control, co-ordination, demeanor, deportment, direction, discharge, escort, guidance, guide, leadership, management, manners, mien, orchestration, organization, running, supervision, ways.
v. accompany, acquit, act, administer, attend, bear, behave, carry, chair, comport, control, convey, demean, deport, direct, escort, govern, guide, handle, lead, manage, orchestrate, organize, pilot, regulate, run, solicit, steer, supervise, transact, usher.

confederate *adj.* allied, associated, combined, federal, federated.
n. abettor, accessory, accomplice, ally, assistant, associate, collaborator, colleague, conspirator, friend, leaguer, partner, practisant, supporter.
v. ally, amalgamate, associate, bind, combine, federate, join, merge, unite, weld.

confer *v.* accord, award, bestow, consult, converse, deliberate, discourse, discuss, give, grant, impart, lay heads together, lend, parley, powwow, present, talk, vouchsafe.

confess *v.* acknowledge, admit, affirm, agnize, allow, assert, attest, aver, betray, concede, confide, confirm, declare, disclose, divulge, evince, expose, grant, manifest, own, own up, profess, prove, recognize, reveal, show.
antonyms conceal, deny.

confession *n.* acknowledgment, admission, affirmation, assertion, attestation, averment, avowal, confidences, confiteor, declaration, disclosure, divulgence, exposé, exposure, profession, revelation, unbosoming, unburdening, verbal.
antonyms concealment, denial.

confidence *n.* aplomb, assurance, belief, boldness, calmness, communication, composure, confession, coolness, courage, credence, dependence, disclosure, divulgence, faith, firmness, nerve, reliance, savoir-faire, secret, self-assurance, self-confidence, self-possession, self-reliance, trust.
antonyms diffidence, distrust.

confident *adj.* assured, bold, certain, composed, convinced, cool, dauntless, fearless, persuaded, positive, sanguine, satisfied, secure, self-assured, self-confident, self-possessed, self-reliant, sure, unabashed, unbashful, unselfconscious.
antonyms diffident, sceptical.

confidential *adj.* classified, close, closed, faithful, familiar, hush-hush, in camera, intimate, private, privy, secret, tête-à-tête, trusted, trustworthy, trusty.
antonyms common, public.

confine *v.* bind, bound, cage, chamber, circumscribe, constrain, cramp, crib, emmew, enclose, immew, immure, imprison, incarcerate, inhibit, intern, keep, keep prisoner, limit, mew, repress, restrain, restrict, shackle, shut up, thirl, trammel.
antonym free.

confirm *v.* approve, assure, attest, authenticate, back, buttress, clinch, corroborate, endorse, establish, evidence, fix, fortify, homologate, prove, ratify, reinforce, sanction, settle, strengthen, substantiate, support, validate, verify, witness to.
antonym deny.

confirmation *n.* acceptance, agreement, approval, assent, attestation, authentication, backing, clincher, corroboration, endorsement, evidence, proof, ratification, sanction, substantiation, support, testimony, validation, verification, witness.
antonym denial.

confirmed *adj.* authenticated, chronic, committed, corroborated, deep-dyed, dyed-in-the-wool, entrenched, established, habitual, hardened, incorrigible, incurable, ingrained, inured, inveterate, irredeemable, long-established, long-standing, proved, proven, rooted, seasoned, substantiated, unredeemed.
antonyms uncommitted, unconfirmed.

conflict *n.* agony, ambivalence, antagonism, antipathy, Armageddon, battle, brawl, clash, collision, combat, confrontation, contention, contest, difference, disagreement, discord, dissension, encounter, engagement, feud, fight, fracas, friction, hostility, interference, opposition, quarrel, set-to, skirmish, strife, turmoil, unrest, variance, war, warfare.
antonyms agreement, concord.
v. battle, clash, collide, combat, contend, contest, contradict, differ, disagree, fight, interfere, oppose, strive, struggle, war, wrangle.
antonym agree.

conform *v.* accommodate, accord, adapt, adjust, agree, assimilate, comply, correspond, follow, harmonize, match, obey, quadrate, square, suit, tally, yield.
antonym differ.

conformity *n.* affinity, agreement, allegiance, Babbitry, compliance, congruity, consonance, conventionalism, conventionality, correspondence, Gleichschaltung, harmony, likeness, observance, orthodoxy, resemblance, similarity, traditionalism.
antonyms difference, nonconformity.

comfound *v.* abash, amaze, astonish, astound, baffle, bamboozle, bewilder, confuse, contradict, demolish, destroy, discombobulate, dismay, dumbfound, flabbergast, mystify, nonplus, overthrow, overwhelm, perplex, ruin, startle, stupefy, surprise, thwart, unshape, upset.

confront *v.* accost, address, appose, beard, brave, challenge, defy, encounter, face, front, oppose.
antonym evade.

confuse *v.* abash, addle, baffle, befuddle, bemuse, bewilder, buffalo, burble, confound, darken, demoralize, disarrange, discomfit, discompose, disconcert, discountenance, disorder, disorient, disorientate, embarrass, embrangle, flummox, fluster, intermingle, involve, jumble, maze, mingle, mistake, mix up, mortify, muddle, mystify, nonplus, obscure, perplex, puzzle, rattle, shame, tangle, tie in knots, upset.
antonyms clarify, enlighten, reassure.

confused *adj.* addle-brained, addle(d), addle-headed, addlepated, baffled, bewildered, bushed, chaotic, dazed, désorienté, disarranged, discombobulated, disordered, disorderly, disorganized, disorientated, distracted, embarrassed, flummoxed, fuddled, higgledy-piggledy, jumbled, maffled, mistaken, misunderstood, muddled, muddle-headed, muzzy, nonplused, perplexed, puzzled, puzzle-headed, streaked, topsy-turvy, tosticated, untidy, upset.
antonym clear.

confusion *n.* abashment, Babel, befuddlement, bemusement, bewilderment, bustle, chagrin, chaos, clutter, combustion, commotion, demoralization, disarrangement, discomfiture, disorder, disorganization, disorientation, distraction, égarement, embarrassment, embroglio, embroilment, fluster, foul-up, hotchpotch, hubble-bubble, hugger-mugger, imbroglio, jumble, mess, mix-up, muddle, mystification, overthrow, palaver, perdition, perplexity, perturbation, pie, puzzlement, screw-up, shambles, shame, tangle, tizz(y), topsyturviness, topsyturvy, topsyturvydom, toss, turmoil, untidiness, upheaval, welter.
antonyms clarity, composure, order.

congratulate *v.* compliment, felicitate, gratulate.
antonym commiserate.

congregate *v.* accumulate, assemble, bunch, clump, cluster, collect, concentrate, conglomerate, convene, converge, convoke, crowd, flock, foregather, gather, mass, meet, muster, rally, rendezvous, throng.
antonyms dismiss, disperse.

congress *n.* assembly, conclave, conference, convention, convocation, council, diet, forum, legislature, meeting, parliament, synod.

congruity *n.* agreement, coincidence, compatibility, concinnity, concurrence, conformity, congruence, congruousness, consistency, correspondence, harmony, identity, match, parallelism.
antonym incongruity.

conjecture *v.* assume, estimate, extrapolate, fancy, guess, hypothesize, imagine, infer, opine, reckon, speculate, suppose, surmise, suspect, theorize.
n. assumption, conclusion, estimate, extrapolation, fancy, guess, guesstimate, guesswork, hypothesis, inference, notion, opinion, presumption, projection, speculation, supposition, surmise, theorizing, theory.

conjunction *n.* amalgamation, association, coincidence, combination, concurrence, juxtaposition, syzygy, unification, union, unition.

connect *v.* affix, ally, associate, cohere, combine, compaginate, concatenate, couple, enlink, fasten, join, link, relate, unite.
antonym disconnect.

connection *n.* acquaintance, affinity, alliance, ally, arthrosis, associate, association, attachment, bond, catenation, coherence, commerce, communication, compagination, conjunction, contact, context, correlation, correspondence, coupling, fastening, friend, hook-up, intercourse, interrelation, intimacy, junction, kin, kindred, kinsman, kith, link, marriage, reference, relation, relationship, relative, relevance, sponsor, tie, tie-in, union.
antonym disconnection.

conquer *v.* acquire, annex, beat, best, checkmate, crush, defeat, discomfit, get the better of, humble, master, obtain, occupy, overcome, overpower, overrun, overthrow, prevail, quell, rout, seize, subdue, subjugate, succeed, surmount, triumph, vanquish, win, worst.
antonyms surrender, yield.

conquest *n.* acquisition, annexation, appropriation, captivation, coup, defeat, discomfiture, enchantment, enthralment, enticement, invasion, inveiglement, mastery, occupation, overthrow, rout, seduction, subjection, subjugation, takeover, triumph, vanquishment, victory.

conscientious *adj.* careful, diligent, exact, faithful, hard-working, high-minded, high-principled, honest, honorable, incorruptible, just, meticulous, moral, painstaking, particular, punctilious, responsible, scrupulous, solicitous, straightforward, strict, through, upright.
antonyms careless, irresponsible.

conscious *adj.* alert, alive, awake, aware, calculated, cognizant, deliberate, heedful, intentional, knowing, mindful, percipient, premeditated, rational, reasoning, reflective, regardful, responsible, responsive, self-conscious, sensible, sentient, studied, wilful, witting.
antonym unconscious.

consecrate *v.* beatify, dedicate, devote, exalt, hallow, ordain, revere, sanctify, venerate.

consecutive *adj.* chronological, continuous, following, running, sequential, seriatim, succeeding, successive, unbroken, uninterrupted.
antonym discontinuous.

consent *v.* accede, acquiesce, admit, agree, allow, approve, assent, comply, concede, concur, grant, homologate, permit, yield.
antonyms oppose, refuse.
n. accordance, acquiescence, agreement, approval, assent, compliance, concession, concurrence, consentience, go-ahead, green light, permission, sanction.
antonyms opposition, refusal.

consequence *n.* account, concern, distinction, effect, eminence, end, event, fall-out, import, importance, interest, issue, moment, notability, note, outcome, portent, rank, repercussion, repute, result, side effect, significance, standing, status, upshot, value, weight.
antonym cause.

consequential *adj.* arrogant, bumptious, conceited, consequent, eventful, far-reaching, grave, important, impressive, indirect, inflated, momentous, noteworthy, pompous, pretentious, resultant, self-important, serious, significant, supercilious, vainglorious, weighty.
antonyms inconsequential, unimportant.

consequently *adv.* accordingly, consequentially, ergo, hence, inferentially, necessarily, subsequently, therefore, thus.

conservative *adj.* cautious, conventional, die-hard, establishmentarian, guarded, hidebound, middle-of-the-road, moderate, quiet, reactionary, right-wing, sober, Tory, traditional, unexaggerated, unprogressive, verkrampte.
antonyms left-wing, radical.
n. diehard, moderate, moss-back, reactionary, right-winger, stick-in-the-mud, Tory, traditionalist.
antonyms left-winger, radical.

conserve *v.* guard, hoard, husband, keep, maintain, nurse, preserve, protect, save.
antonyms squander, use, waste.

consider *v.* believe, bethink, cogitate, consult, contemplate, count, deem, deliberate, discuss, examine, judge, meditate, mull over, muse, perpend, ponder, rate, reflect, regard, remember, respect, revolve, ruminate, study, think, weigh.
antonym ignore.

considerable *adj.* abundant, ample, appreciable, big, comfortable, distinguished, goodly, great, important, influential, large, lavish, marked, much, noteworthy, noticeable, plentiful, reasonable, renowned, significant, sizable, substantial, tidy, tolerable, venerable.
antonyms insignificant, slight.

considerate *adj.* attentive, charitable, circumspect, concerned, discreet, forbearing, gracious, kind, kindly, mindful, obliging, patient, solicitous, tactful, thoughtful, unselfish.
antonyms selfish, thoughtless.

consideration *n.* analysis, attention, cogitation, concern, considerateness, contemplation, deliberation, discussion, examination, factor, fee, friendliness, issue, kindliness, kindness, meditation, payment, perquisite, point, recompense, reflection, regard, remuneration, respect, review, reward, rumination, scrutiny, solicitude, study, tact, thought, thoughtfulness, tip.
antonyms disdain, disregard.

consistent *adj.* accordant, agreeing, coherent, compatible, congruous, consonant, constant, dependable, harmonious, logical, of a piece, persistent, regular, steady, unchanging, undeviating, unfailing, uniform.
antonyms erratic, inconsistent.

consolation *n.* aid, alleviation, assuagement, cheer, comfort, ease, easement, encouragement, help, relief, solace, succor, support.
antonym discouragement.

console *v.* assuage, calm, cheer, comfort, encourage, hearten, solace, soothe.
antonyms agitate, upset.

consolidate *v.* affiliate, amalgamate, cement, combine, compact, condense, confederate, conjoin, federate, fortify, fuse, harden, join, reinforce, secure, solidify, stabilize, strengthen, thicken, unify, unite.

consort *n.* associate, companion, fellow, helpmate, helpmeet, husband, partner, spouse, wife.
v. accord, agree, associate, correspond, fraternize, harmonize, jibe, mingle, mix, square, tally.

conspicuous *adj.* apparent, blatant, clear, discernible, evident, flagrant, flashy, garish, glaring, kenspeck(le), manifest, noticeable, obvious, patent, perceptible, remarked, showy, visible.
antonym inconspicuous.

conspiracy *n.* cabal, collusion, complot, confederacy, fix, frame-up, intrigue, league, machination, plot, scheme, treason.

conspire *v.* cabal, collude, combine, complot, concur, conduce, confederate, contribute, contrive, co-operate, devise, hatch, intrigue, machinate, maneuver, plot, scheme, tend, treason.

constancy *n.* determination, devotion, faithfulness, fidelity, firmness, fixedness, loyalty, permanence, perseverance, regularity, resolution, stability, steadfastness, steadiness, tenacity, uniformity.
antonyms inconstancy, irregularity.

constant *adj.* attached, ceaseless, changeless, continual, continuous, dependable, determined, devoted, dogged, endless, eternal, even, everlasting, faithful, firm, fixed, habitual, immutable, incessant, interminable, invariable, loyal, never-ending, non-stop, permanent, perpetual, persevering, persistent, regular, relentless, resolute, stable, staunch, steadfast, steady, sustained, tried-and-true, true, trustworthy, trusty, unalterable, unbroken, unchangeable, unfailing, unflagging, uniform, uninterrupted, unrelenting, unremitting, unshaken, unvarying, unwavering.
antonyms fickle, fitful, irregular, occasional, variable.

constantly *adv.* always, continually, continuously, endlessly, everlastingly, incessantly, interminably, invariably, non-stop, perpetually, relentlessly, steadfastly, uniformly.
antonym occasionally.

consternation *n.* alarm, amazement, anxiety, awe, bewilderment, confusion, dismay, disquietude, distress, dread, fear, fright, horror, panic, perturbation, shock, terror, trepidation.
antonym composure.

constitute *v.* appoint, authorize, commission, compose, comprise, create, delegate, depute, empower, enact, establish, fix, form, found, inaugurate, make, name, nominate, ordain.

constitution *n.* build, character, composition, configuration, construction, disposition, establishment, form, formation, habit, health, make-up, nature, organization, physique, structure, temper, temperament.

constrain *v.* bind, bulldoze, chain, check, coerce, compel, confine, constrict, curb, drive, force, impel, necessitate, oblige, pressure, pressurize, railroad, restrain, urge.

construct *v.* assemble, build, compose, create, design, elevate, engineer, erect, establish, fabricate, fashion, form, formulate, found, frame, knock together, make, manufacture, model, organize, raise, shape.
antonyms demolish, destroy.

construction *n.* assembly, building, composition, constitution, creation, edifice, erection, fabric, fabrication, figure, form, formation, model, organization, shape, structure.
antonym destruction.

constructive *adj.* advantageous, beneficial, helpful, positive, practical, productive, useful, valuable.
antonyms destructive, negative, unhelpful.

construe *v.* analyze, decipher, deduce, explain, expound, infer, interpret, parse, read, render, take, translate.

consult *v.* ask, commune, confer, consider, debate, deliberate, interrogate, parley, powwow, question, regard, respect.

consume *v.* absorb, annihilate, decay, demolish, deplete, destroy, devastate, devour, discuss, dissipate, drain, eat, employ, engulf, envelop, exhaust, expend, gobble, guzzle, lessen, ravage, spend, squander, swallow, use (up), utilize, vanish, waste, wear out.

consumer *n.* buyer, customer, end-user, purchaser, shopper, user.

consummate *v.* accomplish, achieve, cap, compass, complete, conclude, crown, effectuate, end, finish, fulfil, perfect, perform, terminate.
adj. absolute, accomplished, complete, conspicuous, distinguished, finished, matchless, perfect, polished, practised, skilled, superb, superior, supreme, total, transcendent, ultimate, unqualified, utter.
antonym imperfect.

consummation *n.* achievement, actualization, completion, culmination, end, fulfilment, perfection, realization, termination.

contact *n.* acquaintance, approximation, association, communication, connection, contiguity, contingence, impact, junction, juxtaposition, meeting, tangency, touch, union.
v. approach, call, get hold of, notify, phone, reach, ring.

contagious *adj.* catching, communicable, epidemic, epizootic, infectious, pestiferous, pestilential, spreading, transmissible, zymotic.

contain *v.* accommodate, check, comprehend, comprise,

control, curb, embody, embrace, enclose, entomb, hold, include, incorporate, involve, limit, repress, restrain, seat, stifle.
antonym exclude.

contaminate *v.* adulterate, befoul, besmirch, corrupt, debase, defile, deprave, infect, pollute, soil, stain, sully, taint, tarnish, vitiate.
antonym purify.

contemplate *v.* behold, cerebrate, consider, deliberate, design, envisage, examine, expect, eye, foresee, inspect, intend, mean, meditate, mull over, observe, plan, ponder, propose, reflect on, regard, ruminate, scrutinize, study, survey, view.

contemplative *adj.* cerebral, intent, introspective, meditative, musing, pensive, rapt, reflective, ruminative, thoughtful.
antonyms impulsive, thoughtless.

contemporary *adj.* à la mode, coetaneous, coeval, coexistent, co-existing, concurrent, contemporaneous, conterminous, coterminous, current, latest, modern, newfangled, present, present-day, recent, synchronous, ultra-modern, up-to-date, up-to-the-minute, with it.
antonyms preceding, succeeding.

contempt *n.* condescension, contemptuousness, contumely, derision, despite, detestation, disdain, disgrace, dishonor, disregard, disrespect, humiliation, loathing, mockery, neglect, scorn, shame, slight.
antonyms admiration, regard.

contemptible *adj.* abject, base, cheap, degenerate, despicable, detestable, ignominious, loathsome, low, low-down, mean, paltry, pitiful, scurvy, shabby, shameful, vile, worthless, wretched.
antonyms admirable, honorable.

contemptuous *adj.* arrogant, cavalier, condescending, contumacious, contumelious, cynical, derisive, disdainful, haughty, high and mighty, insolent, insulting, scornful, sneering, supercilious, tossy, withering.
antonyms humble, polite, respectful.

contend *v.* affirm, allege, argue, assert, aver, avow, clash, compete, contest, cope, debate, declare, dispute, emulate, grapple, hold, jostle, litigate, maintain, skirmish, strive, struggle, vie, wrestle.

content[1] *v.* appease, delight, gladden, gratify, humor, indulge, mollify, pacify, placate, please, reconcile, satisfy, suffice.
antonym displease.
n. comfort, contentment, delight, ease, gratification, happiness, peace, pleasure, satisfaction.
antonym discontent.
adj. agreeable, comfortable, contented, fulfilled, pleased, satisfied, untroubled.
antonym dissatisfied.

content[2] *n.* burden, capacity, essence, gist, ideas, load, matter, meaning, measure, significance, size, subject matter, substance, text, thoughts, volume.

contented *adj.* cheerful, comfortable, complacent, content, glad, gratified, happy, placid, pleased, relaxed, satisfied, serene, thankful.
antonym discontented.

contention *n.* affirmation, allegation, argument, assertion, asseveration, belief, claim, competition, contest, controversy, debate, declaration, discord, dispute, dissension, enmity, feuding, ground, hostility, idea, opinion, position, profession, rivalry, stand, strife, struggle, thesis, view, wrangling.

contentment *n.* comfort, complacency, content, contentedness, ease, equanimity, fulfilment, gladness, gratification, happiness, peace, peacefulness, placidity, pleasure, repletion, satisfaction, serenity.
antonym dissatisfaction.

contest *n.* affray, altercation, battle, combat, competition, concours, conflict, controversy, debate, discord, dispute, encounter, fight, game, match, olympiad, set-to, shock, struggle, tournament, trial.
v. argue against, challenge, compete, contend, debate, deny, dispute, doubt, fight, litigate, oppose, question, refute, strive, vie.

continence *n.* abstemiousness, abstinence, asceticism, celibacy, chastity, moderation, self-control, self-restraint, sobriety, temperance.
antonym incontinence.

contingency *n.* accident, arbitrariness, chance, emergency, event, eventuality, fortuity, happening, incident, juncture, possibility, randomness, uncertainty.

contingent *n.* batch, body, bunch, company, complement, deputation, detachment, group, mission, quota, section, set.

continual *adj.* ceaseless, constant, continuous, endless, eternal, everlasting, frequent, incessant, interminable, oft-repeated, perpetual, recurrent, regular, repeated, repetitive, unbroken, unceasing, uninterrupted, unremitting.
antonyms intermittent, occasional, temporary.

continue *v.* abide, aby(e), adjourn, carry on, endure, extend, go on, last, lengthen, maintain, persevere, persist, proceed, project, prolong, pursue, reach, recommence, remain, rest, resume, stay, stick at, survive, sustain.
antonyms discontinue, stop.

continuous *adj.* connected, consecutive, constant, continued, extended, non-stop, prolonged, unbroken, unceasing, undivided, uninterrupted.
antonyms discontinuous, intermittent, sporadic.

contract *v.* abbreviate, abridge, acquire, agree, arrange, bargain, catch, clinch, close, compress, condense, confine, constrict, constringe, covenant, curtail, develop, dwindle, engage, epitomize, incur, lessen, narrow, negotiate, pledge, purse, reduce, shrink, shrivel, stipulate, tighten, wither, wrinkle.
antonyms enlarge, expand, lengthen.
n. agreement, arrangement, bargain, bond, commission,

commitment, compact, concordat, convention, covenant, deal, engagement, handfast, instrument, pact, settlement, stipulation, transaction, treaty, understanding.

contraction *n.* abbreviation, astringency, compression, constriction, diminution, elision, narrowing, reduction, retrenchment, shortening, shrinkage, shriveling, tensing, tightening.
antonyms expansion, growth.

contradict *v.* belie, challenge, contravene, controvert, counter, counteract, deny, disaffirm, dispute, gainsay, impugn, negate, oppose.
antonyms agree, confirm, corroborate.

contradictory *adj.* antagonistic, antithetical, conflicting, contrary, discrepant, dissident, double-mouthed, incompatible, inconsistent, irreconcilable, opposed, opposite, paradoxical, repugnant, unreconciled.
antonym consistent.

contrary *adj.* adverse, antagonistic, arsy-versy, awkward, balky, cantankerous, clashing, contradictory, counter, cross-grained, cussed, difficult, discordant, disobliging, froward, hostile, inconsistent, inimical, intractable, intractible, obstinate, opposed, opposite, paradoxical, perverse, stroppy, thrawn, unaccommodating, wayward, wilful.
antonyms like, obliging, similar.
n. antithesis, converse, opposite, reverse.

contrast *n.* comparison, contraposition, contrariety, counter-view, difference, differentiation, disparity, dissimilarity, distinction, divergence, foil, opposition, set-off.
antonym similarity.
v. compare, differ, differentiate, discriminate, distinguish, oppose, set off.

contribute *v.* add, afford, bestow, conduce, dob in, donate, furnish, give, help, kick in, lead, provide, subscribe, supply, tend.
antonyms subtract, withhold.

contribution *n.* addition, bestowal, donation, gift, grant, gratuity, handout, input, offering, subscription.

contrive *v.* arrange, compass, concoct, construct, create, design, devise, effect, engineer, excogitate, fabricate, frame, improvise, invent, manage, maneuver, plan, plot, scheme, wangle.

control *v.* boss, bridle, check, command, conduct, confine, constrain, contain, curb, determine, direct, dominate, govern, lead, limit, manage, manipulate, master, monitor, oversee, pilot, regiment, regulate, repress, restrain, rule, run, stage-manage, steer, subdue, superintend, supervise, suppress, verify.
n. authority, brake, charge, check, clutches, command, curb, direction, dirigism(e), discipline, governance, government, guidance, jurisdiction, leading-strings, leash, limitation, management, mastery, oversight, regulation, rule, superintendence, supervision, supremacy.

controversy *n.* altercation, argument, contention, debate, disagreement, discussion, dispute, dissension, polemic, quarrel, squabble, strife, war of words, wrangle, wrangling.
antonyms accord, agreement.

convenience *n.* accessibility, accommodation, advantage, amenity, appliance, appropriateness, availability, benefit, chance, comfort, ease, enjoyment, facility, fitness, handiness, help, leisure, opportuneness, opportunity, satisfaction, service, serviceability, suitability, timeliness, use, usefulness, utility.

convenient *adj.* accessible, adapted, advantageous, appropriate, at hand, available, beneficial, commodious, fit, fitted, handy, helpful, labor-saving, nearby, opportune, seasonable, serviceable, suitable, suited, timely, useful, utile, well-timed.
antonyms awkward, inconvenient.

convention *n.* agreement, assembly, bargain, code, compact, conclave, concordat, conference, congress, contract, convocation, council, custom, delegates, etiquette, formality, matter of form, meeting, pact, practice, propriety, protocol, representatives, stipulation, synod, tradition, treaty, understanding, usage.

conventional *adj.* accepted, arbitrary, bourgeois, common, commonplace, copybook, correct, customary, decorous, expected, formal, habitual, hackneyed, hidebound, iconic, nomic, normal, ordinary, orthodox, pedestrian, prevailing, prevalent, proper, prosaic, regular, ritual, routine, run-of-the-mill, standard, stereotyped, straight, stylized, traditional, unoriginal, uptight, usual, wonted.
antonyms exotic, unconventional, unusual.

conversant with acquainted with, apprised of, au fait with, experienced in, familiar with, informed about, knowledgeable about, practiced in, proficient in, skilled in, versant with, versed in.
antonym ignorant of.

conversation *n.* chat, chinwag, chitchat, colloquy, communication, communion, confab, confabulation, conference, converse, dialogue, discourse, discussion, exchange, gossip, intercourse, interlocution, powwow, talk, tête-à-tête.

converse[1] *v.* chat, colloquize, commune, confabulate, confer, discourse, talk.

converse[2] *n.* antithesis, contrary, counterpart, obverse, opposite, reverse.
adj. antipodal, antipodean, contrary, counter, opposite, reverse, reversed, transposed.

conversion *n.* adaptation, alteration, change, metamorphosis, metanoia, modification, permutation, proselytization, rebirth, reconstruction, reformation, regeneration, remodeling, reorganization, transfiguration, transformation, transmogrification, transmutation.

convert *v.* adapt, alter, apply, appropriate, baptize, change, convince, interchange, metamorphose, modify, permute, proselytize, reform, regenerate, remodel, reorganize, restyle, revise, save, transform, transmogrify, transmute, transpose, turn.

n. catechumen, disciple, neophyte, proselyte, vert.

convey *v.* bear, bequeath, bring, carry, cede, communicate, conduct, deliver, demise, devolve, disclose, fetch, forward, grant, guide, impart, lease, move, relate, reveal, send, steal, support, tell, transfer, transmit, transport, waft, will.

conveyance *n.* carriage, movement, shipment, transfer, transference, transmission, transport, transportation, tran(s)shipment, vehicle, wagonage.

convict *v.* attaint, condemn, imprison, sentence.
n. con, criminal, culprit, felon, forçat, jail-bird, lag, malefactor, prisoner.

conviction *n.* assurance, belief, certainty, certitude, confidence, convincement, creed, earnestness, faith, fervor, firmness, opinion, persuasion, plerophory, principle, reliance, tenet, view.

convince *v.* assure, confirm, persuade, reassure, satisfy, sway, win over.

convivial *adj.* back-slapping, cheerful, festive, friendly, fun-loving, gay, genial, hearty, hilarious, jolly, jovial, lively, merry, mirthful, sociable.
antonym taciturn.

convoy *n.* attendance, attendant, escort, fleet, guard, protection, train.

cool *adj.* aloof, apathetic, audacious, bold, brazen, calm, cheeky, chilled, chilling, chilly, coldish, collected, composed, cosmopolitan, dégagé, deliberate, dispassionate, distant, down-beat, elegant, frigid, impertinent, imperturbable, impudent, incurious, indifferent, laid-back, level-headed, lukewarm, nippy, offhand, placid, pleasant, presumptuous, quiet, refreshing, relaxed, reserved, satisfying, self-controlled, self-possessed, serene, shameless, sophisticated, stand-offish, together, uncommunicative, unconcerned, unemotional, unenthusiastic, unexcited, unfriendly, unheated, uninterested, unresponsive, unruffled, unwelcoming, urbane.
antonyms excited, friendly, hot, warm.
v. abate, allay, assuage, calm, chill, dampen, defuse, fan, freeze, lessen, moderate, quiet, refrigerate, temper.
antonyms excite, heat, warm. *n.* calmness, collectedness, composure, control, poise, sangfroid, self-control, self-discipline, self-possession, temper.

co-operate *v.* abet, aid, assist, collaborate, combine, concur, conduce, conspire, contribute, co-ordinate, help, play along, play ball.

co-ordinate *v.* codify, correlate, grade, graduate, harmonize, integrate, match, mesh, organize, relate, synchronize, systematize, tabulate.
adj. coequal, correlative, correspondent, equal, equipotent, equivalent, parallel, reciprocal.

copious *adj.* abundant, ample, bounteous, bountiful, extensive, exuberant, full, generous, great, huge, inexhaustible, lavish, liberal, luxuriant, overflowing, plenteous, plentiful, profuse, rich, superabundant.
antonyms meager, scarce.

copy *n.* apograph, archetype, autotype, borrowing, calque, carbon copy, counterfeit, crib, duplicate, ectype, engrossment, exemplar, facsimile, flimsy, forgery, image, imitation, likeness, loan translation, loan-word, model, Ozalid®;, pattern, photocopy, Photostat®;, plagiarization, print, replica, replication, representation, reproduction, tracing, transcript, transcription, Xerox®;.
antonym original.
v. ape, borrow, counterfeit, crib, duplicate, echo, emulate, engross, exemplify, extract, facsimile, follow, imitate, mimic, mirror, parrot, personate, photocopy, Photostat®;, plagiarize, repeat, replicate, reproduce, simulate, transcribe, Xerox®;.

cordial *adj.* affable, affectionate, agreeable, cheerful, earnest, friendly, genial, heartfelt, hearty, invigorating, pleasant, restorative, sociable, stimulating, warm, warm-hearted, welcoming, whole-hearted.
antonyms aloof, cool, hostile.

core *n.* center, crux, essence, germ, gist, heart, kernel, nitty-gritty, nub, nucleus, pith.
antonyms exterior, perimeter, surface.

corporation^1 *n.* association, authorities, body, combine, conglomerate, council, society.

corporation^2 *n.* beer belly, paunch, pod, pot, pot-belly, spare tire.

corpse *n.* body, cadaver, carcass, deader, remains, skeleton, stiff.

corpulent *adj.* adipose, beefy, bulky, burly, fat, fattish, fleshy, large, lusty, obese, overweight, plump, poddy, podgy, portly, pot-bellied, pudgy, roly-poly, rotund, stout, tubby, well-padded.
antonym thin.

correct *v.* adjust, admonish, amend, blue-pencil, chasten, chastise, chide, counterbalance, cure, debug, discipline, emend, emendate, improve, punish, rectify, redress, reform, regulate, remedy, reprimand, reprove, right.
adj. acceptable, accurate, appropriate, comme il faut, diplomatic, equitable, exact, faultless, fitting, flawless, jake, just, OK, precise, proper, regular, right, seemly, standard, strict, true, well-formed, word-perfect.
antonyms inaccurate, incorrect, wrong.

correction *n.* adjustment, admonition, alteration, amendment, castigation, chastisement, discipline, emendation, improvement, modification, punishment, rectification, reformation, reproof, righting.

correlation *n.* alternation, correspondence, equivalence, interaction, interchange, interdependence, interrelationship, link, reciprocity, relationship.

correspond *v.* accord, agree, answer, coincide, communicate, complement, concur, conform, correlate, dovetail, fit, harmonize, match, square, tally, write.

correspondent *n.* contributor, journalist, penpal, reporter, writer.

adj. analogous, comparable, equivalent, like, matching, parallel, reciprocal, similar.

corridor *n.* aisle, ambulatory, foyer, hallway, lobby, passage, passageway, vestibule.

corrode *v.* canker, consume, corrupt, crumble, deteriorate, disintegrate, eat away, erode, fret, impair, oxidize, rust, waste, wear away.

corrupt *adj.* abandoned, adulterate(d), altered, bent, bribed, contaminated, crooked, debased, decayed, defiled, degenerate, demoralized, depraved, dishonest, dishonored, dissolute, distorted, doctored, falsified, fraudulent, infected, polluted, profligate, putrescent, putrid, rotten, shady, tainted, unethical, unprincipled, unscrupulous, venal, vicious.
antonyms honest, trustworthy, upright.
v. adulterate, barbarize, bribe, canker, contaminate, debase, debauch, defile, demoralize, deprave, doctor, empoison, entice, fix, infect, lure, pervert, putrefy, seduce, spoil, square, suborn, subvert, taint, vitiate.
antonym purify.

corruption *n.* adulteration, baseness, bribery, bribing, crookedness, debasement, decadence, decay, defilement, degeneration, degradation, demoralization, depravity, dishonesty, distortion, doctoring, evil, extortion, falsification, fiddling, foulness, fraud, fraudulence, fraudulency, graft, immorality, impurity, infection, iniquity, jobbery, leprosy, malversation, perversion, pollution, profiteering, profligacy, putrefaction, putrescence, rot, rottenness, shadiness, sinfulness, turpitude, ulcer, unscrupulousness, venality, vice, viciousness, virus, wickedness.
antonyms honesty, purification.

cost *n.* amount, charge, damage, deprivation, detriment, disbursement, expenditure, expense, figure, harm, hurt, injury, loss, outlay, payment, penalty, price, rate, sacrifice, worth.

costly *adj.* catastrophic, damaging, dear, deleterious, disastrous, excessive, exorbitant, expensive, extortionate, gorgeous, harmful, highly-priced, lavish, loss-making, luxurious, opulent, precious, priceless, pricy, rich, ruinous, sacrificial, splendid, steep, sumptuous, valuable.
antonyms cheap, inexpensive.

costume *n.* apparel, attire, clothing, dress, ensemble, garb, get-up, livery, outfit, raiment, robes, uniform, vestment.

cough *n.* bark, hack, tussis.
v. bark, hack, harrumph, hawk, hem, hoast.

council *n.* assembly, board, cabinet, chamber, committee, conclave, conference, congress, consistory, consult, convention, convocation, diet, divan, ministry, panchayat, panel, parliament, soviet, syndicate, synod, volost.

counsel *n.* admonition, advice, advocate, attorney, barrister, caution, consideration, consultation, deliberation, direction, forethought, guidance, information, lawyer, plan, purpose, recommendation, solicitor, suggestion, warning. *v.* admonish, advise, advocate, caution, direct, exhort, guide, instruct, recommend, suggest, urge, warn.

count *v.* add, ascribe, calculate, check, compute, consider, deem, enumerate, esteem, estimate, hold, impute, include, judge, list, matter, number, rate, reckon, regard, score, signify, tally, tell, think, tot up, total, weigh.
n. addition, calculation, computation, enumeration, numbering, poll, reckoning, sum, tally, total.

countenance *n.* acquiescence, aid, air, appearance, approval, aspect, assistance, backing, demeanor, endorsement, expression, face, favor, features, help, look, mien, physiognomy, sanction, support, visage.
v. abet, acquiesce, agree to, aid, approve, back, brook, champion, condone, encourage, endorse, endure, help, sanction, support, tolerate.

counteract *v.* act against, annul, check, contravene, counterbalance, countervail, cross, defeat, foil, frustrate, hinder, invalidate, negate, neutralize, offset, oppose, resist, thwart, undo.
antonyms assist, support.

counterfeit *v.* copy, fabricate, fake, feign, forge, imitate, impersonate, phony, pretend, sham, simulate.
adj. bogus, copied, ersatz, faked, false, feigned, forged, fraudulent, imitation, phony, postiche, pretend(ed), pseud, pseudo, sham, simular, simulated, simulate(d), spurious, supposititious.
antonym genuine.
n. copy, fake, forgery, fraud, imitant, imitation, phantasm(a), phony, reproduction, sham.

country *n.* backwoods, boondocks, citizenry, citizens, clime, commonwealth, community, countryside, electors, farmland, fatherland, green belt, homeland, inhabitants, kingdom, land, motherland, nation, nationality, outback, outdoors, part, people, populace, provinces, public, realm, region, society, sovereign state, state, sticks, terrain, territory, voters.
adj. agrarian, agrestic, arcadian, bucolic, georgic, landed, pastoral, provincial, rude, rural, rustic.
antonyms oppidan, urban.

couple *n.* brace, Darby and Joan, duo, dyad, pair, span, team, twain, twosome, yoke.
v. accompany, buckle, clasp, conjoin, connect, copulate, fornicate, hitch, join, link, marry, pair, unite, wed, yoke.

courage *n.* boldness, bottle, bravery, daring, dauntlessness, fearlessness, firmness, fortitude, gallantry, grit, guts, hardihood, heroism, mettle, nerve, pluck, resolution, spirit, spunk, stomach, valor.
antonym cowardice.

courageous *adj.* audacious, bold, brave, daring, dauntless, dreadless, fearless, gallant, gutsy, hardy, heroic, high-hearted, indomitable, intrepid, lion-hearted, plucky, resolute, stout-hearted, valiant, valorous.
antonym cowardly.

course *n.* advance, advancement, channel, circuit, circus, classes, continuity, current, curriculum, development, diadrom, direction, duration, flight-path, flow, furtherance, hippodrome, lap, lapse, lectures, line, march, method, mode, movement, orbit, order, passage, passing, path, piste, plan, policy, procedure, program, progress, progression, race, race-course, racetrack, raik, regimen, road, round, route, schedule, sequence, series, studies, succession, sweep, syllabus, tack, term, time, track, trail, trajectory, unfolding, vector, voyage, way, wheel.
v. chase, dash, flow, follow, gush, hunt, move, pour, pursue, race, run, scud, scurry, speed, stream, surge, tumble.

courteous *adj.* affable, attentive, ceremonious, civil, considerate, courtly, debonair, elegant, gallant, gracious, mannerly, obliging, polished, polite, refined, respectful, urbane, well-bred, well-mannered.
antonyms discourteous, rude.

courtesy *n.* affability, attention, benevolence, breeding, civility, comity, consent, consideration, courteousness, courtliness, elegance, favor, gallantness, gallantry, generosity, gentilesse, graciousness, indulgence, kindness, manners, polish, politeness, urbanity.
antonyms discourtesy, rudeness.

covenant *n.* arrangement, bargain, bond, commitment, compact, concordat, contract, convention, deed, engagement, pact, pledge, promise, stipulation, treaty, trust, undertaking.
v. agree, bargain, contract, engage, pledge, promise, stipulate, undertake.

cover *v.* balance, camouflage, canopy, clad, cloak, clothe, coat, compensate, comprehend, comprise, conceal, consider, contain, counterbalance, curtain, daub, defend, describe, detail, disguise, dress, eclipse, embody, embrace, encase, encompass, enshroud, envelop, examine, guard, hide, hood, house, include, incorporate, insure, invest, investigate, involve, layer, mantle, mask, narrate, obscure, offset, overlay, overspread, protect, recount, reinforce, relate, report, screen, secrete, shade, sheathe, shelter, shield, shroud, suffuse, survey, veil.
n. bedspread, binding, camouflage, canopy, cap, case, cloak, clothing, coating, compensation, concealment, confederate, covering, cover-up, defence, disguise, dress, envelope, façade, front, guard, indemnity, insurance, jacket, lid, mask, payment, pretense, pretext, protection, refuge, reimbursement, sanctuary, screen, sheath, shelter, shield, smoke, spread, top, undergrowth, veil, woods, wrapper.

covert *adj.* clandestine, concealed, disguised, dissembled, hidden, private, secret, sneaky, stealthy, subreptitious, surreptitious, ulterior, under the table, underhand, unsuspected, veiled.
antonym open.

covetous *adj.* acquisitive, avaricious, close-fisted, envious, grasping, greedy, insatiable, jealous, mercenary, rapacious, thirsting, yearning. *antonyms* generous, temperate.

coward *n.* caitiff, chicken, craven, dastard, faint-heart, funk, hilding, nithing, poltroon, recreant, renegade, scaredy-cat, skulker, sneak, yellow-belly, yellow-dog.
antonym hero.

cowardice *n.* faint-heartedness, fear, funk, gutlessness, pusillanimity, spinelessness.
antonyms courage, valor.

cowardly *adj.* base, caitiff, chicken, chicken-hearted, chicken-livered, craven, dastard(ly), faint-hearted, fearful, gutless, hilding, lily-livered, nesh, nithing, pusillanimous, recreant, scared, shrinking, soft, spineless, timorous, unheroic, weak, weak-kneed, white-livered, yellow, yellow-bellied.
antonym courageous.

cower *v.* cringe, crouch, flinch, grovel, quail, ruck, shake, shiver, shrink, skulk, tremble.

coy *adj.* arch, backward, bashful, coquettish, demure, diffident, evasive, flirtatious, kittenish, maidenly, modest, prudish, reserved, retiring, self-effacing, shrinking, shy, skittish, timid, virginal.
antonyms forward, impudent, sober.

crack *v.* break, buffet, burst, chap, chip, chop, cleave, clip, clout, collapse, crackle, crash, craze, cuff, decipher, detonate, explode, fathom, fracture, pop, ring, rive, slap, snap, solve, splinter, split, succumb, thump, wallop, whack, yield.
n. attempt, blow, breach, break, buffet, burst, chap, chink, chip, clap, cleft, clip, clout, cranny, crash, craze, crevasse, crevice, cuff, dig, expert, explosion, fent, fissure, flaw, fracture, gag, gap, go, insult, interstice, jibe, joke, moment, opportunity, pop, quip, report, rift, slap, smack, snap, stab, thump, try, wallop, whack, wisecrack, witticism.
adj. ace, choice, élite, excellent, first-class, first-rate, hand-picked, superior, top-notch.

craft *n.* ability, aircraft, aptitude, art, artfulness, artifice, artistry, barque, boat, business, calling, cleverness, contrivance, craftiness, cunning, deceit, dexterity, duplicity, employment, expertise, expertness, guile, handicraft, handiwork, ingenuity, knack, know-how, line, occupation, plane, pursuit, ruse, scheme, ship, shrewdness, skill, spacecraft, spaceship, stratagem, subterfuge, subtlety, technique, trade, trickery, vessel, vocation, wiles, work, workmanship.
antonyms naïvety, openness.

craftiness *n.* artfulness, astuteness, canniness, cunning, deceit, deviousness, double-dealing, duplicity, foxiness, guile, shrewdness, slyness, subtlety, trickiness, underhandedness, vulpinism, wiliness.
antonyms naïvety, openness.

crafty *adj.* artful, astute, calculating, canny, cunning, deceitful, designing, devious, duplicitous, foxy, fraudulent, guileful, insidious, knowing, machiavellian, scheming, sharp, shrewd, sly, subtle, tricksy, tricky, versute, vulpine, wily.
antonyms naïve, open.

craggy *adj.* broken, brusque, cragged, jagged, jaggy, precipitous, rocky, rough, rugged, stony, surly, uneven.
antonyms pleasant, smooth.

crank *n.* eccentric, loony, madman, nutter.

cranky *adj.* bizarre, capricious, crabbed, cross, crotchety, dotty, eccentric, erratic, freakish, freaky, funny, idiosyncratic, irritable, odd, peculiar, prickly, queer, quirky, strange, surly, viewy, wacky.
antonyms normal, placid, sensible.

crash *n.* accident, bang, bankruptcy, boom, bump, clang, clash, clatter, clattering, collapse, collision, debacle (débâcle), depression, din, downfall, failure, fragor, jar, jolt, pile-up, prang, racket, ruin, smash, smashing, smash-up, thud, thump, thunder, wreck.
v. bang, break, bump, collapse, collide, dash, disintegrate, fail, fall, fold (up), fracture, fragment, go bust, go under, hurtle, lurch, overbalance, pitch, plunge, prang, shatter, shiver, smash, splinter, sprawl, topple.
adj. concentrated, emergency, immediate, intensive, round-the-clock, telescoped, urgent.

crave *v.* ask, beg, beseech, desire, entreat, fancy, hanker after, hunger after, implore, long for, need, petition, pine for, require, seek, solicit, supplicate, thirst for, want, yearn for, yen for.
antonyms dislike, spurn.

craving *n.* appetence, appetency, appetite, cacoethes, desire, hankering, hunger, longing, lust, thirst, urge, yearning, yen.
antonyms dislike, distaste.

crazy *adj.* absurd, ardent, bananas, barmy, bats, batty, berserk, bird-brained, bizarre, bonkers, cockeyed, cracked, crazed, cuckoo, daffy, daft, delirious, demented, deranged, derisory, devoted, dippy, eager, eccentric, enamored, enthusiastic, fanatical, fantastic, fatuous, foolhardy, foolish, fruity, half-baked, hysterical, idiotic, ill-conceived, impracticable, imprudent, inane, inappropriate, infatuated, insane, irresponsible, ludicrous, lunatic, mad, maniacal, mental, nonsensical, nuts, nutty, odd, off one's rocker, outrageous, passionate, peculiar, pixil(l)ated, potty, preposterous, puerile, quixotic, ridiculous, scatty, senseless, short-sighted, silly, smitten, strange, touched, unbalanced, unhinged, unrealistic, unwise, unworkable, up the pole, wacky, weird, wild, zany, zealous.
antonyms sane, sensible.

creak *v.* grate, grind, groan, rasp, scrape, scratch, screak, screech, squeak, squeal.

create *v.* appoint, beget, cause, coin, compose, concoct, constitute, design, develop, devise, engender, establish, form, formulate, found, generate, hatch, initiate, install, institute, invent, invest, make, occasion, originate, produce, set up, sire, spawn.
antonym destroy.

creative *adj.* adept, artistic, clever, fertile, gifted, imaginative, ingenious, inspired, inventive, original, productive, resourceful, stimulating, talented, visionary.
antonym unimaginative.

credence *n.* belief, confidence, credit, dependence, faith, reliance, support, trust.
antonym distrust.

credible *adj.* believable, conceivable, convincing, dependable, honest, imaginable, likely, persuasive, plausible, possible, probable, reasonable, reliable, sincere, supposable, tenable, thinkable, trustworthy, trusty.
antonyms implausible, unreliable.

credit *n.* acclaim, acknowledgment, approval, belief, character, clout, commendation, confidence, credence, distinction, esteem, estimation, faith, fame, glory, honor, influence, kudos, merit, position, praise, prestige, recognition, regard, reliance, reputation, repute, standing, status, thanks, tribute, trust.
antonym discredit.
v. accept, believe, buy, subscribe to, swallow, trust.
antonym disbelieve.

creditable *adj.* admirable, commendable, deserving, estimable, excellent, exemplary, good, honorable, laudable, meritorious, praiseworthy, reputable, respectable, sterling, worthy.
antonyms blameworthy, shameful.

credulous *adj.* dupable, green, gullible, naïve, trusting, uncritical, unsuspecting, unsuspicious, wide-eyed.
antonym skeptical.

creed *n.* articles, belief, canon, catechism, confession, credo, doctrine, dogma, faith, persuasion, principles, tenets.

creek *n.* bay, bight, brook, cove, fiord, firth, frith, inlet, rivulet, stream, streamlet, tributary, voe, water-course.

creepy *adj.* awful, direful, disturbing, eerie, frightening, ghoulish, gruesome, hair-raising, horrible, macabre, menacing, nightmarish, ominous, scary, sinister, spookish, spooky, terrifying, threatening, unearthly, unpleasant, weird.
antonyms normal, pleasant.

crime *n.* atrocity, corruption, delinquency, fault, felony, flagitiousness, guilt, illegality, iniquity, law-breaking, malefaction, malfeasance, misconduct, misdeed, misdemeanor, offense, outrage, sin, transgression, trespass, unrighteousness, vice, villainy, violation, wickedness, wrong, wrongdoing.

criminal *n.* con, convict, crook, culprit, delinquent, evildoer, felon, infractor, jail-bird, law-breaker, malefactor, offender, sinner, transgressor.
adj. bent, corrupt, crooked, culpable, deplorable, felonious, flagitious, foolish, illegal, immoral, indictable, iniquitous, lawless, malfeasant, nefarious, peccant, preposterous, ridiculous, scandalous, senseless, unlawful, unrighteous, vicious, villainous, wicked, wrong.
antonyms honest, upright.

cripple *v.* cramp, damage, debilitate, destroy, disable, enfeeble, halt, hamstring, impair, incapacitate, lame, maim, mutilate, paralyze, ruin, sabotage, spoil, vitiate, weaken.

crippled *adj.* deformed, disabled, enfeebled, handicapped, incapacitated, invalid, lame, paralyzed.

crisis *n.* calamity, catastrophe, climacteric, climax, confrontation, conjuncture, crunch, crux, culmination, difficulty, dilemma, disaster, emergency, exigency, extremity, height, impasse, mess, pinch, plight, predicament, quandary, strait, trouble.

crisp *adj.* bracing, brief, brisk, brittle, brusque, clear, crispy, crumbly, crunchy, decisive, firm, forthright, fresh, incisive, invigorating, neat, orderly, pithy, refreshing, short, smart, snappy, spruce, succinct, tart, terse, tidy, vigorous.
antonyms flabby, limp, vague.

criterion *n.* bench-mark, canon, gauge, measure, norm, precedent, principle, proof, rule, shibboleth, standard, test, touchstone, yardstick.

critic *n.* analyst, animadverter, arbiter, Aristarch, attacker, authority, carper, caviler, censor, censurer, commentator, connoisseur, detractor, expert, expositor, fault-finder, feuilletonist, judge, knocker, Momus, pundit, reviewer, reviler, vilifier, Zoilist.

critical *adj.* accurate, all-important, analytical, captious, carping, caviling, censorious, climacteric, crucial, dangerous, deciding, decisive, derogatory, diagnostic, disapproving, discerning, discriminating, disparaging, fastidious, fault-finding, grave, hairy, high-priority, judicious, momentous, nagging, niggling, nit-picking, penetrating, perceptive, perilous, pivotal, precarious, precise, pressing, psychological, risky, serious, sharp-tongued, uncomplimentary, urgent, vital, Zoilean.
antonyms uncritical, unimportant.

criticize *v.* analyze, animadvert, appraise, assess, badmouth, blame, carp, censure, condemn, crab, decry, disparage, evaluate, excoriate, judge, knock, pan, review, roast, scarify, slag, slam, slash, slate, snipe.
antonym praise.

critique *n.* analysis, appraisal, assessment, commentary, essay, evaluation, examination, review.

crony *n.* accomplice, ally, associate, buddy, china, chum, colleague, companion, comrade, follower, friend, henchman, mate, pal, sidekick.

crooked[1] *adj.* bent, corrupt, crafty, criminal, deceitful, discreditable, dishonest, dishonorable, dubious, fraudulent, illegal, knavish, nefarious, questionable, shady, shifty, treacherous, underhand, unethical, unlawful, unprincipled, unscrupulous.
antonym honest.

crooked[2] *adj.* anfractuous, angled, askew, asymmetric, awry, bent, bowed, crank, cranky, crippled, crump, curved, deformed, deviating, disfigured, distorted, hooked, irregular, lopsided, meandering, misshapen, off-center, skew-whiff, slanted, slanting, squint, tilted, tortuous, twisted, twisting, uneven, warped, winding, zigzag.
antonym straight.

crop[1] *n.* fruits, gathering, growth, harvest, ingathering, produce, vintage, yield.
v. browse, clip, collect, curtail, cut, garner, gather, graze, harvest, lop, mow, nibble, pare, pick, prune, reap, reduce, shear, shingle, shorten, snip, top, trim, yield.

crop[2] *n.* craw, gizzard, gullet, maw, oesophagus, throat.

cross *adj.* adverse, angry, annoyed, cantankerous, captious, churlish, contrary, cranky, crosswise, crotchety, crusty, disagreeable, displeased, fractious, fretful, grouchy, grumpy, hybrid, ill-humored, ill-tempered, impatient, interchanged, intersecting, irascible, irritable, oblique, opposed, opposing, opposite, peeved, peevish, pettish, petulant, querulous, reciprocal, shirty, short, snappish, snappy, splenetic, sullen, surly, testy, transverse, unfavorable, vexed, waspish.
antonyms calm, placid, pleasant.
v. annoy, bestride, blend, block, bridge, cancel, criss-cross, crossbreed, cross-fertilize, cross-pollinate, decussate, deny, foil, ford, frustrate, hinder, hybridize, impede, interbreed, intercross, interfere, intersect, intertwine, lace, meet, mix, mongrelize, obstruct, oppose, resist, span, thwart, traverse, zigzag.
n. affliction, amalgam, blend, burden, combination, cross-breed, crossing, crossroads, crucifix, cur, grief, holy-rood, hybrid, hybridization, intersection, load, misery, misfortune, mixture, mongrel, rood, trial, tribulation, trouble, woe, worry.

crouch *v.* bend, bow, cower, cringe, duck, hunch, kneel, ruck, squat, stoop.

crow *v.* bluster, boast, brag, exult, flourish, gloat, prate, rejoice, triumph, vaunt.

crowd *n.* army, assembly, attendance, audience, boodle, bunch, caboodle, circle, clique, company, concourse, flock, gate, group, herd, hoi polloi, horde, host, house, lot, many-headed beast/monster, mass, masses, mob, multitude, pack, people, populace, press, proletariat, public, rabble, riff-raff, set, spectators, squash, swarm, the many, throng, troupe.
v. bundle, cluster, compress, congest, congregate, cram, elbow, flock, for(e)gather, gather, huddle, jostle, mass, muster, pack, pile, press, push, shove, squeeze, stream, surge, swarm, throng.

crown *n.* acme, apex, bays, chaplet, circlet, coronal, coronet, crest, diadem, distinction, forehead, garland, head, honor, kudos, laurel wreath, laurels, monarch, monarchy, pate, perfection, pinnacle, prize, royalty, ruler, skull, sovereign, sovereignty, summit, tiara, tip, top, trophy, ultimate, zenith.
v. adorn, biff, box, cap, clout, complete, consummate, cuff, dignify, festoon, finish, fulfil, honor, instal, perfect, punch, reward, surmount, terminate, top.

crude *adj.* amateurish, blue, boorish, clumsy, coarse, crass, dirty, earthy, gross, half-baked, immature, inartistic,

indecent, lewd, makeshift, natural, obscene, outline, primitive, raw, rough, rough-hewn, rude, rudimentary, sketchy, smutty, tactless, tasteless, uncouth, undeveloped, undigested, unfinished, unformed, unpolished, unprepared, unprocessed, unrefined, unsubtle, vulgar.
antonyms finished, polite, refined, tasteful.

cruel *adj.* atrocious, barbarous, bitter, bloodthirsty, brutal, brutish, butcherly, callous, cold-blooded, cutting, depraved, excruciating, fell, ferocious, fierce, flinty, grim, hard, hard-hearted, harsh, heartless, heathenish, hellish, immane, implacable, inclement, inexorable, inhuman, inhumane, malevolent, marble-breasted, merciless, murderous, painful, pitiless, poignant, ravening, raw, relentless, remorseless, ruthless, sadistic, sanguinary, savage, severe, spiteful, stony-hearted, unfeeling, ungentle, unkind, unmerciful, unnatural, unrelenting, vengeful, vicious.
antonyms compassionate, kind, merciful.

cruelty *n.* barbarity, bestiality, bloodthirstiness, brutality, brutishness, callousness, depravity, ferocity, fiendishness, hard-heartedness, harshness, heartlessness, immanity, inhumanity, mercilessness, murderousness, ruthlessness, sadism, savagery, severity, spite, spitefulness, tyranny, ungentleness, venom, viciousness.
antonyms compassion, kindness, mercy.

crumb *n.* atom, bit, grain, iota, jot, mite, morsel, particle, scrap, shred, sliver, snippet, soupçon, speck.

crunch *v.* champ, chomp, grind, masticate, munch, scranch.
n. crisis, crux, emergency, pinch, test.

crush *v.* abash, break, browbeat, bruise, chagrin, champ, comminute, compress, conquer, contuse, crease, crumble, crumple, crunch, embrace, enfold, extinguish, hug, humiliate, mash, mortify, overcome, overpower, overwhelm, pound, press, pulverize, quash, quell, rumple, shame, smash, squabash, squeeze, squelch, steamroller, subdue, vanquish, wrinkle.
n. check, crowd, huddle, jam.

cry *v.* advertise, announce, bark, bawl, beg, bellow, beseech, bewail, blubber, boo-hoo, broadcast, bruit, call, caterwaul, clamor, ejaculate, entreat, exclaim, greet, hail, halloo, hawk, holler, howl, implore, keen, lament, mewl, miaow, miaul, noise, plead, pray, proclaim, promulgate, pule, roar, scream, screech, shout, shriek, snivel, sob, squall, squeal, trumpet, vociferate, wail, weep, whimper, whine, whinge, whoop, yell, yowl.
n. announcement, appeal, battle-cry, bawl(ing), bellow, blubber(ing), call, caterwaul, caterwaul(ing), ejaculation, entreaty, exclamation, greet, holler, hoot, howl, keening, lament, lamentation, miaow, miaul, outcry, petition, plaint, plea, prayer, proclamation, report, roar, rumor, scream, screech, shriek, slogan, snivel(ing), sob(bing), sorrowing, squall, squawk, squeal, supplication, utterance, wail(ing), watch-word, weep(ing), whoop, yell, yelp, yoo-hoo.

cryptic *adj.* abstruse, ambiguous, aprocryphal, arcane, bizarre, cabbalistic, dark, Delphic, enigmatic, equivocal, esoteric, hidden, mysterious, obscure, occult, oracular, perplexing, puzzling, recondite, secret, strange, vague, veiled.
antonyms clear, obvious, straightforward.

cuddly *adj.* buxom, cosy, cuddlesome, curvaceous, huggable, lovable, plump, soft, warm.

cull *v.* amass, choose, collect, decimate, destroy, gather, glean, kill, pick, pick out, pluck, select, sift, thin, winnow.

culpable *adj.* answerable, blamable, blameworthy, censurable, guilty, liable, offending, peccant, reprehensible, sinful, to blame, wrong.
antonyms blameless, innocent.

culprit *n.* criminal, delinquent, evil-doer, felon, guilty party, law-breaker, malefactor, miscreant, offender, rascal, sinner, transgressor, wrong-doer.

cultivate *v.* aid, ameliorate, better, cherish, civilize, court, develop, discipline, elevate, encourage, enrich, farm, fertilize, forward, foster, further, harvest, help, improve, patronize, plant, plow, polish, prepare, promote, pursue, refine, school, support, tend, till, train, work.
antonym neglect.

cultivation *n.* advancement, advocacy, agronomy, breeding, civilization, civility, culture, development, discernment, discrimination, education, encouragement, enhancement, enlightenment, farming, fostering, furtherance, gardening, gentility, help, husbandry, learning, letters, manners, nurture, patronage, planting, plowing, polish, promotion, pursuit, refinement, schooling, study, support, taste, tillage, tilling, tilth, working.

cultural *adj.* aesthetic, artistic, arty, broadening, civilizing, developmental, edifying, educational, educative, elevating, enlightening, enriching, humane, humanizing, liberal.

culture *n.* accomplishment, aestheticism, agriculture, agronomy, art, breeding, civilization, cultivation, customs, education, elevation, enlightenment, erudition, farming, gentility, husbandry, improvement, Kultur, lifestyle, mores, polish, politeness, refinement, society, taste, the arts, urbanity.

cultured *adj.* accomplished, advanced, aesthetic, arty, civilized, educated, enlightened, erudite, genteel, highbrow, knowledgeable, polished, refined, scholarly, urbane, versed, well-bred, well-informed, well-read.
antonyms ignorant, uncultured.

cumbersome *adj.* awkward, bulky, burdensome, clumsy, cumbrous, embarrassing, heavy, hefty, incommodious, inconvenient, onerous, oppressive, ponderous, unmanageable, unwieldy, weighty.
antonyms convenient, manageable.

cunning *adj.* adroit, arch, artful, astute, canny, crafty, deep, deft, devious, dexterous, foxy, guileful, imaginative, ingenious, knowing, leery, Machiavellian, rusé,

sharp, shifty, shrewd, skilful, sneaky, subtle, tricky, vulpine, wily. *antonyms* gullible, naïve.
n. ability, adroitness, art, artfulness, artifice, astuteness, cleverness, craftiness, deceitfulness, deftness, deviousness, dexterity, finesse, foxiness, guile, ingenuity, policy, shrewdness, skill, slyness, subtlety, trickery, vulpinism, wiliness.
antonyms openness, simplicity.

curb *v.* bit, bridle, check, constrain, contain, control, hamper, hinder, hobble, impede, inhibit, moderate, muzzle, repress, restrain, restrict, retard, subdue, suppress.
antonyms encourage, foster, goad.
n. brake, bridle, check, control, deterrent, hamper, hobble, limitation, rein, restraint.

cure[1] *v.* alleviate, correct, ease, heal, help, mend, rehabilitate, relieve, remedy, restore.
n. alleviation, antidote, corrective, detoxicant, febrifuge, healing, medicine, panacea, panpharmacon, recovery, remedy, restorative, specific, treatment, vulnerary.

cure[2] *v.* brine, dry, kipper, pickle, preserve, salt, smoke.

curiosity *n.* bibelot, bygone, celebrity, curio, freak, inquisitiveness, interest, knick-knack, marvel, nosiness, novelty, object of virtu, objet d'art, objet de vertu, oddity, phenomenon, prying, rarity, sight, snooping, spectacle, trinket, wonder.

curious *adj.* bizarre, enquiring, exotic, extraordinary, funny, inquisitive, interested, marvelous, meddling, mysterious, nosy, novel, odd, peculiar, peeping, peering, prying, puzzled, puzzling, quaint, queer, questioning, rare, searching, singular, snoopy, strange, unconventional, unexpected, unique, unorthodox, unusual, wonderful.
antonyms incurious, indifferent, normal, ordinary, uninterested.

current *adj.* accepted, circulating, common, contemporary, customary, extant, fashionable, general, on-going, popular, present, present-day, prevailing, prevalent, reigning, rife, trendy, up-to-date, up-to-the-minute, widespread.
antonyms antiquated, old-fashioned.
n. atmosphere, course, draft, drift, feeling, flow, inclination, jet, juice, mood, progression, river, stream, tendency, thermal, tide, trend, undercurrent.

curse *n.* affliction, anathema, ban, bane, blasphemy, burden, calamity, cross, damn, denunciation, disaster, evil, excommunication, execration, expletive, imprecation, jinx, malediction, malison, misfortune, oath, obscenity, ordeal, plague, scourge, swearing, swear-word, torment, tribulation, trouble, vexation, woe.
antonyms advantage, blessing.
v. accurse, afflict, anathematize, blaspheme, blight, blind, blow, burden, cuss, damn, destroy, doom, excommunicate, execrate, fulminate, imprecate, plague, scourge, swear, torment, trouble, vex.
antonym bless.

cursory *adj.* brief, careless, casual, desultory, fleeting, hasty, hurried, offhand, passing, perfunctory, quick, rapid, slap-dash, slight, summary, superficial.
antonyms painstaking, thorough.

curt *adj.* abrupt, blunt, brief, brusque, concise, gruff, laconic, offhand, pithy, rude, sharp, short, short-spoken, snappish, succinct, summary, tart, terse, unceremonious, uncivil, ungracious.
antonym voluble.

curtail *v.* abbreviate, abridge, circumscribe, contract, cut, decrease, dock, lessen, lop, pare, prune, reduce, restrict, retrench, shorten, trim, truncate.
antonyms extend, lengthen, prolong.

curtain *v.* conceal, drape, hide, screen, shield, shroud, shutter, veil.
n. arras, backdrop, drapery, hanging, portière, tab, tapestry, vitrage.

curve *v.* arc, arch, bend, bow, coil, hook, incurvate, incurve, inflect, spiral, swerve, turn, twist, wind.
n. arc, bend, camber, curvature, half-moon, incurvation, incurvature, inflexure, loop, trajectory, turn.

cushion *n.* bean-bag, bolster, buffer, hassock, headrest, pad, pillion, pillow, shock absorber, squab. *v.* allay, bolster, buttress, cradle, dampen, deaden, lessen, mitigate, muffle, pillow, protect, soften, stifle, support, suppress.

custodian *n.* caretaker, castellan, chatelaine, claviger, conservator, curator, guardian, keeper, overseer, protector, superintendent, warden, warder, watch-dog, watchman.

custody *n.* aegis, arrest, auspices, care, charge, confinement, custodianship, detention, durance, duress, guardianship, holding, imprisonment, incarceration, keeping, observation, possession, preservation, protection, retention, safe-keeping, supervision, trusteeship, tutelage, ward, wardship, watch.

custom *n.* consuetude, convention, customers, etiquette, fashion, form, formality, habit, habitude, manner, mode, observance, observation, patronage, policy, practice, praxis, procedure, ritual, routine, rule, style, thew, trade, tradition, usage, use, way, wont.

customary *adj.* accepted, accustomed, acknowledged, common, confirmed, conventional, established, everyday, familiar, fashionable, favorite, general, habitual, nomic, normal, ordinary, popular, prevailing, regular, routine, traditional, usual, wonted.
antonyms occasional, rare, unusual.

customer *n.* buyer, client, consumer, habitué, patron, prospect, punter, purchaser, regular, shopper, vendee.

cut *v.* abbreviate, abridge, avoid, bisect, carve, castrate, chip, chisel, chop, cleave, clip, cold-shoulder, condense, contract, cross, curtail, decrease, delete, dissect, divide, dock, edit, engrave, excise, fashion, fell, form, gash, gather, gride, grieve, hack, harvest, hew, hurt, ignore, incise, insult, interrupt, intersect, lacerate, lop, lower, mow, nick, notch, pain, pare, part, penetrate, pierce, précis, prune, rationalize, reap,

reduce, saw, scissor, score, sculpt, sculpture, segment, sever, shape, share, shave, shorten, slash, slice, slight, slim, slit, sned, snub, split, spurn, sting, sunder, trim, truncate, whittle, wound.
n. abscission, blow, chop, configuration, cutback, decrease, decrement, diminution, division, economy, fall, fashion, form, gash, graze, groove, incision, incisure, insection, kickback, laceration, look, lowering, mode, nick, percentage, piece, portion, race, rake-off, reduction, rent, rip, saving, section, shape, share, slash, slice, slit, snick, stroke, style, wound.

cut back check, crop, curb, decrease, economize, lessen, lop, lower, prune, reduce, retrench, slash, trim.

cut in interjaculate, interject, interpose, interrupt, intervene, intrude.

cut off abscind, block, disconnect, discontinue, disinherit, disown, end, excide, excise, exscind, halt, intercept, interclude, interrupt, intersect, isolate, obstruct, prescind, renounce, separate, sever, stop, suspend.

cut short abbreviate, abort, arrest, check, crop, curtail, dock, halt, interrupt, postpone, prune, reduce, stop, terminate.
antonym prolong.

cut-throat *n.* assassin, bravo, butcher, executioner, hatchet man, hit-man, homicide, killer, liquidator, murderer, slayer, thug.
adj. barbarous, bloodthirsty, bloody, brutal, competitive, cruel, dog-eat-dog, ferine, ferocious, fierce, homicidal, murderous, relentless, ruthless, savage, thuggish, unprincipled, vicious, violent.

cutting *adj.* acid, acrimonious, barbed, biting, bitter, caustic, chill, hurtful, incisive, keen, malicious, mordant, numbing, penetrating, piercing, pointed, raw, sarcastic, sardonic, scathing, severe, sharp, stinging, trenchant, wounding.
n. bit, cleavage, clipping, piece, scion, scission, slice.

cynical *adj.* contemptuous, derisive, distrustful, ironic, mephistophelian, mephistophilic, misanthropic(al), mocking, mordant, pessimistic, sarcastic, sardonic, sceptical, scoffing, scornful, sharp-tongued, sneering.

D

dab[1] *v.* blot, daub, pat, stipple, swab, tap, touch, wipe.
n. bit, dollop, drop, fingerprint, fleck, flick, pat, peck, smear, smidgen, smudge, speck, spot, stroke, tap, touch, trace.

dab[2] ace, adept, dab hand, dabster, expert, pastmaster, wizard.

dabble *v.* dally, dip, fiddle, guddle, moisten, paddle, potter, spatter, splash, sprinkle, tinker, toy, trifle, wet.

daft *adj.* absurd, asinine, berserk, besotted, crackers, crazy, daffy, delirious, demented, deranged, dop(e)y, doting, dotty, foolish, giddy, hysterical, idiotic, inane, infatuated, insane, lunatic, mad, mental, nuts, nutty, potty, scatty, screwy, silly, simple, stupid, touched, unhinged, witless.
antonyms bright, sane.

daily *adj.* circadian, common, commonplace, customary, day-to-day, diurnal, everyday, normal, ordinary, quotidian, regular, routine.

dainty *adj.* charming, choice, choos(e)y, delectable, delicate, delicious, dinky, elegant, exquisite, fastidious, fine, finical, finicking, finicky, friand(e), fussy, genty, graceful, lickerish, liquorish, meticulous, mignon(ne), mincing, minikin, neat, nice, palatable, particular, petite, pretty, refined, savory, scrupulous, tasty, tender, toothsome.
antonyms clumsy, gross.
n. bonbon, bonne-bouche, delicacy, fancy, sweetmeat, tidbit.

dally *v.* canoodle, dawdle, delay, dilly-dally, fiddle-faddle, flirt, frivol, linger, loiter, play, procrastinate, sport, tamper, tarry, toy, trifle.
antonyms hasten, hurry.

dam *n.* an(n)icut, barrage, barrier, blockage, embankment, hindrance, obstruction, wall.
v. barricade, block, check, choke, confine, obstruct, restrict, stanch, staunch, stem.

damage *n.* destruction, detriment, devastation, disprofit, harm, hurt, impairment, injury, loss, mischief, mutilation, scathe, suffering.
antonym repair.
v. deface, harm, hurt, impair, incapacitate, injure, mar, mutilate, play havoc with, play hell with, ruin, spoil, tamper with, weaken, wreck.
antonyms fix, repair.

dame *n.* baroness, broad, dowager, female, lady, matron, noblewoman, peeress, woman.

damn *v.* abuse, anathematize, blaspheme, blast, castigate, censure, condemn, criticize, curse, dang, darn, dash, denounce, denunciate, doom, excoriate, execrate, imprecate, pan, revile, sentence, slam, slate, swear.
antonym bless.
n. brass farthing, darn, dash, hoot, iota, jot, monkey's, tinker's cuss, two hoots, whit.

damnable *adj.* abominable, accursed, atrocious, culpable, cursed, despicable, detestable, execrable, hateful, horrible, iniquitous, offensive, sinful, wicked.
antonyms admirable, praiseworthy.

damp *n.* clamminess, dampness, dankness, dew, drizzle, fog, humidity, mist, moisture, muzziness, vapor, wet.
antonym dryness.
adj. clammy, dank, dewy, dripping, drizzly, humid, misty, moist, muggish, muggy, sodden, soggy, sopping, vaporous, vaporish, vapory, wet.
antonyms arid, dry.
v. allay, bedew, check, chill, cool, curb, dampen, dash, deaden, deject, depress, diminish, discourage, dispirit, dull, inhibit, moderate, moisten, restrain, stifle, wet.
antonym dry.

dampen *v.* bedew, besprinkle, check, dash, deaden, decrease, depress, deter, diminish, dishearten, dismay, dull, lessen, moderate, moisten, muffle, reduce, restrain, smother, spray, stifle, wet.
antonyms dry, encourage.

dance *v.* caper, frolic, gambol, hoof it, hop, jig, juke, kantikoy, prance, rock, skip, spin, stomp, sway, swing, tread a measure, whirl.
n. bal masqué, bal paré, ball, hop, kantikoy, kick-up, knees-up, prom, shindig, social.

danger *n.* endangerment, hazard, insecurity, jeopardy, liability, menace, peril, precariousness, risk, threat, trouble, venture, vulnerability.
antonyms safety, security.

dangerous *adj.* alarming, breakneck, chancy, critical, daring, exposed, grave, hairy, harmful, hazardous, insecure, menacing, nasty, parlous, perilous, precarious, reckless, risky, serious, severe, threatening, tickly, treacherous, ugly, unsafe, vulnerable.
antonyms harmless, safe, secure.

dangle *v.* droop, flap, flaunt, flourish, hang, lure, sway, swing, tantalize, tempt, trail, wave.

dank *adj.* chilly, clammy, damp, dewy, dripping, moist, rheumy, slimy, soggy.
antonym dry.

dapper *adj.* active, brisk, chic, dainty, natty, neat, nimble, smart, spiffy, spruce, spry, stylish, trig, trim, well-dressed, well-groomed.
antonyms disheveled, dowdy, scruffy, shabby, sloppy.

dappled *adj.* bespeckled, brindled, checkered, dotted,

flecked, freckled, mottled, piebald, pied, speckled, spotted, stippled, variegated.

dare *v.* adventure, brave, challenge, defy, endanger, gamble, goad, have the gall, hazard, presume, provoke, risk, stake, taunt, venture.
n. challenge, gauntlet, provocation, taunt.

daredevil *n.* adventurer, desperado, exhibitionist, Hotspur, madcap, stuntman.
antonym coward.
adj. adventurous, audacious, bold, daring, death-defying, fearless, madcap, rash, reckless.
antonyms cautious, prudent, timid.

daring *adj.* adventurous, audacious, bold, brave, brazen, dauntless, fearless, game, impulsive, intrepid, plucky, rash, reckless, valiant, venturesome.
antonyms afraid, timid.
n. audacity, boldness, bottle, bravery, bravura, courage, defiance, derring-do, fearlessness, gall, grit, guts, intrepidity, nerve, pluck, prowess, rashness, spirit, spunk, temerity.
antonyms cowardice, timidity.

dark *adj.* abstruse, angry, aphotic, arcane, atrocious, benighted, black, bleak, brunette, caliginous, cheerless, cloudy, concealed, cryptic, damnable, darkling, dark-skinned, darksome, deep, dim, dingy, dismal, doleful, dour, drab, dusky, ebony, enigmatic, evil, forbidding, foul, frowning, gloomy, glowering, glum, grim, hellish, hidden, horrible, ignorant, indistinct, infamous, infernal, joyless, lightless, melanic, melanous, midnight, mirk, mirky, morbid, morose, mournful, murk, murky, mysterious, mystic, nefarious, obscure, occult, ominous, overcast, pitch-black, pitchy, puzzling, recondite, sable, satanic, scowling, secret, shadowy, shady, sinful, sinister, somber, sulky, sullen, sunless, swarthy, tenebr(i)ous, threatening, uncultivated, unenlightened, unillumed, unilluminated, unlettered, unlit, vile, wicked.
antonyms bright, happy, light, lucid.
n. concealment, darkness, dimness, dusk, evening, gloom, ignorance, mirk, mirkiness, murk, murkiness, night, nightfall, night-time, obscurity, secrecy, twilight, yin.
antonyms brightness, light.

darling *n.* acushla, apple of one's eye, asthore, beloved, blue-eyed boy, dear, dearest, fair-haired boy, favorite, jo(e), lady-love, love, lovey, machree, mavourneen, minikin, pet, poppet, sweetheart, true-love.
adj. adored, beloved, cherished, dear, precious, treasured, white-headed.

dart *v.* bound, cast, dartle, dash, flash, fling, flit, fly, hurl, launch, propel, race, run, rush, scoot, send, shoot, sling, spring, sprint, start, tear, throw, whistle, whizz.
n. arrow, barb, bolt, flight, shaft.

dash[1] *v.* abash, blight, break, cast, chagrin, confound, crash, dampen, destroy, ding, disappoint, discomfort, discourage, fling, foil, frustrate, hurl, ruin, shatter, shiver, slam, sling, smash, splinter, spoil, throw, thwart.
n. bit, bravura, brio, da(u)d, drop, élan, flair, flavor, flourish, hint, little, panache, pinch, smack, soupçon, spirit, sprinkling, style, suggestion, tinge, touch, verve, vigor, vivacity.

dash[2] *v.* be off like a shot, bolt, bound, dart, dartle, fly, haste(n), hurry, race, run, rush, speed, spring, sprint, tear.
n. bolt, dart, race, run, rush, sprint, spurt.

dashing *adj.* bold, dapper, daring, dazzling, debonair, doggy, elegant, exuberant, flamboyant, gallant, impressive, jaunty, lively, plucky, showy, smart, spirited, sporty, stylish, swashbuckling, swish.
antonym drab.

dastardly *adj.* base, caitiff, contemptible, cowardly, craven, despicable, faint-hearted, lily-livered, low, mean, niddering, pusillanimous, recreant, sneaking, sneaky, spiritless, timorous, underhand, vile.
antonyms heroic, noble.

data *n.* details, documents, dope, facts, figures, info, information, input, materials, statistics.

date[1] *n.* age, epoch, era, period, point, point in time, stage, time.

date[2] *n.* appointment, assignation, engagement, escort, friend, meeting, partner, rendezvous, steady, tryst.

dated *adj.* antiquated, archaic, démodé, obsolescent, obsolete, old hat, old-fashioned, out, outdated, outmoded, out-of-date, passé, superseded, unfashionable.
antonyms fashionable, up-to-the-minute.

daub *v.* begrime, besmear, blur, coat, cover, dedaub, deface, dirty, gaum, grime, paint, plaster, smear, smirch, smudge, spatter, splatter, stain, sully.
n. blot, blotch, smear, splash, splodge, splotch, spot, stain.

daunt *v.* alarm, appal, cow, deter, discourage, dishearten, dismay, dispirit, frighten, intimidate, overawe, put off, scare, shake, subdue, terrify, unnerve.
antonyms encourage, hearten.

dauntless *adj.* bold, brave, courageous, daring, doughty, fearless, gallant, game, heroic, indomitable, intrepid, lion-hearted, plucky, resolute, stout-hearted, undaunted, unflinching, valiant, valorous.
antonyms discouraged, disheartened.

dawn *n.* advent, aurora, beginning, birth, cock-crow(ing), dawning, daybreak, daylight, day-peep, dayspring, emergence, genesis, inception, morning, onset, origin, outset, peep of day, rise, start, sunrise, sun-up.
antonyms dusk, sundown, sunset.
v. appear, begin, break, brighten, develop, emerge, gleam, glimmer, hit, initiate, lighten, occur, open, originate, register, rise, strike, unfold.

daydream *n.* castles in Spain, castles in the air, dream, dwa(l)m, fantasy, figment, fond hope, imagining, musing, phantasm, pipe dream, reverie, star-gazing, vision, wish, wool-gathering.
v. dream, fancy, fantasize, hallucinate, imagine, muse, stargaze.

daze *v.* amaze, astonish, astound, befog, benumb, bewilder, blind, confuse, dazzle, dumbfound, flabbergast, numb, paralyze, perplex, shock, stagger, startle, stun, stupefy, surprise.
n. bewilderment, confusion, distraction, dwa(l)m, shock, stupor, trance.

dazzle *v.* amaze, astonish, awe, bedazzle, blind, blur, confuse, daze, fascinate, hypnotize, impress, overawe, overpower, overwhelm, scintillate, sparkle, stupefy.

dead[1] *adj.* ad patres, apathetic, barren, boring, breathless, callous, cold, dead-and-alive, dead-beat, deceased, defunct, departed, dull, exhausted, extinct, flat, frigid, glassy, glazed, gone, inactive, inanimate, indifferent, inert, inoperative, insipid, late, lifeless, lukewarm, napoo, numb, obsolete, paralyzed, perished, spent, spiritless, stagnant, stale, sterile, stiff, still, tasteless, tired, torpid, unemployed, uninteresting, unprofitable, unresponsive, useless, vapid, wooden, worn out.
antonyms active, alive, animated.

dead[2] *adj.* absolute, complete, downright, entire, outright, perfect, thorough, total, unqualified, utter.
adv. absolutely, completely, entirely, exactly, perfectly, quite, totally.

deaden *v.* abate, allay, alleviate, anesthetize, benumb, blunt, check, cushion, damp, dampen, desensitize, diminish, dull, hush, impair, lessen, muffle, mute, numb, obtund, paralyze, quieten, reduce, smother, stifle, suppress, weaken.
antonym enliven.

deadlock *n.* halt, impasse, stalemate, standstill.

deadly *adj.* accurate, ashen, baleful, baneful, boring, cruel, dangerous, death-dealing, deathful, deathlike, deathly, destructive, devastating, dull, effective, exact, fatal, feral, funest, ghastly, ghostly, grim, implacable, lethal, malignant, monotonous, mortal, noxious, pallid, pernicious, pestilent, poisonous, precise, ruthless, savage, sure, tedious, thanatoid, true, unerring, unfailing, uninteresting, unrelenting, venomous, wearisome, white.
antonyms harmless, healthy.

deaf *adj.* hard of hearing, heedless, indifferent, oblivious, stone-deaf, unconcerned, unmindful, unmoved.
antonyms aware, conscious.

deafening *adj.* booming, dinning, ear-piercing, ear-splitting, fortissimo, piercing, resounding, ringing, roaring, thunderous.
antonyms pianissimo, quiet.

deal *v.* allot, apportion, assign, bargain, bestow, dispense, distribute, divide, dole out, give, mete out, negotiate, reward, sell, share, stock, trade, traffic, treat.
n. agreement, amount, arrangement, bargain, buy, contract, degree, distribution, extent, hand, pact, portion, quantity, round, share, transaction, understanding.

dear *adj.* beloved, cherished, close, costly, darling, esteemed, expensive, familiar, favorite, high-priced, intimate, loved, overpriced, precious, pric(e)y, prized, respected, treasured, valued.
antonyms cheap, hateful.
n. angel, beloved, darling, dearie, deary, loved one, precious, treasure.

dearth *n.* absence, barrenness, deficiency, exiguousness, famine, inadequacy, insufficiency, lack, need, paucity, poverty, scantiness, scarcity, shortage, sparseness, sparsity, want.
antonyms abundance, excess.

death *n.* annihilation, bane, bereavement, cessation, curtains, decease, demise, departure, destruction, dissolution, dormition, downfall, dying, end, eradication, exit, expiration, extermination, extinction, fatality, finish, grave, loss, obliteration, passing, quietus, release, ruin, ruination, undoing.
antonyms birth, life.

debase *v.* abase, adulterate, allay, bastardize, cheapen, contaminate, corrupt, defile, degrade, demean, depreciate, devalue, diminish, disgrace, dishonor, embase, humble, humiliate, impair, lower, pollute, reduce, shame, taint, vitiate.
antonyms elevate, upgrade.

debate *v.* argue, cogitate, consider, contend, contest, controvert, deliberate, discuss, dispute, logicize, meditate on, mull over, ponder, question, reflect, revolve, ruminate, weigh, wrangle.
antonym agree.
n. altercation, argument, cogitation, consideration, contention, controversy, deliberation, discussion, disputation, dispute, meditation, polemic, quodlibet, reflection.
antonym agreement.

debauched *adj.* abandoned, corrupt, corrupted, debased, degenerate, degraded, depraved, dissipated, dissolute, immoral, intemperate, lewd, licentious, perverted, profligate, raddled, rakehell, rakehelly, wanton.
antonyms decent, pure, virtuous.

debonair *adj.* affable, breezy, buoyant, charming, cheerful, courteous, dashing, elegant, gay, jaunty, lighthearted, refined, smooth, sprightly, suave, urbane, well-bred.

debris *n.* bits, brash, detritus, drift, dross, duff, eluvium, exuviae, fragments, litter, moraine, pieces, remains, rubbish, rubble, ruins, sweepings, trash, waste, wreck, wreckage.

debt *n.* arrears, bill, claim, commitment, debit, due, duty, indebtedness, liability, obligation, score, sin.
antonyms asset, credit.

decay *v.* atrophy, canker, corrode, crumble, decline, decompose, decompound, degenerate, deteriorate, disintegrate, dissolve, dote, dwindle, mortify, molder, perish, putrefy, rot, shrivel, sink, spoil, wane, waste away, wear away, wither.
antonyms flourish, grow, ripen.
n. atrophy, caries, collapse, consenescence, decadence,

decline, decomposition, decrepitness, decrepitude, degeneracy, degeneration, deterioration, disintegration, dying, fading, failing, gangrene, labefactation, labefaction, mortification, perishing, putrefaction, putrescence, putridity, putridness, rot, rotting, wasting, withering.

deceased *adj.* dead, defunct, departed, expired, extinct, finished, former, gone, late, lifeless, lost.
n. dead, decedent, departed.

deceit *n.* abuse, artifice, blind, cheat, cheating, chicanery, con, cozenage, craftiness, cunning, deceitfulness, deception, dissimulation, double-dealing, duplicity, fake, feint, fraud, fraudulence, guile, hypocrisy, imposition, imposture, misrepresentation, pretense, ruse, sham, shift, slyness, stratagem, subterfuge, swindle, treachery, trick, trickery, underhandedness, wile.
antonyms honesty, openness.

deceitful *adj.* collusive, counterfeit, crafty, deceiving, deceptive, designing, dishonest, disingenuous, double-dealing, duplicitous, elusory, fallacious, false, fraudulent, guileful, hypocritical, illusory, insincere, knavish, prestigious, Punic, rusé, sneaky, treacherous, tricky, two-faced, underhand, untrustworthy.
antonyms honest, open, trustworthy.

deceive *v.* abuse, bamboozle, befool, beguile, betray, camouflage, cheat, cog, con, cozen, delude, diddle, disappoint, dissemble, dissimulate, double-cross, dupe, ensnare, entrap, flam, fool, gag, gammon, gull, have on, hoax, hood-wink, impose upon, lead on, mislead, outwit, seel, swindle, take for a ride, take in, trick, two-time.
antonym enlighten.

decency *n.* appropriateness, civility, correctness, courtesy, decorum, etiquette, fitness, good form, good manners, helpfulness, modesty, propriety, respectability, seemliness, thoughtfulness.
antonyms discourtesy, indecency.

decent *adj.* acceptable, accommodating, adequate, ample, appropriate, average, becoming, befitting, chaste, comely, comme il faut, competent, courteous, decorous, delicate, fair, fit, fitting, friendly, generous, gracious, gradely, helpful, kind, modest, nice, obliging, passable, polite, presentable, proper, pure, reasonable, respectable, satisfactory, seemly, sufficient, suitable, thoughtful, tolerable.
antonyms disobliging, indecent, poor.

deception *n.* artifice, bluff, cheat, conning, craftiness, cunning, deceifulness, deceit, deceptiveness, decoy, defraudation, defraudment, dissembling, dissimulation, duplicity, false-pretences, feint, flim-flam, fraud, fraudulence, guile, gullery, hoax, hype, hypocrisy, illusion, imposition, imposture, insincerity, legerdemain, leg-pull, lie, ruse, sell, sham, snare, stratagem, subterfuge, take-in, treachery, trick, trickery, wile.
antonyms artlessness, openness.

deceptive *adj.* ambiguous, catchy, delusive, delusory, dishonest, elusory, fake, fallacious, false, fraudulent, illusive, illusory, misleading, mock, specious, spurious, unreliable.
antonyms artless, genuine, open.

decide *v.* adjudge, adjudicate, choose, conclude, decree, determine, dijudicate, elect, end, fix, judge, opt, purpose, reach a decision, resolve, settle.

decipher *v.* construe, crack, decode, decrypt, deduce, explain, figure out, interpret, make out, read, solve, transliterate, uncipher, understand, unfold, unravel, unscramble.
antonym encode.

decision *n.* arbitrament, arbitration, arrêt, conclusion, decisiveness, determination, fetwa, finding, firmness, judgment, outcome, parti, purpose, purposefulness, resoluteness, resolution, resolve, result, ruling, settlement, verdict.

decisive *adj.* absolute, conclusive, critical, crucial, crunch, decided, definite, definitive, determinate, determined, fateful, final, firm, forceful, forthright, incisive, influential, momentous, positive, resolute, significant, strong-minded, supreme, trenchant.
antonyms indecisive, insignificant.

declaration *n.* acknowledgment, affirmation, announcement, assertion, asseveration, attestation, averment, avouchment, avowal, deposition, disclosure, edict, manifesto, notification, proclamation, profession, promulgation, pronouncement, pronunciamento, protestation, revelation, statement, testimony.

declare *v.* affirm, announce, assert, attest, aver, avouch, avow, certify, claim, confess, confirm, convey, disclose, maintain, manifest, nuncupate, proclaim, profess, pronounce, reveal, show, state, swear, testify, validate, witness.

decline[1] *v.* avoid, balk, decay, decrease, degenerate, deny, deteriorate, deviate, diminish, droop, dwindle, ebb, fade, fail, fall, fall off, flag, forgo, languish, lessen, pine, refuse, reject, shrink, sink, turn down, wane, weaken, worsen.
n. abatement, consumption, decay, declension, decrepitude, degeneration, deterioration, deviation, diminution, downturn, dwindling, enfeeblement, failing, falling-off, lessening, paracme, phthisis, recession, senility, slump, tuberculosis, weakening, worsening.

decline[2] *v.* descend, dip, sink, slant, slope.
n. brae, declination, declivity, descent, deviation, dip, divergence, hill, incline, obliqueness, obliquity, slope.

decompose *v.* analyze, atomize, break down, break up, crumble, decay, decompound, degrade, disintegrate, dissolve, distil, fall apart, fester, fractionate, putrefy, rot, separate, spoil.
antonyms combine, unite.

decorate[1] *v.* adorn, beautify, bedeck, color, deck, do up, embellish, enrich, furbish, grace, impearl, miniate, ornament, paint, paper, prettify, renovate, tart up, trick out, trim, wallpaper.

decorate[2] *v.* bemedal, cite, crown, garland, honor.
decoration[1] *n.* adornment, arabesque, bauble, beautification, curlicue, elaboration, embellishment, enrichment, falderal, flounce, flourish, frill, frou-frou, furbelow, garnish, ornament, ornamentation, pass(e)ment, passementerie, scroll, spangle, trimming, trinket.
decoration[2] *n.* award, badge, colors, crown, emblem, garland, garter, laurel, laurel-wreath, medal, order, ribbon, star.
decoy *n.* attraction, bait, ensnarement, enticement, inducement, lure, pretence, roper(-in), trap.
v. allure, attract, bait, beguile, deceive, draw, ensnare, entice, entrap, inveigle, lead, lure, seduce, tempt.
decrease *v.* abate, ablate, contract, curtail, cut down, decline, diminish, drop, dwindle, ease, fall off, lessen, lower, peter out, reduce, shrink, slacken, slim, subside, taper, wane.
antonym increase.
n. abatement, ablation, contraction, cutback, decline, decrement, degression, diminution, downturn, dwindling, ebb, falling-off, lessening, loss, reduction, shrinkage, step-down, subsidence.
antonym increase.
decree *n.* act, command, decretal, dictum, edict, enactment, firman, hatti-sherif, indiction, interlocution, interlocutor, law, mandate, order, ordinance, precept, proclamation, regulation, ruling, statute, ukase.
v. command, decide, determine, dictate, enact, lay down, ordain, order, prescribe, proclaim, pronounce, rescript, rule.
decrepit *adj.* aged, antiquated, battered, broken-backed, broken-down, crippled, debilitated, deteriorated, dilapidated, doddering, doddery, feeble, frail, incapacitated, infirm, ramshackle, rickety, run-down, superannuated, tumble-down, warby, wasted, weak, worn-out.
antonyms fit, well-cared-for, youthful.
decry *v.* abuse, belittle, blame, censure, condemn, criticize, cry down, declaim against, denounce, depreciate, derogate, detract, devalue, discredit, disparage, inveigh against, rail against, run down, traduce, underestimate, underrate, undervalue.
antonyms praise, value.
dedicate *v.* address, assign, bless, commit, consecrate, devote, give over to, hallow, inscribe, offer, pledge, present, sacrifice, sanctify, set apart, surrender.
dedicated *adj.* committed, devoted, enthusiastic, given over to, purposeful, single-hearted, single-minded, sworn, whole-hearted, zealous.
antonyms apathetic, uncommitted.
deduct *v.* decrease by, knock off, reduce by, remove, subduct, subtract, take away, withdraw.
antonym add.
deed[1] *n.* achievement, act, action, exploit, fact, factum, feat, gest(e), performance, reality, truth.
deed[2] *n.* contract, document, indenture, instrument, record, title, transaction.
deem *v.* account, adjudge, believe, conceive, consider, esteem, estimate, hold, imagine, judge, reckon, regard, suppose, think.
deep *adj.* absorbed, abstract, abstruse, abyssal, acute, arcane, artful, astute, bass, booming, bottomless, broad, canny, cryptic, cunning, dark, designing, devious, discerning, engrossed, esoteric, extreme, far, fathomless, full-toned, grave, great, hidden, immersed, insidious, intense, knowing, learned, lost, low, low-pitched, mysterious, obscure, penetrating, preoccupied, profound, rapt, recondite, resonant, rich, sagacious, scheming, secret, shrewd, sonorous, strong, unfathomable, unfathomed, unplumbed, unsoundable, unsounded, vivid, wide, wise, yawning.
antonyms open, shallow.
n. briny, drink, high seas, main, ocean, sea.
deface *v.* blemish, damage, deform, destroy, disfeature, disfigure, impair, injure, mar, mutilate, obliterate, spoil, sully, tarnish, vandalize.
antonym repair.
defamation *n.* aspersion, calumny, denigration, derogation, disparagement, innuendo, libel, mud-slinging, obloquy, opprobrium, scandal, slander, slur, smear, traducement, vilification.
antonym praise.
default *n.* absence, defalcation, defect, deficiency, dereliction, failure, fault, lack, lapse, neglect, non-payment, omission, want.
v. backslide, bilk, defraud, dodge, evade, fail, levant, neglect, rat, swindle, welsh.
defeat *v.* baffle, balk, beat, best, checkmate, clobber, confound, conquer, counteract, crush, disappoint, discomfit, down, foil, frustrate, get the better of, outbargain, overpower, overthrow, overwhelm, psych out, quell, repulse, rout, ruin, stump, subdue, subjugate, tank, thump, thwart, trounce, vanquish, vote down, whop.
n. beating, conquest, débâcle, disappointment, discomfiture, failure, frustration, overthrow, rebuff, repulse, reverse, rout, setback, thwarting, trouncing, vanquishment, Waterloo.
defect *n.* absence, blemish, bug, default, deficiency, error, failing, fault, flaw, frailty, hamartia, imperfection, inadequacy, lack, mistake, shortcoming, spot, taint, want, weakness.
v. apostatize, break faith, desert, rebel, renegue, revolt, tergiversate.
defective *adj.* abnormal, broken, deficient, faulty, flawed, imperfect, inadequate, incomplete, insufficient, kaput, out of order, retarded, scant, short, subnormal.
antonyms normal, operative.
defend *n.* assert, bulwark, champion, contest, cover, endorse, espouse, fortify, guard, justify, maintain, plead, preserve, protect, safeguard, screen, secure, shelter, shield, speak up for, stand by, stand up for, support, sustain, uphold, vindicate, watch over.
antonym attack.

defensive *adj.* apologetic, aposematic, averting, cautious, defending, opposing, protective, safeguarding, self-justifying, wary, watchful, withstanding.
antonym bold.

defer[1] *v.* adjourn, delay, hold over, postpone, procrastinate, prorogue, protract, put off, put on ice, shelve, suspend, waive.

defer[2] *v.* accede, bow, capitulate, comply, give way, kowtow, respect, submit, yield.

deference *n.* acquiescence, attention, capitulation, civility, complaisance, compliance, consideration, courtesy, esteem, homage, honor, morigeration, obedience, obeisance, obsequiousness, politeness, regard, respect, reverence, submission, submissiveness, thoughtfulness, veneration, yielding.

defiant *adj.* aggressive, audacious, bold, challenging, contumacious, daring, disobedient, insolent, insubordinate, intransigent, mutinous, obstinate, provocative, rebellious, recalcitrant, refractory, truculent, uncooperative.
antonyms acquiescent, submissive.

deficient *adj.* defectible, defective, exiguous, faulty, flawed, impaired, imperfect, inadequate, incomplete, inferior, insufficient, lacking, meager, scanty, scarce, short, skimpy, unsatisfactory, wanting, weak.
antonyms excessive, superfluous.

defile[1] *v.* abuse, befoul, besmirch, contaminate, corrupt, debase, deflower, defoul, degrade, desecrate, dirty, disgrace, dishonor, inquinate, make foul, molest, pollute, profane, rape, ravish, seduce, smear, soil, stain, sully, taint, tarnish, violate, vitiate.
antonym cleanse.

defile[2] *n.* gorge, gulch, gully, pass, passage, ravine.

define *v.* bound, characterize, circumscribe, delimit, delimitate, delineate, demarcate, describe, designate, detail, determine, explain, expound, interpret, limit, mark out, outline, specify, spell out.

definite *adj.* assured, certain, clear, clear-cut, decided, determined, exact, explicit, express, fixed, guaranteed, marked, obvious, particular, positive, precise, settled, specific, substantive, sure.
antonyms indefinite, vague.

definitely *adv.* absolutely, beyond doubt, categorically, certainly, clearly, decidedly, doubtless, doubtlessly, easily, finally, indeed, indubitably, obviously, plainly, positively, surely, undeniably, unequivocally, unmistakably, unquestionably, without doubt, without fail.

definition[1] *n.* clarification, delimitation, delineation, demarcation, description, determination, elucidation, explanation, exposition, interpretation, outlining, settling.

definition[2] *n.* clarity, clearness, contrast, distinctness, focus, precision, sharpness.

deft *adj.* able, adept, adroit, agile, clever, dexterous, expert, feat, habile, handy, neat, nifty, nimble, proficient, skilful.
antonym clumsy.

defunct *adj.* dead, deceased, departed, expired, extinct, gone, inoperative, invalid, kaput, non-existent, obsolete, passé.
antonyms alive, live, operative.

defy *v.* baffle, beard, beat, brave, challenge, confront, contemn, dare, defeat, despise, disregard, elude, face, flout, foil, frustrate, outdare, provoke, repel, repulse, resist, scorn, slight, spurn, thwart, withstand.
antonyms flinch, quail, yield.

degenerate *adj.* base, corrupt, debased, debauched, decadent, degenerated, degraded, depraved, deteriorated, dissolute, effete, fallen, immoral, low, mean, perverted.
antonyms upright, virtuous.
v. age, decay, decline, decrease, deteriorate, fall off, lapse, regress, retrogress, rot, sink, slip, worsen. *antonym* improve.

degrade *v.* abase, adulterate, break, brutalize, cashier, cheapen, corrupt, debase, declass, demean, demote, depose, deprive, deteriorate, discredit, disennoble, disgrace, disgrade, dishonor, disrank, disrate, downgrade, embase, humble, humiliate, impair, injure, lower, pervert, shame, unfrock, ungown, vitiate, weaken.
antonyms enhance, improve.

degree *n.* caliber, class, division, doctorate, extent, gradation, grade, intensity, interval, level, limit, mark, masterate, measure, notch, order, point, position, proportion, quality, quantity, range, rank, rate, ratio, run, scale, scope, severity, stage, standard, standing, station, status, step, unit.

deign *v.* condescend, consent, demean oneself, lower oneself, stoop, vouchsafe.

dejected *adj.* abattu, alamort, blue, cast down, crestfallen, depressed, despondent, disconsolate, disheartened, dismal, doleful, down, downcast, downhearted, gloomy, glum, jaw-fallen, low, low-spirited, melancholy, miserable, morose, sad, spiritless, woebegone, wretched.
antonyms bright, happy, high-spirited.

delectable *adj.* adorable, agreeable, ambrosial, ambrosian, appetizing, charming, dainty, delicious, delightful, enjoyable, enticing, flavorsome, gratifying, inviting, luscious, lush, palatable, pleasant, pleasurable, satisfying, scrumptious, tasty, toothsome, yummy.
antonyms horrid, unpleasant.

delegate *n.* agent, ambassador, commissioner, deputy, envoy, legate, messenger, nuncio, representative.
v. accredit, appoint, assign, authorize, charge, commission, consign, depute, designate, devolve, empower, entrust, give, hand over, mandate, name, nominate, pass on, relegate, transfer.

delete *v.* blot out, blue-pencil, cancel, cross out, dele, edit, edit out, efface, erase, expunge, obliterate, remove, rub out, strike, strike out.
antonym add in.

deleterious *adj.* bad, damaging, destructive, detrimental,

harmful, hurtful, injurious, noxious, pernicious, prejudicial, ruinous.
antonyms enhancing, helpful.

deliberate *v.* cogitate, consider, consult, debate, discuss, meditate, mull over, ponder, reflect, ruminate, think, weigh.
adj. advised, calculated, careful, cautious, circumspect, conscious, considered, designed, heedful, intentional, measured, methodical, planned, ponderous, prearranged, premeditated, prudent, purposeful, slow, studied, thoughtful, unhurried, volitive, voulu, wary, wilful, willed, witting.
antonyms chance, unintentional.

delicate *adj.* accurate, ailing, careful, choice, considerate, critical, dainty, debilitated, deft, delicious, detailed, diaphanous, difficult, diplomatic, discreet, discriminating, eggshell, elegant, elfin, exquisite, faint, fastidious, fine, flimsy, fragile, frail, friand(e), gauzy, graceful, hazardous, kid-glove, minikin, minute, muted, pastel, precarious, precise, prudish, pure, refined, risky, savory, scrupulous, sensible, sensitive, sickly, skilled, slender, slight, soft, softly-softly, squeamish, sticky, subdued, subtle, tactful, tender, ticklish, touchy, weak.
antonyms harsh, imprecise, strong.

delicious *adj.* agreeable, ambrosial, ambrosian, appetizing, charming, choice, dainty, delectable, delightful, enjoyable, entertaining, exquisite, flavorsome, goluptious, luscious, mouthwatering, nectareous, palatable, pleasant, pleasing, savory, scrummy, scrumptious, tasty, toothsome, yummy.
antonym unpleasant.

delight *n.* bliss, ecstasy, enjoyment, felicity, gladness, gratification, happiness, heaven, joy, jubilation, pleasure, rapture, transport.
antonyms dismay, displeasure.
v. amuse, charm, cheer, divert, enchant, gladden, gratify, please, ravish, rejoice, satisfy, thrill, tickle.
antonyms dismay, displease.

delightful *adj.* agreeable, amusing, captivating, charming, congenial, delectable, delightsome, enchanting, engaging, enjoyable, entertaining, fascinating, fetching, gratifying, heavenly, pleasant, pleasing, pleasurable, rapturous, ravishing, scrummy, scrumptious, sweet, thrilling, wizard.
antonym horrible.

delirious *adj.* bacchic, beside oneself, corybantic, crazy, demented, deranged, ecstatic, excited, frantic, frenzied, hysterical, incoherent, insane, light-headed, mad, maenadic, raving, unhinged, wild.
antonym sane.

deliver *v.* acquit, administer, aim, announce, bear, bring, carry, cart, cede, commit, convey, deal, declare, direct, discharge, dispense, distribute, emancipate, feed, free, give, give forth, give up, grant, hand over, inflict, launch, liberate, loose, make over, pass, present, proclaim, pronounce, publish, ransom, read, redeem, release, relinquish, rescue, resign, save, strike, supply, surrender, throw, transfer, transport, turn over, utter, yield.

deluge *n.* avalanche, barrage, cataclysm, downpour, flood, hail, inundation, rush, spate, torrent.
v. bury, douse, drench, drown, engulf, flood, inundate, overload, overrun, overwhelm, soak, submerge, swamp.

delusion *n.* deception, error, fallacy, fancy, fata Morgana, hallucination, illusion, mirage, misapprehension, misbelief, misconception, mistake, phantasm.

demand *v.* ask, call for, challenge, claim, exact, expect, inquire, insist on, interrogate, involve, necessitate, need, order, question, request, require, take, want.
antonyms cede, supply.
n. bidding, call, charge, claim, desire, inquiry, interrogation, necessity, need, order, question, request, requirement, requisition, want.
antonym supply.

demean *v.* abase, condescend, debase, degrade, deign, descend, humble, lower, stoop.
antonym enhance.

demeanor *n.* air, bearing, behavior, carriage, comportment, conduct, deportment, manner, mien, port.

demented *adj.* crazed, crazy, deranged, distracted, distraught, dotty, foolish, frenzied, idiotic, insane, lunatic, mad, maenadic, maniacal, manic, non compos mentis, nutty, unbalanced, unhinged.
antonym sane.

demolish *v.* annihilate, bulldoze, consume, defeat, destroy, devour, dilapidate, dismantle, down, eat, flatten, gobble, gulp, guzzle, knock down, level, overthrow, overturn, pull down, pulverize, raze, ruin, tear down, unbuild, undo, wreck.
antonym build up.

demolition *n.* bulldozing, destruction, dismantling, leveling, razing, wrecking.

demon[1] *n.* afrit, daemon, daimon, devil, evil spirit, fallen angel, fiend, genius, goblin, guardian spirit, incubus, monster, numen, rakshas, rakshasa, succubus, villain, warlock.

demon[2] *n.* ace, addict, dab hand, fanatic, fiend, master, pastmaster, wizard.

demonstrate[1] *v.* describe, display, establish, evidence, evince, exhibit, explain, expound, illustrate, indicate, manifest, prove, show, substantiate, teach, testify to.

demonstrate[2] *v.* march, parade, picket, protest, rally, sit in.

demonstration[1] *n.* affirmation, confirmation, deixis, description, display, evidence, exhibition, explanation, exposition, expression, illustration, manifestation, presentation, proof, substantiation, test, testimony, trial, validation.

demonstration[2] *v.* demo, march, parade, picket, protest, rally, sit-in, work-in.

demur *v.* balk, cavil, disagree, dispute, dissent, doubt, hesitate, object, pause, protest, refuse, take exception, waver.

n. arrière pensée, compunction, demurral, demurrer, dissent, hesitation, misgiving, objection, protest, qualm, reservation, scruple.

demure *adj.* coy, decorous, diffident, grave, maidenly, modest, priggish, prim, prissy, prudish, reserved, reticent, retiring, sedate, shy, sober, staid, strait-laced. *antonym* forward.

den *n.* cave, cavern, cloister, cubby-hole, earth, haunt, hide-away, hide-out, hole, lair, retreat, sanctuary, sanctum, set(t), shelter, study.

denial *n.* abjuration, abnegation, contradiction, denegation, disaffirmance, disaffirmation, disavowal, disclaimer, dismissal, dissent, gainsay, negation, prohibition, rebuff, refusal, rejection, renunciation, repudiation, repulse, retraction, veto.

denounce *v.* accuse, anathematize, arraign, assail, attack, brand, castigate, censure, condemn, declaim, against, decry, denunciate, fulminate, hereticate, impugn, inveigh against, proscribe, revile, stigmatize, vilify, vilipend. *antonym* praise.

dense *adj.* blockish, close, close-knit, compact, compressed, condensed, crass, crowded, dull, heavy, impenetrable, jam-packed, obtuse, opaque, packed, slow, slow-witted, solid, stolid, stupid, substantial, thick, thickset, thick-witted. *antonyms* clever, sparse.

dent *n.* bang, chip, concavity, crater, depression, dimple, dint, dip, dunt, hollow, impression, indentation, pit. *v.* depress, dint, gouge, indent, push in.

deny *v.* abjure, begrudge, contradict, decline, disaffirm, disagree with, disallow, disavow, discard, disclaim, disown, disprove, forbid, gainsay, negative, oppose, rebuff, recant, refuse, refute, reject, renounce, repudiate, revoke, traverse, turn down, veto, withhold. *antonyms* admit, allow.

depart *v.* absent oneself, decamp, deviate, differ, digress, disappear, diverge, escape, exit, go, leave, levant, make off, migrate, mizzle, quit, remove, retire, retreat, set forth, stray, swerve, take one's leave, toddle, vanish, vary, veer, withdraw. *antonyms* arrive, keep to.

departure *n.* abandonment, branching, branching, out, change, decession, deviation, difference, digression, divergence, exit, exodus, going, innovation, leave-taking, leaving, lucky, novelty, removal, retirement, shift, variation, veering, withdrawal. *antonym* arrival.

depend on anticipate, bank on, build upon, calculate on, count on, expect, hang on, hinge on, lean on, reckon on, rely upon, rest on, revolve around, trust in, turn to.

dependable *adj.* certain, conscientious, faithful, gilt-edged, honest, reliable, responsible, steady, sure, trustworthy, trusty, unfailing. *antonyms* undependable, unreliable.

dependent *adj.* adjective, conditional, contingent, defenceless, depending, determined by, feudal, helpless, immature, liable to, relative, reliant, relying on, subject, subject to, subordinate, tributary, vulnerable, weak. *antonym* independent.

depict *v.* caricature, characterize, delineate, describe, detail, draw, illustrate, limn, narrate, outline, paint, picture, portray, render, reproduce, sculpt, sketch, trace.

deplore *v.* abhor, bemoan, bewail, censure, condemn, denounce, deprecate, grieve for, lament, mourn, regret, repent of, rue. *antonym* praise.

deport[1] *v.* banish, exile, expatriate, expel, extradite, ostracize, oust.

deport[2] *v.* acquit, act, bear, behave, carry, comport, conduct, hold, manage.

deportment *n.* air, appearance, aspect, bearing, behavior, carriage, cast, comportment, conduct, demeanor, etiquette, manner, mien, pose, posture, stance.

deposit[1] *v.* drop, dump, lay, locate, park, place, precipitate, put, settle, sit. *n.* accumulation, alluvium, deposition, dregs, hypostasis, lees, precipitate, sediment, silt.

deposit[2] *v.* amass, bank, consign, depone, entrust, file, hoard, lodge, reposit, save, store. *n.* bailment, down payment, instalment, money, part payment, pledge, retainer, security, stake, warranty.

depreciate *v.* belittle, decrease, decry, deflate, denigrate, deride, derogate, detract, devaluate, devalue, disparage, downgrade, drop, fall, lessen, lower, minimize, misprize, reduce, ridicule, scorn, slump, traduce, underestimate, underrate, undervalue. *antonyms* appreciate, overrate, praise.

depress *v.* burden, cheapen, chill, damp, daunt, debilitate, deject, depreciate, devaluate, devalue, devitalize, diminish, discourage, dishearten, dispirit, downgrade, drain, enervate, engloom, exhaust, flatten, hip, impair, lessen, level, lower, oppress, overburden, press, reduce, sadden, sap, squash, tire, undermine, upset, weaken, weary. *antonym* cheer.

depression[1] *n.* blues, cafard, decline, dejection, demission, despair, despondency, doldrums, dolefulness, downheartedness, dullness, dumps, exanimation, gloominess, glumness, hard times, heart-heaviness, hopelessness, inactivity, low spirits, lowness, mal du siècle, megrims, melancholia, melancholy, panophobia, recession, sadness, slump, stagnation, vapors. *antonyms* cheerfulness, prosperity.

depression[2] *n.* basin, bowl, cavity, concavity, dent, dimple, dint, dip, dish, excavation, fossa, fossula, fovea, foveola, hollow, hollowness, impression, indentation, pit, sag, sink, umbilicus, valley. *antonyms* convexity, prominence, protuberance.

deprive *v.* amerce, bereave, denude, deny, despoil,

dispossess, divest, expropriate, mulct, rob, starve, strip.
antonyms bestow.

deputation *n.* appointment, assignment, commission, delegates, delegation, deputies, deputing, designation, embassy, legation, mission, nomination, representatives.

derelict *adj.* abandoned, deserted, desolate, dilapidated, discarded, forlorn, forsaken, neglected, ruined.
n. dosser, down-and-out, drifter, hobo, outcast, toe-rag, tramp, vagrant, wastrel.

dereliction *n.* abandonment, abdication, apostasy, betrayal, delinquency, desertion, evasion, failure, faithlessness, fault, forsaking, neglect, negligence, relinquishment, remissness, renegation, renunciation.
antonyms devotion, faithfulness, fulfilment.

derision *n.* contempt, contumely, dicacity, disdain, disparagement, disrespect, insult, irrision, laughter, mockery, raillery, ridicule, satire, scoffing, scorn, sneering.
antonym praise.

derivation *n.* acquisition, ancestry, basis, beginning, deduction, descent, etymology, extraction, foundation, genealogy, inference, origin, root, source.

derive *v.* acquire, arise, borrow, collect, crib, deduce, descend, develop, draw, elicit, emanate, extract, flow, follow, gain, gather, get, glean, grow, infer, issue, lift, obtain, originate, proceed, procure, receive, spring, stem, trace.

descend *v.* alight, arrive, assail, assault, attack, condescend, degenerate, dégringoler, deign, derive, deteriorate, develop, dip, dismount, drop, fall, gravitate, incline, invade, issue, leap, originate, plummet, plunge, pounce, proceed, raid, sink, slant, slope, spring, stem, stoop, subside, swoop, tumble.

descendants *n.* children, epigones, epigoni, epigons, family, issue, line, lineage, offspring, posterity, progeny, race, scions, seed, sons, and daughters, successors.

describe *v.* characterize, define, delineate, depict, detail, draw, enlarge on, explain, express, illustrate, mark out, narrate, outline, portray, present, recount, relate, report, sketch, specify, tell, trace.

description *n.* account, brand, breed, category, characterization, class, delineation, depiction, detail, explanation, exposition, genre, genus, hypotyposis, ilk, kidney, kind, narration, narrative, order, outline, portrayal, presentation, report, representation, sketch, sort, species, specification, type, variety, word-painting, word-picture.

desecration *n.* blasphemy, debasement, defilement, dishonoring, impiety, insult, invasion, pollution, profanation, sacrilege, violation.

desert[1] *n.* solitude, vacuum, vast, void, waste, wasteland, wilderness, wilds.
adj. arid, bare, barren, desolate, droughty, dry, eremic, infertile, lonely, solitary, sterile, uncultivated, uninhabited, unproductive, untilled, waste, waterless, wild.

desert[2] *v.* abandon, abscond, apostatize, backslide, betray, decamp, deceive, defect, forsake, give up, jilt, leave, leave in the lurch, maroon, quit, rat on, relinquish, renegue, renounce, resign, strand, tergiversate, vacate.

desert[3] *n.* come-uppance, demerit, deserts, due, guerdon, meed, merit, payment, recompense, remuneration, requital, retribution, return, reward, right, virtue, worth.

deserter *n.* absconder, apostate, backslider, betrayer, defector, delinquent, escapee, fugitive, rat, renegade, runaway, traitor, truant.

deserve *v.* ask for, earn, gain, incur, justify, merit, procure, rate, warrant, win.

design *n.* aim, arrangement, blueprint, composition, configuration, conformation, conspiracy, construction, contrivance, delineation, draft, drawing, end, enterprise, exemplar, figure, form, goal, guide, intent, intention, intrigue, machination, maneuver, meaning, model, motif, object, objective, organization, outline, pattern, plan, plot, project, prototype, purpose, schema, schema, shape, sketch, structure, style, target, undertaking.
v. aim, conceive, construct, contrive, create, delineate, describe, destine, develop, devise, draft, draw, draw up, fabricate, fashion, form, intend, invent, make, mean, model, originate, outline, plan, project, propose, purpose, scheme, shape, sketch, structure, tailor, trace.

designate *v.* allot, appoint, assign, bill, call, characterize, choose, christen, code-name, deem, define, delegate, denominate, denote, depute, describe, docket, dub, earmark, entitle, indicate, label, name, nickname, nominate, select, show, specify, stipulate, style, term, ticket, title.

desirable *adj.* adorable, advantageous, advisable, agreeable, alluring, appetible, appropriate, attractive, beneficial, captivating, covetable, eligible, enviable, expedient, fascinating, fetching, good, nubile, pleasing, plummy, preferable, profitable, seductive, sensible, sexy, tempting, worthwhile. *antonyms* undesirable.

desire *v.* ask, aspire to, beg, covet, crave, desiderate, entreat, fancy, hanker after, hunger for, importune, lack, long for, need, petition, request, solicit, want, wish for, yearn for.
n. appeal, appetence, appetency, appetite, ardor, aspiration, besoin, concupiscence, covetousness, craving, cupidity, desideration, entreaty, greed, hankering, hot pants, importunity, kama, kamadeva, lasciviousness, lechery, libido, longing, lust, lustfulness, month's mind, need, passion, petition, request, solicitation, supplication, velleity, want, wish, yearning, yen.

desist *v.* abstain, break off, cease, come to a halt, discontinue, end, forbear, give over, give up, halt, leave off, pause, peter out, refrain, remit, stop, suspend.
antonyms continue, resume.

desolate *adj.* abandoned, arid, bare, barren, benighted, bereft, bleak, cheerless, comfortless, companionless,

dejected, depopulated, depressed, depressing, desert, desolated, despondent, disconsolate, disheartened, dismal, dismayed, distressed, downcast, dreary, forlorn, forsaken, gloomy, god-forsaken, grieved, inconsolable, lonely, melancholy, miserable, ravaged, ruined, solitary, unfrequented, uninhabited, unpopulous, unsolaced, waste, wild, wretched.
antonym cheerful.
v. denude, depopulate, despoil, destroy, devastate, lay waste, pillage, plunder, ravage, ruin, spoil, waste, wreck.

despair *v.* capitulate, collapse, crumple, despond, give in, give up, lose heart, lose hope, quit, surrender.
antonym hope.
n. anguish, dejection, depression, desperation, despond, despondency, emptiness, gloom, hopelessness, inconsolableness, melancholy, misery, ordeal, pain, resourcelessness, sorrow, trial, tribulation, wretchedness.
antonyms cheerfulness, resilience.

desperado *n.* bandit, brigand, cateran, criminal, cutthroat, dacoit, gangster, gunman, heavy, hood, hoodlum, lawbreaker, mugger, outlaw, ruffian, thug.

desperate *adj.* grave, abandoned, acute, audacious, critical, dangerous, daring, despairing, despondent, determined, dire, do-or-die, drastic, extreme, foolhardy, forlorn, frantic, frenzied, furious, great, hasty, hazardous, headlong, headstrong, hopeless, impetuous, inconsolable, irremediable, irretrievable, madcap, precipitate, rash, reckless, risky, serious, severe, temerarious, urgent, violent, wild, wretched.

despicable *adj.* abhorrent, abject, base, cheap, contemptible, degrading, detestable, disgraceful, disgusting, disreputable, hateful, ignoble, ignominious, infamous, low, mean, reprehensible, reprobate, scurvy, shameful, sordid, unprincipled, vile, worthless, wretched.
antonyms laudable, noble.

despise *v.* abhor, condemn, deplore, deride, detest, disdain, dislike, disregard, ignore, loathe, misprize, revile, scorn, slight, spurn, undervalue, vilipend.
antonyms appreciate, prize.

despite *prep.* against, defying, heedless of, in spite of, in the face of, in the teeth of, notwithstanding, regardless of, undeterred by.

despoil *v.* bereave, denude, depredate, deprive, destroy, devastate, disgarnish, dispossess, divest, loot, maraud, pillage, plunder, ransack, ravage, rifle, rob, spoliate, strip, vandalize, wreck.
antonyms adorn, enrich.

despondent *adj.* blue, broken-hearted, dejected, depressed, despairing, disconsolate, discouraged, disheartened, dispirited, doleful, down, downcast, downhearted, gloomy, glum, hopeless, inconsolable, low, low-spirited, melancholy, miserable, morose, mournful, overwhelmed, sad, sorrowful, woebegone, wretched.
antonyms cheerful, hopeful.

despot *n.* absolutist, autocrat, boss, dictator, monocrat, oppressor, tyrant.
antonyms democrat, egalitarian, liberal.

despotic *adj.* absolute, absolutist, arbitrary, arrogant, authoritarian, autocratic, bossy, dictatorial, domineering, imperious, monocratic, oppressive, overbearing, peremptory, tyrannical.
antonyms democratic, egalitarian, liberal, tolerant.

destiny *n.* cup, doom, fate, fortune, joss, karma, kismet, lot, Moira, portion, predestiny, weird.

destitute *adj.* bankrupt, beggared, bereft, deficient, depleted, deprived, devoid of, distressed, down and out, impecunious, impoverished, indigent, innocent of, insolvent, lacking, necessitous, needy, penniless, penurious, poor, poverty-stricken, skint, strapped, wanting.
antonyms prosperous, wealthy.

destroy *v.* annihilate, banjax, break, canker, crush, demolish, destruct, devastate, dismantle, dispatch, eliminate, eradicate, extinguish, extirpate, gut, kill, level, nullify, overthrow, ravage, raze, ruin, sabotage, scuttle, shatter, slay, slight, smash, stonker, thwart, torpedo, undermine, undo, unshape, vaporize, waste, wreck, zap.
antonym create.

destruction *n.* annihilation, bane, confutation, crushing, defeat, demolition, depopulation, desolation, devastation, downfall, elimination, end, eradication, estrepement, extermination, extinction, extirpation, havoc, liquidation, massacre, nullification, overthrow, ravagement, ruin, ruination, shattering, slaughter, undoing, wastage, wrack, wreckage.
antonym creation.

destructive *adj.* adverse, antagonistic, baleful, baneful, calamitous, cataclysmic, catastrophic, contrary, damaging, deadly, deathful, deleterious, derogatory, detrimental, devastating, disastrous, discouraging, disparaging, disruptive, fatal, harmful, hostile, hurtful, injurious, invalidating, lethal, malignant, mischievous, negative, noxious, nullifying, pernicious, pestful, pestiferous, pestilent, pestilential, ruinous, slaughterous, subversive, undermining, vexatious, vicious.
antonyms creative, positive, productive.

detach *v.* abstract, alienate, cut off, deglutinate, disconnect, disengage, disentangle, disjoin, dissociate, disunite, divide, estrange, free, isolate, loosen, remove, segregate, separate, sever, uncouple, undo, unfasten, unfix, unhitch.
antonym attach.

detail *n.* aspect, attribute, complexity, complication, component, count, elaborateness, elaboration, element, fact, factor, feature, ingredient, intricacy, item, meticulousness, nicety, particular, particularity, point, refinement, respect, specific, specificity, technicality, thoroughness, triviality.
v. allocate, appoint, assign, catalog, charge, commission,

delegate, delineate, depict, depute, describe, detach, enarrate, enumerate, individualize, itemize, list, narrate, overname, particularize, portray, recount, rehearse, relate, send, specify.

detain *v.* arrest, buttonhole, check, confine, delay, hinder, hold, hold up, impede, intern, keep, prevent, restrain, retard, slow, stay, stop.
antonym release.

detect *v.* ascertain, catch, descry, discern, disclose, discover, distinguish, espy, expose, find, identify, note, notice, observe, perceive, recognize, reveal, scent, sight, spot, spy, track down, uncover, unmask.

deterioration *n.* atrophy, corrosion, debasement, decline, degeneration, degradation, dégringolade, depreciation, descent, dilapidation, disintegration, downturn, drop, failing, fall, falling-off, lapse, pejoration, retrogression, slump, tabes, tabescence, vitiation, wastage, worsening.
antonym improvement.

determination *n.* backbone, conclusion, constancy, conviction, decision, dedication, doggedness, drive, firmness, fortitude, indomitability, insistence, intention, judgment, obstinacy, perseverance, persistence, pertinacity, purpose, resoluteness, resolution, resolve, result, settlement, single-mindedness, solution, steadfastness, stubbornness, tenacity, verdict, will, willpower.
antonym irresolution.

determine *v.* affect, arbitrate, ascertain, certify, check, choose, conclude, control, decide, detect, dictate, direct, discover, elect, end, establish, finish, fix, govern, guide, identify, impel, impose, incline, induce, influence, intend, lead, learn, modify, ordain, point, purpose, regulate, resolve, rule, settle, shape, terminate, undertake, verify.

detest *v.* abhor, abominate, deplore, despise, dislike, execrate, hate, loathe, recoil from.
antonym adore.

detour *n.* bypass, bypath, byroad, byway, circumbendibus, deviation, digression, diversion, excursus.

detriment *n.* damage, disadvantage, disservice, evil, harm, hurt, ill, impairment, injury, loss, mischief, prejudice.
antonym advantage.

detrimental *adj.* adverse, baleful, damaging, deleterious, destructive, disadvantageous, harmful, hurtful, inimical, injurious, mischievous, noxious, pernicious, prejudicial, unfavorable, untoward.
antonym advantageous.

develop *v.* acquire, advance, amplify, augment, begin, bloom, blossom, branch out, breed, broaden, commence, contract, cultivate, dilate, diversify, elaborate, engender, enlarge, ensue, establish, evolve, expand, flourish, follow, form, foster, generate, grow, happen, invent, make headway, mature, move on, originate, pick up, progress, promote, prosper, result, ripen, sprout, start, unfold.

development *n.* advance, advancement, blooming, blossoming, change, circumstance, detail, elaboration, event, evolution, expansion, extension, furtherance, growth, happening, improvement, incident, increase, issue, maturation, maturity, occurrence, outcome, phenomenon, phylogenesis, phylogeny, progress, progression, promotion, refinement, result, ripening, situation, spread, unfolding, unraveling, upbuilding, upshot.

deviate *v.* aberrate, depart, differ, digress, divagate, diverge, drift, err, go astray, go off the rails, part, stray, swerve, turn, turn aside, vary, veer, wander, yaw.

device *n.* apparatus, appliance, artifice, badge, blazon, colophon, contraption, contrivance, crest, design, dodge, emblem, episemon, expedient, figure, gadget, gambit, gimmick, gismo, implement, improvisation, insignia, instrument, invention, logo, machination, maneuver, motif, motto, plan, plot, ploy, project, ruse, scheme, shield, shift, stratagem, strategy, stunt, symbol, tactic, token, tool, trick, utensil, wile.

devilish *adj.* accursed, black-hearted, damnable, demoniac, demoniacal, diabolic, diabolical, execrable, fiendish, hellish, impious, infernal, iniquitous, mischievous, monstrous, nefarious, satanic, wicked.

devious *adj.* calculating, circuitous, confusing, crooked, cunning, deceitful, deviating, dishonest, disingenuous, double-dealing, erratic, evasive, excursive, indirect, insidious, insincere, misleading, rambling, roundabout, scheming, slippery, sly, subtle, surreptitious, tortuous, treacherous, tricky, underhand, wandering, wily, winding.
antonyms artless, candid, straightforward.

devise *v.* arrange, compass, compose, conceive, concoct, construct, contrive, design, excogitate, forge, form, formulate, frame, imagine, invent, plan, plot, prepare, project, scheme, shape.

devote *v.* allocate, allot, apply, appropriate, assign, commit, consecrate, dedicate, enshrine, give, oneself, pledge, reserve, sacrifice, set apart, set aside, surrender.

devoted *adj.* ardent, attentive, caring, committed, concerned, constant, dedicated, devout, faithful, fond, loving, loyal, staunch, steadfast, tireless, true, unremitting, unswerving.
antonyms inconstant, indifferent, negligent.

devotion *n.* adherence, adoration, affection, allegiance, ardor, assiduity, attachment, commitment, consecration, constancy, dedication, devoutness, earnestness, faith, faithfulness, fervor, fidelity, fondness, godliness, holiness, indefatigability, love, loyalty, partiality, passion, piety, prayer, regard, religiousness, reverence, sanctity, sedulousness, spirituality, steadfastness, support, worship, zeal.
antonyms inconstancy, negligence.

devour *v.* absorb, annihilate, bolt, consume, cram,

destroy, dispatch, down, eat, engulf, feast on, feast one's eyes on, gluttonize, gobble, gorge, gormandize, gulp, guzzle, polish off, ravage, relish, revel in, spend, stuff, swallow, waste, wolf.

devout *adj.* ardent, constant, deep, devoted, earnest, faithful, fervent, genuine, godly, heartfelt, holy, intense, orthodox, passionate, pious, prayerful, profound, pure, religious, reverent, saintly, serious, sincere, staunch, steadfast, unswerving, whole-hearted, zealous.
antonyms insincere, uncommitted.

dexterity *n.* ability, address, adroitness, agility, aptitude, art, artistry, cleverness, cunning, deftness, effortlessness, expertise, expertness, facility, finesse, handiness, ingenuity, knack, legerdemain, mastery, neatness, nimbleness, proficiency, readiness, skilfulness, skill, smoothness, tact, touch.
antonyms clumsiness, ineptitude.

dexterous *adj.* able, active, acute, adept, adroit, agile, apt, clever, cunning, deft, expert, facile, feat, habile, handy, ingenious, light-handed, masterly, neat, neat-handed, nifty, nimble, nimble-fingered, nippy, proficient, prompt, quick, skilful.
antonyms clumsy, inept.

dialect *n.* accent, diction, Doric, idiom, jargon, language, lingo, localism, patois, pronunciation, provincialism, regionalism, speech, tongue, vernacular.

dialogue *n.* causerie, colloquy, communication, confabulation, conference, conversation, converse, debate, discourse, discussion, duologue, exchange, interchange, interlocution, lines, script, stichomythia, table talk, talk.

diary *n.* appointment book, chronicle, commonplace book, day-book, diurnal, engagement book, journal, journal intime, logbook, year-book.

diatribe *n.* abuse, attack, castigation, criticism, denunciation, flyting, harangue, insult, invective, onslaught, philippic, reviling, stricture, tirade, upbraiding, vituperation.
antonyms bouquet, encomium, praise.

dictate *v.* announce, command, decree, direct, enjoin, impose, instruct, ordain, order, prescribe, pronounce, rule, say, speak, transmit, utter.
n. behest, bidding, code, command, decree, dictation, dictum, direction, edict, fiat, injunction, law, mandate, order, ordinance, precept, principle, requirement, ruling, statute, ultimatum, word.

dictator *n.* autarch, autocrat, Big Brother, boss, despot, supremo, tyrant.

die *v.* breathe one's last, croak, decay, decease, decline, depart, desire, disappear, dwindle, ebb, end, expire, fade, finish, fizzle out, gangrene, go over to the majority, go to one's (long) account, hunger, kick in, kick it, kick the bucket, languish, lapse, long for, pass, pass away, pass over, peg out, perish, peter out, pine for, pop off, run down, sink, slip the cable, snuff it, starve, stop, subside, succumb, suffer, vanish, wane, wilt, wither, yearn.

difference *n.* alteration, argument, balance, change, clash, conflict, contention, contrariety, contrast, contretemps, controversy, debate, deviation, differentia, differentiation, difformity, disagreement, discordance, discrepancy, discreteness, disparateness, disparity, dispute, dissimilarity, distinction, distinctness, divergence, diversity, exception, idiosyncrasy, jizz, particularity, peculiarity, quarrel, remainder, rest, set-to, singularity, strife, tiff, unlikeness, variation, variety, wrangle.
antonyms agreement, conformity, uniformity.

different *adj.* altered, anomalous, assorted, at odds, at variance, atypical, bizarre, changed, clashing, contrasting, deviating, discrepant, discrete, disparate, dissimilar, distinct, distinctive, divergent, divers, diverse, eccentric, extraordinary, inconsistent, individual, manifold, many, miscellaneous, multifarious, numerous, opposed, original, other, peculiar, rare, separate, several, singular, special, strange, sundry, unalike, uncommon, unconventional, unique, unlike, unusual, varied, various.
antonyms conventional, normal, same, similar, uniform.

differentiate *v.* adapt, alter, change, contrast, convert, demarcate, discern, discriminate, distinguish, individualize, mark off, modify, particularize, separate, tell apart, transform.
antonyms assimilate, associate, confuse, link.

difficult *adj.* abstract, abstruse, arduous, Augean, baffling, burdensome, captious, complex, complicated, dark, delicate, demanding, difficile, disruptive, enigmatical, fastidious, formidable, fractious, fussy, Gordian, grim, hard, herculean, iffy, intractable, intricate, involved, knotty, laborious, obscure, obstinate, obstreperous, onerous, painful, perplexing, perverse, problematic, problematical, recalcitrant, refractory, rigid, steep, sticky, stiff, straitened, strenuous, stubborn, thorny, ticklish, tiresome, toilsome, tough, troublesome, trying, unamenable, unco-operative, unmanageable, uphill, wearisome.
antonyms easy, straightforward.

difficulty *n.* a bad patch, arduousness, awkwardness, block, complication, dilemma, distress, embarrassment, fix, hang-up, hardship, hiccup, hindrance, hole, hurdle, impediment, jam, labor, laboriousness, mess, nineholes, objection, obstacle, opposition, pain, painfulness, perplexity, pickle, pinch, pitfall, plight, predicament, problem, protest, quandary, scruple, spot, strain, strait, straits, strenuousness, stumbling-block, trial, tribulation, trouble, vexata quaestio, vexed question.
antonyms advantage, ease.

diffidence *n.* abashment, backwardness, bashfulness, constraint, doubt, fear, hesitancy, hesitation, humility, inhibition, insecurity, meekness, modesty, reluctance, reserve, self-consciousness, self-distrust, self-doubt,

self-effacement, shamefacedness, shamefast, sheepishness, shyness, tentativeness, timidity, timidness, timorousness, unassertiveness.
antonym confidence.

diffuse *adj.* ambagious, circuitous, circumlocutory, copious, diffused, digressive, disconnected, discursive, dispersed, long-winded, loose, maundering, meandering, prolix, rambling, scattered, unconcentrated, uncoordinated, vague, verbose, waffling, wordy.
antonyms concentrated, succinct.
v. circulate, dispense, disperse, disseminate, dissipate, distribute, propagate, scatter, spread, winnow.
antonyms concentrate, suppress.

dig[1] *v.* burrow, delve, drive, excavate, go into, gouge, graft, grub, hoe, howk, investigate, jab, mine, penetrate, pierce, poke, probe, prod, punch, quarry, research, scoop, search, spit, thrust, till, tunnel.
n. aspersion, barb, crack, cut, gibe, insinuation, insult, jab, jeer, poke, prod, punch, quip, sneer, taunt, thrust, wisecrack.
antonym compliment.

dig[2] *v.* adore, appreciate, be into, enjoy, fancy, follow, get a kick out of, get off on, go a bundle on, go for, go overboard about, groove, have the hots for, like, love, understand, warm to.
antonym hate.

digest *v.* abridge, absorb, arrange, assimilate, classify, codify, compress, condense, consider, contemplate, dispose, dissolve, grasp, incorporate, ingest, macerate, master, meditate, methodize, ponder, process, reduce, shorten, stomach, study, summarize, systematize, tabulate, take in, understand.
n. abbreviation, abridgment, abstract, compendium, compression, condensation, epitome, précis, reduction, résumé, summary, synopsis.

dignified *adj.* august, decorous, distinguished, exalted, formal, grave, honorable, imposing, impressive, lofty, lordly, majestic, noble, oro(ro)tund, reserved, solemn, stately, upright.
antonym undignified.

dignify *v.* adorn, advance, aggrandize, apotheosize, distinguish, elevate, ennoble, exalt, glorify, honor, promote, raise.
antonyms degrade, demean.

dignity *n.* amour-propre, courtliness, decorum, elevation, eminence, excellence, glory, grandeur, gravitas, gravity, greatness, hauteur, honor, importance, loftiness, majesty, nobility, nobleness, pride, propriety, rank, respectability, self-esteem, self-importance, self-possession, self-regard, self-respect, solemnity, standing, stateliness, station, status.

digress *v.* depart, deviate, divagate, diverge, drift, excurse, expatiate, go off at a tangent, ramble, stray, wander.

dilate *v.* amplify, broaden, descant, detail, develop, distend, dwell on, elaborate, enlarge, expand, expatiate, expound, extend, increase, puff out, spin out, stretch, swell, widen.
antonyms abbreviate, constrict, curtail.

dilemma *n.* bind, corner, difficulty, embarrassment, fix, jam, mess, perplexity, pickle, pinch, plight, predicament, problem, puzzle, quandary, spot, strait.

diligent *adj.* active, assiduous, attentive, busy, careful, conscientious, constant, dogged, earnest, hard-working, indefatigable, industrious, laborious, painstaking, persevering, persistent, pertinacious, sedulous, studious, tireless.
antonyms dilatory, lazy.

dim *adj.* bleary, blurred, caliginous, cloudy, confused, dark, darkish, dense, depressing, dingy, discouraging, dull, dumb, dusky, faint, feeble, foggy, fuzzy, gloomy, gray, hazy, ill-defined, imperfect, indistinct, intangible, lackluster, misty, muted, obscure, obscured, obtuse, opaque, overcast, pale, remote, shadowy, slow, somber, stupid, sullied, tarnished, tenebrious, thick, unclear, unfavorable, unilluminated, unpromising, vague, weak.
antonyms bright, distinct.
v. becloud, bedim, blear, blur, cloud, darken, dull, fade, lower, obscure, tarnish.
antonyms brighten, illuminate.

dimension(s) *n.* amplitude, bulk, capacity, extent, greatness, importance, largeness, magnitude, measure, range, scale, scope, size.

diminish *v.* abate, bate, belittle, cheapen, contract, curtail, cut, deactivate, decline, decrease, demean, depreciate, devalue, dwindle, ebb, fade, lessen, lower, minify, peter out, recede, reduce, retrench, shrink, shrivel, sink, slacken, subside, taper off, wane, weaken.
antonyms enhance, enlarge, increase.

diminutive *adj.* bantam, dinky, Lilliputian, little, midget, mini, miniature, minute, petite, pint-size(d), pocket(-sized), pygmy, small, tiny, undersized, wee.
antonyms big, great, huge, large.
n. hypocorisma, pet-name.

din *n.* babble, chirm, clamor, clangor, clash, clatter, commotion, crash, hubbub, hullabaloo, noise, outcry, pandemonium, racket, randan, row, shout, uproar.
antonyms calm, quiet.

dine *v.* banquet, break bread, eat, feast, feed, lunch, sup.

dingy *adj.* bedimmed, colorless, dark, dim, dirty, discolored, drab, dreary, dull, dusky, faded, fuscous, gloomy, grimy, murky, obscure, run-down, seedy, shabby, soiled, somber, tacky, worn.
antonyms bright, clean.

dip *v.* bathe, decline, descend, disappear, dook, dop, douse, droop, drop, duck, dunk, fade, fall, immerse, ladle, lower, plunge, rinse, sag, scoop, set, sink, slope, slump, souse, spoon, subside, tilt.
n. basin, bathe, concavity, concoction, decline, depression, dilution, dive, dook, douche, drenching, ducking, fall, hole, hollow, immersion, incline, infusion, lowering,

mixture, plunge, preparation, sag, slip, slope, slump, soaking, solution, suspension, swim.

diplomacy *n.* artfulness, craft, delicacy, discretion, finesse, maneuvering, savoir-faire, skill, statecraft, statesmanship, subtlety, tact, tactfulness.

diplomatic *adj.* discreet, judicious, polite, politic, prudent, sagacious, sensitive, subtle, tactful.
antonyms rude, tactless, thoughtless.

dire *adj.* alarming, appalling, awful, calamitous, cataclysmic, catastrophic, critical, crucial, cruel, crying, desperate, disastrous, dismal, distressing, drastic, dreadful, exigent, extreme, fearful, gloomy, grave, grim, horrible, horrid, ominous, portentous, pressing, ruinous, terrible, urgent, woeful.

direct[1] *v.* address, administer, advise, aim, bid, case, charge, command, conduct, control, dictate, dispose, enjoin, fix, focus, govern, guide, handle, indicate, instruct, intend, label, lead, level, mail, manage, mastermind, mean, order, oversee, point, regulate, route, rule, run, send, show, stage-manage, superintend, superscribe, supervise, train, turn.

direct[2] *adj.* absolute, blunt, candid, categorical, downright, explicit, express, face-to-face, first-hand, frank, head-on, honest, immediate, man-to-man, matter-of-fact, non-stop, open, outright, outspoken, personal, plain, plain-spoken, point-blank, shortest, sincere, straight, straightforward, through, unambiguous, unbroken, undeviating, unequivocal, uninterrupted.
antonyms crooked, devious, indirect.

direction *n.* address, administration, aim, approach, bearing, bent, bias, charge, command, control, course, current, drift, end, government, guidance, label, leadership, line, management, mark, order, orientation, oversight, path, proclivity, purpose, road, route, superintendence, superscription, supervision, tack, tendency, tenor, track, trend, way.

directions *n.* briefing, guidance, guidelines, indication, instructions, orders, plan, recipe, recommendations, regulations.

directly *adv.* bluntly, candidly, dead, due, exactly, face-to-face, forthwith, frankly, honestly, immediately, instantaneously, instantly, openly, personally, plainly, point-blank, precisely, presently, promptly, pronto, quickly, right away, soon, speedily, straight, straightaway, straight-forwardly, truthfully, unequivocally, unerringly, unswervingly.
antonym indirectly.

dirt *n.* clay, crud, dust, earth, excrement, filth, grime, impurity, indecency, loam, mire, muck, mud, obscenity, ordure, pornography, slime, smudge, smut, smutch, soil, sordor, stain, tarnish, vomit, yuck.
antonyms cleanliness, cleanness.

dirty *adj.* angry, base, beggarly, begrimed, bitter, blue, clouded, contemptible, corrupt, cowardly, crooked, cruddy, dark, despicable, dishonest, dull, filthy, foul, fraudulent, grimy, grubby, ignominious, illegal, indecent, low, low-down, maculate, manky, mean, messy, miry, mucky, muddy, nasty, obscene, off-color, piggish, polluted, pornographic, risqué, salacious, scruffy, scurvy, shabby, sluttish, smutty, soiled, sordid, squalid, sullied, treacherous, unclean, unfair, unscrupulous, unsporting, unsterile, unswept, vile, vulgar, yucky.
antonyms clean, spotless.
v. bedaub, begrime, besmear, besmirch, besmut, bespatter, blacken, defile, foul, mess up, muddy, pollute, smear, smirch, smudge, soil, soss, spoil, stain, sully.
antonyms clean, cleanse.

disability *n.* affliction, ailment, complaint, crippledom, defect, disablement, disorder, disqualification, handicap, impairment, impotency, inability, incapacitation, incapacity, incompetency, infirmity, malady, unfitness, weakness.

disable *v.* cripple, damage, debilitate, disenable, disqualify, enfeeble, hamstring, handicap, immobilize, impair, incapacitate, invalidate, lame, paralyze, prostrate, unfit, unman, weaken.

disabled *adj.* bedridden, crippled, handicapped, hors de combat, immobilized, incapacitated, infirm, lame, maimed, mangled, mutilated, paralyzed, weak, weakened, wrecked.
antonyms able, able-bodied.

disadvantage *n.* burden, damage, debit, detriment, disservice, drawback, flaw, fly in the ointment, handicap, hardship, harm, hindrance, hurt, impediment, inconvenience, injury, liability, loss, minus, nuisance, prejudice, privation, snag, trouble, unfavorableness, weakness.
antonyms advantage, benefit.
v. hamper, handicap, hinder, inconvenience, wrong-foot.
antonyms aid, help.

disagree *v.* altercate, argue, bicker, bother, clash, conflict, contend, contest, contradict, counter, depart, deviate, differ, discomfort, dissent, distress, diverge, fall out, hurt, nauseate, object, oppose, quarrel, run counter to, sicken, spat, squabble, take issue with, tiff, trouble, upset, vary, wrangle.
antonym agree.

disagreement *n.* altercation, argument, clash, conflict, debate, difference, discord, discrepancy, disparity, dispute, dissent, dissimilarity, dissimilitude, divergence, diversity, division, falling-out, incompatibility, incongruity, misunderstanding, quarrel, squabble, strife, tiff, unlikeness, variance, wrangle.
antonym agreement.

disappear *v.* cease, dematerialize, depart, dissolve, ebb, end, escape, evanesce, evaporate, expire, fade, flee, fly, go, pass, perish, recede, retire, scarper, vamoose, vanish, wane, withdraw.
antonym appear.

disappoint *v.* baffle, balk, chagrin, dash, deceive, defeat, delude, disconcert, disenchant, disgruntle, dishearten, disillusion, dismay, dissatisfy, fail, foil, frustrate, hamper, hinder, let down, miff, sadden, thwart, vex.
antonyms delight, please, satisfy.

disappointment[1] *n.* bafflement, chagrin, discontent, discouragement, disenchantment, disillusionment, displeasure, dissatisfaction, distress, failure, frustration, mortification, regret.
antonyms delight, pleasure, satisfaction.

disappointment[2] *n.* blow, calamity, comedown, disaster, drop, failure, fiasco, frost, lemon, let-down, misfortune, setback, swiz, swizzle.
antonyms boost, success.

disapprove of blame, censure, condemn, denounce, deplore, deprecate, disallow, discountenance, dislike, disparage, object to, reject, spurn, take exception to.
antonym approve of.

disarm[1] *v.* deactivate, demilitarize, demobilize, disable, disband, unarm, unweapon. *antonym* arm.

disarm[2] appease, conciliate, modify, persuade, win over.

disaster *n.* accident, act of God, blow, calamity, cataclysm, catastrophe, curtains, debacle, misadventure, mischance, misfortune, mishap, reverse, ruin, ruination, stroke, tragedy, trouble.
antonyms success, triumph.

disband *v.* break up, demobilize, dismiss, disperse, dissolve, part company, retire, scatter, separate.
antonyms assemble, band, combine.

disbelief *n.* distrust, doubt, dubiety, incredulity, mistrust, rejection, scepticism, suspicion, unbelief.
antonym belief.

discard *v.* abandon, cashier, cast aside, dispense with, dispose of, ditch, drop, dump, jettison, leave off, reject, relinquish, remove, repudiate, scrap, shed.
antonyms adopt, embrace, espouse.

discern *v.* ascertain, behold, descry, detect, determine, differentiate, discover, discriminate, distinguish, espy, judge, make out, notice, observe, perceive, recognize, see, wot.

discernment *n.* acumen, acuteness, ascertainment, astuteness, awareness, clear-sightedness, cleverness, discrimination, ingenuity, insight, intelligence, judgment, keenness, penetration, perception, perceptiveness, percipience, perspicacity, sagacity, sharpness, understanding, wisdom.

discharge *v.* absolve, accomplish, acquit, carry out, cashier, clear, detonate, disburden, discard, disembogue, dismiss, dispense, drum out, effectuate, egest, eject, emit, empty, excrete, execute, exonerate, expel, explode, exude, fire, free, fulfil, give off, gush, honor, leak, let off, liberate, meet, offload, ooze, oust, pardon, pay, perform, release, relieve, remove, sack, satisfy, set off, settle, shoot, unburden, unload, vent, void, volley.
antonyms employ, engage, hire.
n. accomplishment, achievement, acquittal, acquittance, blast, burst, clearance, congé, defluxion, demobilization, detonation, disburdening, discharging, dismissal, effluent, ejecta, ejectamenta, ejection, emission, emptying, excretion, execution, exoneration, explosion, firing, flight, flow, flux, fluxion, fulfilment, fusillade, gleet, glit, liberation, mittimus, observance, ooze, pardon, payment, performance, pus, quietus, quittance, release, remittance, report, salvo, satisfaction, secretion, seepage, settlement, shot, suppuration, the boot, the sack, unburdening, unloading, vent, voidance, voiding, volley, whiff.

disciple *n.* acolyte, adherent, apostle, believer, catechumen, chela, convert, devotee, follower, learner, partisan, proselyte, pupil, student, supporter, votary.

discipline *n.* castigation, chastisement, conduct, control, correction, course, curriculum, drill, exercise, martinetism, method, orderliness, practice, punishment, regimen, regulation, restraint, self-control, specialty, strictness, subject, training.
antonyms carelessness, negligence.
v. break in, castigate, chasten, chastise, check, control, correct, drill, educate, exercise, form, govern, habituate, instruct, inure, penalize, prepare, punish, regulate, reprimand, reprove, restrain, toughen, train.

disclaim *v.* abandon, abjure, abnegate, decline, deny, disacknowledge, disaffirm, disallow, disavow, disown, forswear, reject, renounce, repudiate.
antonyms accept, acknowledge, claim.

disclose *v.* broadcast, communicate, confess, discover, divulge, exhibit, expose, impart, lay, lay bare, leak, let slip, propale, publish, relate, reveal, show, tell, unbare, unbosom, unburden, uncover, unfold, unveil, utter.
antonyms conceal, hide.

discomfit *v.* abash, baffle, balk, beat, checkmate, confound, confuse, defeat, demoralize, discompose, disconcert, embarrass, faze, flurry, fluster, foil, frustrate, humble, humiliate, outwit, overcome, perplex, perturb, rattle, ruffle, thwart, trump, unsettle, vanquish, worry, worst.

discomfort *n.* ache, annoyance, disquiet, distress, hardship, hurt, inquietude, irritant, irritation, malaise, trouble, uneasiness, unpleasantness, unpleasantry, vexation.
antonyms comfort, ease.

disconcerted *adj.* annoyed, bewildered, confused, discombobulated, discomfited, distracted, disturbed, embarrassed, fazed, flurried, flustered, mixed-up, nonplused, perturbed, rattled, ruffled, taken aback, thrown, troubled, unsettled, upset.

disconnect *v.* cut off, detach, disengage, divide, part, separate, sever, uncouple, ungear, unhitch, unhook, unlink, unplug, unyoke.
antonyms attach, connect, engage.

disconsolate *adj.* crushed, dejected, desolate, despairing, dispirited, forlorn, gloomy, grief-stricken, heartbroken, heavy-hearted, hopeless, inconsolable,

melancholy, miserable, sad, unhappy, unsolaced, woeful, wretched.
antonyms cheerful, cheery.

discontent *n.* discontentment, displeasure, disquiet, dissatisfaction, envy, fretfulness, impatience, regret, restlessness, uneasiness, unhappiness, unrest, vexation.
antonym content.

discontinue *v.* abandon, break off, cancel, cease, drop, end, finish, halt, interrupt, pause, quit, stop, suspend, terminate.
antonym continue.

discord *n.* cacophony, clashing, conflict, contention, difference, din, disagreement, discordance, disharmony, dispute, dissension, dissonance, disunity, division, friction, harshness, incompatibility, jangle, jarring, opposition, racket, rupture, split, strife, tumult, variance, wrangling.
antonyms agreement, concord, harmony.

discourage *v.* abash, awe, check, chill, cow, curb, damp, dampen, dash, daunt, deject, demoralize, deprecate, depress, deter, discountenance, disfavor, dishearten, dismay, dispirit, dissuade, frighten, hinder, inhibit, intimidate, overawe, prevent, put off, restrain, scare, unman, unnerve.
antonyms encourage, favor, hearten, inspire.

discourteous *adj.* abrupt, bad-mannered, boorish, brusque, curt, disrespectful, ill-bred, ill-mannered, impolite, insolent, offhand, rude, slighting, unceremonious, uncivil, uncourteous, ungracious, unmannerly.
antonyms courteous, polite, respectful.

discover *v.* ascertain, conceive, contrive, descry, design, detect, determine, devise, dig up, discern, disclose, espy, find, invent, learn, light on, locate, notice, originate, perceive, pioneer, realize, recognize, reveal, see, spot, suss out, uncover, unearth.
antonyms conceal, hide.

discredit *v.* blame, censure, challenge, defame, degrade, deny, disbelieve, discount, disgrace, dishonor, disparage, dispute, distrust, doubt, explode, mistrust, question, reproach, slander, slur, smear, vilify.
antonyms believe, credit.
n. aspersion, blame, censure, disgrace, dishonor, disrepute, distrust, doubt, ignominy, ill-repute, imputation, mistrust, odium, opprobium, question, reproach, scandal, shame, skepticism, slur, smear, stigma, suspicion.
antonym credit.

discreet *adj.* careful, cautious, circumspect, considerate, delicate, diplomatic, discerning, guarded, judicious, politic, prudent, reserved, sagacious, sensible, softly-softly, tactful, wary.
antonyms careless, indiscreet, tactless.

discrepancy *n.* conflict, contrariety, difference, disagreement, discordance, disparity, dissimilarity, dissonance, divergence, imparity, incongruity, inconsistency, inequality, variance, variation.

discretion *n.* acumen, care, carefulness, caution, choice, circumspection, consideration, diplomacy, discernment, disposition, heedfulness, inclination, judgment, judiciousness, liking, maturity, mind, option, pleasure, predilection, preference, prudence, responsibility, sagacity, tact, volition, wariness, will, wisdom, wish.
antonym indiscretion.

discriminating *adj.* acute, astute, critical, cultivated, discerning, discriminant, fastidious, nasute, particular, perceptive, selective, sensitive, tasteful.

discrimination[1] *n.* bias, bigotry, favoritism, inequity, intolerance, Jim Crow, prejudice, unfairness.

discrimination[2] *n.* acumen, acuteness, discernment, insight, judgment, keenness, penetration, perception, percipience, refinement, sagacity, subtlety, taste.

discuss *v.* argue, confer, consider, consult, converse, debate, deliberate, examine, lay heads together, rap.

discussion *n.* analysis, argument, colloquium, colloquy, confabulation, conference, consideration, consultation, conversation, debate, deliberation, dialogue, discourse, examination, exchange, gabfest, moot, quodlibet, rap, review, scrutiny, seminar, symposium, talkfest.

disdain *v.* belittle, contemn, deride, despise, disavow, disregard, misprize, pooh-pooh, rebuff, reject, scorn, slight, sneer at, spurn, undervalue.
antonyms admire, respect.
n. arrogance, contempt, contumely, deprecation, derision, dislike, haughtiness, hauteur, imperiousness, indifference, scorn, sneering, snobbishness, superciliousness.
antonyms admiration, respect.

disdainful *adj.* aloof, arrogant, contemptuous, derisive, haughty, hoity-toity, imperious, insolent, proud, scornful, sneering, supercilious, superior, uppish.
antonyms admiring, respectful.

disease *n.* affection, affliction, ailment, blight, cancer, canker, complaint, condition, contagion, contamination, disorder, distemper, epidemic, epizootic, idiopathy, ill-health, illness, indisposition, infection, infirmity, malady, malaise, murrain, pest, plague, sickness, upset.
antonym health.

disentangle *v.* clarify, debarrass, detach, disconnect, disembarrass, disengage, disentwine, disinvolve, extricate, free, loose, ravel out, resolve, separate, sever, simplify, unfold, unravel, unsnarl, untangle, untwine, untwist.
antonym entangle.

disfigured *adj.* damaged, defaced, deformed, flawed, ruined, scarred, spoilt, ugly.
antonym adorned.

disgrace *n.* aspersion, attaint, baseness, blemish, blot, contempt, defamation, degradation, discredit, disesteem, disfavor, dishonor, disrepute, dog-house, ignominy, infamy, obloquy, odium, opprobium, reproach, scandal, shame, slur, stain, stigma.
antonyms esteem, honor, respect.

v. abase, attaint, defame, degrade, discredit, disfavor, dishonor, disparage, humiliate, reproach, scandalize, shame, slur, stain, stigmatize, sully, taint.
antonyms honor, respect.

disgraceful *adj.* appalling, blameworthy, contemptible, degrading, detestable, discreditable, dishonorable, disreputable, dreadful, ignominious, infamous, low, mean, opprobrious, scandalous, shameful, shocking, unworthy.
antonyms honorable, respectable.

disguise *v.* camouflage, cloak, conceal, cover, deceive, dissemble, dissimulate, dress up, explain away, fake, falsify, fudge, hide, mask, misrepresent, screen, secrete, shroud, veil.
antonyms expose, reveal, uncover.
n. camouflage, cloak, concealment, costume, cover, coverture, deception, dissimulation, façade, front, getup, mask, masquerade, pretence, screen, semblance, travesty, trickery, veil, veneer, visor.

disgust *v.* displease, nauseate, offend, outrage, put off, repel, revolt, scandalize, scunner, sicken.
antonyms delight, gratify, tempt.
n. abhorrence, abomination, antipathy, aversion, detestation, dislike, disrelish, distaste, hatefulness, hatred, loathing, nausea, odium, repugnance, repulsion, revulsion.
antonyms admiration, liking.

disgusting *adj.* abominable, detestable, distasteful, foul, gross, hateful, loathsome, nasty, nauseating, nauseous, objectionable, obnoxious, obscene, odious, offensive, repellent, repugnant, revolting, shameless, sickening, sickmaking, stinking, ugsome, unappetizing, vile, vulgar. *antonyms* attractive, delightful, pleasant.

dish[1] *n.* bowl, fare, food, plate, platter, porringer, ramekin, recipe, salver, trencher.

dish[2] *v.* finish, ruin, spoil, torpedo, wreck.

dishearten *v.* cast down, crush, damp, dampen, dash, daunt, deject, depress, deter, discourage, dismay, dispirit, frighten, weary.

disheartened *adj.* crestfallen, crushed, daunted, dejected, depressed, disappointed, discouraged, dismayed, dispirited, downcast, downhearted, frightened, weary.
antonyms encouraged, heartened.

disheveled *adj.* bedraggled, blowsy, disarranged, disordered, frowsy, messy, mussy, ruffled, rumpled, slovenly, tousled, uncombed, unkempt, untidy.
antonyms neat, spruce, tidy.

dishonest *adj.* bent, cheating, corrupt, crafty, crooked, deceitful, deceiving, deceptive, designing, disreputable, double-dealing, false, fraudulent, guileful, immoral, knavish, lying, mendacious, perfidious, shady, snide, swindling, treacherous, unethical, unfair, unprincipled, unscrupulous, untrustworthy, untruthful, wrongful.
antonym fair, honest, scrupulous, trustworthy.

dishonor *v.* abase, blacken, corrupt, debase, debauch, defame, defile, deflower, degrade, demean, discredit, disgrace, disparage, pollute, rape, ravish, seduce, shame, sully.
antonym honor.
n. abasement, abuse, affront, aspersion, degradation, discourtesy, discredit, disfavor, disgrace, disrepute, ignominy, imputation, indignity, infamy, insult, obloquy, odium, offence, opprobrium, outrage, reproach, scandal, shame, slight, slur.
antonym honor.

disinclined *adj.* antipathetic, averse, hesitant, indisposed, loath, opposed, reluctant, resistant, undisposed, unenthusiastic, unwilling.
antonyms inclined, willing.

disingenuous *adj.* artful, cunning, deceitful, designing, devious, dishonest, duplicitous, guileful, insidious, insincere, shifty, two-faced, uncandid, wily.
antonyms artless, frank, ingenuous, naive.

disintegrate *v.* break up, crumble, decompose, disunite, fall apart, molder, rot, separate, shatter, splinter.
antonyms combine, merge, unite.

disinterested *adj.* candid, detached, dispassionate, equitable, even-handed, impartial, impersonal, neutral, openminded, unbiased, uninvolved, unprejudiced, unselfish.
antonyms biased, concerned, interested, prejudiced.

dislike *n.* animosity, animus, antagonism, antipathy, aversion, detestation, disapprobration, disapproval, disgust, disinclination, displeasure, disrelish, distaste, dyspathy, enmity, hatred, hostility, loathing, repugnance.
antonyms attachment, liking, predilection.
v. abhor, abominate, despise, detest, disapprove, disfavor, disrelish, hate, keck, loathe, scorn, shun.
antonyms favor, like, prefer.

disloyal *adj.* apostate, disaffected, faithless, false, perfidious, seditious, subversive, traitorous, treacherous, treasonable, two-faced, unfaithful, unleal, unpatriotic, untrustworthy, unwifely.
antonym loyal.

dismal *adj.* black, bleak, burdan, cheerless, dark, depressing, despondent, discouraging, doleful, dolorous, dowie, dreary, dreich, forlorn, funereal, ghostful, gloomy, gruesome, hopeless, incompetent, inept, lac(h)rymose, lonesome, long-faced, long-visaged, lowering, low-spirited, lugubrious, melancholy, poor, sad, sepulchral, somber, sorrowful, stupid, thick, useless.
antonyms bright, cheerful.

dismantle *v.* demolish, demount, disassemble, dismount, raze, strike, strip, unrig.
antonym assemble.

dismay *v.* affright, alarm, appal, consternate, daunt, depress, disappoint, disconcert, discourage, dishearten, disillusion, dispirit, distress, frighten, horrify, paralyze, put off, scare, terrify, unnerve, unsettle.
antonym encourage.
n. agitation, alarm, anxiety, apprehension, consternation,

disappointment, distress, dread, fear, fright, funk, horror, panic, terror, trepidation, upset.
antonyms boldness, encouragement.

dismiss *v.* ax, banish, bounce, bowler-hat, cashier, chassé, chuck, disband, discharge, discount, dispel, disperse, disregard, dissolve, drop, fire, free, give (someone) the push, lay off, let go, oust, pooh-pooh, reject, release, relegate, remove, repudiate, sack, send packing, set aside, shelve, spurn.
antonyms accept, appoint.

disobedient *adj.* contrary, contumacious, defiant, disorderly, froward, insubordinate, intractable, mischievous, naughty, obstreperous, refractory, unruly, wayward, wilful.
antonym obedient.

disobey *v.* contravene, defy, disregard, flout, ignore, infringe, overstep, rebel, resist, transgress, violate.
antonym obey.

disorder *n.* affliction, ailment, brawl, chaos, clamor, clutter, commotion, complaint, confusion, derangement, disarray, disease, disorderliness, disorganization, disturbance, fight, fracas, hubbub, hullabaloo, illness, indisposition, irregularity, jumble, malady, mess, misarrangement, misarray, misorder, misrule, muddle, muss(e), mussiness, quarrel, riot, rumpus, shambles, sickness, tumult, untidiness, uproar.
antonym order.
v. clutter, confound, confuse, derange, disarrange, discompose, disorganize, disrank, disturb, jumble, mess up, misorder, mix up, muddle, scatter, unsettle, upset.
antonyms arrange, organize.

disorganization *n.* chaos, confusion, derangement, disarray, disjointedness, dislocation, disorder, disruption, incoherence, unconnectedness.
antonyms order, tidiness.

disorganized *adj.* chaotic, confused, disordered, haphazard, jumbled, muddled, shambolic, shuffled, topsy-turvy, unmethodical, unorganized, unregulated, unsifted, unsorted, unstructured, unsystematic, unsystematized.
antonyms organized, tidy.

disown *v.* abandon, abnegate, cast off, deny, disacknowledge, disallow, disavow, disclaim, reject, renounce, repudiate, unget.
antonym accept.

disparage *v.* belittle, criticize, decry, defame, degrade, denigrate, deprecate, depreciate, deride, derogate, detract from, discredit, disdain, dishonor, dismiss, disvalue, malign, minimize, ridicule, run down, scorn, slander, traduce, underestimate, underrate, undervalue, vilify, vilipend.
antonym praise.

disparagement *n.* aspersion, belittlement, condemnation, contempt, contumely, criticism, debasement, decrial, decrying, degradation, denunciation, deprecation, depreciation, derision, derogation, detraction, discredit, disdain, ridicule, scorn, slander, underestimation, vilification.
antonym praise.

dispassionate *adj.* calm, candid, collected, composed, cool, detached, disinterested, fair, impartial, impersonal, imperturbable, indifferent, moderate, neutral, objective, quiet, serene, sober, temperate, unbiased, unemotional, unexcitable, unexcited, uninvolved, unmoved, unprejudiced, unruffled.
antonyms biased, emotional.

dispatch[1], **despatch** *v.* accelerate, conclude, discharge, dismiss, dispose of, expedite, finish, hasten, hurry, perform, quicken, settle.
antonym impede.
n. alacrity, celerity, dépêche, expedition, haste, precipitateness, promptitude, promptness, quickness, rapidity, speed, swiftness.
antonym slowness.

dispatch[2], **despatch** *v.* consign, express, forward, remit, send, transmit.
n. account, bulletin, communication, communiqué, document, instruction, item, letter, message, missive, news, piece, report, story.

dispatch[3], **despatch** *v.* assassinate, bump off, execute, kill, murder, rub out, slaughter, slay, waste.

dispel *v.* allay, banish, discuss, dismiss, disperse, dissipate, drive off, eliminate, expel, melt away, resolve, rout, scatter.
antonym give rise to.

dispense *v.* administer, allocate, allot, apply, apportion, assign, deal out, direct, disburse, discharge, distribute, dole out, enforce, except, excuse, execute, exempt, exonerate, implement, let off, measure, mete out, mix, operate, prepare, release, relieve, reprieve, share, supply, undertake.

disperse *v.* broadcast, circulate, diffuse, disappear, disband, dismiss, dispel, disseminate, dissipate, dissolve, distribute, drive off, evanesce, melt away, rout, scatter, separate, spread, strew, vanish.
antonym gather.

dispirited *adj.* brassed off, browned off, cast down, crestfallen, dejected, depressed, despondent, discouraged, disheartened, down, downcast, fed up, gloomy, glum, low, morose, sad.
antonym encouraged.

displace *v.* cashier, crowd out, depose, derange, disarrange, discard, discharge, dislocate, dislodge, dismiss, dispossess, disturb, eject, evict, fire, luxate, misplace, move, oust, remove, replace, sack, shift, succeed, supersede, supplant, transpose, unsettle.

display *v.* betray, blazon, boast, demonstrate, disclose, evidence, evince, exhibit, expand, expose, extend, flash, flaunt, flourish, manifest, model, parade, present, reveal, show, show off, showcase, splash, sport, unfold, unfurl, unveil, vaunt, wear.
antonym hide.

n. array, demonstration, étalage, exhibition, exposition, exposure, flourish, manifestation, ostentation, pageant, parade, pomp, presentation, revelation, show, spectacle, splurge.

displeasure *n.* anger, annoyance, disapprobation, disapproval, discontent, disfavor, disgruntlement, dudgeon, huff, indignation, irritation, offense, pique, resentment, vexation, wrath.
antonyms gratification, pleasure.

disposal *n.* arrangement, array, assignment, authority, bequest, bestowal, clearance, conduct, consignment, control, conveyance, determination, direction, discarding, discretion, dispensation, disposition, distribution, dumping, ejection, gift, government, jettisoning, management, ordering, position, regulation, relinquishment, removal, responsibility, riddance, scrapping, settlement, transfer.
antonym provision.

dispose *v.* actuate, adapt, adjust, align, arrange, array, bias, condition, determine, dispone, distribute, fix, group, incline, induce, influence, lay, lead, marshal, motivate, move, order, place, position, predispose, prompt, put, range, rank, regulate, set, settle, situate, stand, tempt.

disposition *n.* adjustment, arrangement, bent, bias, character, classification, constitution, control, direction, disposal, distribution, grain, grouping, habit, inclination, kidney, leaning, make-up, management, nature, ordering, organization, placement, predisposition, proclivity, proneness, propensity, readiness, regulation, spirit, temper, temperament, tendency, velleity.

dispossess *v.* deprive, dislodge, disseize, divest, eject, evict, expel, oust, rob, strip, unhouse.
antonyms give, provide.

disprove *v.* answer, confute, contradict, controvert, discredit, explode, expose, invalidate, negate, rebut, refute.
antonym prove.

dispute *v.* altercate, argue, brawl, challenge, clash, contend, contest, contradict, controvert, debate, deny, discuss, doubt, gainsay, impugn, litigate, moot, oppugn, quarrel, question, spar, squabble, traverse, wrangle.
antonym agree.
n. altercation, argument, brawl, conflict, contention, controversy, debate, disagreement, discord, discussion, dissension, disturbance, feud, friction, quarrel, spar, squabble, strife, wrangle.
antonym agreement.

disqualify *v.* debar, disable, disauthorize, disentitle, dishabilitate, disprivilege, incapacitate, invalidate, preclude, prohibit, rule out, unfit.
antonyms accept, allow.

disregard *v.* brush aside, cold-shoulder, contemn, despise, discount, disdain, disobey, disparage, ignore, laugh off, make light of, neglect, overlook, pass over, pooh-pooh, slight, snub, turn a blind eye to.
antonyms note, pay attention to.
n. brush-off, contempt, disdain, disesteem, disrespect, heedlessness, ignoring, inattention, indifference, neglect, negligence, oversight, slight.
antonym attention.

disrepair *n.* collapse, decay, deterioration, dilapidation, ruin, ruination, shabbiness, unrepair.
antonyms good repair, restoration.

disreputable *adj.* base, contemptible, derogatory, discreditable, disgraceful, dishonorable, disorderly, disrespectable, ignominious, infamous, louche, low, mean, notorious, opprobrious, scandalous, seedy, shady, shameful, shocking, unprincipled.
antonyms decent, honorable.

disrespectful *adj.* bad-tempered, cheeky, contemptuous, discourteous, impertinent, impolite, impudent, insolent, insulting, irreverent, rude, uncivil, unmannerly.
antonym respectful.

dissect *v.* analyze, anatomize, break down, dismember, examine, explore, inspect, investigate, pore over, scrutinize, study.

disseminate *v.* broadcast, circulate, diffuse, disperse, dissipate, distribute, evangelize, proclaim, promulgate, propagate, publicize, publish, scatter, sow, spread.

dissent *v.* decline, differ, disagree, disconsent, object, protest, quibble, refuse.
antonyms agree, consent.
n. difference, disagreement, discord, dissension, dissidence, nonconformity, objection, opposition, quibble, refusal, resistance.
antonym agreement.

dissertation *n.* critique, discourse, disquisition, essay, exposition, monograph, paper, prolegomena, propaedeutic, thesis, treatise.

dissident *adj.* differing, disagreeing, discordant, dissentient, dissenting, heterodox, nonconformist, recusant, schismatic.
antonyms acquiescent, agreeing.
n. agitator, dissenter, protestor, rebel, recusant, refus(e)nik, schismatic.
antonym assenter.

dissimilar *adj.* different, disparate, divergent, diverse, heterogeneous, incompatible, mismatched, unlike, unrelated, various.
antonyms compatible, similar.

dissimulation *n.* act, affectation, concealment, deceit, deception, dissembling, double-dealing, duplicity, feigning, hypocrisy, play-acting, pretence, sham, wile.
antonym openness.

dissipate *v.* burn up, consume, deplete, disappear, dispel, disperse, dissolve, evaporate, expend, fritter away, lavish, rig, scatter, spend, squander, vanish, wanton, waste.
antonym accumulate.

dissolute *adj.* abandoned, corrupt, debauched, degenerate, depraved, dissipated, immoral, lax, lewd, libertine,

licentious, loose, profligate, rakehell, rakehelly, rakish, unrestrained, vicious, wanton, wide, wild.
antonym virtuous.

dissolve *v.* break up, crumble, decompose, deliquesce, destroy, diffuse, disappear, discontinue, disintegrate, dismiss, disorganize, disperse, dissipate, disunite, divorce, dwindle, end, evanesce, evaporate, fade, flux, fuse, liquefy, loose, melt, overthrow, perish, ruin, separate, sever, soften, suspend, terminate, thaw, vanish, wind up.

dissuade *v.* dehort, deter, discourage, disincline, divert, expostulate, put off, remonstrate, warn.
antonym persuade.

distant *adj.* abroad, afar, aloof, apart, ceremonious, cold, cool, disparate, dispersed, distinct, faint, far, faraway, far-flung, far-off, formal, haughty, indirect, indistinct, isolated, obscure, outlying, out-of-the-way, remote, removed, reserved, restrained, reticent, scattered, separate, slight, stand-offish, stiff, unapproachable, uncertain, unfriendly, withdrawn.
antonyms close, friendly.

distasteful *adj.* abhorrent, aversive, disagreeable, displeasing, dissatisfying, loathsome, nasty, nauseous, objectionable, obnoxious, offensive, repugnant, repulsive, undesirable, uninviting, unpalatable, unpleasant, unsavory.
antonym pleasing.

distend *v.* balloon, bloat, bulge, dilate, enlarge, expand, fill out, increase, inflate, intumesce, puff, stretch, swell, widen.
antonym deflate.

distinct *adj.* apparent, clear, clear-cut, decided, definite, detached, different, discrete, dissimilar, evident, individual, lucid, manifest, marked, noticeable, obvious, palpable, patent, plain, recognizable, separate, several, sharp, unambiguous, unconnected, unmistakable, well-defined.
antonyms fuzzy, hazy, indistinct.

distinction[1] *n.* characteristic, contradistinction, contrast, difference, differential, differentiation, diorism, discernment, discrimination, dissimilarity, distinctiveness, division, feature, individuality, mark, nuance, particularity, peculiarity, penetration, perception, quality, separation.

distinction[2] *n.* account, celebrity, consequence, credit, eminence, excellence, fame, glory, greatness, honor, importance, merit, name, note, prestige, prominence, quality, rank, renown, reputation, repute, significance, superiority, worth.
antonym insignificance.

distinctive *adj.* characteristic, different, discriminative, discriminatory, distinguishing, extraordinary, idiosyncratic, individual, inimitable, original, peculiar, singular, special, typical, uncommon, unique.
antonym common.

distinguish *v.* ascertain, categorize, celebrate, characterize, classify, decide, determine, differentiate, dignify, discern, discriminate, honor, immortalize, individualize, judge, know, make out, mark, perceive, pick out, recognize, see, separate, signalize, tell, tell apart.

distinguished *adj.* acclaimed, celebrated, conspicuous, distingué, eminent, eximious, extraordinary, famed, famous, illustrious, marked, nameworthy, notable, noted, outstanding, renowned, signal, striking, well-known.
antonyms insignificant, ordinary.

distort *v.* bend, bias, buckle, color, contort, deform, disfigure, falsify, garble, miscolor, misrepresent, misshape, pervert, skew, slant, torture, twist, warp, wrench, wrest, wring.

distract *v.* agitate, amuse, beguile, bewilder, confound, confuse, derange, discompose, disconcert, disturb, divert, engross, entertain, faze, harass, madden, occupy, perplex, puzzle, sidetrack, torment, trouble.

distracted *adj.* agitated, bemused, bewildered, confounded, confused, crazy, deranged, distraught, éperdu(e), flustered, frantic, frenzied, grief-stricken, harassed, hassled, insane, mad, maddened, overwrought, perplexed, puzzled, raving, troubled, wild, worked up, wrought up.
antonyms calm, untroubled.

distraction *n.* aberration, abstraction, agitation, alienation, amusement, beguilement, bewilderment, commotion, confusion, delirium, derangement, desperation, discord, disorder, disturbance, diversion, divertissement, entertainment, frenzy, hallucination, harassment, incoherence, insanity, interference, interruption, mania, pastime, recreation.

distress *n.* adversity, affliction, agony, anguish, anxiety, calamity, depravation, desolation, destitution, difficulties, discomfort, grief, hardship, heartache, indigence, katzenjammer, misery, misfortune, need, pain, pauperism, poverty, privation, sadness, sorrow, strait(s), suffering, torment, torture, trial, trouble, woe, worry, wretchedness.
antonyms comfort, ease, security. *v.* afflict, agonize, bother, constrain, cut up, disturb, grieve, harass, harrow, pain, perplex, sadden, straiten, torment, trouble, upset, worry, wound.
antonyms assist, comfort.

distribute *v.* administer, allocate, allot, apportion, arrange, assign, assort, bestow, carve up, categorize, circulate, class, classify, convey, deal, deliver, diffuse, dish out, dispense, disperse, dispose, disseminate, divide, dole, file, give, group, hand out, mete, scatter, share, spread, strew.
antonyms collect, gather in.

district *n.* area, canton, cantred, cantret, community, gau, hundred, locale, locality, neighborhood, parish, precinct, quarter, region, sector, vicinity, ward.

distrust *v.* disbelieve, discredit, doubt, misbelieve, miscredit, misdeem, mistrust, question, suspect.
antonym trust.

n. disbelief, doubt, misfaith, misgiving, mistrust, qualm, question, skepticism, suspicion, untrust, wariness.
antonym trust.

disturb *v.* affray, agitate, alarm, annoy, bother, concuss, confound, confuse, derange, disarrange, discompose, disorder, order, disorganize, disrupt, distract, distress, excite, fluster, harass, interrupt, muddle, perturb, pester, rouse, ruffle, shake, startle, trouble, unsettle, upset, worry.
antonyms calm, quiet, reassure.

disturbance *n.* agitation, annoyance, bother, brawl, breeze, broil, burst-up, bust-up, commotion, confusion, derangement, disorder, distraction, fracas, fray, hindrance, hubbub, interruption, intrusion, katzenjammer, kick-up, misarrangement, molestation, muss(e), perturbation, riot, ruckus, ruction, shake-up, stour, stramash, tumult, turmoil, unrest, upheaval, uproar, upset, upturn.
antonyms peace, quiet.

disturbed *adj.* agitated, anxious, apprehensive, bothered, concerned, confused, discomposed, disordered, disquieted, flustered, maladjusted, neurotic, troubled, unbalanced, uneasy, unrestful, upset, worried.
antonyms calm, sane.

disuse *n.* abandonment, decay, desuetude, discontinuance, disusage, idleness, neglect.
antonym use.

diverge *v.* bifurcate, branch, conflict, depart, deviate, differ, digress, disagree, dissent, divaricate, divide, fork, part, radiate, separate, split, spread, stray, vary, wander.
antonyms agree, come together, join.

diverse *adj.* assorted, different, differing, discrete, disparate, dissimilar, distinct, divergent, diversified, heterogeneous, manifold, many, miscellaneous, multifarious, multiform, numerous, separate, several, some, sundry, unlike, varied, various, varying.
antonym identical.

diversify *v.* alter, assort, branch out, change, expand, mix, spread out, variegate, vary.

diversion *n.* alteration, amusement, beguilement, change, deflection, delight, departure, detour, deviation, digression, disportment, distraction, divertissement, enjoyment, entertainment, game, gratification, pastime, play, pleasure, recreation, relaxation, sport, variation.

divert *v.* amuse, avert, beguile, deflect, delight, detract, distract, entertain, gratify, hive off, recreate, redirect, regale, side-track, switch, tickle.
antonyms direct, irritate.

divide *v.* alienate, allocate, allot, apportion, arrange, bisect, break up, categorize, classify, cleave, cut, deal out, detach, disconnect, dispense, distribute, disunite, divvy, estrange, grade, group, part, partition, portion, segment, segregate, separate, sever, share, shear, sort, split, subdivide, sunder.
antonyms collect, gather, join.

divide out allocate, allot, apportion, dole out, measure out, morsel, parcel out, share, share out.

divine *adj.* angelic, beatific, beautiful, blissful, celestial, consecrated, exalted, excellent, glorious, godlike, heavenly, holy, marvelous, mystical, perfect, rapturous, religious, sacred, sanctified, spiritual, splendid, superhuman, superlative, supernatural, supreme, transcendent, transcendental, transmundane, wonderful.
n. churchman, clergyman, cleric, ecclesiastic, minister, parson, pastor, prelate, priest, reverend.
v. apprehend, conjecture, deduce, foretell, guess, hariolate, haruspicate, infer, intuit, perceive, prognosticate, suppose, surmise, suspect, understand.

division *n.* allotment, apportionment, bisection, border, boundary, branch, breach, category, class, compartment, cutting, demarcation, department, detaching, dichotomy, disagreement, discord, distribution, disunion, divide, divider, dividing, estrangement, feud, group, head, part, partition, portion, rupture, schism, scission, section, sector, segment, separation, sept, sharing, side, split, splitting, stream, variance, wapentake, ward, watershed, wing.
antonyms agreement, multiplication, unification.

divorce *n.* annulment, breach, break, break-up, decree nisi, diffarreation, dissolution, disunion, rupture, separation, severance, split-up.
v. annul, cancel, disconnect, dissever, dissociate, dissolve, disunite, divide, part, separate, sever, split up, sunder.
antonyms marry, unify.

divulge *v.* betray, broadcast, communicate, confess, declare, disclose, evulgate, exhibit, expose, impart, leak, let slip, proclaim, promulgate, publish, reveal, spill, tell, uncover.

dizzy *adj.* befuddled, bemused, bewildered, capricious, confused, dazed, dazzled, faint, fickle, flighty, foolish, frivolous, giddy, light-headed, lofty, muddled, reeling, scatterbrained, shaky, staggering, steep, swimming, vertiginous, wobbly, woozy.

do *v.* accomplish, achieve, act, adapt, answer, arrange, behave, carry out, cause, cheat, complete, con, conclude, cover, cozen, create, deceive, decipher, decode, defraud, discharge, dupe, effect, end, execute, explore, fare, fix, fleece, give, hoax, implement, make, manage, organize, pass muster, perform, prepare, present, proceed, produce, put on, render, resolve, satisfy, serve, solve, suffice, suit, swindle, tour, transact, translate, transpose, travel, trick, undertake, visit, work, work out.
n. affair, event, function, gathering, occasion, party.

docile *adj.* amenable, biddable, complaisant, compliant, ductile, manageable, obedient, obliging, pliable, pliant, submissive, teachable, tractable, unmurmuring, unprotesting, unquestioning.
antonyms truculent, unco-operative.

dock[1] *n.* boat-yard, harbor, marina, pier, quay, waterfront, wharf.

v. anchor, berth, drop anchor, join up, land, link up, moor, put in, rendezvous, tie up, unite.

dock[2] *v.* clip, crop, curtail, cut, decaudate, decrease, deduct, diminish, lessen, reduce, shorten, subtract, truncate, withhold.

doctor *n.* clinician, doctoress, doctress, general practitioner, GP, hakim, internist, leech, medic, medical officer, medical practitioner, medicaster, medico, physician, pill(s).
v. adulterate, alter, botch, change, cobble, cook, cut, dilute, disguise, falsify, fix, fudge, hocus, load, medicate, mend, misrepresent, patch, pervert, repair, spike, tamper with, treat.

doctrine *n.* belief, canon, concept, conviction, creed, dogma, ism, opinion, precept, principle, teaching, tenet.

document *n.* certificate, chirograph, deed, form, instrument, paper, parchment, record, report.
v. authenticate, back, certify, cite, corroborate, detail, enumerate, instance, list, particularize, prove, substantiate, support, validate, verify.

dodge *v.* avoid, dart, deceive, duck, elude, equivocate, evade, fend off, fudge, hedge, parry, shift, shirk, shuffle, side-step, skive, swerve, swing the lead, trick.
n. chicane, contrivance, device, feint, machination, maneuver, ploy, ruse, scheme, stratagem, subterfuge, trick, wheeze, wile.

dogged *adj.* determined, firm, indefatigable, indomitable, obstinate, persevering, persistent, pertinacious, relentless, resolute, single-minded, staunch, steadfast, steady, stubborn, tenacious, unflagging, unshakable, unyielding.
antonym irresolute.

dogma *n.* article, article of faith, belief, conviction, credendum, credo, creed, doctrine, opinion, precept, principle, teaching, tenet.

dogmatic *adj.* affirmative, arbitrary, assertive, authoritative, canonical, categorical, dictatorial, didactic, doctrinaire, doctrinal, downright, emphatic, ex cathedra, high-dried, imperious, magisterial, obdurate, opinionated, oracular, overbearing, peremptory, pontific(al), positive.

doings *n.* actions, activities, acts, adventures, affairs, concerns, dealings, deeds, events, exploits, goings-on, handiwork, happenings, proceedings, transactions.

dole *n.* allocation, allotment, allowance, alms, apportionment, benefit, dispensation, dispersal, distribution, division, donation, gift, grant, gratuity, issuance, modicum, parcel, pittance, portion, quota, share.

doleful *adj.* blue, cheerless, depressing, dismal, distressing, dolorous, dreary, forlorn, funereal, gloomy, lugubrious, melancholy, mournful, painful, pathetic, pitiful, rueful, sad, somber, sorrowful, woebegone, woeful, wretched.
antonym cheerful.

dolt *n.* ass, beetlebrain, beetlehead, besom-head, blockhead, bonehead, booby, boodle, bufflehead, bull-calf, calf, chump, clod, clodhopper, clodpate, clodpoll, clot, clunk, dimwit, dope, dullard, dunce, fool, galoot, half-wit, idiot, ignoramus, leather-head, loggerhead, loghead, lurdan(e), lurden, mutt, mutton-head, nitwit, nutcase, palooka, sheep's-head, simpleton, turnip.

domain *n.* area, authority, bailiwick, business, concern, demesne, department, discipline, dominion, empire, estate, field, jurisdiction, kingdom, lands, orbit, pidgin, policies, power, province, realm, region, scope, specialty, sphere, sway, territory.

domestic *adj.* autochthonic, domal, domesticated, domiciliary, family, home, home-bred, home-loving, homely, house, household, house-trained, housewifely, indigenous, internal, native, pet, private, stay-at-home, tame, trained.
n. au pair, char, charwoman, daily, daily help, help, maid, scullery maid, servant, slavey, woman.

domesticate *v.* acclimatize, accustom, break, domesticize, familiarize, habituate, house-train, naturalize, tame, train.

domicile *n.* abode, dwelling, habitation, home, house, lodging(s), mansion, quarters, residence, residency, settlement.

dominate *v.* bestride, control, direct, domineer, dwarf, eclipse, govern, have the whip hand, keep under one's thumb, lead, master, monopolize, outshine, overbear, overgang, overlook, overrule, overshadow, predominate, prevail, rule, tyrannize.

domination *n.* ascendancy, authority, command, control, despotism, dictatorship, hegemony, influence, leadership, mastery, oppression, power, repression, rule, subjection, subordination, superiority, suppression, supremacy, sway, tyranny.

domineering *adj.* arrogant, authoritarian, autocratic, bossy, coercive, despotic, dictatorial, harsh, high-handed, imperious, iron-handed, magisterial, masterful, oppressive, overbearing, severe, tyrannical.
antonyms meek, obsequious, servile.

don *v.* affect, assume, clothe oneself in, dress in, get into, put on.
antonym doff.

donate *v.* bequeath, bestow, chip in, confer, contribute, cough up, fork out, gift, give, impart, present, proffer, subscribe.

donation *n.* alms, benefaction, boon, conferment, contribution, gift, grant, gratuity, largess(e), offering, present, presentation, subscription.

done *adj.* acceptable, accomplished, advised, agreed, completed, concluded, consummated, conventional, cooked, cooked to a turn, de rigueur, depleted, drained, ended, executed, exhausted, fatigued, finished, OK, over, perfected, proper, ready, realized, settled, spent, terminated, through, used up.

doom *n.* Armageddon, catastrophe, condemnation, death, death-knell, decision, decree, destiny, destruction, Doomsday, downfall, fate, fortune, judgment,

Judgment Day, karma, kismet, lot, portion, ruin, sentence, the Last Judgment, the last trump, verdict.
v. condemn, consign, damn, decree, destine, foredoom, foreordain, judge, predestine, preordain, sentence, threaten.

doomed *adj.* accursed, bedeviled, bewitched, condemned, cursed, fated, fey, hopeless, ill-fated, ill-omened, ill-starred, luckless, star-crossed.

dormant *adj.* asleep, comatose, fallow, hibernating, inactive, inert, inoperative, latent, latescent, quiescent, sleeping, sluggish, slumbering, suspended, torpid, undeveloped, unrealized.
antonyms active.

dose *n.* dosage, draught, drench, hit, measure, portion, potion, prescription, quantity, shot, slug.
v. administer, dispense, drench, medicate, treat.

doting *adj.* adoring, devoted, fond, foolish, indulgent, lovesick, soft.

double *adj.* bifarious, bifold, binate, coupled, diploid, doubled, dual, duple, duplex, duplicate, paired, twice, twin, twofold.
v. duplicate, enlarge, fold, geminate, grow, increase, magnify, multiply, repeat.
n. clone, copy, counterpart, dead ringer, dead spit, Doppelgänger, duplicate, fellow, image, impersonator, lookalike, mate, replica, ringer, spitting image, twin.

double-cross *v.* betray, cheat, con, cozen, defraud, hoodwink, mislead, swindle, trick, two-time.

double-dealer *n.* betrayer, cheat, con man, cozener, deceiver, dissembler, double-crosser, fraud, hypocrite, Machiavellian, rogue, swindler, traitor, two-timer.

doubt *v.* be dubious, be uncertain, demur, discredit, distrust, dubitate, fear, fluctuate, hesitate, misgive, mistrust, query, question, scruple, suspect, vacillate, waver.
antonyms believe, trust.
n. ambiguity, apprehension, arrière pensée, confusion, difficulty, dilemma, disquiet, distrust, dubiety, fear, hesitancy, hesitation, incredulity, indecision, irresolution, misgiving, mistrust, perplexity, problem, qualm, quandary, reservation, skepticism, suspense, suspicion, uncertainty, vacillation.
antonyms belief, certainty, confidence, trust.

doubtful *adj.* ambiguous, debatable, disreputable, distrustful, dubious, dubitable, equivocal, hazardous, hesitant, hesitating, inconclusive, indefinite, indeterminate, irresolute, litigious, obscure, perplexed, precarious, problematic, problematical, questionable, sceptical, shady, suspect, suspicious, tentative, uncertain, unclear, unconfirmed, unconvinced, undecided, unresolved, unsettled, unsure, vacillating, vague, wavering.
antonyms certain, definite.

doubtless *adv.* apparently, assuredly, certainly, clearly, indisputably, most likely, of course, ostensibly, out of question, precisely, presumably, probably, questionless, seemingly, supposedly, surely, truly, undoubtedly, unquestionably, without doubt.

doughty *adj.* able, bold, brave, courageous, daring, dauntless, fearless, gallant, game, hardy, heroic, intrepid, redoubtable, resolute, stout-hearted, strong, valiant, valorous.
antonyms cowardly, weak.

douse, dowse *v.* blow out, dip, drench, duck, dunk, extinguish, immerge, immerse, plunge, put out, saturate, smother, snuff, soak, souse, steep, submerge.

dowdy *adj.* dingy, drab, frowzy, frumpish, frumpy, ill-dressed, old-fashioned, scrubby, shabby, slovenly, tacky, tatty, unfashionable, unmodish, unsmart.
antonyms dressy, smart, spruce.

downcast *adj.* cheerless, chopfallen, crestfallen, daunted, dejected, depressed, despondent, disappointed, disconsolate, discouraged, disheartened, dismayed, dispirited, down, miserable, sad, unhappy. *antonyms* cheerful, elated, happy.

downfall *n.* breakdown, cloudburst, collapse, comedown, come-uppance, debacle, deluge, descent, destruction, disgrace, downpour, failure, fall, humiliation, overthrow, rainstorm, ruin, undoing, Waterloo.

downgrade *v.* belittle, decry, degrade, demote, denigrate, detract from, disparage, humble, lower, reduce in rank, run down.
antonyms improve, upgrade.

downhearted *adj.* blue, chopfallen, crestfallen, dejected, depressed, despondent, discouraged, disheartened, dismayed, dispirited, downcast, gloomy, glum, jaw-fallen, low-spirited, sad, sorrowful, unhappy.
antonyms cheerful, enthusiastic, happy.

downpour *n.* cloudburst, deluge, downcome, flood, inundation, rainstorm, torrent, water-spout.

downright *adj.* absolute, blatant, blunt, candid, categorical, clear, complete, explicit, forthright, frank, honest, open, out-and-out, outright, outspoken, plain, positive, simple, sincere, straightforward, thoroughgoing, total, undisguised, unequivocal, unqualified, utter, wholesale.

dowry *n.* dot, dower, endowment, faculty, gift, inheritance, legacy, portion, provision, share, talent, wedding-dower.

drab *adj.* cheerless, colorless, dingy, dismal, dreary, dull, dun-colored, flat, gloomy, gray, lackluster, mousy, shabby, somber, uninspired, vapid.
antonym bright.

draft[1] *v.* compose, delineate, design, draw, draw up, formulate, outline, plan, sketch.
n. abstract, delineation, ébauche, outline, plan, protocol, rough, sketch, version.

draft[2] *n.* bill, check, order, postal order.

draft[3] *n.* cup, current, dose, dragging, drawing, drench, drink, flow, haulage, influx, movement, portion, potation, puff, pulling, quantity, traction.

drag *v.* crawl, creep, dawdle, draggle, draw, hale, harl,

haul, inch, lag, linger, loiter, lug, pull, schlep, shamble, shuffle, straggle, sweep, tow, trail, tug, yank.
n. annoyance, bore, bother, brake, drogue, nuisance, pain, pest, pill.

drain *v.* bleed, consume, deplete, discharge, dissipate, down, draw off, drink up, dry, effuse, empty, emulge, evacuate, exhaust, exude, finish, flow out, lade, leak, milk, ooze, quaff, remove, sap, seep, strain, swallow, tap, tax, trickle, use up, weary, withdraw.
antonym fill.
n. channel, conduit, culvert, depletion, ditch, drag, duct, exhaustion, expenditure, grip, outlet, pipe, reduction, sap, sewer, sink, sough, stank, strain, trench, watercourse, withdrawal.

drama *n.* acting, crisis, dramatics, dramatization, dramaturgy, excitement, histrionics, kabuki, kathakali, melodrama, play, scene, show, spectacle, stage-craft, theater, theatricals, Thespian art, turmoil.

dramatist *n.* comedian, dramaturge, dramaturgist, playwright, play-writer, screen-writer, scriptwriter, tragedian.

drape *v.* adorn, array, cloak, cover, dangle, droop, drop, enrap, fold, hang, suspend, swathe, vest, wrap.

drastic *adj.* desperate, dire, draconian, extreme, far-reaching, forceful, harsh, heroic, radical, severe, strong.
antonym mild.

draw[1] *v.* allure, attenuate, attract, borrow, breathe in, bring forth, choose, deduce, delineate, depict, derive, design, drag, drain, elicit, elongate, engage, entice, entrain, evoke, extend, extort, extract, get, haul, induce, infer, influence, inhale, inspire, invite, lengthen, make, map out, mark out, outline, paint, pencil, persuade, pick, portray, puff, pull, respire, select, sketch, stretch, suck, take, tow, trace, tug, unsheathe.
antonyms propel, push.
n. appeal, attraction, bait, enticement, interest, lure, pull.

draw[2] *v.* be equal, be even, be neck and neck, dead-heat, tie. *n.* dead-heat, deadlock, impasse, stalemate, tie.

drawback *n.* block, defect, deficiency, désagrément, detriment, difficulty, disability, disadvantage, fault, flaw, fly in the ointment, handicap, hindrance, hitch, impediment, imperfection, nuisance, obstacle, pull-back, snag, stumbling, trouble.
antonym advantage.

drawing *n.* cartoon, delineation, depiction, graphic, illustration, outline, picture, portrait, portrayal, representation, sketch, study.

drawn *adj.* fatigued, fraught, haggard, harassed, harrowed, hassled, pinched, sapped, strained, stressed, taut, tense, tired, worn.

dread *v.* cringe at, fear, flinch, quail, shrink from, shudder, shy, tremble.
n. alarm, apprehension, aversion, awe, dismay, disquiet, fear, fright, funk, heebie-jeebies, horror, misgiving, terror, trepidation, worry.
antonyms confidence, security.
adj. alarming, awe-inspiring, awful, dire, dreaded, dreadful, frightening, frightful, ghastly, grisly, gruesome, horrible, terrible, terrifying.

dreadful *adj.* alarming, appalling, awful, dire, distressing, fearful, formidable, frightful, ghastly, grievous, grisly, gruesome, harrowing, hideous, horrendous, horrible, monstrous, shocking, terrible, tragic, tremendous.
antonym comforting.

dream *n.* ambition, aspiration, beauty, castle in Spain, castle in the air, daydream, delight, delusion, design, desire, fantasy, goal, hallucination, hope, illusion, imagination, joy, marvel, notion, phantasm, pipe-dream, pleasure, reverie, speculation, trance, treasure, vagary, vision, wish.
v. conjure, daydream, envisage, fancy, fantasize, hallucinate, imagine, muse, star-gaze, think, visualize.

dreamer *n.* daydreamer, Don Quixote, fantasist, fantasizer, fantast, idealist, John o'dreams, Johnny-head-in-the-air, romancer, star-gazer, theorizer, utopian, visionary, Walter Mitty, wool-gatherer.
antonyms pragmatist, realist.

dreary *adj.* bleak, boring, cheerless, colorless, comfortless, commonplace, depressing, dismal, doleful, downcast, drab, drear, dreich, dull, forlorn, gloomy, glum, humdrum, joyless, lifeless, lonely, lonesome, melancholy, monotonous, mournful, routine, sad, solitary, somber, sorrowful, tedious, trite, uneventful, uninteresting, wearisome, wretched.
antonyms bright, interesting.

dregs *n.* canaille, deposit, draff, dross, excrement, faeces, fag-end, fecula, grounds, lags, lees, left-overs, mother, outcasts, rabble, residue, residuum, riff-raff, scourings, scum, sediment, tailings, trash, waste.

drench *v.* douse, drouk, drown, duck, flood, imbrue, imbue, immerse, inundate, saturate, soak, souse, steep, wet.

dress *n.* apparel, attire, caparison, clothes, clothing, costume, ensemble, frock, garb, garment, garments, gear, getup, gown, guise, habiliments, habit, outfit, raiment, rigout, robe, suit, togs, vestment.
v. accouter, adjust, adorn, align, apparel, arrange, array, attire, bandage, bedeck, bedizen, betrim, bind up, boun, busk, caparison, change, clothe, deck, decorate, dispose, don, drape, embellish, fit, furbish, garb, garnish, groom, habilitate, habit, ornament, plaster, prepare, put on, rig, robe, set, straighten, tend, treat, trim.
antonyms disrobe, strip, undress.

dressing *n.* bandage, compress, emplastron, emplastrum, ligature, pad, plaster, pledget, poultice, spica, tourniquet.

dressy *adj.* classy, elaborate, elegant, formal, natty, ornate, ritzy, smart, stylish, swanky, swish.
antonyms dowdy, scruffy.

dribble *v.* drip, drivel, drool, drop, leak, ooze, run, saliva, seep, slaver, slobber, sprinkle, trickle.
n. drip, droplet, gobbet, leak, seepage, sprinkling, trickle.

drift *v.* accumulate, amass, coast, drive, float, freewheel, gather, meander, pile up, stray, waft, wander.
n. accumulation, aim, bank, course, current, design, direction, dune, flow, gist, heap, implication, import, impulse, intention, mass, meaning, mound, movement, object, pile, purport, ridge, rush, scope, significance, sweep, tendency, tenor, thrust, trend.

drifter *n.* beachcomber, hobo, intinerant, rolling stone, rover, swagman, tramp, vagabond, vagrant, wanderer.

drill[1] *v.* coach, discipline, exercise, instruct, practice, rehearse, teach, train, tutor.
n. coaching, discipline, exercise, instruction, practice, preparation, repetition, training, tuition.

drill[2] *v.* bore, penetrate, perforate, pierce, puncture, transpierce.
n. awl, bit, borer, gimlet.

drink *v.* absorb, bib, booze, carouse, down, drain, dram, gulp, guzzle, hit the bottle, imbibe, indulge, knock back, liquefy, liquor up, partake of, quaff, revel, sip, suck, sup, swallow, swig, swill, tank up, tipple, tope, toss off, wassail, water.
n. alcohol, ambrosia, beverage, bev(v)y, booze, deochandoris, dose, dram, draught, glass, gulp, hooch, liquid, liquor, noggin, plonk, potion, refreshment, sensation, sip, slug, snifter, snort, spirits, stiffener, suck, swallow, swig, swizzle, taste, the bottle, tickler, tiff, tipple, toss, tot.

drip *v.* dribble, drizzle, drop, exude, filter, plop, splash, sprinkle, trickle, weep.
n. dribble, dripping, drop, leak, milk-sop, ninny, softy, stillicide, trickle, weakling, weed, wet.

drive *v.* actuate, bear, coerce, compel, constrain, dash, dig, direct, force, goad, guide, hammer, handle, harass, herd, hurl, impel, manage, motivate, motor, oblige, operate, overburden, overwork, plunge, press, prod, propel, push, ram, ride, rush, send, sink, spur, stab, steer, task, tax, thrust, travel, urge.
n. action, advance, ambition, appeal, campaign, crusade, determination, effort, energy, enterprise, excursion, get-up-and-go, hurl, initiative, jaunt, journey, motivation, outing, pressure, push, ride, run, spin, surge, trip, turn, vigor, vim, zip.

drivel *n.* blathering, bunkum, eyewash, gibberish, gobbledegook, guff, gush, jive, mumbo-jumbo, nonsense, slush, stultiloquy, twaddle, waffle.

driver *n.* cabbie, cabman, charioteer, chauffeur, coachman, Jehu, motorist, trucker, vetturino, voiturier, wagoner.

droll *adj.* amusing, clownish, comic, comical, diverting, eccentric, entertaining, farcical, funny, humorous, jocular, laughable, ludicrous, pawky, quaint, ridiculous, risible, waggish, whimsical, witty.

drone *v.* bombilate, bombinate, buzz, chant, drawl, hum, intone, purr, thrum, vibrate, whirr.
n. buzz, chant, hum, murmuring, purr, thrum, vibration, whirr, whirring.

drool *v.* dote, dribble, drivel, enthuse, fondle, gloat, gush, rave, salivate, slaver, slobber, water at the mouth.

droop *v.* bend, dangle, decline, despond, diminish, drop, fade, faint, fall down, falter, flag, hang (down) sag, languish, lose heart, sink, slouch, slump, stoop, wilt, wither.
antonyms rise, straighten.

drop *n.* abyss, bead, bubble, chasm, cut, dab, dash, decline, declivity, decrease, descent, deterioration, downturn, drib, driblet, drip, droplet, fall, falling-off, glob, globule, globulet, goutte, gutta, lowering, mouthful, nip, pearl, pinch, plunge, precipice, reduction, shot, sip, slope, slump, spot, taste, tear, tot, trace, trickle.
v. abandon, cease, chuck, decline, depress, descend, desert, diminish, discontinue, disown, dive, dribble, drip, droop, fall, forsake, give up, jilt, kick, leave, lower, plummet, plunge, quit, reject, relinquish, remit, renounce, repudiate, sink, stop, terminate, throw over, trickle, tumble.
antonyms mount, rise.

drop-out *n.* Bohemian, deviant, dissenter, dissentient, hippie, loner, malcontent, non-conformist, rebel, renegade.

droppings *n.* dung, egesta, excrement, excreta, faeces, fumet, guano, manure, ordure, spraint, stools.

dross *n.* crust, debris, dregs, impurity, lees, recrement, refuse, remains, rubbish, scoria, scum, trash, waste.

drove *n.* collection, company, crowd, drift, flock, gathering, herd, horde, mob, multitude, press, swarm, throng.

drown *v.* deaden, deluge, drench, engulf, extinguish, flood, go under, immerse, inundate, muffle, obliterate, overcome, overpower, overwhelm, silence, sink, stifle, submerge, swallow up, swamp, wipe out.

drowsiness *n.* dopeyness, doziness, grogginess, lethargy, narcosis, oscitancy, sleepiness, sluggishness, somnolence, torpor.

drowsy *adj.* comatose, dazed, dopey, dozy, dreamy, drugged, heavy, lethargic, lulling, nodding, restful, sleepy, somniculous, somnolent, soothing, soporific, tired, torpid.
antonyms alert, awake.

drubbing *n.* beating, clobbering, defeat, flogging, hammering, licking, pounding, pummeling, thrashing, trouncing, walloping, whipping, whitewash.

drudge *n.* afterguard, devil, dogsbody, factotum, galley-slave, hack, jackal, lackey, maid-of-all-work, man-of-all-work, menial, scullion, servant, skivvy, slave, toiler, worker.
v. beaver, droil, grind, labor, moil, plod, plug away, slave, toil, work.
antonyms idle, laze.

drudgery *n.* chore, collar-work, donkey-work, drudgism, fag, faggery, grind, hack-work, labor, labor improbus, skivvying, slavery, slog, sweat, sweated labor, toil.

drug *n.* depressant, dope, kef, medicament, medication,

medicine, Mickey, Mickey Finn, narcotic, opiate, physic, poison, potion, remedy, stimulant.
v. anesthetize, deaden, dope, dose, drench, knock out, load, medicate, numb, poison, stupefy, treat.

drug-addict *n.* acid head, dope-fiend, head, hop-head, hype, junkie, tripper.

drugged *adj.* comatose, doped, dopey, high, looped, spaced out, stoned, stupefied, tripping, turned on, zonked.

druggist *n.* apothecary, chemist, pharmacologist.

drunk *adj.* a peg too low, a sheet (three sheets) in the wind, bevvied, blind, blotto, bonkers, bottled, canned, cockeyed, corked, corny, drunken, fou, fuddled, half-seas-over, in liquor, inebriate, inebriated, intoxicated, legless, liquored, lit up, loaded, lushy, maggoty, maudlin, merry, moony, moppy, mops and brooms, mortal, muddled, nappy, obfuscated, paralytic, pickled, pie-eyed, pissed, pixilated, plastered, shickered, sloshed, soaked, sottish, soused, sowdrunk, sozzled, stewed, stoned, stotious, tanked up, temulent, tiddly, tight, tipsy, up the pole, well-oiled, wet.
antonym sober.
n. boozer, drunkard, inebriate, lush, soak, sot, toper, wino.

drunkard *n.* alcoholic, bacchant, carouser, dipsomaniac, drinker, drunk, lush, soak, sot, souse, sponge, tippler, toper, tosspot, wino.

dry *adj.* arid, barren, boring, cutting, cynical, deadpan, dehydrated, desiccated, dreary, dried up, droll, droughty, drouthy, dull, juiceless, keen, low-key, moistureless, monotonous, parched, pawky, plain, sapless, sarcastic, sec, secco, sharp, sly, tedious, thirsty, tiresome, torrid, uninteresting, waterless, withered, xeric.
antonyms interesting, sweet, wet.
v. dehumidify, dehydrate, desiccate, drain, exsiccate, harden, mummify, parch, sear, shrivel, welt, wilt, wither, wizen.
antonyms soak, wet.

dub *v.* bestow, call, christen, confer, denominate, designate, entitle, knight, label, name, nickname, style, tag, term.

dubious *adj.* ambiguous, debatable, doubtful, equivocal, fishy, hesitant, iffy, indefinite, indeterminate, obscure, problematical, questionable, shady, skeptical, speculative, suspect, suspicious, uncertain, unclear, unconvinced, undecided, undependable, unreliable, unsettled, unsure, untrustworthy, wavering.
antonyms certain, reliable, trustworthy.

duck[1] *v.* avoid, bend, bob, bow, crouch, dodge, drop, escape, evade, lower, shirk, shun, sidestep, squat, stoop.

duck[2] *v.* dip, dive, dook, douse, dunk, immerse, plunge, souse, submerge, wet.

duct *n.* blood, canal, channel, conduit, fistula, funnel, passage, pipe, tube, vas, vessel.

due *adj.* adequate, ample, appropriate, becoming, bounden, deserved, enough, expected, fit, fitting, in arrears, just, justified, mature, merited, obligatory, outstanding, owed, owing, payable, plenty of, proper, requisite, returnable, right, rightful, scheduled, sufficient, suitable, unpaid, well-earned.
n. birthright, come-uppance, deserts, merits, prerogative, privilege, right(s).
adv. dead, direct, directly, exactly, precisely, straight.

duel *n.* affair of honor, clash, competition, contest, duello, encounter, engagement, fight, monomachia, monomachy, rivalry, single combat, struggle.
v. battle, clash, compete, contend, contest, fight, rival, struggle, vie.

dues *n.* charge(s), contribution, fee, levy, subscription.

duffer *n.* blunderer, bonehead, booby, bungler, clod, clot, dolt, galoot, lubber, lummox, muff, oaf.

dull *adj.* apathetic, blank, blockish, blunt, blunted, Boeotian, boring, bovine, callous, cloudy, commonplace, corny, dead, dead-and-alive, dense, depressed, dim, dimwitted, dismal, doltish, drab, dreary, dry, dulled, edgeless, empty, faded, featureless, feeble, flat, gloomy, heavy, humdrum, inactive, indifferent, indistinct, insensible, insensitive, insipid, lackluster, leaden, lifeless, listless, monotonous, mopish, muffled, mumpish, murky, muted, opaque, overcast, passionless, pedestrian, plain, prosaic, run-of-the-mill, slack, sleepy, slow, sluggish, somber, stodgy, stolid, stultifying, stupid, subdued, subfusc, sullen, sunless, tame, tedious, thick, tiresome, toneless, torpid, turbid, uneventful, unexciting, unfunny, ungifted, unidea'd, unimaginative, unintelligent, uninteresting, unlively, unresponsive, unsharpened, unsunny, unsympathetic, untalented, vacuous, vapid.
antonyms alert, bright, clear, exciting, sharp.
v. allay, alleviate, assuage, blunt, cloud, dampen, darken, deject, depress, dim, discourage, disedge, dishearten, dispirit, fade, hebetate, lessen, mitigate, moderate, muffle, obscure, obtund, opiate, palliate, paralyze, rebate, relieve, sadden, soften, stain, stupefy, subdue, sully, tarnish.
antonyms brighten, sharpen, stimulate.

dullard *n.* blockhead, bonehead, chump, clod, clot, dimwit, dolt, dope, dummy, dunce, dunderhead, flat tire, idiot, ignoramus, imbecile, moron, nitwit, noodle, numskull, oaf, simpleton, vegetable.
antonym brain.

dumb *adj.* aphonic, aphonous, dense, dimwitted, dull, foolish, inarticulate, mum, mute, silent, soundless, speechless, stupid, thick, tongue-tied, unintelligent, voiceless, wordless.
antonym intelligent.

dum(b)founded *adj.* amazed, astonished, astounded, bewildered, bowled over, breathless, confounded, confused, dumb, flabbergasted, floored, knocked sideways, nonplused, overcome, overwhelmed, paralyzed, speechless, staggered, startled, stunned, taken aback, thrown, thunderstruck.

dump *v.* deposit, discharge, dispose of, ditch, drop, empty out, get rid of, jettison, let fall, offload, park, scrap, throw away, throw down, tip, unload.
n. coup, hole, hovel, joint, junk-yard, landhill, mess, midden, pigsty, rubbish-heap, rubbish-tip, shack, shanty, slum, tip.

dunce *n.* ass, blockhead, bonehead, dimwit, dolt, donkey, duffer, dullard, dunderhead, goose, half-wit, ignoramus, loggerhead, log-head, loon, moron, nincompoop, numskull, simpleton.
antonyms brain, intellectual.

dungeon *n.* cage, cell, donjon, lock-up, oubliette, pit, prison, vault.

dupe *n.* cat's-paw, fall guy, flat, geck, gull, instrument, mug, pawn, pigeon, puppet, push-over, sap, simpleton, sitter, soft mark, stooge, sucker, tool, victim.
v. bamboozle, beguile, cheat, con, cozen, deceive, defraud, delude, gammon, grift, gudgeon, gull, hoax, hoodwink, humbug, outwit, overreach, pigeon, rip off, swindle, trick.

duplicate *adj.* corresponding, geminate, identical, matched, matching, twin, twofold.
n. carbon copy, copy, facsimile, match, photocopy, Photostat®;, replica, reproduction, Xerox®;.
v. clone, copy, ditto, double, echo, geminate, photocopy, Photostat®;, repeat, replicate, reproduce, Xerox®;.

duplicity *n.* artifice, chicanery, deceit, deception, dishonesty, dissimulation, double-dealing, falsehood, fraud, guile, hypocrisy, mendacity, perfidy, treachery.

durability *n.* constancy, durableness, endurance, imperishability, lastingness, longevity, permanence, persistence, stability, strength.
antonyms fragility, impermanence, weakness.

durable *adj.* abiding, constant, dependable, enduring, fast, firm, fixed, hard-wearing, lasting, long-lasting, perdurable, permanent, persistent, reliable, resistant, sound, stable, strong, sturdy, substantial, tough, unfading.
antonyms fragile, impermanent, perishable, weak.

duration *n.* continuance, continuation, extent, fullness, length, period, perpetuation, prolongation, span, spell, stretch, term-time.
antonym shortening.

duress *n.* bullying, captivity, coaction, coercion, compulsion, confinement, constraint, force, hardship, imprisonment, incarceration, pressure, restraint, threat.

dusky *adj.* caliginous, cloudy, crepuscular, dark, dark-hued, darkish, dim, fuliginous, gloomy, murky, obscure, overcast, sable, shadowy, shady, sooty, subfusc, swarthy, tenebr(i)ous, twilight, twilit, umbrose, veiled.
antonyms bright, light, white.

dusty *adj.* chalky, crumbly, dirty, filthy, friable, granular, grubby, powdery, pulverous, sandy, sooty, unswept.
antonyms clean, hard, polished, solid.

dutiful *adj.* acquiescent, complaisant, compliant, conscientious, deferential, devoted, docile, duteous, filial, obedient, punctilious, regardful, respectful, reverential, submissive.

duty *n.* allegiance, assignment, business, calling, charge, chore, customs, debt, deference, devoir, due, engagement, excise, function, impost, job, levy, loyalty, mission, obedience, obligation, office, onus, province, respect, responsibility, reverence, role, service, tariff, task, tax, toll, work.

dwarf *n.* droich, durgan, elf, gnome, goblin, homuncle, homuncule, homunculus, hop-o'-my-thumb, Lilliputian, manikin, midget, pygmy, Tom Thumb.
adj. baby, bonsai, diminutive, dwarfed, dwarfish, Lilliputian, mini, miniature, petite, pint-size(d), pocket, small, tiny, undersized.
antonym large.
v. check, dim, diminish, dominate, lower, minimize, overshadow, retard, stunt.

dwell *v.* abide, bide, hang out, inhabit, live, lodge, people, populate, quarter, remain, reside, rest, settle, sojourn, stay, stop, tenant.

dwelling *n.* abode, domicile, dwelling-house, establishment, habitation, home, house, lodge, lodging, quarters, residence, tent, tepee.

dwindle *v.* abate, contract, decay, decline, decrease, die, die out, diminish, disappear, ebb, fade, fall, lessen, peter out, pine, shrink, shrivel, sink, subside, tail off, taper off, vanish, wane, waste away, weaken, wither.
antonym increase.

dying *adj.* at death's door, declining, disappearing, ebbing, expiring, fading, failing, final, going, in articulo mortis, in extremis, moribund, mortal, not long for this world, obsolescent, passing, perishing, sinking, vanishing.
antonyms coming, reviving.

dynamic *adj.* active, driving, electric, energetic, forceful, go-ahead, go-getting, high-powered, lively, powerful, self-starting, spirited, vigorous, vital, zippy.
antonyms apathetic, inactive, slow.

E

eager *adj.* agog, anxious, ardent, athirst, avid, desirous, earnest, empressé, enthusiastic, fervent, fervid, fervorous, freck, greedy, gung-ho, hot, hungry, impatient, intent, keen, longing, perfervid, raring, unshrinking, vehement, yearning, zealous.
antonyms apathetic, unenthusiastic.

early *adj.* advanced, forward, matutinal, matutine, prehistoric, premature, primeval, primitive, primordial, undeveloped, untimely, young.
adv. ahead of time, beforehand, betimes, in advance, in good time, prematurely, too soon.
antonym late.

earmark *v.* allocate, designate, keep back, label, put aside, reserve, set aside, tag.

earn *v.* acquire, attain, bring in, collect, deserve, draw, gain, get, gross, make, merit, net, obtain, procure, rate, realize, reap, receive, warrant, win.
antonyms lose, spend.

earnest *adj.* ardent, close, constant, determined, devoted, eager, enthusiastic, fervent, fervid, firm, fixed, grave, heartfelt, impassioned, intent, keen, passionate, purposeful, resolute, resolved, serious, sincere, solemn, stable, staid, steady, thoughtful, urgent, vehement, warm, zealous.
antonyms apathetic, flippant, unenthusiastic.
n. assurance, deposit, determination, down payment, guarantee, pledge, promise, resolution, security, seriousness, sincerity, token, truth.

earnings *n.* emoluments, gain, income, pay, proceeds, profits, receipts, remuneration, return, revenue, reward, salary, stipend, takings, wages.
antonyms expenses, outgoings.

earth[1] *n.* geosphere, globe, middle-earth, middle-world, Midgard, orb, planet, sphere, world.

earth[2] *n.* clay, clod, dirt, ground, humus, land, loam, mold, sod, soil, topsoil.

earthly *adj.* base, carnal, conceivable, earthern, feasible, fleshly, gross, human, imaginable, likely, low, material, materialistic, mortal, mundane, physical, possible, practical, profane, secular, sensual, slight, slightest, sordid, sublunar, sublunary, tellurian, telluric, temporal, terrene, terrestrial, vile, worldly.
antonyms heavenly, spiritual.

earthy *adj.* bawdy, blue, coarse, crude, down-to-earth, homely, indecorous, lusty, natural, raunchy, ribald, robust, rough, simple, uninhibited, unrefined, unsophisticated, vulgar.
antonyms cultured, refined.

ease *n.* affluence, aplomb, calmness, comfort, composure, content, contentment, deftness, dexterity, easiness, effortlessness, enjoyment, facileness, facility, flexibility, freedom, happiness, informality, insouciance, leisure, liberty, naturalness, nonchalance, peace, peace of mind, poise, quiet, quietude, readiness, relaxation, repose, rest, restfulness, serenity, simplicity, solace, tranquility, unaffectedness, unconstraint, unreservedness.
antonyms difficulty, discomfort.
v. abate, aid, allay, alleviate, appease, assist, assuage, calm, comfort, disburden, edge, expedite, facilitate, forward, further, guide, inch, lessen, lighten, maneuver, mitigate, moderate, mollify, pacify, palliate, quiet, relax, relent, relieve, simplify, slacken, slide, slip, smooth, solace, soothe, speed up, squeeze, steer, still, tranquilize.
antonyms hinder, retard, torment.

easily[1] *adv.* comfortably, effortlessly, facilely, readily, simply, smoothly, standing on one's head, with one arm tied behind one's back.
antonym laboriously.

easily[2] *adv.* absolutely, by far, certainly, clearly, definitely, doubtlessly, far and away, indisputably, indubitably, plainly, probably, simply, surely, undeniably, undoubtedly, unequivocally, unquestionably, well.

easy *adj.* a doddle, a piece of cake, a pushover, accommodating, affable, amenable, biddable, calm, carefree, casual, child's play, clear, comfortable, compliant, contented, cushy, docile, easeful, easy-going, effortless, facile, flexible, friendly, gentle, graceful, gracious, gullible, idiot-proof, indulgent, informal, leisurely, lenient, liberal, light, manageable, mild, moderate, natural, no bother, open, painless, peaceful, permissive, pleasant, pliant, quiet, relaxed, satisfied, serene, simple, smooth, soft, straightforward, submissive, suggestible, susceptible, temperate, tolerant, tractable, tranquil, trusting, unaffected, unburdensome, unceremonious, uncomplicated, unconstrained, undemanding, undisturbed, unexacting, unforced, unhurried, unlabored, unoppressive, unpretentious, untroubled, unworried, well-to-do, yielding.
antonyms demanding, difficult, fast, impossible, intolerant.

easy-going *adj.* amenable, calm, carefree, casual, complacent, easy, easy-osy, even-tempered, flexible, happy-go-lucky, indulgent, insouciant, laid-back, lenient, liberal, mild, moderate, nonchalant, permissive, placid, relaxed, serene, tolerant, unconcerned, uncritical, undemanding, unhurried, unworried.
antonyms fussy, intolerant.

eat *v.* banquet, break bread, chew, chop, consume,

corrode, crumble, decay, devour, dine, dissolve, erode, feed, grub, ingest, knock back, manducate, munch, pig, rot, scoff, swallow, wear away.

eavesdrop *v.* bug, earwig, listen in, monitor, overhear, snoop, spy, tap.

eavesdropper *n.* listener, monitor, snoop, snooper, spy.

ebb *v.* abate, decay, decline, decrease, degenerate, deteriorate, diminish, drop, dwindle, fade away, fall away, fall back, flag, flow back, go out, lessen, peter out, recede, reflow, retire, retreat, retrocede, shrink, sink, slacken, subside, wane, weaken, withdraw.
antonyms increase, rise.
n. decay, decline, decrease, degeneration, deterioration, diminution, drop, dwindling, ebb tide, flagging, lessening, low tide, low water, reflow, refluence, reflux, regression, retreat, retrocession, shrinkage, sinking, slackening, subsidence, wane, waning, weakening, withdrawal.
antonyms flow, increase, rising.

ebullient *adj.* boiling, breezy, bright, bubbling, buoyant, chirpy, effervescent, effusive, elated, enthusiastic, excited, exhilarated, exuberant, foaming, frothing, frothy, gushing, irrepressible, seething, vivacious, zestful.
antonyms apathetic, dull, lifeless.

eccentric *adj.* aberrant, abnormal, anomalous, bizarre, capricious, dotty, erratic, fey, freakish, fruity, idiosyncratic, irregular, nuts, nutty, odd, offbeat, outlandish, peculiar, queer, quirky, screwball, screwy, singular, spac(e)y, strange, uncommon, unconventional, way-out, weird, whimsical.
antonyms normal, sane.
n. case, character, crank, freak, fruit-cake, nonconformist, nut, nutter, oddball, oddity, queer fish, screwball, weirdie, weirdo.

eccentricity *n.* aberration, abnormality, anomaly, bizarreness, bizarrerie, caprice, capriciousness, foible, freakishness, idiosyncrasy, irregularity, nonconformity, oddity, outlandishness, peculiarity, queerness, quirk, singularity, strangeness, unconventionality, waywardness, weirdness, whimsicality.
antonyms normalcy, normality, ordinariness.

ecclesiastic(al) *adj.* church, churchly, churchy, clerical, divine, holy, pastoral, priestly, religious, spiritual, templar.

echelon *n.* degree, grade, level, place, position, rank, status, step, tier.

echo *v.* ape, copy, echoize, imitate, mimic, mirror, parallel, parrot, recall, reflect, reiterate, repeat, reproduce, resemble, resound, reverberate, ring, second.
n. allusion, answer, copy, evocation, hint, image, imitation, intimation, memory, mirror image, parallel, reflection, reiteration, reminder, repetition, reproduction, reverberation, suggestion, sympathy, trace.

eclectic *adj.* all-embracing, broad, catholic, comprehensive, dilettantish, diverse, diversified, general, heterogeneous, liberal, many-sided, multifarious, selective, varied, wide-ranging.
antonyms narrow, one-sided.

eclipse *v.* blot out, cloud, darken, dim, dwarf, exceed, excel, extinguish, obscure, outdo, outshine, overshadow, shroud, surpass, transcend, veil.
n. darkening, decline, deliquium, diminution, dimming, extinction, failure, fall, loss, obscuration, occultation, overshadowing, shading.

economical *adj.* careful, cheap, cost-effective, economic, economizing, efficient, fair, frugal, inexpensive, labor-saving, low, low-priced, modest, prudent, reasonable, saving, scrimping, sparing, thrifty, time-saving.
antonyms expensive, uneconomical.

economize *v.* cut back, cut corners, husband, retrench, save, scrimp, tighten one's belt.
antonym squander.

economy *n.* frugality, frugalness, husbandry, parsimony, providence, prudence, restraint, retrenchment, saving, scrimping, sparingness, thrift, thriftiness.
antonym improvidence.

ecstasy *n.* bliss, delight, ecstasis, elation, enthusiasm, euphoria, exaltation, fervor, frenzy, joy, rapture, ravishment, rhapsody, seventh heaven, sublimation, trance, transport.
antonym torment.

ecstatic *adj.* blissful, delirious, elated, enraptured, enthusiastic, entranced, euphoric, exultant, fervent, frenzied, joyful, joyous, on cloud nine, over the moon, overjoyed, rapturous, rhapsodic, transported.
antonym downcast.

edge *n.* acuteness, advantage, animation, arris, ascendancy, bezel, bite, border, bound, boundary, brim, brink, cantle, contour, dominance, effectiveness, force, fringe, incisiveness, interest, keenness, lead, limit, line, lip, margin, outline, perimeter, periphery, point, pungency, rim, sharpness, side, sting, superiority, threshold, upper hand, urgency, verge, zest.
v. bind, border, creep, drib, ease, fringe, gravitate, hem, hone, inch, rim, shape, sharpen, sidle, steal, strop, trim, verge, whet, work, worm.

edgy *adj.* anxious, ill at ease, irascible, irritable, keyed-up, nervous, on edge, prickly, restive, tense, testy, touchy.
antonym calm.

edict *n.* act, command, decree, dictate, dictum, enactment, fiat, injunction, law, mandate, manifesto, order, ordinance, proclamation, pronouncement, pronunciamento, regulation, rescript, ruling, statute, ukase.

edifice *n.* building, construction, erection, structure.

edit *v.* adapt, annotate, assemble, blue-pencil, bowdlerize, censor, check, compose, condense, correct, emend, polish, rearrange, redact, reorder, rephrase, revise, rewrite, select.

educate *v.* catechize, civilize, coach, cultivate, develop, discipline, drill, edify, exercise, improve, indoctrinate, inform, instruct, learn, mature, rear, school, teach, train, tutor.

education *n.* breeding, civilization, coaching, cultivation, culture, development, discipline, drilling, edification, enlightenment, erudition, guidance, improvement, indoctrination, instruction, knowledge, nurture, scholarship, schooling, teaching, training, tuition, tutelage, tutoring.

eerie *adj.* awesome, chilling, creepy, eldritch, fearful, frightening, ghastly, ghostly, mysterious, scary, spectral, spine-chilling, spooky, strange, uncanny, unearthly, unnatural, weird.
antonyms natural, ordinary.

efface *v.* annihilate, blank out, blot out, blue-pencil, cancel, cross out, delete, destroy, dim, eliminate, eradicate, erase, excise, expunge, extirpate, humble, lower, obliterate, raze, remove, rub out, wipe out, withdraw.

effect *n.* action, aftermath, clout, conclusion, consequence, drift, éclat, effectiveness, efficacy, efficiency, enforcement, essence, event, execution, fact, force, fruit, impact, implementation, import, impression, influence, issue, meaning, operation, outcome, power, purport, purpose, reality, result, sense, significance, strength, tenor, upshot, use, validity, vigor, weight, work. *v.* accomplish, achieve, actuate, cause, complete, consummate, create, effectuate, execute, fulfil, initiate, make, perform, produce, wreak.

effective *adj.* able, active, adequate, capable, cogent, compelling, competent, convincing, current, effectual, efficacious, efficient, emphatic, energetic, forceful, forcible, implemental, impressive, moving, operative, perficient, persuasive, potent, powerful, productive, real, serviceable, striking, telling, useful.
antonyms ineffective, useless.

efficiency *n.* ability, adeptness, capability, competence, competency, economy, effectiveness, efficacy, mastery, power, productivity, proficiency, readiness, skilfulness, skill.
antonym inefficiency.

efficient *adj.* able, adept, businesslike, capable, competent, economic, effective, effectual, powerful, productive, proficient, ready, skilful, streamlined, well-conducted, well-ordered, well-organized, well-regulated, workmanlike.
antonym inefficient.

effort *n.* accomplishment, achievement, application, attempt, conatus, creation, deed, endeavor, energy, essay, exertion, feat, force, go, job, labor, molimen, nisus, pains, power, product, production, shot, stab, strain, stress, stretch, striving, struggle, toil, travail, trouble, try, work.

effortless *adj.* easy, facile, painless, simple, smooth, uncomplicated, undemanding, unlabored.
antonym difficult.

egg on coax, encourage, exhort, goad, incite, prick, prod, prompt, push, spur, stimulate, urge, wheedle.
antonym discourage.

egghead *n.* brain, Einstein, genius, headpiece, intellect, intellectual, scholar.

egoism *n.* amour-propre, egocentricity, egomania, egotism, narcissism, self-absorption, self-centeredness, self-importance, self-interest, selfishness, self-love, self-regard, self-seeking.
antonym altruism.

eject *v.* banish, belch, boot out, bounce, deport, discharge, disgorge, dislodge, dismiss, dispossess, drive out, emit, evacuate, evict, exile, expel, fire, kick out, oust, remove, sack, spew, spout, throw out, turn out, unhouse, vomit.

elaborate *adj.* careful, complex, complicated, daedal(ic), decorated, dedal(ian), detailed, exact, extravagant, fancy, fussy, intricate, involved, labored, minute, ornamental, ornate, ostentatious, painstaking, perfected, precise, showy, skilful, studied, thorough.
antonyms plain, simple.
v. amplify, complicate, decorate, detail, develop, devise, embellish, enhance, enlarge, expand, expatiate, explain, flesh out, garnish, improve, ornament, polish, refine.
antonyms précis, simplify.

elapse *v.* go by, lapse, pass, slip away.

elastic *adj.* accommodating, adaptable, adjustable, bouncy, buoyant, complaisant, compliant, distensible, ductile, flexible, irrepressible, plastic, pliable, pliant, resilient, rubbery, springy, stretchable, stretchy, supple, tolerant, variable, yielding.
antonym rigid.

elated *adj.* animated, blissful, cheered, delighted, ecstatic, euphoric, excited, exhilarated, exultant, gleeful, joyful, joyous, jubilant, on the high ropes, over the moon, overjoyed, pleased, proud, roused.
antonym downcast.

elder *adj.* aîné(e), ancient, eigne, first-born, older, senior.
antonym younger.
n. deacon, presbyter, senior.

elderly *adj.* aged, aging, badgerly, hoary, old, senile.
antonyms young, youthful.

elect *v.* adopt, appoint, choose, designate, determine, opt for, pick, prefer, select, vote.
adj. choice, chosen, designate, designated, elite, hand-picked, picked, preferred, presumptive, prospective, select, selected, to be.

electrify *v.* amaze, animate, astonish, astound, excite, fire, galvanize, invigorate, jolt, rouse, shock, stagger, startle, stimulate, stir, stun, thrill.
antonym bore.

elegant *adj.* à la mode, appropriate, apt, artistic, beautiful, chic, choice, clever, comely, concinnous, courtly, cultivated, debonair, delicate, effective, exquisite, fashionable, fine, genteel, graceful, handsome, ingenious,

luxurious, modish, neat, nice, polished, refined, simple, smooth, stylish, sumptuous, tasteful.
antonym inelegant.

elementary *adj.* basic, clear, easy, elemental, facile, fundamental, initial, introductory, original, plain, primary, principial, rudimentary, simple, straightforward, uncomplicated.
antonyms advanced, complex.

elevate *v.* advance, aggrandize, animate, augment, boost, brighten, buoy up, cheer, elate, exalt, excite, exhilarate, hearten, heighten, hoist, increase, intensify, lift, magnify, prefer, promote, raise, rouse, sublimate, swell, upgrade, uplift, upraise.
antonyms lessen, lower.

elfin *adj.* arch, charming, delicate, elfish, elflike, elvish, frolicsome, impish, mischievous, petite, playful, puckish, small, sprightly.

elicit *v.* cause, derive, draw out, educe, evoke, evolve, exact, extort, extract, fish, mole out, obtain, wrest, wring.

eligible *adj.* acceptable, appropriate, available, desirable, fit, proper, qualified, suitable, suited, worthy.
antonym ineligible.

eliminate *v.* annihilate, bump off, cut out, delete, dispense with, dispose of, disregard, do away with, drop, eject, eradicate, exclude, expel, expunge, exterminate, extinguish, get rid of, ignore, kill, knock out, liquidate, murder, omit, reject, remove, rub out, slay, stamp out, take out, terminate, waste.
antonym accept.

elite *n.* aristocracy, best, cream, crème de la crème, elect, establishment, flower, gentry, high society, meritocracy, nobility, pick.
adj. aristocratic, best, choice, crack, exclusive, first-class, noble, pick, selected, top, top-class, upper-class.
antonyms ordinary, run-of-the-mill.

elongated *adj.* extended, lengthened, long, prolonged, protracted, stretched.

elope *v.* abscond, bolt, decamp, disappear, do a bunk, escape, leave, run away, run off, slip away, steal away.

eloquent *adj.* articulate, Demosthenic, expressive, fluent, forceful, graceful, honeyed, meaningful, moving, persuasive, plausible, pregnant, revealing, silver-tongued, stirring, suggestive, telling, vivid, vocal, voluble, well-expressed.
antonyms inarticulate, tongue-tied.

elude *v.* avoid, baffle, beat, circumvent, confound, dodge, duck, escape, evade, flee, foil, frustrate, outrun, puzzle, shirk, shun, stump, thwart.

emaciated *adj.* atrophied, attenuate, attenuated, cadaverous, gaunt, haggard, lank, lean, meager, pinched, scrawny, skeletal, tabefied, tabescent, thin, wasted.
antonyms plump, well-fed.

emancipate *v.* deliver, discharge, disencumber, disenthral, enfranchise, free, liberate, manumit, release, set free, unbind, unchain, unfetter, unshackle.
antonym enslave.

embankment *n.* bund, causeway, causey, defenses, earthwork, levee, rampart.

embargo *n.* ban, bar, barrier, blockage, check, hindrance, impediment, interdict, interdiction, prohibition, proscription, restraint, restriction, seizure, stoppage.
v. ban, bar, block, check, embar, impede, interdict, prohibit, proscribe, restrict, seize, stop.
antonym allow.

embark *v.* board ship, emplane, entrain, take ship.
antonym disembark.

embarrass *v.* abash, chagrin, confuse, discomfit, discomfort, discompose, disconcert, discountenance, distress, fluster, mortify, shame, show up.

embassy *n.* consulate, delegation, deputation, embassade, embassage, legation, mission.

embed *v.* fix, imbed, implant, insert, plant, root, set, sink.

embellish *v.* adorn, beautify, bedeck, deck, decorate, dress up, elaborate, embroider, enhance, enrich, exaggerate, festoon, garnish, gild, grace, ornament, trim, varnish.
antonyms denude, simplify.

embezzle *v.* abstract, appropriate, defalcate, filch, misapply, misappropriate, misuse, peculate, pilfer, pinch, purloin, steal, sting.

embitter *v.* acerbate, aggravate, alienate, anger, disaffect, disillusion, empoison, envenom, exacerbate, exasperate, poison, sour, worsen.
antonym pacify.

emblem *n.* badge, crest, device, figure, ichthys, image, insignia, mark, representation, sigil, sign, symbol, token, type.

embody *v.* codify, collect, combine, comprehend, comprise, concentrate, concretize, consolidate, contain, encarnalize, exemplify, express, incarnate, include, incorporate, integrate, manifest, organize, personify, realize, reify, represent, stand for, symbolize, systematize, typify.

embrace *v.* accept, canoodle, clasp, complect, comprehend, comprise, contain, cover, cuddle, dally, embody, embosom, encircle, enclose, encompass, enfold, enlace, espouse, grab, grasp, halse, hold, hug, inarm, include, incorporate, involve, neck, receive, seize, snog, squeeze, subsume, take up, welcome.
n. accolade, clasp, clinch, cuddle, hug, squeeze.

embroidery *n.* fancywork, needle-point, needlework, sewing, tapestry, tatting.

embroil *v.* confound, confuse, distract, disturb, encumber, enmesh, ensnare, entangle, implicate, incriminate, involve, mire, mix up, muddle, perplex, trouble.

emerge *v.* appear, arise, crop up, debouch, develop, eclose, emanate, issue, materialize, proceed, rise, surface, transpire, turn up.
antonyms disappear, fade.

emergency *n.* crisis, crunch, danger, difficulty, exigency, extremity, necessity, pass, pinch, plight, predicament, quandary, scrape, strait.

adj. alternative, back-up, extra, fall-back, reserve, spare, substitute.

eminent *adj.* august, celebrated, conspicuous, distinguished, elevated, esteemed, exalted, famous, grand, great, high, high-ranking, illustrious, important, notable, noted, noteworthy, outstanding, paramount, preeminent, prestigious, prominent, renowned, reputable, respected, revered, signal, superior, well-known.
antonyms unimportant, unknown.

emissary *n.* agent, ambassador, courier, delegate, deputy, envoy, herald, legate, messenger, nuncio, plenipotentiary, representative, scout, spy.

emit *v.* diffuse, discharge, eject, emanate, exhale, exude, give off, give out, issue, radiate, shed, vent.
antonym absorb.

emotion *n.* affect, agitation, ardor, excitement, feeling, fervor, passion, perturbation, reaction, sensation, sentiment, vehemence, warmth.

emotional *adj.* affecting, ardent, demonstrative, emotive, enthusiastic, excitable, exciting, feeling, fervent, fervid, fiery, heart-warming, heated, hot-blooded, impassioned, moved, moving, overcharged, passionate, pathetic, poignant, responsive, roused, sensitive, sentimental, stirred, stirring, susceptible, tear-jerking, temperamental, tempestuous, tender, thrilling, touching, volcanic, warm, zealous.
antonyms calm, cold, detached, emotionless, unemotional.

emphasis *n.* accent, accentuation, attention, force, import, importance, impressiveness, insistence, intensity, mark, moment, positiveness, power, pre-eminence, priority, prominence, significance, strength, stress, underscoring, urgency, weight.

emphatic *adj.* absolute, categorical, certain, decided, definite, direct, distinct, earnest, energetic, forceful, forcible, graphic, important, impressive, insistent, marked, momentous, positive, powerful, pronounced, punctuated, resounding, significant, striking, strong, telling, trenchant, unequivocal, unmistakable, vigorous, vivid.
antonyms quiet, understated, unemphatic.

employ *v.* apply, apprentice, bring to bear, commission, engage, enlist, exercise, exert, fill, hire, indent(ure), occupy, ply, retain, spend, take on, take up, use, utilize.
n. employment, hire, pay, service.

employee *n.* hand, job-holder, member of staff, staffer, wage-earner, worker, workman.

employer *n.* boss, business, company, establishment, firm, gaffer, organization, outfit, owner, padrone, patron, proprietor, taskmaster, workmaster, workmistress.

employment *n.* application, avocation, business, calling, craft, employ, engagement, enlistment, errand, exercise, exercitation, exertion, hire, job, line, métier, occupation, profession, pursuit, service, trade, use, utilization, vocation, work.
antonym unemployment.

empower *v.* accredit, allow, authorize, commission, delegate, enable, enfranchise, entitle, license, permit, qualify, sanction, warrant.

empty *adj.* absent, aimless, banal, bare, blank, bootless, cheap, clear, deserted, desolate, destitute, expressionless, famished, frivolous, fruitless, futile, hollow, hungry, idle, inane, ineffective, insincere, insubstantial, meaningless, purposeless, ravenous, senseless, silly, starving, superficial, trivial, unfed, unfilled, unfrequented, unfurnished, uninhabited, unintelligent, unoccupied, unreal, unsatisfactory, unsubstantial, untenanted, vacant, vacuous, vain, valueless, viduous, void, waste, worthless.
antonyms filled, full, replete.
v. clear, consume, deplete, discharge, drain, dump, evacuate, exhaust, gut, lade, pour out, unburden, unload, vacate, void.
antonym fill.

emulate *v.* challenge, compete with, contend with, copy, echo, follow, imitate, match, mimic, rival, vie with.

enable *v.* accredit, allow, authorize, capacitate, commission, empower, endue, equip, facilitate, fit, license, permit, prepare, qualify, sanction, warrant.
antonyms inhibit, prevent.

enact *v.* act (out), authorize, command, decree, depict, establish, impersonate, legislate, ordain, order, pass, perform, personate, play, portray, proclaim, ratify, represent, sanction.
antonym repeal.

enchant *v.* becharm, beguile, bewitch, captivate, charm, delight, enamor, enrapture, enravish, ensorcell, enthral, fascinate, hypnotize, mesmerize, spellbind.
antonyms bore, disenchant.

encircle *v.* begird, circle, circumscribe, compass, enclose, encompass, enfold, engird, engirdle, enlace, enring, envelop, environ, enwreathe, gird, girdle, hem in, ring, surround.

enclose *v.* bound, circumscribe, compass, comprehend, confine, contain, cover, embale, embosom, embrace, encase, encircle, encompass, enlock, environ, fence, hedge, hem in, hold, inclose, include, incorporate, insert, pen, shut in, wall in, wrap.

encompass *v.* admit, begird, bring about, cause, circle, circumscribe, comprehend, comprise, contain, contrive, cover, devise, effect, embody, embrace, encircle, enclose, envelop, environ, girdle, hem in, hold, include, incorporate, involve, manage, ring, subsume, surround.

encounter *v.* chance upon, clash with, combat, come upon, confront, contend, cross swords with, engage, experience, face, fight, grapple with, happen on, meet, rencontre, rencounter, run across, run into, strive, struggle.
n. action, battle, brush, clash, collision, combat, conflict, confrontation, contest, dispute, engagement, fight, meeting, rencontre, rencounter, run-in, set-to, skirmish.

encourage *v.* abet, advance, advocate, aid, animate, boost,

buoy up, cheer, comfort, console, egg on, embolden, embrave, favor, forward, foster, further, hearten, help, incite, inspire, inspirit, promote, rally, reassure, rouse, second, spirit, spur, stimulate, strengthen, succor, support, urge.
antonyms depress, discourage, dissuade.

encroach *v.* appropriate, arrogate, impinge, infringe, intrude, invade, make inroads, muscle in, obtrude, overstep, trench, trespass, usurp.

encumber *v.* burden, clog, cramp, cumber, embarrass, hamper, handicap, hinder, impede, incommode, inconvenience, lumber, obstruct, oppress, overload, retard, saddle, slow down, trammel, weigh down.

end *n.* aim, annihilation, aspiration, attainment, bit, bound, boundary, butt, cessation, close, closure, completion, conclusion, consequence, consummation, culmination, curtain, death, demise, dénouement, design, destruction, dissolution, doom, downfall, drift, edge, ending, expiration, expiry, extent, extermination, extinction, extreme, extremity, finale, fine, finis, finish, fragment, goal, intent, intention, issue, left-over, limit, object, objective, outcome, part, pay-off, piece, point, portion, purpose, reason, remainder, remnant, resolution, responsibility, result, ruin, ruination, scrap, share, side, stop, stub, telos, termination, terminus, tip, upshot, wind-up.
antonyms beginning, opening, start.
v. abate, abolish, annihilate, cease, close, complete, conclude, culminate, destroy, dissolve, expire, exterminate, extinguish, fetch up, finish, resolve, ruin, sopite, stop, terminate, wind up.
antonyms begin, start.

endanger *v.* compromise, expose, hazard, imperil, jeopardize, risk, threaten.
antonyms protect, shelter, shield.

endearing *adj.* adorable, attractive, captivating, charming, delightful, enchanting, engaging, lovable, sweet, winning, winsome.

endeavor *n.* aim, attempt, conatus, crack, effort, enterprise, essay, go, nisus, shot, stab, trial, try, undertaking, venture.
v. aim, aspire, attempt, essay, labor, strive, struggle, take pains, try, undertake, venture.

endless *adj.* boundless, ceaseless, constant, continual, continuous, eternal, everlasting, immortal, incessant, infinite, interminable, interminate, limitless, measureless, monotonous, overlong, perpetual, Sisyphean, termless, unbounded, unbroken, undivided, undying, unending, uninterrupted, unlimited, whole.

endorse *v.* adopt, advocate, affirm, approve, authorize, back, champion, confirm, countenance, countersign, favor, indorse, ratify, recommend, sanction, sign, subscribe to, superscribe, support, sustain, undersign, vouch for, warrant.
antonyms denounce, disapprove.

endow *v.* award, bequeath, bestow, confer, donate, dower, endue, enrich, favor, finance, fund, furnish, give, grant, invest, leave, make over, present, provide, settle on, supply, will.
antonym divest.

endowment *n.* ability, aptitude, attribute, award, benefaction, bequest, bestowal, boon, capability, capacity, donation, dotation, dowry, faculty, flair, fund, genius, gift, grant, income, largesse, legacy, power, presentation, property, provision, qualification, quality, revenue, talent.

endure *v.* abear, abide, aby(e), allow, bear, brave, brook, continue, cope with, countenance, digest, experience, go through, hold, last, live, perdure, permit, persist, prevail, put up with, remain, stand, stay, stick, stomach, submit to, suffer, support, survive, sustain, swallow, thole, tolerate, undergo, weather, withstand.
antonyms cease, end.

enemy *n.* adversary, antagonist, competitor, foe, foeman, opponent, opposer, Philistine, rival, the opposition.
antonyms ally, friend.

energy *n.* activity, animation, ardor, brio, drive, efficiency, élan, exertion, fire, force, forcefulness, get-up-and-go, intensity, inworking, jism, juice, life, liveliness, pluck, power, spirit, stamina, steam, strength, strenuousness, verve, vigor, vim, vitality, vivacity, vroom, zeal, zest, zip.
antonyms inertia, lethargy, weakness.

enervate *v.* debilitate, deplete, devitalize, enfeeble, exhaust, fatigue, incapacitate, paralyze, prostrate, sap, tire, unman, unnerve, weaken, wear out.
antonyms activate, energize.

enfold *v.* clasp, embrace, encircle, enclose, encompass, envelop, enwrap, fold, hold, hug, shroud, swathe, wimple, wrap (up).

enforce *v.* administer, apply, carry out, coact, coerce, compel, constrain, discharge, exact, execute, implement, impose, insist on, oblige, prosecute, reinforce, require, urge.

engage *v.* absorb, activate, affiance, agree, allure, apply, appoint, arrest, assail, attach, attack, attract, bespeak, betroth, bind, book, busy, captivate, catch, charm, charter, combat, commission, commit, contract, covenant, draw, embark, employ, enamor, enchant, encounter, energize, engross, enlist, enrol, enter, fascinate, fit, fix, gain, grip, guarantee, hire, interact, interconnect, interlock, involve, join, lease, meet, mesh, obligate, oblige, occupy, operate, partake, participate, pledge, practice, prearrange, preoccupy, promise, rent, reserve, retain, secure, take on, tie up, undertake, vouch, vow, win.
antonyms discharge, disengage, dismiss.

engaged *adj.* absorbed, affianced, betrothed, busy, committed, employed, engrossed, immersed, involved, occupied, pledged, preoccupied, promised, spoken for, tied up, unavailable.

engaging *adj.* agreeable, appealing, attractive, beguiling,

captivating, charming, enchanting, fascinating, fetching, likable, lovable, pleasant, pleasing, prepossessing, winning, winsome.
antonyms boring, loathsome.

engender *v.* beget, breed, bring about, cause, create, encourage, excite, father, foment, generate, give rise to, hatch, incite, induce, instigate, lead to, make, nurture, occasion, precipitate, procreate, produce, propagate, provoke, sire, spawn.

engineer *n.* architect, contriver, designer, deviser, driver, inventor, operator, originator, planner.
v. cause, concoct, contrive, control, create, devise, effect, encompass, finagle, machinate, manage, maneuver, manipulate, mastermind, originate, plan, plot, scheme, wangle.

engrave *v.* blaze, carve, chase, chisel, cut, embed, enchase, etch, fix, grave, impress, imprint, infix, ingrain, inscribe, lodge, mark, print.

engross *v.* absorb, arrest, corner, engage, engulf, fixate, hold, immerse, involve, monopolize, occupy, preoccupy, rivet.

engulf *v.* absorb, bury, consume, deluge, drown, encompass, engross, envelop, flood, immerse, ingulf, inundate, overrun, overwhelm, plunge, submerge, swallow up, swamp.

enhance *v.* amplify, augment, boost, complement, elevate, embellish, escalate, exalt, heighten, improve, increase, intensify, lift, magnify, raise, reinforce, strengthen, swell.
antonyms decrease, minimize.

enigma *n.* brain-teaser, conundrum, mystery, poser, problem, puzzle, riddle.

enigmatic *adj.* ambiguous, cryptic, Delphic, doubtful, enigmatical, equivocal, impenetrable, incomprehensible, indecipherable, inexplicable, inscrutable, mysterious, obscure, perplexing, puzzling, recondite, riddling, strange, uncertain, unfathomable, unintelligible.
antonyms simple, straightforward.

enjoy *v.* appreciate, delight in, dig, experience, have, like, make a meal of, own, possess, rejoice in, relish, revel in, savor, take pleasure in, use.
antonyms abhor, detest.

enjoyment *n.* advantage, amusement, benefit, comfort, delectation, delight, diversion, ease, entertainment, exercise, fun, gaiety, gladness, gratification, gusto, happiness, indulgence, jollity, joy, ownership, pleasure, possession, recreation, relish, satisfaction, use, zest.
antonyms displeasure, dissatisfaction.

enlarge *v.* add to, amplify, augment, blow up, broaden, descant, develop, diffuse, dilate, distend, elaborate, elongate, expand, expatiate, extend, greaten, grow, heighten, increase, inflate, intumesce, jumboize, lengthen, magnify, multiply, stretch, swell, wax, widen.
antonyms decrease, diminish, shrink.

enlighten *v.* advise, apprise, civilize, counsel, edify, educate, illuminate, indoctrinate, inform, instruct, teach, undeceive.
antonyms confuse, puzzle.

enlist *v.* conscript, employ, engage, enrol, enter, gather, join (up), muster, obtain, procure, recruit, register, secure, sign up, volunteer.

enliven *v.* animate, brighten, buoy up, cheer (up), excite, exhilarate, fire, gladden, hearten, inspire, inspirit, invigorate, kindle, liven (up), pep up, perk up, quicken, rouse, spark, stimulate, vitalize, vivify, wake up.
antonyms subdue.

enmity *n.* acrimony, animosity, animus, antagonism, antipathy, aversion, bad blood, bitterness, feud, hate, hatred, hostility, ill-will, invidiousness, malevolence, malice, malignity, rancor, spite, venom.
antonyms amity, friendship.

enormity *n.* abomination, atrociousness, atrocity, crime, depravity, disgrace, evil, evilness, flagitiousness, heinousness, horror, iniquity, monstrosity, monstrousness, nefariousness, outrage, outrageousness, turpitude, viciousness, vileness, villainy, wickedness.
antonyms triviality, unimportance.

enormous *adj.* abominable, astronomic(al), atrocious, Brobdingnagian, colossal, cyclopean, depraved, disgraceful, evil, excessive, gargantuan, gigantic, gross, heinous, herculean, huge, hulking, immense, jumbo, leviathan, mammoth, massive, monstrous, mountainous, nefarious, odious, outrageous, prodigious, titanic, tremendous, vast, vasty, vicious, vile, villainous, wicked.
antonyms small, tiny.

enough *adj.* abundant, adequate, ample, enow, plenty, sufficient.
n. abundance, adequacy, plenitude, plenty, repletion, sufficiency.
adv. abundantly, adequately, amply, aplenty, enow, fairly, moderately, passably, reasonably, satisfactorily, sufficiently, tolerably.

enquiry, inquiry *n.* examination, exploration, inquest, inspection, investigation, probe, query, quest, question, research, scrutiny, search, study, survey.

enrage *v.* acerbate, aggravate, anger, exasperate, incense, incite, inflame, infuriate, irritate, madden, make someone's hackles rise, provoke.
antonyms calm, placate, soothe.

enrich *v.* adorn, aggrandize, ameliorate, augment, cultivate, decorate, develop, embellish, endow, enhance, fortify, grace, improve, ornament, prosper, refine, supplement.
antonym impoverish.

enrol(l) *v.* accept, admit, chronicle, empanel, engage, enlist, enregister, inscribe, join up, list, matriculate, note, record, recruit, register, sign on, sign up, take on.
antonyms leave, reject.

enshrine *v.* apotheosize, cherish, consecrate, dedicate, embalm, exalt, hallow, idolize, preserve, revere, sanctify, treasure.

ensign *n.* badge, banner, colors, flag, gonfalon, jack, oriflamme, pennant, pennon, standard, streamer.

enslave *v.* bind, conquer, dominate, enchain, enthrall, overcome, subject, subjugate, yoke.
antonyms emancipate, free.

ensue *v.* arise, attend, befall, derive, eventuate, flow, follow, happen, issue, proceed, result, stem, succeed, supervene, turn out, turn up.
antonym precede.

ensure *v.* certify, clinch, confirm, effect, guarantee, guard, insure, protect, safeguard, secure, warrant.

entangle *v.* ball, bewilder, catch, complicate, compromise, confuse, embroil, enlace, enmesh, ensnare, entoil, entrap, foul, implicate, involve, jumble, knot, mat, mix up, muddle, perplex, puzzle, ravel, snag, snare, snarl, tangle, trammel, trap, twist.
antonym disentangle.

entanglement *n.* complication, confusion, difficulty, embarrassment, ensnarement, entoilment, entrapment, imbroglio, involvement, jumble, knot, liaison, mesh, mess, mix-up, muddle, predicament, snare, snarl-up, tangle, tie, toils, trap.
antonym disentanglement.

enter *v.* arrive, begin, board, commence, embark upon, enlist, enrol, inscribe, insert, introduce, join, list, log, note, offer, participate, participate in, penetrate, pierce, present, proffer, record, register, set about, set down, sign up, start, submit, take down, take up, tender.
antonyms delete, issue, leave.

enterprise *n.* activity, adventure, adventurousness, alertness, audacity, boldness, business, company, concern, daring, dash, drive, eagerness, effort, emprise, endeavor, energy, enthusiasm, essay, establishment, firm, get-up-and-go, gumption, imagination, initiative, operation, plan, program, project, push, readiness, resource, resourcefulness, spirit, undertaking, venture, vigor, zeal.
antonyms apathy, inertia.

enterprising *adj.* active, adventurous, alert, ambitious, aspiring, audacious, bold, daring, dashing, eager, energetic, enthusiastic, go-ahead, imaginative, intrepid, keen, pushful, ready, resourceful, self-reliant, spirited, stirring, up-and-coming, venturesome, vigorous, zealous.
antonyms lethargic, unadventurous.

entertain *v.* accommodate, accourt, amuse, charm, cheer, cherish, conceive, consider, contemplate, countenance, delight, divert, fête, foster, harbor, hold, imagine, lodge, maintain, occupy, please, ponder, put up, recreate, regale, support, treat.
antonyms bore, reject.

enthral(l) *v.* beguile, captivate, charm, enchant, enrapture, enravish, entrance, fascinate, grip, hypnotize, intrigue, mesmerize, rivet, spellbind, thrill.
antonyms bore, weary.

enthusiasm *n.* ardor, avidity, craze, devotion, eagerness, earnestness, empressement, entraînement, estro, excitement, fad, fervor, frenzy, hobby, hobby-horse, interest, keenness, mania, oomph, passion, rage, relish, spirit, vehemence, warmth, zeal, zest.
antonym apathy.

enthusiastic *adj.* ardent, avid, devoted, eager, earnest, ebullient, empressé, excited, exuberant, fervent, fervid, forceful, gung-ho, hearty, keen, keen as mustard, lively, passionate, spirited, unstinting, vehement, vigorous, warm, whole-hearted, zealous.
antonyms apathetic, reluctant, unenthusiastic.

entice *v.* allure, attract, beguile, blandish, cajole, coax, decoy, draw, induce, inveigle, lead on, lure, persuade, prevail on, seduce, sweet-talk, tempt, wheedle.

entire *adj.* absolute, all-in, complete, continuous, full, intact, integrated, outright, perfect, sound, thorough, total, unabridged, unbroken, uncut, undamaged, undiminished, undivided, unified, unmarked, unmarred, unmitigated, unreserved, unrestricted, whole.
antonyms impaired, incomplete, partial.

entirely *adv.* absolutely, altogether, completely, every inch, exclusively, fully, hook line and sinker, in toto, lock stock and barrel, only, perfectly, solely, thoroughly, totally, unreservedly, utterly, wholly, without exception, without reservation.
antonym partially.

entitle *v.* accredit, allow, authorize, call, christen, denominate, designate, dub, empower, enable, enfranchise, label, license, name, permit, style, term, title, warrant.

entourage *n.* associates, attendants, claque, companions, company, cortège, coterie, court, escort, followers, following, retainers, retinue, staff, suite, train.

entrance[1] *n.* access, admission, admittance, appearance, arrival, atrium, avenue, beginning, commencement, debut, door, doorway, entrée, entry, gate, ingress, initiation, inlet, introduction, opening, outset, passage, portal, start.
antonyms departure, exit.

entrance[2] *v.* bewitch, captivate, charm, delight, enchant, enrapture, enravish, enthrall, fascinate, gladden, hypnotize, magnetize, mesmerize, ravish, spellbind, transport.
antonyms bore, repel.

entreat *v.* appeal to, ask, beg, beseech, conjure, crave, enjoin, exhort, flagitate, implore, importune, invoke, petition, plead with, pray, request, sue, supplicate.

entreaty *n.* appeal, entreatment, exhortation, importunity, invocation, petition, plea, prayer, request, solicitation, suing, suit, supplication.

entrust *v.* assign, authorize, charge, commend, commit, confide, consign, delegate, deliver, depute, invest, trust, turn over.

enumerate *v.* calculate, cite, count, detail, itemize, list, mention, name, number, quote, recapitulate, recite, reckon, recount, rehearse, relate, specify, spell out, tell.

enunciate *v.* articulate, broadcast, declare, enounce, proclaim, promulgate, pronounce, propound, publish, say, sound, speak, state, utter, vocalize, voice.

envelop *v.* blanket, cloak, conceal, cover, embrace, encase, encircle, enclose, encompass, enfold, engulf, enshroud, enwrap, enwreathe, hide, obscure, sheathe, shroud, surround, swaddle, swathe, veil, wrap.

environment *n.* ambience, atmosphere, background, conditions, context, domain, element, entourage, habitat, locale, medium, milieu, scene, setting, situation, surroundings, territory.

envisage *v.* anticipate, conceive of, conceptualize, contemplate, envision, fancy, foresee, ideate, image, imagine, picture, preconceive, predict, see, visualize.

envoy *n.* agent, ambassador, courier, delegate, deputy, diplomat, elchi, emissary, intermediary, legate, messenger, minister, nuncio, plenipotentiary, representative.

envy *n.* covetousness, cupidity, dissatisfaction, enviousness, grudge, hatred, ill-will, jealousy, malice, malignity, resentfulness, resentment, spite.
v. begrudge, covet, crave, grudge, resent.

epicure *n.* arbiter elegantiae, bon vivant, bon viveur, connoisseur, epicurean, gastronome, glutton, gourmand, gourmet, hedonist, sensualist, sybarite, voluptuary.

epidemic *adj.* epizootic, general, pandemic, prevailing, prevalent, rampant, rife, sweeping, wide-ranging, widespread.
n. growth, outbreak, pandemic, plague, rash, spread, upsurge, wave.

episode *n.* adventure, affaire, business, chapter, circumstance, event, experience, happening, incident, instalment, matter, occasion, occurrence, part, passage, scene, section.

epitomize *v.* abbreviate, abridge, abstract, compress, condense, contract, curtail, cut, embody, encapsulate, exemplify, illustrate, incarnate, personify, précis, reduce, represent, shorten, summarize, symbolize, typify.
antonyms elaborate, expand.

epoch *n.* age, date, epocha, era, period, time.

equal *adj.* able, adequate, alike, balanced, capable, commensurate, competent, corresponding, egalitarian, equable, equivalent, even, even-handed, evenly-balanced, evenly-matched, evenly-proportioned, fair, fifty-fifty, fit, identical, impartial, just, level-pegging, like, matched, proportionate, ready, regular, sufficient, suitable, symmetrical, tantamount, the same, unbiased, uniform, unvarying, up to.
antonyms different, inequitable, unequal.
n. brother, coequal, compeer, counterpart, equivalent, fellow, match, mate, parallel, peer, rival, twin.
v. balance, commeasure, correspond to, equalize, equate, even, level, match, parallel, rival, square with, tally with.

equanimity *n.* aplomb, calm, calmness, composure, coolness, equability, equableness, imperturbability, levelheadedness, peace, phlegm, placidity, poise, presence of mind, sang-froid, self-possession, serenity, steadiness, tranquility.
antonyms alarm, anxiety, discomposure.

equilibrium *n.* balance, calm, calmness, collectedness, composure, cool, coolness, counterpoise, equanimity, equipoise, equiponderance, evenness, poise, rest, self-possession, serenity, stability, steadiness, symmetry.
antonym imbalance.

equip *v.* accouter, arm, array, attire, bedight, deck out, dight, dress, endow, fit out, fit up, furnish, habilitate, kit out, outfit, prepare, provide, rig, stock, supply.

equipment *n.* accessories, accouterments, apparatus, appurtenances, baggage, equipage, furnishings, furniture, gear, graith, impedimenta, implements, material, matériel, muniments, outfit, paraphernalia, rig-out, stuff, supplies, tackle, things, tools, traps.

equitable *adj.* disinterested, dispassionate, due, ethical, even-handed, fair, fair-and-square, honest, impartial, just, legitimate, objective, proper, proportionate, reasonable, right, rightful, square, unbiased, unprejudiced.
antonyms inequitable, unfair.

equity *n.* disinterestedness, equality, equitableness, evenhandedness, fair play, fair-mindedness, fairness, honesty, impartiality, integrity, justice, justness, objectivity, reasonableness, rectitude, righteousness, uprightness.
antonym inequity.

equivalent *adj.* alike, commensurate, comparable, convertible, correlative, correspondent, corresponding, equal, equipollent, equipotent, even, homologous, homotypal, homotypic, interchangeable, same, similar, substitutable, synonymous, tantamount, twin.
antonyms dissimilar, unlike.
n. correlative, correspondent, counterpart, equal, homologue, homotype, match, opposite number, parallel, peer, twin.

equivocal *adj.* ambiguous, ambivalent, casuistical, confusing, Delphic, doubtful, dubious, evasive, indefinite, indeterminate, misleading, oblique, obscure, oracular, questionable, suspicious, uncertain, vague.
antonyms clear, unequivocal.

equivocate *v.* dodge, evade, fence, fudge, hedge, mislead, palter, parry, prevaricate, pussyfoot, quibble, shift, shuffle, sidestep, tergiversate, weasel.

era *n.* age, century, cycle, date, day, days, eon, epoch, generation, period, stage, time.

eradicate *v.* abolish, annihilate, deracinate, destroy, efface, eliminate, erase, expunge, exterminate, extinguish, extirpate, get rid of, obliterate, raze, remove, root out, stamp out, suppress, unroot, uproot, weed out.

erase *v.* blot out, cancel, cleanse, delete, efface, eliminate, eradicate, expunge, get rid of, obliterate, remove, rub out.

erect *adj.* elevated, engorged, firm, hard, perpendicular, pricked, raised, rigid, standing, stiff, straight, taut, tense, tumescent, upright, upstanding, vertical.
antonyms limp, relaxed.
v. assemble, build, constitute, construct, create, elevate, establish, fabricate, form, found, initiate, institute, lift, mount, organize, pitch, put up, raise, rear, set up.

erection *n.* assembly, building, construction, creation, edifice, elevation, establishment, fabrication, manufacture, pile, raising, rigidity, stiffness, structure, tumescence.

erode *v.* abrade, consume, corrade, corrode, denude, destroy, deteriorate, disintegrate, eat away, grind down, spoil, wear away, wear down.

erotic *adj.* amatorial, amatorious, amatory, amorous, aphrodisiac, carnal, concupiscent, erogenic, erogenous, erotogenic, erotogenous, libidinous, lustful, rousing, seductive, sensual, sexy, stimulating, suggestive, titillating, venereal, voluptuous.

err *v.* blunder, deviate, fail, go astray, lapse, misapprehend, misbehave, miscalculate, misjudge, mistake, misunderstand, offend, sin, slip up, stray, stumble, transgress, trespass, trip up, wander.

errand *n.* assignment, charge, commission, duty, job, message, mission, task.

errant *adj.* aberrant, deviant, erring, itinerant, journeying, loose, nomadic, offending, peccant, peripatetic, rambling, roaming, roving, sinful, sinning, stray, straying, vagrant, wandering, wayward, wrong.

erratic *adj.* aberrant, abnormal, capricious, changeable, desultory, directionless, eccentric, fitful, fluctuating, inconsistent, inconstant, irregular, meandering, planetary, shifting, unpredictable, unreliable, unstable, variable, wandering, wayward.
antonyms consistent, reliable, stable, straight.

erroneous *adj.* amiss, fallacious, false, faulty, flawed, illogical, inaccurate, incorrect, inexact, invalid, mistaken, specious, spurious, unfounded, unsound, untrue, wrong.
antonym correct.

error *n.* barbarism, bêtise, bish, bloomer, blunder, boner, boob, corrigendum, delinquency, delusion, deviation, erratum, fallacy, fault, faux pas, flaw, gaucherie, howler, ignorance, ignoratio elenchi, illusion, inaccuracy, inexactitude, lapse, lapsus calami, lapsus linguae, lapsus memoriae, literal, malapropism, misapprehension, miscalculation, misconception, miscopy, miscorrection, misdeed, misprint, mistake, misunderstanding, mumpsimus, offence, omission, oversight, overslip, sin, slip, slip-up, solecism, transgression, trespass, wrong, wrongdoing.

erudite *adj.* academic, cultivated, cultured, educated, highbrow, knowledgeable, learned, lettered, literate, profound, recondite, scholarly, scholastic, well-educated, well-read, wise.
antonym unlettered.

erupt *v.* belch, break, break out, burst, discharge, eruct, eructate, explode, flare, gush, rift, spew, spout, vent, vomit.

escalate *v.* accelerate, amplify, ascend, climb, enlarge, expand, extend, grow, heighten, increase, intensify, magnify, mount, raise, rise, spiral, step up.
antonym diminish.
antonym inevitable.

escapade *n.* adventure, antic, caper, doing, escapado, exploit, fling, fredaine, gest, lark, prank, romp, scrape, spree, stunt, trick.

escape *v.* abscond, avoid, baffle, bolt, break free, break loose, break off, break out, circumvent, decamp, discharge, do a bunk, dodge, drain, duck, elude, emanate, evade, flee, flit, flow, fly, foil, get away, gush, issue, leak, ooze, pass, pour forth, scape, scarper, seep, shake off, shun, skedaddle, skip, slip, slip away, spurt, take it on the run, take to one's heels, trickle, vamoose.
n. abscondence, avoidance, bolt, break, break-out, circumvention, decampment, discharge, distraction, diversion, drain, effluence, effluent, efflux, effluxion, elusion, emanation, emission, escapism, evasion, flight, flit, getaway, gush, jail-break, leak, leakage, meuse, out, outflow, outlet, outpour, pastime, recreation, relaxation, relief, safetyvalve, seepage, spurt, vent.

escort *n.* aide, attendant, beau, bodyguard, chaperon, cicisbeo, companion, company, convoy, cortège, entourage, gigolo, guard, guardian, guide, partner, pilot, procession, protection, protector, retinue, safeguard, squire, suite, train.
v. accompany, chaperon, chum, company, conduct, convoy, guard, guide, lead, partner, protect, shepherd, squire, usher.

especially *adv.* chiefly, conspicuously, eminently, exceedingly, exceptionally, exclusively, expressly, extraordinarily, mainly, markedly, notably, noticeably, outstandingly, particularly, passing, peculiarly, pre-eminently, principally, remarkably, signally, singularly, specially, specifically, strikingly, supremely, uncommonly, uniquely, unusually, very.

espousal *n.* adoption, advocacy, affiance, alliance, backing, betrothal, betrothing, bridal, championing, championship, defence, embracing, engagement, espousing, maintenance, marriage, matrimony, nuptials, plighting, spousal, support, wedding.

essay[1] *n.* article, assignment, commentary, composition, critique, discourse, disquisition, dissertation, essayette, leader, paper, piece, review, thesis, tract, treatise.

essay[2] *n.* attempt, bash, bid, crack, effort, endeavor, exertion, experiment, go, shot, stab, struggle, test, trial, try, undertaking, venture, whack, whirl.
v. attempt, endeavor, go for, have a bash, have a crack,

have a go, have a stab, strain, strive, struggle, tackle, take on, test, try, undertake.

essence *n.* alma, attar, attributes, being, center, character, characteristics, concentrate, core, crux, decoction, decocture, distillate, elixir, ens, entity, esse, extract, fragrance, haecceity, heart, hypostasis, inscape, kernel, life, lifeblood, marrow, meaning, nature, perfume, pith, principle, properties, qualities, quality, quiddit, quiddity, quintessence, scent, significance, soul, spirit, spirits, substance, tincture, virtuality, whatness.

essential[1] *adj.* absolute, basic, cardinal, characteristic, complete, constituent, constitutional, constitutive, crucial, definitive, elemental, elementary, formal, fundamental, ideal, important, indispensable, inherent, innate, intrinsic, key, main, necessary, needed, perfect, principal, quintessential, required, requisite, typical, vital.
antonym inessential.
n. basic, fundamental, must, necessary, necessity, prerequisite, principle, qualification, quality, requirement, requisite, rudiment, sine qua non.
antonym inessential.

essential[2] *adj.* concentrated, decocted, distilled, ethereal, extracted, pure, purified, rectified, refined, volatile.

establish *v.* affirm, attest to, authenticate, authorize, base, certify, confirm, constitute, corroborate, create, decree, demonstrate, enact, ensconce, entrench, fix, form, found, ground, implant, inaugurate, install, institute, introduce, invent, lodge, ordain, organize, plant, prove, radicate, ratify, root, sanction, seat, secure, set up, settle, show, start, station, substantiate, validate, verify.

esteem *v.* account, adjudge, admire, believe, calculate, cherish, consider, count, deem, estimate, hold, honor, include, judge, like, love, prize, rate, reckon, regard, regard highly, respect, revere, reverence, think, treasure, value, venerate, view.
n. account, admiration, consideration, count, credit, estimation, good opinion, honor, judgment, love, reckoning, regard, respect, reverence, veneration.

estimate *v.* appraise, approximate, assess, believe, calculate, compute, conjecture, consider, count, evaluate, gauge, guess, judge, number, opine, rank, rate, reckon, surmise, think, value.
n. appraisal, appraisement, approximation, assessment, belief, computation, conceit, conception, conjecture, estimation, evaluation, guess, guesstimate, judgment, opinion, reckoning, surmise, valuation.

estimation *n.* account, admiration, appraisal, appreciation, assessment, belief, calculation, computation, conception, consideration, credit, esteem, estimate, evaluation, good opinion, honor, judgment, opinion, rating, reckoning, regard, respect, reverence, veneration, view.

etch *v.* bite, burn, carve, corrode, cut, dig, engrave, furrow, grave, groove, hatch, impress, imprint, incise, ingrain, inscribe, stamp.

eternal *adj.* abiding, ceaseless, changeless, constant, deathless, durable, endless, enduring, eonian, eterne, everlasting, eviternal, illimitable, immortal, immutable, imperishable, incessant, indestructible, infinite, interminable, lasting, limitless, never-ending, perennial, permanent, perpetual, sempiternal, timeless, unbegotten, unceasing, unchanging, undying, unending, unextinguishable, unremitting.
antonyms changeable, ephemeral, temporary.

ethical *adj.* commendable, conscientious, correct, decent, fair, fitting, good, honest, honorable, just, meet, moral, noble, principled, proper, right, righteous, seemly, upright, virtuous.
antonym unethical.

etiquette *n.* ceremony, civility, code, convention, conventionalities, correctness, courtesy, customs, decency, decorum, formalities, manners, politeness, politesse, propriety, protocol, rules, seemliness, usage, use.

eulogy *n.* acclaim, acclamation, accolade, applause, commendation, compliment, encomium, exaltation, glorification, laud, laudation, laudatory, paean, panegyric, plaudit, praise, tribute.
antonym condemnation.

euphemism *n.* evasion, fig-leaf, genteelism, hypocorism, hypocorisma, polite term, politeness, substitution, under-statement.

euphoria *n.* bliss, buoyancy, cheerfulness, cloud nine, ecstasy, elation, enthusiasm, euphory, exaltation, exhilaration, exultation, glee, high, high spirits, intoxication, joy, joyousness, jubilation, rapture, transport.
antonym depression.

evacuate[1] *v.* abandon, clear, clear out, decamp, depart, desert, forsake, leave, quit, relinquish, remove, retire from, vacate, withdraw.

evacuate[2] *v.* defecate, discharge, eject, eliminate, empty, excrete, expel, purge, void.

evade *v.* avert, avoid, balk, blink, chicken out of, circumvent, cop out, decline, dodge, duck, elude, equivocate, escape, fence, fend off, fudge, hedge, parry, prevaricate, quibble, scrimshank, shirk, shun, sidestep, skive, steer clear of, temporize.
antonym face.

evaluate *v.* appraise, assay, assess, calculate, compute, estimate, gauge, judge, rank, rate, reckon, size up, value, weigh.

evaporate *v.* condense, dehydrate, dematerialize, desiccate, disappear, dispel, disperse, dissipate, dissolve, distil, dry, evanesce, exhale, fade, melt (away), vanish, vaporize, vapor.

evasive *adj.* ambiguous, cag(e)y, casuistic, casuistical, cunning, deceitful, deceptive, devious, disingenuous, dissembling, elusive, elusory, equivocating, indirect, misleading, oblique, prevaricating, secretive, shifty, shuffling, slippery, sophistical, tricky, unforthcoming, vacillating.
antonyms direct, frank.

even *adj.* abreast, alongside, balanced, calm, coequal, commensurate, comparable, complanate, composed, constant, cool, disinterested, dispassionate, drawn, equable, equal, equalized, equanimous, equitable, even-tempered, fair, fair and square, fifty-fifty, flat, fluent, flush, horizontal, identical, impartial, impassive, imperturbable, just, level, level-pegging, like, matching, metrical, monotonous, neck and neck, on a par, parallel, peaceful, placid, plane, plumb, proportionate, quits, regular, rhythmical, serene, side by side, similar, smooth, square, stable, steady, straight, symmetrical, tied, tranquil, true, unbiased, unbroken, undisturbed, unexcitable, unexcited, uniform, uninterrupted, unprejudiced, unruffled, unvarying, unwavering, well-balanced.
antonyms unequal, uneven.
adv. all the more, also, although, as well, at all, directly, exactly, hardly, including, just, much, scarcely, so much as, still, yet.
v. align, balance, equal, equalize, flatten, flush, level, match, regularize, regulate, smooth, square, stabilize, steady, straighten.

evening *n.* crepuscule, dusk, eve, even, eventide, forenight, gloaming, Hesper, Hesperus, nightfall, sundown, sunset, twilight, vesper.
adj. crepuscular, twilight, vesperal, vespertinal, vespertine.

event *n.* adventure, affair, bout, business, case, circumstance, competition, conclusion, consequence, contest, effect, end, engagement, episode, eventuality, experience, fact, game, happening, incident, issue, match, matter, milestone, occasion, occurrence, outcome, possibility, result, termination, tournament, upshot.

even-tempered *adj.* calm, composed, cool, cool-headed, equable, equanimous, impassive, imperturbable, level-headed, peaceable, peaceful, placid, serene, stable, steady, tranquil, unexcitable, unfussed, unruffled.
antonym excitable.

eventual *adj.* concluding, consequent, ensuing, final, future, impending, last, later, overall, planned, projected, prospective, resulting, subsequent, ultimate.

eventually *adv.* after all, at last, at length, finally, in one's own good time, sooner or later, subsequently, ultimately.

ever *adv.* always, at all, at all times, at any time, ceaselessly, constantly, continually, endlessly, eternally, everlastingly, evermore, for ever, in any case, in any circumstances, incessantly, on any account, perpetually, unceasingly, unendingly.

everlasting *adj.* abiding, boring, ceaseless, changeless, constant, continual, continuous, deathless, durable, endless, enduring, eternal, immarcescible, immortal, imperishable, incessant, indestructible, infinite, interminable, lasting, monotonous, never-ending, perdurable, permanent, perpetual, relentless, tedious, timeless, unceasing, unchanging, undying, unfading, uninterrupted, unremitting.
antonyms temporary, transient.

evermore *adv.* always, eternally, ever, ever after, for aye, for ever, for ever and a day, for ever and ever, henceforth, hereafter, in perpetuum, in saecula saeculorum, till doomsday, to the end of time, unceasingly.

everyday *adj.* accustomed, banal, boring, circadian, common, common-or-garden, commonplace, conventional, customary, daily, diurnal, dull, familiar, frequent, habitual, informal, monotonous, mundane, normal, ordinary, plain, prosaic, quotidian, regular, routine, run-of-the-mill, simple, stock, unexceptional, unimaginative, usual, wonted, workaday.
antonyms exceptional, special.

evict *v.* boot out, cast out, chuck out, defenestrate, dislodge, dispossess, disseize, eject, expel, expropriate, give the bum's rush, kick out, oust, put out, remove, show the door, turf out.

evidence *n.* affirmation, attestation, betrayal, confirmation, corroboration, data, declaration, demonstration, deposition, documentation, grounds, hint, indication, manifestation, mark, pledge, proof, sign, substantiation, suggestion, testimony, token, voucher, witness.
v. affirm, attest, betray, confirm, demonstrate, denote, display, establish, evince, exhibit, indicate, manifest, prove, reveal, show, signify, testify to, witness.

evident *adj.* apparent, clear, clear-cut, confessed, conspicuous, detectable, discernible, distinct, incontestable, incontrovertible, indisputable, manifest, noticeable, obvious, ostensible, palpable, patent, perceptible, plain, tangible, undeniable, unmistakable, visible.
antonym uncertain.

evil *adj.* adverse, bad, baleful, baneful, base, blackguardly, black-hearted, calamitous, catastrophic, corrupt, cruel, deadly, deleterious, depraved, destructive, detrimental, devilish, dire, disastrous, facinorous, flagitious, foul, ghastly, grim, harmful, heinous, hurtful, immoral, inauspicious, inimical, iniquitous, injurious, knavish, malefactory, malefic, maleficent, malevolent, malicious, malignant, mephitic, mischievous, miscreant, nefarious, nefast, nocuous, noisome, noxious, offensive, painful, perfidious, pernicious, pestiferous, pestilential, poisonous, putrid, reprobate, ruinous, sinful, sorrowful, ugly, unfortunate, unlucky, unpleasant, unspeakable, vicious, vile, villainous, wicked, woeful, wrong.
n. adversity, affliction, amiss, badness, bane, baseness, blow, calamity, catastrophe, corruption, curse, demonry, depravity, disaster, distress, facinorousness, flagitiousness, foulness, harm, heinousness, hurt, hydra, ill, immorality, impiety, improbity, iniquity, injury, knavery, maleficence, malignity, mischief, misery, misfortune, pain, perfidy, ruin, sin, sinfulness, sorrow, suffering, turpitude, ulcer, vice, viciousness, villainy, wickedness, woe, wrong, wrong-doing.

evoke *v.* activate, actuate, arouse, awaken, call, call forth, call up, conjure up, educe, elicit, excite, induce, invoke, produce, provoke, raise, recall, rekindle, stimulate, stir, summon, summon up.
antonyms quell, suppress.

evolve *v.* derive, descend, develop, disclose, elaborate, emerge, enlarge, expand, grow, increase, mature, progress, result, unravel.

exact *adj.* accurate, blow-by-blow, careful, close, correct, definite, detailed, explicit, express, factual, faithful, faultless, finical, finicky, flawless, identical, letter-perfect, literal, methodical, meticulous, nice, orderly, painstaking, particular, perfectionist, perjink, precise, punctilious, right, rigorous, scrupulous, severe, specific, square, strict, true, unambiguous, unequivocal, unerring, veracious, very, word-perfect.
antonym inexact.
v. bleed, claim, command, compel, demand, extort, extract, force, impose, insist on, milk, require, requisition, squeeze, wrest, wring.

exactly *adv.* absolutely, accurately, bang, carefully, correctly, dead, definitely, explicitly, expressly, faithfully, faultlessly, just, literally, literatim, methodically, particularly, plumb, precisely, punctiliously, quite, rigorously, scrupulously, severely, specifically, strictly, to the letter, truly, truthfully, unambiguously, unequivocally, unerringly, veraciously, verbatim.
interj. absolutely, agreed, certainly, indeed, just so, of course, precisely, quite, right, true.

exaggerate *v.* amplify, bounce, caricature, distend, embellish, embroider, emphasize, enlarge, exalt, hyperbolize, inflate, magnify, overdo, overdraw, overemphasize, overestimate, oversell, overstate, pile it on.
antonyms belittle, understate.

exalt *v.* acclaim, advance, aggrandize, animate, apotheosize, applaud, arouse, bless, crown, deify, delight, dignify, elate, electrify, elevate, enliven, ennoble, enthrone, excite, exhilarate, extol, fire, glorify, heighten, honor, idolize, inspire, inspirit, laud, magnify, praise, promote, raise, revere, reverence, stimulate, sublimize, thrill, upgrade, uplift, venerate, worship.
antonym debase.

examination *n.* analysis, appraisal, assay, audit, catechism, check, check-up, critique, cross-examination, cross-questioning, docimasy, exam, exploration, inquiry, inquisition, inspection, interrogation, investigation, observation, once-over, perusal, probe, questioning, quiz, research, review, scan, scrutinization, scrutiny, search, sift, study, survey, test, trial, visitation, viva.

examine *v.* analyze, appraise, assay, audit, case, catechize, check (out), consider, cross-examine, cross-question, explore, grill, inquire, inspect, interrogate, investigate, jerque, peruse, ponder, pore over, probe, question, quiz, review, scan, scrutinize, sift, study, survey, sus out, test, vet, visit, weigh.

example *n.* admonition, archetype, case, case in point, caution, citation, ensample, exemplar, exemplification, exemplum, ideal, illustration, instance, lesson, mirror, model, occurrence, paradigm, paragon, parallel, pattern, praxis, precedent, prototype, sample, specimen, standard, type, warning.

exasperate *v.* aggravate, anger, annoy, bug, enrage, exacerbate, excite, exulcerate, gall, get, get in someone's hair, get on someone's nerves, get on someone's wick, get to, goad, incense, inflame, infuriate, irk, irritate, madden, needle, nettle, peeve, pique, plague, provoke, rankle, rile, rouse, vex.
antonyms calm, soothe.

excavate *v.* burrow, cut, delve, dig, dig out, dig up, disinter, drive, exhume, gouge, hollow, mine, quarry, sap, scoop, stope, trench, tunnel, uncover, undermine, unearth.

exceed *v.* beat, better, cap, contravene, eclipse, excel, out-distance, outdo, outreach, outrival, outrun, outshine, outstrip, overdo, overstep, overtake, pass, surmount, surpass, take liberties with, top, transcend, transgress.

exceedingly *adv.* amazingly, astonishingly, enormously, especially, exceeding, exceptionally, excessively, extraordinarily, extremely, greatly, highly, hugely, inordinately, passing, superlatively, surpassingly, unprecedentedly, unusually, vastly, very.

excel *v.* beat, better, cap, eclipse, exceed, outclass, outdo, outperform, outrank, outrival, outshine, outstrip, overshadow, pass, predominate, shine, stand out, surmount, surpass, top, transcend, trump.

excellence *n.* distinction, eminence, fineness, goodness, greatness, merit, perfection, pre-eminence, purity, quality, superiority, supremacy, transcendence, virtue, water, worth.
antonym inferiority.

excellent *adj.* A1, admirable, beaut, bosker, boss, brave, bully, capital, champion, choice, commendable, copacetic, corking, crack, cracking, distinguished, estimable, exemplary, eximious, exquisite, fine, first-class, first-rate, good, great, hot stuff, laudable, meritorious, nonpareil, notable, noted, noteworthy, outstanding, peerless, prime, remarkable, ripping, select, splendid, sterling, stunning, superb, supereminent, superior, superlative, surpassing, tipping, tiptop, top-flight, top-notch, topping, unequaled, unexceptionable, up to dick, way-out, wonderful, worthy.
antonym inferior.

except *prep.* apart from, bar, barring, besides, but, except for, excepting, excluding, exclusive of, leaving out, less, minus, not counting, omitting, other than, save, saving.
v. ban, bar, debar, disallow, eliminate, exclude, leave out, omit, pass over, reject, rule out.

exception *n.* abnormality, anomaly, curiosity, debarment, departure, deviation, disallowment, eccentricity, excepting, exclusion, exemption, freak, inconsistency, irregularity, oddity, omission, peculiarity, prodigy, quirk, rarity, rejection, special case.

exceptional *adj.* aberrant, abnormal, anomalous, atypical, curious, deviant, eccentric, excellent, extraordinary, freakish, inconsistent, irregular, marvelous, notable, noteworthy, odd, outstanding, peculiar, phenomenal, prodigious, quirky, rare, remarkable, singular, special, strange, superior, superlative, uncommon, unconventional, unequaled, unexpected, unusual.
antonyms mediocre, unexceptional.

excerpt *n.* citation, extract, fragment, gobbet, part, passage, pericope, portion, quotation, quote, scrap, section, selection.
v. borrow, cite, crib, cull, extract, lift, mine, quarry, quote, select.

excess *n.* debauchery, diarrhoea, dissipation, dissoluteness, excesses, exorbitance, extravagance, glut, gluttony, immoderateness, immoderation, intemperance, left-over, libertinism, licentiousness, overabundance, overdose, overflow, overflush, overindulgence, overkill, overload, plethora, prodigality, remainder, superabundance, superfluity, surfeit, surplus, unrestraint.
antonym dearth.
adj. additional, extra, left-over, redundant, remaining, residual, spare, superfluous, supernumerary, surplus.

exchange *v.* bandy, bargain, barter, change, commute, convert, interchange, reciprocate, replace, substitute, swap, switch, toss about, trade, truck.
n. bargain, barter, bourse, brush, chat, commerce, conversation, converse, conversation, dealing, interchange, intercourse, market, quid pro quo, reciprocity, replacement, substitution, swap, switch, tit for tat, trade, traffic, truck.

excite *v.* activate, actuate, aerate, affect, agitate, animate, arouse, awaken, discompose, disturb, elate, electrify, elicit, engender, evoke, fire, foment, galvanize, generate, ignite, impress, incite, induce, inflame, initiate, inspire, instigate, kindle, motivate, move, provoke, quicken, rouse, stimulate, stir up, suscitate, sway, thrill, titillate, touch, turn on, upset, waken, warm, whet.
antonyms bore, quell.

excitement *n.* action, activity, ado, adventure, agitation, animation, brouhaha, clamor, commotion, deliriousness, delirium, discomposure, eagerness, elation, enthusiasm, excitation, ferment, fever, flurry, furore, fuss, heat, hubbub, hue and cry, hurly-burly, kerfuffle, kicks, passion, perturbation, restlessness, stimulation, stimulus, tew, thrill, titillation, tumult, unrest, urge.
antonyms apathy, calm.

exclaim *v.* blurt, call, cry, declare, ejaculate, interject, proclaim, shout, utter, vociferate.

exclamation *n.* call, cry, ecphonesis, ejaculation, expletive, interjection, outcry, shout, utterance, vociferation.

exclude *v.* anathematize, ban, bar, blackball, blacklist, bounce, boycott, debar, disallow, eject, eliminate, embargo, evict, except, excommunicate, expel, forbid, ignore, include out, interclude, interdict, keep out, leave out, omit, ostracize, oust, preclude, prohibit, proscribe, refuse, reject, remove, repudiate, rule out, shut out, veto.
antonyms admit, allow, include.

exclusion *n.* ban, bar, boycott, debarment, disfellowship, ejection, elimination, embargo, eviction, exception, expulsion, forbiddal, forbiddance, interdict, non-admission, omission, ostracization, preclusion, prohibition, proscription, refusal, rejection, removal, repudiation, veto.
antonyms admittance, allowance, inclusion.

exclusive *adj.* absolute, arrogant, chic, choice, clannish, classy, cliquey, cliquish, closed, complete, confined, discriminative, elegant, entire, esoteric, exclusory, fashionable, full, limited, luxurious, monopolistic, narrow, only, peculiar, posh, private, restricted, restrictive, select, selective, selfish, single, snobbish, sole, total, undivided, unique, unshared, whole.

excruciating *adj.* acute, agonizing, atrocious, bitter, burning, exquisite, extreme, harrowing, insufferable, intense, intolerable, painful, piercing, racking, savage, searing, severe, sharp, tormenting, torturing, torturous, unbearable, unendurable.

excursion *n.* airing, breather, day trip, detour, deviation, digression, divagation, ecbole, episode, excursus, expedition, jaunt, journey, outing, ramble, ride, sashay, tour, trip, walk, wandering, wayzgoose.

excuse *v.* absolve, acquit, apologize for, condone, defend, discharge, exculpate, exempt, exonerate, explain, extenuate, forgive, free, ignore, indulge, justify, let off, liberate, mitigate, overlook, palliate, pardon, release, relieve, sanction, spare, tolerate, vindicate, warrant, wink at.
n. alibi, apology, cop-out, defence, disguise, evasion, exculpation, exoneration, expedient, explanation, extenuation, grounds, justification, makeshift, mitigation, mockery, palliation, parody, plea, pretense, pretext, put-off, reason, semblance, shift, substitute, subterfuge, travesty, vindication.

execrate *v.* abhor, abominate, anathematize, blast, condemn, curse, damn, denounce, denunciate, deplore, despise, detest, excoriate, fulminate, hate, imprecate, inveigh against, loathe, revile, vilify.
antonyms commend, praise.

execute[1] *v.* behead, burn, crucify, decapitate, decollate, electrocute, guillotine, hang, kill, liquidate, put to death, shoot.

execute[2] *v.* accomplish, achieve, administer, complete, consummate, deliver, discharge, dispatch, do, effect, effectuate, enact, enforce, expedite, finish, fulfil, implement, perform, prosecute, realize, render, seal, serve, sign, validate.

executive *n.* administration, administrator, controller,

director, directorate, directors, government, hierarchy, leadership, management, manager, official, organizer.
adj. administrative, controlling, decision-making, directing, directorial, governing, gubernatorial, guiding, leading, managerial, organizational, organizing, regulating, supervisory.

exemplify *v.* demonstrate, depict, display, embody, ensample, epitomize, evidence, example, exhibit, illustrate, instance, manifest, represent, show, typify.

exempt *v.* absolve, discharge, dismiss, except, excuse, exonerate, free, let off, liberate, make an exception of, release, relieve, spare.
adj. absolved, clear, discharged, excepted, excluded, excused, favored, free, immune, liberated, released, spared.
antonym liable.

exercise *v.* afflict, agitate, annoy, apply, burden, discharge, discipline, distress, disturb, drill, employ, enjoy, exert, habituate, inure, occupy, operate, pain, perturb, practice, preoccupy, train, trouble, try, upset, use, utilize, vex, wield, work out, worry.
n. accomplishment, action, activity, aerobics, application, assignment, daily dozen, discharge, discipline, drill, drilling, effort, employment, enjoyment, exercitation, exertion, fulfilment, implementation, krieg(s)spiel, labor, lesson, operation, physical jerks, practice, problem, schooling, school-work, task, toil, training, use, utilization, war-game, work, work-out.

exertion *n.* action, application, assiduity, attempt, diligence, effort, employment, endeavor, exercise, industry, labor, operation, pains, perseverance, sedulousness, strain, stretch, struggle, toil, travail, trial, use, utilization, work.
antonyms idleness, rest.

exhale *v.* breathe (out), discharge, eject, emanate, emit, evaporate, expel, expire, give off, issue, respire, steam.
antonym inhale.

exhaust *v.* bankrupt, beggar, consume, cripple, debilitate, deplete, disable, dissipate, drain, dry, empty, enervate, enfeeble, expend, fatigue, finish, impoverish, overtax, overtire, overwork, prostrate, run through, sap, spend, squander, strain, tax, tire (out), use up, void, waste, weaken, wear out, weary.
antonym refresh.
n. discharge, education, effluvium, emanation, emission, exhalation, fumes.

exhaustive *adj.* all-embracing, all-inclusive, all-out, complete, comprehensive, definitive, detailed, encyclopedic, expansive, extensive, far-reaching, full, full-scale, in-depth, intensive, sweeping, thorough, thoroughgoing, total.
antonym incomplete.

exhibit *v.* air, demonstrate, disclose, display, evidence, evince, expose, express, flaunt, indicate, manifest, offer, parade, present, reveal, show, showcase, sport.
antonym hide.
n. display, exhibition, illustration, model, show.

exhilarate *v.* animate, cheer, delight, elate, energize, enhearten, enliven, exalt, excite, gladden, hearten, inspirit, invigorate, lift, stimulate, thrill, vitalize.
antonyms bore, discourage.

exhort *v.* admonish, advise, beseech, bid, call upon, caution, counsel, encourage, enjoin, entreat, goad, implore, incite, inflame, inspire, instigate, persuade, press, spur, urge, warn.

exigent *adj.* acute, arduous, constraining, critical, crucial, demanding, difficult, exacting, exhausting, hard, harsh, imperative, importunate, insistent, necessary, needful, pressing, rigorous, severe, stiff, strict, stringent, taxing, tough, urgent.
antonym mild.

exile *n.* banishment, deportation, deportee, émigré, exilement, expatriate, expatriation, expulsion, galut(h), ostracism, outcast, proscription, refugee, separation.
v. banish, deport, drive out, expatriate, expel, ostracize, oust, proscribe.

exist *v.* abide, be, be available, be extant, breathe, continue, endure, happen, have one's being, last, live, obtain, occur, prevail, remain, stand, subsist, survive.

exit *n.* adieu, aperture, congé, departure, door, doorway, egress, evacuation, exodus, farewell, gate, going, leave-taking, outlet, retirement, retreat, vent, way out, withdrawal.
antonym entrance.
v. arrive, depart, enter, issue, leave, retire, retreat, take one's leave, withdraw.

exodus *n.* departure, evacuation, exit, flight, hegira, leaving, long march, migration, retirement, retreat, withdrawal.

exonerate *v.* absolve, acquit, clear, discharge, disculpate, dismiss, except, exculpate, excuse, exempt, free, justify, let off, liberate, pardon, release, relieve, vindicate.
antonym incriminate.

exorbitant *adj.* enormous, excessive, extortionate, extravagant, extreme, immoderate, inordinate, monstrous, out-rageous, preposterous, unconscionable, undue, unreasonable, unwarranted.
antonyms fair, reasonable.

exorcism *n.* adjuration, deliverance, expulsion, exsufflation, purification.

exotic *adj.* alien, bizarre, colorful, curious, different, external, extraneous, extraordinary, extrinsic, fascinating, foreign, foreign-looking, glamorous, imported, introduced, mysterious, naturalized, outlandish, outré, peculiar, recherché, strange, striking, unfamiliar, unusual.
antonym ordinary.

expand *v.* amplify, augment, bloat, blow up, branch out, broaden, develop, diffuse, dilate, dispread, distend, diversify, elaborate, embellish, enlarge, expatiate, expound, extend, fatten, fill out, flesh out, grow, heighten,

increase, inflate, lengthen, magnify, multiply, open, outspread, prolong, protract, snowball, spread, stretch, swell, thicken, unfold, unfurl, unravel, unroll, wax, widen.
antonyms contract, précis.

expansive *adj.* affable, all-embracing, broad, communicative, comprehensive, dilating, distending, easy, effusive, elastic, expanding, expatiative, expatiatory, extendable, extensive, far-reaching, free, friendly, garrulous, genial, inclusive, loquacious, open, outgoing, sociable, stretching, stretchy, swelling, talkative, thorough, unreserved, voluminous, warm, wide, wide-ranging, widespread.
antonyms cold, reserved.

expect *v.* anticipate, assume, await, bank on, bargain for, believe, calculate, conjecture, contemplate, count on, demand, envisage, forecast, foresee, hope for, imagine, insist on, look for, look forward to, predict, presume, project, reckon, rely on, require, suppose, surmise, think, trust, want, wish.

expectant *adj.* agog, anticipating, anxious, apprehensive, awaiting, curious, eager, enceinte, expecting, gravid, hopeful, in suspense, pregnant, ready, watchful.

expecting *adj.* enceinte, expectant, gravid, in the club, in the family way, pregnant, with child.

expedient *adj.* advantageous, advisable, appropriate, beneficial, convenient, desirable, effective, fit, helpful, judicious, meet, opportune, politic, practical, pragmatic, profitable, proper, prudent, serviceable, suitable, useful, utilitarian, worthwhile.
antonym inexpedient.
n. contrivance, device, dodge, makeshift, maneuver, means, measure, method, resort, resource, ruse, scheme, shift, stop-gap, stratagem, substitute.

expedition[1] *n.* company, crusade, enterprise, excursion, exploration, explorers, hike, journey, mission, pilgrimage, quest, raid, ramble, safari, sail, team, tour, travelers, trek, trip, undertaking, voyage, voyagers.

expedition[2] *n.* alacrity, briskness, celerity, dispatch, expeditiousness, haste, hurry, immediacy, promptness, quickness, rapidity, readiness, speed, swiftness.
antonym delay.

expel *v.* ban, banish, bar, belch, blackball, cast out, disbar, discharge, dislodge, dismiss, drive out, drum out, egest, eject, evict, exclude, exile, expatriate, hoof out, oust, proscribe, remove, send packing, spew, throw out, turf out.
antonym admit.

expend *v.* consume, disburse, dissipate, employ, exhaust, fork out, pay, shell out, spend, use, use up.
antonym save.

expense *n.* charge, consumption, cost, damage, disbursement, expenditure, loss, outlay, output, payment, sacrifice, spending, toll, use.

expensive *adj.* costly, dear, excessive, exorbitant, extortionate, extravagant, high-priced, inordinate, lavish, overpriced, rich, steep, stiff.
antonyms cheap, inexpensive.

experience *n.* adventure, affair, assay, contact, doing, encounter, episode, event, evidence, exposure, familiarity, happening, incident, involvement, know-how, knowledge, observation, occurrence, ordeal, participation, practice, proof, taste, test, training, trial, understanding.
antonym inexperience.
v. apprehend, behold, empathize, encounter, endure, face, feel, have, know, meet, observe, perceive, sample, sense, suffer, sustain, taste, try, undergo.

experienced *adj.* accomplished, adept, capable, competent, expert, familiar, knowing, knowledgeable, master, mature, practiced, professional, qualified, schooled, seasoned, skilful, sophisticated, tested, trained, travailed, traveled, tried, veteran, well-versed, wise, worldly, worldly-wise.
antonym inexperienced.

experiment *n.* assay, attempt, ballon d'essai, examination, experimentation, heurism, investigation, procedure, proof, research, test, trial, trial and error, trial run, venture.
v. assay, examine, investigate, research, sample, test, try, verify.

expert *n.* ace, adept, authority, boffin, connoisseur, dab hand, dabster, deacon, dean, maestro, master, pastmaster, pro, professional, specialist, virtuoso, wizard.
adj. able, adept, adroit, apt, clever, crack, deft, dexterous, experienced, facile, handy, knowledgeable, master, masterly, practiced, professional, proficient, qualified, skilful, skilled, trained, virtuoso.
antonym novice.

expire *v.* cease, close, conclude, decease, depart, die, discontinue, emit, end, exhale, finish, lapse, perish, run out, stop, terminate.
antonyms begin, continue.

explain *v.* account for, clarify, clear up, construe, decipher, decode, define, demonstrate, describe, disclose, elucidate, enucleate, excuse, explicate, expound, gloss, gloze, illustrate, interpret, justify, resolve, simplify, solve, spell out, teach, translate, unfold, unravel, untangle.
antonyms obfuscate, obscure.

explanation *n.* account, answer, cause, clarification, definition, demonstration, description, éclaircissement, elucidation, enucleation, excuse, exegesis, explication, exposition, gloss, illustration, interpretation, justification, legend, meaning, mitigation, motive, reason, resolution, sense, significance, solution, vindication, voice-over.

explicit *adj.* absolute, accurate, categorical, certain, clear, declared, definite, detailed, direct, distinct, exact, express, frank, open, outspoken, patent, plain, positive,

precise, specific, stated, straightforward, unambiguous, unequivocal, unqualified, unreserved.
antonyms inexplicit, vague.

exploit *n.* accomplishment, achievement, adventure, attainment, deed, feat, gest(e), stunt.
v. abuse, bleed, capitalize on, cash in on, fleece, impose on, make capital out of, manipulate, milk, misuse, profit by, rip off, skin, soak, take advantage of, turn to account, use, utilize.

explore *v.* analyze, case, examine, inspect, investigate, probe, prospect, reconnoiter, research, scout, scrutinize, search, survey, tour, travel, traverse.

explosion *n.* bang, blast, burst, clap, crack, debunking, detonation, discharge, discrediting, eruption, fit, outbreak, outburst, paroxysm, refutation, report.

explosive *adj.* charged, dangerous, fiery, hazardous, overwrought, perilous, stormy, tense, touchy, ugly, unstable, vehement, violent, volatile, volcanic.
antonym calm.
n. cordite, dynamite, gelignite, gun-powder, jelly, lyddite, melinite, nitroglycerine, TNT.

exponent *n.* advocate, backer, champion, commentator, defender, demonstrator, elucidator, example, executant, exegetist, exemplar, expositor, expounder, illustration, illustrator, indication, interpreter, model, performer, player, presenter, promoter, propagandist, proponent, representative, sample, specimen, spokesman, spokeswoman, supporter, type, upholder.

expose *v.* air, betray, bring to light, denounce, detect, disclose, display, divulge, endanger, exhibit, hazard, imperil, jeopardize, manifest, present, reveal, risk, show, uncover, unearth, unmask, unveil, wash one's dirty linen in public.
antonym cover.

exposition *n.* account, commentary, critique, demonstration, description, discourse, display, elucidation, exegesis, exhibition, explanation, explication, expo, fair, illustration, interpretation, monograph, paper, presentation, show, study, thesis.

expound *v.* describe, elucidate, explain, explicate, illustrate, interpet, preach, sermonize, set forth, spell out, unfold.

express *v.* articulate, assert, asseverate, bespeak, communicate, conceive, convey, couch, declare, denote, depict, designate, disclose, divulge, embody, enunciate, evince, exhibit, extract, force out, formulate, formulize, indicate, intimate, manifest, phrase, pronounce, put, put across, represent, reveal, say, show, signify, speak, stand for, state, symbolize, tell, testify, utter, verbalize, voice, word.
adj. accurate, categorical, certain, clear, clear-cut, definite, direct, distinct, especial, exact, explicit, fast, high-speed, manifest, non-stop, outright, particular, plain, pointed, precise, quick, rapid, singular, special, speedy, stated, swift, unambiguous, unqualified.
antonym vague.

expression *n.* air, announcement, appearance, aspect, assertion, asseveration, communication, countenance, declaration, delivery, demonstration, diction, embodiment, emphasis, enunciation, execution, exhibition, face, idiom, indication, intonation, language, locution, look, manifestation, mention, mien, phrase, phraseology, phrasing, pronouncement, reflex, remark, representation, set phrase, show, sign, speaking, speech, statement, style, symbol, term, token, turn of phrase, utterance, verbalism, verbalization, voicing, word, wording.

expressive *adj.* allusive, demonstrative, eloquent, emphatic, energetic, forcible, indicative, informative, lively, meaningful, mobile, moving, poignant, pointed, pregnant, representative, revealing, significant, striking, strong, suggestive, sympathetic, telling, thoughtful, vivid.
antonyms expressionless, poker-faced.

expressly *adv.* absolutely, categorically, clearly, decidedly, definitely, distinctly, especially, exactly, explicitly, intentionally, manifestly, on purpose, outright, particularly, plainly, pointedly, positively, precisely, purposely, specially, specifically, unambiguously, unequivocally.

expulsion *n.* banishment, debarment, disbarment, discharge, dislodgment, dislodging, dismissal, ejection, ejectment, eviction, exclusion, exile, expatriation, extrusion, proscription, removal.

expunge *v.* abolish, annihilate, annul, blot out, cancel, delete, destroy, efface, eradicate, erase, exterminate, extinguish, extirpate, obliterate, raze, remove, uncreate, unmake, wipe out.

expurgate *v.* blue-pencil, bowdlerize, censor, clean up, cut, emend, purge, purify, sanitize.

exquisite *adj.* acute, admirable, alembicated, appreciative, attractive, beautiful, charming, choice, comely, consummate, cultivated, dainty, delicate, delicious, discerning, discriminating, elegant, excellent, excruciating, fastidious, fine, flawless, impeccable, incomparable, intense, keen, lovely, matchless, meticulous, outstanding, peerless, perfect, piercing, pleasing, poignant, polished, precious, rare, refined, select, selective, sensitive, sharp, splendid, striking, superb, superlative, too-too.
antonyms flawed, imperfect, poor, ugly.

extant *adj.* alive, existent, existing, in existence, living, remaining, subsistent, subsisting, surviving.
antonyms dead, extinct, non-existent.

extemporary *adj.* ad-lib, expedient, extemporaneous, extempore, free, impromptu, improvisatory, improvised, jazz, made-up, makeshift, offhand, off-the-cuff, on-the-spot, spontaneous, temporary, unplanned, unpremeditated, unprepared, unrehearsed.
antonym planned.

extemporize *v.* ad-lib, autoschediaze, improvise, make up, play by ear.

extend *v.* advance, amplify, attain, augment, bestow, broaden, confer, continue, develop, dilate, drag out, draw out, elongate, enhance, enlarge, expand, give, grant, hold out, impart, increase, last, lengthen, offer, present, proffer, prolong, protract, pull out, reach, spin out, spread, stretch, supplement, take, uncoil, unfold, unfurl, unroll, widen, yield.
antonym shorten.

extension *n.* accretion, addendum, addition, adjunct, amplification, annexe, appendage, appendix, augmentation, branch, broadening, continuation, delay, development, dilatation, distension, el, elongation, enhancement, enlargement, expansion, extent, increase, lengthening, postponement, prolongation, protraction, spread, stretching, supplement, widening, wing.

extensive *adj.* all-inclusive, broad, capacious, commodious, comprehensive, expanded, expansive, extended, far-flung, far-reaching, general, great, huge, large, large-scale, lengthy, long, pervasive, prevalent, protracted, roomy, spacious, sweeping, thorough, thoroughgoing, universal, unrestricted, vast, voluminous, wholesale, wide, wide-spread.
antonyms narrow, restricted.

extent *n.* amount, amplitude, area, bounds, breadth, bulk, compass, degree, dimension(s), duration, expanse, expansion, length, magnitude, measure, play, proportions, quantity, range, reach, scope, size, sphere, spread, stretch, sweep, term, time, volume, width.

extenuating *adj.* exculpatory, extenuative, extenuatory, justifying, mitigating, moderating, palliative, qualifying.

exterior *n.* appearance, aspect, coating, covering, externals, façade, face, finish, outside, shell, skin, superficies, surface.
antonym interior.
adj. alien, exotic, external, extraneous, extrinsic, foreign, outer, outermost, outside, outward, peripheral, superficial, surface, surrounding.
antonym interior.

exterminate *v.* abolish, annihilate, deracinate, destroy, eliminate, eradicate, extirpate, massacre, wipe out.

external *adj.* alien, apparent, exoteric, exotic, exterior, extern, externe, extramural, extraneous, extrinsic, foreign, independent, outer, outermost, outside, outward, superficial, surface, visible.
antonym internal.

extinct *adj.* abolished, dead, defunct, doused, ended, exterminated, extinguished, gone, inactive, lost, obsolete, out, quenched, terminated, vanished, void.
antonyms extant, living.

extinction *n.* abolition, annihilation, death, destruction, eradication, excision, extermination, extinguishment, extirpation, obliteration, oblivion, quietus.

extinguish *v.* abolish, annihilate, destroy, douse, dout, eliminate, end, eradicate, erase, expunge, exterminate, extirpate, kill, obscure, put out, quench, remove, slake, smother, snuff out, stifle, suppress.

extol *v.* acclaim, applaud, celebrate, commend, cry up, eulogize, exalt, glorify, laud, magnify, panegyrize, praise, puff.
antonyms blame, denigrate.

extort *v.* blackmail, bleed, bully, coerce, exact, extract, force, milk, squeeze, wrest, wring.

extra *adj.* accessory, added, additional, ancillary, auxiliary, excess, extraneous, for good measure, fresh, further, gash, inessential, leftover, more, needless, new, other, redundant, reserve, spare, supererogatory, superfluous, super-numerary, supplemental, supplementary, surplus, unnecessary, unneeded, unused.
antonym integral.
n. accessory, addendum, addition, adjunct, affix, appendage, appurtenance, attachment, bonus, complement, extension, lagniappe, plus(s)age, supernumerary, supplement.
adv. especially, exceptionally, extraordinarily, extremely, particularly, remarkably, uncommonly, unusually.

extract *v.* abstract, choose, cite, cull, decoct, deduce, derive, develop, distil, draw, draw out, educe, elicit, enucleate, evoke, evolve, evulse, exact, express, extirpate, gather, get, glean, obtain, quote, reap, remove, select, uproot, withdraw, wrest, wring.
antonym insert.
n. abstract, apozem, citation, clip, clipping, concentrate, cutting, decoction, decocture, distillate, distillation, essence, excerpt, juice, passage, quotation, selection.

extraordinary *adj.* amazing, bizarre, curious, exceptional, fantastic, marvelous, notable, noteworthy, odd, outstanding, particular, peculiar, phenomenal, rare, remarkable, significant, singular, special, strange, striking, surprising, uncommon, uncontemplated, unfamiliar, unheard-of, unimaginable, unique, unprecedented, unusual, unwonted, weird, wonderful.
antonyms commonplace, ordinary.

extravagant *adj.* absurd, costly, exaggerated, excessive, exorbitant, expensive, extortionate, fanciful, fancy, fantastic, flamboyant, flashy, foolish, garish, gaudy, grandiose, hyperbolic, hyperbolical, immoderate, improvident, imprudent, inordinate, lavish, ornate, ostentatious, outrageous, outré, overpriced, preposterous, pretentious, prodigal, profligate, reckless, showy, spendthrift, steep, thriftless, unreasonable, unrestrained, unthrifty, wasteful, wild.
antonyms moderate, thrifty.

extreme *adj.* acute, deep-dyed, dire, double-dyed, downright, Draconian, drastic, egregious, exaggerated, exceptional, excessive, exquisite, extraordinary, extravagant, fanatical, faraway, far-off, farthest, final, great, greatest, harsh, high, highest, immoderate, inordinate, intemperate, intense, last, maximum, out-and-out, outermost, outrageous, radical, red-hot, remarkable, remotest, rigid, severe, sheer, stern, strict, supreme,

terminal, ultimate, ultra, unbending, uncommon, uncompromising, unconventional, unreasonable, unusual, utmost, utter, uttermost, worst, zealous.
antonyms mild, moderate.
n. acme, apex, apogee, boundary, climax, consummation, depth, edge, end, excess, extremity, height, limit, maximum, minimum, nadir, peak, pinnacle, pole, termination, top, ultimate, utmost, zenith.

extremism *n.* fanaticism, radicalism, terrorism, ultraism, zeal, zealotism, zealotry.
antonym moderation.

extricate *v.* clear, deliver, disembarrass, disembrangle, disembroil, disengage, disentangle, disintricate, free, liberate, release, relieve, remove, rescue, withdraw.
antonym involve.

exuberant *adj.* abundant, animated, baroque, buoyant, cheerful, copious, eager, ebullient, effervescent, effusive, elated, energetic, enthusiastic, exaggerated, excessive, excited, exhilarated, fulsome, high-spirited, lavish, lively, lush, luxuriant, overdone, overflowing, plenteous, plentiful, prodigal, profuse, rambunctious, rank, rich, sparkling, spirited, sprightly, superabundant, superfluous, teeming, vigorous, vivacious, zestful.
antonyms apathetic, lifeless, scant.

exult *v.* boast, brag, celebrate, crow, delight, gloat, glory, jubilate, rejoice, relish, revel, taunt, triumph.

eye *n.* appreciation, belief, discernment, discrimination, eyeball, glim, judgment, keeker, mind, opinion, optic, orb, peeper, perception, recognition, taste, viewpoint.
v. contemplate, examine, eye up, gaze at, glance at, inspect, leer at, look at, make eyes at, observe, ogle, peruse, regard, scan, scrutinize, stare at, study, survey, view, watch.

F

fable *n.* allegory, apologue, fabliau, fabrication, fairy story, falsehood, fantasy, fib, fiction, figment, invention, legend, lie, Märchen, myth, narrative, old wives' tale, parable, romance, saga, story, tale, tall story, untruth, yarn.

fabled *adj.* fabulous, famed, famous, feigned, fictional, legendary, mythical, renowned, storied.
antonym unknown.

fabric *n.* cloth, constitution, construction, foundations, framework, infrastructure, make-up, material, organization, structure, stuff, textile, texture, web.

fabricate *v.* assemble, build, coin, concoct, construct, create, devise, erect, fake, falsify, fashion, feign, forge, form, frame, invent, make, manufacture, shape, trump up.

fabrication *n.* assemblage, assembly, building, cock-and-bull story, concoction, construction, erection, fable, fairy story, fake, falsehood, fiction, figment, forgery, frame-up, invention, lie, manufacture, myth, production, story, untruth.
antonym truth.

fabulous *adj.* amazing, apocryphal, astounding, breathtaking, fabled, false, fantastic, feigned, fictitious, imaginary, immense, inconceivable, incredible, invented, legendary, marvelous, mythical, phenomenal, renowned, spectacular, superb, unbelievable, unreal, wonderful.
antonyms moderate, real, small.

façade *n.* appearance, cloak, cover, disguise, exterior, face, front, frontage, guise, mask, pretense, semblance, show, veil, veneer.

face *n.* air, appearance, aspect, assurance, audacity, authority, boatrace, boldness, brass neck, cheek, confidence, countenance, cover, dial, dignity, disguise, display, effrontery, expression, exterior, façade, facet, favor, features, front, frown, gall, grimace, honor, image, impudence, kisser, lineaments, look, mask, metope, moue, mug, nerve, outside, phiz, phizog, physiognomy, pout, prestige, presumption, pretence, reputation, sauce, scowl, self-respect, semblance, show, side, smirk, snoot, standing, status, surface, visage.
v. clad, coat, confront, cope with, cover, deal with, defy, dress, encounter, experience, finish, front, give on to, level, line, meet, oppose, overlay, overlook, sheathe, surface, tackle, veneer.

facet *n.* angle, aspect, characteristic, face, feature, part, phase, plane, point, side, slant, surface.

facetious *adj.* amusing, comical, droll, facete, flippant, frivolous, funny, humorous, jesting, jocose, jocular, merry, playful, pleasant, tongue-in-cheek, unserious, waggish, witty.
antonym serious.

facile *adj.* adept, adroit, complaisant, cursory, dexterous, easy, effortless, fluent, glib, hasty, light, plausible, proficient, quick, ready, shallow, simple, skilful, slick, smooth, superficial, uncomplicated, yielding.
antonyms clumsy, implausible, profound.

facilitate *v.* assist, ease, expedite, forward, further, grease, help, promote, speed up.

facilities *n.* amenity, appliance, convenience, equipment, means, mod cons, opportunity, prerequisites, resource.

facility *n.* ability, adeptness, adroitness, bent, dexterity, ease, efficiency, effortlessness, expertness, fluency, gift, knack, proficiency, quickness, readiness, skilfulness, skill, smoothness, talent, turn.

facsimile *n.* carbon, carbon copy, copy, duplicate, image, mimeograph, photocopy, Photostat®;, print, replica, repro, reproduction, transcript, Xerox®;.

fact *n.* act, actuality, certainty, circumstance, datum, deed, detail, event, fait accompli, feature, gospel, happening, incident, item, occurrence, particular, point, reality, specific, truth.

faction[1] *n.* band, bloc, cabal, cadre, camp, caucus, clique, coalition, combination, confederacy, contingent, coterie, crowd, division, gang, ginger group, group, junta, lobby, minority, party, pressure group, ring, section, sector, set, splinter group, splinter party, troop.

faction[2] *n.* conflict, disagreement, discord, disharmony, dissension, disunity, division, divisiveness, fighting, friction, infighting, quarreling, rebellion, sedition, strife, tumult, turbulence.
antonyms agreement, peace.

factitious *adj.* affected, artificial, assumed, contrived, counterfeit, engineered, fabricated, fake, false, imitation, insincere, made-up, manufactured, mock, phony, pinchbeck, pretended, put-on, sham, simulated, spurious, supposititious, synthetic, unnatural, unreal.
antonym genuine.

factor *n.* agent, aspect, cause, circumstance, component, consideration, deputy, determinant, element, estate manager, influence, item, joker, middleman, parameter, part, point, reeve, steward, thing, unknown quantity.

factory *n.* hacienda, manufactory, mill, plant, shop, shop-floor, works.

factual *adj.* accurate, authentic, circumstantial, close, correct, credible, detailed, exact, faithful, genuine, literal, objective, precise, real, straight, sure, true, unadorned, unbiased, veritable.
antonym false.

faculty[1] *n.* academics, department, discipline, lecturers, profession, school, staff.

faculty[2] *n.* ability, adroitness, aptitude, bent, brainpower, capability, capacity, cleverness, dexterity, facility, gift, knack, power, propensity, readiness, skill, talent, turn.

faculty[3] *n.* authorization, authority, license, prerogative, privilege, right.

fad *n.* affectation, craze, crotchet, fancy, fashion, mania, mode, rage, trend, vogue, whim.

fade *v.* blanch, bleach, blench, decline, die, dim, diminish, disappear, discolor, disperse, dissolve, droop, dull, dwindle, ebb, etiolate, evanesce, fail, fall, flag, languish, pale, perish, shrivel, vanish, wane, wilt, wither, yellow.

fagged *adj.* all in, beat, exhausted, fatigued, jaded, jiggered, knackered, on one's last legs, wasted, weary, worn out, zonked.
antonym refreshed.

fail *v.* abandon, cease, come to grief, conk out, crack up, crash, cut out, decline, desert, die, disappoint, droop, dwindle, fade, fall, flop, flub, flunk, fold, forget, forsake, founder, fudge, give out, give up, go bankrupt, go bust, go to the wall, go under, gutter, languish, lay an egg, let down, miscarry, misfire, miss, miss one's trip, neglect, omit, peter out, plow, sink, smash, underachieve, underperform, wane, weaken.
antonyms gain, improve, prosper, succeed.

failing *n.* blemish, blind spot, decay, decline, defect, deficiency, deterioration, drawback, error, failure, fault, flaw, foible, frailty, hamartia, imperfection, lapse, miscarriage, misfortune, peccadillo, shortcoming, weakness.
antonyms advantage, strength.
adj. collapsing, decaying, declining, deteriorating, drooping, dwindling, dying, flagging, languishing, moribund, waning, weak, weakening.
antonyms thriving, vigorous.
prep. in default of, in the absence of, lacking, wanting, without.

failure *n.* abortion, also-ran, bankruptcy, breakdown, bummer, collapse, crash, cropper, damp squib, dead duck, decay, decline, default, defeat, deficiency, dereliction, deterioration, disappointment, downfall, dud, failing, fiasco, flivver, flop, folding, frost, frustration, goner, incompetent, insolvency, loser, loss, miscarriage, neglect, negligence, no-hoper, non-performance, omission, remissness, ruin, shortcoming, slip-up, stoppage, turkey, unsuccess, wash-out, wreck.
antonym success.

faint *adj.* bleached, delicate, dim, distant, dizzy, drooping, dull, enervated, exhausted, faded, faltering, fatigued, feeble, feint, giddy, hazy, hushed, ill-defined, indistinct, languid, lethargic, light, light-headed, low, muffled, muted, muzzy, remote, slight, soft, subdued, thin, unenthusiastic, vague, vertiginous, weak, whispered, woozy.
antonyms clear, strong.
v. black out, collapse, droop, drop, flag, flake out, keel over, pass out, swoon.
n. blackout, collapse, deliquium, swoon, syncope, unconsciousness.

fair[1] *adj.* adequate, all right, average, beauteous, beautiful, bonny, bright, clean, clear, clement, cloudless, comely, decent, disinterested, dispassionate, dry, equal, equitable, even-handed, favorable, fine, handsome, honest, honorable, impartial, just, lawful, legitimate, lovely, mediocre, middling, moderate, not bad, objective, OK, on the level, passable, pretty, proper, reasonable, respectable, satisfactory, so-so, square, sunny, sunshiny, tolerable, trustworthy, unbiased, unclouded, unprejudiced, upright, well-favored.
antonyms cloudy, inclement, poor, unfair.

fair[2] *adj.* blond(e), fair-haired, fair-headed, flaxen, light, tow-headed.
antonym dark.

fair[3] *n.* bang, bazaar, carnival, expo, exposition, festival, fête, gaff, gala, kermis, market, show.

fairly *adv.* absolutely, adequately, deservedly, equitably, ex aequo, fully, honestly, impartially, justly, moderately, objectively, plainly, positively, pretty, properly, quite, rather, really, reasonably, somewhat, tolerably, unbiasedly, veritably.
antonym unfairly.

fairness *n.* decency, disinterestedness, equitableness, equity, impartiality, justice, legitimacy, legitimateness, rightfulness, rightness, unbiasedness, uprightness.
antonym unfairness.

fairy *n.* brownie, buggane, elf, fay, fée, hob, hobgoblin, leprechaun, Mab, peri, pisky, pixie, Robin Goodfellow, rusalka, sprite.

faith *n.* allegiance, assurance, belief, church, communion, confidence, constancy, conviction, credence, credit, creed, denomination, dependence, dogma, faithfulness, fealty, fidelity, honesty, honor, loyalty, persuasion, pledge, promise, reliance, religion, sincerity, trust, truth, truthfulness, uberrima fides, vow, word, word of honor.
antonyms mistrust, treachery, unfaithfulness.

faithful *adj.* accurate, attached, card-carrying, close, constant, convinced, dependable, devoted, exact, just, leal, loyal, precise, reliable, soothfast, soothful, staunch, steadfast, strict, true, true-blue, true-hearted, trusty, truthful, unswerving, unwavering.
antonyms disloyal, inaccurate, treacherous.
n. adherents, believers, brethren, communicants, congregation, followers, supporters.

faithless *adj.* adulterous, delusive, disloyal, doubting, false, false-hearted, fickle, inconstant, perfidious, punic, recreant, traitorous, treacherous, unbelieving, unfaithful, unreliable, untrue, untrustworthy, untruthful.
antonyms believing, faithful.

fake *v.* affect, assume, copy, counterfeit, fabricate, feign, forge, phony, pretend, put on, sham, simulate.

n. charlatan, copy, forgery, fraud, hoax, imitant, imitation, impostor, mountebank, phony, reproduction, sham, simulation.
adj. affected, artificial, assumed, bastard, bogus, counterfeit, ersatz, false, forged, hyped up, imitation, mock, phony, pinchbeck, pretended, pseudo, reproduction, sham, simulated, spurious.
antonym genuine.

fall *v.* abate, backslide, become, befall, capitulate, cascade, chance, collapse, come about, come to pass, crash, decline, decrease, depreciate, descend, die, diminish, dive, drop, drop down, dwindle, ebb, err, fall away, fall off, fall out, flag, give in, give up, give way, go a purler, go astray, go down, happen, incline, keel over, lapse, lessen, measure one's length, meet one's end, nose-dive, occur, offend, perish, pitch, plummet, plunge, push, resign, settle, sin, sink, slope, slump, souse, stumble, subside, succumb, surrender, take place, topple, transgress, trespass, trip, trip over, tumble, yield, yield to temptation.
antonym rise.
n. capitulation, collapse, cropper, cut, death, decline, declivity, decrease, defeat, degradation, descent, destruction, diminution, dip, dive, downfall, downgrade, drop, dwindling, failure, incline, lapse, lessening, lowering, nose-dive, overthrow, plummet, plunge, pusher, reduction, resignation, ruin, sin, slant, slip, slope, slump, souse, spill, surrender, transgression, tumble, voluntary.
antonym rise.

fallacious *adj.* casuistical, deceptive, delusive, delusory, erroneous, false, fictitious, illogical, illusory, incorrect, misleading, mistaken, sophistic, sophistical, spurious, untrue, wrong.
antonyms correct, true.

fallacy *n.* casuistry, deceit, deception, deceptiveness, delusion, error, falsehood, faultiness, flaw, illusion, inconsistency, misapprehension, misconception, mistake, sophism, sophistry, untruth.
antonym truth.

fallow *adj.* dormant, idle, inactive, inert, resting, uncultivated, undeveloped, unplanted, unsown, untilled, unused.

false *adj.* artificial, bastard, bogus, concocted, counterfeit, deceitful, deceiving, deceptive, delusive, dishonest, dishonorable, disloyal, double-dealing, double-faced, duplicitous, erroneous, ersatz, faithless, fake, fallacious, false-hearted, faulty, feigned, fictitious, forged, fraudulent, hypocritical, illusive, imitation, improper, inaccurate, incorrect, inexact, invalid, lying, mendacious, misleading, mistaken, mock, perfidious, postiche, pretended, pseud, pseudo, sham, simulated, spurious, synthetic, treacherous, treasonable, trumped-up, truthless, two-faced, unfaithful, unfounded, unreal, unreliable, unsound, untrue, untrustworthy, untruthful, wrong.
antonyms honest, reliable, true.

falsehood *n.* deceit, deception, dishonesty, dissimulation, fable, fabrication, fib, fiction, inexactitude, inveracity, lie, mendacity, misstatement, perjury, prevarication, pseudery, story, unfact, untruth, untruthfulness.
antonyms truth, truthfulness.

falsify *v.* adulterate, alter, belie, cook, counterfeit, distort, doctor, fake, forge, garble, misrepresent, misstate, pervert, sophisticate, take liberties with, tamper with.

falter *v.* break, fail, flag, flinch, halt, hem and haw, hesitate, shake, stammer, stumble, stutter, totter, tremble, vacillate, waver.

fame *n.* celebrity, credit, eminence, esteem, glory, honor, illustriousness, kudos, name, prominence, renown, reputation, repute, stardom.

famed *adj.* acclaimed, celebrated, famous, noted, recognized, renowned, well-known, widely-known.
antonym unknown.

familiar *adj.* abreast, accustomed, acquainted, amicable, au courant, au fait, aware, bold, chummy, close, common, common-or-garden, confidential, conscious, conventional, conversant, cordial, customary, disrespectful, domestic, easy, everyday, forward, free, free-and-easy, frequent, friendly, household, impudent, informal, intimate, intrusive, knowledgeable, mundane, near, open, ordinary, overfree, presuming, presumptuous, private, recognizable, relaxed, repeated, routine, stock, unceremonious, unconstrained, unreserved, versed, well-known.
antonyms formal, reserved, unfamiliar, unversed.

familiarity *n.* acquaintance, acquaintanceship, awareness, boldness, cheek, closeness, conversance, disrespect, ease, experience, fellowship, forwardness, freedom, friendliness, grasp, impertinence, impudence, informality, intimacy, liberties, liberty, license, naturalness, openness, presumption, sociability, unceremoniousness, understanding.
antonyms formality, reservation, unfamiliarity.

familiarize *v.* acclimatize, accustom, brief, coach, habituate, instruct, inure, prime, school, season, train.

family *n.* ancestors, ancestry, birth, blood, brood, children, clan, class, classification, descendants, descent, dynasty, extraction, folk, forebears, forefathers, genealogy, genre, group, house, household, issue, kin, kind, kindred, kinsmen, kith and kin, line, lineage, ménage, network, offspring, parentage, pedigree, people, progeny, quiverful, race, relations, relatives, sept, stemma, stirps, strain, subdivision, system, tribe.

family tree ancestry, extraction, genealogy, line, lineage, pedigree, stemma, stirps.

famine *n.* dearth, destitution, hunger, scarcity, starvation, want.
antonym plenty.

famous *adj.* acclaimed, celebrated, conspicuous, distinguished, eminent, excellent, famed, far-famed, glorious, great, honored, illustrious, legendary, lionized,

notable, noted, prominent, remarkable, renowned, signal, well-known.
antonym unknown.

fan[1] *v.* aggravate, agitate, air-condition, air-cool, arouse, blow, cool, enkindle, excite, impassion, increase, provoke, refresh, rouse, stimulate, stir up, ventilate, whip up, winnow, work up.
n. air-conditioner, blower, extractor fan, flabellum, propeller, punkah, vane, ventilator.

fan[2] *n.* adherent, admirer, aficionado, buff, devotee, enthusiast, fiend, follower, freak, groupie, lover, rooter, supporter, zealot.

fanatic *n.* activist, addict, bigot, demoniac, devotee, energumen, enthusiast, extremist, fiend, freak, militant, visionary, zealot.

fancy *v.* be attracted to, believe, conceive, conjecture, crave, desire, dream of, favor, go for, guess, hanker after, have an eye for, imagine, infer, like, long for, lust after, picture, prefer, reckon, relish, suppose, surmise, take a liking to, take to, think, think likely, whim, wish for, yearn for, yen for.
antonym dislike.
n. caprice, chim(a)era, conception, daydream, delusion, desire, dream, fantasy, fondness, hankering, humor, idea, image, imagination, impression, impulse, inclination, liking, nightmare, notion, partiality, penchant, phantasm, predilection, preference, relish, thought, urge, vapor, velleity, vision, whim.
antonyms dislike, fact, reality.
adj. baroque, capricious, chimerical, decorated, decorative, delusive, elaborate, elegant, embellished, extravagant, fanciful, fantastic, far-fetched, illusory, ornamented, ornate, rococo, whimsical.
antonym plain.

fantastic *adj.* absurd, ambitious, capricious, chimerical, comical, eccentric, enormous, excellent, exotic, extravagant, extreme, fanciful, fantasque, far-fetched, first-rate, freakish, grandiose, great, grotesque, illusory, imaginative, implausible, incredible, irrational, ludicrous, mad, marvelous, odd, out of this world, outlandish, outré, overwhelming, peculiar, phantasmagorical, preposterous, quaint, queer, ridiculous, rococo, sensational, severe, strange, superb, tremendous, unlikely, unreal, unrealistic, visionary, weird, whimsical, wild, wonderful.
antonyms ordinary, plain, poor.

fantasy *n.* apparition, caprice, creativity, daydream, delusion, dream, dreamery, fancy, fantasia, fantasque, flight of fancy, hallucination, illusion, imagination, invention, mirage, nightmare, originality, phantasy, pipe-dream, reverie, vision, whimsy.
antonym reality.

far *adv.* a good way, a long way, afar, considerably, decidedly, deep, extremely, greatly, incomparably, miles, much.
antonym near.
adj. distal, distant, faraway, far-flung, far-off, far-removed, further, god-forsaken, long, opposite, other, outlying, out-of-the-way, remote, removed.
antonyms close, nearby.

fare[1] *n.* charge, cost, fee, passage, passenger, pick-up, price, traveler.

fare[2] *n.* board, commons, diet, eatables, food, meals, menu, provisions, rations, sustenance, table, victuals.

fare[3] *v.* be, do, get along, get on, go, go on, happen, make out, manage, proceed, prosper, turn out.

farewell *n.* adieu, departure, good-bye, leave-taking, parting, send-off, valediction.
antonym hello.
adj. final, parting, valedictory.
interj. aloha, bye-bye, cheers, ciao, good-bye.

farm *n.* acreage, acres, bowery, croft, farmstead, grange, holding, homestead, kolkhoz, land, mains, plantation, ranch, smallholding, station.
v. cultivate, operate, plant, till, work the land.

fascinate *v.* absorb, allure, beguile, bewitch, captivate, charm, delight, enchant, engross, enrapture, enravish, enthrall, entrance, hypnotize, infatuate, intrigue, mesmerize, rivet, spellbind, transfix.
antonym bore.

fashion *n.* appearance, attitude, beau monde, configuration, convention, craze, custom, cut, demeanor, dernier cri, description, fad, figure, form, guise, haut ton, haute couture, high society, jet set, kind, latest, line, look, make, manner, method, mode, model, mold, pattern, rage, shape, sort, style, trend, type, usage, vogue, way.
v. accommodate, adapt, adjust, alter, construct, contrive, create, design, fit, forge, form, make, manufacture, mold, shape, suit, tailor, work.

fashionable *adj.* à la mode, alamode, all the rage, chic, chichi, contemporary, current, customary, funky, genteel, in, in vogue, latest, modern, modish, popular, prevailing, smart, snazzy, stylish, swagger, tippy, tony, tonish, trend-setting, trendy, up-to-date, up-to-the-minute, usual, with it.
antonym unfashionable.

fast[1] *adj.* accelerated, brisk, fleet, flying, hasty, hurried, mercurial, nippy, quick, rapid, spanking, speedy, swift, winged.
antonym slow.
adv. apace, hastily, hell for leather, hurriedly, like a flash, like a shot, posthaste, presto, quickly, rapidly, speedily, swiftly, ventre à terre.
antonym slowly.

fast[2] *adj.* close, constant, fastened, firm, fixed, fortified, immovable, impregnable, lasting, loyal, permanent, secure, sound, staunch, steadfast, tight, unflinching, unwavering.
antonyms impermanent, loose.
adv. close, deeply, firmly, fixedly, near, rigidly, securely, soundly, sound(ly), tightly, unflinchingly.
antonym loosely.

fast[3] *adj.* dissipated, dissolute, extravagant, immoral, intemperate, licentious, loose, profligate, promiscuous, rakehell, rakehelly, rakish, reckless, self-indulgent, wanton, whorish, wild.
antonyms chaste, moral.

fast[4] *v.* abstain, bant, diet, go hungry, starve.
n. abstinence, diet, fasting, starvation, xerophagy.
antonyms gluttony, self-indulgence.

fasten *v.* affix, aim, anchor, attach, belay, bend, bind, bolt, chain, clamp, concentrate, connect, direct, fix, focus, grip, infibulate, join, lace, link, lock, nail, rivet, seal, secure, spar, tie, unite.
antonym unfasten.

fastidious *adj.* choosy, critical, dainty, difficult, discriminating, finical, finicky, fussy, hypercritical, meticulous, overnice, particular, pernickety, picky, precise, punctilious, squeamish.
antonym undemanding.

fat *adj.* abdominous, adipose, affluent, beefy, blowzy, corpulent, cushy, elephantine, fatling, fatty, fertile, fleshed, fleshy, flourishing, fozy, fruitful, greasy, gross, heavy, jammy, lucrative, lush, obese, oily, oleaginous, overweight, paunchy, pinguid, plump, poddy, podgy, portly, pot-bellied, productive, profitable, prosperous, pudgy, remunerative, rich, roly-poly, rotund, round, solid, squab, stout, suety, thriving, tubbish, tubby, well-upholstered.
antonyms thin, unproductive.
n. adipose tissue, blubber, brown fat, cellulite, corpulence, degras, embonpoint, fatness, flab, obesity, overweight, paunch, pot (belly), speck.

fatal *adj.* baleful, baneful, calamitous, catastrophic, deadly, destructive, disastrous, final, incurable, killing, lethal, malignant, mortal, mortiferous, mortific, pernicious, ruinous, terminal, vital.
antonym harmless.

fatality *n.* casualty, deadliness, death, disaster, lethalness, loss, mortality, unavoidability.

fate *n.* chance, cup, death, destiny, destruction, divine will, doom, downfall, end, fortune, future, horoscope, issue, joss, karma, kismet, lot, Moira, nemesis, outcome, portion, predestination, predestiny, providence, ruin, stars, upshot, weird.

father *n.* abbé, ancestor, architect, author, begetter, confessor, creator, curé, dad, daddy, elder, forebear, forefather, founder, generant, genitor, governor, inventor, leader, maker, old boy, old man, originator, pa, padre, papa, pappy, parent, pastor, pater, paterfamilias, patriarch, patron, pop, poppa, pops, predecessor, priest, prime mover, procreator, progenitor, senator, sire.
v. beget, conceive, create, dream up, engender, establish, found, get, institute, invent, originate, procreate, produce, sire.

fatherland *n.* home, homeland, mother-country, motherland, native land, old country.

fatherly *adj.* affectionate, avuncular, benevolent, benign, forbearing, indulgent, kind, kindly, paternal, patriarchal, protective, supportive, tender.
antonyms cold, harsh, unkind.

fathom *v.* comprehend, deduce, divine, estimate, gauge, get to the bottom of, grasp, interpret, measure, penetrate, plumb, plummet, probe, see, sound, understand, work out.

fatigue *v.* do in, drain, exhaust, fag, jade, knacker, overtire, shatter, tire, weaken, wear out, weary, whack.
antonym refresh.
n. debility, decay, degeneration, ennui, failure, heaviness, languor, lethargy, listlessness, overtiredness, tiredness.
antonyms energy, freshness.

fault *n.* accountability, blemish, blunder, boner, boob, booboo, culpability, defect, deficiency, delict, delinquency, demerit, dislocation, drawback, error, failing, flaw, frailty, goof, hamartia, imperfection, inaccuracy, indiscretion, infirmity, lack, lapse, liability, misconduct, misdeed, misdemeanor, mistake, negligence, offense, omission, oversight, peccadillo, responsibility, shortcoming, sin, slip, slip-up, snag, solecism, transgression, trespass, weakness, wrong.
antonyms advantage, strength.
v. blame, call to account, censure, criticize, find fault with, impugn, pick a hole in someone's coat, pick at, pick holes in.
antonym praise.

faulty *adj.* bad, blemished, broken, casuistic, damaged, defective, erroneous, fallacious, flawed, illogical, impaired, imperfect, imprecise, inaccurate, incorrect, invalid, malfunctioning, out of order, specious, unsound, weak, wrong.

favor *n.* acceptance, approbation, approval, backing, badge, benefit, bias, boon, championship, courtesy, decoration, esteem, favoritism, friendliness, gift, good turn, goodwill, grace indulgence, keepsake, kindness, knot, love-token, memento, obligement, partiality, patronage, present, regard, rosette, service, smile, souvenir, support, token.
antonym disfavor.
v. abet, accommodate, advance, advocate, aid, approve, assist, back, befriend, champion, choose, commend, countenance, ease, encourage, esteem, extenuate, facilitate, fancy, have in one's good books, help, indulge, like, oblige, opt for, pamper, patronize, prefer, promote, resemble, spare, spoil, succor, support, take after, take kindly to, value.
antonyms disfavor, hinder, thwart.

favorite *adj.* best-loved, choice, dearest, esteemed, favored, pet, preferred.
antonyms hated, unfavorite.
n. beloved, blue-eyed boy, choice, darling, dear, form horse, idol, pet, pick, preference, teacher's pet, the apple of one's eye, whitehead, whiteheaded boy.
antonym pet hate.

favoritism *n.* bias, biasedness, injustice, jobs for the boys, nepotism, old school tie, one-sidedness, partiality, partisanship, preference, preferential treatment.
antonym impartiality.

fear *n.* agitation, alarm, anxiety, apprehension, apprehensiveness, awe, bogey, bugbear, concern, consternation, cravenness, danger, dismay, disquietude, distress, doubt, dread, foreboding(s), fright, funk, heart-quake, horror, likelihood, misgiving(s), nightmare, panic, phobia, phobism, qualms, reverence, risk, solicitude, specter, suspicion, terror, timidity, tremors, trepidation, unease, uneasiness, veneration, wonder, worry.
antonyms courage, fortitude.
v. anticipate, apprehend, dread, expect, foresee, respect, reverence, shudder at, suspect, take fright, tremble, venerate, worry.

fearless *adj.* aweless, bold, brave, confident, courageous, daring, dauntless, doughty, gallant, game, gutsy, heroic, impavid, indomitable, intrepid, lion-hearted, plucky, unabashed, unafraid, unapprehensive, unblenching, unblinking, undaunted, unflinching, valiant, valorous.
antonyms afraid, timid.

feast *n.* banquet, barbecue, beanfeast, beano, binge, blowout, carousal, carouse, celebration, delight, dinner, enjoyment, entertainment, epulation, festival, fête, gala day, gaudy, gratification, holiday, holy day, jollification, junket, pig, pleasure, repast, revels, saint's day, spread, treat.
v. delight, eat one's fill, entertain, gladden, gorge, gormandize, gratify, indulge, overindulge, regale, rejoice, stuff, stuff one's face, thrill, treat, wine and dine.

feat *n.* accomplishment, achievement, act, attainment, deed, exploit, gest(e), performance.

feature *n.* article, aspect, attraction, attribute, character, characteristic, column, comment, draw, facet, factor, hallmark, highlight, innovation, item, lineament, mark, peculiarity, piece, point, property, quality, report, special, specialty, story, trait.
v. accentuate, emphasize, headline, highlight, play up, present, promote, push, recommend, show, spotlight, star.

fee *n.* account, bill, charge, compensation, emolument, hire, honorarium, pay, payment, recompense, remuneration, retainer, terms, toll.

feeble *adj.* debilitated, delicate, doddering, effete, enervated, enfeebled, exhausted, failing, faint, flat, flimsy, forceless, frail, fushionless, inadequate, incompetent, indecisive, ineffective, ineffectual, inefficient, inform, insignificant, insufficient, lame, languid, paltry, poor, powerless, puny, shilpit, sickly, silly, slight, tame, thin, unconvincing, vacillating, weak, weakened, weakly.
antonyms strong, worthy.

feed *v.* augment, bolster, cater for, dine, eat, encourage, fare, foster, fuel, graze, grub, nourish, nurture, pasture, provide for, provision, strengthen, subsist, supply, sustain, victual.
n. banquet, feast, fodder, food, forage, meal, nosh, pasturage, pasture, provender, repast, silage, spread, tuck-in, victuals.

feed in inject, input, key in, supply.

feed on consume, devour, eat, exist on, live on, partake of.

feel *v.* appear, believe, caress, consider, deem, empathize, endure, enjoy, experience, explore, finger, fondle, fumble, go through, grope, handle, have, have a hunch, hold, intuit, judge, know, manipulate, maul, notice, observe, paw, perceive, reckon, resemble, seem, sense, sound, stroke, suffer, take to heart, test, think, touch, try, undergo.
n. bent, feeling, finish, gift, impression, knack, quality, sense, surface, texture, touch, vibes.

feeling *n.* (a)esthesia, (a)esthesis, affection, air, ambience, appreciation, apprehension, ardor, atmosphere, aura, compassion, concern, consciousness, emotion, empathy, Empfindung, feel, fervor, fondness, heat, hunch, idea, impression, inclination, inkling, instinct, intensity, mood, notion, opinion, passion, perception, pity, point of view, presentiment, quality, sensation, sense, sensibility, sensitivity, sentiment, sentimentality, suspicion, sympathy, touch, understanding, vibes, vibrations, view, warmth.

fellowship *n.* amity, association, brotherhood, camaraderie, club, communion, companionability, companionableness, companionship, endowment, familiarity, fraternization, fraternity, guild, intercourse, intimacy, kindliness, league, order, sisterhood, sociability, society, sodality.

feminine *adj.* delicate, effeminate, effete, gentle, girlish, graceful, ladylike, modest, petticoat, sissy, soft, tender, unmanly, unmasculine, weak, womanish, womanly.
antonym masculine.

ferocious *adj.* barbaric, barbarous, bloodthirsty, bloody, brutal, brutish, catamountain, cruel, fearsome, feral, fiendish, fierce, homicidal, inhuman, merciless, murderous, pitiless, predatory, rapacious, ravening, relentless, ruthless, sadistic, sanguinary, savage, truculent, vicious, violent, wild.
antonyms gentle, mild.

fertile *adj.* abundant, fat, fecund, feracious, flowering, fructiferous, fructuous, frugiferous, fruit-bearing, fruitful, generative, lush, luxuriant, plenteous, plentiful, potent, productive, prolific, rich, teeming, uberous, virile, yielding.
antonyms arid, barren.

festival *n.* anniversary, carnival, celebration, commemoration, eisteddfod, entertainment, feast, festa, festivities, fête, field day, fiesta, gala, holiday, holy day, jubilee, junketing, merry-make, merrymaking, merry-night, mod, puja, saint's day, treat.

festive *adj.* carnival, celebratory, cheery, Christmassy, convivial, cordial, en fête, festal, festivous, gala, gay, gleeful, happy, hearty, holiday, jolly, jovial, joyful, joyous, jubilant, merry, mirthful, rollicking, sportive, uproarious.
antonyms gloomy, sober, somber.

fetch *v.* be good for, bring, bring in, carry, conduct, convey, deliver, draw, earn, elicit, escort, evoke, get, go for, lead, make, obtain, produce, realize, retrieve, sell for, transport, uplift, utter, yield.

fetching *adj.* alluring, attractive, beguiling, captivating, charming, cute, disarming, enchanting, enticing, fascinating, pretty, sweet, taking, winning, winsome.
antonym repellent.

feud *n.* animosity, antagonism, argument, bad blood, bickering, bitterness, conflict, contention, disagreement, discord, dispute, dissension, enmity, estrangement, faction, feuding, grudge, hostility, ill will, quarrel, rivalry, row, strife, variance, vendetta.
antonyms agreement, peace.
v. altercate, argue, be at odds, bicker, brawl, clash, contend, dispute, duel, fight, quarrel, row, squabble, war, wrangle.
antonym agree.

fever *n.* agitation, calenture, delirium, ecstasy, excitement, febricity, febricula, febricule, ferment, fervor, feverishness, flush, frenzy, heat, intensity, passion, pyrexia, restlessness, temperature, turmoil, unrest.

fiber *n.* backbone, bast, caliber, character, courage, determination, essence, fibril, filament, filasse, funicle, grit, guts, nature, nerve, pile, pluck, quality, resolution, sinew, spirit, stamina, staple, strand, strength, substance, temperament, tenacity, tendril, texture, thread, toughness.

fickle *adj.* capricious, changeable, disloyal, dizzy, erratic, faithless, fitful, flighty, fluctuating, inconstant, irresolute, mercurial, mutable, quicksilver, treacherous, unfaithful, unpredictable, unreliable, unstable, unsteady, vacillating, variable, volage, volageous, volatile, wind-changing.
antonym constant.

fiction *n.* canard, cock-and-bull story, concoction, fable, fabrication, falsehood, fancy, fantasy, feuilleton, fib, figment, imagination, improvisation, invention, legend, lie, myth, novel, parable, romance, story, story-telling, tale, tall story, untruth, whopper, yarn.
antonym truth.

fictitious *adj.* aprocryphal, artificial, assumed, bogus, counterfeit, fabricated, false, fanciful, feigned, fictive, fraudulent, imaginary, imagined, improvised, invented, made-up, make-believe, mythical, non-existent, spurious, supposed, suppositional, supposititious, unreal, untrue.
antonyms genuine, real.

fidelity *n.* accuracy, adherence, allegiance, authenticity, closeness, constancy, correspondence, dedication, dependability, devotedness, devotion, dutifulness, exactitude, exactness, faith, faithfulness, fealty, incorruptibility, integrity, lealty, loyalty, preciseness, precision, reliability, scrupulousness, staunchness, steadfastness, true-heartedness, trustworthiness.
antonyms inaccuracy, inconstancy, treachery.

fidget *v.* bustle, chafe, fiddle, fidge, fike, fret, jerk, jiggle, jitter, jump, mess about, play around, squirm, toy, twitch, worry.
n. agitation, anxiety, creeps, discomposure, edginess, fidgetiness, fidgets, heebie-jeebies, jimjams, jitteriness, jitters, jumpiness, nerves, nerviness, nervousness, restlessness, shakes, twitchiness, unease, uneasiness, willies.

fierce *adj.* baleful, barbarous, blustery, boisterous, brutal, cruel, cut-throat, dangerous, fearsome, fell, feral, ferocious, fiery, frightening, furious, grim, howling, intense, keen, menacing, merciless, murderous, passionate, powerful, raging, relentless, savage, stern, stormy, strong, tempestuous, threatening, truculent, tumultuous, uncontrollable, unrelenting, untamed, vicious, violent, wild.
antonyms calm, gentle, kind.

fiercely *adv.* ardently, bitterly, fanatically, ferociously, furiously, implacably, intensely, keenly, menacingly, mercilessly, murderously, passionately, relentlessly, savagely, sternly, tempestuously, tigerishly, tooth and nail, viciously, violently, wildly, zealously.
antonyms gently, kindly.

fight *v.* altercate, argue, assault, battle, bear arms against, bicker, box, brawl, clash, close, combat, conduct, conflict, contend, contest, cross swords, defy, dispute, do battle, engage, exchange, blows, fence, feud, grapple, joust, lock horns, measure strength, measure swords, mell, mix it, oppose, prosecute, quarrel, resist, scrap, scuffle, skirmish, spar, squabble, stand up to, strive, struggle, take the field, tilt, tussle, wage, wage war, war, withstand, wrangle, wrestle.
n. action, affray, altercation, argument, barney, battle, belligerence, bicker, bout, brawl, brush, clash, combat, conflict, contest, courage, dispute, dissension, dogfight, duel, encounter, engagement, fisticuffs, fracas, fray, free-for-all, gameness, hostilities, joust, luctation, mêlée, mettle, militancy, monomachy, passage of arms, pluck, pugnacity, quarrel, rammy, resilience, resistance, riot, row, ruck, rumble, scrap, scuffle, set-to, skirmish, spirit, strength, struggle, tenacity, tussle, war.

fighter *n.* adventurer, antagonist, battler, belligerent, boxer, brave, bruiser, champion, combatant, contender, contestant, disputant, fighting man, filibuster, free lance, gladiator, man-at-arms, mercenary, militant, prize-fighter, pugilist, soldier, soldier of fortune, swordsman, trouper, warrior, wrestler.

figment *n.* concoction, creation, deception, delusion, fable, fabrication, falsehood, fancy, fiction, illusion, improvisation, invention, mare's nest, production, work.

figure *n.* amount, body, build, celebrity, character, chassis, cipher, configuration, conformation, cost, depiction, design, device, diagram, digit, dignitary, drawing, embellishment, emblem, form, frame, illustration, image, leader, motif, notability, notable, number, numeral, outline, pattern, personage, personality, physique, presence, price, proportions, representation, shadow, shape, sign, silhouette, sketch, somebody, sum, symbol, torso, total, trope, value.
v. act, add, appear, believe, calculate, compute, count, estimate, feature, guess, judge, opine, reckon, sum, surmise, tally, think, tot up, work out.

file[1] *v.* abrade, burnish, furbish, grate, hone, pare, plane, polish, rasp, refine, rub (down), sand, scour, scrape, shape, shave, smooth, trim, whet.

file[2] *n.* binder, cabinet, case, date, documents, dossier, folder, information, portfolio, record.
v. capture, document, enter, memorize, pigeonhole, process, record, register, slot in, store.

file[3] *n.* column, cortège, line, list, procession, queue, row, stream, string, trail, train.
v. defile, march, parade, stream, trail, troop.

fill *v.* assign, block, bung, charge, clog, close, congest, cork, cram, crowd, discharge, drench, engage, englut, engorge, execute, fulfil, furnish, glut, gorge, hold, imbue, impregnate, inflate, load, occupy, officiate, overspread, pack, perform, permeate, pervade, plug, replenish, sate, satiate, satisfy, saturate, seal, soak, stock, stop, stuff, suffuse, supply, surfeit, swell, take up.
antonyms clear, empty.
n. abundance, ample, enough, plenty, sufficiency, sufficient.

fillip *n.* boost, flick, goad, impetus, incentive, prod, push, shove, spice, spur, stimulus, zest.
antonym damper.

filter *v.* clarify, dribble, escape, exude, filtrate, leach, leak, ooze, penetrate, percolate, purify, refine, screen, seep, sieve, sift, strain, transpire, transude, trickle, well. *n.* colander, gauze, membrane, mesh, riddle, sieve, sifter, strainer.

filth *n.* bilge, carrion, coarseness, colluvies, contamination, coprolalia, coprophilia, corruption, crud, defilement, dirt, dirty-mindedness, dung, excrement, excreta, faex, feces, filthiness, foulness, garbage, grime, grossness, gunge, impurity, indecency, muck, nastiness, obscenity, ordure, pollution, pornography, putrefaction, putrescence, refuse, scatology, sewage, slime, sludge, smut, smuttiness, soil, sordes, sordidness, squalor, sullage, uncleanness, vileness, vulgarity.
antonyms cleanliness, decency, purity.

filthy *adj.* Augean, base, bawdy, begrimed, black, blackened, blue, coarse, contemptible, coprolaliac, coprophilous, corrupt, depraved, despicable, dirty, dirty-minded, fecal, feculent, foul, foul-mouthed, grimy, gross, grubby, impure, indecent, lavatorial, lewd, licentious, low, mean, miry, mucky, muddy, nasty, nasty-minded, obscene, offensive, polluted, pornographic, putrid, scatological, scurrilous, slimy, smoky, smutty, sooty, sordid, squalid, suggestive, swinish, unclean, unwashed, vicious, vile, vulgar.
antonyms clean, decent, inoffensive, pure.

final *adj.* absolute, clinching, closing, concluding, conclusive, conclusory, decided, decisive, definite, definitive, desinent, desinential, determinate, dying, eleventh-hour, end, eventual, finished, incontrovertible, irrefragable, irrefutable, irrevocable, last, last-minute, latest, settled, terminal, terminating, ultimate, undeniable.

finalize *v.* agree, clinch, complete, conclude, decide, dispose of, finish, get signed and sealed, get taped, resolve, round off, seal, settle, sew up, tie up, work out, wrap up.

finally *adv.* absolutely, at last, at length, completely, conclusively, convincingly, decisively, definitely, eventually, for ever, for good, for good and all, in conclusion, in the end, inescapably, inexorably, irreversibly, irrevocably, lastly, once and for all, permanently, ultimately.

find *v.* achieve, acquire, ascertain, attain, bring, catch, chance on, come across, consider, contribute, cough up, descry, detect, discover, earn, encounter, espy, experience, expose, ferret out, furnish, gain, get, hit on, judge, learn, light on, locate, meet, note, notice, observe, obtain, perceive, procure, provide, reach, realize, recognize, recover, rediscover, regain, remark, repossess, retrieve, spot, stumble on, supply, think, track down, turn up, uncover, unearth, win.
n. acquisition, asset, bargain, catch, coup, discovery, good buy, unconsidered trifle.

fine[1] *adj.* abstruse, acceptable, acute, admirable, agreeable, all right, attractive, balmy, beau, beaut, beautiful, bonny, brave, braw, bright, brilliant, choice, clear, clement, cloudless, convenient, critical, cutting, dainty, dandy, delicate, diaphanous, discriminating, dry, elegant, elusive, excellent, exceptional, expensive, exquisite, fair, fastidious, fine-drawn, first-class, first-rate, flimsy, four-square, fragile, gauzy, good, good-looking, goodly, gorgeous, gossamer, great, hair-splitting, handsome, honed, hunky-dory, impressive, intelligent, jake, keen, light, lovely, magnificent, masterly, minute, nice, OK, ornate, outstanding, pleasant, polished, powdery, precise, pure, quick, rare, refined, robust, satisfactory, select, sensitive, sharp, sheer, showy, skilful, skilled, slender, small, smart, solid, splendid, sterling, strong, sturdy, stylish, sublime, subtle, suitable, sunny, superior, supreme, tasteful, tenuous, thin, tickety-boo, unalloyed, virtuoso, well-favored, wiredrawn.

fine[2] *v.* amerce, mulct, penalize, punish, sting.

n. amercement, amerciament, damages, forfeit, forfeiture, mulct, penalty, punishment.

finesse *n.* address, adeptness, adroitness, artfulness, artifice, cleverness, craft, deftness, delicacy, diplomacy, discretion, elegance, expertise, gracefulness, know-how, neatness, polish, quickness, refinement, savoir-faire, skill, sophistication, subtlety, tact.
v. bluff, evade, manipulate, maneuver, trick.

finicky *adj.* choosy, critical, dainty, delicate, difficult, fastidious, finical, finicking, fussy, hypercritical, meticulous, nice, nit-picking, overnice, particular, pernickety, scrupulous, squeamish, tricky.
antonyms easy, easy-going.

finish *v.* accomplish, achieve, annihilate, best, buff, burnish, cease, close, coat, complete, conclude, consume, consummate, culminate, deal with, defeat, destroy, devour, discharge, dispatch, dispose of, do, drain, drink, eat, elaborate, empty, encompass, end, execute, exhaust, expend, exterminate, face, finalize, fulfil, get rid of, gild, hone, kill, lacquer, overcome, overpower, overthrow, perfect, polish, put an end to, put the last hand to, refine, round off, rout, ruin, settle, smooth, smooth off, sophisticate, spend, stain, stop, terminate, texture, use (up), veneer, wax, wind up, worst, zap.
n. annihilation, appearance, bankruptcy, burnish, cessation, close, closing, completion, conclusion, coup de grâce, culmination, cultivation, culture, curtain, curtains, death, defeat, dénouement, elaboration, end, end of the road, ending, finale, gloss, grain, liquidation, luster, patina, perfection, polish, refinement, ruin, shine, smoothness, sophistication, surface, termination, texture, wind-up.

fire *n.* animation, ardor, bale-fire, barrage, blaze, bombardment, bonfire, brio, broadside, burning, cannonade, combustion, conflagration, dash, eagerness, earnestness, élan, enthusiasm, excitement, feeling, fervency, fervidity, fervidness, fervor, feu de joie, fierceness, flak, flames, force, fusillade, hail, heat, impetuosity, inferno, intensity, life, light, luster, passion, radiance, salvo, scintillation, shelling, sniping, sparkle, spirit, splendor, verve, vigor, virtuosity, vivacity, volley, warmth, zeal.
v. activate, animate, arouse, boot out, cashier, depose, detonate, discharge, dismiss, eject, electrify, enkindle, enliven, excite, explode, galvanize, give marching orders, give the bum's rush, hurl, ignite, impassion, incite, inflame, inspire, inspirit, kindle, launch, let off, light, loose, put a match to, quicken, rouse, sack, send off, set alight, set fire to, set off, set on fire, shell, shoot, show the door, stimulate, stir, touch off, trigger off, whet.

firm[1] *adj.* abiding, adamant, anchored, balanced, braced, cast-iron, cemented, changeless, committed, compact, compressed, concentrated, congealed, constant, convinced, crisp, definite, dense, dependable, determined, dogged, durable, embedded, enduring, established, fast, fastened, fixed, grounded, hard, hardened, immovable, impregnable, indurate, inelastic, inflexible, iron-hearted, jelled, jellified, motionless, obdurate, reliable, resolute, resolved, rigid, robust, secure, secured, set, settled, solid, solidified, stable, stationary, staunch, steadfast, steady, stiff, strict, strong, sturdy, substantial, sure, taut, tight, true, unalterable, unassailable, unbending, unchanging, undeviating, unfaltering, unflinching, unmoved, unmoving, unshakable, unshakeable, unshaken, unshifting, unswerving, unwavering, unyielding, well-knit.
antonyms infirm, soft, unsound.

firm[2] *n.* association, business, company, concern, conglomerate, corporation, enterprise, establishment, house, institution, organization, outfit, partnership, set-up, syndicate.

first *adj.* basic, cardinal, chief, earliest, eldest, elementary, embryonic, foremost, fundamental, head, highest, initial, introductory, key, leading, maiden, main, oldest, opening, original, paramount, predominant, pre-eminent, premier, primal, primary, prime, primeval, primitive, primordial, principal, prior, pristine, rudimentary, ruling, senior, sovereign, uppermost.
adv. at the outset, before all else, beforehand, early on, firstly, in preference, in the beginning, initially, originally, primarily, rather, sooner, to begin with, to start with.

fishy *adj.* doubtful, dubious, fish-like, funny, glassy, implausible, improbable, irregular, odd, piscatorial, piscatory, pisciform, piscine, queer, questionable, rummy, shady, suspect, suspicious, unlikely, vacant.
antonyms honest, legitimate.

fissile *adj.* cleavable, divisible, easily split, fissionable, fissive, flaky, scissile, separable, severable.

fission *n.* breaking, cleavage, division, parting, rending, rupture, schism, scission, severance, splitting.

fit[1] *adj.* able, able-bodied, adapted, adequate, apposite, appropriate, apt, becoming, blooming, capable, commensurate, competent, condign, convenient, correct, deserving, due, eligible, equipped, expedient, fit as a fiddle, fitted, fitting, hale, hale and hearty, healthy, in fine fettle, in good form, in good nick, in good shape, in good trim, in the pink, meet, prepared, proper, qualified, ready, right, robust, satisfactory, seemly, sound, strapping, strong, sturdy, suitable, suited, trained, trim, well, well-suited, worthy.
antonym unfit.
v. accommodate, accord, adapt, adjust, agree, alter, arrange, assimilate, belong, change, concur, conform, correspond, dispose, dovetail, fashion, fay, figure, follow, gee, go, harmonize, interlock, join, match, meet, modify, place, position, reconcile, shape, suit, tally.

fit[2] *n.* access, attack, bout, burst, caprice, convulsion, eruption, exies, explosion, fancy, humor, mood, outbreak, outburst, paroxysm, seizure, spasm, spell, storm, surge, whim.

fitful *adj.* broken, desultory, disturbed, erratic, fluctuating, haphazard, intermittent, irregular, occasional, spasmodic, sporadic, uneven, unstable, unsteady, variable.
antonyms regular, steady.

fitting *adj.* apposite, appropriate, apt, becoming, comme il faut, condign, correct, decent, decorous, deserved, desirable, harmonious, meet, merited, proper, right, seasonable, seemly, suitable.
antonym unsuitable.
n. accessory, attachment, component, connection, fitment, fixture, part, piece, unit.

fix[1] *v.* adjust, agree on, anchor, appoint, arrange, arrive at, attach, bind, cement, conclude, confirm, congeal, connect, consolidate, correct, couple, decide, define, determine, direct, embed, establish, fasten, fiddle, finalize, firm, focus, freeze, glue, harden, implant, inculcate, influence, install, irradicate, limit, link, locate, make, manipulate, maneuver, mend, nail, name, ordain, pin, place, plant, point, position, prearrange, preordain, produce, regulate, repair, resolve, restore, rigidify, rigidize, rivet, root, seal, seat, secure, see to, set, settle, solidify, sort, sort out, specify, stabilize, stick, stiffen, straighten, swing, thicken, tidy, tie.
n. corner, difficulty, dilemma, embarrassment, hole, jam, mess, muddle, nineholes, pickle, plight, predicament, quagmire, quandary, scrape, spot.

fix[2] *n.* dose, hit, injection, jag, score, shot, slug.

fixation *n.* complex, compulsion, fetish, hang-up, idée fixe, infatuation, mania, monomania, obsession, preoccupation, thing.

flabbergasted *adj.* amazed, astonished, astounded, bowled over, confounded, dazed, disconcerted, dumbfounded, nonplused, overcome, overwhelmed, speechless, staggered, stunned, stupefied.

flagrant *adj.* arrant, atrocious, audacious, barefaced, blatant, bold, brazen, conspicuous, crying, egregious, enormous, flagitious, flaunting, glaring, heinous, immodest, infamous, notorious, open, ostentatious, outrageous, overt, rank, scandalous, shameless, unashamed, undisguised.
antonyms covert, secret.

flair *n.* ability, accomplishment, acumen, aptitude, chic, dash, discernment, elegance, facility, faculty, feel, genius, gift, knack, mastery, nose, panache, skill, style, stylishness, talent, taste.
antonym ineptitude.

flamboyant *adj.* baroque, brilliant, colorful, dashing, dazzling, elaborate, exciting, extravagant, flashy, florid, gaudy, glamorous, jaunty, ornate, ostentatious, rich, showy, striking, stylish, swashbuckling, theatrical.
antonyms modest, restrained.

flame *v.* beam, blaze, burn, flare, flash, glare, glow, radiate, shine.
n. affection, ardor, beau, blaze, brightness, enthusiasm, fervency, fervor, fire, flake, flammule, heart-throb, intensity, keenness, light, lover, passion, radiance, sweetheart, warmth, zeal.

flash *v.* blaze, bolt, brandish, coruscate, dart, dash, display, exhibit, expose, flare, flaunt, flicker, flourish, fly, fulgurate, fulminate, glare, gleam, glint, glisten, glitter, light, race, scintillate, shimmer, shoot, show, sparkle, speed, sprint, streak, sweep, twinkle, whistle.
n. blaze, bluette, burst, coruscation, dazzle, demonstration, display, flare, flaught, flicker, fulguration, gleam, hint, instant, jiff, jiffy, manifestation, moment, outburst, ray, scintillation, second, shaft, shake, shimmer, show, sign, spark, sparkle, split second, streak, touch, trice, twinkle, twinkling.

flashy *adj.* bold, brassy, cheap, flamboyant, flash, garish, gaudy, glamorous, glittery, glitzy, jazzy, loud, meretricious, obtrusive, ostentatious, raffish, rakish, ritzy, showy, snazzy, tacky, tasteless, tawdry, tig(e)rish, tinselly, vulgar.
antonyms plain, simple, tasteful.

flat[1] *adj.* even, horizontal, lamellar, lamelliform, level, leveled, low, outstretched, planar, plane, prone, prostrate, reclining, recumbent, smooth, spread-eagled, supine, unbroken, uniform.
n. lowland, marsh, morass, moss, mud flat, plain, shallow, shoal, strand, swamp.

flat[2] *adj.* bored, boring, burst, collapsed, dead, deflated, depressed, dull, empty, flavorless, insipid, jejune, lackluster, lifeless, monotonous, pointless, prosaic, punctured, spiritless, stale, tedious, uninteresting, unpalatable, vapid, watery, weak.

flat[3] *adj.* absolute, categorical, direct, downright, explicit, final, fixed, out-and-out, peremptory, plain, point-blank, positive, straight, total, uncompromising, unconditional, unequivocal, unqualified.
antonym equivocal.
adv. absolutely, categorically, completely, entirely, exactly, point-blank, precisely, totally, utterly.

flat[4] *n.* apartment, bed-sit, bed-sitter, maison(n)ette, pad, penthouse, pied-à-terre, rooms, tenement.

flatly *adv.* absolutely, categorically, completely, peremptorily, point-blank, positively, uncompromisingly, unconditionally, unhesitatingly.

flattery *n.* adulation, backscratching, blandishment, blarney, bootlicking, butter, cajolement, cajolery, eulogy, fawning, flannel, flapdoodle, fleechment, fulsomeness, ingratiation, obsequiousness, servility, soap, soft sawder, soft soap, sugar, sweet talk, sycophancy, sycophantism, taffy, toadyism, unctuousness.
antonym criticism.

flaunt *v.* air, boast, brandish, dangle, display, disport, exhibit, flash, flourish, parade, show off, sport, vaunt, wield.

flavor *n.* aroma, aspect, character, essence, extract, feel, feeling, flavoring, hint, odor, piquancy, property, quality, relish, sapidity, savor, savoriness, seasoning,

smack, soupçon, stamp, style, suggestion, tang, taste, tastiness, tinge, tone, touch, zest, zing.
v. contaminate, ginger up, imbue, infuse, lace, leaven, season, spice, taint.

flaw *n.* blemish, breach, break, cleft, crack, craze, crevice, defect, disfigurement, failing, fallacy, fault, fissure, fracture, hamartia, imperfection, lapse, macula, mark, mistake, rent, rift, shortcoming, slip, speck, split, spot, tear, weakness, wreath.

flee *v.* abscond, avoid, beat a hasty retreat, bolt, bunk (off), cut and run, decamp, depart, escape, fly, get away, leave, make off, make oneself scarce, scarper, scram, shun, skedaddle, split, take flight, take it on the lam, take off, take to one's heels, vamoose, vanish, withdraw.
antonyms stand, stay.

fleece *v.* bilk, bleed, cheat, clip, con, defraud, diddle, mulct, overcharge, plunder, rifle, rip off, rob, rook, shear, skin, soak, squeeze, steal, sting, swindle.

fleet[1] *n.* argosy, armada, escadrille, flota, flotilla, navy, squadron, task force.

fleet[2] *adj.* expeditious, fast, flying, light-footed, mercurial, meteoric, nimble, quick, rapid, speedy, swift, velocipede, winged.
antonym slow.

fleeting *adj.* brief, disappearing, ephemeral, evanescent, flitting, flying, fugacious, fugitive, impermanent, momentary, passing, short, short-lived, temporary, transient, transitory, vanishing.
antonym lasting.

fleshy *adj.* ample, beefy, brawny, carneous, carnose, chubby, chunky, corpulent, fat, flabby, hefty, meaty, obese, overweight, paunchy, plump, podgy, portly, rotund, stout, tubby, well-padded.
antonym thin.

flexible *adj.* accommodating, adaptable, adjustable, agreeable, amenable, bendable, biddable, complaisant, compliant, discretionary, docile, double-jointed, ductile, elastic, flexile, gentle, limber, lissome, lithe, loose-limbed, manageable, mobile, moldable, open, plastic, pliable, pliant, responsive, springy, stretchy, supple, tensile, tractable, variable, whippy, willowy, withy, yielding.
antonym inflexible.

flighty *adj.* bird-brained, bird-witted, capricious, changeable, dizzy, fickle, frivolous, giddy, hare-brained, impetuous, impulsive, inconstant, irresponsible, light-headed, mercurial, rattle-brained, rattle-headed, rattle-pated, scatterbrained, silly, skittish, thoughtless, unbalanced, unstable, unsteady, volage, volageous, volatile, whisky-frisky, wild.
antonym steady.

flimsy *adj.* cardboard, chiffon, cobwebby, delicate, diaphanous, ethereal, feeble, fragile, frail, frivolous, gauzy, gimcrack, gossamer, implausible, inadequate, insubstantial, light, makeshift, meager, poor, rickety, shaky, shallow, sheer, slight, superficial, thin, transparent, trivial, unconvincing, unsatisfactory, unsubstantial, vaporous, weak.
antonym sturdy.

fling *v.* bung, cant, cast, catapult, chuck, heave, hurl, jerk, let fly, lob, pitch, precipitate, propel, send, shoot, shy, sling, slug, souse, throw, toss.
n. attempt, bash, binge, cast, crack, gamble, go, heave, indulgence, lob, pitch, shot, spree, stab, throw, toss, trial, try, turn, venture, whirl.

flippant *adj.* brash, cheeky, cocky, disrespectful, flip, frivolous, glib, impertinent, impudent, irreverent, malapert, nonchalant, offhand, pert, pococurante, rude, saucy, superficial, unserious.
antonym earnest.

flit *v.* beat, bob, dance, dart, elapse, flash, fleet, flutter, fly, pass, skim, slip, speed, volitate, whisk, wing.

flock *v.* bunch, cluster, collect, congregate, converge, crowd, gather, gravitate, group, herd, huddle, mass, swarm, throng, troop.
n. assembly, bevy, collection, colony, company, congregation, convoy, crowd, drove, flight, gaggle, gathering, group, herd, horde, host, mass, multitude, pack, shoal, skein, swarm, throng.

flog *v.* beat, birch, breech, chastise, drive, drub, flagellate, flay, hide, knout, k(o)urbash, larrup, lash, overexert, overtax, overwork, punish, push, scourge, strain, swish, tat, tax, thrash, trounce, vapulate, verberate, welt, whack, whale, whang, whip, whop.

flood *v.* bog down, brim, choke, deluge, drench, drown, engulf, fill, flow, glut, gush, immerse, inundate, overflow, oversupply, overwhelm, pour, rush, saturate, soak, submerge, surge, swamp, swarm, sweep.
n. abundance, alluvion, bore, cataclysm, debacle, deluge, diluvion, diluvium, downpour, eagre, flash flood, flow, freshet, glut, inundation, multitude, outpouring, overflow, plethora, profusion, rush, spate, stream, superfluity, tide, torrent.
antonyms dearth, drought, trickle.

florid *adj.* baroque, blowzy, bombastic, busy, coloratura, elaborate, embellished, euphuistic, figurative, flamboyant, flourishy, flowery, flushed, fussy, grandiloquent, high-colored, high-falutin(g), high-flown, melismatic, ornate, over-elaborate, purple, raddled, red, rococo, rubicund, ruddy. *antonyms* pale, plain.

flourish[1] *v.* advance, bloom, blossom, boom, burgeon, develop, do well, flower, get on, grow, increase, mushroom, progress, prosper, succeed, thrive, wax.
antonyms fail, languish.

flourish[2] *v.* brandish, display, flaunt, flutter, parade, shake, sweep, swing, swish, twirl, vaunt, wag, wave, wield.
n. arabesque, brandishing, ceremony, curlicue, dash, decoration, display, élan, embellishment, fanfare, ornament, ornamentation, panache, parade, paraph, pizzazz, plume, shaking, show, sweep, twirling, wave.

flout *v.* affront, contemn, defy, deride, disregard, insult, jeer at, mock, outrage, reject, ridicule, scoff at, scorn, scout, spurn, taunt.
antonym respect.

flow *v.* arise, bubble, cascade, circulate, course, deluge, derive, distil, drift, emanate, emerge, flood, glide, gush, inundate, issue, move, originate, overflow, pour, proceed, purl, result, ripple, roll, run, rush, slide, slip, spew, spill, spring, spurt, squirt, stream, surge, sweep, swirl, teem, well, whirl.
n. abundance, cascade, course, current, deluge, drift, effluence, efflux, effusion, emanation, flood, flowage, flux, fluxion, gush, outflow, outpouring, plenty, plethora, spate, spurt, stream, succession, tide, train, wash.

fluctuate *v.* alter, alternate, change, ebb and flow, float, hesitate, oscillate, pendulate, rise and fall, seesaw, shift, shuffle, sway, swing, undulate, vacillate, vary, veer, waver.

fluent *adj.* articulate, easy, effortless, eloquent, facile, flowing, fluid, glib, mellifluous, natural, ready, smooth, smooth-talking, voluble, well-versed.
antonym tongue-tied.

fluff *n.* down, dust, dustball, floccus, flosh, floss, flue, fug, fuzz, lint, nap, oose, pile.
v. balls up, botch, bungle, cock up, fumble, mess up, muddle, muff, screw up, spoil.
antonym bring off.

fluid *adj.* adaptable, adjustable, aqueous, changeable, diffluent, easy, elegant, feline, flexible, floating, flowing, fluctuating, fluent, fluidal, fluidic, graceful, inconstant, indefinite, liquefied, liquid, melted, mercurial, mobile, molten, mutable, protean, running, runny, shifting, sinuous, smooth, unstable, watery.
antonyms solid, stable.
n. humor, juice, liquid, liquor, sanies, sap, solution.

fluke *n.* accident, blessing, break, chance, coincidence, fortuity, freak, lucky break, quirk, serendipity, stroke, windfall.

flummoxed *adj.* at a loss, at sea, baffled, befuddled, bewildered, confounded, confused, foxed, mystified, nonplused, perplexed, puzzled, stumped, stymied.

flush[1] *v.* blush, burn, color, crimson, flame, glow, go red, mantle, redden, rouge, suffuse.
antonym pale.
n. bloom, blush, color, freshness, glow, redness, rosiness, rud, vigor.

flush[2] *v.* cleanse, douche, drench, eject, empty, evacuate, expel, hose, rinse, swab, syringe, wash.
adj. abundant, affluent, full, generous, in funds, lavish, liberal, moneyed, overflowing, prodigal, prosperous, rich, rolling, wealthy, well-heeled, well-off, well-supplied, well-to-do.

flush[3] *adj.* even, flat, level, plane, smooth, square, true.

flush[4] *v.* discover, disturb, drive out, force out, rouse, run to earth, start, uncover.

fluster *v.* abash, agitate, bother, bustle, confound, confuse, discombobulate, disconcert, discountenance, disturb, embarrass, excite, faze, flurry, hassle, heat, hurry, perturb, pother, pudder, rattle, ruffle, unnerve, unsettle, upset.
antonym calm.
n. agitation, bustle, commotion, discomposure, distraction, disturbance, dither, embarrassment, faze, flap, flurry, flutter, furore, kerfuffle, perturbation, ruffle, state, tizzy, turmoil.
antonym calm.

fly[1] *v.* abscond, aviate, avoid, bolt, career, clear out, dart, dash, decamp, disappear, display, elapse, escape, flap, flee, flit, float, flutter, get away, glide, hare, hasten, hasten away, hedge-hop, hightail it, hoist, hover, hurry, light out, mount, operate, pass, pilot, race, raise, retreat, roll by, run, run for it, rush, sail, scamper, scarper, scoot, shoot, show, shun, skim, soar, speed, sprint, take flight, take off, take to one's heels, take wing, tear, vamoose, volitate, wave, whisk, whiz, wing, zoom.

fly[2] *adj.* alert, artful, astute, canny, careful, cunning, knowing, nobody's fool, on the ball, prudent, sagacious, sharp, shrewd, smart, wide-awake.

foam *n.* barm, bubbles, effervescence, foaminess, froth, frothiness, head, lather, scum, spume, spumescence, suds.
v. boil, bubble, effervesce, fizz, froth, lather, spume.

foe *n.* adversary, antagonist, enemy, foeman, ill-wisher, opponent, rival.
antonym friend.

fog *n.* bewilderment, blanket, blindness, brume, confusion, daze, gloom, haze, London particular, miasma, mist, muddle, murk, murkiness, obscurity, pea-souper, perplexity, puzzlement, smog, stupor, trance, vagueness.
v. becloud, bedim, befuddle, bewilder, blanket, blind, cloud, confuse, darken, daze, dim, dull, mist, muddle, obfuscate, obscure, perplex, shroud, steam up, stupefy.

foible *n.* crotchet, defect, eccentricity, failing, fault, habit, idiosyncrasy, imperfection, infirmity, oddity, oddness, peculiarity, quirk, shortcoming, strangeness, weakness.

foist *v.* fob off, force, get rid of, impose, insert, insinuate, interpolate, introduce, palm off, pass off, thrust, unload, wish on.

fold *v.* bend, clasp, close, collapse, crash, crease, crimp, crumple, dog-ear, double, embrace, enclose, enfold, entwine, envelop, fail, fake, gather, go bust, hug, intertwine, overlap, pleat, ply, shut down, tuck, wrap, wrap up.
n. bend, corrugation, crease, crimp, duplicature, furrow, knife-edge, layer, overlap, pleat, ply, turn, wimple, wrinkle.

follow *v.* accompany, accord, act according to, appreciate, arise, attend, catch, catch on, chase, come after,

come next, comply, comprehend, conform, cultivate, dangle, develop, dog, emanate, ensue, escort, fathom, get, get the picture, grasp, haunt, heed, hound, hunt, imitate, keep abreast of, live up to, mind, note, obey, observe, pursue, realize, regard, result, second, see, shadow, stag, stalk, succeed, supersede, supervene, supplant, support, tag along, tail, track, trail, twig, understand, watch.
antonyms desert, precede.

follower *n.* acolyte, adherent, admirer, Anthony, apostle, attendant, backer, believer, buff, cohort, companion, convert, devotee, disciple, emulator, fan, fancier, freak, galloglass, habitué, hanger-on, heeler, helper, henchman, imitator, lackey, minion, partisan, poodle-dog, poursuivant, pupil, representative, retainer, running dog, servitor, sidekick, supporter, tantony, votary, worshipper.
antonyms leader, opponent.

following *adj.* coming, consecutive, consequent, consequential, ensuing, later, next, resulting, sequent, subsequent, succeeding, successive.
n. audience, backing, circle, claque, clientèle, coterie, entourage, fans, followers, patronage, public, retinue, suite, support, supporters, train.

folly[1] *n.* absurdity, craziness, daftness, fatuity, foolishness, idiocy, illogicality, imbecility, imprudence, indiscretion, insanity, irrationality, irresponsibility, lunacy, madness, moonraking, moria, nonsense, preposterousness, rashness, recklessness, senselessness, silliness, stupidity, unreason, unwisdom.
antonym prudence.

folly[2] *n.* belvedere, gazebo, monument, tower, whim.

fond *adj.* absurd, adoring, affectionate, amorous, caring, credulous, deluded, devoted, doting, empty, foolish, indiscreet, indulgent, loving, naive, over-optimistic, sanguine, tender, uxorious, vain, warm.
antonyms hostile, realistic.

fondness *n.* affection, attachment, devotion, engouement, enthusiasm, fancy, inclination, kindness, leaning, liking, love, partiality, penchant, predilection, preference, soft spot, susceptibility, taste, tenderness, weakness.
antonym aversion.

food *n.* aliment, ambrosia, board, bread, cheer, chow, comestibles, commons, cooking, cuisine, diet, eatables, eats, edibles, fare, feed, fodder, foodstuffs, forage, grub, larder, meat, menu, nosh, nourishment, nouriture, nutriment, nutrition, pabulum, pap, prog, provand, provend, provender, proviant, provisions, rations, refreshment, scoff, scran, stores, subsistence, sustenance, table, tack, tommy, tuck, tucker, viands, victuals, vittles, vivers.

fool *n.* ass, bécasse, berk, besom-head, bête, bird-brain, blockhead, bonehead, boodle, buffethead, buffoon, burk, butt, capocchia, Charlie, chump, clodpate, clot, clown, cluck, comic, coxcomb, cuckoo, daftie, daw, dawcock, dimwit, dizzard, Dogberry, dolt, dope, dottle, droll, drongo, dumb-bell, dumb-cluck, dumbo, dunce, dunderhead, dunderpate, dupe, easy mark, fall guy, fathead, fon, galah, gaupus, git, goon, goop, goose, greenhorn, gudgeon, gull, halfwit, harlequin, idiot, ignoramus, illiterate, imbecile, jackass, Jack-fool, jerk, jester, jobernowl, josh, joskin, leather-head, loggerhead, log-head, loon, madhaun, merryandrew, mooncalf, moron, motley, mug, nig-nog, nincompoop, ninny, nit, nitwit, nong, noodle, numskull, pierrot, pot-head, prat, prick, punchinello, sap, saphead, sawney, schmo, schmuck, silly, silly-billy, simpleton, soft, softhead, softie, softy, stooge, stupe, stupid, sucker, tomfool, Tom-noddy, turnip, twerp, twit, wally, want-wit, wimp, witling, wooden-head, yap, zany, zombie.
v. act dido, act the fool, act up, bamboozle, be silly, beguile, bluff, cavort, cheat, clown, con, cozen, cut capers, daff, deceive, delude, diddle, dupe, feign, fiddle, fon, frolic, gull, have on, hoax, hoodwink, horse around, jest, joke, kid, lark, meddle, mess, mess about, mislead, monkey, play, play the fool, play the goat, play up, pretend, put one over on, string, string along, swindle, take in, tamper, tease, toy, trick, trifle.

foolish *adj.* absurd, brainless, cockle-brained, crazy, daft, desipient, doited, doltish, dotish, dottled, dunderheaded, étourdi(e), fatuous, glaikit, gudgeon, half-baked, half-witted, hare-brained, idiotic, idle-headed, ill-advised, illaudable, ill-considered, ill-judged, imbecile, imbecilic, imprudent, incautious, indiscreet, inept, injudicious, insipient, lean-witted, ludicrous, mad, moronic, nonsensical, potty, ridiculous, senseless, short-sighted, silly, simple, simple-minded, sottish, stupid, tomfool, unintelligent, unreasonable, unwise, weak, wet, witless.
antonym wise.

footing *n.* base, basis, condition, conditions, establishment, foot-hold, foundation, grade, ground, groundwork, installation, position, purchase, rank, relations, relationship, settlement, standing, state, status, terms.

footnotes *n.* annotations, apparatus criticus, commentary, marginalia, notes, scholia.

footprint *n.* footmark, spoor, trace, track, trail, vestige.

footstep *n.* footfall, plod, step, tramp, tread, trudge.

fop *n.* beau, coxcomb, dandy, dude, exquisite, Jack-a-dandy, Jessie, macaroni, muscadin, musk-cat, pansy, peacock, petit maître, popinjay, spark, swell.

forbearance *n.* abstinence, avoidance, clemency, endurance, indulgence, leniency, lenity, longanimity, long-suffering, mildness, moderation, patience, refraining, resignation, restraint, self-control, sufferance, temperance, tolerance, toleration.
antonym intolerance.

forbid *v.* ban, block, contraindicate, debar, deny, disallow, exclude, hinder, inhibit, interdict, outlaw, preclude, prevent, prohibit, proscribe, refuse, rule out, veto. *antonym* allow.

forbidding *adj.* abhorrent, awesome, daunting, formidable, frightening, gaunt, grim, hostile, inhospitable, menacing, off-putting, ominous, repellent, repulsive, sinister, threatening, unapproachable, unfriendly.
antonyms approachable, congenial.

force[1] *n.* aggression, arm-twisting, beef, big stick, bite, coercion, cogency, compulsion, constraint, drive, duress, dynamism, effect, effectiveness, efficacy, emphasis, energy, enforcement, fierceness, foison, forcefulness, fushion, impact, impetus, impulse, incentive, influence, intensity, jism, life, mailed fist, might, momentum, motivation, muscle, persistence, persuasiveness, potency, power, pressure, punch, shock, steam, stimulus, strength, stress, validity, vehemence, vigor, violence, vis, vitality, weight.
v. bulldoze, coerce, compel, constrain, drag, drive, exact, extort, impel, impose, lean on, make, necessitate, obligate, oblige, press, press-gang, pressure, pressurize, prize, propel, push, strong-arm, thrust, urge, wrench, wrest, wring.

force[2] *n.* army, battalion, body, corps, detachment, detail, division, effective, enomoty, host, legion, patrol, phalanx, regiment, squad, squadron, troop, unit, Wehrmacht.

forceful *adj.* cogent, compelling, convincing, domineering, drastic, dynamic, effective, emphatic, energetic, persuasive, pithy, potent, powerful, strong, telling, urgent, vigorous, weighty.
antonym feeble.

forcible *adj.* active, aggressive, coercive, cogent, compelling, compulsory, drastic, effective, efficient, energetic, forceful, impressive, mighty, pithy, potent, powerful, strong, telling, urgent, vehement, violent, weighty.
antonym feeble.

forebear *n.* ancestor, antecedent, antecessor, father, forefather, forerunner, predecessor, primogenitor, progenitor.
antonym descendant.

foreboding *n.* anticipation, anxiety, apprehension, apprehensiveness, augury, boding, chill, dread, fear, foreshadowing, foretoken, hoodoo, intuition, misgiving, omen, portent, prediction, prefigurement, premonition, presage, presentiment, prodrome, prodromus, prognostication, sign, token, warning, worry.

forecast *v.* augur, bode, calculate, conjecture, divine, estimate, expect, foresee, foretell, plan, predict, prognosticate, prophesy.
n. augury, conjecture, foresight, forethought, guess, guesstimate, outlook, planning, prediction, prognosis, prognostication, projection, prophecy.

foregoing *adj.* above, aforementioned, antecedent, anterior, earlier, former, preceding, previous, prior, prodromal, prodromic.

foreign *adj.* adventitious, adventive, alien, borrowed, distant, exotic, external, extraneous, extrinsic, fremd, imported, incongruous, irrelevant, outlandish, outside, overseas, remote, strange, tramontane, unassimilable, uncharacteristic, unfamiliar, unknown, unnative, unrelated.
antonym native.

foreigner *n.* alien, Ausländer, barbarian, dago, étranger, étrangère, immigrant, incomer, metic, newcomer, outlander, stranger, uitlander, wog, wop.
antonym native.

foreman *n.* charge-hand, charge-man, gaffer, ganger, gangsman, overman, overseer, oversman, steward, straw boss, supervisor.

foremost *adj.* cardinal, central, chief, first, front, headmost, highest, inaugural, initial, leading, main, paramount, preeminent, primary, prime, principal, salient, supreme, uppermost.

forerunner *n.* ancestor, announcer, antecedent, antecessor, envoy, forebear, foregoer, foretoken, harbinger, herald, indication, omen, portent, precursor, predecessor, premonition, prodrome, prodromus, progenitor, prognostic, prototype, sign, token, vaunt-courier.
antonyms aftermath, result.

foreshadow *v.* adumbrate, anticipate, augur, betoken, bode, forebode, forepoint, foreshow, foresignify, foretoken, imply, import, indicate, omen, portend, predict, prefigure, presage, promise, prophesy, signal.

foresight *n.* anticipation, care, caution, circumspection, farsightedness, forethought, perspicacity, precaution, preparedness, prescience, prevision, providence, provision, prudence, readiness, vision.
antonym improvidence.

forestall *v.* anticipate, avert, balk, circumvent, frustrate, head off, hinder, intercept, obstruct, obviate, parry, preclude, pre-empt, prevent, thwart, ward off.
antonyms encourage, facilitate.

foretell *v.* adumbrate, augur, bode, forebode, forecast, foresay, foreshadow, foreshow, forespeak, forewarn, portend, predict, presage, presignify, prognosticate, prophesy, signify, soothsay, vaticinate.

forever *adv.* always, ceaselessly, constantly, continually, endlessly, eternally, everlastingly, evermore, for all time, for good and all, for keeps, in perpetuity, in saecula saeculorum, incessantly, interminably, permanently, perpetually, persistently, till the cows come home, till the end of time, unremittingly, world without end.

forewarn *v.* admonish, advise, alert, apprize, caution, dissuade, previse, tip off.

forfeit *n.* amercement, damages, escheat, fine, forfeiture, loss, mulct, penalization, penalty, surrender.
v. abandon, forgo, give up, lose, relinquish, renounce, sacrifice, surrender.

forge[1] *v.* beat out, cast, coin, construct, contrive, copy, counterfeit, create, devise, fabricate, fake, falsify, fashion, feign, form, frame, hammer out, imitate, invent, make, mold, shape, simulate, work.

forge[2] *v.* advance, gain ground, improve, make great strides, make headway, press on, proceed, progress, push on.

forget *v.* consign to oblivion, discount, dismiss, disregard, fail, ignore, lose sight of, misremember, neglect, omit, overlook, think no more of, unlearn.
antonym remember.

forgetful *adj.* absent-minded, amnesiac, amnesic, careless, dreamy, heedless, inattentive, lax, neglectful, negligent, oblivious, unmindful, unretentive.
antonyms attentive, heedful.

forgive *v.* absolve, acquit, condone, exculpate, excuse, exonerate, let off, overlook, pardon, remit, shrive.
antonym censure.

forgiving *adj.* clement, compassionate, forbearing, humane, indulgent, lenient, magnanimous, merciful, mild, remissive, soft-hearted, sparing, tolerant.
antonym censorious.

forgo, forego *v.* abandon, abjure, abstain from, cede, do without, eschew, forfeit, give up, pass up, refrain from, relinquish, renounce, resign, sacrifice, surrender, waive, yield.
antonyms claim, indulge in, insist on.

forgotten *adj.* blotted out, buried, bygone, disregarded, ignored, irrecoverable, irretrievable, lost, neglected, obliterated, omitted, out of mind, overlooked, past, past recall, past recollection, unrecalled, unremembered, unretrieved.
antonym remembered.

forlorn *adj.* abandoned, abject, bereft, cheerless, comfortless, deserted, desolate, desperate, destitute, disconsolate, forgotten, forsaken, friendless, helpless, homeless, hopeless, lonely, lost, miserable, pathetic, piteous, pitiable, pitiful, unhappy, woebegone, woeful, wretched.
antonym hopeful.

form *v.* accumulate, acquire, appear, arrange, assemble, bring up, build, combine, compose, comprise, concoct, constitute, construct, contract, contrive, create, crystallize, cultivate, design, develop, devise, discipline, dispose, draw up, educate, establish, evolve, fabricate, fashion, forge, formulate, found, frame, group, grow, hatch, instruct, invent, make, make up, manufacture, materialize, model, mold, organize, pattern, plan, produce, put together, rear, rise, school, serve as, settle, shape, take shape, teach, train. *n.* anatomy, appearance, application, arrangement, behavior, being, body, build, cast, ceremony, character, class, condition, conduct, configuration, construction, convention, custom, cut, description, design, document, etiquette, fashion, fettle, figure, fitness, formality, format, formation, frame, framework, genre, Gestalt, grade, guise, harmony, health, kind, manifestation, manner, manners, matrix, method, mode, model, mold, nature, nick, order, orderliness, organization, outline, paper, pattern, person, physique, plan, practice, procedure, proportion, protocol, questionnaire, rank, ritual, rule, schedule, semblance, shape, sheet, silhouette, sort, species, spirits, stamp, structure, style, symmetry, system, trim, type, variety, way.

formal *adj.* academic, aloof, approved, ceremonial, ceremonious, conventional, correct, exact, explicit, express, fixed, full-dress, impersonal, lawful, legal, methodical, nominal, official, perfunctory, precise, prescribed, prim, punctilious, recognized, regular, reserved, rigid, ritualistic, set, solemn, starch, starched, starchy, stiff, stiff-necked, stilted, strict, unbending.
antonym informal.

formality *n.* ceremoniousness, ceremony, convenance, convention, conventionality, correctness, custom, decorum, etiquette, form, formalism, gesture, matter of form, politeness, politesse, procedure, propriety, protocol, punctilio, red tape, rite, ritual.
antonym informality.

former *adj.* above, aforementioned, aforesaid, ancient, antecedent, anterior, bygone, departed, earlier, erstwhile, ex-, first mentioned, foregoing, late, long ago, of yore, old, old-time, one-time, past, preceding, preexistent, previous, prior, pristine, quondam, sometime, umwhile, whilom.
antonyms current, future, later, present, prospective, subsequent.

formidable *adj.* alarming, appalling, arduous, awesome, challenging, colossal, dangerous, daunting, difficult, dismaying, dreadful, enormous, fearful, frightening, frightful, great, horrible, huge, impressive, indomitable, intimidating, leviathan, mammoth, menacing, mighty, onerous, overwhelming, powerful, puissant, redoubtable, shocking, staggering, terrific, terrifying, threatening, toilsome, tremendous.
antonyms easy, genial.

forsake *v.* abandon, abdicate, cast off, desert, discard, disown, forgo, forswear, give up, jettison, jilt, leave, leave in the lurch, quit, reject, relinquish, renounce, repudiate, surrender, throw over, turn one's back on, vacate, yield.
antonyms resume, revert to.

forte *n.* aptitude, bent, gift, long suit, métier, skill, specialty, strength, strong point, talent.
antonyms inadequacy, weak point.

forthcoming[1] *adj.* accessible, approaching, at hand, available, coming, expected, future, imminent, impending, obtainable, projected, prospective, ready.

forthcoming[2] *adj.* chatty, communicative, conversational, expansive, frank, free, informative, loquacious, open, sociable, talkative, unreserved.
antonyms bygone, distant, lacking, reserved.

forthright *adj.* above-board, blunt, bold, candid, direct, four-square, frank, open, outspoken, plain-speaking, plain-spoken, straightforward, straight-from-the-shoulder, trenchant, unequivocal.
antonyms devious, tactful.

forthwith *adv.* at once, directly, eftsoons, immediately, incontinent, instanter, instantly, posthaste, pronto, quickly, right away, straightaway, tout de suite, without delay.

fortify *v.* boost, brace, bulwark, buttress, cheer, confirm, embattle, embolden, encourage, entrench, garrison, hearten, invigorate, lace, load, mix, munify, protect, reassure, reinforce, secure, shore up, spike, steel, stiffen, strengthen, support, sustain.
antonyms dilute, weaken.

fortuitous *adj.* accidental, adventitious, arbitrary, casual, chance, coincidental, contingent, felicitous, fluky, fortunate, happy, incidental, lucky, providential, random, serendipitous, unexpected, unforeseen, unintentional, unplanned.
antonym intentional.

fortunate *adj.* advantageous, auspicious, blessed, bright, convenient, encouraging, favorable, favored, felicitous, fortuitous, golden, happy, helpful, lucky, opportune, profitable, promising, propitious, prosperous, providential, rosy, serendipitous, successful, timely, well-off, well-timed.
antonym unfortunate.

fortune[1] *n.* affluence, assets, bomb, bundle, estate, income, king's ransom, means, mint, opulence, packet, pile, possessions, property, prosperity, riches, treasure, wealth.

fortune[2] *n.* accident, adventures, chance, circumstances, contingency, cup, destiny, doom, expectation, experience, fate, fortuity, hap, happenstance, hazard, history, kismet, life, lot, luck, portion, providence, star, success, weird.

fortune-telling *n.* augury, chiromancy, crystal-gazing, divination, dukkeripen, palmistry, prediction, prognostication, prophecy, second sight.

forward[1] *adj.* advance, advanced, early, enterprising, first, fore, foremost, forward-looking, front, go-ahead, head, leading, onward, precocious, premature, progressive, well-advanced, well-developed.
antonym retrograde.
adv. ahead, en avant, forth, forwards, into view, on, onward, out, outward, to light, to the fore, to the surface.
antonym backward.
v. accelerate, advance, aid, assist, back, dispatch, encourage, expedite, facilitate, favor, foster, freight, further, hasten, help, hurry, post, promote, route, send, send on, ship, speed, support, transmit.
antonyms impede, obstruct.

forward[2] *adj.* assertive, assuming, audacious, bare-faced, bold, brash, brass-necked, brazen, brazen-faced, cheeky, confident, familiar, fresh, impertinent, impudent, malapert, officious, overweening, pert, presuming, presumptuous, pushy.
antonym diffident.

fossilized *adj.* anachronistic, antediluvian, antiquated, archaic, archaistic, dead, démodé, extinct, exuvial, inflexible, obsolete, old-fashioned, old-fog(e)yish, ossified, out of date, outmoded, passé, petrified, prehistoric, stony, superannuated.
antonym up-to-date.

foul *adj.* abhorrent, abominable, abusive, bad, base, blasphemous, blue, blustery, choked, coarse, contaminated, crooked, despicable, detestable, dirty, disagreeable, disfigured, disgraceful, disgusting, dishonest, dishonorable, entangled, fetid, filthy, foggy, foul-mouthed, fraudulent, gross, hateful, heinous, impure, indecent, inequitable, infamous, iniquitous, lewd, loathsome, low, malodorous, mephitic, murky, nasty, nauseating, nefarious, noisome, notorious, obscene, offensive, polluted, profane, putrid, rainy, rank, repulsive, revolting, rotten, rough, scandalous, scatological, scurrilous, shady, shameful, smutty, squalid, stinking, stormy, sullied, tainted, unclean, underhand, unfair, unfavorable, unjust, unsportsmanlike, untidy, vicious, vile, virose, vulgar, wet, wicked, wild.
antonyms clean, fair, pure, worthy.
v. befoul, begrime, besmear, besmirch, block, catch, choke, clog, contaminate, defile, dirty, ensnare, entangle, foul up, jam, pollute, smear, snarl, soil, stain, sully, taint, twist.
antonyms clean, clear, disentangle.

found *v.* base, bottom, build, constitute, construct, create, endow, erect, establish, fix, ground, inaugurate, initiate, institute, organize, originate, plant, raise, rest, root, set up, settle, start, sustain.

foundation *n.* base, basis, bedrock, bottom, endowment, establishment, fond, footing, ground, groundwork, inauguration, institution, organization, setting up, settlement, substance, substratum, substructure, underpinning.

foxy *adj.* artful, astute, canny, crafty, cunning, devious, fly, guileful, knowing, sharp, shrewd, sly, tricky, vulpine, wily.
antonyms naïve, open.

fractious *adj.* awkward, captious, choleric, crabbed, crabby, cross, crotchety, fretful, froward, grouchy, irritable, peevish, pettish, petulant, quarrelsome, querulous, recalcitrant, refractory, testy, touchy, unruly.
antonyms complaisant, placid.

fracture *n.* breach, break, cleft, crack, fissure, gap, opening, rent, rift, rupture, schism, scission, split.
v. break, crack, rupture, splinter, split.
antonym join.

fragile *adj.* breakable, brittle, dainty, delicate, feeble, fine, flimsy, frail, frangible, infirm, insubstantial, shattery, slight, weak.
antonyms durable, robust, tough.

fragment *n.* bit, cantlet, chip, flinder, fraction, frazzle, fritter, morceau, morsel, ort, part, particle, piece, portion, remnant, scrap, shard, shatter, sheave, shiver, shred, sliver.

v. break, break up, come apart, come to pieces, crumble, disintegrate, disunite, divide, fractionalize, fritter, shatter, shiver, splinter, split, split up.
antonyms hold together, join.

fragrance *n.* aroma, balm, balminess, bouquet, fragrancy, odor, perfume, redolence, scent, smell.

fragrant *adj.* aromatic, balmy, balsamy, odoriferous, odorous, perfumed, redolent, suaveolent, sweet, sweet-scented, sweet-smelling.
antonyms smelly, unscented.

frail *adj.* breakable, brittle, decrepit, delicate, feeble, flimsy, fragile, frangible, infirm, insubstantial, puny, slight, tender, unchaste, unsound, vulnerable, weak.
antonyms firm, robust, strong, tough.

frame *v.* assemble, block out, build, case, compose, conceive, concoct, constitute, construct, contrive, cook up, devise, draft, draw up, enclose, enframe, fabricate, fashion, forge, form, formulate, hatch, institute, invent, make, manufacture, map out, model, mold, mount, plan, put together, redact, set up, shape, sketch, surround, trap, victimize.
n. anatomy, body, bodyshell, bodywork, build, carcass, casing, chassis, construction, fabric, flake, form, framework, monture, morphology, mount, mounting, physique, scaffolding, scheme, setting, shell, skeleton, structure, system.

frank *adj.* artless, blunt, candid, direct, downright, forthright, four-square, free, honest, ingenuous, open, outright, outspoken, plain, plain-spoken, simple-hearted, sincere, straight, straightforward, transparent, truthful, unconcealed, undisguised, unreserved, unrestricted.

frantic *adj.* berserk, beside oneself, desperate, distracted, distraught, fraught, frenetic, frenzied, furious, hairless, hectic, mad, overwrought, raging, raving, wild.
antonym calm.

fraternize *v.* affiliate, associate, concur, consort, cooperate, forgather, hobnob, mingle, mix, socialize, sympathize, unite.
antonyms ignore, shun.

fraud[1] *n.* artifice, cheat, chicane, chicanery, craft, deceit, deception, double-dealing, duplicity, fake, forgery, guile, hoax, humbug, imposture, sham, sharp practice, spuriousness, swindling, swiz, swizzle, take-in, treachery, trickery.

fraud[2] *n.* bluffer, charlatan, cheat, counterfeit, double-dealer, hoaxer, impostor, malingerer, mountebank, phony, pretender, pseud, quack, swindler.

fraudulent *adj.* bogus, counterfeit, crafty, criminal, crooked, deceitful, deceptive, dishonest, double-dealing, duplicitous, false, knavish, phony, sham, specious, spurious, swindling, treacherous.
antonyms genuine, honest.

fray *n.* affray, bagarre, barney, battle, brawl, broil, clash, combat, conflict, disturbance, Donnybrook, dust-up, fight, free-for-all, mêlée, quarrel, rammy, riot, row, ruckus, ruction, rumble, rumpus, scuffle, set-to, shindy.

freak[1] *n.* aberration, abnormality, abortion, anomaly, caprice, crotchet, fad, fancy, folly, grotesque, humor, irregularity, lusus naturae, malformation, misgrowth, monster, monstrosity, mutant, oddity, queer fish, quirk, rara avis, sport, teratism, turn, twist, vagary, weirdie, weirdo, whim, whimsy. *adj.* aberrant, abnormal, atypical, bizarre, capricious, erratic, exceptional, fluky, fortuitous, odd, queer, surprise, unaccountable, unexpected, unforeseen, unparalleled, unpredictable, unpredicted, unusual.
antonyms common, expected.

freak[2] *n.* addict, aficionado, buff, devotee, enthusiast, fan, fanatic, fiend, monomaniac, nut, votary.

freckle *n.* fernitickle, heatspot, lentigo.

free *adj.* able, allowed, at large, at leisure, at liberty, autarchic, autonomous, available, bounteous, bountiful, buckshee, casual, charitable, clear, complimentary, cost-free, dégagé, democratic, disengaged, eager, easy, emancipated, empty, extra, familiar, footloose, forward, frank, free and easy, free of charge, generous, gratis, hospitable, idle, independent, informal, laid-back, lavish, lax, leisured, liberal, liberated, loose, munificent, natural, off the hook, on the house, on the loose, open, open-handed, permitted, prodigal, relaxed, self-governing, self-ruling, solute, sovereign, spare, spontaneous, unattached, unbidden, unbowed, unceremonious, uncommitted, unconstrained, unemployed, unencumbered, unengaged, unfettered, unforced, unhampered, unhindered, unimpeded, uninhabited, uninhibited, unobstructed, unoccupied, unpaid, unpent, unpreoccupied, unregimented, unregulated, unrestrained, unrestricted, unsparing, unstinting, untrammeled, unused, vacant, willing, without charge.
antonyms attached, confined, costly, formal, mean, niggardly, restricted, tied.
adv. abundantly, copiously, for free, for love, for nothing, freely, gratis, idly, loosely, without charge.
antonym meanly.
v. absolve, affranchise, clear, debarrass, declassify, decolonize, decontrol, deliver, disburden, discage, discharge, disembarrass, disembrangle, disenchain, disengage, disenslave, disentangle, disenthral, disimprison, disprison, emancipate, exempt, extricate, let go, liberate, loose, manumit, ransom, release, relieve, rescue, rid, set free, turn loose, unbind, unburden, uncage, unchain, undo, unfetter, unhand, unleash, unlock, unloose, unmanacle, unmew, unpen, unshackle, unstick, untether, untie, unyoke.
antonyms confine, enslave, imprison.

freedom *n.* abandon, ability, affranchisement, autonomy, boldness, brazenness, candor, carte-blanche, deliverance, directness, discretion, disrespect, ease, elbow-room, emancipation, exemption, facility, familiarity,

flexibility, forwardness, frankness, free rein, home rule, immunity, impertinence, impunity, independence, informality, ingenuousness, lack of restraint or reserve, latitude, laxity, leeway, liberty, Liberty Hall, license, manumission, openness, opportunity, overfamiliarity, play, power, presumption, privilege, range, release, scope, self-government, uhuru, unconstraint.
antonyms confinement, reserve, restriction.

freely *adv.* abundantly, amply, bountifully, candidly, cleanly, copiously, easily, extravagantly, frankly, generously, lavishly, liberally, loosely, of one's own accord, open-handedly, openly, plainly, readily, smoothly, spontaneously, sponte sua, unchallenged, unreservedly, unstintingly, voluntarily, willingly.
antonyms evasively, meanly, roughly, under duress.

freight *n.* bulk, burden, cargo, carriage, charge, consignment, contents, conveyance, fee, goods, haul, lading, load, merchandise, pay-load, shipment, tonnage, transportation.

frenzy *n.* aberration, agitation, bout, burst, convulsion, delirium, derangement, distraction, estrus, fit, fury, hysteria, insanity, lunacy, madness, mania, must, outburst, paroxysm, passion, rage, seizure, spasm, transport, turmoil.
antonyms calm, placidness.

frequent[1] *adj.* common, commonplace, constant, continual, customary, everyday, familiar, habitual, incessant, numerous, persistent, recurrent, recurring, regular, reiterated, repeated, usual.
antonym infrequent.

frequent[2] *v.* associate with, attend, crowd, hang about, hang out at, haunt, haunt about, patronize, resort, visit.

fresh *adj.* added, additional, alert, artless, auxiliary, blooming, bold, bouncing, bracing, brazen, bright, brisk, callow, cheeky, chipper, clean, clear, cool, crisp, crude, dewy, different, disrespectful, energetic, extra, fair, familiar, flip, florid, forward, further, glowing, green, hardy, healthy, impudent, inexperienced, innovative, insolent, inventive, invigorated, invigorating, keen, latest, lively, malapert, modern, modernistic, more, natural, new, new-fangled, novel, original, other, pert, presumptuous, pure, raw, recent, refreshed, refreshing, renewed, rested, restored, revived, rosy, ruddy, saucy, span, spanking, sparkling, spick, sprightly, spry, stiff, supplementary, sweet, unblown, unconventional, uncultivated, undimmed, unhackneyed, unjaded, unjaundiced, unpolluted, unsoured, unspoilt, untrained, untried, unusual, unwarped, unwearied, up-to-date, verdant, vernal, vigorous, virescent, vital, vivid, warm, wholesome, young, youthful.
antonyms experienced, faded, old hat, polite, stale, tired.

fret *v.* abrade, agitate, agonize, annoy, bother, brood, chafe, chagrin, corrode, distress, disturb, eat into, erode, fray, gall, goad, grieve, harass, irk, irritate, nag, nettle, peeve, pique, provoke, rankle, repine, rile, ripple, rub, ruffle, torment, trouble, vex, wear, wear away, worry.
antonym calm.

fretful *adj.* cantankerous, captious, complaining, cross, crotchety, edgy, fractious, irritable, peevish, petulant, querulous, short-tempered, snappish, snappy, splenetic, testy, thrawn, touchy, uneasy.
antonym calm.

friction *n.* abrasion, animosity, antagonism, attrition, bad blood, bad feeling, bickering, chafing, conflict, contention, disagreement, discontent, discord, disharmony, dispute, dissension, erosion, fretting, grating, hostility, ill-feeling, incompatibility, irritation, limation, opposition, quarreling, rasping, resentment, resistance, rivalry, rubbing, scraping, wearing away, wrangling, xerotripsis.

friend *n.* Achates, adherent, advocate, ally, alter ego, associate, backer, benefactor, boon companion, bosom friend, buddy, china, chum, cobber, companion, comrade, confidant, crony, familiar, gossip, intimate, mate, paisano, pal, partisan, partner, patron, playmate, sidekick, soul mate, supporter, well-wisher.
antonym enemy.

friendly *adj.* affable, affectionate, amiable, amicable, approachable, attached, attentive, auspicious, beneficial, benevolent, benign, chummy, close, clubby, companionable, comradely, conciliatory, confiding, convivial, cordial, familiar, Favonian, favorable, fond, fraternal, gemütlich, genial, good, helpful, intimate, kind, kindly, maty, neighborly, outgoing, palsy-walsy, peaceable, propitious, receptive, sociable, sympathetic, thick, welcoming, well-disposed.
antonyms cold, unsociable.

friendship *n.* affection, affinity, alliance, amity, attachment, benevolence, closeness, concord, familiarity, fellowship, fondness, friendliness, goodwill, harmony, intimacy, love, neighborliness, rapport, regard.
antonym enmity.

fright *n.* alarm, apprehension, consternation, dismay, dread, eyesore, fear, fleg, funk, horror, mess, monstrosity, panic, quaking, scare, scarecrow, shock, sight, spectacle, sweat, terror, the shivers, trepidation.

frighten *v.* affray, affright, affrighten, alarm, appal, cow, daunt, dismay, fleg, intimidate, petrify, scare, scare stiff, shock, spook, startle, terrify, terrorize, unman, unnerve.
antonyms calm, reassure.

frigid *adj.* aloof, arctic, austere, brumous, chill, chilly, cold, cold-hearted, cool, forbidding, formal, frore, frostbound, frosty, frozen, gelid, glacial, icy, lifeless, passionless, passive, repellent, rigid, stand-offish, stiff, unanimated, unapproachable, unbending, unfeeling, unloving, unresponsive, wintry.
antonyms responsive, warm.

fringe *n.* borderline, edge, fimbriation, frisette, limits, march, marches, margin, outskirts, perimeter, periphery. *adj.* alternative, unconventional, unofficial, unorthodox.
v. border, edge, enclose, fimbriate, skirt, surround, trim.

frisky *adj.* bouncy, buckish, coltish, frolicsome, gamesome, high-spirited, kittenish, lively, playful,

rollicking, romping, skittish, spirited, sportive.
antonym quiet.

frolic *v.* caper, cavort, cut capers, frisk, gambol, gammock, lark, make merry, play, rollick, romp, skylark, sport, wanton.
n. amusement, antic, drollery, escapade, fun, gaiety, gambado, gambol, game, gammock, gilravage, high jinks, lark, merriment, prank, razzle-dazzle, revel, rig, romp, skylarking, sport, spree.

front *n.* air, anterior, appearance, aspect, bearing, beginning, blind, countenance, cover, cover-up, demeanor, disguise, expression, exterior, façade, face, facing, fore, forefront, foreground, forepart, front line, frontage, head, lead, manner, mask, metope, mien, obverse, pretence, pretext, show, top, van, vanguard.
antonym back.
adj. anterior, anticous, first, fore, foremost, head, lead, leading.
antonyms back, last, least, posterior.
v. confront, face, look over, meet, oppose, overlook.

frontier *n.* borderland, borderline, bound, boundary, bourn(e), confines, edge, limit, march, marches, perimeter, verge.
adj. backwoods, limitrophe, outlying, pioneering.

frown *v.* glare, glower, grimace, lower, scowl.
n. dirty look, glare, glower, grimace, moue, scowl.

frugal *adj.* abstemious, careful, cheese-paring, economical, meager, niggardly, parsimonious, penny-wise, provident, prudent, saving, sparing, Spartan, thrifty, ungenerous.
antonym wasteful.

fruitful *adj.* abundant, advantageous, beneficial, copious, effective, fecund, feracious, fertile, flush, fructiferous, fructuous, gainful, plenteous, plentiful, productive, profitable, profuse, prolific, rewarding, rich, spawning, successful, teeming, uberous, useful, well-spent, worthwhile.
antonyms barren, fruitless.

fruitfulness *n.* fecundity, feracity, fertility, productiveness, profitability, uberty, usefulness.
antonym fruitlessness.

fruitless *adj.* abortive, barren, bootless, futile, hopeless, idle, ineffectual, pointless, profitless, unavailing, unfruitful, unproductive, unprofitable, unsuccessful, useless, vain.
antonyms fruitful, successful.

frustrate *v.* baffle, balk, block, bugger, check, circumvent, confront, counter, countermine, crab, defeat, depress, disappoint, discourage, dishearten, foil, forestall, inhibit, neutralize, nullify, scotch, spike, stymie, thwart.
antonyms fulfil, further, promote.

fuddled *adj.* bemused, confused, drunk, groggy, hazy, inebriated, intoxicated, muddled, mused, muzzy, sozzled, stupefied, tipsy, woozy.
antonyms clear, sober.

fuel *n.* ammunition, eilding, encouragement, fodder, food, incitement, material, means, nourishment, provocation.
v. charge, encourage, fan, feed, fire, incite, inflame, nourish, stoke up, sustain.
antonyms damp down, discourage.

fugitive *n.* deserter, escapee, refugee, runagate, runaway.
adj. brief, elusive, ephemeral, evanescent, fleeing, fleeting, flitting, flying, fugacious, intangible, momentary, passing, short, short-lived, temporary, transient, transitory, unstable.
antonym permanent.

fulfill *v.* accomplish, achieve, answer, carry out, complete, comply with, conclude, conform to, consummate, discharge, effect, effectuate, execute, fill, finish, implement, keep, meet, obey, observe, perfect, perform, realize, satisfy.
antonyms break, defect, fail, frustrate.

full *adj.* abundant, adequate, all-inclusive, ample, baggy, brimful, brimming, broad, buxom, capacious, chock-a-block, chock-full, clear, complete, comprehensive, copious, crammed, crowded, curvaceous, deep, detailed, distinct, entire, exhaustive, extensive, filled, generous, gorged, intact, jammed, large, loaded, loud, maximum, occupied, orotund, packed, plenary, plenteous, plentiful, plump, replete, resonant, rich, rounded, sated, satiated, satisfied, saturated, stocked, sufficient, taken, thorough, unabbreviated, unabridged, uncut, unedited, unexpurgated, voluminous, voluptuous.
antonyms empty, incomplete.

full-blooded *adj.* gusty, hearty, lusty, mettlesome, red-blooded, thoroughbred, vigorous, virile, whole-hearted.

full-grown *adj.* adult, developed, full-aged, full-blown, full-scale, grown-up, marriageable, mature, nubile, of age, ripe.
antonyms undeveloped, young.

fullness *n.* abundance, adequateness, ampleness, broadness, clearness, completeness, comprehensiveness, copiousness, curvaceousness, dilation, distension, enlargement, entirety, extensiveness, fill, glut, loudness, orotundity, plenitude, plenty, pleroma, profusion, repletion, resonance, richness, roundness, satiety, saturation, strength, sufficiency, swelling, totality, tumescence, vastness, voluptuousness, wealth, wholeness.
antonyms emptiness, incompleteness.

full-scale *adj.* all-encompassing, all-out, comprehensive, exhaustive, extensive, full-dress, in-depth, intensive, major, proper, sweeping, thorough, thoroughgoing, wide-ranging.
antonym partial.

fulminate *v.* animadvert, criticize, curse, denounce, detonate, fume, inveigh, protest, rage, rail, thunder, vilipend, vituperate.
antonym praise.

fulsome *adj.* adulatory, cloying, effusive, excessive, extravagant, fawning, gross, immoderate, ingratiating, inordinate, insincere, nauseating, nauseous, offensive, overdone, rank, saccharine, sickening, smarmy, sycophantic, unctuous.
antonym sincere.

fume *v.* boil, chafe, fizz, get steamed up, give off, rage, rant, rave, reek, seethe, smoke, smolder, storm.

fun *n.* amusement, buffoonery, cheer, clowning, distraction, diversion, enjoyment, entertainment, foolery, frolic, gaiety, game, gammock, high jinks, horseplay, jesting, jocularity, joking, jollification, jollity, joy, junketing, merriment, merrymaking, mirth, nonsense, play, playfulness, pleasure, recreation, romp, skylarking, sport, teasing, tomfoolery, treat, waggery, whoopee.

function[1] *n.* activity, business, capacity, charge, concern, duty, employment, exercise, faculty, job, mission, occupation, office, operation, part, post, province, purpose, raison d'être, responsibility, role, situation, task.
v. act, be in running order, behave, do duty, functionate, go, officiate, operate, perform, run, serve, work.

function[2] *n.* affair, dinner, do, gathering, junket, luncheon, party, reception, shindig.

fundamental *adj.* axiomatic, basal, basic, basilar, cardinal, central, constitutional, crucial, elementary, essential, first, important, indispensable, integral, intrinsic, key, keynote, necessary, organic, primal, primary, prime, principal, rudimentary, underlying, vital.
antonym advanced.
n. axiom, basic, cornerstone, essential, first principle, law, principle, rudiment, rule, sine qua non.

funereal *adj.* dark, deathlike, depressing, dirgelike, dismal, dreary, exequial, feral, funebral, funebrial, gloomy, grave, lamenting, lugubrious, mournful, sad, sepulchral, solemn, somber, woeful.
antonyms happy, lively.

funny *adj.* a card, a caution, a scream, absurd, amusing, comic, comical, curious, diverting, droll, dubious, entertaining, facetious, farcical, funny ha-ha, funny peculiar, hilarious, humorous, jocose, jocular, jolly, killing, laughable, ludicrous, mirth-provoking, mysterious, odd, peculiar, perplexing, puzzling, queer, remarkable, rich, ridiculous, riotous, risible, side-splitting, silly, slapstick, strange, suspicious, unusual, waggish, weird, witty.
antonyms sad, solemn, unamusing, unfunny.

furious *adj.* acharné, agitated, angry, boiling, boisterous, enraged, fierce, fizzing, frantic, frenzied, fuming, furibund, impetuous, incensed, infuriated, intense, livid, mad, maddened, maenadic, raging, savage, stormy, tempestuous, tumultuous, turbulent, up in arms, vehement, violent, waxy, wild, wrathful, wroth.
antonyms calm, pleased.

furnish *v.* afford, appoint, bedight, bestow, decorate, endow, equip, fit out, fit up, give, grant, offer, outfit, present, provide, provision, reveal, rig, stake, stock, store, suit, supply.
antonym divest.

furore *n.* commotion, craze, disturbance, enthusiasm, excitement, flap, frenzy, fury, fuss, hullabaloo, mania, outburst, outcry, rage, stir, to-do, tumult, uproar.
antonym calm.

furtherance *n.* advancement, advancing, advocacy, backing, boosting, carrying-out, championship, promoting, promotion, prosecution, pursuit.

furthermore *adv.* additionally, also, as well, besides, further, in addition, into the bargain, likewise, moreover, not to mention, to boot, too, what's more.

furtive *adj.* back-door, backstairs, clandestine, cloaked, conspiratorial, covert, hidden, secret, secretive, skulking, slinking, sly, sneaking, sneaky, stealthy, surreptitious, underhand.
antonym open.

fury[1] *n.* anger, desperation, ferocity, fierceness, force, frenzy, impetuosity, intensity, ire, madness, passion, power, rage, savagery, severity, tempestuousness, turbulence, vehemence, violence, wax, wrath.
antonym calm.

fury[2] *n.* bacchante, hag, harridan, hell-cat, shrew, spitfire, termagant, virago, vixen.

fuss *n.* ado, agitation, bother, brouhaha, bustle, coil, commotion, confusion, difficulty, display, doodah, excitement, fantigue, fash, fidget, fikery, flap, flurry, fluster, flutter, furore, hassle, hoo-ha, hurry, kerfuffle, objection, palaver, pother, pudder, row, squabble, stew, stir, to-do, trouble, unrest, upset, worry.
antonym calm.
v. bustle, chafe, complain, emote, fash, fidget, flap, fret, fume, niggle, pother, pudder, take pains, worry.

futile *adj.* abortive, barren, bootless, empty, forlorn, fruitless, hollow, idle, ineffectual, nugatory, otiose, pointless, profitless, Sisyphean, sterile, trifling, trivial, unavailing, unimportant, unproductive, unprofitable, unsuccessful, useless, vain, valueless, worthless.
antonyms fruitful, profitable.

futility *n.* aimlessness, bootlessness, emptiness, fruitlessness, hollowness, idleness, ineffectiveness, otioseness, pointlessness, triviality, unimportance, uselessness, vanity.
antonyms fruitfulness, profitability.

future *n.* expectation, futurition, futurity, hereafter, outlook, prospects.
antonym past.
adj. approaching, coming, designate, destined, eventual, expected, fated, forthcoming, impending, in the offing, later, prospective, rising, subsequent, to be, to come, ultimate, unborn.
antonym past.

fuzzy *adj.* bleary, blurred, blurry, distanceless, distorted, downy, faint, fluffy, frizzy, hazy, ill-defined, indistinct, linty, muffled, napped, shadowy, unclear, unfocused, vague, woolly.
antonyms base, distinct.

G

gab *v.* babble, blabber, blather, blether, buzz, chatter, drivel, gossip, jabber, jaw, prattle, talk, tattle, yabber, yak, yatter. *n.* blab, blarney, blethering, blethers, chat, chatter, chitchat, conversation, drivel, gossip, loquacity, palaver, prattle, prattling, small talk, tête-à-tête, tittle-tattle, tongue-wagging, yabber, yackety-yak, yak, yatter.

gabble *v.* babble, blab, blabber, blether, cackle, chatter, gaggle, gibber, gush, jabber, prattle, rattle, splutter, spout, sputter, yabber, yatter.
n. babble, blabber, blethering, cackling, chatter, drivel, gibberish, jargon, nonsense, prattle, twaddle, waffle, yabber, yatter.

gad about dot about, gallivant, ramble, range, roam, rove, run around, stray, traipse, wander.

gadabout *n.* gallivanter, pleasure-seeker, rambler, rover, runabout, stravaiger, wanderer.

gadget *n.* appliance, contraption, contrivance, device, doodad, gimmick, gismo, gizmo, invention, jiggumbob, jigjam, jigmaree, novelty, thing, thingumajig, tool, widget.

gaffer *n.* boss, foreman, ganger, manager, overman, overseer, superintendent, supervisor.

gag[1] *v.* choke, choke up, curb, disgorge, gasp, heave, muffle, muzzle, puke, quiet, retch, silence, spew, stifle, still, stop up, suppress, throttle, throw up, vomit.

gag[2] *n.* funny, hoax, jest, joke, one-liner, pun, quip, wisecrack, witticism.

gaiety *n.* animation, blitheness, blithesomeness, brightness, brilliance, celebration, cheerfulness, color, colorfulness, conviviality, effervescence, elation, exhilaration, festivity, fun, galliardize, gaudiness, glee, glitter, good humor, high spirits, hilarity, joie de vivre, jollification, jollity, joviality, joyousness, lightheartedness, liveliness, merriment, merrymaking, mirth, revelry, revels, show, showiness, sparkle, sprightliness, vivacity.
antonyms drabness, dreariness, sadness.

gain *v.* achieve, acquire, advance, arrive at, attain, avail, bag, bring in, capture, clear, collect, come to, earn, enlist, gather, get, get to, glean, harvest, impetrate, improve, increase, make, net, obtain, pick up, procure, produce, profit, progress, reach, realize, reap, secure, win, win over, yield.
antonym lose.
n. accretion, achievement, acquisition, advance, advancement, advantage, attainment, benefit, bunce, dividend, earnings, emolument, growth, headway, improvement, income, increase, increment, lucre, proceeds, produce, profit, progress, pudding, return, rise, winnings, yield.
antonyms loss, losses.

gainful *adj.* advantageous, beneficial, feracious, fructuous, fruitful, lucrative, moneymaking, paying, productive, profitable, remunerative, rewarding, useful, worthwhile.
antonym useless.

gainsay *v.* contradict, contravene, controvert, deny, disaffirm, disagree with, dispute, nay-say.
antonym agree.

gait *n.* bearing, carriage, manner, pace, step, stride, tread, walk.

gala *n.* carnival, celebration, festival, festivity, fête, glorification, jamboree, jubilee, Mardi Gras, pageant, party, procession.

gale *n.* blast, burst, cyclone, eruption, explosion, fit, howl, hurricane, outbreak, outburst, peal, ripsnorter, shout, shriek, squall, storm, tempest, tornado, typhoon.

gall[1] *n.* acrimony, animosity, animus, antipathy, assurance, bad blood, bile, bitterness, brass, brass neck, brazenness, cheek, effrontery, enmity, hostility, impertinence, impudence, insolence, malevolence, malice, malignity, neck, nerve, presumption, presumptuousness, rancor, sauciness, sourness, spite, spleen, venom, virulence.
antonyms friendliness, modesty, reserve.

gall[2] *v.* abrade, aggravate, annoy, bark, bother, chafe, exasperate, excoriate, fret, get, get to, graze, harass, hurt, irk, irritate, nag, nettle, peeve, pester, plague, provoke, rankle, rile, rub raw, ruffle, scrape, skin, vex.

gallant *adj.* attentive, august, bold, brave, chivalrous, courageous, courteous, courtly, daring, dashing, dauntless, dignified, doughty, elegant, fearless, game, gentlemanly, glorious, gracious, grand, heroic, high-spirited, honorable, imposing, indomitable, intrepid, lionhearted, lofty, magnanimous, magnificent, manful, manly, mettlesome, noble, plucky, polite, splendid, stately, valiant, valorous.
antonyms cowardly, craven, ungentlemanly.
n. admirer, adventurer, beau, blade, boyfriend, buck, cavalier, champion, cicisbeo, dandy, daredevil, escort, fop, hero, knight, ladies' man, lady-killer, lover, paramour, suitor, wooer.

gallantry *n.* attention, attentiveness, audacity, boldness, bravery, chivalry, courage, courageousness, courteousness, courtesy, courtliness, daring, dauntlessness, derring-do, elegance, fearlessness, gentlemanliness, graciousness, heroism, intrepidity, manliness, mettle,

nerve, nobility, pluck, politeness, politesse, prowess, spirit, valiance, valor.
antonyms cowardice, ungentlemanliness.

gallery *n.* arcade, art-gallery, balcony, circle, gods, grandstand, loggia, museum, passage, pawn, spectators, walk.

galling *adj.* aggravating, annoying, bitter, bothersome, exasperating, harassing, humiliating, infuriating, irksome, irritating, nettling, plaguing, provoking, rankling, vexatious, vexing.
antonym pleasing.

galore *adv.* aplenty, everywhere, heaps of, in abundance, in numbers, in profusion, lots of, millions of, stacks of, to spare, tons of.
antonym scarce.

gamble *v.* back, bet, chance, gaff, game, have a flutter, hazard, play, punt, risk, speculate, stake, stick one's neck out, take a chance, try one's luck, venture, wager.
n. bet, chance, flutter, leap in the dark, lottery, punt, risk, speculation, uncertainty, venture, wager.

gambol *v.* bounce, bound, caper, cavort, curvet, cut a caper, frisk, frolic, hop, jump, prance, rollick, skip.
n. antic, bound, caper, frisk, frolic, gambado, hop, jump, prance, skip, spring.

game[1] *n.* adventure, amusement, business, competition, contest, design, device, distraction, diversion, enterprise, entertainment, event, frolic, fun, jest, joke, lark, line, main, match, meeting, merriment, merry-making, occupation, pastime, plan, play, plot, ploy, proceeding, recreation, romp, round, scheme, sport, stratagem, strategy, tactic, tournament, trick, undertaking.

game[2] *n.* animals, bag, flesh, game-birds, meat, prey, quarry, spoils.

game[3] *adj.* bold, brave, courageous, dauntless, desirous, disposed, dogged, eager, fearless, gallant, gamy, heroic, inclined, interested, intrepid, persevering, persistent, plucky, prepared, ready, resolute, spirited, spunky, unflinching, valiant, valorous, willing.
antonyms cowardly, unwilling.

game[4] *adj.* bad, crippled, deformed, disabled, gammy, gouty, hobbling, incapacitated, injured, lame, maimed.

gamut *n.* area, catalog, compass, field, range, scale, scope, series, spectrum, sweep.

gang *n.* band, circle, clique, club, coffle, company, core, coterie, crew, crowd, group, herd, horde, lot, mob, pack, party, ring, set, shift, squad, team, troupe.

gangling *adj.* angular, awkward, bony, gangly, gauche, gawky, lanky, loose-jointed, rangy, raw-boned, skinny, spindly, tall, ungainly.

gangster *n.* bandit, brigand, crook, desperado, heavy, hood, hoodlum, mobster, racketeer, robber, rough, ruffian, thug, tough.

gap *n.* blank, breach, break, chink, cleft, crack, cranny, crevice, diastema, difference, disagreement, discontinuity, disparateness, disparity, divergence, divide, hiatus, hole, inconsistency, interlude, intermission, interruption, interspace, interstice, interval, lacuna, lull, opening, pause, recess, rent, rift, space, vacuity, void.

gape *v.* crack, dehisce, gawk, gawp, goggle, open, split, stare, wonder, yawn.

garb *n.* accouterments, apparel, appearance, array, aspect, attire, clothes, clothing, costume, covering, cut, dress, fashion, garment, gear, guise, habiliment, habit, look, mode, outfit, raiment, robes, style, uniform, vestments, wear.
v. apparel, array, attire, clothe, cover, dress, habilitate, rig out, robe.

garbage *n.* bits and pieces, debris, detritus, dross, filth, gash, junk, litter, muck, odds and ends, offal, refuse, rubbish, scourings, scraps, slops, sweepings, swill, trash, waste.

garble *v.* confuse, corrupt, distort, doctor, edit, falsify, jumble, misinterpret, misquote, misreport, misrepresent, misstate, mistranslate, mix up, muddle, mutilate, pervert, slant, tamper with, twist.
antonym decipher.

gargantuan *adj.* big, Brobdingnag(ian), colossal, elephantine, enormous, giant, gigantic, huge, immense, large, leviathan, mammoth, massive, monstrous, monumental, mountainous, prodigious, titanic, towering, tremendous, vast.
antonym small.

garments *n.* apparel, array, attire, clothes, clothing, costume, dress, duds, garb, gear, get-up, habiliment, habit, outfit, raiment, robes, togs, uniform, vestments, wear.

garnish *v.* adorn, beautify, bedeck, deck, decorate, embellish, enhance, furnish, grace, ornament, set off, trim.
antonym divest.
n. adornment, decoration, embellishment, enhancement, garnishment, garnishry, garniture, ornament, ornamentation, relish, trim, trimming.

garrulous *adj.* babbling, chattering, chatty, diffuse, effusive, gabby, gassy, glib, gossiping, gushing, long-winded, loquacious, mouthy, prating, prattling, prolix, prosy, talkative, verbose, voluble, windy, wordy, yabbering.
antonyms taciturn, terse.

gash *v.* cleave, cut, gouge, incise, lacerate, nick, notch, rend, score, slash, slit, split, tear, wound.
n. cleft, cut, gouge, incision, laceration, nick, notch, rent, score, slash, slit, split, tear, wound.

gasp *v.* blow, breathe, choke, ejaculate, gulp, pant, puff, utter.
n. blow, breath, ejaculation, exclamation, gulp, pant, puff.

gather *v.* accumulate, amass, assemble, assume, build, clasp, collect, conclude, congregate, convene, crop, cull, deduce, deepen, draw, embrace, enfold, enlarge, expand, flock, fold, foregather, garner, glean, group, grow, harvest, heap, hear, heighten, hoard, hold, hug, increase, infer, intensify, learn, make, marshal, mass, muster,

pick, pile up, pleat, pluck, pucker, rake up, reap, rise, round up, ruche, ruffle, select, shirr, stockpile, surmise, swell, thicken, tuck, understand, wax.
antonyms dissipate, scatter.

gathering *n.* accumulation, acquisition, aggregate, assemblage, assembly, collection, company, concentration, conclave, concourse, congregation, congress, convention, convocation, crowd, fest, flock, gain, galère, get-together, group, heap, hoard, jamboree, kgotla, knot, mass, meeting, moot, muster, omnium-gatherum, party, pile, procurement, rally, round-up, rout, stock, stockpile, throng, turn-out.
antonym scattering.

gaudy *adj.* bright, brilliant, chintzy, flash, flashy, florid, garish, gay, glaring, glitzy, loud, meretricious, ostentatious, raffish, showy, tasteless, tawdry, tinsel(ly), vulgar.
antonyms drab, plain, quiet.

gaunt *adj.* angular, attenuated, bare, bleak, bony, cadaverous, desolate, dismal, dreary, emaciated, forbidding, forlorn, grim, haggard, hagged, harsh, hollow-eyed, lank, lean, meager, pinched, rawboned, scraggy, scrawny, skeletal, skinny, spare, thin, wasted.
antonyms hale, plump.

gay[1] *adj.* animated, blithe, boon, bright, brilliant, carefree, cavalier, cheerful, colorful, convivial, debonair, festive, flamboyant, flashy, fresh, frivolous, frolicsome, fun-loving, gamesome, garish, gaudy, glad, gleeful, happy, hilarious, insouciant, jolly, jovial, joyful, joyous, lifesome, lighthearted, lightsome, lively, merry, playful, pleasure-seeking, rakish, riant, rich, rollicking, rorty, showy, sparkish, sparkling, sportive, sunny, tit(t)upy, vivacious, vivid, waggish.
antonyms gloomy, sad.

gay[2] *adj.* bent, dikey, homosexual, lesbian, queer.
antonyms heterosexual, straight.
n. dike, homo, homosexual, lesbian, poof, queer, sapphist.
antonym heterosexual.

gaze *v.* contemplate, gape, gaup, gawp, look, ogle, regard, stare, view, watch.
n. gaup, gawp, look, stare.

gear *n.* accessories, accouterments, affair, apparatus, apparel, armor, array, attire, baggage, belongings, business, clothes, clothing, cog, costume, doings, dress, effects, equipment, garb, garments, gearing, get-up, habit, harness, instruments, kit, luggage, machinery, matter, mechanism, outfit, paraphernalia, possessions, rigging, rig-out, stuff, supplies, tackle, things, togs, tools, trappings, traps, wear, works.
v. adapt, adjust, equip, fit, harness, rig, suit, tailor.

gel *v.* coagulate, congeal, crystallize, finalize, form, gee, gel, gelatinate, gelatinize, harden, jelly, materialize, set, solidify, take form, take shape, thicken.
antonym disintegrate.

gem *n.* angel, bijou, brick, flower, honey, jewel, masterpiece, pearl, pick, pièce de résistance, precious stone, prize, stone, treasure.

general *adj.* accepted, accustomed, across-the-board, all-inclusive, approximate, blanket, broad, catholic, collective, common, comprehensive, conventional, customary, ecumenic, ecumenical, encyclopedic, everyday, extensive, generic, habitual, ill-defined, imprecise, inaccurate, indefinite, indiscriminate, inexact, loose, miscellaneous, normal, ordinary, panoramic, popular, prevailing, prevalent, public, regular, sweeping, total, typical, universal, unspecific, usual, vague, widespread.
antonyms limited, novel, particular.
n. chief, c-in-c, commander, commander in chief, generalissimo, hetman, leader, marshal, officer.

generally *adv.* approximately, as a rule, broadly, by and large, characteristically, chiefly, commonly, conventionally, customarily, extensively, for the most part, habitually, in the main, largely, mainly, mostly, normally, on average, on the whole, ordinarily, popularly, predominantly, principally, publicly, regularly, typically, universally, usually, widely.
antonym rarely.

generate *v.* beget, breed, bring about, cause, create, engender, father, form, gender, give rise to, initiate, make, originate, procreate, produce, propagate, spawn, whip up.
antonym prevent.

generation *n.* age, age group, begetting, breed, breeding, creation, crop, day, days, engendering, engenderment, engend(r)ure, epoch, era, formation, generating, genesis, geniture, origination, period, procreation, production, progeniture, propagation, reproduction, time, times.

generosity *n.* beneficence, benevolence, big-heartedness, bounteousness, bounty, charity, goodness, high-mindedness, kindness, large-heartedness, liberality, magnanimity, munificence, nobleness, open-handedness, soft-heartedness, unselfishness, unsparingness.
antonyms meanness, selfishness.

generous *adj.* abundant, ample, beneficent, benevolent, big-hearted, bounteous, bountiful, charitable, copious, disinterested, free, full, good, high-minded, hospitable, kind, large-hearted, large-minded, lavish, liberal, lofty, magnanimous, munificent, noble, open-handed, overflowing, plentiful, princely, rich, soft-boiled, soft-hearted, ungrudging, unreproachful, unresentful, unselfish, unsparing, unstinted, unstinting.
antonyms mean, selfish.

genesis *n.* beginning, birth, commencement, creation, dawn, engendering, formation, foundation, founding, generation, inception, initiation, origin, outset, propagation, root, source, start.
antonym end.

genius[1] *n.* adept, brain, expert, intellect, maestro, master, master-hand, mastermind, pastmaster, virtuoso.

genius[2] *n.* ability, aptitude, bent, brightness, brilliance, capacity, endowment, faculty, flair, gift, inclination, intellect, knack, propensity, talent, turn.

genius[3] *n.* daemon, double, genie, ka, spirit.

genre *n.* brand, category, character, class, fashion, genus, group, kind, race, school, sort, species, strain, style, type, variety.

genteel *adj.* aristocratic, civil, courteous, courtly, cultivated, cultured, elegant, fashionable, formal, gentlemanly, graceful, ladylike, mannerly, polished, polite, refined, respectable, stylish, urbane, well-bred, well-mannered.
antonyms crude, rough, unpolished.

gentle *adj.* amiable, aristocratic, balmy, benign, biddable, bland, broken, calm, canny, clement, compassionate, courteous, cultured, docile, easy, elegant, genteel, gentleman-like, gentlemanly, gradual, high-born, humane, imperceptible, kind, kindly, ladylike, lamb-like, lenient, light, low, maidenly, manageable, meek, merciful, mild, moderate, muted, noble, pacific, peaceful, placid, polished, polite, quiet, refined, serene, slight, slow, smooth, soft, soothing, sweet, sweet-tempered, tame, temperate, tender, tractable, tranquil, untroubled, upper-class, well-born, well-bred.
antonyms crude, rough, unkind, unpolished.

genuine *adj.* actual, artless, authentic, bona fide, candid, earnest, frank, heartfelt, honest, kosher, legitimate, natural, original, pukka, pure, real, simon-pure, sincere, sound, sterling, sure-enough, true, unadulterate(d), unaffected, unalloyed, unfeigned, unsophisticated, veritable.
antonyms artificial, insincere.

genus *n.* breed, category, class, division, genre, group, kind, order, race, set, sort, species, taxon, type.

germ *n.* bacterium, beginning, bud, bug, cause, egg, embryo, microbe, micro-organism, nucleus, origin, ovule, ovum, root, rudiment, seed, source, spark, spore, sprout, virus, zyme.

germinate *v.* bud, develop, generate, grow, originate, pullulate, root, shoot, sprout, swell, vegetate.

gesture *n.* act, action, gesticulation, indication, motion, sign, signal, wave.
v. gesticulate, indicate, motion, point, sign, signal, wave.

get *v.* achieve, acquire, affect, annoy, arouse, arrange, arrest, arrive, attain, baffle, bag, become, bother, bring, bug, capture, catch, coax, collar, come, come by, come down with, communicate with, comprehend, confound, contact, contract, contrive, convince, earn, excite, fathom, fetch, fix, follow, gain, glean, grab, grow, hear, impetrate, impress, induce, influence, inherit, irk, irritate, make, make it, manage, move, mystify, net, nonplus, notice, obtain, perceive, perplex, persuade, pick up, pique, prevail upon, procure, puzzle, reach, realize, reap, receive, secure, see, seize, stimulate, stir, stump, succeed, sway, take, touch, trap, turn, twig, understand, upset, vex, wangle, wax, wheedle, win.
antonyms lose, misunderstand, pacify.

ghastly *adj.* ashen, cadaverous, deathlike, deathly, dreadful, frightful, ghostly, grim, grisly, gruesome, hideous, horrendous, horrible, horrid, livid, loathsome, lurid, pale, pallid, repellent, shocking, spectral, terrible, terrifying, wan.
antonym delightful.

ghost *n.* apparition, astral body, duppy, eidolon, fetch, glimmer, gytrash, hint, jumby, larva, lemur, manes, phantasm, phantom, possibility, revenant, semblance, shade, shadow, simulacrum, soul, specter, spirit, spook, suggestion, trace, umbra, visitant, white-lady.

ghoulish *adj.* grisly, gruesome, macabre, morbid, revolting, sick, unhealthy, unwholesome.

giant *n.* behemoth, colossus, Goliath, Hercules, jotun, leviathan, monster, Patagonian, titan.
adj. Atlantean, Babylonian, Brobdingnag(ian), colossal, cyclopean, elephantine, enormous, gargantuan, gigantean, gigantesque, gigantic, huge, immense, jumble, king-size, large, leviathan, mammoth, monstrous, Patagonian, prodigious, rounceval, titanic, vast.

giddy *adj.* capricious, careless, changeable, changeful, dizzy, dizzying, erratic, faint, fickle, flighty, frivolous, heedless, impulsive, inconstant, irresolute, irresponsible, lightheaded, reckless, reeling, scatterbrained, scatty, silly, thoughtless, unbalanced, unstable, unsteady, vacillating, vertiginous, volage, volageous, volatile, wild.
antonyms sensible, sober.

gift *n.* ability, aptitude, attribute, benefaction, benificence, bent, bequest, bonus, boon, bounty, cadeau, capability, capacity, contribution, cumshaw, deodate, dolly, donary, donation, donative, douceur, earnest, endowment, faculty, flair, foy, freebie, genius, grant, gratuity, knack, largess(e), legacy, manna, offering, power, present, sop, talent, turn, xenium.

gigantic *adj.* Atlantean, Babylonian, Brobdingnag(ian), colossal, cyclopean, elephantine, enormous, gargantuan, giant, herculean, huge, immense, leviathan, mammoth, monstrous, Patagonian, prodigious, rounceval, stupendous, titanic, tremendous, vast.
antonym small.

giggle *v.* chortle, chuckle, laugh, snigger, tee-hee, titter.
n. chortle, chuckle, fou rire, laugh, snigger, tee-hee, titter.

gild *v.* adorn, array, beautify, bedeck, brighten, coat, deck, dress up, embellish, embroider, enhance, enrich, festoon, garnish, grace, ornament, paint, trim.

gingerly *adv.* carefully, cautiously, charily, circumspectly, daintily, delicately, fastidiously, gently, hesitantly, reluctantly, squeamishly, suspiciously, timidly, warily.
antonyms carelessly, roughly.

gird *v.* belt, bind, blockade, brace, encircle, enclose, encompass, enfold, engird, environ, enzone, fortify, girdle, hem in, pen, prepare, ready, ring, steel, surround.

girdle *n.* band, belt, ceinture, cestus, cincture, cingulum, corset, cummerbund, fillet, sash, waistband, zona, zone, zonule.
v. bind, bound, encircle, enclose, encompass, engird, environ, enzone, gird, gird round, go round, hem, ring, surround.

girl *n.* backfisch, bird, chick, chicken, chit, colleen, damsel, daughter, demoiselle, filly, fizgig, flapper, flibbertigibbet, floosie, fluff, fräulein, gal, giglet, girl-friend, gouge, grisette, judy, lass, lassie, maid, maiden, miss, moppet, peach, piece, popsy(-wopsy), quean, quine, sheila, sweetheart, wench.

girth *n.* band, belly-band, bulk, circumference, measure, saddle-band, size, strap.

gist *n.* core, direction, drift, essence, force, idea, import, marrow, matter, meaning, nub, pith, point, quintessence, sense, significance, substance.

give *v.* accord, administer, admit, allow, announce, award, bend, bestow, break, cause, cede, collapse, commit, communicate, concede, confer, consign, contribute, deliver, demonstrate, devote, display, do, donate, emit, engender, entrust, evidence, fall, furnish, grant, hand, hand over, impart, indicate, issue, lead, lend, make, make over, manifest, notify, occasion, offer, pay, perform, permit, present, produce, proffer, pronounce, provide, publish, recede, relinquish, render, retire, set forth, show, sink, state, supply, surrender, transmit, utter, vouchsafe, yield.
antonyms hold out, take, withstand.

given *adj.* addicted, admitted, agreed, apt, bestowed, disposed, granted, inclined, liable, likely, prone, specified.

glacial *adj.* antagonistic, arctic, biting, bitter, brumous, chill, chilly, cold, freezing, frigid, frore, frosty, frozen, gelid, hostile, icy, inimical, piercing, polar, raw, Siberian, stiff, unfriendly, wintry.
antonym warm.

glad *adj.* animated, blithe, blithesome, bright, cheerful, cheering, cheery, chuffed, contented, delighted, delightful, felicitous, gay, gleeful, gratified, gratifying, happy, jocund, jovial, joyful, joyous, merry, over the moon, overjoyed, pleasant, pleased, pleasing, willing.
antonym sad.

gladness *n.* animation, blitheness, blithesomeness, brightness, cheerfulness, delight, felicity, gaiety, glee, happiness, high spirits, hilarity, jollity, joy, joyousness, mirth, pleasure.
antonym sadness.

glamor *n.* allure, appeal, attraction, beauty, bewitchment, charm, enchantment, fascination, magic, magnetism, prestige, ravishment, witchery.

glamorous *adj.* alluring, attractive, beautiful, bewitching, captivating, charming, classy, dazzling, elegant, enchanting, entrancing, exciting, fascinating, glittering, glossy, gorgeous, lovely, prestigious, smart.
antonyms boring, drab, plain.

glance[1] *v.* browse, dip, flip, gaze, glimpse, leaf, look, peek, peep, riffle, scan, skim, thumb, touch on, view.
n. allusion, coup d'oeil, dekko, gander, glimpse, look, mention, once over, peek, peep, reference, squint, view.

glance[2] *v.* bounce, brush, cannon, carom, coruscate, flash, gleam, glimmer, glint, glisten, glister, glitter, graze, rebound, reflect, ricochet, shimmer, shine, skim, twinkle.

glare *v.* blaze, coruscate, dazzle, flame, flare, frown, glower, look daggers, lower, scowl, shine.
n. black look, blaze, brilliance, dazzle, dirty look, flame, flare, flashiness, floridness, frown, gaudiness, glow, glower, light, look, loudness, lower, scowl, showiness, stare, tawdriness.

glaring *adj.* audacious, blatant, blazing, bright, conspicuous, dazzling, dreadful, egregious, flagrant, flashy, florid, garish, glowing, gross, horrendous, loud, manifest, obvious, open, outrageous, outstanding, overt, patent, rank, terrible, unconcealed, visible.
antonyms dull, hidden, minor.

glass *n.* beaker, crystal, goblet, lens, looking-glass, magnifying glass, pane, pocket-lens, roemer, rummer, schooner, tumbler, vitrics, window.

glassy *adj.* blank, clear, cold, dazed, dull, empty, expressionless, fixed, glasslike, glazed, glazy, glossy, hyaline, icy, lifeless, shiny, slick, slippery, smooth, transparent, vacant, vitreous, vitriform.

glaze *v.* burnish, coat, crystallize, enamel, furbish, gloss, lacquer, polish, varnish.
n. coat, enamel, finish, gloss, lacquer, luster, patina, polish, shine, varnish.

gleam *n.* beam, brightness, brilliance, coruscation, flash, flicker, glimmer, glint, gloss, glow, hint, inkling, luster, ray, sheen, shimmer, sparkle, splendor, suggestion, trace.
v. coruscate, flare, flash, glance, glimmer, glint, glisten, glister, glitter, glow, scintillate, shimmer, shine, sparkle.

glean *v.* accumulate, amass, collect, cull, find out, garner, gather, harvest, learn, pick (up), reap, select.

glee *n.* cheerfulness, delight, elation, exhilaration, exuberance, exultation, fun, gaiety, gladness, gratification, hilarity, jocularity, jollity, joviality, joy, joyfulness, joyousness, liveliness, merriment, mirth, pleasure, sprightliness, triumph, verve.

gleeful *adj.* beside oneself, cheerful, cock-a-hoop, delighted, elated, exuberant, exultant, gay, gleesome, gratified, happy, jovial, joyful, joyous, jubilant, merry, mirthful, over the moon, overjoyed, pleased, triumphant.
antonym sad.

glib *adj.* artful, easy, facile, fast-talking, fluent, garrulous, insincere, logodaedalic, plausible, quick, ready, slick, slippery, smooth, smooth-spoken, smooth-tongued, suave, talkative, voluble.
antonyms implausible, tongue-tied.

glide *v.* coast, drift, float, flow, fly, glissade, roll, run, sail, skate, skim, slide, slip, soar, volplane.

glimmer *v.* blink, flicker, gleam, glint, glisten, glitter, glow, shimmer, shine, sparkle, twinkle.
n. blink, flicker, gleam, glimmering, glint, glow, grain, hint, inkling, ray, shimmer, sparkle, suggestion, trace, twinkle.

glimpse *n.* glance, gliff, glim, glisk, look, peek, peep, sight, sighting, squint.
v. descry, espy, sight, spot, spy, view.

glint *v.* flash, gleam, glimmer, glitter, reflect, shine, sparkle, twinkle.
n. flash, gleam, glimmer, glimmering, glitter, shine, sparkle, twinkle, twinkling.

glisten *v.* coruscate, flash, glance, glare, gleam, glimmer, glint, glister, glitter, scintillate, shimmer, shine, sparkle, twinkle.

glitter *v.* coruscate, flare, flash, glare, gleam, glimmer, glint, glisten, scintillate, shimmer, shine, spangle, sparkle, twinkle.
n. beam, brightness, brilliance, clinquant, display, flash, gaudiness, glamor, glare, gleam, luster, pageantry, radiance, scintillation, sheen, shimmer, shine, show, showiness, sparkle, splendor, tinsel.

gloat *v.* crow, exult, eye, glory, ogle, rejoice, relish, revel in, rub it in, triumph, vaunt.

global *adj.* all-encompassing, all-inclusive, all-out, comprehensive, encyclopedic, exhaustive, general, globular, international, pandemic, planetary, spherical, thorough, total, unbounded, universal, unlimited, world, world-wide.
antonyms limited, parochial.

globe *n.* ball, earth, orb, planet, round, roundure, sphere, world.

gloom *n.* blackness, blues, cloud, cloudiness, damp, dark, darkness, dejection, depression, desolation, despair, despondency, dimness, downheartedness, dullness, dusk, duskiness, gloominess, glumness, low spirits, melancholy, misery, murk, murkiness, obscurity, sadness, shade, shadow, sorrow, twilight, unhappiness, woe.
antonym brightness.

gloomy *adj.* bad, black, blue, chapfallen, cheerless, comfortless, crepuscular, crestfallen, dark, darksome, dejected, delightless, depressing, despondent, dim, disheartening, dismal, dispirited, dispiriting, down, down in the dumps, down in the mouth, down-beat, downcast, downhearted, dreary, dreich, dull, dusky, gloomful, glum, joyless, long-faced, long-visaged, low-spirited, melancholy, mirk(y), miserable, moody, morose, murk(y), obscure, overcast, pessimistic, sad, saddening, saturnine, sepulchral, shadowy, somber, Stygian, sullen, tenebrous.
antonym bright.

glorify *v.* adore, adorn, aggrandize, apotheosize, augment, beatify, bless, canonize, celebrate, deify, dignify, elevate, enhance, ennoble, enshrine, eulogize, exalt, extol, honor, hymn, idolize, illuminate, immortalize, laud, lift up, magnify, panegyrize, praise, raise, revere, sanctify, venerate, worship.
antonyms denounce, vilify.

glorious *adj.* beautiful, bright, brilliant, celebrated, dazzling, delightful, distinguished, divine, drunk, effulgent, elated, elevated, eminent, enjoyable, excellent, famed, famous, fine, gorgeous, grand, great, heavenly, honored, illustrious, intoxicated, magnificent, majestic, marvelous, noble, noted, pleasurable, radiant, renowned, resplendent, shining, splendid, sublime, superb, tipsy, triumphant, wonderful.
antonyms dreadful, inglorious, plain, unknown.

glory *n.* adoration, beauty, benediction, blessing, brightness, brilliance, celebrity, dignity, distinction, effulgence, eminence, exaltation, fame, gloire, gloria, gorgeousness, grandeur, gratitude, greatness, heaven, homage, honor, illustriousness, immortality, kudos, laudation, luster, magnificence, majesty, nobility, pageantry, pomp, praise, prestige, radiance, renown, resplendence, richness, splendor, sublimity, thanksgiving, triumph, veneration, worship.
antonyms blame, restraint.
v. boast, crow, delight, exult, gloat, pride oneself, rejoice, relish, revel, triumph.

gloss[1] *n.* appearance, brightness, brilliance, burnish, façade, front, gleam, luster, mask, polish, semblance, sheen, shine, show, surface, varnish, veneer, window-dressing.

gloss[2] *n.* annotation, comment, commentary, elucidation, explanation, footnote, interpretation, note, postillation, scholion, scholium, translation.
v. annotate, comment, construe, elucidate, explain, interpret, postil, postillate, translate.

glossary *n.* dictionary, idioticon, lexicon, phrase-book, vocabulary, word-book, word-list.

glossy *adj.* bright, brilliant, burnished, enameled, glacé, glassy, glazed, lustrous, polished, sheeny, shining, shiny, silken, silky, sleek, smooth.
antonym mat(t).

glow *n.* ardor, bloom, blush, brightness, brilliance, burning, earnestness, effulgence, enthusiasm, excitement, fervor, flush, gleam, glimmer, gusto, impetuosity, incandescence, intensity, lambency, light, luminosity, passion, phosphorescence, radiance, reddening, redness, rosiness, splendor, vehemence, vividness, warmth.
v. blush, brighten, burn, color, fill, flush, gleam, glimmer, glowing, radiate, redden, shine, smolder, thrill, tingle.

glower *v.* frown, glare, look daggers, lower, scowl.
n. black look, dirty look, frown, glare, look, lower, scowl, stare.

glowing *adj.* adulatory, aglow, beaming, bright, complimentary, ecstatic, enthusiastic, eulogistic, flaming,

florid, flushed, gleamy, lambent, laudatory, luminous, panegyrical, rave, red, rhapsodic, rich, ruddy, suffused, vibrant, vivid, warm.
antonyms dull, restrained.

glue *n.* adhesive, cement, fish-glue, gum, isinglass, mucilage, paste, size.
v. affix, agglutinate, cement, fix, gum, paste, seal, stick.

glum *adj.* chapfallen, churlish, crabbed, crestfallen, dejected, doleful, down, gloomy, glumpish, glumpy, gruff, grumpy, ill-humored, low, moody, morose, pessimistic, saturnine, sour, sulky, sullen, surly.
antonyms ecstatic, happy.

glut *n.* excess, overabundance, oversupply, pleroma, saturation, superabundance, superfluity, surfeit, surplus.
antonyms lack, scarcity.
v. choke, clog, cram, deluge, englut, fill, flesh, flood, gorge, inundate, overfeed, overload, oversupply, sate, satiate, saturate, stuff.

glutton *n.* cormorant, free-liver, gannet, gobbler, gorger, gormandizer, gourmand, guzzler, hog, omnivore, pig, trencherman, whale.
antonym ascetic.

gluttony *n.* edacity, esurience, gormandize, gormandizing, gormandism, greed, greediness, gulosity, insatiability, omnivorousness, piggishness, rapaciousness, rapacity, voraciousness, voracity.
antonyms abstinence, asceticism.

gnarled *adj.* contorted, distorted, gnarly, gnarred, knarred, knotted, knotty, knurled, leathery, rough, rugged, twisted, weather-beaten, wrinkled.

gnaw *v.* bite, chew, consume, devour, distress, eat, erode, fret, harry, haunt, munch, nag, nibble, niggle, plague, prey, trouble, wear, worry.

go *v.* accord, advance, agree, avail, beat it, blend, chime, complement, concur, conduce, connect, contribute, correspond, decamp, decease, depart, develop, die, disappear, elapse, eventuate, expire, extend, fare, fit, flow, function, gee, happen, harmonize, incline, jib, journey, lapse, lead, lead to, leave, levant, make for, match, mosey, move, naff off, nip, operate, pass, pass away, perform, perish, proceed, progress, rate, reach, repair, result, retreat, roll, run, sally, scram, serve, shift, shove off, slip, span, spread, stretch, suit, take one's leave, tend, travel, trot, vanish, wag, walk, wend, withdraw, work.
n. animation, attempt, bid, crack, drive, dynamism, effort, energy, essay, force, get-up-and-go, life, oomph, pep, shot, spirit, stab, try, turn, verve, vigor, vim, vitality, vivacity, whack, whirl, zest.

goad *n.* fillip, impetus, incentive, incitement, irritation, jab, motivation, poke, pressure, prod, push, spur, stimulation, stimulus, thrust, urge.
v. annoy, arouse, badger, bullyrag, chivvy, drive, egg on, exasperate, exhort, harass, hassle, hector, hound, impel, incite, infuriate, instigate, irritate, lash, madden, nag, needle, persecute, prick, prod, prompt, propel, push, spur, stimulate, sting, urge, vex, worry.

go-ahead *n.* agreement, assent, authorization, clearance, consent, fiat, green light, leave, OK, permission, sanction.
antonyms ban, embargo, moratorium, veto.
adj. ambitious, avant-garde, enterprising, goey, go-getting, pioneering, progressive, up-and-coming.
antonyms sluggish, unenterprising.

goal *n.* aim, ambition, aspiration, bourn(e), design, destination, destiny, end, grail, intention, limit, mark, object, objective, purpose, target.

gobble *v.* bolt, consume, cram, devour, gorge, gulp, guttle, guzzle, hog, put away, shovel, slabber, stuff, swallow, wire into, wolf.

go-between *n.* agent, broker, contact, dealer, factor, informer, intermediary, internuncio, liaison, mediator, medium, messenger, middleman, ombudsman, pander, pimp, procuress.

goblet *n.* balloon glass, brandy-glass, chalice, drinking-cup, hanap, Paris, goblet, quaich, rummer, tass, wine-glass.

goblin *n.* barghest, bogey, bogle, brownie, bugbear, demon, esprit follet, fiend, gremlin, hobgoblin, imp, kelpie, kobold, lubber fiend, nis, nix, nixie, red-cap, red-cowl, spirit, sprite.

God, god *n.* Allah, avatar, Brahma, deity, divinity, genius, Godhead, Holy One, idol, Jah, Jehovah, joss, Jove, kami, lar, Lord, Lord God, monad, Mumbo-jumbo, numen, penates, power, Providence, spirit, the Almighty, the Creator, tutelar, tutelary, Yahweh, Zeus.

godlike *adj.* celestial, deiform, divine, exalted, heavenly, saintly, sublime, superhuman, theomorphic, transcendent.

godly *adj.* blameless, devout, god-fearing, good, holy, innocent, pious, pure, religious, righteous, saintly, virtuous.
antonyms godless, impious.

golden *adj.* advantageous, aureate, auric, auspicious, best, blissful, blond(e), bright, brilliant, delightful, excellent, fair, favorable, favored, flaxen, flourishing, glorious, happy, inaurate, invaluable, joyful, lustrous, opportune, precious, priceless, promising, propitious, prosperous, resplendent, rich, rosy, shining, successful, timely, valuable, xanthous, yellow.

gone *adj.* absent, astray, away, broken, bygone, closed, concluded, consumed, dead, deceased, defunct, departed, disappeared, done, elapsed, ended, extinct, finished, kaput, lacking, lost, missed, missing, over, over and done with, past, pregnant, spent, used, vanished, wanting.

good *adj.* able, acceptable, accomplished, adept, adequate, admirable, adroit, advantageous, agreeable, altruistic, amiable, ample, appropriate, approved, approving, auspicious, authentic, balmy, beneficent, beneficial, benevolent, benign, bona fide, bonzer, boshta, bosker,

bright, brotherly, budgeree, buoyant, calm, capable, capital, charitable, cheerful, choice, clear, clever, cloudless, commendable, competent, complete, congenial, considerate, convenient, convivial, correct, decorous, dependable, deserving, dexterous, dutiful, eatable, efficient, enjoyable, entire, estimable, ethical, excellent, exemplary, expert, extensive, fair, favorable, fine, first-class, first-rate, fit, fitting, friendly, full, genuine, gracious, gratifying, great, happy, healthy, helpful, honest, honorable, humane, kind, kindly, large, legitimate, long, loyal, mannerly, merciful, meritorious, mild, moral, nice, noble, nourishing, nutritious, obedient, obliging, opportune, orderly, pious, pleasant, pleasing, pleasurable, polite, positive, praiseworthy, precious, presentable, professional, proficient, profitable, proper, propitious, rattling, real, reliable, right, righteous, safe, salubrious, salutary, satisfactory, satisfying, seemly, serviceable, sizeable, skilful, skilled, solid, sound, special, splendid, substantial, sufficient, suitable, sunny, super, superior, sustaining, talented, tested, thorough, tranquil, true, trustworthy, uncorrupted, untainted, upright, useful, valid, valuable, virtuous, well-behaved, well-disposed, well-mannered, whole, wholesome, worthwhile, worthy.
n. advantage, avail, behalf, behoof, benefit, boon, convenience, excellence, gain, goodness, interest, merit, morality, probity, profit, rectitude, right, righteousness, service, uprightness, use, usefulness, virtue, weal, welfare, well-being, worth, worthiness.

good-bye *n., interj.* adieu, adiós, arrivederci, au revoir, auf Wiedersehen, chin-chin, ciao, farewell, leave-taking, parting, valediction, valedictory.

good-humored *adj.* affable, amiable, approachable, blithe, cheerful, congenial, expansive, genial, good-tempered, happy, jocund, jovial, pleasant.
antonym ill-humored.

good-looking *adj.* attractive, beautiful, bonny, comely, easy on the eye, fair, handsome, personable, presentable, pretty, well-favored, well-looking, well-proportioned, well-set-up.
antonyms ill-favored, plain, ugly.

good-natured *adj.* agreeable, amenable, approachable, benevolent, broad-minded, friendly, gentle, good-hearted, helpful, kind, kind-hearted, kindly, neighborly, open-minded, sympathetic, tolerant, warm-hearted.
antonym ill-natured.

goodness *n.* advantage, altruism, beneficence, benefit, benevolence, condescension, excellence, fairness, friendliness, generosity, goodwill, graciousness, honesty, honor, humaneness, humanity, integrity, justness, kindliness, kindness, mercy, merit, morality, nourishment, nutrition, piety, probity, quality, rectitude, righteousness, salubriousness, superiority, unselfishness, uprightness, value, virtue, wholesomeness, worth.
antonyms badness, inferiority, wickedness.

goods *n.* appurtenances, bags and baggage, belongings, chattels, commodities, effects, furnishings, furniture, gear, merchandise, movables, paraphernalia, plenishing, possessions, property, stock, stuff, traps, vendibles, wares.

goodwill *n.* altruism, amity, benevolence, compassion, earnestness, favor, friendliness, friendship, generosity, heartiness, kindliness, loving-kindness, sincerity, sympathy, zeal.
antonym ill-will.

gooseflesh *n.* creeps, duck bumps, formication, goose bumps, goose-pimples, grue, heebie-jeebies, horripilation, horrors, shivers, shudders.

gore[1] *n.* blood, bloodiness, bloodshed, butchery, carnage, cruor, grume, slaughter.

gore[2] *v.* impale, penetrate, pierce, rend, spear, spit, stab, stick, transfix, wound.
n. flare, gair, godet, gusset.

gorge[1] *n.* abyss, barranca, canyon, chasm, cleft, clough, defile, fissure, gap, gulch, gully, pass, ravine.

gorge[2] *v.* bolt, cram, devour, feed, fill, fill one's face, glut, gluttonize, gobble, gormandize, gulp, guzzle, hog, make a pig of oneself, overeat, sate, satiate, stuff, surfeit, swallow, wolf.
antonym abstain.

gorgeous *adj.* attractive, beautiful, bright, brilliant, dazzling, delightful, elegant, enjoyable, exquisite, fine, flamboyant, glamorous, glittering, glorious, good, good-looking, grand, lovely, luxuriant, luxurious, magnificent, opulent, pleasing, ravishing, resplendent, rich, showy, splendid, splendiferous, stunning, sumptuous, superb.
antonyms dull, plain, seedy.

gory *adj.* blood-soaked, bloodstained, bloodthirsty, bloody, brutal, ensanguined, murderous, sanguinary, sanguineous, sanguinolent, savage.

gossamer *adj.* airy, cobwebby, delicate, diaphanous, fine, flimsy, gauzy, insubstantial, light, sheer, shimmering, silky, thin, translucent, transparent.
antonyms heavy, opaque, thick.

gossip[1] *n.* blether, bush telegraph, causerie, chinwag, chitchat, clash, clish-clash, clishmaclaver, gup, hearsay, idle talk, jaw, newsmongering, prattle, report, rumor, scandal, schmooze, small talk, tittle-tattle, yackety-yak.

gossip[2] *n.* babbler, blatherskite, blether, bletherskate, busybody, chatterbox, chatterer, gossip-monger, newsmonger, nosy parker, prattler, quidnunc, rumorer, scandalmonger, tabby, talebearer, tattler, telltale, whisperer.
v. blather, blether, bruit, chat, clash, gabble, jaw, prattle, rumor, tattle, tell tales, whisper.

gouge *v.* chisel, claw, cut, dig, extract, force, gash, grave, groove, hack, hollow, incise, scoop, score, scratch, slash.
n. cut, furrow, gash, groove, hack, hollow, incision, notch, scoop, score, scratch, slash, trench.

gourmand *n.* cormorant, free-liver, gannet, glutton,

gorger, gormandizer, guzzler, hog, omnivore, pig, trencherman, whale.
antonym ascetic.

gourmet *n.* arbiter elegantiae, arbiter elegantiarum, bon vivant, bon viveur, connoisseur, dainty eater, epicure, epicurean, gastronome, gastronomer, gastrosoph, gastrosopher.
antonym omnivore.

govern *v.* administer, allay, bridle, check, command, conduct, contain, control, curb, decide, determine, direct, discipline, guide, influence, inhibit, lead, manage, master, order, oversee, pilot, preside, quell, regulate, reign, restrain, rule, steer, subdue, superintend, supervise, sway, tame, underlie.

government *n.* administration, authority, charge, command, conduct, control, direction, domination, dominion, Establishment, executive, governance, guidance, kingcraft, law, management, ministry, polity, powers-that-be, raj, régime, regimen, regulation, restraint, rule, sovereignty, state, statecraft, superintendence, supervision, surveillance, sway.

governor *n.* adelantado, administrator, alcalde, alderman, boss, chief, commander, commissioner, comptroller, controller, corrector, director, executive, gubernator, hakim, head, leader, manager, naik, overseer, ruler, superintendent, supervisor, vali.

gown *n.* costume, creation, dress, dressing-gown, frock, garb, garment, habit, kirtle, négligé, robe.

grab *v.* affect, annex, appropriate, bag, capture, catch, catch hold of, clutch, collar, commandeer, grasp, grip, impress, latch on to, nab, pluck, ramp, rap, seize, snap up, snatch, strike, usurp.

grace[1] *n.* attractiveness, beauty, benefaction, beneficence, benevolence, benignity, benison, breeding, charity, charm, clemency, comeliness, compassion, compassionateness, consideration, courtesy, cultivation, decency, decorum, deftness, ease, elegance, eloquence, etiquette, favor, finesse, fluency, forgiveness, generosity, goodness, goodwill, gracefulness, graciousness, indulgence, kindliness, kindness, leniency, lenity, love, loveliness, mannerliness, manners, mercifulness, mercy, merit, pardon, pleasantness, poise, polish, propriety, quarter, refinement, reprieve, shapeliness, tact, tastefulness, unction, virtue.
v. adorn, beautify, bedeck, deck, decorate, dignify, distinguish, dress, elevate, embellish, enhance, enrich, favor, garnish, glorify, honor, ornament, prettify, set off, trim.
antonyms deface, detract from, spoil.

grace[2] *n.* benediction, benedictus, blessing, consecration, prayer, thanks, thanksgiving.

graceful *adj.* agile, balletic, beautiful, becoming, charming, comely, deft, easy, elegant, facile, feat, feline, fine, flowing, fluid, gainly, genty, gracile, lightsome, natural, pleasing, pliant, slender, smooth, suave, supple, tasteful, willowish, willowy.
antonym graceless.

gracious *adj.* accommodating, affable, affluent, amenable, amiable, beneficent, benevolent, benign, benignant, charitable, chivalrous, civil, compassionate, complaisant, condescending, considerate, cordial, courteous, courtly, elegant, friendly, grand, hospitable, indulgent, kind, kindly, lenient, loving, luxurious, merciful, mild, obliging, pleasant, pleasing, polite, refined, sweet, well-mannered.
antonym ungracious.

grade *n.* acclivity, bank, brand, category, class, condition, dan, declivity, degree, downgrade, echelon, gradation, gradient, group, hill, incline, level, mark, notch, order, place, position, quality, rank, rise, rung, size, slope, stage, station, step, upgrade.
v. arrange, blend, brand, categorize, class, classify, docket, evaluate, group, label, mark, order, pigeonhole, range, rank, rate, shade, size, sort, type, value.

gradual *adj.* cautious, continuous, deliberate, even, gentle, graduated, leisurely, measured, moderate, piecemeal, progressive, regular, slow, steady, step-by-step, successive, unhurried.
antonyms precipitate, sudden.

graduate[1] *v.* arrange, calibrate, classify, grade, group, make the grade, mark off, measure out, order, pass, proportion, qualify, range, rank, regulate, sort.

graduate[2] *n.* alumna, alumnus, bachelor, diplomate, diplômé, diplômée, doctor, fellow, graduand, licentiate, literate, master, member.

graft *n.* bud, engraft, engraftation, engraftment, heteroplasty, imp, implant, implantation, insert, scion, shoot, splice, sprout, transplant.
v. engraft, implant, insert, join, splice, transplant.

grain *n.* atom, bit, cereals, corn, crumb, doit, fiber, fragment, granule, grist, grits, iota, jot, kernel, marking, mite, modicum, molecule, morsel, mote, nap, ounce, panic, particle, pattern, piece, scintilla, scrap, scruple, seed, smidgeon, spark, speck, surface, suspicion, texture, trace, weave, whit.

grand *adj.* A1, admirable, affluent, ambitious, august, chief, condescending, dignified, elevated, eminent, exalted, excellent, fine, first-class, first-rate, glorious, gracious, grandiose, great, haughty, head, highest, illustrious, imperious, imposing, impressive, large, leading, lofty, lordly, luxurious, magnificent, main, majestic, marvelous, monumental, noble, opulent, ostentatious, outstanding, palatial, patronizing, pompous, pre-eminent, pretentious, princely, principal, regal, senior, smashing, splendid, stately, striking, sublime, sumptuous, super, superb, supreme, wonderful.

grandeur *n.* augustness, dignity, graciousness, gravitas, greatness, hauteur, imperiousness, importance, loftiness, magnificence, majesty, morgue, nobility, pomp, splendor, state, stateliness, sublimity.
antonyms humbleness, lowliness, simplicity.

grandiose *adj.* affected, ambitious, bombastic, euphuistic, extravagant, flamboyant, grand, high-flown,

imposing, impressive, lofty, magnificent, majestic, monumental, ostentatious, pompous, ponderous, pretentious, showy, stately, Wagnerian, weighty.
antonym unpretentious.

grant *v.* accede to, accord, acknowledge, admit, agree to, allocate, allot, allow, apportion, assign, award, bestow, cede, concede, confer, consent to, convey, deign, dispense, donate, give, impart, permit, present, provide, transfer, transmit, vouchsafe, yield.
antonyms deny, refuse.
n. accord, admission, allocation, allotment, allowance, annuity, award, benefaction, bequest, boon, bounty, bursary, concession, donation, endowment, gift, honorarium, present, scholarship, subsidy, subvention.

granular *adj.* crumbly, grainy, granulase, granulated, granulous, gravelly, gritty, murly, rough, sabulose, sabulous, sandy.

graphic *adj.* blow-by-blow, clear, cogent, delineated, delineative, descriptive, detailed, diagrammatic, drawn, explicit, expressive, forcible, illustrative, lively, lucid, pictorial, picturesque, representational, seen, specific, striking, telling, visible, visual, vivid.
antonyms impressionistic, vague.

grapple *v.* attack, battle, catch, clash, clasp, clinch, close, clutch, combat, come to grips, confront, contend, cope, deal with, encounter, engage, face, fasten, fight, grab, grasp, grip, gripe, hold, hug, lay hold, make fast, seize, snatch, struggle, tackle, tussle, wrestle.
antonyms avoid, evade.

grasping *adj.* acquisitive, avaricious, close-fisted, covetous, greedy, mean, mercenary, miserly, niggardly, parsimonious, penny-pinching, rapacious, selfish, stingy, tight-fisted, usurious.
antonym generous.

grass[2] *n.* ganja, hash, hay, hemp, joint, marijuana, pot, reefer.

grate *v.* aggravate, annoy, chafe, comminute, creak, exasperate, fret, gall, get on one's nerves, granulate, gride, grind, irk, irritate, jar, mince, nettle, peeve, pulverize, rankle, rasp, rub, scrape, scratch, set one's teeth on edge, shred, triturate, vex.

grateful *adj.* appreciative, aware, beholden, indebted, mindful, obligated, obliged, sensible, thankful.
antonym ungrateful.

gratify *v.* appease, cater to, content, delight, favor, fulfil, gladden, humor, indulge, pander to, please, pleasure, recompense, requite, satisfy, thrill.
antonyms frustrate, thwart.

grating[1] *adj.* annoying, cacophonous, disagreeable, discordant, displeasing, grinding, harsh, horrisonant, irksome, irritating, jarring, rasping, raucous, scraping, squeaky, strident, unharmonious, unmelodious, unpleasant, vexatious.
antonyms harmonious, pleasing.

grating[2] *n.* grid, grill, grille, hack, heck, lattice, latticework, treillage, treille, trellis, trelliswork.

gratitude *n.* acknowledgment, appreciation, awareness, gratefulness, indebtedness, mindfulness, obligation, recognition, thankfulness, thanks.
antonym ingratitude.

gratuity *n.* baksheesh, beer-money, benefaction, bonus, boon, bounty, dash, donation, donative, douceur, drink-money, gift, lagniappe, largess, perquisite, pourboire, present, recompense, reward, tip, Trinkgeld.

grave[1] *n.* barrow, burial-place, burying-place, cairn, cist, crypt, long home, mausoleum, pit, sepulcher, tomb, vault.

grave[2] *adj.* acute, Catonian, critical, crucial, dangerous, depressing, dignified, disquieting, dour, dull, earnest, exigent, gloomy, grim, grim-faced, hazardous, heavy, important, leaden, long-faced, momentous, muted, perilous, ponderous, preoccupied, pressing, quiet, reserved, restrained, sad, sage, saturnine, sedate, serious, severe, significant, sober, solemn, somber, staid, subdued, thoughtful, threatening, unsmiling, urgent, vital, weighty.
antonyms cheerful, light, slight, trivial.

gravel *n.* chesil, grail, hogging, shingle.

gravitate *v.* descend, drop, fall, head for, incline, lean, move, precipitate, settle, sink, tend.

gravity *n.* acuteness, consequence, demureness, dignity, earnestness, exigency, gloom, gravitas, grimness, hazardousness, importance, magnitude, moment, momentousness, perilousness, ponderousness, reserve, restraint, sedateness, seriousness, severity, significance, sobriety, solemnity, somberness, thoughtfulness, urgency, weightiness.
antonyms gaiety, levity, triviality.

gray *adj.* aged, ancient, anonymous, ashen, bloodless, characterless, cheerless, cloudy, colorless, dark, depressing, dim, dismal, drab, dreary, dull, elderly, experienced, glaucous, gloomy, grège, greige, griseous, grizzle, grizzled, hoar, hoary, indistinct, leaden, liard, livid, mature, murksome, murky, neutral, old, overcast, pale, pallid, sunless, uncertain, unclear, unidentifiable, venerable, wan.

graze[1] *v.* batten, browse, crop, feed, fodder, pasture.

graze[2] *v.* abrade, bark, brush, chafe, gride, rub, scart, score, scotch, scrape, scratch, shave, skim, skin, touch.
n. abrasion, score, scrape, scratch.

grease *n.* dope, dripping, fat, gunge, lard, oil, ointment, sebum, tallow, unction, unguent, wax.

greasy *adj.* fatty, fawning, glib, groveling, ingratiating, lardy, oily, oleaginous, sebaceous, slick, slimy, slippery, smarmy, smeary, smooth, sycophantic, tallowy, toadying, unctuous, waxy.

great *adj.* able, ace, active, adept, admirable, adroit, august, big, bulky, capital, celebrated, chief, colossal, consequential, considerable, crack, critical, crucial, decided, devoted, dignified, distinguished, eminent, enormous, enthusiastic, exalted, excellent, excessive, expert, extended, extensive, extravagant, extreme, fab,

fabulous, famed, famous, fantastic, fine, finished, first-rate, generous, gigantic, glorious, good, grand, grave, great-hearted, grievous, heavy, heroic, high, high-minded, huge, idealistic, illustrious, immense, important, impressive, inordinate, invaluable, jake, keen, large, leading, lengthy, lofty, long, magnanimous, main, major, mammoth, manifold, marked, marvelous, massive, masterly, momentous, multitudinous, munificent, noble, nonpareil, notable, noteworthy, noticeable, outstanding, paramount, ponderous, precious, pre-eminent, priceless, primary, princely, principal, prodigious, proficient, prolific, prolonged, prominent, pronounced, protracted, remarkable, renowned, senior, serious, significant, skilful, skilled, strong, stupendous, sublime, superb, superior, superlative, swingeing, talented, terrific, tremendous, valuable, vast, virtuoso, voluminous, weighty, wonderful, zealous.
antonyms insignificant, pusillanimous, small, unimportant.

greed *n.* acquisitiveness, anxiety, avidity, covetousness, craving, cupidity, desire, eagerness, edacity, esurience, esuriency, gluttony, gormandizing, gormandism, gourmandize, greediness, gulosity, hunger, insatiability, insatiableness, itchy palm, land-hunger, longing, plutolatry, rapacity, ravenousness, selfishness, voraciousness, voracity.
antonym abstemiousness.

greedy *adj.* acquisitive, anxious, avaricious, avid, covetous, craving, curious, desirous, eager, edacious, esurient, gare, gluttonish, gluttonous, gormandizing, grasping, gripple, gutsy, hoggery, hoggish, hungry, impatient, insatiable, itchy-palmed, land-grabbing, piggish, rapacious, ravenous, selfish, ventripotent, voracious.
antonym abstemious.

green *adj.* blooming, budding, callow, covetous, credulous, emerald, envious, flourishing, fresh, glaucous, grassy, grudging, gullible, ignorant, ill, immature, inexperienced, inexpert, ingenuous, innocent, jealous, leafy, naive, nauseous, new, pale, pliable, raw, recent, resentful, sick, starry-eyed, supple, tender, unhealthy, unpracticed, unripe, unseasoned, unsophisticated, untrained, untried, unversed, verdant, verdurous, vert, virescent, virid, viridescent, vitreous, wan, wet behind the ears, young.
n. common, grass, greensward, lawn, sward, turf.

greenhorn *n.* apprentice, beginner, catechumen, fledgling, ignoramus, ingénué, initiate, Johnnie raw, learner, naïf, neophyte, newcomer, novice, novitiate, recruit, rookie, simpleton, tenderfoot, tyro.
antonyms old hand, veteran.

greenhouse *n.* conservatory, glasshouse, hothouse, nursery, pavilion, vinery.

greet *v.* accost, acknowledge, address, compliment, hail, hallo, halloo, meet, receive, salute, wave to, welcome.
antonym ignore.

gregarious *adj.* affable, chummy, companionable, convivial, cordial, extrovert, friendly, outgoing, pally, sociable, social, warm.
antonym unsociable.

grief *n.* ache, affliction, agony, anguish, bereavement, blow, burden, dejection, desiderium, desolation, distress, dole, grievance, heartache, heartbreak, lamentation, misery, mournfulness, mourning, pain, regret, remorse, sadness, sorrow, suffering, tragedy, trial, tribulation, trouble, woe.
antonym happiness.

grief-stricken *adj.* afflicted, agonized, broken, broken-hearted, crushed, desolate, despairing, devastated, disconsolate, distracted, grieving, heartbroken, inconsolable, mourning, overcome, overwhelmed, sad, sorrowful, sorrowing, stricken, unhappy, woebegone, wretched.
antonym overjoyed.

grievance *n.* affliction, beef, bitch, charge, complaint, damage, distress, gravamen, grief, gripe, grouse, hardship, injury, injustice, moan, peeve, resentment, sorrow, trial, tribulation, trouble, unhappiness, wrong.

grieve *v.* ache, afflict, agonize, bemoan, bewail, complain, crush, cut to the quick, deplore, distress, disturb, eat one's heart out, harrow, hurt, injure, lament, mourn, pain, regret, rue, sadden, sorrow, suffer, upset, wail, weep, wound.

grieved *adj.* abashed, affronted, ashamed, desolated, displeased, distressed, horrified, hurt, injured, offended, pained, sad, saddened, shocked, sorry, upset, wounded.

grievous *adj.* appalling, atrocious, burdensome, calamitous, damaging, deplorable, devastating, distressing, dreadful, flagrant, glaring, grave, harmful, heart-rending, heavy, heinous, hurtful, injurious, intolerable, lamentable, monstrous, mournful, offensive, oppressive, outrageous, overwhelming, painful, pitiful, plightful, severe, shameful, shocking, sorrowful, tragic, unbearable, wounding.

grim *adj.* adamant, cruel, doom-laden, dour, fearsome, ferocious, fierce, forbidding, formidable, frightening, frightful, ghastly, grisly, gruesome, harsh, hideous, horrible, horrid, implacable, merciless, morose, relentless, repellent, resolute, ruthless, severe, shocking, sinister, stern, sullen, surly, terrible, unpleasant, unrelenting, unwelcome, unyielding.
antonyms benign, congenial, pleasant.

grimace *n.* face, fit of the face, frown, moue, mouth, pout, scowl, smirk, sneer, wry face.
v. fleer, frown, girn, make a face, mop, mop and mow, mouth, mow, mug, pout, scowl, smirk, sneer.

grimy *adj.* begrimed, besmeared, besmirched, contaminated, dirty, filthy, foul, grubby, murky, reechy, smudgy, smutty, soiled, sooty, squalid.
antonyms clean, pure.

grind *v.* abrade, beaver, bray, comminute, crush, drudge, file, gnash, granulate, grate, grit, kibble, labor, levigate,

lucubrate, mill, polish, pound, powder, pulverize, sand, scrape, sharpen, slave, smooth, sweat, swot, toil, triturate, whet.
n. chore, drudgery, exertion, grindstone, labor, round, routine, slavery, sweat, task, toil.

grip *n.* acquaintance, clasp, clutches, comprehension, control, domination, embrace, grasp, handclasp, hold, influence, keeping, mastery, perception, possession, power, purchase, sway, tenure, understanding.
v. absorb, catch, clasp, clutch, compel, divert, engross, enthrall, entrance, fascinate, grasp, hold, involve, latch on to, mesmerize, rivet, seize, spellbind, thrill, vice.

gripe *v.* beef, bellyache, bitch, carp, complain, groan, grouch, grouse, grumble, moan, nag, whine, whinge.
n. ache, aching, affliction, beef, bitch, colic, collywobbles, complaint, cramps, distress, grievance, griping, groan, grouch, grouse, grumble, moan, objection, pain, pang, pinching, spasm, stomach-ache, twinge.

grit[1] *n.* chesil, dust, grail, gravel, hogging, pebbles, sand, shingle, swarf.
v. clench, gnash, grate, grind, lock.

grit[2] backbone, bottle, bravery, courage, determination, doggedness, foison, fortitude, fushion, gameness, guts, hardihood, mettle, nerve, perseverance, pluck, resolution, spine, spirit, spunk, stamina, staying power, tenacity, toughness.

groan *n.* complaint, cry, moan, objection, outcry, protest, sigh, wail.
antonym cheer.
v. complain, cry, lament, moan, object, protest, sigh, wail.
antonym cheer.

groggy *adj.* befuddled, confused, dazed, dizzy, dopey, faint, fuddled, knocked-up, muzzy, punch-drunk, reeling, shaky, stunned, stupefied, unsteady, weak, wobbly, woozy.
antonym lucid.

groom *v.* brush, clean, coach, curry, dress, drill, educate, neaten, nurture, preen, prepare, prime, primp, prink, ready, school, smarten, spruce up, tart up, tend, tidy, titivate, train, turn out, tutor.

groove *n.* canal, cannelure, chamfer, channel, chase, cut, cutting, flute, furrow, gutter, hollow, indentation, kerf, rabbet, rebate, rigol, rut, score, scrobe, sulcus, trench, vallecula. *antonym* ridge.

grope *v.* cast about, feel, feel about, feel up, finger, fish, flounder, fumble, goose, grabble, probe, scrabble, search.

gross[1] *adj.* apparent, arrant, bawdy, bestial, big, blatant, blue, boorish, broad, brutish, bulky, callous, coarse, colossal, corpulent, crass, crude, cumbersome, dense, downright, dull, earthy, egregious, fat, flagrant, foul, glaring, great, grievous, heavy, heinous, huge, hulking, ignorant, immense, imperceptive, improper, impure, indecent, indelicate, insensitive, large, lewd, low, lumpish, manifest, massive, obese, obscene, obtuse, obvious, offensive, outrageous, outright, overweight, plain, rank, ribald, rude, sensual, serious, shameful, shameless, sheer, shocking, slow, sluggish, smutty, tasteless, thick, uncivil, uncouth, uncultured, undiscriminating, undisguised, unfeeling, unmitigated, unseemly, unsophisticated, unwieldy, utter, vulgar.
antonyms delicate, fine, seemly, slight.

gross[2] *n.* aggregate, bulk, entirety, sum, total, totality, whole.
adj. aggregate, all-inclusive, complete, entire, inclusive, total, whole.
v. accumulate, aggregate, bring, earn, make, rake in, take, total.

grotesque *adj.* absurd, antic, bizarre, deformed, distorted, extravagant, fanciful, fantastic, freakish, gruesome, hideous, incongruous, laughable, ludicrous, macabre, malformed, misshapen, monstrous, odd, outlandish, preposterous, ridiculous, rococo, strange, ugly, unnatural, unsightly, weird.
n. bizarrerie, extravaganza, fantastic figure, gargoyle, gobbo, grotesquerie, manikin.

grotto *n.* catacomb, cave, cavern, chamber, dene-hole, grot, souterrain, subterranean (chamber), subterrene, underground chamber.

grouch *v.* beef, bellyache, bitch, carp, complain, find fault, gripe, grouse, grumble, moan, whine, whinge.
antonym acquiesce.
n. belly-acher, churl, complainer, complaint, crab, crosspatch, crotcheteer, curmudgeon, fault-finder, grievance, gripe, grouse, grouser, grumble, grumbler, malcontent, moan, moaner, murmer, murmurer, mutterer, objection, whiner, whinge, whinger.

grouchy *adj.* bad-tempered, cantankerous, captious, churlish, complaining, cross, crotchety, discontented, dissatisfied, grumbling, grumpy, ill-tempered, irascible, irritable, mutinous, peevish, petulant, querulous, sulky, surly, testy, truculent.
antonym contented.

ground *n.* arena, background, ball-park, bottom, clay, clod, deck, dirt, dry land, dust, earth, field, foundation, land, loam, mold, park, pitch, sod, soil, solum, stadium, surface, terra firma, terrain, turf.
v. acquaint with, base, build up, coach, drill, establish, familiarize with, fix, found, inform, initiate, instruct, introduce, prepare, set, settle, teach, train, tutor.

groundless *adj.* absurd, baseless, chimerical, empty, false, gratuitous, idle, illusory, imaginary, irrational, unauthorized, uncalled-for, unfounded, unjustified, unproven, unprovoked, unreasonable, unsubstantiated, unsupported, unwarranted.
antonyms justified, reasonable.

grounds[1] *n.* acres, area, country, district, domain, estate, fields, gardens, habitat, holding, land, park, property, realm, surroundings, terrain, territory, tract.

grounds[2] *n.* account, argument, base, basis, call, cause, excuse, factor, foundation, inducement, justification, motive, occasion, premise, pretext, principle, rationale, reason, score, vindication.

grounds[3] *n.* deposit, dregs, grouts, lees, precipitate, precipitation, sediment, settlings.

groundwork *n.* base, basis, cornerstone, essentials, footing, foundation, fundamentals, homework, preliminaries, preparation, research, spadework, underpinnings.

group *n.* accumulation, aggregation, assemblage, association, band, batch, bracket, bunch, category, caucus, circle, class, classification, classis, clique, clump, cluster, clutch, cohort, collection, collective, combination, company, conclave, conglomeration, congregation, constellation, core, coterie, covey, crowd, detachment, faction, formation, front, galère, gang, gathering, Gemeinschaft, genus, grouping, knot, lot, nexus, organization, pack, parti, party, pop-group, set, shower, species, squad, squadron, team, troop.
v. arrange, assemble, associate, assort, band, bracket, categorize, class, classify, cluster, collect, congregate, consort, deploy, dispose, fraternize, gather, get together, link, marshal, mass, order, organize, range, sort.

grouse *v.* beef, belly-ache, bitch, carp, complain, find fault, fret, fuss, gripe, grouch, grumble, moan, mutter, whine, whinge.
antonym acquiesce.
n. belly-ache, complaint, grievance, gripe, grouch, grumble, moan, murmur, mutter, objection, peeve, whine, whinge.

grovel *v.* abase oneself, backscratch, bootlick, cower, crawl, creep, cringe, crouch, defer, demean oneself, fawn, flatter, kowtow, sneak, sycophantize, toady.

groveling *adj.* backscratching, bootlicking, fawning, flattering, ingratiating, obsequious, sycophantic, wormy.
antonyms outspoken, straightforward.

grow *v.* advance, arise, augment, become, branch out, breed, broaden, burgeon, cultivate, develop, diversify, enlarge, evolve, expand, extend, farm, flourish, flower, germinate, get, heighten, improve, increase, issue, mature, multiply, nurture, originate, produce, progress, proliferate, propagate, prosper, raise, ripen, rise, shoot, spread, spring, sprout, stem, stretch, succeed, swell, thicken, thrive, turn, vegetate, wax, widen.
antonyms decrease, fail, halt.

grown-up *adj.* adult, full-grown, fully-fledged, fully-grown, mature, of age.
antonyms childish, immature.
n. adult, gentleman, lady, man, woman.
antonym child.

growth *n.* accrescence, accretion, advance, advancement, aggrandizement, augmentation, auxesis, broadening, change, crop, cultivation, development, diversification, enlargement, evolution, excrement, excrescence, expansion, extension, flowering, gall, germination, growing, heightening, improvement, increase, intumescence, lump, maturation, multiplication, outgrowth, produce, production, progress, proliferation, prosperity, protuberance, ripening, rise, shooting, sprouting, stretching, success, swelling, thickening, transformation, tumor, vegetation, waxing, widening.
antonyms decrease, failure, stagnation, stoppage.

grub[1] *v.* burrow, delve, dig, explore, ferret, forage, grout, hunt, investigate, nose, probe, pull up, root, rootle, rummage, scour, uproot.
n. caterpillar, chrysalis, larva, maggot, nymph, pupa, worm.

grub[2] *n.* chow, commons, eats, edibles, fodder, food, nosh, provisions, rations, scoff, sustenance, victuals.

grubby *adj.* crummy, dirty, filthy, fly-blown, frowzy, grimy, manky, mean, messy, mucky, scruffy, seedy, shabby, slovenly, smutty, soiled, sordid, squalid, unkempt, untidy, unwashed.
antonyms clean, smart.

grudge *n.* animosity, animus, antagonism, antipathy, aversion, bitterness, dislike, enmity, envy, grievance, hard feelings, hate, ill-will, jealousy, malevolence, malice, pique, rancor, resentment, spite.
antonyms favor, regard.
v. begrudge, covet, dislike, envy, mind, niggard, object to, regret, repine, resent, stint, take exception to.
antonyms applaud, approve.

grueling *adj.* arduous, backbreaking, brutal, crushing, demanding, difficult, exhausting, fatiguing, fierce, grinding, hard, hard-going, harsh, laborious, punishing, severe, stern, stiff, strenuous, taxing, tiring, tough, trying, uphill, wearing, wearying.
antonym easy.

gruesome *adj.* abominable, awful, chilling, eldritch, fearful, fearsome, ghastly, grim, grisly, grooly, hideous, horrible, horrid, horrific, horrifying, loathsome, macabre, monstrous, repellent, repugnant, repulsive, shocking, sick, spine-chilling, terrible, weird.
antonyms charming, congenial.

gruff *adj.* abrupt, bad-tempered, bearish, blunt, brusque, churlish, crabbed, croaking, crusty, curt, discourteous, gravelly, grouchy, grumpy, guttural, harsh, hoarse, husky, ill-humored, ill-natured, impolite, low, rasping, rough, rude, sour, sullen, surly, throaty, uncivil, ungracious, unmannerly.
antonyms clear, courteous, sweet.

grumble *v.* beef, bellyache, bitch, bleat, carp, chunter, complain, croak, find fault, gripe, grouch, grouse, growl, gurgle, moan, murmur, mutter, nark, repine, roar, rumble, whine.
antonym acquiesce.
n. beef, bitch, bleat, complaint, grievance, gripe, grouch, grouse, growl, gurgle, moan, murmur, muttering, objection, roar, rumble, whinge.

grumpy *adj.* bad-tempered, cantankerous, churlish, crabbed, cross, crotchety, discontented, grouchy,

grumbling, ill-tempered, irritable, mutinous, peevish, petulant, querulous, sulky, sullen, surly, testy, truculent.
antonyms civil, contented.

guarantee *n.* assurance, attestation, bond, certainty, collateral, covenant, earnest, endorsement, guaranty, insurance, oath, pledge, promise, security, surety, testimonial, undertaking, voucher, warranty, word, word of honor.
v. answer for, assure, avouch, certify, ensure, insure, maintain, make certain, make sure of, pledge, promise, protect, secure, swear, underwrite, vouch for, warrant.

guarantor *n.* angel, backer, bailsman, bondsman, covenanter, guarantee, referee, sponsor, supporter, surety, underwriter, voucher, warrantor.

guard *v.* be on the qui vive, be on the watch, beware, conserve, cover, defend, escort, keep, look out, mind, oversee, patrol, police, preserve, protect, safeguard, save, screen, secure, sentinel, shelter, shield, supervise, tend, ward, watch.
n. attention, backstop, barrier, buffer, bulwark, bumper, care, caution, convoy, custodian, defense, defender, escort, guarantee, heed, lookout, minder, pad, patrol, picket, precaution, protection, protector, rampart, safeguard, screen, security, sentinel, sentry, shield, vigilance, wall, warder, wariness, watch, watchfulness, watchman.

guarded *adj.* cagey, careful, cautious, circumspect, discreet, disingenuous, non-committal, prudent, reserved, restrained, reticent, secretive, suspicious, uncommunicative, unforthcoming, wary, watchful.
antonyms frank, whole-hearted.

guardian *n.* attendant, champion, conservator, curator, custodian, defender, depositary, depository, escort, fiduciary, guard, keeper, minder, preserver, protector, trustee, warden, warder.

guess *v.* assume, believe, conjecture, dare say, deem, divine, estimate, fancy, fathom, feel, guesstimate, hazard, hypothesize, imagine, intuit, judge, opine, penetrate, predict, reckon, solve, speculate, suppose, surmise, suspect, think, work out.
n. assumption, belief, conjecture, fancy, feeling, guesstimate, hypothesis, intuition, judgment, notion, opinion, prediction, reckoning, shot (in the dark), speculation, supposition, surmise, suspicion, theory.

guest *n.* boarder, caller, company, freeloader, habitué, lodger, parasite, regular, roomer, visitant, visitor.

guide *v.* accompany, advise, attend, command, conduct, control, convoy, counsel, direct, educate, escort, govern, handle, head, influence, instruct, lead, manage, maneuver, oversee, pilot, point, regulate, rule, shape, shepherd, steer, superintend, supervise, sway, teach, train, usher, vector.
n. ABC, adviser, attendant, beacon, catalog, chaperon, cicerone, clue, companion, conductor, controller, counselor, courier, criterion, director, directory, dragoman, escort, example, exemplar, guide-book, guideline, handbook, ideal, index, indication, informant, inspiration, instructions, key, landmark, leader, lodestar, manual, mark, marker, master, mentor, model, monitor, paradigm, pilot, pointer, praxis, sign, signal, signpost, standard, steersman, teacher, template, usher, vade-mecum.

guild *n.* association, brotherhood, chapel, club, company, corporation, fellowship, fraternity, incorporation, league, lodge, order, organization, society, union.

guile *n.* art, artfulness, artifice, cleverness, craft, craftiness, cunning, deceit, deception, deviousness, disingenuity, duplicity, gamesmanship, knavery, ruse, slyness, treachery, trickery, trickiness, wiliness.
antonyms artlessness, guilelessness.

guileless *adj.* artless, candid, direct, frank, genuine, honest, ingenuous, innocent, naïve, natural, open, simple, sincere, straightforward, transparent, trusting, truthful, unreserved, unsophisticated, unworldly.
antonyms artful, guileful.

guilt *n.* blamability, blame, blameworthiness, compunction, conscience, contrition, criminality, culpability, delinquency, disgrace, dishonor, guiltiness, guilty conscience, infamy, iniquity, mens rea, regret, remorse, responsibility, self-condemnation, self-reproach, self-reproof, shame, sinfulness, stigma, wickedness, wrong.
antonyms innocence, shamelessness.

guilty *adj.* ashamed, blamable, blameworthy, compunctious, conscience-stricken, contrite, convicted, criminal, culpable, delinquent, errant, erring, evil, felonious, guilt-ridden, hangdog, illicit, iniquitous, nefarious, nocent, offending, penitent, regretful, remorseful, repentant, reprehensible, responsible, rueful, shamefaced, sheepish, sinful, sorry, wicked, wrong.
antonyms guiltless, innocent.

guise *n.* air, appearance, aspect, behavior, custom, demeanor, disguise, dress, façade, face, fashion, features, form, front, likeness, manner, mask, mode, pretense, semblance, shape, show.

gulf *n.* abyss, basin, bay, bight, breach, chasm, cleft, gap, gorge, opening, rent, rift, separation, split, void, whirlpool.

gullible *adj.* born yesterday, credulous, foolish, glaikit, green, innocent, naïve, trusting, unsuspecting, verdant.
antonym astute.

gully *n.* channel, ditch, donga, geo, gio, gulch, gutter, ravine, watercourse.

gulp *v.* bolt, choke, devour, gasp, gobble, gollop, gormandize, guzzle, knock back, quaff, stifle, stuff, swallow, swig, swill, toss off, wolf.
antonyms nibble, sip.
n. draft, mouthful, slug, swallow, swig.

gun *n.* equalizer, gat, heater, peacemaker, persuader, piece, pistol, shooter, shooting-iron, tool.

gush *v.* babble, blather, burst, cascade, chatter, drivel,

effuse, enthuse, flood, flow, jabber, jet, pour, run, rush, spout, spurt, stream, yatter.
n. babble, burst, cascade, chatter, ebullition, effusion, eruption, exuberance, flood, flow, jet, outburst, outflow, rush, spout, spurt, stream, tide, torrent.

gust *n.* blast, blow, breeze, burst, flaught, flaw, flurry, gale, puff, rush, squall, williwaw.
v. blast, blow, bluster, breeze, puff, squall.

gutter *n.* channel, conduit, ditch, drain, duct, grip, kennel, pipe, rigol(l), sluice, trench, trough, tube.

gypsy *n.* Bohemian, diddicoy, faw, gipsy, gitana, gitano, nomad, rambler, roamer, Romany, rover, tink, tinker, traveler, tsigane, tzigany, vagabond, vagrant, wanderer, Zigeuner, Zincalo, Zingaro.

H

habit[1] *n.* accustomedness, addiction, assuetude, bent, constitution, convention, custom, dependence, diathesis, disposition, fixation, frame of mind, habitude, inclination, make-up, manner, mannerism, mode, mores, nature, obsession, practice, proclivity, propensity, quirk, routine, rule, second nature, tendency, usage, vice, way, weakness, wont.

habit[2] *n.* apparel, attire, clothes, clothing, dress, garb, garment, habiliment.

habitation *n.* abode, cottage, domicile, dwelling, dwelling-place, home, house, hut, inhabitance, inhabitancy, inhabitation, living quarters, lodging, mansion, occupancy, occupation, quarters, residence, tenancy.

habitual *adj.* accustomed, chronic, common, confirmed, constant, customary, established, familiar, fixed, frequent, hardened, ingrained, inveterate, natural, normal, ordinary, persistent, recurrent, regular, routine, standard, traditional, usual, wonted.
antonym occasional.

habituate *v.* acclimatize, accustom, break in, condition, discipline, familiarize, harden, inure, school, season, tame, train.

hack[1] *v.* bark, chop, cough, cut, gash, haggle, hew, kick, lacerate, mangle, mutilate, notch, rasp, slash.
n. bark, chop, cough, cut, gash, notch, rasp, slash.

hack[2] *adj.* banal, hackneyed, mediocre, pedestrian, poor, stereotyped, tired, undistinguished, uninspired, unoriginal.
n. crock, drudge, horse, jade, journalist, nag, paper-stainer, penny-a-liner, scribbler, slave.

hackneyed *adj.* banal, clichéd, common, commonplace, corny, hack, hand-me-down, overworked, pedestrian, percoct, played-out, run-of-the-mill, second-hand, stale, stereotyped, stock, threadbare, time-worn, tired, trite, unoriginal, worn-out.
antonyms arresting, new.

hag *n.* battle-ax, beldame, crone, fury, harpy, harridan, ogress, shrew, termagant, virago, vixen, witch.

haggard *adj.* cadaverous, careworn, drawn, emaciated, gaunt, ghastly, hagged, hollow-eyed, pinched, shrunken, thin, wan, wasted, wrinkled.
antonym hale.

haggle *v.* bargain, barter, bicker, cavil, chaffer, dicker, dispute, higgle, palter, quarrel, squabble, wrangle.

hail[1] *n.* barrage, bombardment, rain, shower, storm, torrent, volley.
v. assail, barrage, batter, bombard, pelt, rain, shower, storm, volley.

hail[2] *v.* acclaim, accost, acknowledge, address, applaud, call, cheer, exalt, flag down, glorify, greet, halloo, honor, salute, shout, signal to, wave, welcome.
n. call, cry, halloo, holla, shout.

hair-do *n.* coiffure, cut, haircut, hairstyle, perm, set, style.

hairdresser *n.* barber, coiffeur, coiffeuse, friseur, hairstylist, stylist.

hairless *adj.* bald, bald-headed, beardless, clean-shaven, depilated, desperate, frantic, glabrate, glabrous, shorn, tonsured.
antonym hairy.

hair-raising *adj.* alarming, bloodcurdling, breathtaking, creepy, eerie, exciting, frightening, ghastly, ghostly, horrifying, petrifying, scary, shocking, spine-chilling, startling, terrifying, thrilling.
antonym calming.

hairy *adj.* bearded, bewhiskered, bushy, crinigerous, crinite, crinose, dangerous, dicey, difficult, fleecy, furry, hazardous, hirsute, hispid, lanuginose, lanuginous, perilous, pilose, pilous, risky, scaring, shaggy, stubbly, tricky, villose, villous, woolly.
antonyms bald, clean-shaven.

hale *adj.* able-bodied, athletic, blooming, fit, flourishing, healthy, hearty, in fine fettle, in the pink, robust, sound, strong, vigorous, well, youthful.
antonym ill.

half-baked *adj.* brainless, crazy, foolish, harebrained, illconceived, ill-judged, impractical, senseless, short-sighted, silly, stupid, unplanned.
antonym sensible.

half-hearted *adj.* apathetic, cool, indifferent, lackadaisical, lackluster, listless, lukewarm, neutral, passive, perfunctory, uninterested.
antonym enthusiastic.

half-wit *n.* cretin, dimwit, dolt, dullard, dunce, dunderhead, fool, gaupus, idiot, imbecile, moron, nitwit, nut, simpleton, underwit, witling.
antonym brain.

hall *n.* assembly-room, auditorium, aula, basilica, chamber, concert-hall, concourse, corridor, entrance-hall, entry, foyer, hallway, lobby, salon, saloon, vestibule.

hallowed *adj.* age-old, beatified, blessed, consecrated, dedicated, established, holy, honored, inviolable, revered, sacred, sacrosanct, sanctified.

hallucination *n.* aberration, apparition, delusion, dream, fantasy, figment, illusion, mirage, phantasmagoria, pink elephants, vision.

halt *v.* arrest, block, break off, call it a day, cease, check, curb, desist, draw up, end, impede, obstruct, pack it in, quit, rest, stem, stop, terminate, wait.
antonyms assist, continue, start.

n. arrest, break, close, end, étape, impasse, interruption, pause, stand, standstill, stop, stoppage, termination, way point.
antonyms continuation, start.

halting *adj.* awkward, broken, faltering, hesitant, imperfect, labored, stammering, stumbling, stuttering, uncertain.
antonym fluent.

hammer *v.* bang, beat, clobber, defeat, din, dolly, drive, drive home, drub, drum, form, grind, hit, impress upon, instruct, knock, make, malleate, pan, repeat, shape, slate, thrash, trounce, worst.
n. beetle, gavel, madge, mall, mallet, maul, monkey.

hamper *v.* bind, cramp, cumber, curb, curtail, distort, embarrass, encumber, entangle, fetter, frustrate, hamshackle, hamstring, handicap, hinder, hobble, hold up, impede, interfere with, obstruct, pinch, prevent, restrain, restrict, shackle, slow down, tangle, thwart, trammel.
antonyms aid, expedite.

hamstrung *adj.* balked, crippled, disabled, foiled, frustrated, handicapped, helpless, hors de combat, incapacitated, paralyzed, stymied.

hand[1] *n.* ability, agency, aid, applause, art, artistry, assistance, calligraphy, cheirography, clap, daddle, direction, fist, flipper, handwriting, help, influence, mitt, ovation, palm, part, participation, paw, penmanship, pud, puddy, script, share, skill, support.
v. aid, assist, conduct, convey, deliver, give, guide, help, lead, offer, pass, present, provide, transmit, yield.

hand[2] *n.* artificer, artisan, craftsman, employee, farmhand, hired man, hireling, laborer, operative, orra man, redneck, worker, workman.

handicap *n.* barrier, block, defect, disability, disadvantage, drawback, encumbrance, hindrance, impairment, impediment, impost, limitation, millstone, obstacle, odds, penalty, restriction, shortcoming, stumbling-block.
antonyms assistance, benefit.
v. burden, disadvantage, encumber, hamper, hamstring, hinder, impede, limit, restrict, retard.
antonyms assist, further.

handiness *n.* accessibility, adroitness, aptitude, availability, cleverness, closeness, convenience, deftness, dexterity, efficiency, expertise, knack, practicality, proficiency, proximity, skill, usefulness, workability.
antonym clumsiness.

handkerchief *n.* fogle, handkercher, hanky, monteith, mouchoir, nose-rag, romal, rumal, sudary, wipe.

handle *n.* ear, grip, haft, handfast, handgrip, heft, helve, hilt, knob, lug, stock, wythe.
v. administer, carry, conduct, control, cope with, deal in, deal with, direct, discourse, discuss, feel, finger, fondle, grasp, guide, hold, manage, manipulate, maneuver, market, maul, operate, paw, pick up, poke, sell, steer, stock, supervise, touch, trade, traffic in, treat, use, wield.

hand-out[1] *n.* alms, charity, dole, freebie, issue, largess(e), share, share-out.

hand-out[2] *n.* bulletin, circular, free sample, leaflet, literature, press release, statement.

handsome *adj.* abundant, admirable, ample, attractive, beau, becoming, bountiful, braw, comely, considerable, elegant, feat(e)ous, featuous, featurely, fine, generous, good-looking, graceful, gracious, large, liberal, magnanimous, majestic, personable, plentiful, seemly, sizeable, stately, well-favored, well-looking, well-proportioned, well-set-up.
antonyms mean, stingy, ugly.

handy *adj.* accessible, adept, adroit, at hand, available, clever, close, convenient, deft, dexterous, expert, helpful, manageable, near, nearby, neat, nimble, practical, proficient, ready, serviceable, skilful, skilled, useful.
antonyms clumsy, inconvenient, unwieldy.

hang *v.* adhere, attach, bow, cling, cover, dangle, deck, decorate, depend, drape, drift, droop, drop, execute, fasten, fix, float, furnish, gibbet, hold, hover, incline, lean, loll, lower, remain, rest, sag, stick, string up, suspend, supercollate, swing, trail, weep.

hanker for/after covet, crave, desire, hunger for, itch for, long for, lust after, pine for, thirst for, want, wish, yearn for, yen for.
antonym dislike.

haphazard *adj.* accidental, aimless, arbitrary, careless, casual, chance, disorderly, disorganized, flukey, hit-or-miss, indiscriminate, promiscuous, random, slapdash, slipshod, unmethodical, unsystematic.
antonyms deliberate, planned.

hapless *adj.* cursed, ill-fated, ill-starred, jinxed, luckless, miserable, star-crossed, unfortunate, unhappy, unlucky, wretched.
antonym lucky.

happen *v.* appear, arise, befall, chance, come about, crop up, develop, ensue, eventuate, fall out, follow, materialize, occur, result, supervene, take place, transpire, turn out.

happening *n.* accident, adventure, affair, case, chance, circumstance, episode, event, experience, incident, occasion, occurrence, phenomenon, proceeding, scene.

happiness *n.* beatitude, blessedness, bliss, cheer, cheerfulness, cheeriness, chirpiness, contentment, delight, ecstasy, elation, enjoyment, exuberance, felicity, gaiety, gladness, high spirits, joy, joyfulness, jubilation, light-heartedness, merriment, pleasure, satisfaction, well-being.
antonym unhappiness.

happy *adj.* advantageous, appropriate, apt, auspicious, befitting, blessed, blest, blissful, blithe, chance, cheerful, content, contented, convenient, delighted, ecstatic, elated, enviable, favorable, felicitous, fit, fitting, fortunate, glad, gratified, gruntled, idyllic, jolly, joyful,

joyous, jubilant, lucky, merry, opportune, over the moon, overjoyed, pleased, promising, propitious, satisfactory, Saturnian, seasonable, starry-eyed, successful, sunny, thrilled, timely, well-timed.
antonym unhappy.

happy-go-lucky *adj.* blithe, carefree, casual, cheerful, devil-may-care, easy-going, heedless, improvident, insouciant, irresponsible, light-hearted, nonchalant, reckless, unconcerned, untroubled, unworried.
antonyms anxious, wary.

harangue *n.* address, declamation, diatribe, discourse, exhortation, homily, lecture, oration, paternoster, peroration, philippic, sermon, speech, spiel, tirade.
v. address, declaim, descant, exhort, hold forth, lecture, monolog(u)ize, orate, perorate, preach, rant, rhetorize, sermonize, spout.

harass *v.* annoy, badger, bait, beleaguer, bother, chivvy, distress, disturb, exasperate, exhaust, fatigue, harry, hassle, hound, perplex, persecute, pester, plague, tease, tire, torment, trash, trouble, vex, wear out, weary, worry.
antonym assist.

harbinger *n.* avant-courier, forerunner, foretoken, herald, indication, messenger, omen, portent, precursor, presage, sign, warning.

harbor *n.* anchorage, asylum, covert, destination, haven, marina, port, refuge, roadstead, sanctuary, sanctum, security, shelter.
v. believe, cherish, cling to, conceal, entertain, foster, hide, hold, imagine, lodge, maintain, nurse, nurture, protect, retain, secrete, shelter, shield.

hard *adj.* acrimonious, actual, adamantine, alcoholic, angry, antagonistic, arduous, backbreaking, baffling, bare, bitter, burdensome, calamitous, callous, cast-iron, cold, compact, complex, complicated, cruel, crusty, dark, definite, dense, difficult, disagreeable, disastrous, distressing, driving, exacting, exhausting, fatiguing, fierce, firm, flinty, forceful, formidable, grievous, grim, habit-forming, hard-hearted, harsh, heavy, Herculean, hostile, impenetrable, implacable, indisputable, inflexible, intolerable, intricate, involved, irony, knotty, laborious, marbly, obdurate, painful, perplexing, pitiless, plain, powerful, puzzling, rancorous, resentful, rigid, rigorous, ruthless, sclerous, severe, shrewd, solid, stern, stiff, stony, strenuous, strict, strong, stubborn, tangled, thorny, toilsome, tough, undeniable, unfathomable, unfeeling, ungentle, unjust, unkind, unpleasant, unrelenting, unsparing, unsympathetic, unvarnished, unyielding, uphill, verified, violent, wearying.
antonyms harmless, kind, mild, non-alcoholic, pleasant, pleasing, soft, yielding.
adv. agonizingly, assiduously, badly, bitterly, close, completely, determinedly, diligently, distressingly, doggedly, earnestly, energetically, fiercely, forcefully, forcibly, fully, hardly, harshly, heavily, industriously, intensely, intently, keenly, laboriously, near, painfully, persistently, powerfully, rancorously, reluctantly, resentfully, roughly, severely, sharply, slowly, sorely, steadily, strenuously, strongly, uneasily, untiringly, vigorously, violently, with difficulty.
antonyms gently, mildly, moderately, unenthusiastically.

harden *v.* accustom, anneal, bake, brace, brutalize, buttress, cake, case-harden, concrete, fortify, freeze, gird, habituate, indurate, inure, nerve, reinforce, sclerose, season, set, solidify, steel, stiffen, strengthen, toughen, train.
antonym soften.

hard-headed *adj.* astute, clear-thinking, cool, hard-boiled, level-headed, practical, pragmatic, realistic, sensible, shrewd, tough, unsentimental.
antonym unrealistic.

hard-hearted *adj.* callous, cold, cruel, hard, heartless, indifferent, inhuman, insensitive, intolerant, iron-hearted, marble-breasted, marble-hearted, merciless, pitiless, stony, uncaring, uncompassionate, unfeeling, unkind, unsympathetic.
antonyms kind, merciful.

hardly *adv.* barely, by no means, faintly, harshly, infrequently, just, no way, not at all, not quite, only, only just, roughly, scarcely, severely, with difficulty.
antonyms easily, very.

hardship *n.* adversity, affliction, austerity, burden, calamity, destitution, difficulty, fatigue, grievance, labor, misery, misfortune, need, oppression, persecution, privation, strait, suffering, toil, torment, trial, tribulation, trouble, want.
antonym ease.

hardy *adj.* audacious, bold, brave, brazen, courageous, daring, firm, fit, foolhardy, hale, headstrong, healthy, hearty, heroic, impudent, intrepid, lusty, manly, plucky, rash, reckless, resolute, robust, rugged, sound, Spartan, stalwart, stout, stout-hearted, strong, sturdy, tough, valiant, valorous, vigorous.
antonyms unhealthy, weak.

harm *n.* abuse, damage, detriment, disservice, evil, hurt, ill, immorality, impairment, iniquity, injury, loss, mischief, misfortune, scathe, sin, sinfulness, vice, wickedness, wrong.
antonyms benefit, service.
v. abuse, blemish, damage, hurt, ill-treat, ill-use, impair, injure, maltreat, mar, molest, ruin, scathe, spoil, wound.
antonyms benefit, improve.

harmful *adj.* baleful, baneful, damaging, deleterious, destructive, detrimental, disadvantageous, evil, hurtful, injurious, noxious, pernicious, pestful, pestiferous, pestilent, scatheful.
antonym harmless.

harmless *adj.* gentle, innocent, innocuous, innoxious, inoffensive, non-toxic, safe, scatheless, unharmed, uninjured, unobjectionable, unscathed.
antonym harmful.

harmonious *adj.* according, agreeable, amicable, compatible, concinnous, concordant, congenial, congruous, consonant, consonous, co-ordinated, cordial, correspondent, dulcet, euharmonic, euphonic, euphonious, eurhythmic, friendly, harmonic, harmonizing, matching, mellifluous, melodious, musical, sweet-sounding, sympathetic, symphonious, tuneful.
antonym inharmonious.

harmony *n.* accord, agreement, amicability, amity, balance, chime, compatibility, concinnity, concord, conformity, congruity, consensus, consistency, consonance, co-operation, co-ordination, correspondence, correspondency, diapason, euphony, eurhythmy, fitness, friendship, goodwill, like-mindedness, melodiousness, melody, parallelism, peace, rapport, suitability, symmetry, sympathy, tune, tunefulness, unanimity, understanding, unity.
antonym discord.

harness *n.* equipment, gear, reins, straps, tack, tackle, trappings.
v. apply, channel, control, couple, employ, exploit, make use of, mobilize, saddle, turn to account, use, utilize, yoke.

harry *v.* annoy, badger, bedevil, chivvy, depredate, despoil, devastate, disturb, fret, harass, hassle, maraud, molest, persecute, pester, pillage, plague, plunder, raid, ravage, rob, sack, tease, torment, trouble, vex, worry.
antonyms aid, calm.

harsh *adj.* abrasive, abusive, austere, bitter, bleak, brutal, coarse, comfortless, croaking, crude, cruel, discordant, dissonant, dour, Draconian, glaring, grating, grim, guttural, hard, jarring, pitiless, punitive, rasping, raucous, relentless, rough, ruthless, scabrous, severe, sharp, Spartan, stark, stern, strident, stringent, unfeeling, ungentle, unkind, unmelodious, unpleasant, unrelenting.
antonyms mild, smooth, soft.

harvest *n.* collection, consequence, crop, effect, fruition, harvesting, harvest-time, hockey, ingathering, inning, produce, product, reaping, result, return, vendage, yield.
v. accumulate, acquire, amass, collect, garner, gather, mow, pick, pluck, reap.

haste *n.* alacrity, briskness, bustle, celerity, dispatch, expedition, fleetness, hastiness, hurry, hustle, impetuosity, nimbleness, precipitance, precipitancy, precipitateness, precipitation, promptitude, quickness, rapidity, rapidness, rashness, recklessness, rush, speed, swiftness, urgency, velocity.
antonyms care, deliberation, slowness.

hasten *v.* accelerate, advance, bolt, dash, dispatch, expedite, fly, gallop, goad, haste, have it on one's toes, hightail it, hurry, make haste, precipitate, press, quicken, race, run, rush, scurry, scuttle, speed, speed up, sprint, step on it, step up, tear, trot, urge.
antonym dawdle.

hasty *adj.* brief, brisk, brusque, cursory, eager, excited, expeditious, fast, fiery, fleet, fleeting, foolhardy, headlong, heedless, hot-headed, hot-tempered, hurried, impatient, impetuous, impulsive, indiscreet, irascible, irritable, passing, passionate, perfunctory, precipitant, precipitate, prompt, quick-tempered, rapid, rash, reckless, rushed, short, snappy, speedy, subitaneous, superficial, swift, thoughtless, urgent.
antonyms careful, deliberate, placid, slow.

hat *n.* beret, biretta, boater, bonnet, bowler, cap, lid, night-cap, poke-bonnet, skull-cap, sombrero, sou'wester, top-hat, trilby, yarmulka.

hatch *v.* breed, brood, conceive, concoct, contrive, cook up, design, develop, devise, dream up, incubate, originate, plan, plot, project, scheme, think up.

hate *v.* abhor, abominate, despise, detest, dislike, execrate, loathe, spite.
antonym like.
n. abhorrence, abomination, animosity, animus, antagonism, antipathy, averseness, aversion, detestation, dislike, enmity, execration, hatred, hostility, loathing, odium, odium theologicum.
antonym like. **hateful** *adj.* abhorrent, abominable, damnable, despicable, detestable, disgusting, execrable, forbidding, foul, hate-worthy, heinous, horrible, loathsome, obnoxious, odious, offensive, repellent, repugnant, repulsive, revolting, vile.
antonym pleasing.

hatred *n.* abomination, animosity, animus, antagonism, antipathy, aversion, despite, detestation, dislike, enmity, execration, hate, ill-will, misandry, misanthropy, odium, repugnance, revulsion.
antonym like.

haughtiness *n.* airs, aloofness, arrogance, conceit, contempt, contemptuousness, disdain, hauteur, insolence, loftiness, pomposity, pride, snobbishness, snootiness, superciliousness.
antonyms friendliness, humility.

haughty *adj.* arrogant, assuming, cavalier, conceited, contemptuous, disdainful, fastuous, high, high and mighty, highty-tighty, hoity-toity, imperious, lofty, overweening, proud, scornful, snobbish, snooty, stiff-necked, stomachful, stuck-up, supercilious, superior, uppish.
antonyms friendly, humble.

haul *v.* bouse, carry, cart, convey, drag, draw, hale, heave, hump, lug, move, pull, tow, trail, transport, trice, tug.
n. booty, bunce, catch, drag, find, gain, harvest, heave, loot, pull, spoils, swag, takings, tug, yield.

have *v.* accept, acquire, allow, bear, beget, cheat, comprehend, comprise, consider, contain, deceive, deliver, dupe, embody, endure, enjoy, entertain, experience, feel, fool, gain, get, give birth to, hold, include, keep, obtain, occupy, outwit, own, permit, possess, procure, produce, put up with, receive, retain, secure, suffer, sustain, swindle, take, tolerate, trick, undergo.

havoc *n.* carnage, chaos, confusion, damage, depopulation, desolation, despoliation, destruction, devastation, disorder, disruption, mayhem, rack and ruin, ravages, ruin, shambles, slaughter, waste, wreck.

hazard *n.* accident, chance, coincidence, danger, deathtrap, endangerment, fluke, imperilment, jeopardy, luck, mischance, misfortune, mishap, peril, risk, threat.
antonym safety.
v. advance, attempt, chance, conjecture, dare, endanger, expose, gamble, imperil, jeopardize, offer, presume, proffer, risk, speculate, stake, submit, suggest, suppose, threaten, venture, volunteer.

hazardous *adj.* chancy, dangerous, dicey, difficult, fraught, hairy, haphazard, insecure, perilous, precarious, risky, thorny, ticklish, uncertain, unpredictable, unsafe.
antonyms safe, secure.

hazy *adj.* blurry, clouded, cloudy, dim, distanceless, dull, faint, foggy, fuzzy, ill-defined, indefinite, indistinct, loose, milky, misty, muddled, muzzy, nebulous, obscure, overcast, smoky, uncertain, unclear, vague, veiled.
antonyms clear, definite.

head *n.* ability, apex, aptitude, bean, beginning, bonce, boss, brain, brains, branch, capacity, cape, captain, caput, category, chief, chieftain, chump, class, climax, commander, commencement, conclusion, conk, cop, cranium, crest, crisis, crown, culmination, department, director, division, end, faculty, flair, fore, forefront, foreland, front, godfather, head teacher, heading, headland, headmaster, headmistress, height, intellect, intelligence, knowledge box, leader, manager, master, mastermind, mentality, mind, nab, napper, nob, noddle, nut, origin, pate, peak, pitch, point, principal, promontory, rise, sconce, section, skull, source, start, subject, summit, super, superintendent, supervisor, talent, tête, thought, tip, top, topic, top-knot, turning-point, understanding, upperworks, van, vanguard, vertex.
antonyms foot, subordinate, tail.
adj. arch, chief, dominant, first, foremost, front, highest, leading, main, pre-eminent, premier, prime, principal, supreme, top, topmost.
v. aim, cap, command, control, crown, direct, govern, guide, lead, make a beeline, make for, manage, oversee, point, precede, rule, run, steer, superintend, supervise, top, turn.

headstrong *adj.* bull-headed, contrary, foolhardy, fractious, froward, heedless, imprudent, impulsive, intractable, mulish, obstinate, perverse, pig-headed, rash, reckless, self-willed, stubborn, ungovernable, unruly, wilful.
antonyms biddable, docile, obedient.

headway *n.* advance, improvement, inroad(s), progress, progression, way.

heady *adj.* exciting, exhilarating, hasty, impetuous, impulsive, inconsiderate, inebriant, intoxicating, overpowering, potent, precipitate, rash, reckless, spirituous, stimulating, strong, thoughtless, thrilling.

heal *v.* alleviate, ameliorate, balsam, compose, conciliate, cure, harmonize, mend, patch up, physic, reconcile, regenerate, remedy, restore, salve, settle, soothe, treat.

healthy *adj.* active, beneficial, blooming, bracing, fine, fit, flourishing, good, hale (and hearty), hardy, healthful, health-giving, hearty, hygienic, in fine feather, in fine fettle, in fine form, in good condition, in good shape, in the pink, invigorating, nourishing, nutritious, physically fit, robust, salubrious, salutary, salutiferous, sound, strong, sturdy, vigorous, well, wholesome.
antonyms diseased, ill, infirm, sick, unhealthy.

heap *n.* accumulation, acervation, aggregation, bing, clamp, cock, collection, cumulus, hoard, lot, mass, mound, mountain, pile, ruck, stack, stockpile, store.
v. accumulate, amass, assign, augment, bank, bestow, build, burden, collect, confer, gather, hoard, increase, lavish, load, mound, pile, shower, stack, stockpile, store.

hear *v.* acknowledge, ascertain, attend, catch, discover, eavesdrop, examine, find, gather, hark, hearken, heed, investigate, judge, learn, listen, overhear, pick up, try, understand.

heart *n.* affection, benevolence, boldness, bravery, center, character, compassion, concern, core, courage, crux, disposition, emotion, essence, feeling, fortitude, guts, hub, humanity, inclination, kernel, love, marrow, mettle, middle, mind, nature, nerve, nerve center, nub, nucleus, pith, pity, pluck, purpose, quintessence, resolution, root, sentiment, soul, spirit, spunk, sympathy, temperament, tenderness, ticker, understanding, will.

heart and soul absolutely, completely, devotedly, eagerly, entirely, gladly, heartily, unreservedly, wholeheartedly.

heartache *n.* affliction, agony, anguish, bitterness, dejection, despair, despondency, distress, grief, heartbreak, heart-sickness, pain, remorse, sorrow, suffering, torment, torture.

heartbroken *adj.* broken-hearted, crestfallen, crushed, dejected, desolate, despondent, disappointed, disconsolate, disheartened, dispirited, down, downcast, grieved, heart-sick, miserable, woebegone.
antonyms delighted, elated.

hearten *v.* animate, assure, buck up, buoy up, cheer, comfort, console, embolden, encourage, gladden, incite, inspire, inspirit, pep up, reassure, revivify, rouse, stimulate.
antonym dishearten.

heartless *adj.* brutal, callous, cold, cold-blooded, cold-hearted, cruel, hard, hard-hearted, harsh, inhuman, merciless, pitiless, stern, uncaring, unfeeling, unkind.
antonyms considerate, kind, merciful, sympathetic.

heart-rending *adj.* affecting, distressing, harrowing, heart-breaking, moving, pathetic, piteous, pitiful, poignant, sad, tear-jerking, tragic.

hearty *adj.* active, affable, ample, ardent, cordial, doughty, eager, earnest, ebullient, effusive, energetic, enthusiastic, exuberant, filling, friendly, generous, genial, genuine, hale, hardy, healthy, heartfelt, honest, jovial, nourishing, real, robust, sincere, sizeable, solid, sound, square, stalwart, strong, substantial, true, unfeigned, unreserved, vigorous, warm, well, whole-hearted.
antonyms cold, emotionless.

heat *n.* agitation, ardor, calefaction, earnestness, excitement, fervor, fever, fieriness, fury, hotness, impetuosity, incandescence, intensity, passion, sizzle, sultriness, swelter, torridity, vehemence, violence, warmness, warmth, zeal.
antonyms cold(ness), coolness.
v. animate, calefy, chafe, excite, flush, glow, impassion, inflame, inspirit, reheat, rouse, stimulate, stir, toast, warm up.
antonyms chill, cool.

heated *adj.* acrimonious, angry, bitter, excited, fierce, fiery, frenzied, furious, impassioned, intense, passionate, perfervid, raging, stormy, tempestuous, vehement, violent.
antonym dispassionate.

heave *v.* billow, breathe, cast, chuck, dilate, drag, elevate, exhale, expand, fling, gag, groan, haul, heft, hitch, hoist, hurl, let fly, lever, lift, palpitate, pant, pitch, puff, pull, raise, retch, rise, send, sigh, sling, sob, spew, surge, suspire, swell, throb, throw, throw up, toss, tug, vomit, yomp.

heaven *n.* bliss, ecstasy, Elysian fields, Elysium, empyrean, enchantment, ether, felicity, fiddler's green, firmament, happiness, happy hunting-ground(s), hereafter, Land of the Leal, next world, nirvana, paradise, rapture, sky, Swarga, transport, utopia, Valhalla, welkin, Zion.
antonym hell.

heavenly *adj.* alluring, ambrosial, angelic, beatific, beautiful, blessed, blest, blissful, celestial, delightful, divine, empyrean, entrancing, exquisite, extra-terrestrial, glorious, godlike, holy, immortal, lovely, paradisaic(al), paradisal, paradisean, paradisial, paradisian, paradisic, rapturous, ravishing, seraphic, sublime, superhuman, supernal, supernatural, Uranian, wonderful.
antonym hellish.

heavy *adj.* abundant, apathetic, boisterous, bulky, burdened, burdensome, clumpy, complex, considerable, copious, crestfallen, deep, dejected, depressed, despondent, difficult, disconsolate, downcast, drowsy, dull, encumbered, excessive, gloomy, grave, grieving, grievous, hard, harsh, hefty, inactive, indolent, inert, intolerable, laborious, laden, large, leaden, listless, loaded, lumping, lumpish, massive, melancholy, onerous, oppressed, oppressive, ponderous, portly, profound, profuse, rough, sad, serious, severe, slow, sluggish, solemn, sorrowful, squabbish, stodgy, stormy, stupid, tedious, tempestuous, torpid, turbulent, vexatious, violent, wearisome, weighted, weighty, wild, wooden.
antonyms airy, insignificant, light.

heckle *v.* bait, barrack, catcall, disrupt, gibe, interrupt, jeer, pester, shout down, taunt.

heed *n.* animadversion, attention, care, caution, consideration, ear, heedfulness, mind, note, notice, reck, regard, respect, thought, watchfulness.
antonyms inattention, indifference, unconcern.
v. animadvert, attend, consider, follow, listen, mark, mind, note, obey, observe, regard, take notice of.
antonyms disregard, ignore.

heedless *adj.* careless, étourdi(e), foolhardy, imprudent, inattentive, incautious, incurious, inobservant, neglectful, negligent, oblivious, precipitate, rash, reckless, thoughtless, uncaring, unconcerned, unheedful, unheedy, unmindful, unobservant, unthinking.
antonym heedful.

height *n.* acme, altitude, apex, apogee, ceiling, celsitude, climax, crest, crown, culmination, degree, dignity, elevation, eminence, exaltation, extremity, grandeur, highness, hill, limit, loftiness, maximum, mountain, ne plus ultra, peak, pinnacle, prominence, stature, summit, tallness, top, ultimate, utmost, uttermost, vertex, zenith.
antonym depth.

heighten *v.* add to, aggrandize, aggravate, amplify, augment, elevate, enhance, ennoble, exalt, greaten, improve, increase, intensify, magnify, raise, sharpen, strengthen, uplift.
antonyms decrease, diminish.

heinous *adj.* abhorrent, abominable, atrocious, awful, evil, execrable, facinorous, flagrant, grave, hateful, hideous, immitigable, infamous, iniquitous, monstrous, nefarious, odious, outrageous, revolting, shocking, unspeakable, vicious, villainous.

hello *interj.* chin-chin, ciao, hail, hi, hiya, how-do-you-do, howdy, salve, what cheer, wotcher.
antonym good-bye.

help[1] *v.* abet, abstain, aid, alleviate, ameliorate, assist, avoid, back, befriend, bestead, control, co-operate, cure, ease, eschew, facilitate, forbear, heal, hinder, improve, keep from, lend a hand, mitigate, prevent, promote, rally round, refrain from, relieve, remedy, resist, restore, save, second, serve, shun, stand by, succor, support, withstand.
antonym hinder.
n. adjuvant, advice, aid, aidance, assistance, avail, benefit, co-operation, guidance, leg up, service, support, use, utility.
antonym hindrance.

help[2] *n.* assistant, daily, employee, hand, helper, worker.

helper *n.* abettor, adjutant, aide, aider, ally, assistant, attendant, auxiliary, coadjutor, collaborator, colleague, deputy, girl Friday, helpmate, man Friday, mate, PA, partner, person Friday, right-hand man, Samaritan, second, subsidiary, supporter.

helpful *adj.* accommodating, adjuvant, advantageous, beneficent, beneficial, benevolent, caring, considerate, constructive, co-operative, favorable, fortunate, friendly, furthersome, kind, neighborly, practical, productive, profitable, serviceable, supportive, sympathetic, timely, useful.
antonyms futile, useless, worthless.

helpless *adj.* abandoned, adynamic, aidless, debilitated, defenceless, dependent, destitute, disabled, exposed, feeble, forlorn, friendless, impotent, incapable, incompetent, infirm, paralyzed, powerless, unfit, unprotected, vulnerable, weak.
antonyms competent, enterprising, independent, resourceful, strong.

helter-skelter *adv.* carelessly, confusedly, hastily, headlong, hurriedly, impulsively, pell-mell, rashly, recklessly, wildly.
adj. anyhow, confused, disordered, disorganized, haphazard, higgledy-piggledy, hit-or-miss, jumbled, muddled, random, topsy-turvy, unsystematic.

hem *n.* border, edge, fringe, margin, skirt, trimming.
v. beset, border, circumscribe, confine, edge, enclose, engird, environ, fimbriate, gird, hedge, restrict, skirt, surround.

hemerrhoids *n.* emerods, piles.

hence *adv.* accordingly, ergo, therefore, thus.

herald *n.* courier, crier, forerunner, harbinger, indication, messenger, omen, precursor, sign, signal, token, vaunt-courier.
v. advertise, announce, broadcast, forebode, foretoken, harbinger, indicate, pave the way, portend, precede, presage, proclaim, prognosticate, promise, publicize, publish, show, trumpet, usher in.

herculean *adj.* arduous, athletic, brawny, colossal, daunting, demanding, difficult, enormous, exacting, exhausting, formidable, gigantic, great, grueling, hard, heavy, huge, husky, laborious, large, mammoth, massive, mighty, muscular, onerous, powerful, prodigious, rugged, sinewy, stalwart, strapping, strenuous, strong, sturdy, titanic, toil-some, tough, tremendous.

herd *n.* assemblage, canaille, collection, cowherd, crowd, crush, drove, flock, herdboy, herdsman, horde, mass, mob, multitude, populace, press, rabble, riff-raff, shepherd, swarm, the hoi polloi, the masses, the plebs, throng, vulgus.
v. assemble, associate, collect, congregate, drive, flock, force, gather, goad, guard, guide, huddle, lead, muster, protect, rally, shepherd, spur, watch.

heretic *n.* apostate, dissenter, dissident, free-thinker, non-conformist, renegade, revisionist, schismatic, sectarian, separatist.
antonym conformist.

heritage *n.* bequest, birthright, deserts, due, endowment, estate, history, inheritance, legacy, lot, past, patrimony, portion, record, share, tradition.

hermit *n.* anchoret, anchorite, ascetic, eremite, monk, recluse, solitaire, solitarian, solitary, stylite.

hero *n.* celebrity, champion, conqueror, exemplar, goody, heart-throb, idol, male lead, paragon, protagonist, star, superstar, victor.

heroic *adj.* bold, brave, classic, classical, courageous, daring, dauntless, doughty, elevated, epic, exaggerated, extravagant, fearless, gallant, game, grand, grandiose, gritty, high-flown, Homeric, inflated, intrepid, legendary, lion-hearted, mythological, spunky, stout-hearted, undaunted, valiant, valorous.
antonyms cowardly, pusillanimous, timid.

heroism *n.* boldness, bravery, courage, courageousness, daring, derring-do, fearlessness, fortitude, gallantry, gameness, grit, intrepidity, prowess, spirit, valor.
antonyms cowardice, pusillaniminity, timidity.

hesitant *adj.* diffident, dilatory, doubtful, half-hearted, halting, hesitating, hesitative, hesitatory, irresolute, reluctant, sceptical, shy, swithering, timid, uncertain, unsure, vacillating, wavering.
antonyms resolute, staunch.

hesitate *v.* balk, be reluctant, be uncertain, be unwilling, boggle, delay, demur, dither, doubt, dubitate, falter, fumble, halt, haver, pause, scruple, shillyshally, shrink from, stammer, stumble, stutter, swither, think twice, vacillate, wait, waver.

hesitation *n.* delay, demurral, doubt, dubiety, faltering, fumbling, hesitancy, indecision, irresolution, misdoubt, misgiving(s), qualm(s), reluctance, scruple(s), second thought(s), stammering, stumbling, stuttering, swithering, uncertainty, unwillingness, vacillation.
antonyms alacrity, assurance, eagerness.

hidden *adj.* abstruse, cabbalistic(al), clandestine, close, concealed, covered, covert, cryptic, dark, de(a)rn, delitescent, doggo, hermetic, hermetical, latent, mysterious, mystic, mystical, obscure, occult, recondite, secret, shrouded, ulterior, unapparent, unseen, veiled.
antonyms open, showing.

hide[1] *v.* abscond, bury, cache, camouflage, cloak, conceal, cover, disguise, earth, eclipse, ensconce, feal, go to ground, go underground, hole up, keep dark, lie low, mask, obscure, occult, screen, secrete, shadow, shelter, shroud, stash, suppress, take cover, tappice, veil, withhold.
antonyms display, reveal, show.

hide[2] *n.* deacon, fell, flaught, nebris, pelt, skin.

hideous *adj.* abominable, appalling, awful, detestable, disgusting, dreadful, frightful, gash, gashful, gashly, ghastly, grim, grisly, grotesque, gruesome, horrendous, horrible, horrid, loathsome, macabre, monstrous, odious, repulsive, revolting, shocking, sickening, terrible, terrifying, ugly, ugsome, unsightly.
antonym beautiful.

high *adj.* acute, altissimo, alto, arch, arrogant, boastful, boisterous, bouncy, bragging, capital, cheerful, chief, consequential, costly, dear, delirious, despotic, distinguished, domineering, elated, elevated, eminent, euphoric, exalted, excessive, excited, exhilarated, exorbitant, expensive, extraordinary, extravagant, extreme, exuberant, freaked out, gamy, grand, grave, great, haughty, high-pitched, important, inebriated, influential, intensified, intoxicated, joyful, lavish, leading, light-hearted, lofty, lordly, luxurious, merry, mountain(s)-high, niffy, orthian, ostentatious, overbearing, penetrating, piercing, piping, pongy, powerful, prominent, proud, rich, ruling, serious, sharp, shrill, significant, soaring, soprano, spaced out, steep, stiff, stoned, strident, strong, superior, tainted, tall, towering, treble, tripping, tumultuous, turbulent, tyrannical, vainglorious, whiffy.
antonyms deep, low, lowly, short.
n. apex, apogee, delirium, ecstasy, euphoria, height, intoxication, level, peak, record, summit, top, trip, zenith.
antonyms low, nadir.

highbrow *n.* aesthete, boffin, Brahmin, brain, egghead, intellectual, long-hair, mandarin, mastermind, savant, scholar.
adj. bookish, brainy, cultivated, cultured, deep, intellectual, long-haired, serious, sophisticated.
antonym lowbrow.

highly *adv.* appreciatively, approvingly, considerably, decidedly, eminently, enthusiastically, exceptionally, extraordinarily, extremely, favorably, greatly, immensely, supremely, tremendously, vastly, very, warmly, well.

high-minded *adj.* elevated, ethical, fair, good, honorable, idealistic, lofty, magnanimous, moral, noble, principled, pure, righteous, scrupulous, upright, virtuous, worthy.
antonyms immoral, unscrupulous.

high-priced *adj.* costly, dear, excessive, exorbitant, expensive, extortionate, high, pricy, steep, stiff, unreasonable.
antonym cheap.

high-spirited *adj.* animated, boisterous, bold, bouncy, daring, dashing, ebullient, effervescent, energetic, exuberant, frolicsome, lively, mettlesome, peppy, sparkling, spirited, spunky, vibrant, vital, vivacious.
antonyms downcast, glum.

highwayman *n.* bandit, bandolero, footpad, knight of the road, land-pirate, rank-rider, robber.

hilarious *adj.* amusing, comical, convivial, entertaining, funny, gay, happy, humorous, hysterical, jolly, jovial, joyful, joyous, killing, merry, mirthful, noisy, rollicking, side-splitting, uproarious.
antonyms grave, serious.

hinder *v.* arrest, check, counteract, debar, delay, deter, embar, encumber, forelay, frustrate, hamper, hamstring, handicap, hold back, hold up, impede, interrupt, obstruct, oppose, prevent, retard, slow down, stop, stymie, thwart, trammel.
antonyms aid, assist, help.

hindrance *n.* bar, barrier, check, demurrage, deterrent, difficulty, drag, drawback, encumbrance, handicap, hitch, impediment, interruption, limitation, obstacle, obstruction, pull-back, remora, restraint, restriction, snag, stoppage, stumbling-block, trammel.
antonyms aid, assistance, help.

hinge *v.* be contingent, center, depend, hang, pivot, rest, revolve around, turn.
n. articulation, condition, foundation, garnet, joint, premise, principle.

hint *n.* advice, allusion, breath, clue, dash, help, implication, indication, inkling, innuendo, insinuation, intimation, mention, pointer, reminder, scintilla, sign, signal, soupçon, speck, subindication, suggestion, suspicion, taste, tinge, tip, tip-off, touch, trace, undertone, whiff, whisper, wrinkle.
v. allude, imply, indicate, inkle, innuendo, insinuate, intimate, mention, prompt, subindicate, suggest, tip off.

hire *v.* appoint, book, charter, commission, employ, engage, lease, let, rent, reserve, retain, sign up, take on.
antonyms dismiss, fire.
n. charge, cost, fare, fee, price, rent, rental, toll.

history *n.* account, annals, antecedents, antiquity, autobiography, biography, chronicle, chronology, days of old, days of yore, genealogy, memoirs, narration, narrative, olden days, recapitulation, recital, record, relation, saga, story, tale, the past.

hit *v.* accomplish, achieve, affect, arrive at, attain, bang, bash, batter, beat, belt, bump, clip, clobber, clock, clonk, clout, collide with, crown, cuff, damage, devastate, flog, frap, fustigate, gain, impinge on, influence, knock, lob, move, overwhelm, prop, punch, reach, secure, slap, slog, slosh, slug, smack, smash, smite, sock, strike, swat, thump, touch, volley, wallop, whack, wham, whap, w(h)op, wipe.
n. blow, bump, clash, clout, collision, cuff, impact, knock, rap, sell-out, sensation, shot, slap, slog, slosh, smack, smash, sock, stroke, success, swipe, triumph, venue, wallop, winner.

hitch *v.* attach, connect, couple, fasten, harness, heave, hike (up), hitch-hike, hoi(c)k, hoist, jerk, join, pull, tether, thumb a lift, tie, tug, unite, yank, yoke.
antonyms unfasten, unhitch.
n. catch, check, delay, difficulty, drawback, hiccup, hindrance, hold-up, impediment, mishap, problem, snag, stick, stoppage, trouble.

hoard *n.* accumulation, cache, fund, heap, mass, pile, profusion, reserve, reservoir, stockpile, store, supply, treasure-trove. *v.* accumulate, amass, cache, coffer, collect, deposit, garner, gather, hive, husband, lay up, put by, reposit, save, stash away, stockpile, store, treasure.
antonyms spend, squander, use.

hoarse *adj.* croaky, discordant, grating, gravelly, growling, gruff, guttural, harsh, husky, rasping, raspy, raucous, rough, throaty.
antonyms clear, smooth.

hoax *n.* bam, cheat, cod, con, deception, fast one, fraud, grift, hum, huntiegowk, hunt-the-gowk, imposture, joke, josh, leg-pull, practical joke, prank, put-on, quiz, ruse, spoof, string, swindle, trick.
v. bam, bamboozle, befool, bluff, cod, con, deceive, delude, dupe, fool, gammon, gull, have on, hoodwink, hornswoggle, hum, lead on, pull someone's leg, spoof, string, stuff, swindle, take for a ride, trick.

hobble *v.* clog, dodder, falter, fasten, fetter, halt, hamshackle, hamstring, hirple, limp, restrict, shackle, shamble, shuffle, stagger, stumble, tie, totter.

hobby *n.* avocation, diversion, pastime, pursuit, recreation, relaxation, sideline.

hoist *v.* elevate, erect, heave, jack up, lift, raise, rear, uplift, upraise.
n. crane, davit, elevator, jack, lift, tackle, winch.

hold *v.* accommodate, account, adhere, apply, arrest, assemble, assume, be in force, be the case, bear, believe, bond, brace, call, carry, carry on, celebrate, check, clasp, cleave, clinch, cling, clip, clutch, comprise, conduct, confine, consider, contain, continue, convene, cradle, curb, deem, delay, detain, embrace, endure, enfold, entertain, esteem, exist, grasp, grip, have, hold good, imprison, judge, keep, last, maintain, occupy, operate, own, persevere, persist, possess, preside over, presume, prop, reckon, regard, remain, remain true, remain valid, resist, restrain, retain, run, seat, shoulder, solemnize, stand up, stay, stick, stop, summon, support, suspend, sustain, take, think, view, wear.
n. anchorage, asendancy, authority, clasp, clout, clutch, control, dominance, dominion, foothold, footing, grasp, grip, holt, influence, leverage, mastery, prop, pull, purchase, stay, support, sway, vantage.

hold-up[1] *n.* bottle-neck, delay, difficulty, gridlock, hitch, obstruction, setback, snag, stoppage, (traffic) jam, trouble, wait.

hold-up[2] *n.* heist, robbery, stick-up.

hole *n.* aperture, breach, break, burrow, cave, cavern, cavity, chamber, covert, crack, defect, den, depression, dilemma, dimple, discrepancy, dive, dump, earth, error, excavation, eyelet, fallacy, fault, fissure, fix, flaw, foramen, fovea, gap, hollow, hovel, imbroglio, inconsistency, jam, joint, lair, loophole, mess, nest, opening, orifice, outlet, perforation, pit, pocket, pore, predicament, puncture, quandary, rent, retreat, scoop, scrape, shaft, shelter, slum, split, spot, tangle, tear, tight spot, vent, ventage.

hollow *adj.* artificial, cavernous, concave, coreless, cynical, deaf, deceitful, deceptive, deep, deep-set, depressed, dished, dull, empty, expressionless, faithless, false, famished, flat, fleeting, flimsy, fruitless, futile, gaunt, glenoid(al), hungry, hypocritical, indented, insincere, lanternjawed, low, meaningless, muffled, muted, pointless, Pyrrhic, ravenous, reverberant, rumbling, sepulchral, specious, starved, sunken, toneless, treacherous, unavailing, unfilled, unreal, unreliable, unsound, useless, vacant, vain, void, weak, worthless.
n. basin, bottom, bowl, cave, cavern, cavity, channel, concave, concavity, coomb, crater, cup, dale, dell, den, dent, depression, dimple, dingle, dint, dish, druse, excavation, fossa, fossula, fovea, foveola, foveole, geode, glen, groove, hole, hope, how(e), indentation, invagination, pit, trough, umbilicus, vacuity, valley, vlei, well, womb.
v. burrow, channel, dent, dig, dint, dish, excavate, furrow, gouge, groove, indent, pit, scoop.

holocaust *n.* annihilation, carnage, conflagration, destruction, devastation, extermination, extinction, flames, genocide, hecatomb, immolation, inferno, mass murder, massacre, pogrom, sacrifice, slaughter.

holy *adj.* blessed, consecrated, dedicated, devout, divine, evangelical, evangelistic, faithful, god-fearing, godly, good, hallowed, perfect, pietistic, pious, pure, religiose, religious, righteous, sacred, sacrosanct, saintly, sanctified, sanctimonious, spiritual, sublime, unctuous, venerable, venerated, virtuous.
antonyms impious, unsanctified, wicked.

homage *n.* acknowledgment, admiration, adoration, adulation, allegiance, awe, deference, devotion, duty, esteem, faithfulness, fealty, fidelity, honor, loyalty, obeisance, praise, recognition, regard, respect, reverence, service, tribute, veneration, worship.

home *n.* abode, almshouse, asylum, birthplace, blighty, clinic, domicile, dwelling, dwelling-place, element, environment, family, fireside, habitat, habitation, haunt, hearth, home ground, home town, homestead, hospice, hospital, house, household, institution, native heath, nest, nursing-home, old people's home, pad, pied-à-terre, range, residence, roof, sanatorium, stamping-ground, territory.
adj. candid, central, direct, domestic, domiciliary, familiar, family, household, incisive, inland, internal, intimate, local, national, native, penetrating, plain, pointed, unanswerable, uncomfortable, wounding.

homely *adj.* comfortable, comfy, congenial, cosy, domestic, easy, everyday, familiar, folksy, friendly, gemütlich, homelike, homespun, hom(e)y, informal, intimate, modest, natural, ordinary, plain, relaxed, simple, snug, unaffected, unassuming, unpretentious, unsophisticated, welcoming.
antonyms formal, unfamiliar.

homesickness *n.* Heimweh, mal du pays, nostalgia, nostomania.
antonym wanderlust.

homicide *n.* assassin, assassination, bloodshed, cutthroat, killer, killing, liquidator, manslaughter, murder, murderer, slayer, slaying.

homily *n.* address, discourse, harangue, heart-to-heart, lecture, postil, preachment, sermon, spiel, talk.

honest *adj.* above-board, authentic, bona fide, candid, chaste, conscientious, decent, direct, equitable, ethical, fair, fair and square, forthright, four-square, frank, genuine, high-minded, honorable, humble, impartial, ingenuous, jake, just, law-abiding, legitimate, modest, objective, on the level, open, outright, outspoken, plain, plain-hearted, proper, real, reliable, reputable, respectable, scrupulous, seemly, simple, sincere, soothfast, square, straight, straightforward, true, trustworthy, trusty, truthful, undisguised, unequivocal, unfeigned, unreserved, upright, veracious, virtuous, well-gotten, well-won, white.
antonyms covert, devious, dishonest, dishonorable.

honestly *adv.* by fair means, candidly, cleanly, conscientiously, directly, dispassionately, equitably, ethically, fairly, frankly, honorably, in all sincerity, in good faith, justly, lawfully, legally, legitimately, objectively, on the level, openly, outright, plainly, really, scrupulously, sincerely, straight, straight out, truly, truthfully, undisguisedly, unreservedly, uprightly, verily.
antonyms dishonestly, dishonorably.

honesty *n.* artlessness, bluntness, candor, equity, even-handedness, explicitness, fairness, faithfulness, fidelity, frankness, genuineness, honor, incorruptibility, integrity, justness, morality, objectivity, openness, outspokenness, plain-heartedness, plainness, plain-speaking, probity, rectitude, reputability, scrupulousness, sincerity, sooth, squareness, straightforwardness, straightness, trustworthiness, truthfulness, unreserve, uprightness, veracity, verity, virtue.
antonyms deviousness, dishonesty.

honor *n.* acclaim, accolade, acknowledgment, admiration, adoration, chastity, commendation, compliment, credit, decency, deference, dignity, distinction, duty, elevation, esteem, fairness, favor, good name, goodness, homage, honesty, honorableness, honorificabilitudinity, innocence, integrity, kudos, laudation, laurels, loyalty, modesty, morality, pleasure, praise, principles, privilege, probity, purity, rank, recognition, rectitude, regard, renown, reputation, repute, respect, reverence, righteousness, self-respect, tribute, trust, trustworthiness, uprightness, veneration, virginity, virtue, worship. *antonyms* disgrace, dishonor, obloquy.
v. accept, acclaim, acknowledge, admire, adore, applaud, appreciate, carry out, cash, celebrate, clear, commemorate, commend, compliment, credit, crown, decorate, dignify, discharge, esteem, exalt, execute, fulfil, glorify, hallow, homage, keep, laud, laureate, lionize, observe, pass, pay, pay homage, perform, praise, prize, remember, respect, revere, reverence, take, value, venerate, worship.
antonyms betray, debase, disgrace, dishonor.

honorable *adj.* creditable, distinguished, eminent, equitable, estimable, ethical, fair, great, high-minded, honest, illustrious, irreproachable, just, meritorious, moral, noble, prestigious, principled, proper, renowned, reputable, respectable, respected, right, righteous, sincere, straight, true, trustworthy, trusty, unexceptionable, upright, upstanding, venerable, virtuous, worthful, worthy.
antonyms dishonest, dishonorable, unworthy.

honorary *adj.* complimentary, ex officio, formal, honorific, honoris causa, in name only, nominal, titular, unofficial, unpaid, virtute officii.
antonyms gainful, paid, salaried, waged.

hop *v.* bound, caper, dance, fly, frisk, hitch, hobble, jump, leap, limp, nip, prance, skip, spring, vault.
n. ball, barn-dance, bounce, bound, crossing, dance, flight, jump, leap, skip, social, spring, step, trip, vault.

hope *n.* ambition, anticipation, aspiration, assumption, assurance, belief, confidence, conviction, desire, dream, expectancy, expectation, faith, hopefulness, longing, optimism, promise, prospect, wish.
antonyms apathy, despair, pessimism.
v. anticipate, aspire, assume, await, believe, contemplate, desire, expect, foresee, long, reckon on, rely, trust, wish.
antonym despair.

hopeful *adj.* assured, auspicious, bright, bullish, buoyant, cheerful, confident, encouraging, expectant, favorable, heartening, optimistic, promising, propitious, reassuring, rosy, sanguine.
antonyms despairing, discouraging, pessimistic.
n. great white hope, white hope, wunderkind.

hopeless *adj.* defeatist, dejected, demoralized, despairing, desperate, despondent, disconsolate, downhearted, foolish, forlorn, futile, helpless, impossible, impracticable, inadequate, incompetent, incorrigible, incurable, ineffectual, irredeemable, irremediable, irreparable, irreversible, lost, madcap, past cure, pessimistic, pointless, poor, reckless, unachievable, unattainable, useless, vain, woebegone, worthless, wretched.
antonyms curable, hopeful, optimistic.

horde *n.* band, bevy, concourse, crew, crowd, drove, flock, gang, herd, host, mob, multitude, pack, press, swarm, throng, troop.

horizon *n.* compass, ken, perspective, prospect, purview, range, realm, scope, skyline, sphere, stretch, verge, vista.

horrible *adj.* abhorrent, abominable, appalling, atrocious, awful, beastly, bloodcurdling, cruel, disagreeable, dreadful, fearful, fearsome, frightful, ghastly, grim, grisly, gruesome, heinous, hideous, horrid, horrific, loathsome, macabre, nasty, repulsive, revolting, shameful, shocking, terrible, terrifying, unkind, unpleasant, weird.
antonyms agreeable, pleasant.

horrid *adj.* abominable, alarming, appalling, awful, beastly, bloodcurdling, cruel, despicable, disagreeable, disgusting, dreadful, formidable, frightening, hair-raising,

harrowing, hateful, hideous, horrible, horrific, mean, nasty, odious, offensive, repulsive, revolting, shocking, terrible, terrifying, unkind, unpleasant.
antonyms agreeable, lovely, pleasant.

horror *n.* abhorrence, abomination, alarm, antipathy, apprehension, aversion, awe, awfulness, consternation, detestation, disgust, dismay, dread, fear, fright, frightfulness, ghastliness, gooseflesh, goose-pimples, grimness, hatred, hideousness, horripilation, loathing, outrage, panic, repugnance, revulsion, shock, terror.

horseplay *n.* buffoonery, capers, clowning, desipience, fooling, fooling around, fun and games, high jinks, pranks, romping, rough-and-tumble, rough-housing, rough-stuff, rumpus, skylarking.

hospitable *adj.* accessible, amenable, amicable, approachable, bountiful, congenial, convivial, cordial, couthie, friendly, gemütlich, generous, genial, gracious, kind, liberal, liv(e)able, open-minded, receptive, responsive, sociable, tolerant, welcoming.
antonyms hostile, inhospitable.

hospital *n.* clinic, lazaret, lazaretto, leprosarium, leproserie, leprosery, sanatorium.

hospitality *n.* cheer, congeniality, conviviality, cordiality, friendliness, generosity, graciousness, openhandedness, sociability, warmth, welcome.
antonyms hostility, inhospitality.

hostile *adj.* adverse, alien, antagonistic, anti, antipathetic, bellicose, belligerent, contrary, ill-disposed, inhospitable, inimical, malevolent, opposed, opposite, oppugnant, rancorous, unfriendly, ungenial, unkind, unpropitious, unsympathetic, unwelcoming, warlike.
antonyms friendly, sympathetic.

hostility *n.* abhorrence, animosity, animus, antagonism, antipathy, aversion, breach, detestation, disaffection, dislike, enmity, estrangement, hate, hatred, ill-will, malevolence, malice, opposition, resentment, unfriendliness.
antonyms friendliness, sympathy.

hot *adj.* acrid, animated, approved, ardent, biting, blistering, boiling, burning, candent, clever, close, dangerous, eager, excellent, excited, exciting, favored, febrile, fervent, fervid, fevered, feverish, fierce, fiery, flaming, fresh, heated, hotheaded, impetuous, impulsive, in demand, in vogue, incandescent, inflamed, intense, irascible, latest, lustful, near, new, passionate, peppery, perfervid, piping, piquant, popular, pungent, quick, raging, recent, risky, roasting, scalding, scorching, searing, sensual, sharp, sizzling, skilful, sought-after, spicy, steaming, stormy, strong, sultry, sweltering, torrid, touchy, tropical, vehement, violent, voluptuous, warm, zealous.
antonyms calm, cold, mild, moderate.

hotbed *n.* breeding-ground, cradle, den, forcing-house, hive, nest, nidus, nursery, school, seedbed.

hot-blooded *adj.* ardent, bold, eager, excitable, fervent, fiery, heated, high-spirited, homothermous, impetuous, impulsive, lustful, lusty, passionate, perfervid, precipitate, rash, sensual, spirited, temperamental, warm-blooded, wild.
antonyms cool, dispassionate.

hotel *n.* auberge, boarding-house, doss-house, flophouse, Gasthaus, Gasthof, guest-house, hostelry, hydro, hydropathic, inn, motel, pension, pub, public house, tavern.

hotheaded *adj.* daredevil, fiery, foolhardy, hasty, headstrong, hot-tempered, impetuous, impulsive, intemperate, madcap, over-eager, precipitate, quick-tempered, rash, reckless, unruly, volatile.
antonyms calm, cool.

hound *v.* badger, chase, chivvy, drive, dun, goad, harass, harry, hunt (down), impel, importune, persecute, pester, prod, provoke, pursue.

house *n.* abode, ancestry, biggin, blood, building, business, clan, company, concern, domicile, dwelling, dynasty, edifice, establishment, family, family tree, firm, gens, habitation, home, homestead, hostelry, hotel, household, inn, kindred, line, lineage, lodgings, maison, maison(n)ette, ménage, organization, outfit, parliament, partnership, pied-à-terre, public house, race, residence, roof, stem, tavern, tribe.
v. accommodate, bed, billet, board, contain, cover, domicile, domiciliate, harbor, hold, keep, lodge, place, protect, put up, quarter, sheathe, shelter, store, take in.

household *n.* establishment, family, family circle, home, house, ménage, set-up.
adj. common, domestic, domiciliary, established, everyday, familiar, family, home, ordinary, plain, well-known.

householder *n.* franklin, freeholder, goodman, head of the household, home-owner, house-father, landlord, occupant, occupier, owner, property owner, proprietor, resident, tenant.

housing *n.* accommodation, case, casing, container, cover, covering, dwellings, enclosure, habitation, holder, homes, houses, living quarters, matrix, protection, roof, sheath, shelter.

hovel *n.* bothy, but-and-ben, cabin, cot, croft, den, doghole, dump, hole, hut, hutch, shack, shanty, shed.

hover *v.* alternate, dally, dither, drift, falter, flap, float, fluctuate, flutter, fly, hang, hang about, hesitate, impend, linger, loom, menace, oscillate, pause, poise, seesaw, threaten, vacillate, waver.

however *conj.* anyhow, but, even so, howbeit, in spite of that, natheless, nevertheless, nonetheless, notwithstanding, still, though, yet.

howl *n.* bay, bellow, clamor, cry, groan, holler, hoot, outcry, roar, scream, shriek, ululation, wail, yell, yelp, yowl.
v. bellow, cry, holler, hoot, lament, quest, roar, scream, shout, shriek, ululate, wail, waul, weep, yawl, yell, yelp.

hub *n.* axis, center, core, focal point, focus, heart, linchpin, middle, nave, nerve center, pivot.

hubbub *n.* ado, agitation, babel, bedlam, brouhaha, chaos, clamor, coil, confusion, din, disorder, disturbance, hue and cry, hullabaloo, hurly-burly, kerfuffle, noise, palaver, pandemonium, racket, riot, rowdedow, rowdydow, ruckus, ruction, rumpus, tumult, turbulence, uproar, upset.
antonym calm.

huckster *n.* barker, chapman, dealer, haggler, hawker, packman, pedlar, pitcher, salesman, tinker, vendor.

huddle *n.* clump, clutch, conclave, confab, conference, confusion, crowd, discussion, disorder, heap, jumble, knot, mass, meeting, mess, muddle.
v. cluster, conglomerate, congregate, converge, crouch, crowd, cuddle, curl up, flock, gather, gravitate, hunch, nestle, press, ruck, snuggle, throng.
antonym disperse.

hue *n.* aspect, cast, character, color, complexion, dye, light, nuance, shade, tincture, tinge, tint, tone.

huffy *adj.* angry, crabbed, cross, crotchety, crusty, disgruntled, grumpy, hoity-toity, huffish, irritable, miffed, miffy, moody, moping, morose, offended, peevish, pettish, petulant, querulous, resentful, shirty, short, snappy, sulky, surly, testy, touchy, waspish.
antonyms cheery, happy.

hug *v.* cherish, clasp, cling to, cuddle, embrace, enclose, enfold, follow, grip, hold, lock, nurse, retain, skirt, squeeze.
n. clasp, clinch, cuddle, embrace, squeeze.

huge *adj.* Babylonian, Brobdingnagian, bulky, colossal, Cyclopean, enormous, extensive, gargantuan, giant, gigantean, gigantesque, gigantic, great, gross, immense, jumbo, large, leviathan, mammoth, massive, monumental, mountainous, Patagonian, prodigious, rounceval, stupendous, swingeing, thundering, titanic, tremendous, unwieldy, vast, walloping, whacking.
antonyms dainty, tiny.

hulking *adj.* awkward, bulky, cloddish, clodhopping, clumsy, cumbersome, galumphing, gross, hulky, loutish, lubberly, lumbering, lumpish, massive, oafish, overgrown, ponderous, ungainly, unwieldy.
antonyms delicate, small.

hullabaloo *n.* agitation, babel, bedlam, brouhaha, chaos, clamor, commotion, confusion, din, disturbance, furore, fuss, hubbub, hue and cry, hurly-burly, kerfuffle, noise, outcry, pandemonium, panic, racket, ruckus, ruction, rumpus, to-do, tumult, turmoil, uproar.

hum *v.* bombilate, bombinate, bum, bustle, buzz, croon, drone, lilt, move, mumble, murmur, pulsate, pulse, purr, sing, stir, susurrate, throb, thrum, vibrate, whirr, zoom.
n. bombilation, bombination, bustle, busyness, buzz, drone, mumble, murmur, noise, pulsation, pulse, purr, purring, singing, stir, susurration, susurrus, throb, thrum, vibration, whirr.

human *adj.* anthropoid, approachable, compassionate, considerate, fallible, fleshly, forgivable, hominoid, humane, kind, kindly, man-like, mortal, natural, reasonable, susceptible, understandable, understanding, vulnerable. *antonym* inhuman.
n. body, child, creature, hominid, homo sapiens, human being, individual, living soul, man, mortal, person, soul, wight, woman.

humane *adj.* beneficent, benevolent, benign, charitable, civilizing, clement, compassionate, forbearing, forgiving, gentle, good, good-natured, human, humanizing, kind, kind-hearted, kindly, lenient, loving, magnanimous, merciful, mild, sympathetic, tender, understanding.
antonym inhumane.

humanitarian *adj.* altruistic, beneficent, benevolent, charitable, compassionate, humane, philanthropic, philanthropical, public-spirited.
n. altruist, benefactor, do-gooder, Good Samaritan, philanthrope, philanthropist.
antonyms egoist, self-seeker.

humanitarianism *n.* beneficence, benevolence, charitableness, charity, compassionateness, do-goodery, generosity, goodwill, humanism, loving-kindness, philanthropy.
antonyms egoism, self-seeking.

humanity *n.* altruism, benevolence, benignity, brotherly love, charity, compassion, everyman, fellow-feeling, flesh, generosity, gentleness, goodwill, Homo sapiens, human nature, human race, humankind, humaneness, kind-heartedness, kindness, loving-kindness, man, mandom, mankind, men, mercy, mortality, people, philanthropy, sympathy, tenderness, tolerance, understanding.
antonym inhumanity.

humble *adj.* common, commonplace, courteous, deferential, demiss, docile, homespun, humdrum, insignificant, low, low-born, lowly, mean, meek, modest, obedient, obliging, obscure, obsequious, ordinary, plebeian, polite, poor, respectful, self-effacing, servile, simple, submissive, subservient, supplicatory, unassertive, unassuming, undistinguished, unimportant, unostentatious, unpretending, unpretentious.
antonyms assertive, important, pretentious, proud.
v. abase, abash, break, bring down, bring low, chagrin, chasten, confound, crush, debase, deflate, degrade, demean, discomfit, discredit, disgrace, humiliate, lower, mortify, reduce, shame, sink, subdue, take down a peg.
antonyms exalt, raise.

humbly *adv.* deferentially, diffidently, docilely, heepishly, meekly, modestly, obsequiously, respectfully, servilely, simply, submissively, subserviently, unassumingly, unpretentiously.
antonyms confidently, defiantly.

humbug *n.* baloney, blague, bluff, bounce, bullshit, bunk, bunkum, cant, charlatan, charlatanry, cheat, claptrap, con, con man, deceit, deception, dodge, eyewash, faker,

feint, fraud, fudge, gaff, gammon, hoax, hollowness, hype, hypocrisy, imposition, impostor, imposture, mountebank, nonsense, phony, pretense, pseud, quack, quackery, rubbish, ruse, sham, shenanigans, swindle, swindler, trick, trickery, trickster, wile.
v. bamboozle, befool, beguile, cajole, cheat, cozen, deceive, delude, dupe, fool, gammon, gull, hoax, hoodwink, impose, mislead, swindle, trick.

humdrum *adj.* boring, commonplace, dreary, droning, dull, everyday, humble, monotonous, mundane, ordinary, prosy, repetitious, routine, tedious, tiresome, uneventful, uninteresting, unvaried, wearisome.
antonyms exceptional, unusual.

humid *adj.* clammy, damp, dank, moist, muggy, soggy, steamy, sticky, sultry, vaporous, watery, wet.
antonym dry.

humiliate *v.* abase, abash, bring low, chagrin, chasten, confound, crush, debase, deflate, degrade, discomfit, discredit, disgrace, embarrass, humble, mortify, shame, subdue, undignify.
antonyms boost, dignify, exalt, vindicate.

humiliation *n.* abasement, affront, chagrin, condescension, deflation, degradation, discomfiture, discrediting, disgrace, dishonor, embarrassment, humbling, ignominy, indignity, mortification, put-down, rebuff, resignation, shame, snub.
antonyms gratification, triumph.

humor *n.* amusement, badinage, banter, bent, bias, caprice, choler, comedy, conceit, disposition, drollery, facetiousness, fancy, farce, frame of mind, fun, funniness, gags, jesting, jests, jocoseness, jocosity, jocularity, jokes, joking, ludicrousness, melancholy, mood, phlegm, pleasantries, propensity, quirk, raillery, repartee, spirits, temper, temperament, vagary, vein, whim, wisecracks, wit, witticisms, wittiness.
v. accommodate, appease, coax, comply with, cosset, favor, flatter, go along with, gratify, indulge, mollify, pamper, spoil.
antonym thwart.

humorous *adj.* absurd, amusing, comic, comical, entertaining, facetious, farcical, funny, hilarious, humoristic, jocose, jocular, laughable, ludicrous, merry, playful, pleasant, Rabelaisian, satirical, side-splitting, waggish, whimsical, wisecracking, witty, zany.
antonym humorless.

hunger *n.* appetence, appetency, appetite, craving, desire, emptiness, esurience, esuriency, famine, greediness, hungriness, itch, lust, rapacity, ravenousness, starvation, voracity, yearning, yen, yird-hunger.
antonyms appeasement, satisfaction.
v. ache, crave, desire, hanker, itch, long, lust, pine, starve, thirst, want, wish, yearn.

hungry *adj.* aching, appetitive, athirst, avid, covetous, craving, desirous, eager, empty, esurient, famished, famishing, greedy, hollow, hungerful, keen, lean, longing, peckish, ravenous, sharp-set, starved, starving, underfed, undernourished, voracious, yearning.
antonyms replete, satisfied.

hunt *v.* chase, chevy, course, dog, ferret, forage, gun for, hound, investigate, look for, pursue, rummage, scour, search, seek, stalk, track, trail.
n. battue, chase, chevy, hue and cry, hunting, investigation, pursuit, quest, search, venation.

hurl *v.* cast, catapult, chuck, dash, fire, fling, heave, launch, let fly, pitch, project, propel, send, shy, sling, throw, toss.

hurried *adj.* breakneck, brief, careless, cursory, hasty, headlong, hectic, passing, perfunctory, precipitate, quick, rushed, shallow, short, slapdash, speedy, superficial, swift, unthorough.
antonym leisurely.

hurry *v.* accelerate, belt, bustle, dash, dispatch, expedite, festinate, fly, get a move on, goad, hasten, hightail it, hump, hustle, jump to it, look lively, move, pike, quicken, rush, scoot, scurry, scutter, scuttle, shake a leg, shift, speed up, step on it, step on the gas, urge.
antonyms dally, delay.
n. bustle, celerity, commotion, dispatch, expedition, flurry, haste, precipitance, precipitancy, precipitation, promptitude, quickness, rush, scurry, speed, sweat, urgency.
antonyms calm, leisureliness.

hurt *v.* abuse, ache, afflict, aggrieve, annoy, bruise, burn, damage, disable, distress, grieve, harm, impair, injure, maim, maltreat, mar, pain, sadden, smart, spoil, sting, throb, tingle, torture, upset, wound.
n. abuse, bruise, damage, detriment, disadvantage, discomfort, distress, harm, injury, lesion, loss, mischief, pain, pang, scathe, sore, soreness, suffering, wound, wrong.
adj. aggrieved, annoyed, bruised, crushed, cut, damaged, displeased, grazed, harmed, huffed, injured, maimed, miffed, offended, pained, piqued, rueful, sad, saddened, scarred, scraped, scratched, wounded.

hurtful *adj.* catty, cruel, cutting, damaging, derogatory, destructive, detrimental, disadvantageous, distressing, harmful, humiliating, injurious, malefactory, malefic, maleficent, malicious, malificious, malignant, mean, mischievous, nasty, nocuous, pernicious, pestful, pestiferous, pestilent(ial), pointed, prejudicial, scathing, spiteful, unkind, upsetting, vicious, wounding.
antonyms helpful, kind.

hurtle *v.* bowl, charge, chase, crash, dash, fly, plunge, race, rattle, rush, scoot, scramble, shoot, speed, spin, spurt, tear.

husband[1] *v.* budget, conserve, economize, eke out, hoard, ration, save, save up, store, use sparingly.
antonyms squander, waste.

husband[2] *n.* Benedick, consort, goodman, hubby, man, married man, mate, old man, spouse.

hush *v.* calm, compose, mollify, mute, muzzle, quieten, settle, shush, silence, soothe, still.

antonyms disturb, rouse.
n. calm, calmness, peace, peacefulness, quiet, quietness, repose, serenity, silence, still, stillness, tranquility.
antonyms clamor, uproar.
interj. belt up, euphemeite, favete linguis, hold your tongue, leave it out, not another word, pipe down, quiet, say no more, shush, shut up, ssh, stow it, unberufen, wheesht, whisht.

husk *n.* bark, bract, bran, case, chaff, covering, glume, hull, pod, rind, shell, shuck, tegmen.

husky[1] *adj.* croaking, croaky, gruff, guttural, harsh, hoarse, low, rasping, raucous, rough, roupy, throaty.

husky[2] *adj.* beefy, brawny, burly, hefty, muscular, powerful, rugged, stocky, strapping, strong, sturdy, thickset, tough.

hustle *v.* bustle, crowd, elbow, force, frog-march, haste, hasten, hurry, impel, jog, jostle, pressgang, pressure, push, rush, shove, thrust.

hut *n.* booth, bothan, bothy, cabin, caboose, crib, den, hogan, hovel, kraal, lean-to, shack, shanty, shebang, shed, shelter, shiel, shieling, tilt.

hybrid *n.* amalgam, combination, composite, compound, conglomerate, cross, crossbreed, half-blood, half-breed, heterogeny, mixture, mongrel, mule, pastiche.
adj. bastard, combined, composite, compound, cross, heterogeneous, hybridous, hyphenated, mixed, mongrel, mule, patchwork.
antonyms pure, pure-bred.

hygiene *n.* asepsis, cleanliness, disinfection, hygienics, purity, salubriousness, salubrity, salutariness, sanitariness, sanitation, sterility, wholesomeness.
antonyms filth, insanitariness.

hygienic *adj.* aseptic, clean, cleanly, disinfected, germfree, healthy, pure, salubrious, salutary, sanitary, sterile, wholesome.
antonym unhygenic.

hyperbole *n.* enlargement, exaggeration, excess, extravagance, magnification, overkill, overplay, overstatement.
antonyms meiosis, understatement.

hypercritical *adj.* captious, carping, caviling, censorious, exceptious, fault-finding, finicky, fussy, hair-splitting, niggling, nit-picking, over-particular, pedantic, pernickety, quibbling, strict, ultracrepidarian, Zoilean.
antonyms tolerant, uncritical.

hypnotic *adj.* compelling, dazzling, fascinating, irresistible, magnetic, mesmeric, mesmerizing, narcotic, opiate, sleep-inducing, somniferous, soothing, soporific, spellbinding.

hypnotize *v.* bewitch, captivate, dazzle, entrance, fascinate, magnetize, mesmerize, spellbind, stupefy.

hypocrisy *n.* cant, deceit, deceitfulness, deception, dissembling, double-talk, duplicity, falsity, imposture, insincerity, lip-service, pharisaicalness, pharisaism, phariseeism, phoneyness, pietism, pretense, quackery, sanctimoniousness, self-righteousness, speciousness, Tartuffism, two-facedness.
antonyms humility, sincerity.

hypocrite *n.* canter, charlatan, deceiver, dissembler, fraud, Holy Willie, impostor, mountebank, Pharisee, phony, pretender, pseud, pseudo, Tartuffe, whited sepulcher.

hypocritical *adj.* canting, deceitful, deceptive, dissembling, double-faced, duplicitous, false, fraudulent, hollow, insincere, Pecksniffian, pharisaic(al), phony, pietistic, sanctimonious, self-pious, self-righteous, specious, spurious, Tartuffian, Tartuffish, two-faced.
antonyms genuine, humble, sincere.

hypothesis *n.* assumption, conjecture, guess, postulate, postulatum, premise, premiss, presumption, proposition, starting-point, supposition, theory, thesis.

hypothetical *adj.* academic, assumed, conjectural, imaginary, postulated, proposed, putative, speculative, supposed, suppositional, theoretical.
antonyms actual, real.

I

idea *n.* abstraction, aim, approximation, archetype, belief, clue, conceit, concept, conception, conceptualization, conclusion, conjecture, construct, conviction, design, doctrine, end, essence, estimate, fancy, form, guess, guesstimate, hint, hypothesis, idée fixe, image, import, impression, inkling, intention, interpretation, intimation, judgment, meaning, monomania, notion, object, opinion, pattern, perception, plan, purpose, reason, recept, recommendation, scheme, sense, significance, solution, suggestion, surmise, suspicion, teaching, theory, thought, type, understanding, view, viewpoint, vision.

ideal *n.* archetype, criterion, dreamboat, epitome, example, exemplar, image, last word, model, ne plus ultra, nonpareil, paradigm, paragon, pattern, perfection, pink of perfection, principle, prototype, standard, type.
adj. abstract, archetypal, best, classic, complete, conceptual, consummate, fanciful, highest, hypothetical, imaginary, impractical, model, optimal, optimum, perfect, quintessential, supreme, theoretical, transcendent, transcendental, unattainable, unreal, Utopian, visionary.

idealistic *adj.* impracticable, impractical, optimistic, perfectionist, quixotic, romantic, starry-eyed, unrealistic, utopian, visionary.
antonyms pragmatic, realistic.

identify *v.* catalog, classify, detect, diagnose, distinguish, finger, know, label, make out, name, pick out, pinpoint, place, recognize, single out, specify, spot, tag.

identity *n.* accord, coincidence, correspondence, empathy, existence, haecceity, individuality, oneness, particularity, personality, quiddity, rapport, sameness, self, selfhood, singularity, unanimity, uniqueness, unity.

ideology *n.* belief(s), convictions, creed, doctrine(s), dogma, ethic, faith, ideas, metaphysics, philosophy, principles, speculation, tenets, Weltanschauung, world view.

idiom *n.* colloquialism, expression, idiolect, idiotism, jargon, language, locution, parlance, phrase, regionalism, set phrase, style, talk, turn of phrase, usage, vernacular.

idiot *n.* ament, ass, blockhead, booby, cretin, cuckoo, dimwit, dolt, dumbbell, dummy, dunderhead, fat-head, featherbrain, fool, golem, half-wit, imbecile, mental defective, mooncalf, moron, natural, nidget, nig-nog, nincompoop, nitwit, noodle, saphead, schlep, schmo, schmuck, simpleton, thick, thickhead.

idiotic *adj.* asinine, crazy, cretinous, daft, dumb, fatheaded, fatuous, foolhardy, foolish, hair-brained, half-witted, harebrained, idiotical, imbecile, imbecilic, inane, insane, loony, lunatic, moronic, nutty, screwy, senseless, simple, stupid, tomfool, unintelligent.
antonyms sane, sensible.

idle *adj.* abortive, bootless, dead, dormant, dronish, empty, foolish, frivolous, fruitless, futile, good-for-nothing, groundless, inactive, indolent, ineffective, ineffectual, inoperative, jobless, lackadaisical, lazy, mothballed, nugatory, of no avail, otiose, pointless, purposeless, redundant, shiftless, slothful, sluggish, stationary, superficial, torpid, trivial, unavailing, unbusy, unemployed, unproductive, unsuccessful, unused, useless, vain, work-shy, worthless.
antonyms active, effective, purposeful.
v. coast, dally, dawdle, drift, fool, fritter, kill time, lally-gag, laze, lie up, loiter, lounge, potter, rest on one's laurels, shirk, skive, slack, take it easy, tick over, vegetate, waste, while.
antonyms act, work.

idol *n.* beloved, darling, deity, favorite, fetish, god, graven image, hero, icon, image, joss, ju-ju, Mumbo-jumbo, pet, pin-up, superstar.

idolize *v.* admire, adore, apotheosize, deify, dote on, exalt, glorify, hero-worship, iconize, lionize, love, revere, reverence, venerate, worship. *antonym* vilify.

ignoble *adj.* abject, base, base-born, caddish, common, contemptible, cowardly, craven, dastardly, degenerate, degraded, despicable, disgraceful, dishonorable, heinous, humble, infamous, low, low-born, lowly, mean, petty, plebeian, shabby, shameless, unworthy, vile, vulgar, worthless, wretched.
antonyms honorable, noble.

ignominious *adj.* abject, crushing, degrading, despicable, discreditable, disgraceful, dishonorable, disreputable, humiliating, indecorous, inglorious, mortifying, scandalous, shameful, sorry, undignified.
antonyms honorable, triumphant.

ignorant *adj.* as thick as two short planks, benighted, blind, bookless, clueless, crass, dense, green, gross, half-baked, idealess, ill-informed, illiterate, ill-versed, inexperienced, innocent, innumerate, insensitive, know-nothing, naïve, nescient, oblivious, pig-ignorant, stupid, thick, unacquainted, unaware, unconscious, uncultivated, uneducated, unenlightened, unidea'd, uninformed, uninitiated, uninstructed, unknowing, unlearned, unlettered, unread, unscholarly, unschooled, untaught, untrained, untutored, unwitting.
antonyms knowlegeable, wise.

ignore *v.* blink, cold-shoulder, cut, disregard, neglect, omit, overlook, pass over, pay no attention to,

pigeon-hole, reject, send to Coventry, set aside, shut one's eyes to, slight, take no notice of, turn a blind eye to, turn a deaf ear to, turn one's back on.
antonym note.

ill[1] *adj.* ailing, dicky, diseased, frail, funny, indisposed, infirm, laid up, not up to snuff, off-color, on the sick list, out of sorts, peelie-wally, poorly, queasy, queer, seedy, sick, under the weather, unhealthy, unwell, valetudinarian.
antonym well.
n. affliction, ailment, complaint, disease, disorder, illness, indisposition, infection, infirmity, malady, malaise, sickness.

ill[2] *adj.* acrimonious, adverse, antagonistic, bad, cantankerous, cross, damaging, deleterious, detrimental, difficult, disturbing, evil, foul, harmful, harsh, hateful, hostile, hurtful, inauspicious, incorrect, inimical, iniquitous, injurious, malevolent, malicious, ominous, reprehensible, ruinous, sinister, sullen, surly, threatening, unfavorable, unfortunate, unfriendly, unhealthy, unkind, unlucky, unpromising, unpropitious, unwholesome, vile, wicked, wrong.
antonyms beneficial, fortunate, good, kind.
n. abuse, affliction, badness, cruelty, damage, depravity, destruction, evil, harm, hurt, ill-usage, injury, malice, mischief, misery, misfortune, pain, sorrow, suffering, trial, tribulation, trouble, unpleasantness, wickedness, woe.
antonym benefit.
adv. amiss, badly, by no means, hard, hardly, inauspiciously, insufficiently, poorly, scantily, scarcely, unfavorably, unluckily, wrongfully.
antonym well.

ill-advised *adj.* daft, foolhardy, foolish, hasty, hazardous, ill-considered, ill-judged, impolitic, imprudent, inappropriate, incautious, indiscreet, injudicious, misguided, overhasty, rash, reckless, short-sighted, thoughtless, unseemly, unwise, wrong-headed.
antonym sensible.

ill-assorted *adj.* discordant, incompatible, incongruous, inharmonious, misallied, mismatched, uncongenial, unsuited.
antonym harmonious.

illegal *adj.* actionable, banned, black-market, contraband, criminal, felonious, forbidden, illicit, outlawed, pirate, prohibited, proscribed, unauthorized, unconstitutional, under-the-counter, unlawful, unlicensed, wrongful, wrongous.
antonym legal.

ill-fated *adj.* blighted, doomed, forlorn, hapless, ill-omened, ill-starred, infaust, luckless, star-crossed, unfortunate, unhappy, unlucky.
antonym lucky.

illiberal *adj.* bigoted, close-fisted, hidebound, intolerant, mean, miserly, narrow-minded, niggardly, parsimonious, petty, prejudiced, reactionary, small-minded, sordid, stingy, tight, tightfisted, uncharitable, ungenerous, verkrampte.
antonym liberal.

illicit *adj.* black, black-market, bootleg, clandestine, contraband, criminal, felonious, forbidden, furtive, guilty, illegal, illegitimate, ill-gotten, immoral, improper, inadmissible, prohibited, unauthorized, unlawful, unlicensed, unsanctioned, wrong.
antonyms legal, licit.

illiterate *adj.* analphabetic, benighted, ignorant, uncultured, uneducated, unlettered, untaught, untutored.
antonym literate.

ill-natured *adj.* bad-tempered, churlish, crabbed, cross, cross-grained, disagreeable, disobliging, malevolent, malicious, malignant, mean, nasty, perverse, petulant, spiteful, sulky, sullen, surly, unfriendly, unkind, unpleasant, vicious, vindictive.
antonym good-natured.

illness *n.* affliction, ailment, attack, complaint, disability, disease, disorder, distemper, dyscrasia, idiopathy, ill-being, ill-health, indisposition, infirmity, malady, malaise, sickness.
antonym health.

illogical *adj.* absurd, fallacious, faulty, illegitimate, inconclusive, inconsistent, incorrect, invalid, irrational, meaningless, senseless, sophistical, specious, spurious, unreasonable, unscientific, unsound.
antonym logical.

ill-tempered *adj.* bad-tempered, choleric, cross, curt, grumpy, ill-humored, ill-natured, impatient, irascible, irritable, sharp, spiteful, testy, tetchy, touchy, vicious, vixenish, vixenly.
antonym good-tempered.

ill-treatment *n.* abuse, damage, harm, ill-use, injury, maltreatment, manhandling, mishandling, mistreatment, misuse, neglect.
antonym care.

illuminate *v.* adorn, beacon, brighten, clarify, clear up, decorate, edify, elucidate, enlighten, explain, illumine, illustrate, instruct, irradiate, light, light up, limn, miniate, ornament.
antonyms darken, deface, divest.

illusion *n.* apparition, chimera, daydream, deception, delusion, error, fallacy, fancy, fantasy, figment, hallucination, ignis fatuus, maya, mirage, misapprehension, misconception, phantasm, semblance, will-o'-the-wisp.
antonym reality.

illusory *adj.* apparent, Barmecidal, beguiling, chimerical, deceitful, deceptive, deluding, delusive, fallacious, false, hallucinatory, illusive, misleading, mistaken, seeming, sham, unreal, unsubstantial, untrue, vain.
antonym real.

illustrate *v.* adorn, clarify, decorate, demonstrate, depict, draw, elucidate, emphasize, exemplify, exhibit, explain, illuminate, instance, interpret, miniate, ornament, picture, show, sketch.

illustration *n.* adornment, analogy, case, case in point, clarification, decoration, delineation, demonstration, drawing, elucidation, example, exemplification, explanation, figure, graphic, half-tone, instance, interpretation, photograph, picture, plate, representation, sketch, specimen.

illustrious *adj.* brilliant, celebrated, distinguished, eminent, exalted, excellent, famed, famous, glorious, great, magnificent, noble, notable, noted, outstanding, prominent, remarkable, renowned, resplendent, signal, splendid.
antonyms inglorious, shameful.

image *n.* appearance, conceit, concept, conception, counterpart, dead ringer, Doppelgänger, double, effigies, effigy, eidolon, eikon, facsimile, figure, icon, idea, idol, impression, likeness, perception, picture, portrait, reflection, replica, representation, semblance, similitude, simulacrum, spit, spitting image, statue, trope.

imaginary *adj.* assumed, Barmecidal, chimerical, dreamlike, fancied, fanciful, fictional, fictitious, hallucinatory, hypothetical, ideal, illusive, illusory, imagined, insubstantial, invented, legendary, made-up, mythological, non-existent, phantasmal, shadowy, supposed, unreal, unsubstantial, visionary.
antonym real.

imagination *n.* chimera, conception, creativity, enterprise, fancy, idea, ideality, illusion, image, imaginativeness, ingenuity, innovativeness, innovatoriness, insight, inspiration, invention, inventiveness, notion, originality, resourcefulness, supposition, unreality, vision, wit, wittiness.
antonyms reality, unimaginativeness.

imaginative *adj.* clever, creative, dreamy, enterprising, fanciful, fantastic, fertile, ingenious, innovative, inspired, inventive, original, poetical, resourceful, visionary, vivid.
antonym unimaginative.

imagine *v.* apprehend, assume, believe, conceive, conceptualize, conjecture, conjure up, create, deduce, deem, devise, dream up, envisage, envision, fancy, fantasize, frame, gather, guess, ideate, infer, invent, judge, picture, plan, project, realize, scheme, suppose, surmise, suspect, take it, think, think of, think up, visualize.

imbecile *n.* ament, blockhead, bungler, clown, cretin, dolt, dotard, fool, half-wit, idiot, moron, thickhead.
adj. anile, asinine, doltish, fatuous, feeble-minded, foolish, idiotic, imbecilic, inane, ludicrous, moronic, senile, simple, stupid, thick, witless.
antonyms intelligent, sensible.

imbibe *v.* absorb, acquire, assimilate, consume, drink, drink in, gain, gather, gulp, ingest, knock back, lap up, quaff, receive, sink, sip, soak in, soak up, swallow, swig, take in.

imitate *v.* affect, ape, burlesque, caricature, clone, copy, copy-cat, counterfeit, do, duplicate, echo, emulate, follow, follow suit, forge, impersonate, mimic, mirror, mock, monkey, parody, parrot, personate, repeat, reproduce, send up, simulate, spoof, take off, travesty.

imitation *n.* apery, aping, copy, counterfeit, counterfeiting, duplication, echoing, echopraxia, echopraxis, fake, forgery, impersonation, impression, likeness, mimesis, mimicry, mockery, parody, reflection, replica, reproduction, resemblance, sham, simulation, substitution, take-off, travesty.
adj. artificial, dummy, ersatz, man-made, mock, phony, pinchbeck, pseudo, repro, reproduction, sham, simulated, synthetic.
antonym genuine.

immaculate *adj.* blameless, clean, faultless, flawless, guiltless, impeccable, incorrupt, innocent, neat, perfect, pure, scrupulous, sinless, spick-and-span, spotless, spruce, stainless, trim, unblemished, uncontaminated, undefiled, unexceptionable, unpolluted, unsullied, untainted, untarnished, virtuous.
antonyms contaminated, spoiled.

immature *adj.* adolescent, babyish, callow, childish, crude, green, immatured, imperfect, inexperienced, infantile, jejune, juvenile, premature, puerile, raw, under-age, undeveloped, unfinished, unfledged, unformed, unripe, unseasonable, untimely, young.
antonym mature.

immeasurable *adj.* bottomless, boundless, endless, illimitable, immense, immensurable, incalculable, inestimable, inexhaustible, infinite, limitless, measureless, unbounded, unfathomable, unlimited, unmeasurable, vast.
antonym limited.

immediate *adj.* actual, adjacent, close, contiguous, current, direct, existing, extant, instant, instantaneous, near, nearest, neighboring, next, on hand, present, pressing, primary, prompt, proximate, recent, unhesitating, up-to-date, urgent.
antonym distant.

immediately *adv.* at once, closely, directly, forthwith, incontinent, instantly, lickety-split, nearly, now, off the top of one's head, on the instant, posthaste, promptly, pronto, right away, straight away, straight off, straight way, tout de suite, unhesitatingly, without delay.
antonyms eventually, never.

immense *adj.* Brobdingnag(ian), colossal, cyclopean, elephantine, enormous, extensive, giant, gigantic, great, herculean, huge, illimitable, immeasurable, infinite, interminable, jumbo, large, limitless, mammoth, massive, monstrous, monumental, prodigious, rounceval, stupendous, Titanesque, titanic, tremendous, vast.
antonym minute.

immensity *n.* bulk, enormousness, expanse, extent, greatness, hugeness, infinity, magnitude, massiveness, scope, size, sweep, vastness.
antonym minuteness.

immerse *v.* bathe, demerge, demerse, dip, douse, duck, dunk, plunge, sink, submerge, submerse.
immigrate *v.* come in, migrate, move in, remove, resettle, settle.
antonym emigrate.
imminent *adj.* afoot, approaching, at hand, brewing, close, coming, forthcoming, gathering, impending, in the air, in the offing, looming, menacing, near, nigh, overhanging, threatening.
antonym far-off.
immoderately *adv.* exaggeratedly, excessively, exorbitantly, extravagantly, extremely, inordinately, unduly, unjustifiably, unreasonably, unrestrainedly, wantonly, without measure.
antonym moderately.
immoral *adj.* abandoned, bad, corrupt, debauched, degenerate, depraved, dishonest, dissolute, evil, foul, impure, indecent, iniquitous, lecherous, lewd, licentious, nefarious, obscene, pornographic, profligate, reprobate, sinful, unchaste, unethical, unprincipled, unrighteous, unscrupulous, vicious, vile, wanton, wicked, wrong.
antonym moral.
antonym morality.
immortal *adj.* abiding, ambrosial, constant, deathless, endless, enduring, eternal, everlasting, imperishable, incorruptible, indestructible, lasting, perennial, perpetual, sempiternal, timeless, undying, unfading, unforgettable.
antonym mortal.
n. deity, divinity, genius, god, goddess, great, hero, Olympian.
immortalize *v.* apotheosize, celebrate, commemorate, deify, enshrine, eternalize, eternize, exalt, glorify, hallow, memorialize, perpetuate, solemnize.
immune *adj.* clear, exempt, free, insusceptible, insusceptive, invulnerable, proof, protected, resistant, safe, unaffected, unsusceptible.
antonym susceptible.
immutable *adj.* abiding, changeless, constant, enduring, fixed, inflexible, invariable, lasting, permanent, perpetual, sacrosanct, solid, stable, steadfast, unalterable, unchangeable.
antonym mutable.
impact *n.* aftermath, bang, blow, brunt, bump, burden, collision, concussion, consequences, contact, crash, effect, force, impression, influence, jolt, knock, knock-on effect, meaning, power, repercussions, shock, significance, smash, stroke, thrust, thump, weight.
v. clash, collide, crash, crush, fix, hit, press together, strike, wedge.
impair *v.* blunt, craze, damage, debilitate, decrease, deteriorate, devalue, diminish, enervate, enfeeble, harm, hinder, injure, lessen, mar, reduce, spoil, undermine, vitiate, weaken, worsen.
antonym enhance.
impart *v.* accord, afford, bestow, communicate, confer, contribute, convey, disclose, discover, divulge, give, grant, hand over, lend, make known, offer, pass on, relate, reveal, tell, yield.
impartial *adj.* detached, disinterested, dispassionate, equal, equitable, even-handed, fair, just, neutral, non-discriminating, non-partisan, objective, open-minded, uncommitted, unbiased, unprejudiced.
antonym biased.
impartiality *n.* detachment, disinterest, disinterestedness, dispassion, equality, equity, even-handedness, fairness, neutrality, non-partisanship, objectivity, open-mindedness, unbiasedness.
antonym bias.
impasse *n.* blind alley, cul-de-sac, dead end, deadlock, halt, nonplus, stalemate, stand-off, standstill.
impassioned *adj.* animated, ardent, blazing, enthusiastic, excited, fervent, fervid, fiery, furious, glowing, heated, inflamed, inspired, intense, passionate, rousing, spirited, stirring, vehement, vigorous, violent, vivid, warm.
antonyms apathetic, mild.
impassive *adj.* aloof, apathetic, blockish, callous, calm, composed, cool, dispassionate, emotionless, expressionless, immobile, impassible, imperturbable, indifferent, inscrutable, insensible, insusceptible, laid back, phlegmatic, poker-faced, reserved, serene, stoical, stolid, unconcerned, unemotional, unexcitable, unfeeling, unimpressible, unmoved, unruffled.
antonyms moved, responsive, warm.
impede *v.* bar, block, brake, check, clog, curb, delay, disrupt, hamper, hinder, hobble, hold up, let, obstruct, restrain, retard, slow, stop, thwart, trammel.
antonym aid.
impediment *n.* bar, barrier, block, burr, check, clog, curb, defect, difficulty, encumbrance, hindrance, let, log, obstacle, obstruction, snag, stammer, stumbling-block, stutter.
antonym aid.
impel *v.* actuate, chivvy, compel, constrain, drive, excite, force, goad, incite, induce, influence, inspire, instigate, motivate, move, oblige, poke, power, prod, prompt, propel, push, spur, stimulate, urge.
antonym dissuade.
impending *adj.* approaching, brewing, close, collecting, coming, forthcoming, gathering, hovering, imminent, in store, looming, menacing, near, nearing, threatening.
antonym remote.
impenetrable *adj.* arcane, baffling, cabbalistic, cryptic, dark, dense, enigmatic(al), fathomless, hermetic, hidden, impassable, impermeable, impervious, incomprehensible, indiscernible, inexplicable, inscrutable, inviolable, mysterious, obscure, solid, thick, unfathomable, unintelligible, unpiercable.
antonyms intelligible, penetrable.
imperative *adj.* authoritative, autocratic, bossy, commanding,

compulsory, crucial, dictatorial, domineering, essential, exigent, high-handed, imperious, indispensable, insistent, lordly, magisterial, obligatory, peremptory, pressing, tyrannical, tyrannous, urgent, vital.
antonyms humble, optional.

imperceptible *adj.* faint, fine, gradual, impalpable, inapparent, inappreciable, inaudible, inconsensequential, indiscernible, indistinguishable, infinitesimal, insensible, invisible, microscopic, minute, shadowy, slight, small, subtle, tiny, undetectable, unnoticeable.
antonym perceptible.

imperfection *n.* blemish, blot, blotch, crack, defect, deficiency, dent, failing, fallibility, fault, flaw, foible, frailty, glitch, inadequacy, incompleteness, insufficiency, peccadillo, shortcoming, stain, taint, weakness.
antonyms asset, perfection.

imperil *v.* compromise, endanger, expose, hazard, jeopardize, risk, threaten.

impersonal *adj.* aloof, bureaucratic, businesslike, cold, detached, dispassionate, faceless, formal, frosty, glassy, inhuman, neutral, official, remote, unfriendly, unsympathetic.
antonym friendly.

impersonate *v.* act, ape, caricature, do, imitate, masquerade as, mimic, mock, parody, personate, pose as, take off.

impertinence *n.* assurance, audacity, backchat, boldness, brass, brazenness, cheek, discourtesy, disrespect, effrontery, forwardness, impoliteness, impudence, incivility, insolence, malapertness, nerve, pertness, politeness, presumption, rudeness, sauce, sauciness.

impertinent *adj.* bold, brattish, brazen, bumptious, cheeky, discourteous, disrespectful, forward, fresh, ill-mannered, impolite, impudent, insolent, interfering, malapert, pert, presumptuous, rude, saucy, uncivil, unmannerly.
antonym polite.

impetuous *adj.* ardent, bull-headed, eager, furious, hasty, headlong, impassioned, impulsive, overhasty, passionate, precipitate, rash, spontaneous, tearaway, unplanned, unpremeditated, unreflecting, unrestrained, unthinking.
antonym circumspect.

implacable *adj.* cruel, immovable, inappeasable, inexorable, inflexible, intractable, intransigent, irreconcilable, merciless, pitiless, rancorous, relentless, remorseless, ruthless, unappeasable, unbending, uncompromising, unforgiving, unrelenting, unyielding.
antonym placable.

implausible *adj.* dubious, far-fetched, flimsy, improbable, incredible, suspect, thin, transparent, unbelievable, unconvincing, unlikely, unplausible, unreasonable, weak.
antonym plausible.

implicate *v.* associate, compromise, connect, embroil, entangle, include, incriminate, inculpate, involve, throw suspicion on.
antonyms absolve, exonerate.

implicit *adj.* absolute, constant, contained, entire, firm, fixed, full, implied, inherent, latent, presupposed, steadfast, tacit, total, undeclared, understood, unhesitating, unqualified, unquestioning, unreserved, unshakable, unshaken, unspoken, wholehearted.
antonym explicit.

implore *v.* ask, beg, beseech, crave, entreat, importune, plead, pray, solicit, supplicate, wheedle.

imply *v.* betoken, connote, denote, entail, evidence, hint, import, indicate, insinuate, intimate, involve, mean, point to, presuppose, require, signify, suggest.
antonym state.

impolite *adj.* abrupt, bad-mannered, boorish, churlish, clumsy, coarse, cross, discourteous, disrespectful, gauche, ill-bred, ill-mannered, indecorous, indelicate, inept, insolent, loutish, rough, rude, uncivil, uncourteous, ungallant, ungentlemanly, ungracious, unladylike, unmannerly, unrefined.
antonym polite.

import *n.* bearing, consequence, drift, essence, gist, implication, importance, intention, magnitude, meaning, message, moment, nub, purport, sense, significance, substance, thrust, weight.
v. betoken, bring in, imply, indicate, introduce, mean, purport, signify.

important *adj.* basic, eminent, essential, far-reaching, foremost, grave, heavy, high-level, high-ranking, influential, key, keynote, large, leading, material, meaningful, momentous, notable, noteworthy, on the map, outstanding, powerful, pre-eminent, primary, prominent, relevant, salient, seminal, serious, signal, significant, substantial, urgent, valuable, valued, weighty.
antonym unimportant.

impose[1] *v.* appoint, burden, charge (with), decree, dictate, encumber, enforce, enjoin, establish, exact, fix, impone, inflict, institute, introduce, lay, levy, ordain, place, prescribe, promulgate, put, saddle, set.

impose[2] *v.* butt in, encroach, foist, force oneself, gate crash, horn in, impone, interpose, intrude, obtrude, presume, take liberties, trespass.

imposing *adj.* august, commanding, dignified, distinguished, effective, grand, grandiose, impressive, majestic, ortund, pompous, stately, striking.
antonyms modest, unimposing.

imposition[1] *n.* application, decree, exaction, infliction, introduction, levying, promulgation.

imposition[2] *n.* burden, charge, cheek, constraint, deception, duty, encroachment, intrusion, levy, liberty, lines, presumption, punishment, task, tax.

impossible *adj.* absurd, hopeless, impracticable, inadmissible, inconceivable, insoluble, intolerable, ludicrous, outrageous, preposterous, unacceptable, unachievable, unattainable, ungovernable, unobtainable,

unreasonable, untenable, unthinkable, unviable, unworkable.
antonym possible.
impractical *adj.* academic, idealistic, impossible, impracticable, inoperable, ivory-tower, non-viable, romantic, starry-eyed, unbusinesslike, unrealistic, unserviceable, unworkable, visionary, wild. *antonym* practical.
impregnable *adj.* fast, fortified, immovable, impenetrable, impugnable, indestructible, invincible, invulnerable, secure, solid, strong, unassailable, unbeatable, unconquerable.
antonym vulnerable.
impress *v.* affect, emboss, emphasize, engrave, excite, fix, grab, imprint, inculcate, indent, influence, inspire, instil, make one's mark, mark, move, namedrop, print, slay, stamp, stand out, stir, strike, sway, touch, wow.
impression[1] *n.* awareness, belief, concept, consciousness, conviction, effect, fancy, feeling, hunch, idea, impact, influence, memory, notion, opinion, reaction, recollection, sense, suspicion, sway.
impression[2] *n.* dent, edition, engram, engramma, hollow, impress, imprint, imprinting, incuse, indentation, issue, mark, niello, outline, pressure, printing, stamp, stamping.
impression[3] *n.* apery, aping, burlesque, imitation, impersonation, parody, send-up, take-off.
impressive *adj.* affecting, effective, exciting, forcible, foudroyant, frappant, imposing, moving, powerful, stirring, striking, touching.
antonym unimpressive.
impromptu *adj.* ad-lib, autoschediastic, extemporaneous, extempore, extemporised, improvised, off the cuff, off-hand, offhand, spontaneous, unpremeditated, unprepared, unrehearsed, unscripted, unstudied.
antonyms planned, rehearsed.
adv. ad lib, extempore, off the cuff, off the top of one's head, on the spur of the moment, spontaneously.
n. autoschediasm, extemporisation, improvisation, voluntary.
improper *adj.* abnormal, erroneous, false, illegitimate, illtimed, impolite, inaccurate, inadmissible, inapplicable, inapposite, inappropriate, inapt, incongruous, incorrect, indecent, indecorous, indelicate, infelicitous, inopportune, irregular, malapropos, off-color, out of place, risqué, smutty, suggestive, unbecoming, uncalled-for, unfit, unfitting, unmaidenly, unparliamentary, unprintable, unquotable, unrepeatable, unseasonable, unseemly, unsuitable, unsuited, untoward, unwarranted, vulgar, wrong.
antonym proper.
improve *v.* advance, ameliorate, amend, augment, better, correct, culture, develop, embourgeoise, enhance, gentrify, help, increase, look up, meliorate, mend, mend one's ways, perk up, pick up, polish, progress, rally, recover, rectify, recuperate, reform, rise, touch up, turn over a new leaf, turn the corner, up, upgrade.
antonyms decline, diminish.
improvement *n.* advance, advancement, amelioration, amendment, augmentation, bettering, betterment, correction, development, embourgeoisement, enhancement, furtherance, gain, gentrification, increase, melioration, progress, rally, recovery, rectification, reformation, rise, upswing.
improvident *adj.* careless, feckless, heedless, imprudent, Micawberish, negligent, prodigal, profligate, reckless, shiftless, spendthrift, thoughtless, thriftless, underprepared, uneconomical, unprepared, unthrifty, wasteful.
antonym thrifty.
improvisation *n.* ad-lib, ad-libbing, autoschediasm, expedient, extemporising, impromptu, invention, makeshift, spontaneity, vamp.
imprudent *adj.* careless, foolhardy, foolish, hasty, heedless, ill-advised, ill-considered, ill-judged, impolitic, improvident, incautious, inconsiderate, indiscreet, injudicious, irresponsible, overhasty, rash, reckless, short-sighted, temerarious, unthinking, unwise.
antonym prudent.
impudence *n.* assurance, audacity, backchat, boldness, brass neck, brazenness, cheek, chutzpah, effrontery, face, impertinence, impudicity, insolence, lip, malapertness, neck, nerve, pertness, presumption, presumptuousness, rudeness, sauciness, shamelessness.
antonym politeness.
impudent *adj.* audacious, bold, bold-faced, brazen, brazen-faced, cheeky, cocky, forward, fresh, immodest, impertinent, insolent, malapert, pert, presumptuous, rude, saucy, shameless.
antonym polite.
impulse *n.* caprice, catalyst, conatus, desire, drive, feeling, force, impetus, incitement, inclination, influence, instinct, momentum, motive, movement, notion, passion, pressure, push, resolve, stimulus, surge, thrust, urge, whim, wish.
impulsive *adj.* hasty, headlong, impetuous, instinctive, intuitive, passionate, precipitant, precipitate, quick, rash, reckless, spontaneous, unconsidered, unpredictable, unpremeditated.
antonym cautious.
impure *adj.* admixed, adulterated, alloyed, carnal, coarse, contaminated, corrupt, debased, defiled, dirty, feculent, filthy, foul, gross, immodest, immoral, indecent, indelicate, infected, lascivious, lewd, licentious, lustful, mixed, obscene, polluted, prurient, salacious, smutty, sullied, tainted, turbid, unchaste, unclean, unrefined, unwholesome, vicious, vitiated.
antonyms chaste, pure.
imputation *n.* accusation, arrogation, ascription, aspersion, attribution, blame, censure, charge, insinuation, reproach, slander, slur, suggestion.
in abeyance dormant, hanging fire, on ice, pending, shelved, suspended.

in camera behind closed doors, hugger-mugger, in private, in secret, privately, secretly, sub rosa, under the rose.
antonym openly.

in confidence in private, privately, secretly, sub rosa, under the rose.

in depth comprehensively, exhaustively, extensively, in detail, intensively, thoroughly.
antonyms broadly, superficially.

in effect actually, effectively, essentially, for practical purposes, in actuality, in fact, in reality, in the end, in truth, really, to all intents and purposes, virtually, when all is said and done.

in force binding, current, effective, gregatim, in crowds, in droves, in flocks, in hordes, in large numbers, in operation, in strength, on the statute, book, operative, valid, working.
antonym inoperative.

in good part cheerfully, cordially, good-naturedly, laughingly, well.
antonyms angrily, touchily.

in keeping appropriate, befitting, fit, fitting, harmonious, in harmony, of a piece, suitable.
antonym inappropriate.

in motion afoot, functioning, going, in progress, moving, on the go, operational, running, sailing, traveling, under way.
antonym stationary.

in order acceptable, all right, allowed, appropriate, arranged, called for, correct, done, fitting, in sequence, neat, OK, orderly, permitted, right, shipshape, suitable, tidy.
antonyms disallowed, out of order.

in order to intending to, so that, to, with a view to, with the intention of, with the purpose of.

in part a little, in some measure, part way, partially, partly, slightly, somewhat, to a certain extent, to some degree.
antonym wholly.

in passing accidentally, by the by(e), by the way, en passant, incidentally.

in person as large as life, bodily, in propria persona, personally.

in principle en principe, ideally, in essence, in theory, theoretically.

in spite of despite, notwithstanding.

in the light of bearing/keeping in mind, because of, considering, in view of, taking into account.

in the money affluent, flush, loaded, opulent, prosperous, rich, rolling in it, wealthy, well-heeled, well-off, well-to-do.
antonym poor.

in the mood disposed, in the right frame of mind, inclined, interested, keen, minded, of a mind, willing.

in the offing at hand, close at hand, coming up, imminent, in sight, on the horizon, on the way. *antonym* far off.

in the red bankrupt, in arrears, in debt, insolvent, on the rocks, overdrawn.
antonym in credit.

in two minds dithering, hesitant, hesitating, shilly-shallying, swithering, uncertain, undecided, unsure, vacillating, wavering.
antonym certain.

in vain bootlessly, fruitlessly, ineffectually, to no avail, unsuccessfully, uselessly, vainly.
antonym successfully.

inability *n.* disability, disqualification, handicap, impotence, inadequacy, incapability, incapacity, incompetence, ineptitude, ineptness, powerlessness, weakness.
antonym ability.

inaccurate *adj.* careless, defective, discrepant, erroneous, faulty, imprecise, in error, incorrect, inexact, loose, mistaken, out, unfaithful, unreliable, unrepresentative, unsound, wide of the mark, wild, wrong.
antonym accurate.

inactive *adj.* abeyant, dormant, dull, idle, immobile, indolent, inert, inoperative, jobless, kicking one's heels, latent, lazy, lethargic, low-key, mothballed, out of service, out of work, passive, quiet, sedentary, sleepy, slothful, slow, sluggish, somnolent, stagnant, stagnating, torpid, unemployed, unoccupied, unused.
antonym active.

inactivity *n.* abeyance, abeyancy, dilatoriness, dolce far niente, dormancy, dullness, heaviness, hibernation, idleness, immobility, inaction, indolence, inertia, inertness, languor, lassitude, laziness, lethargy, passivity, quiescence, sloth, sluggishness, stagnation, stasis, torpor, unemployment, vegetation.
antonym activeness.

inadequate *adj.* defective, deficient, faulty, imperfect, inapt, incapable, incommensurate, incompetent, incomplete, ineffective, ineffectual, inefficacious, inefficient, insubstantial, insufficient, leaving a little/a lot/much to be desired, meager, niggardly, scanty, short, sketchy, skimpy, sparse, unequal, unfitted, unqualified, wanting.
antonym adequate.

inadvertent *adj.* accidental, careless, chance, heedless, inattentive, negligent, thoughtless, unguarded, unheeding, unintended, unintentional, unplanned, unpremeditated, unthinking, unwitting.
antonym deliberate.

inane *adj.* asinine, daft, drippy, empty, fatuous, foolish, frivolous, futile, idiotic, imbecilic, mindless, nutty, puerile, senseless, silly, stupid, trifling, unintelligent, vacuous, vain, vapid, worthless.
antonym sensible.

inanimate *adj.* abiotic, dead, defunct, dormant, dull, exanimate, extinct, heavy, inactive, inert, inorganic, insensate, insentient, leaden, lifeless, listless, slow, spiritless, stagnant, torpid.
antonyms alive, animate, lively, living.

inappropriate *adj.* disproportionate, ill-fitted, ill-suited, ill-timed, improper, incongruous, infelicitous, malapropos, out of place, tactless, tasteless, unbecoming, unbefitting, unfit, unfitting, unseemly, unsuitable, untimely.
antonym appropriate.

inarticulate *adj.* blurred, dumb, dysarthric, dysphasic, dyspraxic, faltering, halting, hesitant, incoherent, incomprehensible, indistinct, muffled, mumbled, mute, silent, speechless, tongue-tied, unclear, unintelligible, unspoken, unuttered, unvoiced, voiceless, wordless.
antonym articulate.

inattentive *adj.* absent-minded, careless, deaf, distracted, distrait, dreaming, dreamy, heedless, inadvertent, neglectful, negligent, preoccupied, regardless, remiss, unheeding, unmindful, unobservant, vague.
antonym attentive.

inaugurate *v.* begin, christen, commence, commission, consecrate, dedicate, enthrone, han(d)sel, induct, initiate, install, instate, institute, introduce, invest, kick off, launch, open, ordain, originate, set up, start, start off, usher in.

incapable *adj.* disqualified, drunk, feeble, helpless, impotent, inadequate, incompetent, ineffective, ineffectual, inept, insufficient, powerless, tipsy, unable, unfit, unfitted, unqualified, weak.
antonyms capable, sober.

incarcerate *v.* cage, commit, confine, coop up, detain, encage, gaol, immure, impound, imprison, intern, jail, lock up, put away, restrain, restrict, send down, wall in.
antonym free.

incense[1] *n.* adulation, aroma, balm, bouquet, fragrance, homage, joss-stick, perfume, scent, worship.

incense[2] *v.* anger, enrage, exasperate, excite, inflame, infuriate, irritate, madden, make one see red, make one's blood boil, make one's hackles rise, provoke, raise one's hackles, rile.
antonym calm.

incentive *n.* bait, carrot, cause, consideration, encouragement, enticement, impetus, impulse, inducement, lure, motivation, motive, reason, reward, spur, stimulant, stimulus.
antonym disincentive.

inception *n.* beginning, birth, commencement, dawn, inauguration, initiation, installation, kick-off, origin, outset, rise, start.
antonym end.

incessant *adj.* ceaseless, constant, continual, continuous, endless, eternal, everlasting, interminable, never-ending, non-stop, perpetual, persistent, relentless, unbroken, unceasing, unending, unrelenting, unremitting, weariless.
antonym intermittent.

incident *n.* adventure, affair(e), brush, circumstance, clash, commotion, confrontation, contretemps, disturbance, episode, event, fight, happening, mishap, occasion, occurrence, scene, skirmish.

incidental *adj.* accidental, accompanying, ancillary, attendant, casual, chance, concomitant, contingent, contributory, fortuitous, incident, inconsequential, inessential, irrelevant, minor, non-essential, occasional, odd, random, related, secondary, subordinate, subsidiary.
antonym essential.

incidentally *adv.* accidentally, by chance, by the by(e), by the way, casually, digressively, en passant, fortuitously, in passing, parenthetically.

incinerate *v.* burn, char, cremate, reduce to ashes.

incisive *adj.* acid, acute, astucious, astute, biting, caustic, cutting, keen, mordant, penetrating, perceptive, perspicacious, piercing, sarcastic, sardonic, satirical, severe, sharp, tart, trenchant.
antonym woolly.

incite *v.* abet, animate, drive, egg on, encourage, excite, foment, goad, impel, inflame, instigate, prompt, provoke, put up to, rouse, set on, solicit, spur, stimulate, stir up, urge, whip up.
antonym restrain.

incitement *n.* abetment, agitation, encouragement, goad, hortation, impetus, impulse, inducement, instigation, motivation, motive, prompting, provocation, spur, stimulus.
antonyms check, discouragement.

inclination[1] *n.* affection, aptitude, bent, bias, clinamen, desire, disposition, fancy, fondness, ingenium, leaning, liking, month's mind, partiality, penchant, predilection, predisposition, prejudice, proclivity, proneness, propensity, stomach, taste, tendency, turn, turn of mind, velleity, wish.
antonym disinclination.

inclination[2] *n.* angle, bend, bending, bow, bowing, clinamen, deviation, gradient, incline, leaning, nod, pitch, slant, slope, tilt.

incline[1] *v.* affect, bias, dispose, influence, nod, persuade, predispose, prejudice, stoop, sway.

incline[2] *v.* bend, bevel, bow, cant, deviate, diverge, lean, slant, slope, tend, tilt, tip, veer.
n. acclivity, ascent, brae, declivity, descent, dip, grade, gradient, hill, ramp, rise, slope.

inclose *see* **enclose**.

include *v.* add, allow for, comprehend, comprise, connote, contain, cover, embody, embrace, enclose, encompass, incorporate, involve, number among, rope in, subsume, take in, take into account.
antonyms exclude, ignore.

incoherent *adj.* confused, disconnected, disjointed, dislocated, disordered, inarticulate, inconsequent, inconsistent, jumbled, loose, muddled, rambling, stammering, stuttering, unconnected, unco-ordinated, unintelligible, unjointed, wandering, wild.
antonym coherent.

income *n.* earnings, gains, interest, means, pay, proceeds, profits, receipts, returns, revenue, salary, takings, wages, yield.
antonym expenses.

incomparable *adj.* brilliant, inimitable, matchless, paramount, peerless, superb, superlative, supreme, transcendent, unequaled, unmatched, unparalleled, unrivaled.
antonyms poor, run-of-the-mill.

incompetence *n.* bungling, inability, inadequacy, incapability, incapacity, incompetency, ineffectiveness, ineffectuality, ineffectualness, inefficiency, ineptitude, ineptness, insufficiency, stupidity, unfitness, uselessness.
antonym competence.

incomprehensible *adj.* above one's head, all Greek, arcane, baffling, beyond one's comprehension, beyond one's grasp, double-Dutch, enigmatic, impenetrable, inapprehensible, inconceivable, inscrutable, mysterious, obscure, opaque, perplexing, puzzling, unfathomable, unimaginable, unintelligible, unthinkable.
antonym comprehensible.

inconceivable *adj.* implausible, incogitable, incredible, mind-boggling, out of the question, staggering, unbelievable, unheard-of, unimaginable, unknowable, unthinkable.
antonym conceivable.

incongruous *adj.* absurd, conflicting, contradictory, contrary, disconsonant, discordant, dissociable, extraneous, improper, inappropriate, inapt, incoherent, incompatible, inconcinnous, inconsistent, out of keeping, out of place, unbecoming, unsuitable, unsuited.
antonyms consistent, harmonious.

inconsiderate *adj.* careless, imprudent, indelicate, insensitive, intolerant, rash, rude, self-centered, selfish, tactless, thoughtless, unconcerned, ungracious, unkind, unthinking.
antonym considerate.

inconsistency *n.* changeableness, contrariety, disagreement, discrepancy, disparity, divergence, fickleness, incompatibility, incongruity, inconsonance, inconstancy, instability, paradox, unpredictability, unreliability, unsteadiness, variance.
antonym consistency.

inconsistent *adj.* at odds, at variance, capricious, changeable, conflicting, contradictory, contrary, discordant, discrepant, erratic, fickle, incoherent, incompatible, incongruous, inconstant, irreconcilable, irregular, unpredictable, unstable, unsteady, variable, varying.
antonym constant.

inconspicuous *adj.* camouflaged, hidden, insignificant, lowkey, modest, muted, ordinary, plain, quiet, retiring, unassuming, unnoticeable, unobtrusive, unostentatious.
antonym conspicuous.

inconstant *adj.* capricious, changeable, changeful, erratic, fickle, fluctuating, inconsistent, irresolute, mercurial, moonish, mutable, uncertain, undependable, unreliable, unsettled, unstable, unsteady, vacillating, variable, varying, volatile, wavering, wayward.
antonym constant.

inconvenient *adj.* annoying, awkward, bothersome, cumbersome, difficult, disadvantageous, disturbing, embarrassing, inopportune, tiresome, troublesome, unhandy, unmanageable, unseasonable, unsocial, unsuitable, untimely, untoward, unwieldy, vexatious.
antonym convenient.

incorrect *adj.* erroneous, false, faulty, flawed, illegitimate, imprecise, improper, inaccurate, inappropriate, inexact, mistaken, out, specious, ungrammatical, unidiomatic, unsuitable, untrue, wrong.
antonym correct.

incorruptible *adj.* everlasting, honest, honorable, imperishable, incorrupt, just, straight, trustworthy, unbribable, undecaying, upright.
antonym corruptible.

increase *v.* add to, advance, aggrandize, amplify, augment, boost, build up, develop, dilate, eke, eke out, enhance, enlarge, escalate, expand, extend, greaten, grow, heighten, inflate, intensify, magnify, mount, multiply, proliferate, prolong, pullulate, raise, snowball, soar, spread, step up, strengthen, swell, wax.
antonym decrease.
n. accrescence, addition, augment, augmentation, auxesis, boost, development, enlargement, escalation, expansion, extension, gain, growth, increment, intensification, proliferation, rise, step-up, surge, upsurge, upsurgence, upturn.
antonym decrease.

incredible *adj.* absurd, amazing, astonishing, astounding, extraordinary, fabulous, far-fetched, great, implausible, impossible, improbable, inconceivable, inspired, marvelous, preposterous, prodigious, superb, superhuman, unbelievable, unimaginable, unthinkable, wonderful.
antonyms believable, run-of-the-mill.

incriminate *v.* accuse, arraign, blame, charge, criminate, impeach, implicate, inculpate, indict, involve, point the finger at, recriminate, stigmatize.
antonym exonerate.

incurious *adj.* apathetic, careless, inattentive, indifferent, unconcerned, uncurious, unenquiring, uninquiring, uninquisitive, uninterested, unreflective.
antonym curious.

indebted *adj.* beholden, grateful, in debt, obligated, obliged, thankful.

indecency *n.* bawdiness, coarseness, crudity, foulness, grossness, immodesty, impropriety, impurity, indecorum, indelicacy, lewdness, licentiousness, obscenity, outrageousness, pornography, Rabelaisianism, smut, smuttiness, unseemliness, vileness, vulgarity.
antonyms decency, modesty.

indecent *adj.* blue, coarse, crude, dirty, filthy, foul, gross, immodest, improper, impure, indecorous, indelicate, lewd, licentious, near the knuckle, offensive, outrageous, pornographic, Rabelaisian, salacious, scatological, smutty, tasteless, unbecoming, uncomely, unseemly, vile, vulgar.
antonyms decent, modest.

indecisive *adj.* doubtful, faltering, hesitating, hung, in two minds, inconclusive, indefinite, indeterminate, irresolute, pussyfooting, swithering, tentative, uncertain, unclear, undecided, undetermined, unsure, vacillating, wavering.
antonym decisive.

indeed *adv.* actually, certainly, doubtlessly, forsooth, positively, really, strictly, to be sure, truly, undeniably, undoubtedly, verily, veritably.

indefinite *adj.* ambiguous, confused, doubtful, equivocal, evasive, general, ill-defined, imprecise, indeterminate, indistinct, inexact, loose, obscure, uncertain, unclear, undecided, undefined, undetermined, unfixed, unfocus(s)ed, unformed, unformulated, unknown, unlimited, unresolved, unsettled, vague.
antonyms clear, limited.

indelicate *adj.* blue, coarse, crude, embarrassing, gross, immodest, improper, indecent, indecorous, low, obscene, off-color, offensive, risqué, rude, suggestive, tasteless, unbecoming, unmaidenly, unseemly, untoward, vulgar, warm.
antonym delicate.

indemnity *n.* amnesty, compensation, excusal, exemption, guarantee, immunity, impunity, insurance, privilege, protection, redress, reimbursement, remuneration, reparation, requital, restitution, satisfaction, security.

independent *adj.* absolute, autarchical, autocephalous, autogenous, autonomous, bold, crossbench, decontrolled, free, individualistic, liberated, non-aligned, one's own man, self-contained, self-determining, self-governing, self-reliant, self-sufficient, self-supporting, separate, separated, sovereign, unaided, unbiased, unconnected, unconstrained, uncontrolled, unconventional, unrelated, upon one's legs.
antonyms conventional, dependent, timid.

indestructible *adj.* abiding, durable, enduring, eternal, everlasting, immortal, imperishable, incorruptible, indissoluble, infrangible, lasting, permanent, unbreakable, unfading.
antonyms breakable, mortal.

indicate *v.* add up to, bespeak, betoken, denote, designate, display, evince, express, imply, manifest, mark, point out, point to, read, record, register, reveal, show, signify, specify, suggest, telegraph, tip.

indication *n.* clue, endeixis, evidence, explanation, forewarning, hint, index, inkling, intimation, manifestation, mark, note, omen, portent, prognostic, sign, signal, signpost, suggestion, symptom, warning.

indict *v.* accuse, arraign, charge, criminate, impeach, incriminate, prosecute, recriminate, summon, summons, tax.
antonym exonerate.

indictment *n.* accusation, allegation, charge, crimination, impeachment, incrimination, prosecution, recrimination, summons.
antonym exoneration.

indifference *n.* aloofness, apathy, callousness, coldness, coolness, detachment, disinterestedness, dispassion, disregard, equity, heedlessness, impartiality, inattention, insignificance, irrelevance, latitudinarianism, negligence, neutrality, objectivity, pococurant(e)ism, stoicalness, unconcern, unimportance.
antonyms bias, interest.

indifferent *adj.* aloof, apathetic, average, callous, careless, cold, cool, detached, disinterested, dispassionate, distant, equitable, fair, heedless, immaterial, impartial, impervious, inattentive, incurious, insignificant, jack easy, mediocre, middling, moderate, neutral, non-aligned, objective, ordinary, passable, perfunctory, pococurante, regardless, so-so, unbiased, uncaring, unconcerned, undistinguished, unenquiring, unenthusiastic, unexcited, unimportant, unimpressed, uninspired, uninterested, uninvolved, unmoved, unprejudiced, unresponsive, unsympathetic.
antonyms biased, interested.

indigence *n.* deprivation, destitution, distress, necessity, need, penury, poverty, privation, want.
antonym affluence.

indigenous *adj.* aboriginal, autochthonous, home-grown, indigene, local, native, original.
antonym foreign.

indigent *adj.* destitute, impecunious, impoverished, in forma pauperis, in want, necessitous, needy, penniless, penurious, poor, poverty-stricken, straitened.
antonym affluent.

indignant *adj.* angry, annoyed, disgruntled, exasperated, fuming, furibund, furious, heated, huffy, in a paddy, in a wax, incensed, irate, livid, mad, marked, miffed, peeved, provoked, resentful, riled, scornful, sore, waxy, wrathful, wroth.
antonym pleased.

indignation *n.* anger, exasperation, fury, ire, pique, rage, resentment, scorn, umbrage, wax, wrath.
antonym pleasure.

indignity *n.* abuse, affront, contempt, contumely, disgrace, dishonor, disrespect, humiliation, incivility, injury, insult, obloquy, opprobrium, outrage, reproach, slight, snub.
antonym honor.

indirect *adj.* ancillary, backhanded, circuitous, circumlocutory, collateral, contingent, crooked, devious, incidental, meandering, mediate, oblique, periphrastic, rambling, roundabout, secondary, slanted, subsidiary, tortuous, unintended, wandering, winding, zigzag.
antonym direct.

indiscretion *n.* boob, brick, error, faux pas, folly, foolishness, gaffe, imprudence, mistake, rashness, recklessness, slip, slip of the tongue, tactlessness, temerarity.
antonym discretion.

indispensable *adj.* basic, crucial, essential, imperative, key, necessary, needed, needful, required, requisite, vital.
antonym unnecessary.

indistinct *adj.* ambiguous, bleary, blurred, confused, dim, distant, doubtful, faint, fuzzy, hazy, ill-defined, indefinite, indeterminate, indiscernible, indistinguishable, misty, muffled, mumbled, obscure, shadowy, slurred, unclear, undefined, unintelligible, vague.
antonym distinct.

indistinguishable *adj.* alike, identical, interchangeable, same, tantamount, twin.
antonyms distinguishable, unalike.

individual *n.* being, bloke, body, chap, character, creature, fellow, individuum, mortal, party, person, personage, punter, soul.
adj. characteristic, discrete, distinct, distinctive, exclusive, identical, idiosyncratic, own, particular, peculiar, personal, personalized, proper, respective, separate, several, single, singular, special, specific, unique.

individuality *n.* character, discreteness, distinction, distinctiveness, haecceity, originality, peculiarity, personality, separateness, singularity, unicity, uniqueness.
antonym sameness.

indolent *adj.* fainéant, idle, inactive, inert, lackadaisical, languid, lazy, lethargic, listless, lumpish, slack, slothful, slow, sluggard, sluggish, torpid.
antonyms active, enthusiastic, industrious.

indomitable *adj.* bold, intrepid, invincible, resolute, staunch, steadfast, unbeatable, unconquerable, undaunted, unflinching, untameable, unyielding.
antonyms compliant, timid.

induce *v.* actuate, bring about, cause, convince, draw, effect, encourage, engender, generate, get, give rise to, impel, incite, influence, instigate, lead to, move, occasion, persuade, press, prevail upon, produce, prompt, talk into.

inducement *n.* attraction, bait, carrot, cause, come-on, consideration, encouragement, impulse, incentive, incitement, influence, lure, motive, reason, reward, spur, stimulus.
antonym disincentive.

induct *v.* consecrate, enthrone, inaugurate, initiate, install, introduce, invest, ordain, swear in.

indulge *v.* baby, cocker, coddle, cosset, favor, foster, give in to, go along with, gratify, humor, mollycoddle, pamper, pander to, pet, regale, satiate, satisfy, spoil, treat (oneself), yield to.

indulge in give free rein to, give oneself up to, give way to, luxuriate in, revel in, wallow in.

indulgent *adj.* complaisant, compliant, easy-going, favorable, fond, forbearing, gentle, gratifying, intemperate, kind, kindly, lenient, liberal, mild, permissive, prodigal, self-indulgent, tender, tolerant, understanding.
antonyms moderate, strict.

industrious *adj.* active, assiduous, busy, conscientious, deedy, diligent, energetic, hard-working, laborious, persevering, persistent, productive, purposeful, sedulous, steady, tireless, zealous.
antonym indolent.

industriously *adv.* assiduously, conscientiously, diligently, doggedly, hard, perseveringly, sedulously, steadily, with one's nose to the grindstone.
antonym indolently.

inebriated *adj.* befuddled, blind drunk, blotto, drunk, glorious, half seas over, half-cut, half-drunk, in one's cups, incapable, inebriate, intoxicated, legless, merry, paralytic, pie-eyed, plastered, sloshed, smashed, sozzled, stoned, stotious, three sheets in the wind, tight, tipsy, tired and emotional, under the influence.
antonym sober.

ineffective, ineffectual *adj.* abortive, barren, bootless, emasculate, feeble, fruitless, futile, idle, impotent, inadequate, incompetent, ineffective, ineffectual, inefficacious, inefficient, inept, lame, powerless, unavailing, unproductive, useless, vain, void, weak, worthless.
antonyms effective, effectual.

inefficient *adj.* incompetent, inept, inexpert, money-wasting, negligent, slipshod, sloppy, time-wasting, unworkmanlike, wasteful.
antonym efficient.

ineligible *adj.* disqualified, improper, inappropriate, incompetent, objectionable, unacceptable, undesirable, unequipped, unfit, unfitted, unqualified, unsuitable, unworthy.
antonym eligible.

inept *adj.* absurd, awkward, bungling, cack-handed, clumsy, fatuous, futile, gauche, improper, inappropriate, inapt, incompetent, inexpert, infelicitous, irrelevant, maladroit, malapropos, meaningless, ridiculous, unfit, unhandy, unskilful, unworkmanlike.
antonyms adroit, apt.

inequity *n.* abuse, bias, discrimination, injustice, maltreatment, mistreatment, one-sidedness, partiality, prejudice, unfairness, unjustness.
antonym equity.

inert *adj.* apathetic, dead, dormant, dull, idle, immobile, inactive, inanimate, indolent, insensible, lazy, leaden, lifeless, motionless, nerveless, numb, passive, quiescent, senseless, slack, sleepy, slothful, sluggish, somnolent, static, still, torpid, unmoving, unreacting, unresponsive.
antonyms alive, animated.

inertia *n.* accedia, accidie, apathy, deadness, drowsiness, dullness, idleness, immobility, inactivity, indolence,

insensibility, languor, lassitude, laziness, lethargy, listlessness, nervelessness, numbness, passivity, sleepiness, sloth, sluggishness, somnolence, stillness, stupor, torpor, unresponsiveness.
antonyms activity, liveliness.

inevitable *adj.* assured, automatic, certain, compulsory, decreed, destined, fated, fixed, ineluctable, inescapable, inexorable, irrevocable, mandatory, necessary, obligatory, ordained, settled, sure, unalterable, unavertable, unavoidable, unpreventable, unshunnable.
antonyms alterable, avoidable, uncertain.

inexorable *adj.* adamant, cruel, hard, harsh, immovable, implacable, ineluctable, inescapable, inflexible, intransigent, irreconcilable, irresistible, irrevocable, merciless, obdurate, pitiless, relentless, remorseless, severe, unalterable, unappeasable, unavertable, unbending, uncompromising, unrelenting, unyielding.
antonyms flexible, lenient, yielding.

inexperienced *adj.* amateur, callow, fresh, green, immature, inexpert, innocent, nescient, new, raw, unaccustomed, unacquainted, unbearded, unfamiliar, unpractical, unpracticed, unschooled, unseasoned, unskilled, unsophisticated, untrained, untraveled, untried, unused, unversed, verdant.
antonym experienced.

inexplicable *adj.* baffling, enigmatic, impenetrable, incomprehensible, incredible, inscrutable, insoluble, intractable, miraculous, mysterious, mystifying, puzzling, strange, unaccountable, unexplainable, unfathomable, unintelligible, unsolvable.
antonym explicable.

infallibility *n.* accuracy, dependability, faultlessness, impeccability, inerrancy, inevitability, irrefutability, irreproachability, omniscience, perfection, reliability, safety, supremacy, sureness, trustworthiness, unerringness.
antonym fallibility.

infamous *adj.* abhorrent, abominable, atrocious, base, dastardly, despicable, detestable, discreditable, disgraceful, dishonorable, disreputable, egregious, execrable, facinorous, flagitious, hateful, heinous, ignoble, ignominious, illfamed, iniquitous, knavish, loathsome, monstrous, nefarious, notorious, odious, opprobrious, outrageous, scandalous, scurvy, shameful, shocking, vile, villainous, wicked.
antonym glorious.

infantile *adj.* adolescent, babyish, childish, immature, juvenile, puerile, tender, undeveloped, young, youthful.
antonyms adult, mature.

infatuation *n.* besottedness, crush, dotage, engouement, fascination, fixation, folly, fondness, intoxication, madness, mania, obsession, passion, possession.
antonyms disenchantment, indifference.

infect *v.* affect, blight, canker, contaminate, corrupt, defile, enthuse, influence, inject, inspire, pervert, poison, pollute, taint, touch, vitiate.

infection *n.* contagion, contamination, corruption, defilement, disease, epidemic, illness, inflammation, influence, miasma, pestilence, poison, pollution, sepsis, septicity, taint, virus.

infectious *adj.* catching, communicable, contagious, contaminating, corrupting, deadly, defiling, epidemic, infective, miasmic, miasmous, pestilential, poisoning, poisonous, polluting, spreading, transmissible, transmittable, venemous, virulent, vitiating.

infer *v.* assume, conclude, conjecture, construe, deduce, derive, extract, extrapolate, gather, presume, surmise, understand.

inference *n.* assumption, conclusion, conjecture, consequence, construction, corollary, deduction, extrapolation, illation, interpretation, presumption, reading, surmise.

inferior *adj.* bad, crummy, dog, grotty, humble, imperfect, indifferent, junior, lesser, low, lower, low-grade, mean, mediocre, menial, minor, one-horse, paravail, poor, poorer, provant, schlock, secondary, second-class, secondrate, shoddy, slipshod, slovenly, subordinate, subsidiary, substandard, under, underneath, undistinguished, unsatisfactory, unworthy, worse.
antonym superior.
n. junior, menial, minion, subordinate, underling, understrapper, vassal.
antonym superior.

inferiority *n.* badness, baseness, deficiency, humbleness, imperfection, inadequacy, insignificance, lowliness, meanness, mediocrity, shoddiness, slovenliness, subordination, subservience, unimportance, unworthiness, worthlessness.
antonym superiority.

infernal *adj.* accursed, Acherontic, chthonian, chthonic, damnable, damned, demonic, devilish, diabolical, fiendish, Hadean, hellish, malevolent, malicious, Mephistophelian, Plutonian, satanic, Stygian, Tartarean, underworld.
antonym heavenly.

infiltrator *n.* entr(y)ist, insinuator, intruder, penetrator, seditionary, spy, subversive, subverter.

infinite *adj.* absolute, bottomless, boundless, countless, enormous, eternal, everlasting, fathomless, illimitable, immeasurable, immense, incomputable, inestimable, inexhaustible, interminable, limitless, measureless, never-ending, numberless, perpetual, stupendous, total, unbounded, uncountable, uncounted, unfathomable, untold, vast, wide.
antonym finite.

infinitesimal *adj.* atomic, exiguous, imperceptible, inappreciable, inconsiderable, insignificant, microscopic, minuscule, minute, negligible, paltry, teeny, tiny, unnoticeable, wee.
antonyms significant, substantial.

infirm *adj.* ailing, crippled, debilitated, decrepit, dicky, doddering, doddery, enfeebled, failing, faltering, feeble,

fickle, frail, hesitant, indecisive, insecure, irresolute, lame, poorly, sickly, unreliable, wavering, weak, wobbly.
antonyms healthy, strong.

infirmity *n.* ailment, complaint, debility, decrepitude, defect, deficiency, dickiness, disease, disorder, failing, fault, feebleness, foible, frailty, ill health, illness, imperfection, instability, malady, sickliness, sickness, vulnerability, weakness.
antonyms health, strength.

inflame *v.* aggravate, agitate, anger, arouse, embitter, enkindle, enrage, exacerbate, exasperate, excite, fan, fire, foment, fuel, galvanize, heat, ignite, impassion, incense, increase, infatuate, infuriate, intensify, intoxicate, kindle, madden, provoke, ravish, rile, rouse, stimulate, worsen.
antonyms cool, quench.

inflammation *n.* abscess, burning, empyema, erythema, heat, infection, painfulness, rash, redness, sepsis, septicity, sore, soreness, tenderness.

inflammatory *adj.* anarchic, demagogic, explosive, fiery, incendiary, incitative, inflaming, instigative, insurgent, intemperate, provocative, rabble-rousing, rabid, riotous, seditious.
antonyms calming, pacific.

inflate *v.* aerate, aggrandize, amplify, balloon, bloat, blow out, blow up, bombast, boost, dilate, distend, enlarge, escalate, exaggerate, expand, increase, puff out, puff up, pump up, swell, tumefy.
antonym deflate.

inflexible *adj.* adamant, dyed-in-the-wool, entrenched, fast, firm, fixed, hard, hardened, immovable, immutable, implacable, inelastic, inexorable, intractable, intransigent, iron, non-flexible, obdurate, obstinate, relentless, resolute, rigid, rigorous, set, steadfast, steely, stiff, strict, stringent, stubborn, taut, unaccommodating, unadaptable, unbending, unchangeable, uncompromising, unpliable, unpliant, unsupple, unyielding.
antonym flexible.

inflict *v.* administer, afflict, apply, burden, deal, deliver, enforce, exact, force, impose, lay, levy, mete, perpetrate, visit, wreak.

influence *n.* agency, ascendancy, authority, bias, charisma, clout, connections, control, credit, direction, domination, drag, effect, éminence grise, good offices, guidance, hold, importance, leverage, magnetism, mastery, power, pressure, prestige, pull, reach, rule, scope, spell, standing, strength, string-pulling, sway, teaching, training, weight, wire-pulling.
v. affect, alter, arouse, bias, change, control, direct, dispose, dominate, edge, guide, head, impel, impress, incite, incline, induce, instigate, maneuver, manipulate, modify, motivate, move, persuade, point, predispose, prompt, pull, pull wires, rouse, strings, sway, teach, train, weigh with.

influential *adj.* ascendant, authoritative, charismatic, cogent, compelling, controlling, dominant, dominating, effective, efficacious, forcible, guiding, important, instrumental, leading, momentous, moving, persuasive, potent, powerful, significant, strong, telling, weighty, well-placed.
antonym ineffectual.

inform[1] *v.* acquaint, advise, apprize, brief, clue up, communicate, enlighten, fill in, illuminate, impart, instruct, intimate, leak, notify, teach, tell, tip off, wise up.

inform[2] *v.* animate, characterize, endue, fill, illuminate, imbue, inspire, invest, irradiate, light up, permeate, suffuse, typify.

informal *adj.* approachable, casual, colloquial, congenial, cosy, easy, familiar, free, homely, irregular, natural, relaxed, relaxing, simple, unbuttoned, unceremonious, unconstrained, unofficial, unorthodox, unpretentious, unsolemn.
antonym formal.

informality *n.* approachability, casualness, congeniality, cosiness, ease, familiarity, freedom, homeliness, irregularity, naturalness, relaxation, simplicity, unceremoniousness, unpretentiousness.
antonym formality.

information *n.* advices, blurb, briefing, bulletin, bumf, clues, communiqué, data, databank, database, dope, dossier, enlightenment, facts, gen, illumination, info, input, instruction, intelligence, knowledge, low-down, message, news, notice, report, tidings, word.

informative *adj.* chatty, communicative, constructive, edifying, educational, enlightening, forthcoming, gossipy, illuminating, informatory, instructive, newsy, revealing, revelatory, useful, valuable.
antonym uninformative.

informer *n.* betrayer, canary, denouncer, denunciator, fink, fiz(z)gig, grass, Judas, nark, singer, sneak, snitch(er), snout, squeak, squealer, stool pigeon, stoolie, supergrass.

infrequent *adj.* exceptional, intermittent, occasional, rare, scanty, sparse, spasmodic, sporadic, uncommon, unusual.
antonym frequent.

infringement *n.* breach, contravention, defiance, encroachment, evasion, infraction, intrusion, invasion, non-compliance, non-observance, transgression, trespass, violation.

ingenious *adj.* adroit, bright, brilliant, clever, crafty, creative, cunning, daedal, Daedalian, daedalic, dedalian, deft, dexterous, fertile, Gordian, imaginative, innovative, intricate, inventive, masterly, original, pretty, ready, resourceful, shrewd, skilful, sly, subtle.
antonyms clumsy, unimaginative.

ingenuity *n.* adroitness, cleverness, cunning, deftness, faculty, flair, genius, gift, ingeniousness, innovativeness, invention, inventiveness, knack, originality, resourcefulness, sharpness, shrewdness, skill, slyness, turn.
antonyms clumsiness, dullness.

ingenuous *adj.* artless, candid, childlike, frank, guileless, honest, innocent, naïf, naïve, open, plain, simple, sincere, trustful, trusting, unreserved, unsophisticated, unstudied.
antonyms artful, sly.

ingratiating *adj.* bland, bootlicking, crawling, fawning, flattering, obsequious, servile, smooth-tongued, suave, sycophantic, time-serving, toadying, unctuous, whilly, whillywha(w).

ingratitude *n.* thanklessness, unappreciativeness, ungraciousness, ungratefulness.
antonym gratitude.

ingredient *n.* component, constituent, element, factor, part.

inhabit *v.* abide, bide, dwell, habit, live, lodge, make one's home, occupy, people, populate, possess, reside, settle, settle in, stay, take up one's abode, tenant.

inhabitant *n.* aborigine, autochthon, burgher, citizen, denizen, dweller, habitant, indigene, indweller, inmate, lodger, native, occupant, occupier, resident, residentiary, resider, settler, tenant.

inherent *adj.* basic, characteristic, congenital, connate, essential, fundamental, hereditary, immanent, inborn, inbred, inbuilt, ingrained, inherited, innate, instinctive, intrinsic, inwrought, native, natural.

inheritance *n.* accession, bequest, birthright, descent, heredity, heritage, heritament, legacy, patrimony, succession.

inhibit *v.* arrest, bar, bridle, check, constrain, cramp, curb, debar, discourage, forbid, frustrate, hinder, hold, impede, interfere with, obstruct, prevent, prohibit, repress, restrain, stanch, stem, stop, suppress, thwart.

inhuman *adj.* animal, barbaric, barbarous, bestial, brutal, brutish, callous, cold-blooded, cruel, diabolical, fiendish, heartless, inhumane, insensate, merciless, pitiless, remorseless, ruthless, savage, sublime, unfeeling, vicious.
antonym human.

inimical *adj.* adverse, antagonistic, antipathetic, contrary, destructive, disaffected, harmful, hostile, hurtful, ill-disposed, inhospitable, injurious, intolerant, noxious, opposed, oppugnant, pernicious, repugnant, unfavorable, unfriendly, unwelcoming.
antonyms favorable, friendly, sympathetic.

inimitable *adj.* consummate, distinctive, exceptional, incomparable, matchless, nonpareil, peerless, sublime, superlative, supreme, unequaled, unexampled, unique, unmatched, unparalleled, unrivaled, unsurpassable, unsurpassed.

iniquitous *adj.* abominable, accursed, atrocious, awful, base, criminal, dreadful, evil, facinorous, flagitious, heinous, immoral, infamous, nefarious, nefast, reprehensible, reprobate, sinful, unjust, unrighteous, vicious, wicked.
antonym virtuous.

iniquity *n.* abomination, baseness, crime, enormity, evil, evil-doing, heinousness, impiety, infamy, injustice, misdeed, offence, sin, sinfulness, ungodliness, unrighteousness, vice, viciousness, wickedness, wrong, wrong-doing.
antonym virtue.

initial *adj.* beginning, commencing, early, embryonic, first, formative, inaugural, inauguratory, inceptive, inchoate, incipient, infant, introductory, opening, original, primary.
antonym final.

initiate *v.* activate, actuate, begin, cause, coach, commence, inaugurate, indoctrinate, induce, induct, instate, institute, instruct, introduce, invest, launch, open, originate, prompt, start, stimulate, teach, train.
n. authority, beginner, catechumen, cognoscente, connoisseur, convert, entrant, epopt, expert, insider, learner, member, newcomer, novice, novitiate, probationer, proselyte, recruit, sage, savant, tenderfoot, tiro.

initiative *n.* advantage, ambition, drive, dynamism, energy, enterprise, forcefulness, get-up-and-go, goeyness, innovativeness, inventiveness, lead, move, originality, prompting, push, recommendation, resource, resourcefulness, suggestion.

injure *v.* abuse, aggrieve, blemish, blight, break, cripple, damage, deface, disable, disfigure, disserve, harm, hurt, ill-treat, impair, maim, maltreat, mar, ruin, scathe, spoil, tarnish, undermine, vandalize, vitiate, weaken, wound, wrong.

injurious *adj.* adverse, bad, baneful, calumnious, corrupting, damaging, deleterious, destructive, detrimental, disadvantageous, harmful, hurtful, iniquitous, insulting, libelous, mischievous, noxious, pernicious, prejudicial, ruinous, slanderous, unconducive, unhealthy, unjust, wrongful.
antonyms beneficial, favorable.

injury *n.* abuse, annoyance, damage, damnification, detriment, disservice, evil, grievance, harm, hurt, ill, impairment, injustice, insult, lesion, loss, mischief, noyance, prejudice, ruin, scathe, trauma, vexation, wound, wrong.

injustice *n.* bias, discrimination, disparity, favoritism, imposition, inequality, inequitableness, inequity, iniquity, onesidedness, oppression, partiality, partisanship, prejudice, unevenness, unfairness, unjustness, unlawfulness, unreason, wrong.
antonym justice.

inn *n.* albergo, alehouse, auberge, caravanserai, hostelry, hotel, howff, khan, local, public, public house, roadhouse, saloon, serai, tavern.

innate *adj.* basic, congenital, connate, constitutional, essential, fundamental, immanent, inborn, inbred, ingenerate, ingrained, inherent, inherited, instinctive, intrinsic, intuitive, native, natural.

innocent *adj.* Arcadian, artless, benign, bereft of, blameless, canny, chaste, childlike, clear, credulous, dewy-eyed, faultless, frank, free of, fresh, green, guileless, guiltless, gullible, harmless, honest, immaculate,

impeccable, incorrupt, ingenuous, innocuous, inoffensive, intact, irreproachable, naïve, natural, nescient, open, pristine, pure, righteous, simple, sinless, spotless, stainless, trustful, trusting, unblemished, uncontaminated, unimpeachable, unobjectionable, unoffending, unsullied, unsuspicious, untainted, untouched, unworldly, verdant, virginal, well-intentioned, well-meaning, well-meant.
antonyms experienced, guilty, knowing.
n. babe, babe in arms, beginner, child, greenhorn, infant, ingénu, ingénue, neophyte, tenderfoot.
antonyms connoisseur, expert.

innocuous *adj.* bland, harmless, hypo-allergenic, innocent, innoxious, inoffensive, non-irritant, safe, unimpeachable, unobjectionable.
antonym harmful.

innovative *adj.* adventurous, bold, daring, enterprising, fresh, go-ahead, goey, imaginative, inventive, modernizing, new, on the move, original, progressive, reforming, resourceful, revolutionary.
antonyms conservative, unimaginative.

innuendo *n.* aspersion, hint, implication, imputation, insinuation, intimation, overtone, slant, slur, suggestion, whisper.

inoperative *adj.* broken, broken-down, defective, hors de combat, idle, ineffective, ineffectual, inefficacious, invalid, non-active, non-functioning, nugatory, out of action, out of commission, out of order, out of service, unserviceable, unused, unworkable, useless.
antonym operative.

inopportune *adj.* clumsy, ill-chosen, ill-timed, inappropriate, inauspicious, inconvenient, infelicitous, malapropos, mistimed, tactless, unfortunate, unpropitious, unseasonable, unsuitable, untimely, wrong-timed.
antonym opportune.

inquire *v.* ask, catechize, delve, enquire, examine, explore, inspect, interrogate, investigate, look into, probe, query, quest, question, reconnoiter, scout, scrutinize, search, speir.

inquiring *adj.* analytical, curious, doubtful, eager, inquisitive, interested, interrogatory, investigative, investigatory, nosy, outward-looking, probing, prying, questing, questioning, searching, skeptical, wondering, zetetic.
antonym incurious.

inquiry *n.* enquiry, examination, exploration, inquest, interrogation, investigation, perquisition, post-mortem, probe, query, question, research, scrutiny, search, study, survey, witch-hunt, zetetic.

inquisitive *adj.* curious, eager, inquiring, intrusive, investigative, meddlesome, nosy, peeping, peering, probing, prying, questing, questioning, snooping, snoopy.
antonym incurious.

insane *adj.* barmy, batty, bizarre, bonkers, brainsick, cracked, crackers, crazed, cuckoo, daft, delirious, demented, deranged, distracted, disturbed, fatuous, foolish, idiotic, impractical, irrational, irresponsible, loony, loopy, lunatic, mad, manic, mental, mentally ill, non compos mentis, nuts, nutty, preposterous, psychotic, queer, schizoid, schizophrenic, screwy, senseless, stupid, touched, unbalanced, unhinged.
antonym sane.

insanity *n.* aberration, alienation, amentia, brainsickness, brainstorm, craziness, delirium, dementia, derangement, folly, frenzy, infatuation, irresponsibility, lunacy, madness, mania, mental illness, neurosis, preposterousness, psychoneurosis, psychosis, senselessness, stupidity.
antonym sanity.

insatiable *adj.* esurient, gluttonous, greedy, immoderate, incontrollable, inordinate, insatiate, intemperate, persistent, quenchless, rapacious, ravenous, unappeasable, uncurbable, unquenchable, unsatisfiable, voracious.
antonym moderate.

inscrutable *adj.* baffling, blank, cryptic, dead-pan, deep, enigmatic, esoteric, expressionless, hidden, impassive, impenetrable, incomprehensible, inexplicable, mysterious, poker-faced, sphinx-like, undiscoverable, unexplainable, unfathomable, unintelligible, unknowable, unsearchable.
antonyms clear, comprehensible, expressive.

insecure *adj.* afraid, anxious, apprehensive, dangerous, defenseless, diffident, exposed, expugnable, flimsy, frail, hazardous, insubstantial, jerry-built, loose, nervous, perilous, precarious, pregnable, rickety, rocky, shaky, shoogly, uncertain, unconfident, uneasy, unguarded, unprotected, unsafe, unshielded, unsound, unstable, unsteady, unsure, vulnerable, weak, wobbly, worried.
antonyms confident, safe, secure.

insensible[1] *adj.* anesthetized, apathetic, blind, callous, cataleptic, cold, deaf, dull, hard-hearted, impassive, impercipient, impervious, indifferent, inert, insensate, marble, nerveless, numb, numbed, oblivious, senseless, stupid, torpid, unaffected, unaware, unconscious, unfeeling, unmindful, unmoved, unnoticing, unobservant, unresponsive, unsusceptible, untouched.
antonyms conscious, sensible.

insensible[2] *adj.* imperceivable, imperceptible, inappreciable, minuscule, minute, negligible, tiny, unnoticeable.
antonym appreciable.

insensitive *adj.* blunted, callous, crass, dead, hardened, immune, impenetrable, imperceptive, impercipient, impervious, indifferent, insusceptible, obtuse, pachydermatous, proof, resistant, tactless, thick-skinned, tough, unaffected, uncaring, unconcerned, unfeeling, unimpressionable, unmoved, unreactive, unresponsive, unsensitive, unsusceptible.
antonym sensitive.

insight *n.* acumen, acuteness, apprehension, awareness, comprehension, discernment, grasp, ingenuity, intelligence, intuition, intuitiveness, judgment, knowledge, observation, penetration, perception, percipience, perspicacity, sensitivity, shrewdness, understanding, vision, wisdom.

insignificant *adj.* dinky, flimsy, humble, immaterial, inappreciable, inconsequential, inconsiderable, insubstantial, irrelevant, meager, meaningless, Mickey Mouse, minor, negligible, nondescript, nonessential, nugatory, paltry, petty, piddling, scanty, scrub, tiny, trifling, trivial, unimportant, unsubstantial.
antonym significant.

insincere *adj.* artificial, canting, deceitful, deceptive, devious, dishonest, disingenuous, dissembling, dissimulating, double-dealing, duplicitous, evasive, faithless, false, hollow, hypocritical, lip-deep, lying, mendacious, perfidious, phony, pretended, synthetic, two-faced, unfaithful, ungenuine, untrue, untruthful.
antonym sincere.

insinuate *v.* allude, get at, hint, imply, indicate, innuendo, intimate, suggest.

insipid *adj.* anemic, banal, bland, characterless, colorless, dilute, drab, dry, dull, fade, flat, flavorless, insulse, jejune, lash, lifeless, limp, missish, missy, monotonous, pointless, prosaic, prosy, savorless, spiritless, stale, tame, tasteless, trite, unappetizing, unimaginative, uninteresting, unsavory, vapid, watery, weak, wearish, weedy, wishy-washy.
antonyms appetizing, piquant, punchy, tasty.

insist *v.* assert, asseverate, aver, claim, contend, demand, dwell on, emphasize, harp on, hold, maintain, persist, reiterate, repeat, request, require, stand firm, stress, swear, urge, vow.

insolence *n.* abuse, arrogance, assurance, audacity, backchat, boldness, cheek, cheekiness, chutzpah, contemptuousness, contumely, defiance, disrespect, effrontery, forwardness, gall, gum, hubris, impertinence, impudence, incivility, insubordination, lip, malapertness, offensiveness, pertness, presumption, presumptuousness, rudeness, sauce, sauciness.
antonyms politeness, respect.

insolent *adj.* abusive, arrogant, bold, brazen, cheeky, contemptuous, contumelious, defiant, disrespectful, forward, fresh, hubristic, impertinent, impudent, insubordinate, insulting, malapert, pert, presumptuous, rude, saucy, uncivil.
antonyms polite, respectful.

insoluble *adj.* baffling, impenetrable, indecipherable, inexplicable, inextricable, intractable, mysterious, mystifying, obscure, perplexing, unaccountable, unexplainable, unfathomable, unsolvable.
antonym explicable.

insolvent *adj.* bankrupt, broke, bust, defaulting, destitute, failed, flat broke, in queer street, on the rocks, ruined.
antonym solvent.

inspect *v.* audit, check, examine, give the once-over, investigate, look over, oversee, peruse, reconnoiter, scan, scrutinize, search, study, superintend, supervise, survey, vet, visit.

inspection *n.* audit, autopsy, check, check-up, examination, investigation, once-over, post-mortem, reconnaissance, review, scan, scrutiny, search, superintendence, supervision, surveillance, survey, vidimus, visitation.

inspiration *n.* afflation, afflatus, Aganippe, arousal, awakening, brainstorm, brain-wave, creativity, elevation, encouragement, enthusiasm, estro, exaltation, genius, Hippocrene, illumination, influence, insight, muse, Muse, revelation, spur, stimulation, stimulus, Svengali, taghairm.

inspire *v.* activate, animate, arouse, encourage, enkindle, enliven, enthuse, excite, fill, galvanize, hearten, imbue, influence, infuse, inhale, inspirit, instil, motivate, produce, quicken, spark off, spur, stimulate, stir, trigger.

inspiring *adj.* affecting, emboldening, encouraging, exciting, exhilarating, heartening, inspiriting, invigorating, moving, rousing, stimulating, stirring, uplifting.
antonyms dull, uninspiring.

instal(l) *v.* consecrate, ensconce, establish, fix, inaugurate, induct, instate, institute, introduce, invest, lay, locate, lodge, ordain, place, plant, position, put, set, set up, settle, site, situate, station.

installation *n.* base, consecration, equipment, establishment, fitting, inauguration, induction, instalment, instatement, investiture, location, machinery, ordination, placing, plant, positioning, post, siting, station, system.

instance[1] *n.* case, case in point, citation, example, illustration, occasion, occurrence, precedent, sample, situation, time.
v. adduce, cite, mention, name, point to, quote, refer to, specify.

instance[2] *n.* advice, application, behest, demand, entreaty, exhortation, importunity, impulse, incitement, initiative, insistence, instigation, pressure, prompting, request, solicitation, urging.

instant *n.* flash, jiffy, juncture, minute, mo, moment, occasion, point, second, shake, split second, tick, time, trice, twinkling, two shakes.
adj. convenience, direct, fast, immediate, instantaneous, on-the-spot, precooked, prompt, quick, rapid, ready-mixed, split-second, unhesitating, urgent.

instantaneous *adj.* direct, immediate, instant, on-the-spot, prompt, rapid, unhesitating.
antonym eventual.

instantly *adv.* at once, directly, forthwith, immediately, instantaneously, now, on the spot, pronto, quick-sticks, right away, straight away, there and then, tout de suite, without delay.
antonym eventually.

instigate *v.* actuate, cause, encourage, excite, foment, generate, impel, incite, influence, initiate, inspire, kindle, move, persuade, prompt, provoke, rouse, set on, spur, start, stimulate, stir up, urge, whip up.

instinct *n.* ability, aptitude, faculty, feel, feeling, flair, gift, gut feeling, gut reaction, id, impulse, intuition, knack, nose, predisposition, proclivity, sixth sense, talent, tendency, urge.

instinctive *adj.* automatic, gut, immediate, impulsive, inborn, inherent, innate, instinctual, intuitional, intuitive, involuntary, mechanical, native, natural, reflex, spontaneous, unlearned, unpremeditated, unthinking, visceral.
antonyms conscious, deliberate, voluntary.

institute[1] *v.* appoint, begin, commence, constitute, create, enact, establish, fix, found, inaugurate, induct, initiate, install, introduce, invest, launch, open, ordain, organize, originate, pioneer, set up, settle, start.
antonyms abolish, cancel, discontinue.

institute[2] *n.* custom, decree, doctrine, dogma, edict, firman, indiction, irade, law, maxim, precedent, precept, principle, regulation, rescript, rule, tenet, ukase.

institute[3] *n.* academy, association, college, conservatory, foundation, guild, institution, organization, poly, polytechnic, school, seminary, society.

instruct *v.* acquaint, advise, apprize, bid, brief, catechize, charge, coach, command, counsel, direct, discipline, drill, educate, enjoin, enlighten, ground, guide, inform, mandate, notify, order, school, teach, tell, train, tutor.

instruction *n.* apprenticeship, briefing, catechesis, catechizing, coaching, command, direction, directive, discipline, drilling, education, enlightenment, grounding, guidance, information, injunction, lesson(s), mandate, order, preparation, ruling, schooling, teaching, training, tuition, tutelage.

instructions *n.* advice, book of words, commands, directions, guidance, handbook, information, key, legend, orders, recommendations, rules.

instrument *n.* agency, agent, apparatus, appliance, cat'spaw, channel, contraption, contrivance, device, doodad, dupe, factor, force, gadget, implement, means, mechanism, medium, organ, pawn, puppet, tool, utensil, vehicle, way, widget.

insubordinate *adj.* contumacious, defiant, disobedient, disorderly, fractious, impertinent, impudent, insurgent, mutinous, rebellious, recalcitrant, refractory, riotous, rude, seditious, turbulent, undisciplined, ungovernable, unruly.
antonyms docile, obedient.

insubstantial *adj.* chimerical, ephemeral, false, fanciful, feeble, flimsy, frail, idle, illusory, imaginary, immaterial, incorporeal, moonshine, poor, slight, tenuous, thin, unreal, vaporous, weak, windy, yeasty.
antonyms real, strong.

insufficient *adj.* deficient, inadequate, incapable, incommensurate, lacking, scanty, scarce, short, sparse, wanting.
antonyms excessive, sufficient.

insulation *n.* cushioning, deadening, deafening, padding, protection, stuffing.

insult *v.* abuse, affront, call names, fling/throw mud at, give offence to, injure, libel, miscall, offend, outrage, revile, slag, slander, slight, snub, vilify, vilipend.
antonyms compliment, honor.
n. abuse, affront, aspersion, contumely, indignity, insolence, libel, offence, outrage, rudeness, slander, slap in the face, slight, snub.
antonyms compliment, honor.

insulting *adj.* abusive, affronting, contemptuous, degrading, disparaging, insolent, libelous, offensive, rude, scurrilous, slanderous, slighting.
antonyms complimentary, respectful.

insurance *n.* assurance, cover, coverage, guarantee, indemnification, indemnity, policy, premium, protection, provision, safeguard, security, warranty.

insure *v.* assure, cover, guarantee, indemnify, protect, underwrite, warrant.

intact *adj.* all in one piece, complete, entire, inviolate, perfect, scatheless, sound, together, unbroken, undamaged, undefiled, unharmed, unhurt, unimpaired, uninjured, unscathed, untouched, unviolated, virgin, whole.
antonyms broken, damaged, harmed.

integrated *adj.* cohesive, concordant, connected, desegregated, harmonious, interrelated, part and parcel, unified, unsegregated, unseparated.
antonym unintegrated.

integration *n.* amalgamation, assimilation, blending, combining, commingling, desegregation, fusing, harmony, incorporation, mixing, unification.
antonym separation.

integrity *n.* candor, coherence, cohesion, completeness, entireness, goodness, honesty, honor, incorruptibility, principle, probity, purity, rectitude, righteousness, soundness, unity, uprightness, virtue, wholeness.
antonyms dishonesty, incompleteness, unreliability.

intellect *n.* brain, brain power, brains, egghead, genius, highbrow, intellectual, intelligence, judgment, mind, nous, reason, sense, thinker, understanding.
antonym dunce.

intellectual *adj.* bookish, cerebral, deep-browed, discursive, highbrow, intelligent, mental, noetic, rational, scholarly, studious, thoughtful.
antonym low-brow.
n. academic, egghead, headpiece, highbrow, mastermind, thinker.
antonym low-brow.

intelligence *n.* acuity, acumen, advice, alertness, aptitude, brain power, brains, brightness, capacity, cleverness, comprehension, data, discernment, disclosure, facts, findings, gen, gray matter, information, intellect, intellectuality, knowledge, low-down, mind, news, notice, notification, nous, penetration, perception,

quickness, reason, report, rumor, tidings, tip-off, understanding, word.
antonym foolishness.

intelligent *adj.* acute, alert, apt, brainy, bright, clever, deep-browed, discerning, enlightened, instructed, knowing, penetrating, perspicacious, quick, quick-witted, rational, razor-sharp, sharp, smart, thinking, well-informed.
antonyms foolish, unintelligent.

intend *v.* aim, consign, contemplate, design, destine, determine, earmark, have a mind, mark out, mean, meditate, plan, project, propose, purpose, scheme, set apart.

intense *adj.* acute, agonizing, ardent, burning, close, concentrated, consuming, eager, earnest, energetic, fanatical, fervent, fervid, fierce, forceful, forcible, great, harsh, heightened, impassioned, intensive, keen, passionate, powerful, profound, severe, strained, strong, vehement.
antonyms apathetic, mild.

intensify *v.* add to, aggravate, boost, concentrate, deepen, emphasize, enhance, escalate, exacerbate, fire, fuel, heighten, hot up, increase, magnify, quicken, redouble, reinforce, sharpen, step up, strengthen, whet, whip up.
antonyms damp down, die down.

intensity *n.* accent, ardor, concentration, depth, earnestness, emotion, energy, excess, extremity, fanaticism, fervency, fervor, fierceness, fire, force, intenseness, keenness, passion, potency, power, severity, strain, strength, tension, vehemence, vigor, voltage.

intent *adj.* absorbed, alert, attentive, bent, committed, concentrated, concentrating, determined, eager, earnest, engrossed, fixed, hell-bent, industrious, intense, mindful, occupied, piercing, preoccupied, rapt, resolute, resolved, set, steadfast, steady, watchful, wrapped up.
antonyms absent-minded, distracted.
n. aim, design, end, goal, intention, meaning, object, objective, plan, purpose.

intention *n.* aim, concept, design, end, end in view, goal, idea, intent, meaning, object, objective, plan, point, purpose, scope, target, view.

intentional *adj.* calculated, deliberate, designed, intended, meant, planned, prearranged, preconcerted, premeditated, purposed, studied, wilful.
antonym accidental.

intentionally *adv.* by design, deliberately, designedly, meaningly, on purpose, wilfully, with malice aforethought.
antonym accidentally.

intercept *v.* arrest, block, catch, check, cut off, deflect, delay, frustrate, head off, impede, interrupt, obstruct, retard, seize, stop, take, thwart.

intercourse[1] *n.* association, commerce, communication, communion, congress, connection, contact, conversation, converse, correspondence, dealings, intercommunication, traffic, truck.

intercourse[2] *n.* carnal knowledge, coition, coitus, copulation, embraces, intimacy, love-making, sex, sexual relations, venery.

interest *n.* activity, advantage, affair, affection, attention, attentiveness, attraction, authority, bag, benefit, business, care, claim, commitment, concern, consequence, curiosity, diversion, finger, gain, good, hobby, importance, influence, investment, involvement, line of country, matter, moment, note, notice, participation, pastime, portion, preoccupation, profit, pursuit, regard, relaxation, relevance, right, share, significance, stake, study, suspicion, sympathy, weight.
antonyms boredom, irrelevance.
v. affect, amuse, attract, concern, divert, engage, engross, fascinate, intrigue, involve, move, touch, warm.
antonym bore.

interested *adj.* affected, attentive, attracted, biased, concerned, curious, drawn, engrossed, fascinated, implicated, intent, involved, keen, partisan, predisposed, prejudiced, responsive, simulated.
antonyms apathetic, indifferent, unaffected.

interesting *adj.* absorbing, amusing, amusive, appealing, attractive, compelling, curious, engaging, engrossing, entertaining, gripping, intriguing, provocative, stimulating, thought-provoking, unusual, viewable, visitable.
antonym boring.

interfere *v.* block, butt in, clash, collide, conflict, cramp, frustrate, hamper, handicap, hinder, impede, inhibit, interlope, intermeddle, interpose, intervene, intrude, meddle, obstruct, poke one's nose in, stick one's oar in, tamper, trammel.
antonyms assist, forbear.

interference *n.* clashing, collision, conflict, do-goodery, do-goodism, impedance, intervention, intrusion, meddlesomeness, meddling, mush, obstruction, opposition, prying, statics, white noise.
antonyms assistance, forbearance.

interior *adj.* central, domestic, hidden, home, inland, inly, inner, inside, internal, intimate, inward, mental, pectoral, personal, private, remote, secret, spiritual, up-country.
antonyms exterior, external.
n. bowels, center, core, heart, heartland, hinterland, inside, up-country.

interject *v.* call, cry, exclaim, interjaculate, interpolate, interpose, interrupt, introduce, shout.

interlude *n.* break, breathing-space, breathing-time, breathing-while, delay, episode, halt, hiatus, intermission, interval, pause, respite, rest, spell, stop, stoppage, wait.

intermediate *adj.* halfway, in-between, intermediary, interposed, intervening, mean, medial, median, mid, middle, midway, transitional.
antonym extreme.

interminable *adj.* boundless, ceaseless, dragging, endless,

everlasting, immeasurable, infinite, limitless, long, long-drawn-out, long-winded, never-ending, perpetual, prolix, protracted, unbounded, unlimited, wearisome.
antonym limited.

intermittent *adj.* broken, discontinuous, fitful, irregular, occasional, periodic, periodical, punctuated, recurrent, recurring, remittent, spasmodic, sporadic, stop-go.
antonym continuous.

internal *adj.* domestic, in-house, inner, inside, interior, intimate, inward, private, subjective.
antonym external.

interpose *v.* come between, insert, intercede, interfere, interjaculate, interject, interrupt, intervene, introduce, intrude, mediate, offer, place between, step in, thrust in.
antonym forbear.

interpret *v.* adapt, clarify, construe, decipher, decode, define, elucidate, explain, explicate, expound, paraphrase, read, render, solve, take, throw light on, translate, understand, unfold.

interpretation *n.* anagoge, anagogy, analysis, clarification, construction, diagnosis, elucidation, exegesis, explanation, explication, exposition, meaning, performance, portrayal, reading, rendering, rendition, sense, signification, translation, understanding, version.

interrogate *v.* ask, catechize, cross-examine, cross-question, debrief, enquire, examine, give (someone) the third degree, grill, inquire, investigate, pump, question, quiz.

interrupt *v.* barge in, break, break in, break off, butt in, check, cut, cut off, cut short, delay, disconnect, discontinue, disjoin, disturb, disunite, divide, heckle, hinder, hold up, interfere, interjaculate, interject, intrude, obstruct, punctuate, separate, sever, stay, stop, suspend.
antonym forbear.

interruption *n.* break, cessation, disconnection, discontinuance, disruption, dissolution, disturbance, disuniting, division, halt, hiatus, hindrance, hitch, impediment, intrusion, obstacle, obstruction, pause, separation, severance, stop, stoppage, suspension.

interval *n.* break, delay, distance, entr'acte, gap, hiatus, inbetween, interim, interlude, intermission, interspace, interstice, meantime, meanwhile, opening, pause, period, playtime, rest, season, space, spell, term, time, wait.

intervene *v.* arbitrate, befall, ensue, happen, intercede, interfere, interpose oneself, interrupt, intrude, involve, mediate, occur, step in, succeed, supervene, take a hand.

interview *n.* audience, conference, consultation, dialogue, enquiry, evaluation, inquisition, meeting, oral, oral examination, press conference, talk, viva.
v. examine, interrogate, question, viva.

intimacy *n.* brotherliness, closeness, coition, coitus, confidence, confidentiality, copulating, copulation, familiarity, fornication, fraternization, friendship, intercourse, sexual intercourse, sisterliness, understanding.

intimate[1] *v.* allude, announce, communicate, declare, hint, impart, imply, indicate, insinuate, state, suggest, tell.

intimate[2] *adj.* as thick as thieves, bosom, cherished, close, confidential, cosy, dear, deep, deep-seated, detailed, exhaustive, friendly, gremial, informal, innermost, internal, near, palsy-walsy, penetrating, personal, private, privy, profound, secret, warm.
antonyms cold, distant, unfriendly.
n. Achates, associate, bosom buddy, buddy, china, chum, comrade, confidant, confidante, crony, familiar, friend, mate, mucker, pal, repository.
antonym stranger.

intimation *n.* allusion, announcement, communication, declaration, hint, indication, inkling, insinuation, notice, reminder, statement, suggestion, warning.

intimidate *v.* alarm, appal, browbeat, bulldoze, bully, coerce, cow, daunt, dishearten, dismay, dispirit, frighten, lean on, overawe, psych out, put the frighteners on, scare, subdue, terrify, terrorize, threaten.
antonym persuade.

intolerant *adj.* bigoted, chauvinistic, dictatorial, dogmatic, fanatical, illiberal, impatient, narrow, narrow-minded, opinionated, opinionative, opinioned, persecuting, prejudiced, racialist, racist, small-minded, uncharitable.
antonym tolerant.

intoxicated *adj.* blotto, canned, cut, disguised in liquor, dizzy, drunk, drunken, ebriate, ebriated, ebriose, elated, enraptured, euphoric, excited, exhilarated, fuddled, glorious, half seas over, high, in one's cups, incapable, inebriate, inebriated, infatuated, legless, lit up, looped, pickled, pissed, pixil(l)ated, plastered, sent, sloshed, smashed, sozzled, stewed, stiff, stimulated, stoned, stotious, three sheets in the wind, tight, tipsy, under the influence, up the pole, zonked.
antonym sober.

intransigent *adj.* hardline, immovable, intractable, irreconcilable, obdurate, obstinate, stubborn, tenacious, tough, unamenable, unbending, unbudgeable, uncompromising, unpersuadable, unyielding, uppity.
antonym amenable.

intrepid *adj.* audacious, bold, brave, courageous, daring, dashing, dauntless, doughty, fearless, gallant, game, gutsy, heroic, lion-hearted, nerveless, plucky, resolute, stalwart, stout-hearted, unafraid, undashed, undaunted, unflinching, valiant, valorous.
antonyms cowardly, timid.

intricate *adj.* Byzantine, complex, complicated, convoluted, daedal(e), Daedalian, daedalic, dedal, dedalian, difficult, elaborate, entangled, fancy, Gordian, involved, knotty, labyrinthine, perplexing, rococo, sophisticated, tangled, tortuous.
antonym simple.

intrigue[1] *v.* attract, charm, fascinate, interest, puzzle, rivet, tantalize, tickle one's fancy, titillate.
antonym bore.

intrigue[2] *n.* affair, amour, brigue, cabal, chicanery, collusion, conspiracy, double-dealing, intimacy, knavery, liaison, machination, machination(s), maneuver, manipulation, plot, romance, ruse, scheme, sharp practice, stratagem, string-pulling, trickery, wheeler-dealing, wile, wire-pulling.
v. connive, conspire, machinate, maneuver, plot, scheme.

intrinsic *adj.* basic, basically, built-in, central, congenital, constitutional, constitutionally, elemental, essential, essentially, fundamental, fundamentally, genuine, inborn, inbred, inherent, intrinsically, inward, native, natural, underlying.
antonym extrinsic.

introduce *v.* acquaint, add, advance, air, announce, begin, bring in, bring up, broach, commence, conduct, establish, familiarize, found, inaugurate, initiate, inject, insert, institute, interpolate, interpose, launch, lead in, lead into, moot, offer, open, organize, pioneer, preface, present, propose, put forward, put in, recommend, set forth, start, submit, suggest, throw in, ventilate.
antonym take away.

introduction *n.* addition, baptism, commencement, debut, establishment, exordium, foreword, inauguration, induction, initiation, insertion, institution, interpolation, intro, launch, lead-in, opening, overture, pioneering, preamble, preface, preliminaries, prelude, presentation, prodrome, prodromus, proem, prolegomena, prolegomenon, prologue, prooemion, prooemium.
antonym withdrawal.
vation, soul-searching.

introverted *adj.* indrawn, intervertive, introspective, introversive, inward-looking, self-centered, self-contained, withdrawn.
antonym extroverted.

intrude *v.* aggress, butt in, encroach, infringe, interfere, interrupt, meddle, obtrude, trespass, violate.
antonyms stand back, withdraw.

intruder *n.* burglar, gate-crasher, infiltrator, interloper, invader, prowler, raider, snooper, trespasser.

intuition *n.* discernment, feeling, gut feeling, hunch, insight, instinct, perception, presentiment, sixth sense.
antonym reasoning.

invade *v.* assail, assault, attack, burst in, come upon, descend upon, encroach, enter, fall upon, infest, infringe, irrupt, occupy, overrun, overspread, penetrate, pervade, raid, rush into, seize, swarm over, violate.
antonym withdraw.

invalid[1] *adj.* ailing, bedridden, disabled, feeble, frail, ill, infirm, invalidish, poorly, sick, sickly, valetudinarian, valetudinary, weak.
antonym healthy.
n. case, convalescent, patient, sufferer, valetudinarian, valetudinary.

invalid[2] *adj.* baseless, fallacious, false, ill-founded, illogical, incorrect, inoperative, irrational, nugatory, null, null and void, unfounded, unscientific, unsound, untrue, void, worthless.
antonym valid.

invalidate *v.* abrogate, annul, cancel, nullify, overrule, overthrow, quash, rescind, undermine, undo, vitiate, weaken.
antonym validate.

invaluable *adj.* costly, exquisite, inestimable, precious, priceless, valuable.
antonym worthless.

invariable *adj.* changeless, consistent, constant, fixed, immutable, inflexible, permanent, regular, rigid, set, static, unalterable, unchangeable, unchanging, unfailing, uniform, unvarying, unwavering.
antonym variable.

invasion *n.* aggression, assault, attack, breach, encroachment, foray, incursion, infiltration, infraction, infringement, inroad, intrusion, irruption, offensive, onslaught, raid, seizure, usurpation, violation.
antonym withdrawal.

invective *n.* abuse, berating, castigation, censure, contumely, denunciation, diatribe, flyting, obloquy, philippic, philippic(s), reproach, revilement, sarcasm, scolding, tirade, tongue-lashing, vilification, vituperation.
antonym praise.

invent *v.* coin, conceive, concoct, contrive, cook up, create, design, devise, discover, dream up, fabricate, formulate, frame, imagine, improvise, make up, originate, think up, trump up.

invention *n.* brainchild, coinage, contraption, contrivance, contrivement, creation, creativeness, creativity, deceit, design, development, device, discovery, excogitation, fabrication, fake, falsehood, fantasy, fib, fiction, figment of (someone's) imagination, forgery, gadget, genius, imagination, ingenuity, inspiration, inventiveness, inveracity, lie, originality, prevarication, resourcefulness, sham, story, tall story, untruth, yarn.
antonym truth.

inventive *adj.* creative, daedal(e), Daedalian, daedalic, dedal, excogitative, fertile, gifted, imaginative, ingenious, innovative, inspired, original, resourceful.
antonym uninventive.

inventor *n.* architect, author, builder, coiner, creator, designer, father, framer, inventress, maker, originator.

inventory *n.* account, catalog, equipment, file, list, listing, record, register, roll, roster, schedule, stock.

invert *v.* capsize, introvert, inverse, overturn, reverse, transpose, turn turtle, turn upside down, upset, upturn.
antonym right.

invest *v.* adopt, advance, authorize, charge, consecrate, devote, empower, endow, endue, enthrone, establish,

inaugurate, induct, install, lay out, license, ordain, provide, put in, sanction, sink, spend, supply, vest.
antonym divest.

investigate *v.* consider, enquire into, examine, explore, go into, inspect, look into, probe, scrutinize, search, see how the land lies, sift, study, suss out.

investigation *n.* analysis, enquiry, examination, exploration, fact finding, hearing, inquest, inquiry, inspection, probe, research, review, scrutiny, search, study, survey, witch-hunt, zetetic.

investment *n.* ante, asset, besieging, blockade, contribution, investing, investiture, siege, speculation, stake, transaction, venture.

invidious *adj.* discriminating, discriminatory, hateful, objectionable, obnoxious, odious, offensive, repugnant, slighting, undesirable.
antonym desirable.

invigorating *adj.* bracing, energizing, exhilarating, fresh, generous, healthful, inspiriting, refreshing, rejuvenating, rejuvenative, restorative, salubrious, stimulating, tonic, uplifting, vivifying.
antonyms disheartening, wearying.

invincible *adj.* impenetrable, impregnable, indestructible, indomitable, inseparable, insuperable, invulnerable, irreducible, unassailable, unbeatable, unconquerable, unreducible, unsurmountable, unyielding.
antonym beatable.

invisible *adj.* concealed, disguised, hidden, imperceptible, inappreciable, inconspicuous, indetectable, indiscernible, infinitesimal, microscopic, out of sight, unperceivable, unseeable, unseen.
antonym visible.

invite *v.* allure, ask, ask for, attract, beckon, beg, bid, bring on, call, court, draw, encourage, entice, lead, provoke, request, seek, solicit, summon, tempt, welcome.
antonyms force, order.

inviting *adj.* alluring, appealing, appetizing, attractive, beguiling, captivating, delightful, engaging, enticing, fascinating, intriguing, magnetic, mouthwatering, pleasing, seductive, tantalizing, tempting, warm, welcoming, winning.
antonym uninviting.

involuntary *adj.* automatic, blind, compulsory, conditioned, forced, instinctive, instinctual, obligatory, reflex, reluctant, spontaneous, unconscious, uncontrolled, unintentional, unthinking, unwilled, unwilling, vegetative.
antonym voluntary.

involve *v.* absorb, affect, associate, bind, commit, comprehend, comprise, compromise, concern, connect, contain, cover, draw in, embrace, engage, engross, entail, grip, hold, implicate, imply, include, incorporate, incriminate, inculpate, mean, mix up, necessitate, number among, preoccupy, presuppose, require, rivet, take in, touch.

involved *adj.* anfractuous, caught up/in, complex, complicated, concerned, confusing, convoluted, difficult, elaborate, implicated, in on, intricate, knotty, labyrinthine, mixed up in/with, occupied, participating, sophisticated, tangled, tortuous.
antonyms simple, uninvolved.

invulnerable *adj.* impenetrable, indestructible, insusceptible, invincible, proof against, safe, secure, unassailable, unwoundable.
antonym vulnerable.

inward *adj.* confidential, entering, hidden, inbound, incoming, inflowing, ingoing, inly, inmost, inner, innermost, inpouring, inside, interior, internal, penetrating, personal, private, privy, secret.
antonyms external, outward.

inwardly *adv.* at heart, deep down, in gremio, in pectore, in petto, inly, inside, privately, secretly, to oneself, within.
antonyms externally, outwardly.

irate *adj.* angered, angry, annoyed, enraged, exasperated, fuming, furibund, furious, gusty, in a paddy, incensed, indignant, infuriated, ireful, irritated, livid, mad, piqued, provoked, riled, up in arms, waxy, worked up, wrathful, wroth.
antonym calm.

ire *n.* anger, annoyance, choler, displeasure, exasperation, fury, indignation, passion, rage, wax, wrath.
antonym calmness.

irk *v.* aggravate, annoy, bug, disgust, distress, gall, get, get to, irritate, miff, nettle, peeve, provoke, put out, rile, rub up the wrong way, ruffle, vex, weary.
antonym please.

irksome *adj.* aggravating, annoying, boring, bothersome, burdensome, disagreeable, exasperating, infuriating, irritating, tedious, tiresome, troublesome, vexatious, vexing, wearisome.
antonym pleasing.

ironic *adj.* contemptuous, derisive, incongruous, ironical, irrisory, mocking, paradoxical, sarcastic, sardonic, satirical, scoffing, scornful, sneering, wry.

irrational *adj.* aberrant, absurd, alogical, brainless, crazy, demented, foolish, illogical, injudicious, insane, mindless, muddle-headed, nonsensical, preposterous, raving, senseless, silly, unreasonable, unreasoning, unsound, unstable, unthinking, unwise, wild.
antonym rational.

irreconcilable *adj.* clashing, conflicting, hardline, implacable, incompatible, incongruous, inconsistent, inexorable, inflexible, intransigent, opposed, unappeasable, uncompromising, unreconcilable.
antonym reconcilable.

irregular *adj.* abnormal, anomalistic(al), anomalous, asymmetrical, broken, bumpy, capricious, craggy, crooked, difform, disconnected, disorderly, eccentric, erratic, exceptional, extraordinary, extravagant, fitful, fluctuating, fragmentary, haphazard, holey, immoderate, improper, inappropriate, incondite, inordinate,

intermittent, jagged, lopsided, lumpy, occasional, odd, patchy, peculiar, pitted, queer, quirky, ragged, random, rough, serrated, shifting, snatchy, spasmodic, sporadic, uncertain, unconventional, unequal, uneven, unofficial, unorthodox, unprocedural, unpunctual, unsteady, unsuitable, unsymmetrical, unsystematic, unusual, variable, wavering.
antonyms conventional, regular, smooth.

irregularity *n.* abberation, abnormality, anomaly, asymmetry, breach, bumpiness, confusion, crookedness, desultoriness, deviation, difformity, disorderliness, disorganization, eccentricity, freak, haphazardness, heterodoxy, jaggedness, lop-sidedness, lumpiness, malfunction, malpractice, oddity, patchiness, peculiarity, raggedness, randomness, roughness, singularity, uncertainty, unconventionality, unevenness, unorthodoxy, unpunctuality, unsteadiness.
antonyms conventionality, regularity, smoothness.

irrelevant *adj.* alien, extraneous, foreign, immaterial, impertinent, inapplicable, inapposite, inappropriate, inapt, inconsequent, inessential, peripheral, tangential, unapt, unconnected, unnecessary, unrelated.
antonym relevant.

irrepressible *adj.* boisterous, bubbling over, buoyant, ebullient, effervescent, inextinguishable, insuppressible, resilient, uncontainable, uncontrollable, ungovernable, uninhibited, unmanageable, unquenchable, unrestrainable, unstoppable.
antonyms depressed, depressive, despondent, resistible.

irresistible *adj.* alluring, beckoning, beguiling, charming, compelling, enchanting, fascinating, imperative, ineluctable, inescapable, inevitable, inexorable, overmastering, overpowering, overwhelming, potent, pressing, ravishing, resistless, seductive, tempting, unavoidable, uncontrollable, urgent. *antonyms* avoidable, resistible.

irresolute *adj.* dithering, doubtful, faint-hearted, fickle, fluctuating, half-hearted, hesitant, hesitating, indecisive, infirm, shifting, shilly-shallying, swithering, tentative, undecided, undetermined, unsettled, unstable, unsteady, vacillating, variable, wavering, weak.
antonym resolute.

irresponsible *adj.* carefree, careless, feather-brained, feckless, flibbertigibbit, flighty, foot-loose, giddy, hare-brained, harum-scarum, heedless, ill-considered, immature, lighthearted, madcap, negligent, rash, reckless, scatter-brained, shiftless, thoughtless, undependable, unreliable, untrustworthy, wild.
antonym responsible.

irreverent *adj.* blasphemous, cheeky, contemptuous, derisive, discourteous, disrespectful, flip, flippant, godless, iconoclastic, impertinent, impious, impudent, mocking, profane, rude, sacrilegious, saucy, tongue-in-cheek.
antonym reverent.

irrevocable *adj.* changeless, fated, fixed, hopeless, immutable, inexorable, invariable, irremediable, irrepealable, irretrievable, irreversible, predestined, predetermined, settled, unalterable, unchangeable.
antonyms alterable, flexible, mutable, reversible.

irritable *adj.* bad-tempered, cantankerous, captious, choleric, crabbed, crabby, cross, crotchety, crusty, edgy, feisty, fractious, fretful, hasty, hypersensitive, ill-humored, ill-tempered, impatient, irascible, narky, peevish, petulant, prickly, querulous, short, short-tempered, snappish, snappy, snarling, sore, tense, testy, te(t)chy, thin-skinned, touchy.
antonyms cheerful, complacent.

irritant *n.* annoyance, bore, bother, goad, menace, nuisance, pain, pest, pin-prick, plague, provocation, rankle, tease, thorn in the flesh, trouble, vexation.
antonyms pleasure, sop, sweetness.

irritate *v.* acerbate, aggravate, anger, annoy, bedevil, bother, bug, chafe, emboil, enrage, exacerbate, exasperate, faze, fret, get on one's nerves, get to, give the pip, gravel, grig, harass, incense, inflame, infuriate, intensify, irk, needle, nettle, offend, pain, peeve, pester, pique, provoke, put out, rankle, rile, rouse, rub, ruffle, vex.
antonyms gratify, mollify, placate, please.

irritation *n.* aggravation, anger, annoyance, crossness, displeasure, dissatisfaction, exasperation, fury, goad, impatience, indignation, irritability, irritant, nuisance, pain, pain in the neck, pest, pin-prick, provocation, rankle, resentment, shortness, snappiness, tease, testiness, vexation, wrath.
antonyms pleasure, satisfaction.

isolate *v.* abstract, cut off, detach, disconnect, divorce, exclude, identify, insulate, keep apart, ostracize, pinpoint, quarantine, remove, seclude, segregate, separate, sequester, set apart.
antonyms assimilate, incorporate.

isolated *adj.* abnormal, anomalous, atypical, backwoods, deserted, detached, dissociated, eremitic, exceptional, freak, godforsaken, hermitical, hidden, incommunicado, insular, lonely, monastic, outlying, out-of-the-way, random, reclusive, remote, retired, secluded, single, solitary, special, sporadic, unfrequented, unique, unrelated, untrodden, untypical, unusual, unvisited.
antonyms populous, typical.

isolation *n.* aloofness, detachment, disconnection, dissociation, exile, insularity, insulation, lazaretto, loneliness, quarantine, reclusion, remoteness, retirement, seclusion, segregation, self-sufficiency, separation, solitariness, solitude, withdrawal.

issue[1] *n.* affair, argument, concern, controversy, crux, debate, matter, point, problem, question, subject, topic.

issue[2] *n.* announcement, broadcast, circulation, copy, delivery, dispersal, dissemination, distribution, edition, emanation, flow, granting, handout, impression, instalment, issuance, issuing, number, printing,

promulgation, propagation, publication, release, supply, supplying, vent.
v. announce, broadcast, circulate, deal out, deliver, distribute, emit, give out, mint, produce, promulgate, publicize, publish, put out, release, supply.

issue[3] *n.* conclusion, consequence, culmination, dénouement, effect, end, finale, outcome, pay-off, product, result, termination, upshot.
v. arise, burst forth, debouch, emanate, emerge, flow, leak, originate, proceed, rise, spring, stem.

issue[4] *n.* brood, children, descendants, heirs, offspring, progeny, scions, seed, young.

itemize *v.* count, detail, document, enumerate, instance, inventory, list, mention, number, overname, particularize, record, specify, tabulate.

itinerant *adj.* ambulatory, drifting, journeying, migratory, nomadic, peregrinatory, peripatetic, rambling, roaming, rootless, roving, traveling, vagabond, vagrant, wandering, wayfaring.
antonyms settled, stationary.
n. diddicoy, dusty-foot, gypsy, hobo, nomad, perigrinator, peripatetic, piepowder, pilgrim, Romany, tinker, toe-rag, tramp, traveler, vagabond, vagrant, wanderer, wayfarer.

itinerary *n.* circuit, course, journey, line, plan, program, route, schedule, tour.

J

jab *v.* dig, elbow, jag, lunge, nudge, poke, prod, punch, push, shove, stab, tap, thrust.

jabber *v.* babble, blather, blether, chatter, drivel, gab, gabble, gash, jaw, mumble, prate, rabbit, ramble, tattle, witter, yap.

jacket *n.* blouson, case, casing, coat, cover, covering, envelope, folder, jerkin, jupon, mackinaw, sheath, shell, skin, wrap, wrapper, wrapping.

jackpot *n.* award, big time, bonanza, kitty, pool, pot, prize, reward, stakes, winnings.

jade *n.* baggage, broad, draggle-tail, floosie, harridan, hussy, nag, shrew, slattern, slut, strumpet, tart, trollop, vixen, wench.

jaded *adj.* blunted, bored, cloyed, dulled, effete, exhausted, fagged, fatigued, played-out, satiated, spent, surfeited, tired, tired out, weary.
antonyms fresh, refreshed.

jag *n.* barb, denticle, dentil, notch, point, projection, protrusion, snag, spur, tooth.

jagged *adj.* barbed, broken, craggy, denticulate, hackly, indented, irregular, notched, pointed, ragged, ridged, rough, saw-edged, serrate, serrated, snagged, snaggy, spiked, spiky, toothed, uneven.
antonyms smooth.

jail, gaol *n.* borstal, bridewell, brig, calaboose, can, cells, choky, clink, cooler, coop, custody, guardhouse, hoos(e)gow, house of correction, inside, jailhouse, jankers, jug, lock-up, nick, pen, penitentiary, pokey, prison, quod, reformatory, slammer, stir, tollbooth.
v. confine, detain, immure, impound, imprison, incarcerate, intern, lock up, quod, send down.

jailer, gaoler *n.* captor, guard, keeper, prison officer, screw, turnkey, warden, warder.

jam[1] *v.* block, clog, compact, confine, congest, cram, crowd, crush, force, obstruct, pack, press, ram, sandwich, squash, squeeze, stall, stick, stuff, throng, thrust, vice, wedge.
n. bottle-neck, concourse, crowd, crush, gridlock, herd, horde, mass, mob, multitude, pack, press, swarm, throng, traffic jam.

jam[2] *n.* bind, contretemps, difficulty, dilemma, fix, hitch, hole, hot water, imbroglio, impasse, pickle, plight, predicament, quandary, scrape, spot, straits, tangle, tight corner, trouble.

jam[3] *n.* confiture, confyt, conserve, jelly, marmalade, preserve, spread.

jamboree *n.* carnival, carouse, celebration, convention, festival, festivity, fête, field day, frolic, gathering, get-together, jubilee, junket, merriment, party, potlatch, rally, revelry, shindig, spree.

jangle *v.* chime, clank, clash, clatter, jar, jingle, rattle, upset, vibrate.
n. cacophony, clang, clangor, clash, din, dissonance, jar, racket, rattle, reverberation, stridence, stridency, stridor.
antonyms euphony, harmony.

janitor *n.* caretaker, concierge, custodian, doorkeeper, doorman, janitress, janitrix, ostiary, porter.

jar[1] *n.* amphora, aquamanile, bellarmine, can, carafe, container, crock, cruet, cruse, ewer, flagon, jug, kang, mug, olla, pitcher, pot, receptacle, stamnos, stoup, urn, vase, vessel.

jar[2] *v.* agitate, annoy, clash, convulse, disagree, discompose, disturb, grate, grind, interfere, irk, irritate, jangle, jolt, nettle, offend, quarrel, rasp, rattle, rock, shake, upset, vibrate.
n. clash, disagreement, discord, dissonance, grating, irritation, jangle, jolt, quarrel, rasping, wrangling.

jargon *n.* argot, balderdash, bunkum, cant, dialect, diplomatese, double-Dutch, drivel, gabble, gibberish, gobbledegook, gobbledygook, Greek, idiom, jive, lingo, mumbojumbo, nonsense, palaver, parlance, patois, rigmarole, slang, tongue, twaddle, vernacular.

jaundiced *adj.* biased, bitter, cynical, disbelieving, distorted, distrustful, envious, hostile, jaded, jealous, misanthropic, partial, pessimistic, preconceived, prejudiced, resentful, skeptical, suspicious.
antonyms fresh, naïve, optimistic.

jaunty *adj.* airy, breezy, buoyant, carefree, cheeky, chipper, dapper, debonair, gay, high-spirited, insouciant, lively, perky, self-confident, showy, smart, sparkish, sprightly, spruce, trim.
antonyms anxious, depressed, dowdy, seedy.

jazzy *adj.* animated, avant-garde, bold, fancy, flashy, gaudy, goey, lively, smart, snazzy, spirited, stylish, swinging, vivacious, wild, zestful.
antonyms conservative, prosaic, square.

jealous *adj.* anxious, apprehensive, attentive, careful, covetous, desirous, emulous, envious, green, green-eyed, grudging, guarded, heedful, invidious, mistrustful, possessive, proprietorial, protective, resentful, rival, solicitous, suspicious, vigilant, wary, watchful, zealous.

jealousy *n.* covetousness, distrust, emulation, envy, grudge, heart-burning, ill-will, mistrust, possessiveness, resentment, spite, suspicion, vigilance, watchfulness, zelotypia.

jeer *v.* banter, barrack, chaff, contemn, deride, explode, fleer, flout, flyte, gibe, heckle, hector, knock, mock, rail, razz, ridicule, scoff, sneer, taunt, twit.

n. abuse, aspersion, catcall, chaff, derision, dig, fleer, flyte, flyting, gibe, hiss, hoot, mockery, raillery, raspberry, ridicule, scoff, sneer, taunt, thrust.

jeopardize *v.* chance, endanger, expose, gamble, hazard, imperil, jeopard, menace, risk, stake, threaten, venture.
antonyms protect, safeguard.

jerk[1] *n.* bounce, jog, jolt, lurch, pluck, pull, shrug, throw, thrust, tug, tweak, twitch, wrench, yank.
v. bounce, flirt, jigger, jog, jolt, jounce, lurch, peck, pluck, pull, shrug, throw, thrust, tug, tweak, twitch, wrench, yank.

jerk[2] *n.* bum, clod, clot, clown, creep, dimwit, dolt, dope, fool, halfwit, idiot, klutz, ninny, prick, schlep, schmo, schmuck, twit.

jerky *adj.* bouncy, bumpy, convulsive, disconnected, fitful, incoherent, jolting, jumpy, rough, shaky, spasmodic, tremulous, twitchy, uncontrolled, unco-ordinated.
antonym smooth.

jest *n.* banter, bon mot, clowning, cod, crack, desipience, foolery, fooling, fun, gag, hoax, jape, jeu d'esprit, joke, josh, kidding, leg-pull, pleasantry, prank, quip, sally, sport, trick, trifling, waggery, wisecrack, witticism.
v. banter, chaff, clown, deride, fool, gibe, jeer, joke, josh, kid, mock, quip, scoff, tease, trifle.

jester *n.* buffoon, clown, comedian, comic, droll, fool, goliard, harlequin, humorist, joculator, joker, juggler, merry-andrew, merryman, motley, mummer, pantaloon, patch, prankster, quipster, wag, wit, zany.

jet[1] *n.* atomizer, flow, fountain, gush, issue, nose, nozzle, rose, rush, spout, spray, sprayer, spring, sprinkler, spurt, squirt, stream, surge.

jet[2] *adj.* atramentous, black, coal-black, ebon, ebony, inky, jetty, pitch-black, pitchy, raven, sable, sloe, sooty.

jetsam *n.* jetsom, jetson, lagan, waif, wreckage.

jettison *v.* abandon, chuck, discard, ditch, dump, eject, expel, heave, offload, scrap, unload.
antonyms load, take on.

jetty *n.* breakwater, dock, groyne, jutty, mole, pier, quay, wharf.

jewel *n.* bijou, brilliant, charm, find, flower, gaud, gem, gemstone, humdinger, locket, masterpiece, ornament, paragon, pearl, precious stone, pride, prize, rarity, rock, sparkler, stone, treasure, wonder.

jib *v.* back off, balk, recoil, refuse, retreat, shrink, stall, stop short.

jibe, gibe *v.* deride, fleer, flout, jeer, mock, rail, ridicule, scoff, scorn, sneer, taunt, twit.
n. barb, crack, derision, dig, fleer, fling, jeer, mockery, poke, quip, raillery, ridicule, sarcasm, scoff, slant, sneer, taunt, thrust.

jig *v.* bob, bobble, bounce, caper, hop, jerk, jiggle, jounce, jump, prance, shake, skip, twitch, wiggle, wobble.

jiggle *v.* agitate, bounce, fidget, jerk, jig, jog, joggle, shake, shift, shimmy, twitch, waggle, wiggle, wobble.

jilt *v.* abandon, betray, brush off, chuck, deceive, desert, discard, ditch, drop, forsake, reject, repudiate, spurn, throw over.
antonym cleave to.

jingle[1] *v.* chime, chink, clatter, clink, jangle, rattle, ring, tink, tinkle, tintinnabulate.
n. clang, clangor, clink, rattle, reverberation, ringing, tink, tinkle, tintinnabulation.

jingle[2] *n.* chant, chime, chorus, couplet, ditty, doggerel, limerick, melody, poem, rhyme, song, tune, verse.

jinx *n.* black magic, charm, curse, evil eye, gremlin, hex, hoodoo, jettatura, Jonah, plague, spell, voodoo.
v. bedevil, bewitch, curse, doom, hex, hoodoo, plague.

jittery *adj.* agitated, anxious, edgy, fidgety, flustered, jumpy, nervous, panicky, perturbed, quaking, quivering, shaky, shivery, trembling, uneasy.
antonyms calm, composed, confident.

job *n.* activity, affair, allotment, assignment, batch, business, calling, capacity, career, charge, chore, commission, concern, consignment, contract, contribution, craft, duty, employment, enterprise, errand, function, livelihood, lot, message, métier, mission, occupation, office, output, part, piece, place, portion, position, post, proceeding, product, profession, project, province, pursuit, responsibility, role, share, situation, stint, task, trade, undertaking, venture, vocation, work.

jobless *adj.* idle, inactive, laid off, on the dole, out of work, unemployed, unoccupied, unused, workless.
antonym employed.

jocularity *n.* absurdity, comicality, desipience, drollery, facetiousness, fooling, gaiety, hilarity, humor, jesting, jocoseness, jocosity, jolliness, joviality, laughter, merriment, playfulness, pleasantry, roguishness, sport, sportiveness, teasing, waggery, waggishness, whimsicality, whimsy, wit.

jog[1] *v.* activate, arouse, bounce, jar, jerk, joggle, jolt, jostle, jounce, nudge, poke, prod, prompt, push, remind, rock, shake, shove, stimulate, stir.
n. jerk, jiggle, jolt, nudge, poke, prod, push, reminder, shake, shove.

jog[2] *v., n.* bump, canter, dogtrot, jogtrot, lope, lumber, pad, run, trot.

join *v.* abut, accompany, accrete, add, adhere, adjoin, affiliate, alligate, amalgamate, annex, append, associate, attach, border, border on, butt, cement, coincide, combine, compaginate, conglutinate, conjoin, conjugate, connect, couple, dock, enlist, enrol, enter, fasten, knit, link, march with, marry, meet, merge, reach, sign up, splice, team, tie, touch, unite, verge on, yoke.
antonyms leave, separate.

joint[1] *n.* articulation, commissure, connection, geniculation, gimmal, ginglymus, gomphosis, hinge, intersection, junction, juncture, knot, nexus, node, seam, union.
adj. adjunct, amalgamated, collective, combined, communal, concerted, consolidated, co-operative, co-ordinated, joined, mutual, shared, united.

v. articulate, carve, connect, couple, cut up, dismember, dissect, divide, fasten, fit, geniculate, join, segment, sever, sunder, unite.

joint[2] *n.* dance-hall, dive, haunt, honky-tonk, jerry-shop, night-club, place, pub.

joint[3] *n.* reefer, roach, stick.

joke *n.* buffoon, butt, clown, conceit, concetto, frolic, fun, funny, gag, guy, hoot, jape, jest, jeu d'esprit, lark, laughing-stock, play, pun, quip, quirk, sally, simpleton, sport, target, whimsy, wisecrack, witticism, yarn, yell.
v. banter, chaff, clown, deride, fool, frolic, gambol, jest, kid, laugh, mock, quip, ridicule, spoof, taunt, tease, wisecrack.

joker *n.* buffoon, card, character, clown, comedian, comic, droll, humorist, jester, joculator, jokesmith, kidder, prankster, sport, trickster, wag, wit.

jolly *adj.* blithe, blithesome, buxom, carefree, cheerful, cheery, convivial, exuberant, festive, frisky, frolicsome, funny, gay, gladsome, happy, hearty, hilarious, jaunty, jocund, jovial, joyful, joyous, jubilant, merry, mirthful, playful, sportive, sprightly, sunny.
antonym sad.

jolt *v.* astonish, bounce, bump, discompose, disconcert, dismay, disturb, jar, jerk, jog, jostle, jounce, knock, nonplus, perturb, push, shake, shock, shove, stagger, startle, stun, surprise, upset.
n. blow, bolt from the blue, bombshell, bump, hit, impact, jar, jerk, jog, jump, lurch, quiver, reversal, setback, shake, shock, start, surprise, thunderbolt.

jostle *v.* bump, butt, crowd, elbow, force, hustle, jog, joggle, jolt, press, push, rough up, scramble, shake, shoulder, shove, squeeze, throng, thrust.

jot *n.* ace, atom, bit, detail, fraction, gleam, glimmer, grain, hint, iota, mite, morsel, particle, scintilla, scrap, smidgen, speck, tittle, trace, trifle, whit.

journal *n.* book, chronicle, commonplace, daily, daybook, diary, ephemeris, gazette, log, magazine, monthly, newspaper, organ, paper, periodical, publication, record, register, review, tabloid, waste-book, weekly.

journey *n.* career, course, excursion, expedition, eyre, hadj, itinerary, jaunt, odyssey, outing, passage, peregrination, pilgrimage, progress, raik, ramble, route, safari, tour, travel, trek, trip, voyage, wanderings.
v. fare, fly, gallivant, go, jaunt, peregrinate, proceed, ramble, range, roam, rove, safari, tour, tramp, travel, traverse, trek, voyage, wander, wend.

joust *n.* contest, encounter, engagement, pas d'armes, skirmish, tilt, tournament, tourney, trial.

jovial *adj.* affable, airy, animated, blithe, buoyant, cheery, convivial, cordial, ebullient, expansive, Falstaffian, gay, glad, happy, hilarious, jaunty, jocose, jocund, jolly, jubilant, merry, mirthful.
antonyms morose, sad, saturnine.

joy *n.* blessedness, bliss, charm, delight, ecstasy, elation, exaltation, exultation, felicity, festivity, gaiety, gem, gladness, gladsomeness, glee, gratification, happiness, hilarity, jewel, joyance, joyfulness, joyousness, pleasure, pride, prize, rapture, ravishment, satisfaction, seel, transport, treasure, treat, triumph, wonder.
antonyms mourning, sorrow.

joyful *adj.* blithe, blithesome, delighted, ecstatic, elated, enraptured, glad, gladsome, gratified, happy, jocund, jolly, jovial, jubilant, light-hearted, merry, pleased, rapturous, satisfied, seely, transported, triumphant.
antonyms mournful, sorrowful.

joyous *adj.* cheerful, ecstatic, festal, festive, frabjous, glad, gladsome, gleeful, happy, joyful, jubilant, merry, rapturous.
antonym sad.

jubilant *adj.* celebratory, delighted, elated, enraptured, euphoric, excited, exuberant, exultant, flushed, glad, gratified, joyous, over the moon, overjoyed, rejoicing, thrilled, triumphal, triumphant.
antonyms defeated, depressed.

jubilee *n.* anniversary, carnival, celebration, commemoration, festival, festivity, fête, gala, holiday.

judge *n.* adjudicator, alcalde, arbiter, arbiter elegantiae, arbitrator, arbitratrix, assessor, authority, beak, connoisseur, critic, Daniel, deemster, dempster, doomster, elegantiarum, evaluator, expert, hakim, justice, justiciar, justiciary, Law Lord, magistrate, mediator, moderator, pundit, referee, umpire, virtuoso, wig.
v. adjudge, adjudicate, appraise, appreciate, arbitrate, ascertain, assess, conclude, condemn, consider, criticize, decern, decide, decree, determine, dijudicate, discern, distinguish, doom, esteem, estimate, evaluate, examine, find, gauge, mediate, opine, rate, reckon, referee, review, rule, sentence, sit, try, umpire, value.

judgment *n.* acumen, appraisal, arbitration, arrêt, assessment, assize, award, belief, common sense, conclusion, conviction, damnation, decision, decree, decreet, deduction, determination, diagnosis, discernment, discretion, discrimination, doom, enlightenment, estimate, expertise, fate, fetwa, finding, intelligence, mediation, misfortune, opinion, order, penetration, perceptiveness, percipience, perspicacity, prudence, punishment, result, retribution, ruling, sagacity, sense, sentence, shrewdness, taste, understanding, valuation, verdict, view, virtuosity, wisdom.

judicial *adj.* critical, decretory, discriminating, distinguished, forensic, impartial, judiciary, juridical, legal, magisterial, magistral, official.

judicious *adj.* acute, astute, canny, careful, cautious, circumspect, considered, diplomatic, discerning, discreet, discriminating, enlightened, expedient, informed, percipient, perspicacious, politic, prescient, prudent, rational, reasonable, sagacious, sage, sane, sapient, sensible, shrewd, skilful, sober, sound, thoughtful, wary, well-advised, well-judged, well-judging, wise.
antonym injudicious.

jug *n.* amphora, aquamanile, bellarmine, blackjack, carafe, churn, container, crock, ewer, flagon, jar, pitcher, stoup, urn, vessel.

juice *n.* essence, extract, fluid, latex, liquid, liquor, nectar, sap, secretion, serum, succus.

jumble *v.* confuse, disarrange, disarray, disorder, disorganize, mingle-mangle, mix, mix up, muddle, shuffle, tangle, tumble, wuzzle.
antonym order.
n. agglomeration, chaos, clutter, collection, confusion, congeries, conglomeration, disarrangement, disarray, disorder, farrago, gallimaufry, hotch-potch, medley, mess, mingle-mangle, miscellany, mishmash, mixture, mix-up, muddle, olio, olla-podrida, pastiche, potpourri, raffle, salad.

jump[1] *v.* bounce, bound, caper, clear, dance, frisk, frolic, gambol, hop, hurdle, jig, leap, pounce, prance, skip, spring, vault.
n. bounce, bound, capriole, curvet, dance, frisk, frolic, gambado, hop, jeté, leap, pounce, prance, saltation, skip, spring, vault.

jump[2] *v.* avoid, bypass, digress, disregard, evade, ignore, leave out, miss, omit, overshoot, pass over, skip, switch.
n. breach, break, gap, hiatus, interruption, interval, lacuna, lapse, omission, saltation, saltus, switch.

jump[3] *v.* advance, appreciate, ascend, boost, escalate, gain, hike, increase, mount, rise, spiral, surge.
n. advance, ascent, augmentation, boost, escalation, increase, increment, mounting, rise, upsurge, upturn.

jump[4] *v.* flinch, jerk, jump out of one's skin, leap in the air, quail, recoil, resile, shrink, start, wince.
n. jar, jerk, jolt, lurch, quiver, shiver, shock, spasm, start, swerve, twitch, wrench.

jump[5] *n.* barricade, barrier, fence, gate, hedge, hurdle, impediment, obstacle, pons asinorum, rail.

jumpy *adj.* agitated, anxious, apprehensive, discomposed, edgy, fidgety, jittery, nervous, nervy, restive, restless, shaky, tense, tremulous, uneasy.
antonyms calm, composed.

junction *n.* abutment, combination, confluence, conjunction, connection, coupling, disemboguement, intersection, interstice, join, joining, joint, juncture, linking, meeting-point, nexus, seam, union.

junior *adj.* inferior, lesser, lower, minor, puisne, secondary, subordinate, subsidiary, younger.
antonyms senior.

junk *n.* clutter, debris, detritus, dregs, garbage, litter, oddments, refuse, rejectamenta, rubbish, rummage, scrap, trash, waste, wreckage.

jurisdiction *n.* area, authority, bailiwick, bounds, cognizance, command, control, domination, dominion, field, influence, judicature, orbit, power, prerogative, province, range, reach, rule, scope, sovereignty, sphere, sway, verge, zone.

just *adj.* accurate, apposite, appropriate, apt, blameless, condign, conscientious, correct, decent, deserved, disinterested, due, equitable, even-handed, exact, fair, fairminded, faithful, fitting, four-square, good, honest, honorable, impartial, impeccable, irreproachable, justified, lawful, legitimate, merited, normal, precise, proper, pure, reasonable, regular, right, righteous, rightful, sound, suitable, true, unbiased, unimpeachable, unprejudiced, upright, virtuous, well-deserved.
antonym unjust.

justice[1] *n.* amends, appositeness, appropriateness, compensation, correction, dharma, equitableness, equity, fairness, honesty, impartiality, integrity, justifiableness, justness, law, legality, legitimacy, nemesis, penalty, propriety, reasonableness, recompense, rectitude, redress, reparation, requital, right, rightfulness, rightness, satisfaction.
antonym injustice.

justice[2] *n.* JP, judge, Justice of the Peace, justiciar, magistrate.

justifiable *adj.* acceptable, allowable, defensible, excusable, explainable, explicable, fit, forgivable, justified, lawful, legitimate, licit, maintainable, pardonable, proper, reasonable, right, sound, tenable, understandable, valid, vindicable, warrantable, warranted, well-founded.
antonyms culpable, illicit, unjustifiable.

justify *v.* absolve, acquit, condone, confirm, defend, establish, exculpate, excuse, exonerate, explain, forgive, legalize, legitimize, maintain, pardon, substantiate, support, sustain, uphold, validate, vindicate, warrant.

jut *v.* beetle, bulge, extend, impend, overhang, poke, project, protrude, stick out.
antonym recede.

juvenile *n.* adolescent, boy, child, girl, halfling, infant, kid, minor, young person, youngster, youth.
antonym adult.
adj. adolescent, babyish, boyish, callow, childish, girlish, immature, impressionable, inexperienced, infantile, jejune, puerile, tender, undeveloped, unsophisticated, young, youthful.
antonym mature.

K

keen *adj.* acid, acute, anxious, ardent, argute, assiduous, astute, avid, biting, brilliant, canny, caustic, clever, cutting, devoted, diligent, discerning, discriminating, eager, earnest, ebullient, edged, enthusiastic, fervid, fierce, fond, forthright, impassioned, incisive, industrious, intense, intent, mordant, penetrating, perceptive, perfervid, perspicacious, piercing, pointed, pungent, quick, razorlike, sagacious, sapient, sardonic, satirical, scathing, sedulous, sensitive, sharp, shrewd, shrill, tart, trenchant, wise, zealous. *antonyms* apathetic, blunt, dull.

keep[1] *v.* accumulate, amass, carry, collect, conserve, control, deal in, deposit, furnish, garner, hang on to, heap, hold, hold on to, maintain, pile, place, possess, preserve, retain, stack, stock, store.

keep[2] *v.* be responsible for, board, care for, defend, feed, foster, guard, have charge of, have custody of, look after, maintain, manage, mind, nourish, nurture, operate, protect, provide for, provision, safeguard, shelter, shield, subsidize, support, sustain, tend, victual, watch, watch over.
n. board, food, livelihood, living, maintenance, means, nourishment, nurture, subsistence, support, upkeep.

keep[3] *v.* arrest, block, check, constrain, control, curb, delay, detain, deter, hamper, hamstring, hinder, hold, hold back, hold up, impede, inhibit, interfere with, keep back, limit, obstruct, prevent, restrain, retard, shackle, stall, trammel, withhold.

keep[4] *v.* adhere to, celebrate, commemorate, comply with, fulfil, hold, honor, keep faith with, keep up, maintain, obey, observe, perform, perpetuate, recognize, respect, ritualize, solemnize.

keep[5] *n.* castle, citadel, donjon, dungeon, fastness, fort, fortress, motte, peel-house, peel-tower, stronghold, tower.

keeper *n.* attendant, caretaker, conservator, conservatrix, curator, custodian, defender, gaoler, governor, guard, guardian, inspector, jailer, mahout, nab, overseer, steward, superintendent, supervisor, surveyor, warden, warder.

keepsake *n.* emblem, favor, memento, pledge, relic, remembrance, reminder, souvenir, token.

keg *n.* barrel, butt, cask, drum, firkin, hogshead, puncheon, round, rundlet, tierce, tun, vat.

ken *n.* acquaintance, appreciation, awareness, cognizance, compass, comprehension, field, grasp, knowledge, notice, perception, range, reach, realization, scope, sight, understanding, view, vision.

kerchief *n.* babushka, bandana, cravat, fichu, headscarf, headsquare, kaffiyeh, madras, neck-cloth, neckerchief, scarf, shawl, square, sudary, veronica.

kernel *n.* core, essence, germ, gist, grain, heart, marrow, nitty-gritty, nub, pith, seed, substance.

key *n.* answer, clavis, clue, code, crib, cue, digital, explanation, glossary, guide, index, indicator, interpretation, lead, means, pointer, secret, sign, solution, table, translation.
adj. basic, cardinal, central, chief, core, crucial, decisive, essential, fundamental, hinge, important, leading, main, major, pivotal, principal, salient.

keynote *n.* accent, center, core, emphasis, essence, flavor, flavor of the month, gist, heart, kernel, leitmotiv, marrow, motif, pith, stress, substance, theme.

kick *v.* abandon, boot, break, desist from, drop, foot, give up, leave off, leave out, punt, quit, spurn, stop, toe.
n. bite, buzz, dash, élan, enjoyment, excitement, feeling, force, fun, gratification, gusto, intensity, panache, pep, pizzazz, pleasure, power, punch, pungency, relish, snap, sparkle, stimulation, strength, tang, thrill, verve, vitality, zest, zing, zip.

kick-off *n.* beginning, bully-off, commencement, face-off, inception, introduction, opening, outset, start, word go.

kid[1] *n.* babe, baby, bairn, bambino, boy, child, dandiprat, girl, halfling, infant, juvenile, kiddy, lad, nipper, shaver, stripling, teenager, tot, wean, whippersnapper, youngster, youth.

kid[2] *v.* bamboozle, befool, beguile, con, cozen, delude, dupe, fool, gull, have on, hoax, hoodwink, humbug, jest, joke, josh, mock, pretend, pull someone's leg, put one over on, rag, ridicule, tease, trick.

kidnap *v.* abduct, capture, hijack, rape, remove, seize, skyjack, snatch, steal.

kill *v.* abolish, annihilate, assassinate, beguile, bump off, butcher, cancel, cease, deaden, defeat, destroy, dispatch, do away with, do in, do to death, eliminate, eradicate, execute, exterminate, extinguish, extirpate, fill, finish off, halt, kibosh, knock off, knock on the head, liquidate, mar, martyr, massacre, murder, napoo, neutralize, nip in the bud, nullify, obliterate, occupy, pass, pip, put to death, quash, quell, rub out, ruin, scotch, slaughter, slay, smite, smother, spoil, stifle, still, stonker, stop, suppress, top, veto, vitiate, while away, zap.
n. climax, conclusion, coup de grâce, death, death-blow, dénouement, dispatch, end, finish, mop-up, shoot-out.

killing[1] *n.* assassination, bloodshed, carnage, elimination,

ethnocide, execution, extermination, fatality, fratricide, homicide, infanticide, liquidation, mactation, manslaughter, massacre, matricide, murder, parricide, patricide, pogrom, regicide, slaughter, slaying, sororicide, thuggee, uxoricide.
adj. deadly, death-dealing, deathly, debilitating, enervating, exhausting, fatal, fatiguing, final, lethal, lethiferous, mortal, mortiferous, murderous, prostrating, punishing, tiring, vital.

killing[2] *n.* big hit, bonanza, bunce, clean-up, coup, fortune, gain, hit, lucky break, profit, smash, success, windfall, winner.

killing[3] *adj.* absurd, amusing, comical, funny, hilarious, ludicrous, side-splitting, uproarious.

killjoy *n.* complainer, cynic, dampener, damper, grouch, misery, moaner, pessimist, prophet of doom, skeptic, spoilsport, trouble-mirth, wet blanket, whiner.
antonyms enthusiast, optimist, sport.

kin *n.* affines, affinity, blood, clan, connection, connections, consanguinity, cousins, extraction, family, flesh and blood, kindred, kinsfolk, kinship, kinsmen, kith, lineage, people, relations, relationship, relatives, stock, tribe.
adj. affine, akin, allied, close, cognate, congener, connected, consanguine, consanguineous, interconnected, kindred, linked, near, related, similar, twin.

kind[1] *n.* brand, breed, category, character, class, description, essence, family, genus, habit, ilk, kidney, manner, mold, nature, persuasion, race, set, sort, species, stamp, style, temperament, type, variety.

kind[2] *adj.* accommodating, affectionate, altruistic, amiable, amicable, avuncular, beneficent, benevolent, benign, benignant, bonhomous, boon, bounteous, bountiful, brotherly, charitable, clement, compassionate, congenial, considerate, cordial, courteous, diplomatic, fatherly, friendly, generous, gentle, giving, good, gracious, hospitable, humane, indulgent, kind-hearted, kindly, lenient, loving, mild, motherly, neighborly, obliging, philanthropic, propitious, sisterly, soft-boiled, soft-hearted, sweet, sympathetic, tactful, tender-hearted, thoughtful, understanding.
antonyms cruel, inconsiderate, unhelpful.

kindle *v.* activate, actuate, agitate, animate, arouse, awaken, deflagrate, enkindle, exasperate, excite, fan, fire, foment, ignite, incite, induce, inflame, initiate, inspire, inspirit, light, provoke, rouse, set alight, sharpen, stimulate, stir, thrill.

kindly *adj.* benefic, beneficent, beneficial, benevolent, benign, charitable, comforting, compassionate, cordial, favorable, generous, genial, gentle, giving, good-natured, good-willy, hearty, helpful, indulgent, kind, mild, patient, pleasant, polite, sympathetic, tender, warm.
adv. agreeably, charitably, comfortingly, considerately, cordially, generously, gently, graciously, indulgently, patiently, politely, tenderly, thoughtfully.
antonyms cruel, inconsiderate, uncharitable, unpleasant.

kindred *n.* affines, affinity, clan, connections, consanguinity, family, flesh, folk, kin, kinsfolk, kinship, kinsmen, lineage, people, relations, relationship, relatives.
adj. affiliated, affine, akin, allied, cognate, common, congenial, connected, corresponding, kin, like, matching, related, similar.

king *n.* boss, chief, chieftain, doyen, emperor, kingpin, leading light, luminary, majesty, monarch, overlord, paramount, patriarch, potentate, prince, royalet, ruler, sovereign, supremo, suzerain.

kingdom *n.* area, commonwealth, country, division, domain, dominion, dynasty, empire, field, land, monarchy, nation, palatinate, principality, province, realm, reign, royalty, sovereignty, sphere, state, territory, tract.

kingly *adj.* august, basilical, glorious, grand, grandiose, imperial, imperious, imposing, lordly, majestic, monarchical, noble, regal, royal, sovereign, splendid, stately, sublime, supreme.

kink[1] *n.* bend, coil, complication, corkscrew, crick, crimp, defect, dent, difficulty, entanglement, flaw, hitch, imperfection, indentation, knot, loop, tangle, twist, wrinkle.
v. bend, coil, crimp, curl, tangle, twist, wrinkle.

kink[2] *n.* caprice, crotchet, eccentricity, fetish, foible, freak, idiosyncracy, idiosyncrasy, oddity, quirk, singularity, vagary, whim.

kinship *n.* affinity, alliance, association, bearing, community, conformity, connection, consanguinity, correspondence, kin, relation, relationship, similarity.

kismet *n.* destiny, doom, fate, fortune, joss, karma, lot, portion, predestiny, providence, weird.

kiss[1] *v.* buss, canoodle, neck, osculate, peck, salute, smooch, snog.
n. buss, osculation, peck, plonker, salute, smack, smacker, snog.

kiss[2] *v.* brush, caress, fan, glance, graze, lick, scrape, touch.

kit *n.* accouterments, apparatus, appurtenances, baggage, effects, equipage, equipment, gear, impedimenta, implements, instruments, luggage, matériel, muniments, outfit, paraphernalia, provisions, rig, rig-out, set, supplies, tackle, tools, trappings, traps, utensils.

knack *n.* ability, adroitness, aptitude, bent, capacity, dexterity, expertise, expertness, facility, faculty, flair, forte, genius, gift, handiness, hang, ingenuity, propensity, quickness, skilfulness, skill, talent, trick, trick of the trade, turn.

knave *n.* bastard, blackguard, blighter, bounder, cheat, dastard, drôle, fripon, rapscallion, rascal, reprobate, rogue, rotter, scallywag, scamp, scapegrace, scoundrel, stinker, swindler, swine, varlet, villain.

knead *v.* form, knuckle, manipulate, massage, mold, ply, press, rub, shape, squeeze, work.

knick-knack *n.* bagatelle, bauble, bibelot, bric-à-brac, gadget, gaud, gewgaw, gimcrack, gismo, jimjam, kickshaw, object of virtu, plaything, pretty, pretty-pretty, quip, rattle-trap, toy, trifle, trinket, whigmaleerie, whim-wham.

knife *n.* blade, carver, chiv, cutter, dagger, dah, flick-knife, jack-knife, machete, parang, pen-knife, pocket-knife, skean, skene, skene-dhu, skene-occle, switchblade, whittle.
v. cut, impale, lacerate, pierce, rip, slash, stab, wound.

knightly *adj.* bold, chivalrous, courageous, courtly, dauntless, gallant, gracious, heroic, honorable, intrepid, noble, soldierly, valiant, valorous.
antonyms cowardly, ignoble, ungallant.

knit *v.* ally, bind, connect, crease, crotchet, fasten, furrow, heal, interlace, intertwine, join, knot, link, loop, mend, secure, tie, unite, weave, wrinkle.

knob *n.* boll, boss, bump, caput, door-handle, knot, knub, knurl, lump, nub, projection, protrusion, protuberance, snib, stud, swell, swelling, tuber, tumor, umbo.

knock[1] *v.* buffet, clap, cuff, ding, hit, knobble, (k)nubble, punch, rap, slap, smack, smite, strike, thump, thwack.
n. blow, box, chap, clip, clout, con, cuff, hammering, rap, slap, smack, thump.

knock[2] *v.* abuse, belittle, carp, cavil, censure, condemn, criticize, deprecate, disparage, find fault, lambaste, run down, slam, vilify, vilipend.
n. blame, censure, condemnation, criticism, defeat, failure, rebuff, rejection, reversal, setback, stricture.
antonyms boost, praise.

knockout *n.* bestseller, coup de grâce, hit, kayo, KO, sensation, smash, smash-hit, stunner, success, triumph, winner. *antonyms* flop, loser.

knoll *n.* barrow, hill, hillock, hummock, knowe, koppie, mound.

knot *v.* bind, entangle, entwine, knit, loop, secure, tangle, tether, tie, weave.
n. aggregation, bond, bow, braid, bunch, burl, clump, cluster, collection, connection, gnar, gnarl, heap, hitch, joint, knag, knar, knarl, ligature, loop, mass, pile, rosette, tie, tuft.

know *v.* apprehend, comprehend, discern, distinguish, experience, fathom, identify, intuit, ken, learn, make out, notice, perceive, realize, recognize, see, tell, undergo, understand, wist.

knowing *adj.* acute, astute, aware, clever, competent, conscious, cunning, discerning, downy, eloquent, experienced, expert, expressive, gnostic, gnostical, hep, intelligent, meaningful, perceptive, qualified, sagacious, shrewd, significant, skilful, well-informed.
antonyms ignorant, obtuse.

knowledge *n.* ability, acquaintance, acquaintanceship, apprehension, book-learning, booklore, cognition, cognizance, comprehension, consciousness, cum-savvy, discernment, education, enlightenment, erudition, familiarity, gnosis, grasp, information, instruction, intelligence, intimacy, judgment, know-how, learning, multiscience, notice, pansophy, recognition, scholarship, schooling, science, tuition, understanding, wisdom.
antonym ignorance.

knowledgeable *adj.* acquainted, au courant, au fait, aware, book-learned, bright, cognizant, conscious, conversant, educated, erudite, experienced, familiar, in the know, intelligent, learned, lettered, scholarly, well-informed.
antonym ignorant.

kowtow *v.* bow, court, cringe, defer, fawn, flatter, genuflect, grovel, kneel, pander, suck up, toady, truckle.

kudos *n.* acclaim, applause, distinction, esteem, fame, glory, honor, laudation, laurels, plaudits, praise, prestige, regard, renown, repute.

L

label *n.* badge, brand, categorization, characterization, classification, company, description, docket, epithet, mark, marker, sticker, tag, tally, ticket, trademark.
v. brand, call, categorize, characterize, class, classify, define, describe, designate, docket, dub, identify, mark, name, stamp, tag.

labor[1] *n.* chore, donkey-work, drudgery, effort, employees, exertion, grind, hands, industry, job, labor improbus, laborers, moil, pains, painstaking, slog, sweat, task, toil, undertaking, work, workers, workforce, workmen.
antonyms ease, leisure, relaxation, rest.
v. drudge, endeavor, grind, heave, moil, pitch, plod, roll, slave, strive, struggle, suffer, sweat, toil, toss, travail, work.
antonyms idle, laze, loaf, lounge.

labor[2] *n.* birth, childbirth, contractions, delivery, labor pains, pains, parturition, throes, travail.
v. dwell on, elaborate, overdo, overemphasize, overstress, strain.

labored *adj.* affected, awkward, complicated, contrived, difficult, forced, heavy, overdone, overwrought, ponderous, stiff, stilted, strained, studied, unnatural.
antonyms easy, natural.

laborer *n.* drudge, farm-hand, hand, hireling, hobbler, hobo, hodman, hunky, husbandman, manual worker, redneck, worker, working man, workman.

laborious *adj.* arduous, assiduous, backbreaking, burdensome, difficult, diligent, fatiguing, forced, hard, hard-working, heavy, herculean, indefatigable, industrious, labored, onerous, operose, painstaking, persevering, ponderous, sedulous, strained, strenuous, tireless, tiresome, toilsome, tough, unflagging, uphill, wearing, wearisome.
antonyms easy, effortless, relaxing, simple.

labyrinth *n.* circumvolution, coil, complexity, complication, convolution, entanglement, Gordian knot, intricacy, jungle, maze, perplexity, puzzle, riddle, tangle, windings.

lace[1] *n.* crochet, dentelle, filigree, mesh-work, netting, open-work, tatting.

lace[2] *n.* bootlace, cord, lanyard, shoe-lace, string, thong, tie.
v. attach, bind, close, do up, fasten, intertwine, interweave, interwork, string, thread, tie.

lace[3] *v.* add to, fortify, intermix, mix in, spike.

lacerate *v.* afflict, claw, cut, distress, gash, ga(u)nch, harrow, jag, lancinate, maim, mangle, rend, rip, slash, tear, torment, torture, wound.

laceration *n.* cut, gash, injury, lancination, maim, mutilation, rent, rip, slash, tear, wound.

lack *n.* absence, dearth, deficiency, deprivation, destitution, emptiness, insufficiency, need, privation, scantiness, scarcity, shortage, shortcoming, shortness, vacancy, void, want.
antonyms abundance, profusion.
v. miss, need, require, want.

lackey *n.* attendant, creature, fawner, flatterer, flunky, footman, gofer, hanger-on, instrument, manservant, menial, minion, parasite, pawn, servitor, sycophant, toady, tool, valet, yes-man.

lacking *adj.* defective, deficient, flawed, impaired, inadequate, minus, missing, needing, sans, short of, wanting, without.

lackluster *adj.* boring, dim, drab, dry, dull, flat, leaden, lifeless, lusterless, mundane, muted, prosaic, somber, spiritless, unimaginative, uninspired, vapid.
antonyms brilliant, polished.

laconic *adj.* brief, close-mouthed, compact, concise, crisp, curt, pithy, sententious, short, succinct, taciturn, terse.
antonyms garrulous, verbose, wordy.

lad *n.* boy, bucko, callant, chap, fellow, guy, halfling, juvenile, kid, laddie, schoolboy, shaver, stripling, youngster, youth.

laden *adj.* burdened, charged, chock-a-block, chock-full, encumbered, fraught, full, hampered, jammed, loaded, oppressed, packed, stuffed, taxed, weighed down, weighted.
antonym empty.

ladle *v.* bail, dip, dish, lade, scoop, shovel, spoon.

lady *n.* begum, dame, damsel, don(n)a, Frau, gentlewoman, hidalga, madam(e), matron, memsahib, milady, noblewoman, Señora, signora, woman.

ladylike *adj.* courtly, cultured, decorous, elegant, genteel, matronly, modest, polite, proper, queenly, refined, respectable, well-bred.

lag *v.* dawdle, delay, hang back, idle, linger, loiter, mosey, saunter, shuffle, straggle, tarry, trail.
antonym lead.

laggard *n.* dawdler, idler, lingerer, loafer, loiterer, lounger, saunterer, slowcoach, slowpoke, slug-a-bed, sluggard, snail, straggler.
antonyms dynamo, go-getter, livewire.

lair *n.* burrow, den, earth, form, hideout, hole, nest, refuge, retreat, roost, sanctuary, stronghold.

lake *n.* lagoon, loch, lochan, lough, mere, reservoir, tarn.

lambaste *v.* beat, berate, bludgeon, castigate, censure, cudgel, drub, flay, flog, leather, rebuke, reprimand, roast, scold, strike, thrash, upbraid, whip.

lame *adj.* crippled, defective, disabled, disappointing,

feebl, flimsy, game, half-baked, halt, handicapped, hobbling, inadequate, insufficient, limping, poor, thin, unconvincing, unsatisfactory, weak.
v. cripple, damage, disable, hamstring, hobble, hurt, incapacitate, injure, maim, wing.

lament *v.* bemoan, bewail, beweep, complain, deplore, grieve, keen, mourn, regret, sorrow, wail, weep, yammer.
antonyms celebrate, rejoice.
n. complaint, coronach, dirge, dumka, elegy, jeremiad, keening, lamentation, moan, moaning, monody, plaint, requiem, threnody, ululation, wail, wailing.

lamentable *adj.* deplorable, disappointing, distressing, funest, grievous, inadequate, insufficient, low, meager, mean, miserable, mournful, pitiful, poor, regrettable, sorrowful, tragic, unfortunate, unsatisfactory, woeful, wretched.

lamp *n.* beacon, flare, floodlight, lampad, lantern, light, limelight, searchlight, torch, veilleuse.

lampoon *n.* burlesque, caricature, mickey-take, parody, Pasquil, Pasquin, pasquinade, satire, send-up, skit, spoof, squib, take-off.
v. burlesque, caricature, make fun of, mock, parody, Pasquil, Pasquin, pasquinade, ridicule, satirize, send up, spoof, squib, take off, take the mickey out of.

land[1] *n.* country, countryside, dirt, district, earth, estate, farmland, fatherland, ground, grounds, loam, motherland, nation, property, province, real estate, realty, region, soil, terra firma, territory, tract.
v. alight, arrive, berth, bring, carry, cause, come to rest, debark, deposit, disembark, dock, drop, end up, plant, touch down, turn up, wind up.

land[2] *v.* achieve, acquire, capture, gain, get, net, obtain, secure, win.

landlord *n.* freeholder, host, hotelier, hotel-keeper, innkeeper, lessor, letter, owner, proprietor, publican.
antonym tenant.

landmark *n.* beacon, boundary, cairn, feature, milestone, monument, signpost, turning-point, watershed.

landscape *n.* aspect, countryside, outlook, panorama, prospect, scene, scenery, view, vista.

landslide *n.* avalanche, earthfall, éboulement, landslip, rock-fall.
adj. decisive, emphatic, overwhelming, runaway.

lane *n.* alley(way), avenue, boreen, byroad, byway, channel, driveway, footpath, footway, gut, loan, passage(way), path(way), towpath, vennel, way, wynd.

language *n.* argot, cant, conversation, dialect, diction, discourse, expression, idiolect, idiom, interchange, jargon, langue, lingo, lingua franca, parlance, parole, patois, phraseology, phrasing, speech, style, talk, terminology, tongue, utterance, vernacular, vocabulary, wording.

languid *adj.* debilitated, drooping, dull, enervated, faint, feeble, heavy, inactive, indifferent, inert, lackadaisical, languorous, lazy, lethargic, limp, listless, pining, sickly, slow, sluggish, spiritless, torpid, unenthusiastic, uninterested, weak, weary.
antonyms alert, lively, vivacious.

languish *v.* brood, decline, desire, despond, droop, fade, fail, faint, flag, grieve, hanker, hunger, long, mope, pine, repine, rot, sicken, sigh, sink, sorrow, suffer, sulk, want, waste, waste away, weaken, wilt, wither, yearn.
antonym flourish.

languor *n.* apathy, asthenia, calm, debility, dreaminess, drowsiness, enervation, ennui, faintness, fatigue, feebleness, frailty, heaviness, hush, indolence, inertia, lassitude, laziness, lethargy, listlessness, lull, oppressiveness, relaxation, silence, sleepiness, sloth, stillness, torpor, weakness, weariness.
antonyms alacrity, gusto.

lanky *adj.* angular, bony, gangling, gangly, gaunt, loose-jointed, rangy, rawboned, scraggy, scrawny, spare, tall, thin, twiggy, weedy.
antonyms short, squat.

lap[1] *v.* drink, lick, sip, sup, tongue.

lap[2] *v.* gurgle, plash, purl, ripple, slap, slosh, splash, swish, wash.

lap[3] *n.* ambit, circle, circuit, course, distance, loop, orbit, round, tour.
v. cover, encase, enfold, envelop, fold, surround, swaddle, swathe, turn, twist, wrap.

lapse *n.* aberration, backsliding, break, caducity, decline, descent, deterioration, drop, error, failing, fall, fault, gap, indiscretion, intermission, interruption, interval, lull, mistake, negligence, omission, oversight, passage, pause, relapse, slip.
v. backslide, decline, degenerate, deteriorate, drop, end, expire, fail, fall, run out, sink, slide, slip, stop, terminate, worsen.

larceny *n.* burglary, expropriation, heist, misappropriation, pilfering, piracy, purloining, robbery, stealing, theft.

large *adj.* abundant, ample, big, broad, bulky, capacious, colossal, comprehensive, considerable, copious, decuman, enormous, extensive, full, generous, giant, gigantic, goodly, grand, grandiose, great, huge, immense, jumbo, king-sized, liberal, man-sized, massive, monumental, Patagonian, plentiful, plonking, roomy, sizeable, spacious, spanking, substantial, sweeping, swingeing, tidy, vast, wide.
antonyms diminutive, little, slight, small, tiny.

largely *adv.* abundantly, by and large, chiefly, considerably, extensively, generally, greatly, highly, mainly, mostly, predominantly, primarily, principally, widely.

largess(e) *n.* aid, allowance, alms, benefaction, bequest, bounty, charity, donation, endowment, generosity, gift, grant, handout, liberality, munificence, openhandedness, philanthropy, present.
antonym meanness.

lark *n.* antic, caper, escapade, fling, fredaine, frolic, fun,

gambol, game, gammock, guy, jape, mischief, prank, revel, rollick, romp, skylark, spree.
v. caper, cavort, frolic, gambol, gammock, play, rollick, romp, skylark, sport.

lascivious *adj.* bawdy, blue, coarse, crude, dirty, horny, indecent, lecherous, lewd, libidinous, licentious, lustful, obscene, offensive, Paphian, pornographic, prurient, randy, ribald, salacious, scurrilous, sensual, smutty, suggestive, tentiginous, unchaste, voluptuous, vulgar, wanton.

lash[1] *n.* blow, cat, cat-o'-nine-tails, hit, quirt, stripe, stroke, swipe, whip.
v. attack, beat, belabor, berate, birch, buffet, castigate, censure, chastize, criticize, dash, drum, flagellate, flay, flog, hammer, hit, horsewhip, knock, lace, lam, lambaste, lampoon, larrup, pound, ridicule, satirize, scold, scourge, smack, strike, tear into, thrash, upbraid, welt, whip.

lash[2] *v.* affix, bind, fasten, join, make fast, rope, secure, strap, tether, tie.

lass *n.* bird, chick, colleen, damsel, girl, lassie, maid, maiden, miss, quean, quine, schoolgirl.

last[1] *adj.* aftermost, closing, concluding, conclusive, definitive, extreme, final, furthest, hindmost, latest, rearmost, remotest, terminal, ultimate, utmost.
antonyms first, initial.
adv. after, behind, finally, ultimately.
antonyms first, firstly.
n. close, completion, conclusion, curtain, end, ending, finale, finish, termination.
antonyms beginning, start.

last[2] *v.* abide, carry on, continue, endure, hold on, hold out, keep (on), perdure, persist, remain, stand up, stay, survive, wear.

latch *n.* bar, bolt, catch, fastening, hasp, hook, lock, sneck.

late[1] *adj.* behind, behind-hand, belated, delayed, dilatory, last-minute, overdue, slow, tardy, unpunctual.
antonyms early, punctual.
adv. behind-hand, belatedly, dilatorily, formerly, recently, slowly, tardily, unpunctually.
antonyms early, punctually.

late[2] *adj.* dead, deceased, defunct, departed, ex-, former, old, past, preceding, previous.

lately *adv.* formerly, heretofore, latterly, recently.

latent *adj.* concealed, delitescent, dormant, hidden, inherent, invisible, lurking, potential, quiescent, secret, underlying, undeveloped, unexpressed, unrealized, unseen, veiled.
antonyms active, live, patent.

lather[1] *n.* bubbles, foam, froth, shampoo, soap, soapsuds, suds.
v. foam, froth, shampoo, soap, whip up.

lather[2] *n.* agitation, dither, fever, flap, fluster, flutter, fuss, pother, state, stew, sweat, tizzy, twitter.

lather[3] *v.* beat, cane, drub, flog, lambaste, lash, leather, strike, thrash, whip.

latitude *n.* breadth, clearance, compass, elbow-room, extent, field, freedom, indulgence, laxity, leeway, liberty, license, play, range, reach, room, scope, space, span, spread, sweep, width.

latter *adj.* closing, concluding, ensuing, last, last-mentioned, later, latest, modern, recent, second, succeeding, successive.
antonym former.

lattice *n.* espalier, fret-work, grate, grating, grid, grille, lattice-work, mesh, network, open-work, reticulation, tracery, trellis, web.

laud *v.* acclaim, applaud, approve, celebrate, extol, glorify, hail, honor, magnify, praise.
antonyms blame, condemn, curse, damn.

laudable *adj.* admirable, commendable, creditable, estimable, excellent, exemplary, meritorious, of note, praiseworthy, sterling, worthy.
antonyms damnable, execrable.

laudation *n.* acclaim, acclamation, accolade, adulation, blessing, celebrity, commendation, devotion, encomion, encomium, eulogy, extolment, glorification, glory, homage, kudos, paean, panegyric, praise, reverence, tribute, veneration.
antonyms condemnation, criticism.

laugh *v.* cachinnate, chortle, chuckle, crease up, fall about, giggle, guffaw, snicker, snigger, split one's sides, te(e)hee, titter.
antonym cry.
n. belly-laugh, card, case, caution, chortle, chuckle, clown, comedian, comic, cure, entertainer, giggle, guffaw, hoot, humorist, joke, lark, scream, snicker, snigger, te(e)hee, titter, wag, wit.

laughable *adj.* absurd, amusing, comical, derisive, derisory, diverting, droll, farcical, funny, gelastic, hilarious, humorous, laughworthy, ludicrous, mirthful, mockable, nonsensical, preposterous, ridiculous, risible.
antonyms impressive, serious, solemn.

launch *v.* begin, cast, commence, discharge, dispatch, embark on, establish, fire, float, found, inaugurate, initiate, instigate, introduce, open, project, propel, send off, set in motion, start, throw.

lavatory *n.* bathroom, bog, can, cloakroom, closet, cludge, comfort station, convenience, dike, draught-house, dunnakin, dunny, dyke, garderobe, Gents, George, head(s), jakes, john, Ladies, latrine, lav, office, powder-room, privy, public convenience, restroom, smallest room, toilet, urinal, washroom, water-closet, WC.

lavish *adj.* abundant, bountiful, copious, effusive, exaggerated, excessive, extravagant, exuberant, free, generous, gorgeous, immoderate, improvident, intemperate, liberal, lush, luxuriant, munificent, open-handed, opulent, plentiful, princely, prodigal, profuse, prolific, sumptuous, thriftless, unlimited, unreasonable, unrestrained, unstinting, wasteful, wild.
antonyms economical, frugal, parsimonious, scanty, sparing, thrifty.

v. bestow, deluge, dissipate, expend, heap, pour, shower, spend, squander, waste.

law *n.* act, axiom, brocard, canon, charter, code, command, commandment, constitution, consuetudinary, covenant, criterion, decree, dharma, edict, enactment, formula, institute, jurisprudence, order, ordinance, precept, principle, regulation, rule, standard, statute.
antonym chance.

lawful *adj.* allowable, authorized, constitutional, hal(l)al, kosher, legal, legalized, legitimate, licit, permissible, proper, rightful, valid, warranted.
antonyms illegal, illicit, lawless, unlawful.

lawless *adj.* anarchic(al), chaotic, disorderly, felonious, insubordinate, insurgent, mutinous, rebellious, reckless, riotous, ruleless, seditious, unbridled, ungoverned, unrestrained, unruly, wild.
antonym lawful.

lawlessness *n.* anarchy, chaos, disorder, insurgency, mobocracy, mob-rule, ochlocracy, piracy, racketeering, rent-a-mob.
antonym order.

lawyer *n.* advocate, attorney, barrister, counsel, counsellor, jurisconsult, law-agent, lawmonger, legist, solicitor.

lax *adj.* broad, careless, casual, derelict, easy-going, flabby, flaccid, general, imprecise, inaccurate, indefinite, inexact, lenient, loose, neglectful, negligent, overindulgent, remiss, shapeless, slack, slipshod, soft, vague, wide, wide-open, yielding.
antonyms rigid, strict, stringent.

lay[1] *v.* advance, allay, alleviate, allocate, allot, appease, apply, arrange, ascribe, assess, assign, assuage, attribute, bet, burden, calm, charge, concoct, contrive, deposit, design, devise, dispose, encumber, establish, gamble, hatch, hazard, impose, impute, leave, locate, lodge, offer, organize, place, plan, plant, plot, posit, position, prepare, present, put, quiet, relieve, risk, saddle, set, set down, set out, settle, soothe, spread, stake, still, submit, suppress, tax, wager, work out.

lay[2] *adj.* amateur, inexpert, laic, laical, non-professional, non-specialist, secular.

lay[3] *n.* ballad, canzone(t), lyric, madrigal, ode, poem, roundelay, song.

lay-off *n.* discharge, dismissal, redundancy, unemployment.

layout *n.* arrangement, blueprint, design, draft, formation, geography, map, outline, plan, sketch.

lazy *adj.* dormant, drowsy, idle, inactive, indolent, inert, languid, languorous, lethargic, otiose, remiss, shiftless, slack, sleepy, slobby, slothful, slow, slow-moving, sluggish, somnolent, torpid, work-shy.
antonyms active, diligent, energetic, industrious.

leach *v.* drain, extract, filter, filtrate, lixiviate, osmose, percolate, seep, strain.

lead *v.* antecede, cause, command, conduct, direct, dispose, draw, escort, exceed, excel, experience, govern, guide, have, head, incline, induce, influence, live, manage, outdo, outstrip, pass, persuade, pilot, precede, preside over, prevail, prompt, spend, steer, supervise, surpass, transcend, undergo, usher.
antonym follow.
n. advance, advantage, clue, direction, edge, example, first place, guidance, guide, hint, indication, leadership, margin, model, precedence, primacy, principal, priority, protagonist, starring role, start, suggestion, supremacy, tip, title role, trace, van, vanguard.
adj. chief, first, foremost, head, leading, main, premier, primary, prime, principal, star.

leader *n.* bell-wether, boss, captain, chief, chieftain, commander, conductor, coryphaeus, counselor, director, doyen, figurehead, flagship, guide, head, mahatma, principal, ringleader, ruler, skipper, superior, supremo.
antonym follower.

leading *adj.* chief, dominant, first, foremost, governing, greatest, highest, main, number one, outstanding, paramount, pre-eminent, primary, principal, ruling, superior, supreme.
antonyms subordinate.

league *n.* alliance, association, band, Bund, cartel, category, class, coalition, combination, combine, compact, confederacy, confederation, consortium, federation, fellowship, fraternity, group, guild, level, partnership, sorority, syndicate, union.
v. ally, amalgamate, associate, band, collaborate, combine, confederate, consort, join forces, unite.

leak *n.* aperture, chink, crack, crevice, disclosure, divulgence, drip, fissure, hole, leakage, leaking, oozing, opening, percolation, perforation, puncture, seepage.
v. discharge, disclose, divulge, drip, escape, exude, give away, let slip, let the cat out of the bag, make known, make public, make water, ooze, pass, pass on, percolate, reveal, seep, spill, spill the beans, tell, trickle, weep.

lean[1] *v.* bend, confide, count on, depend, favor, incline, list, prefer, prop, recline, rely, repose, rest, slant, slope, tend, tilt, tip, trust.

lean[2] *adj.* angular, bare, barren, bony, emaciated, gaunt, inadequate, infertile, lank, meager, pitiful, poor, rangy, scanty, scragged, scraggy, scrawny, skinny, slender, slim, slink(y), spare, sparse, thin, unfruitful, unproductive, wiry.
antonyms fat, fleshy.

lean on force, persuade, pressurize, put pressure on.

leaning *n.* aptitude, bent, bias, disposition, inclination, liking, partiality, penchant, predilection, proclivity, proneness, propensity, susceptibility, taste, tendency, velleity.

leap *v.* advance, bounce, bound, caper, capriole, cavort, clear, curvet, escalate, frisk, gambol, hasten, hop, hurry, increase, jump, jump (over), reach, rocket, rush, skip, soar, spring, surge, vault.
antonyms drop, fall, sink.

n. bound, caper, capriole, curvet, escalation, frisk, hop, increase, jump, rise, sally, skip, spring, surge, upsurge, upswing, vault, volt(e).

learn *v.* acquire, ascertain, assimilate, attain, cognize, con, detect, determine, discern, discover, find out, gather, get off pat, grasp, hear, imbibe, learn by heart, master, memorize, pick up, see, understand.

learned *adj.* academic, adept, blue, cultured, erudite, experienced, expert, highbrow, intellectual, lettered, literate, proficient, sage, scholarly, skilled, versed, well-informed, well-read, wise.
antonyms ignorant, illiterate, uneducated.

learning *n.* acquirements, attainments, culture, edification, education, enlightenment, erudition, information, knowledge, letters, literature, lore, research, scholarship, schoolcraft, schooling, study, tuition, wisdom.

lease *v.* charter, farm out, hire, let, loan, rent, sublet.

leash *n.* check, control, curb, discipline, hold, lead, lyam, rein, restraint, tether.

least *adj.* fewest, last, lowest, meanest, merest, minimum, minutest, poorest, slightest, smallest, tiniest.
antonym most.

leave[1] *v.* abandon, allot, assign, bequeath, cause, cease, cede, commit, consign, decamp, depart, deposit, desert, desist, disappear, do a bunk, drop, entrust, exit, flit, forget, forsake, generate, give over, give up, go, go away, hand down, leave behind, levant, move, produce, pull out, quit, refer, refrain, relinquish, renounce, retire, set out, stop, surrender, take off, transmit, will, withdraw.
antonyms arrive.

leave[2] *n.* allowance, authorization, concession, consent, dispensation, exeat, freedom, furlough, holiday, indulgence, liberty, permission, sabbatical, sanction, time off, vacation.
antonyms refusal, rejection.

lecherous *adj.* carnal, concupiscent, goatish, lascivious, lewd, libidinous, licentious, lickerish, liquorish, lubricous, lustful, prurient, randy, raunchy, salacious, unchaste, wanton, womanizing.

lecture *n.* address, castigation, censure, chiding, discourse, disquisition, dressing-down, going-over, harangue, instruction, lesson, prelection, rebuke, reprimand, reproof, scolding, speech, talk, talking-to, telling-off, wigging.
v. address, admonish, berate, carpet, castigate, censure, chide, discourse, expound, harangue, hold forth, lucubrate, prelect, rate, reprimand, reprove, scold, speak, talk, teach, tell off.

ledge *n.* berm, mantle, projection, ridge, shelf, shelve, sill, step.

leech *n.* bloodsucker, freeloader, hanger-on, parasite, sponger, sycophant, usurer.

leer *v.* eye, fleer, gloat, goggle, grin, ogle, smirk, squint, stare, wink.
n. grin, ogle, smirk, squint, stare, wink.

leeway *n.* elbow-room, latitude, play, room, scope, space.

left-overs *n.* dregs, fag-end, leavings, oddments, odds and ends, orts, refuse, remainder, remains, remnants, residue, scraps, surplus, sweepings.

legacy *n.* bequest, birthright, devise, endowment, estate, gift, heirloom, hereditament, heritage, heritance, inheritance, patrimony.

legal *adj.* above-board, allowable, allowed, authorized, constitutional, forensic, judicial, juridical, lawful, legalized, legitimate, licit, permissible, proper, rightful, sanctioned, valid, warrantable.
antonym illegal.

legalize *v.* allow, approve, authorize, decriminalize, legitimate, legitimize, license, permit, sanction, validate, warrant.

legate *n.* ambassador, delegate, depute, deputy, emissary, envoy, exarch, messenger, nuncio.

legend *n.* caption, celebrity, cipher, code, device, fable, fiction, folk-tale, household name, inscription, key, luminary, marvel, motto, myth, narrative, phenomenon, prodigy, saga, spectacle, story, tale, tradition, wonder.

legendary *adj.* apocryphal, celebrated, fabled, fabulous, famed, famous, fanciful, fictional, fictitious, illustrious, immortal, mythical, renowned, romantic, storied, storybook, traditional, unhistoric(al), well-known.

legible *adj.* clear, decipherable, discernible, distinct, intelligible, neat, readable.
antonym illegible.

legion *n.* army, battalion, brigade, cohort, company, division, drove, force, horde, host, mass, multitude, myriad, number, regiment, swarm, throng, troop.
adj. countless, illimitable, innumerable, multitudinous, myriad, numberless, numerous.

legislation *n.* act, authorization, bill, charter, codification, constitutionalization, enactment, law, law-making, measure, prescription, regulation, ruling, statute.

legislator *n.* law-giver, law-maker, nomothete, parliamentarian.

legitimate *adj.* acknowledged, admissible, authentic, authorized, correct, genuine, just, justifiable, kosher, lawful, legal, legit, licit, logical, proper, real, reasonable, rightful, sanctioned, sensible, statutory, true, true-born, valid, warranted, well-founded.
antonym illegitimate.
v. authorize, charter, entitle, legalize, legitimize, license, permit, sanction.

leisure *n.* breather, ease, freedom, holiday, let-up, liberty, opportunity, pause, quiet, recreation, relaxation, respite, rest, retirement, spare time, time off, vacation.
antonyms toil, work.

leisurely *adj.* carefree, comfortable, deliberate, easy, gentle, indolent, laid-back, lazy, lingering, loose, relaxed, restful, slow, tranquil, unhasty, unhurried.
antonyms hectic, hurried, rushed.

lend *v.* add, advance, afford, bestow, confer, contribute, furnish, give, grant, impart, lease, loan, present, provide, supply.
antonym borrow.

length *n.* distance, duration, elongation, extensiveness, extent, lengthiness, longitude, measure, operoseness, operosity, period, piece, portion, prolixity, protractedness, reach, section, segment, space, span, stretch, tediousness, term.

lengthen *v.* continue, draw out, eke, eke out, elongate, expand, extend, increase, pad out, prolong, prolongate, protract, spin out, stretch.
antonym shorten.

leniency *n.* clemency, compassion, forbearance, gentleness, indulgence, lenience, lenity, mercy, mildness, moderation, permissiveness, soft-heartedness, softness, tenderness, tolerance.
antonym severity.

lenient *adj.* clement, compassionate, easy-going, forbearing, forgiving, gentle, indulgent, kind, merciful, mild, soft, soft-hearted, sparing, tender, tolerant.
antonym severe.

lessen *v.* abate, abridge, bate, contract, curtail, deaden, decrease, de-escalate, degrade, die down, diminish, dwindle, ease, erode, fail, flag, impair, lighten, lower, minimize, moderate, narrow, reduce, shrink, slack, slow down, weaken.
antonym increase.

lesson *n.* admonition, assignment, censure, chiding, class, coaching, deterrent, drill, example, exemplar, exercise, homework, instruction, lection, lecture, message, model, moral, pericope, period, practice, precept, punishment, reading, rebuke, recitation, reprimand, reproof, schooling, scolding, task, teaching, tutorial, tutoring, warning.

let[1] *v.* agree to, allow, authorize, cause, charter, consent to, empower, enable, entitle, give leave, give permission, give the go-ahead, give the green light, grant, hire, lease, make, OK, permit, rent, sanction, tolerate.
antonym forbid.

let[2] *n.* check, constraint, hindrance, impediment, interference, obstacle, obstruction, prohibition, restraint, restriction.
antonym assistance.

let-down *n.* anticlimax, betrayal, blow, desertion, disappointment, disillusionment, frustration, lemon, setback, wash-out.
antonym satisfaction.

lethal *adj.* baleful, dangerous, deadly, deathful, deathly, destructive, devastating, fatal, lethiferous, mortal, mortiferous, murderous, noxious, pernicious, poisonous, virulent.
antonym harmless.

lethargic *adj.* apathetic, comatose, debilitated, drowsy, dull, enervated, heavy, hebetant, hebetated, hebetudinous, inactive, indifferent, inert, languid, lazy, listless, sleepy, slothful, slow, sluggish, somnolent, stupefied, torpid.
antonym lively.

lethargy *n.* apathy, drowsiness, dullness, hebetation, hebetude, hebetudinosity, inaction, indifference, inertia, languor, lassitude, listlessness, sleepiness, sloth, slowness, sluggishness, stupor, torpidity, torpor.
antonym liveliness.

letter[1] *n.* acknowledgment, answer, billet, chit, communication, da(w)k, dispatch, encyclical, epistle, epistolet, line, message, missive, note, reply.

letter[2] *n.* character, grapheme, lexigram, logogram, logograph, sign, symbol.

let-up *n.* abatement, break, breather, cessation, interval, lessening, lull, pause, recess, remission, respite, slackening.
antonym continuation.

level[1] *adj.* aligned, balanced, calm, champaign, commensurate, comparable, consistent, equable, equal, equivalent, even, even-tempered, flat, flush, horizontal, neck and neck, on a par, plain, proportionate, smooth, stable, steady, uniform.
antonyms behind, uneven, unstable.
v. aim, beam, bulldoze, couch, demolish, destroy, devastate, direct, equalize, even out, flatten, flush, focus, knock down, lay low, plane, point, pull down, raze, smooth, tear down, train, wreck.
n. altitude, bed, class, degree, echelon, elevation, floor, grade, height, horizontal, layer, plain, plane, position, rank, stage, standard, standing, status, story, stratum, zone.

level[2] *v.* admit, avow, come clean, confess, divulge, open up, tell.
antonym prevaricate.

level-headed *adj.* balanced, calm, collected, commonsensical, composed, cool, dependable, even-tempered, reasonable, sane, self-possessed, sensible, steady, together, unflappable.

leverage *n.* advantage, ascendancy, authority, clout, force, influence, pull, purchase, rank, strength, weight.

levity *n.* buoyancy, facetiousness, fickleness, flightiness, flippancy, frivolity, giddiness, irreverence, lightheartedness, silliness, skittishness, triviality, whifflery.
antonyms seriousness, sobriety.

levy *v.* assemble, call, call up, charge, collect, conscript, demand, exact, gather, impose, mobilize, muster, press, raise, summon, tax.
n. assessment, collection, contribution, duty, exaction, excise, fee, gathering, imposition, impost, subscription, tariff, tax, toll.

lewd *adj.* bawdy, blue, Cyprian, dirty, harlot, impure, indecent, lascivious, libidinous, licentious, loose, lubric, lubrical, lubricious, lubricous, lustful, obscene, pornographic, profligate, salacious, smutty, unchaste, vile, vulgar, wanton, wicked.
antonyms chaste, polite.

liability *n.* accountability, albatross, answerability, arrears, burden, culpability, debit, debt, disadvantage, drag, drawback, duty, encumbrance, handicap, hindrance, impediment, inconvenience, indebtedness, likeliness, millstone, minus, nuisance, obligation, onus, responsibility.
antonyms asset(s), unaccountability.

liable *adj.* accountable, amenable, answerable, apt, bound, chargeable, disposed, exposed, inclined, likely, obligated, open, predisposed, prone, responsible, subject, susceptible, tending, vulnerable.
antonyms unaccountable, unlikely.

liaison *n.* affair, amour, communication, conjunction, connection, contact, entanglement, interchange, intermediary, intrigue, link, love affair, romance, union.

liar *n.* Ananias, bouncer, deceiver, fabricator, falsifier, fibber, perjurer, prevaricator, storyteller.

libel *n.* aspersion, calumny, defamation, denigration, obloquy, slander, slur, smear, vilification, vituperation.
antonym praise.
v. blacken, calumniate, defame, derogate, malign, revile, slander, slur, smear, traduce, vilify, vilipend, vituperate.
antonym praise.

liberal *adj.* abundant, advanced, altruistic, ample, beneficent, bounteous, bountiful, broad, broad-minded, catholic, charitable, copious, enlightened, flexible, free, free-handed, general, generous, handsome, high-minded, humanistic, humanitarian, indulgent, inexact, kind, large-hearted, latitudinarian, lavish, lenient, libertarian, loose, magnanimous, munificent, open-handed, open-hearted, permissive, plentiful, profuse, progressive, radical, reformist, rich, tolerant, unbiased, unbigoted, unprejudiced, unstinting, verligte, Whig, Whiggish.
antonyms conservative, illiberal, mean, narrow-minded.

liberality *n.* altruism, beneficence, benevolence, bounty, breadth, broad-mindedness, candor, catholicity, charity, free-handedness, generosity, impartiality, kindness, large-heartedness, largess(e), latitude, liberalism, libertarianism, magnanimity, munificence, open-handedness, open-mindedness, permissiveness, philanthropy, progressivism, tolerance, toleration.
antonyms illiberality, meanness.

liberate *v.* affranchise, deliver, discharge, disenthral, emancipate, free, let go, let loose, let out, manumit, ransom, redeem, release, rescue, set free, uncage, unchain, unfetter, unpen, unshackle.
antonyms enslave, imprison, restrict.

liberation *n.* deliverance, emancipation, enfranchisement, freedom, freeing, liberating, liberty, manumission, ransoming, redemption, release, uncaging, unchaining, unfettering, unpenning, unshackling.
antonyms enslavement, imprisonment, restriction.

liberty *n.* authorization, autonomy, carte-blanche, dispensation, emancipation, exemption, franchise, free rein, freedom, immunity, independence, latitude, leave, liberation, license, permission, prerogative, privilege, release, right, sanction, self-determination, sovereignty.
antonyms imprisonment, restriction, slavery.

libretto *n.* book, lines, lyrics, script, text, words.

license[1] *n.* authorization, authority, carte blanche, certificate, charter, dispensation, entitlement, exemption, freedom, immunity, imprimatur, independence, indult, latitude, tude, leave, liberty, permission, permit, privilege, right, self-determination, warrant.
antonyms banning, dependence, restriction.

license[2] *n.* abandon, amorality, anarchy, debauchery, disorder, dissipation, dissoluteness, excess, immoderation, impropriety, indulgence, intemperance, irresponsibility, lawlessness, laxity, profligacy, unruliness.
antonyms decorum, temperance.

license[3] *v.* accredit, allow, authorize, certificate, certify, commission, empower, entitle, permit, sanction, warrant.
antonym ban.

lick[1] *v.* brush, dart, flick, lap, play over, smear, taste, tongue, touch, wash.
n. bit, brush, dab, hint, little, sample, smidgeon, speck, spot, stroke, taste, touch.

lick[2] *v.* beat, best, defeat, excel, flog, outdo, outstrip, overcome, rout, skelp, slap, smack, spank, strike, surpass, thrash, top, trounce, vanquish, wallop.

lick[3] *n.* clip, gallop, pace, rate, speed.

lie[1] *v.* dissimulate, equivocate, fabricate, falsify, fib, forswear oneself, invent, misrepresent, perjure, prevaricate.
n. bam, bounce, caulker, cram, crammer, cretism, deceit, fabrication, falsehood, falsification, falsity, fib, fiction, flam, invention, inveracity, mendacity, plumper, prevarication, stretcher, tar(r)adiddle, untruth, whacker, white lie, whopper.
antonym truth.

lie[2] *v.* be, belong, couch, dwell, exist, extend, inhere, laze, loll, lounge, recline, remain, repose, rest, slump, sprawl, stretch out.

life *n.* activity, animation, autobiography, behavior, being, biography, breath, brio, career, conduct, confessions, continuance, course, creatures, duration, élan vital, energy, entity, essence, existence, fauna, flora and fauna, get-up-and-go, go, growth, heart, high spirits, history, life story, life-blood, life-style, lifetime, liveliness, memoirs, oomph, organisms, sentience, soul, span, sparkle, spirit, story, the world, this mortal coil, time, verve, viability, vigor, vita, vital flame, vital spark, vitality, vivacity, way of life, wildlife, zest.

lift[1] *v.* advance, ameliorate, annul, appropriate, arrest, ascend, boost, buoy up, cancel, climb, collar, copy, countermand, crib, dignify, disappear, disperse, dissipate, draw up, elevate, end, enhance, exalt, half-inch, heft, hoist, improve, mount, nab, nick, pick up, pilfer,

pinch, pirate, plagiarize, pocket, promote, purloin, raise, rear, relax, remove, rescind, revoke, rise, steal, stop, take, terminate, thieve, up, upgrade, uplift, upraise, vanish.
antonyms drop, fall, impose, lower.
n. boost, encouragement, fillip, pick-me-up, reassurance, shot in the arm, spur, uplift.
antonym discouragement.

lift[2] *n.* drive, hitch, ride, run, transport.

light[1] *n.* beacon, blaze, brightness, brilliance, bulb, candle, cockcrow, dawn, day, daybreak, daylight, daytime, effulgence, flame, flare, flash, glare, gleam, glim, glint, glow, illumination, incandescence, lambency, lamp, lampad, lantern, lighter, lighthouse, luminescence, luminosity, luster, match, morn, morning, phosphorescence, radiance, ray, refulgence, scintillation, shine, sparkle, star, sunrise, sunshine, taper, torch, window, Yang.
antonym darkness.
v. animate, beacon, brighten, cheer, fire, floodlight, ignite, illuminate, illumine, inflame, irradiate, kindle, light up, lighten, put on, set alight, set fire to, switch on, turn on.
antonyms darken, extinguish.
adj. bleached, blond, bright, brilliant, faded, faint, fair, glowing, illuminated, lightful, lightsome, lucent, luminous, lustrous, pale, pastel, shining, sunny, well-lit.
antonym dark.

light[2] *n.* angle, approach, aspect, attitude, awareness, clue, comprehension, context, elucidation, enlightenment, example, exemplar, explanation, hint, illustration, information, insight, interpretation, knowledge, model, paragon, point of view, slant, understanding, viewpoint.

light[3] *adj.* agile, airy, amusing, animated, blithe, buoyant, carefree, cheerful, cheery, crumbly, delicate, delirious, digestible, diverting, dizzy, easy, effortless, entertaining, facile, faint, fickle, flimsy, friable, frivolous, frugal, funny, gay, gentle, giddy, graceful, humorous, idle, imponderous, inconsequential, inconsiderable, indistinct, insignificant, insubstantial, light-footed, light-headed, light-hearted, lightweight, lithe, lively, loose, manageable, merry, mild, minute, moderate, modest, nimble, pleasing, porous, portable, reeling, restricted, sandy, scanty, simple, slight, small, soft, spongy, sprightly, sunny, superficial, thin, tiny, trifling, trivial, unchaste, undemanding, underweight, unexacting, unheeding, unsteady, unsubstantial, untaxing, volatile, wanton, weak, witty, worthless.
antonyms clumsy, harsh, heavy, important, sad, severe, sober, solid, stiff.

lighten[1] *v.* beacon, brighten, illume, illuminate, illumine, light up, shine.
antonym darken.

lighten[2] *v.* alleviate, ameliorate, assuage, brighten, buoy up, cheer, disburden, disencumber, ease, elate, encourage, facilitate, gladden, hearten, inspire, inspirit, lessen, lift, mitigate, perk up, reduce, relieve, revive, unload, uplift.
antonyms burden, depress, oppress.

light-hearted *adj.* blithe, blithesome, bright, carefree, cheerful, effervescent, elated, frolicsome, gay, glad, gleeful, happy-go-lucky, insouciant, jocund, jolly, jovial, joyful, joyous, light-spirited, merry, perky, playful, sunny, untroubled, upbeat.
antonym sad.

like[1] *adj.* akin, alike, allied, analogous, approximating, cognate, corresponding, equivalent, homologous, identical, parallel, related, relating, resembling, same, similar.
antonym unlike.
n. counterpart, equal, fellow, match, opposite number, parallel, peer, twin.
prep. in the same manner as, on the lines of, similar to.

like[2] *v.* admire, adore, appreciate, approve, care to, cherish, choose, choose to, delight in, desire, dig, enjoy, esteem, fancy, feel inclined, go a bundle on, go for, hold dear, love, prefer, prize, relish, revel in, select, take a shine to, take kindly to, take to, want, wish.
antonym dislike.
n. favorite, liking, love, partiality, penchant, poison, predilection, preference.
antonym dislike.

likely *adj.* acceptable, agreeable, anticipated, appropriate, apt, befitting, believable, bright, credible, disposed, expected, fair, favorite, feasible, fit, foreseeable, hopeful, inclined, liable, odds-on, on the cards, plausible, pleasing, possible, predictable, probable, promising, prone, proper, qualified, reasonable, suitable, tending, up-and-coming, verisimilar.
antonyms unlikely, unsuitable.
adv. doubtlessly, in all probability, like as not, like enough, no doubt, odds on, presumably, probably, very like.

likeness *n.* affinity, appearance, copy, correspondence, counterpart, delineation, depiction, effigies, effigy, facsimile, form, guise, image, model, photograph, picture, portrait, replica, representation, reproduction, resemblance, semblance, similarity, similitude, simulacrum, study.
antonym unlikeness.

likewise *adv.* also, besides, by the same token, eke, further, furthermore, in addition, moreover, similarly, too.
antonym contrariwise.

liking *n.* affection, affinity, appreciation, attraction, bent, bias, desire, favor, fondness, inclination, love, partiality, penchant, predilection, preference, proneness, propensity, satisfaction, soft spot, stomach, taste, tendency, weakness.
antonym dislike.

limb *n.* appendage, arm, bough, branch, extension, extremity, fork, leg, member, offshoot, part, projection, ramus, spur, wing.

limber *adj.* agile, elastic, flexible, flexile, graceful, lissom, lithe, loose-jointed, loose-limbed, plastic, pliable, pliant, supple. *antonym* stiff.

limelight *n.* attention, big time, celebrity, fame, prominence, public notice, publicity, recognition, renown, stardom, the public eye, the spotlight.

limit *n.* bitter end, border, bound, boundary, bourne(e), brim, brink, ceiling, check, compass, confines, curb, cut-off point, deadline, edge, end, extent, frontier, limitation, maximum, mete, obstruction, outrance, perimeter, periphery, precinct, restraint, restriction, rim, saturation point, termination, terminus, terminus a quo, terminus ad quem, threshold, ultimate, utmost, verge.
v. bound, check, circumscribe, condition, confine, constrain, curb, delimit, delimitate, demarcate, fix, hem in, hinder, ration, restrain, restrict, specify.
antonyms extend, free.

limp[1] *v.* dot, falter, halt, hamble, hirple, hitch, hobble, hop, shamble, shuffle.
n. claudication, hitch, hobble, lameness.

limp[2] *adj.* debilitated, drooping, enervated, exhausted, flabby, flaccid, flexible, flexile, floppy, hypotonic, lax, lethargic, limber, loose, pliable, pooped, relaxed, slack, soft, spent, tired, toneless, weak, worn out.
antonym strong.

limpid *adj.* bright, clear, comprehensible, crystal-clear, crystalline, glassy, hyaline, intelligible, lucid, pellucid, pure, still, translucent, transparent, unruffled, untroubled.
antonyms muddy, ripply, turbid, unintelligible.

line[1] *n.* band, bar, border, borderline, boundary, cable, chain, channel, column, configuration, contour, cord, crease, crocodile, crow's foot, dash, demarcation, disposition, edge, features, figure, filament, file, firing line, formation, front, front line, frontier, furrow, groove, limit, mark, outline, position, procession, profile, queue, rank, rope, row, rule, score, scratch, sequence, series, silhouette, stipe, strand, streak, string, stroke, tail, thread, trail, trenches, underline, wire, wrinkle.
v. border, bound, crease, cut, draw, edge, fringe, furrow, hatch, inscribe, mark, rank, rim, rule, score, skirt, verge.

line up align, arrange, array, assemble, dispose, engage, fall in, form ranks, hire, lay on, marshal, obtain, order, organize, prepare, procure, produce, queue up, range, regiment, secure, straighten.

line[2] *n.* activity, approach, area, avenue, axis, belief, business, calling, course, course of action, department, direction, employment, field, forte, ideology, interest, job, line of country, method, occupation, path, policy, position, practice, procedure, profession, province, pursuit, route, scheme, specialism, specialization, specialty, system, track, trade, trajectory, vocation.

line[3] *n.* ancestry, breed, family, lineage, pedigree, race, stirps, stock, strain, succession.

line[4] *n.* card, clue, hint, indication, information, lead, letter, memo, memorandum, message, note, postcard, report, word.

line[5] *v.* ceil, cover, encase, face, fill, reinforce, strengthen, stuff.

lineage *n.* ancestors, ancestry, birth, breed, descendants, descent, extraction, family, forebears, forefathers, genealogy, heredity, house, line, offspring, pedigree, progeny, race, stirp(s), stock, succession.

linger *v.* abide, continue, dally, dawdle, delay, dilly-dally, endure, hang around, hang on, hold out, idle, lag, last out, loiter, persist, procrastinate, remain, stay, stop, survive, tarry, wait.
antonyms leave, rush.

lingo *n.* argot, cant, dialect, idiom, jargon, language, parlance, patois, patter, speech, talk, terminology, tongue, vernacular, vocabulary.

link *n.* association, attachment, bond, communication, component, connection, constituent, division, element, joint, knot, liaison, member, part, piece, relationship, tie, tie-up, union.
v. associate, attach, bind, bracket, catenate, concatenate, connect, couple, fasten, identify, join, relate, tie, unite, yoke.
antonyms separate, unfasten.

lip[1] *n.* border, brim, brink, edge, margin, rim, verge.

lip[2] *n.* backchat, cheek, effrontery, impertinence, impudence, insolence, rudeness, sauce.
antonym politeness.

liquid *n.* drink, fluid, juice, liquor, lotion, potation, sap, solution.
adj. aqueous, clear, convertible, dulcet, flowing, fluid, limpid, liquefied, mellifluent, mellifluous, melted, molten, negotiable, running, runny, serous, shining, smooth, soft, sweet, thawed, translucent, transparent, watery, wet.
antonyms harsh, solid.

liquidate *v.* abolish, annihilate, annul, assassinate, bump off, cancel, cash, clear, destroy, discharge, dispatch, dissolve, do away with, do in, eliminate, exterminate, finish off, honor, kill, massacre, murder, pay, pay off, realize, remove, rub out, sell off, sell up, settle, silence, square, terminate, wipe out.

liquor[1] *n.* aguardiente, alcohol, booze, drink, fire-water, grog, hard stuff, hooch, intoxicant, juice, jungle juice, potation, rotgut, spirits, strong drink, tape.

liquor[2] *n.* broth, essence, extract, gravy, infusion, juice, liquid, stock.

lissom(e) *adj.* agile, flexible, graceful, light, limber, lithe, lithesome, loose-jointed, loose-limbed, nimble, pliable, pliant, supple, willowy.
antonym stiff.

list[1] *n.* catalog, directory, enumeration, file, index, inventory, invoice, leet, listing, litany, matricula, record, register, roll, schedule, series, syllabus, table, tabulation, tally.

v. alphabeticize, bill, book, catalog, enrol, enter, enumerate, file, index, itemize, note, record, register, schedule, set down, tabulate, write down.

list[2] *v.* cant, careen, heel, heel over, incline, lean, slope, tilt, tip.
n. cant, leaning, slant, slope, tilt.

listen *v.* attend, get a load of, give ear, give heed to, hang on (someone's) words, hang on (someone's) lips, hark, hear, hearken, heed, keep one's ears open, lend an ear, mind, obey, observe, pay attention, pin back one's ears, prick up one's ears, take notice.

listless *adj.* apathetic, bored, depressed, enervated, ennuyed, heavy, impassive, inattentive, indifferent, indolent, inert, languid, languishing, lethargic, lifeless, limp, lymphatic, mopish, sluggish, spiritless, supine, torpid, uninterested, vacant.
antonym lively.

literal *adj.* accurate, actual, boring, close, colorless, down-to-earth, dull, exact, factual, faithful, genuine, matter-of-fact, plain, prosaic, prosy, real, simple, strict, true, unexaggerated, unimaginative, uninspired, unvarnished, verbatim, word-for-word.
antonym loose.

literally *adv.* actually, closely, exactly, faithfully, literatim, plainly, precisely, really, simply, strictly, to the letter, truly, verbatim, word for word.
antonym loosely.

literary *adj.* bookish, cultivated, cultured, erudite, formal, learned, lettered, literate, refined, scholarly, well-read.
antonym illiterate.

literature *n.* belles-lettres, blurb, brochure(s), bumf, circular(s), hand-out(s), information, leaflet(s), letters, lore, pamphlet(s), paper(s), writings.

lithe *adj.* double-jointed, flexible, flexile, limber, lissom(e), lithesome, loose-jointed, loose-limbed, pliable, pliant, supple.
antonym stiff.

litigious *adj.* argumentative, belligerent, contentious, disputable, disputatious, quarrelsome.
antonym easy-going.

litter[1] *n.* clutter, confusion, debris, detritus, disarray, disorder, fragments, jumble, mess, muck, refuse, rubbish, scatter, scoria, shreds, untidiness, wastage.
v. bestrew, clutter, derange, disarrange, disorder, mess up, scatter, strew.
antonym tidy.

litter[2] *n.* brood, family, offspring, progeny, quiverful, young.

litter[3] *n.* couch, palanquin, stretcher.

little *adj.* babyish, base, brief, cheap, diminutive, dwarf, elfin, fleeting, hasty, immature, inconsiderable, infant, infinitesimal, insignificant, insufficient, junior, Lilliputian, meager, mean, microscopic, miniature, minor, minute, negligible, paltry, passing, petite, petty, piccaninny, pintsize(d), pygmy, scant, short, short-lived, skimpy, slender, small, sparse, tiny, transient, trifling, trivial, undeveloped, unimportant, wee, young.
antonyms important, large, long.
adv. barely, hardly, infrequently, rarely, scarcely, seldom.
antonyms frequently, greatly.
n. bit, dab, dash, drib, fragment, hint, modicum, particle, pinch, snippet, speck, spot, taste, touch, trace, trifle.
antonym lot.

liturgy *n.* celebration, ceremony, form, formula, office, rite, ritual, sacrament, service, usage, worship.

live[1] *v.* abide, breathe, continue, draw breath, dwell, earn a living, endure, exist, fare, feed, get along, hang out, inhabit, last, lead, lodge, make ends meet, pass, persist, prevail, remain, reside, settle, stay, subsist, survive.
antonyms cease, die.

live[2] *adj.* active, alert, alight, alive, animate, blazing, breathing, brisk, burning, connected, controversial, current, dynamic, earnest, energetic, existent, glowing, hot, ignited, lively, living, pertinent, pressing, prevalent, relevant, sentient, smoldering, topical, unsettled, vigorous, vital, vivid, wide-awake.
antonyms apathetic, dead, out.

livelihood *n.* employment, income, job, living, maintenance, means, occupation, subsistence, support, sustenance, work.

lively *adj.* active, agile, alert, animated, astir, blithe, blithesome, breezy, bright, brisk, buckish, bustling, busy, buxom, buzzing, canty, cheerful, chipper, chirpy, colorful, crowded, energetic, eventful, exciting, forceful, frisky, frolicsome, galliard, gay, invigorating, keen, lifesome, lightsome, merry, moving, nimble, perky, quick, racy, refreshing, skittish, sparkling, spirited, sprightly, spry, stimulating, stirring, swinging, tit(t)upy, vigorous, vivacious, vivid, zippy.
antonyms apathetic, inactive, moribund.

livid[1] *adj.* angry, beside oneself, boiling, enraged, exasperated, fuming, furibund, furious, incensed, indignant, infuriated, irate, ireful, mad, outraged, waxy.
antonym calm.

livid[2] *adj.* angry, ashen, black-and-blue, blanched, bloodless, bruised, contused, discolored, doughy, grayish, leaden, pale, pallid, pasty, purple, wan, waxen, waxy.
antonyms healthy, rosy.

living *adj.* active, alive, animated, breathing, existing, live, lively, strong, vigorous, vital.
antonyms dead, sluggish.
n. being, benefice, existence, income, job, life, livelihood, maintenance, occupation, profession, property, subsistence, support, sustenance, way of life, work.

load *n.* affliction, albatross, bale, burden, cargo, consignment, encumbrance, freight, goods, lading, millstone, onus, oppression, pressure, shipment, trouble, weight, worry.
v. adulterate, burden, charge, cram, doctor, drug,

encumber, fill, fortify, freight, hamper, heap, lade, oppress, overburden, pack, pile, prime, saddle with, stack, stuff, trouble, weigh down, weight, worry.

loafer *n.* beachcomber, bludger, bum, bummer, burn, corner-boy, do-nothing, drone, idler, layabout, lazybones, lounge-lizard, lounger, ne'er-do-well, shirker, skiver, sluggard, time-waster, wastrel. *antonym* worker.

loan *n.* accommodation, advance, allowance, calque, credit, lend-lease, loan translation, loan-word, mortgage, touch.
v. accommodate, advance, allow, credit, lend, let out, oblige.
antonym borrow.

loath *adj.* against, averse, backward, counter, disinclined, grudging, hesitant, indisposed, opposed, reluctant, resisting, unwilling.
antonym willing.

loathe *v.* abhor, abominate, despise, detest, dislike, execrate, hate, keck.
antonym like.

loathsome *adj.* abhorrent, abominable, detestable, disgusting, execrable, hateful, horrible, loathful, nasty, nauseating, obnoxious, odious, offensive, repellent, repugnant, repulsive, revolting, vile.
antonym likeable.

lob *v.* chuck, fling, heave, launch, lift, loft, pitch, shy, throw, toss.

lobby[1] *v.* call for, campaign for, demand, influence, persuade, press for, pressure, promote, pull strings, push for, solicit, urge.
n. ginger group, pressure group.

lobby[2] *n.* anteroom, corridor, entrance hall, foyer, hall, hallway, passage, passageway, porch, vestibule, waiting-room.

local *adj.* community, confined, district, limited, narrow, neighborhood, parish, parochial, provincial, pump, regional, restricted, small-town, vernacular, vicinal.
antonym far-away.
n. denizen, inhabitant, native, resident, yokel.
antonym incomer.

locality *n.* area, district, locale, location, neck of the woods, neighborhood, place, position, region, scene, settings, site, spot, vicinity, zone.

locate *v.* detect, discover, establish, find, fix, identify, lay one's hands on, pin-point, place, put, run to earth, seat, set, settle, situate, track down, unearth.

location *n.* bearings, locale, locus, place, point, position, site, situation, spot, ubiety, venue, whereabouts.

lock[1] *n.* bolt, clasp, fastening, padlock, sneck.
v. bolt, clasp, clench, close, clutch, disengage, embrace, encircle, enclose, engage, entangle, entwine, fasten, grapple, grasp, hug, join, latch, link, mesh, press, seal, secure, shut, sneck, unite, unlock.

lock out ban, bar, debar, exclude, keep out, ostracize, refuse admittance to, shut out.

lock together interdigitate, interlock.

lock up cage, close up, confine, detain, enlock, imprison, incarcerate, jail, pen, secure, shut, shut in, shut up.
antonym free.

lock[2] *n.* curl, plait, ringlet, strand, tress, tuft.

locomotion *n.* action, ambulation, headway, motion, movement, moving, progress, progression, travel, traveling.

locution *n.* accent, articulation, cliché, collocation, diction, expression, idiom, inflection, intonation, phrase, phrasing, style, term, turn of phrase, wording.

lodge *n.* abode, assemblage, association, branch, cabin, chalet, chapter, club, cot, cot-house, cottage, den, ganghut, gatehouse, group, haunt, house, hunting-lodge, hut, lair, meeting-place, retreat, shelter, society.
v. accommodate, billet, board, deposit, dig, entertain, file, get stuck, harbor, imbed, implant, lay, place, put, put on record, put up, quarter, register, room, set, shelter, sojourn, stay, stick, stop, submit.

lodger *n.* boarder, guest, inmate, paying guest, renter, resident, roomer, tenant.

lofty *adj.* arrogant, condescending, dignified, disdainful, distinguished, elevated, esteemed, exalted, grand, haughty, high, high and mighty, illustrious, imperial, imposing, lordly, majestic, noble, patronizing, proud, raised, renowned, sky-high, snooty, soaring, stately, sublime, supercilious, superior, tall, toffee-nosed, towering. *antonyms* humble, low(ly), modest.

log[1] *n.* billet, block, bole, chunk, loggat, stump, timber, trunk.

log[2] *n.* account, chart, daybook, diary, journal, listing, logbook, record, tally.
v. book, chart, note, record, register, report, tally, write down, write in, write up.

logic *n.* argumentation, deduction, dialectic(s), ratiocination, rationale, rationality, reason, reasoning, sense.

logistics *n.* co-ordination, engineering, management, masterminding, orchestration, organization, planning, plans, strategy.

loiter *v.* dally, dawdle, delay, dilly-dally, hang about, idle, lag, lallygag, linger, loaf, loll, lollygag, mooch, mouch, saunter, skulk, stroll.

loll *v.* dangle, depend, droop, drop, flap, flop, hang, lean, loaf, lounge, recline, relax, sag, slouch, slump, sprawl.

lone *adj.* deserted, isolated, lonesome, one, only, separate, separated, single, sole, solitary, unaccompanied, unattached, unattended.
antonym accompanied.

loneliness *n.* aloneness, desolation, forlornness, friendlessness, isolation, lonesomeness, seclusion, solitariness, solitude.

lonely *adj.* abandoned, alone, apart, companionless, destitute, estranged, forlorn, forsaken, friendless, isolated, lonely-heart, lonesome, outcast, out-of-the-way, remote, secluded, sequestered, solitary, unfrequented, uninhabited, untrodden.

loner *n.* hermit, individualist, lone wolf, maverick, outsider, pariah, recluse, solitary, solitudinarian.

lonesome *adj.* cheerless, companionless, deserted, desolate, dreary, forlorn, friendless, gloomy, isolated, lone, lonely, solitary.

long *adj.* dragging, elongated, expanded, expansive, extended, extensive, far-reaching, interminable, late, lengthy, lingering, long-drawn-out, marathon, prolonged, protracted, slow, spread out, stretched, sustained, tardy.
antonyms abbreviated, brief, fleeting, short.

long-standing *adj.* abiding, enduring, established, fixed, hallowed, long-established, long-lasting, long-lived, time-honored, traditional.

long-winded *adj.* circumlocutory, diffuse, discursive, garrulous, lengthy, long-drawn-out, overlong, prolix, prolonged, rambling, repetitious, tedious, verbose, voluble, wordy.
antonyms brief, compact, curt, terse.

look *v.* appear, behold, consider, contemplate, display, evidence, examine, exhibit, eye, gape, gawk, gawp, gaze, get a load of, glance, goggle, inspect, observe, ogle, peep, regard, rubberneck, scan, scrutinize, see, seem, show, stare, study, survey, view, watch.
n. air, appearance, aspect, bearing, cast, complexion, countenance, decko, demeanor, effect, examination, expression, eyeful, eye-glance, face, fashion, gaze, glance, glimpse, guise, inspection, look-see, manner, mien, observation, once-over, peek, review, semblance, sight, squint, survey, view.

loom *v.* appear, bulk, dominate, emerge, hang over, hover, impend, materialize, menace, mount, overhang, overshadow, overtop, rise, soar, take shape, threaten, tower.

loop *n.* arc, bend, circle, coil, convolution, curl, curve, eyelet, hoop, kink, loophole, noose, ring, spiral, turn, twirl, twist, whorl.
v. bend, braid, circle, coil, connect, curl, curve round, encircle, fold, gird, join, knot, roll, spiral, turn, twist.

loose[1] *adj.* baggy, crank, diffuse, disconnected, disordered, easy, floating, free, hanging, ill-defined, imprecise, inaccurate, indefinite, indistinct, inexact, insecure, loosened, movable, rambling, random, relaxed, released, shaky, slack, slackened, sloppy, solute, unattached, unbound, unconfined, unfastened, unfettered, unrestricted, unsecured, untied, vague, wobbly.
antonyms close, compact, precise, strict, taut, tense, tight.
v. absolve, detach, disconnect, disengage, ease, free, let go, liberate, loosen, release, set free, slacken, unbind, unbrace, unclasp, uncouple, undo, unfasten, unhand, unleash, unlock, unloose, unmew, unmoor, unpen, untie.
antonyms bind, fasten, fix, secure.

loose[2] *adj.* abandoned, careless, debauched, disreputable, dissipated, dissolute, fast, heedless, immoral, imprudent, lax, lewd, libertine, licentious, negligent, profligate, promiscuous, rash, thoughtless, unchaste, unmindful, wanton.
antonyms strict, stringent, tight.

loosen *v.* deliver, detach, free, let go, let out, liberate, release, separate, set free, slacken, unbind, undo, unfasten, unloose, unloosen, unstick, untie.
antonym tighten.

loot *n.* boodle, booty, cache, goods, haul, plunder, prize, riches, spoils, swag.
v. burglarize, despoil, maraud, pillage, plunder, raid, ransack, ravage, rifle, rob, sack.

lope *v.* bound, canter, gallop, lollop, run, spring, stride.

lop-sided *adj.* askew, asymmetrical, awry, cockeyed, crooked, disproportionate, ill-balanced, off balance, one-sided, out of true, squint, tilting, unbalanced, unequal, uneven, warped.
antonyms balanced, straight, symmetrical.

loquacious *adj.* babbling, blathering, chattering, chatty, gabby, garrulous, gassy, gossipy, multiloquent, multiloquous, talkative, voluble, wordy.
antonyms succinct, taciturn, terse.

lord *n.* baron, commander, count, daimio, duke, earl, governor, Herr, king, leader, liege, liege-lord, master, monarch, noble, nobleman, overlord, peer, potentate, prince, ruler, seigneur, seignior, sovereign, superior, suzerain, viscount.

lore *n.* beliefs, doctrine, erudition, experience, know-how, knowledge, learning, letters, mythus, saws, sayings, scholarship, schooling, teaching, traditions, wisdom.

lose *v.* capitulate, come a cropper, come to grief, consume, default, deplete, displace, dissipate, dodge, drain, drop, duck, elude, escape, evade, exhaust, expend, fail, fall short, forfeit, forget, get the worst of, give (someone) the slip, lap, lavish, leave behind, lose out on, misfile, mislay, misplace, miss, misspend, outdistance, outrun, outstrip, overtake, pass, pass up, shake off, slip away, squander, stray from, suffer defeat, take a licking, throw off, use up, wander from, waste, yield.
antonyms gain, make, win.

loss *n.* bereavement, cost, damage, debit, debt, defeat, deficiency, deficit, depletion, deprivation, destruction, detriment, disadvantage, disappearance, failure, forfeiture, harm, hurt, impairment, injury, losing, losings, misfortune, privation, ruin, shrinkage, squandering, waste, write-off.
antonyms benefit, gain.

lost *adj.* abandoned, abolished, absent, absorbed, abstracted, adrift, annihilated, astray, baffled, bewildered, confused, consumed, corrupt, damned, demolished, depraved, destroyed, devastated, disappeared, disoriented, dissipated, dissolute, distracted, dreamy, engrossed, entranced, eradicated, exterminated, fallen, forfeited, frittered away, irreclaimable, licentious, misapplied, misdirected, mislaid, misplaced, missed, missing, misspent, misused, mystified, obliterated,

off-course, off-track, perished, perplexed, preoccupied, profligate, puzzled, rapt, ruined, spellbound, squandered, strayed, unrecallable, unrecapturable, unrecoverable, untraceable, vanished, wanton, wasted, wayward, wiped out, wrecked.
antonym found.

lot *n.* accident, allowance, assortment, batch, chance, collection, consignment, crowd, cut, destiny, doom, fate, fortune, group, hazard, jing-bang, parcel, part, percentage, piece, plight, portion, quantity, quota, ration, set, share, weird.

lottery *n.* chance, draw, gamble, hazard, raffle, risk, sweep-stake, toss-up, uncertainty, venture.

loud *adj.* blaring, blatant, boisterous, booming, brash, brassy, brazen, clamorous, coarse, crass, crude, deafening, ear-piercing, ear-splitting, flamboyant, flashy, garish, gaudy, glaring, high-sounding, loud-mouthed, lurid, noisy, offensive, ostentatious, piercing, raucous, resounding, rowdy, showy, sonorous, stentorian, streperous, strepitant, strident, strong, tasteless, tawdry, thundering, tumultuous, turbulent, vehement, vocal, vociferous, vulgar.
antonyms low, quiet, soft.

lounge *v.* dawdle, idle, kill time, laze, lie about, lie back, loaf, loiter, loll, potter, recline, relax, slump, sprawl, take it easy, waste time.
n. day-room, drawing-room, parlor, sitting-room.

louring, lowering *adj.* black, brooding, browning, clouded, cloudy, dark, darkening, forbidding, foreboding, gloomy, glowering, gray, grim, heavy, impending, menacing, minatory, ominous, overcast, scowling, sullen, surly, threatening.

lousy *adj.* awful, bad, base, contemptible, crap, despicable, dirty, hateful, inferior, lice-infested, lice-ridden, low, mean, miserable, no good, pedicular, pediculous, poor, rotten, second-rate, shoddy, slovenly, terrible, trashy, vicious, vile.
antonyms excellent, superb.

lovable *adj.* adorable, amiable, attractive, captivating, charming, cuddly, delightful, enchanting, endearing, engaging, fetching, likable, lovely, pleasing, sweet, taking, winning, winsome.
antonym hateful.

love *v.* adore, adulate, appreciate, cherish, delight in, desire, dote on, enjoy, fancy, hold dear, idolize, like, prize, relish, savor, take pleasure in, think the world of, treasure, want, worship.
antonyms detest, hate, loathe.
n. adoration, adulation, affection, agape, aloha, amity, amorosity, amorousness, ardor, attachment, delight, devotion, enjoyment, fondness, friendship, inclination, infatuation, liking, partiality, passion, rapture, regard, relish, soft spot, taste, tenderness, warmth, weakness.
antonyms detestation, hate, loathing.

loveless *adj.* cold, cold-hearted, disliked, forsaken, friendless, frigid, hard, heartless, icy, insensitive, lovelorn, passionless, unappreciated, uncherished, unfeeling, unfriendly, unloved, unloving, unresponsive, unvalued.
antonym passionate.

lovely *adj.* admirable, adorable, agreeable, amiable, attractive, beautiful, captivating, charming, comely, delightful, enchanting, engaging, enjoyable, exquisite, graceful, gratifying, handsome, idyllic, nice, pleasant, pleasing, pretty, sweet, taking, winning.
antonyms hideous, ugly, unlovely.

lover *n.* admirer, amoretto, amorist, amoroso, beau, beloved, bon ami, boyfriend, Casanova, fancy man, fancy woman, fiancé(e), flame, gigolo, girlfriend, inamorata, inamorato, mistress, paramour, philanderer, suitor, swain, sweetheart.

loving *adj.* affectionate, amative, amatorial, amatorian, amatorious, amorous, ardent, cordial, dear, demonstrative, devoted, doting, fond, friendly, kind, passionate, solicitous, tender, warm, warm-hearted.

low[1] *adj.* abject, base, base-born, blue, brassed off, browned off, cheap, coarse, common, contemptible, crude, dastardly, debilitated, deep, deficient, degraded, dejected, depleted, depraved, depressed, despicable, despondent, disgraceful, disheartened, dishonorable, disreputable, down, down in the dumps, downcast, dying, economical, exhausted, fed up, feeble, forlorn, frail, gloomy, glum, gross, humble, hushed, ignoble, ill, ill-bred, inadequate, inexpensive, inferior, insignificant, little, low-born, low-grade, lowly, low-lying, meager, mean, mediocre, meek, menial, miserable, moderate, modest, morose, muffled, muted, nasty, obscene, obscure, paltry, plain, plebeian, poor, prostrate, puny, quiet, reasonable, reduced, rough, rude, sad, scant, scurvy, second-rate, servile, shallow, shoddy, short, simple, sinking, small, soft, sordid, sparse, squat, stricken, stunted, subdued, substandard, sunken, trifling, unbecoming, undignified, unhappy, unpretentious, unrefined, unworthy, vile, vulgar, weak, whispered, worthless.
antonyms elevated, high, lofty, noble.

lower[1] *adj.* inferior, insignificant, junior, lesser, low-level, lowly, minor, secondary, second-class, smaller, subordinate, subservient, under, unimportant.
v. abase, abate, belittle, condescend, couch, curtail, cut, debase, decrease, degrade, deign, demean, demolish, depress, devalue, diminish, discredit, disgrace, downgrade, drop, fall, humble, humiliate, lessen, let down, minimize, moderate, prune, raze, reduce, sink, slash, soften, stoop, submerge, take down, tone down.
antonyms elevate, increase, raise, rise.

lower[2] *see* **lour**.

low-key *adj.* low-pitched, muffled, muted, quiet, restrained, slight, soft, subdued, understated.

lowly *adj.* average, common, docile, dutiful, homespun, humble, ignoble, inferior, low-born, mean, mean-born,

meek, mild, modest, obscure, ordinary, plain, plebeian, poor, proletarian, simple, submissive, subordinate, unassuming, unexalted, unpretentious.
antonyms lofty, noble.

loyal *adj.* attached, constant, dependable, devoted, dutiful, faithful, honest, leal, patriotic, sincere, staunch, steadfast, true, true-blue, true-hearted, trustworthy, trusty, unswerving, unwavering.
antonyms disloyal, traitorous.

loyalty *n.* allegiance, constancy, dependability, devotion, faithfulness, fealty, fidelity, honesty, lealty, patriotism, reliability, sincerity, staunchness, steadfastness, true-heartedness, trueness, trustiness, trustworthiness.
antonyms disloyalty, treachery.

lubricate *v.* grease, lard, oil, smear, wax.

lucid *adj.* beaming, bright, brilliant, clear, clear-cut, clear-headed, compos mentis, comprehensible, crystalline, diaphanous, distinct, effulgent, evident, explicit, glassy, gleaming, intelligible, limpid, luminous, obvious, pellucid, perspicuous, plain, pure, radiant, rational, reasonable, resplendent, sane, sensible, shining, sober, sound, translucent, transparent.
antonyms dark, murky, unclear.

luck *n.* accident, blessing, break, chance, destiny, fate, fluke, fortuity, fortune, godsend, good fortune, hap, happenstance, hazard, jam, joss, prosperity, serendipity, stroke, success, windfall.
antonym misfortune.

lucky *adj.* advantageous, adventitious, auspicious, blessed, canny, charmed, favored, fluky, fortuitous, fortunate, jammy, opportune, propitious, prosperous, providential, serendipitous, successful, timely.
antonyms luckless, unlucky.

lucky dip bran tub, grab-bag.

lucrative *adj.* advantageous, fecund, fertile, fruitful, gainful, paying, productive, profitable, remunerative, well-paid.
antonym unprofitable.

ludicrous *adj.* absurd, amusing, burlesque, comic, comical, crazy, drôle, droll, farcical, funny, incongruous, laughable, nonsensical, odd, outlandish, preposterous, ridiculous, risible, silly, zany.

lug *v.* carry, drag, haul, heave, hump, humph, pull, tote, tow, yank.

lugubrious *adj.* dismal, doleful, dreary, funereal, gloomy, glum, melancholy, morose, mournful, sad, sepulchral, serious, somber, sorrowful, Wertherian, woebegone, woeful.
antonyms cheerful, jovial, merry.

lukewarm *adj.* apathetic, cold, cool, half-hearted, indifferent, laodicean, Laodicean, lew, phlegmatic, tepid, unconcerned, unenthusiastic, uninterested, unresponsive, warm.

lull *v.* abate, allay, calm, cease, compose, decrease, diminish, dwindle, ease off, hush, let up, lullaby, moderate, pacify, quell, quiet, quieten down, sedate, slacken, soothe, still, subdue, subside, tranquilize, wane.
antonym agitate.
n. calm, calmness, hush, let-up, pause, peace, quiet, respite, silence, stillness, tranquility.
antonym agitation.

lumber[1] *n.* bits and pieces, clutter, jumble, junk, odds and ends, refuse, rubbish, trash, trumpery.
v. burden, charge, encumber, hamper, impose, land, load, saddle.

lumber[2] *v.* clump, galumph, plod, shamble, shuffle, stump, trudge, trundle, waddle.

luminous *adj.* bright, brilliant, glowing, illuminated, lighted, lit, lucent, luminescent, luminiferous, lustrous, radiant, resplendent, shining, vivid.

lump[1] *n.* ball, bulge, bump, bunch, cake, chuck, chump, chunk, clod, cluster, cyst, dab, daud, dod, gob, gobbet, group, growth, hunch, hunk, (k)nub, (k)nubble, lob, mass, nugget, piece, protrusion, protuberance, spot, swelling, tuber, tumescence, tumor, wedge, wen, wodge.
v. coalesce, collect, combine, consolidate, group, mass, unite.

lump[2] *v.* bear (with), brook, endure, put up with, stand, stomach, suffer, swallow, take, thole, tolerate.

lunacy *n.* aberration, absurdity, craziness, dementia, derangement, folly, foolhardiness, foolishness, idiocy, imbecility, insanity, madness, mania, moon-madness, moonraking, psychosis, senselessness, stupidity, tomfoolery.
antonym sanity.

lunge *v.* bound, charge, cut, dash, dive, fall upon, grab (at), hit (at), jab, leap, pitch into, plunge, poke, pounce, set upon, stab, strike (at), thrust.
n. charge, cut, jab, pass, pounce, spring, stab, swing, swipe, thrust, venue.

lurch *v.* heave, lean, list, pitch, reel, rock, roll, stagger, stumble, sway, tilt, totter, wallow, weave, welter.

lure *v.* allure, attract, beckon, decoy, draw, ensnare, entice, inveigle, invite, lead on, seduce, tempt, trepan.
n. allurement, attraction, bait, carrot, come-on, decoy, enticement, inducement, magnet, siren, song, temptation, train.

lurid *adj.* ashen, bloody, disgusting, exaggerated, fiery, flaming, ghastly, glaring, glowering, gory, graphic, grim, grisly, gruesome, intense, livid, loud, macabre, melodramatic, pale, pallid, revolting, sallow, sanguine, savage, sensational, shocking, startling, unrestrained, violent, vivid, wan.

lurk *v.* crouch, hide, hide out, lie in wait, lie low, prowl, skulk, slink, sneak, snook, snoop.

luscious *adj.* appetizing, delectable, delicious, honeyed, juicy, luxuriant, luxurious, mouth-watering, palatable, rich, savory, scrumptious, succulent, sweet, tasty, toothsome, yummy.
antonym austere.

lush *adj.* abundant, dense, elaborate, extravagant, flourishing, grand, green, juicy, lavish, luxuriant, luxurious, opulent, ornate, overgrown, palatial, plush, prolific, rank, ripe, ritzy, succulent, sumptuous, superabundant, teeming, tender, verdant.

lust *n.* appetence, appetency, appetite, avidity, carnality, concupiscence, covetousness, craving, cupidity, desire, greed, Kama, Kamadeva, lasciviousness, lechery, lewdness, libido, licentiousness, longing, passion, prurience, randiness, salaciousness, sensuality, thirst, wantonness.

luster *n.* brightness, brilliance, burnish, dazzle, distinction, effulgence, fame, gleam, glint, glitter, glory, gloss, glow, gorm, honor, illustriousness, lambency, luminousness, prestige, radiance, renown, resplendence, sheen, shimmer, shine, sparkle, water.

lustful *adj.* carnal, concupiscent, craving, goatish, hankering, horny, lascivious, lecherous, lewd, libidinous, licentious, passionate, prurient, randy, raunchy, ruttish, sensual, unchaste, venerous, wanton.

lusty *adj.* blooming, brawny, energetic, gutsy, hale, healthy, hearty, in fine fettle, muscular, powerful, red-blooded, robust, rugged, stalwart, stout, strapping, strong, sturdy, vigorous, virile.
antonyms effete, weak.

luxuriant *adj.* abundant, ample, baroque, copious, dense, elaborate, excessive, extravagant, exuberant, fancy, fecund, fertile, festooned, flamboyant, florid, flowery, lavish, lush, opulent, ornate, overflowing, plenteous, plentiful, prodigal, productive, profuse, prolific, rank, rich, riotous, rococo, sumptuous, superabundant, teeming, thriving.
antonyms barren, infertile.

luxurious *adj.* comfortable, costly, deluxe, epicurean, expensive, hedonistic, lavish, magnificent, opulent, pampered, plush, plushy, rich, ritzy, self-indulgent, sensual, splendid, sumptuous, sybaritic, voluptuous, well-appointed.
antonyms ascetic, austere, economical, frugal, scant(y), spartan.

luxury *n.* affluence, bliss, comfort, delight, dolce vita, enjoyment, extra, extravagance, flesh-pots, flesh-pottery, frill, gratification, hedonism, indulgence, milk and honey, non-essential, opulence, pleasure, richness, satisfaction, splendor, sumptuousness, treat, voluptuousness, well-being.
antonym essential.

lying *adj.* accumbent, deceitful, decumbent, dishonest, dissembling, double-dealing, duplicitous, false, guileful, mendacious, perfidious, treacherous, two-faced, untruthful.
antonyms honest, truthful.
n. deceit, dishonesty, dissimulation, double-dealing, duplicity, fabrication, falsity, fibbing, guile, mendacity, perjury, prevarication, pseudology, untruthfulness.
antonyms honesty, truthfulness.

lyrical *adj.* carried away, ecstatic, effusive, emotional, enthusiastic, expressive, impassioned, inspired, musical, passionate, poetic, rapturous, rhapsodic.

M

macabre *adj.* cadaverous, deathlike, deathly, dreadful, eerie, frightening, frightful, ghastly, ghostly, ghoulish, grim, grisly, gruesome, hideous, horrible, horrid, morbid, sick, weird.

macerate *v.* blend, liquefy, mash, pulp, soak, soften, steep.

Machiavellian *adj.* amoral, artful, astute, calculating, crafty, cunning, cynical, deceitful, designing, double-dealing, foxy, guileful, intriguing, opportunist, perfidious, scheming, shrewd, sly, underhand, unscrupulous, wily.

machine *n.* agency, agent, apparatus, appliance, automaton, contraption, contrivance, device, engine, gadget, gizmo, instrument, machinery, mechanism, organization, party, puppet, robot, set-up, structure, system, tool, zombi(e).

mad *adj.* abandoned, aberrant, absurd, agitated, angry, ardent, avid, bananas, barmy, bats, batty, berserk, boisterous, bonkers, crackers, crazed, crazy, cuckoo, daft, delirious, demented, deranged, devoted, distracted, dotty, ebullient, enamored, energetic, enraged, enthusiastic, exasperated, excited, fanatical, fond, foolhardy, foolish, frantic, frenetic, frenzied, fuming, furious, gay, have bats in the belfry, hooked, impassioned, imprudent, in a paddy, incensed, infatuated, infuriated, insane, irate, irrational, irritated, keen, livid, loony, loopy, ludicrous, lunatic, madcap, mental, moon-stricken, moon-struck, non compos mentis, nonsensical, nuts, nutty, off one's chump, off one's head, off one's nut, off one's rocker, off one's trolley, out of one's mind, possessed, preposterous, psychotic, rabid, raging, raving, resentful, riotous, round the bend, round the twist, screwball, screwy, senseless, unbalanced, uncontrolled, unhinged, unreasonable, unrestrained, unsafe, unsound, unstable, up the pole, waxy, wild, wrathful, zealous.
antonyms lucid, rational, sane.

madden *v.* annoy, craze, dement, dementate, derange, enrage, exasperate, incense, inflame, infuriate, irritate, provoke, unhinge, upset, vex.
antonyms calm, pacify, please.

madness *n.* abandon, aberration, absurdity, agitation, anger, ardor, craze, craziness, daftness, delusion, dementia, demoniacism, demonomania, derangement, distraction, enthusiasm, exasperation, excitement, fanaticism, folie, folly, fondness, foolhardiness, foolishness, frenzy, furore, fury, infatuation, insanity, intoxication, ire, keenness, lunacy, lycanthropy, mania, monomania, moon-madness, moonraking, nonsense, passion, preposterousness, psychopathy, psychosis, rage, raving, riot, unrestraint, uproar, wildness, wrath, zeal.
antonym sanity.

maelstrom *n.* bedlam, chaos, Charybdis, confusion, disorder, mess, pandemonium, tumult, turmoil, uproar, vortex, whirlpool.

magic *n.* allurement, black art, charm, conjuring, conjury, diablerie, enchantment, fascination, glamor, goety, gramary(e), hocus-pocus, hoodoo, illusion, jiggery-pokery, jugglery, legerdemain, magnetism, medicine, necromancy, occultism, prestidigitation, sleight of hand, sorcery, sortilege, spell, thaumaturgics, thaumaturgism, thaumaturgy, theurgy, trickery, voodoo, witchcraft, wizardry, wonder-work.
adj. bewitching, charismatic, charming, enchanting, entrancing, fascinating, goetic, hermetic, magical, magnetic, marvelous, miraculous, mirific, mirifical, sorcerous, spellbinding, spellful.

magician *n.* archimage, conjurer, conjuror, enchanter, enchantress, genius, illusionist, maestro, mage, Magian, magus, marvel, miracle-worker, necromancer, prestidigitator, prestigiator, sorcerer, spellbinder, thaumaturge, theurgist, virtuoso, warlock, witch, witch-doctor, wizard, wonder-monger, wonder-worker.

magistrate *n.* aedile, bailiff, bail(l)ie, beak, JP, judge, jurat, justice, justice of the peace, mittimus, stipendiary, tribune.

magnanimous *adj.* altruistic, beneficent, big, big-hearted, bountiful, charitable, free, generous, great-hearted, handsome, high-minded, kind, kindly, large-hearted, large-minded, liberal, munificent, noble, open-handed, philanthropic, selfless, ungrudging, unselfish, unstinting.
antonyms mean, paltry, petty.

magnate *n.* aristocrat, baron, bashaw, big cheese, big noise, big shot, big wheel, bigwig, captain of industry, chief, fat cat, grandee, leader, magnifico, merchant, mogul, nabob, noble, notable, personage, plutocrat, prince, tycoon, VIP.

magnet *n.* appeal, attraction, bait, draw, enticement, lodestone, lure, solenoid.
antonym repellent.

magnetic *adj.* absorbing, alluring, attractive, captivating, charismatic, charming, enchanting, engrossing, entrancing, fascinating, gripping, hypnotic, irresistible, mesmerizing, seductive.
antonyms repellent, repugnant, repulsive.

magnetism *n.* allure, appeal, attraction, attractiveness, charisma, charm, draw, drawing power, enchantment, fascination, grip, hypnotism, lure, magic, mesmerism, power, pull, seductiveness, spell.

magnificence *n.* brilliance, glory, gorgeousness, grandeur,

grandiosity, impressiveness, luxuriousness, luxury, majesty, nobility, opulence, pomp, resplendence, splendor, stateliness, sublimity, sumptuousness.
antonyms modesty, plainness, simplicity.

magnificent *adj.* august, brilliant, elegant, elevated, exalted, excellent, fine, glorious, gorgeous, grand, grandiose, imposing, impressive, lavish, luxurious, majestic, noble, opulent, outstanding, plush, posh, princely, regal, resplendent, rich, ritzy, splendid, stately, sublime, sumptuous, superb, superior, transcendent.
antonyms humble, modest, plain, simple.

magnify *v.* aggrandize, aggravate, amplify, augment, blow up, boost, build up, deepen, dilate, dramatize, enhance, enlarge, exaggerate, expand, greaten, heighten, increase, inflate, intensify, lionize, overdo, overemphasize, overestimate, overplay, overrate, overstate, praise.
antonyms belittle, play down.

magnitude *n.* amount, amplitude, bigness, brightness, bulk, capacity, consequence, dimensions, eminence, enormousness, expanse, extent, grandeur, greatness, hugeness, immensity, importance, intensity, largeness, mark, mass, measure, moment, note, proportions, quantity, significance, size, space, strength, vastness, volume, weight.
antonym smallness.

maid *n.* abigail, bonne, damsel, dresser, femme de chambre, fille de chambre, gentlewoman, girl, handmaiden, housemaid, lady's maid, lass, lassie, maiden, maid-of-all-work, maid-servant, miss, nymph, servant, serving-maid, soubrette, tirewoman, tiring-woman, virgin, waitress, wench.

maiden *n.* damozel, damsel, demoiselle, girl, lass, lassie, maid, may, miss, nymph, virgin, wench.
adj. chaste, female, first, fresh, inaugural, initial, initiatory, intact, introductory, new, pure, unbroached, uncaptured, undefiled, unmarried, unpolluted, untapped, untried, unused, unwed, virgin, virginal.
antonyms defiled, deflowered, unchaste.

mail *n.* correspondence, da(w)k, delivery, letters, packages, parcels, post.
v. air-mail, dispatch, forward, post, send.

maim *v.* cripple, disable, hack, haggle, hamstring, hurt, impair, incapacitate, injure, lame, mangle, mar, mutilate, savage, wound.
antonyms heal, repair.

main[1] *adj.* absolute, brute, capital, cardinal, central, chief, critical, crucial, direct, downright, entire, essential, extensive, first, foremost, general, great, head, leading, mere, necessary, outstanding, paramount, particular, predominant, pre-eminent, premier, primary, prime, principal, pure, sheer, special, staple, supreme, undisguised, utmost, utter, vital.
antonyms minor, unimportant.
n. effort, foison, force, might, potency, power, puissance, strength, vigor.
antonym weakness.

main[2] *n.* cable, channel, conduit, duct, line, pipe.

mainstay *n.* anchor, backbone, bulwark, buttress, linchpin, pillar, prop, support.

maintain *v.* advocate, affirm, allege, argue, assert, asseverate, aver, avouch, avow, back, care for, carry on, champion, claim, conserve, contend, continue, declare, defend, fight for, finance, hold, insist, justify, keep, keep up, look after, make good, nurture, observe, perpetuate, plead for, practice, preserve, profess, prolong, provide, retain, stand by, state, supply, support, sustain, take care of, uphold, vindicate.
antonyms deny, neglect, oppose.

maintenance *n.* aliment, alimony, allowance, care, conservation, continuance, continuation, defense, food, keep, keeping, livelihood, living, nurture, perpetuation, preservation, prolongation, protection, provision, repairs, retainment, subsistence, supply, support, sustainment, sustenance, sustention, upkeep.
antonym neglect.

majestic *adj.* august, awesome, dignified, distinguished, elevated, exalted, grand, grandiose, imperial, imperious, imposing, impressive, kingly, lofty, magisterial, magnificent, monumental, noble, pompous, princely, queenly, regal, royal, splendid, stately, sublime, superb.
antonyms unimportant, unimpressive.

majesty *n.* augustness, awesomeness, dignity, exaltedness, glory, grandeur, impressiveness, kingliness, loftiness, magnificence, majesticness, nobility, pomp, queenliness, regalness, resplendence, royalty, splendor, state, stateliness, sublimity.
antonyms unimportance, unimpressiveness.

major *adj.* better, bigger, chief, critical, crucial, elder, grave, great, greater, higher, important, key, keynote, larger, leading, main, most, notable, older, outstanding, pre-eminent, radical, senior, serious, significant, superior, supreme, uppermost, vital, weighty.
antonym minor.

make *v.* accomplish, acquire, act, add up to, amount to, appoint, arrive at, assemble, assign, attain, beget, bring about, build, calculate, carry out, catch, cause, clear, coerce, compel, compose, conclude, constitute, constrain, construct, contract, contribute, convert, create, designate, do, dragoon, draw up, drive, earn, effect, elect, embody, enact, engage in, engender, establish, estimate, execute, fabricate, fashion, fix, flow, force, forge, form, frame, gain, gar, gauge, generate, get, give rise to, impel, induce, install, invest, judge, lead to, manufacture, meet, mold, net, nominate, oblige, obtain, occasion, ordain, originate, pass, perform, practise, press, pressurize, prevail upon, proceed, produce, prosecute, put together, reach, reckon, render, require, secure, shape, smith(y), suppose, synthesize, take in, tend, think, turn, win.
antonyms dismantle, lose, persuade.
n. brand, build, character, composition, constitution,

construction, cut, designation, disposition, form, formation, humor, kind, make-up, manner, manufacture, mark, model, nature, shape, sort, stamp, structure, style, temper, temperament, texture, type, variety.

make-believe *n.* charade, dream, fantasy, imagination, play-acting, pretense, role-play, unreality.
antonym reality.
adj. dream, fantasized, fantasy, feigned, imaginary, imagined, made-up, mock, pretend, pretended, sham, simulated, unreal.
antonym real.

maker *n.* architect, author, builder, constructor, contriver, creator, director, fabricator, framer, manufacturer, producer.
antonym dismantler.

makeshift *adj.* band-aid, expedient, haywire, improvised, make-do, provisional, rough and ready, stop-gap, substitute, temporary.
antonyms finished, permanent.
n. band-aid, expedient, fig-leaf, shift, stop-gap, substitute.

make-up[1] *n.* cosmetics, fard, fucus, greasepaint, maquillage, paint, powder, war paint, white-face.

make-up[2] *n.* arrangement, assembly, build, cast, character, complexion, composition, configuration, constitution, construction, disposition, figure, form, format, formation, make, nature, organization, stamp, structure, style, temper, temperament.

maladroit *adj.* awkward, bungling, cack-handed, clumsy, gauche, graceless, ham-fisted, ill-timed, inconsiderate, inelegant, inept, inexpert, insensitive, tactless, thoughtless, undiplomatic, unhandy, unskilful, untoward.
antonyms adroit, tactful.

malady *n.* affliction, ailment, breakdown, complaint, disease, disorder, illness, indisposition, infirmity, malaise, sickness.
antonym health.

malaise *n.* angst, anguish, anxiety, depression, discomfort, disquiet, distemper, doldrums, enervation, future shock, illness, indisposition, lassitude, melancholy, sickness, unease, uneasiness, weakness.
antonyms happiness, well-being.

malcontent *adj.* belly-aching, disaffected, discontented, disgruntled, dissatisfied, dissentious, factious, ill-disposed, morose, rebellious, resentful, restive, unhappy, unsatisfied.
antonym contented.
n. agitator, belly-acher, complainer, grouch, grouser, grumbler, mischief-maker, moaner, rebel, troublemaker.

male *adj.* bull, cock, dog, manlike, manly, masculine, virile.
antonym female.
n. boy, bull, cock, daddy, dog, father, man.
antonym female.

malefactor *n.* convict, criminal, crook, culprit, delinquent, evil-doer, felon, law-breaker, miscreant, misfeasor, offender, outlaw, transgressor, villain, wrong-doer.

malevolence *n.* bitterness, hate, hatred, hostility, ill-will, malice, maliciousness, malignance, malignancy, malignity, rancor, spite, spitefulness, vengefulness, venom, viciousness, vindictiveness.
antonym benevolence.

malfunction *n.* breakdown, defect, failure, fault, flaw, glitch, impairment.
v. break down, fail, go wrong, misbehave.

malice *n.* animosity, animus, bad blood, bitterness, despite, enmity, hate, hatred, ill-will, malevolence, maliciousness, malignity, rancor, spite, spitefulness, spleen, vengefulness, venom, viciousness, vindictiveness.
antonym kindness.

malicious *adj.* baleful, bitchy, bitter, catty, despiteful, evilminded, hateful, ill-natured, injurious, malevolent, malignant, mischievous, pernicious, rancorous, resentful, sham, spiteful, vengeful, venomous, vicious.
antonyms kind, thoughtful.

malign *adj.* bad, baleful, baneful, deleterious, destructive, evil, harmful, hostile, hurtful, injurious, malevolent, malignant, noxious, pernicious, venomous, vicious, wicked.
antonym benign.
v. abuse, badmouth, blacken the name of, calumniate, defame, denigrate, derogate, disparage, harm, injure, libel, revile, run down, slander, smear, traduce, vilify, vilipend.
antonym praise.

malignant *adj.* baleful, bitter, cancerous, cankered, dangerous, deadly, destructive, devilish, evil, fatal, harmful, hostile, hurtful, inimical, injurious, irremediable, malevolent, malicious, malign, pernicious, spiteful, uncontrollable, venomous, vicious, viperish, viperous, virulent.
antonyms harmless, kind.

malingerer *n.* dodger, lead-swinger, loafer, shirker, skiver, slacker.
antonym toiler.

malleable *adj.* adaptable, biddable, compliant, ductile, governable, impressionable, manageable, plastic, pliable, pliant, soft, tractable, tractile, workable.
antonyms intractable, unworkable.

malodorous *adj.* evil-smelling, fetid, foul-smelling, mephitic, miasmal, miasmatic, miasmatous, miasmic, miasmous, nauseating, niffy, noisome, offensive, putrid, rank, reeking, smelly, stinking.
antonym sweet-smelling.

malpractice *n.* abuse, dereliction, malversation, misbehavior, misconduct, misdeed, mismanagement, negligence, offence, transgression.

maltreat *v.* abuse, bully, damage, harm, hurt, ill-treat, injure, mistreat, misuse, mousle.
antonym care for.

maltreatment *n.* abuse, bullying, harm, ill-treatment, ill-usage, ill-use, injury, mistreatment, misuse.
antonym care.

mammoth *adj.* Brobdingnag, Brobdingnagian, colossal, enormous, formidable, gargantuan, giant, gigantic, herculean, huge, immense, leviathan, massive, mighty, monumental, mountainous, prodigious, rounceval, stupendous, titanic, vast.
antonym small.

man[1] *n.* adult, attendant, beau, bloke, body, boyfriend, cat, chap, employee, fellow, follower, gentleman, guy, hand, hireling, hombre, human, human being, husband, individual, lover, male, manservant, partner, person, retainer, servant, soldier, spouse, subject, subordinate, valet, vassal, worker, workman.
v. crew, fill, garrison, occupy, operate, people, staff, take charge of.

man[2] *n.* Homo sapiens, human race, humanity, humankind, humans, mankind, mortals, people.

manacle *v.* bind, chain, check, clap in irons, confine, constrain, curb, fetter, gyve, hamper, hamstring, handcuff, inhibit, put in chains, restrain, shackle, trammel.
antonym unshackle.

manage *v.* accomplish, administer, arrange, bring about, bring off, carry on, command, concert, conduct, contrive, control, cope, cope with, deal with, direct, dominate, effect, engineer, fare, get along, get by, get on, govern, guide, handle, influence, make do, make out, manipulate, muddle through, operate, oversee, pilot, ply, preside over, rule, run, shift, solicit, stage-manage, steer, succeed, superintend, supervise, survive, train, use, wield.
antonym fail.

manageable *adj.* amenable, biddable, complaint, controllable, convenient, docile, easy, governable, handy, submissive, tamable, tractable, wieldable, wieldy.
antonym unmanageable.

management *n.* administration, board, bosses, care, charge, command, conduct, control, direction, directorate, directors, employers, executive, executives, governance, government, governors, guidance, handling, managers, manipulation, operation, oversight, rule, running, stewardry, superintendence, supervision, supervisors.

manager *n.* administrator, boss, comptroller, conductor, controller, director, executive, factor, gaffer, governor, head, impresario, organizer, overseer, proprietor, steward, superintendent, supervisor.

mandate *n.* authorization, authority, bidding, charge, command, commission, decree, dedimus, directive, edict, fiat, firman, injunction, instruction, irade, order, precept, rescript, right, sanction, ukase, warrant.

mandatory *adj.* binding, compulsory, imperative, necessary, obligatory, required, requisite.
antonym optional.

maneuver *n.* action, artifice, device, dodge, exercise, gambit, intrigue, machination, move, movement, operation, plan, plot, ploy, ruse, scheme, stratagem, subterfuge, tactic, trick.
v. contrive, deploy, devise, direct, drive, engineer, exercise, guide, handle, intrigue, jockey, machinate, manage, manipulate, move, navigate, negotiate, pilot, plan, plot, pull strings, scheme, steer, wangle.

mangle *v.* butcher, crush, cut, deform, destroy, disfigure, distort, hack, haggle, lacerate, maim, mar, maul, mutilate, rend, ruin, spoil, tear, twist, wreck.

mangy *adj.* dirty, grotty, mean, moth-eaten, ratty, scabby, scruffy, seedy, shabby, shoddy, squalid, tatty.
antonyms clean, neat, spruce.

manhandle *v.* carry, haul, heave, hump, knock about, lift, maltreat, maneuver, maul, mishandle, mistreat, misuse, paw, pull, push, rough up, shove, tug.

manhood *n.* adulthood, bravery, courage, determination, firmness, fortitude, hardihood, machismo, manfulness, manliness, masculinity, maturity, mettle, resolution, spirit, strength, valor, virility.
antonym timidness.

mania *n.* aberration, cacoethes, compulsion, craving, craze, craziness, delirium, dementia, derangement, desire, disorder, enthusiasm, fad, fetish, fixation, frenzy, infatuation, insanity, itch, lunacy, madness, obsession, partiality, passion, preoccupation, rage, thing.

manifest *adj.* apparent, clear, conspicuous, distinct, evident, glaring, noticeable, obvious, open, palpable, patent, plain, unconcealed, undeniable, unmistakable, visible.
antonym unclear.
v. demonstrate, display, establish, evidence, evince, exhibit, expose, illustrate, prove, reveal, set forth, show.
antonym hide.

manifesto *n.* declaration, platform, policies, policy, pronunciamento.

manifold *adj.* abundant, assorted, copious, diverse, diversified, kaleidoscopic, many, multifarious, multifold, multiple, multiplex, multiplied, multitudinous, numerous, varied, various.
antonym simple.

manipulate *v.* conduct, control, cook, direct, employ, engineer, gerrymander, guide, handle, influence, juggle with, maneuver, negotiate, operate, ply, shuffle, steer, use, wield, work.

manly *adj.* bold, brave, courageous, daring, dauntless, fearless, gallant, hardy, heroic, macho, male, manful, masculine, muscular, noble, powerful, resolute, robust, stalwart, stout-hearted, strapping, strong, sturdy, valiant, valorous, vigorous, virile.
antonyms timid, unmanly.

man-made *adj.* artificial, ersatz, imitation, manufactured, simulated, synthetic.
antonym natural.

manner *n.* address, air, appearance, approach, aspect,

bearing, behavior, brand, breed, category, character, comportment, conduct, custom, demeanor, deportment, description, fashion, form, genre, habit, kind, line, look, means, method, mien, mode, nature, practice, presence, procedure, process, routine, sort, style, tack, tenor, tone, type, usage, variety, way, wise, wont.

mannerism *n.* characteristic, feature, foible, habit, idiosyncrasy, peculiarity, quirk, stiltedness, trait, trick.

mannerly *adj.* civil, civilized, courteous, decorous, deferential, formal, genteel, gentlemanly, gracious, ladylike, polished, polite, refined, respectful, well-behaved, well-bred, well-mannered.
antonym unmannerly.

mantle *n.* blanket, canopy, cape, cloak, cloud, cover, covering, curtain, envelope, hood, mantlet, pall, pelerine, pelisse, screen, shawl, shroud, veil, wrap.

manual[1] *n.* bible, book of words, companion, enchi(e)ridion, guide, guide-book, handbook, instructions, primer, vademecum.

manual[2] *adj.* hand, hand-operated, human, physical.

manufacture *v.* assemble, build, churn out, compose, concoct, construct, cook up, create, devise, fabricate, forge, form, hatch, invent, make, make up, mass-produce, mold, process, produce, shape, think up, trump up, turn out.
n. assembly, construction, creation, fabrication, facture, formation, making, mass-production, production.

manure *n.* compost, droppings, dung, fertilizer, guano, muck, ordure.

manuscript *n.* autograph, deed, document, handwriting, holograph, palimpsest, parchment, scroll, text, vellum.

many *adj.* abundant, copious, countless, divers, frequent, innumerable, manifold, multifarious, multifold, multitudinous, myriad, numerous, profuse, sundry, umpteen, umpty, varied, various, zillion.
antonym few.

map *n.* atlas, chart, graph, mappemond, plan, plot, street plan.

mar *v.* blemish, blight, blot, damage, deface, detract from, disfigure, foul up, harm, hurt, impair, injure, maim, mangle, mutilate, pollute, ruin, scar, spoil, stain, sully, taint, tarnish, temper, vitiate, wreck.
antonym enhance.

maraud *v.* depredate, despoil, forage, foray, harry, loot, pillage, plunder, raid, ransack, ravage, reive, sack, spoliate.

march *v.* countermarch, file, flounce, goose-step, pace, parade, slog, stalk, stride, strut, stump, tramp, tread, walk.
n. advance, career, demo, demonstration, development, evolution, footslog, gait, hike, pace, parade, passage, procession, progress, progression, step, stride, tramp, trek, walk.

margin *n.* allowance, border, bound, boundary, brim, brink, compass, confine, edge, extra, latitude, leeway, limit, marge, perimeter, periphery, play, rand, rim, room, scope, side, skirt, space, surplus, verge.
antonyms center, core.

marginal *adj.* bordering, borderline, doubtful, infinitesimal, insignificant, low, minimal, minor, negligible, peripheral, slight, small.
antonyms central, core.

marina *n.* dock, harbor, mooring, port, yacht station.

marine *adj.* maritime, nautical, naval, ocean-going, oceanic, pelagic, salt-water, sea, seafaring, sea-going, thalassian, thalassic.
n. galoot, leather-neck, sailor.

mariner *n.* bluejacket, deckhand, hand, Jack Tar, matelot, matlo(w), navigator, sailor, salt, sea-dog, seafarer, seaman, tar.

marital *adj.* conjugal, connubial, hymeneal, hymenean, married, matrimonial, nuptial, sponsal, sponsal, wedded.

maritime *adj.* coastal, littoral, marine, nautical, naval, oceanic, pelagic, sea, seafaring, seaside, thalassian, thalassic.

mark *n.* aim, badge, blaze, blemish, blot, blotch, brand, bruise, character, characteristic, consequence, criterion, dent, device, dignity, distinction, earmark, emblem, eminence, end, evidence, fame, feature, fingermark, footmark, footprint, goal, hallmark, importance, impression, incision, index, indication, influence, label, level, line, lineament, marque, measure, nick, norm, notability, note, noteworthiness, notice, object, objective, pock, prestige, print, proof, purpose, quality, regard, scar, scratch, seal, sign, smudge, splotch, spot, stain, stamp, standard, standing, streak, symbol, symptom, target, token, trace, track, trail, vestige, yardstick.
v. appraise, assess, attend, betoken, blemish, blot, blotch, brand, bruise, characterize, correct, denote, dent, distinguish, evaluate, evince, exemplify, grade, hearken, heed, identify, illustrate, impress, imprint, label, list, listen, mind, nick, note, notice, observe, print, regard, remark, scar, scratch, show, smudge, splotch, stain, stamp, streak, take to heart, traumatize, watch.

marked *adj.* apparent, clear, considerable, conspicuous, decided, distinct, doomed, emphatic, evident, glaring, indicated, manifest, notable, noted, noticeable, obvious, outstanding, patent, prominent, pronounced, remarkable, salient, signal, striking, strong, suspected, watched.
antonyms slight, unnoticeable.

market *n.* bazaar, demand, fair, market-place, mart, need, outlet, shop, souk.
v. hawk, peddle, retail, sell, vend.
antonym buy.

maroon *v.* abandon, cast away, desert, isolate, leave, put ashore, strand.
antonym rescue.

marriage *n.* alliance, amalgamation, association, confederation, coupling, espousal, link, match, matrimony, matronage, matronhood, merger, nuptials, spousage, spousals, union, wedding, wedlock.
antonym divorce.

marrow *n.* core, cream, essence, gist, heart, kernel, nub, pith, quick, quintessence, soul, spirit, stuff, substance.

marry *v.* ally, bond, espouse, get hitched, get spliced, join, jump the broomstick, knit, link, match, merge, splice, tie, tie the knot, unify, unite, wed, wive, yoke.
antonyms divorce, separate.

marsh *n.* bayou, bog, carr, fen, maremma, marshland, morass, moss, muskeg, quagmire, slough, slump, soak, swale, swamp, wetland.

marshal *v.* align, arrange, array, assemble, collect, conduct, convoy, deploy, dispose, draw up, escort, gather, group, guide, lead, line up, muster, order, organize, rank, shepherd, take, usher.

martial *adj.* bellicose, belligerent, brave, combative, heroic, militant, military, soldierly, warlike.
antonym pacific.

martyrdom *n.* agony, anguish, death, excruciation, ordeal, persecution, suffering, torment, torture, witness.

marvel *n.* genius, miracle, non(e)such, phenomenon, portent, prodigy, sensation, spectacle, whiz, wonder.
v. gape, gaze, goggle, wonder.

marvelous *adj.* amazing, astonishing, astounding, beyond belief, breathtaking, épatant, excellent, extraordinary, fabulous, fantastic, glorious, great, implausible, improbable, incredible, magnificent, miraculous, mirific(al), phenomenal, prodigious, remarkable, sensational, singular, smashing, spectacular, splendid, stupendous, super, superb, surprising, terrific, unbelievable, unlikely, wonderful, wondrous.
antonyms ordinary, plausible, run-of-the-mill.

masculine *adj.* bold, brave, butch, gallant, hardy, macho, male, manlike, manly, mannish, muscular, powerful, redblooded, resolute, robust, stout-hearted, strapping, strong, tomboyish, vigorous, virile.
antonym feminine.

mash *v.* beat, champ, comminute, crush, grind, pound, pulverize, pummel, smash, triturate.

mask *n.* blind, camouflage, cloak, concealment, cover, cover-up, disguise, domino, façade, false face, front, guise, pretense, screen, semblance, show, veil, veneer, visardmask, visor, vizard.
v. camouflage, cloak, conceal, cover, disguise, hide, obscure, screen, shield, veil.
antonym uncover.

masquerade *n.* cloak, costume, costume ball, counterfeit, cover, cover-up, deception, disguise, dissimulation, domino, fancy dress party, front, guise, imposture, mask, masked ball, masque, mummery, pose, pretense, put-on, revel, screen, subterfuge.
v. disguise, dissemble, dissimulate, impersonate, mask, pass oneself off, play, pose, pretend, profess.

mass[1] *n.* accumulation, aggregate, aggregation, assemblage, band, batch, block, body, bulk, bunch, chunk, collection, combination, concretion, congeries, conglomeration, crowd, dimension, entirety, extensity, group, heap, horde, host, hunk, lion's share, load, lot, lump, magnitude, majority, mob, number, piece, pile, preponderance, quantity, size, stack, sum, sum total, throng, totality, troop, welter, whole.
adj. across-the-board, blanket, comprehensive, extensive, general, indiscriminate, large-scale, pandemic, popular, sweeping, wholesale, widespread.
antonym limited.
v. assemble, cluster, collect, congregate, crowd, for(e)gather, gather, muster, rally.
antonym separate.

mass[2] *n.* communion, eucharist, holy communion, Lord's Supper, Lord's Table.

massacre *n.* annihilation, blood bath, butchery, carnage, decimation, extermination, holocaust, killing, murder, slaughter.
v. annihilate, butcher, decimate, exterminate, kill, mow down, murder, slaughter, slay, wipe out.

massage *n.* effleurage, kneading, malaxage, malaxation, manipulation, petrissage, rubbing, rub-down.
v. knead, manipulate, rub, rub down.

massive *adj.* big, bulky, colossal, cyclopean, enormous, extensive, gargantuan, gigantic, great, heavy, hefty, huge, hulking, immense, imposing, impressive, jumbo, mammoth, monster, monstrous, monumental, ponderous, rounceval, solid, substantial, titanic, vast, weighty, whacking, whopping.
antonyms slight, small.

master *n.* ace, adept, baas, boss, bwana, captain, chief, commander, controller, dab hand, deacon, director, doyen, employer, expert, genius, governor, guide, guru, head, Herr, instructor, lord, maestro, manager, overlord, overseer, owner, past master, pedagogue, preceptor, principal, pro, ruler, schoolmaster, skipper, superintendent, swami, teacher, tutor, virtuoso, wizard.
antonyms amateur, learner, pupil, servant, slave.
adj. ace, adept, chief, controlling, crack, expert, foremost, grand, great, leading, main, masterly, predominant, prime, principal, proficient, skilful, skilled.
antonyms copy, subordinate, unskilled.
v. acquire, bridle, check, command, conquer, control, curb, defeat, direct, dominate, get the hang of, govern, grasp, learn, manage, overcome, quash, quell, regulate, rule, subdue, subjugate, suppress, tame, triumph over, vanquish.

masterful *adj.* adept, adroit, arrogant, authoritative, autocratic, bossy, clever, consummate, crack, deft, despotic, dexterous, dictatorial, domineering, excellent, expert, exquisite, fine, finished, first-rate, high-handed, imperious, magisterial, masterly, overbearing, overweening, peremptory, powerful, professional, self-

willed, skilful, skilled, superior, superlative, supreme, tyrannical.
antonyms clumsy, humble, unskilful.

masterly *adj.* adept, adroit, clever, consummate, crack, dexterous, excellent, expert, exquisite, fine, finished, first-rate, magistral, masterful, skilful, skilled, superb, superior, superlative, supreme.
antonyms clumsy, poor, unskilled.

mastermind *v.* conceive, design, devise, direct, dream up, forge, frame, hatch, manage, organize, originate, plan.
n. architect, authority, brain(s), creator, director, engineer, genius, intellect, manager, organizer, originator, planner, prime mover, virtuoso.

masterpiece *n.* chef d'oeuvre, classic, jewel, magnum opus, master-work, museum-piece, pièce de résistance, tour de force.

mastery *n.* ability, acquirement, advantage, ascendancy, attainment, authority, cleverness, command, comprehension, conquest, control, conversancy, deftness, dexterity, domination, dominion, expertise, familiarity, finesse, grasp, know-how, knowledge, pre-eminence, proficiency, prowess, rule, skill, superiority, supremacy, sway, triumph, understanding, upper hand, victory, virtuosity, whip-hand.
antonyms clumsiness, unfamiliarity.

masticate *v.* champ, chew, crunch, eat, knead, manducate, munch, ruminate.

mat *n.* carpet, doormat, drugget, felt, rug, under-felt, underlay.

match[1] *n.* bout, competition, contest, game, main, test, trial, venue.
v. compete, contend, oppose, pit against, rival, vie.

match[2] *n.* affiliation, alliance, combination, companion, complement, copy, counterpart, couple, dead ringer, double, duet, duplicate, equal, equivalent, fellow, like, look-alike, marriage, mate, pair, pairing, parallel, partnership, peer, replica, ringer, rival, spit, spitting image, tally, twin, union.
v. accompany, accord, adapt, agree, ally, blend, combine, compare, co-ordinate, correspond, couple, emulate, equal, fit, gee, go together, go with, harmonize, join, link, marry, mate, measure up to, pair, relate, rival, suit, tally, team, tone with, unite, yoke.
antonyms clash, separate.

match[3] *n.* Congreve-match, fuse, fusee, light, lucifer, lucifer-match, safety match, spill, taper, vesta, vesuvian.

matchless *adj.* consummate, excellent, exquisite, incomparable, inimitable, nonpareil, peerless, perfect, superlative, supreme, unequaled, unique, unmatched, unparalleled, unrivaled, unsurpassed.
antonyms commonplace, poor.

mate *n.* assistant, associate, better half, buddy, china, chum, colleague, companion, compeer, comrade, confidant(e), coworker, crony, double, fellow, fellow-worker, fere, friend, gossip, helper, helpmate, helpmeet, husband, match, pal, partner, repository, side-kick, spouse, subordinate, twin, wife.
v. breed, copulate, couple, join, marry, match, pair, wed, yoke.

material *n.* body, cloth, constituents, data, element, evidence, fabric, facts, information, literature, matter, notes, stuff, substance, textile, work.
adj. applicable, apposite, apropos, bodily, central, concrete, consequential, corporeal, essential, fleshly, germane, grave, gross, hylic, important, indispensable, key, meaningful, momentous, non-spiritual, palpable, pertinent, physical, relevant, serious, significant, substantial, tangible, vital, weighty, worldly.
antonyms ethereal, immaterial.

materialize *v.* appear, arise, happen, occur, take shape, turn up.
antonym disappear.

maternal *adj.* loving, matronal, motherly, protective.
antonym paternal.

matrimony *n.* espousals, marriage, nuptials, sponsalia, spousage, spousal, wedlock.

matron *n.* dame, dowager, matriarch.

matted *adj.* knotted, tangled, tangly, tousled, uncombed.
antonyms tidy, untangled.

matter[1] *n.* affair, amount, argument, body, business, complication, concern, consequence, context, difficulty, distress, episode, event, hyle, import, importance, incident, issue, material, moment, note, occurrence, problem, proceeding, purport, quantity, question, sense, significance, situation, stuff, subject, substance, sum, text, thesis, thing, topic, transaction, trouble, upset, weight, worry.
antonym insignificance.
v. count, make a difference, mean something, signify.

matter[2] *n.* discharge, purulence, pus, secretion, suppuration.
v. discharge, secrete.

mature *adj.* adult, complete, due, fit, full-blown, full-grown, fully fledged, grown, grown-up, matured, mellow, nubile, perfect, perfected, prepared, ready, ripe, ripened, seasoned, well-thought-out.
antonym immature.
v. accrue, age, bloom, come of age, develop, fall due, grow up, maturate, mellow, perfect, ripen, season.

maudlin *adj.* drunk, emotional, fuddled, half-drunk, icky, lachrymose, mawkish, mushy, sentimental, sickly, slushy, soppy, tearful, tipsy, weepy.
antonym matter-of-fact.

maul *v.* abuse, batter, beat, beat up, claw, ill-treat, knock about, lacerate, maltreat, mangle, manhandle, molest, paw, pummel, rough up, thrash.

mawkish *adj.* disgusting, emotional, feeble, flat, foul, gushy, icky, insipid, jejune, loathsome, maudlin, mushy, nauseous, offensive, schmaltzy, sentimental, sickly, slushy, soppy, squeamish, stale, vapid.
antonyms matter-of-fact, pleasant.

maxim *n.* adage, aphorism, apophthegm, axiom, byword, epigram, gnome, mot, motto, precept, proverb, rule, saw, saying, sentence.

maximum *adj.* biggest, greatest, highest, largest, maximal, most, paramount, supreme, topmost, utmost.
antonym minimum.
n. apogee, ceiling, crest, extremity, height, most, ne plus ultra, peak, pinnacle, summit, top (point), upper limit, utmost, zenith.
antonym mimimum.

maybe *adv.* haply, happen, mayhap, peradventure, perchance, perhaps, possibly.
antonym definitely.

maze *n.* confusion, convolutions, imbroglio, intricacy, labyrinth, meander, mesh, mizmaze, puzzle, snarl, tangle, web.

meadow *n.* field, haugh, holm, inch, lea, ley, mead, pasture.

meager *adj.* barren, bony, deficient, emaciated, exiguous, gaunt, hungry, inadequate, infertile, insubstantial, lank, lean, little, negligible, paltry, penurious, poor, puny, scanty, scraggy, scrawny, scrimpy, short, skimpy, skinny, slender, slight, small, spare, sparse, starved, thin, underfed, unfruitful, unproductive, weak.
antonyms fertile, substantial.

meal[1] *n.* banquet, barbecue, beanfeast, beano, blow-out, breakfast, brunch, collation, déjeuner, déjeuner à la fourchette, dinner, feast, lunch, luncheon, nosh, nosh-up, petit déjeuner, picnic, repast, scoff, snack, supper, tea, tuck-in.

meal[2] *n.* farina, flour, grits, oatmeal, powder.

mean[1] *adj.* abject, bad-tempered, base, base-born, beggarly, callous, cheese-paring, churlish, close, close-fisted, close-handed, common, contemptible, degraded, despicable, disagreeable, disgraceful, dishonorable, down-at-heel, excellent, fast-handed, good, great, hard-hearted, hostile, humble, ignoble, illiberal, inconsiderable, inferior, insignificant, low, low-born, lowly, malicious, malignant, meanspirited, menial, mercenary, mingy, miserable, miserly, modest, narrow-minded, nasty, near, niggardly, obscure, one-horse, ordinary, paltry, parsimonious, penny-pinching, penurious, petty, plebeian, poor, proletarian, pusillanimous, rude, run-down, scrub, scurvy, seedy, selfish, servile, shabby, shameful, skilful, slink, small-minded, snippy, sordid, sour, squalid, stingy, tawdry, tight, tight-fisted, undistinguished, unfriendly, ungenerous, ungiving, unhandsome, unpleasant, vicious, vile, vulgar, wretched.
antonyms generous, kind, noble, superior.

mean[2] *v.* adumbrate, aim, aspire, augur, betoken, cause, connote, contemplate, convey, denote, design, desire, destine, drive at, engender, entail, express, fate, fit, foreshadow, foretell, get at, give rise to, herald, hint, imply, indicate, insinuate, intend, involve, lead to, make, match, necessitate, omen, plan, portend, predestine, preordain, presage, produce, promise, propose, purport, purpose, represent, result in, say, set out, signify, spell, stand for, suggest, suit, symbolize, want, wish.

mean[3] *adj.* average, half-way, intermediate, medial, median, medium, middle, middling, moderate, normal, standard.
antonym extreme.
n. aurea mediocritas, average, balance, compromise, golden mean, happy medium, median, middle, middle course, middle way, mid-point, norm, via media.
antonym extreme.

meander *v.* amble, curve, ramble, snake, stravaig, stray, stroll, turn, twist, wander, wind, zigzag.

meaning *n.* aim, connotation, construction, denotation, design, drift, end, explanation, force, gist, goal, idea, implication, import, intention, interpretation, matter, message, object, plan, point, purport, purpose, sense, significance, signification, substance, thrust, trend, upshot, validity, value, worth.

meaningful *adj.* eloquent, expressive, important, material, meaningful, pointed, pregnant, purposeful, relevant, serious, significant, speaking, suggestive, useful, valid, warning, worthwhile.

meaningless *adj.* absurd, aimless, empty, expressionless, futile, hollow, inane, inconsequential, insignificant, insubstantial, nonsense, nonsensical, nugatory, pointless, purposeless, senseless, trifling, trivial, unmeaning, useless, vain, valueless, worthless.
antonym meaningful.

means *n.* ability, affluence, agency, avenue, capacity, capital, channel, course, estate, expedient, fortune, funds, income, instrument, machinery, measure, medium, method, mode, money, process, property, resources, riches, substance, way, wealth, wherewithal.

measly *adj.* beggarly, contemptible, meager, mean, mingy, miserable, miserly, niggardly, paltry, pathetic, petty, piddling, pitiful, poor, puny, scanty, skimpy, stingy, trivial, ungenerous.

measure *n.* act, action, allotment, allowance, amount, amplitude, beat, bill, bounds, cadence, capacity, control, course, criterion, deed, degree, démarche, enactment, example, expedient, extent, foot, gauge, jigger, law, limit, limitation, magnitude, maneuver, means, method, meter, model, moderation, norm, portion, procedure, proceeding, proportion, quantity, quota, range, ration, reach, resolution, restraint, rhythm, rule, scale, scope, share, size, standard, statute, step, system, test, touchstone, verse, yardstick.
v. admeasure, appraise, assess, calculate, calibrate, choose, compute, determine, estimate, evaluate, fathom, gauge, judge, mark out, measure off, measure out, plumb, quantify, rate, size, sound, step, survey, value, weigh.

measureless *adj.* bottomless, boundless, endless,

immeasurable, immense, incalculable, inestimable, infinite, innumerable, limitless, unbounded, vast.
antonym measurable.

meat[1] *n.* aliment, charqui, cheer, chow, comestibles, eats, fare, flesh, food, grub, jerk, nourishment, nutriment, provender, provisions, rations, subsistence, sustenance, viands, victuals.

meat[2] *n.* core, crux, essence, fundamentals, gist, heart, kernel, marrow, nub, nucleus, pith, point, substance.

mechanic *n.* artificer, engineer, machinist, mechanician, operative, operator, opificer, repairman, technician.

mechanism *n.* action, agency, apparatus, appliance, components, contrivance, device, execution, functioning, gadgetry, gears, innards, instrument, machine, machinery, means, medium, method, motor, operation, performance, procedure, process, structure, system, technique, tool, workings, works.

medal *n.* award, decoration, gong, honor, medalet, medallion, prize, reward, trophy.

meddle *v.* interfere, interlope, interpose, intervene, intrude, mell, pry, put one's oar in, tamper.

meddlesome *adj.* interfering, intruding, intrusive, meddling, mischievous, officious, prying, ultracrepidarian.

mediate *v.* arbitrate, conciliate, incubate, intercede, interpose, intervene, moderate, negotiate, reconcile, referee, resolve, settle, step in, umpire.

medicinal *adj.* adjuvant, analeptic, curative, healing, homeopathic, medical, medicamental, medicamentary, remedial, restorative, roborant, sanatory, therapeutic.

medicine[1] *n.* cure, diapente, diatessaron, drug, electuary, elixir, febrifuge, Galenical, materia medica, medicament, medication, nostrum, panacea, physic, remedy, specific, tincture, vermifuge.

medicine[2] *n.* acupuncture, allopathy, homeopathy, leechcraft, surgery, therapeutics.

mediocre *adj.* amateurish, average, commonplace, indifferent, inferior, insignificant, mean, medium, middling, ordinary, passable, pedestrian, run-of-the-mill, second-rate, so-so, undistinguished, unexceptional, uninspired.
antonyms excellent, exceptional, extraordinary.

meditate *v.* be in a brown study, cerebrate, cogitate, consider, contemplate, deliberate, devise, excogitate, intend, mull over, muse, plan, ponder, purpose, reflect, ruminate, scheme, speculate, study, think, think over.

medium[1] *adj.* average, fair, intermediate, mean, medial, median, mediocre, middle, middling, midway, standard.
n. aurea mediocritas, average, center, compromise, golden mean, happy medium, mean, middle, middle ground, midpoint, via media, way.

medium[2] *n.* agency, avenue, base, channel, excipient, form, instrument, instrumentality, means, mode, organ, vehicle, way.

medium[3] *n.* clairvoyant, psychic, spiritist, spiritualist.

medium[4] *n.* ambience, atmosphere, circumstances, conditions, element, environment, habitat, influences, milieu, setting, surroundings.

medley *n.* assortment, collection, confusion, conglomeration, farrago, galimatias, gallimaufry, hodge-podge, hotchpotch, jumble, macaroni, macédoine, mélange, mingle-mangle, miscellany, mishmash, mixture, olio, ollapodrida, omnium-gatherum, pastiche, patchwork, potpourri, quodlibet, salmagundi.

meek *adj.* acquiescent, compliant, deferential, docile, forbearing, gentle, humble, long-suffering, mild, modest, patient, peaceful, resigned, slavish, soft, spineless, spiritless, subdued, submissive, tame, timid, unambitious, unassuming, unpretentious, unresisting, weak, yielding.
antonyms arrogant, rebellious.

meet *v.* abut, adjoin, answer, assemble, bear, bump into, chance on, collect, come across, come together, comply, confront, congregate, connect, contact, convene, converge, cross, discharge, encounter, endure, equal, experience, face, find, forgather, fulfil, gather, go through, gratify, handle, happen on, intersect, join, link up, match, measure up to, muster, perform, rally, rencontre, rencounter, run across, run into, satisfy, suffer, touch, undergo, unite.

melancholy *adj.* blue, dejected, depressed, despondent, disconsolate, dismal, dispirited, doleful, down, down in the dumps, down in the mouth, downcast, downhearted, gloomy, glum, heavy-hearted, hipped, joyless, low, low-spirited, lugubrious, melancholic, miserable, moody, mournful, pensieroso, pensive, sad, somber, sorrowful, splenific, unhappy, woebegone, woeful.
antonyms cheerful, gay, happy, joyful.
n. blues, dejection, depression, despondency, dole, dolor, gloom, gloominess, glumness, low spirits, pensiveness, sadness, sorrow, unhappiness, woe.
antonym exhilaration.

mêlée *n.* affray, battle royal, brawl, broil, dogfight, donnybrook, fight, fracas, fray, free-for-all, ruckus, ruction, rumpus, scrimmage, scrum, scuffle, set-to, stramash, tussle.

mellow *adj.* cheerful, cordial, delicate, dulcet, elevated, expansive, full, full-flavored, genial, happy, jolly, jovial, juicy, mature, mellifluous, melodious, merry, perfect, placid, relaxed, rich, ripe, rounded, serene, smooth, soft, sweet, tipsy, tranquil, well-matured.
antonyms immature, unripe.
v. improve, mature, perfect, ripen, season, soften, sweeten, temper.

melodious *adj.* arioso, canorous, concordant, dulcet, euphonious, harmonious, melodic, musical, silvery, sonorous, sweet-sounding, tuneful.
antonyms discordant, grating, harsh.

melodramatic *adj.* blood-and-thunder, exaggerated, hammy, histrionic, overdone, overdramatic, overemotional, overwrought, sensational, stagy, theatrical.

melody *n.* air, aria, arietta, arriette, euphony, harmony, melisma, melodiousness, music, musicality, refrain, song, strain, theme, tune, tunefulness.

melt *v.* deliquesce, diffuse, disarm, dissolve, flux, fuse, liquate, liquefy, mollify, relax, soften, thaw, touch, uncongeal, unfreeze.
antonyms freeze, harden, solidify.

member *n.* appendage, arm, associate, component, constituent, element, extremity, fellow, initiate, leg, limb, organ, part, portion, representative.

membrane *n.* diaphragm, fell, film, hymen, integument, partition, septum, skin, tissue, veil, velum.

memento *n.* keepsake, memorial, record, relic, remembrance, reminder, souvenir, token, trophy.

memoirs *n.* annals, autobiography, chronicles, confessions, diary, experiences, journals, life, life story, memories, personalia, recollections, records, reminiscences, transactions.

memorable *adj.* catchy, celebrated, distinguished, extraordinary, famous, historic, illustrious, important, impressive, marvelous, momentous, notable, noteworthy, outstanding, remarkable, signal, significant, striking, unforgettable.
antonym forgettable.

memorial *n.* cairn, cromlech, dolmen, martyry, mausoleum, memento, menhir, monument, plaque, record, remembrance, souvenir, stone.
adj. celebratory, commemorative, monumental.

memorize *v.* con, learn, learn by heart, learn by rote, learn off, mug up, swot up.
antonym forget.

memory *n.* celebrity, commemoration, fame, glory, honor, memorial, name, recall, recollection, remembrance, reminiscence, renown, reputation, repute, retention.
antonym forgetfulness.

menace *v.* alarm, browbeat, bully, comminate, cow, frighten, impend, intimidate, loom, lour (lower), terrorize, threaten.
n. annoyance, commination, danger, hazard, intimidation, jeopardy, nuisance, peril, pest, plague, scare, terror, threat, troublemaker, warning.

mend *v.* ameliorate, amend, better, bushel, cobble, convalesce, correct, cure, darn, emend, fix, heal, improve, patch, recover, rectify, recuperate, refit, reform, remedy, renew, renovate, repair, restore, retouch, revise, solder.
antonyms break, destroy, deteriorate.
n. clout, darn, patch, repair, stitch.

mendacious *adj.* deceitful, deceptive, dishonest, duplicitous, fallacious, false, fraudulent, insincere, inveracious, lying, perfidious, perjured, untrue, untruthful, unveracious.
antonyms honest, truthful.

mendicant *adj.* begging, cadging, petitionary, scrounging, supplicant.
n. almsman, beachcomber, beggar, bum, cadger, hobo, moocher, panhandler, pauper, scrounger, tramp, vagabond, vagrant.

menial *adj.* abject, attending, base, boring, degrading, demeaning, dull, fawning, groveling, helping, humble, humdrum, ignoble, ignominious, low, lowly, mean, obsequious, routine, servile, slavish, sorry, subservient, sycophantic, unskilled, vile.
n. attendant, creature, dog's-body, domestic, drudge, eta, flunky, laborer, lackey, peon, serf, servant, skivvy, slave, underling.

mental[1] *adj.* abstract, cerebral, cognitive, conceptual, ideational, ideative, intellectual, noetic, rational, theoretical.
antonym physical.

mental[2] *adj.* crazy, deranged, disturbed, insane, loony, loopy, lunatic, mad, psychiatric, psychotic, unbalanced, unstable.
antonyms balanced, sane.

mentality *n.* attitude, brains, capacity, character, comprehension, disposition, endowment, faculty, frame of mind, intellect, IQ, make-up, mind, outlook, personality, psychology, rationality, understanding, wit.

mentally *adv.* emotionally, intellectually, inwardly, psychologically, rationally, subjectively, temperamentally.

mention *v.* acknowledge, adduce, advise, allude to, apprize, bring up, broach, cite, communicate, declare, disclose, divulge, hint at, impart, intimate, make known, name, point out, recount, refer to, report, reveal, speak of, state, tell, touch on.
n. acknowledgment, allusion, announcement, citation, indication, notification, observation, recognition, reference, remark, tribute.

mentor *n.* adviser, coach, counselor, guide, guru, instructor, pedagogue, swami, teacher, tutor.

merchandise *n.* cargo, commodities, freight, goods, produce, products, shipment, staples, stock, stock in trade, truck, vendibles, wares.
v. carry, deal in, distribute, market, peddle, retail, sell, supply, trade, traffic in, vend.

merchant *n.* broker, dealer, jobber, négociant, retailer, salesman, seller, shopkeeper, trader, tradesman, trafficker, vendor, wholesaler.

merciful *adj.* beneficent, benignant, clement, compassionate, condolent, forbearing, forgiving, generous, gracious, humane, humanitarian, kind, lenient, liberal, mild, pitying, soft, sparing, sympathetic, tender-hearted.
antonyms cruel, merciless.

merciless *adj.* barbarous, callous, cruel, hard, hard-hearted, harsh, heartless, implacable, inexorable, inhuman, inhumane, pitiless, relentless, remorseless, ruthless, severe, unappeasable, unforgiving, unmerciful, unpitying, unsparing.
antonym merciful.

mercurial *adj.* active, capricious, changeable, erratic, fickle, flighty, gay, impetuous, impulsive, inconstant, irrepressible, light-hearted, lively, mobile, spirited, sprightly, temperamental, unpredictable, unstable, variable, volatile.
antonym saturnine.
mercy *n.* benevolence, blessing, boon, charity, clemency, compassion, favor, forbearance, forgiveness, godsend, grace, humanitarianism, kindness, leniency, pity, quarter, relief.
antonyms cruelty, revenge.
mere *adj.* absolute, bare, common, complete, entire, paltry, petty, plain, pure, pure and simple, sheer, simple, stark, unadulterated, unmitigated, unmixed, utter, very.
merge *v.* amalgamate, blend, coalesce, combine, commingle, confederate, consolidate, converge, fuse, incorporate, intermix, join, liquesce, meet, meld, melt into, mingle, mix, unite.
merger *n.* amalgamation, coalescence, coalition, combination, confederation, consolidation, fusion, incorporation, union.
merit *n.* advantage, asset, claim, credit, desert, due, excellence, good, goodness, integrity, justification, quality, right, strong point, talent, value, virtue, worth, worthiness.
antonyms demerit, fault.
v. deserve, earn, incur, justify, rate, warrant.
merited *adj.* appropriate, condign, deserved, due, earned, entitled, fitting, just, justified, rightful, warranted, worthy.
antonyms inappropriate, unjustified.
meritorious *adj.* admirable, commendable, creditable, deserving, estimable, excellent, exemplary, good, honorable, laudable, praiseworthy, right, righteous, virtuous, worthful, worthy.
antonym unworthy.
merry *adj.* amusing, blithe, blithesome, boon, carefree, cheerful, chirpy, comic, comical, convivial, crank, elevated, facetious, festive, frolicsome, fun-loving, funny, gay, glad, gleeful, happy, heartsome, hilarious, humorous, jocular, jocund, jolly, joyful, joyous, light-hearted, mellow, mirthful, rollicking, rorty, saturnalian, sportful, sportive, squiffy, tiddly, tipsy, vivacious.
antonyms gloomy, glum, grave, melancholy, serious, sober, somber.
mesh *n.* entanglement, lattice, net, netting, network, plexus, reticulation, snare, tangle, toils, tracery, trap, web.
v. catch, combine, come together, connect, co-ordinate, dovetail, engage, enmesh, entangle, fit, harmonize, inmesh, interlock, knit.
mesmerize *v.* benumb, captivate, enthral, entrance, fascinate, grip, hypnotize, magnetize, spellbind, stupefy.
mess *n.* botch, chaos, clutter, cock-up, confusion, difficulty, dilemma, dirtiness, disarray, disorder, disorganization, fiasco, fix, guddle, hash, imbroglio, jam, jumble, litter, mishmash, mix-up, muddle, muss(e), perplexity, pickle, plight, predicament, shambles, shemozzle, soss, stew, turmoil, untidiness, yuck.
antonyms order, tidiness.
v. befoul, besmirch, clutter, dirty, disarrange, disarray, dishevel, foul, litter, muss(e), pollute, tousle.
antonyms order, tidy.
message *n.* bulletin, cable, commission, communication, communiqué, dépêche, dispatch, errand, idea, import, intimation, job, letter, meaning, memorandum, mission, missive, moral, note, notice, point, purport, send, task, theme, tidings, word.
messenger *n.* agent, ambassador, bearer, carrier, courier, delivery boy, emissary, envoy, errand-boy, go-between, harbinger, herald, in-between, internuncio, mercury, nuncio, runner, send, vaunt-courier.
messy *adj.* chaotic, cluttered, confused, dirty, disheveled, disordered, disorganized, grubby, littered, muddled, shambolic, sloppy, slovenly, unkempt, untidy, yucky.
antonyms neat, ordered, tidy.
metamorphosis *n.* alteration, change, change-over, conversion, modification, mutation, rebirth, transfiguration, transformation, translation, transmogrification, transmutation, transubstantiation.
mete out administer, allot, apportion, assign, deal out, dispense, distribute, divide out, dole out, hand out, measure out, parcel out, portion, ration out, share out.
meteoric *adj.* brief, brilliant, dazzling, fast, instantaneous, momentary, overnight, rapid, spectacular, speedy, sudden, swift.
method *n.* approach, arrangement, course, design, fashion, form, manner, mode, modus operandi, order, orderliness, organization, pattern, plan, planning, practice, procedure, process, program, purpose, regularity, routine, rule, scheme, structure, style, system, technique, way.
methodical *adj.* business-like, deliberate, disciplined, efficient, meticulous, neat, ordered, orderly, organized, painstaking, planned, precise, punctilious, regular, scrupulous, structured, systematic, tidy.
antonyms confused, desultory, irregular.
meticulous *adj.* accurate, detailed, exact, fastidious, fussy, microscopic, nice, painstaking, particular, perfectionist, precise, punctilious, scrupulous, strict, thorough.
antonyms careless, slapdash.
mettle *n.* ardor, boldness, bottle, bravery, caliber, character, courage, daring, disposition, fire, fortitude, gallantry, gameness, ginger, grit, guts, hardihood, heart, indomitability, kidney, life, make-up, nature, nerve, pith, pluck, quality, resolution, resolve, spirit, spunk, stamp, temper, temperament, valor, vigor.
microscopic *adj.* imperceptible, indiscernible, infinitesimal, invisible, minuscule, minute, negligible, tiny.
antonyms huge, vast.
middle *adj.* central, halfway, inner, inside, intermediate,

intervening, mean, medial, median, mediate, medium, mid, middle-bracket.
n. aurea mediocritas, center, focus, golden mean, halfway mark, halfway point, happy medium, heart, inside, mean, middle way, midpoint, midriff, midsection, midst, thick, via media, waist.
antonyms beginning, border, edge, end, extreme.

middleman *n.* broker, distributor, entrepreneur, fixer, go-between, intermediary, negotiator, retailer.

midget *n.* dwarf, gnome, homuncule, homunculus, manikin, minikin, minnow, pygmy, shrimp, Tom Thumb.
antonym giant.
adj. dwarf, Lilliputian, little, miniature, pocket, pocketsized, pygmy, small, teeny, tiny.
antonym giant.

midst *n.* bosom, center, core, depths, epicenter, heart, hub, interior, middle, mid-point, thick.

midway *adv.* betwixt and between, halfway, in the middle, partially.

mien *n.* air, appearance, aspect, aura, bearing, carriage, complexion, countenance, demeanor, deportment, look, manner, presence, semblance.

miffed *adj.* aggrieved, annoyed, chagrined, disgruntled, displeased, hurt, in a huff, irked, irritated, narked, nettled, offended, piqued, put out, resentful, upset, vexed.
antonyms chuffed, delighted, pleased.

might *n.* ability, capability, capacity, clout, efficacy, efficiency, energy, force, heftiness, muscularity, potency, power, powerfulness, prowess, puissance, strength, sway, valor, vigor.

mighty *adj.* bulky, colossal, doughty, enormous, forceful, gigantic, grand, great, hardy, hefty, huge, immense, indomitable, large, lusty, manful, massive, monumental, muscular, potent, powerful, prodigious, puissant, robust, stalwart, stout, strapping, strenuous, strong, stupendous, sturdy, titanic, towering, tremendous, vast, vigorous.
antonyms frail, weak.

migrant *n.* drifter, emigrant, globe-trotter, gypsy, immigrant, itinerant, land-louper, nomad, rover, tinker, transient, traveler, vagrant, wanderer.
adj. drifting, globe-trotting, gypsy, immigrant, itinerant, migratory, nomadic, roving, shifting, transient, traveling, vagrant, wandering.

migrate *v.* drift, emigrate, journey, move, roam, rove, shift, transhume, travel, trek, voyage, wander.

migratory *adj.* gipsy, itinerant, migrant, nomadic, peripatetic, roving, shifting, transient, transitory, traveling, vagrant, wandering.

mild *adj.* amiable, balmy, bland, calm, clement, compassionate, docile, easy, easy-going, equable, forbearing, forgiving, gentle, indulgent, kind, lenient, meek, mellow, merciful, moderate, pacific, passive, peaceable, placid, pleasant, serene, smooth, soft, temperate, tender, tranquil, warm. *antonyms* fierce, harsh, stormy, strong, violent.

milieu *n.* arena, background, element, environment, locale, location, medium, scene, setting, sphere, surroundings.

militant *adj.* active, aggressive, assertive, belligerent, combating, combative, contending, embattled, fighting, hawkish, pugnacious, vigorous, warring.
n. activist, aggressor, belligerent, combatant, fighter, partisan, struggler, warrior.

military *adj.* armed, martial, service, soldier-like, soldierly, warlike.
n. armed forces, army, forces, services, soldiers, soldiery.

milksop *n.* chinless wonder, coward, milquetoast, Miss Nancy, molly, mollycoddle, namby-pamby, pansy, sissy, weakling.

mill[1] *n.* ball-mill, crusher, grinder, quern.
v. comminute, crush, granulate, grate, grind, pound, powder, press, pulverize, roll.

mill[2] *n.* factory, foundry, plant, shop, works.

mill[3] *v.* crowd, scurry, seethe, swarm, throng, wander.

millstone *n.* affliction, burden, drag, encumbrance, grindstone, load, quernstone, weight.

mimic *v.* ape, caricature, echo, imitate, impersonate, look like, mirror, parody, parrot, personate, resemble, simulate, take off.
n. caricaturist, copy, copy-cat, imitator, impersonator, impressionist, parodist, parrot.
adj. echoic, fake, imitation, imitative, make-believe, mimetic, mock, pseudo, sham, simulated.

mince[1] *v.* chop, crumble, cut, dice, grind, hash.
n. hachis, hash.

mince[2] *v.* diminish, euphemize, extenuate, hold back, moderate, palliate, play down, soften, spare, suppress, tone down, weaken.

mince[3] *v.* attitudinize, ponce, pose, posture, simper.

mind[1] *n.* attention, attitude, belief, bent, brains, concentration, desire, disposition, fancy, feeling, genius, gray matter, head, imagination, inclination, inner, intellect, intellectual, intelligence, intention, judgment, leaning, marbles, memory, mentality, notion, opinion, outlook, point of view, psyche, purpose, rationality, reason, recollection, remembrance, sanity, sense, senses, sensorium, sensory, sentiment, spirit, tendency, thinker, thinking, thoughts, understanding, urge, view, will, wish, wits.

mind[2] *v.* care, demur, disapprove, dislike, object, resent, take offense.

mind[3] *v.* adhere to, attend, attend to, be careful, be on one's guard, comply with, ensure, follow, guard, have charge of, heed, keep an eye on, listen to, look after, make certain, mark, note, notice, obey, observe, pay attention, pay heed to, regard, respect, take care, take care of, take heed, tend, watch.

mindful *adj.* alert, alive (to), attentive, aware, careful, chary, cognizant, compliant, conscious, heedful, obedient, regardful, remindful, respectful, sensible, thoughtful, wary, watchful.
antonyms heedless, inattentive, mindless.

mine[1] *n.* abundance, coalfield, colliery, deposit, excavation, fund, hoard, lode, pit, reserve, sap, shaft, source, stock, store, supply, treasury, trench, tunnel, vein, wealth, wheal.
v. delve, dig for, dig up, excavate, extract, hew, quarry, remove, sap, subvert, tunnel, undermine, unearth, weaken.

mine[2] *n.* bomb, depth charge, egg, explosive, land-mine.

mingle *v.* alloy, associate, blend, circulate, coalesce, combine, commingle, compound, hobnob, intermingle, intermix, interweave, join, marry, mell, merge, mix, rub shoulders, socialize, unite.

miniature *adj.* baby, diminutive, dwarf, Lilliputian, little, midget, mini, minuscule, minute, pint-size(d), pocket, pocket-sized, pygmy, reduced, scaled-down, small, tiny, toy, wee.
antonym giant.

minimize *v.* abbreviate, attenuate, belittle, curtail, decrease, decry, deprecate, depreciate, diminish, discount, disparage, make light of, make little of, play down, prune, reduce, shrink, underestimate, underrate.
antonym maximize.

minimum *n.* bottom, least, lowest point, nadir, slightest.
antonym maximum.
adj. least, littlest, lowest, minimal, slightest, smallest, tiniest, weeniest, weest.
antonym maximum.

minister *n.* administrator, agent, aide, ambassador, assistant, churchman, clergyman, cleric, delegate, diplomat, divine, ecclesiastic, envoy, executive, Levite, office-holder, official, parson, pastor, plenipotentiary, preacher, priest, servant, subordinate, underling, vicar, vizier.
v. accommodate, administer, attend, cater to, nurse, pander to, serve, take care of, tend.

minor *adj.* inconsequential, inconsiderable, inferior, insignificant, junior, lesser, light, negligible, paltry, petty, piddling, secondary, second-class, slight, small, smaller, subordinate, trifling, trivial, unclassified, unimportant, younger.
antonym major.

minstrel *n.* bard, joculator, jongleur, musician, rhymer, rimer, singer, troubadour.

mint *v.* cast, coin, construct, devise, fabricate, fashion, forge, invent, make, make up, manufacture, monetize, produce, punch, stamp, strike.
adj. brand-new, excellent, first-class, fresh, immaculate, perfect, unblemished, undamaged, untarnished.
n. bomb, bundle, fortune, heap, million, packet, pile, stack.

minute[1] *n.* flash, instant, jiff, jiffy, mo, moment, sec, second, shake, tick, trice.

minute[2] *adj.* close, critical, detailed, diminutive, exact, exhaustive, fine, inconsiderable, infinitesimal, itsy-bitsy, Lilliputian, little, meticulous, microscopic, miniature, minim, minuscule, negligible, painstaking, paltry, petty, picayune, piddling, precise, punctilious, puny, slender, slight, small, tiny, trifling, trivial, unimportant.
antonyms gigantic, huge, immense.

miraculous *adj.* amazing, astonishing, astounding, extraordinary, incredible, inexplicable, magical, marvelous, otherworldly, phenomenal, preternatural, prodigious, stupendous, superhuman, supernatural, thaumaturgic, unaccountable, unbelievable, wonderful, wondrous.
antonyms natural, normal.

mirage *n.* fata Morgana, hallucination, illusion, optical illusion, phantasm.

mire *n.* bog, difficulties, dirt, fen, glaur, marsh, morass, muck, mud, ooze, quag, quagmire, slime, swamp, trouble.

mirror *n.* copy, double, glass, hand-glass, image, keeking-glass, likeness, looking-glass, pocket-glass, reflection, reflector, replica, representation, speculum, spit and image, spitting image, twin.
v. copy, depict, echo, emulate, follow, imitate, mimic, reflect, represent, show.

mirth *n.* amusement, cheerfulness, festivity, frolic, fun, gaiety, gladness, glee, hilarity, jocosity, jocularity, jocundity, jollity, joviality, joyousness, laughter, levity, merriment, merrymaking, pleasure, rejoicing, revelry, sport.
antonyms gloom, gl&udot;mness, melancholy.

misadventure *n.* accident, calamity, cataclysm, catastrophe, debacle, disaster, failure, ill fortune, ill luck, mischance, misfortune, mishap, reverse, setback, tragedy.

misappropriate *v.* abuse, defalcate, embezzle, misapply, misspend, misuse, peculate, pervert, pocket, steal, swindle.

misbehave *v.* act up, carry on, get up to mischief, kick over the traces, mess about, muck about, offend, transgress, trespass.
antonym behave.

miscalculate *v.* blunder, boob, err, get wrong, misjudge, overestimate, overrate, overvalue, slip up, underestimate, underrate, undervalue.

miscarriage *n.* abortion, botch, breakdown, casualty, disappointment, error, failure, misadventure, mischance, misfire, mishap, mismanagement, perversion, thwarting, undoing.
antonym success.

miscarry *v.* abort, bite the dust, come to grief, come to nothing, fail, fall through, flounder, gang agley, misfire, warp.
antonym succeed.

miscellaneous *adj.* assorted, confused, diverse, diversified, farraginous, heterogeneous, indiscriminate, jumbled, manifold, many, mingled, mixed, motley, multifarious, multiform, omnifarious, promiscuous, sundry, varied, various.

miscellany *n.* anthology, assortment, collection, diversity, farrago, gallimaufry, hash, hotch-potch, jumble, medley, mélange, mixed bag, mixture, olla-podrida, omniumgatherum, pot-pourri, salmagundi, variety.

mischief[1] *n.* bane, damage, detriment, devilment, deviltry, diablerie, disruption, evil, harm, hurt, impishness, injury, misbehavior, misfortune, monkey business, naughtiness, pranks, roguery, roguishness, shenanigans, trouble, waggery, waywardness.

mischief[2] *n.* devil, imp, monkey, nuisance, pest, rapscallion, rascal, rascallion, rogue, scallywag, scamp, tyke, villain.
antonym angel.

mischievous *adj.* arch, bad, damaging, deleterious, destructive, detrimental, elfish, elvan, elvish, evil, exasperating, frolicsome, harmful, hurtful, impish, injurious, malicious, malignant, naughty, pernicious, playful, puckish, rascally, roguish, sinful, spiteful, sportive, teasing, tricksy, troublesome, vexatious, vicious, wayward, wicked.
antonyms good, well-behaved.

misconduct *n.* delinquency, dereliction, hanky-panky, immorality, impropriety, malfeasance, malpractice, malversation, misbehavior, misdemeanor, misfeasance, mismanagement, naughtiness, rudeness, transgression, wrong-doing.

miscreant *n.* blackguard, caitiff, criminal, dastard, evildoer, knave, malefactor, mischief-maker, profligate, rascal, reprobate, rogue, scallywag, scamp, scapegrace, scoundrel, sinner, trouble-maker, vagabond, varlet, villain, wretch, wrong-doer.
antonym worthy.

misdemeanor *n.* delict, fault, indiscretion, infringement, lapse, malfeasance, misbehavior, misconduct, misdeed, offense, peccadillo, transgression, trespass.

miser *n.* cheapskate, curmudgeon, hunks, mammonist, meanie, money-grubber, muck-worm, niggard, penny-pincher, pinchfist, pinchgut, pinchpenny, save-all, screw, Scrooge, skinflint, snudge, tightwad.
antonym spendthrift.

miserable *adj.* abject, anguished, bad, broken-hearted, caitiff, cheerless, contemptible, crestfallen, crushed, dejected, deplorable, depressed, depressive, desolate, despicable, despondent, destitute, detestable, disconsolate, disgraceful, dismal, distressed, doleful, dolorous, down, downcast, dreary, forlorn, gloomy, glum, grief-stricken, hapless, heartbroken, ignominious, impoverished, indigent, joyless, lachrymose, lamentable, low, luckless, lugubrious, meager, mean, melancholic, melancholy, mournful, needy, niggardly, paltry, pathetic, penniless, piteous, pitiable, pitiful, poor, sad, scanty, scurvy, shabby, shameful, sordid, sorrowful, sorrowing, sorry, squalid, star-crossed, stricken, tearful, unhappy, vile, woebegone, worthless, wretched.
antonyms cheerful, comfortable, generous, honorable, noble.

miserly *adj.* avaricious, beggarly, cheese-paring, close, close-fisted, close-handed, covetous, curmudgeonly, gare, grasping, grudging, illiberal, mean, mercenary, mingy, money-grubbing, near, niggardly, parsimonious, penny-pinching, penurious, sordid, sparing, stingy, thrifty, tight-fisted, ungenerous.
antonyms generous, lavish, prodigal, spendthrift.

misery[1] *n.* abjectness, adversity, affliction, agony, anguish, bale, bane, bitter pill, blow, burden, calamity, catastrophe, cross, curse, depression, desolation, despair, destitution, disaster, discomfort, distress, dole, dolor, extremity, gloom, grief, hardship, heartache, heartbreak, humiliation, indigence, living death, load, melancholia, melancholy, misfortune, mortification, need, oppression, ordeal, penury, poverty, privation, prostration, sadness, sordidness, sorrow, squalor, suffering, torment, torture, trial, tribulation, trouble, unhappiness, want, woe, wretchedness.

misery[2] *n.* grouch, Jeremiah, Job's comforter, killjoy, moaner, pessimist, prophet of doom, ray of sunshine, sourpuss, spoil-sport, Weary Willie, wet blanket, whiner, whinger.
antonym sport.

misfit *n.* drop-out, eccentric, fish out of water, horse marine, individualist, lone wolf, loner, maverick, nonconformist, odd man out, oddball, rogue, square peg in a round hole, weirdo.
antonym conformist.

misfortune *n.* accident, adversity, affliction, bad luck, blow, buffet, calamity, catastrophe, disaster, failure, grief, hardship, harm, ill-luck, infelicity, infortune, loss, misadventure, mischance, misery, mishap, reverse, setback, sorrow, tragedy, trial, tribulation, trouble, woe.
antonyms luck, success.

misgiving *n.* anxiety, apprehension, backward glance, compunction, distrust, doubt, dubiety, fear, hesitation, misdoubt, niggle, presentiment, qualm, reservation, scruple, second thoughts, suspicion, uncertainty, unease, worry.
antonym confidence.

misguided *adj.* deluded, erroneous, foolish, ill-advised, ill-considered, ill-judged, imprudent, incautious, injudicious, misconceived, misled, misplaced, mistaken, rash, unreasonable, unsuitable, unwarranted, unwise.
antonym sensible.

mishap *n.* accident, adversity, balls-up, calamity, contretemps, disaster, hiccup, ill-fortune, ill-luck, misadventure, mischance, misfortune, misventure, setback.

mishmash *n.* conglomeration, farrago, gallimaufry, hash, hotchpotch, jumble, medley, mess, muddle, olio, olla-podrida, pastiche, pot-pourri, salad, salmagundi.

misjudge *v.* miscalculate, miscount, misestimate, misinterpret, misprize, mistake, overestimate, overrate, underestimate, underrate, undervalue.

mislay *v.* lose, lose sight of, misplace, miss.

mislead *v.* beguile, bluff, deceive, delude, fool, give a bum steer, hoodwink, lead up the garden path, misadvise, misdirect, misguide, misinform, mizzle, pull the wool over someone's eyes, snow, take for a ride, take in.

misleading *adj.* ambiguous, biased, casuistical, confusing, deceitful, deceptive, delusive, delusory, disingenuous, distorted, equivocatory, evasive, fallacious, false, falsidical, loaded, mendacious, sophistical, specious, spurious, tricky, unreliable.
antonyms authentic, authoritative, informative, plain, unequivocal.

mismatched *adj.* antipathetic, clashing, discordant, disparate, ill-assorted, incompatible, incongruous, irregular, misallied, mismated, unmatching, unreconcilable, unsuited.
antonyms compatible, matching.

misplace *v.* lose, misapply, misassign, misfile, mislay, miss.

misrepresent *v.* belie, bend, disguise, distort, exaggerate, falsify, garble, load, minimize, miscolor, misconstrue, misinterpret, misquote, misstate, pervert, slant, twist.

miss[1] *v.* avoid, bypass, circumvent, err, escape, evade, fail, forego, jump, lack, leave out, let go, let slip, lose, miscarry, mistake, obviate, omit, overlook, pass over, pass up, side-step, skip, slip, trip.
n. blunder, error, failure, fault, fiasco, flop, lack, lacuna, loss, mistake, need, omission, oversight, want.

miss[2] *v.* grieve for, lack, lament, long for, mourn, need, pine for, regret, sorrow for, want, wish, yearn for.

miss[3] *n.* backfisch, child, damsel, demoiselle, flapper, Fraülein, girl, girly, Jungfrau, junior miss, kid, lass, lassie, mademoiselle, maid, maiden, missy, Ms, nymphet, school-girl, spinster, teenager, young thing.

misshapen *adj.* contorted, crippled, crooked, deformed, distorted, grotesque, ill-made, ill-proportioned, malformed, monstrous, thrawn, twisted, ugly, ungainly, unshapely, unsightly, warped, wry.
antonyms regular, shapely.

missile *n.* arrow, ball, bomb, dart, flying bomb, grenade, projectile, rocket, shaft, shell, shot, torpedo, V-bomb, weapon.

missing *adj.* absent, astray, disappeared, gone, lacking, lost, minus, misgone, mislaid, misplaced, strayed, unaccounted-for, wanting.
antonyms found, present.

mission *n.* aim, assignment, business, calling, campaign, charge, commission, crusade, delegation, deputation, duty, embassy, errand, goal, job, legation, mandate, ministry, object, office, operation, purpose, pursuit, quest, raison d'être, remit, task, task force, trust, undertaking, vocation, work.

missionary *n.* ambassador, apostle, campaigner, champion, crusader, emissary, envoy, evangelist, exponent, gospeller, preacher, promoter, propagandist, proselytizer, teacher.

mist *n.* brume, cloud, condensation, dew, dimness, drizzle, exhalation, film, fog, haar, haze, mizzle, roke, smir, smog, spray, steam, vapor, veil, water-smoke.
v. becloud, bedim, befog, blur, cloud, dim, film, fog, glaze, obscure, steam up, veil.
antonym clear.

mistake *n.* aberration, bêtise, bish, bloomer, blunder, boner, boob, boo-boo, clanger, clinker, corrigendum, erratum, error, fallacy, false move, fault, faux pas, floater, folly, gaffe, gaucherie, goof, howler, inaccuracy, indiscretion, inexactitude, lapse, lapsus, lapsus calami, lapsus linguae, lapsus memoriae, literal, malapropism, misapprehension, miscalculation, misconception, misjudgment, misprint, misprision, mispronunciation, misreading, misspelling, misunderstanding, mumpsimus, oversight, scape, slip, slip-up, solecism, stumer, tactlessness, trespass.
v. blunder, confound, confuse, err, get the wrong end of the stick, goof, misapprehend, miscalculate, misconceive, misconstrue, misinterpret, misjudge, misobserve, misprize, misrate, misread, misreckon, misunderstand, slip up.

mistaken *adj.* deceived, deluded, erroneous, fallacious, false, faulty, ill-judged, inaccurate, inappropriate, inauthentic, incorrect, inexact, misguided, misinformed, misinstructed, mislead, misprized, off base, unfair, unfounded, unjust, unsound, untrue, wide of the mark, wrong.
antonyms correct, justified.

mistreat *v.* abuse, batter, brutalize, bully, harm, hurt, ill-treat, ill-use, injure, knock about, maltreat, manhandle, maul, mishandle, misuse, molest, rough up.
antonym pamper.

mistrust *n.* apprehension, caution, chariness, distrust, doubt, dubiety, fear, hesitancy, misdoubt, misgiving, reservations, skepticism, suspicion, uncertainty, wariness.
antonym trust.
v. be wary of, beware, disbelieve, distrust, doubt, fear, fight shy of, look askance at, misdoubt, mislippen, question, suspect.
antonym trust.

misunderstand *v.* get the wrong end of the stick, get wrong, misapprehend, miscomprehend, misconceive, misconstrue, misesteem, mishear, misinterpret, misjudge, misknow, misprize, misread, miss the point, mistake, take up wrong(ly).
antonyms grasp, understand.

misunderstanding *n.* argument, breach, clash, conflict, difference, difficulty, disagreement, discord, disharmony, dispute, dissension, error, malentendu, misacceptation, misapprehension, misconception, misconstruction, misinterpretation, misjudgment, misknowledge, misprision, misreading, mistake, mix-up, quarrel, rift, rupture, squabble, variance.
antonyms agreement, reconciliation.

misuse *n.* abusage, abuse, barbarism, catachresis, corruption, desecration, dissipation, distortion, exploitation,

harm, ill-treatment, ill-usage, injury, malappropriation, malapropism, maltreatment, manhandling, misapplication, misappropriation, misemployment, mistreatment, misusage, perversion, profanation, prostitution, solecism, squandering, wastage, waste.
v. abuse, brutalize, corrupt, desecrate, dissipate, distort, exploit, harm, ill-treat, ill-use, injure, malappropriate, maltreat, manhandle, maul, misapply, misappropriate, misemploy, mistreat, molest, overload, overtax, pervert, profane, prostitute, squander, strain, waste, wrong.

mite *n.* atom, grain, iota, jot, modicum, morsel, ounce, scrap, smidgen, spark, trace, whit.

mitigate *v.* abate, allay, alleviate, appease, assuage, attemper, blunt, calm, check, decrease, diminish, dull, ease, extenuate, lenify, lessen, lighten, moderate, modify, mollify, pacify, palliate, placate, quiet, reduce, remit, slake, soften, soothe, still, subdue, temper, tone down, weaken.
antonyms aggravate, exacerbate, increase.

mix *v.* allay, alloy, amalgamate, associate, blend, coalesce, combine, commingle, commix, compound, consort, contemper, cross, dash, fold in, fraternize, fuse, hobnob, homogenize, immingle, incorporate, intermingle, intermix, interweave, join, jumble, mell, merge, mingle, shuffle, socialize, synthesize, unite.
antonym separate.
n. alloy, amalgam, assortment, blend, combination, composite, compound, conglomerate, fusion, medley, mishmash, mixture, pastiche, synthesis.

mixture *n.* admixture, alloy, amalgam, amalgamation, association, assortment, blend, brew, coalescence, combination, combine, composite, compost, compound, concoction, conglomeration, cross, fusion, galimatias, gallimaufry, half-breed, hotchpotch, hybrid, jumble, macédoine, medley, mélange, miscegen, miscegenation, miscellany, mix, mixed bag, mongrel, olio, olla-podrida, omnium-gatherum, pastiche, pot-pourri, salad, salmagundi, synthesis, union, variety.

moan *n.* beef, belly-ache, bitch, complaint, gripe, groan, grouch, grouse, grumble, howl, keen, lament, lamentation, sigh, snivel, sob, sough, ululation, wail, whimper, whine, whinge.
v. beef, belly-ache, bemoan, bewail, bitch, carp, complain, deplore, grieve, gripe, groan, grouch, grouse, grumble, howl, keen, lament, mourn, sigh, snivel, sob, sough, ululate, wail, weep, whimper, whine, whinge, wuther.
antonym rejoice.

mob *n.* assemblage, bevy, body, canaille, class, collection, common herd, commonalty, company, crew, crowd, drove, faex populi, flock, galère, gang, gathering, great unwashed, group, herd, hoi polloi, horde, host, jingbang, lot, many-headed beast, many-headed monster, mass, masses, mobile, multitude, pack, plebs, populace, press, rabble, rent-a-crowd, rent-a-mob, riff-raff, rout, scum, set, swarm, throng, tribe, troop, vulgus.
v. besiege, charge, cram, crowd, crowd round, descend on, fill, jam, jostle, overrun, pack, pester, set upon, surround, swarm round.
antonym shun.

mobile *adj.* active, agile, ambulatory, animated, changeable, changing, energetic, ever-changing, expressive, flexible, fluid, itinerant, lively, locomobile, locomotive, mercurial, migrant, motile, movable, moving, nimble, peripatetic, portable, roaming, roving, supple, traveling, vagile, vivacious, wandering.
antonym immobile.

mock *v.* ape, baffle, befool, burlesque, caricature, chaff, cheat, counterfeit, debunk, deceive, defeat, defy, delude, deride, disappoint, disparage, dupe, elude, explode, fleer, flout, foil, fool, frustrate, guy, imitate, insult, jeer, lampoon, laugh at, laugh in (someone's) face, laugh to scorn, make fun of, make sport of, mimic, parody, parrot, poke fun at, queer, quiz, ridicule, satirize, scoff, scorn, send up, sneer, take the mickey, taunt, tease, thwart, travesty, twit.
antonyms flatter, praise.
adj. artificial, bogus, counterfeit, dummy, ersatz, fake, faked, false, feigned, forged, fraudulent, imitation, phony, pinchbeck, pretended, pseudo, sham, simulated, spurious, synthetic.

mockery *n.* apology, burlesque, caricature, contempt, contumely, deception, derision, disappointment, disdain, disrespect, farce, fleer, gibes, iconoclasm, imitation, insults, invective, irrision, jeering, joke, lampoon, lampoonery, let-down, mickey-taking, mimesis, mimicry, misrepresentation, parody, pasquinade, pretence, quiz, ridicule, sarcasm, satire, scoffing, scorn, send-up, sham, spoof, take-off, travesty, wisecracks.

mode *n.* approach, condition, convention, course, craze, custom, dernier cri, fad, fashion, form, latest thing, look, manner, method, plan, practice, procedure, process, quality, rage, rule, state, style, system, technique, trend, vein, vogue, way.

model *n.* archetype, configuration, copy, criterion, design, draft, dummy, embodiment, epitome, example, exemplar, facsimile, form, gauge, ideal, image, imitation, kind, lodestar, manikin, mannequin, maquette, mark, miniature, mock-up, mode, mold, original, paradigm, paragon, pattern, personification, plan, poser, praxis, prototype, replica, representation, sitter, sketch, standard, style, subject, template, touchstone, type, variety, version, yardstick.
adj. archetypal, complete, consummate, dummy, exemplary, facsimile, ideal, illustrative, imitation, miniature, par excellence, paradigmatic, perfect, prototypal, prototypical, representative, standard, typical.
v. base, carve, cast, create, design, display, fashion, form, make, mold, pattern, plan, sculpt, shape, show off, sport, wear, work.

moderate *adj.* abstemious, average, calm, centrist, continent, controlled, cool, deliberate, disciplined, equable, fair, fairish, frugal, gentle, indifferent, judicious, limited, mediocre, medium, middle-of-the-road, middling, mild, modest, non-extreme, ordinary, passable, peaceable, quiet, rational, reasonable, restrained, sensible, sober, soft-shell(ed), so-so, steady, temperate, unexceptional, well-regulated.
v. abate, allay, alleviate, appease, assuage, attemper, blunt, calm, chasten, check, control, curb, cushion, decrease, diminish, dwindle, ease, lenify, lessen, mitigate, modify, modulate, pacify, palliate, play down, quiet, regulate, repress, restrain, slake, soften, soft-pedal, subdue, subside, tame, temper, tone down.

moderation *n.* abatement, abstemiousness, alleviation, aurea mediocritas, calmness, caution, chastity, composure, continence, control, coolness, decrease, diminution, discipline, discretion, easing, equanimity, extenuation, fairness, golden mean, judiciousness, justice, justness, let-up, mildness, mitigation, moderateness, modification, modulation, palliation, reasonableness, reduction, restraint, self-control, sobriety, temperance, via media.
antonyms increase, intemperance.

modern *adj.* advanced, avant-garde, contemporary, current, emancipated, fashionable, fresh, go-ahead, goey, innovative, inventive, jazzy, late, latest, mod, modernistic, modish, neoteric, new, newfangled, novel, present, present-day, progressive, recent, stylish, trendy, twentieth-century, up-to-date, up-to-the-minute, with-it.
antonyms antiquated, old.

modernize *v.* do up, improve, modify, neoterize, progress, redesign, reform, refresh, refurbish, regenerate, rejuvenate, remake, remodel, renew, renovate, revamp, streamline, tart up, transform, update.
antonym regress.

modest *adj.* bashful, blushing, chaste, chastened, coy, demure, diffident, discreet, fair, humble, limited, maidenly, meek, middling, moderate, ordinary, proper, quiet, reserved, reticent, retiring, seemly, self-conscious, self-effacing, shamefaced, shy, simple, small, timid, unassuming, unexceptional, unpresuming, unpresumptuous, unpretending, unpretentious, verecund.
antonyms conceited, immodest, pretentious, vain.

modesty *n.* aidos, bashfulness, coyness, decency, demureness, diffidence, discreetness, humbleness, humility, meekness, propriety, quietness, reserve, reticence, seemliness, self-effacement, shamefacedness, shamefastness, shyness, simplicity, timidity, unobtrusiveness, unpretentiousness.
antonyms conceit, immodesty, vanity.

modicum *n.* atom, bit, crumb, dash, drop, fragment, grain, hint, inch, iota, little, mite, ounce, particle, pinch, scrap, shred, speck, suggestion, tinge, touch, trace.

modification *n.* adjustment, alteration, change, limitation, moderation, modulation, mutation, qualification, refinement, reformation, restriction, revision, tempering, variation.

modify *v.* abate, adapt, adjust, allay, alter, attemper, change, convert, improve, lessen, limit, lower, moderate, modulate, qualify, recast, redesign, redo, reduce, refashion, reform, remodel, reorganize, reshape, restrain, restrict, revise, rework, soften, temper, tone down, transform, vary.

modish *adj.* à la mode, all the rage, avant-garde, chic, contemporary, current, fashionable, goey, hip, in, jazzy, latest, mod, modern, modernistic, now, smart, stylish, trendy, up-to-the-minute, vogue, voguish, with-it.
antonyms dowdy, old-fashioned.

modulate *v.* adjust, alter, attune, balance, harmonize, inflect, lower, moderate, regulate, soften, tone, tune, vary.
antonyms increase, raise.

modus operandi manner, method, operation, plan, practice, praxis, procedure, process, rule, rule of thumb, system, technique, way.

mogul *n.* baron, bashaw, big cheese, big gun, big noise, big pot, big shot, big wheel, bigwig, grandee, magnate, magnifico, Mr Big, nabob, notable, panjandrum, personage, potentate, supremo, top dog, tycoon, VIP.
antonym nobody.

moist *adj.* clammy, damp, dampish, dampy, dank, dewy, dripping, drizzly, humid, marshy, muggy, rainy, soggy, swampy, tearful, vaporous, watery, wet, wettish.
antonyms arid, dry.

moisten *v.* bedew, damp, dampen, embrocate, humect, humectate, humidify, humify, imbue, irrigate, lick, madefy, moistify, moisturize, slake, soak, water, wet.
antonym dry.

moisture *n.* damp, dampness, dankness, dew, humidity, humor, liquid, mugginess, perspiration, sweat, tears, vapor, water, wateriness, wet, wetness.
antonym dryness.

mold[1] *n.* arrangement, brand, build, caliber, cast, character, configuration, construction, cut, design, die, fashion, form, format, frame, framework, ilk, kidney, kind, line, make, matrix, model, nature, pattern, quality, shape, sort, stamp, structure, style, template, type. *v.* affect, carve, cast, construct, control, create, design, direct, fashion, fit, forge, form, hew, influence, make, model, sculpt, sculpture, shape, stamp, work.

mold[2] *n.* black, black spot, blight, fungus, mildew, moldiness, must, mustiness, rust.

mold[3] *n.* clods, dirt, dust, earth, ground, humus, loam, soil.

moldy *adj.* bad, blighted, corrupt, decaying, fusty, mildewed, mucedinous, mucid, muggish, muggy, musty, putrid, rotten, rotting, spoiled, stale, vinewed.
antonyms fresh, wholesome.

molest *v.* abuse, accost, afflict, annoy, assail, attack, badger, beset, bother, bug, disturb, faze, harass, harm, harry, hassle, hector, hound, hurt, ill-treat, injure, irritate, maltreat, manhandle, mistreat, persecute, pester, plague, tease, torment, trouble, upset, vex, worry.

mollify *v.* abate, allay, appease, assuage, blunt, calm, compose, conciliate, cushion, ease, lessen, lull, mellow, mitigate, moderate, modify, pacify, placate, propitiate, quell, quiet, relax, relieve, soften, soothe, sweeten, temper.
antonyms aggravate, anger.

moment[1] *n.* breathing-while, flash, hour, instant, jiff, jiffy, juncture, less than no time, minute, mo, point, second, shake, split second, stage, tick, time, trice, twink, twinkling.

moment[2] *n.* concern, consequence, gravity, import, importance, note interest, seriousness, significance, substance, value, weight, weightiness, worth.
antonym insignificance.

momentary *adj.* brief, elusive, ephemeral, evanescent, fleeting, flying, fugitive, hasty, momentaneous, passing, quick, short, short-lived, temporary, transient, transitory.
antonyms lasting, permanent.

momentous *adj.* apocalyptic, consequential, critical, crucial, decisive, earth-shaking, epoch-making, eventful, fateful, grave, historic, important, major, pivotal, serious, significant, tremendous, vital, weighty.
antonym insignificant.

momentum *n.* drive, energy, force, impact, impetus, impulse, incentive, power, propulsion, push, speed, stimulus, strength, thrust, urge, velocity.

monarch *n.* despot, dynast, emperor, empress, king, potentate, prince, princess, queen, ruler, sovereign, tyrant.

money *n.* baksheesh, banco, banknotes, bankroll, boodle, brass, bread, capital, cash, chips, coin, currency, dough, dumps, fat, filthy lucre, fonds, funds, gelt, gold, gravy, greens, hard cash, hard money, legal tender, lolly, loot, mazuma, mint-sauce, money of account, moolah, oof, pelf, readies, ready money, riches, scrip, shekels, siller, silver, specie, spondulix (spondulicks), stumpy, sugar, the needful, the ready, the wherewithal, tin, wealth.

mongrel *n.* bigener, cross, crossbreed, half-breed, hybrid, lurcher, mule, mutt, yellow-dog.
adj. bastard, crossbred, half-breed, hybrid, ill-defined, mixed, mongrelly, nondescript.
antonyms pedigree, pure-bred.

monitor *n.* adviser, detector, guide, invigilator, overseer, prefect, recorder, scanner, screen, supervisor, watchdog.
v. check, detect, follow, keep an eye on, keep track of, keep under surveillance, note, observe, oversee, plot, record, scan, supervise, survey, trace, track, watch.
ite, contemplative, conventual, frate, frater, friar, gyrovague, hermit, mendicant, monastic, religieux, religionary, religioner, religious.

monkey[1] *n.* ape, primate, simian.

monkey[2] *n.* ass, butt, devil, dupe, fool, imp, jackanapes, laughing-stock, mug, rapscallion, rascal, rogue, scallywag, scamp.
v. fiddle, fidget, fool, interfere, meddle, mess, play, potter, tamper, tinker, trifle.

monogamous *adj.* monandrous, monogamic, monogynous.
antonyms bigamous, polygamous.

monologue *n.* harangue, homily, lecture, oration, sermon, soliloquy, speech, spiel.
antonyms conversation, dialogue, discussion.

monomania *n.* bee in one's bonnet, fanaticism, fetish, fixation, hobby-horse, idée fixe, mania, neurosis, obsession, ruling passion, thing.

monopoly *n.* ascendancy, control, corner, domination, exclusive right, monopsony, sole right.

monotonous *adj.* boring, colorless, droning, dull, flat, humdrum, monochrome, plodding, prosaic, repetitious, repetitive, routine, samey, soul-destroying, tedious, tiresome, toneless, unchanging, uneventful, uniform, uninflected, unvaried, unvarying, wearisome.
antonyms colorful, lively, varied.

monster *n.* abortion, barbarian, basilisk, beast, behemoth, bogeyman, brute, centaur, chimera, cockatrice, colossus, Cyclops, demon, devil, fiend, freak, giant, Gorgon, harpy, hellhound, hippocampus, hippogriff, Hydra, jabberwock, kraken, lamia, leviathan, lindworm, mammoth, manticore, Medusa, Minotaur, miscreation, monstrosity, mutant, ogre, ogress, prodigy, rye-wolf, savage, Sphinx, teratism, titan, villain, wivern.
adj. Brobdingnagian, colossal, cyclopean, enormous, gargantuan, giant, gigantic, huge, immense, jumbo, mammoth, massive, monstrous, prodigious, rounceval, stupendous, titanic, tremendous, vast.
antonym minute.

monstrous *adj.* abhorrent, abnormal, atrocious, colossal, criminal, cruel, cyclopean, deformed, devilish, diabolical, disgraceful, dreadful, egregious, elephantine, enormous, evil, fiendish, foul, freakish, frightful, gargantuan, giant, gigantic, great, grotesque, gruesome, heinous, hellish, hideous, horrendous, horrible, horrific, horrifying, huge, hulking, immense, infamous, inhuman, intolerable, loathsome, malformed, mammoth, massive, miscreated, misshapen, monster, obscene, odious, outrageous, prodigious, rounceval, satanic, scandalous, shocking, stupendous, teratoid, terrible, titanic, towering, tremendous, unnatural, vast, vicious, villainous, wicked.

monument *n.* ancient monument, antiquity, barrow, cairn, cenotaph, commemoration, cross, dolmen, evidence, gravestone, headstone, marker, martyry, mausoleum, memento, memorial, obelisk, pillar, prehistoric monument, record, relic, remembrance, reminder, shaft, shrine, statue, testament, token, tombstone, tumulus, witness.

monumental *adj.* abiding, awe-inspiring, awesome, catastrophic, classic, colossal, commemorative, conspicuous, cyclopean, durable, egregious, enduring, enormous, epoch-making, funerary, gigantic, great, historic, horrible, huge, immense, immortal, important, imposing, impressive, indefensible, lasting, magnificent, majestic, massive, memorable, memorial, monolithic, notable, outstanding, overwhelming, prodigious, significant, staggering, statuary, stupendous, terrible, tremendous, vast, whopping.
antonyms insignificant, unimportant.

mood *n.* blues, caprice, depression, disposition, doldrums, dumps, fit, frame of mind, grumps, humor, melancholy, pique, spirit, state of mind, sulk, temper, tenor, the sulks, vein, whim.

moody *adj.* angry, atrabilious, broody, cantankerous, capricious, cast-down, changeable, choleric, crabbed, crabby, cranky, cross, crotchety, crusty, dejected, depressive, dismal, doleful, dour, downcast, erratic, faddish, fickle, fitful, flighty, gloomy, glum, huffish, huffy, ill-humored, impulsive, inconstant, introspective, introvert, irascible, irritable, lugubrious, melancholy, mercurial, miserable, mopy, morose, peevish, pensive, petulant, piqued, sad, saturnine, short-tempered, splenetic, sulky, sullen, temperamental, testy, touchy, unpredictable, unsociable, unstable, unsteady, volatile, waspish.
antonyms cheerful, equable.

moor[1] *v.* anchor, berth, bind, dock, drop anchor, fasten, fix, hitch, lash, secure, tie up.
antonym loose.

moor[2] *n.* brae, downs, fell, heath, moorland, muir, upland, wold.

moot *v.* advance, argue, bring up, broach, debate, discuss, introduce, pose, propose, propound, put forward, submit, suggest, ventilate.
adj. academic, arguable, contestable, controversial, crucial, debatable, disputable, disputed, doubtful, insoluble, knotty, open, open to debate, problematic, questionable, undecided, undetermined, unresolvable, unresolved, unsettled, vexed.

mop *n.* head of hair, mane, mass, mat, shock, sponge, squeegee, swab, tangle, thatch.
v. absorb, clean, soak, sponge, swab, wash, wipe.

mope *v.* agonize, boody, brood, despair, despond, droop, fret, grieve, idle, languish, mooch, moon, pine, sulk.
n. depressive, grouch, grump, introvert, killjoy, melancholic, melancholic, misery, moaner, moper, mopus, pessimist, Weary Willie.

moral *adj.* blameless, chaste, clean-living, decent, equitable, ethical, good, high-minded, honest, honorable, incorruptible, innocent, just, meritorious, moralistic, noble, principled, proper, pure, responsible, right, righteous, square, straight, temperate, upright, upstanding, virtuous.
antonym immoral.
n. adage, aphorism, apophthegm, dictum, epigram, gnome, import, lesson, maxim, meaning, message, motto, point, precept, proverb, saw, saying, significance, teaching.

morale *n.* confidence, esprit de corps, heart, mettle, mood, resolve, self-esteem, spirit, spirits, state of mind, temper.

morality *n.* chastity, conduct, decency, deontology, equity, ethicality, ethicalness, ethics, ethos, goodness, habits, honesty, ideals, integrity, justice, manners, morals, mores, philosophy, principle, principles, probity, propriety, rationale, rectitude, righteousness, standards, tightness, uprightness, virtue.
antonym immorality.

morals *n.* behavior, conduct, deontics, deontology, equity, ethics, ethos, habits, ideals, integrity, manners, morality, mores, principles, probity, propriety, rectitude, scruples, standards.

morass *n.* bog, can of worms, chaos, clutter, confusion, fen, flow, jam, jumble, marsh, marshland, mess, mire, mix-up, moss, muddle, quag, quagmire, quicksand, slough, swamp, tangle.

morbid *adj.* ailing, brooding, corrupt, deadly, diseased, dreadful, ghastly, ghoulish, gloomy, grim, grisly, gruesome, hideous, horrid, hypochondriacal, infected, lugubrious, macabre, malignant, melancholy, neurotic, pathological, peccant, pessimistic, putrid, sick, sickly, somber, unhealthy, unsalubrious, unsound, unwholesome, vicious, Wertherian.

more *adj.* added, additional, alternative, extra, fresh, further, increased, new, other, renewed, repeated, spare, supplementary.
adv. again, better, further, longer.

moreover *adv.* additionally, also, as well, besides, further, furthermore, in addition, into the bargain, likewise, may I add, more, more to the point, to boot, too, what is more, withal.

moron *n.* ass, blockhead, bonehead, clot, cretin, daftie, dimwit, dolt, dope, dumbbell, dummy, dunce, dunderhead, fool, halfwit, idiot, imbecile, klutz, mental defective, mooncalf, muttonhead, natural, numbskull, schmo, schmuck, simpleton, thickhead, vegetable, zombie.

morose *adj.* blue, cheerless, churlish, crabbed, crabby, cross, crusty, depressed, dour, down, gloomy, glum, grim, grouchy, gruff, grum, huffy, humorless, ill-humored, ill-natured, ill-tempered, low, melancholy, misanthropic, moody, mournful, perverse, pessimistic, saturnine, sour, stern, sulky, sullen, surly, taciturn, testy, unsociable.
antonyms cheerful, communicative.

morsel *n.* atom, bit, bite, bonne-bouche, crumb, fraction, fragment, grain, modicum, morceau, mouthful, nibble, part, piece, scrap, segment, slice, smidgen, snack, soupçon, taste, titbit.

mortal *adj.* agonizing, awful, bodily, corporeal, deadly, deathful, dire, earthly, enormous, ephemeral, extreme,

fatal, fleshly, grave, great, human, impermanent, implacable, intense, irreconcilable, lethal, lethiferous, mortiferous, passing, perishable, relentless, remorseless, severe, sublunary, sworn, temporal, terrible, transient, unrelenting, worldly.
antonym immortal.
n. being, body, creature, earthling, human, human being, individual, man, person, sublunar, sublunary, woman.
antonyms god, immortal.

mortgage *v.* dip, pawn, pledge, put in hock.
n. bond, debenture, lien, loan, pledge, security, wadset.

mortified *adj.* abashed, affronted, annoyed, ashamed, chagrined, chastened, confounded, crushed, dead, decayed, deflated, discomfited, displeased, embarrassed, gangrenous, humbled, humiliated, necrotic, put out, put to shame, putrefied, putrid, rotted, rotten, shamed, vexed.
antonyms elated, jubilant.

mortify *v.* abase, abash, affront, annoy, chagrin, chasten, confound, conquer, control, corrupt, crush, deflate, deny, die, disappoint, discipline, discomfit, embarrass, fester, gangrene, humble, humiliate, macerate, necrose, put to shame, putrefy, shame, subdue, vex.

mortuary *n.* deadhouse, funeral home, funeral parlor, morgue.

mostly *adv.* as a rule, characteristically, chiefly, commonly, customarily, feckly, for the most part, generally, largely, mainly, normally, on the whole, particularly, predominantly, primarily, principally, typically, usually.

mother *n.* dam, generatrix, genetrix, ma, mam, mama, mamma, mammy, mater, materfamilias, mom, momma, mommy, mum, mummy, old lady, old woman.
v. baby, bear, care for, cherish, cosset, foster, fuss over, indulge, nurse, nurture, overprotect, pamper, produce, protect, raise, rear, spoil, tend.
antonym neglect.

motif *n.* concept, decoration, design, device, figure, form, idea, leitmotiv, logo, notion, ornament, pattern, shape, strain, subject, theme.

motion *n.* action, change, dynamics, flow, flux, gesticulation, gesture, inclination, kinesics, kinetics, locomotion, mechanics, mobility, motility, move, movement, nod, passage, passing, progress, proposal, proposition, recommendation, sign, signal, submission, suggestion, transit, travel, wave.
v. beckon, direct, gesticulate, gesture, nod, sign, signal, usher, wave.

motionless *adj.* at a standstill, at rest, calm, fixed, frozen, halted, immobile, inanimate, inert, lifeless, moveless, paralyzed, resting, rigid, stagnant, standing, static, stationary, still, stock-still, transfixed, unmoved, unmoving.
antonym active.

motivate *v.* actuate, arouse, bring, cause, draw, drive, encourage, impel, incite, induce, inspire, inspirit, instigate, kindle, lead, move, persuade, prompt, propel, provoke, push, spur, stimulate, stir, trigger, urge.
antonyms deter, prevent.

motive *n.* cause, consideration, design, desire, encouragement, ground(s), impulse, incentive, incitement, inducement, influence, inspiration, intention, mainspring, motivation, object, occasion, purpose, rationale, reason, spur, stimulus, thinking, urge.
antonyms deterrent, discouragement, disincentive.
adj. activating, actuating, agential, driving, impelling, initiating, motivating, moving, operative, prompting, propellent.
antonyms deterrent, inhibitory, preventive.

motley *adj.* assorted, checkered, disparate, dissimilar, diverse, diversified, haphazard, heterogeneous, ill-assorted, kaleidoscopic, mingled, miscellaneous, mixed, multicolored, particolored, patchwork, polychromatic, polychrome, polychromous, promiscuous, rainbow, unlike, varied, variegated.
antonyms homogeneous, monochrome, uniform.

mottled *adj.* blotchy, brindled, checkered, dappled, flecked, freaked, freckled, jaspé, marbled, piebald, pied, poikilitic, skewbald, speckled, spotted, stippled, streaked, tabby, variegated, veined, watered.
antonyms monochrome, plain, uniform.

motto *n.* adage, apophthegm, byword, catchword, cry, dictum, epigraph, formula, gnome, golden rule, ichthys, maxim, precept, proverb, rule, saw, saying, sentence, slogan, watchword.

mound *n.* agger, bank, barrow, bing, bulwark, drift, dune, earthwork, elevation, embankment, heap, hill, hillock, hummock, knoll, mote, motte, pile, rampart, rick, ridge, rise, stack, tuffet, tumulus, tussock, yardang.

mount *v.* accumulate, arise, ascend, bestride, build, clamber up, climb, climb on, climb up on, copulate, cover, deliver, display, emplace, enchase, escalade, escalate, exhibit, fit, frame, get astride, get on, get up, get up on, go up, grow, horse, increase, install, intensify, jump on, launch, lift, multiply, pile up, place, position, prepare, produce, put in place, put on, ready, ride, rise, rocket, scale, set, set in motion, set off, set up, soar, stage, straddle, swell, tower, tread.
n. backing, base, fixture, foil, frame, horse, monture, mounting, pedestal, podium, setting, stand, steed, support.

mountain *n.* abundance, alp, backlog, ben, berg, elevation, eminence, fell, heap, height, mass, massif, mound, mount, Munro, peak, pile, reserve, stack, ton.

mountebank *n.* charlatan, cheat, con man, confidence, fake, fraud, huckster, impostor, phony, pretender, pseud, quack, quacksalver, rogue, spieler, swindler, trickster.

mourn *v.* bemoan, bewail, beweep, deplore, grieve, keen, lament, miss, regret, rue, sorrow, wail, weep.
antonyms bless, rejoice.

mournful *adj.* afflicting, broken-hearted, calamitous, cast-down, cheerless, chopfallen, dearnful, dejected,

deplorable, depressed, desolate, disconsolate, dismal, distressing, doleful, dolorous, downcast, funereal, gloomy, grief-stricken, grieving, grievous, heartbroken, heavy, heavy-hearted, joyless, lachrymose, lamentable, long-faced, long-visaged, lugubrious, melancholy, miserable, painful, piteous, plaintive, plangent, rueful, sad, somber, sorrowful, stricken, tragic, unhappy, woeful, woesome.
antonyms cheerful, joyful.

mourning *n.* bereavement, black, desolation, grief, grieving, keening, lamentation, sackcloth and ashes, sadness, sorrow, wailing, weeds, weeping, widow's weeds, woe.
antonym rejoicing.

mousy *adj.* brownish, characterless, colorless, diffident, drab, dull, indeterminate, ineffectual, mouse-like, plain, quiet, self-effacing, shy, timid, timorous, unassertive, unforthcoming, uninteresting, withdrawn.
antonyms assertive, bright, extrovert, irrepressible.

move *v.* activate, actuate, adjust, advance, advise, advocate, affect, agitate, budge, carry, cause, change, cover the ground, decamp, depart, disturb, drift, drive, ease, edge, excite, flit, get, give rise to, go, go away, gravitate, impel, impress, incite, induce, influence, inspire, instigate, jiggle, lead, leave, locomote, make strides, march, migrate, motivate, move house, operate, persuade, proceed, progress, prompt, propel, propose, pull, push, put forward, quit, recommend, relocate, remove, rouse, run, set going, shift, shove, start, stimulate, stir, submit, suggest, switch, take, touch, transfer, transport, transpose, turn, urge, walk.
n. act, action, deed, démarche, dodge, draft, flit, flitting, go, maneuver, measure, migration, motion, movement, ploy, relocation, removal, ruse, shift, step, stratagem, stroke, tack, tactic, transfer, turn.

movement *n.* act, action, activity, advance, agitation, beat, cadence, campaign, change, crusade, current, development, displacement, division, drift, drive, evolution, exercise, faction, flow, front, gesture, ground swell, group, grouping, innards, machinery, maneuver, measure, mechanism, meter, motion, move, moving, operation, organization, pace, part, party, passage, progress, progression, rhythm, section, shift, steps, stir, stirring, swing, tempo, tendency, transfer, trend, workings, works.

moving *adj.* affecting, ambulant, ambulatory, arousing, dynamic, emotional, emotive, exciting, impelling, impressive, inspirational, inspiring, locomobile, mobile, motile, motivating, movable, pathetic, persuasive, poignant, portable, propelling, running, stimulating, stimulative, stirring, touching, unfixed.
antonyms fixed, stationary, unemotional.

mow *v.* clip, crop, cut, scythe, shear, trim.

much *adv.* considerably, copiously, decidedly, exceedingly, frequently, greatly, often.
adj. a lot of, abundant, ample, considerable, copious, great, plenteous, plenty of, sizable, substantial.
n. heaps, lashings, loads, lots, oodles, plenty, scads.
antonym little.

muck *n.* dirt, droppings, dung, feces, filth, gunge, gunk, manure, mire, mud, ooze, ordure, scum, sewage, slime, sludge.

muddle *v.* befuddle, bewilder, confound, confuse, daze, disarrange, disorder, disorganize, disorient(ate), fuddle, fuzzle, jumble, make a mess of, mess, mix up, mull, perplex, scramble, spoil, stupefy, tangle.
n. balls up, chaos, clutter, cock-up, confusion, daze, disarray, disorder, disorganization, fankle, guddle, jumble, mess, mix-up, mull, perplexity, pie, plight, predicament, puddle, snarl-up, tangle.

muddled *adj.* at sea, befuddled, bewildered, chaotic, confused, dazed, disarrayed, disordered, disorganized, disorient(at)ed, higgledy-piggledy, incoherent, jumbled, loose, messy, mixed-up, muddle-headed, perplexed, puzzle-headed, scrambled, stupefied, tangled, unclear, vague, woolly.

muff *v.* botch, bungle, fluff, mess up, mishit, mismanage, miss, spoil.

muffle *v.* cloak, conceal, cover, damp down, dampen, deaden, disguise, dull, envelop, gag, hood, hush, mask, mute, muzzle, quieten, shroud, silence, soften, stifle, suppress, swaddle, swathe, wrap up.
antonym amplify.

mug[1] *n.* beaker, cup, flagon, jug, pot, stoup, tankard, toby jug.

mug[2] *n.* chump, fool, gull, innocent, mark, muggins, sap, saphead, simpleton, soft touch, sucker.

mug[3] *n.* clock, countenance, dial, face, features, mush, phiz(og), puss, visage.

mug[4] *v.* attack, bash, batter, beat up, garrotte, jump (on), mill, rob, roll, set upon, steal from, waylay.

muggy *adj.* clammy, close, damp, humid, moist, oppressive, sticky, stuffy, sudorific, sultry, sweltering.
antonym dry.

mulish *adj.* bull-headed, cross-grained, defiant, difficult, headstrong, inflexible, intractable, intransigent, obstinate, perverse, pig-headed, recalcitrant, refractory, rigid, self-willed, stiff-necked, stubborn, unreasonable, wilful, wrong-headed.

multifarious *adj.* different, diverse, diversified, legion, manifold, many, miscellaneous, multiform, multiple, multiplex, multitudinous, numerous, sundry, varied, variegated.

multiply *v.* accumulate, augment, boost, breed, build up, expand, extend, increase, intensify, proliferate, propagate, reproduce, spread.
antonyms decrease, lessen.

multitude *n.* army, assemblage, assembly, collection, commonalty, concourse, congregation, crowd, herd, hive, hoi polloi, horde, host, legion, lot, lots, mass, mob, myriad, people, populace, proletariat, public, rabble, sea, swarm, throng.
antonyms handful, scattering.

mum *adj.* close-lipped, close-mouthed, dumb, mute, quiet, reticent, secretive, silent, tight-lipped, uncommunicative, unforthcoming.

mundane *adj.* banal, commonplace, day-to-day, earthly, everyday, fleshly, human, humdrum, material, mortal, ordinary, prosaic, routine, secular, subastral, sublunar(y), temporal, terrestrial, workaday, worldly. *antonyms* cosmic, extraordinary, supernatural.

municipal *adj.* borough, burgh(al), city, civic, community, public, town, urban.

munificent *adj.* beneficent, benevolent, big-hearted, bounteous, bountiful, free-handed, generous, hospitable, lavish, liberal, magnanimous, open-handed, philanthropical, princely, rich, unstinting. *antonym* mean.

murder *n.* agony, assassination, bloodshed, butchery, carnage, danger, deicide, difficulty, filicide, fractricide, hell, homicide, infanticide, killing, manslaughter, massacre, misery, ordeal, parricide, patricide, slaying, trial, trouble. *v.* abuse, assassinate, bump off, burke, butcher, destroy, dispatch, do in, drub, eliminate, hammer, hit, kill, mangle, mar, massacre, misuse, rub out, ruin, slaughter, slay, spoil, thrash, waste.

murderer *n.* assassin, butcher, cut-throat, filicide, hitman, homicide, killer, matricide, parricide, patricide, slaughterer, slayer.

murky *adj.* cloudy, dark, dim, dismal, dreary, dull, dusky, enigmatic, foggy, gloomy, gray, misty, mysterious, obscure, overcast, veiled.
antonyms bright, clear.

murmur *n.* babble, brool, burble, buzz, buzzing, complaint, croon, drone, grumble, humming, moan, mumble, muttering, purl, purling, purr, rumble, susurrus, undertone, whisper, whispering.
v. babble, burble, burr, buzz, drone, gurgle, hum, mumble, mutter, purl, purr, rumble.

muscle *n.* brawn, clout, depressor, force, forcefulness, levator, might, potency, power, sinew, stamina, strength, sturdiness, tendon, thew, weight.

muse *v.* brood, chew, cogitate, consider, contemplate, deliberate, dream, meditate, mull over, ponder, reflect, review, ruminate, speculate, think, think over, weigh.

mushroom *v.* boom, burgeon, expand, flourish, grow, increase, luxuriate, proliferate, shoot up, spread, spring up, sprout.
n. champignon, chanterelle, fungus, morel, pixy-stool, puffball, toadstool.

musical *adj.* canorous, dulcet, euphonious, Euterpean, harmonious, lilting, lyrical, melodic, melodious, sweet-sounding, tuneful.
antonym unmusical.

musician *n.* accompanist, bard, composer, conductor, instrumentalist, minstrel, performer, player, singer, vocalist.

musing *n.* absent-mindedness, abstraction, brown study, cerebration, cogitation, contemplation, daydreaming, dreaming, introspection, meditation, ponderment, reflection, reverie, rumination, thinking, wool-gathering.

must *n.* basic, duty, essential, fundamental, imperative, necessity, obligation, prerequisite, provision, requirement, requisite, sine qua non, stipulation.

muster *v.* assemble, call together, call up, collect, come together, congregate, convene, convoke, enrol, gather, group, marshal, mass, meet, mobilize, rally, round up, summon, throng.
n. assemblage, assembly, collection, concourse, congregation, convention, convocation, gathering, mass, meeting, mobilization, rally, round-up, throng.

musty *adj.* airless, ancient, antediluvian, antiquated, banal, clichéd, dank, decayed, dull, frowsty, fusty, hackneyed, hoary, mildewed, mildewy, moth-eaten, moldy, mucedinous, mucid, obsolete, old, old-fashioned, smelly, stale, stuffy, threadbare, trite, vinewed, worn-out.

mute *adj.* aphonic, dumb, mum, noiseless, silent, speechless, unexpressed, unpronounced, unspeaking, unspoken, voiceless, wordless.
antonyms articulate, vocal, voluble.
v. dampen, deaden, lower, moderate, muffle, silence, soften, soft-pedal, subdue, tone down.

mutilate *v.* adulterate, amputate, bowdlerize, butcher, censor, cut, cut to pieces, cut up, damage, detruncate, disable, disfigure, dismember, distort, expurgate, hack, hamble, injure, lacerate, lame, maim, mangle, mar, spoil.

mutinous *adj.* bolshie, bolshy, contumacious, disobedient, insubordinate, insurgent, rebellious, recusant, refractory, revolutionary, riotous, seditious, subversive, turbulent, ungovernable, unmanageable, unruly.
antonyms compliant, dutiful, obedient.

mutiny *n.* defiance, disobedience, insubordination, insurrection, putsch, rebellion, resistance, revolt, revolution, riot, rising, strike, uprising.
v. disobey, protest, rebel, resist, revolt, rise up, strike.

mutter *v.* chunter, complain, grouch, grouse, grumble, mumble, murmur, mussitate, rumble.

mutual *adj.* common, communal, complementary, exchanged, interchangeable, interchanged, joint, reciprocal, reciprocated, requited, returned, shared.

muzzle *n.* bit, curb, gag, guard, jaws, mouth, nose, snaffle, snout.
v. censor, choke, curb, gag, mute, restrain, silence, stifle, suppress.

myopic *adj.* half-blind, near-sighted, short-sighted.
antonym far-sighted.

myriad *adj.* boundless, countless, immeasurable, incalculable, innumerable, limitless, multitudinous, untold.
n. army, flood, horde, host, millions, mountain, multitude, scores, sea, swarm, thousands, throng.

mysterious *adj.* abstruse, arcane, baffling, concealed, covert, cryptic, curious, dark, enigmatic, furtive, hidden, impenetrable, incomprehensible, inexplicable, inscrutable, insoluble, mystical, mystifying, obscure, perplexing, puzzling, recondite, secret, secretive, strange, uncanny, unfathomable, unsearchable, veiled, weird.

antonyms comprehensible, frank, straightforward.

mystery *n.* arcanum, conundrum, enigma, problem, puzzle, question, riddle, secrecy, secret.

mystical *adj.* abstruse, arcane, cab(b)alistic(al), cryptic, enigmatical, esoteric, hidden, inscrutable, metaphysical, mysterious, mystic, occult, otherworldly, paranormal, preternatural, supernatural, transcendental.

mystify *v.* baffle, bamboozle, beat, befog, bewilder, confound, confuse, escape, perplex, puzzle, stump.

myth *n.* allegory, delusion, fable, fairy tale, fancy, fantasy, fiction, figment, illusion, legend, old wives' tale, parable, saga, story, superstition, tradition, untruism.

N

nag[1] *v.* annoy, badger, berate, chivvy, goad, harass, harry, henpeck, irritate, kvetch, pain, pester, plague, scold, torment, upbraid, vex.
n. harpy, harridan, kvetch(er), scold, shrew, tartar, termagant, virago.

nag[2] *n.* hack, horse, jade, plug, rip, Rosinante.

nail *v.* apprehend, attach, beat, capture, catch, clinch, collar, fasten, fix, hammer, join, nab, nick, pin, secure, seize, tack.
n. brad, hobnail, peg, pin, rivet, screw, skewer, spike, staple, tack, tacket.

naïve *adj.* artless, callow, candid, childlike, confiding, credulous, dewy-eyed, facile, frank, green, guileless, gullible, ingenuous, innocent, jejune, natural, open, simple, simplistic, trusting, unaffected, uncritical, unpretentious, unsophisticated, unsuspecting, unsuspicious, unworldly, verdant, wide-eyed.
antonyms experienced, sophisticated.

naked *adj.* adamic, bare, blatant, defenseless, denuded, disrobed, divested, evident, exposed, helpless, in puris naturalibus, in the altogether, in the buff, insecure, manifest, mother-naked, nude, open, overt, patent, plain, simple, skyclad, stark, starkers, stark-naked, stripped, unadorned, unarmed, unclothed, unconcealed, uncovered, undisguised, undraped, undressed, unexaggerated, unguarded, unmistakable, unprotected, unqualified, unvarnished, vulnerable.
antonyms clothed, concealed, covered.

name *n.* acronym, agname, agnomen, appellation, character, cognomen, compellation, compellative, credit, denomination, designation, distinction, eminence, epithet, esteem, fame, handle, honor, moni(c)ker, nickname, note, praise, renown, reputation, repute, sobriquet, stage name, term, title, to-name.
v. appoint, baptize, bename, betitle, call, choose, christen, cite, classify, cognominate, commission, denominate, designate, dub, entitle, identify, label, mention, nominate, select, specify, style, term, title.

nap[1] *v.* catnap, doze, drop off, drowse, kip, nod, nod off, rest, sleep, snooze.
n. catnap, forty winks, kip, rest, shuteye, siesta, sleep.

nap[2] *n.* down, downiness, fuzz, grain, pile, shag, weave.

narcissistic *adj.* conceited, egocentric, egomaniacal, ego(-t)istic, self-centered, self-loving, vain.

narcotic *n.* anesthetic, analgesic, anodyne, drug, hop, kef, opiate, pain-killer, sedative, tranquilizer.
adj. analgesic, calming, dulling, hypnotic, Lethean, numbing, pain-killing, sedative, somniferous, somnific, soporific, stupefacient, stupefactive, stupefying.

narrate *v.* chronicle, describe, detail, recite, recount, rehearse, relate, repeat, report, set forth, state, tell, unfold.

narrative *n.* account, chronicle, detail, history, parable, report, statement, story, tale.

narrow *adj.* attenuated, avaricious, biased, bigoted, circumscribed, close, confined, constricted, contracted, cramped, dogmatic, exclusive, fine, illiberal, incapacious, intolerant, limited, meager, mean, mercenary, narrow-minded, near, niggardly, partial, pinched, prejudiced, reactionary, restricted, scanty, select, simplistic, slender, slim, small-minded, spare, straitened, tapering, thin, tight, ungenerous.
antonyms broad, liberal, tolerant, wide.
v. circumscribe, constrict, constringe, diminish, limit, reduce, simplify, straiten, tighten.
antonyms broaden, increase, loosen, widen.
antonyms broadening, widening.

narrow-minded *adj.* biased, bigoted, blinkered, borné, conservative, hidebound, illiberal, insular, intolerant, mean, opinionated, parochial, petty, prejudiced, provincial, reactionary, short-sighted, small-minded, strait-laced.
antonym broad-minded.
antonyms breadth, width.

nascent *adj.* advancing, budding, developing, embryonic, evolving, growing, incipient, naissant, rising, young.
antonym dying.

nasty *adj.* abusive, annoying, bad, bad-tempered, base, critical, dangerous, despicable, dirty, disagreeable, disgusting, distasteful, filthy, foul, gross, horrible, impure, indecent, lascivious, lewd, licentious, loathsome, low-down, malicious, malodorous, mean, mephitic, nauseating, noisome, objectionable, obnoxious, obscene, odious, offensive, painful, polluted, pornographic, repellent, repugnant, ribald, serious, severe, sickening, smutty, spiteful, unappetizing, unpleasant, unsavory, vicious, vile, waspish.
antonyms agreeable, clean, decent, pleasant.

nation *n.* citizenry, commonwealth, community, country, people, population, race, realm, society, state, tribe.

native *adj.* aboriginal, autochthonous, built-in, congenital, domestic, endemic, genuine, hereditary, home, home-born, home-bred, home-grown, home-made, inborn, inbred, indigene, indigenous, ingrained, inherent, inherited, innate, instinctive, intrinsic, inveterate, local, mother, natal, natural, original, real, vernacular.
n. aborigine, autochthon, citizen, countryman, dweller, indigene, inhabitant, national, resident.
antonyms foreigner, outsider, stranger.

natty *adj.* chic, dapper, elegant, fashionable, neat, ritzy, smart, snazzy, spruce, stylish, swanky, trim.

natural *adj.* artless, candid, characteristic, common, congenital, constitutional, essential, everyday, frank, genuine, inborn, indigenous, ingenuous, inherent, innate, instinctive, intuitive, legitimate, logical, natal, native, normal, open, ordinary, organic, plain, pure, real, regular, simple, spontaneous, typical, unaffected, unbleached, unforced, unlabored, unlearned, unmixed, unpolished, unpretentious, unrefined, unsophisticated, unstudied, untaught, usual, whole.
antonyms abnormal, affected, alien, artificial, pretended, unnatural.

naturally *adj.* absolutely, artlessly, as a matter of course, candidly, certainly, customarily, frankly, genuinely, informally, normally, of course, plainly, simply, spontaneously, typically, unaffectedly, unpretentiously.

nature[1] *n.* attributes, category, character, complexion, constitution, cosmos, creation, description, disposition, earth, environment, essence, features, humor, inbeing, inscape, kind, make-up, mood, outlook, quality, sort, species, style, temper, temperament, traits, type, universe, variety, world.

nature[2] *n.* country, countryside, landscape, natural history, scenery.

naught *n.* nil, nothing, nothingness, nought, zero, zilch.

naughty *adj.* annoying, bad, bawdy, blue, disobedient, exasperating, fractious, impish, improper, lewd, misbehaved, mischievous, obscene, off-color, perverse, playful, refractory, remiss, reprehensible, ribald, risqué, roguish, sinful, smutty, teasing, vulgar, wayward, wicked, worthless.
antonyms good, polite, well-behaved.

nausea *n.* abhorrence, aversion, biliousness, disgust, loathing, motion sickness, qualm(s), queasiness, repugnance, retching, revulsion, sickness, squeamishness, vomiting.

nauseating *adj.* abhorrent, detestable, disgusting, distasteful, fulsome, loathsome, nauseous, offensive, repugnant, repulsive, revolting, sickening.

nautical *adj.* boating, marine, maritime, naval, oceanic, sailing, seafaring, sea-going, yachting.

naval *adj.* marine, maritime, nautical, sea.

navigate *v.* con, cross, cruise, direct, drive, guide, handle, helm, journey, maneuver, pilot, plan, plot, sail, skipper, steer, voyage.

near *adj.* accessible, adjacent, adjoining, akin, allied, alongside, approaching, at close quarters, attached, beside, bordering, close, connected, contiguous, dear, familiar, forthcoming, handy, imminent, impending, in the offing, intimate, looming, near-at-hand, nearby, neighboring, next, nigh, on the cards, proximal, related, touching.
antonyms distant, far, remote.

near thing close shave, narrow escape, nasty moment, near miss.

nearly *adv.* about, all but, almost, approaching, approximately, as good as, closely, just about, not quite, practically, pretty much, pretty well, roughly, virtually, well-nigh.

neat *adj.* accurate, adept, adroit, agile, apt, clean-cut, clever, dainty, deft, dexterous, dinky, efficient, effortless, elegant, expert, fastidious, genty, graceful, handy, methodical, nice, nimble, orderly, practiced, precise, pure, shipshape, skilful, smart, spick-and-span, spruce, straight, stylish, systematic, tiddley, tidy, trig, trim, uncluttered, undi *antonyms* disordered, disorderly, messy, untidy.

nebulous *adj.* ambiguous, amorphous, cloudy, confused, dim, fuzzy, hazy, imprecise, indefinite, indeterminate, indistinct, misty, murky, obscure, shadowy, shapeless, uncertain, unclear, unformed, unspecific, vague.
antonym clear.

necessary *adj.* certain, compulsory, de rigueur, essential, fated, imperative, indispensable, ineluctable, inescapable, inevitable, inexorable, mandatory, needed, needful, obligatory, required, requisite, unavoidable, vital.
antonyms inessential, unimportant, unnecessary.

necessity *n.* ananke, compulsion, demand, desideratum, destiny, destitution, essential, exigency, extremity, fate, fundamental, indigence, indispensability, inevitability, inexorableness, necessary, need, needfulness, obligation, penury, poverty, prerequisite, privation, requirement, requisite, sine qua non, want.

necromancy *n.* black art, black magic, conjuration, demonology, divination, enchantment, hoodoo, magic, sorcery, thaumaturgy, voodoo, witchcraft, witchery, wizardry.

need *v.* call for, crave, demand, lack, miss, necessitate, require, want.
n. besoin, demand, deprivation, desideratum, destitution, distress, egence, egency, emergency, essential, exigency, extremity, impecuniousness, inadequacy, indigence, insufficiency, lack, longing, necessity, neediness, obligation, paucity, penury, poverty, privation, requirement, requisite, shortage, urgency, want, wish.
antonym sufficiency.

needed *adj.* called for, compulsory, desired, essential, lacking, necessary, obligatory, required, requisite, wanted.
antonyms unnecessary, unneeded.

needle *v.* aggravate, annoy, bait, goad, harass, irk, irritate, nag, nettle, pester, prick, prod, provoke, rile, ruffle, spur, sting, taunt, torment.

needless *adj.* causeless, dispensable, excessive, expendable, gratuitous, groundless, inessential, non-essential, pointless, purposeless, redundant, superfluous, uncalled-for, unessential, unnecessary, unwanted, useless.
antonyms necessary, needful.

needy *adj.* deprived, destitute, disadvantaged, impecunious,

impoverished, indigent, penniless, penurious, poor, poverty-stricken, underprivileged.
antonyms affluent, wealthy, well-off.

nefarious *adj.* abominable, atrocious, base, criminal, depraved, detestable, dreadful, evil, execrable, foul, heinous, horrible, infamous, infernal, iniquitous, monstrous, odious, opprobrious, satanic, shameful, sinful, unholy, vicious, vile, villainous, wicked. *antonym* exemplary.

negate *v.* abrogate, annul, cancel, contradict, countermand, deny, disallow, disprove, gainsay, invalidate, neutralize, nullify, oppose, quash, refute, repeal, rescind, retract, reverse, revoke, void, wipe out.
antonym affirm.
antonyms optimistic, positive.
n. contradiction, denial, opposite, refusal.

neglect *v.* contemn, disdain, disprovide, disregard, forget, ignore, leave alone, let slide, omit, overlook, pass by, pigeon-hole, rebuff, scorn, shirk, skimp, slight, spurn.
antonyms cherish, nurture, treasure.
n. carelessness, default, dereliction, disdain, disregard, disrespect, failure, forgetfulness, heedlessness, inattention, indifference, laches, laxity, laxness, neglectfulness, negligence, oversight, slackness, slight, slovenliness, unconcern.

negligent *adj.* careless, cursory, disregardful, forgetful, inattentive, indifferent, lax, neglectful, nonchalant, offhand, regardless, remiss, slack, thoughtless, uncareful, uncaring, unmindful, unthinking.
antonyms attentive, careful, heedful, scrupulous.

negligible *adj.* imperceptible, inconsequential, insignificant, minor, minute, neglectable, nugatory, petty, small, trifling, trivial, unimportant.
antonym significant.

negotiate *v.* adjudicate, arbitrate, arrange, bargain, broke, clear, conciliate, confer, consult, contract, cross, deal, debate, discuss, get past, handle, manage, mediate, parley, pass, settle, surmount, transact, traverse, treat, work out.

neighborhood *n.* community, confines, district, environs, locale, locality, precincts, proximity, purlieus, quarter, region, surroundings, vicinage, vicinity.

neighboring *adj.* abutting, adjacent, adjoining, bordering, connecting, contiguous, near, nearby, nearest, next, surrounding, vicinal.
antonyms distant, faraway, remote.

neighborly *adj.* amiable, chummy, civil, companionable, considerate, friendly, genial, helpful, hospitable, kind, obliging, sociable, social, solicitous, well-disposed.

nerve *n.* audacity, boldness, bottle, brass, bravery, brazenness, cheek, chutzpah, coolness, courage, daring, determination, effrontery, endurance, energy, fearlessness, firmness, force, fortitude, gall, gameness, grit, guts, hardihood, impertinence, impudence, insolence, intrepidity, mettle, might, pluck, resolution, sauce, spirit, spunk, steadfastness, temerity, vigor, will.
antonyms cowardice, weakness.
v. bolster, brace, embolden, encourage, fortify, hearten, invigorate, steel, strengthen.
antonym unnerve.

nervous *adj.* agitated, anxious, apprehensive, edgy, excitable, fearful, fidgety, flustered, hesitant, highly-strung, high-strung, hysterical, jittery, jumpy, nervy, neurotic, on edge, shaky, tense, timid, timorous, twitchy, uneasy, uptight, weak, windy, worried.
antonyms bold, calm, confident, cool, relaxed.

nest *n.* breeding-ground, burrow, den, drey, earth, form, formicary, haunt, hideaway, hotbed, nid(e), nidus, refuge, resort, retreat.

nestle *v.* cuddle, curl up, ensconce, huddle, nuzzle, snuggle.

net[1] *n.* drag, drag-net, drift, drift-net, drop-net, lattice, mesh, netting, network, open-work, reticulum, tracery, web.
v. apprehend, bag, benet, capture, catch, enmesh, ensnare, entangle, nab, trap.

net[2] *adj.* after tax, clear, final, lowest, nett.
v. accumulate, bring in, clear, earn, gain, make, obtain, realize, reap, receive, secure.

nettle *v.* annoy, chafe, discountenance, exasperate, fret, goad, harass, incense, irritate, needle, pique, provoke, ruffle, sting, tease, vex.

neurotic *adj.* abnormal, anxious, compulsive, deviant, disordered, distraught, disturbed, maladjusted, manic, morbid, nervous, obsessive, overwrought, unhealthy, unstable, wearisome.
antonyms normal, stable.

neutral *adj.* colorless, disinterested, dispassionate, dull, even-handed, expressionless, impartial, indeterminate, indifferent, indistinct, indistinguishable, intermediate, non-aligned, non-committal, nondescript, non-partisan, unbia(s)sed, uncommitted, undecided, undefined, uninvolved, unprejudiced.
antonyms biased, prejudiced.

nevertheless *adv.* anyhow, anyway, but, even so, however, nonetheless, notwithstanding, regardless, still, yet.

new *adj.* added, advanced, altered, changed, contemporary, current, different, extra, fresh, improved, latest, modern, modernistic, modernized, modish, more, newborn, newfangled, novel, original, recent, redesigned, renewed, restored, supplementary, topical, trendy, ultra-modern, unfamiliar, unknown, unused, unusual, up-to-date, up-to-the-minute, virgin.
antonyms hackneyed, old, outdated, out-of-date, usual.

newcomer *n.* alien, arrival, arriviste, beginner, colonist, foreigner, immigrant, incomer, Johnny-come-lately, novice, outsider, parvenu, settler, stranger.

news *n.* account, advice, bulletin, communiqué, disclosure, dispatch, exposé, gen, gossip, hearsay, information, intelligence, latest, leak, release, report, revelation, rumor, scandal, statement, story, tidings, update, word.

next *adj.* adjacent, adjoining, closest, consequent, ensuing, following, later, nearest, neighboring, sequent, sequential, subsequent, succeeding.
antonyms preceding, previous.
adv. afterwards, later, subsequently, then, thereafter.

nibble *n.* bit, bite, crumb, morsel, peck, piece, snack, soupçon, taste, titbit.
v. bite, eat, gnaw, knap, knapple, munch, nip, nosh, peck, pickle.

nice *adj.* accurate, agreeable, amiable, attractive, careful, charming, commendable, courteous, critical, cultured, dainty, delicate, delightful, discriminating, exact, exacting, fastidious, fine, finical, friendly, genteel, good, kind, likable, meticulous, neat, particular, pleasant, pleasurable, polite, precise, prepossessing, punctilious, purist, refined, respectable, rigorous, scrupulous, strict, subtle, tidy, trim, virtuous, well-bred, well-mannered.
antonyms careless, disagreeable, haphazard, nasty, unpleasant.

niche[1] *n.* alcove, corner, cubby, cubby-hole, hollow, nook, opening, recess.

niche[2] *n.* calling, métier, pigeon-hole, place, position, slot, vocation.

nick[1] *n.* chip, cut, damage, dent, indent, indentation, mark, notch, scar, score, scratch, snick.
v. chip, cut, damage, dent, indent, mark, notch, scar, score, scratch, snick.

nick[2] *v.* finger, knap, knock off, lag, pilfer, pinch, snitch, steal.

nickname *n.* cognomen, diminutive, epithet, familiarity, label, moni(c)ker, pet name, sobriquet.

niggardly *adj.* avaricious, beggarly, cheese-paring, close, covetous, frugal, grudging, hard-fisted, inadequate, insufficient, meager, mean, mercenary, miserable, miserly, near, paltry, parsimonious, penurious, scanty, skimpy, small, sordid, sparing, stinging, stingy, tight-fisted, ungenerous, ungiving, wretched.
antonyms bountiful, generous.

nightmare *n.* bad dream, ephialtes, hallucination, horror, incubus, ordeal, succubus, torment, trial, tribulation.

nil *n.* duck, goose-egg, love, naught, nihil, none, nothing, zero.

nimble *adj.* active, agile, alert, brisk, deft, dexterous, lightfoot(ed), lissom(e), lively, nippy, proficient, prompt, quick, quick-witted, ready, smart, sprightly, spry, swift, volant.
antonyms awkward, clumsy.

nincompoop *n.* blockhead, dimwit, dolt, dunce, fool, idiot, ignoramus, ninny, nitwit, noodle, numskull, sap, saphead, simpleton.

nip[1] *v.* bite, catch, check, clip, compress, grip, nibble, pinch, snag, snap, sneap, snip, squeeze, tweak, twitch.

nip[2] *n.* dram, draught, drop, finger, mouthful, peg, portion, shot, sip, slug, snifter, soupçon, sup, swallow, taste.

nippy[1] *adj.* astringent, biting, chilly, nipping, pungent, sharp, stinging.

nippy[2] *adj.* active, agile, fast, nimble, quick, speedy, sprightly, spry.
antonym slow.

nit-picking *adj.* captious, carping, caviling, finicky, fussy, hair-splitting, hypercritical, pedantic, pettifogging, quibbling.

noble *n.* aristocrat, baron, gentilhomme, grand seigneur, lord, nobleman, patrician, peer.
antonyms pleb, prole.
adj. aristocratic, august, blue-blooded, dignified, distinguished, elevated, eminent, excellent, generous, gentle, grand, great, high-born, honorable, honored, imposing, impressive, lofty, lordly, magnanimous, magnificent, majestic, patrician, splendid, stately, titled, upright, virtuous, worthy.
antonyms base, ignoble, low-born.

nobody *n.* also-ran, cipher, lightweight, man of straw, menial, minnow, nonentity, no-one, nothing, Walter Mitty.
antonym somebody.

nod *v.* acknowledge, agree, assent, beckon, bob, bow, concur, dip, doze, droop, drowse, duck, gesture, indicate, nap, salute, sign, signal, sleep, slip up, slump.
n. acknowledgment, beck, cue, gesture, greeting, indication, salute, sign, signal.

node *n.* bud, bump, burl, caruncle, growth, knob, knot, lump, nodule, process, protuberance, swelling.

noise *n.* babble, ballyhoo, blare, brattle, chirm, clamor, clash, clatter, coil, commotion, cry, din, fracas, hubbub, outcry, pandemonium, racket, row, sound, talk, tumult, uproar.
antonyms quiet, silence.
v. advertise, announce, bruit, circulate, gossip, publicize, repeat, report, rumor.

noisome *adj.* bad, baneful, deleterious, disgusting, fetid, foul, fulsome, harmful, hurtful, injurious, malodorous, mephitic, mischievous, noxious, offensive, pernicious, pestiferous, pestilential, poisonous, putrid, reeking, smelly, stinking, unhealthy, unwholesome.
antonyms balmy, pleasant, wholesome.

noisy *adj.* boisterous, cacophonous, chattering, clamorous, clangorous, deafening, ear-piercing, ear-splitting, horrisonant, loud, obstreperous, piercing, plangent, rackety, riotous, strepitant, strident, tumultuous, turbulent, uproarious, vocal, vociferous.
antonyms peaceful, quiet, silent.

nomad *n.* drifter, itinerant, migrant, rambler, roamer, rover, traveler, vagabond, vagrant, wanderer.

nominate *v.* appoint, assign, choose, commission, designate, elect, elevate, empower, mention, name, present, propose, put up, recommend, select, submit, suggest, term.

nomination *n.* appointment, choice, designation, election, proposal, recommendation, selection, submission, suggestion.

nominee *n.* appointee, assignee, candidate, contestant, entrant, protégé, runner.

nonchalant *adj.* airy, apathetic, blasé, calm, careless, casual, collected, cool, detached, dispassionate, impassive, indifferent, insouciant, offhand, pococurante, unconcerned, unemotional, unperturbed.
antonyms anxious, careful, concerned, worried.

non-committal *adj.* ambiguous, careful, cautious, circumspect, cunctatious, cunctative, cunctatory, discreet, equivocal, evasive, guarded, indefinite, neutral, politic, reserved, tactful, temporizing, tentative, unrevealing, vague, wary.

nonconformist *n.* deviant, dissenter, dissentient, eccentric, heretic, iconoclast, individualist, maverick, oddball, protester, radical, rebel, seceder, secessionist.
antonym conformist.

nondescript *adj.* commonplace, dull, featureless, indeterminate, mousy, ordinary, plain, unclassified, undistinctive, undistinguished, unexceptional, uninspiring, uninteresting, unmemorable, unremarkable, vague.

nonentity *n.* cipher, dandiprat, drip, drongo, earthworm, gnatling, lightweight, mediocrity, nobody.

non-essential *adj.* dispensable, excessive, expendable, extraneous, extrinsic(al), inessential, peripheral, superfluous, supplementary, unimportant, unnecessary.
antonym essential.

non-existent *adj.* chimerical, fancied, fictional, hallucinatory, hypothetical, illusory, imaginary, imagined, immaterial, incorporeal, insubstantial, legendary, missing, mythical, null, unreal.
antonyms actual, existing, real.

nonplus *v.* astonish, astound, baffle, bewilder, confound, confuse, discomfit, disconcert, discountenance, dismay, dumbfound, embarrass, flabbergast, flummox, mystify, perplex, puzzle, stump, stun, take aback.

nonsense *n.* absurdity, balderdash, balls, baloney, bilge, blah, blather, blethers, bollocks, bombast, bosh, bull, bullshit, bunk, bunkum, claptrap, cobblers, codswallop, crap, double-Dutch, drivel, fadaise, faddle, fandangle, fatuity, fiddle-de-dee, fiddle-faddle, fiddlesticks, flapdoodle, folly, foolishness, fudge, gaff, galimatias, gammon, gas and gaiters, gibberish, gobbledygook, havers, hogwash, hooey, inanity, jabberwock(y), jest, ludicrousness, moonshine, nomeaning, piffle, pulp, ridiculousness, rot, rubbish, senselessness, silliness, squish, squit, stuff, stultiloquence, stupidity, tar(r)adiddle, tommy-rot, tosh, trash, twaddle, twattle, unreason, waffle.
antonym sense.

nonsensical *adj.* absurd, crazy, daft, fatuous, foolish, inane, incomprehensible, irrational, ludicrous, meaningless, ridiculous, senseless, silly.
antonyms logical, sensible.

non-stop *adj.* ceaseless, constant, continuous, direct, endless, incessant, interminable, never-ending, on-going, relentless, round-the-clock, steady, unbroken, unceasing, unending, unfaltering, uninterrupted, unrelenting, unremitting.
antonyms intermittent, occasional.
adv. ceaselessly, constantly, continuously, directly, endlessly, incessantly, interminably, relentlessly, round-the-clock, steadily, unbrokenly, unceasingly, unendingly, unfalteringly, uninterruptedly, unrelentingly, unremittingly.
antonyms imtermittently, occasionally.

nook *n.* alcove, cavity, corner, cranny, crevice, cubbyhole, hide-out, ingle-nook, nest, niche, opening, recess, retreat, shelter.

normal *adj.* accustomed, acknowledged, average, common, common-or-garden, conventional, habitual, mainstream, natural, ordinary, par for the course, popular, rational, reasonable, regular, routine, run-of-the-mill, sane, standard, straight, typical, usual, well-adjusted.
antonyms abnormal, irregular, odd, peculiar.

normally *adv.* as a rule, characteristically, commonly, habitually, ordinarily, regularly, straight, typically, usually.
antonym abnormally.

nos(e)y *adj.* curious, eavesdropping, inquisitive, interfering, intermeddling, intrusive, meddlesome, officious, prying, snooping.

nostalgia *n.* homesickness, longing, mal du pays, pining, regret, regretfulness, remembrance, reminiscence, wistfulness, yearning.

notable *adj.* celebrated, conspicuous, distinguished, eminent, evident, extraordinary, famous, impressive, manifest, marked, memorable, noteworthy, noticeable, notorious, outstanding, overt, pre-eminent, pronounced, rare, remarkable, renowned, signal, striking, uncommon, unusual, well-known.
antonyms commonplace, ordinary, usual.
n. celebrity, dignitary, luminary, notability, personage, somebody, VIP, worthy.
antonyms nobody, nonentity.

notch *n.* cleft, cut, degree, grade, incision, indentation, insection, kerf, level, mark, nick, score, sinus, snip, step.
v. cut, gimp, indent, mark, nick, raffle, scallop, score, scratch.

note *n.* annotation, apostil(le), billet, celebrity, character, comment, communication, consequence, distinction, eminence, epistle, epistolet, fame, gloss, heed, indication, jotting, letter, line, mark, memo, memorandum, message, minute, notice, observation, prestige, record, regard, remark, reminder, renown, reputation, signal, symbol, token.
v. denote, designate, detect, enter, indicate, mark, mention, notice, observe, perceive, record, register, remark, see, witness.

noted *adj.* acclaimed, celebrated, conspicuous, distinguished, eminent, famous, great, illustrious, notable, notorious, prominent, recognized, renowned, respected, well-known. **noteworthy** *adj.* exceptional, extraordinary, important, notable, on the map, outstanding, remarkable, significant, unusual, visitable.
antonyms commonplace, ordinary, unexceptional, usual.

notice *v.* descry, detect, discern, distinguish, espy, heed, mark, mind, note, observe, perceive, remark, see, spot.
antonyms ignore, overlook.
n. advertisement, advice, affiche, announcement, attention, bill, civility, cognizance, comment, communication, consideration, criticism, heed, instruction, intelligence, intimation, news, note, notification, observation, order, poster, regard, respect, review, sign, warning.

notify *v.* acquaint, advise, alert, announce, apprize, declare, disclose, inform, publish, reveal, tell, warn.

notion *n.* apprehension, belief, caprice, conceit, concept, conception, concetto, construct, desire, fancy, idea, image, impression, impulse, inclination, inkling, judgment, knowledge, opinion, sentiment, understanding, view, whim, wish.

notorious *adj.* arrant, blatant, dishonorable, disreputable, egregious, flagrant, infamous, obvious, open, opprobrious, overt, patent, scandalous, undisputed.

nourish *v.* attend, cherish, comfort, cultivate, encourage, feed, foster, furnish, harbor, maintain, nurse, nurture, promote, supply, support, sustain, tend.

nourishment *n.* aliment, diet, food, goodness, nutriment, nutrition, pabulum, provender, sustenance, viands, victuals.

novel *adj.* different, fresh, imaginative, innovative, new, original, rare, singular, strange, surprising, uncommon, unconventional, unfamiliar, unusual.
antonyms familiar, ordinary.
n. fiction, narrative, romance, saga, story, tale, yarn.

novice *n.* amateur, apprentice, beginner, catechumen, convert, cub, griffin, Johnny-raw, learner, neophyte, newcomer, novitiate, probationer, proselyte, pupil, tiro.
antonyms doyen, expert, professional.

now *adv.* at once, at present, directly, immediately, instanter, instantly, next, nowadays, presently, promptly, straightaway, these days.

noxious *adj.* baneful, corrupting, deadly, deleterious, destructive, detrimental, foul, harmful, hurtful, injurious, insalubrious, mephitic(al), morbiferous, morbific, noisome, pernicious, pestilential, poisonous, unhealthy, unwholesome.
antonyms innocuous, wholesome.

nucleus *n.* basis, center, core, crux, focus, heart, heartlet, kernel, nub, pivot.

nude *adj.* au naturel, bare, disrobed, exposed, in one's birthday suit, in puris naturalibus, in the altogether, in the buff, naked, starkers, stark-naked, stripped, unattired, unclad, unclothed, uncovered, undraped, undressed, without a stitch.
antonyms clothed, covered, dressed.

nudge *v., n.* bump, dig, jog, poke, prod, prompt, push, shove, touch.

nugget *n.* chunk, clump, hunk, lump, mass, piece, wodge.

nuisance *n.* annoyance, bore, bother, désagrément, drag, drawback, inconvenience, infliction, irritation, offence, pain, pest, plague, problem, trouble, vexation.

nullify *v.* abate, abolish, abrogate, annul, cancel, counteract, countervail, invalidate, negate, neutralize, quash, repeal, rescind, revoke, undermine, veto, vitiate, void.
antonym validate.

numb *adj.* benumbed, dead, deadened, frozen, immobilized, insensate, insensible, insensitive, paralyzed, stunned, stupefied, torpid, unfeeling.
antonym sensitive.
v. anesthetize, benumb, deaden, dull, freeze, immobilize, obtund, paralyze, stun, stupefy.
antonym sensitize.

number[1] *n.* aggregate, amount, character, collection, company, count, crowd, digit, figure, folio, horde, index, integer, many, multitude, numeral, quantity, several, sum, throng, total, unit.
v. account, add, apportion, calculate, compute, count, enumerate, include, inventory, reckon, tell, total.

number[2] *n.* copy, edition, impression, imprint, issue, printing, volume.

numeral *n.* character, cipher, digit, figure, folio, integer, number.

numerous *adj.* abundant, copious, divers, many, multitudinous, myriad, plentiful, profuse, several, sundry.
antonyms few, scanty.

numskull *n.* blockhead, bonehead, buffoon, clot, dimwit, dolt, dope, dullard, dummy, dunce, dunderhead, fathead, fool, sap, saphead, simpleton, thickhead, twit.

nuptials *n.* bridal, espousal, marriage, matrimony, spousals, wedding.

nurse *v.* breast-feed, care for, cherish, cultivate, encourage, feed, foster, harbor, keep, nourish, nurture, preserve, promote, succor, suckle, support, sustain, tend, treat, wetnurse.
n. amah, district-nurse, home-nurse, mammy, nanny, nursemaid, sister of mercy, wet nurse.

nurture *n.* care, cultivation, development, diet, discipline, education, food, instruction, nourishment, rearing, training, upbringing.
v. bring up, care for, cultivate, develop, discipline, educate, feed, instruct, nourish, nurse, rear, school, support, sustain, tend, train.

nutriment *n.* aliment, diet, food, foodstuff, nourishment, nutrition, pabulum, provender, subsistence, support, sustenance.

nutrition *n.* eutrophy, food, nourishment, nutriment, sustenance.

O

oaf *n.* baboon, blockhead, bonehead, booby, brute, clod, dolt, dullard, dummy, dunce, fool, galoot, gawk, goon, gorilla, half-wit, hick, hobbledehoy, hulk, idiot, imbecile, lout, lummox, moron, nincompoop, oik, sap, schlemiel, schlep, simpleton, yob.

oasis *n.* enclave, haven, island, refuge, resting-place, retreat, sanctuary, sanctum, watering-hole.

oath *n.* affirmation, assurance, avowal, blasphemy, bond, curse, cuss, expletive, imprecation, malediction, pledge, plight, profanity, promise, swear-word, vow, word, word of honor.

obdurate *adj.* adamant, callous, dogged, firm, fixed, flinty, hard, hard-hearted, harsh, immovable, implacable, inexorable, inflexible, intransigent, iron, mulish, obstinate, perverse, pig-headed, relentless, stiff-necked, stony, stubborn, unbending, unfeeling, unrelenting, unshakable, unyielding.
antonyms submissive, tender.

obedience *n.* accordance, acquiescence, agreement, allegiance, amenableness, compliance, conformability, deference, docility, dutifulness, duty, observance, passivity, respect, reverence, submission, submissiveness, subservience, tractability.
antonym disobedience.

obedient *adj.* acquiescent, amenable, biddable, compliant, deferential, docile, duteous, dutiful, law-abiding, observant, passive, regardful, respectful, sequacious, submissive, subservient, tractable, unquestioning, unresisting, well-trained, yielding.
antonyms disobedient, rebellious, refractory, unruly, wilful.

obese *adj.* bulky, corpulent, Falstaffian, fat, fleshy, gross, heavy, outsize, overweight, paunchy, plump, podgy, ponderous, portly, pursy, roly-poly, rotund, stout, tubby.
antonyms skinny, slender, thin.

obey *v.* abide by, act upon, adhere to, be ruled by, bow to, carry out, comply, conform, defer (to), discharge, embrace, execute, follow, fulfil, give in, give way, heed, implement, keep, knuckle under, mind, observe, perform, respond, serve, submit, surrender, take orders from, toe the line, yield.
antonym disobey.

object[1] *n.* aim, article, body, butt, design, end, entity, fact, focus, goal, idea, intent, intention, item, motive, objective, phenomenon, point, purpose, raison d'être, reality, reason, recipient, target, thing, victim, visible.

object[2] *v.* argue, complain, demur, dissent, expostulate, oppose, protest, rebut, refuse, repudiate, take exception.
antonyms accede, acquiesce, agree, assent.

objection *n.* cavil, censure, challenge, complaint, counter-argument, demur, doubt, exception, niggle, opposition, protest, remonstrance, scruple.
antonyms agreement, assent.

objectionable *adj.* abhorrent, antisocial, deplorable, despicable, detestable, disagreeable, dislikable, displeasing, distasteful, exceptionable, indecorous, insufferable, intolerable, loathsome, noxious, obnoxious, offensive, regrettable, repugnant, unacceptable, undesirable, unpleasant, unseemly.
antonyms acceptable, pleasant, welcome.

objective *adj.* calm, detached, disinterested, dispassionate, equitable, even-handed, fair, impartial, impersonal, judicial, just, open-minded, sensible, sober, unbiased, uncolored, unemotional, unimpassioned, uninvolved, unprejudiced.
antonyms biased, subjective.
n. aim, ambition, aspiration, design, destination, end, goal, intention, mark, object, prize, purpose, target.

objectivity *n.* detachment, disinterest, disinterestedness, dispassion, equitableness, even-handedness, impartiality, impersonality, open mind, open-mindedness.
antonyms bias, subjectivity.

obligation *n.* accountability, accountableness, agreement, bond, burden, charge, commitment, compulsion, contract, debt, duty, engagement, indebtedness, liability, must, obstriction, onus, promise, requirement, responsibility, stipulation, trust, understanding.
antonyms choice, discretion.

obligatory *adj.* binding, bounden, coercive, compulsory, de rigueur, enforced, essential, imperative, mandatory, necessary, required, requisite, statutory, unavoidable.
antonym optional.

oblige *v.* accommodate, assist, benefit, bind, coerce, compel, constrain, do a favor, favor, force, gratify, help, impel, indulge, make, necessitate, obligate, please, require, serve.

obliging *adj.* accommodating, agreeable, aidful, amiable, civil, complaisant, considerate, co-operative, courteous, eager, friendly, good-natured, helpful, kind, polite, willing.
antonyms inconsiderate, unhelpful, unkind.

obliterate *v.* annihilate, blot out, cancel, delete, destroy, efface, eradicate, erase, expunge, extirpate, rub out, vaporize, wipe out.

oblivious *adj.* blind, careless, comatose, deaf, disregardful, forgetful, heedless, ignorant, inattentive, insensible, neglectful, negligent, nescient, regardless, unaware, unconcerned, unconscious, unmindful, unobservant.
antonyms aware, conscious.

obloquy *n.* abuse, animadversion, aspersion, attack, bad press, blame, calumny, censure, contumely, criticism, defamation, detraction, discredit, disfavor, disgrace, dishonor, humiliation, ignominy, infamy, invective, odium, opprobrium, reproach, shame, slander, stigma, vilification.

obnoxious *adj.* abhorrent, abominable, detestable, disagreeable, disgusting, dislikable, foul, fulsome, hateful, horrid, insufferable, loathsome, nasty, nauseating, nauseous, noisome, objectionable, odious, offensive, repellent, reprehensible, repugnant, repulsive, revolting, sickening, unpleasant.
antonyms agreeable, likable, pleasant.

obscene *adj.* atrocious, barrack-room, bawdy, blue, coarse, dirty, disgusting, evil, Fescennine, filthy, foul, gross, heinous, immodest, immoral, improper, impure, indecent, lewd, licentious, loathsome, loose, offensive, outrageous, pornographic, prurient, Rabelaisian, ribald, salacious, scabrous, scurrilous, shameless, shocking, sickening, smutty, suggestive, unchaste, unwholesome, vile, wicked.
antonyms clean, decent, decorous.

obscure *adj.* abstruse, ambiguous, arcane, blurred, caliginous, clear as mud, clouded, cloudy, concealed, confusing, cryptic, deep, Delphic, dim, doubtful, dusky, enigmatic, esoteric, faint, gloomy, hazy, hermetic, hidden, humble, incomprehensible, inconspicuous, indefinite, indistinct, inglorious, intricate, involved, little-known, lowly, minor, misty, murky, mysterious, nameless, obfuscated, occult, opaque, oracular, out-of-the-way, recondite, remote, riddling, shadowy, shady, somber, tenebr(i)ous, tenebrose, twilight, unclear, undistinguished, unheard-of, unhonored, unimportant, unknown, unlit, unnoted, unobvious, unrenowned, unseen, unsung, vague, veiled.
antonyms clear, definite, explicit, famous, lucid.
v. bedim, befog, block out, blur, cloak, cloud, conceal, cover, darken, dim, disguise, dull, eclipse, hide, mask, muddy, obfuscate, overshadow, screen, shade, shadow, shroud, veil.
antonyms clarify, illuminate.

obsequious *adj.* abject, cringing, deferential, dough-faced, fawning, flattering, groveling, ingratiating, knee-crooking, menial, oily, servile, slavish, slimy, smarmy, submissive, subservient, sycophantic, toadying, unctuous.
antonym assertive.

observant *adj.* alert, attentive, eagle-eyed, eagle-sighted, falcon-eyed, heedful, mindful, perceptive, percipient, quick, sharp-eyed, vigilant, watchful, wide-awake.
antonyms inattentive, unobservant.

observation *n.* annotation, attention, cognition, comment, consideration, discernment, examination, experience, finding, information, inspection, knowledge, monitoring, note, notice, obiter dictum, opinion, perception, pronouncement, reading, reflection, remark, review, scrutiny, study, surveillance, thought, utterance, watching.

observe *v.* abide by, adhere to, animadvert, celebrate, commemorate, comment, comply, conform to, contemplate, declare, detect, discern, discover, espy, follow, fulfil, heed, honor, keep, keep an eye on, keep tabs on, mention, mind, monitor, note, notice, obey, opine, perceive, perform, regard, remark, remember, respect, say, scrutinize, see, solemnize, spot, state, study, surveille, survey, view, watch, witness.
antonyms break, miss, overlook, violate.

observer *n.* beholder, bystander, commentator, discerner, eyewitness, looker-on, noter, onlooker, spectator, spotter, viewer, watcher, witness.

obsession *n.* bee in one's bonnet, complex, enthusiasm, fetish, fixation, hang-up, idée fixe, infatuation, mania, monomania, phobia, preoccupation, ruling passion, thing, zelotypia.

obsolete *adj.* anachronistic, ancient, antediluvian, antiquated, antique, archaic, bygone, dated, dead, démodé, discarded, disused, extinct, fogram, horse-and-buggy, musty, old, old hat, old-fashioned, out, out of date, outmoded, outworn, passé, superannuated.
antonyms contemporary, current, modern, new, up-to-date.

obstacle *n.* bar, barrier, boyg, catch, check, chicane, difficulty, drawback, hindrance, hitch, hurdle, impediment, interference, interruption, obstruction, pons asinorum, remora, snag, stop, stumbling-block, stumbling-stone.
antonyms advantage, help.

obstinate *adj.* bullet-headed, bull-headed, bullish, camelish, contumacious, determined, dogged, firm, headstrong, immovable, inflexible, intractable, intransigent, mulish, obdurate, opinionated, persistent, pertinacious, perverse, pervicacious, pig-headed, recalcitrant, refractory, restive, rusty, self-willed, steadfast, stomachful, strong-minded, stubborn, sturdy, tenacious, unadvisable, unyielding, uppity, wilful, wrong-headed.
antonyms co-operative, flexible, pliant, submissive.

obstruct *v.* arrest, bar, barricade, block, check, choke, clog, crab, cumber, curb, cut off, frustrate, hamper, hamstring, hide, hinder, hold up, impede, inhibit, interfere with, interrupt, mask, obscure, occlude, prevent, restrict, retard, shield, shut off, slow down, stall, stonewall, stop, stuff, thwart, trammel.
antonym help.

obstruction *n.* bar, barricade, barrier, blockage, check, difficulty, filibuster, hindrance, impediment, snag, stop, stoppage, trammel, traverse.
antonym help.

obtain[1] *v.* achieve, acquire, attain, come by, compass, earn, gain, get, impetrate, procure, secure.

obtain[2] *v.* be in force, be prevalent, be the case, exist, hold, prevail, reign, rule, stand.

obtrusive *adj.* blatant, forward, importunate, interfering, intrusive, manifest, meddling, nosy, noticeable, obvious, officious, prominent, protruding, protuberant, prying, pushy.
antonym unobtrusive.

obtuse *adj.* blunt, boneheaded, crass, dense, dopey, dull, dull-witted, dumb, imperceptive, impercipient, inattentive, insensitive, retarded, rounded, slow, stolid, stupid, thick, thick-skinned, uncomprehending, unintelligent.
antonyms bright, sharp.

obviate *v.* anticipate, avert, counter, counteract, divert, forestall, preclude, prevent, remove.

obvious *adj.* apparent, clear, conspicuous, discernible, distinct, evident, glaring, indisputable, manifest, noticeable, open, open-and-shut, overt, palpable, patent, perceptible, plain, prominent, pronounced, recognizable, self-evident, self-explanatory, straightforward, transparent, unconcealed, undeniable, undisguised, unmistakable, unsubtle, visible.
antonyms obscure, unclear.

obviously *adv.* certainly, clearly, distinctly, evidently, manifestly, of course, palpably, patently, plainly, undeniably, unmistakably, unquestionably, visibly, without doubt.

occasion *n.* affair, call, case, cause, celebration, chance, convenience, event, excuse, experience, ground(s), incident, inducement, influence, instance, justification, moment, motive, occurrence, opening, opportunity, prompting, provocation, reason, time.
v. bring about, bring on, cause, create, effect, elicit, engender, evoke, generate, give rise to, induce, influence, inspire, lead to, make, originate, persuade, produce, prompt, provoke.

occasional *adj.* casual, desultory, fitful, incidental, infrequent, intermittent, irregular, odd, periodic, rare, scattered, sporadic, uncommon.
antonym frequent.

occasionally *adv.* at intervals, at times, every so often, from time to time, infrequently, irregularly, now and again, now and then, off and on, on and off, on occasion, once in a while, periodically, sometimes, sporadically.
antonym frequently.

occult *adj.* abstruse, arcane, cabbalistic, concealed, esoteric, faint, hidden, impenetrable, invisible, magical, mysterious, mystic, mystical, mystifying, obscure, preternatural, recondite, secret, supernatural, unknown, unrevealed, veiled.
v. conceal, cover (up), enshroud, hide, mask, obscure, screen, shroud, veil.
antonym reveal.

occupant *n.* addressee, denizen, holder, householder, incumbent, indweller, inhabitant, inmate, lessee, occupier, resident, squatter, tenant, user.

occupation[1] *n.* absorption, activity, business, calling, craft, employment, job, line, post, profession, pursuit, trade, vocation, walk of life, work.

occupation[2] *n.* billet, conquest, control, habitation, holding, invasion, occupancy, possession, residence, seizure, subjugation, takeover, tenancy, tenure, use.

occupy *v.* absorb, amuse, beguile, busy, capture, conquer, cover, divert, dwell in, employ, engage, engross, ensconce oneself in, entertain, establish oneself in, fill, garrison, hold, immerse, inhabit, interest, invade, involve, keep, keep busy, live in, monopolize, overrun, own, permeate, pervade, possess, preoccupy, reside in, seize, stay in, take over, take possession of, take up, tenant, tie up, use, utilize.

occur *v.* appear, arise, be found, be met with, be present, befall, betide, chance, come about, come off, come to pass, crop up, develop, eventuate, exist, happen, intervene, manifest itself, materialize, obtain, result, show itself, take place, transpire, turn up.

occur to come to mind, come to one, cross one's mind, dawn on, enter one's head, present itself, spring to mind, strike one, suggest itself.

occurrence *n.* action, adventure, affair, appearance, case, circumstance, development, episode, event, existence, happening, incident, instance, manifestation, materialization, proceeding, transaction. **ocean** *n.* briny, main, profound, sea, the deep, the drink.

odd[1] *adj.* abnormal, atypical, bizarre, curious, deviant, different, eccentric, exceptional, extraordinary, fantastic, freak, freakish, freaky, funky, funny, irregular, kinky, outlandish, peculiar, quaint, queer, rare, remarkable, singular, strange, uncanny, uncommon, unconventional, unexplained, unusual, weird, whimsical.
antonym normal.

odd[2] *adj.* auxiliary, casual, fragmentary, ill-matched, incidental, irregular, left-over, lone, miscellaneous, occasional, periodic, random, remaining, seasonal, single, solitary, spare, sundry, surplus, uneven, unmatched, unpaired, varied, various.

odious *adj.* abhorrent, abominable, annoying, detestable, disgusting, execrable, foul, hateful, heinous, horrible, horrid, insufferable, loathsome, obnoxious, offensive, repellent, repugnant, repulsive, revolting, unpleasant, vile.
antonym pleasant.

odium *n.* abhorrence, animosity, antipathy, censure, condemnation, contempt, detestation, disapprobation, disapproval, discredit, disfavor, disgrace, dishonor, dislike, disrepute, execration, hatred, infamy, obloquy, opprobrium, reprobation, shame.

odor *n.* air, aroma, atmosphere, aura, bouquet, breath, emanation, essence, exhalation, flavor, fragrance, perfume, quality, redolence, scent, smell, spirit, stench, stink.

odyssey *n.* journey, travels, wandering.

off *adj.* abnormal, absent, bad, below par, canceled, decomposed, disappointing, disheartening, displeasing,

finished, gone, high, inoperative, moldy, poor, postponed, quiet, rancid, rotten, slack, sour, substandard, turned, unavailable, unsatisfactory, wrong.
adv. apart, aside, at a distance, away, elsewhere, out.

off-color *adj.* faded, ill, indecent, indisposed, off form, out of sorts, pasty-faced, peaky, peelie-wally, poorly, queasy, sick, under the weather, unwell.

offend *v.* affront, annoy, disgruntle, disgust, displease, fret, gall, hip, hurt, insult, irritate, miff, nauseate, outrage, pain, pique, provoke, repel, repulse, rile, sicken, slight, snub, transgress, turn off, upset, vex, violate, wound, wrong.
antonym please.

offender *n.* criminal, culprit, delinquent, guilty party, lawbreaker, malefactor, miscreant, misfeasor, sinner, transgressor, wrong-doer.

offense *n.* affront, anger, annoyance, crime, delict, delinquency, displeasure, fault, hard feelings, harm, huff, hurt, indignation, indignity, infraction, infringement, injury, injustice, insult, ire, lapse, misdeed, misdemeanor, needle, outrage, peccadillo, pique, putdown, resentment, sin, slight, snub, transgression, trespass, umbrage, violation, wrath, wrong, wrong-doing.

offensive *adj.* abominable, abusive, aggressive, annoying, attacking, detestable, disagreeable, discourteous, disgusting, displeasing, disrespectful, embarrassing, grisly, impertinent, insolent, insulting, intolerable, invading, irritating, loathsome, nasty, nauseating, noisome, objectionable, obnoxious, odious, rank, repellent, repugnant, revolting, rude, sickening, uncivil, unmannerly, unpalatable, unpleasant, unsavory, vile.
antonyms defensive, pleasing.
n. attack, drive, onslaught, push, raid, sortie, thrust.

offer *v.* advance, afford, bid, extend, furnish, give, hold out, make available, move, present, proffer, propose, propound, provide, put forth, put forward, show, submit, suggest, tender, volunteer.
n. approach, attempt, bid, endeavor, essay, overture, presentation, proposal, proposition, submission, suggestion, tender.

offhand *adj.* abrupt, aloof, brusque, careless, casual, cavalier, curt, glib, informal, offhanded, perfunctory, take-it-or-leave-it, unappreciative, uncaring, unceremonious, unconcerned, uninterested.
antonyms calculated, planned.
adv. at once, extempore, immediately, off the cuff, off the top of one's head, straightaway.

office *n.* appointment, bath, business, capacity, charge, commission, duty, employment, function, obligation, occupation, place, post, responsibility, role, room, service, situation, station, trust, work.

officiate *v.* adjudicate, chair, conduct, emcee, manage, oversee, preside, referee, serve, superintend, umpire.

offset *v.* balance out, cancel out, compare, compensate for, counteract, counterbalance, counterpoise, countervail, juxtapose, make up for, neutralize.
n. balance, compensation, counterbalance, counterweight, equipoise, equivalent, redress.

offshoot *n.* adjunct, appendage, arm, branch, by-product, development, embranchment, limb, outgrowth, spin-off, sprout, spur.

offspring *n.* brood, child, children, creation, descendant, descendants, family, fry, heir, heirs, issue, kids, litter, progeny, quiverful, result, scion, seed, spawn, successor, successors, young.
antonym parent(s).

often *adv.* again and again, frequently, generally, habitually, many a time, much, oft, over and over, regularly, repeatedly, time after time, time and again.
antonym seldom.

ogle *v.* eye, eye up, leer, look, make eyes at, stare.

ogre *n.* bogey, bogeyman, bogle, boyg, bugaboo, bugbear, demon, devil, giant, humgruffi(a)n, monster, specter.

ointment *n.* balm, balsam, cerate, cream, demulcent, embrocation, emollient, liniment, lotion, salve, unction, unguent.

old *adj.* aboriginal, aged, age-old, ancient, antediluvian, antiquated, antique, archaic, bygone, cast-off, crumbling, dated, decayed, decrepit, done, earlier, early, elderly, erstwhile, ex-, experienced, familiar, former, gray, gray-haired, grizzled, hackneyed, hardened, hoary, immemorial, long-established, long-standing, mature, obsolete, of old, of yore, Ogygian, olden, old-fashioned, one-time, original, out of date, outdated, outmoded, over the hill, passé, patriarchal, practiced, preadamic(al), prehistoric, previous, primeval, primitive, primordial, pristine, quondam, remote, senescent, senile, skilled, stale, superannuated, time-honored, time-worn, traditional, unfashionable, unoriginal, venerable, versed, veteran, vintage, worn-out.
antonym young.

old-fashioned *adj.* ancient, antiquated, archaic, arriéré, behind the times, corny, dated, dead, démodé, fog(e)yish, fusty, horse-and-buggy, musty, neanderthal, obsolescent, obsolete, old hat, old-fog(e)yish, old-time, out of date, outdated, outmoded, passé, past, retro, square, superannuated, unfashionable.
antonyms contemporary, modern, up-to-date.

old-world *adj.* archaic, ceremonious, chivalrous, conservative, courtly, formal, gallant, old-fashioned, picturesque, quaint, traditional.

omen *n.* augury, auspice, boding, foreboding, foretoken, indication, portent, premonition, presage, prognostic, prognostication, sign, straw in the wind, warning, writing on the wall.

ominous *adj.* baleful, bodeful, dark, fateful, inauspicious, menacing, minatory, portentous, premonitory, presageful, sinister, threatening, unpromising, unpropitious.
antonym auspicious.

omission *n.* avoidance, bowdlerization, default, ellipsis, exclusion, failure, forgetfulness, gap, lack, neglect, oversight.
antonyms addition, inclusion.

omit *v.* disregard, drop, edit out, eliminate, exclude, fail, forget, give something a miss, leave out, leave undone, let slide, miss out, neglect, overlook, pass over, pretermit, skip.
antonyms add, include.

omnipotent *adj.* all-powerful, almighty, plenipotent, supreme.
antonym impotent.

omnipresent *adj.* pervasive, ubiquitary, ubiquitous, universal.

omniscient *adj.* all-knowing, all-seeing, pansophic.

once *adv.* at one time, formerly, heretofore, in the old days, in the past, in times gone by, in times past, long ago, once upon a time, previously.

oncoming *adj.* advancing, approaching, forthcoming, gathering, imminent, impending, looming, onrushing, upcoming.

oneness *n.* completeness, consistency, distinctness, identicalness, identity, individuality, sameness, singleness, unicity, unity, wholeness.

onerous *adj.* backbreaking, burdensome, crushing, demanding, difficult, exacting, exhausting, exigent, formidable, grave, hard, heavy, herculean, laborious, oppressive, responsible, taxing, troublesome, weighty.
antonyms easy, light.

one-sided *adj.* asymmetrical, biased, colored, discriminatory, inequitable, lopsided, partial, partisan, prejudiced, unequal, unfair, unilateral, unjust.
antonym impartial.

ongoing *adj.* advancing, continuing, continuous, current, developing, evolving, extant, growing, in progress, lasting, progressing, successful, unfinished, unfolding.

onlooker *n.* bystander, eye-witness, looker-on, observer, rubber-neck, spectator, viewer, watcher, witness.

only *adv.* at most, barely, exclusively, just, merely, purely, simply, solely.
adj. exclusive, individual, lone, single, sole, solitary, unique.

onset *n.* assault, attack, beginning, charge, commencement, inception, kick-off, onrush, onslaught, outbreak, outset, start.
antonyms end, finish.

onslaught *n.* assault, attack, barrage, blitz, bombardment, charge, offensive, onrush, onset.

onus *n.* burden, duty, encumbrance, liability, load, obligation, responsibility, task.

onward(s) *adv.* ahead, beyond, forth, forward, frontward(s), in front, on.
antonym backward(s).

ooze *v.* bleed, discharge, drain, dribble, drip, drop, emit, escape, exude, filter, leach, leak, osmose, overflow with, percolate, seep, strain, sweat, transude, weep.
n. alluvium, deposit, mire, muck, mud, sediment, silt, slime, sludge.

opacity *n.* cloudiness, density, dullness, filminess, impermeability, milkiness, murkiness, obfuscation, obscurity, opaqueness, unclearness.
antonym transparency.

opaque *adj.* abstruse, baffling, clouded, cloudy, cryptic, difficult, dim, dull, enigmatic, filmy, fuliginous, hazy, impenetrable, incomprehensible, inexplicable, lusterless, muddied, muddy, murky, obfuscated, obscure, turbid, unclear, unfathomable, unintelligible.
antonym transparent.

open *adj.* above-board, accessible, agape, airy, ajar, apparent, arguable, artless, available, avowed, bare, barefaced, blatant, bounteous, bountiful, candid, champaign, clear, conspicuous, debatable, disinterested, downright, evident, expanded, exposed, extended, extensive, fair, filigree, flagrant, frank, free, fretted, gaping, general, generous, guileless, holey, honest, honeycombed, impartial, ingenuous, innocent, lacy, liberal, lidless, loose, manifest, moot, munificent, natural, navigable, noticeable, objective, obvious, overt, passable, plain, porous, public, receptive, revealed, rolling, sincere, spacious, spongy, spread out, sweeping, transparent, unbarred, unbiased, unclosed, uncluttered, uncommitted, unconcealed, unconditional, uncovered, uncrowded, undecided, undefended, undisguised, unenclosed, unengaged, unfastened, unfenced, unfolded, unfortified, unfurled, unlidded, unlocked, unobstructed, unoccupied, unprejudiced, unprotected, unqualified, unreserved, unresolved, unrestricted, unroofed, unsealed, unsettled, unsheltered, unwalled, vacant, visible, wide, wide-open, yawning.
antonyms closed, shut.
v. begin, clear, come apart, commence, crack, disclose, divulge, exhibit, explain, expose, inaugurate, initiate, launch, lay bare, ope, pour out, rupture, separate, set in motion, show, split, spread (out), start, throw wide, unbar, unbare, unblock, unclose, uncork, uncover, undo, unfasten, unfold, unfurl, unlatch, unlid, unlock, unroll, unseal, unshutter.
antonyms close, shut.

open-handed *adj.* bountiful, eleemosynary, free, generous, large-hearted, lavish, liberal, munificent, unstinting.
antonym tight-fisted.

opening *n.* adit, aperture, beginning, birth, breach, break, chance, chasm, chink, cleft, commencement, crack, dawn, fissure, fistula, foramen, gap, hole, inauguration, inception, initiation, interstice, kick-off, launch, launching, occasion, onset, opportunity, orifice, ostiole, outset, perforation, place, rent, rupture, slot, space, split, start, vacancy, vent, vista.
antonyms closing, closure.
adj. beginning, commencing, early, first, inaugural,

inauguratory, inceptive, initial, initiatory, introductory, maiden, primary.
antonym closing.

openly *adv.* blatantly, brazenly, candidly, face to face, flagrantly, forthrightly, frankly, glaringly, in full view, in public, overtly, plainly, publicly, shamelessly, unabashedly, unashamedly, unhesitatingly, unreservedly, wantonly.
antonyms secretly, slyly.

open-minded *adj.* broad, broad-minded, catholic, dispassionate, enlightened, free, impartial, latitudinarian, liberal, objective, reasonable, receptive, tolerant, unbiased, unprejudiced. *antonyms* bigoted, intolerant, prejudiced.

operate *v.* act, function, go, handle, manage, maneuver, perform, run, serve, use, utilize, work.

operation *n.* action, activity, affair, agency, assault, business, campaign, course, deal, effect, effort, employment, enterprise, exercise, force, influence, instrumentality, maneuver, manipulation, motion, movement, performance, procedure, proceeding, process, surgery, transaction, undertaking, use, utilization, working.

operative *adj.* active, crucial, current, effective, efficient, engaged, functional, functioning, important, in action, in force, in operation, indicative, influential, key, operational, relevant, serviceable, significant, standing, workable.
antonym inoperative.
n. artisan, employee, hand, laborer, machinist, mechanic, operator, worker.

operator *n.* administrator, conductor, contractor, dealer, director, driver, handler, machinator, machinist, manager, manipulator, mechanic, mover, operant, operative, practitioner, punter, shyster, speculator, technician, trader, wheeler-dealer, worker.

opiate *n.* anodyne, bromide, depressant, downer, drug, narcotic, nepenthe, pacifier, sedative, soporific, stupefacient, tranquilizer.

opinion *n.* assessment, belief, conception, conjecture, conventional wisdom, doxy, estimation, feeling, idea, idée reçue, impression, judgment, mind, notion, perception, persuasion, point of view, sentiment, stance, tenet, theory, view, voice, vox pop, vox populi.

opinionated *adj.* adamant, biased, bigoted, bull-headed, cocksure, dictatorial, doctrinaire, dogmatic, high-dried, inflexible, obdurate, obstinate, overbearing, partisan, pig-headed, prejudiced, self-assertive, single-minded, stubborn, uncompromising, wilful.
antonym open-minded.

opponent *n.* adversary, antagonist, challenger, competitor, contestant, disputant, dissentient, dissident, enemy, foe, objector, opposer, opposition, rival.
antonyms ally, proponent.

opportune *adj.* advantageous, appropriate, apt, auspicious, convenient, favorable, felicitous, fit, fitting, fortunate, good, happy, lucky, pertinent, proper, propitious, seasonable, suitable, timely, well-timed.
antonym inopportune.

opportunity *n.* break, chance, convenience, hour, moment, occasion, opening, scope, shot, time, turn.

oppose *v.* bar, beard, breast, check, combat, compare, confront, contradict, contrary, contrast, contravene, controvert, counter, counterattack, counterbalance, defy, face, fight, fly in the face of, gainsay, hinder, obstruct, pit against, play off, prevent, recalcitrate, resist, stand up to, take a stand against, take issue with, thwart, withstand.
antonyms favor, support.

opposed *adj.* against, agin, antagonistic, anti, antipathetic, antithetical, clashing, conflicting, contrary, contrasted, dissentient, hostile, in opposition, incompatible, inimical, opposing, opposite.
antonym in favor.

opposite *adj.* adverse, antagonistic, antipodal, antipodean, antithetical, conflicting, contradictory, contrary, contrasted, corresponding, different, differing, diverse, facing, fronting, hostile, inconsistent, inimical, irreconcilable, opposed, reverse, unlike.
antonym same. *n.* antipode(s), antipole, antithesis, contradiction, contrary, converse, inverse, reverse.
antonym same.

opposition *n.* antagonism, antagonist, clash, colluctation, competition, contraposition, contrariety, counteraction, counter-stand, counter-time, counter-view, disapproval, foe, hostility, obstruction, obstructiveness, opponent, other side, polarity, prevention, resistance, rival, syzygy, unfriendliness.
antonyms co-operation, support.

oppress *v.* abuse, afflict, burden, crush, depress, dispirit, harass, harry, lie hard on, lie heavy on, maltreat, overpower, overwhelm, persecute, sadden, subdue, subjugate, suppress, torment, trample, tyrannize, vex, weigh heavy.

oppression *n.* abuse, brutality, calamity, cruelty, hardship, harshness, injury, injustice, jackboot, liberticide, maltreatment, misery, persecution, severity, subjection, suffering, tyranny.

oppressive *adj.* airless, brutal, burdensome, close, cruel, despotic, grinding, harsh, heavy, inhuman, intolerable, muggy, onerous, overbearing, overpowering, overwhelming, repressive, severe, stifling, stuffy, suffocating, sultry, torrid, tyrannical, unendurable, unjust.
antonym gentle.

oppressor *n.* autocrat, bully, coercionist, despot, dictator, harrier, intimidator, liberticide, persecutor, scourge, slave-driver, taskmaster, tormentor, tyrant.
olic, vituperative.

opprobrium *n.* calumny, censure, contumely, debasement, degradation, discredit, disfavor, disgrace, dishonor, disrepute, ignominy, infamy, obloquy, odium, reproach, scurrility, shame, slur, stigma.

opt *v.* choose, decide (on), elect, go for, plump for, prefer, select, single out.

optimistic *adj.* assured, bright, bullish, buoyant, cheerful, confident, encouraged, expectant, heartened, hopeful, idealistic, Panglossian, Panglossic, positive, sanguine, upbeat, Utopian.
antonym pessimistic.

option *n.* alternative, choice, election, possibility, preference, selection.

optional *adj.* discretionary, elective, extra, open, possible, unforced, voluntary.
antonym compulsory.

opulence *n.* abundance, affluence, copiousness, cornucopia, easy street, fortune, fullness, lavishness, luxuriance, luxury, plenty, pleroma, profusion, prosperity, riches, richness, sumptuousness, superabundance, wealth.
antonyms penury, poverty.

opulent *adj.* abundant, affluent, copious, lavish, luxuriant, luxurious, moneyed, plentiful, profuse, prolific, prosperous, rich, sumptuous, superabundant, wealthy, well-heeled, well-off, well-to-do.
antonyms penurious, poor.

oracle *n.* adviser, answer, augur, augury, authority, divination, guru, high priest, mastermind, mentor, prediction, prognostication, prophecy, prophet, pundit, python, revelation, sage, seer, sibyl, soothsayer, vision, wizard.

oral *adj.* acroamatic(al), spoken, unwritten, verbal, vocal.
antonym written.

orate *v.* declaim, discourse, harangue, hold forth, pontificate, sermonize, speak, speechify, talk.

oration *n.* address, declamation, discourse, éloge, harangue, homily, lecture, sermon, speech, spiel.

orb *n.* ball, circle, globe, globule, mound, ring, round, sphere, spherule.

orbit *n.* ambit, circle, circumgyration, circumvolution, compass, course, cycle, domain, ellipse, influence, path, range, reach, revolution, rotation, scope, sphere, sphere of influence, sweep, track, trajectory.
v. circle, circumnavigate, circumvolve, encircle, revolve.

orchestrate *v.* arrange, compose, concert, co-ordinate, fix, integrate, organize, prepare, present, score, stage-manage.

ordain *v.* anoint, appoint, call, consecrate, decree, destine, dictate, elect, enact, enjoin, fate, fix, foredoom, foreordain, frock, instruct, intend, invest, lay down, legislate, nominate, order, predestine, predetermine, prescribe, pronounce, require, rule, set, will.

ordeal *n.* affliction, agony, anguish, nightmare, pain, persecution, suffering, test, torture, trial, tribulation(s), trouble(s).

order[1] *n.* application, arrangement, array, behest, booking, calm, categorization, chit, classification, codification, command, commission, control, cosmos, decree, dictate, diktat, direction, directive, discipline, disposal, disposition, eutaxy, grouping, harmony, injunction, instruction, law, law and order, layout, line, line-up, mandate, method, neatness, ordering, orderliness, ordinance, organization, pattern, peace, placement, plan, precept, progression, propriety, quiet, regularity, regulation, request, requisition, reservation, rule, sequence, series, stipulation, structure, succession, symmetry, system, tidiness, tranquility.
antonym disorder.
v. adjure, adjust, align, arrange, authorize, bid, book, catalog, charge, class, classify, command, conduct, control, decree, direct, dispose, enact, engage, enjoin, group, instruct, lay out, manage, marshal, neaten, ordain, organize, prescribe, put to rights, regulate, request, require, reserve, sort out, systematize, tabulate, tidy.
antonym disorder.

order[2] *n.* association, breed, brotherhood, cast, caste, class, community, company, degree, family, fraternity, genre, genus, grade, guild, hierarchy, ilk, kind, league, lodge, organization, pecking order, phylum, position, rank, sect, sisterhood, society, sodality, sort, species, status, subclass, tribe, type, union.

orderly *adj.* businesslike, controlled, cosmic, decorous, disciplined, in order, law-abiding, methodical, neat, nonviolent, peaceable, quiet, regular, restrained, ruly, scientific, shipshape, systematic, systematized, tidy, trim, well-behaved, well-organized, well-regulated.
antonym disorderly.

ordinarily *adv.* as a rule, commonly, conventionally, customarily, familiarly, generally, habitually, in general, normally, usually.

ordinary *adj.* accustomed, average, common, common-or-garden, commonplace, conventional, customary, established, everyday, fair, familiar, habitual, homespun, household, humble, humdrum, inconsequential, indifferent, inferior, mean, mediocre, modest, normal, pedestrian, plain, prevailing, prosaic, quotidian, regular, routine, run-of-the-mill, settled, simple, standard, stock, typical, undistinguished, unexceptional, unmemorable, unpretentious, unremarkable, usual, wonted, workaday.
antonyms extraordinary, special, unusual.

ordnance *n.* arms, artillery, big guns, cannon, guns, matériel, missil(e)ry, munitions, weapons.

organ *n.* agency, channel, device, element, forum, harmonium, hurdy-gurdy, implement, instrument, journal, kist of whistles, means, medium, member, mouthpiece, newspaper, paper, part, periodical, process, publication, structure, tool, unit, vehicle, viscus, voice.

organic *adj.* anatomical, animate, biological, biotic, constitutional, formal, fundamental, inherent, innate, integral, integrated, live, living, methodical, natural, ordered, organized, structural, structured, systematic, systematized.

organization *n.* arrangement, assembling, assembly,

association, body, business, chemistry, combine, company, composition, concern, confederation, configuration, conformation, consortium, constitution, construction, co-ordination, corporation, design, disposal, federation, firm, format, formation, formulation, framework, group, grouping, institution, league, make-up, management, method, methodology, organism, outfit, pattern, plan, planning, regulation, running, standardization, structure, structuring, syndicate, system, unity, whole.
antonym disorganization.

organize *v.* arrange, catalog, classify, codify, constitute, construct, co-ordinate, dispose, establish, form, frame, group, marshal, pigeonhole, regiment, run, see to, set up, shape, structure, systematize, tabulate.
antonym disorganize.

organized *adj.* arranged, neat, orderly, planned.
antonym disorganized.

orient *v.* acclimatize, accommodate, adapt, adjust, align, familiarize, get one's bearings, habituate, orientate.

orifice *n.* aperture, cleft, hole, inlet, mouth, opening, perforation, pore, rent, slit, vent.

origin *n.* ancestry, base, basis, beginning, beginnings, birth, cause, commencement, creation, dawning, derivation, descent, emergence, etymology, etymon, extraction, family, fons et origo, font, foundation, fountain, fountainhead, genesis, heritage, inauguration, inception, incunabula, launch, lineage, occasion, origination, outset, parentage, paternity, pedigree, provenance, root, roots, source, spring, start, stirps, stock, wellspring.
antonyms end, termination.

original *adj.* aboriginal, archetypal, authentic, autochthonous, commencing, creative, earliest, early, embryonic, fertile, first, first-hand, fresh, genuine, imaginative, infant, ingenious, initial, innovative, innovatory, introductory, inventive, master, new, novel, opening, primal, primary, primigenial, primitical, primitive, primordial, pristine, prototypical, resourceful, rudimentary, seminal, starting, unborrowed, unconventional, unhackneyed, unprecedented, unusual.
antonym unoriginal.
n. archetype, case, character, cure, eccentric, master, model, nonconformist, oddity, paradigm, pattern, prototype, queer fish, standard, type, weirdo.

originality *n.* boldness, cleverness, creative spirit, creativeness, creativity, daring, eccentricity, freshness, imagination, imaginativeness, individuality, ingenuity, innovation, innovativeness, inventiveness, newness, novelty, resourcefulness, singularity, unconventionality, unorthodoxy.

originate *v.* arise, be born, begin, come, commence, conceive, create, derive, develop, discover, emanate, emerge, establish, evolve, flow, form, formulate, generate, give birth to, inaugurate, initiate, institute, introduce, invent, issue, launch, pioneer, proceed, produce, result, rise, set up, spring, start, stem.
antonyms end, terminate.

originator *n.* architect, author, creator, designer, father, founder, generator, innovator, inventor, mother, pioneer, prime mover, the brains.

ornament *n.* accessory, adornment, bauble, decoration, doodah, embellishment, fallal, fandangle, figgery, flower, frill, furbelow, garnish, gaud, honor, jewel, leading light, pride, treasure, trimming, trinket.
v. adorn, beautify, bedizen, bespangle, brighten, caparison, deck, decorate, dress up, embellish, festoon, garnish, gild, grace, prettify, prink, trim.

ornamental *adj.* attractive, beautifying, decorative, embellishing, flashy, for show, grandiose, showy.

ornate *adj.* arabesque, aureate, baroque, beautiful, bedecked, busy, convoluted, decorated, elaborate, elegant, fancy, florid, flowery, fussy, ornamented, rococo, sumptuous.
antonyms austere, plain.

orthodox *adj.* accepted, approved, conformist, conventional, correct, customary, doctrinal, established, kosher, official, received, sound, traditional, true, usual, well-established.
antonym unorthodox.

oscillate *v.* fluctuate, librate, seesaw, sway, swing, vacillate, vary, vibrate, waver, wigwag, yo-yo.

ostentation *n.* affectation, boasting, display, exhibitionism, flamboyance, flashiness, flaunting, flourish, foppery, pageantry, parade, pomp, pretension, pretentiousness, show, showiness, showing off, swank, tinsel, trappings, vaunting, window-dressing.
antonym unpretentiousness.

ostentatious *adj.* aggressive, boastful, conspicuous, extravagant, fastuous, flamboyant, flash, flashy, garish, gaudy, loud, obtrusive, pretentious, self-advertising, showy, splashy, swanking, swanky, vain, vulgar.
antonyms quiet, restrained.

ostracize *v.* avoid, banish, bar, black, blackball, blacklist, boycott, cast out, cold-shoulder, cut, debar, disfellowship, exclude, excommunicate, exile, expatriate, expel, reject, segregate, send to Coventry, shun, snub.
antonyms accept, receive, reinstate, welcome.

other *adj.* added, additional, alternative, auxiliary, contrasting, different, differing, dissimilar, distinct, diverse, extra, fresh, further, more, new, remaining, separate, spare, supplementary, unrelated.

oust *v.* depose, disinherit, dislodge, displace, dispossess, drive out, eject, evict, expel, overthrow, replace, supplant, throw out, topple, turn out, unseat, upstage.
antonyms ensconce, install, reinstate, settle.

out[1] *adj.* abroad, absent, away, disclosed, elsewhere, evident, exposed, gone, manifest, not at home, outside, public, revealed.

out[2] *adj.* antiquated, banned, blacked, dated, dead,

démodé, disallowed, ended, excluded, exhausted, expired, extinguished, finished, forbidden, impossible, not on, old hat, old-fashioned, out of date, passé, square, taboo, unacceptable, unfashionable, used up.
antonyms acceptable, fashionable, in.

outbreak *n.* burst, ebullition, epidemic, eruption, excrescence, explosion, flare-up, flash, outburst, pompholyx, rash, spasm, upsurge.

outburst *n.* access, attack, boutade, discharge, eruption, explosion, fit, fit of temper, flare-up, gale, gush, outbreak, outpouring, paroxysm, seizure, spasm, storm, surge, volley.

outcast *n.* abject, castaway, derelict, exile, leper, outsider, pariah, persona non grata, refugee, reject, reprobate, unperson, untouchable, vagabond, wretch.
antonyms favorite, idol.

outclass *v.* beat, eclipse, excel over, leave standing, outdistance, outdo, outrank, outrival, outshine, outstrip, overshadow, put in the shade, surpass, top, transcend.

outcome *n.* after-effect, aftermath, conclusion, consequence, effect, end, end result, harvest, issue, pay-off, result, sequel, upshot.

outcry *n.* clamor, commotion, complaint, cry, exclamation, flap, howl, hue and cry, hullaballoo, noise, outburst, protest, row, scream, screech, uproar, vociferation, yell.

outdated *adj.* antediluvian, antiquated, antique, archaic, behind the times, dated, démodé, fogram, obsolescent, obsolete, old-fashioned, out of date, out of style, outmoded, passé, square, unfashionable, unmodish.
antonyms fashionable, modern, modish.

outdo *v.* beat, best, eclipse, excel over, get the better of, outclass, outdistance, outfox, out-Herod, outmaneuver, outshine, outsmart, outstrip, outwit, overcome, surpass, top, transcend.

outer *adj.* distal, distant, exterior, external, further, outlying, outside, outward, peripheral, remote, superficial, surface.
antonyms central, inner, mesial, proximal.

outfit[1] *n.* accouterments, clothes, costume, ensemble, equipage, equipment, garb, gear, get-up, kit, paraphernalia, rig, rig-out, set-out, suit, togs, trappings, turn-out.
v. accouter, apparel, appoint, attire, equip, fit out, fit up, furnish, kit out, provision, stock, supply, turn out.

outfit[2] *n.* business, clan, clique, company, corps, coterie, crew, firm, galère, gang, group, organization, set, set-out, set-up, squad, team, unit.

outgoing *adj.* affable, approachable, chatty, communicative, cordial, demonstrative, departing, easy, ex-, expansive, extrovert, former, friendly, genial, gregarious, informal, last, open, past, retiring, sociable, sympathetic, unreserved, warm, withdrawing.
antonyms incoming, introvert, new, unsociable.

outgrowth *n.* consequence, effect, emanation, excrescence, offshoot, product, protuberance, shoot, sprout, swelling.

outing *n.* excursion, expedition, jaunt, picnic, pleasure trip, ramble, spin, trip, wayzgoose.

outlandish *adj.* alien, barbarous, bizarre, eccentric, exotic, extraordinary, fantastic, foreign, grotesque, odd, outré, preposterous, queer, strange, unheard-of, weird.
antonyms familiar, ordinary.

outlandishness *n.* bizarreness, eccentricity, exoticness, grotesqueness, oddness, peregrinity, queerness, strangeness, weirdness.
antonyms commonplaceness, familiarity.

outlast *v.* come through, outlive, outstay, ride, survive, weather.

outlaw *n.* bandit, brigand, bushranger, cateran, dacoit, desperado, freebooter, fugitive, highwayman, marauder, outcast, outsider, pariah, proscript, robber.
v. ban, banish, bar, condemn, debar, decitizenize, disallow, embargo, exclude, excommunicate, forbid, illegalize, illegitimate, interdict, prohibit, proscribe, waive.
antonyms allow, legalize.

outlay *n.* cost, disbursal, disbursement, expenditure, expenses, investment, outgoings, payment, price.
antonym income.

outlet *n.* avenue, channel, débouché, debouchment, duct, egress, emissary, exit, femerall, market, opening, orifice, outfall, release, safety valve, vent, way out.
antonyms entry, inlet.

outline *n.* bare facts, configuration, contorno, contour, croquis, delineation, draft, drawing, figure, form, frame, framework, lay-out, lineament(s), plan, profile, recapitulation, résumé, rough, run-down, scenario, schema, shape, silhouette, skeleton, sketch, summary, synopsis, thumbnail sketch, tracing.
v. adumbrate, delineate, draft, plan, recapitulate, rough out, sketch, summarize, trace.

outlook *n.* angle, aspect, attitude, expectations, forecast, frame of mind, future, look-out, panorama, perspective, point of view, prognosis, prospect, scene, slant, standpoint, vantage-point, view, viewpoint, views, vista.

outlying *adj.* distant, far-away, far-flung, far-off, further, outer, outlandish, peripheral, provincial, remote.
antonyms central, inner.

outmoded *adj.* anachronistic, antediluvian, antiquated, antique, archaic, behind the times, bygone, dated, démodé, fogram, fossilized, horse-and-buggy, obsolescent, obsolete, olden, old-fashioned, old-fogeyish, out of date, outworn, passé, square, superannuated, superseded, unfashionable, unmodish, unusable.
antonyms fashionable, fresh, modern, modish, new.

output *n.* achievement, manufacture, outturn, print-out, product, production, productivity, read-out, yield.
antonyms input, outlay.

outrage *n.* hurt, abuse, affront, anger, atrocity, barbarism, crime, desecration, disgrace, enormity, evil, fury, grand guignol, horror, indignation, indignity, inhumanity,

injury, insult, offence, profanation, rape, ravishing, resentment, scandal, shock, violation, violence, wrath.
v. abuse, affront, astound, defile, desecrate, disgust, épater le bourgeois, incense, infuriate, injure, insult, madden, make someone's blood boil, maltreat, offend, rape, ravage, ravish, repel, scandalize, shock, violate.

outrageous *adj.* abominable, atrocious, barbaric, beastly, disgraceful, egregious, excessive, exorbitant, extortionate, extravagant, flagrant, godless, heinous, horrible, immoderate, infamous, inhuman, iniquitous, inordinate, monstrous, nefarious, offensive, preposterous, scandalous, shocking, steep, turbulent, unconscionable, ungodly, unholy, unreasonable, unspeakable, villainous, violent, wicked.
antonyms acceptable, irreproachable.

outright *adj.* absolute, arrant, categorical, complete, consummate, definite, direct, downright, flat, out-and-out, perfect, point-blank, pure, straightforward, thorough, thoroughgoing, total, uncompromising, unconditional, undeniable, unequivocal, unmitigated, unqualified, utter, wholesale.
antonyms ambiguous, indefinite, provisional.
adv. absolutely, at once, cleanly, completely, directly, explicitly, immediately, instantaneously, instantly, on the spot, openly, positively, straight away, straightaway, straightforwardly, there and then, thoroughly, unhesitatingly, without restraint.

outset *n.* beginning, commencement, early days, forthgoing, inauguration, inception, kick-off, opening, start.
antonyms conclusion, end, finish.

outside[1] *adj.* exterior, external, extramural, extraneous, extreme, outdoor, outer, outermost, outward, superficial, surface.
antonym inside.
n. cover, exterior, façade, face, front, skin, superficies, surface, topside.
antonym inside.
prep. furth, outwith, without.

outside[2] *adj.* distant, faint, infinitesimal, marginal, minute, negligible, remote, slight, slim, small, unlikely.
antonyms likely, real, substantial.

outsider *n.* alien, foreigner, immigrant, incomer, interloper, intruder, layman, misfit, newcomer, non-member, non-resident, observer, odd man out, outcast, outlander, outlier, settler, stranger.
antonyms inhabitant, insider, local, member, native, resident, specialist.

outsmart *v.* beat, best, deceive, dupe, get the better of, outfox, outmaneuver, outperform, out-think, outwit, trick.

outspoken *adj.* abrupt, blunt, candid, direct, explicit, forthright, frank, free, open, plain-spoken, pointed, Rabelaisian, rude, sharp, trenchant, unceremonious, unequivocal, unreserved.
antonyms diplomatic, tactful.

outstanding[1] *adj.* ace, arresting, celebrated, conspicuous, distinguished, egregious, eminent, excellent, exceptional, extraordinary, eye-catching, great, important, impressive, marked, memorable, notable, noteworthy, pre-eminent, prominent, prosilient, remarkable, salient, signal, singular, special, striking, superior, superlative, surpassing.
antonyms ordinary, unexceptional.

outstanding[2] *adj.* due, left, ongoing, open, over, owing, payable, pending, remaining, uncollected, undone, unpaid, unresolved, unsettled.

outward *adj.* alleged, apparent, avowed, evident, exterior, external, noticeable, observable, obvious, ostensible, outer, outside, professed, public, superficial, supposed, surface, visible.
antonyms inner, private.

outweigh *v.* cancel out, compensate for, eclipse, make up for, outbalance, overcome, override, overrule, predominate, preponderate, prevail over, take precedence over, tip the scales in favor of, transcend.

outwit *v.* beat, best, better, cheat, circumvent, deceive, defraud, dupe, get the better of, gull, make a monkey of, outfox, outmaneuver, outsmart, outthink, swindle, trick.

oval *adj.* egg-shaped, ellipsoidal, elliptical, lens-shaped, lenticular, lentiform, lentoid, obovate, obovoid, ovate, oviform, ovoid, ovoidal, vulviform.

ovation *n.* acclaim, acclamation, applause, bravos, cheering, cheers, clapping, éclat, laudation, plaudits, praises, tribute.
antonyms abuse, boos, catcalls, mockery.

over[1] *adj.* accomplished, bygone, closed, completed, concluded, done with, ended, finished, forgotten, gone, in the past, past, settled, up.

over[2] *prep.* above, exceeding, in charge of, in command of, in excess of, more than, on, on top of, superior to, upon.
adv. above, aloft, beyond, extra, in addition, in excess, left, on high, overhead, remaining, superfluous, surplus, unclaimed, unused, unwanted.

overall *adj.* all-embracing, all-inclusive, all-over, blanket, broad, complete, comprehensive, general, global, inclusive, total, umbrella.
antonyms narrow, short-term.
adv. by and large, generally speaking, in general, in the long term, on the whole.

overbearing *adj.* arrogant, autocratic, bossy, cavalier, despotic, dictatorial, dogmatic, domineering, haughty, high and mighty, high-handed, imperious, lordly, magisterial, officious, oppressive, overweening, peremptory, pompous, supercilious, superior, tyrannical.
antonyms modest, unassertive, unassuming.

overcast *adj.* black, clouded, clouded over, cloudy, dark, darkened, dismal, dreary, dull, gray, hazy, leaden, lowering, murky, somber, sunless, threatening.
antonyms bright, clear, sunny.

overcome *v.* beat, best, better, conquer, crush, defeat, expugn, lick, master, overpower, overthrow, overwhelm, prevail, rise above, subdue, subjugate, surmount, survive, triumph over, vanquish, weather, worst.
adj. affected, beaten, bowled over, broken, defeated, exhausted, overpowered, overwhelmed, speechless, swept off one's feet.

over-confident *adj.* arrogant, brash, cocksure, cocky, foolhardy, hubristic, incautious, over-optimistic, overweening, presumptuous, rash, sanguine, temerarious, uppish.
antonyms cautious, diffident.

overdo *v.* do to death, exaggerate, gild the lily, go to extremes, go too far, labor, lay it on thick, overact, overexert, overindulge, overplay, overreach, overstate, overtax, overuse, overwork.
antonyms neglect, underuse.

overdue *adj.* behind schedule, behindhand, belated, delayed, late, owing, slow, tardy, unpunctual.
antonym early.

overemphasize *v.* belabor, exaggerate, labor, overdramatize, overstress.
antonyms belittle, minimize, underplay, understate.

overflow *v.* brim over, bubble over, cover, deluge, discharge, drown, flood, inundate, pour over, shower, soak, spill, spray, submerge, surge, swamp, well over.
n. flood, inundation, overabundance, overspill, spill, superfluity, surplus.

overflowing *adj.* abounding, bountiful, brimful, copious, inundant, plenteous, plentiful, profuse, rife, superabundant, swarming, teeming, thronged.
antonyms lacking, scarce.

overhang *v.* beetle, bulge, extend, impend, jut, loom, menace, project, protrude, stick out, threaten.

overhaul[1] *v.* check, do up, examine, fix, inspect, mend, recondition, re-examine, repair, restore, service, survey.
n. check, check-up, examination, going-over, inspection, reconditioning, repair, restoration, service.

overhaul[2] *v.* gain on, outpace, outstrip, overtake, pass, pull ahead of.

overhead *adv.* above, aloft, on high, up above, upward.
antonyms below, underfoot.
adj. aerial, elevated, overhanging, roof, upper.
antonyms floor, ground, underground.

overjoyed *adj.* delighted, delirious, ecstatic, elated, enraptured, euphoric, in raptures, joyful, jubilant, on cloud nine, over the moon, rapturous, thrilled, tickled pink, transported.
antonyms disappointed, sad.

overlap *v.* coincide, cover, flap over, imbricate, overlay, overlie, shingle.

overload *v.* burden, encumber, oppress, overburden, overcharge, overtax, saddle, strain, surcharge, tax, weigh down.

overlook[1] *v.* condone, disregard, excuse, forget, forgive, ignore, let pass, let ride, miss, neglect, omit, pardon, pass, pass over, skip, slight, turn a blind eye to, wink at.
antonyms animadvert, note, notice, penalize, record, remember.

overlook[2] *v.* command a view of, face, front on to, give upon, look on to.

overly *adv.* exceedingly, excessively, immoderately, inordinately, over, too, unduly, unreasonably.
antonyms inadequately, insufficiently.

overpower *v.* beat, best, conquer, crush, defeat, floor, immobilize, master, overcome, overthrow, overwhelm, quell, subdue, subjugate, vanquish.

overpowering *adj.* compelling, convincing, extreme, forceful, insuppressible, invincible, irrefutable, irrepressible, irresistible, nauseating, oppressive, overwhelming, powerful, sickening, strong, suffocating, telling, unbearable, uncontrollable.

overrate *v.* blow up, magnify, make too much of, overestimate, overpraise, overprize, oversell, overvalue.
antonym underrate.

override *v.* abrogate, annul, cancel, countermand, disregard, ignore, nullify, outweigh, overrule, quash, rescind, reverse, ride roughshod over, set aside, supersede, trample, upset, vanquish.

overrule *v.* abrogate, annul, cancel, countermand, disallow, invalidate, outvote, override, overturn, recall, repeal, rescind, reverse, revoke, set aside, veto, vote down.
antonyms allow, approve.

overrun[1] *v.* choke, infest, inundate, invade, occupy, overflow, overgrow, overspread, overwhelm, permeate, ravage, run riot, spread over, surge over, swamp, swarm over.
antonyms desert, evacuate.

overrun[2] *v.* exceed, overdo, overshoot, overstep.

overseas *adj.* exotic, foreign, outland, outlandish, ultramarine.
antonyms domestic, home.
adv. abroad, in/to foreign climes, in/to foreign parts.
n. foreign climes, foreign parts, outland, outremer.
antonym home.

overseer *n.* boss, chief, foreman, forewoman, gaffer, headman, manager, master, super, superintendent, superior, supervisor, surveyor, workmaster, workmistress.

overshadow *v.* adumbrate, becloud, bedim, blight, cloud, darken, dim, dominate, dwarf, eclipse, excel, mar, obfuscate, obscure, outshine, outweigh, protect, put in the shade, rise above, ruin, shelter, spoil, surpass, tower above, veil.

oversight[1] *n.* administration, care, charge, control, custody, direction, guidance, handling, inspection, keeping, management, responsibility, superintendence, supervision, surveillance.

oversight[2] *n.* blunder, boob, carelessness, delinquency, error, fault, inattention, lapse, laxity, mistake, neglect, omission, slip, slip-up.

overt *adj.* apparent, avowed, evident, manifest, observable, obvious, open, patent, plain, professed, public, unconcealed, undisguised, visible.
antonyms covert, secret.

overtake *v.* befall, catch up with, come upon, draw level with, engulf, happen, hit, outdistance, outdo, outstrip, overhaul, pass, pull ahead of, strike.

overthrow *v.* abolish, beat, bring down, conquer, crush, defeat, demolish, depose, destroy, dethrone, displace, knock down, level, master, oust, overcome, overpower, overturn, overwhelm, raze, ruin, subdue, subjugate, subvert, topple, unseat, upset, vanquish.
antonyms install, reinstate.
n. bouleversement, confounding, defeat, deposition, destruction, dethronement, discomfiture, disestablishment, displacement, dispossession, downfall, end, fall, humiliation, labefactation, labefaction, ousting, prostration, rout, ruin, subjugation, subversion, suppression, undoing, unseating.

overture *n.* advance, approach, introduction, invitation, motion, move, offer, opening, (opening) gambit, opening move, prelude, proposal, proposition, signal, suggestion, tender.

overturn *v.* abolish, abrogate, annul, capsize, countermand, depose, destroy, invalidate, keel over, knock down, knock over, overbalance, overset, overthrow, quash, repeal, rescind, reverse, set aside, spill, tip over, topple, tumble, unseat, upend, upset, upturn.

overweight *adj.* ample, bulky, buxom, chubby, chunky, corpulent, fat, flabby, fleshy, gross, heavy, hefty, huge, massive, obese, outsize, plump, podgy, portly, pot-bellied, stout, tubby, well-padded, well-upholstered.
antonyms emaciated, skinny, thin, underweight.

overwhelm *v.* bowl over, bury, confuse, crush, cut to pieces, defeat, deluge, destroy, devastate, engulf, floor, inundate, knock for six, massacre, overcome, overpower, overrun, prostrate, rout, snow under, stagger, submerge, swamp.

overwrought *adj.* agitated, beside oneself, distracted, emotional, excited, frantic, keyed up, on edge, overcharged, overexcited, overheated, overworked, stirred, strung up, tense, uptight, worked up, wound up.
antonyms calm, cool, impassive.

owing *adj.* due, in arrears, outstanding, overdue, owed, payable, unpaid, unsettled.

own[1] *adj.* idiosyncratic, individual, inimitable, particular, personal, private.

own[2] *v.* acknowledge, admit, agree, allow, avow, concede, confess, disclose, enjoy, grant, have, hold, keep, possess, recognize, retain.

owner *n.* franklin, freeholder, holder, laird, landlady, landlord, lord, master, mistress, possessor, proprietor, proprietress, proprietrix.

P

pace *n.* celerity, clip, gait, lick, measure, momentum, motion, movement, progress, quickness, rapidity, rate, speed, step, stride, tempo, time, tread, velocity, walk.
v. count, determine, march, mark out, measure, pad, patrol, pound, step, stride, tramp, tread, walk.

pacific *adj.* appeasing, calm, complaisant, conciliatory, diplomatic, dovelike, dovish, eirenic, equable, friendly, gentle, halcyon, irenic, mild, nonbelligerent, nonviolent, pacificatory, pacifist, peaceable, peaceful, peace-loving, peacemaking, placatory, placid, propitiatory, quiet, serene, smooth, still, tranquil, unruffled.
antonyms aggressive, belligerent, contentious, pugnacious.

pacify *v.* allay, ameliorate, appease, assuage, calm, chasten, compose, conciliate, crush, humor, lull, moderate, mollify, placate, propitiate, put down, quell, quiet, repress, silence, smooth down, soften, soothe, still, subdue, tame, tranquilize.
antonyms aggravate, anger.

pack *n.* assemblage, back-pack, bale, band, boodle, bunch, bundle, burden, collection, company, crew, crowd, deck, drove, fardel, flock, galère, gang, group, haversack, herd, kit, kitbag, knapsack, load, lot, Matilda, mob, outfit, package, packet, parcel, rucksack, set, troop, truss.
v. batch, bundle, burden, charge, compact, compress, cram, crowd, empocket, fill, jam, load, mob, package, packet, press, ram, steeve, store, stow, stuff, tamp, throng, thrust, wedge.

package *n.* agreement, amalgamation, arrangement, bale, box, carton, combination, consignment, container, deal, entity, kit, pack, packet, parcel, proposal, proposition, unit, whole.
v. batch, box, pack, pack up, packet, parcel, parcel up, wrap, wrap up.

packed *adj.* brimful, brim-full, chock-a-block, chock-full, congested, cram-full, crammed, crowded, filled, full, hotching, jammed, jam-packed, overflowing, overloaded, seething, swarming.
antonyms deserted, empty.

packet[1] *n.* bag, carton, case, container, pack, package, packing, parcel, poke, wrapper, wrapping.

packet[2] *n.* bomb, bundle, fortune, king's ransom, lot, lots, mint, pile, pot, pots, pretty penny, small fortune, tidy sum.

pact *n.* agreement, alliance, arrangement, bargain, bond, cartel, compact, concord, concordat, contract, convention, covenant, deal, entente, league, protocol, treaty, understanding.
antonyms breach, disagreement, quarrel.

pad[1] *n.* block, buffer, cushion, jotter, notepad, pillow, protection, pulvillus, pulvinar, stiffening, stuffing, tablet, wad, writing-pad.
v. cushion, fill, line, pack, protect, shape, stuff, wrap.

pad[2] *n.* foot, footprint, paw, print, sole.

pad[3] *n.* apartment, flat, hang-out, home, penthouse, place, quarters, room, rooms.

pad[4] *v.* lope, move, run, step, tiptoe, tramp, tread, trudge, walk.

padding *n.* bombast, circumlocution, filling, hot air, packing, perissology, prolixity, stuffing, verbiage, verbosity, wadding, waffle, wordiness.

paddle[1] *n.* oar, scull, sweep.
v. oar, ply, propel, pull, row, scull, steer.

paddle[2] *v.* dabble, plash, slop, splash, stir, trail, wade.

pageant *n.* display, extravaganza, masque, parade, play, procession, representation, ritual, scene, show, spectacle, tableau, tableau vivant.

pain *n.* ache, affliction, aggravation, agony, anguish, annoyance, bitterness, bore, bother, burden, cramp, discomfort, distress, dole, dolor, drag, grief, gyp, headache, heartache, heartbreak, hurt, irritation, lancination, misery, nuisance, pang, pest, smart, soreness, spasm, suffering, tenderness, throb, throe, torment, torture, tribulation, trouble, twinge, vexation, woe, wretchedness.
v. afflict, aggrieve, agonize, annoy, chagrin, cut to the quick, disappoint, disquiet, distress, exasperate, gall, grieve, harass, hurt, irritate, nettle, rile, sadden, torment, torture, vex, worry, wound, wring.
antonyms gratify, please.

painful *adj.* aching, achy, afflictive, agonizing, arduous, difficult, disagreeable, distasteful, distressing, doloriferous, dolorific, excruciating, grievous, hard, harrowing, laborious, lancinating, saddening, severe, smarting, sore, tedious, tender, troublesome, trying, unpleasant, vexatious.
antonyms easy, painless.

painstaking *adj.* assiduous, careful, conscientious, dedicated, devoted, diligent, earnest, exacting, hardworking, industrious, meticulous, perfectionist, persevering, punctilious, scrupulous, sedulous, strenuous, thorough, thoroughgoing.
antonyms careless, negligent.

painting *n.* aquarelle, daubery, depiction, fresco, illustration, kakemono, landscape, miniature, mural, oil, oil-painting, picture, portrait, portraiture, portrayal, representation, scene, seascape, still life, tablature, water-color.

pair *n.* brace, combination, couple, doublet, doubleton,

duad, duo, dyad, match, span, twins, two of a kind, two-some, yoke.
v. bracket, couple, join, link, marry, match, match up, mate, pair off, put together, splice, team, twin, wed, yoke.
antonyms dissever, sever.

pal *n.* amigo, buddy, chum, companion, comrade, confidant(e), crony, friend, gossip, intimate, mate, partner, side-kick, soul mate.
antonym enemy.

palatial *adj.* de luxe, grand, grandiose, illustrious, imposing, luxurious, magnificent, majestic, opulent, plush, posh, regal, spacious, splendid, stately, sumptuous, swanky.
antonyms cramped, poky.

pale *adj.* anemic, ashen, ashy, bleached, bloodless, chalky, colorless, dim, etiolated, faded, faint, feeble, inadequate, light, lily-livered, pallid, pasty, poor, sallow, thin, wan, washed-out, waxy, weak, whey-faced, white, white-livered, whitish.
antonym ruddy.
v. blanch, decrease, dim, diminish, dull, etiolate, fade, lessen, whiten.
antonyms blush, color.

pallid *adj.* anemic, ashen, ashy, bloodless, cadaverous, colorless, doughy, etiolated, insipid, lifeless, livid, pale, pasty, pasty-faced, peelie-wally, sallow, spiritless, sterile, tame, tired, uninspired, vapid, wan, waxen, waxy, whey-faced, whitish.
antonyms high-complexioned, ruddy, vigorous.

pally *adj.* affectionate, chummy, close, familiar, friendly, intimate, palsy, palsy-walsy, thick.
antonym unfriendly.

palpable *adj.* apparent, blatant, clear, concrete, conspicuous, evident, manifest, material, obvious, open, overt, patent, plain, real, solid, substantial, tangible, touchable, unmistakable, visible.
antonyms elusive, impalpable, imperceptible, intangible.

paltry *adj.* base, beggarly, contemptible, derisory, despicable, inconsiderable, insignificant, jitney, low, meager, mean, minor, miserable, negligible, pettifogging, petty, picayunish, piddling, piffling, pimping, pitiful, poor, puny, rubbishy, slight, small, sorry, tinpot, trifling, trivial, two-bit, unimportant, worthless, wretched.
antonyms significant, substantial.

pamper *v.* baby, cocker, coddle, cosset, fondle, gratify, humor, indulge, mollycoddle, mother, overindulge, pet, spoil.
antonyms ill-treat, neglect.

pamphlet *n.* booklet, broadside, brochure, chapbook, folder, leaflet, tract, tractate, treatise.

panacea *n.* catholicon, cure-all, diacatholicon, elixir, nostrum, panpharmacon, theriac, treacle.

panache *n.* brio, dash, élan, enthusiasm, flair, flamboyance, flourish, grand manner, ostentation, pizzazz, spirit, style, swagger, theatricality, verve, vigor, zest.

pang *n.* ache, agony, anguish, crick, discomfort, distress, gripe, pain, prick, spasm, stab, sting, stitch, throe, twinge, twitch, wrench.

panic *n.* agitation, alarm, consternation, dismay, fear, fright, hassle, horror, hysteria, scare, terror, tizzy, to-do.
antonyms assurance, confidence.
v. alarm, get one's knickers in a twist, go to pieces, lose one's cool, lose one's nerve, overreact, put the wind up, scare, startle, terrify, unnerve.
antonyms reassure, relax.

pant *v.* ache, blow, breathe, covet, crave, desire, flaff, gasp, hanker, heave, huff, hunger, long, palpitate, pine, puff, sigh, thirst, throb, want, wheeze, yearn, yen.
n. gasp, huff, puff, throb, wheeze.

pants *n.* briefs, drawers, knickers, panties, shorts, slacks, trews, trousers, trunks, underpants, undershorts, Y-fronts.

paper *n.* analysis, archive, article, assignment, authorization, certificate, composition, credential, critique, daily, deed, diary, dissertation, document, dossier, essay, examination, file, gazette, instrument, journal, letter, monograph, news, newspaper, notepaper, organ, rag, record, report, script, stationery, study, thesis, treatise.

papery *adj.* delicate, flimsy, fragile, frail, insubstantial, light, lightweight, paper-thin, thin, translucent.

parable *n.* allegory, apologue, exemplum, fable, homily, lesson, story.

parade *n.* array, cavalcade, ceremony, column, corso, display, exhibition, flaunting, march, motorcade, ostentation, pageant, panache, pizzazz, pomp, procession, promenade, review, show, spectacle, train, vaunting.
v. air, brandish, defile, display, exhibit, flaunt, make a show of, march, peacock, process, show, show off, strut, swagger, vaunt.

paradise *n.* bliss, City of God, delight, Eden, Elysian fields, Elysium, felicity, garden of delights, Garden of Eden, heaven, heavenly kingdom, Land o' the Leal, Olympus, Promised Land, seventh heaven, utopia, Valhalla, Zion.
antonyms Hades, hell.

paradoxical *adj.* absurd, ambiguous, baffling, conflicting, confounding, contradictory, enigmatic, equivocal, Gilbertian, illogical, impossible, improbable, incongruous, inconsistent, puzzling, self-contradictory.

paragon *n.* apotheosis, archetype, crème de la crème, criterion, cynosure, epitome, exemplar, ideal, jewel, masterpiece, model, non(e)such, nonpareil, paradigm, pattern, prototype, quintessence, standard, the bee's knees.

parallel *adj.* akin, aligned, alongside, analogous, co-extensive, collateral, connate, correspondent, corresponding, equidistant, homologous, like, matching, resembling, similar, uniform.
antonyms divergent, separate.

n. analog, analogy, comparison, corollary, correlation, correspondence, counterpart, duplicate, equal, equivalent, homologue, likeness, match, parallelism, resemblance, similarity, twin.
v. agree, compare, conform, correlate, correspond, duplicate, emulate, equal, match.
antonyms diverge, separate.

paramount *adj.* capital, cardinal, chief, dominant, eminent, first, foremost, highest, main, outstanding, predominant, pre-eminent, premier, primary, prime, principal, superior, supreme, topmost, top-rank.
antonyms inferior, last, lowest.

paraphernalia *n.* accessories, accouterments, apparatus, appurtenances, baggage, belongings, bits and pieces, clobber, clutter, effects, equipage, equipment, gear, impedimenta, material, odds and ends, stuff, tackle, things, trappings, traps.

parasite *n.* bloodsucker, cadger, endophyte, endozoon, entozoon, epiphyte, epizoan, epizoon, free-loader, hanger-on, leech, lick-trencher, scrounger, sponge, sponger, sucker.

parcel *n.* band, batch, bunch, bundle, carton, collection, company, crew, crowd, da(w)k, gang, group, lot, pack, package, packet, plot, portion, property, quantity, set, tract.
v. bundle, collect, pack, package, tie up, wrap.

parched *adj.* arid, dehydrated, dried up, drouthy, dry, scorched, shriveled, thirsty, waterless, withered.

pardon *v.* absolve, acquit, amnesty, condone, emancipate, exculpate, excuse, exonerate, forgive, free, let off, liberate, overlook, release, remit, reprieve, respite, vindicate.
n. absolution, acquittal, allowance, amnesty, compassion, condonation, discharge, excuse, exoneration, forgiveness, grace, humanity, indulgence, mercy, release, remission, reprieval, reprieve.

pare *v.* clip, crop, cut, cut back, decrease, diminish, dock, flaught, float, lop, peel, prune, reduce, retrench, shave, shear, skin, skive, trim.

parent *n.* architect, author, begetter, cause, creator, father, forerunner, generant, genetrix, genitor, guardian, mother, origin, originator, procreator, progenitor, progenitress, progenitrix, prototype, root, sire, source.

pariah *n.* black sheep, castaway, exile, Ishmael, leper, outcast, outlaw, undesirable, unperson, untouchable.

parity *n.* affinity, agreement, analogy, conformity, congruence, congruity, consistency, consonance, correspondence, equality, equivalence, likeness, par, parallelism, resemblance, sameness, semblance, similarity, similitude, uniformity, unity.

parley *n.* colloquy, confab, conference, council, deliberation, dialogue, discussion, get-together, meeting, negotiation, palaver, powwow, talk(s), tête-à-tête.
v. confabulate, confer, consult, deliberate, discuss, get together, negotiate, palaver, powwow, speak, talk.

parody *n.* burlesque, caricature, imitation, lampoon, mimicry, pasquinade, satire, send-up, skit, spoof, take-off.
v. burlesque, caricature, lampoon, mimic, pasquinade, satirize, send up, spoof, take off, travesty.

paroxysm *n.* attack, convulsion, eruption, explosion, fit, flare-up, outbreak, outburst, seizure, spasm, tantrum.

parry *v.* avert, avoid, block, circumvent, deflect, divert, dodge, duck, evade, fence, fend off, field, forestall, obviate, rebuff, repel, repulse, shun, sidestep, stave off, ward off.

parsimonious *adj.* cheese-paring, close, close-fisted, close-handed, frugal, grasping, mean, mingy, miserable, miserly, money-grubbing, niggardly, penny-pinching, penny-wise, penurious, saving, scrimpy, sparing, stingy, stinting, tight-fisted.
antonyms generous, liberal, open-handed.

part *n.* airt, area, behalf, bit, branch, business, capacity, cause, character, charge, clause, complement, component, concern, constituent, department, district, division, duty, element, faction, factor, fraction, fragment, function, heft, ingredient, interest, involvement, limb, lines, lot, member, module, neck of the woods, neighborhood, office, organ, particle, partwork, party, piece, place, portion, quarter, region, responsibility, role, scrap, section, sector, segment, share, side, slice, task, territory, tip of the iceberg, unit, vicinity, work.
v. break, break up, cleave, come apart, depart, detach, disband, disconnect, disjoin, dismantle, disperse, disunite, divide, go, go away, leave, part company, quit, rend, scatter, separate, sever, split, split up, sunder, take leave, tear, withdraw.

partake *v.* be involved, engage, enter, participate, share, take part.

partial[1] *adj.* fragmentary, imperfect, incomplete, inexhaustive, limited, part, uncompleted, unfinished.
antonyms complete, exhaustive, total.

partial[2] *adj.* affected, biased, colored, discriminatory, exparte, influenced, interested, one-sided, partisan, predisposed, prejudiced, tendentious, unfair, unjust.
antonyms disinterested, fair, unbiased.

partiality *n.* affinity, bias, discrimination, favoritism, fondness, inclination, liking, love, partisanship, penchant, predilection, predisposition, preference, prejudice, proclivity, propensity, soft spot, taste, weakness.
antonyms dislike, justice.

partially *adv.* fractionally, in part, incompletely, partly, somewhat.

participant *n.* associate, contributor, co-operator, helper, member, partaker, participator, party, shareholder, worker.

participation *n.* a piece of the action, assistance, contribution, co-operation, involvement, mucking in, partaking, partnership, sharing.

particle *n.* atom, atom(y), bit, corn, crumb, drop, electron, grain, iota, jot, kaon, mite, molecule, morsel, mote, neutrino, neutron, piece, pion, proton, scrap, shred, sliver, smidgen, speck, tittle, whit.

particular[1] *adj.* blow-by-blow, circumstantial, detailed, distinct, especial, exact, exceptional, express, itemized, marked, minute, notable, noteworthy, painstaking, peculiar, precise, remarkable, selective, several, singular, special, specific, thorough, uncommon, unique, unusual, very.
antonym general.
n. circumstance, detail, fact, feature, item, point, specific, specification.

particular[2] *adj.* choosy, critical, dainty, demanding, discriminating, exacting, fastidious, finical, finicky, fussy, meticulous, nice, overnice, perjink, pernickety, picky.
antonym casual.

particularity *n.* accuracy, carefulness, characteristic, choosiness, circumstance, detail, distinctiveness, fact, fastidiousness, feature, fussiness, idiosyncrasy, individuality, instance, item, mannerism, meticulousness, peculiarity, point, precision, property, quirk, singularity, thoroughness, trait, uniqueness.

particularly *adv.* decidedly, distinctly, especially, exceptionally, explicitly, expressly, extraordinarily, in particular, markedly, notably, noticeably, outstandingly, peculiarly, remarkably, singularly, specifically, surprisingly, uncommonly, unusually.

partisan *n.* adherent, backer, champion, devotee, disciple, factionary, factionist, follower, guerrilla, irregular, partyman, stalwart, supporter, upholder, votary.
adj. biased, discriminatory, factional, guerrilla, interested, irregular, one-sided, partial, predisposed, prejudiced, resistance, sectarian, tendentious, underground.

partisanship *n.* bias, factionalism, fanaticism, partiality, partyism, sectarianism.

partition[1] *n.* allocation, allotment, apportionment, distribution, dividing, division, part, portion, rationing, out, section, segregation, separation, severance, share, splitting.
v. allocate, allot, apportion, assign, divide, parcel out, portion, section, segment, separate, share, split up, subdivide.

partition[2] *n.* barrier, diaphragm, dissepiment, divider, membrane, room-divider, screen, septum, traverse, wall.
v. bar, divide, fence off, screen, separate, wall off.

partly *adv.* halfway, in part, incompletely, moderately, partially, relatively, slightly, somewhat, to a certain degree, to a certain extent, up to a point.
antonyms completely, in toto, totally.

partner *n.* accomplice, ally, associate, bedfellow, butty, collaborator, colleague, companion, comrade, confederate, consort, co-partner, gigolo, helper, helpmate, helpmeet, husband, mate, participant, side-kick, spouse, team-mate, wife.

party[1] *n.* assembly, at-home, bash, beanfeast, beano, ceilidh, celebration, do, drag, drum, entertainment, -fest, festivity, function, gathering, get-together, hooley, hoot(e)nanny, housewarming, hurricane, jollification, knees-up, rave-up, reception, rout, shindig, social, soirée, thrash.

party[2] *n.* alliance, association, band, body, bunch, cabal, caucus, clique, coalition, combination, company, confederacy, contingent, contractor, coterie, crew, defendant, detachment, faction, gang, gathering, group, grouping, individual, junto, league, litigant, participant, person, plaintiff, set, side, squad, team, unit.

pass[1] *v.* accept, adopt, answer, approve, authorize, beat, befall, beguile, blow over, cease, come up, come up to scratch, convey, declare, decree, defecate, delate, deliver, depart, develop, devote, die, die away, disappear, discharge, disregard, dissolve, do, dwindle, ebb, elapse, eliminate, employ, empty, enact, end, establish, evacuate, evaporate, exceed, excel, exchange, excrete, expel, experience, expire, express, fade, fall out, fill, flow, get through, give, go, go beyond, go by, go past, graduate, hand, happen, ignore, impersonate, lapse, leave, legislate, melt away, miss, move, neglect, occupy, occur, omit, ordain, outdistance, outdo, outstrip, overlook, overtake, pass muster, proceed, pronounce, qualify, ratify, roll, run, sanction, send, serve as, skip, spend, succeed, suffer, suffice, suit, surmount, surpass, take place, terminate, throw, transcend, transfer, transmit, undergo, utter, validate, vanish, void, waft, wane, while away.

pass[2] *n.* advances, approach, authorization, chit, condition, feint, identification, jab, juncture, laissez-passer, license, lunge, overture, passport, permission, permit, pinch, play, plight, predicament, proposition, push, safe-conduct, situation, stage, state, state of affairs, straits, suggestion, swing, thrust, ticket, warrant.

pass[3] *n.* canyon, col, defile, gap, gorge, nek, ravine.

passable *adj.* acceptable, adequate, admissible, all right, allowable, average, clear, fair, mediocre, middling, moderate, navigable, OK, open, ordinary, presentable, so-so, tolerable, traversable, unblocked, unexceptional, unobstructed.

passage *n.* acceptance, access, adit, advance, allowance, authorization, avenue, change, channel, citation, clause, close, communication, conduit, conversion, corridor, course, crossing, deambulatory, doorway, drift, dromos, duct, enactment, entrance, entrance hall, establishment, excerpt, exit, extract, fistula, flow, freedom, gallery, gut, hall, hallway, journey, lane, legalization, legislation, lobby, motion, movement, opening, orifice, paragraph, part, passageway, passing, path, permission, piece, portion, progress, progression, quotation, ratification, reading, right, road, route, safe-conduct, section, sentence, spiracle, text, thorough, thoroughfare, tour, transit, transition, trek, trip, vent, verse, vestibule, visa, vista, voyage, warrant, way.

passenger *n.* commuter, fare, hitch-hiker, pillionist, pillion-rider, rider, traveler.

passer-by *n.* bystander, looker-on, onlooker, spectator, witness.

passion *n.* adoration, affection, anger, animation, ardor, attachment, avidity, bug, chafe, concupiscence, craving, craze, dander, desire, eagerness, emotion, enthusiasm, excitement, fancy, fascination, feeling, fervency, fervor, fire, fit, flare-up, fondness, frenzy, fury, heat, idol, indignation, infatuation, intensity, ire, itch, joy, keenness, love, lust, mania, monomania, obsession, outburst, paroxysm, rage, rapture, resentment, spirit, storm, transport, vehemence, verve, vivacity, warmth, wax, wrath, zeal, zest.
antonyms calm, coolness, self-possession.

passionate *adj.* amorous, animated, ardent, aroused, choleric, desirous, eager, emotional, enthusiastic, erotic, excitable, excited, fervent, fervid, fierce, fiery, frenzied, heart-felt, hot, hot-headed, hot-tempered, impassioned, impetuous, impulsive, incensed, inflamed, inspirited, intense, irascible, irate, irritable, loving, lustful, peppery, quick-tempered, sensual, sexy, stormy, strong, sultry, tempestuous, torrid, vehement, violent, wanton, warm, wild, zealous.
antonyms frigid, laid-back, phlegmatic.

passive *adj.* acquiescent, compliant, docile, enduring, impassive, inactive, indifferent, indolent, inert, lifeless, long-suffering, non-participating, non-violent, patient, quiescent, receptive, resigned, submissive, supine, unaffected, unassertive, uninvolved, unresisting.
antonyms active, involved, lively.

password *n.* countersign, open sesame, parole, shibboleth, signal, watchword.

past *adj.* accomplished, ancient, bygone, completed, defunct, done, early, elapsed, ended, erstwhile, extinct, finished, foregone, forgotten, former, gone, gone by, late, long-ago, no more, olden, over, over and done with, preceding, previous, prior, quondam, recent, spent, vanished.
n. antiquity, auld lang syne, background, days of yore, dossier, experience, former times, good old days, history, life, old times, olden days, track record, yesteryear.

pastiche *n.* blend, composition, farrago, gallimaufry, hotch-potch, medley, mélange, miscellany, mixture, motley, ollapodrida, patchwork, pot-pourri.

pastime *n.* activity, amusement, avocation, distraction, diversion, divertisement, entertainment, game, hobby, play, recreation, relaxation, sport.
antonyms business, employment, occupation, vocation, work.

pat *v.* caress, clap, dab, fondle, pet, rub, slap, stroke, tap, touch.
n. cake, caress, clap, dab, lump, piece, portion, slap, stroke, tap, touch.
adv. exactly, faultlessly, flawlessly, fluently, glibly, just right, off pat, opportunely, perfectly, plumb, precisely, relevantly, seasonably.
antonyms imprecisely, wrongly.
adj. apposite, appropriate, apropos, apt, automatic, easy, facile, felicitous, fitting, glib, happy, neat, pertinent, ready, relevant, right, simplistic, slick, smooth, spot-on, suitable, to the point, well-chosen.
antonyms irrelevant, unsuitable.

patch *n.* area, bit, clout, ground, land, lot, parcel, piece, plot, scrap, shred, spot, stretch, tract.
v. botch, cover, fix, mend, reinforce, repair, sew up, stitch, vamp.

patent *adj.* apparent, blatant, clear, clear-cut, conspicuous, downright, evident, explicit, flagrant, glaring, indisputable, manifest, obvious, open, ostensible, overt, palpable, transparent, unconcealed, unequivocal, unmistakable.
antonyms hidden, opaque.
n. certificate, copyright, invention, license, privilege, registered trademark.

path *n.* avenue, course, direction, footpath, footway, gate, pad, passage, pathway, procedure, ridgeway, road, route, towpath, track, trail, walk, walkway, way.

pathetic *adj.* affecting, contemptible, crummy, deplorable, dismal-looking, distressing, feeble, heartbreaking, heart-rending, inadequate, lamentable, meager, melting, miserable, moving, paltry, petty, piteous, pitiable, pitiful, plaintive, poignant, poor, puny, rubbishy, sad, sorry, tender, touching, trashy, uninteresting, useless, woebegone, woeful, worthless.
antonyms admirable, cheerful.

patience *n.* calmness, composure, constancy, cool, diligence, endurance, equanimity, forbearance, fortitude, long-suffering, perseverance, persistence, resignation, restraint, self-control, serenity, stoicism, submission, sufferance, tolerable, toleration.
antonyms impatience, intolerance.

patient[1] *adj.* accommodating, calm, composed, enduring, even-tempered, forbearing, forgiving, indulgent, lenient, long-suffering, mild, persevering, persistent, philosophical, quiet, resigned, restrained, self-controlled, self-possessed, serene, stoical, submissive, tolerant, uncomplaining, understanding, untiring.
antonyms impatient, intolerant.

patient[2] *n.* case, client, invalid, sufferer.

patriotism *n.* chauvinism, flag-waving, jingoism, loyalty, nationalism.

patrol *n.* defence, garrison, guard, guarding, policing, protecting, roundvigilance, sentinel, surveillance, watch, watching, watchman.
v. cruise, go the rounds, guard, inspect, perambulate, police, range, tour.

patron *n.* advocate, backer, benefactor, buyer, champion, client, customer, defender, fautor, frequenter, friend, guardian, habitué, helper, Maecenas, partisan, philanthropist, protector, regular, shopper, sponsor, subscriber, supporter, sympathizer.

patronize *v.* assist, back, befriend, encourage, foster, frequent, fund, habituate, help, humor, maintain, promote, shop at, sponsor, support, talk down to.

pattern *n.* archetype, arrangement, criterion, cynosure, decoration, delineation, design, device, diagram, examplar, example, figuration, figure, Gestalt, guide, instructions, kind, method, model, motif, norm, order, orderliness, original, ornament, ornamentation, paradigm, paragon, plan, prototype, sample, sequence, shape, sort, specimen, standard, stencil, style, system, template, type, variety.
v. copy, decorate, design, emulate, follow, form, imitate, match, model, mold, order, shape, stencil, style, trim.

paunchy *adj.* adipose, corpulent, fat, podgy, portly, pot-bellied, pudgy, rotund, tubby.

pause *v.* break, cease, cut, delay, desist, discontinue, halt, hesitate, interrupt, rest, take a break, take a breather, take five, wait, waver.
n. abatement, break, breather, caesura, cessation, delay, discontinuance, dwell, gap, halt, hesitation, interlude, intermission, interruption, interval, let-up, lull, respite, rest, slackening, stay, stoppage, suspension, wait.

pawn[1] *n.* cat's-paw, creature, dupe, instrument, plaything, puppet, stooge, tool, toy.

pawn[2] *v.* deposit, dip, gage, hazard, hock, impawn, impignorate, lay in lavender, mortgage, pledge, pop, stake, wager.
n. hostage, security.

pay *v.* ante, benefit, bestow, bring in, clear, compensate, cough up, disburse, discharge, extend, foot, get even with, give, grant, honor, indemnify, liquidate, meet, offer, pay out, present, produce, proffer, profit, punish, reciprocate, recompense, reimburse, remit, remunerate, render, repay, requite, return, reward, serve, settle, square, square up, yield.
n. allowance, compensation, consideration, earnings, emoluments, fee, hire, honorarium, income, payment, recompense, reimbursement, remuneration, reward, salary, stipend, takings, wages.

payable *adj.* due, in arrears, mature, obligatory, outstanding, owed, owing, receivable, unpaid.

peace *n.* accord, agreement, amity, armistice, calm, calmness, cease-fire, composure, conciliation, concord, contentment, frith, harmony, hush, pacification, pax, peacefulness, placidity, quiet, quietude, relaxation, repose, rest, serenity, silence, stillness, tranquility, treaty, truce.
antonyms disagreement, disturbance, war

peace studies irenology.

peaceable *adj.* amiable, amicable, compatible, conciliatory, douce, dovish, easy-going, friendly, gentle, inoffensive, mild, non-belligerent, pacific, peaceful, peace-loving, placid, unwarlike.
antonyms belligerent, offensive.

peaceful *adj.* amicable, at peace, becalmed, calm, conciliatory, friendly, gentle, halcyon, harmonious, irenic (eirenic), non-violent, pacific, peaceable, peace-loving, placatory, placid, quiet, restful, serene, still, tranquil, unagitated, undisturbed, unruffled, untroubled, unwarlike.
antonyms disturbed, noisy, troubled.

peak *n.* acme, aiguille, apex, apogee, brow, climax, crest, crown, culmination, cuspid, high point, maximum, ne plus ultra, pinnacle, point, summit, tip, top, visor, zenith.
antonyms nadir, trough.
v. climax, come to a head, culminate, spire, tower.

peccadillo *n.* boob, delinquency, error, fault, indiscretion, infraction, lapse, misdeed, misdemeanor, slip, slip-up.

peculiar[1] *adj.* abnormal, bizarre, curious, eccentric, exceptional, extraordinary, far-out, freakish, funky, funny, odd, offbeat, outlandish, out-of-the-way, quaint, queer, singular, strange, uncommon, unconventional, unusual, wayout, weird.
antonyms normal, ordinary.

peculiar[2] *adj.* appropriate, characteristic, discriminative, distinct, distinctive, distinguishing, endemic, idiosyncratic, individual, local, particular, personal, private, quintessential, restricted, special, specific, unique.
antonyms general, uncharacteristic.

peculiarity *n.* abnormality, attribute, bizarreness, characteristic, distinctiveness, eccentricity, exception, feature, foible, freakishness, idiosyncrasy, kink, mannerism, mark, oddity, particularity, property, quality, queerness, quirk, singularity, specialty, trait, whimsicality.

pedantic *adj.* abstruse, academic, bookish, caviling, didactic, donnish, erudite, finical, formal, fussy, hair-splitting, learned, nit-picking, particular, pedagogic, perfectionist, pompous, precise, punctilious, scholastic, schoolmasterly, sententious, stilted.
antonyms casual, imprecise, informal.

peddle *v.* dilly-dally, flog, hawk, huckster, idle, loiter, market, piddle, push, retail, sell, tout, trade, trifle, vend.

pedestrian *n.* footslogger, foot-traveler, voetganger, walker.
adj. banal, boring, commonplace, dull, flat, humdrum, indifferent, mediocre, mundane, ordinary, plodding, prosaic, run-of-the-mill, stodgy, tolerable, unimaginative, uninspired, uninteresting.
antonyms bright, brilliant, exciting, imaginative.

pedigree *n.* ancestry, blood, breed, derivation, descent, dynasty, extraction, family, family tree, genealogy, heritage, line, lineage, parentage, race, stemma, stirps, stock, succession.

peek *v.* glance, keek, look, peep, peer, spy.
n. blink, dekko, gander, glance, glimpse, keek, look, look-see, peep.

peel *v.* decorticate, denude, desquamate, flake (off), pare, scale, skin, strip (off), undress.

n. epicarp, exocarp, integument, peeling, rind, skin, zest.

peep *v.* blink, emerge, glimpse, issue, keek, peek, peer.
n. blink, dekko, gander, glim, glimpse, keek, look, look-see, peek.

peer[1] *v.* appear, blink, emerge, examine, gaze, inspect, peep, scan, scrutinize, snoop, spy, squint.

peer[2] *n.* aristocrat, baron, count, duke, earl, lord, marquess, marquis, noble, nobleman, thane, viscount.

peer[3] *n.* compeer, counterpart, equal, equipollent, equivalent, fellow, like, match.

peevish *adj.* acrimonious, cantankerous, captious, childish, churlish, crabbed, cross, crotchety, crusty, fractious, franzy, fretful, grumpy, hipped, ill-natured, ill-tempered, irritable, miffy, perverse, pettish, petulant, querulous, ratty, short-tempered, snappy, splenetic, sulky, sullen, surly, testy, touchy, waspish.
antonym good-tempered.

peevishness *n.* acrimony, captiousness, ill-temper, irritability, perversity, pet, petulance, pique, protervity, querulousness, testiness.

peg *v.* attach, control, fasten, fix, freeze, insert, join, limit, mark, pierce, score, secure, set, stabilize.
n. dowel, hook, knob, marker, pin, post, stake, thole(-pin), toggle.

pejorative *adj.* bad, belittling, condemnatory, damning, debasing, deprecatory, depreciatory, derogatory, detractive, detractory, disparaging, negative, slighting, uncomplimentary, unflattering, unpleasant. *antonyms* complimentary, laudatory.

pen *n.* cage, coop, crib, cru(i)ve, enclosure, fold, hutch, stall, sty.
v. cage, confine, coop, corral, crib, enclose, fence, hedge, hem in, hurdle, mew (up), shut up.

penalize *v.* amerce, correct, disadvantage, discipline, handicap, mulct, punish.
antonym reward.

penalty *n.* amende, amercement, disadvantage, fine, forfeit, forfeiture, handicap, mulct, price, punishment, retribution.
antonym reward.

penchant *n.* affinity, bent, bias, disposition, fondness, inclination, leaning, liking, partiality, predilection, predisposition, preference, proclivity, proneness, propensity, soft spot, taste, tendency, turn.
antonym dislike.

penetrate *v.* affect, bore, come across, come home, comprehend, decipher, diffuse, discern, enter, fathom, get through to, get to the bottom of, grasp, impress, infiltrate, perforate, permeate, pervade, pierce, prick, probe, seep, sink, stab, strike, suffuse, touch, understand, unravel.

penetrating *adj.* acute, astute, biting, carrying, critical, discerning, discriminating, harsh, incisive, intelligent, intrusive, keen, observant, penetrative, perceptive, percipient, perspicacious, pervasive, piercing, profound, pungent, quick, sagacious, searching, sharp, sharp-witted, shrewd, shrill, stinging, strong.
antonyms gentle, obtuse, soft.

peninsula *n.* cape, chersonese, doab, mull, point, tongue.

penitent *adj.* abject, apologetic, atoning, conscience-stricken, contrite, humble, in sackcloth and ashes, regretful, remorseful, repentant, rueful, sorrowful, sorry.
antonym unrepentant.

penniless *adj.* bankrupt, broke, bust(ed), cleaned out, destitute, flat broke, impecunious, impoverished, indigent, moneyless, necessitous, needy, obolary, on one's uppers, on the rocks, penurious, poor, poverty-stricken, ruined, skint, stony-broke, strapped.
antonyms rich, wealthy.

pensive *adj.* absent-minded, absorbed, cogitative, contemplative, dreamy, grave, meditative, melancholy, musing, preoccupied, reflective, ruminative, serious, sober, solemn, thoughtful, wistful.

penurious *adj.* beggarly, bust(ed), cheeseparing, close, close-fisted, deficient, destitute, flat broke, frugal, grudging, impecunious, impoverished, inadequate, indigent, meager, mean, miserable, miserly, near, needy, niggardly, obolary, paltry, parsimonious, penniless, poor, poverty-stricken, scanty, skimping, stingy, tight-fisted, ungenerous.
antonyms generous, wealthy.

penury *n.* beggary, dearth, deficiency, destitution, indigence, lack, mendicancy, mendicity, need, paucity, pauperism, poverty, privation, scantiness, scarcity, shortage, sparseness, straitened circumstances, straits, want.
antonym prosperity.

people *n.* citizens, clan, commonalty, community, crowd, demos, family, folk, general public, gens, grass roots, hoi polloi, human beings, humanity, humans, inhabitants, mankind, many-headed beast, many-headed monster, masses, mob, mortals, multitude, nation, persons, plebs, populace, population, public, punters, rabble, race, rank and file, the herd, the million, tribe.
v. colonize, inhabit, occupy, populate, settle, tenant.

perceive *v.* appreciate, apprehend, be aware of, behold, catch, comprehend, conclude, deduce, descry, discern, discover, distinguish, espy, feel, gather, get, grasp, intuit, know, learn, make out, note, observe, realize, recognize, remark, see, sense, spot, understand.

perceptible *adj.* apparent, appreciable, clear, conspicuous, detectable, discernible, distinct, distinguishable, evident, noticeable, observable, obvious, palpable, perceivable, recognizable, salient, tangible, visible.
antonym imperceptible.

perception *n.* apprehension, awareness, conception, consciousness, discernment, feeling, grasp, idea, impression, insight, intellection, notion, observation, recognition, sensation, sense, taste, understanding, uptake.

perceptive *adj.* able to see through a millstone, acute,

alert, astute, aware, discerning, insightful, observant, penetrating, percipient, perspicacious, quick, responsive, sagacious, sapient, sensitive, sharp.
antonym unobservant.

percipient *adj.* alert, alive, astute, aware, discerning, discriminating, intelligent, judicious, knowing, penetrating, perceptive, perspicacious, quick-witted, sharp, wide-awake.
antonyms obtuse, unaware.

perfect *adj.* absolute, accomplished, accurate, adept, blameless, close, complete, completed, consummate, copybook, correct, entire, exact, excellent, experienced, expert, faithful, faultless, finished, flawless, full, ideal, immaculate, impeccable, irreproachable, masterly, model, polished, practiced, precise, pure, right, sheer, skilful, skilled, splendid, spotless, spot-on, strict, sublime, superb, superlative, supreme, true, unadulterated, unalloyed, unblemished, unerring, unimpeachable, unmarred, unmitigated, untarnished, utter, whole.
antonyms flawed, imperfect.
v. accomplish, achieve, carry out, complete, consummate, effect, elaborate, finish, fulfil, perfectionate, perform, realize, refine.

perfection *n.* accomplishment, achievement, acme, completeness, completion, consummation, crown, evolution, exactness, excellence, exquisiteness, flawlessness, fulfilment, ideal, integrity, maturity, nonpareil, paragon, perfectness, pinnacle, precision, purity, realization, sublimity, superiority, wholeness.
antonyms flaw, imperfection.

perfectly *adv.* absolutely, admirably, altogether, completely, consummately, entirely, exquisitely, faultlessly, flawlessly, fully, ideally, impeccably, incomparably, irreproachably, quite, superbly, superlatively, supremely, thoroughly, to perfection, totally, unimpeachably, utterly, wholly, wonderfully.
antonyms imperfectly, partially.

perform *v.* accomplish, achieve, act, appear as, bring about, bring off, carry out, complete, depict, discharge, do, effect, enact, execute, fulfil, function, functionate, manage, observe, play, present, produce, pull off, put on, render, represent, satisfy, stage, transact, work.

performance *n.* accomplishment, account, achievement, act, acting, action, appearance, behavior, bother, business, carrying out, carry-on, completion, conduct, consummation, discharge, efficiency, execution, exhibition, exploit, feat, fulfilment, functioning, fuss, gig, implementation, interpretation, melodrama, operation, play, portrayal, practice, presentation, production, rendition, representation, rigmarole, running, show, to-do, work, working.

performer *n.* actor, actress, artiste, moke, mummer, play-actor, player, Thespian, trouper.

perfume *n.* aroma, attar, balm, balminess, bouquet, cologne, essence, fragrance, incense, odor, redolence, scent, smell, sweetness, toilet water.

perfunctory *adj.* automatic, brief, careless, cursory, heedless, hurried, inattentive, indifferent, mechanical, negligent, offhand, routine, sketchy, slipshod, slovenly, stereo-typed, superficial, wooden.
antonym cordial.

perhaps *adv.* conceivably, feasibly, happen, maybe, mayhap, peradventure, perchance, possibly, you never know.

peril *n.* danger, exposure, hazard, imperilment, insecurity, jeopardy, menace, pitfall, risk, threat, uncertainty, vulnerability.
antonyms safety, security.

perilous *adj.* chancy, dangerous, desperate, dicey, difficult, dire, exposed, hairy, hazardous, menacing, parlous, precarious, risky, threatening, unsafe, unsure, vulnerable.
antonyms safe, secure.

period[1] *n.* age, course, cycle, date, days, end, eon, epoch, era, generation, interval, season, space, span, spell, stage, stint, stop, stretch, term, time, turn, while, years.

period[2] *n.* menses, menstrual flow, menstruation, monthlies, the curse.

periodical *n.* gazette, journal, magazine, monthly, organ, paper, publication, quarterly, review, serial, weekly.

perish *v.* collapse, croak, crumble, decay, decline, decompose, decrease, die, disappear, disintegrate, end, expire, fall, molder, pass away, rot, vanish, waste, wither.

perishable *adj.* biodegradable, corruptible, decomposable, destructible, fast-decaying, fast-deteriorating, short-lived, unstable.

perjury *n.* false oath, false statement, false swearing, false witness, falsification, forswearing, mendacity.

permanent *adj.* abiding, constant, durable, enduring, everlasting, fixed, immutable, imperishable, indestructible, ineffaceable, ineradicable, inerasable, invariable, lasting, long-lasting, perennial, perpetual, persistent, stable, standing, steadfast, unchanging, unfading.
antonyms ephemeral, fleeting, temporary.

permeate *v.* charge, fill, filter through, imbue, impenetrate, impregnate, infiltrate, interfuse, interpenetrate, pass through, penetrate, percolate, pervade, saturate, seep through, soak through.

permissible *adj.* acceptable, admissible, all right, allowable, allowed, authorized, kosher, lawful, leal, legit, legitimate, licit, OK, permitted, proper, sanctioned.
antonym prohibited.

permission *n.* allowance, approval, assent, authorization, consent, dispensation, freedom, go-ahead, green light, imprimatur, indult, leave, liberty, license, permit, sanction, sufferance.
antonym prohibition.

permissive *adj.* acquiescent, complaisant, easy-going, forbearing, free, indulgent, latitudinarian, lax, lenient, liberal, open-minded, overindulgent, tolerant.
antonym strict.

permit *v.* admit, agree, allow, authorize, consent, empower, enable, endorse, endure, give leave, grant, let, warrant.
antonym prohibit.
n. authorization, carnet, liberty, license, pass, passport, permission, sanction, visa, warrant. *antonym* prohibition.

perpetrate *v.* carry out, commit, do, effect, enact, execute, inflict, perform, practice, wreak.

perpetual *adj.* abiding, ceaseless, constant, continual, continuous, deathless, endless, enduring, eternal, everlasting, immortal, incessant, infinite, interminable, lasting, never-ending, never-failing, perennial, permanent, persistent, recurrent, repeated, sempiternal, unceasing, unchanging, undying, unending, unfailing, unflagging, uninterrupted, unremitting, unvarying.
antonyms ephemeral, intermittent, transient.

perpetuate *v.* commemorate, continue, eternalize, immortalize, keep alive, keep up, maintain, preserve, protract, sustain.

perplex *v.* baffle, befuddle, beset, bewilder, complicate, confound, confuse, dumbfound, embrangle, encumber, entangle, gravel, hobble, involve, jumble, mix up, muddle, mystify, nonplus, pother, pudder, puzzle, stump, tangle, thicken, throw.

perplexed *adj.* at a loss, baffled, bamboozled, bewildered, confounded, disconcerted, fuddled, muddled, mystified, puzzled, worried.

perplexing *adj.* amazing, baffling, bewildering, complex, complicated, confusing, difficult, distractive, enigmatic, hard, inexplicable, intricate, involved, knotty, labyrinthine, mysterious, mystifying, paradoxical, puzzling, strange, taxing, thorny, unaccountable, vexatious, weird.
antonyms easy, simple.

persecute *v.* afflict, annoy, badger, bait, bother, castigate, crucify, distress, dragoon, harass, haze, hound, hunt, ill-treat, injure, maltreat, martyr, molest, oppress, pester, pursue, tease, torment, torture, tyrannize, vex, victimize, worry.
antonyms accommodate, humor, indulge, pamper.

persevere *v.* adhere, carry on, continue, endure, go on, hang on, hold fast, hold on, keep going, persist, plug away, pursue, remain, soldier on, stand firm, stick at.
antonyms desist, discontinue, give up, stop.

persist *v.* abide, carry on, continue, endure, insist, keep at it, last, linger, perdure, persevere, remain, stand fast, stand firm.
antonyms desist, stop.

persistence *n.* assiduity, assiduousness, constancy, determination, diligence, doggedness, endurance, grit, indefatigableness, perseverance, pertinacity, pluck, resolution, sedulity, stamina, steadfastness, tenacity, tirelessness.

persistent *adj.* assiduous, constant, continual, continuous, determined, dogged, endless, enduring, fixed, hydra-headed, immovable, incessant, indefatigable, indomitable, interminable, never-ending, obdurate, obstinate, perpetual, persevering, pertinacious, relentless, repeated, resolute, steadfast, steady, stubborn, tenacious, tireless, unflagging, unrelenting, unremitting, zealous.

person *n.* being, bod, body, cat, character, codger, cookie, customer, human, human being, individual, individuum, living soul, party, soul, specimen, type, wight.

personable *adj.* affable, agreeable, amiable, attractive, charming, good-looking, handsome, likable, nice, outgoing, pleasant, pleasing, presentable, warm, winning.
antonyms disagreeable, unattractive.

personal *adj.* bodily, corporal, corporeal, derogatory, disparaging, exclusive, exterior, idiosyncratic, individual, inimitable, insulting, intimate, material, nasty, offensive, own, particular, peculiar, pejorative, physical, private, privy, slighting, special, tête-à-tête. *antonyms* general, public, universal.

personality *n.* attraction, attractiveness, celebrity, character, charisma, charm, disposition, dynamism, humor, identity, individuality, likableness, magnetism, makeup, nature, notable, personage, pleasantness, psyche, selfhood, selfness, star, temper, temperament, traits.

perspicacity *n.* acuity, acumen, acuteness, brains, cleverness, discernment, discrimination, insight, keenness, penetration, perceptiveness, percipience, perspicaciousness, perspicuity, sagaciousness, sagacity, sharpness, shrewdness, wit.

persuade *v.* actuate, advise, allure, bring round, cajole, coax, convert, convince, counsel, entice, impel, incite, induce, influence, inveigle, lead on, lean on, prevail upon, prompt, satisfy, sway, sweet-talk, talk into, urge, win over.
antonyms discourage, dissuade.

persuasion *n.* belief, blandishment, cajolery, camp, certitude, cogency, come-on, conversion, conviction, credo, creed, cult, denomination, enticement, exhortation, faction, faith, force, inducement, influence, inveiglement, opinion, party, persuasiveness, potency, power, pull, school (of thought), sect, side, suasion, sweet talk, tenet, views, wheedling.

persuasive *adj.* cogent, compelling, convincing, credible, effective, eloquent, forceful, honeyed, impelling, impressive, inducing, influential, logical, moving, persuasory, plausible, potent, sound, telling, touching, valid, weighty, whilly, whillywha(w), winning.

pertain *v.* appertain, apply, be appropriate, be part of, be relevant, bear on, befit, belong, come under, concern, refer, regard, relate.

pertinacious *adj.* determined, dogged, headstrong, inflexible, intractable, mulish, obdurate, obstinate, persevering, persistent, perverse, purposeful, relentless, resolute, self-willed, strong-willed, stubborn, tenacious, uncompromising, unyielding, wilful.

pertinent *adj.* ad rem, admissible, analogous, applicable,

apposite, appropriate, apropos, apt, befitting, fit, fitting, germane, material, pat, proper, relevant, suitable, to the point, to the purpose.
antonyms inappropriate, irrelevant, unsuitable.

perturbed *adj.* agitated, alarmed, anxious, discomposed, disconcerted, disturbed, fearful, flurried, flustered, nervous, restless, shaken, troubled, uncomfortable, uneasy, unsettled, upset, worried.
antonym unperturbed.

pervade *v.* affect, charge, diffuse, extend, fill, imbue, infuse, osmose, overspread, penetrate, percolate, permeate, saturate, suffuse.

perverse *adj.* abnormal, balky, cantankerous, churlish, contradictory, contrary, contumacious, crabbed, cross, cross-grained, cussed, delinquent, depraved, deviant, disobedient, dogged, fractious, froward, headstrong, ill-natured, ill-tempered, improper, incorrect, intractable, intransigent, miscreant, mulish, obdurate, obstinate, peevish, petulant, pig-headed, rebellious, recalcitrant, refractory, spiteful, stroppy, stubborn, surly, thrawn, thwart, troublesome, unhealthy, unmanageable, unreasonable, unyielding, uppity, wayward, wilful, wrong-headed, wry.
antonyms normal, reasonable.

perversion *n.* aberration, abnormality, anomaly, corruption, debauchery, depravity, deviance, deviancy, deviation, distortion, falsification, immorality, kink, kinkiness, misapplication, misinterpretation, misrepresentation, misuse, paraphilia, twisting, unnaturalness, vice, vitiation, wickedness.

pervert *v.* abuse, bend, corrupt, debase, debauch, degrade, deprave, distort, divert, falsify, garble, lead astray, misapply, misconstrue, misinterpret, misrepresent, misuse, subvert, twist, vitiate, warp, wrest.
n. debauchee, degenerate, deviant, paraphiliac, vert, weirdo.

perverted *adj.* aberrant, abnormal, corrupt, debased, debauched, depraved, deviant, distorted, evil, freakish, immoral, impaired, kinky, misguided, queer, sick, twisted, unhealthy, unnatural, vicious, vitiated, warped, wicked.

pest *n.* annoyance, bane, blight, bore, bother, bug, canker, curse, irritation, nuisance, pain (in the neck), scourge, thorn in one's flesh, trial, vexation.

pester *v.* annoy, badger, bedevil, bother, bug, chivvy, disturb, dog, drive round the bend, drive up the wall, fret, get at, harass, harry, hassle, hector, hound, irk, nag, pick on, plague, ride, torment, worry.

pet *n.* darling, dilling, doll, duck, ewe-lamb, favorite, idol, jewel, treasure, whitehead.
adj. cherished, dearest, favored, favorite, particular, preferred, special.
v. baby, canoodle, caress, coddle, cosset, cuddle, dote on, fondle, indulge, kiss, mollycoddle, neck, pamper, pat, smooch, snog, spoil, stroke.

petition *n.* address, appeal, application, boon, entreaty, imploration, invocation, plea, prayer, request, rogation, round robin, solicitation, suit, supplication.
v. appeal, ask, beg, beseech, bid, call upon, crave, entreat, implore, memorialize, plead, pray, press, solicit, sue, supplicate, urge.

petrify *v.* amaze, appal, astonish, astound, benumb, calcify, confound, dumbfound, fossilize, gorgonize, harden, horrify, immobilize, numb, paralyze, set, solidify, stun, stupefy, terrify, transfix, turn to stone.

petty *adj.* cheap, contemptible, grudging, inconsiderable, inessential, inferior, insignificant, junior, lesser, little, lower, mean, measly, minor, negligible, one-horse, paltry, picayune, picayunish, piddling, pimping, poking, poky, secondary, shabby, slight, small, small-minded, spiteful, stingy, subordinate, trifling, trivial, ungenerous, unimportant.
antonyms generous, important, large-hearted, significant, vital.

petulant *adj.* bad-tempered, captious, caviling, crabbed, cross, crusty, fretful, ill-humored, impatient, irascible, irritable, moody, peevish, perverse, pettish, procacious, querulous, snappish, sour, sulky, sullen, ungracious, waspish.

phantom *n.* apparition, chimera, eidolon, figment (of the imagination), ghost, hallucination, illusion, manes, phantasm(a), revenant, shade, simulacrum, specter, spirit, spook, vision, wraith.

phase *n.* aspect, chapter, condition, development, juncture, period, point, position, season, spell, stage, state, step, time.

phenomenon *n.* appearance, circumstance, curiosity, episode, event, fact, happening, incident, marvel, miracle, occurrence, prodigy, rarity, sensation, sight, spectacle, wonder.

philanthropy *n.* agape, alms-giving, altruism, beneficence, benevolence, benignity, bounty, brotherly love, charitableness, charity, generosity, humanitarianism, kind-heartedness, liberality, munificence, open-handedness, patronage, public-spiritedness, unselfishness.

philosophical *adj.* abstract, analytical, calm, collected, composed, cool, dispassionate, equanimous, erudite, impassive, imperturbable, learned, logical, metaphysical, patient, philosophic, rational, resigned, sagacious, serene, stoical, theoretical, thoughtful, tranquil, unruffled, wise.

phlegmatic *adj.* apathetic, bovine, cold, dull, frigid, heavy, impassive, imperturbable, indifferent, lethargic, listless, lymphatic, matter-of-fact, nonchalant, placid, sluggish, stoical, stolid, unconcerned, undemonstrative, unemotional.
antonyms demonstrative, passionate.

phony *adj.* affected, assumed, bogus, counterfeit, fake, false, forged, imitation, pseudo, put-on, quack, quack-salving, sham, spurious, trick.
antonyms real, true.

n. counterfeit, fake, faker, forgery, fraud, humbug, impostor, mountebank, pretender, pseud, quack, sham.

phrase *n.* construction, expression, idiom, locution, mention, motto, remark, saying, tag, utterance.
v. couch, express, formulate, frame, present, pronounce, put, say, style, term, utter, voice, word.

physical *adj.* actual, bodily, carnal, concrete, corporal, corporeal, earthly, fleshly, incarnate, material, mortal, natural, palpable, real, sensible, solid, somatic, substantial, tangible, visible.
antonyms mental, spiritual.

physique *n.* body, build, chassis, constitution, figure, form, frame, make-up, shape, structure.

pick *v.* break into, break open, choose, collect, crack, cull, cut, decide on, elect, embrace, espouse, fix upon, foment, gather, harvest, incite, instigate, opt for, pluck, prize, provoke, pull, screen, select, settle on, sift out, single out, start.
antonym reject.
n. best, brightest and best, choice, choicest, choosing, cream, crème de la crème, decision, elect, élite, flower, option, preference, pride, prize, selection, tops.

picket *n.* demonstrator, dissenter, guard, look-out, outpost, pale, paling, palisade, patrol, peg, picketer, post, protester, scout, sentinel, sentry, spotter, stake, stanchion, upright, vedette, watchman.
v. blockade, boycott, corral, demonstrate, enclose, fence, hedge in, palisade, pen in, protest.

pictorial *adj.* diagrammatic, expressive, graphic, illustrated, picturesque, representational, scenic, schematic, striking, vivid.

picture *n.* account, archetype, carbon copy, copy, dead ringer, delineation, depiction, description, double, drawing, duplicate, effigy, embodiment, engraving, epitome, essence, film, flick, graphic, illustration, image, impression, kakemono, likeness, living image, lookalike, motion picture, movie, painting, personification, photograph, portrait, portrayal, print, re-creation, replica, report, representation, ringer, scene, similitude, sketch, spit, spitting image, tablature, table, twin, vraisemblance.
v. conceive of, delineate, depict, describe, draw, envisage, envision, illustrate, image, imagine, paint, photograph, portray, render, represent, see, show, sketch, visualize.

piece *n.* allotment, article, bit, case, chunk, component, composition, constituent, creation, division, element, example, fraction, fragment, instance, item, length, mammock, morsel, mouthful, objet d'art, occurrence, offcut, part, piecemeal, portion, production, quantity, sample, scrap, section, segment, share, shred, slice, snippet, specimen, stroke, study, work, work of art.

piecemeal *adv.* at intervals, bit by bit, by degrees, fitfully, in dribs and drabs, in penny numbers, intermittently, little by little, parcel-wise, partially, slowly.
antonyms completely, entirely, wholly. *adj.* discrete, fragmentary, intermittent, interrupted, partial, patchy, scattered, unsystematic.
antonyms complete, entire, whole, wholesale.

pierce *v.* affect, barb, bore, comprehend, discern, discover, drift, drill, enter, excite, fathom, grasp, gride, hurt, impale, lancinate, move, pain, penetrate, perforate, pink, prick, probe, prog, puncture, realize, rouse, run through, see, spike, stab, stick into, sting, stir, strike, thrill, thrust, touch, transfix, transpierce, understand, wound.

piercing *adj.* acute, agonizing, alert, algid, arctic, aware, biting, bitter, cold, ear-piercing, ear-splitting, excruciating, exquisite, fierce, freezing, frore, frosty, gelid, high-pitched, intense, keen, loud, nipping, nippy, numbing, painful, penetrating, perceptive, perspicacious, powerful, probing, quick-witted, racking, raw, searching, severe, sharp, shattering, shooting, shrewd, shrill, Siberian, stabbing, wintry.

pig-headed *adj.* bull-headed, contrary, cross-grained, dense, froward, inflexible, intractable, intransigent, mulish, obstinate, perverse, self-willed, stiff-necked, stubborn, stupid, unyielding, wilful, wrong-headed.
antonyms flexible, tractable.

pigment *n.* color, colorant, coloring, coloring matter, dye, dyestuff, hue, paint, stain, tempera, tincture, tint.

pile[1] *n.* accumulation, assemblage, assortment, bing, bomb, building, cock, collection, edifice, erection, fortune, heap, hoard, mass, mint, money, mound, mountain, mow, packet, pot, stack, stockpile, structure, wealth.
v. accumulate, amass, assemble, build up, charge, climb, collect, crowd, crush, flock, flood, gather, heap, hoard, jam, load up, mass, pack, rush, stack, store, stream.

pile[2] *n.* bar, beam, column, foundation, pier, piling, pill, post, rib, stanchion, support, upright.

pile[3] *n.* down, fur, fuzz, fuzziness, hair, nap, plush, shag.

pilgrim *n.* crusader, hadji, palmer, peregrine, traveler, wanderer, wayfarer.

pilgrimage *n.* crusade, excursion, expedition, hadj, journey, mission, odyssey, peregrination, tour, trip.

pillar *n.* balluster, bastion, cippus, column, leader, leading light, mainstay, mast, pier, pilaster, piling, post, prop, rock, shaft, stanchion, support, supporter, tower of strength, upholder, upright, worthy.

pilot *n.* airman, aviator, captain, conductor, coxswain, director, flier, guide, helmsman, hobbler, leader, lodesman, navigator, steersman.
v. boss, conduct, control, direct, drive, fly, guide, handle, lead, manage, navigate, operate, run, shepherd, steer.
adj. experimental, model, test, trial.

pimp *n.* bawd, fancy man, fleshmonger, go-between, mack, pander, panderer, procurer, white-slaver, whoremaster, whoremonger.

pin *v.* affix, attach, fasten, fix, hold down, hold fast, immobilize, join, nail, pinion, press, restrain, secure, tack.

n. bolt, breastpin, brooch, clip, fastener, nail, peg, rivet, screw, spike, spindle, stick pin, tack, tie-pin.

pinch *v.* afflict, apprehend, arrest, bust, chafe, check, collar, compress, confine, cramp, crush, distress, do, economize, filch, grasp, hurt, knap, knock off, lay, lift, nab, nick, nip, oppress, pain, pick up, pilfer, press, prig, pull in, purloin, rob, run in, scrimp, skimp, snaffle, snatch, sneap, snitch, spare, squeeze, steal, stint, swipe, tweak.

n. bit, crisis, dash, difficulty, emergency, exigency, hardship, jam, jot, mite, necessity, nip, oppression, pass, pickle, plight, predicament, pressure, soupçon, speck, squeeze, strait, stress, taste, tweak.

pinion *v.* bind, chain, confine, fasten, fetter, hobble, immobilize, manacle, pin down, shackle, tie, truss.

pinnacle *n.* acme, apex, apogee, cap, cone, crest, crown, eminence, height, needle, obelisk, peak, pyramid, spire, steeple, summit, top, turret, vertex, zenith.

pioneer *n.* colonist, colonizer, developer, explorer, founder, founding father, frontiersman, innovator, leader, settler, trail-blazer, voortrekker, way-maker.

v. blaze a trail, create, develop, discover, establish, found, initiate, instigate, institute, invent, launch, lead, open up, originate, prepare, start.

pious *adj.* dedicated, devoted, devout, God-fearing, godly, good, goody-goody, holier-than-thou, holy, hypocritical, moral, pietistic, religiose, religious, reverent, righteous, saintly, sanctimonious, self-righteous, spiritual, unctuous, virtuous.

antonyms impious.

piquant *adj.* biting, interesting, lively, peppery, poignant, provocative, pungent, racy, salty, savory, scintillating, sharp, sparkling, spicy, spirited, stimulating, stinging, tangy, tart, zesty.

antonyms banal, jejune.

pirate *n.* buccaneer, corsair, filibuster, freebooter, infringer, marauder, marque, picaroon, plagiarist, plagiarizer, raider, rover, sallee-man, sea-rat, sea-robber, sea-rover, sea-wolf, water-rat.

v. appropriate, borrow, copy, crib, lift, nick, pinch, plagiarize, poach, reproduce, steal.

pistol *n.* dag, derringer, gat, gun, hand-gun, iron, Luger, piece, revolver, rod, sidearm, six-shooter.

pit *n.* abyss, alveole, alveolus, cavity, chasm, coal-mine, crater, dent, depression, dimple, excavation, gulf, hole, hollow, indentation, mine, oubliette, pock-mark, pothole, trench, variole.

pitch *v.* bung, cast, chuck, dive, drop, erect, fall headlong, fix, fling, flounder, heave, hurl, launch, lob, locate, lurch, peck, place, plant, plunge, raise, roll, set up, settle, sling, stagger, station, throw, topple, toss, tumble, wallow, welter.

n. angle, cant, degree, dip, gradient, ground, harmonic, height, incline, level, line, modulation, park, patter, playing-field, point, sales talk, slope, sound, spiel, sports field, steepness, summit, tilt, timbre, tone.

pitcher *n.* bottle, can, container, crock, ewer, jack, jar, jug, urn, vessel.

piteous *adj.* affecting, deplorable, distressing, doleful, doloriferous, dolorific, grievous, heartbreaking, heart-rending, lamentable, miserable, mournful, moving, pathetic, pitiable, pitiful, plaintive, poignant, sad, sorrowful, touching, woeful, wretched.

pitfall *n.* catch, danger, difficulty, downfall, drawback, hazard, peril, pit, snag, snare, stumbling-block, trap.

pitiable *adj.* contemptible, distressed, distressful, distressing, doleful, grievous, lamentable, miserable, mournful, pathetic, piteous, poor, sad, sorry, woeful, woesome, wretched.

pitiful *adj.* abject, base, beggarly, contemptible, deplorable, despicable, distressing, grievous, heartbreaking, heart-rending, hopeless, inadequate, insignificant, lamentable, low, mean, miserable, paltry, pathetic, piteous, pitiable, ruthful, sad, scurvy, shabby, sorry, vile, woeful, worthless, wretched.

pitiless *adj.* brutal, callous, cold-blooded, cold-hearted, cruel, flinty, hard-hearted, harsh, heartless, implacable, inexorable, inhuman, merciless, obdurate, relentless, ruthless, uncaring, unfeeling, unmerciful, unpitying, unsympathetic.

antonyms compassionate, gentle, kind, merciful.

pity *n.* charity, clemency, commiseration, compassion, condolence, crime, crying shame, fellow-feeling, forbearance, kindness, mercy, misfortune, regret, ruth, shame, sin, sympathy, tenderness, understanding.

antonyms cruelty, disdain, scorn.

v. absolve, bleed for, commiserate with, condole with, feel for, forgive, grieve for, pardon, reprieve, sympathize with, weep for.

pivotal *adj.* axial, central, climactic, critical, crucial, decisive, determining, focal, vital.

place *n.* abode, accommodation, affair, apartment, appointment, area, berth, billet, charge, city, concern, district, domicile, duty, dwelling, employment, flat, function, grade, home, house, job, locale, locality, location, locus, manor, mansion, neighborhood, pad, point, position, post, prerogative, property, quarter, rank, region, residence, responsibility, right, role, room, seat, site, situation, space, spot, station, status, stead, town, venue, vicinity, village, whereabouts.

v. allocate, appoint, arrange, assign, associate, bung, charge, class, classify, commission, deposit, dispose, dump, entrust, establish, fix, give, grade, group, identify, install, know, lay, locate, order, plant, position, put, put one's finger on, rank, recognize, remember, rest, set, settle, situate, sort, stand, station, stick.

placid *adj.* calm, collected, composed, cool, equable, even, even-tempered, gentle, halcyon, imperturbable, level-headed, mild, peaceful, quiet, reposeful, restful,

self-possessed, serene, still, tranquil, undisturbed, unexcitable, unmoved, unruffled, untroubled.
antonyms agitated, jumpy.

plagiarize *v.* appropriate, borrow, counterfeit, crib, infringe, lift, pirate, reproduce, steal, thieve.

plague *n.* affliction, aggravation, annoyance, bane, blight, bother, calamity, cancer, contagion, curse, death, disease, epidemic, evil, infection, irritant, nuisance, pain, pandemic, pest, pestilence, problem, scourge, thorn in the flesh, torment, trial, vexation, visitation.
v. afflict, annoy, badger, bedevil, bother, distress, disturb, fret, harass, harry, hassle, haunt, hound, molest, pain, persecute, pester, tease, torment, torture, trouble, vex.

plain *adj.* apparent, artless, austere, bare, basic, blunt, candid, clear, clinical, common, commonplace, comprehensible, direct, discreet, distinct, downright, even, everyday, evident, flat, forthright, frank, frugal, guileless, homebred, homely, homespun, honest, ill-favored, ingenuous, legible, level, lowly, lucid, manifest, modest, muted, obvious, open, ordinary, outspoken, patent, penny-plain, plane, pure, restrained, self-colored, severe, simple, sincere, smooth, Spartan, stark, straightforward, transparent, ugly, unadorned, unaffected, unambiguous, unattractive, unbeautiful, understandable, undistinguished, unelaborate, unembellished, unfigured, unhandsome, unlovely, unmistakable, unobstructed, unornamented, unpatterned, unprepossessing, unpretentious, untrimmed, unvarnished, visible, whole-colored, workaday.
antonyms abstruse, attractive, elaborate, exaggerated, ostentatious, rich, striking, unclear.
n. flat, grassland, llano, lowland, maidan, plateau, prairie, steppe, tableland, vega, veld(t).

plan *n.* blueprint, chart, contrivance, delineation, design, device, diagram, drawing, idea, illustration, layout, map, method, plot, procedure, program, project, proposal, proposition, representation, scenario, schedule, scheme, sketch, strategy, suggestion, system.
v. aim, arrange, complot, concoct, conspire, contemplate, contrive, design, devise, draft, envisage, foreplan, foresee, formulate, frame, intend, invent, mean, organize, outline, plot, prepare, propose, purpose, represent, scheme.

plane[1] *n.* class, condition, degree, echelon, footing, level, position, rank, rung, stage, stratum.
adj. even, flat, flush, horizontal, level, plain, planar, regular, smooth, uniform.

plane[2] *n.* aircraft, airliner, airplane, bomber, fighter, glider, jet, jumbo, jumbo jet, sea-plane, swing-wing, VTOL.
v. fly, glide, sail, skate, skim, volplane, wing.

plastic *adj.* compliant, docile, ductile, fictile, flexible, impressionable, malleable, manageable, moldable, pliable, pliant, receptive, responsive, soft, supple, tractable.
antonyms inflexible, rigid.

plasticity *n.* flexibility, malleability, pliability, pliableness, pliancy, softness, suppleness, tractability.
antonyms inflexibility, rigidity.

platform *n.* dais, estrade, gantry, manifesto, objective(s), party line, podium, policy, principle, program, rostrum, stage, stand, tenet(s).

platitude *n.* banality, bromide, chestnut, cliché, common-place, inanity, stereotype, truism.

plausible *adj.* believable, colorable, conceivable, convincing, credible, facile, fair-spoken, glib, likely, persuasive, possible, probable, reasonable, smooth, smooth-talking, smooth-tongued, specious, tenable, voluble.
antonyms implausible, improbable, unlikely.

play *v.* act, bet, caper, challenge, chance, compete, contend, execute, fiddle, fidget, flirt, fool around, frisk, frolic, gamble, gambol, hazard, impersonate, interfere, lilt, participate, perform, personate, portray, punt, represent, revel, risk, rival, romp, speculate, sport, string along, take, take on, take part, take the part of, trifle, vie with, wager.
antonym work.
n. action, activity, amusement, caper, comedy, diversion, doodle, drama, elbowroom, employment, entertainment, exercise, farce, foolery, frolic, fun, function, gambling, gambol, game, gaming, give, humor, jest, joking, lark, latitude, leeway, margin, masque, motion, movement, operation, pastime, performance, piece, prank, range, recreation, romp, room, scope, show, space, sport, sweep, swing, teasing, tragedy, transaction, working.

playful *adj.* arch, cheerful, coltish, coquettish, coy, espiègle, flirtatious, frisky, frolicsome, gamesome, gay, good-natured, humorous, impish, jesting, jokey, joking, joyous, kittenish, kitteny, larkish, larky, lively, merry, mischievous, puckish, reasing, roguish, rollicking, spirited, sportive, sprightly, tongue-in-cheek, toyish, toysome, vivacious, waggish.
antonyms serious, stern.

plaything *n.* amusement, bauble, game, gewgaw, gimcrack, pastime, puppet, toy, trifle, trinket.

playwright *n.* dramatist, dramaturge, dramaturgist, screenwriter, scriptwriter.

plea *n.* action, allegation, apology, appeal, begging, cause, claim, defense, entreaty, excuse, explanation, extenuation, imploration, intercession, invocation, justification, overture, petition, placit(um), prayer, pretext, request, suit, supplication, vindication.

plead *v.* adduce, allege, appeal, argue, ask, assert, beg, beseech, crave, entreat, implore, importune, maintain, moot, petition, put forward, request, solicit, supplicate.

pleasant *adj.* acceptable, affable, agreeable, amene, amiable, amusing, charming, cheerful, cheery, congenial, cool, delectable, delightful, delightsome, engaging, enjoyable, fine, friendly, genial, good-humored, gratifying, likable,

listenable, lovely, nice, pleasing, pleasurable, refreshing, satisfying, sunshiny, toothsome, welcome, winsome.
antonyms distasteful, nasty, repugnant, unpleasant.

please *v.* amuse, captivate, charm, cheer, choose, content, delight, desire, enchant, entertain, gladden, go for, gratify, humor, indulge, like, opt, prefer, rejoice, satisfy, see fit, suit, think fit, tickle, tickle pink, want, will, wish.
antonyms anger, annoy, displease.

pleasing *adj.* acceptable, agreeable, amiable, amusing, attractive, charming, congenial, delightful, engaging, enjoyable, entertaining, good, gratifying, likable, nice, pleasurable, polite, satisfying, welcome, winning.
antonym unpleasant.

pleasure *n.* amusement, bliss, choice, comfort, command, complacency, contentment, delectation, delight, desire, diversion, ease, enjoyment, gladness, gratification, happiness, inclination, joy, mind, option, preference, purpose, recreation, satisfaction, solace, will, wish.
antonyms displeasure, pain, sorrow, trouble.

plebiscite *n.* ballot, poll, referendum, straw poll, vote.

pledge *n.* assurance, bail, bond, collateral, covenant, deposit, earnest, gage, guarantee, health, oath, pawn, promise, security, surety, toast, undertaking, vow, warrant, word, word of honor.
v. bind, contract, drink to, engage, ensure, gage, guarantee, mortgage, plight, promise, secure, swear, toast, undertake, vouch, vow.

plentiful *adj.* abounding, abundant, ample, bounteous, bountiful, bumper, complete, copious, fertile, fruitful, generous, inexhaustible, infinite, lavish, liberal, luxuriant, overflowing, plenteous, productive, profuse, prolific.
antonyms rare, scanty, scarce.

plenty *n.* abundance, affluence, copiousness, enough, fertility, fruitfulness, fund, heap(s), lots, luxury, mass, masses, milk and honey, mine, mountain(s), oodles, opulence, pile(s), plenitude, plenteousness, plentifulness, plethora, profusion, prosperity, quantities, quantity, stack(s), store, sufficiency, volume, wealth.
antonyms lack, need, scarcity, want.

pliable *adj.* accommodating, adaptable, bendable, bendy, compliant, docile, ductile, flexible, impressionable, influenceable, limber, lithe, malleable, manageable, persuadable, plastic, pliant, receptive, responsive, suggestible, supple, susceptible, tractable, yielding.
antonyms inflexible, rigid.

pliant *adj.* adaptable, bendable, bendy, biddable, compliant, ductile, easily led, flexible, impressionable, influenceable, lithe, manageable, persuadable, plastic, pliable, supple, susceptible, tractable, whippy, yielding.
antonyms inflexible, intractable.

plight[1] *n.* case, circumstances, condition, difficulty, dilemma, extremity, galère, hole, jam, perplexity, pickle, predicament, quandary, scrape, situation, spot, state, straits, trouble.

plight[2] *n.* affiance, contract, covenant, engage, guarantee, pledge, promise, propose, swear, vouch, vow.

plot[1] *n.* action, cabal, conspiracy, covin, design, intrigue, machination(s), narrative, outline, plan, scenario, scheme, story, story line, stratagem, subject, theme, thread.
v. brew, cabal, calculate, chart, collude, compass, compute, conceive, concoct, conspire, contrive, cook up, design, devise, draft, draw, frame, hatch, imagine, intrigue, lay, locate, machinate, maneuver, map, mark, outline, plan, project, scheme.

plot[2] *n.* allotment, area, green, ground, lot, parcel, patch, tract.

plotter *n.* caballer, conspirator, intriguer, Machiavellian, machinator, schemer, strategist.

ploy *n.* artifice, contrivance, device, dodge, gambit, game, maneuver, move, ruse, scheme, strategem, subterfuge, tactic, trick, wile.

pluck[1] *n.* backbone, boldness, bottle, bravery, courage, determination, fortitude, gameness, grit, guts, hardihood, heart, intrepidity, mettle, nerve, resolution, spirit, spunk, tenacity.

pluck[2] *v.* catch, clutch, collect, depilate, deplume, displume, draw, evulse, gather, harvest, jerk, pick, plunk, pull, pull off, pull out, snatch, strum, thrum, tug, twang, tweak, unplume, yank.

plug *n.* advert, advertisement, bung, cake, chew, cork, dossil, dottle, good word, hype, mention, pigtail, publicity, puff, push, quid, spigot, spile, stopper, stopple, studdle, tamp(i)on, twist, wad.
v. advertise, block, build up, bung, choke, close, cork, cover, drudge, fill, grind, hype, labor, mention, pack, peg away, plod, promote, publicize, puff, push, seal, slog, stop, stop up, stopper, stopple, stuff, tamp, toil.

plump[1] *adj.* beefy, burly, buxom, chopping, chubby, corpulent, dumpy, embonpoint, endomorphic, fat, fleshy, full, matronly, obese, podgy, portly, roly-poly, rotund, round, stout, tubby, well-upholstered.
antonyms skinny, thin.

plump[2] *v.* collapse, descend, drop, dump, fall, flop, sink, slump.
adv. abruptly, directly, straight.

plunder *v.* depredate, despoil, devastate, loot, pillage, raid, ransack, ravage, reive, rifle, rob, sack, spoil, spoliate, steal, strip.
n. booty, despoilment, ill-gotten gains, loot, pickings, pillage, prey, prize, rapine, spoils, swag.

plunge *v.* career, cast, charge, dash, demerge, demerse, descend, dip, dive, dive-bomb, dook, douse, drop, fall, go down, hurtle, immerse, jump, lurch, nose-dive, pitch, plummet, rush, sink, submerge, swoop, tear, throw, tumble.
n. collapse, descent, dive, dook, drop, fall, immersion, jump, submersion, swoop, tumble.

plurality *n.* bulk, diversity, galaxy, majority, mass, most, multiplicity, multitudinousness, numerousness, preponderance, profusion, variety.

pocketbook *n.* bag, handbag, purse, wallet.

podium *n.* dais, platform, rostrum, stage, stand.

poem *n.* acrostic, ballad(e), dit(t), ditty, eclogue, elegy, epicede, epicedium, epinicion, epithalamion, epithalamium, fabliau, genethliac(on), idyll, jingle, lay, limerick, lipogram, lyric, madrigal, monody, ode, palinode, rhyme, song, sonnet, verse, verselet, verset, versicle.

poetry *n.* free verse, gay science, iambics, lyrics, macaronics, muse, Parnassus, pennill, poems, poesy, rhyme, rhyming, vers libre, verse, versing.

poignant *adj.* acrid, acute, affecting, agonizing, biting, bitter, caustic, distressing, heartbreaking, heart-rending, intense, keen, moving, painful, pathetic, penetrating, piercing, piquant, pointed, pungent, sad, sarcastic, severe, sharp, stinging, tender, touching, upsetting.

point[1] *n.* aim, aspect, attribute, burden, characteristic, circumstance, condition, core, crux, degree, design, detail, dot, drift, end, essence, extent, facet, feature, full stop, gist, goal, import, instance, instant, intent, intention, item, juncture, location, mark, marrow, matter, meaning, moment, motive, nicety, nub, object, objective, particular, peculiarity, period, pith, place, position, property, proposition, purpose, quality, question, reason, respect, score, side, site, speck, spot, stage, station, stop, subject, tally, text, theme, thrust, time, trait, unit, use, usefulness, utility.
v. aim, denote, designate, direct, draw attention to, hint, indicate, level, show, signal, signify, suggest, train.

point[2] *n.* apex, bill, cacumen, cape, end, fastigium, foreland, head, headland, neb, ness, nib, promontory, prong, spike, spur, summit, tang, tine, tip, top.

pointed *adj.* accurate, acicular, aciform, aculeate(d), acuminate, acute, barbed, biting, cuspidate, cutting, edged, fastigiate(d), incisive, keen, lanceolate(d), lancet, lanciform, mucronate, penetrating, pertinent, sharp, telling, trenchant.

pointless *adj.* absurd, aimless, bootless, fruitless, futile, inane, ineffectual, irrelevant, meaningless, nonsensical, profitless, senseless, silly, stupid, unavailing, unbeneficial, unproductive, unprofitable, useless, vague, vain, worthless.
antonyms meaningful, profitable.

poise *n.* aplomb, assurance, calmness, collectedness, composure, cool, coolness, dignity, elegance, equanimity, equilibrium, grace, presence, presence of mind, sangfroid, savoir-faire, self-possession, serenity.
v. balance, float, hang, hold, hover, librate, position, support, suspend.

poison *n.* aconite, aconitum, bane, blight, cancer, canker, contagion, contamination, corruption, malignancy, miasma, toxin, venom, virus.
v. adulterate, contaminate, corrupt, defile, deprave, empoison, envenom, infect, kill, murder, pervert, pollute, subvert, taint, undermine, vitiate, warp.

poke *v.* butt, butt in, dig, elbow, hit, interfere, intrude, jab, meddle, nose, nudge, peek, prod, prog, pry, punch, push, shove, snoop, stab, stick, tamper, thrust.
n. butt, dig, dunt, jab, nudge, prod, punch, shove, thrust.

pole[1] *n.* bar, lug, mast, post, rod, shaft, spar, staff, stake, standard, stang, stick.

pole[2] *n.* antipode, extremity, limit, terminus, (ultima) Thule.

policy *n.* action, approach, code, course, custom, discretion, good sense, guideline, line, plan, position, practice, procedure, program, protocol, prudence, rule, sagacity, scheme, shrewdness, stance, stratagem, theory, wisdom.

polish *v.* brighten, brush up, buff, burnish, clean, correct, cultivate, emend, emery, enhance, file, finish, furbish, improve, luster, perfect, planish, refine, rub, rub up, shine, shine up, slick, slicken, smooth, touch up, wax.
antonyms dull, tarnish.
n. breeding, brightness, brilliance, class, cultivation, elegance, eutrapelia, expertise, finesse, finish, glaze, gloss, grace, luster, perfectionism, politesse, proficiency, refinement, savoir-faire, sheen, smoothness, sophistication, sparkle, style, suavity, urbanity, varnish, veneer, wax.
antonyms clumsiness, dullness, gaucherie.

polished *adj.* accomplished, adept, bright, burnished, civilized, courtly, cultivated, educated, elegant, expert, faultless, fine, finished, flawless, furbished, genteel, glassy, gleaming, glossy, graceful, gracious, impeccable, lustrous, masterly, outstanding, perfected, polite, professional, refined, sheeny, shining, skilful, slippery, smooth, sophisticated, suave, superlative, urbane, well-bred.
antonyms clumsy, dull, gauche, inexpert, tarnished.

polite *adj.* affable, attentive, civil, civilized, complaisant, considerate, cordial, courteous, courtly, cultured, deferential, diplomatic, discreet, elegant, genteel, gentlemanly, gracious, ladylike, mannerly, obliging, polished, refined, respectful, tactful, thoughtful, urbane, well-behaved, well-bred, well-mannered.
antonyms impolite, uncultivated.

politic *adj.* advantageous, advisable, artful, astute, canny, crafty, cunning, designing, diplomatic, discreet, expedient, ingenious, intriguing, judicious, Machiavellian, opportune, prudent, sagacious, sage, scheming, sensible, shrewd, sly, subtle, tactful, unscrupulous, wise.
antonym impolitic.

pollute *v.* adulterate, befoul, besmirch, canker, contaminate, corrupt, debase, debauch, defile, deprave, desecrate, dirty, dishonor, foul, infect, mar, poison, profane, soil, spoil, stain, sully, taint, violate, vitiate.

pomp *n.* ceremonial, ceremoniousness, ceremony, display, éclat, flourish, formality, grandeur, grandiosity,

magnificence, ostentation, pageant, pageantry, parade, pomposity, ritual, show, solemnity, splendor, state, vainglory.
antonyms austerity, simplicity.

pompous *adj.* affected, aldermanlike, aldermanly, arrogant, bloated, bombastic, budge, chesty, euphuistic, flatulent, fustian, grandiloquent, grandiose, high-flown, imperious, inflated, magisterial, magniloquent, oro(ro)tund, ostentatious, overbearing, overblown, pontifical, portentous, pretentious, prosy, ranting, self-important, stilted, supercilious, turgid, vainglorious, windy.
antonyms economical, modest, simple, unaffected, unassuming.

ponder *v.* analyze, brood, cerebrate, cogitate, contemplate, consider, deliberate, examine, excogitate, give thought to, incubate, meditate, mull over, muse, ponderate, puzzle over, ratiocinate, reason, reflect, ruminate over, study, think, volve, weigh.

ponderous *adj.* awkward, bulky, clumsy, cumbersome, cumbrous, dreary, dull, elephantine, graceless, heavy, heavy-footed, heavy-handed, hefty, huge, humorless, labored, laborious, lifeless, long-winded, lumbering, massive, pedantic, pedestrian, plodding, portentous, prolix, slow-moving, stilted, stodgy, stolid, tedious, unwieldy, verbose, weighty.
antonyms delicate, light, simple.

pool[1] *n.* dub, lake, lasher, leisure pool, linn, mere, pond, puddle, splash, stank, swimming bath, swimming pool, tarn, water-hole, watering-hole.

pool[2] *n.* accumulation, bank, cartel, collective, combine, consortium, funds, group, jackpot, kitty, pot, purse, reserve, ring, stakes, syndicate, team, trust.
v. amalgamate, chip in, combine, contribute, dob in, merge, muck in, put together, share.

poor[1] *adj.* badly off, bankrupt, beggared, beggarly, broke, deficient, destitute, distressed, embarrassed, exiguous, hard up, impecunious, impoverished, in reduced circumstances, inadequate, indigent, insufficient, lacking, meager, miserable, moneyless, necessitious, needy, niggardly, obolary, on one's beam-ends, on one's uppers, on the rocks, pauperized, penniless, penurious, pinched, pitiable, poverty-stricken, reduced, scanty, skimpy, skint, slight, sparse, stony-broke, straitened, without means, without the where-withal.
antonyms affluent, opulent, rich, wealthy.

poor[2] *adj.* bad, bare, barren, below par, depleted, exhausted, faulty, feeble, fruitless, grotty, humble, imperfect, impoverished, inferior, infertile, insignificant, jejune, lowgrade, lowly, mean, mediocre, modest, paltry, pathetic, pitiful, plain, ropy, rotten, rubbishy, second-rate, shabby, shoddy, sorry, spiritless, sterile, substandard, third-rate, trivial, unfruitful, unimpressive, unproductive, unsatisfactory, valueless, weak, worthless.
antonym superior.

poor[3] *adj.* accursed, cursed, forlorn, hapless, ill-fated, luckless, miserable, pathetic, pitiable, star-crossed, unfortunate, unhappy, unlucky, wretched.
antonym lucky.

poppycock *n.* babble, balderdash, balls, baloney, bullshit, bunk, bunkum, drivel, eyewash, gibberish, gobbledegook, guff, hooey, nonsense, rot, rubbish, tommyrot, tosh, trash, twaddle.
antonym sense.

popular *adj.* accepted, approved, celebrated, common, conventional, current, democratic, demotic, famous, fashionable, favored, favorite, fêted, general, household, idolized, in, in demand, in favor, liked, lionized, modish, overpopular, overused, prevailing, prevalent, public, sought-after, standard, stock, trite, ubiquitous, universal, vernacular, voguey, voguish, vulgar, well-liked, widespread.
antonyms exclusive, unpopular, unusual.

popularity *n.* acceptance, acclaim, adoration, adulation, approbation, approval, celebrity, currency, esteem, fame, favor, glory, idolization, kudos, lionization, mass appeal, recognition, regard, renown, reputation, repute, vogue, worship.
antonym unpopularity.

population *n.* citizenry, citizens, community, denizens, folk, inhabitants, natives, occupants, people, populace, residents, society.

pornographic *adj.* bawdy, blue, coarse, dirty, filthy, girlie, gross, indecent, lewd, nudie, obscene, off-color, offensive, porn, porno, prurient, risqué, salacious, smutty.
antonyms innocent, inoffensive.

port *n.* anchorage, harbor, harborage, haven, hithe, roads, roadstead, seaport.

portable *adj.* carriageable, compact, convenient, handy, light, lightweight, manageable, movable, portatile, portative, transportable.
antonyms fixed, immovable.

portend *v.* adumbrate, announce, augur, bespeak, betoken, bode, forebode, forecast, foreshadow, foretell, foretoken, forewarn, harbinger, herald, indicate, omen, point to, predict, presage, prognosticate, promise, signify, threaten, warn of.

portentous *adj.* alarming, amazing, astounding, awe-inspiring, bloated, charged, consequential, crucial, earth-shaking, epoch-making, extraordinary, fateful, heavy, important, menacing, minatory, miraculous, momentous, ominous, phenomenal, pompous, ponderous, pontifical, pregnant, prodigious, remarkable, significant, sinister, solemn, threatening.
antonyms insignificant, unimportant, unimpressive.

portion *n.* allocation, allotment, allowance, assignment, bit, cup, destiny, division, fate, fortune, fraction, fragment, helping, kismet, lot, luck, measure, meed, moiety, morsel, parcel, part, piece, quantity, quota, rake-off, ration, scrap, section, segment, serving, share, slice, something, tranche, whack.

v. allocate, allot, apportion, assign, carve up, deal, distribute, divide, divvy up, dole, parcel, partion, partition, share out, slice up.

portly *adj.* ample, beefy, bulky, chubby, corpulent, dumpy, embonpoint, fat, fleshy, full, heavy, large, obese, overweight, paunchy, plump, rotund, round, stout, tubby.
antonyms slight, slim.

portrait *n.* account, caricature, characterization, depiction, description, icon, image, likeness, miniature, mug shot, painting, photograph, picture, portraiture, portrayal, profile, representation, sketch, thumbnail, vignette.

portray *v.*. act, capture, characterize, delineate, depict, describe, draw emblazon, encapsulate, evoke figure, illustrate, impersonate, limn, paint, personate, personify, picture, play, present, render, represent, sketch, suggest.

pose *v.* advance, affect, arrange, assert, attitudinize, claim, feign, impersonate, masquerade, model, pass oneself off, place, posit, position, posture, present, pretend, profess to be, propound, put, put forward, put on an act, set, sham, sit, state, strike an attitude, submit.
n. act, affectation, air, attitude, bearing, con, façade, front, mark, masquerade, mien, position, posture, pretense, role, sham, stance, take-in.

poseur *n.* attitudinizer, charlatan, con, exhibitionist, impostor, masquerader, mountebank, phony, poser, poseuse, posturer, posturist, pseud, quack.

position *n.* angle, area, arrangement, attitude, bearings, belief, berth, billet, capacity, character, circumstances, condition, deployment, disposition, duty, employment, function, grade, importance, job, level, locale, locality, location, niche, occupation, office, opinion, outlook, pass, perspective, pinch, place, placement, placing, plight, point, point of view, pose, positioning, post, posture, predicament, prestige, rank, reference, reputation, role, set, setting, site, situation, slant, slot, spot, stance, stand, standing, standpoint, state, station, stature, status, ubiety, view, viewpoint, whereabouts.
v. arrange, array, deploy, dispose, fix, lay out, locate, place, pose, put, range, set, settle, stand, stick.

positive *adj.* absolute, actual, affirmative, arrant, assertive, assured, authoritative, beneficial, categorical, certain, clear, clear-cut, cocksure, complete, conclusive, concrete, confident, constructive, consummate, convinced, decided, decisive, definite, direct, dogmatic, downright, effective, efficacious, emphatic, explicit, express, firm, forceful, forward-looking, helpful, hopeful, incontestable, incontrovertible, indisputable, irrefragable, irrefutable, open-and-shut, opinionated, optimistic, out-and-out, peremptory, perfect, practical, productive, progressive, promising, rank, real, realistic, resolute, secure, self-evident, sheer, stubborn, sure, thorough, thoroughgoing, uncompromising, undeniable, unequivocal, unmistakable, unmitigated, unquestioning, useful, utter.
antonyms indecisive, indefinite, negative, uncertain.

positively *adv.* absolutely, assuredly, authoritatively, categorically, certainly, conclusively, constructively, decisively, definitely, dogmatically, emphatically, expressly, finally, firmly, incontestably, incontrovertibly, indisputably, surely, uncompromisingly, undeniably, unequivocally, unmistakably, unquestionably.

possess *v.* acquire, be endowed with, control, dominate, enjoy, have, hold, obtain, occupy, own, possess oneself of, seize, take, take over, take possession of.

possessed *adj.* bedeviled, berserk, besotted, bewitched, consumed, crazed, cursed, demented, dominated, enchanted, frenzied, hag-ridden, haunted, infatuated, maddened, mesmerized, obsessed, raving.

possession *n.* colony, control, custody, dependency, dominion, enjoyment, fruition, hold, mandate, occupancy, occupation, ownership, proprietorship, protectorate, province, tenure, territory, title.

possessions *n.* assets, belongings, chattels, effects, estate, goods, goods and chattels, junk, meum et tuum, movables, paraphernalia, property, riches, stuff, things, traps, wealth, worldly wealth.

possibility *n.* achievability, chance, conceivability, feasibility, hazard, hope, liability, likelihood, odds, plausibility, potentiality, practicability, probability, prospect, realizability, risk, workableness.
antonym impossibility.

possible *adj.* accomplishable, achievable, alternative, attainable, available, conceivable, credible, doable, feasible, hopeful, hypothetical, imaginable, likely, on, potential, practicable, probable, promising, realizable, tenable, viable, workable.
antonym impossible.

possibly *adv.* at all, by any chance, by any means, Deo volente, DV, God willing, haply, happen, hopefully, in any way, maybe, mayhap, peradventure, perchance, perhaps, very like(ly).

post[1] *n.* baluster, banister, column, leg, newel, pale, palisade, picket, pier, pillar, pin, pole, shaft, stake, stanchion, standard, stock, strut, support, upright.
v. advertise, affix, announce, denounce, display, make known, placard, preconize, proclaim, promulgate, publicize, publish, report, stick up.

post[2] *n.* appointment, assignment, beat, berth, billet, employment, incumbency, job, office, place, position, situation, station, vacancy.
v. appoint, assign, establish, locate, move, place, position, put, second, send, shift, situate, station, transfer.

post[3] *n.* collection, delivery, dispatch, mail, postal service, uplifting.
v. acquaint, advise, apprize, brief, dispatch, fill in on, inform, keep posted, mail, notify, report to, send, transmit.

postpone *v.* adjourn, defer, delay, freeze, hold over,

pigeonhole, prorogue, put back, put off, put on ice, shelve, suspend, table, waive.
antonyms advance, forward.

postulate *v.* advance, assume, hypothesize, lay down, posit, predicate, presuppose, propose, stipulate, suppose, take for granted, theorize.

posture *n.* attitude, bearing, carriage, decubitus, disposition, mien, port, pose, position, set, stance.
v. affect, attitudinize, pose, put on airs, show off, strike attitudes, strut.

potency *n.* authority, capacity, cogency, control, effectiveness, efficaciousness, efficacy, energy, force, headiness, influence, kick, might, muscle, persuasiveness, potential, power, puissance, punch, strength, sway, vigor.
antonyms impotence, weakness.

potential *adj.* budding, concealed, conceivable, dormant, embryonic, future, hidden, imaginable, in embryo, in posse, inherent, latent, likely, possible, probable, promising, prospective, undeveloped, unrealized.
n. ability, aptitude, capability, capacity, flair, possibility, potentiality, power, talent, the makings, what it takes, wherewithal.

potion *n.* beverage, brew, concoction, cup, dose, draught, drink, electuary, elixir, medicine, mixture, philter, potation, tonic, treacle.

pouch *n.* bag, container, marsupium, pocket, poke, purse, reticule, sac, sack, sporran, wallet.

pounce *v.* ambush, attack, dash at, dive on, drop, fall upon, grab, jump, leap at, lunge at, snatch, spring, strike, swoop.
n. assault, attack, bound, dive, grab, jump, leap, lunge, spring, swoop.

pound[1] *v.* bang, bash, baste, batter, beat, belabor, bray, bruise, clobber, clomp, clump, comminute, crush, drum, hammer, levigate, march, palpitate, pelt, powder, pulsate, pulse, pulverize, pummel, smash, stomp, strike, strum, thrash, throb, thrum, thud, thump, thunder, tramp, triturate.

pound[2] *n.* compound, corral, enclosure, fank, fold, pen, yard.

pour *v.* bucket, cascade, course, crowd, decant, effuse, emit, exude, flow, gush, rain, rain cats and dogs, run, rush, sheet, spew, spill, spout, stream, swarm, teem, throng, tumble.

pout *v.* glower, grimace, lower, mope, pull a face, scowl, sulk.
antonyms grin, smile.
n. glower, grimace, long face, moue, scowl.
antonyms grin, smile.

poverty *n.* aridity, bareness, barrenness, beggary, dearth, deficiency, depletion, destitution, distress, exhaustion, hardship, ill-being, impoverishment, inadequacy, indigence, infertility, insolvency, insufficiency, jejuneness, lack, meagerness, necessitousness, necessity, need, paucity, pauperism, pennilessness, penury, poorness, privation, proletarianism, scarcity, shortage, sterility, thinness, unfruitfulness, want.
antonyms affluence, fertility, fruitfulness, riches, richness.

power *n.* ability, ascendancy, autarchy, authorization, authority, brawn, capability, capacity, clout, clutches, command, competence, competency, control, dominance, domination, dominion, efficience, energy, faculty, force, forcefulness, heavy metal, hegemony, imperium, influence, intensity, juice, kami, license, mana, mastery, might, muscle, omnipotence, plenipotence, potency, potential, prerogative, privilege, right, rule, sovereignty, strength, supremacy, sway, teeth, vigor, virtue, vis, voltage, vroom, warrant, weight.
dominant, effective, effectual, energetic, forceful, forcible, impressive, influential, leading, masterful, mighty, muscular, omnipotent, persuasive, plutocratic, potent, pre-eminent, prepotent, prevailing, puissant, robust, souped-up, sovereign, stalwart, strapping, strong, sturdy, supreme, telling, vigorous, weighty, winning.
antonyms impotent, ineffective, weak.

practical *adj.* accomplished, active, applicative, applied, businesslike, commonsense, commonsensical, down-to-earth, efficient, empirical, everyday, expedient, experienced, experimental, factual, feasible, functional, hard-headed, hard-nosed, material, matter-of-fact, mundane, nuts-and-bolts, ordinary, practicable, practive, pragmatic, proficient, qualified, realistic, seasoned, sensible, serviceable, skilled, sound, trained, unsentimental, useful, utilitarian, workable, workaday, working.
antonym impractical.

practically[1] *adv.* actually, all but, almost, essentially, fundamentally, in effect, in practice, in principle, just about, nearly, not quite, pretty nearly, pretty well, very nearly, virtually, well-nigh.

practically[2] *adv.* clearly, from a commonsense angle, matter-of-factly, rationally, realistically, reasonably, sensibly, unsentimentally.

practice[1] *n.* action, application, business, career, clientèle, convention, custom, discipline, drill, dry run, dummy run, effect, exercise, experience, habit, ism, method, mode, modus operandi, operation, patronage, performance, policy, practic, practicalities, practicum, praxis, preparation, procedure, profession, rehearsal, repetition, routine, rule, run-through, study, system, tradition, training, usage, use, vocation, way, wont, work, work-out.

practice[2] *v.* apply, carry out, discipline, do, drill, enact, engage in, execute, exercise, follow, implement, live up to, observe, perfect, perform, ply, prepare, pursue, put into practice, rehearse, repeat, run through, study, train, undertake, warm up.

practiced *adj.* able, accomplished, consummate, experienced, expert, finished, highly-developed, knowing,

knowledgeable, perfected, proficient, qualified, refined, seasoned, skilled, trained, versed, veteran, well-trained.
antonyms inexpert, unpracticed.

pragmatic *adj.* businesslike, efficient, factual, hard-headed, opportunistic, practical, realistic, sensible, unidealistic, unsentimental, utilitarian.
antonyms idealistic, romantic, unrealistic.

praise *n.* acclaim, acclamation, accolade, acknowledgment, adoration, adulation, applause, approbation, approval, bouquet, cheering, commend, commendation, compliment, compliments, congratulation, devotion, encomium, eulogium, eulogy, extolment, flattery, glory, homage, honor, kudos, laud, laudation, ovation, panegyric, plaudit, puff, rave, recognition, salvoes, testimonial, thanks, thanksgiving, tribute, worship.
antonyms criticism, revilement.
v. acclaim, acknowledge, admire, adore, applaud, approve, belaud, bless, celebrate, cheer, compliment, congratulate, cry up, eulogize, exalt, extol, flatter, give thanks to, glorify, hail, honor, laud, magnify, panegyrize, pay tribute to, promote, puff, rave over, recognize, tout, wax lyrical, worship.
antonyms criticize, revile.

praiseworthy *adj.* admirable, commendable, creditable, deserving, estimable, excellent, exemplary, fine, honorable, laudable, meritorious, reputable, sterling, worthy.
antonyms discreditable, dishonorable, ignoble.

pray *v.* adjure, ask, beg, beseech, call on, crave, entreat, implore, importune, invoke, obsecrate, petition, plead, press, request, solicit, sue, supplicate, urge.

prayer *n.* appeal, collect, communion, devotion, entreaty, invocation, kyrie, kyrie eleison, litany, orison, paternoster, petition, plea, request, solicitation, suffrage, suit, supplication.

preach *v.* address, admonish, advocate, ethicize, evangelize, exhort, harangue, lecture, moralize, orate, pontificate, pontify, preachify, prose, sermonize, urge.

preamble *n.* exordium, foreword, introduction, lead-in, overture, preface, preliminaries, prelude, preparation, proem, prolegomenon, prologue.
antonyms epilogue, postscript.

precarious *adj.* chancy, dangerous, delicate, dicey, dodgy, doubtful, dubious, hairy, hazardous, iffy, insecure, parlous, periculous, perilous, problematic, risky, shaky, slippery, ticklish, tricky, uncertain, unpredictable, unreliable, unsafe, unsettled, unstable, unsteady, unsure, vulnerable.
antonyms certain, safe, secure.

precaution *n.* anticipation, backstop, buffer, care, caution, circumspection, foresight, forethought, insurance, preparation, prophylaxis, protection, providence, provision, prudence, safeguard, safety measure, security, surety, wariness.

precedence *n.* antecedence, first place, lead, pre-eminence, preference, pride of place, primacy, priority, rank, seniority, superiority, supremacy.

precedent *n.* antecedent, authority, citation, criterion, example, exemplar, guideline, instance, judgment, model, paradigm, past instance, pattern, prototype, ruling, standard, yardstick.

precept *n.* axiom, behest, bidding, byword, canon, charge, command, commandment, convention, decree, dictum, direction, directive, guideline, injunction, institute, instruction, law, mandate, maxim, motto, order, ordinance, principle, regulation, rubric, rule, saying, sentence, statute.

precious *adj.* adored, affected, artificial, beloved, cherished, chichi, choice, costly, darling, dear, dearest, expensive, exquisite, fastidious, favorite, fine, flowery, greenery-yallery, idolized, inestimable, invaluable, irreplaceable, loved, namby-pamby, overnice, over-refined, priceless, prized, rare, recherché, treasured, twee, valuable, valued.

precipice *n.* bluff, brink, cliff, cliff face, crag, drop, escarp, escarpment, height, scarp, steep.

precipitate *v.* accelerate, advance, bring on, cast, cause, chuck, discharge, drive, expedite, fling, further, hasten, hurl, hurry, induce, launch, occasion, pitch, press, project, quicken, speed, throw, trigger.
adj. abrupt, breakneck, brief, frantic, Gadarene, hasty, headlong, heedless, hot-headed, hurried, impatient, impetuous, impulsive, incautious, indiscreet, madcap, pell-mell, plunging, precipitous, quick, quixotic, rapid, rash, reckless, rushing, sudden, swift, unannounced, unexpected, violent.
antonym cautious.

precise *adj.* absolute, accurate, actual, authentic, blow-by-blow, buckram, careful, ceremonious, clear-cut, correct, definite, delimitative, determinate, distinct, exact, explicit, express, expressis verbis, factual, faithful, fastidious, finical, finicky, fixed, formal, identical, literal, meticulous, minute, nice, particular, prim, punctilious, puritanical, rigid, scrupulous, specific, strict, succinct, unequivocal, verbatim, word-for-word.
antonym imprecise.

precisely *adv.* absolutely, accurately, bang, blow by blow, correctly, dead, distinctly, exactly, expressis verbis, just, just so, literally, minutely, plumb, slap, smack, square, squarely, strictly, verbatim, word for word.

precision *n.* accuracy, care, correctness, definiteness, detail, exactitude, exactness, explicitness, expressness, faithfulness, fastidiousness, fidelity, meticulousness, minuteness, neatness, niceness, nicety, particularity, preciseness, punctilio, punctiliousness, rigor, scrupulosity, specificity.
antonym imprecision.

preclude *v.* avoid, check, debar, eliminate, exclude, forestall, hinder, inhibit, obviate, prevent, prohibit, restrain, rule out, stop.
antonyms incur, involve.

precocious *adj.* advanced, ahead, bright, clever, developed,

fast, forward, gifted, mature, precocial, premature, quick, smart.
antonym backward.

predatory *adj.* acquisitive, avaricious, carnivorous, covetous, despoiling, greedy, hunting, lupine, marauding, pillaging, plundering, predacious, predative, preying, rapacious, raptatorial, raptorial, ravaging, ravening, thieving, voracious, vulturine, vulturous, wolfish.

predestination *n.* ananke, destiny, doom, election, fate, foreordainment, foreordination, karma, lot, necessity, portion, predestiny, predetermination, preordainment, preordination, weird.

predicament *n.* can of worms, corner, crisis, dilemma, embarrassment, emergency, fix, galère, hole, hot water, impasse, jam, kettle of fish, mess, pickle, pinch, plight, quandary, scrape, situation, spot, state, trouble.

predict *v.* augur, auspicate, divine, forebode, forecast, foresay, foresee, foreshow, forespeak, foretell, portend, presage, prognosticate, project, prophesy, second-guess, soothsay, vaticinate.

prediction *n.* augury, auspication, divination, forecast, fortune-telling, prognosis, prognostication, prophecy, second sight, soothsaying, vaticination.

predilection *n.* affection, affinity, bent, bias, enthusiasm, fancy, fondness, inclination, leaning, liking, love, partiality, penchant, predisposition, preference, proclivity, proneness, propensity, soft spot, taste, tendency, weakness.
antonyms antipathy, disinclination.

predisposed *adj.* agreeable, amenable, biased, disposed, favorable, inclined, liable, minded, not unwilling, nothing loth, prejudiced, prepared, prone, ready, subject, susceptible, well-disposed, willing.

predominant *adj.* ascendant, capital, chief, controlling, dominant, forceful, important, influential, leading, main, paramount, potent, powerful, prepollent, preponderant, prepotent, prevailing, prevalent, primary, prime, principal, prominent, ruling, sovereign, strong, superior, supreme.
antonyms ineffective, lesser, minor, weak.

predominate *v.* dominate, obtain, outnumber, outweigh, override, overrule, overshadow, preponderate, prevail, reign, rule, tell, transcend.

pre-eminent *adj.* chief, consummate, distinguished, excellent, exceptional, facile princeps, foremost, incomparable, inimitable, leading, matchless, nonpareil, outstanding, paramount, passing, peerless, predominant, prominent, renowned, superior, superlative, supreme, surpassing, transcendent, unequaled, unmatched, unrivaled, unsurpassed.
antonyms undistinguished, unknown.

pre-empt *v.* acquire, anticipate, appropriate, arrogate, assume, bag, forestall, secure, seize, usurp.

preface *n.* exordium, foreword, intro, introduction, preamble, preliminaries, prelims, prelude, proem, prolegomena, prolegomenon, prologue, prooemion, prooemium.
antonyms afterthought, epilogue, postscript.
v. begin, introduce, launch, lead up to, open, precede, prefix, prelude, premise, start.
antonyms append, complete, finish.

prefer[1] *v.* adopt, advocate, back, be partial to, choose, desire, elect, endorse, fancy, favor, go for, incline towards, like better, opt for, pick, plump for, recommend, select, single out, support, want, wish, would rather, would sooner.
antonym reject.

prefer[2] *v.* bring, file, lodge, place, present, press.

prefer[3] *v.* advance, aggrandize, dignify, elevate, exalt, promote, raise, upgrade.
antonym demote.

preference[1] *n.* choice, desire, election, fancy, favorite, first choice, inclination, liking, option, partiality, pick, predilection, selection, wish.

preference[2] *n.* advantage, favor, favoritism, precedence, preferential treatment, priority, special consideration, special treatment.

pregnant[1] *adj.* big, big-bellied, enceinte, expectant, expecting, gravid, impregnated, in an interesting condition, in the club, in the family way, in the pudding club, parturient, preggers, teeming, with child.

pregnant[2] *adj.* charged, eloquent, expressive, full, heavy, loaded, meaning, meaningful, ominous, pithy, pointed, significant, suggestive, telling, weighty.
antonym jejune.

prejudice[1] *n.* bias, bigotry, chauvinism, discrimination, injustice, intolerance, narrow-mindedness, partiality, partisanship, preconception, prejudgment, racism, sexism, unfairness, viewiness, warp.
antonyms fairness, tolerance.
v. bias, color, condition, distort, incline, indoctrinate, influence, jaundice, load, poison, predispose, prepossess, slant, sway, warp, weight.

prejudice[2] *n.* damage, detriment, disadvantage, harm, hurt, impairment, injury, loss, mischief, ruin, vitiation, wreck.
antonyms advantage, benefit.
v. damage, harm, hinder, hurt, impair, injure, mar, ruin, spoil, undermine, vitiate, wreck.
antonyms advance, benefit, help.

prejudiced *adj.* biased, bigoted, chauvinist, conditioned, discriminatory, distorted, ex parte, illiberal, influenced, intolerant, jaundiced, loaded, narrow-minded, one-sided, opinionated, partial, partisan, prepossessed, racist, sexist, subjective, unenlightened, unfair, verkrampte, viewy, warped, weighted.
antonyms fair, tolerant.

preliminary *adj.* earliest, early, embryonic, exordial, experimental, exploratory, first, inaugural, initial, initiative, initiatory, introductory, opening, pilot, precursory, prefatory, prelusive, preparatory, primary, prior, qualifying, test, trial.
antonyms closing, final.

premature *adj.* abortive, early, embryonic, forward, green, half-formed, hasty, ill-considered, ill-timed, immature, imperfect, impulsive, incomplete, inopportune, overhasty, precipitate, precocious, preterm, previous, rash, raw, undeveloped, unfledged, unripe, unseasonable, untimely.
antonyms late, tardy.

premeditated *adj.* aforethought, calculated, cold-blooded, conscious, considered, contrived, deliberate, intended, intentional, planned, plotted, prearranged, predetermined, prepense, preplanned, studied, wilful.
antonyms spontaneous, unpremeditated.

premeditation *n.* deliberateness, deliberation, design, determination, forethought, intention, malice, aforethought, planning, plotting, prearrangement, predetermination, purpose, scheming.
antonyms impulse, spontaneity.

premise *v.* assert, assume, hypothesize, lay down, posit, postulate, predicate, presuppose, state, stipulate, take as true.
n. argument, assertion, assumption, ground, hypothesis, postulate, postulation, predication, premiss, presupposition, proposition, statement, stipulation, supposition, thesis.

preoccupied *adj.* absent-minded, absorbed, abstracted, day-dreaming, distracted, distrait, engrossed, entêté, faraway, fixated, heedless, immersed, intent, oblivious, obsessed, pensive, rapt, taken up, unaware, visited, wrapped up.

preparation[1] *n.* alertness, anticipation, arrangement, assignment, basics, development, expectation, foresight, foundation, groundwork, homework, imposition, lesson, measure, plan, precaution, preliminaries, prep, preparedness, provision, readiness, revision, rudiments, safeguard, schoolwork, study, task.

preparation[2] *n.* application, composition, compound, concoction, lotion, medicine, mixture, potion, tincture.

prepare *v.* accouter, adapt, adjust, anticipate, arrange, assemble, boun, brace, brief, busk, coach, compose, concoct, confect, construct, contrive, develop, devise, dispose, do one's homework, draft, draw up, dress, equip, fashion, fettle, fit, fit out, fix up, forearm, form, fortify, furnish, get up, gird, groom, instruct, limber up, make, make ready, outfit, plan, practice, predispose, prime, produce, provide, psych up, ready, rehearse, rig out, steel, strengthen, supply, train, trim, warm up.

prepared *adj.* able, arranged, briefed, disposed, expectant, fit, forearmed, inclined, minded, planned, predisposed, primed, psyched up, ready, set, waiting, well-rehearsed, willing, word-perfect.
antonyms unprepared, unready.

preponderance *n.* ascendancy, bulk, dominance, domination, dominion, extensiveness, force, lion's share, majority, mass, power, predominance, prevalence, superiority, supremacy, sway, weight.

prepossessing *adj.* alluring, amiable, appealing, attractive, beautiful, bewitching, captivating, charming, delightful, disarming, enchanting, engaging, fair, fascinating, fetching, good-looking, handsome, inviting, likable, lovable, magnetic, pleasing, striking, taking, winning, winsome.
antonyms unattractive, unprepossessing.

preposterous *adj.* absurd, asinine, bizarre, crazy, derisory, excessive, exorbitant, extravagant, extreme, fatuous, foolish, imbecile, impossible, inane, incredible, insane, intolerable, irrational, laughable, ludicrous, monstrous, nonsensical, outrageous, ridiculous, risible, senseless, shocking, unbelievable, unconscionable, unreasonable, unthinkable.
antonym reasonable.

prerequisite *adj.* basic, essential, fundamental, imperative, indispensable, mandatory, necessary, needed, needful, obligatory, required, requisite, vital.
antonym unnecessary.
n. condition, essential, imperative, must, necessity, precondition, provision, proviso, qualification, requirement, requisite, sine qua non.
antonym extra.

prerogative *n.* advantage, authority, birthright, carte blanche, choice, claim, droit, due, exemption, immunity, liberty, license, perquisite, privilege, right, sanction, title.

prescribe *v.* appoint, assign, command, decree, define, dictate, direct, enjoin, fix, impose, lay down, limit, ordain, order, require, rule, set, set bounds to, specify, stipulate.

presence *n.* air, apparition, appearance, aspect, attendance, aura, bearing, carriage, closeness, companionship, company, comportment, demeanor, ease, existence, ghost, habitation, inhabitance, manifestation, mien, nearness, neighborhood, occupancy, personality, poise, propinquity, proximity, residence, revenant, self-assurance, shade, specter, spirit, statuesqueness, vicinity.
antonym absence.

present[1] *adj.* at hand, attending, available, contemporary, current, existent, extant, here, immediate, instant, near, ready, there, to hand.
antonyms absent, out-of-date, past.

present[2] *v.* acquaint with, adduce, advance, award, bestow, confer, declare, demonstrate, display, donate, entrust, exhibit, expound, extend, furnish, give, grant, hand over, hold out, introduce, mount, offer, porrect, pose, produce, proffer, put on, raise, recount, relate, show, stage, state, submit, suggest, tender.
antonym take.
n. benefaction, boon, bounty, cadeau, compliment, donation, endowment, favor, gift, grant, gratuity, largess, nuzzer, offering, prezzie, refresher.

presentable *adj.* acceptable, becoming, clean, decent, neat, passable, proper, respectable, satisfactory, suitable, tidy, tolerable.
antonyms unpresentable, untidy.

presently *adv.* anon, before long, by and by, directly, immediately, in a minute, shortly, soon.

preserve *v.* care for, confect, conserve, continue, defend, embalm, entreasure, guard, keep, maintain, perpetuate, protect, retain, safeguard, save, secure, shelter, shield, store, sustain, uphold.
antonyms destroy, ruin.
n. area, confection, confiture, conserve, domain, field, game park, game reserve, jam, jelly, konfyt, marmalade, realm, reservation, reserve, safari park, sanctuary, specialism, specialty, sphere, thing.

preside *v.* administer, chair, conduct, control, direct, govern, head, lead, manage, officiate, run, supervise.

press[1] *v.* adpress, afflict, appress, assail, beg, beset, besiege, calendar, clasp, cluster, compel, compress, condense, constrain, crowd, crush, demand, depress, disquiet, dun, embrace, encircle, enfold, enforce, enjoin, entreat, exhort, finish, flatten, flock, force, force down, gather, harass, hasten, herd, hug, hurry, implore, importune, insist on, iron, jam, mangle, mash, mill, petition, plague, plead, pressurize, push, reduce, rush, seethe, smooth, squeeze, steam, stuff, sue, supplicate, surge, swarm, throng, torment, trouble, urge, vex, worry.
antonyms expand, hang back, lighten, relieve.
n. bunch, bustle, crowd, crush, demand, flock, hassle, herd, horde, host, hurry, mob, multitude, pack, pressure, push, strain, stress, swarm, throng, urgency.

press[2] *n.* columnists, correspondents, fourth estate, hacks, journalism, journalists, news media, newsmen, newspapers, paparazzi, papers, photographers, pressmen, reporters, writers.

pressing *adj.* burning, constraining, crowding, crucial, essential, exigent, high-priority, imperative, important, importunate, serious, thronging, urgent, vital.
antonyms trivial, unimportant.

pressure *n.* adversity, affliction, burden, coercion, compressing, compression, compulsion, constraint, crushing, demands, difficulty, distress, exigency, force, hassle, heat, heaviness, hurry, influence, load, obligation, power, press, pression, squeezing, strain, stress, sway, urgency, weight. *v.* browbeat, bulldoze, bully, coerce, compel, constrain, dragoon, drive, force, impel, induce, lean on, oblige, persuade, press, pressurize, squeeze.

prestige *n.* authority, cachet, celebrity, clout, credit, distinction, eminence, esteem, fame, honor, importance, influence, kudos, pull, regard, renown, reputation, standing, stature, status, weight.
antonyms humbleness, unimportance.

presume *v.* assume, bank on, believe, conjecture, count on, dare, depend on, go so far, have the audacity, hypothesize, hypothetize, infer, make bold, make so bold, posit, postulate, presuppose, rely on, suppose, surmise, take for granted, take it, take the liberty, think, trust, undertake, venture.

presumption[1] *n.* assurance, audacity, boldness, brass, brass neck, cheek, effrontery, forwardness, gall, impudence, insolence, neck, nerve, presumptuousness, temerity.
antonyms humility, politeness.

presumption[2] *n.* anticipation, assumption, basis, belief, chance, conjecture, grounds, guess, hypothesis, likelihood, opinion, plausibility, premiss, presupposition, probability, reason, supposition, surmise.

presumptuous *adj.* arrogant, audacious, big-headed, bold, conceited, foolhardy, forward, impertinent, impudent, insolent, over-confident, over-familiar, overweening, presuming, pushy, rash, uppish.
antonym modest.

presupposition *n.* assumption, belief, hypothesis, preconception, premise, premiss, presumption, supposition, theory.

pretend *v.* act, affect, allege, aspire, assume, claim, counterfeit, dissemble, dissimulate, fake, falsify, feign, go through the motions, imagine, impersonate, make believe, pass oneself off, profess, purport, put on, sham, simulate, suppose.

pretense *n.* acting, affectation, aim, allegation, appearance, artifice, blague, bounce, charade, claim, cloak, color, cover, deceit, deception, display, excuse, fabrication, façade, faking, falsehood, feigning, garb, guise, humbug, invention, make-believe, mask, masquerade, posing, posturing, pretentiousness, pretext, profession, pseudery, purpose, ruse, semblance, sham, show, simulation, subterfuge, trickery, veil, veneer, wile.
antonyms honesty, openness, reason.

pretentious *adj.* affected, ambitious, assuming, bombastic, chichi, conceited, euphemistic, exaggerated, extravagant, flaunting, grandiloquent, grandiose, high-falutin, high-flown, high-sounding, hollow, inflated, magniloquent, mannered, oro(ro)tund, ostentatious, overambitious, overassuming, pompous, showy, snobbish, specious, uppish, vainglorious.
antonyms humble, modest, simple, straightforward.

pretty *adj.* appealing, attractive, beautiful, bijou, bonny, charming, comely, cute, dainty, delicate, elegant, fair, fine, good-looking, graceful, lovely, neat, nice, personable, pleasing, sightly, tasteful, trim.
antonyms tasteless, ugly.
adv. fairly, moderately, passably, quite, rather, reasonably, somewhat, tolerably.

prevail *v.* abound, obtain, overcome, overrule, predominate, preponderate, reign, rule, succeed, triumph, win.
antonym lose.

prevailing *adj.* common, controlling, current, customary, dominant, established, fashionable, general, in style, in vogue, influential, main, mainstream, operative, ordinary, popular, predominating, preponderating, prepotent, prevalent, principal, ruling, set, usual, widespread.
antonyms minor, uncommon.

prevalent *adj.* accepted, ascendant, common, commonplace, compelling, current, customary, dominant, epidemic, established, everyday, extensive, frequent, general, governing, habitual, popular, powerful, predominant, prevailing, rampant, regnant, rife, successful, superior, ubiquitous, universal, usual, victorious, widespread.
antonyms subordinate, uncommon.

prevaricate *v.* cavil, deceive, dodge, equivocate, evade, fib, hedge, lie, palter, quibble, shift, shuffle, temporize, tergiversate.

prevent *v.* anticipate, avert, avoid, balk, bar, block, check, counteract, debar, defend against, foil, forestall, frustrate, hamper, head off, hinder, impede, inhibit, intercept, obstruct, obviate, preclude, restrain, stave off, stop, stymie, thwart, ward off.
antonyms cause, foster, help.

preventive *adj.* counteractive, deterrent, hampering, hindering, impeding, inhibitory, obstructive, precautionary, prevenient, preventative, prophylactic, protective, shielding.
antonyms causative, fostering.
n. block, condom, deterrent, hindrance, impediment, neutralizer, obstacle, obstruction, prevention, prophylactic, protection, protective, remedy, safeguard, shield.
antonyms cause, encouragement, incitement.

previous *adj.* antecedent, anterior, arranged, earlier, erstwhile, ex-, foregoing, former, one-time, past, preceding, precipitate, premature, prior, quondam, sometime, umwhile, untimely, whilom.
antonyms later, timely.

prey *n.* booty, dupe, fall guy, game, kill, mark, mug, plunder, quarry, target, victim.

prey on blackmail, bleed, bully, burden, devour, distress, eat, eat away, exploit, feed on, gnaw at, haunt, hunt, intimidate, live off, moth-eat, oppress, seize, take advantage of, terrorize, trouble, victimize, waste, weigh down, weigh heavily, worry.

price *n.* amount, assessment, bill, bounty, charge, consequences, cost, damage, estimate, expenditure, expense, fee, figure, levy, odds, outlay, payment, penalty, rate, reward, sacrifice, sum, toll, valuation, value, worth.
v. assess, cost, estimate, evaluate, offer, put, rate, valorize, value.

priceless[1] *adj.* beyond price, cherished, costly, dear, expensive, incalculable, incomparable, inestimable, invaluable, irreplaceable, precious, prized, rare, rich, treasured, without price.
antonyms cheap, run-of-the-mill.

priceless[2] *adj.* a hoot, a scream, absurd, amusing, comic, droll, funny, hilarious, killing, rib-tickling, ridiculous, riotous, risible, side-splitting.

pride *n.* amour-propre, arrogance, best, big-headedness, boast, choice, conceit, cream, delight, dignity, egotism, élite, flower, gem, glory, gratification, haughtiness, hauteur, high spirits, honor, hubris, jewel, joy, loftiness, magnificence, mettle, morgue, ostentation, pick, pleasure, presumption, pretension, pretensiousness, pride and joy, prize, satisfaction, self-esteem, self-importance, self-love, self-respect, smugness, snobbery, splendor, superciliousness, treasure, vainglory, vanity.
antonym humility.

prim *adj.* demure, fastidious, formal, fussy, governessy, old-maidish, old-maidist, particular, perjink, po-faced, precise, priggish, prissy, proper, prudish, pudibund, puritanical, school-marmish, sedate, starchy, stiff, strait-laced.
antonyms broad-minded, informal.

primarily *adv.* at first, basically, chiefly, especially, essentially, fundamentally, generally, initially, mainly, mostly, originally, principally.
antonym secondarily.

primary *adj.* aboriginal, basic, beginning, best, capital, cardinal, chief, dominant, earliest, elemental, elementary, essential, first, first-formed, first-made, fundamental, greatest, highest, initial, introductory, leading, main, original, paramount, primal, prime, primeval, primigenial, primitial, primitive, primordial, principal, pristine, radical, rudimentary, simple, top, ultimate, underlying.
antonym secondary.

prime[1] *adj.* basic, best, capital, chief, choice, earliest, excellent, first-class, first-rate, fundamental, highest, leading, main, original, predominant, pre-eminent, primary, principal, pal, quality, ruling, select, selected, senior, superior, top, underlying.
antonyms minor, secondary, second-rate.
n. beginning, flowering, height, heyday, maturity, morning, opening, peak, perfection, spring, springtide, springtime, start, zenith.

prime[2] *v.* brief, charge, clue up, coach, cram, fill, fill in, gen up, groom, inform, notify, post up, prepare, train.

primeval *adj.* ancient, earliest, early, first, Ogygian, old, original, prehistoric, primal, primitial, primitive, primordial, pristine.
antonyms developed, later, modern.

primitive *adj.* aboriginal, barbarian, barbaric, childlike, crude, earliest, early, elementary, first, naïve, neanderthal, original, primal, primary, primeval, primordial, pristine, rough, rude, rudimentary, savage, simple, uncivilized, uncultivated, undeveloped, unrefined, unsophisticated, untrained, untutored.
antonyms advanced, civilized, developed.

primordial *adj.* basic, earliest, elemental, first, first-formed, first-made, fundamental, original, prehistoric, primal, primeval, primigenial, primitial, primitive, pristine, radical.
antonyms developed, later, modern.

principal[1] *adj.* capital, cardinal, chief, controlling, decuman, dominant, essential, first, foremost, highest, key, leading, main, paramount, pre-eminent, primary, prime, strongest, truncal.
antonyms least, lesser, minor.

n. boss, chief, dean, director, first violin, head, head teacher, headmaster, headmistress, lead, leader, master, prima ballerina, prima donna, rector, star, superintendent.

principal[2] *n.* assets, capital, capital funds, money.

principle *n.* assumption, attitude, axiom, belief, canon, code, conscience, credo, criterion, dictum, doctrine, dogma, duty, element, ethic, formula, fundamental, golden rule, honor, institute, integrity, law, maxim, moral, morality, morals, opinion, precept, principium, probity, proposition, rectitude, rule, scruples, standard, tenet, truth, uprightness, verity.
antonyms corruption, wickedness.

print *v.* engrave, impress, imprint, issue, mark, produce, publish, put to bed, reproduce, run off, stamp, write.
n. book, characters, copy, dab, engraving, face, fingerprint, font, fount, impression, lettering, letters, magazine, mold, newspaper, newsprint, periodical, photo, photograph, picture, publication, reproduction, stamp, type, typeface, typescript.

prior *adj.* aforementioned, antecedent, anterior, earlier, foregoing, former, preceding, pre-existent, previous.
antonym later.

prison *n.* bagnio, bastille, brig, cage, calaboose, can, cell, chok(e)y, clink, confinement, cooler, coop, dungeon, glass-house, guardhouse, gulag, hoos(e)gow, house of correction, house of detention, imprisonment, jail, jug, lock-up, panopticon, penal institution, penitentiary, pokey, prison-house, prison-ship, quod, reformatory, slammer, slink, stalag, stir, stockade, tank.

pristine *adj.* earliest, first, former, initial, original, primal, primary, primeval, primigenial, primitial, primitive, primordial, uncorrupted, undefiled, unspoiled, unsullied, untouched, virgin.
antonyms developed, later, spoiled.

private *adj.* clandestine, closet, concealed, confidential, exclusive, home-felt, hush-hush, in camera, independent, individual, inside, intimate, intraparietal, inward, isolated, off the record, own, particular, personal, privy, reserved, retired, secluded, secret, separate, sequestrated, solitary, special, unofficial, withdrawn.
antonyms open, public.
n. buck private, common soldier, enlisted man, private soldier.

privation *n.* affliction, austerity, destitution, distress, hard-ship, indigence, lack, loss, misery, necessary, need, neediness, penury, poverty, suffering, want.
antonyms affluence, wealth.

privilege *n.* advantage, benefit, birthright, claim, concession, droit, due, entitlement, franchise, freedom, immunity, liberty, license, prerogative, right, sanction, title.
antonym disadvantage.

prize[1] *n.* accolade, aim, ambition, award, conquest, desire, gain, goal, haul, honor, hope, jackpot, premium, purse, reward, stake(s), trophy, windfall, winnings.
adj. award-winning, best, champion, excellent, first-rate, outstanding, top, top-notch, winning.
antonym second-rate.
v. appreciate, cherish, esteem, hold dear, revere, reverence, set store by, treasure, value.
antonyms despise, undervalue.

prize[2] *n.* booty, capture, loot, pickings, pillage, plunder, spoils, trophy.

prize[3], prise *v.* force, jemmy, lever, pry, winkle.

probable *adj.* apparent, credible, feasible, likely, odds-on, on the cards, plausible, possible, presumed, reasonable, seeming, verisimilar.
antonym improbable.

probe *v.* examine, explore, go into, investigate, look into, pierce, poke, prod, query, scrutinize, search, sift, sound, test, verify.
n. bore, detection, drill, examination, exploration, inquest, inquiry, investigation, research, scrutiny, study, test.

problem *n.* boyg, brain-teaser, complication, conundrum, difficulty, dilemma, disagreement, dispute, doubt, enigma, no laughing matter, poser, predicament, puzzle, quandary, question, riddle, trouble, vexata quaestio, vexed question.
adj. delinquent, difficult, intractable, perverse, refractory, uncontrollable, unmanageable, unruly.
antonyms manageable, well-behaved.

procedure *n.* action, conduct, course, custom, form, formula, method, modus operandi, move, operation, performance, plan of action, policy, practice, process, routine, scheme, step, strategy, system, transaction.

proceed *v.* advance, arise, carry on, come, continue, derive, emanate, ensue, flow, follow, go ahead, issue, move on, originate, press on, progress, result, set in motion, spring, start, stem.
antonyms retreat, stop.

proceedings *n.* account, action, affair, affairs, annals, archives, business, course of action, dealings, deeds, doings, event(s), matters, measures, minutes, moves, procedure, process, records, report, steps, transactions, undertaking.

proceeds *n.* earnings, emoluments, gain, income, motser, motza, produce, products, profit, receipts, returns, revenue, takings, yield.
antonyms losses, outlay.

process[1] *n.* action, advance, case, course, course of action, development, evolution, formation, growth, manner, means, measure, method, mode, movement, operation, performance, practice, procedure, proceeding, progress, progression, stage, step, suit, system, transaction, trial, unfolding.
v. alter, convert, deal with, digitize, dispose of, fulfil, handle, prepare, refine, transform, treat.

process[2] *n.* node, nodosity, nodule, projection, prominence, protuberance, protusion.

procession *n.* cavalcade, column, concatenation, cortege, course, cycle, file, march, motorcade, parade, run, sequence, series, string, succession, train.

proclaim *v.* advertise, affirm, announce, annunciate, blaze, blazon, circulate, declare, enounce, enunciate, give out, herald, indicate, make known, preconize, profess, promulgate, publish, show, testify, trumpet.

proclamation *n.* announcement, annunciation, ban, declaration, decree, edict, indiction, interlocution, irade, manifesto, notice, notification, proclaim, promulgation, pronouncement, pronunciamento, publication, ukase.

procrastinate *v.* adjourn, dally, defer, delay, dilly-dally, drag one's feet, gain time, penelopize, play for time, postpone, prolong, protract, put off, retard, stall, temporize.
antonyms advance, proceed.

procreate *v.* beget, breed, conceive, engender, father, generate, mother, produce, propagate, reproduce, sire, spawn.

procure *v.* acquire, appropriate, bag, buy, come by, earn, effect, find, gain, get, induce, lay hands on, obtain, pander, pick up, pimp, purchase, secure, win.
antonym lose.

prod *v.* dig, drive, egg on, elbow, goad, impel, incite, jab, motivate, move, nudge, poke, prick, prog, prompt, propel, push, rouse, shove, spur, stimulate, urge.
n. boost, cue, dig, elbow, jab, nudge, poke, prog, prompt, push, reminder, shove, signal, stimulus.

prodigious *adj.* abnormal, amazing, astounding, colossal, enormous, exceptional, extraordinary, fabulous, fantastic, flabbergasting, giant, gigantic, huge, immeasurable, immense, impressive, inordinate, mammoth, marvelous, massive, miraculous, monstrous, monumental, phenomenal, remarkable, spectacular, staggering, startling, striking, stupendous, tremendous, unusual, vast, wonderful.
antonyms commonplace, small, unremarkable.

produce[1] *v.* advance, afford, bear, beget, breed, bring forth, cause, compose, construct, create, deliver, demonstrate, develop, direct, effect, engender, exhibit, fabricate, factify, factuate, furnish, generate, give, give rise to, invent, make, manufacture, mount, occasion, offer, originate, present, provoke, put forward, put on, render, result in, show, stage, supply, throw, yield.
antonyms consume, result from. *n.* crop, harvest, product, yield.

produce[2] *v.* continue, elongate, extend, lengthen, prolong, protract.

product *n.* artefact, commodity, concoction, consequence, creation, effect, facture, fruit, goods, invention, issue, legacy, merchandise, offshoot, offspring, outcome, output, produce, production, result, returns, spin-off, upshot, work, yield.
antonym cause.

productive *adj.* advantageous, beneficial, constructive, creative, dynamic, effective, energetic, fecund, fertile, fructiferous, fructuous, fruitful, gainful, generative, gratifying, inventive, plentiful, producing, profitable, prolific, rewarding, rich, teeming, uberous, useful, valuable, vigorous, voluminous, worthwhile.
antonyms fruitless, unproductive.

profanity *n.* abuse, blasphemy, curse, cursing, execration, expletive, four-letter word, impiety, imprecation, inquination, irreverence, malediction, obscenity, profaneness, sacrilege, swearing, swear-word.
antonyms politeness, reverence.

profess *v.* acknowledge, admit, affirm, allege, announce, assert, asseverate, aver, avow, certify, claim, confess, confirm, declare, enunciate, fake, feign, maintain, make out, own, pretend, proclaim, propose, propound, purport, sham, state, vouch.

profession *n.* acknowledgment, affirmation, assertion, attestation, avowal, business, calling, career, claim, confession, declaration, employment, job, line (of work), manifesto, métier, occupation, office, position, sphere, statement, testimony, vocation, vow, walk of life.

professional *adj.* adept, competent, crack, efficient, experienced, expert, finished, masterly, polished, practiced, proficient, qualified, skilled, slick, trained, virtuose, virtuosic, well-skilled.
antonyms amateur, unprofessional.
n. adept, authority, dab hand, expert, maestro, master, pastmaster, pro, proficient, specialist, virtuoso, wizard.

proffer *v.* advance, extend, hand, hold out, offer, present, propose, propound, submit, suggest, tender, volunteer.

proficient *adj.* able, accomplished, adept, apt, capable, clever, competent, conversant, efficient, experienced, expert, gifted, masterly, qualified, skilful, skilled, talented, trained, versed, virtuose, virtuosic.
antonyms clumsy, incompetent.

profile *n.* analysis, biography, biopic, characterization, chart, contour, diagram, drawing, examination, figure, form, graph, outline, portrait, review, shape, side view, silhouette, sketch, study, survey, table, thumbnail sketch, vignette.

profit *n.* a fast buck, advancement, advantage, avail, benefit, boot, bottom line, bunce, earnings, emoluments, fruit, gain, gelt, good, graft, gravy, grist, interest, melon, percentage, proceeds, receipts, return, revenue, surplus, takings, use, value, velvet, winnings, yield.
antonym loss.
v. advance, advantage, aid, avail, benefit, better, boot, contribute, gain, help, improve, line one's pockets, promote, serve, stand in good stead.
antonyms harm, hinder.

profitable *adj.* advantageable, advantageous, beneficial, commercial, cost-effective, emolumental, emolumentary, fruitful, gainful, lucrative, money-making, paying, plummy, productive, remunerative,

rewarding, serviceable, useful, utile, valuable, worthwhile.
antonym unprofitable.

profligate *adj.* abandoned, corrupt, Cyprian, debauched, degenerate, depraved, dissipated, dissolute, extravagant, immoderate, immoral, improvident, iniquitous, libertine, licentious, loose, prodigal, promiscuous, reckless, shameless, spendthrift, squandering, unprincipled, vicious, vitiated, wanton, wasteful, whorish, wicked, wild.
antonyms moral, parsimonious, thrifty, upright.
n. debauchee, degenerate, libertine, prodigal, racketeer, rake, reprobate, roué, spendthrift, squanderer, waster, wastrel.

profound *adj.* abject, absolute, abstruse, abysmal, acute, awful, bottomless, cavernous, complete, consummate, deep, deep-seated, discerning, erudite, exhaustive, extensive, extreme, far-reaching, fathomless, great, heartfelt, heart-rending, hearty, intense, keen, learned, penetrating, philosophical, pronounced, recondite, sagacious, sage, serious, sincere, skilled, subtle, thoroughgoing, thoughtful, total, utter, weighty, wise, yawning.
antonyms mild, shallow, slight.

profuse *adj.* abundant, ample, bountiful, copious, excessive, extravagant, exuberant, fulsome, generous, immoderate, large-handed, lavish, liberal, luxuriant, open-handed, over the top, overflowing, plentiful, prodigal, prolific, teeming, unstinting.
antonyms sparing, sparse.

profusion *n.* abundance, bounty, copiousness, cornucopia, excess, extravagance, exuberance, glut, lavishness, luxuriance, multitude, plenitude, pleroma, plethora, prodigality, quantity, riot, superabundance, superfluity, surplus, wealth.
antonyms sparingness, sparsity.

program *n.* agenda, broadcast, curriculum, design, lineup, list, listing, order of events, order of the day, performance, plan, plan of action, presentation, procedure, production, project, schedule, scheme, show, syllabus, transmission.
v. arrange, bill, book, brainwash, design, engage, formulate, itemize, lay on, line up, list, map out, plan, prearrange, schedule, work out.

progress *n.* advance, advancement, amelioration, betterment, breakthrough, circuit, continuation, course, development, gain, growth, headway, improvement, increase, journey, movement, passage, procession, progression, promotion, step forward, way.
antonyms decline, deterioration.
v. advance, ameliorate, better, blossom, come on, continue, develop, forge ahead, gain, gather momentum, grow, improve, increase, make headway, make strides, mature, proceed, prosper, travel.
antonyms decline, deteriorate.

progression *n.* advance, advancement, chain, concatenation, course, cycle, furtherance, gain, headway, order, progress, sequence, series, string, succession.
antonyms decline, deterioration.

prohibit *v.* ban, bar, constrain, debar, disallow, forbid, hamper, hinder, impede, interdict, obstruct, outlaw, preclude, prevent, proscribe, restrict, rule out, stop, veto.
antonym permit.

prohibition *n.* ban, bar, constraint, disallowance, embargo, exclusion, forbiddal, forbiddance, injunction, interdict, interdiction, negation, obstruction, prevention, proscription, restruction, veto.
antonym permission.

prohibitive *adj.* excessive, exorbitant, extortionate, forbidding, impossible, preposterous, prohibiting, prohibitory, proscriptive, repressive, restraining, restrictive, sky-high, steep, suppressive.
antonyms encouraging, reasonable.

project *n.* activity, assignment, conception, design, enterprise, idea, job, occupation, plan, program, proposal, purpose, scheme, task, undertaking, venture, work.
v. beetle, bulge, calculate, cast, contemplate, contrive, design, devise, discharge, draft, estimate, exsert, extend, extrapolate, extrude, fling, forecast, frame, gauge, hurl, jut, launch, map out, outline, overhang, plan, predetermine, predict, propel, prophesy, propose, protrude, purpose, reckon, scheme, shoot, stand out, stick out, throw, transmit.

prolific *adj.* abounding, abundant, bountiful, copious, fecund, fertile, fertilizing, fruitful, generative, luxuriant, productive, profuse, rank, reproductive, rich, teeming, voluminous.
antonyms infertile, scarce.

prolong *v.* continue, delay, drag out, draw out, extend, lengthen, lengthen out, perpetuate, produce, protract, spin out, stretch.
antonym shorten.

prominent *adj.* beetling, bulging, celebrated, chief, conspicuous, distinguished, eminent, eye-catching, famous, foremost, important, jutting, leading, main, noted, noticeable, obtrusive, obvious, outstanding, popular, pre-eminent, projecting, pronounced, protruding, protrusive, protuberant, remarkable, renowned, respected, salient, standing out, striking, top, unmistakable, weighty, well-known.
antonyms inconspicuous, unimportant.

promiscuity *n.* abandon, amorality, debauchery, depravity, dissipation, immorality, laxity, laxness, lechery, libertinism, licentiousness, looseness, permissiveness, profligacy, promiscuousness, protervity, wantonness, whoredom, whoring, whorishness.
antonym chastity.

promise *v.* assure, augur, bespeak, betoken, bid fair, contract, denote, engage, guarantee, hint at, indicate,

look like, pledge, plight, predict, presage, prophesy, stipulate, suggest, swear, take an oath, undertake, vouch, vow, warrant.
n. ability, aptitude, assurance, bond, capability, capacity, commitment, compact, covenant, engagement, flair, guarantee, oath, pledge, pollicitation, potential, talent, undertaking, vow, word, word of honor.

promote *v.* advance, advertise, advocate, aggrandize, aid, assist, back, blazon, boost, champion, contribute to, develop, dignify, elevate, encourage, endorse, espouse, exalt, forward, foster, further, help, honor, hype, kick upstairs, nurture, plug, popularize, prefer, publicize, puff, push, raise, recommend, sell, sponsor, stimulate, support, trumpet, upgrade, urge.
antonyms demote, disparage, obstruct.

prompt[1] *adj.* alert, brisk, eager, early, efficient, expeditious, immediate, instant, instantaneous, on time, punctual, quick, rapid, ready, responsive, smart, speedy, swift, timely, timeous, unhesitating, willing.
antonym slow.
adv. exactly, on the dot, promptly, punctually, sharp, to the minute.

prompt[2] *v.* advise, assist, call forth, cause, cue, elicit, evoke, give rise to, impel, incite, induce, inspire, instigate, motivate, move, occasion, prod, produce, provoke, remind, result in, spur, stimulate, urge.
antonym dissuade. *n.* cue, help, hint, instigation, jog, jolt, prod, reminder, spur, stimulus.

promptly *adv.* directly, forthwith, immediately, instantly, on time, posthaste, pronto, punctually, quickly, speedily, swiftly, unhesitatingly.

promulgate *v.* advertise, announce, broadcast, circulate, communicate, declare, decree, disseminate, issue, notify, preconize, proclaim, promote, publicize, publish, spread.

prone[1] *adj.* apt, bent, disposed, given, inclined, liable, likely, predisposed, propense, subject, susceptible, tending, vulnerable.
antonym unlikely.

prone[2] *adj.* face down, flat, full-length, horizontal, procumbent, prostrate, recumbent, stretched.
antonym upright.

pronounce *v.* accent, affirm, announce, articulate, assert, breathe, declaim, declare, decree, deliver, enunciate, judge, proclaim, say, sound, speak, stress, utter, vocalize, voice.

pronounced *adj.* broad, clear, conspicuous, decided, definite, distinct, evident, marked, noticeable, obvious, positive, striking, strong, unmistakable.
antonyms unnoticeable, vague.

proof *n.* assay, attestation, authentication, certification, confirmation, corroboration, demonstration, documentation, evidence, examination, experiment, ordeal, scrutiny, substantiation, test, testimony, trial, verification, voucher.
adj. impenetrable, impervious, proofed, rainproof, repellent, resistant, strong, tight, treated, waterproof, weather-proof, windproof.
antonyms permeable, untreated.

propagate *v.* beget, breed, broadcast, circulate, diffuse, disseminate, engender, generate, increase, multiply, proclaim, procreate, produce, proliferate, promote, promulgate, publicize, publish, reproduce, spawn, spread, transmit.

propel *v.* drive, force, impel, launch, push, send, shoot, shove, start, thrust, waft.
antonyms slow, stop.

propensity *n.* aptness, bent, bias, disposition, foible, inclination, leaning, liability, penchant, predisposition, proclivity, proneness, readiness, susceptibility, tendency, weakness.
antonym disinclination.

proper *adj.* accepted, accurate, appropriate, apt, becoming, befitting, characteristic, conventional, correct, decent, decorous, established, exact, fit, fitting, formal, genteel, gentlemanly, gradely, individual, kosher, ladylike, legitimate, mannerly, meet, orthodox, own, particular, peculiar, perjink, personal, polite, precise, prim, prissy, punctilious, refined, respectable, respective, right, sedate, seemly, special, specific, suitable, suited, well-becoming, well-beseeming.
antonyms common, general, improper.

property[1] *n.* acres, assets, belongings, building(s), capital, chattels, effects, estate, freehold, goods, holding, holdings, house(s), land, means, meum et tuum, possessions, real estate, realty, resources, riches, title, wealth.

property[2] *n.* ability, affection, attribute, characteristic, feature, hallmark, idiosyncrasy, mark, peculiarity, quality, trait, virtue.

prophecy *n.* augury, divination, forecast, foretelling, hariolation, prediction, prognosis, prognostication, revelation, second-sight, soothsaying, taghairm, vaticination.

prophesy *v.* augur, divine, forecast, foresee, foretell, forewarn, hariolate, predict, presage, prognosticate, soothsay, vaticinate.

prophet *n.* augur, Cassandra, clairvoyant, divinator, diviner, forecaster, foreteller, Nostradamus, oracle, prognosticator, prophesier, seer, sibyl, soothsayer, tipster, vaticinator.

propitious *adj.* advantageous, auspicious, beneficial, benevolent, benign, bright, encouraging, favorable, fortunate, friendly, gracious, happy, kindly, lucky, opportune, promising, prosperous, reassuring, rosy, timely, well-disposed.
antonym inauspicious.

proportion *n.* agreement, amount, balance, congruity, correspondence, cut, distribution, division, eurhythmy, fraction, harmony, measure, part, percentage, quota, ratio, relationship, segment, share, symmetry.
antonyms disproportion, imbalance.

proportional *adj.* balanced, commensurate, comparable, compatible, consistent, correspondent, corresponding, equitable, even, fair, just, logistical, proportionate.
antonyms disproportionate, unjust.

proposal *n.* bid, design, draft, manifesto, motion, offer, outline, overture, plan, platform, presentation, proffer, program, project, proposition, recommendation, scheme, sketch, suggestion, suit, tender, terms.

propose *v.* advance, aim, bring up, design, enunciate, have in mind, intend, introduce, invite, lay before, mean, move, name, nominate, pay suit, plan, pop the question, present, proffer, propound, purpose, put forward, put up, recommend, scheme, submit, suggest, table, tender.
antonyms oppose, withdraw.

proposition *n.* manifesto, motion, plan, program, project, proposal, recommendation, scheme, suggestion, tender.
v. accost, solicit.

propound *v.* advance, advocate, contend, enunciate, lay down, move, postulate, present, propose, put forward, set forth, submit, suggest.
antonym oppose.

proprietor *n.* châtelaine, deed holder, freeholder, landlady, landlord, landowner, owner, possessor, proprietary, proprietress, proprietrix, title-holder.

prosaic *adj.* banal, boring, bromidic, commonplace, dry, dull, everyday, flat, hackneyed, humdrum, matter-of-fact, mundane, ordinary, pedestrian, routine, stale, tame, trite, unimaginative, uninspired, uninspiring, unpoetical, vapid, workaday.
antonyms imaginative, interesting.

proscribe *v.* attaint, ban, banish, bar, black, blackball, boycott, censure, condemn, damn, denounce, deport, doom, embargo, exclude, excommunicate, exile, expatriate, expel, forbid, interdict, ostracize, outlaw, prohibit, reject.
antonyms admit, allow.

prosecute *v.* arraign, bring suit against, bring to trial, carry on, conduct, continue, direct, discharge, engage in, execute, follow through, indict, litigate, manage, perform, persevere, persist, practice, prefer charges, pursue, put on trial, see through, sue, summon, take to court, try, work at.
antonym desist.

prospect *n.* calculation, chance, contemplation, expectation, future, hope, landscape, likelihood, odds, opening, outlook, panorama, perspective, plan, possibility, presumption, probability, promise, proposition, scene, sight, spectacle, thought, view, vision, vista.
antonym unlikelihood.
v. explore, fossick, nose, quest, search, seek, survey.

prospective *adj.* anticipated, approaching, awaited, coming, designate, designated, destined, eventual, expected, forthcoming, future, imminent, intended, likely, possible, potential, soon-to-be, to come, -to-be.
antonyms agreed, current.

prosper *v.* advance, bloom, boom, burgeon, fare well, flourish, flower, get on, grow rich, make good, progress, succeed, thrive, turn out well.
antonym fail.

prosperous *adj.* affluent, blooming, booming, burgeoning, flourishing, fortunate, in the money, lucky, moneyed, opulent, palmy, profitable, rich, successful, thriving, wealthy, well-heeled, well-off, well-to-do.
antonym poor.

prostrate *adj.* abject, brought to one's knees, crushed, defenseless, dejected, depressed, desolate, disarmed, done, drained, exhausted, fagged, fallen, flat, helpless, horizontal, impotent, inconsolable, knackered, kowtowing, overcome, overwhelmed, paralyzed, pooped, powerless, procumbent, prone, reduced, shattered, spent, worn out.
antonyms elated, erect, hale, happy, strong, triumphant.
v. crush, depress, disarm, drain, exhaust, fag out, fatigue, knacker, lay low, overcome, overthrow, overturn, overwhelm, paralyze, poop, reduce, ruin, sap, shatter, tire, wear out, weary.
antonyms elate, exalt, strengthen.

protagonist *n.* advocate, champion, chief character, exponent, hero, heroine, lead, leader, mainstay, prime mover, principal, proponent, standard-bearer, supporter.

protect *v.* care for, chaperon, convoy, cover, cover up for, defend, escort, guard, harbor, keep, look after, preserve, safeguard, save, screen, secure, shelter, shield, stand guard over, support, watch over.
antonyms attack, threaten.

protection *n.* aegis, armor, backstop, barrier, buffer, bulwark, care, charge, cover, custody, defense, guard, guardianship, guarding, preservation, protecting, refuge, safe-guard, safekeeping, safety, screen, security, shelter, shield, umbrella, wardship.
antonyms attack, threat.

protest *n.* complaint, declaration, demur, demurral, dharna, disapproval, dissent, formal complaint, objection, obtestation, outcry, protestation, remonstrance.
antonym acceptance.
v. affirm, argue, assert, asseverate, attest, avow, complain, contend, cry out, declare, demonstrate, demur, disagree, disapprove, expostulate, insist, maintain, object, obtest, oppose, profess, remonstrate, squawk, take exception, testify, vow.
antonym accept.

prototype *n.* archetype, example, exemplar, mock-up, model, original, paradigm, pattern, precedent, standard, type.

protract *v.* continue, draw out, extend, keep going, lengthen, prolong, spin out, stretch out, sustain.
antonym shorten.

protuberance *n.* apophysis, bulb, bulge, bump, excrescence, knob, lump, mamelon, mamilla, outgrowth, process, projection, prominence, protrusion, swelling, tuber, tubercle, tumor, umbo, venter, wart, welt.

proud *adj.* appreciative, arrogant, august, boastful, conceited, content, contented, disdainful, distinguished, egotistical, eminent, exalted, glad, glorious, grand, gratified, gratifying, great, haughty, high and mighty, honored, illustrious, imperious, imposing, lofty, lordly, magnificent, majestic, memorable, misproud, noble, orgulous, overbearing, overweening, pleased, pleasing, presumptuous, prideful, red-letter, rewarding, satisfied, satisfying, self-important, self-respecting, snobbish, snobby, snooty, splendid, stately, stuck-up, supercilious, toffee-nosed, vain.
antonym humble.

prove *v.* analyze, ascertain, assay, attest, authenticate, bear out, check, confirm, corroborate, demonstrate, determine, document, establish, evidence, evince, examine, experience, experiment, justify, show, substantiate, suffer, test, try, turn out, verify.
antonyms discredit, disprove, falsify.

proverb *n.* adage, aphorism, apophthegm, bromide, byword, dictum, gnome, maxim, precept, saw, saying.

proverbial *adj.* accepted, acknowledged, apophthegmatic, archetypal, axiomatic, bromidic, conventional, current, customary, famed, famous, legendary, notorious, self-evident, time-honored, traditional, typical, unquestioned, well-known.

provide *v.* accommodate, add, afford, anticipate, arrange for, bring, cater, contribute, determine, equip, forearm, furnish, give, impart, lay down, lend, outfit, plan for, prepare for, present, produce, provision, render, require, serve, specify, state, stipulate, stock up, suit, supply, take measures, take precautions, yield.
antonyms remove, take.

provident *adj.* canny, careful, cautious, discreet, economical, equipped, far-seeing, far-sighted, frugal, imaginative, long-sighted, prudent, sagacious, shrewd, thrifty, vigilant, wary, well-prepared, wise.
antonym improvident.

provision *n.* accouterment, agreement, arrangement, catering, clause, condition, demand, equipping, fitting out, furnishing, plan, prearrangement, precaution, preparation, prerequisite, providing, proviso, purveyance, purveying, requirement, specification, stipulation, supplying, term, victualing.
antonyms neglect, removal.

provisions *n.* comestibles, eatables, eats, edibles, fare, food, foodstuff, groceries, grub, piece, prog, provand, provender, proviant, rations, stores, supplies, sustenance, viands, viaticum, victualage, victuals, vittles.

proviso *n.* clause, condition, limitation, provision, qualification, requirement, reservation, restriction, rider, small print, stipulation.

provoke *v.* affront, aggravate, anger, annoy, cause, chafe, elicit, enrage, evoke, exasperate, excite, fire, gall, generate, give rise to, incense, incite, induce, inflame, infuriate, inspire, instigate, insult, irk, irritate, kindle, madden, motivate, move, occasion, offend, pique, precipitate, produce, promote, prompt, put out, rile, rouse, stimulate, stir, vex.
antonyms pacify, please, result.

prowess *n.* ability, accomplishment, adeptness, adroitness, aptitude, attainment, bravery, command, daring, dauntlessness, dexterity, doughtiness, excellence, expertise, expertness, facility, genius, heroism, mastery, skill, talent, valor.
antonyms clumsiness, mediocrity.

prowl *v.* creep, cruise, hunt, lurk, nose, patrol, range, roam, rove, scavenge, search, skulk, slink, sneak, snook, stalk, steal.

proximity *n.* adjacency, closeness, contiguity, juxtaposition, nearness, neighborhood, propinquity, proximation, vicinity. *antonym* remoteness.

proxy *n.* agent, attorney, delegate, deputy, factor, representative, stand-in, substitute, surrogate.

prudence *n.* canniness, care, caution, circumspection, common sense, discretion, economy, far-sightedness, foresight, forethought, frugality, good sense, heedfulness, husbandry, judgment, judiciousness, planning, policy, precaution, preparedness, providence, sagacity, saving, thrift, vigilance, wariness, wisdom.
antonym imprudence.

prudent *adj.* canny, careful, cautious, circumspect, discerning, discreet, economical, far-sighted, frugal, judicious, politic, provident, sagacious, sage, sensible, shrewd, sparing, thrifty, vigilant, wary, well-advised, wise, wise-hearted.
antonym imprudent.

prudish *adj.* demure, narrow-minded, old-maidish, overmodest, overnice, po-faced, priggish, prim, prissy, proper, pudibund, puritanical, school-marmish, squeamish, starchy, strait-laced, stuffy, ultra-virtuous, Victorian.
antonyms easy-going, lax.

pry *v.* delve, dig, ferret, interfere, intrude, meddle, nose, peep, peer, poke, poke one's nose in, snoop.
antonym mind one's own business.

prying *adj.* curious, inquisitive, interfering, intrusive, meddlesome, meddling, nosy, peering, peery, snooping, snoopy, spying.
antonym uninquisitive.

psyche *n.* anima, awareness, consciousness, individuality, intellect, intelligence, mind, personality, pneuma, self, soul, spirit, subconscious, understanding.

psychiatrist *n.* analyst, headshrinker, psychoanalyzer, psychoanalyst, psychologist, psychotherapist, shrink, therapist, trick-cyclist.

psychic *adj.* clairvoyant, cognitive, extra-sensory, intellectual, mental, mystic, mystical, occult, preternatural, psychogenic, psychological, spiritual, spiritualistic, supernatural, telekinetic, telepathic.

psychological *adj.* affective, cerebral, cognitive,

emotional, imaginary, intellectual, irrational, mental, psychosomatic, subconscious, subjective, unconscious, unreal.

psychotic *adj.* certifiable, demented, deranged, insane, lunatic, mad, mental, psychopathic, unbalanced.
antonym sane.

public *adj.* accessible, acknowledged, circulating, civic, civil, common, communal, community, exposed, general, important, known, national, notorious, obvious, open, overt, patent, plain, popular, prominent, published, recognized, respected, social, state, universal, unrestricted, well-known, widespread.
antonym private.
n. audience, buyers, citizens, clientèle, commonalty, community, country, electorate, everyone, followers, following, masses, multitude, nation, patrons, people, populace, population, punters, society, supporters, voters.

publicize *v.* advertise, blaze, blazon, broadcast, hype, plug, promote, puff, push, spotlight, spread about, write off.
antonym keep secret.

publish *v.* advertise, announce, bring out, broadcast, circulate, communicate, declare, diffuse, disclose, distribute, divulgate, divulge, evulgate, issue, leak, part, print, proclaim, produce, promulgate, publicize, reveal, spread, vent.
antonym keep secret.

puerile *adj.* babyish, childish, foolish, immature, inane, infantile, irresponsible, jejune, juvenile, naïve, petty, ridiculous, silly, trifling, trivial, weak.
antonym mature.

pugnacious *adj.* aggressive, antagonistic, argumentative, bellicose, belligerent, choleric, combative, contentious, disputatious, hostile, hot-tempered, irascible, petulant, quarrelsome.
antonym easy-going.

pull *v.* attract, cull, dislocate, drag, draw, draw out, entice, extract, gather, haul, jerk, lure, magnetize, pick, pluck, remove, rend, rip, schlep, sprain, strain, stretch, take out, tear, tow, track, trail, tug, tweak, uproot, weed, whang, wrench, yank.
antonyms deter, push, repel.
n. advantage, allurement, attraction, clout, drag, drawing power, effort, exertion, force, forcefulness, influence, inhalation, jerk, leverage, lure, magnetism, muscle, power, puff, seduction, tug, twitch, weight, yank.
antonyms deterring, push, repelling.

pulsate *v.* beat, drum, hammer, oscillate, palpitate, pound, pulse, quiver, throb, thud, thump, tick, vibrate.

pulse *n.* beat, beating, drumming, oscillation, pulsation, rhythm, stroke, throb, throbbing, thudding, vibration.
v. beat, drum, pulsate, throb, thud, tick, vibrate.

pummel *v.* bang, batter, beat, fib, hammer, knock, nevel, pound, punch, strike, thump.

pump *v.* catechize, cross-examine, debrief, drive, force, grill, inject, interrogate, pour, probe, push, question, quiz, send, supply.

pun *n.* clinch, double entendre, equivoke, jeu de mots, paronomasia, paronomasy, play on words, quip, witticism.

punch[1] *v.* bash, biff, bop, box, clout, fib, hit, plug, pummel, slam, slug, smash, sock, strike, wallop.
n. bash, biff, bite, blow, bop, clout, drive, effectiveness, force, forcefulness, hit, impact, jab, knock, knuckle sandwich, lander, muzzler, panache, pizzazz, plug, point, sock, thump, verve, vigor, wallop.
antonym feebleness.

punch[2] *v.* bore, cut, drill, perforate, pierce, pink, prick, puncture, stamp.

punctilious *adj.* careful, ceremonious, conscientious, exact, finicky, formal, formalist, fussy, meticulous, nice, overnice, particular, precise, proper, scrupulous, strict.
antonyms boorish, easy-going, informal.

punctual *adj.* early, exact, in good time, on the dot, on time, precise, prompt, punctilious, strict, timely, up to time.
antonym unpunctual.

pungent *adj.* acid, acrid, acrimonious, acute, aromatic, barbed, biting, bitter, caustic, cutting, fell, hot, incisive, keen, mordant, painful, penetrating, peppery, piercing, piquant, poignant, pointed, sarcastic, scathing, seasoned, sharp, sour, spicy, stinging, stringent, strong, tangy, tart, telling, trenchant.
antonyms feeble, mild, tasteless.

punish *v.* abuse, amerce, batter, beat, castigate, chasten, chastise, correct, crucify, discipline, flog, give a lesson to, give someone laldie, harm, hurt, injure, keelhaul, kneecap, lash, maltreat, manhandle, masthead, misuse, oppress, penalize, rough up, scour, scourge, sort, strafe, trounce.

punishment *n.* abuse, beating, chastening, chastisement, come-uppance, correction, damnation, deserts, discipline, jankers, knee-capping, laldie, maltreatment, manhandling, medicine, pain, pay-off, penalty, penance, punition, retribution, sanction, toco, torture, victimization.

puny *adj.* diminutive, dwarfish, feeble, frail, inconsequential, inferior, insignificant, little, meager, minor, paltry, petty, piddling, pimping, reckling, runted, runtish, runty, sickly, stunted, tiny, trifling, trivial, underfed, undersized, undeveloped, weak, weakly, worthless.
antonyms important, large, strong.

pupil *n.* beginner, catechumen, disciple, learner, neophyte, novice, protégé, scholar, schoolboy, schoolgirl, student, tiro, tutee.
antonym teacher.

purchase *v.* achieve, acquire, attain, buy, earn, gain, invest in, obtain, pay for, procure, ransom, realize, secure, win.
antonym sell.

n. acquisition, advantage, asset, buy, edge, emption, foot-hold, footing, gain, grasp, grip, hold, influence, investment, lever, leverage, possession, property, ransoming, support, toehold.
antonym sale.

pure *adj.* absolute, abstract, academic, antiseptic, authentic, blameless, chaste, clean, clear, disinfected, flawless, genuine, germ-free, guileless, high-minded, honest, hygienic, immaculate, innocent, intemerate, maidenly, modest, natural, neat, pasteurized, perfect, philosophical, real, refined, sanitary, Saturnian, sheer, simple, sincere, snow-white, speculative, spiritous, spotless, stainless, sterile, sterilized, straight, taintless, theoretical, thorough, true, unadulterate, unadulterated, unalloyed, unblemished, uncontaminated, uncorrupted, undefiled, unmingled, unmitigated, unmixed, unpolluted, unqualified, unsoiled, unspoilt, unspotted, unstained, unsullied, untainted, untarnished, upright, utter, virgin, virginal, virginly, virtuous, wholesome.
antonyms adulterated, applied, defiled, immoral, impure, polluted, tainted.

purely *adv.* absolutely, completely, entirely, exclusively, just, merely, only, plainly, sheerly, simply, solely, thoroughly, totally, utterly, wholly.

purify *v.* absolve, beneficiate, catharize, chasten, clarify, clean, cleanse, decontaminate, deodorize, depurate, desalinate, disinfect, epurate, filter, fumigate, furbish, lustrate, mundify, redeem, refine, sanctify, sanitize, shrive, sublimize, wash.
antonyms contaminate, defile, pollute.

purist *n.* Atticist, classicist, formalist, grammaticaster, grammatist, mandarin, nit-picker, pedant, precisian, precisianist, precisionist, quibbler, stickler, vocabularian.
antonym liberal.
adj. austere, captious, fastidious, finicky, fussy, hypercritical, nit-picking, over-exact, over-fastidious, over-meticulous, over-particular, over-precise, pedantic, puristic, quibbling, strict, uncompromising.
antonyms liberal, open-minded, tolerant.

puritanical *adj.* abstemious, abstinent, ascetic, austere, bigoted, disapproving, disciplinarian, fanatical, narrow, narrow-minded, prim, proper, prudish, puritan, rigid, severe, stern, stiff, strait-laced, strict, stuffy, uncompromising, zealous.
antonyms broad-minded, hedonistic, indulgent, liberal.

purity *n.* blamelessness, chasteness, chastity, clarity, classicism, cleanliness, clearness, decency, faultlessness, fineness, genuineness, immaculateness, incorruption, innocence, integrity, morality, piety, pureness, rectitude, refinement, sanctity, simplicity, sincerity, spotlessness, stainlessness, truth, unspottedness, untaintedness, uprightness, virginity, virtue, virtuousness, wholesomeness.
antonyms immorality, impurity.

purloin *v.* abstract, appropriate, filch, finger, half-inch, lift, nick, nobble, palm, pilfer, pinch, pocket, prig, remove, rob, snaffle, snitch, steal, swipe, take, thieve.

purport *v.* allege, argue, assert, betoken, claim, convey, declare, denote, express, give out, imply, import, indicate, intend, maintain, mean, portend, pose as, pretend, proclaim, profess, seem, show, signify, suggest.
n. bearing, direction, drift, gist, idea, implication, import, meaning, point, significance, spirit, substance, tendency, tenor, theme, thrust.

purpose *n.* advantage, aim, ambition, aspiration, assiduity, avail, benefit, constancy, contemplation, decision, dedication, design, determination, devotion, drive, effect, end, firmness, function, gain, goal, good, hope, idea, ideal, intention, motive, object, objective, outcome, persistence, pertinacity, plan, point, principle, profit, project, rationale, reason, resolution, resolve, result, return, scheme, service, single-mindedness, steadfastness, target, telos, tenacity, use, usefulness, utility, view, vision, will, wish, zeal.
v. aim, aspire, contemplate, decide, design, desire, determine, ettle, intend, mean, meditate, plan, propose, resolve.

purposely *adv.*. by design, calculatedly, consciously, deliberately, designedly, expressly, intentionally, knowingly, on purpose, premeditatedly, specifically, wilfully, with malice aforethought.
antonyms impulsively, spontaneously, unpremeditatedly.

pursue *v.* accompany, adhere to, aim at, aim for, aspire to, attend, bedevil, beset, besiege, carry on, chase, check out, conduct, continue, course, court, cultivate, desire, dog, engage in, follow, follow up, go for, gun for, harass, harry, haunt, hold to, hound, hunt, inquire into, investigate, keep on, maintain, perform, persecute, persevere in, persist in, plague, ply, practice, proceed, prosecute, purpose, seek, set one's cap at, shadow, stalk, strive for, tackle, tail, track, trail, try for, wage, woo.
antonyms eschew, shun.

pursuit[1] *n.* chase, chevy, hounding, hue and cry, hunt, hunting, inquiry, investigation, quest, search, seeking, stalking, tracking, trail, trailing.

pursuit[2] *n.* activity, craft, hobby, interest, line, occupation, parergon, pastime, pleasure, side-line, specialty, vocation.

push *v.* advance, advertise, boost, browbeat, bulldoze, bully, coerce, constrain, depress, dragoon, drive, edge, egg on, elbow, encourage, expedite, force, hurry, hype, incite, influence, inveigle, jockey, jog, joggle, jostle, maneuver, manhandle, oblige, peddle, persuade, plug, poke, press, prod, promote, propagandize, propel, publicize, puff, ram, shoulder, shove, speed, spur, squeeze, thrust, urge, wedge, whang.
n. advance, ambition, assault, attack, bunt, butt, charge, determination, discharge, dismissal, drive, dynamism, effort, energy, enterprise, go, impetus, impulse, initia-

tive, jolt, knock, notice, nudge, offensive, one's books, one's cards, one's marching orders, onset, onslaught, poke, pressure, prod, shove, the axe, the boot, the bum's rush, the chop, the sack, thrust, vigor, vim, vitality, zip.

push-over *n.* child's play, cinch, doddle, dupe, easy mark, fall guy, gull, mug, picnic, piece of cake, sinecure, sitting duck, sitting target, soft mark, soft touch, stooge, sucker, walk-over. *antonyms* challenge, labor.

pushy *adj.* aggressive, ambitious, arrogant, assertive, assuming, bold, bossy, brash, bumptious, forceful, forward, loud, obtrusive, offensive, officious, overconfident, presumptuous, pushing, self-assertive.
antonyms quiet, restrained, unassertive, unassuming.

pusillanimous *adj.* caitiff, chicken, chicken-hearted, cowardly, craven, faint-hearted, fearful, feeble, gutless, lily-livered, mean-spirited, poltroon, recreant, scared, spineless, timid, timorous, unassertive, unenterprising, weak, weak-kneed, yellow.
antonyms ambitious, courageous, forceful, strong.

put *v.* advance, apply, assign, bring, bring forward, cast, commit, condemn, consign, constrain, couch, deploy, deposit, dispose, drive, employ, enjoin, establish, express, fit, fix, fling, force, formulate, forward, frame, heave, hurl, impel, impose, induce, inflict, land, lay, levy, lob, make, oblige, offer, park, phrase, pitch, place, plonk, pose, position, post, present, propose, push, render, require, rest, send, set, set down, settle, situate, state, station, subject, submit, suggest, tender, throw, thrust, toss, utter, voice, word, write.

putative *adj.* alleged, assumed, conjectural, hypothetical, imputed, presumed, presumptive, reported, reputative, reputed, supposed, suppositional, supposititious.

put-down *n.* affront, dig, disparagement, gibe, humiliation, insult, rebuff, sarcasm, slap in the face, slight, sneer, snub.

putrefy *v.* addle, corrupt, decay, decompose, deteriorate, fester, foost, gangrene, go bad, mortify, mold, necrose, perish, rot, spoil, stink, taint.

putrid *adj.* addle, addled, bad, contaminated, corrupt, decayed, decomposed, fetid, foosty, foul, gangrenous, mephitic, moldy, necrosed, noisome, off, putrefied, rancid, rank, reeking, rotten, rotting, sphacelate(d), spoiled, stinking, tainted.
antonyms fresh, wholesome.

puzzle[1] *v.* baffle, bamboozle, beat, bewilder, confound, confuse, fickle, floor, flummox, metagrobolize, mystify, non-plus, perplex, pother, stump, worry.
n. acrostic, anagram, brain-teaser, confusion, conundrum, crossword, difficulty, dilemma, enigma, knot, koan, logogram, logograph, logogriph, maze, mind-bender, mystery, paradox, poser, problem, quandary, question, rebus, riddle, Sphinx, tickler.

puzzle[2] *v.* brood, cogitate, consider, deliberate, figure, meditate, mull over, muse, ponder, rack one's brains, ratiocinate, reason, ruminate, study, think, wonder, worry.

puzzled *adj.* at a loss, at sea, baffled, bamboozled, beaten, bemused, bewildered, confounded, confused, disorientated, doubtful, flummoxed, in a haze, lost, mixed up, mizzled, mystified, nonplused, perplexed, stuck, stumped, stymied, uncertain.
antonyms certain, clear.

puzzling *adj.* abstruse, ambiguous, baffling, bewildering, bizarre, cabalistic, circuitous, confusing, cryptic, curious, enigmatic, equivocal, impenetrable, inexplicable, intricate, involved, knotty, labyrinthine, mind-bending, mind-boggling, misleading, mysterious, mystical, mystifying, peculiar, perplexing, queer, riddling, Sphynx-like, strange, tangled, tortuous, unaccountable, unclear, unfathomable.

Q

quack *n.* charlatan, cowboy, empiric, fake, fraud, humbug, impostor, masquerader, medicaster, mountebank, phony, pretender, pseud, quacksalver, sham, spieler, swindler, trickster, witch-doctor.
adj. bogus, counterfeit, fake, false, fraudulent, phony, pretended, sham, so-called, spurious, supposed, unqualified.
antonym genuine.

quackery *n.* charlatanism, charlatanry, empiricism, fraud, fraudulence, humbug, imposture, mountebankery, mountebankism, phoniness, sham.

quaff *v.* booze, carouse, down, drain, drink, gulp, guzzle, imbibe, knock back, swallow, swig, swill, tipple, tope, toss off.
n. bevvy, cup, dram, draught, drink, jorum, slug, snifter, swig.

quagmire *n.* bog, everglade, fen, marsh, mire, morass, moss, mudflat, quag, quicksand, slough, swamp.

quail *v.* back away, blanch, blench, cower, droop, faint, falter, flinch, quake, recoil, shake, shrink, shudder, shy away, tremble, wince.

quaint *adj.* absurd, antiquated, antique, bizarre, charming, curious, droll, eccentric, fanciful, fantastic, freaky, funky, ingenious, odd, old-fashioned, old-time, old-world, peculiar, picturesque, queer, rum, singular, strange, unconventional, unusual, weird, whimsical.

quake *v.* convulse, heave, jolt, move, pulsate, quail, quiver, rock, shake, shiver, shudder, sway, throb, totter, tremble, vibrate, waver, wobble.

qualification[1] *n.* ability, accomplishment, adequacy, aptitude, attribute, capability, capacity, certification, competence, eligibility, fitness, skill, suitability, suitableness, training.

qualification[2] *n.* adaptation, adjustment, allowance, caveat, condition, criterion, exception, exemption, limitation, modification, objection, provision, proviso, reservation, restriction, stipulation.

qualified[1] *adj.* able, accomplished, adept, adequate, capable, certificated, certified, competent, efficient, eligible, equipped, experienced, expert, fit, habilitated, knowledgeable, licensed, practiced, proficient, skilful, talented, trained.
antonym unqualified.

qualified[2] *adj.* bounded, cautious, circumscribed, conditional, confined, contingent, equivocal, guarded, limitative, limited, modificatory, modified, provisional, qualificatory, reserved, restricted.

qualify[1] *v.* authorize, capacitate, certificate, empower, endow, equip, fit, graduate, habilitate, permit, prepare, sanction, shape, train.
antonym unfit.

qualify[2] *v.* abate, adapt, adjust, alleviate, assuage, categorize, characterize, circumscribe, classify, define, delimit, describe, designate, diminish, distinguish, ease, lessen, limit, mitigate, moderate, modify, modulate, reduce, regulate, restrain, restrict, soften, temper, vary, weaken.

quality *n.* aspect, attribute, caliber, character, characteristic, class, complexion, condition, constitution, deal, description, distinction, essence, excellence, feature, fineness, grade, kidney, kind, make, mark, merit, nature, peculiarity, position, pre-eminence, property, rank, refinement, sort, standing, status, superiority, talent, timbre, tone, trait, value, water, worth.

qualm *n.* anxiety, apprehension, compunction, disquiet, doubt, fear, hesitation, misgiving, pang, presentiment, regret, reluctance, remorse, scruple, twinge, uncertainty, unease, uneasiness, worry.

quandary *n.* bewilderment, confusion, corner, difficulty, dilemma, doubt, embarrassment, entanglement, fix, hole, imbroglio, impasse, jam, kettle of fish, mess, perplexity, plight, predicament, problem, puzzle, uncertainty.

quantity *n.* aggregate, allotment, amount, breadth, bulk, capacity, content, dosage, expanse, extent, greatness, length, lot, magnitude, mass, measure, number, part, portion, proportion, quantum, quota, share, size, spread, strength, sum, total, volume, weight.

quarantine *n.* detention, isolation, lazaret, lazaretto, segregation.

quarrel *n.* affray, altercation, argument, barney, beef, bicker, brattle, brawl, breach, breeze, broil, clash, commotion, conflict, contention, controversy, coolness, debate, difference, disagreement, discord, disputation, dispute, dissension, dissidence, disturbance, dust-up, estrangement, feud, fight, fracas, fray, misunderstanding, row, rupture, schism, scrap, shouting match, slanging match, spat, split, squabble, strife, tiff, tumult, vendetta, wrangle.
antonyms agreement, harmony.
v. altercate, argue, be at loggerheads, be at variance, bicker, brawl, carp, cavil, clash, contend, differ, disagree, dispute, dissent, fall out, fight, find fault, object, pick holes, question, row, spar, spat, squabble, take exception, tiff, vitilitigate, wrangle.
antonym agree.

quarrelsome *adj.* altercative, antagonistic, argumentative, bellicose, belligerent, cantankerous, captious, choleric, combative, contentious, contrary, cross, disputatious, fractious, ill-tempered, irascible, irritable, peevish, perverse, petulant, pugnacious, querulous,

stroppy, testy, truculent, turbulent, wranglesome.
antonyms peaceable, placid.

quarry *n.* game, goal, kill, object, objective, prey, prize, target, victim.

quarter[1] *n.* area, direction, district, division, locality, location, neighborhood, part, place, point, position, province, quartier, region, section, sector, side, spot, station, territory, vicinity, zone.

quarter[2] *n.* clemency, compassion, favor, forgiveness, grace, indulgence, leniency, mercy, pardon, pity.

quarter[3] *n.* fourth, quartern, term.
v. decussate, divide in four, quadrisect.

quarter[4] *v.* accommodate, bed, billet, board, house, install, lodge, place, post, put up, shelter, station.

quarters *n.* abode, accommodation, apartment, barracks, billet, cantonment, caserne, chambers, digs, domicile, dwelling, habitation, lodging, lodgings, post, quarterage, residence, rooms, station.

quash *v.* annul, cancel, crush, declare null and void, defeat, disannul, disenact, invalidate, nullify, overrule, overthrow, quell, repress, rescind, reverse, revoke, set aside, squash, subdue, suppress, void.
antonyms confirm, justify, reinstate, vindicate.

quaver *v.* break, crack, flicker, flutter, oscillate, pulsate, quake, quiver, shake, shudder, tremble, trill, twitter, vibrate, warble.
n. break, quaveriness, quiver, shake, sob, throb, tremble, trembling, tremolo, tremor, trill, vibration, vibrato, warble.

quay *n.* dock, harbor, jetty, levee, pier, wharf.

queasy *adj.* bilious, dizzy, faint, giddy, green, groggy, ill, indisposed, nauseated, off-color, qualmish, qualmy, queer, sick, sickened, squeamish, unwell.

queen *n.* beauty, belle, consort, diva, doyenne, empress, goddess, grande dame, idol, maharani, mistress, monarch, nonpareil, prima donna, princess, rani, ruler, sovereign, star, sultana, tsarina, Venus.

queer *adj.* aberrant, abnormal, absurd, anomalous, atypical, bizarre, cranky, crazy, curious, daft, demented, deranged, deviant, disquieting, dizzy, doubtful, droll, dubious, eccentric, eerie, eldritch, erratic, exceptional, extraordinary, faint, fanciful, fantastic, fey, fishy, freakish, funny, giddy, grotesque, homosexual, idiosyncratic, ill, irrational, irregular, light-headed, mad, mysterious, odd, offbeat, outlandish, outré, peculiar, preternatural, puzzling, quaint, queasy, questionable, reeling, remarkable, rum, screwy, shady, shifty, singular, strange, suspect, suspicious, touched, unaccountable, unbalanced, uncanny, uncommon, unconventional, uneasy, unhinged, unnatural, unorthodox, unusual, unwell, unwonted, weird.
antonyms common, ordinary, straightforward, unexceptional, usual.
v. botch, cheat, endanger, foil, frustrate, harm, impair, imperil, injure, jeopardize, mar, ruin, spoil, stymie, thwart, upset, wreck.

queerness *n.* aberrance, abnormality, absurdity, anomalousness, atypicalness, bizarreness, crankiness, craziness, curiousness, deviance, drollness, dubiety, dubiousness, eccentricity, eeriness, fishiness, grotesqueness, idiosyncrasy, individuality, irrationality, irregularity, light-headedness, madness, mysteriousness, mystery, oddity, oddness, outlandishness, peculiarity, puzzle, quaintness, shadiness, shiftiness, singularity, strangeness, suspiciousness, uncanniness, uncommonness, unconventionality, unnaturalness, unorthodoxy, unusualness, unwontedness.

quell *v.* allay, alleviate, appease, assuage, blunt, calm, compose, conquer, crush, deaden, defeat, dull, extinguish, hush, mitigate, moderate, mollify, overcome, overpower, pacify, put down, quash, quench, quiet, reduce, silence, soothe, squash, stifle, subdue, subjugate, suppress, vanquish.

quench *v.* allay, appease, check, cool, crush, damp down, destroy, douse, end, extinguish, overcome, put out, quash, quell, sate, satisfy, silence, slake, smother, snuff out, stifle, suppress.

querulous *adj.* cantankerous, captious, carping, caviling, censorious, complaining, crabbed, critical, cross, cross-grained, crusty, discontented, dissatisfied, exacting, fault-finding, fretful, fussy, grouchy, grumbling, hypercritical, intolerant, irascible, irritable, peevish, perverse, petulant, plaintive, quarrelsome, querimonious, sour, testy, thrawn, waspish, whingeing, whining.
antonyms contented, equable, placid, uncomplaining.

query *v.* ask, be skeptical of, call in question, challenge, disbelieve, dispute, distrust, doubt, enquire, misdoubt, mistrust, quarrel with, question, suspect.
antonym accept.
n. demand, doubt, hesitation, inquiry, misdoubt, misgiving, objection, problem, quaere, question, quibble, reservation, skepticism, suspicion, uncertainty.

quest *n.* adventure, crusade, enterprise, expedition, exploration, hunt, inquiry, investigation, journey, mission, pilgrimage, pursuit, search, undertaking, venture, voyage.

question *v.* ask, be skeptical of, catechize, challenge, controvert, cross-examine, debrief, disbelieve, dispute, distrust, doubt, enquire, examine, grill, impugn, interpellate, interrogate, interview, investigate, misdoubt, mistrust, oppose, probe, pump, quarrel with, query, quiz, suspect.
n. argument, confusion, contention, controversy, debate, difficulty, dispute, doubt, dubiety, erotema, erotesis, examination, inquiry, interpellation, interrogation, investigation, issue, misdoubt, misgiving, motion, point, problem, proposal, proposition, quaere, query, quibble, skepsis, subject, theme, topic, uncertainty.

questionable *adj.* arguable, borderline, controversial, debatable, disputable, doubtful, dubious, dubitable, equivocal, fishy, iffy, impugnable, moot, problematical,

queer, shady, suspect, suspicious, uncertain, undetermined, unproven, unreliable, unsettled, vexed.
antonyms certain, indisputable, straightforward.

queue *n.* file, line, line-up, order, procession, sequence, series, string, succession, tail, tail-back, train.

quibble *v.* carp, cavil, chop logic, equivocate, pettifog, prevaricate, shift, split hairs.
n. carriwitchet, casuistry, cavil, complaint, criticism, equivocation, equivoke, evasion, niggle, objection, pettifoggery, prevarication, query, quiddit, quiddity, quillet, quip, quirk, sophism, subterfuge.

quibbler *n.* casuist, caviler, chop-logic, criticaster, equivocator, hair-splitter, logic-chopper, niggler, nit-picker, pettifogger, sophist.

quick *adj.* able, active, acute, adept, adroit, agile, alert, animated, apt, astute, awake, brief, bright, brisk, clever, cursory, deft, dexterous, discerning, energetic, expeditious, express, fast, fleet, flying, hasty, headlong, hurried, immediate, instant, instantaneous, intelligent, keen, lively, nifty, nimble, nippy, penetrating, perceptive, perfunctory, precipitate, prompt, quick-witted, rapid, ready, receptive, responsive, sharp, shrewd, skilful, smart, snappy, speedy, spirited, sprightly, spry, sudden, summary, swift, unhesitating, vivacious, wide-awake, winged.
antonyms dull, slow.

quicken *v.* accelerate, activate, advance, animate, arouse, dispatch, energize, enliven, excite, expedite, galvanize, hasten, hurry, impel, incite, inspire, invigorate, kindle, precipitate, reactivate, refresh, reinvigorate, resuscitate, revitalize, revive, revivify, rouse, sharpen, speed, stimulate, strengthen, vitalize, vivify.
antonyms dull, retard.

quickly *adv.* abruptly, at a rate of knots, at the double, before you can say Jack Robinson, briskly, by leaps and bounds, cursorily, expeditiously, express, fast, hastily, hell for leather, hotfoot, hurriedly, immediately, instantaneously, instantly, lickety-split, like a bat out of hell, perfunctorily, posthaste, promptly, pronto, quick, rapidly, readily, soon, speedily, swiftly, unhesitatingly.
antonyms slowly, tardily, thoroughly.

quickness *n.* acuteness, agility, alertness, aptness, astuteness, briskness, deftness, dexterity, expedition, hastiness, immediacy, instantaneousness, intelligence, keenness, liveliness, nimbleness, penetration, precipitation, promptitude, promptness, quick-wittedness, rapidity, readiness, receptiveness, sharpness, shrewdness, speed, speediness, suddenness, summariness, swiftness, turn of speed.
antonyms dullness, slowness, tardiness.

quick-witted *adj.* acute, alert, astute, bright, clever, crafty, ingenious, intelligent, keen, nimble-witted, penetrating, perceptive, ready-witted, resourceful, sharp, shrewd, smart, wide-awake, witty.
antonyms dull, slow, stupid.

quiescent *adj.* asleep, calm, dormant, in abeyance, inactive, inert, latent, motionless, passive, peaceful, placid, quiet, reposeful, resting, serene, silent, sleeping, smooth, still, tranquil, undisturbed, untroubled.
antonym active.

quiet *adj.* calm, composed, conservative, contemplative, contended, docile, dumb, even-tempered, gentle, hushed, inaudible, isolated, lonely, low, low-pitched, meek, mild, modest, motionless, noiseless, pacific, passive, peaceable, peaceful, placid, plain, private, removed, reserved, restful, restrained, retired, retiring, secluded, secret, sedate, self-contained, sequestered, serene, shy, silent, simple, smooth, sober, soft, soundless, still, stilly, subdued, taciturn, thoughtful, tranquil, uncommunicative, unconversable, undisturbed, uneventful, unexcitable, unexciting, unforthcoming, unfrequented, uninterrupted, unobtrusive, untroubled.
antonyms busy, noisy, obtrusive.
n. calm, calmness, ease, hush, lull, peace, quiescence, quietness, quietude, repose, rest, serenity, silence, stillness, tranquility.
antonyms bustle, disturbance, noise.

quietness *n.* calm, calmness, composure, dullness, hush, inactivity, inertia, lull, peace, placidity, quiescence, quiet, quietude, repose, serenity, silence, still, stillness, tranquility, uneventfulness.
antonyms activity, bustle, commotion, disturbance, noise, racket.

quintessence *n.* core, distillation, embodiment, essence, exemplar, extract, gist, heart, kernel, marrow, pattern, pith, quiddity, soul, spirit, sum and substance.

quip *n.* bon mot, carriwitchet, crack, epigram, gag, gibe, jest, jeu d'esprit, joke, mot, one-liner, pleasantry, quirk, retort, riposte, sally, wisecrack, witticism.
v. gag, gibe, jest, joke, quirk, retort, riposte, wisecrack.

quirk *n.* aberration, caprice, characteristic, curiosity, eccentricity, fancy, fetish, foible, freak, habit, idiosyncrasy, kink, mannerism, oddity, oddness, peculiarity, singularity, trait, turn, twist, vagary, warp, whim.

quit *v.* abandon, abdicate, apostatize, cease, conclude, decamp, depart, desert, disappear, discontinue, drop, end, exit, forsake, give up, go, halt, leave, relinquish, renege, renounce, repudiate, resign, retire, stop, surrender, suspend, vamoose, vanish, withdraw.

quite *adv.* absolutely, comparatively, completely, entirely, exactly, fairly, fully, moderately, perfectly, precisely, rather, relatively, somewhat, totally, utterly, wholly.

quits *adj.* equal, even, level, square.

quitter *n.* apostate, defector, delinquent, deserter, rat, recreant, renegade, shirker, skiver.

quiver *v.* agitate, bicker, convulse, flichter, flicker, flutter, oscillate, palpitate, pulsate, quake, quaver, shake, shiver, shudder, tremble, vibrate, wobble.
n. convulsion, flicker, flutter, oscillation, palpitation, pulsation, shake, shiver, shudder, spasm, throb, tic, tremble, tremor, vibration, wobble.

quixotic *adj.* chivalrous, extravagant, fanciful, fantastical, idealistic, impetuous, impracticable, impulsive, romantic, starry-eyed, unrealistic, unworldly, Utopian, visionary.
antonyms hard-headed, practical, realistic.

quiz *n.* catechism, examination, investigation, questioning, questionnaire, test.
v. ask, catechize, cross-examine, cross-question, debrief, examine, grill, interrogate, investigate, pump, question.

quizzical *adj.* amused, arch, bantering, curious, humorous, inquiring, mocking, questioning, sardonic, satirical, skeptical, teasing, waggish, whimsical.

quota *n.* allocation, allowance, assignment, cut, part, percentage, portion, proportion, quotum, ration, share, slice, whack.

quotation[1] *n.* citation, crib, cutting, excerpt, extract, gobbet, locus classicus, passage, piece, quote, reference, remnant.

quotation[2] *n.* charge, cost, estimate, figure, price, quote, rate, tender.

quote *v.* adduce, attest, cite, detail, echo, instance, name, parrot, recall, recite, recollect, refer to, repeat, reproduce, retell.

R

rabble *n.* canaille, clamjamphrie, colluvies, commonalty, commoners, crowd, doggery, dregs, faex populi, galère, herd, hoi polloi, horde, masses, mob, peasantry, plebs, populace, proles, proletariat, raffle, raggle-taggle, ragtag (and bobtail), rascality, riffraff, scum, swarm, tagrag, throng, trash.
antonyms aristocracy, elite, nobility.

rabid *adj.* berserk, bigoted, crazed, extreme, fanatical, fervent, frantic, frenzied, furious, hydrophobic, hysterical, infuriated, intemperate, intolerant, irrational, mad, maniacal, narrow-minded, obsessive, overzealous, raging, unreasoning, violent, wild, zealous.

race[1] *n.* chase, competition, contention, contest, corso, dash, derby, foot-race, marathon, pursuit, quest, rat race, regatta, rivalry, scramble, sprint, steeplechase.
v. career, compete, contest, dart, dash, fly, gallop, hare, hasten, hurry, run, rush, speed, sprint, tear, zoom.

race[2] *n.* ancestry, blood, breed, clan, descent, family, folk, house, issue, kin, kindred, line, lineage, nation, offspring, people, progeny, seed, stirps, stock, strain, tribe, type.

racial *adj.* ancestral, avital, ethnic, ethnological, folk, genealogical, genetic, inherited, national, tribal.

rack[1] *n.* frame, framework, gantry, gondola, hack, shelf, stand, structure.

rack[2] *n.* affliction, agony, anguish, distress, misery, pain, pangs, persecution, suffering, torment, torture.
v. afflict, agonize, convulse, crucify, distress, excruciate, harass, harrow, lacerate, oppress, pain, shake, strain, stress, stretch, tear, torment, torture, wrench, wrest, wring.

racket[1] *n.* babel, ballyhoo, clamor, clangor, commotion, din, disturbance, fuss, hubbub, hullabaloo, hurly-burly, kerfuffle, noise, outcry, pandemonium, row, shouting, tumult, uproar.

racket[2] *n.* business, con, deception, dodge, fiddle, fraud, game, scheme, swindle, trick.

racy *adj.* animated, bawdy, blue, boisterous, breezy, broad, buoyant, distinctive, doubtful, dubious, dynamic, ebullient, energetic, entertaining, enthusiastic, exciting, exhilarating, gamy, heady, immodest, indecent, indelicate, jaunty, lewd, lively, naughty, piquant, pungent, Rabelaisian, ribald, rich, risqué, salacious, sharp, smutty, sparkling, spicy, spirited, stimulating, strong, suggestive, tangy, tasty, vigorous, zestful.
antonyms dull, ponderous.

radiance *n.* brightness, brilliance, delight, effulgence, gaiety, glare, gleam, glitter, glow, happiness, incandescence, joy, lambency, light, luminosity, luster, pleasure, rapture, refulgence, resplendence, shine, splendor, warmth.

radiant *adj.* aglow, alight, beaming, beamish, beamy, beatific, blissful, bright, brilliant, delighted, ecstatic, effulgent, gleaming, glittering, glorious, glowing, happy, illuminated, incandescent, joyful, joyous, lambent, luminous, lustrous, profulgent, rapturous, refulgent, resplendent, shining, sparkling, splendid, sunny.
antonym dull.

radiate *v.* branch, diffuse, disseminate, divaricate, diverge, emanate, emit, eradiate, gleam, glitter, issue, pour, scatter, shed, shine, spread, spread out.

radical *adj.* basic, complete, comprehensive, constitutional, deep-seated, entire, essential, excessive, extreme, extremist, fanatical, far-reaching, fundamental, inherent, innate, intrinsic, native, natural, organic, primary, profound, revolutionary, rooted, severe, sweeping, thorough, thorough-going, total, violent.
antonym superficial.
n. extremist, fanatic, jacobin, left-winger, militant, reformer, reformist, revolutionary.

rag *v.* badger, bait, bullyrag, chaff, haze, jeer, mock, rib, ridicule, taunt, tease, torment, twit.

ragamuffin *n.* dandiprat, gamin, guttersnipe, mudlark, scarecrow, street arab, tatterdemalion, urchin, waif.

rage *n.* agitation, anger, bate, chafe, conniption, craze, dernier cri, enthusiasm, fad, fashion, frenzy, fury, ire, madness, mania, obsession, paddy, passion, style, tantrum, vehemence, violence, vogue, wrath.
v. chafe, explode, fret, fulminate, fume, inveigh, ramp, rampage, rant, rave, seethe, storm, surge, thunder.

raging *adj.* enraged, fizzing, frenzied, fulminating, fuming, furibund, furious, incensed, infuriated, irate, ireful, mad, rabid, rampageous, raving, seething, wrathful.

raid *n.* attack, break-in, bust, descent, foray, incursion, inroad, invasion, irruption, onset, onslaught, sally, seizure, sortie, strike, swoop.
v. attack, bust, descend on, do, forage, foray, invade, loot, maraud, pillage, plunder, ransack, reive, rifle, rush, sack.

rail *v.* abuse, arraign, attack, castigate, censure, criticize, decry, denounce, fulminate, inveigh, jeer, mock, revile, ridicule, scoff, upbraid, vituperate, vociferate.

railing *n.* balustrade, barrier, fence, paling, parapet, rail, rails.

rain *n.* cloudburst, deluge, downpour, drizzle, fall, flood, hail, mizzle, precipitation, raindrops, rainfall, rains, serein, shower, spate, squall, stream, torrent, volley.
v. bestow, bucket, deluge, deposit, drizzle, drop, expend, fall, heap, lavish, mizzle, pour, shower, spit, sprinkle, teem.

raise *v.* abandon, activate, advance, aggrade, aggrandize,

aggravate, amplify, arouse, assemble, augment, awaken, boost, breed, broach, build, cause, collect, construct, create, cultivate, develop, discontinue, elate, elevate, emboss, embourgeoise, end, engender, enhance, enlarge, erect, escalate, evoke, exaggerate, exalt, excite, foment, form, foster, gather, gentrify, get, grow, heave, heighten, hoist, incite, increase, inflate, instigate, intensify, introduce, kindle, levy, lift, loft, magnify, mass, mobilize, moot, motivate, muster, nurture, obtain, occasion, originate, pose, prefer, produce, promote, propagate, provoke, rally, rear, recruit, reinforce, relinquish, remove, sky, start, strengthen, sublime, suggest, terminate, up, upgrade, uplift.
antonyms debase, decrease, degrade, dismiss, lower, reduce, suppress.

rakish *adj.* abandoned, breezy, dapper, dashing, debauched, debonair, degenerate, depraved, devil-may-care, dissipated, dissolute, flamboyant, flashy, immoral, jaunty, lecherous, libertine, licentious, loose, natty, prodigal, profligate, raffish, sharp, sinful, smart, snazzy, sporty, stylish, wanton.

rally[1] *v.* assemble, bunch, cheer, cluster, collect, congregate, convene, embolden, encourage, gather, hearten, improve, marshal, mass, mobilize, muster, organize, pick up, rally round, reassemble, recover, recuperate, re-form, regroup, reorganize, revive, round up, summon, unite.
n. assembly, comeback, concourse, conference, congregation, convention, convocation, gathering, improvement, jamboree, meeting, recovery, recuperation, regrouping, renewal, reorganization, resurgence, reunion, revival, stand.

rally[2] *v.* chaff, mock, rag, rib, ridicule, send up, taunt, tease, twit.

ramble *v.* amble, babble, chatter, digress, divagate, dodder, drift, expatiate, maunder, meander, perambulate, peregrinate, range, roam, rove, saunter, snake, straggle, stravaig, stray, stroll, traipse, walk, wander, wind, zigzag.
n. divagation, excursion, hike, perambulation, peregrination, roaming, roving, saunter, stroll, tour, traipse, trip, walk.

rambling *adj.* circuitous, desultory, diffuse, digressive, disconnected, discursive, disjointed, excursive, incoherent, irregular, long-drawn-out, long-winded, periphrastic, prolix, sprawling, spreading, straggling, trailing, wordy.
antonym direct.

ramification *n.* branch, complication, consequence, development, dichotomy, divarication, division, excrescence, extension, fork, offshoot, outgrowth, ramulus, ramus, result, sequel, subdivision, upshot.

rampage *v.* rage, rant, rave, run amuck, run riot, run wild, rush, storm, tear.
n. destruction, frenzy, furore, fury, rage, storm, tempest, tumult, uproar, violence.

rampant *adj.* aggressive, dominant, epidemic, erect, excessive, exuberant, fierce, flagrant, luxuriant, outrageous, prevalent, prodigal, profuse, raging, rampaging, rank, rearing, rife, riotous, standing, unbridled, unchecked, uncontrollable, uncontrolled, ungovernable, unrestrained, upright, vehement, violent, wanton, widespread, wild.

ramshackle *adj.* broken-down, crumbling, decrepit, derelict, dilapidated, flimsy, haywire, jerry-built, rickety, shaky, tottering, tumbledown, unsafe, unsteady.
antonyms solid, stable.

rancid *adj.* bad, fetid, foul, frowsty, fusty, musty, off, putrid, rank, reasty, rotten, sour, stale, strong-smelling, tainted.
antonym sweet.

rancor *n.* acrimony, animosity, animus, antipathy, bitterness, enmity, grudge, hate, hatred, hostility, ill-feeling, ill-will, malevolence, malice, malignity, resentfulness, resentment, spite, spleen, venom, vindictiveness.

random *adj.* accidental, adventitious, aimless, arbitrary, casual, chance, desultory, fortuitous, haphazard, incidental, indiscriminate, purposeless, scattershot, spot, stray, unfocused, unplanned, unpremeditated. *antonyms* deliberate, systematic.

range *n.* amplitude, area, assortment, band, bounds, chain, class, collection, compass, confines, diapason, distance, domain, extent, field, file, gamut, kind, latitude, limits, line, lot, orbit, order, palette, parameters, province, purview, radius, raik, rank, reach, row, scale, scope, selection, sequence, series, sort, span, spectrum, sphere, string, sweep, tessitura, tier, variety.
v. aim, align, arrange, array, bracket, catalog, categorize, class, classify, cruise, direct, dispose, explore, extend, file, fluctuate, go, grade, group, level, order, pigeonhole, point, raik, ramble, rank, reach, roam, rove, run, straggle, stravaig, stray, stretch, stroll, sweep, train, traverse, wander.

rank[1] *n.* caste, class, classification, column, condition, degree, dignity, division, echelon, estate, état, file, formation, grade, group, level, line, nobility, order, position, quality, range, row, series, sort, standing, station, status, stratum, tier, type.
v. align, arrange, array, class, classify, dispose, grade, locate, marshal, order, organize, place, position, range, sort.

rank[2] *adj.* absolute, abundant, abusive, arrant, atrocious, bad, blatant, coarse, complete, crass, dense, disagreeable, disgusting, downright, egregious, excessive, extravagant, exuberant, fetid, filthy, flagrant, flourishing, foul, fusty, gamy, glaring, gross, indecent, lush, luxuriant, mephitic, musty, nasty, noisome, noxious, obscene, off, offensive, out-and-out, outrageous, productive, profuse, pungent, putrid, rampant, rancid, repulsive, revolting, scurrilous, sheer, shocking, stale, stinking, strong-smelling, thorough, thoroughgoing, total, undisguised, unmitigated, utter, vigorous, vulgar.
antonyms sparse, sweet.

ransack *v.* comb, depredate, despoil, explore, gut, loot, maraud, pillage, plunder, raid, rake, ravage, rifle, rummage, sack, scour, search, strip.

ransom *n.* deliverance, liberation, money, payment, payoff, price, redemption, release, rescue.
v. buy out, deliver, extricate, liberate, redeem, release, rescue.

rant *v.* bellow, bluster, cry, declaim, mouth it, rave, roar, shout, slang-whang, spout, vociferate, yell.
n. bluster, bombast, declamation, diatribe, fanfaronade, harangue, philippic, rhetoric, storm, tirade, vociferation.

rap *v.* bark, castigate, censure, chat, confabulate, converse, crack, criticize, discourse, flirt, hit, knock, pan, reprimand, scold, strike, talk, tap.
n. blame, blow, castigation, censure, chat, chiding, clout, colloquy, confabulation, conversation, crack, dialogue, discourse, discussion, knock, punishment, rebuke, reprimand, responsibility, sentence, talk, tap.

rapacious *adj.* avaricious, esurient, extortionate, grasping, greedy, insatiable, marauding, plundering, predatory, preying, ravening, ravenous, usurious, voracious, vulturine, vulturish, vulturous, wolfish, wolvish.

rapid *adj.* brisk, expeditious, express, fast, fleet, flying, hasty, headlong, hurried, precipitate, prompt, quick, speedy, swift, tantivy.
antonyms leisurely, slow, sluggish.

rapidity *n.* alacrity, briskness, celerity, dispatch, expedition, expeditiousness, fleetness, haste, hurry, precipitateness, promptitude, promptness, quickness, rush, speed, speediness, swiftness, velocity. *antonym* slowness.

rapids *n.* dalles, white water, wild water.

rapine *n.* depredation, despoilment, despoliation, looting, marauding, pillage, plunder, ransacking, rape, ravaging, robbery, sack, sacking, seizure, spoliation, theft.

rapport *n.* affinity, bond, compatibility, empathy, harmony, link, relationship, sympathy, understanding.

rapture *n.* beatitude, bliss, delectation, delight, ecstasy, enthusiasm, entrancement, euphoria, exaltation, felicity, happiness, joy, ravishment, rhapsody, spell, transport.

rare *adj.* admirable, choice, curious, excellent, exceptional, exquisite, extreme, few, fine, great, incomparable, infrequent, invaluable, peerless, precious, priceless, recherché, rich, scarce, singular, sparse, sporadic, strange, superb, superlative, uncommon, unusual.
antonyms abundant, common, usual.

rarely *adv.* atypically, exceptionally, extraordinarily, finely, hardly, infrequently, little, notably, remarkably, seldom, singularly, uncommonly, unusually.
antonyms frequently, often.

rascal *n.* blackguard, caitiff, cullion, devil, disgrace, good-for-nothing, hellion, imp, knave, loon, miscreant, ne'er-do-well, rake, ra(p)scallion, reprobate, rogue, scallywag, scamp, scoundrel, skeesicks, spalpeen, toe-rag, toe-ragger, varmint, villain, wastrel, wretch.

rash[1] *adj.* adventurous, audacious, brash, careless, foolhardy, harebrained, harum-scarum, hasty, headlong, headstrong, heedless, helter-skelter, hot-headed, ill-advised, ill-considered, impetuous, imprudent, impulsive, incautious, indiscreet, injudicious, insipient, madcap, precipitant, precipitate, premature, reckless, slapdash, temerarious, temerous, thoughtless, unguarded, unthinking, unwary, venturesome.
antonyms calculating, careful, considered, wary.

rash[2] *n.* epidemic, eruption, exanthem(a), flood, hives, nettlerash, outbreak, plague, pompholyx, series, spate, succession, urticaria, wave.

rashness *n.* adventurousness, audacity, brashness, carelessness, foolhardiness, hastiness, heedlessness, incaution, incautiousness, indiscretion, precipitance, precipitation, precipitency, recklessness, temerity, thoughtlessness.
antonyms carefulness, cautiousness.

rasp *n.* croak, grating, grinding, harshness, hoarseness, scrape, scratch.
v. abrade, croak, excoriate, file, grate, grind, irk, irritate, jar, rub, sand, scour, scrape.

rasping *adj.* creaking, croaking, croaky, grating, gravelly, gruff, harsh, hoarse, husky, jarring, raspy, raucous, rough, scratchy, stridulant.

rate[1] *n.* basis, charge, class, classification, cost, degree, dues, duty, fee, figure, gait, grade, hire, measure, pace, percentage, position, price, proportion, quality, rank, rating, ratio, reckoning, relation, scale, speed, standard, status, tariff, tax, tempo, time, toll, value, velocity, worth.
v. adjudge, admire, appraise, assess, class, classify, consider, count, deserve, esteem, estimate, evaluate, figure, grade, judge, measure, measure up, merit, perform, rank, reckon, regard, respect, value, weigh.

rate[2] *v.* admonish, berate, blame, castigate, censure, chide, criticize, lecture, rebuke, reprimand, reprove, roast, scold, tongue-lash, upbraid.

ratify *v.* affirm, approve, authenticate, authorize, bind, certify, confirm, corroborate, endorse, establish, homologate, legalize, recognize, sanction, sign, uphold, validate.
antonyms reject, repudiate.

rating[1] *n.* class, classification, degree, designation, estimate, evaluation, grade, grading, order, placing, position, rank, rate, sort, sorting, standing, status.

rating[2] *n.* castigation, chiding, dressing-down, lecture, rebuke, reprimand, reproof, roasting, row, scolding, telling-off, ticking-off, tongue-lashing, upbraiding, wigging.

ration *n.* allocation, allotment, allowance, amount, dole, helping, measure, part, portion, provision, quota, share.
v. allocate, allot, apportion, budget, conserve, control, deal, dispense, distribute, dole, issue, limit, mete, restrict, save, supply.

rational *adj.* balanced, cerebral, cognitive, compos mentis,

dianoetic, enlightened, intelligent, judicious, logical, lucid, normal, ratiocinative, realistic, reasonable, reasoning, sagacious, sane, sensible, sound, thinking, well-founded, well-grounded, wise.
antonyms crazy, illogical, irrational.

rationalize *v.* elucidate, excuse, extenuate, justify, reason out, reorganize, resolve, streamline, trim, vindicate.

raucous *adj.* grating, harsh, hoarse, husky, loud, noisy, rasping, rough, rusty, strident.

ravage *v.* demolish, depredate, desolate, despoil, destroy, devastate, gut, lay waste, loot, pillage, plunder, ransack, raze, ruin, sack, shatter, spoil, wreck.
n. damage, defilement, demolition, depredation, desecration, desolation, destruction, devastation, havoc, pillage, plunder, rapine, ruin, ruination, spoliation, waste, wreckage.

rave *v.* babble, declaim, fulminate, fume, harangue, rage, ramble, rant, roar, splutter, storm, thunder.
adj. ecstatic, enthusiastic, excellent, fantastic, favorable, laudatory, wonderful.

ravenous *adj.* avaricious, covetous, devouring, esurient, famished, ferocious, gluttonous, grasping, greedy, insatiable, insatiate, predatory, rapacious, ravening, starved, starving, voracious, wolfish, wolvish.

ravine *n.* arroyo, canyon, chine, clough, defile, flume, gap, gorge, grike, gulch, gully, kloof, linn, lin(n), pass.

ravish *v.* abuse, captivate, charm, deflorate, deflower, delight, enchant, enrapture, entrance, fascinate, outrage, overjoy, rape, spellbind, transport, violate.

ravishing *adj.* alluring, beautiful, bewitching, charming, dazzling, delightful, enchanting, entrancing, gorgeous, lovely, radiant, seductive, stunning.

raw *adj.* abraded, bare, basic, biting, bitter, bleak, bloody, blunt, brutal, callow, candid, chafed, chill, chilly, coarse, cold, crude, damp, frank, freezing, fresh, grazed, green, harsh, ignorant, immature, inexperienced, naked, natural, new, open, organic, piercing, plain, realistic, rough, scraped, scratched, sensitive, skinned, sore, tender, unadorned, uncooked, undisciplined, undisguised, undressed, unfinished, unpleasant, unpracticed, unprepared, unprocessed, unrefined, unripe, unseasoned, unskilled, untrained, untreated, untried, unvarnished, verdant, wet.
antonyms cooked, experienced, refined.

ray *n.* bar, beam, flash, flicker, gleam, glimmer, glint, hint, indication, scintilla, shaft, spark, stream, trace.

raze *v.* bulldoze, delete, demolish, destroy, dismantle, efface, erase, expunge, extinguish, extirpate, flatten, level, obliterate, remove, ruin. **reach** *v.* amount to, arrive at, attain, contact, drop, fall, get to, grasp, hand, land at, make, move, pass, rise, sink, stretch, strike, touch.
n. ambit, capacity, command, compass, distance, extension, extent, grasp, influence, jurisdiction, latitude, mastery, power, purview, range, scope, spread, stretch, sweep.

react *v.* acknowledge, act, answer, behave, emote, function, operate, proceed, reply, respond, work.

reaction *n.* acknowledgment, answer, antiperistasis, backwash, compensation, conservatism, counteraction, counter-balance, counterbuff, counterpoise, counter-revolution, feedback, obscurantism, recoil, reply, response, swing-back.

readable *adj.* clear, compelling, comprehensible, compulsive, decipherable, enjoyable, entertaining, enthralling, gripping, intelligible, interesting, legible, plain, pleasant, understandable, unputdownable.
antonyms illegible, unreadable.

readily *adv.* cheerfully, eagerly, easily, effortlessly, fain, freely, gladly, lief, promptly, quickly, smoothly, speedily, unhesitatingly, voluntarily, willingly.

ready *adj.* à la main, about, accessible, acute, ad manum, adroit, agreeable, alert, apt, arranged, astute, available, bright, clever, close, completed, convenient, deft, dexterous, disposed, eager, expert, facile, fit, game, glad, handy, happy, inclined, intelligent, keen, liable, likely, minded, near, on call, on tap, organized, overflowing, perceptive, predisposed, prepared, present, primed, prompt, prone, quick, quick-witted, rapid, resourceful, ripe, set, sharp, skilful, smart, willing.
antonyms unprepared, unready.
v. alert, arrange, equip, order, organize, prepare, prime, set.

real *adj.* absolute, actual, authentic, bona fide, certain, dinkum, dinky-di(e), essential, existent, factual, genuine, heartfelt, honest, intrinsic, legitimate, positive, right, rightful, simon-pure, sincere, substantial, substantive, sure-enough, tangible, thingy, true, unaffected, unfeigned, valid, veritable.
antonyms imaginary, unreal.

realization *n.* accomplishment, achievement, actualization, appreciation, apprehension, awareness, cognizance, completion, comprehension, conception, consciousness, consummation, effectuation, fulfilment, grasp, imagination, perception, recognition, understanding.

realize *v.* accomplish, achieve, acquire, actualize, appreciate, apprehend, catch on, clear, complete, comprehend, conceive, consummate, do, earn, effect, effectuate, fulfil, gain, get, grasp, imagine, implement, make, net, obtain, perform, produce, recognize, reify, take in, twig, understand.

really *adv.* absolutely, actually, assuredly, categorically, certainly, essentially, genuinely, indeed, intrinsically, positively, surely, truly, undoubtedly, verily.

realm *n.* area, bailiwick, branch, country, department, domain, dominion, empire, field, jurisdiction, kingdom, land, monarchy, orbit, principality, province, region, sphere, state, territory, world, zone.

reap *v.* acquire, collect, crop, cut, derive, gain, garner, gather, get, harvest, mow, obtain, realize, secure, win.

rear[1] *n.* back, backside, bottom, buttocks, croup, end,

hind-quarters, posterior, rearguard, rump, stern, tail. *antonym* front.
adj. aft, after, back, following, hind, hindmost, last. *antonym* front.

rear[2] *v.* breed, build, construct, cultivate, educate, elevate, erect, fabricate, foster, grow, hoist, lift, loom, nurse, nurture, parent, raise, rise, soar, tower, train.

reason *n.* aim, apologia, apology, apprehension, argument, basis, bounds, brains, case, cause, common sense, comprehension, consideration, defense, design, end, excuse, explanation, exposition, goal, ground, grounds, gumption, impetus, incentive, inducement, intellect, intention, judgment, justification, limits, logic, mentality, mind, moderation, motive, nous, object, occasion, propriety, purpose, ratiocination, rationale, rationality, reasonableness, reasoning, sanity, sense, sensibleness, soundness, target, understanding, vindication, warrant, wisdom.
v. conclude, deduce, infer, intellectualize, ratiocinate, resolve, solve, syllogize, think, work out.

reasonable *adj.* acceptable, advisable, arguable, average, believable, credible, equitable, fair, fit, honest, inexpensive, intelligent, judicious, just, justifiable, logical, moderate, modest, OK, passable, plausible, possible, practical, proper, rational, reasoned, right, sane, satisfactory, sensible, sober, sound, tenable, tolerable, viable, well-advised, well-thought-out, wise.
antonyms crazy, extravagant, irrational, outrageous, unreasonable.

rebel *v.* defy, disobey, dissent, flinch, kick over the traces, mutiny, recoil, resist, revolt, rise up, run riot, shrink.
n. apostate, dissenter, heretic, insurgent, insurrectionary, Jacobin, malcontent, mutineer, nonconformist, revolutionary, revolutionist, schismatic, secessionist.
adj. insubordinate, insurgent, insurrectionary, malcontent(ed), mutinous, rebellious, revolutionary.

rebellion *n.* apostasy, defiance, disobedience, dissent, heresy, insubordination, insurgence, insurgency, insurrection, Jacquerie, mutiny, nonconformity, resistance, revolt, revolution, rising, schism, uprising.

rebellious *adj.* contumacious, defiant, difficult, disaffected, disloyal, disobedient, disorderly, incorrigible, insubordinate, insurgent, insurrectionary, intractable, malcontent(ed), mutinous, obstinate, rebel, recalcitrant, refractory, resistant, revolutionary, seditious, turbulent, ungovernable, unmanageable, unruly.
antonyms obedient, submissive.

rebirth *n.* reactivation, reanimation, regeneration, reincarnation, rejuvenation, renaissance, renascence, renewal, restoration, resurgence, resurrection, revitalization, revival.

rebuff *v.* cold-shoulder, cut, decline, deny, discourage, put someone's nose out of joint, refuse, reject, repulse, resist, slight, snub, spurn, turn down.
n. brush-off, check, cold shoulder, defeat, denial, discouragement, flea in one's ear, noser, opposition, refusal, rejection, repulse, rubber, set-down, slight, snub.

rebuild *v.* reassemble, reconstruct, re-edify, refashion, remake, remodel, renovate, restore.
antonyms demolish, destroy.

rebuke *v.* admonish, berate, blame, carpet, castigate, censure, chide, countercheck, jobe, keelhaul, lecture, lesson, rate, reprehend, reprimand, reproach, reprove, scold, slap down, tell off, tick off, trim, trounce, upbraid.
antonyms compliment, praise.
n. admonition, blame, castigation, censure, countercheck, dressing-down, lecture, reprimand, reproach, reproof, reproval, row, slap, telling-off, ticking-off, tongue-lashing, wigging. *antonyms* compliment, praise.

rebuttal *n.* confutation, defeat, disproof, invalidation, negation, overthrow, refutation.

recall *v.* abjure, annul, cancel, cast one's mind back, countermand, evoke, mind, nullify, place, recognize, recollect, remember, repeal, rescind, retract, revoke, withdraw.
n. abrogation, annulment, cancellation, memory, nullification, recision, recollection, remembrance, repeal, rescission, retraction, revocation, withdrawal.

recapitulate *v.* give a resumé, recap, recount, reiterate, repeat, restate, review, summarize.

recede *v.* abate, decline, decrease, diminish, dwindle, ebb, fade, lessen, regress, retire, retreat, retrogress, return, shrink, sink, slacken, subside, wane, withdraw.
antonyms advance, proceed.

receive *v.* accept, accommodate, acquire, admit, apprehend, bear, collect, derive, encounter, entertain, experience, gather, get, greet, hear, meet, obtain, perceive, pick up, react to, respond to, suffer, sustain, take, undergo, welcome.
antonyms donate, give.

recent *adj.* contemporary, current, fresh, late, latter, latter-day, modern, neoteric(al), new, novel, present-day, up-to-date, young.
antonyms dated, old, out-of-date.

reception *n.* acceptance, acknowledgment, admission, do, durbar, entertainment, function, greeting, levee, party, reaction, receipt, receiving, recipience, recognition, response, shindig, soirée, treatment, welcome.

recess *n.* alcove, apse, apsidiole, bay, break, cavity, cessation, closure, corner, depression, embrasure, holiday, hollow, indentation, intermission, interval, loculus, niche, nook, oriel, respite, rest, vacation.

recession *n.* decline, depression, downturn, slump, stagflation.
antonyms boom, upturn.

recipe *n.* directions, formula, ingredients, instructions, method, prescription, procedure, process, program, receipt, system, technique.

recital *n.* account, convert, description, detailing, enumeration, interpretation, narration, narrative, performance, reading, recapitulation, recitation, rehearsal, relation, rendering, rendition, repetition, statement, story, tale, telling.

recite *v.* articulate, declaim, deliver, describe, detail, enumerate, itemize, narrate, orate, perform, recapitulate, recount, rehearse, relate, repeat, speak, tell.

reckless *adj.* careless, daredevil, devil-may-care, foolhardy, harebrained, hasty, headlong, heedless, ill-advised, imprudent, inattentive, incautious, indiscreet, irresponsible, madcap, mindless, negligent, precipitate, rantipole, rash, regardless, tearaway, thoughtless, wild.
antonyms calculating, careful, cautious.

recklessness *n.* carelessness, foolhardiness, gallowsness, heedlessness, imprudence, inattention, incaution, irresponsibleness, irresponsibility, madness, mindlessness, negligence, rashness, thoughtlessness.
antonym carefulness.

reckon *v.* account, add up, adjudge, appraise, assess, assume, believe, calculate, compute, conjecture, consider, count, deem, enumerate, esteem, estimate, evaluate, expect, fancy, gauge, guess, hold, imagine, judge, number, opine, rate, regard, suppose, surmise, tally, think, total.

reclaim *v.* impolder, recapture, recover, redeem, reform, regain, regenerate, reinstate, rescue, restore, retrieve, salvage.

recline *v.* couch, lean, lie, loll, lounge, repose, rest, sprawl, stretch out.

recluse *n.* anchoress, anchoret, anchorite, ancress, ascetic, eremite, hermit, monk, solitaire, solitarian, solitary, stylite.

recognize *v.* accept, acknowledge, admit, allow, appreciate, approve, avow, concede, confess, grant, greet, honor, identify, know, notice, own, perceive, place, realize, recall, recollect, remember, respect, salute, see, spot, understand, wot.

recollect *v.* call up, cast one's mind back, mind, place, recall, remember, reminisce.

recollection *n.* image, impression, memory, recall, remembrance, reminiscence, souvenir.

recommend *v.* advance, advise, advocate, approve, commend, counsel, endorse, enjoin, exhort, plug, praise, propose, puff, suggest, urge, vouch for.
antonyms disapprove, veto.

recommendation *n.* advice, advocacy, approbation, approval, blessing, commendation, counsel, endorsement, plug, praise, proposal, puff, reference, sanction, suggestion, testimonial, urging.
antonyms disapproval, veto.

reconcile *v.* accept, accommodate, accord, adjust, appease, compose, conciliate, harmonize, pacify, placate, propitiate, rectify, resign, resolve, reunite, settle, square, submit, yield.
antonym estrange.

recondition *v.* fix, overhaul, refurbish, remodel, renew, renovate, repair, restore, revamp, sort.

reconsider *v.* modify, reassess, re-examine, rethink, review, revise, think better of, think over, think twice.

record *n.* account, album, annals, archives, background, career, chronicle, curriculum vitae, diary, disc, document, documentation, dossier, entry, EP, evidence, file, form, forty-five, gramophone record, history, journal, log, LP, memoir, memorandum, memorial, minute, noctuary, performance, platter, recording, register, release, remembrance, report, single, talkie, testimony, trace, tracing, track record, witness.
v. annalize, chalk up, chronicle, contain, cut, diarize, document, enregister, enrol, enter, indicate, inscribe, log, minute, note, preserve, read, register, report, say, score, show, tape, tape-record, transcribe, video, videotape, wax.

recount *v.* communicate, delineate, depict, describe, detail, enumerate, narrate, portray, recite, rehearse, relate, repeat, report, tell.

recoup *v.* compensate, indemnify, make good, recover, redeem, refund, regain, reimburse, remunerate, repay, requite, retrieve, satisfy.

recover *v.* convalesce, heal, improve, mend, pick up, pull through, rally, recapture, reclaim, recoup, recuperate, redeem, regain, repair, replevy, repossess, restore, retake, retrieve, revive.
antonyms forfeit, lose, worsen.

recreation *n.* amusement, distraction, diversion, enjoyment, entertainment, exercise, fun, games, hobby, leisure activity, pastime, play, pleasure, refreshment, relaxation, relief, sport.

recrimination *n.* accusation, bickering, counter-attack, counterblast, countercharge, name-calling, quarrel, retaliation, retort, squabbling.

recruit *v.* augment, draft, engage, enlist, enrol, gather, headhunt, impress, levy, mobilize, muster, obtain, procure, proselytize, raise, refresh, reinforce, renew, replenish, restore, strengthen, supply, trawl.
n. apprentice, beginner, conscript, convert, draftee, green-horn, helper, initiate, learner, neophyte, novice, proselyte, rookie, trainee, tyro, yob.

recuperate *v.* convalesce, get better, improve, mend, pick up, rally, recoup, recover, regain, revive.
antonym worsen.

recur *v.* persist, reappear, repeat, return.

redeem *v.* absolve, acquit, atone for, cash (in), change, compensate for, defray, deliver, discharge, emancipate, exchange, extricate, free, fulfil, keep, liberate, make good, make up for, meet, offset, outweigh, perform, ransom, reclaim, recoup, recover, recuperate, redress, regain, rehabilitate, reinstate, repossess, repurchase, rescue, retrieve, salvage, satisfy, save, trade in.

redolent *adj.* aromatic, evocative, fragrant, odorous, perfumed, remindful, reminiscent, scented, suggestive, sweet-smelling.

reduce *v.* abate, abridge, bankrupt, break, cheapen, conquer, contract, curtail, cut, debase, decimate, decrease,

degrade, demote, deoxidate, deoxidize, depress, diet, dilute, diminish, discount, downgrade, drive, force, humble, humiliate, impair, impoverish, lessen, lower, master, moderate, overpower, pauperize, rebate, ruin, scant, shorten, slake, slash, slenderize, slim, subdue, trim, truncate, vanquish, weaken.
antonyms boost, fatten, increase, upgrade.

reduction *n.* abbreviation, abridgment, abstraction, alleviation, attenuation, compression, condensation, constriction, contraction, curtailment, cut, cutback, decline, decrease, deduction, degradation, demotion, deoxidation, deoxidization, deposal, depreciation, devaluation, diminution, discount, drop, easing, ellipsis, limitation, loss, miniature, mitigation, moderation, modification, muffling, muting, narrowing, rebate, rebatement, refund, restriction, shortening, shrinkage, slackening, softening, subtraction, summarization, summary, syncope.
antonyms enlargement, improvement, increase.

redundant *adj.* de trop, diffuse, excessive, extra, inessential, inordinate, padded, periphrastic, pleonastical, prolix, repetitious, supererogatory, superfluous, supernumerary, surplus, tautological, unemployed, unnecessary, unneeded, unwanted, verbose, wordy.
antonyms concise, essential, necessary.

reek *v.* exhale, fume, hum, pong, smell, smoke, stink.
n. effluvium, exhalation, fetor, fume(s), malodor, mephitis, odor, pong, smell, smoke, stench, stink, vapor.

refer *v.* accredit, adduce, advert, allude, apply, ascribe, assign, attribute, belong, cite, commit, concern, consign, consult, credit, deliver, direct, go, guide, hint, impute, invoke, look up, mention, pertain, point, recommend, relate, send, speak of, submit, touch on, transfer, turn to.

referee *n.* adjudicator, arbiter, arbitrator, arbitratrix, arbitress, judge, ref, umpire.
v. adjudicate, arbitrate, judge, ref, umpire.

reference *n.* allusion, applicability, bearing, certification, character, citation, concern, connection, consideration, credentials, endorsement, illustration, instance, mention, note, quotation, recommendation, regard, relation, remark, respect, testimonial.

refine *v.* chasten, civilize, clarify, cultivate, distil, elevate, exalt, filter, hone, improve, perfect, polish, process, purify, rarefy, spiritualize, sublimize, subtilize, temper.

refined *adj.* Attic, Augustan, civil, civilized, clarified, clean, courtly, cultivated, cultured, delicate, discerning, discriminating, distilled, elegant, exact, fastidious, filtered, fine, genteel, gentlemanly, gracious, ladylike, nice, polished, polite, precise, processed, punctilious, pure, purified, sensitive, sophisticated, sublime, subtle, urbane, well-bred, well-mannered.
antonyms brutish, coarse, earthy, rude, vulgar.

refinement *n.* breeding, chastity, civilization, civility, clarification, cleansing, courtesy, courtliness, cultivation, culture, delicacy, discrimination, distillation, elegance, fastidiousness, filtering, fineness, finesse, finish, gentility, grace, graciousness, manners, nicety, nuance, polish, politeness, politesse, precision, processing, purification, rarefaction, rectification, sophistication, style, subtlety, taste, urbanity.
antonyms coarseness, earthiness, vulgarity.

reflect *v.* bespeak, cogitate, communicate, consider, contemplate, deliberate, demonstrate, display, echo, evince, exhibit, express, imitate, indicate, manifest, meditate, mirror, mull (over), muse, ponder, reproduce, return, reveal, ruminate, show, think, wonder.

reflection *n.* aspersion, censure, cerebration, cogitation, consideration, contemplation, counterpart, criticism, deliberation, derogation, echo, idea, image, impression, imputation, meditation, musing, observation, opinion, pondering, reflex, reproach, rumination, slur, study, thinking, thought, view.

reform *v.* ameliorate, amend, better, correct, emend, improve, mend, purge, rebuild, reclaim, reconstitute, reconstruct, rectify, regenerate, rehabilitate, remodel, renovate, reorganize, repair, restore, revamp, revolutionize.
n. amelioration, amendment, betterment, correction, improvement, purge, rectification, rehabilitation, renovation, shake-out.

refractory *adj.* balky, cantankerous, contentious, contumacious, difficult, disobedient, disputatious, headstrong, intractable, mulish, obstinate, perverse, recalcitrant, resistant, restive, stubborn, uncontrollable, unco-operative, unmanageable, unruly, wilful.
antonyms co-operative, malleable, obedient.

refrain[1] *v.* abstain, avoid, cease, desist, eschew, forbear, leave off, quit, renounce, stop, swear off.

refrain[2] *n.* burden, chorus, epistrophe, falderal, melody, song, tune, undersong, wheel.

refresh *v.* brace, cheer, cool, energize, enliven, freshen, inspirit, jog, prod, prompt, reanimate, reinvigorate, rejuvenate, renew, renovate, repair, replenish, restore, revitalize, revive, revivify, stimulate.
antonyms exhaust, tire.

refreshing *adj.* bracing, cooling, different, energizing, fresh, inspiriting, invigorating, new, novel, original, refrigerant, restorative, revivifying, stimulating, thirst-quenching.
antonyms exhausting, tiring.

refreshment *n.* enlivenment, freshening, reanimation, reinvigoration, renewal, renovation, repair, restoration, revitalization, revival, stimulation.

refuge *n.* asylum, bolthole, funk-hole, harbor, haven, hide-away, hideout, holt, protection, resort, retreat, sanctuary, security, shelter.

refuse[1] *v.* decline, deny, nay-say, reject, repel, repudiate, spurn, withhold.
antonyms accept, allow.

refuse[2] *n.* chaff, dregs, dross, excrementa, garbage, hogwash, husks, junk, lag(s), landfill, leavings, lees, left-overs, litter, mullock, offscourings, rejectamenta, riddlings, rubbish, scum, sediment, slops, sordes, sullage, sweepings, tailings, trash, waste, wastrel.

refute *v.* confute, counter, discredit, disprove, give the lie to, negate, overthrow, rebut, silence.

regain *v.* reattain, recapture, reclaim, recoup, recover, redeem, re-establish, repossess, retake, retrieve, return to.

regal *adj.* kingly, magnificent, majestic, monarch(i)al, monarchic(al), noble, princely, proud, queenly, royal, sovereign, stately.

regale *v.* amuse, captivate, delight, divert, entertain, fascinate, feast, gratify, ply, refresh, serve.

regard *v.* account, adjudge, attend, behold, believe, concern, consider, deem, esteem, estimate, eye, heed, hold, imagine, interest, judge, mark, mind, note, notice, observe, pertain to, rate, relate to, remark, respect, scrutinize, see, suppose, think, treat, value, view, watch.
antonyms despise, disregard.
n. account, advertence, advertency, affection, aspect, attachment, attention, bearing, care, concern, connection, consideration, deference, detail, esteem, feature, gaze, glance, heed, honor, item, look, love, matter, mind, note, notice, particular, point, reference, relation, relevance, reputation, repute, respect, scrutiny, stare, store, sympathy, thought.
antonyms contempt, disapproval, disregard.

regardless *adj.* disregarding, heedless, inattentive, inconsiderate, indifferent, neglectful, negligent, nonchalant, rash, reckless, remiss, uncaring, unconcerned, unmindful.
antonyms attentive, heedful, regardful.
adv. anyhow, anyway, come what may, despite everything, in any case, nevertheless, no matter what, nonetheless, willy-nilly.

regards *n.* compliments, devoirs, greetings, respects, salutations.

regenerate *v.* change, inspirit, invigorate, reawaken, reconstitute, reconstruct, re-establish, refresh, reinvigorate, rejuvenate, renew, renovate, reproduce, restore, revive, revivify, uplift.

regime *n.* administration, command, control, establishment, government, leadership, management, reign, rule, system.

regimented *adj.* controlled, co-ordinated, disciplined, methodical, ordered, organized, regulated, severe, standardized, stern, strict, systematic.
antonyms disorganized, free, lax, loose.

region *n.* area, clime, country, district, division, domain, expanse, field, land, locality, neighborhood, part, place, province, quarter, range, realm, scope, section, sector, sphere, terrain, terrene, territory, tract, vicinity, world, zone.

register *n.* almanac, annals, archives, catalog, chronicle, diary, file, ledger, list, log, matricula, memorandum, notitia, record, roll, roster, schedule.
v. bespeak, betray, catalog, chronicle, display, enlist, enrol, enter, exhibit, express, indicate, inscribe, list, log, manifest, mark, note, read, record, reflect, reveal, say, score, show, sign on.

regress *v.* backslide, degenerate, deteriorate, ebb, lapse, recede, relapse, retreat, retrocede, retrogress, return, revert, wane.
antonym progress.

regret *v.* bemoan, bewail, deplore, grieve, lament, miss, mourn, repent, rue, sorrow.
n. bitterness, compunction, contrition, disappointment, grief, lamentation, penitence, remorse, repentance, ruefulness, self-reproach, shame, sorrow.

regrettable *adj.* deplorable, disappointing, distressing, ill-advised, lamentable, pitiable, sad, shameful, sorry, unfortunate, unhappy, unlucky, woeful, wrong.
antonyms fortunate, happy.

regular *adj.* approved, balanced, bona fide, classic, common, commonplace, consistent, constant, consuetudinary, conventional, correct, customary, daily, dependable, efficient, established, even, everyday, fixed, flat, formal, habitual, level, methodical, normal, official, ordered, orderly, ordinary, orthodox, periodic, prevailing, proper, rhythmic, routine, sanctioned, set, smooth, standard, standardized, stated, steady, straight, symmetrical, systematic, time-honored, traditional, typical, uniform, unvarying, usual.
antonyms irregular, sporadic, unconventional.

regulate *v.* adjust, administer, arrange, balance, conduct, control, direct, fit, govern, guide, handle, manage, moderate, modulate, monitor, order, organize, oversee, regiment, rule, run, settle, square, superintend, supervise, systematize, tune.

regulation *n.* adjustment, administration, arrangement, commandment, control, decree, dictate, direction, edict, governance, government, law, management, modulation, order, ordinance, precept, prodecure, regimentation, requirement, rule, statute, supervision, tuning.
adj. accepted, customary, mandatory, normal, official, prescribed, required, standard, stock, usual.

rehabilitate *v.* adjust, clear, convert, mend, normalize, rebuild, recondition, reconstitute, reconstruct, redeem, redintegrate, re-establish, reform, reinstate, reintegrate, reinvigorate, renew, renovate, restore, save.

rehearse *v.* act, delineate, depict, describe, detail, drill, enumerate, list, narrate, practice, prepare, ready, recite, recount, relate, repeat, review, run through, spell out, study, tell, train, trot out.

reign *n.* ascendancy, command, control, dominion, empire, hegemony, influence, monarchy, power, rule, sovereignty, supremacy, sway.
v. administer, authority, command, govern, influence, kingship, obtain, predominate, prevail, rule.

reimburse *v.* compensate, indemnify, recompense, refund, remunerate, repay, requite, restore, return, square up.

rein *n.* brake, bridle, check, check-rein, control, curb, harness, hold, overcheck, restraint, restriction.
v. arrest, bridle, check, control, curb, halt, hold, hold back, limit, restrain, restrict, stop.

reinforce *v.* augment, bolster, buttress, emphasize, fortify, harden, increase, prop, recruit, steel, stiffen, strengthen, stress, supplement, support, toughen, underline.
antonyms undermine, weaken.

reiterate *v.* ding, iterate, recapitulate, repeat, resay, restate, retell.

reject *v.* athetize, condemn, decline, deny, despise, disallow, discard, eliminate, exclude, explode, jettison, jilt, pip, rebuff, refuse, renounce, repel, reprobate, repudiate, repulse, scrap, spike, spurn, veto.
antonyms accept, select.
n. cast-off, discard, failure, second.

rejection *n.* athetesis, brush-off, dear John letter, denial, dismissal, elimination, exclusion, rebuff, refusal, renunciation, repudiation, veto.
antonyms acceptance, selection.

rejoice *v.* celebrate, delight, exult, glory, joy, jubilate, revel, triumph.

rejuvenate *v.* reanimate, recharge, refresh, regenerate, reinvigorate, rekindle, renew, restore, revitalize, revivify.

relapse *v.* backslide, degenerate, deteriorate, fade, fail, lapse, regress, retrogress, revert, sicken, sink, weaken, worsen.
n. backsliding, deterioration, hypostrophe, lapse, recidivism, recurrence, regression, retrogression, reversion, setback, weakening, worsening.

relate *v.* ally, appertain, apply, associate, chronicle, concern, connect, co-ordinate, correlate, couple, describe, detail, empathize, feel for, identify with, impart, join, link, narrate, pertain, present, recite, recount, refer, rehearse, report, sympathize, tell, understand.

relation *n.* account, affiliation, affine, affinity, agnate, agnation, application, bearing, bond, comparison, connection, consanguinity, correlation, description, german, interdependence, kin, kindred, kinship, kinsman, kinswoman, link, narration, narrative, pertinence, propinquity, recital, recountal, reference, regard, relationship, relative, report, sib, similarity, story, tale, tie-in.

relationship *n.* affaire, association, bond, communications, conjunction, connection, contract, correlation, dealings, exchange, intercourse, kinship, liaison, link, parallel, proportion, rapport, ratio, similarity, tie-up.

relative *adj.* allied, applicable, apposite, appropriate, appurtenant, apropos, associated, comparative, connected, contingent, correlative, corresponding, dependent, germane, interrelated, pertinent, proportionate, reciprocal, related, relevant, respective.
n. cognate, connection, german, kinsman, kinswoman, relation, sib.

relatively *adv.* comparatively, fairly, quite, rather, somewhat.

relax *v.* abate, diminish, disinhibit, ease, ebb, lessen, loosen, lower, mitigate, moderate, reduce, relieve, remit, rest, slacken, soften, tranquilize, unbend, unclench, unwind, weaken.
antonyms intensify, tighten.

relaxation *n.* abatement, amusement, délassement, détente, diminution, disinhibition, distraction, easing, emollition, enjoyment, entertainment, fun, leisure, lessening, let-up, moderation, pleasure, recreation, reduction, refreshment, rest, slackening, weakening.
antonyms intensification, tension.

relaxed *adj.* calm, carefree, casual, collected, composed, cool, down-beat, easy-going, even-tempered, happy-go-lucky, informal, insouciant, laid-back, mellow, mild, nonchalant, placid, serene, together, tranquil, unhurried.
antonyms edgy, nervous, stiff, tense, uptight.

release *v.* absolve, acquit, break, circulate, declassify, decontrol, deliver, discage, discharge, disengage, disenthral, disimprison, disinhibit, disoblige, dispense, disprison, disseminate, distribute, drop, emancipate, exempt, excuse, exonerate, extricate, free, furlough, issue, launch, liberate, loose, manumit, present, publish, unbind, uncage, unchain, undo, unfasten, unfetter, unhand, unleash, unloose, unmew, unpen, unshackle, untie, unveil.
antonyms check, detain.
n. absolution, acquittal, acquittance, announcement, deliverance, delivery, discharge, disimprisonment, disinhibition, dispensation, emancipation, exemption, exoneration, freedom, issue, let-off, liberation, liberty, manumission, offering, proclamation, publication, quittance, relief.
antonym detention.

relegate *v.* assign, banish, consign, delegate, demote, deport, dispatch, downgrade, eject, entrust, exile, expatriate, expel, refer, transfer.
antonym promote.

relent *v.* acquiesce, capitulate, drop, ease, fall, forbear, give in, melt, relax, slacken, slow, soften, unbend, weaken, yield.

relentless *adj.* cruel, fierce, grim, hard, harsh, implacable, incessant, inexorable, inflexible, merciless, nonstop, persistent, pitiless, punishing, remorseless, ruthless, stern, sustained, unabated, unbroken, uncompromising, undeviating, unfaltering, unflagging, unforgiving, unrelenting, unrelieved, unremitting, unstoppable, unyielding.
antonyms submissive, yielding.

relevant *adj.* ad rem, admissible, applicable, apposite, appropriate, appurtenant, apt, congruous, fitting, germane, material, pertinent, proper, related, relative, significant, suitable, suited.
antonym irrelevant.

reliable *adj.* certain, constant, copper-bottomed,

dependable, faithful, honest, predictable, regular, responsible, safe, solid, sound, stable, staunch, sure, true, trustworthy, trusty, unfailing, upright, white.
antonyms doubtful, suspect, unreliable, untrustworthy.

reliance *n.* assurance, belief, confidence, credence, credit, dependence, faith, trust.

relic *n.* fragment, keepsake, memento, potsherd, remembrance, remnant, scrap, souvenir, survival, token, trace, vestige.

relief *n.* abatement, aid, alleviation, assistance, assuagement, balm, break, breather, comfort, cure, deliverance, diversion, ease, easement, help, let-up, load off one's mind, mitigation, palliation, refreshment, relaxation, release, remedy, remission, respite, rest, solace, succor, support, sustenance.

relieve *v.* abate, aid, alleviate, appease, assist, assuage, break, brighten, calm, comfort, console, cure, deliver, diminish, discharge, disembarrass, disencumber, dull, ease, exempt, free, help, interrupt, lighten, mitigate, mollify, palliate, relax, release, salve, slacken, soften, solace, soothe, spell, stand in for, substitute for, succor, support, sustain, take over from, take the place of, unburden, vary.
antonyms aggravate, intensify.

religious *adj.* church-going, conscientious, devotional, devout, divine, doctrinal, exact, faithful, fastidious, God-fearing, godly, holy, meticulous, pious, punctilious, pure, reverent, righteous, rigid, rigorous, sacred, scriptural, scrupulous, sectarian, spiritual, strict, theological, unerring, unswerving.
antonyms irreligious, lax, ungodly.

relinquish *n.* abandon, abdicate, cede, desert, discard, drop, forgo, forsake, hand over, leave, quit, release, renounce, repudiate, resign, surrender, vacate, waive, yield.
antonyms keep, retain.

relish *v.* appreciate, degust, enjoy, fancy, lap up, like, prefer, revel in, savor, taste.
n. appetizer, appetite, appreciation, condiment, enjoyment, fancy, flavor, fondness, gout, gusto, liking, love, partiality, penchant, piquancy, predilection, sauce, savor, seasoning, smack, spice, stomach, tang, taste, trace, zest.

reluctance *n.* aversion, backwardness, disinclination, dislike, distaste, hesitancy, indisposition, loathing, recalcitrance, repugnance, unwillingness.
antonyms eagerness, willingness.

reluctant *adj.* averse, backward, disinclined, grudging, hesitant, indisposed, loath, loathful, loth, recalcitrant, renitent, slow, squeamish, unenthusiastic, unwilling.
antonyms eager, willing.

rely *v.* bank, bet, count, depend, lean, reckon, swear by, trust.

remain *v.* abide, bide, cling, continue, delay, dwell, endure, last, linger, persist, prevail, rest, sojourn, stand, stay, survive, tarry, wait.
antonyms depart, go, leave.

remainder *n.* balance, dregs, excess, leavings, remanent, remanet, remnant, residuum, rest, surplus, trace, vestige(s).

remains *n.* ashes, balance, body, cadaver, carcass, corpse, crumbs, debris, detritus, dregs, fragments, leavings, leftovers, oddments, pieces, relics, reliquiae, remainder, remnants, residue, rest, scraps, traces, vestiges.

remark *v.* animadvert, comment, declare, espy, heed, mark, mention, note, notice, observe, perceive, reflect, regard, say, see, state.
n. acknowledgment, assertion, attention, comment, consideration, declaration, heed, mention, notice, observation, opinion, recognition, reflection, regard, say, statement, thought, utterance, word.

remarkable *adj.* amazing, conspicuous, distinguished, exceptional, extraordinary, famous, impressive, miraculous, notable, noteworthy, odd, outstanding, phenomenal, pre-eminent, prominent, rare, signal, singular, strange, striking, surprising, unco, uncommon, unusual, wonderful.
antonyms average, commonplace, ordinary.

remedy *n.* antidote, corrective, counteractive, countermeasure, cure, magistery, medicament, medicine, nostrum, panacea, physic, prescript, redress, relief, restorative, solution, specific, therapy, treatment.
v. alleviate, ameliorate, assuage, control, correct, counteract, cure, ease, fix, heal, help, mitigate, palliate, put right, rectify, redress, reform, relieve, repair, restore, solve, soothe, treat.

remember *v.* commemorate, place, recall, recognize, recollect, reminisce, retain, summon up, think back.
antonym forget.

remembrance *n.* anamnesis, commemoration, keepsake, memento, memorial, memory, mind, monument, recall, recognition, recollection, recordation, regard, relic, remembrancer, reminder, reminiscence, retrospect, souvenir, testimonial, thought, token.

remiss *adj.* careless, culpable, delinquent, derelict, dilatory, fainéant, forgetful, heedless, inattentive, indifferent, lackadaisical, lax, neglectful, negligent, regardless, slack, slipshod, sloppy, slothful, slow, tardy, thoughtless, unmindful.
antonyms careful, scrupulous.

remit *v.* abate, alleviate, cancel, decrease, defer, delay, desist, desist from, diminish, dispatch, dwindle, forbear, forward, halt, mail, mitigate, moderate, post, postpone, put back, reduce, relax, repeal, rescind, send, send back, shelve, sink, slacken, soften, stop, suspend, transfer, transmit, wane, weaken.
n. authorization, brief, guidelines, instructions, orders, responsibility, scope, terms of reference.

remittance *n.* allowance, consideration, dispatch, fee, payment, sending.

remnant *n.* balance, bit, end, fent, fragment, hangover, leftovers, piece, remainder, remains, remane(n)t, residue, residuum, rest, rump, scrap, shred, survival, trace, vestige.

remonstrate *v.* argue, challenge, complain, dispute, dissent, expostulate, gripe, object, protest.

remorse *n.* anguish, bad conscience, compassion, compunction, contrition, grief, guilt, penitence, pity, regret, repentance, ruefulness, ruth, self-reproach, shame, sorrow.

remorseless *adj.* callous, cruel, hard, hard-hearted, harsh, implacable, inexorable, inhumane, merciless, pitiless, relentless, ruthless, savage, stern, undeviating, unforgiving, unmerciful, unrelenting, unremitting, unstoppable.
antonyms remorseful, sorry.

remote *adj.* abstracted, alien, aloof, backwoods, cold, detached, distant, doubtful, dubious, extraneous, extrinsic, faint, far, faraway, far-off, foreign, god-forsaken, immaterial, implausible, inaccessible, inconsiderable, indifferent, introspective, introverted, irrelevant, isolated, lonely, meager, negligible, outlying, out-of-the-way, outside, poor, removed, reserved, secluded, slender, slight, slim, small, standoffish, unconnected, uninterested, uninvolved, unlikely, unrelated, withdrawn.
antonyms adjacent, close, nearby, significant.

remove *v.* ablate, abolish, abstract, amove, amputate, assassinate, delete, depart, depose, detach, dethrone, discharge, dislodge, dismiss, displace, doff, efface, eject, eliminate, erase, execute, expunge, extract, flit, flit (move house), guy, kill, liquidate, move, murder, oust, purge, quit, relegate, relocate, shave, shear, shed, shift, sideline, strike, subduct, transfer, transmigrate, transport, unseat, vacate, withdraw.

remuneration *n.* compensation, earnings, emolument, fee, guerdon, income, indemnity, pay, payment, profit, recompense, reimbursement, remittance, reparation, repayment, retainer, return, reward, salary, stipend, wages.

render *v.* act, cede, clarify, construe, contribute, deliver, depict, display, do, evince, exchange, exhibit, explain, furnish, give, give back, give up, hand over, interpret, leave, make, make up, manifest, melt, pay, perform, play, portray, present, provide, put, relinquish, repay, represent, reproduce, restate, restore, return, show, show forth, submit, supply, surrender, swap, tender, trade, transcribe, translate, yield.

rendition *n.* arrangement, construction, delivery, depiction, execution, explanation, interpretation, metaphrase, metaphrasis, performance, portrayal, presentation, reading, rendering, transcription, translation, version.

renegade *n.* apostate, backslider, betrayer, defector, deserter, dissident, mutineer, outlaw, rebel, recreant, renegado, renegate, runaway, tergiversator, traitor, turncoat.
antonyms adherent, disciple, follower.
adj. apostate, backsliding, disloyal, dissident, mutinous, outlaw, perfidious, rebel, rebellious, recreant, runaway, traitorous, unfaithful.

renege *v.* apostatize, cross the floor, default, renegue, renig, repudiate, welsh.

renew *v.* continue, extend, mend, modernize, overhaul, prolong, reaffirm, recommence, recreate, re-establish, refashion, refit, refresh, refurbish, regenerate, rejuvenate, remodel, renovate, reopen, repair, repeat, replace, replenish, restate, restock, restore, resume, revitalize, transform.

renounce *v.* abandon, abdicate, abjure, abnegate, decline, deny, discard, disclaim, disown, disprofess, eschew, forgo, forsake, forswear, put away, quit, recant, reject, relinquish, repudiate, resign, spurn.

renovate *v.* do up, furbish, improve, modernize, overhaul, recondition, reconstitute, recreate, refit, reform, refurbish, rehabilitate, remodel, renew, repair, restore, revamp.

renown *n.* acclaim, celebrity, distinction, eminence, fame, glory, honor, illustriousness, kudos, luster, mark, note, reputation, repute, stardom.
antonyms anonymity, obscurity.

renowned *adj.* acclaimed, celebrated, distinguished, eminent, esteemed, famed, famous, illustrious, notable, noted, pre-eminent, supereminent, well-known.
antonyms anonymous, obscure, unknown.

rent[1] *n.* fee, gale, hire, lease, payment, rental, tariff.
v. charter, farm out, hire, lease, let, sublet, take.

rent[2] *n.* breach, break, chink, cleavage, crack, dissension, disunion, division, flaw, gash, hole, opening, perforation, rift, rip, rupture, schism, slash, slit, split, tear.

repair[1] *v.* debug, fix, heal, mend, patch up, recover, rectify, redress, renew, renovate, restore, retrieve, square.
n. adjustment, condition, darn, fettle, form, improvement, mend, nick, overhaul, patch, restoration, shape, state.

repair[2] *v.* go, wend one's way, move, remove, resort, retire, turn, withdraw.

repartee *n.* badinage, banter, jesting, persiflage, pleasantry, raillery, riposte, sally, waggery, wit, witticism, wittiness, wordplay.

repast *n.* collation, feed, food, meal, nourishment, refection, snack, spread, victuals.

repeal *v.* abolish, abrogate, annul, cancel, countermand, invalidate, nullify, quash, recall, rescind, reverse, revoke, set aside, void, withdraw.
antonyms enact, establish.
n. abolition, abrogation, annulment, cancellation, invalidation, nullification, quashing, rescinding, rescindment, rescission, reversal, revocation, withdrawal.
antonyms enactment, establishment.

repeat *v.* duplicate, echo, iterate, quote, rebroadcast, recapitulate, recite, re-do, rehearse, reiterate, relate, renew, replay, reproduce, rerun, reshow, restate, retell.

n. duplicate, echo, rebroadcast, recapitulation, reiteration, repetition, replay, reproduction, rerun, reshowing.

repeatedly *adv.* again and again, frequently, often, oftentimes, ofttimes, over and over, recurrently, time after time, time and (time) again.

repel *v.* check, confront, decline, disadvantage, disgust, fight, hold off, nauseate, offend, oppose, parry, rebuff, refuse, reject, repulse, resist, revolt, sicken, ward off.
antonym attract.

repellent *adj.* abhorrent, abominable, discouraging, disgusting, distasteful, hateful, horrid, loathsome, nauseating, noxious, obnoxious, odious, offensive, off-putting, rebarbative, repugnant, repulsive, revolting, sickening.
antonym attractive.

repent *n.* atone, bewail, deplore, lament, regret, relent, rue, sorrow.

repentance *n.* compunction, contrition, grief, guilt, metanoia, penitence, regret, remorse, self-reproach, sorriness, sorrow.

repentant *adj.* apologetic, ashamed, chastened, compunctious, contrite, penitent, regretful, remorseful, rueful, sorry.
antonym unrepentant.

repetitious *adj.* battological, long-winded, pleonastic(al), prolix, redundant, tautological, tedious, verbose, windy, wordy.

repine *v.* beef, brood, complain, fret, grieve, grouse, grumble, lament, languish, moan, mope, murmur, sulk.

replace *v.* deputize, follow, make good, oust, re-establish, reinstate, restore, substitute, succeed, supersede, supplant, supply.

replacement *n.* double, fill-in, proxy, replacer, stand-in, substitute, succedaneum, successor, surrogate, understudy.

replenish *v.* fill, furnish, provide, recharge, recruit, refill, reload, renew, replace, restock, restore, stock, supply, top up.

replica *n.* clone, copy, duplicate, facsimile, imitation, model, reproduction.

reply *v.* acknowledge, answer, counter, echo, react, reciprocate, rejoin, repartee, respond, retaliate, retort, return, riposte.
n. acknowledgment, answer, comeback, counter, echo, reaction, reciprocation, rejoinder, repartee, response, retaliation, retort, return, riposte.

report *n.* account, announcement, article, bang, blast, boom, bruit, character, communication, communiqué, crack, crash, declaration, description, detail, detonation, discharge, dispatch, esteem, explosion, fame, gossip, hearsay, information, message, narrative, news, noise, note, paper, piece, procès-verbal, recital, record, regard, relation, reputation, repute, reverberation, rumor, sound, statement, story, summary, tale, talk, tidings, version, word, write-up.
v. air, announce, appear, arrive, broadcast, bruit, circulate, come, communicate, cover, declare, describe, detail, document, mention, narrate, note, notify, proclaim, publish, recite, record, recount, relate, relay, state, tell.

reporter *n.* announcer, correspondent, hack, journalist, legman, newscaster, newshound, newspaperman, newspaperwoman, pressman, stringer, writer.

repose[1] *n.* aplomb, calm, calmness, composure, dignity, ease, equanimity, inactivity, peace, poise, quiet, quietness, quietude, relaxation, respite, rest, restfulness, self-possession, serenity, sleep, slumber, stillness, tranquility.
antonyms activity, strain, stress.
v. laze, recline, relax, rest, sleep, slumber.

repose[2] *v.* confide, deposit, entrust, invest, lodge, place, put, set, store.

reprehensible *adj.* bad, blamable, blameworthy, censurable, condemnable, culpable, delinquent, discreditable, disgraceful, errant, erring, ignoble, objectionable, opprobrious, remiss, shameful, unworthy.
antonyms creditable, good, praiseworthy.

represent *v.* act, appear as, be, betoken, delineate, denote, depict, depicture, describe, designate, embody, enact, epitomize, equal, evoke, exemplify, exhibit, express, illustrate, mean, outline, perform, personify, picture, portray, produce, render, reproduce, show, sketch, stage, symbolize, typify.

representation *n.* account, argument, bust, committee, delegates, delegation, delineation, depiction, description, embassy, exhibition, explanation, exposition, expostulation, icon, idol, illustration, image, likeness, model, narration, narrative, performance, petition, picture, play, portrait, portrayal, production, relation, remonstrance, resemblance, show, sight, sketch, spectacle, statue.

representative *n.* agent, archetype, commissioner, congressman, congresswoman, councillor, delegate, depute, deputy, embodiment, epitome, exemplar, member, personification, proxy, rep, representant, salesperson, senator, spokesperson, traveler, type.
adj. archetypal, characteristic, chosen, delegated, elected, elective, emblematic, evocative, exemplary, illustrative, normal, symbolic, typical, usual.
antonyms atypical, unrepresentative.

repress *v.* bottle up, chasten, check, control, crush, curb, hamper, hinder, impede, inhibit, master, muffle, overcome, overpower, quash, quell, reprime, restrain, silence, smother, stifle, subdue, subjugate, suppress, swallow.

reprimand *n.* admonition, blame, castigation, censure, dressing-down, jawbation, jobation, lecture, rebuke, reprehension, reproach, reproof, row, schooling, talking-to, telling-off, ticking-off, tongue-lashing, wigging.
v. admonish, bawl out, blame, bounce, castigate, censure, check, chide, jobe, keelhaul, lecture, lesson,

rebuke, reprehend, reproach, reprove, scold, slate, tongue-lash, upbraid.

reproach *v.* abuse, blame, censure, chide, condemn, criticize, defame, discredit, disparage, dispraise, rebuke, reprehend, reprimand, reprove, scold, upbraid.
n. abuse, blame, blemish, censure, condemnation, contempt, disapproval, discredit, disgrace, dishonor, disrepute, ignominy, indignity, nayword, obloquy, odium, opprobrium, reproof, scorn, shame, slight, slut, stain, stigma, upbraiding.

reproduction *n.* amphimixis, breeding, copy, duplicate, ectype, facsimile, fructuation, gamogenesis, generation, imitation, increase, multiplication, picture, print, procreation, proliferation, propagation, replica.
antonym original.

reproof *n.* admonition, blame, castigation, censure, chiding, condemnation, criticism, dressing-down, rebuke, reprehension, reprimand, reproach, reproval, reproving, scolding, ticking-off, tongue-lashing, upbraiding.
antonym praise.

repugnance *n.* abhorrence, abhorring, antipathy, aversion, disgust, dislike, disrelish, distaste, hatred, inconsistency, loathing, reluctance, repugnancy, repulsion, revulsion.
antonyms liking, pleasure.

repulsive *adj.* abhorrent, abominable, cold, disagreeable, disgusting, distasteful, forbidding, foul, hateful, hideous, horrid, ill-faced, loathsome, nauseating, objectionable, obnoxious, odious, offensive, repellent, reserved, revolting, sickening, ugly, unpleasant, vile.
antonyms friendly, pleasant.

reputable *adj.* creditable, dependable, estimable, excellent, good, honorable, honored, irreproachable, legitimate, principled, reliable, respectable, trustworthy, unimpeachable, upright, worthy.
antonyms disreputable, infamous.

reputation *n.* bad name, character, credit, distinction, esteem, estimation, fame, good name, honor, infamy, name, opinion, renown, repute, standing, stature.

repute *n.* celebrity, distinction, esteem, estimation, fame, good name, name, renown, reputation, standing, stature.
antonym infamy.

request *v.* ask, ask for, beg, beseech, demand, desire, entreat, impetrate, importune, petition, pray, requisition, seek, solicit, supplicate.
n. appeal, application, asking, begging, call, demand, desire, entreaty, impetration, petition, prayer, representation, requisition, solicitation, suit, supplication.

require *v.* ask, beg, beseech, bid, command, compel, constrain, crave, demand, desire, direct, enjoin, exact, force, instruct, involve, lack, make, miss, necessitate, need, oblige, order, request, take, want, wish.

requirement *n.* demand, desideratum, essential, lack, must, necessity, need, precondition, prerequisite, provision, proviso, qualification, requisite, sine qua non, specification, stipulation, term, want.
antonym inessential.

requisite *adj.* essential, imperative, indispensable, mandatory, necessary, needed, needful, obligatory, prerequisite, required, vital.
antonyms inessential, optional.
n. condition, desiderative, desideratum, essential, must, necessity, need, precondition, prerequisite, requirement, sine qua non.
antonym inessential.

rescind *v.* abrogate, annul, cancel, countermand, invalidate, negate, nullify, overturn, quash, recall, repeal, retract, reverse, revoke, void.
antonym enforce.

rescue *v.* deliver, extricate, free, liberate, ransom, recover, redeem, release, salvage, save.
antonym capture.
n. deliverance, delivery, extrication, liberation, recovery, redemption, release, relief, salvage, salvation, saving.
antonym capture.

research *n.* analysis, delving, examination, experimentation, exploration, fact-finding, groundwork, inquiry, investigation, probe, quest, scrutiny, search, study.
v. analyze, examine, experiment, explore, ferret, investigate, probe, scrutinize, search, study.

resemblance *n.* affinity, analogy, assonance, closeness, comparability, comparison, conformity, correspondence, counterpart, facsimile, image, kinship, likeness, parallel, parity, sameness, semblance, similarity, similitude.
antonym dissimilarity.

resemble *v.* approach, duplicate, echo, favor, mirror, parallel, take after.
antonym differ from.

resentful *adj.* aggrieved, angry, bitter, embittered, exasperated, grudging, huffish, huffy, hurt, incensed, indignant, irate, ireful, jealous, miffed, offended, peeved, piqued, put out, resentive, revengeful, stomachful, unforgiving, wounded.
antonym contented.

resentment *n.* anger, animosity, bitterness, disaffection, discontentment, displeasure, fury, grudge, huff, hurt, ill-feeling, ill-will, indignation, ire, irritation, malice, pique, rage, rancor, umbrage, vexation, vindictiveness, wrath.
antonym contentment.

reservation[1] *n.* arrière pensée, condition, demur, doubt, hesitancy, hesitation, inhibition, proviso, qualification, restraint, scruple, second thought, skepticism, stipulation.

reservation[2] enclave, homeland, park, preserve, reserve, sanctuary, territory, tract.

reserve[1] *v.* bespeak, book, conserve, defer, delay, engage, hoard, hold, husband, keep, postpone, prearrange,

preserve, retain, save, secure, set apart, spare, stockpile, store, withhold.
antonym use up.
n. backlog, cache, capital, fund, hoard, park, preserve, reservation, reservoir, sanctuary, savings, stock, stockpile, store, substitute, supply, tract.

reserve[2] aloofness, constraint, coolness, formality, limitation, modesty, reluctance, reservation, restraint, restriction, reticence, secretiveness, shyness, silence, taciturnity.
antonyms friendliness, informality.
adj. additional, alternate, auxiliary, extra, secondary, spare, substitute.

reserved[1] *adj.* booked, bound, designated, destined, earmarked, engaged, fated, held, intended, kept, meant, predestined, restricted, retained, set aside, spoken for, taken.
antonym unreserved.

reserved[2] aloof, cautious, close-mouthed, cold, cool, demure, formal, modest, prim, restrained, reticent, retiring, secretive, shy, silent, stand-offish, taciturn, unapproachable, unclub(b)able, uncommunicative, uncompanionable, unconversable, undemonstrative, unforthcoming, unresponsive, unsociable.
antonyms friendly, informal.

reside *v.* abide, consist, dwell, exist, inhabit, inhere, lie, live, lodge, remain, settle, sit, sojourn, stay.

residence *n.* abode, country-house, country-seat, domicile, dwelling, habitation, hall, home, house, household, lodging, manor, mansion, occupancy, occupation, pad, palace, place, quarters, seat, sojourn, stay, tenancy, villa.

residue *n.* balance, difference, dregs, excess, extra, leftovers, overflow, overplus, remainder, remains, remnant, residuum, rest, surplus.
antonym core.

resign *v.* abandon, abdicate, cede, forgo, forsake, leave, quit, relinquish, renounce, sacrifice, stand down, surrender, vacate, waive, yield.
antonyms join, maintain.

resignation *n.* abandonment, abdication, acceptance, acquiescence, compliance, defeatism, demission, departure, endurance, forbearing, fortitude, leaving, nonresistance, notice, passivity, patience, relinquishment, renunciation, retirement, submission, sufferance, surrender.
antonym resistance.

resigned *adj.* acquiescent, compliant, defeatist, long-suffering, patient, stoical, subdued, submissive, unprotesting, unresisting.
antonym resisting.

resilience *n.* adaptability, bounce, buoyancy, elasticity, flexibility, give, hardiness, plasticity, pliability, recoil, spring, springiness, strength, suppleness, toughness, unshockability.
antonyms inflexibility, rigidity.

resist *v.* avoid, battle, check, combat, confront, counteract, countervail, curb, defy, dispute, fight back, forbear, forgo, hinder, oppose, recalcitrate, refuse, repel, thwart, weather, withstand.
antonyms accept, submit.

resolute *adj.* bold, constant, determined, dogged, firm, fixed, indissuadable, indivertible, inflexible, obstinate, persevering, purposeful, relentless, set, staunch, steadfast, stout, strong-minded, strong-willed, stubborn, sturdy, tenacious, unbending, undaunted, unflinching, unshakable, unshaken, unwavering.
antonym irresolute.

resolution *n.* aim, answer, boldness, constancy, courage, decision, declaration, dedication, dénouement, determination, devotion, doggedness, earnestness, end, energy, finding, firmness, fortitude, intent, intention, judgment, motion, obstinacy, outcome, perseverance, pertinacity, purpose, relentlessness, resoluteness, resolve, settlement, sincerity, solution, solving, staunchness, steadfastness, stubbornness, tenacity, unraveling, verdict, will power, zeal.
antonym indecision.

resolve *v.* agree, alter, analyze, anatomize, answer, banish, break up, change, clear, conclude, convert, crack, decide, design, determine, disentangle, disintegrate, dispel, dissect, dissipate, dissolve, elucidate, explain, fathom, fix, intend, liquefy, melt, metamorphose, purpose, reduce, relax, remove, separate, settle, solve, transform, transmute, undertake, unravel.
antonyms blend, waver.
n. boldness, conclusion, conviction, courage, decision, design, determination, earnestness, firmness, intention, objective, project, purpose, resoluteness, resolution, sense of purpose, steadfastness, undertaking, will power.
antonym indecision.

resort *v.* frequent, go, haunt, hie, repair, visit.
antonym avoid.
n. alternative, chance, course, expedient, haunt, health resort, hope, howf(f), possibility, recourse, reference, refuge, retreat, spa, spot, watering-place.

resound *v.* boom, echo, re-echo, resonate, reverberate, ring, sound, thunder.

resource *n.* ability, appliance, cache, capability, cleverness, contrivance, course, device, expedient, hoard, ingenuity, initiative, inventiveness, means, quick-wittedness, reserve, resort, resourcefulness, shift, source, stockpile, supply, talent.
antonym unimaginativeness.

resourceful *adj.* able, bright, capable, clever, creative, fertile, imaginative, ingenious, innovative, inventive, originative, quick-witted, sharp, slick, talented.

respect *n.* admiration, appreciation, approbation, aspect, bearing, characteristic, connection, consideration, deference, detail, esteem, estimation, facet, feature, homage, honor, matter, particular, point, recognition,

reference, regard, relation, reverence, sense, veneration, way.
antonym disrespect.
v. admire, appreciate, attend, esteem, follow, heed, honor, notice, obey, observe, pay homage to, recognize, regard, revere, reverence, value, venerate.
antonym scorn.

respectable *adj.* admirable, ample, appreciable, clean-living, considerable, decent, decorous, dignified, estimable, fair, good, goodly, honest, honorable, large, passable, presentable, proper, reasonable, reputable, respected, seemly, sizable, substantial, tidy, tolerable, upright, venerable, well-to-do, worthy.
antonyms disreputable, miserly, unseemly.

respectful *adj.* civil, courteous, courtly, deferential, dutiful, filial, gracious, humble, mannerly, obedient, polite, regardful, reverent, reverential, self-effacing, solicitous, submissive, subservient, well-mannered.
antonym disrespectful.

respite *n.* adjournment, break, breather, cessation, delay, gap, halt, hiatus, intermission, interruption, interval, letup, lull, moratorium, pause, postponement, recess, relaxation, relief, remission, reprieve, rest, stay, suspension.

response *n.* acknowledgment, answer, comeback, counterblast, feedback, reaction, rejoinder, reply, respond, retort, return, riposte.
antonym query.

responsibility *n.* accountability, amenability, answerability, authority, blame, burden, care, charge, conscientiousness, culpability, dependability, duty, fault, guilt, importance, level-headedness, liability, maturity, obligation, onus, power, rationality, reliability, sense, sensibleness, soberness, stability, trust, trustworthiness.
antonym irresponsibility.

responsible *adj.* accountable, adult, amenable, answerable, authoritative, bound, chargeable, conscientious, culpable, decision-making, dependable, duty-bound, ethical, executive, guilty, high, important, level-headed, liable, mature, public-spirited, rational, reliable, right, sensible, sober, sound, stable, steady, subject, trustworthy.
antonym irresponsible.

rest[1] *n.* base, break, breather, breathing-space, breathing-time, breathing-while, calm, cessation, cradle, doze, halt, haven, holiday, idleness, inactivity, interlude, intermission, interval, leisure, lie-down, lie-in, lodging, lull, motionlessness, nap, pause, prop, refreshment, refuge, relaxation, relief, repose, retreat, shelf, shelter, shut-eye, siesta, sleep, slumber, snooze, somnolence, spell, stand, standstill, stillness, stop, support, tranquility, trestle, vacation.
antonyms action, activity, restlessness.
v. alight, base, cease, continue, depend, desist, discontinue, doze, found, halt, hang, hinge, idle, keep, land, lay, laze, lean, lie, lie back, lie down, lie in, perch, prop, recline, relax, rely, remain, repose, reside, settle, sit, sleep, slumber, snooze, spell, stand, stay, stop, turn.
antonyms change, continue, work.

rest[2] *n.* balance, core, excess, left-overs, majority, others, remainder, remains, remnants, residue, residuum, rump, surplus.

restful *adj.* calm, calming, comfortable, easeful, languid, pacific, peaceful, placid, quiet, relaxed, relaxing, serene, sleepy, soothing, tranquil, tranquilizing, undisturbed, unhurried.
antonyms disturbed, disturbing.

restitution *n.* amends, compensation, damages, indemnification, indemnity, recompense, redress, refund, reimbursement, remuneration, reparation, repayment, requital, restoration, restoring, return, satisfaction.

restive *adj.* agitated, edgy, fidgety, fractious, fretful, impatient, jittery, jumpy, nervous, obstinate, recalcitrant, refractory, restless, uneasy, unquiet, unruly.
antonyms calm, relaxed.

restless *adj.* active, agitated, anxious, bustling, changeable, disturbed, edgy, fidgety, fitful, footloose, fretful, hurried, inconstant, irresolute, jumpy, moving, nervous, nomadic, restive, roving, shifting, sleepless, transient, troubled, turbulent, uneasy, unquiet, unresting, unruly, unsettled, unstable, unsteady, wandering, worried.
antonyms calm, relaxed.

restore *v.* fix, mend, reanimate, rebuild, recondition, reconstitute, reconstruct, recover, recruit, redintegrate, re-enforce, re-establish, refresh, refurbish, rehabilitate, reimpose, reinstate, reintroduce, rejuvenate, renew, renovate, repair, replace, retouch, return, revitalize, revive, revivify, strengthen.
antonyms damage, remove, weaken.

restrain *v.* arrest, bind, bit, bridle, chain, check, cohibit, confine, constrain, control, curb, curtail, debar, detain, fetter, govern, hamper, hamshackle, handicap, harness, hinder, hold, imprison, inhibit, jail, keep, limit, manacle, muzzle, pinion, prevent, repress, restrict, stay, subdue, suppress, tie.
antonyms encourage, liberate.

restraint *n.* arrest, ban, bondage, bonds, bridle, captivity, chains, check, coercion, cohibition, command, compulsion, confinement, confines, constraint, control, cramp, curb, curtailment, dam, detention, embargo, fetters, grip, hindrance, hold, imprisonment, inhibition, interdict, lid, limit, limitation, manacles, moderation, pinions, prevention, rein, restriction, self-control, self-discipline, self-possession, self-restraint, stint, straitjacket, suppression, taboo, tie.
antonym freedom.

restrict *v.* astrict, bound, circumscribe, condition, confine, constrain, contain, cramp, demarcate, hamper, handicap, impede, inhibit, limit, regulate, restrain, restringe, scant, thirl, tie.
antonyms broaden, encourage, free.

restriction *n.* check, condition, confinement, constraint, containment, control, curb, demarcation, handicap, inhibition, limitation, regulation, restraint, rule, squeeze, stint, stipulation.
antonyms broadening, encouragement, freedom.

result *n.* conclusion, consequence, decision, development, effect, end, end-product, event, fruit, issue, outcome, produce, reaction, sequel, termination, upshot.
antonyms beginning, cause.
v. appear, arise, culminate, derive, develop, emanate, emerge, end, ensue, eventuate, finish, flow, follow, happen, issue, proceed, spring, stem, terminate.
antonyms begin, cause.

resume *v.* continue, pick up, proceed, recommence, re-institute, reopen, restart, take up.
antonym cease.

resurgence *n.* rebirth, recrudescence, re-emergence, renaissance, renascence, resumption, resurrection, return, revival, revivification, risorgimento.
antonym decrease.

resuscitate *v.* quicken, reanimate, reinvigorate, renew, rescue, restore, resurrect, revitalize, revive, revivify, save.

retain *v.* absorb, commission, contain, detail, employ, engage, grasp, grip, hire, hold, hold back, keep, keep in mind, keep up, maintain, memorize, pay, preserve, recall, recollect, remember, reserve, restrain, save.
antonyms release, spend.

retainer[1] *n.* attendant, dependant, domestic, galloglass, henchman, lackey, minion, servant, satellite, subordinate, supporter.

retainer[2] *n.* advance, deposit, fee, retaining fee.

retaliate *v.* fight back, get back at, get even with, get one's own back, give as good as one gets, hit back, reciprocate, repay in kind, return like for like, revenge oneself, strike back, take revenge.
antonyms accept, submit.

retard *v.* arrest, brake, check, clog, decelerate, defer, delay, detain, encumber, handicap, hinder, impede, keep back, obstruct, slow, stall.
antonym advance.

reticent *adj.* boutonné, close-lipped, close-mouthed, mum, mute, quiet, reserved, restrained, secretive, silent, taciturn, tight-lipped, uncommunicative, unforthcoming, unspeaking.
antonyms communicative, forward, frank.

retire *v.* decamp, depart, draw back, ebb, exit, leave, recede, remove, retreat, withdraw.
antonyms enter, join.

retiring *adj.* bashful, coy, demure, diffident, humble, meek, modest, mousy, quiet, reclusive, reserved, reticent, self-effacing, shamefaced, shrinking, shy, timid, timorous, unassertive, unassuming.
antonyms assertive, forward.

retort *v.* answer, counter, rejoin, repartee, reply, respond, retaliate, return, riposte.
n. answer, backword, come-back, quip, rejoinder, repartee, reply, response, riposte, sally.

retreat *v.* depart, ebb, leave, quit, recede, recoil, retire, shrink, turn tail, withdraw.
antonym advance.
n. asylum, den, departure, ebb, evacuation, flight, funk-hole, growlery, haunt, haven, hibernacle, hibernaculum, hideaway, privacy, refuge, resort, retirement, sanctuary, seclusion, shelter, withdrawal.
antonyms advance, company, limelight.

retrench *v.* curtail, cut, decrease, diminish, economize, husband, lessen, limit, pare, prune, reduce, save, slim down, trim.
antonym increase.

retribution *n.* compensation, justice, Nemesis, payment, punishment, reckoning, recompense, redress, repayment, reprisal, requital, retaliation, revenge, reward, satisfaction, talion, vengeance.

retrieve *v.* fetch, make good, recall, recapture, recoup, recover, redeem, regain, repair, repossess, rescue, restore, return, salvage, save.
antonym lose.

retrograde *adj.* backward, declining, degenerative, denigrating, deteriorating, downward, inverse, negative, regressive, relapsing, retreating, retrogressive, reverse, reverting, waning, worsening.
antonym progressive.

return *v.* announce, answer, choose, communicate, convey, deliver, earn, elect, make, net, pick, reappear, rebound, reciprocate, recoil, recompense, recur, redound, re-establish, refund, reimburse, reinstate, rejoin, remit, render, repair, repay, replace, reply, report, requite, respond, restore, retort, retreat, revert, send, submit, transmit, volley, yield.
antonyms leave, take.
n. account, advantage, answer, benefit, comeback, compensation, form, gain, home-coming, income, interest, list, proceeds, profit, quip, reappearance, rebound, reciprocation, recoil, recompense, recrudescence, recurrence, redound, re-establishment, reimbursement, reinstatement, rejoinder, reparation, repayment, replacement, reply, report, requital, response, restoration, retaliation, retort, retreat, revenue, reversion, reward, riposte, sally, statement, summary, takings, yield.
antonyms disappearance, expense, loss, payment.

reveal *v.* announce, bare, betray, broadcast, communicate, disbosom, disclose, dismask, display, divulge, exhibit, expose, impart, leak, lift the lid off, manifest, open, proclaim, publish, show, tell, unbare, unbosom, uncover, unearth, unfold, unmask, unshadow, unveil.
antonym hide.

revel *v.* carouse, celebrate, live it up, make merry, paint the town red, push the boat out, raise the roof, roist, roister, whoop it up.
n. bacchanal, carousal, carouse, celebration, comus,

debauch, festivity, gala, jollification, merry-make, merry-making, party, saturnalia, spree.

revel in bask, crow, delight, gloat, glory, indulge, joy, lap up, luxuriate, rejoice, relish, savor, take pleasure, thrive on, wallow.
antonym dislike.

revelation *n.* announcement, apocalypse, betrayal, broadcasting, communication, disclosure, discovery, display, exhibition, exposé, exposition, exposure, giveaway, leak, manifestation, news, proclamation, publication, telling, uncovering, unearthing, unveiling.

revelry *n.* carousal, carouse, celebration, debauch, debauchery, festivity, fun, jollification, jollity, merry-making, party, revel-rout, riot, roistering, saturnalia, spree, wassail, wassailing, wassailry.
antonym sobriety.

revenge *n.* a dose/taste of one's own medicine, ravanche, reprisal, requital, retaliation, retribution, revengement, satisfaction, ultion, vengeance, vindictiveness.
v. avenge, even the score, get one's own back, get satisfaction, repay, requite, retaliate, vindicate.

revenue *n.* gain, income, interest, proceeds, profits, receipts, returns, rewards, take, takings, yield.
antonym expenditure.

revere *v.* adore, defer to, exalt, honor, pay homage to, respect, reverence, venerate, worship.
antonyms despise, scorn.

reverence *n.* admiration, adoration, awe, deference, devotion, dulia, esteem, genuflection, homage, honor, hyperdulia, latria, respect, veneration, worship.
antonym scorn.
v. acknowledge, admire, adore, honor, respect, revere, venerate, worship.
antonyms despise, scorn.

reverent *adj.* adoring, awed, decorous, deferential, devout, dutiful, humble, loving, meek, pious, respectful, reverential, solemn, submissive.
antonym irreverent.

reverse *v.* alter, annul, back, backtrack, cancel, change, countermand, hark back, invalidate, invert, negate, overrule, overset, overthrow, overturn, quash, repeal, rescind, retract, retreat, revert, revoke, transpose, undo, up-end, upset.
antonym enforce.
n. adversity, affliction, antithesis, back, blow, check, contradiction, contrary, converse, defeat, disappointment, failure, hardship, inverse, misadventure, misfortune, mishap, opposite, rear, repulse, reversal, setback, trial, underside, verso, vicissitude, woman.
adj. backward, contrary, converse, inverse, inverted, opposite, verso.

revert *v.* backslide, lapse, recur, regress, relapse, resume, retrogress, return, reverse.
antonym progress.

review *v.* assess, criticize, discuss, evaluate, examine, inspect, judge, reassess, recall, recapitulate, recollect, reconsider, re-evaluate, re-examine, rehearse, remember, rethink, revise, scrutinize, study, weigh.
n. analysis, assessment, commentary, criticism, critique, evaluation, examination, journal, judgment, magazine, notice, periodical, reassessment, recapitulation, recension, reconsideration, re-evaluation, re-examination, report, rethink, retrospect, revision, scrutiny, study, survey.

revile *v.* abuse, blackguard, calumniate, defame, denigrate, libel, malign, miscall, reproach, scorn, slander, smear, traduce, vilify, vilipend, vituperate.
antonym praise.

revise *v.* alter, amend, change, correct, edit, emend, memorize, modify, recast, recense, reconsider, reconstruct, redo, re-examine, reread, revamp, review, rewrite, study, swot up, update. **revision** *n.* alteration, amendment, change, correction, editing, emendation, homework, memorizing, modification, recast, recasting, recension, reconstruction, re-examination, rereading, review, rewriting, rifacimento, studying, swotting, updating.

revival *n.* awakening, quickening, reactivation, reanimation, reawakening, rebirth, recrudescence, renaissance, renascence, renewal, restoration, resurgence, resurrection, resuscitation, revitalization, revivification, risorgimento.
antonym suppression.

revive *v.* animate, awaken, cheer, comfort, invigorate, quicken, rally, reactivate, reanimate, recover, refresh, rekindle, renew, renovate, restore, resuscitate, revitalize, revivify, rouse.
antonyms suppress, weary.

revoke *v.* abolish, abrogate, annul, cancel, countermand, disclaim, dissolve, invalidate, negate, nullify, quash, recall, recant, renounce, repeal, repudiate, rescind, retract, reverse, withdraw.
antonym enforce.

revolt[1] *n.* breakaway, defection, insurgency, insurrection, Jacquerie, mutiny, putsch, rebellion, revolution, rising, secession, sedition, uprising.
v. defect, mutiny, rebel, resist, riot, rise.
antonym submit.

revolt[2] *v.* disgust, nauseate, offend, outrage, repel, repulse, scandalize, shock, sicken.
antonym please.

revolting *adj.* abhorrent, abominable, appalling, disgusting, distasteful, fetid, foul, horrible, horrid, loathsome, nasty, nauseating, nauseous, noisome, obnoxious, obscene, offensive, repellent, repugnant, repulsive, shocking, sickening, sickly.
antonym pleasant.

revolution *n.* cataclysm, change, circle, circuit, coup, coup d'état, cycle, gyration, innovation, insurgency, Jacquerie, lap, metamorphosis, metanoia, mutiny, orbit, putsch, rebellion, reformation, revolt, rising, rotation, round, shift, spin, transformation, turn, upheaval, uprising, volution, wheel, whirl.

revolutionary *n.* anarchist, insurgent, insurrectionary, insurrectionist, Jacobin, mutineer, rebel, revolutionist, Trot, Trotskyite.
adj. anarchistic, avant-garde, different, drastic, experimental, extremist, fundamental, innovative, insurgent, insurrectionary, mutinous, new, novel, progressive, radical, rebel, seditious, subversive, thoroughgoing.
antonyms commonplace, establishment.

revolve *v.* circle, circumgyrate, circumvolve, gyrate, orbit, rotate, spin, turn, wheel, whirl.

revolver *n.* air-gun, firearm, gun, hand-gun, heater, peacemaker, piece, pistol, rod, shooter, six-shooter.

revulsion *n.* abhorrence, abomination, aversion, detestation, disgust, dislike, distaste, hatred, loathing, recoil, repugnance, repulsion.
antonym pleasure.

reward *n.* benefit, bonus, bounty, come-up(p)ance, compensation, desert, gain, guerdon, honor, meed, merit, payment, pay-off, premium, prize, profit, punishment, recompense, remuneration, repayment, requital, retribution, return, wages.
antonym punishment.
v. compensate, guerdon, honor, pay, recompense, remunerate, repay, requite.
antonym punish.

rewarding *adj.* advantageous, beneficial, edifying, enriching, fruitful, fulfilling, gainful, gratifying, pleasing, productive, profitable, remunerative, rewardful, satisfying, valuable, worthwhile.
antonym unrewarding.

rhetorical *adj.* artificial, bombastic, declamatory, false, flamboyant, flashy, florid, flowery, grandiloquent, high-flown, high-sounding, hyperbolic, inflated, insincere, linguistic, magniloquent, oratorical, over-decorated, pompous, pretentious, rhetoric, showy, silver-tongued, stylistic, verbal, verbose, windy.
antonyms simple.

rhythm *n.* accent, beat, cadence, cadency, eurhythmy, flow, lilt, measure, meter, movement, pattern, periodicity, pulse, rhythmicity, swing, tempo, time.

ribald *adj.* base, bawdy, blue, broad, coarse, derisive, earthy, filthy, foul-mouthed, gross, indecent, irrisory, jeering, licentious, low, mean, mocking, naughty, obscene, off-color, Rabelaisian, racy, risqué, rude, scurrilous, smutty, vulgar.
antonym polite.

rich *adj.* abounding, abundant, affluent, ample, bright, copious, costly, creamy, deep, delicious, dulcet, elaborate, elegant, expensive, exquisite, exuberant, fatty, fecund, fertile, fine, flavorsome, flush, fruitful, full, full-bodied, full-flavored, full-toned, gay, gorgeous, heavy, highly-flavored, humorous, in the money, intense, juicy, laughable, lavish, loaded, ludicrous, luscious, lush, luxurious, mellifluous, mellow, moneyed, opulent, palatial, pecunious, plenteous, plentiful, plutocratic, precious, priceless, productive, prolific, propertied, property, prosperous, resonant, ridiculous, risible, rolling, savory, side-splitting, spicy, splendid, strong, succulent, sumptuous, superb, sweet, tasty, uberous, valuable, vibrant, vivid, warm, wealthy, well-heeled, well-off, well-provided, well-stocked, well-supplied, well-to-do.
antonyms harsh, miserly, plain, poor, simple, tasteless, thin, unfertile.

rickety *adj.* broken, broken-down, decrepit, derelict, dilapidated, feeble, flimsy, frail, imperfect, infirm, insecure, jerry-built, precarious, ramshackle, shaky, shoogly, tottering, tottery, unsound, unstable, unsteady, weak, wobbly.
antonyms stable, strong.

rid *v.* clear, deliver, disabuse, disburden, disembarrass, disencumber, expel, free, purge, relieve, unburden.
antonym burden.

riddle[1] *n.* brain-teaser, charade, conundrum, enigma, logogram, logograph, logogriph, mystery, poser, problem, puzzle, rebus.

riddle[2] *v.* corrupt, damage, fill, filter, impair, infest, invade, mar, pepper, perforate, permeate, pervade, pierce, puncture, screen, sieve, sift, spoil, strain, winnow.
n. sieve, strainer.

ride *v.* control, dominate, enslave, float, grip, handle, haunt, hurl, journey, manage, move, oppress, progress, sit, survive, travel, weather.
n. drive, hurl, jaunt, journey, lift, outing, spin, trip, whirl.

ridge *n.* arête, band, costa, crinkle, drum, drumlin, escarpment, eskar, hill, hog's back, hummock, lump, reef, ripple, saddle, wale, weal, welt, zastruga.

ridicule *n.* banter, chaff, derision, gibe, irony, irrision, jeering, jeers, laughter, mockery, raillery, sarcasm, satire, scorn, sneers, taunting.
antonym praise.
v. banter, burlesque, caricature, cartoon, chaff, crucify, deride, humiliate, jeer, josh, lampoon, mock, parody, pillory, pooh-pooh, queer, quiz, rib, satirize, scoff, send up, sneer at, take the mickey out of, taunt.
antonym praise.

ridiculous *adj.* absurd, comical, contemptible, damfool, derisory, farcical, foolish, funny, hilarious, incredible, laughable, laughworthy, ludicrous, nonsensical, outrageous, preposterous, risible, silly, stupid, unbelievable.
antonym sensible.

rife *adj.* abounding, abundant, common, commonplace, current, epidemic, frequent, general, plentiful, prevailing, prevalent, raging, rampant, teeming, ubiquitous, universal, widespread.
antonym scarce.

rifle[1] *v.* burgle, despoil, gut, loot, maraud, pillage, plunder, ransack, rob, rummage, sack, strip.

rifle[2] *n.* air-gun, carbine, firearm, firelock, flintlock, fusil, gun, musket, shotgun.

rift *n.* alienation, beach, breach, break, chink, cleavage, cleft, crack, cranny, crevice, difference, disaffection, disagreement, dissure, division, estrangement, fault, flaw, fracture, gap, opening, quarrel, schism, separation, space, split.
antonym unity.

right *adj.* absolute, accurate, admissible, advantageous, appropriate, authentic, balanced, becoming, characteristic, comme il faut, complete, compos mentis, conservative, correct, deserved, desirable, dexter, dextral, direct, done, due, equitable, ethical, exact, factual, fair, favorable, fine, fit, fitting, genuine, good, healthy, honest, honorable, ideal, just, lawful, lucid, moral, normal, opportune, out-and-out, perpendicular, precise, proper, propitious, rational, reactionary, real, reasonable, righteous, rightful, rightist, rightward, right-wing, sane, satisfactory, seemly, sound, spot-on, straight, suitable, thorough, thoroughgoing, Tory, true, unerring, unimpaired, upright, utter, valid, veracious, veritable, virtuous, well.
antonyms left, left-wing, mad, unfit, wrong.
adv. absolutely, accurately, advantageously, altogether, appropriate, aptly, aright, bang, befittingly, beneficially, completely, correctly, directly, entirely, ethically, exactly, factually, fairly, favorably, fittingly, fortunately, genuinely, honestly, honorably, immediately, instantly, justly, morally, perfectly, precisely, promptly, properly, quickly, quite, righteously, rightward(s), satisfactorily, slap-bang, squarely, straight, straightaway, suitably, thoroughly, totally, truly, utterly, virtuously, well, wholly.
antonyms incorrectly, left, unfairly, wrongly.
n. authority, business, claim, droit, due, equity, freedom, good, goodness, honor, integrity, interest, justice, lawfulness, legality, liberty, licence, morality, permission, power, prerogative, privilege, propriety, reason, rectitude, righteousness, rightfulness, rightness, title, truth, uprightness, virtue.
antonyms depravity, wrong.
v. avenge, correct, fix, rectify, redress, repair, righten, settle, stand up, straighten, vindicate.

righteous *adj.* blameless, equitable, ethical, fair, God-fearing, good, guiltless, honest, honorable, incorrupt, just, law-abiding, moral, pure, saintly, sinless, upright, virtuous.
antonym unrighteous.
n. Holy Willies, just, Pharisees, saints, unco guid, welldoers.
antonym unrighteous.

rigid *adj.* adamant, austere, cast-iron, exact, fixed, harsh, inflexible, intransigent, invariable, rigorous, set, severe, starch(y), stern, stiff, stony, strict, stringent, tense, unalterable, unbending, uncompromising, undeviating, unrelenting, unyielding.
antonym flexible.

rigorous *adj.* accurate, austere, challenging, conscientious, demanding, exact, exacting, extreme, firm, hard, harsh, inclement, inflexible, inhospitable, meticulous, nice, painstaking, precise, punctilious, Rhadamanthine, rigid, scrupulous, severe, stern, strict, stringent, thorough, tough, unsparing.
antonyms lenient, mild.

rile *v.* anger, annoy, bug, exasperate, gall, get, irk, irritate, miff, nark, nettle, peeve, pique, provoke, put out, upset, vex.
antonym soothe.

rim *n.* border, brim, brink, circumference, edge, lip, margin, skirt, verge.
antonym center.

rind *n.* crust, epicarp, husk, integument, peel, skin, zest.

ring[1] *n.* annulation, annulet, annulus, arena, association, band, cabal, cartel, cell, circle, circuit, circus, clique, collar, collet, combine, coterie, crew, enclosure, gang, group, gyre, halo, hoop, knot, loop, mob, organization, rink, round, rundle, syndicate.
v. circumscribe, encircle, enclose, encompass, gash, gird, girdle, mark, score, surround.

ring[2] *v.* bell, buzz, call, chime, clang, clink, peal, phone, resonate, resound, reverberate, sound, tang, telephone, ting, tinkle, tintinnabulate, toll.
n. buzz, call, chime, clang, clink, knell, peal, phone-call, tang, ting, tinkle, tintinnabulation.

ringleader *n.* bell-wether, brains, chief, fugleman, leader, spokesman.

rinse *v.* bathe, clean, cleanse, dip, sluice, splash, swill, synd, wash, wet.
n. bath, dip, dye, splash, tint, wash, wetting.

riot *n.* anarchy, bagarre, boisterousness, carousal, commotion, confusion, debauchery, disorder, display, disturbance, Donnybrook, émeute, excess, extravaganza, festivity, flourish, fray, frolic, high, insurrection, jinks, jollification, lawlessness, merry-make, merrymaking, quarrel, revelry, riotousness, riotry, romp, rookery, rout, row, ruction, ruffle, shindig, shindy, show, splash, strife, tumult, turbulence, turmoil, uproar.
antonyms calm, order.
v. carouse, frolic, rampage, rebel, revel, revolt, rise up, roister, romp, run riot, run wild.

riotous *adj.* anarchic, boisterous, disorderly, insubordinate, insurrectionary, lawless, loud, luxurious, mutinous, noisy, orgiastic, rambunctious, rampageous, rebellious, refractory, roisterous, rollicking, rowdy, saturnalian, side-splitting, tumultuous, ungovernable, unrestrained, unruly, uproarious, violent, wanton, wild.
antonyms orderly, restrained.

rip *v.* burst, claw, cut, gash, hack, lacerate, rend, rupture, score, separate, slash, slit, split, tear.
n. cleavage, cut, gash, hole, laceration, rent, rupture, slash, slit, split, tear.

ripe *adj.* accomplished, auspicious, complete, developed, favorable, finished, grown, ideal, mature, mellow, opportune, perfect, prepared, promising, propitious, ready, right, ripened, seasoned, suitable, timely. *antonyms* inopportune, untimely.

ripen *v.* age, burgeon, develop, mature, mellow, prepare, season.

rip-off *n.* cheat, con, con trick, daylight robbery, diddle, exploitation, fraud, robbery, sting, swindle, theft.

riposte *n.* answer, come-back, quip, rejoinder, repartee, reply, response, retort, return, sally.
v. answer, quip, reciprocate, rejoin, reply, respond, retort, return.

ripple *n.* babble, burble, disturbance, eddy, gurgle, lapping, pirl, purl, ripplet, undulation, wave, wimple.

rise *v.* advance, appear, arise, ascend, buoy, climb, crop up, emanate, emerge, enlarge, eventuate, flow, get up, grow, happen, improve, increase, intensify, issue, levitate, lift, mount, mutiny, occur, originate, progress, prosper, rebel, resist, revolt, slope, slope up, soar, spring, spring up, stand up, surface, swell, tower, volume, wax.
antonyms descend, fall.
n. acclivity, advance, advancement, aggrandizement, ascent, climb, elevation, hillock, improvement, incline, increase, increment, origin, progress, promotion, raise, rising, upsurge, upswing, upturn, upward turn.
antonyms descent, fall.

risk *n.* adventure, chance, danger, gamble, hazard, jeopardy, peril, possibility, speculation, uncertainty, venture.
antonyms certainty, safety.
v. adventure, chance, dare, endanger, gamble, hazard, imperil, jeopardize, speculate, venture.

risky *adj.* chancy, dangerous, dicey, dodgy, fraught, hazardous, perilous, precarious, riskful, touch-and-go, tricky, uncertain, unsafe.
antonym safe.

rite *n.* act, ceremonial, ceremony, custom, form, formality, liturgy, mystery, observance, office, ordinance, practice, procedure, ritual, sacrament, service, solemnity, usage, worship.

ritual *n.* ceremonial, ceremony, communion, convention, custom, form, formality, habit, liturgy, mystery, observance, ordinance, practice, prescription, procedure, rite, routine, sacrament, service, solemnity, tradition, usage, wont.
adj. ceremonial, ceremonious, conventional, customary, formal, formulary, habitual, prescribed, procedural, routine, stereotyped.
antonyms informal, unusual.

rival *n.* adversary, antagonist, challenger, collateral, compeer, competitor, contender, contestant, corrival, emulator, equal, equivalent, fellow, match, opponent, peer, rivaless.
antonyms associate, colleague, co-worker.
adj. competing, competitive, conflicting, corrival, emulating, emulous, opposed, opposing.
antonyms associate, co-operating.
v. compete, contend, emulate, equal, match, oppose, rivalize, vie with.
antonym co-operate.

rivalry *n.* antagonism, competition, competitiveness, conflict, contention, contest, duel, emulation, opposition, rivality, rivalship, struggle, vying.
antonym co-operation.

river *n.* beck, burn, creek, ea, flood, flow, gush, riverway, rush, spate, stream, surge, tributary, waterway.
adj. fluvial, riverain, riverine.

riveting *adj.* absorbing, arresting, captivating, engrossing, enthralling, fascinating, gripping, hypnotic, magnetic, spellbinding. *antonym* boring.

road *n.* Autobahn, autopista, autoroute, autostrada, avenue, boulevard, camino real, carriageway, clearway, course, crescent, direction, drift, drive, driveway, freeway, highway, lane, path, pathway, roadway, route, street, thoroughfare, thruway, track, way.

roam *v.* drift, meander, peregrinate, prowl, ramble, range, rove, squander, stravaig, stray, stroll, travel, walk, wander.
antonym stay.

roar *v.* bawl, bay, bell, bellow, blare, clamor, crash, cry, guffaw, hoot, howl, rumble, shout, thunder, vociferate, wuther, yell.
antonym whisper.
n. bellow, belly-laugh, blare, clamor, crash, cry, guffaw, hoot, howl, outcry, rumble, shout, thunder, yell.
antonym whisper.

rob *v.* bereave, bunko, cheat, con, defraud, deprive, despoil, dispossess, do, flake, flimp, gyp, heist, hold up, loot, mill, pillage, plunder, raid, ramp, ransack, reive, rifle, rip off, roll, sack, sting, strip, swindle.
antonyms give, provide.

robbery *n.* burglary, dacoitage, dacoity, depredation, embezzlement, filching, fraud, heist, hold-up, larceny, pillage, plunder, purse-snatching, purse-taking, raid, rapine, rip-off, spoliation, stealing, stick-up, swindle, theft, thievery.

robe *n.* bathrobe, costume, dressing-gown, gown, habit, housecoat, peignoir, vestment, wrap, wrapper.
v. apparel, attire, clothe, drape, dress, garb, vest.

robot *n.* android, automaton, golem, machine, zombie.

robust *adj.* able-bodied, athletic, boisterous, brawny, coarse, down-to-earth, earthy, fit, hale, hard-headed, hardy, healthy, hearty, husky, indecorous, lusty, muscular, over-hearty, powerful, practical, pragmatic, raw, realistic, robustious, roisterous, rollicking, rough, rude, rugged, sensible, sinewy, sound, staunch, sthenic, stout, straight-forward, strapping, strong, sturdy, thick-set, tough, unsubtle, vigorous, well.
antonyms mealy-mouthed, unhealthy, unrealistic, weak.

rock[1] *n.* anchor, boulder, bulwark, cornerstone, danger, foundation, hazard, logan, log(g)an-stone, mainstay, obstacle, pebble, problem, protection, stone, support.

rock[2] *v.* astonish, astound, daze, dumbfound, jar, lurch, pitch, reel, roll, shake, shock, stagger, stun, surprise, sway, swing, tilt, tip, toss, wobble.

rocky[1] *adj.* craggy, flinty, hard, pebbly, rocklike, rough, rugged, stony.
antonyms smooth, soft.

rocky[2] *adj.* dizzy, doubtful, drunk, ill, inebriated, intoxicated, rickety, shaky, sick, sickly, staggering, tipsy, tottering, uncertain, undependable, unpleasant, unreliable, unsatisfactory, unstable, unsteady, unwell, weak, wobbly, wonky.
antonyms dependable, steady, well.

rod *n.* bar, baton, birch, cane, dowel, ferula, ferule, mace, pole, scepter, shaft, spoke, staff, stick, strut, switch, verge, wand.

rogue *n.* blackguard, charlatan, cheat, con man, crook, deceiver, devil, fraud, knave, miscreant, mountebank, nasty piece/bit of work, ne'er-do-well, picaroon, rapscallion, rascal, reprobate, scamp, scapegallows, scoundrel, sharper, swindler, vagrant, villain, wag.
antonym saint.

roguish *adj.* arch, bantering, cheeky, confounded, coquettish, criminal, crooked, deceitful, deceiving, dishonest, espiègle, fraudulent, frolicsome, hempy, impish, knavish, mischievous, playful, puckish, raffish, rascally, roguing, shady, sportive, swindling, unprincipled, unscrupulous, villainous, waggish.
antonyms honest, serious.

roister *v.* bluster, boast, brag, carouse, celebrate, frolic, make merry, paint the town red, revel, roist, rollick, romp, strut, swagger, whoop it up.

role *n.* capacity, character, duty, function, impersonation, job, job of work, part, portrayal, position, post, representation, task.

roll *v.* billow, bind, boom, coil, curl, drum, echo, elapse, enfold, entwine, envelop, even, flatten, flow, furl, grumble, gyrate, level, lumber, lurch, pass, peel, pivot, press, reel, resound, reverberate, revolve, roar, rock, rotate, rumble, run, smooth, spin, spread, stagger, swagger, swathe, sway, swing, swivel, thunder, toss, trill, trindle, trundle, tumble, turn, twirl, twist, undulate, volume, waddle, wallow, wander, welter, wheel, whirl, wind, wrap.
n. annals, ball, bobbin, boom, catalog, census, chronicle, cycle, cylinder, directory, drumming, growl, grumble, gyration, index, inventory, list, notitia, record, reel, register, resonance, reverberation, revolution, roar, roller, roster, rotation, rumble, run, schedule, scroll, spin, spool, table, thunder, turn, twirl, undulation, volume, wheel, whirl.

rollicking *adj.* boisterous, carefree, cavorting, devil-may-care, exuberant, frisky, frolicsome, hearty, jaunty, jovial, joyous, lively, merry, playful, rip-roaring, roisterous, roisting, romping, spirited, sportive, sprightly, swashbuckling.
antonyms restrained, serious.

romance *n.* absurdity, adventure, affair(e), amour, attachment, charm, color, exaggeration, excitement, fabrication, fairy tale, falsehood, fantasy, fascination, fiction, gest(e), glamor, idyll, intrigue, invention, legend, liaison, lie, love affair, love story, melodrama, mystery, novel, passion, relationship, sentiment, story, tale, tear-jerker.
v. exaggerate, fantasize, lie, overstate.

romantic *adj.* amorous, charming, chimerical, colorful, dreamy, exaggerated, exciting, exotic, extravagant, fabulous, fairy-tale, fanciful, fantastic, fascinating, fictitious, fond, glamorous, high-flown, idealistic, idyllic, imaginary, imaginative, impractical, improbable, legendary, lovey-dovey, loving, made-up, mushy, mysterious, passionate, picturesque, quixotic, romantical, sentimental, sloppy, soppy, starry-eyed, tender, unrealistic, utopian, visionary, whimsical, wild.
antonyms humdrum, practical, real, sober, unromantic.
n. Don Quixote, dreamer, idealist, romancer, sentimentalist, utopian, visionary.
antonym realist.

romp *v.* caper, cavort, frisk, frolic, gambol, revel, rig, roister, rollick, skip, sport.
n. caper, frolic, lark, rig, spree.

room *n.* allowance, apartment, area, capacity, chamber, chance, compartment, compass, elbow-room, expanse, extent, house-room, latitude, leeway, margin, occasion, office, opportunity, play, range, salon, saloon, scope, space, territory, volume.

roomy *adj.* ample, broad, capacious, commodious, extensive, generous, large, sizable, spacious, voluminous, wide.
antonym cramped.

root[1] *n.* base, basis, beginnings, bottom, cause, core, crux, derivation, essence, foundation, fountainhead, fundamental, germ, heart, mainspring, more, nub, nucleus, occasion, origin, radicle, radix, rhizome, root-cause, rootlet, seat, seed, source, starting point, stem, tuber.
v. anchor, embed, entrench, establish, fasten, fix, ground, implant, moor, set, sink, stick.

root[2] *v.* burrow, delve, dig, ferret, forage, grout, hunt, nose, poke, pry, rootle, rummage.

rooted *adj.* confirmed, deep, deeply, deep-seated, entrenched, established, felt, firm, fixed, ingrained, radical, rigid, root-fast.
antonyms superficial, temporary.

rope *n.* cable, cord, fake, hawser, lariat, lasso, line, marline, strand, warp, widdy.
v. bind, catch, fasten, hitch, lash, lasso, moor, pinion, tether, tie.

ropy *adj.* below par, deficient, inadequate, indifferent, inferior, off-color, poorly, rough, sketchy, stringy, substandard, unwell.
antonyms good, well.

roster *n.* bead-roll, list, listing, register, roll, rota, schedule, table.

rosy *adj.* auspicious, blooming, blushing, bright, cheerful, encouraging, favorable, fresh, glowing, healthy-looking, hopeful, optimistic, pink, promising, reassuring, red, reddish, rose, roseate, rose-colored, rose-hued, roselike, rose-pink, rose-red, rose-scented, rosy-fingered, rubicund, ruddy, sunny.
antonyms depressed, depressing, sad.

rot *v.* corrode, corrupt, crumble, decay, decline, decompose, degenerate, deteriorate, disintegrate, fester, go bad, languish, molder, perish, putrefy, ret, spoil, taint.
n. balderdash, blight, bosh, bunk, bunkum, canker, claptrap, codswallop, collapse, corrosion, corruption, decay, decomposition, deterioration, disintegration, drivel, flap-doodle, guff, hogwash, moonshine, mold, nonsense, poppycock, putrefaction, putrescence, rubbish, tommyrot, tosh, twaddle.

rotary *adj.* gyrating, gyratory, revolving, rotating, rotational, rotatory, spinning, turning, whirling.
antonym fixed.

rotate *v.* alternate, gyrate, interchange, pirouette, pivot, reel, revolve, spell, spin, switch, swivel, turn, twiddle, wheel.

rotation *n.* alternation, cycle, gyration, interchanging, orbit, pirouette, reel, revolution, sequence, spin, spinning, succession, switching, turn, turning, volution, wheel.

rotten *adj.* addle(d), bad, base, below par, bent, contemptible, corroded, corrupt, crooked, crumbling, crummy, decayed, decaying, deceitful, decomposed, decomposing, degenerate, deplorable, despicable, dirty, disagreeable, disappointing, dishonest, dishonorable, disintegrating, disloyal, faithless, festering, fetid, filthy, foul, grotty, ill-considered, ill-thought-out, immoral, inadequate, inferior, lousy, low-grade, manky, mean, mercenary, moldering, moldy, nasty, off-color, perfidious, perished, poor, poorly, punk, putid, putrescent, putrid, rank, regrettable, ropy, rough, scurrilous, sick, sorry, sour, stinking, substandard, tainted, treacherous, unacceptable, unfortunate, unlucky, unpleasant, unsatisfactory, unsound, untrustworthy, unwell, venal, vicious, vile, wicked.
antonyms good, honest, practical, sensible, well.

rotund *adj.* bulbous, chubby, corpulent, fat, fleshy, full, globular, grandiloquent, heavy, magniloquent, obese, orbed, orbicular, orby, oro(ro)tund, plump, podgy, portly, resonant, rich, roly-poly, rotundate, round, rounded, sonorous, spheral, spheric, spherical, spherular, sphery, stout, tubby.
antonyms flat, gaunt, slim.

rough *adj.* agitated, amorphous, approximate, arduous, austere, basic, bearish, bluff, blunt, boisterous, bristly, broken, brusque, bumpy, bushy, cacophonous, choppy, churlish, coarse, craggy, crude, cruel, cursory, curt, discordant, discourteous, disheveled, disordered, drastic, estimated, extreme, foggy, formless, fuzzy, general, grating, gruff, hairy, hard, harsh, hasty, hazy, husky, ill, ill-bred, ill-mannered, imperfect, impolite, imprecise, inclement, incomplete, inconsiderate, indelicate, inexact, inharmonious, irregular, jagged, jarring, loutish, nasty, off-color, poorly, quick, rasping, raspy, raucous, raw, rocky, ropy, rotten, rough-and-ready, rowdy, rude, rudimentary, rugged, rusty, scabrous, severe, shaggy, shapeless, sharp, sick, sketchy, spartan, squally, stony, stormy, tangled, tempestuous, tough, tousled, tousy, turbulent, unceremonious, uncivil, uncomfortable, uncouth, uncultured, uncut, undressed, uneven, unfeeling, unfinished, ungracious, unjust, unmannerly, unmusical, unpleasant, unpolished, unprocessed, unrefined, unshaven, unshorn, untutored, unwell, unwrought, upset, vague, violent, wild.
antonyms accurate, calm, harmonious, mild, polite, smooth, well.
n. boor, bruiser, bully, hooligan, keelie, lout, mock-up, model, outline, roughneck, rowdy, ruffian, sketch, thug, tough, yob, yobbo.

round *adj.* ample, annular, ball-shaped, blunt, bowed, bulbous, candid, circular, complete, curved, curvilinear, cylindrical, direct, discoid, disc-shaped, entire, fleshy, frank, full, full-fleshed, globular, mellifluous, orbed, orbicular, orby, orotund, outspoken, plain, plump, resonant, rich, ring-shaped, roly-poly, rotund, rotundate, rounded, solid, sonorous, spheral, spheric, spherical, spherular, sphery, straightforward, unbroken, undivided, unmodified, whole.
antonyms evasive, niggardly, partial, thin.
n. ambit, ball, band, beat, bout, bullet, cartridge, circle, circuit, compass, course, cycle, disc, discharge, division, globe, lap, level, orb, period, ring, routine, schedule, sequence, series, session, shell, shot, sphere, spheroid, spherule, stage, succession, tour, turn.
v. bypass, circle, circumnavigate, encircle, flank, sail round, skirt, turn.

roundabout *adj.* ambagious, circuitous, circumlocutory, devious, discursive, evasive, indirect, meandering, oblique, periphrastic, tortuous, twisting, winding.
antonyms direct, straight, straightforward.

roundly *adv.* bluntly, completely, fiercely, forcefully, frankly, intensely, openly, outspokenly, rigorously, severely, sharply, thoroughly, vehemently, violently.
antonym mildly.

rouse *v.* agitate, anger, animate, arouse, awaken, bestir, call, disturb, enkindle, excite, exhilarating, firk, flush, galvanize, incite, inflame, instigate, move, provoke, rise, start, startle, stimulate, stir, suscitate, unbed, wake, whip up.
antonym calm.

rousing *adj.* brisk, electrifying, excitant, excitative, excitatory, exciting, exhilarating, hypnopompic, inflammatory, inspiring, lively, moving, spirited, stimulating, stirring, vigorous.
antonym calming.

rout *n.* beating, brawl, clamor, crowd, debacle, defeat,

disturbance, Donnybrook, drubbing, flight, fracas, fuss, herd, hiding, licking, mob, overthrow, pack, rabble, riot, rookery, ruffle, ruin, shambles, stampede, thrashing. *antonyms* calm, win.
v. beat, best, chase, conquer, crush, defeat, destroy, discomfit, dispel, drub, hammer, lick, overthrow, scatter, thrash, worst.

route *n.* avenue, beat, circuit, course, direction, flightpath, itinerary, journey, passage, path, road, round, run, way.
v. convey, direct, dispatch, forward, send.

routine *n.* act, bit, custom, formula, grind, groove, heigh, jog-trot, line, method, order, pattern, performance, piece, practice, procedure, program, spiel, usage, way, wont.
adj. banal, boring, clichéd, conventional, customary, day-by-day, dull, everyday, familiar, habitual, hackneyed, humdrum, mundane, normal, ordinary, predictable, run-of-the-mill, standard, tedious, tiresome, typical, unimaginative, uninspired, unoriginal, usual, wonted, workaday.
antonyms exciting, unusual.

rover *n.* drifter, gadabout, gypsy, itinerant, nomad, rambler, ranger, stravaiger, transient, traveler, vagrant, wanderer.
antonym stay-at-home.

row[1] *n.* bank, colonnade, column, file, line, queue, range, rank, sequence, series, string, tier.

row[2] *n.* altercation, brawl, castigation, commotion, controversy, dispute, disturbance, Donnybrook, dressing-down, falling-out, fracas, fray, fuss, lecture, noise, quarrel, racket, rammy, reprimand, reproof, rhubarb, rollicking, rookery, rout, ruckus, ruction, ruffle, rumpus, scrap, shemozzle, shindig, shindy, slanging match, squabble, talking-to, telling-off, ticking-off, tiff, tongue-lashing, trouble, tumult, uproar.
antonym calm.
v. argue, argufy, brawl, dispute, fight, scrap, squabble, wrangle.

rowdy *adj.* boisterous, disorderly, loud, loutish, noisy, obstreperous, roisterous, roisting, rorty, rough, rumbustious, stroppy, unruly, uproarious, wild.
antonyms quiet, restrained.
n. brawler, hoodlum, hooligan, keelie, lout, rough, ruffian, tearaway, tough, yahoo, yob, yobbo.

royal *adj.* august, basilical, grand, imperial, impressive, kinglike, kingly, magnificent, majestic, monarchical, princely, queenlike, queenly, regal, sovereign, splendid, stately, superb, superior.

rub *v.* abrade, apply, caress, chafe, clean, embrocate, fray, grate, knead, malax, malaxate, massage, polish, put, scour, scrape, shine, smear, smooth, spread, stroke, wipe.
n. caress, catch, difficulty, drawback, hindrance, hitch, impediment, kneading, malaxage, malaxation, massage, obstacle, polish, problem, shine, snag, stroke, trouble, wipe.

rubbish *n.* balderdash, balls, baloney, bosh, bunkum, clamjamphrie, claptrap, cobblers, codswallop, crap, dead-wood, debris, draff, drivel, dross, flotsam and jetsam, garbage, gibberish, gobbledegook, guff, havers, hogwash, junk, kibosh, kitsch, landfill, leavings, litter, lumber, moonshine, mullock, nonsense, offal, offscourings, offscum, piffle, poppycock, raffle, refuse, riddlings, rot, scoria, scrap, stuff, sullage, sweepings, tommyrot, tosh, trash, trashery, truck, trumpery, twaddle, vomit, waste.
antonym sense.

ruddy *adj.* blooming, blushing, crimson, flammulated, florid, flushed, fresh, glowing, healthy, pink, red, reddish, roseate, rose-hued, rose-pink, rosy, rosy-cheeked, rubicund, rubineous, rubious, ruby, sanguine, scarlet, sunburnt.
antonyms pale, unhealthy.

rude *adj.* abrupt, abusive, artless, barbarous, blunt, boorish, brusque, brutish, cheeky, churlish, coarse, crude, curt, discourteous, disrespectful, graceless, gross, harsh, ignorant, illiterate, ill-mannered, impertinent, impolite, impudent, inartistic, inconsiderate, inelegant, insolent, insulting, loutish, low, makeshift, oafish, obscene, offhand, peremptory, primitive, raw, rough, savage, scurrilous, sharp, short, simple, startling, sudden, uncivil, uncivilized, uncouth, uncultured, uneducated, ungracious, unmannerly, unpleasant, unpolished, unrefined, untutored, violent, vulgar.
antonyms graceful, polished, polite, smooth.

rudimentary *adj.* abecedarian, basic, early, elementary, embryonic, fundamental, germinal, immature, inchoate, initial, introductory, primary, primitive, primordial, undeveloped, vestigial.
antonyms advanced, developed.

rue *v.* bemoan, bewail, beweep, deplore, grieve, lament, mourn, regret, repent.
antonym rejoice.

ruffian *n.* apache, bruiser, brute, bully, bully-boy, cutthroat, hoodlum, hooligan, keelie, lout, miscreant, Mohock, myrmidon, plug-ugly, rascal, rogue, rough, roughneck, rowdy, scoundrel, thug, tough, villain, yob, yobbo.

ruffle *v.* agitate, annoy, confuse, derange, disarrange, discompose, disconcert, dishevel, disorder, disquiet, disturb, fluster, harass, irritate, mess up, muss up, muss(e), nettle, peeve, perturb, rattle, rumple, stir, torment, tousle, trouble, unsettle, upset, vex, worry, wrinkle.
antonym smooth.

rugged *adj.* arduous, austere, barbarous, beefy, blunt, brawny, broken, bumpy, burly, churlish, crabbed, craggy, crude, demanding, difficult, dour, exacting, graceless, gruff, hale, hard, hard-featured, hardy, harsh, husky, irregular, jagged, laborious, muscular, ragged, rigorous, robust, rocky, rough, rude, severe, sour, stark, stern, strenuous, strong, sturdy, surly, taxing, tough,

trying, uncompromising, uncouth, uncultured, uneven, unpolished, unrefined, vigorous, weather-beaten, weathered, worn.
antonyms easy, refined, smooth.

ruin *n.* bankruptcy, bouleversement, breakdown, collapse, crash, damage, decay, defeat, destitution, destruction, devastation, disintegration, disrepair, dissolution, downfall, failure, fall, havoc, heap, insolvency, nemesis, overthrow, ruination, subversion, undoing, Waterloo, wreck, wreckage.
antonyms development, reconstruction.
v. banjax, bankrupt, botch, break, crush, damage, defeat, demolish, destroy, devastate, disfigure, impoverish, injure, jigger, mangle, mar, mess up, overthrow, overturn, overwhelm, pauperize, raze, scupper, scuttle, shatter, smash, spoil, unmake, unshape, wreck.
antonyms develop, restore.

ruinous *adj.* baleful, baneful, broken-down, calamitous, cataclysmic, catastrophic, crippling, deadly, decrepit, deleterious, derelict, destructive, devastating, dilapidated, dire, disastrous, extravagant, fatal, immoderate, injurious, murderous, noxious, pernicious, ramshackle, ruined, shattering, wasteful, withering.
antonym beneficial.

rule *n.* administration, ascendancy, authority, axiom, canon, command, condition, control, convention, course, criterion, custom, decree, direction, domination, dominion, empire, form, formula, governance, government, guide, guideline, habit, influence, institute, jurisdiction, law, leadership, mastery, maxim, method, order, ordinance, policy, power, practice, precept, prescript, principle, procedure, raj, regime, regulation, reign, routine, ruling, standard, supremacy, sway, tenet, way, wont.
v. adjudge, adjudicate, administer, command, control, decide, decree, determine, direct, dominate, establish, find, govern, guide, judge, lead, manage, obtain, predominate, preponderate, prevail, pronounce, regulate, reign, resolve, settle.

ruler *n.* commander, controller, emperor, empress, gerent, governor, gubernator, head of state, imperator, king, leader, lord, monarch, potentate, prince, princess, queen, sovereign, suzerain.
antonym subject.

ruling *n.* adjudication, decision, decree, finding, indiction, interlocution, irade, judgment, pronouncement, resolution, ukase, verdict.
adj. boss, chief, commanding, controlling, dominant, governing, leading, main, predominant, pre-eminent, preponderant, prevailing, prevalent, principal, regnant, reigning, supreme, upper.

ruminate *v.* brood, chew over, chew the cud, cogitate, consider, contemplate, deliberate, meditate, mull over, muse, ponder, reflect, revolve, think.

rummage *v.* delve, examine, explore, hunt, poke around, ransack, root, rootle, rout, search.

rumor *n.* breeze, bruit, bush telegraph, buzz, canard, fame, gossip, grapevine, hearsay, kite, news, on-dit, report, story, talk, tidings, underbreath, whisper, word.
v. bruit, circulate, gossip, publish, put about, report, say, tell, whisper.

rumple *v.* crease, crinkle, crumple, crush, derange, dishevel, disorder, muss up, muss(e), pucker, ruffle, scrunch, tousle, wrinkle.
antonym smooth.

rumpus *n.* bagarre, barney, brouhaha, commotion, confusion, disruption, disturbance, Donnybrook, fracas, furore, fuss, kerfuffle, noise, rhubarb, rookery, rout, row, ruction, shemozzle, shindig, shindy, tumult, uproar.
antonym calm.

run *v.* abscond, administer, bear, beat it, bleed, bolt, boss, career, carry, cascade, challenge, circulate, clear out, climb, compete, conduct, contend, continue, control, convey, co-ordinate, course, creep, dart, dash, decamp, depart, direct, discharge, display, dissolve, drive to, escape, extend, feature, flee, flow, function, fuse, gallop, glide, go, gush, hare, hasten, head, hie, hotfoot, hurry, issue, jog, ladder, last, lead, leak, lie, liquefy, lope, manage, maneuver, mastermind, melt, mix, move, operate, oversee, own, pass, perform, ply, pour, print, proceed, propel, publish, race, range, reach, regulate, roll, rush, scamper, scarper, scramble, scud, scurry, skedaddle, skim, slide, speed, spill, spout, spread, sprint, stand, stream, stretch, superintend, supervise, tear, tick, trail, transport, unravel, work.
antonyms stay, stop.
n. application, category, chain, class, coop, course, current, cycle, dash, demand, direction, drift, drive, enclosure, excursion, flow, gallop, jaunt, jog, journey, joy, kind, ladder, lift, motion, movement, order, outing, passage, path, pen, period, pressure, progress, race, ride, rip, round, rush, season, sequence, series, snag, sort, spell, spin, sprint, spurt, streak, stream, stretch, string, tear, tendency, tenor, tide, trend, trip, type, variety, way.

runaway *n.* absconder, deserter, escapee, escaper, fleer, fugitive, refugee, truant.
adj. escaped, fleeing, fugitive, loose, uncontrolled, wild.

rundown *n.* briefing, cut, decrease, drop, lessening, outline, précis, recap, reduction, résumé, review, run-through, sketch, summary, synopsis.

run-down *adj.* broken-down, debilitated, decrepit, dilapidated, dingy, drained, enervated, exhausted, fatigued, grotty, peaky, ramshackle, scabby, seedy, shabby, tumble-down, unhealthy, weak, weary, worn-out.
antonym well-kept.

rupture *n.* altercation, breach, break, breaking, burst, bustup, cleavage, cleft, contention, crack, disagreement, disruption, dissolution, estrangement, falling-out, feud, fissure, fracture, hernia, hostility, quarrel, rent, rift, schism, split, splitting, tear.

v. break, burst, cleave, crack, disrupt, dissever, divide, fracture, puncture, rend, separate, sever, split, sunder, tear.

rural *adj.* agrarian, agrestic, agricultural, Arcadian, bucolic, countrified, country, forane, pastoral, predial, rustic, sylvan, yokelish.
antonym urban.

ruse *n.* artifice, blind, deception, device, dodge, hoax, imposture, maneuver, ploy, sham, stall, stratagem, subterfuge, trick, wile.

rush *v.* accelerate, attack, bolt, capture, career, charge, dart, dash, dispatch, expedite, fly, hasten, hightail it, hotfoot, hurry, hustle, overcome, press, push, quicken, race, run, scour, scramble, scurry, shoot, speed, speed up, sprint, stampede, storm, tear, wallop, w(h)oosh.
n. assault, charge, dash, dispatch, expedition, flow, haste, hurry, onslaught, push, race, scramble, speed, stampede, storm, streak, surge, swiftness, tantivy, tear, urgency.
adj. brisk, careless, cursory, emergency, expeditious, fast, hasty, hurried, prompt, quick, rapid, superficial, swift, urgent.

S

sabotage *v.* cripple, damage, destroy, disable, disrupt, incapacitate, mar, nullify, ratten, scupper, subvert, thwart, undermine, vandalize, vitiate, wreck.
n. damage, destruction, disablement, disruption, impairment, marring, rattening, subversion, treachery, treason, undermining, vandalism, vitiation, wrecking.

sack[1] *v.* axe, discharge, dismiss, fire, lay off, make redundant.
n. discharge, dismissal, notice, one's books, one's cards, one's marching orders, the ax, the boot, the bum's rush, the chop, the elbow, the push.

sack[2] *v.* demolish, depredate, desecrate, despoil, destroy, devastate, lay waste, level, loot, maraud, pillage, plunder, raid, rape, ravage, raze, rifle, rob, ruin, spoil, strip, waste.
n. depredation, desecration, despoliation, destruction, devastation, leveling, looting, marauding, pillage, plunder, plundering, rape, rapine, ravage, razing, ruin, waste.

sacred *adj.* blessed, consecrated, dedicated, devotional, divine, ecclesiastical, godly, hallowed, heavenly, holy, inviolable, inviolate, invulnerable, priestly, protected, religious, revered, sacrosanct, saintly, sanctified, secure, solemn, venerable, venerated.
antonyms mundane, profane, temporal.

sad *adj.* bad, blue, calamitous, cheerless, chopfallen, crestfallen, crushed, dark, dejected, deplorable, depressed, depressing, desolated, despondent, disastrous, disconsolate, dismal, dispirited, distressed, distressing, doleful, dolesome, doloriferous, dolorific, doughy, dour, dowie, downcast, down-hearted, drear, dreary, gloomy, glum, grave, grief-stricken, grieved, grieving, grievous, heart-rending, heavy, heavy-hearted, jaw-fallen, joyless, lachrymose, lamentable, long-faced, low, low-spirited, lugubrious, melancholy, miserable, mournful, moving, painful, pathetic, pensive, piteous, pitiable, pitiful, poignant, regrettable, serious, shabby, sober, sober-minded, somber, sorrowful, sorry, sportless, stiff, tearful, touching, tragic, triste, uncheerful, unfortunate, unhappy, unsatisfactory, upsetting, wan, wistful, woebegone, woeful, wretched.
antonyms cheerful, fortunate, happy, lucky.

safe *adj.* alive and well, all right, cautious, certain, circumspect, conservative, dependable, discreet, foolproof, guarded, hale, harmless, immune, impregnable, innocuous, intact, invulnerable, non-poisonous, non-toxic, OK, out of harm's way, protected, proven, prudent, pure, realistic, reliable, scatheless, secure, sound, sure, tame, tested, tried, trustworthy, unadventurous, uncontaminated, undamaged, unfailing, unharmed, unhurt, uninjured, unscathed, wholesome.
antonyms exposed, harmful, unsafe, vulnerable.
n. cash-box, chest, coffer, deposit box, peter, repository, strongbox, vault.

safeguard *v.* assure, defend, guard, insure, preserve, protect, screen, secure, shelter, shield.
antonyms endanger, jeopardize.
n. armor, assurance, bulwark, convoy, cover, defense, escort, guarantee, guard, insurance, long-stop, Palladium, precaution, preventive, protection, security, shield, surety.

sag *v.* bag, decline, dip, drag, droop, drop, dwindle, fail, fall, flag, give, give way, hang, settle, sink, slide, slip, slump, wane, weaken, wilt.
antonyms bulge, rise.
n. decline, depression, dip, downturn, drop, dwindling, fall, low, low point, reduction, slide, slip, slump.
antonyms peak, rise.

sagacity *n.* acumen, acuteness, astuteness, canniness, discernment, foresight, insight, judgment, judiciousness, knowingness, penetration, percipience, perspicacity, prudence, sapience, sense, sharpness, shrewdness, understanding, wariness, wiliness, wisdom.
antonyms folly, foolishness, obtuseness.

sage *adj.* astute, canny, discerning, intelligent, judicious, knowing, knowledgeable, learned, perspicacious, politic, prudent, sagacious, sapient, sensible, wise.
antonym foolish.
n. authority, elder, expert, guru, hakam, maharishi, mahatma, master, Nestor, oracle, philosopher, pundit, rishi, savant, Solomon, Solon, teacher, wise man.
antonym ignoramus.

saintly *adj.* angelic, beatific, blameless, blessed, blest, celestial, devout, god-fearing, godly, holy, immaculate, innocent, pious, pure, religious, righteous, sainted, saintlike, seraphic, sinless, spotless, stainless, upright, virtuous, worthy.
antonyms godless, unholy, unrighteous, wicked.

sake *n.* account, advantage, aim, behalf, benefit, cause, consideration, end, gain, good, interest, motive, object, objective, principle, profit, purpose, reason, regard, respect, score, welfare, wellbeing.

salary *n.* earnings, emolument, honorarium, income, pay, remuneration, screw, stipend, wage, wages.

salient *adj.* arresting, chief, conspicuous, important, jutting, main, marked, noticeable, obvious, outstanding, principal, projecting, prominent, pronounced, protruding, remarkable, signal, significant, striking.

salubrious *adj.* beneficial, bracing, healthful, health-giving, healthy, hygienic, invigorating, refreshing, restorative, salutary, sanitary, wholesome.
antonyms insalubrious, unwholesome.

salutary *adj.* advantageous, beneficial, good, healthful, healthy, helpful, much-needed, practical, profitable, salubrious, seasonable, timely, useful, valuable, wholesome.

salute *v.* accost, acknowledge, address, bow, greet, hail, honor, kiss, knuckle, nod, recognize, salaam, wave, welcome.
n. acknowledgment, address, bow, gesture, greeting, hail, handclap, handshake, hello, kiss, nod, obeisance, recognition, reverence, salaam, salutation, salve, salvo, tribute, wave.

salvage *v.* conserve, glean, preserve, reclaim, recover, recuperate, redeem, repair, rescue, restore, retrieve, salve, save.
antonyms abandon, lose, waste.

salvation *n.* deliverance, escape, liberation, lifeline, preservation, reclamation, redemption, rescue, restoration, retrieval, safety, saving, soteriology.
antonyms damnation, loss.

same *adj.* aforementioned, aforesaid, alike, analogous, changeless, comparable, consistent, corresponding, duplicate, equal, equivalent, homologous, identical, indistinguishable, interchangeable, invariable, matching, mutual, reciprocal, selfsame, similar, substitutable, synonymous, twin, unaltered, unchanged, undiminished, unfailing, uniform, unvarying, very.
antonyms changeable, different, incompatible, inconsistent, variable.
n. ditto, the above-mentioned, the above-named, the aforementioned, the aforesaid.

sample *n.* cross-section, demonstration, ensample, example, exemplification, foretaste, free sample, freebie, illustration, indication, instance, model, pattern, representative, sign, specimen, swatch.
v. experience, inspect, investigate, pree, sip, taste, test, try.
adj. demonstration, illustrative, pilot, representative, specimen, test, trial.

sanction *n.* accreditation, agreement, allowance, approbation, approval, authorization, authority, backing, cachet, confirmation, countenance, endorsement, go-ahead, green light, imprimatur, license, OK, permission, ratification, seal, support.
antonyms disapproval, veto.
v. accredit, allow, approve, authorize, back, confirm, countenance, countersign, endorse, fiat, license, permit, ratify, support, underwrite, warrant.
antonyms disallow, disapprove, veto.

sanctuary *n.* adytum, altar, ark, asylum, chancel, church, delubrum, frith, grith, harborage, haven, holy of holies, naos, presbytery, protection, refuge, retreat, sacrarium, sanctum, sanctum sanctorum, seclusion, shelter, shrine, tabernacle, temple.

sane *adj.* all there, balanced, compos mentis, dependable, judicious, level-headed, lucid, moderate, normal, rational, reasonable, reliable, right-minded, sensible, sober, sound, stable.

sanguinary *adj.* bloodied, bloodthirsty, bloody, brutal, cruel, fell, gory, grim, merciless, murderous, pitiless, ruthless, savage.

sanguine[1] *adj.* animated, ardent, assured, buoyant, cheerful, confident, expectant, hopeful, lively, optimistic, over-confident, over-optimistic, Panglossian, roseate, spirited, unabashed, unappalled, unbowed.
antonyms cynical, depressive, gloomy, melancholy, pessimistic, realistic.

sanguine[2] *adj.* florid, flushed, fresh, fresh-complexioned, pink, red, rosy, rubicund, ruddy.
antonyms pale, sallow.

sanitary *adj.* aseptic, clean, disinfected, germ- free, healthy, hygienic, pure, salubrious, uncontaminated, unpolluted, wholesome.
antonyms insanitary, unwholesome.

sap *v.* bleed, deplete, devitalize, diminish, drain, enervate, exhaust, impair, reduce, rob, undermine, weaken.
antonyms build up, increase, strengthen.

sarcastic *adj.* acerbic, acid, acrimonious, biting, caustic, contemptuous, cutting, cynical, derisive, disparaging, incisive, ironical, mocking, mordant, sardonic, sarky, satirical, scathing, sharp, sharp-tongued, sneering, taunting, withering.

sardonic *adj.* biting, bitter, cynical, derisive, dry, heartless, ironical, jeering, malevolent, malicious, malignant, mocking, mordant, quizzical, sarcastic, satirical, scornful, sneering, wry.

satanic *adj.* accursed, black, demoniac, demoniacal, demonic, devilish, diabolic, diabolical, evil, fell, fiendish, hellish, infernal, inhuman, iniquitous, malevolent, malignant, Mephistophelian, satanical, wicked.
antonyms benevolent, benign, divine, godlike, godly, heavenly, holy.

sate *v.* cloy, fill, glut, gorge, gratify, overfill, satiate, satisfy, saturate, sicken, slake, surfeit, weary.
antonyms deprive, dissatisfy, starve.

satiate *v.* cloy, engorge, glut, gorge, jade, nauseate, overfeed, overfill, sate, satisfy, slake, stuff, surfeit.
antonyms deprive, dissatisfy, underfeed.

satire *n.* burlesque, caricature, diatribe, invective, irony, lampoon, parody, Pasquil, Pasquin, pasquinade, raillery, ridicule, sarcasm, send-up, skit, spoof, squib, takeoff, travesty, wit.

satirical *adj.* biting, bitter, burlesque, caustic, cutting, cynical, derisive, Hudibrastic, iambic, incisive, ironical, irreverent, mocking, mordant, pungent, sarcastic, sardonic, satiric, taunting.

satisfaction *n.* achievement, amends, appeasing, assuaging, atonement, comfort, compensation, complacency, content, contentedness, contentment, conviction, damages, ease, enjoyment, fulfilment, fullness, gratification, guerdon, happiness, indemnification, justice, payment, pleasure, pride, quittance, recompense, redress, reimbursement, remuneration, reparation, repleteness, repletion, requital, resolution, restitution, reward,

satiety, self-satisfaction, sense of achievement, settlement, vindication, well-being.
antonyms discontent, displeasure, dissatisfaction, frustration.

satisfactory *adj.* acceptable, adequate, all right, average, competent, fair, fit, OK, passable, proper, sufficient, suitable, tickety-boo, up to the mark.
antonyms inadequate, unacceptable, unsatisfactory.

satisfy *v.* answer, appease, assuage, assure, atone, compensate, content, convince, delight, discharge, do, fill, fulfil, glut, gratify, guerdon, indemnify, indulge, meet, mollify, pacify, pay, persuade, placate, please, qualify, quench, quiet, reassure, recompense, reimburse, remunerate, replete, requite, reward, sate, satiate, serve, settle, slake, square up, suffice, surfeit.
antonyms disappoint, dissatisfy, fail, frustrate, thwart.

saturate *v.* douse, drench, drouk, imbue, impregnate, infuse, permeate, ret, soak, souse, steep, suffuse, waterlog.

saucy *adj.* arch, audacious, cheeky, dashing, disdainful, disrespectful, flip, flippant, forward, fresh, gay, impertinent, impudent, insolent, irreverent, jaunty, lippy, malapert, natty, perky, pert, presumptuous, provocative, rakish, rude, sassy, sporty.
antonyms polite, respectful.

savage *adj.* barbarous, beastly, bestial, blistering, bloodthirsty, bloody, brutal, brutish, catamountain, cruel, devilish, diabolical, dog-eat-dog, fell, feral, ferocious, fierce, harsh, immane, inhuman, merciless, murderous, pitiless, primitive, ravening, rough, rude, rugged, ruthless, sadistic, sanguinary, uncivilized, uncultivated, undomesticated, uneducated, unenlightened, unsparing, untamed, untaught, vicious, wild.
antonyms benign, civilized, humane.
n. aboriginal, aborigine, ape, autochthon, barbarian, bear, beast, boor, brute, fiend, heathen, illiterate, indigene, lout, monster, native, oaf, philistine, primitive, roughneck, yahoo, yobbo.
v. attack, claw, hammer, lacerate, mangle, maul, pan, scarify, tear.

save *v.* cache, collect, conserve, cut back, deliver, economize, free, gather, guard, hinder, hoard, hold, husband, keep, lay up, liberate, obviate, preserve, prevent, protect, put aside, put by, reclaim, recover, redeem, rescue, reserve, retain, retrench, safeguard, salt away, salvage, screen, shield, spare, squirrel, stash, store.
antonyms discard, spend, squander, waste.

savory *adj.* agreeable, appetizing, aromatic, dainty, decent, delectable, delicious, edifying, full-flavored, gamy, good, gusty, honest, luscious, mouthwatering, palatable, piquant, reputable, respectable, rich, salubrious, scrumptious, spicy, tangy, tasty, toothsome, wholesome.
antonyms insipid, tasteless, unappetizing.
n. appetizer, bonne bouche, canapé, hors d'oeuvre.

say *v.* add, affirm, allege, announce, answer, assert, assume, bruit, claim, comment, communicate, conjecture, convey, declare, deliver, disclose, divulge, do, enunciate, estimate, express, guess, imagine, imply, intimate, judge, maintain, mention, opine, orate, perform, presume, pronounce, read, recite, reckon, rehearse, rejoin, remark, render, repeat, reply, report, respond, retort, reveal, rumor, signify, speak, state, suggest, surmise, tell, utter, voice.
n. authority, chance, clout, crack, go, influence, power, sway, turn, voice, vote, weight, word.

saying *n.* adage, aphorism, apophthegm, axiom, byword, dictum, gnome, maxim, mot, motto, precept, proverb, remnant, saw, slogan.

scald *v.* blister, burn, sear.

scale[1] *n.* calibration, compass, continuum, degree, degrees, extent, gamut, gradation, grading, graduation, hierarchy, ladder, measure, order, progression, proportion, range, ranking, ratio, reach, register, scope, sequence, series, spectrum, spread, steps.
v. adjust, level, move, proportion, prorate, regulate, shift.

scale[2] *n.* crust, encrustation, film, flake, furfur, lamella, lamina, layer, plate, scutellum, shield, squama, squamella, squamula, squamule.
v. clean, desquamate, exfoliate, flake, peel, scrape.

scale[3] *v.* ascend, clamber, climb, escalade, mount, scramble, shin up, surmount, swarm.

scamp *n.* blighter, caitiff, devil, fripon, imp, knave, mischief-maker, monkey, prankster, rascal, rogue, ruffian, scallywag, scapegrace, tyke, whippersnapper, wretch.

scan *v.* check, con, examine, glance through, investigate, pan, pan over, scrutinize, search, skim, survey, sweep.
n. check, examination, investigation, probe, review, screening, scrutiny, search, survey.

scandal *n.* abuse, aspersion, backbiting, calumniation, calumny, crime, defamation, detraction, dirt, discredit, disgrace, dishonor, embarrassment, enormity, evil, furore, gossip, gossiping, ignominy, infamy, muck-raking, obloquy, odium, offense, opprobrium, outcry, outrage, reproach, rumors, shame, sin, slander, stigma, talk, tattle, traducement, uproar, Watergate, wrongdoing.

scandalize *v.* affront, appal, astound, disgust, dismay, horrify, nauseate, offend, outrage, repel, revolt, shock, sicken.

scandalous *adj.* abominable, atrocious, calumnious, defamatory, disgraceful, disreputable, evil, exorbitant, extortionate, gamy, gossiping, immoderate, improper, infamous, libelous, monstrous, odious, opprobrious, outrageous, scurrilous, shameful, shocking, slanderous, unseemly, unspeakable, untrue.

scant *adj.* bare, deficient, hardly any, inadequate, insufficient, limited, little, little or no, minimal, sparse.
antonyms adequate, ample, sufficient.

scanty *adj.* bare, beggarly, deficient, exiguous, inadequate, insubstantial, insufficient, light, meager, narrow, parsimonious, poor, restricted, scant, scrimp, scrimpy, short, shy, skimped, skimpy, slender, sparing, sparse, thin.
antonyms ample, plentiful, substantial.

scarce *adj.* deficient, few, infrequent, insufficient, lacking, rare, scanty, sparse, thin on the ground, uncommon, unusual, wanting.
antonyms common, copious, plentiful.

scarcely *adv.* barely, hardly, just and no more, not readily, not willingly, only just, scarce.

scarcity *n.* dearth, deficiency, infrequency, insufficiency, lack, niggardliness, paucity, poverty, rareness, rarity, scantiness, shortage, sparseness, uncommonness, want.
antonyms abundance, enough, glut, plenty, sufficiency.

scare *v.* affright, alarm, appal, daunt, dismay, frighten, gally, intimidate, panic, shock, startle, terrify, terrorize, unnerve.
antonym reassure.
n. agitation, alarm, alarm and despondency, alert, consternation, dismay, fright, hysteria, panic, shock, start, terror.
antonym reassurance.

scared *adj.* affrighted, affrightened, agitated, anxious, appalled, dismayed, fearful, frightened, nervous, panicky, panic-stricken, petrified, shaken, startled, terrified, worried.
antonyms confident, reassured.

scarf *n.* babushka, boa, cravat, fichu, headscarf, headsquare, kerchief, muffler, neckerchief, necktie, shawl, stole, tawdry-lace.

scatter *v.* bestrew, break up, broadcast, diffuse, disband, disintegrate, disject, dispel, disperse, disseminate, dissipate, disunite, divide, fling, flurr, litter, propagate, separate, shower, sow, spatter, splutter, spread, sprinkle, squander, strew.
antonyms collect, concentrate.

scene *n.* act, area, arena, backdrop, background, business, carry-on, chapter, circumstances, commotion, confrontation, display, disturbance, division, drama, environment, episode, exhibition, focus, fuss, incident, landscape, locale, locality, location, melodrama, milieu, mise en scène, outburst, pageant, panorama, part, performance, picture, place, position, prospect, representation, row, set, setting, show, sight, site, situation, spectacle, spot, stage, tableau, tantrum, to-do, upset, view, vista, whereabouts, world.

scent *n.* aroma, bouquet, fragrance, fumet, odor, perfume, redolence, smell, spoor, trace, track, trail, waft, whiff.
antonym stink.
v. detect, discern, nose, nose out, perceive, recognize, sense, smell, sniff, sniff out.

schedule *n.* agenda, calendar, catalog, diary, form, inventory, itinerary, list, plan, program, scheme, scroll, table, timetable.
v. appoint, arrange, book, list, organize, plan, program, slot, table, time.

scheme *n.* arrangement, blueprint, chart, codification, configuration, conformation, conspiracy, contrivance, dart, design, device, diagram, disposition, dodge, draft, game, idea, intrigue, lay-out, machinations, maneuver, method, outline, pattern, plan, plot, ploy, procedure, program, project, proposal, proposition, racket, ruse, schedule, schema, shape, shift, stratagem, strategy, subterfuge, suggestion, system, tactics, theory.
v. collude, conspire, contrive, design, devise, frame, imagine, intrigue, machinate, manipulate, maneuver, mastermind, plan, plot, project, pull strings, pull wires, work out.

scheming *adj.* artful, calculating, conniving, crafty, cunning, deceitful, designing, devious, duplicitous, foxy, insidious, Machiavellian, slippery, sly, tricky, underhand, unscrupulous, wily.
antonyms artless, honest, open, transparent.

scholar *n.* academe, academic, authority, bookman, bookworm, egghead, intellectual, man of letters, pupil, savant, scholastic, schoolboy, schoolchild, schoolgirl, schoolman, student.
antonyms dullard, dunce, ignoramus, illiterate, philistine.

scholarly *adj.* academic, analytical, bookish, clerk-like, clerkly, conscientious, critical, erudite, intellectual, knowledgeable, learned, lettered, scholastic, scientific, studious, well-read, wissenschaftlich.
antonyms illiterate, unscholarly.

scholarship[1] *n.* attainments, book- learning, education, erudition, insight, knowledge, learnedness, learning, lore, scholarliness, wisdom, Wissenschaft.

scholarship[2] *n.* award, bursary, endowment, exhibition, fellowship, grant.

science *n.* art, discipline, knowledge, ology, proficiency, skill, specialization, technique, technology, Wissenschaft.

scoff[1] *v.* belittle, deride, despise, fleer, flout, geck, gibe, jeer, knock, mock, poke fun, pooh-pooh, rail, revile, rib, ridicule, scorn, sneer, taunt, twit.
antonyms compliment, flatter, praise.

scoff[2] *v.* bolt, consume, cram, devour, fill one's face, gobble, gulp, guzzle, pig, put away, shift, wolf.
antonym abstain.
n. chow, comestibles, commons, eatables, eats, edibles, fare, feed, fodder, food, grub, meal, nosh, nosh-up, provisions, rations, scran, tuck, victuals.

scold *v.* admonish, bawl out, berate, blame, castigate, censure, chide, find fault with, flyte, jaw, lecture, nag, rate, rebuke, remonstrate, reprimand, reproach, reprove, take to task, tell off, tick off, upbraid, vituperate, wig.
antonyms commend, praise.
n. battle-ax, beldam, fishwife, Fury, harridan, nag, shrew, termagant, virago, vixen, Xanthippe.

scope *n.* ambit, application, area, breadth, capacity, compass, competence, confines, coverage, elbow-room, extent, freedom, latitude, liberty, opportunity, orbit, outlook, purview, range, reach, remit, room, space, span, sphere, terms of reference, tessitura.

scorch *v.* blacken, blister, burn, char, parch, roast, scald, sear, shrivel, singe, sizzle, torrefy, wither.

score *n.* a bone to pick, account, amount, basis, bill, cause, charge, debt, due, gash, grade, gravamen, grievance, ground, grounds, grudge, injury, injustice, line, mark, notch, obligation, outcome, points, reason, reckoning, record, result, scratch, sum total, tab, tally, total, wrong.
v. achieve, adapt, amass, arrange, attain, be one up, benefit, chalk up, count, cut, deface, earn, engrave, furrow, gain, gouge, grave, graze, groove, hatch, have the advantage, have the edge, impress, incise, indent, knock up, make, make a hit, mark, nick, notch, notch up, orchestrate, profit, realize, record, register, scrape, scratch, set, slash, tally, total, win.

scorn *n.* contempt, contemptuousness, contumely, derision, despite, disdain, disgust, dismissiveness, disparagement, geck, mockery, sarcasm, scornfulness, slight, sneer.
antonyms admiration, respect.
v. contemn, deride, despise, disdain, dismiss, flout, hold in contempt, laugh at, laugh in the face of, look down on, misprize, pooh-pooh, refuse, reject, scoff at, slight, sneer at, spurn.
antonyms admire, respect.

scornful *adj.* arrogant, contemptuous, contumelious, defiant, derisive, disdainful, dismissive, disparaging, haughty, insulting, jeering, mocking, sarcastic, sardonic, scathing, scoffing, slighting, sneering, supercilious, withering.
antonyms admiring, complimentary, respectful.

scoundrel *n.* blackguard, blighter, bounder, caitiff, cheat, cur, dastard, good-for-nothing, heel, hound, knave, louse, miscreant, ne'er-do-well, picaroon, rascal, rat, reprobate, rogue, rotter, ruffian, scab, scallywag, scamp, scapegrace, stinker, swine, vagabond, villain.

scour[1] *v.* abrade, buff, burnish, clean, cleanse, flush, furbish, polish, purge, rub, scrape, scrub, wash, whiten.

scour[2] *v.* beat, comb, drag, forage, go over, hunt, rake, ransack, search, turn upside-down.

scourge *n.* affliction, bane, cat, cat-o'-nine- tails, curse, evil, flagellum, infliction, knout, lash, menace, misfortune, penalty, pest, pestilence, plague, punishment, strap, switch, terror, thong, torment, visitation, whip.
antonyms benefit, blessing, boon, godsend.
v. afflict, beat, belt, cane, castigate, chastize, curse, devastate, discipline, excoriate, flagellate, flail, flog, harass, horsewhip, lambaste, lash, lather, leather, plague, punish, tan, terrorize, thrash, torment, trounce, verberate, visit, wallop, whale, whip.

scowl *v.* frown, glare, glower, grimace, lower.
n. frown, glare, glower, grimace, moue.
antonyms beam, grin, smile.

scramble *v.* clamber, climb, contend, crawl, hasten, jostle, jumble, push, run, rush, scale, scrabble, shuffle, sprawl, strive, struggle, swarm, vie.
n. climb, commotion, competition, confusion, contention, free-for-all, hustle, mêlée, muddle, race, rat race, rivalry, rush, strife, struggle, trek, trial, tussle.

scrap[1] *n.* atom, bit, bite, crumb, fraction, fragment, grain, iota, junk, mite, modicum, morsel, mouthful, part, particle, piece, portion, remnant, shard, shred, sliver, snap, snatch, snippet, trace, vestige, waste, whit.
v. abandon, ax, break up, cancel, chuck, demolish, discard, ditch, drop, jettison, junk, shed, throw out, write off.
antonyms reinstate, restore, resume.

scrap[2] *n.* argument, bagarre, barney, battle, brawl, disagreement, dispute, dust-up, fight, quarrel, row, ruckus, ruction, rumpus, scuffle, set-to, shindy, squabble, tiff, wrangle.
antonyms agreement, peace.
v. argue, argufy, bicker, clash, fall out, fight, spat, squabble, wrangle.
antonym agree.

scrape *v.* abrade, bark, claw, clean, erase, file, grate, graze, grind, pinch, rasp, remove, rub, save, scour, scrabble, scratch, screech, scrimp, scuff, skimp, skin, squeak, stint.
n. abrasion, difficulty, dilemma, distress, fix, graze, mess, pickle, plight, predicament, pretty kettle of fish, rub, scratch, scuff, shave, spot, trouble.

scratch *v.* annul, cancel, claw, curry, cut, damage, delete, eliminate, erase, etch, grate, graze, incise, lacerate, mark, race, retire, rub, scarify, score, scrab, scrabble, scrape, withdraw.
n. blemish, claw mark, gash, graze, laceration, mark, race, scrape, streak.
adj. haphazard, impromptu, improvised, rough, rough-and-ready, unrehearsed.
antonym polished.

scrawny *adj.* angular, bony, emaciated, gaunt, lanky, lean, rawboned, scraggy, skeletal, skinny, thin, underfed, under-nourished.
antonym plump.

scream[1] *v.* bawl, clash, cry, holler, jar, roar, screak, screech, shriek, shrill, squeal, wail, yell, yelp, yowl.
n. howl, outcry, roar, screak, screech, shriek, squeal, wail, yell, yelp, yowl.
antonym whisper.

scream[2] *n.* card, caution, character, comedian, comic, cure, hoot, joker, laugh, riot, sensation, wit.
antonym bore.

screech *v.* cry, screak, scream, shriek, squawk, squeal, ululate, yelp.
antonym whisper.

screen *v.* broadcast, cloak, conceal, cover, cull, defend, evaluate, examine, filter, gauge, grade, guard, hide, mask, present, process, protect, riddle, safeguard, scan, shade, shelter, shield, show, shroud, sieve, sift, sort, veil, vet.
n. abat-jour, awning, canopy, cloak, concealment, cover, divider, guard, hallan, hedge, hoarding, mantle, mesh, net, partition, shade, shelter, shield, shroud, uncover.

scrimp *v.* curtail, economize, limit, pinch, reduce, restrict, save, scrape, shorten, skimp, stint.
antonym spend.

script *n.* book, calligraphy, cheirography, copy, hand, hand-writing, letters, libretto, lines, longhand, manuscript, penmanship, text, words, writing.

scrounge *v.* beg, bludge, bum, cadge, freeload, purloin, sponge, wheedle.

scrub *v.* abandon, abolish, cancel, clean, cleanse, delete, discontinue, ditch, drop, forget, give up, rub, scour.

scrupulous *adj.* careful, conscientious, conscionable, exact, fastidious, honorable, meticulous, minute, moral, nice, painstaking, precise, principled, punctilious, rigorous, strict, upright.
antonym careless.

scrutinize *v.* analyze, dissect, examine, explore, give a onceover, inspect, investigate, peruse, probe, scan, search, sift, study.

scurrilous *adj.* abusive, coarse, defamatory, Fescennial, foul, foul-mouthed, gross, indecent, insulting, low, nasty, obscene, offensive, Rabelaisian, ribald, rude, salacious, scabrous, scandalous, slanderous, vituperative, vulgar.
antonym polite.

scurry *v.* dart, dash, fly, hurry, race, scamper, scoot, scud, scuttle, skedaddle, skelter, skim, sprint, trot, whisk.
antonym stroll.
n. flurry, hustle and bustle, scampering, whirl.
antonym calm.

scuttle *v.* bustle, hare, hasten, hurry, run, rush, scamper, scoot, scramble, scud, scurry, scutter, trot.
antonym stroll.

seal *v.* assure, attest, authenticate, bung, clinch, close, conclude, confirm, consummate, cork, enclose, establish, fasten, finalize, plug, ratify, secure, settle, shake hands on, shut, stamp, stop, stopper, validate, waterproof.
antonym unseal.
n. assurance, attestation, authentication, bulla, confirmation, imprimatur, insignia, notification, ratification, sigil, signet, stamp.

search *v.* check, comb, examine, explore, ferret, frisk, inquire, inspect, investigate, jerque, look, probe, pry, quest, ransack, rifle, rummage, scour, scrutinize, sift, test.
n. examination, exploration, going-over, hunt, inquiry, inspection, investigation, perquisition, perscrutation, pursuit, quest, researches, rummage, scrutiny, zetetic.

searching *adj.* close, intent, keen, minute, penetrating, piercing, probing, quizzical, severe, sharp, thorough, zetetic.
antonyms superficial, vague.

season *n.* division, interval, period, span, spell, term, time.
v. acclimatize, accustom, anneal, color, condiment, condition, discipline, enliven, flavor, habituate, harden, imbue, inure, lace, leaven, mature, mitigate, moderate, prepare, qualify, salt, spice, temper, toughen, train.

seasoned *adj.* acclimatized, battle-scarred, experienced, hardened, long-serving, mature, old, practiced, time-served, veteran, weathered, well-versed.
antonym novice.

secede *v.* apostatize, disaffiliate, leave, quit, resign, retire, separate, split off, withdraw.
antonyms join, unite with.

secluded *adj.* claustral, cloistered, cloistral, cut off, isolated, lonely, out-of-the-way, private, reclusive, remote, retired, sequestered, sheltered, solitary, umbratile, umbratilous, unfrequented.
antonyms busy, public.

seclusion *n.* concealment, hiding, isolation, privacy, purdah, recluseness, remoteness, retirement, retreat, shelter, solitude.

secondary *adj.* alternate, auxiliary, back-up, consequential, contingent, derivative, derived, extra, indirect, inferior, lesser, lower, minor, relief, reserve, resultant, resulting, second, second-hand, second-rate, spare, subordinate, subsidiary, supporting, unimportant.
antonym primary.

secret *adj.* abstruse, arcane, back-door, backstairs, cabbalistic(al), camouflaged, clandestine, classified, cloak-and-dagger, close, closet, concealed, conspiratorial, covered, covert, cryptic, deep, discreet, disguised, esoteric, furtive, hidden, hole-and-corner, hush-hush, inly, mysterious, occult, out-of-the-way, private, privy, recondite, reticent, retired, secluded, secretive, sensitive, shrouded, sly, stealthy, tête-à-tête, undercover, underground, underhand, under-the-counter, undisclosed, unfrequented, unknown, unpublished, unrevealed, unseen.
antonyms open, public.
n. arcanum, code, confidence, enigma, formula, key, mystery, recipe.

secrete[1] *v.* appropriate, bury, cache, conceal, cover, disguise, harbor, hide, screen, secure, shroud, stash away, stow, veil.
antonym reveal.

secrete[2] *v.* emanate, emit, extravasate, extrude, exude, osmose, secern, separate.

sect *n.* camp, denomination, division, faction, group, party, school, splinter group, subdivision, wing.

section *n.* area, article, component, cross section, department, district, division, fraction, fractionlet, fragment, instalment, part, passage, piece, portion, region, sample, sector, segment, slice, subdivision, wing, zone.
antonym whole.

secular *adj.* civil, laic, laical, lay, non- religious, profane, state, temporal, worldly.
antonym religious.

secure *adj.* absolute, assured, certain, conclusive, confident, definite, dependable, easy, fast, fastened, firm,

fixed, fortified, immovable, immune, impregnable, on velvet, overconfident, protected, reassured, reliable, safe, sheltered, shielded, solid, stable, steadfast, steady, sure, tight, unassailable, undamaged, unharmed, well-founded.
antonyms insecure, uncertain.
v. acquire, assure, attach, batten down, bolt, chain, ensure, fasten, fix, gain, get, get hold of, guarantee, insure, land, lash, lock, lock up, moor, nail, obtain, padlock, procure, rivet, seize.
antonyms lose, unfasten.

security *n.* assurance, asylum, care, certainty, collateral, confidence, conviction, cover, custody, defense, gage, guarantee, guards, hostage, immunity, insurance, pawn, pledge, positiveness, precautions, preservation, protection, refuge, reliance, retreat, safeguards, safe-keeping, safety, sanctuary, sureness, surety, surveillance, warranty.
antonym insecurity.

sedate *adj.* calm, collected, composed, cool, decorous, deliberate, demure, dignified, douce, earnest, grave, imperturbable, middle-aged, placed, proper, quiet, seemly, serene, serious, slow-moving, sober, solemn, staid, tranquil, unflappable, unruffled.
antonyms flippant, hasty, undignified.

sediment *n.* deposit, draff, dregs, feces, fecula, grounds, lees, precipitate, residium, settlings, warp.

seductive *adj.* alluring, attractive, beguiling, bewitching, captivating, come-hither, come-on, enticing, flirtatious, honeyed, inviting, irresistible, provocative, ravishing, seducing, sexy, siren, specious, tempting. *antonym* unattractive.

see *v.* accompany, anticipate, appreciate, ascertain, attend, behold, comprehend, consider, consult, court, date, decide, deem, deliberate, descry, determine, discern, discover, distinguish, divine, encounter, ensure, envisage, escort, espy, experience, fathom, feel, follow, foresee, foretell, get, glimpse, grasp, guarantee, heed, identify, imagine, interview, investigate, judge, know, lead, learn, look, make out, mark, meet, mind, note, notice, observe, perceive, picture, realize, receive, recognize, reflect, regard, show, sight, spot, take, understand, usher, view, visit, visualize, walk, witness.

seek *v.* aim, ask, aspire to, attempt, beg, busk, desire, endeavor, entreat, essay, follow, hunt, inquire, invite, petition, pursue, request, solicit, strive, try, want.

seem *v.* appear, look, look like, pretend, sound like.

seemly *adj.* appropriate, attractive, becoming, befitting, comely, comme il faut, decent, decorous, fit, fitting, handsome, maidenly, meet, nice, proper, suitable, suited.
antonym unseemly.

segment *n.* articulation, bit, compartment, division, part, piece, portion, section, slice, wedge.
antonym whole.
v. anatomize, cut up, divide, halve, separate, slice, split.

segregate *v.* cut off, discriminate against, dissociate, isolate, quarantine, separate, set apart.
antonym unite.

seize *v.* abduct, annex, apprehend, appropriate, arrest, capture, catch, claw, clutch, cly, collar, commandeer, confiscate, crimp, distrain, distress, fasten, fix, get, grab, grasp, grip, hijack, impound, nab, prehend, smug, snatch, take.
antonym let go.

seldom *adv.* infrequently, occasionally, rarely, scarcely.
antonym often.

select *v.* choose, cull, pick, prefer, single out.
adj. choice, élite, excellent, exclusive, first-class, first-rate, hand-picked, limited, picked, posh, preferable, prime, privileged, rare, selected, special, superior, top, top- notch.
antonyms general, second-rate.

selection *n.* anthology, assortment, choice, choosing, collection, line-up, medley, miscellany, option, palette, pick, potpourri, preference, range, variety.

self-confident *adj.* assured, confident, fearless, poised, secure, self-assured, self-collected, self-possessed, self-reliant.
antonyms humble, unsure.

self-conscious *adj.* affected, awkward, bashful, coy, diffident, embarrassed, ill at ease, insecure, nervous, retiring, self-effacing, shamefaced, sheepish, shrinking, uncomfortable.
antonyms natural, unaffected.

self-denial *n.* abstemiousness, asceticism, moderation, renunciation, self-abandonment, self-abnegation, selflessness, self-renunciation, self-sacrifice, temperance, unselfishness.
antonym self-indulgence.

self-evident *adj.* axiomatic, clear, incontrovertible, inescapable, manifest, obvious, undeniable, unquestionable.

self-important *adj.* arrogant, big-headed, bumptious, cocky, conceited, consequential, overbearing, pompous, pushy, self-consequent, strutting, swaggering, swollen-headed, vain.
antonym humble.

self-indulgence *n.* dissipation, dissoluteness, excess, extravagance, high living, incontinence, intemperance, profligacy, self-gratification, sensualism.
antonym self-denial.

selfish *adj.* egoistic, egoistical, egotistic, egotistical, greedy, mean, mercenary, narrow, self-centered, self-interested, self-seeking, self-serving.
antonym unselfish.

self-possessed *adj.* calm, collected, composed, confident, cool, poised, self-assured, self-collected, together, unruffled.
antonym worried.

self-respect *n.* amour-propre, dignity, pride, self- assurance, self-confidence, self-esteem, self-pride, self-regard.
antonym self-doubt.

self-righteous *adj.* complacent, goody-goody, holier-than-thou, hypocritical, pharisaical, pi, pietistic(al), pious, priggish, sanctimonious, self-satisfied, smug, superior, Tartuffian, Tartuffish.
antonym understanding.

self-sacrifice *n.* altruism, generosity, self- abandonment, self-abnegation, self-denial, selflessness, self- renunciation.
antonym selfishness.

self-satisfied *adj.* complacent, puffed up, self- approving, self-congratulatory, self-righteous, smug.
antonym humble.

self-seeking *adj.* acquisitive, calculating, careerist, fortune-hunting, gold-digging, mercenary, on the make, opportunistic, self-endeared, self-interested, selfish, self- loving, self-serving.
antonym altruistic.

sell *v.* barter, cheat, convince, deal in, exchange, handle, hawk, impose on, market, merchandise, peddle, persuade, promote, retail, sell out, stock, surrender, trade, trade in, traffic in, trick, vend.
antonym buy.

send *v.* broadcast, cast, charm, communicate, consign, convey, delight, deliver, direct, discharge, dispatch, electrify, emit, enrapture, enthrall, excite, exude, fire, fling, forward, grant, hurl, intoxicate, move, please, propel, radiate, ravish, remit, shoot, stir, thrill, titillate, transmit.

senile *adj.* anile, decrepit, doddering, doited, doting, failing, imbecile, senescent.

senior *adj.* aîné(e), elder, first, higher, high- ranking, major, older, superior.
antonym junior.

sensation *n.* agitation, awareness, commotion, consciousness, emotion, Empfindung, excitement, feeling, furore, hit, impression, perception, scandal, sense, stir, surprise, thrill, tingle, vibes, vibrations, wow.

sensational *adj.* amazing, astounding, blood-and- thunder, breathtaking, dramatic, electrifying, excellent, exceptional, exciting, fabulous, gamy, hair-raising, horrifying, impressive, lurid, marvelous, melodramatic, mind-blowing, revealing, scandalous, sensationalistic, shocking, smashing, spectacular, staggering, startling, superb, thrilling.
antonym run-of-the-mill.

sense *n.* advantage, appreciation, atmosphere, aura, awareness, brains, clear-headedness, cleverness, consciousness, definition, denotation, direction, discernment, discrimination, drift, faculty, feel, feeling, gist, good, gumption, implication, import, impression, intelligence, interpretation, intuition, judgment, logic, marbles, meaning, message, mother wit, nous, nuance, opinion, perception, point, premonition, presentiment, purport, purpose, quickness, reason, reasonableness, sagacity, sanity, savvy, sensation, sensibility, sentiment, sharpness, significance, signification, smeddum, substance, tact, understanding, use, value, wisdom, wit(s), worth.
antonym foolishness.
v. appreciate, comprehend, detect, divine, feel, grasp, notice, observe, perceive, realize, suspect, understand.

senseless *adj.* absurd, anesthetized, asinine, crazy, daft, deadened, dotty, fatuous, foolish, halfwitted, idiotic, illogical, imbecilic, inane, incongruous, inconsistent, insensate, insensible, irrational, ludicrous, mad, meaningless, mindless, moronic, nonsensical, numb, numbed, out, out for the count, pointless, ridiculous, silly, simple, stunned, stupid, unconscious, unfeeling, unintelligent, unreasonable, unwise.
antonym sensible.

sensibility *n.* appreciation, awareness, delicacy, discernment, insight, intuition, perceptiveness, responsiveness, sensitiveness, sensitivity, susceptibility, taste.
antonym insensibility.

sensible *adj.* appreciable, canny, considerable, delicate, discernible, discreet, discriminating, down-to-earth, far-sighted, intelligent, judicious, level-headed, matter-of-fact, noticeable, palpable, perceptible, practical, prudent, rational, realistic, reasonable, right-thinking, sagacious, sage, sane, senseful, shrewd, significant, sober, solid, sound, tangible, visible, well-advised, well-thought-out, wise.
antonyms imperceptible, senseless.

sensible of acquainted with, alive to, aware of, cognizant of, conscious of, convinced of, mindful of, observant of, sensitive to, understanding.
antonym unaware of.

sensitive *adj.* acute, controversial, delicate, fine, hyperesthesic, hyperesthetic, hyperconscious, impressionable, irritable, keen, perceptive, precise, reactive, responsive, secret, sensitized, sentient, susceptible, temperamental, tender, thin-skinned, touchy, umbrageous.
antonym insensitive.

sensual *adj.* animal, bodily, carnal, epicurean, erotic, fleshly, lascivious, lecherous, lewd, libidinous, licentious, lustful, luxurious, pandemian, physical, randy, raunchy, self-indulgent, sexual, sexy, voluptuous, worldly.
antonyms ascetic, Puritan.

sentence *n.* aphorism, apophthegm, condemnation, decision, decree, doom, gnome, judgment, maxim, opinion, order, pronouncement, ruling, saying, verdict.
v. condemn, doom, judge, pass judgment on, penalize, pronounce judgment on.

sentiment *n.* attitude, belief, emotion, emotionalism, feeling, idea, judgment, mawkishness, maxim, opinion, persuasion, romanticism, saying, sensibility,

sentimentalism, sentimentality, slush, soft-heartedness, tenderness, thought, view.
antonyms hard-heartedness, straightforwardness.

sentimental *adj.* corny, dewy-eyed, drippy, emotional, gushing, gushy, gutbucket, impressionable, lovey-dovey, maudlin, mawkish, mushy, nostalgic, pathetic, romantic, rose-water, schmaltzy, simpering, sloppy, slushy, soft-hearted, tearful, tear-jerking, tender, too-too, touching, treacly, weepy, Wertherian.
antonym unsentimental.

separate *v.* abstract, bifurcate, deglutinate, departmentalize, detach, disaffiliate, disally, discerp, disconnect, disentangle, disjoin, dislink, dispart, dissever, distance, disunite, divaricate, diverge, divide, divorce, eloi(g)n, estrange, exfoliate, isolate, part, part company, prescind, remove, secede, secern, seclude, segregate, sever, shear, split, split up, sunder, uncouple, winnow, withdraw.
antonyms join, unite.
adj. alone, apart, autonomous, detached, disconnected, discrete, disjointed, disjunct, disparate, distinct, divided, divorced, independent, individual, isolated, particular, several, single, solitary, sundry, unattached, unconnected.
antonyms attached, together.

separation *n.* break, break-up, detachment, diaeresis, dialysis, diaspora, diastasis, discerption, disconnection, disengagement, disgregation, disjunction, disjuncture, disseverance, disseveration, disseverment, dissociation, disunion, division, divorce, estrangement, farewell, gap, leave-taking, parting, rift, segregation, severance, solution, split, split-up.
antonyms togetherness, unification.

sequence *n.* arrangement, chain, consequence, course, cycle, order, procession, progression, series, set, succession, track, train.

serene *adj.* calm, composed, cool, halcyon, imperturbable, peaceful, placid, tranquil, unclouded, undisturbed, unflappable, unruffled, untroubled.
antonym troubled.

serenity *n.* calm, calmness, composure, cool, peace, peacefulness, placidity, quietness, quietude, stillness, tranquility, unflappability.
antonyms anxiety, disruption.

series *n.* arrangement, catena, chain, concatenation, consecution, course, cycle, enfilade, line, order, progression, run, scale, sequence, set, string, succession, train.

serious *adj.* acute, alarming, critical, crucial, dangerous, deep, deliberate, determined, difficult, earnest, far-reaching, fateful, genuine, grave, grim, heavy, honest, humorless, important, long-faced, momentous, pensive, pressing, resolute, resolved, sedate, severe, significant, sincere, sober, solemn, staid, stern, thoughtful, unsmiling, urgent, weighty, worrying.
antonyms facetious, light, slight, smiling, trivial.

servant *n.* aia, amah, ancillary, attendant, ayah, bearer, boy, butler, daily, day, day-woman, domestic, drudge, flunky, footman, garçon, gentleman's gentleman, gossoon, gyp, haiduk, handmaid, handmaiden, help, helper, hind, hireling, Jeeves, kitchen-maid, knave, lackey, lady's maid, livery- servant, maid, maid of all work, maître d'hôtel, major-domo, man, manservant, menial, ministrant, retainer, scout, seneschal, servitor, skivvy, slave, slavey, steward, valet, vassal, woman.
antonyms master, mistress.

serve *v.* act, aid, answer, arrange, assist, attend, avail, complete, content, dance attendance, deal, deliver, discharge, distribute, do, fulfil, further, handle, help, minister to, oblige, observe, officiate, pass, perform, present, provide, satisfy, succor, suffice, suit, supply, undergo, wait on, work for.

service *n.* advantage, assistance, avail, availability, benefit, business, ceremony, check, disposal, duty, employ, employment, expediting, function, help, labor, maintenance, ministrations, observance, office, overhaul, performance, rite, servicing, set, supply, use, usefulness, utility, work, worship.
v. check, maintain, overhaul, recondition, repair, tune.

serviceable *adj.* advantageous, beneficial, convenient, dependable, durable, efficient, functional, hard- wearing, helpful, operative, plain, practical, profitable, simple, strong, tough, unadorned, usable, useful, utilitarian.
antonym unserviceable.

servile *adj.* abject, base, bootlicking, controlled, craven, cringing, fawning, groveling, humble, low, mean, menial, obsequious, slavish, subject, submissive, subservient, sycophantic, toadying, toadyish, unctuous.
antonyms aggressive, bold.

servitude *n.* bondage, bonds, chains, enslavement, obedience, serfdom, slavery, subjugation, thraldom, thrall, vassalage, villeinage.
antonym freedom.

set[1] *v.* adjust, aim, allocate, allot, apply, appoint, arrange, assign, cake, conclude, condense, congeal, coordinate, crystallize, decline, decree, deposit, designate, determine, dip, direct, disappear, embed, establish, fasten, fix, fix up, gelatinize, harden, impose, install, jell, lay, locate, lodge, mount, name, ordain, park, place, plant, plonk, plump, position, prepare, prescribe, propound, put, rectify, regulate, resolve, rest, schedule, seat, settle, sink, situate, solidify, specify, spread, stake, station, stick, stiffen, subside, synchronize, thicken, turn, vanish.
n. attitude, bearing, carriage, fit, hang, inclination, miseen-scène, position, posture, scene, scenery, setting, turn.
adj. agreed, appointed, arranged, artificial, conventional, customary, decided, definite, deliberate, entrenched, established, firm, fixed, formal, hackneyed, immovable, inflexible, intentional, prearranged,

predetermined, prescribed, regular, rehearsed, rigid, routine, scheduled, settled, standard, stereotyped, stock, strict, stubborn, traditional, unspontaneous, usual.
antonyms free, movable, spontaneous, undecided.

set[2] *n.* apparatus, assemblage, assortment, band, batch, circle, class, clique, collection, company, compendium, coterie, covey, crew, crowd, faction, gang, group, kit, outfit, sect, sequence, series.

settle *v.* adjust, agree, alight, appoint, arrange, bed, calm, choose, clear, colonize, compact, complete, compose, conclude, confirm, decide, decree, descend, determine, discharge, dispose, dower, drop, dwell, endow, establish, fall, fix, found, hush, inhabit, land, light, liquidate, live, lower, lull, occupy, ordain, order, pacify, pay, people, pioneer, plant, plump, populate, quell, quiet, quieten, quit, reassure, reconcile, relax, relieve, reside, resolve, sedate, sink, soothe, square, square up, subside, tranquilize.

settlement[1] *n.* accommodation, adjustment, agreement, allowance, arrangement, clearance, clearing, completion, conclusion, confirmation, decision, defrayal, diktat, discharge, disposition, establishment, income, liquidation, payment, resolution, satisfaction, termination.

settlement[2] *n.* colonization, colony, community, encampment, hamlet, immigration, kibbutz, nahal, occupation, outpost, peopling, plantation, population.

settlement[3] *n.* compacting, drop, fall, sinkage, subsidence.

sever *v.* alienate, bisect, cleave, cut, detach, disconnect, disjoin, dissever, dissociate, dissolve, dissunder, disunite, divide, estrange, part, rend, separate, split, sunder, terminate.
antonyms join, unite.

several *adj.* assorted, different, discrete, disparate, distinct, divers, diverse, individual, many, particular, respective, separate, single, some, some few, specific, sundry, various.

severe *adj.* acute, arduous, ascetic, astringent, austere, biting, bitter, Catonian, caustic, chaste, classic, classical, cold, critical, cruel, cutting, dangerous, demanding, difficult, disapproving, distressing, dour, Draconian, Draconic, Dracontic, eager, exacting, extreme, fierce, flinty, forbidding, functional, grave, grim, grinding, hard, harsh, inclement, inexorable, intense, iron-handed, oppressive, pitiless, plain, punishing, relentless, restrained, Rhadamanthine, rigid, rigorous, satirical, scathing, serious, shrewd, simple, sober, Spartan, stern, strait-laced, strict, stringent, taxing, tight- lipped, tough, trying, unadorned, unbending, unembellished, ungentle, unrelenting, unsmiling, unsparing, unsympathetic, violent.
antonyms compassionate, kind, lenient, mild, sympathetic.

sex *n.* coition, coitus, congress, copulation, desire, fornication, gender, intercourse, intimacy, libido, lovemaking, nookie, reproduction, screw, sexual intercourse, sexual relations, sexuality, union, venery.

sexual *adj.* carnal, coital, erotic, gamic, genital, intimate, procreative, reproductive, sensual, sex, sex-related, venereal.
antonym asexual.

sexy *adj.* arousing, beddable, come-hither, cuddly, curvaceous, epigamic, erotic, flirtatious, inviting, kissable, naughty, nubile, pornographic, provocative, provoking, seductive, sensual, sensuous, slinky, suggestive, titillating, virile, voluptuous.
antonym sexless.

shabby *adj.* cheap, contemptible, dastardly, despicable, dilapidated, dingy, dirty, dishonorable, disreputable, dog-eared, down-at-heel, faded, frayed, ignoble, low, low-down, low-life, low-lived, mangy, mean, moth-eaten, neglected, paltry, poking, poky, poor, ragged, raunchy, rotten, run-down, scruffy, seedy, shameful, shoddy, tacky, tattered, tatty, threadbare, ungentlemanly, unworthy, worn, worn-out.
antonyms honorable, smart.

shack *n.* bothy, but and ben, cabin, dump, hole, hovel, hut, hutch, lean-to, shanty, shed, shiel, shieling.

shackle *n.* bond, bracelets, chain, darbies, fetter, gyve, hamper, handcuff, hobble, iron, leg-iron, manacle, rope, shackles, tether, trammel.
v. bind, chain, constrain, embarrass, encumber, fetter, gyve, hamper, hamstring, handcuff, handicap, hobble, hogtie, impede, inhibit, limit, manacle, obstruct, pinion, restrain, restrict, secure, tether, thwart, tie, trammel.

shade *n.* amount, apparition, blind, canopy, color, coolness, cover, covering, curtain, darkness, dash, degree, difference, dimness, dusk, eidolon, ghost, gloaming, gloom, gloominess, gradation, hint, hue, manes, murk, nuance, obscurity, phantasm, phantom, screen, semblance, semidarkness, shadiness, shadow, shadows, shelter, shield, shroud, specter, spirit, stain, suggestion, suspicion, tinge, tint, tone, trace, twilight, umbra, umbrage, variation, variety, veil, wraith.
v. cloud, conceal, cover, darken, dim, hide, inumbrate, mute, obscure, overshadow, protect, screen, shadow, shield, shroud, veil.

shadowy *adj.* caliginous, crepuscular, dark, dim, dreamlike, dusky, faint, ghostly, gloomy, half-remembered, hazy, illusory, imaginary, impalpable, indistinct, intangible, murky, nebulous, obscure, shaded, shady, spectral, tenebrious, tenebrose, tenebrous, umbratile, umbratilous, undefined, unreal, unsubstantial, vague, wraithlike.

shady[1] *adj.* bosky, bowery, caliginous, cool, dark, dim, leafy, shaded, shadowy, tenebrous, umbrageous, umbratile, umbratilous, umbriferous, umbrose, umbrous.
antonyms bright, sunlit, sunny.

shady[2] *adj.* crooked, discreditable, dishonest, disreputable, dubious, fishy, louche, questionable, shifty, slippery, suspect, suspicious, underhand, unethical, unscrupulous, untrustworthy.
antonyms honest, trustworthy.

shaggy *adj.* crinose, hairy, hirsute, long-haired, nappy, rough, tousled, tousy, unkempt, unshorn.
antonyms bald, shorn.

shake *n.* agitation, convulsion, disturbance, instant, jar, jerk, jiffy, jolt, jounce, moment, no time, pulsation, quaking, second, shiver, shock, shudder, tick, trembling, tremor, trice, twitch, vellication, vibration.
v. agitate, brandish, bump, churn, concuss, convulse, didder, discompose, distress, disturb, flourish, fluctuate, frighten, heave, impair, intimidate, jar, joggle, jolt, jounce, move, oscillate, quake, quiver, rattle, rock, rouse, shimmy, shiver, shock, shog, shudder, split, stir, succuss, sway, totter, tremble, twitch, undermine, unnerve, unsettle, upset, vellicate, vibrate, wag, waggle, wave, waver, weaken, wobble.

shaky *adj.* dubious, faltering, inexpert, insecure, precarious, questionable, quivery, rickety, rocky, shoogly, suspect, tottering, tottery, uncertain, undependable, unreliable, unsound, unstable, unsteady, unsupported, untrust-worthy, weak, wobbly.
antonyms firm, strong.

shallow *adj.* empty, flimsy, foolish, frivolous, idle, ignorant, meaningless, puerile, simple, skin-deep, slight, superficial, surface, trivial, unanalytical, unintelligent, unscholarly.
antonyms analytical, deep.

sham *n.* charlatan, counterfeit, feint, forgery, fraud, goldbrick, hoax, humbug, imitation, impostor, imposture, mountebank, phony, pretense, pretender, pseud, stumer.
adj. artificial, bogus, counterfeit, ersatz, faked, false, feigned, imitation, mock, pasteboard, phony, pinchbeck, pretended, pseud, pseudo, put-on, simulated, snide, spurious, synthetic.
antonym genuine.
v. affect, counterfeit, fake, feign, malinger, pretend, put on, simulate.

shame *n.* aidos, bashfulness, blot, chagrin, compunction, contempt, degradation, derision, discredit, disgrace, dishonor, disrepute, embarrassment, humiliation, ignominy, infamy, mortification, obloquy, odium, opprobrium, reproach, scandal, shamefacedness, stain, stigma.
antonyms distinction, honor, pride.
v. abash, blot, confound, debase, defile, degrade, discomfit, disconcert, discredit, disgrace, dishonor, embarrass, humble, humiliate, mortify, put to shame, reproach, ridicule, show up, smear, stain, sully, taint.
interj. fi donc, fie, fie upon you, for shame, fy, shame on you.

shameful *adj.* abominable, atrocious, base, contemptible, dastardly, degrading, discreditable, disgraceful, dishonorable, embarrassing, humiliating, ignominious, indecent, infamous, low, mean, mortifying, outrageous, reprehensible, scandalous, shaming, unbecoming, unworthy, vile, wicked.
antonyms creditable, honorable.

shameless *adj.* abandoned, abashless, audacious, barefaced, blatant, brash, brazen, corrupt, defiant, depraved, dissolute, flagrant, hardened, immodest, improper, impudent, incorrigible, indecent, insolent, ithyphallic, profligate, reprobate, unabashed, unashamed, unblushing, unprincipled, unscrupulous, wanton.
antonyms ashamed, contrite, shamefaced.

shape *n.* apparition, appearance, aspect, build, condition, configuration, conformation, contours, cut, dimensions, fettle, figure, form, format, frame, Gestalt, guise, health, kilter, likeness, lines, make, model, mold, outline, pattern, physique, profile, semblance, silhouette, state, template, trim.
v. accommodate, adapt, construct, create, define, develop, devise, embody, fashion, forge, form, frame, guide, make, model, modify, mold, plan, prepare, produce, redact, regulate, remodel.

shapeless *adj.* amorphous, asymmetrical, battered, characterless, dumpy, embryonic, formless, inchoate, indeterminate, indigest, irregular, misshapen, nebulous, undeveloped, unformed, unshapely, unstructured.
antonym shapely.

shapely *adj.* comely, curvaceous, elegant, featous, gainly, graceful, neat, pretty, trim, voluptuous, well-formed, well-proportioned, well-set-up, well-turned.
antonym shapeless.

share *v.* allot, apportion, assign, chip in, distribute, divide, divvy, divvy up, go Dutch, go fifty-fifty, go halves, muck in, partake, participate, split, whack.
n. a piece of the action, allotment, allowance, contribution, cut, dividend, division, divvy, due, finger, lot, part, portion, proportion, quota, ration, snap, snip, stint, whack.

sharp *adj.* abrupt, acerbic, acicular, acid, acidulous, acrid, acrimonious, acute, alert, apt, artful, astute, barbed, biting, bitter, bright, burning, canny, caustic, chic, chiseled, classy, clear, clear-cut, clever, crafty, crisp, cunning, cutting, discerning, dishonest, distinct, dressy, eager, edged, excruciating, extreme, fashionable, fierce, fit, fly, harsh, honed, hot, hurtful, incisive, intense, jagged, keen, knife-edged, knifelike, knowing, long-headed, marked, natty, nimble-witted, noticing, observant, painful, penetrating, peracute, perceptive, piercing, piquant, pointed, pungent, quick, quick-witted, rapid, razor-sharp, ready, sarcastic, sardonic, saw-edged, scathing, serrated, severe, sharpened, shooting, shrewd, sly, smart, snappy, snazzy, sour, spiky, stabbing, stinging, stylish, subtle, sudden, tart, trenchant, trendy, unblurred, undulled, unscrupulous, vinegary, violent, vitriolic, waspish, wily.
antonyms blunt, dull, mild, obtuse, slow, stupid.
adv. abruptly, exactly, on the dot, out of the blue, precisely, promptly, punctually, suddenly, unexpectedly.

sharpen *v.* acuminate, edge, file, grind, hone, strop, taper, whet.
antonym blunt.

shatter *v.* blast, blight, break, burst, crack, crush, demolish, destroy, devastate, disable, disshiver, dumbfound, exhaust, explode, impair, implode, overturn, overwhelm, pulverize, ruin, shiver, smash, split, stun, torpedo, undermine, upset, wreck.

shattered *adj.* all in, crushed, dead beat, devastated, dog-tired, done in, exhausted, jiggered, knackered, overwhelmed, undermined, weary, worn out, zonked.

sheepish *adj.* abashed, ashamed, chagrined, chastened, embarrassed, foolish, mortified, self-conscious, shamefaced, silly, uncomfortable.
antonym unabashed.

sheer[1] *adj.* abrupt, absolute, arrant, complete, downright, mere, out-and-out, perpendicular, precipitous, pure, rank, steep, thorough, thoroughgoing, total, unadulterated, unalloyed, unmingled, unmitigated, unqualified, utter, vertical.

sheer[2] diaphanous, fine, flimsy, gauzy, gossamer, pellucid, see-through, thin, translucent, transparent.
antonyms heavy, thick.

sheet *n.* blanket, broadsheet, broadside, circular, coat, covering, expanse, film, flyer, folio, handbill, handout, lamina, layer, leaf, leaflet, membrane, nappe, newssheet, overlay, pane, panel, piece, plate, shroud, skin, slab, stratum, surface, veneer.

shelf *n.* bank, bar, bench, bracket, ledge, mantel, mantelpiece, platform, projection, reef, sandbank, sand-bar, shoal, step, terrace.

shelter *v.* accommodate, cover, defend, ensconce, guard, harbor, hide, protect, put up, safeguard, screen, shade, shadow, shield, shroud, skug.
antonym expose.
n. accommodation, aegis, asylum, bield, bunker, cover, covert, coverture, defense, dugout, funk-hole, guard, harborage, haven, lean-to, lee, lodging, protection, refuge, retreat, roof, safety, sanctuary, sconce, screen, screening, security, shade, shadow, shiel, umbrage, umbrella.
antonym exposure.

shield *n.* aegis, ancile, buckler, bulwark, cover, defense, escutcheon, guard, pelta, protection, rampart, safeguard, screen, scutum, shelter, targe, ward.
v. cover, defend, guard, protect, safeguard, screen, shade, shadow, shelter.
antonym expose.

shift *v.* adjust, alter, budge, change, dislodge, displace, fluctuate, maneuver, move, quit, rearrange, relocate, remove, reposition, rid, scoff, swallow, swerve, switch, transfer, transpose, vary, veer, wolf.
n. alteration, artifice, change, contrivance, craft, device, displacement, dodge, equivocation, evasion, expedient, fluctuation, maneuver, modification, move, permutation, rearrangement, removal, resource, ruse, shifting, sleight, stratagem, subterfuge, switch, transfer, trick, veering, wile.

shifty *adj.* contriving, crafty, deceitful, devious, dishonest, disingenuous, dubious, duplicitous, evasive, fly-by-night, furtive, scheming, shady, slippery, tricky, underhand, unprincipled, untrustworthy, wily.
antonyms honest, open.

shilly-shally *v.* dilly-dally, dither, falter, fluctuate, haver, hem and haw, hesitate, mess about, prevaricate, seesaw, shuffle, swither, teeter, vacillate, waver.

shimmer *v.* coruscate, gleam, glisten, glitter, phosphoresce, scintillate, twinkle.
n. coruscation, gleam, glimmer, glitter, glow, incandescence, iridescence, luster, phosphorescence.

shine *v.* beam, brush, buff, burnish, coruscate, effulge, excel, flash, glare, gleam, glimmer, glisten, glitter, glow, luster, polish, radiate, resplend, scintillate, shimmer, sparkle, stand out, star, twinkle.
n. brightness, burnish, effulgence, glare, glaze, gleam, gloss, glow, lambency, light, luminosity, luster, patina, polish, radiance, sheen, shimmer, sparkle.

shining *adj.* beaming, bright, brilliant, celebrated, conspicuous, distinguished, effulgent, eminent, fulgent, gleaming, glistening, glittering, glorious, glowing, illustrious, lamping, leading, lucent, luminous, nitid, outstanding, profulgent, radiant, resplendent, rutilant, shimmering, sparkling, splendid, twinkling.

shiny *adj.* agleam, aglow, bright, burnished, gleaming, glistening, glossy, lustrous, nitid, polished, satiny, sheeny, shimmery, sleek.
antonyms dark, dull.

shipshape *adj.* businesslike, neat, orderly, seamanlike, spick-and-span, spruce, tidy, trig, trim, well- organized, well-planned, well-regulated.
antonyms disorderly, untidy.

shiver *v.* palpitate, quake, quiver, shake, shudder, tremble, vibrate.
n. flutter, frisson, grue, quiver, shudder, start, thrill, tremble, trembling, tremor, twitch, vibration.

shock *v.* agitate, appal, astound, confound, disgust, dismay, disquiet, horrify, jar, jolt, nauseate, numb, offend, outrage, paralyze, revolt, scandalize, shake, sicken, stagger, stun, stupefy, traumatize, unnerve, unsettle.
antonyms delight, gratify, please, reassure.
n. blow, bombshell, breakdown, clash, collapse, collision, concussion, consternation, dismay, distress, disturbance, encounter, fright, impact, jarring, jolt, perturbation, prostration, stupefaction, stupor, succussion, thunderbolt, trauma, turn, upset.
antonyms delight, pleasure.

shocking *adj.* abhorrent, abominable, appalling, astounding, atrocious, deplorable, detestable, disgraceful, disgusting, disquieting, distressing, dreadful, execrable, foul, frightful, ghastly, hideous, horrible, horrific, horrifying, insufferable, intolerable, loathsome, monstrous, nauseating, nefandous, odious, offensive, outrageous, repugnant, repulsive, revolting, scandalous, sickening, stupefying, unbearable, unspeakable.
antonyms acceptable, delightful, pleasant, satisfactory.

shore[1] *n.* beach, coast, foreshore, lakeside, littoral, margin, offing, promenade, rivage, sands, seaboard, seafront, sea-shore, strand, waterfront, water's edge, waterside.

shore[2] *v.* brace, buttress, hold, prop, reinforce, shore up, stay, strengthen, support, underpin.

short *adj.* abbreviated, abridged, abrupt, blunt, brief, brittle, brusque, compendious, compressed, concise, crisp, crumbly, crusty, curt, curtailed, deficient, diminutive, direct, discourteous, dumpy, ephemeral, evanescent, fleeting, friable, gruff, impolite, inadequate, insufficient, lacking, laconic, limited, little, low, meager, momentary, murly, offhand, passing, petite, pithy, poor, précised, sawn-off, scant, scanty, scarce, sententious, sharp, shortened, short-handed, short-lived, short- term, slender, slim, small, snappish, snappy, sparse, squat, straight, succinct, summarized, summary, tart, terse, tight, tiny, transitory, uncivil, understaffed, unplentiful, wanting, wee.
antonyms adequate, ample, expansive, large, lasting, long, long-lived, polite, tall.

shortage *n.* absence, dearth, deficiency, deficit, failure, inadequacy, insufficiency, lack, leanness, meagerness, paucity, poverty, scantiness, scarcity, shortfall, sparseness, want, wantage.
antonyms abundance, sufficiency.

shortcoming *n.* defect, drawback, faible, failing, fault, flaw, foible, frailty, imperfection, inadequacy, weakness.

shorten *v.* abbreviate, abridge, crop, curtail, cut, decrease, diminish, dock, foreshorten, lessen, lop, précis, prune, reduce, take up, telescope, trim, truncate.
antonyms amplify, enlarge, lengthen.

short-lived *adj.* brief, caducous, ephemeral, evanescent, fleeting, fugacious, impermanent, momentary, passing, short, temporary, transient, transitory.
antonyms abiding, enduring, lasting, long-lived.

shortly *adv.* abruptly, anon, briefly, concisely, curtly, directly, laconically, presently, sharply, soon, succinctly, tartly, tersely.

short-sighted *adj.* careless, hasty, ill-advised, ill-considered, impolitic, impractical, improvident, imprudent, injudicious, myopic, near-sighted, unimaginative, unthinking.
antonyms far-sighted, hypermetropic, long-sighted.

short-tempered *adj.* choleric, crusty, fiery, hot- tempered, impatient, irascible, irritable, peppery, quick-tempered, ratty, testy, touchy.
antonyms calm, patient, placid.

shout *n.* bay, bellow, belt, call, cheer, cry, roar, scream, shriek, yell.
v. bawl, bay, bellow, call, cheer, cry, holler, roar, scream, shriek, yell.

shove *v.* barge, crowd, drive, elbow, force, impel, jostle, press, propel, push, shoulder, thrust.

shovel *n.* backhoe, bail, bucket, scoop, spade.
v. convey, dredge, heap, ladle, load, move, scoop, shift, spade, spoon, toss.

show *v.* accompany, accord, assert, attend, attest, bestow, betray, clarify, conduct, confer, demonstrate, disclose, display, divulge, elucidate, escort, evidence, evince, exemplify, exhibit, explain, grant, guide, illustrate, indicate, instruct, lead, manifest, offer, present, prove, register, reveal, teach, usher, witness.
n. affectation, air, appearance, array, dash, demonstration, display, éclat, élan, entertainment, exhibition, exhibitionism, expo, exposition, extravaganza, façade, fair, féerie, flamboyance, gig, illusion, indication, likeness, manifestation, ostentation, pageant, pageantry, panache, parade, performance, pizzazz, plausibility, pose, presentation, pretence, pretext, production, profession, razzle-dazzle, representation, semblance, sight, sign, spectacle, swagger, view.

show-down *n.* clash, climax, confrontation, crisis, culmination, dénouement, exposé, face-off.

show-off *n.* boaster, braggadocio, braggart, egotist, exhibitionist, peacock, self-advertiser, swaggerer, swanker, vaunter.

showy *adj.* epideictic, euphuistic, flamboyant, flash, flashy, florid, flossy, garish, gaudy, glitzy, loud, ostentatious, pompous, pretentious, sparkish, specious, splashy, swanking, swanky, tawdry, tinselly.
antonyms quiet, restrained.

shred *n.* atom, bit, fragment, grain, iota, jot, mammock, mite, piece, rag, ribbon, scrap, sliver, snippet, tatter, trace, whit, wisp.

shrewd *adj.* acute, arch, argute, artful, astucious, astute, calculated, calculating, callid, canny, clever, crafty, cunning, discerning, discriminating, downy, far-seeing, far- sighted, fly, gnostic, intelligent, judicious, keen, knowing, long-headed, observant, perceptive, perspicacious, sagacious, sharp, sly, smart, well-advised, wily.
antonyms naïve, obtuse, unwise.

shriek *v.* bellow, caterwaul, cry, holler, howl, scream, screech, shout, squeal, wail, yell.
n. bellow, caterwaul, cry, howl, scream, screech, shout, squeal, wail.

shrill *adj.* acute, argute, carrying, ear-piercing, ear-splitting, high, high-pitched, penetrating, piercing, piping, screaming, screeching, screechy, sharp, strident, treble.
antonyms gentle, low, soft.

shrink *v.* back away, balk, contract, cower, cringe, decrease, deflate, diminish, dwindle, flinch, lessen, narrow, quail, recoil, retire, shorten, shrivel, shun, shy away, wince, withdraw, wither, wrinkle.
antonyms embrace, expand, stretch, warm to.

shrivel *v.* burn, dehydrate, desiccate, dwindle, frizzle, gizzen, parch, pucker, scorch, sear, shrink, wilt, wither, wizen, wrinkle.

shun *v.* avoid, cold-shoulder, elude, eschew, evade, ignore, ostracize, shy away from, spurn, steer clear of.
antonyms accept, embrace.

shut *v.* bar, bolt, cage, close, fasten, latch, lock, seal, secure, slam, spar.
antonym open.

shy *adj.* backward, bashful, cautious, chary, coy, diffident, distrustful, farouche, hesitant, inhibited, modest, mousy, nervous, reserved, reticent, retiring, self-conscious, self-effacing, shrinking, suspicious, timid, unassertive, wary.
antonyms bold, confident.
v. back away, balk, buck, flinch, quail, rear, recoil, shrink, start, swerve, wince.

sick *adj.* ailing, black, blasé, bored, diseased, disgusted, displeased, dog-sick, fed up, feeble, ghoulish, glutted, ill, indisposed, jaded, laid up, morbid, mortified, nauseated, pining, poorly, puking, qualmish, queasy, sated, satiated, sickly, tired, under the weather, unwell, vomiting, weak, weary.
antonyms healthy, well.

sickness *n.* affliction, ailment, bug, complaint, derangement, disease, disorder, dwam, ill-health, illness, indisposition, infirmity, insanity, malady, nausea, pestilence, qualmishness, queasiness, vomiting.
antonym health.

side *n.* airs, angle, arrogance, aspect, bank, border, boundary, brim, brink, camp, cause, department, direction, division, edge, elevation, face, facet, faction, flank, flitch, fringe, gang, hand, insolence, light, limit, margin, opinion, ostentation, page, part, party, perimeter, periphery, position, pretentiousness, quarter, region, rim, sect, sector, slant, stand, standpoint, surface, team, twist, verge, view, viewpoint.
adj. flanking, incidental, indirect, irrelevant, lateral, lesser, marginal, minor, oblique, roundabout, secondary, subordinate, subsidiary.

sidle *v.* creep, edge, inch, ingratiate, insinuate, slink, sneak, steal, wriggle.

sieve *v.* boult, remove, riddle, separate, sift, strain.
n. boulter, colander, riddle, screen, sifter, strainer.

sight *n.* appearance, apprehension, decko, display, estimation, exhibition, eye, eyes, eye-shot, eyeshot, eyesight, eyesore, field of vision, fright, gander, glance, glimpse, judgment, ken, look, mess, monstrosity, observation, opinion, pageant, perception, range, scene, seeing, show, spectacle, view, viewing, visibility, vision, vista.
v. behold, discern, distinguish, glimpse, observe, perceive, see, spot.

sightseer *n.* excursionist, holidaymaker, rubber- neck, tourist, tripper, visitor.

sign *n.* augury, auspice, badge, beck, betrayal, board, character, cipher, clue, device, emblem, ensign, evidence, figure, foreboding, forewarning, gesture, giveaway, grammalogue, hierogram, hint, indication, indicium, insignia, intimation, lexigram, logo, logogram, logograph, manifestation, mark, marker, miracle, note, notice, omen, placard, pointer, portent, presage, proof, reminder, representation, rune, signal, signature, signification, signpost, spoor, suggestion, symbol, symptom, token, trace, trademark, vestige, warning.
v. autograph, beckon, endorse, gesticulate, gesture, indicate, initial, inscribe, motion, signal, subscribe, wave.

signal *n.* alarm, alert, beacon, beck, cue, flare, flash, gesture, go-ahead, griffin, impulse, indication, indicator, light, mark, OK, password, rocket, sign, tip-off, token, transmitter, waft, warning, watchword.
adj. conspicuous, distinguished, eminent, exceptional, extraordinary, famous, glorious, impressive, memorable, momentous, notable, noteworthy, outstanding, remarkable, significant, striking.
v. beckon, communicate, gesticulate, gesture, indicate, motion, nod, sign, telegraph, waft, wave.

significance *n.* consequence, consideration, force, implication, implications, import, importance, impressiveness, interest, matter, meaning, message, moment, point, purport, relevance, sense, signification, solemnity, weight.
antonym unimportance.

significant *adj.* critical, denoting, eloquent, expressing, expressive, important, indicative, knowing, material, meaning, meaningful, momentous, noteworthy, ominous, pregnant, senseful, serious, solemn, suggestive, symbolic, symptomatic, vital, weighty.
antonyms meaningless, unimportant.

signify *v.* announce, augur, betoken, carry weight, communicate, connote, convey, count, denote, evidence, exhibit, express, imply, indicate, intimate, matter, mean, omen, portend, presage, proclaim, represent, show, stand for, suggest, symbolize, transmit.

silence *n.* calm, dumbness, hush, lull, muteness, noiselessness, obmutescence, peace, quiescence, quiet, quietness, reserve, reticence, secretiveness, speechlessness, stillness, taciturnity, uncommunicativeness.
v. deaden, dumbfound, extinguish, gag, muffle, muzzle, quell, quiet, quieten, stifle, still, strike dumb, subdue, suppress.

silent *adj.* aphonic, aphonous, dumb, hushed, idle, implicit, inaudible, inoperative, mum, mute, muted, noiseless, quiet, reticent, soundless, speechless, still, stilly, tacit, taciturn, tongue-tied, uncommunicative, understood, unexpressed, unforthcoming, unpronounced, unsounded, unspeaking, unspoken, voiceless, wordless.
antonyms loud, noisy, talkative.

silhouette *n.* configuration, delineation, form, outline, profile, shadow-figure, shadowgraph, shape.

silly *adj.* absurd, addled, asinine, benumbed, bird- brained, brainless, childish, cuckoo, daft, dazed, dopey, drippy, fatuous, feather-brained, flighty, foolhardy, foolish, frivolous, giddy, groggy, hen-witted, idiotic, illogical, immature, imprudent, inane, inappropriate, inept, irrational, irresponsible, meaningless, mindless, muzzy,

pointless, preposterous, puerile, ridiculous, scatter-brained, senseless, spoony, stunned, stupefied, stupid, unwise, witless.
antonyms collected, mature, sane, sensible, wise.
n. clot, dope, duffer, goose, half-wit, ignoramus, ninny, silly-billy, simpleton, twit, wally.

similar *adj.* alike, analogous, close, comparable, compatible, congruous, corresponding, homogeneous, homogenous, homologous, related, resembling, self-like, uniform.
antonym different.

similarity *n.* affinity, agreement, analogy, closeness, coincidence, comparability, compatibility, concordance, congruence, correspondence, equivalence, homogeneity, likeness, relation, resemblance, sameness, similitude, uniformity.
antonym difference.

simple *adj.* artless, bald, basic, brainless, childlike, classic, classical, clean, clear, credulous, dense, direct, dumb, easy, elementary, feeble, feeble-minded, foolish, frank, green, guileless, half-witted, homely, honest, humble, idiot-proof, inelaborate, ingenuous, innocent, inornate, intelligible, lowly, lucid, manageable, modest, moronic, naïf, naive, naïve, naked, natural, obtuse, one-fold, plain, pure, rustic, Saturnian, shallow, silly, sincere, single, slow, Spartan, stark, straightforward, stupid, thick, unadorned, unaffected, unalloyed, unblended, uncluttered, uncombined, uncomplicated, undeniable, understandable, undisguised, undivided, unelaborate, unembellished, unfussy, uninvolved, unlearned, unmixed, unornate, unpretentious, unschooled, unskilled, unsophisticated, unsuspecting, unvarnished.
antonyms artful, clever, complicated, difficult, fancy, intricate.

simpleton *n.* Abderite, blockhead, booby, daftie, dizzard, dolt, dope, dullard, dunce, dupe, flat, flathead, fool, gaby, gander, gomeril, goon, goop, goose, goose-cap, goosy, Gothamist, Gothamite, green goose, greenhorn, gump, gunsel, idiot, imbecile, jackass, Johnny, juggins, maffling, moron, nincompoop, ninny, ninny-hammer, numskull, soft-head, spoon, stupid, twerp.
antonym brain.

simulate *v.* act, affect, assume, counterfeit, duplicate, echo, fabricate, fake, feign, imitate, mimic, parrot, pretend, put on, reflect, reproduce, sham.

sin *n.* crime, damnation, debt, error, evil, fault, guilt, hamartia, impiety, iniquity, lapse, misdeed, offense, sinfulness, transgression, trespass, ungodliness, unrighteousness, wickedness, wrong, wrongdoing.
v. err, fall, fall from grace, go astray, lapse, misbehave, offend, stray, transgress, trespass.

sincere *adj.* artless, bona fide, candid, deep-felt, earnest, frank, genuine, guileless, heartfelt, heart-whole, honest, natural, open, plain-hearted, plain-spoken, pure, real, serious, simple, simple-hearted, single-hearted, soulful, straightforward, true, true-hearted, truthful, unadulterated, unaffected, unfeigned, unmixed, wholehearted.
antonym insincere.

sincerity *n.* artlessness, bona fides, candor, earnestness, frankness, genuineness, good faith, guilelessness, honesty, plain-heartedness, probity, seriousness, straightforwardness, truth, truthfulness, wholeheartedness.
antonym insincerity.

sinful *adj.* bad, corrupt, criminal, depraved, erring, fallen, guilty, immoral, impious, iniquitous, irreligious, peccable, peccant, ungodly, unholy, unrighteous, unvirtuous, wicked, wrongful.
antonyms righteous, sinless.

sing *v.* betray, bizz, blow the whistle, cantillate, carol, caterwaul, chant, chirp, croon, finger, fink, grass, hum, inform, intone, lilt, melodize, peach, pipe, purr, quaver, rat, render, serenade, spill the beans, squeal, talk, trill, vocalize, warble, whine, whistle, yodel.

singe *v.* blacken, burn, cauterize, char, scorch, sear.

single *adj.* celibate, distinct, exclusive, free, individual, lone, man-to-man, one, one-fold, one-to-one, only, particular, separate, simple, sincere, single-minded, singular, sole, solitary, unattached, unblended, unbroken, uncombined, uncompounded, undivided, unique, unmarried, unmixed, unshared, unwed, wholehearted.

singular *adj.* atypical, conspicuous, curious, eccentric, eminent, exceptional, extraordinary, individual, noteworthy, odd, out-of-the-way, outstanding, peculiar, pre- eminent, private, prodigious, proper, puzzling, queer, rare, remarkable, separate, single, sole, strange, uncommon, unique, unparalleled, unusual.
antonyms normal, usual.

sink *v.* abandon, abate, abolish, bore, collapse, conceal, decay, decline, decrease, defeat, degenerate, degrade, delapse, descend, destroy, dig, diminish, dip, disappear, drill, drive, droop, drop, drown, dwindle, ebb, engulf, excavate, fade, fail, fall, finish, flag, founder, invest, lapse, lay, lessen, lower, merge, overwhelm, pay, penetrate, plummet, plunge, relapse, retrogress, ruin, sag, scupper, slip, slope, slump, stoop, submerge, subside, succumb, suppress, weaken, worsen.
antonyms float, rise, uplift.

sinless *adj.* faultless, guiltless, immaculate, impeccable, innocent, pure, unblemished, uncorrupted, undefiled, unspotted, unsullied, virtuous.
antonym sinful.

sip *v.* delibate, sample, sup, taste.
n. drop, mouthful, spoonful, swallow, taste, thimbleful.

sit *v.* accommodate, assemble, befit, brood, contain, convene, deliberate, hold, meet, officiate, perch, pose, preside, reside, rest, seat, settle.

site *n.* ground, location, lot, place, plot, position, setting, spot, station.
v. dispose, install, locate, place, position, set, situate, station.

situation *n.* ball-game, berth, case, circumstances, condition, employment, galère, job, kettle of fish, lie of the land, locale, locality, location, office, place, plight, position, post, predicament, rank, scenario, seat, setting, setup, site, sphere, spot, state, state of affairs, station, status.

size *n.* amount, amplitude, bigness, bulk, dimensions, extent, greatness, height, hugeness, immensity, largeness, magnitude, mass, measurement(s), proportions, range, vastness, volume.

skeletal *adj.* cadaverous, drawn, emaciated, fleshless, gaunt, haggard, hollow-cheeked, shrunken, skin-and-bone, wasted.

sketch *v.* block out, delineate, depict, draft, draw, outline, paint, pencil, plot, portray, represent, rough out.
n. croquis, delineation, design, draft, drawing, ébauche, esquisse, outline, plan, scenario, skeleton, vignette.

sketchy *adj.* bitty, crude, cursory, imperfect, inadequate, incomplete, insufficient, outline, perfunctory, rough, scrappy, skimpy, slight, superficial, unfinished, vague.
antonym full.

skill *n.* ability, accomplishment, adroitness, aptitude, art, cleverness, competence, dexterity, experience, expertise, expertness, facility, finesse, handiness, ingenuity, intelligence, knack, proficiency, quickness, readiness, savoir- faire, savvy, skilfulness, talent, technique, touch.

skilled *adj.* able, accomplished, crack, experienced, expert, masterly, practiced, professional, proficient, schooled, skilful, trained.
antonym unskilled.

skimpy *adj.* beggarly, exiguous, inadequate, insufficient, meager, measly, miserly, niggardly, scanty, short, sketchy, sparse, thin, tight.
antonym generous.

skin *n.* casing, coating, crust, deacon, epidermis, fell, film, hide, husk, integument, membrane, outside, peel, pellicle, pelt, rind, tegument.
v. abrade, bark, excoriate, flay, fleece, graze, peel, scrape, strip.

skinny *adj.* attenuate(d), emaciated, lean, scragged, scraggy, skeletal, skin-and-bone, thin, twiggy, underfed, under-nourished, weedy.
antonym fat.

skip *v.* bob, bounce, caper, cavort, cut, dance, eschew, flisk, flit, frisk, gambol, hop, miss, omit, overleap, play truant, prance, trip.

skirmish *n.* affair, affray, battle, brush, clash, combat, conflict, contest, dust-up, encounter, engagement, fracas, incident, scrap, scrimmage, set-to, spat, tussle, velitation.
v. clash, collide, pickeer, scrap, tussle.

slack *adj.* baggy, crank, dull, easy, easy-going, flaccid, flexible, idle, inactive, inattentive, lax, lazy, limp, loose, neglectful, negligent, permissive, quiet, relaxed, remiss, slow, slow-moving, sluggish, tardy.
antonyms busy, diligent, quick, rigid, stiff, taut.
n. excess, give, inactivity, leeway, looseness, play, relaxation, room.
v. dodge, idle, malinger, neglect, relax, shirk, slacken.

slander *n.* aspersion, backbiting, calumniation, calumny, defamation, detraction, libel, misrepresentation, muckraking, obloquy, scandal, smear, traducement, traduction.
v. asperse, backbite, calumniate, decry, defame, detract, disparage, libel, malign, muck-rake, scandalize, slur, smear, traduce, vilify, vilipend.
antonyms glorify, praise.

slang *v.* abuse, berate, castigate, excoriate, insult, lambaste, malign, revile, scold, slag, vilify, vituperate.
antonym praise.

slant *v.* angle, bend, bevel, bias, cant, color, distort, incline, lean, list, shelve, skew, slope, tilt, twist, warp, weight.
n. angle, attitude, bias, camber, declination, diagonal, emphasis, gradient, incline, leaning, obliquity, pitch, prejudice, rake, ramp, slope, tilt, viewpoint.

slanting *adj.* angled, askew, aslant, asymmetrical, bent, canted, cater-cornered, diagonal, inclined, oblique, sideways, skew-whiff, slanted, slantwise, sloping, tilted, tilting.
antonyms level.

slap-dash *adj.* careless, clumsy, disorderly, haphazard, hasty, hurried, last-minute, messy, negligent, offhand, perfunctory, rash, slipshod, sloppy, slovenly, thoughtless, thrown-together, untidy.
antonyms careful, orderly.

slash *v.* criticize, cut, drop, gash, hack, lacerate, lash, lower, reduce, rend, rip, score, slit.
n. cut, gash, incision, laceration, lash, rent, rip, slit.

slaughter *n.* battue, blood-bath, bloodshed, butchery, carnage, extermination, holocaust, killing, liquidation, massacre, murder, slaying.
v. butcher, crush, defeat, destroy, exterminate, halal, hammer, kill, liquidate, massacre, murder, overwhelm, rout, scupper, slay, thrash, trounce, vanquish. **slave** *n.* abject, bondservant, bond-slave, bond(s)man, bond(s)woman, captive, drudge, peon, scullion, serf, servant, skivvy, slavey, thrall, vassal, villein.
v. drudge, grind, labor, skivvy, slog, struggle, sweat, toil.

slavery *n.* bondage, captivity, duress(e), enslavement, impressment, serfdom, servitude, subjugation, thraldom, thrall, vassalage, yoke.
antonym freedom.

slay *v.* amuse, annihilate, assassinate, butcher, destroy, dispatch, eliminate, execute, exterminate, impress, kill, massacre, murder, rub out, slaughter, wow.

sleek *adj.* glossy, insinuating, lustrous, plausible, shiny, smooth, smug, well-fed, well-groomed.

sleep *v.* catnap, doss (down), doze, drop off, drowse, hibernate, nod off, repose, rest, slumber, snooze, snore.

n. coma, dormancy, doss, doze, forty winks, hibernation, nap, repose, rest, shut-eye, siesta, slumber(s), snooze, sopor.

sleepy *adj.* drowsy, dull, heavy, hypnotic, inactive, lethargic, quiet, slow, sluggish, slumb(e)rous, slumbersome, slumbery, somnolent, soporific, soporose, soporous, torpid.
antonyms alert, awake, restless, wakeful.

slender *adj.* acicular, faint, feeble, flimsy, fragile, gracile, inadequate, inconsiderable, insufficient, lean, little, meager, narrow, poor, remote, scanty, slight, slim, small, spare, svelte, sylph-like, tenuous, thin, thready, wasp- waisted, weak, willowish, willowy.
antonyms considerable, fat, thick.

slide *v.* coast, glide, glissade, lapse, skate, skim, slidder, slip, slither, toboggan, veer.

slight *adj.* delicate, feeble, flimsy, fragile, gracile, inconsiderable, insignificant, insubstantial, meager, minor, modest, negligible, paltry, scanty, slender, slim, small, spare, superficial, trifling, trivial, unimportant, weak.
antonyms considerable, large, major, significant.
v. affront, cold-shoulder, cut, despise, disdain, disparage, disrespect, ignore, insult, neglect, scorn, snub.
antonyms compliment, flatter.
n. affront, contempt, discourtesy, disdain, disregard, disrespect, inattention, indifference, insult, neglect, rebuff, rudeness, slur, snub.

slim *adj.* ectomorphic, faint, gracile, lean, narrow, poor, remote, slender, slight, svelte, sylph-like, thin, trim.
antonyms chubby, fat, strong.
v. bant, diet, lose weight, reduce, slenderize.

slip[1] *v.* blunder, boob, conceal, creep, disappear, discharge, dislocate, elude, err, escape, fall, get away, glide, hide, lapse, loose, miscalculate, misjudge, mistake, skate, skid, slidder, slide, slink, slither, sneak, steal, trip.
n. bloomer, blunder, boob, error, failure, fault, imprudence, indiscretion, lapsus, lapsus calami, lapsus linguae, lapsus memoriae, mistake, omission, oversight, slip-up.

slip[2] *n.* certificate, coupon, cutting, offshoot, pass, piece, runner, scion, shoot, sliver, sprig, sprout, strip.

slipshod *adj.* careless, casual, loose, negligent, slap-dash, sloppy, slovenly, unsystematic, untidy.
antonyms careful, fastidious, neat, tidy.

slit *v.* cut, gash, knife, lance, pierce, rip, slash, slice, split.
n. cut, fent, fissure, gash, incision, opening, rent, split, tear, vent. *adj.* cut, pertusate, pertuse(d), rent, split, torn.

slogan *n.* battle-cry, catch-phrase, catchword, chant, jingle, motto, rallying-cry, war cry, watchword.

slope *v.* batter, delve, fall, incline, lean, pitch, rise, slant, tilt, verge, weather.
n. bajada, brae, cant, declination, declivity, descent, downgrade, escarp, glacis, gradient, inclination, incline, ramp, rise, scarp, slant, tilt, versant.

sloth *n.* accidie, acedia, fainéance, idleness, inactivity, indolence, inertia, laziness, listlessness, slackness, slothfulness, sluggishness, torpor.
antonyms diligence, industriousness, sedulity.

slothful *adj.* do-nothing, fainéant, idle, inactive, indolent, inert, lazy, listless, slack, sluggish, torpid, workshy.
antonyms diligent, industrious, sedulous.

slouching *adj.* careless, disorderly, heedless, loose, negligent, shambling, shuffling, slack, slap-dash, slatternly, slipshod, sloppy, unkempt, untidy.

slow *adj.* adagio, backward, behind, behindhand, boring, bovine, conservative, creeping, dawdling, dead, dead-and- alive, delayed, deliberate, dense, dilatory, dim, dull, dull- witted, dumb, easy, gradual, inactive, lackadaisical, laggard, lagging, late, lazy, leaden, leisurely, lingering, loitering, long-drawn-out, measured, obtuse, one-horse, pedetentous, plodding, ponderous, prolonged, protracted, quiet, retarded, slack, sleepy, slow-moving, slow-witted, sluggardly, sluggish, stagnant, stupid, tame, tardy, tedious, thick, time-consuming, uneventful, unhasty, unhurried, uninteresting, unproductive, unprogressive, unpunctual, unresponsive, wearisome.
antonyms active, fast, quick, rapid, swift.
v. brake, check, curb, decelerate, delay, detain, draw rein, handicap, hold up, lag, relax, restrict, retard.

sluggish *adj.* dull, heavy, inactive, indolent, inert, lethargic, lifeless, listless, lurdan, lymphatic, phlegmatic, slothful, slow, slow-moving, torpid, unresponsive.
antonyms brisk, dynamic, eager, quick, vigorous.

slumber *v.* doze, drowse, nap, repose, rest, sleep, snooze.

slump *v.* bend, collapse, crash, decline, deteriorate, droop, drop, fall, hunch, loll, plummet, plunge, sag, sink, slip, slouch, worsen.
n. collapse, crash, decline, depreciation, depression, downturn, drop, failure, fall, falling-off, low, recession, reverse, stagnation, trough, worsening.
antonym boom.

sly *adj.* arch, artful, astute, canny, clever, conniving, covert, crafty, cunning, devious, foxy, furtive, guileful, impish, insidious, knowing, mischievous, peery, roguish, scheming, secret, secretive, shifty, sleeky, stealthy, subtle, surreptitious, underhand, vulpine, wily.
antonyms frank, honest, open, straightforward.

small *adj.* bantam, base, dilute, diminutive, dwarf(ish), grudging, humble, illiberal, immature, inadequate, incapacious, inconsiderable, insignificant, insufficient, itsybitsy, lesser, limited, little, meager, mean, mignon(ne), mini, miniature, minor, minuscule, minute, modest, narrow, negligible, paltry, petite, petty, pigmean, pintsize(d), pocket, pocket-sized, puny, pygmaean, pygmean, scanty, selfish, slight, small-scale, tiddl(e)y, tiny, trifling, trivial, undersized, unimportant, unpretentious, wee, young.
antonyms big, huge, large.

smart[1] *adj.* acute, adept, agile, apt, astute, bright, brisk, canny, chic, clever, cracking, dandy, effective, elegant, fashionable, fine, impertinent, ingenious, intelligent, jaunty, keen, lively, modish, natty, neat, nimble, nimble-witted, nobby, pert, pointed, quick, quick-witted, rattling, ready, ready-witted, saucy, sharp, shrewd, smart- alecky, snappy, spanking, spirited, spruce, stylish, swagger, swish, tippy, trim, vigorous, vivacious, well-appointed, witty.
antonyms dowdy, dumb, slow, stupid, unfashionable, untidy.

smart[2] *v.* burn, hurt, nip, pain, sting, throb, tingle, twinge.
adj. hard, keen, nipping, nippy, painful, piercing, resounding, sharp, stinging.
n. nip, pain, pang, smarting, soreness, sting, twinge.

smash *v.* break, collide, crash, crush, defeat, demolish, destroy, disintegrate, lay waste, overthrow, prang, pulverize, ruin, shatter, shiver, squabash, wreck.
n. accident, collapse, collision, crash, defeat, destruction, disaster, downfall, failure, pile-up, prang, ruin, shattering, smash-up.

smear *v.* asperse, bedaub, bedim, besmirch, blacken, blur, calumniate, coat, cover, dab, daub, dirty, drag (someone's) name through the mud, gaum, malign, patch, plaster, rub on, slubber, smarm, smudge, soil, spread over, stain, sully, tarnish, traduce, vilify.
n. blot, blotch, calumny, daub, defamation, gaum, libel, mudslinging, slander, smudge, splodge, streak, vilification, whispering campaign.

smell *n.* aroma, bouquet, fetor, fragrance, fumet(te), funk, malodor, mephitis, nose, odor, perfume, pong, redolence, scent, sniff, stench, stink, whiff.
v. be malodorous, hum, inhale, nose, pong, reek, scent, sniff, snuff, stink, stink to high heaven, whiff.

smelly *adj.* bad, evil-smelling, fetid, foul, foul- smelling, frowsty, funky, graveolent, high, malodorous, mephitic, noisome, off, pongy, putrid, reeking, stinking, strong, strong- smelling, whiffy.

smitten *adj.* afflicted, beguiled, beset, bewitched, bowled over, burdened, captivated, charmed, enamored, infatuated, plagued, struck, troubled.

smoke *n.* exhaust, film, fog, fume, funk, gas, mist, reek, roke, smog, vapor.
v. cure, dry, fume, fumigate, reek, roke, smolder, vent.

smooth *adj.* agreeable, bland, calm, classy, easy, effortless, elegant, equable, even, facile, fair-spoken, flat, flowing, fluent, flush, frictionless, glassy, glib, glossy, hairless, horizontal, ingratiating, level, levigate, mellow, mild, mirror-like, peaceful, persuasive, plain, plane, pleasant, polished, regular, rhythmic, serene, shiny, silken, silky, sleek, slick, slippery, smarmy, smug, soft, soothing, steady, suave, tranquil, unbroken, unctuous, undisturbed, uneventful, uniform, uninterrupted, unpuckered, unruffled, unrumpled, untroubled, unwrinkled, urbane, velvety, well-ordered.
antonyms coarse, harsh, irregular, rough, unsteady.
v. allay, alleviate, appease, assuage, calm, dub, ease, emery, extenuate, facilitate, flatten, iron, level, levigate, mitigate, mollify, palliate, plane, polish, press, slicken, soften, unknit, unwrinkle.
antonym roughen.

smother *v.* choke, cocoon, conceal, cover, envelop, extinguish, heap, hide, inundate, muffle, overlie, overwhelm, repress, shower, shroud, snuff, stifle, strangle, suffocate, suppress, surround.

smug *adj.* cocksure, complacent, conceited, holierthanthou, priggish, self-opinionated, self-righteous, self- satisfied, superior, unctuous. *antonym* modest.

smutty *adj.* bawdy, blue, coarse, crude, dirty, filthy, gross, improper, indecent, indelicate, lewd, obscene, off-color, pornographic, prurient, racy, raunchy, ribald, risqué, salacious, suggestive, vulgar.
antonyms clean, decent.

snag *n.* bug, catch, complication, difficulty, disadvantage, drawback, hitch, inconvenience, obstacle, problem, snub, stick, stumbling block.
v. catch, hole, ladder, rip, tear.

snap *v.* bark, bite, break, catch, chop, click, crack, crackle, crepitate, flash, grip, growl, knap, nip, pop, retort, seize, separate, snarl, snatch.
n. bite, break, crack, crackle, energy, fillip, flick, get-up-and-go, go, grabe, liveliness, nip, pizazz, pop, vigor, zip.
adj. abrupt, immediate, instant, offhand, on-the-spot, sudden, unexpected, unpremeditated.

snappy *adj.* brusque, chic, crabbed, cross, dapper, edgy, fashionable, hasty, ill-natured, irritable, modish, natty, quick-tempered, smart, snappish, stylish, tart, testy, touchy, trendy, up-to-the-minute, waspish.

snare *v.* catch, ensnare, entrap, illaqueate, net, seize, springe, trap, trepan, wire.
n. catch, cobweb, gin, lime, lime-twig, net, noose, pitfall, springe, springle, toils, trap, wire.

snarl[1] *v.* complain, gnarl, gnar(r), growl, grumble, knar.

snarl[2] *v.* complicate, confuse, embroil, enmesh, entangle, entwine, jam, knot, muddle, ravel, tangle.

snatch *v.* clutch, gain, grab, grasp, grip, kidnap, nab, pluck, pull, ramp, rap, rescue, seize, spirit, take, win, wrench, wrest.
n. bit, fraction, fragment, part, piece, section, segment, smattering, snippet, spell.

sneak *v.* cower, cringe, grass on, inform on, lurk, pad, peach, sidle, skulk, slink, slip, smuggle, spirit, steal, tell tales.
n. informer, snake in the grass, sneaker, telltale.
adj. clandestine, covert, furtive, quick, secret, stealthy, surprise, surreptitious.

sneer *v.* deride, disdain, fleer, gibe, jeer, laugh, look down on, mock, ridicule, scoff, scorn, sniff at, snigger.
n. derision, disdain, fleer, gibe, jeer, mockery, ridicule, scorn, smirk, snidery, snigger.

sniff *v.* breathe, inhale, nose, smell, snuff, snuffle, vent.

snigger *v., n.* giggle, laugh, sneer, snicker, snort, titter.

sniveling *adj.* blubbering, crying, girning, grizzling, mewling, moaning, sniffling, snuffling, weeping, whimpering, whingeing, whining.

snobbish *adj.* arrogant, condescending, high and mighty, high-hat, hoity-toity, lofty, lordly, patronizing, pretentious, snooty, stuck-up, superior, toffee-nosed, uppish, uppity, upstage.

snoop *v.* interfere, pry, sneak, spy.

snooze *v.* catnap, doze, drowse, kip, nap, nod off, sleep.
n. catnap, doze, forty winks, kip, nap, shut-eye, siesta, sleep.

snub *v.* check, cold-shoulder, cut, humble, humiliate, mortify, rebuff, rebuke, shame, slight, sneap, squash, squelch, wither.
n. affront, brush-off, check, humiliation, insult, put-down, rebuff, rebuke, slap in the face, sneap.

snug *adj.* close, close-fitting, comfortable, comfy, compact, cosy, homely, intimate, neat, sheltered, trim, warm.

soak *v.* bathe, damp, drench, imbue, immerse, infuse, interfuse, marinate, moisten, penetrate, permeate, saturate, sog, souse, steep, wet.

soar *v.* ascend, climb, escalate, fly, mount, plane, rise, rocket, tower, wing.
antonym plummet.

sob *v.* bawl, blubber, boohoo, cry, greet, howl, mewl, moan, shed tears, snivel, weep.

sober *adj.* abstemious, abstinent, calm, clear- headed, cold, composed, cool, dark, dispassionate, douce, drab, grave, level-headed, lucid, moderate, peaceful, plain, practical, quiet, rational, realistic, reasonable, restrained, sedate, serene, serious, severe, solemn, somber, sound, staid, steady, subdued, temperate, unexcited, unruffled.
antonyms drunk, excited, frivolous, gay, intemperate, irrational.

sobriety *n.* abstemiousness, abstinence, calmness, composure, continence, coolness, gravity, level-headedness, moderation, reasonableness, restraint, sedateness, self- restraint, seriousness, soberness, solemnity, staidness, steadiness, temperance.
antonyms drunkenness, excitement, frivolity.

social *adj.* collective, common, communal, community, companionable, friendly, general, gregarious, group, neighborly, organized, public, sociable, societal.
n. ceilidh, do, gathering, get-together, hoolly, hoot(e)nanny, party.

society *n.* association, beau monde, brotherhood, camaraderie, circle, civilization, club, companionship, company, corporation, culture, elite, fellowship, fraternity, fratry, friendship, gentry, Gesellschaft, group, guild, haut monde, humanity, institute, league, mankind, organization, people, population, sisterhood, the public, the smart set, the swells, the top drawer, the world, union, upper classes, upper crust, Verein.

soft *adj.* balmy, bendable, bland, caressing, comfortable, compassionate, cottony, creamy, crumby, cushioned, cushiony, cushy, daft, delicate, diffuse, diffused, dim, dimmed, doughy, downy, ductile, dulcet, easy, easy-going, effeminate, elastic, faint, feathery, feeble-minded, flabby, flaccid, fleecy, flexible, flowing, fluid, foolish, furry, gelatinous, gentle, impressible, indulgent, kind, lash, lax, lenient, liberal, light, limp, low, malleable, mellifluous, mellow, melodious, mild, moldable, murmured, muted, namby-pamby, non-alcoholic, overindulgent, pale, pampered, pastel, permissive, pitying, plastic, pleasant, pleasing, pliable, pulpy, quaggy, quiet, restful, sensitive, sentimental, shaded, silky, silly, simple, smooth, soothing, soppy, spineless, spongy, squashy, subdued, supple, swampy, sweet, sympathetic, temperate, tender, tender- hearted, undemanding, understated, unprotected, velvety, weak, whispered, yielding.
antonyms hard, harsh, heavy, loud, rigid, rough, severe, strict.

soften *v.* abate, allay, alleviate, anneal, appease, assuage, calm, cushion, digest, diminish, ease, emolliate, intenerate, lessen, lighten, lower, macerate, malax, malaxate, melt, mitigate, moderate, modify, mollify, muffle, palliate, quell, relax, soothe, still, subdue, temper.

soil[1] *n.* clay, country, dirt, dust, earth, glebe, ground, humus, land, loam, region, terra firma.

soil[2] *v.* bedaggle, bedraggle, befoul, begrime, besmirch, besmut, defile, dirty, foul, maculate, muddy, pollute, smear, spatter, spot, stain, sully, tarnish.

solace *n.* alleviation, assuagement, comfort, consolation, relief, succor, support.
v. allay, alleviate, comfort, console, mitigate, soften, soothe, succor, support.

sole *adj.* alone, exclusive, individual, one, only, single, singular, solitary, unique.
antonyms multiple, shared.

solemn *adj.* august, awed, awe-inspiring, ceremonial, ceremonious, devotional, dignified, earnest, formal, glum, grand, grave, hallowed, holy, imposing, impressive, majestic, momentous, pompous, portentous, religious, reverential, ritual, sacred, sanctified, sedate, serious, sober, somber, staid, stately, thoughtful, venerable.
antonyms frivolous, gay, light-hearted.

solicit *v.* ask, beg, beseech, canvass, crave, entreat, implore, importune, petition, pray, seek, sue, supplicate.

solicitous *adj.* anxious, apprehensive, ardent, attentive, careful, caring, concerned, eager, earnest, fearful, troubled, uneasy, worried, zealous.

solicitude *n.* anxiety, attentiveness, care, concern, considerateness, consideration, disquiet, regard, uneasiness, worry.

solid *adj.* agreed, compact, complete, concrete, constant, continuous, cubic(al), decent, dense, dependable, estimable, firm, genuine, good, hard, law-abiding, level-headed,

massed, pure, real, reliable, sensible, serious, sober, sound, square, stable, stocky, strong, sturdy, substantial, trusty, unalloyed, unanimous, unbroken, undivided, uninterrupted, united, unmixed, unshakeable, unvaried, upright, upstanding, wealthy, weighty, worthy.
antonyms broken, insubstantial, liquid.

solitary *adj.* alone, cloistered, companionless, de(a)rnful, desolate, friendless, hermitical, hidden, isolated, lone, lonely, lonesome, out-of-the-way, reclusive, remote, retired, secluded, separate, sequestered, single, sole, unfrequented, unsociable, unsocial, untrodden, unvisited.
antonyms accompanied, gregarious.

solitude *n.* aloneness, desert, emptiness, isolation, loneliness, privacy, reclusiveness, retirement, seclusion, waste, wasteland, wilderness.
antonym companionship.

solution *n.* answer, blend, clarification, compound, decipherment, dénouement, disconnection, dissolution, elucidation, emulsion, explanation, explication, key, liquefaction, melting, mix, mixture, resolution, result, solvent, solving, suspension, unfolding, unraveling.

solve *v.* answer, clarify, crack, decipher, disentangle, dissolve, elucidate, explain, expound, interpret, resolve, settle, unbind, unfold, unravel, work out.

somber *adj.* dark, dim, dismal, doleful, drab, dull, dusky, funereal, gloomy, grave, joyless, lugubrious, melancholy, mournful, obscure, sad, sepulchral, shadowy, shady, sober, sombrous, subfusc.
antonyms bright, cheerful, happy.

sometimes *adv.* at times, from time to time, now and again, now and then, occasionally, off and on, once in a while, otherwhiles.
antonyms always, never.

soon *adv.* anon, betimes, in a minute, in a short time, in the near future, presently, shortly.

soothe *v.* allay, alleviate, appease, assuage, calm, coax, comfort, compose, ease, hush, lull, mitigate, mollify, pacify, quiet, relieve, salve, settle, soften, still, tranquilize.
antonyms annoy, irritate, vex.

soothing *adj.* anetic, assuasive, balmy, balsamic, calming, demulcent, easeful, emollient, lenitive, palliative, relaxing, restful.
antonyms annoying, irritating, vexing.

sophisticated *adj.* advanced, blasé, citified, complex, complicated, cosmopolitan, couth, cultivated, cultured, delicate, elaborate, highly-developed, intricate, jet-set, multifaceted, refined, seasoned, subtle, urbane, worldly, worldlywise, world-weary.
antonyms artless, naïve, simple, unsophisticated.

sorcery *n.* black art, black magic, charm, diablerie, divination, enchantment, hoodoo, incantation, magic, necromancy, pishogue, spell, voodoo, warlockry, witchcraft, witchery, witching, wizardry.

sordid *adj.* avaricious, base, corrupt, covetous, debauched, degenerate, degraded, despicable, dingy, dirty, disreputable, filthy, foul, grasping, low, mean, mercenary, miserly, niggardly, rapacious, seamy, seedy, selfish, self- seeking, shabby, shameful, sleazy, slovenly, slummy, squalid, tawdry, unclean, ungenerous, venal, vicious, vile, wretched.

sore *adj.* acute, afflicted, aggrieved, angry, annoyed, annoying, burning, chafed, critical, desperate, dire, distressing, extreme, grieved, grievous, harrowing, hurt, inflamed, irked, irritable, irritated, pained, painful, peeved, pressing, raw, reddened, resentful, sensitive, severe, sharp, smarting, stung, tender, touchy, troublesome, upset, urgent, vexed.
n. abscess, boil, canker, carbuncle, chafe, gathering, inflammation, swelling, ulcer, wound.

sorrow *n.* affliction, anguish, blow, distress, dole, grief, hardship, heartache, heartbreak, lamentation, misery, misfortune, mourning, regret, ruth, sadness, trial, tribulation, trouble, unhappiness, woe, worry.
antonyms happiness, joy.
v. agonize, bemoan, bewail, beweep, grieve, lament, moan, mourn, pine, weep.
antonym rejoice.

sorrowful *adj.* affecting, afflicted, dejected, depressed, disconsolate, distressing, doleful, grievous, heartbroken, heart-rending, heavy-hearted, lamentable, lugubrious, melancholy, miserable, mournful, painful, piteous, rueful, ruthful, sad, sorry, tearful, unhappy, wae, woebegone, woeful, wretched.
antonyms happy, joyful.

sorry *adj.* abject, apologetic, base, commiserative, compassionate, conscience-stricken, contrite, deplorable, disconsolate, dismal, distressed, distressing, grieved, guiltridden, mean, melancholy, miserable, mournful, moved, paltry, pathetic, penitent, piteous, pitiable, pitiful, pitying, poor, regretful, remorseful, repentant, ruthful, sad, self- reproachful, shabby, shamefaced, sorrowful, sympathetic, unhappy, unworthy, vile, wretched.
antonym glad.

sort *n.* brand, breed, category, character, class, denomination, description, family, genre, genus, group, ilk, kidney, kind, make, nature, order, quality, race, species, stamp, style, type, variety.
v. arrange, assort, catalog, categorize, choose, class, classify, distribute, divide, file, grade, group, neaten, order, rank, screen, select, separate, systematize, tidy.

sound[1] *n.* description, din, earshot, hearing, idea, implication, impression, look, noise, range, report, resonance, reverberation, tenor, tone, utterance, voice. *v.* announce, appear, articulate, chime, declare, echo, enunciate, express, knell, look, peal, pronounce, resonate, resound, reverberate, ring, seem, signal, toll, utter, voice.

sound[2] *adj.* complete, copper-bottomed, correct, deep,

entire, established, fair, fere, firm, fit, hale, healthy, hearty, intact, just, level-headed, logical, orthodox, peaceful, perfect, proper, proven, prudent, rational, reasonable, recognized, reliable, reputable, responsible, right, right- thinking, robust, safe, secure, sensible, solid, solvent, stable, sturdy, substantial, thorough, tried-and-true, true, trustworthy, unbroken, undamaged, undisturbed, unhurt, unimpaired, uninjured, untroubled, valid, vigorous, wakeless, well-founded, well- grounded, whole, wise.
antonyms shaky, unfit, unreliable, unsound.

sound[3] *v.* examine, fathom, inspect, investigate, measure, plumb, probe, test.

sound[4] *n.* channel, estuary, firth, fjord, inlet, passage, strait, voe.

sour *adj.* acerb(ic), acetic, acid, acidulated, acrid, acrimonious, bad, bitter, churlish, crabbed, curdled, cynical, disagreeable, discontented, embittered, fermented, grouchy, grudging, ill-natured, ill-tempered, inharmonious, jaundiced, off, peevish, pungent, rancid, rank, sharp, tart, turned, ungenerous, unpleasant, unsavory, unsuccessful, unsweet, unwholesome, vinegarish, vinegary, waspish.
antonyms good-natured, sweet.
v. alienate, curdle, disenchant, embitter, envenom, exacerbate, exasperate, spoil.

source *n.* author, authority, begetter, beginning, cause, commencement, derivation, fons et origo, fountainhead, informant, klondike, milch-cow, mine, origin, originator, primordium, quarry, rise, spring, waterhead, well-head, ylem.

souvenir *n.* fairing, gift, keepsake, memento, memory, relic, remembrance(r), reminder, token.

sovereign *n.* autarch, chief, dynast, emperor, empress, kaiser, king, monarch, potentate, prince, queen, ruler, shah, tsar.
adj. absolute, august, chief, dominant, effectual, efficacious, efficient, excellent, imperial, kingly, majestic, monarch(ic)al, paramount, predominant, principal, queenly, regal, royal, ruling, supreme, unlimited.

sovereignty *n.* ascendancy, domination, imperium, kingship, primacy, raj, regality, supremacy, suzerainty, sway.

space *n.* accommodation, amplitude, berth, blank, capacity, chasm, diastema, distance, duration, elbowroom, expanse, extension, extent, gap, house-room, interval, lacuna, leeway, margin, omission, period, place, play, room, scope, seat, spaciousness, span, time, volume.

spacious *adj.* ample, big, broad, capacious, comfortable, commodious, expansive, extensive, huge, large, roomy, sizable, uncrowded, vast, wide.
antonyms confined, cramped, narrow, small.

span *n.* amount, compass, distance, duration, extent, length, period, reach, scope, spell, spread, stretch, term.
v. arch, bridge, cover, cross, encompass, extend, link, overarch, traverse, vault.

spare *adj.* additional, economical, emergency, extra, free, frugal, gash, gaunt, lank, lean, leftover, meager, modest, odd, over, remaining, scanty, slender, slight, slim, sparing, superfluous, supernumerary, surplus, unoccupied, unused, unwanted, wiry.
antonyms corpulent, necessary, profuse.
v. afford, allow, bestow, give quarter, grant, leave, let off, pardon, part with, refrain from, release, relinquish.

sparing *adj.* careful, chary, cost-conscious, economical, frugal, lenten, prudent, saving, thrifty.
antonyms lavish, liberal, unsparing.

sparkle *v.* beam, bubble, coruscate, dance, effervesce, emicate, fizz, fizzle, flash, gleam, glint, glisten, glister, glitter, glow, scintillate, shimmer, shine, spark, twinkle, wink.
n. animation, brilliance, coruscation, dash, dazzle, effervescence, élan, emication, flash, flicker, gaiety, gleam, glint, glitter, life, panache, pizzazz, radiance, scintillation, spark, spirit, twinkle, vim, vitality, vivacity, wit, zip.

spartan *adj.* abstemious, abstinent, ascetic, austere, bleak, disciplined, extreme, frugal, hardy, joyless, plain, rigorous, self-denying, severe, stern, strict, stringent, temperate, unflinching.

spasm *n.* access, burst, contraction, convulsion, eruption, fit, frenzy, jerk, outburst, paroxysm, seizure, throe, twitch.

speak *v.* address, advert to, allude to, argue, articulate, breathe, comment on, communicate, converse, deal with, declaim, declare, discourse, discuss, enunciate, express, harangue, lecture, mention, plead, pronounce, refer to, say, speechify, spiel, state, talk, tell, utter, voice.

special *adj.* appropriate, certain, characteristic, chief, choice, detailed, distinctive, distinguished, especial, exceptional, exclusive, extraordinary, festive, gala, important, individual, intimate, main, major, memorable, momentous, particular, peculiar, precise, primary, red-letter, select, significant, specialized, specific, uncommon, unique, unusual.
antonyms common, normal, ordinary, usual.

specialist *n.* adept, authority, connoisseur, consultant, expert, master, professional, proficient.

species *n.* breed, category, class, collection, denomination, description, genus, group, kind, sort, type, variety.

specific *adj.* characteristic, clear-cut, definite, delimitative, distinguishing, especial, exact, explicit, express, limited, particular, peculiar, precise, special, unambiguous, unequivocal.
antonyms general, vague.

specify *v.* cite, define, delineate, describe, designate, detail, enumerate, indicate, individualize, itemize, list, mention, name, particularize, spell out, stipulate.

specimen *n.* copy, embodiment, ensample, example,

exemplar, exemplification, exhibit, illustration, individual, instance, model, paradigm, pattern, person, proof, representative, sample, type.

speck *n.* atom, bit, blemish, blot, defect, dot, fault, flaw, fleck, grain, iota, jot, macula, mark, mite, modicum, mote, particle, shred, speckle, spot, stain, tittle, trace, whit.

spectacle *n.* curiosity, display, event, exhibition, extravaganza, marvel, pageant, parade, performance, phenomenon, scene, show, sight, wonder.

spectator *n.* beholder, bystander, eye-witness, looker-on, observer, onlooker, passer-by, viewer, watcher, witness.
antonyms contestant, participant, player.

speculate *v.* cogitate, conjecture, consider, contemplate, deliberate, gamble, guess, hazard, hypothesize, meditate, muse, reflect, risk, scheme, suppose, surmise, theorize, venture, wonder.

speech *n.* address, articulation, colloquy, communication, conversation, dialect, dialogue, diction, discourse, discussion, disquisition, enunciation, harangue, homily, idiom, intercourse, jargon, language, lecture, lingo, oration, parlance, parole, peroration, say, spiel, talk, tongue, utterance, voice, winged words.

speed *n.* acceleration, celerity, dispatch, expedition, fleetness, haste, hurry, lick, momentum, pace, precipitation, quickness, rapidity, rush, swiftness, tempo, velocity.
v. advance, aid, assist, belt, bomb, boost, bowl along, career, dispatch, expedite, facilitate, flash, fleet, further, gallop, hasten, help, hurry, impel, lick, press on, promote, put one's foot down, quicken, race, rush, sprint, step on it, step on the gas, step on the juice, tear, urge, vroom, zap, zoom.
antonyms delay, hamper, restrain, slow.

spell[1] *n.* bout, course, innings, interval, patch, period, season, stint, stretch, term, time, turn.

spell[2] *n.* abracadabra, allure, bewitchment, charm, conjuration, enchantment, exorcism, fascination, glamor, hex, incantation, jettatura, love-charm, magic, open sesame, paternoster, philter, rune, sorcery, trance, weird, witchery.

spell[3] *v.* augur, herald, imply, indicate, mean, portend, presage, promise, signal, signify, suggest.

spellbound *adj.* bemused, bewitched, captivated, charmed, enchanted, enthralled, entranced, fascinated, gripped, hooked, mesmerized, possessed, rapt, transfixed, transported.

spend *v.* apply, bestow, blow, blue, concentrate, consume, cough up, deplete, devote, disburse, dispense, dissipate, drain, employ, empty, exhaust, expend, fill, fork out, fritter, invest, lavish, lay out, occupy, pass, pay out, shed, shell out, splash out, squander, use, use up, waste.
antonyms hoard, save.

spendthrift *n.* big spender, prodigal, profligate, spendall, spender, squanderer, unthrift, waster, wastrel.
antonyms hoarder, miser, saver.
adj. extravagant, improvident, prodigal, profligate, thriftless, wasteful.

sphere *n.* ball, capacity, circle, compass, department, domain, employment, field, function, globe, globule, milieu, orb, province, range, rank, realm, scope, spheroid, spherule, station, stratum, territory.

spherical *adj.* globate, globed, globe-shaped, globoid, globose, globular, orbicular, rotund, round.

spicy *adj.* aromatic, flavorsome, fragrant, hot, improper, indecorous, indelicate, off-color, piquant, pointed, pungent, racy, ribald, risqué, savory, scandalous, seasoned, sensational, showy, suggestive, tangy, titillating, unseemly.
antonym bland.

spin *v.* birl, concoct, develop, gyrate, gyre, hurtle, invent, narrate, pirouette, purl, recount, reel, relate, revolve, rotate, spirt, swim, swirl, tell, turn, twirl, twist, unfold, wheel, whirl.
n. agitation, commotion, drive, flap, gyration, hurl, panic, pirouette, revolution, ride, roll, run, state, tizzy, turn, twist, whirl.

spine *n.* backbone, barb, needle, quill, rachis, ray, spicule, spiculum, spike, spur, vertebrae, vertebral column.

spineless *adj.* cowardly, faint-hearted, feeble, gutless, inadequate, ineffective, irresolute, lily-livered, soft, spiritless, squeamish, submissive, vacillating, weak, weak-kneed, weak-willed, wet, wishy-washy, yellow.
antonyms brave, strong.

spirit *n.* air, animation, apparition, ardor, Ariel, atmosphere, attitude, backbone, bravura, breath, brio, character, complexion, courage, daemon, dauntlessness, deva, disposition, div, djinni, earnestness, energy, enterprise, enthusiasm, entrain, Erdgeist, esprit follet, essence, familiar, faun, feeling, feelings, fire, foison, force, gameness, geist, genie, genius, genius loci, ghost, ghoul, gist, grit, guts, humor, intent, intention, jinnee, jinni, ka, kobold, life, liveliness, manito(u), marid, meaning, mettle, mood, morale, motivation, outlook, phantom, pneuma, psyche, purport, purpose, python, quality, resolution, resolve, revenant, sense, shade, shadow, soul, sparkle, specter, spook, sprite, spunk, stout-heartedness, substance, sylph, temper, temperament, tenor, tone, verve, vigor, vision, vivacity, warmth, water-horse, water-nymph, water-rixie, water-sprite, Weltgeist, wili, will, will power, Zeitgeist, zest.
v. abduct, abstract, capture, carry, convey, kidnap, purloin, remove, seize, snaffle, steal, whisk.

spirited *adj.* active, animated, ardent, bold, courageous, energetic, game, gamy, high-spirited, lively, mettlesome, plucky, sparkling, sprightly, spunky, stomachful, vigorous, vivacious.
antonyms lazy, spiritless, timid.

spiritless *adj.* anemic, apathetic, dejected, depressed,

despondent, dispirited, droopy, dull, lackluster, languid, lifeless, listless, low, melancholic, melancholy, mopy, torpid, unenthusiastic, unmoved, wishy-washy.
antonym spirited.

spiritual *adj.* aery, devotional, divine, ecclesiastical, ethereal, ghostly, holy, immaterial, incorporeal, otherwordly, pneumatic, pure, religious, sacred, unfleshly, unworldly.
antonyms material, physical.

spit *v.* discharge, drizzle, eject, expectorate, hawk, hiss, spew, splutter, sputter.
n. dribble, drool, expectoration, phlegm, saliva, slaver, spittle, sputum.

spite *n.* animosity, bitchiness, despite, gall, grudge, hate, hatred, ill-nature, malevolence, malice, malignity, pique, rancor, spitefulness, spleen, venom, viciousness.
antonyms affection, goodwill.
v. annoy, discomfit, gall, harm, hurt, injure, irk, irritate, needle, nettle, offend, peeve, pique, provoke, put out, vex.

spiteful *adj.* barbed, bitchy, catty, cruel, ill- disposed, ill-natured, malevolent, malicious, malignant, nasty, rancorous, snide, splenetic, vengeful, venomous, vindictive, waspish.
antonyms affectionate, charitable.

splendid *adj.* admirable, beaming, bright, brilliant, costly, dazzling, excellent, exceptional, fantastic, fine, first-class, glittering, glorious, glowing, gorgeous, grand, great, heroic, illustrious, imposing, impressive, lavish, lustrous, luxurious, magnificent, marvelous, ornate, outstanding, pontific(al), radiant, rare, refulgent, remarkable, renowned, resplendent, rich, splendiferous, splend(o)rous, sterling, sublime, sumptuous, superb, supreme, tiptop, top-hole, top-notch, topping, wonderful.
antonyms drab, ordinary, run-of-the-mill.

splendor *n.* brightness, brilliance, ceremony, dazzle, display, effulgence, fulgor, glory, gorgeousness, grandeur, luster, magnificence, majesty, pomp, radiance, refulgence, renown, resplendence, richness, show, solemnity, spectacle, stateliness, sumptuousness.

splinter *n.* chip, flake, flinder, fragment, needle, paring, shaving, sliver, spall, spicule, stob.
v. disintegrate, fracture, fragment, shatter, shiver, smash, split.

split *v.* allocate, allot, apportion, betray, bifurcate, branch, break, burst, cleave, crack, delaminate, disband, distribute, disunite, divaricate, diverge, divide, divulge, fork, gape, grass, halve, inform on, open, parcel out, part, partition, peach, rend, rip, separate, share out, slash, slice up, slit, sliver, snap, spell, splinter, squeal.
n. breach, break, break-up, cleft, crack, damage, dichotomy, difference, discord, disruption, dissension, disunion, divergence, division, estrangement, fissure, gap, partition, race, rent, rift, rip, rupture, schism, scissure, separation, slash, slit, tear.
adj. ambivalent, bisected, broken, cleft, cloven, cracked, divided, dual, fractured, ruptured, twofold.

spoil *v.* addle, baby, blemish, bugger, butcher, cocker, coddle, cosset, curdle, damage, debase, decay, decompose, deface, despoil, destroy, deteriorate, disfigure, go bad, go off, harm, impair, indulge, injure, jigger, louse up, mar, mildew, mollycoddle, pamper, plunder, putrefy, queer, rot, ruin, screw, spoon-feed, turn, upset, wreck.

spoken *adj.* declared, expressed, oral, phonetic, said, stated, told, unwritten, uttered, verbal, viva voce, voiced.
antonyms unspoken, written.

spontaneous *adj.* extempore, free, impromptu, impulsive, instinctive, natural, ultroneous, unbidden, uncompelled, unconstrained, unforced, unhesitating, unlabored, unpremeditated, unprompted, unstudied, untaught, voluntary, willing.
antonyms forced, planned, studied.

sport *n.* activity, amusement, badinage, banter, brick, buffoon, butt, dalliance, derision, diversion, entertainment, exercise, fair game, frolic, fun, game, jest, joking, kidding, laughing-stock, merriment, mirth, mockery, pastime, play, plaything, raillery, recreation, ridicule, sportsman, teasing.
v. caper, dally, display, disport, exhibit, flirt, frolic, gambol, philander, play, romp, show off, toy, trifle, wear.

sporting *adj.* considerate, fair, gentlemanly, sportsmanlike.
antonyms unfair, ungentlemanly, unsporting.

spot *n.* bit, blemish, blot, blotch, daub, difficulty, discoloration, flaw, little, locality, location, macula, maculation, macule, mark, mess, morsel, pimple, place, plight, plook, point, position, predicament, pustule, quandary, scene, site, situation, smudge, speck, splash, stain, stigma, taint, trouble.
v. besmirch, blot, descry, detect, dirty, discern, dot, espy, fleck, identify, maculate, mark, mottle, observe, recognize, see, sight, soil, spatter, speckle, splodge, splotch, stain, sully, taint, tarnish.

spotty *adj.* blotchy, pimpled, pimply, plooky, speckled, spotted.

spout *v.* declaim, discharge, emit, erupt, expatiate, gush, jet, orate, pontificate, rabbit on, ramble (on), rant, sermonize, shoot, speechify, spiel, spray, spurt, squirt, stream, surge.
n. chute, fistula, fountain, gargoyle, geyser, jet, nozzle, outlet, rose, spray.

spray[1] *v.* atomize, diffuse, douse, drench, scatter, shower, sprinkle, wet.
n. aerosol, atomizer, drizzle, droplets, foam, froth, mist, moisture, spindrift, spoondrift, sprinkler.

spray[2] *n.* bough, branch, corsage, garland, shoot, sprig, wreath.

spread *v.* advertise, arrange, array, blazon, bloat, broadcast, broaden, bruit, cast, circulate, couch, cover, diffuse,

dilate, dispread, disseminate, distribute, divulgate, divulge, effuse, escalate, expand, extend, fan out, furnish, lay, metastasize, multiply, mushroom, open, overlay, prepare, proclaim, proliferate, promulgate, propagate, publicize, publish, radiate, scatter, set, shed, sprawl, stretch, strew, swell, transmit, unfold, unfurl, unroll, widen.
antonyms close, compress, contain, fold.
n. advance, advancement, array, banquet, blow-out, compass, cover, development, diffusion, dispersion, dissemination, divulgation, divulgence, escalation, expanse, expansion, extent, feast, increase, period, proliferation, ranch, reach, repast, span, spreading, stretch, suffusion, sweep, term, transmission.

sprightly *adj.* active, agile, airy, alert, animated, blithe, brisk, cheerful, energetic, frolicsome, gamesome, gay, hearty, jaunty, joyous, lively, nimble, perky, playful, spirited, sportive, spry, vivacious.
antonym inactive.

spring[1] *v.* appear, arise, bounce, bound, burgeon, come, dance, derive, descend, develop, emanate, emerge, grow, hop, issue, jump, leap, mushroom, originate, proceed, rebound, recoil, shoot up, sprout, start, stem, vault.
n. bounce, bounciness, bound, buck, buoyancy, elasticity, flexibility, gambado, give, hop, jump, leap, rebound, recoil, resilience, saltation, springiness, vault.

spring[2] *n.* beginning, cause, eye, fountain-head, origin, root, source, well, well-spring.

sprinkle *v.* asperge, diversify, dot, dredge, dust, pepper, powder, scatter, seed, shower, sparge, spatter, spray, strew.

spruce *adj.* dainty, dapper, elegant, natty, neat, sleek, slick, smart, smirk, trig, trim, well-groomed, well-turned-out.
antonyms disheveled, untidy.

spry *adj.* active, agile, alert, brisk, energetic, nimble, nippy, peppy, quick, ready, sprightly, supple.
antonyms doddering, inactive, lethargic.

spur *v.* animate, drive, goad, impel, incite, poke, press, prick, prod, prompt, propel, stimulate, urge.
antonym curb.
n. fillip, goad, impetus, impulse, incentive, incitement, inducement, motive, prick, rowel, stimulus.
antonym curb.

spurious *adj.* adulterate, adulterine, apocryphal, artificial, bastard, bogus, contrived, counterfeit, deceitful, dog, fake, false, feigned, forged, illegitimate, imitation, mock, phony, pretended, pseudo, sham, simulated, specious, suppositious, unauthentic.
antonyms authentic, genuine, real.

squabble *v.* argue, bicker, brawl, clash, dispute, fall out, fight, quarrel, row, scrap, spat, tiff, wrangle.
n. argument, barney, clash, disagreement, dispute, fight, rhubarb, row, scrap, set-to, spat, tiff.

squalid *adj.* broken-down, decayed, dingy, dirty, disgusting, fetid, filthy, foul, low, nasty, neglected, poverty-stricken, repulsive, run-down, seedy, sleazy, slovenly, slummy, sordid, uncared-for, unclean, unkempt.
antonyms clean, pleasant.

squander *v.* blow, blue, consume, dissipate, expend, fritter away, lavish, misspend, misuse, scatter, spend, splurge, throw away, waste.

square *v.* accommodate, accord, adapt, adjust, agree, align, appease, balance, bribe, conform, correspond, corrupt, discharge, fit, fix, harmonize, level, liquidate, match, quit, reconcile, regulate, rig, satisfy, settle, suborn, suit, tailor, tally, true.
adj. above-board, bourgeois, broad, complete, conservative, conventional, decent, equitable, ethical, even, exact, fair, fitting, full, genuine, honest, just, old-fashioned, on the level, opposed, orthodox, quadrate, right-angled, satisfying, solid, straight, straightforward, strait-laced, stuffy, suitable, thick-set, traditional, true, unequivocal, upright.
n. antediluvian, conformer, conformist, conservative, conventionalist, die-hard, fuddy-duddy, (old) fogy, stick-in-the- mud, traditionalist.

squeamish *adj.* coy, delicate, fastidious, finicky, nauseous, particular, prissy, prudish, punctilious, qualmish, queasy, queer, reluctant, scrupulous, sick, sickish, strait- laced.

squeeze *v.* bleed, chirt, clasp, clutch, compress, cram, crowd, crush, cuddle, embrace, enfold, extort, force, grip, hug, jam, jostle, lean on, milk, nip, oppress, pack, pinch, press, pressurize, ram, scrounge, squash, strain, stuff, thrust, wedge, wrest, wring.
n. clasp, congestion, crowd, crush, embrace, grasp, handclasp, hold, hug, jam, press, pressure, restriction, squash.

stability *n.* constancy, durability, firmness, fixity, permanence, solidity, soundness, steadfastness, steadiness, strength, sturdiness.
antonyms insecurity, instability, unsteadiness, weakness.

stable *adj.* abiding, constant, deep-rooted, durable, enduring, established, fast, firm, fixed, immutable, invariable, lasting, permanent, reliable, secure, self-balanced, sound, static, steadfast, steady, strong, sturdy, sure, unalterable, unchangeable, unwavering, well-founded.
antonyms shaky, unstable, weak, wobbly.

stack *n.* accumulation, clamp, cock, heap, hoard, load, mass, mound, mountain, pile, ruck, stockpile.
v. accumulate, amass, assemble, gather, load, pile, save, stockpile, store.

staff *n.* caduceus, cane, crew, employees, lecturers, lituus, officers, organization, personnel, pole, prop, rod, stave, teachers, team, wand, workers, workforce.

stage *n.* division, floor, juncture, lap, leg, length, level, period, phase, point, shelf, step, story, subdivision, tier.

v. arrange, do, engineer, give, mount, orchestrate, organize, perform, present, produce, put on, stage-manage.

stagger *v.* alternate, amaze, astonish, astound, confound, daddle, daidle, dumbfound, falter, flabbergast, hesitate, lurch, nonplus, overlap, overwhelm, reel, shake, shock, step, stun, stupefy, surprise, sway, teeter, titubate, totter, vacillate, waver, wobble, zigzag.

staid *adj.* calm, composed, decorous, demure, grave, quiet, sedate, self-restrained, serious, sober, sober-blooded, solemn, steady, Victorian.
antonyms debonair, frivolous, jaunty, sportive.

stain *v.* bedye, besmirch, blacken, blemish, blot, color, contaminate, corrupt, defile, deprave, dirty, discolor, disgrace, distain, dye, imbue, mark, smutch, soil, spot, sully, taint, tarnish, tinge.
n. blemish, blot, discoloration, disgrace, dishonor, dye, infamy, reproach, shame, slur, smirch, smutch, soil, splodge, spot, stigma, tint.

stake[1] *n.* loggat, pale, paling, picket, pile, pole, post, spike, standard, stang, stave, stick.
v. brace, fasten, pierce, prop, secure, support, tether, tie, tie up.

stake[2] *n.* ante, bet, chance, claim, concern, hazard, interest, investment, involvement, peril, pledge, prize, risk, share, venture, wager.
v. ante, bet, chance, gage, gamble, hazard, imperil, jeopardize, pledge, risk, venture, wager.

stale *adj.* antiquated, banal, cliché'd, cliché- ridden, common, commonplace, decayed, drab, dry, effete, faded, fetid, flat, fozy, fusty, hackneyed, hard, insipid, musty, old, old hat, overused, platitudinous, repetitious, sour, stagnant, stereotyped, tainted, tasteless, threadbare, trite, unoriginal, vapid, worn-out.
antonym fresh.

stalk[1] *v.* approach, follow, haunt, hunt, march, pace, pursue, shadow, stride, strut, tail, track.

stalk[2] *n.* bole, branch, kex, shoot, spire, stem, sterigma, trunk.

stall[1] *v.* delay, equivocate, hedge, obstruct, penelopize, play for time, prevaricate, stonewall, temporize.
antonym advance.

stall[2] *n.* bay, bench, booth, compartment, cowshed, pew, seat, stable, table.

stammer *v.* falter, gibber, hesitate, splutter, stumble, stutter.

stamp *v.* beat, brand, bray, categorize, characterize, crush, engrave, exhibit, fix, identify, impress, imprint, inscribe, label, mark, mint, mold, pound, print, pronounce, reveal, strike, trample.
n. attestation, authorization, brand, breed, cast, character, cut, description, earmark, evidence, fashion, form, hallmark, impression, imprint, incuse, kind, mark, mold, sign, signature, sort, stomp, type.

stand *v.* abide, allow, bear, belong, brook, continue, cost, countenance, demur, endure, erect, exist, experience, halt, handle, hold, mount, obtain, pause, place, position, prevail, put, rank, remain, rest, rise, scruple, set, stay, stomach, stop, suffer, support, sustain, take, thole, tolerate, undergo, wear, weather, withstand.
antonym advance.
n. attitude, base, booth, bracket, cradle, dais, determination, erection, frame, grandstand, halt, holder, loss, opinion, place, platform, position, rack, rank, resistance, rest, stage, staging, stall, stance, standpoint, standstill, stay, stop, stop-over, stoppage, support, table, tub, vat, witness-box.
antonym progress.

standard[1] *n.* average, bench-mark, canon, criterion, example, exempler, gauge, grade, guide, guideline, level, measure, model, norm, norma, pattern, principle, requirement, rule, sample, specification, touchstone, type, yardstick.
adj. accepted, approved, authoritative, average, basic, classic, customary, definitive, established, mainstream, normal, official, orthodox, popular, prevailing, recognized, regular, set, staple, stock, typical, usual.
antonyms abnormal, irregular, unusual.

standard[2] *n.* banner, colors, ensign, flag, gonfalon, gonfanon, labarum, pennant, pennon, rallying- point, streamer, vexillum.

standing *n.* condition, continuance, credit, duration, eminence, estimation, existence, experience, footing, position, rank, reputation, repute, seniority, station, status.
adj. erect, fixed, lasting, on one's feet, permanent, perpendicular, perpetual, rampant, regular, repeated, upended, upright, vertical.
antonyms horizontal, lying.

standpoint *n.* angle, point of view, position, post, stance, station, vantage-point, viewpoint, Weltanschauung.

staple *adj.* basic, chief, essential, fundamental, key, leading, main, major, predominant, primary, principle.
antonym minor.

stare *v.* gape, gawk, gawp, gaze, glare, goggle, look, watch.
n. fish-eye, gaze, glare, glower, leer, look, ogle, scowl.

stark *adj.* absolute, arrant, austere, bald, bare, barren, bleak, blunt, cold, consummate, depressing, desolate, downright, drear, dreary, entire, flagrant, forsaken, grim, harsh, out-and-out, palpable, patent, plain, pure, severe, sheer, simple, solitary, stern, stiff, strong, unadorned, unalloyed, unmitigated, unyielding, utter.
antonyms mild, slight.
adv. absolutely, altogether, clean, completely, entirely, quite, stoutly, totally, utterly, wholly.
antonyms mildly, slightly.

start *v.* activate, appear, arise, begin, blench, break away, commence, create, dart, depart, engender, establish, father, flinch, found, inaugurate, initiate, instigate, institute, introduce, issue, jerk, jump, kick off, launch, leave, open, originate, pioneer, recoil, sally forth, set off, set out, set up, shoot, shy, spring forward, twitch.
antonyms finish, stop.

n. advantage, backing, beginning, birth, break, chance, commencement, convulsion, dawn, edge, fit, foundation, inauguration, inception, initiation, introduction, jar, jump, kick-off, lead, onset, opening, opportunity, outburst, outset, spasm, sponsorship, spurt, twitch.
antonyms finish, stop.

startle *v.* affray, agitate, alarm, amaze, astonish, astound, electrify, flush, frighten, scare, shock, spook, start, surprise.
antonym calm.

starving *adj.* famished, hungering, hungry, ravenous, sharpset, starved, underfed, undernourished.
antonym fed.

state[1] *v.* affirm, articulate, assert, asseverate, aver, declare, enumerate, explain, expound, express, formalize, formulate, formulize, present, propound, put, report, say, specify, voice.
n. attitude, bother, case, category, ceremony, circumstances, condition, dignity, display, flap, glory, grandeur, humor, majesty, mode, mood, panic, pass, phase, plight, pomp, position, pother, predicament, shape, situation, spirits, splendor, stage, station, style, tizzy.
antonym calmness.

state[2] *n.* body politic, commonwealth, country, federation, government, kingdom, land, leviathan, nation, republic, territory.
adj. ceremonial, ceremonious, formal, governmental, magnificent, national, official, pompous, public, solemn.

stately *adj.* august, ceremonious, deliberate, dignified, elegant, grand, imperial, imposing, impressive, Junoesque, kingly, lofty, majestic, measured, noble, pompous, princely, queenly, regal, royal, solemn.
antonyms informal, unimpressive.

statement *n.* account, announcement, bulletin, communication, communiqué, constatation, declaration, explanation, ipse dixit, ipsissima verba, proclamation, recital, relation, report, testimony, utterance, verbal.

station *n.* appointment, base, business, calling, depot, employment, grade, habitat, head-quarters, location, occupation, office, place, position, post, rank, seat, situation, sphere, stance, standing, standing-place, status, stopping-place.
v. appoint, assign, establish, fix, garrison, install, locate, post, send, set.

statuesque *adj.* dignified, imposing, majestic, regal, stately, statuary.
antonym small.

status *n.* character, condition, consequence, degree, distinction, eminence, grade, importance, position, prestige, rank, standing, state, weight.
antonym unimportance.

statute *n.* act, decree, edict, enactment, indiction, interlocution, irade, law, ordinance, regulation, rescript, rule, ukase.

staunch[1] *adj.* constant, dependable, faithful, firm, hearty, loyal, reliable, resolute, sound, steadfast, stout, strong, sure, true, true-blue, trustworthy, trusty, watertight, yeomanly, zealous.
antonyms unreliable, wavering, weak.

staunch[2] *same as* **stanch**.

stay[1] *v.* abide, adjourn, allay, arrest, check, continue, curb, defer, delay, detain, discontinue, dwell, endure, halt, hinder, hold, hold out, hover, impede, last, linger, live, lodge, loiter, obstruct, pause, prevent, prorogue, remain, reside, restrain, settle, sojourn, stand, stop, suspend, tarry, visit, wait.
antonyms advance, leave.
n. continuance, deferment, delay, halt, holiday, pause, postponement, remission, reprieve, sojourn, stop, stopover, stopping, suspension, visit.

stay[2] *n.* brace, buttress, prop, reinforcement, shoring, stanchion, support.
v. buttress, prop, prop up, shore up, support, sustain.

steadfast *adj.* constant, dedicated, dependable, established, faithful, fast, firm, fixed, intent, loyal, perseverant, persevering, reliable, resolute, single-minded, stable, staunch, steady, unfaltering, unflinching, unswerving, unwavering.
antonyms unreliable, wavering, weak.

steady *adj.* balanced, calm, ceaseless, confirmed, consistent, constant, continuous, dependable, equable, even, faithful, firm, fixed, habitual, immovable, imperturbable, incessant, industrious, level-headed, nonstop, persistent, regular, reliable, rhythmic, safe, sedate, sensible, serene, serious-minded, settled, sober, stable, staid, steadfast, substantial, unbroken, unchangeable, unfaltering, unfluctuating, unhasting, unhasty, unhurried, uniform, uninterrupted, unremitting, unswerving, unvarying, unwavering.
antonyms unsteady, wavering.
v. balance, brace, firm, fix, secure, stabilize, support.

steal *v.* appropriate, bone, cly, convey, creep, embezzle, filch, flit, half-inch, heist, knap, knock off, lag, lift, mill, misappropriate, nab, nick, peculate, pilfer, pinch, pirate, plagiarize, poach, purloin, relieve someone of, rip off, shoplift, slink, slip, smouch, smug, snaffle, snatch, sneak, snitch, swipe, take, thieve, tiptoe.
antonym return.

stealthy *adj.* cat-like, clandestine, covert, furtive, quiet, secret, secretive, skulking, sly, sneaking, sneaky, surreptitious, underhand. *antonym* open.

steamy *adj.* close, damp, gaseous, hazy, humid, misty, muggy, roky, steaming, stewy, sticky, sultry, sweaty, sweltering, vaporiform, vaporous, vaporish, vapory.

steep[1] *adj.* abrupt, bluff, excessive, exorbitant, extortionate, extreme, headlong, high, overpriced, precipitious, sheer, stiff, uncalled-for, unreasonable.
antonyms gentle, moderate.

steep[2] *v.* brine, damp, drench, fill, imbrue, imbue, immerse, infuse, macerate, marinate, moisten, permeate, pervade, pickle, saturate, seethe, soak, souse, submerge, suffuse.

steer *v.* con, conduct, control, direct, govern, guide, pilot.

stem[1] *n.* axis, branch, family, house, line, lineage, peduncle, race, shoot, stalk, stock, trunk.

stem[2] *v.* check, contain, curb, dam, oppose, resist, restrain, stanch, stay, stop, tamp.
antonyms encourage, increase.

stench *n.* mephitis, odor, pong, reek, stink, whiff.

step *n.* act, action, advance, advancement, deed, degree, demarche, doorstep, expedient, footfall, footprint, footstep, gait, halfpace, impression, level, maneuver, means, measure, move, pace, phase, point, print, procedure, proceeding, process, progression, rank, remove, round, rung, stage, stair, stride, trace, track, tread, walk.
v. move, pace, stalk, stamp, tread, walk.

stereotyped *adj.* banal, cliché'd, cliché-ridden, conventional, corny, hackneyed, mass-produced, overused, platitudinous, stale, standard, standardized, stock, threadbare, tired, trite, unoriginal.
antonyms different, unconventional.

sterile *adj.* abortive, acarpous, antiseptic, aseptic, bare, barren, disinfected, dry, empty, fruitless, germ- free, infecund, pointless, sterilized, unfruitful, unimaginative, unproductive, unprofitable, unprolific.
antonyms fruitful, septic.

stern *adj.* austere, authoritarian, bitter, cruel, flinty, forbidding, frowning, grim, hard, harsh, inflexible, relentless, rigid, rigorous, serious, severe, stark, steely, strict, unrelenting, unsmiling, unsparing, unyielding.
antonym mild.

stew *v.* agonize, boil, braise, fret, fricassee, fuss, jug, perspire, seethe, simmer, sweat, swelter, worry.
n. agitation, bother, bouillabaisse, chowder, daube, fluster, fret, fuss, goulash, hash, lobscouse, pot-au-feu, pother, ragout, tizzy, worry.

stick[1] *v.* abid, adhere, affix, attach, bind, bond, bulge, catch, cement, cleave, cling, clog, deposit, dig, drop, endure, extend, fasten, fix, fuse, glue, gore, hold, insert, install, jab, jam, join, jut, lay, linger, lodge, obtrude, paste, penetrate, persist, pierce, pin, place, plant, plonk, poke, position, prod, project, protrude, puncture, put, put up with, remain, set, show, snag, spear, stab, stand, stay, stomach, stop, store, stuff, take, thole, thrust, tolerate, transfix, weld.
antonym unstick.

stick[2] *n.* baton, bavin, birch, bludgeon, branch, cane, lathi, lug, pole, quarterstaff, rod, scepter, staff, stake, stave, switch, twig, wand, whip, withy.

stick[3] *n.* abuse, blame, criticism, flak, hostility, punishment, reproof.
antonym praise.

stickler *n.* fanatic, fusspot, maniac, martinet, nut, pedant, perfectionist, precisianist, purist.

sticky *adj.* adhesive, awkward, claggy, clammy, clinging, clingy, cloggy, close, dauby, delicate, difficult, discomforting, embarrassing, gluey, glutinous, gooey, gummy, hairy, humid, muggy, nasty, oppressive, painful, smeary, sultry, sweltering, syrupy, tacky, tenacious, thorny, tricky, unpleasant, viscid, viscous.
antonyms cool, dry, easy.

stiff *adj.* arduous, arthritic, artificial, austere, awkward, brisk, brittle, buckram, budge, ceremonious, chilly, clumsy, cold, constrained, creaky, crude, cruel, difficult, drastic, exacting, excessive, extreme, fatiguing, firm, forced, formal, formidable, fresh, graceless, great, hard, hardened, harsh, heavy, inelastic, inelegant, inexorable, inflexible, jerky, laborious, labored, mannered, oppressive, pertinacious, pitiless, pokerish, pompous, powerful, priggish, prim, punctilious, resistant, rheumaticky, rigid, rigorous, severe, sharp, solid, solidified, stand-offish, starch(y), stark, stilted, strict, stringent, strong, stubborn, taut, tense, tight, toilsome, tough, trying, unbending, uneasy, ungainly, ungraceful, unnatural, unrelaxed, unsupple, unyielding, uphill, vigorous, wooden.
antonyms flexible, graceful, informal, mild.

stifle *v.* asphyxiate, check, choke, curb, dampen, extinguish, hush, muffle, prevent, repress, restrain, silence, smother, stop, strangle, suffocate, suppress.
antonym encourage.

stigma *n.* blemish, blot, brand, disgrace, dishonor, imputation, mark, reproach, shame, slur, smirch, spot, stain.
antonym credit.

still *adj.* calm, hushed, inert, lifeless, motionless, noiseless, pacific, peaceful, placid, quiet, restful, serene, silent, smooth, stagnant, stationary, stilly, tranquil, undisturbed, unruffled, unstirring.
antonyms agitated, busy, disturbed, noisy.
v. allay, alleviate, appease, calm, hold back, hush, lull, pacify, quiet, quieten, restrain, settle, silence, smooth, soothe, subdue, tranquilize.
antonyms agitate, stir up.
n. hush, peace, peacefulness, quiet, quietness, silence, stillness, tranquility.
antonyms agitation, disturbance, noise.
adv. but, even so, even then, however, nevertheless, nonetheless, notwithstanding, yet.

stimulate *v.* animate, arouse, encourage, fan, fire, foment, get psyched up, goad, hop up, hype up, impel, incite, inflame, instigate, jog, prompt, provoke, psych oneself up, quicken, rouse, spur, titillate, urge, whet.
antonym discourage.

stimulus *n.* carrot, encouragement, fillip, ginger, goad, incentive, incitement, inducement, prick, provocation, spur.
antonym discouragement.

stingy *adj.* avaricious, cheeseparing, close-fisted, covetous, illiberal, inadequate, insufficient, meager, mean, measly, mingy, miserly, near, niggardly, parsimonious,

penny- pinching, penurious, save-all, scanty, scrimping, small, tightfisted, ungenerous, ungiving.
antonym generous.

stinking *adj.* boozed, canned, contemptible, disgusting, drunk, fetid, foul-smelling, graveolent, grotty, ill- smelling, intoxicated, low, low-down, malodorous, mean, mephitic, noisome, pissed, plastered, pongy, reeking, rotten, smashed, smelly, sozzled, stenchy, stewed, stoned, unpleasant, vile, whiffy, wretched.
antonyms good, pleasant, sober.

stipulate *v.* agree, contract, covenant, engage, guarantee, insist upon, lay down, pledge, postulate, promise, provide, require, settle, specify.
antonym imply.

stir *v.* affect, agitate, beat, bestir, budge, disturb, electrify, emove, excite, fire, flutter, hasten, inspire, look lively, mix, move, quiver, rustle, shake, shake a leg, thrill, touch, tremble.
antonyms bore, calm, stay.
n. activity, ado, agitation, bustle, commotion, disorder, disturbance, excitement, ferment, flurry, fuss, hustle and bustle, movement, to-do, toing and froing, tumult, uproar.
antonym calm.

stock *n.* ancestry, array, assets, assortment, background, beasts, block, breed, cache, capital, cattle, choice, commodities, descent, equipment, estimation, extraction, family, flocks, forebears, fund, funds, goods, handle, herds, hoard, horses, house, inventory, investment, kindred, line, lineage, livestock, log, merchandise, parentage, pedigree, post, property, race, range, repertoire, repute, reserve, reservoir, selection, sheep, source, stem, stockpile, store, strain, stump, supply, trunk, type, variety, wares.
adj. banal, basic, bromidic, clichéd, commonplace, conventional, customary, formal, hackneyed, ordinary, overused, regular, routine, run-of-the-mill, set, standard, staple, stereotyped, traditional, trite, usual, worn-out.
antonym original.
v. deal in, handle, keep, sell, supply, trade in.

stoical *adj.* calm, cool, dispassionate, impassive, imperturbable, indifferent, long-suffering, patient, philosophic(al), phlegmatic, resigned, stoic, stolid.
antonyms anxious, depressed, furious, irascible.

stolid *adj.* apathetic, beefy, blockish, bovine, doltish, dull, heavy, impassive, lumpish, obtuse, slow, stoic(al), stupid, unemotional, wooden.
antonyms interested, lively.

stone *n.* boulder, cobble, concretion, endocarp, flagstone, gem, gemstone, gravestone, headstone, jewel, kernel, lapis, pebble, pip, pit, rock, seed, set(t), slab, tombstone.

stony *adj.* adamant, blank, callous, chilly, expressionless, frigid, hard, heartless, hostile, icy, indifferent, inexorable, lapideous, lapilliform, lithoid(al), merciless, obdurate, pitiless, steely, stonelike, unfeeling, unforgiving, unresponsive.
antonyms forgiving, friendly, soft-hearted.

stoop *v.* bend, bow, couch, crouch, descend, duck, hunch, incline, kneel, lean, squat.
n. droop, inclination, round-shoulderedness, sag, slouch, slump.

stop *v.* arrest, bar, block, break, cease, check, close, conclude, desist, discontinue, embar, end, finish, forestall, frustrate, halt, hinder, impede, intercept, intermit, interrupt, knock off, leave off, lodge, obstruct, pack (it) in, pack in, pack up, pause, plug, poop out, prevent, quit, refrain, repress, rest, restrain, scotch, seal, silence, sojourn, stall, staunch, stay, stem, stymie, suspend, tarry, terminate.
antonyms advance, continue, start.
n. bar, block, break, bung, cessation, check, conclusion, control, depot, destination, discontinuation, end, finish, halt, hindrance, impediment, plug, rest, sojourn, stage, standstill, station, stay, stop-over, stoppage, termination, terminus, ventage, visit.
antonyms continuation, start.
interj. avast, cease, cut it out, desist, easy, give over, halt, hang on, hold it, hold on, hold your horses, lay off, leave it out, refrain, stop it, wait, wait a minute, whoa.

store *v.* accumulate, cupboard, deposit, garner, hive, hoard, husband, keep, lay aside, lay by, lay in lavender, lay up, put aside, reserve, salt away, save, stash, stock, stockpile, treasure.
antonym use.
n. abundance, accumulation, cache, cupboard, depository, emporium, esteem, fund, hoard, keeping, lot, market, mart, mine, outlet, panary, plenty, plethora, provision, quantity, repository, reserve, reservoir, shop, stock, stockpile, storehouse, storeroom, supermarket, supply, value, warehouse, wealth.
antonym scarcity.

storm *n.* agitation, anger, assault, attack, blast, blitz, blitzkrieg, blizzard, clamor, commotion, cyclone, disturbance, dust-devil, furore, gale, gust, hubbub, hurricane, offensive, onset, onslaught, outbreak, outburst, outcry, paroxysm, passion, roar, row, rumpus, rush, sandstorm, squall, stir, strife, tempest, tornado, tumult, turmoil, violence, whirlwind.
antonym calm.
v. assail, assault, beset, bluster, charge, complain, expugn, flounce, fly, fume, rage, rant, rave, rush, scold, stalk, stamp, stomp, thunder.

stormy *adj.* blustering, blustery, boisterous, choppy, dirty, foul, gustful, gusty, oragious, raging, rough, squally, tempestuous, turbulent, wild, windy.
antonym calm.

story[1] *n.* account, ancedote, article, chronicle, episode, fable, fairy-tale, falsehood, feature, fib, fiction, historiette, history, legend, lie, Märchen, myth, narration, narrative, news, novel, plot, recital, record, relation, report, romance, scoop, spiel, tale, untruth, version, yarn.

story[2] *n.* deck, étage, flight, floor, level, stage, stratum, tier.

stout *adj.* able-bodied, athletic, beefy, big, bold, brave, brawny, bulky, burly, chopping, corpulent, courageous, dauntless, doughty, embonpoint, enduring, fat, fearless, fleshy, gallant, hardy, heavy, hulking, husky, intrepid, lion-hearted, lusty, manly, muscular, obese, overweight, plucky, plump, portly, resolute, robust, rotund, stalwart, strapping, strong, sturdy, substantial, thick, tough, tubby, valiant, valorous, vigorous.
antonyms slim, timid, weak.

straight *adj.* accurate, aligned, arranged, authentic, balanced, blunt, bourgeois, candid, consecutive, conservative, continuous, conventional, decent, direct, downright, equitable, erect, even, fair, forthright, frank, honest, honorable, horizontal, just, law-abiding, level, near, neat, nonstop, normal, orderly, organized, orthodox, outright, perpendicular, plain, plumb, point-blank, pure, reliable, respectable, right, running, settled, shipshape, short, smooth, solid, square, straightforward, successive, sustained, through, tidy, traditional, true, trustworthy, unadulterated, undeviating, undiluted, uninterrupted, unmixed, unqualified, unrelieved, unswerving, upright, vertical.
antonyms circuitous, dilute, dishonest, evasive, indirect, roundabout.
adv. candidly, directly, frankly, honestly, outspokenly, point-blank, upright.

straightforward *adj.* candid, clear-cut, direct, easy, elementary, forthright, genuine, guileless, honest, open, open-and-shut, penny-plain, routine, simple, sincere, truthful, uncomplicated, undemanding.
antonyms complicated, devious, evasive.

strain[1] *v.* compress, distend, drive, embrace, endeavor, exert, express, extend, fatigue, filter, injure, labor, overtax, overwork, percolate, pull, purify, restrain, retch, riddle, screen, seep, separate, sieve, sift, sprain, squeeze, stretch, strive, struggle, tauten, tax, tear, tighten, tire, tug, twist, weaken, wrench, wrest, wrick.
n. anxiety, burden, effort, exertion, force, height, injury, key, pitch, pressure, pull, sprain, stress, struggle, tautness, tension, wrench.

strain[2] *n.* ancestry, blood, descent, extraction, family, humor, lineage, manner, pedigree, race, spirit, stem, stock, streak, style, suggestion, suspicion, temper, tendency, tone, trace, trait, vein, way.

strained *adj.* artificial, awkward, constrained, difficult, embarrassed, epitonic, false, forced, labored, self- conscious, stiff, tense, uncomfortable, uneasy, unnatural, unrelaxed.
antonym natural.

straitened *adj.* difficult, distressed, embarrassed, impoverished, limited, poor, reduced, restricted.
antonyms easy, well-off.

strait-laced *adj.* moralistic, narrow, narrow- minded, oldmaidish, prim, proper, prudish, puritanical, strict, stuffy, upright, Victorian.
antonyms broad-minded, easy-going.

strange *adj.* abnormal, alien, astonishing, awkward, bewildered, bizarre, curious, disorientated, disoriented, eccentric, eerie, exceptional, exotic, extraordinary, fantastic(al), foreign, funny, irregular, lost, marvelous, mystifying, new, novel, odd, out-of-the-way, peculiar, perplexing, queer, rare, remarkable, remote, singular, sinister, unaccountable, unacquainted, uncanny, unco, uncomfortable, uncommon, unexplained, unexplored, unfamiliar, unheard of, unknown, untried, unversed, weird, wonderful.
antonyms comfortable, common, familiar, ordinary.

stranger *n.* alien, foreigner, guest, incomer, newcomer, non-member, outlander, unknown, visitor.
antonyms local, native.

strap *n.* belt, leash, thong, tie, vitta.
v. beat, belt, bind, buckle, fasten, flog, lash, scourge, secure, tie, truss, whip.

stratagem *n.* artifice, device, dodge, feint, fetch, intrigue, maneuver, plan, plot, ploy, ruse, ruse de guerre, scheme, subterfuge, trick, wile.

strategy *n.* approach, design, maneuvering, plan, planning, policy, procedure, program, scheme, way.

stray *v.* deviate, digress, diverge, drift, err, get lost, meander, ramble, range, roam, rove, straggle, wander (off).
adj. abandoned, accidental, chance, erratic, forwandered, freak, homeless, lost, odd, random, roaming, scattered, vagrant.

stream *n.* beck, brook, burn, course, creek, current, drift, flow, freshet, ghyll, gill, gush, outpouring, rill, rillet, river, rivulet, run, runnel, rush, surge, tide, torrent, tributary.
v. cascade, course, emit, flood, flow, glide, gush, issue, pour, run, shed, spill, spout, surge, well out.

streamer *n.* banner, ensign, flag, gonfalon, gonfanon, pennant, pennon, plume, ribbon, standard.

street *n.* avenue, boulevard, corso, crescent, drive, expressway, freeway, highway, lane, main drag, parkway, road, roadway, row, terrace, thoroughfare, thruway, turnpike.

strength *n.* advantage, anchor, asset, backbone, brawn, brawniness, cogency, concentration, courage, effectiveness, efficacy, energy, firmness, foison, force, fortitude, fushion, health, intensity, lustiness, mainstay, might, muscle, potency, power, resolution, robustness, security, sinew, spirit, stamina, stoutness, sturdiness, thew, toughness, vehemence, vigor, virtue.
antonyms timidness, weakness.

strengthen *v.* afforce, bolster, brace, buttress, confirm, consolidate, corroborate, edify, encourage, enhance, establish, fortify, harden, hearten, heighten, increase, intensify, invigorate, justify, nerve, nourish, reinforce, rejuvenate, restore, steel, stiffen, substantiate, support, toughen.
antonym weaken.

strenuous *adj.* active, arduous, bold, demanding, determined, eager, earnest, energetic, exhausting, hard, Herculean, laborious, persistent, resolute, spirited, strong,

taxing, tireless, toilful, toilsome, tough, uphill, urgent, vigorous, warm, zealous.
antonyms easy, effortless.

stress *n.* accent, accentuation, anxiety, beat, burden, emphasis, emphaticalness, force, hassle, importance, oppression, pressure, significance, strain, tautness, tension, trauma, urgency, weight, worry.
antonym relaxation.
v. accentuate, belabor, emphasize, repeat, strain, tauten, underline, underscore.
antonym relax.

stretch *n.* area, bit, distance, exaggeration, expanse, extensibility, extension, extent, period, reach, run, space, spell, spread, stint, strain, sweep, term, time, tract.
v. cover, distend, elongate, expand, extend, inflate, lengthen, pull, rack, reach, spread, strain, swell, tauten, tighten, unfold, unroll.
antonyms relax, squeeze.

strict *adj.* absolute, accurate, austere, authoritarian, close, complete, exact, faithful, firm, harsh, meticulous, no-nonsense, particular, perfect, precise, religious, restricted, rigid, rigorous, scrupulous, severe, stern, stringent, thoroughgoing, total, true, unsparing, utter, Victorian.
antonyms easy-going, flexible, mild.

strident *adj.* cacophonous, clamorous, clashing, discordant, grating, harsh, jangling, jarring, loud, rasping, raucous, screeching, shrill, stridulant, stridulous, unmusical, vociferous.
antonyms quiet, sweet.

strife *n.* animosity, battle, bickering, brigue, colluctation, combat, conflict, contention, contest, contestation, controversy, discord, dissension, friction, quarrel, rivalry, row, squabbling, struggle, warfare, wrangling.
antonym peace.

strike *n.* attack, buffet, hit, mutiny, raid, refusal, stoppage, thump, walk-out, wallop, work-to-rule.
v. achieve, affect, afflict, arrange, assail, assault, assume, attack, attain, bang, beat, bop, box, buff, buffet, cancel, chastise, clap, clash, clobber, clout, clump, cob, coin, collide with, cuff, dart, dash, delete, devastate, discover, dismantle, douse, down tools, drive, dunt, effect, encounter, find, force, hammer, hit, impel, impress, interpose, invade, knock, mutiny, penetrate, pierce, pound, print, punish, ratify, reach, register, remove, revolt, seem, shoot, slap, slat, smack, smite, sock, stamp, stumble across, stumble upon, surrender, swap, swipe, swop, thrust, thump, touch, trap, turn up, uncover, unearth, walk out, wallop, wham, work to rule, zap.

striking *adj.* arresting, astonishing, conspicuous, dazzling, distingué(e), extraordinary, forcible, foudroyant, frappant, impressive, memorable, noticeable, outstanding, salient, stunning, wonderful.
antonym unimpressive.

stringent *adj.* binding, demanding, exacting, flexible, inflexible, mild, rigid, rigorous, severe, strict, tight, tough.

strip[1] *v.* bare, clear, defoliate, denude, deprive, despoil, devest, disadorn, disembellish, disgarnish, disinvest, disleaf, disleave, dismantle, displenish, disrobe, divest, doff, empty, excoriate, excorticate, expose, gut, husk, lay bare, loot, peel, pillage, plunder, ransack, rob, sack, skin, spoil, unclothe, uncover, undress, widow.
antonyms cover, provide.

strip[2] *n.* band, belt, bit, fillet, lath, list, piece, ribbon, sash, screed, shred, slat, slip, spline, strake, strap, swathe, thong, tongue, vitta.

stripe *n.* band, bar, belt, chevron, flash, fleck, striation, vitta.

strive *v.* attempt, compete, contend, endeavor, fight, labor, push oneself, strain, struggle, toil, try, work.

stroke *n.* accomplishnment, achievement, apoplexy, attack, blow, clap, collapse, effleurage, feat, fit, flourish, hit, knock, move, movement, pat, rap, seizure, shock, swap, swop, thump.
v. caress, clap, fondle, pat, pet, rub.

stroll *v.* amble, dander, dawdle, mosey, promenade, ramble, saunter, stooge, toddle, wander.
n. airing, constitutional, dawdle, excursion, promenade, ramble, saunter, toddle, turn, walk.

strong *adj.* acute, aggressive, athletic, beefy, biting, bold, brave, brawny, bright, brilliant, burly, capable, clear, clear-cut, cogent, compelling, competent, concentrated, convincing, courageous, dazzling, dedicated, deep, deep-rooted, determined, distinct, drastic, durable, eager, effective, efficient, emphasized, excelling, extreme, fastmoving, fervent, fervid, fierce, firm, forceful, forcible, formidable, glaring, great, grievous, gross, hale, hard, hard-nosed, hard-wearing, hardy, heady, healthy, hearty, heavy-duty, Herculean, highly-flavored, highly-seasoned, hot, intemperate, intense, intoxicating, keen, loud, lusty, marked, muscular, nappy, numerous, offensive, overpowering, persuasive, petrous, piquant, pithy, plucky, pollent, potent, powerful, pungent, pure, rank, redoubtable, reinforced, resilient, resolute, resourceful, robust, self-assertive, severe, sharp, sinewy, sound, spicy, stalwart, stark, staunch, steadfast, sthenic, stout, stout- hearted, strapping, stressed, sturdy, substantial, telling, tenacious, thewy, tough, trenchant, undiluted, unmistakable, unseemly, unyielding, urgent, vehement, violent, virile, vivid, weighty, well-armed, well-built, well-established, well-founded, well-knit, well-protected, well-set, well-versed, zealous.
antonyms mild, weak.

structure *n.* arrangement, building, compages, configuration, conformation, construction, contexture, design, edifice, erection, fabric, form, formation, make-up, organization, pile, set-up.
v. arrange, assemble, build, construct, design, form, organize, shape.

struggle *v.* agonize, battle, compete, contend, fight, grapple, labor, scuffle, strain, strive, toil, work, wrestle.
antonyms give in, rest.

n. agon, agony, battle, brush, clash, combat, conflict, contest, effort, encounter, exertion, grind, hostilities, labor, luctation, pains, scramble, skirmish, strife, toil, tussle, work. *antonyms* ease, submission.

stubborn *adj.* bull-headed, contumacious, cross- grained, difficult, dogged, dour, fixed, headstrong, inflexible, intractable, intransigent, mulish, obdurate, obstinate, opinionated, persistent, pertinacious, pig-headed, recalcitrant, refractory, rigid, self-willed, stiff, stiff-necked, tenacious, unbending, unmanageable, unshakable, unyielding, wilful.
antonym compliant.

student *n.* apprentice, bajan, bejant, bookman, chela, coed, collegianer, contemplator, disciple, fresher, freshman, learner, observer, pupil, scholar, seminarist, soph, sophomore, undergraduate, undergraduette.

studio *n.* atelier, school, workroom, workshop.

study *v.* analyze, cogitate, con, consider, contemplate, cram, deliberate, dig, examine, investigate, learn, lucubrate, meditate, mug up, peruse, ponder, pore over, read, read up, research, scan, scrutinize, survey, swot.
n. analysis, application, attention, cogitation, consideration, contemplation, cramming, critique, examination, inclination, inquiry, inspection, interest, investigation, learning, lessons, lucubration, memoir, monograph, prolusion, reading, report, research, reverie, review, scrutiny, survey, swotting, thesis, thought, zeal.

stuff *v.* binge, bombast, compress, cram, crowd, fill, force, gobble, gorge, gormandize, guzzle, jam, load, overindulge, pack, pad, push, ram, sate, satiate, shove, squeeze, steeve, stodge, stow, trig, wedge.
antonyms nibble, unload.
n. belongings, clobber, cloth, effects, equipment, essence, fabric, furniture, gear, goods, impedimenta, junk, kit, luggage, material, materials, matériel, matter, objects, paraphernalia, pith, possessions, provisions, quintessence, staple, substance, tackle, textile, things, trappings.

stumble *v.* blunder, fall, falter, flounder, fluff, hesitate, lurch, reel, slip, stagger, stammer, stutter, titubate, trip.

stun *v.* amaze, astonish, astound, bedeafen, bewilder, confound, confuse, daze, deafen, dumbfound, flabbergast, overcome, overpower, shock, stagger, stupefy.

stunning *adj.* beautiful, brilliant, dazing, dazzling, devastating, gorgeous, great, heavenly, impressive, lovely, marvelous, ravishing, remarkable, sensational, smashing, spectacular, stotting, striking, wonderful.
antonyms poor, ugly.

stunt[1] *n.* act, campaign, deed, enterprise, exploit, feat, feature, gest(e), performance, tour de force, trick, turn.

stunt[2] *v.* arrest, check, dwarf, hamper, hinder, impede, restrict, slow, stop.
antonym promote.

stupefy *v.* amaze, astound, baffle, benumb, bewilder, confound, daze, drowse, dumbfound, hocus, numb, shock, stagger, stun.

stupid *adj.* anserine, asinine, beef-brained, beef- witted, blockish, Boeotian, boobyish, boring, bovine, brainless, clueless, crackbrained, cretinous, cuckoo, damfool, dazed, deficient, dense, dim, doltish, dopey, dovie, dozy, drippy, dull, dumb, fat-witted, foolish, fozy, futile, gaumless, glaikit, gormless, groggy, gullible, half-baked, half-witted, hammer- headed, idiotic, ill-advised, imbecilic, inane, indiscreet, insensate, insensible, insulse, irrelevant, irresponsible, laughable, ludicrous, lumpen, lurdan, meaningless, mindless, moronic, naïve, nonsensical, obtuse, opaque, pointless, puerile, punch-drunk, rash, semiconscious, senseless, short-sighted, simple, simple-minded, slow, slow-witted, sluggish, stolid, stunned, stupefied, thick, thick-headed, thick-witted, trivial, unintelligent, unthinking, vacuous, vapid, witless, wooden- headed.
antonyms alert, clever.

stupor *n.* coma, daze, inertia, insensibility, kef, lethargy, numbness, stupefaction, torpor, trance, unconsciousness, wonder.
antonym alertness.

sturdy *adj.* athletic, brawny, determined, durable, firm, flourishing, hardy, hearty, husky, lusty, muscular, obstinate, powerful, resolute, robust, secure, solid, stalwart, staunch, steadfast, stout, strong, substantial, vigorous, well- built, well-made.
antonyms decrepit, puny.

style *n.* affluence, appearance, approach, bon ton, category, chic, comfort, cosmopolitanism, custom, cut, dash, design, diction, dressiness, dress-sense, ease, élan, elegance, expression, fashion, fashionableness, flair, flamboyance, form, genre, grace, grandeur, hand, haut ton, kind, luxury, manner, method, mode, panache, pattern, phraseology, phrasing, pizzazz, polish, rage, refinement, savoir-faire, smartness, sophistication, sort, spirit, strain, stylishness, taste, technique, tenor, tone, treatment, trend, type, urbanity, variety, vein, vogue, way, wording.
antonym inelegance.
v. adapt, address, arrange, call, christen, create, cut, denominate, design, designate, dress, dub, entitle, fashion, label, name, shape, tailor, term, title.

suave *adj.* affable, agreeable, bland, charming, civilized, courteous, diplomatic, gracious, obliging, pleasing, polite, smooth, smooth-tongued, soft-spoken, sophisticated, unctuous, urbane, worldly.
antonym unsophisticated.

subdue *v.* allay, break, check, conquer, control, crush, damp, dampen, daunt, defeat, discipline, humble, master, mellow, moderate, overcome, overpower, overrun, quell, quieten, reduce, repress, soften, soft-pedal, subact, subject, suppress, tame, trample, vanquish.
antonym arouse.

subject *n.* affair, business, case, chapter, citizen, client,

dependant, ground, issue, liegeman, matter, mind, national, object, participant, patient, point, question, subordinate, substance, theme, topic, vassal, victim.
antonym master.
adj. answerable, captive, cognizable, conditional, contingent, dependent, disposed, enslaved, exposed, heteronomous, inferior, liable, obedient, open, prone, satellite, subjugated, submissive, subordinate, subservient, susceptible, vulnerable.
antonyms free, insusceptible, superior.
v. expose, lay open, subdue, submit, subordinate, treat.

sublime *adj.* Dantean, Dantesque, elevated, eminent, empyreal, empyrean, exalted, glorious, grand, great, high, imposing, lofty, magnificent, majestic, noble, transcendent.
antonym lowly.

submerge *v.* deluge, demerge, dip, drown, duck, dunk, engulf, flood, immerse, implunge, inundate, overflow, overwhelm, plunge, sink, submerse, swamp.
antonym surface.

submissive *adj.* abject, accommodating, acquiescent, amenable, biddable, bootlicking, complaisant, compliant, deferential, docile, dutiful, humble, ingratiating, malleable, meek, obedient, obeisant, obsequious, passive, patient, pliant, resigned, subdued, subservient, supine, tractable, uncomplaining, unresisting, yielding. *antonym* intractable.

submit *v.* accede, acquiesce, advance, agree, argue, assert, bend, bow, capitulate, claim, commit, comply, contend, defer, endure, knuckle under, move, present, proffer, propose, propound, put, refer, state, stoop, succumb, suggest, surrender, table, tender, tolerate, volunteer, yield.
antonym struggle.

subordinate *adj.* ancillary, auxiliary, dependent, inferior, junior, lesser, lower, menial, minor, secondary, servient, subject, subservient, subsidiary, supplementary.
antonym superior.
n. adjunct, aide, assistant, attendant, dependant, inferior, junior, second, second banana, stooge, sub, subaltern, underdog, underling, underman, under-workman, weakling.
antonym superior.
antonym superiority.

subpoena *n.* court order, decree, summons, writ.

subsequent *adj.* after, consequent, consequential, ensuing, following, later, postliminary, postliminous, resulting, succeeding.
antonym previous.

subside *v.* abate, collapse, decline, decrease, descend, diminish, drop, dwindle, ease, ebb, fall, lessen, lower, moderate, quieten, recede, settle, sink, slacken, slake, wane.
antonym increase.

subsidy *n.* aid, allowance, assistance, backing, contribution, finance, grant, help, sponsorship, subvention, support.

subsist *v.* continue, endure, exist, hold out, inhere, last, live, remain, survive.

substance *n.* actuality, affluence, assets, body, burden, concreteness, consistence, element, entity, essence, estate, fabric, force, foundation, gist, gravamen, ground, hypostasis, import, material, matter, meaning, means, nitty- gritty, pith, property, reality, resources, significance, solidity, stuff, subject, subject-matter, texture, theme, wealth.

substantial *adj.* actual, ample, big, bulky, considerable, corporeal, durable, enduring, essential, existent, firm, full-bodied, generous, goodly, hefty, important, large, massive, material, positive, real, significant, sizable, solid, sound, stout, strong, sturdy, tidy, true, valid, weighty, well- built, worthwhile.
antonyms insignificant, small.

substantiate *v.* affirm, authenticate, confirm, corroborate, embody, establish, prove, support, validate, verify.
antonym disprove.

substitute *v.* change, commute, exchange, interchange, replace, subrogate, swap, switch.
n. agent, alternate, depute, deputy, equivalent, ersatz, locum, locum tenens, makeshift, proxy, relief, replacement, replacer, reserve, stand-by, stop-gap, sub, succedaneum, supply, surrogate, temp, vicar.
adj. acting, additional, alternative, ersatz, proxy, replacement, reserve, second, surrogate, temporary, vicarious.

substitution *n.* change, exchange, interchange, replacement, swap, swapping, switch, switching.

subterfuge *n.* artifice, deception, deviousness, dodge, duplicity, evasion, excuse, expedient, machination, maneuver, ploy, pretense, pretext, quibble, ruse, scheme, shift, stall, stratagem, trick.
antonyms honesty, openness.

subtle *adj.* artful, astute, crafty, cunning, deep, delicate, designing, devious, discriminating, elusive, faint, fine-drawn, fine-spun, impalpable, implied, indirect, ingenious, insinuated, intriguing, keen, Machiavellian, nice, obstruse, over-refined, penetrating, profound, rarefied, refined, scheming, shrewd, slight, sly, sophisticated, tenuous, understated, wily.
antonyms open, unsubtle.

subtract *v.* debit, deduct, detract, diminish, remove, withdraw.
antonyms add, add to.

subvert *v.* confound, contaminate, corrupt, debase, demolish, demoralize, deprave, destroy, disrupt, invalidate, overturn, pervert, poison, raze, ruin, sabotage, undermine, upset, vitiate, wreck.
antonyms boost, uphold.

succeed *v.* arrive, ensue, fadge, flourish, follow, make good, make it, prosper, result, supervene, thrive, triumph, work.
antonyms fail, precede.

success *n.* ascendancy, bestseller, celebrity, eminence,

fame, fortune, happiness, hit, luck, prosperity, sensation, somebody, star, triumph, VIP, well-doing, winner.
antonym failure.

successful *adj.* acknowledged, bestselling, booming, efficacious, favorable, flourishing, fortunate, fruitful, lucky, lucrative, moneymaking, paying, profitable, prosperous, rewarding, satisfactory, satisfying, thriven, thriving, top, unbeaten, victorious, wealthy, well-doing.
antonym unsuccessful.

succession *n.* accession, assumption, chain, concatenation, continuation, course, cycle, descendants, descent, elevation, flow, inheritance, line, lineage, order, procession, progression, race, run, sequence, series, train.

successive *adj.* consecutive, following, in succession, sequent, succeeding.

succinct *adj.* brief, compact, compendious, concise, condensed, gnomic, laconic, pithy, short, summary, terse.
antonym wordy.

succor *v.* aid, assist, befriend, comfort, encourage, foster, help, help out, nurse, relieve, support.
antonym undermine.
n. aid, assistance, comfort, help, helping hand, ministrations, relief, support.

sudden *adj.* abrupt, hasty, hurried, impulsive, prompt, quick, rapid, rash, snap, startling, subitaneous, swift, unexpected, unforeseen, unusual.
antonym slow.

suffer *v.* ache, agonize, allow, bear, brook, deteriorate, endure, experience, feel, grieve, hurt, let, permit, sorrow, support, sustain, tolerate, undergo.

suffering *n.* ache, affliction, agony, anguish, discomfort, distress, hardship, martyrdom, misery, ordeal, pain, pangs, torment, torture.

sufficient *adj.* adequate, competent, effective, enough, satisfactory, sufficing, well-off, well-to-do.
antonyms insufficient, poor.

suffocate *v.* asphyxiate, choke, smother, stifle, strangle, throttle.

suggest *v.* advise, advocate, connote, evoke, hint, imply, indicate, inkle, innuendo, insinuate, intimate, move, propose, recommend.
antonyms demonstrate, order.

suggestion *n.* breath, hint, incitement, indication, innuendo, insinuation, intimation, motion, plan, proposal, proposal, proposition, recommendation, suspicion, temptation, trace, whisper.
antonyms demonstration, order.

suit *v.* accommodate, adapt, adjust, agree, answer, become, befit, correspond, do, fashion, fit, gee, gratify, harmonize, match, modify, please, proportion, satisfy, tailor, tally.
antonyms clash, displease.
n. action, addresses, appeal, attentions, case, cause, clothing, costume, courtship, dress, ensemble, entreaty, get-up, habit, invocation, kind, lawsuit, outfit, petition, prayer, proceeding, prosecution, request, rig-out, series, trial, type.

suitable *adj.* acceptable, accordant, adequate, applicable, apposite, appropriate, apt, becoming, befitting, competent, conformable, congenial, congruent, consonant, convenient, correspondent, due, fit, fitting, opportune, pertinent, proper, relevant, right, satisfactory, seemly, square, suited, well-becoming, well-beseeming.
antonym unsuitable.

sulky *adj.* aloof, churlish, cross, disgruntled, grouty, ill-humored, moody, morose, perverse, pettish, petulant, put out, resentful, sullen.
antonym cheerful.

sullen *adj.* baleful, brooding, cheerless, cross, dark, dismal, dull, farouche, gloomy, glowering, glum, heavy, lumpish, malignant, moody, morose, obstinate, perverse, silent, somber, sour, stubborn, sulky, surly, unsociable.
antonym cheerful.

sultry *adj.* close, come-hither, erotic, hot, humid, indecent, lurid, muggy, oppressive, passionate, provocative, seductive, sensual, sexy, sticky, stifling, stuffy, sweltering, torrid, voluptuous.
antonyms cold, cool.

sum *n.* aggregate, amount, completion, culmination, entirety, height, quantity, reckoning, result, score, substance, sum total, summary, tally, total, totality, whole.

summarize *v.* abbreviate, abridge, condense, encapsulate, epitomize, outline, précis, review, shorten, sum up.
antonym expand (on).

summary *n.* abridgment, abstract, compendium, digest, epitome, essence, extract, outline, précis, recapitulation, résumé, review, rundown, summation, summing-up, synopsis.
adj. arbitrary, brief, compact, compendious, concise, condensed, cursory, expeditious, hasty, laconic, perfunctory, pithy, short, succinct.
antonym lengthy.

summit *n.* acme, apex, apogee, crown, culmination, head, height, peak, pinnacle, point, top, zenith.
antonyms bottom, nadir.

summon *v.* accite, arouse, assemble, beckon, bid, call, cite, convene, convoke, gather, hist, invite, invoke, mobilize, muster, preconize, rally, rouse.
antonym dismiss.

sundry *adj.* a few, assorted, different, divers, miscellaneous, separate, several, some, varied, various.

sunny *adj.* beaming, blithe, bright, brilliant, buoyant, cheerful, cheery, clear, cloudless, fine, genial, happy, joyful, light-hearted, luminous, optimistic, pleasant, radiant, smiling, summery, sun-bright, sunlit, sunshiny.
antonym gloomy.

superannuated *adj.* aged, antiquated, decrepit, fogram,

moribund, obsolete, old, past it, pensioned off, put out to grass, retired, senile, superannuate.
antonym young.

superb *adj.* admirable, breathtaking, choice, clipping, excellent, exquisite, fine, first-rate, gorgeous, grand, magnificent, marvelous, splendid, superior, unrivaled.
antonym poor.

supercilious *adj.* arrogant, condescending, contemptuous, disdainful, haughty, highty-tighty, hoity-toity, imperious, insolent, lofty, lordly, overbearing, patronizing, proud, scornful, snooty, snotty, snouty, stuck-up, toffee-nosed, uppish, uppity, upstage, vainglorious.
antonym humble.

superficial *adj.* apparent, casual, cosmetic, cursory, desultory, empty, empty-headed, evident, exterior, external, frivolous, hasty, hurried, lightweight, nodding, ostensible, outward, passing, perfunctory, peripheral, seeming, shallow, silly, sketchy, skin-deep, slapdash, slight, surface, trivial, unanalytical, unreflective.
antonym detailed.

superintend *v.* administer, control, direct, guide, inspect, manage, overlook, oversee, run, steer, supervise.

superintendence *n.* administration, care, charge, control, direction, government, guidance, inspection, management, supervision, surveillance.

superintendent *n.* administrator, chief, conductor, controller, curator, director, gaffer, governor, inspector, manager, overseer, supervisor.

superior *adj.* admirable, airy, better, choice, condescending, de luxe, disdainful, distinguished, excellent, exceptional, exclusive, fine, first-class, first-rate, good, grander, greater, haughty, high-class, higher, highty-tighty, hoity-toity, lofty, lordly, par excellence, patronizing, predominant, preferred, pretentious, prevailing, respectable, snobbish, snooty, snotty, snouty, stuck-up, supercilious, superordinate, surpassing, top-flight, top-notch, transcendent, unrivaled, upper, uppish, uppity, upstage, worthy.
antonyms humble, inferior.
n. boss, chief, director, foreman, gaffer, manager, principal, senior, supervisor.
antonyms inferior, junior.

superiority *n.* advantage, ascendancy, edge, excellence, lead, predominance, pre-eminence, preponderance, prevalence, supremacy, vis major.
antonym inferiority.

superlative *adj.* consummate, crack, excellent, greatest, highest, magnificent, matchless, nonpareil, outstanding, peerless, supreme, surpassing, transcendent, unbeatable, unbeaten, unparalleled, unrivaled, unsurpassed.
antonym poor.

supernatural *adj.* abnormal, dark, ghostly, hidden, hyperphysical, metaphysical, miraculous, mysterious, mystic, occult, paranormal, phantom, preternatural, psychic, spectral, spiritual, superlunary, supersensible, supersensory, uncanny, unearthly, unnatural.
antonym natural.

supervise *v.* administer, conduct, control, direct, general, handle, inspect, keep tabs on, manage, oversee, preside over, run, superintend.

supervision *n.* administration, auspices, care, charge, control, direction, guidance, instruction, leading-strings, management, oversight, stewardship, superintendence, surveillance.

supervisor *n.* administrator, boss, chief, foreman, gaffer, inspector, manager, overseer, steward, superintendent.

supplant *v.* displace, dispossess, oust, overthrow, remove, replace, supersede, topple, undermine, unseat.

supple *adj.* bending, double-jointed, elastic, flexible, limber, lithe, loose-limbed, plastic, pliable, pliant, whippy, willowish, willowy.
antonym rigid.

supplement *n.* addendum, addition, appendix, codicil, complement, extra, insert, postscript, pull-out, sequel, supplemental, supplementary, suppletion.
v. add, add to, augment, complement, eke, eke out, extend, fill up, reinforce, supply, top up.
antonym deplete.

supplication *n.* appeal, entreaty, invocation, orison, petition, plea, pleading, prayer, request, rogation, solicitation, suit, supplicat.

supply *v.* afford, contribute, endow, equip, fill, furnish, give, grant, minister, outfit, produce, provide, purvey, replenish, satisfy, stock, store, victual, yield.
antonym take.
n. cache, fund, hoard, materials, necessities, provender, provisions, quantity, rations, reserve, reservoir, service, source, stake, stock, stockpile, store, stores.
antonym lack.

support *v.* adminiculate, advocate, aid, appui, appuy, assist, authenticate, back, bear, bolster, brace, brook, buttress, carry, champion, cherish, confirm, corroborate, countenance, crutch, defend, document, endorse, endure, finance, foster, fund, help, hold, keep, maintain, nourish, promote, prop, rally round, reinforce, second, stand (for), stay, stomach, strengthen, strut, submit, subsidize, substantiate, succor, suffer, sustain, take (someone's) part, thole, tolerate, underpin, underwrite, uphold, verify.
antonyms contradict, oppose.
n. abutment, adminicle, aid, aidance, approval, appui, assistance, back, backbone, backer, backing, backstays, backstop, blessing, brace, championship, comfort, comforter, crutch, encouragement, foundation, friendship, fulcrum, furtherance, help, jockstrap, keep, lining, livelihood, loyalty, mainstay, maintenance, patronage, pillar, post, prop, protection, relief, second, sheet-anchor, shore, stanchion, stay, stiffener, subsistence, succor, supporter, supportment, supporture,

sustenance, sustenance, underpinning, upkeep.
antonym opposition.

supporter *n.* adherent, advocate, ally, apologist, bottle-holder, champion, co-worker, defender, fan, follower, friend, heeler, helper, patron, seconder, sponsor, upholder, well-wisher.
antonym opponent.

suppose *v.* assume, believe, calculate, conceive, conclude, conjecture, consider, expect, fancy, guess, hypothesize, hypothetize, imagine, infer, judge, opine, posit, postulate, presume, presuppose, pretend, surmise, think.
antonym know.

supposition *n.* assumption, conjecture, doubt, guess, guesstimate, guesswork, hypothesis, idea, notion, opinion, postulate, presumption, speculation, surmise, theory.
antonym knowledge.

suppress *v.* censor, check, conceal, conquer, contain, crush, extinguish, muffle, muzzle, overpower, overthrow, quash, quell, repress, restrain, silence, smother, snuff out, squelch, stamp out, stifle, stop, strangle, subdue, submerge, vote down, withhold.
antonyms encourage, incite.

supremacy *n.* ascendancy, dominance, domination, dominion, hegemony, lordship, mastery, paramountcy, predominance, pre-eminence, primacy, sovereignty, sway.

supreme *adj.* cardinal, chief, consummate, crowning, culminating, extreme, final, first, foremost, greatest, head, highest, incomparable, leading, matchless, nonpareil, paramount, peerless, predominant, pre-eminent, prevailing, prime, principal, second-to-none, sovereign, superlative, surpassing, top, transcendent, ultimate, unbeatable, unbeaten, unsurpassed, utmost, world-beating. *antonyms* lowly, poor, slight.

sure *adj.* accurate, assured, bound, certain, clear, confident, convinced, decided, definite, dependable, effective, fast, firm, fixed, foolproof, guaranteed, honest, indisputable, ineluctable, inescapable, inevitable, infallible, irrevocable, persuaded, positive, precise, reliable, safe, satisfied, secure, solid, stable, steadfast, steady, sure-fire, trustworthy, trusty, undeniable, undoubted, unerring, unfailing, unmistakable, unswerving, unwavering.
antonyms doubtful, unsure.

surface *n.* covering, day, exterior, façade, face, facet, grass, outside, plane, side, skin, superficies, top, veneer, working-surface, worktop.
antonym interior.
adj. apparent, exterior, external, outer, outside, outward, superficial.
antonym interior.
v. appear, come to light, emerge, materialize, rise, transpire.
antonyms disappear, sink.

surge *v.* billow, eddy, gush, heave, rise, roll, rush, seethe, swell, swirl, tower, undulate.
n. access, billow, breaker, efflux, flood, flow, gurgitation, gush, intensification, outpouring, roller, rush, swell, uprush, upsurge, wave.

surly *adj.* bearish, brusque, chuffy, churlish, crabbed, cross, crusty, curmudgeonly, grouchy, gruff, grum, gurly, ill-natured, morose, perverse, sulky, sullen, testy, uncivil, ungracious.
antonym pleasant.

surmise *v.* assume, conclude, conjecture, consider, deduce, fancy, guess, imagine, infer, opine, presume, speculate, suppose, suspect.
antonym know.
n. assumption, conclusion, conjecture, deduction, guess, hypothesis, idea, inference, notion, opinion, possibility, presumption, speculation, supposition, suspicion, thought.
antonym certainty.

surmount *v.* conquer, exceed, get over, master, overcome, surpass, triumph over, vanquish.

surpass *v.* beat, best, ding, eclipse, exceed, excel, outdo, outshine, outstrip, override, overshadow, surmount, top, tower above, transcend.

surplus *n.* balance, excess, overplus, remainder, residue, superabundance, superfluity, surfeit, surplusage.
antonym lack.
adj. excess, extra, odd, redundant, remaining, spare, superfluous, unused.
antonym essential.

surprise *v.* amaze, astonish, astound, bewilder, confuse, disconcert, dismay, flabbergast, nonplus, stagger, startle, stun.
n. amazement, astonishment, bewilderment, bombshell, dismay, eye-opener, incredulity, jolt, revelation, shock, start, stupefaction, wonder.
antonym composure.

surrender *v.* abandon, capitulate, cede, concede, forego, give in, give up, quit, relinquish, remise, renounce, resign, submit, succumb, waive, yield.
antonyms fight on.
n. appeasement, capitulation, déchéance, delivery, Munich, relinquishment, remise, rendition, renunciation, resignation, submission, white flag, yielding.

surreptitious *adj.* behind-door, clandestine, covert, fraudulent, furtive, secret, sly, sneaking, stealthy, unauthorized, underhand, veiled.
antonym open.

surround *v.* begird, besiege, compass, embosom, encase, encincture, encircle, enclose, encompass, envelop, environ, girdle, invest, ring.

surveillance *n.* care, charge, check, control, direction, guardianship, inspection, monitoring, observation, regulation, scrutiny, stewardship, superintendence, supervision, vigilance, watch.

survey *v.* appraise, assess, consider, contemplate, estimate,

examine, inspect, measure, observe, peruse, plan, plot, prospect, reconnoiter, research, review, scan, scrutinize, study, supervise, surview, triangulate, view.
n. appraisal, assessment, conspectus, examination, geodesy, inquiry, inspection, measurement, overview, perusal, review, sample, scrutiny, study, triangulation.

survive *v.* endure, exist, last, last out, live, live out, live through, outlast, outlive, ride, stay, subsist, weather, withstand.
antonym succumb.

susceptible *adj.* defenseless, disposed, given, impressible, impressionable, inclined, liable, open, predisposed, pregnable, prone, receptive, responsive, sensitive, subject, suggestible, tender, vulnerable.
antonyms impregnable, resistant.

suspect *v.* believe, call in question, conclude, conjecture, consider, distrust, doubt, fancy, feel, guess, infer, mistrust, opine, speculate, suppose, surmise.
adj. debatable, dodgy, doubtful, dubious, fishy, questionable, suspicious, unauthoritative, unreliable.
antonyms acceptable, innocent, straightforward.

suspend *v.* adjourn, append, arrest, attach, cease, dangle, debar, defer, delay, disbar, discontinue, dismiss, expel, freeze, hang, hold off, interrupt, postpone, shelve, sideline, stay, swing, unfrock, withhold.
antonyms continue, expedite, reinstate, restore.

suspicious *adj.* apprehensive, chary, distrustful, dodgy, doubtful, dubious, fishy, incredulous, irregular, jealous, louche, mistrustful, peculiar, queer, questionable, shady, skeptical, suspect, suspecting, unbelieving, uneasy, wary.
antonyms innocent, trustful, unexceptionable.

sustain *v.* aid, approve, assist, bear, carry, comfort, confirm, continue, endorse, endure, experience, feel, foster, help, hold, keep going, maintain, nourish, nurture, prolong, protract, provide for, ratify, relieve, sanction, stay, suffer, support, survive, sustenate, undergo, uphold, validate, verify, withstand.

sustenance *n.* aliment, board, comestibles, commons, eatables, edibles, étape, fare, food, freshments, livelihood, maintenance, nourishment, nutriment, pabulum, provender, provisions, rations, refection, subsistence, support, viands, victuals.

swagger *v.* bluster, boast, brag, brank, bully, cock, crow, gasconade, hector, parade, prance, roist, roister, strut, swank.
n. arrogance, bluster, boastfulness, boasting, braggadocio, display, fanfaronade, gasconade, gasconism, ostentation, rodomontade, show, showing off, swank, vainglory.
antonyms diffidence, modesty, restraint.

swallow *v.* absorb, accept, assimilate, believe, buy, consume, devour, down, drink, eat, englut, engulf, gulp, imbibe, ingest, ingurgitate, knock back, quaff, stifle, suppress, swig, swill, wash down.

swamp *n.* bog, dismal, everglades, fen, marsh, mire, morass, moss, quagmire, quicksands, slough, vlei. *v.* beset, besiege, capsize, deluge, drench, engulf, flood, inundate, overload, overwhelm, saturate, sink, submerge, waterlog.

swank *v.* attitudinize, boast, parade, posture, preen oneself, show off, strut, swagger.
n. boastfulness, conceit, conceitedness, display, ostentation, pretentiousness, self-advertisement, show, showing- off, swagger, vainglory.
antonyms modesty, restraint.

swarm *n.* army, bevy, concourse, crowd, drove, flock, herd, horde, host, mass, mob, multitude, myriad, shoal, throng.
v. congregate, crowd, flock, flood, mass, stream, throng.

swarthy *adj.* black, brown, dark, dark-complexioned, dark-skinned, dusky, swart, swarth, tawny.
antonyms fair, pale.

sway *v.* affect, bend, control, direct, divert, dominate, fluctuate, govern, guide, incline, induce, influence, lean, lurch, oscillate, overrule, persuade, rock, roll, swerve, swing, titter, veer, wave.
n. ascendency, authority, cloud, command, control, dominion, government, hegemony, influence, jurisdiction, leadership, power, predominance, preponderance, rule, sovereignty, sweep, swerve, swing.

swear[1] *v.* affirm, assert, asseverate, attest, avow, declare, depose, insist, promise, testify, vow, warrant.

swear[2] *v.* blaspheme, blind, curse, cuss, eff, imprecate, maledict, take the Lord's name in vain, turn the air blue.

sweat *n.* agitation, anxiety, chore, dew, diaphoresis, distress, drudgery, effort, exudation, fag, flap, hidrosis, labor, panic, perspiration, strain, sudation, sudor, worry.
v. agonize, chafe, exude, fret, glow, perspirate, perspire, swelter, worry.

sweeping *adj.* across-the-board, all-embracing, all- inclusive, blanket, broad, comprehensive, exaggerated, extensive, far-reaching, global, indiscriminate, overdrawn, oversimplified, overstated, radical, simplistic, thoroughgoing, unanalytical, unqualified, wholesale, wide, wide-ranging.

sweet[1] *adj.* affectionate, agreeable, amiable, appealing, aromatic, attractive, balmy, beautiful, beloved, benign, charming, cherished, clean, cloying, darling, dear, dearest, delightful, dulcet, engaging, euphonic, euphonious, fair, fragrant, fresh, gentle, gracious, harmonious, honeyed, icky, kin, lovable, luscious, mellow, melodious, melting, mild, musical, new, perfumed, pet, precious, pure, redolent, saccharine, sickly, silver-toned, silvery, soft, suave, sugary, sweetened, sweet-smelling, sweet-sounding, sweet- tempered, syrupy, taking, tender, toothsome, treasured, tuneful, unselfish, wholesome, winning, winsome.
antonyms acid, bitter, cacophonous, discordant, malodorous, salty, sour, unpleasant.
n. afters, dessert, pudding, second course, sweet course.

sweet[2] *n.* bonbon, candy, comfit, confect, confection, confectionery, sweetie, sweetmeat.

swell[1] *v.* aggravate, augment, balloon, belly, billow, blab, bloat, boll, bulb, bulge, dilate, distend, enhance, enlarge, expand, extend, fatten, grow, heave, heighten, hove, increase, intensify, intumesce, louden, mount, protrude, reach a crescendo, rise, strout, surge, tumefy, volume.
antonyms contract, dwindle, shrink. *n.* billow, bore, bulge, distension, eagre, enlargement, loudening, rise, surge, swelling, undulation, wave.

swell[2] *n.* adept, beau, bigwig, blade, cockscomb, dandy, dude, fop, nob, popinjay, toff.
antonyms down-and-out, scarecrow, tramp.
adj. de luxe, dude, exclusive, fashionable, flashy, grand, posh, ritzy, smart, stylish, swanky.
antonyms seedy, shabby.

swift *adj.* abrupt, agile, expeditious, express, fast, fleet, fleet-footed, flying, hurried, light-heeled, light- legged, limber, nimble, nimble-footed, nippy, precipitate, prompt, quick, rapid, ready, short, spanking, speedy, sudden, winged.
antonyms slow, sluggish, tardy.

swindle *v.* bamboozle, bilk, bunko, cheat, chicane, chouse, con, deceive, defraud, diddle, do, dupe, finagle, financier, fleece, grift, gyp, hand someone a lemon, hornswoggle, overcharge, ramp, rip off, rook, sell smoke, sell someone a pup, skelder, trick.
n. chicanery, con, deceit, deception, double-dealing, fiddle, fraud, gold-brick, grift, gyp, imposition, knavery, racket, rip-off, roguery, scam, sharp practice, shenanigans, skingame, swizz, swizzle, trickery.

swing *v.* arrange, brandish, control, dangle, fix, fluctuate, hang, hurl, influence, librate, oscillate, pendulate, rock, suspend, sway, swerve, vary, veer, vibrate, wave, whirl.
n. fluctuation, impetus, libration, motion, oscillation, rhythm, scope, stroke, sway, swaying, sweep, sweeping, vibration, waving.

switch[1] *v.* change, change course, change direction, chop and change, deflect, deviate, divert, exchange, interchange, put, rearrange, replace, shift, shunt, substitute, swap, trade, turn, veer.
n. about-turn, alteration, change, change of direction, exchange, interchange, shift, substitution, swap.

switch[2] *v.* birch, flog, jerk, lash, swish, twitch, wave, whip, whisk.
n. birch, cane, jerk, rod, whip, whisk.

swivel *v.* gyrate, pirouette, pivot, revolve, rotate, spin, swing round, turn, twirl, wheel.

sycophantic *adj.* ass-licking, backscratching, bootlicking, cringing, fawning, flattering, groveling, ingratiating, obsequious, parasitical, servile, slavish, slimy, smarmy, timeserving, toad-eating, toadying, truckling, unctuous.

symbol *n.* badge, character, emblem, figure, grammalogue, ideogram, ideograph, image, logo, logogram, logograph, mandala, mark, representation, rune, sign, token, type.

symmetry *n.* agreement, balance, correspondence, evenness, form, harmony, isometry, order, parallelism, proportion, regularity.
antonyms asymmetry, irregularity.

sympathetic *adj.* affectionate, agreeable, appreciative, caring, comforting, commiserating, companionable, compassionate, compatible, concerned, congenial, consoling, empathetic, empathic, exorable, feeling, friendly, interested, kind, kindly, like-minded, pitying, responsive, supportive, tender, understanding, warm, warm-hearted, well-intentioned.
antonyms antipathetic, callous, indifferent, unsympathetic.

sympathize *v.* agree, commiserate, condole, empathize, feel for, identify with, pity, rap, respond to, side with, understand.
antonyms disapprove, dismiss, disregard, ignore, oppose.

sympathy *n.* affinity, agreement, comfort, commiseration, compassion, condolement, condolence, condolences, congeniality, correspondence, empathy, fellow-feeling, harmony, pity, rapport, responsiveness, tenderness, thoughtfulness, understanding, warmth.
antonyms callousness, disharmony, incompatibility, indifference.

symptom *n.* concomitant, diagnostic, evidence, expression, feature, indication, manifestation, mark, note, sign, syndrome, token, warning.

symptomatic *adj.* associated, characteristic, indicative, suggestive, typical.

synonymous *adj.* co-extensive, comparable, corresponding, equal, equivalent, exchangeable, identical, identified, interchangeable, parallel, similar, substitutable, tantamount, the same.
antonyms antonymous, dissimilar, opposite.

synopsis *n.* abridgment, abstract, aperçu, compendium, condensation, conspectus, digest, epitome, outline, précis, recapitulation, résumé, review, run-down, sketch, summary, summation.

synthetic *adj.* artificial, bogus, ersatz, fake, imitation, manmade, manufactured, mock, pseud, pseudo, put-on, sham, simulated.
antonyms genuine, real.

system *n.* arrangement, classification, co- ordination, logic, method, methodicalness, methodology, mode, modus operandi, orderliness, organization, plan, practice, procedure, process, regularity, routine, rule, scheme, set-up, structure, systematization, tabulation, taxis, taxonomy, technique, theory, usage.

systematic *adj.* businesslike, efficient, habitual, intentional, logical, methodical, ordered, orderly, organized, planned, precise, standardized, systematical, systematized, well- ordered, well-planned.
antonyms disorderly, inefficient, unsystematic.

T

table *n.* agenda, altar, bench, board, catalog, chart, counter, diagram, diet, digest, fare, flat, flatland, food, graph, index, inventory, list, mahogany, paradigm, plain, plan, plateau, record, register, roll, schedule, slab, spread, stall, stand, syllabus, synopsis, tableland, victuals.
v. postpone, propose, put forward, submit, suggest.

tableau *n.* diorama, picture, portrayal, representation, scene, spectacle, tableau vivant, vignette.

taboo *adj.* accursed, anathema, banned, forbidden, inviolable, outlawed, prohibited, proscribed, sacrosanct, unacceptable, unmentionable, unthinkable, verboten.
antonym acceptable.
n. anathema, ban, curse, disapproval, interdict, interdiction, prohibition, proscription, restriction.

tacit *adj.* implicit, implied, inferred, silent, ulterior, undeclared, understood, unexpressed, unprofessed, unspoken, unstated, unuttered, unvoiced, voiceless, wordless.
antonyms explicit, express, spoken, stated.

taciturn *adj.* aloof, antisocial, cold, distant, dumb, mute, quiet, reserved, reticent, saturnine, silent, tight- lipped, uncommunicative, unconversable, unforthcoming, withdrawn.
antonyms communicative, forthcoming, sociable, talkative.

tack *n.* approach, attack, bearing, course, direction, drawing-pin, heading, line, loop, method, nail, path, pin, plan, procedure, route, staple, stitch, tactic, thumbtack, tin-tack, way. *v.* add, affix, annex, append, attach, baste, fasten, fix, join, nail, pin, staple, stitch, tag.

tackle[1] *n.* accouterments, apparatus, equipment, gear, harness, implements, outfit, paraphernalia, rig, rigging, tackling, tools, trappings.
v. harness.

tackle[2] *n.* attack, block, challenge, interception, intervention, stop.
v. attempt, begin, block, challenge, clutch, confront, deal with, embark upon, encounter, engage in, essay, face up to, grab, grapple with, grasp, halt, intercept, seize, set about, stop, take on, throw, try, undertake, wade into.
antonyms avoid, side-step.

tacky *adj.* adhesive, cheap, gimcrack, gluey, gummy, messy, nasty, scruffy, seedy, shabby, shoddy, sleazy, sticky, tasteless, tatty, tawdry, vulgar, wet.

tact *n.* address, adroitness, consideration, delicacy, diplomacy, discernment, discretion, finesse, grace, judgment, perception, prudence, savoir-faire, sensitivity, skill, thoughtfulness, understanding.
antonyms clumsiness, indiscretion, tactlessness.

tactful *adj.* careful, considerate, delicate, diplomatic, discerning, discreet, graceful, judicious, perceptive, polished, polite, politic, prudent, sensitive, skilful, subtle, thoughtful, understanding.
antonym tactless.

tactical *adj.* adroit, artful, calculated, clever, cunning, diplomatic, judicious, politic, prudent, shrewd, skilful, smart, strategic.
antonym impolitic.

tactics *n.* approach, campaign, game plan, line of attack, maneuvers, moves, plan, plan of campaign, plans, ploys, policy, procedure, shifts, stratagems, strategy.

tag[1] *n.* aglet, aiglet, aiguillette, appellation, dag, designation, docket, epithet, flap, identification, label, mark, marker, name, note, slip, sticker, tab, tally, ticket.
v. add, adjoin, affix, annex, append, call, christen, designate, dub, earmark, fasten, identify, label, mark, name, nickname, style, tack, term, ticket.

tag[2] *n.* dictum, fadaise, gnome, gobbet, maxim, moral, motto, proverb, quotation, quote, remnant, saw, saying.

tail *n.* appendage, backside, behind, bottom, bum, buttocks, conclusion, croup, detective, empennage, end, extremity, file, follower, fud, line, posterior, queue, rear, rear end, retinue, rump, scut, suite, tailback, tailpiece, tailplane, train.
v. dog, follow, keep with, shadow, spy on, stalk, track, trail.

tailor *n.* clothier, costumer, costumier, couturier, couturière, dressmaker, modiste, outfitter, seamstress, whipcat, whip-stitch.
v. accommodate, adapt, adjust, alter, convert, cut, fashion, fit, modify, mold, shape, style, suit, trim.

taint *v.* adulterate, besmirch, blacken, blemish, blight, blot, brand, contaminate, corrupt, damage, defile, deprave, dirty, disgrace, dishonor, envenom, foul, infect, muddy, poison, pollute, ruin, shame, smear, smirch, soil, spoil, stain, stigmatize, sully, tarnish, vitiate.
n. blemish, blot, contagion, contamination, corruption, defect, disgrace, dishonor, fault, flaw, infamy, infection, obloquy, odium, opprobium, pollution, shame, smear, smirch, spot, stain, stigma.

take *v.* abduct, abide, abstract, accept, accommodate, accompany, acquire, adopt, appropriate, arrest, ascertain, assume, attract, bear, believe, betake, bewitch, blight, book, brave, bring, brook, buy, call for, captivate, capture, carry, cart, catch, charm, clutch, conduct, consider, consume, contain, convey, convoy, deduct, deem, delight, demand, derive, detract, do, drink, eat, effect, eliminate, enchant, endure, engage,

ensnare, entrap, escort, execute, fascinate, ferry, fetch, filch, gather, glean, grasp, grip, guide, haul, have, have room for, hire, hold, imbibe, ingest, inhale, lead, lease, make, measure, misappropriate, necessitate, need, nick, observe, obtain, operate, perceive, perform, photograph, pick, pinch, please, pocket, portray, presume, purchase, purloin, receive, regard, remove, rent, require, reserve, secure, seize, select, stand, steal, stomach, strike, subtract, succeed, suffer, swallow, swipe, thole, tolerate, tote, transport, undergo, understand, undertake, usher, weather, win, withstand, work.
n. catch, gate, haul, income, proceeds, profits, receipts, return, revenue, takings, yield.

take-off *n.* burlesque, caricature, imitation, lampoon, mickey-take, mimicry, parody, spoof, travesty.

taking *adj.* alluring, appealing, attractive, beguiling, captivating, catching, charming, compelling, delightful, enchanting, engaging, fascinating, fetching, intriguing, pleasing, prepossessing, winning, winsome.
antonyms repellent, repulsive, unattractive.
n. agitation, alarm, coil, commotion, consternation, flap, fuss, panic, passion, pother, state, sweat, tiz-woz, tizzy, turmoil, wax.

tale *n.* account, anecdote, fable, fabrication, falsehood, fib, fiction, legend, lie, Märchen, Munchausen, myth, narration, narrative, old wives' tale, relation, report, rigmarole, romance, rumor, saga, spiel, story, superstition, tall story, tradition, untruth, yarn.

talent *n.* ability, aptitude, bent, capacity, endowment, faculty, feel, flair, forte, genius, gift, knack, long suit, nous, parts, power, strength.
antonyms inability, ineptitude, weakness.

talented *adj.* able, accomplished, adept, adroit, apt, artistic, brilliant, capable, clever, deft, gifted, ingenious, inspired, well-endowed.
antonyms clumsy, inept, maladroit.

talk *v.* articulate, blab, blether, chat, chatter, chinwag, commune, communicate, confabulate, confer, converse, crack, gab, gossip, grass, inform, jaw, natter, negotiate, palaver, parley, prate, prattle, rap, say, sing, speak, squeak, squeal, utter, verbalize, witter.
n. address, argot, bavardage, blather, blether, causerie, chat, chatter, chinwag, chitchat, clash, claver, colloquy, conclave, confab, confabulation, conference, consultation, conversation, crack, dialect, dialogue, discourse, discussion, disquisition, dissertation, gab, gossip, harangue, hearsay, jargon, jaw, jawing, language, lecture, lingo, meeting, natter, negotiation, oration, palabra, palaver, parley, patois, rap, rumor, seminar, sermon, slang, speech, spiel, symposium, tittle-tattle, utterance, words.

talkative *adj.* chatty, communicative, conversational, effusive, expansive, forthcoming, gabby, garrulous, gossipy, long-tongued, long-winded, loquacious, prating, prolix, unreserved, verbose, vocal, voluble, wordy.
antonyms reserved, taciturn.

tall *adj.* absurd, big, dubious, elevated, embellished, exaggerated, far-fetched, giant, grandiloquent, great, high, implausible, improbable, incredible, lanky, leggy, lofty, overblown, preposterous, remarkable, soaring, steep, topless, towering, unbelievable, unlikely. *antonyms* low, reasonable, short, small.

tally *v.* accord, agree, coincide, compute, concur, conform, correspond, figure, fit, harmonize, jibe, mark, match, parallel, reckon, record, register, square, suit, tie in, total.
antonyms differ, disagree.
n. account, count, counterfoil, counterpart, credit, duplicate, label, mark, match, mate, notch, reckoning, record, score, stub, tab, tag, tick, total.

tame *adj.* amenable, anemic, biddable, bland, bloodless, boring, broken, compliant, cultivated, disciplined, docile, domesticated, dull, feeble, flat, gentle, humdrum, insipid, lifeless, manageable, meek, obedient, prosaic, spiritless, subdued, submissive, tedious, tractable, unadventurous, unenterprising, unexciting, uninspired, uninspiring, uninteresting, unresisting, vapid, wearisome.
antonyms exciting, rebellious, unmanageable, wild.
v. break in, bridle, calm, conquer, curb, discipline, domesticate, enslave, gentle, house-train, humble, master, mellow, mitigate, mute, pacify, quell, repress, soften, subdue, subjugate, suppress, temper, train.

tamper *v.* alter, bribe, cook, corrupt, damage, fiddle, fix, influence, interfere, intrude, juggle, manipulate, meddle, mess, rig, tinker.

tang *n.* aroma, bite, flavor, hint, kick, overtone, piquancy, pungency, reek, savor, scent, smack, smell, suggestion, taste, tinge, touch, trace, whiff.

tangible *adj.* actual, concrete, corporeal, definite, discernible, evident, manifest, material, objective, observable, palpable, perceptible, physical, positive, real, sensible, solid, substantial, tactile, touchable.
antonym intangible.

tangle *n.* burble, coil, complication, confusion, convolution, embroglio, embroilment, entanglement, fankle, fix, imbroglio, jam, jumble, jungle, knot, labyrinth, mass, mat, maze, mesh, mess, mix-up, muddle, raffle, snarl, snarl-up, twist, web.
v. catch, coil, confuse, convolve, embroil, enmesh, ensnare, entangle, entrap, hamper, implicate, interlace, interlock, intertwine, intertwist, interweave, involve, jam, knot, mat, mesh, muddle, snarl, trap, twist.
antonym disentangle.

tangy *adj.* biting, bitter, fresh, gamy, piquant, pungent, savory, sharp, spicy, strong, tart.
antonym insipid.

tantalize *v.* baffle, bait, balk, disappoint, entice, frustrate, lead on, play upon, provoke, taunt, tease, thwart, titillate, torment, torture.
antonym satisfy.

tantrum *n.* bate, fit, flare-up, fury, hysterics, outburst, paddy, paroxysm, rage, scene, storm, temper, wax.

tap[1] *v.* beat, chap, drum, knock, pat, rap, strike, tat, touch.
n. beat, chap, knock, pat, rap, rat-tat, touch.

tap[2] *n.* bug, bung, faucet, plug, receiver, spigot, spile, spout, stop-cock, stopper, valve.
v. bleed, broach, bug, drain, exploit, milk, mine, open, pierce, quarry, siphon, unplug, use, utilize, wiretap.

tape *n.* band, binding, magnetic tape, riband, ribbon, strip, tape-measure.
v. assess, bind, measure, record, seal, secure, stick, tape-record, video, wrap.

taper[1] *v.* attenuate, decrease, die away, die out, dwindle, fade, lessen, narrow, peter out, reduce, slim, subside, tail off, thin, wane, weaken.
antonyms increase, swell, widen.

taper[2] *n.* bougie, candle, spill, wax- light, wick.

tardy *adj.* backward, behindhand, belated, dawdling, delayed, dilatory, eleventh-hour, lag, last-minute, late, loitering, overdue, procrastinating, retarded, slack, slow, sluggish, unpunctual.
antonyms prompt, punctual.

target *n.* aim, ambition, bull's-eye, butt, destination, end, goal, intention, jack, mark, object, objective, prey, prick, purpose, quarry, scapegoat, victim.

tariff *n.* assessment, bill of fare, charges, customs, duty, excise, impost, levy, menu, price list, rate, schedule, tax, toll.

tarnish *v.* befoul, blacken, blemish, blot, darken, dim, discolor, disluster, dull, mar, rust, soil, spoil, spot, stain, sully, taint.
antonyms brighten, enhance, polish up.
n. blackening, blemish, blot, discoloration, film, patina, rust, spot, stain, taint.
antonyms brightness, polish.

tarry *v.* abide, bide, dally, dawdle, delay, dwell, lag, linger, loiter, pause, remain, rest, sojourn, stay, stop, wait.

tart[1] *n.* pastry, pie, quiche, tartlet.

tart[2] *adj.* acerb, acerbic, acid, acidulous, acrimonious, astringent, barbed, biting, bitter, caustic, cutting, incisive, piquant, pungent, sardonic, scathing, sharp, short, sour, tangy, trenchant, vinegary.

tart[3] *n.* broad, call girl, drab, fallen woman, fille de joie, fille publique, floosie, harlot, hooker, prostitute, slut, street-walker, strumpet, tramp, trollop, whore.

task *n.* assignment, aufgabe, burden, business, charge, chore, darg, duty, employment, enterprise, exercise, imposition, job, job of work, labor, mission, occupation, pensum, toil, undertaking, work.
v. burden, charge, commit, encumber, entrust, exhaust, load, lumber, oppress, overload, push, saddle, strain, tax, test, weary.

taste *n.* appetite, appreciation, bent, bit, bite, choice, correctness, cultivation, culture, dash, decorum, delicacy, desire, discernment, discretion, discrimination, drop, elegance, experience, fancy, finesse, flavor, fondness, gout, grace, gustation, inclination, judgment, leaning, liking, morsel, mouthful, nibble, nicety, nip, palate, partiality, penchant, perception, polish, politeness, predilection, preference, propriety, refinement, relish, restraint, sample, sapor, savor, sensitivity, sip, smack, smatch, soupçon, spoonful, style, swallow, tact, tactfulness, tang, tastefulness, titbit, touch.
v. assay, degust, degustate, differentiate, discern, distinguish, encounter, experience, feel, know, meet, nibble, perceive, relish, sample, savor, sip, smack, test, try, undergo.

tasteful *adj.* aesthetic, artistic, beautiful, charming, comme il faut, correct, cultivated, cultured, delicate, discreet, discriminating, elegant, exquisite, fastidious, graceful, handsome, harmonious, judicious, polished, refined, restrained, smart, stylish, well-judged.
antonym tasteless.

tasteless *adj.* barbaric, bland, boring, cheap, coarse, crass, crude, dilute, dull, flashy, flat, flavorless, garish, gaudy, graceless, gross, improper, inartistic, indecorous, indelicate, indiscreet, inelegant, inharmonious, insipid, low, mild, rude, stale, tacky, tactless, tame, tatty, tawdry, thin, uncouth, undiscriminating, uninspired, uninteresting, unseemly, untasteful, vapid, vulgar, watered-down, watery, weak, wearish.
antonym tasteful.

tasty *adj.* appetizing, delectable, delicious, flavorful, flavorous, flavorsome, gusty, luscious, mouthwatering, palatable, piquant, sapid, saporous, savory, scrumptious, succulent, toothsome, yummy.
antonyms disgusting, insipid, tasteless.

tattered *adj.* duddie, frayed, in shreds, lacerated, ragged, raggy, rent, ripped, tatty, threadbare, torn.
antonyms neat, trim.

tattle *v.* babble, blab, blather, blether, chat, chatter, clash, claver, gab, gash, gossip, jabber, natter, prate, prattle, talk, tittle-tattle, yak, yap.
n. babble, blather, blether, chat, chatter, chitchat, clash, claver, gossip, hearsay, jabber, prattle, rumor, talk, tittle-tattle, yak, yap.

taunt *v.* bait, chiack, deride, fleer, flout, flyte, gibe, insult, jeer, mock, provoke, reproach, revile, rib, ridicule, sneer, tease, torment, twit.
n. barb, catcall, censure, cut, derision, dig, fling, gibe, insult, jeer, poke, provocation, reproach, ridicule, sarcasm, sneer, teasing.

taut *adj.* contracted, rigid, strained, stressed, stretched, tense, tensed, tight, tightened, unrelaxed.
antonyms loose, relaxed, slack.

tautology *n.* duplication, iteration, otioseness, perissology, pleonasm, redundancy, repetition, repetitiousness, repetitiveness, superfluity.
antonyms economy, succinctness.

tavern *n.* alehouse, bar, boozer, bush, dive, doggery, fonda, hostelry, inn, joint, local, pub, roadhouse, saloon, taphouse.

tawdry *adj.* cheap, cheap-jack, flashy, garish, gaudy, gimcrack, gingerbread, glittering, meretricious, pinchbeck,

plastic, raffish, showy, tacky, tasteless, tatty, tinsel, tinsely, vulgar.
antonyms excellent, fine, superior.

tax *n.* agistment, assessment, burden, charge, contribution, customs, demand, drain, duty, excise, geld, imposition, impost, levy, load, octroi, pressure, rate, scat, scot, strain, tariff, tithe, toll, tribute, weight.
v. accuse, arraign, assess, blame, burden, censure, charge, demand, drain, enervate, exact, exhaust, extract, geld, impeach, impose, impugn, incriminate, load, overburden, overtax, push, rate, reproach, sap, strain, stretch, task, tithe, try, weaken, weary.

taxi *n.* cab, fiacre, hack, hansom-cab, taxicab.

teach *v.* accustom, advise, coach, counsel, demonstrate, direct, discipline, drill, edify, educate, enlighten, ground, guide, impart, implant, inculcate, inform, instil, instruct, school, show, train, tutor, verse.

teacher *n.* abecedarian, coach, dominie, don, educator, guide, guru, instructor, khodja, kindergartener, kindergärtner, lecturer, luminary, maharishi, master, mentor, mistress, pedagogue, professor, pundit, school-marm, schoolmaster, schoolmistress, schoolteacher, trainer, tutor, usher.

team *n.* band, body, bunch, company, crew, écurie, équipe, gang, group, line-up, pair, set, shift, side, span, squad, stable, troupe, yoke.
v. combine, couple, join, link, match, yoke.

teamwork *n.* collaboration, co-operation, co- ordination, esprit de corps, fellowship, joint effort, team spirit.
antonyms disharmony, disunity.

tear *v.* belt, bolt, career, charge, claw, dart, dash, dilacerate, divide, drag, fly, gallop, gash, grab, hurry, lacerate, mangle, mutilate, pluck, pull, race, rend, rip, rive, run, rupture, rush, scratch, seize, sever, shoot, shred, snag, snatch, speed, split, sprint, sunder, wrench, wrest, yank, zoom.
n. hole, laceration, rent, rip, run, rupture, scratch, snag, split.

tearful *adj.* blubbering, crying, distressing, dolorous, emotional, lachrymose, lamentable, maudlin, mournful, pathetic, pitiable, pitiful, poignant, sad, sobbing, sorrowful, upsetting, weeping, weepy, whimpering, woeful.

tease *v.* aggravate, annoy, badger, bait, banter, bedevil, chaff, chip, gibe, goad, grig, guy, irritate, josh, mock, needle, pester, plague, provoke, rag, rib, ridicule, take a rise out of, tantalize, taunt, torment, twit, vex, worry.

technique *n.* address, adroitness, approach, art, artistry, course, craft, craftsmanship, delivery, executancy, execution, expertise, facility, fashion, knack, know-how, manner, means, method, mode, modus operandi, performance, procedure, proficiency, skill, style, system, touch, way.

tedious *adj.* annoying, banal, boring, deadly, drab, dreary, dreich, dull, fatiguing, humdrum, irksome, laborious, lifeless, long-drawn-out, longsome, long-spun, monotonous, prosaic, prosy, soporific, tiring, unexciting, uninteresting, vapid, wearisome.
antonyms exciting, interesting.

tedium *n.* banality, boredom, drabness, dreariness, dullness, ennui, lifelessness, monotony, prosiness, routine, sameness, tediousness, vapidity.

teem *v.* abound, bear, brim, bristle, burst, increase, multiply, overflow, overspill, produce, proliferate, pullulate, swarm.
antonyms lack, want.

teeming *adj.* abundant, alive, brimful, brimming, bristling, bursting, chock-a-block, chock-full, crawling, fruitful, full, numerous, overflowing, packed, pregnant, proliferating, pullulating, replete, swarming, thick.
antonyms lacking, rare, sparse.

teeter *v.* balance, lurch, pitch, pivot, rock, seesaw, stagger, sway, titubate, totter, tremble, waver, wobble.

teetotaller *n.* abstainer, nephalist, non-drinker, Rechabite, water-drinker.

telephone *n.* blower, handset, line, phone.
v. buzz, call, call up, contact, dial, get in touch, get on the blower, give someone a tinkle, phone, ring (up).

telescope *v.* abbreviate, abridge, compress, concertina, condense, contract, crush, curtail, cut, reduce, shorten, shrink, squash, trim, truncate.

television *n.* boob tube, goggle-box, idiot box, receiver, set, small screen, the box, the tube, TV, TV set.

tell *v.* acquaint, announce, apprize, authorize, bid, calculate, chronicle, command, communicate, comprehend, compute, confess, count, depict, describe, differentiate, direct, discern, disclose, discover, discriminate, distinguish, divulge, enjoin, enumerate, express, foresee, identify, impart, inform, instruct, mention, militate, narrate, notify, number, order, portray, predict, proclaim, reckon, recount, register, rehearse, relate, report, require, reveal, say, see, speak, state, summon, tally, understand, utter, weigh.

temerity *n.* assurance, audacity, boldness, brass neck, chutzpah, daring, effrontery, forwardness, gall, heedlessness, impudence, impulsiveness, intrepidity, nerve, pluck, rashness, recklessness.
antonym caution.

temper *n.* anger, annoyance, attitude, bate, calm, calmness, character, composure, constitution, cool, coolness, disposition, equanimity, fury, heat, humor, ill-humor, irascibility, irritability, irritation, mind, moderation, mood, nature, paddy, passion, peevishness, pet, petulance, rage, resentment, sang-froid, self-control, surliness, taking, tantrum, temperament, tenor, tranquility, vein, wax, wrath.
v. abate, admix, allay, anneal, assuage, calm, harden, indurate, lessen, mitigate, moderate, modify, mollify, palliate, restrain, soften, soothe, strengthen, toughen.

temperament *n.* anger, bent, character, complexion,

constitution, crasis, disposition, excitability, explosiveness, hot-headedness, humor, impatience, make-up, mettle, moodiness, moods, nature, outlook, personality, petulance, quality, soul, spirit, stamp, temper, tendencies, tendency, volatility.

temperamental *adj.* capricious, congenital, constitutional, emotional, erratic, excitable, explosive, fiery, highly-strung, hot-headed, hypersensitive, impatient, inborn, inconsistent, ingrained, inherent, innate, irritable, mercurial, moody, natural, neurotic, over-emotional, passionate, petulant, sensitive, touchy, undependable, unpredictable, unreliable, volatile, volcanic.
antonyms calm, serene, steady.

temperance *n.* abstemiousness, abstinence, continence, discretion, forbearance, moderation, prohibition, restraint, self-abnegation, self-control, self-denial, self-discipline, self-restraint, sobriety, teetotalism.
antonyms excess, intemperance.

temperate *adj.* abstemious, abstinent, agreeable, balanced, balmy, calm, clement, composed, continent, controlled, cool, dispassionate, equable, even-tempered, fair, gentle, mild, moderate, pleasant, reasonable, restrained, sensible, sober, soft, stable.
antonyms excessive, extreme, intemperate.

tempest *n.* bourasque, commotion, cyclone, disturbance, ferment, furore, gale, hurricane, squall, storm, tornado, tumult, typhoon, upheaval, uproar.

tempo *n.* beat, cadence, measure, meter, pace, pulse, rate, rhythm, speed, time, velocity.

temporal *adj.* carnal, civil, earthly, evanescent, fleeting, fleshly, fugacious, fugitive, impermanent, lay, material, momentary, mortal, mundane, passing, profane, secular, short-lived, sublunary, temporary, terrestrial, transient, transitory, unspiritual, worldly.
antonym spiritual.

temporary *adj.* brief, ephemeral, evanescent, fleeting, fugacious, fugitive, impermanent, interim, makeshift, momentary, passing, pro tem, pro tempore, provisional, short- lived, stop-gap, transient, transitory.
antonyms everlasting, permanent.

tempt *v.* allure, attract, bait, coax, dare, decoy, draw, enamor, entice, incite, inveigle, invite, lure, provoke, risk, seduce, tantalize, test, try, woo.
antonyms discourage, dissuade.

tenacious *adj.* adamant, adhesive, clinging, coherent, cohesive, determined, dogged, fast, firm, forceful, gluey, glutinous, inflexible, intransigent, mucilaginous, obdurate, obstinate, persistent, pertinacious, resolute, retentive, single-minded, solid, staunch, steadfast, sticky, strong, strong-willed, stubborn, sure, tight, tough, unshakeable, unswerving, unwavering, unyielding, viscous.
antonyms loose, slack, weak.

tenacity *n.* adhesiveness, application, clinginess, coherence, cohesiveness, determination, diligence, doggedness, fastness, firmness, force, forcefulness, indomitability, inflexibility, intransigence, obduracy, obstinacy, perseverance, persistence, pertinacity, power, resoluteness, resolution, resolve, retention, retentiveness, single-mindedness, solidity, solidness, staunchness, steadfastness, stickiness, strength, stubbornness, toughness, viscosity.
antonyms looseness, slackness, weakness.

tenant *n.* gavelman, inhabitant, landholder, leaseholder, lessee, occupant, occupier, renter, resident.

tend[1] *v.* affect, aim, bear, bend, conduce, contribute, go, gravitate, head, incline, influence, lead, lean, move, point, trend, verge.

tend[2] *v.* attend, comfort, control, cultivate, feed, guard, handle, keep, maintain, manage, minister to, nurse, nurture, protect, serve, succor.
antonym neglect.

tendency *n.* bearing, bent, bias, conatus, course, direction, disposition, drift, drive, heading, inclination, leaning, liability, movement, partiality, penchant, predilection, predisposition, proclivity, proneness, propensity, purport, readiness, susceptibility, tenor, thrust, trend, turning.

tender[1] *adj.* aching, acute, affectionate, affettuoso, amoroso, amorous, benevolent, breakable, bruised, callow, caring, chary, compassionate, complicated, considerate, dangerous, delicate, difficult, emotional, evocative, feeble, fond, fragile, frail, gentle, green, humane, immature, impressionable, inexperienced, inflamed, irritated, kind, loving, merciful, moving, new, painful, pathetic, pitiful, poignant, raw, risky, romantic, scrupulous, sensitive, sentimental, smarting, soft, soft-hearted, sore, sympathetic, tender-hearted, ticklish, touching, touchy, tricky, vulnerable, warm, warm-hearted, weak, young, youthful.
antonyms callous, chewy, hard, harsh, rough, severe, tough.

tender[2] *v.* advance, extend, give, offer, present, proffer, propose, submit, suggest, volunteer.
n. bid, currency, estimate, medium, money, offer, payment, proffer, proposal, proposition, specie, submission, suggestion.

tender-hearted *adj.* affectionate, benevolent, benign, caring, compassionate, considerate, feeling, fond, gentle, humane, kind, kind-hearted, kindly, loving, merciful, mild, pitying, responsive, sensitive, sentimental, soft-hearted, sympathetic, warm, warm-hearted.
antonyms callous, cruel, hard-hearted, unfeeling.

tenderness *n.* ache, aching, affection, amorousness, attachment, benevolence, bruising, callowness, care, compassion, consideration, delicateness, devotion, discomfort, feebleness, fondness, fragility, frailness, gentleness, greenness, humaneness, humanity, immaturity, impressionableness, inexperience, inflammation, irritation, kindness, liking, love, loving-kindness, mercy, newness, pain, painfulness, pity, rawness, sensitiveness,

sensitivity, sentimentality, soft- heartedness, softness, soreness, sweetness, sympathy, tender- heartedness, vulnerability, warm-heartedness, warmth, weakness, youth, youthfulness.
antonyms cruelty, hardness, harshness.

tenet *n.* article of faith, belief, canon, conviction, credo, creed, doctrine, dogma, maxim, opinion, precept, presumption, principle, rule, teaching, thesis, view.

tense *adj.* anxious, apprehensive, edgy, electric, exciting, fidgety, jittery, jumpy, moving, nerve-racking, nervous, overwrought, restless, rigid, strained, stressful, stretched, strung up, taut, tight, uneasy, uptight, worrying.
antonyms calm, lax, loose, relaxed.
v. brace, contract, strain, stretch, tauten, tighten.
antonyms loosen, relax.

tension *n.* anxiety, apprehension, edginess, hostility, nervousness, pressure, restlessness, rigidity, stiffness, strain, straining, stress, stretching, suspense, tautness, tightness, tone, unease, worry.
antonyms calm(ness), laxness, looseness, relaxation.

tentative *adj.* cautious, conjectural, diffident, doubtful, experimental, faltering, hesitant, indefinite, peirastic, provisional, speculative, timid, uncertain, unconfirmed, undecided, unformulated, unsettled, unsure.
antonyms conclusive, decisive, definite, final.

tenure *n.* habitation, holding, incumbency, occupancy, occupation, possession, proprietorship, residence, tenancy, term, time.

tepid *adj.* apathetic, cool, half-hearted, indifferent, lew, lukewarm, unenthusiastic, warmish.
antonyms animated, cold, hot, passionate.

term[1] *n.* appellation, denomination, designation, epithet, epitheton, expression, locution, name, phrase, title, word.
v. call, denominate, designate, dub, entitle, label, name, style, tag, title.

term[2] *n.* bound, boundary, close, conclusion, confine, course, culmination, duration, end, finish, fruition, half, interval, limit, period, season, semester, session, space, span, spell, terminus, time, while.

terminal *adj.* bounding, concluding, deadly, desinent, desinential, extreme, fatal, final, incurable, killing, last, lethal, limiting, mortal, ultimate, utmost.
antonym initial.
n. boundary, depot, end, extremity, limit, termination, terminus.

terminate *v.* abort, cease, close, complete, conclude, cut off, discontinue, drop, end, expire, finish, issue, lapse, result, stop, wind up.
antonyms begin, initiate, start.

terminology *n.* argot, cant, jargon, language, lingo, nomenclature, patois, phraseology, terms, vocabulary, words.

terms *n.* agreement, charges, compromise, conditions, fees, footing, language, particulars, payment, phraseology, position, premises, price, provisions, provisos, qualifications, rates, relations, relationship, specifications, standing, status, stipulations, terminology, understanding.

terrible *adj.* abhorrent, appalling, awful, bad, beastly, dangerous, desperate, dire, disgusting, distressing, dread, dreaded, dreadful, extreme, fearful, foul, frightful, godawful, gruesome, harrowing, hateful, hideous, horrendous, horrible, horrid, horrific, horrifying, loathsome, monstrous, obnoxious, odious, offensive, outrageous, poor, repulsive, revolting, rotten, serious, severe, shocking, unpleasant, vile.
antonyms great, pleasant, superb, wonderful.

terrific *adj.* ace, amazing, awesome, awful, breathtaking, brilliant, dreadful, enormous, excellent, excessive, extreme, fabulous, fantastic, fearful, fierce, fine, gigantic, great, harsh, horrific, huge, intense, magnificent, marvelous, monstrous, outstanding, prodigious, sensational, severe, smashing, stupendous, super, superb, terrible, tremendous, wonderful.

terrify *v.* affright, alarm, appal, awe, dismay, frighten, horrify, intimidate, petrify, scare, shock, terrorize.

territory *n.* area, bailiwick, country, dependency, district, domain, jurisdiction, land, park, preserve, province, region, sector, state, terrain, tract, zone.

terror *n.* affright, alarm, anxiety, awe, blue funk, bogeyman, bugbear, consternation, devil, dismay, dread, fear, fiend, fright, horror, intimidation, monster, panic, rascal, rogue, scourge, shock, tearaway. **terse** *adj.* abrupt, aphoristic, brief, brusque, clipped, compact, concise, condensed, crisp, curt, economical, elliptical, epigrammatic, gnomic, incisive, laconic, neat, pithy, sententious, short, snappy, succinct.
antonyms long-winded, prolix, repetitious.

test *v.* analyze, assay, assess, check, examine, experiment, investigate, prove, screen, try, verify.
n. analysis, assessment, attempt, catechism, check, evaluation, examination, hurdle, investigation, moment of truth, ordeal, pons asinorum, probation, proof, shibboleth, trial, try- out.

testify *v.* affirm, assert, asseverate, attest, avow, certify, corroborate, declare, depone, depose, evince, show, state, swear, vouch, witness.

testimony *n.* affidavit, affirmation, asseveration, attestation, avowal, confirmation, corroboration, declaration, demonstration, deposition, evidence, indication, information, manifestation, profession, proof, statement, submission, support, verification, witness.

testy *adj.* bad-tempered, cantankerous, captious, carnaptious, crabbed, cross, crusty, fretful, grumpy, impatient, inflammable, irascible, irritable, peevish, peppery, petulant, quarrelsome, quick-tempered, short-tempered, snappish, snappy, splenetic, sullen, tetchy, touchy, waspish.
antonyms even-tempered, good-humored.

tether *n.* bond, chain, cord, fastening, fetter, halter, lead, leash, line, restraint, rope, shackle.

v. bind, chain, fasten, fetter, lash, leash, manacle, picket, restrain, rope, secure, shackle, tie.

text *n.* argument, body, contents, lection, libretto, matter, motif, paragraph, passage, reader, reading, script, sentence, source, subject, textbook, theme, topic, verse, wordage, wording, words.

texture *n.* character, composition, consistency, constitution, fabric, feel, grain, quality, structure, surface, tissue, weave, weftage, woof.

thankful *adj.* appreciative, beholden, contented, grateful, indebted, obliged, pleased, relieved.
antonyms thankless, unappreciative, ungrateful.

thaw *v.* defreeze, defrost, dissolve, liquefy, melt, soften, unbend, uncongeal, unfreeze, unthaw, warm.
antonym freeze.

theater *n.* amphitheater, auditorium, hall, lyceum, odeon, opera house, playhouse.

theatrical *adj.* affected, artificial, ceremonious, dramatic, dramaturgic, exaggerated, extravagant, hammy, histrionic, mannered, melodramatic, ostentatious, overdone, pompous, scenic, showy, stagy, stilted, theatric, Thespian, unreal.

theft *n.* abstraction, embezzlement, fraud, heist, kleptomania, larceny, pilfering, plunderage, purloining, rip-off, robbery, stealing, thievery, thieving.

theme *n.* argument, burden, composition, dissertation, essay, exercise, idea, keynote, leitmotiv, lemma, matter, motif, mythos, paper, subject, subject-matter, text, thesis, topic, topos.

theoretical *adj.* abstract, academic, conjectural, doctrinaire, doctrinal, hypothetical, ideal, impractical, on paper, pure, speculative.
antonyms applied, concrete, practical.

theory *n.* abstraction, assumption, conjecture, guess, hypothesis, ism, philosophy, plan, postulation, presumption, proposal, scheme, speculation, supposition, surmise, system, thesis.
antonyms certainty, practice.

therefore *adv.* accordingly, as a result, consequently, ergo, for that reason, hence, so, then, thence, thus.

thick *adj.* abundant, brainless, brimming, bristling, broad, bulky, bursting, chock-a-block, chock-full, chummy, close, clotted, coagulated, compact, concentrated, condensed, confidential, covered, crass, crawling, crowded, decided, deep, dense, devoted, dim-witted, distinct, distorted, dopey, dull, excessive, familiar, fat, foggy, frequent, friendly, full, gross, guttural, heavy, hoarse, husky, impenetrable, inarticulate, indistinct, insensitive, inseparable, intimate, marked, matey, moronic, muffled, numerous, obtuse, opaque, packed, pally, pronounced, replete, rich, slow, slow-witted, solid, soupy, squabbish, strong, stupid, substantial, swarming, teeming, thick-headed, throaty, turbid, wide.
antonyms brainy, clever, slender, slight, slim, thin, watery.
n. center, focus, heart, hub, middle, midst.

thief *n.* abactor, Autolycus, bandit, burglar, cheat, cracksman, crook, cut-purse, embezzler, filcher, housebreaker, kleptomaniac, ladrone, land-rat, larcener, larcenist, latron, mugger, pickpocket, pilferer, plunderer, prigger, purloiner, robber, shop-lifter, snatch-purse, St Nicholas's clerk, stealer, swindler.

thin *adj.* attenuate, attenuated, bony, deficient, delicate, diaphanous, dilute, diluted, emaciated, feeble, filmy, fine, fine-drawn, flimsy, gaunt, gossamer, inadequate, insubstantial, insufficient, lanky, lean, light, meager, narrow, poor, rarefied, runny, scant, scanty, scarce, scattered, scragged, scraggy, scrawny, see-through, shallow, sheer, skeletal, skimpy, skinny, slender, slight, slim, spare, sparse, spindly, superficial, tenuous, translucent, transparent, unconvincing, undernourished, underweight, unsubstantial, washy, watery, weak, wishy-washy, wispy.
antonyms broad, dense, fat, solid, strong, thick.
v. attenuate, decrassify, dilute, diminish, emaciate, extenuate, prune, rarefy, reduce, refine, trim, water down, weaken, weed out.

think *v.* anticipate, be under the impression, believe, brood, calculate, cerebrate, cogitate, conceive, conclude, consider, contemplate, deem, deliberate, design, determine, envisage, esteem, estimate, expect, foresee, hold, ideate, imagine, intellectualize, judge, meditate, mull over, muse, ponder, presume, purpose, ratiocinate, reason, recall, reckon, recollect, reflect, regard, remember, revolve, ruminate, suppose, surmise.
n. assessment, cogitation, consideration, contemplation, deliberation, meditation, reflection.

thirst *n.* appetite, craving, desire, drought, drouth, drouthiness, dryness, eagerness, hankering, hunger, hydromania, keenness, longing, lust, passion, thirstiness, yearning, yen.

thirsty *adj.* adry, appetitive, arid, athirst, avid, burning, craving, dehydrated, desirous, drouthy, dry, dying, eager, greedy, hankering, hungry, hydropic, itching, longing, lusting, parched, thirsting, yearning.

thorn *n.* acantha, affliction, annoyance, bane, barb, bother, curse, doorn, irritant, irritation, nuisance, pest, plague, prickle, scourge, spike, spine, torment, torture, trouble.

thorough *adj.* absolute, all-embracing, all- inclusive, arrant, assiduous, careful, complete, comprehensive, conscientious, deep-seated, downright, efficient, entire, exhaustive, full, in-depth, intensive, meticulous, out-and-out, pains-taking, perfect, pure, root-and-branch, scrupulous, sheer, sweeping, thoroughgoing, total, unmitigated, unqualified, utter.
antonyms careless, haphazard, partial.

thoroughfare *n.* access, avenue, boulevard, concourse, expressway, freeway, highway, motorway, passage, passageway, road, roadway, street, thruway, turnpike, way.

though *conj.* albeit, allowing, although, even if, granted, howbeit, notwithstanding, while.

adv. all the same, even so, for all that, however, in spite of that, nevertheless, nonetheless, notwithstanding, still, yet.

thought *n.* aim, anticipation, anxiety, aspiration, assessment, attention, attentiveness, belief, brainwork, care, cerebration, cogitation, compassion, concept, conception, concern, conclusion, conjecture, considerateness, consideration, contemplation, conviction, dash, deliberation, design, dream, estimation, excogitation, expectation, heed, hope, idea, intention, introspection, jot, judgment, kindness, little, meditation, mentation, muse, musing, notion, object, opinion, plan, prospect, purpose, reflection, regard, resolution, rumination, scrutiny, solicitude, study, sympathy, thinking, thoughtfulness, touch, trifle, view, whisker.

thoughtful *adj.* absorbed, abstracted, astute, attentive, canny, careful, caring, cautious, circumspect, considerate, contemplative, deliberate, deliberative, discreet, heedful, helpful, introspective, kind, kindly, meditative, mindful, musing, pensieroso, pensive, prudent, rapt, reflective, ruminative, serious, solicitous, studious, thinking, unselfish, wary, wistful.
antonym thoughtless.

thoughtless *adj.* absent-minded, careless, étourdi(e), foolish, heedless, ill-considered, impolite, imprudent, inadvertent, inattentive, inconsiderate, indiscreet, injudicious, insensitive, mindless, neglectful, negligent, rash, reckless, regardless, remiss, rude, selfish, silly, stupid, tactless, uncaring, undiplomatic, unkind, unmindful, unobservant, unreflecting, unthinking.
antonym thoughtful.

thrash *v.* beat, belt, bethump, bethwack, birch, cane, chastise, clobber, crush, defeat, drub, flagellate, flail, flog, hammer, heave, horse-whip, jerk, lam, lambaste, larrup, lather, lay into, leather, maul, overwhelm, paste, plunge, punish, quilt, rout, scourge, slaughter, spank, squirm, swish, tan, thresh, toss, towel, trim, trounce, wallop, whale, whap, whip, writhe.

thread *n.* cotton, course, direction, drift, fiber, filament, film, fimbria, line, motif, plot, story-line, strain, strand, string, tenor, theme, yarn.
v. ease, inch, meander, pass, string, weave, wind.

threadbare *adj.* clichéd, cliché-ridden, commonplace, conventional, corny, down-at-heel, frayed, hackneyed, moth-eaten, old, overused, overworn, ragged, scruffy, shabby, stale, stereotyped, stock, tattered, tatty, tired, trite, used, well-worn, worn, worn-out.
antonyms fresh, luxurious, new, plush.

threat *n.* commination, danger, foreboding, foreshadowing, frighteners, hazard, menace, omen, peril, portent, presage, risk, saber-rattling, warning.

threaten *v.* browbeat, bully, comminate, cow, endanger, forebode, foreshadow, impend, imperil, intimidate, jeopardize, menace, portend, presage, pressurize, terrorize, warn.

threatening *adj.* baleful, bullying, cautionary, comminatory, Damoclean, grim, inauspicious, intimidatory, menacing, minacious, minatory, ominous, sinister, terrorizing, warning.

threshold *n.* beginning, brink, dawn, door, door- sill, door-stead, doorstep, doorway, entrance, inception, minimum, opening, outset, sill, start, starting-point, verge.

thrift *n.* carefulness, conservation, economy, frugality, husbandry, parsimony, prudence, saving, thriftiness.
antonyms profligacy, waste.

thrifty *adj.* careful, conserving, economical, frugal, parsimonious, provident, prudent, saving, sparing.
antonyms prodigal, profligate, thriftless, wasteful.

thrill *n.* adventure, buzz, charge, flutter, fluttering, frisson, glow, kick, pleasure, quiver, sensation, shudder, stimulation, throb, tingle, titillation, tremble, tremor, vibration.
v. arouse, electrify, excite, flush, flutter, glow, move, quake, quiver, send, shake, shudder, stimulate, stir, throb, tingle, titillate, tremble, vibrate, wow.

thrive *v.* advance, bloom, blossom, boom, burgeon, develop, flourish, gain, grow, increase, profit, prosper, succeed, wax.
antonyms die, fail, languish, stagnate.

throb *v.* beat, palpitate, pound, pulsate, pulse, thump, vibrate.
n. beat, palpitation, pounding, pulsating, pulsation, pulse, thump, thumping, vibration, vibrato.

throe *n.* convulsion, fit, pain, pang, paroxysm, seizure, spasm, stab.

throng *n.* assemblage, bevy, concourse, congregation, crowd, crush, flock, herd, horde, host, jam, mass, mob, multitude, pack, press, swarm.
v. bunch, congregate, converge, cram, crowd, fill, flock, herd, jam, mill around, pack, press, swarm.

throttle *v.* asphyxiate, choke, control, gag, garrotte, inhibit, silence, smother, stifle, strangle, strangulate, suppress.

through *prep.* as a result of, because of, between, by, by means of, by reason of, by virtue of, by way of, during, in, in and out of, in consequence of, in the middle of, past, thanks to, throughout, using, via.
adj. completed, direct, done, ended, express, finished, nonstop, terminated.

throughout *adv.* everywhere, extensively, ubiquitously, widely.

throw *v.* astonish, baffle, bemuse, bring down, cast, chuck, confound, confuse, defeat, discomfit, disconcert, dislodge, dumbfound, elance, execute, fell, fling, floor, heave, hurl, jaculate, launch, lob, overturn, perform, perplex, pitch, produce, project, propel, put, send, shy, sling, slug, toss, unhorse, unsaddle, unseat, upset, whang.
n. attempt, cast, chance, essay, fling, gamble, hazard, heave, lob, pitch, projection, put, shy, sling, spill, toss, try, venture, wager.

thrust *v.* bear, butt, drive, force, impel, intrude, jab, jam, lunge, pierce, plunge, poke, press, prod, propel, push, ram, shove, stab, stick, urge, wedge.
n. drive, flanconade, impetus, lunge, momentum, poke, prod, prog, push, shove, stab, stoccado.

thug *n.* animal, assassin, bandit, bangster, bruiser, bullyboy, cut-throat, gangster, goon, gorilla, heavy, highbinder, hood, hoodlum, hooligan, killer, mugger, murderer, robber, ruffian, tough.

thump *n.* bang, blow, box, clout, clunk, crash, cuff, knock, rap, smack, thud, thwack, wallop, whack.
v. bang, batter, beat, belabor, box, clout, crash, cuff, daud, ding, dunt, dush, hit, knock, lambaste, pound, rap, smack, strike, thrash, throb, thud, thwack, wallop, whack.

thunderstruck *adj.* agape, aghast, amazed, astonished, astounded, dazed, dumbfounded, flabbergasted, floored, flummoxed, nonplused, open-mouthed, paralyzed, petrified, shocked, staggered, stunned.

thus *adv.* accordingly, as follows, consequently, ergo, hence, in this way, like so, like this, so, then, therefore, thuswise.

thwart *v.* baffle, balk, check, defeat, foil, frustrate, hinder, impede, obstruct, oppose, outwit, prevent, spite, stonker, stop, stymie, transverse, traverse.
antonyms abet, aid, assist.

ticket *n.* card, certificate, coupon, docket, label, marker, pass, slip, sticker, tab, tag, tessera, token, voucher.

tickle *v.* amuse, cheer, delight, divert, enchant, entertain, excite, gratify, please, thrill, titillate.

ticklish *adj.* awkward, critical, delicate, difficult, dodgy, hazardous, nice, precarious, risky, sensitive, thorny, touchy, tricky, uncertain, unstable, unsteady.
antonyms easy, straightforward.

tidings *n.* advice, bulletin, communication, dope, gen, greetings, information, intelligence, message, news, report, word.

tidy *adj.* ample, businesslike, clean, cleanly, considerable, fair, generous, good, goodly, handsome, healthy, large, largish, methodical, neat, ordered, orderly, respectable, shipshape, sizable, spick, spick-and-span, spruce, substantial, systematic, trim, uncluttered, well-groomed, well-kept.
antonyms disorganized, untidy.
v. arrange, clean, fettle, groom, neaten, order, spruce up, straighten.

tie *v.* attach, bind, confine, connect, draw, equal, fasten, hamper, hinder, hold, interlace, join, knot, lash, ligature, limit, link, match, moor, oblige, restrain, restrict, rope, secure, strap, tether, truss, unite.
n. affiliation, allegiance, band, bond, commitment, connection, contest, copula, cord, dead heat, deadlock, draw, duty, encumbrance, fastening, fetter, fixture, game, hindrance, joint, kinship, knot, liaison, ligature, limitation, link, match, obligation, relationship, restraint, restriction, rope, stalemate, string.

tier *n.* band, belt, echelon, floor, gradin(e), layer, level, line, rank, row, stage, story, stratification, stratum, zone.

tiff *n.* barney, difference, disagreement, dispute, falling-out, huff, ill-humor, pet, quarrel, row, scrap, set-to, spat, squabble, sulk, tantrum, temper, words.

tight[1] *adj.* close, close-fitting, compact, competent, constricted, cramped, dangerous, difficult, even, evenly-balanced, fast, firm, fixed, grasping, harsh, hazardous, hermetic, impervious, inflexible, mean, miserly, narrow, near, niggardly, parsimonious, penurious, perilous, precarious, precise, problematic, proof, rigid, rigorous, sealed, secure, severe, snug, sound, sparing, stern, sticky, stiff, stingy, stretched, strict, stringent, taut, tense, ticklish, tight-fisted, tough, tricky, trig, troublesome, uncompromising, unyielding, watertight, well-matched, worrisome.
antonyms lax, loose, slack.

tight[2] *adj.* blotto, drunk, half cut, half-seas-over, in one's cups, inebriated, intoxicated, pickled, pie-eyed, pissed, plastered, smashed, sozzled, stewed, stoned, three sheets in the wind, tiddly, tipsy, under the influence.
antonym sober.

till *v.* cultivate, dig, dress, plow, work.

tilt *v.* attack, cant, clash, contend, duel, encounter, fight, heel, incline, joust, lean, list, overthrow, pitch, slant, slope, spar, tip.
n. angle, cant, clash, combat, duel, encounter, fight, inclination, incline, joust, list, lists, pitch, set-to, slant, slope, thrust, tournament, tourney.

timber *n.* beams, boarding, boards, forest, logs, planking, planks, trees, wood.

time *n.* age, beat, chronology, date, day, duration, epoch, era, generation, heyday, hour, instance, interval, juncture, life, lifespan, lifetime, measure, meter, occasion, peak, period, point, rhythm, season, space, span, spell, stage, stretch, tempo, term, tide, while.
v. clock, control, count, judge, measure, meter, regulate, schedule, set.

timeless *adj.* abiding, ageless, amaranthine, ceaseless, changeless, deathless, endless, enduring, eternal, everlasting, immortal, immutable, imperishable, indestructible, lasting, permanent, perpetual, persistent, undying.

timely *adj.* appropriate, convenient, judicious, opportune, prompt, propitious, punctual, seasonable, suitable, tempestive, well-timed.
antonym ill-timed, inappropriate, unfavorable.

timetable *n.* agenda, calendar, curriculum, diary, list, listing, program, roster, rota, schedule.

time-worn *adj.* aged, ancient, broken-down, bromidic, clichéd, dated, decrepit, dog-eared, hackneyed, hoary, lined, old hat, out of date, outworn, passé, ragged, ruined, rundown, shabby, stale, stock, threadbare, tired, trite, weathered, well-worn, worn, wrinkled.
antonyms fresh, new.

timid *adj.* afraid, apprehensive, bashful, cowardly, coy, diffident, faint-hearted, fearful, hen-hearted, irresolute, modest, mousy, nervous, pavid, pusillanimous, retiring, shrinking, shy, spineless, timorous.
antonyms audacious, bold, brave.

tinge *n.* bit, cast, color, dash, drop, dye, flavor, pinch, shade, smack, smatch, smattering, sprinkling, stain, suggestion, tinct, tincture, tint, touch, trace, wash.
v. color, dye, encolor, imbue, shade, stain, suffuse, tint.

tingle *v.* dindle, itch, prickle, ring, sting, thrill, throb, tickle, vibrate.
n. frisson, gooseflesh, goose-pimples, itch, itching, pins and needles, prickling, quiver, shiver, stinging, thrill, tickle, tickling.

tinker *v.* dabble, fiddle, meddle, monkey, play, potter, putter, toy, trifle.
n. botcher, bungler, diddicoy, fixer, itinerant, mender.

tint *n.* cast, color, dye, hint, hue, rinse, shade, stain, streak, suggestion, tinct, tincture, tinge, tone, touch, trace, wash.
v. affect, color, dye, influence, rinse, stain, streak, taint, tincture, tinge.

tiny *adj.* diminutive, dwarfish, infinitesimal, insignificant, itsy-bitsy, Lilliputian, little, microscopic, mini, miniature, minute, negligible, petite, pint-size(d), pocket, puny, pygmy, slight, small, teensy, teentsy, teeny, teeny-weeny, tiddl(e)y, tottie, totty, trifling, wee, weeny.
antonyms big, immense.

tip[1] *n.* acme, apex, cap, crown, end, extremity, ferrule, head, nib, peak, pinnacle, point, summit, top.
v. cap, crown, finish, pinnacle, poll, pollard, prune, surmount, top.

tip[2] *v.* cant, capsize, ditch, dump, empty, heel, incline, lean, list, overturn, pour out, slant, spill, tilt, topple over, unload, up-end, upset.
n. bing, coup, dump, midden, refuse-heap, rubbish-heap, slag-heap.

tip[3] *n.* baksheesh, clue, forecast, gen, gift, gratuity, hint, information, inside information, lagniappe, perquisite, pointer, pourboire, refresher, suggestion, tip-off, warning, word, word of advice, wrinkle.
v. advise, caution, forewarn, inform, remunerate, reward, suggest, tell, warn.

tipsy *adj.* a peg too low, a pip out, cockeyed, corny, drunk, elevated, fuddled, happy, mellow, merry, moony, moppy, mops and brooms, nappy, pixil(l)ated, rocky, screwed, screwy, slewed, sprung, squiff(y), tiddled, tiddley, tiddly, tight, totty, wet, woozy.
antonym sober.

tirade *n.* abuse, denunciation, diatribe, fulmination, harangue, invective, lecture, outburst, philippic, rant.

tire *v.* annoy, betoil, bore, cook, drain, droop, enervate, exasperate, exhaust, fag, fail, fatigue, flag, harass, irk, irritate, jade, knacker, sink, weary.
antonyms energize, enliven, exhilarate, invigorate, refresh.

tired *adj.* all in, awearied, aweary, beat, bone- weary, bushed, clapped-out, clichéd, conventional, corny, dead- beat, disjaskit, dog-tired, drained, drooping, drowsy, enervated, épuisé(e), exhausted, fagged, familiar, fatigued, flagging, forfairn, forfough(t)en, forjeskit, hackneyed, jaded, knackered, old, outworn, shagged, shattered, sleepy, spent, stale, stock, threadbare, trite, weary, well-worn, whacked, worn out.
antonyms active, energetic, fresh, lively, rested.

tireless *adj.* determined, diligent, energetic, indefatigable, industrious, resolute, sedulous, unflagging, untiring, unwearied, vigorous.
antonyms tired, unenthusiastic, weak.

tiresome *adj.* annoying, boring, bothersome, dull, exasperating, fatiguing, flat, irksome, irritating, laborious, monotonous, pesky, tedious, troublesome, trying, uninteresting, vexatious, wearing, wearisome.
antonyms easy, interesting, stimulating.

tiring *adj.* arduous, demanding, draining, enervating, enervative, exacting, exhausting, fagging, fatiguing, laborious, strenuous, tough, wearing, wearying.

titan *n.* Atlas, colossus, giant, Hercules, leviathan, superman.

titillating *adj.* arousing, captivating, exciting, interesting, intriguing, lewd, lurid, provocative, sensational, stimulating, suggestive, teasing, thrilling.

title *n.* appellation, caption, championship, claim, crown, denomination, designation, entitlement, epithet, handle, heading, inscription, label, laurels, legend, letterhead, moniker, name, nickname, nom de plume, ownership, prerogative, privilege, pseudonym, right, sobriquet, style, term.
v. call, christen, designate, dub, entitle, label, name, style, term.

toast[1] *v.* broil, brown, grill, heat, roast, warm.

toast[2] *n.* compliment, darling, drink, favorite, grace cup, health, hero, heroine, pledge, salutation, salute, tribute, wassail.

together *adv.* all at once, arranged, as one, as one man, at the same time, cheek by jowl, closely, collectively, concurrently, consecutively, contemporaneously, continuously, en masse, fixed, hand in glove, hand in hand, in a body, in a row, in concert, in co-operation, in fere, in mass, in succession, in unison, jointly, mutually, on end, ordered, organized, pari passu, settled, shoulder to shoulder, side by side, simultaneously, sorted out, straight, successively.
antonym separately.
adj. calm, commonsensical, composed, cool, down-to- earth, level-headed, sensible, stable, well-adjusted, well- balanced, well-organized.

toil *n.* application, donkey-work, drudgery, effort, elbow grease, exertion, graft, industry, labor, labor improbus, pains, slog, sweat, travail.

v. drudge, graft, grind, grub, labor, persevere, plug away, slave, slog, strive, struggle, sweat, tew, work.

token *n.* badge, clue, demonstration, earnest, evidence, expression, index, indication, keepsake, manifestation, mark, memento, memorial, note, proof, remembrance, reminder, representation, sign, souvenir, symbol, tessera, testimony, voucher, warning.
adj. emblematic, hollow, inconsiderable, minimal, nominal, perfunctory, superficial, symbolic.

tolerant *adj.* biddable, broad-minded, catholic, charitable, complaisant, compliant, easy-going, fair, forbearing, indulgent, kind-hearted, latitudinarian, lax, lenient, liberal, long-suffering, magnanimous, open-minded, patient, permissive, soft, sympathetic, understanding, unprejudiced.
antonyms biased, bigoted, intolerant, prejudiced, unsympathetic.

tolerate *v.* abear, abide, accept, admit, allow, bear, brook, condone, connive at, countenance, endure, indulge, permit, pocket, put up with, receive, sanction, stand, stomach, suffer, swallow, take, thole, turn a blind eye to, undergo, wear, wink at.

toll[1] *v.* announce, call, chime, clang, knell, peal, ring, send, signal, sound, strike, summon, warn.

toll[2] *n.* assessment, charge, cost, customs, damage, demand, duty, fee, impost, inroad, levy, loss, payment, penalty, rate, tariff, tax, tithe, tribute.

tomb *n.* burial-place, catacomb, cenotaph, crypt, dolmen, grave, mastaba, mausoleum, sepulcher, sepulture, speos, vault.

tone *n.* accent, air, approach, aspect, attitude, cast, character, color, drift, effect, emphasis, feel, force, frame, grain, harmony, hue, inflection, intonation, klang, manner, modulation, mood, note, pitch, quality, shade, spirit, strength, stress, style, temper, tenor, timbre, tinge, tint, tonality, vein, volume.
v. blend, harmonize, intone, match, sound, suit.

tongue *n.* argot, articulation, clack, clapper, dialect, discourse, idiom, language, languet(te), lath, lingo, parlance, patois, red rag, speech, talk, utterance, vernacular, voice.

tongue-tied *adj.* dumb, dumbstruck, inarticulate, mute, silent, speechless, voiceless.
antonyms garrulous, talkative, voluble.

too[1] *adv.* also, as well, besides, further, in addition, into the bargain, likewise, moreover, to boot, what's more.

too[2] *adv.* excessively, exorbitantly, extremely, immoderately, inordinately, over, overly, ridiculously, to excess, to extremes, unduly, unreasonably, very.

tool *n.* agency, agent, apparatus, appliance, cat's-paw, contraption, contrivance, creature, device, dupe, flunkey, front, gadget, hireling, implement, instrument, intermediary, jackal, lackey, machine, means, medium, minion, pawn, puppet, stooge, toady, utensil, vehicle, weapon, widget. *v.* chase, cut, decorate, fashion, machine, ornament, shape, work.

top *n.* acme, apex, apogee, cacumen, cap, cop, cork, cover, crest, crown, culmen, culmination, head, height, high point, hood, lead, lid, meridian, peak, pinnacle, roof, stopper, summit, upside, vertex, zenith.
antonyms base, bottom, nadir.
adj. best, chief, crack, crowning, culminating, dominant, elite, finest, first, foremost, greatest, head, highest, lead, leading, pre-eminent, prime, principal, ruling, sovereign, superior, topmost, upmost, upper, uppermost.
v. ascend, beat, best, better, cap, climb, command, cover, crest, crown, decorate, eclipse, exceed, excel, finish, finish off, garnish, head, lead, outdo, outshine, outstrip, roof, rule, scale, surmount, surpass, tip, transcend.

topic *n.* issue, lemma, matter, motif, point, question, subject, subject-matter, talking-point, text, theme, thesis.

topical *adj.* contemporary, current, familiar, newsworthy, popular, relevant, up-to-date, up-to-the-minute.

topple *v.* capsize, collapse, oust, overbalance, overthrow, overturn, totter, tumble, unseat, upset.

torment *v.* afflict, agitate, agonize, annoy, bedevil, bother, chivvy, crucify, devil, distort, distress, excruciate, harass, harrow, harry, hound, irritate, nag, pain, persecute, pester, plague, provoke, rack, tease, torture, trouble, vex, worry, wrack.
n. affliction, agony, angst, anguish, annoyance, bane, bother, distress, harassment, hassle, hell, irritation, misery, nag, nagging, nuisance, pain, persecution, pest, plague, provocation, scourge, suffering, torture, trouble, vexation, worry.

torpid *adj.* apathetic, benumbed, dormant, drowsy, dull, fainéant, hebetudinous, inactive, indolent, inert, lackadaisical, languid, languorous, lazy, lethargic, listless, lymphatic, motionless, numb, passive, slothful, slow, slow- moving, sluggish, somnolent, stagnant, supine.
antonyms active, lively, vigorous.

torpor *n.* accidie, acedia, apathy, dormancy, drowsiness, dullness, hebetude, inactivity, inanition, indolence, inertia, inertness, languor, laziness, lethargy, listlessness, numbness, passivity, sloth, sluggishness, somnolence, stagnancy, stupidity, stupor, torpidity.
antonyms activity, animation, vigor.

torrent *n.* barrage, cascade, deluge, downpour, effusion, flood, flow, gush, outburst, rush, spate, stream, tide, volley.

torrid *adj.* ardent, arid, blistering, boiling, broiling, burning, dried, dry, emotional, erotic, fervent, fiery, hot, intense, parched, parching, passionate, scorched, scorching, sexy, sizzling, steamy, stifling, sultry, sweltering, tropical.
antonym arctic.

tortuous *adj.* ambagious, ambiguous, bent, Byzantine, circuitous, complicated, convoluted, crooked, cunning, curved, deceptive, devious, indirect, involved, mazy,

meandering, misleading, roundabout, serpentine, sinuous, tricky, twisted, twisting, winding, zigzag.
antonyms straight, straightforward.

torture *v.* afflict, agonize, crucify, distress, excruciate, harrow, lacerate, martyr, martyrize, pain, persecute, rack, torment, wrack.
n. affliction, agony, anguish, distress, gyp, hell, laceration, martyrdom, misery, pain, pang(s), persecution, rack, suffering, torment.

toss *v.* agitate, cant, cast, chuck, disturb, fling, flip, heave, hurl, jiggle, joggle, jolt, labor, launch, lob, lurch, pitch, project, propel, rock, roll, shake, shy, sling, thrash, throw, tumble, wallow, welter, wriggle, writhe.
n. cast, chuck, fling, lob, pitch, shy, sling, throw.

total *n.* aggregate, all, amount, ensemble, entirety, lot, mass, sum, totality, whole.
adj. absolute, all-out, complete, comprehensive, consummate, downright, entire, full, gross, integral, out-and- out, outright, perfect, root-and-branch, sheer, sweeping, thorough, thoroughgoing, unconditional, undisputed, undivided, unmitigated, unqualified, utter, whole, whole-hog.
antonyms limited, partial, restricted.
v. add (up), amount to, come to, count (up), reach, reckon, sum (up), tot up.

totalitarian *adj.* authoritarian, despotic, dictatorial, monocratic, monolithic, omnipotent, one-party, oppressive, tyrannous, undemocratic.
antonym democratic.

totter *v.* daddle, daidle, falter, lurch, quiver, reel, rock, shake, stagger, stumble, sway, teeter, titter, tremble, waver.

touch *n.* ability, acquaintance, adroitness, approach, art, artistry, awareness, bit, blow, brush, caress, characteristic, command, communication, contact, correspondence, dash, deftness, detail, direction, drop, effect, facility, familiarity, feel, feeling, flair, fondling, hand, handiwork, handling, hint, hit, influence, intimation, jot, knack, manner, mastery, method, palpation, pat, pinch, push, skill, smack, smattering, soupçon, speck, spot, stroke, style, suggestion, suspicion, tactility, tap, taste, technique, tig, tincture, tinge, trace, trademark, understanding, virtuosity, way, whiff.
v. abut, adjoin, affect, attain, border, brush, caress, cheat, compare with, concern, consume, contact, converge, disturb, drink, eat, equal, feel, finger, fondle, graze, handle, hit, hold a candle to, impress, influence, inspire, interest, mark, match, meet, melt, move, palp, palpate, parallel, pat, pertain to, push, reach, regard, rival, soften, stir, strike, stroke, tap, tat, tinge, upset, use, utilize.

touch-and-go *adj.* close, critical, dangerous, dodgy, hairy, hazardous, near, nerve-racking, offhand, parlous, perilous, precarious, risky, sticky, tricky.

touching *adj.* affecting, emotional, emotive, haptic, heartbreaking, libant, melting, moving, pathetic, piteous, pitiable, pitiful, poignant, sad, stirring, tender.

touchy *adj.* bad-tempered, captious, crabbed, cross, feisty, grouchy, grumpy, huffy, irascible, irritable, miffy, peevish, pettish, petulant, querulous, quick-tempered, snippety, snuffy, sore, splenetic, surly, testy, tetchy, thin-skinned.
antonyms calm, imperturbable, serene, unflappable.

tough *adj.* adamant, arduous, bad, baffling, brawny, butch, callous, cohesive, difficult, durable, exacting, exhausting, firm, fit, hard, hard-bitten, hard-boiled, hardened, hardnosed, hardy, herculean, inflexible, intractable, irksome, knotty, laborious, lamentable, leathery, merciless, obdurate, obstinate, perplexing, pugnacious, puzzling, refractory, regrettable, resilient, resistant, resolute, rigid, rough, ruffianly, rugged, ruthless, seasoned, severe, solid, stalwart, stern, stiff, stout, strapping, strenuous, strict, strong, stubborn, sturdy, tenacious, thorny, troublesome, unbending, unforgiving, unfortunate, unlucky, unyielding, uphill, vicious, vigorous, violent.
antonyms brittle, delicate, fragile, liberal, soft, tender, vulnerable, weak.
n. bravo, bruiser, brute, bully, bully-boy, bully- rook, gorilla, hooligan, rough, roughneck, rowdy, ruffian, thug, yob, yobbo.

toughness *n.* arduousness, callousness, difficulty, durability, firmness, fitness, grit, hardiness, hardness, inflexibility, intractability, laboriousness, obduracy, obstinacy, pugnacity, resilience, resistance, rigidity, roughness, ruggedness, ruthlessness, severity, solidity, sternness, stiffness, strength, strenuousness, strictness, sturdiness, tenacity, viciousness.
antonyms fragility, liberality, softness, vulnerability, weakness.

tour *n.* circuit, course, drive, excursion, expedition, jaunt, journey, outing, peregrination, progress, ride, round, trip.
v. drive, explore, journey, ride, sightsee, travel, visit.

tourist *n.* excursionist, globe-trotter, holidaymaker, journeyer, rubber-neck, sightseer, sojourner, traveler.

tournament *n.* championship, competition, contest, event, joust, lists, match, meeting, series, tourney.

tousled *adj.* disarranged, disheveled, disordered, messed up, ruffled, rumpled, tangled, tumbled.

tow *v.* drag, draw, haul, lug, pull, tote, trail, transport, trawl, tug, yank.

towering *adj.* burning, colossal, elevated, excessive, extra-ordinary, extreme, fiery, gigantic, great, high, immoderate, imposing, impressive, inordinate, intemperate, intense, lofty, magnificent, mighty, monumental, outstanding, overpowering, paramount, passionate, prodigious, soaring, sublime, superior, supreme, surpassing, tall, transcendent, vehement, violent.
antonyms minor, small, trivial.

town *n.* borough, bourg, burg, burgh, city, metropolis, municipality, settlement, township.
antonym country.

toxic *adj.* baneful, deadly, harmful, lethal, morbific, noxious, pernicious, pestilential, poisonous, septic, unhealthy.
antonym harmless.

toy *n.* bauble, doll, game, gewgaw, kickshaw(s), knick-knack, plaything, trifle, trinket.
v. dally, fiddle, flirt, play, potter, putter, sport, tinker, trifle, wanton.

trace *n.* bit, dash, drop, evidence, footmark, footprint, footstep, hint, indication, iota, jot, mark, path, record, relic, remains, remnant, scintilla, shadow, sign, smack, soupçon, spoor, spot, suggestion, survival, suspicion, tincture, tinge, token, touch, track, trail, trifle, vestige, whiff.
v. ascertain, chart, copy, delineate, depict, detect, determine, discover, draw, find, follow, map, mark, outline, pursue, record, seek, shadow, show, sketch, stalk, track, trail, traverse, unearth, write.

track *n.* course, drift, footmark, footprint, footstep, line, mark, orbit, path, pathway, piste, rail, rails, ridgeway, road, scent, sequence, slot, spoor, tack, trace, trail, train, trajectory, wake, wavelength, way.
v. chase, dog, follow, hunt, pursue, shadow, spoor, stalk, tail, trace, trail, travel, traverse.

tract[1] *n.* area, district, estate, expanse, extent, lot, plot, quarter, region, section, stretch, territory, zone.

tract[2] *n.* booklet, brochure, discourse, disquisition, dissertation, essay, homily, leaflet, monograph, pamphlet, sermon, tractate, treatise.

tractable *adj.* amenable, biddable, complaisant, compliant, controllable, docile, ductile, fictile, governable, malleable, manageable, obedient, persuadable, plastic, pliable, pliant, submissive, tame, tractile, willing, workable, yielding.
antonyms headstrong, intractable, obstinate, refractory, stubborn, unruly, wilful.

trade *n.* avocation, barter, business, calling, clientele, commerce, commodities, craft, custom, customers, deal, dealing, employment, exchange, interchange, job, line, market, métier, occupation, patrons, profession, public, pursuit, shopkeeping, skill, swap, traffic, transactions, truck.
v. bargain, barter, commerce, deal, do business, exchange, peddle, swap, switch, traffic, transact, truck.

trademark *n.* badge, brand, crest, emblem, hallmark, identification, idiograph, insignia, label, logo, logotype, name, sign, symbol.

tradition *n.* convention, custom, customs, folklore, habit, institution, lore, praxis, ritual, usage, usance, way, wony.

traduce *v.* abuse, asperse, blacken, calumniate, decry, defame, denigrate, deprecate, depreciate, detract, disparage, knock, malign, misrepresent, revile, run down, slag, slander, smear, vilify.

tragedy *n.* adversity, affliction, blow, calamity, catastrophe, disaster, misfortune, unhappiness.
antonyms prosperity, success, triumph.

tragic *adj.* anguished, appalling, awful, calamitous, catastrophic, deadly, dire, disastrous, doleful, dreadful, fatal, grievous, heartbreaking, heart-rending, ill- fated, ill-starred, lamentable, miserable, mournful, pathetic, pitiable, ruinous, sad, shocking, sorrowful, thespian, unfortunate, unhappy, woeful, wretched.
antonyms comic, successful, triumphant.

trail *v.* chase, dangle, dawdle, drag, draw, droop, extend, follow, hang, haul, hunt, lag, linger, loiter, pull, pursue, shadow, stalk, straggle, stream, sweep, tail, tow, trace, track, traipse.
n. abature, appendage, drag, footpath, footprints, footsteps, mark, marks, path, road, route, scent, spoor, stream, tail, trace, track, train, wake, way.

train *v.* aim, coach, direct, discipline, drill, educate, exercise, focus, guide, improve, instruct, lesson, level, point, prepare, rear, rehearse, school, teach, tutor.
n. appendage, attendants, caravan, chain, choo-choo, column, concatenation, convoy, cortege, course, court, entourage, file, followers, following, household, lure, order, process, procession, progression, retinue, sequence, series, set, staff, string, succession, suite, tail, trail.

traipse *v.* plod, slouch, trail, tramp, trudge.
n. plod, slog, tramp, trek, trudge.

trait *n.* attribute, characteristic, feature, idiosyncrasy, lineament, mannerism, peculiarity, quality, quirk, thew.

traitor *n.* apostate, back-stabber, betrayer, deceiver, defector, deserter, double-crosser, fifth columnist, informer, Judas, miscreant, nithing, proditor, quisling, rebel, renegade, turncoat.

traitorous *adj.* apostate, dishonorable, disloyal, double-crossing, double-dealing, faithless, false, perfidious, proditorious, renegade, seditious, treacherous, treasonable, unfaithful, untrue.
antonyms faithful, loyal, patriotic.

trajectory *n.* course, flight, line, path, route, track, trail.

tramp *v.* crush, footslog, hike, march, plod, ramble, range, roam, rove, slog, stamp, stomp, stump, toil, traipse, trample, tread, trek, trudge, walk, yomp.
n. call girl, clochard, derelict, dosser, down-and- out, drifter, drummer, footfall, footstep, hike, hobo, hooker, march, piker, plod, ramble, slog, stamp, street walker, toerag(ger), tread, trek, vagabond, vagrant, weary willie.

trample *v.* crush, flatten, hurt, infringe, insult, squash, stamp, tread, violate.

tranquil *adj.* at peace, calm, composed, cool, disimpassioned, dispassionate, pacific, peaceful, placid, quiet, reposeful, restful, sedate, serene, still, undisturbed, unexcited, unperturbed, unruffled, untroubled.
antonyms agitated, disturbed, noisy, troubled.

tranquility *n.* ataraxia, ataraxy, calm, calmness, composure, coolness, equanimity, hush, imperturbability, peace, peacefulness, placidity, quiet, quietness, quietude, repose, rest, restfulness, sedateness, serenity, silence, stillness.
antonyms agitation, disturbance, noise.

transact *v.* accomplish, carry on, carry out, conclude, conduct, discharge, dispatch, do, enact, execute, handle, manage, negotiate, perform, prosecute, settle.

transaction *n.* action, affair, arrangement, bargain, business, coup, deal, deed, enterprise, event, execution, matter, negotiation, occurrence, proceeding, undertaking.

transcend *v.* eclipse, exceed, excel, outdo, outrival, outshine, outstrip, overleap, overstep, overtop, surmount, surpass.

transcribe *v.* copy, engross, exemplify, interpret, note, record, render, reproduce, rewrite, take down, tape, tape- record, transfer, translate, transliterate.

transfer *v.* carry, cede, change, consign, convey, decal, decant, demise, displace, grant, hand over, move, relocate, remove, second, shift, translate, transmit, transplant, transport, transpose.
n. change, changeover, crossover, decantation, displacement, handover, move, relocation, removal, shift, switch, switch-over, transference, translation, transmission, transposition, virement.

transform *v.* alter, change, convert, metamorphose, reconstruct, remodel, renew, revolutionize, transfigure, translate, transmogrify, transmute, transverse.
antonym preserve.

transgression *n.* breach, contravention, crime, debt, encroachment, error, fault, infraction, infringement, iniquity, lapse, misbehavior, misdeed, misdemeanor, offence, peccadillo, peccancy, sin, trespass, violation, wrong, wrongdoing.

transient *adj.* brief, caducous, deciduous, ephemeral, evanescent, fleeting, flying, fugacious, fugitive, impermanent, momentary, passing, short, short-lived, short-term, temporary, transitory.
antonym permanent.

transition *n.* alteration, change, changeover, conversion, development, evolution, flux, metabasis, metamorphosis, metastasis, passage, passing, progress, progression, shift, transformation, transit, transmutation, upheaval.
antonyms beginning, end.

translate *v.* alter, carry, change, construe, convert, convey, decipher, decode, do, do up, elucidate, enrapture, explain, improve, interpret, metamorphose, move, paraphrase, remove, render, renovate, send, simplify, spell out, transcribe, transfer, transfigure, transform, transliterate, transmogrify, transmute, transplant, transport, transpose, turn.

translucent *adj.* clear, diaphanous, limpid, lucent, pellucid, translucid, transparent.
antonym opaque.

transmit *v.* bear, broadcast, carry, communicate, convey, diffuse, dispatch, disseminate, forward, impart, network, radio, relay, remit, send, spread, traject, transfer, transport.
antonym receive.

transparent *adj.* apparent, candid, clear, crystalline, diaphanous, dioptric, direct, distinct, easy, evident, explicit, filmy, forthright, frank, gauzy, hyaline, hyaloid, ingenuous, limpid, lucent, lucid, manifest, obvious, open, patent, pellucid, perspicuous, plain, plain-spoken, recognizable, see-through, sheer, straight, straightforward, translucent, transpicuous, unambiguous, understandable, undisguised, unequivocal, visible.
antonyms ambiguous, opaque, unclear.

transpire *v.* appear, arise, befall, betide, chance, come out, come to light, emerge, happen, leak out, occur, take place, turn up.

transport *v.* banish, bear, bring, captivate, carry, carry away, convey, delight, deport, ecstasize, electrify, enchant, enrapture, entrance, exile, fetch, haul, move, ravish, remove, run, ship, spellbind, take, transfer, waft.
antonyms bore, leave.
n. bliss, carriage, cartage, carting, conveyance, delight, ecstasy, enchantment, euphoria, happiness, haulage, heaven, rapture, ravishment, removal, shipment, shipping, transference, transportation, vehicle, waterage.
antonym boredom.

transpose *v.* alter, change, exchange, interchange, metathesize, move, rearrange, relocate, reorder, shift, substitute, swap, switch, transfer.
antonym leave.

trap *n.* ambush, artifice, bunker, danger, deception, device, gin, hazard, net, noose, pitfall, ruse, snare, spring, springe, springle, strategem, subterfuge, toils, trapdoor, trepan, trick, trickery, wile.
v. ambush, beguile, benet, catch, corner, deceive, dupe, enmesh, ensnare, entrap, illaqueate, inveigle, lime, snare, take, tangle, trepan, trick.

trash *n.* balderdash, draff, dregs, drivel, dross, garbage, hogwash, inanity, junk, kitsch, litter, nonsense, offscourings, offscum, refuse, riddlings, rot, rubbish, scoria, sullage, sweepings, trashery, tripe, trumpery, twaddle, waste.
antonym sense.

trashy *adj.* catchpenny, cheap, cheap-jack, flimsy, grotty, inferior, kitschy, meretricious, pinchbeck, rubbishy, shabby, shoddy, tawdry, third-rate, tinsel, worthless.
antonym first-rate.

trauma *n.* agony, anguish, damage, disturbance, hurt, injury, jolt, lesion, ordeal, pain, scar, shock, strain, suffering, torture, upheaval, upset, wound.
antonyms healing, relaxation.

travail *n.* birth-pangs, childbirth, distress, drudgery, effort, exertion, grind, hardship, labor, labor pains, pain, slavery, slog, strain, stress, suffering, sweat, tears, throes, toil, tribulation.
antonym rest.

travel *v.* carry, commute, cross, excursionize, go, journey, locomote, move, peregrinate, proceed, progress, ramble, roam, rove, tour, traverse, trek, voyage, walk, wander, wayfare, wend.
antonym stay.

travesty *n.* apology, botch, burlesque, caricature, distortion, lampoon, mockery, parody, perversion, send-up, sham, take-off. *v.* burlesque, caricature, deride, distort, lampoon, mock, parody, pervert, pillory, ridicule, send up, sham, spoof, take off.

treachery *n.* betrayal, disloyalty, double-cross, double-dealing, duplicity, faithlessness, falseness, infidelity, Judaskiss, laesa majestas, Medism, perfidiousness, perfidy, Punic faith, Punica fides, trahison, treason.
antonyms dependability, loyalty.

treason *n.* disaffection, disloyalty, duplicity, laesa majestas, lese-majesty, mutiny, perfidy, sedition, subversion, trahison, traitorousness, treachery.
antonym loyalty.

treasure *n.* cash, darling, ewe-lamb, flower, fortune, funds, gem, gold, jewel, jewels, money, nonpareil, paragon, pearl, precious, pride and joy, prize, riches, valuables, wealth.
v. adore, cherish, esteem, idolize, love, preserve, prize, revere, value, venerate, worship.
antonym disparage.

treat *n.* banquet, celebration, delight, enjoyment, entertainment, excursion, feast, fun, gift, gratification, joy, outing, party, pleasure, refreshment, satisfaction, surprise, thrill, wayzgoose.
antonym drag.
v. attend to, bargain, care for, confer, consider, contain, deal with, discourse upon, discuss, doctor, entertain, feast, give, handle, manage, medicament, medicate, medicine, negotiate, nurse, parley, provide, regale, regard, stand, use.

treaty *n.* agreement, alliance, bargain, bond, compact, concordat, contract, convention, covenant, entente, negotiation, pact.

trek *n.* expedition, footslog, hike, journey, march, migration, odyssey, safari, slog, tramp, walk.
v. footslog, hike, journey, march, migrate, plod, range, roam, rove, slog, traipse, tramp, trudge, yomp.

tremble *v.* heave, oscillate, quake, quiver, rock, shake, shiver, shudder, teeter, totter, vibrate, wobble.
n. heart-quake, oscillation, quake, quiver, shake, shiver, shudder, tremblement, tremor, vibration.
antonym steadiness.

trembling *n.* heart-quake, oscillation, quaking, quavering, quivering, rocking, shakes, shaking, shivering, shuddering, tremblement, trepidation, vibration.
antonym steadiness.

tremendous *adj.* ace, amazing, appalling, awe- inspiring, awesome, awful, colossal, deafening, dreadful, enormous, excellent, exceptional, extraordinary, fabulous, fantastic, fearful, formidable, frightful, gargantuan, gigantic, great, herculean, huge, immense, incredible, mammoth, marvelous, monstrous, prodigious, sensational, spectacular, stupendous, super, terrible, terrific, titanic, towering, vast, whopping, wonderful.
antonyms boring, dreadful, run-of-the-mill, tiny.

tremor *n.* agitation, earthquake, quake, quaking, quaver, quavering, quiver, quivering, shake, shaking, shiver, shock, thrill, tremble, trembling, trepidation, trillo, vibration, wobble.
antonym steadiness.

tremulous *adj.* afraid, agitated, agog, anxious, aspen, excited, fearful, frightened, jittery, jumpy, nervous, quavering, quivering, quivery, scared, shaking, shivering, timid, trembling, trembly, tremulant, trepid, trepidant, vibrating, wavering.
antonyms calm, firm.

trenchant *adj.* acerbic, acid, acidulous, acute, astringent, biting, caustic, clear, clear-cut, cogent, crisp, cutting, distinct, driving, effective, effectual, emphatic, energetic, explicit, forceful, forthright, hurtful, incisive, keen, mordant, penetrating, piquant, pointed, potent, powerful, pungent, sarcastic, scratching, severe, sharp, strong, tart, unequivocal, vigorous.
antonym woolly.

trend *n.* bias, course, crazed, current, dernier cri, direction, fad, fashion, flow, inclination, leaning, look, mode, rage, style, tendency, thing, vogue.

trendy *adj.* fashionable, funky, groovy, in, latest, modish, stylish, up to the minute, voguish, with it.
antonym unfashionable.

trepidation *n.* agitation, alarm, anxiety, apprehension, butterflies, cold sweat, consternation, dismay, disquiet, disturbance, dread, emotion, excitement, fear, fright, jitters, misgivings, nervousness, palpitation, perturbation, qualms, quivering, shaking, trembling, tremor, unease, uneasiness, worry.
antonym calm.

trespass *v.* encroach, err, infringe, injure, intrude, invade, obtrude, offend, poach, sin, transgress, violate, wrong.
antonyms keep to, obey.
n. breach, contravention, crime, debt, delinquency, encroachment, error, evil-doing, fault, infraction, infringement, iniquity, injury, intrusion, invasion, misbehavior, misconduct, misdeed, misdemeanor, offense, poaching, sin, transgression, wrong-doing.

trespasser *n.* criminal, debtor, delinquent, evil- doer, infringer, interloper, intruder, invader, malefactor, offender, poacher, sinner, transgressor, wrong-doer.

tribe *n.* blood, branch, caste, clan, class, division, dynasty, family, gens, group, house, ilk, nation, people, phratry, race, seed, sept, stock.

tribulation *n.* adversity, affliction, blow, burden, care, curse, distress, grief, heartache, misery, misfortune, ordeal, pain, reverse, sorrow, suffering, travail, trial, trouble, unhappiness, vexation, woe, worry, wretchedness.
antonyms happiness, rest.

tribunal *n.* bar, bench, court, examination, hearing, inquisition, trial.

tribute *n.* accolade, acknowledgment, annates, applause,

charge, commendation, compliment, contribution, cornage, credit, customs, duty, encomium, esteem, eulogy, excise, first-fruits, gavel, gift, gratitude, homage, honor, horngeld, impost, laudation, offering, panegyric, payment, praise, ransom, recognition, respect, subsidy, tax, testimonial, testimony, toll.
antonyms blame.

trick *n.* antic, art, artifice, cantrip, caper, characteristic, chicane, command, con, craft, deceit, deception, device, dodge, dog-trick, expedient, expertise, feat, feint, foible, fraud, frolic, gag, gambol, gift, gimmick, habit, hang, hoax, idiosyncrasy, imposition, imposture, jape, joke, josh, knack, know-how, legerdemain, leg-pull, maneuver, mannerism, peculiarity, ploy, practical joke, practice, prank, put-on, quirk, quiz, rig, ruse, secret, shot, skill, sleight, spell, stall, stratagem, stunt, subterfuge, swindle, technique, toy, trait, trap, trinket, turn, wile.
adj. artificial, bogus, counterfeit, ersatz, fake, false, feigned, forged, imitation, mock, pretend, sham.
antonym genuine.
v. bamboozle, beguile, cheat, con, cozen, deceive, defraud, delude, diddle, dupe, fool, gull, hoax, hocus-pocus, hoodwink, hornswoggle, illude, lead on, mislead, outwit, pull a fast one on, pull someone's leg, sell, swindle, trap.

trickle *v.* dribble, drip, drop, exude, filter, gutter, leak, ooze, percolate, run, seep.
antonyms gush, stream.
n. drib, dribble, driblet, dribs and drabs, drip, seepage.
antonyms gush, stream.

tricky *adj.* artful, complicated, crafty, cunning, deceitful, deceptive, delicate, devious, difficult, foxy, Gordian, knotty, legerdemain, problematic, risky, scheming, slippery, sly, sticky, subtle, thorny, ticklish, touch-and-go, trickish, tricksome, tricksy, wily.
antonyms easy, honest.

trifling *adj.* empty, footling, foozling, fribbling, fribblish, frivolous, idle, inconsiderable, insignificant, minuscule, negligible, nugatory, paltry, petty, piddling, piffling, puny, shallow, silly, slight, small, tiny, trivial, unimportant, valueless, worthless.
antonym important.
n. desipience, fiddling, fooling, footling, frivolity, piddling, piffling, whifflery.

trigger *v.* activate, actuate, cause, elicit, generate, initiate, produce, prompt, provoke, set off, spark off, start.
n. catch, goad, lever, release, spur, stimulus, switch.

trim *adj.* clean-limbed, compact, dapper, natty, neat, orderly, shipshape, slender, slim, smart, smirk, soigné, spick-and-span, spruce, streamlined, svelte, trig, well-dressed, well-groomed, willowy.
antonym scruffy.
v. adjust, adorn, arrange, array, balance, barb, barber, beautify, bedeck, clip, crop, curtail, cut, decorate, distribute, dock, dress, dub, embellish, embroider, garnish, lop, order, ornament, pare, prepare, prune, settle, shave, shear, tidy, trick.
n. adornment, array, attire, border, clipping, condition, crop, cut, decoration, disposition, dress, edging, embellishment, equipment, fettle, fitness, fittings, form, frill, fringe, garnish, gear, health, humor, nick, order, ornament, ornamentation, piping, pruning, repair, shape, shave, shearing, situation, state, temper, trappings, trimming.

trimmings *n.* accessories, accompaniments, additions, appurtenances, clippings, cuttings, ends, extras, frills, garnish, ornaments, paraphernalia, parings, remnants, shavings, trappings.

trinket *n.* bagatelle, bauble, bibelot, bijou, doodad, fairing, gewgaw, gimcrack, kickshaws, knick-knack, nothing, ornament, toy, trifle, trinkum-trankum, whigmaleerie, whim-wham.

trio *n.* terzetto, threesome, triad, trilogy, trine, trinity, triple, triplet, triptych, triumvirate, triune.

trip *n.* blunder, boob, errand, error, excursion, expedition, fall, faux pas, foray, indiscretion, jaunt, journey, lapse, misstep, outing, ramble, run, skip, slip, step, stumble, tour, travel, voyage.
v. activate, blunder, boob, caper, confuse, dance, disconcert, engage, err, fall, flip, flit, frisk, gambol, go, hop, lapse, miscalculate, misstep, pull, ramble, release, set off, skip, slip, slip up, spring, stumble, switch on, throw, tilt up, tip up, tour, trap, travel, tumble, unsettle, voyage.

trite *adj.* banal, bromidic, clichéd, common, commonplace, corny, dull, hack, hackneyed, Mickey Mouse, ordinary, overworn, pedestrian, routine, run-of-the-mill, stale, stereotyped, stock, threadbare, tired, uninspired, unoriginal, well-trodden, well-worn, worn, worn out.
antonym original.

triumph *n.* accomplishment, achievement, ascendancy, attainment, conquest, coup, elation, exultation, feat, happiness, hit, joy, jubilation, masterstroke, mastery, pride, rejoicing, sensation, smash, smash-hit, success, tour de force, victory, walk-away, walk-over, win.
antonym disaster.
v. best, celebrate, crow, defeat, dominate, exult, gloat, glory, have the last laugh, humble, humiliate, jubilate, overcome, overwhelm, prevail, prosper, rejoice, revel, subdue, succeed, swagger, vanquish, win.
antonym fail.

triumphant *adj.* boastful, celebratory, cock-a-hoop, conquering, dominant, elated, epinikian, exultant, gloating, glorious, joyful, jubilant, proud, rejoicing, successful, swaggering, triumphal, undefeated, victorious, winning.
antonyms defeated, humble.

trivial *adj.* commonplace, dinky, everyday, frivolous, incidental, inconsequential, inconsiderable, insignificant, little, meaningless, Mickey Mouse, minor, negligible, nugatory, paltry, pettifogging, petty, piddling,

piffling, puny, slight, small, snippety, trifling, trite, unimportant, valueless, worthless.
antonym significant.

troops *n.* army, forces, men, military, servicemen, soldiers, soldiery.

trophy *n.* award, booty, cup, laurels, memento, memorial, prize, souvenir, spoils.

tropical *adj.* equatorial, hot, humid, lush, luxuriant, steamy, stifling, sultry, sweltering, torrid.
antonyms arctic, cold, cool, temperate.

trouble *n.* affliction, agitation, ailment, annoyance, anxiety, attention, bother, care, commotion, complaint, concern, danger, defect, difficulty, dilemma, disability, discontent, discord, disease, disorder, disquiet, dissatisfaction, distress, disturbance, effort, exertion, failure, grief, heartache, illness, inconvenience, irritation, labor, malfunction, mess, misfortune, nuisance, pain, pains, pest, pickle, predicament, problem, row, scrape, solicitude, sorrow, spot, strife, struggle, suffering, thought, torment, travail, trial, tribulation, tumult, uneasiness, unrest, upheaval, upset, vexation, woe, work, worry.
antonyms calm, peace.
v. afflict, agitate, annoy, bother, burden, discomfort, discommode, discompose, disconcert, disquiet, distress, disturb, fash, fret, grieve, harass, incommode, inconvenience, molest, muddy, pain, perplex, perturb, pester, plague, sadden, torment, upset, vex, worry.
antonyms help, reassure.

troublemaker *n.* agent provocateur, agitator, bellwether, bolshevik, firebrand, heller, incendiary, instigator, meddler, mischief-maker, rabble-rouser, ringleader, stirrer, tub- thumper.
antonym peace-maker.

troublesome *adj.* annoying, arduous, bothersome, burdensome, demanding, difficult, disorderly, fashious, harassing, hard, importunate, inconvenient, insubordinate, irksome, irritating, laborious, oppressive, pestilential, plaguesome, plaguey, rebellious, recalcitrant, refractory, rowdy, spiny, taxing, thorny, tiresome, tricky, trying, turbulent, uncooperative, undisciplined, unruly, upsetting, vexatious, violent, wearisome, worrisome, worrying.
antonyms easy, helpful, polite.

trounce *v.* beat, best, censure, clobber, crush, drub, hammer, lick, overwhelm, paste, punish, rebuke, rout, slaughter, thrash, whale, whitewash.

truant *n.* absentee, deserter, dodger, hookey, malingerer, runaway, shirker, skiver, wag.
adj. absent, malingering, missing, runaway, skiving.
v. desert, dodge, malinger, play truant, shirk.

truce *n.* armistice, break, cease-fire, cessation, intermission, interval, let-up, lull, moratorium, peace, respite, rest, stay, suspension, treaty, Truce of God.
antonym hostilities.

truculent *adj.* aggressive, antagonistic, bad- tempered, bellicose, belligerent, combative, contentious, cross, defiant, fierce, hostile, ill-tempered, obstreperous, pugnacious, quarrelsome, savage, scrappy, sullen, violent.
antonyms co-operative, good-natured.

trudge *v.* clump, footslog, hike, labor, lumber, march, mush, plod, slog, stump, traipse, tramp, trek, walk.
n. footslog, haul, hike, march, mush, slog, traipse, tramp, trek, walk.

true *adj.* absolute, accurate, actual, apod(e)ictic, authentic, bona fide, confirmed, conformable, constant, correct, corrected, dedicated, devoted, dutiful, exact, factual, faithful, fast, firm, genuine, honest, honorable, legitimate, loyal, natural, perfect, precise, proper, pure, real, right, rightful, sincere, sooth, spot-on, square, staunch, steady, true-blue, true-born, true-hearted, trustworthy, trusty, truthful, typical, unerring, unswerving, upright, valid, veracious, veridical, veritable.
antonyms faithless, false, inaccurate.
adv. accurately, correctly, exactly, faithfully, honestly, perfectly, precisely, properly, rightly, truly, truthfully, unerringly, veraciously, veritably.
antonyms falsely, inaccurately.

truly *adv.* accurately, authentically, constantly, correctly, devotedly, dutifully, en verité, exactly, exceptionally, extremely, factually, faithfully, firmly, genuinely, greatly, honestly, honorably, in good sooth, in reality, in truth, indeed, indubitably, legitimately, loyally, precisely, properly, really, rightly, sincerely, soothly, staunchly, steadfastly, steadily, truthfully, undeniably, veraciously, verily, veritably, very.
antonyms faithlessly, falsely, incorrectly, slightly.

truncate *v.* abbreviate, clip, crop, curtail, cut, cut short, lop, maim, pare, prune, shorten, trim.
antonym lengthen.

truss *v.* bind, bundle, fasten, hogtie, pack, pinion, secure, strap, tether, tie.
antonym untie.
n. bale, bandage, beam, binding, brace, bundle, buttress, joist, prop, shore, stanchion, stay, strut, support.

trust *n.* affiance, assurance, belief, care, certainty, certitude, charge, confidence, conviction, credence, credit, custody, duty, expectation, faith, fidelity, guard, guardianship, hope, obligation, protection, reliance, responsibility, safe-keeping, trusteeship, uberrima fides.
antonym mistrust.
v. assign, assume, bank on, believe, command, commit, confide, consign, count on, credit, delegate, depend on, entrust, expect, give, hope, imagine, presume, rely on, suppose, surmise, swear by.
antonym mistrust.

trusting *adj.* confiding, credulous, gullible, innocent, naïve, optimistic, simple, trustful, unguarded, unquestioning, unsuspecting, unsuspicious, unwary.
antonyms cautious, distrustful.

trustworthy *adj.* authentic, dependable, ethical, four-square, honest, honorable, level-headed, mature, principled, reliable, responsible, righteous, sensible, steadfast, true, trusty, truthful, upright.
antonym unreliable.

truth *n.* accuracy, actuality, axiom, candor, certainty, constancy, dedication, devotion, dutifulness, exactness, fact, facts, factuality, factualness, faith, faithfulness, fidelity, frankness, genuineness, historicity, honesty, integrity, law, legitimacy, loyalty, maxim, naturalism, precision, realism, reality, sooth, truism, truthfulness, uprightness, validity, veracity, verdicality, verity.
antonym falsehood.

truthful *adj.* accurate, candid, correct, exact, faithful, forthright, frank, honest, literal, naturalistic, plain-spoken, precise, realistic, reliable, sincere, sooth, soothfast, soothful, straight, straightforward, true, trustworthy, veracious, veridicous, verist, veristic, veritable.
antonym untruthful.

try *v.* adjudge, adjudicate, afflict, aim, annoy, appraise, attempt, catechize, endeavor, essay, evaluate, examine, experiment, hear, inconvenience, inspect, investigate, irk, irritate, pain, plague, prove, sample, seek, strain, stress, strive, struggle, taste, tax, test, tire, trouble, undertake, upset, venture, vex, wear out, weary.
n. appraisal, attempt, bash, crack, effort, endeavor, essay, evaluation, experiment, fling, go, inspection, sample, shot, stab, taste, taster, test, trial, whack.

trying *adj.* aggravating, annoying, arduous, bothersome, difficult, distressing, exasperating, fatiguing, hard, irksome, irritating, searching, severe, stressful, taxing, testing, tiresome, tough, troublesome, upsetting, vexing, wearisome.
antonym calming.

tub *n.* back, barrel, basin, bath, bathtub, bucket, butt, cask, hogshead, keeve, keg, kid, kit, pail, puncheon, stand, tun, vat.

tube *n.* channel, conduit, cylinder, duct, hose, inlet, main, outlet, pipe, shaft, spout, trunk, valve, vas.

tubular *adj.* pipelike, pipy, tubate, tubelike, tubiform, tubulate, tubulous, vasiform.

tuck[1] *v.* cram, crease, fold, gather, insert, push, stuff.
n. crease, fold, gather, pinch, pleat, pucker.

tuck[2] *n.* comestibles, eats, food, grub, nosh, prog, scoff, victuals, vittles.

tuft *n.* beard, bunch, clump, cluster, collection, crest, dag, daglock, dollop, floccule, flocculus, floccus, flock, knot, shock, tassle, topknot, truss, tussock.

tug *v.* drag, draw, haul, heave, jerk, jigger, lug, pluck, pull, tow, wrench, yank.
n. drag, haul, heave, jerk, pluck, pull, tow, traction, wrench, yank.

tuition *n.* education, instruction, lessons, pedagogics, pedagogy, schooling, teaching, training, tutelage, tutoring.

tumble *v.* disorder, drop, fall, flop, jumble, overthrow, pitch, plummet, roll, rumple, stumble, topple, toss, trip up.
n. collapse, drop, fall, flop, plunge, roll, spill, stumble, toss, trip.

tumbledown *adj.* broken-down, crumbling, crumbly, decrepit, dilapidated, disintegrating, ramshackle, rickety, ruined, ruinous, shaky, tottering.
antonym well-kept.

tumult *n.* ado, affray, agitation, altercation, bedlam, brattle, brawl, brouhaha, bustle, clamor, coil, commotion, deray, din, disorder, disturbance, Donnybrook, émeute, excitement, fracas, hubbub, hullabaloo, outbreak, pandemonium, quarrel, racket, riot, rookery, rout, row, ruction, ruffle, stir, stramash, strife, turmoil, unrest, upheaval, uproar.
antonym calm.

tune *n.* agreement, air, attitude, concert, concord, consonance, demeanor, disposition, euphony, frame of mind, harmony, melisma, melody, mood, motif, pitch, song, strain, sympathy, temper, theme, unison.
v. adapt, adjust, attune, harmonize, pitch, regulate, set, synchronize, temper.

tunnel *n.* burrow, channel, chimney, drift, flue, gallery, hole, passage, passageway, sap, shaft, subway, underpass.
v. burrow, dig, excavate, mine, penetrate, sap, undermine.

turbid *adj.* clouded, cloudy, confused, dense, dim, disordered, feculent, foggy, foul, fuzzy, hazy, impure, incoherent, muddled, muddy, murky, opaque, roily, thick, unclear, unsettled.
antonym clear.

turbulent *adj.* agitated, anarchic, blustery, boiling, boisterous, choppy, confused, disordered, disorderly, foaming, furious, insubordinate, lawless, mutinous, obstreperous, raging, rebellious, refractory, riotous, rough, rowdy, seditious, stormy, tempestuous, tumultuous, unbridled, undisciplined, ungovernable, unruly, unsettled, unstable, uproarious, violent, wild.
antonym calm.

turf *n.* clod, divot, glebe, grass, green, sod, sward.

turmoil *n.* agitation, bedlam, brouhaha, bustle, chaos, combustion, commotion, confusion, disorder, disquiet, disturbance, Donnybrook, dust, émeute, ferment, flurry, hubbub, hubbuboo, noise, pandemonium, pother, pudder, rookery, rout, row, ruffle, stir, stour, stramash, strife, tracasserie, trouble, tumult, turbulence, uproar, violence, welter.
antonym calm.

turn *v.* adapt, alter, apostatize, appeal, apply, approach, become, caracol, change, circle, construct, convert, corner, curdle, defect, deliver, depend, desert, divert, double, execute, fashion, fit, form, frame, go, gyrate, hang, hinge, infatuate, influence, issue, look, make, metamorphose, mold, move, mutate, nauseate, negotiate,

pass, perform, persuade, pivot, prejudice, remodel, renege, resort, retract, return, reverse, revolve, roll, rotate, shape, shift, sicken, sour, spin, spoil, swerve, switch, swivel, taint, transfigure, transform, translate, transmute, twirl, twist, upset, veer, wheel, whirl, write.
n. act, action, airing, aptitude, bend, bent, bias, bout, caracol, cast, chance, change, circle, circuit, constitutional, crack, crankle, crisis, culmination, curve, cycle, deed, departure, deviation, direction, distortion, drift, drive, excursion, exigency, fashion, favor, fling, form, format, fright, gesture, go, guise, gyration, heading, innings, jaunt, make-up, manner, mode, mold, occasion, opportunity, outing, performance, performer, period, pivot, promenade, reversal, revolution, ride, rotation, round, saunter, scare, service, shape, shift, shock, shot, spell, spin, start, stint, stroll, style, succession, surprise, swing, tendency, time, trend, trick, try, turning, twist, uey, U-turn, vicissitude, walk, warp, way, whack, whirl.

turncoat *n.* apostate, backslider, blackleg, defector, deserter, fink, rat, recreant, renegade, renegate, scab, seceder, tergiversator, traitor.

turning *n.* bend, crossroads, curve, flexure, fork, junction, turn, turn-off.

turning-point *n.* change, climacteric, crisis, crossroads, crux, cusp, moment of truth, watershed.

turnover *n.* business, change, flow, income, movement, output, outturn, production, productivity, profits, replacement, volume, yield.

tussle *v.* battle, brawl, compete, contend, fight, grapple, scramble, scrap, scuffle, struggle, vie, wrestle.
n. battle, bout, brawl, competition, conflict, contention, contest, dust-up, fight, fracas, fray, mêlée, punch-up, race, scramble, scrap, scrimmage, scrum, scuffle, set-to, struggle.

tutor *n.* coach, director of studies, educator, governor, guardian, guide, guru, instructor, lecturer, master, mentor, preceptor, répétiteur, supervisor, teacher.
v. coach, control, direct, discipline, drill, edify, educate, guide, instruct, lecture, school, supervise, teach, train.

tweak *v., n.* jerk, nip, pull, punch, snatch, squeeze, tug, twist, twitch.

twig[1] *n.* branch, offshoot, ramulus, shoot, spray, spring, stick, wattle, whip, withe, withy.

twig[2] *v.* catch on, comprehend, cotton on, fathom, get, grasp, rumble, savvy, see, tumble to, understand.

twilight *n.* crepuscle, crepuscule, decline, demi- jour, dimness, dusk, ebb, evening, eventide, gloaming, half-light, sundown, sunset.
adj. crepuscular, darkening, declining, dim, dying, ebbing, evening, final, last, shadowy.

twin *n.* clone, corollary, counterpart, doppelgänger, double, duplicate, fellow, gemel, likeness, lookalike, match, mate, ringer.
adj. balancing, corresponding, didymous, double, dual, duplicate, geminate, geminous, identical, matched, matching, paired, parallel, symmetrical, twofold.
v. combine, couple, join, link, match, pair, yoke.

twine *n.* cord, string, twist, yarn.
v. bend, braid, coil, curl, encircle, entwine, interlace, interweave, knit, loop, meander, plait, snake, spiral, splice, surround, tie, twist, weave, wind, wrap, wreathe, wriggle, zigzag.

twinge *n.* bite, gripe, pain, pang, pinch, prick, qualm, spasm, stab, stitch, throb, throe, tweak, twist, twitch.

twinkle *v.* blink, coruscate, flash, flicker, gleam, glint, glisten, glitter, scintillate, shimmer, shine, sparkle, vibrate, wink.
n. amusement, blink, coruscation, flash, flicker, gleam, glimmer, glistening, glitter, glittering, light, quiver, scintillation, shimmer, shine, spark, sparkle, wink.

twirl *v.* birl, coil, gyrate, gyre, pirouette, pivot, revolve, rotate, spin, swivel, turn, twiddle, twist, wheel, whirl, wind.
n. coil, convulution, gyration, gyre, helix, pirouette, revolution, rotation, spin, spiral, turn, twiddle, twist, wheel, whirl, whorl.

twist *v.* alter, change, coil, contort, corkscrew, crankle, crinkle, crisp, curl, distort, encircle, entangle, entwine, garble, intertwine, misquote, misrepresent, pervert, pivot, revolve, rick, screw, spin, sprain, squirm, strain, swivel, turn, tweak, twine, warp, weave, wigwag, wind, wrap, wreathe, wrench, wrest, wrick, wriggle, wring, writhe. *n.* aberration, arc, bend, bent, braid, break, change, characteristic, coil, confusion, contortion, convolution, crankle, curl, curlicue, curve, defect, deformation, development, distortion, eccentricity, entanglement, fault, flaw, foible, hank, idiosyncrasy, imperfection, intortion, jerk, kink, knot, meander, mess, mix-up, nuance, oddity, peculiarity, plug, proclivity, pull, quid, quirk, revelation, roll, screw, slant, snarl, spin, sprain, squiggle, surprise, swivel, tangle, tortion, trait, turn, twine, undulation, variation, warp, wind, wrench, wrest, zigzag.

twitch *v.* blink, flutter, jerk, jump, pinch, pluck, pull, snatch, tug, tweak, vellicate, yank.
n. blink, convulsion, flutter, jerk, jump, pluck, pull, spasmytic, subsultus, tremor, tweak, twinge, vellication.

two-faced *adj.* deceitful, deceiving, devious, dissembling, double-dealing, double-tongued, duplicitous, false, hypocritical, insincere, Janus-faced, lying, mendacious, perfidious, treacherous, untrustworthy.
antonyms candid, frank, honest.

tycoon *n.* baron, big cheese, big noise, big shot, capitalist, captain of industry, Croesus, Dives, entrepreneur, fat cat, financier, gold-bug, industrialist, magnate, mogul, nabob, plutocrat, potentate, supremo.

type[1] *n.* archetype, breed, category, class, classification, description, designation, emblem, embodiment, epitome, essence, example, exemplar, form, genre, group, ilk, insignia, kidney, kind, mark, model, order, original, paradigm, pattern, personification, prototype, quintessence, sort, species, specimen, stamp, standard, strain, subdivision, variety.

type[2] *n.* case, characters, face, font, fount, lettering, print, printing.

typhoon *n.* baguio, cordonazo, cyclone, hurricane, squall, storm, tempest, tornado, twister, whirlwind, willy-willy.

typical *adj.* archetypal, average, characteristic, classic, conventional, distinctive, essential, illustrative, indicative, model, normal, orthodox, quintessential, representative, standard, stock, symptomatic, usual, vintage.
antonyms atypical, untypical.

typify *v.* characterize, embody, encapsulate, epitomize, exemplify, illustrate, incarnate, personify, represent, symbolize.

tyrannical *adj.* absolute, arbitrary, authoritarian, autocratic, coercive, despotic, dictatorial, domineering, high-handed, imperious, inexorable, iron-handed, magisterial, Neronian, oppressive, overbearing, overpowering, overweening, peremptory, ruthless, severe, tyrannous, unjust, unreasonable.
antonyms liberal, tolerant.

tyrannize *v.* browbeat, bully, coerce, crush, dictate, domineer, enslave, intimidate, lord it, oppress, subjugate, terrorize.

U

ubiquitous *adj.* all-over, common, commonly- encountered, ever-present, everywhere, frequent, global, omnipresent, pervasive, universal.
antonym rare.

ugly *adj.* angry, bad-tempered, dangerous, dark, disagreeable, disgusting, distasteful, evil, evil-favored, forbidding, frightful, hagged, haggish, hard-favored, hard-featured, hideous, homely, horrid, ill-faced, ill-favored, ill- looking, malevolent, menacing, misshapen, monstrous, nasty, objectionable, offensive, ominous, plain, repugnant, repulsive, revolting, shocking, sinister, spiteful, sullen, surly, terrible, threatening, truculent, unattractive, unlovely, unpleasant, unprepossessing, unsightly, vile.
antonyms beautiful, charming, good, pretty.

ultimate *adj.* basic, conclusive, consummate, decisive, elemental, end, eventual, extreme, final, fundamental, furthest, greatest, highest, last, maximum, paramount, perfect, primary, radical, remotest, superlative, supreme, terminal, topmost, utmost.
n. consummation, culmination, daddy of them all, dinger, epitome, extreme, granddaddy, greatest, height, peak, perfection, summit.

umbrage *n.* anger, chagrin, disgruntlement, displeasure, grudge, high dudgeon, huff, indignation, offence, pique, resentment, sulks.

umpire *n.* adjudicator, arbiter, arbitrator, daysman, judge, linesman, mediator, moderator, ref, referee.
v. adjudicate, arbitrate, call, control, judge, moderate, ref, referee.

umpteen *adj.* a good many, a thousand, considerable, countless, innumerable, millions, numerous, plenty, uncounted.
antonym few.

unabashed *adj.* blatant, bold, brazen, composed, confident, unawed, unblushing, unconcerned, undaunted, undismayed, unembarrassed.
antonyms abashed, sheepish.

unaccountable *adj.* astonishing, baffling, extraordinary, impenetrable, incomprehensible, inexplicable, inscrutable, mysterious, odd, peculiar, puzzling, singular, strange, uncommon, unexplainable, unfathomable, unheard-of, unintelligible, unusual, unwonted.
antonyms accountable, explicable.

unaffected[1] *adj.* aloof, impervious, naïf, natural, proof, spontaneous, unaltered, unchanged, unimpressed, unmoved, unresponsive, untouched.
antonyms affected, unnatural.

unaffected[2] *adj.* artless, blasé, genuine, honest, indifferent, ingenuous, naive, plain, simple, sincere, straightforward, unassuming, unconcerned, unpretentious, unsophisticated, unspoilt, unstudied.
antonyms affected, impressed, moved.

unalterable *adj.* final, fixed, immutable, inflexible, invariable, permanent, rigid, steadfast, unchangeable, unchanging, unyielding.
antonyms alterable, flexible.

unanimous *adj.* agreed, common, concerted, concordant, harmonious, in accord, in agreement, joint, united.
antonyms disunited, split.

unapproachable *adj.* aloof, distant, forbidding, formidable, frigid, godforsaken, inaccessible, remote, reserved, standoffish, unbending, unfriendly, un-get-at-able, unreachable, unsociable, withdrawn.
antonym approachable.

unassailable *adj.* absolute, conclusive, impregnable, incontestable, incontrovertible, indisputable, invincible, inviolable, invulnerable, irrefutable, positive, proven, sacrosanct, secure, sound, undeniable, well-armed, well- fortified.
antonym assailable.

unassuming *adj.* diffident, humble, meek, modest, natural, quiet, restrained, retiring, self-effacing, simple, unassertive, unobtrusive, unostentatious, unpresuming, unpretentious.
antonyms assuming, presumptuous, pretentious.

unattached *adj.* autonomous, available, fancy-free, footloose, free, independent, non-aligned, single, unaffilated, uncommitted, unengaged, unmarried, unspoken for. *antonyms* attached, committed, engaged.

unavailing *adj.* abortive, barren, bootless, fruitless, futile, idle, ineffective, ineffectual, inefficacious, pointless, unproductive, unprofitable, unsuccessful, useless, vain.
antonyms productive, successful.

unavoidable *adj.* certain, compulsory, fated, ineluctable, inescapable, inevitable, inexorable, mandatory, necessary, obligatory.
antonym avoidable.

unawares *adv.* aback, abruptly, accidentally, by surprise, imperceptibly, inadvertently, insidiously, mistakenly, off guard, on the hop, suddenly, unconsciously, unexpectedly, unintentionally, unknowingly, unprepared, unthinkingly, unwittingly.

unbalanced *adj.* asymmetrical, biased, crazy, demented, deranged, disturbed, dysharmonic, eccentric, erratic, inequitable, insane, irrational, irregular, lopsided, lunatic, mad, off-balance, off-center, one-sided, partial, partisan, prejudiced, shaky, touched, unequal, uneven, unfair, unhinged, unjust, unsound, unstable, unsteady, wobbly.
antonym balanced.

unbearable *adj.* insufferable, insupportable, intolerable, outrageous, unacceptable, unendurable, unspeakable.
antonyms acceptable, bearable.

unbecoming *adj.* discreditable, dishonorable, ill- suited, improper, inappropriate, incongruous, indecorous, indelicate, offensive, tasteless, unattractive, unbefitting, unfit, unflattering, unmaidenly, unmeet, unseemly, unsightly, unsuitable, unsuited.
antonyms becoming, seemly.

unbelievable *adj.* astonishing, far-fetched, implausible, impossible, improbable, inconceivable, incredible, outlandish, preposterous, questionable, staggering, unconvincing, unimaginable, unlikely, unthinkable.
antonyms believable, credible.

unbending *adj.* aloof, distant, firm, forbidding, formal, formidable, hard-line, inflexible, intransigent, reserved, resolute, Rhadamanthine, rigid, severe, stiff, strict, stubborn, tough, uncompromising, unyielding.
antonyms approachable, friendly, relaxed.

unbiased *adj.* disinterested, dispassionate, equitable, evenhanded, fair, fair-minded, impartial, independent, just, neutral, objective, open-minded, uncolored, uninfluenced, unprejudiced.
antonym biased.

unbidden *adj.* free, spontaneous, unasked, unforced, uninvited, unprompted, unsolicited, unwanted, unwelcome, voluntary, willing.
antonyms invited, solicited.

unblemished *adj.* clear, flawless, immaculate, irreproachable, perfect, pure, spotless, unflawed, unimpeachable, unspotted, unstained, unsullied, untarnished.
antonyms blemished, flawed, imperfect.

unbosom *v.* admit, bare, confess, confide, disburden, disclose, divulge, lay bare, let out, pour out, reveal, tell, unburden, uncover.
antonyms conceal, suppress.

unbridled *adj.* excessive, immoderate, intemperate, licentious, profligate, rampant, riotous, unchecked, unconstrained, uncontrolled, uncurbed, ungovernable, ungoverned, unrestrained, unruly, violent, wanton.

unbroken *adj.* ceaseless, complete, constant, continuous, endless, entire, incessant, intact, integral, perpetual, progressive, serried, solid, successive, total, unbowed, unceasing, undivided, unimpaired, uninterrupted, unremitting, unsubdued, untamed, whole.
antonyms cowed, fitful, intermittent.

unburden *v.* confess, confide, disburden, discharge, disclose, discumber, disencumber, empty, lay bare, lighten, offload, pour out, relieve, reveal, tell all, unbosom, unload.
antonyms conceal, hide, suppress.

uncalled-for *adj.* gratuitous, inappropriate, needless, undeserved, unheeded, unjust, unjustified, unmerited, unnecessary, unprovoked, unwanted, unwarranted, unwelcome.
antonym timely.

uncanny *adj.* astonishing, astounding, bizarre, creepy, eerie, eldritch, exceptional, extraordinary, fantastic, incredible, inspired, miraculous, mysterious, preternatural, prodigious, queer, remarkable, scary, singular, spooky, strange, supernatural, unaccountable, unco, unearthly, unerring, unheard- of, unnatural, unusual, weird.

uncertain *adj.* ambiguous, ambivalent, chancy, changeable, conjectural, dicky, doubtful, dubious, erratic, fitful, hazardous, hazy, hesitant, iffy, in the lap of the gods, incalculable, inconstant, indefinite, indeterminate, indistinct, insecure, irregular, irresolute, on the knees of the gods, precarious, problematic, questionable, risky, shaky, slippy, speculative, unclear, unconfirmed, undecided, undetermined, unfixed, unforeseeable, unpredictable, unreliable, unresolved, unsettled, unsure, vacillating, vague, variable, wavering.
antonym certain.

uncertainty *n.* ambiguity, bewilderment, confusion, diffidence, dilemma, doubt, dubiety, hesitancy, hesitation, incalculability, inconclusiveness, indecision, insecurity, irresolution, misgiving, peradventure, perplexity, puzzlement, qualm, quandary, risk, skepticism, unpredictability, vagueness.
antonym certainty.

uncharitable *adj.* callous, captious, cruel, hard- hearted, hypercritical, inhumane, insensitive, mean, merciless, pitiless, stingy, unchristian, unfeeling, unforgiving, unfriendly, ungenerous, unkind, unsympathetic.
antonym charitable.

uncharted *adj.* foreign, mysterious, new, novel, strange, undiscovered, unexplored, unfamiliar, unknown, unplumbed, virgin.
antonyms familiar, well-known.

uncivil *adj.* abrupt, bad-mannered, bearish, boorish, brusque, churlish, curt, discourteous, disrespectful, gruff, ill-bred, ill-mannered, impolite, rude, surly, uncouth, ungracious, unmannerly.
antonym civil.

uncivilized *adj.* antisocial, barbarian, barbaric, barbarous, boorish, brutish, churlish, coarse, gross, heathenish, ill-bred, illiterate, philistine, primitive, savage, tramontane, uncouth, uncultivated, uncultured, uneducated, unpolished, unsophisticated, untamed, vulgar, wild.
antonym civilized.

unclean *adj.* contaminated, corrupt, defiled, dirty, evil, filthy, foul, impure, insalubrious, nasty, polluted, soiled, spotted, stained, sullied, tainted, unhygienic, unwholesome.
antonym clean.

uncomfortable *adj.* awkward, bleak, confused, conscience-stricken, cramped, disagreeable, discomfited, discomfortable, discomposed, disquieted, distressed, disturbed, embarrassed, hard, ill-fitting, incommodious, irritating, painful, poky, self-conscious, sheepish, troubled, troublesome, uneasy.
antonyms comfortable, easy.

uncommon *adj.* abnormal, atypical, bizarre, curious, distinctive, exceptional, extraordinary, incomparable, infrequent, inimitable, notable, noteworthy, novel, odd, outstanding, peculiar, queer, rare, recherché, remarkable, scarce, singular, special, strange, superior, unfamiliar, unparalleled, unprecedented, unusual, unwonted. *antonym* common.

uncompromising *adj.* decided, die-hard, firm, hard- core, hard-line, hardshell, inexorable, inflexible, intransigent, obdurate, obstinate, rigid, steadfast, strict, stubborn, tough, unaccommodating, unbending, unyielding. *antonyms* flexible, open-minded.

unconcerned *adj.* aloof, apathetic, blithe, callous, carefree, careless, complacent, composed, cool, detached, dispassionate, distant, easy, incurious, indifferent, insouciant, joco, nonchalant, oblivious, pococurante, relaxed, serene, uncaring, uninterested, uninvolved, unmoved, unperturbed, unruffled, unsympathetic, untroubled, unworried. *antonym* concerned.

unconditional *adj.* absolute, categorical, complete, downright, entire, full, implicit, out-and-out, outright, plenary, positive, thoroughgoing, total, unequivocal, unlimited, unqualified, unreserved, unrestricted, utter, whole-hearted. *antonym* conditional.

uncongenial *adj.* antagonistic, antipathetic, disagreeable, discordant, displeasing, distasteful, incompatible, unappealing, unattractive, uninviting, unpleasant, unsavory, unsuited, unsympathetic. *antonym* congenial.

unconscious *adj.* accidental, automatic, blind to, comatose, concussed, deaf to, heedless, ignorant, inadvertent, innate, insensible, instinctive, involuntary, knocked out, latent, oblivious, out, out cold, out for the count, reflex, repressed, senseless, stunned, subconscious, subliminal, suppressed, unaware, unintended, unintentional, unknowing, unmindful, unsuspecting, unwitting. *antonym* conscious.

unconventional *adj.* abnormal, alternative, atypical, bizarre, bohemian, different, eccentric, freakish, idiosyncratic, individual, individualistic, informal, irregular, nonconforming, odd, offbeat, original, spacy, unconformable, unorthodox, unusual, way-out, wayward. *antonym* conventional.

uncouth *adj.* awkward, barbarian, barbaric, boorish, clownish, clumsy, coarse, crude, gauche, gawky, graceless, gross, ill-mannered, loutish, lubberly, oafish, rough, rude, rustic, uncivilized, uncultivated, ungainly, unrefined, unseemly, vulgar. *antonyms* polished, polite, refined, urbane.

uncover *v.* bare, detect, disclose, discover, dismask, disrobe, divulge, exhume, expose, leak, lift the lid off, open, reveal, show, strip, unearth, unmask, unveil, unwrap. *antonyms* conceal, cover, suppress.

unctuous *adj.* fawning, glib, greasy, gushing, ingratiating, insincere, obsequious, oily, pietistic, plausible, religiose, sanctimonious, slick, smarmy, smooth, suave, sycophantic.

undaunted *adj.* bold, brave, courageous, dauntless, fearless, gallant, indomitable, intrepid, resolute, steadfast, unbowed, undashed, undeterred, undiscouraged, undismayed, unfaltering, unflinching, unperturbed, unshrinking. *antonyms* cowed, timorous.

undefined *adj.* formless, hazy, ill-defined, imprecise, indefinite, indeterminate, indistinct, inexact, nebulous, shadowy, tenuous, unclear, unexplained, unspecified, vague, woolly. *antonyms* definite, precise.

undependable *adj.* capricious, changeable, erratic, fair-weather, fickle, inconsistent, inconstant, irresponsible, mercurial, treacherous, uncertain, unpredictable, unreliable, unstable, untrustworthy, variable. *antonyms* dependable, reliable.

under *prep.* belonging to, below, beneath, governed by, included in, inferior to, junior to, lead by, less than, lower than, secondary to, subject to, subordinate to, subservient to, underneath. *adv.* below, beneath, down, downward, less, lower.

undercover *adj.* clandestine, concealed, confidential, covert, furtive, hidden, hush-hush, intelligence, private, secret, spy, stealthy, surreptitious, underground. *antonyms* open, unconcealed.

undercurrent *n.* atmosphere, aura, cross-current, drift, eddy, feeling, flavor, hint, movement, murmur, overtone, rip, riptide, sense, suggestion, tendency, tenor, tide, tinge, trend, underflow, undertone, undertow, vibes, vibrations.

undergo *v.* bear, brook, endure, experience, run the gauntlet, stand, submit to, suffer, sustain, weather, withstand.

underhand *adj.* clandestine, crafty, crooked, deceitful, deceptive, devious, dishonest, dishonorable, fraudulent, furtive, immoral, improper, shady, shifty, sly, sneaky, stealthy, surreptitious, treacherous, underhanded, unethical, unscrupulous. *antonym* above board.

undermine *v.* debilitate, disable, erode, excavate, impair, mar, mine, sabotage, sap, subvert, threaten, tunnel, undercut, vitiate, weaken, wear away. *antonyms* fortify, strengthen.

underprivileged *adj.* deprived, destitute, disadvantaged, impecunious, impoverished, needy, poor, poverty-stricken. *antonyms* affluent, fortunate, privileged.

understand *v.* accept, appreciate, apprehend, assume, believe, commiserate, comprehend, conceive, conclude, cotton on, discern, fathom, follow, gather, get, get the message, get the picture, grasp, hear, know, learn, penetrate, perceive, presume, realize, recognize, savvy, see, see daylight, suppose, sympathize, think, tolerate, tumble, twig. *antonym* misunderstand.

understanding *n.* accord, agreement, appreciation, awareness, belief, comprehension, conclusion, discernment, estimation, grasp, idea, impression, insight, intellect, intellection, intelligence, interpretation, judgment, knowledge, notion, opinion, pact, penetration, perception, reading, sense, view, viewpoint, wisdom.
adj. accepting, compassionate, considerate, discerning, forbearing, forgiving, kind, kindly, loving, patient, perceptive, responsive, sensitive, sympathetic, tender, tolerant.
antonyms impatient, insensitive, intolerant, unsympathetic.

understudy *n.* alternate, deputy, double, fill-in, replacement, reserve, stand-in, substitute.

undertake *v.* accept, agree, assume, attempt, bargain, begin, commence, contract, covenant, embark on, endeavor, engage, guarantee, pledge, promise, shoulder, stipulate, tackle, try.

undertaking *n.* adventure, affair, assurance, attempt, business, commitment, effort, emprise, endeavor, enterprise, game, operation, pledge, project, promise, task, venture, vow, word.

undervalue *v.* depreciate, discount, dismiss, disparage, disprize, minimize, misjudge, misprice, misprize, underestimate, underrate.
antonyms exaggerate, overrate.

underwrite *v.* approve, authorize, back, consent, countenance, countersign, endorse, finance, fund, guarantee, initial, insure, okay, sanction, sign, sponsor, subscribe, subsidize, validate.

undesirable *adj.* disagreeable, disliked, disreputable, distasteful, dreaded, objectionable, obnoxious, offensive, repugnant, unacceptable, unattractive, unpleasant, unpopular, unsavory, unsuitable, unwanted, unwelcome, unwished- for.
antonym desirable.

undignified *adj.* foolish, improper, inappropriate, indecorous, inelegant, infra dig, petty, unbecoming, ungentlemanly, unladylike, unrefined, unseemly, unsuitable.
antonym dignified.

undisciplined *adj.* disobedient, disorganized, obstreperous, uncontrolled, unpredictable, unreliable, unrestrained, unruly, unschooled, unsteady, unsystematic, untrained, wayward, wild, wilful.
antonym disciplined.

undivided *adj.* combined, complete, concentrated, concerted, entire, exclusive, full, individuate, solid, thorough, tight-knit, unanimous, unbroken, united, whole, whole-hearted.

undoing *n.* besetting sin, blight, collapse, curse, defeat, destruction, disgrace, downfall, hamartia, humiliation, misfortune, overthrow, overturn, reversal, ruin, ruination, shame, tragic fault, trouble, weakness.

undoubtedly *adv.* assuredly, certainly, definitely, doubtless, indubitably, of course, surely, undeniably, unmistakably, unquestionably.

undreamed-of *adj.* astonishing, inconceivable, incredible, miraculous, undreamt, unexpected, unforeseen, unheardof, unhoped-for, unimagined, unsuspected.

undulating *adj.* billowing, flexuose, flexuous, rippling, rolling, sinuous, undate, undulant, wavy.
antonym flat.

unduly *adv.* disproportionately, excessively, extravagantly, immoderately, inordinately, over, overly, overmuch, too, unjustifiably, unnecessarily, unreasonably.
antonym reasonably.

undying *adj.* abiding, constant, continuing, deathless, eternal, everlasting, immortal, imperishable, indestructible, inextinguishable, infinite, lasting, perennial, permanent, perpetual, sempiternal, undiminished, unending, unfading.
antonyms impermanent, inconstant.

unearthly *adj.* abnormal, eerie, eldritch, ethereal, extraordinary, ghostly, haunted, heavenly, nightmarish, otherworldly, phantom, preternatural, spectral, spine-chilling, strange, sublime, supernatural, uncanny, ungodly, unreasonable, weird.

uneasy *adj.* agitated, anxious, apprehensive, awkward, constrained, discomposed, disquieting, disturbed, disturbing, edgy, impatient, insecure, jittery, nervous, niggling, on edge, perturbed, precarious, restive, restless, shaky, strained, tense, troubled, troubling, uncomfortable, unquiet, unsettled, unstable, upset, upsetting, worried, worrying.
antonyms calm, composed.

uneconomic *adj.* loss-making, non-profit-making, uncommercial, unprofitable.
antonyms economic, profitable.

unemotional *adj.* apathetic, cold, cool, dispassionate, impassive, indifferent, laid-back, low-key, objective, passionless, phlegmatic, reserved, undemonstrative, unexcitable, unfeeling, unimpassioned, unresponsive.
antonyms emotional, excitable.

unemployed *adj.* idle, jobless, out of employ, out of work, redundant, resting, unoccupied, workless.
antonym employed.

unenviable *adj.* disagreeable, painful, thankless, uncomfortable, uncongenial, undesirable, unpalatable, unpleasant, unsavory.
antonyms desirable, enviable.

unequal *adj.* asymmetrical, different, differing, disparate, disproportionate, dissimilar, ill-equipped, ill-matched, inadequate, incapable, incompetent, insufficient, irregular, unbalanced, uneven, unlike, unmatched, variable, varying.
antonym equal.

unequivocal *adj.* absolute, certain, clear, clear- cut, crystal-clear, decisive, definite, direct, distinct, evident, explicit, express, incontrovertible, indubitable, manifest, plain, positive, straight, unambiguous, uncontestable, unmistakable.
antonyms ambiguous, vague.

unerring *adj.* accurate, certain, dead, exact, faultless, impeccable, infallible, perfect, sure, uncanny, unfailing.
antonym fallible.

unethical *adj.* dirty, discreditable, dishonest, dishonorable, disreputable, illegal, illicit, immoral, improper, shady, underhand, unfair, unprincipled, unprofessional, unscrupulous, wrong.
antonym ethical.

uneven *adj.* accidented, asymmetrical, broken, bumpy, changeable, desultory, disparate, erratic, fitful, fluctuating, ill-matched, inconsistent, intermittent, irregular, jerky, lopsided, odd, one-sided, patchy, rough, spasmodic, unbalanced, unequal, unfair, unsteady, variable.
antonym even.

unexceptional *adj.* average, commonplace, conventional, indifferent, insignificant, mediocre, normal, ordinary, pedestrian, run-of-the-mill, typical, undistinguished, unimpressive, unmemorable, unremarkable, usual.
antonyms exceptional, impressive.

unexpected *adj.* abrupt, accidental, amazing, astonishing, chance, fortuitous, startling, sudden, surprising, unaccustomed, unanticipated, unforeseen, unlooked-for, unpredictable, unusual, unwonted.
antonyms expected, normal, predictable.

unfair *adj.* arbitrary, biased, bigoted, crooked, discriminatory, dishonest, dishonorable, inequitable, one-sided, partial, partisan, prejudiced, uncalled-for, undeserved, unethical, unjust, unmerited, unprincipled, unscrupulous, unsporting, unwarranted, wrongful.
antonym fair.

unfaithful *adj.* adulterous, deceitful, dishonest, disloyal, faithless, false, false-hearted, fickle, godless, inconstant, perfidious, recreant, traitorous, treacherous, treasonable, two-timing, unbelieving, unchaste, unreliable, untrue, untrustworthy.
antonyms faithful, loyal.

unfamiliar *adj.* alien, curious, different, foreign, new, novel, out-of-the-way, strange, unaccustomed, unacquainted, uncharted, uncommon, unconversant, unexplored, unknown, unpracticed, unskilled, unusual, unversed.
antonyms customary, familiar.

unfasten *v.* detach, disconnect, loosen, open, separate, uncouple, undo, unlace, unlock, unloose, unloosen, untie.
antonym fasten.

unfavorable *adj.* adverse, bad, contrary, critical, disadvantageous, discouraging, hostile, ill-suited, inauspicious, infelicitous, inimical, inopportune, low, negative, ominous, poor, threatening, uncomplimentary, unfortunate, unfriendly, unlucky, unpromising, unpropitious, unseasonable, unsuited, untimely, untoward.
antonym favorable.

unfeeling *adj.* apathetic, callous, cold, cruel, hard, hardened, hard-hearted, harsh, heartless, inhuman, insensitive, pitiless, soulless, stony, uncaring, unsympathetic.
antonym concerned.

unfeigned *adj.* frank, genuine, heartfelt, natural, pure, real, sincere, spontaneous, unaffected, unforced, whole- hearted.
antonyms feigned, insincere, pretended.

unfit *adj.* debilitated, decrepit, feeble, flabby, flaccid, hypotonic, ill-adapted, ill-equipped, inadequate, inappropriate, incapable, incompetent, ineffective, ineligible, unequal, unhealthy, unprepared, unqualified, unsuitable, unsuited, untrained, useless.
antonyms competent, fit, suitable.

unfold *v.* clarify, describe, develop, disclose, disentangle, divulge, elaborate, evolve, expand, explain, flatten, grow, illustrate, mature, open, present, reveal, show, spread, straighten, stretch out, uncoil, uncover, undo, unfurl, unravel, unroll, unwrap.
antonyms fold, suppress, withhold, wrap.

unforeseen *adj.* abrupt, accidental, fortuitous, startling, sudden, surprise, surprising, unanticipated, unavoidable, unexpected, unheralded, unlooked-for, unpredicted.
antonyms expected, predictable.

unfortunate *adj.* adverse, calamitous, cursed, deplorable, disadventurous, disastrous, doomed, hapless, hopeless, ill-advised, ill-fated, ill-starred, ill-timed, inappropriate, infelicitous, inopportune, lamentable, luckless, poor, regrettable, ruinous, star-crossed, tactless, unbecoming, unfavorable, unhappy, unlucky, unprosperous, unsuccessful, unsuitable, untimely, untoward, wretched.
antonym fortunate.

unfriendly *adj.* alien, aloof, antagonistic, chilly, cold, critical, disagreeable, distant, hostile, ill-disposed, inauspicious, inhospitable, inimical, quarrelsome, sour, stand- offish, surly, unapproachable, unbending, uncongenial, unfavorable, unneighborly, unsociable, unwelcoming.
antonyms agreeable, amiable, friendly.

ungainly *adj.* awkward, clumsy, gangling, gauche, gawky, inelegant, loutish, lubberly, lumbering, slouching, uncoordinated, uncouth, unwieldy.
antonyms elegant, graceful.

ungodly *adj.* blasphemous, corrupt, depraved, dreadful, godless, horrendous, immoral, impious, intolerable, irreligious, outrageous, profane, sinful, unearthly, unreasonable, unseasonable, unseemly, unsocial, vile, wicked.

ungrateful *adj.* heedless, ill-mannered, ingrate, selfish, thankless, unappreciative, ungracious, unmindful.
antonym grateful.

unguarded[1] *adj.* careless, foolhardy, foolish, heedless, ill-considered, impolitic, imprudent, incautious, indiscreet,

rash, thoughtless, uncircumspect, undiplomatic, unheeding, unthinking, unwary.
antonyms cautious, guarded.

unguarded[2] *adj.* defenseless, exposed, pregnable, undefended, unpatrolled, unprotected, vulnerable.
antonyms guarded, protected.

unhappy *adj.* awkward, blue, clumsy, contentless, crestfallen, cursed, dejected, depressed, despondent, disconsolate, dismal, dispirited, down, downcast, gauche, gloomy, hapless, ill-advised, ill-chosen, ill-fated, ill-omened, ill- timed, inappropriate, inapt, inept, infelicitous, injudicious, long-faced, luckless, lugubrious, malapropos, melancholy, miserable, mournful, sad, sorrowful, sorry, tactless, uneasy, unfortunate, unlucky, unsuitable, wretched.
antonyms fortunate, happy.

unhealthy *adj.* ailing, bad, baneful, corrupt, corrupting, degrading, deleterious, delicate, demoralizing, detrimental, epinosic, feeble, frail, harmful, infirm, insalubrious, insalutary, insanitary, invalid, morbid, noisome, noxious, polluted, poorly, sick, sickly, undesirable, unhygienic, unsound, unwell, unwholesome, weak.
antonyms healthy, hygienic, robust, salubrious.

unheard-of *adj.* disgraceful, extreme, inconceivable, new, novel, obscure, offensive, out of the question, outrageous, preposterous, shocking, singular, unacceptable, unbelievable, undiscovered, undreamed-of, unexampled, unfamiliar, unimaginable, unique, unknown, unprecedented, unregarded, unremarked, unsung, unthinkable, unthought-of, unusual.
antonyms famous, normal, usual.

unhurried *adj.* calm, deliberate, easy, easy-going, laid-back, leisurely, relaxed, sedate, slow.
antonyms hasty, hurried.

uniform *n.* costume, dress, garb, gear, habit, insignia, livery, outfit, regalia, regimentals, rig, robes, suit.
adj. alike, consistent, constant, equable, equal, even, homochromous, homogeneous, homomorphic, homomorphous, identical, like, monochrome, montonous, of a piece, regular, same, selfsame, similar, smooth, unbroken, unchanging, undeviating, unvarying.
antonyms changing, colorful, varied.

unify *v.* amalgamate, bind, combine, confederate, consolidate, federate, fuse, join, marry, merge, unite, weld.
antonyms separate, split.

unimaginable *adj.* fantastic, impossible, inconceivable, incredible, indescribable, ineffable, mind- boggling, unbelievable, undreamed-of, unheard-of, unhoped-for, unknowable, unthinkable.

unimportant *adj.* immaterial, inconsequential, insignificant, irrelevant, low-ranking, Mickey Mouse, minor, minuscule, negligible, nugatory, off the map, paltry, paravail, petty, slight, small-time, trifling, trivial, worthless.
antonym important.

unimpressive *adj.* average, commonplace, dull, indifferent, mediocre, undistinguished, unexceptional, uninteresting, unremarkable, unspectacular.
antonyms impressive, memorable, notable.

uninhibited *adj.* abandoned, candid, emancipated, frank, free, informal, instinctive, liberated, natural, open, relaxed, spontaneous, unbridled, unchecked, unconstrained, uncontrolled, uncurbed, unrepressed, unreserved, unrestrained, unrestricted, unselfconscious.
antonyms constrained, inhibited, repressed.

uninspired *adj.* boring, commonplace, dull, humdrum, indifferent, ordinary, pedestrian, prosaic, stale, stock, trite, undistinguished, unexciting, unimaginative, uninspiring, uninteresting, unoriginal.
antonyms inspired, original.

unintelligent *adj.* brainless, dense, dull, dumb, empty-headed, fatuous, foolish, gormless, half-witted, obtuse, silly, slow, stupid, thick, unreasoning, unthinking.
antonym intelligent.

unintelligible *adj.* double Dutch, garbled, illegible, inapprehensible, inarticulate, incoherent, incomprehensible, indecipherable, indistinct, jumbled, meaningless, muddled, unfathomable.
antonym intelligible.

unintentional *adj.* accidental, fortuitous, inadvertent, involuntary, unconscious, undeliberate, unintended, unpremeditated, unthinking, unwitting.
antonyms deliberate, intentional.

uninviting *adj.* disagreeable, distasteful, offensive, off-putting, repellent, repulsive, unappealing, unappetizing, unattractive, undesirable, unpleasant, unsavory, unwelcoming.
antonyms inviting, welcome.

union *n.* accord, agreement, alliance, amalgam, amalgamation, Anschluss, association, blend, Bund, coalition, coition, coitus, combination, compact, concord, concrescence, concurrence, confederacy, confederation, conjugation, conjunction, copulation, couplement, coupling, enosis, federation, fusion, harmony, intercourse, junction, juncture, league, marriage, matrimony, mixture, symphysis, synthesis, unanimity, unison, uniting, unity, wedlock.
antonyms alienation, disunity, estrangement, separation.

unique *adj.* incomparable, inimitable, lone, matchless, nonpareil, one-off, only, peerless, single, sole, solitary, sui generis, unequaled, unexampled, unmatched, unparalleled, unprecedented, unrivaled.
antonym commonplace.

unison *n.* accord, accordance, aggreement, concert, concord, co-operation, harmony, homophony, monophony, unanimity, unity.
antonyms disharmony, polyphony.

unit *n.* ace, assembly, component, constituent, detachment, element, entity, Gestalt, group, item, measure, measurement, member, module, monad, monas, one, part, piece, portion, quantity, section, segment, system, whole.

unite *v.* accrete, ally, amalgamate, associate, band, blend, coadunate, coalesce, combine, confederate, conglutinate, conjoin, conjugate, consolidate, cooperate, couple, fay, fuse, incorporate, join, join forces, league, link, marry, merge, pool, splice, unify, wed.
antonyms separate, sever.

universal *adj.* across-the-board, all-embracing, all-inclusive, all-round, catholic, common, ecumenic, ecumenical, entire, general, global, omnipresent, total, ubiquitous, unlimited, whole, widespread, worldwide.

unjustifiable *adj.* excessive, immoderate, indefensible, inexcusable, outrageous, steep, unacceptable, unforgivable, unjust, unpardonable, unreasonable, unwarrantable, wrong.
antonym justifiable.

unkempt *adj.* bedraggled, blowsy, disarranged, disheveled, disordered, frowsy, mal soigné, messy, mop-headed, ratty, rumpled, scruffy, shabby, shaggy, slatternly, sloppy, slovenly, sluttish, tousled, uncombed, ungroomed, untidy.
antonyms neat, tidy.

unkind *adj.* callous, cruel, disobliging, hard- hearted, harsh, inconsiderate, inhuman, inhumane, insensitive, malevolent, malicious, mean, nasty, spiteful, thoughtless, unamiable, uncaring, uncharitable, unchristian, unfeeling, unfriendly, unsympathetic. *antonyms* considerate, kind.

unknown *adj.* alien, anonymous, concealed, dark, foreign, hidden, humble, incognito, mysterious, nameless, new, obscure, secret, strange, uncharted, undisclosed, undiscovered, undistinguished, unexplored, unfamiliar, unheard-of, unidentified, unnamed, unrecognized, unsung, untold.
antonyms familiar, known.

unlawful *adj.* actionable, banned, criminal, forbidden, illegal, illegitimate, illicit, outlawed, prohibited, unauthorized, unconstitutional, unlicensed, unsanctioned.
antonym lawful.

unlike *adj.* contrasted, different, difform, disparate, dissimilar, distinct, divergent, diverse, ill-matched, incompatible, opposed, opposite, unequal, unrelated.
antonyms related, similar.

unlimited *adj.* absolute, all-encompassing, boundless, complete, countless, endless, extensive, full, great, illimitable, immeasurable, immense, incalculable, infinite, limitless, total, unbounded, uncircumscribed, unconditional, unconstrained, unfettered, unhampered, unqualified, unrestricted, vast.
antonyms circumscribed, limited.

unlooked-for *adj.* chance, fortuitous, fortunate, lucky, surprise, surprising, unanticipated, undreamed-of, unexpected, unforeseen, unhoped-for, unpredicted, unthought-of.
antonyms expected, predictable.

unlucky *adj.* cursed, disastrous, doomed, hapless, ill-fated, ill-omened, ill-starred, inauspicious, infaust, jinxed, left-handed, luckless, mischanceful, miserable, ominous, unfavorable, unfortunate, unhappy, unsuccessful, untimely, wretched.
antonym lucky.

unmanageable *adj.* awkward, bulky, cumbersome, difficult, disorderly, fractious, inconvenient, intractable, obstreperous, recalcitrant, refractory, stroppy, uncontrollable, unco-operative, unhandy, unruly, unwieldy, wild.
antonyms docile, manageable.

unmannerly *adj.* badly-behaved, bad-mannered, boorish, discourteous, disrespectful, graceless, ill-bred, ill-mannered, impolite, low-bred, rude, uncivil, uncouth, ungracious.
antonym polite.

unmatched *adj.* beyond compare, consummate, incomparable, matchless, nonpareil, paramount, peerless, supreme, unequaled, unexampled, unparalleled, unrivaled, unsurpassed.

unmerciful *adj.* brutal, callous, cruel, hard, heartless, implacable, merciless, pitiless, relentless, remorseless, ruthless, sadistic, uncaring, unfeeling, unrelenting, unsparing.
antonym merciful.

unmistakable *adj.* certain, clear, conspicuous, crystal-clear, decided, distinct, evident, explicit, glaring, indisputable, manifest, obvious, palpable, patent, plain, positive, pronounced, sure, unambiguous, undeniable, undisputed, unequivocal, unquestionable.
antonyms ambiguous, unclear.

unmitigated *adj.* absolute, arrant, complete, consummate, downright, grim, harsh, intense, oppressive, out-and- out, outright, perfect, persistent, pure, rank, relentless, sheer, thorough, thoroughgoing, unabated, unalleviated, unbroken, undiminished, unmodified, unqualified, unredeemed, unrelenting, unrelieved, unremitting, utter.

unnatural *adj.* aberrant, abnormal, absonant, affected, anomalous, artificial, assumed, bizarre, brutal, callous, cataphysical, cold-blooded, contrived, cruel, disnatured, evil, extraordinary, factitious, false, feigned, fiendish, forced, freakish, heartless, inhuman, insincere, irregular, labored, mannered, monstrous, odd, outlandish, perverse, perverted, phony, queer, ruthless, sadistic, savage, self-conscious, stagy, stiff, stilted, strained, strange, studied, supernatural, theatrical, unaccountable, uncanny, unfeeling, unspontaneous, unusual, wicked.
antonyms acceptable, natural, normal.

unnecessary *adj.* dispensable, expendable, inessential, needless, non-essential, otiose, pleonastic, redundant, supererogatory, superfluous, supernumerary, tautological, uncalled-for, unjustified, unneeded, useless.
antonyms indispensable, necessary.

unobtrusive *adj.* humble, inconspicuous, low-key, meek, modest, quiet, restrained, retiring, self-effacing, subdued, unassertive, unassuming, unemphatic, unnoticeable, unostentatious, unpretentious.
antonyms obtrusive, ostentatious.

unoccupied *adj.* disengaged, empty, free, idle, inactive, jobless, unemployed, uninhabited, untenanted, vacant, workless.
antonyms busy, occupied.

unofficial *adj.* confidential, illegal, informal, personal, private, ulterior, unauthorized, unconfirmed, undeclared, wildcat.
antonym official.

unorthodox *adj.* abnormal, alternative, fringe, heterodox, irregular, nonconformist, unconventional, unusual, unwonted.
antonyms conventional, orthodox.

unparalleled *adj.* consummate, exceptional, incomparable, matchless, peerless, rare, singular, superlative, supreme, surpassing, unequaled, unexampled, unique, unmatched, unprecedented, unrivaled, unsurpassed.

unpleasant *adj.* abhorrent, bad, disagreeable, displeasing, distasteful, god-awful, ill-natured, irksome, nasty, objectionable, obnoxious, repulsive, rocky, sticky, traumatic, troublesome, unattractive, unpalatable.
antonym pleasant.

unpopular *adj.* avoided, detested, disliked, hated, neglected, rejected, shunned, undesirable, unfashionable, unloved, unsought-after, unwanted, unwelcome.
antonyms fashionable, popular.

unprecedented *adj.* abnormal, exceptional, extraordinary, freakish, new, novel, original, remarkable, revolutionary, singular, unexampled, unheard-of, unknown, unparalleled, unrivaled, unusual.

unpredictable *adj.* chance, changeable, doubtful, erratic, fickle, fluky, iffy, in the lap of the gods, inconstant, on the knees of the gods, random, scatty, unforeseeable, unreliable, unstable, variable.
antonym predictable.

unprejudiced *adj.* balanced, detached, dispassionate, enlightened, even-handed, fair, fair-minded, impartial, just, non-partisan, objective, open-minded, unbiased, uncolored.
antonyms narrow-minded, prejudiced.

unpremeditated *adj.* extempore, fortuitous, impromptu, impulsive, offhand, off-the-cuff, spontaneous, spur-of-the-moment, unintentional, unplanned, unprepared, unrehearsed.
antonym premeditated.

unprincipled *adj.* amoral, corrupt, crooked, deceitful, devious, discreditable, dishonest, dishonorable, immoral, underhand, unethical, unprofessional, unscrupulous.
antonym ethical.

unprofessional *adj.* amateur, amateurish, improper, inadmissible, incompetent, inefficient, inexperienced, inexpert, lax, negligent, unacceptable, unbecoming, unethical, unfitting, unprincipled, unseemly, unskilled, untrained, unworthy.
antonyms professional, skilful.

unprotected *adj.* defenseless, exposed, helpless, inerm, liable, naked, open, pregnable, unarmed, unattended, undefended, unfortified, unguarded, unsheltered, unshielded, unvaccinated, vulnerable.
antonyms immune, protected, safe.

unqualified *adj.* absolute, categorical, complete, consummate, downright, ill-equipped, incapable, incompetent, ineligible, out-and-out, outright, thorough, thoroughgoing, total, uncertificated, unconditional, unfit, unmitigated, unmixed, unprepared, unreserved, unrestricted, untrained, utter, whole-hearted.
antonyms conditional, tentative.

unreal *adj.* academic, artificial, chimerical, fabulous, fairy-tale, fake, false, fanciful, fantastic, fictitious, hypothetical, illusory, imaginary, immaterial, impalpable, insincere, insubstantial, intangible, made-up, make-believe, mock, moonshiny, mythical, nebulous, ostensible, phantasmagorical, pretended, seeming, sham, storybook, synthetic, vaporous, visionary.
antonyms genuine, real.

unrealistic *adj.* half-baked, idealistic, impracticable, impractical, improbable, quixotic, romantic, starry-eyed, theoretical, unworkable.
antonyms pragmatic, realistic.

unreasonable *adj.* absurd, arbitrary, biased, blinkered, capricious, cussed, erratic, excessive, exorbitant, extortionate, extravagant, far-fetched, foolish, froward, headstrong, illogical, immoderate, inconsistent, irrational, mad, nonsensical, opinionated, perverse, preposterous, quirky, senseless, silly, steep, stupid, thrawn, uncalled-for, undue, unfair, unjust, unjustifiable, unjustified, unwarranted.
antonyms moderate, rational, reasonable.

unregenerate *adj.* abandoned, hardened, impenitent, incorrigible, intractable, obdurate, obstinate, persistent, recalcitrant, refractory, shameless, sinful, stubborn, unconverted, unreformed, unrepentant, wicked.
antonyms reformed, repentant.

unrelenting *adj.* ceaseless, constant, continual, continuous, cruel, endless, implacable, incessant, inexorable, insistent, intransigent, merciless, perpetual, pitiless, relentless, remorseless, ruthless, steady, stern, tough, unabated, unalleviated, unbroken, unceasing, uncompromising, unmerciful, unremitting, unsparing.
antonyms intermittent, spasmodic.

unreliable *adj.* deceptive, delusive, disreputable, erroneous, fair-weather, fallible, false, implausible, inaccurate, inauthentic, irresponsible, mistaken, specious, uncertain, unconvincing, undependable, unsound, unstable, untrustworthy.
antonym reliable.

unrepentant *adj.* callous, hardened, impenitent,

incorrigible, obdurate, shameless, unabashed, unashamed, unregenerate, unremorseful, unrepenting.
antonyms penitent, repentant.

unresponsive *adj.* aloof, apathetic, cool, echoless, indifferent, unaffected, uninterested, unmoved, unsympathetic.
antonyms responsive, sympathetic.

unrest *n.* agitation, anxiety, apprehension, disaffection, discontent, discord, disquiet, dissatisfaction, dissension, distress, perturbation, protest, rebellion, restlessness, sedition, strife, tumult, turmoil, unease, uneasiness, worry.
antonyms calm, peace.

unrestrained *adj.* abandoned, boisterous, free, immoderate, inordinate, intemperate, irrepressible, natural, rampant, unbounded, unbridled, unchecked, unconstrained, uncontrolled, unhindered, uninhibited, unrepressed, unreserved, uproarious.
antonym inhibited.

unruffled *adj.* calm, collected, composed, cool, even, imperturbable, level, peaceful, placid, serene, smooth, tranquil, unbroken, undisturbed, unflustered, unmoved, unperturbed, untroubled.
antonyms anxious, troubled.

unruly *adj.* camstairy, disobedient, disorderly, fractious, headstrong, insubordinate, intractable, lawless, mutinous, obstreperous, rebellious, refractory, riotous, rowdy, ruleless, turbulent, uncontrollable, ungovernable, unmanageable, wayward, wild, wilful.
antonym manageable.

unsafe *adj.* dangerous, exposed, hazardous, insecure, parlous, perilous, precarious, risky, threatening, treacherous, uncertain, unreliable, unsound, unstable, vulnerable.
antonyms safe, secure.

unsatisfactory *adj.* deficient, disappointing, displeasing, dissatisfying, frustrating, inadequate, inferior, insufficient, leaving a lot to be desired, mediocre, poor, rocky, thwarting, unacceptable, unsatisfying, unsuitable, unworthy, weak.
antonym satisfactory.

unscrupulous *adj.* corrupt, crooked, cynical, discreditable, dishonest, dishonorable, immoral, improper, ruthless, shameless, unethical, unprincipled.
antonym scrupulous.

unseemly *adj.* discreditable, disreputable, improper, inappropriate, indecorous, indelicate, shocking, unbecoming, unbefitting, undignified, undue, ungentlemanly, unlady-like, unrefined, unsuitable.
antonyms decorous, seemly.

unselfish *adj.* altruistic, charitable, dedicated, devoted, dis-interested, generous, humanitarian, kind, liberal, magnanimous, noble, philanthropic, self-denying, selfless, self- sacrificing, single-eyed, ungrudging, unstinting.
antonym selfish.

unsentimental *adj.* cynical, hard as nails, hard- headed, level-headed, practical, pragmatic, realistic, shrewd, tough.
antonyms sentimental, soft.

unsettled *adj.* agitated, anxious, changeable, changing, confused, debatable, disorderly, disoriented, disturbed, doubtful, due, edgy, flustered, iffy, inconstant, insecure, moot, open, outstanding, overdue, owing, payable, pending, perturbed, problematical, restive, restless, shaken, shaky, tense, troubled, uncertain, undecided, undetermined, uneasy, unnerved, unpredictable, unresolved, unstable, unsteady, upset, variable.
antonyms certain, composed, settled.

unsightly *adj.* disagreeable, displeasing, hideous, horrid, off-putting, repellent, repugnant, repulsive, revolting, ugly, unattractive, unpleasant, unprepossessing.
antonym pleasing.

unsolicited *adj.* gratuitous, spontaneous, unasked, uncalled-for, unforced, uninvited, unrequested, unsought, unwanted, unwelcome, voluntary.
antonyms invited, solicited.

unsophisticated *adj.* artless, childlike, funky, guileless, hick, homespun, inexperienced, ingenuous, innocent, naïve, natural, plain, simple, straightforward, unaffected, uncomplicated, uninvolved, unpretentious, unrefined, unspecialized, unspoilt, untutored, unworldly.
antonyms complex, pretentious, sophisticated.

unsound *adj.* ailing, defective, delicate, deranged, dicky, diseased, erroneous, fallacious, fallible, false, faulty, flawed, frail, ill, ill-founded, illogical, insecure, invalid, shaky, specious, unbalanced, unhealthy, unhinged, unreliable, unsafe, unstable, unsteady, unwell, weak, wobbly.
antonyms safe, sound.

unspeakable *adj.* abhorrent, abominable, appalling, dreadful, evil, execrable, frightful, heinous, horrible, inconceivable, indescribable, ineffable, inexpressible, loathsome, monstrous, nefandous, odious, overwhelming, repellent, shocking, unbelievable, unimaginable, unutterable, wonderful.

unstable *adj.* astable, capricious, changeable, erratic, fitful, fluctuating, inconsistent, inconstant, insecure, irrational, labile, precarious, rickety, risky, shaky, shoogly, slippy, ticklish, tottering, unpredictable, unsettled, unsteady, untrustworthy, vacillating, variable, volatile, wobbly.
antonyms stable, steady.

unsteady *adj.* changeable, dicky, erratic, flickering, flighty, fluctuating, frail, inconstant, infirm, insecure, irregular, precarious, reeling, rickety, shaky, shoogly, skittish, tittupy, tottering, totty, treacherous, tremulous, unreliable, unsafe, unstable, unsteeled, vacillating, variable, volatile, wavering, wobbly.
antonyms firm, steady.

unsubstantiated *adj.* debatable, dubious, questionable, unattested, unconfirmed, uncorroborated, unestablished, unproved, unproven, unsupported, unverified.
antonyms proved, proven.

unsuccessful *adj.* abortive, bootless, failed, foiled, fruitless, frustrated, futile, ill-fated, inadequate, ineffective, ineffectual, losing, luckless, manqué, otiose, sterile, thwarted, unavailing, unfortunate, unlucky, unproductive, unsatisfactory, useless, vain.
antonyms effective, successful.

unsuitable *adj.* improper, inapposite, inappropriate, inapt, incompatible, incongruous, inconsistent, indecorous, ineligible, infelicitous, malapropos, unacceptable, unbecoming, unbefitting, unfitting, unlikely, unseasonable, unseemly, unsuited.
antonyms seemly, suitable.

unsuspecting *adj.* childlike, confiding, credulous, green, gullible, inexperienced, ingenuous, innocent, naïve, trustful, trusting, unconscious, uncritical, unsuspicious, unwary, unwitting.
antonyms conscious, knowing.

unswerving *adj.* constant, dedicated, devoted, direct, firm, fixed, immovable, resolute, single-minded, staunch, stead-fast, steady, sure, true, undeviating, unfaltering, unflagging, untiring, unwavering.
antonyms irresolute, tentative.

unsympathetic *adj.* antagonistic, antipathetic, apathetic, callous, cold, compassionless, cruel, hard, hard as nails, hard-hearted, harsh, heartless, indifferent, inhuman, insensitive, soulless, stony, uncharitable, uncompassionate, unconcerned, unfeeling, unkind, unmoved, unpitying, unresponsive.
antonyms compassionate, sympathetic.

untamed *adj.* barbarous, ferae naturae, feral, fierce, haggard, savage, unbroken, undomesticated, unmellowed, untameable, wild. *antonyms* domesticated, tame.

untenable *adj.* fallacious, flawed, illogical, indefensible, insupportable, rocky, shaky, unmaintainable, unreasonable, unsound, unsustainable.
antonyms sound, tenable.

untidy *adj.* bedraggled, chaotic, cluttered, disheveled, disorderly, higgledy-piggledy, jumbled, littered, messy, muddled, ratty, raunchy, rumpled, scruffy, shambolic, slatternly, slipshod, sloppy, slovenly, sluttish, topsy-turvy, unkempt, unsystematic.
antonyms systematic, tidy.

untimely *adj.* awkward, early, ill-timed, inappropriate, inauspicious, inconvenient, inopportune, intempestive, malapropos, mistimed, premature, unfortunate, unseasonable, unsuitable.
antonyms opportune, timely.

untold *adj.* boundless, countless, hidden, incalculable, indescribable, inexhaustible, inexpressible, infinite, innumerable, measureless, myriad, numberless, private, secret, uncountable, uncounted, undisclosed, undreamed-of, unimaginable, unknown, unnumbered, unpublished, unreckoned, unrecounted, unrelated, unrevealed, unthinkable, unutterable.

untoward *adj.* adverse, annoying, awkward, contrary, disastrous, ill-timed, improper, inappropriate, inauspicious, inconvenient, indecorous, inimical, inopportune, irritating, ominous, troublesome, unbecoming, unexpected, unfavorable, unfitting, unfortunate, unlucky, unpropitious, unseemly, unsuitable, untimely, vexatious, worrying.
antonyms auspicious, suitable.

untrustworthy *adj.* capricious, deceitful, devious, dishonest, disloyal, dubious, duplicitous, fair-weather, faithless, false, fickle, fly-by-night, shady, slippery, treacherous, tricky, two-faced, undependable, unfaithful, unreliable, unsafe, untrue, untrusty.
antonyms reliable, trustworthy.

untruthful *adj.* crooked, deceitful, deceptive, dishonest, dissembling, false, hypocritical, lying, mendacious, untrustworthy, unveracious.
antonym truthful.

untutored *adj.* artless, ignorant, illiterate, inexperienced, inexpert, simple, uneducated, unlearned, unlessoned, unpracticed, unrefined, unschooled, unsophisticated, untrained, unversed.
antonyms educated, trained.

unusual *adj.* abnormal, anomalous, atypical, bizarre, curious, different, eccentric, exceptional, extraordinary, odd, phenomenal, queer, rare, remarkable, singular, strange, surprising, uncommon, unconventional, unexpected, unfamiliar, unwonted.
antonyms normal, usual.

unutterable *adj.* egregious, extreme, indescribable, ineffable, nefandous, overwhelming, unimaginable, unspeakable.

unwarranted *adj.* baseless, gratuitous, groundless, indefensible, inexcusable, uncalled-for, unjust, unjustified, unprovoked, unreasonable, vain, wrong.
antonyms justifiable, warranted.

unwary *adj.* careless, credulous, hasty, heedless, imprudent, incautious, indiscreet, rash, reckless, thoughtless, unchary, uncircumspect, unguarded, unthinking, unwatchful.
antonyms cautious, wary.

unwieldy *adj.* awkward, bulky, burdensome, clumsy, cumbersome, cumbrous, gangling, hefty, hulking, inconvenient, massive, ponderous, ungainly, unhandy, unmanageable, weighty.
antonyms dainty, neat, petite.

unwilling *adj.* averse, disinclined, grudging, indisposed, laggard, loath, loathful, opposed, reluctant, resistant, slow, unenthusiastic.
antonyms enthusiastic, willing.

unwise *adj.* foolhardy, foolish, ill-advised, ill- considered, ill-judged, impolitic, improvident, imprudent, inadvisable, indiscreet, inexpedient, injudicious,

irresponsible, rash, reckless, senseless, short-sighted, silly, stupid, thoughtless, unintelligent.
antonyms prudent, wise.

unwitting *adj.* accidental, chance, ignorant, inadvertent, innocent, involuntary, unaware, unconscious, unintended, unintentional, unknowing, unmeant, unplanned, unsuspecting, unthinking.
antonyms conscious, deliberate, knowing, witting.

unwonted *adj.* atypical, exceptional, extraordinary, infrequent, peculiar, rare, singular, strange, unaccustomed, uncommon, uncustomary, unexpected, unfamiliar, unheard-of, unusual.
antonyms usual, wonted.

unyielding *adj.* adamant, determined, firm, hardline, immovable, implacable, inexorable, inflexible, intractable, intransigent, obdurate, obstinate, relentless, resolute, rigid, solid, staunch, steadfast, stubborn, tough, unbending, uncompromising, unrelenting, unwavering.
antonyms flexible, yielding.

upbeat *adj.* bright, bullish, buoyant, cheerful, cheery, encouraging, favorable, forward-looking, heartening, hopeful, optimistic, positive, promising, rosy.
antonyms down-beat, gloomy.

upbraid *v.* admonish, berate, blame, carpet, castigate, censure, chide, condemn, criticize, dress down, jaw, lecture, rate, rebuke, reprimand, reproach, reprove, scold, take to task, tell off, tick off.
antonyms commend, praise.

upbringing *n.* breeding, bringing-up, care, cultivation, education, instruction, nurture, parenting, raising, rearing, tending, training.

upgrade *v.* advance, ameliorate, better, elevate, embourgeoise, enhance, gentilize, gentrify, improve, promote, raise.
antonyms degrade, downgrade.

uphold *v.* advocate, aid, back, champion, countenance, defend, encourage, endorse, fortify, hold to, justify, maintain, promote, stand by, stengthen, support, sustain, vindicate.

upkeep *n.* care, conservation, expenditure, expenses, keep, maintenance, oncosts, operating costs, outgoing, outlay, overheads, preservation, repair, running, running costs, subsistence, support, sustenance.
antonym neglect.

uppish *adj.* affected, arrogant, assuming, big- headed, bumptious, cocky, conceited, hoity-toity, impertinent, overweening, presumptuous, self-importan‌t, snobbish, stuck-up, supercilious, swanky, toffee-nosed, uppity.
antonyms diffident, unassertive.

upright *adj.* arrect, bluff, conscientious, erect, ethical, faithful, four-square, good, high-minded, honest, honorable, incorruptible, just, noble, perpendicular, principled, righteous, straight, straightforward, true, trustworthy, unimpeachable, upstanding, vertical, virtuous.
antonyms dishonest, flat, horizontal, prone, supine.

uprising *n.* insurgence, insurgency, insurrection, mutiny, putsch, rebellion, revolt, revolution, rising, sedition, upheaval.

uproar *n.* brawl, brouhaha, clamor, commotion, confusion, din, disorder, furore, hubbub, hullabaloo, hurly-burly, katzenjammer, noise, outcry, pandemonium, racket, rammy, randan, riot, ruckus, ruction, rumpus, stramash, tumult, turbulence, turmoil.

uproarious *adj.* boisterous, clamorous, confused, convulsive, deafening, disorderly, gleeful, hilarious, hysterical, killing, loud, noisy, rib-tickling, riotous, rip-roaring, roistering, rollicking, rowdy, rowdy-dowdy, side- splitting, tempestuous, tumultuous, turbulent, unrestrained, wild.
antonym sedate.

upset *v.* agitate, bother, capsize, change, conquer, defeat, destabilize, discombobulate, discompose, disconcert, dismay, disorder, disorganize, disquiet, distress, disturb, fluster, grieve, hip, overcome, overset, overthrow, overturn, perturb, ruffle, shake, spill, spoil, tip, topple, trouble, unnerve, unsteady.
n. agitation, bother, bug, complaint, defeat, disorder, disruption, disturbance, illness, indisposition, malady, purl, reverse, shake-up, shock, sickness, surprise, trouble, upheaval, worry.
adj. agitated, bothered, capsized, chaotic, choked, confused, disconcerted, dismayed, disordered, disquieted, distressed, disturbed, frantic, gippy, grieved, hurt, ill, messed up, muddled, overturned, overwrought, pained, poorly, qualmish, queasy, ruffled, shattered, sick, spilled, toppled, topsy-turvy, troubled, tumbled, worried.

upshot *n.* conclusion, consequence, culmination, end, event, finale, finish, issue, outcome, pay-off, result.

urbane *adj.* bland, civil, civilized, cosmopolitan, courteous, cultivated, cultured, debonair, easy, elegant, mannerly, polished, refined, smooth, sophisticated, suave, well- bred, well-mannered.
antonyms gauche, uncouth.

urge *v.* advise, advocate, beg, beseech, champion, compel, constrain, counsel, drive, emphasize, encourage, entreat, exhort, force, goad, hasten, hist, impel, implore, incite, induce, instigate, nag, plead, press, propel, push, recommend, solicit, spur, stimulate, support, underline, underscore.
antonyms deter, dissuade.
n. compulsion, desire, drive, eagerness, fancy, impulse, inclination, itch, libido, longing, wish, yearning, yen.
antonym disinclination.

urgency *n.* exigence, exigency, extremity, gravity, hurry, imperativeness, importance, importunity, instancy, necessity, need, pressure, seriousness, stress.

urgent *adj.* clamorous, cogent, compelling, critical, crucial, eager, earnest, emergent, exigent, immediate, imperative, important, importunate, insistent, instant, intense, persistent, persuasive, pressing, top-priority.

usage *n.* application, control, convention, custom, employment, etiquette, form, habit, handling, management, method, mode, operation, practice, procedure, protocol, régime, regulation, routine, rule, running, tradition, treatment, use, wont.

use *v.* apply, bring, consume, employ, enjoy, exercise, exhaust, expend, exploit, handle, manipulate, misuse, operate, ply, practice, spend, treat, usufruct, utilize, waste, wield, work.
n. advantage, application, avail, benefit, call, cause, custom, employment, end, enjoyment, exercise, good, habit, handling, help, meaning, mileage, necessity, need, object, occasion, operation, point, practice, profit, purpose, reason, service, treatment, usage, usefulness, usufruct, utility, value, way, wont, worth.

useful *adj.* advantageous, all-purpose, beneficial, convenient, effective, fruitful, general-purpose, handy, helpful, practical, productive, profitable, salutary, serviceable, valuable, worthwhile.
antonym useless.

useless *adj.* bootless, clapped-out, disadvantageous, effectless, feckless, fruitless, futile, hopeless, idle, impractical, incompetent, ineffective, ineffectual, inefficient, inept, of no use, pointless, profitless, shiftless, stupid, unavailing, unproductive, unworkable, vain, valueless, weak, worthless.
antonym useful.

usher *n.* attendant, doorkeeper, escort, guide, huissier, usherette.
v. conduct, direct, escort, guide, lead, pilot, shepherd, steer.

usual *adj.* accepted, accustomed, common, constant, conventional, customary, everyday, expected, familiar, fixed, general, habitual, nomic, normal, ordinary, recognized, regular, routine, standard, stock, typical, unexceptional, wonted.
antonyms unheard-of, unusual.

usually *adv.* as a rule, by and large, chiefly, commonly, customarily, generally, generally speaking, habitually, in the main, mainly, mostly, normally, on the whole, ordinarily, regularly, routinely, traditionally, typically.
antonym exceptionally.

utensil *n.* apparatus, contrivance, device, gadget, gismo, implement, instrument, tool.

utility *n.* advantage, advantageousness, avail, benefit, convenience, efficacy, expedience, fitness, point, practicality, profit, satisfactoriness, service, serviceableness, use, usefulness, value.
antonym inutility.

utilize *v.* adapt, appropriate, employ, exploit, make use of, put to use, resort to, take advantage of, turn to account, use.

Utopian *adj.* airy, chimerical, dream, Elysian, fanciful, fantastic, ideal, idealistic, illusory, imaginary, impractical, perfect, romantic, unworkable, visionary, wishful.

utter[1] *adj.* absolute, arrant, complete, consummate, dead, downright, entire, out-and-out, perfect, sheer, stark, thorough, thoroughgoing, total, unalleviated, unmitigated, unqualified.

utter[2] *v.* articulate, declare, deliver, divulge, enounce, enunciate, express, proclaim, promulgate, pronounce, publish, reveal, say, sound, speak, state, tell, tongue, verbalize, vocalize, voice.

V

vacancy *n.* accommodation, emptiness, gap, job, opening, opportunity, place, position, post, room, situation, space, vacuity, vacuousness, vacuum, void.

vacant *adj.* absent, absent-minded, abstracted, available, blank, disengaged, dreaming, dreamy, empty, expressionless, free, idle, inane, inattentive, incurious, thoughtless, to let, unemployed, unengaged, unfilled, unoccupied, untenanted, unthinking, vacuous, void.
antonyms engaged, occupied.

vacate *v.* abandon, depart, evacuate, leave, quit, withdraw.

vacillate *v.* fluctuate, haver, hesitate, oscillate, shilly-shally, shuffle, sway, swither, temporize, tergiversate, waver.

vacillating *adj.* hesitant, irresolute, oscillating, shilly-shallying, shuffling, swithering, temporizing, uncertain, unresolved, wavering.
antonyms resolute, unhesitating.

vacuity *n.* apathy, blankness, emptiness, inanity, incognizance, incomprehension, incuriosity, nothingness, space, vacuousness, vacuum, void.

vacuous *adj.* apathetic, blank, empty, idle, inane, incurious, stupid, uncomprehending, unfilled, unintelligent, vacant, void.

vacuum *n.* chasm, emptiness, gap, nothingness, space, vacuity, void.

vagabond *n.* beggar, bo, bum, down-and-out, hobo, itinerant, knight of the road, migrant, nomad, outcast, rascal, rover, runabout, runagate, tramp, vagrant, wanderer, wayfarer.

vagary *n.* caprice, crotchet, fancy, fegary, humor, megrim, notion, prank, quirk, whim, whimsy.

vagrant *n.* beggar, bum, gangrel, hobo, itinerant, rolling stone, stroller, tramp, wanderer.
adj. footloose, homeless, itinerant, nomadic, roaming, rootless, roving, shiftless, traveling, vagabond, wandering.

vague *adj.* amorphous, blurred, dim, doubtful, evasive, fuzzy, generalized, hazy, ill-defined, imprecise, indefinite, indeterminate, indistinct, inexact, lax, loose, misty, nebulous, obscure, shadowy, uncertain, unclear, undefined, undetermined, unknown, unspecific, unspecified, woolly.
antonyms certain, clear, definite.

vain *adj.* abortive, affected, arrogant, baseless, bigheaded, conceited, egotistical, empty, fruitless, futile, groundless, hollow, idle, inflated, mindless, narcissistic, nugatory, ostentatious, overweening, peacockish, pointless, pretentious, proud, purposeless, self-important, self-satisfied, senseless, stuck-up, swaggering, swanky, swollen-headed, time- wasting, trifling, trivial, unavailing, unimportant, unproductive, unprofitable, unsubstantial, useless, vain- glorious, vaporous, worthless.
antonyms modest, self-effacing.

valet *n.* body servant, gentleman's gentleman, man, manservant, valet de chambre.

valiant *adj.* bold, brave, courageous, dauntless, doughty, fearless, gallant, heroic, indomitable, intrepid, plucky, redoubtable, stalwart, staunch, stout, stout-hearted, valorous, worthy.
antonym cowardly.

valid *adj.* approved, authentic, binding, bona fide, cogent, conclusive, convincing, efficacious, efficient, genuine, good, just, lawful, legal, legitimate, logical, official, potent, powerful, proper, rational, reliable, sound, substantial, telling, weighty, well-founded, well-grounded.
antonym invalid.

validate *v.* attest, authenticate, authorize, certify, confirm, corroborate, endorse, legalize, ratify, substantiate, underwrite.

validity *n.* authority, cogency, force, foundation, grounds, justifiability, lawfulness, legality, legitimacy, logic, point, power, soundness, strength, substance, weight.
antonym invalidity.

valley *n.* arroyo, canyon, cwm, dale, dell, depression, dingle, draw, glen, gorge, gulch, hollow, hope, slade, strath, vale.

valor *n.* boldness, bravery, courage, derring-do, doughtiness, fearlessness, fortitude, gallantry, hardiness, heroism, intrepidity, lion-heartedness, mettle, spirit.
antonyms cowardice, weakness.

valuable *adj.* advantageous, beneficial, blue-chip, cherished, costly, dear, esteemed, estimable, expensive, fruitful, handy, helpful, high-priced, important, invaluable, precious, prizable, prized, productive, profitable, serviceable, treasured, useful, valued, worthwhile, worthy.
antonyms useless, valueless.

value *n.* account, advantage, avail, benefit, cost, desirability, equivalent, good, help, importance, merit, price, profit, rate, significance, use, usefulness, utility, worth.
v. account, appraise, appreciate, apprize, assess, cherish, compute, esteem, estimate, evaluate, hold dear, price, prize, rate, regard, respect, survey, treasure.
antonyms disregard, neglect, undervalue.

vanish *v.* dematerialize, depart, die out, disappear, disperse, dissolve, evanesce, evaporate, exit, fade, fizzle out, melt, peter out.
antonyms appear, materialize.

vanity *n.* affectation, airs, arrogance, bigheadedness, conceit, conceitedness, egotism, emptiness, frivolity, fruitlessness, fume, futility, hollowness, idleness, inanity, narcissism, ostentation, peacockery, pointlessness, pretension, pride, self-admiration, self-conceit, self-love, self-satisfaction, swollen-headedness, triviality, unreality, unsubstantiality, uselessness, vainglory, worthlessness.
antonyms modesty, worth.

vanquish *v.* beat, confound, conquer, crush, defeat, humble, master, overcome, overpower, overwhelm, quell, reduce, repress, rout, subdue, subjugate, triumph over.

vapid *adj.* banal, bland, bloodless, boring, colorless, dead, dull, flat, flavorless, insipid, jejune, lifeless, limp, stale, tame, tasteless, tedious, tiresome, trite, uninspiring, uninteresting, watery, weak, wishy-washy.
antonyms interesting, vigorous.

vapor *n.* breath, brume, damp, dampness, exhalation, fog, fumes, halitus, haze, miasm, miasma, mist, reek, roke, smoke, steam.

variable *adj.* capricious, chameleonic, changeable, fickle, fitful, flexible, fluctuating, inconstant, mercurial, moonish, mutable, protean, shifting, temperamental, unpredictable, unstable, unsteady, vacillating, varying, versiform, wavering.
antonym invariable.
n. factor, parameter.

variant *adj.* alternative, derived, deviant, different, divergent, exceptional, modified.
antonyms normal, standard, usual.
n. alternative, development, deviant, modification, rogue, sport, variation.

variation *n.* alteration, change, departure, deviation, difference, discrepancy, diversification, diversity, elaboration, inflection, innovation, modification, modulation, novelty, variety.
antonyms monotony, similitude, uniformity.

variety *n.* array, assortment, brand, breed, category, change, class, collection, difference, discrepancy, diversification, diversity, intermixture, kind, make, manifoldness, many-sidedness, medley, miscellany, mixture, multifariousness, multiplicity, olio, olla-podrida, order, pot- pourri, range, sort, species, strain, type, variation.
antonyms monotony, similitude, uniformity.

various *adj.* assorted, different, differing, disparate, distinct, divers, diverse, diversified, heterogeneous, many, many-sided, miscellaneous, multifarous, omnifarous, several, sundry, varied, variegated, varying.

vary *v.* alter, alternate, change, depart, differ, disagree, diverge, diversify, fluctuate, inflect, intermix, modify, modulate, permutate, reorder, transform.

vassalage *n.* bondage, dependence, serfdom, servitude, slavery, subjection, subjugation, thraldom, villeinage.

vast *adj.* astronomical, boundless, capacious, colossal, cyclopean, enormous, extensive, far-flung, fathomless, gigantic, great, huge, illimitable, immeasurable, immense, limitless, mammoth, massive, measureless, monstrous, monumental, never-ending, prodigious, stupendous, sweeping, tremendous, unbounded, unlimited, vasty, voluminous, wide.

vault[1] *v.* bound, clear, hurdle, jump, leap, leap-frog, spring.

vault[2] *n.* arch, camera, cavern, cellar, concave, crypt, depository, mausoleum, repository, roof, span, strong-room, tomb, undercroft, wine-cellar.

vaunt *v.* blazon, boast, brag, crow, exult in, flaunt, parade, show off, trumpet.
antonyms belittle, minimize.

veer *v.* change, sheer, shift, swerve, tack, turn, wheel.

vehement *adj.* animated, ardent, eager, earnest, emphatic, enthusiastic, fervent, fervid, fierce, forceful, forcible, heated, impassioned, impetuous, intense, passionate, powerful, strong, urgent, violent, zealous.
antonyms apathetic, indifferent.

veil *v.* cloak, conceal, cover, dim, disguise, dissemble, dissimulate, hide, mantle, mask, obscure, screen, shade, shadow, shield.
antonyms expose, uncover.
n. blind, cloak, cover, curtain, disguise, film, humeral, integument, mask, screen, shade, shroud, velum.

venal *adj.* bent, bribable, buyable, corrupt, corruptible, grafting, mercenary, purchasable, simoniacal.
antonym incorruptible.

venerable *adj.* aged, august, dignified, esteemed, grave, honored, respected, revered, reverenced, reverend, sage, sedate, venerated, wise, worshipful.

venerate *v.* adore, esteem, hallow, honor, respect, revere, reverence, worship.
antonyms anathematize, disregard, execrate.

vengeance *n.* avengement, lex talionis, reprisal, requital, retaliation, retribution, revanche, revenge, talion, tit for tat.
antonym forgiveness.

venom *n.* acrimony, bane, bitterness, gall, grudge, hate, hatred, ill-will, malevolence, malice, maliciousness, malignity, poison, rancor, spite, spitefulness, spleen, toxin, venin, vindictiveness, virulence, virus, vitrio.

vent *n.* aperture, blowhole, duct, hole, opening, orifice, outlet, passage, spiracle, split.
v. air, discharge, emit, express, let fly, release, unloose, utter, voice.

venture *v.* advance, adventure, chance, dare, endanger, hazard, imperil, jeopardize, make bold, presume, put forward, risk, speculate, stake, suggest, take the liberty, volunteer, wager.
n. adventure, chance, endeavor, enterprise, fling, gamble, hazard, operation, project, risk, speculation, undertaking.

verbal *adj.* lexical, oral, spoken, unwritten, verbatim, word-of-mouth.

verbatim *adv.* exactly, literally, precisely, to the letter, (verbatim et) literatim, word for word.

verbose *adj.* ambagious, circumlocutory, diffuse, garrulous, long-winded, loquacious, multiloquent, periphrastic, phrasy, pleonastic, prolix, windy, wordy.
antonyms economical, laconic, succinct.

verbosity *n.* garrulity, logorrhoea, long- windedness, loquaciousness, loquacity, multiloquy, prolixity, verbiage, verboseness, windiness, wordiness.
antonyms economy, succinctness.

verdict *n.* adjudication, assessment, conclusion, decision, finding, judgment, opinion, sentence.

verge *n.* border, boundary, brim, brink, edge, edging, extreme, limit, lip, margin, roadside, threshold.

verification *n.* attestation, authentication, checking, confirmation, corroboration, proof, substantiation, validation.

verify *v.* attest, authenticate, check, confirm, corroborate, prove, substantiate, support, testify, validate.
antonyms discredit, invalidate.

vernacular *adj.* colloquial, common, endemic, indigenous, informal, local, mother, native, popular, vulgar.
n. argot, cant, dialect, idiom, jargon, language, lingo, parlance, patois, speech, tongue.

versatile *adj.* adaptable, adjustable, all-round, flexible, functional, general-purpose, handy, many-sided, multifaceted, multipurpose, protean, Renaissance, resourceful, variable.
antonym inflexible.

versed *adj.* accomplished, acquainted, au fait, competent, conversant, experienced, familiar, knowledgeable, learned, practiced, proficient, qualified, seasoned, skilled.

version *n.* account, adaptation, design, form, interpretation, kind, model, paraphrase, portrayal, reading, rendering, rendition, style, translation, type, variant.

vertical *adj.* erect, on end, perpendicular, upright, upstanding.
antonym horizontal.

verve *n.* animation, brio, dash, élan, energy, enthusiasm, force, gusto, life, liveliness, pizzazz, punch, relish, sparkle, spirit, vigor, vim, vitality, vivacity, zeal, zip.
antonym apathy.

very *adv.* absolutely, acutely, awfully, decidedly, deeply, dogged, dooms, eminently, exceeding(ly), excessively, extremely, fell, gey, greatly, highly, jolly, noticeably, particularly, passing, rattling, really, remarkably, superlatively, surpassingly, terribly, truly, uncommonly, unusually, wonderfully.
antonyms hardly, scarcely, slightly.
adj. actual, appropriate, bare, exact, express, identical, mere, perfect, plain, precise, pure, real, same, selfsame, sheer, simple, unqualified, utter.

vessel *n.* barque, boat, canister, container, craft, holder, jar, pot, receptacle, ship, utensil.

vestige *n.* evidence, glimmer, hint, indication, print, relic, remainder, remains, remnant, residue, scrap, sign, suspicion, token, trace, track, whiff.

veto *v.* ban, blackball, disallow, forbid, interdict, kill, negative, prohibit, reject, rule out, turn down.
antonyms approve, sanction.
n. ban, embargo, interdict, prohibition, rejection, thumbs down.
antonyms approval, assent.

vex *v.* afflict, aggravate, agitate, annoy, bother, bug, chagrin, deave, displease, distress, disturb, exasperate, fret, gall, get (to), harass, hump, irritate, molest, needle, nettle, offend, peeve, perplex, pester, pique, plague, provoke, rile, spite, tease, torment, trouble, upset, worry.
antonym soothe.

vexation *n.* aggravation, anger, annoyance, bore, bother, chagrin, difficulty, displeasure, dissatisfaction, exasperation, frustration, fury, headache, irritant, misfortune, nuisance, pique, problem, trouble, upset, worry.

viable *adj.* achievable, applicable, feasible, operable, possible, practicable, usable, workable.
antonyms impossible, unworkable.

vibrate *v.* fluctuate, judder, oscillate, pendulate, pulsate, pulse, quiver, resonate, reverberate, shake, shimmy, shiver, shudder, sway, swing, throb, tremble, undulate.

vice *n.* bad habit, besetting sin, blemish, corruption, defect, degeneracy, depravity, evil, evil-doing, failing, fault, hamartia, immorality, imperfection, iniquity, profligacy, shortcoming, sin, venality, weakness, wickedness.
antonym virtue.

vicinity *n.* area, circumjacency, district, environs, locality, neighborhood, precincts, propinquity, proximity, purlieus, vicinage.

vicious *adj.* abhorrent, atrocious, backbiting, bad, barbarous, bitchy, brutal, catty, corrupt, cruel, dangerous, debased, defamatory, depraved, diabolical, fiendish, foul, heinous, immoral, infamous, malicious, mean, monstrous, nasty, perverted, profligate, rancorous, savage, sinful, slanderous, spiteful, unprincipled, venomous, vile, vindictive, violent, virulent, vitriolic, wicked, worthless, wrong.
antonyms gentle, good, virtuous.

victimize *v.* bully, cheat, deceive, defraud, discriminate against, dupe, exploit, fool, gull, hoodwink, oppress, persecute, pick on, prey on, swindle, use.

victor *n.* champ, champion, conqueror, first, prize- winner, subjugator, top dog, vanquisher, victor ludorum, victrix, winner.
antonyms loser, vanquished.

victory *n.* conquest, laurels, mastery, palm, prize, subjugation, success, superiority, triumph, vanquishment, win.
antonyms defeat, loss.

view *n.* aspect, attitude, belief, contemplation, conviction, display, estimation, examination, feeling, glimpse, impression, inspection, judgment, landscape, look,

notion, opinion, outlook, panorama, perception, perspective, picture, prospect, scan, scene, scrutiny, sentiment, sight, spectacle, survey, viewing, vision, vista.
v. behold, consider, contemplate, deem, examine, explore, eye, inspect, judge, observe, perceive, read, regard, scan, speculate, survey, watch, witness.

viewpoint *n.* angle, Anschauung, attitude, feeling, opinion, perspective, position, slant, stance, standpoint.

vigilant *adj.* alert, Argus-eyed, attentive, careful, cautious, circumspect, guarded, on one's guard, on one's toes, on the alert, on the lookout, on the qui vive, sleepless, unsleeping, wakeful, watchful, wide-awake.
antonyms careless, forgetful, lax, negligent.

vigor *n.* activity, animation, dash, dynamism, energy, force, forcefulness, gusto, health, liveliness, might, oomph, pep, potency, power, punch, robustness, snap, soundness, spirit, stamina, strength, verve, vim, virility, vitality, zip.
antonyms impotence, sluggishness, weakness.

vigorous *adj.* active, brisk, dynamic, effective, efficient, energetic, enterprising, flourishing, forceful, forcible, full-blooded, hale, hardy, healthy, hearty, intense, lively, lusty, mettlesome, powerful, red-blooded, robust, sound, spanking, spirited, stout, strenuous, strong, virile, vital, zippy.
antonyms feeble, lethargic, weak.

vile *adj.* abandoned, abject, appalling, bad, base, coarse, contemptible, corrupt, debased, degenerate, degrading, depraved, despicable, disgraceful, disgusting, earthly, evil, foul, horrid, humiliating, ignoble, impure, loathsome, low, mean, miserable, nasty, nauseating, nefarious, noxious, offensive, perverted, repellent, repugnant, repulsive, revolting, scabbed, scabby, scandalous, scurvy, shocking, sickening, sinful, ugly, vicious, vulgar, wicked, worthless, wretched.

vilify *v.* abuse, asperse, bad-mouth, berate, calumniate, criticize, debase, decry, defame, denigrate, denounce, disparage, malign, revile, slander, smear, stigmatize, traduce, vilipend, vituperate.
antonyms adore, compliment, eulogize, glorify.

village *n.* clachan, community, district, dorp, hamlet, kraal, pueblo, settlement, township.

villain *n.* anti-hero, baddy, blackguard, bravo, caitiff, criminal, devil, evil-doer, heavy, knave, libertine, malefactor, miscreant, profligate, rapscallion, rascal, reprobate, rogue, scoundrel, wretch.
antonyms angel, goody, hero, heroine.

villainous *adj.* atrocious, bad, base, blackguardly, criminal, cruel, debased, degenerate, depraved, detestable, diabolical, disgraceful, evil, fiendish, hateful, heinous, ignoble, infamous, inhuman, malevolent, mean, nefarious, opprobrious, outrageous, ruffianly, scoundrelly, sinful, terrible, thievish, vicious, vile, wicked.
antonyms angelic, good, heroic.

vindication *n.* apology, assertion, defence, exculpation, excuse, exoneration, extenuation, justification, maintenance, plea, rehabilitation, substantiation, support, verification.
antonyms accusation, conviction.

violate *v.* abuse, assault, befoul, break, contravene, debauch, defile, desecrate, dishonor, disobey, disregard, flout, infract, infringe, invade, outrage, pollute, profane, rape, ravish, transgress.
antonyms obey, observe, uphold.

violence *n.* abandon, acuteness, bestiality, bloodshed, bloodthirstiness, boisterousness, brutality, conflict, cruelty, destructiveness, ferocity, fervor, fierceness, fighting, force, frenzy, fury, harshness, hostilities, intensity, murderousness, passion, power, roughness, savagery, severity, sharpness, storminess, terrorism, thuggery, tumult, turbulence, vehemence, wildness.
antonyms passivity, peacefulness.

violent *adj.* acute, agonizing, berserk, biting, bloodthirsty, blustery, boisterous, brutal, cruel, destructive, devastating, excruciating, extreme, fiery, forceful, forcible, furious, harsh, headstrong, homicidal, hot-headed, impetuous, intemperate, intense, maddened, maniacal, murderous, outrageous, painful, passionate, peracute, powerful, raging, riotous, rough, ruinous, savage, severe, sharp, strong, tempestuous, tumultuous, turbulent, uncontrollable, ungovernable, unrestrained, vehement, vicious, wild.
antonyms calm, gentle, moderate, passive, peaceful.

virgin *n.* bachelor, celibate, damsel, girl, maid, maiden, spinster, vestal, virgo intacta.
adj. chaste, fresh, immaculate, intact, maidenly, modest, new, pristine, pure, snowy, spotless, stainless, uncorrupted, undefiled, unsullied, untouched, unused, vestal, virginal.

virile *adj.* forceful, husky, lusty, macho, male, man-like, manly, masculine, potent, red-blooded, robust, rugged, strong, vigorous.
antonyms effeminate, impotent, weak.

virtue *n.* advantage, asset, attribute, chastity, credit, excellence, goodness, high-mindedness, honor, incorruptibility, innocence, integrity, justice, merit, morality, plus, probity, purity, quality, rectitude, redeeming feature, righteousness, strength, uprightness, virginity, worth, worthiness.
antonym vice.

virtuous *adj.* blameless, celibate, chaste, clean- living, continent, ethical, excellent, exemplary, good, high-principled, honest, honorable, incorruptible, innocent, irreproachable, moral, praiseworthy, pure, righteous, spotless, unimpeachable, upright, virginal, worthy.
antonyms bad, dishonest, immoral, vicious, wicked.

virulent *adj.* acrimonious, baneful, bitter, deadly, envenomed, hostile, infective, injurious, lethal, malevolent, malicious, malignant, noxious, pernicious, poisonous, rancorous, resentful, septic, spiteful, splenetic, toxic, venomous, vicious, vindictive, vitriolic.

vision *n.* apparition, chimera, concept, conception,

construct, daydream, delusion, discernment, dream, eyes, eyesight, fantasy, far-sightedness, foresight, ghost, hallucination, idea, ideal, illusion, image, imagination, insight, intuition, mirage, penetration, perception, phantasm, phantasma, phantom, picture, prescience, revelation, seeing, sight, spectacle, specter, view, wraith.

visionary *adj.* chimerical, delusory, dreaming, dreamy, fanciful, fantastic, ideal, idealized, idealistic, illusory, imaginary, impractical, moonshiny, prophetic, quixotic, romantic, speculative, starry-eyed, unreal, unrealistic, unworkable, utopian.
n. daydreamer, Don Quixote, dreamer, enthusiast, fantasist, idealist, mystic, prophet, rainbow-chaser, romantic, seer, theorist, utopian, zealot.
antonym pragmatist.

visit *v.* afflict, assail, attack, befall, call in, call on, drop in on, haunt, inspect, look in, look up, pop in, punish, see, smite, stay at, stay with, stop by, take in, trouble.
n. call, excursion, sojourn, stay, stop.

visitor *n.* caller, company, guest, holidaymaker, tourist, visitant.

vista *n.* enfilade, panorama, perspective, prospect, view.

vital *adj.* alive, animate, animated, animating, basic, cardinal, critical, crucial, decisive, dynamic, energetic, essential, forceful, fundamental, generative, imperative, important, indispensable, invigorating, key, life-giving, life- or-death, live, lively, living, necessary, quickening, requisite, significant, spirited, urgent, vibrant, vigorous, vivacious, zestful.
antonyms inessential, peripheral, unimportant.

vitality *n.* animation, energy, exuberance, foison, go, life, liveliness, lustiness, oomph, pep, robustness, sparkle, stamina, strength, vigor, vim, vivaciousness, vivacity.

vitiate *v.* blemish, blight, contaminate, corrupt, debase, defile, deprave, deteriorate, devalue, harm, impair, injure, invalidate, mar, nullify, pervert, pollute, ruin, spoil, sully, taint, undermine.
antonym purify.

vituperation *n.* abuse, blame, castigation, censure, contumely, diatribe, fault-finding, flak, invective, objurgation, obloquy, phillipic, rebuke, reprimand, reproach, revilement, scurrility, stick, vilification.
antonyms acclaim, eulogy, praise.

vivacious *adj.* animated, bubbling, bubbly, cheerful, chipper, ebullient, effervescent, frisky, frolicsome, gay, high-spirited, jolly, light-hearted, lively, merry, scintillating, sparkling, spirited, sportive, sprightly, vital.
antonym languid.

vivid *adj.* active, animated, bright, brilliant, clear, colorful, distinct, dramatic, dynamic, eidetic, energetic, expressive, flamboyant, glowing, graphic, highly-colored, intense, lifelike, lively, memorable, powerful, quick, realistic, rich, sharp, spirited, stirring, striking, strong, telling, vibrant, vigorous.
antonyms dull, lifeless.

vocal *adj.* articulate, clamorous, eloquent, expressive, forthright, frank, free-spoken, noisy, oral, outspoken, plain-spoken, said, shrill, spoken, strident, uttered, vociferous, voiced.
antonyms inarticulate, quiet.

vocation *n.* bag, business, calling, career, employment, job, métier, mission, niche, office, post, profession, pursuit, role, trade, work.

void *adj.* bare, blank, canceled, clear, dead, drained, emptied, empty, free, inane, ineffective, ineffectual, inoperative, invalid, nugatory, null, tenantless, unenforceable, unfilled, unoccupied, useless, vacant, vain, worthless.
antonyms full, valid.
n. blank, blankness, cavity, chasm, emptiness, gap, hiatus, hollow, lack, opening, space, vacuity, vacuum, want.
v. abnegate, annul, cancel, defecate, discharge, drain, eject, elimate, emit, empty, evacuate, invalidate, nullify, rescind.
antonyms fill, validate.

volatile *adj.* airy, changeable, erratic, explosive, fickle, flighty, gay, giddy, hot-headed, hot-tempered, inconstant, lively, mercurial, sprightly, temperamental, unsettled, unstable, unsteady, variable, volcanic.
antonyms constant, steady.

volition *n.* choice, choosing, determination, discretion, election, option, preference, purpose, resolution, taste, velleity, will.

voluble *adj.* articulate, fluent, forthcoming, garrulous, glib, loquacious, talkative.

volume *n.* aggregate, amount, amplitude, bigness, body, book, bulk, capacity, compass, dimensions, fascic(u)le, heft, mass, part, publication, quantity, tome, total, treatise.

voluminous *adj.* abounding, ample, big, billowing, bulky, capacious, cavernous, commodious, copious, full, large, massive, prolific, roomy, vast.
antonyms scanty, slight.

voluntary *adj.* conscious, deliberate, discretional, free, gratuitous, honorary, intended, intentional, optional, purposeful, purposive, spontaneous, unconstrained, unforced, unpaid, volunteer, wilful, willing.
antonyms compulsory, forced, involuntary, unwilling.

voluptuous *adj.* ample, buxom, curvaceous, effeminate, enticing, epicurean, erotic, goluptious, hedonistic, licentious, luscious, luxurious, pleasure-loving, provocative, seductive, self-indulgent, sensual, shapely, sybaritic.
antonym ascetic.

voracious *adj.* acquisitive, avid, devouring, edacious, gluttonous, greedy, hungry, insatiable, omnivorous, pantophagous, prodigious, rapacious, ravening, ravenous, uncontrolled, unquenchable.

vouch for affirm, assert, asseverate, attest to, avouch, back, certify, confirm, endorse, guarantee, support, swear to, uphold.

vouchsafe *v.* accord, bestow, cede, confer, deign, grant, impart, yield.

vow *v.* affirm, avouch, bename, consecrate, dedicate, devote, maintain, pledge, profess, promise, swear.
n. avouchment, oath, pledge, promise, troth.

voyage *n.* crossing, cruise, expedition, journey, passage, peregrination, travels, trip.

vulgar *adj.* banausic, blue, boorish, cheap and nasty, coarse, common, crude, dirty, flashy, gaudy, general, gross, ill-bred, impolite, improper, indecent, indecorous, indelicate, low, low-life, low-lived, low-minded, low-thoughted, nasty, native, naughty, ordinary, pandemian, plebby, plebeian, ribald, risqué, rude, suggestive, tacky, tasteless, tawdry, uncouth, unmannerly, unrefined, vernacular.
antonyms correct, decent, elegant, noble, polite, refined.

vulnerable *adj.* accessible, assailable, defenseless, exposed, expugnable, pregnable, sensitive, susceptible, tender, thin-skinned, unprotected, weak, wide open.
antonyms protected, strong.

W

wacky *adj.* crazy, daft, eccentric, erratic, goofy, irrational, loony, loopy, nutty, odd, screwy, silly, unpredictable, wild, zany.
antonym sensible.
wad *n.* ball, block, bundle, chunk, hump, hunk, mass, pledget, plug, roll.
waffle *v.* blather, fudge, jabber, prate, prattle, prevaricate, rabbit on, spout, witter on.
n. blather, gobbledegook, guff, jabber, nonsense, padding, prating, prattle, prolixity, verbiage, verbosity, wordiness.
waft *v.* bear, carry, convey, drift, float, ride, transmit, transport, whiffle, winnow.
n. breath, breeze, current, draft, puff, scent, whiff.
wage *n.* allowance, compensation, earnings, emolument, fee, guerdon, hire, pay, payment, penny-fee, recompense, remuneration, reward, salary, screw, stipend, wage- packet, wages.
v. carry on, conduct, engage in, practice, prosecute, pursue, undertake.
wager *n.* bet, flutter, gage, gamble, hazard, pledge, punt, speculation, stake, venture.
v. bet, chance, gamble, hazard, lay, lay odds, pledge, punt, risk, speculate, stake, venture.
waggish *adj.* amusing, arch, bantering, comical, droll, espiègle, facetious, frolicsome, funny, humorous, impish, jesting, jocose, jocular, merry, mischievous, playful, puckish, risible, roguish, sportive, witty.
antonyms grave, serious, staid.
wagon *n.* buggy, carriage, cart, float, pushcart, train, truck, wain.
waif *n.* foundling, orphan, stray, wastrel.
wail *v.* bemoan, bewail, complain, cry, deplore, grieve, howl, keen, lament, mewl, moan, ululate, weep, yammer, yowl.
n. caterwaul, complaint, cry, grief, howl, keen, lament, lamentation, moan, ululation, weeping, yowl.
wait *v.* abide, dally, delay, hang fire, hesitate, hold back, hover, linger, loiter, mark time, pause, remain, rest, stay, tarry.
antonyms depart, go, leave.
n. delay, halt, hesitation, hiatus, hold-up, interval, pause, rest, stay.
waive *v.* abandon, defer, disclaim, forgo, postpone, relinquish, remit, renounce, resign, surrender.
antonyms claim, maintain.
wake[1] *v.* activate, animate, arise, arouse, awake, awaken, bestir, enliven, excite, fire, galvanize, get up, kindle, provoke, quicken, rise, rouse, stimulate, stir, unbed.
antonyms relax, sleep.
n. death-watch, funeral, pernoctation, vigil, watch.
wake[2] *n.* aftermath, backwash, path, rear, track, trail, train, wash, waves.
waken *v.* activate, animate, arouse, awake, awaken, enliven, fire, galvanize, get up, ignite, kindle, quicken, rouse, stimulate, stir, whet.
walk *v.* accompany, advance, amble, convoy, escort, go by Shanks's pony, hike, hoof it, march, move, pace, pedestrianize, perambulate, plod, promenade, saunter, step, stride, stroll, take, traipse, tramp, tread, trek, trog, trudge.
n. aisle, alley, ambulatory, avenue, carriage, constitutional, esplanade, footpath, frescade, gait, hike, lane, mall, march, pace, path, pathway, pavement, pawn, perambulation, promenade, ramble, saunter, sidewalk, step, stride, stroll, trail, traipse, tramp, trek, trudge, turn.
wall *n.* bailey, barricade, barrier, block, breastwork, bulkhead, bulwark, dike, divider, dyke, embankment, enclosure, fence, fortification, hedge, impediment, membrane, obstacle, obstruction, palisade, panel, parapet, partition, rampart, screen, septum, stockade.
wallow *v.* bask, delight, enjoy, flounder, glory, indulge, lie, lurch, luxuriate, relish, revel, roll, splash, stagger, stumble, tumble, wade, welter.
wan *adj.* anemic, ashen, bleak, bloodless, cadaverous, colorless, dim, discolored, faint, feeble, ghastly, livid, lurid, mournful, pale, pallid, pasty, sickly, waxen, weak, weary, whey-faced, white.
wander *v.* aberrate, babble, cruise, depart, deviate, digress, divagate, diverge, drift, err, hump the bluey, lapse, meander, mill around, peregrinate, ramble, range, rave, roam, rove, saunter, squander, straggle, stravaig, stray, stroll, swerve, traipse, veer, wilder.
n. cruise, excursion, meander, peregrination, ramble, saunter, stroll, traipse.
wane *v.* abate, atrophy, contract, decline, decrease, dim, diminish, droop, drop, dwindle, ebb, fade, fail, lessen, shrink, sink, subside, taper off, weaken, wither.
antonyms increase, wax.
n. abatement, atrophy, contraction, decay, decline, decrease, diminution, drop, dwindling, ebb, fading, failure, fall, lessening, sinking, subsidence, tapering off, weakening.
antonym increase.
want *v.* call for, covet, crave, demand, desiderate, desire, fancy, hanker after, hunger for, lack, long for, miss, need, pine for, require, thirst for, wish, yearn for, yen.
n. absence, appetite, besoin, craving, dearth, default, deficiency, demand, desideratum, desire, destitution,

famine, fancy, hankering, hunger, indigence, insufficiency, lack, longing, necessity, need, neediness, paucity, pauperism, penury, poverty, privation, requirement, scantiness, scarcity, shortage, thirst, wish, yearning, yen.
antonyms abundance, plenty, riches.

wanton *adj.* abandoned, arbitrary, careless, coltish, cruel, dissipated, dissolute, evil, extravagant, fast, gratuitous, groundless, heedless, immoderate, immoral, intemperate, lavish, lecherous, lewd, libertine, libidinous, licentious, loose, lubricious, lustful, malevolent, malicious, motiveless, needless, outrageous, promiscuous, rakish, rash, reckless, senseless, shameless, spiteful, uncalled-for, unchaste, unjustifiable, unjustified, unprovoked, unrestrained, vicious, wicked, wild, wilful.
n. baggage, Casanova, debauchee, Don Juan, floozy, harlot, hussy, lecher, libertine, loose woman, profligate, prostitute, rake, roué, slut, strumpet, tart, trollop, voluptuary, wench, whore.

war *n.* battle, bloodshed, combat, conflict, contention, contest, enmity, fighting, hostilities, hostility, jihad, strife, struggle, ultima ratio regum, warfare.
antonym peace.
v. battle, clash, combat, contend, contest, fight, skirmish, strive, struggle, take up arms, wage war.

ward *n.* apartment, area, care, charge, cubicle, custody, dependant, district, division, guardianship, keeping, minor, precinct, protection, protégé, pupil, quarter, room, safe- keeping, vigil, watch, zone.

warden *n.* administrator, captain, caretaker, castellan, châtelaine, concierge, curator, custodian, guardian, janitor, keeper, ranger, steward, superintendent, warder, watchman.

wardrobe *n.* apparel, attire, closet, clothes, cupboard, garderobe, outfit.

warehouse *n.* depository, depot, entrepot, freightshed, godown, hong, repository, stockroom, store, storehouse.

wares *n.* commodities, goods, lines, manufactures, merchandise, produce, products, stock, stuff, vendibles.

wariness *n.* alertness, apprehension, attention, caginess, care, carefulness, caution, circumspection, discretion, distrust, foresight, heedfulness, hesitancy, mindfulness, prudence, suspicion, unease, vigilance, watchfulness.
antonyms heedlessness, recklessness, thoughtlessness.

warlike *adj.* aggressive, antagonistic, bellicose, belligerent, bloodthirsty, combative, hawkish, hostile, inimical, jingoistic, martial, militaristic, military, pugnacious, saber- rattling, truculent, unfriendly.
antonym peaceable.

warm *adj.* affable, affectionate, amiable, amorous, animated, ardent, balmy, calid, cheerful, cordial, dangerous, disagreeable, earnest, effusive, emotional, enthusiastic, excited, fervent, friendly, genial, glowing, happy, hazardous, hearty, heated, hospitable, impassioned, incalescent, intense, irascible, irritable, keen, kindly, lively, loving, lukewarm, passionate, perilous, pleasant, quick, sensitive, short, spirited, stormy, sunny, tender, tepid, thermal, touchy, tricky, uncomfortable, unpleasant, vehement, vigorous, violent, zealous.
antonyms cool, indifferent, unfriendly.
v. animate, awaken, excite, heat, heat up, interest, melt, mull, put some life into, reheat, rouse, stimulate, stir, thaw, turn on.
antonym cool.

warm-hearted *adj.* affectionate, ardent, compassionate, cordial, generous, genial, kind-hearted, kindly, loving, sympathetic, tender, tender-hearted.
antonyms cold, unsympathetic.

warmth *n.* affability, affection, amorousness, animation, ardor, calidity, cheerfulness, cordiality, eagerness, earnestness, effusiveness, empressement, enthusiasm, excitement, fervency, fervor, fire, happiness, heartiness, heat, hospitableness, hotness, intensity, kindliness, love, passion, spirit, tenderness, transport, vehemence, vigor, violence, warmness, zeal, zest.
antonyms coldness, coolness, unfriendliness.

warn *v.* admonish, advise, alert, apprize, caution, counsel, forewarn, inform, notify, put on one's guard, tip off.

warning *n.* admonishment, admonition, advance notice, advice, alarm, alert, augury, caution, caveat, forenotice, foretoken, forewarning, griffin, hint, larum, larumbell, lesson, monition, notice, notification, omen, premonition, presage, prodrome, sign, signal, siren, threat, tip, tip-off, token, vigia, word, word to the wise.
adj. admonitory, aposematic, cautionary, in terrorem, monitive, monitory, ominous, premonitory, prodromal, prodromic, threatening.

warp *v.* bend, contort, deform, deviate, distort, kink, misshape, pervert, twist.
antonym straighten.
n. bend, bent, bias, contortion, deformation, deviation, distortion, irregularity, kink, perversion, quirk, turn, twist.

warranty *n.* assurance, authorization, bond, certificate, contract, covenant, guarantee, justification, pledge.

warrior *n.* champion, combatant, fighter, fighting man, knight, man-at-arms, soldier, wardog, war-horse.

wary *adj.* alert, apprehensive, attentive, cagey, careful, cautious, chary, circumspect, distrustful, guarded, hawk-eyed, heedful, leery, on one's guard, on the lookout, on the qui vive, prudent, suspicious, vigilant, watchful, wide- awake.
antonyms careless, foolhardy, heedless, reckless, unwary.

wash[1] *v.* bath, bathe, clean, cleanse, launder, moisten, rinse, scrub, shampoo, shower, sluice, swill, wet.
n. a lick and a promise, ablution, bath, bathe, cleaning, cleansing, coat, coating, ebb and flow, film, flow, laundering, layer, overlay, rinse, roll, screen, scrub, shampoo, shower, souse, stain, suffusion, surge, sweep, swell, washing, wave.

wash[2] *v.* bear examination, bear scrutiny, carry weight, hold up, hold water, pass muster, stand up, stick.

washed-out *adj.* all in, blanched, bleached, colorless, dead on one's feet, dog-tired, drained, drawn, etiolated, exhausted, faded, fatigued, flat, haggard, knackered, lackluster, mat, pale, pallid, peelie-wally, spent, tired-out, wan, weary, worn-out.

waspish *adj.* bad-tempered, bitchy, cantankerous, captious, crabbed, crabby, cross, crotchety, fretful, grouchy, grumpy, ill-tempered, irascible, irritable, peevish, peppery, pettish, petulant, prickly, snappish, splenetic, testy, touchy, waxy.

waste *v.* atrophy, blow, consume, corrode, crumble, debilitate, decay, decline, deplete, despoil, destroy, devastate, disable, dissipate, drain, dwindle, eat away, ebb, emaciate, enfeeble, exhaust, fade, fritter away, gnaw, lavish, lay waste, misspend, misuse, perish, pillage, prodigalize, rape, ravage, raze, rig, ruin, sack, sink, spend, spoil, squander, tabefy, throw away, undermine, wane, wanton, wear out, wither.
n. debris, desert, desolation, destruction, devastation, dissipation, dregs, dross, effluent, expenditure, extravagance, garbage, havoc, leavings, leftovers, litter, loss, misapplication, misuse, mullock, offal, offscouring(s), prodigality, ravage, recrement, refuse, rubbish, ruin, scrap, slops, solitude, spoilage, squandering, sweepings, trash, void, wastefulness, wasteland, wild, wilderness.
adj. bare, barren, desolate, devastated, dismal, dreary, empty, extra, left-over, superfluous, supernumerary, uncultivated, uninhabited, unproductive, unprofitable, unused, unwanted, useless, wild, worthless.

wasteful *adj.* dissipative, extravagant, improvident, lavish, prodigal, profligate, ruinous, spendthrift, thriftless, uneconomical, unthrifty.
antonyms economical, frugal, thrifty.

watch[1] *v.* attend, contemplate, eye, gaze at, guard, keep, keep an eye open, look, look after, look at, look on, look out, mark, mind, note, observe, ogle, pay attention, peer at, protect, regard, see, spectate, stare at, superintend, take care of, take heed, tend, view, wait.
n. alertness, attention, eye, heed, inspection, lookout, notice, observation, pernoctation, supervision, surveillance, vigil, vigilance, wake, watchfulness.

watch[2] *n.* chronometer, clock, ticker, tick-tick, tick-tock, timepiece, wristwatch.

watch-dog *n.* custodian, guard dog, guardian, house- dog, inspector, monitor, ombudsman, protector, scrutineer, vigilante.

watchful *adj.* alert, attentive, cautious, circumspect, guarded, heedful, observant, on one's guard, on the lookout, on the qui vive, on the watch, suspicious, unmistaking, vigilant, wary, wide awake.
antonym inattentive.

water *n.* Adam's ale, Adam's wine, aqua, lake, ocean, rain, river, saliva, sea, stream, sweat, tears, urine.
v. adulterate, damp, dampen, dilute, douse, drench, drink, flood, hose, irrigate, moisten, soak, souse, spray, sprinkle, thin, water down, weaken.
antonyms dry out, purify, strengthen.

waterfall *n.* cascade, cataract, chute, fall, force, lash, lin(n), torrent.

watery *adj.* adulterated, aqueous, damp, dilute, diluted, flavorless, fluid, humid, hydatoid, insipid, liquid, marshy, moist, poor, rheumy, runny, soggy, squelchy, tasteless, tear-filled, tearful, thin, washy, watered-down, waterish, weak, weepy, wet, wishy-washy.
antonyms solid, strong.

wave[1] *v.* beckon, brandish, direct, flap, flourish, flutter, gesticulate, gesture, indicate, oscillate, quiver, ripple, shake, sign, signal, stir, sway, swing, undulate, waft, wag, waver, weave, wield.

wave[2] *n.* billow, breaker, comber, current, drift, flood, ground swell, movement, outbreak, rash, ripple, roller, rush, stream, surge, sweep, swell, tendency, tidal wave, trend, tsunami, undulation, unevenness, upsurge, water-wave, wavelet, white horse.

waver *v.* blow hot and cold, dither, falter, flicker, fluctuate, haver, hesitate, hum and haw, quiver, reel, rock, seesaw, shake, shilly-shally, sway, swither, totter, tremble, undulate, vacillate, vary, waffle, wave, weave, wobble.
antonyms decide, stand.

wavering *adj.* dithering, dithery, doubtful, doubting, havering, hesitant, in two minds, shilly-shallying.
antonym determined.

wavy *adj.* curly, curvy, flamboyant, ridged, ridgy, rippled, ripply, sinuate(d), sinuous, undate, undulate, undulated, winding, wrinkled, zigzag.
antonyms flat, smooth.

wax *v.* become, develop, dilate, enlarge, expand, fill out, grow, increase, magnify, mount, rise, swell.
antonym wane.

way *n.* access, advance, aim, ambition, approach, aspect, avenue, channel, characteristic, choice, circumstance, condition, conduct, course, custom, demand, desire, detail, direction, distance, elbow-room, fashion, feature, fettle, gate, goal, habit, headway, highway, idiosyncrasy, journey, lane, length, manner, march, means, method, mode, movement, nature, opening, particular, passage, path, pathway, personality, plan, pleasure, point, practice, procedure, process, progress, respect, road, room, route, scheme, sense, shape, situation, space, state, status, street, stretch, style, system, technique, thoroughfare, track, trail, trait, usage, will, wish, wont.

waylay *v.* accost, ambush, attack, buttonhole, catch, hold up, intercept, lie in wait for, seize, set upon, surprise.

way-out *adj.* advanced, amazing, avant-garde, bizarre, crazy, eccentric, excellent, experimental, fantastic, far-out, freaky, great, marvelous, off-beat, outlandish,

progressive, satisfying, tremendous, unconventional, unorthodox, unusual, weird, wild, wonderful.
antonym ordinary.

wayward *adj.* capricious, changeable, contrary, contumacious, cross-grained, disobedient, erratic, fickle, flighty, froward, headstrong, inconstant, incorrigible, insubordinate, intractable, mulish, obdurate, obstinate, perverse, rebellious, refractory, self-willed, stubborn, undependable, ungovernable, unmanageable, unpredictable, unruly, uppity, wilful.
antonyms complaisant, good-natured.

weak *adj.* anemic, asthenic, atonic, cowardly, debile, debilitated, decrepit, defenseless, deficient, delicate, diluted, disturbant, dull, effete, enervated, exhausted, exposed, faint, faulty, feeble, fiberless, flimsy, fragile, frail, helpless, hollow, imperceptible, impotent, inadequate, inconclusive, indecisive, ineffective, ineffectual, infirm, insipid, invalid, irresolute, lacking, lame, languid, low, milk- and-water, muffled, namby-pamby, pathetic, poor, powerless, puny, quiet, runny, shaky, shallow, sickly, slight, small, soft, spent, spineless, substandard, tasteless, tender, thin, timorous, toothless, unconvincing, under-strength, unguarded, unprotected, unresisting, unsafe, unsatisfactory, unsound, unsteady, unstressed, untenable, vulnerable, wanting, wasted, watery, weak- hearted, weak-kneed, weakly, weak-minded, weak-spirited, wishy- washy.
antonym strong.

weaken *v.* abate, adulterate, craze, cut, debase, debilitate, depress, dilute, diminish, disinvigorate, droop, dwindle, ease up, effeminate, effeminize, emasculate, enervate, enfeeble, fade, fail, flag, give way, impair, invalidate, lessen, lower, mitigate, moderate, reduce, sap, soften up, temper, thin, tire, undermine, wane, water down.
antonym strengthen.

weakling *n.* coward, doormat, drip, milksop, mouse, namby-pamby, puff, pushover, sissy, softling, underdog, underling, wally, weed, wet, wimp, wraith.
antonyms hero, stalwart.

weakness *n.* Achilles' heel, asthenia, atonicity, atony, blemish, debility, decrepitude, defect, deficiency, enervation, enfeeblement, faible, failing, faintness, fault, feebleness, flaw, foible, fondness, fragility, frailty, imperfection, impotence, inclination, infirmity, irresolution, lack, liking, passion, penchant, powerlessness, predilection, proclivity, proneness, shortcoming, soft spot, soft underbelly, underbelly, vulnerability, weakpoint, weediness.
antonyms dislike, strength.

wealth *n.* abundance, affluence, assets, bounty, capital, cash, copiousness, cornucopia, estate, fortune, fullness, funds, golden calf, goods, klondike, lucre, mammon, means, money, opulence, pelf, plenitude, plenty, possessions, profusion, property, prosperity, resources, riches, richness, store, substance.
antonym poverty.

wealthy *adj.* affluent, comfortable, easy, filthy rich, flush, living in clover, loaded, moneyed, opulent, prosperous, rich, rolling in it, well-heeled, well-off, well-to- do.
antonym poor.

wear *v.* abrade, accept, allow, annoy, bear, bear up, believe, brook, carry, consume, corrode, countenance, deteriorate, display, don, drain, dress in, endure, enervate, erode, exasperate, exhibit, fall for, fatigue, fly, fray, grind, harass, have on, hold up, irk, last, permit, pester, put on, put up with, rub, show, sport, stand for, stand up, stomach, swallow, take, tax, tolerate, undermine, use, vex, waste, weaken, weary.
n. abrasion, apparel, attire, attrition, clothes, corrosion, costume, damage, depreciation, deterioration, dress, durability, employment, erosion, friction, garb, garments, gear, habit, mileage, outfit, service, things, use, usefulness, utility, wear and tear.

weariness *n.* drowsiness, enervation, ennui, exhaustion, fatigue, languor, lassitude, lethargy, listlessness, prostration, sleepiness, tiredness.
antonym freshness.

wearisome *adj.* annoying, boring, bothersome, burdensome, dreary, dull, ennuying, exasperating, exhausting, fatiguing, humdrum, irksome, monotonous, oppressive, pestilential, prolix, prosaic, protracted, tedious, troublesome, trying, vexatious, weariful, wearing.
antonym refreshing.

weary *adj.* all in, arduous, awearied, aweary, beat, bored, browned-off, dead beat, dead on one's feet, discontented, dog-tired, drained, drooping, drowsy, enervated, enervative, ennuied, ennuyé, exhausted, fagged, fatigued, fed up, flagging, impatient, indifferent, irksome, jaded, knackered, laborious, sick, sick and tired, sleepy, spent, taxing, tired, tiresome, tiring, wayworn, wearied, wearing, wearisome, whacked, worn out.
antonyms excited, fresh, lively.
v. annoy, betoil, bore, bug, burden, debilitate, drain, droop, enervate, ennui, exasperate, fade, fag, fail, fatigue, irk, irritate, jade, plague, sap, sicken, tax, tire, tire out, wear out.

weather *n.* climate, conditions, rainfall, temperature.
v. brave, come through, endure, expose, harden, live through, overcome, pull through, resist, ride out, rise above, season, stand, stick out, suffer, surmount, survive, toughen, weather out, withstand.
antonym succumb.

weave *v.* blend, braid, build, construct, contrive, create, criss-cross, entwine, fabricate, fuse, incorporate, intercross, interdigitate, interlace, intermingle, intertwine, introduce, knit, make, mat, merge, plait, put together, spin, twist, unite, wind, zigzag.

web *n.* interlacing, lattice, mesh, mesh-work, net, netting, network, palama, screen, snare, tangle, tela, texture, toils, trap, weave, webbing, weft.

wed *v.* ally, blend, coalesce, combine, commingle, dedicate, espouse, fuse, get hitched, interweave, join, jump the broomstick, link, marry, merge, splice, tie the knot, unify, unite, wive, yoke.
antonym divorce.

wedlock *n.* holy matrimony, marriage, matrimony, union.

wee *adj.* diminutive, insignificant, itsy-bitsy, Lilliputian, little, microscopic, midget, miniature, minuscule, minute, negligible, small, teeny, teeny-weeny, tiny, weeny.
antonym large.

weep *v.* bemoan, bewail, blub, blubber, boo-hoo, bubble, complain, cry, drip, exude, greet, keen, lament, leak, moan, mourn, ooze, pipe, pipe one's eye, pour forth, pour out, rain, snivel, sob, tune one's pipes, ululate, whimper, whinge.
antonym rejoice.
n. blub, bubble, cry, greet, lament, moan, snivel, sob.

weigh *v.* bear down, burden, carry weight, consider, contemplate, count, deliberate, evaluate, examine, give thought to, impress, matter, meditate on, mull over, oppress, ponder, ponderate, prey, reflect on, study, tell, think over.
antonyms cut no ice, hearten.

weight *n.* authority, avoirdupois, ballast, burden, clout, consequence, consideration, efficacy, emphasis, force, gravity, heaviness, heft, impact, import, importance, impressiveness, influence, load, mass, millstone, moment, onus, oppression, persuasiveness, ponderance, ponderancy, poundage, power, preponderance, pressure, significance, strain, substance, tonnage, value.
antonym lightness.
v. ballast, bias, burden, charge, encumber, freight, handicap, hold down, impede, keep down, load, oppress, overburden, slant, unbalance, weigh down.
antonym lighten.

weird *adj.* bizarre, creepy, eerie, eldritch, freakish, ghostly, grotesque, mysterious, odd, outlandish, preternatural, queer, spooky, strange, superlunar, supernatural, uncanny, unco, unearthly, unnatural, witching.
antonym normal.

welcome *adj.* able, acceptable, accepted, agreeable, allowed, appreciated, delightful, desirable, entitled, free, gratifying, permitted, pleasant, pleasing, refreshing.
antonym unwelcome.
n. acceptance, greeting, hospitality, reception, red carpet, salaam, salutation.
v. accept, approve of, embrace, greet, hail, meet, receive, roll out the red carpet for.
antonyms reject, snub.

weld *v.* bind, bond, cement, connect, fuse, join, link, seal, solder, unite.
antonym separate.
n. bond, joint, seal, seam.

welfare *n.* advantage, benefit, good, happiness, heal, health, interest, profit, prosperity, success, weal, well-being.
antonym harm.

well[1] *n.* bore, cavity, fount, fountain, hole, lift-shaft, mine, pit, pool, repository, shaft, source, spring, waterhole, well-spring.
v. brim over, flood, flow, gush, jet, ooze, pour, rise, run, seep, spout, spring, spurt, stream, surge, swell, trickle.

well[2] *adv.* ably, abundantly, accurately, adeptly, adequately, admirably, agreeably, amply, approvingly, attentively, capitally, carefully, clearly, closely, comfortably, completely, conscientiously, considerably, correctly, deeply, easily, effectively, efficiently, expertly, fairly, famously, favorably, fittingly, flourishingly, fully, glowingly, graciously, greatly, happily, heartily, highly, intimately, justly, kindly, nicely, personally, pleasantly, possibly, proficiently, profoundly, properly, prosperously, readily, rightly, satisfactorily, skilfully, smoothly, splendidly, substantially, successfully, sufficiently, suitably, thoroughly, warmly.
antonym badly.
adj. A1, able-bodied, advisable, agreeable, bright, fine, fit, fitting, flourishing, fortunate, good, great, hale, happy, healthy, hearty, in fine fettle, in good health, lucky, on the top of the world, pleasing, profitable, proper, prudent, right, robust, satisfactory, sound, strong, thriving, up to par, useful.
antonyms bad, ill.

well-being *n.* comfort, contentment, good, happiness, prosperity, weal, welfare.
antonyms discomfort, harm.

well-bred *adj.* aristocratic, blue-blooded, civil, courteous, courtly, cultivated, cultured, gallant, genteel, gentle, gentlemanly, highborn, ladylike, mannerly, noble, patrician, polished, polite, refined, titled, upper-crust, urbane, well-born, well-brought-up, well-mannered.
antonym ill-bred.

well-known *adj.* celebrated, famed, familiar, famous, illustrious, notable, noted, popular, renowned.
antonym unknown.

well-off *adj.* affluent, comfortable, flourishing, flush, fortunate, in the money, loaded, lucky, moneyed, prosperous, rich, successful, thriving, warm, wealthy, well-heeled, well-to-do.
antonym poor.

well-thought-of *adj.* admired, esteemed, highly regarded, honored, reputable, respected, revered, venerated, weighty.
antonym despised.

well-to-do *adj.* affluent, comfortable, flush, loaded, moneyed, prosperous, rich, warm, wealthy, well-heeled, well-off.
antonym poor.

welsh *v.* cheat, defraud, diddle, do, swindle, welch.

wet *adj.* boggy, clammy, damp, dank, drenched, dripping, drizzling, effete, feeble, foolish, humid, ineffectual, irresolute, misty, moist, moistened, namby-pamby, pouring, raining, rainy, saturated, showery, silly, sloppy, soaked, soaking, sodden, soft, soggy, sopping, soppy, soused, spineless, spongy, teeming, timorous, waterlogged, watery, weak, weedy.
antonyms dry, resolute, strong.
n. clamminess, condensation, damp, dampness, drip, drizzle, humidity, liquid, milksop, moisture, rain, rains, sap, water, weakling, weed, wetness, wimp.
antonyms dryness.
v. bedabble, bedew, bedrench, damp, dampen, dip, douse, drench, humidify, imbue, irrigate, moisten, saturate, sluice, soak, splash, spray, sprinkle, steep, water.
antonym dry.

wharf *n.* dock, dockyard, jetty, landing-stage, marina, pier, quay, quayside.

wheedle *v.* cajole, charm, coax, court, draw, entice, flatter, importune, inveigle, persuade, whilly, whillywha(w).
antonym force.

whereabouts *n.* location, place, position, site, situation, vicinity.

wherewithal *n.* capital, cash, funds, means, money, necessary, readies, resources, supplies.

whim *n.* caprice, chimera, conceit, concetto, crank, craze, crotchet, fad, fancy, fizgig, flam, freak, humor, impulse, maggot, notion, quirk, sport, urge, vagary, whims(e)y.

whimper *v.* blub, blubber, cry, girn, grizzle, mewl, moan, pule, snivel, sob, weep, whine, whinge.
n. girn, moan, snivel, sob, whine.

whimsical *adj.* capricious, chimeric(al), crotchety, curious, dotty, droll, eccentric, fanciful, fantastic(al), freakish, funny, maggoty, mischievous, odd, peculiar, playful, quaint, queer, singular, unusual, waggish, weird, whimmy.
antonym sensible.

whine *n.* beef, belly-ache, complaint, cry, girn, gripe, grouch, grouse, grumble, moan, sob, wail, whimper.
v. beef, belly-ache, carp, complain, cry, girn, gripe, grizzle, grouch, grouse, grumble, kvetch, moan, sob, wail, whimper, whinge.

whip *v.* agitate, beat, best, birch, cane, castigate, clobber, compel, conquer, dart, dash, defeat, dive, drive, drub, flagellate, flash, flit, flog, flounce, fly, foment, goad, hammer, hound, incite, instigate, jambok, jerk, knout, lash, leather, lick, outdo, overcome, overpower, overwhelm, paddle, prick, prod, produce, provoke, pull, punish, push, quirt, remove, rout, rush, scourge, shoot, sjambok, snatch, spank, spur, stir, strap, switch, tan, tear, thrash, trounce, urge, whale, whisk, whop, worst.
n. birch, bullwhip, cane, cat, cat-o'-nine-tails, crop, flagellum, horsewhip, jambok, knout, lash, paddle, quirt, rawhide, riding-crop, scourge, sjambok, switch, thong.

whirl *v.* birl, circle, gyrate, gyre, pirouette, pivot, reel, revolve, roll, rotate, spin, swirl, swivel, turn, twirl, twist, wheel.
n. agitation, birl, bustle, circle, commotion, confusion, daze, dither, flurry, giddiness, gyration, gyre, hubbub, hubbuboo, hurly-burly, merry-go-round, pirouette, reel, revolution, roll, rotation, round, series, spin, stir, succession, swirl, tumult, turn, twirl, twist, uproar, vortex, wheel, whorl.
antonym calm.

whisk *v.* beat, brush, dart, dash, flick, fly, grab, hasten, hurry, race, rush, scoot, shoot, speed, sweep, swipe, tear, twitch, whip, wipe.
n. beater, brush, swizzle-stick.

whisk(e)y *n.* barley-bree, bourbon, Canadian, corn, John Barleycorn, Irish, malt, mountain dew, peat-reek, rye, Scotch, usquebaugh.

whisper *v.* breathe, buzz, divulge, gossip, hint, hiss, insinuate, intimate, murmur, rustle, sigh, sough, susurrate, tittle.
antonym shout.
n. breath, buzz, gossip, hint, hiss, innuendo, insinuation, murmur, report, rumor, rustle, shadow, sigh, sighing, soughing, soupçon, suggestion, suspicion, susurration, susurrus, swish, tinge, trace, underbreath, undertone, whiff, word.
antonym roar.

whistle *n.* call, cheep, chirp, hooter, siren, song, warble.
v. call, cheep, chirp, pipe, siffle, sing, warble, wheeze, whiss.

whole *adj.* better, complete, cured, entire, faultless, fit, flawless, full, good, hale, healed, healthy, in one piece, intact, integral, integrate, inviolate, mint, perfect, recovered, robust, sound, strong, total, unabbreviated, unabridged, unbroken, uncut, undamaged, undivided, unedited, unexpurgated, unharmed, unhurt, unimpaired, uninjured, unmutilated, unscathed, untouched, well.
antonyms damaged, ill, partial.
n. aggregate, all, ensemble, entirety, entity, everything, fullness, Gestalt, lot, piece, total, totality, unit, unity.
antonym part.

wholesome *adj.* advantageous, beneficial, clean, decent, edifying, exemplary, good, healthful, health-giving, healthy, helpful, honorable, hygienic, improving, innocent, invigorating, moral, nice, nourishing, nutritious, propitious, pure, respectable, righteous, salubrious, salutary, sanitary, uplifting, virtuous, worthy.
antonym unwholesome.

wholly *adv.* absolutely, all, altogether, completely, comprehensively, entirely, exclusively, fully, in toto, only, perfectly, solely, thoroughly, through and through, totally, utterly.
antonym partly.

wicked *adj.* abandoned, abominable, acute, agonizing, amoral, arch, atrocious, awful, bad, black-hearted,

bothersome, corrupt, debased, depraved, destructive, devilish, difficult, dissolute, distressing, dreadful, egregious, evil, facinorous, fearful, fiendish, fierce, flagitious, foul, galling, guilty, harmful, heinous, immoral, impious, impish, incorrigible, inexpiable, iniquitous, injurious, intense, irreligious, mighty, mischievous, nasty, naughty, nefarious, nefast, offensive, painful, piacular, rascal-like, rascally, roguish, scandalous, severe, shameful, sinful, spiteful, terrible, troublesome, trying, ungodly, unpleasant, unprincipled, unrighteous, vicious, vile, villainous, worthless.
antonyms good, harmless, modest, upright.

wide *adj.* ample, away, baggy, broad, capacious, catholic, commodious, comprehensive, diffuse, dilated, distant, distended, encyclopedic, expanded, expansive, extensive, far- reaching, full, general, immense, inclusive, large, latitudinous, loose, off, off-course, off-target, outspread, outstretched, remote, roomy, spacious, sweeping, vast.
antonyms limited, narrow.
adv. aside, astray, off course, off target, off the mark, out.
antonym on target.

wide-awake *adj.* alert, astute, aware, conscious, fully awake, heedful, keen, observant, on one's toes, on the alert, on the ball, on the qui vive, quick-witted, roused, sharp, vigilant, wakened, wary, watchful.
antonym asleep.

width *n.* amplitude, beam, breadth, compass, diameter, extent, girth, measure, range, reach, scope, span, thickness, wideness.

wield *v.* apply, brandish, command, control, employ, exercise, exert, flourish, handle, have, hold, maintain, manage, manipulate, ply, possess, swing, use, utilize, wave, weave.

wild *adj.* agrest(i)al, brabaric, barbarous, berserk, blustery, boisterous, brutish, chaotic, chimeric(al), choppy, crazed, crazy, daft, delirious, demented, desert, deserted, desolate, disheveled, disordered, disorderly, eager, empty, enthusiastic, excited, extravagant, fantastic, ferae naturae, feral, feralized, ferine, ferocious, fierce, flighty, foolhardy, foolish, frantic, free, frenzied, furious, giddy, god- forsaken, howling, hysterical, ill-considered, impetuous, impracticable, imprudent, inaccurate, indigenous, intense, irrational, lawless, mad, madcap, maniacal, native, natural, noisy, nuts, outrageous, potty, preposterous, primitive, rabid, raging, rash, raving, reckless, riotous, rough, rowdy, rude, savage, self-willed, tempestuous, tousled, trackless, turbulent, unbridled, unbroken, uncheated, uncivilized, uncontrollable, uncontrolled, uncultivated, undisciplined, undomesticated, unfettered, ungovernable, uninhabited, unjustified, unkempt, unmanageable, unpopulated, unpruned, unrestrained, unruly, unsubstantiated, untamed, untidy, uproarious, violent, virgin, wayward, woolly.
antonyms civilized, peaceful, sane, sensible, tame, unenthusiastic.

wilderness *n.* clutter, confusion, congeries, desert, jumble, jungle, mass, maze, muddle, tangle, waste, wasteland, welter, wild, wild-land.

wile *n.* artfulness, artifice, cheating, chicanery, contrivance, craft, craftiness, cunning, deceit, device, dodge, expedient, fraud, guile, hanky-panky, imposition, lure, maneuver, ploy, ruse, slyness, stratagem, subterfuge, trick, trickery.
antonym guilelessness.

wilful *adj.* adamant, bloody-minded, bull-headed, conscious, deliberate, determined, dogged, froward, headstrong, inflexible, intended, intentional, intractable, intransigent, mulish, obdurate, obstinate, persistent, perverse, pig-headed, purposeful, refractory, self-willed, stubborn, thrawn, uncompromising, unyielding, volitional, voluntary.
antonyms complaisant, good-natured.

will *n.* aim, attitude, choice, command, decision, declaration, decree, desire, determination, discretion, disposition, fancy, feeling, inclination, intention, mind, option, pleasure, preference, prerogative, purpose, resolution, resolve, testament, velleity, volition, will power, wish, wishes.
v. bequeath, bid, cause, choose, command, confer, decree, desire, determine, devise, direct, dispose of, elect, give, leave, opt, ordain, order, pass on, resolve, transfer, want, wish.

willing *adj.* agreeable, amenable, biddable, compliant, consenting, content, desirous, disposed, eager, enthusiastic, favorable, game, happy, inclined, nothing lo(a)th, pleased, prepared, ready, so-minded, volitient, willing-hearted.
antonym unwilling.

wilt *v.* atrophy, diminish, droop, dwindle, ebb, fade, fail, flag, flop, languish, melt away, sag, shrivel, sink, wane, weaken, wither.
antonym perk up.

wily *adj.* arch, artful, astute, cagey, crafty, crooked, cunning, deceitful, deceptive, designing, fly, foxy, guileful, intriguing, long-headed, Machiavellian, scheming, sharp, shifty, shrewd, sly, tricky, underhand, versute, wileful.
antonym guileless.

win *v.* accomplish, achieve, acquire, attain, bag, capture, catch, collect, come away with, conquer, earn, gain, get, net, obtain, overcome, pick up, prevail, procure, receive, secure, succeed, sweep the board, triumph.
antonym lose.
n. conquest, mastery, success, triumph, victory.
antonym defeat.

wind[1] *n.* air, air-current, babble, blast, blather, bluster, boasting, breath, breeze, clue, current, cyclone, draft, flatulence, flatus, gab, gale, gas, gust, hint, hot air, humbug, hurricane, idle talk, inkling, intimation, north-easter, notice, puff, report, respiration, rumor, sirocco, southwester, suggestion, talk, tidings, tornado, twister, typhoon, warning, whisper, williwaw, windiness, zephyr.

wind[2] *v.* bend, coil, curl, curve, deviate, encircle, furl, loop, meander, ramble, reel, roll, serpent, serpentine, serpentinize, snake, spiral, turn, twine, twist, wreath, zigzag.
n. bend, curve, meander, turn, twist, zigzag.

windfall *n.* bonanza, find, godsend, jackpot, manna, pennies from heaven, stroke of luck, treasure-trove.

windy *adj.* afraid, blowy, blustering, blustery, boastful, boisterous, bombastic, breezy, changeable, chicken, conceited, cowardly, diffuse, empty, fearful, flatulent, flatuous, frightened, garrulous, gusty, long-winded, loquacious, meandering, nervous, pompous, prolix, rambling, scared, squally, stormy, tempestuous, thrasonic, timid, turgid, ventose, verbose, wild, windswept, wordy.
antonyms calm, fearless, modest.

wing *n.* adjunct, annexe, arm, branch, circle, clique, coterie, extension, faction, fender, flank, group, grouping, pinion, protection, section, segment, set, side.
v. clip, fleet, flit, fly, glide, hasten, hit, hurry, move, nick, pass, race, soar, speed, travel, wound, zoom.

wink *v.* bat, blink, flash, flicker, flutter, gleam, glimmer, glint, nictate, nictitate, pink, sparkle, twinkle.
n. blink, flash, flutter, gleam, glimmering, glint, hint, instant, jiffy, moment, nictation, nictitation, second, sparkle, split second, twinkle, twinkling.

winnow *v.* comb, cull, diffuse, divide, fan, part, screen, select, separate, sift, waft.

winsome *adj.* agreeable, alluring, amiable, attractive, bewitching, captivating, charming, cheerful, comely, delectable, disarming, enchanting, endearing, engaging, fair, fascinating, fetching, graceful, pleasant, pleasing, prepossessing, pretty, sweet, taking, winning.
antonym unattractive.

wire-pulling *n.* clout, conspiring, influence, intrigue, Machiavellianism, manipulation, plotting, pull, scheming.

wisdom *n.* anthroposophy, astuteness, circumspection, comprehension, discernment, enlightenment, erudition, foresight, gnosis, intelligence, judgment, judiciousness, knowledge, learning, penetration, prudence, reason, sagacity, sapience, sense, sophia, understanding.
antonym folly.

wise *adj.* aware, clever, discerning, enlightened, erudite, informed, intelligent, judicious, knowing, long-headed, long-sighted, perceptive, politic, prudent, rational, reasonable, sagacious, sage, sapient, sensible, shrewd, sound, understanding, well-advised, well-informed.
antonym foolish.

wish *v.* ask, aspire, bid, command, covet, crave, desiderate, desire, direct, greet, hanker, hope, hunger, instruct, long, need, order, require, thirst, want, whim, yearn, yen.
antonyms dislike, fear.
n. aspiration, bidding, command, desire, hankering, hope, hunger, inclination, intention, liking, order, request, thirst, urge, velleity, voice, want, whim, will, yearning, yen.
antonyms dislike, fear.

wispy *adj.* attenuate, attenuated, delicate, diaphanous, ethereal, faint, fine, flimsy, flyaway, fragile, frail, gossamer, insubstantial, light, thin, unsubstantial.
antonym substantial.

wistful *adj.* contemplative, disconsolate, dreaming, dreamy, forlorn, longing, meditative, melancholy, mournful, musing, pensive, reflective, sad, soulful, thoughtful, wishful, yearning.

wit *n.* acumen, badinage, banter, brains, card, cleverness, comedian, common sense, comprehension, conceit, discernment, drollery, epigrammatist, eutrapelia, facetiousness, farceur, fun, homme d'esprit, humorist, humor, ingenuity, insight, intellect, intelligence, jocularity, joker, judgment, levity, merum sal, mind, nous, perception, pleasantry, punster, quipster, raillery, reason, repartee, sense, smeddum, understanding, wag, wisdom, wit-cracker, wordplay. *antonyms* seriousness, stupidity.

witch *n.* enchantress, hag, hex, lamia, magician, necromancer, occultist, pythoness, sorceress, sortileger, weird, wise woman, witch-wife.

witchcraft *n.* black magic, conjuration, divination, enchantment, glamor, goety, incantation, invultuation, magic, myalism, necromancy, occultism, pishogue, sorcery, sortilege, sortilegy, spell, the black art, the occult, voodoo, witchery, witching, wizardry.

withdraw *v.* abjure, absent oneself, back out, depart, disavow, disclaim, disengage, disenrol, disinvest, draw back, draw out, drop out, extract, fall back, go, go away, hive off, leave, pull back, pull out, recall, recant, remove, repair, rescind, retire, retract, retreat, revoke, secede, subduct, subtract, take away, take back, take off, unsay, waive.
antonyms advance, deposit, persist.

wither *v.* abash, blast, blight, decay, decline, desiccate, disintegrate, droop, dry, fade, humiliate, languish, miff, mortify, perish, put down, shame, shrink, shrivel, snub, wane, waste, welt, wilt.
antonyms boost, thrive.

withhold *v.* check, conceal, deduct, detain, hide, keen, keep back, refuse, repress, reserve, resist, restrain, retain, sit on, suppress, suspend.
antonyms accord, give.

withstand *v.* bear, brave, combat, confront, cope with, defy, endure, face, grapple with, hold off, hold one's ground, hold out, last out, oppose, put up with, resist, stand, stand fast, stand one's ground, stand up to, survive, take, take on, thwart, tolerate, weather.
antonyms collapse, yield.

witness *n.* attestant, beholder, bystander, corroborator, deponent, eye-witness, looker-on, observer, onlooker,

spectator, testifier, viewer, vouchee, voucher, watcher, witnesser.
v. attend, attest, bear out, bear witness, confirm, corroborate, countersign, depone, depose, endorse, look on, mark, note, notice, observe, perceive, see, sign, testify, view, watch.

wits *n.* acumen, astuteness, brains, cleverness, comprehension, faculties, gumption, ingenuity, intelligence, judgment, marbles, mother-wit, nous, reason, sense, understanding.
antonym stupidity.

witty *adj.* amusing, brilliant, clever, comic, droll, epigrammatic, facetious, fanciful, funny, humorous, ingenious, jocular, lively, original, piquant, salty, sparkling, waggish, whimsical.
antonyms dull, unamusing.

wizard[1] *n.* conjurer, enchanter, mage, magician, magus, necromancer, occultist, shaman, sorcerer, sortileger, thaumaturge, warlock, witch.

wizard[2] *n.* ace, adept, dabster, deacon, expert, genius, hotshot, maestro, master, prodigy, star, virtuoso, whiz.
antonym duffer.
adj. ace, brilliant, enjoyable, fab, fantastic, good, great, marvelous, sensational, smashing, super, superb, terrif, terrific, tiptop, topping, tremendous, wonderful.
antonym rotten.

wizardry *n.* black magic, conjuration, divination, enchantment, glamor, goety, incantation, invultuation, magic, myalism, necromancy, occultism, pishogue, sorcery, sortilege, sortilegy, the black art, the occult, voodoo, warlockry, witchcraft, witchery, witching.

woe *n.* adversity, affliction, agony, anguish, burden, curse, dejection, depression, disaster, distress, dole, dolor, dule, gloom, grief, hardship, heartache, heartbreak, melancholy, misery, misfortune, pain, sadness, sorrow, suffering, tears, trial, tribulation, trouble, unhappiness, wretchedness.
antonym joy.

woebegone *adj.* blue, crestfallen, dejected, disconsolate, dispirited, doleful, down in the mouth, downcast, down-hearted, forlorn, gloomy, grief-stricken, hangdog, long- faced, lugubrious, miserable, mournful, sad, sorrowful, tearful, tear-stained, troubled, wretched.
antonym joyful.

woman *n.* bride, broad, chambermaid, char, charwoman, chick, dame, daughter, domestic, fair, female, feme, femme, Frau, girl, girlfriend, handmaiden, housekeeper, kept woman, lady, lady-in-waiting, ladylove, lass, lassie, maid, maiden, maidservant, mate, miss, mistress, old lady, partner, piece, she, sheila, spouse, sweetheart, vrouw, wife, woman-body.
antonym man.

womanly *adj.* female, feminine, ladylike, matronly, motherly, weak, womanish.
antonym manly.

wonder *n.* admiration, amaze, amazement, astonishment, awe, bewilderment, curiosity, fascination, marvel, miracle, nonpareil, phenomenon, portent, prodigy, rarity, sight, spectacle, stupefaction, surprise, wonderment, wunderkind.
antonyms disinterest, ordinariness.
v. ask oneself, boggle, conjecture, doubt, gape, gaup, gawk, inquire, marvel, meditate, ponder, puzzle, query, question, speculate, stare, think.

wonderful *adj.* ace, admirable, amazing, astonishing, astounding, awe-inspiring, awesome, brilliant, épatant, excellent, extraordinary, fab, fabulous, fantastic, great, incredible, magnificent, marvelous, miraculous, mirific(al), odd, oustanding, peculiar, phenomenal, remarkable, sensational, smashing, staggering, startling, strange, stupendous, super, superb, surprising, terrif, terrific, tiptop, top-hole, topping, tremendous, unheard-of, wizard, wondrous.
antonyms ordinary, rotten.

wont *adj.* accustomed, given, habituated, used.
n. custom, habit, practice, routine, rule, use, way.

wooden *adj.* awkward, blank, clumsy, colorless, deadpan, dense, dim, dim-witted, dull, dull-witted, emotionless, empty, expressionless, gauche, gawky, glassy, graceless, inelegant, inflexible, lifeless, ligneous, maladroit, muffled, oaken, obstinate, obtuse, rigid, slow, spiritless, stiff, stupid, thick, timber, treen, unbending, unemotional, ungainly, unresponsive, unyielding, vacant, woody, xyloid.
antonyms bright, lively.

word *n.* account, advice, affirmation, assertion, assurance, bidding, bulletin, chat, colloquy, command, commandment, comment, communication, communiqué, confab, confabulation, consultation, conversation, countersign, declaration, decree, discussion, dispatch, edict, expression, firman, go-ahead, green light, guarantee, hint, information, intelligence, interlocution, intimation, lexigram, locution, mandate, message, news, notice, oath, order, palabra, parole, password, pledge, promise, remark, report, rescript, rumor, sign, signal, slogan, talk, term, tête-à-tête, tidings, ukase, undertaking, utterance, vocable, vow, warcry, watch-word, will.
v. couch, explain, express, phrase, put, say, write.

wordy *adj.* diffuse, discursive, garrulous, longiloquent, long-winded, loquacious, phrasy, pleonastic, prolix, rambling, verbose, windy.
antonyms concise, laconic.

work *n.* achievement, art, assignment, book, business, calling, chore, commission, composition, craft, creation, darg, deed, doings, drudgery, duty, effort, elbow grease, employ, employment, exertion, graft, grind, handiwork, industry, job, labor, line, livelihood, métier, occupation, oeuvre, office, opus, ouvrage, performance, piece, play, poem, production, profession, pursuit, service, skill, slog, stint, sweat, task, toil, trade, travail, undertaking, workload, workmanship.
antonyms hobby, play, rest.

v. accomplish, achieve, act, arrange, beaver, bring about, bring off, cause, contrive, control, convulse, create, cultivate, dig, direct, drive, drudge, effect, encompass, execute, exploit, farm, fashion, fiddle, fix, force, form, function, go, graft, handle, implement, knead, labor, make, manage, maneuver, manipulate, mold, move, operate, peg away, perform, ply, process, progress, pull off, run, shape, slave, slog, sweat, swing, till, toil, twitch, use, wield, writhe.
antonyms fail, play, rest.

workable *adj.* doable, effectible, feasible, possible, practicable, practical, realistic, viable.
antonym unworkable.

working *n.* action, functioning, manner, method, operation, routine, running.
adj. active, employed, functioning, going, laboring, operational, operative, running.
antonyms idle, inoperative, retired, unemployed.

workmanlike *adj.* adept, careful, efficient, expert, masterly, painstaking, professional, proficient, satisfactory, skilful, skilled, thorough, workmanly.
antonym amateurish.

workmanship *n.* art, artistry, craft, craftsmanship, execution, expertise, facture, finish, handicraft, handiwork, manufacture, skill, technique, work.

world *n.* age, area, class, creation, days, division, domain, earth, environment, epoch, era, existence, field, globe, human race, humanity, humankind, kingdom, life, man, mankind, men, nature, people, period, planet, province, public, realm, society, sphere, star, system, terrene, times, universe, Welt.

worldly *adj.* ambitious, avaricious, blasé, carnal, cosmopolitan, covetous, earthly, experienced, fleshly, grasping, greedy, knowing, lay, materialistic, mundane, physical, politic, profane, secular, selfish, sophisticated, sublunary, temporal, terrene, terrestrial, unspiritual, urbane, worldly-minded, worldly-wise.
antonym unworldly.

worn *adj.* attrite, bromidic, careworn, clichéd, drawn, exhausted, fatigued, frayed, hackneyed, haggard, jaded, lined, pinched, played-out, ragged, shabby, shiny, spent, tattered, tatty, threadbare, tired, trite, wearied, weary, wizened, woe-wearied, woe-worn, worn-out.
antonyms fresh, new.

worried *adj.* afraid, agonized, anxious, apprehensive, bothered, concerned, distracted, distraught, distressed, disturbed, fearful, frabbit, fretful, frightened, ill at ease, nervous, on edge, overwrought, perturbed, strained, tense, tormented, troubled, uneasy, unquiet, upset.
antonyms calm, unconcerned, unworried.

worry *v.* agonize, annoy, attack, badger, bite, bother, brood, disquiet, distress, disturb, faze, fret, get one's knickers in a twist, gnaw at, go for, harass, harry, hassle, hector, importune, irritate, kill, lacerate, nag, perturb, pester, plague, savage, tantalize, tear, tease, torment, trouble, unsettle, upset, vex.
antonyms comfort, reassure. *n.* agitation, annoyance, anxiety, apprehension, care, concern, disturbance, fear, irritation, misery, misgiving, perplexity, pest, plague, problem, stew, tew, tizz, tizzy, torment, trial, trouble, unease, vexation, woe, worriment.
antonyms comfort, reassurance.

worsen *v.* aggravate, damage, decay, decline, degenerate, deteriorate, disimprove, exacerbate, go downhill, pejorate, retrogress, sink, take a turn for the worse.
antonym improve.

worship *v.* adore, adulate, deify, exalt, glorify, honor, idolatrize, idolize, kanticoy, laud, love, misworship, praise, pray to, respect, revere, reverence, venerate.
antonym despise.
n. adoration, adulation, deification, devotion(s), dulia, exaltation, glorification, glory, homage, honor, hyperdulia, image-worship, knee-drill, latria, latry, laudation, love, misdevotion, misworship, monolatry, praise, prayer(s), regard, respect, reverence, will-worship.
antonym vilification.

worth *n.* aid, assistance, avail, benefit, cost, credit, desert(s), excellence, goodness, help, importance, merit, price, quality, rate, significance, use, usefulness, utility, value, virtue, worthiness.
antonym worthlessness.

worthless *adj.* abandoned, abject, base, beggarly, contemptible, depraved, despicable, draffish, draffy, futile, good-for-nothing, grotty, ignoble, ineffectual, insignificant, littleworth, meaningless, miserable, no use, no-account, nugatory, paltry, pointless, poor, rubbishy, scabbed, scabby, screwy, stramineous, trashy, trifling, trivial, unavailing, unimportant, unusable, useless, valueless, vaurien, vile, wretched.
antonym valuable.

worthy *adj.* admirable, appropriate, commendable, creditable, decent, dependable, deserving, estimable, excellent, fit, good, honest, honorable, laudable, meritorious, praise- worthy, reliable, reputable, respectable, righteous, suitable, upright, valuable, virtuous, worthwhile.
antonyms disreputable, unworthy.
n. big cheese, big noise, big pot, big shot, big-wig, dignitary, luminary, name, notable, personage.

wound *n.* anguish, cut, damage, distress, gash, grief, harm, heartbreak, hurt, injury, insult, laceration, lesion, offense, pain, pang, scar, shock, slash, slight, torment, torture, trauma.
v. annoy, bless, cut, cut to the quick, damage, distress, gash, grieve, harm, hit, hurt, injure, irritate, lacerate, mortify, offend, pain, pierce, pip, shock, slash, sting, traumatize, wing, wring someone's withers.

wrangle *n.* altercation, argument, argy-bargy, barney, bickering, brawl, clash, contest, controversy, dispute, quarrel, row, set-to, slanging match, squabble, tiff, tussle.
antonym agreement.

v. altercate, argue, argufy, bicker, brawl, contend, digladiate, disagree, dispute, ergotize, fall out, fight, quarrel, row, scrap, squabble.
antonym agree.

wrap *v.* absorb, bind, bundle up, cloak, cocoon, cover, encase, enclose, enfold, envelop, fold, hap, immerse, muffle, pack, package, roll up, sheathe, shroud, surround, swathe, wind.
antonym unwrap.
n. cape, cloak, mantle, pelisse, robe, shawl, stole.

wrath *n.* anger, bitterness, choler, displeasure, exasperation, fury, indignation, ire, irritation, passion, rage, resentment, spleen, temper.
antonyms calm, pleasure.

wreck *v.* break, crab, demolish, destroy, devastate, mar, play havoc with, ravage, ruin, shatter, smash, spoil, torpedo, write off.
antonyms repair, save.
n. derelict, desolation, destruction, devastation, disruption, hulk, mess, overthrow, ruin, ruination, shipwreck, undoing, write-off.

wrench *v.* distort, force, jerk, pull, rax, rick, rip, sprain, strain, tear, tug, twist, wrest, wring, yank.
n. ache, blow, jerk, monkey-wrench, pain, pang, pliers, pull, sadness, shock, sorrow, spanner, sprain, tear, tug, twist, upheaval, uprooting.

wrestle *v.* battle, combat, contend, contest, fight, grapple, scuffle, strive, struggle, tussle, vie.

wretch *n.* blackguard, cad, caitiff, cullion, cur, good-for-nothing, insect, miscreant, outcast, profligate, rapscallion, rascal, rascallion, rat, rogue, rotter, ruffian, scoundrel, swine, vagabond, villain, wight, worm.

wretched *adj.* abject, base, broken-hearted, caitiff, calamitous, cheerless, comfortless, contemptible, crestfallen, dejected, deplorable, depressed, despicable, disconsolate, distressed, doggone, doleful, downcast, forlorn, gloomy, grotty, hapless, hopeless, inferior, low, low-down, mean, melancholy, miserable, paltry, pathetic, pesky, pitiable, pitiful, poor, ratty, scurvy, shabby, shameful, sorry, unfortunate, unhappy, vile, woebegone, woeful, worthless.
antonyms excellent, happy.

writ *n.* court order, decree, subpoena, summons.

write *v.* compose, copy, correspond, create, draft, draw up, indite, inscribe, jot down, pen, record, screeve, scribble, scribe, set down, take down, tell, transcribe.

writer *n.* amanuensis, author, authoress, clerk, columnist, copyist, crime writer, detectivist, dialogist, diarist, diatribist, dramatist, dramaturg, dramaturgist, elegiast, elegist, encomiast, epigrammatist, epistler, epistolarian, epistoler, epistolist, epitapher, epitaphist, epitomist, essayist, farceur, fictionist, hack, librettist, littérateur, man of letters, memoirist, novelist, panegyrist, paper-stainer, pen, penman, penny-a-liner, penpusher, penwoman, periodicalist, playwright, prosaist, proseman, proser, prose- writer, quill-driver, scribbler, scribe, secretary, wordsmith, writeress.

writhe *v.* coil, contort, jerk, squirm, struggle, thrash, thresh, toss, twist, wiggle, wreathe, wriggle.

wrong *adj.* abusive, amiss, askew, awry, bad, blameworthy, criminal, crooked, defective, dishonest, dishonorable, erroneous, evil, fallacious, false, faulty, felonious, funny, illegal, illicit, immoral, improper, in error, in the wrong, inaccurate, inappropriate, inapt, incongruous, incorrect, indecorous, infelicitous, iniquitous, inner, inside, inverse, malapropos, misinformed, mistaken, off beam, off target, off-base, opposite, out, out of commission, out of order, reprehensible, reverse, sinful, unacceptable, unbecoming, unconventional, under, undesirable, unethical, unfair, unfitting, unhappy, unjust, unlawful, unseemly, unsound, unsuitable, untrue, wicked, wide of the mark, wrongful, wrongous.
antonym right.
adv. amiss, askew, astray, awry, badly, erroneously, faultily, improperly, inaccurately, incorrectly, mistakenly, wrongly.
antonym right.
n. abuse, crime, error, grievance, immorality, inequity, infraction, infringement, iniquity, injury, injustice, misdeed, offense, sin, sinfulness, transgression, trespass, unfairness, wickedness, wrong-doing.
antonym right.
v. abuse, cheat, discredit, dishonor, harm, hurt, ill-treat, ill-use, impose on, injure, malign, maltreat, misrepresent, mistreat, oppress, traduce.

wry *adj.* askew, aslant, awry, contorted, crooked, deformed, distorted, droll, dry, ironic, mocking, pawky, perverse, sarcastic, sardonic, thrawn, twisted, uneven, warped.
antonym straight.

Y

yank *v., n.* haul, heave, jerk, pull, snatch, tug, wrench.

yap *v.* babble, blather, chatter, go on, gossip, jabber, jaw, prattle, talk, tattle, twattle, ya(c)k, yammer, yatter, yelp, yip.

yard *n.* court, court-yard, garden, garth, Hof, hypaethron, quad, quadrangle.

yardstick *n.* benchmark, comparison, criterion, gauge, measure, standard, touchstone.

yarn[1] *n.* abb, fiber, fingering, gimp, lisle, thread.

yarn[2] *n.* anecdote, cock-and-bull story, fable, fabrication, story, tale, tall story.

yawn *v.* gape, ga(u)nt, open, split.

yearly *adj.* annual, per annum, per year.
adv. annually, every year, once a year.

yearn for ache for, covet, crave, desire, hanker for, hunger for, itch for, languish for, long for, lust for, pant for, pine for, want, wish for, yen for.
antonym dislike.

yell *v.* bawl, bellow, holler, hollo, howl, roar, scream, screech, shout, shriek, squawl, squeal, whoop, yelp, yowl.
antonym whisper.
n. bellow, cry, holler, hollo, howl, roar, scream, screech, shriek, squawl, whoop, yelp.
antonym whisper.

yellow *adj.* flavescent, flaxen, fulvid, fulvous, gold, golden, lemon, primrose, saffron, vitellary, vitelline, xanthic, xanthochroic, xanthomelanous, xanthous.

yelp *v.* bark, bay, cry, yap, yell, yip, yowl.
n. bark, cry, yap, yell, yip, yowl.

yen *n.* craving, desire, hankering, hunger, itch, longing, lust, passion, thing, yearning.
antonym dislike.

yield[1] *v.* abandon, abdicate, accede, acquiesce, admit defeat, agree, allow, bow, capitulate, cave in, cede, comply, concede, consent, cry quits, give, give in, give way, go along with, grant, knuckle under, part with, permit, relinquish, resign, resign oneself, submit, succumb, surrender, throw in the towel.
antonym withstand.

yield[2] *v.* afford, bear, bring forth, bring in, earn, fructify, fructuate, fruit, furnish, generate, give, net, pay, produce, provide, return, supply.
n. crop, earnings, harvest, income, output, proceeds, produce, product, profit, return, revenue, takings.

yielding *adj.* accommodating, acquiescent, amenable, biddable, complaisant, compliant, docile, easy, elastic, flexible, obedient, obliging, pliable, pliant, quaggy, resilient, soft, spongy, springy, submissive, supple, tractable, unresisting.
antonyms obstinate, solid.

yoke *n.* bond, bondage, burden, chain, coupling, enslavement, helotry, ligament, link, oppression, serfdom, service, servility, servitude, slavery, subjugation, thraldom, tie, vassalage.
v. bracket, connect, couple, enslave, harness, hitch, inspan, join, link, tie, unite.
antonym unhitch.

yokel *n.* boor, bucolic, bumpkin, clodhopper, corn- ball, country cousin, hick, hillbilly, jake, peasant, rustic.
antonyms sophisticate, towny.

young *adj.* adolescent, baby, callow, cub, early, fledgling, green, growing, immature, infant, junior, juvenile, little, new, recent, unblown, unfledged, youthful.
antonym old.
n. babies, brood, chicks, cubs, family, fledglings, issue, litter, little ones, offspring, progeny, quiverful.
antonym parents.

youngster *n.* boy, girl, juvenile, kid, lad, laddie, lass, lassie, nipper, shaver, teenybopper, urchin, young pup, youth.
antonym oldie.

youthful *adj.* active, boyish, childish, ephebic, fresh, girlish, immature, inexperienced, juvenescent, juvenile, lively, pubescent, puerile, sprightly, spry, vigorous, vivacious, well-preserved, young.
antonyms aged, languorous.

youthfulness *n.* freshness, juvenileness, juvenility, liveliness, sprightliness, spryness, vigor, vivaciousness, vivacity.
antonyms agedness, languor.

yowl *v.* bay, caterwaul, cry, howl, screech, squall, ululate, wail, yell, yelp.
n. cry, howl, screech, wail, yell, yelp.

Z

zany *adj.* amusing, clownish, comical, crazy, daft, droll, eccentric, funny, goofy, kooky, loony, madcap, nutty, screwy, wacky.
antonym serious.
n. buffoon, card, clown, comedian, cure, droll, fool, jester, joker, kook, laugh, merry-andrew, nut, nutcase, nutter, screwball, wag.
zeal *n.* ardor, dedication, devotion, eagerness, earnestness, enthusiasm, fanaticism, fervency, fervor, fire, gusto, keenness, militancy, passion, spirit, verve, warmth, zelotypia, zest.
antonym apathy.
zealot *n.* bigot, devotee, enthusiast, extremist, fanatic, fiend, freak, maniac, militant.
zealous *adj.* ardent, burning, devoted, eager, earnest, enthusiastic, fanatical, fervent, fervid, fired, gung- ho, impassioned, keen, militant, passionate, rabid, spirited.
antonym apathetic.
zenith *n.* acme, apex, apogee, climax, culmination, height, high point, meridian, peak, pinnacle, summit, top, vertex.
antonym nadir.
zero *n.* bottom, cipher, duck, goose-egg, love, nadir, naught, nil, nothing, nought.
zest *n.* appetite, charm, delectation, élan, enjoyment, flavor, gusto, interest, joie de vivre, keenness, kick, peel, piquancy, pungency, relish, rind, savor, smack, spice, tang, taste, zeal, zing.
antonym apathy.
zip *n.* brio, drive, élan, energy, enthusiasm, get- up-and-go, go, gusto, life, liveliness, oomph, pep, pizzazz, punch, sparkle, spirit, verve, vigor, vim, vitality, zest, zing.
antonym listlessness.
v. dash, flash, fly, gallop, hurry, race, rush, scoot, shoot, speed, tear, whiz, whoosh, zoom.
zone *n.* area, belt, district, region, section, sector, sphere, stratum, territory, tract, zona, zonule, zonulet.
zoo *n.* animal park, aquarium, aviary, menagerie, safari park, zoological gardens.

APPENDICES

APPENDIX I

Grammar and Usage

abbreviations are shortened forms of words usually used as a space-saving technique and becoming increasingly common in modern usage. They cause problems with regard to punctuation. The common question asked is whether the letters of an abbreviation should be separated by periods. In modern usage the tendency is to omit periods from abbreviations. This is most true of abbreviations involving initial capital letters, as in TUC, EEC and USA. In such cases periods should definitely not be used if one or some of the initial letters do not belong to a full word. Thus television is abbreviated to TV and educationally subnormal to ESN.

There are usually no periods in abbreviations involving the first and last letters of a word (contractions) Dr, Mr, Rd, St, but this is a matter of taste.

Abbreviations involving the first few letters of a word, as in "Prof" (Professor) are the most likely to have periods, as in "Feb." (February) but again this is now a matter of taste. These are mostly formed by adding lower-case s, as in Drs, JPs, TVs. Note the absence of apostrophes.

antonym refers to a word that is the opposite of another word. Thus "black" is an antonym for "white," "cowardly" is an antonym for "courageous," "dull" is an antonym for "bright" and "fast" is an antonym for "slow."

apostrophe[1] is a figure of speech which takes the form of a rhetorical address to an absent or dead person or to a personified thing, as in "O Romeo! Romeo! wherefore art thou, Romeo?" and "Oh Peace, why have you deserted us?"

apostrophe[2] is a form of punctuation that is mainly used to indicate possession. Many spelling errors center on the position of the apostrophe in relation to *s*.

Possessive nouns are usually formed by adding *'s* to the singular noun, as in "the girl's mother," and "Peter's car"; by adding an apostrophe to plural nouns that end in s, as in "all the teachers' cars"; by adding 's to irregular plural nouns that do not end in s, as in "women's shoes."

In the possessive form of a name or singular noun that ends in *s*, *x* or *z*, the apostrophe may or may not be followed by *s*. In words of one syllable the final s is usually added, as in "James's house," "the fox's lair," "Roz's dress." The final s is most frequently omitted in names, particularly in names of three or more syllables, as in "Euripides' plays." In many cases the presence or absence of final s is a matter of convention.

The apostrophe is also used to indicate omitted letters in contracted forms of words, as in "can't" and "you've." They are sometimes used to indicate missing century numbers in dates, as in "the '60s and '70s," but are not used at the end of decades, etc, as in "1960s," not "1960's."

Generally apostrophes are no longer used to indicate omitted letters in shortened forms that are in common use, as in "phone" and "flu."

Apostrophes are often omitted wrongly in modern usage, particularly in the media and by advertisers, as in "womens hairdressers," "childrens helpings." In addition, apostrophes are frequently added erroneously (as in "potato's for sale" and "Beware of the dog's"). This is partly because people are unsure about when and when not to use them and partly because of a modern tendency to punctuate as little as possible.

brackets are used to enclose information that is in some way additional to the main statement. The information so enclosed is called *parenthesis* and the pair of brackets enclosing it can be known as *parentheses*. The information that is enclosed in the brackets is purely supplementary or explanatory in nature and could be removed without changing the overall basic meaning or grammatical completeness of the statement. **Brackets**, like *commas* and *dashes*, interrupt the flow of the main statement but **brackets** indicate a more definite or clear-cut interruption. The fact that they are more visually obvious emphasizes this.
Material within brackets can be one word, as in "In a local wine bar we had some delicious crepes (pancakes)" and "They didn't have the chutzpah (nerve) to challenge her." It can also take the form of dates, as in "Robert Louis Stevenson (1850–94) wrote *Treasure Island*" and "*Animal Farm* was written by George Orwell (1903–50)."

The material within brackets can also take the form of a phrase, as in "They served lasagne (a kind of pasta) and some delicious veal" and "They were drinking Calvados (a kind of brandy made from apples)" or in the form of a clause, as in "We were to have supper (or so they called it) later in the evening" and "They went for a walk round the loch (as a lake is called in Scotland) before taking their departure."

It can also take the form of a complete sentence, as in "He was determined (we don't know why) to tackle the problem alone" and "She made it clear (nothing could be more clear) that she was not interested in the offer." Sentences that appear in brackets in the middle of a sentence are not usually given an initial capital letter or a period, as in "They very much desired (she had no idea why) to purchase her house." If the material within brackets comes at the end of a sentence the period comes outside the second bracket, as in "For some reason we agreed to visit her at home (we had no idea where she lived)."

If the material in the brackets is a sentence which comes between two other sentences it is treated like a normal sentence with an initial capital letter and a closing period, as in "He never seems to do any studying. (He is always either asleep or watching television.) Yet he does brilliantly in his exams." Punctuation of the main statement is unaffected by the presence of the brackets and their enclosed material except that any punctuation that would have followed the word before the first bracket follows the second bracket, as in "He lives in a place (I am not sure exactly where), that is miles from anywhere.

There are various shapes of brackets. Round brackets are the most common type. Square brackets are sometimes used to enclose information that is contained inside other information already in brackets, as in "(Christopher Marlowe [1564–93] was a contemporary of Shakespeare)" or in a piece of writing where round brackets have already been used for some other purpose. Thus in a dictionary if round brackets are used to separate off the pronunciation, square brackets are sometimes used to separate off the etymologies.

Square brackets are also used for editorial comments in a scholarly work where the material within brackets is more of an intrusion to the flow of the main statement than is normerly the case with bracketed material. Angle brackets and brace brackets tend to be used in more scholarly or technical contexts.

capital letters are much less common than lower-case letters. They are used as the initial letter of proper nouns. Thus names of countries, rivers, mountains, cities, etc. Thus we find Africa, Mount Everest, River Nile, Paris, etc. The first names and surnames of people have initial capital letters, as in John Black and Mary Brown. Initial capital letters are used for the days of the week, as in Tuesday and Wednesday, for the months of the year, as in May and October, public and religious holidays, as in Easter Sunday, Ramadan and Hanaku. Initial capital letters are used for the books of the Bible.

Points of the compass are spelt with an initial capital letter if they are part of a specific geographical feature or region, as in South Africa.

Initial capital letters are usually used in the titles of books. Only the main words are capitalized. Prepositions, determiners and the articles are left in lower-case, unless they form the first word of the title, as in *A Room with a View* and *For Whom the Bell Tolls*.

Initial capital letters are necessary in tradenames, as in Hoover, Jacuzzi, Xerox and Kodak. Note that verbs formed from trade names are not spelt with an initial capital letter.

The first word in a sentence is spelt with a capital letter, as in "We heard them come in. They made very little noise. However, we are light sleepers.."

For capital letters in abbreviation see ABBREVIATIONS.

colon is a punctuation mark (:) which is used within a sentence to explain, interpret, clarify or amplify what has gone before it. "The standard of school work here is extremely high: it is almost university standard," "The fuel bills are giving cause for concern: they are almost double last year's." "We have some new information: the allies have landed." A capital letter is not usually used after the colon in this context.

The **colon** is also used to introduce lists or long quotations, as in "The recipe says we need: tomatoes, peppers, courgettes, garlic, oregano and basil," "The boy has a huge list of things he needs for school: blazer, trousers, shirts, sweater, ties, shoes, tennis shoes, rugby boots, sports clothes and leisure wear" and "One of his favourite quotations was: 'If music be the food of love play on' ."

The **colon** is sometimes used in numerals, as in "7:30 a.m.," "1:20:01" and "a ratio of 7:3." It is used in the titles of some books, for example where there is a subtitle or explanatory title, as in "The Dark Years: the Economy in the 1930s."

In informal writing, the dash is sometimes used instead of the colon, Indeed the dash tends to be overused for this purpose.

comma is a very common punctuation mark. In modern usage there is a tendency to adopt a system of minimal punctuation and the comma is one of the casualties of this new attitude. Most people use the comma considerably less frequently than was formerly the case.

However there are certain situations in which the comma is still commonly used. One of these concerns lists. The individual items in a series of three or more items are separated by commas. Whether a comma is put before the "and" which follows the second-last item is now a matter of choice. Some people dislike the use of a comma after "and" in this situation, and it was formerly considered wrong. Examples of lists include— "At the sports club we can play tennis, squash, badminton and table tennis," "We need to buy bread, milk, fruit and sugar," and "They are studying French, German, Spanish and Russian." The individual items in a list can be quite long, as in "We opened the door, let ourselves in, fed the cat and started to cook a meal" and "They consulted the map, planned the trip, got some foreign currency and were gone before we realized it." Confusion may arise if the last item in the list contains "and" in its own right, as in "In the restaurant they served ham salad, shepherd's pie, pie and chips and omelette. In such cases it as well to put a comma before the "and."

In cases where there is a list of adjectives before a noun, the use of commas is now optional although it was formerly standard practice. Thus both "She wore a long, red, sequinned dress" and "She wore a long red sequinned dress" are used. When the adjective immediately before the noun has a closer relationship with it than the other adjectives no comma should be used, as in "a beautiful old Spanish village."

The **comma** is used to separate clauses or phrases that are parenthetical or naturally cut off from the rest of a sentence, as in "My mother, who was of Irish extraction, was very superstitious." In such a sentence the clause within the commas can be removed without altering the basic meaning. Care should be taken to include both commas. Commas are not normally used to separate main clauses and relative clauses, as in "The woman whom I met was my friend's sister." Nor are they usually used to separate main clauses and subordinate clauses, as in "He left when we arrived" and "They came to the party although we didn't expect them to." If the subordinate clause precedes the main clause, it is sometimes followed by a comma, especially if it is a reasonably long clause, as in "Although we stopped and thought about it, we still made the wrong decision." If the clause is quite short, or if it is a short phrase, a comma is not usually inserted, as in "Although it rained we had a good vacation" and "Although poor they were happy." The use of commas to separate such words and expression from the rest of the sentence to which they are related is optional. Thus one can write "However, he could be right" or "However he could be right." The longer the expression is, the more likely it is to have a comma after it, as in "On the other hand, we may decide not to go."

Commas are always used to separate terms of address, interjections or question tags from the rest of the sentence, as in "Please come this way, Ms Brown, and make yourself at home," "Now, ladies, what can I get you?" and "It's cold today, isn't it?"

Commas may be used to separate main clauses joined by a coordinating conjunction, but this is not usual if the clauses have the same subject or object, as in "She swept the floor and dusted the table." In cases where the subjects are different and the clauses are fairly long, it is best to insert a comma, as in "They took all the furniture with them, and she was left with nothing."

A **comma** can be inserted to avoid repeating a verb in the second of two clauses, as in "he plays golf and tennis, his brother football."

dash is a punctuation mark in the form of a short line that indicates a short break in the continuity of a sentence, as in "He has never been any trouble at school—quite the reverse," "I was amazed when he turned up—I thought he was still abroad." In such situations it serves the same purpose as brackets, except that it is frequently considered more informal. The dash should be used sparingly. Depending on it too much can lead to careless writing with ideas set down at random rather than turned into a piece of coherent prose.

The **dash** can be used to emphasize a word or phrase, as in "They said goodbye then—forever." It can also be used to add a remark to the end of a sentence, as in "They had absolutely no money—a regular state of affairs towards the end of the month." The **dash** can also be used to introduce a statement that amplifies or explains what has been said, as in "The burglars took everything of value—her jewellery, the silver, the TV set, her hi-fi and several hundred pounds." It can be used to summarize what has gone before, as in "Disease, poverty, ignorance—these are the problems facing us."

The **dash** is also used to introduce an afterthought, as in "You can come with me—but you might not want to." It can also introduce a sharp change of subject, as in "I'm just making tea—what was that noise?" It can also be used to introduce some kind of balance in a sentence, as in "It's going to take two of us to get this table out of here—one to move it and one to hold the door open."

Dashes are sometimes found in pairs. A pair of dashes acts in much the same way as a set of round brackets. A pair of dashes can be used to indicate a break in a sentence, as in "We prayed—prayed as we had never prayed before—that the children would be safe," "It was—on reflection—his best performance yet," and "He introduced me to his wife—an attractive pleasant woman—before he left."

Dashes are used to indicate hesitant speech, as in "I don't—well—maybe—you could be right." They can be used to indicate the omission of part of a word or name, as in "It's none of your b— business," "He's having an affair with Mrs D—."

They can also be used between points in time or space, as in "Chicago–New York" and "1750–1790."

ellipsis indicates omission of some kind. It can refer to the omission of words from a statement because they are thought to be obvious from the context. In many cases it involves using an auxiliary verb on its own rather than a full verb, as in "Jane won't accept it but Mary will" and "They would go if they could." In such cases the full form of "Jane won't accept it but Mary will accept it" and "They would go if they could go" would sound unnatural and repetitive. This is common in spoken English. Some sentences containing an ellipsis sound clumsy as well as ungrammatical, as in "This is as good, or perhaps even better than that," where "as" is omitted after "good" and in "People have and still do express their disapproval about it," where "expressed" is omitted after "have." Care should be taken to avoid ellipsis if the use of it is going to be ambiguous or clumsy.

Ellipsis is often used to indicate an omission from a quoted passage. If part of a passage is quoted and there is a gap before the next piece of the same passage is required to be quoted an **ellipsis** is used in the form of three dots. If the part of the passage quoted does not start at the beginning of a sentence the ellipsis precedes it.

exclamation is a word, phrase or sentence called out with strong feeling of some kind. It is marked by an **exclamation mark** which occurs at the end of the **exclamation**, as in "Get lost!," "What a nerve!," "Help!," "Ouch!" "Well I never!," "What a disaster!," "I'm tired of all this!" and "Let me out of here!" An **exclamatory question** is a sentence that is interrogative in form but is an **exclamation** in meaning, as in "Isn't the baby beautiful!" and "Isn't it lovely!"

homonym refers to a word which has the same sound and often the same spelling as another word but which differs in meaning – more correctly classified as homographs or homophones. Examples include:

"bill," a noun meaning "a written statement of money owed," as in "You must pay the bill for the conversion work immediately," or a "written or printed advertisement," as in "We were asked to deliver handbills advertising the play."

"bill," a noun meaning "a bird's beak," as in "The seagull has injured its bill."

"fair," an adjective meaning "attractive," as in "fair young women"; "light in colour," as in "She has fair hair"; "fine, not raining," as in "I hope it keeps fair"; "just, free from prejudice," as in "We felt that the referee came to a fair decision."

"fair," a noun meaning "a market held regularly in the same place, often with stalls, entertainments and rides" (now often simply applying to an event with entertainments and rides without the market), as in "He won a coconut at the fair"; "a trade exhibition," as in "the Frankfurt Book Fair."

hyphen refers to a small stroke used to join two words together or to indicate that a word has been broken at the end of a line because of lack of space. It is used in a variety of situations.

The **hyphen** is used as the prefixed element in a proper noun, as in "pre-Christian," "post-Renaissance," "anti-British," "anti-Semitic," "pro-French" and "pro-Marxism." It is also used before dates or numbers, as in "pre-1914," "pre-1066," "post-1920," "post-1745." It is also used before abbreviations, as in "anti-EEC" and "anti-TUC."

The **hyphen** is used for clarification. Some words are ambiguous without the presence of a hyphen. For example, "re-cover," as in "re-cover a chair," is spelt with a hyphen to differentiate it from "recover," as in "The accident victim is likely to recover." Similarly, it is used in "re-form," meaning "to form again," as in "They have decided to re-form the society which closed last year," to differentiate the word from "reform," meaning "to improve, to become better behaved," as in "He was wild as a young man but he has reformed now." Similarly "re-count" in the sense of "count again" , as in "re-count the number of votes cast," is spelt with a hyphen to differentiate it from "recount" in the sense of "tell," as in "recount what happened on the night of the accident."

The **hyphen** was formerly used to separate a prefix from the main element of a word if the main element begins with a vowel, as in "pre-eminent," but there is a growing tendency in modern usage to omit the hyphen in such cases. At the moment both "pre-eminent" and "preeminent" are found. However, if the omission of the hyphen results in double i, the hyphen is usually retained, as in "anti-inflationary" and "semi-insulated."

The **hyphen** was formerly used in words formed with the prefix non-, as in "non-functional," "non-political," "non-flammable" and "non-pollutant." However there is a growing tendency to omit the **hyphen** in such cases, as in "nonfunctional" and "nonpollutant." At the moment both forms of such words are common.

The **hyphen** is usually used with "ex-" in the sense of "former," as in "ex-wife" and "ex-president."

The **hyphen** is usually used when "self-" is prefixed to words, as in "self-styled," "a self-starter" and "self-evident."

Use or non-use of the **hyphen** is often a matter of choice, house style or frequency of usage, as in "drawing-room" or "drawing room." and "dining-room" or "dining room." There is a modern tendency to punctuate less frequently than was formerly the case and so in modern usage use of the **hyphen** in such expressions is less frequent. The length of compounds often affects the inclusion or omission of the hyphen. Compounds of two short elements that are well-established words tend not to be hyphenated, as in "bedroom" and "toothbrush." Compound words with longer elements are more likely to be hyphenated, as in "engine-driver" and "carpet-layer."

Some fixed compounds of two or three or more words are always hyphenated, as in "son-in-law," "good-for-nothing" and "devil-may-care."

Some compounds formed from phrasal verbs are sometimes hyphenated and sometimes not. Thus both "take-over" and "takeover" are common, and "run-down" and "rundown" are both common. Again the use of the hyphen is a matter of choice. However some words formed from phrasal verbs are usually spelt without a hyphen, as in "breakthrough."

Compound adjectives consisting of two elements, the second of which ends in -ed, are usually hyphenated, as in "heavy-hearted," "fair-haired," "fair-minded" and "long-legged."

Compound adjectives when they are used before nouns are usually hyphenated, as in "gas-fired central heating," "oil-based paints," "solar-heated buildings" and "chocolate-coated cookies."

Compounds containing some adverbs are usually hyphenated, sometimes to avoid ambiguity, as in "his best-known opera," a "well-known singer," "an ill-considered venture" and "a half-planned scheme."

Generally adjectives and participles preceded by an adverb are not hyphenated if the adverb ends in -ly, as in "a highly talented singer," "neatly pressed clothes" and "beautifully dressed young women."

In the case of two or more compound hyphenated adjectives with the same second element qualifying the same noun, the common element need not be repeated but the **hyphen** should be, as in "two- and three-bedroom houses" and "long- and short-haired dogs."

The **hyphen** is used in compound numerals from 21 to 99 when they are written in full, as in "thirty-five gallons," "forty-four years," "sixty-seven kilometers" and "two hundred and forty-five kilometers." Compound numbers such as "three hundred" and "two thousand" are not hyphenated.

Hyphens are used in fractions, as in "three-quarters" and "seven-eighths."

Hyphens are also used in such number phrases as "a seventeenth-century play," "a sixteenth-century church," "a five-year contract" and a "third-year student."

The other use of **hyphens** is to break words at the ends of lines. Formerly people were more careful about where they broke words. Previously, words were broken up according to etymological principles but there is a growing tendency to break words according to how they are pronounced. Some dictionaries or spelling dictionaries give help with the division and hyphenation of individual words. General points are that one-syllable words should not be divided and words should not be broken after the first letter of a word or before the last letter. Care should be taken not to break up words, for example by forming elements that are words in their own right, in such a way as to mislead the reader. Thus divisions such as "the-rapist" and "mans-laughter" should be avoided.

italic type refers to a sloping typeface that is used for a variety of purposes. It is used to differentiate a piece of text from the main text, which is usually in Roman type. For example, it is used sometimes for the titles of books, newspapers, magazines, plays, films, musical works and works of art, as in "he is a regular reader of *The Times*," "She reads *The New Yorker*," "Have you read *Animal Farm* by George Orwell," "He has never seen a production of Shakespeare's *Othello*," "We went to hear Handel's *Messiah*," "*Mona Lisa* is a famous painting." Sometimes such titles are put in quotation marks rather than in italic.

Italic type is also sometimes used for the names of ships, trains, etc, as in "the launch of *The Queen Elizabeth II*," "She once sailed in *The Queen Mary*" and "Their train was called *The Flying Scotsman*."

Italic type is also used for the Latin names of plants and animals, as in "of the genus *Lilium*," "trees of the genus *Pyrus*, *Panthera pardus* and *Canis lupus*."

Italic type is sometimes used for foreign words that have been adopted into the English language but have never been fully integrated. Examples include *bête noire*, *raison d'être*, *inter alia* and *Weltschmerz*.

Italic type can also sometimes be used to draw attention to a particular word, phrase or passage, as in "How do you pronounce *formidable*?," or to emphasize a word or phrase, as in "Is he *still* in the same job?"

numbers can be written in either figures or words. It is largely a matter of taste which method is adopted. As long as the method is consistent it does not really matter. Some establishments, such as a publishing house or a newspaper office, will have a house style. For example, some of them prefer to have numbers up to 10 written in words, as in "They have two boys and three girls." If this system is adopted, guidance should be sought as to whether a mixture of figures and words in the same sentence is acceptable, as in "We have 12 cups but only six saucers," or whether the rule should be broken in such situations as "We have twelve cups but only six saucers."

period is a punctuation mark consisting of a small dot. Its principal use is to end a sentence that is not a question or an exclamation, as in "They spent the money.," "She is studying hard.," "He has been declared redundant and is very upset." and "Because she is shy, she rarely goes to parties."

The **period** is used in decimal fractions, as in "4.5 meters" and "12.2 litres." It can also be used in dates, as in "1.20.01," and times, as in "3.15 tomorrow afternoon."

In modern usage the tendency is to omit **periods** from abbreviations. This is most true of abbreviations involving initial capital letters as in TUC, BBC, EEC and USA. In such cases periods should definitely not be used if one or some of the initial letters do not belong to a full word. Thus, television is abbreviated to TV and educationally subnormal to ESN.

There are usually no periods in abbreviations involving the first and letters of a word (contractions) Dr, Mr, Rd, St, but this is a matter of taste.

Abbreviations involving the first few letters of a word, as in "Prof" (Professor) are the most likely to have periods, as in "Feb." (February), but again this is now a matter of taste.

The **period** can also be called **point** or **period**.

question mark refers to the punctuation mark that is placed at the end of a question or interrogative sentence, as in "Who is he?," "Where are they?," "Why have they gone?," "Whereabouts are they?," "When are you going?" and "What did he say?." The **question mark** is sometimes known as the "query."

quotation marks, also known as inverted commas or quotes, are used in direct speech. **Quotation marks** are also used to enclose titles of newspaper articles, book chapters, short stories, poems, songs, articles in periodicals and essays. **Quotation marks** may consist of a set of single inverted comas or a set of double inverted commas. If a title, etc, is to be enclosed in quotation marks and the title is part of a piece of writing already in quotation marks for some other reason, such as being part of direct speech, then the quotation marks round the title should be in the type of quotation marks opposite to the other ones. Thus if the piece of writing is in single quotation marks then the title should be in double quotation marks. If the piece of prose is in double quotation marks the title should be in single quotation marks. Examples include "Have you read 'My Last Duchess' by Robert Browning?" and "Can you sing 'Auld Lang Syne'?"

semi-colon is a rather formal form of punctuation. It is mainly used between clauses that are not joined by any form of conjunction, as in "We had a wonderful vacation; sadly they did not," "She was my sister; she was also my best friend" and "He was a marvelous friend; he is much missed." A dash is sometimes used instead of a semi-colon but this more informal.

The **semi-colon** is also used to form subsets in a long list or series of names so that the said list seems less complex, as in "The young man who wants to be a journalist has applied everywhere. He has applied to *The Times* in London; *The Globe and Mail* in Toronto; *The Age* in Melbourne; *The Tribune* in Chicago.

The **semi-colon** is also sometimes used before "however," "nevertheless" "hence," etc, as in "We have extra seats for the concert; however you must not feel obliged to come."

synonym refers to a word which has the same meaning as another of the same language, or a word denoting a very similar description but perhaps differing in some senses, or in a range of applications. Synonyms for the verb "believe" would include: "accept," "consider," "count on," "guess," "judge" etc.

Parts of Speech

These define the ways in which words can be used in different contexts:

active voice is one of two voices that verbs are divided into, the other being passive voice. In verbs in the active voice, commonly called active verbs, the subject of the verb performs the action described by the verb. Thus, in the sentence "The boy threw the ball," "throw" is in the active voice since the subject of the verb (the boy) is doing the throwing. Similarly, in the sentence "Her mother was driving the car," "driving" is in the active voice since it is the subject of the sentence (her mother) that is doing the driving. Similarly, in the sentence "We saw the cows in the field," "saw" is the active voice since it is the subject of the sentence (we) that is doing the seeing. *See also* PASSIVE VOICE.

adjective is a word that describes or gives information about a noun or pronoun. It is said to qualify a noun or pronoun since it limits the word it describes in some way, by making it more specific. Thus, adding the adjective "red" to "book" limits "book," since it means we can forget about books of any other color. Similarly, adding "large" to "book" limits it, since it means we can forget about books of any other size.

Adjectives tell us something about the color, size, number, quality, or classification of a noun or pronoun, as in "purple dress," "jet-black hair," "bluish eyes"; "tiny baby," "large houses," "biggish gardens," "massive estates"; five children," "twenty questions," "seventy-five books"; "sad people," "joyful occasions," "delicious food," "civil engineering," "nuclear physics," "modern languages," "Elizabethan drama."

Several **adjectives** may modify one noun or pronoun, as in "the small, black cat," "an enormous, red-brick, Victorian house." The order in which they appear is flexible and can vary according to the emphasis one wishes to place on the various adjectives. However, a common sequence is size, quality, color and classification, as in "a small, beautiful, pink wild rose" and "a large, ugly, grey office building."

Adjectives do not change their form. They remain the same whether the noun to which they refer is singular or plural, or masculine or feminine. All the above examples of adjectives come before the noun, but not all adjectives do so.

Many **adjectives** are formed from either the past participles of verbs, and so end in *-ed*, or from the present participles and so end in *-ing*. Examples of adjectives ending in *-ed* include "annoyed," "blackened," "colored," "damaged," "escaped," "fallen," "guarded," "heated," "identified," "jailed," "knotted," "labeled," "mixed," "numbered," "opened," "pleated," "recorded," "satisfied," "taped," "used," "varied," "walled," "zoned." Examples of adjectives ending in -ing include "amusing," "boring," "captivating," "demanding," "enchanting," "fading," "grating," "horrifying," "identifying," "jarring," "kneeling," "labouring," "manufacturing," "nursing," "operating," "parting," "quivering," "racing," "satisfying," "telling," "undermining," "worrying," "yielding."

Several **adjectives** end in *-ical* and are formed by adding *-al* to certain nouns ending in *-ic*. Examples include "arithmetical," "comical," "critical," "cynical," "fanatical," "logical," "magical," "musical," "mystical" and "sceptical." Sometimes the adjectives ending in *-ical* are formed from nouns that end in *-ics*. These include "acoustical," "ethical," "hysterical," "statistical" and "tropical." Several adjectives end in *-ic* and are formed from nouns ending in *-ics*. These include "acoustic," "acrobatic," "aerobic," "athletic," "economic," "electronic," "genetic," "gymnastic," "histrionic" and "linguistic."

Other common adjectival endings include *-ful*, as in "beautiful," "dreadful," "eventful," "graceful," "hateful," "tearful" and "youthful." They also include *-less*, as in "clueless," "graceless," "hatless," "meaningless" and "sunless."

Many adjectives end in *-able* and many end in *-ible*. There are often spelling problems with such adjectives. The following adjectives are likely to be misspelt:

Some adjectives in *-able*:

abominable	definable	impeccable	readable
acceptable	delectable	implacable	recognizable
adaptable	demonstrable	impracticable	regrettable
adorable	dependable	impressionable	renewable
advisable	desirable	indescribable	reputable
agreeable	discreditable	indispensable	sizeable
amiable	disreputable	inimitable	stoppable
approachable	durable	insufferable	tenable
available	enviable	lamentable	tolerable
bearable	excitable	manageable	transferable
beatable	excusable	measurable	understandable
believable	expendable	memorable	unmistakable
blameable	foreseeable	nameable	usable
calculable	forgettable	non-flammable	variable
capable	forgivable	objectionable	viable
changeable	healable	operable	washable
comfortable	hearable	palpable	wearable
commendable	immovable	pleasurable	winnable
conceivable	impassable	preferable	workable

Some adjectives ending in *-ible*:

accessible	credible	expressible	irascible
admissible	defensible	fallible	negligible
audible	destructible	feasible	perceptible
collapsible	digestible	flexible	permissible
combustible	discernible	forcible	possible
compatible	divisible	gullible	repressible
comprehensible	edible	indelible	reproducible
contemptible	exhaustible	intelligible	

adverb is a word that adds to our information about a verb, as in "work rapidly"; about an adjective, as in "an extremely beautiful young woman"; or about another adverb, as in "sleeping very soundly." **Adverbs** are said to modify the words to which they apply since they limit the words in some way and make them more specific. Thus, adding "slowly" to "walk," as in "They walked slowly down the hill," limits the verb "walk" since all other forms of "walk," such as "quickly," "lazily," etc, have been discarded.

There are several different kinds of adverbs, categorized according to the information they provide about the word they modify. They include adverbs of time, adverbs of place, adverbs of manner, adverbs of degree, adverbs of frequency, adverbs of probability, adverbs of duration, and interrogative adverbs.

Adverbs of time tell us when something happened and include such words as "now," "then," "later," "soon," "afterwards," "yesterday," etc, as in "He is due to arrive now," I will call you later," "She had a rest and went out afterwards," "They left yesterday."

Adverbs of place tell us where something happened and include such words as "there," "here," "somewhere," "anywhere," "thereabouts," "abroad," "outdoors," "overhead," "underground," "hither and thither," etc, as in "I haven"t been there," "They couldn't see her anywhere," "His family live abroad," and "We heard a noise overhead."

Adverbs of manner tell us how something happens and include a wide range of possibilities. Frequently adverbs in this category are formed by adding *-ly* to an adjective. Examples of these include:

adjective	*adverb*	*adjective*	*adverb*
anxious	anxiously	mean	meanly
bad	badly	narrow	narrowly
cautious	cautiously	pale	palely
dumb	dumbly	quick	quickly
elegant	elegantly	soothing	soothingly
fearless	fearlessly	tough	toughly
hot	hotly	unwilling	unwillingly
interested	interestedly	vain	vainly
joking	jokingly	weak	weakly
lame	lamely		

Some adjectives have to be modified in some way before the suffix *-ly* is added to form the adverbs. For example, in adjectives ending in *-y*, the *y* changes to *i* before *-ly* is added. Examples of these include:

adjective	*adverb*	*adjective*	*adverb*
angry	angrily	happy	happily
busy	busily	merry	merrily
canny	cannily	pretty	prettily
dry	drily	silly	sillily
easy	easily	tatty	tattily
funny	funnily	weary	wearily

Note the exceptions "shyly," "slyly," "wryly."

Adjectives ending in *-e* frequently drop the e before adding *-ly*. Examples of these include:

adjective	*adverb*	*adjective*	*adverb*
able	ably	peaceable	peaceably
feeble	feebly	true	truly
gentle	gently	unintelligble	unintelligibly

Suffixes other than *-ly* that may be added to adjectives to form **adverbs of manner** include *-wards*, as in "backwards," "heavenwards"; *-ways*, as in "edgeways," "sideways"; *-wise*, as in "clockwise," "moneywise."

Some **adverbs of manner** may take the same form as the adjectives to which they correspond. These include "fast," "hard," "solo," "straight," "wrong," as in "She took the wrong book" and "Don"t get me wrong."

Adverbs of degree tells us the degree, extent or intensity of something that happens and include "hugely," "immensely," "moderately," "adequately," "greatly," "strongly," "tremendously," "profoundly," "totally," "entirely," "perfectly," "partially," "practically," "virtually," "almost," as in "They enjoyed the show hugely," "The office was not adequately equipped," "We strongly disapprove of such behavior," "He was totally unaware of the facts," "They are virtually penniless."

Adverbs of frequency are used to tell us how often something happens and include "never," "rarely," "seldom," "infrequently," "occasionally," "periodically," "intermittently," "sometimes," "often," "frequently," "regularly," "normally," "always," "constantly," "continually," as in "She never eats breakfast," "We go to the movies occasionally," "He goes to the dentist regularly," "Normally they travel by bus," "He is in pain constantly."

Adverbs of probability tells us how often something happens and include "probably," "possibly," "conceivably," "perhaps," "maybe," "presumably," "hopefully," "definitely," "certainly," "indubitably," "doubtless," as in "You will probably see them there," "He may conceivably pass the exam this time," "Presumably they know that she is leaving," "Hopefully the news will be good," "I am definitely not going," "He is indubitably a criminal."

Adverbs of duration tell us how long something takes or lasts and include "briefly," "temporarily," "long," "indefinitely," "always," "permanently," "forever," as in "We stopped briefly for coffee," "Have you known her long?," "Her face is permanently disfigured," "They have parted forever."

Adverbs of emphasis add emphasis to the action described by the verb and include "absolutely," "certainly," "positively," "quite," "really," "simply," "just," as in "They absolutely detest each other," "He positively adores her," "She really wants to be forgiven," "I simply must go now."

Interrogative adverbs ask questions and include "where," "when," "how," and "why," as in "Where are you going?," "When will you be back?," "How will you get there?," "Why have they asked you to go?" They are placed at the beginning of sentences, and such sentences always end with a question mark.

adverbial clauses are subordinate clauses that modify the main or principal clause by adding information about time, place, concession, condition, manner, purpose and result. They usually follow the main clause but most of them can be put in front of the main clause for reason of emphasis or style.

auxiliary verb refers to a verb which is used in forming tenses, moods and voices of other verbs. These include "be," "do" and "have."

The verb "to be" is used as an **auxiliary verb** with the -ing form of the main verb to form the continuous present tense, as in "They are living abroad just now" and "We were thinking of going on vacation but we changed our minds."

The verb "to be" is used as an **auxiliary verb** with the past participle of the main verb to form the passive voice, as in "Her hands were covered in blood" and "These toys are manufactured in China."

The verb "to have" is used as an **auxiliary verb** along with the past participle of the main verb to form the perfect tenses, as in "They have filled the post," "She had realized her mistake" and "They wished that they had gone earlier."

The verb "to be" is used as an **auxiliary verb** along with the main verb to form negative sentences, as in "She is not accepting the job." The verb "to do" is used as an **auxiliary verb** along with the main verb to form negative sentences, as in "he does not believe her." It is also used along with the main verb to form questions, as in "Does he know that she's gone?" and to form sentences in which the verb is emphasized, as in "She does want to go."

complex sentence refers to a type of sentence in which there is a main clause and one or more subordinate clauses. The sentence "We went to visit him although he had been unfriendly to us" is a complex sentence since it is composed of a main clause and one subordinate clause ("although he had been unfriendly to us"). The sentence "We wondered where he had gone and why he was upset" is a complex sentence since it has a main clause and two subordinate clauses ("where he had gone" and "why he was upset").

conjunctions are of two types. Coordinating conjunctions join units of equal status, as in "bread and butter," "We asked for some food and we got it." A subordinating conjunction joins a dependent or subordinating clause to main verbs: in "We asked him why he was there," "why he was there" is a subordinate clause and thus "why" is a subordinating conjunction.

definite article is a term for "the," which is the most frequently used word in the English language. "The" is used to refer back to a person or thing that has already been mentioned, as in "Jack and Jill built a model. The model was of a ship" and "We've bought a car. It was the cheapest car we could find."

"The" can be used to make a general statement about all things of a particular type, as in "The computer has lead to the loss of many jobs" and "The car has caused damage to the environment." "The" can be used to refer to a whole class or group, as in "the Italians," "the Browns" and "the younger generation."

"The" can also be used to refer to services or systems, as in "They are not on the phone." It can be used to refer to the name of a musical instrument when someone's ability to play it is being referred to, as in "Her son is learning to play the violin."

"The" indicates a person or thing to be the only one, as in the Bible, the King of Spain, the White House, the Palace of Westminster and the President of the United States.

"The" can be used instead of a possessive determiner to refer to parts of the body, as in "She took him by the arm" and "The dog bit him on the leg."

"The" is used in front of superlative adjectives, as in "the largest amount of money" and "the most beautiful woman." It can also be used to indicate that a person or thing is unique or exceptional, as in "the political debater of his generation." In this last sense "the" is pronounced "thee."

finite clause is a clause which contains a "finite verb," as in "when she sees him," "after she had defeated him," and "as they were sitting there."

finite verb is a verb that has a tense and has a subject with which it agrees in number and person. For example "cries" is finite in the sentence "The child cries most of the time," and "looks" is finite in the sentence "The old man looks ill." However "go" in the sentence "He wants to go" is non-finite since it has no variation of tense and does not have a subject. Similarly in the sentence "Sitting on the river-bank, he was lost in thought," "sitting" is non-finite.

first person refers to the person who is speaking or writing when referring to himself or herself. The **first person** pronouns are "I," "me," "myself" and "mine," with the plural forms being "we," "us," "ourselves" and "ours." Examples include "She said, 'I am going home' ," " '*I* am going shopping,' he said' ," " '*We* have very little money left,' she said to her husband," and "He said, '*We* shall have to leave now if we are to get there on time'." The first person determiners are "my" and "our," as in "I have forgotten to bring *my* notebook" and "We must remember to bring *our* books home."

he is a personal pronoun and is used as the subject of a sentence or clause to refer to a man, boy, etc. It is thus said to be a "masculine" personal pronoun. Since he refers to a third party and does not refer to the speaker or the person being addressed, it is a "third-person pronoun." Examples include "James is quite nice but he can be boring," "Bob has got a new job and he is very pleased" and "He is rich but his parents are very poor."

He traditionally was used not only to refer to nouns relating to the masculine sex but also to nouns that are now regarded as being neutral or of "dual gender." Such nouns include "architect," "artist," "athlete," "doctor," "passenger," "parent," "pupil," "singer," "student." Without further information from the context it is impossible to know to which sex such nouns are referring. In modern usage it is regarded as sexist to assume such words to be masculine by using **he** to refer to one of them unless the context indicates that the noun in question refers to a man or boy. Formerly it was considered acceptable to write or say "Send a message to the architect who designed the building that he is to attend the meeting" whether or not the writer or speaker knew that the architect was a man. Similarly it was considered acceptable to write or say "Please tell the doctor that he is to come straight away" whether or not the speaker or writer knew that the doctor was in fact a man. Nowadays this convention is considered sexist. In order to avoid sexism it is possible to use the convention "he/she," as in "Every student was told that he/she was to be smartly dressed for the occasion," "Each passenger was informed that he/she was to arrive ten minutes before the coach was due to leave" and "Tell the doctor that he/she is required urgently." However this convention is regarded by some people as being clumsy, particularly in spoken English or in informal written English. Some people prefer to be ungrammatical and use the plural personal pronoun "they" instead of "he/she" in certain situations, as in "Every passenger was told that they had to arrive ten minutes before the coach was due to leave" and "Every student was advised that they should apply for a college place by March." In some cases it may be possible to rephrase sentences and avoid being either sexist or ungrammatical, as in "All the passengers were told that they should arrive ten minutes before the coach was due to leave" and "All students were advised that they should apply for a college place by March."

her is a personal pronoun. It is the third person singular, is feminine in gender and acts as the object in a sentence, as in "We saw her yesterday," "I don't know her," "He hardly ever sees her," "Please give this book to her," "Our daughter sometimes plays with her" and "We do not want her to come to the meeting." See he.

hers is a personal pronoun. It is the third person singular, feminine in gender and is in the possessive case. "The car is not hers," "I have forgotten my book but I don't want to borrow hers," "This is my seat and that is hers," and "These clothes are hers." See his; her.

him is the third person masculine personal pronoun when used as the object of a sentence or clause, as in "She shot him," "When the police caught the thief they arrested him" and "His parents punished **him** after the boy stole the money." Traditionally him was used to apply not only to masculine nouns, such as "man" and "boy," but also to nouns that are said to be "of dual gender." These include "architect," "artist," "parent," "passenger," "pupil" and "student." Without further information from the context, it is not possible for the speaker or writer to know the sex of the person referred to by one of these words. Formerly it was acceptable to write or say "The artist must bring an easel with him" and "Each student must bring food with him." In modern usage this convention is considered sexist and there is a modern convention that "him/her" should be used instead to avoid sexism, as in "The artist must bring an easel with him/her" and "Each student must bring food with "him/her." This convention is felt by some people to be clumsy, particularly in spoken and in informal English, and some people prefer to be ungrammatical and use the plural personal pronoun "them" instead, as in "The artist must bring an easel with them" and "Each student must bring food with them." In some situations it is possible to avoid being either sexist or ungrammatical by rephrasing the sentence, as in "All artists must bring easels with them" and "All students must bring food with them. See he.

his is the third personal masculine pronoun when used to indicate possession, as in "He has hurt his leg," "The boy has taken his books home" and "Where has your father left his tools?" Traditionally **his** was used to refer not only to masculine nouns, such as "man," "boy," etc, but to what are known as nouns "of dual gender." These include "architect," "artist," "parent," "passenger," "pupil" and "student." Without further information from the context it is not possible for the speaker or the writer to know the sex of the person referred to by one of these words. Formerly it was considered acceptable to use **his** in such situations, as in "Every student has to supply his own sports equipment" and "Every passenger is responsible for his own luggage." In modern usage this is now considered sexist and there is a modern convention that "his/her" should be used instead to avoid sexism, as in "Every student has to supply his/her own sports equipment" and "Every passenger is responsible for his/her own luggage." This convention is felt by some people to be clumsy, particularly when used in spoken or informal written English. Some people prefer to be ungrammatical and use the plural personal pronoun "their," as in "Every student must supply their own sports equipment" and "Every passenger is to be responsible for their own luggage." In some situations it is possible to avoid being sexist, clumsy and ungrammatical by rephrasing the sentence, as in "All students must supply their own sports equipment" and "All passengers are to be responsible for their own luggage."

indefinite article: **a** and **an** are the forms of the indefinite article. The form a is used before words that begin with a consonant sound, as "a box," "a garden," "a road," "a wall." The form **an** is used before words that begin with a vowel sound, as "an apple," "an easel," "an ostrich," "an uncle." Note that it is the sound of the initial letter that matters and not the spelling. Thus **a** is used before words beginning with a *u* when they are pronounced with a *y* sound as though it were a consonant, as "a unit," "a usual occurrence." Similarly, **an** is used, for example, before words beginning with the letter *h* where this is not pronounced, as in "an heir," "an hour," "an honest man."

Formerly it was quite common to use **an** before words that begin with an h sound and also begin with an unstressed syllable, as in "an hotel (ho-tel)," "an historic (his-tor-ik) occasion," "an hereditary (her-ed-it-ary) disease." It is now more usual nowadays to use a in such cases and ignore the question of the unstressed syllable.

intransitive verb refers to a verb that does not take a "direct object," as in "Snow fell yesterday," "The children played in the sand," "The path climbed steeply," "Time will tell," "The situation worsened," "Things improved" and "Prices increased." Many verbs can be either transitive or intransitive, according to the context. Thus "play" is **intransitive** in the sentence "The children played in the sand" but "transitive" in the sentence "The boy plays the piano." Similarly "climb" is intransitive in the sentence "The path climbs steeply" but transitive in the sentence "The mountaineers climbed Everest." Similarly "tell" is **intransitive** in the sentence "Time will tell" but "transitive" in the sentence "He will tell his life story."

irregular verbs are verbs that do not conform to the usual pattern of verbs in that some of their forms deviate from what one would expect if the pattern of regular verbs was being followed. There are four main forms of a regular verb – the infinitive or "base" form, as in "hint," "halt," "hate" and "haul"; the "third-person singular" form as "hints," "halts," "hates" and "hauls"; the *-ing* form or "present participle," as "hinting," halting," "hating" and "hauling"; the *-ed* form or "past tense" or "past participle," as "hinted," halted," "hated" and "hauled.

Irregular verbs deviate in some way from that pattern, in particular from the pattern of adding *-ed* to the past tense and past participle. They fall into several categories.
One category concerns those which have the same form in the past tense and past participle forms as the infinitive and do not end in -ed, like regular verbs. These include:

infinitive	*past tense*	*past participle*
bet	bet	bet
burst	burst	burst
cast	cast	cast
cost	cost	cost
cut	cut	cut
hit	hit	hit
hurt	hurt	hurt
let	let	let
put	put	put
run	run	run
set	set	set
shed	shed	shed
shut	shut	shut
slit	slit	slit
split	split	split
spread	spread	spread

Some **irregular verbs** have two past tenses and two past participles which are the same, as in:

infinitive	past tense	past participle
burn	burned, burnt	burned, burnt
infinitive	past tense	past participle
dream	dreamed, dreamt	dreamed, dreamt
dwell	dwelled, dwelt	dwelled, dwelt
hang	hanged, hung	hanged, hung
kneel	kneeled, knelt	kneeled, knelt
lean	leaned, leant	learned, learnt
leap	leaped, leapt	leaped, leapt
learn	learned, learnt	learned, learnt
light	lighted, lit	lighted, lit
smell	smelled, smelt	smelled, smelt
speed	speeded, sped	speeded, sped
spill	spilled, spilt	spilled, spilt
spoil	spoiled, spoilt	spoiled, spoilt
weave	weaved, woven	weaved, woven
wet	wetted, wet	wetted, wet

Some **irregular verbs** have past tenses which do not end in *-ed* and have the same form as the past participle. These include:

infinitive	*past tense*	*past participle*
become	became	became
bend	bent	bent
bleed	bled	bled
breed	bred	bred
build	built	built
cling	clung	clung
come	came	came
dig	dug	dug
feel	felt	felt
fight	fought	fought
find	found	found
flee	fled	fled
fling	flung	flung
get	got	gotten
grind	ground	ground
hear	heard	heard
hold	held	held
keep	kept	kept
lay	laid	laid
lead	led	led
leave	left	left
lend	lent	lent
lose	lost	lost
make	made	made
mean	meant	meant
meet	met	met
pay	paid	paid
rend	rent	rent
say	said	said
seek	sought	sought
sell	sold	sold
send	sent	sent
shine	shone	shone
shoe	shod	shod
sit	sat	sat
sleep	slept	slept
slide	slid	slid
sling	slung	slung
slink	slunk	slunk
spend	spent	spent
spin	spun	spun

stand	stood	stood
stick	stuck	stuck
sting	stung	stung
strike	struck	struck
string	strung	strung
sweep	swept	swept
swing	swung	swung
teach	taught	taught
tell	told	told
think	thought	thought
understand	understood	understood
weep	wept	wept
win	won	won
wring	wrung	wrung

Some **irregular verbs** have regular past tense forms but two possible past participles, one of which is regular. These include:

infinitive	*past tense*	*past participle*
mow	mowed	mowed, mown
prove	proved	proved, proven
sew	sewed	sewn, sewed
show	showed	showed, shown
sow	sowed	sowed, sown
swell	swelled	swelled, swollen

Some **irregular verbs** have past tenses and past participles that are different from each other and different from the infinitive. These include:

infinitive	*past tense*	*past participle*
arise	arose	arisen
awake	awoke	awoken
bear	bore	borne
begin	began	begun
bid	bade	bidden
bite	bit	bitten
blow	blew	blown
break	broke	broken
choose	chose	chosen
do	did	done
draw	drew	drawn
drink	drank	drunk
drive	drove	driven
eat	ate	eaten
fall	fell	fallen
fly	flew	flown
forbear	forbore	forborne
forbid	forbade	forbidden
forgive	forgave	forgiven
forget	forgot	forgotten
forsake	forsook	forsaken
freeze	froze	frozen
forswear	forswore	forewarn
give	gave	given
go	went	gone
grow	grew	grown
hew	hewed	hewn
hide	hid	hidden
know	knew	known
lie	lay	lain
ride	rode	ridden
ring	rang	rung
saw	sawed	sawn
see	saw	seen
rise	rose	risen
shake	shook	shaken
shrink	shrank	shrunk
slay	slew	slain
speak	spoke	spoken
spring	sprang	sprung
steal	stole	stolen
stink	stank	stunk
strew	strewed	strewn
stride	strode	stridden
strive	strove	striven
swear	swore	sworn
swim	swam	swum
take	took	taken
tear	tore	torn
throw	threw	thrown
tread	trod	trodden
wake	woken	woke
wear	wore	worn
write	written	wrote

major sentence can be used to refer to a sentence that contains at least one subject and a finite verb, as in "We are going" and "They won." They frequently have more elements than this, as in "They bought a car," "We lost the match," "They arrived yesterday" and "We are going away next week." They are sometimes described as "regular" because they divide into certain structural patterns, a subject, finite verb, adverb or adverbial, etc. The opposite of a **major sentence** is called a "minor sentence," "irregular sentence" or "fragmentary sentence." These include interjections such as "Ouch!" and "How terrible"; formula expressions, such as "Good morning" and "Well done"; and short forms of longer expressions, as in "Traffic diverted," "Shop closed," "No dogs" and "Flooding ahead." Such short forms could be rephrased to become "major sentences," as in "Traffic has been diverted because of roadworks," "The shop is closed on Sundays," "The owner does not allow dogs in her shop" and "There was flooding ahead on the motorway."

modal verb refers to a type of "auxiliary verb" that "helps" the main verb to express a range of meanings including, for example, such meanings as possibility, probability, wants, wishes, necessity, permission, suggestions, etc. The main modal verbs are "can," "could"; "may," "might"; "will," "would"; "shall," "should"; "must." Modal verbs have only one form. They have no -s form in the third person singular, no infinitive and no participles. Examples of modal verbs include "He cannot read and write," "She could go if she wanted to" (expressing ability); "You can have another cookie," "You may answer the question" (expressing permission); "We may see her on the way to the station," "We might get there by nightfall" (expressing possibility); "Will you have some wine?," "Would you take a seat?" (expressing an offer or invitation); "We should arrive by dawn," "That must be a record" (expressing probability and certainty); "You may prefer to wait," "You might like to leave instructions" (expressing suggestion); "Can you find the time to phone him for me?," "Could you give him a message?" (expressing instructions and requests); "They must leave at once," "We must get there on time" (expressing necessity).

modifier refers to a word, or group of words, that "modifies" or affects the meaning of another word in some way, usually by adding more information about it. **Modifiers** are frequently used with nouns. They can be adjectives, as in "He works in the *main* building" and "They need a *larger* house." **Modifiers** of nouns can be nouns themselves, as in "the *theatre* profession," "the *publishing* industry" and "singing tuition." They can also be place names, as in "a *Paris* cafe" and "the *London* underground" or adverbs of place and direction, as in "a *downstairs* cloakroom."

Adverbs, adjectives and pronouns can be accompanied by modifiers. Examples of modifiers with adverbs include "walking *amazingly* quickly" and "stopping *incredibly* abruptly." Examples of modifiers with adjectives include "a *really* warm day" and "a *deliriously* happy child." Examples of modifiers with pronouns include "almost no one there" and "*practically* everyone present."

The examples given above are all "pre-modifiers."

mood refers to one of the categories into which verbs are divided. The verb moods are "indicative," "imperative" and "subjunctive." The indicative makes a statement, as in "He lives in France," "They have two children" and "It's starting to rain." The "imperative" is used for giving orders or making requests, as in "Shut that door!," and "Please bring me some coffee." The subjunctive was originally a term in Latin grammar and expressed a wish, supposition, doubt, improbability or other non-factual statement. It is used in English for hypothetical statements and certain formal "that" clauses, as in "If I were you I would have nothing to do with it," "If you were to go now you would arrive on time," and "It was his lawyer who suggested that he sue the firm." The word **mood** arose because it was said to indicate the verb's attitude or viewpoint.

non-finite clause is a clause which contains a "non-finite verb." Thus in the sentence "He works hard to earn a living," "to earn a living" is a non-finite clause since "to earn" is an infinitive and so a non-finite verb. Similarly in the sentence "Getting there was a problem," "getting there" is a non-finite clause, "getting" being a present participle and so a non-finite verb.

non-finite verb is one which shows no variation in tense and which has no subject. The non-finite verb forms include the infinitive form, as in "go," the present participle and gerund, as in "going," and the past participle, as in "gone."

noun indicates the name of something or someone. Thus "anchor," "baker," "cat," "elephant," "foot," "gate," "lake," "pear," "shoe," "trunk" and "wallet" are all nouns. There are various categories of nouns.

noun clause refers to a "subordinate clause" which performs a function in a sentence similar to a noun or noun phrase. It can act as the subject, object or complement of a main clause. In the sentence "Where he goes is his own business," "where he goes" is a **noun clause**. In the sentence "They asked why he objected," "why he objected" is a **noun clause**. A **noun clause** is also known as a nominal clause.

noun phrase refers to a group of words containing a noun as its main word and functioning like a noun in a sentence. Thus it can function as the subject, object or complement of a sentence. In the sentence "The large black dog bit him," "the large black dog" is a noun phrase and in the sentence "They bought a house with a garden," "with a garden" is a noun phrase. In the sentence "She is a complete fool," "a complete fool" is a noun phrase.

passive voice designates the voice of a verb whereby the subject is the recipient of the action of the verb. Thus, in the sentence "Mary was kicked by her brother," "Mary" is the receiver of the "kick" and so "kick" is in the passive voice. Had it been in the active voice it would have been "Her brother kicked Mary." Thus "the brother" is the subject and not the receiver of the action.

personal pronouns are used to refer back to someone or something that has already been mentioned. The personal pronouns are divided into subject pronouns, object, pronouns and possessive pronouns. They are also categorized according to "person." *See* FIRST PERSON, SECOND PERSON and THIRD PERSON.

prepositions are words which relate two elements of a sentence, clause or phrase together. They show how the elements relate in time or space and generally precede the words which they "govern." Words governed by **prepositions** are nouns or pronouns. **Prepositions** are often very short words, as "at," "in," "on," "to," "before" and "after." Some complex prepositions consist of two words, as "ahead of," "instead of," "apart from," and some consist of three, as "with reference to," "in accordance with" and "in addition to." Examples of **prepositions** in sentences include "The cat sat on the mat," "We were at a concert," "They are in shock," "She arrived before me" and "Apart from you she has no friends."

pronoun is a word that takes the place of a noun or a noun phrase.

second person refers to the person or thing to whom one is talking. The term is applied to personal pronouns. The second person singular whether acting as the subject of a sentence is "you," as in "I told you so," "We informed you of our decision" and "They might have asked you sooner." The **second person** personal pronoun does not alter its form in the plural in English, unlike in some languages. The possessive form of the **second person** pronoun is "yours" whether singular or plural, as in "He said to the boys 'These books are not yours' " and "This pen must be yours."

sentence is at the head of the hierarchy of grammar. All the other elements, such as words, phrases and clauses go to make up sentences. It is difficult to define a sentence. In terms of recognizing a sentence visually it can be described as beginning with a capital letter and ending with a period, or with an equivalent to the period, such as an exclamation mark. It is a unit of grammar that can stand alone and make sense and obeys certain grammatical rules, such as usually having a subject and a predicate, as in "The girl banged the door," where "the girl" is the subject and "the door" is the predicate.

simple sentence is a sentence which cannot be broken down into other clauses. It generally contains a finite verb. Simple sentences include "The man stole the car," "She nudged him" and "He kicked the ball."

tense is used to show the time at which the action of a verb takes place. One of the tenses in English is the "present tense." It is used to indicate an action now going on or a state now existing. A distinction can be made between the "habitual present," which marks habitual or repeated actions or recurring events, and the "stative present," which indicates something that is true at all times. Examples of "habitual present" include "He works long hours" and "She walks to work." Examples of the stative tense include "The world is round" and "Everyone must die eventually."

The progressive present or continuous present is formed with the verb "to be" and the present participle, as in, "He is walking to the next village," "They are thinking about leaving" ,'She was driving along the road when she saw him" and "They were worrying about the state of the economy."

The "past tense" refers to an action or state which has taken place before the present time. In the case of "irregular verbs" it is formed by adding *-ed* to the base form of the verb, as in "fear/feared," "look/looked," and "turn/turned." For the past tense of "irregular verbs," *see* IRREGULAR VERBS.

The "future tense" refers to an action or state that will take place at some time in the future. It is formed with "will" and "shall." Traditionally "will" was used with the second and third person pronouns ("you," "he/she/it," "they") and "shall" with the first person ("I" and "we"), as in "You will be bored," "He will soon be home," "They will leave tomorrow," "I shall buy some bread" and "We shall go by train." Also traditionally "shall" was used with the second and third persons to indicate emphasis, insistence, determination, refusal, etc., as in "You shall go to the ball" and "He shall not be admitted." "Will" was used with the first person in the same way, as in "I will get even with him."

In modern usage "will" is generally used for the first person as well as for second and third, as in "I will see you tomorrow" and "We will be there soon" and "shall" is used for emphasis, insistence, etc. for first, second and third persons.

The "future tense" can also be formed with the use of "be about to" or "be going to," as in "We were about to leave" and "They were going to look for a house.

Other tenses include the "perfect tense" which is formed using the verb "to have" and the past participle. In the case of "regular verbs" the "past participle" is formed by adding "ed" to the base form of the verb. For the past participles of "irregular verbs" see irregular verbs. Examples of the "perfect tense" include "He has played his last match," "We have traveled all day" and "They have thought a lot about it."

The "past perfect tense" or "pluperfect tense" is formed using the verb "to have" and the past participle, as in "She had no idea that he was dead," and "They had felt unhappy about the situation."

The "future perfect" is formed using the verb "to have" and the past participle, as in "He will have arrived by now."

third person refers to a third party not the speaker or the person or thing being spoken to. Note that "person" in this context can refer to things or people. "Person" in this sense applies to personal pronouns. The third person singular forms are "he," "she" and "it" when the subject of a sentence or clause, as in "She will win" and "It will be fine." The third person singular forms are "him," "her," "it" when the object, as in "His behavior hurt her" and "She meant it." The third person plural is "they" when the subject, as in "They have left" and "They were angry" and "them" when the object, as in "His words made them angry" and "We accompanied them.

The possessive forms of the singular are "his," "hers" and "its," as in "he played his guitar" and "The dog hurt its leg" and the the possessive form of the plural is theirs,as in "That car is theirs" and "They say that the book is theirs."

transitive verb is a verb which takes a direct object. In the sentence "The boy broke the window" "window" is a "direct object" and so "broke" (break) is a transitive verb. In the sentence "She eats fruit" "fruit" is a "direct object" and so "eat" is a transitive verb. In the sentence "They kill enemy soldiers" "enemy soldiers" is a "direct object" and so "kill" is a transitive verb." *See* INTRANSITIVE VERB.

verb is often known as a "doing" word. Although this is rather restrictive ,since it tends to preclude auxiliary verbs, modal verbs, etc. the verb is the word in a sentence that is most concerned with the action and is usually essential to the structure of the sentence. **Verbs** "inflect" and indicate tense, voice, mood, number, number and person. Most of the information on **Verbs** has been placed under related entries. *See* ACTIVE, PASSIVE, VOICE, AUXILIARY VERB, MODAL VERB, MOOD, FINITE VERB, NON-FINITE VERB, TRANSITIVE VERB, INTRANSITIVE VERB and IRREGULAR VERB.

verb phrase refers to a group of verb forms which has the same function as a single verb. Examples include "have been raining," "must have been lying," should not have been doing and "has been seen doing."

voice is one of the categories that describes verbs. It involves two different ways of looking at the action of verbs. It is divided into "active voice" and "passive voice." *See* ACTIVE VOICE and PASSIVE VOICE.

APPENDIX II

Phrases and Quotations from Latin, Greek and Modern Foreign Languages

A

abiit, excessit, evasit, erupit (L.) he is gone, he is off, he has escaped, he has broken away. — Cicero, *In Catilinam*, II. i. 1.
ab imo pectore (L.) from the bottom of the heart.
à bon chat, bon rat (Fr.) to a good cat, a good rat — well matched: set a thief to catch a thief.
ab ovo usque ad mala (L.) from the egg to the apples — of a Roman banquet: from the beginning to the end.
absens haeres non erit (L.) the absent one will not be the heir — out of sight, out of mind.
ab uno disce omnes (L.) from one (offense) learn all (the race). — Virgil, *Aen.*, I. 65–66: hence, from one example you may know the rest.
abusus non tollit usum (L.) abuse does not do away with use — i.e. an abuse is not a reason for giving up the legitimate use of a thing.
a capite ad calcem (L.) from head to heel.
à chacun son goût (Fr.) to everyone his own taste. See also **chacun (à) son goût**.
à chaque saint sa chandelle (Fr.) every saint his candle: to every patron his meed of service.
Acherontis pabulum (L.) food for Acheron — of a bad person. — Plautus, *Casina*, II. i. 12.
actum est de republica (L.) it is all up with the state.
actum ne agas (L.) do not do what is already done — quoted as a proverb by Terence, *Phormio.*, II. iii. 72 (or 1. 419).
ad Calendas Graecas (L.) at the Greek Calends — i.e. never, as the Greeks had no Calends.
adhuc sub judice lis est (L.) the dispute is still before the court. — Horace, *A.P.*, 78.
ad majorem Dei gloriam (L.) for the greater glory of God — the Jesuit motto.
adscriptus glebae (L.) bound to the soil — of serfs.
ad utrumque paratus (L.) prepared for either case.
ad vitam aut culpam (L.) for life or till fault: of appointments, for life unless misconduct necessitates dismissal.
advocatus diaboli (L.) devil's advocate. See Dict.
aequam memento rebus in arduis servare mentem (L.) remember to keep a calm mind in difficulties. — Horace, *Od.*, II. iii. 1.
aequitas sequitur legem (L.) equity follows law.
age quod agis (L.) do what you are doing — i.e. with all your powers.
aide-toi, le ciel t'aidera (Fr.) help yourself and Heaven will help you.
aliquando bonus dormitat Homerus (L.) See **indignor**.
aliquid haeret (L.) something sticks.
Allah il Allah, a corr. of Ar. *laa ilaaha illaa 'llaah* = there is no God but the God.
Allahu akbar (Ar.) God is great.
alter ipse amicus (L.) a friend is another self.
amabilis insania (L.) a pleasing madness or rapture. — Horace, *Od.*, III. 4. 5–6.
amantium irae amoris integratio est (L.) lovers' quarrels are a renewal of love. — Terence, *Andr.*, III. iii. 23.
amare et sapere vix deo conceditur (L.) to be in love and to be wise is scarce granted even to a god. — Laberius.
amari aliquid (L.) some touch of bitterness. — Lucretius, *De Rer. Nat.*, iv. 1130.
a mensa et toro (L.) from bed and board.

amicus Plato, amicus Socrates, sed magis amica veritas (L.) Plato is dear to me (or is my friend), Socrates is dear, but truth is dearer still. — L. version of saying attributed to Aristotle.
amicus usque ad aras (L.) a friend as far as the altars — i.e. as far as may be without offense to the gods.
amor sceleratus habendi (L.) the accursed love of possessing. — Ovid, *Met.*, I. 131.
amor vincit omnia (L.). See **omnia**.
anathema sit (L.) let him be accursed. — 1 Cor. xvi. 22.
anch' io son pittore (It.) I, too, am a painter (said by Correggio on looking at Raphael's 'St Cecilia').
anearithmon gelasma. See **kymatoan anearithmon gelasma**.
anguis in herba (L.) a snake in the grass. — Virgil, *Ecl.*, III. 93.
anima naturaliter Christiana (L.) a soul naturally Christian, i.e. one who behaves like a Christian without the benefit of Christian revelation. — Tertullian, *Apologia*, xvii.
animula vagula (L.) little soul flitting away — beginning of a poem ascribed to the dying Hadrian, translated or paraphrased by Prior, Pope, Byron, and Dean Merivale.
à nos moutons. See **revenons**.
ante Agamemnona. See **vixere fortes**.
a parte ante (L.) on the side before, from past eternity — opp. to **a parte post**, in future eternity.
a posse ad esse (L.) from the possible to the actual. **après moi (nous) le déluge** (Fr.) after me (us) the deluge: then the deluge may come when it likes — attributed to Mme. de Pompadour and to Louis XV. Cf. **emou thanontos**.
aquila non capit muscas (L.) an eagle does not catch flies.
arbiter elegantiae (L.) judge of good taste — said by Tacitus, *Annals*, XVI. 18, of Gaius Petronius, an exquisite at the court of Nero (prob. same as Petronius Arbiter). — Also quoted as **arbiter elegantiarum**.
Arcades ambo (L.) Arcadians both: two of the same stamp. — Virgil, *Ecl.*, VII. 4. — Rendered by Byron blackguards both, *Don Juan*, IV. xciii.
ariston men hydoar (Gr.) water is best. — Pindar, *Olympian Odes*, i. 1.
ars est celare artem (L.) true art is to conceal art.
ars longa, vita brevis (L.) art is long, life is short. — Seneca, *De Brevitate Vitae*, 1. Cf. **ho bios brachys**.
asbestos geloas (Gr.) inextinguishable laughter. — Homer, *Iliad*, I. 599, etc.
asinus ad lyram (L.) an ass at the lyre, one ignorant of music or art: one unsuited to an occupation. — From a Greek proverbial expression *onos pros lyran*.
astra castra, numen lumen (L.) the stars my camp, God my lamp.
Athanasius contra mundum (L.) Athanasius against the world: one resolute man facing universal opposition.
atra cura (L.) black care. See **post equitem**.
at spes non fracta (L.) but hope is not yet crushed.
au bout de son latin (Fr.) at the end of his Latin, at the end of his knowledge, at his wits' end.
auctor quae pretiosa facit (L.) gifts that the giver adds value to. — Ovid, *Her.*, XVII. 71–2.
audentes fortuna juvat (L.) fortune favors the daring. — Virgil, *Aen.*, X. 284.
audi alteram partem (L.) hear the other side. — St Augustine, *De Duabus Animabus*, XIV. 2.
auditque vocatus Apollo (L.) and Apollo hears when invoked. — Virgil, *Georg.*, IV. 7.
aufgeschoben ist nicht aufgehoben (Ger.) put off is not given up.
aujourd'hui roi, demain rien (Fr.) king today, nothing tomorrow.
au plaisir de vous revoir (Fr.) till I have the pleasure of seeing you again.
auribus teneo lupum (L.) I am holding a wolf by the ears. — Terence, *Phormio*, III. ii. 21.
auri sacra fames (L.) accursed hunger for gold. — Virgil, *Aen.*, III. 57.
au royaume des aveugles les borgnes sont rois (Fr.) in the kingdom of the blind the one-eyed are kings. — As a Latin proverb, *beati monoculi in regione caecorum*.
aurum omnes, victa jam pietate, colunt (L.) all worship gold, piety being overthrown. — Propertius, III. xiii. 48.
auspicium melioris aevi (L.) augury of a better age.
aussitôt dit, aussitôt fait (Fr.) no sooner said than done.
Austriae est imperare orbi universo (L.) it is Austria's part to command the whole world — often **A.E.I.O.U.**
aut amat aut odit mulier, nihil est tertium (L.) a woman either loves or hates, there is no third course. — Syrus, 42.
autant d'hommes (or **de têtes**), **autant d'avis** (Fr.) so many men, so many minds. Cf. **quot homines**.
aut Caesar aut nullus, or **nihil** (L.) either Caesar or nobody (nothing): all or nothing.
aut insanit homo aut versus facit (L.) either the man is mad or he is making verses. — Horace, *Sat.*, II. vii. 117.
aut inveniam viam aut faciam (L.) I shall either find a way or make one.
aut non tentaris aut perfice (L.) either do not attempt or else achieve. — Ovid, *A.A.*, I. 389.
aut prodesse volunt aut delectare poetae (L.) poets seek either to profit or to please. — Horace, *A.P.*, 333.

aut regem aut fatuum nasci oportet (L.) one should be born either king or fool. — Proverb; quoted by Seneca.
autres temps, autres mœurs (Fr.) other times, other manners.
aut vincere aut mori (L.) to conquer or die.
aut vitam aut culpam. An incorrect variant of **ad vitam aut culpam** (q.v.).
aux absents les os (Fr.) the bones to the absent.
aux grands maux les grands remèdes (Fr.) to desperate evils, desperate remedies.
auxilium ab alto (L.) help from on high.
ave, Caesar (or **imperator**), **morituri te salutant** (L.) hail, Caesar, men doomed to die salute thee (said by gladiators).
a verbis ad verbera (L.) from words to blows.
à vieux comptes nouvelles disputes (Fr.) old accounts breed new disputes.
a vinculo matrimonii (L.) from the bond of matrimony.
avi numerantur avorum (L.) ancestors of ancestors are counted [to me].
avis au lecteur (Fr.) notice to the reader.
avise la fin (Fr.) weigh well the end.
avito viret honore (L.) he is green with ancestral honours.
avoir la langue déliée (Fr.) to have the tongue unbound, to be glib of speech.

B

barba tenus sapientes (L.) sages as far as the beard — i.e. with an appearance of wisdom only.
battre la campagne (Fr.) to scour the country, to beat the bush.
bayer aux corneilles (Fr.) to gape at the crows, to stare vacantly.
beatus ille qui procul negotiis . . . paterna rura bobus exercet suis (L.) happy he who, far removed from business . . . tills with his own oxen the fields that were his father's.— Horace, *Epod.*, ii. 1.
bella gerant alii, tu, felix Austria, nube (L.) let others wage wars; do thou, lucky Austria, make marriages. — Matthias Corvinus of Hungary.
bella, horrida bella (L.) wars, horrid wars. — Virgil, *Aen.*, VI. 86.
bellaque matribus detestata (L.) and wars abhorred by mothers. — Horace, *Od.*, I. i. 24–5.
bellum nec timendum nec provacandum (L.) war is neither to be feared nor provoked (Pliny the Younger, *Panegyricus*, 16, **nec times bellum, nec provocas**).
belua multorum capitum (L.) monster with many heads— the irrational mob. — Horace, *Epistolae*, I. i. 76.
beneficium accipere libertatem est vendere (L.) to accept a favor is to sell one's liberty. — Syrus, 49.
bene orasse est bene studuisse (L.) to have prayed well is to have endeavored well.
bene qui latuit bene vixit (L.) he has lived well who has lived obscure. — Ovid, *Trist.*, III. iv. 25.
benigno numine (l.) with favoring godhead. — Horace, *Od.*, III. iv. 74.
bibere venenum in auro (L.) to drink poison from a cup of gold.
biblia abiblia (Gr.) books that are no books.
bis dat qui cito dat (L.) he gives twice who gives promptly. — Proverb; by Bacon.
bis peccare in bello non licet (L.) in war one may not blunder twice.
bis pueri senes (L.) old men are twice boys.
blandae mendacia linguae (L.) falsehoods of a smooth tongue.
bon avocat, mauvais voisin (Fr.) a good lawyer is a bad neighbor.
bon jour, bonne œuvre (Fr.) better day, better deed.
bonnes nouvelles adoucissent le sang (Fr.) good news sweetens the blood.
borgen macht sorgen (Ger.) borrowing makes sorrowing.
boutez en avant (Fr.) push forward.
brevis esse laboro, obscurus fio (L.) I labor to be brief, and I become obscure. — Horace, *A.P.*, 25–26.
briller par son absence (Fr.) to be conspicuous by its absence.
brûler la chandelle par les deux bouts (Fr.) to burn the candle at both ends.
buen principio, la mitad es hecha (Sp.) well begun is half-done.

C

cadit quaestio (L.) the question drops.
caeca invidia est (L.) envy is blind. — Livy, xxxviii. 49.
caelebs quid agam (L.) (you wonder) what I, a bachelor, am about. — Horace, *Od.*, III. viii. 1.
caelum non animum mutant qui trans mare currunt (L.) they change their sky, not their mind, who scour across

the sea. — Horace, *Epist.*, I. xi. 27.
Caesar non supra grammaticos (L.) Caesar has no authority over the grammarians.
ça ira (Fr.) it will go — refrain of a famous song of the French Revolution.
callida junctura (L.) a skilful connection. — Horace, *A.P.*, 47–48.
candida Pax (L.) white-robed Peace. — Tibullus, I. x. 45.
cantabit vacuus coram latrone viator (L.) the empty-handed traveler will sing in presence of the robber. — Juvenal, X. 22.
carent quia vate sacro (L.) because they lack a sacred bard. — Horace, *Od.*, IV. ix. 28.
carpe diem, quam minimum credula postero (L.) enjoy the present day, trust the least possible to the future. — Horace, *Od.*, I. xi. 8.
causa sine qua non (L.) an indispensable cause.
cave quid dicis, quando, et cui (L.) beware what you say, when, and to whom.
cedant arma togae (L.) let arms yield to the gown: let military authority yield to civil. — Cicero, *De Officiis*, I. xxii. 77, *in Pisonem*, xxx. 73.
cela va sans dire (Fr.) that goes without saying: of course.
cela viendra (Fr.) that will come.
celui qui veut, peut (Fr.) who will, can.
ce monde est plein de fous (Fr.) this world is full of madmen.
c'en est fait de lui (Fr.) it is all up with him.
ce n'est que le premier pas qui coûte (Fr.). See **il n'ya**. **certum est quia impossibile est** (L.) it is certain because it is impossible. — Tertullian.
c'est-à-dire (Fr.) that is to say.
c'est égal (Fr.) it's all one (to me): it makes no odds.
c'est le commencement de la fin (Fr.) it is the beginning of the end. — Attrib. to Talleyrand.
c'est magnifique, mais ce n'est pas la guerre (Fr.) it is magnificent, but it is not war (said at Balaklava by a French general watching the charge of the Light Brigade).
c'est pire (or **plus**) **qu'un crime, c'est une faute** (Fr.) it is worse than a crime, it is a blunder (on the execution of the Duc d'Enghien; attributed to various persons, incl. Boulay de la Meurthe).
c'est selon (Fr.) that is according to the circumstances.
c'est (**une**) **autre chose** (Fr.) that is quite another thing.
ceterum censeo (L.) but I think (said of persistent obstruction like that of Cato).
chacun (à) son goût (Fr.) everyone to his taste. Also **à chacun son goût**.
chapeaux bas (Fr.) hats off.
cherchez la femme (Fr.) look for the woman: there's a woman at the bottom of it. — Dumas *père*.
che sarà sarà (It.) what will be will be.
chiesa libera in libero stato (It.) a free church in a free state (Cavour's ideal for Italy).
chi tace confessa (It.) who keeps silence, confesses.
circulus in probando (L.) arguing in a circle, using the conclusion as one of the arguments.
civis Romanus sum (L.) I am a Roman citizen. — Cicero, *In Verrem*, VI. 57.
clarior e tenebris (L.) the brighter from the darkness.
clarum et venerabile nomen (L.) an illustrious and venerable name. — Lucan, IX. 202.
cogito, ergo sum (L.) I think, therefore I am. (Descartes's fundamental basis of philosophy.)
comitas inter gentes, or **comitas gentium** (L.) See **comity** in Dict.
conditio sine qua non (L.) an indispensable condition.
conjunctis viribus (L.) with united powers.
conquiescat in pace (L.) may he [or she] rest in peace.
conscia mens recti (L.) a mind conscious of rectitude. — Ovid, *Fast.*, IV. 311. Cf. **mens sibi**.
consensus facit legem (L.) consent makes law or rule.
consuetudo pro lege servatur (L.) custom is held as a law.
consule Planco (L.) when Plancus was consul, when I was a young man. — Horace, *Od.*, III. xiv. 28.
contraria contrariis curantur (L.) opposites are cured by opposites.
corruptio optimi pessima (L.) the corruption of the best is the worst of all.
cosi fan tutte (It.) so do they all (of women): they are all like that.
coûte que coûte (Fr.) cost what it may.
crambe repetita (L.) cauld kale het again — cold cabbage warmed up. — Juvenal, VII. 154.
credat Judaeus Apella, non ego (L.) let the Jew Apella believe that, for I don't. — Horace, *Sat.*, I. v. 100.

credo quia absurdum (L.) I believe it because it is absurd; — **quia impossibile** because it is impossible (based on Tertullian; see **certum est quia impossibile est**).
crescit eundo (L.) it grows as it goes. — Lucretius VI. 341.
cucullus non facit monachum (L.) the cowl does not make the monk.
cuilibet (or **cuicunque**) **in arte sua** (**perito**) **credendum est** (L.) every (skilled) person is to be trusted in his own art. — Coke.
cujus regio, ejus religio (L.) whose the region, his the religion — the principle that the established religion should be that of the prince in each state.
curiosa felicitas (L.) studied felicity of expression — said by Petronius Arbiter, *Saturae* (*Satyricon*), 118, 5 of Horace's style: (*loosely*) curious felicity.

D

da dextram misero (L.) give the right hand to the unhappy.
da locum melioribus (L.) give place to your betters. — Terence, *Phormio*, III. ii. 37.
damnosa haereditas (L.) an inheritance of debts (*Roman law*): any hurtful inheritance. — Gaius, *Institutes*, ii. 163.
damnum absque injuria (L.) loss without legal injury.
das Ding an sich (Ger.) the thing in itself.
das Ewig-Weibliche zieht uns hinan (Ger.) the eternal feminine draws us upward. — Goethe, *Faust*, at end.
data et accepta (L.) expenditures and receipts.
date obolum Belisario (L.) give a penny to Belisarius (ascribed to the great general when reduced to beggary).
Davus sum, non Oedipus (L.) I am Davus, not Oedipus — no good at riddles. — Terence, *Andria.*, I. ii. 23.
de die in diem (L.) from day to day.
de gustibus non est disputandum (L.) there is no disputing about tastes.
de l'audace, encore de l'audace, et toujours de l'audace (Fr.) to dare, still to dare, and ever to dare (Danton's famous phrase).
delenda est Carthago (L.) Carthage must be wiped out (a saying constantly repeated by Cato).
de mal en pis (Fr.) from bad to worse.
de minimis non curat lex (L.) the law does not concern itself about very small matters. — Bacon, Letter cclxxxii.
de mortuis nil nisi bonum (L.) say nothing but good of the dead.
de nihilo nihilum. See **gigni**.
de omni re scibili et quibusdam aliis (L.) about all things knowable, and some others.
de pis en pis (Fr.) worse and worse.
der grosse Heide (Ger.) the great pagan (Heine's name for Goethe).
desipire in loco. See **dulce**.
desunt cetera (L.) the rest is wanting.
de te fabula narratur (L.) the story is about you. — Horace, *Sat.*, I. i. 69–70.
detur digniori (L.) let it be given to the more worthy; **detur pulchriori** let it be given to the fairer.
deus nobis haec otia fecit (L.) it is a god that hath given us this ease. — Virgil, *Ecl.*, I. 6.
dicamus bona verba (L.) let us speak words of good omen. — Tibullus, II, ii. 1.
Dichtung und Wahrheit (Ger.) poetry and truth.
dictum de dicto (L.) hearsay report.
dictum sapienti sat est (L.) a word to the wise is enough (usu. quoted as **verbum**). — Plautus, *Persa*, IV. vii. 19.
diem perdidi (L.) I have lost a day (said by the Emperor Titus). **Dieu défend le droit** (Fr.) God defends the right; **Dieu vous garde** God keep you.
Die Wacht am Rhein (Ger.) the Watch on the Rhine (a famous German patriotic song).
digito monstrari (L.) to be pointed out with the finger: to be famous. — Persius, I. 28.
dignus vindice nodus (L.) See **nec deus intersit**.
di grado in grado (It.) by degrees.
dis aliter visum (L.) the gods have adjudged otherwise. — Virgil, *Aen.*, II. 428.
disjecta membra (L.) scattered limbs (after Ovid, *Met.*, III. 724); **disjecti membra poetae** limbs of the dismembered poet. — Horace, *Sat.*, I. iv. 62.
distinguo (L.) I distinguish.
divide et impera (L.) divide and rule.
docendo discimus (L.) we learn by teaching.
doctor utriusque legis (L.) doctor of both laws (civil and canon).
doli capax (L.) capable of committing a wrong — opp. to *doli incapax*.

Domine. dirige nos (L.) Lord, direct us (the motto of London).
Dominus illuminatio mea (L.) the Lord is my light.
domus et placens uxor (L.) a home and a pleasing wife. — Horace, *Od.*, II. xiv. 21–22.
dorer la pilule (Fr.) to gild the pill.
dormitat Homerus (L.) See **indignor**.
dos moi pou stoa kai tean gean kineasoa (Gr.) give me where to stand, and I will move the earth (attributed to Archimedes).
do ut des (L.) I give that you may give.
dulce, 'Domum' (L.) sweet strain, 'Homeward' — from a Winchester school song sung before the holidays; **dulce est desipire in loco** it is pleasant to play the fool on occasion. — Horace, *Od.*, IV. xii. 28; **dulce et decorum est pro patria mori** it is sweet and glorious to die for one's country. — Horace, *Od.*, III. ii. 13.
dum casta (L.) while (she is) chaste.
dum spiro, spero (L.) while I breathe, I hope.
dum vivimus, vivamus (L.) let us live while we live.
dux femina facti (L.) a woman was leader in the deed. — Virgil, *Aen.*, I. 364.

E

écrasez l'infâme (Fr.) crush the vile thing. Voltaire against the Roman Catholic Church of his time.
edax rerum. See **tempus**.
ego et rex meus (L.) I and my kng. — Cardinal Wolsey.
ebeu fugaces . . . labuntur anni (L.) alas! the fleeting years slip away. — Horace, *Od.*, II. xiv. 1–2.
eile mit Weile (Ger.) make speed with leisure. Cf. **festina lente**.
ein Mal, kein Mal (Ger.) just once counts nothing.
ek parergou (Gr.) as a by-work.
eali, eali, lama sabachthani (Matt. xxvii. 46), **Eloi, Eloi, lamma sabachthani** (Mark xv. 34) (Gr. transliterations of Aramic) my God, my God, why hast thou forsaken me?
emou thanontos gaia michtheatoa pyri (Gr.) when I am dead let earth be mingled with fire. Cf. **après moi le déluge**.
entbehren sollst du, sollst entbehren (Ger.) thou must abstain, abstain thou must. — Goethe, *Faust*, Part I. (Studierzimmer, ii).
en toutoai nika (Gr.) conquer in this (sign). See **in hoc (signo) vinces**.
epea pteroenta (Gr.) winged words. — Homer (*Iliad*, I, 201, etc.).
ephphatha (Aramaic) be opened (Mark vii. 34).
e pluribus unum (L.) one out of many — before 1956 regarded as motto of the United States.
eppur si muove (It.) it does move all the same (attrib. to Galileo after he had recanted his doctrine that the earth moves round the sun).
erectos ad sidera tollere vultus (L.). See **os homini**.
ergo bibamus (L.) therefore let us drink.
Erin go bragh (Ir.) Erin forever.
errare est humanum (L.) to err is human.
es korakas (Gr.) to the ravens: go and be hanged.
esse quam videri (L.) to be, rather than to seem.
est modus in rebus (L.) there is a mean in (all) things. — Horace, *Sat.*, I. i. 106.
esto perpetua (L.) be lasting.
est quaedam flere voluptas (L.) there is in weeping a certain pleasure. — Ovid, *Trist.*, IV. iii. 37.
et hoc (or **id**) **genus omne** (L.) and all that sort of thing.
et in Arcadia ego (L.) I, too, lived in Arcadia. (Inscription from tomb, used in Poussin's picture 'The Arcadian Shepherds').
et tu, Brute (L.) you too, Brutus. (Caesar's alleged exclamation when he saw Brutus amongst his assassins.)
eventus stultorum magister (L.) the outcome is the schoolmaster of fools. — Livy, XXII, 39.
ex abusu non arguitur ad usum (L.) from the abuse no argument is drawn against the use. Cf. **abusus non**.
exceptio confirmat (or **probat**) **regulam** (L.) the exception proves the rule. (See **except** in Dict.)
exegi monumentum aere perennius (L.) I have reared a monument more lasting than brass. — Horace, *Od.*, III. xxx. 1.
exempla sunt odiosa (L.) examples are hateful.
exitus acta probat (L.) the outcome justifies the deed. — Ovid, *Her.*, II. 85.

ex nihilo (or **nilo**) **nihil** (or **nil**) **fit** (L.) out of nothing nothing comes. See **gigni**.
ex pede Herculem (L.) (we recognise) Hercules from his foot.
experientia docet stultos (L.) experience teaches fools.
experto crede, or (Virgil, *Aen.*, XI. 283) **credite** (L.) trust one who has tried, or had experience.
expertus metuet, or **metuit** (L.) he who has experienced it will fear (or fears). — Horace, *Epist.*, I. xviii, 87.
exstinctus amabitur idem (L.) the same man (maligned living) when dead will be loved. — Horace, *Epist.*, II. i. 14.
ex ungue leonem (L.) (judge, or infer) the lion from his claws.

F

faber est quisque fortunae suae (L.) every man is the fashioner of his own fortunes. — Proverb quoted by Sallust, *De Republica*. I.
fable convenue (Fr.) fable agreed upon — Voltaire's name for history.
facile est inventis addere (L.) it is easy to add to things invented already.
facilis descensus Averno, or **Averni** (L.) descent to Avernus is easy. — Virgil, *Aen.*, VI. 126.
facinus majoris abollae (L.) the crime of a larger cloak, i.e. of a philosopher. — Juvenal, III. 115.
facit indignatio versum (L.) indignation makes verse. — Juvenal. I. 79.
facta non verba (L.) deeds, not words.
factum est (L.) it is done.
facundi. See **fecundi**.
faire bonne mine (Fr.) to put a good face on the matter.
falsus in uno, falsus in omnibus (L.) false in one thing, false in all.
fama nihil est celerius (L.) nothing is swifter than rumour. — Livy.
fama semper vivat (L.) may his (or her) fame live for ever.
far niente (It.) doing nothing.
farrago libelli. See **quicquid**.
fas est et ab hoste doceri (L.) it is right to learn even from an enemy. — Ovid, *Met.*, IV. 428.
Fata obstant (L.) the Fates oppose. — Virgil, *Aen.*, IV. 440.
Fata viam invenient (L.) the Fates will find out a way. — Virgil, *Aen.*, X. 113.
favete linguis (L.) favor me with your tongues — keep silent to avoid ill omen. — Horace, *Od.*, III. i. 2.
fecundi (or **facundi**) **calices quem non fecere disertum**? (L.) whom have not full cups made eloquent? — Horace, *Epist.*, I. v. 19.
felicitas multos habet amicos (L.) prosperity has many friends.
felix qui potuit rerum congnoscere causas (L.) happy is he who has been able to understand the causes of things. — Virgil, *Georg.*, II. 490.
fendre un cheveu en quatre (Fr.) to split a hair in four.
fenum (or **foenum**) **habet in cornu** (L.) he has hay on his horn (sign of a dangerous bull). — Horace, *Sat.*, I. iv. 34.
festina lente (L.) hasten gently.
fiat experimentum in corpore vili (L.) let experiment be made on a worthless body.
fiat justitia, ruat caelum (L.) let justice be done, though the heavens should fall.
fiat lux (L.) let there be light.
fide, sed cui vide (L.) trust, but take care in whom.
fidus Achates (L.) faithful Achates (friend of Aeneas): hence, a close friend. — Virgil.
finem respice (L.) See **respice finem**.
finis coronat opus (L.) the end crowns the work.
fin mot de l'affaire (Fr.) the bottom of the matter, the explanation.
flectere si nequeo superos, Acheronta movebo (L.) if I can't move the gods, I'll stir up hell. — Virgil, *Aen.*, VII. 312.
foenum. See **fenum**.
forsan et haec olim meminisse juvabit (L.) perhaps some day we shall like to remember even these things. — Virgil, *Aen.*, I. 203.
Fors Clavigera (L.) Fortune the club-bearer (used as a title by Ruskin).
fortes Fortuna adjuvat (L.) Fortune helps the brave (Terence, *Phorm.*, I. iv. 26): **forti et fideli nihil difficile** to the brave and faithful nothing is difficult; **fortis cadere, cedere non potest** the brave man may fall, he cannot yield.
fortiter in re, suaviter in modo (L.). See **suaviter**.
Fortuna favet fatuis (L.) Fortune favors fools; **Fortuna favet fortibus** Fortune favors the bold.
frangas, non flectes (L.) you may break, you shall not bend.
fraus est celare fraudem (L.) it is a fraud to conceal a fraud.

frontis nulla fides (L.) no reliance on the face, no trusting appearances. — Juvenal, II. 8.
fruges consumere nati (L.) born to consume the fruits of the soil. — Horace, *Epist.*, I. ii. 27.
fugit hora (L.) the hour flies. — Persius, V. 153.
fuimus Troes; fuit Ilium (L.) we were Trojans; Troy was. — Virgil, *Aen.*, II. 325.
fulmen brutum (L.) a harmless thunderbolt.
furor arma ministrat (L.) rage supplies arms. — Virgil, *Aen.*, I. 150.

G

gaudet tentamine virtus (L.) virtue rejoices in trial.
geflügelte Worte (Ger.) winged words. See **epea**.
genus irritabile vatum (L.) the irritable tribe of poets. — Horace, *Epist.*, II. ii. 102.
gibier de potence (Fr.) gallows-bird.
gigni de nihilo nihilum, in nihilum nil posse reverti (L.) from nothing nothing can come, into nothing nothing can return. — Persius, III. 84.
giovine santo, diavolo vecchio (It.) young saint, old devil.
gli assenti hanno torto (It.) the absent are in the wrong.
gloria virtutis umbra (L.) glory (is) the shadow of virtue.
glückliche Reise (Ger.) prosperous journey to you.
gnoathi seauton (Gr.) know thyself.— Inscribed on the temple of Apollo at Delphi. See also **nosce teipsum**.
Gott mit uns (Ger.) God with us — Hohenzollern motto.
gradu diverso, via una (L.) with different step on the one way.
gradus ad Parnassum (L.) a step, or stairs, to Parnassus, a Latin or Greek poetical dictionary.
Graeculus esuriens (L.) the hungry Greekling. — Juvenal III. 78.
Graecum est: non legitur (L.) this is Greek; it is not read (placed against a Greek word in mediaeval MSS, a permission to skip the hard words).
grande chère et beau feu (Fr.) ample cheer and a fine fire; **grande fortune, grande servitude** great wealth, great slavery.
gratia placendi (L.) the delight of pleasing.
graviora manent (L.) greater dangers remain (Virgil, *Aen.*, VI. 84); **graviora quaedam sunt remedia periculis** some remedies are more grievous than the perils (Syrus).
gravis ira regum est semper (L.) the anger of kings is always serious.
grosse Seelen dulden still (Ger.) great souls suffer in silence. — Schiller, *Don Carlos*, I. iv., end of scene.
grosse tête et peu de sens (Fr.) big head and little wit.
gutta cavat lapidem (L.) the drop wears away the stone. — Ovid, *Pont.*, IV. x. 5.

H

habendum et tenendum (L.) to have and to hold.
habent sua fata libelli (L.) books have their destinies. — Maurus, *De Litteris, Syllabis et Metris.* **hanc veniam petimusque damusque vicissim** (L.) this liberty we ask and grant in turn. — Horace, *A.P.*, 11.
Hannibal ad portas (L.) Hannibal at the gates. — Cicero, *Philippica*, I. v. 11.
haud longis intervallis (L.) at no long intervals.
helluo librorum (L.) a glutton of books.
heu pietas! heu prisca fides! (L.) alas for piety! alas for the ancient faith! — Virgil, *Aen.*, VI. 879.
hiatus valde deflendus (L.) a gap deeply to be deplored.
hic finis fandi (L.) here (was, or let there be) an end of the speaking.
hinc illae lacrumae (L.) hence [came] those tears. — Terence, *Andria*, I. i. 99; also Horace, *Epist.*, I. xix. 41.
hinc lucem et pocula sacra (L.) from this source [we draw] light and draughts of sacred learning.
ho bios brachys, hea de technea makrea (Gr.) life is short and art is long. — Attributed to Hippocrates.
hoc age (L.) this do.
hoc erat in votis (L.) this was the very thing I prayed for. — Horace, *Sat.*, II. vi. 1.
hoc opus, hic labor est (L.) this is the toil, this the labor. — Virgil, *Aen.*, VI. 129.
hoc saxum posuit (L.) placed this stone.
hoc (or **sic**) **volo, sic jubeo, sit pro ratione voluntas** (L.) this (thus) I will, thus I command, be my will sufficient reason. — Juvenal, VI. 223.
hodie mihi, cras tibi (L.) me today, you tomorrow.
hominibus plenum, amicis vacuum (L.) full of men, empty of friends.

hominis est errare (L.) it belongs to man to err.
homo alieni juris (L.) one under control of another; **homo antiqua virtute ac fide** a man of the antique virtue and loyalty (Terence, *Adelphi*, III. iii. 88 or 1. 442); **homo homini lupus** man is a wolf to man; **homo multarum literarum** a man of many literary accomplishments; **homo mullius coloris** a man of no color, one who does not commit himself; **homo sui juris** one who is his own master; **homo sum: humani nihil a me alienum puto** I am a man: I count nothing human indifferent to me (Terence, *Heaut.*, I. i. 25); **homo trium litterarum** man of three letters — i.e. *fur* = thief; **homo unius libri** a man of one book.
hon hoi theoi philousi apothneaskei neos (Gr.) whom the gods love dies young. — Menander. Cf. **quem di diligunt** . . .
honi soit qui mal y pense (O.Fr.) the shame be his who thinks ill of it — the motto of the Order of the Garter.
honneur et patrie (Fr.) honor and native land.
honores mutant mores (L.) honors change manners.
honor virtutis praemium (L.) honor is the reward of virtue.
honos alit artes (L.) honor nourishes the arts (Cicero, *Tusculanae Disputationes*, I. ii. 4); **honos habet onus** honor has its burden.
hora fugit (L.) the hour flies.
horas non numero nisi serenas (L.) I number none but shining hours. [Common on sundials.]
horresco referens (L.) I shudder in relating. — Virgil, *Aen.*, II, 204.
horribile dictu (L.) horrible to relate.
hostis honori invidia (L.) envy is an enemy to honor; **hostis humani generis** enemy of the human race.
humanum est errare (L.) to err is human.
hurtar para dar por Dios (Sp.) to steal in order to give to God.
hypage Satana (Gr.) away Satan. — Matt. iv. 10. **hypotheses non fingo** (L.) I do not frame hypotheses (i.e. unverifiable speculations). — Newton.

I

ich dien (Ger.) I serve.
ici on parle français (Fr.) here French is spoken.
idem velle atque idem nolle ea demum firma amicitia est (L.) to like and dislike the same things is indeed true friendship. — Sallust, *Catalina*, 20.
Iesus Hominum Salvator (L.) Jesus, Saviour of men.
ignorantia legis neminem excusat (L.) ignorance of the law excuses nobody.
ignoti nulla cupido (L.) for a thing unknown there is no desire. — Ovid, *A.A.*, III. 397.
ignotum per ignotius (L.) the unknown by the still more unknown.
i gran dolori sono muti (It.) great griefs are mute.
il a inventé l'histoire (Fr.) he has invented history.
il a le diable au corps (Fr.) the devil is in him: he is full of devilment, or of vivacity, wit, enthusiasm, etc.: he can't sit still.
il a les défauts de ses qualités (Fr.) he has the defects that answer to his good qualities.
il faut de l'argent (Fr.) money is necessary.
il faut laver son linge sale en famille (Fr.) one should wash one's dirty linen in private.
il gran rifiuto (It.) the great refusal (the abdication of Pope Celestine V). — Dante, *Inferno*, III. 60.
Ilias malorum (L.) an Iliad of woes.
ille crucem sceleris pretium tulit, hic diadema (L.) that man got a cross, this man a crown, as the price of his crime. — Juvenal, XIII. 105.
ille terrarum mihi praeter omnes angulus ridet (L.) that corner of the earth to me smiles sweetest of all. — Horace, *Od.*, II. vi. 13–14.
il meglio è l'inimico del bene (It.) the better is the enemy of the good.
il n'y a pas à dire (Fr.) there is nothing to be said.
il n'y a que le premier pas qui coûte (Fr.) it is only the first step that counts. (Mme du Deffand on St Denis walking after decapitation.)
ils n'ont rien appris ni rien oublié (Fr.) they have learned nothing and forgotten nothing [said of the French *Émigrés*, often of the Bourbons].
impar congressus Achilli (L.) unequally matched against Achilles. — Virgil, *Aen.*, I. 475.
incedis per ignis suppositos cineri doloso (L.) you walk on fires covered with treacherous ash. — Horace, *Od.*, II. i. 7–8.

incidis in Scyllam cupiens vitare Charybdim (L.) you fall into Scylla trying to avoid Charybdis. — Philip Gaultier de Lille.
incredulus odi (L.) I hate and disbelieve. — Horace, *A.P.*, 188.
indignor quandoque bonus dormitat Homerus (L.) I am annoyed whenever good Homer slumbers. — Horace, *A.P.*, 359. Usually cited as **aliquando** (=sometimes) **bonus**, etc.
infandum, regina, jubes renovare dolorem (L.) thou bidst me, queen, renew unspeakable woes. — Virgil, *Aen.*, II. 3.
in hoc (signo) vinces (L.) in this sign thou wilt conquer — i.e. in the Cross [the motto of Constantine the Great]. See **en toutoai nika**.
in magnis et voluisse sat est (L.) in great things even to have wished is enough. — Propertius, II. x. 6. **in meditatione fugae** (L.) in contemplation of flight.
inopen me copia fecit (L.) plenty has made me poor. — Ovid, *M.*, III. 466.
integer vitae scelerisque purus (L.) blameless in life and clear of offense. — Horace, *Od.*, I. xxii. 1.
inter arma silent leges (L.) amid wars laws are silent (Cicero).
interdum stultus bene loquitur (L.) sometimes a fool speaks a right.
invita Minerva (L.) against the will of Minerva: uninspired. — Horace, *A.P.*, 385.
ira furor brevis est (L.) rage is a brief madness. — Horace, *Epist.*, I. ii. 62.
Italia irredenta (It.) unredeemed Italy — the parts of Italy still under foreign domination after the war of 1866 — South Tirol, etc.

J

jacta est alea (L.) the die is cast (quoted as said by Caesar at the crossing of the Rubicon).
je n'en vois pas la nécessité (Fr.) I don't see the necessity for that [said by the Comte d'Argental in reply to a man who pleaded, 'But one must live somehow'].
joci causa (L.) for the joke.
judex damnatur cum nocens absolvitur (L.) the judge is condemned when the guilty is acquitted. — Syrus, 247.
Jup(p)iter optimus maximus (L.) Jupiter best and greatest; **Jup(p)iter Pluvius** rain-bringing Jupiter; **Jup(p)iter Tonans** Jupiter the thunderer.
justum et tenacem propositi virum (L.) a man upright and tenacious of purpose. — Horace, *Od.*, III. iii. 1.
j'y suis, j'y reste (Fr.) here I am, here I stay [said by Macmahon at the Malakoff].

K

kai ta leipomena, kai ta loipa (Gr.) and the rest: and so on.
kalos kagathos, kalokagathos (Gr.) good and honorable: a perfect gentleman.
kat' exochean (Gr.) pre-eminently: *par excellence*.
keine Antwort is auch eine Antwort (Ger.) no answer is still an answer: silence gives consent.
Kirche, Küche, Kinder (Ger). church, kitchen, children — said, e.g. during the Nazi period, to be the proper interests of a German woman.
kteama es aei (Gr.) a possession for ever.
kymatoan anearithmon gelasma (Gr.) innumerable smiles of the waves. — Aeschylus, *Prom.*, 89–90.

L

laborare est orare (L.) work is prayer.
labore et honore (L.) by labor and honor.
labuntur et imputantur (L.) [the moments] slip away and are laid to our account (inscription on sundials). Also **pereunt et imputantor** (q.v.).
la donna è mobile (It.) woman is changeable.
la garde meurt et ne se rend pas (Fr.) the guard dies, it does not surrender.
la grande nation (Fr.) the great nation — i.e. France.
laa ilaaha illaa 'llaah (Ar.) there is no god but God.
langage des halles (Fr.) language of the market-place.
l'appétit vient en mangeant (Fr.) appetite comes as you eat.
la propriété c'est le vol (Fr.) property is theft [from Proudhon].
la reyne le veult (s'avisera) (Norm. Fr.). See **le roy**.
lasciate ogni speranza, voi che'ntrate (It.) abandon all hope ye who enter. — Dante, *Inferno*, III. 9. From the inscription over the gate of hell.

latet anguis in herba (L.) there is a snake hidden in the grass. — Virgil, *Ecl.*, III. 93.
laudator temporis acti (L.) one who praises past times. — Horace, *A.P.*, 173.
le génie n'est qu'une grande aptitude à la patience (Fr.) genius is merely a great aptitude for patience (attributed to Buffon).
le grand monarque (Fr.) the great king — i.e. Louis XIV.
le jeu ne vaut pas la chandelle (Fr.) the game is not worth the candle.
l'empire c'est la paix (Fr.) the empire means peace [said by Louis Napoleon in 1852].
le roy (or **la reyne**) **le veult** (Norm. Fr.) the king (or queen) wills it — form of royal assent.
le roy (la reyne) s'avisera (Norm. Fr.) the king (or queen) will deliberate — form of refusal.
le style est l'homme (même) (Fr.) the style is the man himself (from Buffon).
l'état, c'est moi (Fr.) I am the state [alleged to have been said by Louis XIV].
liberté, égalité, fraternité (Fr.) liberty, equality, fraternity — a slogan of the French Revolution.
limae labor (L.) the labor of the file, of polishing. — Horace, *A.P.*, 291.
littera scripta manet (L.) what is written down is permanent. See **vox audita**.
lucri causa (L.) for the sake of gain.
lucus a non lucendo (L.) the grove (*lucus*) (is so named) from its *not* shining (*lucendo*).
ludere cum sacris (L.) to trifle with sacred things.
l'union fait la force (Fr.) union makes strength.
lupus in fabula (L.) the wolf in the fable: talk of the devil. — Terence, *Adelphi.*, IV. i. 21.

M

macte virtute (L.) be honored in your valor, virtue — used by Cicero, Virgil, Livy (**macte virtute esto** — Cato to one coming out of a resort of vice, acc. to Horace, *Sat.*, I. ii. 31–32).
magna est veritas et praevalebit (L.) truth is great and will prevail (Vulgate, **et prevalet**).
magni nominis umbra (L.) the mere shadow of a mighty name. — Lucan, I. 135.
man spricht Deutsch (Ger.) German spoken here.
matre pulchra filia pulchrior (L.) a daughter fairer than her fair mother. — Horace, *Od.*, I. xvi. 1.
maxima debetur puero reverentia (L.) the greatest reverence is due to the boy — i.e. to the innocence of his age. — Juvenal, XIV, 47.
mea virtute me involvo (L.) I wrap myself in my virtue. — Horace, *Od.*, III. xxix. 54–55.
meaden agan (Gr.) [let there be] nothing in excess.
medio tutissimus ibis (L.) thou wilt go safest in the middle. — Ovid, *Met.*, II. 137.
mega biblion, mega kakon (Gr.) big book, great evil.
mea kinei Kamarinan (Gr.) do not stir up Kamarina (a pestilent marsh in Sicily): let well alone.
mens sana in corpore sano (L.) a sound mind in a sound body.— Juvenal, X. 356. **mens sibi conscia recti** (L.) a mind conscious of rectitude. — Virgil, *Aen.*, I. 604. Cf. **conscia mens recti**.
mirabile dictu (L.) wonderful to tell; **mirabile visu**, wonderful to see.
mole ruit sua (L.) falls by its own weight. — Horace, *Od.*, III. iv. 65.
monstrum horrendum, informe, ingens (L.) a frightful monster, ill-shapen, huge. — Virgil, *Aen.*, III. 658.
morituri te salutant. See **ave**.
muet comme un poisson (Fr.) dumb as a fish.

N

natura abhorret vacuum (L.) nature abhors a vacuum.
naturam expellas furca, tamen usque recurret (L.) though you drive out nature with a pitchfork, yet will she always return. — Horace, *Epist.*, I. x. 24.
natura non facit saltus (or **saltum**) (L.) nature does not make leaps (or a leap).
naviget Anticyram (L.) let him sail to Anticyra [where hellebore could be had, to cure madness]. — Horace, *Sat.*, II. iii. 166.
nec cupias, nec metuas (L.) neither desire nor fear.
nec deus intersit nisi dignus vindice nodus inciderit (L.) let not a god intervene unless a knot occur worthy of the untier. — Horace, *A.P.*, 191–2.
ne cede malis (L.) yield not to misfortune. — Virgil, *Aen.*, VI. 95.
necessitas non habet legem (L.) necessity has no law.
nec pluribus impar (L.) no unequal match for several (suns). — Louis XIV's motto.
nec scire fas est omnia (L.) it is not permitted to know all things. — Horace, *Od.*, IV. iv. 22.

ne exeat (L.) let him not depart.
negatur (L.) it is denied.
nemo me impune lacessit (L.) no one provokes me with impunity — the motto of the kings of Scotland and of the Order of the Thistle; **nemo repente fuit turpissimus** no one ever became utterly bad all at once. — Juvenal, II 83.
ne obliviscaris (L.) do not forget.
neque semper arcum tendit Apollo (L.) Apollo does not always bend his bow. — Horace, *Od.*, II. x. 19–20.
ne quid nimis (L.) [let there be] nothing in excess.
nescis, mi fili, quantilla prudentia mundus regatur (L.) you know not, my son, with what a small stock of wisdom the world is governed. — Attributed to Oxenstierna and others.
nescit vox missa reverti (L.) a word published cannot be recalled. — Horace, *A.P.*, 390.
n'est-ce-pas? (Fr.) is it not so?
ne sutor ultra crepidam (L.). See **sutor**.
ne temere (L.) not rashly — a papal decree of 1907 denying recognition to the marriage of a Catholic unless contracted before a priest.
nicht wahr? (Ger.) is it not true? isn't that so?
nihil tetigit quod non ornavit. See **nullum**.
nil actum credens dum quid superesset agendum (L.) thinking nothing done while anything was yet to do. — Lucan, II. 657; **nil admirari** to wonder at nothing. — Horace, *Epist.*, I. vi. 1; **nil desperandum** nothing is to be despaired of. — Horace, *Od.*, I. vii. 27.
n'importe (Fr.) no matter.
nisi Dominus frustra (L.) except the Lord (keep the city, the watchman waketh but) in vain. — Ps. cxxvii — the motto of Edinburgh.
nitor in adversum (L.) I strive in opposition. — Ovid, *Met.*, II. 72.
non amo te, Sabidi, nec possum dicere quare (L.) I do no love thee, Sabidius, nor can I tell you why. — Martial, I. xxxiii.
non compos mentis (L.) not of sound mind.
non est inventus (L.) he has not been found (he has absconded).
non licet (L.) it is not allowed.
non liquet (L.) it is not clear.
non mi ricordo (It.) I don't remember.
non multa, sed multum (L.) not many, but much.
non nobis, Domine (L.) not unto us, O Lord. — Psalm cxv.
non olet pecunia (L.) the money does not stink. — Attributed to Vespasian, of revenue from an unsavoury source.
non omnia possumus omnes (L.) we cannot all do everything. — Virgil, *Ecl.*, viii. 63.
non omnis moriar (L.) I shall not wholly die. — Horace, *Od.*, III. xxx. 6.
non placet (L.) it does not please — a negative vote.
non possumus (L.) we cannot — a form of refusal.
non tali auxilio nec defensoribus istis tempus eget (L.) not for such aid nor for these defenders does the time call. — Virgil, *Aen.*, II. 521.
nonumque prematur in annum (L.) and let it be kept unpublished till the ninth year. — Horace, *A.P.*, 388.
non ut edam vivo sed ut vivam edo (L.) I do not live to eat, but eat to live. — Quintilian.
nosce teipsum (L.) know thyself — a translation of **gnoathi seauton** (q.v.).
nous avons changé tout cela (Fr.) we have changed all that. — Molière, *Le Médecin malgré lui*, II. iv.
nous verrons (ce que nous verrons) (Fr.) we shall see (what we shall see).
nulla dies sine linea (L.) no day without a line, without painting (or writing) a little.
nulla nuova, buona nuova (It.) no news is good news.
nullius addictus (or **adductus**) **jurare in verba magistri** (L.) bound to swear to the words of no master, to follow no one blindly or slavishly. — Horace, *Epist.*, I. i. 14.
nullum (scil. **scribendi genus**) **quod tetigit non ornavit** (L.) he touched no form of literature without adorning it. From Johnson's epitaph on Goldsmith.
nunc est bibendum (L.) now is the time to drink. — Horace, *Od.*, I. xxxvii. 1.

O

obscurum per obscurius (L.) (explaining) the obscure by means of the more obscure.
oderint dum metuant (L.) let them hate so long as they fear. — Accius, *Atreus*, Fragment IV; quoted in Cicero, *Philippica*, I. xiv.

odi profanum vulgus et arceo (L.) I loathe and shun the profane rabble. — Horace, *Od.*, iii. i. 1.
O fortunatos nimium, sua si bona norint, agricolas (L.) Oh too happy farmers, if they but knew their luck. — Virgil, *Georg.*, II. 458.
ohe! jam satis (L.) hold! enough now (a common phrase).
ohne Hast, ohne Rast (Ger.) without haste, without rest. — Goethe's motto.
olim meminisse juvabit. See **forsan**.
omne ignotum pro magnifico (L.) everything unknown (is taken to be) magnificent. — Tacitus, *Agric.*, 30.
omnem crede diem tibi diluxisse supremum (L.) believe each day to have dawned as your last. — Horace, *Epist.*, I. iv. 13.
omne tulit punctum qui miscuit utile dulci (L.) he has carried every vote who has combined the useful with the pleasing. — Horace, *A.P.*, 343.
omne vivum ex ovo (L.) every living thing comes from an egg. — Attributed to Harvey.
omnia mea mecum porto (L.) all I have I carry with me.
omnia mutantur. See **tempora mutantur**.
omnia vincit amor, et nos cedamus amori (L.) love overcomes all things, let us too yield to love. — Virgil, *Ecl.*, X. 69.
ore rotunda (L.) with round, full voice (mouth). — Horace, *A.P.*, 323.
O sancta simplicitas! (L.) O holy simplicity!
os homini sublime dedit caelumque tueri jussit et erectos ad sidera tollere vultus (L.) he gave man an up-turned face and bade contemplate the heavens and raise looks to the stars. — Ovid, *Met.*, I. 85.
O si sic omnia! (L.) Oh that he had done all things thus, or Oh that all things were thus!
O tempora! O mores! (L.) O the times! O the manners! Occurs in Cicero's first speech against Catiline.
otia dant vitia (L.) idleness begets vice.
otium cum dignitate (L.) dignified leisure.
ouk esti? (Gr.) is it not so?
ovem lupo committere (L.) to entrust the sheep to the wolf.

P

pace tua (L.) by your leave.
pallida Mors aequo pulsat pede pauperum tabernas regumque turres (L.) pale Death knocks with impartial foot at poor men's huts and kings' castles. — Horace, *Od.*, I. iv. 13–14.
palmam qui meruit ferat (L.) let him who has won the palm wear it. — Dr Jortin, *Lusus Poetici*, viii. 20.
panem et circenses (L.) bread and (Roman) circus-games — food and amusements at public expense. — Juvenal, X. 81.
panta men kathara tois katharois (Gr.) all things are pure to the pure. — Titus, I. 15.
panta rhei (Gr.) all things are in a flux (a saying of Heraclitus).
parcere subjectis et debellare superbos (L.) to spare the vanquished and put down the proud. — Virgil, *Aen.*, VI. 854.
par nobile fratrum (L.) a noble pair of brothers. — Horace, *Sat.*, II. iii. 243.
parturiunt montes, nascetur ridiculus mus (L.) the mountains are in travail, an absurd mouse will be born. — Horace, *A.P.*, 139.
parva componere magnis. See **si parva**.
pas op (Afrik.) look out.
patheamata matheamata (Gr.) sufferings [are] lessons.
paulo majora canamus (L.) let us sing of rather greater things. — Virgil, *Ecl.*, IV. 1.
pax vobiscum (L.) peace be with you.
peccavi (L.) I have sinned.
pecunia non olet. See **non olet pecunia**.
pereant qui ante nos nostra dixerunt (L.) perish those who have said our good things before us. — Attributed to Donatus and to Augustine.
pereunt et imputantur (L.) [the moments, hours] pass away and are reckoned to our account.
perfervida. See **praefervida**. **per varios casus, per tot discrimina rerum** (L.) through various chances, through so many crises of fortune. — Virgil, *Aen.*, I. 204.
pleon heamisy pantos (Gr.) the half is more than the whole. — Hesiod, *Erga*, 40.
plus ça change, plus c'est la même chose (Fr.) the more that changes the more it is the same thing (no superficial or apparent change alters its essential nature).
poeta nascitur, non fit (L.) the poet is born, not made.
polloan onomatoan mia morphea (Gr.) one shape of many names. — Aeschylus, *Prometheus*, 210.

polyphloisboio thalasseas (Gr.) of the much-sounding sea. — Homer, *Il.*, I. 34; also Hesiod, *Erga*, 648.
populus vult decipi, ergo decipiatur (L.) the public wishes to be fooled, therefore let it be fooled. — Ascribed to Cardinal Caraffa.
poscimur (L.) we are called on [to sing, etc.].
post equitem sedet atra cura (L.) behind the horseman sits black care. — Horace, *Odes*, III. i. 40.
post hoc, ergo propter hoc (L.) after this, therefore because of this (a fallacious reasoning).
pour encourager les autres (Fr.) to encourage the others (Voltaire, *Candide*, on the shooting of Admiral Byng); **pour faire rire**, to raise a laugh; **pour mieux sauter** see **reculer** below; **pour passer le temps** to pass away the time; **pour prendre congé**, or **PPC**, to take leave.
praefervida (misquoted as **perfervida**). See **Scotorum**.
principiis obsta (L.) resist the first beginnings. — Ovid, *R.A.*, 91. Cf. **yenienti**, etc.
probatum est (L.) it has been proved.
probitas laudatur et alget (L.) honesty is commended and left out in the cold. — Juvenal, I. 74.
procul este, profani (L.) keep your distance, uninitiated ones. — Virgil, *Aen.*, VI. 258.
proh pudor! (L.) oh, for shame!
proxime accessit (*pl.* **accesserunt**) (L.) came next [to the prizeman].
pulvis et umbra sumus (L.) we are dust and a shadow. — Horace, *Od.*, IV. vii. 16.
purpureus pannus (L.) a purple patch. — From Horace, *A.P.*, 15–16.

Q

quamdiu se bene gesserit (L.) during good behavior.
quantum mutatus ab illo (L.) how changed from that (Hector who came back clad in Achilles's spoils). — Virgil, *Aen.*, II. 274.
que diable allait-il faire dans cette galère? (Fr.) what the devil was he doing in that galley? — Molière, *Les Fourberies de Scapin*, II. vii.
quem di diligunt adolescens moritur (L.) whom the gods love dies young. — Plautus's translation of **hon hoi theoi** . . .
quem lupiter vult perdere dementat prius, or **quem deus perdere vult, prius dementat** (L.) whom Jupiter (a god) wishes to destroy, he first makes mad.
que sais-je (**sçai-je**)? (Fr.) what do I know? — Montaigne's motto.
que voulez-vous? (Fr.) what would you?
quicquid agunt homines . . . nostri est farrago libelli (L.) whatever men do is the medley of our little book. — Juvenal, I. 85–86.
quicquid delirant reges plectuntur Achivi (L.) whatever madness possesses the chiefs, it is (the common soldiers or people of) the Achaeans who suffer. — Horace, *Epist.*, I. ii. 14.
quicunque vult salvus esse (L.) whosoever will be saved (the beginning of the Athanasian creed).
quid hoc sibi vult? (L.) what does this mean?
quid rides? mutato nomine de te fabula narratur (L.) why do you laugh? with change of name the story is about you. — Horace, *Sat.*, I. i. 69–70.
quién sabe? (Sp.) who knows?
quieta non movere (L.) not to move things that are at rest — to let sleeping dogs lie.
qui facit per alium facit per se (L.) he who acts through another is himself responsible.
quis custodiet ipsos custodes? (L.) who will guard the guards themselves? — Juvenal, VI. 347–8.
quis desiderio sit pudor aut modus tam cari capitis? (L.) what shame or stint should there be in mourning for one so dear? — Horace, *Od.*, I. xxiv. 1.
qui s'excuse s'accuse (Fr.) he who excuses himself accuses himself.
quis separabit? (L.) who shall separate [us]?
qui tacet consentit (L.) who keeps silence consents.
qui va là? (Fr.) who goes there?
quod avertat Deus (L.) which may God avert.
quod bonum, felix, faustumque sit (L.) may it be right, happy, and of good omen.
quod erat demonstrandum (L.), or **Q.E.D.**, which was to be proved or demonstrated; **quod erat faciendum**, or **Q.E.F.**, which was to be done.
quod ubique, quod semper, quod ab omnibus (L.) what everywhere, what always, what by all (has been believed). — St Vincent of Lérin's definition of orthodoxy.
quorum pars magna fui (L.) in which I bore a great share. — Virgil, *Aen.*, II. 6.

quot homines, tot sententiae (L.) as many men, so many minds or opinions. — Terence, *Phormio*, II. iv. 14 (or l. 454).
quousque tandem abutere, Catilina, patientia nostra? (L.) how far, O Catiline, will you abuse our patience?— Cicero, *In Catilinam*.
quo vadis? (L.) whither goest thou?

R

rara avis (L.) a rare bird, rare person or thing. — Juvenal, VI. 165.
rari nantes in gurgite vasto (L.) here and there some swimming in a vast whirlpool. — Virgil, *Aen.*, I. 118.
reculer pour mieux sauter (Fr.) to draw back to take a better leap.
redolet lucerna (L.) it smells of the lamp.
re galantuomo (It.) the honest king — king and gentleman [said of Victor Emmanuel II].
religio loci (L.) the religious spirit of the place. — Virgil, *Aen.*, VIII. 349.
rem acu tetigisti (L.) you have touched the thing with a needle, hit it exactly. — Proverbial expression used by Plautus.
remis velisque (L.) with oars and sails; also **remis ventisque** with oars and winds (Virgil, etc.): with all vigor.
res angusta domi (L.) straitened circumstances at home. — Juvenal, III. 165.
res ipsa loquitur (L.) the thing speaks for itself: the accident is in itself evidence of negligence.
respice finem (L.) look to the end. — Playfully perverted into **respice funem**, beware of the (hangman's) rope.
resurgam (L.) I shall rise again.
retro me, satana (L.) in Vulgate, **vade retro me, satana**, get thee behind me, Satan (Matt. xvi. 23, Mark viii. 33, Luke iv. 8): stop trying to tempt me.
revenons à nos moutons (Fr.) let us return to our sheep, i.e. our subject. — From the mediaeval farce, *L'Avocat Pathelin*.
rhododaktylos Eoas (Gr.) rosy-fingered Dawn. — Homer, *Odyssey*, II. 1.
rien ne va plus (Fr.) lit. nothing goes any more — used by croupiers to indicate that no more bets may be made.
risum teneatis, amici? (L.) could you keep from laughing, friends? — Horace, *A.P.*, 5.
Roma locuta, causa finita (L.) Rome has spoken, the cause is ended.
ruat caelum. See **fiat justitia**.
rudis indigestaque moles (L.) a rude and shapeless mass. — Ovid, *Met.*, I. 7.
ruit. See **mole**.
rus in urbe (L.) the country in town. — Martial, XII. 57, 21.
rusticus expectat dum defluat amnis (L.) waits like the yokel for the river to run by. — Horace, *Epist.*, I. ii. 42.

S

salaam aleikum (Ar.) peace be upon you.
salus populi suprema lex esto (L.) let the welfare of the people be the final law (Cicero, *De Legibus*, III. iiii: **suprema est lex**).
sans peur et sans reproche (Fr.) without fear and without reproach.
sapere aude (L.) dare to be wise. — Horace, *Epist.*, I. ii. 40.
sartor resartus (L.) the tailor retailored.
sauter à pieds joints (Fr.) to take a standing jump.
sauve qui peut (Fr.) save himself who can: every man for himself.
Scotorum praefervida ingenia (L.) the ardent tempers of the Scots. — Buchanan, *Hist. Scot.*, XVI. li.
selon les règles (Fr.) according to the rules.
semel insanivimus omnes (L.) we have all played the fool once. — J. B. Mantuanus, *Ecl.*, i. 217.
se non è vero, è ben trovato (It.) if it is not true, it is cleverly invented.
sero venientibus ossa (L.) the bones to the late-comers.
sic itur ad astra (L.) such is the way to the stars. — Virgil, *Aen.*, IX. 641.
si componere magnis parva, etc. See **si parva, etc.**
sic transit gloria mundi (L.) so passes away earthly glory.
sic volo. See **hoc volo.**
sic vos non vobis (L.) thus do you, not for yourselves. — Ascribed to Virgil.
Sieg heil (Ger.) victory hail!
si jeunesse savait, si vieillesse pouvait (Fr.) if youth but knew, if age but could.
s'il vous plaît (Fr.) if you please.
similia similibus curantur (L.) likes are cured by likes — a hair of the dog that bit one.

si monumentum requiris, circumspice (L.) if you seek (his) monument, look round you (inscription for the architect Christopher Wren's tomb in St Paul's).
simplex munditiis (L.) elegant in simplicity. — Horace, *Od.*, I. v. 5. **sine Cerere et Libero friget Venus** (L.) without Ceres and Bacchus (food and drink) Venus (love) is cold. — Terence, *Eun.*, IV. v. 6.
sine ira et studio (L.) without ill-will and without favor.
sint ut sunt aut non sint (L.) let them be as they are or not at all.
si parla Italiano (It.) Italian spoken.
si parva licet componere magnis (L.; Virgil, *Georg.*, IV. 176); **si componere magnis parva mihi fas est** (Ovid, *Met.*, V. 416–7) if it is permissible to compare small things to great.
siste, viator (L.) stop, traveler.
si vis pacem, para bellum (L.) if you would have peace, be ready for war.
skias onar anthroapos (Gr.) man is a dream of a shadow. — Pindar., *Pyth.*, VIII. 95.
solitudinem faciunt, pacem appellant (L.) they make a desert and call it peace. — Tacitus, *Agric.*, 30.
solventur risu tabulae: tu missus abibis (L.) the bills will be dismissed with laughter — you will be laughed out of court. — Horace, *Sat.*, II. i. 86.
solvitur ambulando (L.) (the problem of reality of motion) is solved by walking — by practical experiment, by actual performance.
spero meliora (L.) I hope for better things.
splendide mendax (L.) splendidly false, nobly lying. — Horace, *Od.*, III. xi. 35.
spretaeque injuria formae (L.) (and) the insult of beauty slighted. — Virgil, *Aen.*, I. 27.
stans pede in uno (L.) standing on one foot. — Horace, *Sat.*, I. iv. 10.
stat pro ratione voluntas (L.) See **hoc volo**.
stet fortuna domus (L.) may the fortune of the house last long.
Sturm und Drang (Ger.) storm and stress.
sua si bona. See **O fortunatos**, etc.
suaviter in modo, fortiter in re (L.) gentle in manner, resolute in deed.
suggestio falsi. See **suppressio veri**, etc.
sunt lacrimae rerum (L.) there are tears for things (unhappy). — Virgil, *Aen.*, I. 462.
suo motu on one's own initiative.
suppressio veri suggestio falsi (L.) suppression of truth is suggestion of the false. (In law, **suppressio veri** is passive, **suggestio falsi** active, misrepresentation.)
sursum corda (L.) lift up your hearts.
surtout, pas de zèle (Fr.) above all, no zeal.
sutor ne supra crepidam judicaret (L.) let not the cobbler criticise (a work of art) above the sandal. See **ultracrepidate** in Dict.

T

tacent, satis laudant (L.) their silence is praise enough. — Terence, *Eun.*, III. ii. 23.
tantae molis erat Romanam condere gentem (L.) a task of such difficulty was it to found the Roman race. — Virgil, *Aen.*, I. 33.
tantaene animis caelestibus irae? (L.) are there such violent passions in celestial minds? — Virgil, *Aen.*, I. 11.
tempora (orig. **omnia) mutantur, nos et mutamur in illis** (L.) the times (all things) change, and we with them.
tempus edax rerum (L.) time, consumer of things. — Ovid, *Met.*, XV. 234.
tempus fugit (L.) time flies.
thalassa, thalassa! or **thalatta thalatta!** (Gr.) the sea, the sea! (the exulting cry of Xenophon's men on beholding the sea). — Xenophon, *Anabasis*, IV. 7.
timeo Danaos et dona ferentes (L.) I fear the Greeks, even when bringing gifts. — Virgil, *Aen.*, II. 49.
tiré à quatre épingles (Fr.) as neat as can be.
ton d'apameibomenos prosephea (Gr.) addressed him in reply. — Homer (*passim*).
totus, teres, atque rotundus (L.) complete, smooth, and round. — Horace, *Satires*, II. vii. 86.
toujours perdrix (Fr.) partridge every day — too much of a good thing.
tout comprendre c'est tout pardonner (Fr.) to understand all is to pardon all; **tout est perdu fors l'honneur** all is lost but honor [attrib. to Francis I after Pavia]; **tout vient (à point) à qui sait attendre** all things come to him who can wait.
traduttore traditore (It.) a translator is a traitor or betrayer: *pl.* **traduttori traditori**.
tria juncta in uno (L.) three things in one.

U

ubi bene, ibi patria (L.) where it goes well with me, there is my fatherland.
ubi saeva indignatio ulterious cor lacerare nequit (L.) where fierce indignation can tear his heart no longer. — Part of Swift's epitaph.
und so weiter (Ger.), or **u.s.w.**, and so forth.
urbi et orbi (L.) to the city (Rome) and to the world, to everyone.
uti possidetis (L.) lit. as you possess — the principle of letting e.g. belligerents keep what they have acquired.

V

vade in pace (L.) go in peace.
vade retro me, satana. See **retro**.
varium et mutabile semper femina (L.) woman is ever a fickle and changeable thing. — Virgil, *Aen.*, IV. 569.
vedi Napoli, e poi muori (It.) see Naples, and die.
veni Creator Spiritus (L.) come, Creator Spirit — the beginning of an early Latin hymn.
venienti occurrite morbo (L.) run to meet disease as it comes. — Persius, III. 63.
veni, vidi, vici (L.) I came, I saw, I conquered. — Ascribed to Caesar on his victory over Pharnaces.
vera incessu patuit dea (L.) the true goddess was revealed by her gait. — Virgil, *Aen.*, I. 405.
verbum sapienti sat est (L.) a word to the wise is enough — often abbrev. *verb. sap.* and *verb. sat.* See **dictum**.
veritas odium parit (L.) truth begets hatred. — Terence, *Andria*, I. i. 41.
vestigia . . . nulla retrorsum (L.) no footprints backwards (at the lion's den): sometimes used to mean no going back. — Horace, *Epist.*, I. i. 74–75.
victrix causa deis placuit, sed victa Catoni (L.) the gods preferred the winning cause, but Cato the losing. — Lucan, I. 128.
video meliora proboque, deteriora sequor (L.) I see the better course and approve it, I follow the worse. — Ovid, *Met.*, VII. 20.
vigilate et orate (L.) watch and pray.
viresque acquirit eundo (L.) (Fama, hearsay personified) gains strenght as she goes. — Virgil, *Aen.*, IV. 175.
Virgilium vidi tantum (L.) I just saw Virgil [and no more]. — Ovid, *Trist.*, IV. x. 51.
virginibus puerisque canto (L.) I sing for maidens and boys — for the young person. — Horace, *Od.*, III. i. 4.
virtus post nummos (L.) virtue after money — i.e. money first. — Horace, *Epist.*, I. i. 54.
vita brevis, ars longa (L.) life is short, art is long (see **ho bios**, etc.); **vita sine litteris mors est** life without literature is death.
vive la bagatelle (quasi-Fr.) long live folly.
vive ut vivas (L.) live that you may live; **vive, valeque** life and health to you
vivit post funera virtus (L.) virtue lives beyond the grave.
vixere fortes ante Agamemnona multi (L.) many brave men lived before Agamemnon. — Horace, *Od.*, IV. ix. 25–26.
vogue la galère! (Fr.) row the boat: row on: come what may!
volenti non fit injuria (L.) no wrong is done to one who consents.
volo, non valeo (L.) I am willing, but unable.
volto sciolto e pensieri stretti (It.) open face, close thoughts.
vous l'avez voulu, George Dandin (Fr.) you would have it so. — Molière, *George Dandin*, Act 1.
vox audita perit, littera scripta manet (L.) the heard word is lost, the written letter abides; **vox et praeterea nihil** a voice and nothing more (of a nightingale).

W

Wahrheit und Dichtung (Ger.) truth and poetry.
Wein, Weib, und Gesang (Ger.) wine, women and song.
wer da? (Ger.) who is there?
wie geht's? (Ger.) how are you?

Z

zonam perdidit (L.) he has lost his money-belt: he is in needy circumstances; **zonam solvere** to loose the virgin zone, i.e. marry.

Appendix III

Words Listed by Suffix

-ast chiliast, diaskeuast, dicast, dikast, dynast, ecclesiast, ecdysiast, elegiast, encomiast, enthusiast, fantast, gymnasiast, gymnast, Hesychast, hypochondriast, iconoclast, idoloclast, metaphrast, orgiast, pancratiast, paraphrast, pederast, peltast, phantasiast, pleonast, scholiast, utopiast.

-aster criticaster, grammaticaster, medicaster, philosophaster, poetaster, politicaster, theologaster.

-cide aborticide, acaricide, algicide, aphicide, aphidicide, bacillicide, bactericide, biocide, deicide, ecocide, ethnocide, feticide, filicide, foeticide, fratricide, fungicide, genocide, germicide, giganticide, herbicide, homicide, infanticide, insecticide, larvicide, liberticide, matricide, menticide, molluscicide, ovicide, parasiticide, parasuicide, parricide, patricide, pesticide, prolicide, regicide, rodenticide, sororicide, spermicide, suicide, taeniacide, trypanocide, tyrannicide, uxoricide, vaticide, verbicide, vermicide, viricide, viticide, vulpicide, weedicide,

-cracy aristocracy, autocracy, bureaucracy, chrysocracy, cottonocracy, democracy, demonocracy, despotocracy, dollarocracy, doulocracy, dulocracy, ergatocracy, Eurocracy, gerontocracy, gynecocracy, hagiocracy, hierocracy, isocracy, kakistocracy, meritocracy, millocracy, mobocracy, monocracy, nomocracy, ochlocracy, pantisocracy, pedantocracy, physiocracy, plantocracy, plutocracy, plutodemocracy, pornocracy, ptochocracy, slavocracy, snobocracy, squattocracy, stratocracy, technocracy, thalassocracy, thalattocracy, theocracy, timocracy.

-crat aristocrat, autocrat, bureaucrat, cosmocrat, democrat, hierocrat, meritocrat, millocrat, mobocrat, monocrat, ochlocrat, pantisocrat, pedantocrat, physiocrat, plutocrat, slavocrat, stratocrat, technocrat, theocrat.

-cratic aristocratic, autocratic, bureaucratic, cosmocratic, democratic, Eurocratic, gerontocratic, gynecocratic, hierocratic, isocratic, meritocratic, mobocratic, monocratic, ochlocratic, pancratic, pantisocratic, pedantocratic, physiocratic, plutocratic, stratocratic, technocratic, theocratic, timocratic, undemocratic.

-cultural accultural, agricultural, arboricultural, crinicultural, cultural, floricultural, horticultural, piscicultural, subcultural, vinicultural, vocicultural.

-culture agriculture, apiculture, aquaculture, aquiculture, arboriculture, aviculture, culture, electroculture, floriculture, horticulture, mariculture, monoculture, ostreiculture, pisciculture, pomiculture, self-culture, sericiculture, sericulture, silviculture, stirpiculture, subculture, sylviculture, viniculture, viticulture, water-culture, zooculture.

-cyte athrocyte, cyte, erythrocyte, fibrocyte, gonocyte, granulocyte, hemocyte, leucocyte, lymphocyte, macrocyte, microcyte, oocyte, phagocyte, poikilocyte, spermatocyte, thrombocyte, thymocyte.

-dom Anglo-Saxondom, apedom, archdukedom, attorneydom, babeldom, babudom, bachelordom, beadledom, beggardom, birthdom, bishopdom, boredom, Bumbledom, chiefdom, Christendom, clerkdom, cockneydom, crippledom, cuckoldom, czardom, demirepdom, devildom, Dogberrydom, dolldom, dufferdom, dukedom, dancedom, earldom, enthraldom, fairydom, fandom, filmdom, flunkeydom, fogydom, freedom, fresherdom, Greekdom, gypsydom, halidom, heathendom, heirdom, hobbledehoydom, hobodom, junkerdom, kaiserdom, kingdom, kitchendom, leechdom, liegedom, mandom, martyrdom, masterdom, newspaperdom, noodledom, noveldom, officialdom, overfreedom, penny-wisdom, popedom, princedom, puppydom, puzzledom, Quakerdom, queendom, queerdom, rascaldom, rebeldom, sachemdom, saintdom, savagedom, Saxondom, scoundreldom, serfdom, sheikdom, sheikhdom, sheriffdom, Slavdom, spinsterdom, squiredom, stardom, subkingdom, swelldom, thanedom, thraldom, thralldom, topsyturvydom, tsardom, underkingdom, unwisdom, villadom, whoredom, wisdom, Yankeedom.

-ferous aluminiferous, amentiferous, antenniferous, argentiferous, auriferous, bacciferous, balsamiferous, bulbiferous, calciferous, carboniferous, celliferous, celluliferous, cheliferous, cobaltiferous, conchiferous, coniferous, coralliferous, corniferous, cruciferous, culmiferous, cupriferous, cupuliferous, diamantiferous, diamondiferous, doloriferous, dorsiferous, ferriferous, flagelliferous, flammiferous, floriferous, foraminiferous, fossiliferous, frondiferous, fructiferous, frugiferous, furciferous, garnetiferous, gemmiferous, glandiferous, glanduliferous, globuliferous, glumiferous, granuliferous, guaniferous, gummiferous, guttiferous, lactiferous, laniferous, laticiferous, lethiferous, luciferous, luminiferous, mammaliferous, mammiferous, manganiferous, manniferous, margaritiferous, melliferous, metalliferous, morbiferous, mortiferous, moschiferous, muciferous, nectariferous, nickeliferous, nubiferous, nuciferous, odoriferous, oleiferous, omniferous, ossiferous, oviferous, ovuliferous, ozoniferous, papilliferous, papuliferous, Permo-Carboniferous, pestiferous, petaliferous, petroliferous, piliferous, platiniferous, plumbiferous, polliniferous, pomiferous, poriferous, proliferous, pyritiferous, quartziferous, reptiliferous, resiniferous, rotiferous, sacchariferous, saliferous, salutiferous, sanguiferous, sebiferous, seminiferous, septiferous, siliciferous, soboliferous, somniferous, soporiferous, spiniferous, spinuliferous, splendiferous, staminiferous, stanniferous, stelliferous, stigmatiferous, stoloniferous, strombuliferous, styliferous, sudoriferous, tentaculiferous, thuriferous, titaniferous, tuberiferous, umbelliferous, umbriferous, unfossiliferous, uriniferous, vitiferous, vociferous, yttriferous, zinciferous, zinkiferous.

-gamy allogamy, apogamy, autogamy, bigamy, chalazogamy, chasmogamy, cleistogamy, clistogamy, cryptogamy, deuterogamy, dichogamy, digamy, endogamy, exogamy, geitonogamy, hercogamy, herkogamy, heterogamy, homogamy, hypergamy, isogamy, misogamy, monogamy, oogamy, pangamy, pantagamy, plasmogamy, plastogamy, polygamy, porogamy, siphonogamy, syngamy, trigamy, xenogamy, zoogamy.

-genesis abiogenesis, agamogenesis, anthropogenesis, autogenesis, biogenesis, blastogenesis, carcinogenesis, chondrogenesis, cytogenesis, diagenesis, diplogenesis, dynamogenesis, ectogenesis, electrogenesis, embryogenesis, epeirogenesis, epigenesis, gametogenesis, gamogenesis, hematogenesis, heterogenesis, histogenesis, homogenesis, hylogenesis, hypogenesis, merogenesis, metagenesis, monogenesis, morphogenesis, mythogenesis, neogenesis, noogenesis, ontogenesis, oogenesis, organogenesis, orogenesis, orthogenesis, osteogenesis, palingenesis, pangenesis, paragenesis, parthenogenesis, pathogenesis, pedogenesis, perigenesis, petrogenesis, phylogenesis, phytogenesis, polygenesis, psychogenesis, pyogenesis, schizogenesis, spermatogenesis, sporogenesis, syngenesis, thermogenesis, xenogenesis.

-genic aesthesiogenic, allergenic, androgenic, anthropogenic, antigenic, biogenic, blastogenic, carcinogenic, cariogenic, cryogenic, dysgenic, ectogenic, electrogenic, endogenic, epeirogenic, erogenic, erotogenic, eugenic, genic, glycogenic, hallucinogenic, histogenic, hypnogenic, hysterogenic, iatrogenic, lactogenic, lysigenic, mammogenic, mutagenic, myogenic, neurogenic, odontogenic, oestrogenic, oncogenic, ontogenic, orogenic, orthogenic, osteogenic, pathogenic, photogenic, phytogenic, polygenic, psychogenic, pyogenic, pyrogenic, pythogenic, radiogenic, rhizogenic, saprogenic, schizogenic, somatogenic, spermatogenic, telegenic, teratogenic, thermogenic, tumorgenic, tumorigenic, visiogenic, zoogenic, zymogenic.

-gon chiliagon, decagon, dodecagon, endecagon, enneagon, hendecagon, heptagon, hexagon, isogon, nonagon, octagon, pentagon, perigon, polygon, tetragon, trigon.

-gram airgram, anagram, anemogram, angiogram, audiogram, ballistocardiogram, barogram, cablegram, calligram, cardiogram, cartogram, centigram, centimeter-gram, chromatogram, chromogram, chronogram, cryptogram, dactylogram, decagram, decigram, dendrogram, diagram, echogram, electrocardiogram, electroencephalogram, encephalogram, engram, epigram, ergogram, ferrogram, harmonogram, hectogram, hexagram, hierogram, histogram, hologram, ideogram, indicator-diagram, isogram, kilogram, lexigram, lipogram, logogram, lymphogram, marconigram, marigram, meteorogram, microgram, monogram, myogram, nanogram, nephogram, neurogram, nomogram, organogram, oscillogram, pangram, paragram, parallelogram, pentagram, phonogram, photogram, phraseogram, pictogram, program, psychogram, pyelogram, radiogram, radiotelegram, röntgenogram, scintigram, seismogram, sialogram, skiagram, sociogram, spectrogram, spectroheliogram, sphenogram, sphymogram, steganogram, stereogram, tachogram, telegram, tephigram, tetragram, thermogram, tomogram, trigram.

-graph Addressograph®;, airgraph, allograph, anemograph, apograph, audiograph, autograph, autoradiograph, ballistocardiograph, bar-graph, barograph, biograph, cardiograph, cathodograph, cerograph, chirograph, choreograph, chromatograph, chromolithograph, chromoxylograph, chronograph, cinematograph, coronagraph, coronograph, cryptograph, cyclograph, cymagraph, cymograph, diagraph, Dictograph®;, digraph, dynamograph, eidograph, electrocardiograph, electroencephalograph, electrograph, electromyograph, ellipsograph, encephalograph, epigraph, ergograph, evaporograph, flannelgraph, glyphograph, harmonograph, hectograph, helicograph, heliograph, hierograph, hodograph, holograph, homograph, hydrograph, hyetograph, hyetometrograph, hygrograph, ideograph, idiograph, jellygraph, keraunograph, kinematograph, kinetograph, kymograph, lithograph, logograph, magnetograph, marconigraph, marigraph, meteorograph, micrograph, microphotograph, microseismograph, mimeograph, monograph, myograph, nephograph, nomograph, odograph, odontograph, oleograph, opisthograph, orthograph, oscillograph, pantograph, paragraph, pentagraph, phonautograph, phonograph, photograph, photolithograph, photomicrograph, phototelegraph, photozincograph, phraseograph, pictograph, planigraph, plethysmograph, polygraph, pseudograph, psychograph, pyrophotograph, radioautograph, radiograph, radiometeorograph, radiotelegraph, rotograph, seismograph, salenograph, serigraph, shadowgraph, skiagraph, spectrograph, spectroheliograph, sphygmograph, spirograph, steganograph, stenograph, stereograph, Stevengraph, stylograph, syngraph, tachograph, tachygraph,

Telautograph®;, telegraph, telephotograph, thermograph, thermometrograph, tomograph, torsiograph, trigraph, vectograph, vibrograph, xylograph, zincograph.

-graphy aerography, ampelography, angiography, anthropogeography, anthropography, areography, autobiography, autography, autoradiography, autotypography, ballistocardiography, bibliography, biogeography, biography, brachygraphy, cacography, calligraphy, cardiography, cartography, cathodography, ceramography, cerography, chalcography, chartography, chirography, cholangiography, choregraphy, choreography, chorography, chromatography, chromolithography, chromotypography, chromoxylography, chronography, cinematography, cinemicrography, climatography, cometography, cosmography, cryptography, crystallography, dactyliography, dactylography, demography, dermatography, dermography, discography, dittography, doxography, echocardiography, ectypography, electrocardiography, electroencephalography, electrography, electromyography, electrophotography, encephalography, enigmatography, epigraphy, epistolography, ethnography, ferrography, filmography, geography, glossography, glyphography, glyptography, hagiography, haplography, heliography, heresiography, hierography, historiography, holography, horography, hydrography, hyetography, hymnography, hypsography, ichnography, ichthyography, iconography, ideography, lexicography, lexigraphy, lipography, lithography, logography, lymphography, mammography, metallography, microcosmography, micrography, microphotography, mimography, monography, morphography, myography, mythography, nomography, nosography, oceanography, odontography, oleography, opisthography, orchesography, oreography, organography, orography, orthography, osteography, paleogeography, paleography, paleontography, pantography, paroemiography, pasigraphy, pathography, petrography, phonography, photography, photolithography, photomicrography, phototelegraphy, photoxylography, photozincography, physiography, phytogeography, phytography, pictography, polarography, polygraphy, pornography, prosopography, pseudepigraphy, pseudography, psychobiography, psychography, pterylography, pyelography, pyrography, pyrophotography, radiography, radiotelegraphy, reprography, rhyparography, röntgenography, scenography, scintigraphy, seismography, selenography, serigraphy, sialography, snobography, spectrography, sphygmography, steganography, stenography, stereography, stratigraphy, stylography, symbolography, tachygraphy, telautography, telegraphy, telephotography, thalassography, thanatography, thaumatography, thermography, tomography, topography, typography, ultrasonography, uranography, urography, ventriculography, xerography, xeroradiography, xylography, xylopyrography, xylotypography, zincography, zoogeography, zoography.

-graphical autobiographical, bathygraphical, bathyorographical, bibliographical, biobibliographical, biogeographical, biographical, cacographical, calligraphical, cartographical, cerographical, chorographical, cinematographical, climatographical, cosmographical, geographical, glossographical, graphical, hagiographical, hierographical, historiographical, hydrographical, hyetographical, hygrographical, ichnographical, ideographical, lexicographical, lexigraphical, lithographical, logographical, monographical, myographical, oceanographical, oreographical, orographical, orthographical, paleographical, paleontographical, pantographical, paragraphical, pasigraphical, petrographical, photographical, physiographical, prosopographical, pseudepigraphical, psychobiographical, psychographical, pterylographical, seismographical, selenographical, spectrographical, stenographical, stereographical, stratigraphical, tachygraphical, topographical, typographical, xylographical, zincographical, zoogeographical, zoographical.

-hedron chiliahedron, decahedron, dihedron, dodecahedron, enneahedron, hemihedron, hexahedron, holohedron, icosahedron, icositetrahedron, leucitohedron, octahedron, octohedron, pentahedron, polyhedron, pyritohedron, rhombohedron, scalenohedron, tetrahedron, tetrakishexahedron, trapezohedron, triakisoctahedron, trihedron, trisoctahedron.

-hood adulthood, angelhood, apehood, apprenticehood, babyhood, bachelorhood, beadlehood, beasthood, bountihood, boyhood, brotherhood, cathood, childhood, Christhood, companionhood, cousinhood, cubhood, deaconhood, dollhood, drearihood, elfhood, fairyhood, falsehood, fatherhood, flapperhood, fleshhood, gawkihood, gentlehood, gentlemanhood, gianthood, girlhood, godhood, hardihood, high-priesthood, hobbledehoyhood, hoghood, hoydenhood, idlehood, invalidhood, jealoshood, kinghood, kinglihood, knighthood, ladyhood, likelihood, livelihood, lustihood, maidenhood, maidhood, manhood, masterhood, matronhood, misshood, monkhood, motherhood, nationhood, needy-hood, neighborhood, novicehood, nunhood, old-maidhood, orphanhood, pagehood, parenthood, popehood, priesthood, princehood, prophethood, puppyhood, queenhood, sainthood, selfhood, serfhood, sisterhood, spinsterhood, squirehood, statehood, swinehood, tabbyhood, thanehood, thinghood, traitorhood, unlikelihood, virginhood, waiterhood, widowerhood, widowhood, wifehood, wivehood, womanhood, youthhood.

-iac ammoniac, amnesiac, anaphrodisiac, anglomaniac, Anglophobiac, antaphrodisiac, anthomaniac, aphasiac, aphrodisiac, archgenethliac, bacchiac, bibliomaniac, cardiac, celiac, Cluniac, coprolaliac, demoniac, dextrocardiac,

Dionysiac, dipsomaniac, dochmiac, dysthymiac, egomaniac, elegiac, endocardiac, erotomaniac, etheromaniac, Genesiac, genethliac, hebephreniac, heliac, hemophiliac, hypochondriac, iliac, insomniac, intracardiac, Isiac, kleptomaniac, maniac, megalomaniac, meloncholiac, melomaniac, monomaniac, morphinomaniac, mythomaniac, necrophiliac, neurastheniac, nymphomaniac, opsomaniac, orchidomaniac, Pandemoniac, paradisiac, paranoiac, paraphiliac, paroemiac, pedophiliac, pericardiac, phrenesiac, pyromaniac, sacroiliac, scopophiliac, scoriac, simoniac, symposiac, Syriac, theomaniac, theriac, timbromaniac, toxiphobiac, zodiac, zygocardiac.

-iatric chemiatric, chemopsychiatric, geriatric, hippiatric, kinesiatric, pediatric, psychiatric, psychogeriatric.

-iatry chemopsychiatry, geriatry, hippiatry, neuropsychiatry, orthopsychiatry, pediatry, podiatry, psychiatry.

-ician academician, acoustician, aeroelastician, aesthetician, arithmetician, audiometrician, beautician, biometrician, clinician, cosmetician, diagnostician, dialectician, dietician, econometrician, ekistician, electrician, geometrician, geopolitician, geriatrician, informatician, linguistician, logician, logistician, magician, magnetician, mathematician, mechanician, metaphysician, metrician, mortician, musician, obstetrician, optician, pediatrician, patrician, Paulician, phonetician, physician, politician, practician, psychogeriatrician, psychometrician, rhetorician, rubrician, statistician, systematician, tactician, technician, theoretician.

-ics acoustics, acrobatics, aerobatics, aerobics, aerodynamics, aeronautics, aerostatics, aesthetics, agogics, agnostics, ambisonics, apologetics, aquabatics, aquanautics, astrodynamics, astronautics, astrophysics, athletics, atmospherics, autonomics, avionics, axiomatics, ballistics, bioastronautics, biodynamics, bioethics, biomathematics, biomechanics, biometrics, bionics, bionomics, biophysics, biorhythmics, biosystematics, cacogenics, calisthenics, callisthenics, catacoustics, catallactics, cataphonics, catechetics, catoptrics, ceroplastics, chemotherapeutics, chremastics, chromatics, civics, cliometrics, conics, cosmonautics, cosmopolitics, cryogenics, cryonics, cryophysics, cybernetics, cytogenetics, deontics, dermatoglyphics, diacoustics, diagnostics, dialectics, dianetics, didactics, dietetics, dioptrics, dogmatics, dramatics, dynamics, dysgenics, eclectics, econometrics, economics, ecumenics, ekistics, electrodynamics, electrokinetics, electromechanics, electronics, electrostatics, electrotechnics, electrotherapeutics, electrothermics, energetics, entoptics, environics, epigenetics, epistemics, epizootics, ergonomics, ethics, ethnolinguistics, eudaemonics, eudemonics, eugenics, eurhythmics, euthenics, exegetics, floristics, fluidics, forensics, genetics, geodetics, geodynamics, geophysics, geopolitics, geoponics, geostatics, geotectonics, geriatrics, gerontotherapeutics, glyptics, gnomonics, gnotobiotics, graphemics, graphics, gyrostatics, halieutics, haptics, harmonics, hedonics, hermeneutics, hermetics, hippiatrics, histrionics, homiletics, hydraulics, hydrodynamics, hydrokinetics, hydromagnetics, hydromechanics, hydroponics, hydrostatics, hydrotherapeutics, hygienics, hypersonics, hysterics, informatics, irenics, isagogics, isometrics, kinematics, kinesics, kinetics, linguistics, lithochromatics, liturgics, logistics, loxodromics, macrobiotics, macroeconomics, magnetics, magneto-hydrodynamics, magneto-optics, maieutics, mathematics, mechanics, melodics, metalinguistics, metamathematics, metaphysics, metapsychics, meteoritics, microeconomics, microelectronics, microphysics, mnemotechnics, mole-electronics, monostrophics, morphemics, morphophonemics, nautics, nucleonics, numismatics, obstetrics, olympics, onomastics, optics, optoelectronics, orchestics, orthodontics, orthodromics, orthogenics, orthopedics, orthoptics, orthotics, paideutics, pantopragmatics, paralinguistics, party-politics, pataphysics, patristics, pedagogics, pedentics, pediatrics, pedodontics, peptics, periodontics, pharmaceutics, pharmacodynamics, pharmacokinetics, phelloplastics, phonemics, phonetics, phonics, phonocamptics, phonotactics, photics, photochromics, photoelectronics, phototherapeutics, photovoltaics, physics, physiotherapeutics, plastics, pneumatics, pneumodynamics, polemics, politico-economics, politics, power- politics, problematics, prosthetics, prosthodontics, psychics, psychodynamics, psychogeriatrics, psycholinguistics, psychometrics, psychonomics, psychophysics, psychosomatics, psychotherapeutics, pyrotechnics, quadraphonics, quadrophonics, radionics, radiophonics, radiotherapeutics, rhythmics, robotics, semantics, semeiotics, semiotics, Semitics, sferics, significs, sociolinguistics, sonics, sophistics, spherics, sphragistics, statics, stereoptics, strategics, stylistics, subatomics, subtropics, syllabics, symbolics, synectics, systematics, tactics, technics, tectonics, telearchics, thaumaturgics, theatrics, therapeutics, thermionics, thermodynamics, thermotics, toponymics, toreutics, transonics, transsonics, ultrasonics, vitrics, zoiatrics, zootechnics, zymotechnics.

-iform aciform, acinaciform, aciniform, aeriform, alphabetiform, amoebiform, anguiform, anguilliform, antenniform, asbestiform, auriform, aviform, bacciform, bacilliform, biform, bursiform, cactiform, calcariform, calceiform, calyciform, cambiform, campaniform, campodeiform, cancriform, capriform, cauliform, cerebriform, cirriform, claviform, clypeiform, cobriform, cochleariform, coliform, colubriform, conchiform, coniform, coralliform, cordiform, corniform, corolliform, cotyliform, crateiform, cribriform, cristiform, cruciform, cteniform, cubiform, cucumiform, culiciform, cultriform, cumuliform, cuneiform, curviform, cyathiform, cylindriform, cymbiform, cystiform, deiform, dendriform, dentiform, digitiform, dolabriform, elytriform, ensiform, equisetiform, eruciform, falciform, fibriform, filiform, flabelliform, flagelliform, floriform, fringilliform, fungiform, fusiform, gangliform, gasiform, glandiform, granitiform, granuliform, hydatidiform, incisiform, infundibuliform, insectiform, janiform, jelliform, lamelliform, lanciform, lapilliform, larviform, lentiform, limaciform, linguiform, lumbriciform, lyriform, malleiform, mamilliform, mammiform, maniform, medusiform, mitriform, monadiform, moniliform, morbilliform, multiform, mummiform, muriform, mytiliform,, napiform, natiform, naupliiform, nubiform, omniform, oviform, paliform, panduriform, papilliform, patelliform, pelviform, penicilliform, penniform, perciform, phialiform, piliform, pisciform, pisiform, placentiform, planuliform, plexiform, poculiform, proteiform, pulvilliform, pyriform, quadriform, radiciform, raduliform, raniform, reniform, restiform, retiform, sacciform, sagittiform, salpiform, scalariform, scalpelliform, scalpriform, scoleciform, scolopendriform, scutiform, scyphiform, securiform, septiform, serpentiform, spiniform, spongiform, squamiform, stalactiform, stalactitiform, stelliform, stratiform, strigiform, strobiliform, strombuliform, styliform, tauriform, tectiform, telescopiform, thalliform, triform, tuberiform, tubiform, tympaniform, umbraculiform, unciform, unguiform, uniform, vaporiform, variform, vasculiform, vasiform, vermiform, verruciform, versiform, villiform, viperiform, vitriform, vulviform, ypsiliform, zeolitiform.

-ism abnormalism, abolitionism, aboriginalism, absenteeism, absolutism, academicalism, academicism, accidentalism, achromatism, acosmism, acrobatism, acotism, actinism, activism, Adamitism, adiaphorism, adoptianism, Adopttionism, adventurism, aeroembolism, aerotropism, aestheticism, Africanism, ageism, agnosticism, agrarianism, Albigensianism, albinism, albinoism, alcoholism, algorism, alienism, allelomorphism, allotropism, alpinism, altruism, amateurism, Americanism, ametabolism, amoralism, amorism, amorphism, anabaptism, anabolism, anachronism, anagrammatism, anarchism, anastigmatism, androdioecism, andromonoecism, aneurism, Anglicanism, anglicism, Anglo-Catholicism, aniconism, animalism, animatism, animism, annihilationism, antagonism, anthropomorphism, anthropomorphitism, anthropopathism, anthropophuism, anthropopsychism, antichristianism, anticivism, anticlericalism, antidisestablishmentarianism, anti-federalism, anti-Gallicanism, anti-Jacobinism, antinomianism, antiochianism, antiquarianism, anti-Semitism, antisepticism, antisocialism, antitheism, antitrinitarianism, antivaccinationism, antivivisectionism, anythingarianism, apheliotropism, aphorism, apism, aplanatism, apochromatism, apogeotropism, apoliticism, Apollinarianism, apostolicism, apriorism, Arabism, Aramaism, Arcadianism, archaicism, archaism, Arianism, aristocratism, Aristotelianism, Aristotelism, Arminianism, asceticism, asepticism, Asiaticism, aspheterism, asteism, asterism, astigmatism, asynchronism, asystolism, atavism, atheism, athleticism, Atlanticism, atomism, atonalism, atropism, Atticism, attorneyism, Augustinianism, Australianism, authorism, authoritarianism, autism, autochthonism, autoeroticism, autoerotism, automatism, automobilism, automorphism, autotheism, avant-gardism, Averrhoism, Averroism, Baalism, Baathism, Ba'athism, Babbitism, Babeeism, babelism, Babiism, Babism, babuism, bacchanalianism, bachelorism, Baconianism, Bahaism, bantingism, baptism, barbarism, bashawism, bastardism, bathmism, bedlamism, behaviorism, Benthamism, Bergsonism, Berkeleianism, bestialism, betacism, biblicism, bibliophilism, bilateralism, bilingualism, bimetallism, bipedalism, blackguardism, blepharism, bogeyism, bogyism, Bohemianism, bolshevism, Bonapartism, bonism, boobyism, Boswellism, botulism, Bourbonism, bowdlerism, bradyseism, braggartism, Brahmanism, Brahminism, Braidism, Briticism, Britishism, Brownism, bruxism, Buchmanism, Buddhism, bullyism, Burschenism, Byronism, Byzantinism, cabalism, cabbalism, Caesarism, caesaropapism, caffeinism, caffeism, Calvinism, cambism, Camorrism, cannibalism, capitalism, Carbonarism, careerism, Carlism, Carlylism, carnalism, Cartesianism, casualism, catabolism, catastrophism, catechism, catechumenism, Catharism, catheterism, catholicism, causationism, cauterism, cavalierism, Celticism, cenobitism, centenarianism, centralism, centripetalism, centrism, cerebralism, ceremonialism, chaldaism, characterism, charism, charlatanism, chartism, Chasidism, Chassidism, Chaucerism, chauvinism, chemism, chemotropism, chloralism, Christianism, chromaticism, churchism, Ciceronianism, cicisbeism, cinchonism, civisim, classicism, clericalism, cliquism, clubbism, coalitionism, Cobdenism, cocainism, cockneyism, collectivism, collegialism, colloquialism, colonialism, commensalism, commercialism, communalism, communism, compatriotism, comstockism, Comtism, conacreism, conceptualism, concettism, concretism, confessionalism, confrontationism, Confucianism, Congregationalism, conservatism, consortism, constitutionalism, constructionism, constructivism, consubstantialism, consumerism, contact-metamorphism, continentalism, contortionism, contrabandism, conventionalism, conversationism, convictism, copyism, corporatism, corporealism, corybantism, cosmeticism, cosmism, cosmopolitanism, cosmopolitism, cosmotheism, cottierism, Couéism, courtierism, creatianism, creationism, cretinism, cretism, criticism, crotalism, cubism, cultism, curialism, cyclicism, cynicism, czarism, Dadaism, Daltonism, dandyism, Darwinism, deaf-mutism, decimalism, defeatism, deism, demagogism, demaguism, demoniacism, demonianism, demonism, denominationalism, departmentalism, descriptivism, depotism, deteriorism, determinism, deviationism, devilism, diabolism, diachronism, diageotropism, diaheliotropism, dialecticism, diamagnetism, diaphototropism, diastrophism, diatropism, dichroism, dichromatism, dichromism, diclinism, dicrotism, didacticism, diffusionism, dilettanteism, dilettantism, dimerism, dimorphism, diocism, diorism, diothelism, diphysitism, dirigism, dissenterism, dissolutionism, disyllabism, ditheism, ditheletism, dithelism, dithelitism, divisionism, Docetism, doctrinairism, doctrinarianism, Dogberryism, dogmatism, do-goodism, dolichocephalism, donatism, donnism, do-nothingism, Doricism, Dorism, dowdyism, draconism, dragonism, dramaticism, drudgism, druidism, dualism, dudism, dufferism, dunderheadism, dynamism, dyotheletism, dyothelism, dysphemism, ebionism, ebionitism, echoism, eclecticism, ecumenicalism, ecumenicism, ecumenism, Edwardianism, egalitarianism, egoism, egotheism, egotism, electromagnetism, electromerism, elementalism, elitism, Elizabethanism, embolism, emotionalism, empiricism, enantiomorphism, Encratism, encyclopedism, endemism, Englishism, entrism, environmentalism, eonism, epicism, Epicureanism, epicurism, epiphenomenalism, epiphytism, epipolism, episcopalianism, episcopalism, equalitarianism, equestrianism, Erastianism, eremitism, erethism, ergotism, eroticism, erotism, erythrism, escapism, esotericism, esoterism, Essenism, essentialism, etacism, etherism, ethicism, ethnicism, ethnocentrism, eudemonism, eugenism, euhemerism, eumerism, eunuchism, eunuchoidism, euphemism, euphuism, Eurocommunism, Europeanism, evangelicalism, evangelicism, evangelism, evolutionism, exclusionism, exclusivism, exhibitionism, existentialism, ex-librism, exorcism, exotericism, exoticism, expansionism, experientialism, experimentalism, expressionism, extensionalism, externalism, extremism, Fabianism, factionalism, faddism, fairyism, fakirism, falangism, familism, fanaticism, fantasticism, faradism, fascism, fatalism, Fauvism, favism, favoritism, Febronianism, federalism, femininism, feminism, Fenianism, fetichism, fetishism, feudalism, feuilletonism, fideism, fifth-monarchism, filibusterism, finalism, fissiparism, flagellantism, flunkeyism, fogyism, formalism, fortuitism, Fourierism, fractionalism, Froebelism, functionalism, fundamentalism, fusionism, futurism, gaelicism, Galenism, Gallicanism, gallicism, galvanism, gamotropism, ganderism, gangsterism, Gargantuism, gargarism, gargoylism, Gasconism, Gaullism, generationism, Genevanism, genteelism, gentilism, geocentricism, geomagnetism, geophagism, geotropism, Germanism, giantism, gigantism, Girondism, Gnosticism, Gongorism, gormandism, Gothicism, gradualism, Graecism, grammaticism, Grangerism, Grecism, gregarianism, griffinism, Grobianism, Grundyism, gynandrism, gynandromophism, gynodioecism, gynomonoecism, gypsyism, gyromagnetism, haptotropism, Hasidism, Hassidism, heathenism, Hebraicism, Hebrewism, hectorism, hedonism, Hegelianism, hegemonism, heliotropism, Hellenism, helotism, hemihedrism, hemimorphism, henotheism, hermaphroditism, heroism, hetaerism, hetairism, heterochronism, heteroecism, heteromorphism, heterostylism, heterothallism, heurism, Hibernianism, Hibernicism, hidalgoism, hierarchism, highbrowism, High-Churchism, Hildebrandism, Hinduism, Hippocratism, hispanicism, historicism, historism, histrionicism, histrionism, Hitlerism, Hobbesianism, Hobbianism, Hobbism, hobbledehoyism, hobbyism, hobgoblinism, hoboism, holism, holohedrism, holometabolism, holophytism, homeomorphism, homoeroticism, homoerotism, homomorphism, homothallism, hooliganism, hoydenism, humanism, humanitarianism, Humism, humoralism, hybridism, hydrargyrism, hydrotropism, hylicism, hylism, hylomorphism, hylopathism, hylotheism, hylozoism, hyperadrenalism, hyperbolism, hypercriticism, hyperthyroidism, hyphenism, hypnotism, hypochondriacism, hypocorism, hypognathism, hypothyroidism, Ibsenism, iconomaticism, iconophilism, idealism, idiotism, idolism, illuminism, illusionism, imagism, immanentism, immaterialism, immediatism, immersionism, immobilism, immoralism, imperialism, impossibilism, impressionism, incendiarism, incivism, incorporealism, indeterminism, indifferentism, individualism, industrialism, infallibilism, infantilism, inflationism, Infralapsarianism, inquilinism, inspirationism, institutionalism, instrumentalism, insularism, insurrectionism, intellectualism, interactionism, internationalism, interventionism, intimism, intransigentism, intuitionalism, intuitionism, intuitivism, invalidism, iodism, Ionism, iotacism, irenicism, Irishism, irrationalism, irredentism, Irvingism, Islamism, ism, Ismailism, isochronism, isodimorphism, isolationism, isomerism, isomorphism, isotropism, itacism, Italianism, italicism, Jacobinism, Jacobitism, Jainism, Jansenism, Jesuitism, jingoism, jockeyism, Johnsonianism, Johnsonism, journalism, Judaism, junkerism, kaiserism, Kantianism, Kantism, katabolism, Kelticism, Keynesianism, klephtism, know-nothingism, Krishnaism, labdacism, labialism, laborism, laconicism, laconism, ladyism, Lamaism, Lamarckianism, Lamarckism, lambdacism, landlordism, Laodiceanism, larrikinism, lathyrism, Latinism, latitudinarianism, laxism, leftism, legalism, leggism, Leibnitzianism, Leibnizianism, Leninism, lesbianism, liberalism, liberationism, libertarianism, libertinism, lichenism, lionism, lipogrammatism, Listerism, literalism, literaryism, localism, Lollardism, Londonism, Low- Churchism, Luddism, luminarism, Lutheranism, Lutherism, lyricism, lyrism, Lysenkoism, macarism, Machiavellianism, Machiavellism, Magianism, Magism, magnetism, Magyarism, Mahdiism, Mahdism, maidism, malapropism, Malthusianism, mammonism, Manichaeism, Manicheanism, Manicheism, mannerism, Maoism, Marcionitism, Marinism, martialism, martinetism, Marxianism, Marxism, masochism, materialism, mathematicism, matriarchalism, maudlinism, Mazdaism, Mazdeism, McCarthyism, mechanism, medievalism, Medism, melanism, meliorism, memoirism, Mendelism, mentalism, mephitism, mercantilism, mercenarism, mercurialism, merism, merycism, mescalism, mesmerism, mesocephalism, mesomerism, Messianism, metabolism, metachronism, metamerism, metamorphism, metasomatism, metempiricism, meteorism, methodism, metopism, Micawberism, Michurinism, micro-organism, microseism, militarism, millenarianism, millenarism, millennianism, millenniarism, Miltonism, minimalism, minimism, misoneism, Mithraicism, Mithraism, mithridatism, modalism, moderatism, modernism, Mohammedanism, Mohammedism, Molinism, monachism, monadism, monarchianism, monarchism, monasticism, monergism, monetarism, mongolism, mongrelism, monism, monkeyism, monochromatism, monoecism, monogenism, monolingualism, monometallism, monophysitism, monorchism, monosyllabism, monotheism, monotheletism, monothelism, monothelitism, Monroeism, Montanism, moralism, Moravianism, Morisonianism, Mormonism, morphinism, mosaicism, Mosaism, Moslemism, mountebankism, multiracialism, Munichism, municipalism, Muslimism, mutism, mutualism, myalism, mysticism, mythicism, mythism, namby- pambyism, nanism, Napoleonism, narcissism, narcotism, nationalism, nativism, naturalism, naturism, navalism, Nazaritism, Naziism, Nazism, necessarianism, necessitarianism, necrophilism, negativism, negroism, negrophilism, neoclassicism, neocolonialism, Neo-Darwinism, Neofascism, Neohellenism, Neo- Impressionism, Neo-Kantianism, Neo-Lamarckism, neologism, Neo- Malthusianism, neo-Nazism, neonomianism, neopaganism, neoplasticism, Neo-Plasticism, Neoplatonism, Neopythagoreanism, neoterism, neovitalism, nephalism, Nestorianism, neuroticism, neutralism, newspaperism, nicotinism, Nietzscheanism, nihilism, noctambulism, Noetianism, nomadism, nominalism, nomism, northernism, notaphilism, nothingarianism, nothingism, Novatianism, novelism, nudism, nyctitropism, obeahism, obeism, obiism, objectivism, obscurantism, obsoletism, Occamism, occasionalism, Occidentalism, occultism, Ockhamism, odism, odylism, officialism, old-maidism, onanism, onirocriticism, Ophism, Ophitism, opportunism, optimism, Orangeism, Orangism, organicism, organism, Orientalism, Origenism, Orleanism, orphanism, Orphism, orthognathism, orthotropism, ostracism, ostrichism, Owenism, pacificism, pacifism, Paddyism, paganism, paleomagnetism, palladianism, paludism, panaesthetism, Pan-Africanism, Pan-Americanism, Pan-Arabian, panchromatism, pancosmism, panderism, panegoism, Pan-Germanism, Panhellenism, panislamism, panlogism, panpsychism, pansexualism, Pan-Slavism, pansophism, panspermatism, panspermism, Pantagruelism, pantheism, papalism, papism, parabaptism, parachronism, paragnathism, paraheliotropism, parallelism, paralogism, paramagnetism, paramorphism, parapsychism, parasitism, Parkinsonism, parliamentarism, Parnassianism, Parnellism, parochialism, Parseeism, Parsiism, Parsism, partialism, particularism, partyism, passivism, pasteurism, pastoralism, paternalism, patrialism, patriarchalism, patriarchism, patriotism, Patripassianism, patristicism, Paulinism, pauperism, pedagogism, pedagoguism, pedanticism, pedantism, pedestrianism, pedobaptism, pedomorphism, Pelagianism, pelmanism, pelorism, pennalism, penny- a-linerism, pentadactylism, pentamerism, pentaprism, peonism, perfectibilism, perfectionism, peripateticism, perpetualism, Persism, personalism, perspectivism, pessmism, petalism, Petrarchianism, Petrarchism, Petrinism, phagocytism, phalansterianism, phalansterism, phallicism, phallism, pharisaism, phariseeism, pheism, phenakism, phenomenalism, phenomenism, philhellenism, philistinism, philosophism, phobism, phoneticism, phonetism, phosphorism, photism, photochromism, photoperiodism, phototropism, physicalism, physicism, physitheism, pianism, pietism, piezomagnetism, Pindarism, Pittism, plagiarism, plagiotropism, Platonicism, Platonism, plebeianism, pleiotropism, pleochroism, pleomorphism, plumbism, pluralism, Plutonism, Plymouthism, pococuranteism, pococurantism, poeticism, pointillism, polonism, polychroism, polycrotism, polydactylism, polygenism, polymastism, polymerism, polymorphism, polynomialism, polysyllabicism, polysyllabism, polysyllogism, polysyntheticism, polysynthetism, polytheism, Pooterism, populism, porism, Porphyrogenitism, positivism, possibilism, Post-Impressionism, post-millennialism, Poujadism, Powellism, practicalism, pragmatism, precisianism, predestinarianism, predeterminism, preferentialism, preformationism, prelatism, premillenarianism, premillennialism, Pre-Raphaelism, Pre- Raphaelitism, Presbyterianism, presentationism, preternaturalism, prettyism, priapism, priggism, primitivism, primordialism, probabiliorism, probablism, prochronism, professionalism, prognathism, progressionism, progressism, progressivism, prohibitionism, proletarianism, propagandism, prophetism, prosaicism, prosaism, proselytism, prostatism, prosyllogism, protectionism, Protestantism, proverbialism, provincialism, prudentialism, Prussianism, psellism, psephism, pseudo-archaism, pseudoclassicism, pseudomorphism, psilanthropism, psychism, psychologism, psychopannychism, psychoticism, ptyalism, puerilism, pugilism, puppyism, purism, puritanism, Puseyism, pyrrhonism, Pythagoreanism, Pythagorism, Quakerism, quattrocentism, quietism, quixotism, rabbinism, Rabaelaisianism, racemism, Rachmanism, racialism, racism, radicalism, Ramism, ranterism, rascalism, rationalism, reactionarism, realism, rebaptism, Rebeccaism, Rechabitism, recidivism, red-tapism, reductionism, reformism, regalism, regionalism, reincarnationism, relationism, relativism, religionism, Rembrandtism, representationalism, representationism, republicanism, restitutionism, restorationism, resurrectionism, reunionism, revanchism, revisionism, revivalism, revolutionism, rheotropism, rheumatism, rhopalism, rhotacism, Ribbonism, rigorism, ritualism, Romanism, romanticism, Rosicrucianism, Rosminianism, Rotarianism, routinism, rowdyism, royalism, ruffianism, ruralism, Russianism, Russophilism, Sabaism, Sabbatarianism, sabbatism, Sabellianism, Sabianism, sacerdotalism, sacramentalism, sacramentarianism, Sadduceeism, Sadducism, sadism, sado-masochism, saintism, Saint- Simonianism, Saint-Simonism, Saivism, Saktism, salvationism, Samaritanism, sanitarianism, sansculottism, sapphism, saprophytism, Saracenism, satanism, saturnism, Saxonism, schematism, scholasticism, scientism, sciolism, Scotism, Scotticism, scoundrelism, scribism, scripturalism, scripturism, secessionism, sectarianism, sectionalism, secularism, self- criticism, self-hypnotism, selfism, semi-Arianism, semi- barbarism, Semi-Pelagianism, Semitism, sensationalism, sensationism, sensism, sensualism, sensuism, sentimentalism, separatism, serialism, servilism, servo-mechanism, sesquipedalianism, sexism, sexualism, Shaivism, shakerism, Shaktism, shamanism, shamateurism, Shiism, Shintoism, Shivaism, shunamitism, sigmatism, Sikhism, simplism, sinapism, sinecurism, singularism, Sinicism, Sinophilism, Sivaism, skepticism, Slavism, snobbism, socialism, Socinianism, sociologism, Sofism, solarism, solecism, sol-faism, solidarism, solidism, solifidianism, solipsism, somatism, somnambulism, somniloquism, sophism, southernism, sovietism, specialism, speciesism, Spencerianism, Spinozism, spiritism, spiritualism, spoonerism, spread-eagleism, Stahlianism, Stahlism, Stakhanovism, Stalinism, stand-pattism, statism, stercoranism, stereoisomerism, stereotropism, stibialism, stigmatism, stoicism, strabism, structuralism, strychninism, strychnism, Stundism, subjectivism, sublapsarianism, subordinationism, substantialism, suburbanism, suffragism, Sufiism, Sufism, suggestionism, supernationalism, supernaturalism, superrealism, Supralapsarianism, supremacism, suprematism, surrealism, sutteeism, Swadeshism, swarajism, Swedenborgianism, swingism, sybaritism, sybotism, syllabism, syllogism, symbolism, symphilism, synaposematism, synchronism, syncretism, syndactylism, syndicalism, synecdochism, synergism, synoecism, syntheticism, Syriarcism, Syrianism, systematism, tachism, tactism, Tammanyism, tantalism, Tantrism, Taoism, tarantism, Tartuffism, Tartufism, tautochronism, tautologism, tautomerism, teetotalism, teleologism, tenebrism, teratism, terminism, territorialism, terrorism, tetramerism, tetratheism, Teutonicism, Teutonism, textualism, thanatism, thaumaturgism, theanthropism, theatricalism, theatricism, theism, theomorphism, Theopaschitism, theophilanthropism, theosophism, therianthropism, theriomorphism, thermotropism, thigmotropism, Thomism, thrombo- embolism, thuggism, tigerism, Timonism, Titanism, Titoism, toadyism, tokenism, Toryism, totalitarianism, totemism, tourism, tractarianism, trade-unionism, traditionalism, Traducianism, traitorism, transcendentalism, transformism, transmigrationism, transsexualism, tranvestism, tranvestitism, traumatism, trialism, tribadism, tribalism, trichroism, trichromatism, tricrotism, triliteralism, trimorphism, Trinitarianism, trinomialism, tripersonalism, tritheism, triticism, trituberculism, trivialism, troglodytism, troilism, trophotropism, tropism, Trotskyism, truism, tsarism, tuism, Turcophilism, tutiorism, tutorism, tychism, ultra-Conservatism, ultraism, ultramontanism, undenominationalism, unicameralism, unidealism, uniformitarianism, unilateralism, unionism, unitarianism, unversalism, unrealism, unsectarianism, unsocialism, untuism, uranism, utilitarianism, utopianism, utopism, Utraquism, vagabondism, Valentinianism, valetudinarianism, vampirism, vandalism, Vansittartism, Vaticanism, Vedism, veganism, vegetarianism, ventriloquism, verbalism, verism, vernacularism, Victorianism, vigilantism, vikingism, virilism, virtualism, vitalism, viviparism, vocalism, vocationalism, volcanism, Voltaireanism, Voltairianism, Voltairism, voltaism, voltinism, voluntarism, voluntaryism, voodooism, vorticism, voyeurism, vulcanism, vulgarism, vulpinism, vulturism, Wagnerianism, Wagnerism, Wahabiism, Wahabism, welfarism, werewolfism, Wertherism, werwolfism, Wesleyanism, westernism, Whiggism, wholism, witticism, Wodenism, Wolfianism, xanthochroism, Yankeeism, yogism, zanyism, Zarathustrianism, Zarathustrism, zealotism, Zionism, Zoilism, zoism, Zolaism, zombiism, zoomagnetism, zoomorphism, zoophilism, zootheism, Zoroastrianism, Zwinglianism, zygodactylism, zygomorphism.

-itis adenitis, antiaditis, aortitis, appendicitis, arteritis, arthritis, balanitis, blepharitis, bronchitis, bursitis, carditis, cellulitis, cephalitis, ceratitis, cerebritis, cholecystitis, colitis, conchitis, conjunctivitis, crystallitis, cystitis, dermatitis, diaphragmatitis, diphtheritis, diverticulitis, duodenitis, encephalitis, endocarditis, endometritis, enteritis, fibrositis, gastritis, gastroenteritis, gingivitis, glossitis, hamarthritis, hepatitis, hysteritis, ileitis, iritis, keratitis, labyrinthitis, laminitis, laryngitis, lymphangitis, mastitis, mastoiditis, meningitis, metritis, myelitis, myocarditis, myositis, myringitis, nephritis, neuritis, onychitis, oophoritis, ophthalmitis, orchitis, osteitis, osteo-arthritis, osteomyelitis, otitis, ovaritis, panarthritis, pancreatitis, panophthalmitis, papillitis, parotiditis, parotitis, pericarditis, perigastritis, perihepatitis, perinephritis, perineuritis, periostitis, peritonitis, perityphlitis, pharnygitis, phlebitis, phrenitis, pleuritis, pneumonitis, poliomyelitis, polyneuritis, proctitis, prostatitis, pyelitis, pyelonephritis, rachitis, rectitis, retinitis, rhachitis, rhinitis, rhinopharyngitis, salpingitis, scleritis, sclerotitis, sinuitis, splenitis, spondylitis, staphylitis, stomatitis, strumitis, synovitis, syringitis, thrombo-phlebitis, thyroiditis, tonsilitis, tonsillitis, tracheitis, trachitis, tympanitis, typhlitis, ulitis, ureteritis, urethritis, uteritis, uveitis, uvulitis, vaginitis, valvulitis, vulvitis.

-latrous bibliolatrous, heliolatrous, ichthyolatrous, idolatrous, litholatrous, Mariolatrous, Maryolatrous, monolatrous, ophiolatrous, zoolatrous.

-latry angelolatry, anthropolatry, astrolatry, autolatry, bardolatry, bibliolatry, Christolatry, cosmolatry, demonolatry, dendrolatry, ecclesiolatry, epeolatry, geolatry, hagiolatry, heliolatry, hierolatry, ichthyolatry, iconolatry, idolatry, litholatry, lordolatry, Mariolatry, Maryolatry, monolatry, necrolatry, ophiolatry, physiolatry, plutolatry, pylolatry, symbololatry, thaumatolatry, theriolatry, zoolatry.

-logical aerobiological, aerological, aetiological, agrobiological, agrological, agrostological, algological, alogical, amphibological, analogical, anthropological, arachnological, archaeological, astrological, atheological, audiological, autecological, axiological, bacteriological, batological, battological, biological, bryological, campanological, carcinological, cartological, chorological, Christological, chronological, climatological, codicological, conchological, cosmological, craniological, cryobiological, cryptological, cytological, demonological, dendrological, deontological, dermatological, dysteleological, ecclesiological, ecological, Egyptological, electrophysiological, embryological, enological, entomological, epidemiological, epistemological, eschatological, ethnological, ethological, etymological, futurological, gastrological, gemmological, gemological, genealogical, genethlialogical, geochronological, geological, geomorphological, gerontological, glaciological, glossological, gnotobiological, graphological, gynecological, hagiological, helminthological, hepaticological, herpetological, histological, histopathological, homological, horological, hydrobiological, hydrological, ichthyological, ideological, illogical, immunological, laryngological, limnological, lithological, logical, malacological, mammalogical, martyrological, metapsychological, meteorological, micrological, mineralogical, monological, morphological, musicological, mycological, myological, myrmecological, mythological, necrological, neological, nephological, nephrological, neurological, nomological, nosological, nostological, oceanological, odontological, ontological, ophiological, ophthalmological, oreological, ornithological, orological, osteological, paleontological, paleozoological, palynological, parapsychological, pathological, pedological, penological, pestological, petrological, phenological, phenomenological, philological, phonological, phraseological, phrenological, phycological, physiological, phytological, phytopathological, pneumatological, pomological, posological, potamological, protozoological, psephological, psychobiological, psychological, radiological, reflexological, rheumatological, rhinological, scatological, sedimentological, seismological, selenological, serological, Sinological, sociobiological, sociological, somatological, soteriological, Sovietological, spectrological, speleological, stoechiological, stoicheiological, stoichiological, synecological, tautological, technological, teleological, teratological, terminological, theological, topological, toxicological, traumatological, trichological, tropological, typological, unlogical, untheological, urological, virological, volcanological, vulcanological, zoological, zoophytological, zymological.

-logous analogous, antilogous, dendrologous, heterologous, homologous, isologous, tautologous.

-logue apologue, collogue, decalogue, dialogue, duologue, eclogue, epilogue, grammalogue, homologue, idealogue, ideologue, isologue, monologue, philologue, prologue, Sinologue, theologue, travelogue, trialogue.

-logy acarology, aerobiology, aerolithology, aerology, aetiology, agriology, agrobiology, agrology, agrostology, algology, amphibology, anesthesiology, analogy, andrology, anemology, angelology, anthology, anthropobiology, anthropology, antilogy, apology, arachnology, archaeology, archology, aristology, Assyriology, astrogeology, astrology, atheology, atmology, audiology, autecology, autology, axiology, bacteriology, balneology, batology, battology, bibliology, bioecology, biology, biotechnology, brachylogy, bryology, bumpology, cacology, caliology, campanology, carcinology, cardiology, carphology, cartology, cetology, cheirology, chirology, choreology, chorology, Christology, chronobiology, chronology, cine-biology, climatology, codicology, cometology, conchology, coprology, cosmetology, cosmology, craniology, criminology, cryobiology, cryptology, cytology, dactyliology, dactylology, deltiology, demology, demonology, dendrochronology, dendrology, deontology, dermatology, diabology, diabolology, dialectology, diplomatology, dittology, docimology, dogmatology, dosiology, dosology, doxology, dyslogy, dysteleology, ecclesiology, eccrinology, ecology, edaphology, Egyptology, electrobiology, electrology, electrophysiology, electrotechnology, elogy, embyology, emmenology, endemiology, endocrinology, enology, entomology, enzymology, epidemiology, epistemology, escapology, eschatology, ethnology, ethnomusicology, ethology, Etruscology, etymology, euchology, eulogy, exobiology, festilogy, festology, folk-etymology, futurology, gastroenterology, gastrology, gemmology, gemology, genealogy, genethlialogy, geochronology, geology, geomorphology, gerontology, gigantology, glaciology, glossology, glottology, gnomonology, gnoseology, gnosiology, gnotobiology, graphology, gynecology, hematology, hagiology, hamartiology, haplology, heliology, helminthology, heorology, hepaticology, hepatology, heresiology, herpetology, heterology, hierology, hippology, histiology, histology, histopathology, historiology, homology, hoplology, horology, hydrobiology, hydrogeology, hydrology, hydrometeorology, hyetology, hygrology, hymnology, hypnology, ichnology, ichthyology, iconology, ideology, immunology, insectology, irenology, kidology, kinesiology, koniology, Kremlinology, laryngology, lepidopterology, lexicology, lichenology, limnology, lithology, liturgiology, macrology, malacology, malariology, mammalogy, Mariology, martyrology, Maryology, Mayology, menology, metapsychology, meteorology, methodology, microbiology, microclimatology, micrology, micro- meteorology, microtechnology, mineralogy, misology, monadology, monology, morphology, muscology, museology, musicology, mycetology, mycology, myology, myrmecology, mythology, necrology, nematology, neology, nephology, nephrology, neurobiology, neurohypnology, neurology, neuropathology, neurophysiology, neuroradiology, neurypnology, nomology, noology, nosology, nostology, numerology, numisatology, oceanology, odontology, olfactology, oncology, onirology, ontology, oology, ophiology, ophthalmology, optology, orchidology, oreology, ornithology, orology, orthopterology, oryctology, osteology, otolaryngology, otology, otorhinolaryngology, ourology, paleanthropology, paleethnology, paleichthyology, paleoclimatology, paleolimnology, paleontology, paleopelology, paleophytology, paleozoology, palillogy, palynology, pantheology, papyrology, paradoxology, paralogy, parapsychology, parasitology, paroemiology, pathology, patrology, pedology, pelology, penology, periodontology, perissology, pestology, petrology, phenology, pharmacology, pharyngology, phenology, phenomenology, philology, phonology, photobiology, photogeology, phraseology, phrenology, phycology, physiology, phytology, phytopathology, planetology, plutology, pneumatology, prodology, pomology, ponerology, posology, potamology, primatology, protistology, protozoology, psephology, pseudology, psychobiology, psychology, psychopathology, psychophysiology, pteridology, pyretology, pyroballogy, radiobiology, radiology, reflexology, rheology, rheumatology, rhinology, röntgenology, sacrology, satanology, scatology, Scientology, sedimentology, seismology, selenology, selenomorphology, semasiology, semeiology, semiology, serology, sexology, sindonology, Sinology, sitiology, sitology, skatology, sociobiology, sociology, somatology, soteriology, spectrology, speleology, sphagnology, sphygmology, spongology, stichology, stoechiology, stoichiology, stomatology, storiology, symbology, symbolology, symptomatology, synchronology, synecology, syphilology, systematology, tautology, technology, teleology, teratology, terminology, terotechnology, tetralogy, thanatology, theology, thermology, therology, thremmatology, timbrology, tocology, tokology, topology, toxicology, traumatology, tribology, trichology, trilogy, trophology, tropology, typhlology, typology, ufology, uranology, urbanology, urinology, urology, venereology, vexillology, victimology, vinology, virology, volcanology, vulcanology, xylology, zoopathology, zoophytology, zoopsychology, zymology.

-lysis analysis, atmolysis, autocatalysis, autolysis, bacteriolysis, catalysis, cryptanalysis, cytolysis, dialysis, electroanalysis, electrolysis, hematolysis, hemodialysis, hemolysis, histolysis, hydrolysis, hypno-analysis, leucocytolysis, microanalysis, nacro-analysis, neurolysis, paralysis, photolysis, plasmolysis, pneumatolysis, proteolysis, psephoanalysis, psychoanalysis, pyrolysis, radiolysis, thermolysis, uranalysis, urinalysis, zincolysis, zymolysis.

-lytic analytic, anxiolytic, autocatalytic, autolytic, bacteriolytic, catalytic, dialytic, electrolytic, hemolytic, histolytic, hydrolytic, paralytic, photolytic, plasmolytic, pneumatolytic, proteolytic, psychoanalytic, pyrolytic, sympatholytic, tachylytic, thermolytic, unanalytic.

-mania acronymania, anglomania, anthomania, balletomania, bibliomania, Celtomania, demonomania, dipsomania, egomania, enomania, erotomania, etheromania, francomania, gallomania, hydromania, hypomania, hysteromania, Keltomania, kleptomania, mania, megalomania, melomania, methomania, metromania, monomania, morphinomania, mythomania, nostomania, nymphomania, opsomania, orchidomania, petalomania, phyllomania, potichomania, pteridomania, pyromania, squandermania, theatromania, theomania, timbromania, toxicomania, tulipomania, typomania, xenomania.

-mancy aeromancy, axinomancy, belomancy, bibliomancy, botanomancy, capnomancy, cartomancy, ceromancy, chiromancy, cleromancy, coscinomancy, crithomancy, crystallomancy, dactyliomancy, enomancy, gastromancy, geomancy, gyromancy, hieromancy, hydromancy, lampadomancy, lithomancy, myomancy, necromancy, nigromancy, omphalomancy, oniromancy, onychomancy, ornithomancy, pyromancy, rhabdomancy, scapulimancy, spodomancy, tephromancy, theomancy, zoomancy.

-mantic chiromantic, geomantic, hydromantic, myomantic, necromantic, ornithomantic, pyromantic, scapulimantic, spodomantic, theomantic, zoomantic.

-mathic chrestomathic, philomathic, polymathic.

-mathy chrestomathy, opsimathy, philomathy, polymathy.

-meter absorptiometer, accelerometer, acidimeter, actinometer, aerometer, alcoholometer, alkalimeter, altimeter, ammeter, anemometer, areometer, arithmometer, atmometer, audiometer, auxanometer, auxometer, barometer, bathometer, bathymeter, bolometer, bomb-calorimeter, calorimeter, cathetometer, centimeter, chlorimeter, chlorometer, chronometer, clinometer, colorimeter, Comptometer®;, coulombmeter, coulometer, craniometer, cryometer, cyanometer, cyclometer, decelerometer, declinometer, dendrometer, densimeter, densitometer, diagometer, diameter, diaphanometer, diffractometer, dimeter, dose-meter, dosimeter, drosometer, dynamometer, effusiometer, electrodynamometer, electrometer, endosmometer, enometer, ergometer, eriometer, evaporimeter, extensimeter, extensometer, fathometer, flowmeter, fluorimeter, fluorometer, focimeter, galactometer, galvanometer, gas-meter, gasometer, geometer, geothermometer, goniometer, gradiometer, gravimeter, harmonometer, heliometer, heptameter, hexameter, hodometer, hydrometer, hyetometer, hygrometer, hypsometer, iconometer, inclinometer, interferometer, isoperimeter, katathermometer, konimeter, kryometer, lactometer, luxmeter, lysimeter, machmeter, magnetometer, manometer, mekometer, meter, micrometer, microseismometer, mileometer, milometer, monometer, nephelometer, Nilometer, nitrometer, octameter, odometer, ohmmeter, ombrometer, oncometer, ophthalmometer, opisometer, opsiometer, optometer, osmometer, oximeter, pachymeter, parameter, passimeter, pedometer, pelvimeter, pentameter, perimeter, permeameter, phonmeter, phonometer, photometer, piezometer, planimeter, planometer, plessimeter, pleximeter, pluviometer, pneumatometer, polarimeter, potentiometer, potometer, psychometer, psychrometer, pulsimeter, pulsometer, pycnometer, pyknometer, pyrheliometer, pyrometer, quantometer, radiogoniometer, radiometer, radiotelemeter, refractometer, rheometer, rhythmometer, saccharimeter, saccharometer, salimeter, salinometer, scintillometer, sclerometer, seismometer, semi- diameter, semiperimeter, sensitometer, slot-meter, solarimeter, spectrophotometer, speedometer, spherometer, sphygmomanometer, sphygmometer, stactometer, stalagometer, stereometer, strabismometer, strabometer, swingometer, sympiesometer, tacheometer, tachometer, tachymeter, taseometer, tasimeter, taximeter, telemeter, tellurometer, tetrameter, thermometer, Tintometer®;, tonometer, torque-meter, tribometer, trigonometer, trimeter, trocheameter, trochometer, tromometer, udometer, urinometer, vaporimeter, variometer, viameter, vibrometer, viscometer, viscosimeter, voltameter, voltmeter, volumenometer, volumeter, volumometer, water-barometer, water- meter, water-thermometer, wattmeter, wavemeter, weathermeter, xylometer, zymometer, zymosimeter.

-metry acidimetry, aerometry, alcoholometry, alkalimetry, anemometry, anthropometry, areometry, asymmetry, barometry, bathymetry, biometry, bolometry, calorimetry, chlorimetry, chlorometry, chronometry, clinometry, colorimetry, coulometry, craniometry, densimetry, densitometry, dissymmetry, dosimetry, dynamometry, electrometry, galvanometry, gasometry, geometry, goniometry, gravimetry, hodometry, horometry, hydrometry, hygometry, hypsometry, iconometry, interferometry, isometry, isoperimetry, micrometry, microseismometry, nephelometry, noometry, odometry, ophthalometry, optometry, pelvimetry, perimetry, photometry, planimetry, plessimetry, pleximetry, polarimetry, pseudosymmetry, psychometry, psychrometry, pyrometry, saccharimetry, seismometry, sociometry, spectrometry, spectrophotometry, spirometry, stalagmometry, stereometry, stichometry, stoechiometry, stoichiometry, symmetry, tacheometry, tachometry, tachymetry, telemetry, tensiometry, thermometry, trigonometry, unsymmetry, uranometry, viscometry, viscosimetry, zoometry.

-monger balladmonger, barber-monger, borough-monger, carpetmonger, cheese-monger, costardmonger, costermonger, fellmonger, fishmonger, flesh-monger, gossip-monger, ironmonger, lawmonger, love-monger, maxim-monger, meal-monger, miracle- monger, mystery-monger, newsmonger, panic-monger, peace-monger, pearmonger, peltmonger, phrasemonger, place-monger, prayer- monger, relic-monger, scandalmonger, scaremonger, sensation- monger, species-monger, starmonger, state-monger, system-monger, verse-monger, warmonger, whoremonger, wit-monger, wonder-monger.

-morphic actinomorphic, allelomorphic, allotriomorphic, anamorphic, anthropomorphic, automorphic, biomorphic, dimorphic, ectomorphic, enantiomorphic, endomorphic, ergatomorphic, gynandromorphic, hemimorphic, heteromorphic, homeomorphic, homomorphic, hylomorphic, idiomorphic, isodimorphic, isomorphic, lagomorphic, mesomorphic, metamorphic, monomorphic, morphic, ophiomorphic, ornithomorphic, paramorphic, pedomorphic, perimorphic, pleomorphic, polymorphic, protomorphic, pseudomorphic, tetramorphic, theomorphic, theriomorphic, trimorphic, xenomorphic, xeromorphic, zoomorphic, zygomorphic.

-morphous amorphous, anamorphous, anthropomorphous, dimorphous, enantiomorphous, gynandromorphous, heteromorphous, homeomorphous, homomorphous, isodimorphous, isomorphous, lagomorphous, mesomorphous, monomorphous, ophiomorphous, perimorphous, pleomorphous, polymorphous, pseudomorphous, rhizomorphous, tauromorphous, theriomorphous, trimorphous, xeromorphous, zygomorphous.

-onym acronym, anonym, antonym, autonym, cryptonym, eponym, exonym, heteronym, homonym, metonym, paronym, polyonym, pseudonym, synonym, tautonym, toponym, trionym.

-onymic acronymic, Hieronymic, homonymic, matronymic, metonymic, metronymic, patronymic, polyonymic, synonymic, toponymic.

-osis abiosis, acidosis, actinobacillosis, actinomycosis, aerobiosis, aeroneurosis, alkalosis, amaurosis, amitosis, anabiosis, anadiplosis, anamorphosis, anaplerosis, anastomosis, anchylosis, anerobiosis, ankylosis, anthracosis, anthropomorphosis, antibiosis, apodosis, aponeurosis, apotheosis, arteriosclerosis, arthrosis, asbestosis, aspergillosis, ateleiosis, atherosclerosis, athetosis, autohypnosis, avitaminosis, bacteriosis, bagassosis, bilharziosis, biocoenosis, bromhidrosis, bromidrosis, brucellosis, byssinosis, carcinomatosis, carcinosis, chlorosis, cirrhosis, coccidiosis, cyanosis, cyclosis, dermatosis, diarthrosis, diorthosis, diverticulosis, dulosis, ecchymosis, enantiosis, enarthrosis, endometriosis, endosmosis, enosis, enteroptosis, epanadiplosis, epanorthosis, exosmosis, exostosis, fibrosis, fluorosis, furunculosis, gliomatosis, gnotobiosis, gomphosis, gummosis, halitosis, hallucinosis, heliosis, hematosis, heterosis, hidrosis, homeosis, homomorphosis, homozygosis, hydronephrosis, hyperhidrosis, hyperidrosis, hyperinosis, hypersacosis, hypervitaminosis, hypinosis, hypnosis, hypotyposis, ichthyosis, kenosis, keratosis, ketosis, kurtosis, kyllosis, kyphosis, leishmaniosis, leptospirosis, leucocytosis, limosis, lipomatosis, lordosis, madarosis, marmarosis, meiosis, melanosis, metachrosis, metamorphosis, metempsychosis, miosis, mitosis, molybdosis, mononucleosis, monosis, morphosis, mucoviscidosis, mycosis, mycotoxicosis, myosis, myxomatosis, narcohypnosis, narcosis, necrobiosis, necrosis, nephroptosis, nephrosis, neurosis, onychocryptosis, ornithosis, osmidrosis, osmosis, osteoarthrosis, osteoporosis, otosclerosis, parabiosis, paraphimosis, parapsychosis, parasitosis, pedamorphosis, pediculosis, phagocytosis, phimosis, pholidosis, phytosis, pneumoconiosis, pneumokoniosis, pneumonokoniosis, pneumonoultramicroscopicsilicovolcanoconiosis, pollenosis, polyposis, porosis, proptosis, psilosis, psittacosis, psychoneurosis, psychosis, pterylosis, ptilosis, ptosis, pyrosis, resinosis, salmonellosis, sarcoidosis, sarcomatosis, sclerosis, scoliosis, self-hypnosis, siderosis, silicosis, sorosis, spirillosis, spirochetosis, steatosis, stegnosis, stenosis, strongylosis, sycosis, symbiosis, symptosis, synarthrosis, synchrondrosis, syndesmosis, synociosis, synostosis, syntenosis, syssarcosis, thanatosis, theriomorphosis, thrombosis, thylosis, thyrotoxicosis, torulosis, toxoplasmosis, trichinosis, trichophytosis, trichosis, trophobiosis, trophoneurosis, tuberculosis, tylosis, ulosis, urosis, virosis, visceroptosis, xerosis, zoonosis, zygosis, zymosis.

-path allopath, homeopath, kinesipath, naturopath, neuropath, osteopath, psychopath, sociopath, telepath.

-pathic allopathic, anthropopathic, antipathic, empathic, homoeopathic, hydropathic, idiopathic, kinesipathic, naturopathic, neuropathic, osteopathic, protopathic, psychopathic, sociopathic, telepathic.

-pathy allopathy, anthropopathy, antipathy, apathy, cardiomyopathy, dyspathy, empathy, enantiopathy, homeopathy, hydropathy, idiopathy, kinesipathy, myocardiopathy, naturopathy, neuropathy, nostopathy, osteopathy, psychopathy, sociopathy, sympathy, telepathy, theopathy, zoopathy.

-phage bacteriophage, macrophage, ostreophage, xylophage.

-phagous anthropophagous, autophagous, carpophagous, coprophagous, creophagous, endophagous, entomophagous, exophagous, geophagous, hippophagous, hylophagous, ichthyophagous, lithophagous, mallophagous, meliphagous, monophagous, myrmecophagous, necrophagous, omophagous ophiophagous, ostreophagous, pantophagous, phyllophagous, phytophagous, polyphagous, rhizophagous, saprophagous, sarcophagous, scatophagous, theophagous, toxicophagous, toxiphagous, xylophagous, zoophagous.

-phagy anthropophagy, autophagy, coprophagy, dysphagy, endophagy, entomophagy, exophagy, hippophagy, ichthyophagy, monophagy, mycophagy, omophagy, ostreophagy, pantophagy, polyphagy, sacrophagy, scatophagy, theophagy, xerophagy.

-phile ailurophile, arctophile, audiophile, bibliophile, cartophile, discophile, enophile, francophile, gallophile, Germanophile, gerontophile, halophile, hippophile, homophile, iodophile, lyophile, myrmecophile, necrophile, negrophile, ombrophile, pedophile, psammophile, Russophile, scripophile, Sinophile, Slavophile, spermophile, thermophile, Turcophile, xenophile, zoophile.

-philia ailurophilia, anglophilia, canophilia, coprophilia, ephebophilia, Germanophilia, gerontophilia, hemophilia, necrophilia, paraphilia, pedophilia, scopophilia, scoptophilia, zoophilia.

-philist bibliophilist, canophilist, cartophilist, Dantophilist, enophilist, iconophilist, negrophilist, notaphilist, ophiophilist, pteridophilist, Russophilist, scripophilist, stegophilist, timbrophilist, zoophilist.

-phily acarophily, anemophily, bibliophily, cartophily, enophily, entomophily, halophily, hydrophily, myrmecophily, necrophily, notaphily, ornithophily, photophily, scripophily, Sinophily, symphily, timbrophily, toxophily, xerophily.

-phobe ailurophobe, anglophobe, francophobe, gallophobe, Germanophobe, hippophobe, hygrophobe, lyophobe, negrophobe, ombrophobe, photophobe, Russophobe, Slavophobe, Turcophobe, xenophobe.

-phobia acrophobia, aerophobia, agoraphobia, ailurophobia, algophobia, anglophobia, astraphobia, astrapophobia, bathophobia, bibliophobia, canophobia, claustrophobia, cynophobia, dromophobia, ecophobia, ergophobia, gallophobia, hydrophobia, hypsophobia, monophobia, mysophobia, necrophobia, negrophobia, neophobia, nosophobia, nyctophobia, ochlophobia, panophobia, pantophobia, pathophobia, phonophobia, photophobia, Russophobia, satanophobia, scopophobia, sitiophobia, sitophobia, symmetrophobia, syphilophobia, taphephobia, taphophobia, thanatophobia, theophobia, toxicophobia, toxiphobia, triskaidecaphobia, triskaidekaphobia, xenophobia, zoophobia.

-phobic aerophobic, agoraphobic, anglophobic, claustrophobic, heliophobic, hydrophobic, lyophobic, monophobic, phobic, photophobic.

-phone aerophone, allophone, anglophone, Ansaphone®;, audiphone, chordophone, detectophone, diaphone, dictaphone, diphone, earphone, Entryphone®;, francophone, geophone, gramophone, harmoniphone, headphone, heckelphone, homophone, hydrophone, idiophone, interphone, kaleidophone, megaphone, metallophone, microphone, monotelephone, optophone, phone, photophone, Picturephone®;, polyphone, pyrophone, radiogramophone, radiophone, radiotelephone, sarrusophone, saxophone, sousaphone, speakerphone, sphygmophone, stentorphone, telephone, theatrophone, triphone, vibraphone, videophone, videotelephone, viewphone, zylophone.

-phonic acrophonic, allophonic, anglophonic, antiphonic, aphonic, cacophonic, cataphonic, chordophonic, dodecaphonic, dysphonic, euphonic, gramophonic, homophonic, microphonic, monophonic, paraphonic, photophonic, quadraphonic, quadrophonic, radiophonic, stentorophonic, stereophonic, symphonic, telephonic, xylophonic.

-phony acrophony, antiphony, aphony, autophony, cacophony, colophony, dodecaphony, euphony, gramophony, homophony, laryngophony, monophony, photophony, polyphony, quadraphony, quadrophony, radiophony, radiotelephony, stereophony, symphony, tautophony, telephony.

-phorous discophorous, Eriophorous, galactophorous, hypophosphorous, mastigophorous, necrophorous, odontophorous, phosphorous, pyrophorous, rhynchophorous, sporophorous.

-phyte aerophyte, bryophyte, cormophyte, dermatophyte, ectophyte, endophyte, entophyte, epiphyte, gametophyte, geophyte, halophyte, heliophyte, heliosciophyte, holophyte, hydrophyte, hygrophyte, hylophyte, lithophyte, mesophyte, microphyte, neophyte, oophyte, osteophyte, phanerophyte, phreatophyte, protophyte, psammophyte, pteridophyte, saprophyte, schizophyte, spermaphyte, spermatophyte, spermophyte, sporophyte, thallophyte, tropophyte, xerophyte, zoophyte, zygophyte.

-saurus Allosaurus, Ankylosaurus, Apatosaurus, Atlantosaurus, brachiosaurus, brontosaurus, Ceteosaurus, Dolichosaurus, Ichthyosaurus, megalosaurus, Plesiosaurus, Stegosaurus, Teleosaurus, Titanosaurus, tyrannosaurus.

-scope aethrioscope, auriscope, baroscope, bathyscope, benthoscope, bioscope, bronchoscope, chromoscope, chronoscope, colposcope, cryoscope, cystoscope, dichrooscope, dichroscope, dipleidoscope, ebullioscope, electroscope, endoscope, engiscope, engyscope, epidiascope, episcope, fluoroscope, galvanoscope, gastroscope, gyroscope, hagioscope, helioscope, hodoscope, horoscope, hydroscope, hygroscope, iconoscope, iriscope, kaleidoscope, kinetoscope, koniscope, lactoscope, laparoscope, laryngoscope, lychnoscope, megascope, microscope, mutoscope, myringoscope, myrioscope, nephoscope, opeidoscope, ophthalmoscope, oscilloscope, otoscope, pantoscope, periscope, pharyngoscope, phenakistoscope, phonendoscope, polariscope, poroscope, praxinoscope, proctoscope, pseudoscope, pyroscope, radarscope, radioscope, rhinoscope, scintilloscope, scope, seismoscope, sigmoidoscope, somascope, spectrohelioscope, spectroscope, sphygmoscope, spinthariscope, statoscope, stereofluoroscope, stereoscope, stethoscope, stroboscope, tachistoscope, teinoscope, telescope, thermoscope, triniscope, ultramicroscope, vectorscope, Vertoscope®;, vitascope.

-scopic autoscopic, bronchoscopic, cryoscopic, deuteroscopic, dichroscopic, ebullioscopic, electroscopic, endoscopic, gyroscopic, hagioscopic, helioscopic, horoscopic, hygroscopic, kaleidoscopic, laryngoscopic, macroscopic, megascopic, metoscopic, microscopic, necroscopic, ophthalmoscopic, orthoscopic, pantoscopic, periscopic, poroscopic, rhinoscopic, seismoscopic, spectroscopic, stethoscopic, stroboscopic, submicroscopic, tachistoscopic, telescopic, thermoscopic, ultramicroscopic, zooscopic.

-scopy autoscopy, bronchoscopy, colposcopy, cranioscopy, cryoscopy, cystoscopy, dactyloscopy, deuteroscopy, ebullioscopy, endoscopy, episcopy, fluoroscopy, hepatoscopy, hieroscopy, horoscopy, laparoscopy, laryngoscopy, metoposcopy, microscopy, necroscopy, omoplatoscopy, oniroscopy, ophthalmoscopy, ornithoscopy, ouroscopy, pharyngoscopy, poroscopy, proctoscopy, radioscopy, retinoscopy, rhinoscopy, röntgenoscopy, skiascopy, spectroscopy, stereoscopy, stethoscopy, telescopy, tracheoscopy, ultramicroscopy, urinoscopy, uroscopy, zooscopy.

-ship abbotship, accountantship, acquaintanceship, administratorship, admiralship, advisership, aedileship, airmanship, aldermanship, amateurship, ambassadorship, apostleship, apprenticeship, archonship, assessorship, associateship, attorneyship, auditorship, augurship, authorship, bachelorship, bailieship, baillieship, bardship, barristership, bashawship, batmanship, beadleship, bedellship, bedelship, benchership, bondmanship, brinkmanship, bursarship, bushmanship, butlership, cadetship, Caesarship, candidateship, captainship, cardinalship, catechumenship, censorship, chairmanship, chamberlainship, championship, chancellorship, chaplainship, chelaship, chiefship, chieftainship, citizenship, clanship, clerkship, clientship, clownship, coadjutorship, colleagueship, collectorship, colonelship, commandantship, commandership, commissaryship, commissionership, committeeship, companionship, compotationship, comradeship, conductorship, confessorship, connoisseurship, conservatorship, constableship, consulship, controllership, copartnership, co-rivalship, corporalship, counsellorship, countship, courtship, cousinship, cowardship, craftmanship, craftsmanship, creatorship, creatureship, curateship, curatorship, custodianship, deaconship, dealership, deanship, demyship, denizenship, devilship, dictatorship, directorship, discipleship, disfellowship, doctorship, dogeship, dogship, dollarship, donship, draftsmanship, dukeship, editorship, eldership, electorship, emperorship, endship, ensignship, entrepreneurship, envoyship, executorship, factorship, fathership, fellowship, foxship, freshmanship, friendship, gamesmanship, generalship, gentlemanship, giantship, gladiatorship, goddess-ship, godship, good-fellowship, governor- generalship, governorship, grandeeship, guardianship, guideship, hardship, headship, hectorship, heirship, heraldship, heroship, hership, hetmanship, horsemanship, hostess-ship, housewifeship, huntsmanship, inspectorship, interpretership, interrelationship, janitorship, jockeyship, judgeship, justiceship, kaisership, keepership, kindredship, kingship, kinship, knaveship, ladyship, lairdship, land-ownership, laureateship, leadership, lectorship, lectureship, legateship, legislatorship, librarianship, lieutenant-commandership, lieutenant-generalship, lieutenant- governorship, lieutenantship, lifemanship, logship, lordship, ludship, mageship, major-generalship, majorship, managership, marshalship, mastership, matronship, mayorship, mediatorship, membership, Messiahship, milk-kinship, minorship, mistress-ship, moderatorship, monitorship, multi-ownership, musicianship, noviceship, nunship, oarsmanship, one-upmanship, overlordship, ownership, partisanship, partnership, pastorship, patroonship, peatship, pendragonship, penmanship, physicianship, poetship, popeship, possessorship, postmastership, praetorship, preachership, precentorship, perfectship, prelateship, premiership, prenticeship, presbytership, presidentship, pretendership, priestship, primateship, primogenitureship, principalship, priorship, probationership, proconsulship, proctorship, procuratorship, professorship, progenitorship, prolocutorship, prophetship, proprietorship, prosectorship, protectorship, provostship, pursership, quaestorship, queenship, rajahship, rajaship, rangership, readership, recordership, rectorship, regentship, registrarship, relationship, residentiaryship, residentship, retainership, rivalship, rogueship, rulership, sachemship, saintship, salesmanship, scholarship, school-friendship, schoolmastership, scrivenership, seamanship, secretaryship, seigniorship, sempstress-ship, senatorship, seneschalship, serfship, sergeantship, serjeantship, servantship, servitorship, sextonship, sheriffship, showmanship, sibship, sizarship, soldiership, solicitorship, sonship, speakership, spectatorship, spinstership, sponsorship, sportsmanship, squireship, statesmanship, stewardship, studentship, subahship, subdeaconship, subeditorship, subinspectorship, subjectship, successorship, suffraganship, sultanship, superintendentship, superiorship, supervisorship, suretyship, surgeonship, surrogateship, surveyorship, survivorship, swordsmanship, teachership, tellership, tenantship, thaneship, thwartship, tide-waitership, township, traineeship, traitorship, treasurership, treeship, tribuneship, truantship, trusteeship, tutorship, twinship, umpireship, uncleship, under- clerkship, undergraduateship, under-secretaryship, unfriendship, ushership, vaivodeship, vergership, vicarship, vice-chairmanship, vice-chancellorship, vice-consulship, viceroyship, virtuosoship, viscountship, viziership, vizirship, voivodeship, waivodeship, wardenship, wardship, watermanship, Whigship, workmanship, worship, wranglership, writership, yachtsmanship.

-sophy anthroposophy, gastrosophy, gymnosophy, pansophy, philosophy, sciosophy, theosophy.

-stat aerostat, antistat, appestat, bacteriostat, barostat, celostat, chemostat, coccidiostat, cryostat, gyrostat, heliostat, hemostat, humidistat, hydrostat, hygrostat, klinostat, pyrostat, rheostat, siderostat, thermostat.

-therapy actinotherapy, balneotherapy, chemotherapy, cryotherapy, curietherapy, electrotherapy, heliotherapy, hydrotherapy, hypnotherapy, immunotherapy, kinesitherapy, musicotherapy, narcotherapy, opotherapy, organotherapy, pelotherapy, phototherapy, physiotherapy, psychotherapy, pyretotherapy, radiotherapy, röntgenotherapy, serotherapy, serum- therapy, zootherapy.

-tomy adenectomy, adenoidectomy, anatomy, anthropotomy, appendectomy, appendicectomy, arteriotomy, autotomy, cephalotomy, cholecystectomy, cholecystotomy, colotomy, cordotomy, craniectomy, craniotomy, cystotomy, dichotomy, duodenectomy, embryotomy, encephalotomy, enterectomy, enterotomy, gastrectomy, gastrotomy, gingivectomy, glossectomy, hepatectomy, herniotomy, hysterectomy, hysterotomy, iridectomy, iridotomy, laparotomy, laryngectomy, laryngotomy, leucotomy, lipectomy, lithotomy, lobectomy, lobotomy, lumpectomy, mastectomy, microtomy, myringotomy, necrotomy, nephrectomy, nephrotomy, neurectomy, neuroanatomy, neurotomy, oophorectomy, orchidectomy, orchiectomy, osteotomy, ovariotomy, pharyngotomy, phlebotomy, phytotomy, pleurotomy, pneumonectomy, pogonotomy, prostatectomy, rhytidectomy, salpingectomy, sclerotomy, splenectomy, stapedectomy, stereotomy, strabotomy, sympathectomy, symphyseotomy, symphsiotomy, syringotomy, tenotomy, tetrachotomy, thymectomy, tonsillectomy, tonsillotomy, topectomy, tracheotomy, trichotomy, tubectomy, ultramicrotomy, uterectomy, uterotomy, varicotomy, vasectomy, zootomy.

-urgy chemurgy, dramaturgy, electrometallurgy, hierurgy, hydrometallurgy, liturgy, metallurgy, micrurgy, theurgy, zymurgy.

-vorous apivorous, baccivorous, carnivorous, fructivorous, frugivorous, graminivorous, granivorous, herbivorous, insectivorous, lignivorous, mellivorous, myristicivorous, nucivorous, omnivorous, ossivorous, piscivorous, radicivorous, ranivorous, sanguinivorous, sanguivorous, vermivorous.

Appendix IV

Classified Word-lists

air and space vehicles aerobus, airdrome, aerodyne, aerohydroplane, airplane, aerostat, air-ambulance, air-bus, airship, all-wing airplane, amphibian, autogiro, balloon, biplane, blimp, bomber, cable-car, camel, canard, chopper, comsat, convertiplane, crate, delta-wing, dirigible, dive bomber, fan-jet, fighter, fire-balloon, flying boat, flying saucer, flying wing, glider, gondola, gyrocopter, gyroplane, helibus, helicopter, hoverbus, hovercar, hovercraft, hovertrain, hydro- airplane, hydrofoil, hydroplane, intercepter, jet, jetliner, jetplane, lem, mictolight, module, monoplane, multiplane, plane, rocket, rocket-plane, runabout, sailplane, satellite, seaplane, space platform, space probe, space shuttle, spacecraft, spaceship, spitfire, sputnik, steprocket, stol, strato-cruiser, stratotanker, swingtail cargo aircraft, swing-wing, tanker, taube, téléférique, tow-plane, tractor, triplane, troop-carrier, tube, tug, turbojet, twoseater, UFO, warplane, zeppelin.

alphabets and writing systems Chalcidian alphabet, cuneiform, Cyrillic, devanagari, estrang(h)elo, finger-alphabet, futhark, Glagol, Glossic, Greek, Gurmukhi, hieroglyphs, hiragana, ideograph, kana, katakana, Kuffic, linear A, linear B, logograph, nagari, naskhi, og(h)am, pictograph, Roman, runic, syllabary.

anatomical abductor, acromion, adductor, alvine, ancon, astragalus, atlas, aural, auricular, axilla, biceps, blade-bone, bone, brachial, bregma, buccal, calcaneum, calcaneus, capitate, cardiac, carpal, carpus, cartilage, cephalic, cerebral, cholecyst, clavicle, coccyx, celiac, collar-bone, concha, coracoid, crural, cuboid, cuneiform, deltoid, dental, derm, derma, dermal, dermic, diaphragm, diencephalon, digital, diploe, diverticulum, dorsal, dorsolumbar, dorsum, duodenal, duodenum, dura mater, earlap, elbow, enarthrosis, encephalic, encephalon, endocardiac, endocardial, endocardium, endocrinal, endocrine, epencephalic, epencephalon, epidermal, epidermic, epidermis, epididymis epigastric, epigastrium, epiglottic, epiglottis, epithelium, eponychium, erythrocyte, esophagus, ethmoid, extensor, Fallopian tubes, false rib, femur, fenestra ovalis, fenestra rotunda, fibula, flexor, floating rib, fontanel(le), fonticulus, foramen magnum, forearm, forebrain, forefinger, foreskin, fourchette, frenum, frontal, funiculus, funny bone, gastric, gastrocnemius, gena, genal, genial, genitalia, genu, gingival, glabella, glabellar, gladiolus, glossa, glossal, glottal, glottic, glottis, gluteus, gnathal, gnathic, gonion, gracilis, gremial, gristle, groin, gula, gular, gullet, guttural, hallux, ham, hamate, hamstring, helix, hemal, hematic, hepatic, hind-brain, hindhead, hip-bone, hip-girdle, hock, huckle-bone, humeral, humerus, hyoid, hypogastrium, hypothalamus, iliac, ilium, incus, inguinal, innominate, innominate bone, intercostal, ischium, jugular, labial, lachrymal, lacrimal, leucocyte, ligament, lumbar, lumbrical, lunate, luz, malar, malleolus, malleus, mamillar(y), mammary, mandible, mandibular, manubrium, marriage-bone, mastoid, maxilla, maxillary, membral, mental, merrythought, metacarpal, metatarsal, mons veneris, mount of Venus, muscle, nasal, nates, navicular, neural, obturators, occipital, occiput, occlusal, occlusion, occlusor, ocular, odontic, omentum, omohyoid, omoplate, optical, orbicularis, orbit(a), origin, os innominatum, oscheal, oscular, ossicle, otic, otolith, palatal, palatine, palpebral, parasphenoid, parietal, paroccipital, parotid, patela, patellar, pecten, pectoral, pedal, pelvic girdle, pelvis, periotic, perone, phalanges, pisiform, plantar, popliteal, poplitic, prefrontal, premaxilla, premaxillary, pronator, prootic, prosencephalon, psoas, pubis, pudenda, pulmonary, quadriceps, radius, renal, rhomboid, rib, rictal, sacrocostal, sacrum, sartorius, scaphoid, scapula, sesamoid, shoulder-blade, shoulder-bone, skull, soleus, spade-bone, sphenoid, spine, splinter-bone, stapes, sternum, stirrup-bone, supinator, sural, talus, tarsal, temporal, tendon, thigh-bone, tibia, trapezium, trapezius, trapezoid, triceps, triquetral, turbinal, tympanic, ulna, umbilicus, unguis, urachus, uterus, uvula, vagus, vas deferens, velum, vermis, vertebra, vertebrae, vertex, vesica, voice-box, vomer, vulva, windpipe, wisdom tooth, womb, wrist, xiphisternum, xiphoid, zygapophysis, zygoma, zygomatic.

architecture and building abacus, abutment, acrolith, acroter, acroterial, acroterion, acroterium, alcove, annulet, anta, antefix, areostyle, architrave, ashlar, ashler, astragal, baguette, bandelet, banderol(e), barge-board, barge-couple, barge-stones, battlement, bellcote, bema, bratticing, canephor, canton, cartouche, caryatid, Catherine-wheel, cavetto, centering, cinque-foil, concha, corbeil, corbel, corner-stone, corona, cradling, crenel, crocket, crossette, cruck, cul-de-four, dado, decorated, demi-bastion, demi-lune, dentil, diaconicon, diaper, diastyle, diglyph, dimension work, dinette, dipteros, distyle, ditriglyph, dodecastyle, dog-leg(ged), dogtooth, dome, domed, domical, donjon, Doric, dormer, double-glazing, doucine, drawbridge, drawing-room, dreamhole, dressing, drip, dripstone, dromic, dromos, drum, dry-stone, duplex, Early English, eaves, echinus, egg-and-anchor, egg-and-dart, egg-and-tongue, egg-box, el, elevation, Elizabethan, embattlement, embrasure, emplection, encarpus, engage, engaged, engrail, enneastyle, entresol, epaule, epaulement, epistyle, eustyle, exedra, extrados, eye-catcher, façade, fan tracery, fan vaulting, fanlight, fascia, fastigium, feathering, fenestella, fenestra, fenestral, fenestration, festoon, fillet, finial, flamboyant, flèche, Flemish bond, fletton, fleuron, foliation, fornicate, fortalice, French sash/window, frieze, fronton, furring, fusarol(e), fust, gable, gablet, galilee, gambrel roof, gargoyle, gatehouse, glacis, glyph, gopura(m), gorgerin, Gothic, gradin(e), griff(e), groin, groundplan, groundsel, guilloche, gutta, hagioscope, half- timbered, hammer-beam, hammer-brace, hance, hanging buttress, harling, haunch, haute époque, headstone, heart, helix, herringbone, hexastyle, hip, hip-knob, holderbat, hood-mold(ing), hypostyle, imbrex, imbricate, imbrication, imperial, impost, impostume, intercolumniation, intrados, jamb, javelin, jerkinhead, knosp, lierne, linen-fold, linen-scroll, lintel, mansard(-roof), mascaron, merlon, metope, modillion, monostyle, mullion, muntin(g), mutule, Norman, oeil-de-boeuf, ogee, opisthodomos, oriel, out-wall, ovolo, ox-eye, pagoda, pantile, pargret, patera, paternoster, patten, pediment, pilaster, pineapple, pinnacle, plafond, platband, plateresque, plinth, poppy-head, predella, propylaeum, propylon, prostyle, pylon, quatrefeuille, quatrefoil, queen-post, quirk, rear-arch, reglet, regula, rere-arch, retrochoir, reredos, revet, rocaille, rococo, Romanesque, rood-loft, rood-screen, rood-steeple, rood tower, roof, roof-tree, rosace, rose, rosette, rotunda, roughcast, sacristy, skew-back, socle, soffit, solidum, spandrel, strap- work, stria, string-course, subbasal, surbase, swag, systyle, tabernacle-work, table, telamon, terrazzo, tierceron, tondino, toroid, torsel, torus, trabeation, tracery, triforium, trumeau, tympanum, vault, vaultage, vaulted, vaulting, Venetian mosaic, vermiculate(d), vice, vitrail, vitrailled, Vitruvian, volute, voussoir, wainscot, wall-plate, water-joint, water-table, weathering, xystus.

art abstract, abstraction, action painting, anaglyph, anastasis, anastatic, anthemion, aquarelle, bas relief, Bauhaus, camaieu, cire perdue, dadaism, decal, decoupage, Der Blaue Reiter, diaglyph, Die Brücke, diptych, dry-point, duotone, écorché, enamel, encaustic, engraving, etch, etchant, faience, fashion-plate, Fauve, Fauvism, fête champêtre, figurine, filigree, flambé, flannelgraph, Flemish, flesh-tint, Florentine, free-hand, fresco, fret, frit, futurism, futurist, gadroon, genre, gesso, glyptics, glyptography, Gobelin, gouache, graphic, graphics, graphium, graticulation, gravure, grecque, grisaille, gumption, hachure, hatch, hatching, haut relief, herm(a), historiated, hound's-tooth, intaglio, linocut, literalism, litho, lithochromatic(s), lithchromy, lithograph, lithoprint, lost wax, mandorla, meander, monotint, monotype, morbidezza, Parian, paysage, phylactery, pietra-dura, piqué, pochoir, pompier, putto, quattrocento, relievo, repoussage, repoussé, reserved, retroussage, rilievo, sculp(t), scumble, sea-piece, seascape, secco, serigraph, statuary, stipple, stylus, surrealism, symbolism, tachism(e), tempera, tenebrism, tessellated, tessera, tondo, trecento, triptych, ukiyo-e, velatura, Venetian mosaic, Venetian red, verditer, verism, vermiculate(d), versal, vitrail, vitraillist, vitrifacture, vitrine, vitro-di-trina, volute, vorticism, woodblock, wood- carving, woodcut, wood-engraving, xoanon, zoomorphic.

canonical hours compline, lauds, matins, none, orthros, prime, sext, terce, undern, vespers.

cattle breeds Africander, Alderney, Angus, Ankole, Ayrshire, Blonde d'Aquitaine, Brahman, Brown Swiss, cattabu, cattalo, Charol(l)ais, Chillingham, Devon, dexter, Durham, Friesian, Galloway, Guernsey, Hereford, Highland, Holstein, Jersey, Latvian, Limousin, Luing, Red Poll, Romagnola, Santa Gertrudis, short-horn, Simmenthaler, Teeswater, Ukrainian, Welsh Black.

cheeses Amsterdam, Bel Paese, Blarney, Bleu d'Auvergne, Blue Vinny, Boursin, Brie, Caboc, Caerphilly, Camembert, Carré, Cheddar, Cheshire, Chevrotin, Colwick, Coulommiers, Crowdie, Danish blue, Derby, Dolcelatte, Dorset Blue, double Gloucester, Dunlop, Edam, Emmental, Emment(h)al(er), Esrom, ewe-cheese, Feta, Fynbo, Gammelost, G(j)etost, Gloucester, Gorgonzola, Gouda, Grana, Grevé, Gruyère, Handkäse, Havarti, Herrgårdsost, Herve, Huntsman, Hushållsost, Islay, Jarlsberg, Killarney, Kryddost, Lancashire, Leicester, Limburg(er), Lymeswold, mouse-trap, mozzarella, Munster, Mysost, Neufchâtel, Parmesan, Petit Suisse, pipo creme, Pont-l'Évеque, Port(-du-)Salut, Prästost, Provolone, Pultost, Raclette, Red Windsor, Reggiano, ricotta, Romadur, Roquefort, sage Derby, Saint-Paulin, Sams_, sapsago, Stilton, stracchino, Tilsit(er), Vacherin, Wensleydale, Wexford.

chemical elements Actinium, Aluminum, Americium, Antimony, Argon, Arsenic, Astatine, Barium, Berkelium, Beryllium, Bismuth, Boron, Bromine, Cadmium, Calcium, Californium, Carbon, Cerium, Cesium, Chlorine, Chromium, Cobalt, Copper, Curium, Dysprosium, Einsteinium, Erbium, Europium, Fermium, Fluorine, Francium, Gadolinium, Gallium, Germanium, Gold, Hafnium, Hahnium, Helium, Holmium, Hydrogen, Indium, Iodine, Iridium, Iron, Krypton, Lanthanum, Lawrencium, Lead, Lithium, Lutetium, Magnesium, Manganese, Mendelevium, Mercury, Molybdenum, Neodymium, Neon, Neptunium, Nickel, Niobium, Nitrogen, Nobelium, Osmium, Oxygen, Palladium, Phosphorus, Platinum, Plutonium, Polonium, Potassium, Praseodymium, Promethium, Protoactinium, Radium, Radon, Rhenium, Rhodium, Rubidium, Ruthenium, Rutherfordium,

Samarium, Scandium, Selenium, Silicon, Silver, Sodium, Strontium, Sulfur, Tantalum, Technetium, Tellurium, Terbium, Thallium, Thorium, Thulium, Tin, Titanium, Tungsten, Uranium, Vanadium, Xenon, Ytterbium, Yttrium, Zinc, Zirconium.

cloths, fabrics abaca, abb, alamonde, alepine, alpaca, American cloth, angora, armozine, armure, arrasene, astrakhan, atlas, baft, bagging, Balbriggan, baldachin, balzarine, barathea, barege, barracan, batiste, batting, bayadère, bearskin, beaver, beige, bengaline, Binca®;, blanket, blanketing, blonde(e)- lace, bobbinet, bobbin-lace, bombasine, bone-lace, botany, bouclé, bolting cloth, box-cloth, broadcloth, brocade, brocatel(le), broché, Brussels lace, buckram, buckskin, budge, buff, bunting, Burberry, burlap, burnet, burrel, butter-cloth, butter-muslin, byssus, caddis, calamanco, calico, cambric, cameline, camlet, candlewick, canvas, carmelite, carpeting, casement-cloth, cashmere, cassimere, catgut, (cavalry) twill, challis, chamois, chantilly (lace), charmeuse, cheesecloth, damask, damassin, delaine, denim, devil's dust, dhoti, d(h)urrie, diamanté, diaper, dimity, doe-skin, doily, domett, dornick, dowlas, drab, drabbet, drap-de-Berry, dreadnought, drill, droguet, drugget, duchesse lace, duck, duffel, dungaree, dupion, durant, Dutch carpet, ecru, éolienne, façonné, faille, far(r)andine, fearnought, felt, ferret, filet, flannel, flannelette, foulard, foulé, frieze, frocking, fustian, gaberdine, galatea, galloon, gambroon, gauze, genappe, georgette, gingham, Gobelini(s), gold-cloth, gold-lace, grass cloth, grenadine, grogram, grosgrain, guipure, gunny, gurrah, habit- cloth, haircloth, harn, Hessian, hodden, holland, homespun, Honiton, hopsack, horsehair, huckaback, humhum, jaconet, Jaeger®;, jamdani, jean, jeanette, jersey, kalamkari, karakul, kente cloth, kersey, kerseymere, khader, khaki, kid, kidskin, kilt, kincob, kip-skin, lamé, lampas, lawn, leather, leather- cloth, leatherette, leghorn, leno, levant, linen, linsey, linsey- woolsey, llama, lockram, loden, longcloth, lovat, Lurex®;, luster, lustring, lutestring, mac(k)intosh, madras, mantling, marcella, marocain, maroquin, marquisette, mazarine, Mechlin, medley, melton, merino, Mexican, mignonette, mohair, moire, moleskin, monk's cloth, moreen, morocco, mourning-stuff, mousseline, mousseline-de-laine, mousseline-de-soie, Moygashel®;, mull, mulmul(l), mungo, musk-rat, muslin, muslinet, musquash, nacarat, nainsook, nankeen, ninon, nitro- silk, nun's-veiling, nylon, oilcloth, organdie, organza, organzine, orleans, osnaburg, orris, ottoman, overcoating, paduasoy, paisley, panne, paper-cloth, paper-muslin, par(r)amatta, peau-de-soie, penistone, percale, percaline, perse, petersham, piña-cloth, pin-stripe, piqué, plaid, plush, point- lace, polycotton, poplin, poplinette, prunella, purple, quilting, rabanna, ratine(ratteen), raven('s)-duck, rep (repp), roan, russel, russel-cord, russet, sackcloth, sacking, sagathy, sail- cloth, samite, sarsenet, satara, sateen, satin, satinette, satin-sheeting, saxony, say, scarlet, schappe, scrim, seersucker, sendal, serge, shagreen, shalloon, shammy(-leather), shantung, sharkskin, sheepskin, Shetland wool, shoddy, Sicilian, sicilienne, silesia, silk, slipper satin, soneri, split, sponge- cloth, spun silk, stammel, strouding, suede, suedette, suiting, surah, surat, swansdown, swan-skin, tabaret, tabbinet, tabby, taffeta, tamin(e), tamise, tammy, tarlatan, tarpaulin, tartan, tat, Tattersall (check), T-cloth, tentage, tent-cloth, terry, Terylene®;, thibet, thickset, thrown-silk, thunder-and- lightning, ticken, tick(ing), tiffany, toile, toilinet(te), torchon lace, toweling, tram, tricot, troll(e)y, tulle, tusser(- silk), tweed, union, Valenciennes, veiling, Velcro®;, velour(s), veloutine, velveret, velvet, velveteen, velveting, vicuña, voile, wadmal, waistcoating, watchet, waterwork, waxcloth, webbing, whipcord, wigan, wild silk, wincey, winceyette, wire gauze, woolsey, worcester, worsted, zanella, zephyr.

coins, currencies agora, antoninianus, as, asper, aureus, baht, balboa, bawbee, bekah, belga, bezant, bit, bod(d)le, bolivar, boliviano, bonnet-piece, broad(piece), buck, cardecu(e), Carolus, cash, cent, centavo, centime, chiao, colon, conto, cordoba, couter, crown, crusado, cruzeiro, dam, daric, deaner, décime, denarius, denier, Deutschmark, didrachm(a), dime, dinar, dirham, doit, dollar, double, doubloon, drachma, ducat, dupondius, duro, eagle, écu, eighteen-penny piece, escudo, farthing, fen, fifty-pence piece, fifty-penny piece, five-pence piece, five-penny piece, florin, forint, franc, geordie, gerah, gourde, groat, groschen, guinea, gulden, haler, half-crown, half- dollar, halfpenny, half-sovereign, heller, jacobus, jane, jitney, joe, joey, jo(h)annes, kina, knife-money, koban(g), kopeck, koruna, kreutzer, krona, krone, Krugerrand, kwacha, kyat, lek, lepton, leu, lev, lion, lira, litre, livre, louis, louis-d'or, mag, maik, make, manch, mancus, maravedi, mark, mawpus, merk, mil, millième, millime, milreis, mina, mite, mna, mohur, moidore, mopus, naira, napoleon, (naya) paisa, (new) cedi, ngwee, nickel, obang, obol, obolus, öre, _re, Paduan, pagoda, paolo, para, patrick, paul, peseta, pesewa, peso, pfennig, piastre, picayune, pice, piece of eight, pine-tree money, pistareen, pistole, pistolet, plack, portague, portcullis, pound, punt, qintar, quetzal, quid, rag, rand, real, red, red cent, reichsmark, reis, rial, rider, riel, ringgit, rix-dollar, riyal, rose-noble, r(o)uble, royal, ruddock, ruddy, rupee, rupiah, ryal, saw-buck, sceat(t), schilling, scudo, semis, semuncia, sen, sequin, sesterce, sestertium, sextans, shekel, shilling, silverling, sixpence, skilling, smacker, sol, soldo, solidus, sou, sovereign, spade-guinea, spur-royal, stater, sterling, stiver, sucre, sword- dollar, sycee, tael, taka, talent, tanner, tenner, tenpence, ten- pence piece, ten-penny piece, tester(n), testo(o)n, testril(l), tetradrachm, thaler, thick'un, thin'un, three-farthings, three-halfpence, threepence, three-penny bit/piece, tical, tick(e)y, tizzy, toman, turner, twenty-pence piece, twenty-penny piece, two bits, twopence, two-pence piece, two-penny piece, unicorn, ure, vellon, wakiki, wampum, won, xerafin, yen, yuan, zack, zecchino, zimbi, zloty, zuz, zwanziger.

collective nouns building of rooks, cast of hawks, cete of badgers, charm of goldfinches, chattering of choughs, clamor of rooks, clowder of cats, covert of coots, covey of partridges, down of hares, drift of swine, drove of cattle, dule of doves, exaltation of larks, fall of woodcock, fesnyng of ferrets, gaggle of geese, gam of whales, gang of elks, grist of bees, husk of hares, kindle of kittens, leap of leopards, leash of bucks, murder of crows, murmuration of starlings, muster of peacocks, mute of hounds, nide of pheasants, pace of asses, pod of seals, pride of lions, school of porpoises, siege (or sedge) of bitterns, skein of geese, skulk of foxes, sloth of bears, sounder of boars, spring of teals, stud of mares, team of ducks, tok of capercailzies, troop of kangaroos, walk of snipe, watch of nightingales.

collectors, enthusiasts abolitionist, ailurophile, antiquary, antivaccinationist, antivivisectionist, arachnologist, arctophile, audiophil(e), balletomane, bibliolatrist, bibliomane, bibliopegist, bibliophagist, bibliophile, bibliophilist, bicameralist, campanologist, canophilist, cartophile, cartophilist, cheirographist, coleopterist, conservationist, cynophilist, Dantophilist, deltiologist, discophile, dog-fancier, ecclesiologist, egger, enophile, enophilist, entomologist, environmentalist, ephemerist, epicure, ex-librist, feminist, Francophile, Gallophile, gastronome, gemmologist, Germanophil(e), gourmet, herpetologist, hippophile, homoeopathist, iconophilist, incunabulist, Kremlinologist, lepidopterist, medallist, miscegenationist, monarchist, myrmecologist, negrophile, negrophilist, notaphilist, numismatist, ophiophilist, orchidomaniac, ornithologist, orthoepist, orthographist, ostreiculturist, pangrammatist, Panhellenist, panislamist, Pan- Slavist, paragrammatist, paroemographer, perfectionist, philanthrope, philatelist, philhellene, phillumenist, philogynist, philologist, philologue, prohibitionist, pteridophilist, reincarnationist, Russophile, Russophilist, scripophile, scripophilist, sericulturist, Sinophile, Slavophile, speleologist, steganographist, stegophilist, supernaturalist, tege(s)tologist, timbrologist, timbromaniac, timbrophilist, tulipomane, tulipomaniac, Turcophile, ufologist, ultramontanist, vexillologist, virtuoso, vulcanologist, xenophile, zoophile, zoophilist.

colors anthochlore, anthocyan(in), anthoxanthin, aquamarine, argent, aurora, avocado, badious, Berlin blue, beryl, biscuit, black, blae, blood-red, blue, bottle-green, brick-red, buff, canary, caramel, carmine, carnation, celadon, celeste, cerise, cerulean, cervine, cesious, champagne, charcoal, cobalt- blue, coral, cyan, dove, drab, dun, Dutch pink, dwale, eau de Nil, ebony, emerald, fawn, feldgrau, ferrugin(e)ous, filemot, flame, flavescent, flaxen, flesh-color, fulvous, fuscous, ginger, glaucous, gold, golden, gray, green, greige (grège), gridelin, griseous, grizzle(d), gules, guly, hoar, horse-flesh, hyacinth, hyacinthine, ianthine, icterine, icteritious, incarnadine, indigo, isabel, isabella, isabelline, jacinth, khaki, lake, lateritious, lemon, lilac, lovat, lurid, luteolous, luteous, lutescent, magenta, mahogany, maize, mandarin(e), maroon, mauve, mazarine, miniate, minium, modena, morel, mouse-color(ed), mous(e)y, mulberry, murrey, nacarat, Naples-yellow, nattier blue, Nile green, nut-brown, ochroleucous, off-white, orange, oxblood, Oxford blue, palatinate, pansy, peach, peach-bloom, peacock, peacock-blue, perse, philomot, piceous, pink, plum, plumbeous, pompadour, ponceau, pongee, porphyry, porraceous, puce, purple, purpure, pyrrhous, red, reseda, roan, rose, rose-colored, rose- pink, rose-red, rosy, rubicund, rubied, rubiginous, rubineous, rubious, ruby, ruby-red, ruddy, rufescent, rufous, russet, rust- colored, rusty, sable, saffron, sage, salmon, sand, sapphire, saxe blue, scarlet, sepia, siena, silver, sky, slate, smalt, straw, tan, taupe, tawny, tenné, Titian, tomato, tusser, Tyrian, ultramarine, vermeil, vermilion, vinous, violet, virescent, vitellary, vitreous, watchet, white, wine, xanthic, xanthous, yellow.

confections, dishes, foods angels-on-horseback, battalia pie, bir(i)yani, blanquette, Bombay duck, borsch(t), bouillabaisse, bubble-and-squeak, bummalo, burgoo, cannelloni, carbon(n)ade, cassoulet, cecils, charlotte russe, chilli con carné, chocolate vermicelli, chop-suey, chowder, chow-mein, cockaleekie, colcannon, consommé, Danish pastry, dariole, devil, devil's food cake, devils-on-horseback, Devonshire cream, diet-bread, dika-bread, dimsum, dough-boy, doughnut, dragée, drammock, duff, dumpling, dunderfunk, Eccles cake, éclair, Edinburgh rock, egg custard, enchilada, eryngo, escalope, escargot, faggot, fancy-bread, farle, fedelini, felafel, fettuc(c)ine, fishball, fishcake, fishfinger, flan, flapjack, floater, flummery, foie gras, fondant, fondue, forcemeat, fortune cookie, fraise, frankfurter, French bread, French dressing, French fry, French stick, French toast, fricandeau, fricassee, friedcake, fritter, fritto misto, friture, froise, fruit cocktail, fruit salad, fruitcake, frumenty, fu yung, fudge, fumado, galantine, game chips, garam masala, Garibaldi biscuit, gateau, gazpacho, gefilte fish, Genoa cake, ghee, ginger nut, gingerbread, gingersnap, gnocchi, gofer, goulash, graham bread, graham crackers, grits, gruel, guacamole, gumdrop, gundy, haberdine, haggis, halva(h), hamburger, hard sauce, hardbake, hardtack, hoe-cake, hominy, hoosh, hot dog, hot-cross-bun, hotpot, howtowdie, humbug, hummus, hundreds-and-thousands, hyson, jemmy, kedgeree, lardy-cake, laverbread, matelote, millefeuille(s), minestrone, mous(s)aka, na(a)n, navarin, olla- podrida, opsonium, paella, panada, pastrami, pavlova, pem(m)ican, pettitoes, pilaff, pilau, pinole, pirozhki, pizza, plowman's lunch, plum-duff, plum-porridge, plum-pudding, poi, polenta, polony, popover, pop(p)adum, porterhouse(-steak), pot-au-feu, prairie-oyster, profiterole, prosciutto, pumpernickel, queen of puddings, queen's pudding, quenelle, quiche, ragout, ramekin, ratatouille, ravioli, remoulade, risotto, roly-poly pudding, Sachertorte, salmagundi, salmi(s), saltimbocca, sauce hollandaise, sauerkraut, scampi, schnitzel, sch(t)chi, Scotch woodcock, shepherd's pie, sm_rbr_d, smörgåsbord, soufflé, spaghetti (alla) bolognese, spotted dick, spring roll, stovies, stroganoff, succotash, sukiyaki, summer pudding, sundae, sup(p)awn, sushi, syllabub, Tabasco®;, tablet, taco, tamal(e), tandoori, tapioca, taramasalata, tempura, timbale, toad-in-the- hole, torte, tortellini, tortilla, trifle, tsamba, turtle-soup, tutti-frutti, tzimmes, velouté sauce, vermicelli, vichyssoise, vienna loaf, vienna steak, vindaloo, vol-au-vent, wafer, waffle, warden pie, wastel-bread, water-biscuit, water-gruel, welsh rabbit (rarebit), white sauce, white-pot, white-pudding, Wiener schnitzel, Wimpy®;, wine-biscuit, wonder, Worcestershire sauce, wurst, yoghurt, Yorkshire pudding, zabaglione, Zwieback.

dances allemande, beguine, belly-dance, bergamask, black bottom, bolero, bossanova, bourree, branle, breakdown, bunny-hug, cachucha, cakewalk, canary, cancan, carioca, carmagnole, carol, cha-cha, chaconne, Charleston, cinque-pace, Circassian, circle, clogdance, conga, coranto, corroboree, cotill(i)on, country- dance, courant, cracovienne, csárdás (czardas), dos-à-dos (dosi- do) dump, écossaise, egg-dance, fading, fado, fandango, farruca, figure-dance, flamenco, fling, flip-flap(-flop), forlana, fox- trot, galliard, gallopade, galop, gavotte, gigue, gopak, habanera, haka, halling, haymaker, hey (hay), hey-de-guy, Highland fling, hoedown, hoolachan, hula-hula, jig, jitterbug, jive, jota, juba, kolo, lancers, loure, malagueña, mambo, matachin, maxixe, mazurka, minuet, Moresco, morris-dance, musette, onestep, Paduan, paso doble, passacaglia, passepied, passy-measure, Paul Jones, pavan(e), petronella, planxty, polacca, polka, polo, polonaise, poule, poussette, quadrille, quickstep, redowa, reel, r(h)umba, rigadoon, ring-dance, romaika, roundel, roundelay, roundle, rumba, saltarello, samba, sand-dance, saraband, schottische, sequidilla, shimmy(-shake), siciliano, spring, square-dance, stomp, strathspey, sword-dance, tamborin, tango, tap-dance, tarantella, the twist, toe-dance, tripudium, turkey-trot, two-step, Tyrolienne, valeta, valse, varsovienne, volta, waltz, war dance, zapateado, ziganka.

dog-breeds affenpinscher, badger-dog, basenji, basset(- hound), Bedlington (terrier), Blenheim spaniel, boar-hound, Border terrier, borzoi, Boston terrier, Briard, Brussels griffon, bull mastiff, bulldog, bull-terrier, cairn terrier, Cavalier King Charles spaniel, chihuahua, chow, clumber spaniel, coach-dog, cocker spaniel, collie, corgi, dachshund, Dalmatian, Dandie Dinmont, Dane, deerhound, dhole, dingo, Doberman(n) pinscher, elkhound, Eskimo dog, foxhound, fox-terrier, German police dog, German Shepherd dog, Great Dane, greyhound, griffon, harlequin, (Irish) water-spaniel, Jack Russell, keeshond, King Charles spaniel, Labrador, laika, lhasa apso, lurcher, lyam-hound, malemute, Maltese, mastiff, peke, Pekin(g)ese, pinscher, pointer, Pomeranian, poodle, pug, pug-dog, retriever, Rottweiler, saluki, Samoyed(e), sausage-dog, schipperke, schnauzer, Scotch-terrier, Sealyham, setter, sheltie, Shetland sheepdog, shih tzu, shough, Skye (terrier), spaniel, Spartan, spitz, St Bernard, staghound, Sussex spaniel, talbot, teckel, terrier, vizsla, volpino, warragal, water-dog, Weimaraner, whippet, wire-hair(ed terrier), wolf-dog, wolf-hound, Yorkshire terrier, zorro.

drinks, alcoholic absinth(e), aguardiente, akvavit, amontillado, anisette, apple-jack, aqua-mirabilis, aquavit, aqua-vitae, arak, Armagnac, arrack, audit ale, ava, bacharach, badminton, barley-bree, Beaujolais, Beaune, Benedictine, bingo, bishop, black velvet, bloody Mary, blue ruin, bourbon, brandy- pawnee, bride-ale, Bristol-milk, bucellas, bumbo, burgundy, Calvados, Campari, canary, catawba, Chablis, chain-lightning, Chambertin, Champagne, Chartreuse, cherry brandy, cherry-bounce, Chianti, chicha, cider, claret, claret-cup, cobbler, cobbler's punch, Cognac, Cointreau®;, cold-without, Constantia, cool- tankard, cooper, cordial, corn-brandy, daiquiri, demerara, dog's nose, dop, eau de vie, eau des creoles, egg-flap, eggnog, enamel, enzian, fine, fino, four-ale, geneva, genevrette, geropiga, gimlet, gin, gin and it, gin-fizz, ginger wine, ginsling, glogg, gooseberry wine, grappa, Graves, grog, haoma, heavy wet, herb-beer, hermitage, hippocras, hock, hollands, hoo(t)ch, it, Johannisberger, John Barleycorn, John Collins, kaoliang, kava, kefir, kirsch, kirschwasser, k(o)umiss, kümmel, kvass, London particular, manzanilla, maraschino, marc brandy, Marcobrunner, Marsala, Martini®;, Médoc, metheglin, mirabelle, mobbie, Moselle, mountain, mountain dew, muscat, muscatel, negus, Nipa, noyau, Old Tom, oloroso, olykoek, Orvieto, ouzo, pastis, peach-brandy, Pernod®;, perry, persico(t), Peter-see-me, pils(e)ner, plottie, pombe, port, pot(h)een, pousse-café, pulque, punch, purl, quetsch, ratafia, resinata, retsina, Rhine-wine, Riesling, Rioja, rosé, Rudesheimer, Rüdesheimer, rum, rumbo, rumfustian, rum-punch, rum-shrub, rye, rye-whisky, sack, sack- posset, sake, samshoo, sangaree, sangria, Sauterne(s), schiedam, schnapps, Scotch, shandy, sherry, sherry-cobbler, shrub, sidecar, Sillery, sling, slivovitz, sloe-gin, small beer, small-ale, sour, spruce-beer, St Julien, Steinberger, stengah, stinger, stingo, swipes, swizzle, tafia, Tarragona, tent, tequil(l)a, tipper, toddy, Tokay, Tom Collins, Tom-and-Jerry, twankay, twopenny, usquebaugh, vermouth, vin blanc, vin ordinaire, vin rosé, vinho verde, vodka, wassail, water-brose, whisk(e)y, whisky toddy, white wine, white-ale, Xeres, zythum.

French Revolutionary calendar Brumaire, Floréal, Frimaire, Fructidor, Germinal, Messidor, Nivôse, Pluviôse, Prairiel, Thermidor, Vendémiaire, Ventôse.

furniture, furnishings andiron, banquette, basket-chair, basketwork, bergama, bergamot, bolster, bonheur-du-jour, box-bed, bracket clock, brise-soleil, buffet, buhl, bureau, cabriolet, camp-bed, canterbury, chair-bed, chaise-longue, chesterfield, cheval-glass, chiffonier, coaster, commode, continental quilt, credence (table/shelf), credenza, davenport, day-bed, desk, dinner-table, dinner-wagon, divan, dos-à-dos, drape, drawer, drawing-table, draw-leaf table, dresser, dressing-table, dumb- waiter, easy-chair, elbow-chair, electrolier, encoignure, escritoire, étagere, faldstool, fauteuil, fender, fender-stool, festoon-blind, fire-dog, fireguard, firescreen, four-poster, gasalier, girandole, girnel, guéridon, hallstand, hassock, hearth-rug, highboy, high-chair, hip-bath, humpty, jardinière, lectern, looking-glass, lounge, lounger, love-seat, lowboy, lug- chair, mirror, mobile, ottoman, overmantel, pelmet, pembroke (table), picture rail, piecrust table, pier-glass, pier-table, plaque, plenishings, pouf(fe), prie-dieu, pulpit, pulvinar, radiator, rocking chair, sag-bag, scatter rug/cushion, sconce, secretaire, settee, settle, settle-bed, sideboard, sidetable, sofa, sofa-bed, sofa-table, squab, standard lamp, studio couch, swivel-chair, table, tallboy, tapestry, tatami, teapoy, tea- service, tea-set, tea-table, tea-tray, tea-trolley, tent-bed, tête-à-tête, toilet-table, toilet(te), torchère, tridarn, tringle, umbrella-stand, Vanitory®;, vanity unit, vargueño, veilleuse, vis-à-vis, vitrine, wall-unit, wardrobe, washhand- stand, wash-stand, water bed, Welsh dresser, whatnot, writing- desk, writing-table.

garments, vestments aba, abaya, abba, abolla, achkan, acton, Afghan, alb, alpargata, amice, anorak, antigropelo(e)s, babouche, babushka, balaclava, Balbriggan, balibuntal, balmoral, bandan(n)a, bania(n), barret, basher, bashlyk, basinet, basque, basquine, bathing-costume, bauchle, beanie, bearskin, beaver, bed-jacket, bedsocks, beetle-crushers, belcher, benjamin, Bermuda shorts, Bermudas, bertha, bikini, billycock, biretta, blanket, blouson, blucher, boa, boater, bobbysock, bodice, body stocking, bolero, bomber jacket, bongrace, bonnet, bonnet-rouge, boob-tube, bootee, bottine, box-coat, bow-tie, bra, brassière, breeches, breeks, breton, broad-brim, brogue(s), buckskins, buff, buffalo- robe, buff-coat, buff-jerkin, bumfreezer, Burberry, burdash, burk(h)a, burnous(e), busby, bush jacket, bush shirt, buskin, bustle, bustle, bycoket, caftan, cagoul(e), calamanco, calash, calceamentum, calotte, calyptra, camiknickers, camise, camisole, capa, cape, capel(l)ine, capote, capuche, capuchin, carcanet, car-coat, cardigan, cardinal, carmagnole, cashmere, casque, cassock, casuals, catsuit, caul, cere-cloth, cerement, chadar, chaparajos, chapeau, chapeau-bras, chaperone, chapka, chaplet, chaps, chasuble, collar of esses, corset, corslet, cummerbund, dalmahoy, Dalmatic, décolletage, derby, diadem, diaper, dick(e)y, dinner-gown, dinner-jacket, dirndl, dishabille, dittos, divided skirt, djellaba(h), djibbah, dog-collar, Dolly Varden, dolman, donkey jacket, doublet, drainpipes, drapesuit, drawers, dreadnought, dress uniform, dress-coat, dress-improver, dressing- gown, dressing-jacket, dressing-sack, dress-shirt, dress-suit, dress-tie, duffel coat, dungarees, earmuffs, encolpion, epaulet(te), ephod, epitrachelion, espadrille, Eton collar, Eton jacket, Etons, evening dress, evening-dress, exomis, faldetta, falling band, fannel(l), fanon, farthingale, fascinator, fatigues, fedora, ferronnière, fez, fibula, fichu, filibeg, fillet, finnesko, flat-cap, flip-flop, fob, fontange, fore-and- after, fraise, French knickers, frock, frock-coat, frog, frontlet, fustanella, gaberdine, gaiter, galligaskins, galoshes, gamash, gambeson, garibaldi, gauchos, gay deceivers, gee-string (G-string), geneva bands, geta, gibus, gi(e), gilet, girandole, gizz, grego, gremial, g-suit, guernsey, gumboot, gum(shoe), habergeon, hacqueton, haik, hair-net, hair-piece, half-boot, hat, hatband, hatpin, hattock, hauberk, havelock, headcloth, head- hugger, headsquare, himation, hip-huggers, hipsters, hogger, Homburg, hood, hotpants, housecoat, hug-me-tight, humeral veil, hummel, hunting cap, ihram, indescribables, jabot, jacket, Jap- silk, jeans, jersey, jiz, jubbah (djibbah), jumper, jump-suit, jupon, kabaya, kaffiyeh, kaftan, kagoul, kalpak, kalyptra, kamees, kanzu, kell, kerchief, k(h)anga, k(h)urta, Kilmarnock, Kilmarnock cowl, kimono, kirtle, kiss-me, kiss-me-quick, knickerbockers, knickers, lammy, lava-lava, lederhosen, leggings, leghorn, leg-warmers, leotard, Levis®;, liberty bodice, lingerie, loden, lounger, lounge-suit, lungi, mac(k), mackinaw, mac(k)intosh, madras, manta, manteau, mantilla, mantle, mantlet, manto, matinee, matinee jacket/coat, maud, mazarine, mazarine hood, middy (blouse), mink, miter, mitt, mitten, mob, mob-cap, mode, modius, mohair, moleskins, monkey-jacket, monteith, montero, montero-cap, morning-dress, morning-gown, mortar-board, Mother Hubbard, mourning-cloak, mousquetaire, moz(z)etta, muff, muffin-cap, muffler, mutch, muu-muu, netherstock, newmarket, nightingale, Nithsdale, Norfolk jacket, nubia, obi, omophorion, orarion, orarium, overcoat, overgarment, Oxonian, paduasoy, paenula, pagri, paletot, pall, palla, pallium, paludament, pantable, pantalets, pantaloons, panties, pantihose, pantof(f)le, panton, pantoufle, pants, pants suit, pea-coat, pea-jacket, pearlies, pectoral, pedal-pushers, pelerine, pelisse, pencil skirt, penitentials, peplos, peplum, petasos, petersham, petticoat, petticoat, petticoat-breeches, ph(a)elonion, Phrygian cap, picture-hat, pierrot, pilch, pileus, pill-box, pinafore, pinafore-dress, pinafore-skirt, pinner, pixie-hood, plaid, plimsoll, plus-fours, plushes, pneumonia-blouse, poke-bonnet, polonaise, polo-neck, poncho, pontificals, pos(h)teen, powdering- gown, pressure-helmet, pressure-suit, pressure-waistcoat, princess(e), pumps, puttee, rabato, raglan, raincoat, rami(e), Ramil(l)ie(s), ra-ra skirt, rat-catcher, rational, rationals, rebater, rebato, redingote, reefer, reefing-jacket, riding- breeches, riding-cloak, riding-clothes, riding-coat, riding- glove, riding-habit, riding-hood, riding-robe, riding-skirt, riding-suit, robe, robe-de-chambre, rochet, roll-neck sweater, roll-on, rompers, romper-suit, roquelaure, ruff, rug-gown, sabot, sack, sack-coat, safari jacket, safari suit, sagum, sailor-hat, sakkos, salopette, samfoo, sanbenito, sandal, sarafan, sari, sarong, sash, sayon, scapular, scarf, scarpetto, schema, scotch bonnet, screen, sea-boots, sealskin, semmit, separates, shako, shaps, shauchle, shawl, shawl-waistcoat, shift, shirt, shirt dress, shirtwaist, shirtwaister, shoe, shooting-jacket, short-clothes, short-coats, shortgown, shorts, shovel-hat, silk-hat, silly-how, singlet, siren suit, skeleton suit, skin-tights, skirt, skullcap, slacks, slicker, sling-back, slip, slip-over, slipper(s), slipslop, sloppy Joe, slop(s), slouch(-hat), small- clothes, smalls, smicket, smock, smock-frock, smoking cap, smoking jacket, sneaker(s), snood, snow-boots, snow-shoe(s), sock, sola(r) topi/helmet, solitaire, solleret, sombrero, sontag, soubise, soutane, sou'-wester, space-suit, spat, spattee, spatterdash, spencer, sphendone, sponge-bags, sporran, sports jacket, sports shirt, start-up, stays, steenkirk, steeple-crown, steeple-hat, stephane, step-in, Stetson, sticharion, stock, stockinet(te), stockingette, stocking(s), stola, stole, stomacher, stovepipe (hat), strait-jacket, strait-waistcoat, straw (hat), string vest, string-tie, strip, stuff-gown, subfusc, subucula, succinctorium, sun-bonnet, sundown, sun-dress, sunhat, sunsuit, superhumeral, surcingle, surcoat, surplice, surtout, suspender-belt, suspenders, swaddling-band/cloth/clothes, swagger-coat, swallow-tail, sweat band, sweat suit, sweater, sweat-shirt, swimming costume, swimsuit, swimwear, sword-belt, tabard, taglioni, tail-coat, tails, taj, talar, talaria, tall hat, tallith, talma, tam, Tam O'Shanter, tammy, tanga, tank top, tarboosh, tarpaulin, tasse, tawdry-lace, tea-gown, Teddy suit, tee-shirt, ten-gallon hat, terai, thrum-cap, tiar(a), tie, tights, tile(-hat), tippet, toga, tonnag, top-boots, topcoat, topee, topi, topper, tops, toque, toreador pants, tournure, tower, toy, tozie, track shoe, track suit, trenchard, trench- coat, trencher-cap, trews, tricorn(e), trilby, trollopee, trot- cozy, trouser suit, trousers, trouse(s), trunk-breeches, trunk- hose, trunks, truss(es), trusty, T-shirt, tube-skirt, tunic, tunicle, tuque, turban, turtle-neck, tuxedo, twin-set, ugly, ulster, ulsterette, undercoat, underpants, undershorts, undervest, upper-stock, Vandyke (collar), vareuse, veil, veld(-)schoen, vest, victorine, visite, vitta, volet, waistcloth, waistcoat, wam(p)us, war bonnet, warm, watch cap, watch chain, Watteau bodice, weeper, wellie, wellington, wet-suit, whisk, white tie, wide-awake, wig, wimple, windcheater, windjammer, wing collar, winkle-pickers, woggle, wrap, wraparound, wrapover, wrapper, wrap-rascal, wristlet, wylie-coat, yarmulka, yashmak, Y- fronts, zamarra, zoot suit, zoster, zucchetto.

heraldry abatement, addorsed, affrontee, Albany Herald, allusive, annulet, armorist, assurgent, augmentation, baton- sinister, bendlet, bend-sinister, bendwise, bendy, bezant, bicorporate, billet, bordure, botoné, brisure, caboched, cabré, cadency, canting, canton, catherine-wheel, champ, chequy, chevron, chevrony, chief, coupé, debased, debruised, declinant, delf, device, dexter, difference, dimidiate, dismembered, displayed, dormant, double, doubling, dragonné, dwale, eightfoil, embattled, emblaze, emblazon, emblazoner, emblazonment, emblazonry, enarched, enarmed, engouled, engrail, engrailed, engrailment, enveloped, escrol(l), escutcheon, extendant, fess(e), fesse-point, fetterlock, field, fimbriate, fitché(e), flanch, flanched, flotant, fracted, fret, fructed, fur, fusil, gale, gamb, garb(e), gemel, gerbe, golp(e), gorged, grieced, g(u)ardant, gules, gyron, gyronny, hatchment, haurient, herisson, honor-point, impale, impalement, increscent, inescutcheon, interfretted, invected, jessant, langued, lioncel, lis, lozenge, lozengy, manche, mantling, martlet, mascle, mascled, masculy, moline, morné, morned, mounted, mullet, naiant, naissant, nombril, nowed, nowy, opinicus, or, orle, palewise, pall, passant, patonce, patté(e), pean, percussant, pheon, pile, point, pommelé, pommeled, pommetty, portate, portcullis, posé, potencé, potent, primrose, quarter, quartering, quarterly, queue, ragged staff, raguled, raguly, rampant, raping, rebate, regardant, respect, respectant, roundel, rustre, saltire, sans nombre, satyral, scarp, segreant, sej(e)ant, semé(e), square-pierced, statant, tenné, trangle, tressure, trippant, umbrated, undee, undifferenced, unguled, urinant, vair, vairé, verdoy, vert, voided, vol, volant, vorant, vuln, vulned, waved, weel, wivern, woodwose (wood-house).

herbs, spices amaracus, basil thyme, caraway seeds, cardamom, cassia, cayenne, chervil, chilli, chive, cinnamon, cloves, coriander, cum(m)in, dill, dittany, endive, eyebright, fennel, fenugreek, finoc(c)hio, galega, garlic, gentian, ginger, groundsel, hellebore, henbane, horehound, horseradish, Hyoscyamus, hyssop, isatis, juniper, lemon thyme, licorice, lovage, lungwort, mace, marjoram, mint, motherwort, mustard, myrrh, nutmeg, oregano, orpine, paprika, parsley, peppermint, purslane, rampion, rape, rosemary, rue, saffron, sage, savory, stacte, tarragon, thyme, turmeric, vanilla, verbena, watercress, wintergreen, wormwood, woundwort, yerba.

jewels, gems agate, amber, amethyst, aquamarine, asteria, balas ruby, baroque, beryl, bloodstone, brilliant, cairngorm, cameo, carbuncle, chalcedony, chrysolite, coral, cornelian, crystal, diamond, draconites, emerald, fire-opal, garnet, girasol(e), grossular(ite), heliodor, hyacinth, hyalite, hydrophane, intaglio, jacinth, jade, jango(o)n, jasper, jet, lapis lazuli, ligure, marcasite, marquise, Mocha stone, moonstone, morganite, mother-of-pearl, nacre, olivet, olivine, onyx, opal, oriental amethyst, paragon, pearl, peridot(e), pyreneite, pyrope, Rhinestone, rhodolite, rose, rose-cut, rose- diamond, ruby, sapphire, sard, sardine, sardonyx, smaragd, topaz, tourmaline, turquoise, water-sapphire, wood-opal, yu, yu-stone, zircon.

Jewish calendar Ab, Abib, Adar, Adar Sheni, Elul, Hes(h)van, Iy(y)ar, Kislev, Nisan, S(h)ebat, Sivan, Tammuz, Tebet(h), Tis(h)ri, Veadar.

languages Aeolic, Afghan, Afrikaans, Akkadian, Albanian, Alemannic, Algonki(a)n, Altaic, Ameslan, Amharic, Anatolian, Anglo-Saxon, Arabic, Aramaic, Armenian, Armoric, Aryan, Assyrian, Attic, Austric, Austroasiatic, Austronesian, Avestan, Bahasa Indonesia, Balinese, Baltoslav(on)ic, Baluch(i), Bantu, Basque, Basuto, Bengali, Berber, Bohemian, bohunk, Breton, Brezonek, British, Brythonic, Bulgarian, Bulgaric, Burmese, B(y)elorussian, Cajun, Carib, Catalan, Celtic, Chaldaic, Cherokee, Chinese, Choctaw, Circassian, Cornish, creole, Croat(ian), Cushitic, Czech, Danish, Dardic, Doric, Dravidian, Dutch, Early English, English, Erse, Eskimo, Esperanto, Est(h)onian, Ethiopic, Etruscan, Euskarian, Fanti, Farsi, Finnish, Finno-Ugric(-Ugrian), Flemish, Franglais, French, Frisian, Gadhelic (Goidelic), Gaelic, Gaulish, Geëz (Giz), Gentoo, Georgian, German, Germanic, Greek, Guarani, Gujarat(h)i, Gullah, Hausa, Hawaiian, Hebrew, Hellenic, Herero, High German, Hindi, Hindustani, Hittite, Hottentot, Hungarian, Icelandic, Idiom Neutral, Ido, I(g)bo, Indian, Indic, Indo-European, Indo-Germanic, In(n)uit, Interlingua, Ionic, Iranian, Iraqi, Irish, Iroquoian, Italian, Italic, Japanese, Kalmuck, Kanarese, Kannada, Karen, Kennick, Khmer, Koine, Kolarian, Kuo-yü, Kurdish, Ladin, Ladino, Lallans, Landsmaal, Langue d'oc, Langue d'oil, Langue d'oui, Laplandish, Lapp, Lappish, Latin, Latvian, Lettic, Lettish, lingua franca, lingua geral, Lithuanian, Low German, Magyar, Malagasy, Malay, Malayala(a)m, Maltese, Manchu, Mandaean, Mandarin, Mandingo, Manx, Maori, Marathi, Median, Melanesian, Mexican, Micmac, Middle English, Moesogothic, Mohawk, Mohican, Mon, Mongolian, Munda, Nahuati, Neo, Newspeak, Norwegian, Novial, Nynorsk, Old English, Old Norse, Oriya, Oscan, Ostyak, Pali, Pawnee, Pehlevi, Pekin(g)ese, Pennsylvania Dutch, Persian, Persic, Phoenician, Pictish, pig Latin, Pilipino, Platt-Deutsch, Polabian, Polish, Portuguese, Prakrit, Provençal Provinçal, Prussian, Punic, Punjabi, Pushtu, Quechua, Rabbinic, Rhaetic, Rhaeto-Romance, Rhaeto-Romanic, Rock English, rogues' Latin, Romaic, Romance, Romanes, Romanic, Roman(n)y, Romans(c)h, Rumanian, Russian, Russniak, Ruthenian, Sakai, Samnite, Samoyed(e), Sanskrit, Saxon, Scots, Scythian, Semitic, Serb(ian), Serbo-Croat(ian), Shan, Shona, Siamese, Sinhalese, Siouan, Slavonic, Slovak, Slovenian, Somali, Sorbian, Sorbish, Spanish, Sudanic, Sumerian, Suomi, Swahili, Swedish, Swiss, Syriac, Taal, Tagálog, Taino, Tamil, Tataric, Telugu, Teutonic, Thai, Tibetan, Tocharian, Tswana, Tuareg, Tungus(ian), Tupi, Turki, Turkish, Twi, Ugrian, Ugrofinnic, Ukrainian, Umbrian, Uralic, Urdu, Uzbeg, Vaudois, Vietnamese, Volapük, Volga-Baltic, Volscian, Welsh, Wendic, Wendish, West-Saxon, Wolof, Xhosa, Yakut, Yiddish, Yoruba, Zulu.

legal abate, abatement, absolvitor, abstract of title, acceptilation, accession, accessory, accessory after the fact, accessory before the fact, Acts of Adjournal, (ad)avizandum, adeem, adhere, adjudication, adminicle, administrator, afforce, alienee, alienor, allenarly, allodial, amicus curiae, amove, appointer, apprize, apprizer, assumpsit, attorn, back-bond, bairn's-part, capias, certiorari, chaud-mellé, cognosce, cognovit, compear, compulsitor, copyhold, cross-examine, decree absolute, decree nisi, decreet, decretals, decretist, dedimus, deed, deed of accession, defalcate, defeasance, defeasanced, defeasible, defendant, defender, deforce, deforcement, deforciant, delapidation, delate, delation, delator, delict, demurrer, deodand, detainer, detinue, devastavit, devest, diet, dimissory, disapply, disbar, disbench, discovert, discoverture, disentail, disgavel, disinherison, dispone, disponee, disposition, disseise, disseisin, disseisor, distinguish, distrain, distrainee, distrainer, distrainment, distrainor, distraint, distress, distringas, dittay, dole, donatary, droit, droit du Seigneur, duplicand, duply, dying declaration, easement, ejectment, embracer, embracery, emendals, emphyteusis, en ventre sa mère, enfeoff, enfeoffment, enjoin, enlevé, enlevement, entry, eric, escheat, escrow (escroll), escuage, esnecy, esrepe, essoin, estate, estop, estoppel, estover, estray, estreat, estrepement, examination, excamb, excambion, excambium, executry, exemplify, expromission, extend, extent, extinguishment, extract, extradition, facile, facility, factorize, faldage, felo de se, felony, feme, feme covert, feme sole, feoff, feoffee, feoffer (feoffor), feoffment, feu, feuar, fief, filacer, fire-bote, fiscal, folio, force and fear, force majeure, foreclose, foreclosure, forinsec, forisfamiliate, forjudge, frankalmoign, french-bench, frontager, fugitation, fungibles, garnishee, garnisheement, garnisher, gavelkind, gavelman, granter (grantor), grassum, hamesucken, hedge-bote, hide, homologation, horning, house-bote, hypothec, hypothecary, hypothecate, hypothecation, improbation, indenture, indict, indictee, indictment, induciae, infangthief, infeft, inquirendo, institorial, insucken, interlocutor, interplead, interpleader, interpose, irrepleviable, irreplevisable, ish, John Doe and Richard Roe, joinder, jointure, jus primae noctis, laches, law-agent, law-burrows, legitim, lenocinium, letters of administration, lien, life-rent, malfeasance, mens rea, mesne, messuage, misdemeanant, misfeasance, misfeasor, misprison, mittimus, mora, mortmain, multiplepoinding, nolle prosequi, nolo contendere, non-access, nonage, non-compearance, non-entry, nonsuit, non-user, notour, novalia, noverint, novodamus, noxal, obligant, obligation, obligor, obreption, onus probandi, ouster, outfangthief, overt act, owelty, oyer, pactum nudum, Pandect, panel, pernancy, personalty, pickery, plaint, plaintiff, porteous roll, portioner, practic, prima facie, privy, prorogate, pupil, quadruply, realty, recaption, recusation, reddendo, relator, relaxation, remise, replevin, replevy, repone, reprobator, res gestae, retour, retroact, retroactive, reverser, right of drip, rout, scutage, stillicide, supersedeas, supplicavit, surrebut, surrebuttal, surrebutter, surrejoin, surrejoinder, terminer, tolt, tort, tortfeasor, tortious, udal, udaller, ultimus haeres, unlaw, uses, usucapient, usucapion (usucaption), usucapt, usucaptible, usufruct, usufructuary, ultimogeniture, vacatur, venire (facias), venter, venue, vert, vest, vested, visne, voidable, voir dire, volunteer, wage, waive, waste, watch, watching brief, water- privilege, wit.

minerals adularia, aegirine, aegirite, alabandine, almandine, alum-shale, alum-slate, alum-stone, alunite, amazonite, amazon-stone, amianthus, amphibole, analcime, anatase, andesine, argil, arkose, asbestos, asparagus-stone, asphalt(um), aventurine, baetyl, balas, Barbados earth, barilla, baryta, barytes, basalt, Bath stone, bath-brick, bezoar, bitter-earth, bitter-spar, bitumen, blackjack, blacklead, blaes, blende, bloodstone, blue ground, blue John, blue vitriol, bluestone, Bologna phosphorous, borane, borax, borazon, boride, bornite, boulder-clay, breccia, Bristol-brick, Bristol-diamond, brown spar, brownstone, buhrstone, cacholong, caen-stone, cairngorm, calamine, calc-sinter, calcspar, calc-tuff, caliche, calp, Carborundum®;, cat's-eye, cat-silver, cauk, celestine, cement-stone, ceruse, chalcedony, chalcedonyx, chalk, chert, Chile saltpeter, china clay, china stone, chrome-alum, chrome- spinel, chrysoberyl, chrysocolla, chrysoprase, chrysotile, cinnabar, cinnamon-stone, cipollino, corundum, cryolite, cymophane, dacite, dendrite, Derbyshire spar, diabase, diallage, dialogite, diaspore, diatomite, dice-coal, diopside, dioptase, diorite, dogger, dogtooth-spar, dolerite, dolomite, dopplerite, dropstone, dunite, dyscrasite, dysodyle, eagle-stone, earthflax, earthwax, eclogite, electric calamine, elvan, emery, encrinite, enhydrite, enhydros, epidiorite, epidosite, epidote, epistilbite, epsomite, erinite, erubescite, erythrite, euclase, eucrite, eudialyte, eutaxite, euxenite, fahlerz, fahlore, fakes, fayalite, fel(d)spar, felsite, felstone, flint, fluorite, fluorspar, franklinite, French chalk, fuchsite, fulgurite, fuller's earth, gabbro, gadolinite, gahnite, galena, galenite, gangue, gan(n)ister, garnet-rock, gibbsite, glance, glauberite, glauconite, glimmer, gmelinite, gneiss, goldstone, goslarite, gossan, göthite, granite, granitite, granodiorite, granophyre, granulite, graphic granite, graphite, green earth, greenockite, greensand, greenstone, greisen, greywacke, gummite, gypsum, hälleflinta, halloysite, harmotome, hatchettite, haüyne, heavy spar, hedyphane, hematite, hemimorphite, hepatite, hercynite, (h)essonite, heulandite, hiddenite, honey-stone, hornblende, hornfels, hornstone, horseflesh ore, humite, hyacinth, hyalophane, hypersthene, ice-spar, ice-stone, idocrase, ironstone, jacinth, keratophyre, kermes, kermesite, kieselguhr, kunkur, kupferschiefer, lamprophyre, lapis lazuli, lepidomelane, limestone, lithomarge, marlstone, meerschaum, mellite, mica, microlite, microlith, mispickel, morion, moss-agate, mundic, nail-head-spar, needle-tin, nepheline, nickel-bloom, nickel- ocher, Norway saltpeter, nosean, noselite, obsidian, omphacite, onyx, onyx-marble, orthoclase, orthophyre, ottrelite, ozokerite, peacock-ore, pencil-ore, pencil-stone, peperino, periclase, pericline, petuntse, pipeclay, pipestone, plagioclose, pleonaste, porphyry, potstone, prase, protogine, pyrites, quartz, realgar, rock-oil, rubicelle, ruby-spinel, rutile, saltpeter, sandstone, sanidine, sapphire, sapphire-quartz, sapphirine, sard, sardonyx, satin-spar, satinstone, scaglia, schalstein, schiller-spar, schist, schorl, serpentine, serpentine(-rock), shale, shell- limestone, shell-marl, silica, silver-glance, sinter, slate, soapstone, spar, speiss-cobalt, spelter, sphene, spiegeleisen, spinel, spinel-ruby, spodumene, stinkstone, sunstone, surturbrand, swinestone, sylvine, tabular spar, tachylite, talc, talc-schist, terne, terpene, terpineol, terra alba, terracotta, terra-japonica, terramara, terrarossa, terra-sigillata, terts, thulia, tiger(s)-eye, till, tin-stone, toad-stone, tombac, touchstone, tourmaline, trass, travertin(e), tripoli, troutstone, tufa, tuff, Turkey hone, Turkey stone, turquoise, tutty, uinta(h)ite, umber, Uralian emerald, uralite, uraninite, uranite, uvarovite, vanadinite, variolite, variscite, veinstone, veinstuff, Venice talc, verd-antique, vesuvianite, vitrain, vivianite, vulpinite, wacke, wad(d), wallsend, wavellite, Wernerite, whet-slate, whewellite, whinstone, white pyrites, willemite, witherite, wolfram, wollastonite, wood-coal, wulfenite, wurtzite, zaratite, zarnich, zeolite, zeuxite, zinkenite, zircon, zoisite, zorgite.

musical instruments aeolian harp, aerophone, alpenhorn, alphorn, althorn, alto, Amati, American organ, apollonicon, archlute, arpeggione, atabal, autoharp, balalaika, bandore, banjulele, baryton(e), bass clarinet, bass drum, bass fiddle, bass horn, bass tuba, bass viol, basset horn, bazooka, bombard, bombardon, bongo (drum), bouzouki, buccina, bugle, buglet, bull fiddle, calliope, castanets, celeste, cello, cembalo, chair- organ, chalumeau, chamber organ, chikara, Chinese pavilion, chitarrone, chordophone, cinema-organ, cithara, cither(n), citole, cittern, clarichord, clarinet, clarion, clarsach, clave, clavichord, crwth, cymbal, cymbalo, decachord, dichord, didgeridoo, digitorium, double bass, drum, dulcimer, Dulcitone®;, dumb-piano, echo, electric guitar, electric organ, euphonium, fagotto, fife, fipple-flute, flageolet, flügel, flügelhorn, flute, flûte-à-bec, flutina, French horn, gamelan, German flute, gimbard, gittern, glass harmonica, glockenspiel, grand piano, gu, guitar, gusla, Hammerklavier, hand-horn, hand- organ, harmonica, harmonicon, harmoniphone, harmonium, harp, harpsichord, hautboy, heckelphone, heptachord, horn, hornpipe, humstrum, hunting-horn, hurdy-gurdy, idiophone, jingling Johnny, kazoo, kent-bugle, keyboard(s), keybugle, klavier, koto, krummhorn, Kuh-horn, langsp(i)el, lituus, lur(e), lyraviol, lyre, mandola, mandolin(e), mandora, maraca, marimba, marine trumpet, melodeon, metallophone, mirliton, monochord, Moog synthesizer, mouth-harp, mouth-organ, musette, musical glasses, naker, nose- flute, nun's-fiddle, oboe, oboe d'amore, oboe di caccia, ocarina, octachord, octave-flute, ophicleide, organ-harmonium, orpharion, orpheorion, pandora, panharmonicon, Pan-pipes, Pan's pipes, pantaleon, pianette, pianino, piano, piano- accordion, pianoforte, Pianola®;, piano-organ, piffero, pipe, pipeless organ, pipe-organ, player piano, polyphon(e), posaune, psaltery, pyrophone, quint(e), racket(t), rebec(k), regal, rote, sackbut, salpinx, sambuca, sancho, sang, santir, sarangi, sarrusophone, sausage-bassoon, saxhorn, saxophone, seraphine, serinette, serpent, s(h)amisen, shawm, side-drum, sitar, small- pipes, sourdeline, sousaphone, spinet(te), squeeze-box, squiffer, steel drum, sticcado, stock-and-horn, strad, Stradivari(us), string bass, sultana, symphonion, symphony, synthesizer, syrinx, tabla, tabor, tabo(u)rin, tabret, tambour, tamboura, tambourine, tam-tam, testudo, tetrachord, theater organ, theorbo, timbal, timbrel, timpano, tin whistle, traps, triangle, trichord, tromba marina, trombone, trump, trumpet, trumpet marine, tuba, tubular bells, tympan, uillean pipes, ukulele, vibraharp, vibraphone, vielle, vihuela, vina, viol, viola, viola da braccio, (viola da) gamba, viola da gamba, viola da spalla, viola d'amore, violin, violoncello, violone, virginal(s), vocalion, waldflute, waldhorn, Welsh harp, xylophone, zambomba, zampogna, zanze, zel, zinke, zither, zufolo.

parliaments Althing (Iceland), Congress (USA), Cortes (Spain, Portugal), Dáil (Ireland), d(o)uma (Russia), ecclesia (Athens), Folketing (Denmark), House of Commons (UK), House of Keys (Isle of Man), House of Lords (UK), Knesset (Israel), Lagt(h)ing (Norway), Lagting (Norway), Landst(h)ing (Denmark), Landtag (Germany), Lok Sabha (India), Majlis (Iran), Odelst(h)ing (Norway), Oireachtas (Ireland), Parliament (UK), Pnyx (Athens), Porte (Turkey), Rajya Sabha (India), Reichsrat(h) (Austria), Reichstag (Germany), Rigsdag (Denmark), Riksdag (Sweden), Seanad (Ireland), Senate (Rome, USA, etc.), Skupshtina (Yugoslavia), Sobranje (Bulgaria), Stort(h)ing (Norway), Tynwald (Isle of Man), witenagemot (England).

prosody Alcaic, alexandrine, amphibrach, amphibrachic, amphimacer, Anacreontic, anacrusis, anacrustic, anapaest, anapaestic, antibacchius, antispast, antispastic, antistrophe, Archilochian, arsis, Asclepiad, asynartete, atonic, bacchius, catalectic, choliamb, choree, choriamb, cinquain, cretic, dactyl, decastich, decasyllabic, decasyllable, dipody, dispondaic, dispondee, distich, disyllable, ditrochean, ditrochee, dizain, dochmiac, dochmius, dodecasyllabic, dodecasyllable, dolichurus, duan, ectasis, ecthlipsis, elide, elision, enjamb(e)ment, envoy, epic, epirrhema, epistrophe, epitrite, epode, epopee, epopoeia, epos, epyllion, extrametrical, eye-rhyme, false quantity, feminine caesura, feminine ending, feminine rhyme, fifteener, free verse, galliambic, g(h)azal, glyconic, gradus, haiku, head- rhyme, hendecasyllabic, hendecasyllable, hephthemimer, heptameter, heptapody, heptasyllabic, heterostrophic, heterostrophy, hexameter, hexametric(al), hexapody, hexastich, Hudibrastic, huitain, hypercatalectic, hypercatalexis, hypermetrical, iamb, iambus, ictus, Ionic, irrational, kyrielle, laisse, Leonine, limerick, limma, linked verse, logaoedic, long- measure, macaronic(s), masculine ending, masculine rhyme, meliboean, miurus, monometer, monorhyme, monostich, monostrophic, mora, outride, oxytone, pantoum, pentameter, pentastich, penthemimer, Pherecratean, Pherecratic, Pindaric, poulters' measure, proceleusmatic, pyrrhic, Pythian, quatorzain, quatrain, reported verses, rhopalic, rhyme-royal, rich rhyme, riding-rhyme, rime riche, rime suffisante, rondeau, rondel, rove-over, rubaiyat, run-on, Sapphics, scazon, semeion, senarius, septenarius, sestina, spondee, strophe, synaphe(i)a, tetrameter, tetrapody, tetrasemic, tetrastich, thesis, tirade, tribrach, trimeter, tripody, triseme, trochee, villanelle, virelay.

ranks in armed forces able seaman, acting sub-lieutenant, admiral, admiral of the fleet, air chief marshal, air commandant, air commodore, air vice marshal, aircraftsman, air-marshal, brigadier, captain, chief officer, chief petty officer, chief technician, colonel, commandant, commander, commodore, corporal, field marshal, first officer, fleet chief petty officer, flight lieutenant, flight officer, flight sergeant, flying officer, general, group captain, group officer, junior seaman, junior technician, lance-corporal, lance-jack, lancesergeant, leading aircraftsman, leading seaman, lieutenant, lieutenant-colonel, lieutenant-commander, lieutenant-general, major, major-general, marshal, marshal of the Royal Air Force, master-at-arms, midshipman, ordinary seaman, petty officer, pilot officer, post- captain, private, purser, quartermaster, quartermaster-general, quartermaster-sergeant, quartermistress, rear-admiral, risaldar, ritt-master, second lieutenant, second officer, senior aircraftsman, sergeant, sergeant-major, squadron leader, squadron officer, staff sergeant, sub-lieutenant, superintendent, third officer, vice admiral, warrant officer, wing commander, wing officer.

rhetoric abscission, alliteration, amoebaean, anacoluthia, anacoluthon, anadiplosis, anaphora, anaphoric, anastrophe, antimetabole, antimetathesis, antiphrasis, antiphrastic(al), antithesis, antithetic(al), antonomasia, aporia, asteism, asyndeton, auxesis, catachresis, chiasmus, climax, diallage, diegesis, dissimile, double entendre, dramatic irony, dysphemism, ecbole, echoic, ecphonesis, ellipsis, enallage, enantiosis, enumeration, epanadiplosis, epanalepsis, epanaphora, epanodos, epanorthosis, epexegesis, epiphonema, epizeuxis, erotema, erotetic, figure, flower, head-rhyme, hendiadys, holophrase, hypallage, hyperbaton, hyperbole, hypobole, hypostrophe, hypotyposis, hysteron-proteron, increment, irony, litotes, meiosis, metalepsis, metaphor, metonym, metonymy, mixed metaphor, onomatopoeia, oxymoron, parabole, paral(e)ipsis, parenthesis, prolepsis, simile, syllepsis, symploce, synchoresis, synchysis, synedoche, synoeciosis, trope, vicious circle, zeugma.

titles of rulers abuna, adelantado, ag(h)a, alderman, amir, amman, amtman, ard-ri(gh), atabeg, atabek, ataman, atheling, ayatollah, Ban, beglerbeg, begum, bey, boyar, burgrave, caboceer, cacique, caliph, caudillo, Cid, Dan, Dauphin, Dauphine, Dauphiness, dey, diadochus, doge, duce, duke, ealdorman, elector, emir, emperor, empress, ethnarch, exarch, gospodar, Graf, Gräfin, grave, Great Mogul, harmost, heptarch, hospodar, huzoor, imperator, Inca, infanta, infante, jarl, kaid, kaiser, kalif, khan, khedive, king, kinglet, kingling, landgrave, landgravine, maharaja(h), maharani, mandarin, marchesa, marchese, marchioness, margrave, margravine, marquess, marquis, marquise, mikado, Mirza, Monseigneur, monsieur, Monsignor, Monsignore, mormaor, mpret, nabob, naik, nawab, nizam, nomarch, omrah, padishah, palatine, palsgrave, pasha, pendragon, pentarch, pharaoh, prince, prince- bishop, prince-imperial, princess, raja(h), rajpramukh, rana, rani, Rhinegrave, Rhinegravine, sachem, sagamore, satrap, shah, sheik(h), sherif, shogun, sirdar, sovereign, stad(t)holder, starosta, suba(h)dar, sultan, suzerain, taoiseach, theocrat, toiseach, toparch, tsar, tuchun, voivode, waldgrave.

tools about-sledge, aiguille, auger, auger-bit, awl, boaster, bodkin, bolster, bradawl, broach, bucksaw, burin, burr, buzz-saw, card, caschrom, caulking-iron, celt, center-bit, chaser, chisel, chopper, clamp, cleaver, cold-chisel, cradle- scythe, crosscut-saw, crown-saw, diamond-drill, dibble, dividers, dolly, drawing-knife, draw-knife, drill, drove, els(h)in, extirpator, fillister, float, forceps, forfex, fork, fraise, frame-saw, fretsaw, gad, gang-saw, gavelock, gimlet, gouge, grapnel, grapple, graver, gurlet, hacksaw, hammer, handsaw, hawk, hay fork, hay knife, helve-hammer, hod, hoe, holing-axe, jackhammer, jack-plane, jointer, laster, level, leveling rod, leveling staff, loy, mace, madge, maker, mall, mallet, mattock, maul, monkey, moon-knife, mortar, muller, oliver, oustiti, pachymeter, pad-saw, palstave, panel saw, panga, paper-cutter, paper-knife, pattle, pecker, peel, pestle, pick, pickaxe, pincers, pinch, pinking-shears, piolet, pitchfork, plane, planer, plessor, plexor, pliers, plow, plugger, plumb, plumb-line, plumb- rule, plummet, pocket-knife, pointel, pricker, priest, priming- iron, priming-wire, probang, probe, probing-scissors, prod, prog, pruning-bill, pruning-hook, pruning-knife, pruning-shears, prunt, punch, puncheon, punty, quadrant, quannet, rabble, rake, raspatory, reed-knife, repositor, retractor, ricker, rickstick, riddle, riffle, ripper, ripping-saw, ripple, rip-saw, risp, router, rule, ruler, sash-tool, saw, sax, scalpel, scauper, scissors, scoop, scooper, scorper, scraper, screwdriver, screwjack, screw-wrench, scribe(r), scutch(er), scythe, seam-set, serving-mallet, shave, shears, shovel, sickle, slane, slate-axe, slater, slicker, smoother, snap, snarling-iron, snarling-rod, snips, soldering-bolt, soldering-iron, spade, spanner, spider, spokeshave, spud, squeegee, stadda, stake, stapler, stapling- machine, steel, stithy, stone-hammer, stretching-iron, strickle, strigil, stubble-rake, style, stylet, swage, swingle(-hand), switch, tedder, tenon-saw, threshel, thresher, thrust-hoe, tint- tool, tongs, trepan, trowel, T-square, turfing-iron, turf-spade, turning-saw, tweezers, twist drill, upright, van, vice, vulsella, waster, whip-saw, widener, wimble, wood-shears, wortle, xyster, Y-level.

units of measurement acre, ampere, angstrom, anker, ardeb, are, arpent, arroba, arshin, as, bar, barleycorn, barn, barrel, bath, baud, becquerel, bel, bigha, bit, board-foot, boll, bolt, braccio, bushel, butt, cab, cable, calorie, candela, candle, candy, carat, catty, cell, cental, centner, chain, chalder, chaldron, chenix, chopin, chronon, clove, co(o)mb, cor, cord, coss, coulumb, cran, crith, cubit, cumec, curie, cusec, cyathus, daraf, Debye (unit), degree, demy, dessiatine, digit, dirham, dra(ch)m, dyne, ell, em, en, epha(h), erg, farad, faraday, fathom, fermium, firkin, firlot, foot, fother, fou, furlong, gal, gallon, gerah, gilbert, gill, grain, gram, hectare, henry, hertz, hin, hogshead, homer, hoppus foot, hundredweight, inch, joule, kaneh, kantar, kelvin, k(h)at, kilderkin, kin, knot, league, leaguer, li, liang, liard, ligne, link, lippy, lire lisp(o)und, liter, log, lux, maneh, maund, meter, mho, micrometer, micron, mile, mil(l), mina, minim, minute, mna, modius, mole, morgen, muid, mutchkin, nail, neper, nepit, newton, nit (information), nit (luminance), noggin, obol, oersted, ohm, oke, omer, ounce, oxgang, parasang, pascal, peck, perch, picul, pin, pint, pipe, poise, pole, pood, pound, poundal, quart, quarter, quartern, quintal, quire, radian, ream, rem, rod, rood, rote, rotolo, run(d)let, rutherford, sabin, s(a)eculum, sazhen, scruple, second, seer, semuncia, shekel, shippound, siemens, sievert, sone, span, square, stadium, steradian, stere, stilb, stoke(s), stone, tael, talent, tare, tesla, therm, tical, tierce, tod, toise, tola, ton, tonne, tonneau, tor, truss, tun, vara, verst, virgate, volt, watt, weber, wey, yard, yardland, yojan.

vehicles aerotrain, air-car, amtrack, araba, arba, aroba, automobile, barouche, Bath chair, berlin(e), bicycle, biga, bobsled, bobsleigh, bogie, boneshaker, brake, britzka, brougham, bubble-car, buckboard, buckcart, buck-wagon, buggy, bus, cab, caboose, cabriolet, caisson, calash, camper, caravan, caravanette, caroche, car(r)iole, carry-all, catafalque, chair, chaise, chaise-cart, chapel cart, charabanc, chariot, clarence, coach, convertible, conveyance, cycle, dandy-cart, dandy-horse, dennet, désobligeante, dhooly, diesel, diligence, dilly, Dodgem(s)®;, dog-cart, dogcart, dolly, doolie, dormitory-car, drag, dray, dros(h)ky, duck, ekka, fiacre, fly, fork-lift truck, four-in-hand, gharri, gig, glass-coach, go-kart, Green Goddess, gyrocar, gyrodyne, hack, hackery, hackney-carriage/coach, hatchback, herdic, honey-cart, honey-wagon, hurley-hacket, ice- yacht, inside-car, jeep, jingle, jinricksha(w), jitney, juggernaut, kago, kajawah, kart, kibitka, landau, landaulet(te), limousine, litter, lorry, mail-cart, minibus, monorail, motor caravan, motor-bicycle, motor-bike, motor-bus, motor-car, motor- coach, motor-cycle, motor-lorry, motor-scooter, norimon, omnibus, outside-car, palanquin (palankeen), palki, pantechnicon, pedal cycle, pedicab, people mover, phaeton, pick-up, pill-box, pincers, post-chaise, prairie schooner, pulka, quadriga, rail-bus, rail-car, rail-motor, ricksha(w), roadster, rockaway, runabout, safety bicycle, saloon-car, saloon-carriage, scooter, sedan, sedan-chair, shandry(dan), shooting-brake, sidecar, single-decker, skateboard, ski-bob, sled, sledge, sleeper, sleeping-car, sleeping-carriage, sleeping-coach, sleigh, slip- carriage, slip-coach, slipe, snowmobile, snowplow, sociable, solo, speedster, spider, spring-carriage, spring-cart, squad car, stage-coach, stage-wagon, stanhope, station-wagon, steam-car, steam-carriage, steamer, steam-roller, stillage, stone boat, straddle carrier, street-car, sulky, surrey, tally-ho, tandem, tank, tank-car, tank-engine, tanker, tank-wagon, tarantas(s), tartana, tax(ed)-cart, taxi, taxicab, T-cart, telega, telpher, tender, thoroughbrace, through-train, tilbury, tim-whisk(e)y, tin Lizzie, tip, tip-cart, tipper, toboggan, tonga, tourer, touring- car, tractor, trailer, train, tram, tramway-car, transporter, transport-rider, trap, tricar, tricycle, trike, triplet, trishaw, troika, trolley, trolley-bus, trolley-car, troop-carrier, truck, tube, tumble-car(t), tumbrel, turbocar, two-decker, twoseater, two-wheeler, velocipede, vettura, victoria, village cart, vis-à- vis, volante, wagon, wagonette, wagon-lit, wain, water-cart, water-wagon, weasel, wheelbarrow, wheel-chair, whisk(e)y, Whitechapel cart.

vessels, ships argosy, barca, barque, barquentine, bateau, bawley, Berthon-boat, bilander, billyboy, bireme, birlinn, boat, bomb-ketch, bomb-vessel, brig, brigantine, Bucentaur, budgerow, bum-boat, buss, butty, cabin cruiser, caique, canal-boat, canoe, caravel, Carley float, carrack, casco, cat, catamaran, catboat, clipper, coaster, cob(b)le, cockboat, cockleshell, cog, collier, commodore, coracle, corocore, corvette, cot, crare, crayer, currach, cutter, dandy, deep-sinker, destroyer, d(h)ow, dinghy, diving-bell, dogger, drake, dreadnought, dredger, drog(h)er, dromond, dugout, East-Indiaman, E-boat, faltboat, felucca, flatboat, floating battery, flyboat, flying bridge, fore-and- after, frigate, frigatoon, funny, gabbart, galleass, galleon, galley, gal(l)iot, gallivat, gay-you, geordie, gondola, grab, hatch-boat, herringer, hooker, hovercraft, hoy, hydrofoil, hydroplane, hydrovane, ice-boat, Indiaman, iron-clad, jigger, jollyboat, junk, kayak, ketch, koff, laker, landing-craft, lapstreak, launch, liberty-ship, lighter, line-of-battle-ship, liner, long-boat, longship, lorcha, lugger, lymphad, mackinaw, masoolah, merchantman, mistico, monitor, monkey-boat, monohull, monoxylon, montaria, motor-boat, motor-launch, motor-ship, motoscafo, mud-boat, mudscow, multihull, nacelle, nuggar, outrigger, packet, packet-boat, packet-ship, pair-oar, patamar, pedalo, penteconter, periagua, peter-boat, pink, pinkie, pinky, pinnace, piragua, pirogue, pleasure-boat, pocket battleship, polacca, polacre, pontoon, powerboat, praam, pra(h)u, pram, privateer, puffer, pulwar, punt, puteli, quadrireme, quinquereme, randan, razee, river-boat, river-craft, row-barge, row-boat, rowing-boat, saic, sail-boat, sailing-boat, sailing-ship, salmon- coble, sampan, schooner, schuit, scooter, scow, scull, sculler, sea-boat, seaplane-carrier, settee, shallop, ship, ship-of-the- line, shore-boat, show-boat, skiff, sloop, sloop-of-war, smack, smuggler, snow, speed-boat, speedster, square rigger, steamboat, steamer, steam-launch, steam-packet, steamship, steam-tug, steam- vessel, steam-yacht, stern-wheeler, stew-can, sub, submarine, super-Dreadnought, supertanker, surface-craft, surf-board, surf- boat, surf-canoe, surfing-board, swamp boat, tanker, tartane(e), tender, tern, three-decker, three-master, tilt-boat, torpedo- boat, torpedo-boat destroyer, track-boat, tracker, trader, train ferry, tramp, transport-ship, trawler, trek-schuit, triaconter, trimaran, trireme, troop-carrier, trooper, troop-ship, tub, tug, tug-boat, turbine-steamer, turret-ship, two-decker, two-master, U-boat, umiak, vaporetto, vedette(-boat), vessel, wager-boat, warship, water-bus, well-boat, well-smack, whaleboat, whaler, wherry, whiff, windjammer, xebec, yacht, yawl, zabra.

weapons, armor A-bomb, ack-ack, aerodart, ailette, air rifle, amusette, an(e)lace, arbalest, arblast, Archibald, Archie, arcubalist, armet, arquebus(e), baldric(k), ballista, ballistic missile, bandolier, Bangalore torpedo, basilisk, baton gun, bazooka, beaver, bill, Biscayan, blackjack, blowgun, blowpipe, bludgeon, blunderbuss, boarding-pike, bodkin, Bofors gun, bolas, bomb, bombard, boomerang, bowie knife, brassard, breastplate, breech-loader, Bren(gun), bricole, brigandine, broadsword, brown Bess, brown bill, buckler, buckshot, bulldog, bullet, bundook, burganet, byrnie, caltrop, cannon, carbine, carronade, casque, cataphract, catapult, chain-armor, chain-mail, chamfrain, Chassepot, chausses, cheval-de-frise, chokebore, claymore, cluster-bomb, coal-box, co(e)horn, Colt, Congreve, corium, dag, dagger, dah, Damascus blade, Damascus sword, demi-cannon, demi- culverin, demi-lance, depth-bomb, depth-charge, dirk, dragoon, elephant gun, épée, escopette, Exocet®;, express rifle, falchion, falconet, field gun, fire-arm, fire-arrow, firebomb, firelock, firepot, fission bomb, flail, flame-thrower, flick- knife, flintlock, foil, fougade, fougasse, four-pounder, fusee, fusil, Garand rifle, gatling-gun, gavelock, genouillère, gisarme, gladius, gorget, grapeshot, greave, Greek fire, grenade, gun, habergeon, hackbut, hacqueton, hailshot, halberd, half-pike, hand-grenade, hand-gun, han(d)jar, handstaff, harquebus, hauberk, H-bomb, heaume, helm, helmet, hielaman, howitzer, jack, jamb(e), jazerant, jesserant, Jethart staff, kris, lamboys, lame, lance, Lochaber-axe, Long Tom, machete, machine-gun, mangonel, martel, Martini(-Henry), matchlock, Mauser, Maxim(-gun), mesail, Mills bomb, Mills grenade, mine, mine-thrower, mini-rocket launcher, minnie, mitrailleur, mitrailleuse, morgenstern, morglay, morning- star, mor(r)ion, mortar, musket, musketoon, nulla-nulla, oerlikon, panga, partisan, pauldron, pavis(e), peasecod-cuirass, pederero, pelican, pelta, perrier, petrary, petronel, pickelhaube, pike, pilum, pistol, pistolet, placket, plastron, plate-armor, pocket-pistol, poitrel, pole-ax(e), poleyn, pompom, poniard, potgun, quarter-staff, queen's-arm, rapier, rerebrace, rest, revolver, rifle, rifle-grenade, sabaton, saber, saker, sallet, saloon-pistol, saloon-rifle, sap, sarbacane, schiavone, schläger, scimitar, scorpion, scutum, serpentine, sharp, shell, shield, shillela(g)h, shortsword, shotgun, shrapnel, siege-artillery, siege-gun, siege-piece, singlestick, six-gun, six-shooter, skean(dhu), sling, slung-shot, small-arm, small-sword, smoke-ball, smoke-bomb, snickersnee, spadroon, sparth(e), spear, spear gun, splint-armor, spontoon, spring-gun, squid, steel, sten gun, Sterling, stern-chaser, stiletto, stone axe, stone-bow, stylet, submachine-gun, sumpit(an), switch-blade (knife), swivel-gun, sword, sword bayonet, sword-cane, sword-stick, tace, targe, target, taslet, tasse, tasset, testudo, three-pounder, threshel, throw-stick, time-bomb, toc emma, toggle-iron, tomahawk, tomboc, tommy-gun, tormentum, torpedo, tortoise, trecento, trench-mortar, trident, truncheon, tuille, tuillette, tulwar, turret-gun, twibill, vambrace, vamplate, V- bomb, visor, vou(l)ge, war-wolf, waster, water-cannon, water- pistol, Welsh hook, white-arm, Winchester (rifle), wind-gun, wo(o)mera(ng), yatag(h)an, zumbooruk.

wine-bottle sizes baby, balthasar, jeroboam, magnum, Methuselah, nebuchadnezzar, nip, rehoboam, Salmanazar.

zodiac signs Aquarius, Aries, Cancer, Capricorn, Gemini, Leo, Libra, Pisces, Sagittarius, Scorpio, Taurus, Virgo.

APPENDIX V

The World

Earth's Vital Statistics

Age:	Approx 4600 million years
Weight:	Approx 5.976 x 1021 tonnes
Diameter:	Pole to Pole through the centre of the Earth 7900 miles (12,713 km)
	Across the Equator through the center of the Earth 7926 miles (12,756 km)
Circumference:	Around the Poles 24 861 miles (40,008 km)
	Around the Equator 40 091 km (24,912 miles)
Area:	Land 57,268,700 sq miles (148,326,000 sq km) 29% of surface
	Water139,667,810 sq miles (361,740,000 sq km) 71% of surface
Volume:	260 160 million cubic miles (1 084 000 million cubic km)
Volume of the oceans:	317 million cubic miles (1321 million cubic km)
Average height of land:	2756 ft (840 m) above sea level
Average depth of ocean:	3808 m (12,493 ft) below sea level
Density:	5.52 times water
Mean temperature:	22°C (72°F)
Length of year:	365.25 days
Length of one rotation:	23 hours 56 minutes
Mean distance from Sun:	149,600,000 km (92 960 000 miles)
Mean velocity in orbit:	18.5 miles (29.8 km) per second
Escape velocity:	6.96 miles (11.2 km) per second
Atmosphere:	Main constituents: nitrogen (78.5%), oxygen (21%)
Crust:	Main constituents: oxygen (47%), silicon (28%), aluminium (8%), iron (5%)
Known satellites:	One (The moon)

Continents of the World

	Highest Point		**Area**	
	(m)	**(ft)**	**(sq km)**	**(sq miles)**
Asia	8848	29,028	43,608,000	16,833,000
Africa	5895	19,340	30,335,000	11,710,000
North & Central America	6194	20,320	25,349,000	9,785,000
South America	6960	22,834	17,611,000	6,798,000
Antarctica	5140	16,863	14,000,000	5,400,000
Europe	5642	18,510	10,498,000	4,052,000
Oceania	4205	13,796	8,900,000	3,400,000

Oceans of the World

	Max. Depth		**Area**	
	metres	**feet**	**sq km**	**sq miles**
Pacific	11 033	36 197	165 384 000	63 860 000
Atlantic	8381	27 496	82,217 000	31 744 000
Indian	8047	26 401	73 481 000	28 371 000
Arctic	5450	17 880	14 056 000	5 427 000

Principal Rivers of the World

Name (location)	Length (km)	(miles)	Name (location)	Length (km)	(miles)
Nile (Africa)	6695	4160	Rio Grande (N Amer)	3034	1885
Amazon (S Amer)	6516	4050	São Francisco (S Amer)	2897	1800
Yangtze (Asia)	6380	3965	Danube (Europe)	2850	1770
Mississippi-Missouri (N Amer)	6019	3740	Brahmaputra (Asia)	2840	1765
Ob-Irtysh (Asia)	5570	3460	Euphrates (Asia)	2815	1750
Yenisel-Angara (Asia)	5553	3450	Pará-Tocantins (S Amer)	2752	1710
Hwang Ho (Asia)	5464	3395	Kolyma (Asia)	2600	1600
Zaïre (Africa)	4667	2900	Ganges (Asia)	2525	1568
Mekong (Asia)	4426	2750	Arkansas (N Amer)	2350	1460
Amur (Asia)	4416	2744	Colorado (N Amer)	2330	1450
Lena (Asia)	4400	2730	Xi Jiang (Asia)	2300	1437
Mackenzie (N Amer)	4250	2640	Dnepr (Europe)	2285	1420
Niger (Africa)	4032	2505	Negro (S Amer)	2254	1400
Paraná (S Amer)	4000	2485	Aldan (Asia)	2242	1393
Missouri (N Amer)	3969	2466	Irrawaddy (Asia)	2150	1335
Mississippi (N Amer)	3779	2348	Ohio (N Amer)	2102	1306
Murray-Darling (Oceania)	3750	2330	Orange (Africa)	2090	1299
Volga (Europe)	3686	2290	Kama (Europe)	2028	1260
Madeira (S Amer)	3203	1990	Xingú (S Amer)	2012	1250
St. Lawrence (N Amer)	3203	1990	Columbia (N Amer)	1950	1210
Yukon (N Amer)	3187	1980	Juruá (S Amer)	1932	1200
Indus (Asia)	3180	1975	Peace (N Amer)	1923	1195
Syr Darya (Asia)	3079	1913	Tigris (Asia)	1900	1180
Darling (Oceania)	3057	1900	Don (Europe)	1870	1165
Salween (Asia)	3060	1901	Pechora (Europe)	1814	1127

Principal Mountains of the World

Name (location)	Height (m)	(ft)	Name (location)	Height (m)	(ft)
Everest (Asia)	8848	29,028	Kailas (Asia)	6714	22,027
Godwin-Austen or K2 (Asia)	8611	28,250	Tengri Khan (Asia)	6695	21,965
Kangchenjunga (Asia)	8586	28,170	Sajama (S Amer)	6542	21,463
Makalu (Asia)	8463	27,766	Chimborazo (S Amer)	6310	20,702
Dhaulagiri (Asia)	8167	26,795	McKinley (N Amer)	6194	20,320
Nanga Parbat (Asia)	8125	26,657	Logan (N Amer)	5951	19,524
Annapurna (Asia)	8091	26,545	Cotopaxi (S Amer)	5896	19,344
Gosainthan (Asia)	8012	26,286	Kilimanjaro (Africa)	5895	19,340
Nanda Devi (Asia)	7816	25,643	Huila (S Amer)	5750	18,865
Kamet (Asia)	7756	25,446	Citlaltepi (C Amer)	5699	18,697
Namcha Barwa (Asia)	7756	25,446	Demavend (Asia)	5664	18,582
Gurla Mandhata (Asia)	7728	25,355	Elbrus (Asia)	5642	18,510
Kongur (Asia)	7720	25,325	St Elias (N Amer)	5489	18,008
Tirich Mir (Asia)	7691	25,230	Popocatepetl (C Amer)	5452	17,887
Minya Kanka (Asia)	7556	24,790	Foraker (N Amer)	5304	17,400
Kula Kangri (Asia)	7555	24,784	Ixtaccihuati (C Amer)	5286	17,342
Muztagh Ata (Asia)	7546	24,757	Dykh Tau (Europe)	5203	17,070
Kommunizma (Asia)	7495	24,590	Kenya (Africa)	5200	17,058
Pobedy (Asia)	7439	24,406	Ararat (Asia)	5165	16,945
Chomo Lhar (Asia)	7313	23,992	Vinson Massif (Antarctica)	5140	16,863
Lenina (Asia)	7134	23,405	Kazbek (Europe)	5047	16,558
Acongagua (S Amer)	6960	22,834	Jaya (Asia)	5030	16,502
Ojos del Salado (S Amer)	6908	22,664	Klyucheveyskava (Asia)	4750	15,584
Tupungato (S Amer)	6801	22,310	Mont Blanc (Europe)	4808	15,774
Huascarán (S Amer)	6769	22,205	Vancouver (N Amer)	4786	15,700
Llullailaco (S Amer)	6723	22,057	Trikora (Asia)	4750	15,584

Principal Waterfalls of the World

Name (location)	Height (m)	(ft)	Name (location)	Height (m)	(ft)
Angel (S Amer)	979	3212	Terni (Europe)	180	590
Yosemite (N Amer)	740	2425	Skjeggedalsfoss (Europe)	160	525
Kukenaãm (S Amer)	610	2000	Marina (S Amer)	153	500
Sutherland (Oceania)	581	1904	Aughrabies (Africa)	147	480
Wolloomombie (Oceania)	519	1700	Tequendama (S Amer)	131	427
Ribbon (N Amer)	492	1612	Guaíra (S Amer)	114	374
Upper Yosemite (N Amer)	436	1430	Illilouette (N Amer)	113	370
Gavarnie (Europe)	422	1384	Victoria (Africa)	108	355
Tugela (Africa)	412	1350	Kegon-no-tali (Asia)	101	330
Takkakau (N Amer)	366	1200	Lower Yosemite (N Amer)	98	320
Staubbach (Europe)	300	984	Cauvery (Asia)	98	320
Trümmelbach (Europe)	290	950	Vernal (N Amer)	97	317
Middle Cascade (N Amer)	278	910	Virginia (N Amer)	96	315
Vettisfoss (Europe)	271	889	Lower Yellowstone (N Amer)	94	308
King Edward VIII (S Amer)	256	840	Churchill (N Amer)	92	302
Gersoppa (Asia)	253	830	Reichenbach (Europe)	91	300
Skykjefos (Europe)	250	820	Sluiskin (N Amer)	91	300
Kajeteur (S Amer)	226	741	Lower Gastein (Europe)	86	280
Kalambo (Africa)	222	726	Paulo Alfonso (S Amer)	84	275
Maradalsfos (Europe)	199	650	Snoqualmie (N Amer)	82	268
Maletsunyane (Africa)	192	630	Seven (N Amer)	81	266
Bridalveil (N Amer)	189	620	Montmorency (N Amer)	77	251
Multnomah (N Amer)	189	620	Handegg (Europe)	76	250
Vöringfoss (Europe)	182	597	Taughannock (N Amer)	66	215
Nevada (N Amer)	181	594	Iguassú (S Amer)	64	210

Principal Lakes of the World

Name (location)	Area sq km	Area sq mi	Length km	Length mi	Max. Depth m	Max. Depth ft
Caspian (Asia-Europe)	371 000	143 205	1172	728	980	3215
Superior (North America)	83 270	32 140	564	350	393	1289
Victoria (Africa)	68 800	26 560	363	225	100	328
Aral (Asia)	65 500	25 285	379	235	68	223
Michigan (North America)	58 020	22 395	495	307	281	922
Tanganyika (Africa)	32 900	12 700	676	420	1435	4708
Great Bear (North America)	31 790	12 270	309	192	319	1047
Baykal (Asia)	30 500	11 775	636	395	1741	5712
Nyasa (Africa)	28 900	11 150	580	360	706	2316
Great Slave (North America)	28 440	10 980	480	298	140	459
Erie (North America)	25 680	9915	388	241	64	210
Winnipeg (North America)	24 510	9460	429	266	21	69
Ontario (North America)	19 230	7425	311	193	237	778
Ladoga (Europe)	18 390	7100	200	124	230	755
Balkhash (Asia)	17 400	6715	605	376	26	85
Chad (Africa)	10-26 000	4-10 000	210	130	4-7	13-23
Onega (Europe)	9600	3705	234	145	124	407
Eyre (Australia)	0-8900	0-3435	145	90	0-21	0-66
Titicaca (South America)	8340	3220	197	122	304	997
Nicaragua (Central America)	8270	3190	165	102	71	230
Athabasca (North America)	8080	3120	335	208	92	299
Turkana (Africa)	7105	2743	248	154	73	240
Reindeer (North America)	6390	2470	250	155		
Issyk-Kul (Asia)	6200	2395	186	115	702	2,303
Urmia (Asia)	5900	2280	145	90	15	49
Torrens (Australia)	5780	2230	210	130		

The areas of some of these lakes are subject to seasonal variations.

APPENDIX VI

Time Zones

At 12:00 noon, Greenwich Mean Time, the standard time is:

Place	Local Time	Place	Local Time
Addis Ababa (Ethiopia)	3pm	Johannesburg (South Africa)	2pm
Alexandria (Egypt)	2pm	Karachi (Pakistan)	5pm
Amsterdam (Netherlands)	1pm	Lima (Peru)	7am
Anchorage (USA)	2am	Lisbon (Portugal)	12 noon
Athens (Greece)	2pm	Los Angeles (USA)	4am
Auckland (New Zealand)	12 midnight	Madrid (Spain)	1pm
Baghdad (Iraq)	3pm	Manila (Philippines)	8pm
Bangkok (Thailand)	7pm	Mecca (Saudi Arabia)	3pm
Barcelona (Spain)	1pm	Melbourne (Australia)	10pm
Beijing (China)	8pm	Mexico City (Mexico)	6am
Belfast (N. Ireland)	12 noon	Montreal (Canada)	7am
Belgrade (Serbia)	1pm	Moscow (Russian Fed.)	3pm
Berlin (Germany)	1pm	New York (USA)	7am
Bogotà (Colombia)	7am	Oslo (Norway)	1pm
Bombay (India)	5.30pm	Paris (France)	1pm
Brussels (Belgium)	1pm	Perth (Australia)	8pm
Bucharest (Romania)	2pm	Prague (Czech Republic)	1pm
Budapest (Hungary)	1pm	Rangoon (Burma)	6.30pm
Buenos Aires (Argentina)	9am	Rio de Janeiro	9am
Cairo (Egypt)	2pm	Rome (Italy)	1pm
Calcutta (India)	5.30pm	St. Petersburg (Russian Fed.)	3pm
Cape Town (South Africa)	2pm	Santiago (Chile)	8am
Caracas (Venezuela)	8am	Seoul (South Korea)	9pm
Casablanca (Morocco)	12 noon	Shanghai (China)	8pm
Chicago (USA)	6am	Singapore (Singapore)	8pm
Copenhagen (Denmark)	2pm	Stockholm (Sweden)	1pm
Dacca (Bangladesh)	6pm	Sydney (Australia)	10pm
Darwin (Australia)	9.30pm	Tashkent (Uzbekistan)	6pm
Delhi (India)	5.30pm	Tehran (Iran)	3.30pm
Denver (USA)	5am	Tel Aviv (Israel)	2pm
Geneva (Switzerland)	1pm	Tokyo (Japan)	9pm
Havana (Cuba)	7am	Valparaíso (Chile)	8am
Helsinki (Finland)	2pm	Vancouver (Canada)	4am
Ho Chi Minh City (Vietnam)	7pm	Vienna (Austria)	1pm
Hong Kong (Hong Kong)	8pm	Vladivostock (Russian Fed.)	10pm
Istanbul (Turkey)	2pm	Warsaw (Poland)	1pm
Jakarta (Indonesia)	7pm	Wellington (New Zealand)	12 midnight
Jerusalem (Israel)	2pm	Zurich (Switzerland)	1pm

APPENDIX VII

Weights and Measures

Measurement of mass or weight

avoirdupois		*metric equivalent*
	1 grain (gr)	= 64.8 mg
	1 dram (dr)	= 1.772 g
16 drams	= 1 ounce (oz.)	= 28.3495 g
16 oz (= 7000 gr.)	= 1 pound (lb)	= 0.4536 kg
100 lb	= 1 short hundredweight	= 45.3592 kg
112 lb	= 1 long hundredweight	= 50.8024 kg
2,000 lb	= 1 short ton	= 0.9072 kg
2,240 lb	= 1 long ton	= 1.01605 tonnes

metric		*avoirdupois equivalent*
	1 milligram (mg)	0.015 gr
10 mg	= 1 centigram	0.154 gr
10 cg	= 1 decigram (dg)	1.543 gr
10 dg	= 1 gram (g)	15.43 gr = 0.035 oz
10 g	= 1 decagram (dag)	= 0.353 oz
10 dag	= 1 hectogram (hg)	= 3.527 oz
10 hg	= 1 kilogram (kg)	= 2.205 lb
1000 kg	= 1 tonne (metric ton)	= 0.984 (long) ton = 2204.62 lb

Troy weight

		metric equivalent
	1 grain	= 0.065 g
4 grains	= 1 carat of gold or silver	= 0.2592 g
6 carats	= 1 pennyweight (dwt)	= 1.5552 g
20 dwt	= 1 ounce (oz)	= 31.1035 g
12 oz	= 1 pound (lb)	= 373.242 g
25 lb	= 1 quarter (qr)	= 9.331 kg
100 lb	= 1 hundredweight (cwt)	= 37.324 kg
20 cwt	= 1 ton of gold or silver	= 746.68 kg

Note: the grain troy is the same as the grain avoirdupois, but the pound troy contains 5760 grains, the pound avoirdupois 7000 grains. Jewels are not weighed by this measure.

Linear measure

		metric equivalent
	1 inch (in)	= 25.4 mm
12 in	= 1 foot (ft)	= 0.305 m
3 ft	= 1 yard (yd)	= 0.914 m
2 yds	= 6 ft = 1 fathom (fm)	= 1.829 m
5.5 yds	= 16.5 ft = 1 rod	= 5.029 m
4 rod	= 22 yds = 66 ft = 1 chain	= 20.12 m
10 chain	= 220 yds = 660 ft = 1 furlong (fur.)	= 0.201 km
8 fur.	= 1760 yds = 5280 ft = 1 (statute) mile (mi)	= 1.609 km
3 mi	= 1 league	= 4.827 km

metric		*U.S. equivalent*
	1 millimeter (mm)	= 0.0394 in
10 mm	= 1 centimeter (cm)	= 0.3937 in
10 cm	= 1 decimeter (dm)	= 3.937 in
10 dm	= 1 meter (m)	= 39.37 in
10 m	= 1 decameter (dam)	= 10.94 yds
10 dam	= 1 hectometer (hm)	= 109.4 yds
10 hm	= 1 kilometer (km)	= 0.621 mi

Surveyor's measure

Surveyor's linear units		*metric equivalent*
1 link	= 7.92 in	= 20.117 cm
25 links = 1 rod	= 5.50 yds	= 5.029 m
100 links = 1 chain	= 22 yds	= 20.12 m
10 chains = 1 furlong (fur.)	= 220 yds	= 0.201 m
80 chains = 8 fur.	= 1 mile (mi)	= 1.609 km

Surveyor's square units — *metric equivalent*

100 x 100 links or 10,000 sq. links = 1 sq. chain = 484 sq. yds = 404.7 m2
4 x 4 poles or 16 sq. poles = 1 sq. chain
22 x 22 yds or 484 sq. yds = 1 sq. chain
100,000 sq. links or 10 sq. chains = 1 acre = 4840 sq. yds = 0.4047 ha

Square measure

		metric equivalent
	1 square inch (sq. in)	= 6.4516 cm2
144 sq. in.	= 1 square foot (sq. ft)	= 0.0929 m2
9 sq. ft.	= 1 square yard (sq. yd)	= 0.8361 m2
301/4 sq. yds.	= 1 square perch	= 25.29 m2
40 sq. perch	= 1 rood	= 0.1012
4 roods or 4840 sq. yds	= 1 acre	= 04.047 ha
640 acres	= 1 square mile (sq. mi)	= 2.5900 km2

metric units		*U.S. equivalent*
	1 square millimeter (mm2)	= 0.0016 sq. in
100 mm2	= 1 square centimeter (cm2)	= 0.1550 sq. in
100 cm2	= 1 square decimeter (dm2)	= 15.500 sq. in
100 dm2	= 1 square meter (m2)	= 10.7639 sq. ft (= 1.1959 sq. yds)
100 m2	= 1 square decameter (dam2)	= 1076.3910 sq. ft
100 dam2	= 1 square hectometer (hm2)	= 0.0039 sq. mi
100 hm2	= 1 square kilometer (km2)	= 0.3861 sq. mi

*Note: The square hectometer is also known as a *hectare* (ha.).

The hectare can be sub-divided into *ares*:

metric units		
100 m2	= 1 are	= 119.59 sq. yds
1000 m2	= 10 ares = 1 dekare	= 1195.9 sq. yds
10,000 m2	= 100 ares = 1 hectare	= 2.471 acres

Cubic measure

		metric equivalent
	1 cubic inch (cu. in)	= 16.39 cm3
1728 cu. in	= 1 cubic foot (cu. ft)	= 0.0283 m3
27 cu. ft	= 1 cubic yard (cu. yd)	= 0.7646 m3

	metric units
1000 cubic millimeters (mm3) = 1 cubic centimeter (cm3)	= 0.0610 cu. in
1000 cubic centimeters (cm3) = 1 cubic decimeter (dm3)	= 610 cu. in
1000 cubic decimeters (dm3) = 1 cubic meter (m3)	= 35.3147 cu. ft

The *stere* is also used, in particular as a unit of measurement for timber:

1 cubic meter	= 1 stere	= 35.3147 cu. ft
10 decisteres	= 1 stere	= 35.3147 cu. ft
10 steres	= 1 decastere	= 353.1467 cu. ft (= 13.0795 cu. yds)

Liquid measure

		metric equivalent
	1 fluid ounce (fl. oz)	= 29.573 ml
4 fl. oz	= 1 gill	= 118.291 ml
4 gills	= 1 pint (pt)	= 473.163 ml
2 pt	= 1 quart (qt)	= 0.9461
4 qt	= 1 gallon (gal)	= 3.7851

U.S. and British equivalents

U.S.	British
1 fluid ounce	1.0408 fl oz
1 pint	0.8327 pt
1 gallon	0.8327 gal

metric units		
10 milliliters (ml)	= 1 centiliter (cl)	= 0.0211 pt
10 cl	= 1 decileter (dl)	= 0.211 pt
10 dl	= 1 liter (l)	= 2.11 pt (= 0.264 gal)
101	= 1 decaliter (dal)	2.64 gal
10 dal	= 1 hectoliter (hl)	26.4 gal
10 hl	= kiloliter (kl)	264.0 gal

Temperature

Equations for conversion

°Fahrenheit = (9/5 x x°C) + 32 °Centigrade = 5/9 x (x°F - 32)

°Kelvin = x°C + 273.15

Some equivalents

	Centigrade	Fahrenheit
Normal temperature of the human body	36.9°C	98.4°F
Freezing point	0°C	32°F
Boiling point	100°C	212°F

Table of equivalents

Fahrenheit	*Centigrade*	*Centigrade*	*Fahrenheit*
100°C	212°C	30°C	86°F
90°C	194°F	20°C	68°F
80°C	176°F	10°C	50°F
70°C	158°F	0°C	32°F
60°C	140°F	-10°C	14°F
50°C	122°F	-20°C	4°F
40°C	104°F	-30°C	-22°F

Approximate oven temperatures

Description	Electric °C	°F	Gas no. (equiv. °F)
very cool	107°	225°	1/4 (240°)
	121°	250°	1/2 (265°)
cool	135°	275°	1 (290°)
	149°	300°	2 (310°)
warm	163°	325°	3 (335°)
moderate	177°	350°	4 (355°)
fairly hot	191°	375°	5 (375°)
	204°	400°	6 (400°)
hot	218°	425°	7 (425°)
very hot	232°	450°	8 (450°)
	246°	475°	9 (470°)

Clothing Sizes

Women: Dresses, Coats, Skirts/Junior Sizes Misses Sizes

American	7	9	11	13	15	8	10	12	14	16	18
British	9	11	13	15	17	10	12	14	16	18	20
Continental	34	36	38	40	42	38	40	42	44	46	48

Women: Blouses, Sweaters

American	10	12	14	16	18	20
British	32	34	36	38	40	42
Continental	38	40	42	44	46	48

Women: Shoes

American	4½	5	5½	6	6½	7	7½	8	8½	9	91/2
British	3	3½	4	4½	5	5½	6	6½	7	7½	8
Continental	35½	36	36½	37	37½	38	38½	39	39½	40	40½

Children:

American	3	4	5	6	6X
British	18	20	22	24	26
Continental	98	104	110	116	122

(For older children, sizes usually correspond with their ages)

Children: Shoes

American	8	9	10	11	12	13	1	2	3
British	7	8	9	10	11	12	13	1	2
Continental	24	25	27	28	29	30	32	33	34

Men: Suits

American	34	35	36	37	38	39	40	41	42
British	34	35	36	37	38	39	40	41	42
Continental	44	46	48	491/2	51	521/2	54	551/2	57

Men: Shirts

American	14½	15	15½	16	16½	17	17½	18
British	14½	15	15½	16	16½	17	17½	18
Continental	37	38	39	41	42	43	44	45

Metric Tyre Pressure Conversion Chart

Pounds per sq in	*Kilograms per sq cm*	*Kilo Pascals (kPa)*	*(Atmospheres)*
14	0.98	96.6	0.95
16	1.12	110.4	1.08
18	1.26	124.2	1.22
20	1.40	138.0	1.36
22	1.54	151.8	1.49
24	1.68	165.6	1.63
26	1.83	179.4	1.76
28	1.96	193.2	1.90
30	2.10	207.0	2.04
32	2.24	220.8	2.16
36	2.52	248.4	2.44
40	2.80	276.0	2.72
50	3.50	345.0	3.40
55	3.85	379.5	3.74
60	4.20	414.0	4.08
65	4.55	448.5	4.42

Mile/kilometer

Miles	*Kilometers*	*Kilometers*	*Miles*
1	1.6	1	0.6
2	3.2	2	1.2
3	4.8	3	1.8
4	6.4	4	2.4
5	8.0	5	3.1
6	9.6	6	3.7
7	11.2	7	4.3
8	12.8	8	4.9
9	14.4	9	5.5
10	16.0	10	6.2
20	32.1	20	12.4
30	48.2	30	18.6
40	64.3	40	24.8
50	80.4	50	31.0
60	96.5	60	37.2
70	112.6	70	43.4
80	128.7	80	49.7
90	144.8	90	55.9
100	160.9	100	62.1
1000	1,609	1,000	621

For approximate conversions:

Miles – Kilometers: divide by 5, then multiply by 8

Kilometers – Miles: divide by 8, multiply by 5

Numeration

Arabic	*Roman*	*Ordinal*	*Binary*
1	I	1st first	1
2	II	2nd second	10
3	III	3rd third	11
4	IV	4th fourth	100
5	V	5th fifth	101
6	VI	6th sixth	110
7	VII	7th seventh	111
8	VIII	8th eighth	1000
9	IX	9th ninth	1001
10	X	10th tenth	1010
11	XI	11th eleventh	1011
12	XII	12th twelfth	1100
13	XIII	13th thirteenth	1101
14	XIV	14th fourteenth	1110
15	XV	15th fifteenth	1111
16	XVI	16th sixteenth	10000
17	XVII	17th seventeenth	10001
18	XVIII	18th eighteenth	10010
19	XIX	19th nineteenth	10011
20	XX	20th twentieth	10100
21	XXI	21st twenty-first	10101
29	XXIX	29th twenty-ninth	11101
30	XXX	30th thirtieth	11110
32	XXXII	32nd thirty-second	100000
40	XL	40th	101000
50	L	50th	110010
60	LX	60th	111100
64	LXIV	64th	1000000
90	XC	90th	1011010
99	XCIX	99th	1100011
100	C	100th	1100100
128	CXXVIII	128th	10000000
200	CC	200th	11001000
256	CCLVI	256th	100000000
300	CCC	300th	100101100
400	CD	400th	110010000
500	D	500th	111110100
900	CM	900th	1110000100
1000	M	1000th thousandth	1111101000
1024	MXXIV	1024th	10000000000
1500	MD	1500th fifteen hundredth	10111011100
4000	MV	4000th	111110100000
5000	V	5000th	1001110001000
10,000	X	10,000th	10011100010000
100,000	C	100,000th	11000011010100000
1,000,000	M	1,000,000th millionth	10500,000

Periods of Time

annual	yearly
biannual	twice a year
bicentennial	every 200 years
biennial	every two years
bimonthly	every two months; twice a month
biweekly	every two weeks; twice a week
centennial	every 100 years
decennial	every 10 years
diurnal	daily
duodecennial	every 12 years
millennial	every 1,000 years
millennium	a thousand years
novennial	every nine years
octennial	every eight years
perennial	year after year
quadrennial	every four years
quadricentennial	every 400 years
quincentennial	every 500 years
quindecennial	every 15 years
quinquennial	every 5 years
semiannual	every six months
semicentennial	every 50 years
semidiurnal	twice a day
semiweekly	twice a week
septennial	every seven years
sesquicentennial	every 150 years
sexennial	every six years
thrice weekly	three times a week
tricennial	every 30 years
triennial	every three years
trimonthly	every three months
triweekly	every three weeks; three times a week
undecennial	every 11 years
vicennial	every 20 years

Traditional Anniversary Names

1st	Paper	14th	Ivory
2nd	Cotton	15th	Crystal
3rd	Leather	20th	China
4th	Fruit, flowers	25th	Silver
5th	Wood	30th	Pearl
6th	Iron, sugar	35th	Coral
7th	Wool, copper	40th	Ruby
8th	Bronze	45th	Sapphire
9th	Pottery	50th	Golden
10th	Tin, aluminium	55th	Emerald
11th	Steel	60th	Diamond
12th	Silk, fine linen	75th	Diamond
13th	Lace		

Birthstones

Month	*Biblical*	*Present*
January	Garnet	Garnet
February	Amethyst	Amethyst
March	Jasper	Aquamarine, Bloodstone
April	Sapphire	Diamond
May	Chalcedony, Carnelian, Agate	Emerald, chrysoprase
June	Emerald	Pearl, moonstone, alexandrite
July	Onyx	Ruby, carnelian
August	Carnelian	Peridot, sardonyx
September	Chrysolite	Sapphire, lapis luzuli
October	Aquamarine, Beryl	Opal, tourmaline
November	Topaz	Topaz
December	Ruby	Turquoise, zircon

Days of the Week

Day	*Derivation*	*Abbreviation*
Sunday	The Sun	Sun. or S.
Monday	The Moon	Mon. or M.
Tuesday	Tiu, Norse God of War	Tues. or T.
Wednesday	Woden, Anglo-Saxon chief of Gods	Wed. or W.
Thursday	Thor, Norse God of Thunder	Thurs. or Th.
Friday	Frigg, Norse Goddess	Fri. or F.
Saturday	Saturn, Roman God of Harvests	Sat. or Sa.

Months of the Year

Month	*Derivation*	*Abbreviation*
January	Janus, Roman God of Doors and Gates	Jan.
February	Februa, Roman period of purification	Feb.
March	Mars, Roman God of War	Mar.
April	Aperire, Latin for "to open"	Apr.
May	Maia, Roman Goddess of Spring and Growth	My.
June	Juno, Roman Goddess of Marriage	Jun. or Je.
July	Julius Caesar	Jul. or Jy.
August	Augustus, First Emperor of Rome	Aug.
September	Septem, Latin for "seven"	Sept. or Sep.
October	Octo, Latin for "eight"	Oct.
November	Novem, Latin for "nine"	Nov.
December	Decem, Latin for "ten"	Dec.

Appendix VIII

Chemical Elements

An element is a substance not separable by ordinary chemical means into substances different from itself. Fewer than a hundred elements occur naturally, the others can only be made artificially.

Name	*Symbol*	*Atomic number*	*Atomic weight*	*Valency*
Actinium	Ac	89	(227)	
Aluminum	Al	13	26.98154	3
Americium	Am	95	(243)	3,4,5,6
Antimony	Sb	51	121.75	3,5
Argon	Ar	18	39.948	0
Arsenic	As	33	74.9216	3.5
Astatine	At	85	(210)	1,3,5,7
Barium	Ba	56	137.34	2
Berkelium	Bk	97	(247)	3,4
Beryllium	Be	4	9.01218	2
Bismuth	Bi	83	208.9804	3,5
Boron	B	5	10.81	3
Bromine	Br	35	79.904	1,3,5,7
Cadmium	Cd	48	112.40	2
Caesium	Cs	55	132.9054	1
Calcium	Ca	20	40.08	2
Californium	Cf	98	(251)	
Carbon	C	6	12.011	2.4
Cerium	Ce	58	140.12	3.4
Chlorine	Cl	17	35.453	1,3,5,7
Chromium	Cr	24	51.996	2,3,6
Cobalt	Co	27	58.9332	2,3
Copper	Cu	29	63.546	1,2
Curium	Cm	96	(247)	3
Dysprosium	Dy	66	162.50	3
Einsteinium	Es	99	(254)	
Erbium	Er	68	167.26	3
Europium	Eu	63	151.96	2,3
Fermium	Fm	100	(257)	
Fluorine	F	9	18.99840	1
Francium	Fr	87	(223)	1
Gadolinium	Gd	64	157.25	3
Gallium	Ga	31	69.72	2,3
Germanium	Ge	32	72.59	4
Gold	Au	79	196.9665	1,3
Hafnium	Hf	72	178.49	4
Hahnium	Ha	105		
Helium	He	2	4.00260	0
Holmium	Ho	67	164.9304	3
Hydrogen	H	1	1.0079	1
Iridium	In	49	114.82	3
Iodine	I	53	126.9045	1,3,5,7
Irdium	Ir	77	192.22	3,4
Iron	Fe	26	55.847	2,3
Krypton	Kr	36	83.80	0
Lanthanum	La	57	138.9055	3
Lawrencium	Lr	103	(260)	
Lead	Pb	82	207.2	2,4
Lithium	Li	3	6.941	1
Lutetium	Lu	71	174.97	3
Magnesium	Mg	12	24.305	2
Manganese	Mn	25	54.9380	2,3,4,6,7
Mendelevium	Md	101	(258)	
Mercury	Hg	80	200.59	1,2
Molybdenum	Mo	42	95.94	3,4,6
Neodymium	Nd	60	144.24	3
Neon	Ne	10	20.179	0
Neptunium	Np	93	237.0482	4,5,6
Nickel	Ni	28	58.70	2,3
Niobium	Nb	41	92.9064	3,5
Nitrogen	N	7	14.0067	3,5
Nobelium	No	102	(255)	
Osmium	Os	76	190.2	2,3,4,8
Oxygen	O	8	15.9994	2
Palladium	Pd	46	106.4	2,4,6
Phosphorus	P	15	30.97376	3,5
Platinum	Pt	78	195.09	2,4
Plutonium	Pu	94	(244)	3,4,5,6
Polonium	Po	84	(209)	
Potassium	K	19	39.098	1
Praseodymium	Pr	59	140.9077	3
Promethium	Pm	61	(145)	3
Protactinium	Pa	91	231.0359	
Radium	Ra	88	226.0254	2
Radon	Rn	86	(222)	0
Rhenium	Re	75	186.207	
Rhodium	Rh	45	102.9055	3
Rubidium	Rb	37	85.4678	1
Ruthenium	Ru	44	101.07	3,4,6,8
Rutherfordium	Ru	104		
Samarium	Sm	62	105.4	2,3
Scandium	Sc	21	44.9559	3
Selenium	Se	34	78.96	2,4,6
Silicon	Si	14	28.086	4
Silver	Ag	47	107.868	1
Sodium	Na	11	22.98977	1
Strontium	Sr	38	87.62	2
Sulphur	S	16	32.06	2,4,6
Tantalum	Ta	73	180.9479	5
Technetium	Tc	43	(97)	6,7
Tellurium	Te	52	127.60	2,4,6
Terbium	Tb	65	158.9254	3
Thallium	Tl	81	204.37	1,3
Thorium	Th	90	232.0381	4
Thulium	Tm	69	168.9342	3
Tin	Sn	50	118.69	2,4
Titanium	Ti	22	47.90	3,4
Tungsten (Wolfram)	W	74	183.85	6
Uranium	U	92	238.029	4,6
Vanadium	V	23	50.9414	3,5
Xenon	Xe	54	131.30	0
Ytterbium	Yb	70	173.04	2,3
Yttrium	Y	39	88.9059	3
Zinc	Zn	30	65.38	2
Zirconium	Zr	40	91.22	4